CLASSIC CINEMA FROM NEW YORKER VIDEO

Jazz On A Summer's Day
This precursor to Woodstock is the granddaddy of all concert films, a chronicle of the Newport Jazz Fest in Rhode Island. 114 min. total.
53-7383   VHS $29.99
D1-6371   DVD $29.99

Mon Oncle D'Amerique
Witty treatise on human behavior from Alain Resnais stars Gerard Depardieu, Nicole Garcia and Roger Pierre. 123 min. In French with English subtitles.
53-1616   VHS Letterboxed $29.99
D1-7975   DVD $29.99

Fire
A forbidden lesbian tryst is the subject of this taboo-breaking erotic tale. Shabana Azmi and Nandita Das star. 104 min. Filmed in English.
53-6281   VHS Letterboxed $29.99
D1-7349   DVD $29.99

Fireworks (Hana-Bi)
Triple-threat Takeshi Kitano's poetic, explosive police saga showcases Kitano as a distraught detective. 103 min. In Japanese with English subtitles.
53-6279   VHS $29.99
D1-7348   DVD $29.99

The Cement Garden
Psychosexual drama focuses on a family who, after their mother dies, seals her body in cement in the basement. Charlotte Gainsbourg and Andrew Robertson. 105 min.
53-8661   VHS $29.99
D1-7974   DVD $29.99

Le Samouraï
Alain Delon, François Périer, and Nathalie Delon star. In French with English subtitles.
53-8959   VHS $29.99

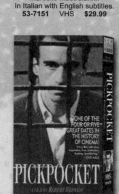

City Of Women
Federico Fellini directs Marcello Mastroianni. In Italian with English subtitles.
53-7151   VHS $29.99

Pickpocket
Robert Bresson's powerful French New Wave crime drama. In French with English subtitles.
53-7256   VHS $29.99

Underground
Yugoslavian history is traced in this drama from Emir Kusturica; winner of the Palm d'Or prize at Cannes. In Serbian with English subtitles.
53-6233   VHS $29.99

Available On DVD For Just $29.99!

N·E·W YORKER VIDEO

After Life
In this heartfelt fantasy from the director of "Maborosi", the newly dead are met by a celestial staff who help them in choosing the memory that will be all they take with them into eternity. Arata, Erika Oda, and Taketoshi Naito star. 118 min. Widescreen; Soundtrack: Japanese stereo; Subtitles: English; theatrical trailers; web links; scene access.
D1-8213   DVD $29.99

Guantanamera!
From Cuba's Tomas Gutirrez Alea ("Strawberry and Chocolate") comes this effervescent social and romantic comedy described as a "road story with a Cuban twist." Mirta Ibarra, and Carlos Cruz star. 104 min. Standard; Soundtrack: Spanish; Subtitles: English; theatrical trailer; scene access.
D1-7973   DVD $29.99

The War Zone
Tim Roth's emotionally raw drama, which Roger Ebert called one of the year's ten best, looks at a family in England being torn apart by incest. Ray Winstone, Tilda Swinton and Freddie Cunliffe star. Uncut, unrated; 99 min. Widescreen; Soundtrack: English; audio commentary; "making of" featurette; theatrical trailer; scene access.
D1-7971   DVD $29.99

The Way of the Samurai

While everyone knows that *The Magnificent Seven* was a remake of *Seven Samurai*, few know that Sergio Leone's famous spaghetti westerns, *Fist Full of Dollars* and *For a Few Dollars More* with Clint Eastwood, were remakes of Kurosawa's *Yojimbo* and *Sanjuro*. Whereas American film icons like Eastwood, Harrison Ford, and Steve McQueen portray the hardened, honor-bound anti-heroes in the remakes, there is one actor - **Toshiro Mifune** - whose presence conveys the breathtaking scope of an epic samurai film.

Akira Kurosawa's
Seven Samurai
Starring: Takashi Shimura and Toshiro Mifune

Venice Film Festival, Silver Lion

"One of the greatest films ever made." Gene Siskel, CHICAGO TRIBUNE

$34.95

Akira Kurosawa's
Sanjuro
Starring: Toshiro Mifune

"Exciting. Plenty of sparkling swordplay." THE FABER COMPANION TO FOREIGN FILMS

$29.95

Kihachi Okamoto's
Sword of Doom
Starring: Toshiro Mifune

"A rousing samurai epic." VIDEOHOUND'S GOLDEN MOVIE RETRIEVER

$29.95

Kenji Mizoguchi's
The 47 Ronin

"For admirers of Japanese cinema, The 47 Ronin is essential." THE VILLAGE VOICE

2 tape set- **$49.95**

Akira Kurosawa's
Yojimbo
Starring: Toshiro Mifune and Takashi Shimura

Venice Film Festival, Best Actor (Toshiro Mifune)

"Explosively comic and exhilarating." Pauline Kael, THE NEW YORKER

$29.95

Masaki Kobayashi's
Samurai Rebellion
Starring: Toshiro Mifune

Venice Film Festival, International Film Critics Award

"The screen explodes into the most slashing since Harakiri." VARIETY

$29.95

Hiroshi Inagaki's
Samurai Trilogy
Starring: Toshiro Mifune

Academy Award™, Best Foreign Language Film

"A masterful and enthralling epic." MOVIES ON TV

3 tape set- **$69.95**

Home Vision Cinema

Creepy slasher flick featuring Margot Kidder *(Superman)* as a psychotic twin with a brand new set of knives. Now with its own cult following, *Sisters* was the film that put director Brian De Palma *(Carrie, The Fury, Dressed to Kill)* on the map. Replete with gore, excellent use of split-screen photography, and cameos from Olympia Dukakis *(Moonstruck, Steel Magnolias)* and Charles Durning *(The Sting, The Hudsucker Proxy),* De Palma's first tribute to Hitchcock also features a spine tingling score from Bernard Herrmann *(Psycho, Vertigo).*

SISTERS

VHS $19.95

1973, Color, 93 min., Aspect Ratio- 1.85:1

DVD $29.95
from THE CRITERION COLLECTION

Long missing from the video marketplace

From Director BRIAN DE PALMA *(Carrie, Mission to Mars)*

Letterboxed in its proper aspect ratio for the first time

Featuring a score by BERNARD HERRMANN *(Psycho, Vertigo)*

THE CLASSIC COLLECTION
A JOINT VENTURE BETWEEN HOME VISION CINEMA AND JANUS FILMS
Design and Summary © 2000 Public Media, Inc. All rights reserved. 092000S

Dear Movie Lover:

You are now holding the future of video in your hands: the 2001 Movies Unlimited Video Catalog, an 816-page guide to the most incredible selection of movies available on video, courtesy of one of the world's oldest and most reliable video retailers.

Boasting expert synopses for nearly 40,000 titles and filled with rare artwork, the 2001 Movies Unlimited Video Catalog puts both the classics and the latest films from Hollywood at your fingertips, and allows movie buffs to have an opportunity to not only read about, but purchase, their favorites. The catalog also offers hundreds of titles at reduced prices, presenting a perfect opportunity for film lovers to start their own collection or add to an already existing library.

We're happy to say that such recent cinematic smashes as *Chicken Run*, *The Perfect Storm*, *Gladiator*, *The Patriot*, *The Nutty Professor II: The Klumps*, *Toy Story 2* and *X-Men* have found their way into the Movies Unlimited Video Catalog, along with such much-requested first-time-on-video titles as *Annie Get Your Gun*, Orson Welles' director's cut of *Touch of Evil*, *The Story of G.I. Joe*, *The Lathe of Heaven* and Disney's *Make Mine Music*.

In addition, we can once again offer many rare titles that have been impossible to find for several years, including *The Conversation* with Gene Hackman, *Gimme Shelter*, the 1967 version of *Bedazzled* and *Aguirre: The Wrath of God* from Werner Herzog, all at collectible prices.

What's more, Movies Unlimited is not just movies. Within these pages you'll find scores of documentaries, Japanese animation, vintage serials and B westerns, and instructional tapes. The TV section this year should merit special attention with such entries as the cult classic *The Prisoner*, the first season of *The Sopranos*, the *Captains and the Kings* mini-series and episodes of the 1960s war series, *The Rat Patrol*.

Yes, there's all this and lots more in the 2001 Movies Unlimited Video Catalog. If you're interested in any titles, or if you just have a question, please call us toll-free at 1-800-4MOVIES or email us at movies@moviesunlimited.com. And if you want to check us out on the World Wide Web, drop by our site at www.moviesunlimited.com. Our ever-expanding website is updated daily, showcasing the latest in video releases and sales items, and you can order directly online as well.

Also, DVD customers, call us to find out how you can obtain a copy of our brand-new, comprehensive DVD Flash! catalog, the most comprehensive listing of titles available in this fast-growing format.

Thank you for choosing us as your one-stop video shop.

Sincerely,

Jerry

Jerry Frebowitz, President

Movies Unlimited VHS Video Catalog

2001 Edition

24-HOUR ORDER LINE:
To order tapes any time, simply call **1-800-4-MOVIES**, toll-free, 24 hours-a-day, and you can charge it to your Visa, MasterCard, American Express or Discover. Please note this number is for placing orders only.

CUSTOMER SERVICE LINE:
To inquire on orders already placed, or if you have any other questions, please feel free to call us toll-free at **1-800-668-4344** weekdays from 9 a.m. to 9 p.m. (ET) and we'll be glad to assist you.

email: movies@moviesunlimited.com • website: www.moviesunlimited.com
Please Note: All titles listed are VHS/NTSC only.

CATALOG EDITORS:
Joseph McLaughlin, Gary Cahall, Irv Slifkin, Jay Steinberg, Brian Sieck

CATALOG LAYOUT:
Jason Marcewicz, Jim Frangos, Matt Torpey.

Cover Design: FP Design Inc. • Cover Artist: Dave Schweitzer

Titles appearing in this catalog with the ☐ symbol are closed captioned. This registered mark identifies programs closed captioned by the National Captioning Institute; used with permission. This catalog and all descriptions, pictures and materials within are property of MOVIES UNLIMITED INC., 3015 Darnell Road, Philadelphia, PA 19154.

OUR VARIETY IS SHOWING!

VCI Home Video is one of the pioneer producers of the home video industry.
We have a library of over 2,000 titles (and still growing). From the obscure and eclectic,
to bona fide critical classics...our variety is showing.

A CHRISTMAS CAROL (1951)
Alastair Sim. "By far the most entertaining of all
the movie versions." - Video Review
(VHS & DVD)

THE LONE RANGER
LONE RANGER &
THE LOST CITY OF GOLD
HI YO SILVER!
The famous masked man and his faithful
companion Tonto together in three classic
westerns. (VHS & DVD)

ADVENTURES OF RED RYDER
Thrilling western action with Red Ryder and Little
Beaver. (VHS & DVD)

FLASH GORDON CONQUERS THE UNIVERSE
Before Luke Skywalker there was Flash Gordon!
(VHS & DVD)

THE PHANTOM
Funny paper hero comes to life battling bad guys in
the jungle. (VHS & DVD)

BUCK ROGERS
Buster Crabbe stars in 12 epic sci-fi
chapters. (VHS & DVD)

JUNGLE GIRL
"The best of the Jungle serials..."
- Alan Barbour (VHS & DVD)

COLLECTORS' BOX SETS

BLOOD & BLACK LACE
THE WHIP & THE BODY
Two chillers from the
Godfather of Horror films,
Mario Bava. Now in
restored, uncut, widescreen
versions. (VHS & DVD)

MY LITTLE MARGIE - BOX SET #1 AND BOX SET #2 (VHS & DVD)
One of America's favorite TV gals. Two Box sets available. 12 episodes on 4 tapes on each set.

MR. WONG
Boris Karloff, or Key Luke as the famous oriental detective. 6 tape box set, or individual tapes.

STORIES OF THE CENTURY
Jim Davis stars in series of real stories about the Old West. Box set contains 12 episodes.

AMERICA AT WAR COLLECTION
Incredible WWII documentaries from Hollywood directors - John Ford, John Huston, William Wyler
and more. Box set or individual tapes.

I MARRIED JOAN - BOX SETS #1 & #2
Classic TV with Joan Davis and Jim Backus - over 24 hilarious episodes in 2 sets.

SECRETS OF THE MILLENNIUM (VHS & DVD)
Four volume series explores the farthest reaches of outer space and the most remote and alien spaces
of our own planet.

PIPPIN
Special edition video of Bob Fosse's Broadway hit.
(VHS & DVD)

GORGO
Lookout Godzilla, Gorgo's back in town. Special Edition
of sci-fi classic. (VHS & DVD)

I Dreamed Of Africa (2000)
In this true story, Kim Basinger is Kuki Gallman, a divorced Italian socialite who weds dashing young adventurer Vincent Perez and, along with her young son, moves with him to Africa, where she once lived. Settling onto a large Kenyan ranch, Basinger struggles to overcome trials ranging from wild animals and ivory poachers to Perez's lengthy absences. Eva Marie Saint, Liam Aiken co-star. 115 min.
02-3454 ❑*$99.99*

Backlash (2000)
When her pursuit of a South American drug cartel reveals a high-level government conspiracy and leaves her partner dead, federal prosecutor Tracey Needham turns to two unlikely allies—convict James Belushi and veteran homicide detective Charles Durning—for help. Explosive actioner also stars JoBeth Williams, Dan Lauria. AKA: "Justice." 103 min.
02-3431 ❑*$99.99*

The Silencer (2000)
FBI agent Brennan Elliot takes on his most dangerous assignment when he fakes his own death and, with a new identity, infiltrates the notorious terrorist group Division 5. As a rookie hit man, Elliott is taken under the wing of veteran Division 5 assassin Michael Dudikoff, but when he's framed for the murder of a U.S. senator he soon learns there was a sinister ulterior motive for his mission. 92 min.
68-2016 ❑*$69.99*

Silicon Towers (2000)
Charlie Cook has just been promoted to a powerful executive position at the Silicon Towers. But he soon finds out that he has walked into a corporate trap of espionage after learning that the company is illegally accessing numerous banks around the world. When Charlie himself is accused of embezzling, he must race to find a way out. With Brian Dennehy, Daniel Baldwin and Robert Guillaume. 95 min.
82-5213 *$89.99*

The Perfect Storm (2000)
Based on a true story, director Wolfgang Petersen's harrowing nautical adventure stars George Clooney, Mark Wahlberg, John C. Reilly and William Fichtner as the captain and crew of the New England fishing vessel Andrea Gail, who found themselves in the fight of their lives when their boat was caught in a record-setting storm in the fall of 1991. With Diane Lane, Mary Elizabeth Mastrantonio.
19-5012 ❑*$22.99*

The Perfect Storm (Letterboxed Version)
Also available in a theatrical, widescreen format.
19-5013 ❑*$22.99*

Reindeer Games (2000)
Newly released from prison, car thief Ben Affleck assumes his late cellmate's identity so he can be with the dead man's pen-pal girlfriend (Charlize Theron). Unfortunately for Affleck, Theron's gun-running brother (Gary Sinise) wants him to supply inside information he doesn't have so Sinise and his cronies can hold up an Indian reservation casino. John Frankenheimer expertly directs this gripping thriller; Clarence Williams III, Dennis Farina also star.
11-2450 Was $99.99 ❑*$19.99*

In The Hood (2000)
High-octane actioner stars Fred "Rerun" Berry as a drug kingpin and strip club owner who hires two losers to watch his business, then finds his turf being encroached upon by rival gangsters. Berry's henchmen have a chance to protect their boss, but when one is involved with a beautiful assassin, matters get complicated. Debbie Rochon, John Paul Fedele co-star. 90 min.
73-9338 *$59.99*

The Ultimate Weapon (2000)
Hulk Hogan is some commando in this no-holds-barred actioner that finds him as a mercenary hired by IRA terrorists posing as Special Forces units. When he discovers the truth, Hogan becomes a universal soldier, flying solo to beat the bad guys as an army of one. With Daniel Pillon, Carl Marotte. 110 min.
82-5195 *$99.99*

Rapid Assault (2000)
An international terrorist is planning to wipe out the Earth's entire population with a biochemical weapon unless he is paid 50 million dollars from the U.S. government. Now it's up to a team of top-secret agents to stop an army of mercenaries before it's too late. Tim Abell, Don Scribner, Jeff Rector and Lisa Mazzetti star. 90 min.
82-5218 *$89.99*

Dead Punkz (2000)
When a troubled teen is sent to prison at the young age of 17 after a brief life of crime, he plans to make a desperate escape from his abusive jailers with the help of his friends. They then decide to wage a war against their old neighborhood. This intense urban film features a bright young cast. 90 min.
82-5219 *$99.99*

Under Oath (2000)
Crackerjack cop thriller starring Jack Scalia and Eddie Velez as cops who decide to temporarily stray to the other side of the law in a scheme involving an arms dealer. But when the criminal is killed, they find themselves in trouble—especially when they are called on to solve the murder! Richard Lynch, Clint Howard and Abraham Benrubi also star. 89 min.
21-9214 *$99.99*

Take It To The Limit (2000)
Leo Fitzpatrick plays a young man who is constantly getting into trouble. Eventually, he is sent off to a wilderness home, run by his uncle, to reform himself. But when he is lured into joining a rock climbing group by a local girl he gets into even more trouble as the crew embarks on a dangerous adventure. Also featuring Gretel Roenfeldt, John Marlo. 87 min.
21-9216 *$99.99*

Termination Man (2000)
Covert secret agent Steve Railsback is called on to save the world when a Serbian terrorist blackmails NATO and the United Nations with a deadly nerve gas. Railsback is joined on his mission by sexy Athena Massey and lethal assassin Eb Lottimer. 92 min.
21-9218 *$59.99*

Tha Eastsidaz (2000)
In this urban actioner, Snoop Dogg is a music exec/gangsta who decides to abandon his ruthless lifestyle after one more heist. But when an arch-rival frames him for murder, Snoop has to take matters into his own hands, straightening things out. Tray Dee, Goldie Loc, Warren G., Darryl Brunson and Xzibit also star.
54-9201 *$24.99*

2 G'S And A Key (2000)
Curtis, just out of the joint for drug possession, finds his life in trouble when Sadd Dog, a dealer he double-crossed, tries to settle an old score. Gritty urban actioner stars Conroe Brooks, Aaron D. Spears. 93 min.
81-9115 *$59.99*

Hangfire (1990)
An all-star cast highlights this gripping thriller about two tough Vietnam veterans who call on their military experience when they try to stop escaped cons from terrorizing a small town. Brad Davis, Jan-Michael Vincent, Yaphet Kotto, Lou Ferrigno, Kim Delaney, Lyle Alzado and George Kennedy star. 89 min.
02-2098 *$89.99*

Blind Fury (1990)
Blinded and left for dead in Vietnam, Rutger Hauer survives and learns to overcome his handicap. Now, he's the deadliest martial arts master around, and some drug dealers who threaten Hauer's friends soon learn it doesn't take two eyes to kill. Mind-blowing action stunts; Terry O'Quinn, Randall "Tex" Cobb co-star. 85 min.
02-2051 *$14.99*

Live Wire (1992)
An ace FBI bomb expert, troubled by his wife's open affair with the U.S. senator he's been hired to protect, is put into the most dangerous situation of his life when he must find and detonate a powerful explosive disguised as water. Pierce Brosnan, Ron Silver, Ben Cross and Lisa Eilbacher star in this action-packed thriller. Unrated version; 87 min.
02-2330 Was $19.99 ❑*$14.99*

Revolver (1992)
Government agent Robert Urich tries to put a stop to a Spanish mobster's stateside encroachment, but an assassination attempt leaves him in a wheelchair. Despite the odds, Urich continues his pursuit in this action-laced thriller. With Dakin Matthews. 96 min.
02-2292 *$79.99*

Write To Kill (1991)
After his brother is killed by a group of seedy counterfeiters, a shy young writer decides to find the killers and get revenge. Turning in his keyboard for a gun, the scribe becomes involved in some risky business...and with a beauty with a mysterious past. Scott Valentine, Joan Severance, Chris Mulkey and G.W. Bailey star. 120 min.
02-2135 *$79.99*

Toy Soldiers (1991)
Suspenseful thriller about a group of South American terrorists who take over a New England military school populated by rebellious teenage boys. Instead of giving in to the terrorists' strong-arm tactics, the boys devise an ingenious plan to fight back. Sean Astin, Wil Wheaton, Keith Coogan, Denholm Elliott and Louis Gossett, Jr. star. 111 min.
02-2136 Was $19.99 ❑*$14.99*

Double Trouble (1991)
Twin musclemen on different sides of the law become involved with rare jewels, beautiful women and smugglers as they attempt to stop a dastardly criminal plot. The unbelievable cast includes the Barbarian Brothers, Roddy McDowall, Troy Donahue, Bill Mumy, James Doohan and David Carradine. 87 min.
02-2178 *$89.99*

The Taking Of Beverly Hills (1991)
When a criminal billionaire hatches an elaborate plot to rob the world's richest city by shutting it down with a phony toxic spill, a former football star and a renegade cop team up to try to stop his devious plan. Ken Wahl, Matt Frewer, Robert Davi and Harley Jane Kozak star in this explosive action saga. 96 min.
02-2185 Was $19.99 ❑*$14.99*

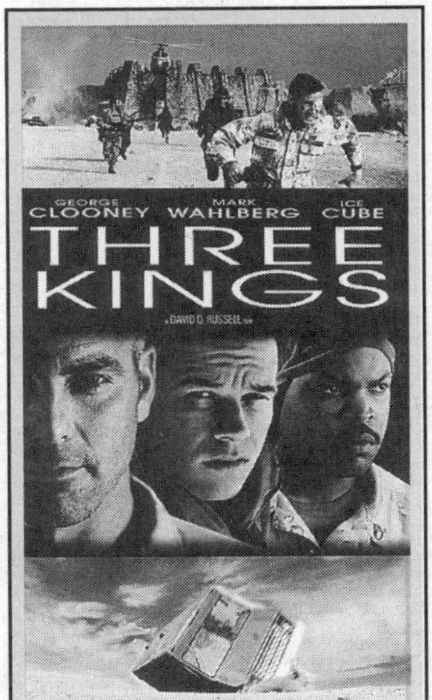

Three Kings (1999)
In the aftermath of Desert Storm, four American soldiers (George Clooney, Mark Wahlberg, Ice Cube, Spike Jonez) stationed in occupied Iraq come upon a map showing where a fortune in stolen Kuwaiti gold sits in an underground bunker. Setting out to help themselves to the gold, the G.I.s find themselves coming to the aid of anti-Hussein civilians under attack by Iraqi forces. Action and dark comedy are mixed in director David O. Russell's acclaimed, offbeat war drama. 115 min.
19-2960 Was $99.99 ❑*$19.99*

Three Kings (Letterboxed Version)
Also available in a theatrical, widescreen format.
19-2999 ❑*$19.99*

Adventures In Spying (1992)
Two teens enjoying a lazy summer day stumble onto a plot involving a hired killer who is believed dead. In order to expose him and get a $50,000 reward, the pair encounters a wacky cop, a brilliant professor and a ruthless drug syndicate. Jill Schoelen, Bernie Coulson, G. Gordon Liddy and Michael Emil star. 91 min.
02-2319 Was $19.99 *$14.99*

Freeze Frame (1992)
Shannen Doherty stars in this high-tech thriller as a high school TV reporter who befriends a cool classmate and the campus nerd in order to capture a biotech company's illegal workings on video. Charles Haid, Robyn Douglass co-star. 78 min.
02-2321 Was $19.99 *$14.99*

The 13th Warrior (1999)
Based on Michael Crichton's "Eaters of the Dead," this medieval adventure stars Antonio Banderas as a 10th-century ambassador from Baghdad who is confronted by Vikings while on a mission in Russia. Banderas is recruited to join them as they fight a supernatural presence destroying the Norsemen's villages. With Omar Sharif, Diane Venora; directed by John McTiernan ("Die Hard"). 103 min.
11-2368 Was $99.99 ❑*$14.99*

Wild Grizzly (1999)
Escaping from its mountain home, a gigantic grizzly bear is stalking the streets of a remote wilderness community, and a teenage boy sets out to find it before local rangers and a hunting party get to the animal first. Daniel Baldwin, Fred Dryer, Riley Smith and Michele Greene star. 90 min.
76-9121 *$49.99*

Confessions Of A Hitman (1993)
After running off with a fortune belonging to his Mafia boss uncle, a killer-for-hire is in for the road trip of his life, as an army of mobsters are hot on his trail. They want the money back safe and sound...him, they're not so picky about! James Remar, Michael Wright, Emily Longstreth star. 93 min.
80-1068 Was $89.99 *$14.99*

Dark Angels (1997)
An African-American couple finds themselves in trouble when they are seduced by the gangsta lifestyle of sex, drugs and power. Angela will try anything to stop her and her lover's downward spiral, but can they pull themselves out of danger before it's too late? With a bright young cast.
81-9039 Was $89.99 *$14.99*

Act Of War (1998)
Jack Scalia, America's most accomplished special agent, is assigned to stop a group of terrorists who have captured nuclear warheads and are threatening the life of the president of the Republic of Bazrakistan. When Scalia finds the launch access disc in his hands, he suddenly becomes the most powerful person in the world.
81-9059 *$89.99*

Misled (1998)
A Chicago cop named Charlie Torres goes undercover to try to stop the drug trade in Chicago, but soon gets seduced by the dope and the dollars. When he dupes "Papo" Charlie, the top drug kingpin, Torres finds himself embroiled in a violent urban war.
81-9066 *$99.99*

In The Name Of Justice (1998)
Four friends who witness their family members' killings by a drug dealer make a pact to exact revenge for the deeds. Their plan? Pose as DEA agents and infiltrate and kill the members of the dealer's gang—and, eventually, the dealer himself. An explosive action yarn!
81-9067 *$99.99*

Men Of Means (1998)
Looking for a way out of his life of crime before his psychotic boss launches a violent mob war, small-time hood Michael Paré hatches a scheme to steal counterfeiting plates. Fast-paced and engrossing action tale also stars Raymond Serra, Kaela Dobkin. 80 min.
81-9071 Was $89.99 *$59.99*

The Rocketeer (1991)
Thrilling comic-book fantasy, set in '30s Los Angeles, about a young stunt pilot who finds a rocket pack that enables him to soar through the skies. However, his discovery also puts him in the middle of a deadly search involving the government, Howard Hughes, gangsters, Nazis and a swashbuckling matinee idol. Bill Campbell, Jennifer Connelly, Alan Arkin and Timothy Dalton star. 109 min.
11-1586 Was $19.99 ❑$14.99

Aspen Extreme (1993)
Spectacular ski action highlights this story about two friends who seek the thrills and spills of Aspen, Colorado, snowcapped playground of the rich and famous. They become ski instructors and experience luxury, romance and danger in the extreme. With Paul Gross, Peter Berg and Teri Polo. 118 min.
11-1686 ❑$14.99

Final Round (1993)
A streetwise boxer, his gorgeous lover and a tough former football player are kidnapped by a wealthy psychotic and sent to a secret location, where audiences watch as they are hunted by high-tech killers. Lorenzo Lamas, Kathleen Kinmont and Clark Johnson star in this awesome actioner. AKA: "Human Target." 90 min.
14-3417 Was $89.99 ❑$14.99

Last Of The Redmen (1947)
James Fenimore Cooper's "The Last of the Mohicans" was adapted by Columbia for this exciting drama set in the American wilderness of the mid-18th century, where British settlers battled French forces and their Indian allies. Jon Hall, Evelyn Ankers, Julie Bishop and Michael O'Shea star. 79 min.
02-2359 $19.99

The Last Tomahawk (1965)
One of the first and greatest American adventure novels, Cooper's "The Last of the Mohicans," served as the basis for this European-made drama loaded with thrilling action sequences. Anthony Steffens, Karin Dor, Dan Martin star. 89 min.
68-8841 $19.99

DANIEL DAY-LEWIS
THE LAST OF THE MOHICANS

The Last Of The Mohicans: Millennium Collection (1992)
The American wilderness of the 1750s is the setting for director/co-scripter Michael Mann's grand adaptation of the James Fenimore Cooper adventure classic. Daniel Day-Lewis stars as frontier scout Hawkeye, defending a band of British settlers from attack during the French and Indian Wars. With Madeleine Stowe, Wes Studi, Russell Means. 114 min. NOTE: This version is presented in a 1.85:1 letterbox ratio.
04-2627 Letterboxed ❑$14.99

The Last Of The Mohicans: Widescreen Series
The film is also available in its original theatrical, widescreen format, presented in a 2.35:1 letterbox ratio. Also includes a "behind-the-scenes" featurette and original trailer.
04-3353 Remastered ❑$19.99

James Fenimore Cooper's Leatherstocking Tales (1979)
Grand PBS dramatization of the classic wilderness saga about frontier hero Natty Bumppo and his partner, Chingachgook, the Delaware Indian; culled from parts of "The Deerslayer" and "The Pathfinder." Each tape runs 60 min.

Leatherstocking Tales, Vol. I
52-1064 Was $69.99 $24.99

Leatherstocking Tales, Vol. II
52-1065 Was $69.99 $24.99

The Criminal Mind (1993)
Two long-separated brothers reunite and find themselves on opposite sides of the law, with one man a Los Angeles D.A. and the other a Mafia member on the run from mobsters and the FBI, in this gripping actioner. Ben Cross, Frank Rossi, Tahnee Welch and Lance Henriksen star. 93 min.
02-2843 Was $89.99 ❑$19.99

Ravenhawk (1996)
Bodybuilding body beautiful Rachel McLish stars in this hard-hitting actioner as a Native American woman framed for murdering her parents by sleazy businessmen after their land for use as a nuclear waste facility. After escaping from prison, McLish sets out to bring the killers her own brand of justice. John Enos, Ed Lauter co-star. 89 min.
02-2991 $99.99

Deadly Heroes (1996)
In this action-packed outing, Michael Paré is a Navy SEAL who joins forces with his former partner, now a CIA official, in order to get his wife back from terrorists who have kidnapped her. Jan-Michael Vincent and Billy Drago also star; directed by Menahem Golan. 104 min.
02-3020 ❑$99.99

Storm And Sorrow (1990)
Hair-raising true story about mountain-climbing legend Molly Higgins, who joins a group of professional climbers seeking to scale Russia's treacherous Pamir Mountains. Her journey includes earthquakes, blizzards, avalanches and rivalries between her partners. Lori Singer, Todd Allen star. 96 min.
14-3335 ❑$89.99

Fatal Skies (1990)
Oh, man, has '60s drug mastermind Timothy Leary lost touch with reality? Seems that way, because he's hatched a diabolical plot to ditch toxic waste in a small town. Coming to the rescue are a group of sky-diving teens who get the news first-hand that Timothy Leary is definitely not dead. With Veronica Carrothers. 88 min.
16-9054 Was $79.99 $29.99

Sudden Thunder (1993)
A sexy blonde cop on Miami's toughest enforcement team goes into action when her father, a small-town sheriff, is murdered. Her enemy: a ruthless drug cartel conspiring to take over America. Andrea Lamatsch and Corwyn Sperry star in an explosive tale. 90 min.
16-9133 $14.99

Miami Beach Cops (1993)
Two Persian Gulf veterans return to their Miami home in hopes of some peace and quiet as sheriff's deputies. But their R&R time is interrupted when a local merchant is murdered, forcing them to begin a danger-filled investigation. Frank Maldonatti and Salvatore Rendimo star. 97 min.
16-9139 $14.99

Showdown (1993)
A small town with a population consisting of retired hoodlums is turned into the center of a drug smuggling ring run by a nasty mobster. The local law agent needs help to stop the ring and calls on his martial arts expert friend to thwart them. Richard Lynch, Leo Fong, Troy Donahue and Frank Martin star. 92 min.
16-9141 $14.99

Kill Or Be Killed (1993)
After being released from an eight-year stint in prison, Michael Julian discovers that his brother has become kingpin of a drug empire and has stolen his girlfriend. The sibling rivalry leads to a million-dollar theft, a deadly ambush, warfare between rival drug gangs, and a final battle to the death between brothers. David Heavener, Joseph Nuzzolo star. 97 min.
16-9142 $14.99

Into The West (1993)
Two poor Dublin boys are given an opportunity to escape from an impoverished existence with their alcoholic father with the arrival of a beautiful white stallion that's followed their grandfather to the city. When the animal is nabbed by an unscrupulous horse breeder, the boys take off on a magical and haunting adventure to reclaim it. Gabriel Byrne, Ellen Barkin star. 97 min.
11-1782 ❑$14.99

By The Sword (1994)
Fierce fencing action highlights this enthralling adventure in which an undefeated Olympic champ and an ex-con cross swords in a duel of mortal combat. F. Murray Abraham, Eric Roberts and Mia Sara star. 91 min.
02-2631 Was $89.99 ❑$14.99

Desperate Crimes (1993)
The boyfriend of a woman killed in the crossfire of a mob war recruits a prostitute to help him infiltrate the underworld and find his lover's killers. Traci Lords, Denise Crosby, Franco Columbu star in this wild actioner. 92 min.
16-9143 $14.99

Extreme Vengeance (1993)
Released from prison after 10 years, a brutal crime kingpin is out for revenge on the former cop who put him in the slammer in this explosive action tale of "eye for an eye" justice. With David A. Cox, Tanya George. 97 min.
16-9150 $14.99

Crime Of Crimes (1990)
A series of abductions of children has the parents of Los Angeles in a panic. One detective's search for the missing kids leads to a shocking discovery and a desperate search to stop the kidnappers before they strike again. David Carradine, Richard Yniguez, Susan Saldivar and Aldo Ray star. 88 min.
08-1508 Was $89.99 $19.99

He moves without sound.
Kills without emotion.
Disappears without trace.
THE PROFESSIONAL

The Professional (1994)
Stylish and poignant actioner from director Luc Besson ("La Femme Nikita") focuses on Leon, a lonely French hit man who lives in a cruddy New York apartment and works for a local mob boss. After a 12-year-old neighbor girl's family is slaughtered by a corrupt cop, she moves in with Leon and asks him to show her the tricks of his "trade." Jean Reno, Natalie Portman and Gary Oldman star. AKA: "Leon." 109 min.
02-2760 Was $19.99 ❑$14.99

The Professional (Letterboxed Version)
Also available in a theatrical, widescreen format.
02-3051 $19.99

Total Force (1998)
The creator of a military weapon that utilizes satellite technology to turn people into killing machines decides to keep control of his invention and use it for his own evil purposes. Frank Stallone and Timothy Bottoms are called on to retrieve the weapon, but they soon realize there are other motives behind their dangerous assignment. With Richard Lynch.
81-9054 $99.99

Deadly Sister (1997)
A female serial killer stalks Los Angeles targeting men. Her motive? Revenge for all who wronged her in her past. As the body count grows, two detectives put their lives on the line to track her down. Joyce Sylvester and Donnie Wilson star.
81-9080 Was $89.99 $14.99

Night Of The Twisters (1996)
While his sleepy Nebraska town faces deadly, unpredictable tornadoes, the son of a football star baby-sitting his young brother must survive the night and rescue his family as the weather gets horrendously worse. John Schneider, Devon Sawa and Amos Crawley star in this special effects-filled story. 91 min.
10-2727 $14.99

Terminal Velocity (1994)
High-flying action movie stars Charlie Sheen as a skydiving instructor whose school is closed after student Nastassja Kinski is killed in an accident...until she shows up, alive and well, and draws Sheen into a complicated web of intrigue involving ex-KGB agents. Amazing parachuting stunts are a highlight. 102 min.
11-1875 Was $19.99 ❑$14.99

Homeboyz II: Crack City (1992)
Down and dirty urban drama set on the gang-ruled streets of Harlem, where two youths who survive by selling drugs find themselves at odds with the godfather of the Spanish Mafia and forced to fight for their lives. With Brian Paul Stuart, McKinley Winston. 90 min.
16-9130 $14.99

Fatal Justice (1993)
When the CIA decides their top assassin is too old for his job, they enlist a beautiful female agent to kill him. What she doesn't know is that her target is the father who abandoned her at birth. When she learns the truth, dad and daughter team up to kill the corrupt agency official who ordered the hit. Joe Estevez, Suzanne Ager star. 90 min.
16-9131 $14.99

Brutal Fury (1993)
A female detective goes undercover at a local high school and discovers an all-girl vigilante group called "the Fury" that takes the law into its own hands, killing drug pushers and a school football star suspected of raping several students. Two-fisted actioner stars Tom Campitelli and Lisa-Gabrielle Green. 97 min.
16-9132 $14.99

The Broken Chain (1993)
True-life adventure saga set during the Revolutionary War and focusing on two Iroquois brothers who stage a brave fight to keep their land from being taken over by settlers. Eric Schweig, Wes Studi, Pierce Brosnan and Graham Greene star. 93 min.
18-7480 Was $89.99 ❑$14.99

Surviving The Game (1994)
A ferocious reworking of "The Most Dangerous Game" with rapper Ice-T as a homeless Seattle man enlisted by a group of hunters to lead them on an expedition in the Pacific Northwest, little realizing that he's slated to be the quarry of the sadistic "sportsmen." Rutger Hauer, Charles S. Dutton, Gary Busey and F. Murray Abraham also star. 94 min.
02-2649 Was $19.99 ❑$14.99

Road Kill USA (1993)
"The Hitcher" warned young people never to give rides to psychopaths along the roadway...now this intense action film offers viewers the flip side, as a college student accepts a lift from a pair of murderous drifters and is in danger of becoming their next victim! Andrew Porter, Sean Bridgers star. 98 min.
16-9151 $14.99

Dirty Games (1993)
A world-famous scientist is brutally murdered by a lethal assassin. Six years later, his daughter discovers that the killer is alive and part of a delegation visiting an African nuclear arms site. Can she stop him and his group of terrorists plotting to destroy the complex? Jan-Michael Vincent, Ronald France and Valentina Vargas star. 97 min.
16-9146 $14.99

Decoy (1995)
A deadly game of deception and danger occurs when two tough former intelligence operatives are hired to protect the daughter of their former commanding officer from a group of high-tech mercenaries. Peter Weller, Robert Patrick and Charlotte Lewis star. 83 min.
18-7575 $99.99

CHiPs '99 (1998)
Freewheeling California Highway Patrolmen Ponch (Erik Estrada) and Jon (Larry Wilcox) are back on their bikes in this reunion movie based on the popular '80s cop series, but will the CHiPs be down when they have to tackle a carjacking ring? Robert Pine, Paul Korver also star, with cameos by Judge Judy Sheindlin and Johnnie Cochran. 94 min.
18-7856 Was $89.99 ❑$14.99

Black Snow (1993)
A deadly and beautiful woman holds Travis Winslow's life in her hands as he frantically searches for his kidnapped daughter. It seems that the police and mobsters are after a drug shipment brought in by Winslow's late brother, and now he's stuck in the middle of the search for the drugs. Jane Badler, Peter Sherayko star. 90 min.
16-9153 $14.99

Roadracers (1994)
Rebellious teenagers, fast cars and rock and roll music all add up to high-octane action when a young man in a small town in the '50s runs afoul of the local lawman and his troublemaking son in this retro rouser from director Robert Rodriguez ("From Dusk Till Dawn"). David Arquette, Salma Hayek, John Hawkes star. 93 min.
11-2170 Was $99.99 ❑$14.99

Silent Trigger (1997)
Ex-Special Forces commando-turned-covert government assassin Dolph Lundgren adds another job title to his resumé—that of target—when he and his beautiful partner become the hunted in a deadly race for their lives in this intense actioner. With Gina Bellman, Conrad Dunn. 93 min.
11-2171 Was $99.99 ❑$14.99

Revenge
is a dish
best served
cold.
KILLING TIME
Two Guns Are Better Than One.

Killing Time (1998)
In order to avenge a colleague's murder, a cop hires the world's deadliest—and sexiest—assassin to take out the mob boss responsible. But when he can't pay the hit woman for her assignment, a violent crossfire is unleashed that leads to an explosive climax. Craig Fairbrass, Kendra Torgan star. 91 min.
02-3161 Was $99.99 ❑$14.99

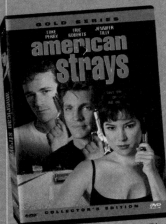

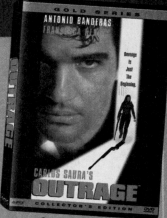

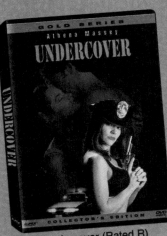
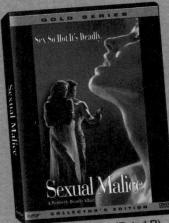
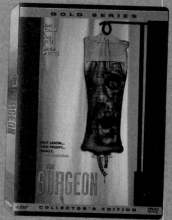
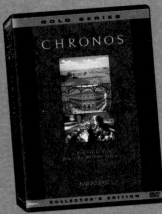

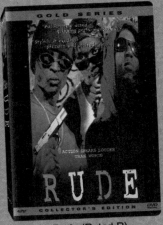
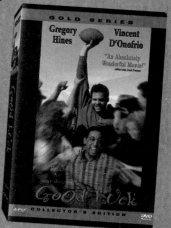

BFS brings you these Classics...

AMERICAN HOME TREASURES

Sharpe's MASTERPIECE THEATRE CLASSIC

Acclaimed actor **Sean Bean** *(James Bond, Patriot Games)* stars in this Masterpiece Theatre Classic, as British officer Richard Sharpe, set in the midst of the desperate missions and battles of the Napoleonic Wars in 19th-century Spain.

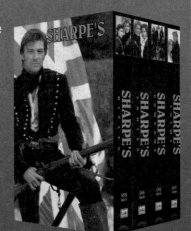

VHS – Collection Set
Cat. #98601-V (4 videos)
approx. 6.5 hrs. col.
UPC 0-66805-98601-7
$69.98 SRP
(also available on individual DVD's
$19.98 SRP each.)

NEW LOWER PRICE ON VHS

"A wonderful melodrama of snobbery and swords, love and hate." – THE GUARDIAN
"Compelling viewing for adventure lovers."
– THE DAILY MAIL

The Six Wives of Henry VIII

Few television series have attracted as much critical and public acclaim as these six triumphant plays, now preserved on video. Each play is a lavish and authentic dramatisation, produced with style and quality. Starring **Keith Michell** as the definitive Henry VIII.

VHS – Collection Set
Cat. #99902-V (6 videos)
approx. 9 hrs. col.
UPC 0-66805-99902-4
$79.98 SRP
(also available on a 3-DVD
Collection Set **$79.98** SRP)

NEW LOWER PRICE ON VHS

"Michell is magnificent; his Henry VIII set the standard against which all others must compare."
– TORONTO STAR

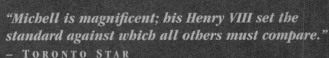

---

and these exciting Best Sellers!

AMERICAN HOME TREASURES

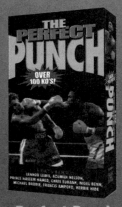

The Perfect Punch
Cat. #30008-V
approx. 76 mins. col.
UPC 0-66805-20008-3
$14.98 SRP
(also available on DVD **$19.98** SRP)

Over 100 of the best knock-out punches ever!

The Three Stooges
Cat. #83012-V
approx. 222 mins. B&W
UPC 0-86624-30012-2
$9.98 SRP
(also available on DVD **$14.98** SRP)

Enjoy these classic movie shorts starring the goofiest characters we ever let into our livingrooms!

Signing Made Easy!
Cat. #83990-V
approx. 55 mins. col.
UPC 6-17873-39903-4
$19.98 SRP
(also available on DVD **$19.98** SRP)

"This is a fabulous piece of work." – LOS ANGELES TIMES
"Fun... excellent."
– LEONARD MALTIN

Play to Win Collection Set
Cat. #83978-V (3 videos)
approx. 123 mins. col.
UPC 6-17873-3978-3-2
$29.98 SRP
(also available on DVD **$19.98** SRP)

Now you can be a winner by knowing the secrets of playing Slots, Blackjack and Craps.

BFS Video and American Home Treasures are divisions of BFS Entertainment & Multimedia Limited, 360 Newkirk Road, Richmond Hill, Ontario, Canada L4C 3G7 Tel (905) 884-2323 Fax (905) 884-8292 www.bfsent.com

Shadow Of The Wolf (1993)
A spectacular adventure set in the Great White North, with Lou Diamond Phillips starring as a young hunter in an Eskimo tribe who is banished by his father, the clan's leader. Struggling to survive against the elements, he later returns to save his people. Toshiro Mifune, Donald Sutherland and Jennifer Tilly also star. 108 min.
02-2413 Was $89.99 ❑*$14.99*

Deadly Ransom (1999)
While on vacation in Rio, a young woman and her Wall Street magnate father are kidnapped by a ruthless gang. It's up to the woman's boyfriend, a Navy SEAL, and a handpicked team of mercenaries to mount a dangerous rescue attempt. Pulse-pounding actioner stars Loren Avedon, John Aprea, Lisa Crosato and Brion James. 90 min.
81-9099 *$59.99*

Sniper (1993)
A tough, thrilling actioner featuring Tom Berenger as a veteran armed forces assassin who is joined by an inexperienced partner from the National Security Council (Billy Zane) while on assignment in the jungles of Panama. Their mission: eliminate a rebel general and a Colombian drug chief. 99 min.
02-2435 Was $19.99 ❑*$14.99*

Money To Burn (1994)
After their friends drop $5 million into their laps, Chad McQueen and Don Swayze can only enjoy spending the loot. It's women, wild thrills and fun in nightclubs and mansions...until the mob comes looking for their cash. Penthouse Pet Julie Strain, Playboy Playmate Kimberly Herrin and Joe Estevez co-star in this action romp. 96 min.
02-2621 Was $19.99 *$14.99*

Eyes Of A Witness (1994)
An American businessman searching for his missing daughter in Kenya gets caught in the middle of a tribal ambush in bush country and is charged with murdering a government official. Can he tackle the legal system, a gang of poachers and the police to save himself and find his daughter? Daniel J. Travanti, Jennifer Grey and Carl Lumbly star. 90 min.
02-2716 Was $89.99 ❑*$19.99*

El Mariachi (1993)
Made for a paltry $7,000 for the Hispanic home video market, Robert Rodriguez's much-acclaimed action-comedy tells the tale of a Mariachi singer who finds himself in the middle of a gang rivalry when he's mistaken for a gun-toting killer. Hip, funny and explosively violent; Carlos Gallardo, Consuelo Gomez star. 81 min. In Spanish with English subtitles.
02-2467 Was $19.99 *$14.99*

El Mariachi (Dubbed Version)
Also available in a dubbed-in-English edition.
02-2468 Was $19.99 *$14.99*

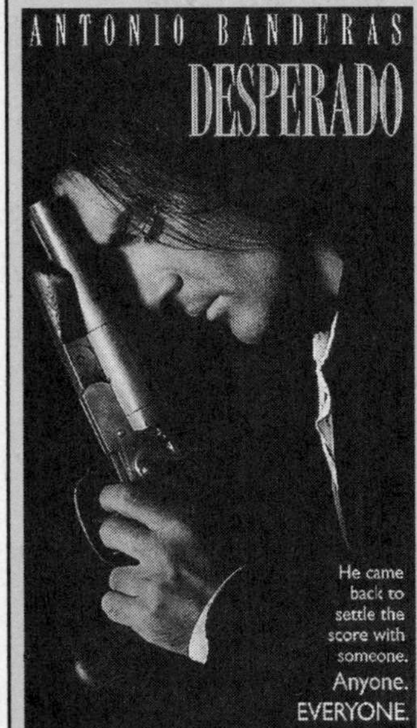

ANTONIO BANDERAS
DESPERADO
He came back to settle the score with someone.
Anyone.
EVERYONE.

Desperado (1995)
Robert Rodriguez's remake of his made-on-pennies sensation "El Mariachi" is an explosive actioner starring Antonio Banderas as the swaggering guitar-player who takes on a series of hombres in a Mexican town ruled by a druglord with whom he has a score to settle. Salma Hayek is his fetching romantic interest; cameos are turned in by Quentin Tarantino and Cheech Marin. 103 min.
02-2839 Was $19.99 ❑*$14.99*

Desperado (Letterboxed Version)
Also available in a theatrical, widescreen format.
02-3052 *$19.99*

Race The Sun (1996)
Lively family adventure featuring Halle Berry as a science teacher at a Hawaiian high school who encourages her disadvantaged students to build a solar-powered car. The students then head to Australia with Berry and cynical shop instructor James Belushi to race the car in an exciting, danger-filled competition. With Casey Affleck, Eliza Dushku. 99 min.
02-2934 Was $19.99 ❑*$14.99*

Excessive Force (1993)
A young Chicago cop (Thomas Ian Griffith) is framed for murder and finds himself caught between mobsters and his own friends on the force in this actioner filled with superior shootouts and martial arts action. Lance Henriksen, James Earl Jones and Charlotte Lewis also star. 87 min.
02-2487 Was $19.99 ❑*$14.99*

Excessive Force II: Force On Force (1995)
A female special agent who once was romantically involved with a fellow agent during the Gulf War now finds herself at the top of her former lover's hit list after he has become the leader of an assassination squad. Stacie Randall, Dan Gauthier star. 88 min.
02-5060 Was $19.99 ❑*$14.99*

Detonator (1993)
A renegade Russian general hijacks a nuclear bomb and sends it toward Iraq on a hijacked train. The situation threatens the world's peace, and only secret agents Pierce Brosnan and Alexandra Paul can halt the dangerous proceedings. Ted Levine, Christopher Lee and Patrick Stewart also star; based on Alistair MacLean's "Death Train." 98 min.
02-2505 ❑*$14.99*

Detonator II: Night Watch (1995)
Alistair MacLean's "Night Watch" is the basis for this sequel to the popular actioner. Pierce Brosnan is a UN special agent who uncovers a North Korean weapon that can destroy global communications systems. There's shoot-outs, chases and stunts galore; with Alexandra Paul, William Devane. 99 min.
02-5071 Was $19.99 ❑*$14.99*

Fortunes Of War (1994)
An American relief worker in Thailand in desperate need of cash is lured into a plot to smuggle medical supplies to a warlord in a jungle fortress. Joining him on his mission are his Cambodian refugee friend and a beautiful French Red Cross worker. Matt Salinger, Michael Ironside, Haing S. Ngor and Martin Sheen star. 107 min.
02-2712 Was $89.99 *$14.99*

American Yakuza (1995)
A rogue undercover agent infiltrating the Japanese secret Mafia known as the Yakuza delves into a deadly underworld to get the goods on some of the organization's most dangerous members. This explosive actioner stars Viggo Mortensen, Michael Nouri, Ryo Ishibashi and Franklyn Ajaye. 96 min.
02-2728 Was $89.99 ❑*$14.99*

Blue Tiger (1994)
A wham-bang actioner starring Virginia Madsen as the mother of a young boy murdered by a Japanese assassin known as the "Blue Tiger." The mother adopts the alter ego of the "Red Tiger" as she infiltrates the Japanese underworld in hopes of getting revenge. With Harry Dean Stanton, Toru Nakamura. 88 min.
02-2739 Was $89.99 ❑*$14.99*

No Contest (1995)
Andrew "No Dice" Clay teams with erotic video queen Shannon Tweed for this actioner in which a legion of deadly terrorists do their dirty work at an international beauty contest, holding the contestants hostage for a $10 million ransom and wiring the building with explosives. Robert Davi and Roddy Piper co-star. 98 min.
02-2784 ❑*$89.99*

Arctic Blue (1995)
In the Alaska wilderness, an environmental biologist squares off against a deadly trapper in a battle for survival against the elements and each other. Rutger Hauer and Dylan Walsh star in this thrilling adventure with action so hot, it could melt the film's icy backdrop. 95 min.
02-2799 Was $19.99 ❑*$14.99*

New York Cop (1995)
Gritty actioner with thrilling shoot-outs and martial arts about a Japanese karate expert who joins the New York Police Department in order to catch a gang of gunrunners dealing with Colombian druglords and the Japanese Yakuza. Chad McQueen, Mira Sorvino and Toru Nakamura star. 88 min.
02-2819 Was $89.99 ❑*$19.99*

Distant Justice (1995)
A gripping actioner about a Japanese family whose visit to Boston turns into tragedy when the mother is murdered and the daughter kidnapped. George Kennedy, the police chief and a friend of the family, launches an investigation that leads right to his own department. With David Carradine. 91 min.
02-2825 *$89.99*

The Stranger (1995)
Action-filled mix of "Pale Rider" and "Easy Rider" about a mysterious woman who arrives in a small desert town ruled by a vicious motorcycle gang and proceeds to take on the bikers in a violent vengeance crusade. Who is she, and what's her link to a brutal crime that occurred there years earlier? Martial artist Kathy Long, Andrew Divoff, Eric Pierpoint star. 98 min.
02-2832 ❑*$89.99*

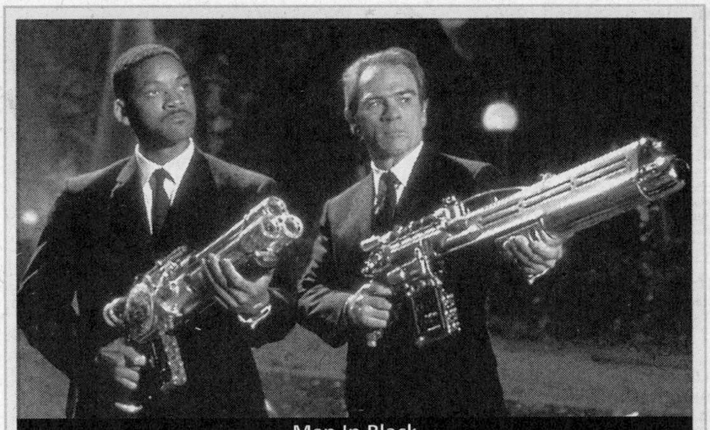

Men In Black

Will Smith

Where The Day Takes You (1992)
Gritty, authentic drama of a group of homeless teens living on the streets of Hollywood. The make-shift family's leader, known as King, is involved in a bitter rivalry with a dangerous pimp. When the pimp is found dead, King and his friends go on the run and take the law into their own hands. Dermot Mulroney, Sean Astin, Lara Flynn Boyle, Ricki Lake, Will Smith and Balthazar Getty star. 107 min.
02-2329 Was $89.99 ❑*$19.99*

Six Degrees Of Separation (1993)
Triumphant translation of John Guare's award-winning play stars Will Smith as Paul, the slick and possibly dangerous con artist who poses as Sidney Poitier's son in order to infiltrate the household of snooty art dealers living on Manhattan's Upper East Side. Donald Sutherland, Stockard Channing, Ian McKellen, Mary Beth Hurt also star. 112 min.
12-2938 Was $19.99 ❑*$14.99*

Six Degrees Of Separation (Letterboxed Version)
Also available in a theatrical, widescreen format.
12-3226 ❑*$14.99*

Bad Boys (1995)
Whatcha' gonna do when the Miami detective duo of family man Martin Lawrence and freewheeling smoothie Will Smith switch identities to investigate missing drug money lifted from police custody? Enthralling chases, wise-cracking dialogue and exciting shoot-outs highlight this comic actioner that co-stars Tea Leoni and Joe Pantoliano. 119 min.
02-2802 Was $19.99 ❑*$14.99*

Bad Boys (Letterboxed Version)
Also available in a theatrical, widescreen format.
02-3236 ❑*$19.99*

Independence Day (1996)
Who will save the Earth after huge alien spacecraft demolish the Empire State Building, the White House, downtown Los Angeles and most of the world's major cities? How about brave pilot Will Smith, satellite specialist Jeff Goldblum and U.S. President Bill Pullman? The smash-hit mixture of sci-fi thrills and disaster movie dramatics also stars Randy Quaid and Robert Loggia. 145 min.
04-3372 Was $19.99 ❑*$14.99*

Independence Day (Letterboxed Version)
Also available in a theatrical, widescreen format.
04-3406 Was $19.99 ❑*$14.99*

Men In Black: Special Edition (1997)
Look out, illegal aliens (and we don't mean the human kind)! Tommy Lee Jones and Will Smith are the nattily-dressed government agents whose top-secret job it is to track down any extraterrestrials landing on Earth and keep tabs on the ones living incognito as humans, all the while keeping the truth hidden from the general public, in this slyly funny, effects-filled sci-fi comedy. With Linda Fiorentino, Vincent D'Onofrio. Special edition includes a "making of" featurette, extended and alternate scenes, and a music video. 98 min.
02-3456 *$14.99*

Men In Black (Letterboxed Version)
Also available in a theatrical, widescreen format.
02-3121 Was $24.99 ❑*$19.99*

Enemy Of The State (1998)
Tightly-wound suspenser starring Will Smith as a labor lawyer who finds himself in the middle of a web of espionage when he accidentally comes into possession of a videotape featuring the assassination of a U.S. congressman. Gene Hackman is the communications expert who tries to help Smith in battling sinister, hi-tech special agents. With Jon Voight, Gabriel Byrne. 132 min.
11-2320 Was $22.99 ❑*$14.99*

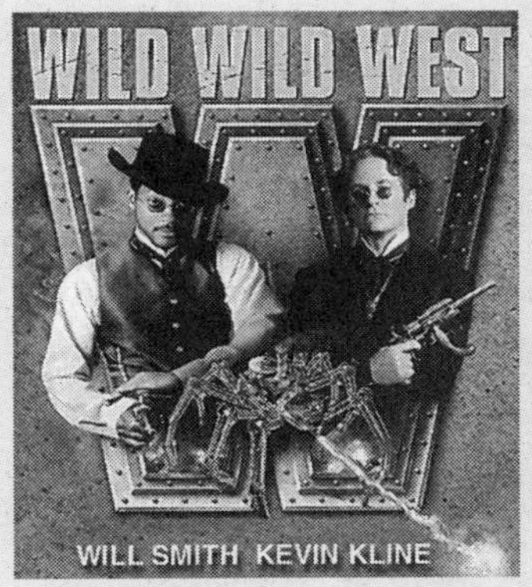

WILD WILD WEST
WILL SMITH KEVIN KLINE

Wild Wild West (1999)
"Men in Black" star Will Smith and director Barry Sonnenfeld reteam for this special effects-filled sagebrusher based on the 1960s TV fave. Smith is government agent James West, who, along with master-of-disguise Artemus Gordon (Kevin Kline), tries to thwart demented handicapped genius Dr. Loveless (Kenneth Branagh) from kidnapping President Grant. Salma Hayek also stars. 105 min.
19-2909 ❑*$22.99*

Wild Wild West (Letterboxed Version)
Also available in a theatrical, widescreen format.
19-2915 ❑*$22.99*

The Will Smith Story
Rapper and actor Will Smith is the "fresh prince" of the entertainment world, winning Grammy Awards for his music and bringing in huge box-office receipts for such hits as "Independence Day" and "Men in Black." This program traces Will's career, including his Philadelphia childhood, his partnership with DJ Jazzy Jeff, breakthrough roles and his personal life. 45 min.
50-8278 *$14.99*

Please see our index for the Will Smith title: *Made In America*

Storm Tracker (1999)
Meteorologist Luke Perry invents a device that can control the direction and intensity of storms, but during a test mission off the Pacific coast maverick general Martin Sheen uses the machine to send a massive hurricane towards Los Angeles. Can Perry stop Sheen and the storm in time? 90 min.
81-9101 *$99.99*

Raw Nerve (1998)
Hard-edged cop Mario Van Peebles' years of flouting the law are beginning to catch up to him, and with Internal Affairs about to expose his shady dealings, his relationship with girlfriend Nicollette Sheridan takes a sinister and deadly turn in this gripping action tale. 102 min.
81-9098 *$99.99*

Hidden Assassin (1996)
U.S. marshal Dolph Lundgren travels to Prague to find the person who has assassinated Cuba's ambassador to the United Nations. The culprit turns out to be a beautiful woman who draws Lundgren into a deadly international conspiracy. Gripping, suspense-filled action tale also stars Maruschka Detmers, John Ashton. 88 min.
11-2044 Was $99.99 ❑$14.99

Mask Of Death (1997)
After his wife is brutally murdered by mobsters, policeman Lorenzo Lamas seeks revenge by undergoing plastic surgery and infiltrating the crooks' world. With help from superior Billy Dee Williams and ex-partner Rae Dawn Chong, Lamas makes the bad guys look not-so-"mahvelous." 89 min.
11-2130 Was $99.99 ❑$14.99

Hawk's Vengeance (1996)
Heavyweight kickboxing champ Gary Daniels flies high in this action-packed thriller about a lieutenant in the British Royal Marines out for revenge against the savage gang responsible for his stepbrother's death. With Jayne Heitmeyer, Cass Magda. 96 min.
11-2180 Was $99.99 ❑$14.99

Bounty Hunters (1997)
At first rivals, a male and female bounty hunter become reluctant partners to track down an escaped criminal that the mob also wants to find—and eliminate—in this action-packed tale starring Michael Dudikoff, Lisa Howard and Benjamin Ratner. 98 min.
11-2202 Was $99.99 ❑$14.99

Royal Deceit (1994)
Set in 6th-century Denmark, this lavish adventure yarn from director Gabriel Axel ("Babette's Feast") tells of the nasty struggle between brothers Gabriel Byrne and Christian Bale over the throne of their father, the murdered king of Jutland. With Helen Mirren, Brian Cox, Kate Beckinsale. AKA: "Prince of Jutland." 85 min.
11-2225 Was $99.99 ❑$19.99

Blackjack (1998)
From screen action master John Woo ("Face/Off") comes a supercharged thriller starring Dolph Lundgren as an agent for the federal Witness Protection Program. His latest assignment, to guard a beautiful supermodel from an expert assassin, could well be his last! Kate Vernon, Philip MacKenzie and Fred Williamson also star. 123 min.
11-2243 Was $19.99 ❑$14.99

The Rage (1998)
Brilliant, psychopathic serial murderer Gary Busey leads a gang of assassins on a brutal cross-country killing spree against political and military leaders, and only FBI agent Lorenzo Lamas can stop them, in this tale filled with action and suspense. Roy Scheider, David Carradine and Kristen Cloke also star. 95 min.
11-2252 Was $99.99 ❑$14.99

Marshal Law (1996)
In the devastating aftermath of an earthquake, former Texas marshal Jimmy Smits must stop a vicious gang from preying on the survivors, including his family and friends, in this explosive actioner. Kristy Swanson, James LeGros also star. 96 min.
12-3099 ❑$99.99

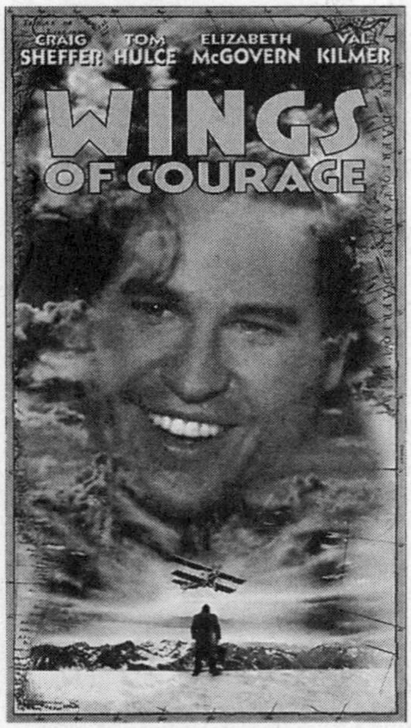

Wings Of Courage (1995)
The first dramatic film to be made for IMAX theaters, this stirring true story, set in South America in the 1930s, follows famed aviators Jean Mermoz and Antoine de Saint-Exupery and the young pilot recruited for their Aeropostale airmail company to fly a dangerous route over the Andes. Craig Sheffer, Tom Hulce, Val Kilmer and Elizabeth McGovern star; Jean-Jacques Annaud ("The Bear") directs. Not in 3-D. 40 min.
02-3066 ❑$19.99

Mercenary 2: Thick And Thin (1999)
While in Latin America, businessman Robert Townsend is kidnapped by a group of commandos working for a military leader. A female associate of the businessman hires a group of mercenaries to retrieve him in this action-packed tale. With Nicolas Turturro, Olivier Gruner and Claudia Christian. 101 min.
11-2331 Was $99.99 ❑$14.99

The Palermo Connection (1991)
James Belushi and Mimi Rogers star in this no-punches-pulled thriller about a tough New Yorker fighting the Mafia-controlled drug trade who travels to Sicily to battle the Mob on their home turf. Joss Ackland, Philippe Noiret also star. 100 min. Please note: Title is available only as a manufacturer's cut-out; though box is new, box has a minor cut on upper flap.
27-6728 Was $89.99 ❑$14.99

Blue Steel (1990)
Novice New York cop Jamie Lee Curtis gets involved with a handsome commodities trader. Little does she know that he's a serial killer who carves her name into bullets and uses her gun to kill innocent people. Ron Silver and Clancy Brown also star in this super-charged, stylish thriller directed by Kathryn Bigelow ("Near Dark"). 102 min.
12-2064 Was $19.99 ❑$14.99

Maximum Security (1996)
After the first group of five inmates arrives at L.A.'s newest prison, it's discovered that the place's real warden and guards have been replaced by international terrorists with a thermonuclear bomb. The prisoners, four crooks and a wrongly convicted policeman, must band together to stop the terrorists before they blow up the city. Paul Michael Robinson and John Lazar star.
21-9130 Was $99.99 $14.99

Fled (1996)
Stephen Baldwin's a movie-obsessed computer expert. Laurence Fishburne is a no-nonsense criminal. Together they're linked on a chain gang, and together they flee following a prison riot, only to find themselves pursued by federal agents and Cuban mobsters. This humorous, action-packed adventure yarn also stars Salma Hayek, Will Patton and Robert John Burke. 98 min.
12-3105 Was $99.99 ❑$19.99

Tidal Wave: No Escape (1997)
A weapons expert and an oceanographer must take down a ruthless terrorist who is planning to destroy portions of the Pacific coastline by creating huge tidal waves unless he gets what he wants. The pair must somehow get to this criminal before time runs out and thousands of lives are lost. Corbin Bernsen, Julianne Phillips and Harve Presnell star. 91 min.
27-7358 ❑$39.99

Sonic Impact (1999)
An FBI agent must lead a force of commandos on a deadly rescue mission after a psychotic criminal takes control of a plane full of innocent civilians and makes plans to crash it into a major city. When the two combatants come face to face, the safety of everyone hangs in the balance in this white-knuckle action ride. James Russo, Ice-T and Mel Harris star. 94 min.
27-7357 ❑$99.99

Masterminds (1997)
Playing like a teenage "Die Hard," this fast-paced action tale is set in an exclusive private school taken over by security expert Patrick Stewart, who plans to hold the students for ransom. It's up to a 14-year-old skateboarding troublemaker and computer whiz to foil Stewart's scheme. Vincent Kartheiser, Matt Craven, Brenda Fricker also star. 120 min.
02-3132 Was $99.99 ❑$14.99

The Substitute (1996)
Mercenary Tom Berenger decides to take matters into his own hands when his teacher girlfriend is brutally assaulted by a thug tied to her school's toughest gang. He poses as a substitute teacher and, in between history classes, uses his soldier-of-fortune skills to try to stop the gang and their drug-dealing activities. Smashing action yarn also stars Ernie Hudson, Diane Venora. 114 min.
27-6979 Was $99.99 ❑$14.99

The Substitute 2: School's Out (1998)
Treat Williams stars in this action-packed sequel as a New York cop who goes undercover as a high school teacher in order to bring the gang members who murdered his brother to justice. With B.D. Wong, Michael Michele and Guru. 90 min.
27-7076 Was $99.99 ❑$14.99

The Substitute 3: Winner Takes All (1999)
When a war buddy's college professor daughter is savagely attacked by some drug-dealing football team members, it's up to the Substitute (Treat Williams) to enter the halls of ivy and, with a team of mercenaries, clean up the campus his own way. Claudia Christian, Rebecca Staab, James Black also star. 90 min.
27-7174 Was $99.99 ❑$14.99

DVD VIDEO
ASK ABOUT OUR GIANT DVD CATALOG!

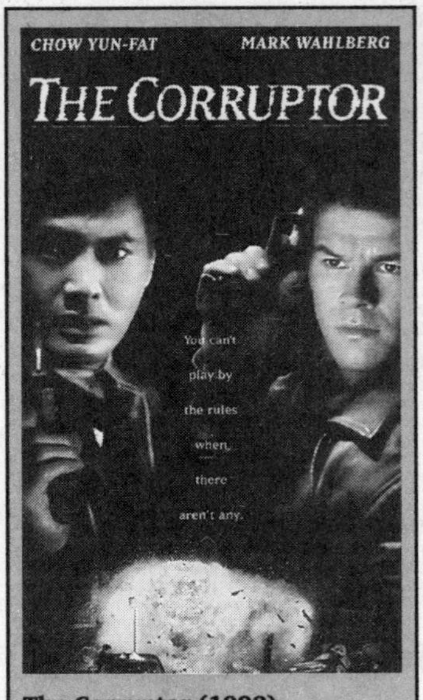

The Corruptor (1999)
In the heart of New York's Chinatown, veteran police detective Chow Yun-Fat and new partner Donnie Wahlberg must stop a violent war between rival crime factions that threatens to tear the city apart. Can this mismatched pair trust each other, or will the secrets they carry cost both their lives? High-octane actioner also stars Ric Young, Brian Cox. 100 min.
02-5213 Was $99.99 ❑$14.99

Anaconda (1997)
A documentary film crew travelling deep into the heart of the Brazilian rain forest becomes the prey for a gigantic, man-eating snake in this slitheringly suspenseful action tale. Jon Voight, Jennifer Lopez, Eric Stoltz, Ice Cube star. 90 min.
02-3107 Was $19.99 ❑$14.99

Anaconda (Letterboxed Version)
Also available in a theatrical, widescreen format.
02-3143 ❑$19.99

Into Thin Air: Death On Everest (1997)
Based on the best-seller by Jon Krakhauer, this intense real-life adventure tells of the disastrous events that occurred on the May, 1996 expedition to the top of Mt. Everest. Two opposing teams led by experienced guides attempt to scale the mountain, but when their trip turns dangerous, they must band together. Christopher McDonald, Peter Horton and Nat Parker star. 90 min.
02-3223 Was $99.99 ❑$19.99

Most Wanted (1997)
Marine officer Keenen Ivory Wayans is chosen to join a secret government security unit and assigned to help guard the First Lady during a visit to Los Angeles. But when the trip ends in assassination and Wayans is framed for murder, he'll need all his combat skills to avoid capture and clear his name. Slam-bang actioner also stars Jon Voight, Jill Hennessy, Eric Roberts. 99 min.
02-5168 Was $19.99 ❑$14.99

In God's Hands (1998)
This change of pace from erotica auteur Zalman King ("Red Shoe Diaries") is an enthralling surfing adventure detailing the lives of three surfers and their quest for perfect waves and perfect women—from Hawaii to Bali to Madagascar. Featuring spectacular surfing footage, the films star real-life pros Patrick Shane Dorian, Matt George and Matty Liu. 97 min.
02-3222 Was $99.99 ❑$14.99

Montana (1998)
Kyra Sedgwick plays a hit woman called on by mobster boss Robbie Coltrane to track down runaway girlfriend Robin Tunney, but forced to team up with her charge when the women are marked for elimination by the crooks, in this intense actioner. Stanley Tucci, John Ritter also star. 97 min.
02-3255 Was $99.99 ❑$19.99

Simon Sez (1999)
Dennis Rodman plays an Interpol agent out to stop an arms deal from happening that could eventually cause mass destruction. Joining him in thwarting the evil gunrunners are two undercover monks and a former operative whose bumbling ways threaten to ruin Rodman's mission. With Dane Cook and Ricky Harris. 86 min.
02-3393 Was $99.99 ❑$14.99

Storm Catcher (1999)
Falsely accused of taking part in the theft of a top-secret, high-tech airplane, Air Force pilot Dolph Lundgren escapes while being transported to prison. Can he catch the renegade general who stole the plane, framed him and kidnapped his daughter? High-flying actioner also stars Robert Miano, Mystro Clark. 95 min.
02-3397 Was $99.99 ❑$14.99

Never Say Die (1995)
Years after he's been declared dead, ex-Marine John Blake returns to seek vengeance against the psychotic renegade commander who ambushed him and to save a general's beautiful kidnapped daughter. Frank Zagarino, Billy Drago and Jennifer Miller star in this all-out action assault. 99 min.
02-5056 Was $89.99 ❑$19.99

Felony (1995)
After a planned police sting operation results in a deadly massacre, a maverick cop looking for the truth behind what happened must track down a telling videotape before the rogue CIA operative behind the sting gets it. Intense actioner stars Leo Rossi, Lance Henriksen, Joe Don Baker, Cory Everson. 90 min.
02-5074 ❑$19.99

Live Wire: Human Timebomb (1995)
A top FBI agent and martial arts expert is captured by a Cuban general who has a mind-controlling computer chip implanted in the American's neck, turning him into a deadly killing machine just waiting to go off. Thrill-packed action tale stars Bryan Genesse, Joe Lara, J. Cynthia Brooks. 98 min.
02-5082 Was $19.99 ❑$14.99

Set It Off (1996)
Tough "Girlz in the Hood" crime drama follows a quartet of inner-city women, best friends since high school, who team up to rob a bank when one of them is unfairly fired from her teller job. Their success leads the foursome to try a few more heists, with tragic results. Jada Pinkett, Queen Latifah, Vivica A. Fox, Kimberly Elise and Blair Underwood star. 83 min.
02-5125 Was $19.99 ❑$14.99

Dangerous Ground (1997)
Returning to his native South Africa for his father's funeral after spending 12 years growing up in America, graduate student and former freedom fighter Ice Cube searches for his missing younger brother and finds that gangs, drugs and street crime have also made their way across the Atlantic. Compelling action tale also stars Elizabeth Hurley, Ving Rhames. 85 min.
02-5130 Was $99.99 ❑$19.99

Made Men (1999)
Former mob member James Belushi, hiding out in the federal witness protection program, is on the run from both sides of the law after stealing $12 million from his ex-employers in this fast-paced actioner. Timothy Dalton, Vanessa Angel, Michael Beach co-star. 90 min.
02-3392 Was $99.99 ❑$14.99

Hard Justice (1995)
Going undercover behind bars in an attempt to find his partner's killer, a two-fisted ATF agent learns that the jail is headquarters for a gunrunning operation and the corruption reaches to the warden's office. Now he must fight to get out with the truth...and his life! Explosive actioner stars David Bradley, Charles Napier, Vernon Wells. 95 min.
02-5084 Was $19.99 ❑$14.99

The Viking Sagas (1996)
When his father is brutally killed and his people forced from their homeland, a young Viking warrior teams with a legendary soldier and a beautiful woman as he fights for vengeance in this thrilling adventure that'll have you pining for the fjords. Ralf Moeller stars. 83 min.
02-5116 Was $99.99 ❑$19.99

Back In Business (1996)
Ex-cop Brian Bosworth gets his chance for revenge when he's contacted by the crooked former colleagues who framed him earlier to take part in a multi-million dollar heroin scheme—but will the hunter become the hunted? In-your-face action tale also stars Joe Torry, Brion James. 93 min.
02-3086 Was $19.99 ❑$14.99

The Mod Squad (1999)
Inspired by the popular '60s TV series, this action effort follows a trio of criminal slackers who use their age and connections to help the L.A. police stop a teen prostitution ring. Claire Danes is Julie, a former heroin addict; Giovanni Ribisi plays rich kid gone wrong Pete; and Omar Epps is Linc, an African-American arsonist. With Dennis Farina, Josh Brolin. 94 min.
12-3279 Was $99.99 ❑$14.99

THE REPLACEMENT KILLERS

The Replacement Killers (1998)
Hong Kong action film icon Chow Yun Fat ("Hard Boiled") makes his Hollywood debut in this stylish, hyper-kinetic thriller. Refusing to complete an assignment from his crimelord boss sends hit man Chow—along with passport forger and reluctant ally Mira Sorvino—on the run from an army of killers as he races to save a child's life and his own family in China. With Kenneth Tsang, Michael Rooker, Jurgen Prochnow. 88 min.
02-3177 Was $99.99 ❑$14.99

The Collectors (1999)
Mob debt collectors Casper Van Dien and Rick Fox find their lives in danger after they scam their crime boss employer by keeping the money for themselves. As they are also pursued by a dedicated female detective, the two must somehow escape New York before someone catches up with them. Catherine Oxenberg also stars. 97 min.
64-9067 $99.99

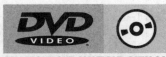

Bruce Willis

Moonlighting (1985)
The slick, sexy, silly adventure that started the hit TV series. Cybill Shepherd is the model-turned-detective and Bruce Willis is her wisecracking partner in a case that involves a punk rock murder, missing diamonds and sadistic Nazis. 93 min.
19-1506 Was $19.99 ***$14.99***

Blind Date (1987)
Blake Edwards' uproarious salute to everyone who's ever been "fixed up" by a friend. Bruce Willis stars as a strait-laced exec, and Kim Basinger is his gorgeous date who wreaks havoc after getting drunk and puts his job, sanity and life in danger. With John Larroquette, Phil Hartman. 93 min.
02-1776 Was $19.99 ***$14.99***

Sunset (1988)
What if movie cowboy Tom Mix teamed up with aging gunslinger Wyatt Earp to solve a murder in 1920s Hollywood? Blake Edwards' engaging comedy/adventure stars Bruce Willis as the cocky matinee idol and James Garner as his world-weary partner. Malcolm McDowell, Mariel Hemingway co-star. 107 min.
02-1874 ***❑$14.99***

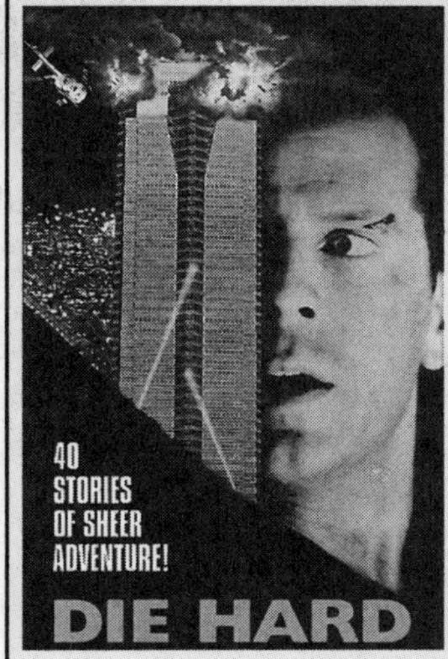

Die Hard (1988)
Terrorists take an L.A. skyscraper and hold everyone inside prisoner...except for New York cop Bruce Willis, who must evade fire from the crooks and the police on his daring one-man rescue mission. Slam-bang action hit also stars Bonnie Bedelia, Alan Rickman and Alexander Gudonov. 131 min.
04-2188 Was $19.99 ***❑$14.99***

Die Hard (Letterboxed Version)
Also available in a theatrical, widescreen format.
04-3447 ***$19.99***

Die Hard II: Die Harder (1990)
Bruce Willis is back as wisecracking Det. John McLane in this spectacular sequel. While awaiting the arrival of his wife's plane at Washington's Dulles Airport, McLane uncovers a terrorist scheme that involves holding the airport at bay and freeing a dictator incarcerated by U.S. troops. Bonnie Bedelia, William Atherton, Franco Nero and John Amos co-star. 124 min.
04-2376 Was $19.99 ***❑$14.99***

Die Hard II: Die Harder (Letterboxed Version)
Also available in a theatrical, widescreen format.
04-3448 ***$19.99***

Die Hard With A Vengeance (1995)
After travelling across America to battle bad guys in the first two films, New York detective Bruce Willis gets to stay on his home turf this time out, as German terrorist leader Jeremy Irons sends Willis and reluctant ally Samuel L. Jackson on a race against time to save several Big Apple sites from being blown to kingdom come. With Graham Greene, Colleen Camp. 131 min.
04-2997 Was $89.99 ***❑$19.99***

Die Hard With A Vengeance (Letterboxed Version)
Also available in a theatrical, widescreen format.
04-3449 ***$19.99***

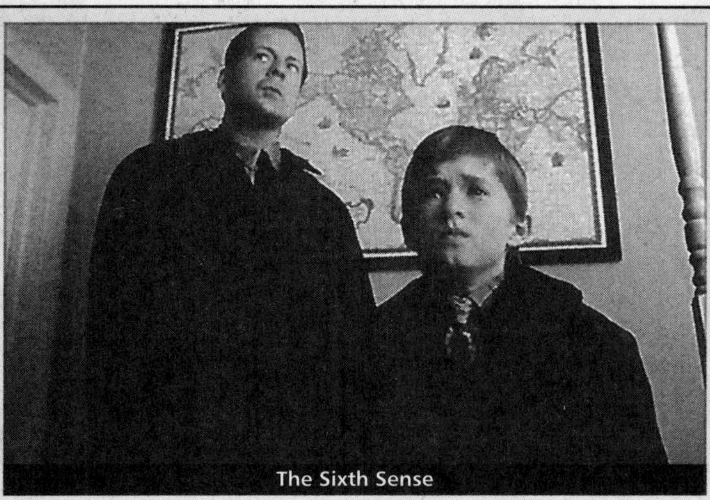
The Sixth Sense

Die Hard Trilogy
Whether it's in a skyscraper, in an airport, or on the streets of New York, Bruce Willis is all action in this boxed set featuring all three "Die Hard" films.
04-3315 Save $5.00! ***$44.99***

Die Hard Trilogy (Letterboxed Version)
The collector's set featuring all three "Die Hard" movies is also available in a theatrical, widescreen format.
04-3316 ***$59.99***

In Country (1989)
Dramatic look at the lives of Vietnam veterans stars Emily Lloyd as a young girl, curious about the war that killed the father she never knew, who attempts to get her uncle, emotionally-scarred vet Bruce Willis, to talk about his experiences. Norman Jewison directs. 120 min.
19-1749 Was $19.99 ***$14.99***

Hudson Hawk (1991)
Globe-trotting action-comedy stars Bruce Willis as a famed former cat burglar drawn into stealing priceless Leonardo Da Vinci artifacts by a group of bizarre characters, who include a pair of neurotic millionaires, an undercover nun and an ex-CIA agent. Danny Aiello, Andie MacDowell, James Coburn, Richard E. Grant and Sandra Bernhard co-star in this wild, stunt-filled ride. 95 min.
02-2119 Was $19.99 ***❑$14.99***

The Last Boy Scout (1991)
A slam-bang actioner with Bruce Willis as a down-on-his-luck private detective who teams with former pro quarterback Damon Wayans to find out who killed a beautiful stripper. The trail leads them to a corrupt football team owner and a sports gambling plot. Chelsea Field, Halle Berry co-star. 105 min.
19-1957 Was $19.99 ***❑$14.99***

Striking Distance (1993)
Gritty suspenser with Bruce Willis as a smart-alecky Pittsburgh cop who accuses his colleagues of corruption and the framing of a man in a serial murder case, and is demoted to the river patrol for his efforts. Two years later, the killings start again, and this time the culprit is targeting women connected with Willis. With Sarah Jessica Parker, Robert Pastorelli, Brion James. 102 min.
02-2533 Was $19.99 ***❑$14.99***

Color Of Night (1994)
In this steamy suspenser, Bruce Willis is a distraught New York psychiatrist who takes over a Los Angeles group therapy session in order to find the killer of his analyst friend. At the same time, Willis is seduced by a mysterious young beauty who may have played a part in the murder. Jane March, Ruben Blades, Lesley Ann Warren co-star; presented in a scorching 140-minute director's cut edition.
11-1858 Was $19.99 ***❑$14.99***

12 Monkeys (1995)
An exciting, intelligent science-fiction adventure from Terry Gilliam starring Bruce Willis as a convict from the year 2035 sent back to 1996, where he attempts to find the cause of a deadly virus that has ravaged his future world. With help from psychiatrist Madeleine Stowe, Willis tracks the germ's invention to mental patient Brad Pitt, the son of a prominent scientist. 130 min.
07-2422 Was $99.99 ***❑$19.99***

12 Monkeys (Letterboxed Version)
Also available in a theatrical, widescreen format.
07-2473 ***$19.99***

Last Man Standing (1996)
An explosive reworking of Akira Kurosawa's "Yojimbo" (which was previously remade as "A Fistful of Dollars") stars Bruce Willis as a mysterious gunslinger who plays the two rival gangs who rule a Depression-era Texas town against each other for his own enjoyment and profit. Christopher Walken, Bruce Dern and Karina Lombard also star in Walter Hill's dynamic mix of the gangster and sagebrush genres. 101 min.
02-5120 Was $19.99 ***❑$14.99***

Last Man Standing (Letterboxed Version)
Also available in a theatrical, widescreen format.
02-5136 ***❑$19.99***

The Fifth Element (1997)
In the 23rd century, a mysterious young woman carries inside her the secret to saving all life on Earth against a sinister enemy, and the key to her survival rests with New York "sky cabby" and reluctant hero Bruce Willis. Writer/co-scripter Luc Besson's visually stunning sci-fi adventure also stars Milla Jovovich, Gary Oldman, Chris Tucker and Luke Perry. 126 min.
02-3111 Was $19.99 ***❑$14.99***

The Fifth Element (Letterboxed Version)
Also available in a theatrical, widescreen format.
02-3158 Was $19.99 ***❑$14.99***

The Jackal (1997)
He's the world's deadliest and most mysterious assassin-for-hire, and someone in the White House is his latest target. Bruce Willis is the ruthless Jackal, and Richard Gere is a jailed IRA terrorist who may be the FBI's only hope of catching Willis before he strikes, in this gripping revamping of Frederick Forsyth's "Day of the Jackal." Sidney Poitier, Diane Venora also star. 125 min.
07-2616 Was $99.99 ***❑$14.99***

The Jackal (Letterboxed Version)
Also available in a theatrical, widescreen format.
07-2619 Was $99.99 ***❑$14.99***

Mercury Rising (1998)
Bruce Willis stars in this nail-biting suspenser as an FBI agent racing to protect a young autistic boy who accidentally cracks a top-secret government code and is targeted for "elimination" by NSA official Alec Baldwin. With Miko Hughes, Kim Dickens; Harold Becker ("Sea of Love") directs. 112 min.
07-2662 Was $99.99 ***❑$14.99***

Mercury Rising (Letterboxed Version)
Also available in a theatrical, widescreen format.
07-2663 Was $99.99 ***❑$19.99***

Armageddon (1998)
A "global killer" asteroid the size of Texas is heading towards Earth, and the future of the planet rests with a misfit group of oil-drilling experts. Their job: land a space shuttle on the rock and plant a nuclear device inside to blow it up. Striking special effects highlight this smash hit that stars Bruce Willis, Ben Affleck, Liv Tyler, Will Patton, Steve Buscemi and Billy Bob Thornton; directed by Michael Bay ("The Rock"). 151 min.
11-2806 Was $19.99 ***❑$14.99***

Armageddon (Letterboxed Version)
Also available in a theatrical, widescreen format.
11-2270 ***❑$22.99***

Breakfast Of Champions (1999)
Dwayne Hoover (Bruce Willis) is Midway City's biggest car dealer, but business success doesn't make up for a stormy private life—with crises ranging from a drug-addled wife (Barbara Hershey) to a cross-dressing sales manager (Nick Nolte)—that has him close to a mental breakdown. Does Dwayne's salvation lie with enigmatic author Kilgore Trout (Albert Finney)? Kurt Vonnegut's classic satirical novel comes to the screen via writer/director Alan Rudolph; with Glenne Headly, Lukas Haas, Omar Epps. 110 min.
11-2394 ***❑$99.99***

The Sixth Sense (1999)
Haunted by his failure to help a former patient who shot him before killing himself a year earlier, Philadelphia child psychologist Bruce Willis sees a chance for redemption when he tries to help 8-year-old Haley Joel Osment, who likewise is haunted—literally, in his case. Writer/director M. Night Shyamalan's eerie supernatural thriller, with a twist ending that demands more than one viewing, also stars Toni Collette, Olivia Williams. 107 min.
11-2397 Was $99.99 ***❑$22.99***

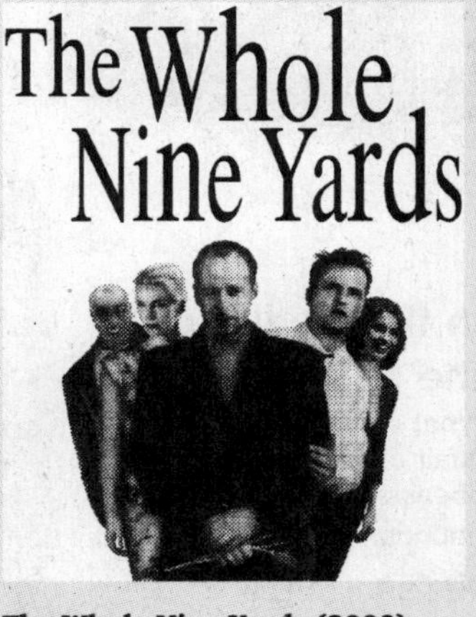

The Whole Nine Yards (2000)
Bruce Willis is a Chicago mob hit man and Witness Protection Program participant who moves into a suburban Montreal neighborhood next to dentist Matthew Perry and wife Rosanna Arquette. When Perry recognizes his new neighbor, Arquette tries to persuade him to turn Willis in to collect a large reward, prompting a series of hilarious complications. Amanda Peet, Natasha Henstridge, Michael Clarke Duncan and Kevin Pollak also star. 98 min.
19-2984 ***❑$99.99***

Please see our index for these other Bruce Willis titles: *The Bonfire Of The Vanities • Death Becomes Her • The First Deadly Sin • Four Rooms • Look Who's Talking • Look Who's Talking Too • Mortal Thoughts • Nobody's Fool • North • Pulp Fiction • The Siege • The Story Of Us*

Heart Of Darkness (1994)
In turn-of-the-century Africa, sea captain Marlow (Tim Roth) pursues Kurtz (John Malkovich), the deranged head of a trading station who is worshipped as a god by the natives. The two face off in an explosive battle of wits in the dangerous jungles of the Congo; Nicolas Roeg directs this powerful adaptation of Joseph Conrad's classic novella, which also served as the inspiration for "Apocalypse Now." 105 min.
18-7473 ***❑$89.99***

Men Of War (1995)
High-octane actioner stars Dolph Lundgren as an ex-Special Forces soldier who's hired to head up a mercenary team charged with getting the inhabitants of a South Pacific island to sign over their land rights...or else. When Lundgren and some of his men decide to support the islanders, an explosive confrontation is sure to follow. With Charlotte Lewis, B.D. Wong, Anthony John Denison. 102 min.
11-1957 Was $89.99 ***❑$14.99***

Plunkett & Macleane (1999)
"Tom Jones" meets "Butch Cassidy and the Sundance Kid" in this witty, action-packed romp set in 18th-century England. "Trainspotting" chums Robert Carlyle and Jonny Lee Miller play a pair of ne'er-do-wells who become coach-robbing highwaymen, lining their pockets with gold, romancing the ladies, and staying one step ahead of the law. Liv Tyler, Ken Stott, Michael Gambon also star. 102 min.
02-9201 Was $99.99 ***❑$14.99***

The Getaway (1994)
This remake of Sam Peckinpah's action favorite stars Alec Baldwin as a slick thief married to partner Kim Basinger who pacts with sleazy crook James Woods to get sprung from jail. Baldwin agrees to participate in a heist at a dog track, but a series of double-crosses sends the couple on the lam from the law and his partners. Michael Madsen co-stars. Steamy unrated version features footage not seen in theaters. 116 min.
07-2121 Was $19.99 ***❑$14.99***

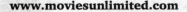

Sensual Adventures

On VHS® and DVD VIDEO

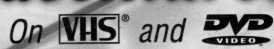

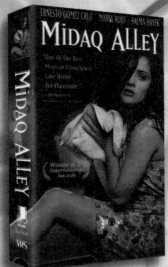

Midaq Alley
The story of three neighbors and the inseparable connection that ties their lives together.

VHS SRP: $19.99
DVD SRP: $29.99

"Intriguing, funny, ...sexy." *—Variety*

1-900
A phone sex rendezvous tests the boundaries of fantasy and power.

VHS SRP: $19.99
DVD SRP: $29.99

Emmanuelle
Sylvia Kristel stars in this groundbreaking exploration of sexual passion.

VHS SRP: $19.99
DVD SRP: $29.99

"EMMANUELLE IS A...CLASSY ENJOYABLE EROTIC FILM." —Roger Ebert

In the Realm of the Senses
What starts as a casual affair escalates into an obsession that knows no bounds.

VHS SRP: $19.99
DVD SRP: $29.99

In the Realm of Passion
The mature ghost story of a jilted husband who returns to haunt his wife and her lover.

VHS SRP: $19.99
DVD SRP: $29.99

Emmanuelle 2
The classic sequel to the erotic blockbuster, starring Sylvia Kristel.

VHS SRP: $19.99
DVD SRP: $29.99

Erotique
A sexually-charged anthology of erotic short films told from a female perspective.

VHS SRP: $19.99
DVD SRP: $29.99

winstar

THE STRANGEST, MOST HORRIFYING COLLECTION EVER COMPILED!

Faces Of Death: Fact Or Fiction?
Unlock some of the mysteries behind one of the most controversial series ever made! Creator/Director Conan Le Cilaire reveals inside information about infamous scenes. VHS exclusives: *Scenes From The Underground* and the *Faces of Death* music video. 60 min.

#50-7555   VHS $19.99

The Strange And The Gruesome
A collection of the oddest and most repulsive events ever captured on film. Watch graphic surgeries, body mutilation, circumcision and animal slaughter. Not for the squeamish! 54 min.

#50-7556   VHS $19.99

Faces Of Death/Faces Of Death: Fact Or Fiction
Re-live the horror of the original *Faces Of Death* through the cleanest crispest version of the cult classic that's ever been released! Also includes *Faces Of Death: Fact Or Fiction*, Gorgon Video trailers and spanish subtitles. 155 min.

#D1-5750   DVD $24.99

ALSO AVAILABLE THE CLASSIC ORIGINALS!

Faces Of Death 15-9046 $19.99	**Faces Of Death IV** 15-9049 $19.99
Faces Of Death II 15-9047 $19.99	**The Worst Of Faces Of Death** 15-9050 $19.99
Faces Of Death III 15-9048 $19.99	**Faces Of Death Boxed Set** 15-9053 $99.99

CULT FAVORITES

Alien Terror
48-1066 $14.99

Beyond Bizarre
7 Volumes Available
$14.99 Each

Come Die With Me
50-7052 $14.99

Cult Of The Dead
48-1032 $14.99

Dan Curtis' Dracula
50-7041 $19.99

Dead Of Night
(1977)
50-7048 $19.99

Death Spa
50-6625 $19.99

Dance Of Death
68-8229 $14.99

Frankenstein
(1973)
50-7044 $14.99

Henry: Portrait Of A Serial Killer
50-6575 $19.99

Henry: Portrait Of A Serial Killer 2
50-7504 $19.99

The Invasion Of Carol Enders
50-7049 $14.99

Mondo Cane
(It's A Dog's World)
50-1170 $19.99

Nightmare at 43 Hillcrest
50-7050 $14.99

The Picture Of Dorian Gray
(1975)
50-7047 $14.99

Shadow Of Fear
50-7053 $14.99

The Strange Case Of Dr. Jekyll & Mr. Hyde
(1968)
50-7045 $14.99

The Texas Chainsaw Massacre
50-7144 $19.99

The Torture Zone
68-8233 $14.99

The Turn Of The Screw
(1974)
50-7046 $14.99

The Magic Stone (1994)
Set during the 10th century, this adventure saga tells of a young Irish slave who escapes from his Viking captors when their ship stops on the shores of North America. While being pursued by a Viking warrior, the slave is befriended by a group of Native Americans involved in their own battles with the Norsemen. Christopher Johnson and Robert McDonough star. AKA: "Kilian's Chronicle." 95 min.
76-9106 Was $99.99 *$14.99*

Heat In The Hood (1997)
A city is threatened by a killer whose victims are all teenage girls. The murderer believes nobody will catch him, but maverick Detective Bo Butler has other plans. Will Butler's crime-solving abilities work against this diabolical killer? With Ben Guillory and Joel Neiss.
81-9081 Was $89.99 *$14.99*

Warrior Brother (1998)
One man out to protect the unprotected wanders the streets looking to solve any criminal problems he faces. When he believes he's found his new love, his life appears to be settled—until he has to deal with the woman's boyfriend. With a bright young cast.
81-9082 Was $89.99 *$14.99*

Crack Down (1998)
A South American drug cartel takes control of a Caribbean island, but expert DEA agents arrest the cartel's leader. The drug kingpin buys his freedom, then claims he will get even with the agents who had him captured. Gerard Anthony and Tricia Lee Keishell star.
81-9083 Was $89.99 *$14.99*

Diamondbacks (1999)
A renegade militia group known as the Diamondbacks seize control of a space tracking station and take an orbiting shuttle and its crew hostage. Two NASA controllers are called in to try to stop the diabolical Diamondbacks and rescue the astronauts before time runs out. Miles O'Keeffe, Chris Mitchum and Timothy Bottoms star. 90 min.
81-9086 *$69.99*

Wanted (1999)
A young man's career as a mob debt collector is permanently sidetracked when his boss is killed in a failed sting operation. On the run from both sides of the law, the hood finds refuge in a Catholic school for troubled boys...but for how long? Fast-paced thriller stars Michael Sutton, Timothy Busfield, Robert Culp, Tracey Gold. 92 min.
81-9093 *$69.99*

Angel's Dance (1999)
High-impact thriller stars Jim Belushi as a top Mafia hit man charged with training neophyte gunman Kyle Chandler to follow in his bloody footsteps. Things go great until the woman picked at random to be Chandler's "final exam"—mysterious Angel Chaste (Sheryl Lee)—proves to be more than a match for them.
81-9096 *$99.99*

Forgotten City (1997)
Stockbroker James Wheeler (Robert Patrick) wishes he'd registered at Crate and Barrel when the antique tray he gets as a gift from his brother turns out to be the key to a lost Mayan civilization. Soon, he's fighting off sickness, archeologists and Fred Ward during an action-packed race to the lost city. Will its treasures be worth the risk? 96 min.
81-9103 *$99.99*

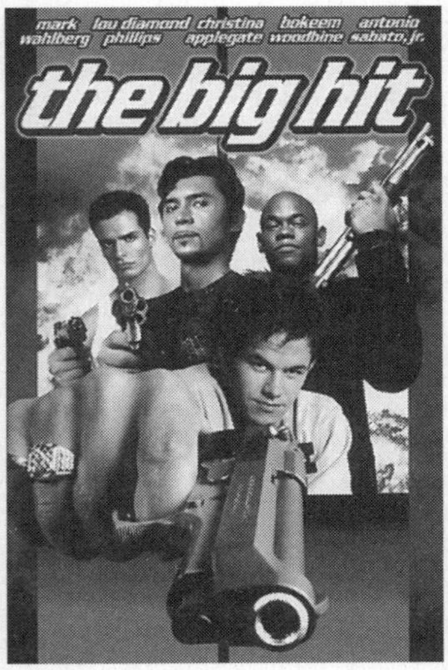

The Big Hit (1998)
Electrifying mix of high-octane action and laughs starring Mark Wahlberg, Lou Diamond Phillips, Bokeem Woodbine and Antonio Sabato, Jr. as a team of fiercely competitive hit men. Phillips gets an idea for some quick "freelance" cash by kidnapping the daughter of a Japanese businessman, unaware that she's their boss's goddaughter. This first American effort from Hong Kong's Kirk Wong ("Crime Story") also features Christina Applegate, Lela Rochon, China Chow and Avery Brooks. 91 min.
02-3226 Was $99.99 ❑*$14.99*

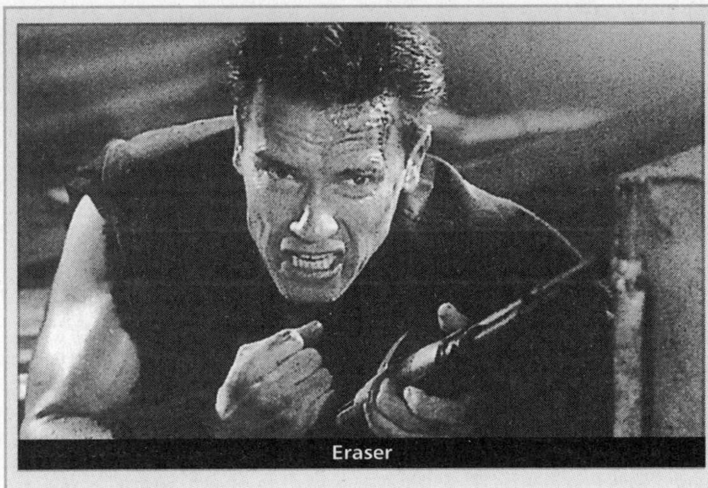

Eraser

Arnold Schwarzenegger

Hercules In New York (1970)
Muscular movie megastar Arnold Schwarzenegger made his film debut (under the name "Arnold Strong") in this Herculean comedy. Bored with life on Mount Olympus, the legendary Greek hero leaves and lands in 20th-century New York, getting mixed up with crooked wrestling promoters and pretzel seller Arnold Stang. With James Karen, Taina Elg. This special edition features Schwarzenegger's own voice on the soundtrack for the first time on home video. AKA: "Hercules Goes Bananas." 91 min.
50-6838 *$14.99*

The Villain (1979)
A wacky western spoof from Hal Needham ("Smokey and the Bandit") starring Kirk Douglas as a calamity-prone outlaw who is continually impeded in his pursuit of "innocent" damsel-in-distress Ann-Margret by white-clad hero Arnold Schwarzenegger. Paul Lynde, Ruth Buzzi, Foster Brooks also star. 88 min.
02-2252 Was $19.99 *$14.99*

Conan The Barbarian (1982)
Sword-and-sorcery fantasy, based on the adventures of Robert E. Howard's pulp novel warrior, ushered in a wave of imitators and launched the career of star Arnold Schwarzenegger. After enduring the murder of his parents and his enslavement by evil leader Thulsa Doom (James Earl Jones), Conan sets out on a mission of vengeance. Co-stars Max von Sydow, Sandahl Bergman; directed by John Milius. 115 min.
07-1116 *$14.99*

Conan The Destroyer (1984)
The titular tower of strength, Arnold Schwarzenegger, returns in this action-filled sequel that finds the Hyborian Age swordsman battling all manner of beasts and brawlers while on a quest to recover a mystical gem. Co-stars Grace Jones, Wilt Chamberlain, Olivia d'Abo and Mako. 103 min.
07-1232 ❑*$14.99*

The Terminator (1984)
Arnold Schwarzenegger is the unstoppable killing machine sent back in time to the 20th century to "terminate" the woman whose child would someday lead a revolt against the mechanical rulers of future Earth. James Cameron's monster sci-fi hit also stars Linda Hamilton, Michael Biehn. 108 min.
27-6928 *$14.99*

The Terminator (Letterboxed Version)
Also available in a theatrical, widescreen format.
27-6929 Was $19.99 *$14.99*

Terminator 2: Judgment Day (1991)
Schwarzenegger the cyborg is "baaack" in a big way, this time defending Sarah Connor (Linda Hamilton) and her young son from a killing machine from the future with the ability to change its shape. Oscar-winning special effects, fine acting, and real heart make this James Cameron production a pulse-pounding classic. With Robert Patrick, Edward Furlong. 135 min.
27-6729 Was $99.99 ❑*$14.99*

Terminator 2: Judgment Day (Letterboxed Version)
Also available in a theatrical, widescreen format.
27-6980 Was $19.99 ❑*$14.99*

Red Sonja (1985)
Fantasy's famed "she-devil with a sword" comes to the screen, as fiery Sonja (Brigitte Nielsen) and warrior Kalidor (Arnold Schwarzenegger) battle all enemies to defeat an evil sorceress who plans to rule the world. Co-stars Sandahl Bergman, Paul Smith, Ernie Reyes, Jr.; directed by Richard Fleischer. 88 min.
12-1158 Was $19.99 ❑*$14.99*

Commando (1985)
Riding the wave of success he attained with "The Terminator," Arnold Schwarzenegger followed with this humor-laden actioner, starring as a former Special Forces colonel who attempts to rescue his kidnapped daughter from South American revolutionaries, who demand he assassinate their country's president. Co-stars Rae Dawn Chong, Vernon Wells and Alyssa Milano. 90 min.
04-3881 ❑*$14.99*

Raw Deal (1986)
That's what ex-FBI agent Arnold Schwarzenegger gives the bad guys in this full-tilt actioner, as he goes undercover to help a former colleague bring down a crime kingpin responsible for the death of a friend's son. Co-stars Kathryn Harrold, Darren McGavin. 97 min.
08-8430 Letterboxed *$14.99*

Raw Deal (1986)
That's what ex-FBI agent Arnold Schwarzenegger gives the bad guys in this full-tilt actioner, as he goes undercover to help a former colleague bring down a crime kingpin responsible for the death of the friend's son. Co-stars Kathryn Harrold, Darren McGavin. 97 min.
44-1420 ❑*$14.99*

Predator (1987)
Schwarzenegger blows the screen apart as the top-kick of a special forces commando unit whose mission to South America has hit a horrifying snag...the presence of a huge, carnivorous extraterrestrial being who turns the hunters into the hunted. Co-stars Carl Weathers, Jesse "the Body" Ventura. 107 min.
04-2114 Was $89.99 ❑*$14.99*

The Running Man (1987)
It's the top-rated TV show in the future, where condemned criminals fight for survival, and the latest contestant is Arnold Schwarzenegger! Can the Austrian Atlas defeat a bizarre succession of adversaries and clear his name? Exciting sci-fi actioner, based on a Stephen King story, co-stars Richard Dawson as the slimy emcee, Maria Conchita Alonso, Jesse "the Body" Ventura. 101 min.
47-1842 *$14.99*

Twins (1988)
Double your pleasure, double your fun, with Arnold Schwarzenegger and Danny DeVito as mismatched siblings, the product of a genetics experiment that went farblondjet. Mental and physical giant Arnold flexes his comedic muscles as he searches for lowlife brother Danny on the streets of L.A. With Chloe Webb, Kelly Preston. 107 min.
07-1612 Was $19.99 ❑*$14.99*

Red Heat (1988)
The "Cold War" was never hotter! Soviet officer Arnold Schwarzenegger teams up with maverick Chicago cop Jim Belushi to bring back a Russian criminal who's tearing up the streets of the Windy City. Fast-paced hit also stars Peter Boyle, Ed O'Ross, Larry Fishburne, Gina Gershon; Walter Hill directs. 104 min.
27-6598 Was $89.99 ❑*$14.99*

Total Recall (1990)
What would you do if all your memories turned out to be lies? For 21st-century laborer Arnold Schwarzenegger, dreams of a life on Mars drive him to journey to the colonized planet, only to find himself a wanted an in the middle of a worldwide rebellion. Outstanding effects and Arnold at his toughest highlight this wild sci-fi blockbuster from "RoboCop" director Paul Verhoeven; with Rachel Ticotin, Sharon Stone, Ronny Cox. 113 min.
27-6684 Was $24.99 ❑*$14.99*

Kindergarten Cop (1990)
In this action-comedy, Arnold Schwarzenegger plays an L.A. cop who poses as a kindergarten teacher in order to track down a vicious drug dealer. The laughs, chases and shoot-outs come fast and furious in this hit from director Ivan Reitman ("Twins"). With Pamela Reed, Penelope Ann Miller, Richard Tyson and Carroll Baker. 110 min.
07-1685 Was $19.99 ❑*$14.99*

Last Action Hero (1993)
Using a magical ticket he received from an elderly projectionist, a movie-obsessed 12-year-old boy finds himself transported into the fictional world of his film hero, macho L.A. cop Jack Slater (Arnold Schwarzenegger). Co-starring Austin O'Brien, Mercedes Ruehl and Charles Dance, this elaborate action-comedy features cameos by Maria Shriver, Jean-Claude Van Damme and others. 131 min.
02-2478 Was $19.99 ❑*$14.99*

Last Action Hero (Letterboxed Version)
Also available in a theatrical, widescreen format.
02-3205 ❑*$19.99*

True Lies (1994)
Arnold Schwarzenegger plays a master spy who can defuse nuclear weapons and speak six languages, although his wife (Jamie Lee Curtis) thinks he's a staid computer salesman. Soon the couple is caught in an adventure filled with danger and excitement. Can it save their troubled marriage? James Cameron's stunt-filled thriller co-stars Tom Arnold, Tia Carrere and Charlton Heston. 141 min.
04-2866 Was $19.99 ❑*$14.99*

True Lies (Letterboxed Version)
Also available in a theatrical, widescreen format.
04-3355 *$19.99*

Junior (1994)
He's been a Barbarian, a cyborg and a spy, but is Arnold Schwarzenegger ready to be...a mother? Thanks to an embryonic implant and an experimental fertility drug he devised with partner Danny DeVito, scientist Arnold gets in touch with his feminine side, and strikes up a romance with fellow researcher Emma Thompson, in this offbeat and touching comedy from director Ivan Reitman ("Twins"). With Frank Langella, Pamela Reed. 110 min.
07-2273 Was $19.99 ❑*$14.99*

Eraser (1996)
In this powerhouse actioner, Arnold Schwarzenegger is a no-nonsense government agent who "wipes out" the pasts of federal witnesses. When a woman working for a powerful arms company decides to blow the whistle on her associates' dirty dealings, Arnold protects her—and uncovers a deadly conspiracy in the process. With Vanessa L. Williams, James Caan and Robert Pastorelli. 115 min.
19-2470 Was $19.99 ❑*$14.99*

Eraser (Letterboxed Version)
Also available in a theatrical, widescreen format.
19-2550 ❑*$19.99*

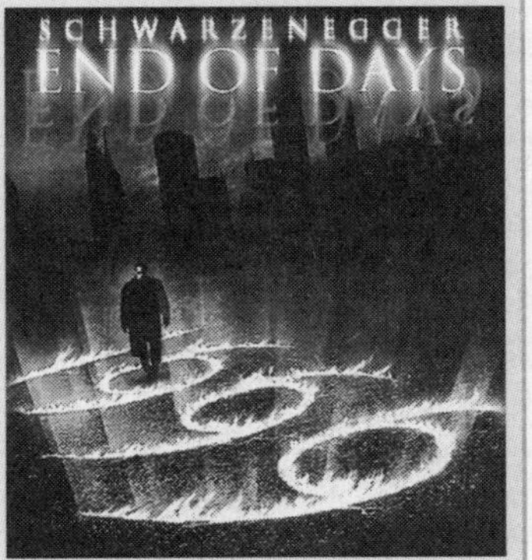

End Of Days (1999)
Embittered ex-cop/security expert Arnold Schwarzenegger becomes the protector of a young woman (Robin Tunney) prophesized to give birth to the Antichrist after she's impregnated by Satan on the last hour of New Year's Eve, 1999. A thrilling race against time and the forces of Hell ensues as Arnold battles an incarnated devil (Gabriel Byrne) in this apocalyptic actioner. With Kevin Pollak, Rod Steiger. 123 min.
07-2847 Was $99.99 ❑*$19.99*

Schwarzenegger Action 5-Pack
Fans of the film world's ultimate action star will love this collection of ultimate action flicks, including "Predator," "The Terminator," "Terminator 2: Judgment Day," "Total Recall" and "True Lies."
04-3850 Save $30.00! *$64.99*

Schwarzenegger Action Three-Pack
Here's a pumped-up package with three of Arnold's biggest action hits in a money-saving gift set. Includes "Red Heat," "The Running Man" and "Total Recall."
27-6739 Save $13.00! *$29.99*

Please see our index for these other Arnold Schwarzenegger titles: *Batman & Robin • Jingle All The Way • The Long Goodbye • Stay Hungry*

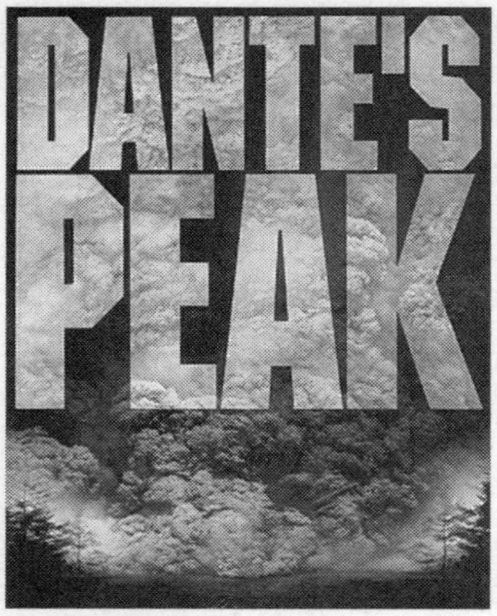

Dante's Peak (1997)
A tranquil town in the Pacific Northwest becomes a Hell on Earth when the long-dormant volcano that gave the community its name becomes active again and erupts, unleashing showers of hot ash and deadly rivers of molten lava, in this (literally) explosive action hit. Pierce Brosnan, Linda Hamilton, Elizabeth Hoffman star. Special video edition includes 15 minutes of behind-the-scenes footage. 109 min.
07-2537 Was $99.99 ❑*$14.99*

Dante's Peak (Letterboxed Version)
Also available in a theatrical, widescreen format.
07-2547 Was $99.99 ❑*$19.99*

Back To Back (1996)
It's action across the Pacific when a down-and-out cop becomes reluctant partners with a killer for the Yakuza in order to take down the enemies who are after both of them in this offbeat "buddy thriller." Michael Rooker, Ryo Ishibashi, Bobcat Goldthwait, Danielle Harris star. 95 min.
02-8656 Was $99.99 ❑*$14.99*

Bloodmoon (1997)
A detective teams up with a "mindhunter" who aids the police in tracking down serial killers in order to capture a demented murderer terrorizing New York City in this thriller loaded with action and suspense. Gary Daniels, Chuck Jeffries, Nina Repeta and Frank Gorshin star. 105 min.
02-8779 Was $99.99 ❑*$14.99*

Body Count (1997)
An ex-con reluctantly returns to a life of crime when a buddy talks him into taking part in a "foolproof" heist at a Boston art gallery, but the easy job turns into a life-or-death run from the police that has the crooks at each other's throats. Action-packed caper tale stars Ving Rhames, Forest Whitaker, David Caruso, John Leguizamo and Linda Fiorentino. 84 min.
02-8834 Was $19.99 ❑*$14.99*

Resurrection Man (1998)
Powerhouse crime drama from Ireland stars Stuart Townsend as a Cagney-fixated hood whose cocaine-fueled violent streak serves him well as he climbs up the ladder of criminal success, until his own excesses and a reporter's investigations start to drag him down. James Nesbitt, Brenda Fricker also star. 102 min.
02-9106 Was $99.99 ❑*$14.99*

Downtown (1990)
White Philadelphia cop Anthony Edwards gets transferred from his cushy suburban beat to the crime-ridden inner city, where he's partnered with black patrolman Forest Whitaker. Together they battle a drug ring and each other in this culture-clash action/comedy. 95 min.
04-2353 Was $89.99 ❑*$19.99*

Back In The USSR (1991)
An action-filled thriller about a young American tourist in Moscow who becomes involved in the Russian underworld when he's framed for murder. Frank Whaley, Natalya Negoda ("Little Vera") and Roman Polanski star in this suspenser that's the first American film to be shot entirely in Moscow. 88 min.
04-2526 Was $89.99 ❑*$19.99*

Hard To Die (1990)
A group of gorgeous young women is trapped in a deserted skyscraper with a maniacal killer close at their high heels. Clothed in leather, lingerie and sometimes nothing, these gals take matters into their own hands, brandishing heavy artillery to stop the culprit. Robyn Harris, Melissa Moore, Lindsay Taylor and Forrest J. Ackerman star. AKA: "Tower of Terror." 81 min.
21-9029 *$89.99*

Volcano (1997)
The "City of Angels" becomes a Hell on Earth when seismic activity beneath the surface of Los Angeles leads to a volcanic eruption, filling the skies with deadly ash and the streets with rivers of fiery lava. Thrill-packed action tale with tremendous effects stars Tommy Lee Jones, Anne Heche, Don Cheadle, Gaby Hoffman. 104 min.
04-3497 Was $99.99 ❑*$14.99*

Volcano (Letterboxed Version)
Also available in a theatrical, widescreen format.
04-3635 *$19.99*

Congo (1995)
Action, adventure, suspense and science fiction combine in this thrilling adaptation of Michael Crichton's best-selling book. A former CIA agent, a primatologist, a greedy fortune seeker, a mercenary and a "speaking" gorilla search for a fabled lost city on a danger-filled African safari. With Dylan Walsh, Laura Linney, Ernie Hudson and Tim Curry. 109 min.
06-2386 Was $89.99 ❑*$14.99*

Congo (Letterboxed Version)
Also available in a theatrical, widescreen format.
06-2505 ❑*$14.99*

The Chase (1994)
Slick thief Charlie Sheen swipes a red BMW from a supermarket lot and takes its owner, sexy heiress Kristy Swanson, hostage, while the police trail them on a high-speed pursuit towards the Mexican border. This energized car chase film offers lots of stunning stuntwork and some nice satirical jabs at TV news coverage. Henry Rollins, Ray Wise, Josh Mostel also star. 88 min.
04-2851 Was $19.99 ❑*$14.99*

The Edge (1997)
When their plane crashes in the Alaskan wilderness, billionaire Anthony Hopkins and photographer Alec Baldwin, whom Hopkins suspects of having an affair with his supermodel wife, must battle the elements, a savage bear that's tracking them, and each other as they fight to stay alive. Gripping adventure/drama, scripted by David Mamet, also stars Elle Macpherson, Harold Perrineau. 120 min.
04-3563 Was $99.99 ❑*$14.99*

The Edge (Letterboxed Version)
Also available in a theatrical, widescreen format.
04-3738 *$14.99*

Cold Around The Heart (1997)
Romance, greed and vengeance all hit the road in this action-packed tale. David Caruso and Kelly Lynch are lovers whose plan to flee with a fortune in stolen gems hits a minor snag when Lynch double-crosses Caruso and leaves him behind in jail...but not for as long as she had hoped. Stacey Dash co-stars. 96 min.
04-3578 ❑*$99.99*

Firestorm (1998)
When some prisoners set a forest fire as a cover for a daring escape plan, "smoke-jumper" Howie Long has to contend with both a natural and a human menace in this explosive action tale. Scott Glenn, William Forsythe, Suzy Amis also star. 99 min.
04-3658 Was $99.99 ❑*$14.99*

Hired To Kill (1991)
A soldier of fortune joins a group of gorgeous fashion models to go on a dangerous mission to free a jailed rebel leader. Brian Thompson, Jose Ferrer, Oliver Reed, George Kennedy star in this thrilling tale spiced with incredible women. 91 min.
06-1911 ❑*$89.99*

K2 (1992)
Sweeping, spectacularly photographed adventure about two ace rock climbers who, after dramatically rescuing the victims of a mountaineering accident, get an opportunity to climb K-2, one of the most treacherous summits in the world. Matt Craven, Michael Biehn and Julia Nickson-Soul star. 104 min.
06-2003 Was $19.99 ❑*$14.99*

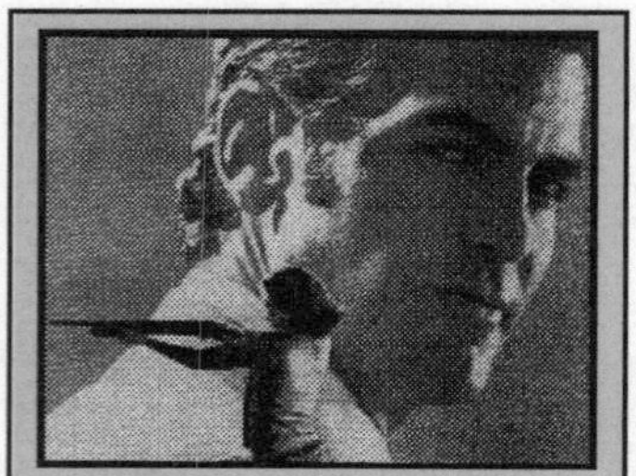

'OUT OF SIGHT'

Out Of Sight (1998)
George Clooney and Jennifer Lopez headline this critically acclaimed crime caper adapted from the Elmore Leonard best-seller. Clooney is a convicted bank robber who escapes from prison with help from partner Ving Rhames, but they're forced to kidnap U.S. marshal Lopez along the way. The romance that blossoms between Clooney and Lopez, however, has to take a back seat to a "can't miss" robbery plan. Don Cheadle, Albert Brooks and Dennis Farina also star, with unbilled cameos by Samuel L. Jackson and Michael Keaton; directed by Steven Soderbergh. 123 min.
07-2671 Was $99.99 ❑*$14.99*

Out Of Sight (Letterboxed Version)
Also available in a theatrical, widescreen format.
07-2700 Was $99.99 ❑*$19.99*

Meteorites! (1998)
Here they come, falling out of the blue...but, unfortunately, they're not tiny arrows. A rural town is reeling from a series of deadly random explosions, and former big-city bomb squad expert Tom Wopat is the only person who can solve the mysterious occurrences...but will anyone believe him? With Roxanne Hart, Pato Hoffmann. 89 min.
06-2822 ❑*$69.99*

The Take (1990)
A tough ex-cop leaves the slammer and vows to get his life back in shape. After trying to rebuild his marriage, he's thrown into a sordid sex murder and into the world of a Cuban drug kingpin. Ray Sharkey, R. Lee Ermey and Lisa Hartman star. 91 min.
07-1672 Was $79.99 *$14.99*

Till There Was You (1991)
In this intense thriller, Mark Harmon stars as an American jazz musician who journeys to a tropical island in search of his brother's killer. Soon, he encounters danger when he carries on an affair with the wife of the island's most powerful figure. Jeroen Krabbe, Deborah Unger co-star. 94 min.
07-1733 Was $89.99 *$19.99*

Fifty/Fifty (1993)
Two happy-go-lucky adventurers (Peter Weller and Robert Hays) are recruited by the CIA to overthrow a dictator on a South Seas island. They have trouble gathering an Army to help them on their mission, but eventually get unexpected help from a beautiful freedom fighter. Charles Martin Smith directs and co-stars. 101 min.
19-7092 Was $19.99 ❑*$14.99*

The Last Hit (1993)
A burned-out CIA assassin refuses a final "assignment" and moves to the mountains of New Mexico. There he falls in love with a beautiful neighbor, but his life becomes dangerous again when he learns that his new girlfriend's father is to be his next target. Bryan Brown, Brooke Adams, Harris Yulin star. 93 min.
07-2001 ❑*$89.99*

Tough And Deadly (1994)
When a major drug bust goes awry, a CIA agent caught in the ambush is left with amnesia and pursued by the crooks, who want to silence him for good. His only chance is to team up with a wisecracking bounty hunter who's after the same drug ring. Awesome action thriller stars Roddy Piper, Billy Blanks, Richard Norton. 92 min.
07-2237 Was $89.99 ❑*$14.99*

Incident At Deception Ridge (1995)
In this hair-raising adventure, ex-con Michael O'Keefe's newfound freedom is in jeopardy when the bus he's on is waylaid by two ruthless kidnappers who don't know the banker they're looking for has already run off with the ransom, and a dangerous hunt through the woods follows. Ed Begley, Jr., Linda Purl, Miguel Ferrer co-star. 94 min.
07-2269 ❑*$89.99*

Militia (1999)
Federal agent Dean Cain goes undercover, joining a militia supervised by a right-wing talk show host. After discovering that the group has swiped warheads containing anthrax, Cain enlists the help of his friend, a current militia member, to stop them from unleashing it. Stacy Keach, Jennifer Beals and Frederic Forrest also star. 97 min.
82-5209 *$99.99*

Impulse (1990)
Intense police thriller stars Theresa Russell as a burned-out L.A. undercover vice cop who becomes increasingly attracted to the temptations she confronts night after night and becomes involved in a botched sting operation and the murder of a Colombian drug dealer. Jeff Fahey, George Dzundza co-star; directed by Sondra Locke. 108 min.
19-1798 *$19.99*

Hurricane Smith (1992)
A Texas cop goes to Australia to stop a band of Aussie mobsters involved in drug dealing and prostitution. Carl Weathers plays the two-fisted enforcer who blows up a storm of action. With Jurgen Prochnow, Cassandra Delany and Tony Bonner. 86 min.
19-1971 Was $19.99 ❑*$14.99*

Point Of No Return (1993)
Action-packed reworking of the 1991 French thriller "Le Femme Nikita" stars Bridget Fonda as a drug-addicted cop killer whose life is spared so she can be transformed into a highly-trained super-assassin by the government. Gabriel Byrne, Dermot Mulroney, Harvey Keitel, Anne Bancroft also star. 109 min.
19-2140 Was $19.99 ❑*$14.99*

True Romance (1993)
Comic book store worker Christian Slater falls in love with hooker Patricia Arquette, kills her pimp and unknowingly swipes a suitcase loaded with cocaine. The couple heads to L.A. to sell the coke for big money, but both the cops and the drug ring's boss are on their trail. Stylishly violent actioner, directed by Tony Scott from Quentin Tarantino's script, also stars Christopher Walken, Dennis Hopper, Brad Pitt, Gary Oldman. Unrated director's cut; 121 min.
19-2159 Was $19.99 ❑*$14.99*

The Young Americans (1993)
Rousing action yarn stars Harvey Keitel as an American cop called to England to halt a crime spree headed by a group of youthful gangsters. Keitel's investigation leads to the unpredictable club scene, and he soon realizes his targets are more dangerous than he initially believed. Ian Glen, Viggo Mortensen co-star. 103 min.
27-6879 Was $19.99 ❑*$14.99*

Hostage (1992)
A British Secret Service agent attempts to leave his job, but his former employers feel he knows too much to be left alive. Now he must fight for his own life and those of his ex-wife, their children, and his lover in this explosive actioner. Sam Neill, Talisa Soto, James Fox star. 100 min.
06-2062 Was $89.99 ❑*$14.99*

Chrome Soldiers (1992)
They were comrades in the jungles of Vietnam, and when one of their number is killed by drug dealers who control the town, five motorcycle-riding vets team up to dispense their own brand of justice. Revved-up actioner stars Gary Busey, Ray Sharkey, Yaphet Kotto. 92 min.
06-2070 Was $89.99 ❑*$14.99*

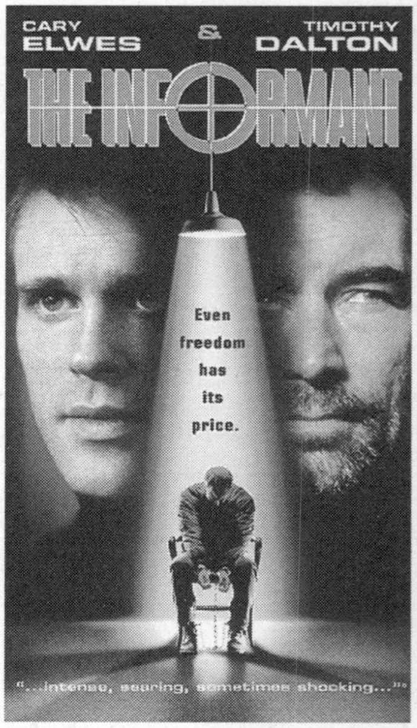

The Informant (1998)
Fiery Northern Ireland is the setting for this political actioner in which a recruit of the Irish Republican Army is captured by the British police. He is caught between his loyalty to his countrymen and the threat of life in prison when he is pressured by an IRA-hating chief inspector to testify against his comrades-in-arms. Cary Elwes, Timothy Dalton and Anthony Brophy star. 106 min.
06-2748 Was $79.99 ❑*$14.99*

Moonshine Highway (1996)
A daredevil moonshiner goes head-to-head against a ruthless sheriff with a personal score to settle in this action-packed adventure that features wild car chases. Kyle MacLachlan, Randy Quaid and Gary Farmer star. 96 min.
06-2477 Was $89.99 ❑*$14.99*

The Phantom (1996)
The masked, purple-clad defender of the jungle leaps from the comics pages to the big screen with this thrilling adventure saga. Billy Zane stars as the "Ghost Who Walks," latest in a line of familial Phantoms, who must battle a scheming businessman in search of the mystical Skulls of Touganda. Kristy Swanson, Treat Williams, Catherine Zeta-Jones also star. 100 min.
06-2528 Was $99.99 ❑*$14.99*

Dead Ahead (1996)
Beset by a pack of vicious fugitives, a woman on a wilderness camping trip with her family must fight to protect her loved ones in this tense action tale. Stephanie Zimbalist, Peter Onorati, Sarah Chalke star. 92 min.
06-2565 ❑*$89.99*

Hard Rain (1998)
As the waters rise, so does the action in this thrill-packed tale set in a flood-ravaged Indiana town. Armored truck driver Christian Slater must protect his multi-million-dollar cargo from a gang of thieves using the town's evacuation as a cover for their crimes. Morgan Freeman, Minnie Driver, Randy Quaid and Ed Asner also star. 98 min.
06-2735 Was $99.99 ❑*$14.99*

His Bodyguard (1997)
When a hearing-impaired young man witnesses the theft of a valuable drug from his father's bio-engineering company, security expert Mitzi Kapture is assigned to serve as his bodyguard and steer him out of danger. Anthony Natale and Robert Guillaume also star. 88 min.
06-2786 Was $69.99 ❑*$14.99*

Double Tap (1997)
Heather Locklear is a dedicated undercover cop, Stephen Rea a cold-blooded vigilante, and when the pursuit of a deadly drug ring brings them together the passion and danger will reach a fever pitch. Steamy, suspense-filled action tale also stars Peter Greene, Mykelti Williamson. 99 min.
06-2821 ❑*$69.99*

Blast (1997)
As provocative as yesterday's headlines, this actioner tells of a group of terrorists who attempt to wreak havoc at the Atlanta Olympic Games. Rutger Hauer, Andrew Divoff, Linden Ashby and Kimberly Warren star. 98 min.
19-2528 Was $99.99 ***$19.99***

Suspicious Agenda (1995)
Tough actioner starring Richard Grieco as a cop with a troubled past assigned to a task force trying to identify a rogue officer who's taking justice into his own hands. Nick Mancuso co-stars. 97 min.
19-3827 ***$89.99***

Chameleon (1995)
When his family is savagely murdered by a powerful drug cartel, a maverick DEA agent uses his mastery of disguise to bring down the ring's leaders. Intense actioner stars Anthony LaPaglia, Kevin Pollack, Melora Hardin, Wayne Knight. 108 min.
19-3889 ***$89.99***

Criminal Hearts (1995)
She's looking for revenge on her ex-lover...he's a fugitive on the run from the law...and when they meet together on the road, they set out on a violent, passionate ride that ends in an explosive climax. Kevin Dillon, Amy Locane, Morgan Fairchild and M. Emmet Walsh star. 92 min.
19-3890 ***$89.99***

Sabotage (1996)
A clandestine operation of high-level government assassins lies at the heart of this thrilling, suspense-filled actioner. Mark Dacascos, Carrie Anne Moss, Graham Greene and Tony Todd star. 99 min.
19-3975 Was $99.99 ***$19.99***

Chain Of Command (1993)
The deserts of the Middle East get even hotter when anti-terrorist agent Michael Dudikoff is sent in to battle a mercenary force trying to take over a country with strategic oil reserves. Todd Curtis, Keren Tishman, R. Lee Ermey co-star. 98 min.
19-7103 Was $89.99 □***$19.99***

The Chain (1996)
An American cop travels to South America to track down an elusive illegal arms dealer, but soon both lawman and villain are chained together in a prison work camp and must work together to stay alive. Thrilling action tale stars Gary Busey, Victor Rivers, Jamie Rose. 95 min.
19-3976 Was $99.99 ***$19.99***

The Assassination Game (1993)
A deadly game with global consequences ensues when two special agents are assigned to protect a prominent world leader from a hired hit man. Can they uncover the mysterious killer in the three days they have? Robert Rusler and Theodore Bikel star. 83 min.
21-9030 ***$89.99***

Steven Seagal

Above The Law (1988)
That's just what martial arts expert Steven Seagal is, as he smashes his way across the screen in his starring debut, a white-hot actioner about a Chicago cop who finds himself in a one-man battle against corrupt colleagues and ruthless drug runners. Co-stars Pam Grier, Henry Silva. 99 min.
19-1653 Was $19.99 □***$14.99***

Marked For Death (1990)
That's just what former DEA Agent Steven Seagal is, and when a Jamaican drug kingpin also threatens to kill his family, Seagal goes on a rampage, teaming with a former Army pal to thwart the voodoo-worshipping posse in this all-kicking, all-shooting action epic. With Keith David, Basil Wallace and Joanna Pacula. 94 min.
04-2419 □***$14.99***

Hard To Kill (1990)
That's just what tough L.A. cop Steven Seagal is, after he's shot and uncovers an assassination plot masterminded by a crooked politician. After spending seven years in a coma, he wakes up and promptly goes to work searching for those who tried to do him in. Smashing action yarn co-stars Kelly LeBrock (Seagal's then real-life wife). 103 min.
19-1771 Was $19.99 □***$14.99***

Out For Justice (1991)
That's just what streetwise Brooklyn cop Steven Seagal is, in this white-hot action flick, tracking down the renegade mob hood who killed his best friend and now is gunning for him. Can Seagal bring him down before the "family" finds him? William Forsythe, Jo Campa co-star. 91 min.
19-1880 Was $19.99 □***$14.99***

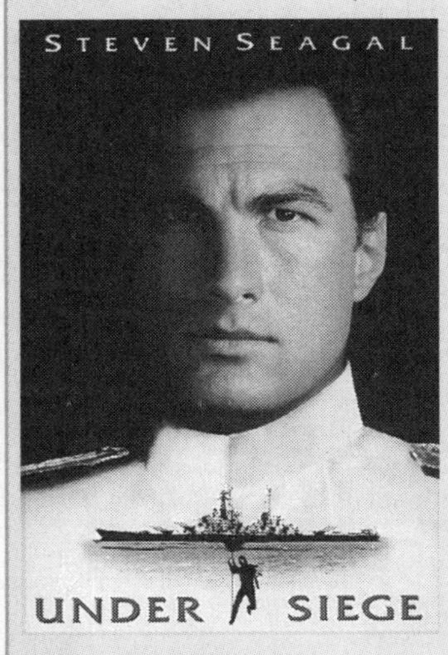

Under Siege (1992)
That's just what cook and ex-Navy SEAL Steven Seagal is, when a group of terrorists led by psychotic CIA operative Tommy Lee Jones commandeers the battleship U.S.S. Missouri and nuclear arsenal, forcing him to use his martial arts and military skills to stop them. Action smash co-stars Erika Eleniak, Gary Busey and Patrick O'Neal. 103 min.
19-2051 Was $19.99 □***$14.99***

Under Siege II: Dark Territory (1995)
Steven Seagal's former Navy SEAL-turned-cook gets help from a porter when he squares off against ruthless mercenaries who have taken his teenage niece hostage on a train excursion through the Rocky Mountains. Led by deranged hi-tech genius Eric Bogosian, the nasties swipe a powerful U.S. satellite, then terrorize the world. With Katherine Heigl, Morris Chestnut. 100 min.
19-2385 Was $19.99 □***$14.99***

ON DEADLY GROUND

On Deadly Ground (1994)
That's just what oil-rig troubleshooter Steven Seagal is, when he discovers that weaselly tycoon Michael Caine's new Alaskan refinery will destroy the surrounding ecosystem. With help from beautiful native woman Joan Chen, Seagal goes up against Caine and his goons and tries to send the refinery sky-high. Environmental actioner co-stars John C. McGinley. 102 min.
19-2232 Was $89.99 □***$14.99***

The Glimmer Man (1996)
Los Angeles cops Steven Seagal and Keenen Ivory Wayans struggle to track down a serial killer who may be connected to the Russian mob, but when Seagal's ex-wife and her new husband are the latest victims he becomes a prime suspect. Action and suspense galore in this hit thriller; with Brian Cox, Bob Gunton. 92 min.
19-2495 Was $19.99 □***$14.99***

The Glimmer Man (Letterboxed Version)
Also available in a theatrical, widescreen format.
19-2592 □***$19.99***

Fire Down Below (1997)
When the corrupt industrialists who are poisoning the hills of Kentucky's Appalachia region kill a federal environmental agent, fellow agent Steven Seagal goes undercover to clean things up and bring the bad guys to justice in this hard-hitting thriller. Kris Kristofferson, Marg Helgenberger, Harry Dean Stanton also star. 105 min.
19-2618 Was $99.99 □***$14.99***

The Patriot (1998)
Steven Seagal is a former government agent-turned-holistic medicine practitioner who has settled into a quiet life in a small Midwestern town. Seagal's serenity is shattered when a local militia group unleashes a deadly disease that begins killing the locals and threatens the life of his daughter. L.Q. Jones, Gailard Sartain and Camilla Belle star. 90 min.
11-2323 Was $99.99 □***$14.99***

Please see our index for these other Steven Seagal titles: *Executive Decision • My Giant*

Airborne (1993)
A young surfer dude from L.A. arrives in Cincinnati to stay with relatives while his parents are away. He runs afoul of neighborhood toughs who don't like his California attitude—until he uses his rollerblading skills to help them beat the school's preppies at roller hockey. Shane McDermott, Brittany Powell and Seth Green star in this stunt-filled film. 91 min.
19-2207 Was $89.99 □***$19.99***

Empire City (1994)
A hot-tempered, maverick New York detective is teamed with a beautiful, no-nonsense partner to investigate a murder amid ritzy Manhattan society, but the steamy affair that erupts between them could put the case—and their lives—in jeopardy. Sizzling actioner stars Michael Paré, Mary Mara. 82 min.
19-2234 Was $79.99 □***$19.99***

Fair Game (1995)
Stunning supermodel Cindy Crawford adds actress to her resumé with her big screen debut in this fast-paced action tale about a lawyer (an admittedly stunning lawyer) who's pursued by Russian mobsters and goes on the run with renegade cop William Baldwin to stop their terroristic plans. 91 min.
19-2429 Was $19.99 □***$14.99***

North Star (1996)
The search for gold in turn-of-the-century Alaska puts sacred Eskimo territory in jeopardy and leads to a deadly confrontation between half-breed fugitive Christopher Lambert and corrupt mining boss James Caan in a thrilling action tale. Catherine McCormack, Burt Young co-star. 89 min.
19-2501 Was $99.99 □***$19.99***

Hostile Intentions (1994)
After crossing the border for a wild weekend party in Tijuana, three young women get caught up in a deadly turn of events that forces them to flee for their lives and attempt a dangerous return to America with a group of illegal immigrants. Offbeat actioner that's been called a distaff "Deliverance" stars Tia Carrere, Tricia Leigh Fisher, Lisa Dean Ryan. 90 min.
19-3912 ***$89.99***

Rescue Me (1993)
In a Nebraska town, a teenager whose father was killed in Vietnam befriends a tough but understanding Vietnam veteran who serves as a surrogate dad and helps him rescue a kidnapped girl he has fallen for. Michael Dudikoff, Stephen Dorff and Ami Dolenz star in this coming-of-age story spiked with exciting chases. 99 min.
19-7097 Was $19.99 ***$14.99***

Midnight Ride (1995)
A deranged killer holding a hostage uses a police car, a bus, a cab and an ambulance to make his escape. Hot on his trail is a no-nonsense policeman whose wife happens to be the hostage! This fast-paced actioner stars Michael Dudikoff, Mark Hamill, Savina Gersak and Robert Mitchum. 93 min.
19-7099 Was $89.99 □***$19.99***

Executive Decision (1996)
When Muslim extremists carrying a lethal nerve gas hijack an Athens-Washington flight, government information expert Kurt Russell joins an elite anti-terrorist unit to try to board the plane before it lands, but a mid-air accident puts the mission in jeopardy. Taut actioner with more than one surprise also stars Halle Berry, John Leguizamo, Oliver Platt, David Suchet and, in a special appearance, Steven Seagal. 133 min.
19-2459 Was $99.99 □***$14.99***

Executive Decision (Letterboxed Version)
Also available in a theatrical, widescreen format.
19-2553 □***$19.99***

The Peacemaker (1997)
International terrorists set off a nuclear explosion on a Russian train carrying warheads earmarked for dismantling in order to cover their theft of the remaining weapons. U.S. Army Special Forces officer George Clooney and scientist Nicole Kidman work together in a desperate global search to find the stolen warheads before they're put to use in this gripping action-thriller, the debut release from the Geffen-Katzenberg-Speilberg Dreamworks studio. Armin Mueller-Stahl, Marcel Iures also star. 124 min.
07-2598 Was $99.99 □***$14.99***

The Peacemaker (Letterboxed Version)
Also available in a theatrical, widescreen format.
07-2599 Was $99.99 □***$14.99***

Chill Factor (1999)
The heat had definitely better not be on in this super-cool actioner, as renegade Army officer Peter Firth tries to hijack a deadly experimental chemical weapon. Dying scientist David Paymer passes the compound to pal Skeet Ulrich with a warning that it must be kept below 50 degrees, forcing Ulrich to commandeer Cuba Gooding, Jr.'s ice cream truck and sending the pair on a wild race to save the weapon from Firth's men. 102 min.
19-2937 Was $89.99 □***$14.99***

Shadow Warriors (1997)
Terry "Hulk" Hogan plays a Navy SEAL who must lead his team against a treacherous druglord and stop a terrorist attack aimed at the U.S. But things go from bad to worse when one of his own betrays him and kidnaps a gymnastics team, keeping them prisoner on a remote island. Now the SEALs must race to save the gymnasts, waging one last, personal battle. With Carl Weathers, Shannon Tweed, Martin Kove and Billy Blanks. AKA: "Assault on Devil's Island." 94 min.
82-5211 ***$99.99***

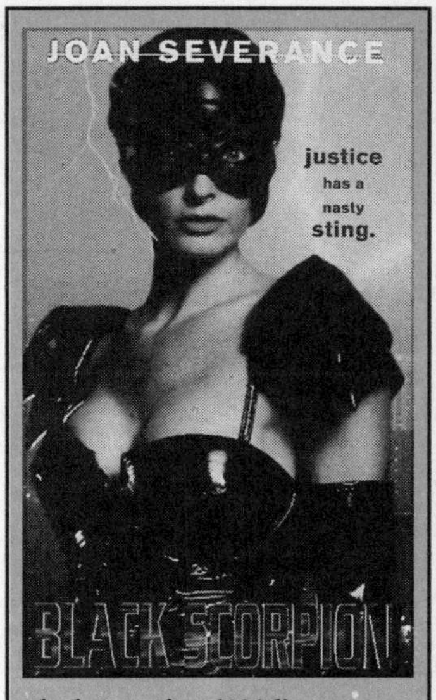

Black Scorpion (1996)
Sexy, fast-paced action tale stars Joan Severance as an undercover cop who decides to take matters into her own hands after her father is murdered. Donning a mask and a tight leather uniform, she becomes the Black Scorpion, policing the city in her Porsche in search of her father's killer. Garrett Morris, Rick Rossovich and Casey Siemaszko also star. 90 min.
21-9118 Was $99.99 ***$14.99***

Black Scorpion II (1997)
That beautiful crimebuster Black Scorpion is back, this time facing two criminal masterminds who present her biggest challenge yet: Gangster Prankster, a demented jokester, and the seismic supervillain AfterShock. Black Scorpion attempts to save the city before the bad guys—or the police—get to her first. Joan Severance, Garrett Morris and Whip Hubley star. 85 min.
21-9136 Was $99.99 ***$14.99***

Urban Crossfire (1994)
After his partner and best friend is murdered by a drug dealer, a New York cop goes ballistic, seeking revenge for the senseless killing. But will he go too far over the edge and use the violence he's sworn to fight against to gain justice? Mario Van Peebles, Ray Sharkey and Peter Boyle star.
21-9068 Was $89.99 ***$14.99***

Born To Run (1993)
Richard Grieco is a hot-shot blacktop racer whose brother gets in trouble with a local mob boss. He steals a car in order to help his brother, but the danger reaches new heights when he discovers that the mobster's book of associates is in the vehicle. Shelli Lether, Joe Cortese co-star. 97 min.
04-2752 Was $89.99 □***$29.99***

The Human Shield (1992)
A war is raging in the Persian Gulf and CIA Marine instructor Michael Dudikoff must save his brother, who has been captured and is being held hostage in Iraq. Soon, the tough leatherneck finds himself going up against a ruthless general who holds an old grudge. Steve Inwood co-stars. 88 min.
19-7089 Was $19.99 □***$14.99***

Red Scorpion 2 (1995)
A rogue secret agent joins forces with fellow operatives in the National Security Commission to stop a neo-Nazi who has stolen the Spear of Destiny, a sacred artifact whose mystical powers will be used in his global campaign of hate. Matt McColm, Michael Ironside, Jennifer Rubin and John Savage star. 94 min.
07-2370 □***$89.99***

The Beast (1996)
A seaside village in the Pacific Northwest is held in a grip of terror—literally and figuratively—when a ferocious and gigantic predator comes up from the depths of the ocean in search of a new food supply. Terrifying action tale from Peter Benchley ("Jaws") stars William Petersen, Charles Martin Smith, Karen Sillas and Larry Drake. Special feature-length version; 116 min.
07-2630 □***$99.99***

Curse Of The Crystal Eye (1993)
A gunrunner goes on a hunt for the mystic Crystal Eye, the key to finding the long-lost treasure of Ali Baba. Trouble is, there's 5,000 savage warriors, diabolical mercenaries, and the Cavern of Death standing in his way. Jameson Parker and Cynthia Rhodes star in this hair-raising adventure. 82 min.
21-9044 Was $89.99 ***$14.99***

Fast Gun (1993)
An embittered ex-CIA agent wants to turn a remote lakeside town into the headquarters for his gunrunning operation, and with a local bigwig in his pocket, only the town's sheriff can stop the mercenaries' plans. All-out action tale stars Rick Hill, Kaz Garas, Robert Dryer and Brenda Bakke. 90 min.
21-9046 ***$89.99***

Twister (1996)

Blockbuster adventure yarn stars Helen Hunt and Bill Paxton as estranged husband/wife scientists who reunite to chase down some of the world's nastiest tornadoes in Oklahoma with help from the special storm-tracking gadget they've developed. Incredible special effects highlight this Steven Spielberg production. With Jami Gertz, Cary Elwes. Directed by Jan DeBont ("Speed"). 113 min.
19-2469   Was $19.99   ❏*$14.99*

Twister (Letterboxed Version)

Also available in a theatrical, widescreen format.
19-2473   ❏*$19.99*

Black Thunder (1998)

When the Air Force's advanced Mach 2 fighter jet is swiped by Libyan forces, ace pilot Michael Dudikoff is called on to get it back. Along with reckless partner Gary Hudson, Dudikoff heads for enemy territory, battling terrorists and a traitorous American pilot in a high-tech battle. Richard Norton, Nancy Valen and Frederic Forrest also star. 88 min.
21-9166   *$59.99*

Stray Bullet (1998)

After being seduced by a beautiful woman, Robert Carradine is mistaken for her husband. The case of mistaken identity leads to him being framed for murder and pursued by both the police and crime boss Fred Dryer. Carradine decides to play one side against another in order to get out of the jam. Rebecca Staab also stars. 90 min.
21-9169   *$59.99*

My Brother's War (1998)

Retired CIA agent James Brolin must put an end to the violence provoked by a renegade IRA terrorist out to sabotage Irish peace talks. Brolin enlists the culprit's brother, a convicted terrorist, to help him on his demanding assignment. Josh Brolin, Patrick Foy and Jennie Garth also star. 84 min.
21-9170   *$59.99*

The Protector (1998)

Ed Marinaro is an assassin trained by the military who attempts to avenge his wife's murder. Soon, he finds himself helping other women in trouble and falls in love with one of them—one whose former lover has mob ties. Kate Rodger and Lee Majors also star in this actioner.
21-9178   *$59.99*

Enemy Action (1999)

When a newly designed "smart bomb" is swiped, a military expert teams with the weapon's builder, a beautiful female officer, to track it down. They find terrorists, CIA double agents and others in their way as the clock ticks—and Washington, D.C. is the target. C. Thomas Howell, Lisa Thornhill and Louis Mandylor star. 84 min.
21-9180   *$59.99*

Desert Thunder (1999)

The Iraqis have developed a deadly biological weapon, and in order to stop them, former Air Force fighter ace Daniel Baldwin is brought out of retirement. He heads a group of military rejects enlisted to take out the Iraqis using F-14s. Now, if they could only survive training camp! Richard Tyson also stars.
21-9198   *$49.99*

Boxcar Blues (1991)

Hard-hitting Depression-era actioner about a down-and-out boxer who teams with a streetwise young hustler to pool their talents into a successful "business project." Paul Coufos, Margaret Langrick, Jesse "the Body" Ventura and M. Emmet Walsh star. 96 min.
23-5047   *$79.99*

Detonator (1998)

A painter who doubles as a hit man decides to rescue a homeless teenage girl rather than kill her. This puts him in jeopardy with a corrupt cop who ordered the hit because she was a witness to his sleazy wheelings and dealings. Scott Baio, Charlene Tilton and Don Stroud star.
21-9159   Was $59.99   *$14.99*

Body Count (1997)

The home of a wealthy art dealer becomes a masterpiece of murderous mayhem when a group of thieves breaks in and attacks the occupants, and two survivors turn the tables on the killers. Ice T, Alyssa Milano, Justin Theroux and Tiny Lister star. 88 min.
27-7063   Was $99.99   ❏*$14.99*

Marked Man (1996)

Roddy Piper slams home the action in this thrill-packed tale of a prisoner who witnesses a murder behind bars and breaks out to avoid becoming the next victim. Pursued by both sides of the law, Piper must stay alive long enough to track the killers and clear his name. With Jane Wheeler, Miles O'Keeffe. 94 min.
27-6996   ❏*$99.99*

Beyond The Law (1994)

Charlie Sheen plays a fearless cop who goes undercover, posing as a reckless biker in order to stop a motorcycle gang notorious for their criminal activity. When Sheen falls for a gorgeous female member of the group, he finds it tough to discern who's the enemy and who's an ally. Michael Madsen, Linda Fiorentino co-star. 101 min.
27-6882   Was $89.99   ❏*$14.99*

The Hard Truth (1994)

An honest cop is lured by his seductive girlfriend into taking part in a multi-million-dollar heist, but when she also enlists the aid of an expert safecracker, the resulting love triangle could blow everything sky-high. Suspenseful, sexy actioner stars Eric Roberts, Michael Rooker, Lysette Anthony. 100 min.
27-6894   Was $89.99   ❏*$19.99*

The Dogfighters (1996)

In this thrill-packed actioner, a former Air Force pilot finds himself in a tough spot, racing against the clock in order to stop a potential nuclear disaster involving a ruthless terrorist leader. Filled with exciting aerial sequences, the film stars Robert Davi, Alexander Godunov and Lara Harris. 96 min.
27-6974   Was $19.99   ❏*$14.99*

The Punisher (1990)

Rip-roaring, action-packed yarn with Dolph Lundgren as Marvel Comics vigilante Frank Castle, a streetwise cop who escapes a Mafia car bomb that kills his entire family. He heads underground to the city's sewers, where he carries out an all-out war against crime. Lou Gossett, Jr., Jeroen Krabbe, Kim Myori co-star. 92 min.
27-6701   Was $89.99   *$14.99*

Pentathlon (1994)

East German athlete Dolph Lundgren defects from his Olympic team to the U.S. following troubles with cruel coach David Soul. At the games years later, Lundgren must compete for his life when Soul, now a neo-Nazi, launches a scheme of vengeance. Roger E. Mosley co-stars. 101 min.
27-6919   Was $89.99   ❏*$12.99*

In Too Deep (1999)

Undercover cop Omar Epps gets an assignment to infiltrate the operation of the city's biggest drug dealer, a charismatic but violent kingpin known as God (LL Cool J), but as the two become friends Epps finds his loyalties tested. Compelling urban tale also stars Stanley Tucci, Nia Long, Pam Grier. 97 min.
11-2388   ❏*$99.99*

Throw Down (1999)

An ex-Marine returns to his Bronx neighborhood and is dismayed to learn that his childhood sweetheart and her sister are mixed up with a ruthless gang of drug dealers. His attempt to save them leads to a brutal showdown in this hard-hitting urban action tale with a bright young cast. 100 min.
81-9111   *$59.99*

GEENA DAVIS   SAMUEL L. JACKSON
THE LONG KISS GOODNIGHT

The Long Kiss Goodnight (1996)

Eight years after she was found suffering from amnesia, mild-mannered teacher and suburban mother Geena Davis discovers she was formerly a top assassin for the CIA...and someone from her past wants her dead. Now Davis must use all her latent and lethal skills as she teams with detective Samuel L. Jackson to uncover her enemies in this slam-bang actioner directed by Davis's husband, Renny Harlin. 120 min.
02-5133   ❏*$14.99*

The Long Kiss Goodnight (Letterboxed Version)

Also available in a theatrical, widescreen format.
02-5137   ❏*$19.99*

Open Fire (1994)

When a mercenary group takes over a city, one man launches a...well, a one-man assault...that turns the streets into a battlefield in this explosive actioner. Jeff Wincott, Mimi Craven star. 93 min.
63-1740   ❏*$89.99*

Deadly Outbreak (1996)

A biochemical research laboratory is seized by terrorists after a deadly virus as part of a blackmail scheme, and one lone soldier stands in their way in this high contagious action tale. Jeff Speakman, Ron Silver, Rochelle Swanson star. 94 min.
27-6985   Was $99.99   ❏*$14.99*

Indio II: The Revolt (1992)

"Marvelous" Marvin Hagler returns as a Marine sergeant called on to unite the Indian tribes of the Amazon jungle against greedy men who want to enslave and slaughter them. Charles Napier co-stars. 104 min.
27-6763   *$14.99*

When The Bullet Hits The Bone (1996)

An emergency doctor disgusted with the horror he sees every day in the hospital decides to take matters into his own hands in this explosive actioner. He believes drugs are the cause of most of the evils he encounters, and soon discovers a government conspiracy involving narcotics and corruption. Jeff Wincott and Michelle Johnson star. 88 min.
21-9120   *$59.99*

Red Snow (1990)

Thrilling ski action and mystery mix in this thrilling story about a handsome ski instructor, new to a fashionable resort, who discovers his predecessor was murdered...and he may be next! Carlos Scandiuzzi stars. 88 min.
23-5048   *$39.99*

The Takeover (1995)

A two-fisted actioner in which an East Coast crime syndicate tries to muscle in on an L.A. cocaine-dealing operation and ignites a violent mob war. Billy Drago, Nick Mancuso and John Savage star. 91 min.
27-6964   ❏*$89.99*

Dead Men Can't Dance (1997)

Gripping action tale, set inside the DMZ that divides North and South Korea, follows a covert American intelligence squad sent into Communist territory to destroy a nuclear reactor that could tip the balance of power in post-Cold War Asia. Michael Biehn, Adrian Paul, Kathleen York and Kelly Jo Minter star. 97 min.
27-7023   Was $99.99   ❏*$14.99*

A Cop For The Killing (1994)

A lieutenant on L.A.'s narcotics squad is about to capture the city's biggest drug dealer when a sting operation goes awry and his partner is killed. The cop takes the events personally and goes on a one-man rampage to bring the mobster down. James Farentino, Charles Haid, Steven Weber star.
21-9080   *$89.99*

Mob Justice (1991)

Nail-biting gangster saga about a man who finds himself caught between the mob, who wants him to be their fall guy for a drug-related murder, and the FBI, who needs him alive as their only witness to the incident. Tony Danza, Ted Levine, Dan Lauria, Nicholas Turturro and Samuel L. Jackson star.
21-9095   *$89.99*

Demolition Day (1997)

Three Southern California teens stumble across an abandoned nuclear weapon and decide to hold the city of Los Angeles up for ransom, but both the FBI and some crooks are hot on their trail. Thrilling mix of action, suspense and laughs stars Joe Mantegna, Joe Piscopo, Martin Sheen, Rod Steiger and Joanna Pacula. AKA: "Captain Nuke and the Bomber Boys." 91 min.
21-9097   *$89.99*

Delta Force 3 (1991)

Brand-new action thrills with a brand-new Delta Force. Joined by two Russian officers, the crack anti-terrorist squad has their work cut out for them when they must locate an atomic bomb that a terrorist has hidden in an American city. Mike Norris, Nick Cassavetes, Eric Douglas star. 97 min.
19-7085   Was $19.99   *$14.99*

Operation Delta Force (1997)

When a South African white extremist group threatens to use a stolen biological weapon, the top-secret American strike team known as the Delta Force must stop them and recover the deadly virus before it can be unleashed. Ernie Hudson, Jeff Fahey, Frank Zagarino and Hal Holbrook star. 93 min.
27-7033   ❏*$99.99*

Operation Delta Force 2 (1997)

When there's trouble, count on the highly-skilled men of "the Delta Force" to take care of it. In this action-packed effort, a terrorist uses an American cruise ship as a shield as he readies a nuclear submarine to destroy America and Russia. Only the Force members can save the day. Michael McGrady, Dale Dye star. 98 min.
50-5652   ❏*$99.99*

Operation Delta Force III: Clear Target (1999)

After his cocaine operation is smashed by the Delta Force, a vengeful drug kingpin hijacks a U.S. submarine and threatens to launch biochemical warheads at New York. Can the Delta members find him in time to stop him? Explosive actioner stars Jim Fitzpatrick, Bryan Genesse, Danny Keogh. 93 min.
68-1950   ❏*$69.99*

Turbulence (1997)

A Christmas Eve Los Angeles-to-New York 747 flight becomes a nightmare in the air when psychotic serial killer Ray Liotta, being transported by federal agents, escapes from custody and kills the plane's pilot, as well as the feds. When a storm leads to the co-pilot's death, flight attendant Lauren Holly must struggle to land the jet as she battles Liotta. With Hector Elizondo, Ben Cross. 101 min.
44-2096   Was $19.99   ❏*$14.99*

Turbulence (Letterboxed Version)

Also available in a theatrical, widescreen format.
44-2151   Was $19.99   ❏*$14.99*

Turbulence 2: Fear Of Flying (2000)

A routine flight aboard a 747 for a therapy group trying to cure their fear of air travel becomes a course in "shock therapy" when violent turbulence rocks the plane, disabling the crew, and a psychotic hijacker with a nerve gas bomb takes control. Can aircraft engineer Craig Sheffer overcome him and ditch the bomb before the plane must be shot down? Jennifer Beals, Tom Berenger also star. 100 min.
68-2015   ❏*$79.99*

SAMUEL L. JACKSON   KEVIN SPACEY
THE NEGOTIATOR
HE FREES HOSTAGES FOR A LIVING.
NOW HE'S TAKING HOSTAGES TO SURVIVE.

The Negotiator: Collector's Edition (1998)

When Chicago police hostage negotiator Samuel L. Jackson is framed for his partner's murder, he takes over the department Internal Affairs division and holds the officials captive. With the SWAT team and feds threatening, Jackson insists on smooth-as-silk outsider Kevin Spacey as the man to negotiate his own dangerous situation. John Spencer, David Morse and J.T. Walsh also star in this intense actioner. Special video version includes a "making of" documentary. 140 min.
19-2758   Was $99.99   ❏*$19.99*

The Negotiator (Letterboxed Version)

Also available in a theatrical, widescreen format.
19-2859   ❏*$19.99*

One Man's Justice (1995)

Army drill sergeant Brian Bosworth wages an all-out war against the ruthless drug- and gun-runners who murdered his wife and daughter in this intense action tale that co-stars rap star Hammer as the bloodthirsty gang leader. With Bruce Payne, DeJuan Guy. 100 min.
27-6978   Was $99.99   ❏*$14.99*

Out Of Sync (1995)

A disc jockey in trouble with tough bookies, their enforcers and the Los Angeles police gets into even more hot water when he falls in love with a dangerous drug dealer's girlfriend. Urban actioner stars L.L. Cool J, Victoria Dillard, Yaphet Kotto and Howard Hesseman. 105 min.
27-6950   Was $89.99   ❏*$14.99*

Timebomb (1991)

Rip-snorting action thriller starring Michael Biehn as a mild-mannered watchmaker haunted by mysterious nightmares. With help from a beautiful psychiatrist (Patsy Kensit), he discovers he is actually a CIA-trained killing machine who has been given a new memory. With Richard Jordan, Robert Culp. 96 min.
12-2399   Was $19.99   ❏*$14.99*

Rumble In The Streets (1997)

Tori has grown up on the means streets of Dallas, where she struggled to survive. Now the teenager finds herself the target of a renegade cop out to kill all of the city's street kids. Joining her to stop the lethal lawman is an aspiring country singer. Kimberly Rowe, David Courtemarche and Patrick Defazio star. 85 min.
21-9138   *$99.99*

Eruption (1998)

While covering a Papal visit to a small South American dictatorship, photojournalist Cyril O'Reilly searches for a rebel leader headquartered in the mountains. While there, O'Reilly learns an active volcano threatens the area, and the government will do nothing. With help from the rebels and a beautiful physician, he combats the ruler's men and tries to alert the people to their danger. F. Murray Abraham also stars. 92 min.
21-9176   *$59.99*

Back Of Beyond (1995)
In the desolation of the Australian Outback, a gas station attendant with a dark secret in his past finds a chance for atonement when a gang of diamond smugglers break down at his place. Intense action tale stars Paul Mercurio, Colin Friels. 85 min.
27-7012 $99.99

Gunmen (1994)
Action-crammed caper thriller starring Christopher Lambert as an unpredictable crook who forms an uneasy alliance with DEA agent Mario Van Peebles to retrieve a load of stolen drug money hidden in Mexico. Hot on their trail is a gang of no-nonsense thugs led by Denis Leary. With Patrick Stewart, Kadeem Hardison and Sally Kirkland. 97 min.
27-6860 Was $19.99 $14.99

Cover-Up (1991)
Here's an action film that's as real and striking as today's headlines! Journalist Dolph Lundgren investigates an attack on a U.S. naval compound near Tel Aviv, and when government official Louis Gossett, Jr. isn't quick to take action, it leads Lundgren to believe a conspiracy is in the works. John Finn and Susan Berkley also star. 89 min.
27-6727 Was $89.99 ❑$12.99

Danger Zone (1996)
In this explosive actioner, Billy Zane plays a mining expert who stumbles upon a secret plot involving nuclear arms that threatens the future of the United States. Now, only he can stop the devious scheme from being carried out. Ron Silver, Robert Downey, Jr., Cary-Hiroyuki Tagawa and Lisa Collins star. 92 min.
27-7003 Was $99.99 ❑$14.99

Caught Up (1998)
Getting off the streets could cost reformed hood Bokeem Woodbine his life, as he is caught up in the middle of a war between gangsters and cops, in this compelling urban action tale. Cynda Williams, Tony Todd star, with special appearances by Snoop Doggy Dogg and LL Cool J. 98 min.
27-7069 Was $99.99 ❑$14.99

Framed (1990)
An art forger gets a taste of his own medicine when he's duped by a female con artist. After years of searching, he catches up with her, but soon becomes involved with her brilliantly conceived art swindle. Jeff Goldblum, Kristin Scott Thomas and Todd Graff star. 87 min.
44-1770 Was $89.99 $14.99

Riding The Edge (1990)
Dirt bike thrills and Middle Eastern espionage mix in this action-packed tale. After a scientist is taken hostage by terrorists, his young, dirt bike-riding son joins a martial arts student to get to the bottom of things. Raphael Sbarge, Catherine Mary Stewart and Peter Haskell star. 100 min.
44-1771 $89.99

Acts Of Betrayal (1998)
When the wife of a powerful Mafia member agrees to testify against her husband and his cronies, a Marine-trained FBI agent is assigned to escort her from the small town where she's been hiding. Some high-ranking official, though, is out to make sure they don't get out alive. Explosive thriller stars Maria Conchita Alonso, Matt McColm, David Groh. 112 min.
27-7107 ❑$89.99

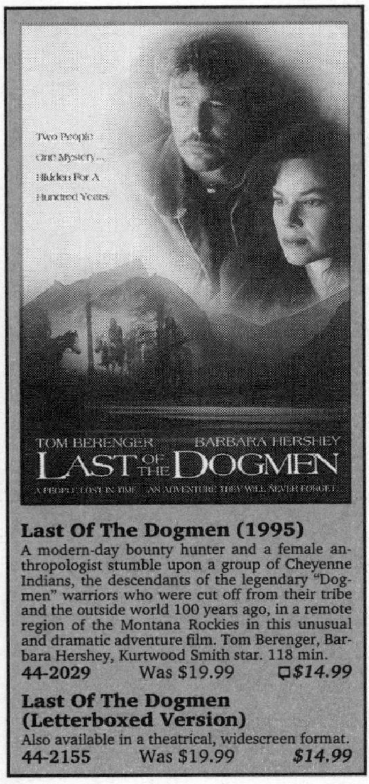

Last Of The Dogmen (1995)
A modern-day bounty hunter and a female anthropologist stumble upon a group of Cheyenne Indians, the descendants of the legendary "Dogmen" warriors who were cut off from their tribe and the outside world 100 years ago, in a remote region of the Montana Rockies in this unusual and dramatic adventure film. Tom Berenger, Barbara Hershey, Kurtwood Smith star. 118 min.
44-2029 Was $19.99 ❑$14.99

Last Of The Dogmen (Letterboxed Version)
Also available in a theatrical, widescreen format.
44-2155 Was $19.99 $14.99

Mission Of Death (1997)
As a child, he helplessly watched as his family was savagely murdered. Twenty-three years later, cop Michael Paré finds himself pursued by both a drug ring that framed him for his partner's death and his fellow officers. What is the shocking secret that links both killings? Riveting actioner also stars Linda Hoffman, Anthony Fridjhon. AKA: "Merchant of Death." 96 min.
27-7115 ❑$99.99

Stealth Fighter (1999)
After faking his own death in order to go into business with an infamous arms dealer, crack Navy pilot Ice-T hatches a plan to hijack a B-2 Stealth Fighter plane from an American base in the Philippines and use it for a campaign of international terrorism. It's up to old rival Costas Mandylor to infiltrate the arms ring and stop them. Andrew Divoff, Ernie Hudson, Erika Eleniak-Goglia also star. 87 min.
27-7177 Was $99.99 ❑$14.99

Final Voyage (1999)
It's "Die Hard" meets "Titanic" in this aquatic actioner. Ice-T and his band of high-tech pirates seize control of a luxury liner, but when an explosion blows a hole in the hull, security guard Dylan Walsh must find a way to stop the crooks and save the passengers and crew before the ship goes down. With Erika Eleniak, Rick Ducommun. 95 min.
27-7206 Was $99.99 ❑$14.99

Dead Boyz Can't Fly (1992)
Three nasty punks, led by a disturbed androgynous man named Goose, go on a wild, bloody killing spree in a high-rise office building. Featuring unsettling action and dark humor, this shocking look at urban violence stars Mark McCulley, Delia Sheppard and Ruth Collins; directed by Howard Winters (adult film director Cecil Howard). Uncut, unrated version; 102 min.
42-1051 Was $59.99 $39.99

Pursuit (1991)
James Ryan ("Kill or Be Killed") stars in this awesome actioner, as a mercenary tracking a cache of stolen gold enlists the aid of a group of renegades, who turn against him and kidnap a female journalist. That's only the beginning of his problems, however, as a cannibal tribe draws closer. Andre Jacobs also stars. 94 min.
44-1828 $89.99

Conflict Of Interest (1993)
Judd Nelson plays a ruthless crime kingpin who runs a drug operation and stolen car ring from his heavy metal club, where a harem of women attend to him. But when a cop discovers that Nelson is behind his wife's murder, the framing of his son and abduction of his son's girl, he'll stop at nothing to get him. Alyssa Milano, Dey Young and Christopher McDonald also star. 88 min.
44-1935 Was $89.99 $14.99

Soldier Boyz (1995)
A tough-as-nails ex-Marine officer who now runs a high-security L.A. prison is recruited to rescue a wealthy heiress who's been kidnapped by a crime ring to taken to Vietnam. The Marine convinces six of his toughest charges to follow him in a danger-filled jungle mission that could mean their freedom...or their death. Michael Dudikoff, Tyrin Turner, Cary-Hiroyuki Tagawa star. 91 min.
44-2028 Was $19.99 $14.99

Spy Games (1999)
In the complicated world of post-Cold War espionage, rival American (Bill Pullman) and Russian (Irene Jacob) agents find themselves engaging in undercover—and under-the-covers—action as they try to retrieve a missing classified videotape. Exciting and often funny actioner also stars Bruno Kirby, Udo Kier. AKA: "History Is Made at Night." 94 min.
68-2003 ❑$69.99

The Hunted (1999)
Neil, a young marine, is joined by girlfriend Kate on a Pacific Northwest vacation that turns deadly when a group of ruthless drug runners kill Neil and try to kidnap Kate. While attempting to escape from the murderers, Kate meets Richard, a hiker she trusts, but who has a true identity she's unaware of. With Sandra Hess, Martin Kove, Rick Aiello, Dale Dye, Renee Estevez. 90 min.
76-7482 $79.99

Lethal Tender (1997)
A Chicago cop suspended from the force finds his boring job as a water plant security guard turn dangerous when terrorists take control of the facility along with a group of hostages. But the terrorists have a master plan involving swiping unsold government bonds, and the guard must disrupt the diabolical scheme before it's too late. Jeff Fahey, Gary Busey star. 93 min.
53-1887 ❑$99.99

Wolverine (1996)
Antonio Sabato, Jr. is Harry Gordini, a college professor and Navy SEAL. When Harry and his family accidentally get drawn into a war between the U.S. government and a highly dangerous drug cartel, he must utilize military tactics to save the lives of his loved ones. Based on the novel by Frederick Forsythe; with Richard Brooks, Traci Lind. AKA: "Code Name: Wolverine." 91 min.
82-5214 $99.99

Fugitive X (1996)
Advertising executive David Heavener has to fight for his life after a clandestine casino computer selects him as the next target in a most dangerous game. Warned that his wife will be killed if he contacts the authorities, Heavener is on the run as wagers are placed on his ability to escape his pursuers. Lynne Holly-Johnson William Windom also star. 97 min.
88-5004 Was $89.99 $14.99

Wesley Snipes

New Jack City (1991)
Explosive modern-day gangster saga starring Wesley Snipes as a crime kingpin who uses high-tech methods to control a ghetto housing project...and New York City's crack trade. Ice-T, Judd Nelson and Mario Van Peebles (who also directed) are the cops trying to halt his operation. 101 min.
19-1871 Was $19.99 ❑$14.99

The Waterdance (1992)
Based on co-director and screenwriter Neal Jimenez's own experiences, this powerful, off-handedly funny story stars Eric Stoltz as a talented writer whose life is shattered when a hiking accident leaves him paralyzed. His rehabilitation takes place in an L.A. clinic where he befriends a biker (William Forsythe) and a hard-living black man (Wesley Snipes). With Helen Hunt. 106 min.
02-2340 Was $19.99 ❑$14.99

White Men Can't Jump (1992)
The hit full-court comedy from writer/director Ron Shelton ("Bull Durham") stars Woody Harrelson and Wesley Snipes as a pair of basketball scam artists who pull their money-making hustles on the playgrounds of Los Angeles. With Rosie Perez, Tyra Ferrell. 115 min.
04-2549 Was $19.99 ❑$14.99

Passenger 57 (1992)
Rip-roaring action yarn starring Wesley Snipes as an airline security expert who gets caught in a plane hijacking masterminded by an infamous terrorist and his band of thugs. Using street smarts and martial arts mastery, Snipes pulls out all the stops to thwart them. With Tom Sizemore, Bruce Payne. 84 min.
19-2058 Was $19.99 ❑$14.99

Boiling Point (1993)
After his partner is killed, U.S. Treasury agent Wesley Snipes searches for the killers among L.A.'s underworld. The culprits turn out to be a veteran con artist (Dennis Hopper) with a penchant for dealing in counterfeit money and his young, trigger-happy partner (Viggo Mortensen). Dan Hedaya, Lolita Davidovich also star in this atmospheric thriller. 93 min.
19-2125 Was $19.99 ❑$14.99

Sugar Hill (1994)
A contemporary gangster epic focusing on the lives of two Harlem siblings (Wesley Snipes, Michael Wright) who become dope dealers, working for the same mobster who maimed their drug-addicted father. When Snipes decides he wants a life away from crime, his brother pulls him into a war against a rival dealer. Clarence Williams III, Ernie Hudson and Abe Vigoda co-star. 123 min.
04-2836 Was $89.99 ❑$14.99

Drop Zone (1994)
Spectacular aerial stunts propel this slam-bang actioner that stars Wesley Snipes as a U.S. marshal who takes to the not-so-friendly skies to find a group of parachuting cons responsible for hijacking an airplane carrying a computer-hacking drug informant. Michael Jeter, Yancy Butler and Gary Busey co-star; John Badham ("Blue Thunder") directs. 101 min.
06-2320 Was $89.99 ❑$14.99

Money Train (1995)
Breathtaking actioner reteams "White Men Can't Jump" stars Wesley Snipes and Woody Harrelson as foster brother transit cops who try to pull off a dangerous heist, robbing a runaway subway train carrying New York transit receipts. Filled with incredible stunts, the film also stars Jennifer Lopez, Robert Blake. 110 min.
02-2874 Was $19.99 ❑$14.99

One Night Stand (1997)
For Los Angeles commercial creator Wesley Snipes, a New York trip for business and to visit estranged friend Robert Downey, Jr., who's been diagnosed with AIDS, leads to a chance sexual encounter with married stranger Nastassja Kinski. The consequences the affair has on Snipes' job and marriage are compellingly portrayed in this sensual drama from director Mike Figgis ("Leaving Las Vegas"). Kyle MacLachlan, Ming-Na Wen also star. 104 min.
02-5171 Was $99.99 ❑$19.99

Murder At 1600 (1997)
When a White House secretary is found murdered inside the executive mansion, veteran D.C. homicide detective Wesley Snipes finds his investigation into the crime meeting with high-level opposition. Snipes teams with Secret Service agent Diane Lane to find the killer, but their search uncovers a shocking secret with global ramifications in this gripping thriller. Alan Alda, Daniel Benzali, Ronny Cox and Dennis Miller also star. 108 min.
19-2572 Was $19.99 ❑$14.99

Futuresport (1998)
In the early 21st century, a deadly team competition known as Futuresport has become the world's most popular sporting event. But when star player Dean Cain uncovers a terrorist plot, he turns to ex-girlfriend Vanessa L. Williams and mentor Wesley Snipes for help in dealing with it the only way he can—in the arena, to the death. Snipes also co-produced this intense sci-fi actioner. 89 min.
02-3301 Was $99.99 ❑$14.99

Blade (1998)
Wesley Snipes is pure dynamite as the Marvel Comics vampire killer, out to cleanse the world of bloodsuckers as he hunts for the vampire who bit his mother during pregnancy and made Snipes a half-human hybrid. With help from sidekick Kris Kristofferson and hematologist N'Bushe Wright, Snipes will need his weapons and martial arts prowess to stop top tooth Stephen Dorff and his nasty minions from taking over the world. 91 min.
02-5193 Was $99.99 ❑$14.99

Blade (Letterboxed Version)
Also available in a theatrical, widescreen format.
02-5204 ❑$14.99

U.S. Marshals (1998)
Tommy Lee Jones returns as unflappable Deputy Marshal Sam Gerard in this sequel to the smash hit "The Fugitive." This time he and his crew are tracking down State Department operative Wesley Snipes, who has been accused of killing two other federal agents. But is Snipes really guilty? Robert Downey, Jr., Kate Nelligan, Irene Jacob, Joe Pantoliano also star. 131 min.
19-2730 Was $99.99 ❑$19.99

U.S. Marshals (Letterboxed Version)
Also available in a theatrical, widescreen format.
19-2786 ❑$19.99

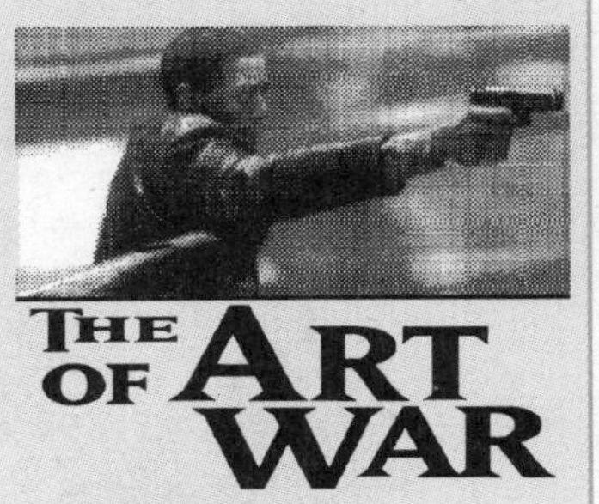

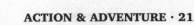

The Art Of War (2000)
Set up as the fall guy in the assassination of a Chinese ambassador to the United Nations, covert U.N. agent Wesley Snipes has to clear his name in order to save his life. After forging an alliance with a pretty translator and an FBI agent, Snipes uncovers the connection between a powerful Chinese businessman, U.S. government agencies and Asia's Triad underworld. Anne Archer, Marie Matiko, Donald Sutherland, Michael Biehn also star.
19-5024 ❑$99.99

Please see our index for these other Wesley Snipes titles: *America's Dream • Demolition Man • Down In The Delta • The Fan • Jungle Fever • Major League • Mo' Better Blues • Rising Sun • To Wong Foo, Thanks For Everything! Julie Newmar • Waiting To Exhale • Wildcats*

Surface To Air (1999)
Michael Madsen and Chad McQueen are brothers stationed in the same Marine Detachment Unit who must put their differences aside when a Persian Gulf mission leaves them stranded behind enemy lines and battling an Iraqi terrorist leader. With Matthew Anderson, Melanie Shatner. 93 min.
27-7121 ❑$99.99

A Rage In Harlem (1991)
Rousing action-comedy, based on a book by Chester Himes ("Cotton Comes to Harlem"), about a mortuary assistant who falls for a Southern vixen trying to fence some stolen gold lifted from her gangster ex-boyfriend. The undertaker will do anything for the girl, even if it means involving his sleazy brother-in-law in the proceedings. Forest Whitaker, Robin Givens, Danny Glover, Gregory Hines star. 115 min.
44-1822 Was $19.99 ❑$14.99

White Mile (1994)
What starts out as a rafting trip/"bonding experience" for some ad executives and their clients turns into a desperate fight for survival on the dangerous white waters...and not everyone will make it. Pulse-pounding adventure saga, based on a true story, stars Alan Alda, Robert Loggia, Peter Gallagher. 96 min.
44-1971 Was $19.99 ❑$14.99

The Ebb-Tide (1998)
Robert Louis Stevenson's tale is given a gripping treatment as "Cracker's" Robbie Coltrane plays a down-and-out sea captain who joins a crew of ex-cons on a voyage which was planned to end in disaster for insurance purposes. Troubles worsen when their ship wrecks on an island inhabited by a mad sea captain and a mute woman. Nigel Terry and Sean Scanlon also star. 100 min.
53-6644 $19.99

Army Of One (1994)
On the run and framed for killing a policeman, car thief Dolph Lundgren kidnaps a beautiful woman who just happens to be a cop. A wild chase ensues, as the police force pursues Lundgren while he seeks to clear his name. George Segal, Kristian Alfonso and Michelle Phillips also star. 102 min.
27-9886 Was $89.99 □*$12.99*

Act Of Piracy (1990)
Gary Busey stars in this thriller as a Vietnam vet who is left adrift on the Mediterranean by a group of terrorists who kidnapped his children. He calls on his expertise at "search-and-destroy" tactics to find the culprits in this tightly woven, action-packed tale. Ray Sharkey and Belinda Bauer also star. 101 min.
40-1414 *$14.99*

Black Cat Run (1998)
When four escaped convicts kill a local sheriff and take his daughter hostage, a young man wrongly pursued by the police for the murder must avoid the law while pursuing the crooks in this high-octane action tale. Patrick Muldoon, Peter Greene, Amelia Heinle and Jake Busey star. 88 min.
44-2182 Was $89.99 □*$14.99*

Bridge Of Dragons (1999)
Intense actioner stars Dolph Lundgren as a man who was adopted as a child by an Asian warlord and trained to be the ultimate fighting machine. When he is joined by a princess who's also a martial arts master, Lundgren must fight for freedom against the warlord's army. Rachel Shane, Cary-Hiroyuki Tagawa also star. 91 min.
44-2206 Was $99.99 □*$14.99*

Exiled In America (1990)
A Central American freedom fighter and his wife escape to the U.S. but find themselves the target of a corrupt CIA agent after she takes a job as a waitress. Complicating matters is a young man who falls for her and a sheriff out for political gain. Edward Albert, Wings Hauser, Kamala Lopez and Stella Stevens star in this actioner. 84 min.
46-5541 *$79.99*

Tomcat Angels (1996)
When one of their cohorts is taken hostage overseas, the sexy fighting femmes known as the "Tomcat Angels" go to work. Using their flying abilities along with their bodies, the gals get down for some hot-and-heavy action in and out of their uniforms. Troma's answer to "Top Gun," this one scores and soars! 95 min.
46-8021 Was $59.99 *$14.99*

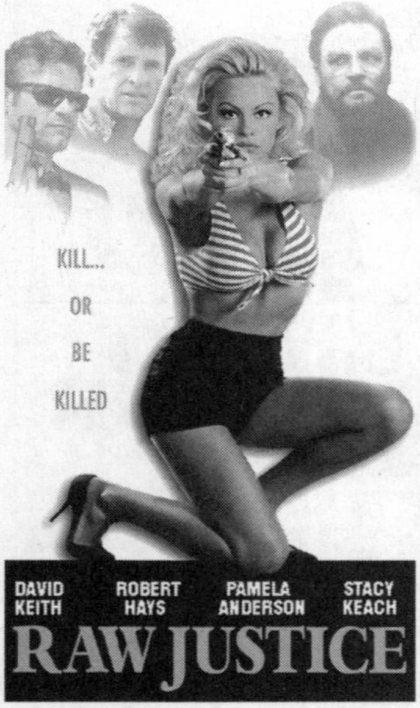
KILL...
OR
BE
KILLED
DAVID KEITH
ROBERT HAYS
PAMELA ANDERSON
STACY KEACH
RAW JUSTICE

Raw Justice (1994)
After the daughter of the mayor is killed, a former cop teams with a gorgeous hooker to find the culprit. The killings mount, leaving this unlikely pair as the next targets in a deadly cat-and-mouse game. David Keith, Pamela Anderson, Charles Napier, Robert Hays, Stacy Keach and Leo Rossi star. AKA: "Good Cop Bad Cop." 92 min.
63-1703 Was $89.99 □*$12.99*

Deadly Descent (1992)
A photographer travels the globe to capture the world's greatest slope stars in this action-packed ski thriller set in the Rocky Mountains and featuring spectacular downhill footage. Damian Lee, Franco Columbu and Paul Coufos star. 85 min.
48-1186 *$59.99*

The Assault (1997)
A female homicide cop and the beautiful murder witness she's assigned to guard hide out in a homeless women's shelter from hit men sent to silence the witness. The shelter's handyman and residents soon help the pair defend themselves from the killers. Stacy Randall, Matt McCoy star. Unrated version; 94 min.
50-5651 *$14.99*

Thunder In Paradise (1993)
Terry "Hulk" Hogan brings his brawn and biceps to this entertaining actioner in which he plays a former Navy SEAL who uses his superboat in a battle against a modern-day pirate. Filled with stunts, comedy and Hulk-sized thrills. With Carol Alt, Patrick Macnee and Chris Lemmon. 104 min.
68-1273 Was $89.99 □*$19.99*

Thunder In Paradise II (1994)
Seaside soldiers-of-fortune Terry "Hulk" Hogan and Chris Lemmon are back aboard their hi-tech boat "Thunder," racing to rescue kidnapped comrade Carol Alt from a foreign prison, in this feature-length adventure taken from the hit TV series. 90 min.
68-1335 □*$89.99*

Thunder In Paradise 3 (1995)
Hulk Hogan's Hurricane and Chris Lemmon's Bru team to save Hurricane's daughter from South American crook Santiago in another feature-length actioner from the hit TV series. There's suspense and wild stunts galore aboard the Thunder. Carol Alt and Patrick Macnee also star. 88 min.
68-1365 □*$89.99*

Master P:
Da Last Don: The Movie (1998)
Gangsta rapper Master P plays Nino Corleone, a man forced into the world of crime after his father, Don Corleone, is gunned down. Master P infiltrates the Cuban mob in order to exact revenge on his father's murderers.
50-8366 *$19.99*

The Great Air Race (1990)
Hair-raising saga set in 1934 in which pilots from around the world converge in London to participate in a 12,000-mile air race to Melbourne, Australia. Barry Bostwick, Helen Slater, Caroline Goodall and David Arnett star. 180 min. on three tapes.
53-6645 Was $99.99 *$39.99*

Bad Attitude (1993)
A streetwise Seattle cop stationed in Chinatown seeks revenge for his partner, who was gunned down in a senseless murder. During his search for the killer, he meets an assassin who works for a drug dealer and a preacher who may hold the keys to the killing. Leon, Gina Lin star. 99 min.
54-9105 Was $69.99 *$19.99*

Urban Jungle (1994)
When a corrupt Harlem housing commissioner devises a scheme to make cash while forcing poor tenants out of their homes, two drug-runners decide to take matters into their own hands, playing contemporary Robin Hoods to help the put-upon tenants and stop the seedy official. Dan Charlton, McKinley Winston star. 90 min.
54-9112 *$79.99*

Kla$h (1996)
A New York photographer takes an assignment in Jamaica, unaware of the danger he will eventually face. He encounters drug dealing and violence, and falls for the girlfriend of a powerful gangster who's plotting to rob the box office take of a reggae contest. Giancarlo Esposito, Jasmine Guy and Cedella Marley star in the reggae-fueled thriller. 90 min.
54-9190 □*$59.99*

The Swordsman (1992)
Swordplay, suspense and science-fantasy mix in this action-packed tale. A detective investigating the theft of an ancient sword from a museum is drawn into the sinister plans of a power-hungry tycoon ready to renew their centuries-spanning battle for the mystical weapon. Lorenzo Lamas, Claire Stansfield and Michael Champion star. 98 min.
63-1586 Was $89.99 □*$12.99*

Gladiator Cop:
The Swordsman II (1994)
Ex-detective Lorenzo Lamas is lured into a deadly game against a man who was executed 2,000 years ago. Both are after a sword once used by Alexander the Great that has been swiped by thugs using it in lethal underground sword-fighting duels. Nicholas Pasco and James Hong also star. 92 min.
76-9076 Was $89.99 *$14.99*

Shadowhunter (1993)
A burned-out Los Angeles cop journeys to a Navajo reservation in Arizona to capture a mystical Native American accused of killing three people. After the murderer escapes from custody, the cop must track him down in the foreboding desert. Scott Glenn, Angela Alvarado and Robert Beltran star in this relentless actioner. 98 min.
63-1608 Was $89.99 □*$14.99*

Bounty Tracker (1993)
A team of assassins led by a criminal mastermind holds Los Angeles at bay. After unsuccessful attempts to stop them, the LAPD calls on a renegade bounty hunter with incredible martial arts expertise to halt the culprits. Lorenzo Lamas, Matthias Hues and Cyndi Pass star in this cinematic powderkeg. 90 min.
63-1622 Was $89.99 □*$14.99*

Direct Hit (1994)
A CIA hit man with plans to retire gets one last assignment from his agency: murder a woman who once had an affair with a senator. When the hired gun discovers that she's only a pawn in a deadly political game, he decides to protect her from being rubbed out. William Forsythe, George Segal, Jo Champa star. 91 min.
63-1738 □*$89.99*

The Heist (1997)
In this intense actioner, an armed robbery leads to a dangerous hostage crisis. Andrew McCarthy and Cynthia Geary star. AKA: "Hostile Force."
50-5684 Was $99.99 *$14.99*

To Die Standing (1991)
A maverick D.E.A. agent teams with a Peruvian cop to track down an international drug kingpin in this pulse-pounding actioner that co-stars Cliff DeYoung, Robert Beltran and Jamie Rose. 87 min.
02-2099 *$89.99*

Deadly Surveillance (1991)
While staking out the apartment of a suspected drug dealer, a detective is drawn into an erotic and deadly triangle involving his ex-partner and a beautiful, seductive blonde. Michael Ironside, Susan Almgren, Christopher Bondy and David Carradine star. 92 min.
63-1476 □*$89.99*

Soldier's Fortune (1991)
A grizzled mercenary adventurer has his work cut out for him when his teenage daughter is abducted by an enemy from his past in this action-laden thriller. Gil Gerard, Charles Napier, P.J. Soles and Dan Haggerty star. 96 min.
63-1491 □*$89.99*

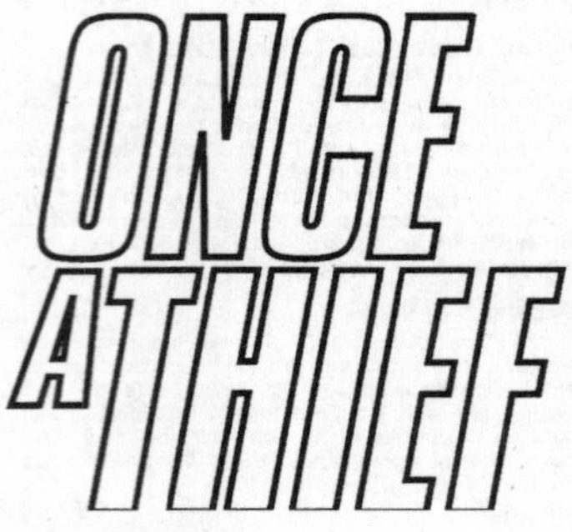
ONCE
A THIEF

Once A Thief
(Director's Cut) (1996)
Director John Woo ("Broken Arrow") adapts his 1991 Hong Kong action film for the small screen. Mac and Li Ann, two expert thieves in the employ of a powerful Asian crime lord, try to break away from him but are ambushed and left for dead. Reunited in America, the pair join up with a top-secret anti-crime task force and face a return encounter with their old boss. Sandrine Holt, Ivan Sergei, Nicholas Lea and Michael Wong star. 99 min.
83-1149 Was $99.99 *$14.99*

Warriors (1994)
Explosive actioner featuring Gary Busey as the leader of a group of former soldiers who serve as America's fiercest anti-terrorist squad. When Busey becomes a fugitive, protégé Michael Paré is called on to stop him in a ruthless battle of wits and wills. Wendii Fulford also stars. 100 min.
63-1743 Was $89.99 □*$12.99*

Clockin' Green (1999)
Mickey and Sonya are a pair of streetwise New York petty crooks and lovers whose relationship—business and personal—takes a serious downswing during a multi-million-dollar bank caper. Sonya betrays Mickey to the law and flees with the money, but it's not long before her ex-partner comes looking for her. With a bright young cast. 105 min.
81-9112 *$59.99*

Bad Blood (1994)
When his estranged brother is marked for death by a ruthless drug kingpin, Lorenzo Lamas goes into action, putting their problematical past behind. This all-out action assault also stars John P. Ryan, Kimberly Kates. 90 min.
27-6922 Was $89.99 □*$12.99*

The Force (1994)
After a maverick L.A. homicide detective is mysteriously killed while investigating a string of murders, a rookie cop encounters the spirit of the deceased detective leading him to a web of corruption in the department. Jason Gedrick, Kim Delaney, Gary Hudson and Cyndi Pass star. 94 min.
63-1744 □*$89.99*

Protector (1998)
After he loses a witness to mobster activities to assassins, an undercover cop is given an ultimatum: find the killers in 10 days or be kicked off the force. Mario Van Peebles, Randy Quaid and Rae Dawn Chong star in this intense actioner.
64-9029 *$99.99*

The Base (1998)
The soldiers of Camp Tillman have been led into dealing drugs by a scheming officer. The Pentagon decides to send a special forces agent to go undercover and investigate. His work brings him into a dangerous situation that threatens his life. Mark Dacascos and Tim Abell star. 101 min.
64-9041 *$69.99*

Supreme Sanction (1998)
She was trained by a secret government organization to be a top assassin, but when she's assigned to kill a reporter about to expose corruption within the agency, which side will she choose? Kristy Swanson, Michael Madsen and David Dukes star in this high-octane actioner. 93 min.
64-9043 *$69.99*

Crackerjack (1994)
A tasty treat for action fans, this thriller that pits a maverick cop on vacation at a Rocky Mountain ski resort against a gang of jewel thieves features the high-popping style of Thomas Ian Griffith, the candy-like sweetness of Nastassja Kinski, and a nutty turn by Christopher Plummer as the crooks' leader. Is there a surprise inside, too? How about an exploding glacier? 96 min.
63-1751 Was $89.99 □*$14.99*

Beyond Forgiveness (1995)
In this action-packed thriller, a tough Chicago cop searches for his brother's killers and is soon thrust into a dangerous battle against international black marketeers dealing with human lives. Thomas Ian Griffith, Rutger Hauer and Joanna Trzepiecinska star. 95 min.
63-1782 Was $89.99 □*$14.99*

The Final Cut (1996)
You'll get blown away by this actioner in which Sam Neill plays a retired bomb specialist called on to stop a sophisticated bomber destroying the city of Seattle with his devastating "craft." Charles Martin Smith, Matt Craven, Anne Ramsay and Amanda Plummer also star. 99 min.
63-1853 □*$99.99*

Hostage Train (1997)
When a terrorist group commandeers a train filled with wealthy passengers, a maverick cop who is the head bad guy's arch-enemy is the only man who can stop them. But what can he do when he learns his girlfriend is among the hostages? Judge Reinhold, Carol Alt and Michael Sarrazin star in this fast-paced actioner. 99 min.
63-1892 □*$99.99*

Shelter (1998)
With his wife in a coma and a price placed on his head by his corrupt boss, ATF agent John Allen Nelson goes on the run and is forced to hide out with the Greek crimelord he had initially been chasing. Their uneasy alliance leads to a deadly and violent showdown in this explosive actioner. Charles Durning, Peter Onorati, Brenda Bakke and Costas Mandylor co-star. 92 min.
64-9024 Was $99.99 □*$14.99*

The Wrecking Crew (1999)
The streets of Detroit are going to explode—literally—with action when Ice-T leads his government-backed anti-crime squad, the Wrecking Crew, against gang boss Snoop Dogg and his minions in this intense mix of martial arts thrills and urban drama. With Ernie Hudson, Jr., TJ Storm.
64-9057 *$99.99*

Reason To Die (1990)
Wings Hauser plays a man who hunts down bail-jumpers and brings them back to the courts for justice. His latest assignment finds him after a killer who murders prostitutes and who threatens the life of a pretty writer specializing in the subject. With Anneline Kriel, Paddy Lister. Uncut, unrated version; 96 min.
68-1159 *$89.99*

Beyond Justice (1992)
After a gorgeous businesswoman's son is kidnapped by his playboy Arab father, she hires a former CIA agent to retrieve him. Taking a commando team into the father's desert homeland, the mission soon becomes a deadly battle with international consequences. Rutger Hauer, Omar Sharif, Carol Alt and Elliott Gould star. 113 min.
68-1246 Was $89.99 □*$12.99*

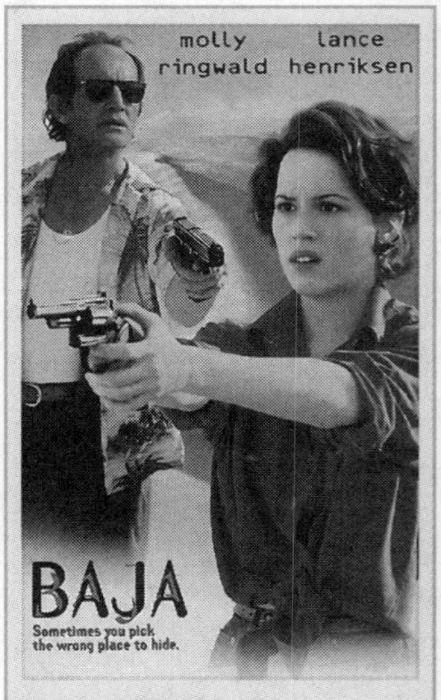
molly ringwald
lance henriksen
BAJA
Sometimes you pick the wrong place to hide.

Baja (1995)
On the run from crooks and the police after a drug deal goes sour, a young woman and her boyfriend hiding out in a trailer in the Baja desert have their problems compounded when the woman's estranged husband comes looking for her, as well as a mob hit man. Molly Ringwald, Michael A. Nickles and Lance Henriksen star. 92 min.
63-1815 Was $89.99 □*$14.99*

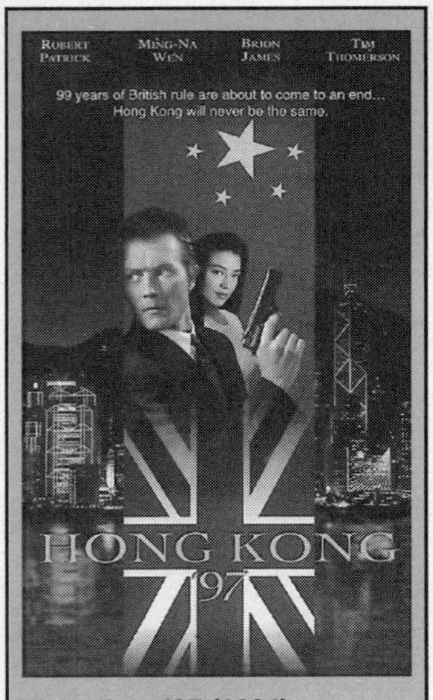

Hong Kong '97 (1994)
Slam-bang thriller about a corporate assassin assigned to murder a Chinese general on the eve of the People's Republic of China's 1997 takeover of Hong Kong from Great Britain. When the hit man discovers that his superiors have set him up and put a $10 million bounty on his head, he must get out of Hong Kong before anyone can collect. Robert Patrick, Ming-Na Wen, Brion James star. 91 min.
68-1327 Was $89.99 ❏*$14.99*

Interceptor (1992)
A group of terrorists attempts to abduct the Air Force's top-secret virtual reality Stealth Fighter plane in transit at 30,000 feet. The hijackers' only obstacles are a determined Air Force captain and the transport plane's tough female pilot. Jurgen Prochnow, Elizabeth Morehead and Andrew Divoff star. 92 min.
68-1251 ❏*$14.99*

Extreme Justice (1993)
Forceful, true-to-life action saga focusing on the Los Angeles Police Department's Special Investigation Section, a secretive branch that will do anything to stop a crime—even step outside the boundaries of the law. Lou Diamond Phillips is the cop wanting out of the squad; Scott Glenn his partner. With Yaphet Kotto, Chelsea Field. 96 min.
68-1276 Was $89.99 ❏*$12.99*

Day Of Atonement (1993)
Christopher Walken, Jennifer Beals and Jill Clayburgh star in this action-packed thriller about a drug kingpin who is released from prison after a 10-year stint, only to find his son's bank is involved in money-laundering and his nephew is running the family's criminal activities. 127 min.
68-1271 Was $89.99 ❏*$12.99*

McCinsey's Island (1998)
Ex-secret agent Hulk Hogan leaves the spy biz to study sea turtles on a remote tropical island. He's lured out of retirement, though, when one of his reptilian charges is found to have the map to a buried treasure engraved on its shell—a treasure that old foe Grace Jones will stop at nothing to claim. Light-hearted action flick also stars Robert Vaughn, Todd Sheeler. 93 min.
76-9112 Was $39.99 *$14.99*

Point Of Impact (1993)
After being accused of killing a fellow agent, a customs agent based in Miami is hired as a bodyguard for a mobster's sexy wife. Sparks ignite between the cop and the wife, leading to a high-risk triangle of danger. Michael Paré, Barbara Carrera and Michael Ironside star. Uncut, unrated version; 98 min.
68-1282 ❏*$89.99*

Teenage Bonnie And Klepto Clyde (1993)
High-powered modern take on the legendary gangster story, focusing on two teenagers who go on a wild crime spree across state lines. Maureen Flannigan, Scott Wolf and Don Novello star in this sexy, fast-paced actioner. 90 min.
68-1284 ❏*$89.99*

Merchants Of War (1990)
Two military commandos experience all sorts of deadly obstacles when one of them falls into the hands of a despicable terrorist, provoking the other friend to carry out a daring escape plan. Asher Brauner, Jesse Vint star. 84 min.
68-1169 *$89.99*

Nightmare At Bittercreek (1990)
A riveting actioner starring Tom Skerritt as the guide to a horseback party consisting of four women. He and his charges are put to the test when a group of sadistic killers hunt them down. Joanna Cassidy co-stars. 92 min.
68-1193 *$89.99*

On The Block (1991)
An erotic thriller set in Baltimore about a stripper trying to rebuild her life and an evil real estate tycoon trying to shut down the red-light district clubs. Marilyn Jones, Howard Rollins and Blaze Starr star. 96 min.
68-1194 *$89.99*

Into The Sun (1992)
Action is mixed with laughs in this tale of a hot-shot Air Force pilot who gets saddled with looking after a movie star researching for a film role. The pair find themselves caught in a real-life dogfight in the Middle East. Michael Paré, Anthony Michael Hall, Terry Kiser star. 101 min.
68-1227 Was $89.99 ❏*$12.99*

Faith (1992)
A teenage girl is faced with a life on the city streets after her parents die and she escapes from a brutal foster home. She's saved by a Mafia tough out for revenge against his own father's killers in this gritty urban thriller. Sylvia Seidel, Richard Maldone and Ami Dolenz star. 104 min.
68-1252 ❏*$89.99*

The Chase (1992)
A young bank robber on the run from the law and an elderly man who becomes involved in his life-or-death chase are the key players in this taut blend of action and suspense. Casey Siemaszko, Ben Johnson star. 93 min.
68-1253 *$89.99*

Killer Instinct (1992)
The streets of New York run red with Mafia blood in this explosive gangster saga, as two brothers rise to the top of the crime world, only to be torn apart when they fall for the same woman. Christopher Bradley, Bruce Nozick, Rachel York star. AKA: "Mad Dog Cole." 101 min.
68-1256 ❏*$89.99*

Hitz (1992)
Thrill-packed urban actioner about a Latino youth who unwillingly kills two rival gang members and finds himself caught in a fight between a liberal judge and her "law and order"-minded colleague. Elliott Gould, Emilia Crow, Richard Coca and Cuba Gooding, Jr. star. 90 min.
68-1236 ❏*$89.99*

Treasure (1993)
Three 12-year-old boys stumble upon clues about the strange disappearance of a lighthouse keeper 30 years earlier. During their investigation, they are hurled into a thrilling adventure with supernatural experiences. John Weisbarth stars. 87 min.
68-1262 *$89.99*

Dead Center (1994)
A street punk arrested in a drug bust is turned into a government assassin. When things go wrong on an assignment and he's framed for the killing of a U.S. senator, he finds himself on the lam...and the only person he can confide in is the lethal female agent who trained him. Justin Lazard, Rachel York star. 90 min.
68-1301 *$89.99*

Freefall (1994)
An undercover crime fighter who thrives on danger by freefalling off mountain cliffs in the rain forest has a romantic liaison with a beautiful photographer, which draws him into a world of danger and international conspiracy. Eric Roberts, Jeff Fahey and Pamela Gidley star. 96 min.
68-1303 ❏*$89.99*

Covert Assassin (1993)
Action and suspense with Roy Scheider as an ex-government agent who specialized in covert tactical operations. Hired by a sexy baroness to head a strike force and eliminate her husband's killers, Scheider's search for the assassins lands him in a deadly battle with more than one twist along the way. Patricia Millardet, Ted McGinley co-star. 114 min.
68-1329 ❏*$89.99*

Spitfire (1994)
When her father is abducted by a crime syndicate after a top-secret computer disc, a beautiful martial arts expert teams up with a hard-nosed reporter to rescue him. Exciting actioner stars Lance Henriksen, Tim Thomerson, Kristie Phillips. 95 min.
68-1338 ❏*$89.99*

Warrior Spirit (1994)
Two young men from contrasting worlds meet at school and, after being forced to leave for different reasons, decide to set out into the Yukon wilderness to search for a fabled fortune in gold inside Rainbow Mountain. Exciting "coming of age" adventure saga stars Lukas Haas, Jimmy Herman, Allan Musy. 94 min.
68-1345 Was $89.99 *$14.99*

Flashfire (1993)
A pair of Los Angeles detectives are assigned to catch a gang of arsonists who've been setting the city ablaze, but one of the cops is murdered by the crooks. His vengeful partner teams up with a prostitute who saw the killing to uncover the shocking truth behind the fires. Intense actioner stars Billy Zane, Louis Gossett, Jr., Kristin Minter. 88 min.
68-1353 Was $89.99 ❏*$14.99*

Night Of The Running Man (1995)
High-powered actioner stars Andrew McCarthy as a down-and-out Las Vegas cab driver who's given a chance to get out of his rut when he finds a cool $1 million on the backseat of his taxi. He's soon pursued by mob hit man Scott Glenn and forced to use his wits to elude him. John Glover, Janet Gunn also star. 93 min.
68-1357 ❏*$89.99*

Eye Of The Wolf (1995)
Rugged adventure set in the Canadian northwoods of 1912, where government zoologist Jeff Fahey stumbles upon a murdered mountie in the wild, and a part-husky, part-wolf hybrid found standing guard over the body may be the only thing that can help find the mountie's killer. With Sophie Duez. 95 min.
68-1377 Was $89.99 *$14.99*

Operation Intercept (1995)
After a scientist who designed technology that can cause airplanes to crash is murdered, his daughter, convinced the death was a government hit, uses the device to take over a plane to bomb Washington. A top pilot takes off in a desperate race to stop her in this fast-paced thriller. Bruce Payne, Natasha Andreichenko, Lance Henriksen star. 94 min.
68-1784 ❏*$89.99*

Northern Passage (1995)
Exciting frontier adventure set in the late 1800s and starring Jeff Fahey ("The Marshal") as a zoologist who must rescue a friend's beautiful daughter when she's abducted by a villainous fur trader. Neve Campbell, Jacques Weber co-star. 97 min.
68-1791 *$89.99*

The Wolves (1995)
When a reckless mining company uses the wilderness home of a family of wolves as a toxic dump site, a brother and sister join with a Native American guide to stop the environmental devastation. Exciting actioner stars Darren Dalton, Kristen Hocking. 87 min.
68-1794 *$89.99*

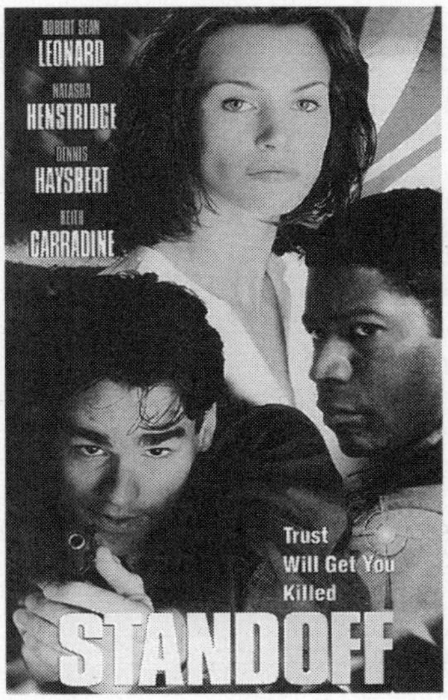

Standoff (1997)
Four federal agents, part from a botched FBI raid on a cult compound in Texas, take refuge in a seemingly empty farmhouse. Tensions rise to the surface and things get deadly when two of the agents capture two female cult members and bring them inside. Gripping and suspenseful actioner stars Robert Sean Leonard, Natasha Henstridge, Dennis Haysbert and Keith Carradine. 91 min.
68-1866 Was $99.99 ❏*$14.99*

Black Out (1996)
The "Boz" is back—and we've got him. Former football ace Brian Bosworth returns to the screen, playing a happily married bank executive whose life changes radically when a car accident leaves him with amnesia. After his wife is brutally murdered, Bosworth pulls out all the stops to find out who killed her and what his past was really like. With Brad Dourif, Clair Yarlett. 98 min.
68-1811 ❏*$99.99*

Hollow Point (1996)
Crime boss John Lithgow plans one last operation before leaving America for good, but finds competing federal agents Tia Carrere and Thomas Ian Griffith in his way. Their rivalry threatens each other's investigation, but eventually they must work with Donald Sutherland, Lithgow's former top hit man, to bring him down. 102 min.
68-1815 Was $99.99 ❏*$14.99*

Virus (1996)
An accidental spill of biochemical warfare specimens in a national park near where the president is due to attend an ecological conference threatens to spread a deadly virus across the country. Only government security chief Brian Bosworth and a local park ranger can stop the disaster in this taut action tale. With Leah Pinsent, Eric Peterson. 90 min.
68-1819 ❏*$99.99*

Warhead (1996)
A renegade Army general in charge of a radical militia group has gained control of an ICBM silo and is threatening to launch the missile at Washington. Only an elite special forces squad, led by Frank Zagarino, and a beautiful scientist can stop the nuclear nightmare in this riveting action tale. With Joe Lara, Elizabeth Giordano. 97 min.
68-1820 ❏*$99.99*

Ordeal In The Arctic (1992)
On a military transport flight to an outpost near the North Pole, a C-130 Hercules crashes in the frozen wilderness. As a search-and-rescue mission is hampered by storms, the crash survivors struggle to survive in sub-zero temperatures. Richard Chamberlain, Melanie Mayron, Catherine Mary Stewart star. 93 min.
68-1835 ❏*$99.99*

Volcano: Fire On The Mountain (1997)
No one will listen to the warnings of a geologist when he discovers that a popular ski resort is sitting on top of a long-dormant volcano that's about to blow—until the mountaintop erupts and threatens everything and everyone in sight! Exciting actioner stars Dan Cortese, Cynthia Gibb and Brian Kerwin. 98 min.
68-1842 Was $89.99 ❏*$12.99*

The Real Thing (1997)
An ex-con, desperate for money to help his dying brother obtain a liver transplant, hooks up with a motley crew of fellow crooks and his former girlfriend for a New Year's Eve nightclub robbery in this action-filled crime drama. James Ruzzo, Gary Busey, Ashley Laurence, Emily Lloyd, Jeremy Piven, Rod Steiger star. 89 min.
68-1859 ❏*$99.99*

Brainsmasher... A Love Story (1993)
Ayyyyyy! It's Andrew Dice Clay as a no-nonsense bouncer who protects gorgeous supermodel Teri Hatcher from a gang of killer ninjas. Hip action-comedy also stars Deborah Van Valkenburgh, Tim Thomerson and Charles Rocket. AKA: "The Bouncer and the Lady." 88 min.
68-1279 Was $89.99 ❏*$12.99*

Mean Guns (1997)
An about-to-be-opened prison becomes a battleground when a gathering of the world's deadliest criminals is forced to fight for their survival by the crime boss who holds them prisoner and offers a $10,000,000 prize to the last three survivors. Ultra-intense actioner stars Ice T, Christopher Lambert, Deborah Van Valkenburgh. 110 min.
68-1876 Was $99.99 ❏*$14.99*

Armstrong (1998)
For hard-hitting action that'll floor you, don't miss this explosive tale of an ex-Navy SEAL who must avenge his friend's murder by Moscow-based thugs who are selling nuclear weapons to international terrorists. Frank Zagarino, Charles Napier, Richard Lynch, Kimberly Kates star. 97 min.
68-1880 ❏*$99.99*

Scarred City (1998)
Policeman Stephen Baldwin is thrilled when he's tabbed to join the city's elite Select Unit Armed Response team, but when he discovers the SCAR squad's lethal tactics include leaving no witnesses, Baldwin rescues call girl Tia Carrere from a deadly drug bust. Together they must fight for their lives in this riveting action tale. Chazz Palminteri also stars. 95 min.
68-1900 ❏*$99.99*

Sweepers (1998)
Years after dropping out of sight following his son's death from a land mine during a mission, mercenary minesweeper Dolph Lundgren is brought back to help a female bomb squad expert stop terrorists from shipping high-tech mines to America. Intense actioner also stars Claire Stansfield, Bruce Payne. 96 min.
68-1910 ❏*$99.99*

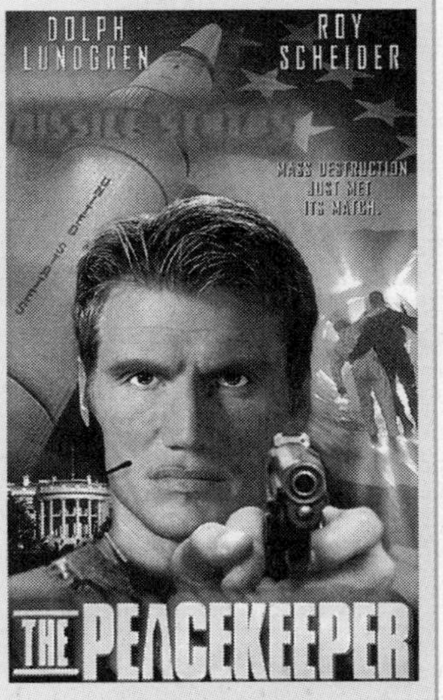

The Peacekeeper (1997)
He's the man who loves peace enough to fight for it. He's Dolph Lundgren, and in this explosive action film he's all that stands between America and a international terrorist who is threatening the country with nuclear blackmail. Roy Scheider, Michael Sarazin and Montel Williams also star. 98 min.
68-1883 Was $99.99 ❏*$14.99*

Desert Steel (1994)
The world of 4x4 racing provides the backdrop for this thrilling story about a driver who must make a choice between his dedication to the sport and the woman he loves. David Naughton, Amanda Wyss and road racing champion Roger Mears star. 89 min.
76-9057 Was $89.99 *$14.99*

L.A. Wars (1994)
A ruthless drug kingpin...a Mafia boss...a rugged bodyguard. These three people find themselves battling each other in a war filled with weapons, amazing martial arts moves and action on the streets of Los Angeles. Vince Murdocco and Rodrigo Obregon star. 94 min.
76-9058 Was $89.99 *$14.99*

Boiler Room (1994)
Two phony phone salesmen who push everything from sex to rare coins in a "boiler room" find their operation coming under the scrutiny of the Attorney General. As the investigation gets tougher, the partners begin cheating each other, which leads to violent altercations. Joe Estevez, Ahley Rhey and Paul Clark star. 84 min.
73-9114 *$29.99*

Sweet Justice (1992)
When their friend is brutally murdered, six lovely, lethal ex-commandos take the law into their own hands and set out to teach the killers that "when revenge is bitter...justice is sweet." High-impact actioner stars Marc Singer, Finn Carter and Kathleen Kinmont. 92 min.
72-9013 Was $89.99 *$14.99*

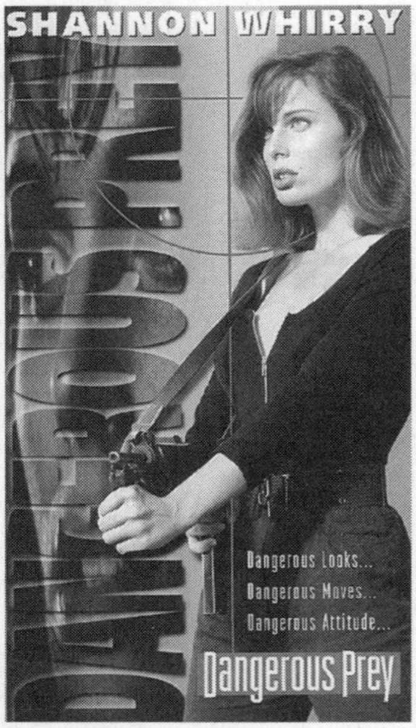

Dangerous Prey (1995)
Sexy actioner starring Shannon Whirry as a woman arrested for gunrunning who is taken to a secret government agency where she is indoctrinated into the Falcons, a team of assassins. With help from a fellow lesbian assassin, Whirry tackles a series of tough assignments until she finds out what her superior's real plans are. With Joseph Laufer, Ciara Hunter and Carol Kartier. 92 min.
76-9102 Was $99.99 *$14.99*

Dark Reign 187 (1998)
Two African-American friends trying to raise cash to shoot their "gangsta" film run into trouble when a series of murders occurs at a house party. Suspense and thrills follow as everyone becomes a suspect in the massacre. Andre Walker, Maurice Sparks and Everette Elliston star. 93 min.
73-9300 *$19.99*

Demolition Highway (1997)
This is one highway action fans will want to get lost on! A man sent to prison after a crime syndicate murdered his girlfriend finds his new girl held by a depraved criminal leader. In order to save her, he must face sadistic henchmen and a biker gang. Danny Fendley, Joe Estevez and Lisa Tyre star.
76-7343 *$39.99*

The Rebel Within (1998)
A peaceful small town is infected with the plague of drugs in this gripping action/drama. When a local man is killed under mysterious circumstances, his son joins forces with his best friend to bring the well-known businessman responsible to justice. Cliff Potts, Susanne LaVelle, Charles Dierkop and India Allen star. 98 min.
76-7410 *$59.99*

Body Count (1996)
A cop from Thailand seeking revenge on a group of Los Angeles criminals gets in trouble and soon has a detective watching him, but the two lawmen join forces to bring the bad guys to justice. Michael Christian, Joe Estevez, Roger Lee and Chris Mitchum star. 90 min.
82-5017 *$79.99*

Clearcut (1992)
Intense adventure story stars Graham Greene ("Dances with Wolves") as an Indian living in Western Canada who is enraged by the ecological devastation of his ancestral homeland. He kidnaps a lawyer and a developer and takes them on a cross-country trek to show them the results of their actions. Michael Hogan, Ron Lea co-star. 98 min.
71-5257 *$12.99*

Twice Under (1991)
Seventeen years after he served in Vietnam, Ed Chambers, a supervisor for the city's sewer system, discovers a string of people have been murdered near the sewers. Now, he and his son are the targets of the killer, who may be connected to Chambers' wartime experiences. Ron Spencer, Amy Lacy, Ian Borger star. 88 min.
72-4001 *$19.99*

Blood Street (1992)
San Francisco cop Joe Wong (writer/director/star Leo Fong) is a no-nonsense detective hired by a gorgeous woman to find her missing husband. Wong is soon thrown between two warring mobsters in a thrilling film highlighted by spectacular action scenes. Richard Norton and Playboy centerfold Kim Paige co-star. 88 min.
72-4011 *$19.99*

Ground Zero L.A. (1991)
Sex and nuclear blackmail mix in this tale of a physicist and his co-worker who hijack a batch of weapons-grade material and launch a billion-dollar ransom scheme against Los Angeles. It's down to a detective and his beautiful partner to stop everything from going ke-bang! Carol Cummings, Wayne Summers and Tabitha Stevens star. AKA: "Radioactive."
72-4020 *$19.99*

Da Vinci's War (1993)
After his sister is murdered, a young man joins a professional assassin and a team of Vietnam veterans to find the culprits. Joey Travolta, Michael Nouri, Vanity and James Russo star in this actioner. 94 min.
72-9015 *$14.99*

Street Wars (1994)
Ferocious actioner from the director of "Penitentiary" about a teenage aviation cadet named Sugarpop with plans to go to West Point thanks to funding from his brother Frank, one of L.A.'s most powerful drug dealers. When Frank is killed, Sugarpop organizes his brother's gang and turns them into a ghetto air force, seeking revenge. Alan Joseph stars. 90 min.
72-9037 Was $89.99 *$14.99*

Hand Gun (1994)
With his dying breath, the lone survivor of a big-money robbery tells his two sons clues to the location of the missing loot. Can the brothers trust each other long enough to outrun the mob and some crooked cops to locate their "family fortune"? Treat Williams, Paul Schulze, Seymour Cassel star. 90 min.
72-9041 Was $89.99 *$14.99*

Street Law (1995)
A brilliant trial lawyer goes into debt with loan sharks to save his firm, but when he loses everything, he calls on his ex-con friend to help him. For his part of the deal, the lawyer must compete in a deadly, illegal martial arts contest. Jeff Wincott and Paco Christian Prieto star in this wild actioner. 98 min.
72-9053 Was $89.99 *$14.99*

Navy SEALs (1990)
They're the elite strike force trained in anti-terrorist tactics, and they're America's secret weapon against Arab commandos armed with stolen Stinger missiles and holding American hostages. Art imitates life, or vice versa, in this slam-bang, rock-and-roll actioner that stars Charlie Sheen, Michael Biehn and Joanne Whalley-Kilmer. 113 min.
73-1091 Was $89.99 *$14.99*

The Expert (1995)
High-kicking Jeff Speakman is a special operations officer who helps police try to nail the criminal with multiple personalities responsible for killing his sister. When the killer is placed in a hospital for rehabilitation, Speakman decides to take matters into his own hands to stop him before he causes more trouble. Michael Shaner, James Brolin also star. 92 min.
73-1202 Was $89.99 *❑$14.99*

Thick As Thieves (1999)
Master thief-for-hire Alec Baldwin is contracted to pull off a heist for ghetto crime boss Michael Jai White, but the simple job turns into a set-up that ignites a bitter and increasingly deadly battle between the two. Intense and stylish actioner also stars André Braugher, Rebecca De Mornay, David Byrd and Janeane Garofalo. 95 min.
02-9218 *$79.99*

Outlaw Drive-In, Vol. 2: Action-Comedy Double Feature
First up is the outrageous action flick "Chick Boxer" (1992), a woman who joins a karate school and discovers the school's owners are mixed up in prostitution and drugs...and then springs into action. With Michelle Bauer. Next, two students with car trouble find themselves trapped in the backwoods, where they meet a beautiful woman, a nasty sheriff and a psychotic survivalist, in "Redneck County Fever" (1992). 120 min. total.
73-9035 Double Feature *$19.99*

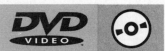

DVD VIDEO
ASK ABOUT OUR GIANT DVD CATALOG!

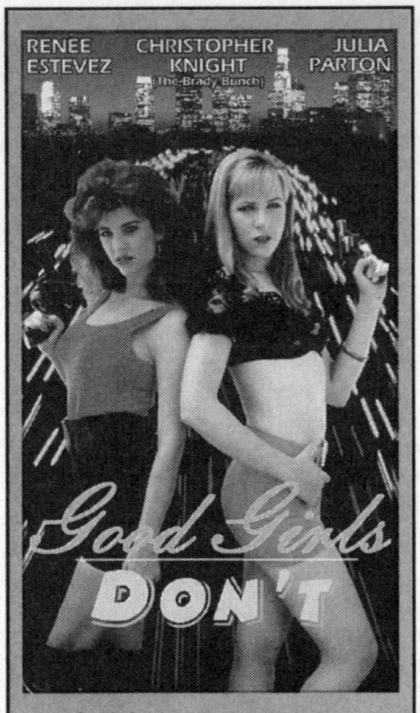

Good Girls Don't (1995)
Renée Estevez and Julia Parton are two sexy babes carrying .45s who are framed for murder. They hightail it from the cops in a slick red convertible, unaware there's $500,000 in stolen loot in the trunk, and in hot pursuit are the law and mobsters in this racy comic actioner. Christopher Knight, Mary Woronov co-star. 90 min.
82-5012 Was $69.99 *$39.99*

Hitman (1999)
High-energy actioner in which boxer Lucky Delon is told to take a fall for a gangster named BMF. When he knocks out his opponent, Delon is forced to go on the run. While in a bar, Delon meets a professional assassin who starts to teach him the finer points of defending himself. With a bright young cast.
73-9342 *$39.99*

Rule #3 (1994)
Con man Travis West plots a brilliant multi-million dollar real estate scam...but so does his gorgeous partner, who hopes to turn the tables on Travis. Soon, the conniving pair are caught between the police, bounty hunters and themselves. Inspired by true events, the film stars Mitchell Cox and Marcia Swayze. 93 min.
74-3006 *$89.99*

Abducted II: The Reunion (1994)
Crazed woodsman Vern is back and up to his old tricks, stalking three women who have come to the woods for a camping trip but wind up in a desperate race to stay alive. Dan Haggerty, Raquel Bianca, Debbie Rochon and Lawrence King star. 85 min.
74-3012 *$49.99*

Bullet Down Under (1993)
An L.A. cop who recently moved to Australia joins the Sydney police force. Teamed with a two-fisted detective, the pair launch a dangerous battle against the ruthless crime ring responsible for the Aussie's partner's murder. Christopher Atkins, Mark ("Jacko") Jackson, Virginia Hey star. 95 min.
74-3026 *$89.99*

One Way Out (1996)
An ex-con hopes to start walking the straight and narrow by returning to his family's farm, but after learning that his brother's sleazy boss has cheated him and caused the farm's foreclosure, a revenge scheme is enacted that leads to kidnaping, murder and a violent crime spree. Jack Gwaltney, Annie Golden and Michael Ironside star. 106 min.
74-3031 *$89.99*

Sacred Cargo (1996)
Two brothers—an ex-U.S. Marine and a priest—get mixed-up in an international gem-smuggling ring operating in Russia in this high-stakes action thriller. Chris Penn, Martin Sheen, J.T. Walsh and Anna Karin star. 93 min.
74-3032 *$89.99*

Behind Enemy Lines (1997)
Thomas Ian Griffith stars as a mercenary who is sent with his friend on a mission to retrieve stolen nuclear weapons from an enemy government. The mission ends in failure and only Griffith escapes, but he returns one year later to finish the job and rescue his buddy. Explosive action tale also stars Chris Mulkey, Mark Carlton. 89 min.
73-1283 *❑$59.99*

Mission Of Mercy (1994)
After his beautiful wife is kidnapped by a Central American gun dealer, an American millionaire hires a squad of expert mercenaries to retrieve her. One of the hired men happens to be an old pal of the kidnapper, but that doesn't stop him from dodging police and L.A. street gangs in order to complete his mission. Gerald Brodin, Jeffrey Orman star.
73-9111 *$29.99*

Atomic Train (1999)
In this high-energy actioner, a freight train carrying a concealed Russian nuclear bomb and hazardous materials is turned into a "fright train" when it becomes a runaway vehicle headed for the city of Denver. Investigator Rob Lowe and a team of experts board the train in hopes of stopping it, while the denizens of Denver riot and evacuate the city. Kristin Davis, Esai Morales also star. 168 min.
68-1942 *❑$69.99*

Tactical Assault (1999)
Shortly after Iraq's 1990 invasion of Kuwait, two U.S. Air Force pilots encounter an Iraqi passenger jet in restricted airspace. When one of the flyers (Rutger Hauer) prepares to attack the defenseless plane, his comrade (Robert Patrick) is forced to shoot him down. Captured and placed in an Iraqi prison, Hauer plans to get back at his former friend in this intense actioner. Ken Howard, Isabel Glasser also star. 89 min.
68-1946 *$69.99*

Jungleground (1995)
Explosive urban action tale stars Roddy Piper as a police officer who is captured by a ruthless drug lord and becomes the prey in a deadly hunt through the burned-out buildings of "Jungleground." If he can't reach freedom by dawn, Piper and his girl will die! With Peter Williams, Torri Higginson. 90 min.
72-9054 Was $89.99 *$14.99*

Under The Gun (1995)
A nightclub owner who's gotten on the wrong side of mobsters and crooked cops is looking to get out of the business, but, caught in the middle, his only way out is to fight with his wits, his fists and his guns. Richard Norton, Kathy Long star. 90 min.
72-9062 Was $89.99 *$14.99*

Shark Attack (1999)
When a marine biologist's friend becomes the latest victim in a series of deadly attacks by man-eating sharks that have terrorized an African fishing village, he teams with his friend's sister to discover what is driving the aquatic killers into a frenzy. Casper Van Dien, Jennifer McShane, Ernie Hudson star. 95 min.
68-1949 *❑$79.99*

The 13th Mission (1991)
This mission was definitely the unluckiest! A group of highly skilled soldiers must complete their most frightening combat campaign in order to escape the jungles of Southeast Asia. Robert Marius, Mike Monty star. 95 min.
68-3001 Was $59.99 *$14.99*

The Bronx War (1991)
Realistic, action-packed story set in the South Bronx, one of the toughest neighborhoods in the country. Here hustlers fight to the death over drugs and power, and only the strong—and the lucky—will survive. This dynamic film was directed by Joseph B. Vasquez ("Hangin' with the Homeboys") and stars Charmaine Cruz and Andre Brown. 91 min.
71-5232 *$12.99*

Delta Heat (1992)
Tracing the source of a deadly drug to the bayous of Louisiana, a Los Angeles detective heads to New Orleans, but finds himself in lots of trouble when his partner is savagely murdered in a voodoo ritual. Anthony Edwards, Lance Henriksen and Betsy Russell star. 91 min.
71-5258 *❑$12.99*

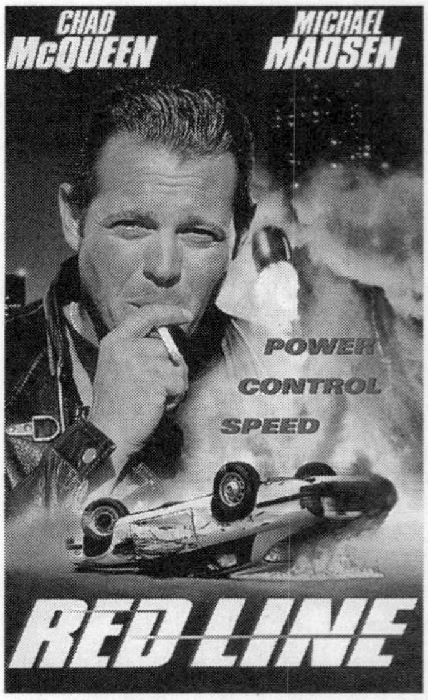

Red Line (1996)
Action-packed tale about a former race car driver who finds himself in big trouble after becoming involved with some underworld figures, and back on track when he teams with a street-smart young woman to take on his adversaries. Chad McQueen, Michael Madsen, Corey Feldman, Roxanna Zal and Jan-Michael Vincent star. 90 min.
72-9072 Was $19.99 *$14.99*

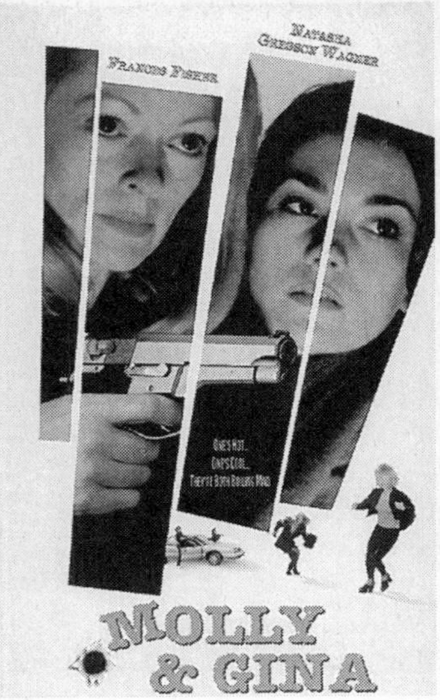

Molly & Gina (1994)
Thelma and Louise...look out! Molly is a heavy-drinking 9-to-5 type who teams with new age nymphomaniac Gina when both of their men are gunned down. They decide to tackle the assassins themselves as they go guns-a-firin' into L.A.'s underworld. Frances Fisher, Natasha Gregson Wagner, Stella Stevens and Peter Fonda star. 93 min.
83-1009 Was $89.99 *$14.99*

Blood, Bullets, Buffoons (1996)
What do you get when you mix explosive action, gorgeous women and hilarious situations? The answer is this effort in which a recent college grad gets out of prison after a bad drug deal and sets out to exact revenge on those who put him there. He goes after mobsters, his sexy girlfriend and a friend who sold him out. Howard Stern fave Amy Lynn Baxter stars with Zachary Winston Snygg. 90 min.
73-9147 Was $49.99 *$29.99*

Panic In The Skies (1996)
A 747 is sent into a nose dive after a lightning strike kills the pilot and co-pilot. Now, with the fuel tanks leaking, the surviving passengers must find a way to save the plane before it either crashes into a city or is shot down over a deserted area by the Air Force. Kate Jackson, Ed Marinaro, Robert Guillaume, Erik Estrada and Maureen McCormick star. 96 min.
85-1509 *$39.99*

Crossfire (1998)
Seeking to avenge his family's killing by government agents, a ruthless arms dealer will strike back at America by blowing up the Statue of Liberty. Only a maverick secret agent with a deadly agenda of his own and an 11-year-old deaf girl who accidentally learns of the terrorist's plan can save the day. Andrew Divoff, Mitchell Cox and Tim Thomerson star. 97 min.
82-5095 *$89.99*

Airspeed (1998)
You have to be fearless to get through this action-packed thriller. When a lightning strike hits an airplane, ripping apart its fuselage, you know it's heading for turbulence. It's zero hour for crew and passengers, and only one thing can save the day from a potentially high and mighty disaster. Joe Mantegna and Elisha Cuthbert star.
82-5096 *$89.99*

Good Cop, Bad Cop (1998)
Lorenzo Lamas looks and acts "mahvelous" as a retired cop called on for one more tough assignment: stop a drug dealer working out of Chaparro, Mexico. But Lamas gets more than he bargained for when he finds the drug dealer calling on a deadly ancient power for help. Lobo Sebastian and Catherine Lazo also star. 102 min.
82-5097 *$89.99*

Counter Measures (1998)
Michael Dudikoff leads an elite American strike team against a Russian submarine manned by nuclear terrorists. The fate of the world rests of the sturdy shoulders of Dudikoff and crew as the clock slowly ticks towards the destruction of the world. 93 min.
82-5113 *□$89.99*

Smalltime (1999)
What starts out as a simple drugs-for-cash swap at a deserted ranch turns into a disaster when the inept hoods charged with guarding the dope use it during a wild party. Glenn Pummer, Jeff Fahey, Rae Dawn Chong and Darren McGavin star in this explosive mix of bullet-riddled action and quirky comedy. 96 min.
82-5117 *□$89.99*

Subterfuge (1998)
When a commercial airplane mysteriously explodes over the Black Sea, it sets off an intense and brutal race to retrieve the plane's "black box." Among those seeking it: CIA agents, spies from the KGB and angry drug dealers. Matt McColm and Amanda Pays star. 95 min
82-5078 *$89.99*

Hitman's Run (1999)
After he's double-crossed by his mob employers, killer-for-hire Eric Roberts has no place else to turn for help but the FBI Witness Protection Program. Before long he's fighting for his life, but are his enemies out to kill him, or his protectors? Hard-hitting actioner also stars Damian Chapa, Esteban Powell. 93 min.
82-5130 *$89.99*

Winner Takes All (1998)
Two friends from the hood get involved in the criminal life. After a botched robbery, one friend is jailed while the other gets away, enters the military and becomes a narcotics agent. Eventually, the two cross paths again. Rappin' 4-Tay, Flesh N' Bone and Robert Hayes star. 103 min.
82-5132 *$89.99*

Rogue Force (1999)
Special agent Michael Rooker joins local police to investigate a series of killings targeting mobsters and criminal organizations. Rooker discovers that the culprits are a specially trained SWAT team dishing out their own brand of justice. With Robert Patrick, Diane DiLascio, Louis Mandylor. 90 min.
82-5148 *$89.99*

Airborne (1999)
Steve Guttenberg goes the action hero route in this high-flying actioner that finds him as the leader of Mach One, a strike force trying to get a lethal biochemical weapon that's been hijacked by terrorists. Sean Bean, Colm Feore and Kim Coates also star. 94 min.
82-5149 *$89.99*

The Contract (1999)
A female assassin who was taught her trade by her covert operations expert father finds herself in trouble after he is killed. It seems that a presidential candidate who once was partners with her father in Vietnam may be responsible for the murder. Billy Dee Williams and Johanna Black star. 90 min.
82-5167 *$89.99*

The Killing Man (1994)
When a top mob assassin-for-hire is double-crossed by his employers, a top-secret government agency gives him a second chance to use his deadly skills. But whose side is in the right, and which will the "killing man" choose? Jeff Wincott, Michael Ironside, Terri Hawkes star. 100 min.
83-1024 Was $89.99 *$14.99*

Bomb Squad (1999)
In this high-octane suspenser, a terrorist with the components of a nuclear bomb zeroes in on Chicago as his target. That would mean no more Sammy Sosa, Tony Amonte or Roger Ebert! A crack team of federal agents has 24 hours before the Windy City is gone with the wind. Michael Ironside, Anthony Michael Hall and Tony Lo Bianco star. 90 min.
82-5169 *$59.99*

The Debt (1998)
When he discovers he's in debt to dangerous bookie Michael Paré, Lorenzo Lamas is forced into helping the crook with an underground counterfeiting operation. Lamas must decide which side to take when he learns that Paré is in deep trouble with mobsters. Heidi Thomas also stars. 92 min.
82-5192 *$99.99*

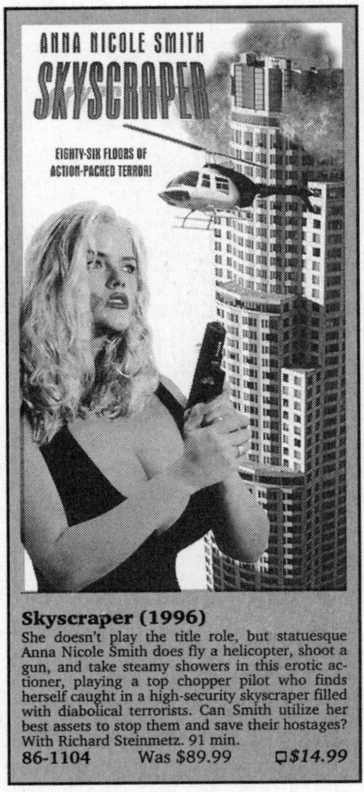

Skyscraper (1996)
She doesn't play the title role, but statuesque Anna Nicole Smith does fly a helicopter, shoot a gun, and take steamy showers in this erotic actioner, playing a top chopper pilot who finds herself caught in a high-security skyscraper filled with diabolical terrorists. Can Smith utilize her best assets to stop them and save their hostages? With Richard Steinmetz. 91 min.
86-1104 Was $89.99 *□$14.99*

Last To Surrender (1998)
Action and wrestling star Roddy Piper is an American cop with a bad attitude who joins forces with Chinese policeman Han Soo Ong. The unlikely team goes into action, trying to stop a narcotics dealer and his group of mercenaries. 95 min.
82-9058 *$89.99*

Deadly Conspiracy (1993)
A ruthless tycoon (John Saxon), who keeps his beautiful wife imprisoned in their home, launches a lethal cover-up when an accidental discovery by an employee reveals an elaborate web of double-dealings. Only the local lawman can stop the magnate's murderous schemes. Wings Hauser, Margaux Hemingway and Frances Fisher also star. AKA: "Frame-Up II: The Cover-Up." 92 min.
76-9039 Was $19.99 *$14.99*

Eye Of The Stranger (1993)
After his brother is mysteriously murdered in a small Western town, a man investigates the crime and discovers a group of frightened citizens and a mayor with a history of corruption. Is he being led to his brother's killer...or to his own death? David Heavener, Sally Kirkland, Martin Landau, Stella Stevens and Don Swayze star. 96 min.
76-9049 Was $89.99 *$14.99*

T.N.T. (1997)
Olivier Gruner is a mercenary working for a government-sponsored agency known as the Organization who suspects his employers have questionable motives. After some dangerous missions, Gruner—now dubbed "Yankee"—tries to settle down, but his past in covert operations just can't be erased. With Randy Travis, Rebecca Staab and Eric Roberts. 87 min.
76-9098 Was $19.99 *$14.99*

Professional Affair (1996)
A former cop-turned-private detective is enlisted by a mobster to help recover $2 million in stolen drug money. The investigation soon thrusts him into a world of Hollywood madams, hookers and producers who will stop at nothing to get what they want. Kim Stetz, Allen Silva and Robert Z'dar star in this sexy actioner. 95 min.
82-5019 Was $79.99 *$19.99*

Perfect Lies (1998)
Two-fisted action thriller in which a tough female detective tries to stay one step ahead of death by outwitting an FBI agent and her blackmailer ex-lover, who has conned her into infiltrating the dangerous lair of a drug dealer. Brettanya Friese, Charis Michelsen star. 87 min.
82-5054 *$59.99*

Perfect Target (1997)
Ex-CIA agent Daniel Bernhardt ("Bloodsport II") turns mercenary when he agrees to protect the president of a Latin American country. Problem is, the guys who hired him intend to use him as the fall guy for the president's murder. Action thriller also stars Robert Englund and Brian Thompson ("The X-Files"). 93 min.
82-5080 Was $99.99 *$14.99*

Killers (1998)
In this Tarantino-styled tale of crime and violence, a drug deal goes awry, leading to danger and mayhem for a group of unsuspecting participants. How can they get out of a warehouse when a Mercedes drops off five killers in search of the goods? Kim Little, Christopher Maleki and Erica Ortega star in this gritty actioner.
82-5086 *$89.99*

Soldier Of Fortune Inc. (1998)
The action-packed pilot to the hit TV series stars Brad Johnson as a renegade Special Forces commander recruited by a secret government agency. His job: lead a group of military experts in missions in which they stop terrorist attacks and infiltrate rebel strongholds. Tim Abell, Melinda Clarke and David Selby also star. 98 min.
82-5093 *$89.99*

Moving Target (1996)
Bounty hunter Michael Dudikoff suddenly finds himself on the opposite side of the law when an easy case backfires and leaves him framed for murder. Billy Dee Williams and Michelle Johnson co-star in this slam-bang actioner. 106 min.
83-1120 Was $99.99 *$14.99*

Border Wars (1999)
A Texas Ranger special forces agent is caught between his duty and his Tejano heritage when his latest assignment—the guarding of a bigoted senator sponsoring anti-immigration legislation—puts him at odds with a deadly Mexican gang. Gripping and dramatic actioner stars Cesar Alejandro, Michael D. Myers. 86 min.
82-5120 *$99.99*

Undercurrent (1999)
Lorenzo Lamas plays a former cop who heads to Puerto Rico, where he's set to oversee the operations at his former partner's nightclub. After Lamas is blackmailed into having an affair with a mobster's beautiful wife, his life is placed in danger. Frank Vincent and Brenda Strong also star in this action-saturated story. 99 min.
82-5122 *$99.99*

DV8 (1999)
This edgy action film follows the exploits of super-assassin Drake Bennet (Nelson Ricardo). He's got three days to save his pal Rizzo (Joe Marino) and find $10 million in diamonds. The only problem: Lisette (Sandrine Le Gallic), his arch-rival, is leading an army of bloodthirsty killers who want the gems for themselves. 90 min.
82-5183 *$99.99*

Love And Action In Chicago (1999)
Courtney B. Vance is an agent whose specialty is eliminating people that the government doesn't want around. Vance is set on leaving his spot to settle down with his girlfriend, but he's told to take out a South American drug cartel leader. Will he take the assignment or risk his life by turning his back on the agency? Regina King, Jason Alexander and Kathleen Turner also star. 97 min.
82-5186 *$89.99*

Marco Polo (1998)
Fictionalized account of Marco Polo, a young Venetian who journeys through Asia to find adventure and his lost father during the 13th century. Along with his teenage brother, Marco encounters danger on a camel caravan, faces off against the warlord Beelzebub and tries to save a beautiful Armenian princess. Donald Diamont, Oliver Reed, Jack Palance star. 97 min.
82-5191 *$99.99*

Desperate Prey (1994)
A woman involved with a noted attorney inadvertently videotapes his brutal murder, and soon she is pursued by the killer in this savage, sexy and suspenseful action film. Claudia Karvan stars. 102 min.
83-1027 Was $89.99 *$14.99*

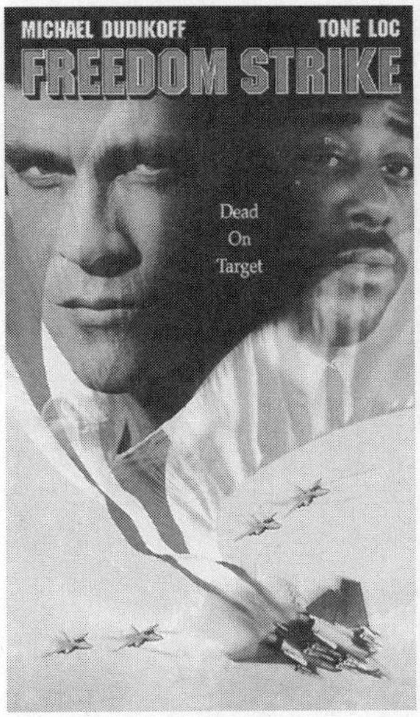

Freedom Strike (1998)
Action takes to the skies, as a special squadron of top gun American pilots undertake a secret mission deep within Iraq to destroy a nuclear reactor. Michael Dudikoff and Tone Loc star. 93 min.
83-1236 Was $99.99 *$14.99*

Showdown (1995)
"Friends" star Matt LeBlanc is a New Yorker who lands at the L.A. home of his Uncle Vinny and is given a job at a bookstore where he works. LeBlanc learns Vinny moved out West to escape a dark, violent secret in his past and live in isolation, but when two of his friends die in a gang shooting, LeBlanc and his uncle seek revenge from the hoods responsible for the deed. With Jay Acovone, Lou Rawls. 100 min.
82-5061 *$79.99*

The Bad Pack (1998)
A town under siege by a miserable group of militia members hires a soldier of fortune to take on the creeps. Among the mercenaries are a fearless race car driver; an ex-spy with super-strength; and a beautiful assassin with a personal agenda. Robert Davi, Ralf Moeller and Roddy Piper star. It's like "Con Air"—on land! 93 min.
82-5074 *$99.99*

Hot Blooded (1998)
An eager and innocent college freshman on his way home to see his family for Thanksgiving gets caught up in a frenzy of deception and death when he rescues a beautiful and mysterious hooker from the men who tried to rape her. Gradually, more and more of her past comes out into the open as she seduces him into doing whatever she wants...even murder. Stars Kari Wuhrer, David Keith, Burt Young.
82-5077 *$89.99*

Sworn Enemies (1997)
Once they were partners, but now two men find themselves on opposite sides of the law, and a remote backroad town where one man serves as sheriff is the setting for their violent showdown. Explosive actioner stars Michael Paré, Peter Greene. 101 min.
83-1140 Was $99.99 *$14.99*

Body Armor (1997)
Secret agent Matt McColm gets a call for ex-lover Annabel Schofield to help track down her missing scientist boyfriend, and soon must stop madman Ron Perlman from unleashing a deadly virus on the world. Stunt-filled action tale also stars Carol Alt, Clint Howard, John Rhys-Davies. 90 min.
83-1182 Was $99.99 *$14.99*

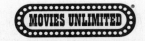

American Cop (1994)
While on a vacation layover at the Moscow airport, the titular lawman gets embroiled in a deadly showdown with the Russian mafia in this thrilling actioner. Wayne Crawford, Daniel Quinn, Ashley Laurence, William Katt star. 87 min.
83-1036 *$89.99*

Body Count (1995)
The count is sure to climb when lovely and lethal hit woman Brigitte Nielsen sets out to take on a squad of special forces agents in this all-out actioner. Robert Davi, Steven Bauer and Sonny Chiba also star. 93 min.
83-1078 Was $99.99 *$14.99*

Crosscut (1996)
Ex-mobster Costas Mandylor, on the run from his former employers, tries to start a new life in a remote logging town, but when the crooks catch up to him, the woodchips and the bullets are going to start flying in this hard-hitting action tale. 90 min.
83-1079 Was $99.99 *$14.99*

Serial Bomber (1998)
A brilliant but demented demolitions expert is threatening to blow a city to bits, and only a resourceful female FBI agent can stop his explosive extortion scheme. Lori Petty, Jason London and James LeGros star in this gripping action tale. 90 min.
83-1228 Was $99.99 *$14.99*

The Killing Grounds (1998)
It's "Cliffhanger" meets "The Treasure of the Sierra Madre" as a group of hikers stumble upon planeload of hijacked gold on a desolate mountaintop. Problem is, a pair of psychotic killers are also on the trail of the loot. Anthony Michael Hall, Courtney Gains, Cynthia Geary and Charles Rocket star. 93 min.
83-1248 Was $29.99 *$14.99*

Drive (1998)
Mark Dacascos and Kadeem Harrison star in this explosive action thriller as two unlikely friends who team up to put an end to the murders being committed by a high-tech killer. Brittany Murphy co-stars. 99 min.
83-1252 Was $99.99 *$14.99*

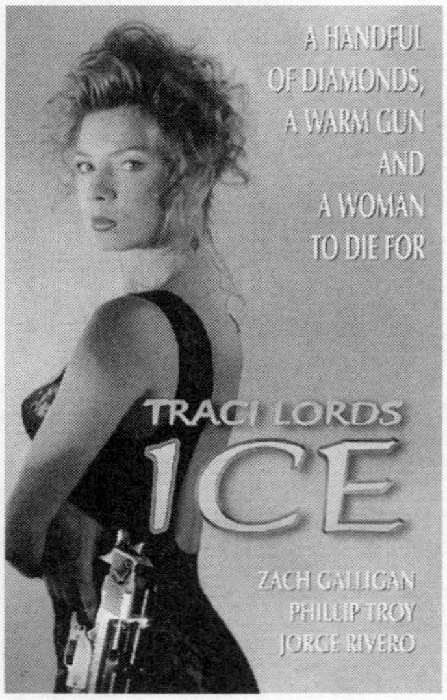
A HANDFUL
OF DIAMONDS,
A WARM GUN
AND
A WOMAN
TO DIE FOR
TRACI LORDS
ICE
ZACH GALLIGAN
PHILLIP TROY
JORGE RIVERO

Ice (1994)
A husband-wife cat burglar duo steals $60 million in diamonds from a powerful mobster, but they're caught in a bloody shoot-out that leaves the man dead and the woman caught in the middle of a battle between rival crime families. Traci Lords, Phillip Troy and Zach Galligan star. 90 min.
86-1077 Was $89.99 □*$14.99*

High Voltage (1998)
Non-stop action thriller with Antonio Sabato, Jr. as one of a group of thieves who attempts to rob a bank, unaware that it's part of an Asian crime boss's money-laundering operation. Things get worse when the mobster's girlfriend (Shannon Lee) falls for Sabato. Lochlyn Monro, George Cheung co-star. 91 min.
83-1255 Was $69.99 *$14.99*

Storm Chasers: Revenge Of The Twister (1998)
Veteran storm tracker Kelly McGillis, whose husband was killed in a lightning strike, teams with FEMA field coordinator Wolf Larson to investigate the devastation left by a series of tornadoes. What they find is a scientific experiment that is indirectly causing the storms and putting their lives in danger. Intense action tale also stars Adrian Zmed, Liz Torres. 96 min.
85-1487 *$39.99*

The Pandora Project (1998)
A renegade former commando breaks into a top-secret military experiment and hijacks an experimental device that can eliminate any living matter while leaving inorganic items untouched, and only the secret operations agent who trained him can stop him before he unleashes it. Intense actioner stars Daniel Baldwin, Richard Tyson and Erika Eleniak.
85-1164 *$89.99*

C.I.A. Code Name: Alexa (1992)
The action nearly explodes off the screen in this slam-bang thriller that pits two-fisted CIA agent Lorenzo Lamas and renegade cop O.J. Simpson against a deadly crime ring whose top killer is the lovely, lethal Alexa (Kathleen Kinmont). With Alex Cord. 90 min.
86-1064 Was $89.99 *$14.99*

C.I.A. II: Target Alexa (1994)
Action-filled follow-up finds former assassin Kathleen Kinmont living in seclusion with her daughter, until government agent Lorenzo Lamas requests her help in recovering a stolen nuclear guidance system. And the man behind the theft is an international terrorist who happens to be Kinmont's former lover. John Savage, John Ryan also star. 90 min.
86-1079 Was $89.99 *$14.99*

Taxman (1999)
The only two certainties in life are death and taxes, and New York tax investigator Joe Pantoliano may be facing both of them when a fraud case involving the Russian mob draws him, NYPD investigator Wade Dominguez and informant's daughter Elizabeth Berkley into a deadly conspiracy. Fast-paced thriller also stars Robert Townsend, Michael Chiklis. 95 min.
86-1147 □*$99.99*

Running Red (1999)
Distraught after his brother's death in a raid on arms dealers, Soviet commando squad member Jeff Speakman leaves Russia and tries to start a new life in America. Years later, Speakman's former boss tracks him down and threatens to kill his family unless he kills three men. Intense actioner also stars Angie Everhart, Elya Baskin, Delane Matthews. 92 min.
86-1148 □*$99.99*

The Underground (1997)
A veteran cop whose partner was gunned down by the same gang responsible for a rap artist's murder is partnered with a young, streetwise black officer to infiltrate a deadly gang war set inside L.A.'s music scene. Gritty actioner stars Jeff Fahey, Michael McCall, Brion James. 92 min.
86-1160 □*$89.99*

Gang In Blue (1996)
Intense actioner starring Mario Van Peebles as a black policeman who tries to blow the whistle on the racism and intimidation he sees around him from white officers. But Van Peebles' efforts soon land him in big trouble with a "gang in blue" as brutal as any gang on the street. With Stephen Lang, Cynda Williams; directed by Mario and dad Melvin Van Peebles. 99 min.
88-1120 Was $99.99 □*$14.99*

Deadly Target (1994)
An L.A. detective is sent to return a notorious Chinese gangster back to Hong Kong to stand trial, but after his prisoner escapes, the detective must team up with a renegade cop and a beautiful Pai Gow poker dealer to recapture the crook before he ignites a Chinatown gang war. Explosive actioner stars Gary Daniels, Susan Byun, Ken McLeod. 91 min.
86-1081 Was $89.99 *$14.99*

Nothing To Lose (1994)
That's what Ramon has left after a life spent on the streets and after his father is killed by the local mob boss. Now Ramon is ready to pay back those who've hurt his family. Paul Gleason, Alexandra Paul, Michael V. Gazzo star in a slam-bang actioner. 85 min.
86-1086 Was $89.99 □*$14.99*

A Dangerous Place (1994)
In order to learn the truth behind his older brother's mysterious death, a high school karate whiz infiltrates a tough martial arts gang and must fight the group's leader in a battle to the death. High-kicking action film stars Ted Jan Roberts, Corey Feldman, Mako, Erin Gray and Dick Van Patten. 97 min.
86-1088 Was $89.99 *$14.99*

To The Limit (1995)
Fashion model and Playboy centerfold Anna Nicole Smith stars as a sexy secret agent in this erotic actioner. After his wedding day is turned into a massacre, a man finds himself in the middle of a battle between rogue CIA agents and mobsters. Guess who's the only one who can help him. With Joey Travolta, Michael Nouri. 96 min.
86-1093 Was $89.99 □*$14.99*

Last Man Standing (1995)
While in pursuit of a gun-happy bank robber, a shootout leaves an L.A. cop dead and his partner convinced that they were set up by corrupt fellow officers. Now he must fight both sides of the law in order to avenge his buddy's murder in this pumped-up actioner. Stars Jeff Wincott, Jonathan Fuller, Jillian McWhirter, Jonathan Banks. 96 min.
86-1098 Was $89.99 □*$14.99*

Dead End (1998)
The murder of police sergeant Eric Roberts' ex-wife is only the beginning of a nightmare that finds both him and his estranged son framed for the crime and running for their lives as they battle a citywide corruption scandal. Jacob Tierney, Eliza Roberts also star. 93 min.
83-1262 Was $69.99 *$14.99*

Last Assassins (1996)
Former CIA agent Nancy Allen thought she left "the agency" behind, but when her daughter is kidnapped she's forced to use her deadly skills one last time. Lance Henriksen also stars in this supercharged action tale. 90 min.
83-1280 Was $99.99 *$14.99*

A Time To Die (1991)
Traci Lords plays a freelance photographer hired by the police department to improve its image. After one of her pictures reveals a murder cover-up within the department, corrupt cops use her young son to get the photo, forcing her to trade in her 35mm camera for a .45 Magnum. Jeff Conaway and Richard Roundtree also star. 90 min.
86-1052 Was $79.99 *$14.99*

No Escape, No Return (1994)
Three Los Angeles policemen are blamed when an undercover drug operation goes sour, leading to a deadly gunfight, two cops dead and $100,000 missing. They soon become targets who must clear their names and elude the attempts made on their lives. Maxwell Caulfield, John Saxon and Michael Nouri star in this action-packed urban thriller. 95 min.
86-1076 Was $89.99 *$14.99*

Forced To Kill (1994)
While trying to deliver a repossessed Jaguar, Corey Michael Eubanks is captured by a backwoods family and forced by a psychotic sheriff to fight in an illegal bare-fist boxing tournament. Michael Ironside, Don Swayze and Clint Howard co-star. 90 min.
86-1078 Was $89.99 □*$14.99*

The Sweeper (1995)
A Los Angeles cop with a record of brutality against suspects is recruited by a secret organization who sends out "sweepers" to take care of criminals the law can't touch, but what is the group's connection to a tragedy in the policeman's past? Intense actioner stars C. Thomas Howell, Jeff Fahey, Ed Lauter, Cynda Williams. 101 min.
86-1103 Was $89.99 □*$14.99*

Pure Danger (1996)
A bag of stolen diamonds is the prize in a deadly contest between two rival groups of bloodthirsty crooks and a short-order cook and his girl, who accidentally come into possession of the gems, in this hard-charging action tale. C. Thomas Howell, Teri Ann Linn, Michael Russo, Leon star. 99 min.
86-1105 Was $89.99 □*$14.99*

Riot (1996)
On Christmas Eve in 1999, riots grip a city where the daughter of a British ambassador is kidnapped and held hostage by Irish Republican Army terrorists. Only an elite British officer has the insight into how to stop the mercenaries, but can he free her in time? Gary Daniels, Sugar Ray Leonard and Charles Napier star. 104 min.
86-1108 Was $89.99 □*$14.99*

Executive Target (1997)
A top Hollywood stunt driver finds himself in a real-life life-or-death situation when he's abducted by a group of mercenaries who need his driving skills in their plan to kidnap the president of the United States. Michael Madsen, Angie Everhart, Keith David and Roy Scheider star. 96 min.
86-1121 □*$89.99*

Recoil (1998)
When his investigation into a violent bank robbery leads him to a powerful crime ring, police detective Gary Daniels is just doing his job. But the job gets personal when the crooks target Daniels' wife and family, forcing him to seek vengeance any way he can. Supercharged actioner also stars Robin Curtis, Gregory A. McKinney. 96 min.
86-1127 □*$89.99*

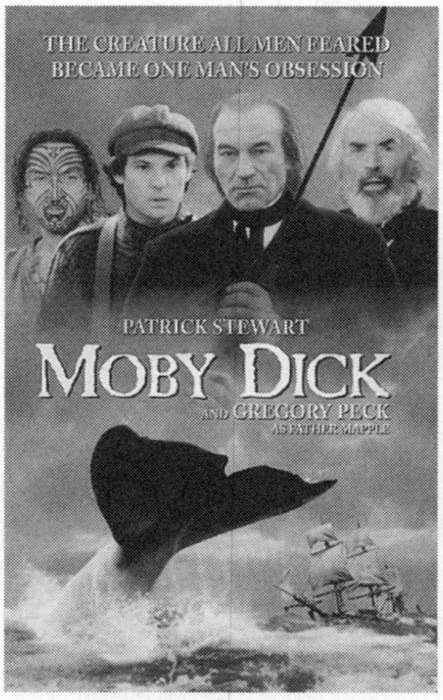
THE CREATURE ALL MEN FEARED
BECAME ONE MAN'S OBSESSION
PATRICK STEWART
MOBY DICK
AND GREGORY PECK
AS FATHER MAPPLE

Moby Dick (1998)
Patrick Stewart gives a stunning performance as peg-legged Captain Ahab, obsessed with tracking down and killing the white whale that cost him a limb and his soul, in this dramatic adaptation of Herman Melville's novel. Henry Thomas co-stars as young sailor Ishmael; with Ted Levine and Gregory Peck (who played Ahab in the 1956 film) as Father Mapple. 120 min.
88-1169 Was $19.99 □*$14.99*

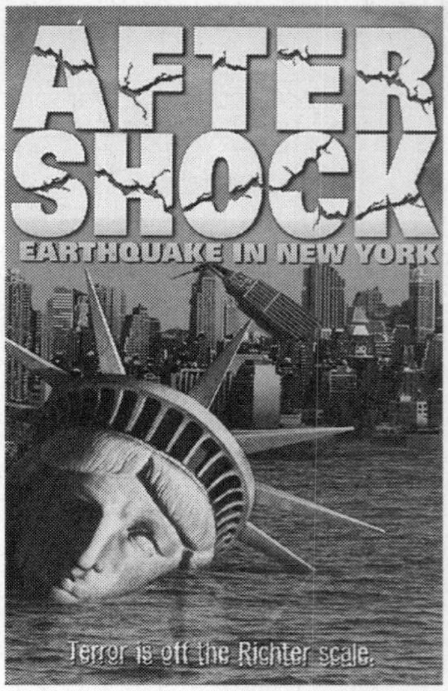
AFTER
SHOCK
EARTHQUAKE IN NEW YORK
Terror is off the Richter scale.

Aftershock: Earthquake In New York (1999)
The Big Apple gets shaken to its core when a devastating temblor rips the city apart, toppling buildings and bridges and flooding tunnels and the subway system, in this action-filled drama of disaster, survival and human courage. Tom Skerritt, Sharon Lawrence, Charles S. Dutton, Lisa Nicole Carson and Erika Eleniak-Goglia star. 139 min.
88-1204 Was $19.99 □*$14.99*

Champions (1998)
A former star in the brutal world of extreme fighting must rejoin the outlawed sport in order to exact revenge when his brother is killed in the ring. Explosive fight footage propels this action tale starring Danny Trejo, Louis Mandylor and UFC/WWF superstar Ken Shamrock. 99 min.
83-1283 Was $69.99 *$14.99*

Thugs (1999)
For small-time hoods Danny, Jake and Joe, their dreams of making it as major players in organized crime may come true when their actions catch the eye of a local mob boss. But is the chance he offers them worth the deadly strings attached? Gripping crime thriller stars Justin Pagel, Michael Egan. 93 min.
83-1525 *$99.99*

Black Male (1999)
A pair of con artists, desperate for money to pay off a loan shark, target a doctor for a blackmail scheme. Little do they know their "victim" is a psychopath who winds up getting them caught in a violent showdown between the law and the loan shark. Gripping urban actioner stars Bokeem Woodbine, Justin Pierce, Roger Rees. 90 min.
83-1527 *$99.99*

The Killer's Edge (1991)
A tough L.A. cop teams with a female FBI agent to hunt down an international counterfeiter who uses deadly methods to keep his business going. Wings Hauser, Karen Black and Robert Z'Dar star in this mesmerizing actioner. 90 min.
86-1045 Was $79.99 *$14.99*

The Killing Zone (1991)
After his brother is viciously murdered, the leader of a drug cartel returns to Los Angeles to even the score. The authorities bring in his arch-enemy, a former DEA agent, to stop the drug kingpin's murderous spree. Daron McBee and Armando Sylvester star. 90 min.
86-1048 Was $29.99 *$14.99*

Driven To Kill (1990)
A quiet dentist has to extract some justice when he battles bikers and mobsters who kidnapped his wife while searching for a stolen fortune. The bad guys have to do more than rinse and spit in this intense actioner. With Jake Jacobs, Chip Campbell.
86-1061 Was $29.99 *$14.99*

Intent To Kill (1992)
Traci Lords turns in a dynamic performance as an undercover detective who uses her looks and smarts to stop a raging drug war. Action, shoot-outs, kickboxing and sexy sequences highlight this thriller. With Yaphet Kotto and Scott Patterson. 93 min.
86-1065 Was $89.99 *$14.99*

Fist Of Honor (1993)
A gang war erupts between two rival "godfathers" when a hot-tempered family member kills two members of the opposing mob. One of those murdered is the fiancée of a young boxer who plans revenge. This over-the-top actioner stars Sam Jones, Harry Guardino, Abe Vigoda, Bubba Smith. 100 min.
86-1068 Was $29.99 *$14.99*

Rage (1995)
An ordinary man is abducted and used as an unwilling guinea pig in an experiment where chemicals are injected into him that trigger uncontrollable outbursts of violence, turning him into a lethal killing machine. Gary Daniels, Jillian McWhirter, Ken Tigar star. 94 min.
86-1100 Was $89.99 □*$14.99*

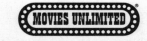

Private Wars (1993)
When an L.A. neighborhood is terrorized by roving gangs, the community hires a private detective to teach them self-defense. The residents join the investigator in a war against a greedy land developer and the corrupt chief of police. Steven Railsback, Stuart Whitman and Michael Champion star.
86-1070 Was $89.99 ❑*$14.99*

Land Of The Free (1998)
When the campaign manager for a charismatic Senate candidate discovers that his boss is part of a far-reaching terrorist plot to seize control of the American government, he must put his life on the line to expose the conspiracy before it's too late. Tense action tale stars Jeff Speakman, William Shatner, Chris Lemmon, Charlie Robinson. 96 min.
86-1139 ❑*$69.99*

Road Ends (1995)
On the run from both his former drug dealer boss and the FBI, a potential informant tries to hide out in a remote town, but brings his troubles with him. Compelling thriller stars Chris Sarandon, Dennis Hopper, Mariel Hemingway and Peter Coyote. 98 min.
86-1144 ❑*$89.99*

Flood: A River's Rampage (1997)
The residents of a small riverside town fight for their lives against the awesome fury of one of nature's most destructive forces—a raging flood—in this exciting action tale. Richard Thomas, Kate Vernon, Jan Rubes star. 92 min.
88-1168 Was $59.99 ❑*$14.99*

Diplomatic Siege (1999)
Now that the Cold War is over, the government wants to get rid of a secret nuclear weapon hidden in the US. embassy in Bucharest. Crack computer expert Peter Weller must defuse the bomb—without causing a diplomatic incident. However, all plans go awry when Serbian nationals seize the building. Can general Tom Berenger save the day? With Daryl Hannah. 94 min.
68-1985 *$79.99*

No Code Of Conduct (1998)
Macho cop Charlie Sheen and partner Mark Dacascos find $50 million in heroin being trafficked across the Mexican border. Further investigation leads them to believe that city leaders and law officials are involved in the smuggling, but after two undercover cops are murdered, Sheen and Dacascos must expose the operation or risk getting killed. Martin Sheen, Joe Lando and Meredith Salenger also star; directed by Poison lead singer Bret Michaels. 93 min.
11-2485 ❑*$99.99*

RPM (1997)
High-octane actioner with David Arquette as a car thief with a desire for danger who pulls off an incredible score, stealing a prototype supercar. Emmanuelle Seigner and Famke Janssen also star. 91 min.
06-3011 ❑*$79.99*

The Highwayman (1999)
Get ready to put the pedal to the metal, as two guys in search of a quick score set out on a wild road trip, accompanied by a gorgeous woman who needs their help in finding her missing father. Stephen McHattie, Jason Priestley, Laura Harris and Louis Gossett, Jr. star. 97 min.
64-9056 *$99.99*

Breach Of Trust (1995)
In this intense actioner, a gorgeous undercover agent teams up with a rogue hood to tackle a powerful drug ring and the crooked cops who support it, but can the "odd couple" trust each other? Michael Biehn, Leilani, Matt Craven star. 96 min.
63-1812 ❑*$89.99*

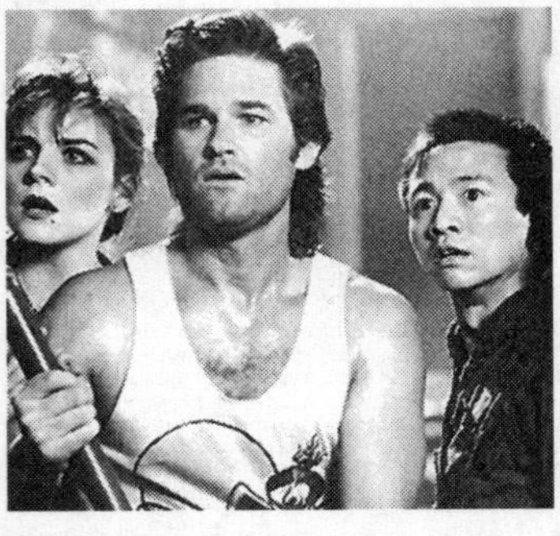

Big Trouble In Little China (1986)
Furiously offbeat, lightning-paced adventure by John Carpenter, blending action, horror, comedy and martial arts, about a ragtag group of heroes out to rescue a kidnapped girl from a 2,000-year-old magician in San Francisco's Chinatown. Kurt Russell, Kim Cattrall, James Hong and Dennis Dun star. 99 min.
04-2032 Was $19.99 ❑*$14.99*

The Island (1980)
While investigating the disappearance of a ship in the Bermuda Triangle, a British journalist (Michael Caine) and his son are forced to crash land on a secluded island, the haven for a band of pirates, who take the pair prisoner and subject them to horrendous acts of torture. With David Warner, Angela Punch McGregor; based on the novel by Peter Benchley. 114 min.
07-1039 *$19.99*

Andy Sidaris

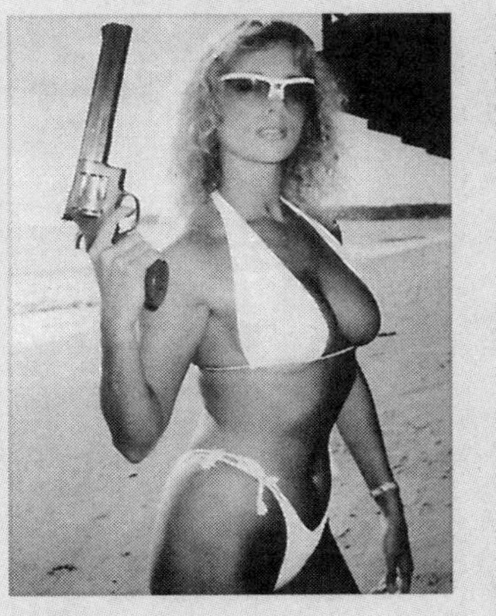

Malibu Express (1985)
Mystery, action and fun in this seaside sizzler that's hotter than a summer day at the beach. Darby Hinton and "Mr. Universe" John Brown supply the beefcake; Sybil Danning and four Playboy Playmates have the cheesecake; Andy Sidaris directs. 101 min.
07-1306 Was $19.99 *$14.99*

Picasso Trigger (1989)
The blood vendetta of a jet-setting assassin against federal agents is squashed by a dashing spy and a crack anti-crime squad composed of seven (count 'em, seven) former Playmates. Scorching sequel to "Malibu Express" stars Steve Bond, Hope Marie Carlton and Dona Speir. 99 min.
19-1699 *$19.99*

Hard Ticket To Hawaii (1987)
The island paradise becomes a Hell for smugglers, as a pair of female undercover agents runs a "sting" operation that soon has a drug ring out to stop them for good. Hot and fast Andy Sidaris saga stars Ronn Moss, Hope Marie Carlton, Dona Speir. 96 min.
40-1347 *$19.99*

Savage Beach (1989)
Thrill-filled Andy Sidaris adventure filled with hot babes and big guns. Former Playboy centerfolds Dona Speir and Hope Marie Carlton are the sexy federal agents who get caught up to their breasts in trouble, as nasty commandos go after a treasure of stolen gold. With Teri Weigel, Patty Duffek. 94 min.
02-2022 Was $79.99 *$29.99*

Return To Savage Beach (1997)
Andy Sidaris scores again with a sex-and-shoot saga in which Penthouse Pet Julie Strain leads the L.E.T.H.A.L. force of curvaceous females in a mission to find a coveted computer disc filled with secrets pertaining to incredible treasures. Shae Marks, Julie K. Smith and wrestling great Marcus "Buff" Bagwell also star. 98 min.
76-9093 Was $19.99 *$14.99*

Guns (1990)
Sexy, tongue-in-cheek actioner from Andy Sidaris ("Picasso Trigger") that stretches from the shores of Hawaii to the neon jungle of Las Vegas. Explosive story stars Dona Speir, Erik Estrada, Phyllis Davis and a bevy of former Playboy Playmates. 96 min.
02-2061 *$79.99*

Do Or Die (1991)
Lovely undercover agents Dona Speir and Roberta Vasquez are the targets of crime lord Pat Morita's revenge when they are forced into a deadly game where only the victors survive. Erik Estrada co-stars in this slick thriller from actionmeister Andy Sidaris. 97 min.
02-2149 *$79.99*

Hard Hunted (1992)
An explosive, erotic joyride from Andy Sidaris about three gorgeous special agents who band together to try to avert a group of high-tech warriors' plot to steal a nuclear trigger. Tony Peck and Playboy Playmates Dona Speir and Roberta Vasquez star. 97 min.
02-2376 *$89.99*

Fit To Kill (1993)
In this lethal mix of wild women and way-out action from Andy Sidaris, a priceless diamond is stolen and finding it falls on the sensuous shoulders of some of the world's hottest undercover agents. Dona Speir, Julie Strain and Roberta Vasquez star. 98 min.
02-2492 *$89.99*

The Dallas Connection (1994)
An international group of scientists meets in Dallas to launch their system for detecting and destroying terrorist weapons, but a team of lovely, lethal enemy agents is also there, seducing and killing the scientists in order to steal the system. Drew Sidaris directed this sexy thriller for producer dad Andy; Julie Strain, Mark Barriere, Samantha Phillips star.
76-9067 Was $19.99 *$14.99*

Day Of The Warrior (1997)
When information regarding a secret agency leaks out, commander Julie Strain and assistant Shae Marks attempt to retrieve the agents out in the field tracking down former CIA agent/pro wrestler/international smuggler Marcus Bagwell. This skin-and-shoot sizzler from Andy Sidaris and family also features Julie K. Smith and Tammy Parks. 97 min.
76-9105 Was $19.99 *$14.99*

White Water Summer (1987)
A young man (Kevin Bacon) takes a group of boys on a wilderness trip in the rugged Sierras, and together they must face a series of challenges from the land around them...and from within themselves. With Sean Astin, K.C. Martel. 90 min.
02-1806 Was $29.99 *$14.99*

Cold Steel (1987)
A tough L.A. cop is marked for death by a sadistic killer whom the cop disfigured years earlier, and a trail of murder leads to a deadly "cat and mouse" game. Nerve-numbing action tale stars Brad Davis, Sharon Stone, Jonathan Banks, Adam Ant. 91 min.
02-1818 Was $79.99 *$19.99*

Deadly Illusion (1987)
Hard-boiled New York detective Billy Dee Williams is framed for murder and must stay ahead of the police and the real killers in order to clear his name in this exciting urban thriller. Co-stars Morgan Fairchild, John Beck, Vanity. 90 min.
02-1824 *$79.99*

Jungle Warriors (1985)
There's blazing action in the wilderness when an all-girl army fights for their lives against a South American drug kingpin. Sybil Danning, Woody Strode, Nina Van Pallandt star. 96 min.
03-1452 *$14.99*

Off Limits (1988)
How do you find a murderer in the middle of a country at war? That's the problem Army policemen Willem Dafoe and Gregory Hines face as they search the streets of Saigon for the killer of prostitutes in this high-tension blend of combat action and suspense. With Amanda Pays, Scott Glenn, Fred Ward. 102 min.
04-1107 Was $19.99 ❑*$14.99*

Quiet Cool (1986)
When his family is brutally slain by a marijuana-growing ring who have taken over a small Northern California town, a young boy teams up with a tough New York cop to bring the killers in, dead or alive. Gritty thriller stars James Remar, Jared Martin. 80 min.
02-1728 Was $79.99 *$14.99*

Streets Of Fire (1984)
A rock music-filled, futuristic adventure with Diane Lane as a rock 'n' roll singer who's kidnapped by the Bombers motorcycle gang. The chase is on to find her—with Michael Paré leading the pack. With Rick Moranis, Amy Madigan, Willem Dafoe; Walter Hill directs. 93 min.
07-1243 Was $19.99 ❑*$14.99*

Scorpion (1987)
Hard-driving action abounds by the pound as a steel-willed intelligence agent (Tonny Tulleners) wreaks his lethal vengeance upon the terrorists responsible for the murder of his best friend. Don Murray, Robert Logan. 98 min.
02-1761 Was $79.99 *$14.99*

The Curse Of King's Tut Tomb (1980)
Unseen by man for over 3,000 years, the discovery of the tomb of King Tut in the 1920s also brought with it a heritage of death and a curse of blood. Join Eva Marie Saint, Raymond Burr, Tom Baker and Wendy Hiller in this exciting historical adventure. 100 min.
02-2625 *$14.99*

BMX Bandits (1989)
A trio of bike-riding teens are up to their handlebars in action and suspense when they get in the middle of a skewed hi-tech crime caper. Loads of daredevil BMX stunts and high-flying excitement; David Argue, John Ley and Nicole Kidman (her first film role) star. AKA: "Short Wave." 90 min.
69-7063 *$14.99*

Blue Thunder (1983)
Climb aboard "Blue Thunder," a space-age helicopter used by the Los Angeles Police Department for top-secret missions. Roy Scheider plays the cop who takes over the craft, going head to head with unscrupulous opponent Malcolm McDowell. Daniel Stern, Warren Oates, Candy Clark. 108 min.
02-1247 *$14.99*

Blue Thunder (Letterboxed Version)
Also available in a theatrical, widescreen format.
02-3237 ❑*$19.99*

The New Kids (1985)
Local teen hoods harass the title characters, a brother and sister, in this violent thriller from Sean Cunningham ("Last House on the Left") that ends in a bloody battle in a carnival midway. Lori Loughlin, James Spader, Eric Stoltz star. 90 min.
02-1459 ❑*$79.99*

Quest For Fire (1982)
An exciting adventure set at the dawn of man, as a tribe of cavemen lose the flame they use for cooking and heat, and three of their number come up against ferocious animals and cannibalistic neighboring tribes while searching for fire. Rae Dawn Chong, Everett McGill star. 100 min.
04-1481 Was $69.99 *$29.99*

Band Of The Hand (1986)
Fast-paced action, a pulsating musical beat and slick production enhance this violent drama from the makers of "Miami Vice." Five rehabilitated street punks turn the tables on a Floridian drug kingpin. Stephen Lang, James Remar, Lauren Holly star. Title track performed by Bob Dylan. 109 min.
02-1648 *$79.99*

High Risk (1981)
Spirited actioner about four American pals who decide to take a chance and make one big score so they can take it easy for the rest of their lives. Their scheme involves stealing cash from an American-born drug lord in Colombia, but they must face one hazard after another in their quest. With James Brolin, James Coburn, Cleavon Little, Anthony Quinn.
53-1130 *$14.99*

Fish Hawk (1981)
Will Sampson, who shined as the Chief in "One Flew Over the Cuckoo's Nest," stars as an alcoholic Indian who changes his life when he meets a young boy. 95 min.
03-1267 *$12.99*

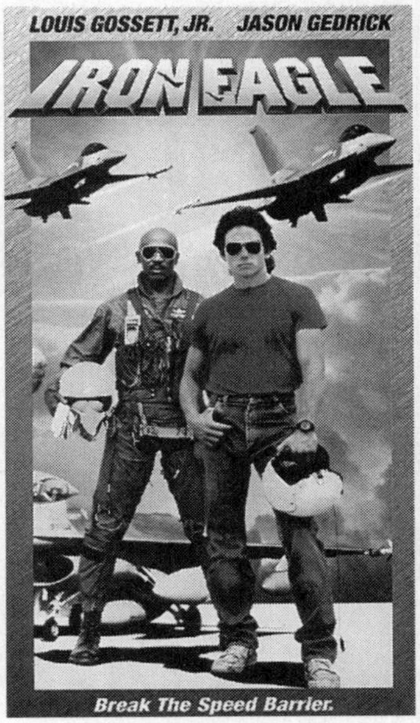

Iron Eagle (1986)
When an American fighter pilot is shot down and held for execution by a fanatical Mideast despot, it's up to his plucky son and a veteran pilot to hijack two F-16s and rescue him themselves! Non-stop action, aerial stunts and rock music galore. Jason Gedrick, Lou Gossett, Jr., Tim Thomerson star. 116 min.
04-1972 *$14.99*

Iron Eagle II (1988)
American and Russian "top gun" pilots must become uneasy allies when a terrorist nation threatens the world, and only ace flier Lou Gossett, Jr. can turn them into a crack squadron in time! High-flying action sequel with a "detente" twist also stars Stuart Margolin, Mark Humphrey. 102 min.
27-6609 Was $89.99 *$12.99*

Iron Eagle III: Aces (1992)
Lou Gossett, Jr. teams with bodybuilding great Rachel McLish for this all-out action assault. They lead a group of former WWII flyers out to save a Peruvian village being held captive by the sadistic German head of a drug cartel. With Horst Buchholz and Sonny Chiba. 98 min.
02-2265 Was $19.99 ❑*$14.99*

Iron Eagle IV (1996)
Retired Air Force general Lou Gossett, Jr. teams with another former flier to open a flight school for troubled teens. When some of the students stumble on a high-level government conspiracy to launch chemical warfare strikes against Cuba, Gossett and his charges go into high-flying action. With Jason Cadieux, Al Waxman. AKA: "Iron Eagle on the Attack." 95 min.
68-1807 Was $99.99 ❑*$14.99*

Duel (1971)
A modern suspense classic that gained director Steven Spielberg instant recognition. While driving along a lonely stretch of road through the backroads of California, salesman Dennis Weaver crosses paths with a sinister tanker truck, whose unseen driver engages him in a deadly game of cat and mouse. Co-stars Tim Herbert, Cary Loftin. 89 min.
07-1132 Was $39.99 *$14.99*

Jaws: 25th Anniversary Collector's Edition (1975)
A relentless, 25-foot-long "killing machine" is on the prowl off the coast of a New England resort town, and no one in the water is safe. Roy Scheider, Richard Dreyfuss and Robert Shaw are the intrepid shark hunters (and Bruce the shark plays himself) in director Steven Spielberg's masterpiece of action and suspense. This special two-tape edition includes previously unseen, unused footage, a 60-minute "making of" documentary, photos, storyboards and trailers.
07-1019 □*$19.99*

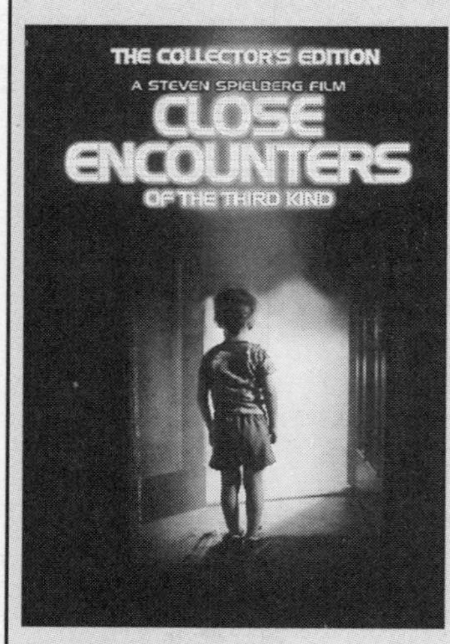

Close Encounters Of The Third Kind: The Collector's Edition (1978)
The newly restored "director's cut" of Steven Spielberg's visually stunning sci-fi masterpiece. Richard Dreyfuss stars as an Indiana electrical lineman whose late-night brush with a UFO overwhelmingly drives him, along with other "encounterees," to a breathtaking meeting at Devil's Tower. With Melinda Dillon, Teri Garr, François Truffaut. Special anniversary edition also includes a 15-minute "making of" documentary featuring interviews with Spielberg and the cast, behind-the-scenes footage and more. 152 min. total.
02-3159 Remastered □*$14.99*

Close Encounters Of The Third Kind: The Collector's Edition (Letterboxed Version)
Also available in a theatrical, widescreen format.
02-3160 □*$19.99*

1941 (1979)
Steven Spielberg's monumental comedy, based on a true incident, about the war panic that erupted in Southern California after a Japanese sub was spotted off the coast six days after the attack on Pearl Harbor. Stars John Belushi, Dan Aykroyd, John Candy, Ned Beatty, Nancy Allen, Robert Stack and many others; written by Robert Zemeckis and Bob Gale ("Back to the Future"). 118 min.
07-1024 Was $19.99 *$14.99*

1941 (Director's Cut)
Also available in a restored version, as edited by Spielberg, in a theatrical, widescreen format. 146 min.
07-2593 Letterboxed □*$14.99*

Raiders Of The Lost Ark (1981)
Adventuring archeologist Indiana Jones (Harrison Ford) circles the globe in an effort to retrieve a priceless religious artifact with untold powers before the Nazis do. Steven Spielberg and George Lucas' heart-racing tribute to the Saturday matinee chapterplay co-stars Karen Allen, Paul Freeman, John Rhys-Davies, Ronald Lacey and Denholm Elliott. 115 min.
06-1200 □*$14.99*

Raiders Of The Lost Ark (Letterboxed Version)
Also available in a theatrical, widescreen format.
06-2895 □*$14.99*

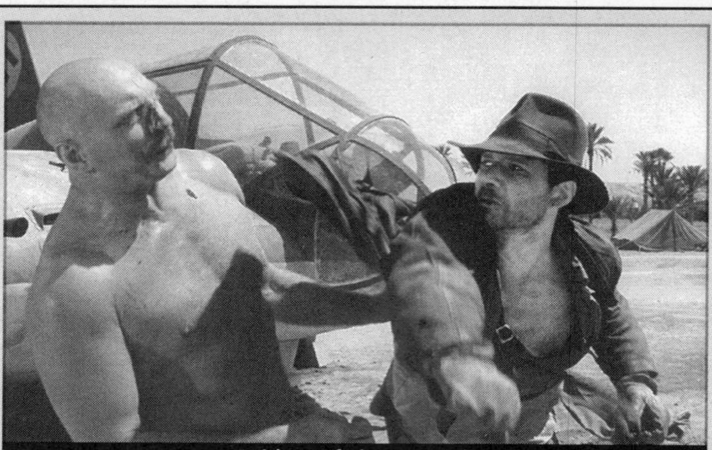
Raiders Of The Lost Ark

Steven Spielberg

Indiana Jones And The Temple Of Doom (1984)
Harrison Ford returns as the whip-wielding archeologist, fighting for his life against a sinister Indian cult. Second slam-bang adventure thriller co-stars Kate Capshaw as Indy's romantic interest and Ke Huy Quan as his sidekick. Thrills, spills and chilled monkey's brains galore. 118 min.
06-1368 □*$14.99*

Indiana Jones And The Temple Of Doom (Letterboxed Version)
Also available in a theatrical, widescreen format.
06-2896 □*$14.99*

Indiana Jones And The Last Crusade (1989)
The third (and final?) chapter in the Indy saga has adventure-seeking antiquarian Harrison Ford joining with his father (Sean Connery) on a search for the fabled Holy Grail, a search that puts them in conflict with the Third Reich. Steven Spielberg directs; with Denholm Elliott, John Rhys-Davies, Alison Doody, and River Phoenix in the "Young Indy" prologue. 127 min.
06-1700 □*$14.99*

Indiana Jones And The Last Crusade (Letterboxed Version)
Also available in a theatrical, widescreen format.
06-2897 □*$14.99*

The Making Of Raiders Of The Lost Ark/Great Movie Stunts
A double-fisted double feature that gives a behind-the-scenes peek at what went into the creation of the action hit, and how Indiana Jones managed all those last-minute escapes, followed by a look at film stuntmen put through their death-defying paces. Wow! 100 min.
06-1130 □*$14.99*

The Adventures Of Indiana Jones Gift Set
For more action than you can crack a whip at, all three of Indy's big-screen sagas have been gathered in a deluxe collector's boxed set that also includes "Treasure of the Peacock's Eye" from "The Adventures of Young Indiana Jones."
06-2898 Save $15.00! *$44.99*

The Adventures Of Indiana Jones Gift Set (Letterboxed Version)
Also available with all three feature films in a theatrical, widescreen format.
06-2899 Save $15.00! *$44.99*

E.T. The Extra-Terrestrial (1982)
One of the most popular films of all time, Steven Spielberg's science-fantasy epic of an alien stranded on Earth and the young boy who befriends him and helps him look for a way home is a warm and wonderful fable for all ages. Henry Thomas, Dee Wallace, Peter Coyote, Robert MacNaughton and Drew Barrymore star. Special limited video edition includes interviews with Spielberg and the cast and crew. 115 min.
07-1321 □*$29.99*

Twilight Zone: The Movie (1983)
Rod Serling's classic TV series lives again, in four tales of suspense and fantasy from top directors John Landis, Steven Spielberg, Joe Dante and George Miller. The cast includes Vic Morrow, Scatman Crothers, Kathleen Quinlan and John Lithgow, with a terrific prologue starring Dan Aykroyd and Albert Brooks. 102 min.
19-1297 Was $19.99 □*$14.99*

The Color Purple (1985)
The award-winning drama about a black woman's struggles to take control of her life in a small Southern town in the early 20th century, based on Alice Walker's novel. Whoopi Goldberg, Danny Glover, Margaret Avery and Oprah Winfrey head an impressive cast, under the direction of Steven Spielberg. 152 min.
19-1566 Letterboxed □*$19.99*

Empire Of The Sun (1987)
Epic "coming of age" war drama from director Steven Spielberg follows a young British boy's harrowing experiences in 1940s Shanghai. Separated from his family during the Japanese invasion and thrown into a prison camp, the boy develops a friendship with a captured American. Christian Bale, John Malkovich, Miranda Richardson star. 152 min.
19-1641 □*$19.99*

Always (1989)
Steven Spielberg's touching remake of "A Guy Named Joe" stars Richard Dreyfuss as a fire-fighting pilot killed in a crash and returned to Earth to serve as "guardian angel" for a young aviator. Holly Hunter co-stars as the feisty dispatcher who falls for both men; with John Goodman, Brad Johnson and Audrey Hepburn. 121 min.
07-1643 Letterboxed □*$19.99*

Hook (1991)
Steven Spielberg's lavish reworking of the "Peter Pan" story stars Robin Williams as the adult Peter, a work-obsessed father whose children are abducted by his old enemy, Captain Hook (Dustin Hoffman). He travels to Never-Never Land and, with help from Tinker Bell (Julia Roberts) and the Lost Boys, battles Hook to retrieve his kids. Maggie Smith and Bob Hoskins also star. 142 min.
02-2230 Was $24.99 □*$14.99*

Jurassic Park: Collector's Edition (1993)
The brontosaurus-sized blockbuster from director Steven Spielberg, based on Michael Crichton's best-seller, is set on a Central American island where millionaire Richard Attenborough has created the ultimate theme park attraction: live genetically-engineered dinosaurs. Scientists Sam Neill, Laura Dern and Jeff Goldblum are among the guests for a test weekend that turns into a fight for survival when the beasts escape from captivity. Special two-tape set also includes a "making of" documentary, original theatrical trailers, pre-production footage and other extras. 127 min.
07-2896 □*$19.99*

The Lost World: Jurassic Park: Collector's Edition (1997)
Using the old "alternate island a few miles away" trick, Steven Spielberg brings his biggest (in every sense of the word) film stars back for a thrilling, visually stunning follow-up. Jeff Goldblum and paleontologist girlfriend Julianne Moore head an expedition to the dino-filled site, where the menaces range from a team of hunters sent to collect specimens to vicious velociraptors and terrifying t-rexes. With Vince Vaughn, Arliss Howard, Pete Postlethwaite. Special two-tape set also includes a "making of" documentary, original theatrical trailers, and deleted scenes. 129 min.
07-2897 □*$19.99*

Schindler's List (1993)
Seven Academy Awards, including Best Picture, Screenplay and Director, went to Steven Spielberg's compelling, harrowing real-life Holocaust drama. Liam Neeson portrays Oskar Schindler, a businessman in Germany who uses his connections to staff his factory in occupied Poland with Jewish refugees, at first as unpaid slave labor, but later in an attempt to save them from extermination. Ben Kingsley, Ralph Fiennes co-star. 197 min.
07-2169 Was $29.99 □*$19.99*

Schindler's List (Letterboxed Version)
Also available in a theatrical, widescreen format.
07-2170 Was $29.99 □*$19.99*

Schindler's List: Limited Edition Collector's Set
This special boxed set includes the letterboxed version of the film, a picture-disc CD of John Williams' Oscar-winning soundtrack score, the novel by Thomas Keneally based on the events that inspired the film, and a special theatrical booklet with an introduction by Steven Spielberg.
07-2171 Was $139.99 □*$79.99*

Amistad (1997)
Director Steven Spielberg turns the camera on a long-neglected but pivotal event in the fight for equality and freedom in America: the 1839 revolt by a group of African captives on board a Spanish slave ship that was stopped off the coast of Long Island. The legal fight to secure the Africans' freedom becomes a bitter struggle that leads to the Supreme Court. Morgan Freeman, Matthew McConaughey, Anthony Hopkins and Djimon Hounsou as Cinque, leader of the rebellion, co-star. 155 min.
07-2637 Was $99.99 □*$14.99*

Amistad (Letterboxed Version)
Also available in a theatrical, widescreen format.
07-2642 Was $99.99 □*$14.99*

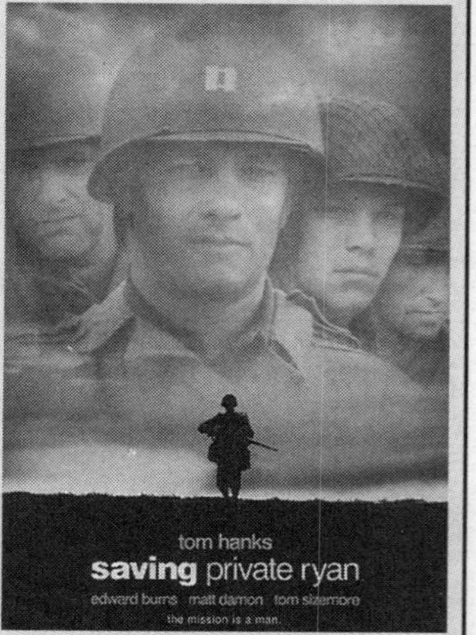

Saving Private Ryan (1998)
Steven Spielberg's WWII epic is a stunning experience, telling the emotional story of an Army captain who, after facing the horrors of Omaha Beach on D-Day, receives orders to lead his troops on a search for a lost paratrooper whose three brothers were killed in combat. Tom Hanks stars as the no-nonsense captain; Edward Burns, Tom Sizemore and Giovanni Ribisi members of his platoon; and Matt Damon is Private Ryan. 169 min.
07-2735 Was $99.99 □*$19.99*

Saving Private Ryan (Letterboxed Version)
Also available in a theatrical, widescreen format.
07-2736 Was $99.99 □*$19.99*

Skinheads: The Second Coming Of Hate (1989)
A group of young hikers are attacked by a gang of shaved-skulled white sumpremacists and take refuge with a WWII vet. Both sides brace for a violent showdown in this action tale of today's hate groups. Jason Culp, Elizabeth Sagal, Chuck Connors, Brian Brophy star. 93 min.
14-6171 *$29.99*

The Clan Of The Cave Bear (1985)
Daryl Hannah stars as a Cro-Magnon girl taken in by a tribe of more primitive Neanderthals, only to find that she cannot conform to their ways, in this drama of prehistoric life, based on the best-selling novel by Jean Auel. James Remar, Pamela Reed co-star; script by John Sayles. 98 min.
19-2193 Was $19.99 *$14.99*

The Chinatown Murders: Man Against The Mob (1989)
Forties Los Angeles is the setting for this fast-paced crime thriller starring George Peppard as the head of a special police unit. The squad has its work cut out for it when they investigate a white slavery ring and come up against the Chinese Mafia. Taut actioner also stars Ursula Andress, Charles Haid. 95 min.
68-1241 □*$89.99*

Treasure Of The Four Crowns (1983)
International superstar Tony Anthony stars in this nailbiting adventure yarn. He's a soldier-of-fortune seeking a coveted gold crown. He enlists a band of helpers that includes a muscleman, a circus performer and a demolitions expert. Not in 3-D. 97 min.
12-1280 *$59.99*

Fast-Walking (1981)
Hard-hitting prison actioner stars James Woods as a crooked prison guard caught in the middle when a jailed black militant offers him $50,000 to help him escape and Woods' cousin wants to have the inmate "accidentally" killed. With Robert Hooks, Tim McIntire, Kay Lenz, M. Emmet Walsh. 115 min.
19-2414 *$19.99*

Storm (1988)
A group of college students takes to the woods to play their favorite wilderness survival game, only to find themselves in a real fight to stay alive when they stumble upon a gang of crooks looking for their hidden loot. David Palfy, Stan Kane. 100 min.
19-7024 Was $79.99 *$19.99*

Cross Mission (1989)
A savage band of bounty hunters joined by a woman journalist take on a crime lord and his army in the South American jungles. Richard Randall heads a mission his government must deny but his drug-running targets will never forget. 90 min.
19-7034 *$59.99*

Miami Cops (1989)
Veteran action star Richard Roundtree follows a trail of heroin and corruption to Naples to trap a psychotic smuggler who killed his partner's father, and mounts a do-or-die assault on an armed drug cartel fortress. 103 min.
19-7049 *$79.99*

River Of Death (1989)
A team of adventurers heads into a remote jungle in order to stop a renegade Nazi scientist from unleashing a deadly germ on the world. Taut actioner stars Michael Dudikoff, Donald Pleasence. 103 min.
19-7068 Was $89.99 *$14.99*

The Dogs Of War (1981)
A fiercely intense actioner from Frederick Forsyth's best-seller about a reckless soldier-of-fortune (Christopher Walken) squaring off against an African dictator holed up in a military outpost. Co-stars Tom Berenger and Colin Blakely. 109 min.
12-1791 *$14.99*

The Dogs Of War (Letterboxed Version)
Also available in a theatrical, widescreen format.
12-3223 *$14.99*

Walking The Edge (1983)
Nancy Kwan and Robert Forster star as two people whose lives have been shattered by criminals and who decide to fight back and become vigilantes. But the men they are after are professional killers, and it will be a fight to the finish! 94 min.
47-3069 Was $79.99 *$14.99*

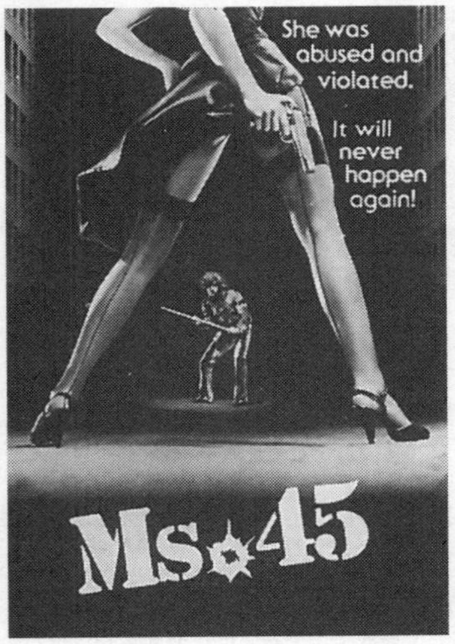
She was abused and violated.
It will never happen again!
Ms.45

Ms. 45 (1981)
An offbeat and well-made independent drama that plays like a distaff "Death Wish." An attractive, mute woman is raped twice in the same night and, after killing the second assailant with his own gun, takes to the streets to dispense vigilante justice. Zoe Tamerlis, Edward Singer star; Abel Ferrara ("Bad Lieutenant") directs. 80 min.
27-6009 *$19.99*

Island Fury (1989)
Two teenage girls are kidnapped by some thugs and taken to a mob-run exotic island. The hoods are after lost Mafia-owned treasure that the girl know the location of, and nothing will stop them from getting their hands on it. When the girls' lives are threatened, a modern-day Robinson Crusoe sets out to save them. Monet Elizabeth, Tanya Louise star. 90 min.
16-9155 *$14.99*

Crossbow (1989)
The true story behind the legend of William Tell is revealed in this thrilling adventure set in 14th-century Europe. Tell, a noted marksman, leads the Swiss resistance against Austria's tyrannical governor. Daring battles, dashing escapes and heroic rescues highlight this historical swashbuckler. With Will Lyman, Jeremy Clyde, Robert Forster. 95 min.
58-5090 *$14.99*

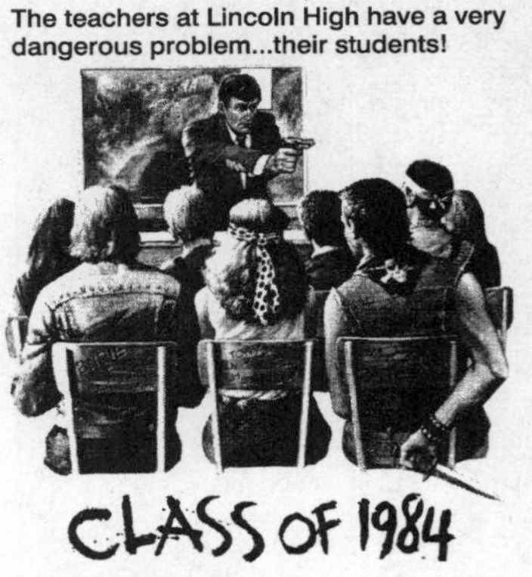
The teachers at Lincoln High have a very dangerous problem...their students!
CLASS OF 1984

Class Of 1984 (1982)
Powerful, violent look at the urban high school jungle like you've never seen it before. Timothy Van Patten is the ruthless head of a student crime ring who leads his charges in an assault on beleaguered teachers Perry King and Roddy McDowall. School's out...forever! With Michael J. Fox in an early role. 93 min.
47-1074 *$24.99*

Fairgame (1985)
Set in the Australian outback, this explosive thriller tells of a young farm woman who becomes an unwilling participant in the dangerous games of three armed marauders and is forced to fend for her life, using makeshift defenses against man and machine. Cassandra Delaney, Peter Ford, Garry Who star. 88 min.
22-9181 *$29.99*

Cold Front (1989)
After a deadly hit man goes on a psychotic warpath, a federal agent and his partner unleash a frenzied attempt to try to find him. The killer soon reciprocates by focusing his sights on the agent's wife. Martin Sheen, Michael Ontkean and Beverly D'Angelo star in this explosive actioner. 94 min.
44-1729 Was $89.99 *$14.99*

3 Kinds Of Heat (1987)
Exciting, stylish actioner follows three hotshot cops—one male, two sexy Amazons—sent by Interpol to halt a deadly crime syndicate. The trail is strewn with vicious deceptions, treachery and romantic entanglements. Stars Robert Ginty ("The Exterminator"), Victoria Barrett and Shakti. 88 min.
19-1611 Was $79.99 *$19.99*

Street Justice (1989)
Returning to his hometown after escaping from 12 years of Eastern European imprisonment, former covert agent Michael Ontkean finds it in the vise-like grip of a crime kingpin. White-hot action tale also stars Catherine Bach. 93 min.
19-1708 *$19.99*

Dead-Bang (1989)
L.A. cop Don Johnson must buck his superiors as he investigates the killing of a fellow officer and a shopkeeper, leading to a life-or-death duel against an interstate white supremacist cabal. Exciting thriller helmed by John Frankenheimer also stars Bob Balaban, Tim Reid, William Forsythe. 100 min.
19-1712 *$14.99*

True Blood (1989)
After a decade on the run, a young man returns to save his brother from membership in a ruthless street gang, the same thugs who set him up for a cop's murder. Jeff Fahey, Chad Lowe, Sherilyn Fenn star. 100 min.
27-9044 Was $19.99 *$14.99*

The Emerald Forest (1985)
John Boorman helmed this unique adventure based on a true story. Powers Boothe stars as an engineer working in the Amazon jungle whose young son disappears. Ten years later, Boothe finds him living in a culture totally foreign to Western civilization. With Charley Boorman, Meg Foster. 110 min.
53-1423 *$14.99*

Two Wrongs Make A Right (1989)
Mobsters slaughtered patrons in his club because he refused to pay protection, but Fletcher Quinn's not the kind to wait for justice; he does his legalizing with a huge cache of firearms and the only judgment he's after is "dead even." Ivan Rogers stars. 85 min.
48-1163 *$79.99*

Treasure Of The Lost Desert (1983)
Exciting action thriller about a Green Beret officer who is sent on a secret mission to stop the world's deadliest terrorist, a mission that no one may leave alive. Bruce Miller, Susan West star. 93 min.
47-3091 *$69.99*

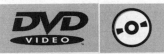

Gleaming The Cube (1989)
A skateboard fanatic from Orange County rounds up his pals-on-wheels and fishtails after the bad skates who killed his Vietnamese half-brother in this balanced mix of stunt riding and suspense. Starring Christian Slater and Steven Bauer. 105 min.
47-1976 *$12.99*

The Baron (1988)
The city streets become a battleground when a ruthless crime kingpin seeks payment on a debt...in blood. Non-stop urban action drama stars Calvin Lockhart, Richard Lynch. 88 min.
55-1184 *$19.99*

Just Before Dawn (1982)
Forest ranger George Kennedy warned those teenagers, but they didn't listen to him. Now they must fend for their lives against some nasty mountain men. Deborah Benson, Chris Lemmon and Mike Kellin also star. 90 min.
58-1046 *$19.99*

Bail Out (1989)
A trio of bail bondsmen, after tracking down bad guys innumerable and bringing them to justice, has to take on their sleazy boss. Great action film stars David Hasselhoff, Linda Blair, John Vernon. 88 min.
47-2013 Was $19.99 *$14.99*

Sno-Line (1984)
Violent, action-filled tale of the drug world, set in a small Texas town where two rival cocaine rings fight an escalating war for power and wealth. Vince Edwards and Paul Smith star. 89 min.
47-3078 Was $69.99 *$19.99*

Deadly Spygames (1989)
Steve Banner is a troubleshooter for the U.S. Special Operations Force, and when he's called on to a case he allows no time for rules or regulations. Troy Donahue, Jack M. Sell and Tippi Hedren star. 86 min.
48-1184 *$59.99*

Tornado Run (1985)
An elite squad of top gun pilots is called on to stop an international terrorist cartel using nuclear devices to threaten the world. Mike Reynolds and Lenny Rose star. 90 min.
50-1433 *$12.99*

Stuntwoman (1981)
Raquel Welch stars in an action-filled tale as a Hollywood stuntperson who takes the falls, crashes, and death-defying smashes for the stars. Lots of thrills, spills and laughs. With Jean-Paul Belmondo. AKA: "L'animal." 95 min.
50-1632 *$14.99*

Lightblast (1985)
San Francisco is the target of a lightblast machine, a weapon that can annihilate an entire city...and Erik Estrada is the only man who stands in the way of its power-hungry creator. 89 min.
47-3134 *$69.99*

The Courier Of Death (1984)
After seeing his wife and best friend murdered, a security guard goes on a rampage in pursuit of revenge. Joey Johnson stars. 77 min.
47-3138 *$69.99*

THE GOONIES

The Goonies (1985)
Dazzling, fun-filled adventure epic from producer Steven Spielberg and writer Chris Columbus about a gang of kids who go on a perilous search for pirate treasure. Plenty of death traps, bumbling crooks, a friendly giant, and non-stop action. Sean Astin, Corey Feldman, Martha Plimpton, Anne Ramsey star. 114 min.
19-1483 Was $19.99 *$14.99*

The Great Gold Swindle (1984)
Three brothers plan and execute a multi-million dollar gold heist in an exciting "Sting"-like action thriller from Down Under. John Hargreaves and Robert Hughes star. 101 min.
47-3160 *$69.99*

Escape From Angola (1989)
A tense, passionate tale of a colonial family trapped between the fickle forces of Nature and the ravages of a rebel army on the attack. Stan Brock, Annie Collins star. AKA: "Return to Africa." 100 min.
50-1792 *$14.99*

Archer's Adventure (1985)
A young apprentice horseman must ride across 600 miles of the Australian wilderness in order to enter his horse in a prestigious race. Exciting drama and adventure in this true story combine for family fun. 120 min.
70-1123 *$12.99*

Deadly Force (1983)
Seventeen people have been murdered and Los Angeles finds itself in the clutches of a diabolical killer who leaves an "X" carved in each victim's head. Hot on his trail is ex-cop "Stoney" Jackson. Wings Hauser stars. 95 min.
53-1100 *$14.99*

Hearts And Armour (1982)
Adventure queen Tanya Roberts ("Sheena") stars in a medieval epic of fierce swordplay, fighting warriors and passion-filled knights who filled the nights with passion. Co-stars Leigh McCloskey, Giovanni Visentin. 101 min.
19-1459 Was $19.99 *$14.99*

Penitentiary (1981)
The original tough-as-nails prison thriller stars Leon Isaac Kennedy as the jailed street tough who must fight to stay alive (and unmolested, if you know what we mean and we think you do) and goes on to become the penitentiary's top boxer. But his toughest battle is yet to come! Gloria Delaney, Thommy Pollard and Wilbur "Hi-Fi" White co-star. 99 min.
54-9100 *$19.99*

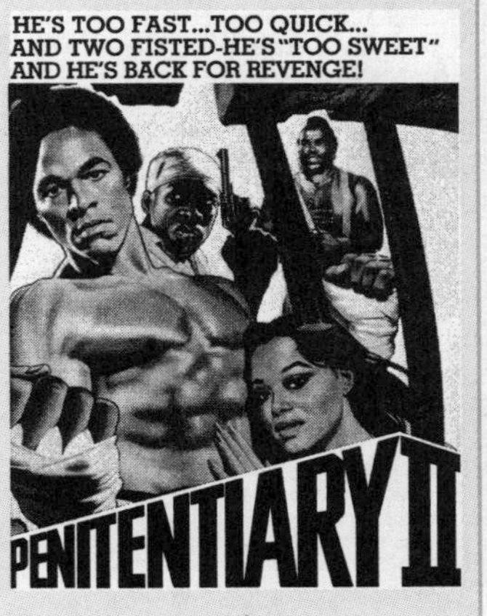
HE'S TOO FAST...TOO QUICK...
AND TWO FISTED-HE'S "TOO SWEET"
AND HE'S BACK FOR REVENGE!
PENITENTIARY II

Penitentiary 2 (1982)
Released from the big house, Leon Isaac Kennedy finds the going in the real world just as dangerous, as his crooked parole officer tries to get him back in the boxing ring and his former prison nemesis is out to get him...period! With Glynn Turman, Ernie Hudson, and Mr. T as Kennedy's trainer. 103 min.
12-1383 Was $69.99 *$19.99*

Penitentiary III (1987)
The stirring saga of maverick boxer Too Sweet (Leon Isaac Kennedy) continues, as he is jailed after accidentally killing an opponent in the ring and finds himself caught between power factions in the slammer. Anthony Geary co-stars. 91 min.
19-1654 Was $79.99 *$14.99*

Nightforce (1986)
When a young woman is abducted and held captive deep in the Central American jungle, five of her friends load up, bear down and head south of the border to kick some terrorist butt. Hot as the tropics action with Linda Blair, James Van Patten, Chad McQueen and Cameron Mitchell. 87 min.
47-3209 Was $29.99 *$12.99*

St. Helens (1982)
Actual footage from the 1980 eruption is featured in this thrilling docudrama based on the true stories of people who lived near the long-dormant Washington volcano and were forced to flee or face its full fury. Art Carney, David Huffman, Cassie Yates star. 90 min.
47-1121 *$14.99*

Gunpowder (1984)
The price of gold takes a tailspin, and the world's economies plunge into chaos! It's the scheme of a demented genius...and if crack Interpol agents Gunn and Powder can't penetrate his fortress, disaster will reign! Stars David Gilliam and Martin Potter. 85 min.
47-1725 *$69.99*

Instant Justice (1986)
Michael Paré stars as a lethally resourceful Marine Corps sergeant who hits the streets in search of vengeance against the drug dealers who murdered his sister. He means business...and he's not taking prisoners. Tawny Kitaen, Charles Napier. 101 min.
19-1552 Was $19.99 *$14.99*

Black Sister's Revenge (1987)
Exciting action drama about a confused teenage girl who moves from her Mississippi home to Southern California, where she falls in with "the wrong crowd" and soon finds herself on the other side of the law. Jerri Hayes, Ernest Williams II star. AKA: "Emma Mae." 100 min.
54-9101 *$19.99*

Vengeance Is Mine (1980)
Ernest Borgnine is a simple, pious farmer whose quiet home is invaded by three armed and dangerous murderers. When his family is threatened, Borgnine turns the tables on them in a brutal manner. Michael J. Pollard, Hollis McLaren co-star. 90 min.
58-1120 *$19.99*

Lethal Obsession (1987)
The streets of the city become a violent battleground for control of a crime empire, and two cops are all that stand between the crooks and total chaos. Exciting action thriller stars Elliott Gould, Tahnee Welch, Michael York. 100 min.
68-1087 *$29.99*

Summer City (1976)
It's "American Graffiti," Aussie-style, as four friends from Sydney set out on a weekend of surfing, racing and girls. Mel Gibson made his screen debut in this seriocomic look at teen life Down Under in the '60s; with Phil Avalon, Steve Bisley. AKA: "Coast of Terror." 83 min.
75-7100 *$19.99*

Tim (1979)
Mel Gibson plays a retarded man who discovers love with an older woman (Piper Laurie) teaching him to read in a thoughtful and touching drama based on a Colleen McCullough novel. 93 min.
03-1188 Was $19.99 *$14.99*

The Road Warrior: Special Edition (1982)
Mel Gibson returns as burned-out adventurer Mad Max, helping a band of refugees across the post-nuclear desert and battling hordes of punkish marauders in a non-stop death race, in one of the most intense action films ever made. With Bruce Spence, Vernon Wells; George Miller directs. Special edition includes behind-the-scenes documentary, two theatrical trailers, a limited edition mini-collector's card reprint, and a new digital transfer. 95 min.
19-2870 □*$19.99*

The Road Warrior: Special Edition (Letterboxed Version)
Also available in a theatrical, widescreen format.
19-2857 □*$19.99*

Mad Max Beyond Thunderdome (1985)
The third film in the futuristic "Road Warrior" series pits Max (Mel Gibson) against the sadistic residents of Bartertown and their leader, Auntie Entity (Tina Turner), while he tries to lead a tribe of wild children to their "promised land." Sci-fi adventure and slam-bang chases galore. 106 min.
19-1468 □*$14.99*

Gallipoli (1981)
Compelling Australian drama by Peter Weir about the friendship between two runners from the Outback, their enlistment in World War I, and the harsh realities and the futility of war they face when they're assigned to fight the Turks in the Dardanelles. Co-stars Mel Gibson, Mark Lee; scored by Brian May. 110 min.
06-1118 □*$14.99*

Gallipoli (Letterboxed Version)
Also available in a theatrical, widescreen format.
06-2707 □*$14.99*

Attack Force Z (1981)
Mel Gibson stars in this rousing, action-packed war saga about a dangerous mission involving the rescue of a defecting Japanese official from an island in the South Pacific in 1945. The mission seems easy for Gibson and fellow soldiers John Phillip Law and Sam Neill, but thousands of Japanese soldiers and the elements provide cause for trouble. 90 min.
74-1003 *$29.99*

The Year Of Living Dangerously (1983)
Adventure, romance and intrigue in a drama from Peter Weir ("Witness") of a reporter and an embassy aide in Indonesia during the 1950s revolution. Mel Gibson, Sigourney Weaver and Linda Hunt, in an Oscar-winning performance as a male cameraman, star. 115 min.
12-1275 Was $19.99 □*$14.99*

The River (1984)
The endless struggle of man versus the land is the theme for this rural drama, with Sissy Spacek and Mel Gibson as a farm couple who must face floods and a government bureaucracy in order to save their crops. Scott Glenn co-stars. 122 min.
07-1289 Was $19.99 □*$14.99*

Mrs. Soffel (1984)
Diane Keaton and Mel Gibson star in a true drama of a prison warden's wife who falls in love with a convict and helps him escape. Together they flee from the law in the wilderness. Directed by Gillian Armstrong ("My Brilliant Career"). 113 min.
12-1432 Was $19.99 □*$14.99*

Mrs. Soffel (Letterboxed Version)
Also available in a theatrical, widescreen format.
12-3136 □*$14.99*

The Bounty (1984)
The fourth screen version of the classic seafaring saga features Anthony Hopkins as the stubborn Captain Bligh and Mel Gibson as mutinous first-mate Fletcher Christian, who forsakes his duties for the pleasures of a South Seas island. Laurence Olivier, Edward Fox and Daniel Day-Lewis co-star in this epic production. 130 min.
47-1282 *$14.99*

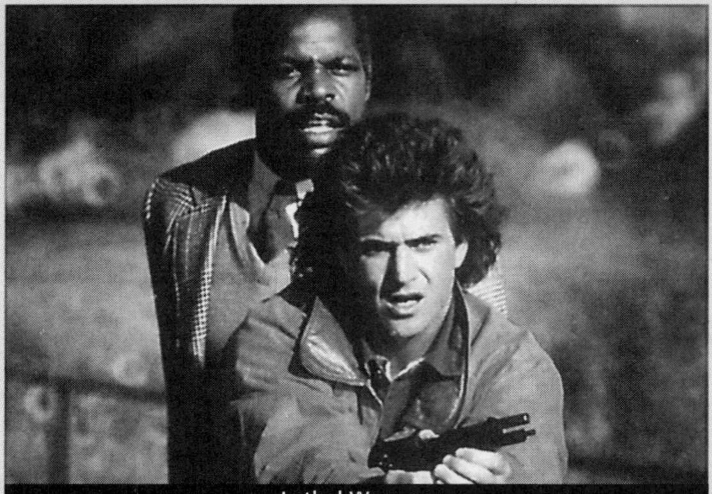
Lethal Weapon

Mel Gibson

Lethal Weapon (1987)
Seminal "buddy" actioner that spawned several sequels stars Danny Glover as a veteran L.A. detective who is less than pleased with new partner Mel Gibson, a gung-ho wildman whose memories of Vietnam and his wife's death are edging him ever closer to psychosis. Can the mismatched pair bring down a heroin ring? With Gary Busey, Mitchell Ryan, Darlene Love; Richard Donner directs. Extended director's cut; 117 min.
19-1596 Was $19.99 □*$14.99*

Lethal Weapon (Letterboxed Version)
Also available in a theatrical, widescreen format.
19-2506 □*$19.99*

Lethal Weapon 2 (1989)
Over-the-edge L.A. cop Mel Gibson and reluctant partner Danny Glover are back, this time taking on a drug operation, backed by South African diplomats whom the law can't touch, while at the same time "babysitting" government witness Joe Pesci. With Patsy Kensit, Derek O'Connor. Extended director's cut; 119 min.
19-1718 Was $19.99 □*$14.99*

Lethal Weapon 2 (Letterboxed Version)
Also available in a theatrical, widescreen format.
19-2507 □*$19.99*

Lethal Weapon 3 (1992)
Third entry in the hit series has Danny Glover counting the days until his retirement from the L.A.P.D., but with manic Mel Gibson as his partner and a stolen weapons ring to bust, it's anybody's guess if he'll live to collect his first pension check! Joe Pesci returns to pester the guys once again, and Rene Russo is a tough female cop who attracts Gibson's eye. Extended director's cut; 121 min.
19-2006 Was $19.99 □*$14.99*

Lethal Weapon 3 (Letterboxed Version)
Also available in a theatrical, widescreen format.
19-2508 □*$19.99*

Lethal Weapon 4: Collector's Edition (1998)
It's been six years since the last "Lethal Weapon" outing, and now Danny Glover's Murtaugh is about to become a grandfather and Mel Gibson's Riggs has settled down with fellow cop Rene Russo. But when trouble comes in the form of Chinese gangsters involved with counterfeiting and immigrant smuggling, the dynamic duo come to the rescue. With Chris Rock, Joe Pesci and Hong Kong action great Jet Li, in his American debut. Special video version includes a "making of" documentary. 127 min.
19-2753 Was $99.99 □*$19.99*

Lethal Weapon 4 (Letterboxed Version)
Also available in a theatrical, widescreen format.
19-2860 □*$19.99*

Tequila Sunrise (1988)
Years ago they were the best of friends. Now, drug dealer Mel Gibson and cop Kurt Russell find themselves on opposite sides of the law and competing for the attentions of Michelle Pfeiffer in an action-filled drama from writer/director Robert Towne ("Chinatown"). With Raul Julia, J.T. Walsh. 116 min.
19-1695 Was $19.99 □*$14.99*

Air America (1990)
It's an airline no one ever heard of, conducting missions that don't officially exist. Mel Gibson and Robert Downey, Jr. star as two pilots who find themselves working for a clandestine air operation in Southwest Asia during the Vietnam War in this high-flying blend of action, war drama and black humor. 112 min.
27-6695 Was $89.99 □*$12.99*

Air America (Letterboxed Version)
Also available in a theatrical, widescreen format.
27-7058 □*$14.99*

Forever Young (1992)
Romantic fantasy stars Mel Gibson as a daredevil Air Force pilot who is cryogenically frozen in 1939 after his girlfriend enters a coma. He reawakens in 1992 and becomes involved in the lives of a fatherless boy and his feisty mother (Jamie Lee Curtis). With Elijah Wood, Isabel Glasser, George Wendt. 102 min.
19-2096 Was $19.99 □*$14.99*

The Man Without A Face (1993)
In Mel Gibson's directing debut, a teenage boy (Nick Stahl) from a troubled family befriends a mysterious, scarred ex-teacher (Gibson) who lives on the outskirts of town. The two outcasts strike a touching friendship in which Gibson tutors the boy, who in turn helps to draw him out of his embittered isolation. Margaret Whitton, Gaby Hoffman co-star. 115 min.
19-2185 Was $19.99 □*$14.99*

Maverick (1994)
Mel Gibson dons cowboy hat, boots and six-guns to play the roguish, sharp-shooting gambler inspired by the classic 1960s TV western. Along with sexy scam artist Jodie Foster and crafty sheriff James Garner (the TV series' Bret Maverick), Gibson enters a high-stakes riverboat poker game. James Coburn and Graham Greene co-star in Richard Donner's amiable sagebrush saga. 127 min.
19-2252 Was $19.99 □*$14.99*

Maverick (Letterboxed Version)
Also available in a theatrical, widescreen format.
19-2509 □*$19.99*

Braveheart (1995)
Director/star Mel Gibson took home Best Picture and Best Director Academy Awards for this historical epic about 13th-century Scottish hero William Wallace, a farmer forced into fighting the forces of England's King Edward I after they kill his father and new wife. Highlighted by amazing battle scenes, the passionate saga also stars Patrick McGoohan, Sophie Marceau and Catherine McCormick. 177 min.
06-2385 Was $89.99 □*$24.99*

Braveheart (Letterboxed Version)
Also available in a theatrical, widescreen format.
06-2499 □*$24.99*

Ransom (1996)
When pilot-turned-airline magnate Mel Gibson's young son is abducted and a rescue attempt by FBI agents fails, Gibson takes matters into his own hands and offers the $2 million ransom as a bounty on the kidnappers. The twists and turns continue to mount in director Ron Howard's hit suspenser, based on the 1956 film of the same name. Rene Russo, Gary Sinise, Delroy Lindo and Lili Taylor also star. 121 min.
11-2116 Was $19.99 □*$14.99*

Ransom (Letterboxed Version)
Also available in a theatrical, widescreen format.
11-2166 □*$19.99*

Conspiracy Theory (1997)
New York cab driver/anti-government ranter Mel Gibson learns that a little paranoia can be a dangerous thing, as his latest conspiracy-busting newsletter brings him to the attention of some sinister CIA agents and puts his life, as well as that of Justice Department worker Julia Roberts, in deadly jeopardy. Director Richard Donner's compelling thriller also stars Patrick Stewart, Cylk Cozart. 135 min.
19-2617 Was $19.99 □*$14.99*

Conspiracy Theory (Letterboxed Version)
Also available in a theatrical, widescreen format.
19-2712 □*$19.99*

Payback (1999)
Based on the same Richard Stark novel that inspired 1967's "Point Blank," this stylish mob actioner stars Mel Gibson as a career criminal double-crossed and left for dead by his partner as well as his wife. Out for both revenge and his $70,000 share of the loot, Gibson goes up against a crime syndicate, crooked cops and Chinese gangsters to claim what's his. Kris Kristofferson, Maria Bello, Gregg Henry, James Coburn and Lucy Liu also star. 101 min.
06-2857 Was $99.99 □*$14.99*

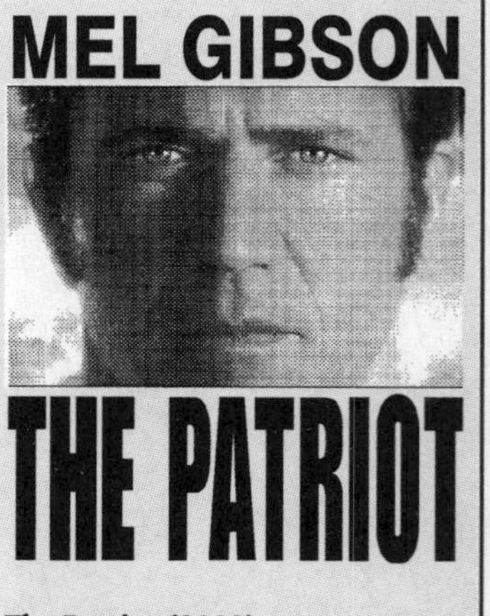

The Patriot (2000)
Mel Gibson is Benjamin Martin, the legendary "Hero of Fort Wilderness" who has left military life to raise his family on his South Carolina farm in 1776. But after a British commander torches his home and kills one of his sons, Gibson joins with oldest son Heath Ledger to lead a ragtag militia against the Redcoats. This stirring, action-packed epic from, appropriately, "Independence Day" director Roland Emmerich also stars Chris Cooper, Joely Richardson and Jason Isaacs. 165 min.
02-3469 □*$99.99*

Please see our index for these other Mel Gibson titles: *Bird On A Wire • Chicken Run • Hamlet • Pocahontas*

Deadly Revenge (1985)
After his best friend is mysteriously slain, a reporter tosses down the gauntlet to an underworld czar...and the crimeboss ups the ante by savagely slaying the reporter's son. Rudolph Rann, Jimmy Grazia. 90 min.
48-1137 *$59.99*

Black Lemons (1985)
No Meadowlark, but plenty of action and suspense when a convict discovers that an open contract has been placed on his head...and he dare not stop watching his back for a moment. Antonio Sabato, Peter Carsten star. 95 min.
48-1124 *$59.99*

Deadly Darling (1985)
After her brutal gang-rape at the hands of a vicious pack of thugs, a beautiful reporter takes the law into her own hands, systematically seducing and slaying her attackers. Fonda Lynn, Warren Chan. 91 min.
48-1128 *$29.99*

Crazed Cop (1988)
When his wife is found raped and murdered, a big city detective is pushed over the brink, firing away at the drug runners responsible for her death. Intense actioner stars Ivan Rogers, Sandy Brooke, Rich Sutherlin and the legendary Abdullah the Great. 85 min.
48-1159 *$29.99*

Lady Street Fighter (1986)
A sexy, tough-as-nails woman holds vital information the Mafia's desperate for, so desperate that they tortured her sister to death to get it. Now she's out for revenge, and nobody better get in her way! Graphic sex and violence with Renee Harmon. 72 min.
48-1145 *$59.99*

Killpoint (1984)
A smash-a-minute action excursion about the night crooks break into an L.A. armory and hold the city at bay. Richard Roundtree, Cameron Mitchell star in this state-of-the-art actioner. 89 min.
47-1276 *$12.99*

One Man Out (1989)
A renegade CIA agent becomes the personal assassin for a ruthless Central American dictator in this fast-paced action thriller. Stephen McHattie, Deborah Van Valkenburgh star. 90 min.
45-5481 *$14.99*

Trained To Kill (1988)
In this arresting actioner, two brothers from different backgrounds combine their fighting skills for a vengeance mission that reaches from the Cambodian jungle to the streets of L.A. Frank Zagarino, Glen Eaton, Ron O'Neal and Chuck Connors star. 94 min.
46-5594 *$79.99*

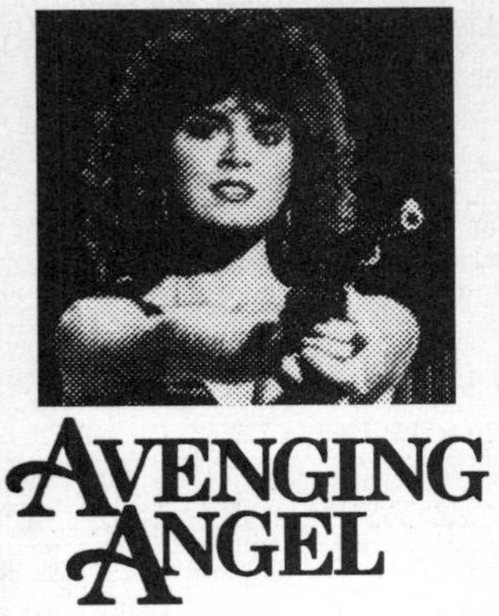
AVENGING
ANGEL

Avenging Angel (1985)
Four years after teenage hooker Angel got off the streets and into law school, she returns to the streets of L.A. to find the mobsters who killed her detective friend. Betsy Russell, Rory Calhoun, Ossie Davis and Susan Tyrrell star in the slam-bang second actioner. 94 min.
70-1008 *$12.99*

Angel III: The Final Chapter (1988)
Now a New York photographer, the "guardian Angel" of teenaged vixens in distress heads back to the West Coast to save her own sister from the clutches of a white slavery ring and its wicked madam. Mitzi Kapture, Maud Adams and Richard Roundtree star. 100 min.
70-1235 *$14.99*

Ellie (1984)
A beautiful farmer's daughter must protect her father from an opportunistic widow with murder on her mind. Shelley Winters, "Penthouse Pet" Sheila Kennedy, George Kennedy and George Gobel star. 89 min.
47-1430 Was $19.99 *$14.99*

Mob War (1989)
A public relations whiz is hired by a New York crime family boss to create a "legitimate" image for him, but what starts as a job becomes a deadly battle when a drug war between rival factions explodes. Crime thriller stars Johnny Stumpter and "Raging Bull" Jake LaMotta. 96 min.
50-1839 *$14.99*

In Your Face (1989)
A powerful, action-laden revenge tale about a man who goes too far to get even. This black-oriented actioner stars Tobar Mayo as the man with "the wisdom of Solomon and the guts of an urban fighter." J. Walter Smith and Connie James also star. 90 min.
54-9015 *$59.99*

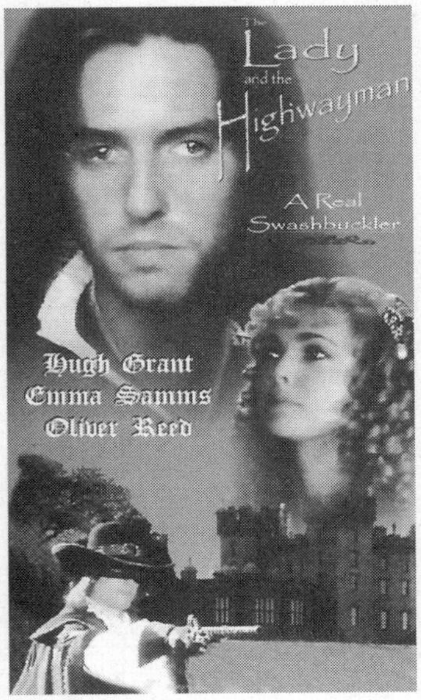
The Lady and the Highwayman
A Real Swashbuckler
Hugh Grant
Emma Samms
Oliver Reed

The Lady And The Highwayman (1989)
Romantic swashbuckler, based on a Barbara Cartland novel, stars Hugh Grant as an English lord-turned-outlaw who helps to restore Charles II to the throne, then faces political intrigue and danger when he falls in love with a noblewoman facing a forced marriage. Emma Samms, Oliver Reed, Lysette Anthony and Michael York also star. 100 min.
78-3031 *$14.99*

Spurs Of Death! (1983)
Fast-paced actioner set amid the violent and illegal sport of cockfighting, where the only thing deadlier than the battling bantams are the men who own them. Vince Van Patten, Jeff Corey, Ruta Lee and Kristine DeBell ("Alice in Wonderland") star. AKA: "Rooster." 90 min.
59-5078 *$14.99*

Cole Justice (1989)
Years ago he watched helplessly as his girl was attacked and murdered. Now, when a similar crime takes place, cowboy-obsessed Coleman Justice takes revolver in hand and dispatches the assailants, becoming a folk hero in the process. Western-style "Death Wish" actioner stars Carl Bartholomew, Amy Robbins. 90 min.
86-1025 *$19.99*

Real Bullets (1989)
When two Hollywood stuntwomen are kidnapped by a sadistic drug lord's guards, their two partners go into action, calling on their athletic and acting abilities to rescue them. Martin Landau stars in this pulse-pounding adventure thriller. 86 min.
68-1149 *$89.99*

American Eagle (1989)
Two decades after they went to war in Vietnam, three friends are engaged in a violent war among themselves. One has become a vicious sadist and kidnapped a group of beautiful models, and the others must use their commando experience to stop him. Asher Brauner, Robert F. Lyons, Vernon Wells star. 92 min.
68-1155 *$89.99*

Intrigue (1988)
Scott Glenn and Robert Loggia star in this tension-filled spy thriller about a U.S. agent with orders to get an old pal out of Russia...then murder him! William Atherton and Eleanor Bron also star in this top-notch suspense yarn. 96 min.
68-1166 *$89.99*

Lockdown (1989)
When he's framed for murder by the gang leader he's trying to bring to justice and his partner is savagely assaulted, a tough cop breaks out of jail and eschews the rules to gain revenge. Top-notch actioner stars Richard Lynch. 86 min.
68-1179 *$89.99*

Code Name: Dancer (1987)
A beautiful, retired spy gives up her new life as a schoolteacher and wife in order to return undercover to Cuba, where she renews a love affair with a foreign spy in order to save a friend's life. Kate Capshaw, Jeroen Krabbe and Gregory Sierra star. 93 min.
68-1203 *$89.99*

Hollywood Vice Squad (1986)
Descend into the seamy bowels of L.A. after dark with this gritty, true-to-life police drama. Great cast includes Carrie Fisher, Frank Gorshin, Leon Isaac Kennedy and Trish Van Devere, under the direction of cult favorite Penelope Spheeris. 108 min.
69-1148 *$19.99*

Hollywood Cop (1987)
When a child is kidnapped and a multi-million dollar ransom is demanded, only one officer of the law is able to rescue him and make the crooks pay a ransom...in bloody revenge! Slam-bang, .38 caliber actioner stars Jim Mitchum, Aldo Ray. 101 min.
69-5019 Was $79.99 *$19.99*

Order Of The Black Eagle (1987)
Look out, Bond! Move over, Helm! Duncan Jax, filmdom's newest superspy, is here. Along with his pet baboon and a bevy of beautiful women, he's out to save the world in this amazing action epic. Ian Hunter, Charles K. Bibby, Anna Rapagna and Flo Hyman star. 93 min.
69-5037 Was $79.99 *$19.99*

Nightmaster (1987)
A group of high school students who've been secretly receiving martial arts training from a tough-as-nails teacher and taking part in weekend paintball "war games" learn that their instructor is using the games as a cover for a drug ring in this tense thriller. Nicole Kidman, Tom Jennings, Joanne Samuel star. 87 min.
71-5119 Was $29.99 *$14.99*

The Rousters (1983)
There's thrills and laughs when carny worker Wyatt Earp III is forced by his crazy family to follow in the footsteps of their famous ancestor by becoming a bounty hunter. Chad Everett, Jim Varney, Hoyt Axton and Mimi Rogers star in this feature-length adventure compiled from the hit TV series. 72 min.
75-7082 *$79.99*

Unmasking The Idol (1987)
Secret agent Duncan Jax returns, along with Boon the baboon, to stop a plot by the arch-fiend combo of Goldtooth and the Scarlet Leader that involves nuclear weapons, death-crazed ninjas and a fortune in gold. Ian Hunter, Charles K. Bibby. 90 min.
69-5040 Was $79.99 *$19.99*

Terminal Entry (1986)
A group of computer whizzes think they're playing the latest simulation game, but they've actually tapped into the command network of a terrorist group...and the bombings they've ordered are real! Stars Yaphet Kotto, Edward Albert. 95 min.
69-5051 *$79.99*

No Justice (1985)
Cameron Mitchell stars in this actioner, playing a rural mayor who chooses his sociopathic nephew to become the new sheriff. The two use threats and violence to keep the citizenry under control, but when their tactics rouse the anger of a rival clan and a rift occurs between the relatives, all hell breaks loose. With Bob Orwig, Camille Keaton.
73-9184 *$39.99*

Women In Prison

Terminal Island (1973)
Four women prisoners...put on an island where violence is the only law...forced to do cruel and sadistic things that you won't believe! It's Terminal Island, land of the unfree and home of the caged! Phyllis Davis, Marta Kristen, and a young Tom Selleck star. 85 min.
14-6028 *$12.99*

Women Unchained (1974)
Five ruthless women break out of their maximum security imprisonment through the swamps to what they think will be freedom, but will their greeds and mistrusts let them escape? Action thriller stars Carolyn Judd, Teri Guzman. AKA: "Escape from Cell Block 3," "5 Angry Women." 82 min.
16-1137 *$14.99*

Caged Heat (1974)
Jonathan Demme's first directorial effort (he also wrote the screenplay) follows two female prisoners who escape from their brutal captivity and then break back in to deliver their own kind of justice. With Russ Meyer fave Erica Gavin, Juanita Brown, Roberta Collins and Barbara Steele as the demented, wheelchair-bound warden; music by The Velvet Underground's John Cale. AKA: "Renegade Girls." 84 min.
53-1206 Was $39.99 *$14.99*

Caged Heat 2: Stripped Of Freedom (1994)
When a gorgeous princess is kidnapped by evil rebel forces, a female CIA agent goes undercover to get her out of one of the most sadistic jails in the world. This blend of action, eroticism and prison drama stars Jewel Shepard, Pamela D'Pella and Chanel Akiko Hirai. 84 min.
21-9061 Was $89.99 *$14.99*

Women In Cell Block 9 (1977)
This kinky girls-behind-bars epic from director Jess Franco tells of a group of female guerrillas who are captured and sent to a South American jungle prison. Refusing to offer any information, the women become subjects of experiments practiced by an evil doctor. A lurid shocker, presented in its unrated version, starring Karine Gampier, Susan Hemingway, Howard Vernon. 90 min.
59-7023 *$89.99*

Escape From Hell (1979)
The Hell is a women's jungle prison camp where the gorgeous inmates are subjected to torture, sexual abuse, and are even made to eat "boiled snake meat." Can they, with help from the camp's new doctor, escape and make their captors pay for their crimes? Footage from this film was later used in the Linda Blair actioner "Savage Island." Ajita Wilson, Christina Lai, Antonio de Teffe star. AKA: "Escape," "Femmine Infernali."
20-1044 *$14.99*

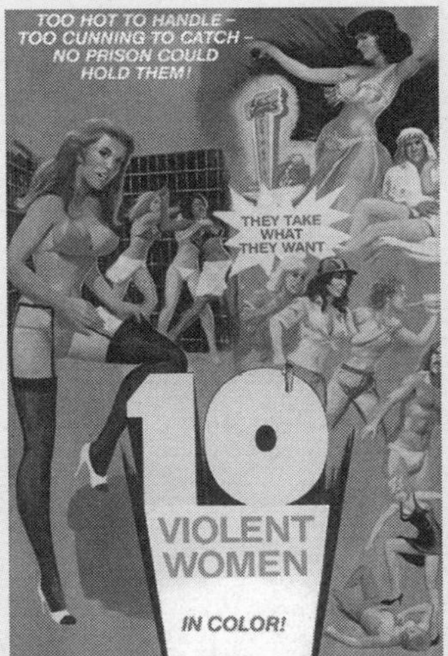
TOO HOT TO HANDLE – TOO CUNNING TO CATCH – NO PRISON COULD HOLD THEM!
THEY TAKE WHAT THEY WANT
10
VIOLENT WOMEN
IN COLOR!

10 Violent Women (1979)
When 10 gorgeous gals go on a crime spree, the action and passion are hot and fast. But after they're caught and sent to a sadistic women's prison, they do anything and everything to escape. Non-stop thrills and sensual tensions galore. Sherri Vernon, Dixie Lauren star. 97 min.
59-5008 *$19.99*

Women's Prison Massacre (1985)
Crazy Ray, Big Sal, Geronimo and Psycho are four maniacal convicts awaiting execution who take advantage of their layover at a woman's prison to ravish and ravage. For women-in-the-slammer film aficionados, violence and nudity are in abundant supply. Stars screen "Emanuelle" Laura Gemser. 89 min.
47-1731 *$24.99*

Caged Fear (1992)
A scorching "babes behind bars" tale about a woman wrongly put into a sadistic prison—and the man who will go to anything to get her out. David Keith, Ray Sharkey, Karen Black and gorgeous newcomer Kristen Cloke star. 94 min.
02-2308 Was $19.99 *$14.99*

Chained Heat 2 (1993)
A woman struggles to stay alive in a prison where guards smuggle heroin, stiletto-heeled wardens use sadistic methods to keep the prisoners in line, and the other inmates have a preference for kinky sex. Brigitte Nielsen, Paul Koslo and Kimberley Kates star in this "concrete jungle" soiree. 98 min.
02-5031 Was $19.99 *$14.99*

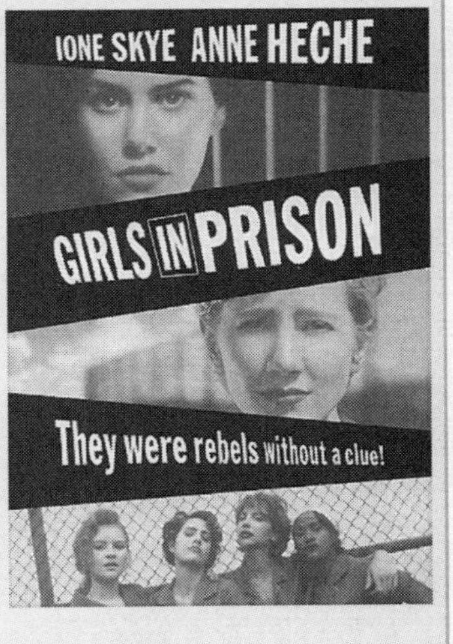
IONE SKYE ANNE HECHE
GIRLS IN PRISON
They were rebels without a clue!

Girls In Prison (1994)
Loosely based on the 1956 drive-in fave of the same name, this satirical tale of caged women tells of an aspiring country singer who comes to California in the 1950s seeking fame, only to wind up in jail for a crime she didn't commit. Anne Heche, Jon Polito, Ione Skye star. Co-written by Sam Fuller, directed by John McNaughton ("Henry: Portrait of a Serial Killer"). 82 min.
11-2790 Was $99.99 *$14.99*

Caged Hearts (1995)
Two beautiful women are framed for murder and sent to a high security prison where they are tortured and humiliated by the inmates and forced into prostitution by a secret organization called "The Shield." With help from a crusading attorney, the women try to expose the group. Carrie Genzel, Tané McClure star.
86-1090 Was $89.99 *$14.99*

Cellblock Sisters: Banished Behind Bars (1995)
Two sisters, separated after their mother's savage murder, grow up on opposite sides of the tracks. They reunite to find their mother's killers, but the "good" sister takes the fall for her wilder sibling's rampage of revenge and is sent to a brutal women's prison. Annie Wood, Gail Harris star. 95 min.
86-1099 Was $89.99 *$14.99*

Fugitive Rage (1996)
A woman is thrown in jail with a bounty on her head after she murders the sleazy criminal responsible for her sister's death. Along with a friend she meets in the pokey, the woman breaks out of the slammer, turning her rage against the mob and the law. Wendy Schumacher and Shauna O'Brien star. 90 min.
83-1117 Was $99.99 *$14.99*

Prison Heat (1997)
The heat's on for two American coeds who find themselves falsely accused by corrupt Turkish border guards and wind up in a brutal prison. Watch the girls make things hot for their captors as they fight to survive in this sizzling look at captive women. Rebecca Chambers, Lori Jo Hendrix, Toni Naples star. 91 min.
19-7105 *$99.99*

Time Served (2000)
Catherine Oxenberg takes a rap for a crime she didn't commit and finds herself in a hellish prison where a treacherous warden and lecherous prison guard dole out their own form of wicked punishment. Jeff Fahey, Bo Hopkins and Louise Fletcher also star. 94 min.
68-1994 *$69.99*

A Fistful Of Dollars (1964)
Director Sergio Leone's landmark "spaghetti western" features Clint Eastwood in his breakthrough role as "the Man with No Name," pitting members of two opposing families in control of a frontier town against each other for his own brand of justice. Based on Kurosawa's "Yojimbo," the brutal drama features an Ennio Morricone score. 100 min.
12-1788 Was $19.99 □*$14.99*

For A Few Dollars More (1967)
Clint squints his way to the top in this slam-bang sequel to "A Fistful of Dollars." Eastwood and Lee Van Cleef star as two wandering gunslingers who must combine forces to track down a wanted killer. Directed by Sergio Leone. 113 min.
12-1895 Was $19.99 *$14.99*

For A Few Dollars More (Letterboxed Version)
Also available in a theatrical, widescreen format.
12-3201 *$14.99*

The Good, The Bad And The Ugly (1967)
Clint Eastwood at his best! Believe it or not, he's the good, while Lee Van Cleef is the bad and Eli Wallach is the ugly. The three are after treasure during the Civil War, and there's no stopping them or their hungry quest. Superb score; a two-fisted Sergio Leone classic. 161 min.
12-1970 Was $24.99 *$14.99*

The Clint Eastwood Gift Set
The complete "Man with No Name" trilogy—"The Good, the Bad, and the Ugly," "For a Few Dollars More" and "A Fistful of Dollars"—is available in a special boxed collection.
12-3281 Save $20.00! *$34.99*

Coogan's Bluff (1968)
Star Clint Eastwood and director Don Siegel's first collaborative effort was this crime drama about an Arizona lawman (Eastwood) who endures culture shock, not to mention a brutal fight in a pool room and the impediments brought on by an uncooperative police lieutenant, while in New York City to bring back a wanted man. Co-stars Lee J. Cobb, Don Stroud and Susan Clark. 93 min.
07-1102 Was $19.99 *$14.99*

Hang 'Em High (1968)
After his "Dollars" trilogy made him an international star, Clint Eastwood returned to America to portray a cattleman who is falsely accused of murdering a local rancher and sets out to exact vengeance on the members of a lynch mob who tried to string him up. Americanized "spaghetti" western co-stars Inger Stevens, Ed Begley, Pat Hingle and Bruce Dern. 115 min.
12-1789 Was $19.99 □*$14.99*

Hang 'Em High (Letterboxed Version)
Also available in a theatrical, widescreen format.
12-3140 *$14.99*

Paint Your Wagon (1969)
Lerner and Loewe's Broadway smash became the first and only musical undertaking for Clint Eastwood, who stars alongside Lee Marvin as two corners of a love triangle involved with beautiful Jean Seberg and partners in a bizarre financial enterprise in Gold Rush-era California. Songs include "They Call the Wind Maria," "I Talk to Trees" and "I'm on My Way"; directed by Joshua Logan. 164 min.
06-1127 *$24.99*

Where Eagles Dare (1969)
WWII action classic has Clint Eastwood and Richard Burton sent to rescue a captured American officer from an impenetrable fortress atop a German mountain. Terrific non-stop thrills from the pen of Alistair MacLean. Co-stars Mary Ure, Patrick Wymark, Michael Hordern. 158 min.
12-1578 Was $19.99 *$14.99*

Two Mules For Sister Sara (1970)
After rescuing Sister Sara (Shirley MacLaine) from the hands of a gang of bandits in the Mexican desert, American mercenary Clint Eastwood and the suspiciously tough-talking, hard-drinking nun embark on a violence-filled effort to assist Mexican guerrilla fighters in their struggle against French exploiters. Directed by Don Siegel. 105 min.
07-1092 Was $19.99 *$14.99*

Kelly's Heroes (1970)
Clint Eastwood stars in this comedy-adventure about a ragtag band of American soldiers robbing a cache of Nazi gold. Telly Savalas, Don Rickles, Carroll O'Connor and Donald Sutherland as a "hippie" tank driver also star. 143 min.
12-1265 Was $19.99 *$14.99*

Play Misty For Me (1971)
Superb suspense story that was Clint Eastwood's directorial debut. Eastwood plays a late-night DJ who has a one-night stand with devoted listener Jessica Walter, but when he attempts to end the affair her love for him turns into a murderous obsession. With Donna Mills, John Larch. 102 min.
07-1042 Was $19.99 *$14.99*

The Beguiled (1971)
Offbeat, entrancing Clint Eastwood film has Clint as a wounded Union soldier during the Civil War, taken into a girls' school to recuperate after getting shot...but his presence stirs up mixed feelings between the women. Geraldine Page, Elizabeth Hartman; Don Siegel directs. 109 min.
07-1153 Was $19.99 □*$14.99*

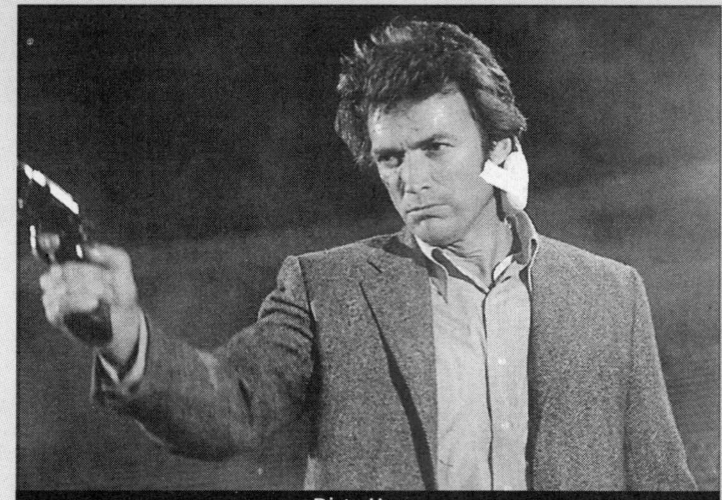
Dirty Harry

Clint Eastwood

Joe Kidd (1971)
Clint Eastwood is in top form as a New Mexico rancher caught in the middle of a land war between the Hispanic settlers and greedy developers. With John Saxon, Robert Duvall; scripted by Elmore Leonard. 88 min.
07-1098 *$14.99*

Dirty Harry (1971)
No-nonsense San Francisco cop Harry Callahan (Clint Eastwood) and his .44 Magnum ("the most powerful handgun in the world") made their debut in director Don Siegel's explosive thriller that pits Eastwood against a brutal murderer terrorizing the city as well as his own superiors and a justice system that lets criminals go free. Harry Guardino, Andy Robinson co-star. 102 min.
19-2584 Was $19.99 *$14.99*

Dirty Harry (Letterboxed Version)
Also available in a theatrical, widescreen format.
19-2574 □*$19.99*

Magnum Force (1973)
A string of shootings of Bay Area criminals which may have been committed by a policeman draws the attention of Clint Eastwood's Harry Callahan, who soon finds himself fighting against a squad of vigilante cops. Hal Holbrook, Mitchell Ryan, David Soul co-star; written by John Milius and Michael Cimino. 124 min.
19-1010 Was $19.99 *$14.99*

The Enforcer (1976)
Clint Eastwood brandishes his .44 Magnum once more as unrestrainable San Francisco detective "Dirty Harry" Callahan, who collides with new female partner Tyne Daly and a group of ruthless terrorists intent on robbing an arms company, then engages in a vicious battle to rescue the kidnapped mayor. Co-stars Harry Guardino, Bradford Dillman. 97 min.
19-1189 Was $19.99 *$14.99*

Sudden Impact (1983)
The film that introduced the phrase "Go ahead...make my day" to the American lexicon, director/star Clint Eastwood's fourth outing as "Dirty Harry" Callahan finds him up against two foes: a San Francisco mob boss and a mysterious killer in a nearby seaside town. With Sondra Locke, Bradford Dillman. 117 min.
19-1310 □*$14.99*

The Dead Pool (1988)
The action is mixed with sly wit in the fifth "Dirty Harry" thriller, as Clint Eastwood investigates a series of murders that are linked to a "celebrity death list" betting game on the set of horror filmmaker Liam Neeson's latest project. Don't miss the "toy car" chase down the San Francisco streets; with Patricia Clarkson, Evan Kim, and Jim Carrey as a rock star. 91 min.
19-1675 □*$14.99*

High Plains Drifter (1973)
A frontier town's residents, fearing the impending return of a trio of escaped convicts, look for help from mysterious new arrival Clint Eastwood. But is he savior or avenging angel? Violent and compelling western, directed by Eastwood, also stars Verna Bloom, Mitchell Ryan, Billy Curtis. 104 min.
07-1082 Was $19.99 *$14.99*

High Plains Drifter (Letterboxed Version)
Also available in a theatrical, widescreen format.
07-2676 □*$19.99*

Thunderbolt And Lightfoot (1974)
Vietnam vet and ex-thief Clint Eastwood teams up with shifty former partners George Kennedy and Geoffrey Lewis, and drifter Jeff Bridges to pull off an elaborate robbery in this exciting caper thriller written and directed by Michael Cimino ("The Deer Hunter"). With Gary Busey, Catherine Bach. 115 min.
12-1790 Was $19.99 *$14.99*

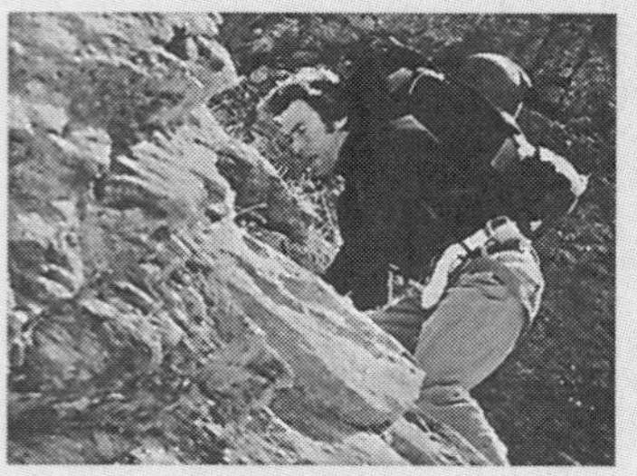

The Eiger Sanction (1975)
Spectacular mountain climbing, fast-paced espionage and steamy romance highlight this rousing adventure, with Clint Eastwood as a former hit man forced out of retirement to "sanction" the man responsible for a co-worker's death. George Kennedy, Vonetta McGee; directed by Eastwood. 128 min.
07-1089 Was $19.99 *$14.99*

The Outlaw Josey Wales: Special Edition (1976)
Director/star Clint Eastwood and co-scripter Phil Kaufman add another dimension to Eastwood's classic insular Western hero, as a Missouri farmer joins Confederate soldiers to pursue the Union renegades who killed his family. Betrayed by his allies, Eastwood begins a vengeance quest that becomes an odyssey of redemption for himself and the people he aids along the way. Sondra Locke, Chief Dan George, John Vernon also star. Special video edition includes a 30-minute "making of" documentary and the original theatrical trailer. 136 min.
19-2898 Was $19.99 □*$14.99*

The Outlaw Josey Wales: Special Edition (Letterboxed Version)
Also available in a theatrical, widescreen format.
19-2899 □*$19.99*

The Gauntlet (1977)
The normally routine exercise of escorting an extradited prisoner (Sondra Locke) from Las Vegas to Phoenix to testify at trial becomes a race for survival for detective Clint Eastwood. On a frantic bus ride to city hall, Eastwood and his charge brave an all-out assault from police and a corrupt mayor, who fears incrimination by the determined witness. Co-stars Pat Hingle, William Prince. 109 min.
19-1182 Was $19.99 *$14.99*

Every Which Way But Loose (1978)
Action star Clint Eastwood drives full throttle into comedy, as an easy-going trucker whose bare-knuckled brawling sideline takes him from honkytonk to honkytonk. Along for the ride are Clyde, a mischievous orangutan; Orville, his lean-witted driving partner; and Echo, an attractive former fruit peddler. Together, they hit the highway in search of Eastwood's one true love, C&W singer Sondra Locke. Co-stars Geoffrey Lewis, Beverly D'Angelo, Ruth Gordon. 105 min.
19-1030 Was $19.99 *$14.99*

Any Which Way You Can (1980)
Continuing where he left off in "Every Which Way But Loose," his most successful film up to that time, Clint Eastwood, as bare-knuckle brawler Philo Beddoe, finds his dreams of settling down with country singer girlfriend Sondra Locke and pet orangutan Clyde evaporate after she is kidnapped by the mob, who want Philo to fight one last time against his arch-rival. Co-stars Geoffrey Lewis, William Smith. 116 min.
19-1171 Was $19.99 *$14.99*

Escape From Alcatraz (1979)
Don Siegel directs this actioner based on the true story of the 1962 breakout from the "escape-proof" island prison. Clint Eastwood, Patrick McGoohan, Fred Ward star; look quickly for Danny Glover. 112 min.
06-1017 *$14.99*

Bronco Billy (1980)
Clint Eastwood plays the owner and star performer in a ragtag Wild West show. His lively companions include a high-strung society girl, a one-armed Indian, and a soft-spoken strongman. Sondra Locke, Scatman Crothers. 116 min.
19-1184 Was $19.99 *$14.99*

Firefox (1982)
Death-defying aerial sequences propel this blend of action, espionage and science-fiction, with Clint Eastwood as an ace fighter pilot lured out of retirement to pierce the Iron Curtain and steal the Soviet's high-tech Firefox superfighter, whose maneuvers and weapons systems are controlled by the pilot's thoughts. Co-stars Freddie Jones, David Huffman. 137 min.
19-1228 *$14.99*

Honkytonk Man (1982)
In contrast to his action and western roles, Clint Eastwood portrays a hope-filled country singer during the Depression who won't let a lack of finances, or battles with the bottle and tuberculosis, hamper his dreams of performing on the Grand Ol' Opry stage. Also stars Clint's son, Kyle, as his supportive nephew; Verna Bloom, John McIntire. 123 min.
19-1249 Was $19.99 *$14.99*

Tightrope (1984)
An intense thriller starring Clint Eastwood as a veteran New Orleans detective searching for the murderer of prostitutes, and as his investigation progresses he begins to realize his own sexual behavior parallels that of the demented killer he's been pursuing. Co-stars Genevieve Bujold, Jennifer Beck, Dan Hedaya. 117 min.
19-1361 Was $19.99 □*$14.99*

Pale Rider (1985)
Clint Eastwood returns to the western as a mysterious stranger, disguised as a priest, who helps the settlers of a small mining town overcome the oppression of a ruthless gold baron. Michael Moriarity, Carrie Snodgress. 116 min.
19-1460 Was $19.99 □*$14.99*

Pale Rider (Letterboxed Version)
Also available in a theatrical, widescreen format.
19-2714 □*$19.99*

Heartbreak Ridge (1986)
Clint Eastwood is dynamic as a grizzled Marine top-kick who's determined to hammer his bottom-of-the-barrel unit into a fighting force—and gets his chance to prove it when the call comes from Grenada. Marsha Mason, Mario Van Peebles co-star. 130 min.
19-1565 □*$14.99*

Pink Cadillac (1989)
He's put some of the biggest, baddest crooks behind bars, but has bounty hunter Clint Eastwood met his match in Bernadette Peters? Slam-bang action/comedy has Clint after Bernadette and the titular car, filled with funny money that belongs to a white supremacist gang. With Timothy Carhart, Jim Carrey. 122 min.
19-1716 Was $19.99 □*$14.99*

White Hunter, Black Heart (1990)
John Huston's on-location filming of "The African Queen" forms the basis of director/star Clint Eastwood's roman a clef adventure saga. Eastwood plays a boisterous filmmaker who takes his crew to the dark continent for the dual purposes of completing the movie and taking part in an elephant safari. This rousing (but overlooked) tale also stars Jeff Fahey, Marisa Berenson. 112 min.
19-1831 Was $19.99 □*$14.99*

The Rookie (1990)
World-weary cop Clint Eastwood teams with spry rookie Charlie Sheen to track down a murderous auto thief in this rock 'em-sock 'em actioner that's filled with car chases and shoot-outs. Raul Julia and Sonia Braga play the dastardly villains. 121 min.
19-1851 Was $19.99 □*$14.99*

Unforgiven (1992)
Four Academy Awards, including Best Picture, Director and Supporting Actor, went to director/star Clint Eastwood's superb revisionist western about a gunslinger-turned-rancher who joins his old partner and a young sharpshooter to capture a pair of cowhands responsible for mutilating a prostitute. With Gene Hackman as a cruel sheriff, Richard Harris, Morgan Freeman and Frances Fisher. 131 min.
19-2064 Was $19.99 □*$14.99*

Unforgiven (Letterboxed Version)
Also available in a theatrical, widescreen format.
19-2588 □*$19.99*

In The Line Of Fire (1993)
Knockout suspenser with Clint Eastwood as a veteran Secret Service agent entwined in a deadly cat-and-mouse game with a brilliant psychotic (John Malkovich) plotting to kill the president. While racing to stop the would-be assassin, Eastwood must overcome the demons haunting him from his days as JFK's bodyguard in Dallas. Rene Russo, Dylan McDermott co-star. 127 min.
02-2483 Was $19.99 ☐*$14.99*

In The Line Of Fire (Letterboxed Version)
Also available in a theatrical, widescreen format.
02-3050 ☐*$19.99*

A Perfect World (1993)
Moody, intense and uniquely poignant drama directed by Clint Eastwood and starring Kevin Costner as a criminal who escapes prison and flees across Texas with an 8-year-old fatherless boy he takes as a hostage. While Costner builds a bond with the boy, Eastwood, a tough Texas Ranger, pursues him. Laura Dern also stars. 138 min.
19-2211 Was $89.99 ☐*$14.99*

The Bridges Of Madison County (1995)
Robert James Waller's monster best-seller about the passionate but doomed love affair between a magazine photographer and a bored farmwife in mid-'60s Iowa is beautifully transferred to the screen by director/star Clint Eastwood, who teams with Meryl Streep for a love story that is moving, funny and unforgettable. Annie Corley, Victor Slezak also star. 135 min.
19-2439 Was $19.99 ☐*$14.99*

Absolute Power (1997)
Top-notch political suspenser directed by and starring Clint Eastwood as a veteran burglar whose last job takes him to the home of the mistress of the President of the United States. After witnessing the woman's murder, Eastwood is caught between the cop investigating the case, nasty Secret Service agents and his own estranged daughter. With Gene Hackman, Laura Linney. 121 min.
19-2537 Was $19.99 ☐*$14.99*

Absolute Power (Letterboxed Version)
Also available in a theatrical, widescreen format.
19-2659 ☐*$19.99*

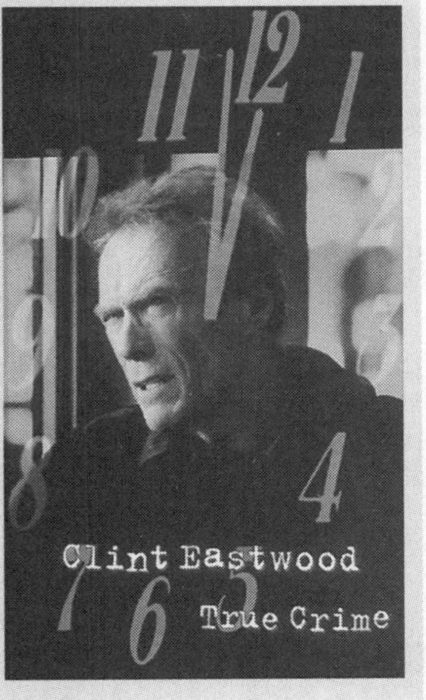

True Crime (1999)
Down-and-out Oakland reporter Clint Eastwood is sent to cover the execution of convicted murderer Isaiah Washington, but when his investigation sheds new evidence regarding his innocence, Eastwood has 12 hours to save him and find the real killer. James Woods, Lisa Gay Hamilton and Denis Leary also star in this top-notch thriller helmed by Eastwood. 127 min.
19-2879 Was $99.99 ☐*$14.99*

True Crime (Letterboxed Version)
Also available in a theatrical, widescreen format.
19-2931 ☐*$19.99*

Eastwood On Eastwood (1998)
Originally shown on TNT, this portrait of Clint Eastwood, actor and filmmaker, is based on Richard Schickel's acclaimed book and is narrated by John Cusack, star of Eastwood's "Midnight in the Garden of Good and Evil." You'll follow the Hollywood icon's career, from contract player to "The Man with No Name" to "Dirty Harry" to Oscar-winning director. 90 min.
19-2774 ☐*$14.99*

Tougher Than Leather (1988)
Rap superstars Run-DMC take over the screen in a drama filled with music and gritty action. When their weasel of a manager rips off their money and murders their friend, Run-DMC take the law into their own hands. With Richard Edson, Jenny Lumet, The Beastie Boys. 92 min.
02-1912 *$14.99*

Hit List (1989)
When a case of mistaken identity lands his wife and son on a mob kidnapper's agenda, Jan-Michael Vincent writes his own list of things to do, and burying the killers who threatened his family shoots straight up to Number One. Rip Torn co-stars. 87 min.
02-1952 *$14.99*

Weekend War (1988)
A group of National Guardsmen take to Honduras for their annual tour of duty, but they soon find themselves caught in the middle of a fierce guerrilla war. Daniel Stern, Charles Haid and Stephen Collins star in this rugged, action-packed story. 91 min.
02-2290 *$59.99*

ffolkes (1980)
Roger Moore is ffolkes, a misogynistic, cat-loving millionaire who moonlights as a counterterrorist. When extortionist Anthony Perkins threatens to blow up North Sea oil platforms, the British government hires ffolkes to save the day. Witty adventure yarn that takes a few digs at the "007" genre co-stars James Mason. 99 min.
07-1305 *$59.99*

The Wild Pair (1987)
Mismatched police officers Beau Bridges and Bubba Smith go undercover to crack a cocaine ring, and uncover a clandestine army being trained for the overthrow of the government. Directed by Bridges and co-stars his father, Lloyd. 89 min.
03-1593 *$29.99*

Troma's War (1988)
After their plane crashes on a deserted Caribbean island, the survivors face an all-new danger from some fanatical terrorists who don't like trespassers. Outrageous actioner stars Sean Bowen, Carolyn Beauchamp. 105 min.
03-1673 *$14.99*

Sky Pirates (1987)
High-flying action epic set in the South Pacific of WWII, with John Hargreaves as a daredevil aviator sent on one danger-filled mission after another, from Australia's Great Barrier Reef to mysterious Easter Island. With Meredith Phillips, Alex Scott. 88 min.
04-1050 Was $79.99 ☐*$29.99*

Edge Of Darkness (1986)
Joe Don Baker stars as a police detective whose investigation into his daughter's murder draws him into a bizarre international plot of global power and environmental extortion in this British mini-series thriller. 307 min.
04-2048 ☐*$29.99*

The Assassination Run (1984)
A retired British intelligence agent is thrust into an assassination plot when his wife is kidnapped by German terrorists. Can he rescue his wife without killing an innocent man? Malcolm Stoddard stars. 111 min.
04-3109 Was $59.99 *$19.99*

Fighting Back (1982)
Tough-as-nails true story about a group of South Philly citizens, headed by delicatessen owner Tom Skerritt, who organize a crime-fighting patrol and get a rude awakening to the scope of the criminals polluting their city's streets. Patti LuPone, Yaphet Kotto, Pat Cooper (who tole you dat?) co-star. 98 min.
06-1147 Was $19.99 *$14.99*

Alice To Nowhere (1986)
An Australian woman is in unknowing possession of a king's ransom in priceless stones...and her pursuers have left her no escape but through the breadth of the desolate Outback. Grueling, thrilling epic stars John Waters, Rosey Jones. 210 min.
06-1458 Was $59.99 *$24.99*

Tropical Snow (1989)
Two young lovers from the Colombian slums are forced into a drug-smuggling scheme and try to escape in this riveting, timely thriller. Madeleine Stowe, Nick Corri and David Carradine star. 87 min.
06-1710 Was $79.99 ☐*$14.99*

The Bad Bunch (1985)
Gritty urban action film set in the streets of Watts, where one white man faces an uphill battle in his efforts to communicate with a black street gang. Stars Tom Johnigarn, Aldo Ray. 82 min.
08-1311 Was $29.99 *$19.99*

Rogue Lion (1986)
The efforts of a team of preservationists to establish a game reserve in South America are thwarted through the interference of a local landowner. Stars Bruce Miller. 95 min.
08-1388 Was $59.99 *$29.99*

Dead Wrong (1980)
Britt Ekland stars as an undercover detective assigned to infiltrate a narcotics ring. She must face a choice between love and duty when she becomes involved with one of the smugglers. With Winston Rekert. 94 min.
03-1359 *$14.99*

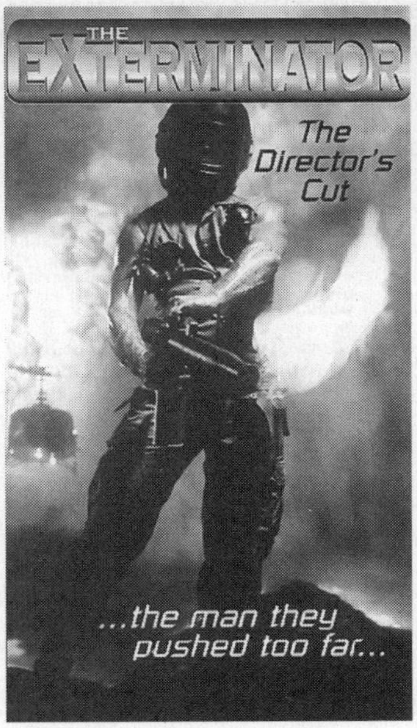

The Exterminator (Collector's Edition) (1980)
A 42nd Street favorite, this no-hold-barred actioner stars Robert Ginty as a troubled Vietnam veteran who has a "death wish" for the street scum of New York after one of his friends is crippled by a gang. Christopher George is a cop out to nab the vigilante; with Samantha Eggar, Steve James. Remastered director's cut includes scenes too intense to be shown in theaters. 104 min.
08-8568 Letterboxed *$14.99*

Street Hawk (1984)
Hunky Rex Smith is a motorcycle cop enlisted by the Feds to become an undercover avenger, astride a super-bike equipped with more crime-crushing gadgetry than you can shake a stick at. Pilot for the hit TV series also stars Christopher Lloyd, Robert Beltran. 60 min.
07-1434 *$39.99*

Runaway Train (1985)
Jon Voight and Eric Roberts are two escaped convicts stowing away on an out of control train barrelling through the Alaskan countryside. Runaway thriller that never lets up also stars Rebecca De Mornay, Kenneth McMillan; co-written by Japanese filmmaker Akira Kurosawa. 108 min.
12-1583 ☐*$14.99*

Project X (1987)
Terrific action/drama stars Matthew Broderick as a maverick Air Force pilot whose stunts get him demoted to "nursemaiding" a group of lab chimps. When he learns of the experiment's fatal consequences, he teams up with the apes' trainer (Helen Hunt) to arrange a breakout. Jonathan Kaplan directs. 108 min.
04-2090 Was $29.99 ☐*$19.99*

The Belarus File (1985)
Who loves ya, kootchie-koo? Theo Kojak does, as Telly Savalas reprises his role as the lollipop-loving scourge of the New York underworld. He must track down a killer who is systematically slaying concentration camp survivors. With Max Von Sydow, Suzanne Pleshette, and George Savalas as Stavros. 95 min.
07-1435 Was $39.99 *$14.99*

Codename: Foxfire (1985)
A gorgeous American spy (Joanna Cassidy) teams up with two other women to retrieve a stolen missile and clear her name in the pilot to the hit TV series. With Robin Johnson. 99 min.
07-1491 *$39.99*

The Rutherford County Line (1987)
Earl Owensby, B-movie legend known as "The South's Roger Corman," produced and stars in this real-life thriller as a rural North Carolina sheriff who must track down the maniac responsible for his deputies' deaths. 98 min.
07-1569 *$59.99*

The Equalizer: Memories Of Manon (1987)
Feature-length adventure from the hit TV series starring Edward Woodward as the crimefighter-for-hire. Here he must locate the kidnapped goddaughter of a government agent, a case that has painful ties to his own past. Melissa Anderson. 96 min.
07-1570 *$39.99*

Cry Of The Innocent (1980)
From the pen of Frederick Forsyth ("Day of the Jackal") comes this gripping story featuring Rod Taylor as a man whose life is destroyed when a plane crashes into his Dublin house, killing his wife and child. Taylor discovers that the crash was part of a terrorist plan and attempts to uncover the culprits. With Joanna Pettet, Nigel Davenport.
03-1240 *$19.99*

Thief (1981)
James Caan is a tough crook trying to go straight, but forced back into a dangerous fold of house-thievery, in director Michael Mann's intense look at crime from both sides of the track. Tuesday Weld, Willie Nelson, Jim Belushi also star. Outstanding Tangerine Dream score. 123 min.
12-1769 Was $19.99 ☐*$14.99*

Thief (Letterboxed Version)
Also available in a theatrical, widescreen format.
12-3081 *$14.99*

Missing Link (1988)
A thrilling, true-to-life adventure set at the dawn of Man's existence, as the last member of a tribe of man-apes wanders across a hostile, danger-filled wilderness in search of others of his kind. Make-up by Rick Baker; stars Peter Elliott, Michael Gambon. 92 min.
07-1613 *$79.99*

Return To Snowy River (1988)
The spectacular Australian wilds are used to good advantage in this sequel to the acclaimed frontier actioner about a cowboy who must fight to save his land and the woman he loves. Tom Burlinson, Sigrid Thornton, Brian Dennehy star. 100 min.
11-1465 ☐*$14.99*

Tripwire (1989)
After a special agent kills the son of the leader of a group of terrorists, incredible violence breaks out leading to an all-out war of wits and weapons. Terence Knox, David Warner, Yaphet Kotto, Charlotte Lewis and some amazing stuntwork share the spotlight in this jolt-a-minute marathon. 92 min.
02-1998 *$89.99*

Corleone (1985)
Two boyhood friends in Italy find themselves on opposite sides of the law in this brutal, "Godfather"-like saga that traces a 40-year battle between Mafia factions. Claudia Cardinale, Giuliano Gemma, Francisco Rabal star. 109 min.
12-1704 *$14.99*

WarGames (1983)
How about a game of Global Thermonuclear War? A teenage computer whiz discovers he can activate a top-secret government computer by way of his home unit and accidentally sets a doomsday program in motion. Matthew Broderick, Ally Sheedy, Dabney Coleman star. 110 min.
12-1770 Was $19.99 ☐*$14.99*

Flesh + Blood (1985)
Dutch director Paul Verhoeven ("RoboCop") creates an authentic look at Medieval life in this drama of a knight's revolt against his king and the royal bride he falls for and kidnaps. Rutger Hauer, Jennifer Jason Leigh and Tom Burlinson star. 126 min.
47-1530 ☐*$19.99*

Taffin (1987)
Dashing Pierce Brosnan stars as a gun for hire who comes to the aid of a small Irish town when they're harassed by a ruthless magnate into accepting a deadly chemical dump. Exciting actioner also stars Alison Doody. 96 min.
12-1799 *$14.99*

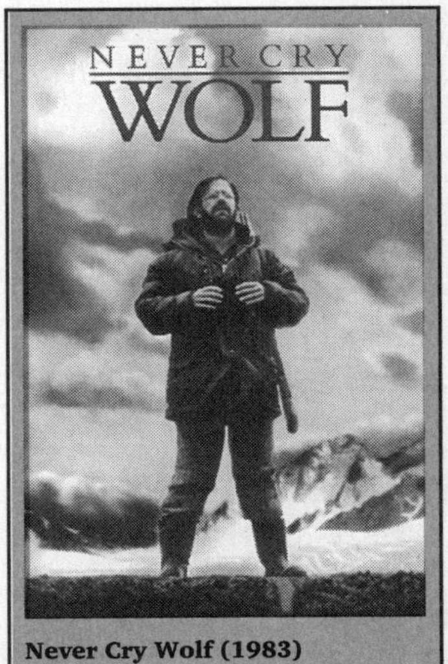

Never Cry Wolf (1983)
Remarkable wilderness adventure saga, based on Farley Mowat's autobiographical book. Biologist Charles Martin Smith travels to Canada's Arctic region to conduct a study of the wolf population. His fight for survival and experiences with the animals make for a funny, moving drama. With Brian Dennehy; Carroll Ballard directs. 105 min.
11-1118 Was $19.99 *$14.99*

Never Cry Wolf (Letterboxed Version)
Also available in a theatrical, widescreen format.
08-8819 *$14.99*

Crack House (1989)
Timely urban thriller set in the gang-ruled L.A. streets, as an ex-gang member turns to a cop for help in freeing his girlfriend from a drug dealer's fortress. Great cast includes Richard Roundtree, Jim Brown, Anthony Geary. 90 min.
12-2591 *$14.99*

Keaton's Cop (1989)
A once-in-a-lifetime cast of Lee Majors, Don Rickles and Abe Vigoda is on hand for this wild Mafia action-comedy. After an elderly man is mistaken for a mob member and rubbed out, a pair of detectives team with a crook to find the killers. Guns are shot, bodies drop and, yup, insults are hurled. 95 min.
12-2593 *$14.99*

The Secret Of The Ice Cave (1989)
Michael Moriarty, Sally Kellerman and David Mendenhall excel in this high-flying adventure saga that mixes comedy, thrills and romance. They're on an expedition to uncover what's really located in the mysterious ice cave. 106 min.
12-2673 *$14.99*

Shark's Paradise (1986)
A trio of American detectives hits the beaches of Australia to stop a blackmailer who claims that he can infest the waters with ferocious sharks unless his demands are met. David Rainey stars. 93 min.
14-3150 *$12.99*

Rage To Kill (1988)
When a tiny Caribbean island is taken over by insurgents and American students are taken hostage, racer/adventurer James Ryan pulls a daring one-man rescue mission and takes on the rebel leader in a battle to the death. James Ryan, Oliver Reed, Cameron Mitchell star. 94 min.
14-3383 *$12.99*

Street Law (1984)
In the mold of "Death Wish" comes this tale of urban revenge. Franco Nero is the man who decides to take the law into his own hands after he's beaten and threatened by mobsters. Barbara Bach is the woman who helps him plot his revenge. 77 min.
15-1133 *$12.99*

Black Cobra (1983)
When a beautiful woman (Laura Gemser) wakes to find her lesbian lover dead beside her, the victim of a venomous attack, she lashes out to trap the murderer in a bizarre and unnatural ritual...a ritual involving the Black Cobra. Jack Palance also stars.
16-1191 *$14.99*

Lust For Freedom (1987)
Arrested and jailed for a crime she didn't commit, a beautiful young woman is attacked and raped by the police until she escapes to take the law into her own hands. Sordid thriller from the Troma studios stars Melanie Coll, William J. Kulzer. 92 min.
16-9115 *$14.99*

The Squeeze (1980)
Hardening his nose for future "Hammer" appearances is Stacy Keach, an ex-cop who stalls his dive into drink by joining the hunt for his former wife's kidnappers. Gritty crime drama co-starring David Hemmings, Stephen Boyd and Edward Fox. 106 min.
19-1557 Was $59.99 *$19.99*

Under Cover (1987)
A young Baltimore cop learns his ex-partner has been killed while working undercover in a high school as a "narc." Determined to get the facts, he travels south to take over his friend's assignment. David Neidorf and Jennifer Jason Leigh star. 95 min.
19-1610 Was $79.99 *$19.99*

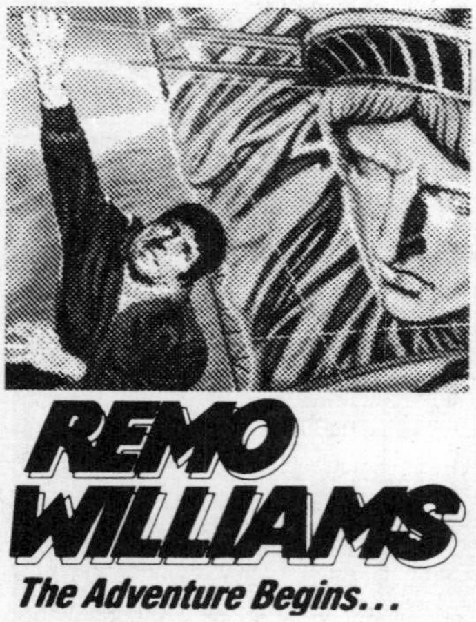

Remo Williams: The Adventure Begins (1985)
Slam-bang action thriller based on the "Destroyer" novels stars Fred Ward as the ex-New York cop who is rescued after being left for dead by a clandestine government group that trains him to be a "super-agent." A showdown on the scaffolded Statue of Liberty is a highlight; with Joel Grey, Wilford Brimley, Kate Mulgrew. 121 min.
44-1362 □*$14.99*

The Lords Of Flatbush (1974)
A cast of then-unknown stars (Sylvester Stallone, Henry Winkler, Susan Blakely and Perry King) head this tale of a street gang in 1957 Brooklyn who must face the one enemy they can't fight: growing up. Action, comedy and a great rock and roll soundtrack. 88 min.
02-1559 *$14.99*

Rocky (1976)
The first and the best! Writer/star Sylvester Stallone is the Philadelphia club boxer who gets a dream shot at fighting the heavyweight champion in this rousing drama that struck a chord with audiences around the world, made Sly a superstar, and won three Academy Awards, including Best Picture. With Talia Shire, Burt Young, Burgess Meredith, Carl Weathers. 119 min.
12-1822 □*$14.99*

Rocky Commemorative Gift Set
It's a knockout deal no Stallone fan can resist: all five "Rocky" films, plus an exclusive, photo-filled collector's insert, in a money-saving boxed set.
50-8642 *$69.99*

F.I.S.T. (1978)
Absorbing social drama stars Sylvester Stallone as a decent, moral trucker who compromises his principles while ascending the union ranks, and in the process, alienates his wife and his best friend and becomes the subject of a government investigation. Co-stars David Huffman, Rod Steiger, Peter Boyle, Tony LoBianco; directed by Norman Jewison. 145 min.
12-1748 *$14.99*

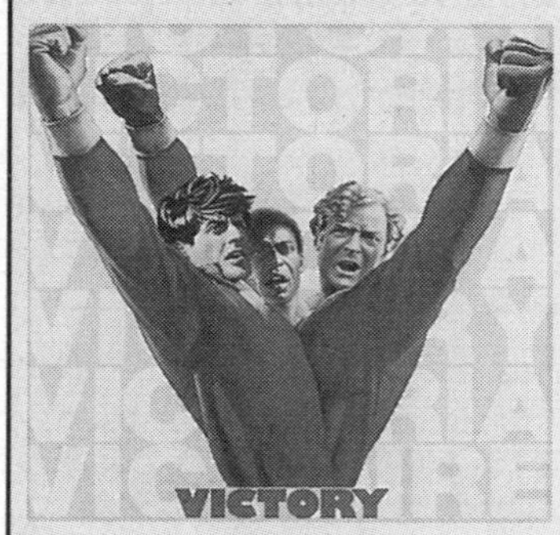

Victory (1981)
Stirring World War II drama centers on a German-sponsored soccer match between the Reich's top players and Allied prisoners. The game, at first the diversion for a planned escape, becomes a symbolic struggle that both sides want to win...at any cost. Sylvester Stallone, Michael Caine, Max Von Sydow and soccer great Pelé star. 110 min.
19-1795 *$14.99*

First Blood (1982)
Rambo (Sylvester Stallone) is an ex-Green Beret who is harassed and jailed by the locals in a North-west town, only to escape and wage a one-man guerrilla war in the mountains. Lightning-fast action film also stars Richard Crenna, Brian Dennehy. 96 min.
27-6682 Was $89.99 *$14.99*

First Blood (Letterboxed Version)
Also available in a theatrical, widescreen format.
27-7085 *$14.99*

Rambo: First Blood Part II (1985)
Stallone returns as Vietnam vet Rambo, returning to Southeast Asia on a "red herring" mission to search for M.I.A.s the government left behind. Once he gets there, though, nothing will stop Rambo from bringin' 'em back alive. Action, action and more action as only Stallone can deliver! 96 min.
27-6587 Was $89.99 □*$14.99*

Rambo: First Blood Part II (Letterboxed Version)
Also available in a theatrical, widescreen format.
44-1295 *$14.99*

Rambo III (1988)
Stallone's a one-man fighting machine who heads to Afghanistan to rescue his former Army commander (Richard Crenna) from Russian captivity in the explosive third entry in the hit action film series. You'll believe a man can shoot down a helicopter with a bow and arrow! 102 min.
27-6597 Was $89.99 *$14.99*

Rambo III (Letterboxed Version)
Also available in a theatrical, widescreen format.
27-7086 *$14.99*

Rambo 3-Pack (Letterboxed Version)
Also available in a theatrical, widescreen format.
27-7087 Save $10.00! *$34.99*

Cobra (1986)
Dull movies are a disease and Stallone is the cure! Watch Sly, as two-fisted, quick-triggered L.A. cop Cobra, as he shoots, blasts, punches and mauls his way through the ranks of a murderous gang terrorizing the streets. With Brigitte Nielsen, Reni Santoni. 87 min.
19-1542 Was $19.99 □*$14.99*

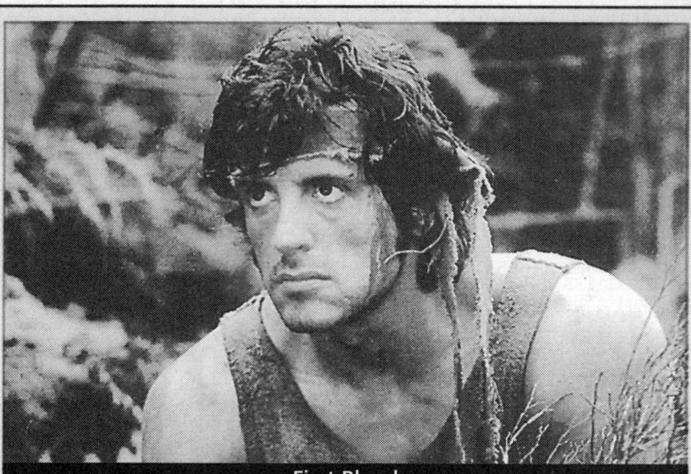

First Blood

Sylvester Stallone

Over The Top (1987)
Stallone stars in this drama as a trucker who struggles as mightily at competition arm-wrestling as he does to bridge the gap between his estranged son and himself. Robert Loggia, Susan Blakely, David Mendenhall co-star. 93 min.
19-1587 □*$14.99*

Tango And Cash (1989)
Slam-bang cop movie pairs slick Sylvester Stallone and sloppy Kurt Russell as mismatched detectives out to stop a mouse-loving drug kingpin played by Jack Palance. Frame jobs, gunplay, high-speed chases and Russell in drag highlight this explosive action-comedy. Brion James and Teri Hatcher also star. 104 min.
19-1761 □*$14.99*

Lock Up (1989)
It's the most hellish prison in America, and when inmate Sylvester Stallone is brought there for six months of torture at the hands of sadistic warden Donald Sutherland, something's got to give! Explosive "big house" thriller also stars Darlanne Fluegel, Sonny Landham. 103 min.
27-6648 Was $89.99 □*$12.99*

Stop! Or My Mom Will Shoot (1992)
A zany action-comedy with Sylvester Stallone as a Los Angeles policeman who gets nothing but trouble when his mother (Estelle Getty) arrives in town for a visit. Problems escalate when Mom witnesses a murder and joins her son on the investigation. JoBeth Williams, Roger Rees co-star. 87 min.
07-1816 Was $19.99 □*$14.99*

Cliffhanger (1993)
Years after a tragic accident in which he was unable to save his best friend's girlfriend, mountain climber Sylvester Stallone attempts to redeem himself by retrieving suitcases of stolen government loot lost in the Colorado Rockies. Spectacular adventure saga also stars John Lithgow as the criminal mastermind behind the heist, Michael Rooker and Janine Turner. 113 min.
02-2481 Was $19.99 □*$14.99*

Cliffhanger (Letterboxed Version)
Also available in a theatrical, widescreen format.
02-3204 □*$19.99*

Demolition Man (1993)
In the late 1990s, maverick L.A. cop Sylvester Stallone and crazed super-criminal Wesley Snipes are put in suspended animation by the state, but when Snipes is revived and escapes into the non-violent, politically correct society of 2032, the authorities have to thaw out Stallone in order to stop his old nemesis. Sandra Bullock, Nigel Hawthorne and Denis Leary co-star in this witty sci-fi actioner. 115 min.
19-2206 Was $89.99 □*$14.99*

The Specialist (1994)
Explosive actioner starring Sylvester Stallone as a former bomb expert for the CIA hired by beautiful Sharon Stone to kill the Miami mobsters who murdered her family. As Stallone starts his assault, he discovers that unpredictable former associate James Woods is working for the hoods. Eric Roberts and Rod Steiger co-star; features steamy Stallone-Stone sex scenes. 110 min.
19-2311 Was $19.99 □*$14.99*

Assassins (1995)
World-weary hit man Sylvester Stallone is ready to retire after one last assignment, but the mission turns out to be a set-up and pits him against cocky young rival Antonio Banderas in a fight for survival. Intense actioner also stars Julianne Moore. 133 min.
19-2431 Was $19.99 □*$14.99*

Judge Dredd (1995)
Sylvester Stallone is Judge Dredd, the comic book-inspired hero who serves as judge, jury and executioner in crime-ridden, futuristic Mega City-One. When arch-enemy Rico escapes from prison, he schemes to have Dredd thrown behind bars and replace the city officials with DNA clones. Rob Schneider, Armand Assante and Diane Lane co-star in this special effects-filled actioner. 96 min.
11-1953 Was $19.99 □*$14.99*

Daylight (1996)
In this explosive disaster epic, Sylvester Stallone is a former Emergency Medical Services worker called on to rescue a group of people trapped inside an underwater New York commuter tunnel after an accident and explosion seal off both ends. Incredible stunts and special effects highlight the film, which also stars Amy Brenneman, Viggo Mortensen and Dan Hedaya. Special video edition also includes behind-the-scenes footage with the cast and director Rob Cohen. 115 min.
07-2503 Was $99.99 □*$14.99*

Daylight (Letterboxed Version)
Also available in a theatrical, widescreen format.
07-2602 *$19.99*

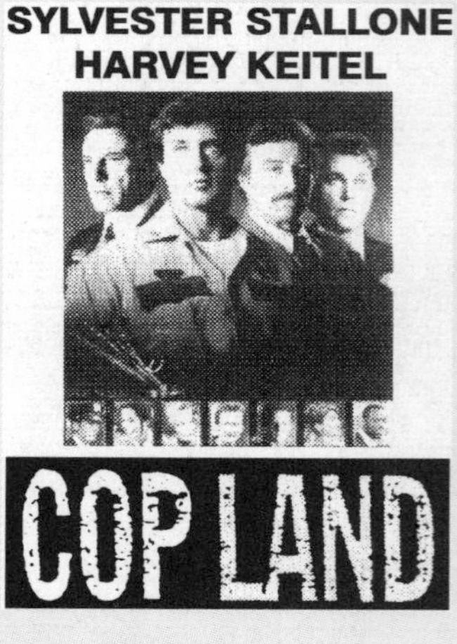

Cop Land (1997)
A controversial shooting by a New York City policeman leads Internal Affairs officer Robert De Niro to a quiet, seemingly trouble-free New Jersey town where a large number of Big Apple cops live. De Niro looks to local sheriff Sylvester Stallone for help in breaking the "wall of silence," but will Stallone stand up to the corrupt lawmen and their leader, veteran cop Harvey Keitel? Ray Liotta, Michael Rapaport, Annabella Sciorra co-star. 105 min.
11-2233 Was $19.99 □*$14.99*

Cop Land (Letterboxed Version)
Also available in a theatrical, widescreen format.
11-2793 □*$19.99*

Please see our index for these other Sylvester Stallone titles: *An Alan Smithee Film: Burn Hollywood Burn • Antz • Bananas • Death Race 2000 • The Prisoner Of Second Avenue*

Night Of The Sharks (1989)
A jewel thief rips off his boss and escapes with a fortune in gems, hiding out with his brother on a tropical island surrounded by sharks. But when the boss comes looking for his property, the fight between human and finned predators becomes deadly. Treat Williams, Antonio Fargas, Steve Elliot star. 85 min.
75-7069 Was $19.99 ***$14.99***

Wild Man (1988)
He's Eric Wilde, ex-CIA agent and gun-for-hire who's come back for a personal vendetta, tracking down the drug kingpin responsible for his former boss's murder. Exciting actioner stars Don Scribner, Michelle Bauer, Ginger (Lynn) Allen. 105 min.
69-5079 ***$79.99***

Cuba Crossing (1980)
A band of expert spies and assassins are hired to put an end to a drug smuggling ring that has its headquarters in Castro's Cuba in this action-filled suspense thriller. Robert Vaughn, Stuart Whitman and Sybill Danning star. AKA: "Kill Castro!," "The Mercenaries," "Sweet Dirty Tony." 92 min.
71-5016 ***$19.99***

Deadly Breed (1988)
A white supremacist group has begun sending its own "police force" on the city streets to get rid of "undesirables," but when they murder the wife of a parole officer opposed to their philosophies he straps on the hardware to teach them a deadly lesson in brotherhood. Timely thriller stars William Smith, Addison Randall. 90 min.
86-1004 Was $69.99 ***$14.99***

Angels Of The City (1989)
Lawrence-Hilton Jacobs heads this steamy thriller about two co-eds who pose as hookers to pass their sorority initiation and get trapped in the Sisterhood of Sleaze by a possessive pimp. With Kelly Galindo and Cynthia Cheston. 90 min.
86-1007 Was $69.99 ***$14.99***

Arizona Heat (1988)
A brutal, no-nonsense cop is teamed with a beautiful new partner to track down a vengeful badge-killer in this explosive actioner. Michael Parks and Denise Crosby star. 91 min.
63-1285 Was $89.99 ***$14.99***

The Soldier (1982)
Russian terrorists are holding the world hostage with a load of stolen plutonium in their clutches. Only the Soldier, a high-priced, lethal assassin, can stop them. Ken Wahl, Klaus Kinski star. 90 min.
53-1040 ***$14.99***

Assignment Skybolt (1984)
Secret agent Don Collins must stop terrorists in Turkey who have a hydrogen bomb. Music by Manos Hadjidakis. 109 min.
64-1020 ***$29.99***

Living To Die (1989)
The Las Vegas gaming commissioner is being blackmailed and turns to a rough ex-cop for help. Soon, the woman the commissioner supposedly murdered turns up, sending the cop into a deadly web of suspense and blackmail in "Glitz City." Wings Hauser, Asher Brauner and Darcy DeMoss star. 84 min.
86-1040 Was $29.99 ***$14.99***

Ruckus (1981)
The arrival in a small Southern town of troubled Vietnam vet Dirk Benedict leads to violent confrontations with local toughs and a showdown with the law. Linda Blair is the war widow who befriends Benedict in this action-packed precursor to "First Blood." Richard Farnsworth, Ben Johnson also star. 92 min.
58-1016 ***$12.99***

Red Surf (1989)
Once they were surfing buddies. Now they're running drugs for a savage street gang, and this time they may really be in over their heads. Brutal action flick stars George Clooney, Dedee Pfeiffer and rock star Gene Simmons. 104 min.
71-5194 Was $19.99 ***$14.99***

Action Jackson (1988)
"Rocky" co-star Carl Weathers takes a solo turn as tough Detroit cop Jericho "Action" Jackson in this hit thriller, taking on a corrupt auto tycoon who has him framed for murder. Craig T. Nelson, Vanity, Sharon Stone also star. 96 min.
40-1394 ***□$14.99***

Gangster Classics

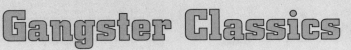

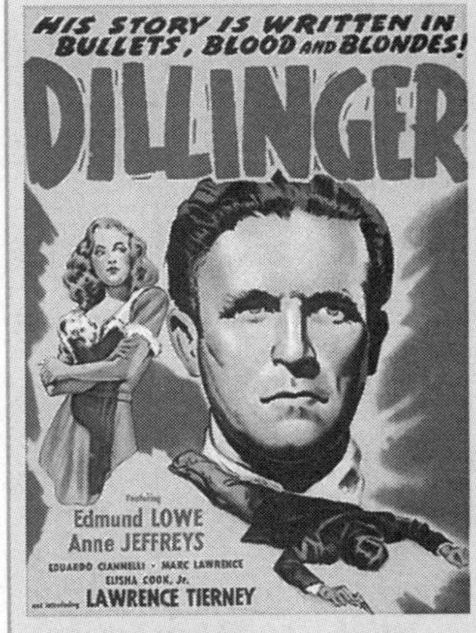
HIS STORY IS WRITTEN IN BULLETS, BLOOD AND BLONDES!
DILLINGER
Featuring
Edmund LOWE
Anne JEFFREYS
EDUARDO CIANNELLI · MARC LAWRENCE
ELISHA COOK, Jr.
and introducing LAWRENCE TIERNEY

Dillinger (1945)
One of the first Hollywood crime dramas based on an actual figure (although the script strays from the true story), this bullet-riddled saga stars Lawrence Tierney as the Indiana farm boy who grew up to rob banks across the Midwest in the 1930s and became "Public Enemy Number One." With Anne Jeffreys, Edmund Lowe, Elisha Cook, Jr. 70 min.
04-1925 ***$19.99***

Dillinger (1973)
Bullet-riddled look at America's most wanted criminal of the '30s follows John Dillinger (Warren Oates) through his bank-robbing career until his violent death outside of the Biograph Theatre in Chicago. Co-stars Michelle Phillips, Ben Johnson, Cloris Leachman, Richard Dreyfuss and Harry Dean Stanton; John Milius directs. 100 min.
47-1117 Was $19.99 ***$12.99***

Dillinger (1991)
Mark Harmon stars as the machine-gunning gangster who terrorized bankers across America in the '30s in this action-filled drama. With Will Patton as G-man Melvin Purvis and Sherilyn Fenn as "the lady in red"; look for former screen Dillinger Lawrence Tierney as a sheriff. 95 min.
19-2379 Was $69.99 ***□$19.99***

Guns Don't Argue (1957)
Some of the world's most notorious gangsters are portrayed in this rambunctious, machine gun-rumbling epic with John Dillinger, Ma Barker, Pretty Boy Floyd, Baby Face Nelson and Bonnie & Clyde battling aggressive G-men. With Myron Healey, Jim Davis and Richard Crane.
68-8733 ***$19.99***

The Rise And Fall Of Legs Diamond (1960)
Jolting gangster fare chronicles the life of the legendary hoodlum with a knack for self-preservation and how he went from two-bit thief to much-feared mob kingpin. Ray Danton electrifies in the title role, with support from Karen Steele, Elaine Stewart, Jesse White, Warren Oates and Dyan Cannon. 101 min.
19-1864 Was $59.99 ***□$19.99***

Ma Barker's Killer Brood (1960)
Before "Big Bad Mama," there was this energetic gangster flick about the meanest Mama of them all. Follow Ma's rise to outlaw legend status, as she leads her sons in bank robberies and dispenses wisdom to John Dillinger and Baby Face Nelson. With Lurene Tuttle, Tris Coffin and Paul Dubov. 82 min.
68-8538 ***$19.99***

Public Enemies (1995)
Rip-roaring, gun-toting gangster yarn with Theresa Russell as Ma Barker, the notorious bank robber who worked with her brood to hold the country in terror in the 1930s. Eric Roberts, Dan Cortese, Alyssa Milano and Frank Stallone also star in this rat-tat-tat actioner. AKA: "Public Enemy #1." 91 min.
68-1817 Was $99.99 ***□$14.99***

The St. Valentine's Day Massacre (1967)
The streets of Chicago become a battlefield in this super-charged drama based on the famed gangster ambush set by Al Capone on Bugs Moran's men. Jason Robards, George Segal, Ralph Meeker star; look for Bruce Dern and Jack Nicholson. Directed by Roger Corman. 100 min.
04-1924 ***$14.99***

The Lost Capone (1990)
Little-known true story focuses on the relationship between ruthless gangster Al Capone (Eric Roberts) and his brother (Adrian Pasdar), a federal marshal in a small Nebraska town. Eventually, a feud erupts between the two and sibling rivalry leads to a showdown between lawbreaker and lawman. Ally Sheedy also stars. 92 min.
18-7253 Was $79.99 ***□$14.99***

Capone (1992)
Ray Sharkey plays the infamous "Scarface" Al Capone in this rip-roaring gangster story. Still ruling his crime empire from jail, Capone engages in a deadly battle against FBI agent Keith Carradine. Debrah Farentino and Charles Haid also star. 97 min.
68-1263 Was $89.99 ***□$12.99***

Dillinger And Capone (1995)
Years after he was supposedly shot down in front of a Chicago movie theatre, retired gangster John Dillinger lives quietly with his wife and son on a California farm...until dying ex-mob boss Al Capone abducts Dillinger's family and forces him to help retrieve a fortune stashed in Capone's infamous secret vault. Rip-roaring gangster epic stars Martin Sheen, F. Murray Abraham and Catherine Hicks.
21-9089 Was $89.99 ***$14.99***

Gangland (1973)
After his mobster kingpin father is knocked off by a rival hood, teenager Rico sets out for revenge by sabotaging the new gangleader's main sources of income, which include counterfeiting, drug trafficking and protection. Christopher Mitchum, Arthur Kennedy, Barbara Bouchet, Claudine Auger and Olivia Hussey star. AKA: "Cauldron of Death," "Dirty Mob," "Mean Machine," "Rico." 90 min.
10-1690 ***$19.99***

Virginia Hill: Mistress To The Mob (1974)
Dyan Cannon stars as the rising Hollywood starlet who caught the eye of gangster Bugsy Siegel and was his lover until his brutal murder in 1947 in this fact-based crime drama. With Allen Garfield, Robby Benson, and Harvey Keitel as Siegel; directed by Joel Schumacher. AKA: "The Virginia Hill Story."
44-2220 ***$14.99***

Gangster Wars (1981)
Feature film version of the gripping TV series noted for its detail and realism. Michael Nouri ("Flashdance") is a fictionalized hood in 1920s New York, in the heyday of gangsters like Bugsy Siegel and Lucky Luciano. 121 min.
07-1099 Was $59.99 ***$14.99***

Mobsters (1991)
Young Hoods with Guns Patrick Dempsey, Christian Slater, Richard Grieco and Costas Mandylor play famed gangsters Meyer Lansky, "Lucky" Luciano, "Bugsy" Siegel and Frank Costello in a smashing shoot-'em-up that chronicles their rise to power on Brooklyn's mean streets. F. Murray Abraham, Lara Flynn Boyle and Anthony Quinn also star. 106 min.
07-1732 Was $19.99 ***□$14.99***

Hit The Dutchman (1992)
The violent rise and fall of '20s gangster Dutch Schultz, who was a protégé and later a rival of Legs Diamond for control of New York, is graphically depicted in this slam-bang mobster drama. Bruce Nozick, Will Kemp and Sally Kirkland star. Uncut, unrated version; 117 min.
68-1249 ***□$89.99***

The Outfit (1993)
The 1930s heyday of infamous gangsters comes alive in this explosive story about an FBI agent who infiltrates Lucky Luciano's mob and orchestrates a war between Luciano and rival hood Dutch Shultz. Lance Henriksen, Martin Kove, Billy Drago and Josh Mosby star. 92 min.
07-2002 ***□$89.99***

Hoodlum (1997)
The streets of 1930s Harlem explode with violence when a war for their control pits black gangster boss Ellsworth "Bumpy" Johnson (Laurence Fishburne) against rival mobsters Dutch Schultz (Tim Roth) and Lucky Luciano (Andy Garcia) in this thrilling true crime drama. Vanessa Williams, Cicely Tyson, Clarence Williams III also star; directed by Bill Duke. 128 min.
12-3210 Was $99.99 ***□$19.99***

Hoodlum (Letterboxed Version)
Also available in a theatrical, widescreen format.
12-3239 ***□$19.99***

Baby Face Nelson (1997)
C. Thomas Howell stars as the diminutive (5'6" in real life) tough guy who came off the streets of '20s Chicago and made a name for himself as part of John Dillinger's mob, rising up the FBI's most wanted list, in this action-packed gangster tale. With Lisa Zane, Martin Kove, and F. Murray Abraham as Al Capone. 88 min.
21-9152 ***$59.99***

The Newton Boys (1998)
Director Richard Linklater ("Dazed and Confused") turns his attention to the disaffected youth of another era in this crime drama that recounts the real-life exploits of four brothers (Vincent D'Onofrio, Ethan Hawke, Matthew McConaughey, Skeet Ulrich) from a Texas farm family who take to bank robbing in the days after World War I and become folk heroes along the way. Juliana Marguiles, Dwight Yoakam also star.
04-3687 Was $99.99 ***□$14.99***

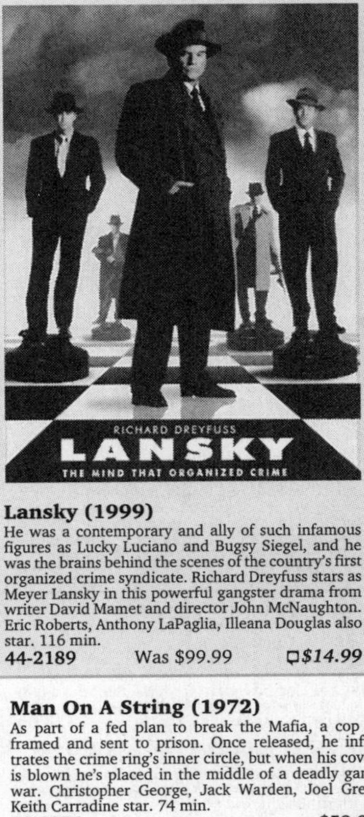
RICHARD DREYFUSS
LANSKY
THE MIND THAT ORGANIZED CRIME

Lansky (1999)
He was a contemporary and ally of such infamous figures as Lucky Luciano and Bugsy Siegel, and he was the brains behind the scenes of the country's first organized crime syndicate. Richard Dreyfuss stars as Meyer Lansky in this powerful gangster drama from writer David Mamet and director John McNaughton. Eric Roberts, Anthony LaPaglia, Illeana Douglas also star. 116 min.
44-2189 Was $99.99 ***□$14.99***

CRIME STORY

Crime Story (1986)
The pilot film to "Miami Vice" creator Michael Mann's gritty 1986-88 TV drama stars Dennis Farina as detective Mike Torello, fighting on the streets of early '60s Chicago against ruthless young hood Anthony Denison, who's making a violent climb up the Mob ladder. Stephen Lang, Darlanne Fluegel also star. 96 min.
70-1161 ***$14.99***

Midnight Warrior (1988)
For a TV news cameraman, the streets of Los Angeles are his beat and battleground, and when he starts getting too involved in the stories, it could mean his life. Drama stars Kevin Bernhardt, Lilly Melgar. 90 min.
86-1005 Was $69.99 ***$14.99***

Shotgun (1988)
When a vice kingpin thinks he owns the streets of Los Angeles, it's up to a team of maverick cops to take him on and dispense "12-gauge justice." Stuart Chapin, Rif Hutton star. 90 min.
86-1003 Was $69.99 ***$14.99***

Gator Bait II: Cajun Justice (1988)
Her beautiful Louisiana swampside wedding is ruined when a vicious gang crashes the ceremony, beats up the groom and rapes her, so this backwoods beauty grabs her guns and a longboat to deliver her own homegrown vengeance. Jan MacKenzie, Paul Muzzcat star. 95 min.
06-1632 ***□$59.99***

L.A. Heat (1988)
A revenge-seeking policeman sets out to find the drug dealers responsible for his partner's death, and no one, not even his fellow officers, will stand in his way. Blazing urban action flick stars Jim Brown and Lawrence-Hilton Jacobs. 90 min.
86-1002 Was $69.99 ***$14.99***

White Line Fever (1975)
Hard-driving action movie focuses on trucker Jan-Michael Vincent and his fight against the hoodlums and racketeers who run the industry. With Kay Lenz, Slim Pickens, Don Porter and the great Dick Miller; Jonathan Kaplan directs. 89 min.
02-1209 ***$59.99***

The Horsemen (1971)
Omar Sharif stars as the rebellious son of Afghan tribal leader Jack Palance. In order to prove his loyalty, Sharif enters a buzkeshi tournament, the grueling native horseback sport that often proves fatal. John Frankenheimer directs. 109 min.
02-1701 ***$69.99***

Man On A String (1972)
As part of a fed plan to break the Mafia, a cop is framed and sent to prison. Once released, he infiltrates the crime ring's inner circle, but when his cover is blown he's placed in the middle of a deadly gang war. Christopher George, Jack Warden, Joel Grey, Keith Carradine star. 74 min.
02-2354 ***$59.99***

The Executioner (1970)
George Peppard is a British agent who must track down and eliminate a colleague-turned-traitor, but finds his job complicated by Joan Collins, his ex-lover and the agent's wife. Top-notch suspense thriller co-stars Keith Michell, Oscar Homolka. 107 min.
02-2690 ***$14.99***

Speedtrap (1977)
A blistering action-smash-em with Joe Don Baker as a private detective on the heels of some nasty car thieves. Lots of fast-paced auto action. Tyne Daly also stars. 98 min.
03-1281 ***$19.99***

Pam Grier

The Big Doll House (1971)
This is the groundbreaking "women behind bars" actioner that became a drive-in classic! When the desperate, abused inmates of an all-female prison rebel against the sadistic warden and his guards, all heck breaks loose! Pam Grier (who also sings the theme song), Judy Collins, Roberta Collins and Sid Haig star. 93 min.
53-1448 Was $59.99 ***$14.99***

Twilight People (1972)
Based on the 1932 horror classic "Island of Lost Souls," this Roger Corman-produced shocker features a mad scientist whose creations include an ape man, antelope man, bat man (no, not that bat man!) and even a tree woman. John Ashley and Jan Merlin star, with Pam Grier as the panther woman. 84 min.
08-1237 Was $29.99 ***$14.99***

The Big Bird Cage (1972)
You'll want to keep this lovely tropical isle off the cruise list...it's a brutally-run work farm for women lorded over by sadistic fey guards. Hit the decks when foxy mercenary Pam Grier arrives to blow the joint wide open. Anitra Ford, Sid Haig and Carol Speed also star in this Roger Corman production. 93 min.
19-1003 Was $39.99 ***$14.99***

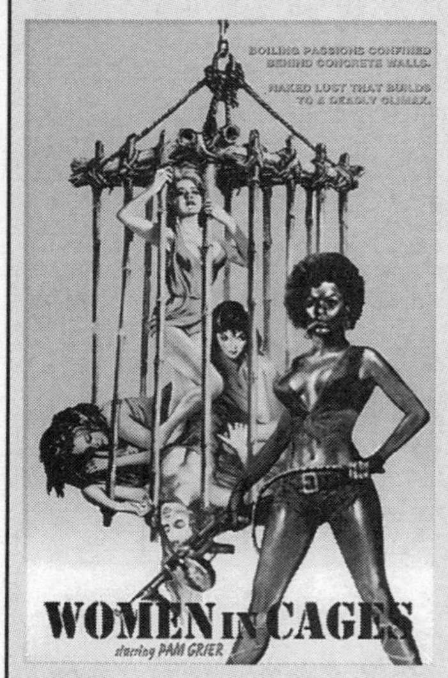

Women In Cages (1972)
Stark, sadistic women-in-prison shocker with a sizzling star turn by Pam Grier as a whip-wielding, lesbian warden named Alabama who enjoys abusing her charges in a gothic torture chamber, "the Playpen." With Judy Brown, Roberta Collins. AKA: "Women's Penitentiary III." 81 min.
53-3065 Was $59.99 ***$14.99***

The Arena (1973)
They were playthings for the vicarious bloodlust of Imperial Rome, slavegirl gladiators forced to fight or die in spectacles of barbarous combat. Pam Grier and Margaret Markov head the cast of sweaty sword-and-sandal sisters who mount a desperate revolt to regain their freedom. AKA: "Naked Warriors." 78 min.
12-1800 Was $19.99 ***$14.99***

Coffy (1973)
A one-woman hit squad who has a heavy score to settle with Vegas' dope peddlers. Guns blasting or talons slashing, when she avenges the ruin of her heroin-addicted baby sister, Pam Grier as Coffy keeps the tension going to the last drop. 91 min.
73-1016 ***$14.99***

Black Mama, White Mama (1973)
Take the racial tension of "The Defiant Ones," mix in a little "women in prison" tease, and you get this outrageous '70s actioner starring Pam Grier and Margaret Markov as chained-together inmates in a Philippines work camp who escape their captors and join up with revolutionaries in the jungle. With Sid Haig, Lynn Borden; Jonathan Demme co-wrote the story. 86 min.
73-1249 ***$14.99***

Foxy Brown (1974)
She's "a chick with drive, who don't take no jive," and when her undercover cop lover is killed by drug pushers, Foxy (Pam Grier) forms a vigilante posse to get revenge on the crime bosses responsible in this ultra-violent thriller. With Anotnio Fargas, Peter Brown. 92 min.
73-1015 ***$14.99***

Friday Foster (1975)
Pam Grier is our gal Friday, a model-turned-photographer caught up in the furious competition between international couturiers, assassins, and the mysterious "Black Widow." Scatman Crothers, Eartha Kitt, Godfrey Cambridge star. 90 min.
73-1013 Was $59.99 ***$14.99***

Sheba, Baby (1975)
Chicago investigator Sheba Shayne returns to her old Kentucky home to help Dad defend his legitimate loan business from mob sharks. Gun-dueling with a .44 Magnum or donning a wet suit to ambush a crimelord's yacht, Pam Grier as Sheba shows why she's queen of the action stars. 90 min.
73-1017 Was $59.99 ❑***$14.99***

Strip Search (1997)
An undercover detective finds himself slowly being seduced into a world of easy money and seductive women, but will he stray over the line to the side of evil? Stylish, hard-hitting actioner stars Michael Paré, Caroline Néron, Maury Chakin, Pam Grier. 90 min.
83-1165 Was $99.99 ***$14.99***

No Tomorrow (1999)
Rap star Master P directs and stars in this explosive action yarn in which criminal Gary Busey and shipping company worker Gary Daniels attempt to pull off a huge arms deal. Word gets out about the transaction in the underworld, and gangster Master P and FBI agent Pam Grier get involved in stopping the scheme. Jeff Fahey also stars. 99 min.
50-8362 ***$39.99***

The Pam Grier Collection
We've got your Grier right here...three of them, in fact, in a boxed collector's set. Pam's all woman and all action in "Coffy," "Foxy Brown" and "Friday Foster."
73-1296 Save $10.00! ***$34.99***

Please see our index for these other Pam Grier titles: *Above The Law • Bucktown • Escape From L.A. • Fort Apache, The Bronx • Fortress 2: Re-Entry • Holy Smoke! • In Too Deep • Jackie Brown • Jawbreaker • Mars Attacks! • Scream, Blacula, Scream • Snow Day • Something Wicked This Way Comes • Tough Enough • The Vindicator*

Outlaw Blues (1977)
Peter Fonda and Susan Saint James team up for action, comedy and romance. An ex-con on the run tries to recover songs he wrote that were stolen by another artist, and along the way becomes a folk hero and is joined by the artist's girlfriend. 100 min.
19-1413 Was $19.99 ***$14.99***

Bobbie Jo And The Outlaw (1976)
Lynda Carter shows off her ample body in this hard-drivin' action tale that has Texas waitress Carter joining smooth-talking auto thief Marjoe Gortner on the run from the law. With Jesse Vint and Gerrit Graham. 90 min.
47-1118 Was $79.99 ***$12.99***

Lady Cocoa (1974)
The beautiful Lola Falana stars as a gorgeous gal involved with sharp-shooting mobsters. The action and excitement of Las Vegas, murder, violence and lovely Lola make this a must-see. Gene Washington, Millie Perkins, "Mean Joe" Greene. 93 min.
48-1046 ***$29.99***

The Florida Connection (1974)
A high-flying adventure in the world's riskiest business: smuggling. Action fans are in for a treat. Dan Pastorini, June Wilkinson. 106 min.
48-1005 ***$14.99***

Erik, The Viking (1970)
Adventure on the high seas with Viking warriors sailing for the New World. Combat scenes abound as the Norsemen deal with enemies within and without. Stars Guiliano Gemma. 86 min.
48-1106 ***$59.99***

Killer Force (1975)
Telly Savalas stars in this wild whiteknuckler as the head of security at a South African diamond mine who enlists the aid of sheriff Peter Fonda to investigate a series of thefts. Co-stars O.J. Simpson, Hugh O'Brian, Maud Adams. 100 min.
47-1109 Was $69.99 ***$14.99***

Sky Heist (1975)
An all-star cast is featured in this action-packed crime story about a husband and wife team who devise a plan to nab $10 million that involves hijacking a police helicopter. Stefanie Powers, Don Meredith, Frank Gorshin, Shelley Fabares star. 96 min.
48-1179 ***$29.99***

Boomerang (1976)
Alain Delon stars as a father who helps his son, sentenced to life for an accidental murder, escape from jail. Their problems are just beginning, however, in this tense action thriller. 102 min.
48-1108 ***$59.99***

Big Bad Mama (1974)
The backroads of Depression-era America run red with blood when lovely lawbreaker Angie Dickinson and her two daughters go on a crime spree in this sexy spin on the "Bonnie and Clyde" genre from producer Roger Corman. With William Shatner, Susan Sennett, Robbie Lee, Sally Kirkland and the great Dick Miller. 83 min.
19-1002 ***$14.99***

Big Bad Mama II (1987)
Angie Dickinson returns as the machine-gun mater of the '30s who teaches her girls the fine arts of romancing men and robbing banks. Slam-bang actioner co-stars Robert Culp, Danielle Brisebois and Playboy cover girl Julie McCullough. 85 min.
12-1773 Was $79.99 ***$14.99***

Probe (1972)
Detective Hugh O'Brian uses high-tech electronic equipment to find $22 million worth of diamonds missing since World War II in this sophisticated thriller, the pilot to the hit TV series "Search." Co-stars Elke Sommer, Sir John Gielgud, Burgess Meredith, Lilia Skala and, in a small part, Jaclyn Smith. 95 min.
48-1178 ***$59.99***

The Black Connection (1974)
Best known for their 1969 soul hit "Black Pearl," The Checkmates LTD boogied into the film world with this incredible blaxploitation epic. It's a "sex heist" film set in Las Vegas in which 'mates Sonny Charles, Bobby Stevens and Sweet Louie battle some jive-ass mobsters over cash. Of course, there's naked chicks, kung fu and Afros. AKA: "Run Nigger Run."
79-6423 Was $24.99 ***$19.99***

Blackjack (1978)
When the crimelord of Vegas sent soul brother Damu King to prison as a patsy for the Mob he gambled that that was the end of it...and lost. King escapes and rides a winning streak against hit squads and double-dealers to collect his revenge. Co-stars William Smith, Tony Burton. 89 min.
76-7014 Was $69.99 ***$19.99***

Black Water Gold (1970)
Fantastic seagoing adventure that follows an intrepid team of treasure hunters in their quest to find a long-sunken galleon off the Florida Keys...and a pack of modern-day pirates following their wake. Ricardo Montalban, Keir Dullea, Bradford Dillman, Lana Wood. 75 min.
78-1007 ***$19.99***

Shaft (1971)
Richard Roundtree's the streetwise private dick who's hired to track down a Harlem ganglord's kidnapped daughter before New York erupts into a gang war zone. Non-stop action hit that spawned two sequels and a TV series also features Moses Gunn, Charles Cioffi, and Isaac Hayes' Oscar-winning theme song. 98 min.
12-1251 Was $19.99 ❑***$14.99***

Shaft's Big Score! (1972)
That bad cat Shaft investigates a friend's murder and finds himself caught in the middle of a bloody feud between rival mobsters. Thrilling chases, exciting shootouts and lively music highlight the second outing in the "Shaft" series. Richard Roundtree and Moses Gunn star. 105 min.
12-2649 Was $19.99 ❑***$14.99***

Shaft In Africa (1973)
New York detective Richard Roundtree goes undercover in the "mother country" to bring down a modern-day slavery ring and its ruthless head. With Frank Finlay, Debebe Eshetu, Vonetta McGee. 112 min.
12-3018 ❑***$14.99***

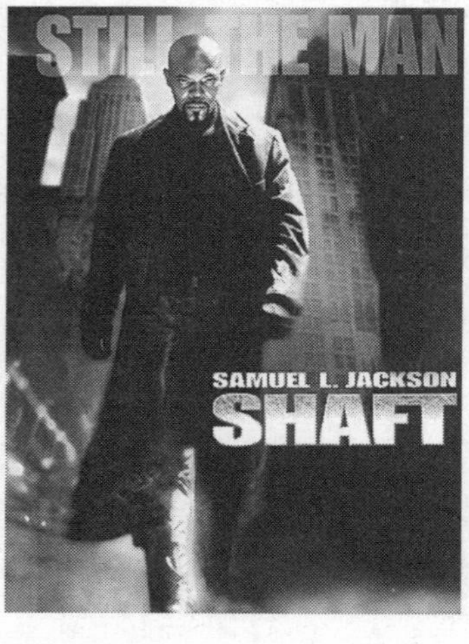

Shaft (2000)
This updating of the 1971 hit stars Samuel L. Jackson as original "Shaft" Richard Roundtree's nephew, an NYPD detective who throws away his badge in order to capture a rich creep responsible for killing a black teen in front of a trendy New York restaurant. Christian Bale, Toni Collette, Jeffrey Wright, Vanessa L. Williams and Roundtree also star in this retro actioner from director John Singleton ("Boyz n the Hood"). 99 min.
06-3048 ❑***$99.99***

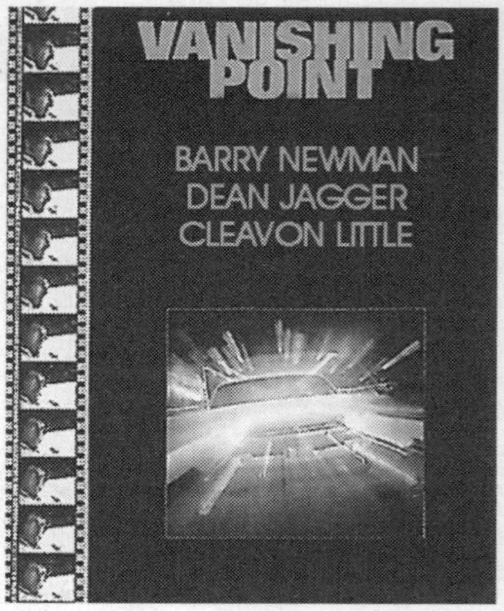

Vanishing Point (1971)
An offbeat mix of road action and existential drama that has earned a cult audience, this chase movie stars Barry Newman as a Vietnam vet and ex-cop who bets a friend he can drive a car from Denver to San Francisco in 15 hours. Soon Newman is pursued across the country by an armada of police and cheered on by a blind D.J. and his listeners. With Cleavon Little, Dean Jagger. 98 min.
04-1173 Was $59.99 ***$14.99***

The Devil And Leroy Bassett (1973)
Gripping drama about an escaped convict who gets more than he bargained for when he is aided by the armed, dangerous and slightly demented Bassett brothers. 85 min.
46-6013 Was $19.99 ***$14.99***

Black Samson (1974)
When a white mob boss wants to extend his drug trade into a black neighborhood, community leader Samson uses his wits and his martial arts skills to run the dope peddlers out. Well-crafted and action-packed urban drama stars Rockne Tarkington, William Smith, Carol Speed. 88 min.
19-2424 ***$19.99***

Eat My Dust! (1976)
Small-town sheriff's son Ron Howard tries to impress a girl by stealing a race car, and the situation soon escalates into a wild, high-octane joyride with more smash-ups than rush hour on the Schuylkill Expressway. Written and directed by "Little Shop of Horrors" scripter Charles B. Griffith; with Christopher Norris, Dave Madden, Clint Howard and a young Corbin Bernsen.
53-1123 Was $19.99 ***$14.99***

The Black Six (1974)
A group of black G.I.s decides to cycle across the country after a tour of duty in Vietnam. Little do they know the violence and danger in store for them. Gene Washington and "Mean Joe" Greene star along with other football greats. 91 min.
48-1049 ***$49.99***

Cobra (1971)
The most villainous of villains, the slimiest of the slimy must be stopped. He's the Cobra, and he'll not stop killing until his thirst for vengeance is quenched. Sterling Hayden stars. 93 min.
48-1120 ***$59.99***

The Black Gestapo (1975)
Hard-hitting black exploitation flick about "The People's Army's" struggles to rid the ghetto of drug pushers and slumlords, while overcoming internal conflicts of power. Stars Rod Perry, Charles P. Robinson and Phil Hoover. 88 min.
48-1132 ***$19.99***

Rip-Off (1977)
Exciting adventure about two mismatched young Greeks who come to America's shores in search of a dream—and wind up in a nightmare of syndicate killers, desperate skyjackers and callous hit men. Michael Benet, Michelle Simone. 78 min.
48-1134 ***$59.99***

The Candy Tangerine Man (1974)
Take a walk on the wild side, down the mean streets of L.A., in this urban thriller about the baddest pimp to work the Sunset Strip. Drugs, sex and gunplay all play a factor as he fights for power. John Daniels, Tom Hankerson star. 93 min.
48-1148 ***$49.99***

Avalanche Express (1979)
Timber! A trans-European train caught in a snowstorm is the setting for intrigue and action in this all-star espionage thriller that features Lee Marvin, Maximilian Schell, Robert Shaw, Linda Evans, Joe Namath and Mike Connors. 88 min.
19-2066 ***$19.99***

Confessions Of A Police Captain (1971)
A gritty urban drama, as a dedicated policeman fights corruption and the establishment to track down an elusive killer. Martin Balsam, Franco Nero and Marilu Tolo star. 102 min.
53-1269 Was $59.99 ***$14.99***

The Hi-Riders (1978)
High-torque action about drag-racing motor jocks who will drive anywhere and through anything in search of adventure, revenge and high-speed thrills. Stars Mel Ferrer, Stephen McNally. 90 min.
08-1326 Was $49.99 *$19.99*

Bad Georgia Road (1977)
Backwoods beauties take on revenuers in a whiz-bang action film of moonshine, fast cars and laugh-filled action. Carol Lynley, Gary Lockwood star. 85 min.
08-1268 Was $49.99 *$19.99*

Evil In The Deep (1974)
A group of treasure hunters looks for gold in the Caribbean and face all sorts of dangers. Cheryl Ladd (billed as "Cheryl Stoppelmoor"), Stephen Boyd, Roosevelt Grier and the great Chuck Woolery star. 81 min.
08-1739 Letterboxed *$14.99*

Funny Car Summer (1978)
A fireman who desires to become a Division Championship racing driver uses an experimental funny car in competition while travelling across the Western United States. Chockfull of exciting racing footage, this four-wall favorite stars Jim Dunn. 98 min.
08-1750 *$14.99*

The Four Deuces (1975)
Rat-a-tat-tat gangster action is mixed with laughs in this tale of Prohibition-era America. Bootlegger Jack Palance and his mob, the Four Deuces, hijack a shipment of "bathtub gin" meant for a rival, and soon a full-blown gang war erupts. With Carol Lynley, Warren Berlinger. 85 min.
09-1129 *$19.99*

The White Dawn (1974)
Fierce action saga set in the Arctic follows three sailors' adventures with Eskimos, fighting fierce weather and wild animals. Lou Gossett, Warren Oates, Timothy Bottoms. 110 min.
06-1145 *$19.99*

Trucker's Woman (1970)
From South Carolina comes this drive-in favorite in which a young man drives the highways in his big rig while investigating his trucker pa's suspicious death. He finds sexy truckstop women and seedy wheeling and dealing behind the wheel. Michael Hawkins, Doodles Weaver and Peggy Linville star. 88 min.
58-1071 Was $24.99 *$19.99*

Mr. Kingstreet's War (1971)
John Saxon and Tippi Hedren star in this unusual adventure film about a game warden in WWII Africa who tries to protect the animals in his care from invading Italian and British armies. With Rossano Brazzi, Brian O'Shaughnessy. AKA: "Heroes Die Hard." 92 min.
08-1435 *$19.99*

Border Cop (1979)
Telly Savalas stars as a patrol officer on the U.S./Mexico border who must take the law into his own hands when his corrupt boss joins forces with a crime boss to exploit illegal immigrants. Eddie Albert, Michael V. Gazzo, Robin Clarke also star. AKA: "Blood Barrier." 88 min.
75-7070 Was $19.99 *$14.99*

The Proud And The Damned (1972)
Five young Civil War veterans find themselves caught in the middle of another revolution when they travel to Central America and are captured by a dictator and forced to fight. War thriller stars Chuck Connors, Aron Kincaid, Cesar Romero. 92 min.
08-1283 Was $19.99 *$14.99*

The Neptune Factor (1973)
A deep-sea lab is thrown into a trench after a sea-quake, trapping three scientists inside and forcing a rescue attempt in an experimental mini-sub. Thrilling aquatic action film stars Ben Gazzara, Yvette Mimieux, Ernest Borgnine and Walter Pidgeon. 94 min.
04-3079 Was $59.99 ❑*$29.99*

Juggernaut (1974)
Superlative suspense film focusing on an extortionist who plants bombs on a luxury ocean liner and the race against time to stop his plan. The top-notch cast includes Omar Sharif as the ship's captain, Richard Harris as a demolitions expert, Anthony Hopkins and Freddie Jones; Richard Lester directs. 109 min.
12-2600 *$14.99*

Standing Tall (1978)
A range war between feuding cattle barons in 1930s Montana erupts into a violent explosion of vandalism, rape and murder. Stars Linda Evans, Chuck Connors, Robert Forster. 100 min.
14-3345 *$12.99*

Irwin Allen

The Lost World (1960)
Filmmaker Irwin Allen's adaptation of the timeless Arthur Conan Doyle novel follows a scientific team led by intrepid Professor Challenger (Claude Rains) to a mysterious plateau in the Amazon jungle where prehistoric animals, giant spiders and a cannibal tribe are just some of the dangers in store. Michael Rennie, Jill St. John, David Hedison and Fernando Lamas co-star. 98 min.
04-3671 *$14.99*

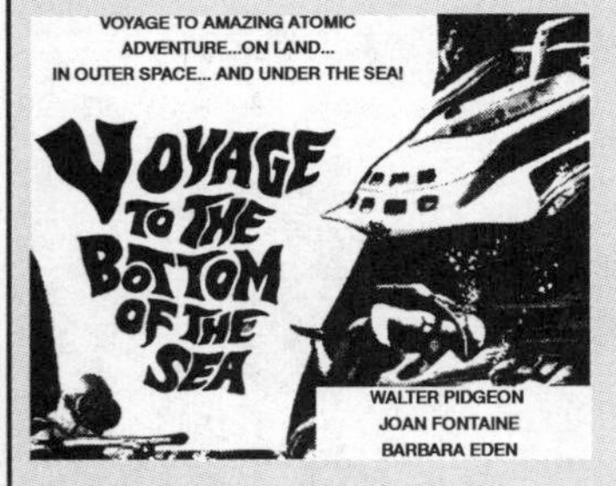
VOYAGE TO AMAZING ATOMIC ADVENTURE...ON LAND... IN OUTER SPACE... AND UNDER THE SEA!
VOYAGE TO THE BOTTOM OF THE SEA
WALTER PIDGEON
JOAN FONTAINE
BARBARA EDEN

Voyage To The Bottom Of The Sea (1961)
When the Earth is endangered by radiation from outer space, the super-submarine Seaview must undertake a dangerous mission to save it. Exciting futuristic adventure stars Walter Pidgeon, Barbara Eden, Peter Lorre and Frankie Avalon. 105 min.
04-3001 ❑*$14.99*

Five Weeks In A Balloon (1962)
From master fantasist Jules Verne comes this tale of a balloon expedition over 19th-century Africa, a trip fraught with dangers both natural and man-made. Sir Cedric Hardwicke, Red Buttons, Peter Lorre, Barbara Eden and Fabian star. 102 min.
04-3006 *$14.99*

The Poseidon Adventure (1972)
Gene Hackman, Ernest Borgnine, Red Buttons, Carol Lynley, Jack Albertson and the buoyant Shelley Winters head the all-star cast in Irwin Allen's highly-charged drama of a capsized ocean liner and the efforts of a group of survivors to escape. 117 min.
04-1123 Was $19.99 *$14.99*

The Poseidon Adventure (Letterboxed Version)
Also available in a theatrical, widescreen format.
04-3397 *$19.99*

Beyond The Poseidon Adventure (1979)
Two salvage crews race to loot the sinking luxury liner Poseidon in a winner-take-all adventure showdown. Action-filled tale of greed on the high seas with Michael Caine, Jack Warden, Sally Field and Telly Savalas. 115 min.
19-1507 Was $19.99 *$14.99*

The Towering Inferno (1974)
The grand opening gala for the world's tallest skyscraper becomes a fiery hell when a massive blaze traps the guests on the top floors. Producer Irwin Allen's Oscar-winning thriller boasts an all-star cast that includes Paul Newman, Steve McQueen, Faye Dunaway, William Holden, Jennifer Jones and Fred Astaire. 165 min.
04-1165 Was $19.99 *$14.99*

The Towering Inferno (Letterboxed Version)
Also available in a theatrical, widescreen format.
04-3396 *$19.99*

Flood! (1976)
Another disaster from filmmaker Irwin Allen, as a poorly constructed dam bursts, threatening a small town in the water's path. Robert Culp, Richard Basehart, Barbara Hershey, Martin Milner and Teresa Wright star. 98 min.
19-1509 Was $19.99 *$14.99*

Fire! (1977)
A convict sets a forest fire to cover his escape. As the fire threatens the neighboring timberland community, emotions burn as hot as the blaze. Tense Irwin Allen thriller with Ernest Borgnine, Patty Duke Astin and Donna Mills. 98 min.
19-1508 Was $19.99 *$14.99*

The Swarm (1978)
A spectacular drama of nature turning against humanity, as millions of killer bees attack the United States. Michael Caine, Katharine Ross, Richard Widmark, Richard Chamberlain, Henry Fonda and Olivia de Havilland head the all-star cast in this Irwin Allen production. Extended video version; 155 min.
19-1099 Was $19.99 *$14.99*

When Time Ran Out (1980)
An all-star epic of disaster and survival which finds a volcano and a tidal wave threatening a lush tropical island. Paul Newman, Jacqueline Bisset, William Holden and Ernest Borgnine star. 144 min.
19-1510 Was $19.99 *$14.99*

Hurricane (1973)
Exciting adventure set against the awesome fury of nature unleashed. Larry Hagman, Patrick Duffy, Martin Milner and Jessica Walter are the people trying to escape. Will they? 74 min.
14-6027 *$14.99*

The Con Artists (1977)
Flashy European heist adventure in which a con fresh out of prison teams with a young protégé to dupe a beautiful but dangerous woman out of her holdings. Anthony Quinn, Capucine and Corrine Clery star in this lively crime tale. AKA: "Bluff," "The Switch." 86 min.
15-1050 *$12.99*

The Kidnap Syndicate (1978)
Two boys (one rich, one poor) are abducted by kidnappers, and when the rich boy's father refuses to pay, the poor child is killed as an example, sending his father on a bloody rampage of vengeance. James Mason stars. 73 min.
15-1072 Was $19.99 *$14.99*

Death Rage (1977)
A former mob assassin comes out of retirement to find and kill the man who murdered his brother, only to learn that the murder was only the bait in a trap set for him. Thriller stars Yul Brynner, Martin Balsam, Barbara Bouchet. 92 min.
15-1100 *$19.99*

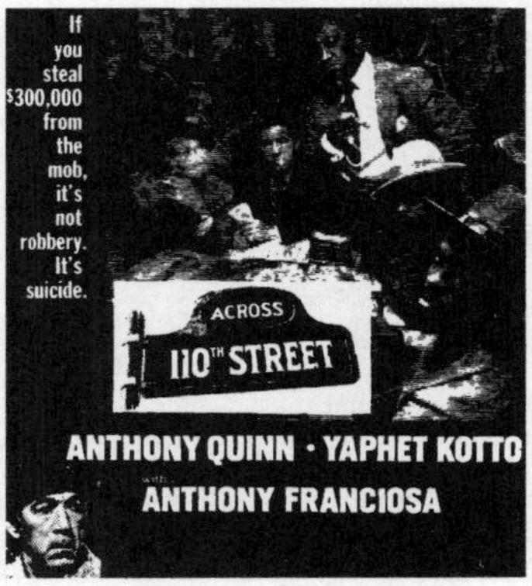
If you steal $300,000 from the mob, it's not robbery. It's suicide.
ACROSS 110TH STREET
ANTHONY QUINN · YAPHET KOTTO
ANTHONY FRANCIOSA

Across 110th Street (1972)
Explosively violent action flick set on the streets of Harlem pits the Mafia against a group of black criminals who ripped off a mob-owned bank, with the police department caught in the middle. Anthony Quinn, Yaphet Kotto, Anthony Franciosa, Richard Ward star. 102 min.
12-2597 *$14.99*

Super Fly T.N.T. (1973)
Ron O'Neal returns as ex-Harlem crime lord Priest, now living in retirement with his lady in Rome. But when an official from a white-ruled African country asks for his help on a gunrunning mission, Priest must use his street smarts to stay alive. Sheila Frazier, Roscoe Lee Browne, Robert Guillaume also star; Alex Haley scripted. 87 min.
06-2076 ❑*$14.99*

The Return Of Superfly (1990)
The king of the streets is back, and ready to reclaim his domain! Harlem becomes a battlefield when Priest finds himself up against drug lords, street gangs and corrupt cops. Explosive action with Nathan Purdee, Margaret Avery, Samuel L. Jackson; music by Curtis Mayfield, Tone Loc. 94 min.
68-1185 Was $89.99 *$14.99*

Ebony, Ivory & Jade (1976)
Three gorgeous American track stars are kidnapped by international terrorists in Hong Kong, and must use their martial arts skills and feminine wiles to escape. Sexy thriller stars Rosanne Katon, Colleen Camp and Sylvia Anderson. AKA: "American Beauty Hostages." 80 min.
14-6086 *$14.99*

The Grissom Gang (1971)
Director Robert Aldrich's offbeat blend of violence, suspense and romance stars Kim Darby as a '20s heiress who is kidnapped by a brutal gang of depraved outlaws. Tensions mount when one of Darby's abductors falls in love with her. Scott Wilson, Tony Musante, Connie Stevens and Robert Lansing co-star. 128 min.
04-1417 *$14.99*

Get Christie Love! (1974)
Teresa Graves plays the sassy, super-sexy Los Angeles cop ("You're under arrest, sugar!") who goes to great lengths to stop a vicious mobster and his drug empire. Harry Guardino co-stars in this action-packed pilot for the hit TV series. 100 min.
54-9025 *$14.99*

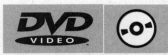

DVD VIDEO
ASK ABOUT OUR GIANT DVD CATALOG!

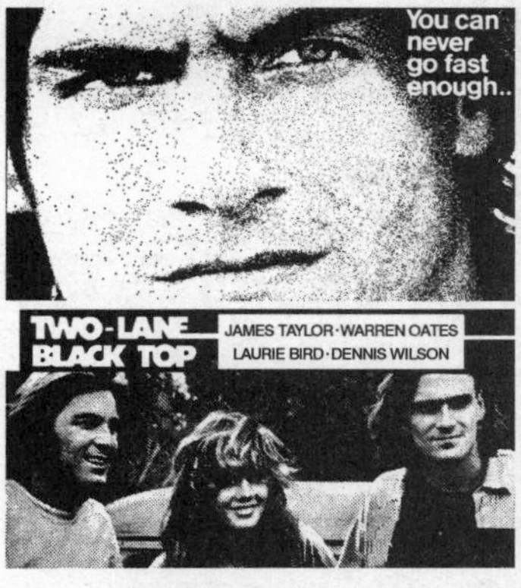
You can never go fast enough..
TWO-LANE BLACK TOP
JAMES TAYLOR · WARREN OATES
LAURIE BIRD · DENNIS WILSON

Two-Lane Blacktop (1971)
Director Monte Hellman's acclaimed road drama features rock stars James Taylor and Dennis Wilson as two car-obsessed wanderers in a '55 Chevy who are challenged to a cross-country race by Warren Oates and his brand-new GTO. Their race turns into a rambling odyssey fueled by an offbeat series of encounters along the way. With Laurie Bird; look for Harry Dean Stanton as a hitchhiker. 103 min.
10-3188 *$14.99*

Two-Lane Blacktop (Letterboxed Version)
Also available in a theatrical, widescreen format.
08-8788 *$14.99*

Gordon's War (1973)
Paul Winfield returns from Vietnam to discover that drug pushers and addicts have taken control of his neighborhood. Outraged, he organizes three friends with whom he fought in the jungle and the war is on! 89 min.
04-2112 Was $59.99 ❑*$29.99*

Lethal Terminator (1978)
Kellog is a professional bounty hunter up against his biggest challenge: a huge black man who is the most dangerous man alive. Kellog uses a new weapon: THE GLOVE, a lethal piece that fits over his fingers. John Saxon, Rosey Grier. 93 min.
03-1195 Was $19.99 *$14.99*

Newman's Law (1974)
Action and suspense abound when honest cop George Peppard is smeared and suspended for cutting too close to the heart of a sensitive case. Peppard then picks up where he left off—and must dodge cop and crook alike to see justice done. 98 min.
07-1432 *$59.99*

The Don Is Dead (1973)
The boss of all the bosses has gone to his reward...who's going to ascend to the throne of power? Anthony Quinn, Frederic Forrest, and Robert Forster all crave it, and the streets will flow crimson with gangland blood before the question is ultimately decided. AKA: "Beautiful But Deadly." 115 min.
07-1433 Was $59.99 *$14.99*

The Hatfields And The McCoys (1975)
What started over 100 years ago as an ill-fated romance erupted over time into America's most infamous feud. Jack Palance and Steve Forrest are the fighting patriarchs in this true-life drama, co-starring Richard Hatch and James Keach. 74 min.
14-3346 *$12.99*

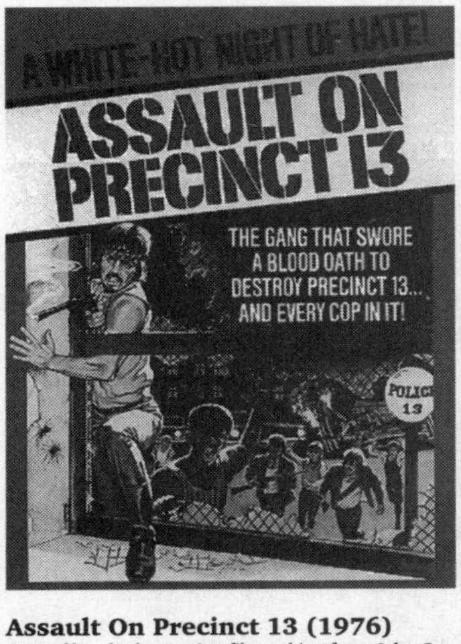
A WHITE-HOT NIGHT OF HATE!
ASSAULT ON PRECINCT 13
THE GANG THAT SWORE A BLOOD OATH TO DESTROY PRECINCT 13... AND EVERY COP IN IT!
POLICE 13

Assault On Precinct 13 (1976)
Gem of low-budget action filmmaking from John Carpenter takes the western classic "Rio Bravo" and moves it to modern-day L.A., where an almost-abandoned police station is under siege from gun-toting street gangs. Austin Stoker, Darwin Joston, Nancy Loomis star. 94 min.
03-1002 Letterboxed ❑*$14.99*

The Lucifer Complex (1978)
A secret island prison is the headquarters for a scheme to replace the world's leaders with identical clones. Shocks, suspense and action, with Robert Vaughn, Keenan Wynn star. 91 min.
08-1259 Was $59.99 *$19.99*

Bunco (1976)
Tom Selleck and Robert Urich team up as a wisecracking pair of L.A. detectives in this exciting thriller, complete with action, gorgeous girls and (believe it or not) car chases. With Donna Mills. 48 min.
40-1047 Was $59.99 *$14.99*

Soul Vengeance (1976)
Free from the penitentiary after serving three years for a crime he didn't commit, a young black man is ready to implement his plan of vengeance against the crooked cop who framed him. Great actioner stars Marlo Monte, Reatha Grey, Tiffany Peters. 91 min.
76-7013 Was $39.99 *$19.99*

Swamp Girl (1971)
Two hot-to-trot Georgia peaches find themselves in lots of trouble when they're stuck in the middle of the Okefenokee Swamp. Ferlin Husky, Claude King and Steve Drexel star. "Filmed in vivid color in the middle of the swamp!" 118 min.
79-5246 *$19.99*

The Death Squad (1974)
It's up to a tough former cop to come back to duty and stop a "vigilannte squad" of policemen who "execute" criminals released on technicalities. Stars Robert Forster, Michelle Phillips. 76 min.
46-5094 Was $19.99 *$14.99*

Puppet On A Chain (1972)
Riveting thriller about an American drug agent who goes to Amsterdam to stop a world-wide narcotics ring. But will it stop him instead? Alexander Knox, Barbara Parkins star. 97 min.
46-5170 *$14.99*

Thunder And Lightning (1977)
When moonshiner David Carradine and spunky girlfriend Kate Jackson run afoul of the Mob, there's sure to be lots of action, fast cars, fast women and good clean comedy. 95 min.
04-1873 Was $59.99 ❑*$29.99*

Dixie Dynamite (1976)
When a Georgia moonshiner is killed by a corrupt town boss, his daughters take over the family business in a rip-roarin' action film. Warren Oates, Christopher George star. 88 min.
08-1053 *$19.99*

A Scream In The Streets (1971)
Rough, adults-only actioner involving two L.A. cops—one a veteran, the other a young, unseasoned type—who search for two criminals: a Peeping Tom and a cross-dressing murderer/rapist. John Kirkpatric, Frank Bannon star. 90 min.
79-5397 Was $24.99 *$19.99*

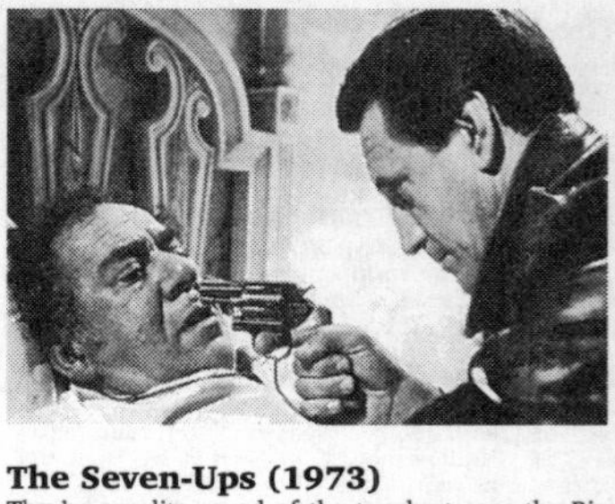

The Seven-Ups (1973)
They're an elite squad of the toughest cops the Big Apple has to offer, and when a drug ring kills one of them, the "Seven-Ups" won't rest until they're behind bars. Urban action à la "The French Connection" with Roy Scheider, Tony LoBianco. 103 min.
04-1842 Was $59.99 ❑*$29.99*

Framed (1975)
Big Joe Don Baker is set up by cops on the take and given a one-way ticket to the slammer vowing never to rest until he pays them back in full. Connie Van Dyke, John Marley and Brock Peters co-star in this gut-slammer. 106 min.
06-1373 Was $24.99 *$14.99*

Moving Violation (1976)
A young couple on vacation in the South must race for their lives when a redneck sheriff with murder on his mind pursues them. Stars Kay Lenz, Eddie Albert, Stephen McHattie. 91 min.
04-1870 Was $59.99 *$29.99*

Oil (1977)
The struggle for power and wealth between an international oil cartel and an Arab state frames this action-packed tale about an oil fire raging in the Sahara desert. Stars Stuart Whitman, Ray Milland, Woody Strode. 95 min.
08-1238 *$19.99*

Stunts (1977)
The brother of a recently murdered stuntman takes his place to investigate his death. Lively action effort filled with incredible stunt-filled sequences stars Robert Forster, Fiona Lewis, Joanna Cassidy. AKA: "Who Is Killing the Stuntman?"
44-1116 *$19.99*

Terror On The 40th Floor (1974)
If you liked "Towering Inferno," you'll want to see the blazing action when seven people are trapped in a burning skyscraper. John Forsythe, Anjanette Comer, Don Meredith and Joseph Campanella head a top cast. 98 min.
46-5061 *$14.99*

Hit Lady (1974)
Sexy Yvette Mimieux stars as a hired killer who uses her body as well as her mind to get her job done. Her involvement with organized crime and the Mob will leave you riveted to your sofa. Clu Gulager, Joseph Campanella. 74 min.
46-5070 *$19.99*

Family Enforcer (1977)
It's "all in the family" for a young, streetwise hood as he becomes a collector for the mob and quickly rises, rung by bloody rung, up the ladder in this violent crime saga. Joe Cortese, Lou Criscuola and a young Joe Pesci star. AKA: "Death Collector." 89 min.
08-1239 Was $19.99 *$14.99*

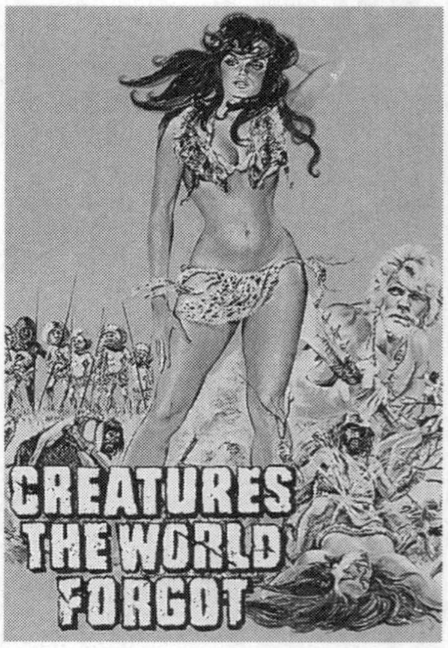

Creatures
The World Forgot (1971)
Exciting thriller set at the dawn of humanity, as two brothers in a caveman clan compete for leadership when the old chief dies. Tony Bonner, Robert John and former Miss Norway Julie Ege star; a Hammer Films production. 95 min.
02-1151 *$69.99*

Fred Williamson

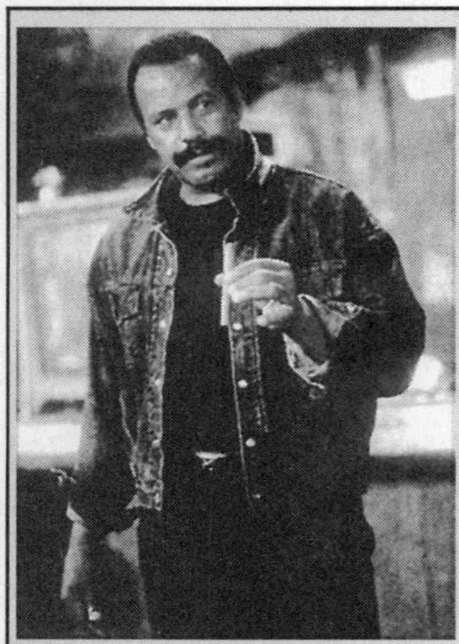

That Man Bolt (1973)
Fred Williamson chop-sockeys his way through this popular blaxploitation adventure as Jefferson Bolt, a Kung Fu expert assigned to deliver a cool $1 million to Mexico City from Hong Kong with a stop in Los Angeles. When Bolt discovers the cash is dirty mob money and his gal has been killed, he heads back to the Far East to get even. Byron Webster, Teresa Graves also star.
07-2819 *$14.99*

Black Caesar (1973)
One of the best of the "urban action" films of the '70s, with Fred Williamson as a power-hungry killer who muscles his way into Mafia territory with his own mob, then must try and survive an all-out gang war on the New York streets. With Art Lund, D'Urville Martin; Larry Cohen directs. 94 min.
73-1005 Was $19.99 *$14.99*

Hell Up In Harlem (1973)
Slam-bang sequel to "Black Caesar" has street king Fred Williamson preparing to regain control of his crime empire. But first he must overcome enemies from without and within. Actioner co-stars D'Urville Martin, Tony King. 98 min.
73-1006 Was $19.99 *$14.99*

Black Eye (1974)
That's just what ex-cop-turned-private investigator Fred Williamson is ready to give a drug ring that may be connected to his sister's overdose death and the murder of his neighbor in this gritty crime drama. Rosemary Forsyth, Teresa Graves and Richard Anderson also star. 98 min.
19-2423 *$19.99*

Mean Johnny Barrows (1974)
He's lean, he's tough, he's mean. Fred Williamson is a macho hero, quick with a gun and Hell with his fists. And when he goes up against the Mob, it's anyone's game! Roddy McDowall, Stuart Whitman, Elliott Gould co-star. 83 min.
48-1015 *$49.99*

Bucktown (1975)
Returning to his Southern hometown for his brother's funeral, Fred Williamson discovers that the black community is held in a grip of graft and fear by the white police chief. He then forms a gang to clean up the town. Pam Grier, Bernie Casey, Carl Weathers co-star. 95 min.
73-1007 Was $59.99 *$14.99*

No Way Back (1976)
Rough, tough, lean, and mean! Fred Williamson's Jesse Crowder is off on a violent adventure that could bring him lots of cash...if he survives!! Tracy Reed and "Soul Train's" Don Cornelius co-star. 92 min.
48-1013 *$29.99*

Death Journey (1976)
Fred Williamson is one mean cat as Jesse Crowder, called on to bring in an informer. The catch, he's 3000 miles away and Jesse's only got 48 hours. D'Urville Martin co-stars. 90 min.
48-1014 *$49.99*

Joshua The Black Rider (1976)
Fred Williamson stars as a Civil War veteran who returns home to find his family massacred by outlaws and no one willing to help him, sending him on a one-man vengeance mission, in this exciting frontier thriller. AKA: "Joshua." 120 min.
69-1089 Was $89.99 *$14.99*

Mr. Mean (1977)
Fred Williamson is Mr. Mean, a hired gun pegged as "the meanest man in the world," who chews his targets up and spits 'em out. His next gig: eliminate a mafioso who embarrassed the Mob. But beware, Mr. Mean, you're next on the hit list. 81 min.
69-1094 *$19.99*

G.I. Bro (1981)
A quintet of Allied soldiers facing court-martial escape and set off across the French countryside in this exciting WWII actioner. Bo Svenson, Fred Williamson, Peter Hooten star. AKA: "Counterfeit Commandos," "Hell's Heroes," "Inglorious Bastards," "Deadly Mission." 99 min.
47-3130 *$19.99*

One Down, Two To Go (1982)
Jim Brown, Fred Williamson, Jim Kelly and Richard Roundtree—four of the greatest black superstars—team up to tackle the Mob. They're out to catch the mobster who fixed a karate tournament and cheated them out of their winnings. 88 min.
03-1202 *$19.99*

White Fire (1982)
"White Fire" is the name of the world's most valuable diamond, a 200-carat gem that becomes the bait in a death duel between some of the world's most cunning and ruthless jewel thieves. Fred Williamson and Robert Ginty star in an action-packed saga. 90 min.
20-5050 Was $19.99 *$14.99*

Vigilante (1982)
Intense urban action film stars Robert Forster as an ex-cop whose family is attacked by a street gang. When the courts let the hoods go free, a frustrated Forster joins with Fred Williamson's neighborhood vigilante group, dedicated to enforcing the law—their own way. With Rutanya Alda, Woody Strode, Joe Spinell. Remastered director's edition also includes original theatrical and TV trailers. 90 min.
47-1113 Letterboxed *$12.99*

The Messenger (1986)
Fred Williamson explodes on the screen as an ex-con out to get the drug runners responsible for his addicted wife's death, a mission that has him fighting around the world and against both sides of the law. With Cameron Mitchell, Joe Spinell. 95 min.
73-1004 Was $79.99 ❑*$14.99*

Black Cobra (1987)
A group of nasty bikers cause all sorts of problems for a female photographer prompting Fred Williamson to take action in this explosive action tale. With Jack Palance, Eva Grimaldi. 87 min.
20-5210 *$19.99*

Black Cobra II (1989)
Fred Williamson returns, coiled and ready to strike as Chicago cop Robert Malone. Here he must act quickly to save a school held hostage by terrorists who've already killed his friend. With Nicholas Hammond. 95 min.
77-1017 *$19.99*

Delta Force Commando (1987)
Fred Williamson and Bo Svenson star in a gripping action tale, as two American fighter pilots on a secret mission in Central America are shot down over the jungle and must fight rebel forces to survive. 90 min.
67-7024 Was $79.99 *$19.99*

The Black Punisher (1990)
Fred Williamson is Malone, an ace detective who tries to stop a group of terrorists from wreaking havoc in the city. At the same time Malone battles the bad guys, a group of refugees seeks freedom in their battle-scarred Yugoslavia homeland. Where the two tales intersect will amaze you! With Donald Foster, Tania Kes. 80 min.
54-9183 Letterboxed *$19.99*

Three Days To A Kill (1992)
After a Colombian drug kingpin kidnaps an international ambassador, a mercenary teams with a weapons expert and a stripper who was once the drug dealer's mistress on a rescue mission. But things get dangerous when someone leaks their moves to the crime lord. Fred Williamson (who also directed), Henry Silva, Chuck Connors star. 90 min.
44-1910 Was $19.99 ❑*$14.99*

South Beach (1992)
Two former football players lead leisurely lives as private detectives in Miami Beach, until an exotic beauty offers them a mysterious challenge. Now they have to be on their toes, as South Beach explodes with danger and thrills. Fred Williamson, Gary Busey, Vanity and Peter Fonda star. 93 min.
46-5567 *$89.99*

Silent Hunter (1994)
After his family is killed by ruthless bank robbers, an undercover cop tries to find solace in a mountain cabin. When those same crooks crash nearby while on the run with a fortune in loot, the cop joins forces with a local sheriff and a beautiful woman to track them down. Miles O'Keeffe and Fred Williamson, who also directed, star. 97 min.
18-7532 Was $89.99 ❑*$14.99*

Foxtrap (1995)
Fred Williamson pulls out all the stops playing a special courier who discovers that he's been doing the dirty work for a European prostitution ring. When a beautiful woman is murdered, Williamson sets out to nail the mobsters responsible for her death. 88 min.
73-1219 ❑*$14.99*

Original Gangstas (1996)
The spirit of 1970s "blaxploitation" films is resurrected in this actioner starring Fred Williamson as a former gangbanger who returns to his Midwest home to battle a group of punks terrorizing his family and his old neighborhood. Joining him are Pam Grier, Jim Brown, Richard Roundtree and Ron O'Neal. With Isabel Sanford, Charles Napier; directed by Larry Cohen ("Black Caesar"). 99 min.
73-1247 Was $99.99 ❑*$14.99*

Night Vision (1997)
When a killer known as "the Video Stalker" terrorizes the city, preying on beautiful young women, motorcycle cop and former detective Fred Williamson gets entangled with the maniac. Joining forces with policewoman Cynthia Rothrock, Williamson tries to catch the killer before he strikes again. Amanda Welles, Frank Pesce also star. 96 min.
50-5686 Was $59.99 *$24.99*

Active Stealth (1999)
A U.S. pilot, on a mission to recover a deadly stealth fighter stolen by Central American terrorists, finds himself in the fight for his life in this wild action yarn. Daniel Baldwin, Hannes Jaenicke and Fred Williamson star in this Fed Olen Ray epic. 99 min.
06-3003 ❑*$99.99*

Submerged (2000)
An airplane carrying a computer capable of launching nuclear weapons has been intentionally crashed into the Pacific after being taken over by terrorists. As the passengers struggle to stay alive, Navy SEALs attempt a rescue mission with time running out and the welfare of the entire world at stake. Fred Williamson, Nicole Eggert, Coolio and Dennis Weaver star. 95 min.
06-3032 ❑*$59.99*

The Fred Williamson Collection
There's three times the action with this boxed collector's set featuring Fred at his fightin' best. "Black Caesar," "Bucktown" and "Hell Up in Harlem" are included.
73-1297 Save $10.00! *$34.99*

Please see our index for these other Fred Williamson titles: *1990: The Bronx Warriors • Adios Amigo • Blackjack • Children Of The Corn V: Fields Of Terror • From Dusk Till Dawn • M*A*S*H • The New Gladiators • Warriors Of The Wasteland • Whatever It Takes*

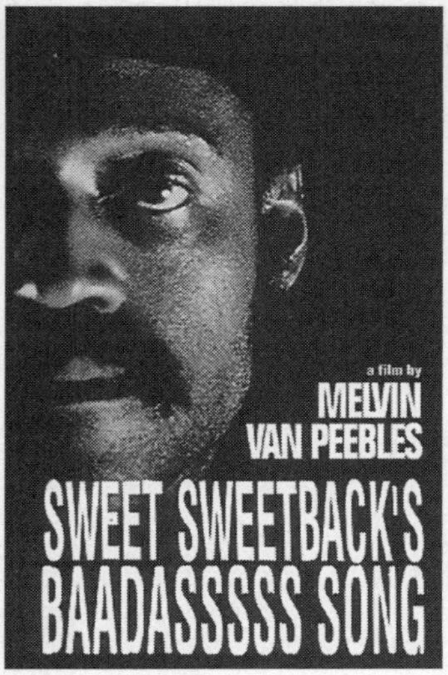

Sweet Sweetback's Baadasssss Song (1973)
Melvin Van Peebles produced, wrote, directed and starred in this groundbreaking black action film, playing a tough and sexually inexhaustible street hustler on the run after witnessing brutality by corrupt police. Violent and intense drama, rated X when first released, also stars Rhetta Hughes, John Amos. Uncut, unrated director's cut includes intro by Van Peebles; 97 min.
69-1006 *$19.99*

Deadly Jaws (1978)
In hopes of retrieving a sunken chest of gold coins, a group of young treasure hunters battle through shark-infested waters. Marius Weyers and Sandra Prinsloo star. 88 min.
09-5181 *$19.99*

Jackson County Jail (1976)
Explosive cult action film stars Yvette Mimieux as a businesswoman wrongly detained in a backwoods jail where she's raped by a deputy. Fellow inmate Tommy Lee Jones helps her escape, and the two lead the law on a violent chase. Severn Darden, Robert Carradine and Mary Woronov co-star, with early appearances by Howard Hesseman and Betty Thomas. 84 min.
19-1135 *$14.99*

Macon County Jail (1998)
Ally Sheedy dumps her unfaithful hubby and heads out on the road. Circumstances land her in Macon County Jail, where she is brutalized by guards and inmates and must defend herself against a rapist. Her only chance comes by way of an escape with fellow prisoner David Carradine in this thrilling revamping of the 1976 actioner "Jackson County Jail." Charles Napier also stars.
21-9177 *$59.99*

T.N.T. Jackson (1974)
Jeanne Bell stars as T.N.T., a karate expert searching for her missing brother. But look out: you don't want to get in her way, 'cause if you do, she'll get in yours! Co-stars Stan Shaw. 73 min.
53-3021 *$19.99*

Mean Mother (1974)
After he's double-crossed by the Mob and his girlfriend is killed, a heroin smuggler vows vengeance—and gets it—in this explosive urban actioner. Clifton Brown, Dennis Safren, Luciana Paluzzi star. 89 min.
54-9132 *$19.99*

Black Heat (1976)
The action is hotter than hot when a small-time crook is wrongly marked for murder and relies on his martial arts skills to stay alive. Timothy Brown, Russ Tamblyn and Regina Carrol star in this Al Adamson thriller. 90 min.
54-9134 *$19.99*

Grand Theft Auto (1977)
A long, long, LONG time before "Cocoon" and "Apollo 13," Ron Howard made his directorial debut with this smash-'em-up actioner for producer Roger Corman in which Howard and his fiancée "borrow" her daddy's Rolls and drive from L.A. to Las Vegas to elope. Soon an armada of autos are out to stop the fast-driving couple, and the highways become a demolition derby. With Nancy Morgan, Howard's "Happy Days" mom Marion Ross, and the interestingly-named Barry Cahill. 84 min.
19-1130 *$14.99*

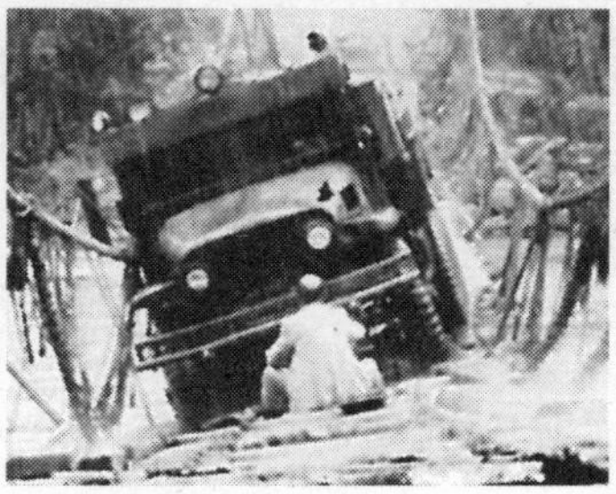

Sorcerer (1977)
William Friedkin's intense adventure film stars Roy Scheider as the leader of a group of cons living in South American squalor who are hired to drive two truckloads of deadly nitroglycerine across miles of rugged terrain. Bruno Cremer, Francisco Rabal and Ramon Bieri also star; inspired by the French classic "The Wages of Fear." 121 min.
07-1664 Was $79.99 *❑$19.99*

Diamond Shaft (1972)
A supposedly "theft-proof" vault in Tel Aviv's famed diamond exchange is the target for a London merchant and an ex-con in this taut crime actioner. Robert Shaw (in a dual role), Richard Roundtree, Shelley Winters and Barbara Seagull (Hershey) star. AKA: "Diamonds." 108 min.
53-3014 Was $59.99 *$19.99*

The Mack (1973)
One of the first black action films, and a much-requested title at Movies Unlimited. Max Julien is the Mack, street hustler and ex-con, out to clean up his city...his way! Helping him are Roger E. Mosley and, in one of his first films, Richard Pryor. 110 min.
53-3035 *❑$14.99*

Detroit 9000 (1974)
The streets of Motown run red with blood in this urban action classic about a gang of ruthless jewel thieves and the cops out to stop their murderous rampage. Alex Rocco, Hari Rhodes, Vonetta McGee and Scatman Crothers star. 107 min.
54-9079 Was $99.99 *❑$14.99*

Double Nickels (1977)
Two highway patrolmen who work as auto repo men on the side discover that their boss has them unknowingly swiping cars. They have to put a stop to the practice, but their superior isn't going to like it. Jack Vacek, Ed Abrams and George Cole star. 89 min.
10-9510 *$14.99*

The Deadly Hunt (1971)
A pair of hired killers are close on the trail of a young couple that they have been recruited to eliminate, but a huge, out-of-control forest fire threatens both hunter and hunted. With Jim Hutton, Anjanette Comer, Anthony Franciosa and Peter Lawford. 74 min.
55-3010 *$19.99*

Escape From Death Row (1976)
Criminal mastermind Lee Van Cleef devises an ingenious way to escape prison on the eve of his execution in this action-packed effort. With James Lane, Barbara Moore. 86 min.
58-1025 *$19.99*

French Intrigue (1976)
Love, espionage and danger in a taut spy thriller that takes you from America to Paris and back in an exciting chase. Curt Jurgens, Jane Birkin star. 90 min.
64-1029 *$29.99*

My Boys Are Good Boys (1977)
Three teenage delinquents break out of prison and rob an armored truck, but their plans to break back into jail go awry. Ralph Meeker, Ida Lupino star in this action crime saga. 90 min.
69-1018 *$14.99*

Alexandre Dumas

The Son Of Monte Cristo (1941)
Sword-slinging action with Louis Hayward as the son of Edmond Dantes, defending the country and the honor of duchess Joan Bennett against scheming George Sanders in a grand Napoleonic saga. 102 min.
17-1036 *$19.99*

Sword Of Venus (1953)
Thrilling swashbuckler with Robert Clarke as the son of the Count of Monte Cristo who finds his wealth is the target of an unscrupulous character, played by Dan O'Herlihy. Catherine McLeod, William Schallert also star. 73 min.
53-6035 Was $29.99 *$19.99*

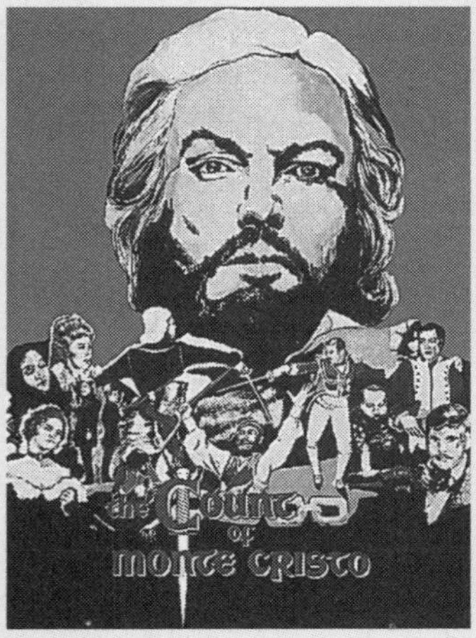

The Count Of Monte Cristo (1975)
Grand treatment of the Dumas adventure classic stars Richard Chamberlain as Edmond Dantes, who escapes from a jail cell after 14 years to claim the woman he loves and vengeance on the enemies who had him unjustly imprisoned. With Tony Curtis, Kate Nelligan, Louis Jourdan and Trevor Howard. 103 min.
27-6808 Was $19.99 *$14.99*

The Three Musketeers (1948)
Swordplay and thrills galore, as D'Artagnan finds romance and adventure when he joins the musketeers to fight intrigue in the court of France's King Louis XIII. Lavish MGM production stars Gene Kelly, Lana Turner, Van Heflin, Gig Young, Robert Coote, June Allyson and Vincent Price. 127 min.
12-1461 *$19.99*

The Fighting Musketeers (1961)
There are duels galore in this European swashbuckling take on the Alexandre Dumas classic. D'Artagnan and his three sword-swinging cronies use their wits and blades to reveal the treacherous ways of Lord Rochefort, Lady D'Winter and Cardinal Richelieu. En gardé! With Gérard Barray, Mylène Demongeot and George Descrières.
79-6546 Was $24.99 *$19.99*

The Secret Mark Of D'Artagnan (1962)
Dashing Musketeer D'Artagnan attempts to stop an assassination attempt on Louis XIII with help from partner Porthos. When they are injured by anarchists, a young noblewoman, whose uncle is behind the plot, and her maid attempt to help them. George Nader, Magali Noel star in this European spectacle.
79-6154 *$19.99*

The Three Musketeers (1974)
It's "one for all, and all for fun" in director Richard Lester's rollicking rendition of the timeless Dumas adventure. Join Aramis, Athos, Porthos and their young ally D'Artagnan (Richard Chamberlain, Oliver Reed, Frank Finlay, Michael York) as they mix heroic exploits with bawdy humor and save their queen from the evil schemes of Cardinal Richelieu. Geraldine Chaplin, Faye Dunaway, Charlton Heston and Raquel Welch also star. 105 min.
27-6053 *$24.99*

The Four Musketeers (1975)
The swordplay- and silliness-filled sequel to "The Three Musketeers" (actually filmed at the same time as the first movie) finds the heroic quartet once again at odds with cunning Cardinal Richelieu and his seductive cohort, Milday De Winter, both of whom are out for revenge. Richard Chamberlain, Faye Dunaway, Frank Finlay, Charlton Heston, Christopher Lee, Oliver Reed, Raquel Welch and Michael York star. 108 min.
27-6083 *$24.99*

The Three Musketeers/ The Four Musketeers Twin Pack
You don't get seven different Musketeers with this money-saving double feature, but you do get "The Three Musketeers" and "The Four Musketeers" in a swashbuckling set.
53-8279 Save $10.00! *$39.99*

The Return Of The Musketeers (1989)
En gardé! Twenty years after they swaskbuckled their way to glory, D'Artagnan and the Three Musketeers return to stop the unscrupulous daughter of Milady De Winter and the conniving Cardinal Mazarin in this action-filled, comic adventure. Michael York, Oliver Reed, Richard Chamberlain, Frank Finlay, Kim Cattrall and Christopher Lee star; directed by Richard Lester. 103 min.
07-2033 Was $89.99 *❑$14.99*

The Three Musketeers (1993)
Raucous adaptation of the Alexandre Dumas classic centering on the adventures of D'Artagnan and his three swashbuckling cohorts, who try to stop the evil Cardinal Richelieu and Milady De Winter from seizing power from King Louis XIII in 17th-century France. Charlie Sheen, Kiefer Sutherland, Oliver Platt, Chris O'Donnell, Tim Curry and Rebecca De-Mornay star. 105 min.
11-1781 Was $19.99 *❑$14.99*

The Sword Of Monte Cristo (1951)
Swashbuckling thriller set in the reign of Napoleon III, as a female adventurer and a rebel army officer unite to rescue the titular weapon, key to a fabulous treasure. George Montgomery, Berry Kroeger, Paula Corday, William Conrad star. 80 min.
23-5041 *$19.99*

The Man In The Iron Mask (1976)
Richard Chamberlain essays dual roles in this adaptation of the Dumas thriller, set in 17th-century France. Who is the mysterious metal-masked prisoner in the Bastille, and why does his identity threaten the fate of the monarchy? With Patrick McGoohan, Sir Ralph Richardson, Louis Jourdan, Jenny Agutter. 108 min.
27-6810 Was $19.99 *$14.99*

The Fifth Musketeer (1979)
In actuality an exciting, swashbuckling reworking of Alexander Dumas' "The Man in the Iron Mask." Beau Bridges takes on a dual role as two royal brothers involved in romance, adventure and swordplay in 17th-century France. Sylvia Kristel, Cornel Wilde, Alan Hale, Jr., Ursula Andress, Rex Harrison co-star. 90 min.
02-1311 Was $19.99 *$14.99*

The Man In The Iron Mask (1998)
They're brothers who share the same face, yet while one sits on the French throne as King Louis XIV, the other—the rightful ruler—languishes in jail, his features hidden behind a metal mask. Edward Albert, Timothy Bottoms, Meg Foster and Nick Richert, in the title role, star in scripter/director William Richert's dramatic rendering of the Alexandre Dumas novel. 85 min.
27-7068 *$49.99*

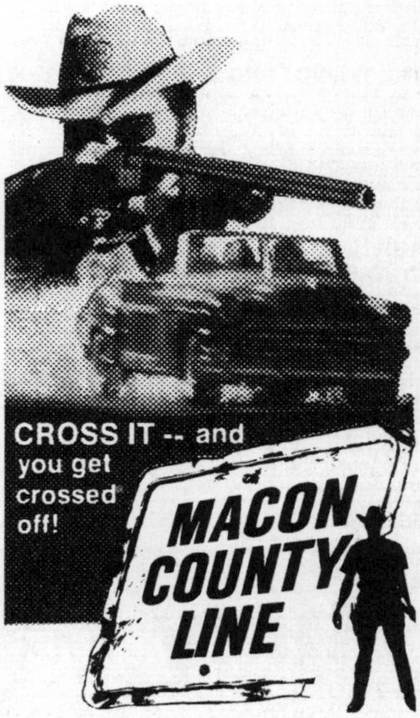

Macon County Line (1974)
Terrific actioner about two brothers travelling through the South in the '50s who are suspected of murdering the wife of sheriff Max Baer, Jr. and are pursued by the vengeful lawman. Co-written and produced by Baer, this drive-in fave also stars Alan Vint, Jesse Vint, Cheryl Waters. 88 min.
53-1124 *$14.99*

Macon County Line (Letterboxed Collector's Edition)
Max Baer, Jr.'s cult classic is available in a theatrical, widescreen edition, which also includes a featurette, audio commentary from the director, cast bios, and the original theatrical trailer.
08-8824 *$14.99*

Cleopatra Jones (1973)
Black, beautiful, brawny Tamara Dobson stars as Cleopatra Jones, the U.S. special agent with a style all her own! Plenty of violence and action as 6'2" Jones goes after the biggest drug dealers and sleazos around...even Shelley Winters! Also stars Antonio Fargas and Brenda Sykes. 89 min.
19-1495 Was $19.99 *$14.99*

Cleopatra Jones And The Casino Of Gold (1975)
Tamara Dobson is back as crack super-agent Cleopatra Jones, up this time against a sinister crime cartel run by the Dragon Lady (Stella Stevens). With Norman Fell, Christopher Hunt. 96 min.
19-1598 Was $19.99 *$14.99*

Switchblade Sisters (1975)
They're the wildest—and sexiest—teen gang to ever hit the mean streets. They're the Dagger Debs, and when a new member sets her sights on the head Deb's fella, you can bet there'll be hell to pay. Tough-as-nails exploitation actioner that gained a cult following 20 years after its release, thanks to filmmaker Quentin Tarantino, stars Robbie Lee, Joanne Nail and Kitty Bruce (Lenny's daughter). 91 min.
27-6016 Was $99.99 *❑$19.99*

Inside Out (1975)
Telly Savalas...James Mason...Robert Culp...all involved in a dangerous plan to unleash a German war criminal from prison. Thrill-a-second suspense. 97 min.
19-1397 Was $59.99 ***$19.99***

Born Losers (1967)
The character of Billy Jack was first introduced in this wild biker flick, with Tom Laughlin helping a young dropout (Elizabeth James) break free from a vicious gang. With a special appearance by Jane Russell; directed by T.C. Frank (Laughlin). 110 min.
47-1076 Was $19.99 ***$14.99***

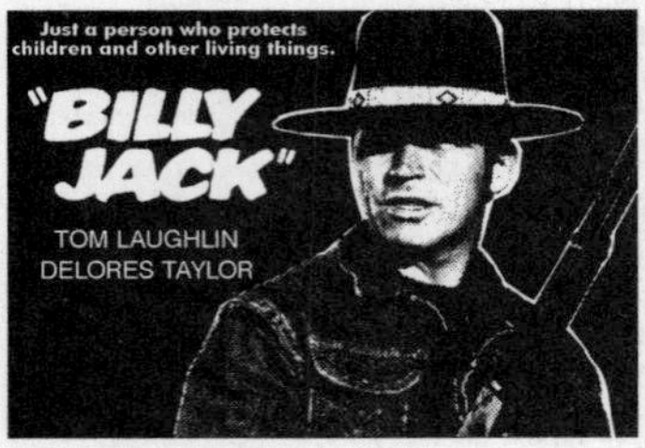
Just a person who protects children and other living things.
"BILLY JACK"
TOM LAUGHLIN
DELORES TAYLOR

Billy Jack (1971)
Tom Laughlin directed, wrote, starred in and probably delivered the film for this legendary saga of a half-breed, karate-trained war hero defending a kids' school from bigoted townspeople. Drama that became a calling-card for pacifism during the '70s co-stars Delores Taylor, Kenneth Tobey; look closely for Howard Hesseman. 114 min.
19-1062 Was $19.99 ***$14.99***

The Trial Of Billy Jack (1974)
Tom Laughlin is back as pacifist Native American martial arts expert Billy Jack in this powerhouse drama. When the Freedom School is occupied by the National Guard, Billy springs into action, battling the military and rednecks who want to take the freedom out of the Freedom School. With Delores Taylor, Master Bong Soo Han and Sacheen Littlefeather. 140 min.
50-8297 ***$19.99***

Billy Jack Goes To Washington (1977)
In this reworking of "Mr. Smith Goes to Washington," Tom Laughlin's Billy Jack fills the unexpired term of a deceased U.S. senator and tries to expose the corruption and conspiracies that engulf the U.S. government. Delores Taylor, Lucie Arnaz, E.G. Marshall and Sam Wanamaker also star; Frank Capra, Jr. co-produced. 110 min.
50-8298 ***$24.99***

The Billy Jack Collection
All four "Billy Jack" movies—"Born Losers," "Billy Jack," "The Trial of Billy Jack" and "Billy Jack Goes to Washington"—are available in a money-saving boxed set.
50-8299 Save $20.00! ***$59.99***

Walking Tall (1973)
The true-life drama that had audiences standing and cheering follows the one-man campaign of Tennessee sheriff Buford Pusser against crime and corruption in his state, a crusade that turns personal when mobsters kill his wife. Joe Don Baker, Elizabeth Hartman, Gene Evans, Noah Beery, Jr. and Leif Garrett star. 126 min.
47-3000 Was $29.99 ***$14.99***

Walking Tall 2 (1975)
Bo Svenson takes over as tough-as-nails lawman Buford Pusser (a role to have been played by Pusser himself before his death in a suspicious auto accident) in this two-fisted actioner that finds Svenson swinging his big stick against mobsters and hit men. With Richard Jaeckel, Leif Garrett, Noah Beery, Jr. AKA: "Part 2, Walking Tall." 113 min.
15-5377 Was $29.99 ***$14.99***

Walking Tall: The Final Chapter (1977)
Buford Pusser (Bo Svenson), the bat-wielding sheriff, is back in this third film based on his struggle to clean up a crime-ridden town. This time, though, the mob is out for blood, and only one side will walk away. Margaret Blye, Forrest Tucker co-star. 116 min.
15-5378 Was $29.99 ***$14.99***

Walking Tall: The Trilogy Set
The first three "Walking Tall" films are also available in a boxed collector's set.
15-5532 ***$29.99***

A Real American Hero (1978)
The real-life saga of "Walking Tall" lawman Buford Pusser continues, with Brian Dennehy starring as the sheriff who speaks softly and carries a big bat. Here he goes up against local moonshiners. With Forrest Tucker, Ken Howard, Sheree North. AKA: "Hard Stick." 94 min.
46-5402 Was $19.99 ***$14.99***

The Ultimate Thrill (1974)
Succumbing to his paranoiac suspicions about his wife's infidelity, a business executive (Barry Brown) follows her to Colorado in order to watch her every move and becomes drawn into murder. Co-stars Britt Ekland, Eric Braeden. 84 min.
16-1110 ***$14.99***

Texas In Flames (1979)
Ronee Blakley stars as a strong-willed woman fighting to protect her land, settling in a small valley on the Texas-Mexico border and fending off both Texan land barons and the forces of Pancho Villa. Dean Stockwell, Scott Glenn co-star. AKA: "She Came to the Valley." 90 min.
16-3014 ***$14.99***

The Warriors (1979)
The Warriors are a street gang from Coney Island, trapped in the Bronx when a city-wide truce explodes. What follows is non-stop suspense and violent action as they try to get through 28 miles of "enemy territory" with 100,000 gang members after them! Michael Beck, Dorsey Wright, James Remar star; directed by Walter Hill. 94 min.
06-1070 ***$14.99***

Rudy Ray Moore

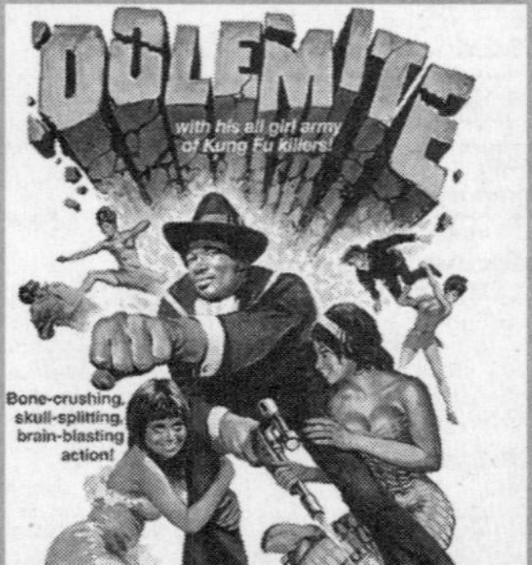
DOLEMITE
with his all girl army of Kung Fu killers!
Bone-crushing, skull-splitting, brain-blasting action!

Dolemite (1975)
The outrageous action-comedy favorite stars Rudy Ray Moore as a nightclub comic released from prison and ready to help the Feds catch the crooks responsible for his imprisonment. With D'Urville Martin, Lady Reed. 88 min.
76-7010 ***$19.99***

The Human Tornado (1976)
He's none other than Rudy Ray Moore, and once he sweeps into town, very little will be left standing. The wild sequel to "Dolemite" finds Moore on the run from the law and hooking up with the residents of a local brothel, protecting the girls from mobsters. With Lady Reed, Glorya De Lani. 98 min.
76-7011 ***$19.99***

Petey Wheatstraw: The Devil's Son-In-Law (1977)
After a stand-up comic is shot to death, Ol' Mr. Scratch pops up and makes him a deal: he'll be returned to life if he marries the Devil's daughter. When he sees the goods, the funnyman tries to back out of the bargain—and all you-know-what breaks loose! Rudy Ray Moore, Jimmy Lynch, and Leroy and Skillet star. AKA: "The Devil's Son-in-Law." 93 min.
54-9103 ***$29.99***

Disco Godfather (1979)
Rudy Ray Moore is the cop-turned-rapmaster owner of a L.A. disco who goes back into action when his nephew is hooked on Angel Dust. Using his martial arts expertise, Rudy goes wild, wreaking vengeance on a drug dealer named Stinger. Carol Speed also stars. AKA: "Avenging Disco Godfather." 93 min.
54-9104 ***$29.99***

The Legend Of Dolemite! (1994)
It's an out-of-sight party compilation featuring action hero and original rapmaster Rudy Ray Moore. Featured on this video are outrageous clips from Rudy's rowdy movies and interviews with performers like Ice-T, Snoop Doggy Dogg, Arsenio Hall and others. 65 min.
54-9115 Was $24.99 ***$19.99***

Shaolin Dolemite (1999)
Rudy Ray Moore's funky, kung fu-fighting Dolemite returns in this wild martial arts adventure that'll take you back to the 1970s. When a cop gets over his head in trouble with crooks, Dolemite has to step in to help. With Harland Williams, "Uncle Floyd" Vivino, Insane Clown Posse's Shaggy 2 Dope and wrestling legend Mick Foley. AKA: "Big Money Hustlas."
54-9188 ***$59.99***

Please see our index for the Rudy Ray Moore title: *Violent New Breed*

Jack London

Wolf Call (1939)
Thrilling adaptation of Jack London's tale about a playboy getting help from trusty dog Smokey while battling corrupt miners. John Carroll, Wheeler Oakman star. 60 min.
09-2131 Was $24.99 ***$19.99***

Torture Ship (1939)
A demented scientist who hopes to cure criminals through an illegal glandular operation fills a boat with convicts he helped escape. Together, they set out for the open sea, with his Annapolis graduate nephew an unwitting aide, in this "B"-actioner starring Lyle Talbot, Irving Pichel and Jacqueline Wells (later Julie Bishop). Inspired by Jack London's short story "A Thousand Deaths." 63 min.
09-3073 ***$19.99***

Mutiny Of The Elsinore (1939)
This exciting Jack London story receives a fine adaptation with Paul Lukas starring as a novelist who finds the ship he's sailing on is taken over by mutineers. The writer must wrestle with the scalawags in order to get control of the ship again. Lyn Harding, Pat Moriarty also star. 80 min.
10-8448 Was $19.99 ***$14.99***

Queen Of The Yukon (1940)
In order to be reunited with her daughter, a woman sells her boating business in the Yukon to a mining company. After the company begins to prevent independent miners from working, the woman's former partner comes to the rescue. Charles Bickford, Irene Rich, Melvin Lang star. 73 min.
17-9067 Was $19.99 ***$14.99***

Sign Of The Wolf (1941)
The panoramic Canadian wilderness enhances this canine adventure based on a short story by Jack London. The unwanted and unruly shepherd of a young woman saves her and her servant after a plane crash and helps another dog being trained to steal fox pelts by thieves. Stars Michael Whalen, Grace Bradley. 69 min.
10-8362 Was $19.99 ***$14.99***

To Build A Fire (1969)
Thrilling outdoor photography and Orson Welles' vibrant narration combine to tell a classic short story by Jack London about a traveller in Alaska's wilderness struggling to survive temperatures 75 degrees below zero. With Ian Hogg. 56 min.
08-1437 Was $19.99 ***$14.99***

The Legend Of Sea Wolf (1975)
Dramatic adaptation of Jack London's novel stars Chuck Connors as Captain Wolf Larsen, a sadistic, obsessed seafarer who must confront his only fear on a danger-filled voyage. With Barbara Bach, Giuseppi Pambieri. AKA: "Wolf Larsen." 92 min.
64-3013 Was $19.99 ***$14.99***

The Sea Wolf (1997)
Stacy Keach gives a memorable performance as tough-as-nails sea captain Wolf Larson in this thrilling adventure that updates the classic Jack London novel. Jaason Simmons is the man rescued at sea who battles Larson in a duel of wills; with Alejandra Cruz, Mako. 85 min.
21-9155 ***$59.99***

White Fang And The Hunter (1975)
Exciting wilderness drama and adventure, as a wounded hunter and his dog are taken in by a trapper's widow and young son. Together they find love and help bring her husband's killer to justice. Robert Wood and Pedro Sanchez star. 87 min.
69-1011 ***$14.99***

The Great Adventure (1976)
A young boy and his trusty dog struggle to survive in Gold Rush-era Alaska but run afoul of a corrupt town boss, in this exciting adaptation of a Jack London story. Jack Palance, Joan Collins, Fred Romer star. 90 min.
03-1150 ***$19.99***

Klondike Fever (1980)
The real-life adventures of Jack London in the Canadian wilderness of the Gold Rush era, adventures that would later inspire him to write "The Call of the Wild" and other classic tales, are depicted in this exciting drama. Jeff East stars as London; with Rod Steiger, Angie Dickinson, Lloyd Bridges. 106 min.
47-3052 ***$14.99***

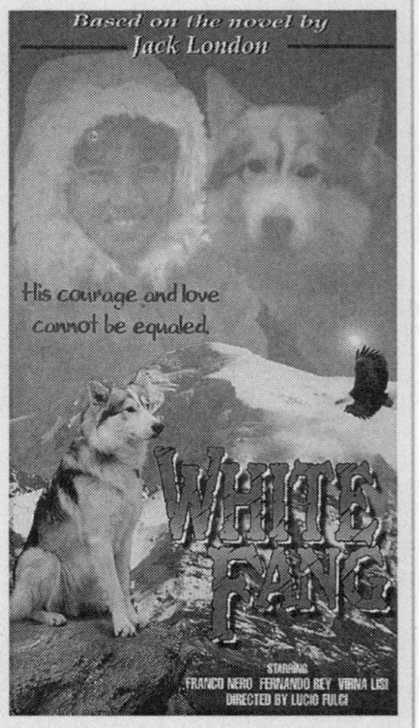
Based on the novel by
Jack London
His courage and love cannot be equaled.
WHITE FANG
STARRING FRANCO NERO FERNANDO REY VIRNA LISI
DIRECTED BY LUCIO FULCI

White Fang (1986)
Jack London's thrilling adventure is brought to life in this scenic adventure from Italian horror maestro Lucio Fulci ("Zombie"). Set in the Yukon, the film centers on a young boy, a newspaper reporter and a nun who are helped by White Fang while defending their city against a greedy businessman. Franco Nero, Virna Lisi star. AKA: "Challenge to White Fang." 105 min.
78-3039 ***$14.99***

Legends Of The North (1994)
Jack London's classic Yukon adventure stars Randy Quaid as an adventurer who teams with an annoying prospector to search for a legendary lake supposedly filled with gold. When his partner dies early in the trek, Quaid calls on the prospector's son for help. Soon, the two men face hostile Indians and fierce weather as their quest continues. With Georges Corraface. 95 min.
68-1359 Was $89.99 ***$14.99***

The Call Of The Wild: Dog Of The Yukon (1997)
Richard Dreyfuss narrates this exciting wilderness adventure, based on the Jack London story of a dog who must fight for survival, first as a member of a sled team in the Yukon, then with a kindly gold prospector. Rutger Hauer, Charles Powell star; Richard Dreyfuss narrates. 105 min.
88-1165 Was $69.99 ***$14.99***

Doc Savage: The Man Of Bronze (1975)
The golden-hued hero of books, comics and radio returns in this exciting, fun-filled adventure saga. Doc and his comrades track a killer to a remote South American nation where a deadly Indian tribe, ruthless villains and a fabulous treasure await. Ron Ely, Pamela Hensley, Paul Wexler star. 100 min.
19-1469 ***$14.99***

Rum Runners (1971)
Set during the Prohibition Era, this adventure stars Lino Ventura and Brigitte Bardot as a smuggler and his film actress girlfriend who encounter U.S. Coast Guard patrols while trying to sneak booze across the Caribbean. Bill Travers, Clive Revill also star. 82 min.
10-5182 ***$19.99***

The Timber Tramps (1975)
Saboteurs want the land owned by a woman for their sawmill operation and call on a ranger to help them out. But the woman has her own set of friends who want to help her against the swindlers. Claude Akins, Tab Hunter, Joseph Cotten, Rosey Grier star in this adventure with beautiful scenery. 90 min.
10-9169 ***$19.99***

The Glove: Black Shampoo (1976)
Mr. Jonathan is a smooth-talking, hard-hitting ladies' man who can curl and kill with equal ease. When his receptionist gets in trouble with the mob, Jonathan teases, cuts and blow-dries his enemies away! Actioner stars John Daniels, Tanya Boyd. 90 min.
08-1312 ***$19.99***

The Outfit (1973)
Newly released from prison, small-time hood Robert Duvall returns home to learn that his brother was killed by Mafia hit men in retaliation for a robbery the pair and partner Joe Don Baker pulled on a mob-run bank. Duvall and Baker become both hunters and hunted as they set out for revenge on crime boss Robert Ryan in this gripping actioner. With Karen Black, Elisha Cook, Jr. 101 min.
12-3035 ***$19.99***

The Long Arm Of The Godfather (1972)
"Thunderball" heavy Adolfo Celi stars in this intense gangster tale about gun smugglers who wreak havoc on the streets of Rome. Peter Lee Lawrence and Erika Blanc also star. 80 min.
10-9992 ***$14.99***

Sean Connery

The Frightened City (1961)
Top-notch British gangster yarn starring Herbert Lom as a mobster who unites London's top crime organizations, but soon finds his idea shattered in a hail of gunplay when one of his associates starts a rival syndicate. Hit man Sean Connery is called on to stop the competition. John Gregson, Alfred Marks also star. 91 min.
10-9375 □*$14.99*

On The Fiddle (1961)
Just before "Dr. No" became an international sensation, Sean Connery co-starred in this comedy, playing a young Gypsy man who joins forces with his conniving pal and enlists in the British Army during World War II. The two small-time crooks pull off a series of scams in the military and become unlikely heroes. With Alfred Lynch. AKA: "Operation Snafu," "War Head." 96 min.
63-1866 □*$14.99*

The Hill (1965)
Intense drama from Sidney Lumet featuring Sean Connery as a British soldier in North Africa who tries to get medical help for a prisoner suffering from his military stockade's grueling punishment. When the prisoner dies, Connery attempts to bring charges against a sadistic sergeant. Harry Andrews, Ian Bannen and Ossie Davis co-star. 122 min.
12-2990 □*$19.99*

A Fine Madness (1966)
Sean Connery excels as an eccentric, rebellious poet who agrees to a temporary stay in the mental ward to avoid bill collectors and alimony lawyers. An offbeat and engaging comedy that was far ahead of its time. Joanne Woodward, Patrick O'Neal, Jean Seberg also star. 104 min.
19-1525 Was $19.99 *$14.99*

Shalako (1968)
Fast-paced frontier action stars Sean Connery as a wandering gunfighter who comes to the aid of a group of travelling European aristocrats when they're stranded in Apache country. Brigitte Bardot, Stephen Boyd, Woody Strode and Connery's "Goldfinger" co-star, Honor Blackman, also star. 113 min.
04-3186 *$14.99*

Shalako (Letterboxed Version)
Also available in a theatrical, widescreen format.
08-8641 *$14.99*

The Molly Maguires (1970)
The personal and professional hardships of Pennsylvania mineworkers circa 1876 explodes in violent confrontation when management's hired infiltrator (Richard Harris) clashes with the underground leader (Sean Connery). Directed by Martin Ritt; with Samantha Eggar and Frank Finlay. 123 min.
06-1370 *$14.99*

The Red Tent (1971)
Gripping adventure epic, based on an actual event, stars Peter Finch as the commander of a dirigible that crashes during an Arctic flight and Sean Connery as explorer Roald Amundsen, who leads a rescue mission. Hardy Kruger, Claudia Cardinale. 121 min.
06-1521 *$19.99*

The Anderson Tapes (1972)
Lightning-fast thriller with Sean Connery as an ex-con who devises an intricate plan to loot a posh New York apartment building, unaware that his every move is being watched by a surveillance system which has been on him since he left prison. Co-stars Dyan Cannon, Martin Balsam, and Christopher Walken in his film debut; directed by Sidney Lumet. 98 min.
02-2606 *$14.99*

The Offence (1973)
Sean Connery gives a daring performance in this powerfully emotional drama as a police detective who, during an interrogation, fatally beats a man accused of child molestation. The dark secret behind Connery's actions leads to a shattering conclusion. With Trevor Howard, Ian Bannen; directed by Sidney Lumet. 108 min.
12-2607 *$14.99*

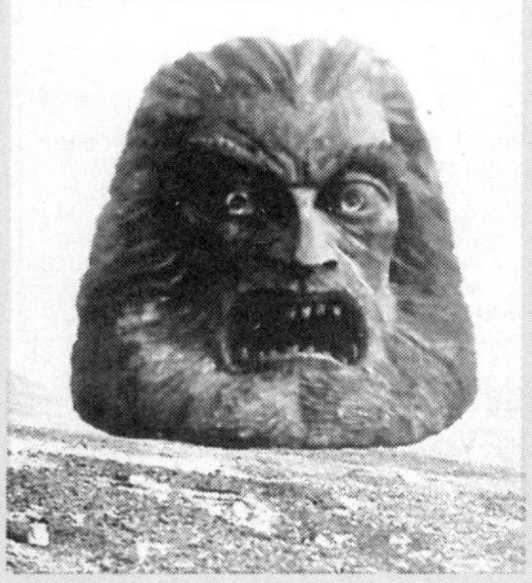

Zardoz (1974)
This cult sensation stars a loincloth-clad Sean Connery as a savage, genetic superman, captured by a race of young, sexless intellectuals during the year 2293. Amazing visuals, bizarre characters and Connery's beefy performance highlight this John Boorman dazzler. 105 min.
04-1678 *$19.99*

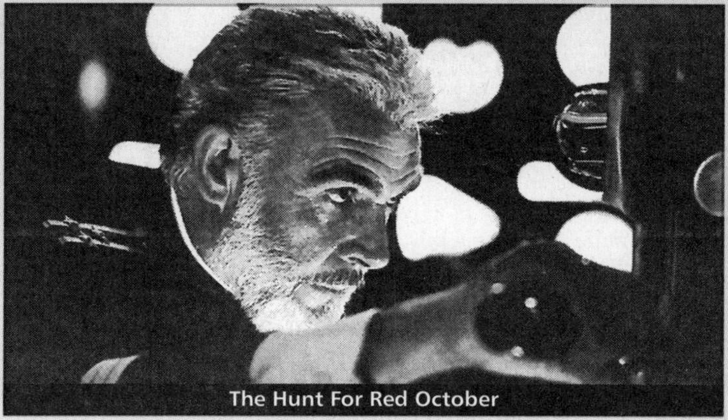
The Hunt For Red October

The Terrorists (1975)
A Scandinavian airport is the setting for global tension when terrorist hijackers kidnap the British ambassador and commandeer a jet. Sean Connery, Ian McShane star. 89 min.
04-2043 Was $59.99 □*$29.99*

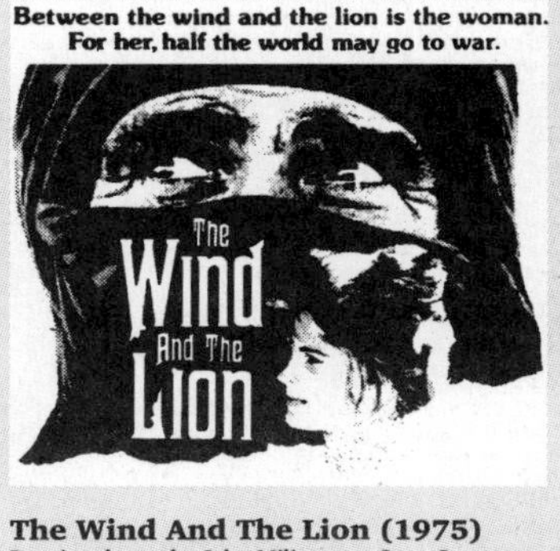
Between the wind and the lion is the woman.
For her, half the world may go to war.
The Wind And The Lion

The Wind And The Lion (1975)
Rousing drama by John Milius stars Sean Connery as a Moroccan chieftain who kidnaps American widow Candice Bergen and her children, and Brian Keith as President Theodore Roosevelt, who puts his country at the brink of war in order to rescue them. 119 min.
12-1563 Was $59.99 *$19.99*

The Man Who Would Be King (1975)
Rousing adventure by John Huston stars Sean Connery and Michael Caine as British soldiers in 1800s India who attempt to dupe a remote village of their gold by passing off Connery as a god. Based on a story by Rudyard Kipling. 129 min.
19-2194 *$19.99*

The Man Who Would Be King (Letterboxed Version)
Also available in a theatrical, widescreen format.
19-2539 □*$19.99*

Robin And Marian (1976)
Exciting and poignant tale of a middle-aged Robin Hood returning to Sherwood Forest after 20 years of fighting in the Crusades to regroup his Merry Men and reunite with Maid Marian. Sean Connery, Audrey Hepburn, Robert Shaw, Richard Harris and Denholm Elliott star. 112 min.
02-1224 Was $19.99 *$14.99*

The Arab Conspiracy (1976)
A Saudi Arabian ambassador's (Sean Connery) attempts to forge a Mideast peace earn him a death sentence from Palestinian hardliners, but the lovely assassin (Cornelia Sharpe) they hire to kill him falls in love with him instead. Gripping, timely thriller co-stars Adolfo Celi, Charles Cioffi. AKA: "Next Man," "Double Hit." 91 min.
78-1053 *$14.99*

The Great Train Robbery (1979)
Based-on-fact tale of the world's first moving train heist, this stylish thriller, written and directed by Michael Crichton, stars Sean Connery and Donald Sutherland as the 1850s British criminals who revolutionize their industry. Lovely Lesley-Anne Down co-stars; Connery performed his own stunts. 110 min.
12-1793 Was $29.99 □*$14.99*

The Great Train Robbery (Letterboxed Version)
Also available in a theatrical, widescreen format.
12-3169 □*$14.99*

Cuba (1979)
Violent action and torrid passion amid the turmoil of the 1959 Cuban Revolution, with Sean Connery as a soldier of fortune fighting for the anti-Castro forces and finding old flame Brooke Adams working for the Communists. Chris Sarandon, Denholm Elliott and Jack Weston co-star; Richard Lester directs. 121 min.
12-2599 *$14.99*

Meteor (1979)
A five-mile-wide meteor races towards Earth, as the world's governments race against time and each other's suspicions to find a way to avert planetary catastrophe. Great special effects in this all-star disaster epic that features Sean Connery, Natalie Wood, Henry Fonda, Karl Malden and Martin Landau. 103 min.
19-1104 Was $19.99 *$14.99*

Outland (1981)
This science-fiction translation of "High Noon" stars Sean Connery as a 21st-century marshal on the third moon of Jupiter who alone stands up to a ruthless mine manager who's been inducing his workers with dangerous drugs to improve their work output. Co-stars Peter Boyle, Frances Sternhagen, Kika Markham. 109 min.
19-1174 *$14.99*

Wrong Is Right (1982)
Writer/director Richard Brooks pulls no punches in this barb-filled satire of international terrorism, the FBI, the CIA, American politics and our television-obsessed global society. Sean Connery stars as a broadcast journalist caught in the middle of Middle East revolutionaries and intelligence agents. Co-stars Katharine Ross, George Grizzard, Robert Conrad. 117 min.
02-1129 *$79.99*

Five Days One Summer (1982)
This romantic drama, set against the backdrop of the Swiss Alps, explores the relationship between a vacationing couple, a mountain climber (Sean Connery) and a young woman who appears to be his wife, and the introduction of a handsome guide into their lives. Director Fred Zinnemann's lush soaper co-stars Betsy Brantley, Lambert Wilson. 108 min.
19-1259 Was $19.99 *$14.99*

The Presidio (1988)
Sean Connery is a veteran Army M.P. officer, Mark Harmon an ex-soldier turned police detective. Together these unwilling allies must investigate a murder at San Francisco's famed military base, and while doing so uncover a dangerous smuggling scheme. Taut thriller also stars Meg Ryan. 97 min.
06-1625 □*$14.99*

The Hunt For Red October (1990)
The world's largest and deadliest submarine, an undetectable Soviet craft codenamed Red October, is hijacked by commander Sean Connery and heading for America, and a race against time begins as both superpowers seek to capture the sub or destroy it. Hit "End of the Cold War" thriller based on Tom Clancy's book also stars Alec Baldwin, Scott Glenn, James Earl Jones. 135 min.
06-1768 Was $19.99 □*$14.99*

The Hunt For Red October (Letterboxed Version)
Also available in a theatrical, widescreen format.
06-2508 □*$14.99*

The Russia House (1990)
Intriguing, intelligent filmization of John le Carré's thriller stars Sean Connery as a British publisher who hopes to snag an important manuscript of Soviet military secrets before the CIA and KGB get to it. Michelle Pfeiffer is the beautiful go-between, Klaus Maria Brandauer the scientist author of the piece, and Roy Scheider an American operative. 126 min.
12-2227 Was $19.99 □*$14.99*

Medicine Man (1992)
A timely adventure saga, with Sean Connery as a biochemist working deep in the Amazon rain forest on a cure for cancer and Lorraine Bracco as a visiting scientist in charge of the institute funding his work. The two clash, but unite when Connery's discoveries are threatened by the jungle's increasing destruction. 105 min.
11-1630 Was $19.99 □*$14.99*

Rising Sun (1993)
Thrilling adaptation of Michael Crichton's controversial novel stars Wesley Snipes as a streetwise Los Angeles detective who teams with Sean Connery, a veteran investigator with expertise in Eastern cultures, to solve the murder of a prostitute in the offices of a powerful Japan-based corporation. Harvey Keitel, Tia Carrere and Kevin Anderson co-star; directed by Philip Kaufman. 129 min.
04-2716 Was $19.99 □*$14.99*

A Good Man In Africa (1994)
This drama with satirical touches focuses on a British official in West Africa who tries to balance his job, which involves carrying out bizarre orders from his superior, his love for a good time, and his romance with the wife of a local politician. The official finds his conscience with help from a well-meaning physician. Colin Friels, Sean Connery, Joanne Whalley-Kilmer star. 95 min.
07-2222 Was $89.99 □*$14.99*

First Knight (1995)
The legend of Camelot is portrayed in this lavish drama starring Sean Connery as King Arthur, the middle-aged ruler of England whose marriage to Queen Guinevere (Julia Ormond) is threatened after she shows interest in dashing Sir Lancelot (Richard Gere). Ben Cross, John Gielgud also star; directed by Jerry Zucker ("Ghost"). 133 min.
02-2811 Was $19.99 □*$14.99*

First Knight (Letterboxed Version)
Also available in a theatrical, widescreen format.
02-3202 □*$19.99*

Just Cause (1995)
Kinetic thriller starring Sean Connery as an eminent lawyer and Harvard professor who tries to save an African-American in the Deep South awaiting execution for raping and killing a young girl. Connery's investigation leads him to a cop with questionable scruples and a serial killer imprisoned in a Florida jail. Laurence Fishburne, Kate Capshaw, Blair Underwood and Ed Harris co-star. 102 min.
19-2364 Was $19.99 □*$14.99*

The Avengers (1998)
The stylish '60s spy series becomes a special effects-filled adventure with Ralph Fiennes as dapper John Steed and Uma Thurman as lithesome Emma Peel, British sleuths teamed to stop Sean Connery's evil Sir August de Wynter, who wreaks havoc with England's weather. With Jim Broadbent, Fiona Shaw, Eddie Izzard and, in a cameo, original Steed Patrick Macnee. 90 min.
19-2782 Was $99.99 □*$14.99*

The Avengers (Letterboxed Version)
Also available in a theatrical, widescreen format.
19-2854 □*$19.99*

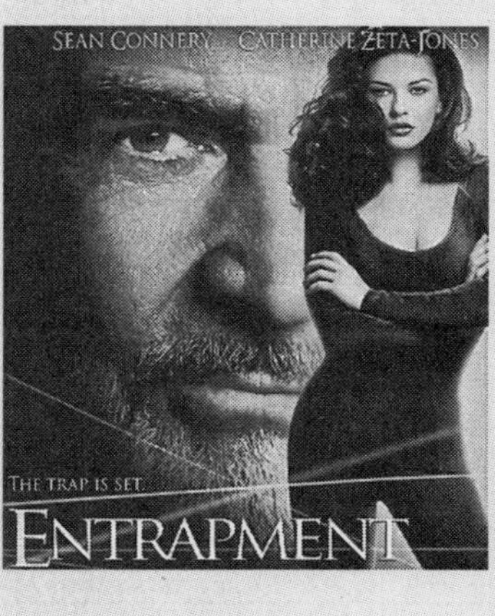
SEAN CONNERY CATHERINE ZETA-JONES
THE TRAP IS SET.
ENTRAPMENT

Entrapment (1999)
Stylish thriller stars Sean Connery as a master thief who is tracked down by insurance investigator Catherine Zeta-Jones after a Rembrandt is swiped from a New York apartment building. The two become partners, first stealing a valuable Chinese mask from a museum, then plotting a New Year's Eve computer heist that will net them billions. Will Patton, Ving Rhames also star. 130 min.
04-3867 Was $99.99 □*$14.99*

Please see our index for these other Sean Connery titles: James Bond films • *A Bridge Too Far* • *Dragonheart* • *Family Business* • *Indiana Jones And The Last Crusade* • *Lilacs In The Spring* • *The Longest Day* • *Marnie* • *Murder On The Orient Express* • *Playing By Heart* • *The Rock* • *Time Bandits* • *Time Lock* • *The Untouchables*

When Hell Broke Loose (1956)
A young Charles Bronson stars in this thrilling WWII adventure, playing a small-time hood in the Army who learns of a plot to kill General Eisenhower, then uses his streetwise style to stop the assassin. Richard Jaeckel, Arvid Nelson, Eddie Foy III co-star. 78 min.
06-2048 *$14.99*

Showdown At Boot Hill (1958)
Charles Bronson is a bounty hunter out to capture an outlaw and collect the reward, only to run afoul of a deputy marshal looking for the same man. With Robert Hutton, John Carradine. 72 min.
63-5031 Was $19.99 *$12.99*

Guns For San Sebastian (1968)
Rousing adventure set in 1746, where Anthony Quinn is a popular bandit posing as a priest with help from Franciscan father Sam Jaffe. Quinn becomes the padre of a small Mexican town and must use his connections to get weapons to help the townspeople fight the Yaqui Indians and half-breed Charles Bronson. Anjanette Comer, Jaime Fernandez also star. 115 min.
12-3085 *$19.99*

Honor Among Thieves (1968)
Charles Bronson is mean and lean in this action-drenched thriller as a former mercenary who takes part in a Marseilles bank robbery with old comrade-turned-doctor Alain Delon, unaware they're being set up. With Brigitte Fossey. AKA: "Farewell, Friend." 93 min.
27-6071 □*$19.99*

Lola (1969)
A bit of a departure for Charles Bronson was this romantic seriocomedy that casts him as a middle-aged writer whose relationship with a 16-year-old nymph (Susan George) hits a snag when they decide to marry. Richard Donner directs; with Orson Bean, Paul Ford and Robert Morley. AKA: "Child Bride." 88 min.
58-1121 *$19.99*

Lola (Letterboxed Version)
Also available in a theatrical, widescreen format.
08-1728 *$14.99*

Hot Lead (Bull Of The West) (1970)
The 1800s American frontier heats up as a violent range war erupts in this action-filled story of men who fight to the death to preserve their way of life. Charles Bronson, Lee J. Cobb, Ben Johnson, George Kennedy star. 94 min.
78-1180 *$14.99*

Cold Sweat (1971)
Talk about action! Charles Bronson gets mistakenly involved in the dangerous drug trade after a ruthless smuggler kidnaps his wife and child. James Mason, Liv Ullmann and Jill Ireland also star in this punch-'em-out thriller. 94 min.
16-1087 Was $19.99 *$14.99*

Red Sun (1971)
The Old West and the Old East collide in this action thriller about train robbers who steal a valuable Japanese sword and are pursued by a samurai warrior. Charles Bronson, Toshiro Mifune star; directed by James Bond vet Terence Young. 112 min.
16-1157 *$19.99*

Someone Behind The Door (1971)
Bizarre psychological drama about a doctor who uses a deranged murderer as his tool in a plot to kill his wife. Charles Bronson, Anthony Perkins and Jill Ireland star. 95 min.
48-1077 Was $19.99 *$14.99*

The Mechanic (1972)
Charles Bronson stars as a steely-eyed "mechanic," an unparalleled professional assassin who takes a cold-hearted apprentice (Jan-Michael Vincent) under his wing. During an adventure-filled tutelage, the pair manage to escape one threat after another, culminating in a nail-biting climax. Co-stars Jill Ireland; directed by Michael Winner. 101 min.
12-1787 Was $19.99 *$14.99*

Chato's Land (1972)
Charles Bronson is at his steely best as an Apache who murders a white man in self-defense in a saloon argument, then finds himself being trailed by a posse headed by nasty tough guy Jack Palance. Co-stars Richard Basehart and James Whitmore. 100 min.
12-2075 *$14.99*

Charles Bronson

Chato's Land (Letterboxed Version)
Also available in a theatrical, widescreen format
12-3255 *$14.99*

The Stone Killer (1973)
Charles Bronson is a cop on the trail of crime kingpin Martin Balsam and his vicious assassination bureau. It's cross-country mayhem and action as only Bronson can dish it out. 95 min.
02-1304 *$59.99*

Chino (Valdez Horses) (1973)
A half-breed horse rancher (Charles Bronson) in New Mexico faces a brutal challenge when he falls for a rival's sister (Jill Ireland) in this two-fisted western drama. 111 min.
19-1116 *$14.99*

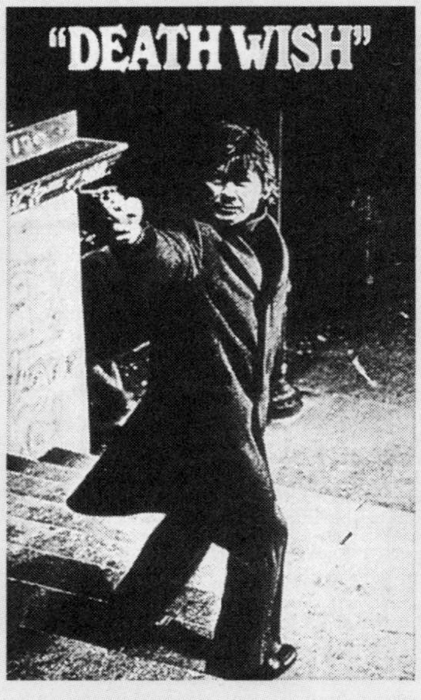

Death Wish (1974)
Original vigilante thriller that spawned a slew of sequels and "copycats" still packs a potent punch. Charles Bronson takes the law into his own fists when his wife is killed and his daughter raped by local toughs. With Hope Lange, Vincent Gardenia. 93 min.
06-1011 *$14.99*

Death Wish II (1982)
Charles Bronson is back...and meaner than ever. His daughter's been assaulted, so once again he goes on a one-man vigilante spree against the crooks, rapists and muggers of the city. Jill Ireland, Vincent Gardenia, J.D. Cannon co-star. 90 min.
19-1225 Was $19.99 *$14.99*

Death Wish 3 (1985)
Crime-busting vigilante Paul Kersey (Charles Bronson) returns in the third action thriller, defending the terrorized residents of a New York apartment building from a horde of marauding gang members and blowing the punks away as only Bronson can. With Ed Lauter, Martin Balsam, Deborah Raffin. 93 min.
12-1543 *$14.99*

Death Wish V: The Face Of Death (1994)
Charles Bronson's Paul Kersey is back, this time returning to New York with girlfriend Lesley-Anne Down. When she's killed in the crossfire of her ex-husband's protection operation, Bronson hunts down the scum responsible in his legendary vigilante style. Michael Parks, Saul Rubinek co-star. 95 min.
68-1306 Was $89.99 □*$14.99*

Mr. Majestyk (1974)
Former Vietnam vet and current Colorado melon farmer Charles Bronson sets out to even the score with an underworld hit man and his associates who have been terrorizing his farmhands and who destroyed his crops. Co-stars Linda Cristal, Al Lettierri, Lee Purcell; scripted by Elmore Leonard from his novel. 103 min.
12-1358 *$14.99*

Breakout (1975)
Rugged action film features Charles Bronson at his daring best, defying the Mexican prison system to rescue an American framed for murder. Robert Duvall, Jill Ireland, John Huston co-star. 96 min.
02-1028 Was $19.99 *$14.99*

Hard Times (1975)
Charles Bronson is a fierce bare-knuckle streetfighter, battling opponents in New Orleans during the 1930s. Fine period detail, smashing fight sequences and gritty direction by Walter Hill make this a memorable winner. With James Coburn, Jill Ireland. 97 min.
02-2696 *$14.99*

Breakheart Pass (1976)
Slam-bang western action with Charles Bronson as a federal agent in the 1870s tracking down gunrunners. The trail leads to a wild train ride and one plot twist after another. Ben Johnson, Charles Durning and Jill Ireland co-star; based on Alistair MacLean's best-selling novel. 95 min.
12-1896 Was $19.99 *$14.99*

From Noon Til Three (1976)
An offbeat Charles Bronson western casts him as a two-bit outlaw who has a brief affair with writer Jill Ireland. Years later, her fictionalized tales of his exploits have made him infamous, but the myth is rudely shattered when he shows up to contradict them. Written and directed by Frank D. Gilroy. 98 min.
12-2609 *$14.99*

St. Ives (1976)
Crime reporter turned crime novelist Charles Bronson plays go-between to recover stolen ledgers that could possibly ignite a gang war between two rival underworld factions and becomes lost in a maze of betrayal and murder. Co-stars John Houseman, Jacqueline Bisset, Maximilian Schell and Harry Guardino. 93 min.
19-1328 Was $59.99 *$14.99*

Telefon (1977)
A Charles Bronson classic, where tough Chuck plays a Russian agent racing against time to stop a spy's deadly sabotage plot. Lee Remick and Tyne Daly also star in this Don ("Dirty Harry") Siegel thriller. 100 min.
12-1343 *$19.99*

The White Buffalo (1977)
Charles Bronson plays legendary gunslinger Wild Bill Hickok, haunted by a vision of a gigantic albino buffalo. He teams with Chief Crazy Horse to search for and destroy the beast in this unusual western adventure that mixes psychology, fantasy and action. With Jack Warden, Will Sampson, Kim Novak. 97 min.
12-2072 *$14.99*

Caboblanco (1980)
Bronson "does Bogart" in this gutsy action-romance based on "Casablanca." He's the proprietor of a South American bar populated by the local authorities, Nazi fugitives and gorgeous women. Here's squinting at you, Chuck. Jason Robards, Dominique Sanda co-star. 87 min.
03-1237 □*$14.99*

Borderline (1980)
Patrolman Charles Bronson, policing the U.S.-Mexican border for aliens, finds himself up against a band of smugglers looking to exploit and rob would-be immigrants. Action-packed Bronson at his best; with Bruno Kirby, Ed Harris, Wilford Brimley. 106 min.
04-1559 *$12.99*

Death Hunt (1981)
Unflinching Mountie Lee Marvin withstands the rugged Canadian wilderness and the passage of time to bring in maverick fur trapper Charles Bronson, who's equally determined not to be punished for a murder he did not commit. Co-stars Angie Dickinson, Andrew Stevens, Carl Weathers. 97 min.
04-1442 *$19.99*

Ten To Midnight (1983)
Charles Bronson plays a cop who throws caution (and ethics) to the wind after a woman-hating serial killer (Andrew Stevens) begins to terrorize his daughter, sending Bronson on a crusade of vengeance. Co-stars Lisa Eilbacher, Gene Davis, Geoffrey Lewis, Wilford Brimley. 101 min.
12-1296 □*$14.99*

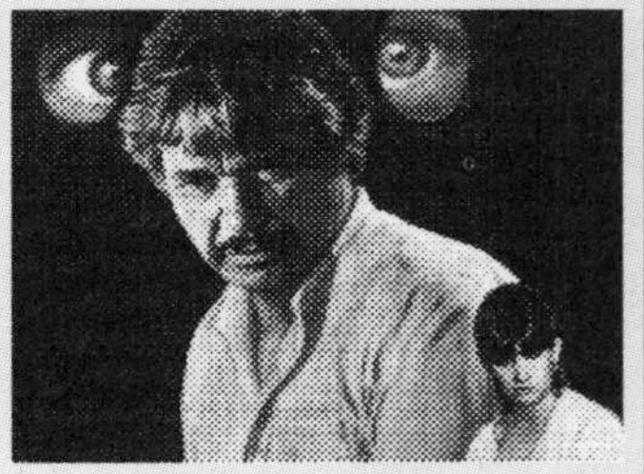

The Evil That Men Do

The Evil That Men Do (1984)
Charles Bronson turns in one of his most rugged performances as a professional assassin out to crash a Central American crime ring. Hard-edged suspense, wild chases and loads of action. Jose Ferrer, Theresa Saldana co-star. 90 min.
02-1381 *$14.99*

Kinjite: Forbidden Subjects (1989)
Hard-edged thriller stars Charles Bronson as a Los Angeles detective who must overcome his own prejudices as he tracks down a Japanese businessman's kidnapped daughter and uncovers a prostitution ring. Perry Lopez, Peggy Lipton. 96 min.
19-1698 *$14.99*

The Sea Wolf (1993)
In this new adaptation of Jack London's classic story, Charles Bronson is a tough ship's captain who finds himself caught in an intense battle of wills with an aristocrat who's been rescued from a shipwreck along with a beautiful con artist. Christopher Reeve, Catherine Mary Stewart and Marc Singer also star. 100 min.
18-7448 Was $89.99 □*$19.99*

Dead To Rights (1993)
Retired detective Charles Bronson joins forces with his police officer daughter (Dana Delaney) to track down a sadistic serial killer preying on nuns in this spine-tingling action thriller. AKA: "Donato and Daughter." 93 min.
68-1788 Was $89.99 □*$14.99*

Family Of Cops (1996)
Police commander Charles Bronson finds himself in the middle of a bizarre homicide case involving a love triangle between a murdered businessman, his seductive wife and Bronson's sexy daughter. The only way for Bronson to prove his daughter's innocence is to get involved with the manipulative widow. Lesley-Anne Down, Daniel Baldwin and Barbara Williams also star. 90 min.
68-1822 Was $99.99 *$14.99*

A Family Of Cops II (1998)
When the brutal murder of a priest in Milwaukee's Russian community appears to be connected to the activities of the Russian mob, police inspector Charles Bronson must return to the neighborhood he grew up in—and thought he left forever—to solve the crime. Diane Ladd, Angela Featherstone, Joe Penny also star. 93 min.
68-1903 □*$99.99*

Please see our index for these other Charles Bronson titles: *Battle Of The Bulge • The Dirty Dozen • 4 For Texas • House Of Wax • How The West Was Won • The Indian Runner • Kid Galahad • The Magnificent Seven • The Marrying Kind • Master Of The World • Never So Few • The Sandpiper • This Property Is Condemned • Vera Cruz*

Firepower (1979)
An all-star cast and stunning locales highlight this lightning-quick action thriller that finds a woman seeking revenge for the murder of her scientist husband by a ruthless drug ring. Sophia Loren, James Coburn, O.J. Simpson, Eli Wallach star. 104 min. Please note: Title is available only as a manufacturer's cut-out; though product is new, box has a minor cut on the upper flap.
04-1610 *$14.99*

Orca, The Killer Whale (1977)
After his mate is killed, a 25-foot killer whale seeks revenge against sailor Richard Harris and follows him to a final showdown in the Arctic. Exciting sea-faring adventure, a reversal of "Moby Dick," also stars Charlotte Rampling, Keenan Wynn and Bo Derek, in one of her first film roles. 92 min.
06-1103 Was $19.99 *$14.99*

Truck Turner (1974)
Isaac Hayes stars as two-fisted bounty hunter Turner, tracking down bail jumpers in the inner city. When his latest quarry is murdered, a contract is taken out on his life, and hunter becomes hunted! Explosive urban actioner, directed by Jonathan Kaplan, also stars Yaphet Kotto, Nichelle Nichols; look for cameos by the great Dick Miller and "Our Gang" alumnus Stymie Beard. 91 min.
73-1100 Was $59.99 *$14.99*

Gold (1974)
Twenty-four-carat adventure saga set in a South African gold mine with Roger Moore as the foreman who learns of a plot to flood the mine, thus raising the world gold price, and fights to save the mine and the workers inside it. Susannah York, Ray Milland, John Gielgud also star. 118 min.
75-7027 *$19.99*

The Doll Squad (1973)
They're beautiful...they're deadly...they're the Doll Squad, and they're America's last chance against a would-be dictator's plans to unleash plague-infested rats on the world's leaders. "Charlie's Angels" meets James Bond in exciting, sexy action. Michael Ansara, Francine York and the legendary Tura Santana star. AKA: "Hustler Squad." 101 min.
59-5016 *$19.99*

Mister Scarface (1977)
A young Italian man who works as a debt collector for a local mobster dreams of a better life, but first he must avenge his father's death at the hands of infamous crime boss "Scarface" (Jack Palance). Al Cliver, Harry Bauer and Edmund Purdom also star. AKA: "Big Boss," "Blood & Bullets," "Rulers of the City," "Scarface Killer." 86 min.
59-5092 *$19.99*

Eagles Attack At Dawn (1975)
Tense action film set in the Middle East, as an Israeli commando undertakes a dangerous mission with an elite squad to infiltrate Arab territory and break into the prison where he was once held. Rick Jason, Peter Brown star in this thrilling Menachem Golan production. AKA: "From Hell to Victory," "Hostages in the Gulf." 93 min.
15-1069 Was $19.99 *$14.99*

Ned Kelly (1970)
Mick Jagger dons a cowboy hat to play Ned Kelly, the legendary outlaw who enlists his family members to fight social injustices levied by Protestant colonialists against Irish-born Catholic settlers in late 19th-century Australia. Tony Richardson directs this exciting, beautifully-lensed film. With Geoff Gilmour, Jeff McManus. 103 min.
12-2668 *$14.99*

Terence Hill & Bud Spencer

A Fistful Of Hell (1975)
Bud Spencer raises hell with both fists as "Flatfoot," a tough Chicago cop who doesn't let the Mob—or his own superiors—get in the way of his breaking up a deadly drug ring. Slam-bang action-comedy also stars Raymond Pellegrini, Angelo Infanti. AKA: "Flatfoot," "The Knock Out Cop," "Trinity: Tracking for Trouble." 95 min.
50-1633 *$29.99*

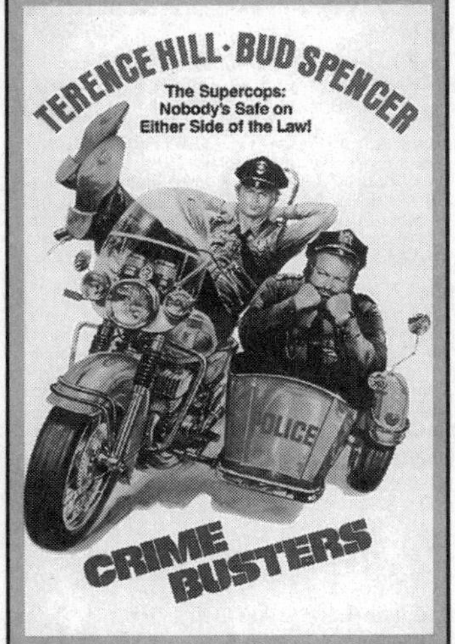

Crime Busters (1978)
Terence Hill and Bud Spencer, two of Europe's favorite action stars, play Miami cops who bust crime and make you chuckle at the same time. Their wild antics will leave you in stitches, as they turn Fairfax Ave. and its environs upside down. AKA: "Two Supercops." 114 min.
19-1810 Was $79.99 *$19.99*

Odds And Evens (1978)
With trouble brewing down Miami way, there's only one pair of coppers to call on to stop crime: Terence Hill and Bud Spencer. Time and luck are running out when the two law enforcers put an end to a Mob-run gambling ring. 109 min.
19-1819 Was $79.99 *$19.99*

Super Fuzz (1981)
A cop suddenly discovers he has amazing powers (super strength, super vision)—until he sees the color red, and uses his newfound gifts to nab some counterfeiters. Terence Hill, Ernest Borgnine, Joanne Dru star. 97 min.
53-1070 Was $69.99 *$29.99*

Go For It (1983)
Two-fisted excitement and fun meet when paisans Terence Hill and Bud Spencer team up. Here the daffy duo are spies out to thwart a plan to ignite a top-secret bomb. 109 min.
19-1818 Was $79.99 *$19.99*

Miami Supercops (1985)
Comic-action superstars Terence Hill and Bud Spencer star in this wacky and wild men-in-blue tale. They're two cops out to find who masterminded a $20 million heist. "Miami Vice" was never this zany! 97 min.
19-1809 Was $79.99 *$19.99*

Please see our index for these other Terence Hill/Bud Spencer titles:
Boot Hil • It Can Be Done Amigo • My Name Is Nobody • They Call Me Trinity • Trinity Is Still My Name

Search For The Gods (1975)
When an archeological dig in New Mexico uncovers a medallion that predates all signs of human inhabitants, a perilous quest ensues for the artifact's shocking origin. Kurt Russell, Ralph Bellamy star in an "ancient astronauts"-flavored adventure saga. 99 min.
48-1176 *$59.99*

Walkabout (1971)
Lost in the Australian Outback after their father takes his own life, two British youngsters are found by an aborigine teenager who shows them how to survive in the wilderness and helps them find their way back to civilization. Nicolas Roeg's solo directorial debut, this moving and lyrically photographed drama stars Jenny Agutter, David Cumpilil, Lucien John. Restored, director's cut includes 5 minutes of additional footage and the original theatrical trailer. 100 min. total.
22-5887 Letterboxed *$29.99*

Wild Riders (1971)
Two thrill-crazed bikers, fleeing from the torture murder of a girl in Florida, happen on two women alone in a mansion and invite themselves in for a party of rape, terror and bloodshed. Alex Rocco, Elizabeth Knowles and Sherry Bain. 91 min.
71-5047 *$14.99*

Evel Knievel (1971)
Entertaining and action-filled biodrama with George Hamilton under the helmet as the famed motorcycle daredevil. The film traces Evel's life, from his early years to some of his wildest stunts. With Sue Lyon, Rod Cameron.
50-6178 *$14.99*

Viva Knievel! (1977)
The world's greatest motorcycle dynamo, Evel Knievel, plays himself in this flick with more wild stunts than you've ever witnessed. Gene Kelly, Lauren Hutton and Red Buttons are on hand for this exciting tale that pits Evel against some nasty drug smugglers. 106 min.
19-1346 Was $19.99 *$14.99*

Mitchell (1975)
My, my, my, my, Mitchell! In a role that makes "Walking Tall's" Buford Pusser look like a wimp, Joe Don Baker plays a two-fisted (albeit slovenly) cop who stops at nothing to crack a drug-dealing operation. Martin Balsam, Linda Evans, Merlin Olsen and John Saxon also star. 97 min.
78-1029 *$14.99*

Bummer (1973)
This group of rockers is in for some heavy-duty action when go-go dancers from the Sunset Strip come out to party with them. But things go wrong, and this weekend turns out to be a major bummer! Carol Speed, Kipp Whitman stars. A David Friedman production.
69-1041 Was $24.99 *$19.99*

The Black Godfather (1974)
The Mafia boys may rule downtown, but uptown the Black Godfather controls the streets, and when the two gangs declare war over drug territories all Hell is sure to break loose. Violent action thriller stars Rod Perry, Damu King, Don Chastain.
69-1066 *$19.99*

Electra Glide In Blue (1973)
Robert Blake shines in this cult favorite action film as a feisty bantam-size motorcycle cop ("Did you know me and Alan Ladd were the same height?") who makes the streets his own personal battleground. Violent, funny and oddly moving; co-stars Jeannine Riley, Mitchell Ryan, Billy Green Bush. 106 min.
12-1740 *$14.99*

The Last Safari (1967)
A tourist on a safari vacation in Africa teams up with a guide racked with guilt over a hunting accident that claimed a friend's life in this gripping action film. Stewart Granger, Kaz Garas, Gabriella Licudi star. 111 min.
06-2059 *$14.99*

The Conqueror Of The Orient (1965)
Gianna Canale stars in this Italian swashbuckler about the son of a sultan who overthrows a traitor to the court. There's action, adventure, swordfights and intrigue. 87 min.
09-5039 *$19.99*

The Naked Prey (1966)
Thrilling adventure classic stars Cornel Wilde as a safari guide in Africa who is captured by a warrior tribe. Stripped of his weapons and clothes, hunter becomes hunted in a desperate race for survival. Co-written and directed by Wilde. 94 min.
06-1329 *$19.99*

Dimension 5 (1966)
Sci-fi spy caper with Jeffrey Hunter and sexy France Nuyen as agents of Espionage, Inc. who must use time-travel belts to stop a Communist organization's plot to nuke Los Angeles. Harold "Oddjob" Sakata, Donald Woods also star. 88 min.
10-9509 *$14.99*

Coast Of Skeletons (1965)
Inspired by Edgar Wallace's "Sanders of the River," this adventure stars Dale Robertson as a shady American who plans to loot the treasures from sunken ships. Investigator Richard Todd, whose employees own the treasures, tries to stop him. Exciting underwater scenes are featured. 91 min.
10-4173 *$19.99*

Password: Kill Agent Gordon (1965)
A tough CIA agent is called in to put a stop to a shipment of weapons to the Viet Cong from an arms smuggling ring in this intercontinental spy thriller. Roger Brown, Helga Line, Frank Ressel and Michel Rivers star.
68-9256 *$19.99*

O.S.S. 117: Double Agent (1969)
When a secret agent has his face surgically altered to look like a notorious killer, he is soon arrested by the police. But then a secret crime organization busts him out of jail and offers him a job. He must make a very important killing! John Gavin, Curt Jurgens and Margaret Lee star.
68-9257 *$19.99*

Requiem For A Secret Agent (1966)
Secret agent adventure with Stewart Granger as spy "Bingo" Merrill, hired to stop an organization out to control the world. Daniela Bianchi, Georgia Moll star. 94 min.
17-9068 Was $19.99 *$14.99*

Strangers At Sunrise (1968)
Exciting action film set around the turn of the century and featuring George Montgomery as an American mining engineer trying to make it rich during the South African gold rush. He runs into trouble when the British accuse him of allegiance to the Boers. With Brian O'Shaugnessy, Deanna Martin. 85 min.
10-9437 *$14.99*

The Bay Of Saint Michel (1963)
First-rate adventure from England involving four veterans of World War II who return to Normandy to seek some loot hidden by the Nazis. Their search leads them to an old castle near a dangerous coastline. Keenan Wynn, Mai Zetterling and Rona Anderson star. AKA: "Pattern for Plunder," "Operation Mermaid." 73 min.
10-9475 *$19.99*

Okefenokee (1960)
This drive-in favorite is a classic of its kind, filmed on location in the swamps. A hooker "with a heart of gumbo" and her boyfriend use airboats and help from Seminole Indians to smuggle illegal aliens and drugs into Southern Florida. After an Indian girl is raped and blinded, her people seek revenge against the white men responsible. Peter Coe stars.
79-6096 Was $24.99 *$19.99*

The Black Archer (1963)
Rousing swordplay highlights this tale of a count's son who plots revenge for his father's death. He discovers that among those involved in his father's murder were two cousins and an evil woman garbed in black. Gerard Landry stars in this Italian-made spectacle. 93 min. Dubbed in English.
09-2255 Was $24.99 *$19.99*

The Night Of The Grizzly (1966)
Clint Walker inherits land in Wyoming and trades in the dangerous life of a lawman for the cushy life of a rancher. But new dangers plague his family: a grizzly on the rampage, neighbors who want his property and outlaws. Exciting action and western adventures! Martha Hyer and Nancy Kulp co-star. 99 min.
06-1282 ◻*$14.99*

Sword Of Lancelot

Sword Of Lancelot (1963)
Grand-scale battles shot on location throughout England highlight this sword-swinging saga based on the Arthurian legend. Sir Lancelot (Cornel Wilde) must choose between his love for Guinevere and his loyalty to the king. 115 min.
07-1421 Was $59.99 *$14.99*

Guns Of The Black Witch (1961)
Swashbuckling saga about two boys who escape from a vicious Spanish tyrant and become pirates in order to seek revenge for themselves and others brutalized by the despot. Don Mergowan, Silvana Pampanini and Livio Lorenzon. 81 min.
68-8747 Was $19.99 *$14.99*

Savage Cycles

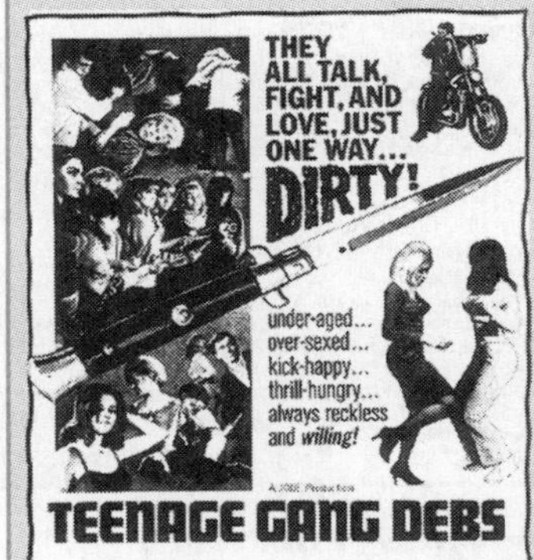

Teenage Gang Debs (1966)
Shot in Brooklyn, this no-budget "teens in trouble" classic follows a conniving female gang member who falls for a fellow J.D. She persuades him to kill the gang's leader, but will the other ruthless toughies discover the murder? Knife fights, rumbles, motorcycles and real gang members are featured, along with Diana Conti and Linda Gale; music by Lee Dowell.
79-5330 Was $24.99 *$19.99*

Wild Rebels (1967)
Rip-snorting look at an ex-stock car driver who helps police bring justice to a group of troublesome motorcycle gang members. Steve Alaimo, Willie Pastrano, Bobbie Byers star. 90 min.
71-5069 *$14.99*

Savages From Hell (1968)
K. Gordon Murray, the importer of kid's flicks from Mexico in the 1960s, produced this brutal story about a creep named High Test, the leader of the Black Angels cycle gang. He kidnaps the sister of a migrant farm worker after he woos the biker's steady gal. With William P. Kelley and Cyril Poitier. AKA: "Big Enough and Old Enough." 79 min.
79-5167 *$19.99*

Cycle Savages (1969)
Chris Robinson is an artist who finds himself on shaky ground when Bruce Dern, the boss of a vicious motorcycle gang running a white slavery ring, wants revenge on Robinson for depicting the gang's crimes in his art. Dern's rage then escalates when he learns that Robinson has taken a liking to his girlfriend in this brutal, action-filled drama. Melody Patterson, Casey Kasem also star. 82 min.
12-3330 *$14.99*

Angel Unchained (1970)
Biker Don Stroud, wandering across the country, is ready to finally settle down when he meets hippie commune member Tyne Daly. But when the neighboring townspeople try to drive the commune out, Stroud calls on his old chopper gang to even the score. With Aldo Ray, Luke Askew. 87 min.
73-1182 *$14.99*

Black Angels (1970)
A rarely seen biker bonanza featuring the Choppers, an African-American gang who essentially play themselves. They encounter racist bikers, corrupt Southern cops, and all sorts of naked bike babes in this action-packed exploiter that stars Des Roberts and Linda Jackson.
79-5959 Was $24.99 *$19.99*

C.C. And Company (1970)
Gridiron legend Joe Namath traded one helmet for another in this savage cycle drama, playing a biker gang leader who must fight rival member William Smith for control of the gang and for lovely hanger-on Ann-Margret. 88 min.
53-1297 Was $19.99 *$14.99*

The Jesus Trip (1971)
A gang of bikers gets more than they bargained for when they hide out from the police in a convent and take a young nun with them as hostage. Exciting and unusual cycle drama stars Robert Porter, Tippy Walker. AKA: "Under Hot Leather." 86 min.
48-1153 *$14.99*

Savage Dawn (1984)
When a small desert town comes under siege by a gang of manic motorcyclists, only a retired special forces Vietnam vet can help save the day. Slam-bang actioner stars George Kennedy, Karen Black and Lance Henriksen. 102 min.
03-1497 *$29.99*

Hellriders (1985)
When an ultra-violent motorcycle gang rides into a small town one morning, you can bet it's not because they're looking for a Holiday Inn. Action-packed biker-townie flick stars Adam West and Tina Louise. 88 min.
19-7025 *$14.99*

Danger Zone III: Steel Horse War (1990)
Harley-riding renegade Jason Williams is back, but in this action-filled tale he may have met his match on the road. An outlaw biker called the Reaper has gathered a gang of toughs in search of hidden treasure in the desert, and the battle between good and evil is on! 91 min.
50-2061 *$79.99*

Running Cool (1993)
When he discovers that a friend in South Carolina is in trouble, a biker joins his cycle club and heads down South to help him. Soon, the cyclist and his pals go head-to-head against a corporate landgrabber and his muscular cronies. Andrew Divoff, Dedee Pfeiffer and Paul Gleason star in this actioner. 106 min.
06-2143 Was $89.99 ◻*$14.99*

Death Riders (1994)
It's a "battle of the bikers" when two cycle-riding adversaries, one good, the other evil, square off in a desert duel that only one will survive. Jason Williams, Robert Brando and Susan Brinkley star. 91 min.
76-9065 Was $19.99 *$14.99*

James Bond

Casino Royale: Collector's Edition (1954)
Ian Fleming's suave super-agent, James Bond, first came to life in this episode from the CBS "Climax!" anthology series, with Barry Nelson as Bond and Peter Lorre as Le Chiffre. Also includes fascinating info on "Casino Royale's" TV and movie versions, original TV ads for the 1967 film, and rare photos and memorabilia presented by 007 expert Lee Pfeiffer. A must for collectors! 70 min.
50-5606 **$19.99**

Dr. No (1962)
The first 007 feature finds Her Majesty's top spy (Sean Connery) investigating mysterious goings-on at a small Jamaican port, where he meets the diabolical Dr. No (Joseph Wiseman) and the first "Bond Bombshell," bikini-clad Honey Rider (Ursula Andress). 111 min.
12-1806 Was $19.99 **$14.99**

From Russia With Love (1963)
Sean Connery's personal favorite of his Bond films is a globe-hopping thriller that pits 007 against Soviet spies and SPECTRE assassins, highlighted by a brutal fight aboard the Orient Express. Robert Shaw, Daniella Bianchi and Lotte Lenya, as blade-booted Rosa Klebb, also star. 118 min.
12-1807 Was $19.99 **$14.99**

Goldfinger (1964)
The quintessential Bond film has it all...Sean Connery, Odd Job and his deadly hat, the beautiful Pussy Galore, the Aston Martin stunt car, John Barry's score and Goldfinger...the man with the plan to irradiate Fort Knox and corner the world's gold market. With Gert Frobe, Honor Blackman, Harold Sakata. 108 min.
12-1808 Was $19.99 **$14.99**

Thunderball (1965)
It's 007 versus SPECTRE when evil agent Largo holds the Bahamas hostage with a nuclear warhead. Sean Connery as Bond must forego his suntan and suit up for an action-packed underwater adventure. Adolfo Celi, Claudine Auger also star. 129 min.
12-1809 Was $19.99 **$14.99**

You Only Live Twice (1967)
"Welcome to Japan, Mr. Bond." Agent 007, played by Sean Connery, is off to the Orient. His mission: smash the evil SPECTRE organization, headed by Blofeld (Donald Pleasence), who plots to incite the world's major powers into war against each other. With Mie Hama, Tetsuro Tamba; scripted by children's author Roald Dahl. 116 min.
12-1810 Was $19.99 **$14.99**

On Her Majesty's Secret Service (1969)
George Lazenby takes over the role as James Bond, Secret Agent 007, in this thrill-a-minute extravaganza. Bond courts contessa Diana Rigg, gets involved in several hair-raising snowbound chases, and matches wits with arch-nemesis Blofeld, played diabolically by Telly Savalas. 140 min.
12-1811 Was $19.99 **$14.99**

Diamonds Are Forever (1971)
Sean Connery returns as James Bond and hits Las Vegas in order to fold the criminal genius Blofeld's diamond-powered extortion scheme. Amazing action scenes include a wild car chase down the Vegas Strip. Co-stars Jill St. John, Charles Gray. 119 min.
12-1812 Was $19.99 **$14.99**

Live And Let Die (1973)
Roger Moore makes his 007 debut, out to smash the plans of Caribbean crime kingpin Yaphet Kotto to take over the U.S. by flooding it with heroin. Wild boat chases, voodoo priests, Jane Seymour as the tarot-dealing love interest and Paul McCartney's title tune highlight this Bond classic. With Geoffrey Holder, Julius Harris. 121 min.
12-1813 Was $19.99 **$14.99**

The Man With The Golden Gun (1975)
James Bond (Roger Moore) may have met his ultimate foe in diabolical master assassin Scaramanga, played to evil perfection by Christopher Lee, in this 007 thriller. With Britt Ekland, Maud Adams, Herve Villechaize. 125 min.
12-1814 **$14.99**

The Spy Who Loved Me (1977)
East meets West, and loves it, when Agent 007 (Roger Moore) teams up with a gorgeous KGB spy (Barbara Bach) to stop a millionaire terrorist from abducting submarines from the superpowers. Spectacular underwater footage, beautiful women, and the first appearance of "Jaws" (Richard Kiel). 125 min.
12-1815 **$14.99**

Moonraker (1979)
The sky's no longer the limit for 007 when Roger Moore, as James Bond, blasts into orbit to bring down an obsessed tycoon with his own space station and a plan for global domination. With Michael Lonsdale, Lois Chiles as Holly Goodhead, and Richard Kiel as "Jaws." 126 min.
12-1816 **$14.99**

For Your Eyes Only (1981)
After "Moonraker," Agent 007 (Roger Moore) returned to terra firma for breathtaking adventures across Europe to retrieve the A.T.A.C. tracking system before it falls into Russian hands, while keeping time with a beautiful young woman (Carole Bouquet) who's out to avenge her parents' murders. Co-stars Topol, Lynn-Holly Johnson; title song performed by Sheena Easton. 128 min.
12-1817 **$14.99**

Octopussy (1983)
Lightning-paced thriller stars Roger Moore as Ian Fleming's superspy, James Bond, this time out to thwart the nefarious efforts of a former Afghan prince and a Russian general to detonate an atomic bomb on an American air base in Berlin. Co-stars Maud Adams, Louis Jourdan, Kristina Wayborn and Steven Berkoff. 130 min.
12-1818 Was $19.99 **$14.99**

Never Say Never Again (1983)
Twelve years after saying "never again," Sean Connery is back as James Bond in a stylish remake of "Thunderball." A little older and wiser, 007 is put back in harness to stop a global extortion plot by SPECTRE's Largo (Klaus Maria Brandauer). Co-stars Kim Basinger and Barbara Carrera. 134 min.
19-1305 Was $19.99 **$14.99**

A View To A Kill (1985)
Has James Bond (Roger Moore) finally met his match in lean, mean female assassin Grace Jones? And if not, will 007 be able to stop high-tech villain Christopher Walken from starting an earthquake that will level California's Silicon Valley? Tanya Roberts co-stars in this action-packed tale that was Moore's series swan song. 131 min.
12-1159 Was $19.99 **$14.99**

The Living Daylights (1987)
Once again, the tuxedo is passed on. Timothy Dalton makes a stylish debut as agent 007, James Bond, in a danger-filled tale of megalomaniacal arms smugglers, Soviet double agents and beautiful cellists. Even the Aston Martin is back! Joe Don Baker, Jeroen Krabbe, Maryam D'Abo co-star. 130 min.
12-2397 Was $19.99 **$14.99**

Licence To Kill (1989)
It's really "license revoked" for James Bond (Timothy Dalton) when he must go against his superiors' orders on a personal vengeance crusade against a Latin American drug kingpin in this dramatic entry in the 007 film saga. Robert Davi, Carey Lowell, Talisa Soto also star. 133 min.
12-2917 **$14.99**

Goldeneye (1995)
The face may be different, but the action, stunts and style are reminiscent of classic 007 outings in Pierce Brosnan's initiation into the James Bond fold. Bond battles Russian mobsters as he tracks down the villians using "leftover" Soviet satellite weapons in a scheme to rob the world's banks. With Sean Bean, Izabella Scorupco, and Famke Janssen as sexy assassin Xenia Onatopp. 130 min.
12-3048 Was $19.99 **$14.99**

Tomorrow Never Dies (1997)
And neither do the adventures of superspy James Bond, as Pierce Brosnan's 007 finds himself going up against megalomaniacal media mogul Jonathan Pryce, who instigates a military incident between England and China as part of his scheme to dominate global communications. Hong Kong action queen Michelle Yeoh co-stars as a Chinese agent who becomes Brosnan's reluctant partner; with Teri Hatcher, Joe Don Baker. 117 min.
12-3233 Was $99.99 **$14.99**

The World Is Not Enough (1999)
There's more than enough action, suspense, chases and sexy women, however, in this James Bond thriller. Charged with protecting a murdered oil tycoon's beautiful daughter, 007 (Pierce Brosnan) must stop a ruthless terrorist—left impervious to pain by a bullet lodged in his skull—who's stolen a Russian nuclear weapon as part of a plan to control the world's oil supply. With Robert Carlyle, Sophie Marceau, Denise Richards, Judi Dench and John Cleese as new gadget man "R." 128 min.
12-3304 **$19.99**

The James Bond Collection
Every fan of the world's most popular secret agent should own this amazing collection of Bond goodies and rarities, featuring Connery, Lazenby, Moore, Dalton and Brosnan. There's trailers galore, plus an early black-and-white intro to the Bond character featuring Sean Connery, behind-the-scenes featurettes and lots, lots more. 120 min. NOTE: The quality of the segments in this video varies, but 007 fans won't want to miss out on this exciting and fun-filled rarity.
50-8374 **$19.99**

The James Bond Story
This is a treat no 007 fan should miss, a gadget- and girl-laden gathering of film clips, interviews and rare footage chronicling the 37-year history of the movies' top superspy. From Connery in "Dr. No" to Brosnan in "The World Is Not Enough," every Bond thriller and actor is featured. 52 min.
53-6760 **$14.99**

The James Bond Collection #1
It's 007 times seven in this boxed collector's set featuring seven classic Bond adventures: "For Your Eyes Only," "Goldeneye," "Goldfinger," Licence to Kill," "Live and Let Die," "Thunderball" and "Tomorrow Never Dies."
12-3282 Save $15.00! **$89.99**

The James Bond Collection #2
The name is Bond...James Bond...and here you can catch him in "Dr. No," "The Man with the Golden Gun," "Moonraker," "On Her Majesty's Secret Service" and "The Spy Who Loved Me," all in a five-tape, boxed collector's set.
12-3310 Save $10.00! **$64.99**

The James Bond Collection #3
Truth be told, most people only live once, so why not live with this money-saving boxed set of six James Bond thrillers: "Diamonds Are Forever," "From Russia with Love," "The Living Daylights," "Octopussy," "A View to a Kill" and "You Only Live Twice"?
12-3323 Save $40.00! **$49.99**

The Mongols (1960)
Large-scale spectacular starring Jack Palance as the son of Genghis Khan whose illicit love affair with rebel beauty Anita Ekberg changes the course of history. Andre de Toth ("House of Wax") directs; the battle scenes are truly impressive. 105 min.
68-8542 **$19.99**

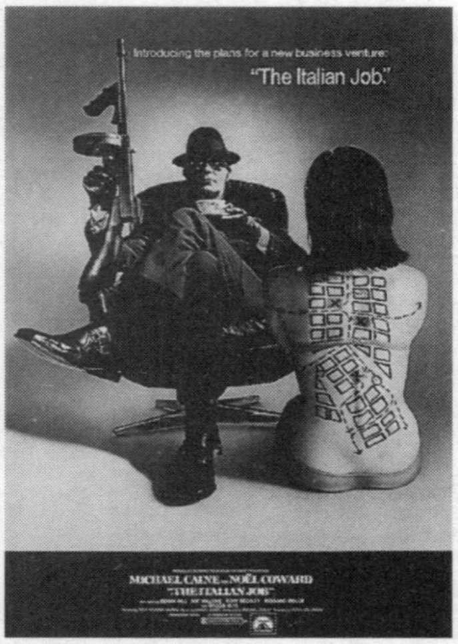

The Italian Job (1969)
Stylish heist yarn starring Michael Caine as the leader of a group of thieves who disguise themselves as football fans to rip off a cache of gold in Turin. Co-stars Noel Coward as the plot's mastermind, Raf Vallone and Benny Hill. Filled with outrageous car chases and stunts. 99 min.
06-1976 **$12.99**

The Drums Of Tabu (1967)
Romantic adventure between a boozy Korean War veteran and a native girl from Fiji who believes that she is off limits to men because of her refusal of a marriage arrangement made by her home island's high priest. With Pietro Ceccarelli, Seyna Seyn, Barta Barri, James Philbrook. 91 min.
55-3013 **$19.99**

Dayton's Devils (1968)
Rory Calhoun, Leslie Nielsen and Lainie Kazan head a group of unlikely thieves who plan a multi-million dollar heist from a U.S. military base in this action-filled thriller. 100 min.
63-5034 **$14.99**

Bloodlust (1961)
A sadistic hunter traps teenage couples on his remote jungle island, then stalks and kills them for pleasure, keeping his gruesome trophies in glass tanks. TV dad Robert Reed appears as one of the hunted, so perhaps this is the answer to the question "Whatever happened to the first Mrs. Brady?" 68 min.
68-8052 **$19.99**

Terror Of The Bloodhunters (1962)
Prison escape adventure about a wrongly condemned French intellectual on Devil's Island who climbs over the frying pan wall and into the fire of Amazon savages. Turgid thrills starring Robert Clarke and Dorothy Haney. 60 min.
68-8406 Was $19.99 **$14.99**

Mask Of The Musketeers (1960)
With five Tarzan pictures behind him, Gordon Scott swung with the Italian film crowd for several years, appearing in this swashbuckler about a masked bandit and a trio of swordsmen who save a French princess. Co-stars Flamenco dancer Jose Greco.
68-8413 **$19.99**

Ali Baba And The Seven Saracens (1964)
Sinbad and his crew enlist the downtrodden subjects of a kingdom ruled by a merciless tyrant in order to overthrow the ruler. Swords fly, Sinbad flexes and gladiator movie fans will delight. With Gordon Mitchell and Don Harrison. AKA: "Hawk of Bagdad." 85 min.
68-8446 **$19.99**

Ali Baba And The Sacred Crown (1962)
Rod Flash Iloosh plays hunky hero Ali Baba in this spectacle that finds him trying to deliver the Sacred Crown of the Desert Kings to a nearby country's ruler who's under the influence of an evil advisor. Ali and pretty Princess Lolo will need some help from the Spirit of Sinbad—and we're not talking the comic here. With Bella Cortez.
79-6040 Was $24.99 **$19.99**

Secret Agent, Super Dragon (1966)
A CIA agent uncovers a diabolical plot by a South American gangster to add lethal drugs to candy and gum and sell it to American college kids. Ray Danton and Marisa Mell star. 95 min.
68-8482 Was $24.99 **$19.99**

Dangerous Charter (1962)
Three fishermen come across an abandoned yacht and claim her, only to find that they have trapped themselves in the nets of an international drug ring. Chris Warfield and Sally Fraser star in a high-excitement high seas adventure! 76 min.
71-5045 **$19.99**

The Sword Of El Cid (1965)
Swordplay extravaganza about the son of a mighty ruler who discovers his uncle has killed his father and, with help from an army from a nearby city, sets out to reclaim his rightful throne. Roland Carey, Sandro Moretti star. 86 min.
68-8746 **$19.99**

River Of Evil (1964)
Thrilling jungle-based tale about a young girl who takes a perilous trip through the Amazon in order to uncover the secret of her father's death. Barbara Rutting, Harold Leipnitz star.
68-8522 **$19.99**

Flight From Singapore (1962)
An air crew travelling over Malaysia with a rare blood plasma crashes in the Asian jungles. It's a race of time for the crew to get through the jungle and save a young girl dying in a hospital. Patrick Allan, Patrick Holt star. 74 min.
68-8519 **$19.99**

The Tartar Invasion (1962)
Romantic adventure featuring Yoko Tani as Prince Steffan, a brave Pole who leads his men against the Tartar invaders of their homeland. After he's captured by his enemies, he tries to settle matters through talk, but his words only have impact on a saucy Tartar princess with whom he falls in love. Ettore Manni, Joe Robinson and Akim Tamiroff also star.
79-6052 Was $24.99 **$19.99**

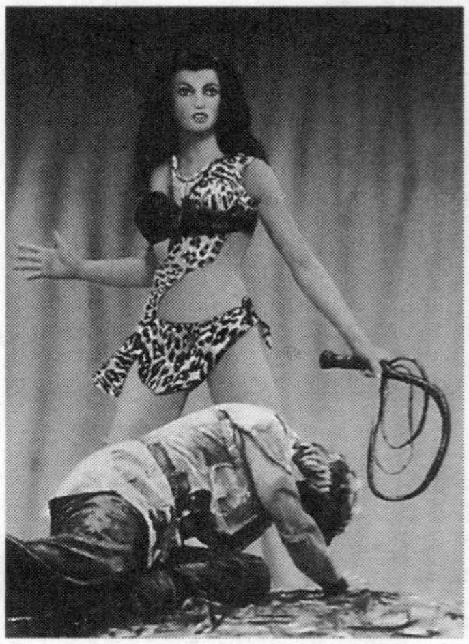

Kilma, Queen Of The Amazons (1965)
A lone shipwrecked sailor is taken prisoner by a tribe of warrior women and becomes the slave of their queen in this brutal adventure thriller. Eva Miller and Claudia Gravy lead the group of gorgeous Amazonian women.
71-1028 **$24.99**

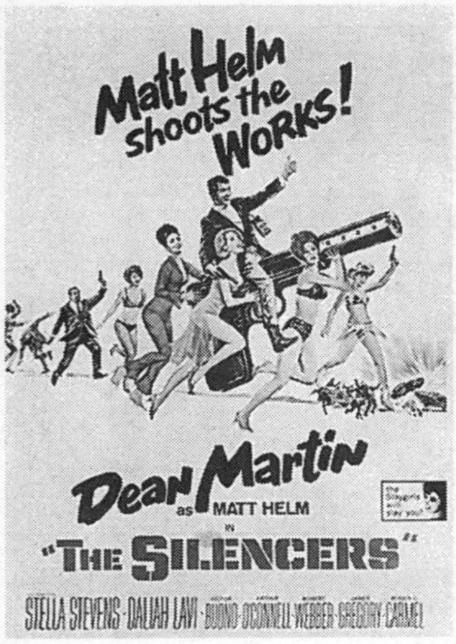
Matt Helm shoots the WORKS!
Dean Martin
as MATT HELM
"THE SILENCERS"
STELLA STEVENS · DALIAH LAVI

The Silencers (1966)
After the success of the James Bond films, Dean Martin swung his way onto the big screen as super-cool secret agent Matt Helm. This debut film in the series finds Martin and klutzy assistant Stella Stevens saving America's nuclear arsenal from Oriental mastermind Victor Buono. With Daliah Lavi, Roger C. Carmel, and Beverly Adams as "Lovey Kravezit." 103 min.
02-2871 *$14.99*

Murderers' Row (1966)
When criminal kingpin Karl Malden threatens to destroy Washington with a hijacked "helio-beam," it's up to ICE agent Matt Helm (Dean Martin) to stop him. Fast-paced follow-up to "The Silencers" also stars Ann-Margret, James Gregory, and Dino, Desi & Billy. 108 min.
02-1050 Was $59.99 *$14.99*

The Ambushers (1968)
Dean Martin, as ace spy and lady-killer Matt Helm, goes to Mexico with a gorgeous female scientist to track down a mysterious flying saucer in this light-hearted spy thriller. With Janice Rule, Senta Berger, Kurt Kasznar. 102 min.
02-1689 *$14.99*

The Wrecking Crew (1968)
The final "Matt Helm" film finds sophisticated super-spy Dean Martin teaming up with sexy sidekick Sharon Tate to track down the criminal genius responsible for a billion-dollar gold hijacking. With Nigel Green, Elke Sommer, Nancy Kwan; look for Chuck Norris, in his film debut, in a bar scene. 105 min.
02-2870 *$14.99*

Matt Helm Gift Set 1
Superspy Dean Martin does double duty with beautiful women and evil villains in this boxed set that includes "The Ambushers" and "Murderer's Row."
02-2872 Save $5.00! *$24.99*

Matt Helm Gift Set 2
Dino wants you to "make it a double" with this action-packed boxed set featuring the Matt Helm thrillers "The Silencers" and "The Wrecking Crew."
02-2962 Save $5.00! *$24.99*

Desert Warrior (1961)
Lively costumer showcasing Ricardo Montalban as an Arabian nobleman who fights for his rightful throne after his sultan father is assassinated. Montalban has his hands full, battling two bad guys, but finds time to fall in love with one of his enemy's pretty daughters. With Carmen Sevilla, Gino Cervi. 90 min.
09-2960 *$19.99*

The Castilian (1963)
Set in 10th-century Spain, this enthralling costume saga centers on a nobleman who leads his followers against an evil king and the Moors who occupy his homeland, with help from the king's beautiful daughter. Colorful spectacle stars Spartaco Santoni, Cesar Romero, Broderick Crawford, Fernando Rey and Frankie Avalon. 129 min.
19-2089 Was $19.99 *$14.99*

Satan's Harvest (1969)
Two-fisted tale stars George Montgomery as an American gumshoe who discovers that the estate he has inherited is being controlled by a group of ruthless dope-smugglers. Tippi Hedren also stars. 104 min.
27-6397 *$14.99*

Samar (1962)
Outstanding adventure stars George Montgomery and Gilbert Roland as two officials so appalled by the cruelties of their Philippine prison system that they lead the inmates to revolt and freedom. 89 min.
27-6441 *$14.99*

Swamp Country (1966)
"Welcome to 'Swamp Country,' where next to lovin' they like fightin' best!" After a mobster's girlfriend is murdered, a hunter becomes the suspect. With the sheriff on his trail, he flees the area and proves himself a swell guy after he saves the sheriff's sister from a panther. And there's music, too! With Rex Allen, Sue Casey and Lyle Waggoner.
30-1036 Was $24.99 *$19.99*

Swords & Sandals

Tharus, Son Of Attila
In this Italian spectacle, brave warrior and son-of-a-Hun Thaurus meets evil head-on when he goes up against the ever-sleazy Prince Cudrum, who not only rules with an iron fist but has secured the hand of lovely Princess Tamal as well. With Jerome Courtland, Lisa Gastoni and Mimmo Palmara.
20-5182 Was $24.99 *$19.99*

Fabiola (1948)
Action-packed epic about the daughter of a Roman senator who converts to Christianity after her father is murdered and receives help from a centurian. Soon, she discovers he is Constantine's secret emissary, and he must engage in battle in the Coliseum to defend her. Michele Morgan, Henri Vidal, Michel Simon star. 96 min.
10-8224 *$19.99*

Sins Of Rome: The Story Of Spartacus (1954)
A valiant gladiator leads a slave revolt against his Roman masters. Italian director Riccardo Freda's boisterous version of the Spartacus story features fine sets and convincing action. Massimo Girotti and Ludmilla Tcherina star.
68-8340 *$19.99*

Roland The Mighty (1958)
He's Roland, Roland, Roland, scourge of western Asia, so hide! A legendary gladiator tames his foes with cruel steel and prodigious pectorals in this Byzantine battle epic starring Rick Battaglia.
68-8332 *$19.99*

Head Of A Tyrant (1959)
Sword, sandals and sadism mix in this lavish adventure about a gorgeous innocent girl who becomes the lover of an Assyrian tyrant who has conquered the city where she lives. She has other plans for her new paramour, though...like cutting off his head! Massimo Girotti and Isabelle Corey star in this Italian production.
68-8873 Letterboxed *$19.99*

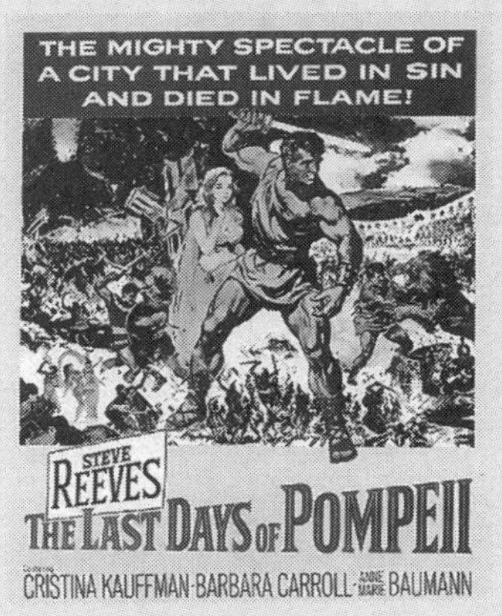
THE MIGHTY SPECTACLE OF A CITY THAT LIVED IN SIN AND DIED IN FLAME!
STEVE REEVES
THE LAST DAYS OF POMPEII
CRISTINA KAUFFMAN · BARBARA CARROLL · BAUMANN

The Last Days Of Pompeii (1960)
Steve Reeves flexes his pecs once more in this epic retelling of the sin and treachery that occurred in the ancient Roman city, under the shadow of the awakening volcano called Vesuvius. Christine Kaufmann, Barbara Carroll also star.
10-2067 Was $24.99 *$19.99*

Thor And The Amazon Women (1960)
Nera, Queen of the Amazons, keeps thousands of beefy men as love slaves for her female warriors and now she's going to get mighty Thor. Joe Robinson stars as the helmeted hero and Suzy Anderson as an ivory-limbed babe. 85 min.
16-9021 *$19.99*

Brennus, Enemy Of Rome (1960)
Rome is attacked by Brennus and his vicious followers. The invader falls in love with a beautiful princess, while holding the city under siege. Gordon Mitchell, Tony Kendell and Ursula Davis star.
68-8543 *$19.99*

Aphrodite, Goddess Of Love (1960)
Set during the reign of Roman emperor Nero, this lavish Italian spectacle centers on a manipulative mistress of a Roman official who uses her seductive powers for revenge against a former lover by persuading the official to persecute Christians. Antonio De Teffe and Isabelle Corey star. In Italian with English subtitles.
68-9248 *$19.99*

The Revolt Of The Slaves (1961)
Rhonda Fleming is Fabiola, the nasty daughter of a Roman aristocrat, who whips a Christian slave after he refuses to partake in a wrestling match. Eventually, she falls in love with the servant and learns of the Christians' hard times in the empire. Lang Jeffries and Gino Cervi also star in this Euro-spectacle. 102 min.
09-5262 *$19.99*

Romulus And Remus (1961)
Musclemen Steve Reeves and Gordon Scott are the siblings raised by wolves whose adventures led to the building of Rome. The brothers fight side by side until they discover they share affections for the daughter of the King of the Sabines. With Virna Lisi. AKA: "Duel of the Titans."
50-5919 Letterboxed *$19.99*

The Invincible Gladiator (1962)
Richard Harrison struts his "cuts" as a brave gladiator helping a 10-year-old king depose a greedy regent. All this, and "the Dwarfs of Death," too! With Isabella Corey. 96 min.
68-8264 *$19.99*

The Son Of Cleopatra (1962)
A sword-and-sandal extravaganza in which El Kabir, the son of Cleopatra and Julius Caesar, leads his Egyptian rebels against Roman oppression. When El Kabir's brother is imprisoned and killed, he kidnaps the daughter of the Roman governor, with whom he falls in love. With Mark Damon, who later became a successful producer, and Scilla Gabel.
79-6049 Was $24.99 *$19.99*

Damon And Pythias (1962)
Guy Williams (Disney's "Zorro") stars in this classic tale from ancient Greece in which he plays Damon, who volunteers himself to die in place of close friend Pythias, who has been accused of plotting the assassination of King Dionysis I. With Don Burnett.
68-9249 *$19.99*

The Centurian (1962)
Ebe, the daughter of an Aegian ruler, falls in love with Vinicius, a Roman centurian wounded in battle. But because of the bad blood between their people and the important suitors they each have, trouble ensues, leading to some nasty battles and problems for the lovers. Jacques Sernas, Genevieve Grad, Gordon Mitchell and John Drew Barrymore star.
79-6093 *$19.99*

Gladiator Of Rome (1963)
Usurpers of the Roman throne imprison the rightful princess and her childhood friend in the dungeons for 14 years. Gaining awesome strength over time, muscleman Gordon Scott frees them and strives to regain the royal birthright. 100 min.
68-8273 *$19.99*

Hero Of Rome (1963)
American bodybuilder Gordon Scott does battle with streams of barbarian scavengers for the honor of the Eternal City. Lithe and lissome Gabriella Pallotta co-stars.
68-8333 *$19.99*

Giants Of Rome (1963)
Spectacular battles highlight this gladiator epic. Rome is menaced by a secret weapon, and the city's top soldiers discover exactly what it is: a big catapult with lots of Gauls. Richard Harrison stars. 98 min.
68-8448 Was $19.99 *$14.99*

Taur The Mighty (1963)
The mighty Taur is out to free a group of young men who have been turned into slaves by an evil emperor. There's some nifty sand-and-sandal action here with battles, brawls and swords. No one's gonna mess with Taur, baby. Joe Robinson, Bella Cortez.
68-8541 *$19.99*

The Three Avengers (1963)
There's three times the action, three times the heroics and three times the beefcake in this costume saga starring screen Hercules Alan Steel as the leader of a trio of adventurers who battle tyranny. With Mimmo Pamera.
68-9094 *$19.99*

The Slave Girls Of Sheba (1963)
A sexy gladiator epic in which the heroic Dimitri attempts to save Japhir, the Captain of the Black Eagle, from death by the tyrant Demitrius. At the same time, a pair of sensuous slave girls get involved in the proceedings. Jose Suarez, Linda Cristal and Cristina Grasoni star; co-written by Sergio Leone!
79-6002 Was $24.99 *$19.99*

Sword Of Damascus (1963)
Comedy and adventure mix as thief Tony Russel swindles most of the denizens of Damascus until he meets the loveliest gal around. When she is captured because of his antics, he frees her, but soon finds himself in hot water when he uses his gift of magic to help rebels fighting Roman soldiers. Luciana Gilli and Gianni Solaro also star.
79-6056 Was $24.99 *$19.99*

Colossus And The Amazon Queen (1964)
A duo of beefy gladiators fresh from the Trojan War are bamboozled into sailing for a secret island, captured by lusty Amazons, and kept as walking sperm banks. Rod Taylor and Ed Fury star in this titillating sheets-and-shackles adventure. 94 min.
09-2079 *$19.99*

Terror Of The Steppes (1964)
Is it Slinky, Toy from Hell? No, but just as fearsome: a bloody tyrant closes his grip on slave girls and dirt farmers until muscleman Kirk Morris puts a kink in his coils. Moira Orfei co-stars.
68-8335 *$19.99*

Two Gladiators (1964)
After Roman Emperor Marcus Aurelius dies, a senator of the Tribune attempts to find the twin brother of the cruel, new emperor. The plan is to have the level-headed sibling take his brother's place, but there are several hurdles to leap before that can occur. Richard Harrison, Moira Ortel star.
68-9250 *$19.99*

The Avenger (1964)
The majestically muscular Steve Reeves slings a lot of bull (literally) in this action-filled tale of a fight for freedom between Etruscan slavedrivers and oppressed Trojans. The bull stampede is not to be missed. AKA: "The Last Glory of Troy." 100 min.
10-2104 *$14.99*

Lion Of Thebes (1964)
This lion's not cowardly. He's actually heroic Mark Forrest, who in this gladitorial saga helps save lovely Helen of Troy from a shipwreck and accompanies her to the city of Thebes, where they find themselves embroiled in court intrigue and conspiracies (proving that there's no honor among Thebes). With Yvonne Furneaux. 88 min.
68-8450 Was $19.99 *$14.99*

Coriolanus, Man Without A Country (1964)
Former Tarzan Gordon Scott leads the Plebians against the evil Roman senate in this gladiator spectacular boasting muscular heroics and expert battle scenes. Alberto Lupo and Lilla Brignone also star.
68-8539 *$19.99*

Revolt Of The Barbarians (1964)
Rome wasn't robbed in a day. At least that's what a gladiator discovers when he learns that the Governor of Gaul is cheating Rome of gold shipments. (Political corruption was rampant centuries before Watergate.) Roland Carey and Gerardo Marini star.
68-8540 *$19.99*

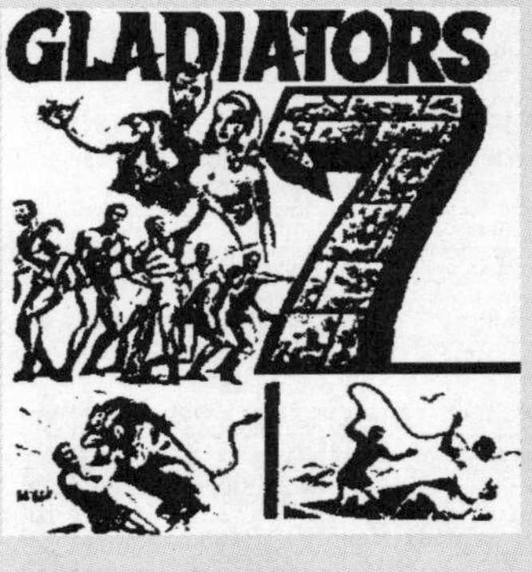
GLADIATORS 7

Gladiators 7 (1964)
Thrilling Imperial Rome opus plays like "The Magnificent Seven in Togas," as seven brave soldiers go up against the cruel tyrants who have been controlling the city of Sparta. When gladiator leader Richard Harrison saves the princess, he gets a "Sparta kiss." With Loredana Nusciak, Livio Lorenzon. 92 min.
68-8737 *$19.99*

Challenge Of The Gladiator (1964)
While Nero rules over his corrupt empire, rebel slave Spartacus saves the day with a revolt. Rock Stevens, Gloria Milland star in this spectacle that'll make you say "I love you, Spartacus."
68-9120 *$19.99*

Triumph Of The Ten Gladiators (1964)
Muscleman fave Dan Vadis leads an army of beefy gladiators into a mission that has them kidnapping a queen. When they discover they've been duped, the men try to change things by battling it out in a series of wild fights (and by, in one scene, disguising themselves as women and flirting with guards!). Truly, this is no mere status quo Vadis. With Stanley Kent, John Heston.
79-6120 *$19.99*

The Viking Queen (1967)
Finnish beauty Carita is the titular character, a scantily-clad Nordic queen who teams with Roman governor Don Murray to keep peace between the Vikings and British tribes. The two leaders fall in love, but a Roman officer sneakily begins calling the shots and captures Carita, starting a war between the different factions. With Adrienne Cori and Donald Houston. 91 min.
08-8720 Letterboxed *$14.99*

Warrior Queen (1987)
Sybil Danning brandishes a lethal sword—and a body to match—in the decadent city of Pompeii, as the Roman emperor's mistress who fights valiantly to rescue a young girl from a den of iniquity. Also stars Donald Pleasance and Penthouse Pet Tally Chanel. 79 min.
47-2133 *$14.99*

Hercules And The Masked Rider (1964)
Suave nobleman Don Juan returns home from a war to find that his beautiful cousin is about to wed a powerful, corrupt neighbor just to keep the local peace. In order to stop the marriage (and because he has the hots for his cousin as well), Don Juan dons a red mask and teams with a Gypsy woman and a strongman named Hercules. Pseudo-Herculean costume drama stars Alan Steel, Mimmo Palmara and Arturo Dominici.
79-6046 Was $24.99 ***$19.99***

Revenge Of The Conquered (1964)
Dracu, the son of a Gypsy queen, saves a beautiful woman from a Gypsy raid. Neither reveals their past—she's the daughter of a prince—but it comes back to haunt them when his mother is tortured and burned at the stake after being accused of murder. Will their love survive all of the bad blood between their ancestors? With Wandisa Guida and Burt Nelson.
79-6048 Was $24.99 ***$19.99***

A Ticket To Die (1966)
I think we're all gonna die. I think it's today, yeah. A madman with nuclear weapons will blow us away, yeah. That is, unless a top secret agent can punch his ticket in time in this tense thriller. Lewis Jordan, Helene Chanel star. AKA: "Regreso de un Espia." 84 min.
76-5002 ***$19.99***

The Hellfire Club (1963)
Thrilling swordplay highlights this epic set in 18th-century England, where the son of the leader of the notorious Hellfire Club returns home years after fleeing as a child to reclaim his father's estate, but crosses swords with his evil cousin. Keith Michell, Adrienne Corri and Peter Cushing star. 88 min.
68-8745 ***$19.99***

The Last Of The Vikings (1961)
Rousing Nordic adventure about two Viking siblings who band together to combat an evil warlord who has taken over their homeland. There's action galore in store with Cameron Mitchell and Edmund Purdom.
68-8886 ***$19.99***

Blazing Sand (1969)
A hot-blooded Israeli beauty holds the key to the Middle East, as she attempts to rescue the legendary Scrolls of Solomon from a group of terrorists. Dahlia Lavi and Gert Hoffman star in this riveting actioner as real as today's headlines. 95 min.
79-1000 Was $24.99 ***$19.99***

Sword Of The Rebellion (1964)
The bitter rivalry between evil Duke Alberto and Count Marco gets nastier when the Duke's niece falls for Marco after he kidnaps and later releases her. There's plenty of exciting swordplay, dangerous double-dealing, and romantic twists in this costume saga. Gerard Landry, Annie Alberti star.
79-6051 Was $24.99 ***$19.99***

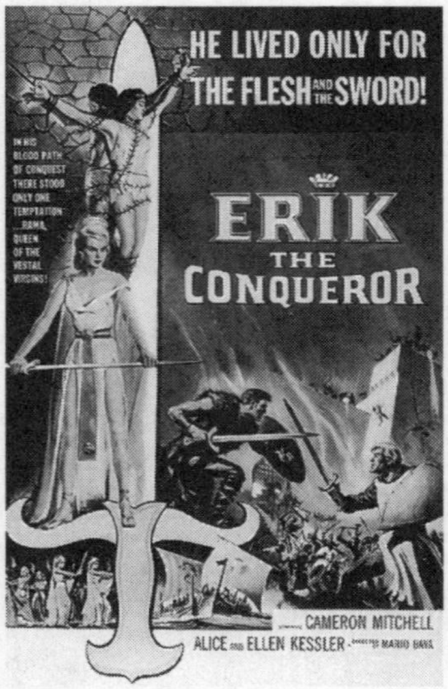

Erik The Conquerer (1963)
Two brothers, separated at birth, find themselves as adults fighting on opposite sides in a deadly struggle between English and Viking forces for control of the seas. Rousing costume actioner from horror director Mario Bava stars Cameron Mitchell, Giorgio Ardisson. AKA: "The Invaders," "Fury of the Vikings."
68-9228 ***$19.99***

Knives Of The Avenger (1965)
Mario Bava's follow-up to his Norseman saga "Erik the Conqueror" presents Cameron Mitchell as a stranger who bravely saves the wife of a Viking leader, then faces off against a warrior who beheaded his wife and children. Fausto Tozzi and Elissa Picelli also star in this colorful, violence-strewn epic. AKA: "Bladestorm," "The Viking Massacre."
50-8400 ***$19.99***

Never Love A Stranger (1958)
Based on the novel by Harold Robbinse (who co-scripted and produced), this compelling gangster drama stars John Drew Barrymore as an embittered, orphaned delinquent who falls in with mobsters and goes on become the ruthless head of a crime syndicate. With Lita Milan, Robert Bray and Steve McQueen in his first featured role. 91 min.
63-1122 ***$19.99***

The Great St. Louis Bank Robbery (1959)
In an early film role, Steve McQueen plays a former football hero who is talked into becoming the getaway driver in an elaborate bank heist scheme that inevitably comes apart. Based on a true story, this drama features the actual police and bank customers involved in the hold-up. With David Clarke, Molly McCarthy. 88 min.
55-9013 Was $29.99 ***$19.99***

The Magnificent Seven (1960)
Star-studded cowboy classic based on the Japanese favorite "The Seven Samurai." Gunslinger Yul Brynner, at the request of Mexican peasants, recruits a band of his fellow mercenaries (Charles Bronson, Horst Buchholz, James Coburn, Brad Dexter, Steve McQueen and Robert Vaughn) to defend their town from bandit Eli Wallach and his gang. Directed by John Sturges. 126 min.
12-1766 Was $19.99 ***$14.99***

The Magnificent Seven (Letterboxed Version)
Also available in a theatrical, widescreen format.
12-3141 ***$14.99***

The Honeymoon Machine (1961)
Fast-paced comedy stars Steve McQueen and Jack Mullaney as two naval officers stationed off the Italian coast who team up with civilian computer whiz Jim Hutton to figure out a way to win at roulette at the Lido casino. With Brigid Bazlen, Paula Prentiss, Dean Jagger. 88 min.
12-2568 ***$19.99***

The War Lover (1962)
Steve McQueen stars as a reckless WWII pilot in England who must compete with rival Robert Wagner for air supremacy, as well as the love of Shirley Anne Field. Exciting war drama with spectacular aerial scenes. 105 min.
02-2608 ***$14.99***

Hell Is For Heroes (1962)
An exhausted, outnumbered American infantry squad is charged with defending a frontline against the Germans in this top-notch WWII drama from director Don Siegel. Steve McQueen, Fess Parker, James Coburn, Bobby Darin, Nick Adams and Bob Newhart lead the company into battle. 90 min.
06-1707 ***$14.99***

The Great Escape (1963)
One of the greatest war films ever made! Steve McQueen is unforgettable as "the Cooler King," leading Allied prisoners in a daring escape from a German POW camp. James Garner, Richard Attenborough, Charles Bronson, James Coburn also star in this superior effort, noted for McQueen's daring motorcycle jump and Elmer Bernstein's triumphant score. 172 min.
12-1825 Was $29.99 ***$24.99***

The Great Escape (Letterboxed Version)
Also available in a theatrical, widescreen format.
12-3080 ***$24.99***

Baby, The Rain Must Fall (1964)
Powerhouse drama stars Steve McQueen as a brawling, guitar-pickin' ex-con who tries to start over with his wife and daughter, but runs into one roadblock after another. With Lee Remick, Don Murray, Paul Fix. 100 min.
02-2538 ***$19.99***

The Cincinnati Kid (1965)
Kid's got 'em. Norman Jewison's acclaimed character study of a young upstart poker player stars Steve McQueen as "the Kid," who sets out to prove he knows his way around the tables, and Edward G. Robinson as the current poker king whose reign is in jeopardy. Co-stars Karl Malden, Ann-Margret, Rip Torn, Tuesday Weld. 104 min.
12-1235 ***$14.99***

Nevada Smith (1966)
The half-breed hero of "The Carpetbaggers" is brought to vivid life by Steve McQueen in this fine Western adventure. Nevada is determined to track down the slayers of his parents and exact his vengeance. Karl Malden, Suzanne Pleshette, Brian Keith, Arthur Kennedy co-star. 135 min.
06-1376 ***$14.99***

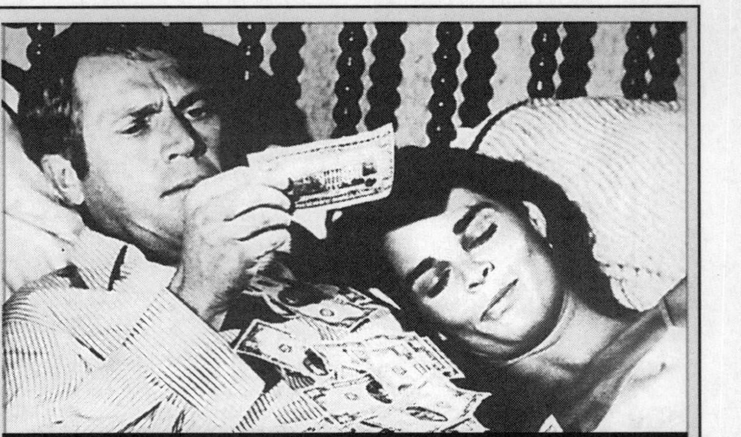
The Getaway

Steve McQueen

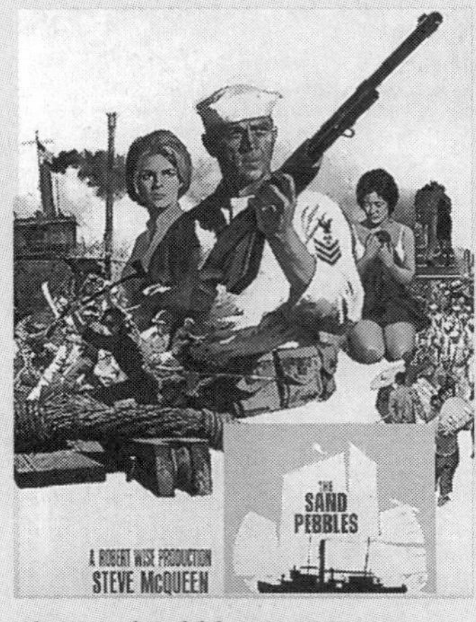

The Sand Pebbles (1966)
A U.S. gunboat stationed in 1920s China is used in a power game between rival warlords in this sprawling adventure saga. Steve McQueen stars as a sailor who must buck his superiors when he sees their mission being endangered. Co-stars Richard Crenna, Candice Bergen, Richard Attenborough. 179 min.
04-1136 ***$29.99***

The Thomas Crown Affair (1968)
Slick, sophisticated romantic caper film starring Steve McQueen as a cool Boston millionaire who masterminds a bank heist, then carries on a torrid romance with beautiful insurance investigator Faye Dunaway. Highlighted by inventive camerawork, chic surroundings and the Oscar-winning song "The Windmills of Your Mind." With Jack Weston, Paul Burke and Yaphet Kotto; directed by Norman Jewison. 102 min.
12-2192 Was $19.99 ***$14.99***

Bullitt (1968)
Steve McQueen stars as a tough, system-bucking police lieutenant who's assigned the task of guarding a government witness set to testify against syndicate bosses. After his charge is killed by two hit men, McQueen embarks on a death-defying car chase through the streets of San Francisco. With Robert Vaughn, Robert Duvall and Jacqueline Bisset; directed by Peter Yates. 114 min.
19-1022 ***$19.99***

The Getaway (1972)
Director Sam Peckinpah's exciting, violent thriller stars Steve McQueen as a Texas ex-con hired by the political boss who arranged for his parole to take part in a bank robbery. The heist falls apart and McQueen, realizing he was set up, flees with the loot and wife Ali McGraw on a run for the Mexican border. With Ben Johnson, Al Lettieri, Sally Struthers. 123 min.
19-1270 Was $19.99 ***$14.99***

Junior Bonner (1972)
A departure for director Sam Peckinpah is this character study of a one-time rodeo star (Steve McQueen) who returns home to re-enter the circuit, thereby gaining self-esteem and rejuvenating his alcoholic father. McQueen and Robert Preston, as his father, are equally great. 101 min.
04-3121 ***$14.99***

Junior Bonner (Letterboxed Version)
Also available in a theatrical, widescreen format.
08-8642 ***$14.99***

Papillon (1973)
A grand (and true) adventure story and a Movies Unlimited favorite. Steve McQueen stars as French thief Henri "Papillon" (French for "butterfly") Charriere, who is imprisoned in South America and repeatedly breaks out, and is finally sent to "inescapable" Devil's Island. Dustin Hoffman co-stars as a fellow prisoner; with Anthony Zerbe, Victor Jory. 150 min.
19-2585 ***$19.99***

Papillon (Letterboxed Version)
Also available in a theatrical, widescreen format.
19-2576 ***$19.99***

Tom Horn (1980)
Steve McQueen stars in a real-life Western adventure as a middle-aged bounty hunter trying to come to grips with the changing face of the early 20th-century West. Linda Evans, Richard Farnsworth, Slim Pickens also star. 98 min.
19-1016 ***$14.99***

The Hunter (1980)
Steve McQueen's last movie casts him as real-life bounty hunter Ralph "Papa" Thorson, trailing criminals on the run from the law. Action, great chases and a strong performance from McQueen make this one a winner. Ben Johnson, Kathryn Harrold, LeVar Burton. 94 min.
06-1078 ***$14.99***

Steve McQueen: Man Behind The Wheel
Actor Steve McQueen's love for cars is chronicled in this thrilling program that includes scenes from "Le Mans" and "Bullitt," two of his films that featured incredible chase and racing footage.
10-8372 Was $19.99 ***$14.99***

Steve McQueen: Man On The Edge
He went from reform schools to the top of the Hollywood heap, rebellious all the way. Here's the inside story of Steve McQueen, filled with clips from his greatest films and comments from his first wife, his children, Chuck Norris and Karl Malden. 60 min.
50-6794 Was $19.99 ***$14.99***

Please see our index for these other Steve McQueen titles: *The Blob • Love With The Proper Stranger • Never So Few • Somebody Up There Likes Me • The Towering Inferno*

Terror Of The Red Mask (1964)
Former screen Tarzan Lex Barker swashes and buckles his way through this adventure yarn, playing a mercenary who offers his service to a treacherous official running a country until his niece is old enough to rule. When Barker realizes the official is into evil, he joins forces with a Gypsy woman and a local vigilante to stop him. With Chelo Alonso.
79-6053 Was $24.99 ***$19.99***

Dark Of The Sun (1968)
Superb action-adventure set in the Congo in the '50s and starring Rod Taylor as a mercenary who accepts a mission to ferry a train with fugitives and a cache of diamonds through rebel-held territory in three days. Filled with expertly-staged action scenes, this gritty film also stars Jim Brown, Yvette Mimieux and Kenneth More. 101 min.
12-2923 ***$19.99***

Swords Without A Country (1967)
When Chino, a simple page boy, is accused of murdering the fiancé of Giniolla, his lover, a woman who was adopted into nobility. The accusation leads the lovers to the hills, where Chino leads freedom fighters against the oppressive noblemen. Leonora Ruffo and Renato Speziali star in this romantic adventure yarn.
79-6156 ***$19.99***

The Violent Patriot (1962)
A violent epic with Vittorio Gassman as a nasty mercenary who believes a war still exists between Italy and France after his friend is murdered by conspirators. A romance with a young woman seems to settle him down a bit, but when she discovers Gassman's background, trouble begins. Anna Mario and Gerard Landry also star in this fine costumer.
79-6054 Was $24.99 **$19.99**

Cleopatra's Daughter (1960)
Debra Paget is Shila, Cleopatra's daughter, who has been brought back to Egypt from Syria to marry a psychotic young king named Nemorat. Shila is blamed for the king's death, but, as she awaits execution, her physician lover concocts an escape plan. Filmed in 1960 but released in 1963 following the Taylor-Burton epic, the film also stars Robert Alda. AKA: "Daughter of Cleopatra."
79-6160 **$19.99**

Adventures In Indochina (1965)
Filmed on location in South Vietnam, this adventure saga tells of four Westerners living in Saigon who are offered $500 each to join an expedition into the jungle where they are slated to dig for gold. Danger awaits them on their thrill-filled odyssey. Dominique Wilms, Jean Gaven star.
79-6143 **$19.99**

The Glass Sphinx (1968)
A famed archeologist travels to Egypt to find a legendary glass sphinx which contains an elixir that guarantees immortality. Joined by his niece and a journalist on his trek, the archeologist finds himself seduced by his secretary—played by Anita Ekberg (grrr-owl)—and facing all sorts of dangerous situations. Robert Taylor, in his last role, stars.
79-6148 **$19.99**

The Shoot (1964)
A ruthless villain named "the Shoot" brings terror to the constituents of a Middle Eastern country he rules. Trying to stop him is good guy (and screen Tarzan) Lex Barker and his comic sidekick. With Chris Howland and Rick Battaglia; directed by Robert Siodmak ("Criss Cross").
79-6155 **$19.99**

Blood On His Sword (1961)
Period adventure yarn in which lovely Lady Jeanne is whisked away by the powerful Duke of Burgundy, much to the dismay of her true love, dashing knight Robert de Neville. De Neville attempts to save the lady, but the Duke's plan to take the throne of France may put a wrench in his rescue plans. Jean Marais, Rosanna Schiaffano stars.
79-6159 **$19.99**

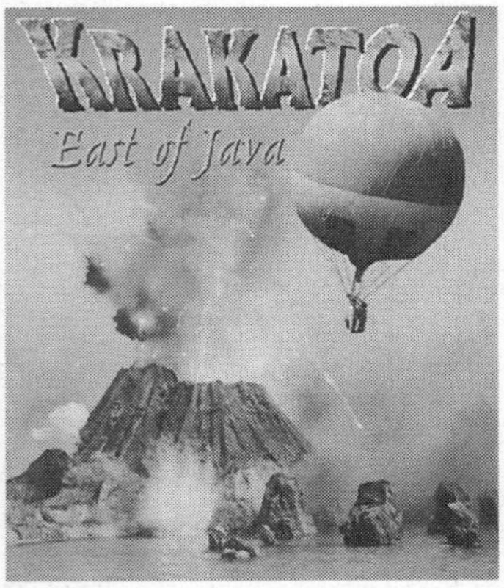

Krakatoa, East Of Java (1969)
In the year 1882, a disparate group of treasure seekers races against time to locate a sunken ship loaded with pearls off the Indonesian coast before the volcanic island of Krakatoa (which, as all you geography buffs know, was really *west* of Java) erupts into one of the biggest natural explosions of all time. Thrilling adventure saga stars Maximilian Schell, Diane Baker, Brian Keith, Sal Mineo and J.D. Cannon. 128 min.
78-3041 Was $19.99 **$14.99**

Krakatoa, East Of Java (Letterboxed Collector's Edition)
Also available in a theatrical, widescreen format.
08-8708 **$14.99**

The Revenge Of The Black Eagle (1965)
Opulent adventure yarn featuring Rossano Brazzi as a bandit-turned-colonel who returns home to Russia after the Crimean War to find his life in shambles: an evil governor has turned the Czar against him, killing his wife and kidnapping his son. Revenge leads Brazzi to kidnap the governor's sister, whom he falls for. Giana Maria Canale co-stars.
79-6152 **$19.99**

Treasure Of The Aztecs (1965)
This film is an edited version of the three hour-long epic that was actually "Treasure of the Aztecs" and "Pyramid of the Sun" spliced together. Lex Barker plays Dr. Sternau, the heroic leader of a group of men trying to help Mexican leader Juarez against the French by finding the legendary treasure of the Incas. Rik Battaglia also stars; Robert Siodmak ("The Killers") directs.
79-6498 **$19.99**

The Desert Renegades (1966)
Genres clash entertainingly in this wild adventure focusing on a swashbuckler named Aldar in the Middle East in the 1930s. Involvement in weapons hijacking leads Aldar into the middle of a desert war and into the arms of a beautiful princess. Robert Hoffman, Marilu Tolo and Pepe Calvo star.
79-6543 Was $24.99 **$19.99**

Dangerous Exile (1957)
Exciting, colorful historical adventure showcasing Louis Jourdan as a nobleman during the French Revolution who befriends the son of Louis XVI and Marie Antoinette after they are beheaded. While serving as a mentor to the 10-year-old, Jourdan falls in love with his benefactor. With Belinda Lee and Keith Michell. 90 min.
10-9507 **$14.99**

Ivanhoe (1952)
A vivid and panoramic portrayal of medieval England was brought forth from Sir Walter Scott's historical romance. Robert Taylor stars as Sir Wilfred of Ivanhoe, the loyal knight in service to King Richard the Lionhearted, who battles fiercely to return the king to the throne, despite the machinations of evil Prince John. Co-stars Elizabeth Taylor, Joan Fontaine, George Sanders. 107 min.
12-1091 **$19.99**

Ivanhoe (1982)
The renowned tale of chivalry and romance in medieval England comes to life in a dramatic rendition. Anthony Andrews is the young knight who comes back from the Crusades to find his true love betrothed to another and the throne in danger. Co-stars Olivia Hussey, James Mason. 142 min.
02-1606 Was $19.99 **$14.99**

Ivanhoe (1997)
Filmed on location in England and Scotland, this lavish BBC adaptation of Sir Walter Scott's historical adventure novel stars Steven Waddington in the title role of the noble knight battling for King Richard (and for the woman he loves) in 12th-century England. With Susan Lynch, Rory Edwards and Ralph Brown as scheming Prince John. 300 min. on two tapes.
53-8892 Was $59.99 **$39.99**

Desert Detour (1958)
The endless sands are the setting for a deadly duel between two foes, with the hand of a beautiful princess and a valuable Uranium mine the prizes, in this thrilling action yarn. Omar Sharif, Jean-Claude Pascal, Gianna Marie Canale star.
68-9232 **$19.99**

Prince Valiant (1954)
The comic strip hero comes alive. Robert Wagner plays the young prince with the wild bangs who falls for lovely Princess Aleta (Janet Leigh) while battling the evil Black Knight during the days of old Camelot. Thrilling, colorful tale co-starring James Mason, Debra Paget and Sterling Hayden. 100 min.
04-2447 **$14.99**

Prince Valiant (1997)
Return to the action, intrigue and magic of Arthurian England with this exciting feature based on Hal Foster's classic adventure comic strip. Young Prince Valiant (Stephen Moyer) teams up with a beautiful, fiery princess (Katherine Heigl) as they battle Viking warriors and the evil sorcery of Morgan Le Fey (Joanna Lumley). With Ron Perlman, Edward Fox. 100 min.
04-3677 ❏**$99.99**

Flame Of Araby (1951)
Arab princess Maureen O'Hara and Bedouin warrior Jeff Chandler compete to capture a prized black stallion—and wind up falling in love in the process—in this lush costume adventure saga. With Lon Chaney, Jr., Buddy Baer, Maxwell Reed. 78 min.
07-2493 **$14.99**

East Of Kilimanjaro (1959)
Marshall Thompson ("Daktari") and real-life hunter Kris Aschan star as two men in an African game preserve who must battle a rare plague and poachers to save the animals. Exciting family adventure.
30-1035 **$14.99**

The Adventurers (1950)
Terrific British adventure yarn in the mold of "The Treasure of the Sierra Madre" starring Jack Hawkins as a Boer War commando who joins forces with three other men to search for gems he buried in South Africa. Greed eventually gets the better part of the men during their dangerous expedition. With Peter Hammond, Dennis Price and Bernard Lee. 82 min.
10-9473 **$19.99**

Mutiny (1952)
Tremendous period adventure, set during the War of 1812, follows a group of American patriots attempting to run the British naval blockade to obtain needed bullion from France. High seas excitement with Mark Stevens, Angela Lansbury, Patric Knowles. 77 min.
64-3054 Was $19.99 **$14.99**

Northwest Frontier (1959)
Thrilling adventure set in rural India, as British forces commandeer a run-down train in order to save a Maharajah's son from Moslem rebels. Kenneth More stars as the Army officer leading the desperate race, and Lauren Bacall is the boy's governess. With Wilfrid Hyde-White, Herbert Lom. AKA: "Flame Over India." 128 min.
53-1013 Was $19.99 **$14.99**

Battles Of Chief Pontiac (1952)
Set in the British occupied wilderness of 1700s Northwest America, this fast-paced actioner stars Lex Barker as a frontiersman who negotiates a peace between the Redcoats and Indian chief Lon Chaney, Jr. When a treacherous officer scuttles the treaty and war erupts, Barker must choose sides. With Helen Westcott, Berry Kroeger. 75 min.
08-1827 ❏**$14.99**

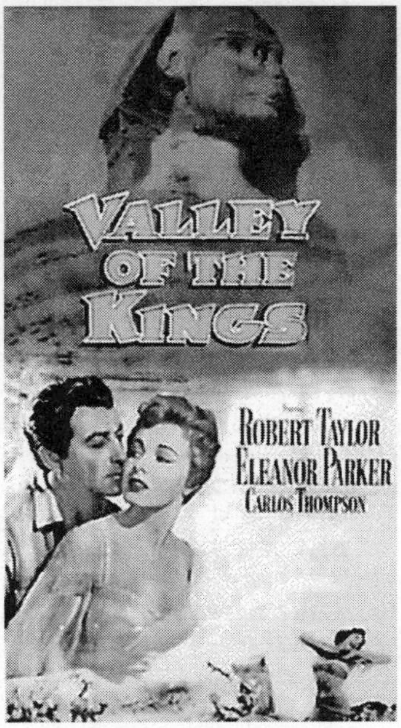

Valley Of The Kings (1954)
Adventure and romance mix on an archeological dig in 1900s Egypt for Robert Taylor, Carlos Thompson and Eleanor Parker, who must cope with desert bandits, as well as a deadly love triangle that grows between the trio, in this exciting action tale that features thrilling location scenery. With Victor Jory, Kurt Kasznar. 86 min.
12-3043 ❏**$19.99**

Sea Fury (1959)
Exciting maritime drama set on a salvage vessel where captain Victor McLaglen and first mate Stanley Baker are pitted in a fight for control of the boat and the heart of lovely landlubber Luciana Paluzzi. 97 min.
58-8040 **$12.99**

King Solomon's Mines (1937)
The classic story of action, danger and fabulous wealth in the wilds of darkest Africa stars Cedric Hardwicke as adventurer Allan Quartermain, with support from Paul Robeson (who sings in the film), Roland Young and Anna Lee. 89 min.
10-1142 **$19.99**

King Solomon's Mines (1950)
One of the greatest jungle adventure films ever made, this grand adaptation of the H. Rider Haggard novel stars Stewart Granger as rugged Allan Quartermain, leading Deborah Kerr and Richard Carlson on a search for a fabled diamond mine deep in the African wilderness. 102 min.
12-1950 **$19.99**

King Solomon's Treasure (1976)
Treasure hunter Allan Quartermain (David McCallum) sets out in search of the lost city of King Solomon in this adventure saga filled with fabulous treasures, prehistoric monsters and erupting volcanoes. Patrick Macnee, Britt Ekland co-star. 90 min.
08-1274 **$14.99**

King Solomon's Mines (1985)
Richard Chamberlain stars as daredevil soldier of fortune Allan Quartermain in this classic tale of breathtaking adventures and split-second escapes. Sharon Stone, Herbert Lom co-star. 101 min.
12-1551 **$14.99**

The Americano (1955)
An American cowboy sent to Brazil to deliver a herd of cattle becomes involved in a deadly feud between ranchers and settlers in this transposed frontier actioner directed by William Castle. Glenn Ford, Cesar Romero, Frank Lovejoy star. 85 min.
63-1099 **$14.99**

Riot In Cell Block 11 (1954)
"Untouchable" bad guys Neville Brand and Leo Gordon star in this riveting prison drama. A single act of violence sparks the revolt, and before long the police and press stand by waiting as the prisoners plan their next move. 80 min.
63-1128 **$19.99**

Mission In Morocco (1959)
After one of his employees is murdered in the Sahara, oil company executive Lex Barker searches for stolen microfilm that reveals the location of precious oil fields. He discovers the Middle Eastern renegades have taken the microfilm, and it's up to him to get it back. Juli Reding co-stars. 79 min.
63-1379 Was $19.99 **$14.99**

The Shadow Of The Eagle (1950)
Empress Catherine the Great of Russia hires an assassin to kill Princess Tarakanova, but when the assassin falls in love with the princess he takes off with her and goes into hiding. The couple must elude the Empress's forces in order to survive. Richard Greene, Valentina Cortesa, Binnie Barnes star. 93 min.
10-8453 Was $19.99 **$14.99**

The Devil's Cavaliers (1958)
After an evil duke causes trouble in the kingdom, a small group of fighters takes it upon themselves to stop him. Frank Latimore, Gianna Canale star. 92 min.
09-5040 **$19.99**

Captain Scarlett (1953)
Richard Greene duels and romances in this action film set in 19th-century France. A nobleman becomes the mysterious Captain to protect citizens from the tyrannical Royalists. With Leonora Amar. 75 min.
59-5024 **$19.99**

The Devil On Wheels (1947)
A teenager takes to the streets, racing hot rods and getting into trouble, after being "inspired" by his father's reckless driving habits. Darryl Hickman, Noreen Nash and Jan Ford star in this rip-roaring youth-in-trouble epic. 67 min.
68-8889 **$19.99**

The Fast And The Furious (1954)
On the run from a bogus murder rap, John Ireland steals a Jaguar with owner Dorothy Malone still inside and joins a Pebble Beach road race to slip across the border. Roger Corman wrote and produced this feature, one of the first releases from AIP. 73 min.
68-8342 Was $19.99 **$14.99**

Hot Rod Girl (1956)
In an attempt to curb teenage drag racing in his town, policeman Chuck Connors sets up a supervised racetrack, but the accidental death of a boy threatens the lives of all involved in this early "teen drama." Mark Andrews, Lori Nelson star. 79 min.
10-2143 **$14.99**

T-Bird Gang (1959)
Exploitation mogul Roger Corman co-produced this Coupe D'Evil about a clean-cut kid who joins a hot-rodding gang to snare his father's killers. Stars Ed Nelson, John Brinkley; music by jazz great Shelley Manne. 75 min.
68-8409 **$19.99**

Wild Ones On Wheels (1962)
Youths in trouble! Cool cars riding fast! Buried treasure! Beautiful babes! They're all here in a story about a gang of sports car enthusiasts who kill a crook, then force his wife to find $240,000 in stolen loot stashed in the desert. Francine York, Edmund Tontini and Robert Blair star. AKA: "Drivers to Hell." 92 min.
68-8751 **$19.99**

Speed Lovers (1968)
The son of a race track mechanic gets into the octane groove and sets out to make a name for himself on the Daytona speedway. David Marcus, Peggy O'Hara and Fred Lorenzen as himself star; music is supplied by Billy Lee Riley of "Red Hot" fame. 102 min.
79-5336 Was $24.99 **$19.99**

Thunder Alley (1967)
Stock car racer Fabian is forced to retire after a blackout on the track leads to the death of another driver. Taking a job with Jan Murray's "thrill circus," he teaches Annette Funicello and boyfriend Warren Berlinger to race, but when Fabian's old girlfriend causes friction between the trio, he must get back behind the wheel and overcome his affliction in this rubber-burning thriller from director Richard Rush ("The Stunt Man"). 90 min.
12-3331 **$14.99**

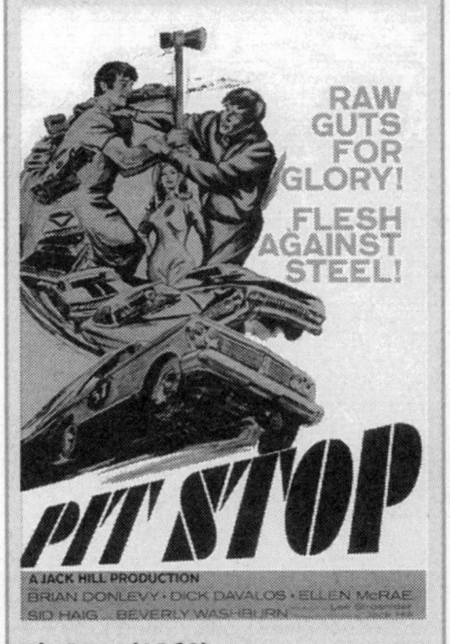

Pit Stop (1969)
Cult classic from director Jack Hill ("Spider Baby") about a young stock-car driver whose ambitions go too far when he decides to run other drivers into accidents so he can swipe their women. Richard Davalos, Brian Donlevy, Ellen McRae (Burstyn) and Sid Haig star. Also includes the featurette "Crash-O-Rama! The Making of Pit Stop" and original theatrical trailers. 91 min.
50-9723 **$14.99**

Ghost Of Zorro (1959)
Screen frontier lawman Clayton Moore sports a different type of mask in this feature version of the 1949 Republic serial, playing the grandson of the original Zorro. Moore dons the black outfit to help a pretty telegraph company owner defend her business from outlaws. Pamela Blake, Eugene Roth, and George J. Lewis as Moccasin, Moore's faithful Indian ally, also star. 69 min.
63-1927   *$14.99*

Zorro Rides Again (Feature Version) (1959)
The masked crusader rides into the 20th century, as Zorro (John Carroll) seeks vengeance for his uncle's murder and goes up against a gang of outlaws trying to seize control of a railroad, in this exciting adventure culled from the 1937 Republic serial. With Helen Christian, Noah Beery, Duncan Renaldo. 68 min.
63-1928   *$14.99*

3 Swords Of Zorro (1963)
It's 1830 in Old California, and, wanting to keep swashbuckling a family business, the legendary Zorro teaches his son and daughter the fine points of the hero trade in this Italian/Spanish actioner. Guy Stockwell, Gloria Milland, Antonio Prieto star.
68-9233   Was $19.99   *$14.99*

Zorro The Avenger (1963)
Don José secretly masks himself as Zorro, the Mexican freedom fighter who tries to protect his people from the wrath of evil revolutionary bandits involved in the murder of a priest. Exciting swordplay and the charismatic Frank Latimore as the legendary hero add spark to this European production. With Marco Tulli. AKA: "Shadow of Zorro."
79-6158   Was $19.99   *$14.99*

Zorro (1975)
En garde! Alain Delon plays the valiant man in the black mask, who uses his slyness and expert swordsmanship to halt mean politicians and evil law enforcers. Lots of action, romance and spectacular riding. With Stanley Baker, Ottavia Piccolo and Moustache. 88 min.
78-1032   *$14.99*

Zorro (Letterboxed Version)
Also available in a theatrical, widescreen format.
08-1795   *$14.99*

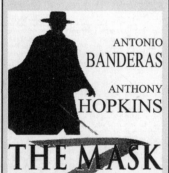

ANTONIO BANDERAS
ANTHONY HOPKINS
THE MASK OF ZORRO

The Mask Of Zorro (1998)
The spirit of Fairbanks, Power, Williams and Hamilton lives on in the guise of Antonio Banderas, the thief who dons a cape and mask when recruited by the aging Don Diego de la Vega (Anthony Hopkins) to adopt his alter-ego of Zorro and take on the evil Spanish governor of Alta California in 1841. Smashing swashbuckling scenes highlight this stylish adventure saga co-starring Catherine Zeta-Jones and Stuart Wilson. 137 min.
02-3218   Was $19.99   *$14.99*

The Mask Of Zorro (Letterboxed Version)
Also available in a theatrical, widescreen format.
02-3243   Was $19.99   *$14.99*

The Many Faces Of Zorro
One of the movie and TV worlds' greatest heroes is given a 10-sword salute in this thrilling program about the screen history of the masked avenger. You'll see clips of famous Zorros from the past, including Guy Williams and Douglas Fairbanks, plus interviews with Antonio Banderas and Anthony Hopkins from 1998's "The Mask of Zorro." 60 min.
05-5081   *$14.99*

Zorro Gift Set
Here's a boxed collector's set that'll put the "Zs" in both your cheeks and some green in your pocket. Included are the 1936 Zorro thriller "The Bold Caballero," starring Bob Livingston, plus "Ghost of Zorro" and "Zorro Rides Again."
63-1930   Save $5.00!   *$39.99*

ROSSANA PODESTA as HELEN   JACK SERNAS as PARIS

Helen of Troy

The Face That Launched a Thousand Ships!

Helen Of Troy (1956)
Lavish swords-and-sandals drama recounting the story of the legendary beauty whose abduction by love-smitten Greek prince Paris drove their countries to war and culminated in the siege of Troy by Greek warriors hidden inside a huge wooden horse. Rossana Podesta is "the face that launched a thousand ships"; Jack Sernas co-stars with a young Brigitte Bardot. Robert Wise directs; features behind-the-scenes footage. 135 min. total.
19-2447   *$19.99*

The Trojan Horse (1962)
Muscles, mythology and history mix in this exciting epic starring Steve Reeves as Aeneas, a Greek warrior who battles leader Paris, tries to find his kidnapped, pregnant wife Creusa and joins fellow fighters in the famous Trojan Horse. With John Drew Barrymore, Juliette Mayniel and Mimmo Palmara. 104 min. Dubbed in English.
10-9923   Was $19.99   *$14.99*

Knights Of The Round Table (1954)
The knights of the Round Table live in this spectacular retelling of the Camelot legend. Romance and adventure, sorcery and treachery combine as King Arthur establishes his kingdom, oblivious to the growing love between Guinevere and Lancelot. Robert Taylor, Mel Ferrer and Ava Gardner star. 117 min.
12-1458   *$19.99*

Scaramouche (1952)
Slickly-rendered swashbuckler set during the French Revolution stars Stewart Granger as a young nobleman whose quest for the identity of his father leads him into a vengeful rivalry with master swordsman Mel Ferrer. The pair's unforgettable climactic duel is the longest in film history; with Janet Leigh, Eleanor Parker, John Dehner. 118 min.
12-2259   *$19.99*

All The Brothers Were Valiant (1953)
Sprawling adventure story stars Robert Taylor and Stewart Granger as feuding New England siblings who battle over wills, wealth and women against the backdrop of their family whaling business. James Whitmore, Ann Blyth and Keenan Wynn also star in this impressive MGM production. 101 min.
12-2921   *$19.99*

The King's Thief (1955)
There's espionage and swashbuckling in the court of England's King Charles II in this lavish adventure starring David Niven as the evil Duke of Brampton, who plans to use his influence to dupe the king out of the Crown Jewels. Edmund Purdom, George Sanders, Ann Blyth and Roger Moore also star. 78 min.
12-2924   *$19.99*

I Died A Thousand Times (1955)
Jack Palance takes the Humphrey Bogart role in this exciting reworking of "High Sierra." He's Mad Dog Earle, a ruthless killer recently released from prison who plots a daring robbery while falling in love with a young, handicapped woman in a mountain retreat. Shelley Winters, Lee Marvin, Lon Chaney, Jr., Earl Holliman, Lori Nelson co-star. 109 min.
19-1863   Was $59.99   *$19.99*

Land Of Fury (1954)
A savvy sailor and his bride walk a perilously narrow path to retain the favor of a tribal king and keep their first-ever white outpost in New Zealand. Jack Hawkins goes shoulder-to-shoulder into the fray with Glynis Johns. AKA: "The Seekers." 90 min.
68-8186   *$19.99*

The Unstoppable Man (1959)
An American businessman living in England refuses help from Scotland Yard when his son is kidnapped, preferring his own Yankee smarts and a nasty flamethrower. Gutsy British actioner stars Cameron Mitchell and Lois Maxwell (Miss Moneypenny in the James Bond series). 68 min.
68-8362   *$19.99*

King Richard And The Crusaders (1954)
Lavish epic detailing the adventures of Sir Kenneth (Laurence Harvey), the brave, trustworthy knight picked by King Richard the Lionhearted (George Sanders) to find the conspirators attempting to overpower him. Rex Harrison and Virginia Mayo also star in this tale filled with rousing swordplay. 113 min.
19-2090   Was $29.99   *$19.99*

Hell Ship Mutiny (1957)
Action and danger in the beautiful South Pacific, as a seafaring adventurer named Captain Knight (Jon Hall) helps the residents of an island paradise overthrow the despotic rule of two foreigners searching for a fortune in pearls. John Carradine, Mike Mazurki and Peter Lorre also star. 66 min.
68-8458   *$19.99*

Men Of Sherwood Forest (1957)
Enthralling swashbuckling adventure featuring Robin Hood attempting to rescue King Richard, who's being held prisoner in Germany. The Merrie Men help Robin after he's blackmailed, and the swordplay is tops. Don Taylor, Reginald Beckwith and Eileen Moore star in this Hammer Studios production. 77 min.
68-8546   Was $19.99   *$14.99*

A Challenge For Robin Hood (1968)
Colorful Robin Hood adventure produced by Hammer Studios and detailing Robin's attempt to wrest power away from his cousin, who has been treating the peasants unfairly. Barrie Ingham, Peter Blythe, John Arnatt, Gay Hamilton and Alfie Bass star. 96 min.
08-8721   Letterboxed   *$14.99*

Robin Hood: The Movie (1991)
Rousing version of the classic tale stars Patrick Bergin as the Saxon nobleman who becomes an outlaw hero and robs from greedy land barons while romancing Maid Marian. Jurgen Prochnow, Jeroen Krabbe and Uma Thurman co-star. 104 min.
04-2446   Was $89.99   *$19.99*

Gun Girls (1956)
Rare exploitation excursion about a misunderstood teenage girl who joins a tough, peroxide blonde for the crime spree of the century. The pair purchase illegal guns and plot to rob a warehouse, but their scheme goes awry. Jeanne Ferghuson, Jean Ann Lewis and Tim Farrell star. 61 min.
79-5132   *$19.99*

The Prisoner Of Zenda (1952)
Conspiracy, romance and swashbuckling swordplay enhance this lively translation of Anthony Hope's grand epic. Stewart Granger essays the dual roles of the future king of Ruritania and his lookalike, an English tourist who is enlisted to pose as the prince after a plot to usurp the throne emerges. Co-stars Deborah Kerr, James Mason, Robert Douglas. 100 min.
12-1206   *$19.99*

Journey To The Lost City (1958)
An architect working in India stumbles across a magnificent city hidden deep in the jungle that's home to feuding princes, man-eating tigers, and a beautiful native dancer, whom he tries to bring back to civilization with him. Paul Christian, Debra Paget and Walter Reyer star in this exciting adventure that was edited together from the German-made films "The Indian Tomb" and "Tiger of Eschnapur"; co-written and directed by Fritz Lang. 95 min.
68-8520   *$19.99*

The White Orchid (1954)
An archeological party explores the Mexican jungle in search of a legendary lost civilization. They find it, but the natives aren't happy about being "discovered"! Exciting thriller stars William Lundigan, Peggie Castle, Armando Silvestre. 80 min.
76-5008   Was $19.99   *$14.99*

Singapore (1947)
Fred MacMurray is an American sailor who returns to Singapore near the end of World War II and gets involved with pearl smuggling. While being pursued by hoodlums in search of the priceless pearls he hid in a hotel during the war, MacMurray discovers that wife Ava Gardner, whom he presumed to be dead, is alive with amnesia. Later remade as "Istanbul." 80 min.
07-2310   *$14.99*

The Black Arrow (1948)
Based on a ripping Robert Louis Stevenson yarn, this glorious medieval drama stars heroic Louis Hayward and villainous George Macready as rivals for the hand of lovely Janet Blair, finishing in a thrilling joust. 76 min.
02-1914   Was $19.99   *$14.99*

Desperate Cargo (1941)
Trouble's brewing for two lovely chorines who've found themselves stranded in a small Latin American town, and whose only escape is aboard a clipper ship harried by hoodlums. Stars Ralph Byrd, Carol Hughes and Julie Duncan. AKA: "S.O.S. Clipper." 67 min.
10-7052   Was $19.99   *$14.99*

Diamond City (1949)
The feud between diamond miners in South Africa in the 1870s is the focus of this exciting adventure yarn in which two factions of gem seekers square off. One group does things in orderly fashion, while the other uses treachery with reckless abandon. David Farrar, Honor Blackman, Diana Dors and Niall MacGinnis star. 90 min.
10-9476   *$19.99*

Drums Of The Desert (1940)
This Foreign Legion saga stars Ralph Byrd and Peter Lynn as Legionnaires battling nasty natives while trying to win the hand of the same woman, played by Adrian Booth (who's billed as "Lorna Gray"). With William Costello and Mantan Moreland. 64 min.
10-9479   *$19.99*

Arabian Nights (1942)
A dazzling spectacle, loosely based on the famous 19th-century fables, focusing on the battle between two brothers over their late father's throne. Evil brother Leif Erickson nearly kills sibling Jon Hall in a fight, but sultry dancing girl Maria Montez nurses the fallen brother back to health. With help from best friend Sabu, an aging Sinbad (Shemp Howard) and Aladdin (John Qualen), Hall sets out to regain his rightful position. 87 min.
07-1985   *$14.99*

WILD NIGHTS OF SHEER DELIGHTS!
Maria MONTEZ
Jon HALL
Turhan BEY
ALI BABA AND THE FORTY THIEVES IN TECHNICOLOR
ANDY DEVINE
and Thousands in Thrilling Spectacles!

Ali Baba And The Forty Thieves (1944)
Lavish adventure starring Jon Hall as the title character, the son of the murdered Caliph of Baghdad who is adopted by a band of thieves opposing an evil Mongol leader. Ali falls in love with the beautiful daughter (Maria Montez) of the tyrant's traitorous advisor, while trying to regain his father's throne and the empire's fortunes. With Turhan Bey, Kurt Katch, Andy Devine. 87 min.
07-1984   *$14.99*

Adventures In Iraq (1943)
Thrilling adventure saga in which a courageous pilot is forced to land in the desert, where he faces a sheik who holds him captive in exchange for the release of his three brothers, who are about to be executed as Nazi spies. John Loder, Ruth Ford and Warren Douglas star. 64 min.
10-9695   *$19.99*

Zanzibar (1940)
A Saturday matinee-flavored adventure saga in which an evil professor swipes the ancient skull of an African sultan in hopes of using it to control the native population. Enter British explorers led by Lola Lane and James Craig who attempt to recover the skull, but find Nazis and a volcano in their way. With Eduardo Ciannelli and Tom Fadden. 70 min.
10-9946   *$14.99*

Devil Monster (1946)
The best friend of a fisherman lost at sea is persuaded by his missing pal's girl, whom he cares deeply about, to search for him. It's a journey filled with such (stock footage) sights as sharks, sea lions and beautiful South Seas maidens, but when the man's ship is found on a strange island, things get more mysterious. Barry Norton stars. 64 min.
09-2380   *$19.99*

Arctic Fury (1949)
Based on a true story, this thrilling adventure stars Del Cambre as an Arctic-based doctor who is forced to survive in the frozen wilderness when his plane crashes while on a mission to a disease-stricken Eskimo village. With Eve Miller, Merrill McCormick. 61 min.
09-5001   *$19.99*

Treasure Island (1934)
Wallace Beery stars as Long John Silver and young Jackie Cooper plays his comrade in adventure in the first sound filming of Robert Louis Stevenson's timeless tale. Pirates, treachery, and a fortune in hidden treasure await the pair. With Lionel Barrymore, Lewis Stone. 105 min.
12-1030 *$19.99*

Treasure Island (Color Version)
"Arrrrrrr, Jim-boy, 'tis colorized we be! If only Blind Pew could see it!"
12-1942 *$19.99*

Long John Silver (1954)
Robert Newton returns as the one-legged buccaneer, out after a hidden treasure in an all-new adventure film for the whole family. Co-stars Grant Taylor, Connie Gilchrist, and Kit Taylor as Jim Hawkins; look closely for Rod Taylor. 109 min.
10-1074 *$19.99*

Treasure Island (1972)
Thrilling cinematic adaptation of Stevenson's pirate classic about young Jim Hawkins' adventures with Long John Silver and his quest for buried gold. Orson Welles, Walter Slezak, Kim Burfield star. 98 min.
19-2302 Was $19.99 *$14.99*

Wallaby Jim Of The Islands (1937)
Danger's afoot for the swashbuckling captain of a pearl fishing boat traversing the South Seas as he crosses swords with merciless freebooters who have their eyes on his prized freight. Stars George Houston and Ruth Coleman. 61 min.
10-7171 Was $19.99 *$14.99*

Frenchman's Creek (1944)
Seventeenth-century England is the setting for this swashbuckling romance on the high seas about a noblewoman, fed up with a failing marriage, who falls in love with a charismatic French pirate. She has to deal not only with her new love's occupation, but also his best friend, who is quite the backstabber. Joan Fontaine, Basil Rathbone and Nigel Bruce star. 112 min.
07-2523 *$14.99*

Frenchman's Creek (1998)
Leaving London to return to her family's estate in 17th-century Cornwall, noblewoman Tara Fitzgerald is shocked to find it, and the surrounding community, under the control of French buccaneers led by Anthony Delon. Romance blooms between the mismatched couple in this sweeping, action-filled adaptation of the Daphne Du Maurier novel. With Tim Dutton, James Fleet. 120 min.
08-8767 ❑*$19.99*

Captain Kidd (1945)
Charles Laughton is superb as one of the most notorious pirates to ever sail the seas, with Randolph Scott as the man charged with bringing him to justice. Barbara Britton, Reginald Owen also star. 89 min.
10-2043 Was $19.99 *$14.99*

Pirate Ship (1949)
Energetic adventure about a band of counterfeiters led by villainous George Reeves who take over a freighter filled with their funny money and hold the crew hostage. Heroic Jon Hall tries to scuttle their scheme. Adele Jergens, Noel Cravat also star. AKA: "The Mutineers." 60 min.
10-9245 Was $19.99 *$14.99*

Captain Sirocco (1949)
Terrific swashbuckling saga with Louis Hayward as an unassuming member of the Naples court who has a secret life as a swordfighting hero who helps a group of rebels attempting to overthrow the queen and her evil police chief. Exciting action scenes with the agile Hayward highlight this tale. Alan Curtis, Rudolph Serato also star. AKA: "Pirates of Capri." 93 min.
53-6078 *$29.99*

The Black Pirates (1954)
High-energy swashbuckler about a group of pirates searching for gold in the West Indies. Anthony Dexter, Martha Roth, Lon Chaney, Jr., Robert Clarke and Alfonso Bedoya star. 70 min.
10-9367 *$14.99*

The Pirate Of The Black Hawk (1958)
Set in the middle of the 15th century, this pirate saga tells of Duke Manfred, an evil ruler of the Duchy of Montefore in France, whose band of pirates rapes, murders and pillages coastal villages. When the pirates kill the former ruler of Montefore, his daughter seeks help from Captain Richard of the Black Hawk. Gerard Landry and Mijanou Bardot (Brigitte's lovely sister) star.
79-6504 *$19.99*

Knights Of The Black Cross (1958)
Highlighted by impressive battle scenes and superior stuntwork, this epic is set at the turn of the 14th century and focuses on events leading to the Battle of Grunwald. The story involves Yurin, a Polish nobleman, and his attempts to free his kidnapped daughter Danuta from the clutches of the Teutonic Knights of East Prussia. Ursula Modrynska stars.
79-6505 *$19.99*

Pirates Of The Coast (1961)
Lex Barker stars as a Spanish naval commander in the 1500s. He risks life, limb, and ship and engages in battles, gunfights, and swordplay all for the love of his beautiful Isabella. Double-crosses and high-seas excitement in this adventure yarn. 102 min.
48-1091 *$29.99*

The Black Lancers (1961)
After he loses a wild weapons tournament to brother André to decide who will become the leader of the Polish army, Sergei joins forces with a barbarian tribe and their sexy queen to get revenge against his sibling. Their epic rivalry involves the use of all sorts of deadly weaponry and torture. With Mel Ferrer, Yvonne Furneaux and Leticia Roman.
79-6503 *$19.99*

Gentlemen Of The Night (1961)
The city of Venice is terrorized by a megalomaniacal tyrant and his hooded aides, the Lords of the Night. At the same time, young freedom-fighting aristocrats try to overthrow the government as well. Enter hero Guy Madison, just back from war, who wants to get to the bottom of the political turmoil—and does, sword in hand. With Lisa Gastoni.
79-6547 Was $24.99 *$19.99*

Women On Devil's Island (1962)
Devil's Island is no paradise for the French prostitutes and political prisoners sentenced to live there. Along with deplorable living conditions and crocodiles, residents are regularly whipped. When pirates attack the island, prisoners must decide whom to side with: the sadistic island officials or the buccaneers. Guy Madison, Michele Mercier star.
79-6157 *$19.99*

Giant Of The Evil Island (1962)
High-spirited adventure with future "Mission Impossible" star Peter Lupus (as Rock Stevens) playing Captain Pedro, swashbuckling head of a Spanish galleon set on destroying the pirate Maloch and his crew on Evil Island. Trouble ensues when bodice-ripping Creole mistress Alma tells Maloch of Pedro's plan, then has fun branding the women Maloch has kidnapped. Dina DeSantis, Halina Zalewski also star.
79-6501 *$19.99*

Avenger Of The Seven Seas (1963)
It's "Mutiny on the Bounty" with pirates, as hunky second mate Richard Harrison seeks revenge against his former captain, a savage scalawag who forced crew members into swimming in shark-infested waters in order to retrieve pearls. Harrison joins pirates to stop the skipper, but soon encounters danger and ferocious, man-eating plants. With Michelle Mercier.
79-6041 Was $24.99 *$19.99*

Son Of The Red Corsair (1963)
Zesty swashbuckler starring Lex Barker as the son of the late Red Pirate who discovers his half-sister, long presumed dead, is still alive. It turns out that not only is she working for a noblewoman with whom Barker is in love, but she's the real Queen of the Darrians. With Sylvia Lopez, Vira Silenti.
79-6095 *$19.99*

The Black Devil (1963)
Action-packed European swashbuckler detailing the efforts of "the Black Devil," a dashing masked avenger, to reunite with Isabella, the niece of traitorous Don Lorenzo whom he vowed to protect years earlier. In order to find Isabella and stop Lorenzo's plot to strengthen his ties to Spain, the Black Devil masquerades as a foppish member of Lorenzo's court. With Gerard Landry.
79-6502 *$19.99*

Sandokan And The Pirates Of Malasia (1964)
In this rarely-seen sequel to his title turn in 1963's "Sandokan the Great," Steve Reeves returns as the heroic East Asian privateer, helping a deposed rajah regain his throne from a greedy British officer. With Jacqueline Sassard, Mimmo Palmara; directed by "Sandokan the Great" helmer Umbero Lenzi. AKA: "Pirates of Malasia." 97 min.
09-5263 *$19.99*

Sandokan Fights Back (1964)
Ray Danton plays the dashing Sandokan, a feared pirate who attempts to claim his rightful throne from an evil European who killed his family and now sits as ruler. Sandokan saves his enemy's niece from a tiger, but when Sandokan's identity is revealed, trouble ensues. With Franco Bettgia.
79-6153 *$19.99*

Attack Of The Normans (1964)
Swords are swinging in this adventure yarn set against the war between the English and the Normans. The story's set in motion when Wilfrid, the Duke of Saxon, attempts to take over the English throne by having his men pose as Norman pirates and ambush the returning king. Can Count Oliver bring peace to the country? Cameron Mitchell, Genevieve Grad star.
79-6097 *$19.99*

Cavalier Of The Devil's Castle (1965)
The mysterious Masked Cavalier is blamed for the disappearance of the popular uncle of Captain Ugonia, an obsessive official who has actually locked him away in a dungeon. The not-so-good Captain plans to marry his beautiful cousin and rule the land, but the Masked Cavalier will have none of that. Massimo Serato, Franco Fantasia and Irene Tunc star.
79-6098 *$19.99*

The Lion Of St. Mark (1967)
Gordon Scott, star of countless gladiator and swashbuckler enterprises, plays a suave aristocrat, forced by law into letting mercenaries defend Venice from ruthless pirates. When the brigands disrupt his engagement party, Scott adopts the name "Lion of St. Mark," joins friends in tackling the invaders, and falls in love with a pirate queen. Gianna Maria Canale also stars.
79-6047 *$19.99*

Swashbuckler (1976)
High seas hijinks highlight this rousing pirate tale set in the 18th-century Caribbean, where buccaneers Robert Shaw and James Earl Jones call on their craftiness and swordfighting talents to stop the terror-of-a-tyrant who rules Jamaica. Genevieve Bujold, Beau Bridges, Geoffrey Holder, Peter Boyle and Anjelica Huston co-star. 101 min.
07-1686 Was $79.99 *$14.99*

Nate And Hayes (1983)
An old-time swashbuckler, filled with daring fights, colorful characters and dangerous escapes, as a missionary teams up with a soldier of fortune to rescue his fiancée, who's been kidnapped by pirates. Tommy Lee Jones, Michael O'Keefe, Jenny Seagrove star. 100 min.
06-1205 *$14.99*

Cutthroat Island (1995)
When her buccaneer father is murdered by his treacherous brother, who's searching for pieces of a map to a fabulous treasure, female freebooter Geena Davis straps on her broadsword and sets sail for revenge in this rousing revisionist pirate adventure filled with laughs, romance and spectacular action scenes. Matthew Modine, Frank Langella also star; Renny Harlin ("Cliffhanger") directs. 118 min.
27-6965 Was $89.99 ❑*$14.99*

Cutthroat Island (Letterboxed Version)
Also available in a theatrical, widescreen format.
27-6966 Was $19.99 ❑*$14.99*

Bush Pilot (1947)
Two pilot brothers, competing in the cargo-flying business, find their lives and loves on the line when one agrees to take the dangerous assignment of transporting nitro. Jack LaRue, Rochelle Hudson, Austin Willis star.
09-5269 *$19.99*

South Of Pago Pago (1940)
First-rate adventure yarn stars Victor McLaglen as the head of a South Seas expedition for pearls who finds resistance from a native tribe and its leader, played by Jon Hall. Frances Farmer is the woman McLaglen uses to lure Hall and land the pearls; Gene Lockhart also stars. 98 min.
27-6506 *$19.99*

Monsoon (1943)
John Carradine has a rare heroic role in this South Seas adventure. A diver hunting for millions in sunken gold must cope with treacherous currents, a full-scale monsoon, and a crooked ship's captain (Sidney Toler of numerable Charlie Chan films). AKA: "Isle of Forgotten Sins." 82 min.
68-8008 *$14.99*

Mercy Plane (1940)
High-flying adventure starring James Dunn as Speed Leslie, an airplane ace who is grounded after the incredible high-tech Mercy Plane is stolen. With help from the pretty sister of a flyer, Speed gets a job at an aircraft factory and learns his employer is behind the Mercy Plane's theft. Frances Gifford, Matty Fain co-star. 73 min.
09-2958 *$19.99*

Sundown (1941)
Dangerous! Intriguing! Fascinating! Gene Tierney plays a beautiful native girl who assists British troops in Africa during WWII. A senses-swooning adventure romance that co-stars Bruce Cabot, George Sanders. 91 min.
08-8071 Was $19.99 *$14.99*

Swamp Fire (1946)
Screen Tarzans Johnny Weissmuller and Buster Crabbe find themselves on opposite sides of the law and rivals for Virginia Grey in this rarely seen actioner set in the Louisiana bayou. Look for a young David Janssen among the alligators. 69 min.
68-8381 Was $19.99 *$14.99*

Amazon Quest (1949)
Set during the early part of the 1900s, this adventure stars Tom Neal ("Detour") as a diamond cutter attempting to retain his rightful share of a rubber empire. He endures panther attacks, piranhas, quicksand and Indians with poison darts while on his journey to Brazil. Carole Mathews, Carole Donne co-star.
79-5958 Was $24.99 *$19.99*

Omoo Omoo, The Shark God (1949)
A fatal curse condemns the captain of a South Sea vessel and threatens his beautiful daughter when he plucks sacred black pearls from a statue of the shark god. Ron Randell stars in this adaptation of the Melville adventure. 58 min.
68-8084 *$19.99*

Adventure Island (1947)
Anchoring on a distant South Pacific island, a party of scruffy adventurers is besieged by a lunatic who rules the natives as a god. Bat-Butler Alan Napier, Rory Calhoun, and Rhonda Fleming team up in this "Ebb Tide" remake. 66 min.
68-8085 Was $19.99 *$14.99*

Outpost In Morocco (1949)
Blazing sands and blazing guns meet in this gritty desert action drama, with George Raft as the defender in love with enemy agent Marie Windsor. Akim Tamiroff also stars. 92 min.
01-1357 *$19.99*

Lure Of The Islands (1942)
Federal agents pose as shipwrecked sailors on a jungle island while snooping for evidence to expose a criminal gang. Robert Lowery and Guinn "Big Boy" Williams head the action. 61 min.
68-8089 Was $19.99 *$14.99*

Bagdad (1949)
Light-hearted look at the costume melodrama genre, with Maureen O'Hara as a beautiful princess who returns to her Arabian homeland and learns an unknown villain killed her father and seized the family fortune. Was it handsome horseman Paul Christian or sinister-looking Vincent Price? Hmmm... O'Hara also sings three songs; with John Sutton, Jeff Corey. 83 min.
07-2492 *$14.99*

The Last Adventurers (1937)
Exciting nautical footage is featured in this tale starring Niall McGinnis as a man who survives two separate shipwrecks. With Roy Emerton, Linden Travers. AKA: "Down to the Sea in Ships." 77 min.
09-5003 *$19.99*

Atlantic Flight (1937)
Dick Merrill, a real-life flyer, was signed by Monogram Pictures to pretty much play himself in this exciting film. He's a plane owner who goes up against an airplane tycoon in a race over London. Jack Lamble, Paula Stone co-star. 70 min.
09-5162 *$19.99*

Yellowstone (1936)
The famed national park becomes the setting for action and drama, as a diverse group of characters search for stolen treasure. Ralph Morgan, Andy Devine, Alan Hale star. 65 min.
08-5058 Was $19.99 *$14.99*

Tundra (1936)
Early "docudrama" set against the rugged and forbidding desolation of the Alaskan tundra, filmed entirely on location. A wilderness doctor who uses an airplane to make his rounds must fight for his own survival when his craft crashes. Del Cambre stars. 72 min.
09-1099 Was $29.99 *$19.99*

Daniel Boone (1936)
America's legendary pioneer leads a group of people out of North Carolina into the unexplored regions of Kentucky, fighting floods and fierce Indians. George O'Brien, Heather Angel and John Carradine star in this superior actioner. 79 min.
17-1068 Was $19.99 *$14.99*

Daniel Boone: Trail Blazer (1957)
Bruce Bennett stars as the coonskin-capped pioneer in this exciting saga about the opening of the American frontier. With Lon Chaney, Jr., Faron Young. 76 min.
21-3038 *$19.99*

Sinners In Paradise (1938)
Bruce Cabot is one of the passengers on an ill-fated airplane, each with his own reason for fleeing the States. Crash-landing on a South Seas isle, the survivors must come to terms with a deadly convict who rules the place, as well as their own pasts. 64 min.
68-8090 *$19.99*

Sea Devils (1931)
A falsely imprisoned man escapes jail and steals aboard a treasure cruise at sea, falling in with a crew on the brink of mutiny. Walter Long and Molly O'Day star. 77 min.
68-8274 *$19.99*

Vengeance Of The Deep (1939)
Thrilling seafaring adventure from Australia about a concert pianist who sets out to win the hand of the girl he loves by going to sea and finding a pearl for her. Lloyd Hughes, Shirley Ann Richards star.
68-9098 *$19.99*

Jungle Thrills

East Of Borneo (1931)
A woman braves the danger of the jungle to find her missing husband in this thrill-a-second tale starring Charles Bickford and Rose Hobert. A great finale featuring the eruption of a volcano is unforgettable. 74 min.
08-5015 Was $19.99 *$14.99*

Adventure Girl (1931)
Female explorer Joan Lowell takes off on a trip to a Central American country on a schooner with her father and two sailors, then faces a hurricane, snakes and hostile natives while following a map leading to buried treasure. Captain Wagner, Bill Sawyer also star in this "fact and fiction" actioner. 65 min.
53-6074 *$29.99*

Hell's Headquarters (1932)
Slam-bang jungle actioner about the race to a secret stash of ivory which pits two African adventurers (Frank Mayo, Jack Mulhall) against one another, one of whom resorts to murder to secure his claim. Co-stars Barbara Weeks. 59 min.
10-7168 Was $19.99 *$14.99*

Savage Girl (1932)
Ingénue Rochelle Hudson is an alluring leopardskin-clad girl discovered by a team of adventurers in the heart of the African jungle. To be worshipped as a goddess by native warriors and forest fauna, or hailed as the Queen of Broadway—what's a savage girl to do? 64 min.
68-8046 Was $19.99 *$14.99*

Jungle Bride (1933)
A devastating shipwreck, a royal rumble between Charles Starrett and a hungry lion, and the loincloth-clad Anita Page spark this jungle adventure about a wrongly-accused Starrett dodging a reporter's pursuit in Africa. With Kenneth Thomson, Eddie Borden. 63 min.
68-8092 *$19.99*

Queen Of The Jungle (1935)
Featurized version of an adventure tale is the exotic story of a girl who is carried to the heart of the African jungle by a runaway balloon, and grows to womanhood revered by the natives as the daughter of the White God. Stars Mary Kornman. 85 min.
09-2013 Was $29.99 *$24.99*

Savage Fury (1935)
Two scientific teams go up against each other in a race to find a secret formula in the African jungle. The search leads them to a lost city where they face a mad priest, dungeons of fire and dangerous electrical rays. Noah Beery, Jr., Walter Miller and Dorothy Short star.
68-8931 Was $19.99 *$14.99*

Wolves Of The Sea (1938)
A sunken ocean liner, a fortune in missing gems, and a young woman stranded on a tropical island with zoo-bound wild animals as her only companions are the elements in this unusual jungle/nautical thriller. Hobart Bosworth, Jeanne Carmen, Pat West star. AKA: "Jungle Island."
68-9234 *$19.99*

Law Of The Jungle (1942)
During an African safari, a singer and an explorer encounter Nazi agents who have started trouble with the natives. Arline Judge, John King, Mantan Moreland and Arthur O'Connell star. 61 min.
10-8252 *$19.99*

Jungle Siren (1942)
Working with the French Underground to oppose Nazi agitators in equatorial Africa, Buster Crabbe is helped by a white woman raised in the wilderness. Billed as a "one-girl love-blitz," burlesque legend Ann Corio plays the jungle queen. 68 min.
68-8087 *$19.99*

Jacaré (1942)
"The first feature picture ever filmed in the wilds of the Amazon jungle" follows famed hunter Frank "Bring 'Em Back Alive" Buck on a danger-filled safari loaded with man-eating crocs, man- and croc-eating piranha, and man-, croc- and piranha-eating natives.
68-8852 *$19.99*

Tiger Fangs (1943)
Real-life great white hunter Frank Buck plays himself in a jungle thriller set in Malaya. Buck must stem the activities of Nazi saboteurs who are using man-eating tigers(!) to stop the Allies' rubber supply. 57 min.
10-7057 Was $19.99 *$14.99*

DOREEN KNOWS NO FEAR . . .
NABONGA KNOWS
NO LOVE
. . . BUT
HIS LOVE
FOR HER.
NABONGA
(GORILLA)
CRABBE
MACLANE
DORSAY
LONDON

Nabonga (1944)
A gorilla named Nabonga warms up to a teenage girl whose plane, which was also carrying a bundle of embezzled cash, crash lands in the Belgian Congo. Years later, Buster Crabbe sets out after the girl and must do battle with villains after the lost booty. With Julie London. 72 min.
10-7056 *$19.99*

White Pongo (1945)
Pongo...is it the scourge of the jungle, the missing link between man and ape, or just a guy in the gorilla suit from 1945's "Nabonga" died white? You be the judge in this drama about a safari searching for the title creature. Richard Fraser, Maris Wrixon, Lionel Royce star; from the director of "The Terror of Tiny Town." 74 min.
01-1372 Was $19.99 *$14.99*

The White Gorilla (1949)
Jungle guide Ray "Crash" Corrigan searches for a treasure in the Cave of the Cyclops on an expedition and faces hippos, stampeding elephants and a young boy with mystical powers over the natives and the animals. But nothing is more frightening than a ferocious albino gorilla, a "seething outcast of ape society."
79-5966 Was $24.99 *$19.99*

Queen Of The Amazons (1946)
A courageous woman organizes a jungle expedition to rescue her fiancé from the clutches of a savage female-ruled tribe. Campy role-reversing adventure stars Patricia Morrison and Robert Lowery. 61 min.
68-8242 *$19.99*

Blonde Savage (1947)
"High Chaparrall" star Leif Erickson is hired to scan unexplored African territories and discovers a white girl raised as a princess by doting native hunters. Gale Sherwood is Meelah in this gender-reversing Tarzan-style adventure. 62 min.
68-8086 *$19.99*

Forbidden Jungle (1950)
A jungle adventure about a great white hunter who journeys to Africa to search for a mysterious "wild boy" whom he thinks may be his own long-lost grandson. Forrest Taylor, Don Harvey and Tamba the chimp star. 67 min.
68-8899 *$19.99*

Perils Of The Jungle (1953)
An expedition headed by animal trainer Clyde Beatty travels to the deepest part of the Belgian Congo in search of lions. They find an animal dealer (Phyllis Coates of "Superman" fame) who loses her catches after a fire breaks out, prompting Beatty to help her by tracking down a gorilla.
79-5977 Was $24.99 *$19.99*

Golden Mistress (1954)
Filmed on location in Haiti, this colorful jungle actioner stars John Agar as a soldier-of-fortune hired by a young woman whose father was struck down by a voodoo curse as they searched for a fabulous lost treasure. With Rosemarie Bowe, Abner Biberman. 82 min.
73-3012 *$19.99*

Black Devils Of Kali (1955)
Former Tarzan Lex Barker stars in this hair-raising jungle adventure. He's joined by a group of explorers in search of the mystery of an idol worshipped by natives in India. Ralph Murray and Jane Maxwell also star. AKA: "Mystery of the Black Jungle." 72 min.
68-8523 *$19.99*

Liane, Jungle Goddess (1956)
Sexy, distaff spin on the Tarzan legend, as an African expedition finds a beautiful (and topless) white jungle queen believed to be a British nobleman's granddaughter and brings her back to England. Marion Michael, Hardy Kruger and Rudolf Forster co-star in this West German production. 86 min.
68-8521 *$19.99*

Walk Into Hell (1957)
Intense adventure in the dense tropical jungles of New Guinea, when an exploratory team finds more than they bargained for at the hands of the restless natives and deadly wildlife. Chips Rafferty, Francoise Christophe. 91 min.
53-3078 Was $59.99 *$19.99*

White Huntress (1957)
Giant pythons, glistening savages, golden lust! A Victorian Diana surpasses dark terrors and deadly sins on the way to an African outpost with two rival brothers. Shot in Kenya with Susan Stephen and John Bentley. 86 min.
68-8407 *$19.99*

Man-Eater (1958)
A big-game hunter has more than just four-legged man-eaters to worry about when a millionaire's spoiled daughter, on safari with her alcoholic husband, begins making a play for his attentions in this offbeat jungle drama, culled from episodes of a British TV series, "White Hunter." Rhodes Reason, Lee Patterson, Magda Miller star. 62 min.
68-9226 *$19.99*

Attack Of The Jungle Women (1959)
A man, his wife and a group of land developers travel to the jungles of Central Panama. While the couple are able to assimilate into a dangerous tribe, the developers get into trouble with headhunting jungle women and are tortured. With Bill and Eve Phillips, Tom Guardia; Paul Frees narrates.
79-5877 Was $24.99 *$19.99*

Gorilla (1964)
Acclaimed Swedish cinematographer Sven Nykvist co-directed this jungle adventure about a game warden and a journalist who fall in love in the Belgian Congo while trying to halt the rampage of an enraged gorilla. Stars Georges Galley and Gio Petre. 79 min.
09-1420 Was $24.99 *$19.99*

Tarzana, The Wild Girl (1972)
Seventeen years after a plane crash, an African expedition searches for the lost granddaughter of a wealthy Englishman. What they discover is a scantily-dressed wild woman (wow!) living freely in the jungle. Lurid adventure saga stars Ken Clark, Fran Poles. 83 min.
68-8876 Letterboxed *$19.99*

Sheena (1984)
Tanya Roberts swings like an angel as the blond-tressed Queen of the Jungle in this exciting adventure. Can Sheena and her animal friends protect her African wilderness home from evil land barons. Co-stars Ted Wass as an American reporter who falls for Roberts. 117 min.
02-2707 *$14.99*

The Scarlet Pimpernel (1934)
Leslie Howard is the foppish English nobleman who leads a double life, and, as the Scarlet Pimpernel, rescues victims of the French Revolution from the guillotine, in this classic screen swashbuckler. Merle Oberon, Raymond Massey, Nigel Bruce co-star. 105 min.
10-2004 Was $19.99 *$14.99*

The Elusive Pimpernel (1950)
David Niven dons the cape to fight France's Reign of Terror in a lavish retelling of the classic saga of the Scarlet Pimpernel. Margaret Leighton, Jack Hawkins and Cyril Cusack also star in this thrilling Michael Powell/Emeric Pressburger adventure yarn that was originally filmed as a musical! 107 min.
22-5439 Was $39.99 *$29.99*

The Scarlet Pimpernel: Book I (1999)
By day he's Percy Blakeney, a dandified English aristocrat in Revolutionary France, but at night he becomes a mysterious swordsman saving the innocent from the Reign of Terror. Richard E. Grant stars as the dashing Pimpernel, and Elizabeth McGovern plays his wife, in this thrilling adaptation of the timeless adventure tale. 94 min.
53-6418 *$19.99*

The Scarlet Pimpernel: Book II: Madame Guillotine (1999)
The further adventures of the Scarlet Pimpernel finds dashing hero Sir Percy Blackeney (Richard E. Grant) joining forces with wife Marguerite (Elizabeth McGovern) to help rescue the young daughter of the Marquis de Rochambeau from the clutches of Madame Guillotine. 100 min.
53-6615 *$19.99*

The Scarlet Pimpernel: Book III: The Kidnapped King (1999)
In the swashbuckling savior of 18th-century France's ultimate mission, the Pimpernel must discover who has abducted young Louis Capet and rescue the heir to the French throne before it's too late. Richard E. Grant, Elizabeth McGovern star. 100 min.
53-6662 *$19.99*

The Scarlet Pimpernel: Boxed Set
All three volumes in the acclaimed mini-series are also available in a boxed collector's set.
53-6663 Save $10.00! *$49.99*

TRADER
HORN
THE MIRACLE OF PICTURES

Trader Horn (1931)
Classic adventure epic set and partially filmed in Africa follows the adventures of Trader Horn (Harry Carey), who encounters incredible danger and malicious natives when he joins a female missionary on a search for her lost daughter in some of the continent's most treacherous areas. Edwina Booth, Duncan Renaldo co-star. 120 min.
12-2926 *$19.99*

In The Wake Of The Bounty (1933)
This rarely-seen Australian seafaring drama, which mixes the first filming of the story of the HMS Bounty and her crew's mutiny with documentary footage of the Pacific locales where the events took place, is also notable for featuring the film debut of Errol Flynn, in the role of rebellious first mate Fletcher Christian. With Mayne Lynton as Captain Bligh. 62 min.
10-9356 ***$19.99***

Captain Blood (1935)
Errol Flynn is the young physician, sentenced to slavery, who's rescued by Olivia de Havilland and begins a life of piracy on the high seas. Superb swordplay, magnetic performances and supporting turns by Basil Rathbone and Lionel Atwill make this a classic. Complete, 119-min. restored version.
12-2232 ***$19.99***

The Charge Of The Light Brigade (1936)
The classic poem of heroism in the face of certain death becomes a timeless adventure epic featuring Errol Flynn and Patric Knowles as sibling cavalry officers competing for the affections of Olivia de Havilland, while battling enemy forces in East India. After Flynn is unable to save a fort from attack, he and his troops fight Russian forces in Crimea. With David Niven. 116 min.
12-2234 ***$19.99***

The Prince And The Pauper (1937)
Mark Twain's classic story of identical boys whose role-swapping ruse leads to calamity and danger in old England. Errol Flynn, Alan Hale, Claude Rains, and Billy and Bobby Mauch, in the title roles, star in this rousing family thriller. 119 min.
12-2044 ***$19.99***

The Adventures Of Robin Hood (1938)
Errol Flynn is in top form as the dashing outlaw, stealing from the rich to give to the poor, romancing Olivia de Havilland and dueling against villainous Basil Rathbone and Claude Rains. Michael Curtiz and William Keighley helmed this colorful classic, with Alan Hale, Eugene Pallette, Ian Hunter, Una O'Connor; score by Erich Wolfgang Korngold. 105 min.
12-1153 Was $19.99 ☐***$14.99***

The Dawn Patrol (1938)
Richly drawn portrayals by Errol Flynn and David Niven as aces in the British air corps during World War I accentuate this dynamic decrial of the futility of war. Basil Rathbone co-stars as the reviled squad commander mindlessly sending his men off to die in the skies over Europe. Features stunning aerial footage, some of which was shot for Howard Hawks' version of the story eight years earlier. 103 min.
12-2611 ☐***$19.99***

Dodge City (1939)
Cattleman Errol Flynn pins on the sheriff's badge and cleans up the Old West's roughest, rowdiest town in this classic frontier saga. A top cast (Olivia de Havilland, Bruce Cabot, Ann Sheridan, Alan Hale), lush Max Steiner music, and one of cinema's all-time barroom brawls add to the fun. 101 min.
12-2168 Was $19.99 ***$14.99***

The Sea Hawk (1940)
Classic high seas action with Errol Flynn as a roguish privateer who takes on the Spanish Armada for Queen Elizabeth I. Rousing action sequences, a cast that also includes Claude Rains, Flora Robson, Brenda Marshall and Alan Hale, and Erich Korngold's score make this a winner. Uncut, 127-min. version.
12-2034 ***$19.99***

The Sea Hawk (Color Version)
See Hawk? Now see him in full, glorious color, as the Errol Flynn swashbuckler takes on a whole new look.
12-2035 ***$19.99***

Captain Blood

Errol Flynn

Virginia City (1940)
Civil War frontier drama stars Errol Flynn as a Union officer who escapes from a Southern prison to the title Nevada town, where he learns of a plan to ship gold to the Confederacy via wagon train. Randolph Scott is Flynn's nemesis, Miriam Hopkins a dance hall girl, and Humphrey Bogart a half-breed Mexican bandit (complete with mustache!). 121 min.
12-2396 ***$19.99***

Santa Fe Trail (1940)
Frontier drama set in pre-Civil War Kansas during John Brown's anti-slavery raids. Errol Flynn is military leader Jeb Stuart, Ronald Reagan is George Armstrong Custer, and Olivia de Havilland is the woman they both love. Sweeping tale co-stars Raymond Massey, Alan Hale; Michael Curtiz directs. 110 min.
12-2734 ☐***$19.99***

They Died With Their Boots On (1941)
While lacking in historical accuracy, Raoul Walsh's depiction of Custer's Last Stand makes for rousing adventure. Errol Flynn shines as the dashing, headstrong general, shown from his West Point and Civil War days to the fateful battle of Little Big Horn. Olivia de Havilland, Arthur Kennedy, Anthony Quinn also star. 140 min.
12-2036 ☐***$19.99***

They Died With Their Boots On (Color Version)
Ah, but didn't you always wonder what color those boots were? With the aid of modern technology, now you can see!
12-2037 ***$19.99***

Dive Bomber (1941)
In order to better understand the problems faced by high-altitude combat fliers, armed forces surgeon Errol Flynn goes through the rigors of pilot training in this fine war-themed drama made shortly before America's entry into World War II. With Ralph Bellamy, Fred MacMurray, Alexis Smith. 130 min.
12-2614 ☐***$19.99***

Footsteps In The Dark (1941)
Comedy and mystery are mixed in the "Thin Man" style in this whodunit starring Errol Flynn as an investment banker who, unknown to his wife, moonlights as a suspense writer and amateur sleuth. Flynn's snooping into a jewel thief's death gets him involved with kooky stripper Lee Patrick. Brenda Marshall, Ralph Bellamy co-star. 96 min.
12-2945 ☐***$19.99***

Desperate Journey (1942)
Spirited Raoul Walsh WWII drama stars Errol Flynn and Ronald Reagan as the leaders of an RAF bomber crew whose plane is shot down over Nazi-occupied Poland. Their perilous trek, dodging the Germans across Europe, makes for a thrilling adventure. With Alan Hale, Raymond Massey. 119 min.
12-2274 ***$19.99***

Gentleman Jim (1942)
An exciting, brawling biodrama that looks at the colorful life of turn-of-the-century boxing champion Jim Corbett, with a typically dashing Errol Flynn in the title role. Able support from Alexis Smith, Alan Hale, Jack Carson and Ward Bond as John L. Sullivan. 104 min.
12-2616 ***$19.99***

Edge Of Darkness (1943)
Superlative wartime drama set in a small Norwegian fishing village under German occupation. Errol Flynn and Ann Sheridan are resistance leaders faced with fighting both the Nazis and local sympathizers. Walter Huston, Judith Anderson, Ruth Gordon co-star; Lewis Milestone directs. 120 min.
12-2613 ***$19.99***

Northern Pursuit (1943)
Errol Flynn is a Mountie in the Canadian woods in this classic wartime suspenser about the search for a downed Nazi pilot. Helmut Dantine gives an excellent portrayal as the young fugitive. With Gene Lockhart, Julie Bishop; directed by Raoul Walsh. 94 min.
12-2947 ☐***$19.99***

Uncertain Glory (1944)
Condemned murderer Errol Flynn escapes the guillotine in occupied Paris when a British air raid destroys the prison and allows him to escape, but police inspector Paul Lukas is hot on his trail in this suspense-filled wartime thriller. With Jean Sullivan, Lucille Watson; Raoul Walsh directs. 102 min.
12-2948 ☐***$19.99***

San Antonio (1945)
The sound of gunfire echoes through the Alamo once more in this two-fisted Errol Flynn western. Here Flynn plays a cattleman who sets out to break the hold rustler Paul Kelly has on the good folk of San Antonio. Alexis Smith provides the love interest, S.Z. Sakall the comedy relief. 107 min.
12-2169 ☐***$19.99***

Objective, Burma! (1945)
One of the most requested films at Movies Unlimited is this classic WWII epic starring Errol Flynn as the commander of American parachutists who go behind enemy lines to destroy an important Japanese communications center. Rugged action scenes and Flynn at his finest highlight Raoul Walsh's stirring drama. With William Prince, James Brown. 142 min.
12-2309 ***$19.99***

Never Say Goodbye (1946)
The rocky marriage between pin-up artist Errol Flynn and understandably jealous spouse Eleanor Parker is salvaged, thanks to the efforts of daughter Patti Brady, in this breezy romantic comedy. With S.Z. Sakall, Lucille Watson; co-scripted by Billy Wilder colleague I.A.L. Diamond. 97 min.
12-2946 ☐***$19.99***

Escape Me Never (1947)
Glossy soaper with Eleanor Parker as a young woman who falls for composer Errol Flynn, who is already involved with widow Ida Lupino. After promising to marry Lupino and care for her young child, Flynn abandons her for Parker. With Gig Young, Reginald Denny. 101 min.
12-2610 ☐***$19.99***

The Adventures Of Don Juan (1948)
Errol Flynn swashes, buckles and romances his way across Europe in this epic costume adventure tale. From swordfights to bedroom trysts, Don Juan is without peer, and this colorful film is without equal. Co-stars Viveca Lindfors, Robert Douglas, Alan Hale. 110 min.
12-1509 Was $59.99 ***$19.99***

Silver River (1948)
Director Raoul Walsh and star Errol Flynn teamed up for the seventh and last time in this frontier drama about a Union Army officer (Flynn) who, after being drummed out of the service, heads west and becomes a ruthless mining baron in the silver trade. With Ann Sheridan, Thomas Mitchell, Bruce Bennett. 109 min.
12-2612 ***$19.99***

That Forsyte Woman (1949)
The first book in John Galsworthy's "Forsyte Saga" trilogy is the basis for this elegant melodrama set in Victorian England. The stormy marriage of aristocratic Errol Flynn and Greer Garson is threatened when she is pursued by cousin Janet Leigh's fiancé, architect Robert Young. Walter Pidgeon, Harry Davenport also star. 112 min.
12-2373 ***$19.99***

Montana (1950)
Sheep rancher Errol Flynn leaves his native Australia to start a new life in America, but upon arriving in the sprawling Montana Territory finds himself in the middle of a violent range war between sheepherders and cattlemen. Fast-paced frontier drama also stars Alexis Smith, Douglas Kennedy, S.Z. Sakall. 77 min.
19-2437 ***$19.99***

Kim (1951)
Children and adults alike will love Rudyard Kipling's classic tale of an English boy raised by the Hindus in 1880s India. The action peaks when the young adventurer is caught between rebellious natives and British soldiers. Errol Flynn and Dean Stockwell star. 112 min.
12-1585 ***$19.99***

The Master Of Ballantrae (1953)
Robert Louis Stevenson's classic adventure is turned into a thrilling screen saga. Errol Flynn wields the steel as the rebellious heir to Scottish royalty who journeys to the Caribbean to help his soldier-of-fortune brother fight pirates and, later, seeks the hand of his true love. Roger Livesey, Anthony Steel and Beatrice Campbell also star. 89 min.
19-1976 Was $19.99 ***$14.99***

Lilacs In The Spring (1954)
World War II entertainer Anna Neagle is injured during an air raid and dreams about which of her two suitors she should marry. Her dreams become fantasies, with her playing courtesan Neil Gwynn, a young Queen Victoria and her own mother. Errol Flynn is the song-and-dance man who marries her mother. With David Farrar, Peter Graves and a young Sean Connery in a bit part. This is the color version. AKA: "Let's Make Up." 93 min.
08-1806 ***$19.99***

The Warriors (1955)
Errol Flynn shines as a British prince defending family and army from the forces of the French in this grand old adventure saga set in medieval times. Co-stars Peter Finch, Joanne Dru, Michael Hordern. 85 min.
04-3075 ***$19.99***

King's Rhapsody (1955)
In one of his last screen roles, Errol Flynn plays the heir to a European throne who chooses the woman he loves over his duty. But the death of his father forces him to become king and marry another. Moving drama co-stars Anna Neagle, Patrice Wymore (the third Mrs. Flynn). 93 min.
53-6016 Was $29.99 ***$14.99***

Istanbul

Istanbul (1957)
In this reworking of 1947's "Singapore," Errol Flynn plays an American pilot who discovers that the bracelet he purchased in Turkey contains 13 priceless diamonds. Smugglers attempt to snag the jewels, but Flynn hides them in a hotel room and, years later, returns to retrieve them. Nat King Cole sings "When I Fall in Love"; Torin Thatcher, Cornell Borchers co-star. 85 min.
07-2309 ☐***$14.99***

The Errol Flynn Theater
Three episodes from Flynn's mid-'50s anthology series. Errol himself stars as a swordsman in "The Duel" and appears with wife Patrice Wymore and son Sean in "The Strange Auction." Also included is "The Sealed Room," with Glynis Johns and Herbert Lom. 80 min.
01-1453 Was $19.99 ***$14.99***

The Errol Flynn Theater/ Man In The Iron Mask
Errol himself stars in "The Duel," a cutlass-wielding tale about a haughty noble who challenges the beloved of his pretty ward, co-starring Ann Silvers. Also, an episode from the adventures of Dumas' classic hero, "The Sword Strikes," with Carl Esmond.
10-7472 Was $19.99 ***$14.99***

The Sword Of Villon/Rescued
Hollywood legend Errol Flynn brings his dashing bravado to these two early TV dramas. "The Sword of Villon," a 1956 episode of "Screen Director's Playhouse," features Flynn's TV acting debut. And "Rescued," from 1957's "The Errol Flynn Theatre," tells of a wounded Lord Alston being rescued from one of Cromwell's officers by his friends. 50 min.
10-9389 ***$14.99***

Errol Flynn: Portrait Of A Swashbuckler
The career and controversial life of Hollywood's leading action star is chronicled in this program that offers anecdotes from friends and family, along with clips from such classics as "The Adventures of Robin Hood," "Captain Blood," and "The Charge of the Light Brigade." Christopher Lee narrates. 50 min.
22-1271 ***$19.99***

Please see our index for these other Errol Flynn titles: *Cry Wolf • The Sisters*

She (1935)
H. Rider Haggard's famed novel was the source for this memorable adventure epic starring Randolph Scott and Nigel Bruce as the leaders of an expedition in search of the secret of eternal life. A spectacular avalanche near Manchuria lands them in the underground world of Kor, where they are captured by the followers of the beautiful, immortal "She-Who-Must-Be-Obeyed" (Helen Gahagan). 95 min.
53-8318 *$24.99*

She (1965)
Lavish Hammer Studios version of H. Rider Haggard's tale stars Ursula Andress as the title character, the ageless beauty who seduces explorer John Richardson, the image of her ancient lover, to take her to a lost city where the Flame of Life is located. Peter Cushing, Christopher Lee also star. 107 min.
12-2998 Letterboxed ❑*$19.99*

The Vengeance Of She (1967)
In this sequel to Hammer Studios' 1967 "She," Olinka Berova plays a dead ringer for the immortal queen who is placed under a spell by the high priest of Kuma. Convinced she is the reincarnation of the undying She, Berova finds herself drawn to the ancient kingdom. Can her boyfriend save her from the Eternal Flame? With Edward Judd, John Richardson. AKA: "The Return of She." 101 min.
08-8719 Letterboxed *$14.99*

Flaming Signal (1933)
Ruthlessly exploited by trader Noah Beery, the native population of a small Pacific island revolts, threatening every white man on the colony. The missionary and his pretty daughter can only be saved by crash-landed pilot John David Horsley and his wondrous dog, Flash. 64 min.
68-8066 *$14.99*

Badge Of Honor (1934)
The heroic Buster Crabbe plays a society boy who poses as a newspaper reporter when he comes to a new city. Soon he's embroiled in a number of exciting situations, ranging from car chases to saloon fights. Guess he's not working the film critic beat. Ruth Hall, Ralph Lewis also star. 62 min.
09-5163 *$19.99*

The Last Stand (1938)
A young Maori girl, raised by the British since the Maori Wars in New Zealand, is kidnapped by Maoris and leads them against her adopted people. Complicating matters is the fact that her former boyfriend has joined the army fighting on England's side. Leo Pilcher, Ramai te Miha and Stanley Knight star.
09-5268 *$19.99*

When Lightning Strikes (1934)
When an unscrupulous timber company owner tries to take over a competitor's land, he doesn't count on meeting resistance from the young man's scrappy canine companion, who puts the bite on the bad guys. Thrill-packed melodrama stars Francis X. Bushman, Jr. and Lightning, the Wonder Dog. 51 min.
09-1541 Was $24.99 *$14.99*

The Lion Man (1936)
Raised in the jungle by a holy man after his father's caravan is slaughtered by an evil Arabian leader, a young man tries to avenge the death by protecting other caravans which may meet a similar fate. Known as "El L'ion," he eventually falls in love with the daughter of a sheik whom he has rescued. Charles Loucher, Kathleen Burke star. 62 min.
10-9481 *$19.99*

Happy Go Lucky (1937)
A top American military flyer is believed to have turned foreign agent after he disappears during a transpacific flight. While his wife's in Shanghai, she sees a singer who looks just like him and tries to convince the crooner he's the missing pilot. Adventure and music mix with Phil Regan, Evelyn Venable and Jed Prouty. 53 min.
09-2409 *$14.99*

Dr. Syn (1937)
George Arliss stars as the kindly 18th-century English parson who at night leads a band of smugglers fighting unjust taxes. Fine adventure drama that inspired "The Scarecrow of Romney Marsh." 90 min.
10-3024 *$19.99*

Stunt Pilot (1939)
Tailspin Tommy and his sky-bound friends zoom off to Hollywood to be in pictures, but land in the soup when, during a dogfight scene, a fellow stunt pilot is killed after someone exchanges live ammo for blanks in Tommy's Tommy gun. Top-flight entertainment stars John Trent and Milburn Stone. 61 min.
10-7160 Was $19.99 *$14.99*

Gangsters Of The Sea (1932)
Shipboard melodrama highlighted by Noah Beery's delightfully villainous portrayal of the devious first mate who signs on to a cargo ship bound for Singapore with plans of blowing up the vessel for the insurance money and seducing the captain's virtuous daughter. Co-stars Montagu Love, Dorothy Burgess, William Moran. AKA: "Out of Singapore." 61 min.
09-3100 *$14.99*

Beau Ideal (1931)
From 1926 "Beau Geste" director Herbert Brenon comes this Foreign Legion adventure in which a man journeys to Arabia to find a boyhood friend. He discovers that the friend is being held in a prison designed for Legionnaires and must battle an evil Emir and the "Angel of Death." Lester Vail, George Rigas and Loretta Young star. 79 min.
08-1749 *$14.99*

The Legion Of Missing Men (1937)
North Africa's burning desert is the setting for this adventure that pits the Foreign Legion against an evil sheik and two brothers-in-arms against one another for the love of a beautiful dancing girl. Stars Ralph Forbes, Ben Alexander, Virginia Sale. 62 min.
09-1296 Was $24.99 *$19.99*

Mystery Plane (1939)
Teenage throttle jockey John Trent (starring in first of four Monogram "Tailspin Tommy" films) and his pals develop a radio-controlled bombing device, then must prevent it from falling into the hands of enemy agents before they can offer it to the U.S. government. With Marjorie Reynolds and Milburn Stone as Skeeter. 60 min.
10-7053 Was $19.99 *$14.99*

Sky Patrol (1939)
Crackerjack adventure tale with John Trent as "Tailspin Tommy," who goes up against a nasty gang of gunrunners attempting to smuggle their weapons to another country by hydroplane. Marjorie Reynolds, Jackie Coogan and Milburn Stone also star. 60 min.
10-8333 *$19.99*

Danger Flight (1939)
Drama based on the comic strip "Tailspin Tommy" concerns a man who works with juvenile delinquents, showing them how to build model airplanes that can skywrite words. Little does he know how soon his life will depend on one boy's "getting the message!" John Trent, Marjorie Reynolds and Milburn Stone star. 60 min.
17-9048 Was $19.99 *$14.99*

The Four Feathers (1939)
A young army officer in Victorian England, branded a coward by his friends and fiancée for refusing to join his regiment on a mission to the strife-torn Sudan, undertakes a dangerous secret campaign in Africa to clear his name. Classic first sound filming of the A.E.W. Mason adventure, courtesy of Zoltan and Alexander Korda, stars John Clements, June Duprez, Ralph Richardson, C. Aubrey Smith. 115 min.
44-1891 Was $19.99 *$14.99*

The Most Dangerous Game (1932)
Leslie Banks is a big game hunter who forces his "guests" to become the quarry in his latest hunt. Exciting jungle thriller made by the creator of "King Kong" features many of the same sets and "Kong" stars Joel McCrea, Fay Wray and Robert Armstrong. 63 min.
10-4022 Was $19.99 *$14.99*

Tarzan, The Ape Man

Tarzan

Tarzan Of The Apes (1918)
The screen legacy of Edgar Rice Burroughs' jungle hero began with this faithful silent version, with Elmo Lincoln as the son of Lord and Lady Greystoke who, after his parents are killed in Africa, is raised by apes and learns to live by the laws of the jungle. Co-stars Enid Markey, True Boardman. 61 min. Silent with music score.
09-1332 *$19.99*

The Adventures Of Tarzan (1921)
Original screen Tarzan Elmo Lincoln returns in this feature version of the classic serial. The ape man has left civilization for his beloved jungle, but Jane is also in Africa and at the mercy of the evil Rokoff, a Russian agent searching for the jeweled city of Opar. Louise Lorraine, Frank Whitson also star. 188 min. Silent with music score.
10-9365 *$39.99*

Tarzan, The Ape Man (1932)
Venturing into the dark depths of the African wilds, a scientific expedition searching for the Elephants' Graveyard instead encounters the untamed Lord of the Apes, who literally sweeps Jane off her feet and into his treetop lair. Johnny Weissmuller, Maureen O'Sullivan co-star. 99 min.
12-1037 *$19.99*

Tarzan And His Mate (1934)
Jungle lord Johnny Weissmuller returns in a hair-raising adventure, the second installment in the MGM series. The Ape Man and his British gal, Jane, see their exotic lifestyle threatened by the arrival of Jane's ex-beau and his ivory-hunting pal. This restored version features Maureen O'Sullivan's long-unseen topless swimming scene. With Neil Hamilton, Paul Cavanagh. 91 min.
12-2230 *$19.99*

Tarzan Escapes (1936)
Action-packed Ape Man outing with Tarzan encountering stampedes and ferocious wild animals while tracking down his beloved Jane, who has been captured by hunters. Johnny Weissmuller, Maureen O'Sullivan, John Buckler and Cheetah the Chimp star. 95 min.
12-2231 *$19.99*

Tarzan Finds A Son! (1939)
Well, the Hollywood censors wouldn't let Johnny Weissmuller and Maureen O'Sullivan have a child out of wedlock, so the jungle-dwelling pair rescue an orphaned 5-year-old from a plane crash and protect him from greedy relatives after his inheritance. Fourth entry in MGM's Tarzan series also stars Ian Hunter and Johnny Sheffield as "Boy." 82 min.
12-2544 *$19.99*

Tarzan's Secret Treasure (1941)
The treasure is a fortune in gold located deep in the bush, and to find it some rapscallions resort to holding Jane and Boy hostage in order to coerce Tarzan into helping them. Want to bet Johnny Weissmuller will deliver some "jungle justice" before too long? With Maureen O'Sullivan, Reginald Owen, Barry Fitzgerald and Johnny Sheffield. 81 min.
12-2545 *$19.99*

Tarzan's New York Adventure (1942)
When Boy is kidnapped by circus owners and taken to America, Tarzan and Jane follow, and the Jungle Lord's first encounter with skyscrapers, traffic jams and suits make a humorous, exciting film. The final MGM entry in the series stars Johnny Weissmuller, Maureen O'Sullivan (her last appearance as Jane), Johnny Sheffield, Charles Bickford; look for first screen Tarzan Elmo Lincoln in a cameo. 70 min.
12-2546 *$19.99*

Tarzan The Fearless (1933)
Olympic great Buster Crabbe dons the loincloth this time as the Lord of the Jungle, helping a young girl find her father, discovering a lost city and fighting treacherous Arabs. Adapted from the serial of the same title. 78 min.
01-1364 Was $19.99 *$14.99*

Tarzan And The Green Goddess (1935)
The animal skin and vine have once again been handed down, this time to another Olympic star, Herman Brix, in this condensed version of the serial "The New Adventures of Tarzan." Two expeditions, each seeking the legendary "Green Goddess," square off with Tarzan trying to heal the breach. 72 min.
01-1278 Was $19.99 *$14.99*

Tarzan's Revenge (1938)
Decathlon champ Glenn Morris takes over the reins as Tarzan, rescuing a young woman from the evil clutches of a demented ruler, who has designs on keeping her for himself in his hidden fortress. Co-stars Eleanor Holm and C. Henry Gordon. 70 min.
01-1272 Was $19.99 *$14.99*

Tarzan And The Trappers (1958)
Enforcing the jungle's code of justice, Tarzan (Gordon Scott) tries to impede the actions of greedy trappers capturing animals for zoos and save a noble chieftain ("Scatman" Crothers) along the way. Also stars Eve Brent. 71 min.
09-1030 Was $19.99 *$14.99*

TARZAN THE APE MAN

Tarzan, The Ape Man (1981)
Bo Derek is the swinging-est Jane yet in this sexy version of the legend. Dry, wet or undressed, Bo will steal your heart and bulge your eyes. No wonder hubby screams, "ah uhh-uhh ah-uh!" Miles O'Keeffe, Richard Harris co-star. 112 min.
12-1114 *$19.99*

Greystoke: The Legend Of Tarzan, Lord Of The Apes (1984)
Faithfully adapted from Burroughs' first Tarzan novel, this film from director Hugh Hudson ("Chariots of Fire") follows the adventures of the jungle lord as he is orphaned as an infant, grows up among the apes, and returns to England to reclaim his heritage. Christopher Lambert, Andie MacDowell, Ralph Richardson star. Special video edition contains footage not show in theatres. 136 min.
19-1340 Was $19.99 ❑*$14.99*

Greystoke: The Legend Of Tarzan, Lord Of The Apes (Letterboxed Version)
Also available in a theatrical, widescreen format.
19-2554 ❑*$19.99*

Tarzan And The Lost City (1998)
Edgar Rice Burroughs' famed hero returns to the screen in this adventure saga which finds him in England, enjoying life as Lord Greystroke and about to marry Lady Jane Porter. When he learns that an explorer's quest for the fabled Lost City of Opar threatens his jungle domain, Tarzan slips back into the loincloth to help. Casper Van Dien and Jane March star. 84 min.
19-2751 Was $99.99 ❑*$14.99*

Skull And Crown (1935)
Breeding will tell, and Rin Tin Tin, Jr. shows the stuff that made his doggie daddy great, when he aids border agent Regis Toomey in the capture of the elusive Zorro. Pick of the litter! Co-stars John Elliott, Lois January, Tom London. 55 min.
09-2073 Was $24.99 *$14.99*

The Test (1935)
After stopping a fur thief from taking his goods, a trapper finds that his furs have been swiped anyway. The ever-popular pooch Rin Tin Tin goes into action, sniffing out the culprit and finding the booty. Monte Blue and Grant Withers star in a film that'll receive mixed reviews from People for the Ethical Treatment of Animals.
68-9010 *$19.99*

Caryl Of The Mountains (1936)
There's no shortage of action in this enthralling tale starring Rin Tin Tin, Jr. as a canine who helps the mounties track down an embezzler and killer responsible for the death of a fur trapper. Lois Wilde and Francis X. Bushman, Jr. also star. 60 min.
68-8971 *$19.99*

Fangs Of The Wild (1938)
A group of fox fur thieves are wanted by forest rangers, but they're tough to find because they use a dog to carry the stolen foxes. The sale of a coat to an undercover agent prompts the rangers to try to stop the thieves with help from Rin-Tin-Tin, Jr. Dennis Moore, Luana Walters and Tom Lundon star. 55 min.
10-9478 *$14.99*

The Drifter (1932)
Effective story of a mysterious, nomadic lumberjack who steps in to resolve the conflicts of two timber magnates who are at loggerheads. Plenty of mystery and adventure with William Farnum, Noah Beery, Phyllis Barrington. 60 min.
10-7184 *$19.99*

Born To Be Wild (1938)
Two truckers attempt to save a town by blowing up a dam, which would thwart underhanded real estate developers. Ralph Byrd, of "Dick Tracy" fame, stars with Doris Weston and Ward Bond in this exciting story written by Nathanael West. 66 min.
10-8207 *$19.99*

Air Police (1931)
Crime in the air doesn't pay. At least that's what pilot/lawman Kenneth Harlan wants to prove when he tries to get the goods on some nasty smugglers who killed his partner. Charles Delaney also stars; features some expert aerial scenes. 65 min.
10-9146 Was $19.99 *$14.99*

King Of The Damned (1936)
There's adventure and intrigue on an island prison when the leader of the convicts stages a revolt against an evil administrator and his ruthless ways. As the administrator's life is endangered, a warship arrives to quell the uprising. Conrad Veidt, Noah Beery, Sr. and Helen Vinson star. 80 min.
10-9234 Was $19.99 *$14.99*

Captain Calamity (1936)
In this exciting adventure, a sea captain's claims that he's discovered a fortune in Spanish treasure draws interest from the area's scalawags. When one of the bad guys puts the captain's girlfriend in danger, Calamity tries to stop the scoundrels. George Houston, Marion Nixon and Crane Wilbur star. 60 min.
10-9255 *$19.99*

Shadow Over Shanghai (1937)
Fast-paced espionage and thrills are in store when a pilot with a gold amulet worth millions is shot down by a Russian delegation while flying over China. Eventually, the amulet is retrieved by the pilot's sister, who lands in Shanghai and is befriended by an American reporter. James Dunn, Ralph Morgan and Linda Gray star.
68-9125 *$19.99*

Island Captives (1937)
A murdered businessman's daughter finds herself stranded on a remote jungle island with, of all people, her pop's killer. They both run afoul of a smuggler who uses the island as his headquarters in this fast-paced actioner. Eddie Nugent, Joan Barclay star.
68-9231 *$19.99*

The Live Wire (1935)
Exciting adventure yarn set on a desert island and starring Richard Talmadge and Alberta Vaughn. Two archaeologists hire a seaman to take them to a remote island in hopes of finding a priceless vase. 57 min.
10-9778 *$19.99*

Found Alive (1934)
It's menacing animals and domestic drama when a woman loses a custody case, kidnaps her baby, and hides with him in the Mexican jungle. Barbara Bedford, Robert Frazer star. 65 min.
68-8091 *$19.99*

Rip Roaring Riley (1935)
Lloyd Hughes is the dynamic Riley, a G-man looking into the production of poison gas by a scientist on a desert island. Riley discovers that dastardly major Grant Withers plans to snag the formula and sell it off to the highest bidder. Filmed in and around Los Angeles, this adventure also stars Ann Baker as the scientist's daughter, with whom Riley has a romance.
79-6456 Was $24.99 *$19.99*

Call Of The Yukon (1938)
In this Klondike adventure, a female reporter heading north for a story gets lost and calls on a handsome guide and wild animals with whom she has a rapport to find her way. During the difficult journey, she and her companions faces many dangers. Richard Arlen, Beverly Roberts and Lyle Talbot star. 70 min.
10-6020 *$14.99*

Night Ride (1937)
When the spoiled daughter of a trucking company owner gets two of the employees fired, they decide to start their own trucking business. They are soon put under pressure by the competition as they fight sabotage while at the same time trying to save trapped miners. Julien Vedey, Jimmy Hanley, Wally Patch and Joan Ponsford star.
68-9254 *$19.99*

Windjammer (1937)
Outstanding adventure stars George O'Brien as a deputy D.A. travelling incognito on a yacht loaded with the rich and powerful that runs afoul of merciless gunrunners! Constance Worth, William Hall co-star. 60 min.
10-7183 *$19.99*

Men Of The Sea (1935)
The first solo directorial effort by Carol Reed ("The Third Man") is a sprawling adventure tale set in the late 18th century and featuring Hughie Green as a young man who enlists in the British Navy. His adventures include rescuing a woman from pirates, capturing an enemy ship and searching for lost treasure. With Margaret Lockwood. AKA: "Midshipman Easy." 70 min.
10-9484 *$19.99*

Mutiny Ahead (1935)
Neil Hamilton, later known as Commissioner Gordon on the "Batman" TV series, stars as a playboy whose involvement with gamblers leads to a search for underwater treasure. Kathleen Burke, Leon Ames and Paul Fix also star. 65 min.
10-9485 *$19.99*

Let 'Em Have It (1935)
Depression-era gangland adventure suggested by J. Edgar Hoover himself about an FBI agent avenging the death of his brother, a fellow officer slain by a Dillinger-like gunman. Richard Arlen and Bruce Cabot star. 96 min.
27-6637 *$19.99*

The Lost Zeppelin (1929)
With special effects and convincing miniatures that were a marvel in its time, this early talkie describes a doomed mission to Antarctica by passengers aboard a futuristic, lighter-than-air colossus. Ricardo Cortez stars. Oh, the humanity! 79 min.
68-8301 *$19.99*

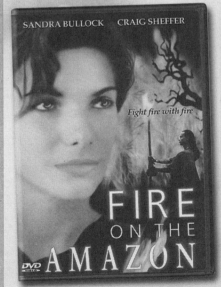

What Planet Are You From? (2000)
A comedy for anyone who thinks men and women come from two different planets, director Mike Nichols' sci-fi satire stars Garry Shandling as an alien dispatched from his all-male homeworld to impregnate an Earth female as a prelude to interplanetary invasion. Coaching a clueless Shandling in the ways of wooing women is smarmy playboy Greg Kinnear, and Annette Bening is a real estate agent who catches Shandling's eye. With John Goodman, Linda Fiorentino. 107 min.
02-3443 ◻*$99.99*

Whatever It Takes (2000)
"Cyrano de Bergerac" gets an updating (and, apparently, a nose job) in this teen romantic comedy. Lovably geeky high schooler Shane West is desperate to date snooty class beauty Jodi Lyn O'Keefe, while jock James Franco wants to woo West's best friend, brainy Marla Sokoloff. The guys agree to coach each other in romancing their "dream girls," but destiny has a surprise in store at the prom. Julia Sweeney also stars. 94 min.
02-3450 ◻*$99.99*

Labor Pains (2000)
A week after she and boyfriend Rob Morrow break up, Kyra Sedgwick learns that she's pregnant. The pregnancy is kept secret until Sedgwick goes into labor and pal Lela Rochon calls her family and friends—including a shocked Morrow—with the news, leading to comical chaos at the hospital. Mary Tyler Moore and Robert Klein also star. 89 min.
02-9209 Was $99.99 ◻*$14.99*

Down To You (2000)
Lively romantic tale stars Freddie Prinze, Jr. as an aspiring chef who meets aspiring artist Julia Stiles while at college. The two hit it off and begin a storybook romance, until questions of infidelity break them up and leave Prinze vowing to win Stiles back. Zak Orth, Selma Blair, Henry Winkler and Lucie Arnaz also star. 89 min.
11-2441 Was $99.99 ◻*$19.99*

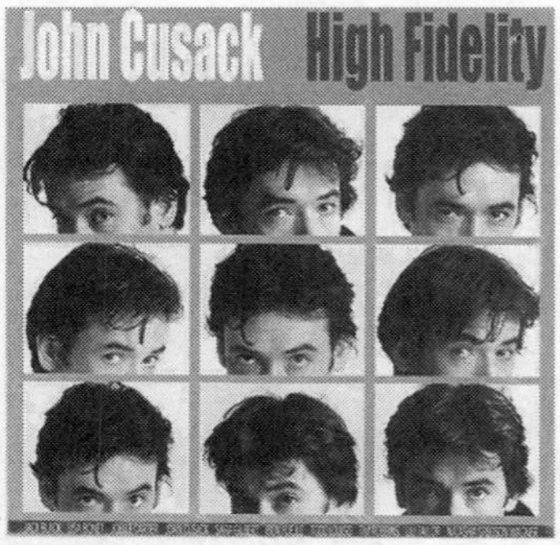
John Cusack
High Fidelity

High Fidelity (2000)
Sharp, witty comedy from Nick Hornby's acclaimed novel stars John Cusack as the music- and list-obsessed proprietor of a funky Chicago record store who reviews his disastrous love life after girlfriend Iben Hjejle leaves him. Catherine Zeta-Jones and Lili Taylor are among the former flames Cusack looks up for advice; Jack Black and Todd Louiso his neurotic coworkers. With Tim Robbins, Lisa Bonet; directed by Stephen Frears ("The Grifters"). 114 min.
11-2460 ◻*$99.99*

3 Strikes (2000)
Fresh out of prison, Brian Hooks finds himself in big trouble when his friend picks him up in a stolen car and an ensuing gunfight with police sends him on the lam. Facing a life in prison, Hooks hilariously seeks help from his parole officer, his girlfriend and his family. With N'Bushe Wright, George Wallace, Faizon Love and David Alan Grier; directed by D.J. Pooh. 82 min.
12-3318 ◻*$99.99*

The Big Tease (2000)
Craig Ferguson plays Cameron Mackenzie, Scotland's finest hairdresser, who travels with a documentary film crew to Los Angeles to compete in the World Freestyle Hairdressing Championship. But when Ferguson realizes he was not invited to take part in the competition, he must find a way to enter and win the coveted Platinum Scissors. With Frances Fisher, David Rasche. 86 min.
19-2985 Was $99.99 ◻*$14.99*

Beautiful People (2000)
A brave mix of dark satire, war horrors and social politics, this acclaimed film from first-time director Jasmin Dizdar is set in London in 1993, where, during the World Cup soccer matches that pit England against Holland, the lives of Balkan refugees collide with Londoners. Charlotte Coleman, Charles Kay and Rosalind Ayres star. 117 min.
68-1999 ◻*$69.99*

It's The Rage (2000)
This scathing, multi-character satire of the American infatuation with guns stars Jeff Daniels as a businessman who shoots his partner for allegedly burglarizing his house. When wife Joan Allen leaves Daniels and winds up working for eccentric computer mogul Gary Sinise, whose previous assistant left to try and land a Hollywood job, a series of violent confrontations follow. With André Braugher, Josh Brolin, Anna Paquin, Giovanni Ribisi and David Schwimmer. AKA: "All the Rage." 103 min.
02-3453 ◻*$99.99*

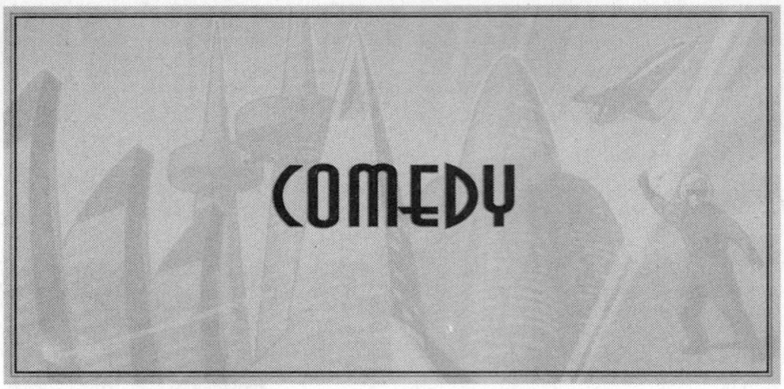
COMEDY

Ready To Rumble (2000)
Wrestling fans David Arquette and Scott Caan leave their tiny Wyoming home to devote themselves to resurrecting the career of Oliver Platt, a washed-up grappler living in a trailer park who has been banned from the World Championship Wrestling promotion by megalomaniacal head Joe Pantoliano. Funny and knowing spoof of the wrassling world also stars Rose McGowan, Martin Landau and real-life wrestlers Diamond Dallas Page, Goldberg and Sting. 106 min.
19-2996 ◻*$99.99*

Bacon Head (2000)
The Troma Team presents a sketch comedy in the Monty Python vein written, directed by and starring Ray Mahoney. Recurring characters humorously satirize popular culture in vignettes on "Land of the People Named Chris," "Tools of Proctology Kitchen Utensils," "The Toast Police," "Gerbil Absorbency Test," and others. Also starring Nick Boicourt, Jr., Terry McNicol, Todd Grundy.
46-8067 *$24.99*

Where The Heart Is (2000)
Pregnant teen Natalie Portman is abandoned in an Oklahoma Wal-Mart by her low-life boyfriend while on a cross-country trip and promptly takes up residence in the store. After making the news with her in-store delivery, Portman sets out to build a life for herself in the quirky small town, with help from local nurse and fellow single mom Ashley Judd, in this heartwarming seriocomedy. Stockard Channing, James Frain and Sally Field also star. 118 min.
04-3986 ◻*$99.99*

Bar-B-Q (2000)
"Ray Ray" West is a pro ball player-turned-hip L.A. actor who has grown tired of the Hollywood rat race and decides that a relaxing trip to his hometown in the South is best for what ails him. However, when the entire town gets word of his bar-B-Q, his backyard is soon infested with the whole neighborhood in this urban comedy with rappers Layzie Bone and Felecia. 96 min.
81-9116 *$59.99*

Soul Talkin' (2000)
James and Kim are about to call it quits until they take part in a college study on relationships to examine what went wrong. However, it seems there are three sides to every story: his, hers and the truth, and despite pressure from their friends, they still can't help but wonder if the truth is that they belong together. Damon Hines, Tamara Lynch and Larry O. Williams star. 91 min.
81-9118 *$59.99*

If You Only Knew (2000)
Johnathon Schaech needs a room after taking a new job in New York. He has also fallen for Alison Eastwood, who only rents her available space to gay men. Schaech decides to lie in order to live with her, but things start to get complicated as their relationship develops, and now he must deal with Eastwood's gay friends whom she is setting him up with! James LeGros, Gabrielle Anwar also star. 111 min.
81-9120 *$99.99*

Deadly Game (2000)
Twelve-year-old Nathan has run away from home, but instead of laying low he's having the time of his life in a hotel suite...thanks to a stolen stash of mob money. However, when the situation becomes too dangerous Nathan decides to help the police catch the crooks before they catch him, in this family comedy. Tim Matheson, Carol Alt, Catherine Oxenberg and Ryan De Boer star. 92 min.
85-1510 *$39.99*

The Big Kahuna (2000)
Kevin Spacey, Danny DeVito and Peter Facinelli are three industrial lubricant salespeople attending a convention in Wichita. As they schmooze with clients in their hotel hospitality suite and await the arrival of a major corporate head whose business they need, the trio discuss their very different views on life, selling, religion and other topics in this unusual, funny character study. 91 min.
07-2901 ◻*$99.99*

Committed (2000)
New Yorker Heather Graham is the epitome of marital strength and fidelity, so when photojournalist hubby Luke Wilson abruptly leaves and moves to Texas, she vows to track him down. Although she learns he's cheating on her, Graham seeks help from brother Casey Affleck and local medicine man Alfonso Arau to salvage their relationship. Lisa Krueger ("Manny & Lo") directs. 96 min.
11-2476 ◻*$99.99*

American Virgin (2000)
"American Beauty" temptress Mena Suvari shines in this cybersex satire about a young woman who's tired of her adult film director dad's lifestyle. She launches a plan to get back at him by signing with his arch-rival to lose her virginity on a webcast event that uses the latest in "interactive technology." Robert Loggia, Bob Hoskins, Sally Kellerman also star. AKA: "Live Virgin." 87 min.
64-9066 *$99.99*

Screwed (2000)
Norm Macdonald is a chauffer who is horribly mistreated by his boss and her evil dog. To get even, he recruits the help of best friend Dave Chappelle and spooky mortician Danny DeVito to kidnap the dog for ransom, but their carefully conceived scheme goes hilariously awry in this screwball comedy. 82 min.
07-2927 ◻*$99.99*

Held Up (2000)
Jamie Foxx is a slick Chicago businessman on a cross-country trip with girlfriend Nia Long. After she dumps him in the desert, he faces a series of comically dangerous situations, encountering carjackers and a robbery at a convenience mart. Barry Corbin, John Cullum and Jake Busey also star. 88 min.
68-2013 ◻*$99.99*

Dish Dogs (2000)
Morgan and Jason are single guys who have no desire to get married. After living the good life as California slacker surfers, they head home for a friend's marriage and soon find their single status threatened when Jason sees an old girlfriend and Morgan has the hots for a stripper. Sean Astin, Matthew Lillard, Brian Dennehy and Shannon Elizabeth star. 96 min.
68-2014 ◻*$69.99*

The Bogus Witch Project (2000)
In a series of short films showcased on a fictitious TV channel, inept film crews with camcorders are getting lost everywhere from the woods to L.A.'s posh Bel Air neighborhood to the ghetto streets, all searching for that elusive spirit. They may be far from Burkittsville, but hopefully not too far from a movie deal, in this wild "Blair Witch" spoof. Pauly Shore, Michael Ian Black star. 85 min.
68-2024 ◻*$69.99*

Return To Me (2000)
It's love at first sight when Chicago architect David Duchovny, whose wife died in an auto accident, meets waitress Minnie Driver in her family's Irish-Italian restaurant. What neither realizes is that Driver received Duchovny's wife's heart in a transplant operation, and the news threatens their blossoming romance. Director/co-writer/co-star Bonnie Hunt's winsome comedy also features Carroll O'Connor, Robert Loggia, James Belushi. 116 min.
12-3325 ◻*$99.99*

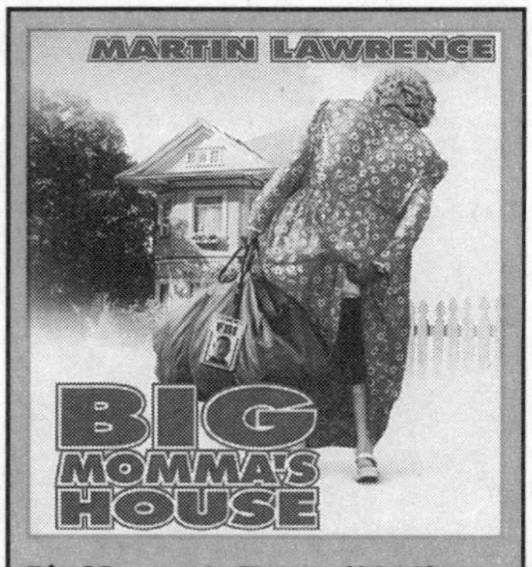
MARTIN LAWRENCE
BIG
MOMMA'S
HOUSE

Big Momma's House (2000)
Side-splitting cross-dressing farce stars Martin Lawrence as a disguise-happy FBI agent who portrays a hefty grandmother in order to gain the confidence of granddaughter Nia Long, the ex-girlfriend of a ruthless bank robber who just broke out of the slammer. While on the case, Lawrence also poses as a handyman with whom Long falls in love, complicating his assignment. With Terrence Howard, Paul Giamatti and Jascha Washington.
04-3989 ◻*$99.99*

East Is East (2000)
Funny, poignant and sometimes downbeat film stars Om Puri as a Pakistani immigrant who runs a fish-and-chip shop in 1970s Manchester, England, with his British wife and seven children. With much opposition, Puri tries to infuse his children with values from his homeland. When two of his sons reject their arranged marriages to Pakistani women, the conflict threatens to tear the family apart. Linda Bassett also stars. 96 min.
11-2461 ◻*$99.99*

American Women
(The Closer You Get) (2000)
After relentless rejection by the native girls, the men of a small Irish town place a personal ad in the Miami Herald in hopes of attracting some American mates. The jealous townswomen counter their move by inviting a band of Spaniards to play at a local dance. A comedic battle of the sexes ensues as the two factions struggle to come to terms with each other. Ian Hart, Cathleen Bradley, Sean McGinley and Niamh Cusack star. 90 min.
04-3987 ◻*$99.99*

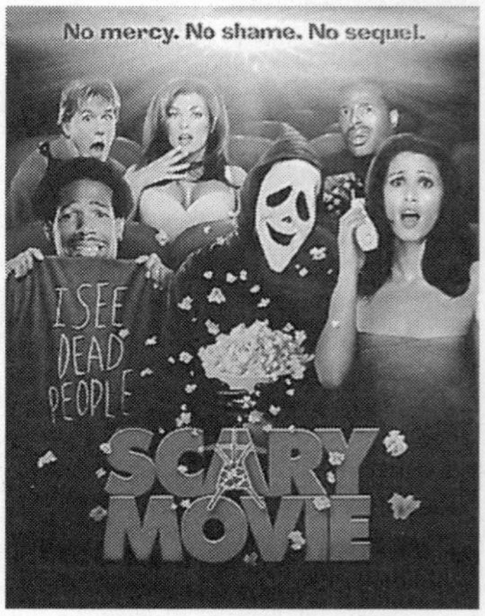
No mercy. No shame. No sequel.
I SEE DEAD PEOPLE
SCARY MOVIE

Scary Movie (2000)
"Scream," "I Know What You Did Last Summer," "The Blair Witch Project" and other horror films are spoofed to outrageous excess by director Keenan Ivory Wayans, whose brothers Shawn and Marlon are among the teenage targets of a white-masked, hooded, hook-handed killer terrorizing B.A. Corpse High School. Shannon Elizabeth, Cheri Oteri and Carmen Electra also star.
11-2488 ◻*$99.99*

Road Trip (2000)
Outrageous road romp about an underachieving college student in upstate New York whose wild romp with an attractive classmate has been videotaped and accidentally sent to his girlfriend in Texas. Now he and his party-loving campus pals are off on a wild cross-country trip to intercept the tape. Breckin Meyer, DJ Qualls, Amy Smart and Tom Green star.
07-2955 ◻*$99.99*

Keeping The Faith (2000)
The directorial debut of Edward Norton is a sweet-natured romantic comedy featuring the actor as a New York priest who has fallen for childhood friend Jenna Elfman, a successful businesswoman and recent Big Apple transplant. Causing problems is the fact that rabbi Ben Stiller, also a childhood pal, has begun a secret affair with Elfman. With Eli Wallach, Anne Bancroft. 129 min.
11-2474 ◻*$99.99*

Don't Hang Up (1990)
A passionate, handicapped New York actress (Rosanna Arquette) starts a long-distance relationship with an emotionally distressed British playwright (David Suchet) that leads to the woman flying to London to continue the romance. A charming, quirky love story. 84 min.
01-1487 Was $59.99 *$29.99*

Little Vegas (1990)
Quirky comedy about a small-time hustler who leaves the big city with the Mob on his tail and finds a safe refuge with some eccentric folk living out in the desert...or so he thinks. Offbeat farce stars Anthony Dennison, Catherine O'Hara, Michael Nouri, Anne Francis, Jerry Stiller. 91 min.
02-2064 *$89.99*

Book Of Love (1991)
Set in 1956, this breezy, nostalgic comedy looks at a shy, imaginative teen who, after moving to a new town, falls for the beautiful blonde girlfriend of a local tough. Chris Young, Keith Coogan, Josie Bisset and Michael McKean star. 86 min.
02-2101 Was $19.99 *$14.99*

Bingo (1991)
A runaway circus canine rescues a little boy who has trouble fitting in with his friends, and soon the two new pals begin playing pinball, riding skateboards and doing homework together. But after the boy's family moves and leaves Bingo behind, the plucky pooch sets out to reunite with his buddy. Cindy Williams and David Rasche star in this hilarious, heartwarming comedy. 90 min.
02-2159 Was $19.99 ◻*$14.99*

Does This Mean We're Married? (1992)
Take "Green Card" and cross it with "Punchline" and you get the idea behind this delightful romantic comedy. Patsy Kensit is an American comic in Paris who needs a work permit in order to perform and winds up "married" to a handsome French musician in need of quick cash. Stephane Freiss co-stars. 93 min.
02-2255 *$14.99*

Medusa: Dare To Be Truthful (1992)
A hilarious spoof of everyone's favorite Material Girl, featuring comedienne Julie Brown as the ever-popular and always-naughty rock diva Medusa, who performs songs like "Expose Yourself," "Vague" and more. With cameos from Chris Elliott, Bobcat Goldthwait and Wink Martindale. 51 min.
02-2286 Was $39.99 *$14.99*

We're Talking Serious Money (1992)
A wild and zany heist comedy about two New York hustlers who find themselves followed by the FBI and the Mob when they attempt to rip off $1 million. Laughs, action and chases abound when Dennis Farina, Leo Rossi and Fran Drescher are around! 92 min.
02-2291 Was $89.99 ❏*$14.99*

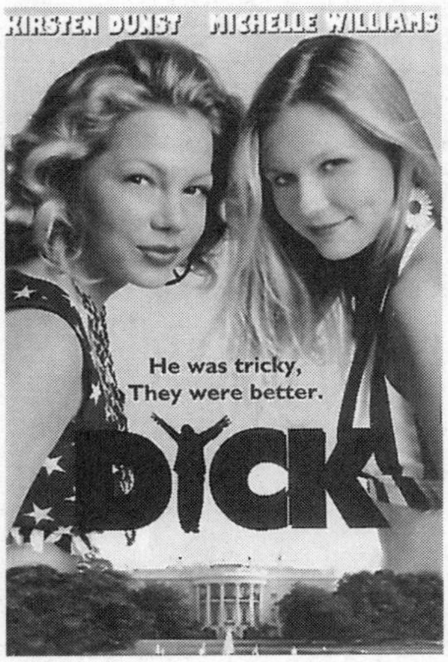

Dick (1999)
Watergate gets comedically whacked in this good-natured satire starring Kirsten Dunst and Michelle Williams as ditsy high school students who become official dog-walkers for President Nixon after they accidentally witness the Watergate burglary. When their friendship with "Tricky Dick" turns sour, they get even by revealing their knowledge of White House shenanigans to a pair of reporters named Woodward and Bernstein. With Dave Foley, Will Ferrell, and Dan Hedaya as Nixon. 94 min.
02-3385 Was $99.99 ❏*$14.99*

Masters Of Menace (1990)
The Road Masters are the roughest, raunchiest and funniest motorcycle gang that ever straddled a hog, and their L.A.-to-Vegas road trip turns into a hilarious ride loaded with beautiful babes, police in pursuit, and zany hi-jinks. David Rasche, David L. Lander, Catherine Bach star. 97 min.
02-2065 Was $89.99 *$19.99*

Me, Myself And I (1993)
George Segal is a New York television writer who falls in love with next-door neighbor JoBeth Williams, unaware that she's a nymphomaniacal pyromaniac with multiple personalities! A wacky romantic farce co-starring Shelley Hack and Don Calfa. 97 min.
02-2509 Was $89.99 *$19.99*

Mr. Nanny (1993)
Hulk Hogan dons a tutu for this family comedy, playing a former pro wrestler who takes a job as a nanny for a group of precocious kids. The youngsters quickly reduce the weight-lifting macho man to rubble as they wreak all sorts of havoc. Sherman Hemsley, Austin Pendelton and David Johansen co-star. 84 min.
02-2525 Was $89.99 ❏*$12.99*

Booty Call (1997)
It's the call that Tommy Davidson hears when he decides it's time he and girlfriend Tamala Jones "get serious" in their relationship. The duo are joined by respective friends Jamie Foxx and Vivica A. Fox for a dinner date at a Chinese restaurant that the men are hoping will lead to a little "booty," while the women are looking for other things, in a sassy, sexy comedy. 79 min.
02-3085 Was $99.99 ❏*$14.99*

Oh, What A Night (1992)
A teenager in 1955 thinks he's in for a boring summer, but winds up having the time of his life when he befriends two guys obsessed with gals, cars and music. The summer turns into a journey of self-discovery for the three friends...especially when it comes to women. Corey Haim, Robbie Coltrane, Barbara Williams and Genevieve Bujold star. 93 min.
02-2324 Was $19.99 *$14.99*

Surf Ninjas (1993)
A wild action-comedy in which teenage California surfer brothers discover that they are princes of a South Seas island and gain magical martial arts skills they use to reclaim their throne from the island's wicked ruler. Ernie Reyes, Jr., Nicolas Cowan, Rob Schneider, Leslie Nielsen and Tone Loc star. 87 min.
02-2514 Was $19.99 ❏*$14.99*

Nervous Ticks (1993)
After planning an escape to Rio de Janeiro with his married lover, an airline employee gets caught in a whirlwind series of wacky misadventures. Bill Pullman, Julie Brown, Peter Boyle and James LeGros star in this farce that's presented entirely in real time. 95 min.
02-2472 *$89.99*

National Lampoon's Attack Of The 5 Ft. 2 Women (1994)
The irrepressible Julie Brown puts her own comic spin on two headline-making "heroines" in this double feature that includes the skating spoof "Tonya: The Battle of Wounded Knee" and a tale of marital discord cutting deep, "He Never Give Me Orgasm: The Lenora Babbitt Story." With Sam McMurray, Rick Overton, Stella Stevens, Khrystyne Haje and the great Dick Miller. 82 min.
06-2300 Was $89.99 ❏*$14.99*

Mo' Money (1992)
Damon Wayans of "In Living Color" stars as a penny-ante scam artist who pulls small crimes with his younger brother (Marlon Wayans). When he is smitten with a credit card company executive (Stacey Dash), he tries to go straight, taking a job in her company mailroom. But the temptation to rip off cardholders gets him mixed up in a big-time scam. Joe Santos, John Diehl also star. 91 min.
02-2338 Was $19.99 ❏*$14.99*

Nickel & Dime (1992)
A charming con artist finds that the IRS is about to impound his fortune and must put up with an obnoxious, by-the-books accountant who is conducting an audit on the crook's goods. When the con man discovers an heiress's life is in danger, he teams with the CPA for a wild caper. C. Thomas Howell, Wallace Shawn and Lise Cutter star. 96 min.
02-2361 Was $89.99 *$19.99*

Ted & Venus (1992)
Bud Cort directed and stars in this quirky romantic farce, playing a poet with a cult following whose obsession with a beautiful woman leads him to go to incredible lengths to strike up a relationship with her. Carol Kane, James Brolin, Martin Mull and Woody Harrelson also star. 100 min.
02-2405 Was $89.99 *$19.99*

Hexed (1993)
A funny spoof of "Fatal Attraction"-type thrillers follows a hotel clerk whose frequent fibs lead him into a whirlwind of daffy danger when Hexina, the world's sexiest (and deadliest) model, stays at the establishment where he works. Arye Gross, Claudia Christian, Adrienne Shelly and Norman Fell star. 93 min.
02-2421 Was $19.99 ❏*$14.99*

The Pickle (1993)
Acclaimed director Harry Stone (Danny Aiello) makes a teenage sci-fi film about a flying cucumber in order to get out of debt. When he comes to New York for its premiere, Harry's encounters with friends, lovers and family lead him to reassess his life. With Dyan Cannon, Shelley Winters, Jerry Stiller and some surprising cameos; Paul Mazursky directs. 103 min.
02-2486 Was $19.99 ❏*$14.99*

Calendar Girl (1993)
Jason Priestley plays a slick teenager who decides to join his two pals on one last fling before he's inducted into the Army in the summer of 1962. The guys decide to head to Hollywood where they plan to meet America's reigning sex symbol, Marilyn Monroe. After several funny near-miss incidents, they come face-to-face with the blonde bombshell. Joe Pantoliano, Jerry O'Connell co-star. 91 min.
02-2528 Was $19.99 ❏*$14.99*

Wilder Napalm (1993)
Two brothers share the amazing ability to set things on fire with their minds. One brother is married to a beautiful, insatiable woman who is under house arrest for arson, while the other is infatuated with her. They square off in an explosive sibling rivalry in this offbeat comedy starring Debra Winger, Dennis Quaid and Arliss Howard. 109 min.
02-2543 Was $89.99 ❏*$14.99*

Jersey Girl (1993)
Lively romantic comedy about a young single woman (Jami Gertz) from Hackensack seeking a nice life in Manhattan with a good-looking Mr. Right. She finds him at a Mercedes car dealership, but is she hip enough to keep him? Dylan McDermott and Sheryl Lee also star. 95 min.
02-2562 Was $19.99 ❏*$14.99*

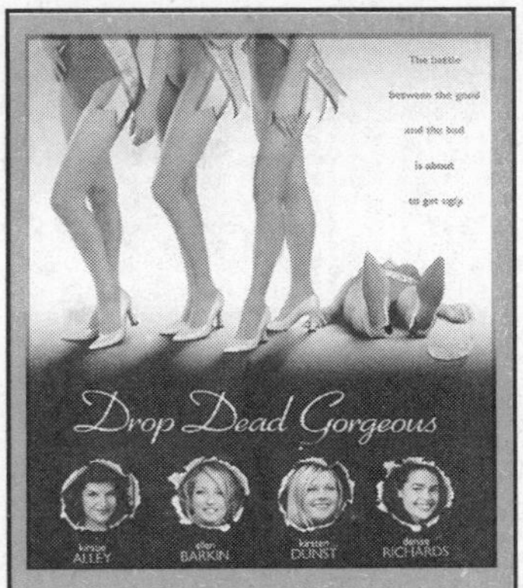

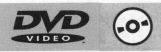

Drop Dead Gorgeous (1999)
Beauty pageants are spoofed to the max in this barbed satire featuring Denise Richards and Kirsten Dunst as rivals vying to represent Minnesota in the Miss Teen Princess America contest. Also battling it out are their mothers: Richards' mom, Kirstie Alley, is a former pageant winner, while Ellen Barkin, Dunst's mother, is a trailer park trash queen. With Nora Dunn and Adam West as himself. 98 min.
02-5219 Was $99.99 ❏*$14.99*

Léolo (1993)
This darkly humorous story set in Montreal centers on the adolescent experiences of a young boy within one of the world's oddest dysfunctional families. His brother is obsessed with body-building, he believes his emotionally troubled sister has floated away, and he's convinced he owes his conception to a tomato. Stars Maxime Collin, Ginetta Reno and Roland Blouin. 107 min. In French with English subtitles.
02-2546 Was $89.99 *$19.99*

Household Saints (1993)
Quirky study of an Italian-American family in New York's Little Italy who experience religious, mystical, gastronomical and sexual revelations over the decades. After butcher Vincent D'Onofrio wins wife Tracey Ullman in a card game, she struggles with overbearing mother-in-law Judith Malina and unpredictable daughter Lili Taylor to keep her brood together. Nancy Savoca ("True Love") directs. 124 min.
02-2622 Was $89.99 *$19.99*

Threesome (1994)
Provocative romantic tale of three students who share the same dorm room at their California college: Eddy (Josh Charles) is a literate transfer student; Stuart (Stephen Baldwin) is a sometimes sensitive jock; and Alex (Lara Flynn Boyle) is a pretty co-ed. The inevitable complex threesome arises when Alex falls for Eddy who, in turn, discovers he really cares for Stuart. 93 min.
02-2646 Was $19.99 ❏*$14.99*

Naked In New York (1994)
Touching romantic comedy about an aspiring young playwright (Eric Stoltz) who recounts his life, career and stormy relationship with a photographer (Mary-Louise Parker). Produced by Martin Scorsese, the film features a fine ensemble cast that includes Ralph Macchio, Tony Curtis, Kathleen Turner and Timothy Dalton. 89 min.
02-2648 Was $89.99 ❏*$19.99*

Widows' Peak (1994)
A witty, atmospheric comedy-mystery set in an Irish village during the 1920s where three women—spinster Mia Farrow, wealthy town matriarch Joan Plowright and Americanized widow Natasha Richardson—carry on a rivalry that leads to the discovery of the dark secrets of their past. With Adrian Dunbar; written by Hugh Leonard ("Da"). 98 min.
02-2659 Was $89.99 ❏*$19.99*

North (1994)
Whimsical comedy centering on a young boy who leaves his work-obsessed mom and dad to find a new set of parents. Along with his "guardian angel" (a bunny-suited Bruce Willis), the lad sets out on a worldwide journey to screen parental prospects. Elijah Wood, Jon Lovitz, Julia Louis-Dreyfus, Jason Alexander and Dan Aykroyd co-star in Rob Reiner's fanciful tale. 87 min.
02-2661 Was $89.99 ❏*$19.99*

Little Big League (1994)
A 12-year-old boy inherits the Minnesota Twins baseball franchise from his grandfather and, because of a lack of on-field success, names himself manager, much to the players' chagrin. Can the school-age skipper lead the team to the World Series? Luke Edwards, Jason Robards and Timothy Busfield star; major leaguers Ken Griffey, Jr., Randy Johnson and Wally Joyner also appear. 120 min.
02-2663 Was $19.99 ❏*$14.99*

The Day My Parents Ran Away (1994)
A quick-talking teen who controls the lives of his parents gets a chance to mature quickly when they leave him on his own. With loads of dirty laundry and a diet that consists of TV dinners, the teen decides to call a parent-finder to help him locate Mom and Dad. Now, if only they wanted to come back home. Matt Frewer, Bobby Jacoby and Blair Brown star. 95 min.
02-2665 Was $19.99 *$14.99*

Even Cowgirls Get The Blues (1994)
The classic counterculture novel by Tom Robbins has been turned into a quirky, surprise-filled comedy by director Gus Van Sant ("My Own Private Idaho"). Uma Thurman plays Sally Hanshaw, the large-thumbed hitchhiker who has an affair with cowgirl Bonanza Jellybean after joining her feminist group at the Rubber Rose Ranch. With Rain Phoenix, Keanu Reeves and John Hurt. 96 min.
02-2679 Was $89.99 ❏*$19.99*

Spanking The Monkey (1994)
Acclaimed coming-of-age "dramady," sparked with dark humor, about an M.I.T. student who carries on an incestuous summer affair with his depressed mother while he helps her after she breaks her leg. Erotic, shocking and funny, this heralded first film from writer-director David O. Russell stars Jeremy Davies and Alberta Watson. 99 min.
02-2715 Was $89.99 ❏*$19.99*

Next Door (1994)
In this outrageous, darkly humorous tale, two suburban neighbors slug it out in an escalating and increasingly dangerous war. Randy Quaid is a butcher who combats college professor James Woods in arm-wrestling, attempted adultery, backyard basketball and, finally, murder. Kate Capshaw, Lucinda Jenney, Miles Fuelner also star. 95 min.
02-2719 *$89.99*

Princess Caraboo (1994)
Delightful comedy, based on a true story, about a mysterious young woman who appears one day in a 19th-century English village and, believed to be a princess from a distant country, is taken in by the townsfolk. But is she actually an impostor who's taking them in? Phoebe Cates, Stephen Rea, John Lithgow and Wendy Hughes star. 96 min.
02-2741 Was $19.99 ❏*$14.99*

Only You (1994)
Lush romantic comedy in the tradition of "Roman Holiday" starring Marisa Tomei as a teacher about to marry who decides to search for the man fate—via a Ouija board—deemed her true love when she was a child. Joined by friend Bonnie Hunt, she takes off to Venice, Italy, and soon finds him...she thinks...in the guise of Robert Downey, Jr. Directed by Norman Jewison ("Moonstruck"). 108 min.
02-2743 Was $19.99 ❏*$14.99*

I Like It Like That (1994)
The acclaimed debut feature from writer-director Darnell Martin is a heartfelt comedy-drama set in a racially mixed section of the Bronx where Lisette, a young Hispanic mother, struggles trying to balance family responsibilities, an unfaithful husband, and a new job with a record company. Lauren Vélez, Jon Seda, Griffin Dunne and Rita Moreno star. 106 min.
02-2754 Was $19.99 ❏*$14.99*

Death In Brunswick (1995)
Short-order cook Sam Neill's obsession with a beautiful barmaid leads him into an unending series of wild events, as he's implicated in a murder and a fire-bombing and soon finds himself involved in a gruesomely funny episode of grave-digging. Zoë Carides co-stars in this unusual, offbeat farce. 106 min.
02-2776 ❏*$89.99*

Nina Takes A Lover (1995)
Insightful comedy about matrimony and its discontents stars Laura San Giacomo as a sexy, unhappily married woman living in San Francisco who has an affair with a handsome, hitched Welsh photographer. At the same time, her reckless best friend becomes involved with a goofy guy from Italy. With Paul Rhys, Cristi Conaway and Michael O'Keefe. 99 min.
02-2803 Was $89.99 ❏*$14.99*

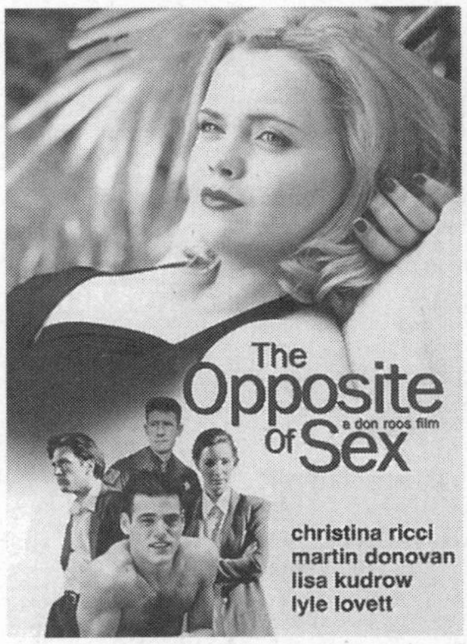

The Opposite Of Sex (1998)
Smart, sassy black comedy features Christina Ricci as a conniving teen who leaves her Louisiana home and moves in with her gay brother in Indiana. Soon, she's not only seducing her sibling's new boyfriend, but coercing him into financing her new baby and going with her to California. Martin Donovan, Lisa Kudrow, Ivan Sergei and Lyle Lovett co-star. 100 min.
02-3227 Was $19.99 ❏*$14.99*

Greetings from PLEASANTVILLE

Pleasantville (1998)
A mysterious remote control zaps contemporary teens Tobey Maguire and Reese Witherspoon into the black-and-white suburban landscape of Maguire's favorite '50s sitcom, "Pleasantville," where their '90s attitudes inspire, agitate, and (literally) put color in the cheeks of the town's befuddledly wholesome citizens. Jeff Daniels, Joan Allen, William H. Macy and Don Knotts also star in this inventive social comedy from "Big" scripter Gary Ross. 124 min.
02-5200   Was $99.99   ☐$19.99

Pleasantville
(Letterboxed Version)
Also available in a theatrical, widescreen format.
02-5209   ☐$19.99

Fools Rush In (1997)
"Friends" star Matthew Perry makes his lead film debut in this funny and wise romantic comedy, playing a New Yorker who meets gorgeous Salma Hayek in Las Vegas while working on a construction project and has a one-night fling with her. When Hayek tells Perry she's pregnant three months later, a wacky wedding and a clash of family cultures soon follow. Jill Clayburgh, Jon Tenney co-star. 110 min.
02-3072   Was $19.99   ☐$14.99

Barcelona (1994)
Driven salesman Taylor Nichols allows his cousin, irresponsible Navy man Chris Eigeman, to stay with him in his Barcelona apartment in the early 1980s. While encountering sexy women, anti-American sentiment and cultural differences, the cousins rekindle their tense childhood relationship. Mira Sorvino co-stars in this wry, erudite tale from Whit Stillman ("Metropolitan"). 102 min.
02-5045   Was $19.99   ☐$14.99

Excess Baggage (1997)
Feeling unnoticed by her rich businessman father, spoiled Alicia Silverstone tries to get his attention by staging a mock kidnapping, only to wind up locked in her car's trunk and taken for a ride by hapless auto thief Benicio Del Toro. The two outcasts wind up on the run from the law together in a fast-paced romantic comedy. Christopher Walken, Harry Connick, Jr. also star. 101 min.
02-3135   Was $99.99   ☐$14.99

Bhaji On The Beach (1994)
A day trip by bus to an English seaside resort becomes a hilarious, cathartic lesson in life and friendship for a group of Indian-born women of various ages and backgrounds in this witty and warm comedy/drama from director Gurinder Chadha. 100 min.
02-2833   ☐$89.99

The Myth Of Fingerprints (1997)
Edgy indie comedy about an uncomfortable Thanksgiving family reunion of a New England brood who haven't seen each other in three years. Parents Roy Scheider and Blythe Danner host the get-together where hidden truths are revealed, resentments come to the surface, and it's proven there are many flaws in the seemingly perfect all-American family. With Noah Wyle, Julianne Moore. 91 min.
02-3145   Was $99.99   ☐$24.99

French Exit (1998)
Jonathan Silverman and Mädchen Amick are Hollywood screenwriters whose lives are changed irrevocably when their cars collide at a busy L.A. intersection. Fueled by ambition, jealousy and genuine affection, their fiery relationship faces many ups and downs as they try to make it in Tinseltown. Molly Hagen, Kurt Fuller and Vince Grant co-star. 88 min.
02-3192   Was $99.99   ☐$24.99

Homegrown (1998)
Billy Bob Thornton heads an all-star cast in this zany new comedy that everyone is toking...er, talking about. When a plantation owner is mysteriously murdered, his $5 million "crop" is up for grabs, employee Thornton and his partners decide that it's theirs for the keeping. Unfortunately, the cops, as well as the mob, will do anything to stop them. Also stars Hank Azaria, Jon Bon Jovi, Jamie Lee Curtis and Kelly Lynch. 102 min.
02-3200   Was $99.99 $14.99

Glory Daze (1997)
With the threat of graduation and entering "the adult world" hanging over their heads, the residents of an infamous college "party house" get ready for a final, all-out celebration in this wild comedy starring Ben Affleck, Megan Ward, Sam Rockwell, French Stewart and Alyssa Milano. 100 min.
02-3108   Was $19.99   ☐$14.99

Snowboard Academy (1997)
Get ready for some wacky, wintry fun in this sexy, zany comedy about a race between skiers and snowboarders to save a favorite winter resort from closing. Corey Haim, Brigitte Nielsen, Jim Varney and Joe Flaherty star. 89 min.
02-3122   ☐$14.99

Twin Sitters (1994)
It's comic calamities times two when the bodybuilding Barbarian Brothers are hired to look after a businessman's obnoxious twin nephews while he testifies against a mob boss. The muscle-bound babysitters have their hands full taking care of the kids...and some gangsters who are after them to keep their uncle quiet. With Jared Martin, Paul Bartel, George Lazenby. 93 min.
02-2829   Was $89.99   ☐$19.99

Idle Hands (1999)
For stoned-out teen slacker Devon Sawa, the old saying about idle extremities and the devil has taken on new meaning, as his right hand is taken over by a demon with its own murderous agenda...and not Sawa's parents, pot-smoking pals or his girlfriend are safe from the deadly digits. Outrageous black comedy/chiller also stars Seth Green, Jessica Alba, Vivica A. Fox. 92 min.
02-3364   Was $99.99   ☐$14.99

To Die For (1995)
An acerbic look at pop celebrity and the drive for fame, this wickedly funny black comedy from scripter Buck Henry and director Gus Van Sant stars Nicole Kidman as a media-obsessed, would-be TV journalist in a small New England town. Eager for success and unwilling to settle for husband Matt Dillon's vision of family life, Kidman seduces a high school student and convinces him to murder her "abusive" spouse. With Joaquin Phoenix, Illeana Douglas. 106 min.
02-2867   Was $19.99   ☐$14.99

Yankee Zulu (1995)
Filmed in South Africa, this comic fable focuses on two former childhood friends (one black, the other white) who reunite after 25 years when circumstances force them into changing personas...and skin colors. Hilarious complications ensue in this family-oriented farce. Leon Schuster, John Matshikiza star. 89 min.
02-2875   ☐$99.99

If Lucy Fell (1996)
Sarah Jessica Parker, a therapist, and Eric Schaeffer, a teacher and painter, are roommates and best friends who made a pact that if they had not found true love by the age of 30, they would jump off the Brooklyn Bridge together. As the clock ticks down, each thinks they've met their perfect companions...or have they? With Elle Macpherson, Ben Stiller; co-written and directed by Schaeffer. 93 min.
02-2935   Was $99.99   ☐$14.99

Friday (1995)
Ice Cube stars as Craig, a lazy fellow living in South Central Los Angeles who spends his time hanging out with pot-smoking pal Smokey (Chris Tucker). Trouble stirs when Ice's gal gets suspicious of his interest in a foxy neighbor and a dope-dealing ice cream man wants some cash from a drug deal he made with Tucker. This outrageous farce also stars Tiny Lister, Jr. and Nia Long. 90 min.
02-5064   Was $19.99   ☐$14.99

Friday
(Letterboxed Special Edition)
The urban comedy is available in a collector's edition featuring deleted scenes and an alternate ending, music videos by Ice Cube and Dr. Dre, and original theatrical trailers. In a theatrical, widescreen format.
02-5221   Was $19.99   ☐$14.99

NEXT friday

the suburbs make the hood look good

Ice Cube

Next Friday (2000)
The laughs don't stop in this hilarious sequel that finds neighborhood bully "Tiny" Lister out of the slammer after a two-year sentence and out for revenge. Ice Cube, the guy that put him behind bars, goes on the run, landing at his uncle's house in the suburbs and finding all sorts of problems. Mike Epps and Don "D.C." Curry also star. 98 min.
02-5230   Was $99.99   ☐$14.99

The Friday Fresh Pack
Looking for something to do between Fridays? Check out this boxed collector's set featuring "Friday" and "Next Friday."
02-5240 $27.99

Bottle Rocket (1996)
Disarming caper comedy about three Texas pals who reluctantly choose a life of crime and proceed to bungle their way through some small-time heists. When they align themselves with a slick professional mobster, they decide to tackle their largest job yet—with surprising results. Owen C. Wilson, Luke Wilson, Robert Musgrave and James Caan star. 92 min.
02-2836   Was $19.99   ☐$14.99

The Last Supper (1996)
Darkly comic satire in which five liberal graduate students share their weekly dinner together with a racist redneck who threatens them. After killing him in self-defense, the quintet soon begin inviting other "societal irritants" for what turn out to be their last meals. Cameron Diaz, Ron Eldard, Annabeth Gish, Courtney B. Vance, Bill Paxton, Charles Durning and Ron Perlman star. 92 min.
02-2942   Was $19.99   ☐$14.99

The Daytrippers (1996)
Daring dark comedy about a Long Island woman who finds a romantic letter that may have been written to her husband. Hoping to find him—and the truth—she and her neurotic family set out for the streets of Manhattan in their station wagon, staging a wacky, soul-searching quest. With Hope Davis, Pat McNamara, Anne Meara, Parker Posey, Liev Schreiber and Stanley Tucci. 87 min.
02-3104   Was $19.99   ☐$14.99

A Modern Affair (1996)
In this romantic farce, a single woman whose biological clock is ticking turns to a sperm bank for help. After becoming pregnant, she sets out to find the anonymous donor, but after she finally locates the handsome, commitment-shy photographer and the pair begin a relationship, will she tell him who she is? Lisa Eichhorn, Stanley Tucci, Caroline Aaron and Tammy Grimes star. 91 min.
02-2943   ☐$99.99

Denise Calls Up (1995)
Witty social comedy based around a series of phone calls from seven New Yorkers who manage to fall in and out of love, have a child and pursue deep, meaningful friendships...all without ever meeting, thanks to their portable phones, PCs, faxes and answering machines. Tim Daly, Caroleen Feeney, Dan Gunther, Alanna Ubach, Dana Wheeler Nicholson star. 80 min.
02-2964   Was $99.99   ☐$19.99

A Midwinter's Tale (1995)
Kenneth Branagh's delightful theatrical comedy focuses on a group of struggling, highly neurotic British actors who, against all odds, decide to stage "Hamlet" in a small-town church hall. The superb ensemble cast includes Michael Maloney, Richard Briers, John Sessions, Joan Collins and "Absolutely Fabulous" stars Julia Sawalha and Jennifer Saunders. 98 min.
02-2965   Was $99.99   ☐$14.99

Welcome To The Dollhouse (1996)
A darkly funny look at that painful period in growing up known as adolescence, writer/director Todd Solondz's acclaimed film follows the hellish life of Dawn Weiner, a gawky, bespectacled and buck-toothed 11-year-old trying to cope with parents who don't understand her, a crush on her older brother's friend, and classmates who call her "Weinerdog." Heather Matarazzo, Brendan Sexton, Jr. and Matthew Faber star. 88 min.
02-2990   Was $24.99   ☐$14.99

Can't Hardly Wait (1998)
Often raucous, sometimes poignant coming-of-age comedy concerns the grads of Huntington Hills High, who hold a blow-out party where beer and tears are spilled as they contemplate their future. For would-be writer Ethan Embry, though, it's also his last chance to act on his four-year crush on class beauty Jennifer Love Hewitt, who was just dumped by her boyfriend. Seth Green, Lauren Ambrose also star. 101 min.
02-3229   Was $99.99   ☐$14.99

The Alarmist (1999)
In this quirky, darkly comic story, David Arquette is a naive young salesman who takes a job selling home security systems for company owner Stanley Tucci. Arquette finds success on and off the job when he falls in love with one of his clients, single mom Kate Capshaw. But when Capshaw and her teenage son are found dead, Arquette grows suspicious of Tucci. 93 min.
02-3272   Was $99.99   ☐$19.99

Blankman (1994)
Nerdy gadget-builder Damon Wayans adopts the alter ego of makeshift superhero Blankman and joins his cameraman brother to battle a nasty mobster responsible for murdering his grandmother in this fanciful spoof. David Alan Grier, Robin Givens and Jon Polito also star. 96 min.
02-2723   Was $89.99   ☐$14.99

Jawbreaker (1999)
In this dark, satiric teen comedy, three beautiful and much-feared students at Reagan High School stage a mock kidnapping of their friend on her 17th birthday. The prank goes awry when the young woman accidentally dies, prompting the trio to concoct a bizarre story to get them out of the jam. Rose McGowan, Rebecca Gayheart, Judy Greer, Julie Benz and Pam Grier star. 91 min.
02-3341   Was $99.99   ☐$14.99

High School High (1996)
There's hilarity in the 'hood when idealistic teacher Jon Lovitz leaves a posh private academy to take a job at crime-riddled inner-city Marion Barry High in this wild spoof of "Blackboard Jungle" and "Dangerous Minds"-style dramas. With Tia Carrere, Mekhi Phifer and Louise Fletcher. 86 min.
02-3029   Was $99.99   ☐$14.99

The Pest (1997)
Zany farce starring multi-talented John Leguizamo as a Miami con artist who owes $50,000 to a group of Spanish mobsters. To erase the debt, Leguizamo agrees to be hunted down by German sharpshooters—and way-out wackiness ensues. Jeffrey Jones, Freddy Rodriguez co-star. 85 min.
02-3068   Was $99.99   ☐$14.99

Dream For An Insomniac (1998)
Ione Skye ("Say Anything") stars in this San Francisco-based coffeehouse comedy as a waitress who finds the man of her dreams in aspiring writer MacKenzie Austin. But there's a slight problem: he's in love with someone else! With Jennifer Aniston, Michael Landes and Seymour Cassel. 87 min.
02-3201   Was $99.99   ☐$14.99

Still Crazy (1998)
Twenty years after drugs, in-fighting and a freak lightning storm during an outdoor concert split them up, the surviving members of the British rock band Strange Fruit are lured out of their middle-class—and worse—lives with plans for a reunion tour. Funny and touching mix of "This Is Spinal Tap" and "The Big Chill" stars Stephen Rea, Billy Connolly, Jimmy Nail, Juliet Aubrey. 97 min.
02-3343   Was $99.99   ☐$21.99

HOLLY HUNTER
DANNY DEVITO
QUEEN LATIFAH

LIVING OUT LOUD

Living Out Loud (1998)
In this sensitive and winning romantic story, Holly Hunter is a lonely, newly divorced New Yorker who learns to pick up the pieces of her life and go on with the help of two new friends: elevator operator Danny DeVito, coping with the break-up of his own marriage and the death of his daughter, and feisty jazz club singer Queen Latifah. Martin Donovan also stars. 103 min.
02-5199   Was $99.99   ☐$19.99

SLC Punk (1999)
In this energetic comedy set in 1985 Salt Lake City, college-age best buddies Stevo (Matthew Lillard) and Heroin Bob (Michael Goorjian) try spiked hair, ripped clothes and punk rocker attitudes to rebel against their staid, conservative hometown, but still find themselves faced with family life, romantic tangles, and an uncertain future. With Annabeth Gish, Jennifer Lien. 98 min.
02-3375   Was $99.99   ☐$14.99

The Velocity Of Gary (1999)
This hip comedy-drama showcases Vincent D'Onofrio as a porn star romantically involved with spicy Times Square waitress Salma Hayek who also finds himself attracted to hustler and phone sex worker Thomas Jane. When D'Onofrio discovers he has contracted AIDS, a complex situation gets even more complicated in this quirky slice-of-life saga. With Ethan Hawke, Olivia d'Abo. 101 min.
02-3379   Was $99.99   ☐$14.99

Fast Getaway (1991)
Teen scene favorite Corey Haim stars in this thrilling action-comedy, playing a slick 16-year-old who masterminds getaways for his bank robber father. Cynthia Rothrock, Leo Rossi and Marcia Strassman also star. 90 min.
02-2111   Was $89.99 $19.99

Rubin & Ed (1992)
Outrageous road farce with neurotic Crispin Glover and real estate agent Howard Hesseman encountering all sorts of wild adventures when they head to the desert to bury a frozen cat. Karen Black and Michael Green also star in this cult-flavored comedy. 82 min.
02-2254 $89.99

Mortuary Academy (1990)
Something funny is happening at Mortuary Academy, a school where students learn about the funeral business in a hilarious way. Join "Eating Raoul's" Paul Bartel and Mary Woronov, Christopher Atkins, Wolfman Jack and Cesar Romero in this wacky spoof. 86 min.
02-2124 $79.99

Desert Blue (1999)
Hip, off-the-wall slice-of-life story set in Baxter, California, a small town "famous" for its 60-foot ice cream cone. Shortly after soap star Kate Hudson and her father, professor John Heard, arrive in town, a soda truck overturns and causes an environmental hazard spill that strands them. While there, Hudson bonds with slacker locals Brendan Sexton III, Christina Ricci and Casey Affleck. 90 min.
02-3386   Was $99.99   ☐$14.99

Orgazmo (1998)
A Mormon missionary becomes an adult film actor/kickboxing superhero? Such a plot could only come from the twisted minds of "South Park" creators Trey Parker and Matt Stone. In this outrageous satire with something to offend everyone, director/scripter Parker plays the naive young evangelist-turned-porn star who saves the day with his secret weapon, the Orgazmorator. With Stone, Dian Bachar and porn legend Ron Jeremy. Theatrical, NC-17 version; 94 min.
02-9074 Was $99.99 *$14.99*

Orgazmo (Unrated Edited Version)
Also available in a less explicit edition. 90 min.
02-9075 Was $99.99 *$14.99*

The Mating Habits Of The Earthbound Human (1999)
This satirical look at dating and lovemaking customs takes the form of a mock TV science documentary with narration by "Frasier's" David Hyde Pierce. Mackenzie Astin and Carmen Elektra are the film's focus, two L.A. singles whose relationship is traced from meeting at a club and their first sexual encounter to an unexpected pregnancy and marriage. With Lucy Liu. 90 min.
02-3394 Was $99.99 ❑*$14.99*

Tinseltown (1999)
A pair of would-be filmmakers, reduced to living in a self-storage warehouse, may have found their ticket to the big time when they become convinced a fellow resident is the "costumed killer" stalking the L.A. streets and pitch a movie based on his future crimes. Darkly funny look at Hollywood moguls and serial killers—and the similarities therein—stars Arye Gross, Tom Wood, Ron Perlman, Joe Pantoliano and Kristy Swanson. 84 min.
02-3398 Was $99.99 ❑*$14.99*

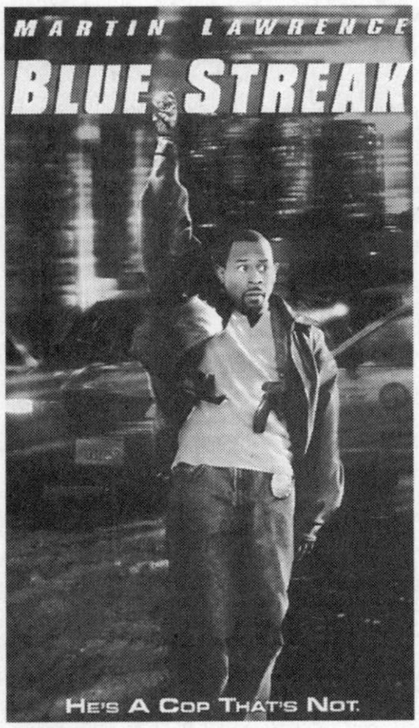

Blue Streak (1999)
Freed from jail after two years, jewel thief Martin Lawrence is dismayed to learn that the building site where he hid a valuable diamond just before his arrest is now home to an LAPD station. Lawrence's solution to getting inside is to impersonate a police detective, but soon he finds himself cleaning up the streets before he can retrieve the gem. Wild action-comedy also stars Luke Wilson, Dave Chappelle. 94 min.
02-3401 Was $19.99 ❑*$14.99*

The Suburbans (1999)
The Suburbans were a "one-hit wonder" band that ranked as a minor footnote in '80s rock history, but an impromptu reunion at one of the group's wedding gives a feisty young music company exec an idea for a high-profile comeback. Director/co-scripter Donal Lardner Ward, Craig Bierko, Will Ferrell, Tony Guma and Jennifer Love Hewitt star in this rocking comedy; with Ben Stiller and Jerry Stiller. 81 min.
02-3399 Was $99.99 ❑*$14.99*

Love Stinks (1999)
To TV sitcom writer French Stewart, new girlfriend Bridgette Wilson seems too good to be true. Unfortunately, that's just what happens when she decides they should get married, as Stewart's fear of commitment turns Wilson into a vengeance-seeking virago. Follow their "romance from Hell" in this wild farce that also stars Bill Bellamy, Tyra Banks. 94 min.
02-3404 Was $99.99 ❑*$14.99*

Crazy In Alabama (1999)
Antonio Banderas turns director with this darkly humorous road movie set against the civil rights movement of the mid-'60s. After beheading her abusive husband, Alabama housewife Melanie Griffith sets out on a cross-country trip to find fame in Hollywood. Back home, her teenage nephew witnesses the murder of a black youth by a racist sheriff. Lucas Black, David Morse, Meat Loaf Aday also star. 113 min.
02-3416 Was $99.99 ❑*$14.99*

A Night At The Roxbury (1998)
The "Saturday Night Live" skit that dares to ask the musical question "What Is Love?" becomes a feature-length comedy. Will Ferrell and Chris Kattan are the slick-dressing, head-bobbing Bubati brothers, who spend their nights trying to gain entry into L.A.'s hottest nightspots and "score" with the ladies, and their days dreaming of opening their own club. Dan Hedaya, Loni Anderson and, as himself, Richard Grieco also star. 82 min.
06-2833 Was $99.99 ❑*$14.99*

Mr. Wrong (1996)
In her first starring film role, Ellen DeGeneres plays the producer of a morning TV talk show unable to find Mr. Right. When she thinks she's met the perfect guy in poet Bill Pullman, she's on cloud nine, but after Pullman proves to be a kleptomaniacal wacko, DeGeneres has to figure out a way to get rid of him. Joan Cusack, Dean Stockwell and Joan Plowright also star. 97 min.
11-2038 Was $19.99 ❑*$14.99*

Spy Hard (1996)
Leslie Nielsen is Dick Steele, Agent WD-40, a famous spy called out of retirement to stop his former nemesis, General Rancor (Andy Griffith), from taking over the world. During his madcap mission, Steele encounters gorgeous Russian agent Nicollette Sheridan, a speeding bus, Dr. Joyce Brothers and a title tune by "Weird Al" Yankovic. With Charles Durning, Marcia Gay Harden. 81 min.
11-2063 Was $19.99 ❑*$14.99*

Flirting With Disaster (1996)
Sexy, hilarious farce stars Ben Stiller as an insecure grown-up adoptee obsessed with finding his real parents. Joined by wife Patricia Arquette and psychologist Téa Leoni, Stiller sets out on a riotous cross-country journey that takes him face-to-face with rednecks, pesky bed-and-breakfast proprietors and, eventually, his outlaw mom and dad. With Alan Alda, Lily Tomlin, Mary Tyler Moore. 92 min.
11-2081 Was $19.99 ❑*$14.99*

Ride (1998)
Malik Yoba and Melissa De Sousa star in this song-filled comedy as the chaperones for a group of up-and-coming rap artists on a New York-to-Florida bus trip for a video shoot. Along the way, the singers learn to put aside their differences and understand each other as a family. Fredo Starr, Kellie Williams, John Witherspoon also star, with cameos by Snoop Doggy Dogg and Luther Campbell. 84 min.
11-2788 Was $99.99 ❑*$19.99*

The Other Sister (1999)
In this sensitive comedy/drama directed by Garry Marshall, Juliette Lewis is a mentally retarded young woman who returns to parents Diane Keaton and Tom Skerritt after spending 10 years in an institution. While attending a vocational college, Lewis meets Giovanni Ribisi, an emotionally handicapped student. The two become involved romantically, which causes problems with Lewis' parents. 130 min.
11-2337 Was $99.99 ❑*$19.99*

Swingers (1996)
Mix yourself a perfectly dry martini and settle back for director Doug Liman's acclaimed seriocomic look at '90s-style Los Angeles lounge lizards who spend their nights going from cocktail bar to cocktail bar and from one girl to another. Jon Favreau, who also scripted, stars as a would-be actor from New York who settles into the swingers' scene in order to forget a failed romance. With Vince Vaughn, Heather Graham. 96 min.
11-2117 Was $99.99 ❑*$19.99*

The 6th Man (1997)
"Ghost" meets "The Fish That Saved Pittsburgh" in this full-court fantasy farce that stars Marlon Wayans and Kadeem Hardison as brothers playing on the University of Washington basketball team whose dreams of winning a championship look to be over when star athlete Hardison dies during a game...until he comes back as a spirit only Wayans can see. With David Paymer, Michael Michelle. 108 min.
11-2179 Was $19.99 ❑*$14.99*

Romy And Michele's High School Reunion (1997)
Mira Sorvino and Lisa Kudrow star in the title roles as two slightly air-headed twentysomethings whose carefree lives in Southern California are shattered with the prospect of returning to their 10-year high school reunion in Tucson as failures and who concoct an elaborate story to impress their old friends and rivals. With Janeane Garofalo, Alan Cumming. 91 min.
11-2181 Was $19.99 ❑*$14.99*

Unstrung Heroes (1995)
Inspired by writer Franz Lidz's autobiographical book and directed by Diane Keaton, this poignant comedy-drama focuses on a 12-year-old son of a wacky inventor and sickly mother who is sent to live with two uncles—one of whom sees conspiracies everywhere and the other who collects junk obsessively. Andie MacDowell, John Turturro, Michael Richards and Nathan Watt star. 93 min.
11-1965 Was $89.99 ❑*$19.99*

Two Girls And A Guy (1998)
When Natasha Gregson Wagner and Heather Graham discover that the boyfriends they're waiting to surprise are in fact the same person—egocentric actor Robert Downey, Jr.—they decide to confront the two-timer with the truth. It's an unforgettable evening of laughs, tears and sexual shenanigans from writer/director James Toback. Uncut, NC-17 version includes footage not shown in theaters. 100 min.
04-3707 ❑*$99.99*

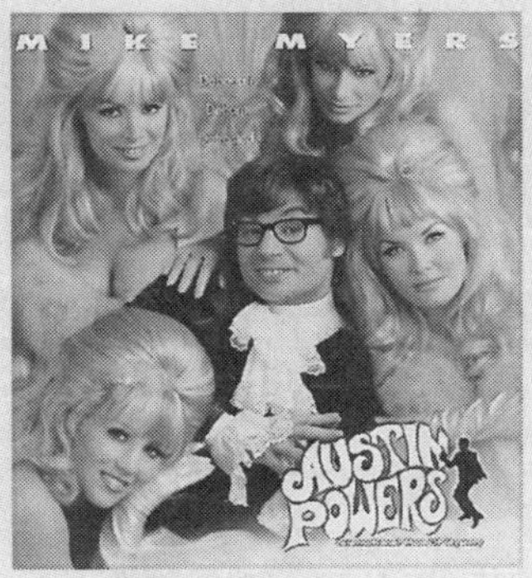

Austin Powers: International Man Of Mystery (1997)
Get ready to groove, baby, with Mike Myers as the psychedelic superspy and ladies' man who was the talk of Swingin' '60s London. Thawed out after 30 years in suspended animation, Austin has to learn about the '90s in a hurry if he's to defeat his arch-enemy, the also-defrosted Dr. Evil (Myers again), in this "shag-a-riffic" hit comedy. Elizabeth Hurley, Michael York, Mimi Rogers also star. 90 min.
02-5151 Was $99.99 ❑*$14.99*

Austin Powers: International Man Of Mystery (Letterboxed Version)
Also available in a theatrical, widescreen format. Special version includes seven deleted scenes, the original theatrical trailer and trailers for "Austin Powers: The Spy Who Shagged Me."
02-5210 ❑*$19.99*

Austin Powers: The Spy Who Shagged Me (1999)
Mike Myers' "groovy" secret agent is back in this riotous sequel in which Austin loses his "mojo" to arch-nemesis Dr. Evil, who's out to terrorize the world with a "frickin' huge" laser cannon, Scottish assassin Fat Bastard and a tiny clone of himself. Will going back to 1969 London and teaming with sexy spy Felicity Shagwell (Heather Graham) help Powers regain his mojo and save the day? With Robert Wagner, Rob Lowe, and Verne J. Troyer as "Mini-Me." 95 min.
02-5216 Was $19.99 ❑*$14.99*

Austin Powers: The Spy Who Shagged Me (Letterboxed Version)
Also available in a theatrical, widescreen format, baby.
02-5217 Was $19.99 ❑*$14.99*

The Powers Pack
"What's that, baby? Both Austin Powers flicks are available in a boxed collector's set? Oh, behave!"
02-5241 *$27.99*

With Friends Like These (1998)
After years of supporting roles in low-budget gangster films and TV shows, character actor Robert Costanzo gets a chance to audition for an upcoming Al Capone biodrama by Martin Scorsese. Once word about the audition gets out to Costanzo's actor buddies, it quickly becomes "every man for himself" in this witty and pointed look at the movie business. Adam Arkin, Beverly D'Angelo, David Strathairn, Jon Tenney also star, with cameos by Scorsese, Bill Murray and others. 105 min.
02-5225 ❑*$99.99*

Woo (1998)
Jada Pinkett Smith heats up the screen as Woo, an outspoken and outrageously sexy New Yorker who has it all...except for a man that she can love and respect. So when a psychic tells Smith that she's about to meet the man of her dreams, she goes out on an outrageous blind date with meek law clerk Tommy Davidson. With David Chappelle and LL Cool J. 80 min.
02-5187 Was $99.99 ❑*$14.99*

Jesus' Son (1999)
Billy Crudup plays a well-meaning but drug-addled young man whose trip across the back roads of '70s America with fellow addict and girlfriend Samantha Morton leads to meetings with a variety of quirky characters, tragedy and, ultimately, redemption. Based on Denis Johnson's collection of short stories, director Alison Maclean's offbeat comedy/drama also stars Dennis Hopper, Holly Hunter, Denis Leary. 109 min.
07-2925 ❑*$99.99*

Canadian Bacon (1995)
In writer/director Michael Moore's ("Roger and Me") zany political comedy, U.S. president Alan Alda and his staff try to boost a sagging post-Cold War economy (and Alda's popularity) through claims of a planned armed invasion by Canada. The plan works, until Niagara Falls sheriff John Candy and his pals launch a "pre-emptive strike" and create an international incident. Rhea Perlman, Rip Torn, Kevin Pollak also star. 95 min.
02-8363 Was $19.99 ❑*$14.99*

Sparkler (1999)
After leaving her cheating husband and their trailer park home behind, a California woman hitches a ride with three young men on their way to Las Vegas. Hip and stylish "road trip" comedy stars Park Overall, Freddie Prinze, Jr., Jamie Kennedy, Don Harvey and Veronica Cartwright. 90 min.
02-3396 Was $99.99 ❑*$14.99*

Virtual Sexuality (1999)
Teenage Justine, eager to find "Mr. Right," learns an important lesson about computer maintenance when a power surge at a science fair causes her to be transformed into Jake, her virtual "perfect male." While trying to regain her real body, Justine/Jake learns important lessons about dealing with the opposite sex in this high-tech comedy. Laura Fraser, Rupert Penry-Jones, Natasha Bell star. 92 min.
02-3428 Was $99.99 ❑*$14.99*

Suburban Commando (1991)
When interplanetary warrior Hulk Hogan finds himself stranded in the middle-class household of Christopher Lloyd and Shelley Duvall, the result is a comedic culture clash and slapstick thrills by the space shipload in this offbeat action-comedy for the whole family. 88 min.
02-5005 Was $89.99 ❑*$12.99*

Riff Raff (1992)
An ex-con from Glasgow attempts to turn his life around by joining a multi-ethnic construction crew in London and taking residence in a squatter's apartment compound. This darkly funny, insightful look at class distinction and "common man" mores in contemporary England was directed by Ken Loach ("Hidden Agenda") and is presented with subtitles because of its array of heavy British accents. 96 min.
02-5026 Was $89.99 *$19.99*

National Lampoon's Loaded Weapon (1993)
In this funny spoof of Hollywood action films, Emilio Estevez and Samuel L. Jackson are "Lethal Weapon"-styled Los Angeles cops who find themselves up against a nefarious creep (William Shatner). Featuring zany car chases, wild shootouts, goofs on flicks like "Basic Instinct" and "The Silence of the Lambs," and Jon Lovitz, Kathy Ireland and Phil Hartman. 82 min.
02-5033 Was $19.99 ❑*$14.99*

National Lampoon's Senior Trip (1995)
Rip-snorting, no-holds-barred hijinks ensues when a group of Ohio high school slackers are invited to Washington to address the president on how the educational system has failed them. But with a drugged-out Tommy Chong driving the bus for the students, their sex-obsessed teacher and the uptight principal, who knows if they'll even make it? With Matt Frewer, Valerie Mahaffey. 91 min.
02-5080 Was $19.99 ❑*$14.99*

Double Happiness (1995)
Appealing "culture clash" comedy centers on a young Chinese woman living with her parents in Canada and trying to juggle dreams of an acting career, a budding romance with a white college student, and her parents' desire to see her marry a "nice Chinese man." Sandra Oh, Johnny Mah, Callum Rennie star in writer/director Mina Shum's acclaimed debut feature. 87 min.
02-5081 ❑*$19.99*

For Better Or Worse... (1995)
Jason Alexander stars in and directs this romantic farce about an insecure loser who has no luck with women or life—in fact, his fiancée hasn't called him in six months. When his brother leaves him to watch his beautiful wife for a few days, love blooms between the in-laws. With James Woods, Lolita Davidovich and Joe Mantegna. 95 min.
02-5096 Was $99.99 ❑*$14.99*

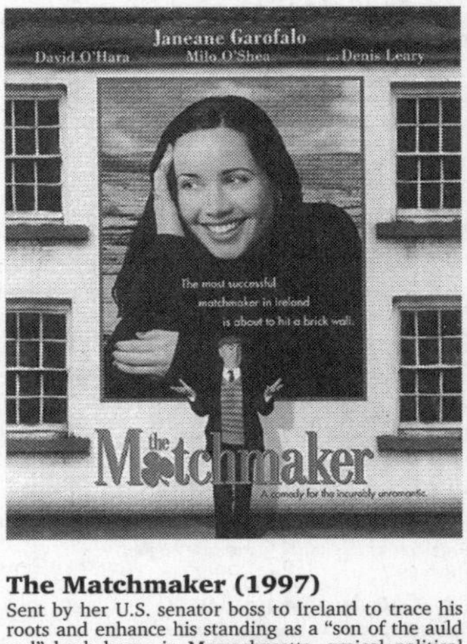

The Matchmaker (1997)
Sent by her U.S. senator boss to Ireland to trace his roots and enhance his standing as a "son of the auld sod" back home in Massachusetts, cynical political aide Janeane Garofalo finds herself surrounded by a host of colorful characters and the "guest of honor" in a coastal town's annual matchmaking festival. Warm and winning comedy also stars David O'Hara, Milo O'Shea. 97 min.
02-8811 Was $19.99 ❑*$14.99*

The Stupids (1996)
Meet the Stupids, a family of Middle American doofuses who take things a bit too literally. When father Tom Arnold sets out to find who stole the garbage from his cans, he thinks he's uncovered a nationwide refuse-robbing conspiracy. But the search gets him into trouble with international arms smugglers, and the whole Stupid clan must save the country in their own unique way. With Jessica Lundy, Christopher Lee. 94 min.
02-5115 Was $99.99 □*$14.99*

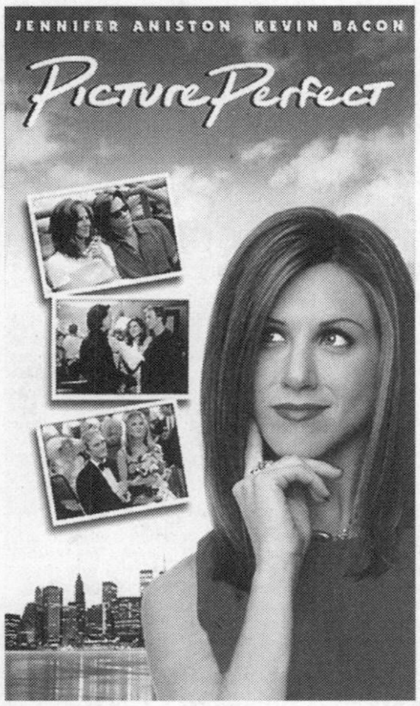

Picture Perfect (1997)
In order to prove her maturity to her bosses (and impress a colleague who likes married women), ad executive Jennifer Aniston passes off a photo of an acquaintance as her fiancé. Comical chaos ensues when she needs to produce her "beau" in the flesh and he decides to make their make-believe romance real. Kevin Bacon, Jay Mohr and Illeana Douglas co-star in this appealing romantic romp. 100 min.
04-3556 Was $99.99 □*$14.99*

The Adventures Of Ford Fairlane (1990)
The outrageous Andrew Dice Clay makes his starring film debut as the hippest rock-and-roll private eye to ever swagger down the streets of L.A. But his latest case, involving crooked record execs, missing groupies, shock deejays and psycho killers, may be his last! Wild action-comedy also stars Priscilla Presley, Wayne Newton, Lauren Holly, Robert Englund. 100 min.
04-2390 Was $89.99 □*$19.99*

Dutch (1991)
Ed O'Neill ("Married...With Children") is Dutch Dooley, a working-class guy whose task is to pick up his girlfriend's arrogant, upper-class son from an Atlanta boarding school and drive him home to Chicago. Sparks and laughs fly during this hilarious road trip from producer John Hughes. JoBeth Williams, Ethan Randall co-star. 107 min.
04-2484 Was $89.99 □*$14.99*

The Super (1991)
Witty social comedy with Joe Pesci as a rich slumlord forced to reside in his own ratty New York tenement by a court order. Soon he's facing the same hardships as the building's residents, and eventually recognizes his insensitivity to their plight. Ruben Blades, Vincent Gardenia, Madolyn Smith Osborne co-star. 86 min.
04-2493 Was $19.99 □*$14.99*

29th Street (1991)
A funny, bittersweet, true-life story about Frank Pesce, Jr., the forever-lucky youngest son of a New York Italian-American family, who finds that winning the state's first lottery brings all sorts of complications involving mobsters and his bet-happy father. Anthony LaPaglia, Danny Aiello, Lanie Kazan and the real Pesce star. 101 min.
04-2494 Was $89.99 □*$19.99*

Let's Talk About Sex (1998)
A Miami newspaper columnist is given the chance to produce a pilot for a TV talk show. With help from her two roommates, she interviews a variety of women throughout the Miami area for their views on sex and romance (much of this footage comes from real interviews), but the project soon has the trio examining their own flawed love lives. Sharp and witty comedy from writer/director/co-star Troy Beyer also stars Paget Brewster, Randi Ingerman. 86 min.
02-5197 Was $99.99 *$19.99*

My Cousin Vinny (1992)
Side-splitting farce stars Joe Pesci as a streetwise but inexperienced lawyer from New York who gets the call to defend his cousin and a friend when they're accused of shooting a convenience store clerk in the Deep South. With Ralph Macchio, Fred Gwynne, and Academy Award-winner Marisa Tomei as Pesci's feisty fiancée. 120 min.
04-2566 Was $19.99 □*$14.99*

Only The Lonely (1991)
A charming romantic comedy with some serious moments from the "Home Alone" team of Chris Columbus and John Hughes. John Candy is an unmarried Chicago cop who falls for a lonely mortuary cosmetician (Ally Sheedy). Humor and problems arise when Candy's acerbic Irish mother (played by Maureen O'Hara, in her first screen role in 20 years) intervenes. Anthony Quinn, James Belushi co-star. 102 min.
04-2464 □*$14.99*

Very Bad Things (1998)
What was supposed to be a simple Las Vegas bachelor party snowballs into a gruesome comedy of errors when a call girl is accidentally killed and the revelers try to cover up the death. Christian Slater, Jon Favreau, Cameron Diaz and Daniel Stern head up the darkly funny goings-on. 100 min.
02-9076 Was $99.99 □*$14.99*

The Naked Man (1998)
Wildly eccentric comedy co-written by Ethan Coen and starring Michael Rapaport as a young man who works his way through chiropractic school as a pro wrestler. When his parents' drug store is threatened by a pharmaceutical kingpin, Rapaport dons his "no-skin" suit, joins forces with a biker chick and sets out for revenge. With Rachael Leigh Cook, Michael Jeter. 98 min.
02-9147 Was $99.99 *$14.99*

Trippin' (1999)
Deon Richmond is a high school senior who can't stop having outrageous fantasies in which he's a rap star and a booty magnet. While his parents urge him to pursue college, Richmond is happy hanging out with his low-life pals. But when his prom date—the class's hottest and smartest girl—looks down on his future plans, he thinks it may be time to change. With Maia Campbell. 92 min.
02-9176 Was $99.99 □*$14.99*

Talkin' Dirty After Dark (1991)
Hilarious, raunchy farce set at Dukie's, an L.A. comedy club where a hip black comic will do anything to get the headlining spot—even mess with the club owner's hot-to-trot wife. Martin Lawrence, John Witherspoon and Jedda Jones star in this outrageous comedy. 89 min.
02-2195 Was $19.99 *$14.99*

Legalese (1998)
In this knife-sharp satire of American jurisprudence, actress Gina Gershon seeks help from top attorney James Garner when she's accused of killing her sister's husband. Eager to win the media circus of a case, Garner appoints an inexperienced but telegenic young lawyer to serve as his in-the-courtroom stand-in. Ed Kerr, Mary-Louise Parker and Kathleen Turner also star. 92 min.
02-5203 Was $99.99 □*$19.99*

This Is My Life (1992)
A sensitive comedy-drama from writer/director Nora Ephron starring Julie Kavner as a New York cosmetics clerk whose life changes radically after she becomes a popular comic. Problems arise after she devotes more time to her career than to her two daughters. Dan Aykroyd, Carrie Fisher, Samantha Mathis and Gaby Hoffman co-star. 94 min.
04-2537 Was $89.99 □*$19.99*

Buffy The Vampire Slayer (1992)
The original horror-action-comedy about a Valley Girl cheerleader who turns out to be the latest in a line of vampire killers and is recruited to stop a band of bloodsuckers who have infiltrated her quiet hometown. Kristy Swanson, Luke Perry, Rutger Hauer, Donald Sutherland and Paul Reubens star. 86 min.
04-2588 Was $19.99 □*$14.99*

Baby's Day Out (1994)
In this John Hughes production, an infant named Bink eludes a group of ornery kidnappers while crawling across the city of Chicago and finding adventure and comedy at every turn. Joe Mantegna, Joe Pantoliano, Lara Flynn Boyle, and Delaware's Adam and Jacob Worton star. 99 min.
04-2887 Was $19.99 □*$14.99*

The Commitments (1991)
An ultra-spirited account of the rise and fall of a ragtag group of Irish musicians who perform American soul tunes. Director Alan Parker's film covers the rifts, romances and friendships of the band and their ever-optimistic manager, and features songs like "Mustang Sally" and "In the Midnight Hour." With Andrew Strong, Johnny Murphy and Robert Arkins. 116 min.
04-2955 Was $19.99 □*$14.99*

The Snapper (1993)
A charming slice-of-life comedy, based on novelist Roddy Doyle's follow-up to "The Commitments," centers on Sharon, the eldest daughter of a North Dublin family, who becomes pregnant and has her siblings, friends, neighbors and cantankerous father trying to figure out who the daddy is. With Tina Kellegher, Colm Meaney and Ruth McCabe; Stephen Frears directs. 95 min.
11-1818 Was $89.99 □*$19.99*

The Van (1996)
The concluding film in writer Roddy Doyle's "Barrytown Trilogy" that centered around the working-class North Dublin neighborhood follows two best friends who think that buying a run-down van and setting up their own mobile fast-food business is their key to success, but aren't prepared for the consequences. Colm Meaney, Donal O'Kelly, Caroline Rothwell star; directed by Stephen Frears. 100 min.
04-3531 □*$99.99*

Rookie Of The Year (1993)
Fun-filled family baseball comedy about a 12-year-old Little Leaguer whose return to the mound after a broken arm is marked by a 100-plus m.p.h. fastball and who is recruited by the Chicago Cubs to help them in their pennant drive. Thomas Ian Nichols, Gary Busey and Daniel Stern, who also directed, star; Pedro Guerrero, Bobby Bonilla and Barry Bonds make cameos. 103 min.
04-2721 Was $89.99 □*$19.99*

Based On An Untrue Story (1993)
Hilarious spoof of made-for-TV dramas, in which perfume mogul Morgan Fairchild loses her sense of smell and seeks help from her separated-at-birth sisters (Ricki Lake and Victoria Jackson). Sexy, surprising lampoon also stars Dyan Cannon, Dan Hedaya, Harvey Korman and Goulet—yeah, Robert Goulet. 90 min.
04-2726 Was $89.99 *$29.99*

Freaked (1993)
Outrageous comedy and weird hijinks ensue when a spoiled teen TV star and his two friends visit an amusement park filled with human oddities. The trio get a much closer look than they bargained for, though, when the park's demented owner turns them into freaks. Alex Winter, Randy Quaid, William Sadler, Mr. T and Megan Ward star. 79 min.
04-2765 Was $89.99 □*$29.99*

The Beverly Hillbillies (1993)
One of the most popular TV shows of all time is turned into a fall-down funny movie, as the Clampett clan strikes "black gold" and moves to Southern California, tries to get Jed hitched and encounters a pair of swindlers out to steal their fortune. Jim Varney stars as Jed, Cloris Leachman is Granny, Erika Eleniak is Elly May and Diedrich Bader is Jethro. With Lily Tomlin, Dabney Coleman. 93 min.
04-2788 Was $19.99 □*$14.99*

PCU (1994)
Outrageous comedy ensues when freshman Tom Lawrence tries to fit in at Port Chester University, a college boasting an array of sensitive special interest groups. While walking the tightrope between Republicans, the anti-meat brigade and "Womynists," Tom decides to hang out with a frat known for their partying abilities. Jeremy Piven, Chris Young and David Spade star. 80 min.
04-2874 Was $29.99 □*$14.99*

Dog Park (1998)
Is the way to a woman's heart through her pet? Recently-dumped thirtysomething Luke Wilson, who shares custody of a neurotic canine with his ex-girlfriend, learns that the newest place for singles to meet is at the local park "dog walk," but his attempt to strike up a relationship with kid's show host Natasha Henstridge leads to some messy situations. Janeane Garofalo, Mark McKinney also star; written and directed by "Kids in the Hall" alum Bruce McCulloch. 92 min.
02-5224 Was $99.99 □*$19.99*

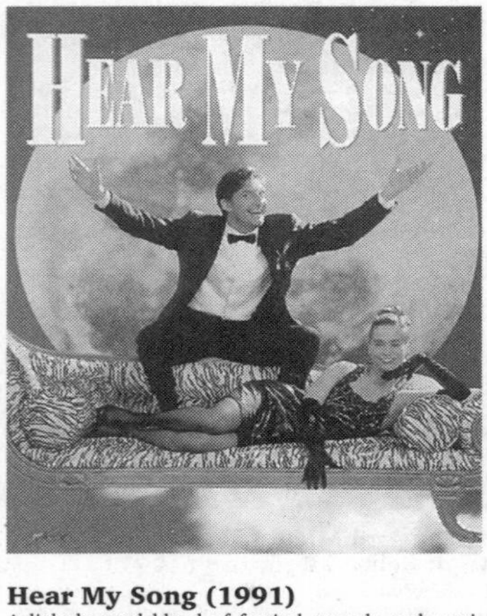

Hear My Song (1991)
A light-hearted blend of farcical comedy and sentimental drama, this acclaimed film follows a fast-talking Liverpool club owner who, in order to keep his dying nightspot and his girlfriend, tries to track down a famous Irish tenor who retired into obscurity decades earlier. Adrian Dunbar, Tara Fitzgerald, David McCallum and Ned Beatty star. 104 min.
06-1986 Was $89.99 *$19.99*

The Scout (1994)
Down-on-his-luck New York Yankees scout Albert Brooks spots the person who could save his job: young fireball pitcher Brendan Fraser, a hero in the Mexican minors. But when the phenom gets to the Big Apple, Brooks discovers that his find has emotional problems and needs a psychiatrist. Dianne Wiest co-stars, with cameos by George Steinbrenner, Bob Costas and Tony Bennett. 101 min.
04-2898 Was $89.99 □*$14.99*

French Kiss (1995)
Winning transatlantic romantic comedy stars Meg Ryan as a recently dumped fiancée who travels to Paris to confront her ex-lover and his new French flame. Along the way she meets Gallic charmer Kevin Kline, who agrees to serve as her guide and mentor...after hiding a stolen necklace in her purse without her knowledge. With Timothy Hutton, Susan Anbeh; Lawrence Kasdan directs. 111 min.
04-2996 Was $19.99 □*$14.99*

Home Alone (1990)
Wild slapstick comedy and sentiment highlight the adventures of 10-year-old Kevin (Macaulay Culkin) as he tries to protect his house from a pair of ornery burglars after he's been mistakenly left behind by his family, who are on their way to Paris for Christmas vacation. Joe Pesci, Daniel Stern, Catherine O'Hara and John Heard star in this smash hit from John Hughes and Chris Columbus. 100 min.
04-2425 □*$14.99*

Home Alone 2: Lost In New York (1992)
Macaulay Culkin returns in the role of Kevin McCallister, the irascible youngster who can't stay out of trouble. This time he's alone in Manhattan when family vacation plans go awry again, and before long Culkin is living it up at a posh hotel, matching wits with the snobby staff, and squaring off again against hapless crooks Daniel Stern and Joe Pesci. With Tim Curry, Catherine O'Hara. 120 min.
04-2672 □*$14.99*

Home Alone 3 (1997)
A new kid and some new crooks add up to another round of hilarious home-defense hi-jinks, as suburban Chicago youngster Alex D. Linz comes up with some ingenious gimmicks to foil a group of industrial spies who are after a stolen computer chip hidden inside Linz's toy car. Lenny Von Dohlen, Olek Krupa, David Thornton also star. 102 min.
04-3654 Was $19.99 □*$14.99*

Home Alone Triple Pack Movie Collection
All three "Home Alone" comedies are also available in a boxed gift set.
04-3969 Save $5.00! *$39.99*

Mr. Jealousy (1998)
Witty independent comedy starring Eric Stoltz as a student teacher and aspiring writer whose jealousy gets the better part of him while dating museum tour guide Anabella Sciorra. Suspicious of Sciorra's relationship with past lovers, Stoltz enrolls in a group therapy session attended by an ex-boyfriend, pretentious writer Chris Eigeman. With Bridget Fonda, Jean-Marie Baptiste, Peter Bogdanovich. 100 min.
02-9028 Was $99.99 *$14.99*

Nine Months (1995)
Get ready for a delightful delivery of laughter when San Francisco child psychologist Hugh Grant tries to cope with girlfriend Julianne Moore's news that she's pregnant. Grant's perfect lifestyle is thrown into an uproar as he braces for fatherhood in this charming hit comedy that also stars Tom Arnold, Joan Cusack, Jeff Goldblum and Robin Williams as a Russian vet-turned-obstetrician. 110 min.
04-3271 Was $89.99 □*$14.99*

Bushwhacked (1995)
After he's framed in the murder of a crooked businessman, loser delivery boy Daniel Stern goes on the lam from the FBI and soon finds himself mistaken for a Ranger Scout leader in charge of taking six youngsters on a camping trip. Hilarity abounds as Stern tries to steer the kids through the rugged wilderness. Jon Polito, Blake Bashoff, Brad Sullivan co-star. 85 min.
04-3281 Was $89.99 □*$14.99*

The Brothers McMullen (1995)
A trio of Irish-American brothers living on Long Island are left to fend for themselves on the choppy seas of love, relationships and marriage, with little help from their Catholic upbringing, after their father dies and their mother moves back to Ireland to be with her true love. Writer/director/co-star Ed Burns' acclaimed independent seriocomedy also features Mike McGlone, Jack Mulcahy, Connie Britton. 98 min.
04-3286 Was $89.99 □*$14.99*

The Dark Backward (1991)
Can a garbageman who moonlights as a hopelessly bad stand-up comic finally hit the big time when a growth on his back turns into a fully-grown third arm? Writer/director Adam Rifkin's ultra-black comedy stars Judd Nelson as the hapless three-handed celebrity, Wayne Newton, Rob Lowe, Lara Flynn Boyle, Bill Paxton and James Caan. 100 min.
02-2166 Was $89.99 *$19.99*

Tokyo Cowboy (1994)
A Japanese fast-food worker decides to fulfill his lifelong dream of becoming a cowboy and heads to the Western Canadian hometown of his female pen pal. Trouble is, she's tired of small-town life, is ready to come out of the closet, and isn't prepared for his arrival. Offbeat and funny culture-clash tale stars Hiromoto Ida, Christina Hirt, Janne Mortil. 94 min.
01-1546 *$39.99*

Spirit Of '76 (1991)
In this comedic blast from the past, a group of futuristic time-travelers try to visit America in 1776 but mistakenly wind up in 1976 at the height of the Disco Era. David Cassidy, Olivia d'Abo, Leif Garrett, Steve and Jeff McDonald (of Redd Kross), Devo, Iron Eyes Cody and Rob Reiner head the cast in a spirited romp filled with great period music and lots of cameos. Get down, get funky! 82 min.
02-2151 *$89.99*

Down Periscope (1996)
It's wackiness beneath the waves when Navy commander Kelsey Grammer takes charge of a rundown WWII-vintage submarine and its ragtag crew in this nutty nautical romp. Lauren Holly, Rob Schneider, Rip Torn and Bruce Dern also star. 92 min.
04-3349 Was $99.99 □*$14.99*

Necessary Roughness (1991)
Wild and wacky gridiron farce about a Texas college that hires a new coach to guide their abysmal football team, and then recruits a star 34-year-old quarterback (Scott Bakula), a beautiful soccer kicker (Kathy Ireland), and an All-American astronomy professor (Sinbad). With Robert Loggia, Hector Elizondo and Harley Jane Kozak. 101 min.
06-1920 Was $19.99 □*$14.99*

Flashback (1990)
"Once we get out of the '80s, the '90s are going to make the '60s look like the '50s," observes Dennis Hopper as the burned-out radical who trades places with straight-arrow FBI agent Kiefer Sutherland during his trek to prison. Their action-packed misadventures on the road will have you yelling "good trip, man!" With Carol Kane and Richard Masur. 108 min.
06-1730 □*$14.99*

Twin Town (1997)
Set in the dingy seaport town of Swansea in West Wales, this raucous dark comedy in the style of "Trainspotting" follows two ne'er-do-well brothers' escalating feud against an affluent local contractor who refuses to compensate their roofer dad after he's injured on the job. A fortune in cocaine, two crooked cops, and a wild karaoke contest add to the extreme fun. Rhys Ifans, Llyr Evans, Dougray Scott star. 99 min.
02-8733 Was $99.99 □*$14.99*

Pronto (1997)
Based on the Elmore Leonard novel, this fast-paced crime comedy stars Peter Falk as a long-time bookie being pursued by both the mob and the feds on a madcap chase from Miami to Italy. James LeGros, Glenne Headly co-star. 100 min.
06-2668 □*$79.99*

National Lampoon's The Don's Analyst (1997)
A psychiatrist gets an offer he can't refuse in this off-the-wall mob comedy, as the sons of a veteran Mafia boss who wants to leave the "family business" persuade the shrink to talk their father out of his plans. Robert Loggia, Kevin Pollack, Joseph Bologna, Sherilyn Fenn and Angie Dickinson star. 103 min.
06-2669 Was $59.99 □*$14.99*

Welcome To Hollywood (1998)
Funny mockumentary on making it in Tinseltown features director Adam Rifkin as a filmmaker whose latest project is chronicling the rise to stardom of a young actor. His subject is Nick Decker (Tony Markes), a struggling thespian who has a series of mishaps, including stepping on a stingray during a "Baywatch" shoot. Features cameos by Sandra Bullock, Nicolas Cage, David Hasselhoff, John Travolta, and Angie Everhart as the celebrity girlfriend Nick recruits to help his career. 90 min.
86-1155 □*$99.99*

But I'm A Cheerleader (1999)
In this knowing satire, Natasha Lyonne is an all-American high school cheerleader whose parents are fearful that she's becoming a lesbian because of her Melissa Etheridge poster and vegetarianism. They ship her to a special camp where they hope she'll get in touch with her heterosexual feelings, but not everything goes as planned. Cathy Moriarty, RuPaul Charles and Clea DuVall co-star. 86 min.
07-2921 □*$99.99*

Waking Ned Devine (1998)
The tiny Irish coastal town of Tully More is thrilled to learn that one of the 53 residents holds a winning national lottery ticket, but their dreams of sharing in the fortune are threatened when ducat-holder Ned Devine is found dead in his home. A pair of elderly local rapscallions launch a scheme to impersonate Ned and claim the money in this warm and winning comedy. Ian Bannen, David Kelly, James Nesbitt and Susan Lynch star. 91 min.
04-3840 Was $99.99 □*$14.99*

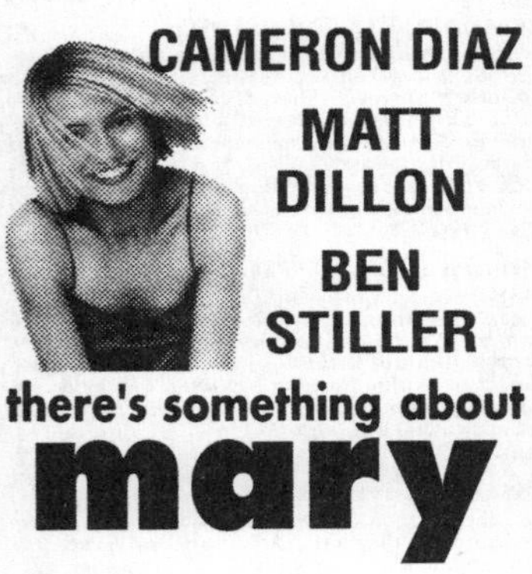

There's Something About Mary (1998)
This outrageous farce stars Ben Stiller as a depressed writer who pines for Cameron Diaz, the beauty he was supposed to take to the prom 13 years earlier. Stiller hires sleazy sleuth Matt Dillon to track her down, but when Dillon locates her in Florida, he gets the hots for her. The laughs come fast and furious from the Farrelly Brothers ("Kingpin") and a cast that includes Chris Elliott and Lee Evans. Special edition includes never-before-seen footage. 119 min.
04-3735 Was $19.99 □*$14.99*

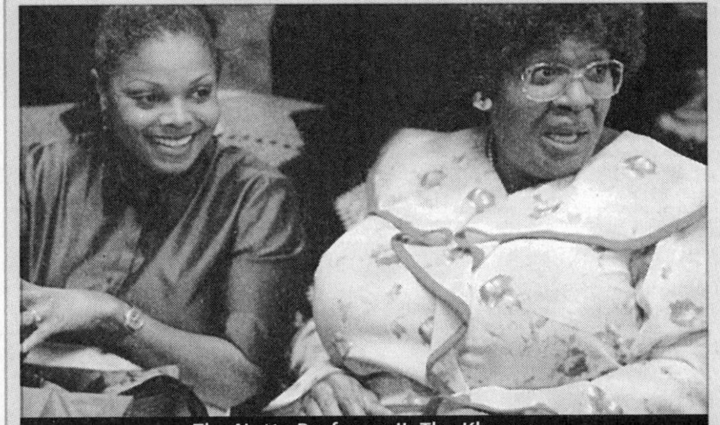
The Nutty Professor II: The Klumps

Eddie Murphy

48 Hrs. (1982)
Boisterous comedy/thriller marked Eddie Murphy's screen debut, with him playing a wisecracking con sprung from prison to help detective Nick Nolte nab a pair of cop killers. With Annette O'Toole, James Remar; Walter Hill directs. 97 min.
06-1179 *$14.99*

Another 48 Hrs. (1990)
That's right, the boys are back! Eddie Murphy and Nick Nolte return as friendly enemies Bannister and Cates, teaming up to clear Nolte of a murder charge and track down the real killer, who's also after them. Also back for this hit sequel is director Walter Hill; Andrew Divoff, David Anthony Marshall co-star. 95 min.
06-1784 Was $19.99 *$14.99*

Trading Places (1983)
Conniving street bum Eddie Murphy and snobby, rich executive Dan Aykroyd wind up switching social positions because of a "heredity vs. environment" bet between corporate bigwig brothers Ralph Bellamy and Don Ameche...and hilarious shenanigans are bound to erupt. The comic cast includes Jamie Lee Curtis, Denholm Elliott. Directed by John Landis. 118 min.
06-1202 □*$14.99*

Best Defense (1984)
It's madness in the military when Eddie Murphy and Dudley Moore star in this wacky comedy. Moore is a weapons designer who builds a "super tank," while Murphy is the hapless gunner who tests it, with hilarious results. 94 min.
06-1236 □*$14.99*

Beverly Hills Cop (1984)
Eddie Murphy is Axel Foley, a Detroit detective who heads to Southern California to track down a friend's killer, only to find resentment from both sides of the law. Action and laughs are mixed perfectly in one of the biggest comedy hits ever. Lisa Eilbacher, Judge Reinhold also star. 105 min.
06-1300 □*$14.99*

Beverly Hills Cop II (1987)
The heat is on...again! Eddie Murphy heads westward once more after police captain Ronny Cox is wounded by a merciless gang of hi-tech robbers. Co-stars Judge Reinhold, John Ashton, Brigitte Nielsen, Dean Stockwell. 102 min.
06-1516 □*$14.99*

Beverly Hills Cop III (1994)
Eddie Murphy's Detroit cop Axel Foley returns to Los Angeles to track down a group of counterfeiters, with the trail leading him to Wonder World, a lavish amusement park where Murphy finds himself in danger...from the bad guys and from some death-defying rides. Judge Reinhold, Bronson Pinchot, Hector Elizondo also star. 105 min.
06-2240 Was $89.99 □*$14.99*

Beverly Hills Cop Collection
Get ready to go "deep, deep, deep undercover" with streetwise Detroit detective Axel Foley (Eddie Murphy) in this boxed set of all three "Beverly Hills Cop" films.
06-2377 *$44.99*

The Golden Child (1986)
Eddie Murphy lights up the screen in this fantastic and funny action-adventure. A Tibetan holy child has been kidnapped by evil forces...and Eddie is the L.A. investigator who has been ordained by fate to bring him back. Charlotte Lewis, Charles Dance co-star. 93 min.
06-1440 □*$14.99*

Coming To America (1988)
Can a 21-year-old African prince find happiness and the girl of his dreams while working incognito at a fast food restaurant in Queens? If the prince is Eddie Murphy, then the answer is a hilarious "yes," as you'll see in this hit comedy. Arsenio Hall, Shari Headley, James Earl Jones also star. 116 min.
06-1628 Was $19.99 □*$14.99*

Harlem Nights (1989)
Gangsters and gunplay run alongside the laughs in writer/director/star Eddie Murphy's comedy set in '30s Harlem. Murphy and Richard Pryor are nightclub owners faced with some dangerous competitors who try to muscle them out of business. Redd Foxx, Della Reese, Jasmine Guy and Danny Aiello co-star. 118 min.
06-1716 Was $19.99 □*$14.99*

Boomerang (1992)
Eddie Murphy elicits non-stop laughs as a fast-tracking cosmetics firm executive and womanizer who finds the tables turned on him when a gorgeous, strong-willed female is named his superior and strings him along romantically. Robin Givens, Halle Berry, Grace Jones and David Allen Grier also star. 115 min.
06-2012 Was $19.99 □*$14.99*

The Distinguished Gentleman (1992)
Small-time con man Eddie Murphy uses his street smarts to get elected to Congress in a get-rich-quick scheme, but soon learns that it's filled with scam artists that make him look like small fry. Can Murphy change his ways and change the way government works? A hilarious, often touching farce in the Frank Capra style, co-starring Sheryl Lee Ralph, Lane Smith and Grant Shaud. 111 min.
11-1683 Was $19.99 □*$14.99*

Vampire In Brooklyn (1995)
Chills and chuckles mix in this toothsome tale starring Eddie Murphy as a Caribbean-born bloodsucker who comes to New York to find a suitable mate. He finds one in detective Angela Bassett, who is seduced by the suave Murphy while investigating a rash of mysterious deaths...and doesn't realize her new paramour is the killer. With Allen Payne, Kadeem Hardison; Wes Craven directs. 102 min.
06-2438 Was $89.99 □*$14.99*

The Nutty Professor (1996)
Eddie Murphy scores "big" laughs in this high-tech updating of the 1963 Jerry Lewis comedy. As good-natured but overweight college instructor Sherman Klump, Murphy concocts a reducing potion that transforms him into the svelte, hip and self-absorbed Buddy Love. Which of Murphy's alter egos will survive to win the hand of love interest Jada Pinkett? With James Coburn, Larry Miller. 96 min.
07-2459 Was $19.99 □*$14.99*

The Nutty Professor II: The Klumps (2000)
The fun continues in this sequel that finds Eddie Murphy's portly Professor Sherman Klump falling for fellow teacher Janet Jackson, only to have super-slick alter-ego Buddy Love re-emerging to spoil the courtship. Klump's solution of removing Love's genetic material from his DNA leads to a series of hilarious disasters. With Larry Miller and an amazingly made-up Murphy in five other roles.
07-2954 □*$22.99*

Metro (1997)
High-octane action-comedy showcasing Eddie Murphy as a San Francisco police hostage negotiation specialist who teams with rookie SWAT sharpshooter Michael Rapaport to track down a vicious jewel thief responsible for killing a police colleague. Features exciting chases, thrilling shoot-outs and quip-filled humor in the best Murphy tradition. With Michael Wincott, Carmen Ejogo. 117 min.
11-2126 Was $19.99 □*$14.99*

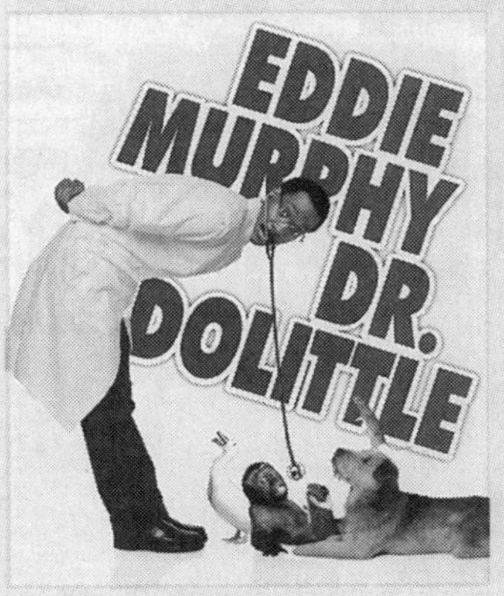

Dr. Dolittle (1998)
Workaholic physician Eddie Murphy turns from two-legged to four-legged patients after an accident restores his childhood ability to communicate with animals. Now Murphy has to cope with complaints from dogs, pigeons, guinea pigs and other critters, while relearning the importance of his family, in this hip updating of the Hugh Lofting stories. Kristen Wilson, Ossie Davis; Albert Brooks, Chris Rock and Garry Shandling are among the animal voices. 85 min.
04-3730 Was $19.99 □*$14.99*

Holy Man (1998)
With his cable TV shopping channel on the verge of bankruptcy, programming executive Jeff Goldblum hires offbeat guru Eddie Murphy as his new on-screen pitchman. Murphy's bizarre style of spiritual hucksterism makes the network a success in this fast-paced satire. With Kelly Preston, Jon Cryer. 114 min.
11-2319 Was $19.99 □*$14.99*

Life (1999)
The comic, raucous and often touching saga of jailbirds Eddie Murphy and Martin Lawrence over five decades begins in Harlem in the 1930s, where hustler Murphy and bank teller Lawrence are wrongly accused of murder. They're placed in a Mississippi prison camp, where they remain bickering pals for decades. Obba Babatunde, Clarence Williams III and Bokeem Woodbine also star. 109 min.
07-2792 Was $99.99 □*$14.99*

Eddie Murphy Collection, Vol. 1
Three of Murphy's funniest films, gathered in a deluxe boxed set. Laugh along as Eddie stars in "48 Hrs.," "Trading Places" and "Beverly Hills Cop."
06-2056 Save $5.00! *$39.99*

Please see our index for these other Eddie Murphy titles: *Bowfinger* • *Mulan*

Funny About Love (1990)
When cartoonist Gene Wilder's biological clock suddenly goes off, his desperate attempts to have a baby with wife Christine Lahti produce nothing but hilarious, heartfelt comedy. Romantic farce directed by Leonard Nimoy also stars Mary Stuart Masterson. 101 min.
06-1826 Was $89.99 □*$14.99*

Almost An Angel (1990)
Paul Hogan puts down the crocodiles to star in this warm, whimsical comedy about an ex-con who lands in a hospital and thinks he's about to become an angel. Soon, he reforms and tries to do good deeds to earn his wings. Linda Kozlowski, Elias Kostas, and Charlton Heston as God star. 98 min.
06-1850 □*$14.99*

Joey Breaker (1993)
An obnoxious, self-absorbed talent agent discovers that there's more to life than wheeling and dealing when he meets a Jamaican waitress who is studying to be a nurse. Richard Edson, Cedella Marley (Reggae star Bob Marley's daughter) and Gina Gershon star in this quirky romantic comedy. 92 min.
06-2141 Was $89.99 □*$14.99*

Milk Money (1994)
"The Courtship of Eddie's Father" meets "Pretty Woman" in this romantic comedy about a young boy who thinks the good-hearted hooker (Melanie Griffith) he meets on a trip to the big city will make a perfect wife for his widowed father (Ed Harris). With Michael Patrick Carter. 110 min.
06-2291 Was $89.99 □*$14.99*

He Said, She Said (1991)
With this unusual romantic farce, two directors (one female, one male), each helming one half of the film, show you the two opposing viewpoints of a stormy love affair that blooms between bickering journalists-turned-TV stars Kevin Bacon and Elizabeth Perkins. Sharon Stone and Anthony LaPaglia co-star. 115 min.
06-1877 Was $89.99 □*$14.99*

A Smile Like Yours (1997)
Winning romantic comedy starring Greg Kinnear and Lauren Holly as a seemingly happily married couple with one problem: they don't have any children, despite much practice. When the couple decides to seek professional help, hilarity ensues. Joan Cusack, Jay Thomas and Jill Hennessy also star. 99 min.
06-2676 Was $99.99 □*$14.99*

The Truth About Cats & Dogs (1996)
In a funny and winsome spin on the "Cyrano" story, witty but shy L.A. veterinarian/radio show host Janeane Garofalo convinces gorgeous friend Uma Thurman to pose as her when a caller eager to take her out shows up at the station. The masquerade grows into a loopy love triangle in this hit romantic comedy that also stars Ben Chaplin. 97 min.
04-3359 Was $99.99 ❑*$14.99*

The Great White Hype (1996)
Hilarious, on-target look at the circus-like world of heavyweight boxing starring Samuel L. Jackson as a flamboyant fight promoter out to find a white "underdog" to take on undefeated champ Damon Wayans. The opponent he selects is rock guitarist Peter Berg, who beat Wayans in an amateur bout years earlier. Jeff Goldblum, Jon Lovitz and Cheech Marin co-star; co-written by Ron Shelton ("Bull Durham"). 95 min.
04-3373 Was $99.99 ❑*$14.99*

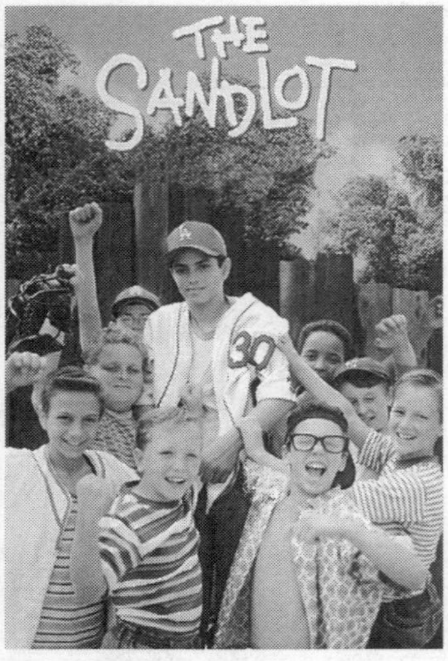
THE SANDLOT

The Sandlot (1993)
Whimsical family comedy set in the summer of 1962 in which a nerdy boy decides to join the neighborhood kids in playing baseball at a decrepit lot. When the boy borrows his stepfather's prize baseball—signed by no less than Babe Ruth—and it lands in a yard inhabited by the mysterious "Beast," it must be retrieved at any cost. Tom Guiry, Karen Allen and James Earl Jones star. 101 min.
04-2707 Was $89.99 ❑*$14.99*

Office Space (1999)
Mike Judge, the creator of "Beavis and Butt-head," tackles flesh-and-blood characters in this satiric look at corporate life. Peter, a computer programmer at a large company, gets heat from his bosses after a miscue. After a session with a hypnotherapist, Peter begins caring less about his job and more about telling the truth—which leads to a promotion! Ron Livingston, Gary Cole and Jennifer Aniston star. 90 min.
04-3852 Was $99.99 ❑*$14.99*

Simply Irresistible (1999)
Lively romantic comedy stars Sarah Michelle Gellar as a struggling cafe owner whose life changes dramatically after she gets a basket of magical crabs from a stranger. First, she meets handsome department store manager Sean Patrick Flanery, then she mysteriously inherits her mother's talent for cooking, which causes crowds to pack Gellar's eatery. With Christopher Durang. 100 min.
04-3853 Was $99.99 ❑*$14.99*

20 Dates (1999)
Filmmaker Myles Berkowitz mixes "my two biggest failures: my professional life and my personal life" in this unusual "docu-comedy" tracing his search for true love in Los Angeles. With backing from a shark-like producer, Berkowitz sets out to film dates with 20 different women. After a string of failures, Berkowitz meets the girl of his dreams...but will she stay through the remaining dates? 92 min.
04-3854 ❑*$99.99*

Drive Me Crazy (1999)
When high schooler Melissa Joan Hart abruptly finds herself without a date for the big centennial dance she's in charge of planning, she makes a deal with her next-door neighbor, scruffy rebel Adrian Grenier: he'll get a makeover and pose as her new beau, which will make his ex-girlfriend jealous. The plan works fine, until the pair wind up falling in love, in this romantic teen romp. With Stephen Collins, Susan May Pratt. 91 min.
04-3921 Was $99.99 ❑*$14.99*

She's The One (1996)
Filmmaker Edward Burns ("The Brothers McMullen") continues to hilariously explore sibling rivalry and the ongoing battle between the sexes in this witty romantic comedy that follows two New York brothers through troubled marriages, an attraction to the same woman, and trying to get along with their father. Jennifer Aniston, Maxine Bahns, Cameron Diaz and Mike McGlone join Burns in the talented ensemble cast. 97 min.
04-3395 Was $99.99 ❑*$14.99*

Among Giants (1999)
Engaging, low-key romantic comedy stars Pete Postlethwaite as a middle-aged British steeplejack who finds himself at uncomfortable heights when free-spirited vagabond Rachel Griffiths enters his work crew and his life. James Thornton co-stars; Simon Beaufoy ("The Full Monty") scripts. 90 min.
04-3862 ❑*$99.99*

Intimate Relations (1996)
A handsome stranger with a dark past takes a room with a quiet family in a small English town in the '50s. Things don't remain quiet when the sexually frustrated landlady, who dotes endlessly on the lodger, draws him into an affair and the family's teenage daughter, who has her own designs on him, learns of the romance. Rupert Graves, Julie Walters and Laura Sadler star in this acclaimed dark comedy, based on a real-life case that rocked Britain. 105 min.
04-3571 ❑*$99.99*

A Life Less Ordinary (1997)
In this off-the-wall romantic comedy from "Trainspotting" director Danny Boyle and scripter John Hodge, laid-off janitor Ewan McGregor's attempt to win back his job turns into an impromptu kidnapping, thanks to some help from his "victim," ex-boss's daughter Cameron Diaz. Adding to the fugitives' problems on the road are a pair of angels (Holly Hunter and Delroy Lindo) charged with bringing the couple together. Ian Holm, Dan Hedaya also star. 96 min.
04-3599 Was $99.99 ❑*$14.99*

Kicked In The Head (1997)
After losing his job and apartment, an aimless twentysomething New Yorker sets out on a "quest for truth," but getting there means navigating through such hazards as a gun-happy beer salesman pal, a con-artist uncle with a "package" to deliver, gun-toting gangsters, and a chance encounter with a beautiful flight attendant. Quirky comedy stars Kevin Corrigan (who co-scripted with director Matthew Harrison), Linda Fiorentino, Michael Rapaport, James Woods and Lili Taylor. 86 min.
04-3600 ❑*$89.99*

The Student Affair (1997)
When fretting over tenure and other mid-life crises push a married college professor into the arms of a sexy student, his wife hires a detective to get the goods on him. Things get more complicated when the private eye falls for his client in this witty, racy comedy. Sally Kellerman, Ed Begley, Jr., Tyne Daly, Stuart Margolin and Howard Stern fave Sandy Taylor star. AKA: "Lay of the Land." 95 min.
04-3660 ❑*$99.99*

The Object Of My Affection (1998)
Jennifer Aniston stars in this winning romantic comedy as a pregnant single woman who knows that gay roommate and best friend Paul Rudd would make a better father to her baby—and a much better husband to her—than her apprehensive boyfriend. What is she to do? Alan Alda, John Pankow and Nigel Hawthorne also star. Scripted by Wendy Wasserstein; Nicholas Hytner ("The Madness of King George") directs. 111 min.
04-3706 Was $99.99 ❑*$14.99*

Driving Me Crazy (1991)
An eccentric German inventor has designed the ultimate car, but the wacky Americans who greet him in his first visit to the States may put a wrench in his innovation's popularity. Dom DeLuise, Billy Dee Williams, George Kennedy, Michelle Johnson and Thomas Gottschalk star. 88 min.
02-2153 *$89.99*

Me Myself I (1999)
Engaging "what if" film from Australia starring Rachel Griffiths as a journalist in her thirties whose depression over her single status leads her to regret a marriage proposal she turned down 13 years earlier. After being hit by a car, Griffiths faces herself—as the married woman who now has three children. David Roberts, Sandy Winton also star. 104 min.
02-3458 ❑*$99.99*

The Addams Family (1991)
The ghoulish clan made famous in Charles Addams' cartoons and the '60s TV show make their big screen debut in this horrifically funny hit comedy. Has long-lost Uncle Fester come back after 20 years in the Bermuda Triangle, or is the bald stranger at the Addams door an impostor? Raul Julia, Anjelica Huston, Christopher Lloyd, Christina Ricci, Dan Hedaya and "Thing" star. 101 min.
06-1925 Was $19.99 ❑*$14.99*

Addams Family Values (1993)
The creepy, kooky, mysterious and spooky brood is back in a hilarious sequel that finds Gomez and Morticia welcoming Pubert, a new Addams, into the world; Uncle Fester getting hitched to a seductive, conniving nanny; and Wednesday and Pugsley disrupting a happy summer camp. Anjelica Huston, Raul Julia, Christopher Lloyd, Christina Ricci and Joan Cusack star. 94 min.
06-2202 Was $19.99 ❑*$14.99*

Addams Family Reunion (1998)
They're back! Gomez, Morticia, Fester and the rest of the frightful family have returned for another outrageous adventure that sends the brood on a search for long-lost relatives, with hilarious results. Tim Curry, Daryl Hannah, Estelle Harris, Ray Walston, and Ed Begley, Jr. star. 90 min.
19-2732 Was $19.99 ❑*$14.99*

Addams Family Gift Set
The first two "Addams Family" feature films are also available in this altogether spooky—and funny—boxed set.
06-2527 Save $10.00! *$19.99*

Pushing Tin (1999)
Set in the ultra-intense world of air traffic controllers, this turbulent comedy/drama stars John Cusack as a high-pressure, highly respected New York area controller whose primacy is threatened by the arrival of laid-back Billy Bob Thornton. When a jealous Cusack retaliates by sleeping with Thornton's wife (Angelina Jolie), his professional and personal lives head into a nosedive. With Kate Blanchett. 124 min.
04-3861 Was $99.99 ❑*$14.99*

Shooting Fish (1998)
Amiable con-artist comedy details the London-based adventures of slicksters Dylan (Dan Futterman), an American, and Jez (Stuart Townsend), a Brit, who make their living bilking fat cats out of cash. When secretary Georgie (Kate Beckinsale) starts collaborating on their criminal activities, sparks fly between her and the guys, complicating business practices. 93 min.
04-3733 ❑*$99.99*

Beavis And Butt-Head Do America (1996)
When their beloved television is stolen ("This sucks more than anything that has sucked before!"), Beavis and Butt-Head get up off their couch and set out on a wild cross-country quest from Las Vegas to the White House to find it—and maybe finally "score" with a woman while they're at it—in the metal-loving MTV cartoon cretins' hit debut feature. Voices by creator Mike Judge, Robert Stack, Cloris Leachman and an unbilled Demi Moore and Bruce Willis. 82 min.
06-2579 Was $99.99 ❑*$14.99*

Private Parts (1997)
Radio bad boy and self-professed "king of all media" Howard Stern lets it all hang out in this alternately hilarious, raunchy and touching filming of his best-selling autobiography. Follow Howard's trauma-filled childhood, his tortuous climb up the radio success ladder and many run-ins with bosses and censors, and his at times stormy relationship with wife Allison (Mary McCormack). Stern show regulars Robin Quivers, Fred Norris, Jackie "the Jokeman" Martling and Gary "Baba Booey" Dell'Abate appear as themselves. 108 min.
06-2608 Was $99.99 ❑*$14.99*

The Beautician And The Beast (1997)
TV's favorite nanny, Fran Drescher, plays a New York beauty school instructor who is mistakenly hired to tutor the children of Eastern European dictator Timothy Dalton. Once there, Drescher proceeds to enlighten the citizenry to her own version of the American way and turn Dalton into a more democratic ruler in this comical spin on "The King and I." 107 min.
06-2611 Was $99.99 ❑*$14.99*

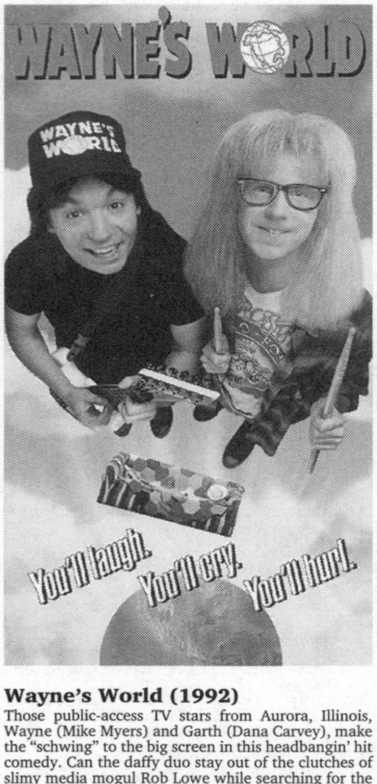
WAYNE'S WORLD
WAYNE'S WORLD
You'll laugh. You'll cry. You'll hurl.

Wayne's World (1992)
Those public-access TV stars from Aurora, Illinois, Wayne (Mike Myers) and Garth (Dana Carvey), make the "schwing" to the big screen in this headbangin' hit comedy. Can the daffy duo stay out of the clutches of slimy media mogul Rob Lowe while searching for the babes of their dreams and hanging out with heroes like Alice Cooper? Tia Carrere, Lara Flynn Boyle co-star. 93 min.
06-1965 Was $24.99 ❑*$14.99*

Wayne's World 2 (1993)
In this sublimely silly sequel, Wayne is summoned by the spirit of Jim Morrison to stage the world's ultimate rock concert, dubbed "Waynestock," and Garth is pursued by a "schwing"-ing blonde. The laughs are fast and furious, and there's spoofing of "Mission: Impossible," "Jurassic Park" and kung-fu films. With Mike Myers, Dana Carvey, Christopher Walken and Kim Basinger. 94 min.
06-2204 Was $89.99 ❑*$14.99*

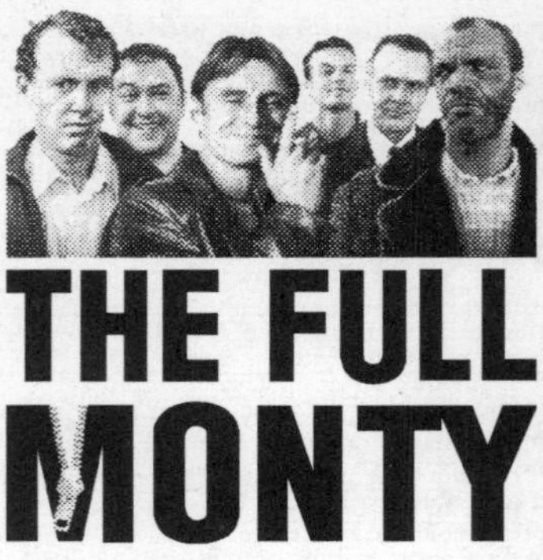
THE FULL MONTY

The Full Monty (1997)
A group of unemployed men in a depressed steel town in England's Yorkshire region hit upon a plan for making quick cash—passing themselves off as a Chippendales-style male stripper revue that dares to go all the way ("the full monty" in British slang) and reveal everything—in the surprise independent hit comedy. Robert Carlyle, Mark Addy, Tom Wilkinson and Lesley Sharp star. 95 min.
04-3562 Was $99.99 ❑*$14.99*

The Full Monty (Letterboxed Version)
Also available in a theatrical, widescreen format.
04-3702 ❑*$19.99*

Polish Wedding (1998)
Set in a blue-collar neighborhood of Detroit, this feisty romantic comedy focuses on the Pzoniaks, a Polish clan thrown into turmoil when daughter Claire Danes announces she's pregnant. The news brings Danes' combative parents—hard-working baker Gabriel Byrne and unfaithful spouse Lena Olin—together as they work to "convince" Danes' boyfriend to do the honorable thing. With Adame Trese, Mili Avital. 107 min.
04-3734 ❑*$99.99*

Slums Of Beverly Hills (1998)
For 15-year-old Vivian Abramowitz, the year 1976 is filled with a series of crises, from her peripatetic family's moves to stay one step ahead of Beverly Hills landlords and the arrival of an older female cousin to the cumbersome brassieres her blossoming body suddenly requires. Writer/director Tamara Jenkins' witty and engaging coming-of-age comedy stars Natasha Lyonne, Alan Arkin, Marisa Tomei and Kevin Corrigan. 91 min.
04-3768 ❑*$99.99*

The Impostors (1998)
In this salute to the screwball and silent comedies of old, Stanley Tucci and Oliver Platt are out-of-work thespians in the 1930s who land on a ship heading for Europe after a run-in with a hammy actor. While trying to evade the authorities, the duo meet a crew of eccentrics and try to stop a plot to blow up the ship. Lili Taylor, Isabella Rossellini, Steve Buscemi also star. 101 min.
04-3832 ❑*$99.99*

Soft Fruit (1999)
Returning home for the first time in years to help care for their terminally ill mother, four siblings—an biker ex-con and his neurotic sisters—must deal with old and new rivalries and their tyrannical father. It's up to the mother to set things right and live out her life the way she wants in this bittersweet seriocomedy from Australia. Jeanie Drynan, Genevieve Lemon, Russell Dykstra star. 101 min.
04-3966 ❑*$99.99*

Antonia And Jane (1991)
Winning, quirky comedy-drama looks at the lifelong friendship between two women: the plain, artistic Jane, who continually changes her lifestyle, and beautiful, bored Antonia, married to Jane's former boyfriend. The pair also happen to share the same psychiatrist. Imelda Staunton, Saskia Reeves and Bill Nighy star in this study of the loving—and not-so loving—bonds between friends. 75 min.
06-1989 ❑*$89.99*

Highway 61 (1992)
A kooky comedic road movie about a Canadian barber who is joined by a female rock-and-roll roadie on a trip to deliver a coffin to New Orleans. The journey brings them face-to-face with a fascist customs agent and a man who claims to buy souls with his bingo winnings. Don McKeller, Valerie Buhagiar and Jello Biafra star. 99 min.
06-1993 Was $89.99 *$14.99*

Brain Donors (1992)
"In the tradition of Abbott and Costello, the Three Stooges, and the Reagan Administration" comes this Zucker Brothers ("The Naked Gun") production starring John Turturro, Mel Smith and Bob Nelson as a trio of zany goofs who band together to help a wealthy widow start a ballet company. With Nancy Marchand, George De La Pena. 79 min.
06-2002 Was $89.99 ❑*$14.99*

Dead Husbands (1998)
Tired of her seemingly storybook marriage to self-help author John Ritter, bored spouse Nicollette Sheridan learns of a unique "club" where wives agree to kill each other's husband. Amy Yasbeck and Donna Pescow also star in this outrageous dark comedy. 90 min.
06-2848 ❑*$69.99*

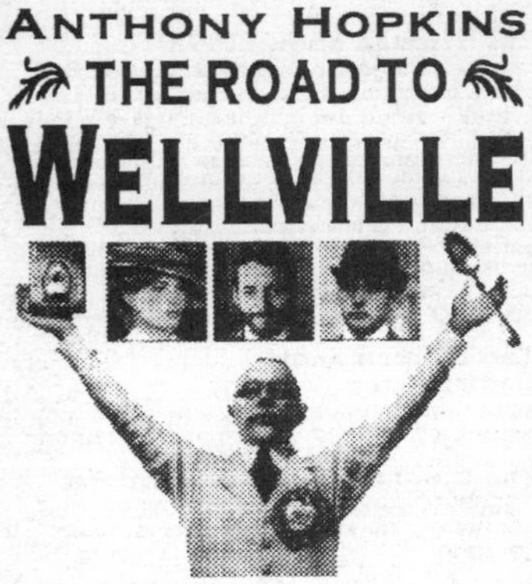

The Road To Wellville (1994)
Writer/director Alan Parker spoofs modern diet crazes with a look back to the early 1900s, when physician/inventor/ce real pioneer Dr. John Kellogg (Anthony Hopkins) lured the rich to his Michigan sanitarium/spa for a bizarre—and sometimes fatal—regimen of exercise, health food, sexual abstinence and enemas. Based on T. Corraghessan Boyle's novel, the offbeat comedy also stars Bridget Fonda, Matthew Broderick, John Cusack and Dana Carvey. 120 min.
02-2756 Was $19.99 *$14.99*

Jon Jost's Frameup (1993)
Acclaimed independent filmmaker Jost ("All the Vermeers in New York") takes a darkly comic look at the "road trip to Hell" taken by a scatterbrained waitress and her ex-con husband across the Pacific Northwest. Howard Swain, Nancy Carlin star. 91 min.
70-3397 Letterboxed *$24.99*

The Boys (1996)
A huge hit in its native Canada, this lively comedy tells of a group of guys who play for an amateur ice hockey team sponsored by a bar. When the watering hole is threatened with closing by a mobster, the team decides to save their hangout by playing the gangster's goons in a big game. Marc Messier (no, not that one) and Patrick Huard star. 110 min. In French with English subtitles.
64-9032 *$99.99*

The Boys (Dubbed Version)
Also available in a dubbed-in-English edition.
64-9033 *$99.99*

National Lampoon's Last Resort (1994)
Sam (Corey Feldman) and Dave (Corey Haim) are recruited to help save Sam's uncle's Caribbean resort island. Acting as CIA agents/scuba instructors, the two guys enlist the help of a wacky mermaid, a Rastafarian flasher and some gorgeous babes to help them stop their uncle's old nemesis. Geoffrey Lewis and First Brother Roger Clinton co-star. 91 min.
68-1298 *$89.99*

The Misery Brothers (1999)
Siblings Michael and Angelo Misery get into trouble with attorney F. Me Weekly for a crime they didn't commit and depend on bombshell public defender Ima Barrister to keep them off Death Row. The courtroom becomes a three-ring circus in this zany, wacky farce. Stars Leo Rossi, Debbie Dunning, Pat Morita, Norm Crosby, Erik Estrada and Stallone...Frank, that is! 88 min.
65-9001 *$99.99*

One Crazy Night (1991)
Five very different teenagers find themselves stranded together with only their love for The Beatles being the common denominator. As time goes on, they share likes, dislikes and secrets, while getting to know each other better. Noah Taylor and Beth Champion star in this spirited Australian production featuring such Fab Four tunes as "I Saw Her Standing There" and "Love Me Do." 92 min.
68-1275 *$89.99*

Getting In (1994)
A young man from a long line of Johns Hopkins Medical School alumni faces disaster when a failed entrance exam lands him on the waiting list. He devises some devious ways to convince his fellow applicants to drop off the list, but when they start turning up dead, he becomes a suspect. Dark comedy stars Stephen Mailer, Kristy Swason, Andrew McCarthy, Matthew Perry and Calista Flockhart. 94 min.
68-1331 Was $89.99 *$14.99*

The Woman Who Loved Elvis (1992)
While waiting for hubby Tom Arnold to dump his live-in girlfriend, Roseanne Arnold becomes obsessed with Elvis Presley and turns her house into a shrine to "the King." A young welfare office worker investigating her becomes her confidante and the two share in laughs and secrets about men and marriage. Cynthia Gibb, Sally Kirkland also star. 104 min.
68-1844 *$99.99*

The Wiz Kid (1993)
A nerdy 14-year-old computer genius wants to get the attention of the rock singer girlfriend of his school's toughest bully, so he uses his science skills to clone a hipper version of himself and lets it turn on the charm. Martin Forbes, Gary Forbes star. 90 min.
68-1278 *$89.99*

Bug Buster (1998)
In this comedy, a pesticide turns fishes into roaches near an idyllic town and a scientist is called on to stop them when a number of terrifying deaths frighten the homespun townspeople. Katherine Heigl, Randy Quaid, June Lockhart, James Doohan, George Takei and Bernie Kopell star. It's "Piranha"—with bugs!
65-9003 Was $89.99 *$19.99*

Trading Mom (1994)
Unhappy with current mother Sissy Spacek, three siblings decide to trade her in, using a magical spell to travel to the Mommy Market and select a new parent—but will any of their new choices (all played by Spacek) be better than the real thing? Heartwarming family comedy also stars Anna Chlumsky, Andre the Giant and Maureen Stapleton. 83 min.
68-1311 Was $89.99 *$14.99*

Late Last Night (1999)
Faced with the disintegration of his marriage, Beverly Hills entertainment lawyer Emilio Estevez looks for solace with buddy Steven Weber in a one-night odyssey of booze, drugs and women through the streets of Los Angeles. Hip and darkly funny tale of '90s relationships also stars Catherine O'Hara, Bobby Edner, Katie Wright. 90 min.
64-9053 *$99.99*

Mob Boss (1990)
It's "The Godfather" gone bonkers, as a devious mistress plots to oust a reigning Mafia don. The don installs his nerdy son to handle family business, and the bullets and laughs fly fast. Eddie Deezen, William Hickey, Stuart Whitman and Morgan Fairchild star. 93 min.
68-1167 *$89.99*

The Stoned Age (1993)
Slip on your best tie-dyed fashions and take a trip back to the '70s, as two high-school buddies out for a night of driving, partying and meeting girls spend the evening...well, driving, partying and meeting girls. Good-natured and evocative comedy stars Michael Kopelow, China Kantner; music by Blue Oyster Cult, Foghat, Ted Nugent and others. 90 min.
68-1333 Was $89.99 *$14.99*

Hostage For A Day (1994)
George Wendt, a man with an overbearing wife, a miserable job and an irascible father-in-law, tries to change his life by devising his own kidnapping. A funny, off-the-wall comedy featuring an appearance by John Candy, who also makes his directorial debut here. With Robin Duke and John Vernon. 92 min.
68-1319 *$89.99*

Sandra Bullock

Hangmen (1987)
Just what is the reason that a band of renegade CIA assassins wants a teenage boy dead, and how can his ex-Green Beret dad save him in time? With Richard Washburn, Doug Thomas and Jake LaMotta; look for Sandra Bullock in her film debut. 88 min.
71-5101 *$14.99*

A Fool And His Money (1988)
A hot-shot ad executive who just lost his job thinks he's found a quick road to riches with a questionable product, but will his greed cost him the woman he loves? Comedic look at romance, finance and other weighty topics stars Jonathan Penner and Sandra Bullock, with cameos by Tama Janowitz, Jerzy Kosinski, and George Plimpton as "God." 84 min.
68-1344 Was $89.99 *$14.99*

Who Shot Pat? (1992)
Set in 1957, this nostalgic comedy-drama focuses on the adventures of a group of seniors at a Brooklyn vocational high school. Trouble erupts when a gunshot wounds one of the teens, and the rest of the group wants to find out who shot him. David Knight, Kevin Otto and Sandra Bullock star. 102 min.
19-2016 Was $89.99 *$19.99*

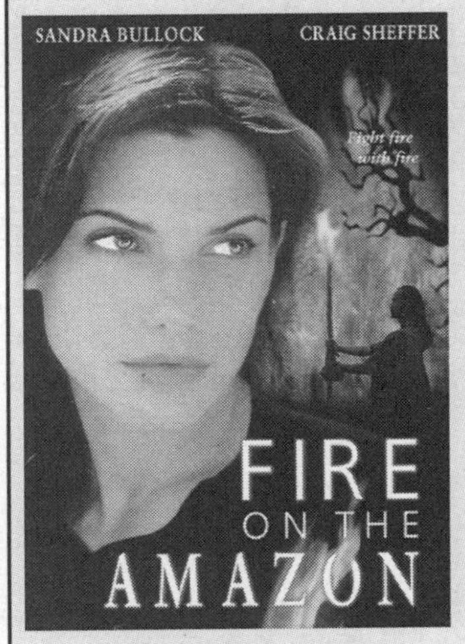

Fire On The Amazon (1993)
Notorious for Sandra Bullock's spunky nude scene, this Roger Corman production stars Craig Sheffer as an adventurous photojournalist who teams with activist Bullock to save the South American rain forest from a reckless lumber company. The much-discussed scene features the two leads in a wild tussle after drinking a drug-spiked potion. AKA: "Lost Paradise." Unrated version; 81 min.
21-9209 Was $99.99 *$14.99*

Love Potion #9 (1993)
A hilarious romantic farce based on the classic pop song, as a pair of nerdish scientists fall in love after taking the title elixir, then take off on a wild adventure to recover it after it's swiped. Tate Donovan, Sandra Bullock and Dale Midkiff star. 97 min.
04-2628 *$14.99*

The Thing Called Love (1993)
The competitive world of the country music business in Nashville is the setting for this romantic drama focusing on four hopefuls who become friends while searching for their big break. There's Miranda (Samantha Mathis) from New York; Connecticut cowboy Kyle (Dermot Mulroney); Southern belle Linda Lue (Sandra Bullock); and a cocky Texan named James (River Phoenix); directed by Peter Bogdanovich. 116 min.
06-2178 Was $89.99 *$19.99*

When The Party's Over (1993)
A group of sophisticated "twentysomethings" living together in an exclusive section of Los Angeles look at life as one big party, rarely paying attention to serious problems. But what happens when the party's over? The answer is pondered in this insightful, sexy serio-comedy with Rae Dawn Chong, Fisher Stevens, Sandra Bullock and Elizabeth Berridge. 114 min.
27-6829 Was $89.99 *$14.99*

Speed (1994)
Electrifying action thriller starring Keanu Reeves as a member of the Los Angeles SWAT team who must rescue the passengers on a bus boobytrapped by deranged bomb expert Dennis Hopper—if the vehicle goes under 50 mph, it explodes! Sandra Bullock is the courageous commuter in charge of driving. With Jeff Daniels, Joe Morton and an amazing array of wild stunts. 115 min.
04-2862 Was $19.99 *$14.99*

Speed (Letterboxed Version)
Also available in a theatrical, widescreen format.
04-3354 *$19.99*

Speed 2: Cruise Control (1997)
A romantic Caribbean cruise for feisty Sandra Bullock and new beau Jason Patric becomes a voyage into danger when deranged computer whiz Willem Dafoe, an ex-employee of the cruise line, takes control of the boat as part of his extortion scheme in this thrill-a-minute action ride helmed by "Speed" director Jan DeBont. 125 min.
04-3529 Was $99.99 *$14.99*

Speed 2: Cruise Control (Letterboxed Version)
Also available in a theatrical, widescreen format.
04-3636 *$19.99*

The Net (1995)
Sleek suspenser with Sandra Bullock as a lonely computer wizard whose Mexican vacation turns dangerous when she meets a British hacker in search of a disc that offers access to secret government files. Back in the U.S., Bullock discovers that her identity has been "deleted" as she is pursued by both police and the disc's mysterious designers. With Jeremy Northam, Dennis Miller and Diane Baker. 114 min.
02-2818 Was $19.99 *$14.99*

While You Were Sleeping (1995)
Lively romantic comedy showcasing the affable Sandra Bullock as a Chicago transit worker who saves the life of a slick lawyer she's smitten with after he falls near an oncoming train. While he's hospitalized in a coma, Bullock is assumed to be the lawyer's fiancée by his eccentric family, but the arrival of a handsome older brother complicates matters. With Bill Pullman, Peter Gallagher.103 min.
11-1939 Was $19.99 *$14.99*

In Love And War (1996)
Based on the real-life WWI exploits of author Ernest Hemingway, director Richard Attenborough's sensitive drama stars Chris O'Donnell as the teenaged Hemingway, whose reckless heroics as a front-line ambulance driver land him in the hospital. There he is cared for and falls in love with American nurse Sandra Bullock, who would later serve as the inspiration for his "A Farewell to Arms." 113 min.
02-5128 Was $99.99 *$14.99*

In Love And War (Letterboxed Version)
Also available in a theatrical, widescreen format.
02-5222 *$14.99*

A Time To Kill (1996)
The best-selling first novel by John Grisham becomes a powerful courtroom drama featuring Samuel L. Jackson as a Mississippi factory worker on trial for killing two racist attackers who raped his young daughter. After taking on the controversial case, white attorney Matthew McConaughey and idealistic law student Sandra Bullock find their lives in danger from the Ku Klux Klan. With Kevin Spacey, Oliver Platt and Donald Sutherland. 150 min.
19-2471 Was $19.99 *$14.99*

A Time To Kill (Letterboxed Version)
Also available in a theatrical, widescreen format.
19-2551 *$19.99*

Two If By Sea (1996)
Off-the-wall romantic romp starring Denis Leary as a thief who swipes a priceless Matisse painting and goes on the lam with adventurous cashier girlfriend Sandra Bullock. While hiding out in a snobby New England coastal town, the two squabble over their future and discover that there may be a real art thief in their midst. 96 min.
19-2442 Was $19.99 *$14.99*

Hope Floats (1998)
Winning romantic story featuring Sandra Bullock as a woman who discovers that her storybook marriage is kaput when she learns of her hubby's indiscretions on a TV talk show. Bullock heads back to her small Texas hometown with her daughter, makes amends with her parents and eventually falls for childhood friend Harry Connick, Jr. With Mae Whitman, Gena Rowlands. 114 min.
04-3731 Was $19.99 *$14.99*

Practical Magic (1998)
The bewitching duo of Sandra Bullock and Nicole Kidman shines in this comedic fantasy/romance, playing sisters who turn to the witchcraft their family's practiced for generations in order to overcome an ancient curse that's responsible for their stagnant love lives. Dianne Wiest, Stockard Channing and Aidan Quinn also star; directed by Griffin Dunne ("Addicted to Love"). 104 min.
19-2814 Was $99.99 *$19.99*

Practical Magic (Letterboxed Version)
Also available in a theatrical, widescreen format.
19-2864 *$19.99*

Forces Of Nature (1999)
With his New York-Savannah flight cancelled and two days to get to Georgia for his wedding, uptight book blurb writer Ben Affleck reluctantly accepts help from another stranded passenger, free spirit Sandra Bullock. Their wild odyssey by car, train and bus includes run-ins with the law, dancing in a nightclub, a hurricane and maybe romance in this winning comedy. Maura Tierney, Steve Zahn, Blythe Danner also star. 106 min.
07-2791 Was $99.99 *$14.99*

Gun Shy (2000)
Anxiety-ridden DEA agent Liam Neeson is eager to retire, but first must complete an undercover assignment in a money-laundering scheme involving a Wall Street hot shot, a Colombian drug cartel and an Italian mobster. Meanwhile, Neeson finds romance (and help for his stressed-out digestive tract) with holistic nurse Sandra Bullock in this offbeat action-comedy. With Oliver Platt, Mary McCormack. 102 min.
11-2433 Was $99.99 *$14.99*

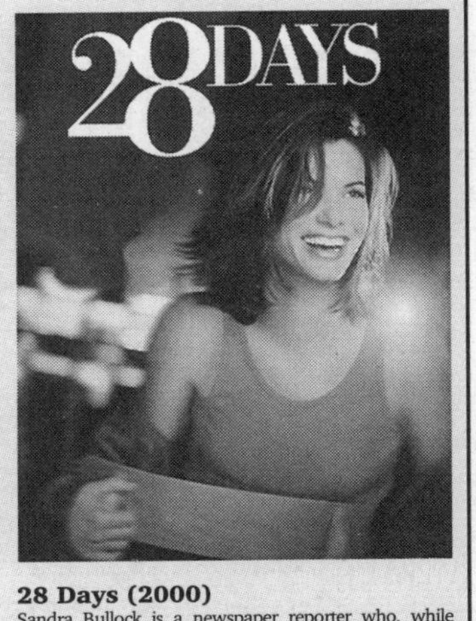

28 Days (2000)
Sandra Bullock is a newspaper reporter who, while intoxicated, crashes a limousine on the day of sister Elizabeth Perkins' wedding. Bullock enters a rehab center where she attempts to fit in with the diverse group of patients—which is difficult when her boyfriend brings her booze and drugs during visits. With Diane Ladd, Viggo Mortensen and Steve Buscemi. 104 min.
02-3457 *$99.99*

Please see our index for these other Sandra Bullock titles: *Demolition Man • Me And The Mob • The Prince Of Egypt • The Vanishing • Wrestling Ernest Hemingway*

Rubberface (1981)
And who better to take the title role than Jim Carrey? A pre-Hollywood Carrey stars in this Canadian-made romp, playing a would-be stage comic who gets help with his act from a shy high school girl. Adah Glassbourg also stars. AKA: "Introducing Janet." 48 min.
68-1372 Was $49.99 ❑*$14.99*

Once Bitten (1985)
What do you get when you cross a teenage male virgin with a need for...well, you know...with a sexy, centuries-old female vampire with a need for young male virgins? Toothsome comedy stars Lauren Hutton, Jim Carrey and Cleavon Little. 93 min.
47-1544 ❑*$14.99*

Earth Girls Are Easy (1989)
When a spaceship crashes into Los Angeles manicurist Geena Davis' swimming pool, she helps the fur-covered, sex-crazed crew (Jim Carrey, Jeff Goldblum, Damon Wayans) disguise themselves as Earthlings and assimilate into the Southern California lifestyle. Zany, song-filled parody of '50s sci-fi and Valley Girl culture also stars Julie Brown, Michael McKean. 100 min.
47-1978 *$14.99*

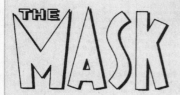

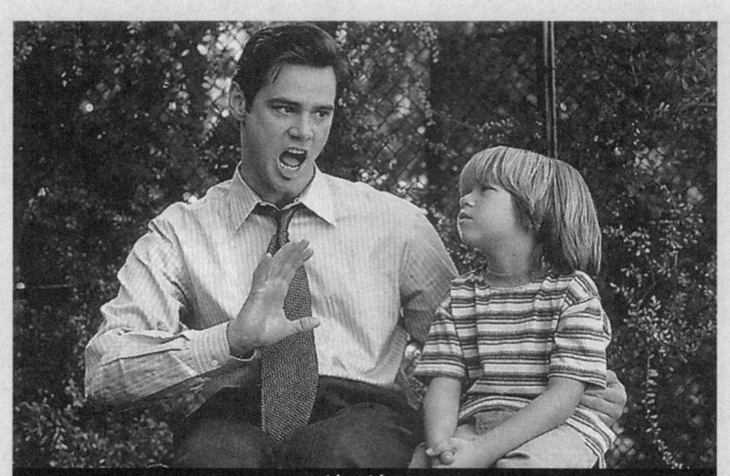
Liar Liar

THE MASK

Jim Carrey

The Truman Show (1998)
After years of idyllic living in a seaside island village, insurance salesman Truman Burbank (Jim Carrey) begins to see signs that things aren't as perfect as they seem. He discovers that he's the "star" of a continuously broadcast TV show that's aired since his infancy, his friends and family are all actors, and his hometown is an elaborate set. Ed Harris, Laura Linney and Noah Emmerich also star in director Peter Weir's compelling satire on truth and freedom in the age of media manipulation. 103 min.
06-2766 Was $99.99 ❑*$14.99*

The Truman Show (Letterboxed Version)
Also available in a theatrical, widescreen format.
06-2851 ❑*$14.99*

The Duh-Lux Collector's Gift Set
"Carrey" on laughing with this "Jim"-dandy boxed set featuring "The Mask" and "Dumb and Dumber."
02-5099 Save $5.00! *$24.99*

Man On The Moon (1999)
In an acclaimed performance that borders on channeling, Jim Carrey plays kamikaze comic genius Andy Kaufman, who delighted in tricking, perplexing, and sometimes annoying his audiences. Director Milos Forman's film follows Kaufman from his early days in stand-up, to his star-making TV turns on "Saturday Night Live" and "Taxi," and to his increasingly strange live shows and feud with pro wrestler Jerry Lawler. Danny DeVito, Courtney Love also star; Tony Clifton appears as himself. 119 min.
07-2866 Was $99.99 ❑*$14.99*

The Mask (1994)
Shy bank clerk Jim Carrey finds a mystical mask that transforms him into a green-faced, zoot-suited madman with super powers and a libido to match. Carrey's wild alter ego runs afoul of the police and mobsters in this effects-filled fantasy/comedy, based on a popular comic book. With Cameron Diaz, Peter Riegert, Peter Greene. 101 min.
02-5042 Was $19.99 ❑*$14.99*

The Mask (Letterboxed Version)
Also available in a theatrical, widescreen format.
02-5139 ❑*$19.99*

Dumb And Dumber (1994)
Outrageously funny hi-jinks ensue when dim-witted pals Jim Carrey and Jeff Daniels set out to find the beautiful socialite who dropped a briefcase filled with loot at a Rhode Island airport. The goofballs' search leads to Aspen, but also on the woman's trail are some nasty kidnappers. Lauren Holly also stars in this wild rib-tickler. 110 min.
02-5049 Was $19.99 ❑*$14.99*

Dumb And Dumber (Letterboxed Version)
Also available in a theatrical, widescreen format.
02-5140 ❑*$19.99*

Ace Ventura: Pet Detective (1994)
This surprise smash stars Jim Carrey as the title character, a goofy gumshoe who specializes in tracking down critters of all sorts. When Snowflake, the mascot of the Miami Dolphins, is swiped, Ace goes to work, using his detective "talents" to save the day. Courteney Cox, Sean Young and Dan Marino also star. 87 min.
19-2227 Was $19.99 ❑*$14.99*

Ace Ventura: When Nature Calls (1995)
Jim Carrey's Ace Ventura is back, big hair and all, this time taking his pet sleuthing expertise to Africa, where he's in search of a sacred white bat being fought over by rival tribes. Ian McNiece, Simon Callow and Maynard Eziashi also star in this wild romp filled with the sort of hilarity you can get "Carrey"-ed away with. 94 min.
19-2432 Was $22.99 ❑*$14.99*

The Cable Guy (1996)
Jim Carrey is at his lunatic best in this dark comedy, playing a media-obsessed cable TV installer who will do just about anything to make friends. Matthew Broderick is the architect who becomes the focus of Carrey's affection and realizes his new pal's wiring isn't all there when he tries to curtail their relationship. With Leslie Mann, George Segal, Janeane Garofalo, Charles Napier. 96 min.
02-2940 Was $19.99 ❑*$14.99*

Liar Liar (1997)
Imagine you're incapable of telling a lie for 24 hours. Now imagine you're unscrupulous attorney Jim Carrey, who's made a career out of stretching the truth but, thanks to a birthday wish made by his estranged son, has to be honest regardless of the cost. Carrey's at his comically contorted funniest (and that's no lie!) in this smash hit that also stars Jennifer Tilly, Maura Tierney, Justin Cooper. 87 min.
07-2542 Was $19.99 ❑*$14.99*

Liar Liar (Letterboxed Version)
Also available in a theatrical, widescreen format.
07-2544 ❑*$19.99*

Me, Myself & Irene

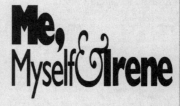

Me, Myself & Irene (2000)
In this comedy from the Farrelly Brothers, Jim Carrey is Charlie, a Rhode Island state trooper whose anger is so repressed that he develops another personality, the maniacal Hank. When Charlie gets the nod to escort Renee Zellweger, a crook's ex-girlfriend, to New York, they must dodge crooks and crooked cops while Carrey's alter egos battle for Irene's hand. With Chris Cooper, Robert Forster and Anna Kournikova.
04-3991 Available 1/01 ❑*$99.99*

Please see our index for these other Jim Carrey titles: *Batman Forever • The Dead Pool • Peggy Sue Got Married • Pink Cadillac • Simon Birch*

Housewife From Hell (1994)
After he kills his slovenly shrew of a wife, a man has the time of his life, drinking, partying and having wild sex...until the wife returns as a sultry ghost with vengeance on her mind! Outrageous comedy stars Lisa Cromshaw, Gregg Bullock and Ron Jeremy. 82 min.
72-9034 Was $89.99 *$14.99*

SWIMMING WITH SHARKS

Swimming With Sharks (1995)
Acidic dark comedy about Guy, a young production assistant at a Hollywood movie studio who is constantly humiliated by his boss, nasty executive Buddy Ackerman. When Guy discovers that Buddy has arranged a date with his producer girlfriend, he goes over the deep end, taking him hostage. Kevin Spacey, Frank Whaley, Michelle Forbes star. 93 min.
68-1376 Was $89.99 ❑*$14.99*

Don't Do It! (1995)
Follow the romantic ups and downs of three twentysomething couples in Los Angeles in this sly and witty "Generation X" comedy. Fine ensemble cast includes Alexis Arquette, Balthazar Getty, Heather Graham, Sheryl Lee, Esai Morales, Sarah Trigger. 90 min.
72-9049 Was $89.99 *$14.99*

Car 54, Where Are You? (1994)
The classic 1960s police sitcom is turned into an all-star comedy featuring David Johansen as easy-going Gunther Tooty and John C. McGinley as by-the-book Francis Muldoon, two New York coppers who keep getting in trouble. Rosie O'Donnell, Fran Drescher, Daniel Baldwin and Al Lewis (yeah!) also star. 89 min.
73-1154 Was $89.99 ❑*$14.99*

8 Heads In A Duffel Bag (1997)
Anyone who's ever had luggage problems at the airport can certainly sympathize with mob hit man Joe Pesci, whose bag contains the noggins of his last eight targets and must be retrieved from the medical student who accidentally picked it up, so Pesci can present the "trophies" to his boss. Outrageous dark comedy also stars Andy Comeau, Kristy Swanson, David Spade. 95 min.
73-1277 Was $99.99 ❑*$14.99*

Prehistoric Bimbos In Armageddon City (1993)
After World War III, Old Chicago City is run by an evil dictator and his cyborg army. Going up against the tyrant in a showdown for survival is the beautiful bimbo Queen Trianna and her battling babes in this wacky, sexy spoof. Holly Star and Stephanie Malone co-star. 75 min.
73-9056 Was $39.99 *$19.99*

Sick Time (1995)
After calling in sick for work, Malcolm has more trouble than he bargained for when he causes himself physical damage and must contend with a wild child raised in a cage, the deranged President of the United States, a sinister hypnotist and some media madness. Darkly humorous effort from the independent shot-on-video world. 40 min.
73-9174 *$19.99*

Working Stiffs (1995)
A sleazy temp agency discovers it can create workaholic, non-complaining zombie employees with a little voodoo. When a woman learns that her late brother has become part of this unearthly work force, she finds herself in the middle of all sorts of ghoulish mayhem. This dark video parody of American work ethics gone awry plays like "Night of the Living Dead" as envisioned by Studs Turkel. 62 min.
73-9176 *$19.99*

Identity Crisis (1990)
When a fashion designer is killed by rivals, his persona is zapped into the body of a streetwise rapper. The "odd couple" are joined by the designer's son as they try to catch the killers and set things right in this wild "body-switching" comedy. Mario Van Peebles, Ilan Mitchell-Smith star. 98 min.
71-5207 *$12.99*

The Big Slice (1991)
Two aspiring novelists decide they need some on-hand experience for their books, so they decide to get involved in a wild adventure that sets them on opposite sides of the law. Casey Siemaszko, Leslie Hope and Heather Locklear star. 86 min.
71-5220 *$12.99*

In The Soup (1993)
Funny and touching seriocomedy about a desperate filmmaker living in a seedy New York apartment who befriends an aging mobster in order to get financing for his movie project. While joining with his new pal in small-time crimes, the filmmaker falls in love with a beautiful next-door neighbor. Steve Buscemi, Seymour Cassel, Jennifer Beals, Will Patton and Stanley Tucci star. Filmed-in-color version. 96 min.
71-5276 ❑*$19.99*

Lovers' Lovers (1994)
Provocative look at love and relationships in the 1990s centering on two couples who wind up sharing beds and partners in a search for happiness and erotic fulfillment. Serge Rodnunsky, Jennifer Ciesar, Cindy Parker star. Uncut, unrated version; 90 min.
72-9030 *$89.99*

Shakes the Clown

Shakes The Clown (1992)
Outrageous clown comedy with writer/director/star Bobcat Goldthwait as an alcoholic harlequin who is framed for murder by a jealous rival. He's rousted by rodeo clowns, mocked by mimes, and must fight for the hand of lady love Julie Brown. With Paul Dooley, Florence Henderson, Adam Sandler and an unbilled Robin Williams. 86 min.
02-2223 Was $89.99 *$14.99*

Medicine River (1994)
A Native American photojournalist of Blackfoot descent returns to his hometown after a 20-year absence to attend his mother's funeral. While struggling with his past and his heritage, the photographer finds himself in a series of hilarious situations. Graham Greene, Tom Jackson and Sheila Tousey star in this sensitive story. 96 min.
71-5312 *$12.99*

The Nutt House (1992)
In this outrageous farce, a lunatic with multiple personalities escapes from a mental hospital to search for his identical twin brother, a successful politician. When the two siblings reunite, unpredictable slapstick wackiness abounds. Traci Lords, Stephen Kearny and Amy Yasbeck star; co-written by Alan Smithee, Jr. and Sr. AKA: "The Nutty Nut." 90 min.
72-9052 Was $89.99 *$14.99*

Sorority Babes In The Dance-A-Thon Of Death (1993)
From the creators of "Sorority Babes in the Slimeball Bowl-A-Rama" comes this sexy farce about four sensuous sorority sisters who mistakenly awaken a hideous demon...and only two elderly antiques dealers can stop it! Holly Star stars. 75 min.
73-9063 *$19.99*

Bikini Drive-In (1994)
When her grandfather's drive-in is about to fall into the hands of a sleazy shopping mall builder, a gorgeous co-ed and her girlfriends don skimpy swimwear for a "grand re-opening" party. Before you can say "dancing hot dogs," business is booming and there's more action off-screen than on! Sexy, zany spoof from cult director Fred Olen Ray stars Ashlie Rhey, Sarah Bellomo, Ross Hagen, with cameos by Michelle Bauer, Forrest J. Ackerman and a host of B-movie legends. Uncut, unrated version; 85 min.
74-3019 *$49.99*

Broadcast Bombshells (1995)
TV station WSEX gets a big rise in its ratings thanks to a gorgeous news anchor, but when a scheming rival plots to put herself behind the newsdesk and a deranged bomber threatens to blow up the station, the zany, racy hi-jinks reach new heights. Wacky, sexy comedy stars Amy Lynn Baxter, Debbie Rochon. Uncut, unrated version; 83 min.
74-3024 *$89.99*

South Park: Bigger, Longer & Uncut (1999)
The foul-mouthed foursome from cable TV's hit series are uncensored at last in their outrageous feature film debut. When a trip to the new "Terrance & Philip" movie has Stan, Kyle, Cartman, Kenny and the rest of the South Park kids cussing a blue streak, the outraged parents start a protest that leads to America declaring war on Canada and the gang trying to stop Satan and Saddam Hussein from taking over the world. All this, and songs, too! 81 min.
06-2916 Was $99.99 ❑***$14.99***

There Goes The Neighborhood (1993)
After a dying inmate tells him where $8.5 million in loot is hidden, a prison psychiatrist tries to find it. The problem is that the cash is buried under the home of a zany divorcée, and some greedy neighbors and escaped convicts are seeking it as well. Jeff Daniels, Catherine O'Hara, Hector Elizondo, Rhea Perlman and Dabney Coleman star. 88 min.
06-2117 Was $89.99 ❑***$14.99***

Dead Man On Campus (1998)
A studious college freshman's scholarship is in jeopardy when, after falling in with his roommate's party animal ways, both find themselves on the verge of flunking out. Salvation lies in a school charter clause that awards straight A's to the roommates of any student that commits suicide—and a series of potential candidates. Outrageous black comedy stars Tom Everett Scott, Mark-Paul Gosselaar, Poppy Montgomery and Alyson Hannigan. 94 min.
06-2826 Was $99.99 ❑***$14.99***

Whiteboyz (1999)
Hip-talking rapper Flip dreams of busting out of the Chicago ghetto and making it big in the urban music scene. Getting there might be a problem, though, because he's a white farmboy from rural Iowa! Follow Flip and his "homiez'" odyssey to live out their MTV-inspired hip-hop fantasies in this phat farce co-written by star Danny Hoch and director Mark Lewin ("Slam"); featuring cameos by Fat Joe, Slick Rick, Doug E. Doug and Snoop Dogg. 88 min.
04-3927 Was $99.99 ❑***$14.99***

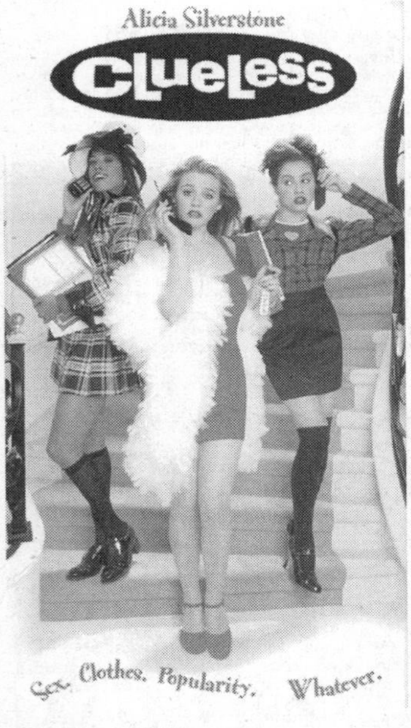
Alicia Silverstone
Clueless
Sex. Clothes. Popularity. Whatever.

Clueless (1995)
Righteous teen comedy starring Alicia Silverstone as Cher, Beverly Hills high school student and pampered daughter of a widowed lawyer, who tries to help her classmates and family with romance and fashion advice, while eventually coming to examine the problems in her own seemingly perfect life. Stacey Dash, Dan Hedaya co-star in director Amy Heckerling's hit film (based on, of all things, Jane Austen's "Emma"). 97 min.
06-2387 Was $89.99 ❑***$14.99***

The Efficiency Expert (1992)
Set in Australia in 1966, this charming film stars Anthony Hopkins as a professional money-saver who is sent to an out-of-date moccasin company in hopes of putting it on the right track. Part of his measures involve laying off more than half of the enterprise's workers, but rather than being angered with Hopkins, they befriend him. With Alwyn Kurts and Bruno Lawrence. AKA: "Spottswood." 97 min.
06-2111 Was $89.99 ❑***$14.99***

I Don't Buy Kisses Anymore (1992)
Chubby Philadelphia shoe salesman Jason Alexander falls head over heels for pretty Italian-American grad student Nia Peeples. The possibility of romance inspires him to lose weight, but things go awry when he learns that he's the subject of her term paper. Lainie Kazan, Lou Jacobi, Eileen Brennan also star in this charming comedy. 112 min.
06-2144 Was $89.99 ❑***$19.99***

Big Girls Don't Cry... They Get Even (1992)
A teenager realizes she's had enough of her wacky step-family, so she decides to run away from home. Soon, her entire clan is out looking for her, and confusion and sibling rivalry reach hilarious new heights. Griffin Dunne, Patricia Kalember, Adrienne Shelly, Margaret Whitton and Hillary Wolf star. 98 min.
02-2322 Was $19.99 ❑***$14.99***

Career Opportunities (1991)
John Hughes wrote and produced this comedy about a young man who takes a job as a department store custodian and gets locked in his first night on the job. He soon discovers that the town beauty has been locked in, too, and the two go on a storewide romp before two crooks arrive on the scene. Frank Whaley, Jennifer Connelly and William Forsythe star. 83 min.
07-1715 Was $89.99 ❑***$19.99***

Pure Luck (1991)
After ace detective Danny Glover has no luck finding a tycoon's klutzy, lost daughter, he teams with the businessman's clumsiest employee (Martin Short) in hopes of completing the assignment. The two men encounter hilarious misadventures while looking for the woman in this reworking of the French film "La Chevrè." With Sheila Kelly, Harry Shearer. 96 min.
07-1736 Was $19.99 ❑***$14.99***

Jimmy Hollywood (1994)
Seriocomic fable about fame and its cost from director Barry Levinson, centering on a failed character actor named Jimmy Alto (Joe Pesci) who goes on a headline-seeking vigilante crusade after his car radio is stolen and becomes a media celebrity. Christian Slater is his dim-witted sidekick. With Victoria Abril. Special re-edited home video version; 118 min.
06-2239 ❑***$89.99***

Galaxies Are Colliding (1992)
Wacky farce in which a man fearful of his impending marriage takes to the road with a friend and heads on a journey through the desert to find the "ultimate truth." What they find are weirdos and beautiful women willing to give advice on life and how to relate to the opposite sex. Kelsey Grammer, Dwier Brown, Susan Walters and Rick Overton star. 97 min.
06-2437 Was $89.99 ❑***$14.99***

Out There (1995)
An award-winning photojournalist stumbles across a 25-year-old roll of film that appears to document an alien encounter. His quest to prove the pictures are real brings him into contact with an array of UFO experts, alien "abductees" and assorted oddballs. Off-the-wall satire stars Bill Campbell, Julie Brown, Rod Steiger, June Lockhart and Bobcat Goldthwait. 98 min.
06-2439 ❑***$89.99***

Wavelength (1996)
An Oxford professor and physicist in love with his wife, in trouble with his girlfriend, and in awe of his idol, Einstein, is given an impossible deadline to unlock the secrets of the universe with his outcast lab crew. But how can he make sense of the cosmos when his personal life is such a mess? Jeremy Piven, Kelli Williams and Richard Attenborough star. AKA: "E Equals MC2." 94 min.
06-2472 ***$89.99***

Solitaire For 2 (1995)
A handsome rogue who counts some of the world's most beautiful women among his conquests meets his match in the form of a gorgeous lady with something extra: the power to read minds. Will the gigolo be able to add the woman, who also happens to have a good punch, to his list? Romantic comedy stars Mark Frankel, Amanda Pays and Maryam D'Abo. 105 min.
06-2535 ❑***$89.99***

Dear God (1996)
In order to avoid a prison sentence, scam artist Greg Kinnear agrees to a postal worker job that lands him in the Dead Letter Office. A mix-up with a letter addressed to God soon has Kinnear and his fellow employees sending gifts and goodwill to the needy in this heartwarming comedy from director Garry Marshall. Laurie Metcalf, Tim Conway, Maria Pitillo also star. 112 min.
06-2567 Was $99.99 ❑***$14.99***

'Til There Was You (1997)
What if you kept missing the chance to meet the person that was destined to be the love of your life? That's the concept behind this winning romantic comedy starring Jeanne Tripplehorn and Dylan McDermott as a struggling writer and architect, respectively, whose hectic lives keep them on the verge of meeting. With Sarah Jessica Parker, Jennifer Aniston, Ken Olin. 114 min.
06-2639 Was $99.99 ❑***$14.99***

National Lampoon's Dad's Week Off (1997)
Stressed-out computer salesman Henry Winkler is looking forward to a quiet week at home when his wife and kids go away on a camping trip, but a wild co-worker introduces him to a sexy, free-spirited girl whose escapades soon have them on the run from the police in this wild comedy. Olivia D'Abo, Richard Jeni co-star. 92 min.
06-2655 ❑***$99.99***

Watch It (1993)
Insightful, comic look at the romantic entanglements of a group of twentysomethings who seek the same partners and play a game in which they try to top each other with elaborate practical jokes. The superb young cast includes Suzy Amis, Lili Taylor, John C. McGinley, Peter Gallagher, Cynthia Stevenson and Tom Sizemore. 102 min.
06-2120 ❑***$89.99***

Tommy Boy (1995)
Chris Farley makes a big impression as the dim-witted son of auto parts tycoon Brian Dennehy who must prove himself worthy of taking over the family business after Dad dies. Along with smart-guy worker David Spade, Farley traverses the country by dilapidated car trying to push parts, while step-mom Bo Derek and "step-brother" Rob Lowe plan to swipe the family fortune. 98 min.
06-2383 Was $89.99 ❑***$14.99***

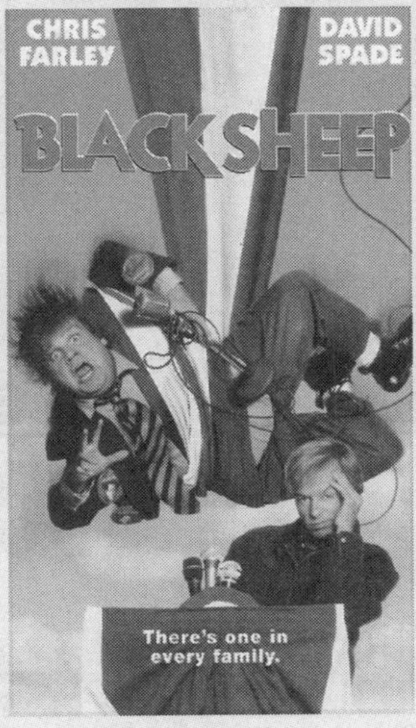
CHRIS FARLEY
DAVID SPADE
BLACK SHEEP
There's one in every family.

Black Sheep (1996)
"SNL" faves and "Tommy Boy" stars Chris Farley and David Spade reteam in this romp with Farley as the accident-prone brother of gubernatorial candidate Tim Matheson. In order to keep his goofy sibling from ruining his campaign, Matheson assigns assistant Spade to keep Farley out of trouble. Christine Ebersole also stars. 86 min.
06-2475 Was $99.99 ❑***$14.99***

Beverly Hills Ninja (1997)
Chris Farley is the bumbling white ninja hired by Nicollette Sheridan, to follow her boyfriend, who's mixed up in a global counterfeiting scheme. When Farley flubs the job in Japan, he heads to sunny California to complete the mission. Wacky kung fu fighting ensues with Farley, adopted brother Robin Shou and hotel bellhop Chris Rock. 89 min.
02-3070 Was $99.99 ❑***$14.99***

Almost Heroes (1998)
Wacky tale of Edwards (Matthew Perry) and Hunt (Chris Farley), a pair of hapless 19th-century explorers on a race against Lewis and Clark to reach the Pacific Ocean. During their expedition, the inept trailblazers encounter all sorts of humorous situations involving bears, Indians and Hidalgo, a conceited conquistador. With Kevin Dunn, Eugene Levy. 90 min.
19-2754 Was $99.99 ❑***$14.99***

Passed Away (1992)
A darkly humorous account of how an offbeat family deals with the death and funeral of the clan patriarch, who dies of a heart attack the same day he returns from the hospital. William Petersen, Bob Hoskins, Blair Brown, Maureen Stapleton, Nancy Travis and Tim Curry head the cast. 97 min.
11-1702 Was $19.99 ❑***$14.99***

Strictly Ballroom (1992)
Delightfully entertaining comedy from Australia centering on the exciting world of ballroom dancing. A brilliant young dancer is forced to find a new partner when his usual accomplice gets tired of his improvising. He chooses a klutzy novice to share steps, but manages to transform her into a first-class carpet-cutter. Paul Mercurio, Tara Morice star. 94 min.
11-1759 ❑***$14.99***

Meeting Daddy (1998)
A liberal and neurotic writer is in for the wildest experience of his life when he's summoned by his girlfriend to join her and her wacky Southern reconstructionist family, headed by her manipulative father, in Georgia. Lloyd Bridges, Josh Charles, Alexandra Wentworth, Kristy Swanson and Beau Bridges star. 91 min.
06-2986 ❑***$89.99***

200 Cigarettes (1999)
A party in Greenwich Village on New Year's Eve, 1981, is the focal point of this hip, ensemble comedy overflowing with eccentric characters. Among the attendees are pals Courtney Love and Paul Rudd; Long Island teenagers Christina Ricci and Gaby Hoffmann; bartender Ben Affleck; womanizer Jay Mohr; performance artist Janeane Garofalo; and Elvis Costello. 101 min.
06-2865 Was $99.99 ❑***$14.99***

Election (1999)
Lacerating satire with Matthew Broderick as a popular Omaha high school history teacher whose animosity towards determined, goody two-shoes student Reese Witherspoon leads him to rig the election for class president towards her dumb jock rival. Broderick's doings lead to a series of disastrous events...which lead to his personal and professional demise. With Chris Klein, Jessica Campbell. 103 min.
06-2913 Was $99.99 ❑***$14.99***

Kids In The Hall: Brain Candy (1996)
The quirky Canadian quintet who delighted TV audiences brought their multiple-role, gender-bending comedy to the big screen with this satire about a scientist who invents the ultimate anti-depression drug and turns the country into "happiness addicts." Scott Thompson, Mark McKinney, Kevin McDonald, Bruce McCulloch and Dave Foley star. 89 min.
06-2511 Was $99.99 ❑***$14.99***

Coneheads (1993)
The ever-popular "Saturday Night Live" skit has been turned into a hilarious feature farce starring Dan Aykroyd and Jane Curtin as Beldar and Prymaat, the Conehead couple with bizarre eating habits whose spaceship crashlands in New Jersey, where they're forced to become part of Earthling society and elude immigration officials. Michelle Burke, Chris Farley, Phil Hartman also star. 87 min.
06-2175 Was $89.99 ❑***$14.99***

Bebe's Kids (1992)
The hellraising children that sprang from the mind of comic Robin Harris come to life in this wild animated comedy. A guy meets the woman of his dreams and agrees to escort her and her son to Fun World amusement park, but when her neighbor's uncontrollable kids decide to tag along, the dream date turns into his worst nightmare. Faizon Love, Tone Loc and Nell Carter supply the voices. 74 min.
06-2072 Was $89.99 ❑***$14.99***

Good Burger (1998)
The stars of Nickelodeon's "Kenan & Kel" show, Kenan Thompson and Kel Mitchell, turn their popular sketch about two off-the-wall fast food clerks into a crazy, condiment-drenched comedy. Can the guys' new "secret sauce" recipe save their boss's restaurant from going under when the evil Mondo Burger chain opens up across the street? Sinbad, Abe Vigoda also star, with a cameo by Shaquille O'Neal. 103 min.
06-2667 Was $99.99 ❑***$14.99***

Kiss Me Guido (1997)
Winning "odd couple" comedy about an Italian-American pizza maker and would-be actor in New York who, thinking "GWM" means "Guy With Money," answers the "roommate wanted" ad of a gay Greenwich Village actor/choreographer. Their at first antagonistic relationship turns into understanding and friendship. Nick Scotti, Anthony Barrile star. 90 min.
06-2671 Was $99.99 ❑***$14.99***

Coupe De Ville (1990)
Heartwarming, often hilarious coming-of-age tale, about three quarrelsome brothers who have to drive a vintage Cadillac from Detroit to Florida, per their father's request. Patrick Dempsey, Arye Gross, Daniel Stern, Alan Arkin and Annabeth Gish star in this winning, wild journey. 98 min.
07-1649 Was $19.99 ***$14.99***

CB4 (1993)
After a local hip-hop club owner is busted by the cops, mild-mannered rapper Chris Rock transforms his group into the hottest in the country by adopting new identities as "gangsta rappers." The newly-named CB4 indulges in non-stop partying and sells millions of records, but the hoods who inspired their success are soon on their trail. With Chris Elliott, Phil Hartman. 89 min.
07-1999 Was $19.99 ❑***$14.99***

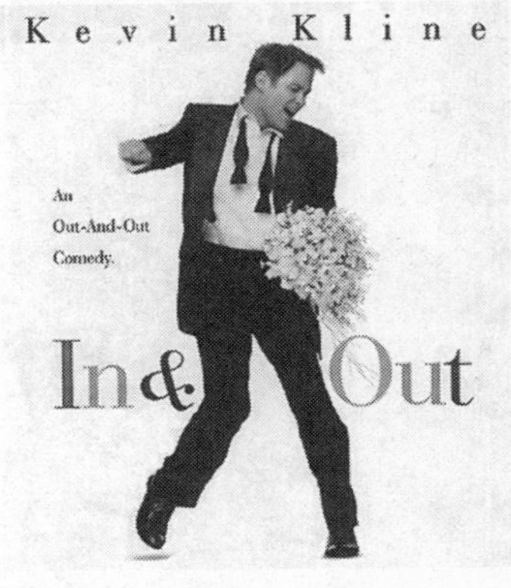
Kevin Kline
An Out-And-Out Comedy.
In & Out

In & Out (1997)
Popular and about-to-be-married high school teacher Kevin Kline is "outed" by a former student during an Academy Award acceptance speech, turning his small Indiana town into a center of national attention. Now Kline is trying to convince everyone—from his parents and fiancée Joan Cusack to his students and tabloid TV reporter Tom Selleck—that he's straight...but is he? Matt Dillon, Bob Newhart and Debbie Reynolds also star in director Frank Oz and scripter Paul Rudnick's riotous "sexual identity crisis" comedy. 92 min.
06-2677 Was $99.99 ❑***$14.99***

Opportunity Knocks (1990)
"Saturday Night Live's" Dana Carvey is a con artist on the run from angry mobsters who poses as a yuppie marketing executive and inadvertently becomes a business whiz. Fast-paced farce also stars Robert Loggia, Julia Campbell, and even "President Bush." 105 min.
07-1651 Was $19.99 *$14.99*

Nightlife (1990)
A beautiful vampire finds love with a human doctor and jealousy from a former romantic interest...who happens to be a vampire, as well. Maryam d'Abo, Ben Cross and Keith Szarabajka star in this haunting comedy/horror. 93 min.
07-1663 Was $79.99 *$14.99*

The Jerky Boys: Don't Hang Up!
The irresponsible, irrepressible duo do their hilarious crank phone calls routine in this outrageous video of lewd, rude and crude tele-fun. You won't see this sort of live, profane shenanigans anywhere else, so tune into the party-like proceedings here. Unedited version; 45 min.
04-5348 *$14.99*

V.I. Warshawski (1991)
Kathleen Turner plays the sexy, streetwise private detective whose life and career are put on the line when she tries to find the killer of a young girl's father. The trail to find the culprit is filled with dangerous chases and encounters with some of Chicago's seediest characters. With Jay O. Sanders, Charles Durning and Angela Goethals. 89 min.
11-1592 Was $19.99 *$14.99*

S.F.W. (1995)
A seething satire on contemporary youth's search for meaning and fascination with the media, starring Stephen Dorff and Reese Witherspoon as disaffected "slackers" who are held hostage for over a month in a convenience store by terrorists. Released as celebrities thanks to their videotaped ordeal, Dorff and Witherspoon use their exposure in unexpected ways. 94 min.
02-8231 *$19.99*

Beethoven (1992)
He's a loveable, huggable, somewhat klutzy St. Bernard that everyone in the family loves...except daddy Charles Grodin, who keeps fighting a losing battle to get rid of the monstrous pooch. Will Beethoven be able to win him over by saving the family and stopping the scheme of a nasty veterinarian? Dean Jones and Bonnie Hunt co-star. 87 min.
07-1852 Was $19.99 *$14.99*

Beethoven's 2nd (1993)
Everyone's favorite trouble-prone St. Bernard is back, and this time he's bringing the family with him! The doggone delightful follow-up to the hit comedy finds Beethoven in love and playing proud papa to a litter of puppies, much to the consternation of Charles Grodin and the delight of his kids. With Bonnie Hunt, Debi Mazar, Chris Penn. 89 min.
07-2119 Was $24.99 *$14.99*

Beethoven's 3rd (2000)
Judge Reinhold, Julia Sweeney and their children find their peaceful vacation plans turned upside-down when the slobbering Saint Bernard named Beethoven enters their lives. The pooch keeps getting into trouble, but he sure comes in handy when some nasty crooks try to dupe Reinhold and his family. Frank Gorshin and Jamie Marsh also star. 99 min.
07-2884 *$99.99*

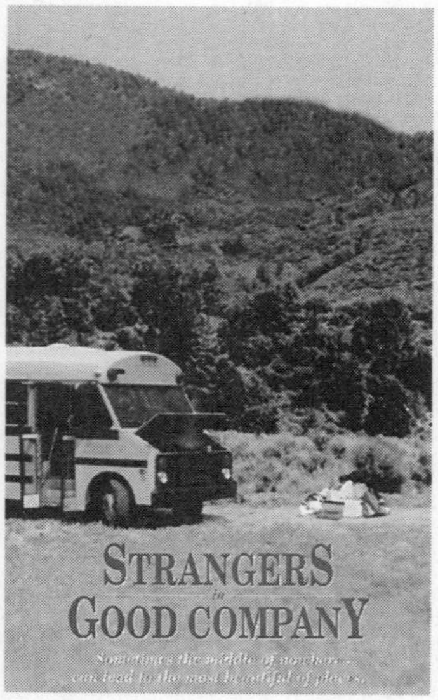

Strangers In Good Company (1990)
Winning, poignant story from Canada centering on seven elderly women who are marooned at an abandoned country house after their bus breaks down. The women soon become friends and learn new things about themselves, each other, and life. Alice Diabo, Constance Garneau star. 101 min.
11-1631 *$19.99*

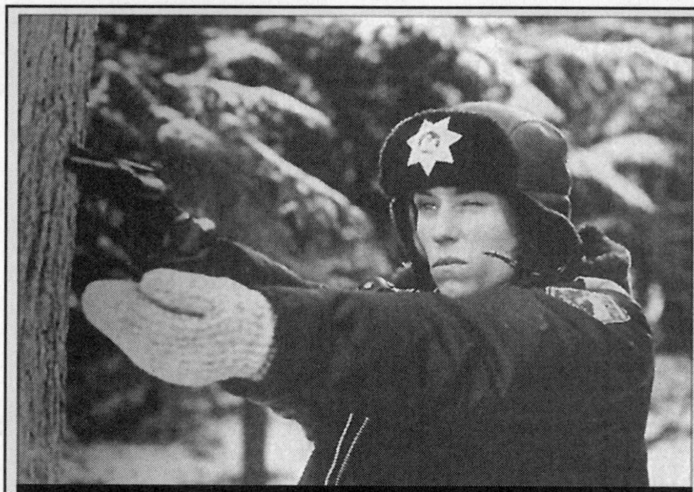

Fargo

Joel & Ethan Coen

Blood Simple (1984)
Double and triple crosses abound in this mystery that is "film noir" Texas style. A love triangle between a bar owner, his wife and a handsome bartender explodes with fatal consequences. John Getz, M. Emmet Walsh, Frances McDormand star; written and directed by Joel and Ethan Coen. 96 min.
07-1304 Was $79.99 *$14.99*

Raising Arizona (1987)
Riotous comedy caper from Joel and Ethan Coen ("Blood Simple") about an infertile couple (ex-con Nicolas Cage and policewoman Holly Hunter) who desperately want children, and figure that the wealthy parents of newborn quints can spare one! With John Goodman, William Forsythe, Randall "Tex" Cobb. 94 min.
04-2089 Was $19.99 *$14.99*

Miller's Crossing (1990)
A compelling, modern twist on the gangster genre, courtesy of Joel and Ethan Coen. Albert Finney is an Irish-American mob boss ready to go to war with a rival gangster, and Gabriel Byrne is a loyal lieutenant who tries to prevent the conflict, until a woman comes between them. Double- and triple-crosses abound in this violent tale of honor among thieves. With John Turturro, Marcia Gay Harden. 114 min.
04-2418 Was $89.99 *$14.99*

Barton Fink (1991)
A perplexing and fascinating mix of psychological drama and black comedy, Joel and Ethan Coen's award-winning film stars John Turturro as a '40s New York playwright hired by a Hollywood studio to write screenplays. His inability to complete the assignment, the rundown hotel he stays in, and a talkative insurance salesman from the next room all play a part in a cinematic descent into Hell. With John Goodman, Judy Davis, Michael Lerner. 116 min.
04-2492 Was $89.99 *$19.99*

The Hudsucker Proxy (1994)
In the Coen Brothers' dazzling pastiche of 1940s comedies á la Frank Capra and Preston Sturges, Tim Robbins plays a nerdy mail clerk enlisted by shifty corporate executive Paul Newman to lead Hudsucker Industries to disaster. Instead, Robbins invents the hula hoop and the company's fortunes rise. Jennifer Jason Leigh is the spitfire reporter for whom Robbins falls. 112 min.
19-2254 Was $89.99 *$14.99*

Fargo (1996)
Joel and Ethan Coen's alternately hilarious and shocking "true crime" drama follows a shady Minneapolis car dealer's plan to have his wife kidnapped and then take part of the ransom from her wealthy father. When the crooks hired to abduct the woman wind up killing a state trooper and two witnesses along a rural Minnesota highway, the very pregnant local police chief begins her own investigation into the murders. Best Actress Oscar-winner Frances McDormand, William H. Macy, Steve Buscemi star. 98 min.
02-8533 Was $19.99 *$14.99*

Fargo (Letterboxed Version)
Also available in a theatrical, widescreen format.
02-8905 *$19.99*

The Big Lebowski (1998)
A comedy about kidnapping, nihilism, the Gulf War and bowling, courtesy of Joel and Ethan Coen. Jeff Bridges plays Jeff "The Dude" Lebowski, a middle-aged slacker whose gutterball existence is disturbed when crooks mistake him for a millionaire industrialist, also named Lebowski, whose wife owes them money. Soon Bridges and bowling buddy John Goodman are mixed up in a complicated abduction scheme and a convoluted mystery. Julianne Moore, David Huddleston, Steve Buscemi and John Turturro also star. 113 min.
02-8864 Was $99.99 *$14.99*

Mixing Nia (1998)
Nia, a young woman of black and white descent, quits her copywriting job at a Manhattan advertising agency in order to pursue her dreams as a novelist. While looking for a topic for her book, Nia encounters a professor with strong African-American ideals, but her attraction to him becomes complicated when she meets a free-spirited white man. Karyn Parsons, Eric Thal and Isaiah Washington star. 93 min.
54-6202 *$59.99*

Cabin Boy (1994)
In this zany comedy, "Late Night with David Letterman" alumnus Chris Elliott plays a foppish finishing school graduate who accidentally boards a scummy ship called "The Filthy Whore" and sets off for a series of fantastic adventures on the high seas with a motley crew that hates him. Co-stars Melora Walters, Brian Doyle-Murray; with cameos by Ann Magnuson and Elliott's former employer. 80 min.
11-1797 Was $19.99 *$14.99*

EDtv (1999)
Matthew McConaughey is a good-natured video store clerk whose life is turned upside-down when he agrees to "star" in a 24-hour-a-day reality TV program conceived by producer Ellen DeGeneres. The show turns into a national hit, but his family's problems become public and his new romance with his brother's girlfriend is threatened. With Woody Harrelson, Jenna Elfman, Rob Reiner, Elizabeth Hurley; directed by Ron Howard. 124 min.
07-2774 Was $99.99 *$14.99*

Friends & Lovers (1999)
In this romantic comedy laced with drama, a group of friends from Los Angeles join Ira Newborn on a road trip to the mountains of Utah, where he's visiting his estranged father. The friends include stud Stephen Baldwin, model Claudia Schiffer, pregnant Suzanne Cryer and gay Danny Nucci, and, over a few days, they'll examine their lives and loves. With Robert Downey, Jr., Alison Eastwood. 104 min.
07-2776 Was $99.99 *$19.99*

Blues Brothers 2000 (1998)
Dan Aykroyd reprises his role as Elwood Blues in this follow-up to the hit 1980 musical comedy. Out of jail and just informed of his brother's death, Elwood gets a new lease on life when he teams up with a streetwise orphan and joins with bartender John Goodman to reform his band. The musical guest stars include James Brown, Eric Clapton, Aretha Franklin, B.B. King and many more. 124 min.
07-2646 Was $99.99 *$14.99*

Home For The Holidays (1995)
Director Jodie Foster's wacky and poignant comedy stars Holly Hunter as a newly-fired art restorer and single mother who travels back to her Maryland home for Thanksgiving dinner. There, Hunter reacquaints herself with homosexual brother Robert Downey, Jr., parents Charles Durning and Anne Bancroft, and zany aunt Geraldine Chaplin. With Dylan McDermott, Claire Danes. 103 min.
02-8424 Was $89.99 *$14.99*

Houseguest (1995)
Con artist Sinbad dodges some mobsters at a Pittsburgh airport where he's mistakenly befriended by nerdy lawyer Phil Hartman, who believes he's his long-lost childhood pal. Sinbad makes himself comfy in Hartman's home, winning over his family and neighbors. Kim Greist, Jeffrey Jones and Stan Shaw co-star. 108 min.
11-1896 Was $19.99 *$14.99*

Cool Runnings (1993)
Loosely based on the real-life formation of the first Olympic bobsled team from Jamaica, this funky farce follows the exploits of an injured sprinter who is forced to find another event to compete in for the 1988 Olympics. The event turns out to be bobsledding, and he hires a down-and-out coach (John Candy) to teach his hapless comrades the sport. Leon, Doug E. Doug star. 98 min.
11-1770 Was $19.99 *$14.99*

Money For Nothing (1993)
Based on the true story of South Philadelphian Joey Coyle, this comedy-drama stars John Cusack as an unemployed blue-collar worker who stumbles upon an instant fortune when he picks up $1.2 million that fell out of an armored car and starts living the good life...until the police catch up with him. Michael Madsen, Debi Mazar co-star. 100 min.
11-1773 Was $19.99 *$14.99*

Green Card (1991)
Andie MacDowell is a sophisticated New Yorker who needs a temporary husband in order to rent the apartment of her dreams, and Gerard Depardieu is a sloppy French musician who must wed an American to stay in this country. Does the marriage of convenience bring these two opposites together? Find out in this winsome romantic comedy from director Peter Weir. With Bebe Neuwirth. 108 min.
11-1558 Was $19.99 *$14.99*

My Boyfriend's Back (1993)
Nothing can stay the course of true love...even an accidental death...for teenager Andrew Lowery, who comes back as a zany zombie in order to keep his prom date with school beauty Traci Lind. Offbeat black comedy also stars Edward Herrmann, Mary Beth Hurt; look for Matthew McConaughey in his film debut. 85 min.
11-1775 *$14.99*

Love And Other Catastrophes (1997)
Mixing screwball-style dialogue with "Generation X" sensibilities, director/co-scripter Emma-Kate Croghan's debut feature tracks the romantic and career crises of a group of Australian college students. The focus is on grad school roommates Mia, who doesn't want her female lover moving into her apartment, and Alice, whose "Doris Day as Feminist Warrior" dissertation is four years overdue. Frances O'Connor, Alice Garner, Matthew Dyktynski star. 76 min.
04-3488 *$99.99*

The Inkwell (1994)
Set in 1976, this funky, heartfelt comedy focuses on a black teenager's coming-of-age experiences during summer vacation in Martha's Vineyard. The young man learns about sex, style and Afros while his former Black Panther father and Republican uncle square off in political debate. Larenz Tate, Joe Morton and Glynn Turman star. 112 min.
11-1815 Was $89.99 *$14.99*

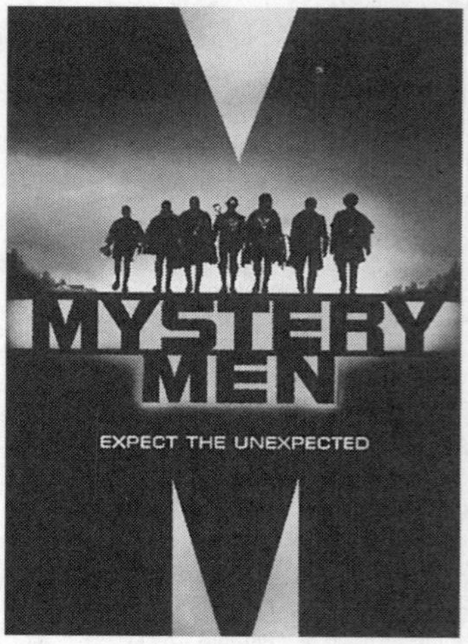

Mystery Men (1999)
When Champion City's top defender, Captain Amazing (Greg Kinnear), falls victim to his own plan to boost his sagging popularity by freeing, then capturing, arch-villain Casanova Frankenstein (Geoffrey Rush), can the city's lesser-known—and decidedly less skilled—costumed crimefighters save the day? Hip and funny superhero satire also stars William H. Macy as the spade-swinging Shoveler, Ben Stiller as the manic Mr. Furious, and Janeane Garofalo as the feisty Bowler; with Hank Azaria, Kel Mitchell, Paul Reubens. 122 min.
07-2800 Was $99.99 *$14.99*

Mystery Men (Letterboxed Version)
Also available in a theatrical, widescreen format.
07-2818 Was $99.99 *$24.99*

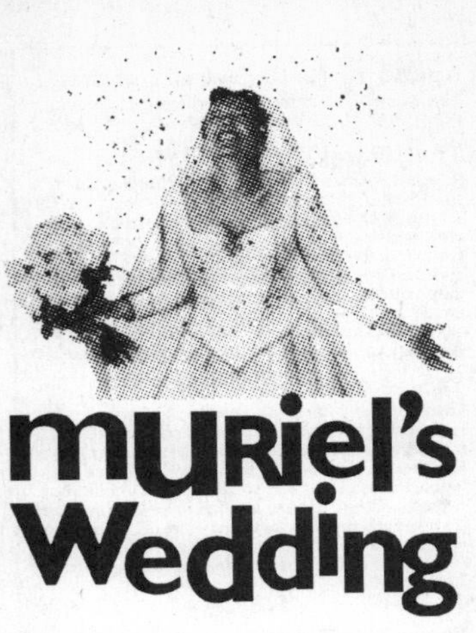

Muriel's Wedding (1995)
Sassy comedy from Australia about an offbeat, overweight young woman who barely passed secretarial school, is obsessed with ABBA, and dreams of finding a husband and leaving her family. A chance encounter with an old schoolmate leads Muriel to join her in Sydney, where her "new lease on life" includes a marriage of convenience with a South African athlete. Toni Collette, Rachel Griffiths star. 105 min.
11-1937 Was $89.99 ❑*$19.99*

Gone Fishin' (1997)
Best buddies and fishing magazine contest winners Danny Glover and Joe Pesci are looking forward to a relaxing angling vacation in the Everglades, but a car thief, some stolen jewels, the women whose jewels were stolen, a hurricane and a hungry alligator turn the trip into a series of comic calamities. Rosanna Arquette, Lynn Whitfield also star. 94 min.
11-2182 Was $19.99 ❑*$14.99*

Cosi (1997)
An out-of-work theatre director signs on to help the patients of a mental hospital put on a production of Mozart's opera "Cosi Fan Tutte," but the rigors of staging the show will test director and cast alike and reveal more than anyone could have imagined in this comedy/drama from Australia. Ben Mendelsohn, Toni Collette, Barry Otto and Rachel Griffiths star.
11-2185 Was $99.99 ❑*$19.99*

Renaissance Man (1994)
Unemployed advertising executive Danny DeVito gets a job teaching a group of misfit Army recruits at a local military base, but his unorthodox lessons on life and "Hamlet" soon cause problems with his superiors. Gregory Hines, Marky Mark, Cliff Robertson and Stacey Dash star in Penny Marshall's heartfelt comedy. 128 min.
11-1848 Was $19.99 ❑*$14.99*

Camp Nowhere (1994)
A junior high student is told by his parents he must attend computer camp, but he has a better idea: he and his pals create their own summer resort, a former hippie commune where no rules apply and a wigged-out ex-drama teacher presides as head counselor. Christopher Lloyd, Joshua G. Mayweather star. 96 min.
11-1862 Was $19.99 ❑*$14.99*

Son-In-Law (1993)
Wacky California dude Pauly Shore befriends a beautiful South Dakota girl while attending U.C.L.A. and agrees to pose as her beau when she goes home to the family farm for Thanksgiving vacation. Can Pauly adjust to country life while his "in-laws" try to adjust to Pauly? Manic culture clash comedy also stars Carla Gugino, Lane Smith, Cindy Pickett. 96 min.
11-1760 Was $89.99 ❑*$14.99*

In The Army Now (1994)
Pauly Shore is an out-of-work slacker who thinks joining the Army reserves would be cool—after all, he helps his country and gets neat stuff for free, too. After a wacky basic training stint, Pauly's shipped to North Africa to fight in a war against Libya. You'll be in stitches as the silly Shore earns his stripes! Andy Dick, David Alan Grier and Lori Petty co-star. 92 min.
11-1859 Was $19.99 ❑*$14.99*

Jury Duty (1995)
Pauly Shore is a slacker looking for a place to live who lucks into a solution when he's assigned to the jury of the high-profile trial of a serial killer. Everyone thinks the defendant is guilty—except Pauly, who enjoys his comfy hotel room, the good food and the company of sexy juror Tina Carrere too much. With Stanley Tucci, Charles Napier. 87 min.
02-2814 Was $19.99 ❑*$14.99*

Bio-Dome (1996)
In this slapstick farce, Pauly Shore and Stephen Baldwin are two Southern California nitwits who are accidentally locked inside an experimental ecological facility with a team of scientists and proceed to wreak more havoc than global warming ever could. Joey Adams, William Atherton co-star. 95 min.
12-3052 Was $99.99 ❑*$14.99*

Nothing To Lose (1997)
Would-be carjacker Martin Lawrence picks the wrong target when he jumps in the car of ad executive Tim Robbins, who had just returned home to find his wife in bed with another man. Robbins turns the tables on his would-be abductor and drives off with a captive Lawrence, sending the odd couple on a comical crime spree, in this offbeat "buddy movie." With Kelly Preston, John C. McGinley, Giancarlo Esposito. 98 min.
11-2186 Was $19.99 ❑*$14.99*

Beautiful Girls (1996)
Winning romantic comedy set during a snowy winter in a small New England town where a group of high school pals gathered for a reunion discuss life, approaching the age of 30, and their relationships (or the lack thereof) with the opposite sex. Among the principals trying to sort it all out are Matt Dillon, Lauren Holly, Timothy Hutton, Rosie O'Donnell, Michael Rapaport, Mira Sorvino, Uma Thurman and teenager Natalie Portman, who dispenses sage advice to her elders. 110 min.
11-2053 Was $19.99 ❑*$14.99*

Celtic Pride (1996)
Hardcore Boston sports fans Dan Aykroyd and Daniel Stern decide that the only way their beloved Celtics have a chance of winning the NBA championship is if the league's top player, trash-talking Utah Jazz star Damon Wayans, doesn't play. But when Aykroyd and Stern kidnap Wayans, they get more than they bargained for. With Gail O'Grady, Christopher McDonald and Larry Bird. 90 min.
11-2054 Was $19.99 ❑*$14.99*

Don't Be A Menace To South Central While Drinking Your Juice In The Hood (1996)
"In Living Color's" Shawn and Marlon Wayans turn their attention to black urban dramas in this hilarious spoof of screen "hood" life. The hero's name is Ashtray; his father's only a few years older than him; and his cousin has color-coordinated his sneakers with his Uzis. Nuff said! With Tracey Cherelle Jones as Ashtray's gal, Dashiki. 89 min.
11-2057 Was $19.99 ❑*$14.99*

The Air Up There (1994)
College basketball coach Kevin Bacon travels to a remote village in Kenya to recruit a 6'10" prospect. But when the player, slated to become the head of his tribe, refuses the offer, Bacon tries to win him over by coaching his village's team in a game against their mining company-sponsored rivals. Inspiring blend of comedy and drama also stars Dennis Patrick, Charles Gitonga Maina. 107 min.
11-1791 Was $19.99 ❑*$14.99*

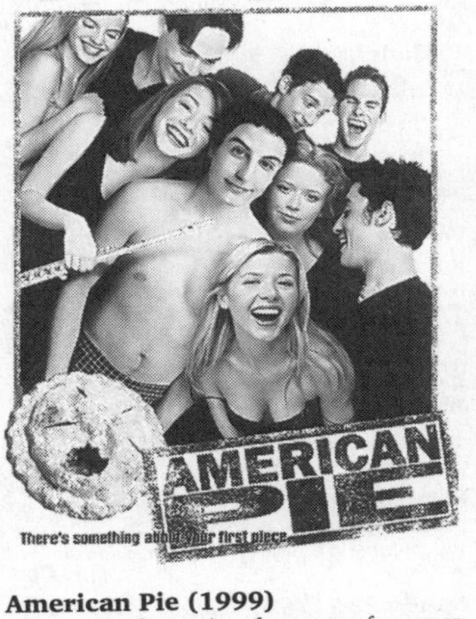

American Pie (1999)
Riotous, raunchy coming-of-age romp focuses on four high school seniors who make a pact to lose their virginity by graduation. Their attempts—ranging from awkward Jason Biggs' Internet-broadcast encounter with foreign exchange student Shannon Elizabeth to jock Chris Klein's joining a singing club to impress studious Mena Suvari—teach the boys hilarious lessons about love. With Thomas Ian Nicholas, Natasha Lyonne, Alyson Hannigan and Tara Reid. Unrated version includes scenes not shown in theatres. 96 min.
07-2798 Was $99.99 ❑*$14.99*

The Brady Bunch Movie (1995)
The relentlessly cheery '70s TV family is spoofed to the max in this hilarious, hip sitcomedy. Faced with life in '90s California, can the Bradys pull together and save the day as their house is threatened by real estate developers, Greg attempts musical stardom, Jan copes with voices in her head, and Marcia tries to get Davy Jones to come to the school dance? Shelley Long, Gary Cole, Michael McKean star; directed by Betty Thomas ("Private Parts"). 88 min.
06-2332 Was $89.99 ❑*$14.99*

A Very Brady Sequel (1996)
Camp out with the every-groovy Bradys in the second send-up of the hit TV series. Here, the household is thrown into an uproar by the sudden appearance of Carol's presumed-dead first husband. But is this interloper who he says he is, why is he so interested in an old knickknack, and will a family trip to Hawaii solve everything? Shelley Long, Gary Cole, Tim Matheson star. 90 min.
06-2555 Was $99.99 ❑*$14.99*

Two Much (1996)
After she saves him from a potentially dangerous hustle, ditzy heiress Melanie Griffith gets engaged to art swindler Antonio Banderas. Just as they're about to get married, however, Banderas falls for sister Daryl Hannah. Since she doesn't like him, Banderas decides to pose as an imaginary twin brother in order to woo both women. With Joan Cusack. 118 min.
11-2046 Was $19.99 ❑*$14.99*

Heart And Souls (1993)
In this magical, heartwarming comedy, Robert Downey, Jr. plays a driven banker who discovers he has four guardian angels, all of whom died in a bus accident at the same time he was born. In order to move from purgatory to heaven, the angels need Downey's help (and body) to solve important unresolved matters in their lives. Charles Grodin, Kyra Sedgwick, Elisabeth Shue also star. 103 min.
07-2042 Was $19.99 ❑*$14.99*

The Cowboy Way (1994)
Free-wheeling action-comedy starring Woody Harrelson and Kiefer Sutherland as former rodeo companions from New Mexico who reunite to find a friend who vanished while searching for his daughter. Their quest leads to New York, where their tough cowboy ways don't always mesh with the city slicker lifestyle. Dylan McDermott, Ernie Hudson co-star. 107 min.
07-2195 Was $19.99 ❑*$14.99*

Radioland Murders (1994)
Someone is killing the employees of a Chicago radio station in 1939 and writer Brian Benben (TV's "Dream On") and estranged wife/secretary Mary Stuart Masterson decide to investigate. Their suspects include the station's wacky workforce: sound effects man Christopher Lloyd, station owner Ned Beatty, and sultry singer Anita Morris. George Burns makes a cameo; produced by George Lucas. 108 min.
07-2253 Was $19.99 ❑*$14.99*

Major Payne (1995)
Damon Wayans is hilarious as Major Benson Winifred Payne, a no-nonsense Marine officer thrust into civilian life who finds himself commander of a Junior ROTC unit. Wayans' tough-guy stance with his misfit kiddie corps leads to a series of funny episodes in this updating of the Charlton Heston film "The Private War of Major Benson." With Karyn Parson, Michael Ironside. 98 min.
07-2336 Was $19.99 ❑*$14.99*

Kissing A Fool (1998)
Contemporary romantic comedy features David Schwimmer as a Chicago sports agent who, in spite of his own womanizing ways, is suspicious about fiancée Mili Avital's fidelity. His plan? Get best friend Jason Lee to come on to her and see if she responds. Lee's not crazy with the idea, but when fate throws him and Avital together, sparks fly. With Bonnie Hunt, Kari Wuhrer. 92 min.
07-2643 Was $99.99 ❑*$14.99*

The Love Letter (1999)
In this sweet romantic comedy, Kate Capshaw is the owner of a small town New England bookstore who has to figure out who wrote the love note she received in the mail. Was it fireman and ex-flame Tom Selleck? Or college student and summer store helper Tom Everett Scott? The problem is that others are receiving the same letter as well. Ellen DeGeneres, Blythe Danner and Gloria Stuart also star. 88 min.
07-2805 Was $99.99 ❑*$19.99*

Captain Ron (1992)
He's the most inept nautical man since Peter "Wrong Way" Peachfuzz, but for the suburban family that hires him to take them on a Caribbean cruise in their new yacht, Captain Ron manages to sail them into a hilariously unforgettable adventure. Kurt Russell, Martin Short, Mary Kay Place star. 99 min.
11-1672 Was $19.99 ❑*$14.99*

The Cemetery Club (1993)
A winning dramedy about three widowed Jewish women who meet regularly to visit their husbands' graves and discuss their experiences with men. When a love affair develops between one of the women and an understanding widower, the group's existence is threatened. Olympia Dukakis, Ellen Burstyn, Diane Ladd and Danny Aiello star. 107 min.
11-1689 Was $19.99 ❑*$14.99*

Sirens (1994)
A free-wheeling, erotic comedy-drama, based on a true story, about an Australian painter in the early '30s whose latest controversial work prompts a liberal minister and his wife to travel to his wilderness home and talk some sense into him. Awaiting the couple is a sensual paradise populated by nude models, a ravishing housemaid and more. Sam Neill, Hugh Grant, Elle Macpherson star. 94 min.
11-1821 Was $89.99 ❑*$14.99*

Holy Matrimony (1994)
After robbing a carnival, Tate Donovan and sexy girlfriend Patricia Arquette flee to Canada to hide out in the Hutterite community where he was raised. The couple marry and try to abide by the colony's strict religious code, but things get worse when Donovan dies and Arquette marries his 12-year-old brother, whom she hopes will lead her to the missing loot. Leonard Nimoy directs. 93 min.
11-1822 ❑*$14.99*

A Low Down Dirty Shame (1994)
Andre Shame (Keenen Ivory Wayans) is a down-on-his-luck private investigator with financial problems and a sassy assistant (Jada Pinkett) who won't let him forget his recent career miscues. Shame decides to take a job from a pal on the DEA, but he soon finds his hands full...with danger. Charles S. Dutton and Salli Richardson also star. 100 min.
11-1878 Was $89.99 ❑*$14.99*

Clerks (1994)
Kevin Smith's engagingly foul-mouthed and funny independent comedy tracks a "typical" day at a New Jersey convenience store, as philosophical counterman Dante serves an array of annoying customers, plays rooftop hockey, and ponders his love life and his future with help from the neighboring video store's clerk, his serious-minded girlfriend, and local ne'er-do-wells Jay and Silent Bob. Brian O'Halloran, Kevin Anderson, Marilyn Ghigliotti star. 92 min.
11-1881 Was $89.99 ❑*$19.99*

Mallrats (1995)
"Clerks" director Kevin Smith moves from the mini-mart to the mall, where slackers Jeremy London and Jason Lee go to forget their romantic woes. But the shoppers' paradise offers little respite, as they encounter a taping of a TV show called "Truth or Date," Marvel Comics guru Stan Lee, the inimitable Jay and Silent Bob, and their ex-girlfriends. With Shannon Doherty, Claire Forlani. 96 min.
07-2387 Was $19.99 ❑*$14.99*

Chasing Amy (1997)
The third (but possibly not last) film in director Kevin Smith's "New Jersey trilogy" is a sharp and emotional look at a most unconventional romance, as comic-book writer Ben Affleck tries to pursue a relationship with fellow comic artist and avowed lesbian Joey Lauren Adams, much to the displeasure of Affleck's creative partner, best friend Jason Lee. With Dwight Ewell, and Jason Mewes and Smith as Jay and Silent Bob. 113 min.
11-2184 Was $99.99 ❑*$19.99*

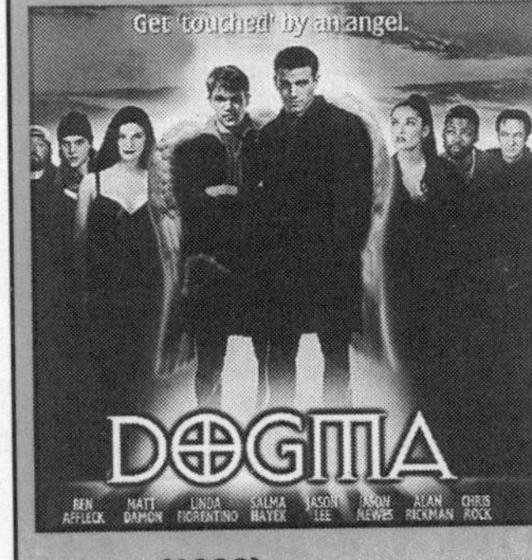

Dogma (1999)
Wayward angels Ben Affleck and Matt Damon, exiled in Wisconsin for millennia, discover that a New Jersey church holds the theological key to their getting back into Heaven. Problem is, if they succeed, all of creation will be obliterated. As faith-affirming as it is controversial, Kevin Smith's off-the-wall satire follows a quirky band of crusaders, from abortion clinic worker Linda Fiorentino and "13th apostle" Chris Rock to the ubiquitous Jay and Silent Bob, trying to keep the angels from reaching their goal. 128 min.
02-3427 Was $99.99 ❑*$14.99*

The Gun In Betty Lou's Handbag (1992)
A shy librarian attempts to escape her boring life and lackluster marriage to a police detective by recovering a murder weapon and claiming she's responsible for the deed. Soon, she learns to enjoy her newfound celebrity after being thrown in jail. Penelope Ann Miller, Cathy Moriarty, Eric Thal and Alfre Woodard star. 89 min.
11-1684 ❑*$14.99*

Leave It To Beaver (1997)
The perennially popular sitcom about the joys and travails of childhood in the '50s gets a modest updating for the '90s in a charming comedy for all ages. Cameron Finley stars as precocious Theodore "Beaver" Cleaver, whose world revolves around his rivalry with big brother Wally (Erik von Detten), playing football to impress parents Ward (Christopher McDonald) and June (Janine Turner), and getting his new bike back from a local bully. 88 min.
07-2582 Was $19.99 ❑*$14.99*

Half-Baked (1998)
"Just say yes" to this smokingly silly comedy about four wigged-out slackers (Jim Breuer, Dave Chappelle, Guillermo Diaz, Harland Williams) whose lives revolve around pot. When Williams accidentally kills a police horse by feeding it junk food, his "buds" must cultivate a scheme to raise bail money. Tommy Chong, Janeane Garofalo, Willie Nelson and Snoop Doggy Dogg are among the cameos in this wacky reefer romp. 73 min.
07-2638 Was $99.99 ❑*$14.99*

The Englishman Who Went Up A Hill But Came Down A Mountain (1995)
Engaging comic fable, set in Wales during World War I, stars Hugh Grant as a British mapmaker who rocks a small town with the news that their treasured "mountain" is 16 feet short of that designation and is merely a hill. The indignant villagers conspire to keep Grant and his boss in town until they raise the hill up to mountain status. Tara Fitzgerald, Colm Meaney also star. 96 min.
11-1941 Was $89.99 ❑*$19.99*

Rona Jaffe's Mazes And Monsters (1982)

Four college students involved in a "dragons and dungeons" fantasy game begin acting out the adventures, only to find reality and make-believe running together into a fatal nightmare. Stars Tom Hanks, Chris Makepeace, Wendy Crewson. 102 min.
40-1139　　Was $19.99　　*$14.99*

Splash (1984)

Tom Hanks is a lonely bachelor in New York; Daryl Hannah is the mystery woman who brings romance into his life. What he doesn't know is that she's a mermaid! John Candy and Eugene Levy co-star in this hilarious and touching comedy/fantasy from director Ron Howard. 109 min.
11-1117　　Was $19.99　　*$14.99*

Bachelor Party (1984)

It's the craziest bash you ever saw, and Tom Hanks is the "guest of honor" who's got to deal with beautiful women, poolside pranks and wild car chases if he hopes to make it to his wedding. Tawny Kitaen, Adrian Zmed co-star. 106 min.
04-1799　　☐*$14.99*

The Man With One Red Shoe (1985)

Average guy Tom Hanks is stuck in the middle of a spy escapade in this rollicking comedy based on the French farce "Tall Blond Man with One Black Shoe." Dabney Coleman, Lori Singer, Carrie Fisher and Jim Belushi co-star. 93 min.
04-1928　　☐*$14.99*

Volunteers (1985)

Ivy League playboy Tom Hanks gets more than he bargained for when he joins the Peace Corps in order to avoid massive gambling debts. Riotous "third world" comedy also stars John Candy, Rita Wilson, Tim Thomerson. 107 min.
44-1341　　Was $19.99　　*$14.99*

The Money Pit (1986)

Sensational slapstick farce features Tom Hanks and Shelley Long as a yuppie couple who have bought their dream house and discover it's more like a nightmare. Gut-busting gags abound as they try to save their domicile from disrepair. 91 min.
07-1438　　☐*$14.99*

Nothing In Common (1986)

Comedy/drama stars Tom Hanks as a successful ad man who finds himself caring for father Jackie Gleason after his parents' divorce. The at-first cold relationship between the two men, strangers for so long, changes in a funny, touching manner. Eva Marie Saint, Bess Armstrong co-star. 118 min.
44-1458　　Was $19.99　　*$14.99*

Dragnet (1987)

Here are the facts, Ma'am: Dan Aykroyd is Sgt. Joe Friday, following in his famed uncle's gumshoed footsteps. Tom Hanks is Friday's unconventional, wise-cracking partner in this spoof of the classic TV series. With Dabney Coleman, Christopher Plummer, Harry Morgan. 103 min.
07-1539　　☐*$14.99*

big

Big (1988)

Tom Hanks stars in this hit comedy as the fast-rising toy company executive whose big success hides an ever-bigger secret: he's really a 13-year-old kid who magically became an adult thanks to a carnival wishing machine. Hit "body-switch" farce also stars Elizabeth Perkins, Robert Loggia, John Heard, Jon Lovitz; directed by Penny Marshall. 104 min.
04-3864　　☐*$14.99*

- You've Got Mail

Tom Hanks

The 'Burbs (1989)

Tom Hanks and his barbecue buddies make like the Hardy Boys sleuth-wise when the weirdness of their night-roaming, trash bag-burying neighbors reaches Munsteresque proportions. Joe Dante's safe-as-lawn-darts suburban vision co-stars Carrie Fisher, Bruce Dern, Brother Theodore. 101 min.
07-1623　　Was $19.99　　*$14.99*

Turner & Hooch (1989)

Pleasurable "policeman's best friend" comedy stars Tom Hanks as a fastidious detective who, to crack a difficult murder investigation, is forced to team with the sole eyewitness: an immense, sloppy, foul-tempered pooch. Co-stars Mare Winningham, Craig T. Nelson and Beasley as Hooch. 100 min.
11-1494　　Was $19.99　　☐*$14.99*

Joe Versus The Volcano (1990)

When hypochondriac Tom Hanks is given six months to live, eccentric millionaire Lloyd Bridges offers him a month of unlimited spending and living it up...if he'll help the natives of a Pacific island appease their fire god by jumping into an active volcano! Quirky, Capraesque fable written and directed by "Moonstruck" scripter John Patrick Shanley also stars Meg Ryan, Abe Vigoda and Ossie Davis. 102 min.
19-1792　　☐*$14.99*

The Bonfire Of The Vanities (1990)

Tom Hanks, Melanie Griffith and Bruce Willis star in the controversial adaptation of Tom Wolfe's acerbic novel. A successful Wall Street trader finds his charmed life turned into a shambles when he accidentally runs over a black youth while driving with his mistress in a tough Bronx neighborhood. With Morgan Freeman, Kim Cattrall; Brian De Palma directs. 126 min.
19-1837　　Was $19.99　　☐*$14.99*

A League Of Their Own (1992)

Crowd-pleasing comedy-drama with Geena Davis and Lori Petty as sisters from Oregon who become rivals when they join an all-woman's baseball league during World War II. Coaching the team is alcoholic former player Tom Hanks, and also on his team are the flirtatious Madonna and brassy Rosie O'Donnell. Jon Lovitz and Garry Marshall also star; Penny Marshall directs. 128 min.
02-2336　　Was $19.99　　☐*$14.99*

A League Of Their Own (Letterboxed Version)

Also available in a theatrical, widescreen format.
02-2348　　Was $89.99　　☐*$14.99*

Sleepless In Seattle: Special Edition (1993)

Sweetly romantic hit comedy starring Tom Hanks as a Seattle widower who draws the attention of scores of women after his son talks about him on a national radio show and Meg Ryan as a soon-to-be-married Baltimore reporter who sets out to meet him. Co-star Rosie O'Donnell, Rob Reiner and Bill Pullman and featuring a slew of classic tunes; directed by Nora Ephron. 105 min.
02-2484　　Remastered　　☐*$14.99*

Sleepless In Seattle (Letterboxed Version)

Also available in a theatrical, widescreen format.
02-3090　　☐*$19.99*

Philadelphia (1993)

Tom Hanks won an Academy Award for Best Actor with his stirring portrayal of a successful attorney stricken with AIDS who sues his powerful Philadelphia firm after they dismiss him. The only lawyer who will take his case is homophobic ambulance-chaser Denzel Washington. With Jason Robards, Mary Steenburgen and Joanne Woodward; Jonathan Demme directs. 125 min.
02-2616　　Was $19.99　　☐*$14.99*

Forrest Gump (1994)

Winner of six Oscars, including Best Picture, Director and Actor, Robert Zemeckis' modern-day "Candide" stars Tom Hanks as the simple-minded but good-hearted Forrest, whose life is a series of accidental encounters with the memorable people and pivotal events of the '50s, '60s and '70s. Endearing mix of comedy and drama also stars Robin Wright, Gary Sinise, Mykelti Williamson and Sally Field as Mama Gump. 142 min.
06-2286　　Was $19.99　　☐*$14.99*

Forrest Gump (Letterboxed Version)

Also available in a theatrical, widescreen format.
06-2507　　☐*$14.99*

Apollo 13 (1995)

It started out as a "routine" trip to the moon, but it became a desperate race against time that had an entire world holding its breath. Tom Hanks, Bill Paxton and Kevin Bacon are the crew of Apollo 13, forced to improvise a return to Earth when an on-board explosion causes them to lose power and oxygen, in director Ron Howard's acclaimed recounting of the 1970 mission. With Gary Sinise, Ed Harris, Kathleen Quinlan. 140 min.
07-2355　　Was $19.99　　☐*$14.99*

Apollo 13 (Letterboxed Version)

Also available in a theatrical, widescreen format.
07-2359　　Was $19.99　　☐*$14.99*

That Thing You Do! (1996)

A bouncy, blast-from-the-past comedy/musical from writer-director Tom Hanks centering on The Wonders, an early '60s pop foursome from Erie, Pa., who become overnight sensations when their recording of the title song rises to the top of the charts, and who eventually self-destruct because of personality conflicts and petty jealousies. With Tom Everett Scott, Johnathon Schaech, Liv Tyler and Hanks as the band's manager. 108 min.
04-3404　　Was $99.99　　☐*$14.99*

You've Got Mail (1998)

The 1940 film "The Shop Around the Corner" gets a high-tech revamping in this romantic computer comedy. Tom Hanks and Meg Ryan star as New York business rivals—a corporate bookstore magnate and the owner of a small children's book shop, respectively—who meet and fall in love, unaware of each other's identity, over the Internet. With Greg Kinnear, Parker Posey, Jean Stapleton; directed and co-scripted by Nora Ephron ("Sleepless in Seattle"). 119 min.
19-2851　　Was $22.99　　☐*$14.99*

From The Earth To The Moon (1998)

Produced by Tom Hanks, the Emmy-winning 12-part mini-series traces America's race against the Soviet Union to put a man on the moon, from Alan Shepard's 1961 suborbital Mercury flight and the Apollo 1 fire that claimed three lives to 1969's triumphant cry of "The Eagle has landed!" and the final Apollo missions. Along with Hanks, the cast includes Tim Daly, Sally Field, Tony Goldwyn, Mark Harmon and Peter Horton. Boxed, six-tape collector's set; 12 hrs. total.
44-2180　　Was $89.99　　*$69.99*

THE GREEN MILE

TOM HANKS

MICHAEL CLARKE DUNCAN

The Green Mile (1999)

This superlative adaptation of Stephen King's novel by "The Shawshank Redemption" scripter/director Frank Darabont boasts Tom Hanks as the head guard in a Louisiana prison's death row in the 1930s who discovers that kindly, convicted murderer Michael Clarke Duncan possesses a magical healing power. David Morse, James Cromwell, Bonnie Hunt and Michael Jeter co-star. 189 min.
19-2978　　Was $99.99　　☐*$19.99*

The Green Mile (Letterboxed Version)

Also available in a theatrical, widescreen format.
19-2998　　☐*$19.99*

Tom Hanks Gift Set

Interested in seeing some movies that *didn't* earn Tom Hanks Academy Award nominations? Check out this collector's set that includes "Bachelor Party," "The Man with One Red Shoe" and "That Thing You Do."
04-3917　　Save $20.00!　　*$24.99*

Please see our index for these other Tom Hanks titles: *Punchline • Radio Flyer • Saving Private Ryan • Toy Story 1 & 2*

Rich In Love (1993)

After his wife leaves him following years of marriage, middle-aged Southerner Albert Finney turns his attentions towards being a father to his two daughters, one of whom is just discovering her sexuality and the other who has returned home married and pregnant. Engaging seriocomedy from the creators of "Driving Miss Daisy" also stars Jill Clayburgh, Kyle MacLachlan and Suzy Amis. 105 min.
12-2740　　Was $19.99　　☐*$14.99*

The Meteor Man (1993)

In this good-natured comic fantasy, Robert Townsend (who also directs) plays a schoolteacher and sometime jazz musician who gains superpowers after he's hit by a meteor. With his new abilities to fly, see through walls, heal wounds and translate dog language, Townsend tackles the gangs that are disrupting his neighborhood. Marla Gibbs, James Earl Jones, Bill Cosby and Sinbad co-star. 99 min.
12-2833　　Was $89.99　　☐*$14.99*

Love Serenade (1997)

A pair of lonely twentysomething sisters in a remote Australian town become bitter rivals for the attention of their new neighbor, a vain, manipulative and middle-aged radio DJ who's arrived from the big city to run the local radio station, in a bitterly funny "anti-romantic" comedy from writer/director Shirley Barrett. Miranda Otto, Rebecca Firth, George Shevtsov star. 101 min.
11-2223　　Was $99.99　　☐*$19.99*

Krippendorf's Tribe (1998)

After spending two years' worth of grant money on raising his family, anthropologist and single dad Richard Dreyfuss is forced to produce evidence of a lost tribe he claims to have discovered in the New Guinea jungle. Dreyfuss' solution: dress up his kids in grass skirts and body paint and film them "in the wild"! Comical romp also stars Jenna Elfman, Lily Tomlin. 94 min.
11-2260　　Was $19.99　　☐*$14.99*

A Slight Case Of Murder (1999)

Film critic William H. Macy's bad day gets even worse when his girlfriend dies from an accidental fall in her apartment. Afraid he'll go from witness to suspect, Macy tries to use his movie knowledge to fool the police, only to have things spin hilariously out of control. Adam Arkin, James Cromwell and Felicity Huffman co-star in this darkly funny comedy thriller, co-scripted by Macy and based on a Donald E. Westlake novel. 94 min.
18-7894　　☐*$99.99*

Undercover Blues (1993)

Romance, comedy and mystery combine in this lighthearted thriller starring Kathleen Turner and Dennis Quaid as husband and wife spies with a new baby girl whose maternity leave in New Orleans is interrupted when they're asked to investigate international terrorists and a stolen arms shipment. Fiona Shaw, Stanley Tucci co-star. 89 min.
12-2869　　Was $89.99　　☐*$14.99*

Fatal Instinct (1994)

In director Carl Reiner's spoof of classic film noirs of the 1940s and contemporary thrillers like "Fatal Attraction" and "Basic Instinct," Armand Assante is Ned Ravine, an inept detective-lawyer involved with three dangerous femme fatales: his adulterous wife (Kate Nelligan), a gorgeous but unpredictable client (Sean Young), and his trusted secretary (Sherilyn Fenn). With Clarence Clemons. 90 min.
12-2904　　Was $89.99　　☐*$14.99*

Clean Slate (1994)

Dana Carvey plays Maurice Pogue, a private detective with a real problem: a case of recurring amnesia that makes each day seem like the first day of the rest of his life. A beautiful femme fatale (Valeria Golino) with a dual identity and a mysterious past brings him into a case filled with danger and laughs. James Earl Jones, Kevin Pollak and Barkley the dog co-star. 106 min.
12-2950　　☐*$14.99*

Wild West (1993)
A young Pakistani man living in London's Little India section desires a career as a country-western singer. Joined by his group, The Honkytonk Cowboys, he tries to overcome neighborhood thugs and dead-end jobs to make it to Nashville. Naveen Andrews, Sarita Choudhury star. 85 min.
68-1360 *$89.99*

Playing Dangerous (1995)
An 11-year-old technology expert uses his wits, remote-controlled car and water gun to stop a gang of thieves out to get a secret fax he has entered in his computer. David Keith Miller, Ali Patrick and Mickey LeBeau star in this fun-filled farce that's like "Home Alone"...with computers! 86 min.
68-1781 *$89.99*

Kicking & Screaming (1995)
A quartet of college buddies graduate and are daunted by the prospects of having to leave their carefree student lifestyles behind and enter the adult world. Sharply written seriocomedy stars Josh Hamilton, Chris Eigman, Olivia D'Abo, Parker Posey and Eric Stoltz. 96 min.
68-1795 Was $89.99 *❑$14.99*

...At First Sight (1995)
When a guy whose luck with the opposite sex has never been good finally meets the girl of his dreams, he goes to his best friend for advice...and promptly winds up on his own again. Outrageous comedy of love, sex and relationships in the '90s stars Jonathan Silverman, Dan Cortese, Allison Smith. 90 min.
68-1801 *❑$99.99*

Sprung (1997)
Hilarious and sensitive farce from writer-director Rusty Cundieff ("Tales from the Hood") that looks at the love lives of four African-Americans: a man-hunting woman and her shy, law clerk pal and a hot-to-trot fast food clerk player and his sensitive friend. Tisha Campbell, Paula Jai Parker, Joe Torry and Cundieff star. 108 min.
68-1849 Was $99.99 *❑$14.99*

Mojave Moon (1997)
When nice guy Danny Aiello offers Angelina Jolie a lift from L.A. to the Mojave Desert, it sets off a chain of bizarre and comical events in this offbeat romantic romp. Anne Archer, Michael Biehn, Alfred Molina also star. 95 min.
68-1858 Was $99.99 *$14.99*

Lawn Dogs (1997)
Daringly different social comedy from Australia's John Duigan ("Wide Sargasso Sea") is set in an affluent Southern community where an outsider—landscaper Sam Rockwell—observes the foibles of the privileged people around him. Rockwell soon forms an unusual friendship with the 10-year-old daughter of one family. Kathleen Quinlan, Christopher McDonald also star. 100 min.
68-1898 *❑$99.99*

Lovelife (1997)
A group of twentysomething friends find themselves facing an uphill struggle together as they try to navigate the dating scene of the '90s in this wistful and witty romantic comedy. Saffron Burrows, Sherilyn Fenn, Carla Gugino, Jon Tenney and Bruce Davison star. 96 min.
68-1861 *❑$99.99*

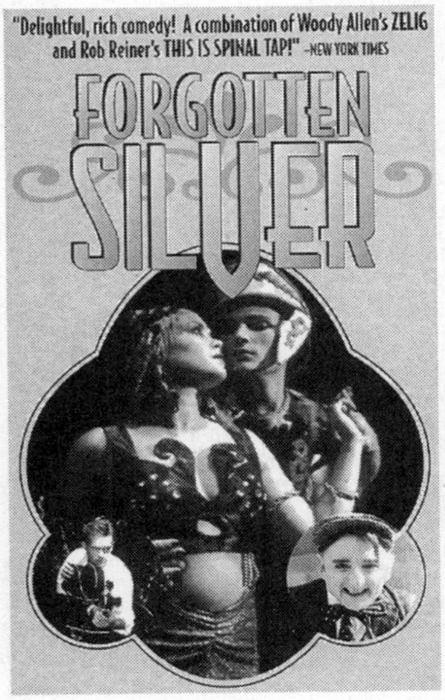
"Delightful, rich comedy! A combination of Woody Allen's ZELIG and Rob Reiner's THIS IS SPINAL TAP!" —NEW YORK TIMES
FORGOTTEN
SILVER

Forgotten Silver (1997)
One part "That's Entertainment!" and one part "This Is Spinal Tap," director Peter Jackson's ("Heavenly Creatures") mock documentary looks at the recently-rediscovered "work" of fellow New Zealander and 1900s filmmaking pioneer Colin McKenzie, who was the actual inventor of color movies, talkies and other innovations. Comments from actor Sam Neill, film critic Leonard Maltin and others help tell McKenzie's hard-luck life story. Also included is the short "Signing Off," about a down under DJ's hectic last day. 70 min. total.
70-5131 Was $59.99 *$29.99*

SO I MARRIED AN AXE MURDERER

So I Married An Axe Murderer (1993)
Mike Myers plays dual roles in this outrageous farce. He's Charlie MacKenzie, a San Francisco bachelor looking to change his luck with women when he decides to wed the beautiful Harriet (Nancy Travis), the co-owner of a butcher shop and a possible serial killer. Myers also plays Charlie's loud Scottish father; with Anthony La Paglia, Amanda Plummer. 93 min.
02-2536 Was $19.99 *❑$14.99*

Teresa's Tattoo (1994)
Teresa is a young woman who becomes the unwilling stand-in hostage for some bumbling kidnappers who accidentally kill their victim before they receive the ransom, and soon she's on the run from both the crooks and the FBI. Hip comedy stars C. Thomas Howell, Nancy McKeon, Lou Diamond Phillips and Adrienne Shelly. 95 min.
68-1340 *❑$89.99*

Chairman Of The Board (1998)
Surf's up...and so is high-energy prop comic Carrot Top, in a frenetic, zany comedy that features the frizzy-haired free spirit as a beach bum/inventor who befriends tycoon and fellow surfer Jack Warden. When Warden dies, he leaves control of his business empire to Carrot Top, who promptly proceeds to turn it upside-down with his wacky gizmos. Courtney Thorne-Smith, Larry Miller and Raquel Welch also star. 95 min.
68-1877 Was $99.99 *❑$14.99*

My Teacher's Wife (1995)
When his admission to Harvard is threatened by a tyrannical calculus teacher, Jeremy London gets help in the form of gorgeous math tutor Tia Carrere. The teacher-pupil relationship blossoms into a romance, but complications ensue when Carrere turns out to be the wife of his calculus instructor. Christopher McDonald, Jeffrey Tambor co-star. AKA: "Learning Curves." 89 min.
68-1909 *❑$99.99*

Sweethearts (1999)
Darkly funny take on the contemporary dating scene finds lonely single Mitch Rouse going to a coffee shop to meet the woman who answered his personal ad. While waiting, he attracts the attention of quirky and neurotic Janeane Garofalo, who has her own reasons for being there...as well as a gun in her purse. With Margaret Cho and Bobcat Goldthwait. 85 min.
68-1922 *❑$69.99*

Twice Upon A Yesterday (1999)
Ever wish you had a second chance to win back the love of your life? Thanks to a pair of mystical garbagemen, struggling London actor Douglas Henshall is sent back to a time before he confessed an affair to girlfriend Lena Headey, who promptly left him. Will history repeat itself, though, when Henshall finds himself attracted to Penélope Cruz? Heather Weeks, Mark Strong also star in this magical romantic comedy. 91 min.
68-1945 *❑$79.99*

The Sex Monster (1999)
In this outrageous romantic romp, a Los Angeles building contractor (writer/director/co-star Mike Binder) tries to persuade his wife (Mariel Hemingway) to let another woman join them in a menage a trois. Not only does Hemingway agree to the idea, but soon she's pursuing every woman that catches her eye! With Stephen Baldwin, Renee Humphrey, Kevin Pollak. 97 min.
68-1959 *❑$69.99*

A Little Stiff (1990)
The real-life relationship and break-up between UCLA film student Caveh Zahedi and an art student was the basis for this witty, quirky independent comedy by Zahedi and Greg Watkins. Its personal, offbeat style has inspired some to call Zahedi "the Persian Woody Allen." Erin McKim co-stars. 85 min.
70-3298 Was $39.99 *$24.99*

Hellcab (1998)
In this off-the-wall comedy-drama from the creators of "Grosse Pointe Blank," a Chicago cab driver's daily routine on a freezing day is enlivened by a steady flow of unusual passengers who have fascinating, funny and sometimes disturbing stories to relate. John Cusack, Gillian Anderson, Julianne Moore, Laurie Metcalf and Paul Dillon star. AKA: "Chicago Cab." 96 min.
68-1919 *❑$99.99*

My Grandpa Is A Vampire (1991)
Al Lewis, who played another Grandpa on "The Munsters," stars in this comic terror tale set in New Zealand, as a bloodsucking old codger shows his grandson and his pals how to be a cool ghoul. Justin Gocke co-stars. AKA: "Moonrise." 90 min.
63-1566 Was $89.99 *❑$14.99*

Aliens Cut My Hair (1992)
Hilarious, slapdash, shot-on-video farce about alien drag queens on a special assignment to find the skipper of the Spaceship Penetrator. Their mission, which they've chosen to accept: restyle his hair! 60 min.
53-9478 *$49.99*

Mob Queen (1999)
A pair of small-time hoods in 1950s Brooklyn try to get in good with their boss by presenting him with a stunning prostitute for his birthday. Things are looking up when the mobster falls for his "present," but when they discover that "Glorice" is really a guy, the hoods must do everything to keep it a secret in this offbeat crime comedy. David Proval, Tony Sirico, Candis Cayne star. 87 min.
70-5178 Was $59.99 *$19.99*

I Don't Hate Las Vegas Anymore (1991)
A filmmaker takes a trip to Las Vegas with his father, teenage half-brother and a two-person crew. He hopes to prove the existence of God and theorizes that if the Almighty exists, he doesn't need a script for his film, as God will take care of its shooting on His own. Hilarity ensues when things go awry in director/star Caveh Zahedi's independent "mockumentary." 74 min.
70-3470 *$79.99*

The Big Dis (1990)
A hip interracial sex comedy about a young black soldier ready for romance while on a weekend pass at his suburban home. Instead of bedroom encounters, the soldier gets "dissed" by a variety of women, while his mother asks him to take care of several errands. James Haig, Allysunn Walker star. 88 min.
70-5034 *$59.99*

Trusting Beatrice (1994)
How do you tell the woman of your dreams that you burned down her home? Find out in this offbeat romantic comedy about a man who accidentally destroys his apartment building and invites a gorgeous French neighbor and her adopted daughter to stay with him and his quirky family. Irene Jacob ("Red"), Mark Evan Jacobs, Steve Buscemi star. 86 min.
70-5080 Was $59.99 *$29.99*

Bad Girls From Mars (1990)
A small-time film studio is filming a softcore sci-fi movie, but the set is also home to a homicidal maniac who is bringing the curtain down on more than one beautiful starlet. Outrageous, racy horror spoof stars the legendary Edy Williams. 86 min.
68-1177 *$12.99*

The Closest Thing To Heaven (1996)
The day-to-day dramas of a variety of Charlotte, North Carolina, residents—including a pair of siblings who are reunited after 15 years, a single mother whose bus stop vigil is interrupted by a would-be Romeo, and a preacher who unknowingly ministers to the husband of his lover—are chronicled in this warm and bittersweet independent film from Tar Heel writer/director Dorne Pentes. 98 min.
70-3474 *$79.99*

Just One Of The Girls (1993)
Teenager Corey Haim is being picked on by the school tough, so he disguises himself as a girl in order to avoid him. After Corey falls for the meanie's sexy sister, will he be able to reveal his incredible secret? Zany farce co-stars Nicole Eggert ("Baywatch") and Gabe Khouth. 94 min.
68-1293 Was $89.99 *❑$12.99*

A Business Affair (1995)
The wife of a successful author comes to a crossroads when, after writing her first novel, she is wooed both professionally and personally by her husband's publisher. Fine romantic comedy stars Carole Bouquet, Jonathan Pryce and Christopher Walken. 105 min.
68-1802 *❑$89.99*

Somewhere In The City (1999)
The professional, romantic and emotional travails of a New York apartment building's diverse residents—among them an exchange student from China, a self-absorbed therapist, and a gay would-be actor—are traced in this funny and revealing comedy. Sandra Bernhard, Robert John Burke, Bai Ling, Ornella Muti and Peter Stormare star. 93 min.
70-5166 Was $79.99 *$19.99*

In The Spirit (1990)
New Age sensibilities are sent up in this funky farce about two women, a businessman's neglected wife and a self-styled mystic and guru, who are stalked by a mysterious killer. Elaine May, Marlo Thomas, Peter Falk star, with cameos by Olympia Dukakis and Melanie Griffith. 94 min.
71-5196 Was $89.99 *$14.99*

Adam Sandler

Going Overboard (1989)
Before he made a splash with "Saturday Night Live" and "Billy Madison," Adam Sandler starred in this zany comedy, playing a cruise ship waiter with aspirations of becoming the ship's comic. When the regular funnyman gets locked in the bathroom, Shecky gets his chance—at success and at getting pretty girls. Billy Zane and Burt Young co-star. AKA: "Babes Ahoy." 99 min.
68-1370 Was $79.99 *$14.99*

Airheads (1994)
Desperate to get their demo tape, a rock band calling themselves The Lone Rangers uses toy pistols to take over the city's top radio station. But when their water guns are mistaken for the real thing, the police are called in and the stunt escalates into a comic "Dog Day Afternoon." Brendan Fraser, Steve Buscemi, Adam Sandler, Joe Mantegna and Amy Locane star in this rock-and-roll farce directed by Michael Lehmann ("Heathers"). 81 min.
04-2889 Was $89.99 *❑$14.99*

Billy Madison (1995)
In this rib-tickling comedy, "Saturday Night Live's" Adam Sandler plays the title character, the moronic, goof-off son of a motel magnate who sets out to prove he's worthy of taking over the family business by going back to school and legitimately passing grades 1 through 12 in six months. Bridgette Wilson and Darren McGavin co-star. 90 min.
07-2323 Was $19.99 *❑$14.99*

Happy Gilmore (1996)
With his grandmother in dire financial trouble, doofus hockey player Adam Sandler discovers he can smash a golf ball 400 yards, so he joins the PGA tour. During his cross-country golf odyssey, he annoys champ Christopher McDonald, gets in a fight with Bob Barker, befriends has-been Carl Weathers, and falls in love with public relations expert Julie Bowen. 92 min.
07-2424 Was $99.99 *❑$14.99*

Bulletproof (1996)
Action and laughs mix as undercover cop Damon Wayans is given the assignment to bust carjacker Adam Sandler, who's working for drug-dealing auto dealer James Caan. But the enemies find themselves forced to work together when both are targeted by Caan and his hit men. Kristen Wilson, James Farentino also star. 85 min.
07-2483 Was $99.99 *❑$14.99*

The Wedding Singer (1998)
The fashions and music of the '80s live on in this winning romantic comedy starring Adam Sandler as the title character, an easy-going wedding reception crooner whose life is thrown into turmoil when his own fiancé leaves him standing at the altar. Drew Barrymore co-stars as the waitress who helps heal Sandler's broken heart; with Allen Covert, Christine Taylor, Steve Buscemi and Ellen Dow as the rapping senior citizen. 97 min.
02-5182 Was $99.99 *❑$14.99*

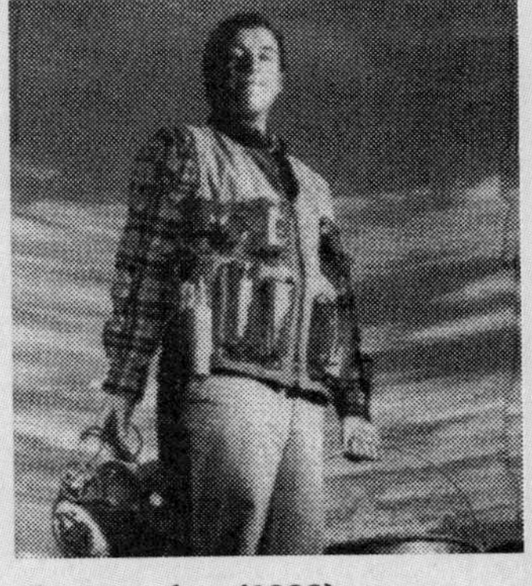
THE
WATERBOY

The Waterboy (1998)
There are bellylaughs by the bucketful in the hit comedy starring Adam Sandler as a crazed Cajun lad who loses his job as waterboy/punching bag for a top Louisiana university football team and is hired by a sadsack college squad. When Sandler's repressed anger explodes, he becomes the team's newest defensive tackle and a gridiron hero. Kathy Bates, Henry Winkler and Fairuza Balk also star. 90 min.
11-2301 Was $19.99 *❑$14.99*

Big Daddy (1999)
When his girlfriend dumps him because of his immaturity, part-time tolltaker and full-time slacker Adam Sandler sets out to prove he's responsible...by adopting a 5-year-old boy. Sandler's attempts to clean up his act and care for his new "son" make for hilarious and heartwarming comedy. With Joey Lauren Adams, Jon Stewart, Kristy Swanson, and Cole and Dylan Sprouse as the child. 93 min.
02-3371 Was $19.99 *❑$14.99*

The Adam Sandler Collection
So drink your gin and tonica and smoke your...oh never mind, just buy this affordable boxed set of Sandler slapstick featuring "Billy Madison," "Bulletproof" and "Happy Gilmore" instead.
07-2935 Save $15.00! *$29.99*

Please see our index for these other Adam Sandler titles: *Mixed Nuts • Shakes The Clown*

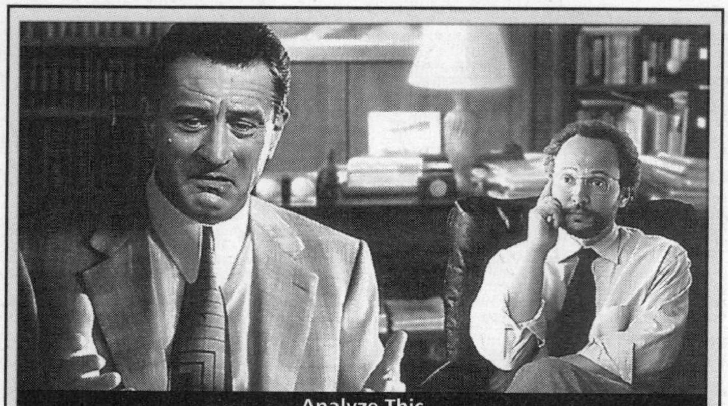

Analyze This

Billy Crystal

Running Scared (1986)
Billy Crystal and Gregory Hines star as two Chicago cops whose final month on the force can be their last month anywhere, if the drug kingpin they're trying to catch has anything to say about it. With Dan Hedaya, Jimmy Smits. 107 min.
12-1641 *$14.99*

Memories Of Me (1988)
Affable and affecting comedy concerning a repressed doctor (Billy Crystal) who heads for Hollywood to make peace with the father he barely knows (Alan King), a carefree film extra who's spent a lifetime trying to win a speaking part. With JoBeth Williams. 105 min.
12-2618 Was $19.99 ❑*$14.99*

When Harry Met Sally... (1989)
Engaging and smartly performed comedy stars Billy Crystal and Meg Ryan as a pair of longtime platonic friends determined not to let sex mess up a great relationship, until... Rob Reiner's wry and winning look at friendship, love and that gray area in between co-stars Carrie Fisher, Bruno Kirby. 95 min.
73-1055 Was $19.99 ❑*$14.99*

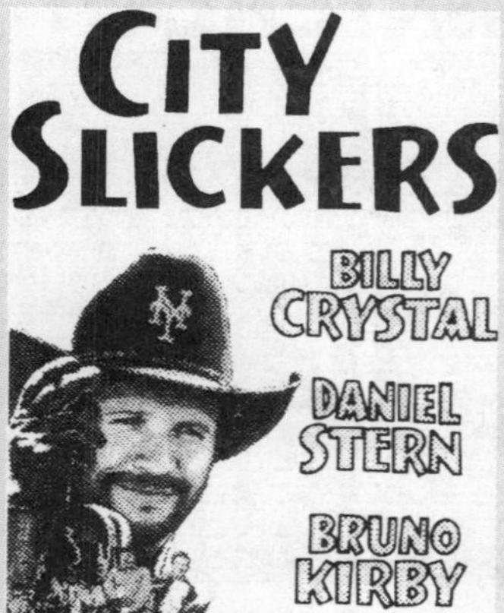

City Slickers (1991)
Hilarious mid-life crisis comedy stars Billy Crystal as a New York radio ad man in his late 30s who joins pals Daniel Stern and Bruno Kirby for a special vacation to re-evaluate their lives, heading to the Southwest to take part in a cattle drive overseen by a crusty cowpoke (Oscar-winner Jack Palance). Helen Slater, Patricia Wettig co-star. 114 min.
02-5003 Was $89.99 ❑*$14.99*

City Slickers II: The Legend Of Curly's Gold (1994)
Laugh-filled sequel to the hit sagebrush farce finds Billy Crystal heading back to the West with pal Daniel Stern and brother Jon Lovitz to search for treasure hidden by their late cowpoke pardner. While hunting for the loot, the trio encounter Curly's twin brother, Duke (played by Jack Palance), and the fun begins. Patricia Wettig co-stars. 115 min.
02-2658 Was $19.99 ❑*$14.99*

Mr. Saturday Night (1992)
Billy Crystal makes his directing debut in this bittersweet chronicle of 50 years in the sometimes hilarious, sometimes sad life of acid-tongued comic Buddy Young, Jr. (played by Crystal), from his early Catskills stints to his relationship with his brother-manager (David Paymer) and his twilight years. Julie Warner, Helen Hunt, Ron Silver co-star. Re-edited video version; 119 min.
02-5012 Was $19.99 ❑*$14.99*

Forget Paris (1995)
In this breezy romantic comedy, Billy Crystal is an NBA ref who falls in love with Paris-based airline executive Debra Winger. After Crystal woos his new girl, they marry, but is the worldly Winger really going to be happy living with Crystal in L.A.? Witty, bittersweet tale also stars Joe Mantegna, along with Kareem Abdul-Jabbar and Charles Barkley as themselves. 101 min.
02-2806 Was $19.99 ❑*$14.99*

Fathers' Day (1997)
When conservative lawyer Billy Crystal and off-the-wall writer Robin Williams are each contacted by ex-flame Nastassja Kinski and told they're the father of her runaway teenage son, this "odd couple" sets out on a comical cross-country search for "their boy." Based on the French film "Les Comperes," this laugh-filled hit also stars Julia Louis-Dreyfus. 99 min.
19-2578 Was $19.99 ❑*$14.99*

My Giant (1998)
A business trip to Romania for career-driven talent agent Billy Crystal takes a surprise detour when an car crash lands him in a monastery that's also home to 7'7" Max (NBA star Gheorghe Muresan). Thinking that this gentle giant could be a hot Hollywood property, Crystal brings Mac back to America to make him a "big" star. Funny and touching comedy also stars Kathleen Quinlan and Steven Seagal in an amusing turn as himself. 104 min.
19-2742 Was $99.99 ❑*$14.99*

Analyze This (1999)
Mirthful mob farce starring Billy Crystal as a New York psychiatrist enlisted to help gangster Robert De Niro, whose recent anxiety has affected his ability to rule with an iron fist. De Niro's dependence on Crystal's therapy soon threatens the doc's life, his Miami vacation and his impending marriage to newscaster Lisa Kudrow. With Chazz Palminteri. 103 min.
19-2877 Was $99.99 ❑*$19.99*

Please see our index for these other Billy Crystal titles: *Deconstructing Harry • Hamlet • The Princess Bride*

Instant Karma (1990)
David Cassidy is the egocentric star of a hit TV series who gets caught up in a comic love triangle with the show's producer, whose luck constantly goes from bad to worse. Hip, sexy farce also stars Craig Sheffer, Chelsea Noble, Marty Ingels. 102 min.
12-2153 Was $89.99 ❑*$19.99*

Delirious (1991)
When TV soap writer John Candy wakes up from a bump on the noggin, he finds himself trapped in the fictional town he's created, able to change events via his typewriter, and caught in a love triangle with Emma Samms and Mariel Hemingway. Offbeat, Mittyesque comedy also stars David Rasche, Raymond Burr. 96 min.
12-2354 Was $89.99 ❑*$14.99*

Once Upon A Crime (1992)
All-star caper farce stars John Candy, Richard Lewis, James Belushi, Cybill Shepherd, Sean Young, George Hamilton and Giancarlo Giannini romping through Europe in a wild-and-wacky story about a prized canine and the mysterious murder of its owner. 94 min.
12-2464 ❑*$14.99*

Office Killer (1998)
Photographer Cindy Sherman's directorial debut is a deliciously dark comedy starring Carol Kane as a put-upon proofreader for Constant Consumer magazine. Going wacko after 14 years on the job, Kane begins killing her co-workers and moving the bodies into her cellar. Molly Ringwald, Jeanne Tripplehorn and Barbara Sukowa also star in this hip, edgy satire. 83 min.
11-2297 Was $99.99 ❑*$14.99*

Since You've Been Gone (1998)
David Schwimmer makes his directorial debut with this ensemble comedy in which a group of old friends and rivals reunite at a Chicago theater for their high school reunion. Lara Flynn Boyle, Teri Hatcher, Marisa Tomei, Liev Schreiber and Molly Ringwald star along with Schwimmer, who plays the reunion's emcee. 96 min.
11-2298 Was $99.99 ❑*$19.99*

Citizen Ruth (1996)
Trenchant satire about the debate over abortion featuring Laura Dern as the white trash, drug-addicted mother of four who finds herself caught between pro-life fundamentalists and ultra-liberal pro-choicers when she becomes pregnant again. Mary Kay Place, Kurtwood Smith, Swoosie Kurtz, Kelly Preston and Burt Reynolds also star. 105 min.
11-2124 Was $99.99 ❑*$19.99*

Miami Rhapsody (1995)
In the tradition of Woody Allen's funniest efforts comes this stylish romantic comedy starring Sarah Jessica Parker as a Miami copywriter who has last-minute reservations about getting hitched when she learns that all of the members of her family are involved in extramarital affairs. Mia Farrow, Paul Mazursky, Gil Bellows and Antonio Banderas also star. 95 min.
11-1895 Was $19.99 ❑*$14.99*

For Richer Or Poorer (1997)
High-living Manhattanites Tim Allen And Kirstie Alley are left holding the bag—and a hefty IRS tax bill—thanks to a crooked accountant. On the run from the feds, the couple winds up in Pennsylvania's Amish country, masquerading as visiting relatives of a farming family. Kooky culture clash comedy also stars Jay O. Sanders, Wayne Knight, Michael Lerner. 116 min.
07-2617 Was $99.99 ❑*$14.99*

Telling You (1999)
Best friends Nolan and Phil are trying to make ends meet while working at a Long Island pizza place. Things get embarrassing and complicated when they encounter Deb and Kristen, their respective ex-girlfriends, who question the paths the guys' lives have taken. Jennifer Love Hewitt, Gina Philips, Peter Facinelli and Dash Mihok star in this witty farce. 94 min.
11-2329 Was $99.99 ❑*$19.99*

Walking And Talking (1996)
Two young women who have been best friends since grade school and helped each other through a series of romantic crises find the future of their relationship up in the air when one of them gets engaged in this warm and witty seriocomedy from writer/director Nicole Holofcener. Catherine Keener, Anne Heche, Todd Field and Kevin Corrigan star. 85 min.
11-2100 Was $99.99 ❑*$19.99*

Senseless (1998)
Short on cash to finish his education and help support his family, college student Marlon Wayans becomes a test subject for an experimental drug that heightens his five senses. Trouble is, he can't control when and where it happens. David Spade, Matthew Lillard and Rip Torn also star in this wild comedy filled with sight (as well as smell, sound, taste and touch) gags. 93 min.
11-2772 Was $99.99 ❑*$19.99*

Summer Fling (1997)
When a 17-year-old Irish student thinks he failed his final exams, he decides to, instead of fretting over them, put grades behind him and have a wild and crazy summer at the beach. Thrown into the mix are an array of love interests and his eccentric family. Jared Leto, Gabriel Byrne, Catherine O'Hara, Christina Ricci star. AKA: "Last of the High Kings." 103 min.
11-2775 Was $99.99 ❑*$19.99*

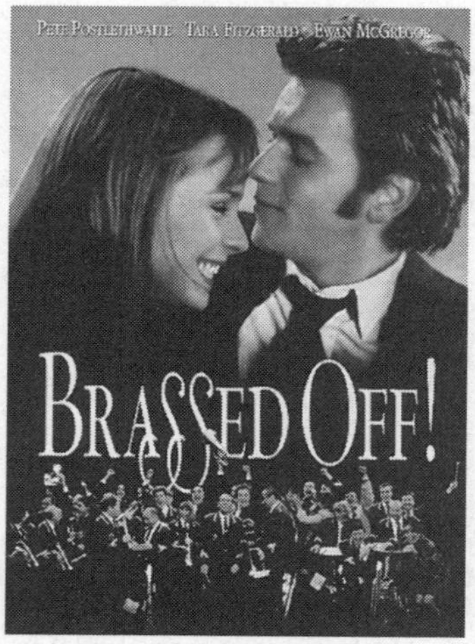

Brassed Off! (1997)
Music may soothe the savage breast, but can a Northern England mining community's brass band soothe the anguish of the residents when the coal mine that is their town's chief source of employment closes? Pete Postlethwaite, Ewan McGregor and Tara Fitzgerald star in this winning mix of comedy and drama. 100 min.
11-2187 Was $99.99 ❑*$19.99*

Stuart Saves His Family (1995)
Al Franken's "Saturday Night Live" self-help guru finds himself sinking into depression and eating too many Fig Newtons, so he decides to investigate the source of his problems when he goes home to attend a relative's funeral. What he discovers is a real dysfunction junction of a family that needs help...and that's...okay. Harris Yulin, Laura San Giacomo and Vincent D'Onofrio co-star. 97 min.
06-2384 Was $89.99 ❑*$19.99*

Smoke Signals (1998)
"It's a good day to be indigenous" in this acclaimed look at modern American Indian life, the first film made by Native Americans. Director Chris Eyre and writer Sherman Alexie present a wryly comic tale of two friends, with very different outlooks on life, who leave their Idaho reservation home for a bus trip to Arizona, where one man has to pick up the remains of his estranged father. Adam Beach, Evan Adams, Irene Bedard star. 89 min.
11-2287 Was $99.99 ❑*$19.99*

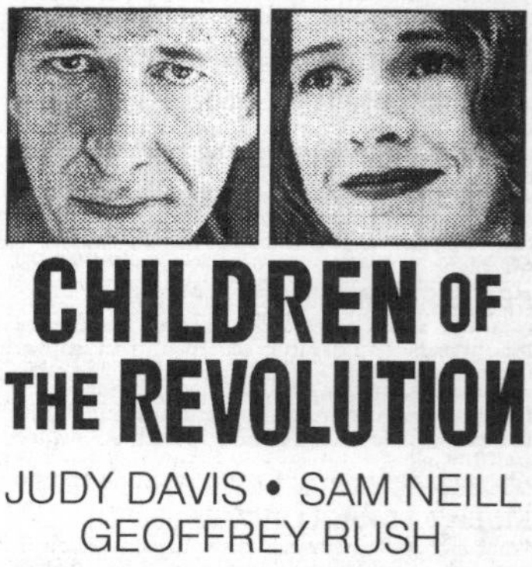

Children Of The Revolution (1997)
An off-the-wall political satire from Down Under, writer/director Peter Duncan's dark comedy stars Judy Davis as a devoted Communist in '40s Australia who is invited to visit Moscow, where she is wooed and made pregnant by Joseph Stalin. Years later, Davis attempts to raise her son in his father's "revolutionary" footsteps, but things take an unexpected turn. Sam Neill, Rachel Griffiths and F. Murray Abraham, as Stalin, also star. 101 min.
11-2188 Was $99.99 ❑*$19.99*

Next Stop, Wonderland (1998)
Fresh romantic comedy starring Hope Davis as a Boston night nurse who, after being dumped by her live-in boyfriend, is coaxed back into the dating scene, thanks to a personal ad placed by her mother. Along the way, Davis' path keeps crossing with plumber Alan Gelfant, who's looking for love, as well as a career in marine biology. Will the two eventually meet? With Holland Taylor, Robert Klein. 96 min.
11-2296 Was $99.99 ❑*$19.99*

All I Wanna Do (1998)
A New England girls' school in the early 1960s is thrown into turmoil when finances force the institution to consider merging with a nearby boys' school, leading a group of students to become activists to preserve their way of life. Bright and funny coming-of-age tale stars Rachael Leigh Cook, Kirsten Dunst, Gaby Hoffmann, Heather Matarazzo and Lynn Redgrave. AKA: "The Hairy Bird," "Strike." 97 min.
11-2306 ❑*$99.99*

She's All That (1999)
"Pygmalion" goes to high school in this sharp, funny tale. After betting he can turn any girl into his school's prom queen, class hunk Freddie Prinze, Jr. has his work cut out for him when his friends select shy, nerdy artist Rachael Leigh Cook. As Prinze woos Cook and makes her over, he becomes genuinely attracted to her, but what happens when Cook learns of the wager? Matthew Lillard, Jodi Lyn O'Keefe co-star. 95 min.
11-2328 Was $19.99 ❑*$14.99*

Entropy (1999)
One part rockumentary and one part romantic comedy, this edgy (in more than one sense of the word) tale stars Stephen Dorff as a director trying to make a documentary on the rock band U2's American tour, even as his personal life is disintegrating around him. Shot during U2's Popmart Tour, the film also stars Judith Godreche and Lauren Holly, with Adam, Bono, Larry and the Edge as themselves. 110 min.
11-2391 Was $99.99 ❑*$19.99*

Wide Awake (1998)
A fifth-grader at a Catholic school undergoes a crisis of faith when his beloved grandfather dies of cancer, and sets out on a mission to find God and restore his beliefs. Set and filmed in the Philadelphia area, writer/director M. Night Shyamalan's touching comedy/drama stars Joseph Cross, Dana Delany, Denis Leary, Robert Loggia and Rosie O'Donnell as the boy's favorite teacher, baseball-loving Sister Terry. 88 min.
11-2786 Was $99.99 ❑*$19.99*

Teenage Exorcist (1993)
A beautiful woman finds her new home is possessed by demons that take over her body and that her only hope for salvation lies with two men: the local priest and...the local pizza boy? Brinke Stevens, Michael Berryman, Robert Quarry, Jasaé and Eddie Deezen star wild horror-comedy mix. 98 min.
16-9149 Was $39.99 *$14.99*

68 · COMEDY MOVIES UNLIMITED CALL · 1-800-4-MOVIES

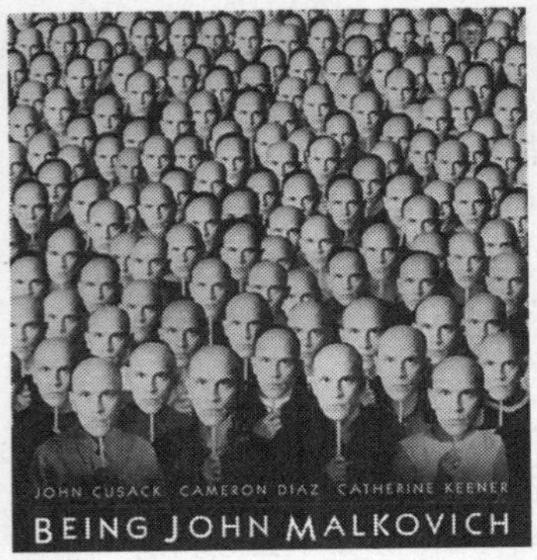

Being John Malkovich (1999)
What would you do if you found a doorway in your workplace that led, via a mysterious portal, into the head of actor John Malkovich, giving you the chance to experience everything he does for 15 minutes? For puppeteer/file clerk John Cusack, pet shop employee wife Cameron Diaz and sexy co-worker Catherine Keener, the find leads to a money-making scheme, a twisted love triangle, and a multi-layered identity crisis. Director Spike Jonze and scripter Charlie Kaufman's outrageously original comedy also stars Orson Bean, and John Malkovich as himself. 113 min.
02-9203 Was $99.99 *$14.99*

Mr. Destiny (1990)
Everybody dreams about going back and fixing mistakes in their life. But for harried executive James Belushi, an encounter with angelic stranger Michael Caine gives him the chance to start over and do things right...or does it? Delightful fantasy/comedy in the manner of "It's a Wonderful Life" also stars Linda Hamilton, Jon Lovitz. 110 min.
11-1556 ❑*$19.99*

Safe Men (1998)
This wild farce features Steve Zahn and Sam Rockwell as struggling musicians who are mistaken for expert thieves and are enlisted by Jewish mobster Michael Lerner to undertake a series of daring break-ins. One of the schemes has them swiping hockey's Stanley Cup from rival hood Harvey Fierstein so Lerner can give it to his son as a Bar Mitzvah present. With Paul Giamatti. 89 min.
07-2726 ❑*$99.99*

Overnight Delivery (1997)
A young man, convinced his girlfriend's been unfaithful, gets his female best friend to help him compose the nastiest possible break-up letter and send it to be delivered the next day—Valentine's Day. When he learns he was wrong, a frantically funny 24-hour quest to stop the poison pen note from reaching its destination ensues. Paul Rudd, Reese Witherspoon and Christine Taylor star. 87 min.
02-5174 Was $99.99 ❑*$19.99*

The Players Club (1998)
Writer/director/star Ice Cube heads a top cast in this comedy/drama about a beautiful college student who turns to work in a strip club in order to pay her tuition. She soon finds out that her dreams have a price, and a sympathetic DJ might be her only hope to avoid the club's sleazy patrons, as well as low-life owner Dollar Bill. Lisa Raye, Jamie Foxx and Bernie Mac co-star. 103 min.
02-5189 Was $99.99 ❑*$19.99*

Welcome To Woop Woop (1998)
From the creator of "The Adventures of Priscilla, Queen of the Desert" comes this way-out tale of an American con artist on the lam in Australia. Captured and imprisoned in a bizarre Outback town, he's drugged and forced to marry the bimbo daughter of the beer-swilling mayor. Johnathon Schaech, Rod Taylor and Susie Porter star. 97 min.
73-1300 Was $59.99 ❑*$14.99*

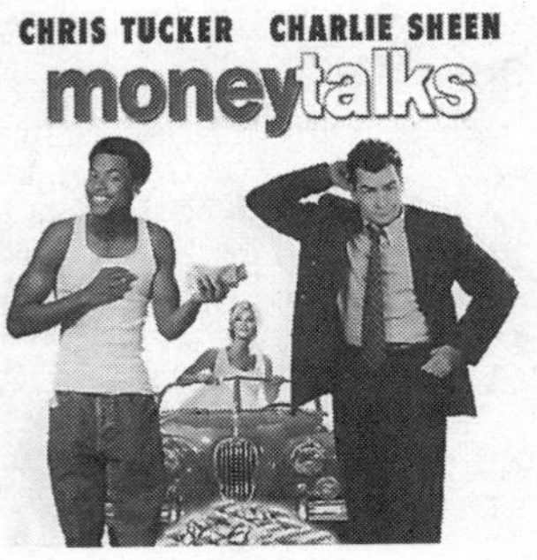

Money Talks (1997)
When story-hungry reporter Charlie Sheen sets up slick-talking ticket-scalper Chris Tucker and has him arrested, it sets off a comic chain reaction of chases and escapes that has the duo on the run from the law as they try to clear their names of a murder charge. Fast-paced buddy comedy also stars Paul Sorvino, Heather Locklear. 95 min.
02-5166 Was $99.99 ❑*$14.99*

Grosse Pointe Blank (1997)
A stylishly hip and dark comedy that hits the bull's-eye, this edgy tale stars John Cusack as an idiosyncratic, jaded hit man whose latest job brings him to his hometown of Grosse Pointe, Michigan, the same time as his 10-year high school reunion. As Cusack tries to put his chaotic life in order and reunite with old flame Minnie Driver, ex-mentor-turned-rival assassin Dan Aykroyd wants Cusack to join him or retire...permanently. Alan Arkin, Joan Cusack also star. 108 min.
11-2178 Was $19.99 ❑*$14.99*

Playing By Heart (1998)
A witty, sexy and touching look at the bonds—both romantic and familial—forged and tested by a diverse group of couples in Los Angeles. Writer/director Willard Carroll's comedy/drama boasts a fine ensemble cast that includes Sean Connery and Gena Rowlands as "old marrieds" facing a crisis on their 40th anniversary; Gillian Anderson as a theatre director whose fear of commitment is tested by suitor Jon Stewart; and Angelina Jolie and Ryan Phillippe as club-hopping twentysomethings. With Madeline Stowe, Dennis Quaid, Jay Mohr. 121 min.
11-2339 Was $99.99 ❑*$19.99*

The Best Man (1999)
A group of college friends reunites for the wedding of one of their number, pro football player Morris Chestnut, but the news that best man and author Taye Diggs has written a novel filled with thinly-veiled accounts of their sexual exploits—including an encounter between Diggs and bride-to-be Monica Calhoun—puts the weekend's events in jeopardy. Called "a black 'Big Chill'" by critics, writer/director Malcolm Lee's (Spike's cousin) winning comedy/drama also stars Nia Long, Terrence Howard, Sanaa Lathan. 121 min.
07-2828 Was $99.99 ❑*$14.99*

Buffalo '66 (1998)
Offbeat dark comedy from writer/director/star Vincent Gallo, who plays a newly-freed ex-con out to kill the Buffalo Bills player whose gridiron miscue got Gallo in trouble with loan sharks and landed him behind bars. Along the way, however, Gallo kidnaps Christina Ricci and convinces her to pose as the "wife" he's talked about to his dysfunctional parents. Ben Gazzara, Anjelica Huston, Rosanna Arquette and Mickey Rourke also star. 110 min.
07-2702 Was $99.99 ❑*$19.99*

The House Of Yes (1997)
Family secrets don't come much deeper—or more outrageous—than this dark comedy of a supremely dysfunctional Washington, D.C., brood. Eldest son Josh Hamilton brings home waitress girlfriend Tori Spelling for a Thanksgiving weekend visit which threatens the already fragile mental state of Hamilton's twin sister, the pink-suited, Kennedy-obsessed "Jackie O" (Parker Posey), whose love for her sibling seems to go beyond the mere familial. Freddie Prinze, Jr. and Genevieve Bujold also star. 85 min.
11-2230 Was $99.99 ❑*$19.99*

Outside Providence (1999)
A change of pace from "There's Something About Mary" creators Peter and Bobby Farrelly, this nostalgic comedy stars Shawn Hatosy ("The Faculty") as a working-class teen in '70s Rhode Island who, after a scrape with the law, is sent by dad Alec Baldwin to an exclusive prep school to "shape up." Once there, Hatosy faces antagonism from his snooty classmates and falls for pretty student Amy Smart. Jonathan Brandis, George Wendt also star. 96 min.
11-2401 Was $99.99 ❑*$19.99*

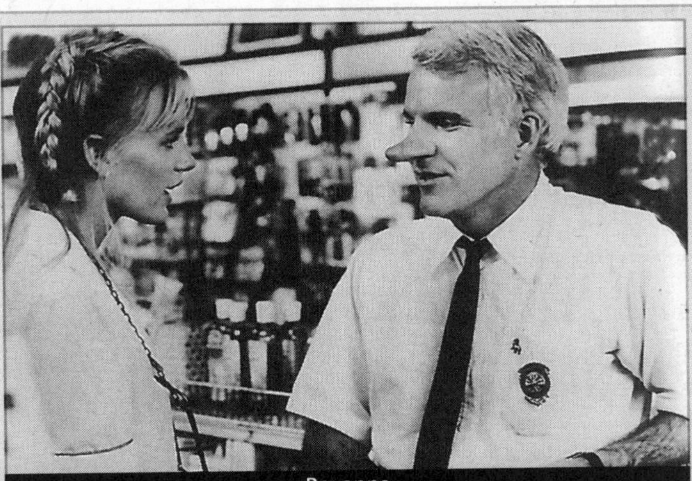
Roxanne

Steve Martin

The Jerk (1979)
Steve Martin in his first starring role is the Jerk, a gullible but likeable boob who rises from a Southern shanty to Beverly Hills, then back to poverty. Bernadette Peters and Jackie Mason co-star in this wild collection of pratfalls and sight gags. Co-written and directed by Carl Reiner. 104 min.
07-1021 Was $19.99 *$14.99*

Pennies From Heaven (1981)
Steve Martin is a sheet music salesman in the 1930s, torn between the two women in his life, in this unique musical drama that combines dazzling dance numbers with a stark look at Depression-era Hollywood. Co-stars Bernadette Peters, Christopher Walken and Jessica Harper; scripted by Dennis Potter from his British TV series. 107 min.
12-1218 *$19.99*

The Man With Two Brains (1983)
Steve Martin is Dr. Michael Hfuhruhurr, a scientist working towards creating the "perfect woman," using the beautiful body of evil wife Kathleen Turner and a very sweet woman's brain he has fallen in love with. With David Warner, Paul Benedict, and the voice of Sissy Spacek. 90 min.
19-1288 Was $19.99 *$14.99*

All Of Me (1984)
Steve Martin's got Lily Tomlin under his skin in this delightful comedy-fantasy. Thanks to a mixed-up mystic ceremony, dying socialite Tomlin's soul takes over half of lawyer Martin's body, and the inner battle for control makes for hilarious complications. With Victoria Tennant, Richard Libertini; Carl Reiner directs. 93 min.
47-7001 ❑*$14.99*

Roxanne (1987)
Steve Martin delivers the performance of his career and scripted this disarming romantic comedy about a modern-day "Cyrano" who must deal with his bumbling firemen's troupe, long-nose jokes, his unrequited love for Roxanne (Daryl Hannah) and the dumbstruck hunk he vicariously lives through. Co-stars Shelley Duvall, Rick Rossovich and Fred Willard. 107 min.
02-1794 Was $19.99 ❑*$14.99*

Planes, Trains And Automobiles (1987)
Every holiday traveller's worst nightmares come to life in this comic odyssey from John Hughes. Steve Martin's struggle to get from New York to Chicago for Thanksgiving is made worse by overbearing lout John Candy, whose presence he can't escape. And remember, "Those aren't PILLOWS!" 93 min.
06-1527 ❑*$14.99*

Dirty Rotten Scoundrels (1988)
Michael Caine and Steve Martin create two marvelously slimy characterizations as a pair of competing con artists who join forces to better take advantage of rich women vacationing on the Riviera. Sly and witty remake of the 1964 comedy "Bedtime Story" also stars Glenne Headly as the scoundrels' ultimate challenge; directed by Frank Oz. 110 min.
73-1038 ❑*$14.99*

Parenthood (1989)
Warm, wise and wonderful comedy from Ron Howard that traces the ups and downs of three generations of a family and celebrates the eternal parent-child relationship. Delightful cast includes Steve Martin, Mary Steenburgen, Rick Moranis, Dianne Wiest, Jason Robards, Martha Plimpton, Keanu Reeves. 120 min.
07-1635 Was $19.99 ❑*$14.99*

My Blue Heaven (1990)
When ex-gangster Steve Martin turns state's evidence and is placed in suburbia under the witness protection program, the result is an uproarious culture clash comedy. Rick Moranis co-stars as the stodgy FBI agent assigned to safeguard Martin and help him adjust to his new life. With Joan Cusack, Melanie Mayron. 95 min.
19-1814 *$14.99*

Father Of The Bride (1991)
In this funny and bittersweet remake of the 1950 Spencer Tracy film, Steve Martin plays the put-upon, overly anxious dad who must deal with all sorts of mishaps and financial demands when his daughter decides to get married. Diane Keaton, Martin Short, Kimberly Williams and B.D. Wong co-star. 105 min.
11-1615 Was $19.99 ❑*$14.99*

Father Of The Bride Part II (1995)
Harried pop Steve Martin is hit with a mid-life crisis when married daughter Kimberly Williams announces she's expecting, but his "baby blues" are doubled when he and wife Diane Keaton learn they have a "bundle of joy" on the way as well. Fast and funny sequel to the remake (or is it remake of a sequel?) also stars Martin Short, George Newbern. 106 min.
11-2013 Was $19.99 ❑*$14.99*

L.A. Story (1991)
Steve Martin salutes Los Angeles in this quirky romantic farce filled with hilarious and heartwarming moments. Martin plays a wacky TV weatherman whose life is changed when a freeway traffic sign miraculously offers him advice. Soon, he falls in love with an eccentric British journalist (played by then real-life wife Victoria Tennant). With Sarah Jessica Parker, Marilu Henner. 98 min.
27-6711 Was $19.99 ❑*$12.99*

Leap Of Faith (1992)
Steve Martin turns in a terrific performance as Jonas Nightengale, a travelling preacher who uses high-tech razzmatazz directed by associate Debra Winger to dupe scores of downtrodden believers in the Midwest. A stop at a small town may change things for the conning couple, as Winger falls for the local lawman (Liam Neeson) and Martin's healing abilities are put to the test. 110 min.
06-2110 Was $19.99 ❑*$14.99*

Housesitter (1992)
Charming, often hilarious farce with Steve Martin as a naive architect who builds a suburban dream house for his long-time girlfriend (Dana Delany). After she turns down his marriage offer, a wacky waitress with a penchant for lying (Goldie Hawn) moves into Martin's home, pretends to be his wife and insinuates her way into his family. Julie Harris, Donald Moffat co-star. 102 min.
07-1890 Was $19.99 ❑*$14.99*

Mixed Nuts (1994)
In this mirthful farce, Steve Martin is the leader of a Venice, California, suicide-prevention center that's facing eviction by its landlord. On a busy and unpredictable Christmas Eve, Martin and his associates are confronted by a transvestite, a serial killer, a homicidal Santa Claus and other zanies. Madeline Kahn, Robert Klein, Adam Sandler, Rita Wilson, Juliette Lewis co-star. 97 min.
02-2774 Was $89.99 ❑*$14.99*

A Simple Twist Of Fate (1994)
Inspired by "Silas Marner," this touching tale features Steve Martin (who also scripted) as a miserly recluse who adopts a cute little girl and soon witnesses his life changing for the better. Ten years later, her biological father, a wealthy politician, appears with plans to take his daughter back. Gabriel Byrne, Catherine O'Hara and Alana Austin co-star. 106 min.
11-1863 Was $89.99 ❑*$14.99*

Sgt. Bilko (1996)
Steve Martin is the scheming master sergeant who specializes in turning his backwater Army base's motor pool into an illegal gambling hall and running one scam after another in this laugh-filled translation of the popular '50s TV series. The cast also includes Dan Aykroyd as the always-oblivious Col. Hall, Phil Hartman as a rival of Martin, and Glenne Headly as Bilko's long-suffering girlfriend. 95 min.
07-2432 Was $99.99 ❑*$14.99*

The Spanish Prisoner (1998)
David Mamet's surprise-filled thriller features Campbell Scott as the inventor of "the Process," a mysterious formula that will make his company extremely rich. While at a conference in the Caribbean, Scott is befriended by businessman Steve Martin, who uses his cunning to make Scott suspicious of his employers' motives. With Rebecca Pidgeon, Ben Gazzara and Ricky Jay. 110 min.
02-3213 Was $99.99 ❑*$19.99*

Bowfinger (1999)
Funny and affecting Hollywood fable featuring (and written by) Steve Martin as a down-and-out producer whose new low-budget sci-fi epic, "Chubby Rain," stars action hero Eddie Murphy. The problem is that Murphy doesn't realize he's in the film, as Martin and crew film him secretly, and that his geeky brother (also played by Murphy) has been recruited to be his stand-in. Heather Graham, Christine Baranski and Jamie Kennedy also star. 97 min.
07-2801 Was $99.99 ❑*$14.99*

Please see our index for these other Steve Martin titles: *Grand Canyon • Joe Gould's Secret • Little Shop Of Horrors • The Out-Of-Towners • The Prince Of Egypt • Sgt. Pepper's Lonely Hearts Club Band • The Three Amigos*

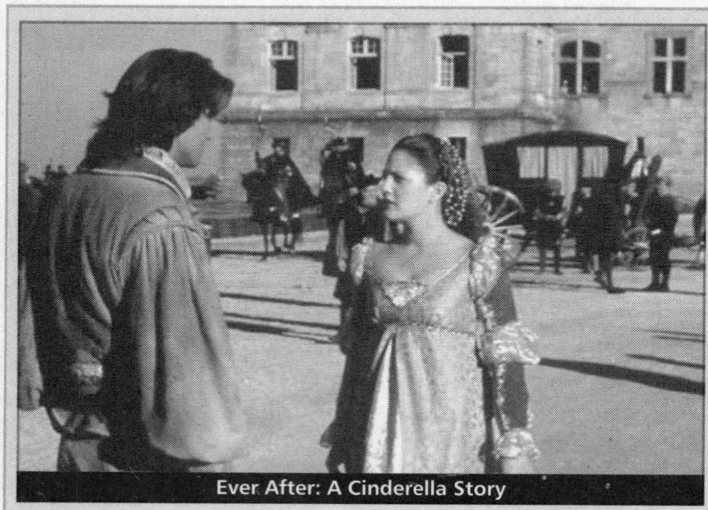

Ever After: A Cinderella Story

Drew Barrymore

Far From Home (1989)
Seedy suspenser stars Matt Frewer and Drew Barrymore as a father and daughter whose cross-country trip is upset when a group of psychotic ruffians terrorize them. Richard Masur, Jennifer Tilly and the great Dick Miller also star in this thriller. 86 min.
47-1979 Was $89.99 ***$12.99***

Guncrazy (1992)
Modern-day "Bonnie and Clyde"-style crime drama stars Drew Barrymore as a lonely Lolita who enters into a strange relationship with convict James Le-Gros. Once he's released he teaches her about guns and leads her into a parade of violence that sends them on the run from the police. With Ione Skye, Billy Drago, Michael Ironside and Joe Dallesandro. 97 min.
71-5264 ***□$12.99***

Motorama (1993)
Unusual comedy, destined for cult status, about a 10-year-old boy who leaves home, steals a car and takes off on a wild road adventure filled with all sorts of wacky characters. The incredible cast includes Garrett Morris, Mary Woronov, Jack Nance, Drew Barrymore, Robert Picardo, Sandy Baron and the great Dick Miller. 89 min.
02-2417 Was $89.99 ***$14.99***

No Place To Hide (1993)
A burned-out cop (Kris Kristofferson) finds himself involved in a brutal murder case that may lead to the upper ranks of the department. His only link to the killer is the victim's sister (Drew Barrymore), a pretty teenager who becomes the bait in a frightening game. Martin Landau, O.J. Simpson, Bruce Weitz also star. 90 min.
19-7094 Was $89.99 ***□$19.99***

Bad Girls (1994)
This action-packed Western set in 19th-century Colorado stars Madeleine Stowe as a prostitute who faces execution after killing an abusive client. She joins three other ladies of the evening (Andie MacDowell, Drew Barrymore and Mary Stuart Masterson) fleeing the law, searching for a new life in Oregon and finding trouble along the trail. Dermot Mulroney co-stars. 100 min.
04-2863 Was $89.99 ***□$14.99***

Mad Love (1995)
This "Generation X" road drama stars Drew Barrymore as the teenager whose free-spirited style draws the attention of Chris O'Donnell, a serious-minded, college-bound young man. During a sexy, thrill-filled trip to Mexico, O'Donnell discovers that his new girlfriend has a mysterious ailment. With Joan Allen, Matthew Lillard. 96 min.
11-1943 Was $19.99 ***□$14.99***

Boys On The Side (1995)
Raucous, heartwarming gals-on-the-road odyssey with lesbian lounge singer Whoopi Goldberg and real estate salesperson Mary-Louise Parker heading on a cross-country car trip. Along the way they're joined by flirtatious Drew Barrymore, and before they reach their Southern California destination, the trio encounters a series of happy and sad surprises. 117 min.
19-2363 Was $19.99 ***□$14.99***

Ever After: A Cinderella Story (1998)
The beloved children's fable gets a lush, more mature revamping in this romantic tale set in 16th-century France. Drew Barrymore stars as an independent young woman whose landowner father dies, leaving the family farm and Barrymore in the not-so-tender care of stepmother Anjelica Huston and her daughters. Dougray Scott plays the handsome prince attracted to Barrymore's feisty spirit, and Patrick Godfrey is "fairy godfather" Leonardo Da Vinci. 120 min.
04-3790 Was $19.99 ***□$14.99***

Home Fries (1998)
Help yourself to some down-home dark comedy with this romantic farce. Drew Barrymore is a single, pregnant fast-food worker who catches the eye of fellow employee Luke Wilson. Unknown to Barrymore, though, Wilson's interested in her because he and brother Jake Busey think she may have overheard them bumping off their philandering father at their crazed mother's request. Catherine O'Hara, Shelley Duvall also star. 93 min.
19-2850 Was $99.99 ***□$14.99***

Best Men (1998)
Offbeat comedy with action and dramatic elements tells of a group of friends heading to a wedding who are caught in the middle of a showdown with police when one of the pals—an ex-con—decides to rob a bank. Wild events soon unfold when the bride-to-be arrives on the scene. Dean Cain, Andy Dick, Luke Wilson, Sean Patrick Flanery and Drew Barrymore star. 89 min.
73-1306 Was $59.99 ***□$14.99***

Never Been Kissed (1999)
Clever comedy stars Drew Barrymore as a twentysomething journalist given the career-making assignment of attending a high school undercover, and who soon discovers that adolescence still hasn't gotten any less traumatic. Leelee Sobieski, David Arquette, Molly Shannon co-star. 108 min.
04-3863 Was $99.99 ***□$14.99***

Wishful Thinking (1999)
James Le Gros is an eccentric movie projectionist who moves in with veterinarian's assistant Jennifer Beals, but can't quite get the feel of a steady relationship. Making things even more complicated is co-worker Drew Barrymore, who draws Le Gros' attention. Jon Stewart and Eric Thal also star in this comedy that features several unusual fantasy scenes. 90 min.
11-2324 Was $99.99 ***□$19.99***

Please see our index for these other Drew Barrymore titles: *Altered States • The Amy Fisher Story • Cat's Eye • E.T. The Extra-Terrestrial • Everyone Says I Love You • Firestarter • Poison Ivy • Scream • See You In The Morning • Titan A.E. • The Wedding Singer*

The Real Howard Spitz (1998)
A down-on-his-luck gumshoe gets a chance at redemption when he meets a spirited 8-year-old who realizes that he would be a natural at writing children's books. However, he makes a promise to help her and her mother find the kid's real father, and that's where the real soul searching begins. Kelsey Grammer and Amanda Donohoe star. 93 min.
27-7079 Was $19.99 ***□$14.99***

Ringmaster (1998)
You'll believe a family can fight on TV. Pop culture phenom Jerry Springer makes his starring film debut, playing, of all things, the host of a syndicated talk show that gives ordinary folks the chance to air their dirty laundry in public. Things get hectic—and hilarious—as unfaithful spouses, cheating boyfriends and assorted misfits arrive for their on-camera showdowns. Molly Hagan, Jaime Pressly, Wendy Raquel Robinson also star. 95 min.
27-7105 Was $99.99 ***□$14.99***

The Breaks (1999)
In one day, Derrick King (Mitch Mullany), a white boy raised in the South Central L.A. hood, has a series of hilarious adventures with his pal Chris (Carl Anthony Payne II) after his mother asks him to get a carton of milk. The two friends encounter drug lords, a gay S&M duo and a pimp being chased by racist cops. With Loretta Devine, basketball star Gary Payton and George Clinton. 86 min.
27-7194 Was $99.99 ***□$14.99***

Deal Of A Lifetime (1999)
Teenage loser Henry Spooner would do just about anything to be one of the popular guys that all the girls go for. So when Satan's agent offers him a date with the queen of the high school in exchange for his soul, Henry jumps at the chance in this comedic tale of temptation and redemption. Kevin Pollak, Michael Goorjian, Jennifer Rubin star. 95 min.
12-3327 ***□$99.99***

The Waiting Game (1999)
Peter's Backyard, a Manhattan restaurant, is the second home for a group of aspiring actors and actresses who wait tables there. While toiling with their jobs the quirky crew must deal with everything from annoying diners to thespian lust and professional disappointment. This New York-flavored comedy stars Will Arnett, Terumi Matthews, Dwight Ewell. 81 min.
22-9049 ***$79.99***

Wirey Spindell (1999)
Wirey Spindell has a problem: he's about to get married, but for some reason he can't make love his fiancée. This compels Wirey to examine his life from childhood to the present—in an array of flashbacks filled with sex, drugs and junk food—to try and make sense of himself. Writer/director/star Eric Schaffer's offbeat comedy also features Callie Thorne, Eric Mabius. 101 min.
53-6940 ***$89.99***

Movie In Your Face (1992)
In the tradition of Woody Allen's classic "What's Up, Tiger Lily?," this gangster epic from Hong Kong has been Americanized with all-new zany dialogue and the appearance of detective comic Tommy Sledge. 85 min.
53-6045 Was $89.99 ***$39.99***

The 24 Hour Woman (1999)
Rosie Perez is a producer of a New York morning TV show whose pregnancy is announced without her knowledge over the air. Her hectic life becomes even more chaotic when she has to deal with her new baby, her workaholic hubby, job responsibilities and a tough boss. This witty domestic fable from Nancy Savoca ("True Love") also stars Marianne Jean-Baptiste, Diego Serrano. 92 min.
27-7119 ***□$99.99***

Exit To Eden (1994)
Strait-laced New York cops Dan Aykroyd and Rosie O'Donnell get laced up in some bizarre leather outfits when they go undercover at an exotic island resort catering to the S&M crowd, in director Garry Marshall's kinky comedy based on a novel by Anne Rice. With Dana Delany, Paul Mercurio, Iman. 120 min.
44-1983 Was $19.99 ***□$14.99***

Nothing (1999)
Part documentary and part comedy, Evan Aaronson's acclaimed film follows the Gen-Xer on a cinematic voyage of self-discovery, trying to figure out why his life "never shaped up like [he] planned" through interviews with family and friends, phone calls and filmed encounters with women. 85 min.
22-9021 ***$29.99***

Wagons East! (1994)
Slapstick reverse-frontier saga stars John Candy as an alcoholic wagon master called on to lead disgruntled settler Richard Lewis and the townsfolk of Prosperity back to the happier environs of St. Louis. Along the route, the wagon train encounters hired guns, Indians and more. Ellen Greene, John C. McGinley and Robert Picardo also star. 107 min.
27-6895 Was $89.99 ***□$14.99***

The Object Of Beauty (1991)
This effervescent comedy about love and money stars John Malkovich and Andie MacDowell as Americans stranded, penniless and over their credit limit, in a luxury hotel in London. Their only way out of the financial predicament is selling a rare Henry Moore statue, but when it disappears, even more complications ensue. Joss Ackland, Peter Riegert and Lolita Davidovich also star. 105 min.
27-6720 Was $89.99 ***□$14.99***

Italian Movie (1994)
Leonardo, a well-meaning Brooklyn guy with financial problems, becomes a male escort in order to get out of trouble. But will he earn enough to keep debt collectors, his fashion-conscious wife, his mother-in-law and others happy? James Gandolfini, Rita Moreno and Caprice Benedetti star in this tale of love, lust and pizza. 95 min.
22-9025 Was $79.99 ***$29.99***

...And God Spoke (1994)
Remember those pretentious religious epics from the '50s and '60s? This sly Hollywood spoof follows a director/producer team who switch from sex comedies to a big-budget Biblical drama. Among the obstacles they face are a Noah's Ark that won't fit on the set, a product placement deal with Coca-Cola, and casting choices like Lou Ferrigno as Cain, Eve Plumb as Noah's wife, and Soupy Sales as Moses. Marvin Handleman, Clive Walton also star. 82 min.
27-6902 Was $89.99 ***□$14.99***

A Little Bit Of Soul (1998)
Science and Satanism down under are the themes of this outrageous dark comedy from Australian filmmaker Peter Duncan ("Children of the Revolution"). David Wenham and Frances O'Connor are rival antiaging researchers and ex-lovers who are invited for a weekend at a potential backer's country estate. Unknown to them, their hosts, aging beauty queen Heather Mitchell and government official Geoffrey Rush, have their own bizarre reasons for funding their projects. 86 min.
22-9037 ***$79.99***

Critical Care (1997)
Cynical young doctor James Spader finds his ideals are among the first things to go—and a patient or two may follow—as he is caught up in a variety of ethical and romantic complications in director Sidney Lumet's darkly funny look at the modern American medical industry. Kyra Sedgwick, Helen Mirren, Anne Bancroft and Albert Brooks also star. 109 min.
27-7055 Was $99.99 ***□$19.99***

Hotel de Love (1997)
Breezy and poignant at the same time, this independent comedy tracks the romantic travails of fraternal twin brothers, one of whom manages a campy, theme-roomed "honeymoon hotel." As if overseeing their parents' wedding-vow renewal wasn't stressful enough, the siblings have to cope with the arrival at the hotel of the woman they both fell in love with 10 years earlier. Aden Young, Simon Bossell and Saffron Burrows star. 93 min.
27-7014 Was $99.99 ***□$14.99***

I Went Down (1998)
Gritty, often hilarious Irish crime story about Git, an ex-con fresh out of the slammer who takes an assignment that has him kidnapping Frank Grogan, a mobster that owes a local hood money. Joining Git is Bunny, a hefty small-time crook with a surprising sensitive streak. The job gets more dangerous and funnier as it goes on. Brendan Gleason, Peter McDonald star. 111 min.
27-7093 ***□$89.99***

Frogs For Snakes (1999)
Off-the-wall dark comedy stars Barbara Hershey as an out-of-work actress who pays the bills by serving as a "debt collector" for her ex, gangster-theatrical producer Robbie Coltrane. When lover John Leguizamo is murdered, Hershey attempts to leave the gang, even as her fellow actors are killing each other to land parts in Coltrane's production of "American Buffalo." With Debi Mazar, Lisa Marie, Harry Hamlin. 98 min.
27-7139 Was $99.99 ***□$14.99***

Short Time (1990)
When police detective Dabney Coleman is erroneously told he has a terminal illness, he throws caution to the wind in order to die in the line of duty and secure pension benefits for his family. His daredevil escapades (and amazing escapes) form the basis of this zippy action/comedy. Teri Garr, Matt Frewer co-star. 97 min.
27-6685 Was $19.99 ***$14.99***

Repossessed (1990)
For laughs that'll have your head spinning, watch what happens when Linda Blair gets caught up in some hellishly hilarious hi-jinks. This outrageous "Exorcist" parody also stars Leslie Nielsen, Ned Beatty. 89 min.
27-6692 Was $89.99 ***$14.99***

Drop Dead Fred (1991)
Comic fantasy starring Phoebe Cates as a recently divorced woman who calls on her imaginary childhood friend to help her out of dire emotional straits. Rik Mayall, Marsha Mason, Tim Matheson and Carrie Fisher co-star in this wild romp. 103 min.
27-6724 Was $19.99 ***□$14.99***

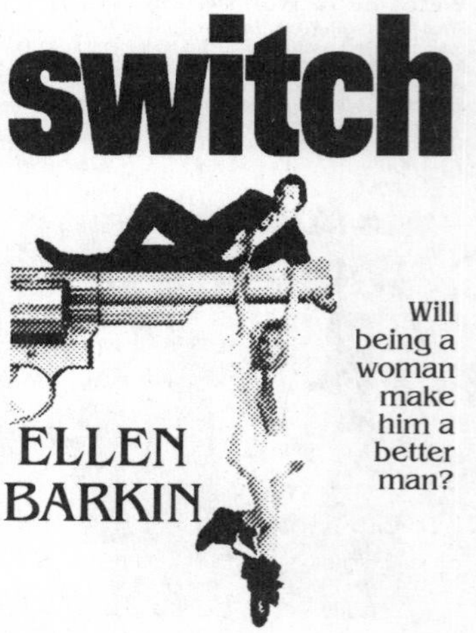
switch
ELLEN
BARKIN
Will being a woman make him a better man?

Switch (1991)
This lively farce from Blake Edwards tells the story of a chauvinistic advertising executive who returns to Earth as a woman after being drowned by a group of hateful girlfriends. The he-in-she clothing and body soon learns an important lesson in relations between the sexes. Ellen Barkin, Jimmy Smits, JoBeth Williams and Lorraine Bracco star. 102 min.
44-1815 Was $19.99 ***□$14.99***

House Of Pancakes (1997)
Twisted Gen-X black comedy about a guy looking to have the perfect first date with the girl of his dreams. However, when a batch of his eccentric friends and roommates show up at his doorstep out of the blue, not only does he find his perfect evening going down the tubes, but one of the "guests" might be a serial killer. Writer/director Onur Tukel's debut feature stars a bright young cast. 80 min.
73-9248 **$59.99**

Cut Throats (1994)
An insomniac thinks he's solved his problems when he uses a sleep-inducing tape featuring the sound of waves. But he soon discovers that he's addicted to the tape, and his working and waking hours quickly take on nightmarish dimensions. A dark, direct-to-video comedy. 80 min.
73-9173 **$19.99**

Snapshots From A .500 Season (1999)
A winning look at mediocrity, this comedy focuses on a college soccer player whose teammates seem to care more about partying than being successful on the field. Despite his new girlfriend's attention, can he adjust to the pervasive "win one, lose one" atmosphere? Daniel Kucan, Soomi Kim star. 90 min.
73-9318 **$59.99**

Sex & The Single Guy (1999)
This witty slacker comedy tells of three roommates desperately in search of Ms. Right. But their luck seems to be changing when one meets a beautiful ballet dancer, another finds a kinky New Age body artist through a personal ad, and roommate number three, a comedian, lives his life vicariously through his pals. Christian Zimmerman and Roger Harrell star. 90 min.
73-9319 **$59.99**

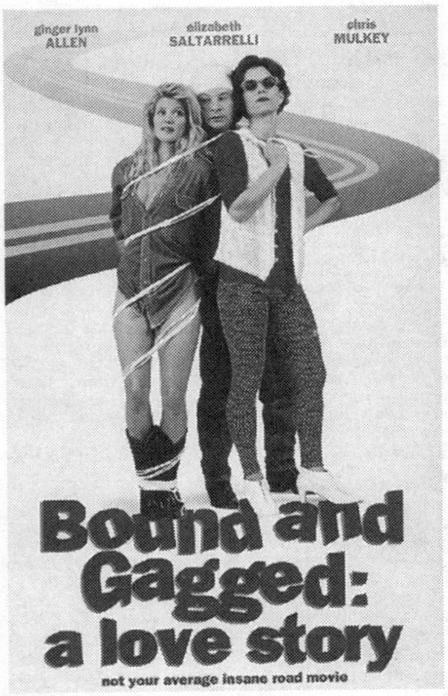

Bound And Gagged: A Love Story (1993)
Sexy, free-spirited road comedy starring former porn starlet Ginger Lynn Allen as a woman who is "saved" from her abusive husband by a couple of friends. The three take off on a raunchy, darkly funny auto odyssey across the state of Minnesota. Chris Mulkey and Karen Black also star. 96 min.
72-9026 Was $89.99 **$14.99**

The Return Of The King (1997)
Wildly inventive mockumentary salute to "the King" in which Elvis Presley is not really dead, he's just heavier and living in Wisconsin. In order to prove its point, the film links supernatural phenomena, coincidence and phone calls. Steve Strangio and Bobby Weill star. 70 min.
73-9220 **$14.99**

Loofa (1998)
After financing for their first movie falters, two neophyte filmmakers decide to shoot the project cheaply and guerrilla style. The unpredictable process of finishing the film with little funds is then chronicled in satiric fashion in this stylish tribute to indie filmmaking. With Mark Hanson, Scarlette McAllister and John Steakley.
73-9290 **$24.99**

Braindrainer (1998)
This sci-fi spoof salutes the classics of the 1950s in its tale of an alien life form, resembling a rock, which falls to Earth and causes all sorts of problems. It feeds on humans, sucking their brains dry, and eventually threatens the scientists who plan to destroy it. Sydelle Pittas, Michelle Leibowitz star.
73-9291 **$24.99**

Apocalypse Bop (1999)
Four years after he disappeared after throwing a wild party, Kurt Swann returns as mysteriously as he vanished. His high school slacker pals gather for the get-together near a graveyard and wild things begin to occur: passion, violence, guests disappearing. This wild black comedy stars Andre Duhamel. 90 min.
73-9306 **$59.99**

Bimbos B.C. (1992)
A group of scantily-clad cave gals are joined by a sword-swinging barbarian beauty as they search for a cure for their queen, who has been poisoned by a radioactive creature. On their journey, they encounter monsters and an evil ruler. Wild fantasy-comedy stars Gina Rydeen, Veronica Orr, Jenny Admire. 85 min.
73-9039 Was $19.99 **$14.99**

Madhouse (1990)
A kooky, outrageous comedy starring Kirstie Alley and John Larroquette as a yuppie couple whose new home is turned into a funhouse of wackiness when they are visited by annoying relatives, zany neighbors and ruthless gang members. With Alison LaPlaca and John Diehl. 90 min.
73-1081 **$14.99**

Mystery Date (1991)
Are you ready for this "Mystery Date," a wacky, high-spirited comic adventure? It's about a shy teenager who uses his brother's advice, hair style and credit cards to date the girl of his dreams and winds up pursued by crooked cops, a zany delivery man and the Chinese mob. With Ethan Hawke, Teri Polo, Fisher Stevens and B.D. Wong. 98 min.
73-1114 Was $89.99 **$14.99**

Married To It (1993)
Delightful comedy-drama about the trials and tribulations of three couples trying to make their marriages work in the stress-filled '90s. Cybill Shepherd, Ron Silver, Beau Bridges, Stockard Channing, Mary Stuart Masterson and Robert Sean Leonard star. 112 min.
73-1134 Was $89.99 **$14.99**

My New Advisor (1999)
Quirky road comedy concerning the adventures of a slacker grad student, a cantankerous professor and the professor's trouble-making teenage daughter during a trip to a conference in a 1960 Oldsmobile. When their car goes kaput, the trio encounter bikers, artists, and a gun-toting waitress on the way to their destination. With a bright young cast.
73-9344 **$39.99**

Jack And His Friends (1993)
A middle-aged shoe salesman has an unforgettable day when his wife throws him out of the house and he's kidnapped at gunpoint by a couple on the run from the law. Lust, murder and other surprises ensue when the odd trio hide out at the salesman's summer home in this off-the-wall satire. Allen Garfield, Judy Reyes and Sam Rockwell star. 93 min.
74-3002 **$79.99**

Me And The Mob (1994)
A would-be author looking for book material desperately tries to join the mob, but his comical bumbling will do more to bring down organized crime than an army of Untouchables! Manic Mafia laughfest features James Lorinz, Tony Darrow and a special appearance by Sandra Bullock. 85 min.
74-3013 **$49.99**

My Life's In Turnaround (1994)
Wacky, off-the-wall, pseudo-documentary comedy detailing the efforts of two best friends, a bartender and a cab driver, who decide to make a movie, but have no idea what the movie should be about or how to go about producing it. Phoebe Cates, Martha Plimpton and Casey Siemaszko play themselves in this screwy satire, written and directed by co-stars Eric Schaeffer and Donal Lardner Ward. 84 min.
74-3016 **$89.99**

The Naked Detective (1996)
It's a wild "film nude-oir" as down-and-out private dick Sam Drake is called on to find out who's trying to murder a wealthy old man. During the investigation, Sam encounters a number of gorgeous women—the old man's wife, nurse, maid and daughter-in-law, among them—who are interested in him. Jim Gardiner, Julia Parton star. Unrated version; 90 min.
74-3038 **$89.99**

Breathing Room (1996)
Set in New York City around Christmastime, this clever romantic tale focuses on Kathy and David, a couple struggling with their relationship who decide to stop seeing each other for a month. During this time, they face some tough decisions about romantic and work-related opportunities. Dan Futterman, Susan Floyd star. 90 min.
74-3040 **$89.99**

Dying To Get Rich (1998)
Deadly funny dark comedy stars Nastassja Kinski as a woman out to cash in on ex-husband Adrian Paul's life insurance by having him bumped off. After boyfriend Billy Zane hires hit men Michael Biehn and Rob Schneider, who promptly bumble the assignment, Kinski sends biker ex-lover Dan Aykroyd to the hospital to finish the job. John Landis ("Animal House") directs. AKA: "Susan's Plan." 90 min.
75-5065 **$89.99**

The Blair Princess Project (1999)
This hilarious spoof of "The Blair Witch Project" concerns three Jewish-American "princesses" who encounter danger while searching for friend Blair Rosenfarb's wedding. The laughs come fast and furious in this right-on satire. Also includes "Crazy Connected Thing," another short by director Paula Goldberg. 20 min.
76-2067 **$14.99**

Slaves Of Hollywood (1999)
Winning independent satire centers on a group of recent college grads who start at the bottom of the ladder in Hollywood, where they aspire to become executives one day. The glitter of Tinseltown soon fades as they take menial jobs, but they hold onto their dreams of becoming players. Hill Harper and Amy Lyndon star. 80 min.
76-2088 **$39.99**

In Between (1992)
Three strangers meet in a mysterious place one morning and soon realize that they've died and are, in fact, in purgatory, and must evaluate their lives before they journey to the next stop. Metaphysical comedy-drama stars Wings Hauser, Robin Mattson, Alexandra Paul and Robert Forster. 92 min.
76-9035 Was $19.99 **$14.99**

Pizza Man (1992)
In this outrageous political satire, an L.A. pizza man meets with shoot-outs, car chases and sexy dames, along with an incredible government conspiracy, while attempting to deliver an extra-large anchovy pie. Annabelle Gurwitch and "Politcally Incorrect" host Bill Maher star; written and directed by "J.D. Athens" (J.F. Lawton, screenwriter of "Pretty Woman"). 90 min.
76-9038 Was $79.99 **$14.99**

Wishman (1993)
A 2-million-year-old genie loses his bottle and finds himself in Beverly Hills in the possession of a Hollywood slickster. The two strike a deal: the hustler will find the genie's bottle if the genie locates the girl of his dreams. Paul LeMat, Geoffrey Lewis, Paul Gleason and Brion James star. 89 min.
76-9046 Was $19.99 **$14.99**

The Magic Bubble (1993)
A woman dreads turning 40, until a birthday gift of a bottle of enchanted bubbles grants her wish of never knowing her age and lets her live life to the fullest. Diane Salinger, Colleen Camp, Wallace Shawn and John Calvin star. 90 min.
76-9051 Was $89.99 **$14.99**

I Didn't Think You Didn't Know I Wasn't Dead (1999)
Edgy independent comedy in which a woman arrives in the Midwest to help her brother with his troubled "okra" farm. After she starts seeing an old flame again, the woman is spied on by a humane society worker and a detective who believe the woman and friend are involved in an illegal cockfighting operation. Zany complications abound in this offbeat essay.
73-9343 **$39.99**

Slacker (1991)
A one-of-a-kind pseudo-documentary about the obsessions of the oddball residents of Austin, Texas, this hilarious film celebrates the lifestyle of "slacking" while commenting subtly on politics, relationships and the media. As captured by director Richard Linklater, Austin's a place where you can purchase Madonna's pap smear, buy a book on JFK called "Conspiracy a-Go-Go" or just hang out. 97 min.
73-1120 Was $19.99 **$14.99**

Dazed And Confused (1993)
"The movie that inhales" is a fractured farce set on the last day of school in 1976 in which a diverse group of Austin, Texas, high school students get stoned, partake in hazing pranks, find romance and contemplate the future. Writer/director Richard Linklater's ("Slacker") far-out flashback stars Jason London, Milla Jovovich, Joey Lauren Adams, Ben Affleck, Parker Posey and Matthew McConaughey and features a great period soundtrack. 94 min.
07-2056 Was $19.99 **$14.99**

Before Sunrise (1995)
American traveller Ethan Hawke and French student Julie Delpy meet while on a Vienna-bound train and share a mutual attraction. With less than 24 hours before having to go their separate ways, the two decide to explore their feelings and Vienna at the same time. A change of pace for director Richard Linklater, this delicate romance features affecting performances and gorgeous scenery. 101 min.
02-2777 Was $19.99 **$14.99**

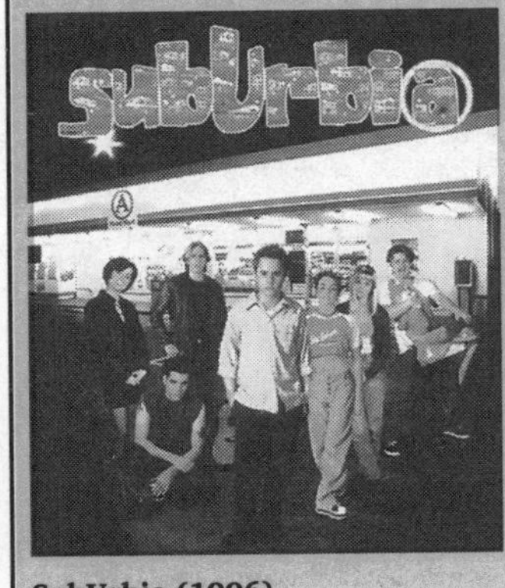

SubUrbia (1996)
Eric Bogosian's stageplay on the seamy underside of suburban life is brought to the screen by twentysomething angstmeister Richard Linklater, and the result is a funny, bitter and compelling look at a group of former high school pals who still hang out in the local convenience store parking lot. Steve Zahn, Nicky Watt, Amie Carey, Giovanni Ribisi and the ubiquitous Parker Posey head the ensemble cast. 118 min.
19-2565 Was $99.99 **$14.99**

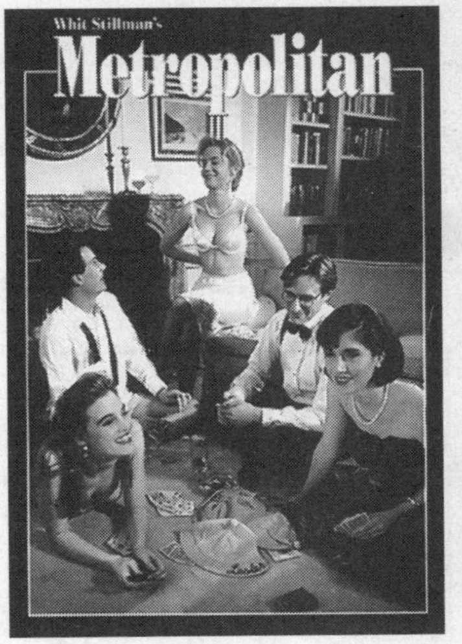

Metropolitan (1990)
Elegant, witty social comedy about a liberal, near-destitute preppie who gets involved with a group of Manhattan debutantes and escorts during the waning days of their popularity. Carolyn Farina, Edward Clements and Christopher Eigeman star in this first effort by writer-director Whit Stillman. 98 min.
02-2087 Was $89.99 **$19.99**

Drop Dead Rock (1995)
Raucous rock-and-roll comedy about a struggling band who decide a quick way to stardom is to kidnap a famous singer and convince him to listen to their music. When the abducted star's wife and manager conspire to hire a hit man to bump him off, a wild series of chases and escapes follows. Adam Ant, Debora Harry, Ian Maynard star. 93 min.
85-1326 **$14.99**

Busted (1996)
This sex-crazed squadroom of comical cops may not be solving many crimes, but they always manage to get their man...or woman. Corey Feldman and Corey Haim lead the racy, wacky, zany fun in this arresting comedy that also stars Mariana Morgan, Ava Fabian and special guest stars Julie Strain and Elliott Gould. 90 min.
86-1109 Was $89.99 **$14.99**

Bandwagon (1997)
This funny and engaging film looks at the rise of Circus Monkey, a neophyte rock group from Raleigh, North Carolina. Hilarity abounds during the group's first gig, while their initial video is being filmed, on tour, when they hire a legendary road manager and during other events. Kevin Corrigan, Matthew Hennessey and Lee Holmes star. 103 min.
85-5100 **$89.99**

Love Is All There Is (1996)
The feud between rival Bronx restaurateur families takes on a new intensity when one couple's son falls in love with the daughter of the other in this comic spin on the "Romeo and Juliet" legend from writer/director/co-stars Joseph Bologna and Renee Taylor. The hilarious ensemble cast also includes Barbara Carrera, Angelina Jolie, Lainie Kazan, Nathaniel Marston and Paul Sorvino. 105 min.
88-1125 Was $99.99 **$14.99**

Just A Little Harmless Sex (1999)
In this witty study of contemporary relationships, Alan's planned party for a friend at a strip club ends in disaster when he's caught with a hooker, leading wife Laura to kick him out. The couple are joined by their respective friends for commiseration and debate on the opposite sex, but fireworks go off when both groups accidentally meet at a nightclub. Alison Eastwood, Robert Mailhouse, Jonathan Silverman and Kimberly Williams star. 98 min.
86-1146 **$99.99**

Witch Academy (1993)
In this sexy farce, devil Robert Vaughn and disciple Priscilla Barnes make a pact with nerdy coed Veronica Carothers. In order to become part of her sorority's in-crowd, Carothers wants to know about sex—and he's the right fellow to teach her! The gal becomes the ultimate sex bomb—as well as a blood-seeking monster. Ruth Collins and Michelle Bauer also star in this scream queen-laden look at lust from Fred Olen Ray. AKA: "Little Witches." Uncut, unrated version.
73-9310 **$29.99**

Mob Story (1990)
From Lois Lane to Mafia dame...Margot Kidder is featured as the moll of a New York mob kingpin whose journey to Canada is complicated by an opposing gang of crooks who want to rub him out. John Vernon, Kate Vernon and Al Waxman also star in this fractured farce. 98 min.
77-5011 **$14.99**

Affairs Of The Heart (1993)
A sexy, zany comedy starring Penthouse Pet and frequent Howard Stern guest Amy Lynn Baxter as a gorgeous advice columnist who has no one to turn to for help but herself when she falls for a handsome stranger while on vacation. With Michael Montana. 90 min.
81-9008 **$89.99**

Pie In The Sky (1996)
An L.A. radio traffic reporter is left up in the air when his new job puts a strain on his relationship with his girlfriend in this high-flying romantic comedy. Josh Charles, Anne Heche, Christine Lahti and John Goodman star. 94 min.
02-5113 Was $99.99 ❑*$19.99*

Frank Finds Out (1999)
Engaging romantic comedy in which stockbroker Frank Johnson learns that his fiancé is cheating on him—with his own boss! For revenge, Johnson devises a plan to cash in on the stock market, ruin the illicit lovers' relationship and meet the girl he spoke to on a wrong number call. Matthew Todd Nolan, Damon Jones star. 90 min.
76-7480 *$79.99*

Bean (1997)
Rowan Atkinson's mischievous, accident-prone Mr. Bean makes the jump from TV to feature film with this slapstick comedy that had audiences laughing around the world. Sent by his London art museum bosses (who were happy to get rid of him) to oversee the moving of "Whistler's Mother" to an L.A. gallery, Bean proceeds to wreak transatlantic havoc on everyone who comes in contact with him. Peter MacNicol, Pamela Reed, Harris Yulin and Burt Reynolds also star. 91 min.
02-8812 Was $19.99 ❑*$14.99*

Bean (Letterboxed Version)
Also available in a theatrical, widescreen format. Includes 17 minutes of exclusive, never-before-seen outtakes.
02-8961 Was $19.99 ❑*$14.99*

Michael Keaton

Night Shift (1982)
Ron Howard's rollicking comedy hit stars Henry Winkler as a straight-arrow city morgue worker whose staid worklife is hilariously disrupted with the arrival of off-the-wall assistant Michael Keaton (his film debut), who uses their workplace to launch a call girl service. Shelley Long co-stars as a hooker with a heart of gold; look for a young Kevin Costner. 105 min.
19-1939 Was $19.99 *$14.99*

Mr. Mom (1983)
What happens when husband Michael Keaton loses his job and wife Teri Garr has to go to work, leaving him with the housework, the neighbors and the kids? Find out in this winning comedy, filled with nutty situations that'll leave you laughing until your toast burns. With Martin Mull, Ann Jillian, Christopher Lloyd. 90 min.
47-1167 *$14.99*

Johnny Dangerously (1984)
The classic gangster films of the '30s are sent up in this hilarious satire that stars Michael Keaton and Joe Piscopo as childhood enemies who later become gangland rivals. Marilu Henner, Peter Boyle and Maureen Stapleton also star. 90 min.
04-1849 ❑*$14.99*

Gung Ho (1986)
Ron Howard's hit comedy stars Michael Keaton as a hustler out to revive his depressed factory town by convincing a Japanese manufacturer to take over the auto plant. The Western workers, though, are dis-Oriented by their Eastern bosses' work habits. Gedde Watanabe, George Wendt. 111 min.
06-1378 ❑*$14.99*

Touch And Go (1986)
Pro hockey player Michael Keaton strikes up a friendship with a young street punk and discovers romance with his single mother (Maria Conchita Alonso) in this funny little sleeper. Co-stars Ajay Naidu, Maria Tucci, Jere Burns. 101 min.
44-1461 ❑*$14.99*

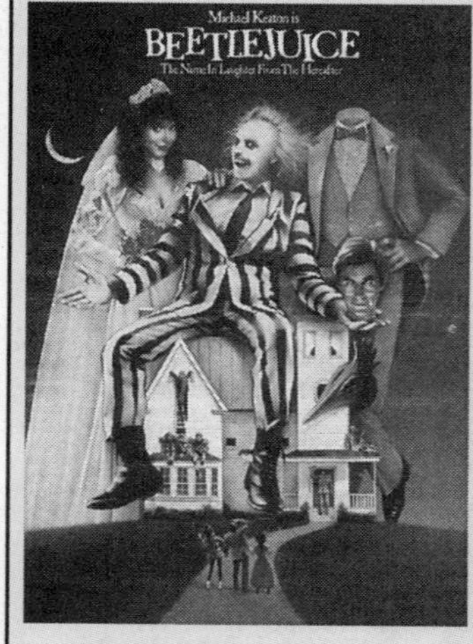
Michael Keaton is
BEETLEJUICE
The Name In Laughter From The Hereafter

Beetlejuice (1988)
Who do two newly-dead spirits go to when their home is taken over by obnoxious humans? The "bio-exorcist" known as "Beetlejuice," of course! Michael Keaton is frighteningly funny as the "ghost with the most" in the hit horror comedy from director Tim Burton. Geena Davis, Alec Baldwin, Catherine O'Hara and Winona Ryder co-star. 92 min.
19-1646 ❑*$14.99*

Clean And Sober (1988)
In a bravura performance, Michael Keaton is a yuppie cocaine user whose obsessive need for the drug and refusal to admit his addiction slowly tears his life apart. One of the finest and most compelling anti-drug films to emerge from modern Hollywood; with Morgan Freeman, Kathy Baker, M. Emmet Walsh. 124 min.
19-1677 ❑*$14.99*

PACIFIC HEIGHTS

Pacific Heights (1990)
Yuppie San Francisco landlords Melanie Griffith and Matthew Modine rent an apartment in their house to Michael Keaton, unaware that his smooth facade hides a sadistic sociopath. He begins terrorizing the couple and drives them into a violent confrontation in order to keep their home. John Schlesinger directs this top-notch thriller. 102 min.
04-2417 Was $19.99 ❑*$14.99*

My Life (1993)
After he's diagnosed with a terminal disease, L.A. public relations man Michael Keaton re-examines his life, reacquaints himself with his family and begins making a video for his unborn child. Nicole Kidman, Haing S. Ngor and Queen Latifah co-star in this poignant film, written and directed by Bruce Joel Rubin, the scripter of "Ghost." 117 min.
02-2605 Was $19.99 ❑*$14.99*

The Paper (1994)
Energized, entertaining look at the newspaper world from Ron Howard centering on a day in the life of the fictional New York Sun tabloid. Metro editor Michael Keaton's struggle to uncover the truth behind a murder story while fighting deadlines puts him at odds with managing editor Glenn Close and pregnant wife Marisa Tomei. With Robert Duvall, Randy Quaid, Jason Alexander. 112 min.
07-2193 Was $19.99 ❑*$14.99*

Speechless (1994)
The old adage "politics makes strange bedfellows" is given a comedic twist in this romantic tale featuring Michael Keaton and Geena Davis as rival speechwriters on opposite sides of the political fence who wind up falling in love. With Bonnie Bedelia, Christopher Reeve. 120 min.
12-2972 Was $89.99 ❑*$14.99*

Multiplicity (1996)
There's loads of laughs—and Michael Keatons—in this sci-fi comedy about a harried construction firm head trying to juggle his career and family life with wife Andie MacDowell and their two kids. A scientist working in the field of cloning produces another Keaton—this one a macho workaholic—but even he's not enough, so it's back to the drawing board for more clones. 117 min.
02-2963 Was $19.99 ❑*$14.99*

Multiplicity (Letterboxed Version)
Also available in a theatrical, widescreen format.
02-3151 ❑*$19.99*

Desperate Measures (1998)
Cop Andy Garcia is caught between his duty and his terminally ill son's life when the only DNA match for a bone marrow transplant the boy needs comes from a convicted murderer, sociopath Michael Keaton, who manages to escape hospital custody. Now Garcia must make sure Keaton stays alive, even as he tries to stop him from killing again, in director Barbet Schroeder's compelling thriller. Marcia Gay Harden, Brian Cox also star. 101 min.
02-3168 Was $99.99 ❑*$14.99*

Jack Frost (1998)
Michael Keaton is a blues musician, struggling to find time for his wife and son and burgeoning music career, who dies in an auto accident during a Christmas snowstorm. A year later, Keaton returns miraculously as a snowman and tries to get to know his son better. Kelly Preston, Mark Addy and Joseph Cross also star in this warm family tale featuring fine special effects. 102 min.
19-2907 Was $19.99 ❑*$14.99*

Please see our index for these other Michael Keaton titles: *Batman • Batman Returns • Jackie Brown • Much Ado About Nothing • Out Of Sight*

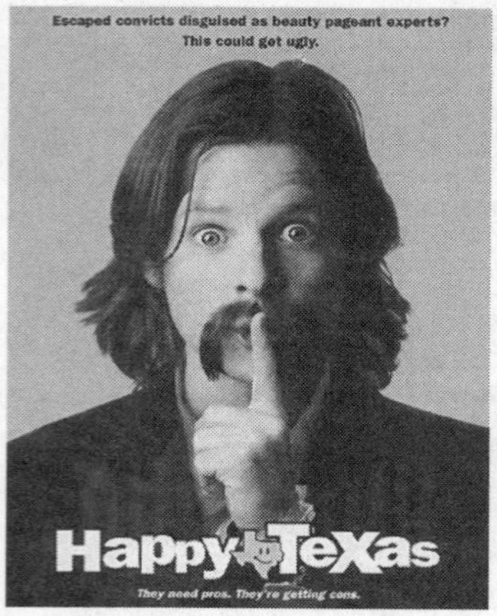
Escaped convicts disguised as beauty pageant experts?
This could get ugly.
Happy Texas
They need pros. They're getting cons.

Happy, Texas (1999)
This Sundance Film Festival hit stars Jeremy Notham and Steve Zahn as escaped cons who land in a small Texas town where they dodge authorities by posing as gay consultants for the annual "Little Miss Fresh Squeezed" beauty contest. The laughs really kick in when Notham falls for bank official Ally Walker while being courted by sheriff William H. Macy. 98 min.
11-2412 Was $99.99 ❑*$14.99*

Trial And Error (1997)
After a bachelor party leaves lawyer Jeff Daniels in no condition to take part in a fraud trial of his boss's relative, Daniels' best friend, out-of-work actor Michael Richards, assumes his identity in the courtroom and manages to set jurisprudence back 100 years. Charlize Theron and Rip Torn also star in this loopy legal comedy. 98 min.
02-5162 Was $99.99 ❑*$14.99*

Detroit Rock City (1999)
It's 1978, and four Ohio teenagers will let nothing, from angry parents to a lack of tickets, stop them from taking a wild road trip to Detroit to see their favorite band, Kiss, in concert. Raucous '70s-flavored comedy stars Edward Furlong, Giuseppe Andrews, James DeBello, Sam Huntington, Natasha Lyonne and, of course, Gene, Ace, Peter and Paul. 95 min.
02-5220 Was $99.99 ❑*$14.99*

Swing (1999)
Returning to his Liverpool home after a prison stint and a gift saxophone from cellmate Clarence Clemons, Hugo Speer ("The Full Monty") tries to form a swing band from among his local buddies and win back his former girlfriend (singer Lisa Stansfield), who wound up marrying the cop who arrested Speer, in this offbeat comedy. Rita Tushingham, Alexei Sayle, Tom Bell also star. 97 min.
11-2405 Was $99.99 ❑*$19.99*

Head Above Water (1997)
Beautiful Cameron Diaz, the new wife of judge Harvey Keitel, is looking forward to a vacation on the coast of Maine with her husband, but when ex-beau Billy Zane shows up while Keitel's away one night and winds up dying in their bed, a series of darkly funny calamities follows. Craig Sheffer also stars. 92 min.
02-5148 Was $99.99 ❑*$19.99*

The Arrangement (1998)
When Jake tells fiancée LuAnn that he had a one-night stand, it opens a can of worms, but he thinks he has it all figured out when he gives LuAnn the go-ahead to start seeing other guys. Jake is less than thrilled when she takes him up on his offer in this hip urban romance. Keith Davis, Billie James star.
82-9063 *$89.99*

Who's The Man? (1993)
Rappers Doctor Dré and Ed Lover, stars of "Yo! MTV Raps," make their big-screen debuts as two Harlem barbers who become cops and investigate why their neighborhood club is being shuttered in this comedic hip-hop whodunit. Guest appearances by Ice-T, Kris Kross, Salt 'n Pepa, Denis Leary and many others. 90 min.
02-5034 Was $19.99 ❑*$14.99*

My New Gun (1993)
Refreshingly offbeat comedy starring Diane Lane as a suburban housewife living a drab existence until her husband purchases a handgun for protection. When her enigmatic neighbor takes the weapon for unknown purposes, she becomes fascinated with it and the neighbor. James LeGros, Stephen Collins also star. 99 min.
02-5035 Was $89.99 *$19.99*

Three Of Hearts (1993)
Provocative romantic story concerning a male escort (William Baldwin) who is hired by a nurse (Kelly Lynch) to break the heart of her former lesbian lover (Sherilyn Fenn) in hopes she'll come back to her. Things get complicated when romance really sparks between the hustler and the hustlee. 103 min.
02-5036 Was $19.99 ❑*$14.99*

Faithful (1996)
Cher is a depressed Westchester, New York, housewife who gets a very unexpected 20th anniversary present from husband Ryan O'Neal: a visit from hit man Chazz Palminteri, hired by O'Neal to kill her, unless she can get him to switch targets. Dark comedy, written by Palminteri and directed by Paul Mazursky. 91 min.
02-5103 Was $99.99 ❑*$14.99*

A Thin Line Between Love & Hate (1996)
Martin Lawrence makes his directorial debut in this comic "Fatal Attraction"-style thriller, in which he plays a smooth-talking ladies' man who adds gorgeous Lynn Whitfield to his list of romantic conquests, but finds this "dream girl" turning his life into a nightmare of jealous rage. With Bobby Brown, Della Reese. 106 min.
02-5106 Was $19.99 ❑*$14.99*

B.A.P.S (1997)
Halle Berry and Natalie Desselle are the "Black American Princesses" who leave their Georgia waitressing jobs behind and fly to Hollywood for a rap video audition, only to wind up as the pampered houseguests of eccentric Beverly Hills millionaire Martin Landau, in this sassy culture-clash comedy from director Robert Townsend. 90 min.
02-5150 Was $99.99 ❑*$14.99*

The Ref (1994)
Rough-edged motormouth comic Denis Leary makes a hilarious starring film debut in this unsettling farce, playing a hostile thief who takes a feuding Connecticut family (including an argumentative husband and wife, their delinquent teenage son, and a nasty grandmother) hostage...and lives to regret it. Judy Davis, Kevin Spacey, Glynis Johns co-star. 97 min.
11-1800 Was $19.99 ❑*$14.99*

For Roseanna (1997)
Devoted husband Jean Reno promises to honor the wish of ailing wife Mercedes Ruehl that she will be buried in their Italian village's local cemetery near their late child. But with only three spaces left, Reno must go to outrageously funny lengths to make sure the town's latest departed don't get one of the precious plots. Offbeat and whimsical comedy also stars Polly Walker. AKA: "Roseanna's Grave." 95 min.
02-5165 Was $99.99 ❑*$19.99*

My Father, The Hero (1994)
In this Americanized version of a French farce, divorced father Gerard Depardieu takes his 14-year-old daughter on a vacation in the Bahamas to help their relationship. But when she claims that Dad is really her older lover in order to impress a resort worker she's fallen for, the lies escalate into comic calamity. Katherine Heigl, Dalton James co-star. 90 min.
11-1794 Was $19.99 ❑*$14.99*

Stiff Upper Lips (1998)
A spoof of costume dramas in the Merchant-Ivory/Jane Austen style, this hilarious comedy is set in 1908 England, where Cambridge graduate Samuel West invites college friend Robert Portal to his estate to meet nubile sister Prunella Scales. The plan to marry Scales off fails when she's rescued from drowning by a local laborer and West and Portal realize they have affections for each other. With Georgina Cates, Peter Ustinov. 87 min.
11-2462 ❑*$99.99*

Captain Jack (1999)
In the tradition of the classic Alec Guinness farces of the 1950s comes this story of Captain Jack (Bob Hoskins), an irascible sea captain trying to trace a voyage from England to the Arctic taken in 1791 by Captain Scorebury, his hero. The journey becomes a wild adventure with lots of laughs with a kooky crew, rough seas, stowaways and more. With Sadie Frost, Peter McDonald. 96 min.
50-8638 *$19.99*

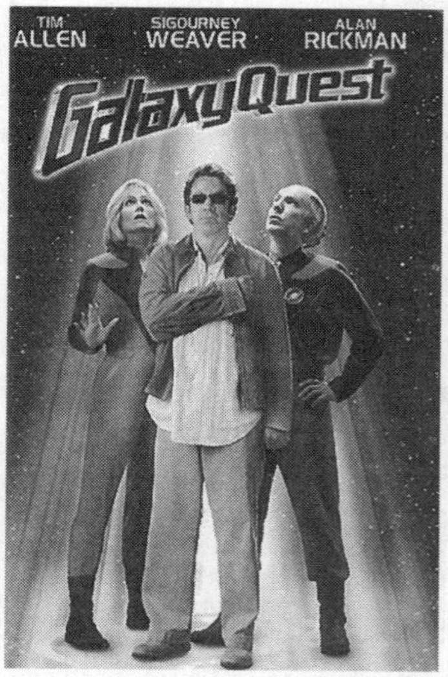
TIM ALLEN
SIGOURNEY WEAVER
ALAN RICKMAN
Galaxy Quest

Galaxy Quest (1999)
The cast of a late '70s sci-fi TV show (Tim Allen, Sigourney Weaver, Alan Rickman, Tony Shaloub, Daryl Mitchell), long since reduced to store openings and fan conventions, gets an unexpected job when they're recruited by aliens who thought the broadcasts were "historical documents" to help save their planet from invasion. Hit mix of action and satire also stars Sam Rockwell, Enrico Colantoni. 102 min.
07-2848 ❑*$22.99*

72 · COMEDY
MOVIES UNLIMITED
CALL · 1-800-4-MOVIES

What's New, Pussycat? (1965)
Zany, very '60s farce, written by Woody Allen, stars Peter O'Toole as a womanizing magazine editor who seeks help from psychiatrist Peter Sellers for his oversexed condition. Romy Schneider, Ursula Andress, Capucine and Woody himself also star; Tom Jones sings the title song. 108 min.
12-2107 *$19.99*

What's Up, Tiger Lily? (1966)
After getting his hands on a 1964 Japanese spy film called "Key of Keys," Woody Allen and his colleagues dubbed in their own dialogue, resulting in a hilarious search between rival gangs for a stolen recipe for "the world's greatest egg salad." Along with a wild barrage of one-liners, there's The Lovin' Spoonful in concert, a snake marrying a chicken, and "Phil Moscowitz, lovable rogue." 90 min.
47-1060 *$14.99*

Take The Money And Run (1969)
Woody Allen's debut as director/writer/star casts him as Virgil Starkweather, a bumbling, small-time crook who manages to fumble his way through a series of heists, from holding up pet stores to armored cars. Told in pseudo-documentary style, the classic crime film spoof co-stars Janet Margolin, Marcel Hillaire; narrated by Jackson Beck. 85 min.
04-1158 Letterboxed *$14.99*

Bananas (1971)
In one of Woody Allen's craziest comedies he plays Fielding Mellish, a sheepish product tester whose feelings for a political activist (then-wife Louise Lasser) draw him into a revolution brewing in the tiny Latin American country of San Marcos...and, ultimately, to the role of president. Co-stars Carlos Montalban and Howard Cosell as himself; look for an unbilled Sylvester Stallone. 82 min.
12-1995 *❑$14.99*

Play It Again, Sam (1972)
A recently divorced film freak (Woody Allen) tries to get back into the singles scene, with some advice on women from the ghost of Humphrey Bogart, in Herbert Ross' film version of Allen's uproarious play. With Diane Keaton, Tony Roberts, Susan Anspach and Jerry Lacy. 87 min.
06-1048 Remastered *$14.99*

Everything You Always Wanted To Know About Sex*... But Were Afraid To Ask (1972)
A frantically fractured look at sexual manners, complete with sexy sheep, giant breasts, chastity belts...and the oddest assortment of characters you'll ever see, all brought to you by Woody Allen. Gene Wilder, Burt Reynolds, Lynn Redgrave co-star. 88 min.
12-1157 Was $19.99 *$14.99*

Sleeper (1973)
It's Woody Allen's hilarious sci-fi romp, as a man frozen alive in 1973, wakes up 200 years later and finds himself an unlikely rebel against a totalitarian society. Diane Keaton co-stars, along with Jewish robots, killer pudding, a dictator's nose, and "a big chicken." Music by Preservation Hall Jazz Band. 88 min.
12-1865 Was $19.99 *❑$14.99*

Love And Death (1975)
Woody Allen takes playful pokes at 19th-century Russian literature and Ingmar Bergman movies with his uproarious satire about an unlikely war hero (Allen) who hopes to bring about an end to the Napoleonic Wars by assassinating the Little Corporal in Moscow. Co-stars Diane Keaton, Harold Gould, James Tolkan, Jessica Harper. 85 min.
12-1997 Was $19.99 *$14.99*

The Front (1976)
In a rare "acting only" turn, Woody Allen plays a hack writer who serves as a "front" for blacklisted TV scripters during the McCarthy era of the mid-'50s. Martin Ritt's acerbic comedic look at the "witch hunts," taken from personal experiences, also stars Andrea Marcovicci and Zero Mostel. 94 min.
02-1105 *$14.99*

Annie Hall (1977)
Winner of four Oscars (Best Picture, Director, Screenplay, Actress), Woody Allen's bittersweet romantic comedy, loosely based on his relationship with co-star Diane Keaton, features classic Allenisms on life in New York and California, cooking lobsters, and love's necessary pains. With Tony Roberts, Paul Simon; look for Jeff Goldblum and Sigourney Weaver. 94 min.
12-1819 Was $19.99 *$14.99*

Interiors (1978)
In his first straight drama, writer/director Woody Allen creates a compelling portrait of a splintered family whose coming together seems to both cause and cure their anxieties. Moody, nervously funny and starkly Bergmanesque. Diane Keaton, E.G. Marshall, Geraldine Page, Maureen Stapleton, Mary Beth Hurt star. 93 min.
12-1324 Was $79.99 *$14.99*

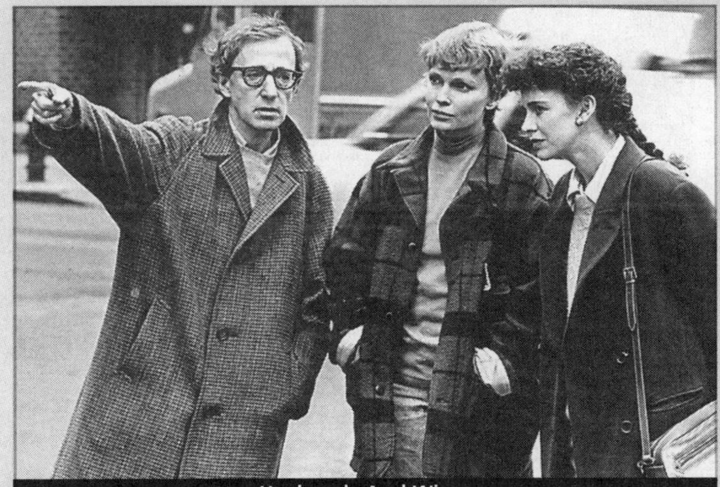
Husbands And Wives

Woody Allen

Manhattan (1979)
Woody Allen's hilarious and poignant look at modern relationships, set against Gershwin music and the splendid backdrop of the Big Apple. He's a TV writer, divorced from his lesbian ex-wife (Meryl Streep), dating a teen-age girl (Mariel Hemingway), and in love with his married best friend's girl (Diane Keaton). 96 min.
12-1369 Letterboxed *$14.99*

Stardust Memories (1980)
While attending a movie seminar weekend, a comedy filmmaker is plagued by sycophantic fans, haunted by past love affairs and thwarted in his attempts to do more serious work. Acerbic (and autobiographical?) Woody Allen film also stars Charlotte Rampling, Jessica Harper, Marie-Christine Barrault and Tony Roberts. 88 min.
12-2675 *$14.99*

Husbands And Wives (1992)
Woody Allen's study of romance and infidelity tells of two couples and their troubled relationships. Allen plays an English professor who falls for young student Juliette Lewis when his marriage to Mia Farrow hits the skids; while Sydney Pollack leaves Judy Davis and takes up with a sexy aerobics instructor, only to have second thoughts. Liam Neeson, Lysette Anthony also star. 107 min.
02-2374 Was $89.99 *❑$19.99*

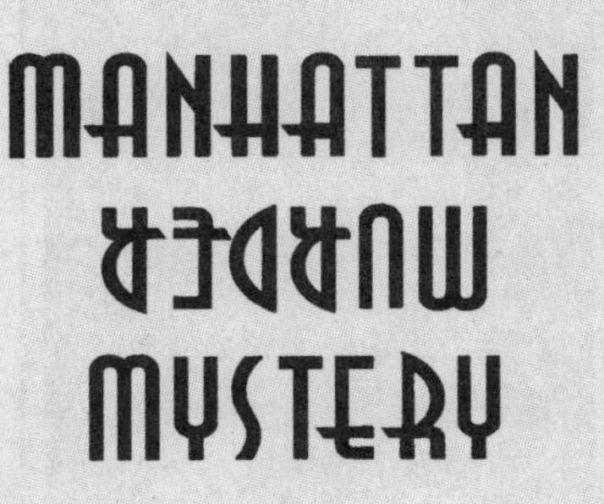

Manhattan Murder Mystery (1993)
In his mirthful tribute to film noir, Woody Allen reteams with Diane Keaton as residents of a New York apartment who investigate the mysterious death of a kindly old neighbor. The neighbor's husband is a prime suspect, but first Woody and Diane must find a motive and evidence, while getting over their own petty jealousies. With Alan Alda, Anjelica Huston, Jerry Adler. 108 min.
02-2535 Was $89.99 *❑$19.99*

Don't Drink The Water (1994)
This second screen adaptation of Woody Allen's play features Woody himself playing a New Jersey caterer who takes a family vacation with wife Julie Kavner and daughter Mayim Bialik in an Eastern European country. Family snapshots lead to espionage accusations, and hilarity ensues. Michael J. Fox, Dom DeLuise and Austin Pendleton also star; directed by Allen. 90 min.
11-2483 *❑$99.99*

Bullets Over Broadway (1994)
Gangsters and the Great White Way collide with comic results in writer/director Woody Allen's Roaring '20s spoof. Struggling author John Cusack manages to get his play on Broadway, but along the way must cope with a mob boss backer who puts his girlfriend in the cast, a famed lead actress who seduces Cusack, and a hit man who advises him on script changes. Jennifer Tilly, Chazz Palminteri, Mary-Louise Parker and Best Supporting Actress Oscar-winner Dianne Wiest co-star. 95 min.
11-1866 Was $19.99 *❑$14.99*

Mighty Aphrodite (1995)
After adopting a baby boy with art gallery owner wife Helena Bonham Carter, sportswriter Woody Allen seeks—and finds—the kid's real mother, a ditzy hooker and part-time porn actress, played by Oscar-winner Mira Sorvino. This discovery prompts Woody to reassess his own life, while a Greek chorus comments on the proceedings. Michael Rapaport and F. Murray Abraham co-star. 95 min.
11-2014 Was $19.99 *❑$14.99*

Everyone Says I Love You (1996)
Offering his own idiosyncratic spin on movie musicals, filmmaker Woody Allen and his co-stars gamely break into song and dance as they trace the romantic foibles of a well-to-do Manhattan family. As happily-married Alan Alda and Goldie Hawn prepare for daughter Drew Barrymore's wedding, Hawn's ex-husband Woody, living in Venice, Italy, is coached by daughter Natasha Lynne in wooing married art student Julia Roberts. Edward Norton, Natalie Portman, Tim Roth co-star; songs include "All My Life," "I'm Through with Love" and "My Baby Just Cares for Me." 105 min.
11-2155 Was $99.99 *❑$19.99*

Deconstructing Harry (1997)
With a series of crises ranging from financial problems and writer's block to a girlfriend who's left him for his closest pal, the last thing self-centered author Harry Block (filmmaker/star Woody Allen) needs on the weekend he's to visit a college to accept a prestigious award is to have the people he's used—in his writing and his life—come back to haunt him. The line between fiction and reality gets erased with an industrial-strength sander in this caustic comedy that also stars Kirstie Alley, Elisabeth Shue and Judy Davis. 95 min.
02-5176 Was $99.99 *❑$19.99*

Deconstructing Harry (Letterboxed Version)
Also available in a theatrical, widescreen format.
02-5229 *❑$19.99*

Celebrity (1998)
Woody Allen's acerbic look at fame and infidelity stars Kenneth Branagh as a "Woody"-like writer who splits from schoolteacher wife Judy Davis, then seeks affection in the arms of a host of women, including movie star Melanie Griffith, supermodel Charlize Theron and waitress/would-be actress Winona Ryder. With Joe Mantegna and Leonardo DiCaprio as a temperamental actor. 110 min.
11-2336 Was $99.99 *❑$19.99*

Sweet And Lowdown (1999)
Woody Allen's affectionate pseudo-documentary centers on Emmet Ray (Sean Penn), "the second-best jazz guitarist in the world," a '30s musical virtuoso with a stormy personal life that includes drunkenness, thievery and failed relationships with socialite writer Uma Thurman and mute laundress Samantha Morton. With Anthony LaPaglia and Gretchen Mol. 95 min.
02-3433 *❑$99.99*

Picking Up The Pieces (2000)
"Like Water for Chocolate's" Alfonso Arau directed this mystical comedy starring Woody Allen as a kosher butcher, relocated from New York to Arizona under the witness protection program, who carves up wife Sharon Stone in a jealous rage. But Allen loses one of her hands, and when a blind Mexican villager thinks the body part has helped her regain her sight, the "miracle" draws the attention of churchgoers, priest David Schwimmer and the authorities. Cheech Marin, Kiefer Sutherland, Maria Grazia Cucinotta and Elliott Gould also star. 95 min.
27-5586 *❑$99.99*

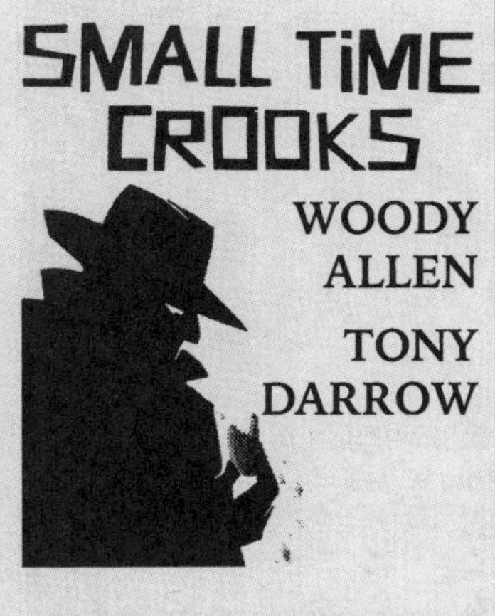

Small Time Crooks (2000)
Woody Allen directs and stars in this amiable comedy, playing a career petty thief who hatches a scheme to buy a cookie store with wife Tracey Ullman, then tunnel into the bank next door with his cronies. But when the cookie business takes off rather than crumbles and leaves Allen and Ullman rolling in dough, a whole new series of funny complications follow. With Hugh Grant, Jon Lovitz, Elaine May, Michael Rapaport.
07-2956 *❑$99.99*

Wild Man Blues (1998)
This documentary from the award-winning Barbara Kopple ("Harlan County, U.S.A.") chronicles the 23-day, 18-city European tour taken by Woody Allen and his New Orleans Jazz Band. The film captures the "real" Allen, playing clarinet, receiving awards from politicians, interacting with his sister and parents and snuggling with Soon-Yi Previn. 103 min.
02-5191 Was $99.99 *❑$19.99*

The Woody Allen Collection
This special boxed collector's set includes "Annie Hall," "Bananas," "Everything You Always Wanted to Know About Sex*," "Interiors," "Love and Death," "Manhattan," "Sleeper" and "Stardust Memories."
12-3312 Save $20.00! *$99.99*

Please see our index for these other Woody Allen titles: *Antz • New York Stories • Scenes From A Mall • The Sunshine Boys*

Plump Fiction (1998)
The films of Quentin Tarantino—along with "Forest Gump," "Waterworld" and others—are spoofed in a wild, bullet-filled burlesque. Follow hit men Tommy Davidson and Paul Dinello through a crisis-filled day that includes sweet-craving mobster's wife Julie Brown, a pair of lethal "Reservoir Nuns," tag-team wrestlers the "Natural Blonde Killers" and other oddballs. With appearances by Sandra Bernhard, Dan Castellaneta, Kevin Meaney, Jennifer Rubin and others. 82 min.
15-5466 *$59.99*

Teaching Mrs. Tingle (1999)
"Scream" writer and "Dawson's Creek" creator Kevin Williamson makes his directorial debut with this darkly comic thriller. Helen Mirren plays a dictatorial high school history teacher who accuses top student Katie Holmes and her pals of cheating, threatening Holmes' chances for a scholarship. A visit to Mirren's house to set things right goes awry and leads the kids to tie her to her bed and hold her captive. With Marisa Coughlan, Barry Watson, Michael McKean and Molly Ringwald. 93 min.
11-2365 Was $99.99 *❑$14.99*

My Life So Far (1999)
Set in a lush country manor in 1920s Scotland, director Hugh Hudson's pastoral comedy/drama follows an inquisitive 10-year-old whose discovery of the opposite sex comes just as the household is thrown into turmoil by the arrival of an uncle and his younger French fiancée. Things get worse when both the boy and his inventor father fall for the attractive houseguest. Robert Norman, Colin Firth, Irene Jacob, Malcolm McDowell and Mary Elizabeth Mastrantonio star. 95 min.
11-2379 Was $99.99 *❑$19.99*

Mumford (1999)
Writer/director Lawrence Kasdan's ("The Big Chill") charming comedy is set in the bucolic small town of Mumford, where new psychologist Loren Dean's offbeat advice wins over some of the area's more neurotic residents. Among his patients are lonely computer mogul Jason Lee, shopping-addicted housewife Mary McDonnell and chronically fatigued Hope Davis, with whom Dean falls in love, but no one can guess the secret their savior is hiding. Alfre Woodard, Ted Danson, Martin Short also star. 112 min.
11-2411 Was $99.99 *❑$14.99*

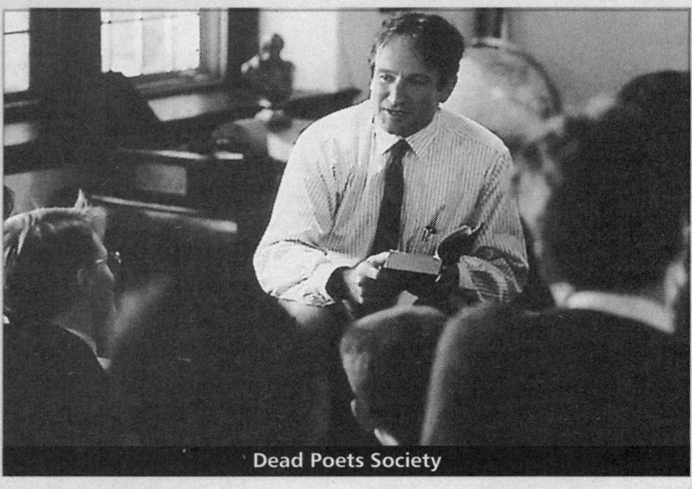
Dead Poets Society

Robin Williams

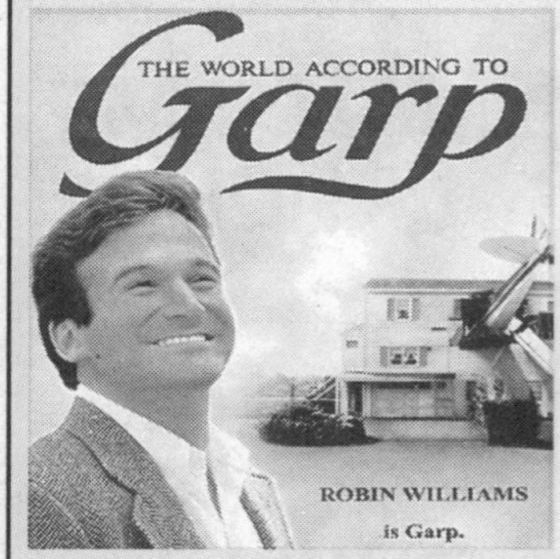
THE WORLD ACCORDING TO
Garp
ROBIN WILLIAMS
is Garp.

The World According To Garp (1982)
John Irving's bestseller about some heartwarmingly offbeat people is brilliantly adapted, with Robin Williams as T.S. Garp, struggling writer, lover and Everyman; Glenn Close as his free-spirited mother; and John Lithgow as best friend Roberta, a transsexual football player. 136 min.
19-1938 Was $19.99 ❑*$14.99*

The Survivors (1983)
After suffering the indignity of being fired by a parrot(!), business executive Robin Williams strikes up an unlikely friendship with former gas station owner Walter Matthau. And when the pair witness a robbery by a mob hit man, only a stint in a survivalist training program can save their keisters. Co-stars Jerry Reed, Kristen Vangard. 102 min.
02-1250 *$14.99*

Moscow On The Hudson (1984)
Robin Williams portrays a Russian saxophone player who defects to America while his troupe tours New York City. He finds romance, muggers and freedom in this warm and often hilarious tale. Maria Conchita Alonso, Alejandro Rey co-star. Paul Mazursky directs. 115 min.
02-1346 Was $19.99 ❑*$14.99*

Club Paradise (1986)
A ramshackle Caribbean resort is the setting for this wild comedy that makes your most harried vacation seem peaceful by comparison. Robin Williams, Peter O' Toole, Jimmy Cliff, Andrea Martin, Rick Moranis, Eugene Levy and Twiggy head the cast. 104 min.
19-1549 Was $19.99 ❑*$14.99*

Seize The Day (1986)
Robin Williams stars in his first dramatic role as a lonely man who refuses to let a failed marriage and financial ruin rob him of his sense of humor and optimism. Based on a Saul Bellow novella, this powerful drama also stars Joseph Wiseman, Tony Roberts and William Hickey. 93 min.
44-1438 *$29.99*

The Best Of Times (1986)
Can you go home again? Robin Williams, who dropped the ball in his high school football team's big game 14 years ago, thinks so, and will do anything to have another chance at winning the game and redeeming his life. Charming comedy about the "hero" in all of us also stars Kurt Russell, Pamela Reed. 105 min.
53-1526 Was $19.99 ❑*$14.99*

Good Morning, Vietnam (1987)
Armed Forces Radio in 1965 Saigon was unprepared for the one-man assault launched on the airwaves by maverick deejay Robin Williams. Williams garnered an Oscar nomination as manic motormouth Adrian Cronauer, whose on-air antics delighted the troops and infuriated his superiors. Co-stars Bruno Kirby, Forest Whitaker, J.T. Walsh, Floyd Vivino. 120 min.
11-1456 Was $19.99 ❑*$14.99*

Dead Poets Society (1989)
Robin Williams turns in a dynamic, Oscar-nominated performance as a literature teacher whose unorthodox methods inspire his students and upset the administration at a boy's boarding school. Ethan Hawke, Robert Sean Leonard, Norman Lloyd also star. Peter Weir directs; filmed in Delaware. 128 min.
11-1496 Was $19.99 ❑*$14.99*

Awakenings (1990)
Powerful, true-life drama stars Robin Williams as a shy neurologist who uses an experimental drug to help the catatonic patients of a Bronx hospital and allow them to function normally for the first time in years. Robert De Niro excels as a patient whose recovery helps draw Williams out of his own shell. Penelope Ann Miller, Julie Kavner also star. 120 min.
02-2097 Was $19.99 ❑*$14.99*

Cadillac Man (1990)
Slick-talking, womanizing car salesman Robin Williams needs all of his oratorical skills to save himself and his co-workers when crazed husband Tim Robbins takes the dealership hostage, looking for the man who seduced his wife. High-test laughfest also stars Pamela Reed, Annabella Sciorra, Fran Drescher and Variety mainstay Zack Norman. 97 min.
73-1082 ❑*$14.99*

The Fisher King (1991)
In Terry Gilliam's enchanting contemporary fable, Jeff Bridges plays a popular radio host who hits the skids after provoking a tragic shooting with his obnoxious on-air banter. In hopes of changing his life, he joins forces with a whimsical but unstable homeless man (Robin Williams) in search of the Holy Grail in downtown Manhattan. Oscar-winner Mercedes Ruehl, Amanda Plummer co-star. 137 min.
02-2168 Was $19.99 ❑*$14.99*

Toys (1992)
A surrealistic comedy from director Barry Levinson starring Robin Williams as a whimsical toymaker who must save his dead father's toy factory from his demented, militaristic uncle. Astounding sets and effects highlight this fanciful anti-war film; co-stars Robin Wright, Michael Gambon and Joan Cusack. 121 min.
04-2633 Was $19.99 ❑*$14.99*

Mrs. Doubtfire (1993)
Family life gets to be a drag, literally, for divorced dad Robin Williams. He's denied custody of his children and decides to impersonate an elderly Englishwoman when estranged wife Sally Field advertises for a nanny. As Mrs. Doubtfire, Williams gets to be with his kids while spoiling Field's new romance. Hit gender-bending farce also stars Pierce Brosnan, Harvey Fierstein. 125 min.
04-2787 Was $19.99 ❑*$14.99*

Jumanji (1995)
Thrilling, special effects-filled fantasy about two orphaned kids who find a mysterious board game in an attic. Once they begin playing, a gateway is opened to a jungle-like world filled with stampeding elephants, mischievous monkeys, and Robin Williams, who was trapped in the game as a boy decades earlier. Now, it's up to Williams, childhood friend Bonnie Hunt, and the kids to finish the game and restore reality. With Kirsten Dunst, Bradley Pierce, David Alan Grier. 104 min.
02-2881 Was $19.99 ❑*$14.99*

The Birdcage (1996)
Smash hit reworking of the classic French comedy "La Cage Aux Folles" stars Robin Williams and Nathan Lane as lovers who operate a Miami gay nightclub where Lane is the drag revue's star. When Williams' son from a long-ago tryst announces he's engaged to the daughter of ultra-conservative senator Gene Hackman, the pair must "straighten up" their act in order to get through a family dinner and save the planned wedding. With Dianne Wiest, Hank Azaria, Calista Flockhart. 118 min.
12-3102 Was $19.99 ❑*$14.99*

The Birdcage (Letterboxed Version)
Also available in a theatrical, widescreen format.
12-3128 ❑*$14.99*

Good Will Hunting (1997)
Real-life pals Matt Damon and Ben Affleck took home an Academy Award for their story about Will Hunting (Damon), a janitor at MIT whose sullen nature masks a genius intellect. Affleck co-stars as his best friend, Minnie Driver is a medical student who falls for Damon, and Best Supporting Actor Oscar-winner Robin Williams is a therapist who tries to help him come to grips with his life; Gus Van Sant ("To Die For") directs. 126 min.
11-2250 Was $19.99 ❑*$14.99*

What Dreams May Come (1998)
Join Robin Williams on a wondrous afterlife odyssey in this visually dazzling fantasy/romance in which he plays a devoted doctor and husband who is killed in a car accident. Taken to a heaven of his own imagining by spiritual guide Cuba Gooding, Jr., Williams must leave the pastoral paradise to attempt to save wife Annabella Sciorra, sent to a hellish netherworld after taking her own life in despair. Max von Sydow also stars. 114 min.
02-9058 Was $99.99 ❑*$14.99*

Patch Adams (1998)
Robin Williams turns in a tour-de-force performance as the real-life title character, a medical student who mixes mirth with medicine, causing a ruckus with university officials. Using a red rubber nose to entertain child and adult patients alike, Williams starts the Gesundheit Institute to further his cause. With Monica Potter, Philip Seymour Hoffman. 116 min.
07-2755 Was $19.99 ❑*$14.99*

Jakob The Liar (1999)
In a world without hope, his lies gave people the courage to dream. Robin Williams plays a resident of a Jewish ghetto in WWII Poland who relates radio news he overhears to his fellow detainees. When they believe he owns a radio, Williams begins making up his own morale-boosting reports and passes them along. Moving drama co-stars Alan Arkin, Liev Schreiber, and Armin Mueller-Stahl (who also appeared in the original 1974 German film). 120 min.
02-3414 Was $99.99 ❑*$14.99*

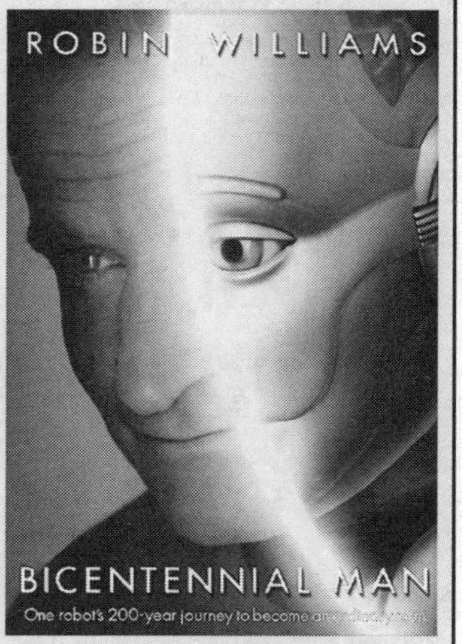
ROBIN WILLIAMS
BICENTENNIAL MAN

Bicentennial Man (1999)
Follow the 200-year quest of robot Robin Williams to become human in this sensitive sci-fi tale, based on an Isaac Asimov story. Purchased as a family domestic and "nanny" by Sam Neill in 2005, Williams displays creativity and a desire to learn that makes him more than a machine. But as the decades pass he encounters difficult human feelings, including love for Embeth Davidtz, Neill's grown daughter (and great-granddaughter). Oliver Platt co-stars. 131 min.
11-2436 Was $99.99 ❑*$19.99*

Please see our index for these other Robin Williams titles: *The Adventures Of Baron Munchausen • Aladdin • Aladdin And The King Of Thieves • Being Human • Can I Do It...'Til I Need Glasses • Dead Again • Deconstructing Harry • Fathers' Day • Flubber • Hamlet • Hook • Jack • Nine Months • Popeye • The Secret Agent • Shakes The Clown*

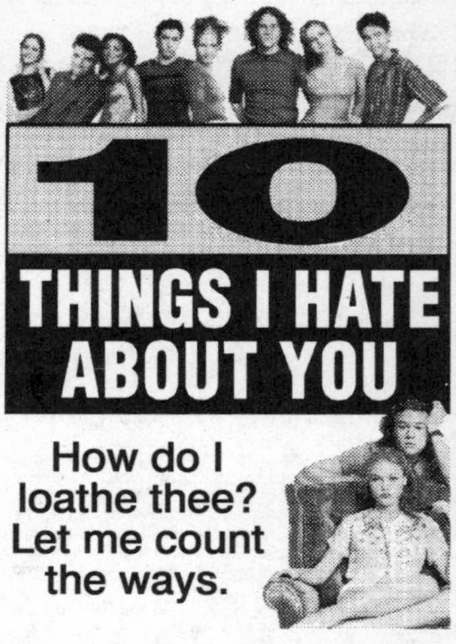
10
THINGS I HATE
ABOUT YOU
How do I loathe thee? Let me count the ways.

10 Things I Hate About You (1999)
Flavorful teen farce, loosely patterned after "The Taming of the Shrew," concerns the would-be suitors of a girl forbidden to start dating before her sullen, standoffish big sister, and their schemes to fix the older sib up with the local rebel. Larisa Oleynik, Joseph Gordon-Levitt, Julia Stiles, Heath Ledger star. 98 min.
11-2350 Was $19.99 ❑*$14.99*

Class Act (1992)
"House Party" stars Kid 'N Play hit the books in this classy comedy. Kid is an out-of-it high schooler whose straight-A records get switched with those of homeboy and remedial student Play. The pair decide to keep the mix-up going while learning about "how the other half lives." Meshach Taylor, Alysia Rogers co-star. 102 min.
19-2013 Was $89.99 ❑*$19.99*

Stay Tuned (1992)
A suburban couple get sucked via satellite dish into a TV underworld where the sinister station boss zaps them into such programs as "Duane's Underworld," "Northern Overexposure" and "Off with His Head," and if they can't last for 24 hours it means permanent "cancellation." John Ritter, Pam Dawber, Jeffrey Jones and Eugene Levy star in this comic, satiric look at the "boob tube." 89 min.
19-2018 Was $19.99 ❑*$14.99*

Singles (1992)
Set in a funky Seattle apartment complex, this lively comedy focuses on the romantic foibles of a group of people in their 20s, struggling to relate with each other in a difficult time. Matt Dillon, Campbell Scott, Kyra Sedgwick and Bridget Fonda star in Cameron Crowe's winning film; music by Paul Westerberg, Pearl Jam, Alice in Chains and others. 100 min.
19-2036 Was $19.99 ❑*$14.99*

Waiting For Guffman (1996)
As the fictitious town of Blaine, Missouri ("Stool Capital of the World"), prepares to celebrate its 150th anniversary, local theater director Christopher Guest is readying his cast of would-be actors for his sesquicentennial offering, a historical musical revue entitled "Red, White and Blaine." Director/co-scripter Guest's hilariously heartwarming salute to big-city dreams and small-town talent also stars Eugene Levy, Catherine O'Hara, Parker Posey and Fred Willard. 84 min.
19-2564 Was $99.99 ❑*$14.99*

Mr. Wonderful (1993)
Winning romantic farce in which Con Ed worker Matt Dillon tries to find a mate for ex-wife Annabella Sciorra so he can put the cash from his alimony payments into his dream project of opening a bowling alley. Vincent D'Onofrio, Mary-Louise Parker and William Hurt co-star in this poignant film from Anthony Minghella ("The English Patient"). 99 min.
19-2205 Was $19.99 ❑*$14.99*

Chasers (1994)
Veteran Navy officer Tom Berenger teams with slick young swabbie William McNamara for military prisoner-transfer detail. But the "seaman" turns out to be gorgeous Erika Eleniak, who'll stop at nothing to escape from her "escorts," in this fast-paced road comedy. With Crispin Glover, Dean Stockwell; Dennis Hopper directs. 100 min.
19-2245 Was $19.99 ❑*$14.99*

Daddy's Dyin'... Who's Got The Will? (1990)
Southern-fried humor, well-done, about a Texas family that goes topsy-turvy when daddy dies and his estate is in question. Beau Bridges, Beverly D'Angelo, Tess Harper, Judge Reinhold, Amy Wright and Keith Carradine star as the family of wackos who get down to some heavy-duty fussin' and feudin'. 96 min.
12-2134 Was $89.99 *$14.99*

Diggstown (1992)
Action- and laugh-filled mix of "The Sting" and "Rocky" starring James Woods as a fast-talking hustler who cooks up a scheme with his friend, ex-boxer Louis Gossett, Jr., to con corrupt town boss Bruce Dern. All Gossett has to do is defeat 10 of Dern's toughest goons in the ring, one after another, in 24 hours! With Oliver Platt, Heather Graham. 98 min.
12-2585 Was $89.99 ❑*$14.99*

74 · COMEDY MOVIES UNLIMITED CALL · 1-800-4-MOVIES

Meet The Deedles (1998)
Nature lovers, look out! Fun-loving, wave-happy beach bums Phil and Stew Deedle find themselves a little out of their element when their wealthy dad sends them to a wilderness "boot camp" to straighten them out, and they winding up posing as national park rangers. Extreme comedy stars Steve Van Wormer, Paul Walker, A.J. Langer and Dennis Hopper. 94 min.
11-2771 Was $19.99 ❑*$14.99*

I Got The Hook-Up (1998)
New Orleans rap artist Master P wrote, produced and stars in this comedy in which two inner-city con artists get busy with a shipment of cellular phones. But because the new phones have old chips in them, the city's entire phone system goes haywire, as communications get hilariously tangled. A.J. Johnson and "Tiny" Lister co-star; features a hit rap soundtrack. 93 min.
11-2799 Was $99.99 ❑*$19.99*

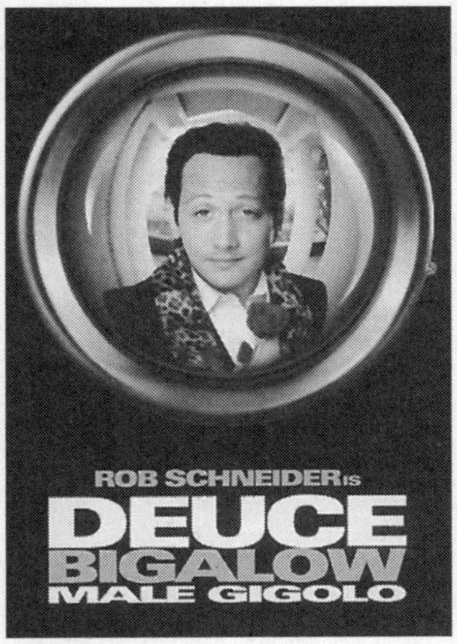

Deuce Bigalow: Male Gigolo (1999)
Rob Schneider is an L.A. fish tank cleaner whose stint as a housesitter for a suave escort turns disastrous when he accidentally destroys a $6,000 aquarium. In order to raise cash, Schneider poses as the "manwhore" and, with help from pimp Eddie Griffin, meets a series of bizarre female clients. Arija Bareikis, Norm MacDonald also star. (FYI: According to Webster, all gigolos are male.) 88 min.
11-2431 Was $99.99 ❑*$19.99*

My Summer Story (1994)
In this sequel to "A Christmas Story," young Ralphie and his eccentric parents encounter a series of hilarious and heartwarming experiences involving fishing trips, top-spinning competitions and Ralphie's unpredictable friends, all based on Jean Shepherd's poignant stories. Charles Grodin, Mary Steenburgen and Kieran Culkin star. AKA: "It Runs in My Family." 85 min.
12-2980 Was $19.99 ❑*$14.99*

Trigger Happy (1996)
A wryly hip and surrealistic gangster comedy, writer/director Larry Bishop's debut effort stars Richard Dreyfuss as a mob boss returning to his nightclub headquarters after a stay in a mental hospital who charges enforcer Gabriel Byrne with eliminating all his rivals, including disloyal assistant Jeff Goldblum. The quirky cast includes Diane Lane, Ellen Barkin, Kyle MacLachlan, Burt Reynolds and Richard Pryor. AKA: "Mad Dog Time." 92 min.
12-3145 Was $99.99 ❑*$14.99*

Play It To The Bone (1999)
Down-and-out L.A. boxers and pals Woody Harrelson and Antonio Banderas get a chance to fight each other for a $100,000 purse in Las Vegas. First, though, they have to survive the car trip to Glitter Gulch with Banderas' current (and Harrelson's ex-) flame, would-be inventor Lolita Davidovich, and drugged-out hitchhiker Lucy Liu. With Tom Sizemore, Robert Wagner; Ron Shelton ("Bull Durham") wrote and directed. 125 min.
11-2432 Was $99.99 ❑*$19.99*

The Extreme Adventures Of Super Dave (1999)
The self-proclaimed world's greatest stuntman, "Super Dave" Osborne, smashes his way onto the screen in his very own movie, but can the super one aid a sick boy by completing—successfully, for once—the most dangerous stunt of his less-than-perfect career? Bob Einstein is the daffy daredevil; with Dan Hedaya, Gia Carides. 91 min.
12-3291 Was $49.99 ❑*$14.99*

Strangest Dreams: Invasion Of The Space Preachers (1991)
Reverend Lash, a radio evangelist who's converting (and making) millions and is really an interplanetary con being, is just one of the bizarre characters in this spaced-out satire from West Virginia independent filmmaker Danny Boyd. Hillbilly gourmets, tourists from Ohio, and the "House of Dung" all figure in the offbeat goings-on. Jim Wolfe, Guy Nelson star. 100 min.
15-5188 Was $79.99 *$19.99*

Touch (1997)
A young person with the power to heal in his hands becomes the prize in a tug-of-war between a sleazy con artist, a fanatical evangelist, and the American mass media in director/scripter Paul Schrader's wicked satirical comedy, based on Elmore Leonard's novel. Skeet Ulrich, Bridget Fonda, Christopher Walken, Tom Arnold and Janeane Garofalo star. 97 min.
12-3146 Was $99.99 ❑*$14.99*

Just The Ticket (1998)
Desperate to keep girlfriend Andie MacDowell from leaving him for cooking school in Paris, ticket scalper and petty con artist Andy Garcia looks to become respectable after his "last big score": cleaning up on ducats to a Papal mass in Yankee Stadium. Winning romantic comedy also stars Richard Bradford, Laura Harris and Chris Lemmon. 112 min.
12-3276 Was $99.99 ❑*$14.99*

The Very Thought Of You (1998)
Lively romantic comedy stars Monica Potter as a Minnesota native whose trip to London brings her into contact with three male friends—a music mogul, a struggling actor and a shy artist—all of whom fall in love with her. Comic and romantic complications ensue when she begins to love one of the suitors. Rufus Sewell and Joseph Fiennes also star. AKA: "Martha, Meet Frank, Daniel and Laurence." 88 min.
11-2373 ❑*$99.99*

Curdled (1996)
First made as a short film by director/co-writer Reb Braddock, this offbeat mix of suspense and black comedy stars Angela Jones as a death-obsessed young woman who takes a job with a cleaning service specializing in tidying up murder scenes in order to learn more about a serial killer preying on society women. Will her fascination with the killer make her his next victim? William Baldwin, Mel Gorham costar. 87 min.
11-2120 Was $19.99 ❑*$14.99*

Getting Even With Dad (1994)
Just when he and his cronies pull a heist that will allow him to retire from the "business," ex-con Ted Danson is left son Macaulay Culkin to look after. The neglected boy finds and hides the loot, forcing Danson to spend time with him and fulfill his parental obligations, in this amusing, heartwarming comedy. Glenne Headly, Saul Rubinek co-star. 108 min.
12-2951 Was $19.99 ❑*$14.99*

Living In Oblivion (1995)
Writer/director Tom DiCillo ("Johnny Suede") follows up that low-budget independent film with this acerbic look at, of all things, the making of a low-budget independent film. Steve Buscemi is a frustrated director who must cope with an egomaniacal leading man set on romancing his female co-star, break-ups and fist fights on the set, a temperamental dwarf actor and other crises. Catherine Keener, James Le Gros, Dermot Mulroney co-star. 92 min.
02-2842 Was $89.99 ❑*$24.99*

Box Of Moonlight (1997)
When the construction job he's working on is abruptly shut down, repressed engineer John Turturro sets out on a road trip that contains more than one detour from his rigidly-structured life, thanks to an encounter with a Davy Crockett-suited free spirit known as the Kid. Director Tom DiCillo's ("Living in Oblivion") off-the-wall comedy also stars Sam Rockwell, Catherine Keener. 111 min.
68-1854 Was $99.99 ❑*$14.99*

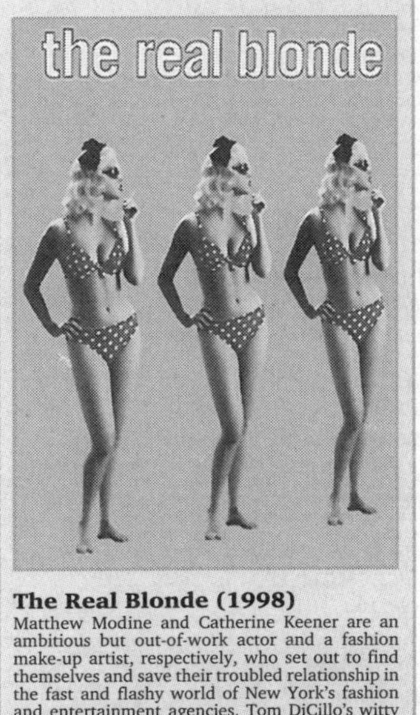

The Real Blonde (1998)
Matthew Modine and Catherine Keener are an ambitious but out-of-work actor and a fashion make-up artist, respectively, who set out to find themselves and save their troubled relationship in the fast and flashy world of New York's fashion and entertainment agencies. Tom DiCillo's witty comedy also stars Daryl Hannah, Kathleen Turner, Christopher Lloyd, Elizabeth Berkley and Maxwell Caulfield. 107 min.
06-2755 Was $99.99 ❑*$14.99*

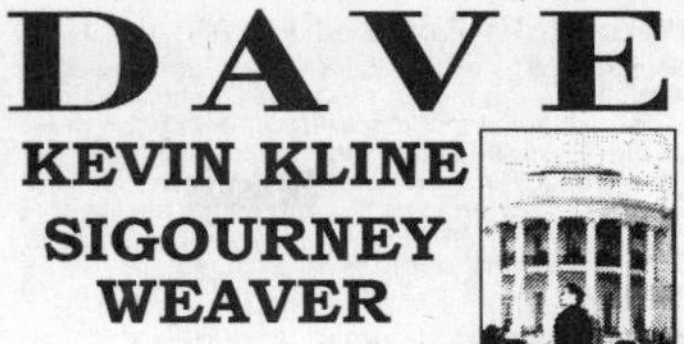

Dave (1993)
Terrific political farce starring Kevin Kline as Dave Kovic, a dead ringer for the President of the United States who is recruited to impersonate the ailing chief executive. Using common sense, idealism and help from accountant friend Charles Grodin, Dave implements new social programs and balances the budget, while bringing romance back into the life of First Lady Sigourney Weaver. With Frank Langella, Ben Kingsley. 110 min.
19-2147 Was $89.99 ❑*$14.99*

T Bone And Weasel (1992)
A wild, action-packed road comedy that pairs Gregory Hines and Christopher Lloyd as a pair of penny-ante crooks who take off in a stolen car on a search for some "easy money," only to encounter rifle-wielding shopkeepers, crooked cops, love-starved women and other oddball types along the way. With Rip Torn and Ned Beatty. 94 min.
18-7423 ❑*$89.99*

Little Giants (1994)
Rick Moranis is the nerdy younger brother of former gridiron star and junior football coach Ed O'Neill who decides to tackle their lifelong rivalry by piloting a competing squad of underdogs. The team Moranis recruits is filled with misfits of all sorts, including his own daughter, whose nickname is "Icebox." John Madden also stars. 106 min.
19-2296 Was $24.99 ❑*$19.99*

The New Age (1994)
Hollywood agent Peter Weller and his wife, graphic artist Judy Davis, are living the good life until Weller quits his job and Davis loses some major clients. Their solution: embrace New Age philosophies, sleep with other people and open a trendy boutique. This darkly humorous tale from Michael Tolkin, creator of "The Player," co-stars Samuel L. Jackson, Adam West. 112 min.
19-2304 Was $89.99 ❑*$19.99*

Empire Records (1995)
The funky young staff of a big-city independent record store try to keep the struggling business afloat while pursuing their own dreams in this hip "Generation X" seriocomedy. Liv Tyler, Ethan Randall, Robin Tunney and Anthony LaPaglia star; music by The Cranberries, Cracker, Toad the Wet Sprocket and others. 91 min.
19-2428 Was $19.99 *$14.99*

Big Bully (1996)
Nerdy Rick Moranis and boorish Tom Arnold are two old-time enemies who find themselves teaching at the same Minnesota school in which they battled as kids. Now, Moranis, a creative writing instructor, and Arnold, a machine shop teacher, continue their rivalry with a hilarious series of malicious pranks. With Julianne Phillips, Carol Kane, Don Knotts and Jeffrey Tambor. 91 min.
19-2461 Was $99.99 ❑*$14.99*

Joe's Apartment (1996)
You've heard all sorts of roommate horror stories, but they pale in comparison to what poor Joe has to put up with when he's forced to share his dilapidated New York apartment with some real "party animals": 50,000 singing, dancing cockroaches! Wild comedy, based on the popular MTV short film, stars Jerry O'Connell and Megan Ward. 82 min.
19-2483 Was $99.99 ❑*$14.99*

Carpool (1996)
Suburban family man David Paymer isn't looking forward to his turn at the morning school carpool, but the trip takes a terrifyingly daffy detour when a bungled convenience store robbery puts fugitive Tom Arnold behind the wheel of Paymer's vanful of rambunctious kids. Fast-lane farce also stars Rhea Perlman, Rod Steiger. 92 min.
19-2484 Was $99.99 ❑*$14.99*

Mars Attacks! (1996)
No one on Earth, from the President of the United States to singer Tom Jones, is safe when an armada of flying saucers arrives and skeletal, bulbous-headed beings from Mars launch an all-out war, blasting the U.S. Congress, destroying world landmarks, and having a good laugh in the process. Director Tim Burton's wickedly funny sci-fi romp, based on the infamous '60s trading cards, features an all-star cast, including Jack Nicholson in a dual role, Annette Bening, Pierce Brosnan, Glenn Close, Michael J. Fox, Lukas Haas, Sarah Jessica Parker and Martin Short. 106 min.
19-2534 Was $19.99 ❑*$14.99*

Mars Attacks! (Letterboxed Version)
Also available in a theatrical, widescreen format.
19-2661 ❑*$19.99*

Foreign Affairs (1993)
Delightful romantic complications ensue when quiet New England teacher Joanne Woodward meets talkative Brian Dennehy on a transatlantic flight to Europe and attempts to evade him. But even after the flight, he turns up wherever she goes, and well-meaning friends try to play matchmaker. With Eric Stoltz, Stephanie Beacham. 100 min.
18-7438 Was $89.99 ❑*$14.99*

Hav Plenty (1998)
Engaging African-American romantic comedy from writer-director Christopher Scott Cherot, who also stars as a struggling New York writer invited to spend Thanksgiving holiday with upper class and engaged Chenoa Maxwell and her family in Washington, D.C. The two have feelings for each other, but Maxwell's sister, friend and fiancé keep getting in the way. With Lauryn Hill. 90 min.
11-2272 Was $99.99 ❑*$19.99*

Little City (1998)
A San Francisco cab driver and struggling painter is having little success with women: one girlfriend left him for another woman, and another went off with his best friend! The arrival of a new girl at the bar where the would-be artist hangs out and his buddy works complicates things even further in this bright comedy. Jon Bon Jovi, Josh Charles, Joanna Going, Penelope Ann Miller and Annabella Sciorra star. 115 min.
11-2286 Was $99.99 ❑*$19.99*

The Castle (1999)
In this acclaimed satire from Australia, a tow-truck driver and his family live on a runway at Melbourne's airport, but find their home threatened when the airport plans to expand. The father, fed up with little guys getting pushed around, takes on the government and the airport in a series of increasingly ridiculous legal battles. With Michael Caton, Anne Tenney.
11-2366 Was $99.99 ❑*$19.99*

Sleep With Me (1994)
Eric Stoltz, Craig Sheffer and Meg Tilly are the sides of a romantic triangle between three best friends that is only made worse by the marriage of Tilly and Stoltz, in this smart, contemporary comedy/drama. With Dean Cameron, Adrienne Shelly and a great cameo by filmmaker Quentin Tarantino. 87 min.
12-2975 Was $89.99 ❑*$14.99*

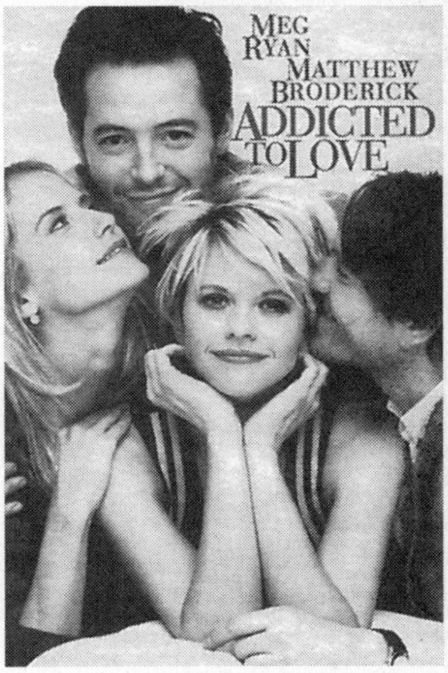

Addicted To Love (1997)
Revenge was never sweeter—or funnier—than in this dark romantic comedy starring Meg Ryan and Matthew Broderick as two strangers with something in common: the former lovers that dumped them have taken up with each other! Holed up in an abandoned apartment across the street from their old flames, Broderick and Ryan's spying on the couple soon escalates into an elaborate vengeance scheme. Kelly Preston, Tcheky Karyo co-star; directed by Griffin Dunne. 99 min.
19-2581 Was $99.99 ❑*$14.99*

Sweet Revenge (1990)
Rosanna Arquette and Carrie Fisher star in this romantic farce about a man who is rewarded alimony until he remarries. He has no intention to walk down the aisle again, so his ex-wife enlists her sexy friend to seduce him. John Sessions also stars in this contemporary comedy. 89 min.
18-7248 *$79.99*

Crazy From The Heart (1991)
A small Texas town is rocked by scandal when the strait-laced high school principal travels across the border and elopes with the school's Mexican-American janitor. Offbeat romantic comedy stars Christine Lahti, Ruben Blades, William Russ. 94 min.
18-7351 ❑*$89.99*

Crazy In Love (1992)
Suburban housewife Holly Hunter gets more than she bargained for during a trip to the city when she meets a handsome stranger who fills her life with the spark and passion missing in her marriage. Lively romantic comedy also stars Julian Sands, Bill Pullman, Gena Rowlands. 93 min.
18-7408 Was $89.99 ❑*$14.99*

Reckless Kelly (1994)
Wildly eccentric comic Yahoo Serious ("Young Einstein") is back, this time putting a wild spin on the tale of sharp-shooting bandit Ned Kelly, known as "Australia's Robin Hood." The outlaw lands in the U.S., and soon skewers Hollywood and Las Vegas in this zany, satiric farce. Melora Hardin co-stars. 81 min.
19-2251 Was $19.99 ❑*$14.99*

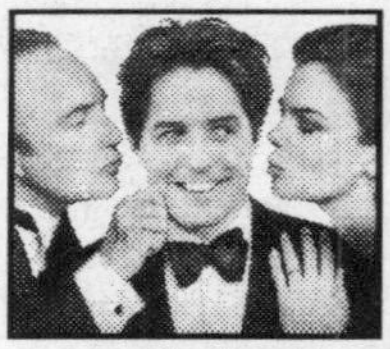

HUGH GRANT
JAMES CAAN

MICKEY BLUE EYES

Mickey Blue Eyes (1999)
When English-born auctioneer Hugh Grant asks New York schoolteacher Jeanne Tripplehorn to marry him, he never expected to become involved in her family's business...and never dreamed that their business is organized crime! James Caan plays the "godfather" who indoctrinates his would-be son-in-law in the ways of Mob life in this comic romp. With Burt Young. 102 min.
19-2924 Was $99.99 ❑*$14.99*

A Perfect Little Murder (1990)
A married couple newly arrived in the suburbs overhear a murder plot on their baby's intercom and, after the authorities ignore their story, play amateur sleuths attempting to figure out which of their neighbors are would-be killers. Teri Garr and Robert Urich star in a comedic whodunit. 94 min.
18-7456 ❑*$89.99*

Under The Hula Moon (1995)
An Arizona couple's dream of making a fortune developing an extra-strong sunblock and moving to Hawaii to raise a family hits a series of comical snags, ranging from an escaped convict and Mexican bandits to DEA agents and the ghost of King Kamehameha, in this fast-paced farce starring Stephen Baldwin, Emily Lloyd and Chris Penn. 96 min.
18-7597 *$89.99*

The Heidi Chronicles (1995)
Jamie Lee Curtis plays the title role, a young woman searching for her place in the world through the social upheavals of the '60s, '70s and '80s, in this marvelous seriocomedy, scripted by Wendy Wasserstein from her own Tony- and Pulitzer Prize-winning play. With Tom Hulce, Kim Cattrall. 94 min.
18-7607 Was $89.99 *$14.99*

Angus (1995)
Can Angus, an overweight but good-hearted high school student, overcome the taunting of his classmates and, with help from his nerdy best friend and cantankerous grandfather, become a football star and impress the girl of his dreams? Winning family comedy stars Charlie Talbert, Chris Owen, Ariana Richards, Kathy Bates and George C. Scott. 87 min.
18-7609 Was $89.99 *$14.99*

If Looks Could Kill (1991)
Hunky Richard Grieco plays a high school student who gets thrown into the world of espionage, secret agents and dangerous chases when he's mistaken for a spy while vacationing in Europe. Linda Hunt, Roger Rees and Gabrielle Anwar also star in this funny, thrilling sleuth spoof. 88 min.
19-1872 Was $19.99 ❑*$14.99*

Eight Days A Week (1999)
"Felicity" sensation Keri Russell is the gorgeous neighbor of nerdy Josh Shaefer, whose obsession with Russell leads him to camp out on her front lawn in hopes of getting a date. Nothing—from Keri's involvement with a thick-headed jock to ridicule from Shaefer's dweeby buddies—will curtail his vigil in this offbeat romantic comedy. With R.D. Robb, Catherine Hicks. 93 min.
19-2880 Was $99.99 ❑*$14.99*

Going Under (1991)
This riotous film does for sailors what "Hot Shots" did for pilots. The U.S. Sub Standard and its wacky crew are off on a top secret assignment, but find a Soviet ship named Pink November threatening their mission. Bill Pullman, Wendy Schaal, Bud Cort, Ned Beatty star. 81 min.
19-1906 Was $89.99 ❑*$19.99*

Welcome To Planet Earth (1996)
After inheriting a boarding house, a young man welcomes some strange new tenants, a human-looking alien family who are using their vacation to expose their beautiful daughter to the ways of Earthlings and are also willing to take on any neighborhood criminals they may encounter. George Wendt, Shanna Reed, Christopher M. Brown and Anastasia Sakelaris star. 85 min.
21-9133 *$99.99*

Aliens Among Us (1998)
This sequel to "Welcome to Planet Earth" features George Wendt and Julie Brown as the alien couple who volunteer to become sheriffs in a western town where people believe outer space beings are responsible for killing three previous lawmen and livestock. Gorgeous Anastasia Sakelaris is back as the couple's daughter. 90 min.
21-9163 Was $59.99 *$14.99*

Wrongfully Accused (1998)
Noted concert violinist Leslie Nielsen must run—and stumble—for his life after he's framed for the murder of the rich hubby of Kelly LeBrock. In order to prove his innocence and find the one-armed, one-legged and one-eyed guy responsible, Nielsen eludes Richard Crenna's tough but inept U.S. marshal in this spoof of "The Fugitive," "Mission: Impossible" and other films, from "Naked Gun" alumnus Pat Proft. 85 min.
19-2781 Was $99.99 ❑*$14.99*

Other People's Money (1991)
Meet "Larry the Liquidator" (Danny DeVito), an irresistibly slimy takeover expert with his eyes on a New England cable company. Standing in his way are the company's patriarch (Gregory Peck) and his sexy lawyer daughter (Penelope Ann Miller), out to out-smart Larry. Norman Jewison's savage satire of corporate greed also stars Piper Laurie, Dean Jones. 101 min.
19-1927 Was $19.99 ❑*$14.99*

Trojan War (1997)
Teenager Will Friedle thinks he has it made when a gorgeous schoolmate promises him a night he'll never forget...as long as he doesn't forget the "protection." His citywide condom quest turns into a series of calamities that best friend Jennifer Love Hewitt—who has a secret crush on Friedle—tries to rescue him from in this fast-paced youth comedy. 84 min.
19-2621 Was $99.99 ❑*$14.99*

The Crazysitter (1994)
This could be called "The Hand That Rocks the Cradle...With Laughter." A scheming con artist gets out of prison and gets a job posing as a babysitter for two children. When she decides to sell the kids, she doesn't realize the comic consequences. Beverly D'Angelo, Ed Begley, Jr., Carol Kane, Phil Hartman, Nell Carter and Mink Stole star. 92 min.
21-9096 *$14.99*

Sour Grapes (1998)
"Seinfeld" co-creator Larry David wrote and directed this farce in which surgeon Steven Weber and cousin Craig Bierko head to Atlantic City with their girlfriends for some gambling fun. When Weber hits $436,000 on the slots with Bierko's borrowed quarter, nasty and hilarious developments ensue. Karen Sillas, Robyn Peterman also star.
19-2755 Was $99.99 ❑*$14.99*

Lost & Found (1999)
David Spade is a restaurant owner who falls for Sophie Marceau, a beautiful French woman who recently moved into his complex. In order to attract Marceau's attention, Spade kidnaps her dog, then sets out to "find" it to impress his new neighbor. When the pooch swallows Spade's pal's wedding ring, the situation gets wacky. With Artie Lange and Martin Sheen. 99 min.
19-2903 Was $99.99 ❑*$14.99*

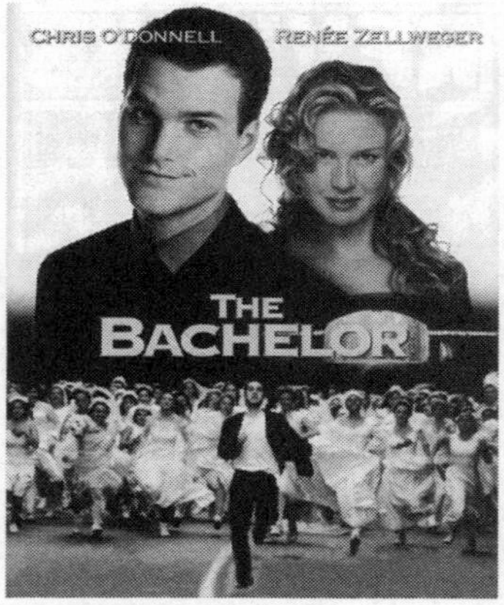

The Bachelor (1999)
Commitment-phobe Chris O'Donnell is told he'll inherit $100 million if he marries by 6:05 p.m. on his 30th birthday. Problem is, that leaves him just 27 hours to get hitched, and girlfriend Renee Zellweger, recipient of a botched prior proposal from O'Donnell, has turned him down. Follow his comical quest to find a bride in this romantic romp, an updating of Buster Keaton's 1925 film "Seven Chances." James Cromwell, Mariah Carey, Brooke Shields and Peter Ustinov also star. 102 min.
19-2963 Was $99.99 ❑*$14.99*

Three To Tango (1999)
Chicago architect Matthew Perry has a chance to win a major commission from builder Dylan McDermott, but there's a catch. Because McDermott mistakenly thinks Perry is gay, he asks him to serve as a "safe" chaperon for his mistress, artist Neve Campbell. It doesn't take long for Perry to fall for Campbell and have to choose between love and money in this romantic comedy. With Oliver Platt. 98 min.
19-2961 Was $99.99 ❑*$14.99*

Curly Sue (1991)
In this adorable comedy from John Hughes, a cute little girl (Alisan Porter) and her homeless guardian (Jim Belushi) pull off little scams to get money and meals. A career-oriented lawyer (Kelly Lynch) takes them in and soon loses her heart to the endearing pair. 102 min.
19-1928 Was $19.99 ❑*$14.99*

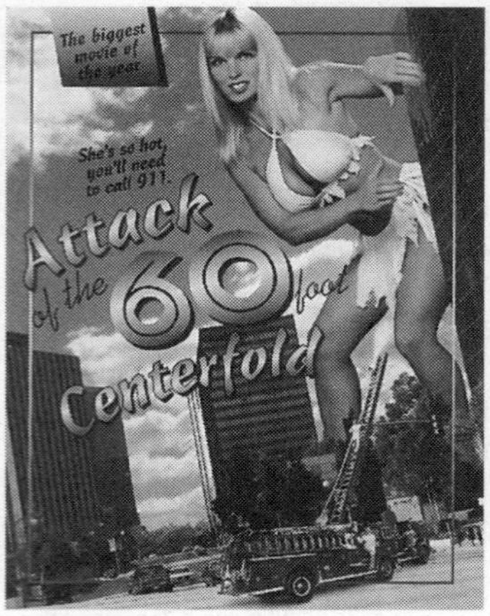

Attack Of The 60 Foot Centerfold (1995)
Angel Grace, one of three women trying to win a Centerfold of the Year competition, attempts to enhance her assets by using a doctor's secret beauty program. But the endowments go awry, and Angel's body, along with her body parts, keep getting bigger. This spoof of 1950s sci-fi epics stars J.J. North, Michelle Bauer; Russ Tamblyn, Tommy Kirk and John ("Z-Man") LaZar provide cameos. 84 min.
21-9086 Was $89.99 *$14.99*

Strictly Business (1991)
In this hilarious satire, a black real estate broker is smitten with a gorgeous waitress, but, alas, he's not hip enough to woo her. For lessons in homeboy coolness, the realtor enlists the help of a workplace pal. Tommy Davidson, Joseph C. Phillips and Halle Berry star. 83 min.
19-1929 Was $89.99 ❑*$19.99*

Liberty Heights (1999)
Barry Levinson returns to his Baltimore roots for a fourth time with this sensitive coming-of-age saga set in the mid-1950s. The focus is on Jewish brothers Ben (Ben Foster), who's smitten with a black girl at his high school, and Van (Adrien Brody), who has grown attached to a gorgeous WASP he met at a party. Joe Mantegna and Bebe Neuwirth are their parents; with Orlando Jones, Rebekah Johnson. 128 min.
19-2976 Was $99.99 ❑*$14.99*

Home For Christmas (1993)
Family caper comedy focusing on a 9-year-old girl who has inherited millions and her search for her real mother. When her wicked stepmother hires a detective to catch her, then tells the feds that the detective has kidnapped her, hilarious developments occur. Howard Hesseman, Anita Morris, (Jennifer) Love Hewitt star. AKA: "Little Miss Millions." 90 min.
21-9042 Was $89.99 *$14.99*

No Dessert Dad, 'Til You Mow The Lawn (1994)
When their unhip parents decide to stop smoking by listening to self-hypnosis tapes, three kids doctor the tapes with suggestions to make them cooler. But as Dad and Mom become hipper and start doing the kids' chores, things get wackier. Joanna Kerns, Robert Hays and Richard Moll star. 93 min.
21-9062 *$14.99*

Archie: Return To Riverdale (1990)
That perennial carrot-topped teenager has finally grown up, but his life hasn't gotten any easier, in this live-action updating of the popular comic books. The Riverdale gang are back for a 15-year high school reunion that finds Betty and Veronica still pursuing Archie—a situation his new fiancée isn't pleased with. Christopher Rich, Lauren Holly, Karen Kopins and Matt McCoy star. AKA: "Archie: To Riverdale and Back Again." 85 min.
21-9103 Was $89.99 *$24.99*

PrimaDonnas (1995)
A posh Beverly Hills debutante ball is turned upside-down when one devilish deb gets back at her snooty girlfriends and transforms the event into a madcap, anything-goes party. Wild comedy stars Shannon Sturges, Bobbie Bresee, Dan Cashman and the great Jack Carter. 98 min.
19-3895 *$89.99*

Younger And Younger (1993)
In this quirky romantic fantasy from director Percy Adlon ("Bagdad Cafe"), Donald Sutherland is the owner of a storage company whose extra-marital affairs drive wife Lolita Davidovich to a fatal heart attack. After taking son Brendan Fraser in as a business partner, Sutherland starts seeing a younger, beautiful incarnation of his wife everywhere. Julie Delpy, Sally Kellerman also star. 97 min.
19-9108 ❑*$14.99*

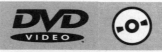

A Man Called Sarge (1990)
An outrageous military comedy that'll leave you saluting in stitches. A strong-willed sarge gets more than he counted on when he commandeers a platoon of misfits against the Nazis. There's laughs aplenty in this spoof that makes "The Dirty Dozen" look clean. With Gary Kroger, Jennifer Runyon and Marc Singer. 88 min.
19-7078 Was $79.99 *$19.99*

Oddball Hall (1991)
Don Ameche and Burgess Meredith play two jewel thieves posing as members in a fraternal organization in Africa. Ten years after pulling off a famous heist they try to cash in their loot, but the son of a local tribe chieftain, impostors and cops complicate matters. Bill Maynard co-stars. 90 min.
19-7087 Was $89.99 *$19.99*

Body Waves (1992)
An outrageously sexy comic farce in which a teen has to prove to his father that he can support himself without the family business. But what to do? He invents a sex cream that makes guys and gals super-stimulated. And soon the bodies begin to wave! Bill Calvert, Leah Lail, Larry Linville and the great Dick Miller star. 80 min.
21-9011 Was $89.99 *$14.99*

Munchie (1992)
A 10-year-old boy with problems at home and in school is befriended by the magical Munchie, a critter from another world who delivers pizzas and knows how to party! The youngster is coached by Munchie and a wacky professor on dancing, romancing and problem-solving. Loni Anderson, Andrew Stevens, Arte Johnson, and Dom DeLuise as the voice of Munchie star. 81 min.
21-9013 Was $89.99 *$14.99*

Munchie Strikes Back (1994)
Munchie, that zany intergalactic creature, causes trouble and is sent back to his astral plane, where the authorities give him one more chance to make good. His new mission is to help a down-on-her-luck single mom and her unhappy son. With Lesley-Anne Down, Andrew Stevens, and Howard Hesseman as the voice of Munchie. 80 min.
21-9060 *$14.99*

Deep In The Heart (Of Texas) (1997)
A documentary filmmaking couple from England delve into the lives of a group of Texans who have fascinating stories to tell in this quirky comedy that started life as a play in an Austin theater. The tales they hear involve a mad dog coach, a pie-maker and an ancient oak tree. Features music by Lyle Lovett, Willie Nelson and Jimmie Dale Gilmore. With Amanda Root, Kenneth Cranham. 91 min.
22-9009 Was $79.99 *$29.99*

Idiot Box (1997)
This edgy black comedy follows the exploits of two unemployed Australian ne'er-do-wells who decide to rid themselves of their teenage ennui by robbing a bank. Unfortunately, it's too late to back out by the time our heroes discover that being in the line of fire in real life is not at all the same as the cop shows they've seen on TV. Ben Mendelsohn, Jeremy Sims star. 85 min.
22-9041 *$79.99*

My Sweet Suicide (1998)
After he has more than he can handle, Kevin Harrison decides to take his own life. But he can't even get that right—until he meets Molly, a bookstore clerk eager to show him the right way to end it all. Matthew Aldrich and Michelle Leigh Thompson star in this off-kilter comedy in the "Harold and Maude" tradition. 78 min.
22-9017 Was $79.99 *$29.99*

BOB ROBERTS

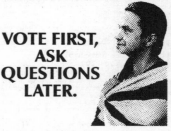

VOTE FIRST, ASK QUESTIONS LATER.

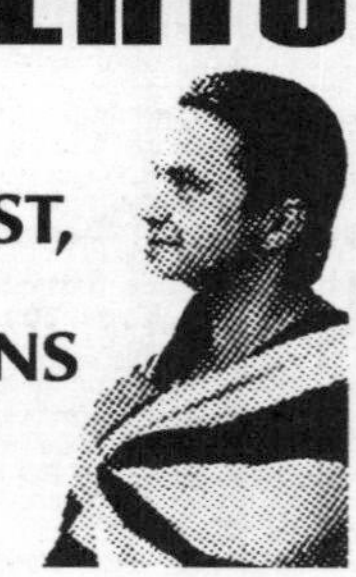

Bob Roberts (1992)
A timely satire of '90s politics and Yuppie conservatism from writer/director Tim Robbins, who stars in the title role of a right wing folksinger and senatorial candidate who mixes Bob Dylan with William F. Buckley and uses the TV cameras following him on the campaign trail to his own advantage. Ray Wise, Gore Vidal and Giancarlo Esposito also star, with cameos from several of Robbins' Hollywood cronies. 102 min.
27-6804 Was $19.99 ❑*$14.99*

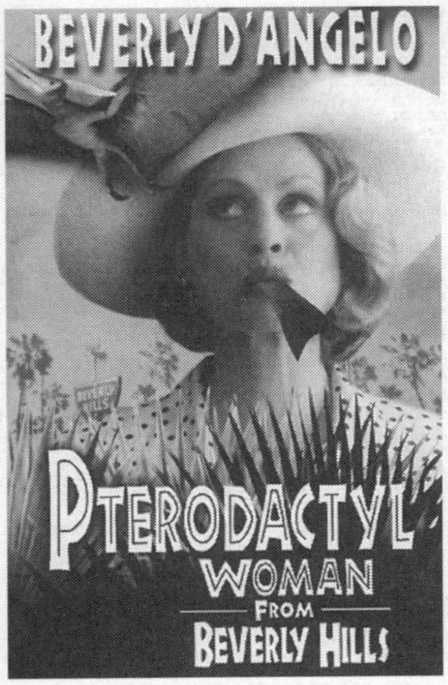
BEVERLY D'ANGELO
PTERODACTYL WOMAN FROM BEVERLY HILLS

Pterodactyl Woman From Beverly Hills (1997)
When her archeologist husband disturbs an ancient burial site and rouses the ire of a witch doctor, eccentric Beverly Hills housewife Beverly D'Angelo is put under a curse that turns her into a half-woman, half-dinosaur creature and has her flying down Rodeo Drive! Wild sci-fi comedy also stars Brion James, Moon Zappa. 97 min.
46-8024 Was $59.99 *$14.99*

Phat Beach (1996)
"Life ain't nothin' but a 'beach' thing" for a pair of girl-crazy homeboys who "borrow" one guy's dad's Mercedes convertible for a wild summer joyride of music, babes and fun. Hip-hop comedy stars Jermaine "Huggy" Hopkins, Brian Hooks and Coolio; music by E-40, Biz Markie and others. 88 min.
27-6995 Was $99.99 □*$14.99*

Foolish (1999)
Brothers Foolish Waise (comedian Eddie Griffin) and Fifty Dollah (rapper Master P, who scripted the film), both dreaming of a show biz career, team to put on a stand-up show that will make them stars and also solve their family's money problems in this hip and edgy urban comedy. With Traci Bingham, Marla Gibbs, Andrew Dice Clay. 84 min.
27-7126 Was $99.99 □*$14.99*

Superstar (1999)
Everyone dreams of stardom, but some have further to go than others...as in the case of tree-kissing, TV movie-obsessed Catholic schoolgirl Mary Katherine Gallagher (Molly Shannon). See if the awkward, anything-but-popular Gallagher can fulfill her dreams of winning a school talent contest and the heart of handsome classmate Will Ferrell in this frenetic farce based on the beloved "Saturday Night Live" sketches. With Glynis Johns, Mark McKinney. 82 min.
06-2949 Was $99.99 □*$14.99*

A Shock To The System (1990)
Much-praised satire on yuppie greed and modern morality (or the lack of it) stars Michael Caine as a Madison Avenue exec who kills the recipient of the promotion he feels he deserved. Soon Caine finds murder an effective method of getting what he wants. Peter Riegert, Elizabeth McGovern and Swoosie Kurtz also star in this clever dark comedy. 87 min.
44-1758 Was $89.99 □*$14.99*

Diamond's Edge (1990)
Here's a delightful detective spoof in the tradition of "Bugsy Malone." A faltering teenage shamus is handed a package to guard, but he's soon visited by a host of strangers who want it in the worst way. Colin Dale, Susannah York and Dursley McLinden star in this miniature salute to "The Maltese Falcon." 83 min.
44-1786 *$79.99*

Ski School (1990)
Wacky, zany farce about an ace ski instructor who rules on the slopes and in the sack. He's given the challenge of his life when a rival teacher tricks him, forcing his team to compete in death-defying competition. Dean Cameron and Playboy Playmate Ava Fabian star. 89 min.
44-1793 Was $89.99 □*$19.99*

Ski School 2 (1994)
"Just when you thought it was safe to go back to the slopes..." Can the hot-dogging dudes of the Ski School save their jobs and make the world safe for bikini skiing? Wacky, sexy sequel stars Dean Cameron and Playboy Playmate Wendy Hamilton.
76-9068 Was $89.99 *$14.99*

Don't Tell Mom The Babysitter's Dead (1991)
"Married...With Children's" Christina Applegate is one of four siblings left at home with a deranged babysitter when their mother goes on an Australian vacation. But when the sitter suddenly suffers a fatal heart attack, the kids have to ditch the corpse and fend for themselves. Funny teen farce co-stars Joanna Cassidy, John Getz, Keith Coogan, David Duchovny. 105 min.
44-1810 Was $19.99 □*$14.99*

Livin' Large (1991)
Hilarious satire of racism, stereotypes and the media tells the tale of a black delivery boy who is thrust into fame after he takes over the story of a murdered TV reporter. Soon, he's an on-air star, wearing expensive suits, exploiting old friends and getting engaged to an "uptown" weathergirl. T.C. Carson, Blanche Baker and Julia Campbell star. 96 min.
44-1865 Was $19.99 □*$14.99*

Hot Under The Collar (1992)
After he mistakenly hypnotizes the girl of his dreams into joining a convent, a young man poses as a priest, then a nun, in order to retrieve her. Complicating matters is a gang of mobsters searching for stolen diamonds in the very same nunnery. Angela Visser, Richard Gabai, Bruce Ly, and Burt Ward as the Pope star. 87 min.
44-1903 Was $89.99 *$19.99*

Mom And Dad Save The World (1992)
A tyrannical dictator from the idiot Planet Spengo (Jon Lovitz) who plans to destroy Earth kidnaps an American housewife (Teri Garr) with hopes of making her his bride. Of course, her husband (Jeffrey Jones) objects to the ruler's advances and must stop his wicked schemes. Eric Idle, Kathy Ireland co-star in this zany sci-fi farce from the creators of "Bill & Ted's Excellent Adventure." 92 min.
44-1914 Was $19.99 □*$14.99*

Running Mates (1992)
A witty farce, Washington-style, starring Ed Harris as a successful senator and presidential hopeful who plans to marry his former girlfriend, spunky children's author Diane Keaton. What disrupts both campaigns is the discovery of some old tapes featuring his bride-to-be in compromising positions. Ed Begley, Jr. co-stars. 88 min.
44-1925 Was $89.99 □*$14.99*

Comrades Of Summer (1992)
After he is fired from the Seattle Mariners, baseball coach Sparky Smith (Joe Mantegna) takes a job as skipper of the Russian Olympic team. His new lineup consists of hockey players and shot-putters, and it's up to Sparky to whip them into shape before a showdown with his old team in the U.S. Natalya Negoda and Michael Lerner also star in this amiable baseball farce. 90 min.
44-1928 Was $89.99 □*$14.99*

Barbarians At The Gate (1993)
Insightful and humorous true-life look at corporate greed starring James Garner as F. Ross Johnson, the CEO of RJR/Nabisco, who plots to buy out the shareholders of his own company. Johnson appears to be heading for a big payday until scheming buyout king Henry Kravis (Jonathan Pryce) gets into the act. Peter Riegert, Joanna Cassidy also star. 107 min.
44-1939 Was $19.99 □*$14.99*

The Positively True Adventures Of The Alleged Texas Cheerleader-Murdering Mom (1993)
The bizarre true story of the Texas woman who hired a hit man to kill her daughter's cheerleading competitor's mom is given a super-charged, satirical treatment from director Michael Ritchie ("Smile"). Holly Hunter plays the mother who takes parental devotion too far; with Beau Bridges, Swoosie Kurtz. 99 min.
44-1940 Was $19.99 *$14.99*

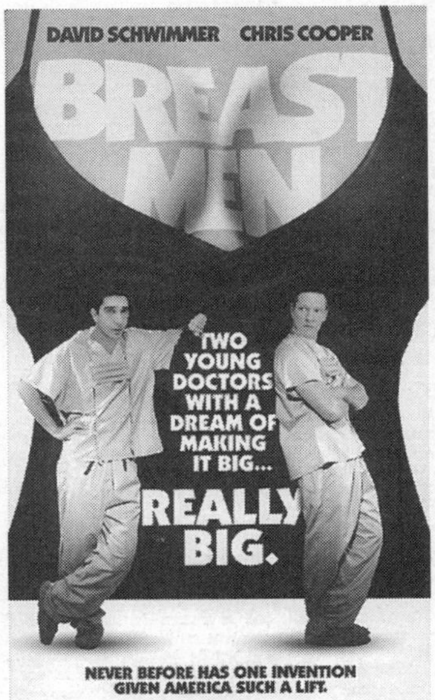
DAVID SCHWIMMER CHRIS COOPER
BREAST MEN
TWO YOUNG DOCTORS WITH A DREAM OF MAKING IT BIG...
REALLY BIG.
NEVER BEFORE HAS ONE INVENTION GIVEN AMERICA SUCH A LIFT.

Breast Men (1998)
Mix "The Story of Louis Pasteur" with "Boogie Nights" and you might get this raucous, lighthearted look at the true story of the Texas plastic surgeons who developed the silicon breast implant, and how their invention changed the look of American womanhood in the '60s and '70s. David Schwimmer, Chris Cooper, Emily Procter and Louise Fletcher star. 95 min.
44-2164 Was $99.99 □*$14.99*

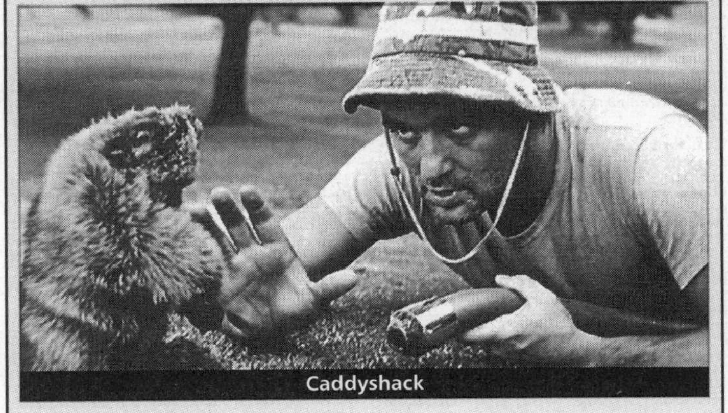
Caddyshack

Bill Murray

Meatballs (1979)
Spend a wild and wacky summer at Camp North Star, where crazed counselor Bill Murray lets his young charges turn the place topsy-turvy. Laugh-packed hit comedy also stars Kate Lynch, Chris Makepeace. 92 min.
47-1046 *$14.99*

Where The Buffalo Roam (1980)
Bill Murray turns in an outrageous performance as gonzo journalist Dr. Hunter S. Thompson. Armed with Wild Turkey, drugs and typewriter, the good Doctor fears and loathes on the campaign trail, covers the Super Bowl and helps out oddball lawyer pal Peter Boyle. 96 min.
07-1219 Was $19.99 *$12.99*

Where The Buffalo Roam (Letterboxed Collector's Edition)
Also available in a theatrical, widescreen format.
08-8697 *$14.99*

Caddyshack: 19th Anniversary Special Edition (1980)
Riotous comedy set in an elite country club features Rodney Dangerfield as a loud and loutish new member, Chevy Chase as the egotistical club pro, Bill Murray as a crazed groundskeeper, and the pesky Mr. Gopher. The plot revolves around a not-so friendly game of golf between Dangerfield, Chase and stuffy judge Ted Knight. Co-stars Michael O'Keefe. Special edition includes an intro by Chase, a documentary which includes never-before-seen outtakes, and more. 130 min. total.
19-2824 □*$19.99*

Stripes (1981)
Ten-hup! Bill Murray deserves a salute for his maniacal performance as a nutty army recruit who turns the military upside down. It's funny...that's the fact, Jack! John Candy, Warren Oates, Harold Ramis, John Larroquette, Sean Young co-star. 105 min.
02-1106 □*$14.99*

The Razor's Edge (1984)
Bill Murray makes his dramatic debut in this engrossing adaptation of Somerset Maugham's classic novel. After experiencing the pain and heartbreak of war and failed relationships, Murray attempts to find direction in his life by visiting a holy man in the Himalayas. With Theresa Russell, Catherine Hicks, Denholm Elliott. 128 min.
02-1403 Was $79.99 □*$14.99*

Ghostbusters (1984)
Dan Aykroyd, Bill Murray and Harold Ramis are the amateur parapsychologists who become spirit catchers-for-hire and soon have all of New York City clamoring for their services in the supernaturally successful comedy. With Sigourney Weaver, Ernie Hudson, Rick Moranis, Annie Potts. 105 min.
02-1483 Was $19.99 □*$14.99*

Ghostbusters (Letterboxed Version)
Also available in a theatrical, widescreen format.
02-3337 □*$14.99*

Ghostbusters II (1989)
It's time to get slimed again, as New York faces a host of horrific menaces...but after five years of forced retirement, can the Ghostbusters still come through? Bill Murray, Dan Aykroyd, Harold Ramis, Sigourney Weaver and the rest return for more hauntingly funny hi-jinks in the hit sequel. 102 min.
02-1963 Was $19.99 □*$14.99*

Quick Change (1990)
Bill Murray co-directed and stars in this calamitous comic caper, as three friends plan and execute the perfect bank robbery...and then face a nightmarish series of obstacles as they try to get from downtown Manhattan to Kennedy Airport. Hilarious look at Big Apple aggravations also stars Geena Davis, Randy Quaid, Jason Robards. 88 min.
19-1813 *$14.99*

What About Bob? (1991)
Hilarity abounds as neurotic Bill Murray discovers that his psychiatrist (Richard Dreyfuss) is about to go on vacation. What's a patient to do but tag along uninvited to New Hampshire? There, amid the splendid New England scenery, Murray befriends Dreyfuss' family while driving him crazy with his wacky behavior. With Julie Hagerty, Charlie Korsmo. 99 min.
11-1585 Was $19.99 □*$14.99*

Groundhog Day

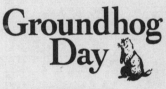

Groundhog Day (1993)
Pittsburgh weatherman Bill Murray finds that his worst nightmare has become a reality when he joins producer Andie McDowell and cameraman Chris Elliott in Punxsutawney, Pennsylvania, to cover the "Groundhog Day" ceremony. Seems that the cynical Murray keeps waking up to the same day, over and over, and he has to find romance and happiness in order to escape this comic time-warp. 101 min.
02-2997 Was $19.99 □*$14.99*

Kingpin (1996)
From the creators of "Dumb & Dumber" comes this hilariously tasteless comedy about hook-handed ex-bowling ace-turned-travelling salesman Woody Harrelson, who joins forces with Amish lane maestro Randy Quaid to enter a big bowling tournament in Reno. Eventually, Harrelson must face his old nemesis, seedy champion Bill Murray. With Vanessa Angel and Chris Elliott. Special video edition features footage not shown in theatres. 117 min.
12-3107 Was $99.99 □*$14.99*

Larger Than Life (1996)
When the circus clown father he never knew dies and leaves him with a four-ton elephant named Vera, Bill Murray sets off on a wild cross-country odyssey to get his new "pet" from New Hampshire to her new home in California in five days. The laughs are as big as...well, elephants...in this slapstick romp. With Matthew McConaughey, Janeane Garofalo. 93 min.
12-3133 Was $19.99 □*$14.99*

The Man Who Knew Too Little (1997)
Video store clerk Bill Murray's London vacation turns into a death-defying adventure—unbeknownst to him—when he accidentally intercepts a phone call meant for a government agent and is thrown into a world of spies, call girls and killers...which he thinks is part of an audience-participation play. Joanne Whalley and Peter Gallagher co-star in the fast-paced cloak-and-dagger comedy. 94 min.
19-2631 Was $19.99 □*$14.99*

Rushmore (1998)
Audaciously witty coming-of-age comedy starring Jason Schwartzman as an ambitious but scholastically challenged student at the private Rushmore Academy who befriends Bill Murray, a successful but troubled businessman alumnus. When Schwartzman discovers Murray has a romantic interest in Olivia Williams, the first-grade teacher he's smitten with, an elaborate battle between the men ensues. 93 min.
11-2326 Was $99.99 □*$19.99*

Please see our index for these other Bill Murray titles: *Caddyshack • Cradle Will Rock • Ed Wood • Hamlet • Little Shop Of Horrors • Scrooged • Shame Of The Jungle • Space Jam • Wild Things • With Friends Like These*

The Pentagon Wars (1998)
Find out what happens when the Pentagon spends 17 years and billions of dollars developing a high-tech tank...and it doesn't work. Colonel Cary Elwes sets out to expose the scandal that general Kelsey Grammar has spent years covering up. Olympia Dukakis and Richard Benjamin (who also directed) co-star in this satire based on James Burton's novel. 104 min.
44-2167 Was $99.99 ❏$14.99

The Old Boy Network (1991)
A pair of British intelligence agents (Tom Conti and John Standing), left to fend for themselves in the wake of post-Cold War budget cuts, use their espionage skills to keep one step ahead of old allies and enemies in this witty political satire. Jayne Brook also stars. 168 min. on two tapes.
44-2234 $24.99

Modern Love (1990)
Robby Benson wrote, directed and stars in this delightful farce about a bachelor who finally gets married...to his urologist, no less. He soon discovers that married life is filled with all sorts of obstacles, like babies, changing diapers and feuding with in-laws. Karla DeVito, Louise Lasser, Burt Reynolds co-star. 110 min.
45-5493 ❏$89.99

Zoo Radio (1991)
Two brothers are left rival radio stations by their tycoon father and battle it out for ratings and control of the $60 million estate in this zany, sexy romp. See a rapping rabbi, outrageous pranks and buxom blondes as the battle for the airwaves gets wilder. Peter Feig, Danielle Villareal star. 89 min.
45-5498 ❏$89.99

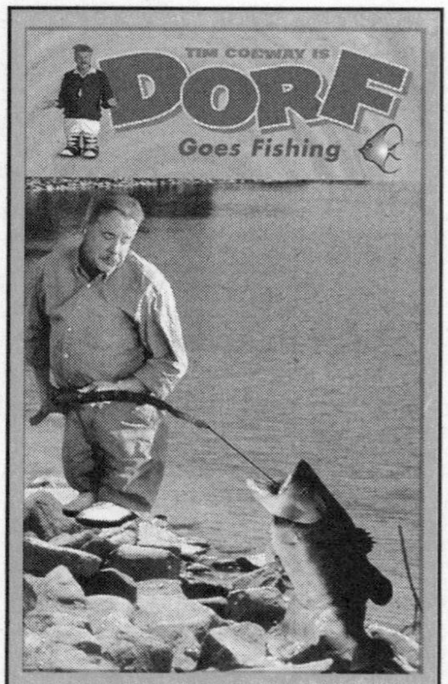

TIM CONWAY IS
DORF
Goes Fishing

Dorf Goes Fishing
The always-wacky Dorf (as played by Tim Conway) goes searching for a big catch and returns with some big laughs in this popular comic salute to fishing.
50-1224 $14.99

Dorf On Golf
If golfing leaves you teed off, sit back and laugh your niblicks off as "master pro" Derk Dorf (Tim Conway) shows you the goofiest greens techniques you've ever seen. Club yourself silly with the first comedy golfing video! 30 min.
50-1486 $14.99

Dorf's Golf Bible
Eighteen hilarious holes with the argyle gargoyle and his guests, Slammin' Sammy Snead, the irrepressible Boom-Boom and Waldo, Dorf's new caddy. Features the hit comedy rap tune, "Different Strokes for Different Folks." 36 min.
50-1679 $14.99

Dorf On The Diamond
Tim Conway's mirthful Dorf tackles the national pastime in this hilarious program that'll have you singing "Take Me Out to the Dorf Tape." The little fella demonstrates—badly—all aspects of the game and covers all of the comedy bases. 40 min.
50-5618 $19.99

Dorf And The First Games Of Mt. Olympus
If you've ever wondered how the Olympics got started, you sure won't find out from this tape! But you're certain to win the gold medal in laughs as Derkus Dorf (Tim Conway) enters one event after another, fouling up as only he can! 35 min.
50-1556 $14.99

Dorf Goes Auto Racing
Tim Conway's famed little man moves from the greens to grease as he takes to the raceway in his own inimitable style. The flags are up and hilarity is non-stop as Tim produces laughs at Indy 500 speed, along with racing superstars Richard Petty, Neil Bonnett and Kenny Schrader. 70 min.
50-4161 $14.99

Breaking The Rules (1992)
Funny and poignant buddy comedy starring C. Thomas Howell, Jonathan Silverman and Jason Bateman as three young men who set out on an Ohio-to-California trip in an attempt to rekindle their friendship. It's a ride filled with mishaps and surprises, not the least of which is feisty waitress Annie Potts, who joins the trio on their journey. 100 min.
44-1926 Was $89.99 ❏$14.99

The Opposite Sex And How To Live With Them (1993)
Winning romantic comedy about sex, love and relationships in the '90s. David (Arye Gross) is a working class guy who meets pretty WASP Carrie (Courteney Cox) in a bar. Funny dating experiences lead to a full-blown relationship and, eventually, discussion of marriage. Kevin Pollak, Julie Brown and Jack Carter also star. 86 min.
44-1942 Was $89.99 ❏$14.99

The Night We Never Met (1993)
Witty comic lark involving the romantic entanglements of three adults who "time-share" a Greenwich Village brownstone apartment and what happens when two of them become attracted to one another...without ever meeting. Matthew Broderick, Annabella Sciorra, Kevin Anderson, Jeanne Tripplehorn and Justine Bateman head up the winning ensemble cast. 98 min.
44-1943 Was $89.99 ❏$14.99

Lightning Jack (1994)
In this amiable western-comedy, Paul Hogan is a dim-witted sharpshooter who wants to be a famous outlaw. So he teams with mute sidekick Cuba Gooding, Jr. to pull off a series of hilarious heists in hopes of achieving fame. Beverly D'Angelo also stars. 96 min.
44-1965 Was $19.99 ❏$14.99

Circle Of Friends (1994)
Funny and touching sleeper hit follows three Irish girls preparing to leave their village for college in Dublin. One of them, plain but self-assured Benny (Minnie Driver), sets her sights on winning the heart of a handsome rugby player (Chris O'Donnell), but the road to true love has several bumps in this romantic comedy/drama. 112 min.
44-1997 Was $19.99 ❏$14.99

Dr. Jekyll And Ms. Hyde (1995)
Sexy and silly spin on the horror classic stars Tim Daly as the infamous doctor's great-grandson whose updating of the family "potion" puts his gender in a blender and changes him into the lovely, lethal Sean Young, who'll stop at nothing to take permanent control of their shared body. Lysette Anthony, Stephen Tobolowsky, Harvey Fierstein co-star. 90 min.
44-2017 Was $19.99 ❏$14.99

Steal Big, Steal Little (1995)
A Capraesque comic adventure featuring Andy Garcia as Mexican twins duelling for control of a Santa Barbara estate owned by their wealthy stepmother. Robby, the conniving brother, wants to sell the land to real estate developers, while Ruben, his sincere sibling, has other, altruistic plans. Alan Arkin, Rachel Ticotin co-star; directed by Andrew Davis ("The Fugitive"). 134 min.
44-2033 Was $89.99 ❏$19.99

The Late Shift (1996)
The film version of Bill Carter's best-seller takes a darkly comic look at the late-night TV war that began between NBC and CBS after Johnny Carson announced his decision to retire as host of "The Tonight Show," and the rivalry between Jay Leno and David Letterman to succeed him. With Daniel Roebuck, John Michael Higgins, Bob Balaban, Rich Little, Treat Williams and Kathy Bates; Betty Thomas ("The Brady Bunch Movie") directs. 95 min.
44-2048 Was $99.99 ❏$14.99

Off And Running (1992)
Hilarity ensues in Miami when performing mermaid Cyndi Lauper falls in love with a horse trainer, but soon discovers that he and his steed are murdered. Who killed them—and who is chasing the mermaid now? Find out in this wacky farce featuring David Keith, Richard Belzer. 91 min.
44-2053 $99.99

House Arrest (1996)
This comedy with a serious message stars Jamie Lee Curtis and Kevin Pollak as parents about to divorce who are tricked by their children and locked in the basement until they work out their differences. The kids' actions prompt their friends to kidnap their bickering folks, too, and bring them over for the same treatment. With Jennifer Tilly and Ray Walston. 111 min.
44-2075 Was $99.99 ❏$14.99

The Second Civil War (1997)
When Idaho governor Beau Bridges refuses to let a group of immigrant orphans settle in his state, a battle of wills with U.S. president Phil Hartman is launched that, fueled by presidential advisors, lobbyists and the media, threatens to turn into a national crisis. Sharply funny satire from director Joe Dante and producer Barry Levinson also stars Elizabeth Peña, James Coburn, Denis Leary. 96 min.
44-2117 Was $19.99 ❏$14.99

Weapons Of Mass Distraction (1997)
It begins as a fight between rival media moguls Gabriel Byrne and Ben Kingsley to own a pro football team, but with each man using bribery, blackmail, innuendo and his newspapers and TV stations to try to crush the other, it escalates into all-out war. Writer Larry Gelbart's darkly funny look at big business also stars Mimi Rogers, Jeffrey Tambor. 96 min.
44-2118 Was $19.99 ❏$14.99

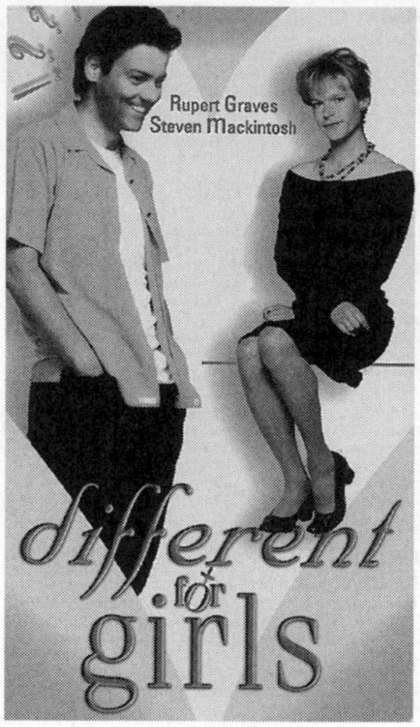

Rupert Graves
Steven Mackintosh
different for girls

Different For Girls (1997)
It's a romantic comedy with a twist when London motorbike courier Paul has a chance meeting with old schoolmate Kim and asks her for a date. The twist: back in school, Kim was Karl! With little in common save a mutual attraction, the friendship they shared as teens becomes a relationship that changes their adult lives in this funny and touching tale. Rupert Graves, Steven Mackintosh and Saskia Reeves star. 101 min.
53-9558 Was $19.99 $14.99

Hangin' With The Homeboys (1991)
A hip, streetwise account of a night on the town with four Bronx ne'er-do-wells, filled with humor, poignancy and compassion. The foursome, comprised of two blacks, a Puerto Rican and an Italian, crash a party, look for women and get into trouble with the police in this fresh look at hangin' out in the '90s. With Mario Joyner, Doug E. Doug, John Leguizamo and Nestor Serrano. 90 min.
45-5522 Was $19.99 ❏$14.99

Destiny Turns On The Radio (1995)
Hip comedy in which an escaped con is rescued in the Nevada desert by a mysterious stranger named Johnny Destiny and taken to Las Vegas, where he's after his share of bank robbery loot and an old flame who's now a lounge singer with a tough casino owner boyfriend. Dylan McDermott, Nancy Travis, James LeGros and Quentin Tarantino as Destiny star. 102 min.
44-1999 Was $19.99 ❏$14.99

Evil Toons (1991)
Live actors and animation mix in this outlandish horror-comedy of four college co-eds who accidentally unleash a mischievous demon from a tome of black magic. David Carradine, Monique Gabrielle, Arte Johnson and the great Dick Miller star in this demented, adult-oriented comedy from director Fred Olen Ray.
46-5522 $29.99

Baby On Board (1991)
When her mob bookkeeper husband is bumped off in a gangland hit, a woman decides to track down the killers herself, only to wind up becoming the pursued instead of the pursuer. Her only allies are a cab driver and her 4-year-old daughter. Wacky comedy stars Carol Kane, Judge Reinhold. 90 min.
46-5550 Was $89.99 $14.99

The Double O Kid (1992)
A teenage intern at a government security agency gets more "on-the-job training" than he bargained for when a maniacal computer genius and his beautiful assistant pursue him for a valuable package he's carrying. Slapstick spy spoof stars Corey Haim, Wallace Shawn, Brigitte Nielsen. 95 min.
46-5556 Was $89.99 $14.99

L.A. Goddess (1992)
Spry and sexy comedy set against the background of a Hollywood studio, where a gorgeous aspiring screenwriter takes a job as a stuntwoman when the alcoholic star of an erotic western can't finish the film. Soon, a steamy affair develops between the woman and the studio's chief. Jeff Conaway, Kathy Shower, James Hong and David Heavener star. Sizzling uncut, unrated version; 93 min.
46-5559 $12.99

Road To Ruin (1992)
A multi-millionaire tries to test his girlfriend's devotion by announcing that he's broke. The joke is on him, though, when he discovers his partner has duped him out of his fortune! Now, he must find a way to get his millions—and his girl—back. Peter Weller and Carey Lowell star. 94 min.
27-6770 Was $89.99 $14.99

Hot Chocolate (1992)
Love is sweet in this comedy starring Bo Derek as a sexy tycoon out to take over a French candy company. Eventually, she falls for the company's manager (Robert Hays), and the more romantic things get, the wackier they get. 93 min.
27-6790 $14.99

Stepmonster (1992)
A boy must go to extraordinary lengths to save his family when he discovers that his father's new wife is really a disguised monster with evil intentions. Outrageously funny fright film stars Alan Thicke, Corey Feldman, Robin Riker, Ami Dolenz and John Astin. 85 min.
21-9026 Was $89.99 $14.99

Hail Caesar (1994)
A young man who works in an eraser factory aspires to be a rock star and live a life filled with fame, fortune and beautiful women. Will he jump over the hurdles that face him on the road to success? Anthony Michael Hall, Robert Downey, Jr., Samuel L. Jackson and Judd Nelson star. 93 min.
46-5588 $14.99

A Million To Juan (1994)
A good-natured comic fable directed by and starring Paul Rodriguez as a hard-working orange salesman struggling to pay his rent, care for his son and avoid deportation. One day, he's offered a chance for a better life when he's mysteriously handed a check for $1 million to be used to start a new business. Edward James Olmos, Polly Draper, Cheech Marin also star. 97 min.
46-5601 Was $89.99 $14.99

Femme Fontaine: Killer Babe For The C.I.A. (1995)
Non-stop action and pro-feminist fury highlight this outrageous comic actioner starring Margot Hope as the title character, a rowdy redhead secret agent out to avenge her late father. With help from former mercenary-turned-monk Master Sun, Femme battles skinheads, female drug dealers and nasty lesbians in an incredible outing. With James Hong.
46-8006 Was $89.99 $14.99

Blondes Have More Guns (1995)
A hilarious spoof of "Basic Instinct" and other erotic thrillers, this romp tells of a detective investigating the chainsaw death of a used car salesman who falls in love with his chief suspect—a mysterious gal named Montana. Michael McGaharin and Elizabeth Key star. 90 min.
46-8007 Was $69.99 $14.99

Viewer Discretion Advised (1998)
Remember your parents saying that too much television was bad for you? Well, it comes true for a tube-obsessed young man in this wild Troma comedy, as he suddenly finds himself trapped in twisted game shows, terrifying horror films, sexy public service announcements and other offbeat programs. Tommy Blaze, Phil Morton, Terri Swift star. 105 min.
46-8029 Was $59.99 $14.99

Buttcrack (1998)
When Brian's girlfriend decides against moving in with him due to roommate Portly Wade's habit of letting his oversized "moon" rise, Brian is forced to kill Portly. But Wade's sister uses voodoo to revive him as a zoned-out zombie, and Brian seeks help from Bible-thumping preacher Mojo Nixon in stopping the menace of the undead derriere in this horror spoof filled with one "crack" after another.
46-8033 Was $59.99 $14.99

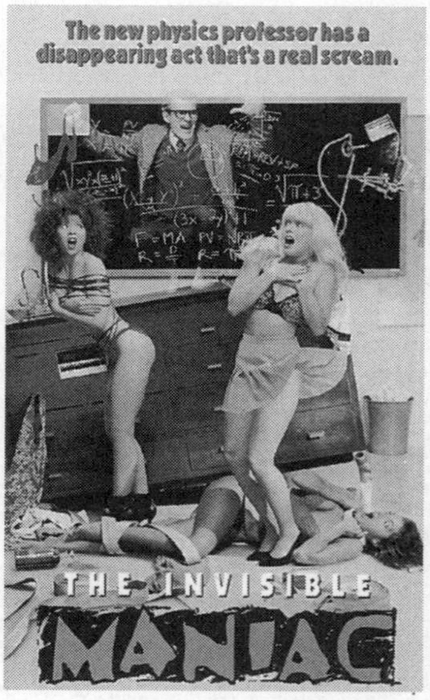

The new physics professor has a disappearing act that's a real scream.
THE INVISIBLE
MANIAC

The Invisible Maniac (1990)
A nerdy physics teacher figures out a way to make himself invisible in order to spy on some of the gorgeous gals in his class. When their teasing gets too sexy, he begins killing them one by one. Noel Peters and Shannon Wilsey (AKA porn star Savannah) star. 87 min.
63-1380 $12.99

And You Thought Your Parents Were Weird (1991)
After their father dies, two teenage boys invent a robot that inherits the spirit of their deceased Dad. The robot reminds the kids and their mother about Dad's good points and also finds itself in trouble when it's nabbed by crooks. Marcia Strassman, Joshua Miller, Edan Gross and the voice of Alan Thicke are featured. 92 min.
68-1220 Was $89.99 ❑*$14.99*

The Favor, The Watch And The Very Big Fish (1992)
A wacky farce set in Paris and featuring Bob Hoskins as a photographer specializing in religious scenes who searches for the perfect Jesus for a photo. He finds the right model in piano-playing ex-con Jeff Goldblum, who soon takes his role way too seriously, and also finds romance with a beautiful woman (Natasha Richardson) who dubs in voices for porno movies. With Michel Blanc. 89 min.
68-1238 Was $89.99 ❑*$12.99*

Raining Stones (1994)
Independent British filmmaker Ken Loach's ("Riff Raff") mix of comedy and pathos follows a working-class English man struggling through a variety of shady and dangerous jobs in order to buy his daughter a Communion dress. Bruce Jones, Ricky Tomlinson, Julie Brown star; music by Stewart Copeland. 90 min.
53-8153 Was $89.99 *$19.99*

National Lampoon's Favorite Deadly Sins (1995)
Three of the seven familiar failings are hilariously depicted in this trilogy of short comedies. Security guard Denis Leary learns the perils of extramarital attractions in "Lust," with Annabella Sciorra; sleazy TV producer Joe Mantegna's "Greed" lands him in a scandal of his own; and temperamental husband Andrew Clay finds his "Anger" carries a price in the afterlife. 99 min.
63-1816 Was $89.99 ❑*$14.99*

Totally F*ed Up (1994)**
From Gregg Araki ("The Living End") comes this no-holds-barred dissection of gay teens in Los Angeles. The film focuses on six homosexual youths—four men and two women—and the crises they face concerning love, romance, AIDS, their future and sex. With James Duval, Alan Boyce and Lance May. 106 min.
53-9738 Was $59.99 *$19.99*

The Doom Generation (1995)
Dazzling, nihilistic road romp from Gregg Araki ("The Living End") concerns a spoiled teenage girl, her well-meaning boyfriend and a creepy drifter who set out on an odyssey of violence and sex after the drifter shoots a convenience store clerk. James Duval, Rose McGowan and Johnathon Schaech star; with Lauren Tewes, Perry Farrell, Parker Posey, Amanda Bearse. Unrated version; 83 min.
68-1796 Was $99.99 ❑*$14.99*

Nowhere (1997)
The concluding chapter in director Gregg Araki's ambisexually anarchic "Teen Apocalypse" trilogy, this stylish dark comedy follows a group of restless L.A. "Gen-Xers" looking for fun, sex, love, and meaning to their lives (not necessarily in that order). All this, plus an alien encounter! James Duval, Rachel True, Ryan Phillippe star, with appearances by Christina Applegate, Shannen Doherty, Heather Graham, and John Ritter as a TV evangelist. 82 min.
02-5160 Was $99.99 ❑*$19.99*

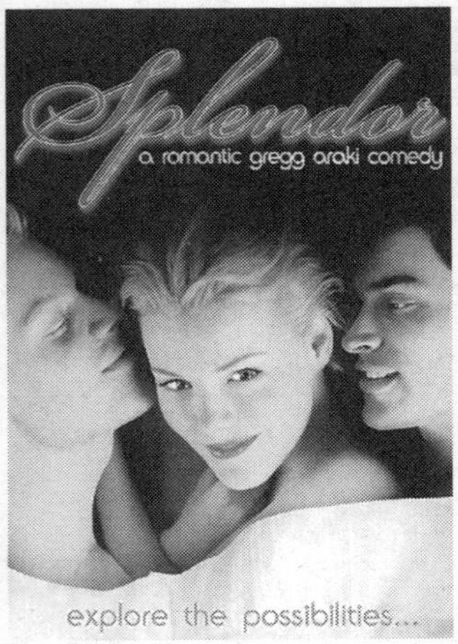

Splendor (1999)
Iconoclastic filmmaker Gregg Araki ("Nowhere") goes the screwball comedy route with this tale centering on the amorous adventures of a blonde named Veronica. She can't decide if she likes a rock critic or punk rock drummer better, so they all move in together. Problems occur when she gets pregnant and can't figure out who's responsible. Kathleen Robertson, Johnathon Schaech and Matt Kesslar star. 93 min.
02-3384 Was $99.99 ❑*$14.99*

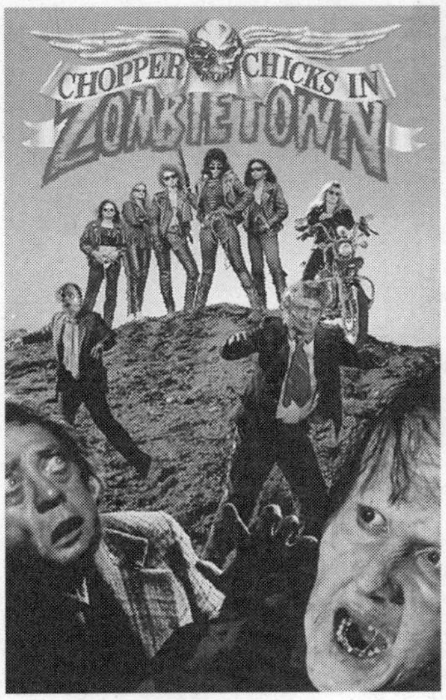

Chopper Chicks In Zombietown (1991)
Outrageous antics from Tromaville as a group of man-hungry motorcycle mamas land in a town where a murderous mortician turns the dim-witted citizens into flesh-eating zombies. Only the biker babes can save the day! Jamie Rose, Martha Quinn and Catherine Carlen star. 86 min.
02-2155 Was $14.99 ❑*$12.99*

Lunatics: A Love Story (1992)
An extremely shy nerd with a fear of spiders falls in love with a gorgeous runaway in this off-the-wall, surrealistic farce produced by Sam Raimi, the director of "Darkman." Theodore Raimi, Deborah Foreman and Bruce Campbell star. 87 min.
45-5533 *$79.99*

Wet And Wild Summer (1993)
A commercial developer has plans to destroy the Mullet Beach Club, home of some of the world's hottest topless sun worshippers. The club's gorgeous owner calls on her surfer friends to go into battle and save their swim, surf and sex paradise. Christopher Atkins, Elliott Gould and Julian McMahon star in this zesty farce. 95 min.
68-1265 *$89.99*

Advising Michael (1998)
Witty romantic story of a romantically-challenged man named Michael who seeks help with women from a group of his supposedly wise friends. When he begins a good relationship with a woman, his pals' advice steers him in the wrong direction, where he discovers the dark side of dating. With Lee Coleman, Tirzah Wise.
46-8046 Was $59.99 *$14.99*

The Suburbanators (1998)
The lives of a group of Calgary slackers collide on what turns out to be a not-just-your-typical day. Deadpan comical complications ensue as three sets of young men find themselves in a series of bizarre and often dangerous situations involving sex, drugs and rock and roll. With Joel McNichol, Stephen Spender and Rogi Masri.
46-8054 Was $59.99 *$14.99*

Left Overs (1996)
A quartet of twentysomething roommates in L.A. have their comfortable, commitment-free lifestyle pulled out from under them when they learn the house they share is about to be sold and they have one week to clear out. Engaging "Gen-X" comedy stars Mark Fite, Jason Oliver, Cyndy Preston.
46-8058 *$59.99*

Shakespeare...In And Out (1998)
Aspiring actor Rich Longfellow moves to L.A. from his Ohio home, hoping to realize his dream of playing Hamlet. In order to pay his dues, he takes a job as the lead actor in the porn film "Aristotle and His Horny Time Travels." But Longfellow is surprised when he becomes well-liked for his physical attributes, rather than his thespian abilities. Wacky spoof in the "Orgazmo" style stars Lee Coleman.
46-8047 *$59.99*

Fatty Drives The Bus (1998)
When Satan has trouble hitting his monthly quota of souls to claim, he decides to play tour guide for a group of unsuspecting passengers on the highway to you-know-where! Little does the Devil know that this bus is filled with obnoxious tourists. Can superhero Jesus Christ save them before it's too late? This devilish farce stars Scot Robinson, Ken Manthey.
46-8051 *$59.99*

Sibling Rivalry (1990)
Kirstie Alley stars as a neglected wife who falls into an afternoon fling with two minor problems: her lover turns out to be her brother-in-law, and he drops dead from a heart attack! Slapstick dark comedy from laughmeister Carl Reiner also stars Sam Elliott, Scott Bakula, Jamie Gertz and Carrie Fisher. 88 min.
53-1792 *$14.99*

The Souler Opposite (1998)
Barry is a comedian struggling in L.A.'s club scene in 1992. When he meets political activist Thea, the unlikely pair wind up falling in love, but their relationship encounters a turning point when Thea leaves to work for Jerry Brown's presidential campaign. Barry soon realizes that his only chance for happiness is to take off across the country to find her. Starring Christopher Meloni, Timothy Busfield and Janel Moloney. 103 min.
82-5216 *$89.99*

Fever Pitch (1997)
Colin Firth is an thirtysomething British teacher and die-hard soccer fan who lives for his Arsenal team. But when he meets and falls for new co-worker Ruth Gemmell, things get complicated because she feels like she's taking a backseat to his obsession. As the championship game draws closer, Firth must decide what's really important to him in this romantic comedy. 102 min.
68-2028 ❑*$69.99*

Man With A Plan (1996)
An offbeat look at American politics, this mock documentary chronicles the 1996 grassroots "campaign" of Fred Tuttle, an outspoken septuagenarian and retired dairy farmer, as he sets out to win his home state of Vermont's seat in the U.S. House of Representatives (Two years after this film, Tuttle became a real-life congressional candidate). 90 min.
50-5886 *$19.99*

Hercules Recycled (1994)
A hilarious reworking of two Steve Reeves classics, "Hercules" and "Hercules Unchained," featuring new dialogue and sound and overall goofiness. Set in 2024, when technology has vanished, the story concerns TV exercise show host Burt Galaxy, who is the only person mighty enough to capture a lost energy formula written on the back of a bath mat. 68 min.
50-5158 *$14.99*

Someone Like You (1990)
A news cameraman who wants to write the greatest love song ever has so many romantic opportunities, he doesn't know whom to settle down with. There's Shelly, a real challenge; Ellen, an overzealous TV reporter; Laurie, an older woman; Carla, his ex-girlfriend; and Jill, who's perfect, but also his roommate's girlfriend. With Jim Bonfield, Rena Davonne. 88 min.
50-5170 Was $19.99 *$14.99*

The Lovemaster (1997)
A hilarious mix of comedy skits and stand-up routine, with comic Craig Shoemaker ("The Magic Hour") as the Lovemaster, a guy with the ability to attract any beautiful woman with ease. Among those involved in the Lovemaster's world are his psychiatrist (George Wendt), wife (Harley Jane Kozak), friend (Courtney Thorne-Smith) and dream girl (Farrah Fawcett). 88 min.
50-5800 *$19.99*

Golfballs! (1999)
Pennytree, a rundown golf club, gets a new life when its owner and his sexy granddaughter decide to populate the place with gorgeous bikini-clad babes and handsome hunks. The owners of rival Bentwood don't take lightly to Pennytree's new attractions, and a tourney takes place pitting the clubs' best golfers against each other. Former Penthouse Pet Amy Lynn Baxter stars. 87 min.
50-8378 *$79.99*

Zack & Reba (1999)
This quirky romantic comedy follows a young woman whose fiancé commits suicide when she calls off their wedding with a week to go. Distraught, Reba returns to her hometown, where an eccentric elderly woman tries to fix her up with her grandson Zack, depressed since his wife's death. Sean Patrick Flanery, Brittany Murphy, Debbie Reynolds and Michael Jeter star. 91 min.
50-8380 *$59.99*

Nudist Colony Of The Dead (1991)
Outrageous horror-comedy-musical-zombie-romance effort about a group of nudists who rise from the dead after a mass suicide and set out to wreak vengeance against the religious zealots who helped close down their beloved nudist colony. Deborah Lynn, Rachel Latt and Forrest J. Ackerman star in this one-of-a-kind spoof shot on 35mm, 16mm and Super 8 formats. 90 min.
53-5172 Was $29.99 *$14.99*

North Shore Fish (1998)
Tony Danza and Mercedes Ruehl star in this heartfelt romantic comedy about two high school sweethearts who struggle with love and the impending closure of their frozen-fish factory on Long Island's North Shore region. With Peter Riegert; from the play by Israel Horovitz. 94 min.
53-6185 Was $89.99 *$19.99*

Bail Jumper (1990)
A Missouri couple tries to leave their life of petty crime behind by moving to New York, but all manner of natural disasters (including floods, tornadoes and locust plagues) seem to follow them on their cross-country odyssey. Bizarre comedy/drama stars Eszter Balint ("Stranger Than Paradise"), B.J. Spalding, Joie Lee. 96 min.
53-7608 Was $79.99 *$19.99*

Unnatural Pursuits (1991)
Alan Bates stars in this song-filled comic romp as a boozing and slightly crazed British playwright who must cope with all sorts of interference when his latest work is brought over to be produced in America. With John Mahoney, Bob Balaban, Nigel Planer. 143 min.
53-8075 Was $39.99 *$19.99*

Let's Get Bizzee (1993)
Rousing hip-hop comedy with music star Doug E. Fresh playing a young rapper who runs for public office against a crooked politician who's out to destroy a local housing project. With Lisa Nicole Carson, Starletta DuBois. 92 min.
54-9130 Was $79.99 *$19.99*

Just Dam' Lucky (1996)
After coming to the aid of an elderly woman, a young black man is amazed when he's rewarded with a large amount of money...and his family and friends all want to share in his good fortune. Fast-paced farce stars Biff Carr, Veronica Pitts. 80 min.
54-9131 *$19.99*

Amanda And The Alien (1995)
An 18-year-old girl finds a really "out-of-this-world" romance when she meets an alien being on the run from the government and helps him blend into Earth culture in this offbeat sci-fi comedy. Nicole Eggert, Michael Dorn, Stacy Keach star. 94 min.
63-1799 *$89.99*

Surviving Desire (1989)
A young woman with dreams of becoming an author begins an affair with her college professor, but while he's falling in love, she's merely using their relationship as inspiration for her writings. Mary Ward, Martin Donovan and Matt Malloy star in writer/director Hal Hartley's sardonic romantic comedy. Also included are two early short films by Hartley, "Theory of Achievement" and "Ambition." 86 min.
53-7728 Was $89.99 *$19.99*

Trust (1991)
Comic and romantic angst courtesy of filmmaker Hal Hartley as a pretty, bratty high school student discovers she's pregnant and is dumped by her football star boyfriend, only to take up with a rebellious computer wizard. Adrienne Shelly, Martin Donovan, John McKay star. 90 min.
63-1487 Was $19.99 ❑*$14.99*

Simple Men (1992)
Long Island auteur Hal Hartley's off-kilter comedy tells the story of two brothers (one's a crook, the other a shy college student) who decide to track down their fugitive father, a former baseball player and 1960s radical accused of bombing the Pentagon. William Sage, Robert Burke and Karen Sillas star. 105 min.
02-2398 Was $89.99 ❑*$19.99*

Amateur (1994)
A former nun who writes pornography. A man with amnesia. A sexy porn queen. An accountant. The lives of these four people eventually collide in upstate New York in this quirky, intellectual comedy from director Hal Hartley. With Isabelle Huppert, Martin Donovan, Damian Young and Elina Lowensohn. 105 min.
02-2807 ❑*$89.99*

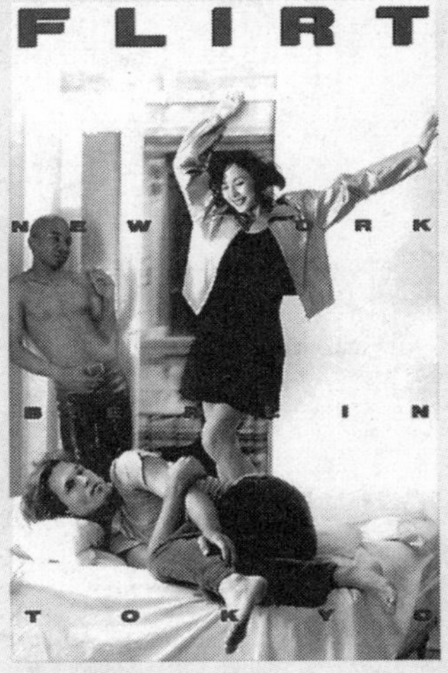

Flirt (1996)
An audacious effort from director Hal Hartley ("Amateur") that looks at romantic triangles in three cities: New York, Berlin and Tokyo. The basic story and dialogue are essentially the same in each locale, although the genders and orientation of the characters change, as Hartley explores the universal search for (and hopelessness of) love. Martin Donovan, Dwight Ewell, Miho Nikaidoh, Parker Posey, Bill Sage star. 84 min.
02-3065 Was $99.99 ❑*$24.99*

Henry Fool (1998)
Hal Hartley's poetic fable concerns the relationship between Henry Fool (Thomas Jay Ryan), a disheveled writer, and Simon Grim (James Urbaniak), an inexpressive garbageman. After becoming unlikely friends, Henry encourages Simon to write a poem. The result is an epic work that soon becomes a controversial sensation. Parker Posey, Maria Potter also star. 137 min.
02-3231 Was $99.99 ❑*$19.99*

Please see our index for the Hal Hartley title: *Book Of Life*

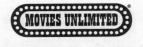

Black Spring Break: The Movie (1998)
Welcome to Daytona Beach, a beautiful Florida spot that hosts Black Spring Break every year. When an All-American football star and his rapper friend hit the sands for some rest and relaxation, the gridiron star discovers gorgeous golddiggers and sports agents want a piece of him. Daron Southboy Fordham, Kenny Flyy star; features a top rap and pop score.
54-9158 *$19.99*

Masala (1993)
Audacious dark comedy about an East Indian junkie living in Canada who, trying to kick his drug habit and overcome his family's death in a plane crash, turns to the god Krishna for help. This politically incorrect satire from writer/director/star Srinivas Krishna also features Saeed Jaffrey, Zohra Segal. 105 min.
53-7838 Was $89.99 *$19.99*

Hijacking Hollywood (1998)
Henry Thomas ("E.T.") stars as a disgruntled Hollywood production assistant in this sharp and funny satire. Fed up with being pushed around by his boss, Thomas decides to steal the undeveloped negative of the producer's latest big-budget project, "Moby Dick 2: Ahab's Revenge," in order to finance his own film. With Scott Thompson, Mark Metcalf and writer/director Neil Mandt. 93 min.
50-5939 *$89.99*

Attention Shoppers (1999)
After losing his job on a hit TV series, actor Nestor Carbonell finds his fame dwindling and his life in a rut until the opportunity arises to do an appearance at the opening of a Houston K-Mart. Carbonell accepts, only to be devastated when he learns that a new teen heartthrob is also appearing across town and is acquiring most of the interest. Luke Perry, Casey Affleck co-star. AKA: "Blue Light Special." 87 min.
12-3339 *□$49.99*

How I Spent My Summer Vacation (1998)
Lively independent comedy about the contemporary African-American dating scene. A group of black college students experiences laughs and love as they try to get together with members of the opposite sex. Ronreaco Lee, Deanna Davis and E. Roger Mitchell star. 90 min.
54-9182 Was $59.99 *$19.99*

Schizopolis (1997)
Writer/director Steven Soderbergh ("sex, lies and videotape") presents a bizarre and darkly comic slice of cinematic surrealism that takes an off-kilter look at religion, cults, romance, family life and exterminators. Soderbergh stars in a dual role, as an aide to the guru of a Scientology-like group and a lovestruck dentist. Betsy Brantley, David Jensen co-star. 96 min.
53-9813 Letterboxed *$19.99*

Secret Agent 00Soul (1990)
Super-smooth spy Billy Dee Williams quits his elite government job in order to realize his dream of opening a detective office in his old urban neighborhood, but being housed above a take-out restaurant and trying to teach his 400-pound son the business isn't what Williams had in mind. Action and comedy mix in this wild spoof; with Tiny Lister, Jr., Marjean Holden, Amanda LeFlore. 71 min.
54-9118 *$89.99*

Open Season (1996)
Satirical swipe at the television industry starring Robert Wuhl (who also wrote and directed) as a tour guide at a TV ratings company who is hired as an advisor at a public television network after it accidentally gets high ratings. Whatever Wuhl says is mistaken as sage advice and he's mistaken for a media guru. With Helen Shaver, Rod Taylor and Gailard Sartain. 102 min.
63-1855 *□$99.99*

Alan Smithee

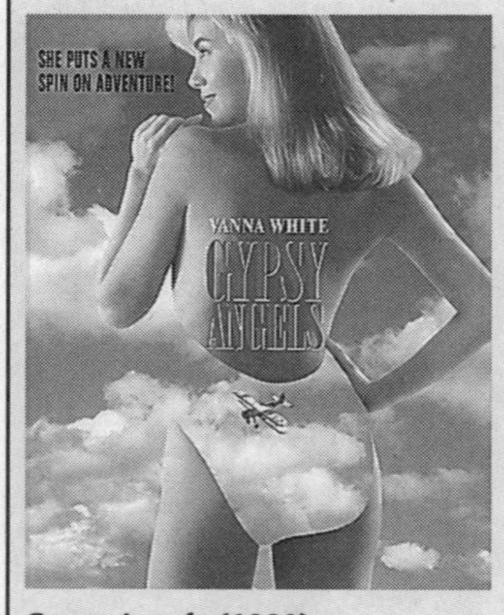

Gypsy Angels (1980)
Long before "Wheel of Fortune," Vanna White played an exotic dancer in director Alan Smithee's high-flying adventure. Vanna's a nightclub stripper who's hoping to land a job as a real dancer, and after she's rescued from a car accident by a lawyer with a passion for stunt planes, romantic sparks fly. Gene Bicknell, Richard Roundtree co-star. 92 min.
68-1296 Was $89.99 *$14.99*

Morgan Stewart's Coming Home (1987)
Enjoyable farce stars Jon Cryer as the unhappy scion of wealthy, politically ambitious parents (Lynn Redgrave, Nicholas Pryor) who's brought home from boarding school just for the media's benefit and discovers that Dad's sleazy campaign manager is up to no good. Directed by Alan Smithee (Terry Winsor and Paul Aaron). 96 min.
44-1503 Was $69.99 *$14.99*

Ghost Fever (1987)
There's frightfully good fun for all ahead when a pair of cops are sent to a mysterious old house to evict the two strange old ladies squatting there. All they find, though, are spooks and spirits...but no way out! Sherman Hemsley, Luis Avalos star; directed by Alan Smithee (Lee Madden). 86 min.
53-3116 Was $19.99 *□$14.99*

The Shrimp On The Barbie (1990)
Cheech Marin plays an enterprising restaurateur who wants to open the first Mexican eatery in Australia. Things don't work out well, and he soon takes an unusual job: posing as a fiancé for rich, beautiful heiress Emma Samms. Vernon Wells, Bruce Spence also star; Alan Smithee (Michael Gottlieb) directs. 87 min.
03-1775 *□$12.99*

Solar Crisis (1992)
In the year 2050, explosions on the surface of the sun threaten to create a solar flare that could destroy all life on Earth, and the crew of an orbiting space station must find a way to avert the disaster. Thrilling sci-fi tale from director Alan Smithee (Richard Sarafian) stars Tim Matheson, Peter Boyle, Jack Palance and Charlton Heston. 111 min.
68-1255 Was $89.99 *□$12.99*

The O.J. Simpson Story (1995)
The life, times and turmoil of football great O.J. Simpson are covered in this controversial movie that includes his illustrious college and pro playing careers, his stints in the entertainment world and the murders of his wife, Nicole Brown Simpson, and her friend, Ronald Goldman. Bobby Hosea, Jessica Tuck and Bruce Weitz star; Alan Smithee (Jerrold Freedman) directs. 90 min.
04-2939 Was $89.99 *$29.99*

Raging Angels (1995)
Two young rock musicians are drawn to a charismatic singer who serves as spokesman for a mysterious organization promoting global unity. What the teens don't realize is that dark supernatural forces are behind the group's success, and they become the pawns in a battle between good and evil. Alan Smithee's unusual shocker stars Sean Patrick Flanery, Monet Mazur, Michael Paré and Diane Ladd. 97 min.
68-1790 *$89.99*

An Alan Smithee Film: Burn Hollywood Burn (1998)
Who better than the writer of "Showgirls," Joe Eszterhas, to pen a scathing satire of Hollywood politics? When he loses creative control of a $200 million action film, director Eric Idle can't have his name pulled off it and substitute the official pseudonym "Alan Smithee," because that's his real name. Idle's solution: steal the only negative from the lab and hold the film hostage. Ryan O'Neal and Richard Jeni co-star. And yes, this comedy's director, Arthur Hiller, had his name replaced with Alan Smithee. 86 min.
11-2776 Was $19.99 *□$14.99*

Sub Down (1998)
A nuclear sub crashes deep below the polar icecap, and it's up to two research scientists in a submersible pod to save the surviving crew before it's too late. Nail-biting suspense and non-stop action abound in director Alan Smithee's (Gregg Champion's) thriller, guaranteed to keep you on the edge of your seat. With Stephen Baldwin, Gabrielle Anwar, Chris Mulkey and Tom Conti. 91 min.
68-1885 *□$99.99*

Please see our index for these other Alan Smithee titles: *Hellraiser: Bloodline • Hostage Hotel • Iron Cowboy*

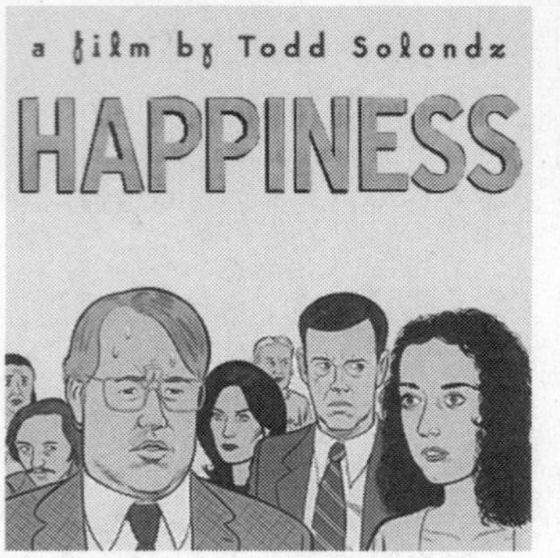

Happiness (1998)
Like a Norman Rockwell painting that covers a Hieronymous Bosch canvas, director Todd Solondz's ("Welcome to the Dollhouse") controversial, jet-black comedy peels back the lives of three suburban New Jersey sisters to reveal a variety of neuroses and crises, from career dissatisfaction and a neighbor's obscene phone calls to a "perfect" husband who's a pedophile. Jane Adams, Dylan Baker, Lara Flynn Boyle, Jared Harris and Cynthia Stevenson star. 139 min.
68-1912 Was $99.99 *$14.99*

Flirting (1992)
Sensitive, funny sequel to "The Year My Voice Broke," following the escapades of a teenage Australian boy who finds romance with a Ugandan girl while attending a strict boarding school in the mid-1960s. Noah Taylor, Thandie Newton and Nicole Kidman star in this refreshing romantic tale. 99 min.
68-1259 Was $89.99 *□$12.99*

Alma's Rainbow (1997)
This hip urban comedy tells of the sexual awakening of a mother and her teenage daughter after a carefree aunt stops in their house for a surprise visit. Filled with fresh insights about middle-class African-American life and lively humor from a female perspective, Ayoka Chenzira's film stars Victoria Gabrielle Platt.
54-9157 *$79.99*

Vermont Is For Lovers (1993)
Lively independent comedy from John O'Brien ("The Big Dis") about a New York couple whose plans to get married at an idyllic New England farm are put in jeopardy when they begin to get cold feet and seek advice on love and life from the Vermont locals. George Thrush and Marya Cohn star. 88 min.
53-8481 *$59.99*

The Wife (1996)
Director/star Tom Noonan's follow-up to his acclaimed "What Happened Was..." features Noonan and Julie Hagerty as husband and wife psychiatrists whose New Age-styled life is disrupted when neurotic patient Wallace Shawn and stripper girlfriend Karen Young pay a surprise visit to their Vermont home. 101 min.
53-8659 Letterboxed *$19.99*

Honey Sweet Love (1994)
Warm and romantic comedy/drama, set in a small town in occupied Sicily during World War II, stars Ben Cross as a by-the-book British colonel who tries to get the villagers to cease their black market operations and elect a mayor. Things get complicated when Cross falls for the new mayor's gorgeous wife. Jo Champa, Eli Wallach also star. 91 min.
53-9666 *$29.99*

Q: The Movie (1999)
In this urban comedy, Cedrick is left in charge of his parents' house and has some rules to follow: no wild parties or babes allowed in the house. But they didn't say anything about the backyard. A wild, babe-filled house party ensues! With Brian Hooks, Keno D. Deary and Ishtar star. 85 min.
54-9189 Was $59.99 *$19.99*

9 1/2 Ninjas (1990)
If you like your ninja action mixed with laughs and sexy fun, this martial arts comedy is your cup of saki. A beautiful woman chased by a gang of black-clad assassins is aided by a dapper karate expert whom she falls for, but can they survive to the wedding night? Michael Phenicie, Andee Gray, Tiny Lister ("No Holds Barred") star. 88 min.
63-1409 Was $89.99 *$12.99*

Bare Essentials (1990)
A New York yuppie couple find themselves accidentally stranded on a remote tropical island. Battling the elements (and each other), the couple soon discovers a handsome beachcomber and his beautiful native gal Friday. Exotic, romantic romp stars Mark Linn-Baker, Gregory Harrison, Lisa Hartman, Charlotte Lewis. 94 min.
63-1433 *□$89.99*

Mastergate (1992)
A hilarious satire of Washington from writer Larry Gelbart ("M*A*S*H"), as cable TV's Total News Network covers Senate hearings on a presidential conspiracy to divert funds through a Hollywood studio to Central American revolutionaries. The terrific cast includes James Coburn, Richard Kiley, Pat Morita, Buck Henry and Ed Begley, Jr. 90 min.
53-8313 Was $89.99 *$19.99*

Clarence (1991)
Clarence, the guardian angel who saved Jimmy Stewart in "It's a Wonderful Life," returns to Earth in order to save a young widow driven to the brink of suicide by a heartless corporate raider out to take over her business. Winning family comedy stars Robert Carradine as Clarence, Kate Trotter. 92 min.
63-1475 Was $19.99 *□$14.99*

Heads (1994)
A small-town newspaper proofreader gets a shot at reporting when he's assigned to cover a murder case. The case soon encompasses several killings—all with victims who are decapitated—and leads the would-be newshound to a mysterious female stranger. Jon Cryer, Jennifer Tilly and Ed Asner star in this dark comedy. 102 min.
63-1675 Was $89.99 *□$14.99*

Sodbusters (1994)
Wacky spoof of western films stars Kris Kristofferson as an enigmatic gunslinger named Destiny who arrives in a small town and immediately finds himself in the middle of a dispute between farmers and cattlemen. As the battle between the two factions gets meaner, the situation gets funnier, thanks to a cast including Fred Willard and John Vernon and direction from Eugene Levy of "SCTV" fame. 97 min.
63-1726 Was $89.99 *□$14.99*

Rent-A-Kid (1995)
Super salesman Leslie Nielsen is asked by his son to take care of an orphanage for a week. Nielsen gets a brilliant idea: start a "rent-a-kid" service for couples unable to decide whether they're ready for the ups and downs of raising children! Hilarious family comedy also stars Christopher Lloyd, Matt McCoy. 90 min.
63-1797 Was $89.99 *$14.99*

Live Nude Girls (1995)
A "bachelorette slumber party" for a group of female friends turns into a funny, emotional and moving evening as the women reveal long-held secrets and bare their souls on love, lust and friendship. Spicy comedy/drama stars Kim Cattrall, Olivia D'Abo, Dana Delany, Laila Robins, Cynthia Stevenson and Lora Zane. 92 min.
63-1826 Was $99.99 *□$14.99*

Ruby Jean And Joe (1996)
Heartwarming comedy/drama stars Tom Selleck as a middle-aged rodeo cowboy who gets a new lease on life when a feisty young hitchhiker joins him on the road and sets out to help him. Rebekah Johnson, JoBeth Williams and Ben Johnson also star. 100 min.
63-1859 *□$99.99*

Bury Me In Niagara (1993)
Ever-controlling mom Jean Stapleton presents problems for her son even after she dies, appearing as a ghost at her own funeral. When her son uses a mystical Japanese stone to keep her alive, he's pursued by hit men and must get Mom back to Niagara within 48 hours in order to get her into heaven. Geraint Wyn Davies also stars. AKA: "Ghost Mom." 96 min.
64-3419 *$14.99*

Sink Or Swim (1998)
A group of friends soon finds their friendship put to the test when they compete for a highly desired writing job in this biting satire on office politics and dirty dealing. Tom Arnold, Illeana Douglas, Dave Foley, Robert Patrick, Stephen Rea and John Ritter star. 111 min.
64-9028 *$99.99*

Hi-Life (1998)
Compulsive gambler Eric Stoltz owes cash to bookie-bartender Charles Durning. He persuades girlfriend Moira Kelly to borrow money from her brother in a complicated plan that eventually spins out of control. All of the elements are eventually revealed at the Hi-Life Bar. Daryl Hannah and Peter Riegert also star. 86 min.
64-9030 *$99.99*

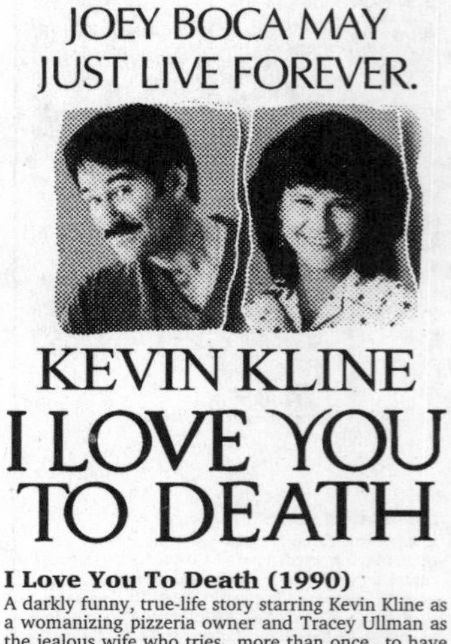

I Love You To Death (1990)
A darkly funny, true-life story starring Kevin Kline as a womanizing pizzeria owner and Tracey Ullman as the jealous wife who tries...more than once...to have him murdered. Lawrence Kasdan's black-hearted look at romance also features Joan Plowright, River Phoenix, and William Hurt and Keanu Reeves as two dim-witted hit men. 96 min.
02-2048 Was $19.99 *□$14.99*

My Girl (1991)
You'll find sunshine on a cloudy day with this bitter-sweet charmer focusing on the delicate relationship between a motherless 10-year-old girl (Anna Chlumsky) and a young boy (Macaulay Culkin). At the same time their friendship grows, so does the romance between the girl's mortician father (Dan Aykroyd) and the free-spirited morgue beautician (Jamie Lee Curtis). Also stars Griffin Dunne, Richard Masur. 102 min.
02-2197 Was $19.99 ☐*$14.99*

My Girl 2 (1994)
Teenager Vada (Anna Chlumsky) is back and feeling unwanted at home with dad Dan Aykroyd and newly expectant stepmom Jamie Lee Curtis. She heads to Los Angeles to find out more about her real mother and, with help from a teenage cousin, discovers revealing things about her family's past. Austin O'Brien, Richard Masur co-star. 99 min.
02-2633 Was $19.99 ☐*$14.99*

Six Ways To Sunday (1998)
Offbeat mobster story with darkly comic touches tells of Harry, a teenager who gets recruited by Jewish mobsters in Youngstown, Ohio, to collect debts owed to them. Harry's devotion and unsparingly violent ways help him get ahead in the criminal world, but his bond with his obsessive mother could cause problems. Norman Reedus, Deborah Harry, Adrien Brody and Isaac Hayes star. 97 min.
83-1395 Was $99.99 *$14.99*

Love Kills (1998)
Fast-paced and darkly funny thriller stars Mario Van Peebles (who also directed and scripted) as a con artist who escapes from jail and attempts to woo Beverly Hills heiress Lesley Ann Warren. Van Peebles quickly finds himself mixed up with Warren's greedy relatives, each trying to double-cross the other for the family fortune. Alexis Arquette, Daniel Baldwin, Lucy Liu co-star. 94 min.
83-1526 *$99.99*

Coming Soon (1999)
A trio of college girlfriends sets out on a comedic quest—to help one of them find the man who can help her reach sexual fulfillment—in this distaff take on "American Pie." Gaby Hoffmann, Bonnie Root and Tricia Vessey star, with appearances by Yasmine Bleeth, Mia Farrow, Spalding Gray and Ryan O'Neal. Unrated version includes scenes not shown in theaters; 96 min.
83-1552 *$99.99*

Kiss And Tell (1999)
A woman is found murdered in Los Angeles International Airport with a carrot wedged in an unlikely place. As detectives investigate the bizarre crime, the victim's "Gen X" friends soon find the killer is one of their crowd. Offbeat black comedy stars Heather Graham, Rose McGowan, Peter Greene, Justine Bateman and David Arquette. 90 min.
83-5168 *$59.99*

The Shot (1996)
Lively Hollywood spoof about two aspiring actors who swipe a copy of a big studio film and hold it hostage. Can the dudes parlay their crime into a shot at stardom? Dan Bell, Michael DeLuise, Mo Gaffney and, in a cameo, Dana Carvey are featured. 85 min.
88-7001 Was $89.99 *$14.99*

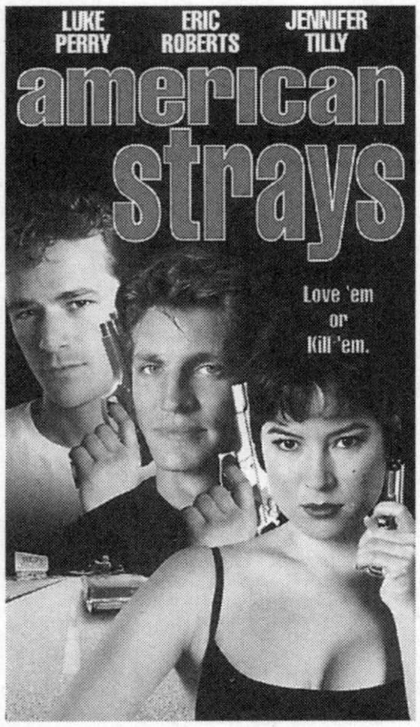

American Strays (1996)
This satiric and unsettling look at violence in America focuses on a group of outlaws and outcasts whose paths cross at a roadside restaurant in the West. Among them: emotionally distressed family man Eric Roberts; Luke Perry, a suicidal masochist; serial killer/vacuum cleaner salesman John Savage; and Carol Kane, the diner's owner. With Jennifer Tilly, Sam Jones. 93 min.
83-1116 Was $99.99 *$14.99*

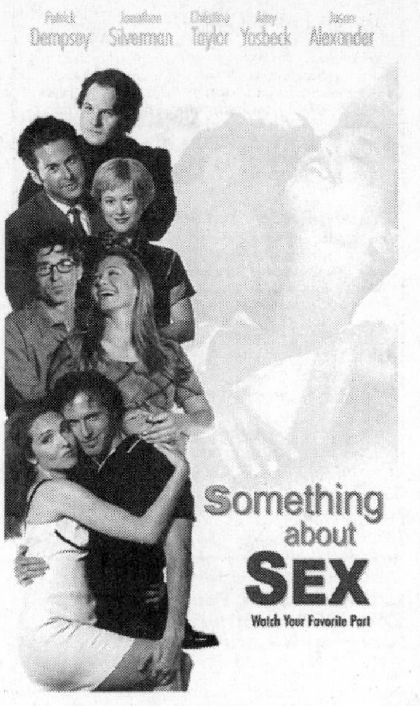

Something About Sex (1998)
A discussion about fidelity at an L.A. dinner party stirs doubts in three couples in this insightful comedy/drama about relationships in the '90s. The ensemble cast includes Jason Alexander, Patrick Dempsey, Jonathan Silverman, Christine Taylor and Amy Yasbeck. AKA: "Denial." 92 min.
83-1385 Was $99.99 *$14.99*

Getting Personal (1998)
A young man meets and falls for a beautiful zoologist after waking up on her porch, but their blossoming relationship is threatened by bad "advice" from friends and his mysterious blackouts, which a psychiatrist thinks are connected to a secret in the man's past, in this romantic comedy/drama. Michael Landes, Hedy Burress, Lane Smith and John Shea star. AKA: "Lost and Found." 82 min.
85-1173 *$59.99*

Deadly Advice (1996)
A shy young English bookseller, constantly nagged by her overbearing mother, is offered help in "eliminating" the problem by such infamous killers as Dr. Crippen and Jack the Ripper. But after committing the crime and getting her sister's aid in dumping the body, the woman can't shake her new "friends." Offbeat black comedy stars Jane Horrocks, Brenda Fricker, Jonathan Pryce and Edward Woodward. 91 min.
88-1077 Was $99.99 ☐*$14.99*

Undercover Angel (1999)
A writer searching for "Miss Right" gets some unexpected help when an old flame asks him to look after her 6-year-old daughter for a few weeks. Soon the youngster is playing matchmaker for her guardian in this fun-filled family comedy. Yasmine Bleeth, Dean Winters, James Earl Jones and Emily Mae Young star. 93 min.
86-1150 ☐*$99.99*

The Perez Family (1995)
A sexy, colorful comedy in which Cuban Alfred Molina heads to America to be reunited with wife Anjelica Huston in Miami after 20 years of separation. In order to win release from detention, however, Molina is convinced by fellow immigrant Marisa Tomei to pose as man and wife. Chazz Palminteri and Trini Alvarado co-star; Mira Nair ("Mississippi Masala") directs. 135 min.
88-1018 Was $19.99 ☐*$14.99*

Eat Your Heart Out (1997)
The lives of three people sharing a loft apartment in Los Angeles take some strange turns when one of them, an up-and-coming chef, gets a job hosting a live TV cooking show and, flushed with success, moves out to be with his agent/lover. Fast and funny look at friendship, California-style, stars Christian Oliver, Pamela Segall, John Craig and Laura San Giacomo. 94 min.
85-1205 *$59.99*

Hoods (1999)
Darkly funny caper comedy stars Joe Mantegna as a put-upon hit man who has six hours to carry out the latest contract from his mob boss father. Trouble is, he doesn't know where to find the target and no one's ever heard of him. Joe Pantoliano, Kevin Pollack, Jennifer Tilly co-star. 92 min.
85-1321 ☐*$59.99*

Bed & Breakfast (1992)
A Nantucket bed-and-breakfast establishment is turned upside-down when a mysterious stranger washes up on a nearby beach. The man's presence affects the lives of the three women (daughter, mother and grandmother) who live there, but soon a group of thugs arrive looking for the new arrival. Roger Moore, Talia Shire, Colleen Dewhurst and Nina Siemaszko star. 96 min.
80-1047 Was $89.99 ☐*$14.99*

Robot In The Family (1993)
Ten-year-old Alec encounters all sorts of danger when he teams up with his family's homemade robot on a search for a valuable relic that could bring his father the $1.5 million he needs. Joe Pantoliano, John Rhys-Davies and Danny Gerard star in this exciting family comedy. 92 min.
83-1002 Was $89.99 *$14.99*

Across The Moon (1994)
A fast and funny road comedy starring Christina Applegate and Elizabeth Peña as two very different women who set out on a road trip across the Southwest to visit their boyfriends in jail, but have trouble remaining faithful when they meet a variety of guys along the way. 88 min.
80-1083 *$14.99*

Round Numbers (1990)
Wacky comedy of marital infidelity, as a woman convinced her "Muffler King" husband is cheating on her winds up at the same spa as her younger rival. Kate Mulgrew, Samantha Eggar, Marty Ingels and Hope Marie Carlton star. 98 min.
80-1026 Was $89.99 *$14.99*

Sorority House Party (1994)
A hunky rock star is held hostage by a group of sexy sorority girls in this crazy campus comedy filled with bodacious babes. Playboy covergirl Avalon Anders, April Lerman and male supermodel Attila star. 95 min.
83-1004 *$14.99*

Never Too Late (1997)
Four elderly people from Quebec discover that a mutual friend was ripped off by the head of a retirement home. The quartet devises a plan to get even that involves pulling off a wild heist. Olympia Dukakis, Cloris Leachman, Jan Rubes, Jean Lapointe and Corey Haim star. 96 min.
82-9059 *$89.99*

Almost Hollywood (1994)
In Hollywood, some people stop at nothing short of murder to get on the big screen, but in this racy, funny comedy-thriller, someone's gone over that line and killed a would-be starlet. Was it the weaselly producer? His jealous wife? The crazed director? Don Short, Rachel Dyer and Playmate of the Year India Allen star.
81-9015 *$14.99*

Mike Leigh

Bleak Moments (1971)
Based on his earlier stageplay, director Mike Leigh's debut feature tracks the life of "quiet desperation" experienced by lonely, overweight Anne Raitt, an office worker who lives with her retarded sister and a guitar-playing hippie who rents out their garage. Mike Bradwell, Sarah Stephenson also star. 110 min.
01-1528 Was $59.99 *$29.99*

Hard Labour (1973)
An early effort from masterful British social satirist Mike Leigh ("Naked") focusing on a poor, elderly woman who faces abuse from her husband, children and employer. Alison Steadman, Clifford Kershaw and Ben Kingsley star in this offhanded look at classism and sexism. 70 min.
01-1490 Was $79.99 *$29.99*

Nuts In May (1976)
A middle-class couple who never abandoned their '60s counterculture ways go on a camping vacation, but their free-love, vegetarian lifestyle is rubbing their fellow campers the wrong way in Mike Leigh's innovative comedy. Roger Sloman, Alison Steadman star. 84 min.
01-1471 Was $79.99 *$29.99*

Abigail's Party (1977)
Filmmaker Mike Leigh's outrageous dark comedy looks at a woman's disastrous attempts to put together a dinner party. The problems that she faces (and that drive her to have more than one drink too many) culminate in her husband's heart attack on her new carpet! Alison Steadman stars. 105 min.
01-1472 Was $89.99 *$29.99*

Kiss Of Death (1977)
The humor of director Mike Leigh is evident in this early whimsical tale of an undertaker's assistant whose attempts at romance make for hilarious, unforgettable moments. David Threlfall, John Wheatley star. 80 min.
01-1491 Was $79.99 *$29.99*

Who's Who (1978)
Satiric slice-of-life look by director Mike Leigh at the members of a British brokerage firm inhabited by weird, socially inept workers. Among the eccentrics examined are two young roommates who throw a dinner party to meet people and a royalty-obsessed boor and his put-upon, cat-loving wife. With Simon Chandler and Adam Norton. 75 min.
01-1477 Was $79.99 *$29.99*

Grown Ups (1980)
A recently married couple moves into their new house and soon discovers such nuisances as the bride's wacky sister and their former high school gym teacher, who happens to live next door. Directed by Mike Leigh; Philip Davis, Sam Kelly star. 95 min.
01-1478 Was $79.99 *$29.99*

Home Sweet Home (1982)
A bitter look at England's problems with class and marriage as seen through the story of a postman who seeks affairs with his co-workers' wives after his spouse leaves him. Eric Richard, Timothy Spall and Kay Stonham star in this film from Mike Leigh. 90 min.
01-1492 Was $79.99 *$29.99*

Four Days In July (1984)
Day-to-day life in Northern Ireland may not seem like the basis for cinema comedy, but director Mike Leigh deftly examines the common and dissimilar troubles of two families (one Catholic, one Protestant) in a film laced with heartfelt, offbeat humor. Brid Brennan, Desmond McAleer star. 99 min.
01-1470 Was $79.99 *$29.99*

Meantime (1985)
Turning his camera on a working-class family living in a squalid apartment in London's East End, writer/director Mike Leigh mixes comedy and drama as he follows the family's growing concern over son Tim Roth's friendship with skinhead Gary Oldman. Phil Daniels, Alfred Molina, Marion Bailey also star. 103 min.
53-9812 Was $79.99 *$19.99*

Life Is Sweet (1991)
This acclaimed quirky comedy from director Mike Leigh centers on an oddball working-class family in London. The father dreams of refurbishing a rundown cafe truck, the mother is a cheerful free spirit, and their twin daughters are an androgynous plumber-to-be and an angry bulimic with a passion for kinky sex. Alison Steadman, Claire Skinner and Jane Horrocks star. 103 min.
63-1559 ☐*$14.99*

Naked (1993)
Lacerating tale of England's disaffected centers on Johnny, a scruffy, loquacious drifter whose visit to London to see an old girlfriend leads him into a whirlwind of wild sex and angry confrontations with other lost souls and different women. David Thewlis' highly-acclaimed, tour-de-force performance is at the center of Mike Leigh's darkly comic drama. 131 min.
02-2617 Was $89.99 ☐*$19.99*

Secrets & Lies (1996)
A 27-year-old black London optometrist decides to seek out the woman who gave her up for adoption after she was born. The search leads to a surprising discovery: her mother is a white factory worker living in the city's grimy East End. Their emotional first meeting is just the beginning of a series of family crises in writer/director Mike Leigh's moving comedy/drama. Brenda Blethyn, Marianne Jean-Baptiste, Timothy Spall star. 142 min.
04-3435 Was $99.99 ☐*$29.99*

Career Girls (1997)
Reuniting for the first time since graduating six years earlier, two young women who were best friends in college spend a day travelling through London, reminiscing about the changes in their lives and encountering a variety of people from the past, in this funny and heartfelt tale from filmmaker Mike Leigh. Katrin Cartlidge, Lynda Steadman, Mark Benton star. 87 min.
04-3557 Was $99.99 ☐*$14.99*

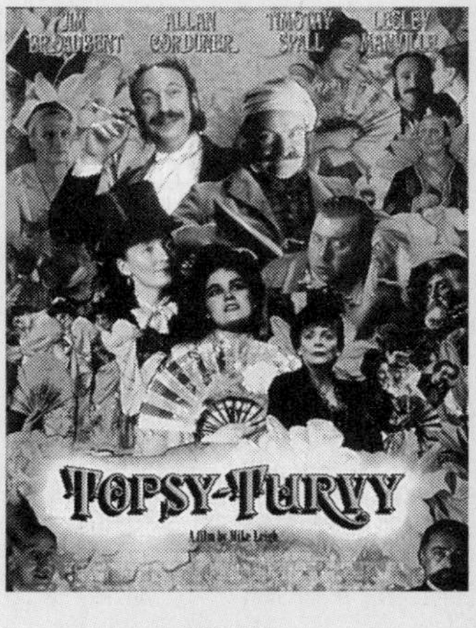

Topsy-Turvy (1999)
Filmmaker Mike Leigh's ("Secrets & Lies") seriocomic spin on the stormy collaboration of operatic masters William S. Gilbert (Jim Broadbent) and Arthur Sullivan (Allan Corduner) is set in 1884, when the failure of "Princess Ida" casts doubts on the duo's future. A chance visit by Gilbert to a Japanese exhibition gives him the idea that will lead to their greatest success—"The Mikado." Ron Cook, Lesley Manville, Timothy Spall. 161 min.
02-9208 Was $99.99 ☐*$14.99*

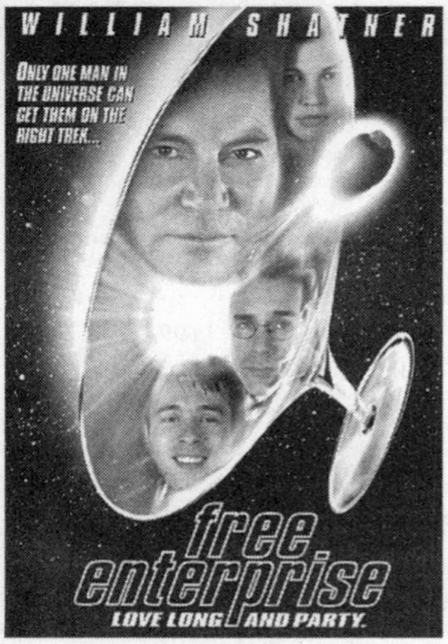
WILLIAM SHATNER
ONLY ONE MAN IN THE UNIVERSE CAN GET THEM ON THE RIGHT TREK...
free enterprise
LOVE LONG AND PARTY.

Free Enterprise (1999)
Two sci-fi obsessed twentysomething pals meet their idol, William Shatner, in a Los Angeles used bookstore. But while the former Captain Kirk tries to interest them in his dream project—a musical version of Shakespeare's "Julius Caesar" in which he tackles all the major roles—the duo have their own romantic and job-related problems to worry about. Rafer Weigel, Eric McCormack and Audie England also star in this zany satirical comedy. 114 min.
85-1322 ❑*$69.99*

Free Enterprise (Letterboxed Version)
Also available in a theatrical, widescreen format.
85-1323 ❑*$69.99*

The All New Adventures Of Laurel And Hardy: For Love Or Mummy (1999)
The beloved comedy duo is re-created for a new generation, as Stan (Bronson Pinchot) and Ollie (Gailard Sartain) serve as escorts for for a museum's Egyptian exhibit. When a 3,000-year-old mummy is missing and they're blamed, the boys find themselves pursued by the the police, the museum authorities, and the now-living mummy. F. Murray Abraham also stars. 84 min.
76-9116 *$99.99*

The Deli (1997)
This slice-of-life comedy centers on Johnny Amico, the owner of a New York deli, who is constantly in trouble because of his gambling debts. With his business in trouble because of his bad betting ways, Johnny takes on bookies, gangsters and neighborhood weirdoes in a last-ditch effort to save his business. Mike Starr, Jerry Stiller, David Johansen, Ice T and Debi Mazar star. 98 min.
81-9035 *$99.99*

Nothin' 2 Lose (1999)
Given an ultimatum by his beautiful girlfriend, would-be hip-hop producer Brian Hooks must prove in 30 days that he can turn from a fun-loving player to a respectable marrying man. Will an old flame's attentions lead him astray, and can his basketball buddies save him? With Yasmine.
81-9106 *$59.99*

Talking About Sex (1996)
Hip, funny and erotic farce starring "In Living Color's" Kim Wayans as an editor whose latest work is a best-seller about sex. Soon, her friends' ideas on the subject become the topic of a TV documentary where their desires are revealed. The revelations lead to changes in their lives and an all-night party where anything can happen. With Marcy Walker. 100 min.
82-5023 *$79.99*

Plan 10 From Outer Space (1996)
In this exercise in kooky cultism, a woman finds an antiquated book that was written by a wacky Mormon prophet and soon is caught in the middle of a plot involving angels, aliens and fanatical Mormons. Karen Black and Stefene Russel star in this sci-fi satire that was banned in Boise.
82-5030 *$79.99*

Movies, Money & Murder (1996)
After a ruthless actress seduces a doctor into helping her finance a movie, wild complications and hilarity ensue when they meet the film's writer and her husband at the doctor's luxurious beach house. Dead bodies, treachery and a chase soon abound in this farce featuring Martin Mull, Lee Purcell and Karen Black. 100 min.
82-5031 *$79.99*

Life In The Fast Lane (1999)
Off-the-wall dark comedy starring Fairuza Balk as a frustrated artist named Mona whose life gets wackier and wackier after she stabs her obsessive graffiti artist boyfriend. Soon, Mona's haunted by his spirit and runs into a group of bizarre characters, including a musical minister and carjacking poet. With Téa Leoni, Debi Mazar, Patrick Dempsey. AKA: "There's No Fish Food in Heaven." 92 min.
82-5181 *$59.99*

Delivery (1998)
Inspired by a real-life company, this raucous comedy centers on a food delivery company that caters to the richest and wackiest residents of Beverly Hills. Set during one unpredictable night, the film follows the exploits of eight delivery service workers and their zany antics. Jim O'Malley, Sam Whipple and Amanda Foreman star. 85 min.
76-7455 *$39.99*

Motorcycle Cheerleading Models (1998)
A group of sexy, young cheerleaders puts their pom-poms down for a while so they can rescue some friends from a demented movie director named Mr. Scardino. Dan Haggerty, Joe Estevez, Chris Mitchum and adult star Brooke Ashley star in this risqué romp.
76-2089 *$39.99*

La Cage Aux Zombies (1996)
It's a "Night of the Living Drag Queens" when the victims of a plane crash turn into flesh-eating, cross-dressing zombies in this outrageous low-budget blend of campy comedy, music, nudity and gore. Gangsters, marital infidelity, cut-rate liposuction...it's all here! Cathy Roubal, Eric Gladsjo star, with a special appearance by Russ Meyer favorite Kitten Natividad. Unrated version; 84 min.
76-7311 *$59.99*

The Windy City (1997)
Energetic independent comedy centering on four black friends who gather for a 10-year high school reunion and soon find how they've changed and drifted apart. Among the attendees are a successful lawyer, a ladies' man, an unstable cop and a comic book writer. Ted Lyde, James Black and Viktor Mack star. 97 min.
76-7400 *$69.99*

Life 101 (1995)
Set in the 1960s, this romantic comedy focuses on a group of college students who get some first-hand lessons on love out of the classroom. With help from roommate Keith Coogan, new student Corey Haim discovers the finer points of college life. Things get really complicated, however, when Haim begins a romance with cute co-ed Ami Dolenz. With Louis Mandylor. 95 min.
76-9078 Was $89.99 *$14.99*

The Man With The Perfect Swing (1995)
In this sports-themed comedy, Babe Lombardo, a former college football star struggling to make ends meet, develops what he thinks is the world's perfect golf swing and tries to market it through an instructional videotape. Lombardo pins his hopes on the efforts of a young golf champ, who signs on in an endorsement deal. James Black, Suzanne Savoy and Bill Dando star. 93 min.
76-9084 Was $19.99 *$14.99*

Plan B (1997)
The "chill" is on for a group of twenty- and thirtysomething friends trying desperately to find their places in the world in the 1990s. There's a struggling novelist, a couple having problems conceiving, a female executive looking for love, and an actor who thinks his time to make a name for himself is running out. Jon Cryer, Lance Guest, Lisa Darr and Mark Matheisen star. 102 min.
76-9094 Was $19.99 *$14.99*

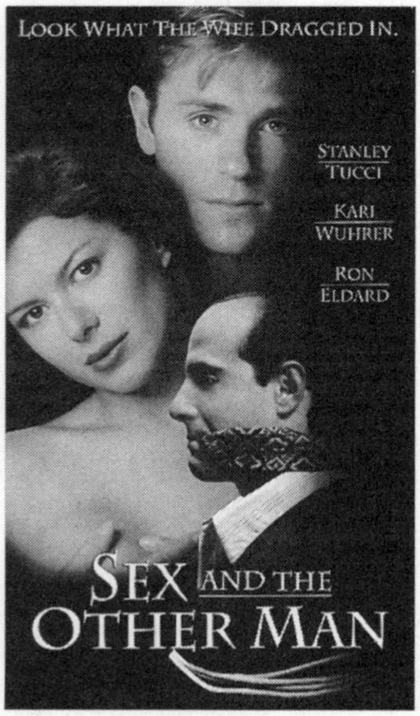
LOOK WHAT THE WIFE DRAGGED IN.
STANLEY TUCCI
KARI WUHRER
RON ELDARD
SEX AND THE OTHER MAN

Sex And The Other Man (1996)
After catching his girlfriend in bed with her married boss, an impotent man ties the interloper up and makes him watch the couple's lovemaking. While this cures his "problem," how long can they keep their unwilling houseguest bound? Steamy sex and dark comedy mix in this acclaimed independent film. Stanley Tucci, Ron Eldard and Kari Wuhrer star. 89 min.
83-1127 Was $99.99 *$14.99*

House Party (1990)
A rambunctious comic rap-attack that turns teenage movie conventions upside-down. After his father grounds him for brawling with a bruiser, a high school kid encounters all sorts of wacky hazards while attempting to get to his pal's party. Kid 'N Play, Martin Lawrence, Robin Harris and Tisha Campbell star in this stylish, music-filled farce. 100 min.
02-2036 *$14.99*

House Party 2 (1991)
Kid 'N Play return for more hip-hop hi-jinks in this funny, fast-moving sequel. After Play blows Kid's college tuition fund in a recording scam, the pair must hold a wild campus "Jammie Jam" to raise money fast. With Martin Lawrence, Tisha Campbell, Queen Latifah and Iman; music by Tony! Toni! Toné! and Bell Biv Devoe. 94 min.
02-2192 Was $19.99 ❑*$14.99*

House Party 3 (1994)
The fun continues in this third party as high-haired Kid decides to get hitched, and Play throws him one wild bachelor party. When Kid's fiancée figures her future hubby's been getting close to a former flame, look out! Bernie Mac, Gilbert Gottfried, Tisha Campbell and TLC co-star. 94 min.
02-2620 Was $89.99 ❑*$14.99*

L.A. Rules (The Pros And Cons Of Breathing) (1994)
Four friends trying to make it big in Hollywood spend their time hanging out in a trendy Los Angeles bar rambling on about life, work and the opposite sex. Joey Lauren Adams ("Chasing Amy") is the waitress who loves them all. 92 min.
82-5083 *$99.99*

Lover Girl (1998)
Produced by Alison Anders ("Gas Food Lodging"), this coming-of-age tale tells of Jake, a teenage girl abandoned by her mother and ignored by her sister, who is taken in by Marcia, the proprietor of a massage parlor. Soon, Jake fits in with the other girls at "Jean's American Spa." Tara Subkoff, Sandra Bernhard and Kristy Swanson star. 87 min.
82-5088 *$89.99*

National Lampoon's Golf Punks (1999)
Down-and-out golf pro Tom Arnold is forced to teach the sport to a group of misfits at a public course. With the group set to play a team from an elite country club headed by his rival, Arnold tries to turn his losing crew into winners. James Kirk and Maureen Webb also star in this laugh ride. 92 min.
82-5126 *$49.99*

14 Ways To Wear Lipstick (1999)
This favorite at the Slamdance Film Festival tells of Carlo, a collector for a loan shark, whose marriage has hit the skids. He doesn't have it in him to tell his wife, so he fakes illness and ignores her. Then he realizes his mistake when she wins a date with a Spanish soap opera star. Michael Tassoni and Tracy Burgard star. 101 min.
82-5138 *$99.99*

Fumbleheads (1999)
Still smarting from the loss of the local pro football team years earlier, former bandleader and diehard fan Ed Asner hatches a scheme to lure them back that involves abducting the team owner and star quarterback. Rousing gridiron gooffest also stars Mark Curry, Barry Corbin. 95 min.
82-5150 *$99.99*

The First To Go (1997)
Lively romantic farce about Adam, an impulsive young man who plans to get married to Carrie after knowing her for only two weeks. Four of Adam's friends question their pal's decision, and decide to take him on one last vacation—and sabotage his nuptials! Zach Galligan, Laurel Holloman, Mark Harmon and Corin Nemec star. 100 min.
82-5152 *$89.99*

Deadlock (1997)
Comedy-horror involving a couple who finally find the perfect house only to discover that it's haunted. Once the couple unknowingly open the portal to "the other side," they are visited by a group of ghosts looking to turn the home's new inhabitants into murderer and victim. John Griffin and Stuart Chapin star. 90 min.
82-5170 *$59.99*

It Came From The Sky (1999)
Quirky comedy-drama about an family whose lives are turned topsy-turvy when eccentric millionaire Christopher Lloyd crash lands his plane on their roof. Lloyd's ridiculously romantic relationship with "dancer" girlfriend Yasmine Bleeth inspire emotionally estranged John Ritter and JoBeth Williams to rediscover their love for each other and help their intellectually impaired son. 92 min.
82-5180 *$99.99*

Floundering (1994)
A darkly humorous account of "twentysomething" angst starring James LeGros as a Venice Beach resident who finds his world in ruins when the IRS freezes his bank account, his brother overdoses on amphetamines and he discovers his girlfriend cheating on him with a fat guy. Ethan Hawke, John Cusack, Steve Buscemi and Kim Wayans appear in cameos. 97 min.
83-1031 Was $89.99 *$14.99*

Palookaville (1996)
This winning, atmospheric heist comedy tells of three best friends who become reluctant criminals when they plan to better their dead-end lives in Jersey City by robbing an armored car. William Forsythe, Vincent Gallo, Adam Trese and Frances McDormand star. 92 min.
88-1129 ❑*$19.99*

The Raffle (1994)
Two girl-crazy guys hit upon a money-making scheme—search the globe for the world's most perfect woman, then raffle off a chance to date her—in this fast and funny romantic comedy. Nicholas Lea, Bobby Dawson, Jennifer Clement star, with a cameo by Mark Hamill. 100 min.
83-1022 Was $89.99 *$14.99*

Back Fire! (1995)
Wacky "Airplane!"-styled spoof of "Backdraft" in which the toilets of New York City are being detonated and an all-woman fire brigade must stop the mad "bomber." Kathy Ireland, Mary McCormack, Shelley Winters and Robert Mitchum star. 88 min.
83-1026 Was $89.99 *$14.99*

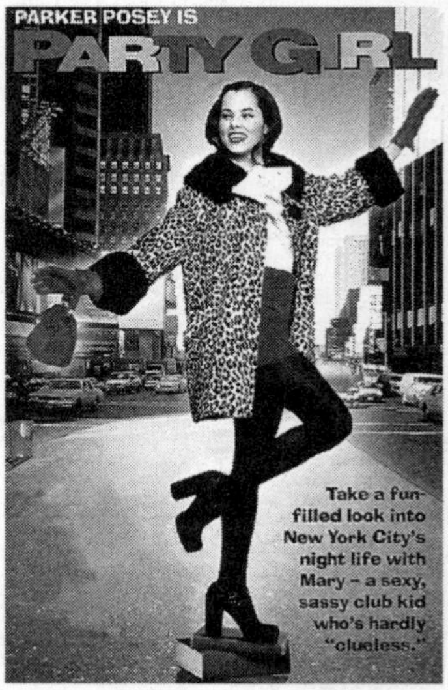
PARKER POSEY IS
PARTY GIRL
Take a fun-filled look into New York City's night life with Mary – a sexy, sassy club kid who's hardly "clueless."

Party Girl (1995)
Engaging comedy starring Parker Posey in a sparkling performance as a hip denizen of Manhattan's party scene who gets arrested for hosting an illegal rave in her loft. Posey's godmother convinces her to get her life in order by taking a library clerk job, and, while immersing herself in the Dewey Decimal System, she falls for a Lebanese falafel vendor. With Omar Townsend, Liev Schreiber. 94 min.
02-2853 Was $19.99 ❑*$14.99*

Running Wild (1995)
A woman about to marry a man twice her age discovers that she's really in love with his handsome son. The woman, her new lover and his friend take a wild ride to Mexico that has them becoming bounty hunters, fugitives and escapees. Daniel Dupont, Jennifer Barker and Daniel Spector star. 97 min.
83-1034 Was $89.99 *$14.99*

Cannes Man (1996)
The glitz and glamour of the Cannes Film Festival are captured in this farce featuring Seymour Cassel as a legendary Hollywood producer who tries to turn a young courier into the next hot thing through hype and chutzpah during the fest. Francesco Quinn, Rebecca Broussard co-star; Johnny Depp, John Malkovich, Dennis Hopper, Treat Williams and Lloyd Kaufman are among the cameos. 88 min.
84-3005 Was $89.99 *$19.99*

Changing Habits (1996)
In this romantic comedy, a talented aspiring artist finds refuge in a dilapidated house populated by nuns after her savings are gone and her rent is raised. But the household chores become more difficult than she originally imagined. Can she find true happiness with an art supply salesman? Moira Kelly, Christopher Lloyd, Teri Garr and Shelley Duvall star. 92 min.
83-1130 Was $99.99 *$14.99*

Misery Loves Company (1998)
Eric thinks he's found the woman of his dreams, but best friends Kevin and Mike want to show him how much trouble one woman can be for a single man...and how far friendship goes! Rockmond Dunbar and Dominick Morales stars in this hip urban comedy. 95 min.
91-9075 *$89.99*

Relax...It's Just Sex! (1999)
The minefield that is relationships in the '90s is the topic of this warm and witty comedy about a group of gay and straight friends who use their regular dinner parties to vent their emotions. Among them: the group's "mother hen" (Jennifer Tilly), who's trying to talk her boyfriend into parenthood; a gay playwright (Mitchell Anderson) looking for "Mr. Right"; and a lesbian couple (Cynda Williams and Serena Scott Thomas) facing a possible break-up. With Lori Petty, Billy Wirth. 100 min.
83-1495 Was $79.99 *$14.99*

BRENDAN FRASER   ALICIA SILVERSTONE

Blast from the Past

Blast From The Past (1999)
After spending his entire life in the elaborate underground bomb shelter his parents retreated into during the 1962 Cuban Missile Crisis, Brendan Fraser emerges into 1990s Los Angeles on a quest to find a nice, non-radioactive girl to marry. Alicia Silverstone is Fraser's guide to the modern world and eventual love interest in this offbeat romantic comedy. Christopher Walken, Sissy Spacek and Dave Foley also star. 106 min.
02-5212   Was $99.99   ☐$14.99

**The Adventures Of
A Gnome Named Gnorm (1993)**
In order to crack a diamond smuggling ring, a Los Angeles police detective teams with a whimsical, smart-talking gnome. Funny, fantastic family adventure stars Anthony Michael Hall, Jerry Orbach, Claudia Christian, and Gnorm as himself. 84 min.
02-8038   Was $89.99   ☐$14.99

Lotto Land (1995)
Lively, sensitive comedy set in a Brooklyn neighborhood where a group of people anxiously await to hear the winner of a $34 million lottery payout. Among the characters showcased are an African-American liquor store clerk, his street musician father, and the clerk's Hispanic, college-bound girlfriend. Larry Gilliard, Jr., Wendell Holmes and Barbara Gonzalez star. 87 min.
02-8479   Was $89.99 $14.99

Edie & Pen (1996)
Heartfelt comedy/drama about two women who meet in Reno while waiting for "quickie" divorces and strike up a friendship with each other and a man whose wife took off with his beloved dog in tow. Stockard Channing, Scott Glenn and Jennifer Tilly star, with a slew of cameos. 98 min.
02-8576   Was $19.99 $14.99

Downhill Willie (1996)
Willie, a dim-witted young man, becomes a dynamo when he puts on skis. And when his best friend gets into business trouble, Willie tries to help him (and himself) by entering a $500,000 skiing contest. Hilarious complications ensue both on and off the slopes. With Keith Coogan, Staci Keanan and Estelle Harris. 90 min.
02-8591   Was $99.99   ☐$14.99

The Pompatus Of Love (1996)
Four male New York friends baffled by the ways of the opposite sex are forced into trying to understand women and their lives better when one of them decides to move in with his new girlfriend. Jon Cryer, Adrian Pasdar, Mia Sara, Kristin Scott Thomas and Jennifer Tilly star in this lively comedy about love in the 1990s. 99 min.
02-8595   Was $99.99 $14.99

The Big Squeeze (1996)
Smart and sexy contemporary "comedy noir" featuring Lara Flynn Boyle as a down-and-out barmaid who devises a plan to dupe her ex-baseball player hubby out of a $130,000 insurance payment. Joining her in the scheme are a slick gambler and a gardener who's in love with her. With Peter Dobson, Danny Nucci. 107 min.
02-8597   Was $99.99 $14.99

**Four Weddings And
A Funeral (1994)**
A surprising box office hit, this charming romantic comedy stars Hugh Grant and Andie MacDowell as two people whose inevitable coming together is followed through a series of encounters at the weddings of mutual friends, a funeral...and even their own weddings. Sharply written and acted, with a great supporting cast that includes Simon Callow, Kristin Scott Thomas and Rowan Atkinson. 117 min.
02-8086   Was $19.99   ☐$14.99

Cadillac Ranch (1996)
A diverse trio of sisters who have been estranged from one another for years come together for a raucous road trip where they learn their late father left them a mysterious bequest buried near Texas's famed tourist attraction, the Cadillac Ranch. Offbeat action-comedy stars Suzy Amis, Caroleen Feeney, Renee Humphrey and Christopher Lloyd. 95 min.
02-8653   Was $99.99   ☐$14.99

Mr. Reliable (1996)
Set in 1968, this hilarious true story depicts Australia's first hostage crisis, as ex-con cab driver Wally Mellish attempts to make a new life for himself with a single mother. But when his theft of some car hood ornaments brings the police to their house, the situation becomes a full-blown siege witnessed on live TV that turns Mellish into a folk hero. Colin Friels, Jacqueline McKenzie star. 110 min.
02-8640   Was $99.99   ☐$14.99

A Couch In New York (1996)
Tired and looking for a change, New York psychiatrist William Hurt arranges to temporarily swap apartments with Paris ballet dancer Juliette Binoche. Once in America, the free-spirited Binoche begins treating Hurt's patients, caring for his dog, and totally rearranging his life in this spirited romantic comedy from Belgian filmmaker Chantal Akerman. 104 min.
02-8655   Was $19.99   ☐$14.99

Wedding Bell Blues (1997)
With their 30th birthdays approaching, girlfriends Illeana Douglas, Paulina Porizkova and Julie Warner decide they'd rather face them as divorcées rather than singles. The trio sets out for Las Vegas to find—and dump—husbands, but find some surprises along the way, in Dana Lustig's smart and funny comedy. John Corbett, Jonathan Penner also star. 101 min.
02-8780   Was $99.99   ☐$14.99

How To Be A Player (1997)
Fast-living and date-juggling ladies' man Bill Bellamy may score big with his buddies by sharing his secrets on becoming a successful "player," but his sister sets out to teach him a lesson by throwing a party—and inviting all his girlfriends to attend!—in this wild comedy. Natalie Desselle, Lark Voorhies, Jermaine Hopkins also star. 94 min.
02-8794   Was $19.99   ☐$14.99

Going All The Way (1997)
Based on the best-selling novel by Dan Wakefield, this coming-of-age seriocomedy stars Jeremy Davies and Ben Affleck as two young Korean War vets from different backgrounds who strike up a life-changing friendship in 1954 Indianapolis. Amy Locane, Rachel Weisz, Lesley Ann Warren and Jill Clayburgh also star. 103 min.
02-8809   Was $19.99 $14.99

Hugo Pool (1997)
Underground director Robert Downey, Sr. ("Putney Swope") returns to off-the-wall form with this way-out dark comedy about sexy pool cleaner Alyssa Milano and her experiences with wacky customers, strange parents and a man stricken with Lou Gehrig's disease. Robert Downey, Jr., Patrick Cassidy, Chuck Barris, Sean Penn, Malcolm McDowell and Richard Lewis also star. 93 min.
02-8859   Was $99.99 $14.99

No Looking Back (1998)
Waitress Lauren Holly is sure that there's got to be more to life than slinging hash in her small New Jersey hometown and settling down with steady beau Jon Bon Jovi, but is the sudden arrival of old flame Edward Burns the answer to her problem? Writer/director Burns' working-class romantic triangle drama also stars Blythe Danner, Connie Britton. 96 min.
02-8862   Was $19.99   ☐$14.99

Clockwatchers (1997)
Four women hired as temp workers in a credit company are united by dissatisfaction with their tenuous job status and the lack of direction in their lives, but can a "temporary" friendship last? Director/co-writer Jill Sprecher's drolly funny comedy/drama of '90s office life stars Toni Collette, Lisa Kudrow, Parker Posey and Alanna Ubach. 96 min.
02-8975   Was $99.99 $14.99

Just Write (1997)
Jeremy Piven is a Hollywood tour bus driver who is mistaken for a hot screenwriter by beautiful actress Sherilyn Fenn. After Piven offers his help on Fenn's new project, the two become romantically involved, but he must find a way to tell her about his real occupation. Sunny, romantic movie industry farce also stars JoBeth Williams, Alex Rocco and Costas Mandylor.
02-9062   Was $99.99 $14.99

PRELUDE TO A KISS

ALEC BALDWIN

MEG RYAN

Prelude To A Kiss (1992)
Bittersweet romantic comedy, based on the hit Broadway play, stars Alec Baldwin as a newlywed whose love for wife Meg Ryan is put to the ultimate test when her soul is mysteriously transferred to the body of a sickly old man on their wedding day. Patty Duke, Ned Beatty, Sydney Walker and Kathy Bates also star. 105 min.
04-2587   Was $89.99 $14.99

Whoopi Goldberg

JUMPIN' JACK FLASH

Jumpin' Jack Flash (1986)
When computer operator Whoopi Goldberg receives a message from a spy being held by enemy agents, the result is comedic cloak and dagger chaos. Wild slapstick thriller co-stars Stephen Collins, Carol Kane and John Wood; directed by Penny Marshall. 100 min.
04-2053   Was $19.99   ☐$14.99

Fatal Beauty (1987)
Streetwise cop Whoopi Goldberg and mob bodyguard Sam Elliott find themselves uneasy allies as they wage a war against the peddlers of a deadly coke strain in this slam-bang actioner. With Brad Dourif, Ruben Blades. 104 min.
12-1780   Was $19.99   ☐$14.99

Burglar (1987)
Fast-rolling comedy actioner stars Whoopi Goldberg as a San Francisco burglar who overhears a murder during a night on the job...and has to race to find the real killer before the police get their hands on her. Co-stars Bob Goldthwait, Lesley Ann Warren. 102 min.
19-1592   Was $19.99   ☐$14.99

Clara's Heart (1988)
Moving drama stars Whoopi Goldberg as a Jamaican woman who leaves her homeland behind to come to America and work for a wealthy family. Soon a special friendship develops between Goldberg and the family's young son. With Kathleen Quinlan, Michael Ontkean, Neil Patrick Harris. 108 min.
19-1685   Was $19.99 $14.99

Kiss Shot (1989)
Whoopi Goldberg excels as a struggling single mom who tries to get some quick cash by shooting pool. Her competitors don't realize it, but Whoopi's a real ace with a cue. Dennis Franz and Dorian Harewood co-star in this fast, funny farce. 88 min.
71-5250 $12.99

The Long Walk Home (1990)
Acclaimed drama takes a powerful look at the beginnings of the modern civil rights movement, as the 1955 Montgomery, Alabama, bus boycott is seen through the eyes of black housekeeper Whoopi Goldberg and well-to-do white employer Sissy Spacek. Their relationship forms a bond that tests each woman's courage. 98 min.
27-6707   Was $19.99   ☐$14.99

Sister Act (1992)
Hilarious habit farce with Whoopi Goldberg as a tough Las Vegas lounge singer who is forced into hiding after she witnesses a mob murder overseen by her gangster boyfriend. She poses as a nun in a San Francisco convent, where she battles the uptight Mother Superior and tries to reorganize the convent choir. Maggie Smith, Harvey Keitel, Mary Wickes and Kathy Najimy co-star. 100 min.
11-1645   Was $19.99   ☐$14.99

**Sister Act 2:
Back In The Habit (1993)**
After leading their choir to international acclaim, Whoopi Goldberg is asked by her singing sister pals to don the habit again in order to give choral lessons to delinquent kids in a San Francisco school. Can she avoid an evil administrator out to reveal her true identity and teach the kids respect and some new tunes in time for the all-state competition? Kathy Najimy, Maggie Smith co-star; with future hip hop star Lauryn Hill. 107 min.
11-1795   Was $19.99   ☐$14.99

Made In America (1993)
When the teenage daughter of a politically correct, African-American single mother (Whoopi Goldberg) is told she is the product of artificial insemination, she learns from sperm bank records that her father is really an obnoxious, politically incorrect used car dealer (Ted Danson). Hilarious interracial romantic comedy also stars Will Smith, Nia Long and Jennifer Tilly. 113 min.
19-2146   Was $19.99   ☐$14.99

Corrina, Corrina (1994)
Set in the early 1960s, this sensitive comedy-drama stars Whoopi Goldberg as a feisty housekeeper-nanny hired by a widowed ad jingle writer (Ray Liotta) to care for his 7-year-old daughter (Tina Majorino), who has been unable to speak since her mother's death. Goldberg uses her magical personality to help the young girl speak again and draw Liotta out of his sadness. 115 min.
02-5043   Was $19.99   ☐$14.99

Theodore Rex (1996)
In this hilarious family fantasy farce, Whoopi Goldberg is a wise-cracking cop who joins forces with Teddy, a meek Tyrannosaurus Rex, in a search for dinosaur murderers in the year 2013. Whoopi at her sassiest and wild special effects highlight this one-of-a-kind movie. With Armin Mueller-Stahl, Juliet Landau. 92 min.
02-5095   Was $99.99   ☐$14.99

Eddie (1996)
Limo driver and hardcore New York basketball fan Whoopi Goldberg is hired by the team's new Texas billionaire owner to coach her beloved Knicks. Stuck with overpaid and lazy players, Whoopi tries to whip the hoopsters into shape using streetwise tactics. Frank Langella, Dennis Farina and Richard Jenkins co-star; features lots of cameos from real players. 100 min.
11-2064   Was $99.99   ☐$19.99

The Associate (1996)
After she's passed over for a promotion in favor of a less qualified male colleague, Wall Street analyst Whoopi Goldberg quits to form her own business, but finds no clients due to her gender. Whoopi's solution is to create a fictitious male partner, but what can she do when she must produce her "associate" in the flesh? Gender-bending business world satire, based on a French film, also stars Dianne Wiest, Tim Daly, Eli Wallach. 114 min.
11-2103   Was $99.99   ☐$19.99

Bogus (1996)
After his mother is killed in a car accident, a 7-year-old boy sets out to build a new family with two very unlikely "parents": his mother's foster sister, a harried businesswoman (Whoopi Goldberg), and a hulking imaginary friend named Bogus (Gerard Depardieu). Sweet and magical comedy/fantasy also stars Haley Joel Osment, Nancy Travis. 112 min.
19-2486   Was $19.99   ☐$14.99

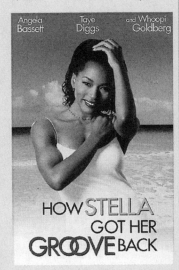

Angela Bassett   Taye Diggs   and Whoopi Goldberg

HOW STELLA GOT HER GROOVE BACK

**How Stella Got
Her Groove Back (1998)**
Angela Bassett stars as Stella, a tightly-wound, 40-year-old stockbroker and single mother who joins best friend Whoopi Goldberg on a much-needed Jamaican vacation and, while there, falls for a striking local man half her age. The reactions to their blossoming romance form the basis for this winning romantic comedy based on Terry McMillan's ("Waiting to Exhale") book. With Taye Diggs, Regina King. 124 min.
04-3775   Was $99.99   ☐$14.99

Please see our index for these other Whoopi Goldberg titles: *Alice In Wonderland • An Alan Smithee Film: Burn Hollywood Burn • Boys On The Side • Cinderella • The Color Purple • The Deep End Of The Ocean • Ghost • Ghosts Of Mississippi • Girl, Interrupted • In The Gloaming • A Knight In Camelot • The Magical Legend Of The Leprechauns • Moonlight And Valentino • Our Friend, Martin*

Folks! (1992)
Riotous comedy with Tom Selleck as a stockbroker who finds his life crumbling after his wife leaves him, and after he brings his parents from Florida to Chicago to live with him, things get even worse. Don Ameche, Anne Jackson also star. 108 min.
04-2567   Was $89.99   ☐$19.99

Frozen Assets (1992)
You can bank on this comedy for outrageous laughs, as ambitious financial executive Corbin Bernsen signs on to save a money-losing institution in a small Oregon town, not knowing it's actually a sperm bank run by biologist Shelley Long. With Larry Miller. 96 min.
04-2671   Was $89.99   ☐$29.99

Cactus Flower (1969)
Walter Matthau, Ingrid Bergman and Oscar-winner Goldie Hawn star in this laugh-filled hit from Broadway, about a lecherous bachelor dentist who enlists the aid of his prudish nurse to pose as his wife and meet his ditzy "mistress." Co-stars Jack Weston, Rick Lenz. 103 min.
02-1116 *$14.99*

There's A Girl In My Soup (1970)
Goldie Hawn played the charmingly daffy heart-stealer to Peter Sellers' lecherous bachelor in this breezy sex romp about a TV gourmet who is willing to give up his bed-hopping ways for a zestful, young beauty. Tony Britton, Nicky Henson, John Comer and Diana Dors co-star; directed by Roy Boulting. 96 min.
02-1243 *$14.99*

Butterflies Are Free (1972)
The entrance of carefree spirit Goldie Hawn into the life of a young blind man (Edward Albert) who's just beginning to spread his wings brings about disapproval, but ultimately acceptance, from his overprotective mother (Oscar-winner Eileen Heckart). Touching translation of the Broadway hit co-stars Michael Glasser. 109 min.
02-1195 *$14.99*

$ (Dollars) (1972)
Warren Beatty and Goldie Hawn team up to steal millions of dollars and laughs in this comedy-adventure about a bank heist in Germany that leads to one of the wildest chases on film. Gert Frobe, Robert Webber co-star; score by Quincy Jones. 119 min.
02-1425 *$14.99*

The Girl From Petrovka (1974)
An American reporter in Moscow falls in love with a Russian ballerina, but finds that their romance is threatened by officials on both sides. Comedy/drama stars Goldie Hawn, Hal Holbrook, Anthony Hopkins. 103 min.
07-1483 Was $59.99 ❑*$14.99*

The Duchess And The Dirtwater Fox (1976)
Flighty dance hall girl Goldie Hawn and sly gambler George Segal team up to take on the frontier in this slapstick western comedy, while dodging a band of outlaws out to retrieve $40,000 stolen from them by Segal. Also stars Conrad Janis, Thayer David and Jennifer Lee. 104 min.
04-1054 ❑*$19.99*

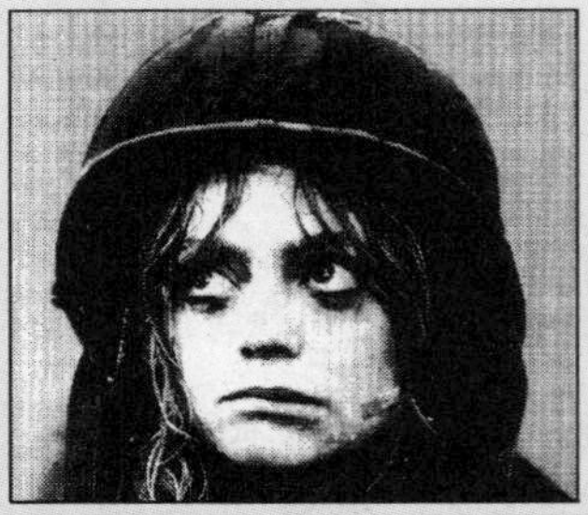

PRIVATE BENJAMIN

Private Benjamin (1980)
Goldie Hawn is delightful as a newly-married (and just-as-newly-widowed) Jewish-American Princess who decides to get away from her life by joining the "new, liberal" Army. Her boot camp misadventures make for great comedy. Eileen Brennan, Armand Assante co-star. 110 min.
19-1169 *$14.99*

Lovers And Liars (1981)
Wacky Italian comedy stars the effervescent Goldie Hawn as an American tourist in Rome who is picked up while hitchhiking by banker Giancarlo Giannini, which leads to wild and romantic misadventures. AKA: "Travels with Anita." 96 min.
53-1104 Was $29.99 *$14.99*

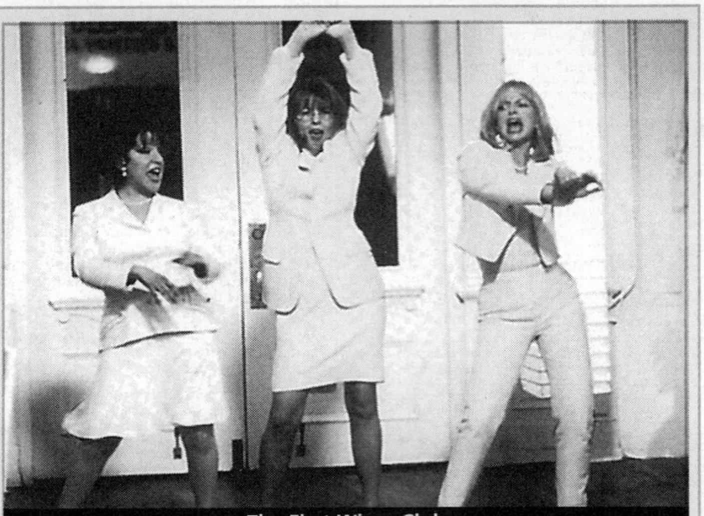

The First Wives Club

Goldie Hawn

Best Friends (1982)
The irresistible pairing of Burt Reynolds and Goldie Hawn elevates this bittersweet comedy about the unexpected effect that marriage has on the relationship between two "best friend" screenwriters. Co-stars Ron Silver, Jessica Tandy, Barnard Hughes; directed by Norman Jewison from Valerie Curtin and Barry Levinson's script. 108 min.
19-1255 *$14.99*

Swing Shift (1984)
When World War II breaks out, housewife Goldie Hawn joins thousands of other women on an airplane factory assembly line. Her offbeat love affair with Kurt Russell, new friends and experiences on the line make this a funny, poignant film. Christine Lahti, Ed Harris, Fred Ward, Holly Hunter co-star; Jonathan Demme directs. 100 min.
19-1335 Was $19.99 *$14.99*

Protocol (1984)
"Ms. Hawn Goes to Washington" and international diplomacy will never be the same. Goldie stars as a ditsy waitress who gets tangled up in red tape and politics after she foils an assassination attempt on an Arab potentate and is given a position as a government protocol officer. Co-stars Chris Sarandon, Andre Gregory, Richard Romanus. 96 min.
19-1414 Was $19.99 ❑*$14.99*

Wildcats (1986)
Giggling Goldie Hawn goes for gridiron greatness as a frustrated gym teacher who finally gets her chance to coach high school football...at the inner city's toughest school. Funny football farce also stars James Keach, Swoosie Kurtz, Wesley Snipes. 107 min.
19-1526 Was $19.99 ❑*$14.99*

Overboard (1987)
When snooty socialite Goldie Hawn takes a tumble off her yacht and wakes up with amnesia, grubby carpenter Kurt Russell, who she snubbed before, convinces her they're married and takes her home to meet their four "children." Wacky class conflict comedy also stars Katherine Helmond, Roddy McDowall. 112 min.
12-2539 Was $19.99 ❑*$14.99*

Bird On A Wire (1990)
A hair-raising action-comedy starring hunky Mel Gibson and hilarious Goldie Hawn. Mel's a former drug dealer who rats on federal agent-turned-pusher David Carradine. Now, Mel's in trouble and Goldie, a former girlfriend, joins him on a cross-country, chase-filled odyssey. With Bill Duke. 106 min.
07-1654 Was $19.99 ❑*$14.99*

Death Becomes Her (1992)
Wild black comedy from director Robert Zemeckis ("Forrest Gump") with Goldie Hawn and Meryl Streep as rivals who'll do anything to stave off growing old, from fighting over plastic surgeon Bruce Willis to obtaining a magical elixir from witch Isabella Rossellini. The potion not only keeps them young, but it allows them to survive "accident" after "accident" without dying! 103 min.
07-1902 Was $19.99 ❑*$14.99*

Crisscross (1992)
A sensitive drama set in Key West, Florida, in 1969, featuring Goldie Hawn as the mother of a 12-year-old son who struggles to make ends meet as a waitress and a stripper in a local bar after her troubled Vietnam vet husband abandons her. Eventually, the boy runs away from home to find his missing father. Keith Carradine, David Arnott also star. 101 min.
12-2530 ❑*$14.99*

The First Wives Club (1996)
The fury of "a woman scorned" was never funnier than in this hit comedy starring Goldie Hawn, Diane Keaton and Bette Midler as former college friends who reunite and set out for revenge on the ex-husbands who, after becoming successful on their spouses' sacrifices, dumped them for younger "trophy wives." With Stephen Collins, Dan Hedaya, Sarah Jessica Parker and Maggie Smith. 104 min.
06-2563 Was $99.99 ❑*$14.99*

Please see our index for these other Goldie Hawn titles: *Everyone Says I Love You • Foul Play • Housesitter • The Out-Of-Towners • Seems Like Old Times • Shampoo*

Nobody's Perfekt (1981)
Three psychiatric patients decide to take on City Hall when the city refuses to pay the damages on their car after a mishap with a pothole. Gabe Kaplan, Robert Klein, Alex Karras, Susan Clark star; directed by Peter Bonerz. 96 min.
02-1103 *$69.99*

Meet The Hollowheads (1989)
Equal parts "Brady Bunch" and "Brazil," this offbeat sci-fi comedy follows the misadventures of a futuristic family trying to impress dad's tyrannical boss at dinner. John Glover, Nancy Mette and Juliette Lewis star. 89 min.
03-1753 *$14.99*

Real Genius (1985)
When some college science whizzes learn that their latest project is to be used as a government weapon, they sabotage the works in this wild comedy. Val Kilmer, Gabe Jarret, Michelle Meyrink and William Atherton star. 106 min.
02-1522 ❑*$14.99*

Big Trouble (1986)
Peter Falk and Alan Arkin star in this zany comedy about two ordinary guys who concoct a wild insurance fraud scheme that will either land them in the life of Riley...or in jail! With Beverly D'Angelo, Charles Durning, Robert Stack. 93 min.
02-1593 Was $29.99 *$19.99*

One More Saturday Night (1986)
"Saturday Night Live" semi-regulars Al Franken and Tom Davis star as rock musicians who head into a small Minnesota town that sleeps six days a week...but on Saturday night, anything goes! Features original songs produced by Jerry Garcia. 96 min.
02-1673 *$14.99*

A Fine Mess (1986)
Ted Danson and Howie Mandel team up for laughs in this wild Blake Edwards farce about a pair of losers who find themselves on the run from gangsters after they win big at the track. Also stars Paul Sorvino, Richard Mulligan, Maria Conchita Alonso. 90 min.
02-1686 Was $19.99 ❑*$14.99*

Armed And Dangerous (1986)
"SCTV" alumni John Candy and Eugene Levy reunite as two bumbling security guards whose investigations into a local mob boss could make their future very insecure. Crazy comedy also stars Robert Loggia, Meg Ryan, Kenneth McMillan. 88 min.
02-1698 *$14.99*

Hardbodies (1984)
It's naughty fun in the sun as a group of businessmen take to the beaches to find nubile girls willing to do "everything." Frankie and Annette were never this open, especially when compared to all the gorgeous nude women who inhabit these beaches. Grant Cramer, Gary Wood star. 88 min.
02-1338 ❑*$14.99*

Hardbodies 2 (1986)
And just when you thought they couldn't get wackier, raunchier, zanier and racier! A film crew on the sun-drenched Greek Isles gets more action off screen than on, thanks to the nubile nymphs who prowl along the beaches, clad only in smiles. Brad Zutaut, James Karen star. 89 min.
02-1682 *$79.99*

Meatballs 4 (1992)
A zany summertime excursion with Corey Feldman as a hot-shot ski instructor who must lead his Lakeside Water Ski Camp against rival Twin Oaks Camp in order to survive. There's outrageous contests, a slew of sultry bikini babes and more in this romp. Are you ready for the summer? With Jack Nance, Sarah Douglas. 91 min.
44-1896 Was $89.99 ❑*$19.99*

Me & Him (1989)
What's a happily married architect to do when his libido develops a mind of its own, and a voice from "down under" steers him towards every beautiful woman in the vicinity? Bizarre comedy of sexual mores from German director Doris Dorrie ("Men") stars Griffin Dunne, Ellen Greene, Carey Lowell, and Mark Linn-Baker as the voice of "man's best friend." 94 min.
02-1984 ❑*$79.99*

The Big Picture (1989)
Savagely funny satire on Hollywood follows the rise and fall of a mediocre young filmmaker (Kevin Bacon) turned mogul's pet. "Spinal Tap" co-creators Christopher Guest and Michael McKean take potshots at the hand that feeds them; with Emily Longstreth, J.T. Walsh, Martin Short. 100 min.
02-1990 Was $89.99 ❑*$19.99*

Look Who's Talking (1989)
Thanks to a sidesplitting voiceover by Bruce Willis, Baby Mikey is, and he has lots to say about unwed mom Kirstie Alley and her post-natal search for the ideal dad. Amy Heckerling's hit comedy co-stars John Travolta as a carefree cabbie and father candidate; with George Segal, Olympia Dukakis. 93 min.
02-1999 Was $19.99 ❑*$14.99*

Look Who's Talking Too (1991)
Ever-loquacious toddler Mikey (voiced by Bruce Willis) is back, but along with problems between mommy Kirstie Alley and new dad John Travolta, he's got to deal with the arrival of a baby sister (with Roseanne Barr doing the talking). Funny sequel also stars Elias Kostas, Gilbert Gottfried. 81 min.
02-2091 Was $19.99 ❑*$14.99*

Look Who's Talking Now! (1993)
Would you believe it's a pair of talking dogs this time around, as marrieds John Travolta and Kirstie Alley have their hands full dealing with kids Mikey and Julie, a gorgeous new boss who's after Travolta, and now two pets sharing their thoughts with the audience? Diane Keaton and Danny DeVito provide the voices of the canine couple. Olympia Dukakis, Lysette Anthony co-star. 95 min.
02-2597 Was $89.99 ❑*$14.99*

Bloodhounds Of Broadway (1989)
The mobsters and molls who populated the "Roaring '20s" New York of writer Damon Runyon come alive in this comic tale of rumrunners, dancehall girls, mad scientists and a wild society party. Matt Dillon, Jennifer Grey, Madonna, Anita Morris, Randy Quaid and Julie Hagerty head the top-notch cast. 90 min.
02-1985 Was $19.99 ❑*$14.99*

Chances Are (1989)
Wistful romantic comedy/fantasy stars Robert Downey, Jr. as a reincarnated reporter who is determined to woo and win his own widow (Cybill Shepherd) and dodge the determined attentions of his now-grown daughter (Mary Stuart Masterson)! Ryan O'Neal co-stars in this captivating charmer. 108 min.
02-1954 Was $19.99 ❑*$14.99*

Just One Of The Guys (1985)
It's the flip side of "Tootsie" when a bright high school girl disguises herself as a boy to prove herself a top-notch investigative reporter. But it's one romantic twist after another when she finds herself falling in love with a sensitive classmate. Joyce Hyser, Clayton Rohner, Bill Jacoby star. 101 min.
02-1491 Was $79.99 ❑*$14.99*

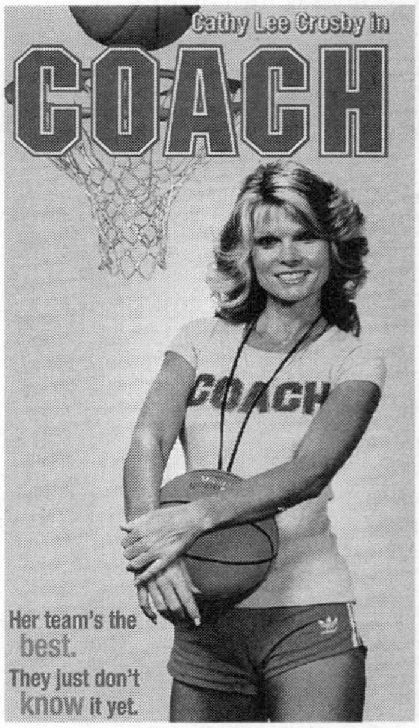

Coach (1981)
A losing high school basketball team hires a new coach chosen by computer, only to learn that "Randy" is gorgeous Cathy Lee Crosby. Can she overcome prejudice from the locals and turn her boys into winners? Winning court comedy also stars Keenan Wynn, Michael Biehn. 100 min.
03-1154 *$14.99*

Joshua Then And Now (1985)
James Woods stars as a rakish, manipulative Canadian author whose carefully constructed life has started falling apart around him. Engaging seriocomedy from the creators of "The Apprenticeship of Duddy Kravitz" also stars Gabrielle Lazure and Alan Arkin as Wood's hoodlum father. 102 min.
04-1946 Was $79.99 ❑*$29.99*

The History Of White People In America (1985)
Join host Martin Mull on a hilarious "documentary" look at America's most overlooked ethnic group. Fred Willard and Mary Kay Place star as an average suburban couple whose lives revolve around lawn furniture, barbecues, TV game shows and mayonnaise. Special guests include Teri Garr, Bob Eubanks. 48 min.
07-1320 *$24.99*

The History Of White People In America, Volume II (1986)
Return to Hawkins Falls, Ohio, with host Martin Mull for another "white riot," as he looks at such Caucasian calamities as White Religion, Stress, Politics, and Crime. Fred Willard, Mary Kay Place star. 100 min.
07-1499 *$39.99*

Portrait Of A White Marriage (1988)
Third entry in Martin Mull's hilarious look at the "mayonnaise set" depicts the stormy crisis that threatens the suburban life of Fred Willard and Mary Kay Place. Can their "white marriage" survive, and if it doesn't, who'll get the patio furniture? 101 min.
07-1598 *$39.99*

Summer Rental (1985)
Heavyweight comedy star John Candy plays a harassed family man whose Summer beach vacation turns into a nightmare in this slapstick hit. Co-stars Rip Torn, Karen Austin and Richard Crenna; directed by Carl Reiner. 88 min.
06-1320 Was $19.99 ❑*$14.99*

Pretty In Pink (1986)
Molly Ringwald and Andrew McCarthy are star-crossed high school lovers from opposite sides of the track. Will their romance survive peer pressure in time for the prom? Seriocomedy written by John Hughes co-stars Jon Cryer as Ringwald's best friend; with Annie Potts, Harry Dean Stanton. 96 min.
06-1382 ❑*$14.99*

Water (1986)
Michael Caine stars as the governor of an isolated Caribbean colony that becomes the object of a worldwide power struggle when a natural mineral water spring is discovered. Satiric comedy also stars Valerie Perrine, Fred Gwynne. 91 min.
06-1404 Was $29.99 *$14.99*

The Whoopee Boys (1986)
Two lovable slobs (Michael O'Keefe, Paul Rodriguez) pass themselves off as members of the "upper crust" in order to impress a beautiful heiress' snooty uncle and ensure her inheritance in this absurd comedy. With Denholm Elliott, Lucinda Jenney. 88 min.
06-1442 Was $79.99 *$14.99*

The Joy Of Sex (1984)
Sexy shenanigans ensue as we take a look at the wacky incidents surrounding high school students losing their virginity. "Based" on Alex Comfort's best-selling book; with Christopher Lloyd, Michelle Meyrink, Colleen Camp. 93 min.
06-1231 Was $79.99 *$19.99*

Rustlers' Rhapsody (1985)
When a dressed-in-white singing cowboy tries to clean up the real Old West, the results are hilarious comedy and a riotous send-up of the '40s Saturday matinees. Tom Berenger, Marilu Henner, Fernando Rey and Andy Griffith star. 98 min.
06-1301 *$14.99*

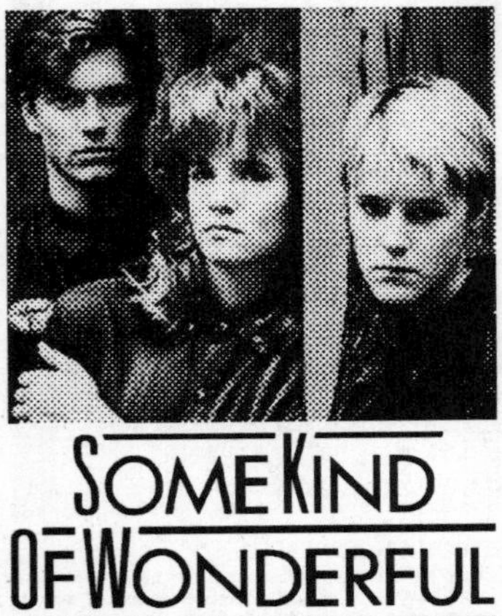

Some Kind Of Wonderful (1987)
Engaging teen comedy/drama as only John Hughes can serve it up, concerning a love triangle between a sensitive young outsider (Eric Stoltz), the rich girl he's got a crush on (Lea Thompson), and the tomboy who's carrying a torch for him (Mary Stuart Masterson). 93 min.
06-1461 Was $19.99 ❑*$14.99*

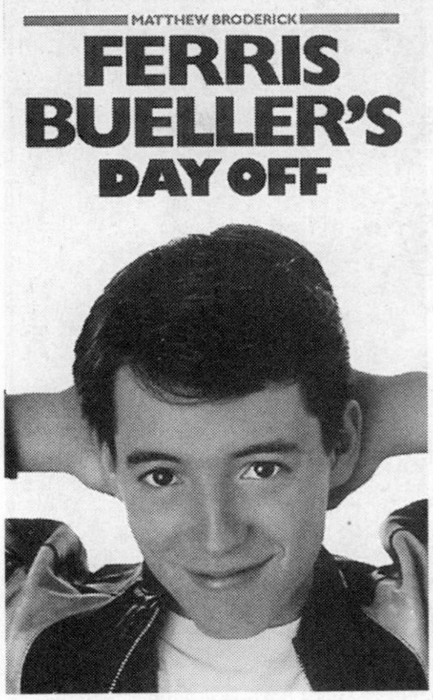

Ferris Bueller's Day Off (1986)
Matthew Broderick is Ferris, a Chicago high school student who's not going to let a little thing like classes get in the way of his enjoying one fine spring day. High-spirited "hooky" comedy from teenmeister John Hughes also stars Mia Sara, Jeffrey Jones. 103 min.
06-1425 ❑*$14.99*

Hot Pursuit (1987)
The laughs fly fast and furious when a harried teenager (John Cusack) misses his girlfriend's vacation ship at the docks...and not even burned-out doperunners, drunken pirates, and trigger-happy banana republic soldiers will keep him from catching up! Robert Loggia, Jerry Stiller, Monte Markham co-star. 101 min.
06-1503 *$19.99*

Campus Man (1987)
An enterprising college student markets a revealing calendar with his hunky pal as the star, and before long both find themselves in hot water with the administration! Far-out, funky comedy stars Miles O'Keeffe, Kim Delaney and Morgan Fairchild. 94 min.
06-1504 Was $79.99 *$14.99*

The Allnighter (1987)
The Bangles' Susanna Hoffs stars in this sexy, zany romp (directed by her mom, Tamar Simon Hoffs) as a vivacious valedictorian hunting for one wild fling before graduating college...and she's got all of one evening to find it! Run (like an Egyptian) to get this one! Michael Ontkean, Joan Cusack, Deedee Pfeiffer also star. 95 min.
07-1531 Was $79.99 *$14.99*

The Allnighter (Letterboxed Collector's Edition)
Also available in a theatrical, widescreen format. Includes Tamar Simon Hoffs' featurette "The Haircut," starring John Cassavetes; the "No TV No Phone" music video; and the theatrical trailer.
08-8780 *$14.99*

Harry And The Hendersons (1987)
Engaging comedy for all ages follows a suburban family who return from their hunting trip with a most unlikely trophy...a live Bigfoot! Sublime Spielberg production stars John Lithgow, Melinda Dillon, Don Ameche, and Kevin Peter Hall as Harry. 110 min.
07-1537 Was $19.99 ❑*$14.99*

The Sting II (1982)
Jackie Gleason and Mac Davis team up to play the double con on Oliver Reed in this sequel to the ever popular you-know-what. Teri Garr is the tootsie involved in the proceedings. 102 min.
07-1152 Was $19.99 *$14.99*

Summer School (1987)
Wacky, zany frolic stars hunky Mark Harmon as a shiftless gym teacher who gets suckered into teaching remedial English over the break to a pack of rejects. Kirstie Alley co-stars in this romp directed by Carl Reiner. 98 min.
06-1501 Was $19.99 ❑*$14.99*

She's Having A Baby (1988)
Those precocious John Hughes teenagers have entered the adult world, with hilarious consequences. Kevin Bacon and Elizabeth McGovern are the newlywed couple who find themselves up against the suburban nesting instinct. With Alec Baldwin, Isabel Lorca. 106 min.
06-1547 ❑*$14.99*

Clue (1985)
The favorite mystery game comes to the screen in a hilarious whodunit that challenges you to guess who killed Mr. Boddy. Was it Eileen Brennan, Tim Curry, Madeline Kahn, Christopher Lloyd, Michael McKean, Martin Mull or Lesley Ann Warren? Special video edition includes all three endings shown in theaters. 98 min.
06-1369 ❑*$14.99*

Amazon Women On The Moon (1987)
From the folks who gave you "Kentucky Fried Movie" and "Gremlins" comes this wild collection of skits. Fifties sci-fi flicks, late night TV commercials, video pirates, film critics and other topics are lampooned by Rosanna Arquette, Ed Begley, Jr., Sybil Danning, Arsenio Hall, Russ Meyer and other stars. 85 min.
07-1554 Was $79.99 *$14.99*

A New Life (1988)
Alan Alda is at his irritable, self-centered best as a recently divorced Wall Street whiz encountering the pitfalls and pratfalls of his new single status. Written and directed by Alda, the film features Ann-Margret as the ex-wife, Veronica Hamel, Mary Kay Place and Hal Linden. 104 min.
06-1588 Was $89.99 ❑*$14.99*

Plain Clothes (1988)
An undercover cop "hits the books" when he masquerades as a high school student in order to solve a teacher's murder. Fast-paced action/comedy stars Arliss Howard, Suzy Amis, George Wendt, Robert Stack. 98 min.
06-1608 Was $89.99 ❑*$14.99*

Haunted Honeymoon (1986)
Gene Wilder and Gilda Radner star in this haunted-house spoof as '40s radio actors who find werewolves, fiendish killers and other strange goings-on at the mansion. Howl-arious comedy also stars Jonathan Pryce, Paul Smith and Dom DeLuise as Aunt Kate; written and directed by Wilder. 82 min.
44-1443 ❑*$19.99*

The Man Who Wasn't There (1983)
A young man (Steve Guttenberg) uncovers a secret disappearing formula and is pursued by American and Russian agents vying for the potion. Light, screwball fun; not in 3-D. 111 min.
06-1193 Was $59.99 *$14.99*

Making Mr. Right (1987)
Romantic sci-fi farce about a woman who teaches an experimental android about emotions...and becomes the apple of his (electronic) eye. John Malkovich stars as both robotic creation and misanthropic creator, with Ann Magnuson as the love interest; Susan Seidelman directs. 95 min.
44-1490 ❑*$14.99*

Going Undercover (1988)
Inept private eye Chris Lemmon gets the case of his life when he's assigned to protect wealthy heiress Lea Thompson from kidnappers...but who'll protect her from him? Zany comedy also stars Jean Simmons. 92 min.
68-1112 Was $29.99 *$14.99*

Just Tell Me What You Want (1980)
It's a witty battle of the sexes as a happily married business tycoon (Alan King) faces a rebellion from his long-time mistress (Ali McGraw), then must try to win her back after she takes up with a handsome playwright. Co-stars Keenan Wynn, Peter Weller, Tony Roberts and, in her final film, Myrna Loy. 114 min.
19-1069 Was $19.99 *$14.99*

Bette Midler

The Rose (1979)
Bette Midler is dynamic in the title role, a Janis Joplin-like pop star who struggles to survive her lonely life on the road but is consumed by drugs, alcohol and her own passions. Co-stars Alan Bates, Frederic Forrest, Harry Dean Stanton and David Keith. 134 min.
04-1134 *$14.99*

Jinxed! (1982)
Fast-paced comedy stars Bette Midler as an unhappily-married Las Vegas lounge singer who enlists the aid of casino dealer Ken Wahl in bumping off her loutish husband. Rip Torn stands out as the pair's would-be victim; Don Siegel directs. 103 min.
12-1261 Was $19.99 *$14.99*

Down And Out In Beverly Hills (1986)
A nouveau riche Beverly Hills family has their lives turned upside-down when they take in a bum who tried to drown himself in their swimming pool. Uproarious culture-clash comedy by Paul Mazursky, based on a 1932 French film, stars Nick Nolte as the derelict, Richard Dreyfuss, Bette Midler, Little Richard and Mike the Dog. 103 min.
11-1339 Was $19.99 ❑*$14.99*

Beaches (1988)
They met at the beach when they were children and formed a friendship that would last a lifetime. Filled with song and sentiment, this seriocomic look at two disparate women and the bonds they forge stars Bette Midler and Barbara Hershey; with John Heard, Lanie Kazan, Spalding Gray. 123 min.
11-1487 Was $19.99 ❑*$14.99*

For The Boys (1991)
Bette Midler and James Caan star in this lavish musical-drama, playing a song-and-dance team specializing in entertaining American troops whose stormy personal and professional relationship spans from World War II through Vietnam. There's lots of high-energy musical numbers and heart-tugging sequences here. With George Segal, Patrick O'Neal and Norman Fell. 145 min.
04-2507 Was $89.99 ❑*$14.99*

Scenes From A Mall (1991)
Bette Midler and Woody Allen team up for an insightful, funny look at the state of marriage in the '90s, courtesy of director Paul Mazursky. On their 16th wedding anniversary, a psychologist and sports attorney take a trip through a Beverly Hills mall and discover that their relationship isn't as solid as they thought. With Bill Irwin and Kamar, the discount magician. 87 min.
11-1577 ❑*$14.99*

Hocus Pocus (1993)
Bette Midler, Sarah Jessica Parker and Kathy Najimy are three 17th-century witches who find themselves in a cauldron of trouble when three kids use an enchanted cat to stop them from terrorizing modern-day Salem, Massachusetts, on Halloween night. This lively, special effects-filled farce also stars Omri Katz, Thora Birch and Vinessa Shaw. 96 min.
11-1746 ❑*$14.99*

Gypsy (1993)
The classic Stephen Sondheim-Jule Styne musical based on the early life of burlesque star Gypsy Rose Lee is given a vibrant treatment, fueled by a bravura turn from Bette Midler as archetypal stage mother Mama Rose. Cynthia Gibb co-stars in the title role; with Peter Riegert, Ed Asner. Songs include "Let Me Entertain You," "Everything's Coming Up Roses," "Small World." 150 min.
58-5128 Was $89.99 *$14.99*

That Old Feeling (1997)
When former spouses Bette Midler and Dennis Farina arrive, each with new mate in tow, to attend their daughter's wedding, the sparks that fly between them quickly change from mutual animosity to mutual passion in this spry romantic romp from director Carl Reiner. With Gail O'Grady, David Rasche, Paula Marshall. 106 min.
07-2541 Was $99.99 ❑*$14.99*

Isn't She Great (2000)
The life and times of trash novelist and "Valley of the Dolls" author Jacqueline Susann is recounted in this comedy featuring Bette Midler as Jackie and Nathan Lane as hot-shot promoter hubby Irving Mansfield. See how Susann, a struggling actress and model, becomes the toast of show biz with her tales of drugs, sex and booze. Stockard Channing, David Hyde Pierce and John Cleese also star; Andrew Bergman ("The Freshman") directs. 96 min.
07-2883 ❑*$99.99*

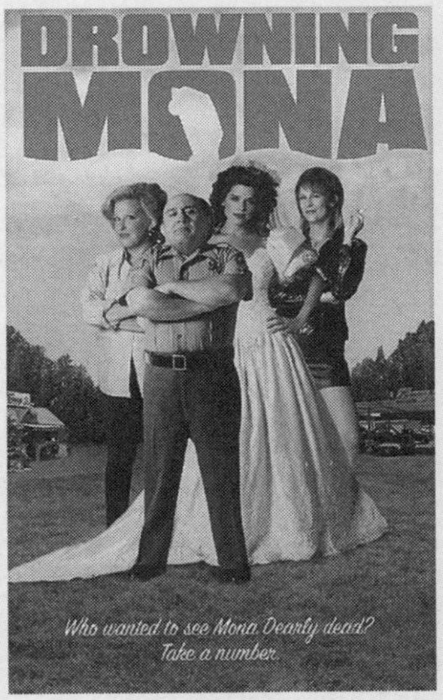

Drowning Mona (2000)
Life in a small upstate New York town is changed, apparently for the better, when local harridan Bette Midler drives her Yugo into the Hudson River. Police chief Danny DeVito discovers the car's brakes were tampered with, but everyone in the town—from Midler's son, landscaper Marcus Thomas, and waitress Jamie Lee Curtis to DeVito's own daughter, bride-to-be Neve Campbell—had a reason to want her dead, in this offbeat black comedy. 96 min.
02-3449 ❑*$99.99*

Please see our index for these other Bette Midler titles: *The First Wives Club • Get Shorty • Oliver & Company*

How To Irritate People (1968)
John Cleese is a master at irritating people, and in this "Monty Python" precursor, he offers a hilarious how-to that shows you the fine art of causing exasperation: in movie theatres and restaurants, at a party, and even on TV. Fellow Pythoners Michael Palin and Graham Chapman join in on this daffy discourse on annoyance. 65 min.
22-1270 *$19.99*

And Now For Something Completely Different (1972)
The madcap members of Monty Python star in this collection of highlights from the "Flying Circus" television series. Lots of laughs, chuckles, spam, guffaws, titters, and spam. 89 min.
02-1120 *$19.99*

Monty Python And The Holy Grail (1974)
The legend of King Arthur will never be the same once the Pythons get through with it. Klutzy knights, killer rabbits, coconut-laden swallows, taunting Frenchmen and other oddities all add up to one of the funniest, most outrageous comedies ever. Graham Chapman, John Cleese, Eric Idle, Terry Gilliam, Terry Jones, Michael Palin star. 90 min.
02-1144 *$19.99*

Monty Python And The Holy Grail (Letterboxed Version)
Also available in a theatrical, widescreen format.
02-3093 *$19.99*

Romance With A Double Bass (1974)
John Cleese stars in this zany slapstick featurette. He's a musician scheduled to perform at a royal wedding. Before long he is skinny dipping in a lake with a princess (Connie Booth), but a sneak thief steals their clothes! 40 min.
07-1246 *$19.99*

The Strange Case Of The End Of Civilization As We Know It (1977)
When the arch-villain Moriarty launches a plan to gain control of the world, the police turn to the bumbling grandson of Sherlock Holmes to rescue mankind. John Cleese stars as the hapless Holmes in this Sherlockian send-up that also features Arthur Lowe and Connie Booth. 55 min.
22-1306 *$19.99*

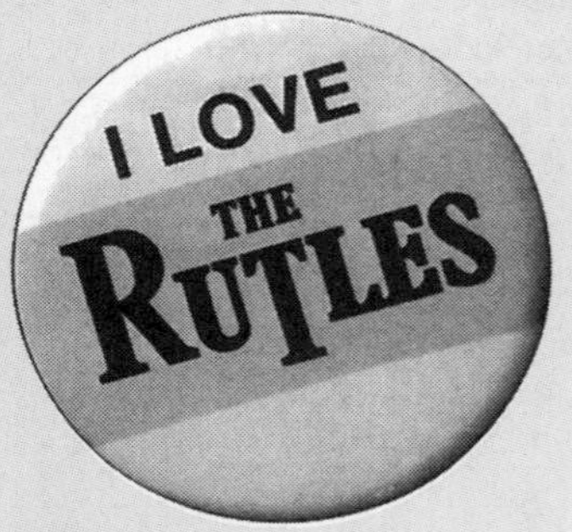

The Rutles: All You Need Is Cash (1978)
That legendary '60s British rock foursome with the suspiciously familiar history is back! Join Dirk, Barry, Stig and Nasty in Monty Python alumnus Eric Idle's hilarious Beatlemania spoof, with guest stars Michael Palin, Bill Murray, John Belushi, Mick Jagger and George Harrison. Songs include "Cheese and Onions," "Get Up and Go," "Ouch!," "Your Mother Should Go." Banned-in-America version; 70 min.
07-8003 Was $19.99 *$14.99*

Monty Python's Life Of Brian (1979)
Brian was a poor little schnook born in the manger next to Jesus, whom, throughout his life, people mistook for the Messiah. This epic farce from the Python gang also takes on revolutionaries, Latin grammar, Roman gladiator movies, religious hypocrisy, "Star Wars" and lisping. 90 min.
06-1870 Was $19.99 *□$14.99*

Monty Python's Life Of Brian (Letterboxed Version)
Also available in a theatrical, widescreen format.
08-8747 *$14.99*

Monty Python's The Meaning Of Life (1983)
Maybe this movie from Britain's loony comic troupe doesn't answer the big questions, but along the way you'll learn why "Every Sperm Is Sacred," see English calm in the midst of war, witness the unfortunate Mr. Creosote's last meal, watch Death join a dinner party, and play "Where's the Fish?" 107 min.
07-1183 Was $19.99 *□$14.99*

A Private Function (1985)
A hilarious and satirical romp set in post-WWII Britain, where food rationing is the law of the land and one tiny village is planning a feast with an illegal pig. Michael Palin and Maggie Smith are a couple who decide to kidnap the contraband porker and use it to increase their social status. With Denholm Elliott, Bill Paterson. 93 min.
06-2005 *$19.99*

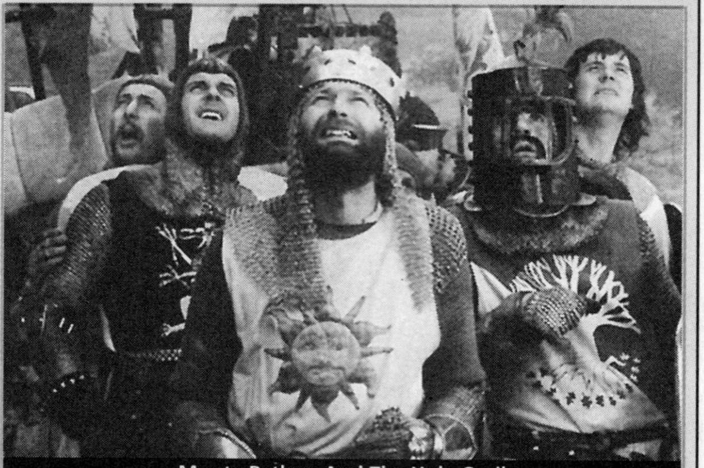

Monty Python And The Holy Grail

Monty Python

A Fish Called Wanda (1988)
Writer/co-star John Cleese and director Charles Crichton ("The Lavender Hill Mob") blend their comic styles in a frantically funny farce. Stodgy barrister Cleese gets involved with a gang of inept robbers (femme fatale Jamie Lee Curtis, sublimely stupid sadist Kevin Kline, and stuttering icthyophile Michael Palin) who needs him to recover a stolen fortune. 108 min.
12-2617 Was $19.99 *□$14.99*

Nuns On The Run (1990)
Eric Idle and Robbie Coltrane star in this high-spirited farce as a pair of bank robbers who, after double-crossing their partners, don habits and hide out in a convent. It's zany British humor at its best; with Janet Suzman, Camille Coduri. 94 min.
04-2362 Was $89.99 *□$19.99*

Too Much Sun (1991)
Outrageous gender-bender farce stars Eric Idle and Andrea Martin as homosexual siblings whose father leaves a healthy inheritance...to whomever can produce a child first! Robert Downey, Jr., Ralph Macchio, Leo Rossi and Howard Duff also star; directed by cult fave Robert Downey, Sr. 87 min.
02-2094 *$89.99*

Missing Pieces (1992)
Funny comedy starring Eric Idle as a man who inherits a riddle containing the clues to a fortune from a distant Chinese relative. He joins forces with friend Robert Wuhl to solve the puzzle, but soon faces a private eye, a one-armed millionaire, a hired killer and other oddballs. Lauren Hutton, Richard Belzer co-star. 93 min.
44-2054 *$99.99*

Splitting Heirs (1993)
Riotously funny mistaken identity farce stars Eric Idle as a man who realizes he was switched at birth and has been living an impoverished existence with a Pakistani family while he should be recognized as a member of British royalty. He hires a shady lawyer to win back his birthright. Rick Moranis, Barbara Hershey, John Cleese, Catherine Zeta Jones co-star; scripted by Idle. 87 min.
07-2032 Was $19.99 *□$14.99*

American Friends (1993)
Michael Palin stars as an Oxford professor who falls in love with both an American woman and her young daughter while on vacation in the Swiss Alps. When the professor returns to school, he finds that a rival teacher also seeks the hand of the mother. Charming and witty romance co-stars Trini Alvarado and Connie Booth ("Fawlty Towers"). 95 min.
68-1268 *$89.99*

Fierce Creatures (1997)
The stars of "A Fish Called Wanda" reunite for a wacky comedy set in and around a London zoo that's acquired by a multinational corporation headed by Australian magnate Kevin Kline. As the mogul's inept son (also played by Kline) and executive Jamie Lee Curtis work on their own plans for the zoo, new manager John Cleese tries to make it profitable by replacing cuddly critters with vicious and dangerous animals. Michael Palin, Carey Lowell also star. 93 min.
07-2506 Was $99.99 *□$14.99*

Fierce Creatures (Letterboxed Version)
Also available in a theatrical, widescreen format.
07-2588 *□$19.99*

Pleasure At Her Majesty's (1976)
The first in a series of all-star benefit concerts for Amnesty International that brought together top British laughmakers, this riotous stage show features the members of Monty Python re-creating some of their most famous skits (including "Dead Parrot" and "Lumberjack Song"), plus appearances by Neil Innes, Peter Cook, the Goodies and others. AKA: "At Her Majesty's Pleasure," "Monty Python Meets Beyond the Fringe." 72 min.
15-5456 *$14.99*

The Secret Policeman's Ball (1979)
Some of the biggest names in British comedy and music came together in this Amnesty International benefit show, taped live at London's Her Majesty's Theatre. The line-up includes Monty Python alums John Cleese, Terry Jones and Michael Palin; Peter Cook; Rowan Atkinson as a menacing headmaster; Pete Townshend performing acoustic versions of "Pinball Wizard" and "Won't Get Fooled Again"; and more. 85 min.
15-5455 *$14.99*

The Secret Policeman's Other Ball (1981)
Taking the stage at the Theatre Royal in London's Drury Lane is a dazzling collection of British comedy stars, including John Cleese Rowan Atkinson, Peter Cook, Alexi Sayle and Dame Edna Everage (Barry Humphries). Music is provided by Eric Clapton, Phil Collins, Bob Geldof, Sting and others. 88 min.
12-1231 *$14.99*

The Secret Policeman's Third Ball (1987)
Mix an array of the biggest names in pop music (Joan Armatrading, Jackson Browne, Kate Bush, Peter Gabriel, Pink Floyd, Lou Reed) with comedy from John Cleese, Stephen Fry and Hugh Laurie, Lenny Henry, Emo Phillips and others, and you get the fifth "Secret Policeman" benefit show for Amnesty International, live from the London Palladium. 92 min.
15-5489 *$14.99*

Amnesty International Box Set
Along with "At Her Majesty's Pleasure," "The Secret Policeman's Ball," "The Secret Policeman's Other Ball" and "The Secret Policeman's Third Ball," this seven-tape collector's set also features three videos unavailable elsewhere: "The Secret Policeman's Biggest Ball," "The Mermaid Frolics" and "The Big Three-O."
15-5568 *$89.99*

Monty Python Gift Set
Friends and family will call you "Two Films" when you get this collector's set featuring the Python classics "And Now for Something Completely Different" and "Monty Python and the Holy Grail."
02-2791 *$34.99*

Please see our index for these other Monty Python titles: *The Adventures Of Baron Munchausen • An Alan Smithee Film: Burn Hollywood Burn • Brazil • Casper • Dudley Do-Right • George Of The Jungle • Isn't She Great • The Jungle Book • Mary Shelley's Frankenstein • Mom And Dad Save The World • National Lampoon's European Vacation • Rudolph The Red-Nosed Reindeer: The Movie • Silverado • The Swan Princess • Time Bandits • The World Is Not Enough*

Revenge Of The Nerds (1984)
You know the Nerds—they've got pens in their shirt pockets, wing-tipped shoes, black-framed glasses and computer programming on their minds. A bunch of them unite and give the college bullies what they deserve. Robert Carradine, Anthony Edwards, Curtis Armstrong star. 90 min.
04-1800 *□$14.99*

Revenge Of The Nerds II: Nerds In Paradise (1987)
Just when you thought it was safe to wear a pocket protector...those "never say die" geeks are back in an all-new riotous comedy, invading a Florida fraternity convention and getting even with the jocks who put them down. Robert Carradine, Barry Sobel and Timothy Busfield star. 89 min.
04-2117 Was $89.99 *□$14.99*

Revenge Of The Nerds III: The Next Generation (1992)
Just when you thought it was safe to go back to the campus, another generation of nerds has arrived at college! And joining them are original nerds Robert Carradine and Anthony Edwards. Ted McGinley and Morton Downey, Jr. also star in this hilarious installment in the series. 93 min.
04-2629 Was $89.99 *$14.99*

Revenge Of The Nerds IV: Nerds In Love (1994)
Good news! Booger's getting married! Unfortunately, his future father-in-law—an aspiring politician—doesn't like this nerdy new addition to his family and attempts to halt the wedding. Can the rest of the nerds save the day? Robert Carradine, Curtis Armstrong, Ted McGinley star. 90 min.
04-2899 Was $89.99 *□$14.99*

Revenge Of The Nerds 4-Pack
Buy yourself a new pocket protector with the money you'll save on this collector's set featuring all four "Nerds" comedies.
04-3929 Save $25.00! *$34.99*

Jocks (1987)
It's a match point for mirth in this wacky, sexy, zany farce! An intercollegiate team of tennis players must defend their alma mater's honor in the Vegas finals. Scott Strader, Mariska Hargitay, Richard Roundtree and Christopher Lee star. 86 min.
02-1767 *$12.99*

Happy New Year (1987)
Catch a gem of a comedy, as Peter Falk and Charles Durning impersonate a rich octogenarian and his chauffeur in order to pull off a jewel heist. With Tom Courtenay, Wendy Hughes. 86 min.
02-1795 *$79.99*

Stewardess School (1986)
Will you have coffee, tea, or a zany, racy, high-flying comedy about the inept, oversexed students who learn to give service in the friendly skies? Risqué romp of the wild blue yonder stars Judy Landers, Sandahl Bergman, Donny Most. 84 min.
02-1727 *$14.99*

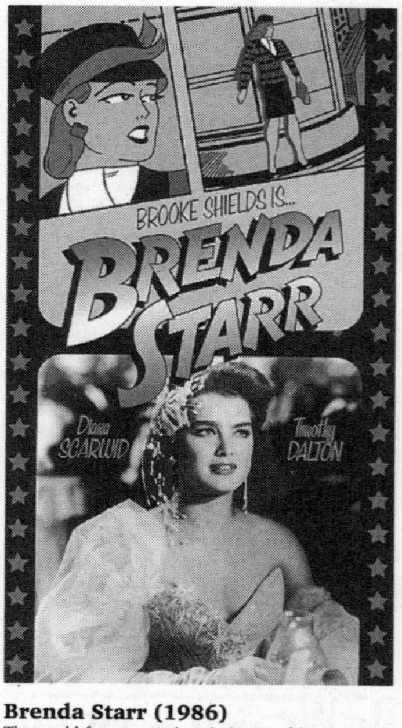

Brenda Starr (1986)
The world-famous comic strip is turned into a stylish comic adventure with Brooke Shields as the ace reporter. With her newspaper about to go bankrupt, Brenda needs a big scoop, so she sails down the Amazon in search of a scientist who has invented a revolutionary new fuel. Timothy Dalton, Diana Scarwid co-star. 94 min.
02-2311 Was $19.99 *$14.99*

Brenda Starr (Letterboxed Version)
Also available in a theatrical, widescreen format.
08-8796 *$14.99*

Coast To Coast (1980)
Silly shenanigans from sea to shining sea with Dyan Cannon as a woman who flies over the cuckoo's nest after her estranged doctor husband tries to commit her to avoid a hefty divorce settlement, and finds romantic adventures with her reluctant rescuer, trucker Robert Blake. Co-stars Michael Lerner, Quinn Redeker. 95 min.
06-1073 Was $49.99 *$14.99*

When Nature Calls (1985)
An urban family says "goodbye" to the big city and takes to the woods in Troma Film's slapstick spoof of "wilderness family" films. Wacky sight gags, fake "coming attractions" trailers and cameos by Willie Mays, G. Gordon Liddy, Morey Amsterdam and Classy Freddie Blassie. 76 min.
03-1461 *$14.99*

Almost You (1985)
Brooke Adams and Griffin Dunne are a Yuppie New York couple whose marriage seems headed for disaster when Adams breaks her hip and Dunne falls for the attractive nurse (Karen Young) hired to care for his wife. Joe Silver, Josh Mostel co-star. 91 min.
04-1936 Was $79.99 ❑*$29.99*

Torch Song Trilogy (1988)
Tony Award-winner Harvey Fierstein brings his acclaimed Broadway play to the screen and re-creates his role as drag queen Arnold Beckoff, a gay man who tries to maintain his old-fashioned dreams of love and "Mr. Right." With Matthew Broderick, Brian Kerwin and Anne Bancroft. 120 min.
02-1937 Was $89.99 ❑*$19.99*

Real Life (1979)
Hilarious satire that was director Albert Brooks' feature film debut takes a lighthearted poke at cinéma vérité filmmaking. A documentarian (Brooks) tries to capture the typical American family on film while remaining uninvolved, but seems to be doing everything but. Co-stars Charles Grodin and Frances Lee McCain. 99 min.
06-1132 Was $19.99 *$14.99*

Lost In America (1985)
Yuppified "Search for America" comedy from co-writer/director/star Albert Brooks has Brooks and wife Julie Hagerty quitting their big city jobs and buying a motor home to "head out on the highway," only to find obstacles that make "Easy Rider's" pale in comparison. With Garry Marshall. 92 min.
19-1453 Was $19.99 ❑*$14.99*

Defending Your Life (1991)
In this warm, witty comedy, writer/director/star Albert Brooks is killed in an auto accident and arrives at a most unusual afterlife: Judgment City, an ethereal resort with great food. There he's put on trial for his life on Earth. If he wins, he moves on to a higher plane of existence; if not, it's back to Earth to try again. Meryl Streep, Rip Torn, Buck Henry, Lee Grant also star. 112 min.
19-1875 Was $19.99 ❑*$14.99*

Mother (1996)
Albert Brooks' funny and poignant comedy features him playing a science-fiction writer who decides to go back to his roots—and mother Debbie Reynolds' house—after his second divorce. The uneasy relationship between mother and son causes much friction, but Brooks eventually learns there's more to Mom's life than he originally envisioned. Rob Morrow, Lisa Kudrow co-star. 104 min.
06-2609 Was $99.99 ❑*$14.99*

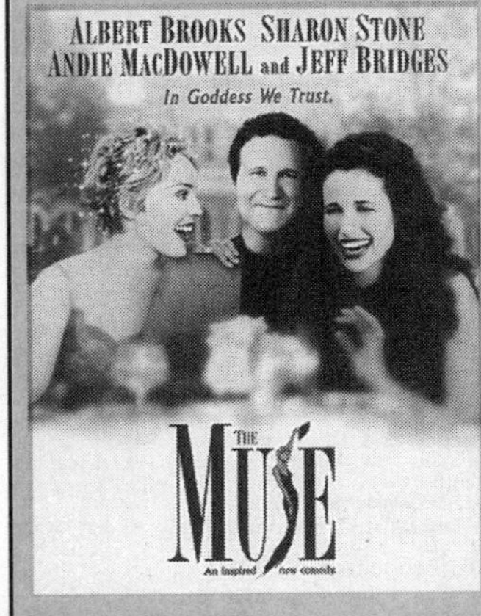
ALBERT BROOKS SHARON STONE
ANDIE MACDOWELL and JEFF BRIDGES
In Goddess We Trust.
THE MUSE

The Muse (1999)
Fearful that he's losing his creativity, screenwriter Albert Brooks seeks help from successful fellow scribe Jeff Bridges. His secret turns out to be gorgeous Sharon Stone, who claims to be one of the Nine Muses of Greek mythology and will provide inspiration to Brooks in exchange for "little gifts" like Tiffany jewelry and a posh hotel suite. Sharp and funny Hollywood satire, directed and co-written by Brooks, also stars Andie MacDowell; cameos by James Cameron, Martin Scorsese and others. 97 min.
02-9170 Was $99.99 ❑*$14.99*

My Bodyguard (1980)
Touching story of a frail high school boy who hires a hulking, withdrawn classmate to protect him from the school bullies, and the friendship that develops between the unlikely allies. Chris Makepeace, Adam Baldwin, Matt Dillon, Martin Mull and Ruth Gordon star. 96 min.
04-1282 Was $59.99 *$14.99*

A Night In The Life Of Jimmy Reardon (1988)
Teen heartthrob River Phoenix stars as teen heartthrob Jimmy Reardon, a smooth high-schooler who sets out to win the rich girl of his dreams, and won't let anything get in his way. Whimsical romantic comedy also stars Meredith Salenger, Ione Skye. 92 min.
04-1101 ❑*$19.99*

Six Pack (1982)
Kenny Rogers' theatrical movie debut casts him as a road-weary racing car driver who must care for six orphans. Diane Lane, Erin Gray, Anthony Michael Hall co-star. 108 min.
04-1492 Was $59.99 *$14.99*

Airplane II: The Sequel (1982)
More fabulous fun with the flight crew that can't keep a good laugh down. Take off into outer space for a second helping of zany sight gags with stars Robert Hays, Julie Hagerty, Peter Graves, William Shatner and Sonny Bono. 85 min.
06-1173 *$14.99*

Gimme An "F" (1985)
Madcap, zany fun as we get a good look at the happenings inside a girl's cheerleading training camp! Watch those sexy young things strut and shake their way into your hearts! Stars Stephen Shellen, Jennifer Cooke and John Karlen. 103 min.
04-1900 Was $79.99 *$29.99*

Key Exchange (1985)
They're young, they're urban, they're professionals and they're in love. But when dime novelist Ben Masters and television producer Brooke Adams determine it's time to exchange apartment keys—a symbol of their "commitment" to one another—romantic entanglements follow. Co-stars Daniel Stern, Danny Aiello. 96 min.
04-1935 Was $79.99 ❑*$29.99*

Partners (1982)
Two cops, one gay and one straight, are assigned to pose as a gay couple in order to trap a murderer in this offbeat, hilarious mix of "48 Hrs." and "La Cage Aux Folles." John Hurt and Ryan O'Neal star as the mismatched roommates. 93 min.
06-1139 Was $79.99 *$14.99*

Jekyll & Hyde... Together Again (1982)
In this comical spin on the familiar horror tale, good Dr. Jekyll discovers a mysterious white powder that, once inhaled, turns him into a wild-haired, girl-chasing, disco-dancing madman. Mark Blankfield, Bess Armstrong, Tim Thomerson star. 87 min.
06-1166 Was $59.99 *$19.99*

Choose Me (1984)
Two dissimilar women—one a bar owner, the other a radio sex therapist—find their lives and relationships intertwined in this witty seriocomedy from writer/director Alan Rudolph. Lesley Ann Warren, Genevieve Bujold, Keith Carradine and Rae Dawn Chong star. 104 min.
03-1369 *$19.99*

Loose Shoes (1980)
Riotous spoof of "coming attractions" features such gems as "The Yid and the Kid," "Skateboarders from Hell" and "Darktown After Dark," among many others. Hilarious, witty fun starring Bill Murray, Howard Hesseman and Buddy Hackett. 74 min.
04-1901 *$14.99*

A Great Wall (1986)
Critically hailed comedy of culture shock follows a Chinese-American family whose visit to their homeland doesn't exactly meet their expectations...nor do the Mainlanders know what to make of them. Director/co-writer Peter Wang stars. 100 min. In English and Mandarin with English subtitles.
07-8097 *$19.99*

Porky's (1982)
Gut-busting comedy about youthful shenanigans in 1950s Florida that follows a group of hormone-driven high school buddies to a rowdy bar named Porky's and through one wacky experience after another. Surprise box office hit stars Roger Wilson, Kim Cattrall, Scott Colomby, Dan Monahan; directed by Bob Clark. 99 min.
04-1550 *$14.99*

Porky's II: The Next Day (1983)
Just when you thought it was safe to go back to the shower room...the whole crew is back! More zany, sexy times in store as the boys tackle a carnival stripper, a mad reverend, the Ku Klux Klan and more. 95 min.
04-1648 *$14.99*

Porky's Revenge (1985)
The ribald fun in filmdom's raunchiest series continues, as the "Porky's" kids graduate from high school, reunite their favorite teacher with her "lost love," and play revenge against Porky himself on his riverboat. Kaki Hunter, Scott Colomby, Dan Monahan, and Chuck Mitchell star. 91 min.
04-1878 *$14.99*

Porky's 3-Pack
You'll be happier than a pig in...mud with this special collector's set featuring all three "Porky's" films.
04-3928 Save $20.00! *$24.99*

Kentucky Fried Movie (1977)
Hilarious compilation of skits spoofing disaster and kung fu films, preview trailers, TV commercials and news shows, and anything else in range, courtesy of scripters David and Jerry Zucker and Jim Abrahams ("Airplane!") and director John Landis ("Animal House"). Cameos by Bill Bixby, Henry Gibson, Donald Sutherland. 90 min.
03-1174 Was $59.99 *$19.99*

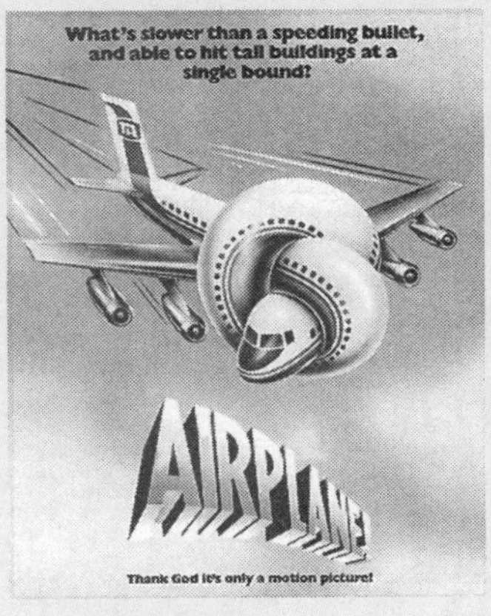
What's slower than a speeding bullet, and able to hit tall buildings at a single bound?
AIRPLANE!
Thank God it's only a motion picture!

Airplane! (1980)
The plot of the 1957 thriller "Zero Hour" had more gags than can be counted attached to it, and the result is the funniest flight ever. The Zucker-Abrahams-Zucker team's hilarious spoof of "Airport"-style disaster films stars Robert Hays, Julie Hagerty, Leslie Nielsen, Robert Stack, Lloyd Bridges, Kareem Abdul-Jabbar and Stephen Stucker as Johnny. 88 min.
06-1076 *$14.99*

Police Squad: Help Wanted (1982)
The zany, short-lived cop show spoof that spawned the "Naked Gun" films stars Leslie Nielsen as inept detective Frank Drebin and Alan North as his partner. These first three episodes feature cameos by Lorne Greene, Tommy Lasorda, Florence Henderson and others. 75 min.
06-1229 *$19.99*

More Police Squad (1982)
The final three episodes from the most offbeat TV detective series ever, courtesy of the creators of "Airplane!" Joining Leslie Nielsen are guest stars Robert Goulet, William Shatner, Dr. Joyce Brothers, William Conrad and the great Dick Miller; some episodes directed by Joe Dante ("Gremlins"). 75 min.
06-1230 *$19.99*

The Naked Gun: From The Files Of Police Squad! (1988)
The cult favorite TV comedy gets transferred to the big screen. Leslie Nielsen stars as relentlessly dizzy detective Frank Drebin, out to stop sinister Ricardo Montalban from having Queen Elizabeth II assassinated. With Priscilla Presley, O.J. Simpson and George Kennedy. 83 min.
06-1670 ❑*$14.99*

Naked Gun 2 1/2: The Smell Of Fear (1991)
Look out, lawbreakers! Lawman Leslie Nielsen is back to stop villainous business mogul Robert Goulet from making a shambles of America's energy policy (shouldn't be too hard!) for his own evil gain. Second hilarious entry in the satirical film series also stars Priscilla Presley, George Kennedy, O.J. Simpson. 85 min.
06-1897 Was $89.99 ❑*$14.99*

Naked Gun 33 1/3: The Final Insult (1994)
A retired Leslie Nielsen is pulled back onto the force when a terrorist threatens to bomb the Academy Awards show. The laughs are non-stop, as Nielsen bumbles his way in and out of trouble, while filmmakers "ZAZ" and company spoof "The Untouchables," "White Heat" and "Thelma and Louise." With George Kennedy, Priscilla Presley, Fred Ward, O.J. Simpson and Anna Nicole Smith. 83 min.
06-2238 Was $89.99 ❑*$14.99*

The Naked Gun Collection
"All three 'Naked Gun' comedies with Leslie Nielsen are now available together in one boxed set? Surely you can't be serious!"
06-2376 *$44.99*

Top Secret! (1984)
Rock 'n' roll singer Val Kilmer is recruited for a dangerous espionage mission in East Germany in an outrageous spoof from the Zucker-Abrahams-Zucker crew that pokes fun at teen musicals and spy thrillers. Co-stars Lucy Gutteridge, Omar Sharif, Peter Cushing. 90 min.
06-1232 ❑*$14.99*

Hot Shots! (1991)
A rip-roaring spoof of "Top Gun" and other fly-boy flicks stars Charlie Sheen as the brave pilot who risks his life and love for sizzling girlfriend Valeria Golino in order to overcome his father's lousy reputation and beat a certain Middle East madman in "Operation Sleepy Weasel." Cary Elwes, Lloyd Bridges, Jon Cryer co-star; Jim Abrahams directs. 83 min.
04-2486 Was $19.99 ❑*$14.99*

Hot Shots! Part Deux (1993)
Hilarious sequel to the hit comedy stars Charlie Sheen as maladroit military man Topper Harley, who fronts a mission to the Middle East to release Americans held hostage after Desert Storm. Along the way, there are spoofs of "Rambo," "Apocalypse Now," "The Wizard of Oz" and other films. With Brenda Bakke, Valeria Golino and Lloyd Bridges. 90 min.
04-2719 Was $19.99 ❑*$14.99*

BASEketball (1998)
"South Park" creators Matt Stone and Trey Parker play slacker pals who invent a bizarre sport that mixes baseball and basketball, minus the running and dribbling, but with ample opportunity for players to psych each other out. Their concoction becomes a national sensation, which offers writer-director David Zucker an opportunity to spoof the contemporary sports business. Yasmine Bleeth, Jenny McCarthy and Robert Vaughn co-star. 104 min.
07-2695 Was $99.99 ❑*$14.99*

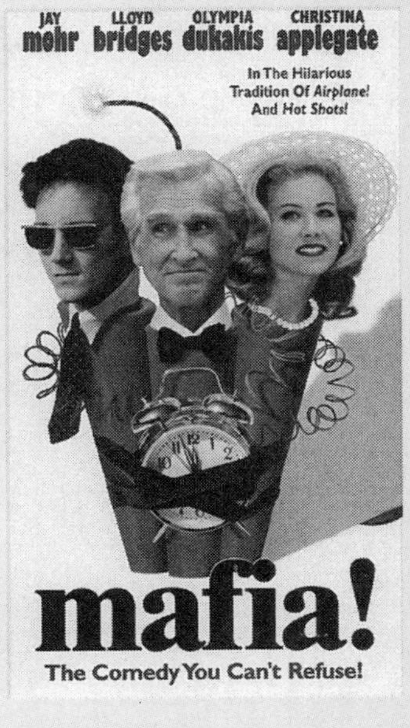
JAY mohr
LLOYD bridges
OLYMPIA dukakis
CHRISTINA applegate
In The Hilarious Tradition Of Airplane! And Hot Shots!
mafia!
The Comedy You Can't Refuse!

Mafia! (1998)
Here's a comedy you can't refuse, as director Jim Abrahams ("Hot Shots!") takes aim at "The Godfather," "Casino" and other crime movies. Jay Mohr stars as the war vet who returns home and must take over his family's "business" when an attempt is made on the life of patriarch Lloyd Bridges. With Christina Applegate, Olympia Dukakis, Billy Burke. 87 min.
11-2288 Was $19.99 ❑*$14.99*

The Decline Of The American Empire (1986)
Acclaimed French Canadian comedy that wittily explores the sexual mores (or the lack thereof) of a college faculty klatch brought together for a dinner party. Dorothy Berryman, Remy Girard star. 102 min. In French with English subtitles.
07-1504 *$79.99*

Playing For Keeps (1986)
A gang of spunky, exuberant teens takes over a dilapidated building and fight an evil chemical company so they can fix it up into "the world's first rock and roll hotel" in this song-filled comedy. Daniel Jordano, Jimmy Baio, Marisa Tomei, Harold Gould star. Notable for being the only directorial effort by future Miramax bigwigs Bob and Harvey Weinstein. 103 min.
07-1505 *$79.99*

Used Cars (1980)
Outrageous comedy from Robert Zemeckis and Bob Gale ("Back to the Future") that depicts the cutthroat feud between rival used car dealerships owned by twin brothers. Kurt Russell and Gerrit Graham are the head salesmen, and Jack Warden is hilarious as the Fuchs brothers; with Michael McKean, David L. Lander, and Al Lewis (yeah!). 111 min.
10-2618 *$14.99*

Moving Violations (1985)
Zany visit to a California school for driving violators stars John Murray (Bill's younger brother), the leader of a group of loopy leadfoots who go up against a couple of cops who will do anything to keep them from getting behind the wheel again. Co-stars Jennifer Tilly, Sally Kellerman, James Keach and Clara ("Where's the beef?") Peller. 90 min.
04-1890 Was $79.99 ❑*$29.99*

Dudley Moore

The Wrong Box (1966)
A top-notch British cast, including Ralph Richardson, John Mills, Michael Caine, Peter Sellers, Dudley Moore and Peter Cook, is featured in this superb comedy about a bunch of loony characters who scramble for an inheritance and turn everything into a hilarious shambles! 105 min.
02-1376 *$19.99*

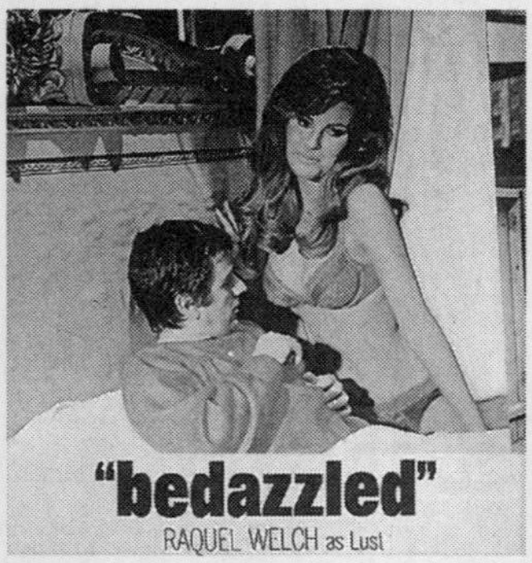

Bedazzled (1967)
The "Faust" legend is hilariously turned on its ear in this classic satirical romp created by and starring Peter Cook and Dudley Moore. Pining away with love for waitress Eleanor Bron, short-order cook Moore receives a devilish offer from otherworldly visitor Cook, who grants him seven wishes relating to the seven deadly sins. With Raquel Welch as Lust and Barry Humphries as Envy.
04-1393 ❑*$14.99*

30 Is A Dangerous Age, Cynthia (1968)
Mid-life crises have never been funnier than in this early Dudley Moore comedy. Moore is a nightclub pianist and aspiring show writer who fears turning 30 while single and unsuccessful. Co-stars Suzy Kendall and Eddie Foy, Jr. 98 min.
02-1305 *$59.99*

"10" (1979)
Blake Edwards' hilarious look at mid-life crises that made Dudley Moore a star and beautiful Bo Derek a sex symbol. Songwriter Moore spies dream girl Derek and follows her from L.A. to a Mexican resort in order to meet her, with surprising results. Julie Andrews, Robert Webber, Brian Dennehy also star, along with Ravel's "Bolero." 122 min.
19-1049 Was $19.99 ❑*$14.99*

Wholly Moses (1980)
The 11th Commandment could've read: "Thou shalt laugh at Dudley Moore, one of the finest funnymen in the land." Here he's Herschell, a Jewish idol carver in Egypt who overhears God speaking to Moses and thinks he's been called upon to lead his people out of bondage. With Dom DeLuise, Jack Gilford, Madeline Kahn, Larraine Newman and Richard Pryor as Pharaoh. 108 min.
02-1079 *$64.99*

Arthur (1981)
Daffy Dudley Moore is Arthur, the tipsy millionaire playboy who is forced to choose between his money (and an arranged marriage) and true love Liza Minnelli. John Gielgud won an Academy Award as Moore's caustic butler in a comedy rich with laughs. With Jill Eikenberry. 97 min.
19-1191 Was $19.99 ❑*$14.99*

Arthur 2 On The Rocks (1988)
Everyone's favorite multimillionaire drunkard is back again in the hit comedy sequel, but will newly-poor Dudley Moore and wife Liza Minnelli be able to make a go of working class life? John Gielgud returns (sort of) as sarcastic butler Hobson; with Cynthia Sikes, Jack Gilford. 113 min.
19-1665 Was $19.99 ❑*$14.99*

Six Weeks (1982)
Heart-tugging weeper about a married politician (Dudley Moore) who strikes up a friendship with a terminally ill little girl and ultimately falls head over heels for her mother (Mary Tyler Moore). Co-stars Katherine Healy. 107 min.
02-1215 *$14.99*

Romantic Comedy (1983)
Follow the witty, hilarious and, yes, romantic relationship between feisty playwriting partners Dudley Moore and Mary Steenburgen in this screen adaptation of the hit stageplay by Bernard Slade. With Ron Leibman, Frances Sternhagen. 103 min.
12-2589 ❑*$14.99*

Lovesick (1983)
A sweet romantic comedy about a New York psychiatrist who falls for a beautiful young female patient. Along the way, he gets advice from the ghost of Sigmund Freud. Dudley Moore, Elizabeth McGovern, John Huston and Alec Guinness star. 94 min.
19-1254 Was $19.99 *$14.99*

Micki & Maude (1984)
Dudley Moore and Blake Edwards team up for the first time since "10" for a fast-paced farce of a man who inadvertently finds himself the father-to-be with two women. Ann Reinking, Amy Irving and Richard Mulligan co-star. 118 min.
02-1434 *$14.99*

Unfaithfully Yours (1984)
Dudley Moore is a symphony conductor, jealous of his wife's presumed extramarital flings. Beautiful Nastassja Kinski is his sexy wife, and Albert Brooks is great as Moore's manager. Based on the 1948 classic. 96 min.
04-1698 Was $79.99 ❑*$29.99*

Like Father, Like Son (1987)
What happens when strait-laced dad Dudley Moore and fun-loving son Kirk Cameron exchange bodies? One hilarious mix-up after another, as the transposed pair must try to live each other's life. With Margaret Colin, Patrick O'Neal. 101 min.
02-1834 Was $19.99 *$14.99*

Crazy People (1990)
Dudley Moore is the disillusioned advertising pro who finds himself committed to a mental hospital after he creates campaigns focusing on the truthful elements of the products he pitches. Soon, his higher-ups want to exploit his new sanitarium pals by passing them off as advertising geniuses. Daryl Hannah, Paul Reiser and J.T. Walsh also star. 90 min.
06-1766 ❑*$14.99*

Blame It On The Bellboy (1992)
In this riotous farce, a bellboy (Bronson Pinchot) at a posh hotel confuses messages for three guests with similar-sounding names, and the plans of realtor Dudley Moore, hit man Bryan Brown and small-town mayor Richard Griffiths are thrown into a tizzy. Patsy Kensit also stars. 79 min.
11-1629 ❑*$14.99*

Please see our index for these other Dudley Moore titles: *Alice's Adventures In Wonderland • Foul Play • The Mighty Kong • Parallel Lives • Santa Claus: The Movie • Those Daring Young Men In Their Jaunty Jalopies*

The Secret Diary Of Sigmund Freud (1984)
You'd have to be crazy to be the father of modern psychiatry...at least, that's how it seems in this wild satire. Bud Cort stars as the young Freud, whose interest in medicine is spurred on by a lusty nurse (Carol Kane), a beautiful neurotic (Marisa Berenson), and a wild schizophrenic (Dick Shawn). 129 min.
04-2037 Was $79.99 ❑*$29.99*

Ferocious Female Freedom Fighters (1989)
It's the funniest Kung Fu flick you've ever seen, courtesy of the good folk at Troma, as the L.A. Connection comedy troupe lend their voices to a typical to a typical martial arts action movie, turning it into a hilarious dubbed-over send-up complete with women wrestlers, Elvis impersonators and Elmer Fudd. 74 min.
03-1723 *$14.99*

Leonard Part 6 (1987)
When the world finds itself in deadly danger, there's only one man to turn to...Bill Cosby! That's right, Cos stars as legendary superspy Leonard Parker, lured out of retirement to foil a dastardly villainess's plans that somehow involve killer lobsters. Tom Courtenay, Gloria Foster, Joe Don Baker. 83 min.
02-1840 Was $89.99 ❑*$14.99*

My Demon Lover (1987)
Monstrously funny farce stars Scott Valentine as a young boy with both a blessing—a cute new girlfriend—and a curse—when he's turned on he not only gets horny, he gets furry, fanged, and grows a tail! With Michelle Little, Robert Trebor. 90 min.
02-1766 Was $79.99 *$14.99*

Vice Versa (1988)
What happens when strait-laced dad Judge Reinhold and fun-loving son Fred Savage exchange bodies? One hilarious mix-up after another, as the transposed pair must try to live each other's life. With Swoosie Kurtz, Corinne Bohrer. 97 min.
02-1865 ❑*$14.99*

Hanky Panky (1982)
Gene Wilder and Gilda Radner make a wacky team of sleuths in this comedic thriller that has Wilder on the run from the cops after being framed for murder. With Richard Widmark, Kathleen Quinlan. 100 min.
02-1136 Was $79.99 ❑*$14.99*

Troop Beverly Hills (1989)
New den mother Shelley Long pampers her daughter's Wilderness Girls troop with shopping trips and expeditions in the L.A. lifestyle in this outrageous comedy. With Betty Thomas, Craig T. Nelson. 105 min.
02-1965 ❑*$14.99*

For Keeps (1987)
Molly Ringwald and Randall Batinkoff are high school sweethearts with everything: good grades, a shot at college...and a baby on the way. Can they face the pressures from family and friends while coping with their decision to keep the child? 98 min.
02-1852 *$14.99*

Stars And Bars (1988)
Witty "culture clash" comedy stars Daniel Day-Lewis as a British art dealer who must negotiate the purchase of a valuable Renoir from a bizarre backwoods Georgia family. With Martha Plimpton, Joan Cusack and Harry Dean Stanton. 94 min.
02-1881 Was $79.99 *$19.99*

Vibes (1988)
We predict you'll love this psychic screwball comedy that stars Jeff Goldblum and rock star Cyndi Lauper as two clairvoyants who join treasure hunter Peter Falk on a South American journey that turns into a bizarre adventure. 99 min.
02-1900 ❑*$89.99*

Wedding Band (1989)
He plays favorites like "The Alley Cat" and "Sunrise, Sunset" in one of the area's top wedding bands. She works as a wedding consultant. Their lives are filled with others' marital bliss, until it's their own time to walk down the aisle. William Katt and Joyce Hyser star. 86 min.
02-2008 Was $89.99 *$19.99*

This Is Spinal Tap: Special Edition (1983)
The hilarious mock-rockumentary from director Rob Reiner and stars/co-scripters Christopher Guest, Michael McKean and Harry Shearer follows the disastrous U.S. tour of Spinal Tap, a raucous British heavy metal band that has seen better days and gone through more than its share of drummers. Biting satire features the songs "Sex Farm Woman," "Big Bottom," "Stonehenge" and more; cameos include Billy Crystal, Fran Drescher, Paul Shaffer. Special edition includes the rare "Bitch School" music video and never-before-seen footage. 83 min.
02-5007 ❑*$14.99*

The Return Of Spinal Tap (1992)
After years off the stage, one of heavy metal's best-known, loudest and funniest bands is back! Get "Tapped" again with David St. Hubbins, Nigel Tufnel and Derek Smalls as they perform hits from their "Break Like the Wind" album like "Majesty of Rock," "Bitch School," "Clam Caravan" and more. Guest stars include Jamie Lee Curtis, Martha Quinn, Martin Short and Mel Torme. 110 min.
50-7040 Was $89.99 *$19.99*

Spinal Tap: Break Like The Wind—The Videos
Rock's venerable heavy metal specialists perform "Bitch School" (both the MTV and original versions) and "The Majesty of Rock" in this program featuring Nigel Tufnel, Derek Smalls and David St. Hubbins. 12 min.
07-4082 *$14.99*

Who's Harry Crumb? (1989)
Hefty John Candy, that's who, as an arrogant-but-inept private detective who stumbles into the perfect test for his skills, a clumsy kidnap and murder plot that's about as transparent as Johnny La Rue's "Jumping For Dollars." Annie Potts, Jeffrey Jones co-star. 87 min.
02-1938 ❑*$14.99*

She's Out Of Control (1989)
What's poor, harried dad Tony Danza to do when his shy, bookish teenage daughter suddenly blossoms into a high school sexpot and drives her male classmates wild? Crazy comedy from the director of "Mr. Mom" co-stars Ami Dolenz, Catherine Hicks, Wallace Shawn. 95 min.
02-1964 Was $19.99 ❑*$14.99*

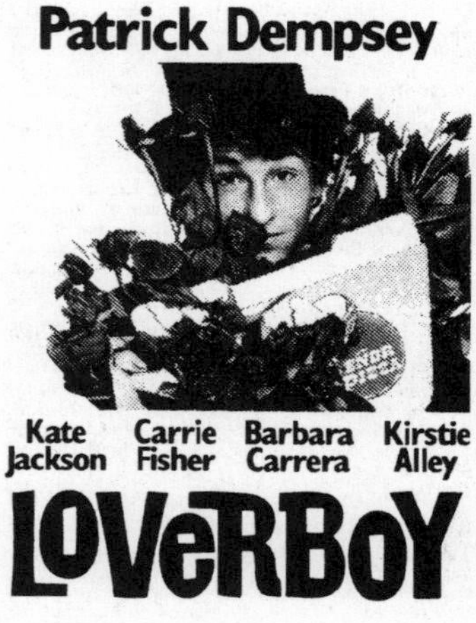

Loverboy (1989)
Saucy farce about a shy young man (Patrick Dempsey) whose pizza job soon has him making some "special deliveries" to the sexiest women in town. With Kirstie Alley, Carrie Fisher, Kate Jackson, Barbara Carrera and Nancy Valen. 108 min.
02-1969 Was $19.99 *$14.99*

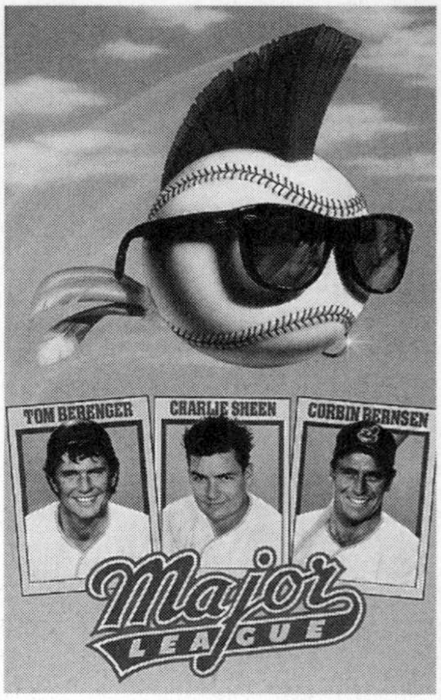

Major League (1989)
Can an ex-con pitcher nicknamed "Wild Thing," a pampered all-star infielder, and a weary itinerant catcher lead the Cleveland Indians to the pennant, against the wishes of the team's new owner? Charlie Sheen, Corbin Bernsen, Tom Berenger, Wesley Snipes and Bob Uecker star. 107 min.
06-1677 ❑*$14.99*

Major League II (1994)
Charlie Sheen, Corbin Bernsen, Tom Berenger and their Cleveland Indians teammates are back for this sequel that's wilder than a Mitch Williams ninth inning. After winning their division the year before, the Tribe has become a group of lazy celebrities who have slacked off on the field. Can they regain their abilities and spirit in time to make the playoffs? Margaret Whitton, Bob Uecker co-star. 105 min.
19-2246 Was $19.99 ❑*$14.99*

Major League: Back To The Minors (1998)
The third entry in the farcical baseball series stars Scott Bakula as a career minor-league pitcher who becomes manager of the Minnesota Twins' AAA affiliate for team owner Corbin Bernsen. Bakula's success at turning around the hapless squad of bush-leaguers and has-beens earns them a game against the big-league club and its arrogant skipper. Dennis Haysbert, Ted McGinley and Bob Uecker also star. 100 min.
19-2750 Was $99.99 ❑*$14.99*

Eat The Rich (1987)
Swift's "Modest Proposal" gets turned around in this outrageous black comedy from Britain, as a group of lower class radicals decides to reduce the aristocracy's numbers by opening a posh restaurant where the main course is murdered aristocrats. Ronald Allen, Lanah Pellay and Nosher Powell star. 92 min.
02-1897 Was $89.99 *$19.99*

The Sure Thing (1985)
Romantic comedy from Rob Reiner about two college students, a strait-laced girl and fun-loving boy, who are forced by circumstances to travel cross-country together...and despite their objections can't help falling in love. Daphne Zuniga, John Cusack, Anthony Edwards and Nicollette Sheridan star; look for Tim Robbins as "Gary Cooper." 94 min.
53-1360 ❑*$14.99*

Educating Rita (1983)
Sentimental comedy stars Julie Walters as a British working-class housewife whose thirst for knowledge brings her under the tutelage of tipsy English professor Michael Caine. In time the delightful pair find there's a lot to learn from each other. Directed by Lewis Gilbert from the hit London stage play. 110 min.
02-1310 *$14.99*

Lucky Stiff (1988)
That's what chubby loner Joe Alaskey feels like when gorgeous Donna Dixon comes on to him and asks him to join her family for dinner. Little does he know he's to be the main course! Anthony Perkins directs this outrageous black comedy. 85 min.
02-1932 Was $89.99 *$14.99*

Monster High (1989)
Its real name is Montgomery Sterling High School, but when this quiet campus becomes the focal point for an invasion from outer space, the plucky student body bands together to save the planet (and their prom plans). Zany sci-fi farce stars Dean Iandoli, Diana Frank. 84 min.
02-1972 *$89.99*

My Wonderful Life (1989)
Gorgeous supermodel Carol Alt stars in this erotic comedy as a woman who will do anything to climb the social ladder and find wealth and true love. She falls for princes, dukes, artists and, finally, journalist Elliott Gould, in her ongoing pursuit. With Jean Rochefort and Capucine. 107 min.
02-2018 *$79.99*

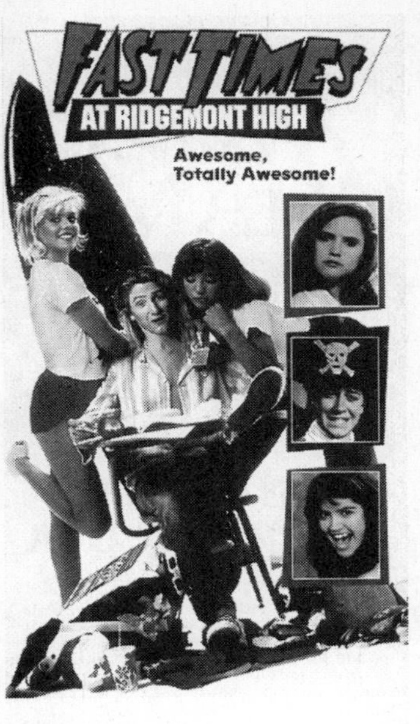

Fast Times At Ridgemont High (1982)
Adapted from Cameron Crowe's book, this fast and funny look at Southern California teen life from high school to the mall is highlighted by Sean Penn's performance as stoned surfer dude Jeff Spicoli. With Phoebe Cates, Judge Reinhold, Jennifer Jason Leigh, Ray Walston; look for Anthony Edwards, Eric Stoltz and Forest Whitaker in their film debuts. 92 min.
07-1133 *$14.99*

The Breakfast Club (1985)
Five disparate high school students spend a Saturday detention together, only to learn they have more in common than they thought in this acclaimed "Little Chill" from John Hughes. Emilio Estevez, Anthony Michael Hall, Judd Nelson, Molly Ringwald and Ally Sheedy star. 97 min.
07-1309 Was $19.99 ❏*$14.99*

Puberty Blues (1980)
Bruce Beresford's seriocomedy of two young girls growing up at the beaches of Sydney, Australia, and refusing to conform to peer pressure from their beach's surfing crowd. Nell Schofield, Jad Capelja star. 86 min.
07-1310 Was $59.99 *$14.99*

Gotcha! (1985)
A college student on vacation in Europe gets more than he bargained for when a sexy "older woman" involves him in espionage, danger and romance in this stylish comedy-thriller. Anthony Edwards, Linda Fiorentino star. 97 min.
07-1315 Was $19.99 *$14.99*

Weird Science (1985)
When two high school "nerds" use their computer skills to create a "perfect woman," the results are wacky, wild and weird comedy! Funny teen tale from John Hughes stars Anthony Michael Hall, Ilan-Mitchell Smith and Kelly LeBrock ("The Woman in Red") as their "creature." 94 min.
07-1378 Was $19.99 ❏*$14.99*

UFOria (1982)
Take a wild look at the flip side of the American Dream in this quirky comedy that mixes small towns, faith healers, UFOs and car thieves. Cindy Williams, Fred Ward and Harry Dean Stanton star in this art house fave. 100 min.
07-1521 *$59.99*

Three O'Clock High (1987)
A high school nerd accidentally rouses the ire of the class bully, and now must fight him after school. His mounting anxiety and desperate attempts to avoid the inevitable make for a wild comedy. Casey Siemaszko, Richard Tyson star. 90 min.
07-1556 *$79.99*

Cross My Heart (1987)
The intros are made, the small talk is over. It's time for the dreaded "third date," and participants Martin Short and Annette O'Toole are afraid that their "little white lies" will come out, in this warm and funny romantic comedy about dating in the '80s. 91 min.
07-1580 Was $79.99 *$14.99*

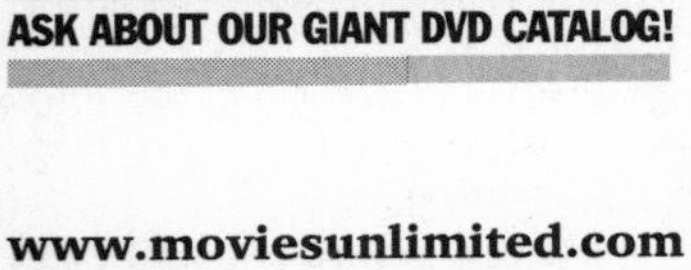

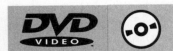

Casual Sex? (1988)
Can two attractive, single women find fulfillment through meaningless relationships in the age of "the new monogamy"? Lea Thompson and Victoria Jackson try to find out in a comedic look at romance in the '80s; with Andrew Dice Clay, Mary Gross. 87 min.
07-1589 Was $19.99 *$14.99*

Private School...For Girls (1983)
Wild, naughty antics and sexy coeds highlight this piquant farce about a rivalry between two girls over a boy from the nearby school. Phoebe Cates, Matthew Modine, Betsy Russell, Sylvia Kristel, and plenty of nubile nymphettes. 89 min.
07-1187 Was $19.99 *$14.99*

Smokey And The Bandit III (1983)
Sheriff Buford T. Justice is hot on the trail of that sly outlaw again, this time played by Jerry Reed. Car chases, sight gags and Jackie Gleason. Colleen Camp, Paul Williams, Pat McCormick co-star. 88 min.
07-1193 Was $59.99 ❏*$14.99*

Shirley Valentine (1989)
Pauline Collins re-creates her Tony-winning stage role as Shirley, a wisecracking English housewife who leaves her husband and two children for a vacation in the Greek islands, where she meets a charming tavern owner (Tom Conti) and gains a new lease on life. 108 min.
06-1711 Was $19.99 ❏*$14.99*

Let It Ride (1989)
Richard Dreyfuss is on a roll and he just can't quit as a racetrack addict who gets a hot tip and lets it ride him to big payoffs. But when will his luck run out? A lively, fractured farce, co-starring Teri Garr, Jennifer Tilly, David Johansen and Michelle Phillips. 86 min.
06-1712 ❏*$14.99*

Heartbeeps (1982)
You've seen lovers that were made for each other before, but never like these two romantic robots (Andy Kaufman, Bernadette Peters) who want go off and find happiness in the Gay 1990s. Futuristic fun with the great Dick Miller, Randy Quaid, Christopher Guest. 79 min.
07-1096 Was $39.99 ❏*$14.99*

Sixteen Candles (1984)
Molly Ringwald stars as a young girl whose 16th birthday has pretty much been a total disaster—her family forgets the day, a boy at school ignores her, and her only confidant is a classmate known as "the Geek." Anthony Michael Hall, Paul Dooley, John Cusack co-star; John Hughes directs. 93 min.
07-1222 Was $19.99 *$14.99*

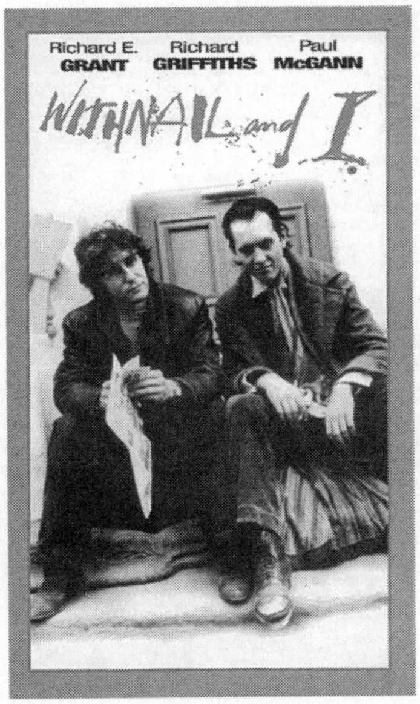

Withnail And I (1987)
Dryly witty, bittersweet comedy from Britain set at the twilight of the '60s, concerning the friendship between two Bohemian Londoners who take a weekend in the country to recover from their dissipating lifestyle. Evocative charmer stars Richard E. Grant, Paul McGann, Richard Griffiths. 104 min.
03-1635 *$14.99*

The Wild Life (1984)
Racy and ribald tale of teens in Southern California on their own for the first time, from the writer of "Fast Times at Ridgemont High." Chris Penn, Eric Stoltz, Lea Thompson and Rick Moranis star. 96 min.
07-1254 Was $79.99 ❏*$14.99*

A Little Sex (1982)
Cute contemporary comedy about an advertising man (Tim Matheson) who walks down the aisle with his live-in lover (Kate Capshaw, in her film debut), hoping to cure his uncontrollable skirt-chasing. Co-stars Edward Herrmann, John Glover and Wallace Shawn. 95 min.
07-1118 Was $59.99 *$14.99*

Crackers (1984)
A madcap farce about a gang of down-and-outers whose pot of gold is a safe in a pawn shop. Donald Sutherland, Sean Penn, Wallace Shawn and Professor Irwin Corey are some of the lead misfits in this hilarious comedy, based on the Italian film "Big Deal on Madonna Street." 92 min.
07-1209 *$59.99*

My Science Project (1985)
What starts out as a high school science fair becomes a harrowing, hilarious chase through history when a student's exhibit—salvaged from a military base junkyard—opens up a time warp! Spaced-out sci-fi comedy stars John Stockwell, Fisher Stevens, Danielle von Zerneck and Dennis Hopper. 95 min.
11-1237 *$14.99*

My Science Project (Letterboxed Version)
Also available in a theatrical, widescreen format.
08-8726 *$14.99*

Ernest Goes To Africa (1997)
Ernest is back and as hilarious as ever in this comic misadventure. The goofy guy unknowingly buys the jeweled eyes of an African idol at a flea market and turns them into a yo-yo. Soon, an adventurer sends Ernest and gal pal Renee to the dark continent in hopes of getting the goods. Linda Kash and Robert Whitehead also star. 90 min.
76-9090 Was $99.99 *$14.99*

Ernest In The Army (1997)
Jim Varney's Ernest P. Worrell gets a dose of military life when an old pal allows him to join the Army Reserves. Soon, Ernest is causing all sorts of havoc—with fellow misfit soldiers and a Middle Eastern dictator alike! 85 min.
76-9092 Was $99.99 *$14.99*

Honey, I Shrunk The Kids (1989)
When klutzy inventor Rick Moranis' latest device accidentally zaps his brood down to dust-mite size, the kids face a danger- and laugh-filled trek across their jungle-sized backyard. Hilarious hit sci-fi comedy from the Disney crew also stars Matt Frewer, Marcia Strassman. BONUS: The wild Roger Rabbit/Baby Herman cartoon "Tummy Trouble" is included! 100 min. total.
11-1493 Was $19.99 ❏*$14.99*

Honey, I Blew Up The Kid (1992)
Bumbling scientist Rick Moranis and his family have a big problem on their hands in this hit sequel, thanks to a growth ray that turns his 2-year-old son into a 100-foot-tall giant. Soon the titanic toddler is creating havoc on the Vegas strip, and a race to catch him before the military does is on. With Marcia Strassman, Lloyd Bridges. 89 min.
11-1646 Was $19.99 ❏*$14.99*

Honey, We Shrunk Ourselves (1997)
The third "Honey" outing is a made-for-video fantasy in which inventor Rick Moranis, his brother and their wives are shrunk to microscopic size and find themselves trying to survive a series of daring adventures—and their teenage kids! See Rick and company in a toy car, swimming in chip dip, in the washer and more! With Stuart Pankin. 75 min.
11-2092 Was $19.99 ❏*$14.99*

Hollywood Shuffle (1987)
Director/co-writer/star Robert Townsend skewers racial stereotyping in show biz with his acclaimed independent comedy. Would-be actor Townsend struggles to find serious roles in a white-run Hollywood that only offers blacks "pimp and hood" parts, while dreaming of fantasy spots for "The Black Acting School," "Sneakin' into the Movies" and "Rambro: First Youngblood." With Anne-Marie Johnson, John Witherspoon, and Keenan Ivory Wayans, who co-scripted. 82 min.
74-1001 Was $24.99 *$14.99*

Riders Of The Storm (1988)
You can't keep a good '60s radical down! At least, not the zonked-out crew of Vietnam vets who've been using a B-29 bomber as their flying guerrilla television station for 20 years, and are now preparing for their ultimate broadcast. Outrageous comedy stars Dennis Hopper, Michael J. Pollard, James Aubrey. 92 min.
53-1740 Was $19.99 *$14.99*

Disorganized Crime (1989)
With their ringleader caught and jailed before he can reveal his plans for a mammoth bank heist, four inept crooks must try to find him and evade a pair of cops even stupider than they are. Comedic crime caper stars Lou Diamond Phillips, Fred Gwynne, Corbin Bernsen, Ruben Blades and Ed O'Neill. 99 min.
11-1488 Was $19.99 ❏*$14.99*

The Great Outdoors (1988)
When John Candy takes his family up to the woods for a peaceful vacation, he doesn't count on the obnoxious clan of brother-in-law Dan Aykroyd tagging along. Stephanie Faracy, Chris Young and Annette Bening co-star. 91 min.
07-1594 Was $19.99 ❏*$14.99*

Desperately Seeking Susan (1985)
Rock queen Madonna is the free-spirited Susan, the girl everyone is seeking...or is housewife Rosanna Arquette really Susan? No one's sure in this dizzy adventure-comedy that blends romance, stolen jewelry, amnesia, mobsters, mystery and rock music. With Aidan Quinn, Steven Wright, Laurie Metcalf, John Turturro; Susan Seidelman directs. 104 min.
73-1169 ❏*$14.99*

Jim Jarmusch

Stranger Than Paradise (1984)
Offbeat and engaging look at the American dream through "foreign" eyes from Jim Jarmusch. The stagnant lives of two New York misfits are changed when the Hungarian cousin of one arrives while on her way to visit an aunt in Cleveland. Witty, starkly filmed "culture clash" comedy/drama stars John Lurie, Eszter Balint, Richard Edson. 90 min.
04-1951 Letterboxed ❏*$14.99*

Mystery Train (1989)
A fleabag Memphis hotel is the setting for three interconnected stories involving Japanese tourists, grieving Italian widows, drunken robbers and even the ghost of Elvis. Wonderfully wry comedy from Jim Jarmusch stars Joe Strummer, Rick Aviles, Nicoletta Braschi, Steve Buscemi, and Screamin' Jay Hawkins and Cinque Lee as the hotel staff. 110 min.
73-1090 Was $79.99 *$14.99*

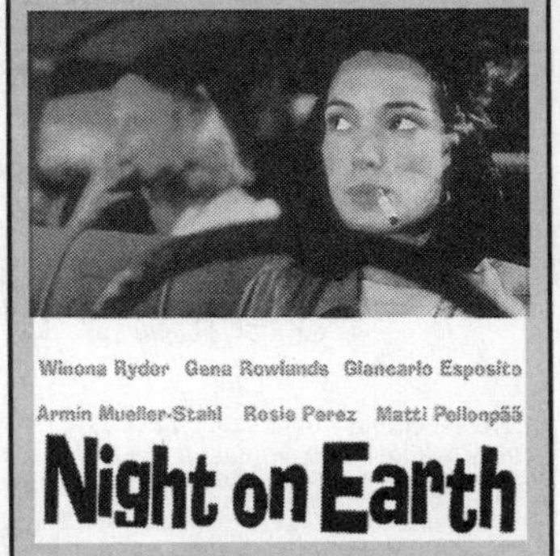

Night On Earth (1992)
Maverick filmmaker Jim Jarmusch casts his camera on the relationships between five taxi drivers and their passengers in this omni-cab comedy that visits L.A., New York, Paris, Rome and Helsinki on the same night. Playing the hacks are Winona Ryder, Roberto Benigni, Isaach De Bankolé, Matti Pellonpää and Armin Mueller-Stahl; their riders include Gena Rowlands, Giancarlo Esposito and Rosie Perez. 128 min.
02-2313 Letterboxed *$14.99*

Dead Man (1996)
Nineteenth-century Ohio accountant Johnny Depp lands a new job at a frontier town called Machine, but before long he kills a man, is pursued by bounty hunters, and is helped by an Indian who thinks he's the reincarnation of poet William Blake. It's a western as only iconoclastic director Jim Jarmusch could make, filled with offbeat humor and mythical symbolism. The supporting cast includes Gary Farmer, Lance Henriksen, Crispin Glover, Iggy Pop and Robert Mitchum. 121 min.
11-2075 Was $19.99 ❏*$14.99*

Dead Man (Letterboxed Version)
Also available in a theatrical, widescreen format.
11-2097 Was $99.99 ❏*$19.99*

Ghost Dog: The Way Of The Samurai (2000)
In Jim Jarmusch's fascinating meshing of gangster story and samurai film, Forest Whitaker is Ghost Dog, a hit man who rubs out opponents for mobsters he's indebted to because one of them saved his life. Living in a rooftop shack and communicating by pigeons, Whitaker abides by an ancient Samurai creed—even when his employers cross him. With John Tormey, Cliff Gorman. 116 min.
27-7225 ❏*$99.99*

Three Men And A Baby (1987)
Tom Selleck, Steve Guttenberg and Ted Danson are the happy-go-lucky swingers whose bachelor pad becomes a slapstick nursery when a "bundle of joy" is left on their doorstep in the hit comedy. With Nancy Travis; Leonard Nimoy directs. 102 min.
11-1459 Was $19.99 ❏*$14.99*

Three Men And A Little Lady (1990)
Lovable bachelor fathers Ted Danson, Steve Guttenberg and Tom Selleck are back, along with their new kindergarten-age charge, in this warm and witty hit sequel. But will their happy "family" be split up when the little lady's mother flies to England to star in a new play and announces plans to marry her director? Nancy Travis, Robin Weisman, Fiona Shaw co-star. 103 min.
11-1557 Was $19.99 ❏*$14.99*

License To Drive (1988)
It's a rite of passage for American teenagers, but when one young man fails his driving test, he's got to do some fast thinking (and illegal driving) to keep a date with the school beauty. Corey Haim, Corey Feldman, Richard Masur, Carol Kane. 90 min.
04-2184 *❑$19.99*

How I Got Into College (1989)
It's an annual rite of passage that sends shivers down the spines of millions of teens. Now follow would-be freshman Corey Parker down the twisted paths of college admissions. Lara Flynn Boyle, Anthony Edwards also star. 89 min.
04-2257 Was $89.99 *❑$14.99*

Bad Medicine (1985)
Steve Guttenberg stars as the new student at a zany "banana republic" medical school where the only anatomies studied are those of the co-eds. Madcap farce also stars Julie Hagerty, Alan Arkin and Julie Kavner. 97 min.
04-3095 Was $79.99 *❑$29.99*

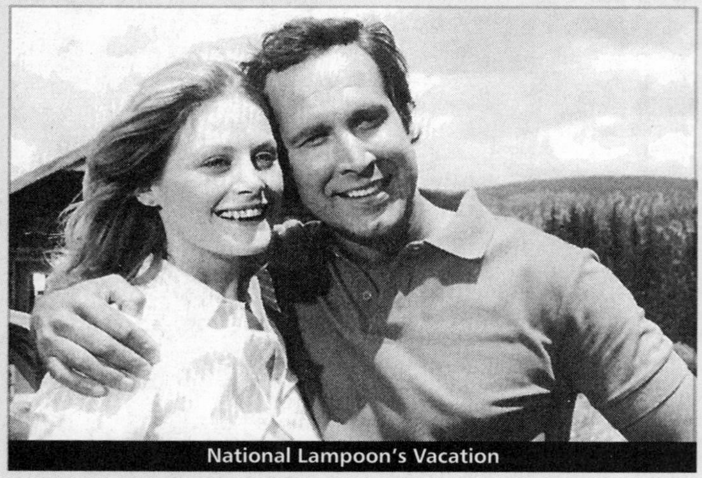
National Lampoon's Vacation

Chevy Chase

The Groove Tube (1974)
Hilarious cult comedy spoofing TV programs and commercials offers wild gags, sexy ladies, witty satire and early appearances by Chevy Chase, Richard Belzer and Paul Bartel, plus singer Buzzy Linhart and porn star Jennifer Welles. There's play-by-play of the "Sexual Olympics"; commercials for "Geritan" and "Butz Beer"; a wild adventure series called "The Dealers"; and a sleazy kid's show. 74 min.
03-1013 *$19.99*

Tunnelvision (1976)
It's the "television of the future" and it's unlike anything you've ever seen! Join Chevy Chase, Franken and Davis, Betty Thomas, Howard Hesseman, Laraine Newman, Ernie Anderson, Phil Proctor, Ron Silver, and Gerrit Graham in this wild look at TV insanity. 68 min.
50-6321 *$19.99*

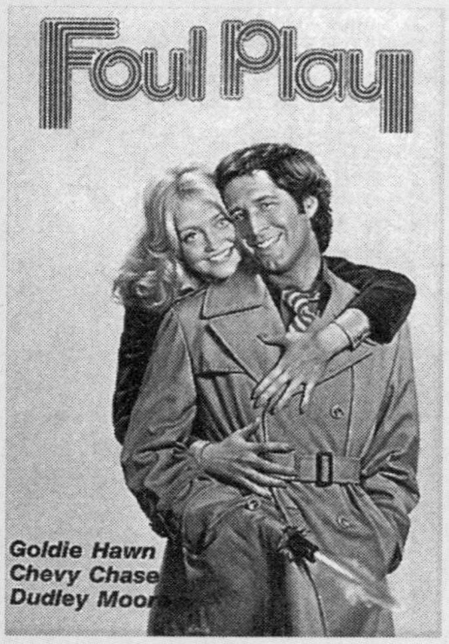

Foul Play (1978)
Hilarious comedy/thriller with Goldie Hawn and Chevy Chase about a shy librarian who realizes an assassination plot is in the works, and a klutzy detective is the only one who believes her. Co-stars Dudley Moore, Burgess Meredith. 116 min.
06-1019 *$14.99*

Modern Problems (1981)
Put-upon air traffic controller Chevy Chase is doused with radioactive goo and develops telekinetic powers in this slapstick comedy that will levitate the laughs out of you. With Dabney Coleman, Patti D'Arbanville, Nell Carter. 91 min.
04-1447 Was $59.99 *$14.99*

Under The Rainbow (1981)
Chevy Chase is a wacky private detective involved with hundreds of midgets during the shooting of "The Wizard of Oz." A small fry comedy with big laughs. Co-stars Carrie Fisher, Eve Arden, Adam Arkin, Billy Barty. 98 min.
19-1186 Was $19.99 *$14.99*

National Lampoon's Vacation (1983)
Join Chevy Chase and family on a madcap vacation trek through the U.S. On this trip, everything happens: cars go out of control, beautiful model Christie Brinkley shows up, along with John Candy, and relatives prove weirder than you'd ever think. Beverly D'Angelo, Imogene Coca, Randy Quaid. 93 min.
19-1294 *❑$14.99*

National Lampoon's European Vacation (1985)
The Griswold family is off on another hilarious holiday, and America is safe, but the continent may never recover! Watch as Chevy Chase, Beverly D'Angelo and their kids raise havoc from London to Rome for a wacky comedy trip. 94 min.
19-1474 Was $19.99 *❑$14.99*

National Lampoon's Christmas Vacation (1989)
It's hilarious holiday havoc for Chevy Chase and his brood, as the Griswolds' plans for an old-fashioned family Christmas go up in smoke (just like their cat!) when a horde of boorish relatives descend upon their home. Comedic carol of calamities also stars Beverly D'Angelo, Randy Quaid, Brian Doyle-Murray, Julia Louis-Dreyfus and Juliette Lewis. 97 min.
19-1759 *❑$14.99*

Vegas Vacation (1997)
It's a sure bet for comical calamity when Chevy Chase, Beverly D'Angelo and their offspring pack up the car and head for the neon lights of Las Vegas. Once there, the Griswold kids get mixed up with mobsters and go-go dancers, D'Angelo is wooed by Wayne Newton, and Chevy winds up on stage with Siegfried and Roy. Randy Quaid also stars. 98 min.
19-2536 Was $19.99 *❑$14.99*

Deal Of The Century (1983)
Chevy Chase gets mixed up in the illegal arms race in this comedy filled with wackiness and zany sight gags, as well as some timely spoofing of nuclear proliferation. Sigourney Weaver, Gregory Hines co-star; directed by William Friedkin. 96 min.
19-1304 Was $19.99 *$14.99*

Fletch (1985)
Chevy Chase plays an unorthodox reporter with a penchant for disguise who gets involved in a murder plot. This thriller, laced with laughs and based on Gregory McDonald's novel, co-stars Tim Matheson, Joe Don Baker and Geena Davis. 96 min.
07-1324 Was $19.99 *❑$14.99*

Fletch Lives (1989)
Irwin Fletcher is back, trying to save the Louisiana plantation he's inherited from a bayou Mr. Big who'll stop at nothing to steal it for himself. Chevy Chase's return as the oft-disguised snoop co-stars Julianne Phillips, Hal Holbrook. 95 min.
07-1624 Was $19.99 *❑$14.99*

Spies Like Us (1985)
Chevy Chase and Dan Aykroyd are two bumbling agents on a top secret assignment to foil a group of international missile maniacs. But they're the ones who get foiled, hung upside down, and lost, a lot, in this frantic comedy feast. Co-stars Donna Dixon, Steve Forrest. 103 min.
19-1505 *❑$14.99*

Three Amigos! (1986)
In the 1910s, the natives of an oppressed Mexican village send a plea for help to their favorite movie star gunslingers (Steve Martin, Chevy Chase and Martin Short). The hapless actors believe they're making a publicity appearance...and get stuck having to face down very real banditos! 103 min.
44-1471 *❑$14.99*

Caddyshack II (1988)
Just when you thought it was safe to head back to the green, those loonies from the links are back in an all-new comedy smash. Jackie Mason, Robert Stack, Dan Aykroyd, Dyan Cannon and Jonathan Silverman star, with Chevy Chase and "Chuck the Rodent" reprising their roles from the original. 93 min.
19-1676 Was $19.99 *❑$14.99*

Funny Farm (1988)
Chevy Chase and Madolyn Smith are two urbanites who decided to try the small town life of a New England farm instead...only to be harassed by strange neighbors, attacked by woodland creatures, and trapped in a decaying house; directed by George Roy Hill. 101 min.
19-1657 *❑$14.99*

Nothing But Trouble (1991)
Dan Aykroyd, Chevy Chase, John Candy and Demi Moore team up for this outrageous farce. A dim-witted New York Yuppie couple are stopped for running a stop sign in a bizarre, run-down village where the demented, 106-year-old justice of the peace sentences them to death! Aykroyd also scripted and directed. 94 min.
19-1873 Was $89.99 *❑$14.99*

Memoirs Of An Invisible Man (1992)
Exciting and funny comic-thriller, with Chevy Chase as a Wall Street analyst who is turned invisible in a freak accident, then dodges the CIA, who wants to recruit him as a spy. He finds help and romance with a sexy filmmaker, played by Daryl Hannah. Co-starring Sam Neill, Michael McKean. 99 min.
19-1978 Was $19.99 *❑$14.99*

Cops And Robbersons (1994)
Funny farce starring Chevy Chase as Norman Robberson, a meek Middle American father with an eccentric family and an adoration for TV cop shows, who plays host and unwanted sidekick to a gruff veteran detective (Jack Palance) and his young partner staking out a counterfeiting neighbor. Dianne Wiest, Robert Davi also star. 93 min.
02-2655 Was $19.99 *❑$14.99*

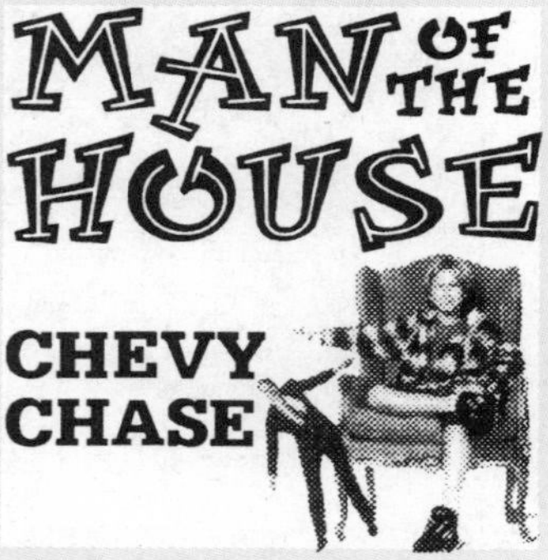

Man Of The House (1995)
In this family comedy, 11-year-old Jonathan Taylor Thomas (TV's "Home Improvement") has a problem with divorced mom Farrah Fawcett's new suitor, nerdy lawyer Chevy Chase. In hopes of marrying Fawcett, Chase tries to bond with the kid. Hilarity abounds when Thomas gets Chase to join the YMCA Indian Guides. George Wendt co-stars. 97 min.
11-1926 Was $89.99 *❑$14.99*

Dirty Work (1998)
"SNL" alumnus Norm MacDonald stars as a guy who is fed up with the stupidity and evil doings of others. Using his lifelong knack for retaliation, he sets up a company dedicated to carrying out the revenge plots of its customers. Artie Lange, Jack Warden, Christopher McDonald and Chevy Chase co-star, with cameos by Chris Farley and Adam Sandler; Philly's own Bob Saget directs. 82 min.
12-3260 Was $99.99 *❑$14.99*

Please see our index for these other Chevy Chase titles: *Hero • Seems Like Old Times • Snow Day*

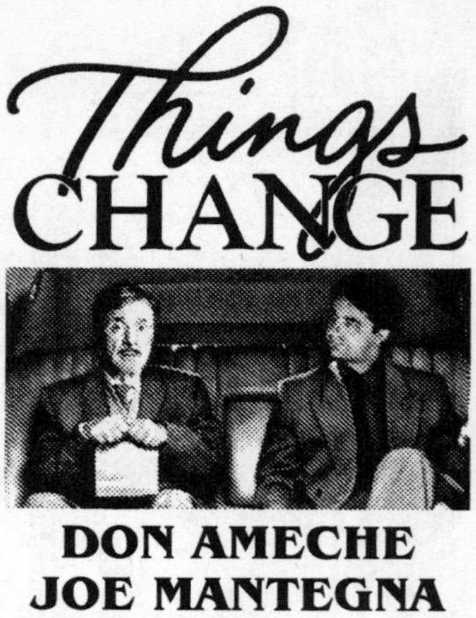

Things Change (1988)
Captivating dark farce follows an elderly Chicago shoeshine (Don Ameche), who's being paid handsomely to go to prison in place of a look-alike mob-lord, and his gunsel "coach" (Joe Mantegna), who decides to treat him to a wild weekend in Tahoe before he goes up. Written and directed by David Mamet ("Glengarry Glen Ross"). 105 min.
02-1913 *❑$14.99*

Broadcast News (1987)
Writer/director James L. Brooks combines a savage look at TV journalism with a hectic love triangle. William Hurt is the not-too-bright but photogenic news anchor who interests driven producer Holly Hunter and angers veteran correspondent Albert Brooks. Also stars Joan Cusack, Robert Prosky, and Jack Nicholson as the network anchorman. 132 min.
04-3865 *❑$14.99*

90 Days (1986)
Delightful comedy from Canada about two buddies who suffer from different "girl problems." One's just been kicked out of his home by his wife, the other is awaiting the arrival of his Asian mail-order bride for a three-month "trial run." Stars Stefan Wodoslawsky and Christine Pak. 100 min.
04-2075 Was3 $79.99 *❑$29.99*

The Pick-Up Artist (1987)
A young man with a line for every girl he meets gets more than he bargained for when his latest "conquest" gives him a taste of his own medicine. Robert Downey, Jr. and Molly Ringwald light up this seriocomedy; Dennis Hopper, Harvey Keitel co-star. 81 min.
04-2127 Was $19.99 *❑$14.99*

Worth Winning (1989)
Mark Harmon stars in this topsy-turvy romantic farce, playing a Philadelphia TV weatherman who bets a friend he can stay engaged to three beautiful women at the same time. Madeleine Stowe, Lesley Ann Warren and Maria Holvöe are the ravishing fiancées who fall for the raging Harmon. 103 min.
04-2310 Was $19.99 *❑$14.99*

Say Anything (1989)
Three-dimensional performances from stars John Cusack and Ione Skye fuel this romantic comedy of a shy high school student trying to win the popular and successful girl of his dreams, over her father's objections. John Mahoney, Lili Taylor, Amy Brooks and Joan Cusack co-star; written and directed by Cameron Crowe. 100 min.
04-2242 Was $19.99 *❑$14.99*

Little Darlings (1980)
Don't let the title fool you. Tatum O'Neal and Kristy McNichol are two adventurous young ladies at summer camp who wager who will become the first to become a "woman" in this wild comedy. Co-stars Matt Dillon and Armand Assante. 95 min.
06-1033 Was $59.99 *$14.99*

Serial (1980)
An all-star comedy cast, including Martin Mull, Sally Kellerman and Tuesday Weld, highlights this hilarious tale about the residents of California's Marin County and their whirlwind search for the ultimate lifestyle. 91 min.
06-1084 Was $49.99 *$14.99*

Going Ape! (1981)
Tony Danza and Danny DeVito, stars of TV's "Taxi," are up to some monkey business in this wild comedy. Danza is in line to inherit five million dollars; all he has to do is care for a trio of orangutans! 91 min.
06-1098 Was $49.99 *$14.99*

Student Bodies (1981)
Scarier than "Porky's"! Funnier than "Friday the 13th"! You've never seen such wacky, bloody, zany, spooky fun as when a typical suburban high school becomes the stalking ground of the murderous "Breather" in this horror/comedy. 86 min.
06-1113 Was $69.99 *$14.99*

Gas (1981)
What happens when a gas shortage gets the best of the residents of a small town? Find out in this deliriously daffy comedy. Donald Sutherland, Susan Anspach, Howie Mandel star. 94 min.
06-1114 Was $69.99 *$14.99*

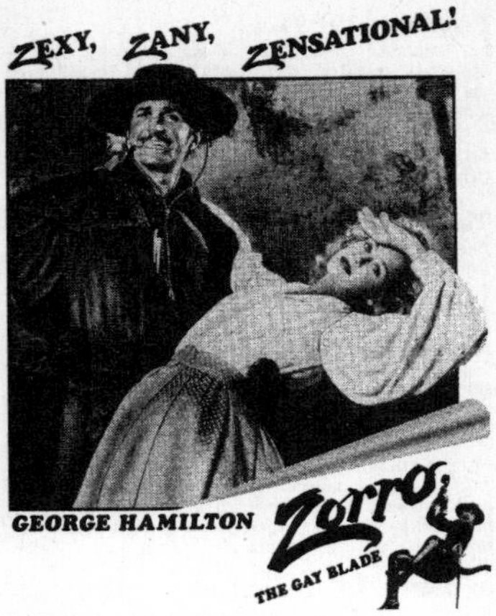

Zorro, The Gay Blade (1981)
A hilarious swish-buckler! Handsome George Hamilton plays dual roles—that of dashing swordsman Zorro and his light-in-the-loafers twin brother Bunny Wigglesworth—with the latter filling in for the former in order to topple the reign of an oppressive dictator. Co-stars Ron Leibman, Lauren Hutton, Brenda Vaccaro. 93 min.
04-1440 Was $29.99 **$14.99**

Gross Anatomy (1989)
It's "The Paper Chase" at medical school as wise guy student Matthew Modine tries to steer through the stormy waters of anatomy class while romancing strong-willed cohort Daphne Zuniga. Christine Lahti co-stars as the strict teacher. 109 min.
11-1497 □**$19.99**

Young Love: Lemon Popsicle 7 (1987)
The "Private Popsicle" boys land jobs as bellhops, socking away tips at a swank beachfront hotel by day, and socking it to the Summertime blues at a wild, non-stop beach party. Stars Zachi Noy, Yftach Katzur. 91 min.
19-1701 Was $79.99 **$19.99**

Walk Like A Man (1987)
That wild and wacky guy, Howie Mandel, really goes to the dogs in this zany comedy, playing a guy raised since infancy by wolves and trying to adjust to life as a human. Doggone funny tale also stars Christopher Lloyd, Cloris Leachman, Amy Steel. 86 min.
12-1747 **$14.99**

Strange Brew (1983)
Those lovable "SCTV" hoseheads, the MacKenzie Brothers (Rick Moranis and Dave Thomas), get into kegfuls of trouble when they meet sinister brewmeister Max Von Sydow in a comedy that's more fun than a mouse in a beer bottle. Koo-Loo-Koo-Koo-Koo-Koo-Koo-Koo! 91 min.
12-1316 Was $19.99 **$14.99**

You Talkin' To Me? (1988)
The line comes from the movie "Taxi Driver," and one diehard De Niro fan who decides to become an actor will do anything to get the agents and filmmakers to talk to him. Jim Young stars in a satire about the constant struggle to make it in Hollywood. 97 min.
12-1857 **$79.99**

Whoops Apocalypse (1986)
Who says World War III won't be a laughing matter? This darkly funny look at "the big one" takes pot shots at everything from the Superpowers to Britain's Royal Family. Loretta Swit, Peter Cook, Herbert Lom, Rik Mayall and Alexi Sayle star. 93 min.
12-1870 Was $79.99 **$14.99**

Hero At Large (1980)
John Ritter is hired to make personal appearances as comic hero Captain Avenger. After foiling a holdup, the public believes him to be the real thing, and he starts to also. Charming comedy about heroism also stars Anne Archer, Kevin McCarthy and Bert Convy. 98 min.
12-1311 **$59.99**

Some Girls (1988)
Cockeyed and very charming comedy starring Patrick Dempsey as a college kid who's invited to spend a family Christmas with the girl of his dreams...but her bizarre, spookily sensual relatives make his visit a sexual nightmare! Also stars Jennifer Connelly, Lila Kedrova, Andre Gregory. 85 min.
12-1891 Was $89.99 **$14.99**

I'm Gonna Git You Sucka (1988)
Director/writer/star Keenen Ivory Wayans takes aim at those black action films of the '70s in a wild satire. Can Wayans coax street heroes Bernie Casey, Jim Brown, Isaac Hayes and Antonio Fargas out of retirement to help him bring down crime boss Mr. Big and his ring of cheap gold chain dealers? 89 min.
12-1898 Was $19.99 **$14.99**

Little Monsters (1989)
What's that lurking under Fred Savage's bed? Why, it's blue-skinned, horned creature Howie Mandel, who promptly takes his charge into his otherworldly home, where all manner of goblins and beasties live. Scaringly funny comedy also stars Daniel Stern, Rick Ducomun. 103 min.
12-2011 Was $19.99 **$14.99**

New York Stories (1989)
Three of today's top filmmakers present a trio of dramatic, funny and touching stories about Big Apple living: Nick Nolte and Rosanna Arquette are a painter and his pupil in Martin Scorsese's "Life Lessons," Francis Coppola depicts a young girl's wondrous adventures in "Life Without Zoe," and Woody Allen faces the ultimate "visit from Mother" in "Oedipus Wrecks," with Mia Farrow and Mae Questel. 126 min.
11-1490 □**$14.99**

True Love (1989)
A raucously funny and perceptive comedy about two Italian kids from the Bronx who are about to wed and must settle questions about tuxedos, guest lists, the color of mashed potatoes at the reception and infidelity before they tie the knot. Annabella Sciorra, Ron Eldard star. 101 min.
12-2019 Was $19.99 **$14.99**

Wise Guys (1986)
Joe Piscopo and Danny De Vito are inept mobster pals whose latest blunder gives them only one way to clear things: bump off the other guy first! Brian DePalma's wild comedy also stars Harvey Keitel and Captain Lou Albano. 91 min.
12-2226 □**$19.99**

Side By Side (1988)
Three legendary laughmakers (Milton Berle, Sid Caesar, Danny Thomas) team up for this heartwarming seriocomedy about a group of retired businessmen who decide sitting in a rest home isn't for them and set up their own clothing company. With Morey Amsterdam, Marjorie Lord. 96 min.
72-9003 Was $79.99 **$14.99**

Dream Date (1989)
A widowed father isn't ready for his "little girl's" first date in this spry romantic comedy that stars Clifton Davis, Tempestt Bledsoe, Kadeem Hardison, Anne Marie Johnson and Pauly Shore. 96 min.
72-9012 Was $89.99 **$14.99**

Johnny Be Good (1988)
Anthony Michael Hall is Johnny Walker, a hotshot high school football hero who's being pursued by every college recruiter in the country, in a funny look at America's obsession with sports. With Robert Downey, Jr., Uma Thurman. 84 min.
73-1018 Was $19.99 □**$14.99**

Under The Biltmore Clock (1985)
Adapted from an F. Scott Fitzgerald short story, this wry romantic comedy stars Sean Young as a husband-hunting flapper in '20s New York whose latest catch comes with a most unusual family. Lenny Von Dohlen, Barnard Hughes also star. 70 min.
73-1060 **$19.99**

The Woman In Red (1984)
"Fooling around" was never funnier than in this romp from Gene Wilder, based on the French comedy "Pardon Mon Affaire." Wilder is a happily-married man who becomes obsessed after seeing beautiful Kelly LeBrock and bumbles every attempt to meet her. With Charles Grodin, Judith Ivey and Gilda Radner as Wilder's love-starved secretary. 87 min.
73-1171 □**$14.99**

Real Men (1987)
A supersuave spy and an average suburban nebbish are the unlikely allies who together must foil enemy agents in this madcap take on the "007" genre. James Belushi, John Ritter, Barbara Barrie star. 86 min.
12-2540 **$19.99**

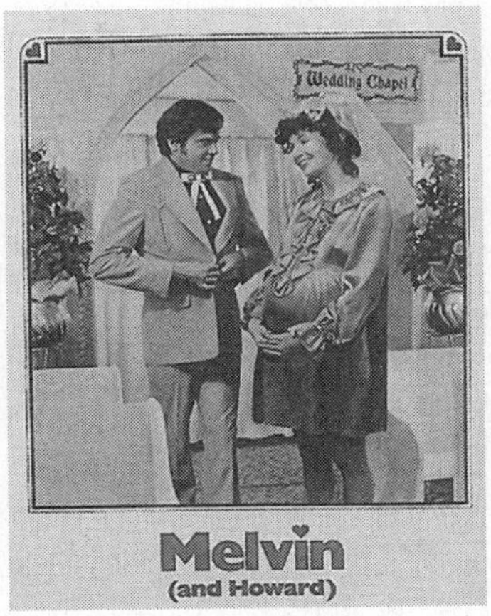

Melvin And Howard (1980)
Irresistible American fable from director Jonathan Demme explores Nevada garage owner Melvin Dummar's claim that he once picked up eccentric billionaire Howard Hughes hitchhiking in the desert, and the skepticism that arose after a will turned up naming Dummar as an heir. Co-star Mary Steenburgen and screenwriter Bo Goldman won Oscars; Paul LeMat and Jason Robards play the title roles. 95 min.
07-1041 **$14.99**

Melvin And Howard (Letterboxed Version)
Also available in a theatrical, widescreen format. Includes the original theatrical trailer.
08-8790 **$14.99**

Michael J. Fox

Midnight Madness (1980)
Follow a group of college students as they turn the streets and tourist sites of L.A. upside-down in an all-night scavenger hunt. This wild romp was notable for being the Disney company's first entry in the "teen comedy" genre (although it was released without the studio's imprint) and for featuring Michael J. Fox in his film debut. David Naughton, Debra Clinger, Stephen Furst and Eddie Deezen star. 112 min.
11-1160 **$14.99**

High School U.S.A. (1984)
Some of the top young TV stars of the '80s (Michael J. Fox, Nancy McKeon, Todd Bridges) and the '60s (Tony Dow, Angela Cartwright, Bob Denver, Dwayne Hickman) star in this laugh-filled look at teenage life in modern America. 96 min.
40-1135 **$12.99**

The Secret Of My Success (1987)
Laugh-getting lark stars Michael J. Fox as an ambitious kid trying to scamper up the corporate ladder in his uncle's business...and scamper out of the lustful clutches of his aunt! Funny tale of yup-ward mobility co-stars Helen Slater, Richard Jordan, Margaret Whitton. 110 min.
07-1538 Was $19.99 □**$14.99**

Bright Lights, Big City (1988)
Michael J. Fox stars as a New York magazine editor whose life is slowly disintegrating, piece by piece, as he sinks into depression and drugs. "Downside" yuppie drama, based on Jay McInerney's novel, also stars Kiefer Sutherland, Phoebe Cates, Dianne Wiest. 108 min.
12-1826 Was $19.99 □**$14.99**

Casualties Of War (1989)
Brian DePalma's searing war drama stars Michael J. Fox as a green recruit in Vietnam who must make an agonizing moral decision when his platoon gang-rapes a village girl. Sean Penn plays the gung-ho sergeant who leads the horrifying assault. A powerful look at a different side of the Vietnam War. 120 min.
02-1997 Was $19.99 □**$14.99**

The Hard Way (1991)
Exciting, action-packed comedy with Michael J. Fox as an obnoxious film star who tunes up for a role as a detective by hanging around tough New York cop James Woods, who's tracking down a serial killer. Laughs, chases and stunts abound. With Stephen Lang, Annabella Sciorra, Penny Marshall. 111 min.
07-1707 Was $19.99 □**$14.99**

Doc Hollywood (1991)
Lively and bittersweet comedy stars Michael J. Fox as a crass young physician who finds himself stuck in a small South Carolina town while his car is being fixed, damaged en route to a new Beverly Hills practice. Soon, the locals are recruiting him to be the town doctor, and he falls for a pretty ambulance driver (Julie Warner). Woody Harrelson, Bridget Fonda and Barnard Hughes co-star. 103 min.
19-1908 Was $19.99 □**$14.99**

For Love Or Money (1993)
Frothy romantic comedy starring Michael J. Fox as a concierge at a posh New York hotel with hopes of opening his own luxury hotel. In order to secure the financing, Fox must take care of an unscrupulous investor's gorgeous mistress (Gabrielle Anwar), but when he falls in love with her, it's a choice between realizing his dream or the woman of his dreams. With Anthony Higgins. 96 min.
07-2055 Was $19.99 □**$14.99**

Life With Mikey (1993)
Endearing comedy about a former child actor-turned-talent agent (Michael J. Fox) who discovers a feisty, streetwise girl (Christina Vidal) he thinks he can help turn into a big star and push him back into the show biz limelight. Cyndi Lauper and Nathan Lane also star. 91 min.
11-1725 □**$14.99**

Greedy (1994)
When the wealthy patriarch of the McTeague family enlists a sexy pizza delivery girl as his live-in nurse, his conniving relatives resort to all sorts of devious means to keep the old man's money where they feel it rightfully belongs—in their pockets! Michael J. Fox, Kirk Douglas, Phil Hartman, Nancy Travis, Olivia d'Abo star. 113 min.
07-2173 Was $19.99 □**$14.99**

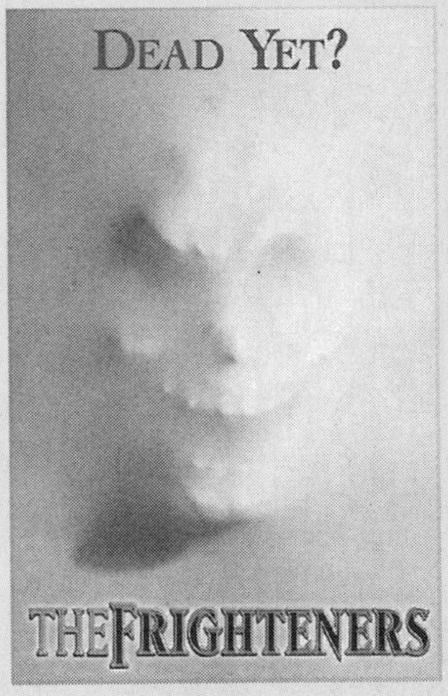

The Frighteners (1996)
Wild horror-comedy from director Peter Jackson ("Heavenly Creatures") starring Michael J. Fox as a psychic con artist who uses a trio of ghosts he's befriended to "haunt" houses he later "cleanses." But when a deadly spirit begins preying on a small town, Fox puts his "powers" to the test to save the locals'—and his—lives. Trini Alvarado, John Astin, Jeffrey Combs also star. 110 min.
07-2467 Was $99.99 □**$14.99**

The Frighteners (Letterboxed Version)
Also available in a theatrical, widescreen format.
07-2551 □**$19.99**

Please see our index for these other Michael J. Fox titles: *The American President • Blue In The Face • Class of 1984 • Homeward Bound I & II • Mars Attacks! • Stuart Little • Where The Rivers Flow North*

Stakeout (1987)
Richard Dreyfuss and Emilio Estevez are two Seattle cops whose assignment to stake out the former girlfriend of an escaped con takes a comical turn after Dreyfuss and she fall in love. Co-stars Madeleine Stowe, Aidan Quinn, Dan Lauria. 115 min.
11-1443 Was $19.99 □**$14.99**

Another Stakeout (1993)
Disaster-prone detectives Richard Dreyfuss and Emilio Estevez are back, this time teaming up with feisty assistant D.A. Rosie O'Donnell. They're posing as a "typical" suburban household while trying to locate a runaway government mob witness, but this family's feuding turns the easy assignment into a comic mess. Engaging sequel also stars Dennis Farina, Madeleine Stowe. 109 min.
11-1778 Was $19.99 □**$14.99**

Moon Over Parador (1988)
When the dictator of a Latin American country suddenly dies, down-and-out New York actor Richard Dreyfuss is "persuaded" to impersonate the ruler by aide Raul Julia. Paul Mazursky's topical farce also stars Sonia Braga, Jonathan Winters. 104 min.
07-1599 Was $19.99 **$14.99**

Screwball Hotel (1988)
Comedian Kelly Monteith stars in this wacky, sexy "service" comedy about a trio of zany bellhops who save a swank Miami hotel from bankruptcy with an outrageous beauty contest. Penthouse Pet Corrine Alphen co-stars. 101 min.
07-1611 **$79.99**

Cold Dog Soup (1989)
A young man's "dream evening" with a beautiful woman turns into a darkly funny nightmare when her mother's beloved dog drops dead. He agrees to take the animal and bury it in a park, but a deranged cabbie takes the man on a riotous quest to find a buyer for the dog's body. Offbeat (to say the least) comedy stars Frank Whaley, Randy Quaid, Christine Harnos. 85 min.
08-8537 **$14.99**

Just The Way You Are (1984)
Funny, touching romantic comedy stars Kristy McNichol as a young woman who finds acceptance and love at a ski resort when she "hides" her crippled leg in a cast, but cannot tell her new boyfriend the truth. Michael Ontkean, Kaki Hunter also star. 95 min.
12-1448 Was $79.99 **$14.99**

Mischief (1985)
A small California town in the mid-'50s is the setting for some good, mostly clean fun in this spry teen comedy that stars Doug McKeon as a nerdy teen who takes the advice of a slick new kid in town to win the heart of the local beauty. With Kelly Preston, Catherine Mary Stewart, Chris Nash. 97 min.
04-1867 Was $79.99 □**$29.99**

Up Your Anchor (1985)
Sail the high seas to sexy and salty comedy with two sailors cruising for nautical nookie in the many ports that they drop anchor. Stars Yftach Katzur, Zachi Noy. 89 min.
12-1675 **$79.99**

John Belushi

National Lampoon's Animal House: Special Edition (1978)
One of the first—and perhaps the greatest—of the "gross-out" comedies, and John Belushi's quintessential screen performance. Watch as the misfits of Delta House use food fights, dead horses, toga parties and other tactics to battle the "straights" and administrators of Faber College in 1962. Tim Matheson, Peter Riegert, Tom Hulce, Karen Allen, Donald Sutherland, and Otis Day and The Knights also star. This special edition version also includes a 15-minute "making of" featurette with interviews with the cast and crew. 109 min.
07-2684 Was $19.99 ❑*$14.99*

National Lampoon's Animal House (Letterboxed Version)
Also available in a theatrical, widescreen format.
07-2685 Was $19.99 ❑*$14.99*

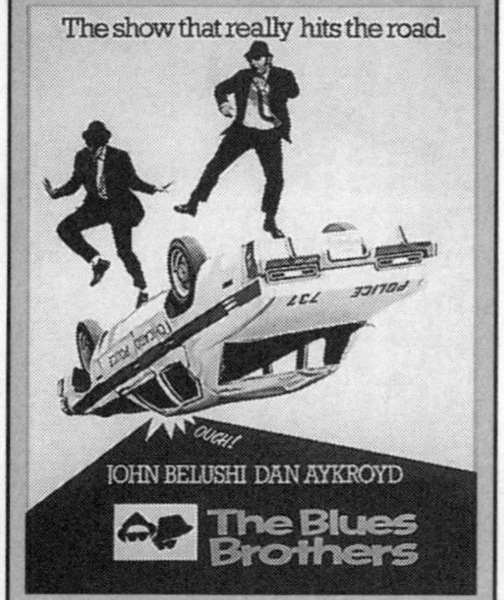

The Blues Brothers (Special Edition) (1980)
John Belushi and Dan Aykroyd bring their "SNL" characters to the big screen, playing Jake and Elwood Blues, two ex-con, music-loving siblings out to reunite their old band so they can raise money to save the Chicago orphanage where they grew up. Filled with wild car chases and songs from such guest stars as James Brown, Cab Calloway, Ray Charles and Aretha Franklin, John Landis' high-octane comedy also stars John Candy, Carrie Fisher, Henry Gibson. Special video version includes 17 minutes of extra footage and interviews with Aykroyd and Landis. 133 min.
07-2742 ❑*$14.99*

The Blues Brothers (Letterboxed Version)
Also available in a theatrical, widescreen format.
07-2743 ❑*$19.99*

Neighbors (1981)
Lock the doors! Here come the neighbors! This psycho-comic look at suburban life tells a hilarious and offbeat tale of how a strange couple annoys the sedate family they move next to. John Belushi, Dan Aykroyd, Cathy Moriarty, Kathryn Walker star. 95 min.
02-2704 *$14.99*

Continental Divide (1981)
John Belushi is a tough Chicago columnist who must "rough it" in the mountains of Colorado as he tries to win the heart of naturalist Blair Brown in a winning romantic comedy; written by Lawrence Kasdan ("The Big Chill"). 103 min.
07-1084 *$14.99*

The Best Of The Blues Brothers
Join host Dan Aykroyd (aka Elwood Blues) as he looks back on his and John Belushi's shades-wearing, blues-singing siblings in rare clips from their only concert tour and appearances on "Saturday Night Live," while recounting the history of the Blues Brothers band. Songs include "Soul Man," "Jailhouse Rock," "Rubber Biscuit" and "Hey, Bartender." 60 min.
58-8104 Was $29.99 *$12.99*

Please see our index for these other John Belushi titles: *1941 • Goin' South • Shame Of The Jungle*

Uncle Buck (1989)
When they leave town for an extended visit, a staid yuppie couple reluctantly taps the family failure, loud and raunchy Uncle Buck, to babysit their under-nurtured brood in the third extra-large hit from director John Hughes and comedy juggernaut John Candy. Amy Madigan, Jean Louisa Kelly, Macaulay Culkin also star. 100 min.
07-1634 Was $19.99 ❑*$14.99*

The Nude Bomb (1980)
Famed "Get Smart" agent Maxwell Smart (Don Adams) is on his most dangerous case ever, trying to stop KAOS from dropping a bomb that would destroy all existing fabric worldwide. And would you believe he only has 48 hours to save the day? Sylvia Kristel, Rhonda Fleming, Vittorio Gassman also star. 94 min.
07-1689 Was $79.99 *$14.99*

There Goes The Bride (1980)
In this wild British farce, Tom Smothers plays a man who bumps his head on his daughter's wedding day and starts to believe he's involved with a 1920s flapper he once saw in a photograph. Twiggy, Martin Balsam, Sylvia Syms, Jim Backus, Phil Silvers, and Broderick Crawford also star. 88 min.
10-1598 *$19.99*

Goddess Of Love (1988)
In her first starring role, Vanna White turns more than letters as Venus, the legendary love goddess, trapped 3,000 years as a statue and now brought back to life in modern-day L.A. David Naughton, David Leisure and Amanda Bearse also star. 92 min.
10-2509 *$12.99*

The Rachel Papers (1989)
A computer whiz has found the high-tech key to meeting and dating any woman he wants...that is, until the beautiful, unpredictable Rachel shows him that love can't be programmed. Ione Skye ("Say Anything"), Dexter Fletcher and James Spader star in a breezy romantic comedy. 95 min.
04-2265 Was $79.99 *$14.99*

Unhinged (1986)
Calvert DeForest, better known as Larry "Bud" Melman from "Late Night with David Letterman," is featured in this kooky comedy about a group of wackos who want to get their goofy show on network TV.
10-7939 Was $19.99 *$14.99*

Doctor Detroit (1983)
Nerdish college professor Dan Aykroyd masquerades as a bizarre, steel-handed pimp named Doctor Detroit in order to help defend a band of hookers from a wicked crime boss named Mom in this slapstick comedy that also stars Howard Hesseman, Donna Dixon, Fran Drescher and James Brown. 89 min.
07-1179 ❑*$14.99*

The Jet Benny Show (1986)
An interstellar spoof in which the evil, power-crazed Lord Zane sets his sights on the planet Altimeera to complete his World Empire. Never fear, though, the avaricious aviator, Jet Benny, and his co-pilot, Rochester, are here to crush Zane. 77 min.
08-1354 Was $19.99 *$14.99*

Down Under (1987)
Two unemployed Southern California beach bums head to Australia to search for gold, and faster than you can say "g'day" they find themselves in one sticky wicket after another. Comedy stars Don Atkinson, Donn Dunlop, Patrick Macnee. 90 min.
08-1414 *$79.99*

Spring Break (1983)
As sure as the swallows fly to Capistrano each year, hundreds of kids pack up their bags and head to Fort Lauderdale for some fun in the sun and sex, sex, sex. Wild antics ensue. With David Knell, Steve Bassett, Corinne Alphen. 101 min.
02-1229 *$14.99*

Mannequin (1987)
Engaging fantasy/comedy starring Andrew McCarthy as a Philadelphia department store window dresser who gets a shock when the fetching figurine he's dressing comes to life as comely Kim Cattrall. With Estelle Getty, James Spader, Meshach Taylor. 89 min.
08-8442 *$14.99*

Mannequin Two: On The Move (1991)
Philadelphia is the backdrop again for romantic adventures of the dummy kind, as a beautiful Bavarian peasant girl is frozen into statue form and comes to life a thousand years later in the arms of a department store employee, the spitting image of her ancient Prince Charming. Kristy Swanson, William Ragsdale and Meshach Taylor star. 95 min.
27-6722 Was $89.99 ❑*$12.99*

In God We Tru$t (1980)
Marty Feldman directed, co-wrote and starred in this divinely funny comedy as a sheltered monk who is sent to Los Angeles to find financial help for his monastery. Along the way Brother Feldman falls for a good-hearted hooker (Louise Lasser), falls in with TV evangelist Armageddon T. Thunderbird (Andy Kaufman), and has an encounter with G.O.D. (Richard Pryor). 97 min.
07-2808 *$14.99*

My Stepmother Is An Alien (1988)
Physicist Dan Aykroyd gets rattled down to his slide rule when a radar beam he sends into deep space accidentally zaps a distant planet whose inhabitants send representative Kim Basinger to pull the plug. Sparks fly (literally) when Aykroyd falls for and weds the amorous alien. Co-stars Jon Lovitz, Alyson Hannigan; look for Juliette Lewis in her feature debut. 108 min.
02-1931 Was $19.99 ❑*$14.99*

"Crocodile" Dundee (1986)
Surprise hit comedy stars Paul Hogan as a roguish poacher from the Australian Outback who finds himself following a beautiful reporter (Linda Kozlowski) to New York, where his easygoing ways make for comedic complications. 102 min.
06-1455 ❑*$14.99*

"Crocodile" Dundee II (1988)
Everyone's favorite Aussie is back for more adventures and laughs, as Mick Dundee (Paul Hogan) must not only cope with life in the Big Apple, but save girlfriend Linda Kozlowski from crooks luring them to his Outback homeland. 110 min.
06-1627 ❑*$14.99*

Cousins (1989)
Hit romantic comedy, based on France's "Cousin, Cousine," stars Ted Danson and Isabella Rossellini as the not-too-happily married "relatives" who meet at a family wedding and embark on an affair. With Sean Young, William Petersen, Lloyd Bridges and Norma Aleandro. 110 min.
06-1676 ❑*$14.99*

The Milagro Beanfield War (1988)
The poor residents of a small Southwestern town find new hope when they band to stop a land mogul's "redevelopment" plans. Wonderfully drawn seriocomedy, directed by Robert Redford, stars John Heard, Ruben Blades, Sonia Braga, Chick Vennera, Daniel Stern; don't miss Paul Newman's "cameo." 118 min.
07-1584 *$14.99*

K-9 (1989)
After teaming with Schwarzenegger in a cop thriller, Jim Belushi is paired with another partner having problems with the language...a narcotics-sniffing German Shepherd named Jerry Lee. Fast-paced action/comedy hit also stars Mel Harris, Kevin Tighe. 102 min.
07-1627 Was $19.99 ❑*$14.99*

K-911 (1999)
This sequel to the popular "K-9" again pairs police detective Jim Belushi and four-footed pal Jerry Lee in a comedy-filled thriller. When Belushi is nearly gunned down, he and the pooch work overtime with two new partners—fellow cop Christine Tucci and Zeus, a daring Doberman—to get the would-be killers. 91 min.
07-2817 Was $99.99 ❑*$14.99*

Henry Jaglom

Tracks (1976)
Dennis Hopper turns in a dynamic portrait of a Vietnam vet escorting his dead buddy home on a long train ride. Disturbing memories from his past and a romance with a young girl make this an unforgettable drama from director Henry Jaglom. With Taryn Power, Michael Emil and Zack Norman (Sammy in "Chief Zabu"). 90 min.
06-1788 Was $19.99 *$14.99*

Sitting Ducks (1980)
An offbeat, fast-paced comedy from writer/director Henry Jaglom about two small-time hoods (Michael Emil and Zack Norman, reprising their roles from 1977's "Tracks") who decide to rip off their mob bosses and skip to Central America. Along the way they meet two women and encounter one calamity after another. Patrice Townsend also stars. 88 min.
03-1165 *$19.99*

Can She Bake A Cherry Pie? (1983)
Quirky romantic comedy by Henry Jaglom, starring Karen Black as a recent divorcee who wants to avoid "further entanglements," but finds herself dating men looking for "commitments." With Michael Emil, Frances Fisher and "Seinfeld" co-creator Larry David. 90 min.
06-1787 ❑*$19.99*

Someone To Love (1987)
Setting his sights once more on the constant search for romantic fulfillment, filmmaker Henry Jaglom creates a witty comedy set at a Valentine's Day party, where a director (Jaglom) shoots footage of guests answering the question, "Why are you alone?" With Sally Kellerman, Michael Emil, Andrea Marcovicci and, in his last role, Orson Welles. 110 min.
06-1619 Was $39.99 ❑*$14.99*

New Year's Day (1989)
Acclaimed tale of contemporary urban "weltschmerz" from creator Henry Jaglom about a man (played by Jaglom) who arrives at his new New York apartment only to find the previous occupants haven't left yet. At a farewell party he (and the audience) watches how the three women react to the changes and trials in their lives. With Maggie Jakobson, Gwen Welles, Melanie Winter and David Duchovny. 85 min.
06-1786 Was $89.99 ❑*$19.99*

Eating (1990)
Director Henry Jaglom turns his cameras on women and their obsession with food in this funny and provocative film. The setting is a birthday party in Southern California, where the female attendees interact, intersect and sometimes collide, but their conversations always leave much food for thought. Nelly Alard, Mary Crosby, Frances Bergen and Gwen Welles star. 110 min.
06-2081 Was $89.99 ❑*$14.99*

Babyfever (1994)
A career woman who thinks she may be pregnant, but isn't sure she wants to settle down with her current beau, attends a baby shower that quickly turns into a discussion group where the attendees offer their opinions, hopes and fears on the "job vs. family" debate, among other topics. Director Henry Jaglom's insightful comedy/drama stars Victoria Foyt, Frances Fisher, Eric Roberts, Matt Salinger. 110 min.
53-8495 Was $89.99 *$19.99*

Venice/Venice (1994)
Henry Jaglom's meditation on reel life and real life features the eccentric director as—you guessed it—an eccentric director who learns that his new film has been chosen to play the Venice Film Festival. His interview with journalist Nelly Alard leads her to contemplate the nature of reality and fantasy. David Duchovny, Melissa Leo co-star. 108 min.
53-8579 Was $89.99 *$19.99*

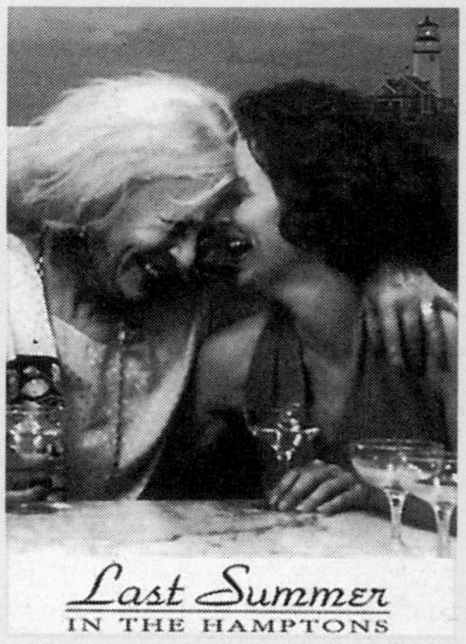

Last Summer In The Hamptons (1997)
The final summer gathering for a New York theatrical family at their Long Island vacation home takes on an added dimension when a popular film actress joins them in this funny and insightful comedy/drama from director Henry Jaglom. The ensemble cast includes Roscoe Lee Browne, Victoria Foyt, Andre Gregory, Melissa Leo, Viveca Lindfors, Roddy McDowall. 108 min.
27-7034 Was $99.99 ❑*$14.99*

Deja Vu (1998)
Henry Jaglom's dreamy romantic tale stars real-life wife Victoria Foyt as a wealthy American businesswoman who keeps bumping into stranger Stephen Dillane when she's trying to return an antique pin to a woman she met in Israel. The woman related a story to Foyt regarding love at first sight, and now Foyt's life is starting to resemble the story. With Vanessa Redgrave, Aviva Marks. 117 min.
19-2927 Was $99.99 ❑*$14.99*

Who Is Henry Jaglom? (1997)
The independent filmmaker who's been both praised and reviled by critics and audiences is the focus of this fascinating retrospective that features clips from such Jaglom movies as "Babyfever," "Eating" and "Someone to Love" and comments from Candice Bergen, Peter Bogdanovich, Milos Forman, Dennis Hopper, Sally Kellerman, Orson Welles and others. 52 min.
70-5129 Was $29.99 *$19.99*

Disorderlies (1987)
Those rotund rappers, The Fat Boys, star as three inept nursing home attendants hired by a greedy nephew to provide "care" for an elderly millionaire. Ralph Bellamy, Anthony Geary co-star. 96 min.
19-1612 $19.99

Feds (1988)
Sexy Rebecca De Mornay and klutzy Mary Gross are the latest recruits to the FBI's training academy, and these girls will become agents if it kills them! Wild comedy also stars Ken Marshall, Larry Cedar. 91 min.
19-1679 $19.99

Take Your Best Shot (1982)
Engaging comedy about a constantly struggling actor (Robert Urich) who must choose between career and family when his wife (Meredith Baxter Birney) tires of supporting him and files for divorce. 96 min.
27-6451 $12.99

Sunset Limousine (1983)
A would-be stand-up comic finds that moonlighting as a limo driver puts him on the outs with his girlfriend and in Dutch with some mobsters in this spry comedy. John Ritter, Susan Dey, Martin Short star. 92 min.
27-6559 $12.99

Up The Academy (1980)
A very undisciplined military school is the stage for a battle between students and teachers in this raucous, mad comedy. Ron Leibman, Ralph Macchio, Barbara Bach star; directed by Robert Downey, Sr. 88 min.
19-1437 $19.99

Doin' Time (1985)
The inmates at this prison don't worry about going "stir crazy"; they already are nuts! Zany comedy of the "big house" that's big on laughs stars Richard Mulligan, Jimmy Walker, John Vernon and Dey Young. 80 min.
19-1478 Was $19.99 $14.99

Army Brats (1984)
Sexy, zany, wacky wild comedy about four siblings who declare war on...their parents! Send-up of military family life will have you laughing so hard, you won't be able to stand at attention! Akkemay, Frank Schaafsma and Peter Faber star. 100 min.
19-1496 Was $59.99 $19.99

French Lesson (1986)
A young English girl is determined to come of age her own way. Set in Paris in the early 1960s this stylish comedy is a nostalgic look at the liberal attitudes just then coming into vogue. Jane Snowden and Alexandre Sterling star. 90 min.
19-1512 Was $19.99 $14.99

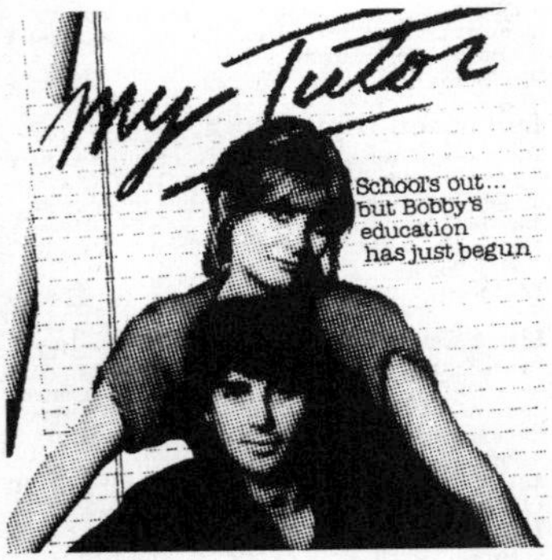

My Tutor (1983)
It's the last year of high school and Matt Lattanzi is flunking French. So his parents hire him a tutor...but the "instructor" turns out to be gorgeous blonde Caren Kaye, who winds up teaching Lattanzi about a lot more than language, in this racy comedy. Kevin McCarthy, Arlene Golonka, Crispin Glover also star. 97 min.
15-5548 $29.99

Mr. Love (1985)
A quiet, mild-mannered British gardener is laid to rest, but at his funeral his widow learns all about a secret past full of beautiful women and romantic entanglements. Charming comedy from England stars Barry Jackson, Margaret Tyzack. 92 min.
19-1547 Was $19.99 $14.99

Seven Minutes In Heaven (1986)
Follow the trials and triumphs of adolescence in this delightful "coming of age" comedy about three high school students searching for acceptance and love. Jennifer Connelly, Byron Thames, Maddie Corman star. 88 min.
19-1548 Was $19.99 $14.99

Cookie (1989)
Emily Lloyd ("Wish You Were Here") is at her sassy best as a Brooklyn punkette who joins forces with her estranged Mafioso father (Peter Falk). Susan Seidelman's off-kilter charmer also features Dianne Wiest, Brenda Vaccaro, Lionel Stander. 93 min.
19-1746 $14.99

Second Sight (1989)
There's a hilarious comedy in your future, as you watch cop John Larroquette and psychic Bronson Pinchot team up to create their own oddball detective agency. Spirited farce also stars Stuart Pankin, Bess Armstrong. 85 min.
19-1748 Was $19.99 $14.99

Police Academy (1984)
An outrageously funny look at the group of misfits who sign up for police academy—where cops are so inept, crime's gotta pay! A riotous beat you won't want to miss! Steve Guttenberg, Kim Cattrall, Bubba Smith, George Gaynes, Michael Winslow; directed by Hugh Wilson ("The First Wives Club"). 96 min.
19-1355 $14.99

Police Academy 2: Their First Assignment (1985)
The misfit peace officers from the academy hit the streets of a crime-ridden city and clean it up, their own way, in this hilarious sequel. With Steve Guttenberg, Bubba Smith, Art Metrano and human sound box Michael Winslow. 87 min.
19-1440 $14.99

Police Academy 3: Back In Training (1986)
Those wacky, zany grads head back to the alma mater to help line up new recruits in the third slapstick cop comedy. Steve Guttenberg, Bubba Smith, Michael Winslow, George Gaynes and Bobcat Goldthwait star. 82 min.
19-1540 $14.99

Police Academy 5: Assignment Miami Beach (1988)
The zoo crew in blue hits the beach in the fifth (Gosh, where have the years gone?) Academy gag fest. Those lovable misfits (Bubba Smith, Michael Winslow, David Graf, George Gaynes) make for arresting comedy once again. 90 min.
19-1642 $14.99

Police Academy 6: City Under Siege (1989)
When mysterious crime boss Mr. Big takes over the town, the citizens know whom to call for help...but Dirty Harry's busy, so they have to turn to Bubba Smith, Michael Winslow, David Graf and the Academy gang, instead. 84 min.
19-1707 $14.99

Police Academy: Mission To Moscow (1994)
You've waited years for their return. And now the men and women from the police academy are back, taking their hilariously inept brand of law and order on a "goodwill mission" to Russia. Michael Winslow, George Gaynes, Leslie Easterbrook, Christopher Lee star. 83 min.
19-2292 Was $89.99 $19.99

Garbo Talks (1984)
With his mother about to die, a young man sets out to fulfill her last request. The trouble is, her last request is to meet her screen idol, reclusive actress Greta Garbo. Anne Bancroft, Ron Silver, Carrie Fisher, Catherine Hicks and Harvey Fierstein star; Sidney Lumet directs. 103 min.
12-2318 $19.99

Baby Boom (1987)
Diane Keaton is hilarious as a successful, yuppified New York executive who inherits a relative's infant and must make the adjustment from "fast track" to "mommy track." Co-stars Sam Shepard, Harold Ramis, Sam Wanamaker. 103 min.
12-2389 $14.99

Electric Dreams (1984)
"Cyrano de Bergerac" meets "PC Magazine" in this sci-fi comedy about a shy California architect who receives advice on romancing his beautiful neighbor from his new and very unusual computer...until his computer begins to fall in love with the young woman, too! Stars Lenny von Dohlen, Virginia Madsen, Maxwell Caulfield and Bud Cort as the voice of Edgar. 98 min.
12-1382 $79.99

Morons From Outer Space (1985)
These aliens can't phone home; they can't even figure out how to *use* a phone! Spaced-out comedy of some offbeat extraterrestrials who come to Earth for shopping and a vacation stars Mel Smith, Griff Rhys Jones and James B. Sikking. 86 min.
12-2594 $14.99

Rockula (1989)
A 300-year-old "teen vampire" with a hankering for blood and babes rises from the tomb with two things on his mind. Can the kooky bloodsucker lick the curse that threatens to keep him a virgin for another three centuries? Dean Cameron, Tawny Feré, Susan Tyrrell and Bo Diddley star in this musical-comedy-horror spoof. 87 min.
12-2595 $14.99

Caveman (1981)
A pre-hysterical comedy featuring Ringo Starr as a thoughtful Stone Age misfit who has to outwit dinosaurs and hulking rivals to win the hand of cave queen Barbara Bach. With Shelley Long, Dennis Quaid, John Matuszak, Jack Gilford. 91 min.
12-2598 $14.99

National Lampoon Goes To The Movies (1981)
Hollywood genres like cop thrillers, "soap opera" melodramas and inspirational biographies are spoofed in this trilogy of outrageous parodies. The great cast includes Robby Benson, Candy Clark, Diane Lane, Christopher Lloyd, Peter Riegert, Richard Widmark and Henny Youngman. 89 min.
12-2606 $14.99

Happy Birthday, Gemini (1980)
Inspired by Albert Innaurato's play, this film takes a bittersweet, often comical look at the sexual crisis faced by a Harvard-educated young man from South Philly who realizes that he's in love with his fiancée's brother. Madeline Kahn, Rita Moreno and Robert Viharo star. 107 min.
12-2662 $14.99

The January Man (1989)
Unconventional New York detective Kevin Kline is called on to track down a calendar-based serial killer in a comedy thriller scripted by John Patrick Shanley ("Moonstruck"). With Rod Steiger, Susan Sarandon, Mary Elizabeth Mastrantonio. 97 min.
12-2774 Was $19.99 $14.99

Illegally Yours (1988)
Rob Lowe stars in this slapstick romantic comedy as a young man who finally meets the girl of his dreams...when he's on the jury for her attempted murder trial! Can he help clear her name? Colleen Camp, Kenneth Mars co-star; Peter Bogdanovich directs. 94 min.
12-2826 $14.99

It Takes Two (1988)
A young man decides to purchase his dream car on the eve of his wedding, but it becomes a nightmare as the four-wheeled lemon leaves him in the bed of a beautiful blonde. Comedy stars George Newbern, Leslie Hope, Kimberly Foster. 79 min.
12-2827 $14.99

Deadly Drifter (1982)
Take a wild cross-country trip with a political revolutionary (Peter Coyote) in this pointed satire of American radicalism that follows his journey from psychedelic '60s Greenwich Village to New Age '80s California. Danny Glover co-stars in an early role; with O'Lan Shepard. AKA: "Out." 83 min.
14-6146 Was $19.99 $14.99

Swimsuit: The Movie (1989)
An ad agency's search for the perfect swimsuit models turns into a comic catastrophe, as gorgeous gals and handsome hunks vie for the honor. Sexy, racy farce stars William Katt, Catherine Oxenberg, Nia Peeples, Jack Wagner. 95 min.
16-9079 $39.99

Dinner At Eight (1989)
A top-notch cast highlights this winning remake of the 1933 George Cukor classic. A swanky dinner party is turned into a circus when a strange assortment of guests arrive. Lauren Bacall, Charles Durning, Marsha Mason, Harry Hamlin, John Mahoney and Ellen Greene star. 90 min.
18-7204 Was $79.99 $14.99

Simon (1980)
Alan Arkin is brainwashed by scientists to pose as an alien come to Earth to tell us how to live. Along the way, he picks up a cult following and angers the military. Madeline Kahn and Wallace Shawn co-star in this witty satire, written and directed by "Annie Hall" collaborator Marshall Brickman. 97 min.
19-1070 $19.99

Die Laughing (1980)
Cab driver and part-time singer Robby Benson is accused of murdering a nuclear scientist in this outrageous comedy-mystery, co-written by Benson. Also stars Bud Cort, Charles Durning and Elsa Lanchester. 108 min.
19-1072 Was $59.99 $19.99

So Fine (1981)
English professor Ryan O'Neal trades "Hamlet" for hemlines to join his clothing manufacturer father's faltering business and "accidentally" comes up with the latest fad in fashion: designer jeans with a bare-bottom bottom! Screwball farce from first time director Andrew Bergman (co-scripter of "Blazing Saddles") also stars Jack Warden, Mariangela Melato, Richard Kiel. 91 min.
19-1194 $19.99

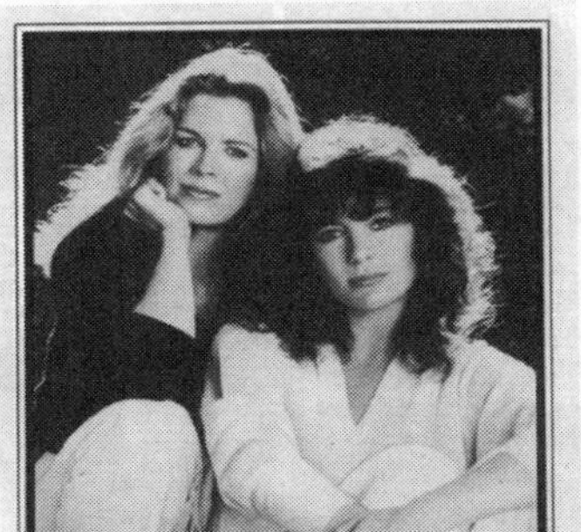

Rich And Famous (1981)
This glossy remake of "Old Acquaintance" chronicles the tempestuous relationship of college classmates Jacqueline Bisset and Candice Bergen over the years. Bisset becomes a respected novelist while Bergen marries, has a child and finds success as a writer of trash fiction. David Selby, Hart Bochner, Meg Ryan (in her film debut) and a young Nicole Eggert also star; George Cukor directs. 111 min.
12-1203 $14.99

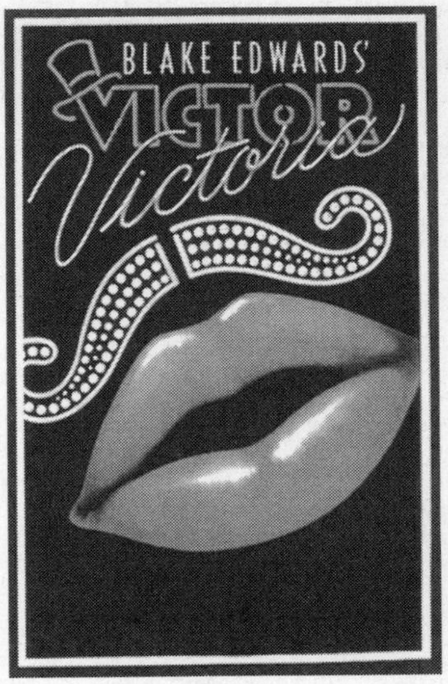

Victor/Victoria (1982)
Sparkling musical comedy stars Julie Andrews as a would-be chanteuse in '30s France who finally obtains a break...by disguising herself as a female impersonator! James Garner, Robert Preston, Alex Karras, Lesley Ann Warren co-star under Blake Edwards' direction. 133 min.
12-1226 Was $19.99 $14.99

Attack From Mars (1988)
The people watching monster movies in a 1950s theater get more than they bargained for when a vampire monster from Mars lands on Earth and begins preying on the audience in this rude, crude and outrageous spoof of vintage horror and sci-fi flicks. Robert Clarke ("The Hideous Sun Demon") and Ann Robinson ("War of the Worlds") star. AKA: "Midnight Movie Massacre."
73-3001 $19.99

Ghosts Can Do It (1989)
Bo Derek said they "can't"; now Pamela Stephenson ("Saturday Night Live") says they "can." She plays a gorgeous but wicked woman who kills her hubby. Soon, he returns to focus his eternal horniness on his wife. Garry McDonald also stars in this outrageous otherwordly farce. 88 min.
21-5038 Was $19.99 $14.99

Goin' All The Way (1982)
And that's just where the wacky, zany, sex-starved teens set out to go in this sexy, zany, wacky comedy. Dan Waldman, Deborah Van Rhyn, Sherie Miller, Joshua Cadman star. 85 min.
27-6014 $39.99

Maid To Order (1987)
Snooty rich girl Ally Sheedy learns how the other half lives when her "fairy godmother" gives her a lesson in humility in this whimsical "riches to rags" tale. Also stars Beverly D'Angelo, Michael Ontkean, Valerie Perrine and Dick Shawn. 93 min.
27-6562 $12.99

Weekend At Bernie's (1989)
Two yuppie ladder-climbers (Andrew McCarthy, Jonathan Silverman) are ready for a weekend party at their boss's beach house, but when he's bumped off by gangsters they have to carry the body around and pretend he's alive in order to salvage the bash. Darkly funny comedy co-stars Catherine Mary Stewart. 100 min.
27-6649 Was $89.99 $14.99

Weekend At Bernie's II (1993)
More wacky shenanigans ensue in this sequel to the hit 1989 comedy. Andrew McCarthy and Jonathan Silverman are back in the leads, this time taking their expired boss Bernie to the Virgin Islands for a wild caper that leads to the corpse's rejuvenation by a voodoo spell. Terry Kiser co-stars as Bernie. 89 min.
02-2485 Was $19.99 $14.99

She'll Be Wearing Pink Pyjamas (1984)
Julie Walters ("Educating Rita") stars in this British comedy about a group of young women who volunteer for a rugged, formerly "men only" survival course in the wilderness to test their spirit. Jane Evers, Anthony Higgins co-star. 87 min.
40-1142 Was $59.99 $19.99

First Family (1980)
Witty White House whimsy from Buck Henry, with Bob Newhart as the put-upon president trying to save flirty First Daughter Gilda Radner from an African tribe about to sacrifice her, as well as keep fuddled First Lady Madeline Kahn off the bottle. With Harvey Korman, Richard Benjamin, Fred Willard. 100 min.
19-1181 Was $19.99 $14.99

Soup For One (1982)
Singles life in '80s New York is the subject for satire in this look at one lovelorn Jewish writer (Saul Rubinek) and his efforts to attain true love with his dream girl. Co-stars Marcia Strassman, Gerrit Graham, Richard Libertini and Teddy Pendergrass. 87 min.
19-1223 Was $39.99 $19.99

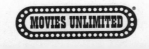

Knights And Emeralds (1987)
Touching British seriocomedy about a British factory town whose two high school bands, from different sides of the tracks, are in the running for a national competition, and the rivalries and romances that develop. Christopher Wild, Warren Mitchell star. 90 min.
19-1578 Was $69.99 ❑*$19.99*

Who's That Girl? (1987)
Why, it's Madonna, of course! And in this fast-paced comedy romp she plays a free-spirited woman who was framed for a crime and sent to prison. Just released, she coaxes the strait-laced lawyer (Griffin Dunne) assigned to escort her into tracking down the real crooks. 94 min.
19-1604 Was $19.99 ❑*$14.99*

High Tide (1987)
Charming comedy/drama from Australia, starring Judy Davis as a backup singer to a nightclub Elvis impersonator who leaves to undertake a voyage of personal discovery after an encounter with the daughter she gave away years earlier. Claudia Karvan, Colin Friels co-star; Gillian Armstrong directs. 102 min.
53-1738 *$14.99*

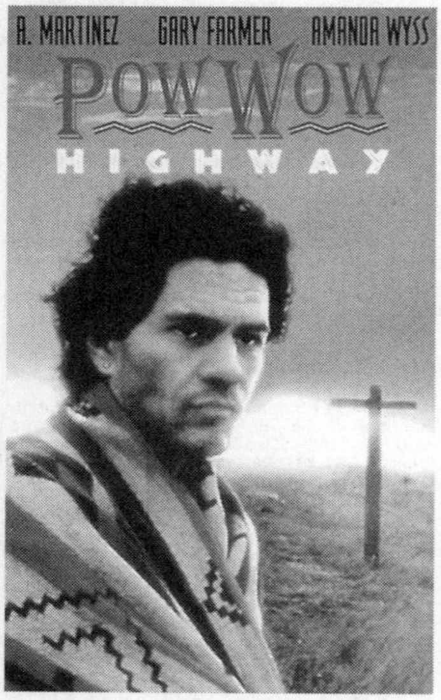

Pow Wow Highway (1989)
A Cheyenne Indian mounts his trusty '64 Buick and seeks the "warrior's vision," a trail that winds through accidental felonies, gunfights with Custer's descendants and other acts of the Great Spirit. Mystical comedy stars Gary Farmer, A Martinez; soundtrack by U2, Robbie Robertson and John Fogerty. 91 min.
19-7058 Was $79.99 *$14.99*

Hot To Trot (1988)
Poor Bob Goldthwait is about to be bounced from the family brokerage business by his greedy stepfather when a fateful encounter with a talking horse changes his life (well, wouldn't it change yours?). With Dabney Coleman, Virginia Madsen, and John Candy as the voice of Don. 83 min.
19-1673 Was $19.99 ❑*$14.99*

Hard Knox (1984)
A by-the-book Marine officer faces his toughest battle yet when he takes the reins of his alma mater, a military academy where the cadets are chaotic and the rules are meant to be broken. Comedy stars Robert Conrad, Bill Erwin, Alan Ruck.
40-1163 *$19.99*

The Cartier Affair (1984)
The glamorous Joan Collins stars in and created her own outfits for this sparkling comedy about a wealthy socialite who romances dashing burglar David Hasselhoff, who has designs on her jewelry collection. Also stars Telly Savalas. 96 min.
40-1250 *$12.99*

P.K. And The Kid (1982)
An unhappy teenager (Molly Ringwald) on the run from her abusive stepfather...a blue-collar worker (Paul LeMat) dreaming of glory at an arm-wrestling tournament...when they link up on the road, there'll be plenty of action and laughs in store. Esther Rolle, John Madden co-star. 90 min.
40-1315 Was $19.99 *$14.99*

Waitress! (1982)
The food's lousy, but the laughs are abundant in this Troma Pictures mirthfest detailing the experiences of three waitresses working in a hectic New York restaurant. Jim Harris, Carol Drake and David Letterman regular Calvert DeForest star.
44-1094 *$14.99*

Long Gone (1987)
Winning baseball comedy/drama stars William Petersen as the skipper of a minor league squad in '50s Florida. They're one win away from a pennant, but a tempting offer from the other team has him stumped. With Virginia Madsen, Larry Riley. 113 min.
40-1411 Was $19.99 *$14.99*

In The Mood (1987)
Poor Sonny Wisecarver wants to meet a nice girl his own age, but the only "girls" he meets are beautiful married women who fall in love with him! A sweet and funny film, based on the true story of the "Woo Woo Kid," teenaged hero of '40s America. With Patrick Dempsey, Beverly D'Angelo, Talia Balsam. 98 min.
40-1355 ❑*$14.99*

Nobody's Fool (1986)
A young woman, ostracized in her smalltown home, falls for an unconventional member of a travelling theater group in this romantic comedy by Beth Henley. Rosanna Arquette, Eric Roberts, Mare Winningham, Louise Fletcher star. 107 min.
40-1263 Was $19.99 *$14.99*

Crossing Delancey (1988)
A winning and heartfelt romantic comedy, with Amy Irving as a young Jewish New Yorker trying to improve her social status and meet Mr. Right, but fixed up by her grandmother and a matchmaker with likable pickle salesman Peter Riegert. Jeroen Krabbe, Reizl Bozyk, Sylvia Miles also star. 97 min.
19-1686 Was $19.99 *$14.99*

The Accidental Tourist (1988)
Acclaimed film adaptation of Anne Tyler's novel stars William Hurt as an emotionally stifled writer of travel books who separates from wife Kathleen Turner following their child's death and is reawakened to life by dog trainer Geena Davis (who won a Best Supporting Actress Oscar). Bill Pullman, Amy Wright, Ed Begley, Jr. co-star. 121 min.
19-1697 Was $19.99 ❑*$14.99*

Her Alibi (1989)
Mystery writer Tom Selleck comes to the aid of accused murderer Paulina Porizkova, but the strange "accidents" occurring in the house since she moved in lead him to believe she may not be as innocent as he first imagined. Light-hearted comedy thriller also stars James Farentino, William Daniels. 94 min.
19-1710 Was $19.99 ❑*$14.99*

Young Einstein (1989)
Albert Einstein: splitter of the beer atom, romancer of Marie Curie, and inventor of rock and roll...you have the word of Yahoo Serious, director, writer and star of this bizarro comedy from down under. Pass the kitten pie and enjoy this riotous romp co-starring Odile Le Clezio, John Howard. 91 min.
19-1743 Was $19.99 ❑*$14.99*

Penn & Teller Get Killed (1989)
The mischievous masters of modern-day magic star in this outrageous black comedy set in Atlantic City. After Penn announces he wants to be killed during a TV show, assassins, Teller and just plain weird people try to rub out the blabbermouth trick artist. With Caitlin Clarke; Arthur Penn directs. 91 min.
19-1757 Was $19.99 ❑*$14.99*

Doin' Time On Planet Earth (1988)
Ryan's lifetime sentence to dull and unusual parents and nerdiness without chance of parole is miraculously commuted when space aliens appear to claim him as one of their own. Nicholas Strouse stars with Adam West. 83 min.
40-1413 Was $79.99 *$19.99*

The First Time (1983)
A shy college freshman is faced with a variety of campus crises, from coping with pretentious film professors to trying to lose his virginity with the unattainable girl of his dreams. Funny and insightful teen comedy that's a notch above most of its genre stars Tim Choate, Wendy Fulton, Wallace Shawn, Wendie Jo Sperber and David Letterman regular Calvert DeForest. 96 min.
44-1114 *$14.99*

The Longshot (1986)
Amiable comedy about four racetrack regulars whose ship has finally come in...if they can just get the money together for the "big bet." Tim Conway, Harvey Korman, Jack Weston co-star. Features a rap song performed by Tim Conway and Ice-T! 110 min.
44-1196 Was $79.99 *$14.99*

Finnegan Begin Again (1985)
Robert Preston and Mary Tyler Moore star in a warm romantic comedy about a reporter in his mid-60s who develops a special relationship with a 40ish teacher having an affair with a married mortician. With Sam Waterston, Sylvia Sidney; Joan Micklin Silver directs. 112 min.
44-1289 Was $79.99 *$29.99*

The Heavy Petting Detective (1994)
The party nerds continue their outrageous, sexy antics in this silly, sensual sequel. Now, one of the nerds is "The Heavy Petting Detective," and when he learns that his nemesis is trying to steal the family business and his wife, he goes into action. Arte Johnson, Burt Ward, Rhonda Shear, Linnea Quigley and Michelle Bauer star. AKA: "Assault of the Party Nerds II." 87 min.
08-1546 *$14.99*

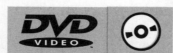

DVD VIDEO
ASK ABOUT OUR GIANT DVD CATALOG!

Secret Admirer (1985)
A passionate unsigned love letter sets off a hilarious chain of events as it gets delivered again and again...but to all the wrong people! Romantic comedy of mistaken delivery stars C. Thomas Howell, Lori Loughlin, Kelly Preston, Cliff De Young. 98 min.
44-1312 Was $19.99 ❑*$14.99*

Bullshot (1985)
The British comedy troupe Low Moan Spectacular brings their hilarious detective thriller stage spoof to film. In 1930s London, ace hero and ladies' man "Bullshot" Crummond must rescue a missing scientist from an evil German count. Alan Shearman, Diz White, Ron House and Billy Connolly star. 84 min.
44-1331 Was $19.99 *$14.99*

Odd Jobs (1984)
Follow the madcap adventures of five wacky college buddies who, with the Mafia's help, form their own trucking company. Paul Reiser, Robert Townsend and Julianne Phillips star, with a cameo by radio's Don Imus. 89 min.
44-1393 Was $19.99 *$14.99*

Head Office (1985)
Wacky comedy centers on the inner workings of a large corporation and the zany characters employed there, including back-stabbing executives, sexy secretaries and a senator's son who uses his contacts to get ahead. Judge Reinhold, Eddie Albert, Richard Masur, Jane Seymour and Danny DeVito star. 90 min.
44-1411 Was $19.99 *$14.99*

My Best Friend Is A Vampire (1988)
Although his last hot date left him with a nasty lovebite and a craving for very rare burgers, creeping vampirism holds no horrors for teenager Robert Sean Leonard. After all, he made it through puberty, didn't he? With Evan Mirand, Cheryl Pollack. 89 min.
44-1559 Was $19.99 ❑*$14.99*

My Mom's A Werewolf (1989)
Like, as if I didn't have enough problems of my own! Now my mom's sprouting fur and fangs, this sinister guy wants her to become his lycanthrope bride, and the whole town's in an uproar! Bogus! Hair-raising comedy stars Susan Blakely, Katrina Caspary, John Schuck, Ruth Buzzi. 90 min.
46-5461 Was $79.99 *$14.99*

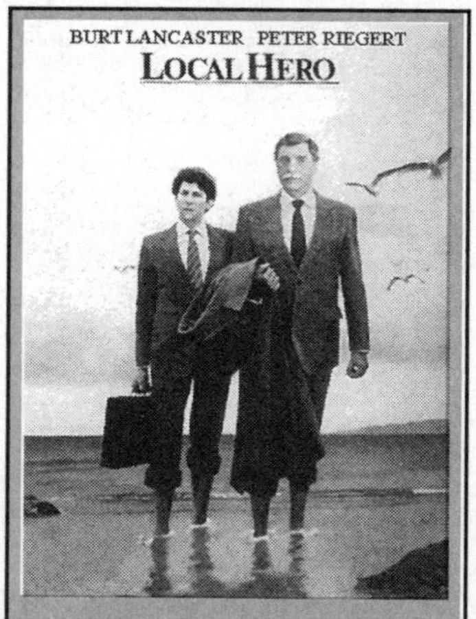

Local Hero (1983)
Wonderfully understated comedy from Bill Forsyth about an American oil executive sent to a Scottish seacoast village to close a land deal, a village filled with offbeat residents and quirky humor. Peter Riegert, Burt Lancaster, Denis Lawson, Jenny Seagrove star; music by Mark Knopfler. 112 min.
19-1293 ❑*$14.99*

Comfort And Joy (1984)
Bill Forsyth's whimsical story of a popular Glasgow deejay whose search for love puts him in the middle of a business war between rival ice cream merchants. Enchanting, bittersweet comedy stars Bill Paterson, Eleanor David. 90 min.
07-1278 Was $69.99 ❑*$14.99*

Housekeeping (1987)
Eccentric aunt Christine Lahti travels to a small Northwest town to care for her orphaned teenage nieces, and immediately puts the locals off with her quirky behavior, in this heartwarming comedy/drama from Scottish filmmaker Bill Forsyth. Sara Walker, Andrea Burchill co-star. 117 min.
02-1841 Was $79.99 ❑*$19.99*

Being Human (1994)
A whimsical fable from Scotland's Bill Forsyth ("Local Hero") featuring Robin Williams as a meek character named Hector who is followed through five historical incarnations: He's a caveman, a slave during the Roman Empire, a medieval traveler, a Portuguese adventurer and a divorced man in modern-day New York. John Turturro, Anna Galiena and Lorraine Bracco also star. 122 min.
19-2256 Was $89.99 ❑*$19.99*

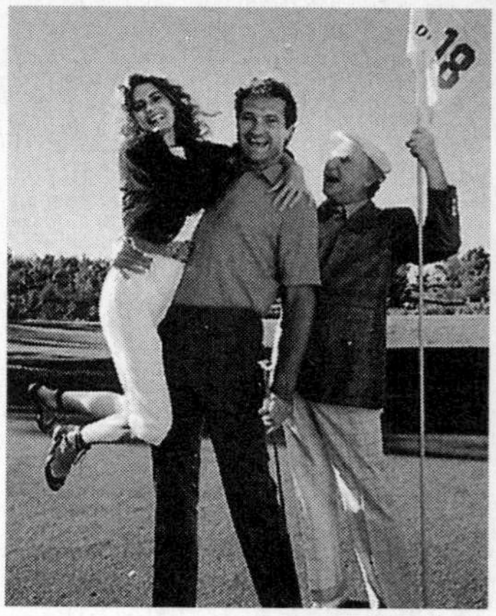

Dead Solid Perfect (1988)
Satiric look at the world of golf, starring Randy Quaid as a second-rate duffer who makes it into a top tournament only to find all sorts of obstacles on and off the course. Kathryn Harrold, Jack Warden and Larry Riley co-star in this clever comedy-drama; based on the novel by Dan Jenkins. 97 min.
19-2100 Was $19.99 *$14.99*

The Trouble With Spies (1987)
Donald Sutherland stars in this romantic adventure about a bungling spy who may yet tilt the balance of power, if his own government lets him live that long. Ned Beatty and Robert Morley co-star. 91 min.
44-1537 Was $79.99 *$14.99*

Collision Course (1989)
Rip-roaring action-comedy teams up Detroit cop Jay Leno with Tokyo detective Pat Morita to take to the streets of Motown to investigate a murder and the theft of plans for a revolutionary new engine developed by the Japanese. With Chris Sarandon, Al Waxman, Tom Noonan. 99 min.
44-1871 Was $19.99 ❑*$14.99*

Million Dollar My$tery (1987)
On his deathbed, Tom Bosley gives a group of misfits clues to four different locales, each the hiding place of a million dollars in cash! And the wackyzanynuttyloony race is on! With Rich Hall, Mona Lyden and the inimitable Eddie Deezen. 95 min.
44-1498 Was $79.99 *$14.99*

Full Moon High (1982)
There'll be howls of laughter in store when teenage werewolf Adam Arkin becomes B.L.O.C. (Big Lycanthrope On Campus) in this frightfully funny comedy that was "Teen Wolf's" precursor. With Ed McMahon, Alan Arkin, Kenneth Mars; Larry Cohen ("It's Alive") directs. 96 min.
44-1516 *$14.99*

Long Shot Kids (1981)
Foosball. That's the game with 3-D players—table soccer! This is about an exciting Foosball tournament. And you thought they could never make a movie about Foosball! Stars Leif Garrett, Linda Manz. AKA: "Long Shot." 100 min.
44-1424 Was $59.99 *$14.99*

Traveling Man (1989)
A veteran traveling salesman (John Lithgow) in the middle of a slump is teamed up with a brash young rival (Jonathan Silverman) for a memorable road trip that opens each man's eyes. Wonderful character comedy also stars Margaret Colin, John Glover. 105 min.
44-1689 Was $89.99 ❑*$19.99*

Something Wild (1986)
Engagingly off-kilter black comedy from director Jonathan Demme concerning an ultrastraight Yuppie (Jeff Daniels) who gets more than he bargains for when he nonchalantly links up with a beautiful, kooky punkette (Melanie Griffith). Co-stars Ray Liotta. 113 min.
44-1470 *$14.99*

Summer Job (1989)
They put the temperature in temporary employment, a sizzling batch of coed cuties who sign on for the summer at a lush tropical resort, half-dressed for success and ready to serve. Fun-filled romp stars Sherrie Rose, Amy Baxter. 92 min.
45-5465 *$14.99*

Fat Guy Goes Nutzoid!! (1986)
What more can we say? He's fat. He's a Fat Guy! And when Fat Guy escapes from the funny farm and joins two wacky teenagers on a zany trip to New York City, the results are—you guessed it—Nutzoid! HE'S SO FAT!! Stars Tibor Feldman, Douglas Stone, and Peter Linari as Fat Guy; score by Leo Kottke. 85 min.
46-5326 *$14.99*

Assault Of The Party Nerds (1988)
It's the wildest, raciest party the campus has ever seen, and it's put on by...the NERDS!? You may have seen "Revenge of the Nerds," but you probably didn't see this comedy with Linnea Quigley, Richard Rifkin and Troy Donahue. 82 min.
46-5449 *$14.99*

Hollywood Zap (1986)
A wide-eyed youngster looking for his long-lost dad...an ex-stockbroker who lost it all (including his marbles) and is now looking for the ultimate video challenge...when these two unlikely allies pair up, look out! Chuck Mitchell stars. 85 min.
46-5329 *$14.99*

Bye Bye Baby (1989)
Sultry superbodies Brigitte Nielsen and Carol Alt star as two women in love with the same man in a zippy romantic farce that also stars Jason Connery. 80 min.
46-5455 *$19.99*

Stuck On You (1983)
Lowdown humor at its most inspired is featured in this zany farce from Troma about two lovers who learn a lesson from a goofy Archangel Gabriel when they consider breaking up. Professor Irwin Corey, Virginia Penta and Mark Mikulski star. 85 min.
53-1240 *$14.99*

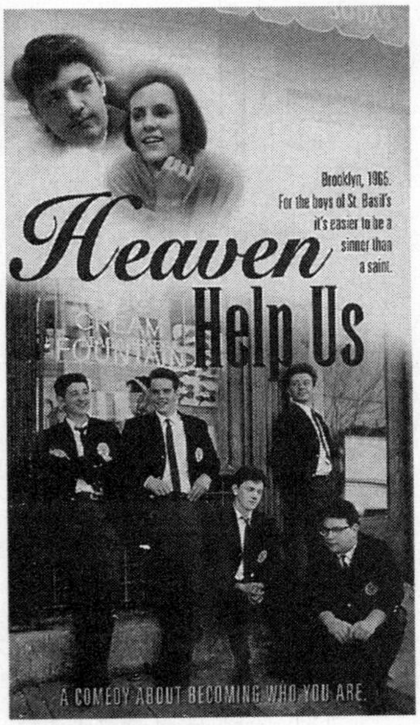

Heaven Help Us (1985)
A new student at a strict Catholic school in the early '60s is shown the ropes of misbehaving in this winning teen comedy. Andrew McCarthy, Kevin Dillon and Malcolm Danare are the prankster students; Wallace Shawn, Donald Sutherland and John Heard are the Brother teachers; and Mary Stuart Masterson runs the local malt shop. 102 min.
44-1271 Was $19.99 *$14.99*

My Chauffeur (1985)
A beautiful young woman is hired by a prestigious limo company as their first female chauffeur and promptly turns the place upside-down in this wacky comedy. Deborah Foreman, Sam Jones, Howard Hesseman, E.G. Marshall star. 97 min.
47-1563 *$29.99*

You Can't Hurry Love (1988)
It's a game of give and take, but when an Ohio farmboy moves to L.A. in search of Miss Right he's got to learn to give those California girls what they want. Madcap farce stars David Packer, Sally Kellerman, Kristy McNichol, Bridget Fonda. 92 min.
47-1869 *$14.99*

Party Favors (1988)
We're not talking "get-the-ball-bearings-in-the-clown's-eyes-and-nose" games here, but the wacky, racy, zany favors that a bevy of beautiful strippers and "party gals" bring to an uproarious get-together. Gail Thackray, Marjorie Miller star. 83 min.
47-1984 Was $79.99 *$14.99*

The First Turn-On (1984)
Join Penthouse Pet of the Year Sheila Kennedy for a wild wilderness romp, as five frisky campers decide to do it the natural way in a wacky, zany farce. Co-stars Jenny Johnstone, Googy Gress, Vincent D'Onofrio. 88 min.
47-3027 Was $79.99 *$14.99*

National Lampoon's Class Reunion (1982)
Lampoon alumnus John Hughes scripted this slasher film parody set in a 10-year high school reunion where the class jocks, jerks, sweethearts and perverts are all in attendance...and all dropping like flies! Gerrit Graham, Michael Lerner, Shelley Smith, Stephen Furst star, with a cameo by Chuck Berry. 86 min.
47-1079 Was $79.99 *$12.99*

Stalag Luft (1985)
Arrogant British officer James Forrester has been recaptured 23 times while trying to escape from a Nazi POW camp. But now he's conceived a plan in which 327 prisoners will escape with him...that is, if "Big F" doesn't make a major mistake. Stephen Fry stars in this raucous war farce. 103 min.
53-9599 Was $49.99 *$24.99*

Class (1983)
Jacqueline Bisset stars as an older woman who has an affair with a young, college-aged boy. Little does she know that the boy is her son's roommate at school! Frantic sexual comedy stars Rob Lowe, Andrew McCarthy, Cliff Robertson. 98 min.
47-1173 *$14.99*

Splitz (1984)
Wacky comedic hijinks ensue when an all-girl rock-and-roll band pulls out all the stops to keep their sorority open. See the gals and their "sisters" partake in wild contests in order to keep the college spirit going. Robin Johnson, Patti Lee and Shirley Stoler star. 88 min.
47-1383 Was $79.99 *$12.99*

Goodbye New York (1985)
Can a New York gentile yuppie adjust to life on an Israeli kibbutz? Julie Hagerty stars in this light-hearted look at culture shock, as a woman running away to Paris to get away from her philandering husband oversleeps on her flight and winds up, minus luggage and money, in Tel Aviv. David Topaz and Amos Kolleck, who also directed, co-star. 90 min.
47-1495 *$14.99*

The Movie Maker (1985)
Fun spoof follows the misadventures of an aspiring filmmaker as he bounces through boardroom and bedroom in Hollywood, trying to finance his dream production. With Zsa Zsa Gabor and Orson Bean. 87 min.
47-3192 *$79.99*

I Was A Teenage T.V. Terrorist (1987)
Two suburban drop-outs get work with a crooked cable company, only to end up poorer than when they were unemployed. Their solution: turn the tables on TV, terrorist style. Adam Nathan stars. 85 min.
47-3220 Was $79.99 *$14.99*

Getting Over (1980)
Crazy comedy and action as a young black singer gets hired by a gangland kingpin to head "Impossible Funky Records," an enterprise designed to fail, but when he puts his heart and soul into it, the surprises never stop! John Daniels, Gwen Brisco. 108 min.
48-1146 *$59.99*

The Occultist (1989)
No, it's not an eye doctor! This devilishly funny (and gory) story follows a young man who inherits a tropical island overflowing with voodoo practitioners, zombie bodyguards and beautiful demon worshippers. Rick Giansi, Jennifer Kanter star. 81 min.
48-1165 *$19.99*

The Imported Bridegroom (1989)
A wealthy, widowed Jewish landlord in turn-of-the-century America returns to the "Old Country" in hopes of erasing his sins through prayer. Once there, he wins a traditional auction for a scholarly bridegroom for his daughter. The fun begins when father and future son-in-law return to the States—and to the daughter who wants to marry an American doctor. Eugene Troobnick stars. 93 min.
48-5105 *$39.99*

Hot Dog...The Movie (1984)
It's "Porky's" in the snow, with wild antics, exciting skiing and gorgeous gals! Two guys from Idaho take to the slopes for some vacation fun, and they also find wet T-shirt contests, nudists and "hot dog" skiers. David Naughton, Shannon Tweed, Patrick Houser star. 96 min.
12-2590 *$14.99*

Forever, Lulu (1987)
German immigrant Hanna Schygulla, an unsuccessful writer on the brink of suicide, becomes the unwitting recipient of a package belonging to the Mob. Her only clue is a photo of the mysterious Lulu. Deborah Harry, Alec Baldwin also star in this madcap farce. AKA: "Crazy Streets." 86 min.
75-7029 Was $19.99 *$14.99*

Checking Out (1989)
When his best friend suddenly dies, fast-track professional Jeff Daniels becomes obsessed with his own health and begins making everyone around him sick with his compulsive behavior. A hilarious comedy that's good for what ails you; with Melanie Mayron, Michael Tucker. 93 min.
74-1064 *$14.99*

Tabloid (1988)
The hilarious "inside story" of sleaze journalism is revealed as renegade publisher Margaret Murdock boosts the readership of the World Investigator with headlines about bearded babies, alien kidnappers, a killer vacuum cleaner, and favorite foods of the Undead. With Glen Coburn. 89 min.
76-7018 *$29.99*

Secret Ingredient (1988)
In this frothy farce, a wealthy American sends his daughter to Yugoslavia to find a long-lost recipe for cognac in a remote monastery. During her journey she meets a handsome monk, a group of Gypsy terrorists and inept state police. Catherine Hicks, Rick Rossovich and Sam Wanamaker star. 95 min.
80-1043 Was $89.99 *$14.99*

Savannah Smiles (1982)
Old-fashioned comedic lark about a young girl who runs away from her rich inattentive parents and falls right into the hands of a pair of escaped cons, who expect to collect a $100,000 ransom...but never expected to grow to love her. Stars Bridgette Andersen, Mark Miller and Donovan Scott. 104 min.
53-1058 *$19.99*

Young Doctors In Love (1982)
A city hospital with an overworked, oversexed staff is the setting for this zany soap opera spoof. Twisted love affairs, crazy characters, outrageous situations abound. With Michael McKean, Sean Young, Patrick Macnee, Dabney Coleman, Michael Richards and many cameos from daytime TV stars (including Demi Moore and Janine Turner). 97 min.
47-1050 *$12.99*

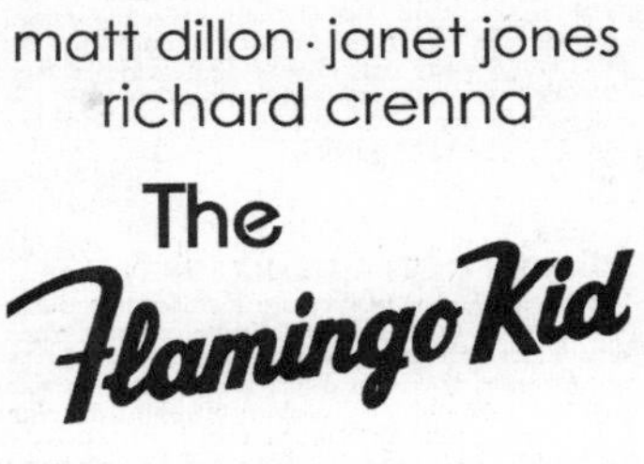

The Flamingo Kid (1984)
A sweet, funny comedy starring Matt Dillon as a high school graduate from the Bronx who learns a lesson or two about life when he lands a summer job at an exclusive Long Island swim club in the early '60s. With Richard Crenna, Hector Elizondo, Janet Jones; look for early turns by Bronson Pinchot, Marisa Tomei and John Turturro. 98 min.
47-1409 Was $29.99 *$14.99*

Jonathan Winters: Gone Fish'n
Jonathan Winters is a wacky riot in this show, playing an elderly resident of the "Home for the Unusual" who talks with interviewer Gary Owens about a comically disastrous fishing trip he made years earlier. Maude Frickett and five other classic Winters creations make appearances. 50 min.
50-2806 *$19.99*

Take This Job And Shove It (1981)
Wacky comedy, based on the hit song, stars Robert Hays as the new exec in a small-town brewery who soon finds himself caught in the middle of a battle between the owner and workers. Also stars Art Carney, Barbara Hershey, Martin Mull. 100 min.
53-1482 Was $39.99 *$14.99*

The Laserman (1989)
After he accidentally kills his assistant in a lab mishap, a nerdy New York laser researcher lands a job at a company with a secret government defense contract. His first assignment is to invent a powerful laser weapon which is to be tested on his crooked brother-in-law. Marc Hayashi, Maryann Urbano and Tony Leung star in Peter Wang's quirky cross-cultural comedy. 92 min.
53-6044 Was $39.99 *$19.99*

West Is West (1989)
A handsome aspiring student from Bombay arrives in San Francisco to find that his college scholarship has fallen through. With the INS on his tail because they think he is a Sikh terrorist, he falls for Sue, a spunky bohemian artist who works at a movie theater. With the clock ticking, he realizes that tying the knot might be his only option. Stars Ashutosh Gowariker and Heidi Carpenter. 80 min.
53-6238 *$89.99*

The Plot Against Harry (1989)
Made in 1969 and unreleased for two decades, this charming low-budget comedy follows the attempts of a former Jewish mobster to go straight after he's released from prison. Michael Roemer's deadpan look at Bronx life stars Martin Priest. 81 min.
53-7516 Was $79.99 *$29.99*

A Year In Provence (1989)
Peter Mayle's international bestsellers, "A Year in Provence" and "Tonjours Provence," are brought to life in this ravishing tale that follows the author and his wife as they relocate from London to Provence in the South of France, where they move into a stone farmhouse and encounter eccentric locals in a series of humorous misadventures. With John Thaw, Lindsay Duncan. 360 min. on four tapes.
53-7793 Was $59.99 *$39.99*

A Night Of Love (1988)
Iconoclastic director Dusan Makavejev ("Montenegro") presents this political satire, set in the Balkans in the 1920s, of a police inspector trying to stop an unknown assassin from killing a king. The inspector confronts an array of suspects, from mysterious women to revolutionaries. Alfred Molina, Eric Stoltz, Camilla Soeberg star. AKA: "Manifesto." 97 min.
53-8332 Was $89.99 *$19.99*

Blat
This BBC comedy has been called "The Russian 'Sting'," as an Italian-Russian gangster goes up against the British financial establishment. Hilarious incidents ensue, with Robert Hardy, Adrienne Cori and Alfred Molina in the leads. 90 min.
53-9363 *$29.99*

The Marquise (1980)
Noel Coward's comedy is set in 1735 in a beautiful chateau outside of Paris where the Compte Raoul De Vriac's celebration of his daughter's wedding to the Duke's son is disrupted when his former mistress arrives on the premises—and decides she is not leaving. Diana Rigg, Richard Johnson and James Villiers star. 55 min.
53-9507 *$29.99*

Super Soul Brother (1989)
Outrageous and uncensored comic Wildman Steve stars as a mild-mannered, down-and-out schnook who accidentally drinks a strange potion that turns him into a suave and successful thief in this wild and racy comedy. AKA: "The Six Thousand Dollar Nigger." 80 min.
54-9024 *$39.99*

King Kung Fu (1987)
Take a well-meaning but misunderstood gorilla, have him learn kung fu at the hands of a martial arts teacher, and put him on top of Wichita's tallest building with a beautiful girl in his arms, and you'll have this off-the-wall comedy that pokes fun at more film genres that you can shake an ape at! 94 min.
55-1241 *$19.99*

Going Steady (1980)
When's the last time you saw a good Zachi Noy movie—we mean a really good Zachi Noy movie? Well, here's that Zachi guy at his best, in a tale of young love, rock and roll and coming of age, courtesy of Cannon Pictures. It's an Israeli "American Graffiti"! With Yiftach Katzur. 88 min.
58-1003 *$19.99*

The Feud (1988)
The rivalry between two families in neighboring communities grows to Hatfield and McCoy-sized proportions in this offbeat satire set in smalltown America in the 1950s. Rene Auberjonois, Joe Grifasi and David Straithairn star. 87 min.
68-1170 *$89.99*

Bad Taste (1989)
Intergalactic gourmands come to Earth in order to use mankind as the latest fast food treat! Can anyone stop these gluttonous aliens, or will Venusian restaurants soon feature People MacNuggets? Pete O'Horne, Mike Minett star in this outrageous gore and gourmet fest from New Zealand director Peter Jackson ("Heavenly Creatures"). 92 min.
69-1140 *$39.99*

Indiscreet (1988)
In this remake of the Cary Grant-Ingrid Bergman classic, Robert Wagner is the purportedly married American diplomat involved in an affair with a glamorous British movie star, played by Lesley-Anne Down. While dodging agents and reporters, the two carry on their funny and charming romance. 94 min.
63-1477 *$79.99*

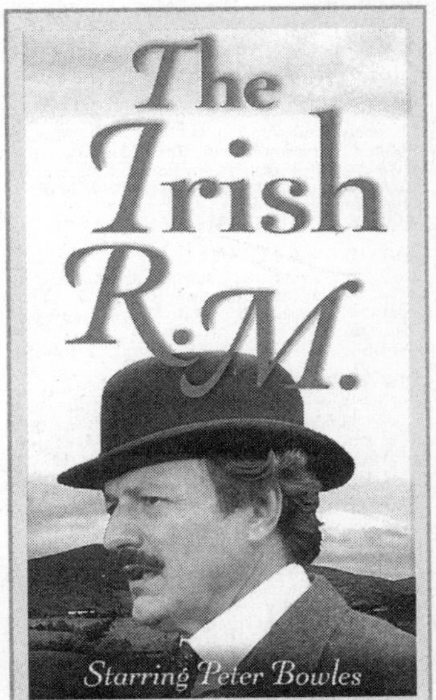

The Irish R.M. (1983)
From the classic stories by Somerville and Ross comes this acclaimed PBS mini-series about a retired English army officer who finds himself appointed Resident Magistrate of the West of Ireland in the late Victorian era. During his term of office, he learns to deal with eccentric town residents as well as the differences between the Irish and their English neighbors. Peter Bowles, Doran Godwin, Byran Murray star. 325 min. on six tapes.
50-5909 *$79.99*

The Irish R.M.: Series 2 (1985)
The professional and personal travails of army man-turned-civil officer Major Sinclair Yeates (Peter Bowles) in rural Ireland at the turn of the 20th century continue in this lively, heartfelt six-part mini-series. Doran Godwin, Faith Brook, Bryan Murray also star. 325 min. on six tapes.
50-8262 *$79.99*

The Irish R.M.: Series 3 (1985)
The concluding episodes of the warm and winning PBS series finds the clash of cultures between Resident Magistrate Peter Bowles and his rural charges reaching a comically fevered pitch, as Bowles' notions of "law and order" run afoul of everyday Irish logic. With Bryan Murray, Anna Manhan. 325 min. on six tapes.
50-8478 *$79.99*

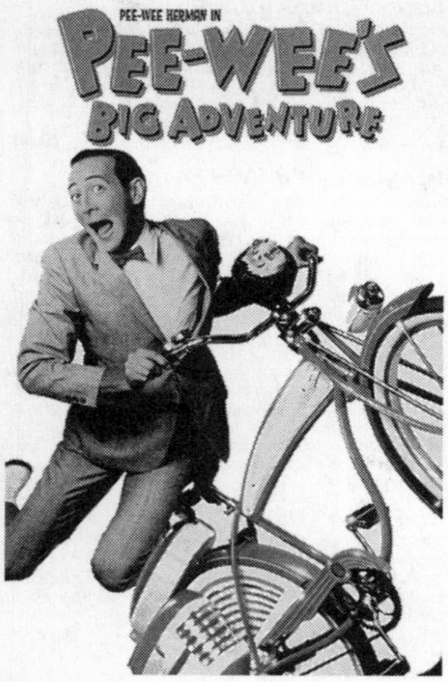

Pee-wee's Big Adventure (1985)
Oh, no! Call the police! Call the FBI! Someone has stolen Pee-wee Herman's prized bike, and he leaves no stone unturned in a wild cross-country search for it. Pee-wee plays himself (no one else possibly could!) in this demented comedy; co-stars Elizabeth Daily, Mark Holton, Speck the Dog; directed by Tim Burton. 90 min.
19-1475 Was $19.99 □$14.99

Big Top Pee-wee (1988)
When a traveling circus troupe winds up on his farm, Pee-wee Herman must stave off the townsfolk's wrath, as well as his fiancée's jealousy over a beautiful trapeze artist who (naturally) falls for him. Kris Kristofferson, Penelope Ann Miller, Valeria Golino and Vance the talking pig co-star. 86 min.
06-1614 □$14.99

Prime Time (1980)
Hilarious "Groove Tube"-style spoof of TV and TV commercials with targets like politics, airline commercials, sports shows and more. Witness "The Charles Whitman Invitational" and "The Sexual Deviation Telethon." With Warren Oates, Kinky Friedman, Harry Shearer, Harris Yulin, George Furth and Fred Dryer. 75 min.
58-1026 Was $19.99 $14.99

Dixie Lanes (1988)
Fast-paced action comedy stars Hoyt Axton as a returning soldier anxious to get back into the family business—moonshine! With Karen Black, Ruth Buzzi, Tina Louise. 90 min.
69-5054 $79.99

Ups & Downs (1981)
Sensitive and funny coming-of-age story, filmed in Canada, concerning the students of a coed prep school who go all out to enjoy the holiday season, which includes the big game and the big dance. With Leslie Hope and Andrew Sabiston. AKA: "Prep School." 98 min.
59-7022 $79.99

Bagdad Cafe (1988)
A sleepy Southwest coffee shop is turned upside-down by the arrival of a feisty German woman who leaves her husband and decides to make the cafe her home. Offbeat comedy from writer/director Percy Adlon reunites him with "Sugarbaby" star Marianne Sägebrecht; with CCH Pounder and Jack Palance as an eccentric desert dweller. 91 min.
74-1044 Was $79.99 $14.99

George And Mildred: The Movie (1980)
This screen version of the popular British TV series showcases the comedic hijinks that occur when George and Mildred Roper take off on a hilarious wedding anniversary trip that finds them facing crooked businessmen, gangsters and a bevy of beautiful women. Brian Murphy, Yootha Joyce and Stratford Johns star. 89 min.
59-7065 $29.99

A Polish Vampire In Burbank (1984)
For years, Dupah's vampiric family has been hunting their victims and bringing him home leftover blood, but they finally decide he has to get out on his own, and set Dupah loose on beautiful downtown Burbank! Unbelievable horror spoof stars Mark Pirro, Lori Sutton, Eddie Deezen. 84 min.
64-3000 $19.99

Rosalie Goes Shopping (1989)
From Percy Adlon, director of "Bagdad Cafe," comes this hilarious satire on consumerism gone out-of-control. When a Bavarian woman living in Arkansas finds herself in deep debt by charging a house full of luxury items to her 37 credit cards, she comes up with a bizarre plan to elude creditors. Marianne Sägebrecht, Brad Davis, Judge Reinhold star. 94 min.
68-1165 $89.99

Can't Buy Me Love (1987)
Funny, charming teen tale of a high school nerd who tries to buy his way into the "in" crowd, even going so far as to hire a popular cheerleader to pose as his girl. Both learn a valuable lesson in the process. Patrick Dempsey and Amanda Peterson star. 94 min.
11-1445 □$19.99

Girls Just Want To Have Fun (1985)
Sarah Jessica Parker has just one desire...to dance! And with the help of her friends and boyfriend, she gets to fulfill every girl's dream: she gets to dance on DTV! Full of laughs, fun and wacky, zany kids who just want to have fun! Also stars Helen Hunt, Lee Montgomery and Shannon Doherty. 90 min.
70-1025 □$14.99

Elvira, Mistress Of The Dark (1988)
TV's campy queen of creature features makes her scream screen debut in an outrageous comedy. When her aunt dies, Elvira (Cassandra Peterson) inherits the family estate, but must deal with hostile townsfolk who don't take kindly to her outrageous lifestyle. With Jeff Conaway, Edie McClurg. 96 min.
70-1247 $14.99

One Minute To Midnight (1988)
A deft blend of real-life drama and black comedy, taken from the actual exploits of writer/star Lawrence Curtin. A bitter divorce and custody trial, a second wife who's "born again" and a cocaine habit are just some of the experiences that push him to the brink of suicide, in a film at once funny and harrowing. 103 min.
72-4008 Was $29.99 $19.99

Rock And The Money Hungry Party Girls (1988)
A detective tracking a stolen relic from the Rock of Ages Museum—the late, great Stan Link's gold-plated nose hairs—faces competition from a mini-skirted girl group who revere the Gabor sisters and have hypnotic powers over men. Raving rock and action parody stars Judi Durand and Paul Sercu. 90 min.
72-5017 $69.99

How To Get Ahead In Advertising (1989)
Years of truth-bending and sycophantic behavior have manifested themselves as a boil on an ad man's neck...a boil that blossoms into a second head, ready to speak out against his counterpart's hypocrisy. Caustic British comedy stars Richard E. Grant as the double-domed exec; with Rachel Ward. 92 min.
74-1067 $14.99

Curse Of The Queerwolf (1989)
The werewolf legend goes gay in this outrageous satire that's been acclaimed as "one of the best horror spoofs" in recent memory. A beer-drinking macho man is in for the surprise of his life when he's bitten on the rear by a Queerwolf, a guy disguised as a girl who inhabits a seedy L.A. nightclub. Michael Palazzolo, Kent Butler and Taylor Whitney star. 90 min.
86-1015 $19.99

Back To School (1986)
Rodney Dangerfield's the B.M.O.C. in this uproarious tale of a self-made millionaire who decides to better himself by entering college with his son. It's an education in laughter for the audience; with Keith Gordon, Sally Kellerman, Robert Downey, Jr. 96 min.
44-1433 Was $19.99 □$14.99

Ladybugs (1992)
Rodney Dangerfield gets no respect as a salesman seeking a promotion, so he decides to coach the company-sponsored girls' soccer team to impress his boss. The problem is, Rodney knows nothing about the sport and the team is filled with inept players. Jackée, Jonathan Brandis co-star. 91 min.
06-1991 Was $19.99 □$14.99

Meet Wally Sparks (1997)
When he's ordered to improve his ratings or get thrown off the air, antagonistic talk show host Rodney Dangerfield wrangles his way into an ritzy party at the governor's mansion in order to get an exclusive interview, but instead proceeds to turn the event into comic chaos. Rodney rules in this wild romp that also stars Debi Mazar, Burt Reynolds, David Ogden Stiers. 105 min.
68-1834 Was $99.99 □$14.99

My 5 Wives (2000)
It's a polygamist's dream come true as real estate developer Rodney Dangerfield inherits five wives when a valuable Utah land deal gets out of control. Now Rodney's got much more than he bargained for with a host of young brides and a crew of dangerous criminals monitoring his every move. Molly Shannon, Jerry Stiller, John Byner and Andrew Dice Clay also star. 100 min.
27-7356 □$99.99

Rodney Dangerfield's Guide To Golf Style & Etiquette
See why Rodney gets no respect when he takes to the links with his breastacular gal pal and a stuffy couple and turns the gentleman's game of golf into a farce. Dangerfield waits impatiently at the tee, orders pizza on the putting green and wreaks havoc all over the place. Can the "Golf Marshal" stop him and his outrageous antics? 38 min.
84-3001 Was $19.99 $14.99

Ricky I (1985)
An uproarious boxing spoof starring Michael Michaud that's almost as funny as "Rocky IV." A New York pug gets a shot at the title when the Mob needs a fall guy, and thanks to positive thinking and plenty of baked beans, he wins. 90 min.
76-7015 $69.99

Zapped! (1982)
Scott Baio is a high school chemistry whiz whose latest discovery gives him the power of mind over matter. Pal Willie Aames guides him in its best uses: getting money and undressing girls. Heather Thomas, Scatman Crothers co-star. 98 min.
53-1033 $14.99

The Bad News Bears (1976)
Hilarious horsehide hoot about a bottom-of-the-barrel Little League team that's raised from dead last with the arrival of a female pitcher (Tatum O'Neal) and a beer-swilling coach (Walter Matthau). Co-stars Vic Morrow, Joyce Van Patten, Jackie Earle Haley; scripted by Bill Lancaster (Burt's son). 102 min.
06-1002 $14.99

The Bad News Bears In Breaking Training (1977)
Smash sequel to the popular pipsqueak baseball comedy, with the Bears off to Houston to play in the Little League championship. Over-the-fence family fun stars William Devane, Jackie Earle Haley, Jimmy Baio, Clifton James. 97 min.
06-1152 $14.99

The Bad News Bears Go To Japan (1978)
And baseball will never be the same! Everybody's favorite Little League squad of misfits, led by coach Tony Curtis, heads to the Land of the Rising Sun in the third Bears comedy. Co-stars Jackie Earle Haley, Tomisaburo Wakayama. 102 min.
06-1564 $14.99

Hot Stuff (1979)
Funny fellow par excellence Dom DeLuise directs and stars in this laugher about a phony fencing operation set up by the cops to put the "sting" on a parade of criminal types. Co-stars Suzanne Pleshette, Jerry Reed, Ossie Davis and many members of the DeLuise family. 91 min.
02-1080 Was $59.99 $14.99

Forty Carats (1973)
Bubbly romantic comedy stars Liv Ullmann as a 40ish Manhattanite who finds love and fulfillment in the arms of a man 20 years her junior while on vacation in Greece. Edward Albert, Deborah Raffin, Binnie Barnes, Nancy Walker and Gene Kelly co-star in this delightful whimsy based on a French stage play. 110 min.
02-1168 $59.99

Fast Break (1979)
Gabe Kaplan stars as a New York delicatessen clerk who leaves his pastrami and corned beef to coach a college basketball team consisting of wacky eccentrics. Mike Warren, Bernard King star. 107 min.
02-1177 $14.99

Getting Straight (1970)
Thirtysomething ex-activist Elliott Gould returns from Vietnam to his old college to earn a master's degree, but finds himself caught up in the battle between students and campus administrators. Candice Bergen is a beautiful coed who falls for Gould in this seriocomic slice of '60s cinema. Look for an early appearance by Harrison Ford. 124 min.
02-1339 Was $59.99 $14.99

Gumshoe (1971)
Albert Finney excels as a Limehouse comic whose fixation with Yank private eye movies leads him to advertise his services as a detective. He soon finds himself caught up in a whirlpool of murder and intrigue in this trenchant trenchcoat tickler. Score by Andrew Webber; Stephen Frears' ("The Grifters") directorial debut. 85 min.
02-1630 $69.99

The One And Only (1977)
Henry Winkler stars as a '50s actor who finds fame not on the stage, but in the wrestling ring as a flamboyant rulebreaker. Carl Reiner's comedy also stars Kim Darby, Harold Gould, Ed Begley, Jr. and Herve Villechaize as Winkler's miniature manager. 98 min.
06-1110 Was $69.99 $14.99

The Big Bus (1976)
Before "Airplane!," there was this outrageous (and overlooked) spoof on disaster movies. A nuclear-powered bus makes its maiden voyage from New York to Denver—with a lockerful of loonies. Joseph Bologna, Stockard Channing, Larry Hagman, Ruth Gordon costar. 88 min.
06-1136 Was $49.99 $19.99

The Big Payoff (1979)
Join Russ Tamblyn, Dean Stockwell, Alex Karras and McLean Stevenson as they try their latest scheme in making it rich: using a para-mutual machine for betting at the racetrack. They're off and running, and you'll be chuckling all the way to the finish line! AKA: "Win, Place or Steal." 88 min.
75-7049 $19.99

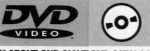

DVD VIDEO
ASK ABOUT OUR GIANT DVD CATALOG!

Law And Disorder (1974)
Ernest Borgnine and Carroll O'Connor live in a working-class town that has become infested with thieves, rapists and other criminals. They decide to put together an auxiliary police force to help clean up the streets, but find out that crimefighting isn't always a good idea for regular citizens to try, in this slapstick comedy. Karen Black also stars. 106 min.
08-8887 Letterboxed $14.99

An Almost Perfect Affair (1979)
Romantic comedy-drama set against the glitter of the Cannes Film Festival stars Keith Carradine as an American filmmaker and Monica Vitti as the bored wife of a French producer. 93 min.
06-1259 Was $59.99 $19.99

Train Ride To Hollywood (1975)
Unusual, song-filled spoof of the Golden Age of Tinseltown follows a young man who is hit on the head and imagines himself in the Hollywood of Bogart, Gable, and Eddy and MacDonald. Harry Williams, Guy Marks, Phyllis Davis star. 90 min.
08-1681 $14.99

Train Ride To Hollywood (Letterboxed Collector's Edition)
Also available in a theatrical, widescreen format.
08-8699 $14.99

Same Time, Next Year (1978)
Touching tale, based on the hit Broadway play, about two happily married people (Alan Alda and Ellen Burstyn) who meet and have a brief tryst at a California resort in the early '50s, then continue the affair one weekend a year for the next 26 years. 117 min.
07-1026 Was $64.99 $14.99

A Guide For The Married Woman (1978)
The woman is sultry Cybill Shepherd, and when she feels her husband is ignoring her she gets a hilarious look at extramarital fun in this frothy comedy. Co-stars Barbara Feldon, Eve Arden, Peter Marshall, John Byner. 104 min.
04-1028 Was $59.99 $29.99

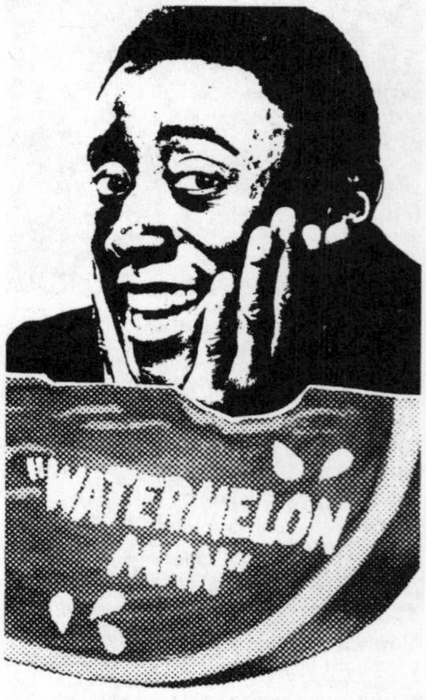

Watermelon Man (1970)
Godfrey Cambridge stars in this offbeat comedy as a bigoted white executive who gets a taste of his own medicine after he awakes one morning and finds he has miraculously turned black. Co-stars Estelle Parsons, Mantan Moreland; directed by Melvin Van Peebles. 97 min.
02-1437 Was $59.99 $14.99

Lovers And Other Strangers (1970)
When a young couple decides to finally tie the knot after living together for a year and a half, neither they nor their harried families can imagine the comic complications that ensue as the wedding day approaches. Wonderfully witty filming of Renee Taylor and Joseph Bologna's stageplay stars Bea Arthur, Bonnie Bedelia, Richard Castellano, Diane Keaton (her film debut), Anne Meara and Gig Young. 104 min.
04-1189 $14.99

Joseph Andrews (1977)
Director Tony Richardson ("Tom Jones") harks back to familiar territory with this irreverent comedy based on a novel by 18th-century author Henry Fielding. Peter Firth is young footman Joseph Andrews, engaged in a series of amorous adventures with the fair sex. Co-stars Ann-Margret, Michael Hordern. 103 min.
06-1150 Was $44.99 $19.99

French Postcards (1979)
A group of American college students touring Paris get an education in life and romance in this tender comedy from the writers of "American Graffiti." Debra Winger, Mandy Patinkin, Miles Chapin and Marie-France Pisier star. 92 min.
06-1260 Was $59.99 $14.99

Burt Reynolds

Armored Command (1961)
Top-notch WWII drama, marked by Burt Reynolds' second screen appearance, stars Howard Keel as the leader of an Allied unit that becomes the target of seductive German spy Tina Louise. With Earl Holliman and Marty Ingels as "Pinhead." 105 min.
04-2332 *$29.99*

Navajo Joe (1967)
After his family and tribe are unmercifully slaughtered by a wicked outlaw and his underlings, Navajo Indian Burt Reynolds plots revenge by defending a town being terrorized by the gang. Aldo Sambrell and Fernando Rey also star in this "Spaghetti western." 89 min.
12-2667 *$14.99*

Shark! (Maneater) (1968)
Burt Reynolds plays a tough American smuggler in the Mediterranean hired by what he thinks a scientific expedition. The voyage turns into a deadly search for undersea treasure in shark-infested waters. Barry Sullivan, Arthur Kennedy, Silvia Pinal also star; Samuel Fuller ("The Big Red One") directs. 90 min.
63-1060 *$14.99*

Iron Cowboy (1968)
Offbeat drama that takes place on the actual set of the 1968 western film "Blue." In an early starring role, Burt Reynolds plays a roughneck actor who gets involved with a beautiful film editor. Barbara Loden co-stars, with cameos by "Blue" players Ricardo Montalban and Terence Stamp. AKA: "Fade-In." 86 min.
75-7017 Was $19.99 *$14.99*

100 Rifles (1969)
Western drama of a Texas lawman, a wily gunrunner and a beautiful half-breed who become involved with Indian revolts in Mexico stars Burt Reynolds, Raquel Welch, Jim Brown and Fernando Lamas. 110 min.
04-3145 *$19.99*

Fuzz (1972)
An Ed McBain "87th Precinct" story served as the basis for this outrageous comedy about a group of incompetent Boston cops, led by Burt Reynolds, who try to stop mysterious bomber Yul Brynner from killing local officials. Jack Weston, Raquel Welch and Tom Skerritt also star. 92 min.
12-2660 *$14.99*

Deliverance (1972)
Four Atlanta businessmen set out on a weekend canoeing trip but must fight for their lives against some sadistic mountain men in John Boorman's riveting adaptation of James Dickey's novel. Burt Reynolds, Jon Voight, Ned Beatty and Ronny Cox star. 109 min.
19-2587 Remastered *$19.99*

Deliverance (Letterboxed Version)
Also available in a theatrical, widescreen format.
19-2575 ❑*$19.99*

Shamus (1973)
Hard-luck private detective Burt Reynolds is hired by a wealthy recluse to recover some stolen diamonds, but soon finds himself running up against dangerous arms smugglers in this slam-bang mystery/adventure. With Dyan Cannon, Joe Santos. 106 min.
02-2706 *$14.99*

White Lightning (1973)
Convicted moonshiner "Gator" McKlusky (Burt Reynolds) is offered a chance to get out of jail if he'll turn in his ex-buddies. He takes it, but instead goes on a mission after the crooked sheriff who killed his brother. Co-stars Ned Beatty, Bo Hopkins. 101 min.
12-1008 Was $29.99 *$14.99*

Gator (1976)
Burt Reynolds' sequel to "White Lightning," this fast-paced hit continues the adventures of moonshine runner "Gator" McKlusky. Here federal agent Jack Weston gets him to help expose some corrupt politicians. Lauren Hutton and Jerry Reed co-star in this good ol' comedy thrller. 116 min.
12-1867 Was $29.99 *$14.99*

The Man Who Loved Cat Dancing (1973)
Romance unfolds between an outlaw (Burt Reynolds) on the run after avenging his wife's murder and a woman (Sarah Miles) running from an abusive husband as they travel, along with his robber pals, across country to find his son. Western drama co-stars Lee J. Cobb, Jack Warden, George Hamilton. 114 min.
12-1371 *$19.99*

The Longest Yard (1974)
Burt Reynolds is an ex-pro quarterback sent to a Florida prison for car theft, where the conniving warden (Eddie Albert) coerces him into organizing an all-con football team to play against the guards' semi-pro squad. The result is a violent and hilarious contest you won't forget. With James Hampton, Michael Conrad. 123 min.
06-1035 *$14.99*

Hustle (1975)
Unnerving police yarn stars Burt Reynolds as a hard-edened cop whose investigation into the death of a young hooker leads him to disturbing revelations in his own personal life. Catherine Deneuve co-stars as Reynolds' high-priced call girl girlfriend; with Ben Johnson, Eddie Albert and Eileen Brennan. Directed by Robert Aldrich. 120 min.
06-1027 *$14.99*

Smokey And The Bandit (1977)
The first film from Hollywood's fastest series stars Burt Reynolds as a scalawag delivering a cross-country shipment of contraband beer and Jackie Gleason as the sheriff obsessed with his capture. Jerry Reed, Sally Field also star. 96 min.
07-1030 Was $19.99 ❑*$14.99*

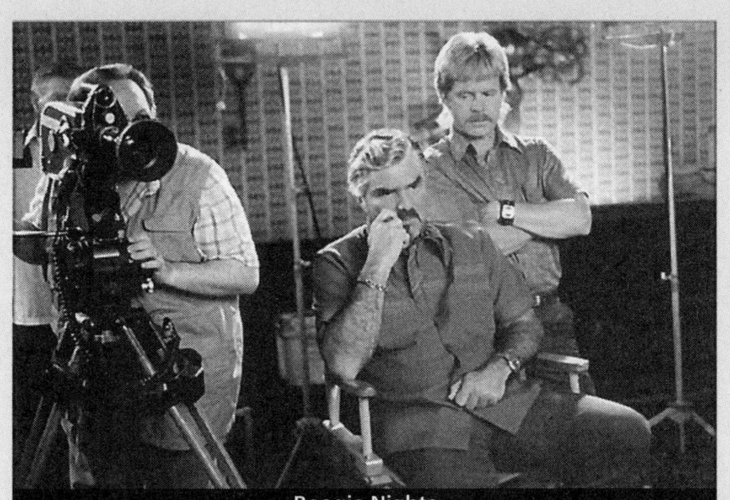

Boogie Nights

Smokey And The Bandit II (1980)
Burt Reynolds puts the pedal to the metal as the Bandit once more. This time he's got to deliver a live elephant to the Republican Convention in Dallas, while trying to dodge the relentless Smokey (Jackie Gleason) and win back girlfriend Sally Field. With Jerry Reed, Dom DeLuise, Paul Williams, Pat McCormick. 96 min.
07-1045 Was $19.99 ❑*$14.99*

Semi-Tough (1977)
Goofy gridiron comedy stars Burt Reynolds and Kris Kristofferson as pro football teammates who find themselves competing for the attentions of team owner's daughter Jill Clayburgh. Rousing adaptation of Dan Jenkins' novel also stars Robert Preston, Roger E. Mosley, Brian Dennehy and Burt Convy as a self-help guru. 108 min.
12-1797 Letterboxed *$14.99*

The End (1978)
In this funny dark comedy, Burt Reynolds plays a man who, after learning he has a fatal illness, tries over and over to kill himself. Eventually, he winds up in a psychiatric hospital, where he enlists the aid of fellow inmate Dom DeLuise, who seems a bit overzealous to complete the job. Sally Field, Robby Benson, Joanne Woodward and Kristy McNichol co-star. 100 min.
12-2658 *$14.99*

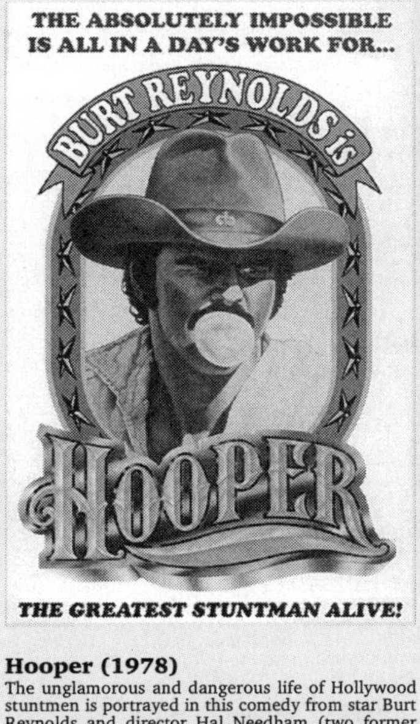
THE ABSOLUTELY IMPOSSIBLE
IS ALL IN A DAY'S WORK FOR...
BURT REYNOLDS is
HOOPER
THE GREATEST STUNTMAN ALIVE!

Hooper (1978)
The unglamorous and dangerous life of Hollywood stuntmen is portrayed in this comedy from star Burt Reynolds and director Hal Needham (two former stuntmen themselves). Burt plays Sonny Hooper, the industry's premier trick driver, whose body has seen better days and who is roped into performing one last death-defying stunt by a young up-and-comer (Jan-Michael Vincent). With Sally Field, Brian Keith. 100 min.
19-1037 Was $19.99 *$14.99*

Starting Over (1979)
Action star Burt Reynolds proved himself equally adept at romantic comedy with this sparkler from director Alan J. Pakula and scripter James L. Brooks. Burt's wife (Candice Bergen) wants her freedom to pursue a sing-ing/songwriting career, so he finds solace in a support group and in the arms of spinster Jill Clayburgh. With Charles Durning, Mary Kay Place. 106 min.
06-1056 Was $69.99 *$14.99*

Rough Cut (1980)
Ultra-suave jewel thief Burt Reynolds is out to make the last heist of his career, and wants to take Lesley-Anne Down for good measure. David Niven is the detective dedicated to catching him. Great fun in this comedy shot on location in England and Holland. 112 min.
06-1077 Was $59.99 *$14.99*

Paternity (1981)
He's on the wrong side of 40, still a bachelor and has no offspring to carry on his name. That's the predicament Burt Reynolds finds himself in, and with a strong desire to sire and dreading a wedding, Burt goes on a search for a potential mother for his child. Mid-life crisis comedy co-stars Beverly D'Angelo, Norman Fell, Paul Dooley. 94 min.
06-1115 Was $39.99 *$14.99*

Sharky's Machine (1981)
After he's demoted as a result of having his cover blown, Atlanta undercover cop Burt Reynolds musters up his new vice squad members to bring down underworld kingpin Vittorio Gassman, who's responsible for a crime wave hitting the city. Action-laden crime thriller directed by Reynolds co-stars Rachel Ward, Brian Keith, Bernie Casey. 122 min.
19-1221 Was $19.99 *$14.99*

The Cannonball Run (1981)
Burt Reynolds leads a pack of wacky racers across the country in this rip-roaring comedy that features zany stunts, loads of crashes, and stars galore. With Roger Moore, Farrah Fawcett, Dom DeLuise, Sammy Davis, Jr., Dean Martin, Jackie Chan and more. 95 min.
44-1863 *$14.99*

The Best Little Whorehouse In Texas (1982)
High-stepping, fast-talking, side-cracking, rib-tickling musical-comedy with Burt Reynolds as the sheriff pressured to force the closing of the Chicken Ranch, a brothel headed by feisty madam Dolly Parton. Songs include "I Will Always Love You." Co-stars Charles Durning, Dom DeLuise, Jim Nabors, Robert Mandan, Noah Beery, Jr. 111 min.
07-1131 Was $19.99 *$14.99*

The Man Who Loved Women (1983)
Burt Reynolds plays a woman-crazed man whose trouble is the ease with which he meets gorgeous ladies. Sexy and sassy comedy by Blake Edwards co-stars Marilu Henner, Kim Basinger, Cynthia Sykes and Julie Andrews. Based on the François Truffaut film. 110 min.
02-1294 Was $79.99 ❑*$19.99*

Stroker Ace (1983)
When Burt Reynolds assembles Jim Nabors, Ned Beatty, Loni Anderson and director Hal Needham for a fast-paced comedy about a champion stock car racer forced to perform some outlandish stunts, such as wearing a chicken costume, for his new sponsor, a fried chicken company, you just gotta laugh! 96 min.
19-1289 Was $19.99 *$14.99*

City Heat (1984)
Burt Reynolds and Clint Eastwood team up in this light-hearted thriller set in 1933 Kansas City, as a wise-cracking private eye and a no-nonsense cop go up against the mob. Co-stars Madeline Kahn, Jane Alexander and Rip Torn. 94 min.
19-1409 Was $19.99 ❑*$14.99*

Switching Channels (1988)
Network news boss Burt Reynolds stalls the resignation and re-marriage of his top reporter and ex-wife (Kathleen Turner) by wheedling her participation on one final story, a sensational execution. The latest "The Front Page"/"His Girl Friday" update also stars Christopher Reeve as the outmaneuvered fiancé. 97 min.
02-1870 *$14.99*

Rent-A-Cop (1988)
Together again for the first time since "Lucky Lady," Burt Reynolds and Liza Minnelli light up the screen as a cop framed for murder during a botched drug bust and a kooky prostitute who can clear him...if they can catch the real killer. James Remar, Dionne Warwick co-star. 95 min.
44-1526 Was $19.99 ❑*$14.99*

Physical Evidence (1989)
Accused of killing a mobster, ex-cop Burt Reynolds' only hope of clearing his name and finding the real murderer rests with defense attorney Theresa Russell. Gripping thriller from Michael Crichton stars Ned Beatty and Kay Lenz. 99 min.
47-1959 Was $89.99 ❑*$12.99*

Cop And A Half (1993)
Family-oriented action farce about a cop-idolizing 8-year-old boy (Norman D. Golden II) who witnesses a mob murder, but refuses to testify until he's allowed to partake in real police work. The youngster is teamed with a burned-out cop (Burt Reynolds) who hates kids, and the two go to work stopping criminals. Ruby Dee, Ray Sharkey also star. 93 min.
07-2023 Was $19.99 ❑*$14.99*

The Maddening (1995)
Ultra-intense suspenser offers a surprising change-of-pace role for Burt Reynolds, as a seemingly helpful gas station owner who brings a woman and her young daughter home when their car breaks down on a remote country road. Upon meeting Reynolds' family, the "guests" are drawn into a sinister secret that could cost them their lives. Angie Dickinson, Mia Sara, Brian Wimmer also star. 97 min.
68-1800 ❑*$99.99*

Raven (1996)
In his first action role in several years, Burt Reynolds plays a soldier-of-fortune whose crack mercenary squad is hired to "procure" a decoder for still-active Soviet defense satellites. But when corrupt government and security officials lead to the mission's downfall, Reynolds escapes to deliver his own brand of justice. With Matt Battaglia, Krista Allen, Richard Gant. 93 min.
02-5159 Was $99.99 ❑*$19.99*

Boogie Nights (1997)
Writer/director Paul Thomas Anderson spun cinematic dross into gold with his acclaimed, disco-filled chronicle of the adult film industry's rise and decline in the late '70s and early '80s. Mark Wahlberg is well-endowed busboy-turned-screen superstud "Dirk Diggler," who becomes part of a close-knit Southern California family of performers and filmmakers that includes auteur-minded director Burt Reynolds, leading lady Julianne Moore, and starlet Heather Graham. Extended version includes 20 minutes of previously unseen footage. 175 min. total.
02-5173 Was $99.99 ❑*$19.99*

Boogie Nights (Letterboxed Version)
Also available in a theatrical, widescreen format.
02-5185 ❑*$19.99*

The Hunter's Moon (1998)
Troubled World War I veteran Keith Carradine falls in love with Hayley Du Mond, a beautiful woman he discovers living in a backwoods mountainside. Carradine finds opposition, however, when Burt Reynolds, Du Mond's father, sees him as a threat to his land and his daughter. With Pat Hingle, Charles Napier and Ann Wedgworth. 104 min.
76-9115 *$99.99*

Hostage Hotel (1999)
Former private eye Burt Reynolds is forced back into the life-or-death struggle when he must rescue a group of hostages, including his ex-partner and the daughter of a U.S. congressman, who've been taken captive by a crazed Vietnam vet. Thrill-a-minute actioner also stars Keith Carradine, Charles Durning; Hal Needham directs as Alan Smithee. AKA: "Hard Time: Hostage Hotel." 89 min.
27-7205 ❑*$99.99*

Big City Blues (1999)
In this wild actioner, Burt Reynolds and William Forsythe are hit men whose lives intersect with beautiful hooker Georgina Cates during one unpredictable night in the big city. A roller coaster of thrills and adventure, the film also stars Balthazar Getty and Arye Gross.
82-5128 *$89.99*

Pups (2000)
Blistering crime drama about two 13-year-old kids who find a .45 Magnum and decide to pull off a bank robbery. The act leads to an intense stand-off with a load of hostages, SWAT team members ready to shoot on rooftops and an encounter with a police negotiator. Directed by Ash ("Bang") and featuring Burt Reynolds, Mischa Barton, Cameron Von Hoy and Kurt Loder. 100 min.
76-9122 *$99.99*

Please see our index for these other Burt Reynolds titles: *All Dogs Go To Heaven • Bean • Best Friends • The Cherokee Kid • Citizen Ruth • Everything You Always Wanted To Know About Sex...But Were Afraid To Ask • Frankenstein & Me • Meet Wally Sparks • Modern Love • Mystery, Alaska • Silent Movie • Striptease • Trigger Happy • Universal Soldier III: Unfinished Business*

Neil Simon

Come Blow Your Horn (1963)
Playboy Frank Sinatra instructs younger brother Tony Bill in the fine art of swinging, only to have his favorite girl stolen from him. TV comedy maven Norman Lear scripted the screen adaptation of Neil Simon's hit play. Co-stars Jill St. John, Lee J. Cobb, Molly Picon, Barbara Rush. 112 min.
06-1871 *$14.99*

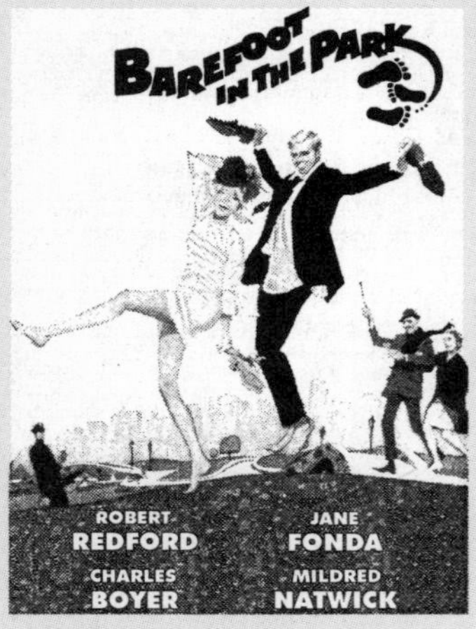

Barefoot In The Park (1967)
The first screen translation by Neil Simon of his own Broadway play was this spirited comedy that portrayed married life in a fifth-floor walk-up apartment in New York for two newlyweds (free spirit Jane Fonda and stiff-shirt lawyer Robert Redford). Co-stars Mildred Natwick, Charles Boyer, Herb Edelman; Gene Saks directs. 105 min.
06-1071 *$14.99*

The Odd Couple (1968)
Neil Simon's Broadway classic (reportedly based on his brother's life) stars Jack Lemmon as the agonizingly neat Felix Ungar and Walter Matthau as the compulsively disheveled Oscar Madison, two divorced men who share a New York apartment...and a desire to wring each other's neck. Co-stars Herb Edelman, John Fiedler, and Monica Evans and Carole Shelley as the Pigeon Sisters. 105 min.
06-1045 *$14.99*

The Odd Couple II (1998)
Thirty years after they made the world laugh hysterically as Oscar Madison and Felix Ungar, Walter Matthau and Jack Lemmon return in a riotous sequel penned by Neil Simon. Can the feuding former roommates tolerate each other long enough to survive a wacky road trip to see Oscar's son marry Felix's daughter? Christine Baranski, Barnard Hughes and Jonathan Silverman also star. 97 min.
06-2764 Was $99.99 □*$14.99*

The Out-Of-Towners (1970)
Neil Simon's witty look at a disaster-prone trip to New York City stars Jack Lemmon and Sandy Dennis as the hapless visitors who lose their luggage, hotel room, money and even shoes. Anne Meara, Sandy Baron co-star. 97 min.
06-1211 *$14.99*

The Out-Of-Towners (1999)
Neil Simon's comedic poison pen letter to the Big Apple is revamped in this hilarious hit starring Steve Martin and Goldie Hawn as the Ohio couple whose New York visit turns into an escalating series of disasters that leave them broke and without a place to sleep. John Cleese co-stars as a smarmy hotel manager. 90 min.
06-2884 Was $99.99 □*$14.99*

Plaza Suite (1971)
Walter Matthau plays three different roles in this Neil Simon comedy about a posh hotel suite and the misadventures that befall its occupants. Maureen Stapleton, Lee Grant, Barbara Harris and Louise Sorel play the various women in Walter's life in this funny trilogy of stories. 115 min.
06-1210 Remastered *$14.99*

Star Spangled Girl (1971)
Sandy Duncan is the ultrasweet, ultrapatriotic miss who gets involved with scruffy, anti-establishment writers Tony Roberts and Todd Susman in this filming of the hilarious Neil Simon play. 92 min.
06-1872 *$14.99*

The Heartbreak Kid (1972)
Hilarious look at love and marriage from the pen of Neil Simon. Charles Grodin plays a newlywed salesman who strays from his sunburn-stricken wife on their honeymoon after meeting sexy Cybill Shepherd on the beach. Eddie Albert, Audra Lindley and Jeannie Berlin (whose mother, Elaine May, directed) co-star; based on a short story by Bruce Jay Friedman. 106 min.
03-1194 *$14.99*

Last Of The Red Hot Lovers (1972)
Alan Arkin is a middle-aged restaurant owner whose hands smell from fish and whose heart aches for a memorable affair. Neil Simon wrote the non-stop array of riotous one-liners. Sally Kellerman, Paula Prentiss. co-star. 98 min.
06-1125 Remastered *$14.99*

The Sunshine Boys (1975)
Two aging and feuding former vaudevillians, played by Walter Matthau and Oscar-winner George Burns (in his first starring role since 1939), reluctantly agree to reteam for a TV special in this witty adaptation of Neil Simon's hit play. Co-stars Richard Benjamin, Lee Meredith, Howard Hesseman; directed by Herbert Ross. 111 min.
12-1019 Was $19.99 *$14.99*

The Sunshine Boys (Letterboxed Version)
Also available in a theatrical, widescreen format.
12-3272 *$14.99*

The Sunshine Boys (1998)
Woody Allen and Peter Falk star as the former comedy partners who, after years of animosity, agree to reunite for a big-budget movie, only to have their long-simmering feud boil over again. Sarah Jessica Parker co-stars in Neil Simon's updating of his hilarious 1975 film. 90 min.
88-1194 Was $19.99 □*$14.99*

The Prisoner Of Second Avenue (1975)
Neil Simon's quips about New York life are on target in this seriocomedy starring Jack Lemmon and Anne Bancroft as an out-of-work executive and his supportive wife. With Elizabeth Wilson; look for early appearances by Sylvester Stallone and F. Murray Abraham. 105 min.
19-1064 Was $19.99 *$14.99*

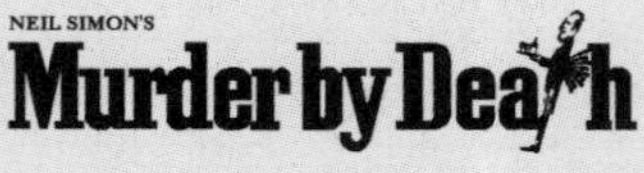

Murder By Death (1976)
An eccentric millionaire invites the world's greatest detectives to his mansion for "dinner and a murder" in Neil Simon's hilarious whodunit. The all-star cast includes Peter Sellers, David Niven, Maggie Smith, Peter Falk, James Coco, Alec Guinness, Truman Capote. 95 min.
02-1049 Was $19.99 □*$14.99*

The Goodbye Girl (1977)
Laugh-filled heart-tugger from Neil Simon about the unpredictable relationship that develops between a struggling actor (Oscar-winner Richard Dreyfuss) and a divorced mother and dancer (Marsha Mason), after circumstances force them to share a New York apartment. Co-stars Quinn Cummings, Paul Benedict. 110 min.
12-1071 Was $19.99 *$14.99*

California Suite (1978)
An array of fine performers make Neil Simon's vignette-styled farce a place you'll want to visit again and again. Alan Alda, Jane Fonda, Richard Pryor, Bill Cosby, Walter Matthau, Elaine May, Michael Caine and Oscar-winning Maggie Smith star. 103 min.
02-1059 *$14.99*

The Cheap Detective (1978)
Neil Simon penned this hilarious homage to Bogey-like detective flicks. Peter Falk plays a wise-cracking gumshoe on a mysterious case who encounters a line-up of zanies that resemble characters out of 1940s movies. Ann-Margret, Eileen Brennan, James Coco, John Houseman, Madeline Kahn and Dom DeLuise head the all-star supporting cast. 92 min.
02-2013 Was $19.99 *$14.99*

Chapter Two (1979)
Drawing from his own life, Neil Simon crafted this comedy-drama about a successful Broadway playwright (James Caan) who struggles with the guilt of falling in love with an attractive actress (Marsha Mason), while still mourning the loss of his beloved first wife. Co-stars Valerie Harper, Joseph Bologna. 124 min.
02-1031 *$14.99*

Seems Like Old Times (1980)
Chevy Chase and Goldie Hawn re-team in this Neil Simon screwballer about a liberal lawyer (Hawn) taking in her trouble-prone ex-husband (Chase) after he is forced to assist bank robbers and becomes the quarry of the cops. Co-stars Charles Grodin as her nerdy D.A. husband, Harold Gould, Robert Guillaume. 121 min.
02-1077 *$19.99*

Only When I Laugh (1981)
Marsha Mason is superb as a reformed alcoholic actress trying to find her way back to a normal, everyday lifestyle. Neil Simon's poignant, bittersweet comedy co-stars James Coco, Kristy McNichol, Joan Hackett. 120 min.
02-1097 Was $79.99 *$19.99*

I Ought To Be In Pictures (1982)
Neil Simon's affectionate look at the relationship between father and daughter. Dinah Manoff hitchhikes from Brooklyn to Hollywood to meet up with her long-lost father (Walter Matthau). Ann-Margret co-stars. 107 min.
04-1493 Was $59.99 *$29.99*

Max Dugan Returns (1983)
This whimsical Neil Simon comic lark tells the story of a long-lost father who comes home, bringing marvelous gifts for his schoolteacher daughter and grandson. Jason Robards is charming as the grandfather. Marsha Mason and Matthew Broderick, in his film debut, co-star. 98 min.
04-1631 Was $59.99 *$29.99*

The Slugger's Wife (1985)
Neil Simon once again explores the wobbly relationship between young marrieds in this comedy about the effect their careers have on the marriage of baseball player Michael O'Keefe and rock singer Rebecca De Mornay. Co-stars Martin Ritt, Randy Quaid; directed by Hal Ashby ("Shampoo"). 105 min.
02-1467 Was $79.99 □*$19.99*

Brighton Beach Memoirs (1986)
New York, the 1930s...and a young man's mind is on the Yankees and sex (not necessarily in that order), as well as trying to deal with his argumentative family. Personal, telling, and touching, Neil Simon's acclaimed comic memoir stars Blythe Danner, Bob Dishy, Judith Ivey and Jonathan Silverman. 108 min.
07-1512 Was $19.99 □*$14.99*

Biloxi Blues (1988)
Neil Simon continues the semi-autobiographical adventures of young Eugene Jerome in this witty comedy, as Eugene (Matthew Broderick) finds bootcamp life in 1942 Alabama full of unexpected hardships and pleasures. Christopher Walken, Penelope Ann Miller co-star. 107 min.
07-1588 □*$12.99*

The Marrying Man (1991)
Sexy romantic comedy with Alec Baldwin as a toothpaste heir, betrothed to the daughter of a Hollywood mogul, who meets sensuous singer Kim Basinger, girlfriend of gangster Bugsy Siegel, while in Las Vegas for his bachelor party. The chemistry between them clicks, and wedding bells ring for the star-crossed lovers...four times before the film is over! Elisabeth Shue, Paul Reiser co-star; Neil Simon scripted. 115 min.
11-1582 □*$19.99*

Neil Simon's Lost In Yonkers (1993)
Set in New York in 1942, Simon's sensitive, often funny award-winning story centers on the dysfunctional family of an elderly, iron-willed candy store owner (Irene Worth). Among the members of her clan are Uncle Louie (Richard Dreyfuss), a brother in trouble with the mob; and Bella (Mercedes Ruehl), her neurotic 36-year-old daughter. David Straithairn also stars. 114 min.
02-2480 Was $89.99 □*$19.99*

Drive-In (1976)
Grab a six-pack, squeeze four or five buddies in the trunk and get ready for the wildest, wackiest and, yes, even sexiest evening you've ever spent at the drive-in, replete with rednecks, rock bands, burglars and a zany disaster flick. What, no dancing hot dogs? Louis Zito, Lisa Lemole star. 96 min.
02-1800 *$69.99*

A Day In The Death Of Joe Egg (1972)
An English couple (Alan Bates, Janet Suzman) contemplate the Christmastime mercy killing of their spastic child in this blackly funny satire from writer Peter Nichols ("Georgy Girl") and director Peter Medak ("The Ruling Class"). 106 min.
02-1866 *$69.99*

If You Don't Stop It... You'll Go Blind (1976)
Some of the all-time funniest (and sexiest) dirty jokes are acted out in rapid-fire ribald fashion in this raunchy laugh riot. Jane Kellen, Dick Stuart and Russ Meyer fave Uschi Digart head the ensemble cast. 82 min.
03-1092 *$59.99*

Can I Do It... 'Till I Need Glasses? (1978)
It's more hilarious dirty jokes, naked gals, jiggle jests and downright zaniness from the same folks who gave you "If You Don't Stop It...You'll Go Blind." A pre-"Mork & Mindy" Robin Williams even makes an appearance, along with the great Vic Dunlop, Roger and Roger, and Walter Olkewicz. 78 min.
03-1053 *$59.99*

The Big Fix (1978)
Offbeat comedy/mystery stars Richard Dreyfuss as Moses Wine, a former '60s college radical-turned-private eye who gets involved in a case of political dirty tricks that ends in murder. Co-stars Susan Anspach, John Lithgow and Bonnie Bedelia. 108 min.
07-1374 *$59.99*

I Love My...Wife (1970)
Irreverent social satire of modern-day marital mayhem stars Elliott Gould as a philandering husband who does love his wife, but nonetheless just can't keep away from other women. Brenda Vaccaro, Angel Tompkins and Dabney Coleman co-star. 98 min.
07-1406 *$59.99*

A Doonesbury Special (1977)
All of your favorites from Garry Trudeau's satiric comic strip are here in this Oscar-nominated animated short, as the Walden residents look back on their lives in the '60s and ponder "splitting up and moving into condominiums." 30 min.
07-8001 *$19.99*

George! (1970)
A carefree bachelor and his beautiful girlfriend get more than they bargained for when their 250-pound St. Bernard gets them into all sorts of wacky trouble. Marshall Thompson, Jack Mullaney and Inge Schoner star in this family comedy. 87 min.
08-1266 Was $19.99 *$14.99*

How Do I Love Thee? (1970)
After years of failing as a father, Jackie Gleason tries to make things right with his son, philosophy professor Rick Lenz, by entering what he thinks is an "original" poem in a contest and donating the $10,000 prize to Lenz's school. Maureen O'Hara and Shelley Winters also star in this heartwarming comedy. 109 min.
08-8754 *$14.99*

FM (1978)
Energetic, music-filled comedy about a progressive radio station that's about to go commercial and how the veteran DJs rally together to fight for its independence. The inspiration for "WKRP in Cincinnati," the film stars Martin Mull, Cleavon Little, Michael Brandon and Alex Karras, with concert appearances by Linda Ronstadt and Jimmy Buffet. 104 min.
07-1717 *$14.99*

FM (Letterboxed Collector's Edition)
Also available in a theatrical, widescreen format.
08-8698 *$14.99*

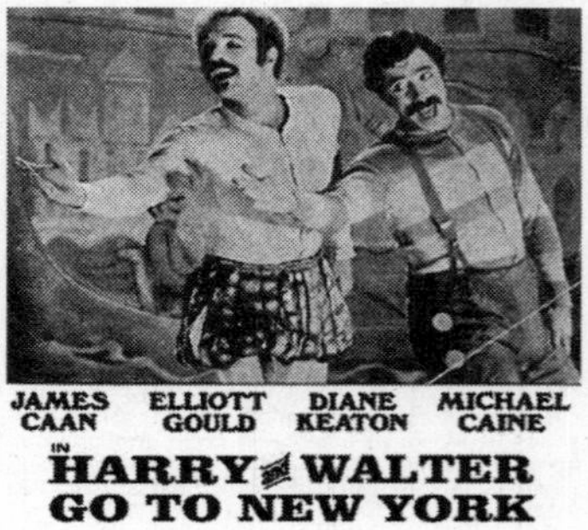

Harry And Walter Go To New York (1976)
James Caan and Elliott Gould are a pair of less-than-successful song-and-dance men in Gay '90s New York who wind up teaming with international safecracker Michael Caine and radical newspaperwoman Diane Keaton to rob a bank in this fast-paced caper comedy. With Charles Durning, Leslie Ann Warren, Carol Kane. 123 min.
02-1042 Was $59.99 *$14.99*

Harry And Tonto (1974)
Art Carney won an Oscar as Harry, an elderly man who is tired of being sent from one relative to another to live. His only friend is his cat, Tonto. Together the pair set out on a cross-country journey in this touching seriocomedy. Chief Dan George, Ellen Burstyn, Larry Hagman co-star; Paul Mazursky directs. 115 min.
04-1276 Was $19.99 □*$14.99*

The Billion Dollar Hobo (1978)
As the sole heir to an unorthodox, free-living millionaire, bumbler Tim Conway must assume the bohemian lifestyle of his deceased relative in order to collect...and hilarity abounds. Co-stars Will Geer, Eric Weston. 96 min.
04-1601 Was $59.99 *$12.99*

The Black Bird (1975)
Smart spoof of "The Maltese Falcon" showcases George Segal as Sam Spade, Jr., who has inherited his dad's detective agency and finds himself involved in a mystery surrounding the famed priceless bird. Stephane Audran, Elisha Cook, Jr. and Lionel Stander co-star. 98 min.
02-2685 *$14.99*

Lost And Found (1979)
"A Touch of Class" stars Glenda Jackson and George Segal reteam for this romantic comedy in which widowed English teacher Segal meets divorced Englishwoman Jackson at a French ski resort, and love—and broken legs—ensue. With Maureen Stapleton. 112 min.
02-2698 *$14.99*

Mr. Billion (1977)
An Italian mechanic is willed a million-dollar business empire, but he has to get from Italy to San Francisco in order to collect! Riotous comedy stars Jackie Gleason, Valerie Perrine and Terence Hill. 93 min.
04-1911 Was $59.99 □*$29.99*

Breaking Away (1979)
Winning story of four college town youths unsure about life after high school and how one boy's obsession with bicycle racing offers an escape from the boredom of daily life. Funny, rousing tale from Oscar-winning screenwriter Steven Tesich stars Dennis Christopher, Daniel Stern, Dennis Quaid, Paul Dooley. 100 min.
04-1019 *$14.99*

Chilly Scenes Of Winter (1979)
Winning serio-comedy about falling in love with the right person at the wrong time stars John Heard and Mary Beth Hurt as ex-lovers whose reunion is complicated by her marriage and his obsessive ways. Peter Riegert, Gloria Grahame. Written and directed by Joan Micklin Silver. AKA: "Head Over Heels." 96 min.
12-1500 *$19.99*

Norman...Is That You? (1976)
Redd Foxx and Pearl Bailey play a married couple who discover that their son is gay and has a white lover. Foxx then takes it on himself to "straighten out" the situation in his inimitable comic style in George Schlatter's fractured farce, shot on video and transferred to film, co-starring Dennis Dugan, Michael Warren, Tamara Dobson and Wayland Flowers. 91 min.
12-2844 Was $19.99 *$14.99*

Travels With My Aunt (1972)
Colorful, unpredictable adaptation of Graham Greene's novel about a young Englishman who is taken on a series of bizarre adventures by his eccentric Aunt Augusta after his mother dies. The young man stops at a number of countries while meeting his relative's lovers and becoming involved in a smuggling plot. Maggie Smith, Alec McCowen and Lou Gossett star; George Cukor directs. 109 min.
12-2988 Letterboxed ☐*$19.99*

Cold Turkey (1971)
Can the entire town of Eagle Rock, Iowa, stop smoking for 30 days and win a $25 million prize offered by a tobacco company? Find out in Norman Lear's slapstick salute to "kicking the habit." Dick Van Dyke, Bob Newhart, Vincent Gardenia, Richard Hughes, Jean Stapleton, and Bob and Ray star. 99 min.
12-2024 *$19.99*

Cotton Comes To Harlem (1970)
An expert blending of crime drama and comedy, this raucous caper film stars Raymond St. Jacques and Godfrey Cambridge as Harlem detectives "Coffin Ed" Johnson and "Gravedigger" Jones, investigating a shady religious leader's "back to Africa" movement. Calvin Lockhart, Redd Foxx, Judy Pace co-star; Ossie Davis directs. 97 min.
12-2604 *$14.99*

Come Back Charleston Blue (1972)
In the second film based on Chester Himes' crime novels, New York cops Godfrey Cambridge and Raymond St. Jacques have to deal with a battle for control of Harlem's drug trade that may involve the ghost of long-dead '30s gangster Charleston Blue. Maxwell Glanville, Jonelle Allen co-star. 101 min.
19-2425 *$19.99*

Slither (1973)
Hilarious, offbeat shenanigans ensue in the world of trailer parks as ex-con James Caan teams with amphetamine addict Sally Kellerman in a search for $300,000 in stolen loot. Cult comedy also stars Louise Lasser, Peter Boyle, Allen Garfield and Alex Rocco. 97 min.
12-2324 *$19.99*

Smile (1975)
Overlooked when first released, Michael Ritchie's satirical look at the goings-on of a California beauty pageant is a marvelous swipe at conniving contestants, smarmy judges and lecherous sponsors. Bruce Dern, Michael Kidd and Barbara Feldon star alongside a parade of contestants that includes Melanie Griffith, Annette O'Toole and Colleen Camp. 113 min.
12-2028 Was $19.99 *$14.99*

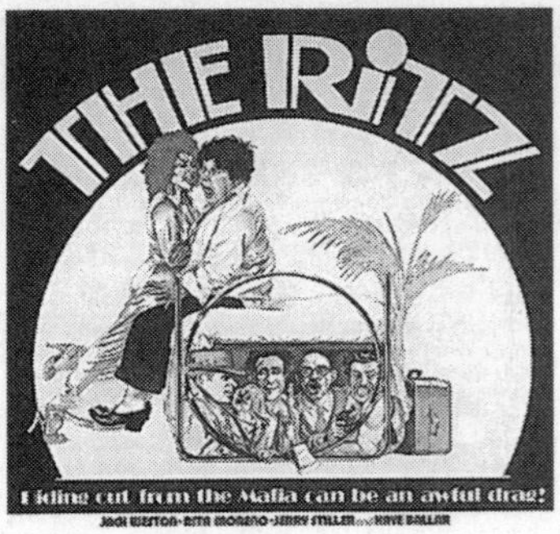

The Ritz (1976)
The heat is on in Terence McNally's ribald farce of a man on the run from the Mob who hides in a gay bathhouse. Jack Weston, Jerry Stiller, Rita Moreno and F. Murray Abraham star in this adaptation of the Broadway hit. 91 min.
19-1416 Was $59.99 *$19.99*

The Hospital (1971)
Lacerating black comedy with George C. Scott in a bravura performance as a New York surgeon struggling with his private and professional life amidst the looniness of the inner workings of the hospital. Diana Rigg, Barnard Hughes and Richard Dysart also star in this acclaimed film; scripted by Paddy Chayefsky. 103 min.
12-2320 Was $19.99 *$14.99*

Cops And Robbers (1973)
Policemen Joseph Bologna and Cliff Gorman turn in their badges for burglary tools, taking advantage of a New York City ticker tape parade to execute a multi-million dollar Wall Street heist, in a comedic caper penned by Donald Westlake. With Dolph Sweet, Joe Spinell. 89 min.
12-2603 *$14.99*

Slumber Party '57 (1978)
At a slumber party, a group of young women swap sexy tales about their "first times." Debra Winger made her screen debut in this sexy comedy co-starring Noelle North, Rainbeaux Smith and Joe E. Ross. 87 min.
12-2674 *$14.99*

The Gamblers (1970)
In this comic caper, a group of pro card sharks tries to swindle an aristocrat of his savings while on a cruise ship, but aren't prepared for what they get instead. Suzy Kendall, Don Gordon and Stuart Margolin head the cast of this international production. 93 min.
08-1770 *$14.99*

The Last Remake Of Beau Geste (1977)
Hysterical parody stars Marty Feldman and Michael York as identical twins in the French Foreign Legion, with the former encountering one madcap mishap after another in the desert after being accused of stealing a priceless gem. First-timer Feldman directs Ann-Margret, Peter Ustinov, James Earl Jones. 83 min.
07-1402 Was $59.99 *$14.99*

Cheech & Chong

Up in Smoke

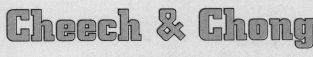

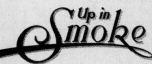

Up In Smoke (1978)
Cheech and Chong's first movie is already a cult classic. A spoiled rich kid and a hippie hitchhiker try to smuggle a van with a marijuana chassis across the Mexican border. Zany, high-flying comedy co-stars Stacy Keach, Tom Skerritt, Strother Martin and Edie Adams. 86 min.
06-1068 *$14.99*

Cheech And Chong's Next Movie (1980)
It's "high times" for all when C.&C., looking for honest work for a change, wreak havoc in a welfare office, a movie studio, a massage parlor, and even wind up in outer space. Co-stars Evelyn Guerrero, Betty Kennedy, Sy Kramer. 95 min.
07-1002 Was $19.99 *$14.99*

Cheech And Chong's Nice Dreams (1981)
HoJo's may have 28 flavors, but C.&C. have the one ice cream flavor that everybody wants! Along their rocky road to riches they are chased by cops, bikers, Hollywood agents, Dr. Timothy Leary and even Pee-wee Herman. 87 min.
02-1130 *$14.99*

Things Are Tough All Over (1982)
The boys are in double trouble in downtown Las Vegas as they play womanizers who run afoul of the Mob and Arab sheiks who don't like to get swindled. Twice the fun and laughs. 92 min.
02-1155 *$14.99*

Cheech And Chong's Still Smokin' (1983)
The organizers of a Dutch film festival want Burt Reynolds and Dolly Parton as their guests of honor; instead they get Cheech and Chong! No one is sorry, though, when the spaced-out duo give a concert of their best comedy sketches. 91 min.
06-1189 Was $19.99 *$14.99*

Ring Of The Musketeers (1993)
The 20th-century descendants of Aramis, Athos, Porthos and D'Artagnan band together to carry on their ancestors' swashbuckling legacy when they attempt a brave rescue of a young boy kidnapped by a Mafia chieftain. Action and comedy are mixed by stars David Hasselhoff, Cheech Marin, Corbin Bernsen, Alison Doody and John Rhys-Davis. 86 min.
02-2598 Was $89.99 ☐*$14.99*

Please see our index for these other Cheech & Chong titles: *After Hours • Charlie's Ghost: The Secret Of Coronado • From Dusk Till Dawn • The Great White Hype • It Came From Hollywood • The Lion King • A Million To Juan • National Lampoon's Senior Trip • Oliver & Company • Paulie • The Shrimp On The Barbie*

Let's Get Laid (1977)
Sexy British farce mixes espionage and erotic moments. A former serviceman recently released from duty discovers a dead man in his borrowed luxury apartment. Complicating matters is a secret device he finds that's desired by a crook and his henchmen and the fact his neighbor is a gorgeous movie star. Fiona Richmond, Robin Askwith and Anthony Steele star. AKA: "Love Trap." 92 min.
59-7072 *$29.99*

The Scalawag Bunch (1973)
A bawdy rendition of the classic tale set in the days of old, when the ever-gallant Robin Hood, along with his spirited Merry Men, clashed with the shiftless Sheriff of Nottingham. Stars Mark Damon. 103 min.
27-6498 *$24.99*

Corvette Summer (1978)
Lively teen comedy-drama starring a post-"Star Wars" Mark Hamill as a car-obsessed high school student who travels to Las Vegas from California in hopes of tracking down a beautifully restored Corvette Stingray that belongs to a teacher. Annie Potts is the fledgling prostitute Hamill befriends. With Eugene Roche, Kim Milford. 105 min.
12-1327 *$19.99*

Antonio (1973)
In return for a favor, a wealthy Texas oilman (interestingly, played by a pre-"Dallas" Larry Hagman), on the run from his wife and her divorce lawyer, hands over the keys to his Mercedes Benz to an impoverished Chilean potter (Trini Lopez), changing the humble man's life forever...but not necessarily for the better. 89 min.
10-1315 Was $19.99 *$14.99*

The Stoolie (1972)
This little-seen crime story features a pre-comeback Jackie Mason as a crook whose deal with the feds to keep out of prison involves trapping other hoods with bait money. But the deal doesn't last long, as he swipes $7,500 and heads to Miami Beach with police and crooks out for him. With Marcia Jean Kurtz; directed by John Avildsen ("Rocky"). 90 min.
10-9532 *$14.99*

Alex In Wonderland (1970)
Surrealistic look at a young filmmaker (Donald Sutherland) trying to decide on what project will follow his successful first effort. Director Paul Mazursky's salute to Federico Fellini's "8 1/2" features Ellen Burstyn and Meg Mazursky, as well as Jeanne Moreau and Fellini in cameos. 109 min.
12-2795 *$19.99*

The Landlord (1970)
Insightful social satire starring Beau Bridges as a sheltered rich kid who inherits a Brooklyn ghetto apartment building and assimilates himself into the lives of his tenants. He falls in love with a black art student who lives there, much to the annoyance of his mother. With Pearl Bailey, Diana Sands, Lee Grant, Lou Gossett; Hal Ashby's directorial debut. 110 min.
12-2993 Was $19.99 ☐*$14.99*

Jeremy (1973)
Sensitive romantic story starring Robby Benson as a cello-playing, horse-loving high school student who falls for pretty Glynnis O'Connor, a newcomer to his New York school who studies ballet. This charming mix of coming-of-age comedy and drama also stars Ned Wilson and Lon Bari. 86 min.
12-3088 *$19.99*

Love At First Sight (1974)
In his first film role, Dan Aykroyd plays an eccentric, independent blind man who works in a china shop and (literally) falls head over heels for a pretty customer. Funny and touching romantic comedy also stars Mary Ann McDonald, George Murray, Barry Morse. 86 min.
14-6111 *$29.99*

The In-Laws (1979)
Alan Arkin is a dentist; Peter Falk is a C.I.A. agent. When they meet at their kids' wedding and get involved in Central American intrigue, the laughs begin. Wild comedy with a slapstick wedding scene; co-starring Arlene Golonka, Richard Libertini, Nancy Dussault. 103 min.
19-1038 Was $19.99 *$14.99*

Oh, God! (1977)
Carl Reiner's delightful and sensitive comedy about God appearing to an ordinary man with the message that He's alive and cares. John Denver is the supermarket manager-turned-prophet, Teri Garr is his distraught wife, and George Burns steals the film as Jehovah. A charmer. 104 min.
19-1044 *$14.99*

Oh, God! Book II (1980)
George Burns returns as the Almighty in this touching sequel to the original hit comedy. This time, Burns picks an 11-year-old girl as the giver of His message. Suzanne Pleshette and David Birney star as her bemused parents. 94 min.
19-1011 ☐*$14.99*

Oh, God! You Devil (1984)
It's double the fun with George Burns this time, as he plays both God and the Devil dueling over the soul of a singer in this funny and touching story. Ted Wass, Roxanne Hart, Eugene Roche co-star; written by Andrew Bergman ("Blazing Saddles"). 96 min.
19-1408 Was $19.99 ☐*$14.99*

Throw Out The Anchor (1975)
In this amiable comedy, an unemployed, widowed public relations worker takes his son and daughter to Florida for a vacation on a houseboat. But when they get there, the houseboat is nowhere to be found. Dina Merrill, Richard Egan star. 89 min.
09-5184 *$19.99*

Hardware Wars (1977)
One of the all-time greatest spoofs, Ernie Fosselius' homage to you-know-what is a coming attraction for the space spectacle that features Fluke Starbucker, Augie "Ben" Doggie, Princess "Ann" Droid, Ham Salad and Darph Nader. See flying spaceship toasters, a robotic vacuum named Arty Deco and lots more. May the farce be with you! 13 min.
76-7342 *$14.99*

The Money (1975)
Laurence Luckinbill, Elizabeth Richards and Danny De Vito star in this satirical salute to "the almighty dollar"...and its effects on people. Sly schemes, baby-sitters and crooked businessmen all play a part in this whimsical comedy. 88 min.
10-1419 *$12.99*

The Prophet (1976)
Ann-Margret is at her grooviest in this cool Seventies comedy, playing a groupie of a famous guru who plans to seduce him in order to add him to her list of sexual conquests. Vittorio Gassman also stars. 90 min.
10-9525 *$14.99*

Blume In Love (1973)
Playful poke at modern marriage and divorce from director Paul Mazursky, with George Segal as an attorney who can't seem to fall out of love with his estranged wife (Susan Anspach). Sparkling supporting cast includes Marsha Mason, Shelley Winters and Kris Kristofferson. 117 min.
19-1110 Was $19.99 *$14.99*

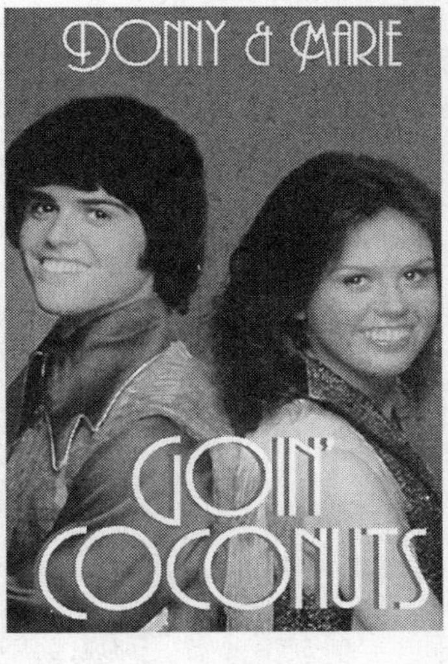

Goin' Coconuts (1979)
America's favorite Mormon sibling singing duo, Donny and Marie Osmond, made their starring film debut in this wacky Waikiki comedy. While on vacation in Hawaii, the kids get mixed up with crooks after a mysterious necklace in Marie's possession. Don't worry, though, they still find time to sing some songs (including "Doctor Dancin'" and "You Bring Me Sunshine." With Kenneth Mars, Ted Cassidy. 96 min.
47-1020 Was $29.99 *$24.99*

On The Buses (1971)
Inspired by a popular British TV series, this feature details the comic adventures of a group of blokes at a bus depot. When the company decides to bring women in as drivers, the fellows try to make life difficult for the ladies. Doris Hare, Michael Robbins and Reg Varney star. 84 min.
59-7055 *$29.99*

Mutiny On The Buses (1972)
Here's the further adventures of the wacky guys at a London transportation terminal where laughter takes precedence over schedules. In this outing, Reg Varney plans to tie the knot—and gets hilarious grief from his family. Doris Hare, Anna Karen also star. 84 min.
59-7056 *$29.99*

Holiday On The Buses (1973)
A series of mishaps leads to the dismissal of Stan, Jack and Inspector Blakey from the bus department. Hilarious adventures ensue when Jack and Stan secure work at a Welsh holiday camp and Blakey is named Camp Security Inspector. With Reg Varney, Bob Grant, Doris Hare and Wilfrid Brambell. 83 min.
59-7063 *$29.99*

Win, Place Or Steal (1979)
Russ Tamblyn, Dean Stockwell and Alex Karras carry out a scheme to get rich quick: use a para-mutual machine for betting at the racetrack. They're off and running, and you'll be chuckling all the way! 88 min.
47-1264 *$14.99*

Silver Bears (1977)
First-rate heist comedy filled with offbeat characters, double-dealings and exotic European locales. Con artist Michael Caine is hired by Vegas mob boss Martin Balsam to launch a money-laundering operation in Switzerland, but once there Caine gets mixed up in an elaborate scheme to corner the world's silver market. With Cybill Shepherd, Louis Jourdan, Tom Smothers and Jay Leno. 113 min.
27-6073 Was $29.99 *$19.99*

Going In Style (1979)
George Burns, Art Carney and Lee Strasberg star as three retirees in their twilight years who rob a bank to stir up the embers in their otherwise boring lives. Heartfelt and hilarious comedy from director Martin Brest ("Beverly Hills Cop"). 90 min.
19-1036 Was $19.99 *$14.99*

Portnoy's Complaint (1972)
The sexual exploits of Alexander Portnoy, a young man who thinks he's living in the middle of a Jewish joke form the basis of this savagely black comedy based on Philip Roth's novel; with Richard Benjamin, Karen Black and Lee Grant. 101 min.
19-1199 Was $19.99 *$14.99*

The Gumball Rally (1976)
Before "Cannonball" there was this smashing car-race comedy about a New York-to California dash with quick cars and wacky characters. Michael Sarrazin, Gary Busey, Raul Julia and others partake in the wild stunt work. 107 min.
19-1345 Was $19.99 *$14.99*

Freebie And The Bean (1974)
Alan Arkin and James Caan make a rip-roaring team of San Francisco-based detectives in this wild comedy. They're out to smash a numbers racket, but first they're gonna crash Frisco to pieces with some of the most incredible car chases you've ever seen! Valerie Harper, Loretta Swit co-star. 113 min.
19-1357 Was $19.99 *$14.99*

Crooks And Coronets (1970)
Entertaining comedy actioner stars Telly Savalas and Warren Oates as a pair of second-story men hired to case and rip-off Dame Edith Evans...and wind up so charmed by her that they can't go through with it! Co-stars Cesar Romero. 106 min.
19-1594 Was $59.99 *$19.99*

Private Lessons (1975)
A young piano student gets an education in more than just music when a sexy instructress arrives and offers him tips on improving his techniques and where to position his fingers...as well as how to play the piano! Wild and racy comedy stars Carroll Baker, Femi Benussi. 90 min.
59-7031 *$89.99*

Please Sir! (1971)
Based on the hit comedy series from England, this feature offers hilarious situations when Fenn Secondary School's 5C class is given a week-long stay at a country recreation center. The unruly group of students get into all sorts of trouble in an orgy of chaos, confusion and catastrophe. With John Alderton, Deryck Guyler and Joan Sanderson. 101 min.
59-7067 *$29.99*

Man About The House: The Movie (1974)
The controversial British sitcom that inspired TV's "Three's Company" was also the basis for this feature film. College student Robin shares his flat with gorgeous coeds Chrissy and Jo. Antics ensue when Chrissy tries to evade Robin's advances, the gals try to cook, and the roommates team to save their building from demolition. Richard O'Sullivan, Paula Wilcox and Sally Thomsett star. 86 min.
59-7078 *$29.99*

Ooh...You Are Awful! (1972)
A con artist battles mobsters when he tries to locate the number of a Swiss bank account where stolen bonds are being kept. Making matters tricky is the fact that he has to find the woman whose bum has the much-desired numbers tattooed to it. Dick Emery, Derren Nesbitt and Pat Coombs star. AKA: "Get Charlie Tully." 93 min.
59-7081 *$29.99*

Playing The Field (1974)
The film Joan Collins fans have been clamoring for is a risqué sex farce from Italy involving an unconventional soccer ref whose passion for the sport—and for gorgeous women—gets him into trouble. Exciting sports sequences and bawdy sexual hi-jinks abound with Joan as one of his sultry conquests. Lando Buzzanca, Daniele Vargas also star. AKA: "The Referee." 90 min.
59-7110 *$29.99*

Sins Within The Family (1975)
In this racy European sex comedy, a young man named Milo decides to take matters into his own hands when his uncle doesn't accept him into the flourishing family business. Milo decides to bed his sexy aunt, but complications ensue when she finds him seducing her daughter. Michele Placido and Simonette Stefanelli (Al Pacino's Sicilian wife in "The Godfather") star. 77 min.
59-7111 *$29.99*

Romance Of A Horse Thief (1971)
Action and comedy are adroitly mixed in this tale set in a Russian village in Czarist Russia, where Cossack ruler Yul Brynner tries to quash a rebellion started by peasant Eli Wallach. With Lainie Kazan, Jane Birkin. 100 min.
75-7026 *$19.99*

Find The Lady (1976)
Inept New York detectives John Candy and Lawrence Dane, reprising their roles from "It Seemed Like a Good Idea at the Time," run into shootouts, car chases and confrontations with female impersonators when they try to nab a kidnapper in this wild romp. Mickey Rooney also stars. AKA: "Call the Cops," "Kopek and Broom." 79 min.
14-6100 Was $19.99 *$14.99*

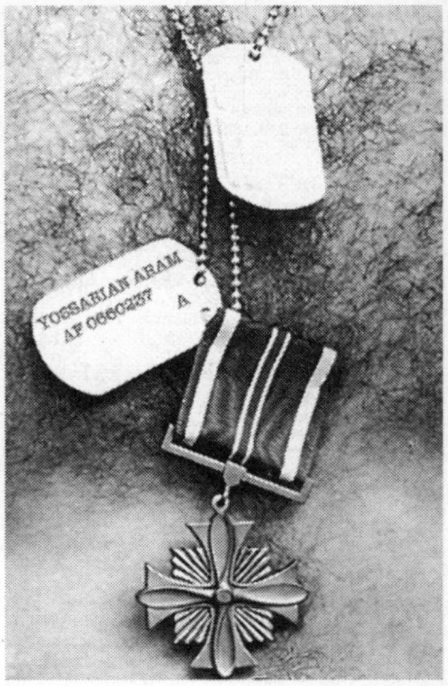

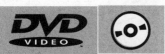

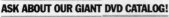

CATCH-22

Catch-22 (1970)
Author Joseph Heller's classic anti-war novel was spun into a gargantuan, surrealistic discourse on the madness of army life by director Mike Nichols. Yossarian (Alan Arkin), a WWII bomber pilot feigning insanity to stop being sent on flying missions, leads a colorful gallery of characters, portrayed by Bob Newhart, Orson Welles, Martin Balsam, Richard Benjamin, Jon Voight and Paula Prentiss. 121 min.
06-1007 *$14.99*

Bless This House: The Movie (1972)
A harried English husband and father tries to cope with the day-to-day struggles of family life, as well as a feud with his neighbors that escalates when his son falls for their daughter, in this comedy based on a popular British TV series. Sidney James, Diana Coupland, Robin Askwith star. 89 min.
59-7027 *$29.99*

Scavenger Hunt (1979)
What happens when Vincent Price dies, leaving his fortune to those who can solve a puzzle that involves collecting all sorts of animals, objects, people? A loony laff-riot that's what. Join the fun with a crew of stars like Tony Randall, James Coco, Cloris Leachman, Willie Aames and Richard Benjamin. 117 min.
04-1642 Was $59.99 *$29.99*

Harper Valley P.T.A. (1978)
Go get 'em, Mrs. Johnson! Bountiful Barbara Eden socks it to those small town hypocrites who hassled her teenage daughter in this hilarious hit comedy, based on the hit novelty song, that later inspired the hit TV series. Nanette Fabray, Pat Paulsen, Louis Nye co-star. 90 min.
44-1807 Was $19.99 *$14.99*

Seniors (1978)
What happens when a group of horny collegians open a sex clinic that becomes a money-making operation? Find out in this racy, zany effort starring Priscilla Barnes, Jeffrey Byron, and a young Dennis Quaid. 87 min.
47-1044 Was $19.99 *$14.99*

Don's Party (1976)
One of director Bruce Beresford's first films, this acclaimed satire focuses on a raunchy, revealing Election Night soiree held by a suburban couple in Australia. Pretenses and defenses come down as the evening wears on, and wicked barbs at Church, State, sex and life Down Under are tossed. John Hargreaves, Graham Kennedy star. 90 min.
47-1216 *$19.99*

Shell Game (1975)
Master con artist John Davidson uses his flim-flamming skills for a good cause when he sets out to pull the rug out from under the corrupt leader of a charity fund who has been stealing money to cover his gambling losses. With Tom Atkins, Joan Van Ark and Robert Sampson. 78 min.
55-3036 *$19.99*

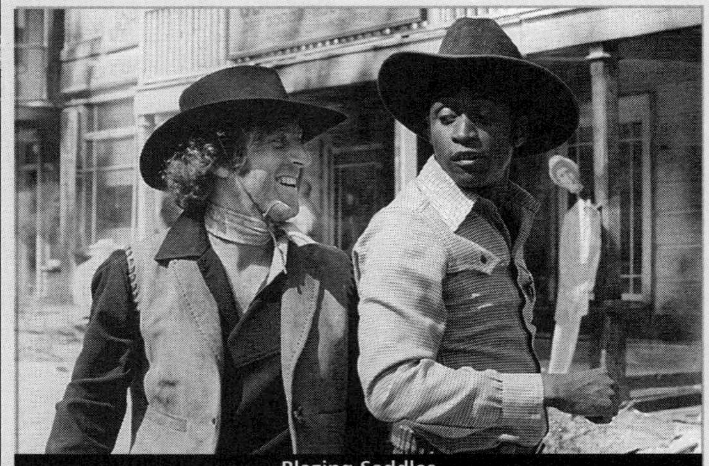
Blazing Saddles

Mel Brooks

The Producers (1967)
Mel Brooks, on his first directorial outing, scores a wild hit. Zero Mostel is a conniving theater producer, Gene Wilder his timid accountant. Together they persuade little old ladies into investing in their play "Springtime for Hitler," which they secretly hope will be a surefire flop. Kenneth Mars and Dick Shawn are marvelous as the play's writer and star. 88 min.
53-1074 ❑*$14.99*

The Twelve Chairs (1970)
Derived from a Russian folk tale, Mel Brooks' fast-paced farce stars Ron Moody as a down-and-out nobleman's son who joins with con artist Frank Langella in a desperate search for a set of 12 chairs, one of which contains a fortune in jewels that once belonged to Moody's family. Dom DeLuise and Brooks, as a tipsy valet, co-star. 94 min.
03-1186 *$14.99*

The 2,000-Year-Old Man (1974)
Mel Brooks and Carl Reiner bring their immortal mensch to life in this hilarious animated comedy. Reiner interviews Brooks, who, as the 2000-year-old man, has met all the greats from Moses and Joan of Arc to Washington and Napoleon. 30 min.
03-1301 *$14.99*

Blazing Saddles (1974)
Hollywood Westerns were never the same after director/co-writer Mel Brooks put them through the comedy wringer with this tasteless, hilarious spoof. Can the frontier town of Rockridge cope with the arrival of Cleavon Little as its new—and black—sheriff? With Gene Wilder, Harvey Korman, Madeline Kahn as Lili Von Shtupp, and Alex Karras as the horse-punching Mongo. 93 min.
19-1019 ❑*$14.99*

Blazing Saddles (Letterboxed Version)
Also available in a theatrical, widescreen format.
19-2820 ❑*$19.99*

Young Frankenstein (Special Edition) (1974)
Mel Brooks' hilarious parody of the Universal horror films stars Gene Wilder as mad doctor Frederick Frankenstein (pronounced "Fron-ken-steen"), Marty Feldman as hunchback aide Ygor (pronounced "eye-gor"), and Peter Boyle as the zipper-necked creature. With Teri Garr, Madeline Kahn, Cloris Leachman. Special video edition includes outtakes and behind-the-scenes footage. 104 min.
04-3860 ❑*$14.99*

Silent Movie (1976)
Manic Mel Brooks is a movie mogul on the skids when he gets a brainstorm: make a modern silent comedy! The only noise you'll hear is laughter when sidekicks Marty Feldman and Dom DeLuise join Mel to sign up stars like Paul Newman, Burt Reynolds, Liza Minnelli and Marcel Marceau for the film. 86 min.
04-1859 ❑*$14.99*

High Anxiety (1977)
With an acute feel for Hitchcock's style, director Mel Brooks provides an uproarious yet loving spoof of the Master's films. Brooks plays a psychiatrist who takes over as head of a sinister sanitarium, inheriting all its troubles. Co-stars Madeline Kahn, Harvey Korman, Dick Van Patten, and Cloris Leachman. 94 min.
04-1321 ❑*$14.99*

History Of The World, Part I (1980)
Take a hilarious trip with Mel through time, with stops at the dawn of Man, Ancient Rome, the Middle Ages and the French Revolution, all with Mel's madcap touch. Brooks, Madeline Kahn, Harvey Korman, Dom DeLuise, Gregory Hines and Sid Caesar head the all-star cast; narrated by Orson Welles. 93 min.
04-1408 ❑*$14.99*

To Be Or Not To Be (1983)
Riotous remake of the 1942 comedy, with real-life husband and wife Mel Brooks and Anne Bancroft (teaming together for the first time on film) as Shakespearean actors caught up in the Polish Resistance against the Nazi occupation of Poland during World War II. Co-stars Tim Matheson, Charles Durning, Jose Ferrer, Christopher Lloyd. 108 min.
04-1688 ❑*$14.99*

Spaceballs (1987)
Such a long time ago, in a galaxy so far away, you don't want to think about it...Mel Brooks lines the "space opera" genre up in his sights and fires away! See Winnebagoes in space, the villainy of Pizza the Hut, and Brooks as Yogurt, master of the Schwartz. Rick Moranis, John Candy, Daphne Zuniga, Bill Pullman star. 96 min.
12-1736 ❑*$14.99*

Life Stinks (1991)
That's the cry of filthy rich business magnate Mel Brooks when he wagers that he can survive a month on the streets of Skid Row L.A. without his millions and mansion. His hapless brush with homelessness makes for manic comedy in the finest Brooksian fashion. With Lesley Ann Warren, Jeffrey Tambor, Howard Morris. 91 min.
12-2355 Was $89.99 ❑*$14.99*

Robin Hood: Men In Tights (1993)
Mel Brooks flings an arrow at the Robin Hood epics of Kevin Costner and Errol Flynn and hits a bull's-eye in the ha-ha department. Cary Elwes is the fearless hero who battles the evil Sheriff of Rottingham (Roger Rees) for the future of England and the hand of Maid Marian (Amy Yasbeck). Richard Lewis, Dom DeLuise and Tracey Ullman co-star. 105 min.
04-2720 Was $19.99 ❑*$14.99*

Dracula: Dead And Loving It (1995)
Count on lots of laughs in this Mel Brooks vampire spoof starring Leslie Nielsen as the legendary bloodsucker, out looking for new necks to conquer. Joining in on the fun are Peter MacNichol as the insect-eating Renfield, Harvey Korman as Dr. Seward, and Brooks as Professor Van Helsing; with Steven Weber, Amy Yasbeck, Lysette Anthony. 90 min.
02-2902 Was $19.99 ❑*$14.99*

Screw Loose (1999)
Italian comedy star Ezio Greggio plays a man trying to fulfill his dying father's final wish to be reunited with an old war buddy. Greggio travels to America to find him—only to discover that he's mental hospital patient Mel Books—and "kidnaps" him back to Europe in this slapstick romp. With Julie Condra, Gianfranco Barra; directed by Greggio. AKA: "Svitavi." 85 min.
02-3461 ❑*$99.99*

The Mel Brooks Collection
There's plenty of babbling Brooks in this boxed collector's set that includes "High Anxiety," "History of the World, Part I," "Robin Hood: Men in Tights," "Silent Movie," "To Be or Not to Be," "The Twelve Chairs" and "Young Frankenstein."
04-3467 Save $30.00! *$59.99*

Down Among The Z-Men (1953)
The stars of Britain's legendary radio program, "The Goon Show" (Spike Milligan, Peter Sellers, Harry Secombe), made a rare film appearance together in this zany WWII spy comedy that features some of their beloved characters. AKA: "Stand Easy." 82 min.
07-8154 *$19.99*

The Case Of The Mukkinese Battle Horn (1956)
"Goon Show" stars Peter Sellers and Spike Milligan sound off on Scotland Yard stereotypes in this hilarious featurette about a bumbling police inspector (guess who?) and a missing 9th-century relic. Filmed in the new "Schizophrenoscope." 28 min.
09-2058 Was $19.99 *$14.99*

The Smallest Show On Earth (1958)
Charming British comedy about a couple who inherit a decrepit movie theatre mere yards away from the train tracks. Margaret Rutherford is the aged ticket seller, Peter Sellers a drunken projectionist. With Virginia McKenna, Bill Travers. 80 min.
08-1469 Was $19.99 *$14.99*

Up The Creek (1958)
An over-eager and accident-prone Navy officer finds himself "seconded" to a ramshackle supply boat where the crew runs a thriving black market in this wacky British service comedy. Peter Sellers, David Tomlinson, Wilfrid Hyde-White star. 83 min.
27-6561 *$39.99*

The Mouse That Roared (1959)
Beloved British satire traces the hilarious efforts of the tiny Grand Duchy of Grand Fenwick to escape bankruptcy by delcaring war on the United States so they can quickly surrender and be repaid in foreign aid...but that's assuming they lose the war! Peter Sellers stars in three roles; with Jean Seberg, Leo McKern. Jack Arnold directs. 83 min.
02-1214 *$19.99*

Orders Are Orders (1959)
The strict routine of a British army barracks is interrupted when a Hollywood movie crew shows up unexpectedly while the commanding officer is away. When the C.O. returns, it's up to a beautiful starlet to "distract" him while the filmmakers continue working. Brian Reece, Sidney James, Margot Grahame and Peter Sellers star. 78 min.
10-9832 *$14.99*

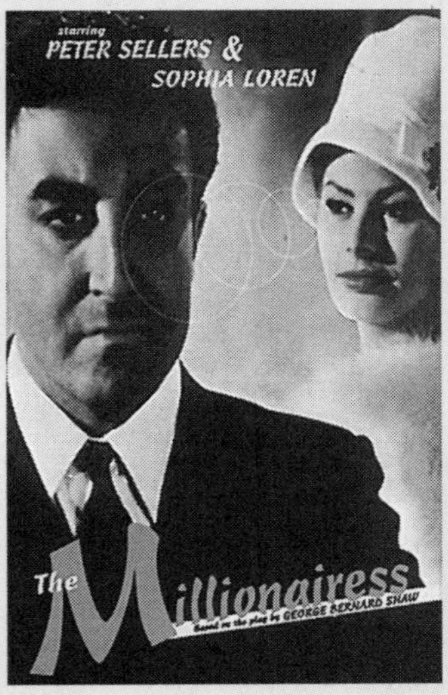

The Millionairess (1960)
George Bernard Shaw's acerbic play served as the basis for this romantic satire starring Sophia Loren as a fabulously wealthy beauty who tires of men pursuing her for her money and sets her sights on Indian doctor Peter Sellers, who has dedicated his life to caring for the poor and needy. With Alastair Sim, Dennis Price, Vittorio De Sica. 90 min.
53-8529 *$19.99*

Only Two Can Play (1962)
A bored library assistant in a small Welsh town is given a chance at a wild extramarital affair with a beautiful woman, but Fate continually conspires against them. Peter Sellers, Mai Zetterling, Richard Attenborough star. 106 min.
02-1815 Was $69.99 *$19.99*

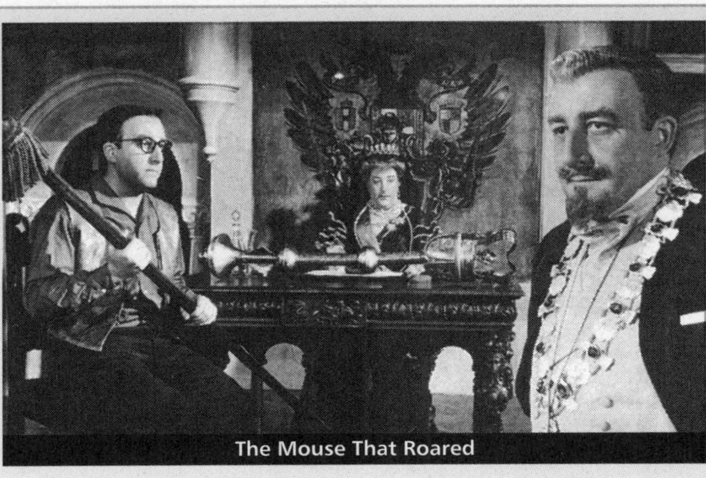
The Mouse That Roared

Peter Sellers

Waltz Of The Toreadors (1962)
Riotous romp based on the sexy stage comedy by Jean Anouilh about a retired general (Peter Sellers) who wiles away his sedentary days on his rich wife's estate pining for a lost love from years before. Co-stars Dany Robin, Margaret Leighton, John Fraser, Prunella Scales. AKA: "The Amorous General." 102 min.
15-1058 *$19.99*

The Wrong Arm Of The Law (1962)
Peter Sellers leads a band of cockeyed crooks on a hilarious caper in this crime-spree comedy. Disguised as police, the gang finds itself chased by both sides of the law! Lionel Jeffries, Bernard Cribbins also star. 94 min.
27-6343 *$39.99*

Trial And Error (1962)
Peter Sellers and Richard Attenborough each tackle multiple roles in this offbeat farce in which an attorney has to defend an accused wife murderer. The pair meticulously rehearses their courtroom maneuvers, but their efforts backfire during the trial. With Beryl Reid, David Lodge and Frank Pettingell. AKA: "The Dock Brief." 78 min.
53-8583 *$19.99*

The Pink Panther (1964)
The original in filmdom's most hilarious series! Peter Sellers is fumble-footed French Inspector Jacques Clouseau, hot on the trail of a jewel thief after the fabulous Pink Panther diamond. David Niven, Capucine, Robert Wagner and Claudia Cardinale head the list of suspects; Blake Edwards directs. 113 min.
12-1821 □*$14.99*

The Pink Panther (Letterboxed Version)
Also available in a theatrical, widescreen format.
12-3161 □*$14.99*

A Shot In The Dark (1964)
After the success of "The Pink Panther," director Blake Edwards and star Peter Sellers brought back bumbling Inspector Clouseau for this wild whodunit comedy, based on a French stageplay, in which Sellers must clear maid Elke Sommer of one murder after another. The nudist camp scene is a classic! With Herbert Lom, George Sanders. 101 min.
12-1155 □*$14.99*

A Shot In The Dark (Letterboxed Version)
Also available in a theatrical, widescreen format.
12-3162 □*$14.99*

The Return Of The Pink Panther (1974)
The relentless Inspector Clouseau (Peter Sellers) is back once more on the trail of the stolen Pink Panther diamond. Ribtickling return of filmdom's most inept sleuth also stars Christopher Plummer, Catherine Schell, Herbert Lom and Burt Kwouk as Cato. 113 min.
27-5442 □*$14.99*

The Pink Panther Strikes Again (1976)
Inspector Clouseau is up to his old tricks again—driving his boss to insanity, blundering his way through an ingenious caper, and having the time of his life with a beautiful Russian spy. Peter Sellers, Herbert Lom, Lesley-Anne Down star. 110 min.
12-1998 □*$14.99*

The Pink Panther Strikes Again (Letterboxed Version)
Also available in a theatrical, widescreen format.
12-3164 □*$14.99*

Revenge Of The Pink Panther (1978)
Peter Sellers returns once more as Inspector Clouseau (his final performance as the maladroit detective) trotting across the globe on a mission to crack a heroin ring, while being helped by a drug lord's former mistress (Dyan Cannon) and hindered by a hired assassin. Co-stars Herbert Lom, Paul Stewart, Robert Webber. 99 min.
12-1999 □*$14.99*

Revenge Of The Pink Panther (Letterboxed Version)
Also available in a theatrical, widescreen format.
12-3163 □*$14.99*

Trail Of The Pink Panther (1982)
Using rare outtakes and never-before-seen footage, director Blake Edwards creates a hilarious tribute to Peter Sellers' most famous screen character, as a TV reporter searches for the missing Inspector Clouseau. With Joanna Lumley, Herbert Lom, Burt Kwouk, Richard Mulligan. 97 min.
12-2875 □*$14.99*

Trail Of The Pink Panther (Letterboxed Version)
Also available in a theatrical, widescreen format.
12-3165 □*$14.99*

The Pink Panther Movie Collection
Make plenty of "rheuuuum" on your shelves for this boxed collector's set that includes "The Pink Panther," "The Pink Panther Strikes Again," "Revenge of the Pink Panther," "A Shot in the Dark" and "Trail of the Pink Panther."
12-3172 Save $10.00! *$64.99*

The World Of Henry Orient (1964)
Delightfully witty farce concerning two teenage girls' infatuation with a playboy concert pianist (Peter Sellers), whom they track all over New York. Their interests lead to a number of hilarious and heartwarming situations involving the pianist's conquests and the girls' friendship. Angela Lansbury, Tom Bosley, Tippy Walker and Merrie Spaeth also star. 106 min.
12-2822 Was $19.99 *$14.99*

After The Fox (1966)
Peter Sellers is Italy's top con man, posing as a film director in order to smuggle a cache of gold into the country. Victor Mature is hilarious as an aging matinee idol; Britt Ekland, Akim Tamiroff also star. Written by Neil Simon; directed by Vittorio De Sica. 103 min.
12-2653 *$14.99*

The Bobo (1967)
Would-be singing matador Peter Sellers must woo lovely Britt Ekland, Barcelona's fairest maiden, in three days in order to win a job in this slapstick comedy that features scenic European locales. With Rossano Brazzi, Adolfo Celi. 105 min.
19-1112 Was $19.99 *$14.99*

The Party (1968)
Peter Sellers is captured in riotous, Clouseauesque form as a klutzy Indian movie star who's imported to Hollywood...and manages to systematically trash both his first production and its wrap party!! Gutbuster helmed by Blake Edwards co-stars Claudine Longet, Marge Champion, Gavin MacLeod. 99 min.
12-1930 Was $19.99 □*$14.99*

I Love You, Alice B. Toklas! (1968)
Razor-sharp satire from co-writers Paul Mazursky and Larry Tucker, with Peter Sellers as a fuddy-duddy lawyer who, after leaving his fiancée at the altar, falls for free-spirit Leigh Taylor-Young and joins the counter-culture. Co-stars Jo Van Fleet, Joyce Van Patten and Herb Edelman. 93 min.
19-1134 Was $19.99 *$14.99*

The Magic Christian (1970)
Wicked British satire stars Peter Sellers and Ringo Starr as the world's richest man, Sir Guy Grand, and his adopted son. Together, they set out to prove the inherent greed of Mankind. Music by Badfinger and Paul McCartney. The cast includes Christopher Lee, Spike Milligan, Raquel Welch and Yul Brynner in drag, singing "Mad About the Boy." 93 min.
63-1310 *$12.99*

The Great McGonagall (1974)
Often hilarious farce about a bad Scottish poet who goes to see Queen Victoria in an attempt to become Britain's poet laureate. "Goon Show" alumni Spike Milligan, in the title role, and Peter Sellers, as Her Royal Majesty, star. 87 min.
20-1003 *$14.99*

The Prisoner Of Zenda (1979)
The timeless adventure is given the Peter Sellers touch in this riotous remake. Sellers stars as the spoiled king and the wanderer who must take his place. Lots of laughs and swashbuckling derring-do. Elke Sommer, Jeremy Kemp co-star. 108 min.
07-1171 Was $39.99 *$14.99*

Being There (1979)
Peter Sellers gives the performance of his career as Chance, a middle-aged gardener whose thoughts and behavior are totally shaped by television. When fate puts him in contact with business and political leaders, his innocence and silence are viewed as genius. Shirley MacLaine, Melvyn Douglas co-star; written by Jerzy Kosinski, from his story. 130 min.
19-1742 *$19.99*

The Fiendish Plot Of Dr. Fu Manchu (1980)
In his last film, Peter Sellers plays the dual role of both the century-old Oriental mastermind and the Scotland Yard detective out to catch him. Outrageous slapsticker also stars Sid Caesar, Helen Mirren. 100 min.
19-1071 Was $19.99 *$14.99*

The Very Best Of Peter Sellers
The funniest moments in the career of the great Peter Sellers are gathered on this masterful tribute tape. See Sellers at his best in clips from the "Pink Panther" series, "Two-Way Stretch," "The Wrong Box" and "What's New, Pussycat?" Also features rare footage from "The Running, Jumping and Standing Still Film" and "The Case of the Mukkinese Battle Horn" with Spike Milligan. 56 min.
59-7077 *$29.99*

The Unknown Peter Sellers (2000)
Britain's beloved funnyman of a thousand voices, Peter Sellers, is saluted in this hilarious retrospective that traces his life and career. Follow Sellers from his days as a member of radio's infamous Goons to his roles in such films as "The Mouse That Roared," "Lolita," "Dr. Strangelove," the "Pink Panther" films and "Being There," plus rare interviews, TV commercials and more. 60 min.
53-7562 *$19.99*

Please see our index for these other Peter Sellers titles: *Alice's Adventures In Wonderland • Dr. Strangelove • John & Julie • Lolita • Murder By Death • The Road To Hong Kong • There's A Girl In My Soup • tom thumb • What's New, Pussycat? • The Wrong Box*

Next Stop, Greenwich Village (1976)
Paul Mazursky's autobiographical comedy centers on an aspiring actor's (Lenny Baker) adventures in Greenwich Village in the 1950s, as he leaves his home in Brooklyn, takes acting lessons and becomes involved with a group of offbeat artists, performers and poets. With Shelley Winters as his overbearing mother, Christopher Walken, Ellen Greene. 109 min.
04-2538 Was $59.99 *$29.99*

The Apprenticeship Of Duddy Kravitz (1974)
Richard Dreyfuss's energetic performance as an aggressive and ambitious young man who's not afraid to step on some toes on his climb out of the Jewish ghettos of 1940s Montreal propels this Canadian comedy-drama, based on Mordecai Richler's novel. Co-stars Jack Warden, Randy Quaid, Micheline Lanctot. 121 min.
06-1129 Was $69.99 *$14.99*

The Wackiest Wagon Train In The West (1976)
If you loved "Dusty's Trail" like Joe McLaughlin did, you'll enjoy this feature-length romp culled from the hit comedy series about a lost group of frontier settlers whose roster includes wagonmaster Forrest Tucker, goofy sidekick Bob Denver, a millionaire and his wife, and the rest. With Jeanine Riley and Lori Saunders. 86 min.
03-1095 Was $19.99 *$14.99*

Quackser Fortune Has A Cousin In The Bronx (1970)
Thoroughly original comedy set in Dublin, Ireland, stars Gene Wilder as the fiercely independent and delightfully eccentric Quackser Fortune, who sells "fertilizer" he sweeps up from accommodating horses, but whose livelihood is threatened by a new law. Margot Kidder co-stars as a wealthy American college student who falls in love with him. 90 min.
08-1488 *$19.99*

Hometown U.S.A. (1979)
Fans of "American Graffiti" will appreciate this look at life in the '50s in which a group of teenage boys who live for chicks and fast cars learn a lesson about friendship. Gary Springer, David Wilson, Brian Kerwin star; directed by Max Baer, Jr. ("The Beverly Hillbillies"). 92 min.
47-1561 Was $69.99 *$14.99*

Hometown U.S.A. (Letterboxed Collector's Edition)
Special edition includes a letterboxed version of the film, cast bios and the original theatrical trailer.
08-8827 *$14.99*

Mastermind (1976)
Zero Mostel pulls out all the stops in this slapstick-riddled spoof of Charlie Chan mysteries, about an Asian super-sleuth who's called in to prevent the theft of an extraordinary robot by a slew of evil foreign governments. Co-stars Sorrell Booke, Gawn Grainger and the great Bradford Dillman. 86 min.
48-1018 *$14.99*

The Hoax (1972)
Two skin divers recover a missing H-bomb and, as a prank, hold the city of Los Angeles hostage in this outrageous caper comedy. Frank Bonner, Bill Ewing star. 85 min.
50-1892 *$19.99*

Richard Pryor

Black Brigade (1969)
Richard Pryor, Billy Dee Williams, Roosevelt Grier and Robert Hooks help comprise an all-black commando squad with no combat experience, a contemptuous white topkick (Stephen Boyd), and a suicide assignment deep behind German lines! AKA: "Carter's Army." 75 min.
16-3001 *$12.99*

Hit! (1973)
A federal agent whose daughter dies from a drug overdose is stymied by the government in his attempts to crack the foreign-based operation responsible, so he assembles his own vigilante team to bring the crime ring down. Thrilling action tale stars Billy Dee Williams, Richard Pryor, Gwen Welles, Sid Melton. 134 min.
06-2073 □*$14.99*

Adios Amigo (1975)
Bumbling cowboys Richard Pryor and Fred Williamson pull off one aborted "sting" after another in this whacked-out western spoof that was also written and directed by Williamson. With James Brown, Thalmus Rasulala. 86 min.
68-1091 Was $19.99 *$14.99*

Silver Streak (1976)
A perfect mix of comedy and Hitchcockian suspense with Gene Wilder as a book editor who finds romance, murder and sneak thief Richard Pryor on a cross-country train journey. Jill Clayburgh, Patrick McGoohan co-star. 113 min.
04-1144 Was $59.99 *$14.99*

The Bingo Long Traveling All-Stars And Motor Kings (1976)
In the 1930s, when major league baseball was a whites-only sport, a squad of top Negro League players break away from the tight-fisted owners and make their way across America, taking on both black and white teams, in this unusual and fun-filled comedy/drama. Billy Dee Williams, Richard Pryor and James Earl Jones star. 110 min.
07-1155 Was $49.99 *$14.99*

Which Way Is Up? (1977)
Richard Pryor offers his take on the Italian comedy "The Seduction of Mimi," and the results are hilarious. He plays a fruit picker, a sex-starved 88-year-old man and a freewheeling preacher who's raising Cain behind his pulpit. Co-stars Lonette McKee, Margaret Avery, Dolph Sweet. 94 min.
07-1033 Was $79.99 *$14.99*

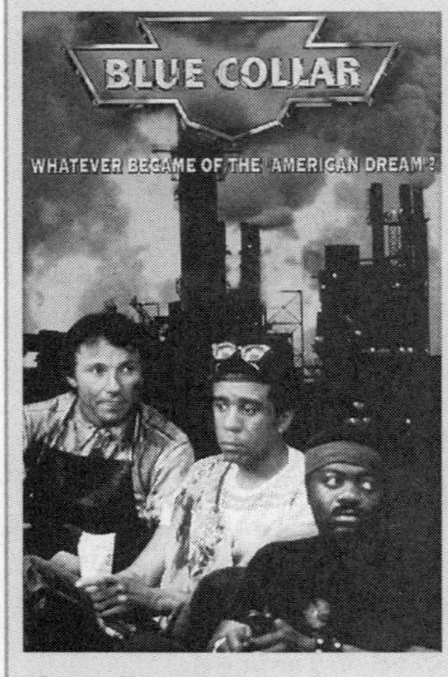

Blue Collar (1978)
Paul Schrader's first film as writer/director is an exciting, underrated comedy/drama. Richard Pryor, Harvey Keitel and Yaphet Kotto are three auto factory workers who "borrow" money from the union till and uncover a deadly combination of corruption and greed. 114 min.
07-1093 Was $69.99 *$14.99*

Blue Collar (Letterboxed Collector's Edition)
Special edition includes a letterboxed version of the film, cast bios, audio commentary by director Schrader, and the original theatrical trailer.
08-8822 *$14.99*

STIR CRAZY

Stir Crazy (1981)
Comedy smash reteams Richard Pryor and Gene Wilder as a wannabe actor and a wannabe playwright from New York who can't even get arrested...until they sport woodpecker costumes for a promotional event on their way to Los Angeles, are mistaken for a pair of bank robbers, and get sent to prison. Co-stars JoBeth Williams, Georg Stanford Brown; directed by Sidney Poitier. 111 min.
02-1087 *$14.99*

The Toy (1982)
Richard Pryor and Jackie Gleason star in an outrageous comedy, based on a French film, about a multimillionaire who hires an unemployed writer to be a human plaything for his bratty son. With Ned Beatty, Teresa Ganzel. 99 min.
02-1190 *$14.99*

Some Kind Of Hero (1982)
In this comedy laced with drama, Richard Pryor plays a P.O.W. returning home from Vietnam. He finds that life has changed for the worse, so he takes up with a hooker and heads for a life of crime. Margot Kidder, Ray Sharkey co-star. 97 min.
06-1138 Was $39.99 *$14.99*

Jo Jo Dancer, Your Life Is Calling (1986)
Richard Pryor mixes hilarity and poignancy in this semi-autobiographical tale of a nightclub comic who looks back on his life and loves after a drug accident leaves him near death. Frank and funny story, co-written and directed by Pryor, also stars Debbie Allen, Barbara Williams and Billy Eckstine. 97 min.
02-1662 *$14.99*

Critical Condition (1987)
Laughs are in store when Richard Pryor feigns insanity to dodge his creditors and winds up committed! Escape's impossible, so he does the next best thing—pass himself off as a doctor! Ruben Blades, Garrett Morris, Joe Mantegna co-star. 99 min.
06-1454 Was $19.99 □*$14.99*

Moving (1988)
Everyone's worst nightmare becomes a comic reality for Richard Pryor and his family, when a job in a new city becomes a cross-country battle with nasty neighbors, manic movers, and other hazards. Co-stars Beverly Todd, Dana Carvey, Dave Thomas, Randy Quaid. 89 min.
19-1637 Was $19.99 □*$14.99*

See No Evil, Hear No Evil (1989)
Together again, Gene Wilder and Richard Pryor are a deaf man and a blind man who become accidental witnesses to mob murder and have to team up to stay alive. Hit slapstick farce also stars Joan Severance, Kevin Spacey. 103 min.
02-1966 Was $19.99 □*$14.99*

Another You (1991)
They're the world's two biggest liars, but while one does it for money, the other can't help himself. Richard Pryor and Gene Wilder reunite for more slapstick hi-jinx in this comic con artist caper. Mercedes Ruehl, Stephen Lang co-star. 94 min.
02-2148 Was $19.99 □*$14.99*

Please see our index for these other Richard Pryor titles: *California Suite • Harlem Nights • In God We Tru$t • Lady Sings The Blues • Lost Highway • The Mack • Superman III • Trigger Happy • Uptown Saturday Night • Wholly Moses • The Wiz*

Paper Moon (1973)
Splendidly-etched portrait of Depression-era mid-America, with Ryan O'Neal as a smooth-talking con man, hustling bibles to recent widows with the help of a precocious little girl (Academy Award-winner Tatum O'Neal). Co-stars Madeline Kahn, John Hillerman; directed by Peter Bogdanovich. 102 min.
06-1046 Was $19.99 *$14.99*

Paper Moon: The Directors' Series
Peter Bogdanovich's beloved comedy is now available with outtakes, behind-the-scenes information and insights by the director. 114 min. total.
06-2316 Letterboxed □*$19.99*

Sunburn (1979)
Larceny and laughter meet head on in this comedy thriller about an insurance investigator (Charles Grodin) who hires an actress (Farrah Fawcett) to pose as his wife in order to solve a murder. Art Carney, Joan Collins co-star. 94 min.
06-1063 Was $49.99 *$19.99*

Start The Revolution Without Me (1970)
A riotous send-up of "The Corsican Brothers," with Donald Sutherland and Gene Wilder as two sets of mismatched twins who find themselves on opposite sides during the French Revolution. With Hugh Griffith, Billie Whitelaw, and Orson Welles as the narrator. 98 min.
19-1354 Was $19.99 *$14.99*

S*P*Y*S (1974)
The wise-cracking "M*A*S*H" team of Donald Sutherland and Elliott Gould reunite in this espionage farce. They play two bumbling CIA agents who are chosen by their superiors for a swap with the KGB. Zouzou, Joss Ackland also star. 87 min.
04-2379 Was $59.99 *$29.99*

Pepper And His Wacky Taxi (1972)
A would-be cab driver sets out to make his fortune in the big city, and isn't about to let a little thing like the lack of a taxi stand in his way! Wacky? What do you think? John Astin, Frank Sinatra, Jr., Allan Sherman star. 80 min.
48-1020 *$19.99*

Cold Comfort Farm (1971)
Stella Gibbons' 1932 satire is the basis for this "Masterpiece Theatre" production about an orphaned, sophisticated woman from London who visits relatives on a farm in Sussex. Her relatives turn out to be a group of neurotics with all sorts of bad manners. Sarah Badel, Alastair Sim, Brian Blessed and Freddie Jones star. 135 min. on three tapes.
50-8402 *$39.99*

Cold Comfort Farm (1996)
After she's left an orphan, tidy, aspiring novelist Kate Beckinsale heads to the country to live on her cousins' farm. She gets a rude awakening when she discovers the family is a sloppy, ill-mannered brood that repulses and fascinates her at the same time. John Schlesinger's witty comedy of manners set in 1930s England also stars Eileen Atkins, Ian McKellen and Joanna Lumley. 104 min.
07-2456 Was $99.99 □*$14.99*

Get To Know Your Rabbit (1972)
Offbeat and quirky tale of a young executive (Tom Smothers) who leaves his corporate job to become a tap-dancing magician under the tutelage of veteran prestidigitator Orson Welles. With Katharine Ross, John Astin and Allen Garfield; directed by Brian De-Palma. 91 min.
19-2080 Was $29.99 *$19.99*

The Fish That Saved Pittsburgh (1979)
Dr. J! Meadowlark Lemon! Jonathan Winters! Flip Wilson! Kareem Abdul-Jabbar! Debbie Allen! With a cast like this you'd expect a wacky basketball comedy—and you get it! The Pittsburgh team is the pits, so they hire an astrologer for spiritual guidance! 102 min.
40-1046 Was $19.99 *$14.99*

Americathon (1979)
America 1998: the country is bankrupt, cars are a thing of the past, and the President (John Ritter) is an inept bumbler who decides to hold a telethon for the U.S. Hilarious satire also stars Harvey Korman and Fred Willard, with special appearances by George Carlin, Elvis Costello and Meat Loaf. 88 min.
40-1060 Was $19.99 *$14.99*

Only With Married Men (1974)
What's a young single lawyer to do when he falls for a woman who avoids involvement by only dating married men? Pretend to be hitched, of course! Spry romantic comedy stars David Birney, Michelle Lee, Dom DeLuise and Judy Carne. 74 min.
40-1078 *$19.99*

King Frat (1979)
Zany antics in the "Animal House" mold ensue when a gang of frat boys at Yellowstone University enlist the aid of their Indian brother to find a flatulence formula that will help them win a "windbreaking" contest. John DeSanti, Dan Chandler star. AKA: "Campus King." 86 min.
41-5024 *$79.99*

Skin Game (1972)
James Garner and Louis Gossett are two con men traveling the early West with their special routine: Gossett is sold as a slave, then helped to escape by Garner. It's a sting that always works...almost. Ed Asner and Susan Clark also star. 102 min.
19-1410 Was $19.99 *$14.99*

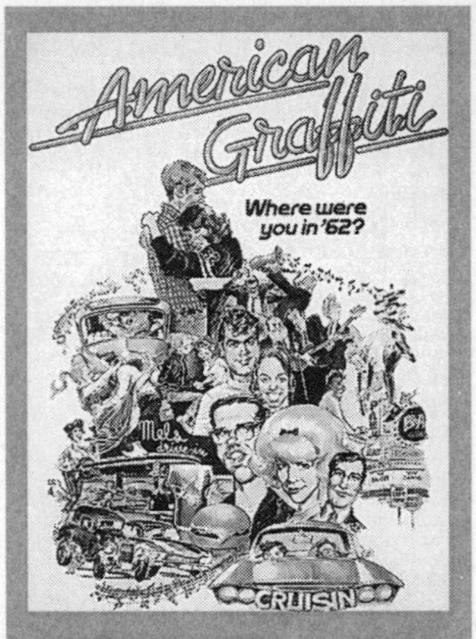

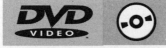

American Graffiti: Special Edition (1973)
Director George Lucas' paean to early '60s youth follows the lives, loves and misadventures of a group of Southern California teens through one memorable Summer night in 1962 as they prepare for the uncertainty of life after high school. The cast of then-unknowns includes Ron Howard, Cindy Williams, Richard Dreyfuss, Paul LeMat, Candy Clark, Harrison Ford, and Suzanne Somers as the blonde in the T-Bird. With Wolfman Jack and a definitive rock and roll soundtrack. Also included is a 10-minute "making of" featurette, with interviews with producer Francis Ford Coppola, Lucas, Howard, Ford and others. 112 min.
07-2682 Was $19.99 □*$14.99*

American Graffiti (Letterboxed Version)
Also available in a theatrical, widescreen format.
07-2683 Was $19.99 □*$14.99*

More American Graffiti (1979)
Inventive sequel to the hit comedy follows the main characters' lives into the late '60s, as they fight in Vietnam, struggle with marital problems and join the flower power movement in San Francisco. Each segment is shot using a different film technique; with Ron Howard, Cindy Williams, Paul LeMat, Candy Clark, Mackenzie Phillips, Charles Martin Smith and Scott Glenn. 111 min.
07-1722 Was $79.99 □*$14.99*

The Great Bank Hoax (1977)
It's the Watergate of the banking industry when a clerk's petty theft snowballs into a million-dollar caper in this madcap comedy. Burgess Meredith, Ned Beatty and Richard Basehart star. 89 min.
19-1417 Was $59.99 *$19.99*

I Wonder Who's Killing Her Now? (1975)
A man who suspects his wife of infidelity hires a hitman to kill her, only to find out later that he was wrong. Now all he has to do is find the killer!! Dark comedy stars Bob Dishy, Joanna Barnes. 87 min.
27-6159 *$14.99*

Rafferty And The Gold Dust Twins (1975)
Two free-spirited females (would-be singer Sally Kellerman and runaway Mackenzie Phillips) kidnap driving instructor Alan Arkin and force him to drive them cross-country in this lighthearted comedy. With Charles Martin Smith, Harry Dean Stanton. 92 min.
19-1418 Was $59.99 *$19.99*

Who Is Killing The Great Chefs Of Europe? (1978)
A feast of laughs and suspense is on the menu with this deliciously dark comedy about a mysterious murderer who is doing away with the cooking world's master chefs, killing each in the manner of their most renowned dish. Robert Morley, George Segal and Jacqueline Bisset star. 112 min.
19-1972 *$19.99*

Citizens Band (1977)
An underrated comedy from director Jonathan Demme and writer Paul Brickman ("Risky Business") that follows the bizarre exploits of a group of truckers, rednecks, town gossips and CB freaks. Paul LeMat, Candy Clark, Bruce McGill, Charles Napier, Ed Begley, Jr. star. AKA: "Handle with Care." 98 min.
06-1558 Was $59.99 *$14.99*

I Wanna Hold Your Hand

I Wanna Hold Your Hand (1978)
Breezy Beatlemania comedy set in New York City on the eve of the Fab Four's "The Ed Sullivan Show" debut, about a group of ticketless teenagers who'll do anything to attend. Co-written and directed by Bob Zemeckis; Nancy Allen, Wendie Jo Sperber, Eddie Deezen and the great Dick Miller. Soundtrack includes 17 Beatles songs. 104 min.
19-1633 Was $19.99 *$14.99*

Is There Sex After Death? (1971)
A rib-ticklingly risqué satire on modern sexual mores, written and directed by infamous hoaxer Alan Abel. Join Dr. Harrison Rogers (Abel) of the Bureau of Sexological Investigation as he visits a nudist colony, a porno film set and other locales for the answers to such mind-boggling questions as "Can a man actually have relations with a vegetable?" With Buck Henry, Holly Woodlawn and Robert Downey. 102 min.
69-1110 *$29.99*

Hollywood High (1976)
A quartet of cuties cruise the California coast looking for sun, surf, suds and studs in this wacky comedy. Four voluptuous schoolgirls frolic in the sun! Marcy Albrecht, Rae Sperling, Sherry Hardin star. 81 min.
47-1361 *$29.99*

Frasier, The Loveable Lion (1973)
He's 95 years old in human years, but this frisky feline is still siring cubs. And if that isn't enough, he's using telepathy to share the secret of his prowess with his keeper! Roaringly outrageous comedy stars Michael Callan, Lori Saunders. 97 min.
46-5408 Was $79.99 *$14.99*

The Girl Who Came Gift-Wrapped (1974)
Romantic comedy about a Hugh Hefner-like girlie magazine publisher who receives a most unusual birthday present on his doorstep: a small-town girl wearing a bikini and a red bow and hoping to become a star. Perky Karen Valentine ("Room 222") stars in the title role; with Richard Long, Tom Bosley and Farrah Fawcett. 74 min.
55-3014 *$19.99*

Good Idea (1975)
Dirt-poor artist Anthony Newley loses golddigger wife Stefanie Powers to a rich uptown bore and, with help from Isaac Hayes, hatches a nutty kidnap and extortion scheme to win her back. John Candy plays a manic policeman in his first film role. AKA: "It Seemed Like a Good Idea at the Time." 90 min.
58-8126 Was $19.99 *$14.99*

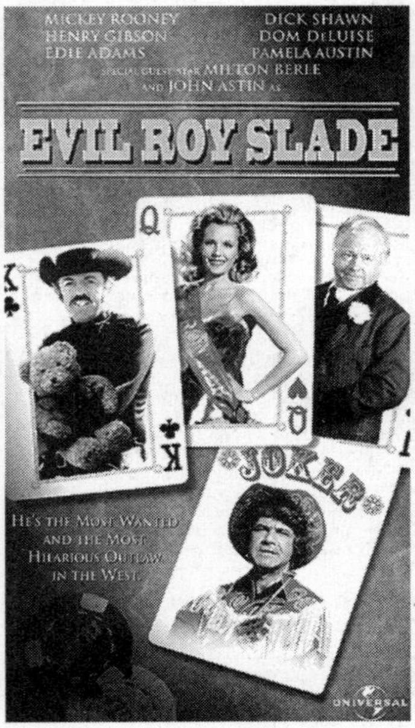

Evil Roy Slade (1972)
John Astin is Evil Roy Slade, the nastiest sidewinder who ever slithered his way across the prairie, in this hilarious western spoof. Can a new schoolmarm's love convince Astin to change his crooked ways and settle down, or will singing sheriff Dick Shawn capture him first? Pamela Austin, Milton Berle, Dom DeLuise and Mickey Rooney also star; co-written by Garry Marshall. 97 min.
07-2865 *$14.99*

Young Wives' Tale (1951)
Hilarious complications abound when Britain's postwar housing crisis forces an assortment of eccentrics to live together in one house. The manners of two married couples collide, nannies repeatedly appear and disappear, and a dog lifts dinner when nobody's looking. Joan Greenwood, Nigel Patrick, Audrey Hepburn star. 79 min.
53-6067 *$29.99*

Roman Holiday (1953)
Audrey Hepburn won an Academy Award for her role as a beautiful princess traveling incognito in the Eternal City. Hard-bitten newspaperman Gregory Peck plans to get a story out of her, but winds up falling in love with her. Co-stars Eddie Albert, Tullio Carminati; William Wyler directs. 119 min.
06-1184 Remastered *$14.99*

Sabrina (1954)
Billy Wilder helmed and co-scripted this spry romantic comedy. Audrey Hepburn is the shy chauffeur's daughter who becomes a stunning beauty, and William Holden and Humphrey Bogart are the socialite brothers who at first ignore, then are entranced by Hepburn. 112 min.
06-1568 Was $19.99 *$14.99*

Love In The Afternoon (1957)
Gary Cooper's an American playboy on holiday in Paris whose string of romantic conquests is in jeopardy when he falls for "worldly" younger woman Audrey Hepburn. Billy Wilder's delightful comedy also stars Maurice Chevalier as Hepburn's private eye father. Includes original theatrical trailer. 133 min.
04-1919 *$19.99*

Green Mansions (1959)
Rima (Audrey Hepburn), a mysterious woman who can communicate with animals, is discovered in the Venezuelan jungles by Abel (Anthony Perkins), a man hoping to avenge the recent death of his father. The two fall in love, but a search for gold and the area's ruthless natives get in the way of their romance. Lee J. Cobb and Sessue Hayakawa co-star; based on the W.H. Hudson book. 104 min.
12-2931 *$19.99*

The Nun's Story (1959)
Sensitive drama by Fred Zinnemann stars Audrey Hepburn as a doctor's daughter who enters a convent in pre-WWII Europe and later serves as a nurse in the Congo. Peter Finch, Dame Edith Evans, Mildred Dunnock and Dean Jagger co-star in a moving story of faith and one woman's devotion. 149 min.
19-1629 *$19.99*

The Unforgiven (1960)
Sprawling, star-laden saga of two families in 1850's Texas in conflict with the neighboring Indians over suspected half-breed Audrey Hepburn. John Huston directs an impressive cast that features Burt Lancaster, Audie Murphy, Lillian Gish, Charles Bickford and Doug McClure. 125 min.
12-1701 Was $19.99 *$14.99*

Breakfast At Tiffany's (1961)
Audrey Hepburn is ever-engaging as Truman Capote's vivacious yet vulnerable heroine, Holly Golightly, "a *real* phony" who's tossed between hobnobbing amongst New York's party set and settling down with her new love, neighbor George Peppard. Co-stars Patricia Neal, Buddy Ebsen, Martin Balsam and Mickey Rooney; directed by Blake Edwards. Henry Mancini's score includes the Oscar-winning "Moon River." 115 min.
06-1006 Was $19.99 *$14.99*

Breakfast At Tiffany's (Letterboxed Version)
Also available in a theatrical, widescreen format.
06-2778 *$14.99*

Breakfast At Tiffany's: Collector's Edition
Fans of Audrey Hepburn, romantic movies and the music of Henry Mancini will all want this special collector's edition of Blake Edwards' gem. Included is a letterboxed, remastered edition of the film; the original theatrical trailer; a soundtrack CD; a copy of Hepburn's own script with her notes; three 8x10 photos; and a brochure with personal notes from Hepburn and Mancini. 115 min.
06-2247 Letterboxed *$59.99*

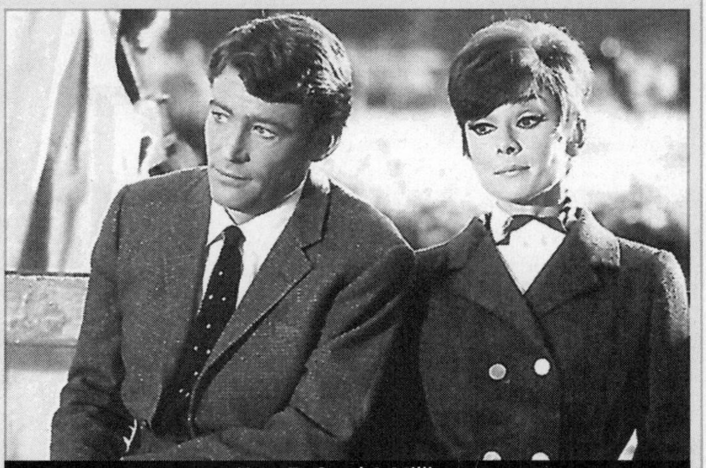

How To Steal A Million

Audrey Hepburn

The Children's Hour (1962)
Lillian Hellman's story of suspected lesbianism in a girls' school gets a provocative filming from director William Wyler (who also made the 1937 version, "These Three"). A student known for lying accuses teachers Audrey Hepburn and Shirley MacLaine of being involved in "an unnatural relationship." With James Garner, Fay Bainter, Karen Balkin, and "These Three" star Miriam Hopkins. 107 min.
12-2111 *$19.99*

CARY GRANT / AUDREY HEPBURN
"CHARADE"

Charade (1963)
Elegant Hitchcock-like thriller has Cary Grant and Audrey Hepburn put through a maze of danger and suspense in Paris, as a group of men pursue Hepburn, thinking she knows the location of a cache of stolen gold. With Walter Matthau, James Coburn. 113 min.
07-1066 *$19.99*

Charade (Letterboxed Version)
Also available in a theatrical, widescreen format.
08-1797 *$19.99*

Paris—When It Sizzles (1964)
Audrey Hepburn and William Holden sizzle, too, in this breezy romantic bon bon, as a screenwriter and his secretary act out film situations in an attempt to get over his writer's block. Co-stars Noel Coward and a cameo by Marlene Dietrich. 110 min.
06-1449 Was $29.99 *$14.99*

How To Steal A Million (1966)
A stylish and witty caper comedy, starring Audrey Hepburn as the daughter of art forger Hugh Griffith, whose latest "project" is about to be exhibited in a museum as the real thing. Fearing discovery, Hepburn enlists the help of burglar Peter O'Toole in stealing the art piece, unaware he's actually a detective. With Eli Wallach, Charles Boyer. 127 min.
04-1075 *$19.99*

Two For The Road (1967)
Called a "cult film for romantics," Stanley Donen's stylish dissection of the 12-year marriage of loutish architect Albert Finney and bored-beyond-tears Audrey Hepburn uses flashbacks to show the good, bad and ugly moments of their relationship. William Daniels, Eleanor Bron and Jacqueline Bisset also star in this much-cherished "dramedy." 111 min.
04-2281 *$19.99*

Wait Until Dark (1967)
Classic suspense story stars Audrey Hepburn as a blind woman terrorized in her apartment by crooks looking for a doll given to her by her husband that, unbeknownest to them, has heroin hidden inside it. With Alan Arkin, Richard Crenna, Jack Weston. 108 min.
19-1157 *$19.99*

Bloodline (1979)
Sidney Sheldon's novel of greed, romance, sex and deceit in a drug corporation is given a big-budget, big-cast treatment. Audrey Hepburn, Ben Gazzara, James Mason, Michelle Phillips, Omar Sharif. 116 min.
06-1004 Was $39.99 *$14.99*

They All Laughed (1981)
A screwball private eye comedy by Peter Bogdanovich about a team of detectives (Ben Gazzara, John Ritter) who are hired to follow, and in turn are followed by, some possibly "unfaithful" wives (Audrey Hepburn, Dorothy Stratten). Colleen Camp, Blaine Novak also star. 115 min.
44-1808 Was $19.99 *$14.99*

Audrey Hepburn Gift Set
This special boxed set, perfect for gift-giving, includes three of Hepburn's best-loved movies: "Breakfast at Tiffany's," "Roman Holiday" and "Sabrina."
06-2015 *$44.99*

Audrey Hepburn: Remembered
This salute to one of Hollywood's most beloved actresses features clips from "Roman Holiday," "Sabrina," "Funny Face," "My Fair Lady," "Breakfast at Tiffany's" and others, as well as a look at Hepburn's tireless work for UNICEF and interviews with Gregory Peck, Billy Wilder, Henry Mancini and Stanley Donen. 66 min.
50-7172 Was $19.99 *$14.99*

Please see our index for these other Audrey Hepburn titles: *Always • Funny Face • Robin And Marian • War And Peace*

Are You Being Served? The Movie (1977)
The cast of the beloved British sitcom with fans on both sides of the Atlantic team up for a rollicking feature-length romp that finds the staff of Grace Brothers going on a Spanish holiday together. Their stay at the carefree and peaceful resort of Costa Plonka, however, is anything but. Mollie Sugden, John Inman, Frank Thornton star. 91 min.
59-7028 *$29.99*

The Battle Of Love's Return (1971)
Before going on to co-found Troma Films ("Surf Nazis Must Die"), auteur Lloyd Kaufman wrote, directed and starred in this independent comedy about a young man who moves to the big city hoping to find love and success, but instead gets into one mess after another. Lynn Lowry, Andy Kay also star; look for an early appearance by future director Oliver Stone!
46-8026 *$14.99*

Congratulations, It's A Boy (1971)
Bill Bixby, in his hip, bell bottoms-wearing days, plays a swinging bachelor who opens his door one morning to find a teenager who claims to be his son as a result of a tryst Bixby had years earlier. Oops. Diane Baker, Jack Albertson, Darrell Larson also star. 73 min.
55-3009 *$19.99*

Enter Laughing (1967)
A Bronx wise guy becomes an actor; it ain't easy but it sure is funny in this semi-autobiographical comedy from Carl Reiner. The all-star cast includes Shelley Winters, Don Rickles, Jose Ferrer, Reni Santoni and Elaine May. 112 min.
02-1597 Was $59.99 *$19.99*

Georgy Girl (1966)
Lynn Redgrave earned an Oscar nomination for her portrayal of an overweight, offbeat London girl in this quirky romantic comedy. James Mason is the middle-aged family man who wants her as his mistress; with Charlotte Rampling, Alan Bates. 100 min.
02-1735 *$19.99*

The Gay Deceivers (1969)
Hilarious look at two young men who pose as homosexuals to avoid being drafted. Funny stuff abounds when an army officer suspects the ploy and the pair move into an all-gay apartment complex to fool him. Kevin Coughlin, Larry Casey and Jack Starrett star. 97 min.
01-1351 *$19.99*

Raising The Wind (1962)
A group of young musicians—all students at the London Academy of Music—find themselves competing against each other for a coveted scholarship. James Robertson Justice, Leslie Phillips and Sidney James star. AKA: "Roommates." 91 min.
09-5031 *$19.99*

She Always Gets Their Man (1962)
Lively British comedy involving a group of girls staying at a youth hostel who attempt to prevent a conniving girl staying with them from conning a wealthy man. Terence Alexander, Ann Sears and Gale Sheridan star. 61 min.
09-5232 *$19.99*

Walter Matthau

The Last Cruise (1952)
A pre-Hollywood Walter Matthau stars in this armed forces-themed early TV drama from "Westinghouse Studio One," scripted by novelist and Navy Commander William Lederer ("The Ugly American") and dedicated to the crews of the USS Cochino and USS Tusk submarines. 56 min.
10-7470   Was $24.99   *$14.99*

Onionhead (1958)
Oklahoma college boy Andy Griffith gives up on school after things don't work out with his girlfriend and enlists in the Coast Guard, where he's soon preparing dishes alongside wise-cracking master cook Walter Matthau. This humorous military comedy also stars Felicia Farr, Ray Danton and Joey Bishop. 110 min.
19-2082   Was $29.99   *$19.99*

Gangster Story (1959)
Walter Matthau's only directorial effort features the actor as a crafty mobster whose independence and style anger the area's reigning crime boss. The two crooks eventually unite, much to the chagrin of Matthau's girlfriend, who's trying to get him to change his life. Carol Grace, Bruce McFarlan also star. 65 min.
53-6053   Was $19.99   *$14.99*

Ensign Pulver (1964)
Robert Walker takes over the title role played by Jack Lemmon in this service farce sequel to "Mister Roberts," teaming with ship's doctor Walter Matthau to make life miserable for hard-nosed captain Burl Ives. The supporting cast includes several future stars, Jack Nicholson, Larry Hagman, James Coco and Nick Adams among them. 104 min.
19-1331   Was $19.99   ❏*$14.99*

The Fortune Cookie (1966)
Jack Lemmon and Oscar-winning Walter Matthau star in Billy Wilder's hilarious, cynical fable about a TV cameraman who is injured while shooting a football game and his brother-in-law, a conniving lawyer who plans to collect $1 million in insurance money. With Ron Rich, Cliff Osmond, Judi West. 125 min.
12-1156   Was $19.99   ❏*$14.99*

The Fortune Cookie (Letterboxed Version)
Also available in a theatrical, widescreen format.
12-3173   Was $19.99   ❏*$14.99*

A Guide For The Married Man (1967)
A delicious farce that finds faithful husband Walter Matthau taking lessons in infidelity from neighbor Robert Morse. The wacky cast includes Lucille Ball, Jack Benny, Jayne Mansfield, Inger Stevens, Phil Silvers and Sid Caesar; directed by Gene Kelly. 91 min.
04-1966   Was $59.99   *$29.99*

The Secret Life Of An American Wife (1968)
A neglected wife cooks up an idea to prove she is still desirable: sleep with her adman husband's celebrity client, "the most physically and sexually attractive man in the world." Walter Matthau and Anne Jackson star in a delightful comedy. 97 min.
04-1964   Was $59.99   *$29.99*

Kotch (1971)
Decades before "Grumpy Old Men," Jack Lemmon directed buddy Walter Matthau in this comedy/drama about an independent septuagenarian whose presence in his son's family's house causes friction. Unwilling to go to a retirement home, Matthau sets out on his own and winds up looking after a pregnant teen runaway. Deborah Winters, Charles Aidman, Felicia Farr also star. 114 min.
04-1188   *$14.99*

A New Leaf (1971)
A wickedly funny story of love and murder, starring Walter Matthau as a bankrupt playboy whose plans to knock off his rich new wife constantly go awry. Writer/director Elaine May is hilarious as the clumsy bride who leads a charmed life. With James Coco, Jack Weston. 102 min.
06-1448   *$14.99*

Pete 'N' Tillie (1972)
The marriage of a spinsterish secretary (Carol Burnett) and an unreliable prankster (Walter Matthau) produces a son, some laughs and a few tears in Martin Ritt's offbeat love story, co-starring Geraldine Page, Barry Nelson. 100 min.
07-1625   Was $79.99   *$14.99*

First Monday In October

The Laughing Policeman (1973)
A madman guns down a busload of people, including a police officer, in San Francisco, and as reluctantly partnered detectives Walter Matthau and Bruce Dern investigate the shooting, a bizarre sex scandal is uncovered. Violent thriller, based on a Per Wahloo/Maj Sjowall novel, also stars Lou Gossett, Albert Paulsen, Cathy Lee Crosby. 111 min.
04-1803   Was $59.99   ❏*$29.99*

The Taking Of Pelham One Two Three (1974)
First-rate crime thriller about a quartet of criminals who commandeer a New York City subway car and hold its occupants hostage for a million-dollar ransom. Walter Matthau, Robert Shaw, Martin Balsam and Hector Elizondo star. 104 min.
12-1868   ❏*$14.99*

Casey's Shadow (1978)
Walter Matthau is a down-and-out horse trainer trying to hold on to his job and his kids in this heartwarming comedy, with all his hopes pinned on one horse—Casey's Shadow. Murray Hamilton and Alexis Smith co-star. 117 min.
02-1142   Was $19.99   *$14.99*

Little Miss Marker (1980)
Bookmaker Walter Matthau is beside himself when a customer's 6-year-old daughter is left as a down payment on a bet and he must care for the child in this fun-filled remake of the Damon Runyon story. With Julie Andrews, Tony Curtis, Bob Newhart and Sara Stimson. 103 min.
07-1136   Was $49.99   *$14.99*

First Monday In October (1981)
The appointment of the first woman to the U.S. Supreme Court is the basis for this comedy, released just before Sandra O'Connor earned the job in real life. Walter Matthau is a veteran liberal justice; Jill Clayburgh, the conservative nominated for the job. 99 min.
06-1116   Was $79.99   *$14.99*

Buddy Buddy (1982)
Master funnymen Walter Matthau and Jack Lemmon reteam with "Fortune Cookie" director Billy Wilder in this blackly funny farce, based on the French film "A Pain in the A—," about a hit man whose latest job goes awry when he gets involved with a cuckolded husband out to kill himself. With Paula Prentiss, Klaus Kinski. 98 min.
12-1211   Was $79.99   *$19.99*

The Couch Trip (1988)
Escaped mental patient Dan Aykroyd winds up impersonating a radio psychiatrist and hobnobbing with the Beverly Hills rich and famous in this barbed look at pop celebrity. Crazy comedy with Walter Matthau, Charles Grodin, Donna Dixon. 98 min.
73-1011   Was $19.99   *$14.99*

Grumpy Old Men (1993)
The long-running feud between small-town Minnesota neighbors Jack Lemmon and Walter Matthau takes on new proportions when sexy redhead Ann-Margret moves onto the block and is pursued by both of them. A fun-filled reteaming of the classic comedy pair offers hilariously salty dialogue and poignant moments. With Kevin Pollak, Daryl Hannah and Burgess Meredith. 104 min.
19-2229   Was $19.99   ❏*$14.99*

Grumpier Old Men (1995)
Riotous hit sequel finds Jack Lemmon happily married to Ann-Margret, while romance enters Walter Matthau's life when Sophia Loren takes over the local bait shop. But when wedding plans of Lemmon's and Matthau's children go awry, the rivalry begins again between the crusty adversaries. With Burgess Meredith, Kevin Pollak and Daryl Hannah. 101 min.
19-2441   Was $19.99   ❏*$14.99*

I.Q. (1994)
Fanciful farce in which Princeton car mechanic Tim Robbins is helped in his romantic pursuit of academic-minded Meg Ryan by her uncle—Albert Einstein (Walter Matthau). A witty script and engaging performances by the leads and supporting players (Gene Saks, Lou Jacobi) help make this a comic winner. 92 min.
06-2330   Was $89.99   ❏*$14.99*

The Grass Harp (1996)
Truman Capote's autobiographical story is turned into a sweet-natured coming-of-age film centered on a young boy who is sent by his widower father to live with his two aunts in a small Southern town in the 1940s. The boy learns a series of important lessons from the women, one of whom is stern and greedy, the other simple and good-natured. The superb cast includes Edward Furlong, Sissy Spacek, Mary Steenburgen, Piper Laurie, Jack Lemmon and Walter Matthau. 107 min.
02-5124   Was $99.99   ❏*$19.99*

I'm Not Rappaport (1996)
In Herb Gardner's adaptation of his hit play, Walter Matthau plays Nat Moyer, an elderly man who spends much of his time telling stories and complaining to pal Midge Carter (Ossie Davis) in Central Park. The men's future is put in jeopardy when Moyer's daughter tries to get him declared legally incompetent and Carter is slated to be fired from his job. Amy Irving also stars. 137 min.
07-2505   Was $99.99   ❏*$14.99*

Out To Sea (1997)
Wheeler-dealer Walter Matthau arranges a free luxury Caribbean vacation for himself and widowed brother-in-law Jack Lemmon, but neglects to tell Lemmon that they'll be earning their keep on the "golden agers" cruise by serving as the ship's dance hosts, in this riotous nautical romp. Dyan Cannon, Gloria De Haven and Brent Spiner also star. 105 min.
04-3530   Was $99.99   *$14.99*

Meg Ryan
Diane Keaton
Lisa Kudrow
and
Walter Matthau

Hanging Up
Every family has a few hang-ups.

Hanging Up (2000)
A trio of sisters—high-powered magazine editor Diane Keaton, housewife and would-be party planner Meg Ryan, and flighty soap actress Lisa Kudrow—have to learn to put their cell phones down and function as a family when aging father Walter Matthau suffers a stroke in this funny and touching seriocomedy. Scripted by Nora and Delia Ephron and directed by Keaton. 95 min.
02-3437   Was $99.99   ❏*$19.99*

Walter Matthau: Diamond In The Rough
Fighting the type-casting that saw him as a character actor, Walter Matthau went on to become an Oscar-winning lead of both comedies and dramas. Matthau serves as narrator for this look back on his acclaimed film work, with clips from such movies as "The Odd Couple," "The Sunshine Boys" and "Grumpier Old Men" and interviews with Jack Lemmon, Neil Simon and Ossie Davis. 55 min.
50-7608   *$14.99*

Please see our index for these other Walter Matthau titles: *The Bad News Bears • Buddy Buddy • Cactus Flower • California Suite • Charade • Dennis The Menace • A Face In The Crowd • Fail-Safe • The Fortune Cookie • Goodbye Charlie • Hello, Dolly! • I Ought To Be In Pictures • JFK • King Creole • Lonely Are The Brave • The Odd Couple • Plaza Suite • The Stingiest Man In Town • The Sunshine Boys • The Survivors • Who's Got The Action?*

The Amorous Mr. Prawn (1964)
When a British army general is close to ending his service time but short of funds to buy a retirement cottage, his industrious wife comes up with a scheme to rent out his military headquarters as a tourist hotel while the general's on maneuvers. Lively comedy stars Cecil Parker, Joan Greenwood, Ian Carmichael, Dennis Price. 89 min.
09-5006   *$19.99*

The Honey Pot (1967)
Three women are summoned to the Venetian deathbed of their former lover (Rex Harrison), all hoping to inherit his fortune. But it's all just a ruse by Harrison, who needs his ex-paramours' cash to get out of debt. Lively, satiric update of "Volpone" from Joseph L. Mankiewicz co-stars Maggie Smith, Cliff Robertson, Susan Hayward, Capucine, Edie Adams. 131 min.
12-2663   *$14.99*

The Wheeler Dealers (1963)
Funny financial farce featuring James Garner as a Texas tycoon who falls in love with stock analyst Lee Remick when he arrives in New York seeking to invest millions he really doesn't have. Remick's unscrupulous boss tells her to sell Garner worthless stock, but an oil strike turns the junk paper into a bonanza! Phil Harris, Chill Wills, Jim Backus and John Astin also star. 110 min.
12-2713   *$19.99*

Kisses For My President (1964)
Funny farce starring Polly Bergen as the first female Chief Executive and Fred MacMurray as her "first man." Can their marriage survive the unusual situation, political pressures and South American dictator Eli Wallach's advances towards Bergen? With Arlene Dahl, Edward Andrews. 113 min.
19-1960   Was $19.99   *$14.99*

Never Too Late (1965)
Preparing to celebrate their golden years after their daughter's marriage, a middle-aged couple are shocked to learn they're going to become parents again in this breezy adaptation of the hit stage comedy. Paul Ford, Maureen O'Sullivan, Connie Stevens and Jim Hutton star; look for a 4-year-old Timothy Hutton. 105 min.
19-2514   ❏*$19.99*

Fitzwilly (1967)
In order to keep his elderly employer from learning that she's broke, loyal butler Dick Van Dyke enlists the aid of the household staff to commit a series of robberies that culminates in a Christmas Eve department store heist. Alternately madcap and touching, this comedy also stars Barbara Feldon, Edith Evans, John McGiver. 102 min.
12-3024   ❏*$19.99*

What A Carve Up! (1961)
The clan of a deceased eccentric gather at his spooky mansion to hear the will and are confronted by every horror cliché known to man. One of the funniest British genre spoofs, this loose remake of 1932's "The Ghoul" stars Kenneth Connor, Donald Pleasence, Shirley Eaton and pop star Adam Faith. AKA: "No Place Like Homicide." 88 min.
68-8320   *$19.99*

The Horizontal Lieutenant (1961)
Military farce meets mirthful romance as klutzy Army officer Jim Hutton searches for a pesky Japanese soldier who's stealing supplies on a Pacific island during World War II. While trying to capture his nemesis, Hutton creates sparks with sexy Army nurse Paula Prentiss. First-rate comic support is offered by Jack Carter, Marty Ingels and Jim Backus. 90 min.
12-2841   *$19.99*

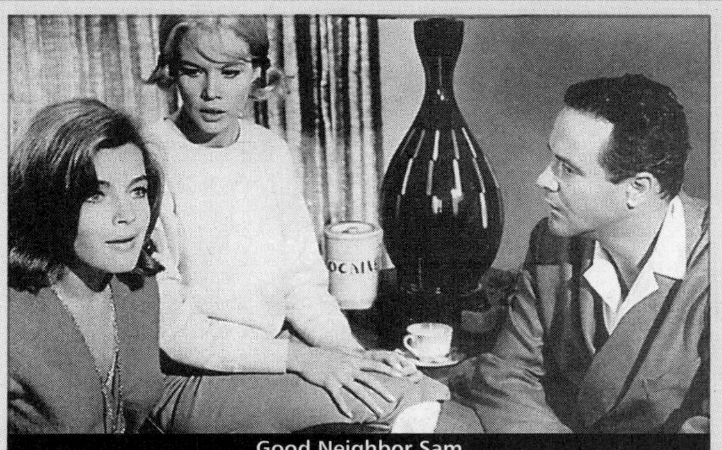

Good Neighbor Sam

Jack Lemmon

It Should Happen To You (1954)
One of Judy Holliday's finest comic performances was in this zippy farce from writer Garson Kanin and director George Cukor. A would-be actress puts her name on a New York billboard and becomes a media celebrity. Fine support from Jack Lemmon (his film debut), Peter Lawford. 88 min.
02-2542 ***$19.99***

My Sister Eileen (1955)
Spry musical adaptation of the hit Broadway comedy stars Janet Leigh and Betty Garrett as two Ohio siblings who move to New York City and take a basement apartment in a Greenwich Village brownstone occupied by offbeat characters. Jack Lemmon, Dick York, Kurt Kaznar, and Bob Fosse (who also served as the film's choreographer) also star; co-scripted by Blake Edwards. 108 min.
02-2383 ***$19.99***

Fire Down Below (1957)
Inflamed passion aboard a small tramp boat divides the friendship of two seafaring adventurers (Robert Mitchum and Jack Lemmon) when they're hired by a mysterious passenger (Rita Hayworth). Co-stars Herbert Lom, Bernard Lee, Anthony Newley. 118 min.
02-1607 ***$19.99***

Cowboy (1958)
The romanticized image of frontier life was examined in this entertaining western drama starring Jack Lemmon as a bored Chicago hotel clerk who loans money to visiting rancher Glenn Ford in exchange for taking part in a cattle drive, where Lemmon's cowboy fantasies don't match reality. With Brian Donlevy, Anna Kashfi. 91 min.
02-2838 ***$14.99***

The Apartment (1960)
Billy Wilder's acerbic look at corporate life stars Jack Lemmon as an ambitious exec who lets his bosses use his bachelor pad for their trysts. Shirley MacLaine, Fred MacMurray, Jack Kruschen also star; winner of five Oscars, including Best Picture, Director and Screenplay. 125 min.
12-1764 Was $19.99 ***$14.99***

The Apartment (Letterboxed Version)
Also available in a theatrical, widescreen format.
12-2848 Was $19.99 ***$14.99***

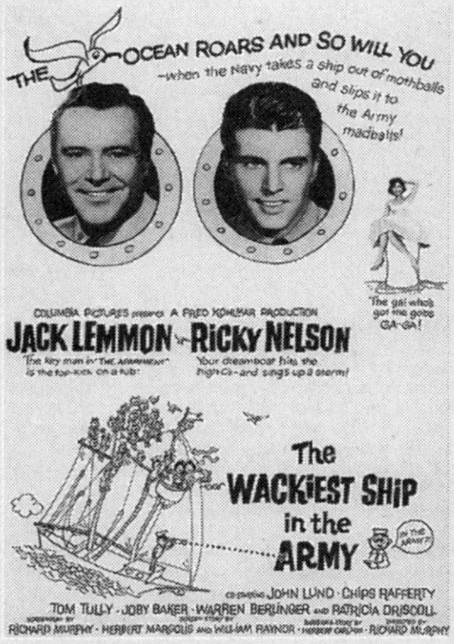

The Wackiest Ship In The Army (1961)
Navy officer Jack Lemmon skippers the title tin can, the USS Echo, during World War II on a mission to escort an Australian enemy craft-tracking expert (Chips Rafferty) through mine-congested Japanese waters. Disarming little comedy co-stars Ricky Nelson, John Lund, Alvy Moore. 99 min.
02-1581 ***$14.99***

Days Of Wine And Roses (1962)
First seen as a TV play, J.P. Miller's searing film look at how alcoholism takes over the lives of a young suburban couple stars Jack Lemmon and Lee Remick in Oscar-nominated turns. With Charles Bickford, Jack Klugman. 117 min.
19-1246 ***$19.99***

Under The Yum Yum Tree (1963)
Breezy and racy (for its time) romantic comedy stars Jack Lemmon as the lothario landlord of an apartment building for single women who sets his sights on new tenant Carol Lynley, unaware of her platonic "live-in" arrangement with fiancé Dean Jones. Edie Adams, Imogene Coca co-star. 110 min.
02-2981 ***$19.99***

Good Neighbor Sam (1964)
Hilarious comedy of suburban marital miscues with Jack Lemmon as a put-upon ad man who masquerades as neighbor Romy Schneider's husband so she can claim an inheritance. A top cast, including Edward G. Robinson, Dorothy Provine and Mike Connors, adds to this frothy free-for-all. 130 min.
02-2694 ***$14.99***

How To Murder Your Wife (1965)
Free-living cartoonist Jack Lemmon awakens one morning after a wild party to find himself married to gorgeous Virna Lisi, who can't speak a word of English. Then finds himself on trial for her murder, an act depicted in his comic strip, which everyone knows is based on his real-life exploits. With Terry-Thomas, Eddie Mayehoff and Claire Trevor. 118 min.
12-1952 ***$19.99***

Luv (1967)
The hit Broadway play becomes a funny movie starring Jack Lemmon as a would-be suicide halted by wealthy eccentric Peter Falk. When Lemmon agrees to repay him by romancing Falk's neurotic wife (Elaine May) so his savior can get cozy with a sexy gym teacher, wild romantic complications ensue. Look quickly for a young Harrison Ford as a hippie. 93 min.
02-2699 ***$14.99***

Avanti! (1972)
Touching and funny romantic farce from Billy Wilder focusing on a stodgy corporate executive (Jack Lemmon) in Italy to claim the body of his father, who has been killed in an accident. There he meets the daughter of his father's mistress (Juliet Mills), and the two begin their own affair on their parents' favorite little island. Clive Revill, Edward Andrews co-star. 144 min.
12-2927 Was $19.99 ***$14.99***

Save The Tiger (1973)
Jack Lemmon won an Oscar for his perceptive portrayal of a decent businessman who, as a matter of necessity, engages in unethical practices and, eventually, finds himself at the end of his rope. Co-stars Jack Gilford, Laurie Heineman, Thayer David and Lara Parker; directed by John Avildsen. 100 min.
06-1111 Was $69.99 ***$14.99***

Tribute (1980)
Jack Lemmon shines as a terminally ill press agent who must come to terms with his life and his estranged son in this touching seriocomedy. Robby Benson, Lee Remick, Colleen Dewhurst, Kim Cattrall also star. 121 min.
44-1809 ***$19.99***

missing.

Missing (1982)
Jack Lemmon and Sissy Spacek star in this exciting, riveting mystery based on a true story. Lemmon plays an American searching for his lost son in a hellish South American country where violence and political chaos have erupted. Directed by Costa-Gavras ("Z"). 122 min.
07-1112 ***$19.99***

Mass Appeal (1984)
Conflicts arise between a highly respected, slightly unconventional priest (Jack Lemmon) and a hot-tempered seminary student (Zeljko Ivanek), whose stance on various religious issues has raised the concern of their rigid Monsignor (Charles Durning), in this dramatic filming of the hit Broadway play. 99 min.
07-1298 Was $19.99 ***□$14.99***

Macaroni (1985)
Two of filmdom's most acclaimed actors, Jack Lemmon and Marcello Mastroianni, team up in this lighthearted tale of old Army buddies who meet after 40 years, only to find that Marcello's been sending his love-starved sister forged letters under Jack's name all those years. 104 min.
06-1352 Was $79.99 ***$14.99***

Dad (1989)
Jack Lemmon turns in a sensational performance in this tear-inducing drama laced with comedy. He plays an elderly man who confronts his son and his own deeply guarded feelings when his wife is hospitalized. Ted Danson, Olympia Dukakis, Ethan Hawke co-star. 117 min.
07-1640 Was $19.99 ***□$14.99***

Glengarry Glen Ross (1992)
David Mamet scripted this forceful adaptation of his award-winning Broadway drama, set in the dingy New York office of a real estate company whose less-than-honest agents will do anything to get their clients to sign on the dotted line. Al Pacino, Jack Lemmon, Ed Harris, Alan Arkin, Kevin Spacey and Alec Baldwin head the ensemble cast. 100 min.
27-6806 Was $19.99 ***□$14.99***

For Richer, For Poorer (1992)
Jack Lemmon plays a wealthy businessman who seems to live a charmed life. Except for his son, who refuses to work, everything is dandy. So Dad decides to relinquish his fortune and start from scratch, just to make a point to his lazy son. Jonathan Silverman, Talia Shire and Joanna Gleason also star. 90 min.
44-1879 Was $19.99 ***□$14.99***

A Life In The Theatre (1993)
Masterful veteran actor Jack Lemmon shares a dressing room with rising star Matthew Broderick, whom he attempts to teach the tricks of the trade. But the competition between the two grows fierce, leading to some poignant and hilarious moments. David Mamet adapted his own play for this production. 78 min.
18-7489 ***□$89.99***

My Fellow Americans (1996)
When Jack Lemmon and James Garner, two former U.S. presidents from opposite sides of the political spectrum, stumble upon a financial scandal involving current chief executive Dan Aykroyd, the ex-rivals find themselves forced to go on the run together from government agents who want to silence them for good. Sharply satirical comedy also stars Lauren Bacall. 101 min.
19-2535 Was $19.99 ***□$14.99***

Getting Away With Murder (1996)
College ethics professor Dan Aykroyd begins to suspect that elderly neighbor Jack Lemmon is a fugitive Nazi death camp commandant and, unable to prove it, poisons him. When evidence comes out that Lemmon was wrongly accused, a guilt-stricken Aykroyd marries the man's spinster daughter, but was he right after all? Outrageous dark comedy also stars Lily Tomlin, Bonnie Hunt. 92 min.
44-2052 Was $99.99 ***□$14.99***

12 Angry Men (1997)
The fate of a young man accused of killing his father rests with 12 jurors who must struggle with the facts of the case, even as their search for the truth puts them at odds with each other. A powerhouse cast that includes Hume Cronyn, Tony Danza, Ossie Davis, Jack Lemmon, Armin Mueller-Stahl, Edward James Olmos and George C. Scott propels director William Friedkin's staging of the Reginald Rose drama. 117 min.
73-1282 Was $59.99 ***□$14.99***

Inherit The Wind (1999)
The third version of the prize-winning play based on the 1925 Scopes Trial features George C. Scott as fundamentalist prosecutor Matthew Harrison Brady and Jack Lemmon as activist defense attorney Henry Drummond, former friends now on opposite sides of a bitter debate over a Tennessee teacher arrested for promoting Darwin's theory of evolution. With Tom Everett Scott, Piper Laurie and Beau Bridges. 113 min.
12-3288 Was $49.99 ***□$14.99***

Jack Lemmon: America's Everyman
As adept with comedic roles as he is with dramatic, the two-time Academy Award-winner is saluted with this wonderful retrospective narrated by Lemmon himself. Along with clips from such films as "Mister Roberts," "The Apartment," "Days of Wine and Roses" and "The Odd Couple," there are interviews with such colleagues as Walter Matthau, Gregory Peck and Kevin Spacey. 53 min.
50-7605 ***$14.99***

Please see our index for these other Jack Lemmon titles: *12 Angry Men • Bell, Book And Candle • The China Syndrome • The Grass Harp • The Great Race • Grumpier Old Men • Grumpy Old Men • Hamlet • Irma La Douce • JFK • Mister Roberts • The Odd Couple • The Out-Of-Towners • Out To Sea • The Prisoner Of Second Avenue • Short Cuts • Some Like It Hot • Three For The Show*

Those Magnificent Men In Their Flying Machines (1965)
Take off with the craziest collection of aircraft and pilots ever assembled in this classic comedy about the first London-to-Paris airplane race in 1910 and the international array of contestants. Stuart Whitman, Sarah Miles, James Fox, Terry-Thomas, Gert Frobe, Benny Hill and (in hilarious framing sequences) Red Skelton star. 138 min.
04-1162 Was $79.99 ***$14.99***

Those Daring Young Men In Their Jaunty Jalopies (1969)
A trans-European road rally in the '20s becomes a comic catastrophe in the hilarious follow-up to "Those Magnificent Men in Their Flying Machines." The all-star cast includes Tony Curtis, Terry-Thomas, Dudley Moore, Peter Cook, Susan Hampshire. 93 min.
06-1792 Was $39.99 ***$19.99***

Papa's Delicate Condition (1963)
Charming period comedy about Corrine Griffith's childhood, and her father's "condition"...perpetual drunkenness! Of course, his prim wife disapproves and delightful comedy ensues. Jackie Gleason, Glynis Johns, Elisha Cook, Jr. star; features the Oscar-winning song "Call Me Irresponsible." 98 min.
06-1909 Was $19.99 ***□$14.99***

Smashing Time: Collector's Edition (1967)
"Swinging London" is where friends Rita Tushingham and Lynn Redgrave head in hopes of finding adventure and excitement among the Mods. Wild situations soon ensue that find Redgrave in continuous trouble and Tushingham the girlfriend and subject of a famous photographer. Michael York co-stars in this satire with slapstick moments. 96 min.
08-8672 Letterboxed ***$14.99***

The Night They Raided Minsky's (1968)
Colorful, quick-paced salute to the world of burlesque and the birth of striptease, as innocent Amish girl Britt Ekland comes to New York, becomes involved with mobsters and eventually performs the world's first strip show. Elliott Gould, Jason Robards, Jr., Forrest Tucker, Norman Wisdom and Joseph Wiseman star. 100 min.
12-2322 ***$19.99***

Buona Sera, Mrs. Campbell (1968)
Three former American GIs—each believing they have fathered an Italian woman's daughter during World War II—learn about one another during a reunion of their old outfit in Italy. Soon, they scramble to seek their grown daughter and keep the secret from their wives. Gina Lollobrigida, Phil Silvers, Peter Lawford, Telly Savalas, Lee Grant, Shelley Winters star. 111 min.
12-2564 Was $19.99 ***□$14.99***

Oh Dad, Poor Dad, Mama's Hung You In The Closet And I'm Feeling So Sad (1967)
This hilariously offbeat farce shows what happens when widow Rosalind Russell and goofy son Robert Morse vacation at a tropical island—along with dad, who's dead in a coffin. Barbara Harris and Hugh Griffith co-star in the wild proceedings. 86 min.
06-1222 Was $49.99 ***$14.99***

A Thousand Clowns (1965)
Hilarious and sensitive comedy about an unconventional (and unemployed) ex-TV writer who must give up his principles and return to the business in order to adopt the 12-year-old nephew who's been living with him for years. Jason Robards, Jr., Barry Gordon, Barbara Harris and Best Supporting Actor Academy Award-winner Martin Balsam star in this touching film. 117 min.
12-2325 ***$14.99***

Son Of Ali Baba (1952)
Colorful adventure in Baghdad greets Tony Curtis, playing the dashing son of a wealthy former thief who gets wise to a scheme hatched by an evil Caliph to force beautiful kidnapped princess Piper Laurie into duping Curtis out of his riches. With Susan Cabot, Victor Jory and Hugh O'Brian. 85 min.
07-1986 □*$14.99*

Houdini (1953)
Lavish (if not always accurate) biodrama of the legendary magician/escape artist/spiritualist stars Tony Curtis as Harry Houdini and Janet Leigh as his wife (the couple's first film together). Many of Houdini's greatest stunts are re-created by director George Pal. With Torin Thatcher, Angela Clark, Tor Johnson. 107 min.
06-1832 □*$14.99*

The Black Shield Of Falworth (1954)
Exciting medieval adventure saga stars Tony Curtis as the son of a disgraced English earl who trains to become a knight. Along the way Curtis also manages to defeat a conspiracy to dethrone King Henry IV, reclaim his family's honor, and win the hand of fair Janet Leigh. Herbert Marshall, David Farrar and Barbara Rush also star. 99 min.
07-2863 □*$14.99*

Sweet Smell Of Success (1957)
A publicity-hungry New York press agent (Tony Curtis) desperate for success tries to ingratiate himself with a powerful columnist (Burt Lancaster) by breaking up an affair between the writer's sister and a jazz musician. Powerful drama of the high cost of fame, co-scripted by Clifford Odets, also stars Martin Milner, Susan Harrison, Barbara Nichols. 96 min.
12-1785 Was $19.99 *$14.99*

The Perfect Furlough (1958)
As part of a morale-building experiment by Army psychologist Janet Leigh, Arctic-stationed G.I. Tony Curtis wins a three-week trip to Paris and beautiful movie star Linda Cristal as an escort. Things don't go as planned, however, as Leigh and Curtis wind up falling for each other in this breezy romantic comedy directed by Blake Edwards. 94 min.
10-3061 *$14.99*

The Defiant Ones (1958)
One of director Stanley Kramer's most important efforts was this provocative drama with a powerful anti-racist message. Sidney Poitier and Tony Curtis, in Oscar-nominated performances, portray shackled escaped convicts who develop a mutual respect despite the deep-rooted hatred they once felt. Co-stars Lon Chaney, Jr. and Cara Williams. 97 min.
12-1894 Was $19.99 □*$14.99*

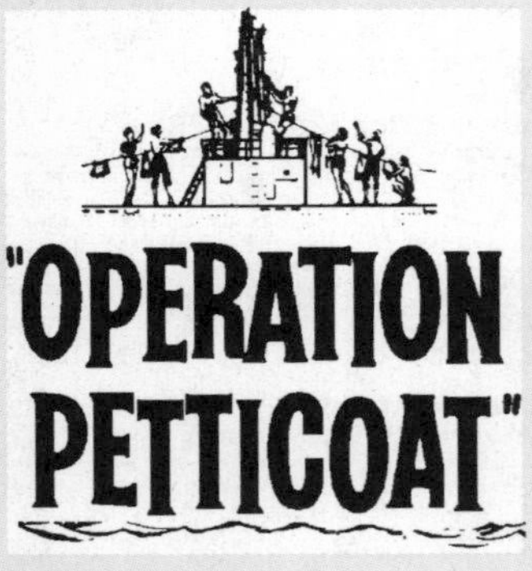

Operation Petticoat (1959)
The crew of a rundown submarine in the WWII Pacific theater rescues a group of stranded Navy nurses, and an undersea battle of the sexes soon follows. Slapstick service comedy stars Cary Grant, Tony Curtis, Joan O'Brien, Dina Merrill. 122 min.
63-1879 Was $19.99 □*$14.99*

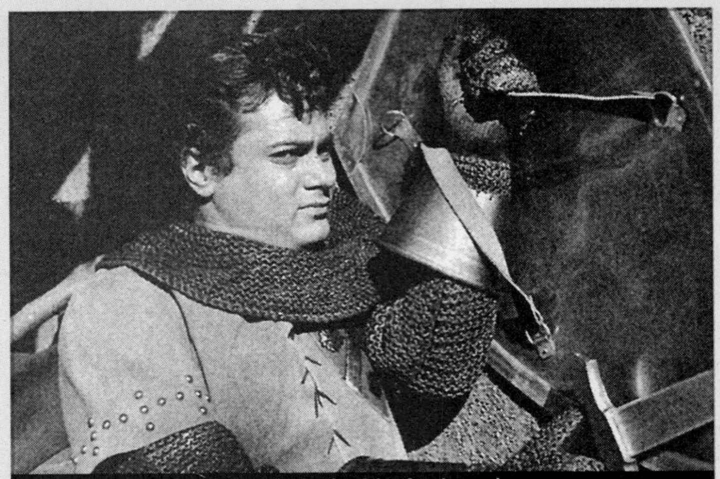
The Black Shield Of Falworth

Tony Curtis

The Great Impostor (1961)
Tony Curtis stars as Ferdinand W. Demara, the colorful hoaxer who pulled off impersonating a school teacher, prison warden, Navy surgeon and Trappist monk, in this amazing true drama. Also stars Edmond O'Brien, Arthur O'Connell. 112 min.
07-1484 Was $59.99 *$14.99*

Taras Bulba (1962)
Yul Brynner is Taras Bulba, feisty Cossack leader and head of a revolt in 16th-century Poland, in this dynamic action saga, based on the Nikolai Gogol novel. Tony Curtis also stars as Brynner's son; with Christine Kaufmann, Sam Wanamaker. 122 min.
12-2912 Letterboxed *$19.99*

40 Pounds Of Trouble (1963)
Winning comedy, based on Damon Runyon's "Little Miss Marker," stars Tony Curtis as a gruff Lake Tahoe nightclub manager saddled with an alimony-seeking ex-wife, a singer in search of a husband, and an indebted friend's mischievous daughter. Highlighted by a whirlwind chase through Disneyland, the film co-stars Suzanne Pleshette, Claire Wilcox, Larry Storch; Norman Jewison's directorial debut. 106 min.
07-2179 □*$14.99*

Goodbye Charlie (1964)
A Hollywood writer and playboy is shot and killed by an angry film producer after being caught with his wife, but gets his chance for revenge—and a lesson in sexism—when he's reincarnated as a beautiful woman. Debbie Reynolds stars as "Charlie," with Tony Curtis as her confused best friend, in this lively filming of George Axelrod's play. With Walter Matthau, Pat Boone.
04-3808 *$14.99*

The Great Race (1965)
"Kitchen sink" comic salute to silent slapstick from Blake Edwards follows a pack of wacky racers, including stalwart hero Tony Curtis, dastardly villain Jack Lemmon, and femme fatale Natalie Wood, on a 22,000-mile road race from New York to Paris in 1908. Peter Falk, Keenan Wynn, Vivian Vance, Larry Storch and Ross Martin also star. Includes original theatrical trailer. 160 min.
19-1308 *$19.99*

Arrivederci, Baby! (1966)
In this darkly humorous farce, Tony Curtis is a suave ladies' man who marries wealthy, beautiful women, then murders them for their inheritance. Filmed in gorgeous locales in England and France, the film also stars Nancy Kwan, Rosanna Schiaffino and Zsa Zsa Gabor. 100 min.
06-2038 □*$12.99*

Not With My Wife, You Don't! (1966)
The stale marriage between Air Force officer Tony Curtis and wife Virna Lisi gets an unexpected twist when George C. Scott, Curtis' old war buddy and Lisi's ex-flame, reappears on the scene in this saucy bedroom farce. With Carroll O'Connor. 118 min.
19-2417 *$19.99*

Don't Make Waves (1967)
Way-out satire on Sixties lifestyles, Southern California-style, with Tony Curtis as a conniving tourist who gets a job selling pools to Malibu hipsters thanks to Claudia Cardinale, a woman who had run his car off the road. Soon, Curtis falls for her and sky-diving Sharon Tate, while trying to stay alive amidst houses sliding towards the ocean. With Robert Webber, Mort Sahl. 96 min.
12-3070 □*$19.99*

Suppose They Gave A War And Nobody Came? (1970)
A dance intended to improve relations between a small Southern town and the Army base located nearby turns into a hilarious showdown between the military and the local militia when sergeant Tony Curtis is arrested in this fun-filled farce. Brian Keith, Tom Ewell, Suzanne Pleshette and Ernest Borgnine co-star. AKA: "War Games." 113 min.
04-1338 Letterboxed *$14.99*

Mission: Monte Carlo (1971)
The dazzling gaming capital is also home to an international business conspiracy, and secret agents Tony Curtis and Roger Moore must play a game where the stakes are life and death. Susan George and Laurence Nesmith are also featured in this featured taken from two episodes of the hit TV series "The Persuaders." 96 min.
04-2143 *$19.99*

Lepke (1975)
Tony Curtis is chilling as Louis "Lepke" Buchalter in this rigorous portrayal of the ruthless gangster's rise from his youth in Manhattan's Lower East Side to his command of "Murder, Inc.," the notorious assassination bureau that served the needs of other underworld figures. Co-stars Anjanette Comer, Michael Callan, Milton Berle. 98 min.
19-1394 Was $19.99 *$14.99*

Some Like It Cool (1979)
Wild sex romp stars Tony Curtis in dual roles: as Casanova, the famed lover who's saddled with sexual problems, and as Casanova's stand-in whose way with the ladies makes him quite popular. Lots of ribald moments and nudity, with the likes of Sylva Koscina, Marisa Berenson and Britt Ekland baring it all. AKA: "Casanova and Co.," "Sex on the Run." 89 min.
27-6716 *$19.99*

Insignificance (1985)
Director Nicolas Roeg's bizarre masterwork depicts four icons of '50s America: thinly veiled, mythic characterizations of Marilyn Monroe (Theresa Russell), Joe DiMaggio (Gary Busey), Joseph McCarthy (Tony Curtis) and Albert Einstein (Michael Emil), coming together in one memorable 24-hour period. 110 min.
40-1137 Was $59.99 *$14.99*

The Last Of Philip Banter (1988)
A self-destructive alcoholic at the end of his rope emerges from a semi-permanent haze and begins to suspect his participation in bizarre and violent events while drunk. Scott Paulin, Irene Miracle and Tony Curtis star in this suspenseful tale. 100 min.
63-1300 *$79.99*

Midnight (1989)
Funny dark comedy stars Lynn Redgrave as a TV horror hostess who has to deal with her greasy boss (Tony Curtis) and an obsessed fan...in a very frightening, very final manner! "Now, this...is dying!" Frank Gorshin, Wolfman Jack co-star. 90 min.
45-5469 *$89.99*

Christmas In Connecticut (1992)
A reworking of the popular 1945 Barbara Stanwyck film, this romantic comedy stars Dyan Cannon as a TV personality who finds her phony lifestyle threatened when she's forced to host a live holiday broadcast with a heroic forest ranger (Kris Kristofferson). Tony Curtis and Richard Roundtree co-star; Arnold Schwarzenegger directs. 93 min.
18-7400 Was $89.99 □*$14.99*

The Mummy Lives (1993)
When treasure-seeking intruders break into an ancient Egyptian crypt, they trigger a curse that sends reincarnated nemesis Tony Curtis out for vengeance (will he say "Yonda lies the pyramid of my fadda, da Pharaoh"?). Greg Wrangler, Leslie Hardy co-star. 97 min.
19-7104 Was $89.99 □*$19.99*

The Immortals (1995)
Eight strangers with a bizarre connection are recruited by a Mafia nightclub owner to recover four suitcases packed with stolen money. As the eight split off into teams and begin their dangerous cross-town search, they realize they're the pawns in a deadly game of double-crosses. Action-filled tale stars Eric Roberts, Tia Carrere, William Forsythe, Chris Rock and Tony Curtis. 92 min.
88-1053 Was $89.99 □*$14.99*

Please see our index for these other Tony Curtis titles: *The Bad News Bears Go To Japan • Boeing Boeing • Captain Newman, M.D. • The Count Of Monte Cristo • Criss Cross • Francis • The Last Tycoon • Little Miss Marker • The Mirror Crack'd • Naked In New York • Sex And The Single Girl • Sextette • Some Like It Hot • Spartacus • Those Daring Young Men In Their Jaunty Jalopies • Trapeze • Winchester '73*

A Jolly Bad Fellow (1964)
Outrageous British farce stars Leo McKern as a brilliant professor who invents an untraceable concoction that drives its victims into hysterical fits of laughter and outrageous behavior before killing them. McKern plans to use the formula for the good of society, but when politics threatens the experiments, he uses it to eliminate his enemies. With Janet Munro. 94 min.
09-5022 *$19.99*

Make Mine A Double (1961)
Two identical Englishmen—a top secret agent and an airman—exchange places during World War II so that new German buzz bombs being tested in France can be investigated...but a mix-up in orders turns the pilot into an inadvertent spy. With Brian Rix, Cecil Parker, William Hartnell. AKA: "The Night We Dropped a Clapper." 86 min.
09-5024 *$19.99*

Never On Sunday (1960)
Classic romantic comedy that blends "Pygmalion" with "Irma La Douce." Melina Mercouri is the earthy prostitute at a Greek resort who is "educated" by an American visitor (director Jules Dassin). 94 min.
12-1450 Was $19.99 *$14.99*

Alice's Restaurant (1969)
You can get anything you want in this classic slice of '60s life, featuring troubadour Arlo Guthrie. The story's about Thanksgiving dinner in a counter-culture Massachusetts church, but there's much more going on: hippie weddings, garbage dumping trials, draft boards, life, death, friendship and music. 111 min.
12-1777 Was $19.99 *$14.99*

The Russians Are Coming, The Russians Are Coming (1966)
An irreverent and wacky "Cold War" comedy about a Russian submarine that strands itself outside a small New England town, throwing people on both sides into a panic. All-star cast includes Alan Arkin, Carl Reiner, Jonathan Winters. 120 min.
12-1866 *$19.99*

The Assassination Bureau (1969)
Lively, off-kilter comedy starring Diana Rigg as a journalist in Victorian England who infiltrates a club comprised of the world's top hit men and killers. She soon turns the club's members against their leader, played by Oliver Reed, who in turn tries to kill them. Telly Savalas, Curt Jurgens also star. 110 min.
06-2039 □*$12.99*

Zotz! (1962)
A mild-mannered college professor finds an ancient coin that can make people move in slow motion, and when enemy spies learn about it a hilarious chase ensues. Tom Poston, Julia Meade, Jim Backus, Margaret Dumont star; directed by horror master William Castle. 87 min.
02-1524 *$59.99*

Wake Me When The War Is Over (1969)
An all-star comedy cast is featured in this Aaron Spelling-Danny Thomas production. Ken Berry is a pilot who falls from his plane and is rescued by a German baroness after World War II. The problem is that Berry thinks the war is still on. With Jim Backus, Eva Gabor, Werner Klemperer and Hans Conried. 73 min.
10-9534 *$14.99*

The Bargee (1964)
British comedy from the creators of "Steptoe and Son" about a freedom-loving playboy who runs his barge up and down the local waterways. When the daughter of a lock-keeper becomes pregnant by him, he faces one of his worst fears...marriage. Harry H. Corbett, Hugh Griffith, Julia Foster star.
09-5009 *$19.99*

Dentist In The Chair (1960)
Wacky British comedy about two goofy dental students who find themselves the guardians of expensive tooth care equipment after they befriend a small-time con. When the cops become suspicious of their actions, they have to figure out a way to get rid of the equipment. Bob Monkhouse, Ronnie Stevens and Peggy Cummins star. 87 min.
08-1754 *$14.99*

The Americanization Of Emily (1964)
WWII-era London is the setting for this sly comedy starring James Garner as a U.S. Navy officer and professed coward whose cushy job as an ambassador's assistant lands him in the arms of war widow Julie Andrews...and possibly on the beaches of Normandy! Co-stars James Coburn, Melvyn Douglas; scripted by Paddy Chayefsky. 115 min.
12-2021 *$19.99*

The Americanization Of Emily (Color Version)
Julie Andrews shows James Garner the true meaning of the "red, white and blue" in this computer-colorized version of the romantic satire.
12-2022 *$19.99*

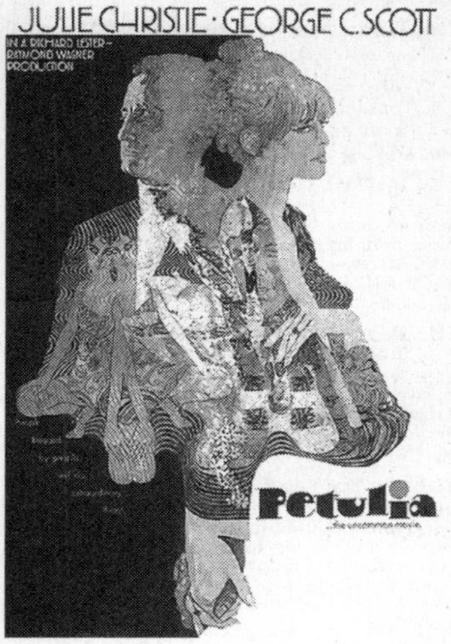
JULIE CHRISTIE · GEORGE C. SCOTT
IN A RICHARD LESTER-RAYMOND WAGNER PRODUCTION
Petulia

Petulia (1968)
Richard Lester's look at mismatched love stars George C. Scott as a divorced San Francisco doctor, Julie Christie as the unhappily married free spirit who sets her sights on him, and Richard Chamberlain as her violent husband. With appearances by The Grateful Dead and Big Brother and the Holding Company. 105 min.
19-1627 Was $19.99 ***$14.99***

Tom Jones (1963)
Director Tony Richardson and scripter John Osborne's sprawling, bawdy romp through 18th-century England earned four Academy Awards, including Best Picture. Albert Finney stars as the titular hero, a shy country boy whose beguiling manner gets him into one hilarious romantic misadventure after another; based on the novel by Henry Fielding. With Susannah York, Hugh Griffith, David Warner, and Edith Evans. 122 min.
44-1852 Letterboxed ***$14.99***

The Bawdy Adventures Of Tom Jones (1976)
English literature's most beloved scamp returns in ribald form in this irreverent farce, trying to outrun over-affectionate ladies in search of the woman of his dreams. Stars Joan Collins, Terry-Thomas and Nicky Henson. 89 min.
07-1488 ***$59.99***

Tom Jones (1997)
Henry Fielding's racy classic of an amiable country bumpkin who makes his way through the bedrooms of 18th-century England as he tries to win the hand of his true love becomes a rollickingly ribald mini-series. Max Beesley stars as Tom; with Samantha Morton, Brian Blessed. 300 min. on six tapes.
53-9987 Was $99.99 ***❑$39.99***

The Tiger And The Pussycat (1967)
Vittorio Gassman is a successful, middle-aged businessman whose contentment ends when he meets luscious young Ann-Margret—and finds out just how spicy a Swedish meatball can be in this sex farce. 110 min.
53-1544 Was $19.99 ***$14.99***

Inspector Clouseau (1968)
Alan Arkin took over for Peter Sellers as the maladroit manhunter from France in this slapstick caper comedy, as Couseau visits England to help Scotland Yard break up a robbery ring...that is, if he doesn't break up England first. With Delia Boccardo, Frank Finlay, Beryl Reid. 98 min.
12-3027 ***❑$19.99***

Son Of The Pink Panther (1993)
Italian comic Roberto Benigni carries on Peter Sellers' legacy, playing the bumbling son of Inspector Clouseau in this funny farce from Blake Edwards. The new Inspector tries to track down a missing Middle Eastern princess and finds himself face to face with Dad's former associates, Cato (Burt Kwouk) and Commissioner Dreyfuss (Herbert Lom). With Robert Davi, Claudia Cardinale. 115 min.
12-2874 Was $89.99 ***❑$14.99***

The Impossible Years (1968)
Hilarious '60s-flavored screwball comedy starring David Niven as a psychiatrist specializing in ironing out differences between parents and teens. Trouble is, his own daughter is arrested for a campus protest, her new friends like loud, groovy music, she poses nude for a portrait, and she gets hitched while on vacation. Lola Albright, Chad Everett, Ozzie Nelson and Christina Ferrare also star. 92 min.
12-2839 ***$19.99***

The Knack... And How To Get It (1965)
Swinging London in the 1960s is the setting for Richard Lester's stylized farce involving a hip young Romeo who tries to teach his schoolteacher landlord the secrets of popularity with the opposite sex. Their meeting with a beautiful young woman leads to romance, obsession and surprises. Michael Crawford, Ray Brooks and Rita Tushingham star. 84 min.
12-2855 Letterboxed ***$14.99***

Lord Love A Duck (1966)
Scathing social satire stars Roddy McDowall as a brilliant high schooler who helps sexy classmate Tuesday Weld get whatever she wants. Among the wishes he "grants" her are high grades, a starring role in a beach party movie, a marriage to a handsome college man—and said husband's eventual murder. Lola Albright, Martin West and Ruth Gordon co-star in this unique gem. 105 min.
12-3001 Was $19.99 ***❑$14.99***

The Biggest Bundle Of Them All (1968)
Funny heist film starring Raquel Welch and Robert Wagner as amateur crooks who kidnap mobster Vittorio de Sica while he's at a funeral in Naples. After they learn he's broke and nobody will pay his ransom, they decide to join him in robbing a train carrying $5 million in gold ingots. With Godfrey Cambridge, Davey Kaye and Edward G. Robinson. 108 min.
12-3074 ***❑$19.99***

Adorable Julia (1964)
Romantic backstage comedy with Charles Boyer and Lilli Palmer as a husband-wife acting team trying to juggle career, marriage and extra-marital affairs. Jean Sorel co-stars; based on a Somerset Maugham play. 97 min.
17-9000 Was $19.99 ***$14.99***

How Sweet It Is! (1968)
James Garner and Debbie Reynolds star as an American couple who fly off on holiday to Europe to chaperone their teenage son and put their love to the test when she attracts the attention of a French playboy and he that of a pretty tour guide. Co-stars Maurice Ronet, Terry-Thomas and Paul Lynde; look for Erin Moran and Penny Marshall, future stars for co-producer/co-writer Garry Marshall. 98 min.
19-1670 Was $59.99 ***$19.99***

The League Of Gentlemen (1961)
Sparkling heist film about a former British Army officer who organizes a group of his friends to pull off a £1,000,000 robbery by using their military expertise. Humorous, tension-filled tale stars Jack Hawkins, Nigel Patrick, Roger Livesey and Richard Attenborough; keep your eyes open for Oliver Reed (as a ballet dancer!). 115 min.
22-5461 Was $39.99 ***$19.99***

The Phony American (1961)
Offbeat comedy-drama about a German WWII orphan adopted by an American pilot who is killed during the Korean War. When the boy grows up, he attempts to join the U.S. Air Force with the aid of false documents, a stolen uniform and a kind sergeant. William Bendix, Christine Kaufmann, Michael Hinz star. 74 min.
53-6090 ***$29.99***

The Mouse On The Moon (1963)
The postage stamp-sized nation of Grand Fenwick decides to enter the space race, with some help from a wine that serves as rocket fuel, in this funny follow-up to "The Mouse That Roared." Margaret Rutherford stars as the Grand Duchess and Ron Moody is the prime minister; with Terry-Thomas, Bernard Cribbins. 85 min.
12-3335 ***❑$14.99***

The Brass Bottle (1964)
Architect Tony Randall is in for a shock when the antique bottle he buys turns out to contain genie Burl Ives, whose attempts to make his new master's life easier erupt into comical chaos. Fun-filled fantasy also stars future TV genie Barbara Eden as Randall's girlfriend. 90 min.
07-2626 ***❑$14.99***

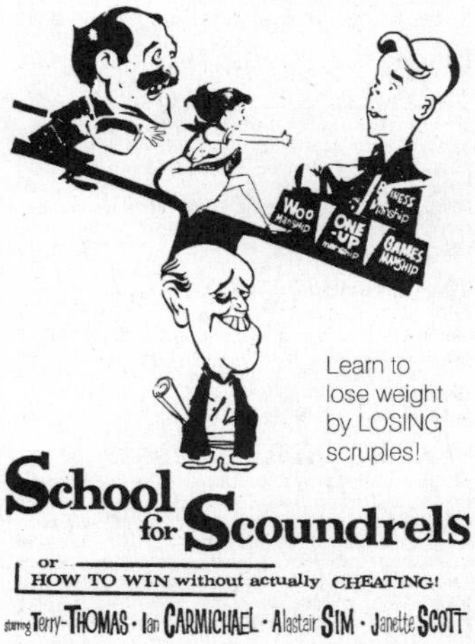
Learn to lose weight by LOSING scruples!
School for Scoundrels
or HOW TO WIN without actually CHEATING!
starring Terry-THOMAS · Ian CARMICHAEL · Alastair SIM · Janette SCOTT

School For Scoundrels (1960)
Deftly funny British satire starring Ian Carmichael as a milquetoast who reaches his limit when snooty rival Terry-Thomas makes off with his girl. He enrolls at the College of Lifemanship, where headmaster Alastair Sim and the faculty teach Carmichael the knack of coming out ahead in any sort of situation, and then returns to seek his revenge. With Janette Scott, Dennis Price. 94 min.
10-9264 Was $19.99 ***$14.99***

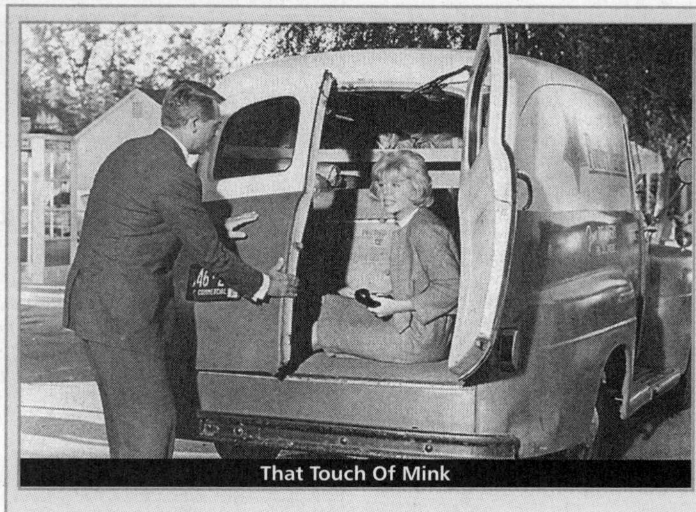
That Touch Of Mink

Doris Day

Julie (1956)
Widowed airline stewardess Doris Day thinks she's found happiness after marrying concert pianist Louis Jourdan. But could the obsessively jealous Jourdan have been her first husband's killer, and will Day be his next target? Fast-paced thriller, with an amazing climax on board a pilotless airplane, also stars Barry Sullivan, Frank Lovejoy. 97 min.
12-3030 ***❑$19.99***

The Tunnel Of Love (1958)
This sparkling romantic comedy teams Doris Day and Richard Widmark as a married couple whose experiences adopting a child result in a series of hilarious episodes. Gig Young, Gia Scala, Elizabeth Wilson and Doodles Weaver star. 98 min.
12-2565 ***$19.99***

Pillow Talk (1959)
Movies Unlimited proudly presents this Doris Day classic. She's an interior decorator who shares a party line with playboy Rock Hudson. Romance ensues with a variety of unpredictable situations thrown in for good measure. Tony Randall, Thelma Ritter. 102 min.
07-1174 Was $19.99 ***$14.99***

Midnight Lace (1960)
A chilling spine-tingler that features Doris Day in the unlikely role of a newlywed harassed by threatening phone calls and plagued by so-called "accidents." Rex Harrison co-stars as her skeptical husband; with John Gavin, Roddy McDowall and Myrna Loy. 108 min.
07-1508 Was $59.99 ***$14.99***

Please Don't Eat The Daisies (1960)
Pleasant comedy stars David Niven and Doris Day as the drama critic and his wife who pack up their brood and move from New York City to a dilapidated old house in the country, only to find old and new problems awaiting them. Janis Paige, Patsy Kelly, Richard Haydn co-star. 111 min.
12-2176 Was $19.99 ***❑$14.99***

Lover Come Back (1961)
Rock Hudson and Doris Day star in this sparkling romantic romp as rival Madison Avenue executives whose feud leads Hudson to create a campaign for a non-existent product, and Day to try to win the "account" away from him. With Tony Randall, Edie Adams, Jack Kruschen. 107 min.
10-3065 ***$14.99***

That Touch Of Mink (1962)
Doris Day and Cary Grant star in this romantic comedy that's an all-time favorite. She's an unemployed young lady; he's a rich, suave bachelor who sees her as another conquest. Gig Young, John Astin, Audrey Meadows. 99 min.
63-1049 ***$19.99***

That Touch Of Mink (Letterboxed Version)
Also available in a theatrical, widescreen format.
63-1555 ***❑$14.99***

The Thrill Of It All (1963)
The quiet domestic life of Doris Day and James Garner is turned upside-down when she becomes a TV spokesperson for a detergent company in this frothy comedy that pokes fun at Madison Avenue, Suburbia and TV, courtesy of scripter Carl Reiner. With Edward Andrews, Arlene Francis, ZaSu Pitts. 108 min.
07-1551 Was $59.99 ***$14.99***

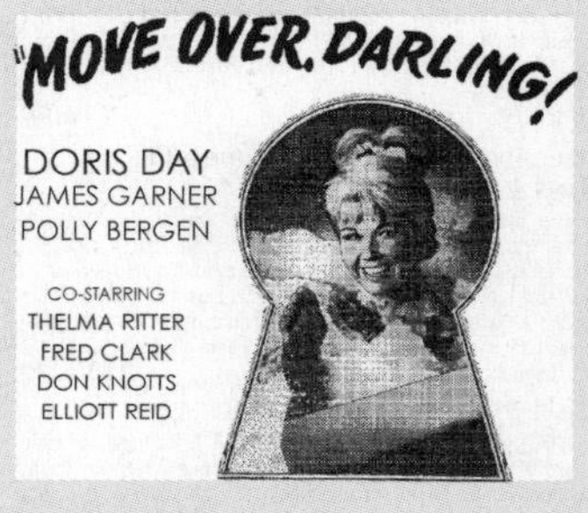
"MOVE OVER, DARLING!"
DORIS DAY
JAMES GARNER
POLLY BERGEN
CO-STARRING
THELMA RITTER
FRED CLARK
DON KNOTTS
ELLIOTT REID

Move Over, Darling (1963)
Originally planned as the Marilyn Monroe vehicle "Something's Got to Give," this remake of 1938's "My Favorite Wife" was revamped for Doris Day. Returning home after being stranded on a remote island for five years, Day is shocked to discover that husband James Garner has remarried. Things get stickier when Garner learns that Doris wasn't on the island alone. With Polly Bergen, Chuck Connors, Don Knotts, Thelma Ritter.
04-3806 ***$14.99***

Send Me No Flowers (1964)
One of the finest Doris Day-Rock Hudson pairings casts Rock as a hypochondriac so sure of impending death that he's trying to fix Doris up with a new love interest. Tony Randall, Paul Lynde, Clint Walker co-star. 100 min.
07-1517 Was $59.99 ***$14.99***

The Glass Bottom Boat (1966)
Comedy mixes with romance in this wacky spy spoof as public relations specialist Doris Day finds that her job in a space lab leads her into a world of zany espionage proceedings and a relationship with boss Rod Taylor. John McGiver, Paul Lynde, Dom DeLuise and Arthur Godfrey also star. 110 min.
12-2319 ***$19.99***

Where Were You When The Lights Were Out? (1968)
After she discovers her husband getting a little too cozy with a secretary during the famous 1965 New York power failure, actress Doris Day decides to relax at her Connecticut home. But things are anything but quiet when she's joined by scheming executive Robert Morse, and, later, inquisitive Patrick O'Neal. With Lola Albright, Terry-Thomas, Steve Allen and Pat Paulsen. 94 min.
12-2569 ***$19.99***

The Rock Hudson/ Doris Day Collection
"Lover Come Back," "Pillow Talk" and "Send Me No Flowers" are all in this deluxe boxed tribute to one of Hollywood's favorite comedic couples.
07-2408 Save $5.00! ***$39.99***

Please see our index for these other Doris Day titles: *April In Paris • Billy Rose's Jumbo • By The Light Of The Silvery Moon • Calamity Jane • Love Me Or Leave Me • Lullaby Of Broadway • The Man Who Knew Too Much • My Dream Is Yours • On Moonlight Bay • Tea For Two • Teacher's Pet • The Winning Team • Young At Heart • Young Man With A Horn*

McHale's Navy (1964)
Conniving commander Quinton McHale (Ernest Borgnine) and the men of the PT 73 made the jump from small screen to big screen with this feature-length laughfest that finds them involved in a horse racing scheme to save a South Pacific orphanage. Tim Conway, Joe Flynn, Carl Ballantine, Claudine Longet also star. 93 min.
07-2605 *$14.99*

McHale's Navy Joins The Air Force (1965)
There's actually no McHale in this, the second film based on the popular WWII sitcom, so Tim Conway's bumbling Ensign Parker takes center stage, as a case of mistaken identity puts him in the cockpit as a would-be ace pilot. Joe Flynn, Bob Hastings, Ted Bessell co-star. 91 min.
07-2606 *$14.99*

McHale's Navy (1997)
Tom Arnold takes the reins of command from Ernest Borgnine in this big-screen updating of the popular '60s service sitcom. Now living in retirement in the Caribbean, Arnold and the hapless crew of the PT 73 are called back into action to defeat international terrorist Tim Curry. David Alan Grier, Dean Stockwell co-star. 109 min.
07-2539 Was $99.99 *$14.99*

The Trouble With Angels (1966)
Hayley Mills and June Harding are two restless, mischief-making students at a convent school in Pennsylvania who run mother superior Rosalind Russell ragged with their crazed exploits. Co-stars Binnie Barnes, Mary Wickes and Gypsy Rose Lee; directed by Ida Lupino. 112 min.
02-1201 Was $59.99 *$14.99*

Where Angels Go... Trouble Follows (1968)
Tradition-minded mother superior Rosalind Russell has her hands full once again, thanks to the unconventional teaching methods of sister Stella Stevens, in this fun-filled sequel to "The Trouble with Angels." With Binnie Barnes, Susan Saint James, Dolores Sutton. 95 min.
02-2470 *$14.99*

The Amorous Adventures Of Moll Flanders (1965)
In the tradition of "Tom Jones" comes this bawdy romp starring Kim Novak as an 18th-century woman who falls in and out of love, beds and marriages until she inherits a fortune from a rich banker and settles with a young highwayman. Richard Johnson, Angela Lansbury and George Sanders co-star. 126 min.
06-1941 *$14.99*

Moll Flanders (1996)
Alex Kingston is both beautiful and feisty as the title heroine in this acclaimed "Masterpiece Theatre" production of the Defoe story. Social satire, bawdy humor and heartfelt drama are blended to tell the tale of young Moll's life of poverty, degradation and eventual redemption. Daniel Craig, Diana Rigg co-star. 210 min. on two tapes.
08-8530 *$29.99*

Moll Flanders (1996)
Rollicking filmization of Daniel Defoe's classic novel showcases Robin Wright as the strong-willed sprite in 18th-century England who goes from prostitute to lover of a tortured painter to social-conscious sweetheart with help from thieving friend Morgan Freeman. Stockard Channing, John Lynch and Brenda Fricker also star. 123 min.
12-3104 Was $19.99 *$14.99*

Divorce American Style (1967)
After 17 years, Dick Van Dyke and Debbie Reynolds decide that their marriage is kaput and, after seeing a counselor, split up. While juggling alimony demands and visits with his kids, Van Dyke befriends Jason Robards, a divorcé who'd love to see him marry ex-wife Jean Simmons. Lee Grant, Martin Gabel co-star; Norman Lear wrote the screenplay. 103 min.
02-2846 *$19.99*

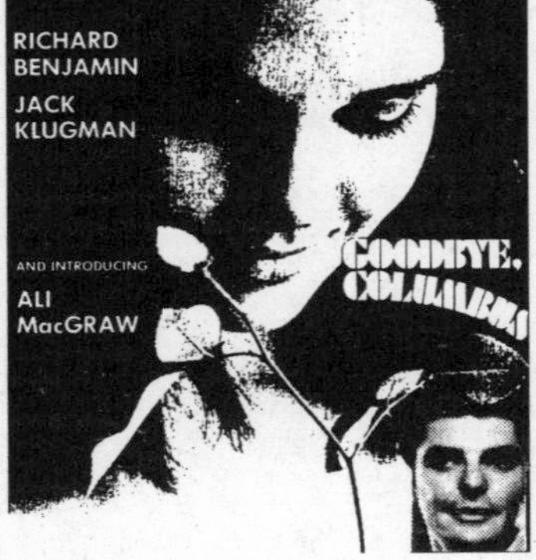

Goodbye, Columbus (1969)
Richard Benjamin is a poor Bronx librarian and Ali McGraw a spoiled Jewish American Princess who fall in love despite their parents' objections. Based on Philip Roth's novella, the film co-stars Jack Klugman, Michael Meyers; look for Jaclyn Smith. 105 min.
06-1090 Was $49.99 *$14.99*

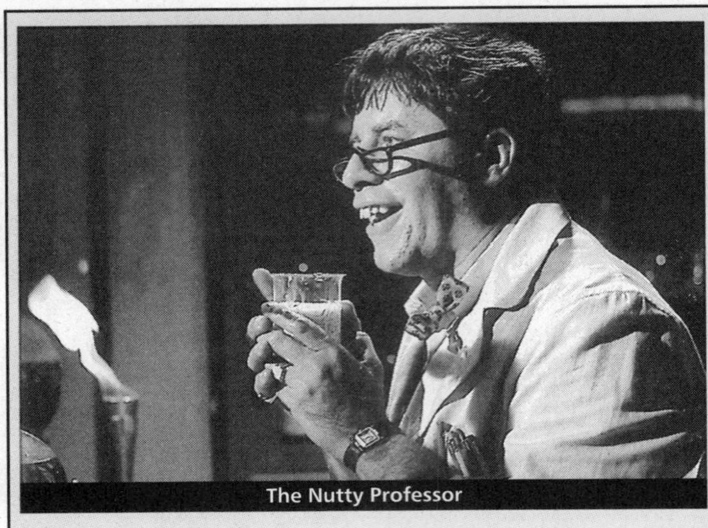

The Nutty Professor

Jerry Lewis

My Friend Irma (1949)
Based on the then-popular radio show, this comedy has since become noteworthy for being the screen debut of Dean Martin and Jerry Lewis. The duo are would-be stage stars who befriend Marie Wilson as the scatterbrained Irma and Diana Lynn as her more sensible roommate, Jane. With John Lund, Hans Conried. 102 min.
06-1995 Was $19.99 *$14.99*

At War With The Army (1950)
Dean Martin and Jerry Lewis' first starring vehicle boosted them to instant fame. Jerry is a not-cut-out-for-the-army private who helps womanizing sergeant Dean Martin iron out some of the wrinkles in his love life. 72 min.
09-1961 *$19.99*

Jumping Jacks (1952)
It's "Geromino!" for Dean and Jerry when the pair play entertainers touring Army bases who wind up as recruits for the paratroop squad. High-flying comedy also stars Don DeFore, Mona Freeman. 96 min.
06-1996 Was $19.99 *$14.99*

The Stooge (1952)
Comic farce with some surprising dramatic and autobiographical moments starring Dean Martin as an accordion-playing vaudevillian who decides to go solo without help from zany, put-upon second banana Jerry Lewis. After Dean has a tough time on the solo route, he tries to reunite with his former pal. Polly Bergen, Eddie Mayehoff also star. 100 min.
06-2208 *$14.99*

The Caddy (1953)
Martin and Lewis break par for laughs in this zany tale of hi-jinx on the golf links, with caddy Jerry trying to help duffer Dean win at Pebble Beach. Donna Reed supplies the romance, there's cameos by Ben Hogan, Sam Snead and other golfers, and Dino sings "That's Amoré." 95 min.
06-1565 *$14.99*

Scared Stiff (1953)
Bob Hope's fright-comedy "The Ghost Breakers" was retooled to fit the talents of Martin and Lewis, and the result was one of Dean and Jerry's funniest films. A haunted castle is the setting for some spooky goings-on, not the least of which is Jerry's impersonation of co-star Carmen Miranda! With Lizabeth Scott, Dorothy Malone, and some surprise guests. 108 min.
06-1997 Was $19.99 *$14.99*

Artists And Models (1955)
Struggling comic book artist Dean Martin begins basing his scripts on the wild dreams of roommate Jerry Lewis and becomes a big success, but the duo winds up getting involved with beautiful models and secret agents. With Shirley MacLaine, Dorothy Malone, Anita Ekberg, Eva Gabor. 108 min.
06-1856 *$14.99*

Pardners (1956)
Lively Martin-Lewis outing with Jerry as a wealthy New York millionaire who teams with ranch foreman Dean to fight a group of ornery cowpokes starting trouble in a Western town. Lots of slapstick, shooting and songs. With Lori Nelson, Jeff Morrow, Agnes Moorehead and Milton Frome. 88 min.
06-2207 *$14.99*

Hollywood Or Bust (1956)
Movie-struck Jerry Lewis travels cross country to get into show business and meet idol Anita Ekberg, picking up hitchhiker Dean Martin along the way. Their hazardous, laugh-filled trek makes for classic comedy in the duo's last film together. 95 min.
06-1445 *$14.99*

The Delicate Delinquent (1957)
In his first solo outing, Jerry Lewis plays a nerdy janitor who gets caught in the middle of a gang rumble and is arrested. Policeman Darren McGavin helps reform the "delinquent" Lewis, who soon becomes a cop. A mirthful mix of silliness and sentiment; with Martha Hyer, Rocky Marciano. 100 min.
06-1736 *$14.99*

The Geisha Boy (1958)
One of Jerry Lewis' funniest romps has him as a third-rate magician on a USO tour of the Orient, where he falls for a Japanese widow, befriends her young son and gets into all sorts of hilarious situations. Sessue Hayakawa, Marie McDonald, Suzanne Pleshette and the L.A. Dodgers co-star, and there's lots of great jokes provided by writer/director Frank Tashlin. 98 min.
06-1907 Was $19.99 *$14.99*

Rock-A-Bye Baby (1958)
Jerry Lewis is a TV repairman smitten with actress Marilyn Maxwell, who has married a Mexican bullfighter. After the matador dies suddenly, a pregnant Maxwell needs someone to look after her child before word leaks out and ruins her image, and Lewis is tapped to serve as "nanny." Things get complicated, though, when she gives birth to triplets! Director Frank Tashlin's take on "The Miracle of Morgan's Creek" also stars Connie Stevens, Salvatore Baccaloni and Reginald Gardiner.
06-3005 *$14.99*

Cinderfella (1960)
The fairy tale classic is given a new look when Jerry Lewis, as put-upon Fella, gets some help from fairy godfather Ed Wynn and meets princess Anna Maria Alberghetti. Will Jerry get to live happily ever after? 85 min.
27-6266 Was $59.99 *$14.99*

The Ladies' Man (1961)
Jerry Lewis is at his zany best playing a woman-hating houseboy at a Hollywood home for wayward girls. Strangely enough, women fawn all over him! Helen Traubel, George Raft and Harry James and His Orchestra (performing "Bang Tail") are also featured in this wacky outing. 106 min.
06-1744 *$14.99*

The Errand Boy (1961)
Le Grand Goofee, Jerry Lewis, is a film studio gopher who turns Tinseltown upside-down with one hilarious misadventure after another. With Brian Donlevy, Fritz Feld, Iris Adrian, and a cameo by the "Bonanza" cast. 95 min.
27-6154 Was $59.99 *$14.99*

The Nutty Professor (1963)
Considered by many to be his best film, writer/director/star Jerry Lewis' slapstick spin on the Jekyll/Hyde story finds him, as nerdy college professor Julius Kelp, inventing a mysterious potion that turns him into hip, conceited stud Buddy Love (whose persona, some say, was based on Dean Martin). Stella Stevens plays his love interest, Miss Purdy. "Vive le Jerry Lewis"—*Paris Times*. 107 min.
06-1203 *$14.99*

Who's Minding The Store? (1963)
Dog walker Jerry Lewis is given a job at a department store owned by the disapproving mother of girlfriend Jill St. John. The always-klutzy Jerry tries his best to finish the tasks he's given by manager Ray Walston and manages to win over St. John's dad, but how about her tough-as-nails mother? Agnes Moorehead, John McGiver also star; Frank Tashlin directs.
06-3006 *$14.99*

The Disorderly Orderly (1964)
The diagnosis is bellylaugh after bellylaugh when Jerry Lewis, as an attendant who experiences "sympathy pains," turns a quiet nursing home upside down. Hilarious hospital hi-jinx with Susan Oliver, Jack E. Leonard. 90 min.
06-1444 *$14.99*

The Patsy (1964)
An inept hotel bellhop is groomed for stardom by a late comedian's management and writing team in this madcap Jerry Lewis feature. Peter Lorre (his last film), Keenan Wynn, Everett Sloane and Ina Balin co-star. 106 min.
27-6156 Was $59.99 *$12.99*

The Family Jewels (1965)
If one Jerry Lewis isn't enough for you, how about seven Jerrys! In this heartwarming comedy he's all six wacky uncles to a 9-year-old heiress who must choose a guardian, as well as the girl's faithful chauffeur. With Sebastian Cabot. 100 min.
06-1566 Was $19.99 *$14.99*

Boeing Boeing (1965)
Jet-setting bedroom farce stars Tony Curtis as a swinging bachelor who juggles three stewardess girlfriends from different airlines, much to the envy of pal Jerry Lewis. The arrangement works perfectly, until schedule changes lead to hilarious complications. With Thelma Ritter, Suzanna Leigh. 102 min.
06-2057 *$14.99*

The Big Mouth (1967)
While on a fishing vacation, angler Jerry Lewis reels in a dying frogman who gives him a map that may provide the location to a fortune in stolen diamonds. When some crooks come looking for the map, a zany chase gets underway that finds Lewis playing one wacky character after another. With Harold J. Stone, Susan Bay, the great Charlie Callas and a cameo by Colonel Sanders. 107 min.
02-1854 Was $69.99 *$19.99*

Don't Raise The Bridge, Lower The River (1968)
Jerry Lewis is in the get-rich-quick business, turning the ancestral home of his English wife into a discotheque and selling the Arabs stolen plans for a new electronic oil drill. With Terry-Thomas. 99 min.
02-1035 Was $59.99 *$19.99*

Which Way To The Front? (1970)
Jerry Lewis is a rich playboy rejected by the Army in WWII. Undaunted, he enlists a gang of other "4-Fs" to form their own commando unit in this wacky war comedy. With Jan Murray, Paul Winchell, Kaye Ballard. 96 min.
19-1439 *$19.99*

Hardly Working (1980)
Jerry Lewis is a fired circus clown who stumbles from one job to another, mucking them up as only Jerry could. Classic comedy from the man about whom *Paris Match* said "Ooo La La!" Susan Oliver, Roger C. Carmel co-star. 91 min.
04-3038 *$59.99*

Cracking Up (1983)
The master of maniacal mirth, Jerry Lewis, plays a hapless sad sack recounting to his psychiatrist how he gets bounced from one job to another...with riotous results. Herb Edelman, Sammy Davis, Jr., Milton Berle co-star. AKA: "Smorgasbord." 87 min.
19-1302 Was $69.99 *$19.99*

FUNNY BONES

Funny Bones (1995)
Off-the-wall tragi-comedy about a famous comedian's son who bombs in his Vegas debut and returns to the English seaside town where he grew up to buy material from local performers. Once there, he learns some surprising facts about his father's work as well as a family secret. Oliver Platt, Jerry Lewis, Leslie Caron and Lee Evans star; directed by Peter Chelsom ("Hear My Song"). 128 min.
11-1935 *$14.99*

Dean Martin And Jerry Lewis Television Party For Muscular Dystrophy (1954)
Before the Telethon, Dean Martin and Jerry Lewis appeared in this special benefit program, singing, mugging and joking with special guest stars. Early TV rarity. 105 min.
01-1157 *$19.99*

Young Jerry Lewis
Hey, ladies...and gentlemen! This tribute to France's favorite comic genius includes rare clips, film footage and segments of Jerry's TV work. You'll also see scenes featuring the classic Martin-Lewis team and lots more. 60 min.
05-5101 *$14.99*

Martin & Lewis Gift Set
Three of the comedy duo's funniest features are here in a money-saving boxed set. "My Friend Irma," "Jumping Jacks" and "Scared Stiff" are included.
06-2013 *$44.99*

Please see our index for these other Jerry Lewis titles: *Arizona Dream* • *Cookie* • *The King Of Comedy*

If It's Tuesday, This Must Be Belgium (1969)
A group of American travellers encounter a number of hilarious and romantic adventures on a bus tour through Europe. The all-star cast includes Suzanne Pleshette, Ian McShane, Peggy Cass, Norman Fell, Joan Collins, Sandy Baron, John Cassavetes, Ben Gazzara and others. 99 min.
12-2563 Was $19.99 🗨***$14.99***

Billie (1965)
Fun family comedy starring Patty Duke as a high school track star who creates a furor when she tries out for the men's team and leaves the male athletes eating her dust. Jim Backus, Jane Greer, Billy DeWolfe, Warren Berlinger also star. 86 min.
12-2275 ***$19.99***

Our Man Flint (1966)
One of Hollywood's first and best "007" spoofs stars James Coburn as ace American agent Derek Flint of Z.O.W.I.E., out to foil a plot to control the world's weather. Lots of action, laughs, gorgeous women and a cigarette lighter with 83 secret weapons; Lee J. Cobb, Edward Mulhare co-star. 107 min.
04-2274 ***$19.99***

In Like Flint (1967)
Super-suave spy James Coburn returns, this time stopping the takeover of an armed space station by an all-girl criminal organization. Second entry in the James Bond send-up series also stars Lee J. Cobb, Andrew Duggan. 114 min.
04-2275 ***$19.99***

The Flim-Flam Man (1967)
George C. Scott is a wily con artist touring the South, but finds that the eager young apprentice he's taken on (Michael Sarrazin) may be a little too honest for him. Fast-paced comedy that predates "The Sting"; directed by Irvin Kershner. 115 min.
04-3008 Was $59.99 🗨***$29.99***

Dear Heart (1964)
Small-town postmistress Geraldine Page, in New York for a post office convention, meets and falls for greeting card salesman Glenn Ford, who is attracted to her although he's engaged to widow Angela Lansbury, in this whimsical romantic comedy. 114 min.
19-2415 ***$19.99***

The Fat Spy (1966)
A camp classic featuring an incredible cast, this spoof details the efforts of a group of people searching for the Fountain of Youth in Florida, uncovering young rock stars and the buxom Jayne Mansfield instead. Jack E. Leonard, Phyllis Diller, Brian Donlevy and The Wild Ones star. 75 min.
17-9050 ***$19.99***

Hot Millions (1968)
Crafty caper comedy starring Peter Ustinov as an embezzler who dupes a computer wizard into leaving the country so he can assume his identity. Soon, Ustinov gets a job at a corporation and uses a computer to issue huge checks to phony companies around the world. Can Ustinov keep one step ahead of boss Karl Malden, who may be on to his scheme? With Maggie Smith, Bob Newhart. 105 min.
12-2842 ***$19.99***

Boys' Night Out (1962)
Writing her thesis on the American male, sociology student Kim Novak decides to pose as a call girl in hopes of dissecting the other sex's psyche. She's soon visited by four men hoping to hook into the swinging suburban scene, but instead of them finding love, they turn to Kim to hear their romantic woes. With James Garner, Tony Randall, Howard Duff and Howard Morris. 115 min.
12-2838 ***$19.99***

The Comic (1969)
Carl Reiner's heartfelt tribute to the silent film laughmakers stars Dick Van Dyke as Billy Bright, a talented but self-centered comedian whose meteoric rise to fame in the '20s is matched by his decline with the advent of "talkies." Co-stars Michele Lee and Mickey Rooney. 96 min.
02-1564 Was $59.99 ***$19.99***

What Did You Do In The War, Daddy? (1966)
A riotous war satire from Blake Edwards about an American troop led by Lt. James Coburn and Capt. Dick Shawn who attempt to overtake an Italian town during World War II and find its inhabitants willing to surrender—if the Americans can wait for the soccer game and wine festival to finish. Aldo Ray, Harry Morgan and Carroll O'Connor also star. 119 min.
12-2681 ***$14.99***

Gidget (1960)
Favorite teen surf comedy stars Sandra Dee as the young beach bunny who must choose between surfer boyfriends Cliff Robertson and James Darren. Arthur O'Connell, Doug McClure and Yvonne Craig co-star. 95 min.
10-2611 ***$14.99***

Gidget Goes Hawaiian (1961)
In the second "Gidget" film, everyone's favorite surfin' girl heads to Waikiki and finds fun and romance. Deborah Walley, James Darren, Michael Callan and Peggy Cass star. 102 min.
02-1458 Was $59.99 ***$14.99***

Gidget Goes To Rome (1963)
The bubbly blonde prima donna of the ocean waves (Cindy Carol) takes the Eternal City by storm in this fluffy romantic misadventure. Moondoggie's got competition from a suave Italian charmer. James Darren, Cesare Danova co-star. 104 min.
02-1653 Was $69.99 ***$14.99***

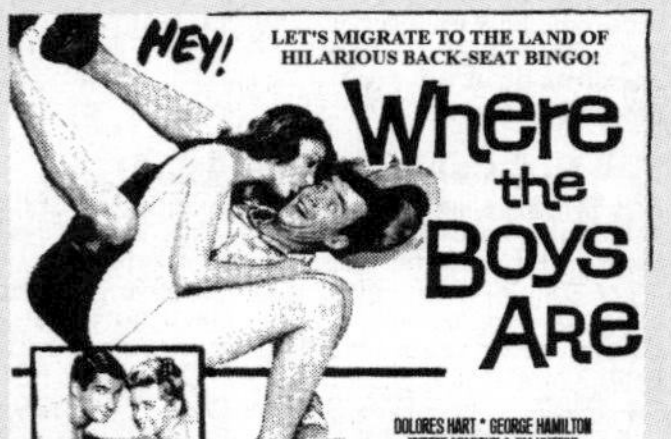

Where The Boys Are (1960)
The original fun-in-the-sun romp, as four young gals head to pleasurable Fort Lauderdale during Easter vacation for tans, music and boys. Connie Francis, Paula Prentiss, Yvette Mimieux, Dolores Hart, Jim Hutton and George Hamilton star. 99 min.
12-1339 ***$19.99***

Beach Party (1963)
The first entry in AIP's beach comedy series stars Bob Cummings as an anthropologist studying teenage mating habits who picks Frankie Avalon and Annette Funicello as his subjects. With Morey Amsterdam, Dorothy Malone, Dick Dale and The Del-Tones, and Harvey Lembeck as Eric Von Zipper. 98 min.
19-1425 Was $19.99 ***$14.99***

Pajama Party (1964)
Whacked-out AIP entry finds Martian Tommy Kirk landing on Earth to scope it out for a future invasion and finding romance with curvaceous Annette Funicello, much to the dismay of boyfriend Jody McCrea. Mix in Harvey Lembeck's Eric Von Zipper, a couple of crooks, Buster Keaton as Chief Rotten Eagle, Dorothy Lamour, and a pajama party thrown by Annette's aunt Elsa Lanchester, and you have a beach party classic minus the sand.
40-5001 ***$14.99***

Muscle Beach Party (1964)
Surf's up! Frankie and Annette sure have their hands full in this one, what with gym owner Don Rickles and his musclemen trying to take over the beach, lovesick heiress Luciana Paluzzi trying to snare Frankie, and Little Stevie Wonder stopping by to perform "Happy Street." With Morey Amsterdam, Buddy Hackett. 94 min.
44-1464 Was $19.99 ***$14.99***

Bikini Beach (1964)
When a wealthy newspaperman wants to turn the local beach into a senior citizen's home, everyone's at arms. What's Annette gonna do—not just about this situation, but about choosing between a British pop star and her jealous boyfriend (Frankie Avalon in two parts)? Don Rickles, Little Stevie Wonder, The Pyramids, Harvey Lembeck and Keenan Wynn star. 100 min.
53-1072 ***$14.99***

How To Stuff A Wild Bikini (1965)
Fearful that buddy Dwayne Hickman will hit on Annette Funicello while he's on Naval Reserve duty, Frankie Avalon gets witch doctor Buster Keaton to send a magical bikini (stuffed with beautiful Beverly Adams) to woo away Hickman. And that's just the start of the hi-jinks in this bouncy beach comedy that also stars Mickey Rooney, The Kingsmen ("Louie Louie"), and Harvey Lembeck; look for Brian Wilson as a (what else?) "beach boy."
19-1266 Was $19.99 ***$14.99***

Beach Blanket Bingo (1965)
The "Beach Party" gang is back again for laughs, rock and roll, surfing and those sexy two-piece bathing suits. The plot, such as it is, involves a missing singing star, a mermaid, and Eric Von Zipper's gang. With Frankie, Annette, Harvey Lembeck, Linda Evans, Paul Lynde, Don Rickles. 98 min.
44-1297 ***$14.99***

Back To The Beach (1987)
Your favorite seaside sweethearts, Frankie Avalon and Annette Funicello, return to the sunny shores of California in this winning spoof of their '60s beach movies. Now married, Frankie and Annette visit the old haunts with their kids and wind up singing, surfing, fighting and making up—just like in the old days. With Lori Loughlin, Connie Stevens and lots of cameos. 92 min.
06-1500 🗨***$14.99***

Palm Springs Weekend (1963)
Easter week brings together college jocks and pretty young women in this lively teenage tale. Romance, brawls and jealousy set the stage for trouble and torrid love affairs with Troy Donahue, Connie Stevens, Ty Hardin, Stefanie Powers and Robert Conrad. 99 min.
19-1778 Was $59.99 ***$19.99***

Ride The Wild Surf (1964)
Columbia attempted to catch the "beach party film" wave with this more serious look at three surf bums in Hawaii whose ambitions revolve around surfing competitions and girls. Tab Hunter, Susan Hart, Fabian, Shelley Fabares, Peter Brown and Barbara Eden star; theme by Jan and Dean. 101 min.
02-2377 Was $19.99 ***$14.99***

Carry On Teacher (1959)
After their favorite teacher decides it's time to move on, a group of students sabotage an inspection by the Ministry of Education in order to keep him at their school. "Carry On" shenanigans reach new comic heights in this outing starring Ted Ray, Charles Hawtrey, Leslie Phillips and Richard O'Sullivan. 86 min.
59-7011 ***$89.99***

Carry On Nurse (1959)
From England's madcap "Carry On" comedy film series comes this tale of hospital hijinks. The workers take on the administration, the interns take on the doctors, and the men's ward takes on the nurses. Stars Kenneth Connor, Shirley Eaton. 90 min.
62-1214 ***$19.99***

Carry On Regardless (1960)
The "Carry On" crew creates more havoc when Sid James runs an employment agency that will supply workers for any job under the sun. That includes chimp walker, underwear model, and babysitter of a married woman—we said "every job"! Kenneth Connor, Joan Sims and Kenneth Williams also star. 90 min.
59-7076 ***$29.99***

Carry On Cruising (1962)
The laughter overflows as the "Carry On" gang sets sail on a madcap adventure on the high seas. Sidney James and Kenneth Williams star in a story about a ship of fools on a Mediterranean cruise. 89 min.
44-1395 ***$29.99***

Carry On Cabby (1963)
The laughs keep "carry-ing on" in this series entry that finds Hattie Jacques, the jealous wife of highly successful cab driver Sid James, deciding to take a stab at competing with her hubby by starting her own taxi fleet. Her marketing catch: she only hires gorgeous female drivers. Jim Dale, Joan Sims and Milo O'Shea also star. 91 min.
59-7075 ***$29.99***

Carry On Spying (1964)
Spies get silly when the "Carry On" crew takes them on in this outrageous spoof in which a secret agent for STENCH (the Society for the Total Extinction of Non-Conforming Humans) and others try to retrieve "Formula X" from evil Dr. Crow. Kenneth Williams, Jim Dale and Barbara Windsor star. 83 min.
59-7061 ***$29.99***

Carry On Cowboy (1965)
It's the Wild West, British-style, when the zany "Carry On" gang moves into Stodge City. Before long, bullets, puns and ribald jokes are flying. Comedy stars Jim Dale, Kenneth Williams, Joan Sims. 91 min.
44-1372 ***$29.99***

Carry On Screaming (1966)
The "Carry On" gang faces shocks and yocks when they try to find some terrifying monsters, leading to a mysterious castle where all manner of eerie mishaps occur. Kenneth Williams, Joan Sims and Jim Dale star. 97 min.
68-8243 ***$29.99***

Carry On... Follow That Camel (1967)
The wacky Brits from the "Carry On" films take their act to the desert in this Foreign Legion spoof, aided by Phil Silvers as conniving Sergeant Novker. The story tells of a Foreign Legion officer who contrives acts of heroism, and is then put on the spot and must prove them. Jim Dale, Anita Harris and Joan Sims star. 91 min.
15-1066 ***$29.99***

Carry On... Don't Lose Your Head (1967)
Hilarity abounds as the "Carry On" crowd spoofs the French Revolution. The peasants may be revolting (you bet, they stink on ice!), but the comedy keeps coming with Sidney James eliciting laughs as the Black Fingernail, a "Scarlet Pimpernel" sort and a master of disguise. Jim Dale, Joan Sims and Kenny Williams also star. 90 min.
59-7074 ***$29.99***

Carry On, Up The Khyber (1968)
The sun does set on the British Empire when the "Carry On" group turns history into hilarity. In this silly series entry, the "Carry On"-ers join forces with the Third Foot and Mouth Regiment to stop an uprising of the native Burpa tribe in India. Sidney James, Kenneth Williams and Roy Castle star. 86 min.
58-7008 ***$89.99***

Carry On Camping (1969)
The "Carry On" series gets campy when the crew heads to the woods in hopes of finding a nudist colony. When they arrive in the great outdoors, there's no nudist colony, but the desirable dollybirds they do find will do just fine. Sidney James, Kenneth Williams, Joan Sims star. 86 min.
84-1005 ***$29.99***

Carry On Loving (1970)
Wild "Carry On" comedy ensues when Sydney and Sophie Bliss run the Wedded Bliss Marriage Agency, where the owners bicker and wacky customers don't stop seeking spouses. Sidney James, Hattie Jacques and Kenneth Williams star. 87 min.
58-7006 ***$89.99***

Carry On Up The Jungle (1970)
There's more than one bungle in the jungle when the "Carry On" crazies go on expedition in search of a rare bird. What they find instead are a lost tribe of female warriors, a love-starved gorilla, headhunters and lots of laughs. Frankie Howerd, Sidney James, Kenneth Connor and Joan Sims star. 87 min.
59-7032 Was $79.99 ***$14.99***

Carry On Henry VIII (1970)
The British aristocracy gets ribbed unmercifully in this funny "Carry On" entry in which the much-married monarch learns that the queen is having an affair right under his nose. Sidney James, Kenneth Williams and Joan Sims star. 87 min.
84-1006 ***$29.99***

Carry On At Your Convenience (1971)
The humor's in the water closet this time, but that's all right, because Britain's "Carry On" zanies are running a toilet factory in a laughfest that's sure to leave you potty. Sidney James, Kenneth Williams star. 90 min.
84-1003 ***$29.99***

Carry On Abroad (1972)
Hilarious entry in the British laugh series finds the "Carry On" crew taking a vacation on the island of Elsbels—and discovering their hotel hasn't been built yet when they arrive. Sidney James, Kenneth Williams star. 86 min.
58-7007 ***$89.99***

Carry On Christmas Capers (1972)
The "Carry On" funsters took their ribald routines to the telly for this TV special in which they recall classic capers from holiday seasons past. It's a bawdy evening of fun that'll have you "ho-ho-ho"-ing all the way through. Barbara Windsor, Joan Sims, Kenneth Connor and Jack Douglas star. AKA: "Carry on Christmas: Carry on Stuffing." 50 min.
59-7082 ***$89.99***

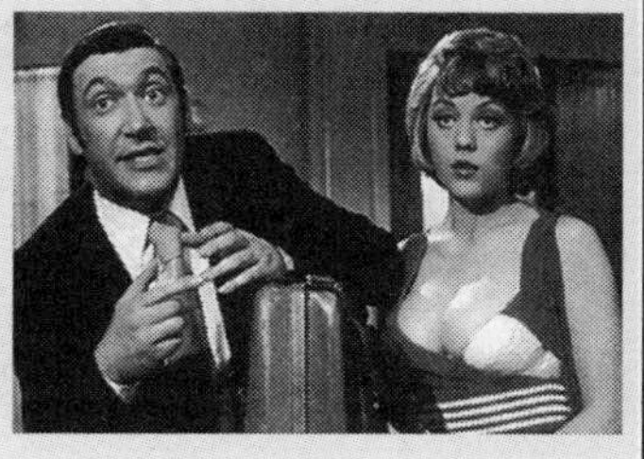

Carry On Girls (1972)
The "Carry On" characters get into some bawdy trouble when they persuade the town council to run a beauty contest to promote their resort. Sidney Fiddler promises all the lovely contestants free lodging at a local hotel. One problem, though: his girlfriend owns it. Sidney James, Barbara Windsor and Kenneth Connor star. 88 min.
84-1004 ***$29.99***

Carry On Christmas (1973)
It's Christmas and the "Carry On" crew of kibbitzers have all sorts of fun with the holidays. See the hilarious situations compound as Sid James plays Father Christmas, Bernard Bresslaw performs a ballet that's unforgettable and even cavemen get into the act, too. With Kenneth Connor, Joan Sim and Jack Douglas. 50 min.
59-7012 ***$89.99***

Carry On Dick (1974)
Highwayman Big Dick Turpin has an alter ego: Reverend Flasher of Upper Dencher village. When Turpin's identity is discovered, the money he has raised for local charities is questioned. Could they be linked to his illegal after-dark activities? Sidney James, Kenneth Williams star. 87 min.
58-7009 ***$89.99***

Carry On Behind (1975)
Sexy Elke Sommer ("grrrrowll!") co-stars in this hilarious entry in the "Carry On" series in which archeologist Kenneth Williams excavates an ancient Roman town that happens to share a site with a holiday caravan. Joan Sims and Sidney James also star. 92 min.
53-1007 ***$29.99***

Carry On Emmanuelle (1978)
It's the sexiest "Carry On" and the funniest "Emmanuelle" film you've ever seen, as the frustrated wife of a stuffy diplomat decides to try some foreign affairs of her own. Suzanne Danielle, Kenneth Connor, Beryl Reid star. 90 min.
30-1023 ***$29.99***

Sid!: The Very Best Of Sid James
One of England's funniest comics is saluted in a program which features clips from his wackiest films, including the "Carry On" series, the "St. Trinian's" films and his TV work in "George and the Dragon." Known as "a lovable rogue" with "the face of an unmade bed" and "the world's dirtiest laugh," James' classic parts are showcased here. 60 min.
59-7057 ***$24.99***

Don Knotts

The Ghost And Mr. Chicken (1966)
In one of his funniest film outings, Don Knotts plays a milquetoast newspaper typesetter whose big chance to become a reporter has arrived—and all he has to do is spend the night in a supposedly haunted house. Chills and chuckles mix in this comedy that also stars Joan Staley, Dick Sargent. 90 min.
07-2389 ◻$14.99

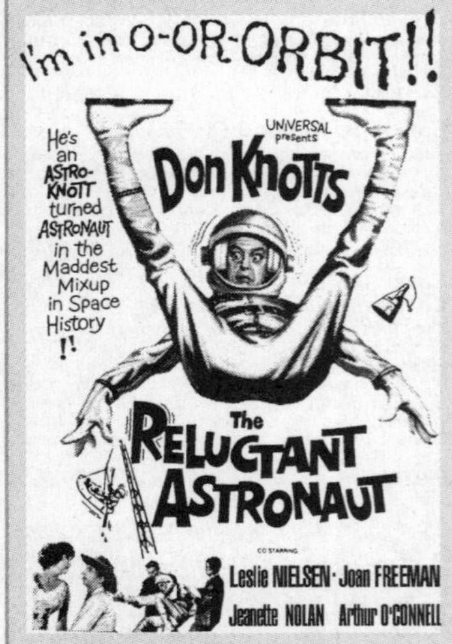

The Reluctant Astronaut (1967)
Amusement park rocket operator Don Knotts has all the "wrong stuff" when his pushy father lands him a slot in the astronaut training program. Knotts' fear of heights grounds him into being a NASA janitor, but a call for the least-qualified subject for a mission soon has him in orbit in this far-out comedy. Leslie Nielsen, Joan Freeman, Arthur O'Connell co-star. 103 min.
07-2388 ◻$14.99

The Shakiest Gun In The West (1968)
Don Knotts rattles, and you'll roll with laughter, as he portrays a cowardly dentist who goes west and gets mistaken for a famous gunslinger! Laughs by the wagonload in this remake of "The Paleface." Jackie Coogan, Barbara Rhoades co-star. 101 min.
07-2445 ◻$14.99

The Love God? (1969)
And who better than Don Knotts to play the title role in this offbeat satire, as the meek editor of a bird-watching magazine becomes a national celebrity when his new publisher, without Knotts' knowledge, turns it into a girlie mag. Anne Francis, Edmond O'Brien also star. 103 min.
07-2390 ◻$14.99

How To Frame A Figg (1971)
Nerdish small-town bookkeeper Don Knotts is framed by a group of corrupt officials for swiping cash from the city till. With Knotts facing charges that could send him to jail, he has to uncover the real culprits. Elaine Joyce, Joe Flynn, Edward Andrews and Yvonne Craig also star. 103 min.
07-2442 ◻$14.99

Mule Feathers (1975)
They're the most outrageous pair of con artists the Wild West has ever seen, Bible-quoting Beauregard and his telepathic mule, Nelson. Rory Calhoun and Don Knotts, as the voice of Nelson, star. 93 min.
08-1434 $19.99

The Private Eyes (1981)
In this wacky comedy thriller, Tim Conway and Don Knotts play clumsy Scotland Yard detectives out to solve a double murder. Their investigation takes them to a creepy mansion inhabited by an heiress and her crew of zany characters, but the slapstick sleuths soon encounter strange happenings of the ghostly kind. Trisha Noble, Bernard Fox co-star.
47-1025 $19.99

The Don Knotts Collection
"Who?" "Don Knotts!," as you'll see in this rib-tickling boxed set that includes "The Ghost and Mr. Chicken," "The Love God?" and "The Reluctant Astronaut."
07-2406 Save $20.00! $24.99

Please see our index for these other Don Knotts titles: *Big Bully • Gus • Herbie Goes To Monte Carlo • Jingle Bells • Move Over, Darling • No Deposit, No Return • No Time For Sergeants • Pleasantville*

If... (1969)
Lindsay Anderson's controversial diatribe of the tyranny of British boarding schools was embraced nationwide in America by anti-authoritarian students in the Sixties. Malcolm McDowell stars as a rebellious youth who leads a student revolt against a despotic headmaster. Co-stars David Wood, Christine Noonan. 110 min.
06-1144 Was $44.99 $19.99

O Lucky Man! (1973)
Cult favorite by director Lindsay Anderson about ambitious coffee salesman Malcolm McDowell and his many surrealistic experiences up and down the "ladder of success." Talented cast, many of whom play multiple roles, includes Rachel Roberts, Ralph Richardson; score by Alan Price. 178 min.
19-1272 Was $29.99 $24.99

Ladies Who Do (1963)
A group of cleaning ladies find their jobs in jeopardy when a nasty realtor plans to raze the buildings in which they work. With help from a retired colonel, they obtain stock tips from brokers' trashcans and "clean up" at the market. British farce stars Robert Morley, Peggy Mount, Harry Corbett. 90 min.
53-8055 $29.99

Rhubarb (1969)
A cavalcade of great British stars can be found in this nearly silent film centering on a golf course where the locals use all sorts of devious tactics to win and ruin the games of their opponents. Harry Secombe, Eric Sykes, Jimmy Edwards and Kenneth Connor star. 36 min.
59-7064 $24.99

I Was A Teenage Mummy (1962)
A campy spoof of horror films, this long-lost effort tells of a professor and his pretty assistant who travel to Egypt to unearth a 3,700-year-old mummy. When the gauze-wrapped guy is brought to the U.S., he comes to life and stalks the streets of Westport, Connecticut. Hosted by Forrest J. Ackerman and featuring an interview with director Ralph C. Bluemke. 72 min.
78-5069 $39.99

Viva Max! (1969)
Frantic farce stars Peter Ustinov as General Maximilian Rodrigues de Santos, latest in a line of Mexican military men, who sets out to prove himself by recapturing the Alamo with his ragtag band of men...120 years after the legendary siege. With Jonathan Winters, Pamela Tiffin, Keenan Wynn. 92 min.
63-1006 $14.99

Support Your Local Sheriff! (1969)
Wanderer James Garner is coerced into serving as a gold rush town's new sheriff. With drunk-turned-deputy Jack Elam at his side, he's got to put outlaw Walter Brennan and his clan behind bars...as soon as the jail is built. Hilarious western spoof also stars Joan Hackett, Bruce Dern. 92 min.
12-1160 Was $19.99 $14.99

Support Your Local Gunfighter (1971)
Pseudo-sequel to "Support Your Local Sheriff!" finds James Garner as a con man mistaken for a gunslinger in a Western town and making the best out of the situation. Laughs and shoot-outs abound in this fun-filled comic western. With Suzanne Pleshette, Jack Elam and Harry Morgan. 93 min.
12-2711 Was $19.99 ◻$14.99

Topkapi (1964)
Director Jules Dassin's elaborate, light-hearted heist film stars Maximilian Schell and Melina Mercouri as lovers who hire a gang of experts to help them lift a priceless jewelled dagger from Istanbul's famed (and heavily-guarded) Topkapi Museum. Robert Morley, Akim Tamiroff, and Best Supporting Actor Academy Award-winner Peter Ustinov co-star. 120 min.
12-3045 Was $19.99 $14.99

A Matter Of WHO (1962)
Terry-Thomas stars in this offbeat farce as a U.N. health investigator trying to track down the source of a smallpox epidemic. Things get complicated when he meets an unscrupulous oilman based in the Middle East. Alex Nichol, Sonja Ziemann and Honor Blackman also star. 92 min.
68-8527 $19.99

Bang, Bang, You're Dead (1966)
Secret agent spoof stars Tony Randall and Senta Berger in a tale about a tourist and a beautiful special agent who find themselves in trouble with ruthlessly funny gangsters in Morocco. With Klaus Kinski, Herbert Lom and Terry-Thomas. 92 min.
75-7034 Was $19.99 $14.99

How I Won The War (1967)
A zany satire on World War II built around the whacked-out experiences of a bumbling British troop leader and his misfit soldiers. Michael Crawford is the put-upon officer, John Lennon a confused infantryman; Richard Lester ("A Hard Day's Night") directs. 109 min.
12-1360 $14.99

St. Benny The Dip (1951)
Dick Haymes, Roland Young and Lionel Stander star as three flim flam men who pose as men of the cloth to evade the pursuit of the law, but are a little too convincing in their guise and are mistaken for real clergymen at a skid row mission. Whimsical comedy also stars Nina Foch, Freddie Bartholomew. 80 min.
01-1247 $19.99

The Secret Of Santa Vittoria (1969)
When German soldiers approaching a small Italian town during World War II threaten to rob the village of its cache of vintage wine, ineffectual mayor Anthony Quinn rises to the occasion and leads the townspeople in an elaborate operation to hide a million bottles in a nearby cave. Director Stanley Kramer's charming comedy also stars Anna Magnani, Virna Lisi, Hardy Kruger. 139 min.
12-3046 $19.99

Cottonpickin' Chickenpickers (1967)
An all-star cast of "Z" movie veterans and country stars populate this zany farce about two easy-going guys who take a train they think is going to Hollywood, California, but is actually headed for Hollywood, Florida. Soon, they're stealing chickens and being chased by moonshiners. With Del Reeves, Sonny Tufts, Slapsy Maxie Rosenbloom, Tommy Noonan; songs include "Dirty Ole Egg Suckin' Dog."
79-5329 Was $24.99 $19.99

The Pink Jungle (1968)
A planned fashion shoot in a South American jungle turns into a wild and comical adventure when photographer James Garner is mistakenly accused of being a CIA spy. On the run with gorgeous model Eva Renzi, Garner must deal with helicopter thieves and murderous crooks after a hidden fortune in diamonds. With George Kennedy, Nigel Green. 104 min.
07-2628 ◻$14.99

The Solid Gold Cadillac (1956)
Judy Holliday turns in a tour-de-force performance in this memorable comedy with satirical barbs hurled at big business and government. She's a minority shareholder in a huge corporation who takes the crooked board of directors to task over some of its doings and enlists former honcho Paul Douglas to help set things right. Fred Clark, John Williams co-star; George Burns narrates. 99 min.
02-2798 $19.99

The President's Analyst (1967)
One of the best political satires on film, with James Coburn as the psychiatrist whose top secret sessions with the president are leading him to a nervous breakdown and making him a target for left- and right-wing assassins. With Godfrey Cambridge, Pat Harrington, Will Geer. 100 min.
06-1450 $14.99

Who's Minding The Mint? (1967)
It's the wackiest heist you ever saw, as a ragtag band of crooks and oddballs break into the U.S. Mint to *replace* accidentally destroyed bills...and maybe make a little extra for themselves. Jim Hutton, Dorothy Provine, Walter Brennan, Milton Berle, Joey Bishop, Bob Denver and Victor Buono star. 97 min.
02-2710 $14.99

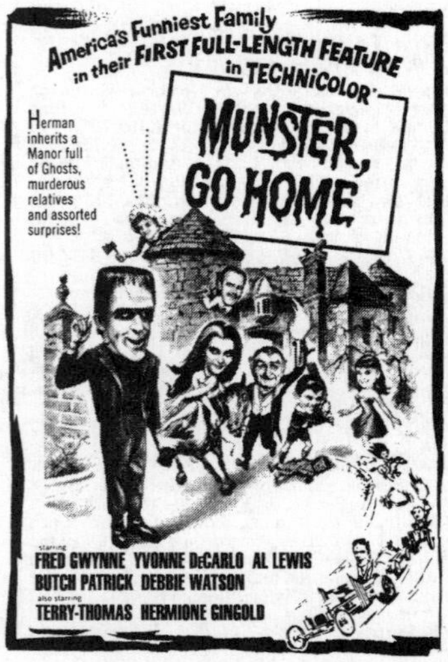

Munster, Go Home! (1966)
The ever-lovable TV family known as the Munsters make their movie debut in this hilarious comedy that takes them to England to claim a castle Herman's inherited. Little do they know that the place is being used as a headquarters for crooks who plan to scare the Munsters out of there. Fred Gwynne, Yvonne De Carlo, Al Lewis, Hermione Gingold, Terry-Thomas star.
10-2746 $14.99

The Munsters' Revenge (1981)
TV's freaky family is back in a howl-arious feature-length comedy. When mad scientist Sid Caesar creates robot doubles of Herman and Grandpa to rob banks, the Munsters catch the real crooks. Fred Gwynne, Yvonne DeCarlo, Al Lewis star. 96 min.
07-1455 $14.99

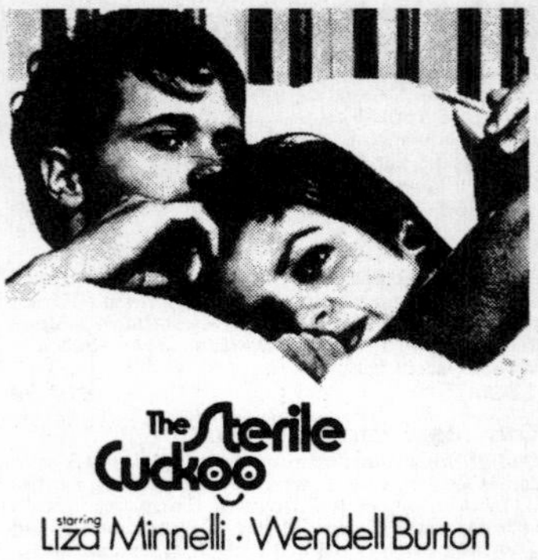

The Sterile Cuckoo (1969)
In this heartfelt portrayal of young love from first-time director Alan J. Pakula, Liza Minnelli is Pookie Adams, an eccentric college girl who dives into a relationship with a naive fellow student (Wendell Burton) that provides both with a lesson in love and heartache. Seriocomedy co-stars Tim McIntire; features the Oscar-nominated song "Come Saturday Morning." 107 min.
06-1250 Was $49.99 $14.99

The Courtship Of Eddie's Father (1963)
Widower Glenn Ford gets more than a little assistance in his love life from Ronnie Howard, his 9-year-old son who wants a say in choosing a new mom, in this winsome family comedy that inspired the popular TV series. With Shirley Jones, Stella Stevens. 117 min.
12-2257 Was $19.99 $14.99

Kiss Me, Stupid (1964)
Billy Wilder's once-controversial farce stars Dean Martin as a Las Vegas crooner who is detoured to a small Nevada town where he meets two amateur songwriters (Cliff Osmond and Ray Walston), who'll do just about anything to get their songs sold, from sabotaging Martin's car to hiring a local hooker to seduce him. Kim Novak, Felicia Farr co-star; songs by Ira and George Gershwin. 126 min.
12-2321 $19.99

Popi (1969)
Warm-hearted comedy stars Alan Arkin as a Puerto Rican widower struggling to make a better life for his two sons in the New York slums. With Rita Moreno. 115 min.
73-5006 $14.99

A Woman Of Distinction (1950)
College dean Rosalind Russell gets a lesson in love when she falls for visiting astronomy professor Ray Milland in this light and lively romantic comedy. With Edmund Gwenn and a cameo by Lucille Ball. 85 min.
02-1685 $69.99

The Marrying Kind (1952)
Laughs and tears were mixed in this story of unhappily married couple Judy Holliday and Aldo Ray telling a judge the reasons behind their wanting to divorce. Through flashbacks, the ups and downs of their life together are traced. George Cukor's witty seriocomedy, with a script by Ruth Gordon and Garson Kanin, also stars Peggy Cass and a young Charles Buchinski (later Bronson). 92 min.
02-2985 $19.99

The Girl Can't Help It (1956)
Sex, gangsters and rock and roll blend in one of the '50s best comedies and the film that made Jayne Mansfield a star. Mob boss Edmond O'Brien coerces agent Tom Ewell into making his talentless girlfriend (Jayne) a singing star. The performances by Little Richard, Gene Vincent and Fats Domino are a highlight. 99 min.
04-1907 Was $59.99 $29.99

Will Success Spoil Rock Hunter? (1957)
Wildly funny spoof of Hollywood and Madison Avenue stars Tony Randall as a struggling New York ad man who saves his company when he convinces screen sexpot Jayne Mansfield to endorse a line of lipstick, only to become a celebrity in his own right when he's assumed to be Mansfield's new beau. Scripter/director Frank Tashlin's adaptation of the George Axelrod play also stars John Williams, Betsy Drake, Mickey Hargitay and a cameo by Groucho Marx. 94 min.
04-3275 ◻$19.99

The Black Orchid (1959)
Lively romantic entanglements ensue when mob widow Sophia Loren falls for businessman Anthony Quinn, much to the dismay of both of their children. Quinn's daughter thinks she's trouble, while Loren's son is already following in father's footsteps, imprisoned on a state farm. Mark Richman and Ina Balin co-star; Martin Ritt directs. 95 min.
06-1943 ◻$14.99

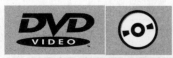

Navy Blue And Gold (1937)
James Stewart, Robert Young and Tom Brown are Navy cadets with different backgrounds who play for the academy football team and form an off-the-field friendship. Stewart, who joined under a phony name, is suspended from the team when he admits a mysterious secret from his past. Can the team beat Army without him? Florence Rice, Lionel Barrymore, Billie Burke co-star. 94 min.
12-2865 *$29.99*

Of Human Hearts (1938)
Civil War-era drama starring James Stewart as the son of strict rural minister Walter Huston. Defying his father's wishes and with help from his mother, Stewart studies medicine in the East and serves as a Union Army physician, ignoring his family until his mother tries to contact him through President Lincoln. John Carradine, Beulah Bondi also star. 100 min.
12-2866 *$29.99*

The Shopworn Angel (1938)
Classic soaper about a Broadway showgirl (Margaret Sullavan) who meets an Army recruit (James Stewart) about to be shipped overseas during World War I. After spending the day together touring the city, the smitten Stewart asks Sullavan to marry him and she reluctantly agrees. Walter Pidgeon, Nat Pendleton and Alan Curtis also star. 81 min.
12-2868 *$29.99*

Destry Rides Again (1939)
One of the most enjoyable westerns of all time features a perfectly-cast James Stewart as the gunless gunslinger-made-sheriff and Marlene Dietrich as Frenchy, the saloon floozy who sings "See What the Boys in the Back Room Will Have." Brian Donlevy, Charles Winninger co-star. 94 min.
07-1457 *$14.99*

Pot O' Gold (1940)
James Stewart and Paulette Goddard co-star in this screwball comedy-musical about a down-and-out music lover who takes a job with a health food company owned by his music-hating uncle, delightfully played by Charles Winninger. Pleasant songs—even Jimmy sings! 86 min.
10-2017 *$14.99*

The Shop Around The Corner (1940)
Classic Ernst Lubitsch charmer stars James Stewart and Margaret Sullavan as co-working clerks that can't stand one another...but don't realize that they're anonymous lonely hearts penpals. Frank Morgan, Joseph Schildkraut star in this beloved comedy. 97 min.
12-1719 *$19.99*

The Mortal Storm (1940)
James Stewart is a farmer in mid-'30s Austria who undertakes a dangerous mission to rescue former girlfriend Margaret Sullavan, whose step-brothers and fiancé have joined the Nazi party even though her father was sent to a concentration camp. Powerful anti-Nazi drama, which led Hitler to ban all MGM films from Germany, co-stars Robert Young, Frank Morgan and Robert Stack. 100 min.
12-2934 *$19.99*

Magic Town (1947)
Frequent Frank Capra scripter Robert Riskin produced and co-wrote this light-hearted satire starring James Stewart as an polling company head who strikes gold when he finds a small town whose residents are a perfect cross-sample of American opinions. With Jane Wyman, Kent Smith, Ned Sparks. 103 min.
63-1010 Was $19.99 *$12.99*

Magic Town (Color Version)
It's not magic, but the modern miracle of computers, that brings James Stewart and Jane Wyman to colorful life in this rendition.
63-1415 *$19.99*

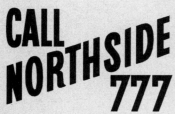

CALL NORTHSIDE 777

Call Northside 777 (1948)
Set and filmed in Chicago, this gritty, based-on-fact newspaper drama stars James Stewart as a cynical reporter who discovers that the wrong man may be behind bars for the killing of a cop that occurred years earlier. Stewart's investigation leads him to the witness to the murder and makes him question the police department's motives. Richard Conte, Lee J. Cobb and E.G. Marshall star. 111 min.
04-2786 *□$19.99*

You Gotta Stay Happy (1948)
When wealthy bride Joan Fontaine decides—on her wedding night—that she's made a mistake, she runs away and wrangles a ride with pilot James Stewart, who owns a near-bankrupt air cargo company, on a wacky cross-country flight that also includes an escaped criminal, a honeymooning couple, a shipment of lobsters and a cigar-smoking chimp! Wild romantic comedy also stars Eddie Albert, Roland Young. 101 min.
07-2625 *□$14.99*

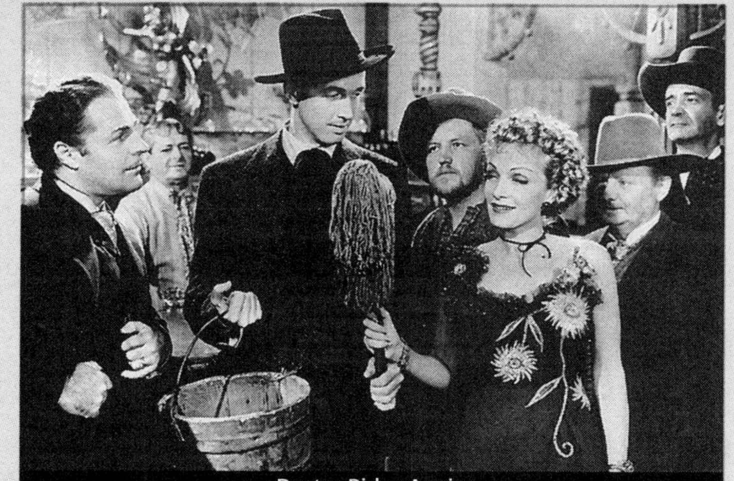
Destry Rides Again

James Stewart

The Stratton Story (1949)
Excellent sports biography starring James Stewart as Monty Stratton, a pitcher with the Chicago White Sox whose career appears over when his leg is amputated after a hunting accident. Using an artificial leg and lots of determination, Stratton attempts to make an amazing comeback to the mound. With June Allyson, Frank Morgan and major leaguers Bill Dickey and Gene Bearden. 106 min.
12-2772 *□$19.99*

Broken Arrow (1950)
Director Delmer Daves ("3:10 to Yuma") deftly handles this sprawling western drama that takes a sympathetic stance towards the plight of the Indians. Peace-seeking frontiersman James Stewart enlists the aid of Cochise (Jeff Chandler) in striking an accord between the Apache and settlers. 93 min.
04-2147 Was $19.99 *□$14.99*

The Jackpot (1950)
Overlooked little gem of a comedy starring James Stewart as an average small-town family man who thinks his dull life will improve when he wins a radio contest. What he gets is a house crammed with unwanted prizes, a live Shetland pony, a boss who's tired of Stewart's notoriety and some unwanted attention from the IRS. With Barbara Hale, James Gleason, Natalie Wood. 85 min.
04-3277 *□$19.99*

Winchester '73 (1950)
Unique western film stars James Stewart as a man searching for his father's killer and the family rifle that was used against him. The gun's new "owners" and their stories are depicted, leading to a dramatic conclusion. Dan Duryea, Rock Hudson, Shelley Winters and a young Tony Curtis are featured. 82 min.
07-1389 *$14.99*

Harvey (1950)
Beloved comedy stars James Stewart as a good-hearted inebriate whose constant companion is a six-foot, invisible rabbit named Harvey. Josephine Hull won an Academy Award as Stewart's sister, who tries to have him put away. With Peggy Down, Jesse White. 104 min.
07-1639 Was $19.99 *$14.99*

No Highway In The Sky (1951)
Aviation scientist James Stewart, sent to investigate the crash of a new plane, becomes convinced the craft's design is unsafe and resorts to sabotage to save lives before a transatlantic flight. Offbeat and provocative drama also features Marlene Dietrich as a famed actress and fellow passenger who believes Stewart's claims; with Glynis Johns, Jack Hawkins. 98 min.
04-2925 *□$19.99*

Bend Of The River (1952)
James Stewart is an outlaw-turned-wagon scout who must help settlers reach Oregon Territory in an exciting frontier action tale. Also stars Arthur Kennedy as Stewart's treacherous rival, Julie Adams, Harry Morgan and Rock Hudson. 91 min.
07-1386 *$14.99*

Thunder Bay (1953)
James Stewart and Dan Duryea are oil wildcatters whose latest search for riches, in a small town along the Gulf of Mexico, sets them against the Cajun fishermen who live there. Action-filled drama co-stars Joanne Dru, Gilbert Roland. 82 min.
07-1388 *$19.99*

The Naked Spur (1953)
This magnificently atmospheric and much-demanded Western stars James Stewart as leader of an impromptu crew of bounty hunters on the trail of killer Robert Ryan. Janet Leigh, Ralph Meeker, Millard Mitchell co-star; Anthony Mann directs. 91 min.
12-1697 *$19.99*

The Man From Laramie (1955)
The final "adult western" to be made by director Anthony Mann and star James Stewart in their mid-'50s collaboration, with Stewart searching for the gunrunners responsible for his brother's death. His quest leads him into the middle of a range war and a bitter power struggle between the sons of a ranchlord. Arthur Kennedy, Donald Crisp, Aline MacMahon co-star. 104 min.
02-1828 Was $19.99 *$14.99*

Strategic Air Command (1955)
The long-lost uncle of "Top Gun" stars James Stewart as a baseball player called back to military duty who finds himself assigned to the Air Force's Strategic Air Command. Contains exciting flying sequences, a '50s view of America's "global peacekeeper" role, and fine support from June Allyson, Barry Sullivan and Frank Lovejoy. 114 min.
06-1422 *$14.99*

The Far Country (1955)
Classic western saga stars James Stewart as a cattleman who moves his herd to Alaska, but encounters nothing but trouble. Action and excitement await in this Northern frontier adventure. Walter Brennan, Ruth Roman, Harry Morgan star. 97 min.
10-3070 Was $19.99 *$14.99*

The Spirit Of St. Louis (1957)
Who better than James Stewart to play America's greatest flying hero, Charles A. Lindbergh, in Billy Wilder's filming of the aviator's autobiography? Follow "Lucky Lindy" from his days as an airmail pilot to his groundbreaking 1927 solo flight across the Atlantic. With Murray Hamilton, Patricia Smith. Includes original theatrical trailers. 135 min.
19-2492 Remastered *□$19.99*

The Spirit Of St. Louis (Letterboxed Version)
Also available in a theatrical, widescreen format.
19-2493 *□$19.99*

Bell, Book And Candle (1958)
About-to-be-married publisher James Stewart finds himself smitten with Kim Novak, but is shocked to find out she's a witch! Jack Lemmon, Hermione Gingold and Ernie Kovacs also star in this enchanting comedy, a hit on Broadway and the indirect basis for TV's "Bewitched." 103 min.
02-1025 *$19.99*

Anatomy Of A Murder (1959)
Consummate courtroom drama by Otto Preminger about an Army officer who is charged with killing a man he claims raped his wife, a claim the defense lawyer must prove. The stellar cast includes James Stewart, George C. Scott, Ben Gazzara, Lee Remick, Arthur O'Connell; score by Duke Ellington. 160 min.
02-1635 *$19.99*

The FBI Story (1959)
Thrilling (and somewhat sanitized) depiction of the FBI's formative years, as seen through the eyes of agent James Stewart. See Stewart take on gangsters like Baby Face Nelson and John Dillinger; the KKK; Nazi spy rings and Communist agents, plus amazing looks inside the bureau's crime labs. With Vera Miles, Murray Hamilton, Nick Adams. 149 min.
19-1834 Was $59.99 *$19.99*

Two Rode Together (1961)
A cynical lawman (James Stewart) and a hard-bitten Cavalry officer (Richard Widmark) join forces to rescue a captive settler party from hostile Indians in this John Ford western adventure. With Shirley Jones, Linda Cristal, Andy Devine. 109 min.
02-1746 *$14.99*

Mr. Hobbs Takes A Vacation (1962)
James Stewart takes his family on a seaside holiday, only to be plagued by a lothario with eyes for his wife, a son who's glued to the TV set, a daughter who refuses to go out in public with braces, and two daughters with marital woes. Warm comedy co-stars Maureen O'Hara. 115 min.
04-2146 *□$19.99*

How The West Was Won (1963)
The sprawling story of three generations of 19th-century pioneers, and their odyssey from New England to the frontier, is a true western classic. The all-star cast includes John Wayne, Henry Fonda, Debbie Reynolds, James Stewart, Carroll Baker, Gregory Peck and Lee J. Cobb, and Spencer Tracy narrates. Co-directed by John Ford, Henry Hathaway and George Marshall. 165 min.
12-1548 Was $29.99 *□$24.99*

How The West Was Won (Letterboxed Version)
Also available in a theatrical, widescreen format.
12-2909 Was $29.99 *□$24.99*

Dear Brigitte (1965)
Charming comedy with Jimmy Stewart as a college professor whose genius son has two passions: handicapping horse races and writing fan letters to Brigitte Bardot. Light-hearted family fare also stars Bill Mumy, Fabian, John Williams, Ed Wynn and a memorable cameo by La Brigitte herself. 100 min.
04-2148 *$19.99*

Shenandoah (1965)
An epic drama set during the Civil War. James Stewart must choose between the Confederacy and the Union when his son is taken as a prisoner of war. Doug McClure, Katharine Ross. 105 min.
07-1059 *$14.99*

The Flight Of The Phoenix (1966)
James Stewart, Richard Attenborough, Peter Finch and Ernest Borgnine star in this saga of a group of men who are stranded in the Sahara when their plane crashes. Their attempts at being rescued fail, and one by one they start dying off. Will their final attempt succeed? 143 min.
04-1891 *□$19.99*

The Rare Breed (1966)
Fine family western stars Jimmy Stewart as a cowboy accompanying heiress Maureen O'Hara and daughter Juliet Mills on a journey across the frontier to deliver a prize bull. Action, comedy and romance; co-stars Brian Keith, Jack Elam, Ben Johnson. 97 min.
07-1387 *□$14.99*

Bandolero! (1968)
Western action with James Stewart and Dean Martin as feuding bandit/brothers who flee across the Mexican border with Raquel Welch as a hostage. George Kennedy, Will Geer also star. 106 min.
04-3082 *□$19.99*

Firecreek (1968)
In the tradition of "High Noon" comes this gripping sagebrusher starring James Stewart as a part-time sheriff who tries to stop a group of ornery crooks led by Henry Fonda from taking over his town. After acts of terrorism and sexual harassment, Western style, Stewart faces the nasties on his own. Inger Stevens, Gary Lockwood, Jack Elam and Dean Jagger co-star. 104 min.
19-2196 Was $29.99 *$19.99*

The Cheyenne Social Club (1970)
Jimmy Stewart and Henry Fonda team in this wry western satire about aging cowpokes who inherit a Wyoming brothel and learn a lesson in the real winning of the West from fancy gals Shirley Jones, Sue Ann Langdon and Jackie Joseph. Gene Kelly directs. 102 min.
19-1660 Was $19.99 *$14.99*

James Stewart: A Wonderful Life
The life and career of one of Hollywood's most beloved actors is celebrated in this wonderful program hosted by Johnny Carson. Clips from Stewart's finest film moments, anecdotes from friends and behind-the-scenes footage comprise this superlative tribute to Jimmy. 111 min.
12-2824 *$19.99*

The James Stewart Western Collection
He's one of the best-loved actors in Hollywood history, and this boxed set features three of Stewart's finest frontier dramas: "Bend of the River," "The Far Country" and "Shenandoah."
07-2407 Save $20.00! *$24.99*

Please see our index for these other James Stewart titles: *After The Thin Man • An American Tail: Fievel Goes West • Born To Dance • Cheyenne Autumn • The Glenn Miller Story • The Greatest Show On Earth • It's A Wonderful Life • Made For Each Other • Malaya • The Man Who Knew Too Much • The Man Who Shot Liberty Valance • Mr. Smith Goes To Washington • On Our Merry Way • The Philadelphia Story • Rope • Rose Marie • The Shootist • Vertigo*

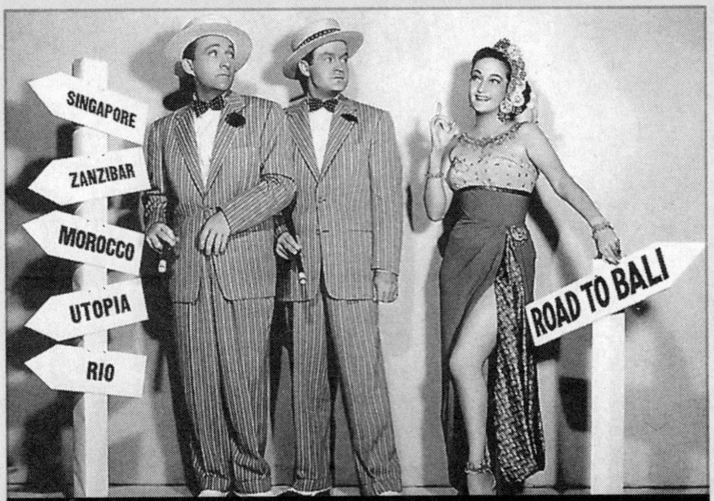

Road To Bali

Bob Hope

College Swing (1938)
An all-star cast is featured in this musical-comedy in which Gracie Allen inherits a small-town school and proceeds to turn it into a hangout for her vaudeville friends. Bob Hope, Martha Raye, Betty Grable and, of course, George Burns are among the students of the "new curriculum." Songs include "I Fall in Love With You Every Day" and "You're a Natural." 86 min.
07-1931 ☐*$14.99*

Give Me A Sailor (1938)
Lively musical-comedy stars Bob Hope and Jack Whiting as sibling sailors who meet sisters Betty Grable and Martha Raye while on leave. Whiting has the hots for Grable, but so does Hope, who tries to fix his brother up with Raye. Songs include "What Goes Here in My Heart?," "A Little Kiss at Twilight." 78 min.
07-2285 ☐*$14.99*

Thanks For The Memory (1938)
After introducing his theme song in "The Big Broadcast of 1938," Bob Hope reteamed with his co-star from that film, Shirley Ross, in this breezy romantic romp. Ross gets a job so author Hope can stay at home to write a novel, but will Bob adjust to his "househusband" role? With Charles Butterworth, Otto Kruger, Hedda Hopper and Eddie "Rochester" Anderson. 79 min.
07-2709 ☐*$14.99*

Never Say Die (1939)
Loony millionaire Bob Hope, under the mistaken belief that he only has one month to live, marries tycoon's daughter Martha Raye so that she will inherit his money and be able to wed her true love. What will happen when Hope's diagnosis is corrected? Lively romantic comedy also stars Andy Devine and Gale Sondergaard and features Raye singing "The Tra La La and Oom Pah Pah." 82 min.
07-2651 ☐*$14.99*

Rhythm Romance (1939)
Bob Hope swings in a song-filled comedy, playing a carnival barker who hooks up with drummer Gene Krupa's band and tries to land the combo an important gig. Shirley Ross, Una Merkel, Dudley Dickerson also star. Songs include "Heart and Soul," "The Lady's in Love with You" and "Some Like It Hot," which was the film's original title. 65 min.
07-2711 ☐*$14.99*

Road To Singapore (1940)
At first planned as a vehicle for Fred MacMurray and Jack Oakie, this light-hearted adventure featured the first screen pairing of Bing Crosby and Bob Hope, and the result was movie history. The two are Americans bumming their way around the world who settle down in Asia and almost immediately begin feuding for the hand of Dorothy Lamour. With Anthony Quinn, Charles Coburn. 84 min.
07-1854 ☐*$14.99*

Road To Zanzibar (1941)
Carnival con men Bob Hope and Bing Crosby find themselves outswindled on a safari scheme by Dorothy Lamour and left to stew in some cannibals' pots in the second "Road" movie. Una Merkel, Eric Blore, Lionel Royce co-star. 92 min.
07-1855 ☐*$14.99*

Road To Morocco (1942)
Shipwreck survivors Bob Hope and Bing Crosby wind up on the Mediterranean coast and take a camel ride into a comedic Arabian Nights-style adventure, as the pair wind up fighting with desert warrior Anthony Quinn for princess Dorothy Lamour. Among the songs featured is the Crosby standard "Moonlight Becomes You." 83 min.
07-1853 ☐*$14.99*

Road To Utopia (1945)
Hope and Crosby lead the rush for gold and laughs in the fourth "Road" howler, playing song-and-dance men searching for a lost mine in the Alaskan wilderness. Perennial co-star Dorothy Lamour joins the boys, along with Douglass Dumbrille and narrator Robert Benchley; look for a cameo by Jim Thorpe. 90 min.
07-1566 Was $29.99 *$14.99*

Road To Rio (1947)
Musicians Bob Hope and Bing Crosby stow away on a boat to Brazil and try to free Dorothy Lamour from hypnotic aunt Gale Sondergaard in the fifth "Road" comedy. With special guests The Andrews Sisters, Frank Faylen, Jerry Colonna, Tor Johnson and the Wiere Brothers. 100 min.
02-1816 *$14.99*

Road To Bali (1953)
The only "Road" movie in color has Bob Hope and Bing Crosby doing their best to dodge trouble, as the pleasure-lovin' pair take jobs as divers in the South Seas. Look for Humphrey Bogart and Katharine Hepburn in a hilarious and unbilled reprise of their "African Queen" roles. Songs include "To See You," "Chicago Style." 90 min.
48-1000 Was $19.99 *$14.99*

The Road To Hong Kong (1962)
This finale to the classic "Road" series features Bob and Bing travelling to the Far East and getting involved with top-secret espionage concerning rocket fuel plans. Joan Collins is their femme foil, and there are cameos by the likes of Peter Sellers, Dean Martin, Zsa Zsa Gabor, Frank Sinatra and, yes, Dorothy Lamour. 91 min.
12-2105 Was $19.99 *$14.99*

The "Road To" Collection
Get ready to hit the "Road" with this money-saving boxed set that includes "Road to Morocco," "Road to Singapore," "Road to Utopia" and "Road to Zanzibar."
07-1856 Save $30.00! *$29.99*

The Ghost Breakers (1940)
After killing a mobster, radio star Bob Hope lands in a haunted house in Cuba where, along with heiress Paulette Goddard, he encounters ghosts, caskets, hidden treasures and the dead gangster's twin brother. Spirited fright farce also stars Richard Carlson, Paul Lukas, Anthony Quinn and Willie Best. 85 min.
07-1930 ☐*$14.99*

Louisiana Purchase (1941)
Zesty comedy with music features Bob Hope getting involved with corrupt politics, shady ladies and righteous senators in Louisiana. Vera Zorina, Victor Moore and Irene Bordoni also star in this engaging political satire with such Irving Berlin tunes as "It's a Lovely Day Tomorrow." 99 min.
07-1929 ☐*$14.99*

Caught In The Draft (1941)
Hilarious service comedy with Bob Hope as a Hollywood star who attempts to evade the draft by marrying the daughter of an Army colonel. When the plan backfires, Hope finds himself in basic training...and in lots of trouble. Dorothy Lamour, Eddie Bracken and Lynne Overman also star. 82 min.
07-1932 ☐*$14.99*

My Favorite Blonde (1942)
Rip-roaring comic yarn starring Bob Hope as a wise-cracking entertainer who becomes involved with a beautiful British woman carrying secret military plans the Nazis are after. Bob and his penguin sidekick join the spy as they dodge the bad guys in a cross-country chase. Madeleine Carroll, Gale Sondergaard and George Zucco co-star. 78 min.
07-1933 ☐*$14.99*

The Princess And The Pirate (1944)
Hapless actor Bob Hope runs afoul of buccaneers on the high seas in this slapstick swashbuckler. Gorgeous Virginia Mayo is the princess, and the pirate crew includes Victor McLaglen and Walter Brennan. With Walter Slezak, Rondo Hatton, and a surprise cameo. 94 min.
44-1832 Was $19.99 *$14.99*

Monsieur Beaucaire (1946)
High-flying costume comedy finds Bob Hope as a barber in the court of Louis XV who is saved from the guillotine by posing as a French nobleman. Political intrigue, sexy romance, hilarious one-liners and daring swashbuckling abound in this Hope gem. With Joan Caulfield, Patric Knowles, Marjorie Reynolds and Joseph Schildkraut. 93 min.
07-1934 ☐*$14.99*

Where There's Life (1947)
Zany comedy romp with Bob Hope as a New York disc jockey talked into believing he's the king of Barovia, a country whose monarch has just been assassinated by revolutionaries. Joined by the kingdom's female general, Hope is pursued throughout the Big Apple by rebels and his fiancée's policeman brother. Signe Hasso, William Bendix and George Coulouris also star. 75 min.
07-2284 ☐*$14.99*

My Favorite Brunette (1947)
While looking after his detective neighbor's office, baby photographer Bob Hope's dream of being a private eye lands him on Death Row in this laugh-a-minute spoof. Hired by lovely Dorothy Lamour to track down her missing uncle, Hope tangles with crooks Charles Dingle, Lon Chaney, Jr. and Peter Lorre and winds up framed for murder. 87 min.
10-2008 Was $19.99 *$14.99*

The Paleface (1948)
Bob Hope is a daffy dentist and a shaky gun; Jane Russell is the gorgeous gunslinger Calamity Jane, and together they tame the Wild West with laughter in one of Bob's best comedies. Features the Oscar-winning song "Buttons and Bows." 91 min.
07-1296 *$14.99*

Sorrowful Jones (1949)
When bookie Bob Hope is left with a client's 5-year-old daughter, he must become a reluctant father in this lively comedy based on Damon Runyon's "Little Miss Marker." Lucille Ball co-stars with William Demarest, Bruce Cabot, Mary Jane Saunders. 88 min.
07-1561 *$14.99*

The Great Lover (1949)
Returning from Europe by steamship, scoutmaster Bob Hope intervenes when a card sharp cleans out an amiable old Duke, making himself the hero of the Duke's beautiful daughter and the target of the crooked gambler's goons. Rhonda Fleming, Roland Young, Jim Backus co-star. 80 min.
02-1869 *$14.99*

Fancy Pants (1950)
Bob Hope and Lucille Ball star in this raucous remake of "Ruggles of Red Gap." Bob's cheery-o impersonation of a proper British lord convi nces Lucy to invite him to her Old West home, where the camouflage continues. With Bruce Cabot and Jack Kirkwood. 92 min.
06-1737 *$14.99*

The Lemon Drop Kid (1951)
When racetrack tout Bob Hope finds himself in hot water with the mob, he hits upon a fast money-making racket: phony Santa Clauses collecting for an "old folk's home." Fast-paced comedy, from Damon Runyon's story, also stars Lloyd Nolan, William Frawley, Marilyn Maxwell. 91 min.
02-1700 *$14.99*

Son Of Paleface (1952)
A hilarious vehicle for Bob Hope, who plays "Junior" Potter, the Harvard graduate who ventures out West to claim the inheritance of his frontier "hero" pa. Jane Russell is the saloon-singing object of Hope's affections—and wisecracks, and Roy Rogers and Trigger play themselves. 95 min.
02-1719 *$14.99*

Here Come The Girls (1953)
A mysterious killer known as "Jack the Slasher" is stalking the members of a musical revue, and his next victim could wind up being "boy" singer Bob Hope in this lively comedy laced with songs. Tony Martin, Arlene Dahl, Rosemary Clooney, William Demarest co-star. 100 min.
06-2058 *$14.99*

Casanova's Big Night (1954)
Who better to portray history's greatest lover than...Bob Hope? Actually, Bob's a tailor who winds up impersonating Casanova and finds himself running from women and court assassins. Lively farce also stars Joan Fontaine, Basil Rathbone. 86 min.
06-1443 *$14.99*

The Seven Little Foys (1955)
Hilarious and heartwarming, the song-filled biodrama of the vaudeville family dance team stars Bob Hope as Eddie Foy, fighting to keep his family together after his wife's death. With Billy Gray, Milly Vitale, and a cameo by James Cagney as George M. Cohan. 93 min.
02-1744 *$14.99*

Paris Holiday (1958)
The City of Lights becomes the City of Laughs when Bob Hope travels to Paris to buy a French playwright's latest work and winds up getting involved with gangsters and lovely Anita Ekberg (What's not to like?). Co-stars French comic Fernandel and director Preston Sturges. 100 min.
48-1001 *$14.99*

Alias Jesse James (1959)
When Eastern insurance salesman Bob Hope inadvertently sells a policy to the infamous outlaw, he heads out West to protect his client, not knowing that James has a plan to get Hope mistaken for him and shot. Hilarious frontier romp also stars Rhonda Fleming and Wendell Corey, with a posse of cameos that includes Gene Autry, Gary Cooper, Roy Rogers and TV gunslingers James Arness, James Garner, Hugh O'Brian, Fess Parker and Jay Silverheels.
12-3147 ☐*$14.99*

The Facts Of Life (1960)
Satire of suburban married life stars Bob Hope and Lucille Ball as the participants in a would-be love affair that never gets off the ground thanks to each other's families. With Don DeFore, Ruth Hussey, Louis Nye. 103 min.
12-3149 ☐*$14.99*

Bachelor In Paradise (1961)
A famous writer (Bob Hope) settles into a small California town to write a book about the opposite sex, and soon finds that the married gals who reside in the area are after him. Lana Turner is the seemingly solo single woman in town; Janis Paige, Paula Prentiss and Jim Hutton also star in this romantic farce. 109 min.
12-2736 *$19.99*

Call Me Bwana (1963)
Explorer Bob Hope and special agent Edie Adams look for an American moon probe that's crashed in Africa and encounter ferocious animals, wacky misadventures and phony missionaries (Anita Ekberg and Lionel Jeffries) along the way. 103 min.
12-2738 *$19.99*

Critic's Choice (1963)
Spirited theatrical farce featuring Bob Hope as a drama critic who must make a decision over whether to review wife Lucille Ball's new play. The problem sends Bob to a psychiatrist and his ex-wife for help. Marilyn Maxwell and Rip Torn also star. 100 min.
19-2079 Was $29.99 *$19.99*

A Global Affair (1964)
Bob Hope springs eternal laughs as a United Nations administrator who finds an abandoned baby and is wooed by a variety of international beauties for the custody of the kid. The attractive supporting cast includes Lilo Pulver, Michelle Mercier, Yvonne De-Carlo, Elga Anderson and Miiko Taka. G-r-r-r-o-w-l! 84 min.
12-2735 *$19.99*

I'll Take Sweden (1965)
Overprotective dad Bob Hope gets transferred to Sweden in order to stop the romance between daughter Tuesday Weld and rock-and-roller Frankie Avalon. But soon she's romanced by a suave playboy, so Bob invites Frankie overseas to stop the liaison. Lively, music-filled comedy co-stars Dina Merrill, Jeremy Slate and The Vulcanes. 96 min.
12-2739 *$19.99*

Boy, Did I Get A Wrong Number! (1967)
And boy, do you get a funny movie! Bob Hope is a slick real estate agent who tries to hide a sexy, runaway movie queen (Elke Sommer), while her film director boyfriend and the studio look for her. Phyllis Diller, Marjorie Lord and Cesare Danova co-star. 99 min.
12-2737 *$19.99*

Eight On The Lam (1967)
When he's wrongly accused of embezzlement, widowed bank clerk Bob Hope and his seven children become fugitives in this wildly comical chase that also stars Jonathan Winters, Phyllis Diller, Jill St. John.
12-3148 ☐*$14.99*

The Private Navy Of Sgt. O'Farrell (1968)
Stuck on a remote Pacific post during World War II, Army sergeant Bob Hope tries to improve his men's morale by bringing in some attractive nurses and winds up with...Phyllis Diller? Thank goodness Gina Lollobrigida shows up on a life raft! Wacky war comedy also stars Jeffrey Hunter, Mako. 92 min.
08-8329 *$14.99*

How To Commit Marriage (1969)
After 20 years of matrimonial life, Bob Hope and Jane Wyman plan to divorce, but when their daughter announces her engagement, only to run off with her fiancé to follow a rock band and a guru, things go from bad to hilarious. Jackie Gleason offers great support as the boyfriend's father in this '60s-flavored comedy that also stars Leslie Nielsen, Tina Louise and Professor Irwin Corey. 98 min.
02-2386 *$14.99*

Golfing With Bing And Bob
You're on the "Road to the 19th Hole" with this collection of classic Hope and Crosby short film appearances. Rare newsreel footage of the duo taking part in golf tournaments is featured, along with the shorts "Swing with Bing" (1940) and "Don't Hook Now" (1942), plus clips of Bing and Bob in "Honor Caddie" (1949). 52 min.
53-6307 *$24.99*

A Bob Hope Christmas/ Bob Hope's Christmas With The Troops '69 World Tour
This two-tape set features Bob Hope at his best in a pair of great holiday programs. "A Bob Hope Christmas" features the beloved comedian in a collection of mirthful moments from his TV shows, with guests Connie Stevens, Lucille Ball, John Wayne and others. And Bob's 19th Yuletide overseas is remembered in the "'69 World Tour" effort. 125 min. total.
50-7580 *$19.99*

Bob Hope's Comedy Classics Four-Pack
The funniest moments from some of Bob Hope's perennially popular NBC specials have been collected in this four-volume set. The 1966 tape features such guests as Milton Berle, Johnny Carson, Soupy Sales and Wally Cox; Steve Allen, Jerry Colonna, Paul Lynde and Don Rickles are spotlighted from 1967; 1968's edition features Phil Silvers, Dean Martin, Angie Dickinson and Carol Burnett; and Danny Thomas, Jimmy Durante, George Gobel, Cyd Charisse and the Smothers Brothers are seen from 1969. Thanks for the memories—and the laughs! 360 min. total.
50-8393 *$59.99*

The Bob Hope Collection
A must-have for fans of America's best-loved comedian, this 10-tape boxed set includes the films "My Favorite Brunette" and "Road to Bali"; the retrospective documentaries "Bob Hope at the Movies" and "Hollywood Remembers Bob Hope"; "Young Bob Hope," with the 1934 short "Going Spanish" and rare WWII "Going GI" programs; "Bob Hope on TV," "The Comedy Hour" and "For Love or Money" from Hope's tube career; and the special "Not So Long Ago," in which Bob looks back on the late 1940s. 9 hrs. total.
05-5041 *$69.99*

Bob Hope Collection: 10 Pack
A special collector's set that includes "The Great Lover," "How to Commit Marriage," "The Lemon Drop Kid," "My Favorite Brunette," "Paris Holiday," "The Private Navy of Sgt. O'Farrell," "Road to Bali," "Road to Rio," "The Seven Little Foys" and "Son of Paleface"? Oh, ho, this *is* big!
05-5121 Save $50.00! *$99.99*

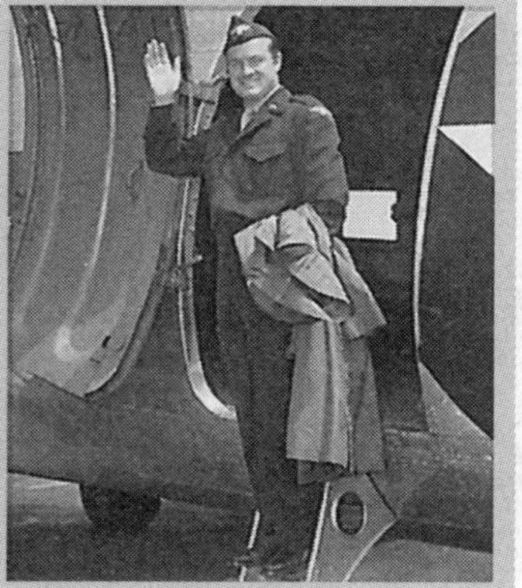

Bob Hope Remembers... World War II: The European Theatre & D-Day
The beloved comic entertainer recalls the events, music and spirit of World War II in this superb package. Along with the video, filled with rare footage and commentary from Bob, Charlton Heston, Dorothy Lamour and others, this package includes a 32-page booklet and the CD "Somewhere in Time: The Songs and Spirit of WWII," in which Dolores Hope sings classic tunes from the 1940s. 50 min.
22-1368 *$49.99*

Bob Hope's Unrehearsed Antics Of The Stars/Bob Hope's Laughing With The Presidents
"Unrehearsed Antics" offers hilarious outtakes from 30 years of Bob Hope specials and includes bloopers from Sammy Davis, Jr., Danny Thomas, Brooke Shields, Lucille Ball and others. Next, "Laughing with the Presidents" is Bob's final TV special, with footage of chief executives from FDR to Clinton, plus Tom Selleck, Don Johnson, Naomi Judd and Tony Danza. 100 min. total.
50-8385 *$19.99*

On The Road With Bing Crosby & Bob Hope
A rare treat for Hope/Crosby fans, this collection of vintage short subjects includes the original theatrical trailer for "Road to Morocco" (1942); the fellas helping GIs readjust to civilian life in "The Road to Home" (1945); Hope entertaining the troops in "Command Performance" (1943); the all-star specials "The Fifth Freedom" (1951), with Bob and Bing joining Perry Como and Arthur Godfrey, and "You Can Change the World" (1954), which also features Jack Benny, William Holden and Loretta Young; and "The Road to Peace" (1949), with Bing and Ann Blyth. 88 min. total.
53-8344 *$24.99*

Bob Hope: Hollywood's Brightest Star
Celebrate the life and career of funnyman Bob Hope, America's king of comedy. See his greatest film moments, classic TV routines and more in this collection. 67 min.
64-3438 *$14.99*

Please see our index for these other Bob Hope titles: *The Big Broadcast Of 1938 • Star Spangled Rhythm*

A Kid For Two Farthings (1956)
Delightful comedy, set in the Jewish section of London's Petticoat Lane, about a boy who buys a one-horned goat he believes is a unicorn with magical powers. When fantastic things begin to happen to people around him, the neighborhood begins to believe the boy's story. Celia Johnson, Diana Dors, Lou Jacobi and Jonathan Ashmore star; Carol Reed directs. 96 min.
22-5460 Was $29.99 *$19.99*

The Happiest Days Of Your Life (1950)
The students and faculty of a London girls' school are evacuated during the Blitz and, thanks to a bureaucratic mix-up, wind up sharing the quarters of a boys' school in the country. Alastair Sim and Margaret Rutherford star as the harried headmaster and headmistress, trying to keep parents and inspectors from discovering the dilemma, in this fast-paced comic gem. 83 min.
22-5728 Was $39.99 *$29.99*

The Admiral Was A Lady (1950)
Wanda Hendrix is the lady, a WAVE officer who finds herself pursued by three war buddies who have sworn to shun all work. Amusing romantic comedy also stars Edmond O'Brien, Rudy Vallee. 87 min.
23-5018 *$19.99*

I Am A Camera (1955)
Serio-comedy that was the basis for "Cabaret" stars Julie Harris and Laurence Harvey as a singer and writer in 1920s Berlin living a life of pleasure and ignoring the signs of encroaching tyranny. Co-stars Shelley Winters and Patrick McGoohan. 99 min.
27-6322 *$24.99*

Three For Bedroom "C" (1952)
Gloria Swanson followed her acclaimed "Sunset Boulevard" turn with this romantic farce in which she again plays an actress. This time she's on a cross-country train journey from New York to Hollywood, along with her precocious daughter. Swanson's publicist and agent provide the laughs and a Harvard professor the love interest. With James Warren, Fred Clark, Hans Conried. 74 min.
27-6503 *$19.99*

Lucky Jim (1957)
Freewheeling British farce starring Ian Carmichael as a lecturer at a university who finds himself in the middle of all sorts of comic adventures during a special weekend in which he attends a colleague's party and a school function. Terry-Thomas and Hugh Griffith also star. 91 min.
44-1075 Was $19.99 *$14.99*

The Great Rupert (1950)
Novel comic excursion finds Jimmy Durante as the patriarch of a down-and-out family who finds fortune when large sums of money begin mysteriously appearing in his home. How did it get there? Why, a little squirrel pilfered the neighbor's savings! George Pal's feature directorial debut also stars Terry Moore, Tom Drake and Frank Cady. 86 min.
53-6022 Was $19.99 *$14.99*

Broth Of A Boy (1959)
Winning comedy about a British TV producer who finds the oldest man in the world, a 110-year-old cantankerous Irish villager, and tries to persuade him to appear on television. Barry Fitzgerald is tops as the centenarian; Tony Wright, Harry Brogan co-star. 77 min.
53-6047 *$29.99*

No Time For Flowers (1952)
Don Siegel's second effort is a reworking of "Ninotchka" with Viveca Lindfors as the secretary for a Czech government official. When her boss tries to test her allegiance to the communist party by showering her with gifts, the secretary begins to like the ways of capitalism—and he begins to like her! Paul Hubschmid, Adrienne Gessner also star. 80 min.
55-3055 *$19.99*

Bachelor In Paris (1952)
Dennis Price is the title Englishman who falls for French singer Anne Vernon but must overcome two obstacles—her French nobleman fiancé and his overbearing mother—in this romantic comedy. With Hermione Baddeley, Mischa Auer. AKA: "Song of Paris." 80 min.
09-5337 *$19.99*

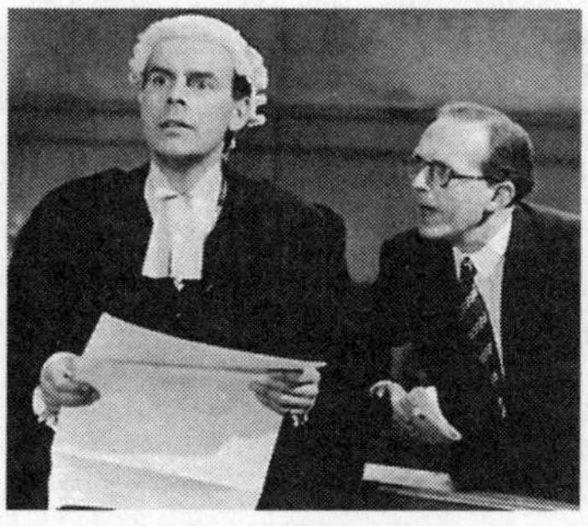

The Brothers In Law (1957)
Neophyte barrister Ian Carmichael learns the peculiarities of the legal system, as well as how to "bend" the law to his advantage, in a sly satiric look at jurisprudence from England's Boulting brothers. Richard Attenborough, Terry-Thomas also star. 94 min.
10-7563 Was $19.99 *$14.99*

Norman Wisdom

Trouble In Store (1953)
Norman Wisdom's first film features the clumsy Cockney comic as a lowly employee at a huge department store with dreams of becoming a window dresser. A number of mishaps get in Wisdom's way while attempting to achieve his goal and get the girl of his dreams. With Margaret Rutherford, Moira Lister. 107 min.
59-7084 *$29.99*

One Good Turn (1954)
Slapstick meets pathos with British comic Norman Wisdom as an orphan who remains at his orphanage to help with odd jobs and promises its charges a model car when he earns some cash. His inept efforts to get the money include stints as a sandwichboard man and a boxer. Joan Rice, Shirley Abicair also star. 90 min.
59-7085 *$29.99*

Man Of The Moment (1955)
Norman Wisdom, the clown with cloth cap and tight clothing, accidentally becomes the British delegate at the Geneva Convention. Comedy abounds as Wisdom conducts negotiations and handles important government affairs. Lana Morris and Belinda Lee co-star. 85 min.
59-7086 *$29.99*

Up In The World (1956)
Popular English funnyman Norman Wisdom takes a job as a window cleaner for Lady Banderville, but constantly gets into trouble with her son, Sir Reggie, who stages wild pranks. Norman decides to try to help the lad by straightening him out. Maureen Swanson and Jerry Desmonde also star. 87 min.
59-7087 *$29.99*

Just My Luck (1957)
Slapstick maven Norman Wisdom is smitten with a nice girl who lives nearby, but he tries to impress her by heading to the local bookie to place a bet. He wins and keeps on winning on the horses until the action whips him into a hilarious frenzy. Margaret Rutherford and Jill Dixon also star. 82 min.
59-7088 *$29.99*

The Square Peg (1958)
English WWII farce finds road mender Norman Wisdom recruited into the army and sent to serve in France. Wisdom accidentally slips behind enemy lines, but is picked up by the Resistance. To show his courage and enthusiasm for Great Britain, Norman leads a mission to rescue prisoners and tackle the German army. Honor Blackman, Edward Chapman also star. 89 min.
59-7089 *$29.99*

Follow A Star (1959)
Norman Wisdom is a tailor with a nice voice hired to do the crooning for a has-been singer. But Norman wants to get a shot at being on stage himself, and finds help from a resourceful music teacher and a handicapped girl. June Laverick and Jerry Desmonde also star. 99 min.
59-7090 *$29.99*

The Bulldog Breed (1960)
Trying to change his life by joining the navy, Norman Wisdom is chosen to be the first test subject for a planned rocket launch. The Cockney comic has to go through all sorts of tests, and people begin to wonder if he has the "right stuff" for the job. With Ian Hunter, David Lodge. 89 min.
59-7091 *$29.99*

The Girl On The Boat (1960)
Zany British jokester Norman Wisdom takes charge of his aunt's cottage during the summer months in the roaring '20s. He decides to invite a group of friends to the place, and the get-together leads to a series of hilarious comic situations. Millicent Martin and Ronald Fraser also star in this adaptation of the P.G. Wodehouse novel. 91 min.
59-7092 *$29.99*

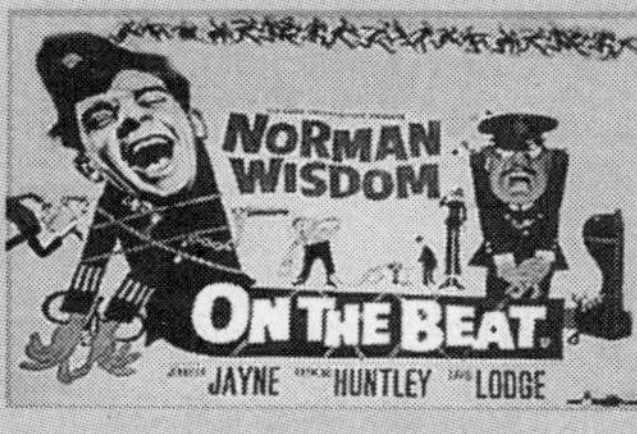

On The Beat (1962)
Diminutive daffy man Norman Wisdom wants desperately to become a policeman, but his height keeps him from joining the force. Instead, he settles for washing police cars—that is, until police superiors realize they can use Wisdom to nab some jewel thieves because of his resemblance to one of the hoods. With Jennifer Jayne, Raymond Huntley and David Lodge. 101 min.
59-7093 *$29.99*

The Early Bird (1965)
With the dairy he works for threatened with closing after a large company moves onto their turf, lone milkman Norman Wisdom decides to take manners into his own hands, sabotaging the corporation head's garden and golf game. Funny slapstick permeates this Wisdom outing, his first color effort. With Edward Chapman, Jerry Desmonde and Paddie O'Neil. 93 min.
59-7095 *$29.99*

Press For Time (1966)
British comic Norman Wisdom pulls a Peter Sellers and plays four different parts in this hilarious escapade. The story centers on Wisdom, a newspaper peddler, whose embarrassed Prime Minister grandfather has him sent to a town to work as a journalist. Rather than reporting the news, Wisdom makes it, getting involved in scandalous adventures. With Derek Bond. 98 min.
59-7096 *$29.99*

A Stitch In Time (1967)
Laughs and sentiments mix as Norman Wisdom plays the assistant to a butcher who has swallowed a watch. While his boss is having surgery, Wisdom gets into trouble with hospital officials and is kicked off the premises. Since Wisdom made an injured orphan girl smile, he tries to get back in the place to see her, but hilarious situations ensue. With Edward Chapman, Jeannette Sterke. 92 min.
59-7094 *$29.99*

What's Good For The Goose (1969)
Norman Wisdom still cranks out the comedies in the 1960s, this time taking a rather risqué approach to humor. He's a meek bank manager who meets a swinging hippie girl at a convention and tries to adapt to her carefree lifestyle, leaving his wife and marriage in the dust. Sally Geeson and Sarah Atkinson star; directed by the great Menahem Golan. 104 min.
59-7097 *$29.99*

The Legendary Norman Wisdom On Stage
Now you can catch one of England's best-loved comics in a stage show filled with his trademark slapstick routines and sensitive characters. He clowns, jokes, sings and even plays several instruments, demonstrating why he has impressed audiences in Great Britain for several decades. 57 min.
59-7098 *$29.99*

Lay That Rifle Down (1955)
Countrified chaos erupts for Judy Canova in this charming "Cinderella" comedy that finds the comedienne enrolled in a correspondence charm school to better herself, then having to outwit con men trying to swindle her aunt out of her small hotel. Corn-fed comedy also stars Robert Lowery, Richard Deacon. 71 min.
10-8486 *$19.99*

Innocents In Paris (1955)
Romantic omnibus film looks at the adventures of five Brits in Paris. There's an Englishman who discovers the only way to negotiate with a Russian official is through drinks; an elderly woman who purchases a phony copy of the Mona Lisa; a young woman charmed by a Parisian Romeo; and more. With Alastair Sim, Claire Bloom, Margaret Rutherford. 95 min.
10-9108 Was $19.99 *$14.99*

One Wild Oat (1951)
The children of two squabbling families try to put an end to the feud by announcing their engagement, but the girl's father tries to dig up dirt on his would-be in-laws to nip the nuptials in the bud, in this breezy British comedy based on a popular stageplay. Robertson Hare, Stanley Holloway star; look quickly for Audrey Hepburn in her film debut. 78 min.
10-9502 *$19.99*

The Reluctant Debutante (1958)
Sparkling comedy stars Rex Harrison and Kay Kendall as a society couple who would like to see daughter Sandra Dee marry a husband from a wealthy, high class British family. Unfortunately, she's head over heels for an American musician with a less-than-sterling reputation. John Saxon and Angela Lansbury also star in Vincente Minnelli's sophisticated gem. 94 min.
12-2323 *$19.99*

The Affairs Of Dobie Gillis (1953)
Max Shulman's comic collegian comes to the big screen in this comedy sparked with big band-styled music. Bobby Van's Dobie gets into romantic and scholastic trouble during freshman year at school, along with pals played by Debbie Reynolds, Barbara Ruick and Bob Fosse. Songs include "I'm Through with Love" and "All I Do Is Dream of You." 74 min.
12-2836 *$19.99*

It Started With A Kiss (1959)
Frothy romantic farce starring Debbie Reynolds as a showgirl who falls for penniless Air Force sergeant Glenn Ford. After he wins a $40,000 car, the two get hitched, but Reynolds tests his love when she forbids him from touching her during their honeymoon in Spain. With Fred Clark, Eva Gabor, Edgar Buchanan. 103 min.
12-2567 ☐*$19.99*

One Night In The Tropics (1940)
Abbott and Costello's screen debut finds them as detectives investigating an insurance scam involving a bride-to-be who runs off with her insurance salesman on their wedding day. Bud and Lou use some of their favorite routines in this musical-comedy that features a score by Jerome Kern, Oscar Hammerstein II and Dorothy Fields. With Allan Jones, Nancy Kelly, Robert Cummings. 82 min.
07-1997 ❑$14.99

Buck Privates (1941)
Boot camp becomes a course in basic comedy training, thanks to Bud Abbott and Lou Costello in the team's first starring film, when they join spoiled rich man Lee Bowman and ex-valet Alan Curtis as reluctant draftees. The Andrews Sisters also get in on the fun, singing "Boogie Woogie Bugle Boy" and "Bounce Me Brother with a Solid Four." With Shemp Howard. 84 min.
07-1170 $14.99

Buck Privates Come Home (1947)
The problems of homecoming G.I.s were spoofed in this sequel to Abbott and Costello's first starring film, as the boys try to sneak a French war orphan into America and find that their old sergeant is now their neighborhood cop! With Nat Pendleton, Beverly Simmons. 77 min.
07-1832 ❑$14.99

In The Navy (1941)
After wrecking the Army in "Buck Privates," Abbott and Costello set sail for seafaring silliness in this service comedy. Joining them on board for laughter and musical numbers are Dick Powell, Shemp Howard and The Andrews Sisters. 85 min.
07-1698 $14.99

Hold That Ghost! (1941)
There are high spirits when Abbott and Costello find themselves trapped in a haunted house along with a cast of eccentrics that includes health nut Richard Carlson, impresario Mischa Auer, and radio "screamer" Joan Davis. 86 min.
07-1134 $14.99

Keep 'Em Flying (1941)
Take off for laughs with Abbott and Costello as the duo play would-be pilots who get mixed up with stunt pilot Dick Foran and Martha Raye (in a dual role). High-flying comedy also includes musical numbers like "I'm Looking for the Boy with the Wistful Eyes" and "Pig Foot Pete." 86 min.
07-1699 $14.99

Who Done It? (1942)
Would you believe Abbott and Costello? What the pair do in this comic mystery is portray private eyes while they "help" the police catch a radio executive's killer. Frantic Bud and Lou farce co-stars William Bendix, Louise Albritton, Shemp Howard. 75 min.
07-1621 $14.99

Pardon My Sarong (1942)
Chicago bus drivers Abbott and Costello take a really wrong turn when their involvement with a wealthy playboy winds up taking them to the South Seas and into a den of jewel thieves. Robert Paige, Lionel Atwill, Virginia Bruce, William Demarest and The Ink Spots co-star. 83 min.
07-1834 ❑$14.99

Ride 'Em Cowboy (1942)
"City slickers" Abbott and Costello wind up working as comic cowhands on a frontier dude ranch in this song-filled gagfest. Highlights include guest star Ella Fitzgerald singing "A Tisket, A Tasket" and a skit with Lou facing constant interruptions while trying to sleep. With Anne Gwynne, Johnny Mack Brown. 86 min.
07-1835 ❑$14.99

Rio Rita (1942)
Lively musical comedy with Abbott and Costello trying to thwart a Nazi spy staying at the Western-styled resort where they work. Kathryn Grayson, John Carroll and Tom Conway co-star; songs include "Sweetheart We Need Each Other" and "Long Before You Came Along." Based on a play and a 1929 Wheeler and Woolsey film. 91 min.
12-2361 $19.99

Hit The Ice (1943)
The laughs snowball when Abbott and Costello get suckered into pulling off a bank heist, and then must track down gang boss Sheldon Leonard before the cops track them down! 89 min.
07-1513 $14.99

In Society (1944)
Inept plumbers Abbott and Costello are accidentally invited to a high society bash and are mistaken as hoity-toity members of the social elite in this farce featuring memorable slapstick stuff, funny dialogue and a great chase sequence. With Marion Hutton, Kirby Grant, Arthur Treacher. 84 min.
07-1996 ❑$14.99

Lost In A Harem (1944)
Abbott and Costello are magicians stranded in a desert kingdom ruled by an evil sheik who are called on to help a dashing prince regain the throne. Marilyn Maxwell, John Conte and Jimmy Dorsey and his Orchestra are featured, along with an elaborate "Scheherazade" ballet segment. 89 min.
12-2360 ❑$19.99

The Naughty Nineties (1945)
As comics on board a paddlewheel showboat, Abbott and Costello come to the aid of their boss when he loses the ship to some shady gamblers in a song-filled "Gay '90s" comedy that features the only big screen appearance of the team's famed "Who's on First?" routine. With Alan Curtis, Rita Johnson. 76 min.
07-1619 $14.99

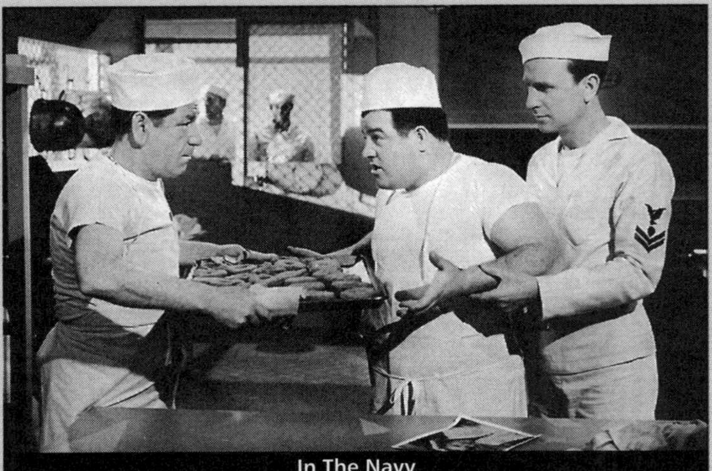
In The Navy

Abbott & Costello

Here Come The Co-Eds (1945)
Funny Abbott and Costello effort with Bud and Lou as caretakers at an all-girl college who go to hilarious lengths to save the school when it's slated to close because of financial trouble. One of the highlights: a wrestling match between Bud and the Masked Marvel (actually the film's bad guy: Lon Chaney, Jr.). With Peggy Ryan, Martha O'Driscoll. 90 min.
07-1998 ❑$14.99

Abbott And Costello In Hollywood (1945)
Bud and Lou are a barber and porter in the movie capital who decide they can make more money by becoming "agents to the stars" and try to get their client, singer Robert Stanton, into a musical film. Cameos by Lucille Ball, Mike Mazurki, Dean Stockwell. 83 min.
12-1075 Was $49.99 $19.99

The Time Of Their Lives (1946)
Considered by many to be their best film, this offbeat Abbott and Costello entry has Lou playing a ghost wrongly accused of treason during the Revolutionary War. Along with fellow spectre Marjorie Reynolds, he must get the new owners of the mansion they haunt to clear their names. Bud co-stars as Lou's 18th-century rival and a 20th-century psychologist. 82 min.
07-1620 $14.99

Little Giant (1946)
A different kind of Abbott and Costello outing with Lou as the star, playing a vacuum cleaner merchant determined to make it as a successful door-to-door salesman in order to earn enough to marry his sweetheart. Bud plays two parts: Lou's boss and the company's president. With Brenda Joyce, Jacqueline De Wit and Marx Brothers foil Margaret Dumont. 91 min.
07-1994 ❑$14.99

The Wistful Widow Of Wagon Gap (1947)
Fun on the frontier with Abbott and Costello as salesmen who accidentally get involved in a gunfight, with Lou being charged with caring for the dead man's family. Since to kill Costello would mean taking on the unruly brood, he becomes the most feared man in town and the new sheriff! Marjorie Main matches the boys laugh for laugh in the title role. 78 min.
07-1836 ❑$14.99

Abbott And Costello Meet Frankenstein (1948)
Universal tossed their most popular ghouls—Dracula, the Wolf Man, and Frankenstein's Monster—in this comedic monster mash, with Abbott and Costello trying to dodge Bela Lugosi (as Dracula), who wants to put Lou's brain inside the Monster's head. With Lon Chaney, Jr., Glenn Strange. 83 min.
07-1115 $14.99

Mexican Hayride (1948)
The Cole Porter Broadway musical was stripped of its score by Universal and turned into a comedy for stars Abbott and Costello, as a stock scheme sends the duo south of the border for laughs amidst the bullfights and señoritas. With Virginia Grey, Luba Malina. 77 min.
07-1833 ❑$14.99

The Noose Hangs High (1948)
Abbott and Costello play a pair of window washers who are mistaken for gamblers and ripped off for $50,000 from a group of thugs. Caper comedy features the sort of hilarious hijinks you'd expect from Bud and Lou, along with their classic "Mudder and Fodder" routine. 77 min.
12-2548 $19.99

Africa Screams (1949)
Mistaken for great hunters and shanghaied to Africa, Abbott and Costello lead crooks on a silly safari for hidden diamonds. Lots of bungles in the jungle, with guest stars like Max and Buddy Baer, Frank Buck and Clyde Beatty, and Shemp Howard and Joe Besser. 79 min.
10-2059 $14.99

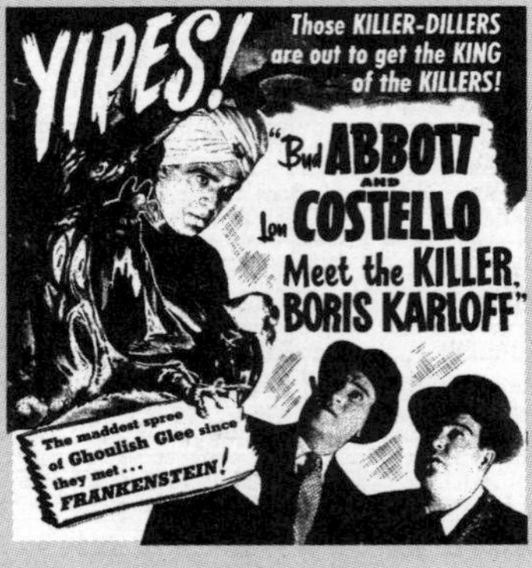

Abbott And Costello Meet The Killer, Boris Karloff (1949)
Funny and suspenseful outing for Bud and Lou casts them as a pair of hotel employees determined to discover why corpses keep popping up around the premises. Is supposed swami Karloff really the killer...or is it someone else? 84 min.
07-2264 ❑$14.99

Abbott And Costello In The Foreign Legion (1950)
Wrestling promoters Abbott and Costello leave their Brooklyn home in search of a missing grappler and are enlisted into the French Foreign Legion after they get involved with a sexy spy. While making mincemeat of the Legion, the boys discover that their sergeant is in cahoots with an evil sheik. Walter Slezak, Patricia Medina, Tor Johnson co-star. 80 min.
07-2114 ❑$14.99

Abbott And Costello Meet The Invisible Man (1951)
"Private eye school" graduates Bud and Lou are hired by a boxer to help clear him of a murder rap put on him by a crooked promoter, but it takes a doctor's invisibility serum and a turn in the ring by Costello to bring the crooks to justice in this laughfest. Arthur Franz, Sheldon Leonard also star. 82 min.
07-1831 ❑$14.99

Comin' Round The Mountain (1951)
Wacky comedy meets hillbilly farce and some lively singing in this Abbott and Costello romp in which the fellows search for gold in backwoods Kentucky and get involved with feuding families and a love potion. Dorothy Shay, Kirby Grant also star. 77 min.
07-2115 ❑$14.99

Lost In Alaska (1952)
After saving a gold prospector from taking his own life, Abbott and Costello go way up North to Alaska in order to help the prospector keep his $2 million fortune away from a devious saloon owner. A wild dogsled chase highlights this funny A&C outing. Tom Ewell, Mitzi Green and Bruce Cabot also star. 87 min.
07-1993 ❑$14.99

Jack And The Beanstalk (1952)
Bud and Lou risk certain death to rescue a beautiful princess from the giant and bring back the hen that lays golden eggs in this musical, magical treatment of the classic fairy tale. Buddy Baer, Dorothy Ford also star. 78 min.
08-1062 Was $19.99 $14.99

Abbott And Costello Meet Dr. Jekyll & Mr. Hyde (1953)
Bud Abbott is Slim and Lou Costello is Tubby, two American cops sent to London who find themselves in the throes of terror when they become mixed up with an equal rights leader (Helen Wescott), her reporter boyfriend (Craig Stevens) and the menacing Dr. Jekyll (Boris Karloff). 77 min.
07-1182 $14.99

Abbott And Costello Go To Mars (1953)
The laughs are out of this world as Abbott and Costello accidentally blast off in a spaceship, land in New Orleans, where they're confronted by some crooks, then take off again to the gal-populated planet of Venus (but not Mars). With Martha Hyer, Jack Kruschen and, in a small role, Anita Ekberg. 77 min.
07-2117 ❑$14.99

Abbott And Costello Meet The Mummy (1955)
Bud Abbott and Lou Costello get wrapped up in riotous comedy when they head to Egypt in search of hidden treasure and have a close encounter with Kharis, the living mummy. Marie Windsor, Richard Deacon, Michael Ansara co-star. 90 min.
07-1995 ❑$14.99

Abbott And Costello Meet The Keystone Kops (1955)
Abbott and Costello are duped into purchasing a ramshackle silent film studio and head from Hollywood to New York to catch the culprit. Wacky car chases, custard pies and zany jokes populate the slapstick proceedings. With Fred Clark, Maxie Rosenbloom, Lynn Bari and Mack Sennett. 79 min.
07-2116 ❑$14.99

Dance With Me Henry (1956)
Abbott and Costello's final film together mixes slapstick and sentiment, as Bud and Lou run an amusement park while playing guardians to a group of orphans for whom a social worker is seeking a permanent home. Mary Wickes, Rusty Hamer co-star. 79 min.
12-2356 ❑$19.99

The 30-Foot Bride Of Candy Rock (1959)
A zany sci-fi comedy with Lou Costello (in his only starring role minus Bud Abbott) as a trashman and part-time inventor who develops a machine that turns curvaceous girlfriend Dorothy Provine into a giant. With Gale Gordon, Charles Lane. 73 min.
02-2681 $14.99

The World Of Abbott And Costello (1964)
A fun-filled salute to two of Hollywood's best-loved laughmakers, this collection of Bud and Lou's greatest movie bits includes many of their classic routines, including "Who's on First?" Jack E. Leonard narrates. 75 min.
07-2265 ❑$14.99

The Abbott & Costello Show (Colgate Comedy Hour)
The beloved screen cut-ups made their starring TV debut as two of the rotating guest hosts of the popular "Colgate Comedy Hour" variety show from 1951 to 1954. Each tape in this nostalgic, laugh-filled series features two episodes and runs about 100 min.

The Abbott & Costello Show: Who's On First?
Guest stars include Lon Chaney, Jr. and Sid Fields.
58-8267 $12.99

The Abbott & Costello Show: Errol Flynn
Guest stars include Errol Flynn, Phil Regan and Gale Storm.
58-8268 $12.99

The Abbott & Costello Show: Victor Borge
Guest stars include Victor Borge and Hoagy Carmichael.
58-8269 $12.99

The Abbott & Costello Show: Jane Russell
Guest stars include Jane Russell and Charles Laughton.
58-8270 $12.99

Colgate Comedy Hour Christmas Show (1952)
Abbott and Costello were the guest hosts for this holiday segment of this early TV variety series. The skits include Bud and Lou trying to raise money for gifts, a cooking lesson on top of Lou's noggin, and more. Also included is a spooky segment from 1955 with the boys meeting the Frankenstein Monster on Universal's back lot. 50 min.
62-1303 $19.99

The Abbott & Costello TV Show
In this situation comedy, which ran from 1951 to 1952, Bud and Lou played unemployed actors who share an apartment together in a rooming house. The team used some of their most famous routines in the show, and supporting characters included Hillary Brooke as Lou's gal, Gordon Jones as Mike the Cop and Joe Besser as Stinky the bratty child. Each tape runs about 110 min.

The Abbott & Costello TV Show, Vol. 1
Includes "Duck Dinner," "Hillary's Birthday," "Million Dollar Refund" and "Actor's Home" (featuring the "Who's on First" sketch).
63-7041 *$19.99*

The Abbott & Costello TV Show, Vol. 2
Includes "Lou's Birthday," "Getting a Job" (with the famous "Susquehana Hat Company" routine), "Uncle Bozzo" and Stolen Skates."
63-7042 *$19.99*

The Abbott & Costello TV Show, Vol. 3
Includes "Lou Falls for Ruby," "Hillary's Father," "Uncle Ruppert" and "Bingo's Troubles."
63-7043 *$19.99*

Abbott & Costello TV Show Set
The first three volumes of the duo's classic TV shenanigans are available in this boxed collection.
63-7083 Save $10.00! *$49.99*

The Abbott & Costello TV Show, Vol. 4
Includes "The Drugstore," "Wife Wanted," "$1,000 Prize" and "Square Meal."
63-7069 *$19.99*

The Abbott & Costello TV Show, Vol. 5
Includes "Police Academy," "Killer's Wife," "Charity Bazaar" and "Well Oiled."
63-7070 *$19.99*

The Abbott & Costello TV Show, Vol. 6
Includes "Wrestling Match," "In Society," "Beauty Contest" and "Lou's Marriage."
63-7071 *$19.99*

The Abbott & Costello TV Show, Vol. 7
Includes "Jail" (featuring the "Niagara Falls" sketch), "Private Eye," "Vacuum Cleaner Salesman" and "Fall Guy."
63-7118 *$19.99*

The Abbott & Costello TV Show, Vol. 8
Includes "Little Old Lady," "Bank Holdup," "Dentist Office" and "Fencing Master."
63-7119 *$19.99*

The Abbott & Costello TV Show, Vol. 9
Includes "Politician," "Public Enemies," "From Bed to Worse" and "Car Trouble."
63-7120 *$19.99*

The Abbott & Costello TV Show, Vol. 10
Includes "The Army Story," "Efficiency Experts," "Peace and Quiet" and "Honeymoon House."
63-7121 *$19.99*

The Abbott & Costello TV Show, Vol. 11
Includes "The Western Story," "Barber Lou," "Las Vegas" and "Pest Exterminators."
63-7122 *$19.99*

The Abbott & Costello TV Show, Vol. 12
Includes "Television," "The Haunted House," "The Vacation" and "South of Dixie."
63-7123 *$19.99*

Abbott & Costello Collector's Set
If you miss out on getting this deluxe boxed set that includes "Abbott and Costello Meet the Killer, Boris Karloff," "The World of Abbott and Costello" and "Abbott and Costello Meet Jerry Seinfeld," then you're a "baaaaad boy."
07-2267 Save $15.00 *$24.99*

Abbott & Costello Meet The Monsters Collection
"Ch...Ch...Ch...." "What, Costello, are ya tryin' ta tell me how cheap this deluxe boxed set is?" Featured are four of Bud and Lou's most frightfully funny films: "Abbott and Costello Meet Dr. Jekyll & Mr. Hyde," "Abbott and Costello Meet Frankenstein," "Abbott and Costello Meet the Invisible Man" and "Abbott and Costello Meet the Mummy."
07-2888 *$59.99*

Legends Of Comedy: Abbott & Costello Gift Set
Their slapstick and snappy patter earned them the title of "Legends of Comedy," and you'll see why with this collector's set that includes "Here Come the Co-Eds," "Hit the Ice," "Hold That Ghost," "The Naughty Nineties," "One Night in the Tropics," "Pardon My Sarong," "The Time of Their Lives" and "Who Done It?," plus the bonus tape "Abbott & Costello Meet Jerry Seinfeld."
07-2830 Save $15.00! *$119.99*

Escapade (1955)
The sons of a famous pacifist break out of his shadow by circulating an anti-war petition and stealing a plane to deliver it to world leaders in Vienna. Thoughtful comedy stars John Mills, Alastair Sim and a young Peter Asher (of Peter and Gordon fame). 88 min.
09-2061 Was $29.99 *$24.99*

The Madame Gambles (1951)
Madcap British farce about Madame Louise, an elderly Mayfair boutique owner who's just lost her shop to a shady bookie named Charlie Trout with a bad bet on the ponies, and her attempts to retrieve it after the new proprietor implements new "modernizing" techniques. Stars Richard Hearne, Hilda Bayley and Petula Clark. 83 min.
09-2274 Was $24.99 *$14.99*

Tony Draws A Horse (1950)
A wry comedy from England about a young boy encouraged by his mother to express himself freely. The lack of discipline turns him into a "problem child" whose behavior leads his parents into heated arguments and threatens their marriage. Cecil Parker, Anne Crawford and Sebastian Cabot star. 90 min.
09-2328 *$24.99*

The Oracle (1953)
A reporter tries to make a story out of a mysterious being he discovers living at the bottom of a well. A disbelieving editor fires him, but the oracle's prophecies come true and soon have the country in an uproar. Robert Beatty, Joseph Tomelty star. AKA: "The Horse's Mouth." 84 min.
09-5029 *$19.99*

Passionate Stranger (1957)
Witty British comedy about a female writer who hires a new, Italian chauffeur to be both her driver and the subject of her new novel. When he reads the manuscript, he believes that she is in love with him, which causes all sorts of complications. Ralph Richardson, Margaret Leighton star. AKA: "A Novel Affair." 97 min.
09-5030 *$19.99*

Second Fiddle (1957)
British romantic farce about a recently wed couple whose marriage is tested when the woman travels to America for business while the husband is tempted by his sexy new secretary. Adrienne Corri, Thorley Walters and Lisa Gastoni star. 73 min.
09-5032 *$19.99*

Into The Blue (1951)
A couple on a yacht bound for Norway discover a mysterious stowaway aboard. Their attempts to get him off the ship and onto dry land are unsuccessful. Could he have fallen in love with the yacht's cook? Michael Wilding, Odile Versois, Jack Hulbert and Constance Cummings star. AKA: "The Man in the Dinghy." 83 min.
09-5152 *$19.99*

Something In The City (1951)
A street artist who has conned his family into thinking he's a successful businessman is forced into having his life revealed when it's believed his alter ego has been murdered. Richard Hearne, Garry Marsh and Ellen Pollock star. 80 min.
09-5234 *$19.99*

The Happy Family (1952)
Fine British satire starring Stanley Holloway and Kathleen Harrison as a married couple who decide to take a stand against the government when their property is desired for a festival site. With Naunton Wayne, Dandy Nichols. AKA: "Mr. Lord Says No." 76 min.
09-5243 *$19.99*

Cheer The Brave (1951)
A henpecked spouse gets an unexpected chance at freedom from his shrewish wife when her first husband shows up at their door in this British domestic comedy. Jack McNaughton, Elsie Randolph, Geoffrey Keen star. 62 min.
09-5335 *$19.99*

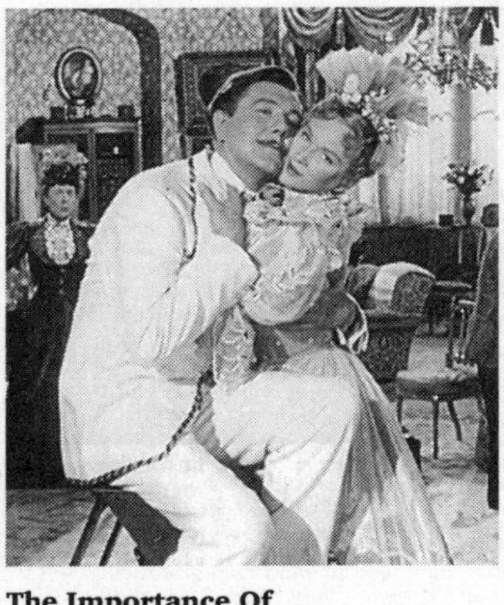

The Importance Of Being Earnest (1952)
Oscar Wilde's classic drawing room comedy of morals and deceptions in Victorian England is faithfully brought to the screen. The talented cast includes Michael Denison, Michael Redgrave, Joan Greenwood, Margaret Rutherford and Edith Evans. 95 min.
06-1535 Was $19.99 *$14.99*

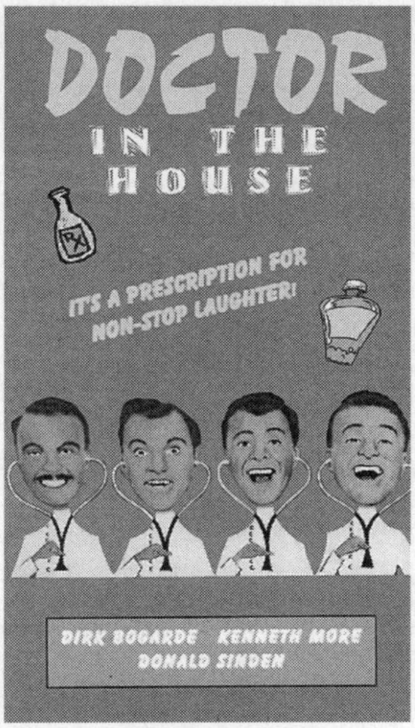
DOCTOR
IN THE
HOUSE
IT'S A PRESCRIPTION FOR NON-STOP LAUGHTER!
DIRK BOGARDE KENNETH MORE
DONALD SINDEN

Doctor In The House (1954)
The original British comedy that spawned a slew of sequels and a popular TV series stars Dirk Bogarde as a medical student who must overcome the womanizing and carousing of his three comrades if any of them hope to graduate. With Kenneth More, Kay Kendall. 89 min.
06-1610 *$29.99*

Doctor At Sea (1955)
Dirk Bogarde returns as young medico Simon Sparrow in this second film in the popular British series, setting out as ship's doctor on a cruise where one of the only two women on board is the stunning Brigitte Bardot. James Robertson Justice co-stars. 93 min.
15-1138 *$29.99*

Doctor At Large (1957)
Dirk Bogarde returns as an eager young surgeon who finds complications at work with his superiors, an attractive lady doctor and a fellow surgeon's wife. Charming comedy stars Shirley Eaton, James Robertson Justice. 94 min.
15-1065 Was $24.99 *$19.99*

Doctor In Love (1960)
Doctors Michael Craig and Leslie Phillips find romance and comedic situations abound when they head to St. Swithin's Hospital in the country to work on the "Foulness Anti-Cold Research Unit." With James Robertson Justice and Carole Lesley. 98 min.
59-7048 *$29.99*

Doctor In Distress (1963)
More British hospital hijinks, as doctor Dirk Bogarde must deal with an amorous actress in his care and two Scandinavian nurses with an eye on his bedside manner. Samantha Eggar, James Robertson Justice star. 98 min.
15-1077 *$29.99*

Doctor In Clover (1966)
When a new doctor with an eye for the ladies take a job at Hampden Cross Hospital, the entire staff is thrown into chaos. Hilarious entry in the sexy and wacky series stars Leslie Phillips, James Robertson Justice and Shirley Ann Field. 98 min.
59-7047 *$29.99*

Doctor In Trouble (1970)
When a TV heartthrob doctor is admitted to St. Swithin's Hospital, he's ordered some special therapy: a cruise on a boat called the Golden Horn. To complicate matters, doctor Leslie Phillips stows away on the ship to chase a woman and eventually becomes the captain's steward. Harry Secombe, James Robertson Justice and Robert Morley also star. 87 min.
59-7049 *$29.99*

Behave Yourself! (1951)
Comedy-thriller stars Shelley Winters and Farley Granger as a couple on the run when the stray dog they take in turns out to be a trained "crime dog" that the bad guys want back. With William Demarest, Sheldon Leonard, Lon Chaney, Jr. 81 min.
08-1310 *$19.99*

Adventures Of Sadie (1955)
Early Joan Collins outing with the sexy star as a woman shipwrecked with three men on an island. All the guys are hot for Joan, and who can blame them? George Cole, Kenneth More and Hermione Gingold co-star. 88 min.
08-1472 Was $19.99 *$14.99*

Carry On Admiral (1956)
Jolly good British comedy, as two members of Her Majesty's Royal Navy trade places, turning the ship into a shambles. The final straw comes when the Admiral's dinghy is destroyed. David Tomlinson, Peggy Cummins star. AKA: "The Ship Was Loaded." 88 min.
08-1473 *$19.99*

Ma And Pa Kettle (1949)
Fresh from their success in "The Egg and I," Marjorie Main and Percy Kilbride reteamed as the hillbilly husband and wife in the initial outing of their popular film series. Just as the Kettles and their 15 kids are about to be run out of their ramshackle house, Pa wins "the home of the future" in a slogan-writing contest. Richard Long, Meg Randall co-star. 76 min.
07-2108 □*$14.99*

Ma And Pa Kettle Go To Town (1950)
Ma and Pa Kettle land in New York City and find themselves helping a crook on the lam when they agree to deliver some stolen cash to a friend. When Pa misplaces the loot, the crooks think he's plotted against them. Percy Kilbride, Marjorie Main, Charles McGraw and Jim Backus star. 80 min.
07-2109 □*$14.99*

Ma And Pa Kettle Back On The Farm (1951)
Ma and Pa head back to their old homestead when they think there's uranium on the premises. Some crooks are also after the priceless element, but the radioactivity turns out to be from Pa's army surplus overalls! Marjorie Main, Percy Kilbride, Edward Sedgwick and Barbara Brown star. 81 min.
07-2111 □*$14.99*

Ma And Pa Kettle At The Fair (1952)
That hilarious backwoods brood heads to the county fair with hopes of winning some tuition money for their college-bound daughter. Ma does some fine baking, Pa enters a wacky horse race, and the homespun fun doesn't stop. Marjorie Main, Percy Kilbride, Richard Long and Jim Backus star. 79 min.
07-2110 □*$14.99*

Ma And Pa Kettle On Vacation (1953)
While on vacation in Paris with their daughter's wealthy in-laws, the Kettles wind up in the middle of an espionage plot involving secret plans. There's lots of laughs as America's most homespun couple get chased through the streets of the world's most sophisticated city. Marjorie Main, Percy Kilbride, Ray Collins and Barbara Brown star. 76 min.
07-2231 □*$14.99*

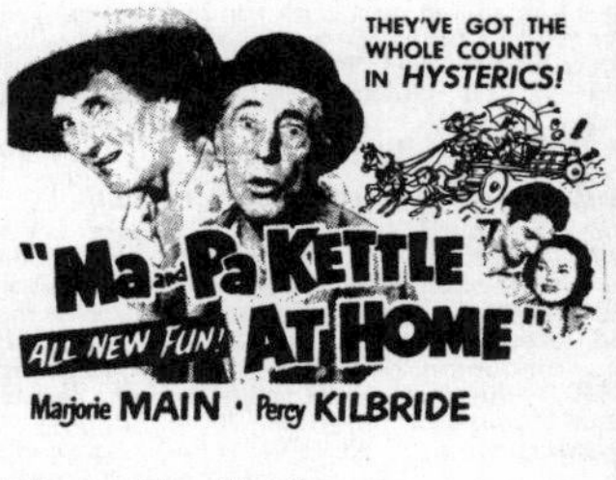
THEY'VE GOT THE WHOLE COUNTY IN HYSTERICS!
"Ma and Pa KETTLE AT HOME"
ALL NEW FUN!
Marjorie MAIN • Percy KILBRIDE

Ma And Pa Kettle At Home (1954)
Elwin Kettle, one of Ma and Pa's 15 kids, has a chance to win a scholarship to an agricultural college. When the school officials decide to investigate their candidate, Ma and Pa try to tidy up the creaky farm, but a rainstorm ruins the place. Will Elwin get to further his education? Marjorie Main, Percy Kilbride, Brett Halsey star. 81 min.
07-2230 □*$14.99*

Ma And Pa Kettle At Waikiki (1955)
When their cousin becomes ill in Hawaii, Ma and Pa Kettle and their daughter Rosie head to the islands to help out in her pineapple factory. Wackiness and intrigue ensue as the family accidentally increases production at the plant and Pa gets kidnapped. Percy Kilbride, Marjorie Main, Lori Nelson and Loring Smith star. 79 min.
07-2254 □*$14.99*

The Kettles In The Ozarks (1956)
Ma Kettle heads to the Ozark Mountains with the kids (but without Pa) to visit Uncle Sedge on his decrepit farm. Soon, the family encounters nasty bootleggers while Uncle Sedge decides what to do with his longtime romance with his housekeeper. Marjorie Main, Arthur Hunnicutt, Una Merkel star. 81 min.
07-2255 □*$14.99*

The Kettles On Old MacDonald's Farm (1957)
The finale to the fractured farm series finds Ma and Pa Kettle (Marjorie Main and Parker Fennelly) playing matchmaker for an amiable lumberjack. But they've got a lot of work ahead of them, as they try to coach his date, a spoiled rich gal, in the ways of the backwoods. Gloria Talbott, John Smith co-star. 82 min.
07-2256 □*$14.99*

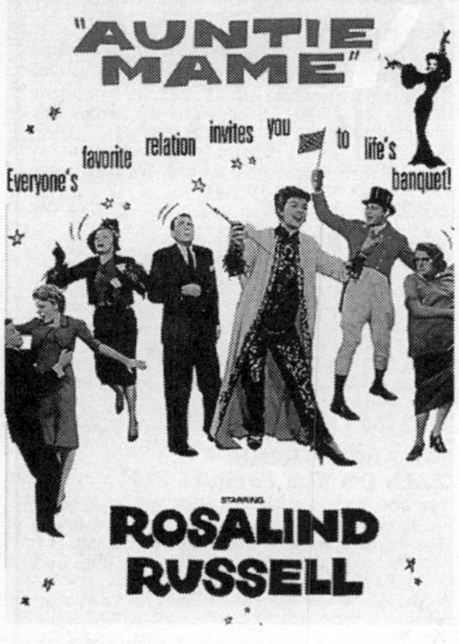
"AUNTIE MAME"
Everyone's favorite relation invites you to life's banquet!
STARRING
ROSALIND RUSSELL

Auntie Mame (1958)
Rosalind Russell re-creates her Broadway triumph as the flashy, lovably eccentric socialite who takes her orphaned nephew under her wing and shows him around the world of the Roaring '20s. Based on Patrick Dennis' novel; with Forrest Tucker, Peggy Cass, Coral Browne and Jan Handzlik. Includes original theatrical trailer. 143 min.
19-1206 $19.99

Auntie Mame (Letterboxed Version)
Also available in a theatrical, widescreen format.
19-2763 $19.99

Uncle Was A Vampire (1959)
An Italian-made vampire satire about the last of a clan of bloodsuckers whose fortunes have sunk so low they are forced to turn the ancestral castle into a hotel. Christopher Lee parodies his famous Count, as the patriarch who brings his not-so-thrilled nephew into the family business. 85 min.
68-8035 $19.99

Girls At Sea (1958)
Three gals are left on a battleship after a party and have to elude the handsome captain before the ship gets called for action. Bright British farce stars Guy Rolfe, Michael Hordern, Anne Kimbell and Daniel Massey. 84 min.
17-9015 Was $19.99 $14.99

Angels In The Outfield (1951)
Heavenly baseball comedy stars Paul Douglas as the brash, loud-mouthed Pittsburgh Pirates skipper who gets some divine intervention to help his team out of the cellar. When a little girl claims to see angels on the field, reporter Janet Leigh turns the story into a national controversy. Named by President Eisenhower as his favorite film; with Donna Corcoran, Keenan Wynn. 102 min.
12-2940 $14.99

Tammy And The Bachelor (1957)
Original entry into the "Tammy" series stars Debbie Reynolds as the ever-cute and perky country gal, here falling in love with the wealthy pilot she nurses back to health after his plane crashes. Leslie Nielsen, Walter Brennan, Fay Wray co-star. 89 min.
07-1404 Was $69.99 $14.99

Tammy And The Doctor (1963)
Look who's here...Sandra Dee, as the effervescent Tammy. This time around, she's off to L.A. to become a nurse, and she turns the hospital upside-down with laughter! Peter Fonda (in his film debut), Beulah Bondi, Macdonald Carey co-star. 88 min.
07-1405 Was $69.99 $14.99

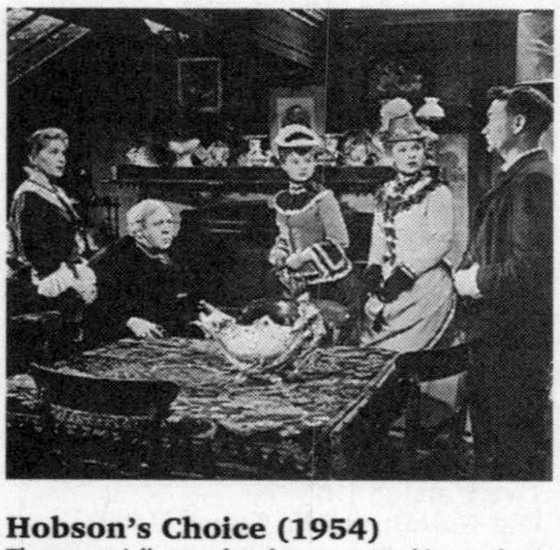

Hobson's Choice (1954)
The perennially popular play was turned into a classic comedy by director/co-scripter David Lean, with a bravura performance by Charles Laughton in the title role of a tyrannical boot-maker who forbids his daughters to marry whom they wish, and how they turn the tables on him. With John Mills, Brenda de Banzie. 107 min.
22-5730 Remastered $29.99

The Caretaker's Daughter (1953)
The jealous wife of a theater impresario suspects him of infidelity, but her jealousy goes haywire when the theater troupe assumes different identities to confuse her. This British farce stars Hugh Wakefield and Derek Bond. 83 min.
53-6079 $29.99

The Baby And The Battleship (1956)
British farce starring John Mills and Richard Attenborough about a sailor on leave in Naples who gets stuck with the baby brother of his buddy's date for the evening, and then sneaks the tot aboard their disembarking warship. 96 min.
10-7561 Was $19.99 $14.99

Full Of Life (1956)
Judy Holliday plays the pregnant wife of struggling writer Richard Conte who comes under duress when hubby's opinionated father tries to ensure that the couple gets a proper, full-blown Italian wedding. Family farce features Esther Minciotti, Joe de Santis and Metropolitan Opera star Salvatore Baccaloni as Papa. 91 min.
10-2324 Was $19.99 $14.99

Navy Heroes (1959)
A tale from Britain about a cynical war hero whose days are brightened after he becomes an athletic director at a boys' camp. With Vincent Ball, John Charlesworth. 93 min.
10-9521 $14.99

The Mating Game (1959)
IRS agent Tony Randall is sent to investigate a backwoods family that owes $50,000 in back taxes, but what he finds is a bizarre bartering economy, a massive moonshine-induced hangover, and romance with gorgeous farmer's daughter Debbie Reynolds. Paul Douglas, Una Merkel, Fred Clark also star. 96 min.
12-2566 $19.99

A Royal Affair (1950)
Charming comedy stars Maurice Chevalier as a king who arrives in Paris and gets a quick indoctrination into the French lifestyle as he romances two women, thanks in part to the efforts of a senator who desperately wants a treaty signed. Annie Ducaux, Sophie Desmarets also star. AKA: "The King." 100 min.
17-9071 $19.99

No Time For Sergeants (1958)
Andy Griffith is hillbilly Army recruit Will Stockdale (a role he first played on Broadway and TV), whose well-meaning attempts to please his harried sergeant make for classic comedy. Murray Hamilton, Myron McCormick and, in an early role, Don Knotts, also star. 119 min.
19-1415 Was $19.99 $14.99

This Could Be The Night (1957)
Charming comedy laced with musical numbers stars Jean Simmons as a prim teacher who moonlights as a secretary for Broadway nightclub owners (Anthony Franciosa and Paul Douglas) and winds up coming between the pair. Julie Wilson, Joan Blondell co-star; directed by Robert Wise. 105 min.
12-2626 $19.99

Our Miss Brooks (1956)
Decades before the Addamses, Clampetts or Flintstones, TV's wisecracking English teacher Connie Brooks (Eve Arden) made the jump to the big screen in this feature-length comedy. Will Madison High's long-suffering single gal finally snare the man of her dreams, biology teacher Phillip Boynton (Robert Rockwell)? Series regulars Gale Gordon and Richard Crenna also star. 84 min.
19-2243 Was $29.99 $19.99

The Lady Says No (1951)
Quick-witted battle-of-the-sexes farce stars David Niven as a photographer assigned to take pictures of author Joan Caulfield, whose latest tome is highly critical of men. James Robertson Justice and Frances Bavier co-star. 80 min.
53-6025 $19.99

Three Guys Named Mike (1951)
Neophyte airline stewardess Jane Wyman has to learn the ropes of working the friendly skies while fending off the friendly advances of a trio of bachelors (Barry Sullivan, Howard Keel, Van Johnson) in this high-flying romantic comedy. 90 min.
62-1337 Was $19.99 $14.99

Hue And Cry (1950)
A sharp cockney lad decodes the messages of a gang of crooks in a weekly children's magazine and gets his East End pals together to halt their scheme. British crime and comedy caper starring Alastair Sim and Harry Fowler. 82 min.
68-8174 $19.99

A Run For Your Money (1950)
High-spirited farce from England's Ealing Studios about two Welsh coal-mining brothers who win a trip to London and find themselves caught in a series of mishaps and hilarious situations. Donald Huston, Moira Lister, Alec Guinness and Hugh Griffith star. 83 min.
17-9022 Was $19.99 $14.99

Last Holiday (1950)
A gem of a comedy with Alec Guinness as a shy man who learns he has a fatal disease and decides to take a long-deserved vacation at a seaside resort. Once there, he is surprised when opportunities for success life denied him appear. Wilfrid Hyde-White and Beatrice Campbell co-star. 88 min.
22-5533 Restored $29.99

The Malta Story (1953)
RAF pilot Alec Guinness leads the fight against a German air raid on a Mediterranean island in this taut WWII thriller, but his love for a local girl puts the mission in jeopardy, thanks to her traitorous brother. Jack Hawkins, Muriel Pavlow also star. 103 min.
10-8415 Was $19.99 $14.99

The Detective (1954)
Alec Guinness is perfectly cast as G.K. Chesterton's amiable priest and would-be crimesolver, Father Brown, in a light-hearted mystery that has the good Father solving the theft of a valuable icon he was taking to Rome. With Peter Finch, Cecil Parker. 91 min.
02-1867 Was $69.99 $19.99

The Prisoner (1955)
Stunning performances by Alec Guinness and Jack Hawkins fuel this intense drama of an Eastern European cardinal held captive by the state authorities and subjected to mental and psychological tortures in an attempt to make him recant his anti-government speeches. 91 min.
02-1929 Was $69.99 $19.99

The Swan (1956)
In the same year she married Prince Rainier of Monaco, Grace Kelly starred as a princess in this sparkling romantic epic set in the early part of the century. She's about to be married off by her mother to a prince when she falls for her dashing tutor. With Alec Guinness, Louis Jourdan, Agnes Moorehead. 112 min.
12-2108 $19.99

The Horse's Mouth (1958)
Alec Guinness wrote the screenplay for and stars in this wry comedy treat. He plays Gully Jimson, an eccentric artist who will do anything for money, including conning his family and friends into buying the same paintings more than once! Based on Joyce Cary's novel; with Kay Walsh, Renee Houston, Ernest Thesiger. 96 min.
22-5729 Letterboxed $24.99

Tunes Of Glory (1960)
Alec Guinness is a fastidious Army colonel and John Mills the brash young officer sent to replace him in this drama that focuses on the emotional clash of wills between the two men. Co-stars Susannah York, Dennis Price. 106 min.
22-5802 $29.99

A Majority Of One (1961)
The popular Broadway play is turned into a sensitive seriocomedy about a Jewish widow from Brooklyn who falls for a wealthy Japanese businessman while on a cruise ship destined for the East. Rosalind Russell and Alec Guinness are the leads; Ray Danton and Madlyn Rhue also star. 153 min.
19-2081 Was $29.99 $19.99

Damn The Defiant! (1962)
Masterful maritime saga stars Alec Guinness as a beleaguered ship's commander in the Napoleonic Wars who must deal with the treachery of his seconds (Dirk Bogarde, Anthony Quayle), as well as the advance of the French Armada. 101 min.
02-1769 Was $19.99 $14.99

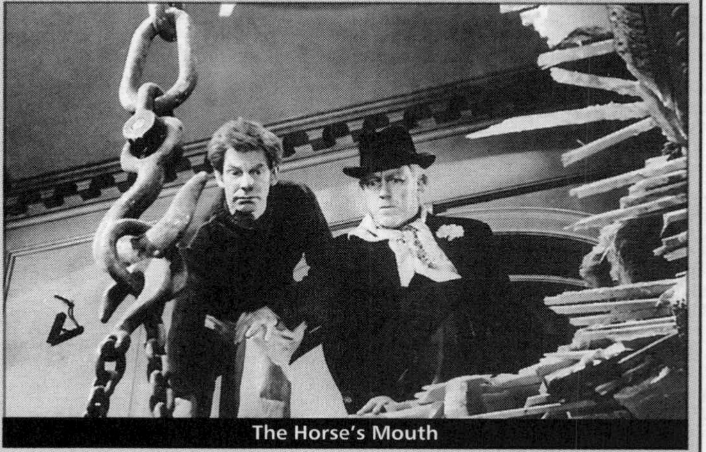
The Horse's Mouth

Alec Guinness

The Quiller Memorandum (1966)
An American agent is charged with tracking down the leaders of a neo-Nazi organization in Berlin, but finds he may have been set up by traitors. Tense espionage thriller stars George Segal, Alec Guinness and Max Von Sydow; screenplay by Harold Pinter. 105 min.
04-2036 Was $59.99 $29.99

Hotel Paradiso (1966)
Side-splitting bedroom farce with the great Alec Guinness as a shy husband with a shrewish wife who carries on a heated affair with a pompous architect's sultry spouse (Gina Lollobrigida). Their rendezvous takes place in a Paris hotel, and when husband Robert Morley arrives there on business, the lovers go to great lengths to avoid getting caught. Akim Tamiroff also stars. 96 min.
12-2843 $19.99

Cromwell (1970)
Richard Harris stars as the Puritan leader who overthrew England's monarchy in the 17th century, only to see his dreams of an "enlightened republic" betrayed by those around him. Epic drama also stars Alec Guinness, Frank Finlay, Robert Morley. 145 min.
02-1738 Was $69.99 $19.99

Hitler: The Last 10 Days (1973)
Alec Guinness shines as the Nazi leader in this realistic, revealing look at the final days in the Berlin bunker. With Simon Ward, Adolfo Celi, Doris Kuntsmann. 108 min.
06-1185 Was $49.99 $14.99

Edwin (1984)
Too much free time and a suspicious mind have led retired High Court judge Alec Guinness to believe that a neighbor had an affair with his wife years earlier and is in fact the true father of Guinness' son, Edwin. An imminent visit by the young man leads Guinness to present his "evidence" to the unseen audience "jury" in this unusual drama. Renée Asherson, Paul Rogers also star. 78 min.
53-6948 $19.99

A Passage To India (1984)
David Lean's visually stunning drama of prejudice and tension in British-ruled India. Friendship between an Indian doctor and English visitors is shattered when he is accused of a shocking crime. Judy Davis, Peggy Ashcroft, Victor Banerjee, James Fox and Alec Guinness star. 163 min.
02-1466 $19.99

Monsignor Quixote (1985)
Alec Guinness stars as an amiable parish priest and ancestor of Don Quixote who embarks on a series of adventures when he's promoted to the rank of Monsignor. Along with pal Sancho Zancas (Leo McKern), he encounters kidnappers and a town whose inhabitants have some very unusual customs. With Ian Richardson. 118 min.
44-1818 Was $59.99 $19.99

A Handful Of Dust (1988)
From the pen of Evelyn Waugh ("Brideshead Revisited") comes an elegant drama that stretches from the parlors and bedrooms of '30s London to the South American jungle, as a married couple find their life together coming apart at the seams. James Wilby, Kristin Scott Thomas, Anjelica Huston, Rupert Graves and Alec Guinness star. 118 min.
02-1907 Was $89.99 $19.99

A Foreign Field (1994)
Poignant tale of love, war and camaraderie in which three vets, an American and two Brits, return to Normandy to recall their World War II experiences and join other friends and relatives in revealing secrets and rekindling memories. Alec Guinness, Jeanne Moreau, Leo McKern, Geraldine Chaplin, Lauren Bacall and John Randolph star. 90 min.
04-2830 Was $89.99 $29.99

Please see our index for these other Alec Guinness titles: *The Bridge On The River Kwai • Brother Sun, Sister Moon • Doctor Zhivago • The Fall Of The Roman Empire • Kafka • Lawrence Of Arabia • Little Dorrit • Lovesick • Murder By Death*

116 · COMEDY
MOVIES UNLIMITED
CALL · 1-800-4-MOVIES

Roogie's Bump (1954)
A baseball-loving kid named Remington "Roogie" Rigsby doesn't have the skills to play with the neighborhood gang, until a mysterious bump on his pitching arm gives him a big-league delivery and a spot on the Brooklyn Dodgers staff. Dodgers greats Roy Campanella, Carl Erskine and Russ Meyer play themselves in this diamond comedy for the whole family. With Robert Marriot, Ruth Warrick. 72 min.
19-2435 *$19.99*

Don't Go Near The Water (1957)
Rip-roaring military farce about Navy press officers on a remote South Seas island during World War II who don't get anywhere near combat action, but are expected to snag new recruits for the service. With Glenn Ford, Anne Francis, Earl Holliman, Fred Clark, and Mickey Shaughnessy as a textbook sailor with a foul mouth. 102 min.
12-2837 *$19.99*

Private's Progress (1956)
Fine farce from the golden days of British comedy about a college student who enlists in the army and has trouble adjusting to military life. Wacky and witty situations abound in this production from the Boulting Brothers, starring Richard Attenborough, Dennis Price, Terry-Thomas and Ian Carmichael. Followed by "I'm All Right, Jack." 99 min.
79-8003 *$19.99*

The Gazebo (1959)
Inventive comedy with darkly humorous touches featuring Glenn Ford as a television writer, the target of a blackmailer who has naked photos of Broadway actress wife Debbie Reynolds taken years earlier. Ford murders the cad, then hides the body near the site of his new gazebo, but things get very confusing when the body appears elsewhere. Carl Reiner and John McGiver also star. 100 min.
12-2840 *$19.99*

The Atomic Kid (1954)
Prospector Mickey Rooney is caught in an A-bomb explosion, but emerges alive (thanks to a peanut butter sandwich) and possessed of mental powers that enable him to win a fortune at Vegas. Blake Edwards wrote this comedy, which added Mickey to Hollywood's '50s nuclear menagerie; with Whit Bissell, Elaine Davis. 86 min.
63-1367 *$14.99*

My Man Godfrey (1957)
Laugh-filled reworking of the 1936 screwball classic stars David Niven as a vagrant taken into the home of wealthy socialite June Allyson and given a job as butler. Niven's wit and understanding soon wins over the eccentric household—except for Allyson's suspicious sister (Martha Hyer). 93 min.
07-2044 *$19.99*

Mister Drake's Duck (1951)
Wacky British farce starring Douglas Fairbanks, Jr. as an American who inherits a farm in England and moves there with new wife Yolande Donlan. One day, Donlan mistakenly purchases 60 ducks, and hilarity ensues when one of them lays a radioactive egg, drawing the attention of the military. Wilfrid Hyde-White also stars; directed by Val Guest ("The Day the Earth Caught Fire"). 80 min.
70-5139 *$24.99*

Blue Murder At St. Trinian's (1958)
Second film in the hilarious British series has a diamond smuggler hiding out at the girls' school by masquerading as the new headmistress. Alastair Sim, Lionel Jeffries, Terry-Thomas star. 86 min.
62-1329 Was $19.99 *$14.99*

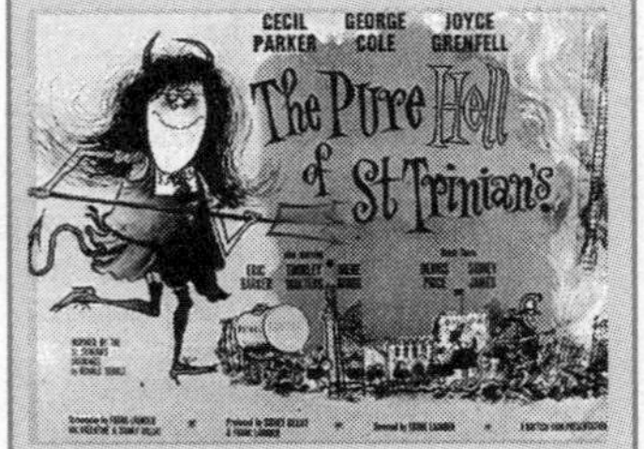

The Pure Hell Of St. Trinian's (1961)
In this entry in the popular Brit comedy series, the always rambunctious gals of St. Trinian's are helped out of trouble by a mysterious professor from the University of Baghdad, and then taken to the Greek Islands aboard a luxury yacht. Little do they know that he's working for a sheik who wants the gals for himself and his sons. Cecil Parker, Joyce Grenfell, George Cole star. 90 min.
59-7083 *$29.99*

The Great St. Trinian's Train Robbery (1966)
A group of crooks stash millions in stolen loot in a decrepit old mansion, but upon returning years later to reclaim their fortune, discover the place has been turned into the St. Trinian School for Girls. When they try to get the cash, the gals stop them—with hockey sticks and more! Frankie Howerd, Desmond Walter and Reg Varney star. 94 min.
44-1077 *$29.99*

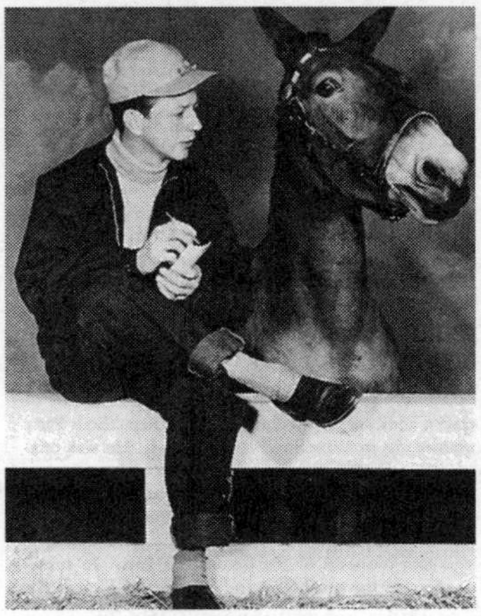

Francis (1949)
While on a mission behind enemy lines in Burma, G.I. Donald O'Connor is rescued by a talking mule named Francis. O'Connor's claim that his four-legged pal speaks lands him in a padded cell before the pair are recognized for their heroic deeds. Debut entry in the "Francis" series co-stars Patricia Medina, with Chill Wills supplying Francis' voice; look quickly for Tony Curtis. 91 min.
07-2084 ❑*$14.99*

Francis Goes To The Races (1951)
The ranch where Francis the Talking Mule resides is in trouble, so the loquacious creature goes to work, helping a race horse get its confidence back and offering some hot tips on the Santa Anita track to pal Donald O'Connor. With Piper Laurie, Cecil Kellaway. 87 min.
07-2085 ❑*$14.99*

Francis Goes To West Point (1952)
After stopping saboteurs at a nuclear plant, Donald O'Connor is given an appointment to West Point, and the new cadet brings Francis along (after all, what's Army without a mule?). A slam-bang finish at the Army-Navy football game highlights this collegiate comedy that also stars Lori Nelson; look for early appearances by David Janssen and Leonard Nimoy. 81 min.
07-2261 ❑*$14.99*

Francis Covers The Big Town (1953)
When Donald O'Connor sets his sights on becoming a major metropolitan newspaper reporter, it's up to his big-eared buddy Francis to come up with some hot scoops and save O'Connor from a murder charge. Gene Lockhart, Yvette Dugay co-star. 86 min.
07-2262 ❑*$14.99*

Francis Joins The WACs (1954)
A clerical miscue lands Donald O'Connor back in the service, but as a WAC, and with equine pal Francis in tow. The Army gals, who are used to strict protocol, soon grow accustomed to all-out wackiness. Julia (Julie) Adams, Mamie Van Doren, ZaSu Pitts and Chill Wills, in voice and in person, also star. 95 min.
07-2086 ❑*$14.99*

Francis In The Navy (1955)
The bombastic burro and human sidekick Donald O'Connor take to the sea in the sixth hee haw-larious Francis comedy. With Martha Hyer, Jim Backus, David Janssen; look quickly for Clint Eastwood in his second film role. 80 min.
07-2087 ❑*$14.99*

Francis In The Haunted House (1956)
Mickey Rooney came aboard to fill in for Donald O'Connor (and Paul Frees took over as the mule's voice) in this seventh and final film in the series. Here Francis gets Rooney out of a scary situation involving spooks and art forgers. With Virginia Welles, Richard Deacon. 80 min.
07-2263 ❑*$14.99*

Never Wave At A Wac (1952)
If you liked "Private Benjamin," wait 'til you see Rosalind Russell as a society woman who joins the WACs, only to find it's not the "easy life" she expected. Sparkling comedy co-stars Marie Wilson, Paul Douglas. 87 min.
08-8014 *$19.99*

The Ambassador's Daughter (1956)
Romantic complications ensue when a G.I. (John Forsythe) stationed in Paris falls head over heels for the daughter (Olivia de Havilland) of the American ambassador in this captivating comedy. Co-stars Adolphe Menjou and Myrna Loy. 102 min.
10-1255 *$19.99*

The Runaway Bus (1954)
Offbeat British comedy/thriller about a stranded bus and its passengers, one of whom just masterminded a daring robbery and hid a fortune in gold aboard the bus. Margaret Rutherford, Frankie Howerd, and a young Petula Clark star. 78 min.
09-1829 Was $24.99 *$14.99*

Murder, He Says (1945)
Pollster Fred MacMurray, stranded in the Ozarks, finds himself up to his ears in homicidal hillbillies, hidden loot and radium deposits in this delightfully daffy dark comedy. Marjorie Main also stars as the head of the sinister Fleagle clan, and Peter Whitney plays her twin sons Mert and Bert (who's got a "trick back"); with Helen Walker, Barbara Pepper. 91 min.
07-2522 *$14.99*

Miss Polly (1941)
In this Hal Roach "streamliner" featurette, ZaSu Pitts plays a blue-nosed busybody who keeps her conservative town behind the times, until Miss Polly sets things right with help from wacky inventor Slim Summerville. 50 min.
09-5411 *$19.99*

Here Comes Mr. Jordan (1941)
Heavenly comedy classic stars Robert Montgomery as the amiable boxer who arrives in Paradise 50 years before his time and is given a second shot at life by the angels. Claude Rains, Evelyn Keyes, Edward Everett Horton co-star in this inspiration for 1978's "Heaven Can Wait." 93 min.
02-1043 *$19.99*

The Doctor Takes A Wife (1940)
Thrown together by chance, medical school teacher Ray Milland and would-be novelist Loretta Young play at being married, only to discover they'd like to try it for real, in this frothy comedy. With Edmund Gwenn, Gail Patrick. 89 min.
02-1842 *$69.99*

A Letter To Three Wives (1948)
A witty dissection of the romance, fears and foibles of matrimony from writer-director Joseph L. Mankiewicz. During a trip on the Hudson River, a trio of wives (Jeanne Crain, Linda Darnell and Ann Sothern) receive a letter telling them that one of their husbands has been unfaithful. Each woman then reviews the ups and downs of their marriages. With Kirk Douglas and Paul Douglas. 103 min.
04-1086 *$19.99*

Three Husbands (1950)
Spry comedy à la "Letter to Three Wives" (from the same co-scripter) about a deceased playboy's written claims to three men that he had affairs with their wives. Eve Arden, Ruth Warrick, Emlyn Williams star. 78 min.
62-1284 *$19.99*

Heaven Can Wait (1943)
Delightful fantasy/comedy from Ernst Lubitsch that despite its title opens in the "other place," where deceased womanizer Don Ameche renews his exploits with the Devil while waiting to learn his afterlife destination. Gene Tierney also stars as Ameche's true love; with Charles Coburn, Marjorie Main, Eugene Pallette, and Laird Cregar as the Satanic "His Excellency." 112 min.
04-2301 ❑*$19.99*

It Happens Every Spring (1949)
Classic baseball farce starring Ray Milland as a college chemistry professor in search of enough money to enable him to propose to sweetheart Jean Peters. He invents a solution that repels wood and uses it to become a pitching phenomenon, striking out scores of batters with his unhittable "screwball." Paul Douglas, Ed Begley, Alan Hale, Jr. co-star. 86 min.
04-2738 ❑*$19.99*

Come To The Stable (1949)
European nuns Celeste Holm and Loretta Young arrive in a small New England town and use their faith and their determination to get a children's hospital built. Charming blend of comedy and drama also stars Elsa Lanchester, Hugh Marlowe, Dooley Wilson. 95 min.
04-2904 ❑*$19.99*

Father Was A Fullback (1949)
College football coach Fred MacMurray has to cope with both a losing team that has angry alumni on his back and two daughters with boy problems in this warm and funny comedy. Maureen O'Hara, Betty Lynn, Natalie Wood, Rudy Vallee and Thelma Ritter also star. 84 min.
04-2945 *$14.99*

Tales Of Manhattan (1942)
A "cursed" formal tailcoat is followed through a series of owners in this six-episode, all-star film that mixes laughter and poignancy. Among the garment's owners: actor and lothario Charles Boyer, unfaithful fiancé Cesar Romero, symphony conductor Charles Laughton, destitute lawyer Edward G. Robinson and, in a newly-restored sequence cut before the movie's release, temperance lecturer W.C. Fields. With Rita Hayworth, Henry Fonda, Ginger Rogers, Elsa Lanchester, George Sanders and Paul Robeson. 130 min.
04-3273 ❑*$19.99*

Abroad With Two Yanks (1944)
Zany comedy hijinks abound when U.S. marines William Bendix and Dennis O'Keefe, stationed in Australia, compete for the affections of pretty local girl Helen Walker. A highlight has the pair disrupting a charity dance after escaping from a guard house in drag. 80 min.
08-1798 *$19.99*

On Approval (1943)
Witty British comedy adapted from a late '20s stage hit. Two upper class couples live together in an isolated Scottish cottage to see if they're compatible for marriage, only to learn they can't stand each other. Clive Brook, Bea Lillie star. 80 min.
01-1175 *$24.99*

Oklahoma Annie (1952)
New deputy Judy Canova sets out to help her sheriff beau clean up a crooked frontier town in a wild western comedy. With John Ruseell, "Fuzzy" Knight, Denver Pyle. 90 min.
63-1213 *$19.99*

Uncle Joe (1941)
A college coed goes to spend summer vacation on her eccentric uncle's farm and joins with some of the local residents in helping to save a neighbor from losing her property in this lively, song-filled comedy. Gale Storm, ZaSu Pitts, Slim Summerville star. 55 min.
01-1640 *$19.99*

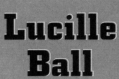

Lucille Ball

Miss Grant Takes Richmond (1949)
Secretary Lucille Ball is hired by William Holden to run his real estate office. Trouble is, she doesn't know the business is a front for Holden's gambling operation and gets the bookie involved in a housing program. Fast-paced Runyonesque treat also stars James Gleason, Janis Carter. 87 min.
02-2072 *$19.99*

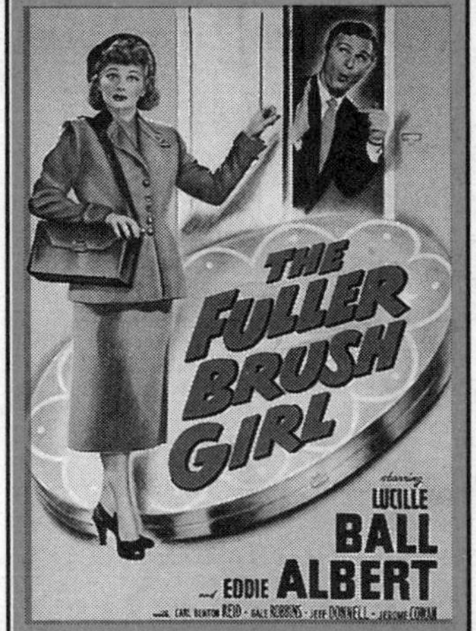

The Fuller Brush Girl (1950)
Door-to-door salesgal Lucille Ball is wrongly accused of murder and, along with boyfriend Eddie Albert, is soon pursued by smugglers, killers and cops. A slapstick sequel-of-sorts to Red Skelton's "The Fuller Brush Man," this Frank Tashlin-penned farce features Jerome Cowan and Red himself in a cameo. 84 min.
02-2434 *$19.99*

The Long, Long Trailer (1954)
Lucille Ball and Desi Arnaz are a laugh riot in this comic lark directed by Vincente Minnelli. They're off on their honeymoon with an expensive, unwieldy trailer, and laughs aplenty are in store. Marjorie Main and Keenan Wynn also star. 96 min.
12-2106 Was $19.99 ❑*$14.99*

Forever Darling (1956)
Lucille Ball, the unhappy wife of workaholic chemist Desi Arnaz, receives marital help from guardian angel James Mason in this offbeat fantasy comedy. The couple's trip to the woods for an insecticide test provides some wacky moments. Louis Calhern, John Hoyt co-star. 96 min.
12-2317 *$19.99*

Yours, Mine And Ours (1968)
Widowed nurse Lucille Ball and widowed Navy man Henry Fonda have a shot at renewed happiness...the only stumbling block being her eight kids and his 10! Endearing family comedy also stars Tom Bosley, Van Johnson, Tim Matheson and Suzanne Cupito (Morgan Brittany). 111 min.
12-1912 ❑*$14.99*

The Funny World Of Lucy
The film career of America's favorite redhead is celebrated in this terrific compilation that traces Lucy's early work in "Room Service" with the Marx Brothers, roles opposite Red Skelton in "DuBarry Was a Lady," Bob Hope in "Sorrowful Jones" and "Fancy Pants," and husband Desi Arnaz in "The Long, Long Trailer" and other movies. 85 min.
10-2561 *$12.99*

Please see our index for these other Lucille Ball titles: *Critic's Choice • DuBarry Was A Lady • Easy To Wed • The Facts Of Life • Fancy Pants • Follow The Fleet • Lured • Sorrowful Jones • Top Hat • The Whole Town's Talking*

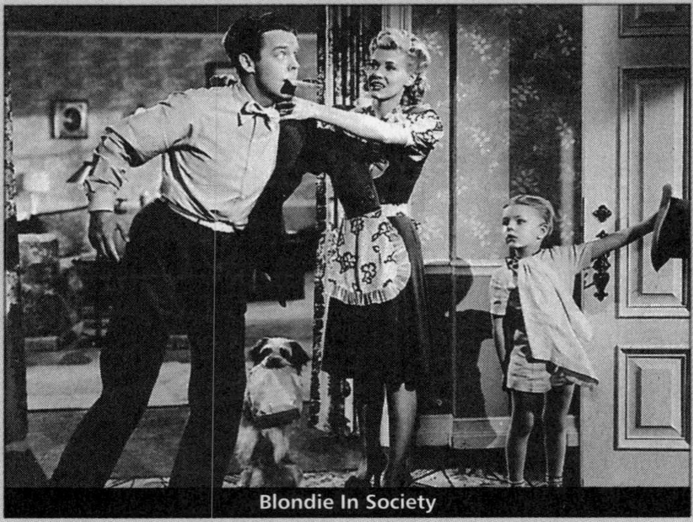

Blondie In Society

Blondie (1938)
The cinematic debut of Chic Young's beloved comic strip characters, featuring Penny Singleton as flighty Blondie, Arthur Lake as ever-bumbling Dagwood and Larry Simms as Baby Dumpling. In this outing, the Bumsteads celebrate their fifth wedding anniversary with Dagwood losing his job, while Blondie suspects him of infidelity. With Gene Lockhart, Ann Doran. 68 min.
80-3000 *$14.99*

Blondie Meets The Boss (1939)
A fishing trip for Dagwood leads to trouble when a picture is snapped of him holding another woman. When Blondie finds the camera and gets the pictures developed, Dagwood has some explaining to do. Arthur Lake, Penny Singleton star. 68 min
66-6080 *$14.99*

Blondie Brings Up Baby (1939)
During Baby Dumpling's first day at school, trusted family canine Daisy is taken in by the dogcatcher and adopted by a politician's handicapped daughter. When Baby Dumpling plays hooky to find her, Blondie and Dagwood think he's been kidnapped. Arthur Lake, Penny Singleton and Jonathan Hale star. 68 min.
66-6081 *$14.99*

Blondie Takes A Vacation (1939)
After being shunned by a classy mountain resort, the Bumsteads help manage a nearby resort in danger of closing. Hilarity ensues as they try to make things click, and Baby Dumpling helps out when he unleashes a skunk in the competing hotel's ventilation system. Penny Singleton, Arthur Lake and Larry Simms star. 68 min.
80-3005 *$14.99*

Blondie On A Budget (1940)
Rita Hayworth can be found in a supporting role in this "Blondie" outing. She's the ex-girlfriend enlisted by Dagwood to help him purchase a fur coat for Blondie with $200 from a contest he entered. At the same time, Blondie tries to use the same cash to get him into a fishing club. Hilarity abounds! With Penny Singleton and Arthur Lake. 68 min.
66-6082 *$14.99*

Blondie Has Servant Trouble (1940)
An estate handled by Dagwood's firm is rumored to be haunted, but the Bumsteads take an offer to stay there because Blondie likes the idea of having servants wait on her. When strange events occur in the mansion, Dagwood and Blondie wonder if the help is human. Penny Singleton and Arthur Lake star. 68 min.
66-6083 *$14.99*

Blondie Plays Cupid (1940)
While travelling to Aunt Hannah's ranch, the Bumsteads run into a couple about to elope. When a series of mishaps threaten their wedding plans, Blondie and Dagwood pitch in to help them. With Penny Singleton and Arthur Lake; Glenn Ford plays the young groom-to-be. 68 min.
66-6084 *$14.99*

Blondie In Society (1941)
When Dagwood brings home a pedigreed Great Dane and Blondie enters it in the local dog show, they get into hot water when one of his clients has an entry in the same competition. Penny Singleton, Arthur Lake, William Frawley and Edgar Kennedy star. 77 min.
80-3003 *$14.99*

Blondie Goes Latin (1942)
Hilarity abounds when Mr. Dithers invites the Bumsteads to join him on a Latin American cruise and Dagwood finds himself trapped in a confusing situation with the ship's orchestra. The predicament leads Dagwood into drag and playing the drums! With Arthur Lake and Penny Singleton. 68 min.
66-6085 *$14.99*

Blondie Goes To College (1942)
When Dagwood decides to enroll in college, Mr. Dithers suggests that Blondie join him. Funny situations don't stop coming as Blondie gets attention from the university's top athlete and Dagwood joins the rowing team and finds favor with a pretty coed. Arthur Lake, Penny Singleton, Janet Blair and Larry Parks star. 68 min.
66-6086 *$14.99*

Blondie For Victory (1942)
The Bumsteads get patriotic when Blondie joins the Housewives of America for the war effort and Dagwood pretends to enlist in the Army after he makes a lousy guinea pig in Blondie's first aid class. Penny Singleton, Arthur Lake and Larry Simms star. 68 min.
66-6087 *$14.99*

Blondie's Blessed Event (1942)
While Blondie is about to give birth to Cookie, Dagwood gets into all sorts of trouble at work when he enlists an avant-garde playwright to write a controversial speech for him. Penny Singleton, Arthur Lake and Hans Conried star in this mirthful movie. 69 min.
80-3007 *$14.99*

It's A Great Life (1943)
In this "Blondie" offering, Dagwood misunderstands Mr. Dithers' instructions to buy a house and winds up purchasing a horse! As luck would have it, Dagwood is soon "riding to hounds" with an eccentric millionaire whom Dithers would like to land as a client, leading to a wild fox hunt. Penny Singleton, Arthur Lake and Hugh Herbert star. 68 min.
66-6088 *$14.99*

Footlight Glamour (1943)
Arthur Lake's Dagwood is hired by a wealthy tool manufacturer to work at a new plant, but his boss gets angry when Penny Singleton's Blondie casts his daughter in a play despite his opposition. Ann Savage and Jonathan Hale co-star. 68 min.
66-6089 *$14.99*

Leave It To Blondie (1945)
Blondie and Dagwood independently enter a songwriting contest in hopes of winning to cover their charitable donations. Funny situations ensue, and they get even wackier when Dagwood is enlisted to schmooze a pretty real estate specialist for a deal. Penny Singleton, Arthur Lake, Larry Simms, Marjorie Weaver and Jonathan Hale star. 74 min.
66-6096 *$14.99*

Life With Blondie (1946)
Top-notch Bumstead frolic in which Daisy, the family pooch, gets lots of attention after winning a contest as a model for a Navy ad campaign. Daisy becomes the canine pin-up answer to Betty Grable, while Dagwood gets jealous and crooks plot to kidnap the dapper doggie. Penny Singleton, Arthur Lake, Marjorie Kent star. 69 min.
66-6097 *$14.99*

Blondie's Lucky Day (1946)
Mr. Dithers takes a leave of absence and leaves Dagwood in charge of the office. When Dagwood decides to hire a former WAC for a job, trouble ensues, eventually leaving Dagwood and the new hire unemployed. Penny Singleton, Arthur Lake, Angelyn Orr and Jonathan Hale star in this lively, late entry in the hit series. 69 min.
66-6098 *$14.99*

Blondie Knows Best (1946)
When Dagwood has to pretend to be Mr. Dithers, all sorts of wacky situations ensue. A fun-filled series entry highlighted by an appearance by Shemp Howard as a myopic process server. With Penny Singleton, Arthur Lake and Jonathan Hale. 69 min.
80-3002 *$14.99*

Blondie's Big Moment (1947)
When Penny Singleton's Blondie decides it's time to take to the spotlight and become a star, the Bumstead household becomes a world of wacky chaos as Arthur Lake's Dagwood gets mighty jealous. With Anita Louise and Jerome Cowan. 69 min.
66-6099 *$14.99*

Blondie's Holiday (1947)
Dagwood tries to ensure his family's finances by getting involved with bookies, but his efforts land him in the pokey. Thankfully, a local bank manager comes to the rescue after Dagwood helps the banker's wife escape a raid on a betting parlor. Some holiday! Arthur Lake, Penny Singleton, Grant Mitchell and Mary Young star. 61 min.
66-6100 *$14.99*

Blondie In The Dough (1947)
Blondie decides to make some extra cash by baking cookies in her kitchen, then selling them. The sales take off, but unusual complications occur that disrupt the Bumstead household. Penny Singleton, Arthur Lake, Hugh Herbert and Larry Simms star. 69 min.
66-6101 *$14.99*

Blondie's Anniversary (1947)
When Blondie finds a watch she thinks is her anniversary gift, Dagwood is in a tizzy trying to find something really special as a "replacement present." Penny Singleton, Arthur Lake, Grant Mitchell and William Frawley star. 67 min.
66-6102 *$14.99*

Blondie's Secret (1948)
It's vacation time for the Bumsteads, but Dagwood's boss, Mr. Radcliffe, needs him at the office, so he hires someone to steal the family luggage in this madcap outing in the popular series. Penny Singleton, Arthur Lake, Jerome Cowan, Thurston Hall star.
09-2975 Was $19.99 *$14.99*

Blondie's Reward (1948)
Dagwood gets into all sorts of trouble in this "Blondie" outing. First, he purchases the wrong property for his boss, then is accused of punching the son of an important client. Arthur Lake, Penny Singleton, Gay Nelson, Ross Ford and Danny Mummert star. 65 min.
66-6103 *$14.99*

Blondie's Big Deal (1949)
Laugh-filled entry in the popular series finds Dagwood inventing a fire-repellent paint and convincing his skeptical boss to allow his fishing cottage to be used as an experimental site. When a rival company schemes to ruin the test by switching paints, hilarity abounds. Arthur Lake, Penny Singleton and Larry Simms star. 67 min.
09-2924 Was $19.99 *$14.99*

Blondie Hits The Jackpot (1949)
Dagwood is in lots of trouble again! After blowing a construction deal for Mr. Radcliffe, he winds up laboring on the site with the hardhats. But Blondie saves the day when she wins a radio quiz show prize. Penny Singleton, Arthur Lake and Jerome Cowan star. 66 min.
80-3001 Was $19.99 *$14.99*

Blondie's Hero (1950)
Dagwood gets into lots of trouble when he mistakenly finds himself in the Army reserve and fumbling through basic training. Blondie stops in to see how her hubby is doing, but witnesses him almost starting a war, then saving the day. Penny Singleton, Arthur Lake, William Frawley and Marjorie Kent star. 67 min.
66-6104 *$14.99*

Beware Of Blondie (1950)
When Mr. Dithers goes on vacation, Dagwood is left in charge of the business, but he soon finds himself in hot water when an attractive con artist tries to pull the wool over his eyes. Luckily, Blondie comes to the rescue! Penny Singleton, Arthur Lake, Adele Jergens and Dick Wessel star. 64 min.
66-6105 *$14.99*

Blondie: Collector's Set 1
This seven-tape set includes "Blondie," "Blondie Meets the Boss," "Blondie Takes a Vacation," "Blondie Brings Up Baby," "Blondie on a Budget," "Blondie Has Servant Trouble" and "Blondie Plays Cupid."
66-6090 Save $35.00! *$69.99*

Blondie: Collector's Set 2
This seven-tape set includes "Blondie Goes Latin," "Blondie in Society," "Blondie Goes to College," "Blondie's Blessed Event," "Blondie for Victory," "It's a Great Life" and "Footlight Glamour."
66-6091 Save $35.00! *$69.99*

Blondie: Collector's Set 3
This seven-tape set includes "Blondie in the Dough," "Blondie Knows Best," "Blondie's Big Moment," "Blondie's Holiday," "Blondie's Lucky Day," "Leave It to Blondie" and "Life with Blondie."
66-6106 Save $35.00! *$69.99*

Blondie: Collector's Set 4
This seven-tape set includes "Blondie's Anniversary," "Blondie's Reward," "Blondie's Secret," "Blondie's Big Deal," "Blondie Hits the Jackpot," "Blondie's Hero" and "Beware of Blondie."
66-6107 Save $35.00! *$69.99*

Twin Beds (1942)
In this zany boudoir romp, newlyweds Joan Bennett and George Brent find their marriage in jeopardy when the next door neighbor, concert singer Mischa Auer, fixes his roving eye on Bennett. With Glenda Farrell, Margaret Hamilton. 85 min.
08-1785 *$19.99*

A Stranger In Town (1943)
Frank Morgan is a Supreme Court justice who decides to take a hunting vacation, only to discover the small town he stops at is riddled with political corruption. Morgan befriends the town's mayoral candidate and attempts to help him by offering advice. Richard Carlson, Jean Rogers, Chill Wills and John Hodiak also star in this lively mix of comedy and drama. 67 min.
08-1826 *$14.99*

I Live In Grosvenor Square (1946)
Post-war comedy in London, involving a love triangle between an English girl, her boyfriend and an American soldier. Rex Harrison, Dean Jagger, Anna Neagle and Robert Morley star. 106 min.
08-8006 Was $19.99 *$14.99*

Molly And Me (1945)
Monty Woolley and Gracie Fields star in a light romp, as a cantankerous recluse hires a new housekeeper, only to have her take over his life. Co-stars Roddy McDowall. 76 min.
08-8027 *$19.99*

Colonel Effingham's Raid (1945)
Delightful comedy of an old Southern colonel (Charles Coburn) who mounts one last battle to save his town's lone historical landmark. Joan Bennett, Allyn Joslyn also star. 70 min.
08-8031 Was $19.99 *$14.99*

That Uncertain Feeling (1941)
The seemingly happy marriage of insurance salesman Melvyn Douglas and neglected wife Merle Oberon, now teetering on the brink of divorce, gets tossed in a flutter with the arrival of eccentric pianist Burgess Meredith, in Ernst Lubitsch's elegantly daffy remake of his silent film "Kiss Me Again." 84 min.
08-8051 *$19.99*

Old Mother Riley's Ghosts (1941)
Arthur Lucan dons skirts once more to play the role of daffy Ma Riley. This entry in the long-running British series is full of spooky gags as Mother Riley resists the crook's efforts to scare her away from an old castle. 82 min.
68-8031 Was $19.99 *$14.99*

Old Mother Riley, Detective (1943)
Old Mother Riley, the English washerwoman played in drag by Arthur Lucan, is pulled into a black market crackdown by the police in this slapstick crime comedy. Kitty McShane, Owen Reynolds also star. 80 min.
10-9374 *$14.99*

Old Mother Riley's New Venture (1949)
Feisty British charwoman Mother Riley (Arthur Lucan) goes from dishwasher to proprietress of a posh London hotel that's been plagued by a string of jewel thefts. But when she becomes the prime suspect, Mrs. Riley and her daughter Kitty (played by Lucan's wife, Kitty McShane) try to find the real culprit in this fast-paced comedy. AKA: "Old Mother Riley." 80 min.
08-1819 *$14.99*

Old Mother Riley, Headmistress (1950)
A girl's school is scarcely ready for the turmoil that erupts when its new top administrator is none other than that Socrates of the scrub board, Mother Riley. Things work out for the best, though, when she saves the institution from being torn down to make way for a railroad. Arthur Lucan, Kitty McShane, Enid Hewitt star. 76 min.
08-1820 *$14.99*

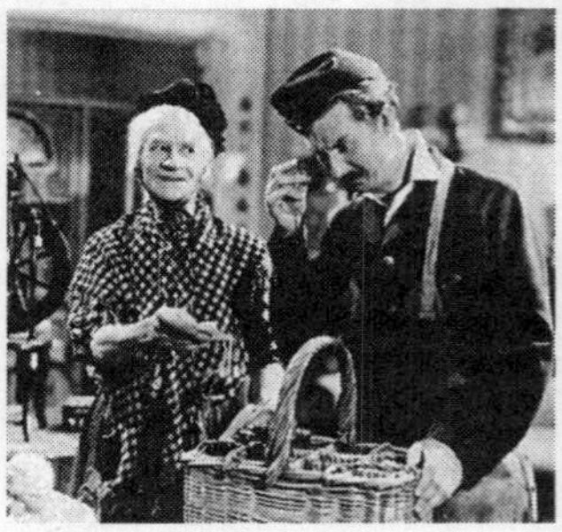

Old Mother Riley's Jungle Treasure (1951)
While working in an antique shop, Old Mother Riley (Arthur Lucan) and daughter Kitty stumble upon a map to the hidden treasure of infamous pirate Henry Morgan, and—with help from the buccaneer's ghost—set sail for the South Seas to find it. Kitty McShane, Roddy Hughes, and Sebastian Cabot as Morgan also star. 75 min.
08-1821 *$14.99*

Jack Benny

The Medicine Man (1930)
Jack Benny (before he struck radio fame) shines in this comedy as a celebrated con artist who peddles a "magic elixir." Benny falls for the town beauty but must first save her from a marriage to an evil brute. 67 min.
09-1884 *$19.99*

Transatlantic Merry Go-Round (1934)
It's "Grand Hotel" on an ocean liner as a host of "characters—including an ex-con, a cheating wife, some gamblers and a crook—find their lives intersecting. It's all played out with satire, thrills and such musical numbers as "It Was Sweet of You," "Moon over Monte Carlo" and "If I Had a Million Dollars." Gene Raymond, Jack Benny, Nancy Carroll lead the top cast. 92 min.
27-6467 *$19.99*

George Washington Slept Here (1941)
Successful translation of the Kaufman and Hart comedy stars Jack Benny as a Manhattan businessman who gets the shock of his life after he moves with wife Ann Sheridan to a rustic Connecticut house. He becomes flustered by a barrage of broken plumbing, kooky neighbors and money problems. With Charles Coburn, Percy Kilbride, Hattie McDaniel and Charles Dingle. 91 min.
12-2485 *$19.99*

To Be Or Not To Be (1942)
The original WWII satire and a comedy classic. Jack Benny is a hammy Shakespearean actor who, along with members of his Polish acting troupe, becomes involved with espionage following the Nazi invasion. Carole Lombard, in her last film, is Benny's unfaithful wife/leading lady. With Sig Rumann, Robert Stack; Ernst Lubitsch directs. 93 min.
19-1775 Was $19.99 *$14.99*

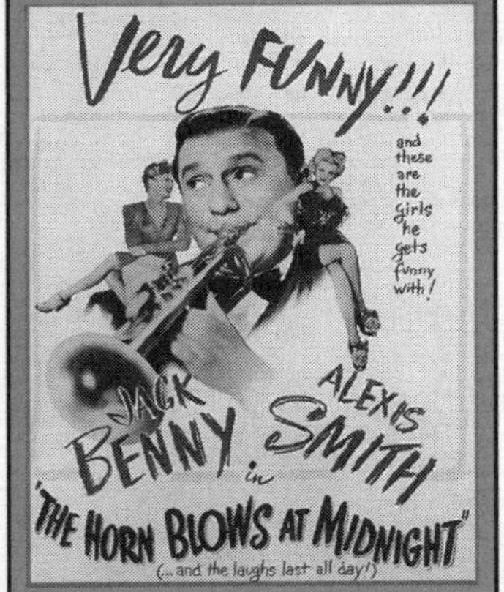

The Horn Blows At Midnight (1945)
Truly funny fantasy comedy (in spite of star Jack Benny's jokes about it years later) about an inept angel (Benny) sent to Earth to trumpet the notes that will bring on Judgment Day. One slapstick mess after another stops him, though, from completing his mission. Alexis Smith, Reginald Gardiner, Margaret Dumont co-star. 78 min.
12-2254 *$19.99*

It's In The Bag (1945)
Radio's famous feuders, Jack Benny and Fred Allen, made their only film appearance together in this riotous farce about a flea circus owner who inherits a fortune...with a catch. Co-stars Jerry Colonna, Robert Benchley and William Bendix. 87 min.
63-5018 *$19.99*

Turned Out Nice Again (1941)
When jealous husband George Formby loses his job as foreman at an underwear factory, his wife begins wearing special see-through underwear made from material he invested in. When she displays the material at a convention, it's a hit, and he gets his job back. Peggy Bryan and Edward Chapman also star. 76 min.
09-5159 *$29.99*

The Adventures Of Jane (1949)
The popular star of British comics makes a memorable jump to the movies in this comic adventure focusing on a phony sea captain involved in gem smuggling who gets in trouble after he tries to slip the diamonds in an actress's bracelet. Chrisbel Leighton-Porter, Stanelli and Sebastain Cabot star. 55 min.
09-5146 *$19.99*

Spring In Park Lane (1949)
Terrific English drawing room comedy about a young man unable to return to his well-to-do family who takes a job as a servant for a rich art patron. Amidst an array of eccentric guests and friends that frequent the art collector's mansion, the young man falls in love with his employer's niece. Anna Neagle, Michael Wilding and Tom Walls star. 91 min.
09-5033 *$19.99*

Lady From Lisbon (1942)
Humor and espionage mix in this British confection about a South American man who decides to help the Nazis on an espionage mission in exchange for the priceless Mona Lisa painting. When different Mona Lisas appear all over the place, a British agent attempts to identify the real one. Francis L. Sullivan, Jane Carr, Martita Hunt star. 75 min.
09-5153 *$19.99*

Meet Me At Dawn (1947)
Set in Paris at the beginning of the 20th century, this romantic comedy tells of a professional duellist who is hired by politicians to insult, then challenge, a prominent senator. The duellist eventually falls in love with a woman he's been chosen to start trouble with—and whose father owns the local newspaper. William Eythe, Stanley Holloway, Hazel Court star. 99 min.
09-5155 *$19.99*

Over The Moon (1940)
Frothy British farce featuring Merle Oberon as an impoverished woman living in a rickety mansion who inherits $90 million from her uncle after he dies. Her physician fiancé (Rex Harrison) isn't fond of Oberon's new social status, so she travels across Europe, where she's wooed by various suitors. Will true love prevail? Ursula Jeans, Robert Douglas co-star. 78 min.
09-5156 *$19.99*

Texas, Brooklyn And Heaven (1948)
Before he turned out such suspense gems as "The Tingler" and "House on Haunted Hill," William Castle directed this screwball comedy about a Texas couple who come to New York in search of fame and fortune and find it when they buy a riding academy. Guy Madison, Diana Lynn, Lionel Stander and Margaret Hamilton star. 76 min.
09-5158 Was $29.99 *$19.99*

The Last Three (The Double-Crossed Fool) (1942)
In this World War II farce, a sailor goes undercover in a captured Nazi submarine to stop the enemy. There's slapstick hijinks galore with Bobby Watson, Joe Devlin, Johnny Arthur. 50 min.
09-5183 *$19.99*

Under Your Hat (1940)
Winning spy comedy starring Jack Hurlbert and Cicely Courtneidge as a married song-and-dance team whose relationship is tested when Courtneidge thinks her spouse is cheating on her. The truth is Hulbert's a special government agent whose mission is to get the goods on a beautiful spy. Courtneidge takes a job as the woman's maid to check up on her husband. 79 min.
09-5236 *$19.99*

Horace Takes Over (1942)
Army recruit John Beal marries sweetheart Wanda McKay and goes to New York for a honeymoon before he's shipped out, but the couple's stay in a hotel is interrupted by gangsters looking for hidden loot in this comedy directed by William "One-Shot" Beaudine. 69 min.
09-5324 *$19.99*

It's That Man Again (1943)
Based on a popular British radio series of the same name, this frenetic wartime comedy stars Tommy Handley as the conniving mayor of the tiny town of Foaming-at-the-Mouth who's out to save his local theater by any means necessary. With Greta Gynt, Jack Train. 84 min.
09-5345 *$19.99*

Treasure Of Fear (1945)
Murder, mayhem and madcap fun combine in this thrill-a-minute comedy, as Jack Haley plays a bumbling newspaper reporter who is sent to cover a wine festival, but has a real story fall into his lap when a passenger on the bus he's riding is murdered. With Ann Savage. AKA: "Scared Stiff." 65 min.
10-3080 *$19.99*

The Ghost Goes Wild (1947)
Engaging farce featuring James Ellison as a cartoonist who, while in trouble with the law for an unauthorized caricature, assumes a disguise as a mystic. Ellison accidentally brings a ghost to life during a seance, which causes all sorts of funny situations, and the spirit eventually helps out the artist in court. Anne Gwynne, Grant Withers also star. 66 min.
10-6004 *$14.99*

Hi Diddle Diddle (1943)
Playful little comedy stars Dennis O'Keefe and Martha Scott as newlyweds whose 48-hour honeymoon is riddled with continuous interruptions from her mother (Billie Burke) and his father (Adolphe Menjou). With Pola Negri. 72 min.
10-7040 *$19.99*

Cracked Nuts (1941)
Slapstick comedy about a country bumpkin who wins $5,000 in a refrigerator slogan contest, then gets duped into investing in a phony robot. Stuart Erwin, Una Merkel and Shemp Howard as "the Robot" star. Also includes the Leon Errol shorts "Home Work," "Hold Your Temper" and "Shocking Affair."
15-9043 Was $19.99 *$14.99*

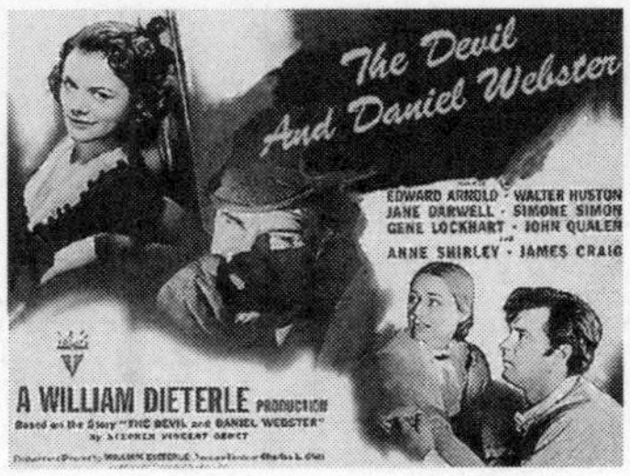

The Devil And Daniel Webster (1941)
Walter Huston and Edward Arnold take the title roles in Stephen Vincent Benet's "New Englandized" Faust story. A young 19th-century farmer sells his soul to Mr. Scratch for seven years of prosperity, but when the Devil shows up to collect, he hires famed lawyer Webster to get him off the hook. With James Craig, Anne Shirley, Simone Simon. AKA: "All That Money Can Buy." Restored version features scenes missing since the film's original run. 106 min.
22-5677 *$24.99*

Baby Face Morgan (1942)
A mobster's son is made head of a phony insurance company by a group of crooks wanting to get back into the biz. The joke is that he doesn't know it's a set-up. With Mary Carlisle, Richard Cromwell and Robert Armstrong. 60 min.
17-3096 Was $19.99 *$14.99*

All-American Co-Ed (1941)
Wacky cross-dressing comedy from Hal Roach Studios. When an all-girl school insults a pack of macho guys from Quinceton University they decide to put one of their own into a dress and have him enter a beauty contest. Frances Langford, Johnny Downs, Harry Langdon star. 51 min.
17-9003 *$19.99*

Broadway Limited (1941)
Hal Roach comedy of three movie stars who travel from Chicago to New York via train with a baby as a publicity stunt. They don't realize the tot is kidnapped, and the police are soon on their trail! Railroad buffs will delight in the many scenes of the title train in all its glory. Victor McLaglen, Marjorie Woodworth, Dennis O'Keefe, Patsy Kelly and ZaSu Pitts star. 75 min.
17-9007 Was $19.99 *$14.99*

I Married A Witch (1942)
A 300-year-old witch returns to Earth to place a curse on the descendant of the man who condemned her, but winds up falling in love with him. Spry, witty comedy stars Veronica Lake, Fredric March, Susan Hayward and Robert Benchley; directed by René Clair. 77 min.
19-1773 Was $19.99 *$14.99*

Hollywood & Vine (1945)
A funny spoof on Hollywood, focusing on the adventures of several characters in Tinseltown. A movie producer tries to make a star out of a dog, a New York down-and-outer finds success as a screenwriter, and the owner of a hamburger stand becomes a studio exec. James Ellison, Wanda McKay, Ralph Morgan and Franklin Pangborn star. 59 min.
50-1910 *$14.99*

Passport To Pimlico (1949)
This, the first of England's Ealing Studios comedies, has become a minor classic. A London neighborhood declares itself independent from England after an unearthed ancient document indicates they actually belong to Burgundy. Margaret Rutherford, Stanley Holloway and Hermione Baddeley star. 84 min.
44-1391 *$19.99*

So's Your Aunt Emma! (1942)
A down-on-his-luck reporter befriends a small-town old maid who arrives in the big city to attend a boxing match. When the unlikely pair discovers that the fight is fixed, they encounter a series of double-crosses, mobsters and more in this lively mix of comedy and melodrama. ZaSu Pitts, Roger Pryor star. AKA: "Meet the Mob." 55 min.
09-2333 *$19.99*

Preston Sturges

The Great McGinty (1940)
Marvelously wicked comedy of political corruption that was Preston Sturges' directorial debut. Brian Donlevy is a bum who gets a job as political boss Akim Tamiroff's "collector" and eventually works his way into the governor's office. With William Demarest. 82 min.
07-1562 *$14.99*

Christmas In July (1940)
Madcap comedy from Preston Sturges about an office worker (Dick Powell) who, thinking he's won a company contest, goes on a wild shopping binge with hilarious complications. Also stars Ellen Drew, William Demarest, Raymond Walburn. 67 min.
07-1332 Was $29.99 *$14.99*

The Lady Eve (1941)
One of Preston Sturges' most engaging and vivacious romantic comedies stars Barbara Stanwyck as a conniving cardsharp who sets her gold digging sights on apparently gullible millionaire Henry Fonda. William Demarest, Charles Coburn and Eugene Pallette provide fine support. 93 min.
07-1496 Was $29.99 *□$14.99*

Sullivan's Travels (1941)
Preston Sturges' gem of Hollywood self-satire stars Joel McCrea as a filmmaker who tires of comedies and light entertainment and wants to make "meaningful" tales of human suffering. To this end, he disguises himself as a bum and sets out across America to experience suffering first-hand. Veronica Lake co-stars. 91 min.
07-1600 Was $29.99 *$14.99*

The Palm Beach Story (1942)
Preston Sturges displays his magic touch for the screwball comedy once again with this hilarious and frantic delight. Claudette Colbert encounters an entourage of zany characters, including "The Ale and Quail Club," after leaving hubby Joel McCrea. Rudy Vallee and Mary Astor co-star. 88 min.
07-1493 Was $29.99 *$14.99*

The Miracle Of Morgan's Creek (1944)
Classic screwball tale with a surprising (for its time) premise. Betty Hutton is a small-town girl who gets drunk at a party and finds herself pregnant a while later, not knowing which of the soldiers she met is the father. Preston Sturges masterpiece also stars Eddie Bracken, Diana Lynn. 99 min.
06-1447 *$14.99*

Hail The Conquering Hero (1944)
4-F Marine reject Eddie Bracken returns to his home town and, thanks to the falsified exploits in his letters to Mom, is declared a war hero in Preston Sturges' hilarious satire. Ella Raines, Raymond Walburn, William Demarest and Freddie Steele co-star. 101 min.
07-1655 Was $29.99 *$14.99*

The Great Moment (1944)
A change of pace for writer-director Preston Sturges, this historical drama laced with humor stars Joel McCrea as Boston dentist William Morton, who invented anesthesia in order to relieve the pain of dental surgery. Betty Field, Harry Carey and William Demarest also star. 83 min.
07-1656 Was $29.99 *$14.99*

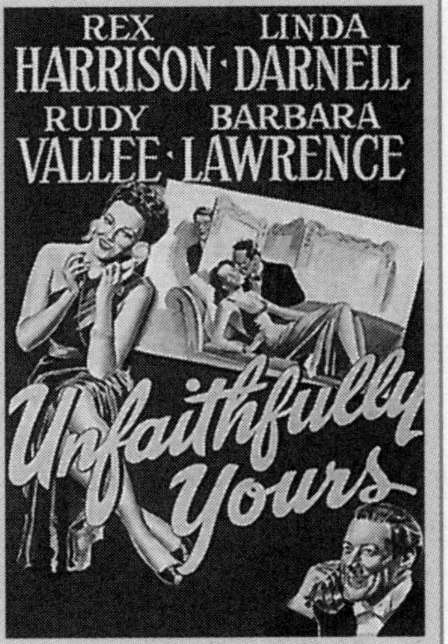

Unfaithfully Yours (1948)
The original version of the classic farce stars Rex Harrison as a symphony conductor seeking revenge against wife Linda Darnell's infidelity. Preston Sturges directs in his signature fast-paced manner. Rudy Vallee, Edgar Kennedy, Lionel Stander co-star. 105 min.
04-1699 Was $59.99 *□$29.99*

The Beautiful Blonde From Bashful Bend (1949)
Rip-roaring western spoof stars Betty Grable as a frontier hellcat on the run from the law who hides out in a small town by masquerading as a prim schoolmarm. With Rudy Vallee, Margaret Hamilton; Preston Sturges' last American film. 76 min.
04-2218 *□$19.99*

Please see our index for the Preston Sturges title: *The Sin Of Harold Diddlebock (Mad Wednesday)*

I'm From Arkansas (1944)
Countrified comedy courtesy of funnyman Slim Summerville that centers around the hilarious havoc that erupts when a Pitchfork, Arkansas, pig gives birth to 10 baby piglets and the money-hungry leeches who try to exploit the joyous occasion. With Ed Brendel. 68 min.
10-7042 *$19.99*

Lost Honeymoon (1947)
Franchot Tone stars in this zesty comedy of the absurd as an amnesia victim who regains his memory but can't recall if he got married in the meantime. Also stars Ann Richards and Una O'Connor. 71 min.
10-7044 Was $19.99 *$14.99*

Road Show (1941)
Affable, wonderfully screwy comedy concerning a run-down carny that discovers aid from its woes in the person of two wealthy mental hospital escapees. Stars Adolphe Menjou, Carole Landis, Charles Butterworth, Patsy Kelly. 87 min.
10-7225 *$19.99*

Misbehaving Husbands (1940)
A woman becomes suspicious of her department store owner husband when he's seen in a compromising position with a beautiful blonde that turns out to be a mannequin. Harry Langdon, Betty Blythe, Ralph Byrd and Gig Young (billed as Byron Barr in his film debut) star in this romantic farce. 65 min.
10-9247 Was $19.99 *$14.99*

It's In The Air (1940)
British comic favorite George Formby plays a humble Army private mistaken for an RAF pilot in this slapstick effort. Polly Ward, Garry Marsh also star. 74 min.
10-9698 *$19.99*

Jeannie (1941)
A romantic comedy delight involving a perky Scottish woman whose inheritance takes her on a series of unusual adventures. She soon gets involved with a gigolo and a washing machine salesman. Edward Chapman, Kay Hammond, Rachel Kempson and Ian Fleming star. AKA: "Girl in Distress." 101 min.
10-9699 *$19.99*

I Didn't Do It (1945)
In this comic thriller, an aspiring actor from London rents a room in a hotel that's populated by other theatrical personalities. When an acrobat is found murdered, he becomes the prime suspect, and must prove himself innocent. George Formby, Billy Caryll and Ian Fleming star. 97 min.
10-9697 *$19.99*

Father Steps Out (1941)
In order to get the scoop on a railroad president, a reporter poses as a doctor's assistant. Later, the high-strung tycoon meets two hoboes who show him how to enjoy life's pleasures. Frank Albertson, Jed Prouty, Frank Faylen and Charles Hall star. 63 min.
10-9303 *$19.99*

Topper Returns (1941)
Roland Young plays detective in a haunted house, helping spectral Joan Blondell track down her own killer. Spook-filled comedy/mystery also stars Billie Burke, Eddie "Rochester" Anderson. 85 min.
17-1031 *$19.99*

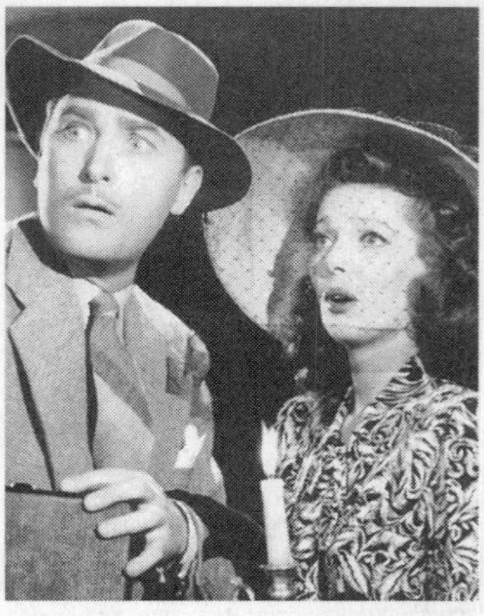

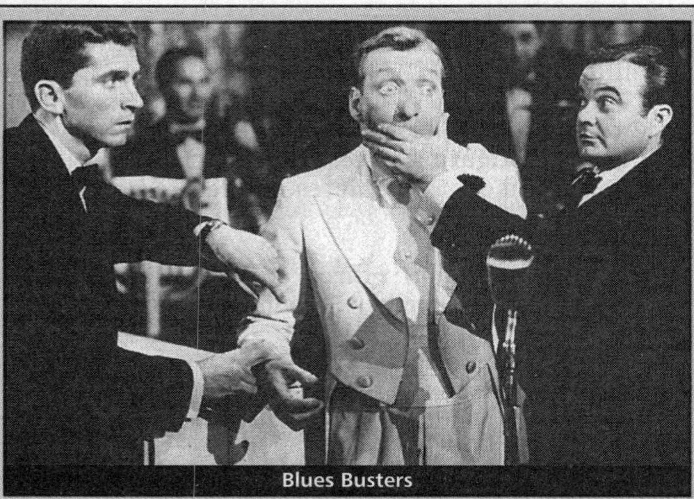

Blues Busters

East Side Kids

Little Tough Guy (1938)
The Dead End Kids star in this social drama of slum life during the Depression about a strike-breaker who is accused of murder and sent to reform school. Stars Billy Halop, Huntz Hall and Gabriel Dell. 84 min.
08-8053 Was $19.99 *$14.99*

Boys Of The City (1940)
Things get scary for Leo Gorcey, Bobby Jordan and the East Side gang when a murder in a creepy old mansion makes them unofficial ghost chasers. 63 min.
01-5106 Was $19.99 *$14.99*

That Gang Of Mine (1940)
One of the East Side Kids becomes a successful jockey, but when he's accused of fixing races, the whole gang has to come to his aid. Leo Gorcey, Bobby Jordan and Clarence Muse star. 62 min.
01-5107 Was $19.99 *$14.99*

Pride Of The Bowery (1940)
The East Side Kids want to get away from city life, so they sign up for a boxing camp that turns out to be a work camp. Leo and David Gorcey, Bobby Jordan star. 61 min.
01-5121 Was $19.99 *$14.99*

East Side Kids (1940)
A gang of streetwise kids gets help from a crook-turned-detective in stopping a counterfeiting ring in the first of Monogram's "East Side Kids" series. Leon Ames, Joyce Bryant, Dave O'Brien star. 62 min.
17-9012 Was $19.99 *$14.99*

Bowery Blitzkrieg (1941)
Fun and danger with the East Side Kids, as Muggsy's chance to win a Golden Gloves boxing match is threatened by crooked fight promoters. Leo Gorcey, Huntz Hall, Bobby Jordan. 62 min.
01-5101 Was $19.99 *$14.99*

Spooks Run Wild (1941)
The East Side Kids (Leo Gorcey, Huntz Hall and crew) meet Bela Lugosi in this haunted-house comedy. 64 min.
08-8045 Was $19.99 *$14.99*

Flying Wild (1941)
It's up to the East Side Kids to ground a ring of saboteurs who are out to obtain airplane blueprints for the Axis. Keep 'em flying with Leo Gorcey, Bobby Jordan. 63 min.
10-7248 Was $19.99 *$14.99*

Hit The Road (1941)
The Dead End Kids and the Little Tough Guys get together for this comedy-drama detailing the Kids' exploits outside of a reformatory and their attempts to find a murderer. Leo Gorcey, Huntz Hall, Billy Halop star, with Shemp Howard as "Dingbat." 60 min.
15-9037 Was $19.99 *$14.99*

'Neath The Brooklyn Bridge (1942)
The East Side Kids find themselves in hot water when they help a young girl in trouble, only to find they're accused of murder. Leo Gorcey and Huntz Hall star. 61 min.
01-5102 Was $19.99 *$14.99*

Let's Get Tough (1942)
The East Side Kids help the home front when they take on a Japanese spy ring. Leo Gorcey, Huntz Hall and Bobby Jordan star. 62 min.
01-5103 Was $19.99 *$14.99*

Mr. Wise Guy (1942)
It's the East Side Kids vs. the Mob when Leo Gorcey, Huntz Hall and all the guys find themselves at odds with gang boss Billy Gilbert. After a few rounds with the boys, the crooks wish they could fight the Untouchables instead.
01-5105 Was $19.99 *$14.99*

Smart Alecks (1942)
Join the East Side Kids (Huntz Hall, Leo Gorcey, Gabriel Dell and co.) in a story concerning the boys' attempt to raise funds to buy baseball uniforms. One of them finds himself in hot water with a gangster, and the rest of the gang comes to his rescue. With Maxie Rosenbloom, Gale Storm. 66 min.
17-9026 Was $19.99 *$14.99*

Kid Dynamite (1943)
Fighter Leo Gorcey is kidnapped by gamblers in hopes of keeping him from boxing in a big match, but when his replacement turns out to be his brother, Gorcey is even less happy about the situation. Bobby Jordan, Huntz Hall and silent star Snub Pollard also star in this East Side Kids romp. 67 min.
08-8010 *$14.99*

Ghosts On The Loose (1943)
Leo Gorcey, Huntz Hall and the East Side Kids stumble into a haunted house used as a hideout by Nazi spy Bela Lugosi in this spooky entry that features a young Ava Gardner as Hall's sister(!). 65 min.
10-2028 Was $19.99 *$14.99*

Clancy Street Boys (1943)
East Side Kids comedy has the gang pretending to be Leo Gorcey's siblings in order to impress a rich uncle from Texas. With Huntz Hall (who gets to play Gorcey's sister!), Bobby Jordan, Noah Beery, Sr. 66 min.
64-3056 Was $19.99 *$14.99*

Million Dollar Kid (1944)
The East Side Kids are plunged into new peccadilloes after they rescue a wealthy man from a mugging, and try to put his punk son on the straight and narrow. Leo Gorcey, Huntz Hall, Gabriel Dell star. 64 min.
09-2040 Was $19.99 *$14.99*

Mr. Hex (1946)
When under hypnosis, Huntz Hall becomes a fighting machine...and the Bowery Boys are quick to hustle him into the boxing ring! Calamity on the canvas with Leo Gorcey, Bobby Jordan, Gabriel Dell. 63 min.
10-7247 Was $19.99 *$14.99*

Spook Busters (1946)
When ghosts are on the loose, who ya gonna call? How about the Bowery Boys, "exterminating school" grads who visit a mansion inhabited by a mad scientist conducting bizarre experiments. Huntz Hall, Douglass Dumbrille and Charles Middleton star. 68 min.
19-1934 *$14.99*

Bowery Buckaroos (1947)
Louie, the sweet shop owner, is in big trouble in the Wild West, and when Slip, Sach and Co. set out to get him off the hook, the West will never be wilder! Huntz Hall, Leo Gorcey, Gabriel Dell and Iron Eyes Cody star; William "One Shot" Beaudine directs. 66 min.
19-1931 *$14.99*

Hard Boiled Mahoney (1947)
The detective genre gets the Bowery Boys treatment, as the fellas turn sleuths and become involved with a phony fortune teller. Huntz Hall, Leo Gorcey, Bobby Jordan and Betty Compson star. 64 min.
19-1933 *$14.99*

Blues Busters (1950)
After a tonsillectomy leaves him with a great singing voice, Sach becomes the star attraction when Louie's Sweet Shop is turned into a nightclub. Leo Gorcey, Huntz Hall, Gabriel Dell, Craig Stevens and Phyllis Coates star. 68 min.
19-1932 *$14.99*

Ghost Chasers (1951)
The zany Bowery Boys try to expose the phony Margo the Medium, and get some help from a 300-year-old spirit. Leo Gorcey, Huntz Hall, Lloyd Corrigan star in this outrageous outing. 70 min.
19-1935 *$14.99*

Here Come The Marines (1952)
The few, the proud...the Bowery Boys? Leo Gorcey, Huntz Hall and crew accidentally join the Marines in this slapstick service comedy that also has the boys busting up a gambling ring. 66 min.
10-7246 Was $19.99 *$14.99*

Clipped Wings (1952)
The always-zany Bowery Boys visit a friend at an Air Force base and proceed to turn things into a shambles...until they help to nab a group of Nazi spies (in 1952?). Leo Gorcey, Huntz Hall, Bernard Gorcey and David Condon are the Bowery-born harbingers of hilarity. 62 min.
19-1930 *$14.99*

The Bowery Boys Scrapbook
The best of the Bowery Boys, AKA Dead End Kids, AKA the East Side Kids. Whatever their names, Huntz Hall, Leo Gorcey, Gabriel Dell, Bobby Jordan, et al. were comedic champions whose slapstick, streetwise antics will leave you laughing. 60 min.
15-9035 Was $19.99 *$14.99*

Bowery Boys Trailers
Previews of the Bowery Boys' funniest films, featuring Huntz Hall, Leo Gorcey and the rest of the zany crew. See slapstick wackiness from their greatest previews. 60 min.
15-9039 Was $19.99 *$14.99*

Please see our index for these other East Side Kids titles: *Angels With Dirty Faces • Dead End • Junior G-Men • Junior G-Men Of The Air*

A Night To Remember (1942)
Brian Aherne and Loretta Young are a successful mystery writer and his wife who relocate in Greenwich Village hoping to inspire his first romantic novel, but when a corpse turns up in their new backyard he gets the sleuthing bug all over again. Comedic whodunit co-stars Gale Sondergaard, Sidney Toler. 91 min.
02-1940 Was $69.99 *$19.99*

The Invisible Woman (1941)
John Barrymore is a demented professor who invents a machine that renders people invisible. His guinea pig is a pretty model (Virginia Bruce) who finds that not being seen isn't all it's cracked up to be when spies go after the machine and her. The supporting cast includes Shemp Howard, Charlie Ruggles, Margaret Hamilton and John Howard. 73 min.
07-1979 *$14.99*

The Perfect Marriage (1946)
Delightful romantic farce featuring David Niven as an airplane factory owner and Loretta Young as his fashion magazine editor wife, who appear to have a perfectly happy union...until their relatives and friends interfere, leading them to divorce. Then their young daughter attempts to get them back together, even though both have new romantic interests. Eddie Albert co-stars. 88 min.
07-2045 *$19.99*

Inside The Law (1942)
The head of a gang of cross-country con artists comes into possession of a letter that lands him a job as a bank manager, and before long he and his cronies are planning to rob the bank—from the inside—in this fast-paced caper comedy. Wallace Ford, Frank Sully, Luana Walters. 56 min.
09-1022 *$14.99*

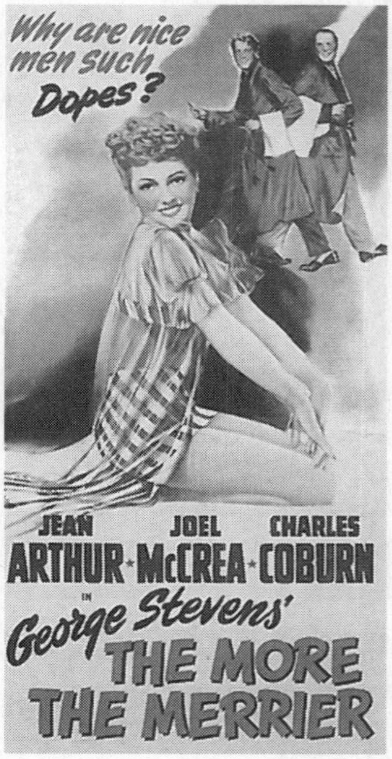

The More The Merrier (1943)
Comic look at Washington's wartime housing shortage has Charles Coburn (who won an Oscar for his role) playing matchmaker for his "roommates," Jean Arthur and Joel McCrea. George Stevens directs this romantic farce, later remade as "Walk, Don't Run." 104 min.
02-1995 *$19.99*

The Eagle And The Hawk (1933)
Compelling WWI aviation drama stars Fredric March as the American commander of a British flying squadron who grows embittered over his sending of men to their deaths and tries to keep old chums Cary Grant and Jack Oakie out of combat. With Carole Lombard, Sir Guy Standing. Includes original theatrical trailer. 73 min.
07-2513 □*$14.99*

Amazing Adventure (1936)
Well-to-do British playboy Cary Grant tires of his wastrel-like existence and wagers that he can earn his own way without touching his inheritance for one year. Amusing social satire from England also stars Mary Brian, Henry Kendall. AKA: "The Amazing Quest of Ernest Bliss," "Romance and Riches." 70 min.
10-2003 *$19.99*

The Awful Truth (1937)
Screwball classic stars Cary Grant and Irene Dunne as a newly-divorced couple who realize, independently of one another, that they're still in love. They must then go and stop each other's latest romances. Fast-paced farce from director Leo McCarey also stars Ralph Bellamy, Cecil Cunningham. 92 min.
02-1591 Was $59.99 *$19.99*

Holiday (1938)
Classic George Cukor comedy stars Cary Grant as a free-spirited young man who is introduced to his fiancée's stuffy society family and falls in love with her sister (Katharine Hepburn). Doris Nolan, Lew Ayres, Edward Everett Horton co-star. 93 min.
02-1741 *$19.99*

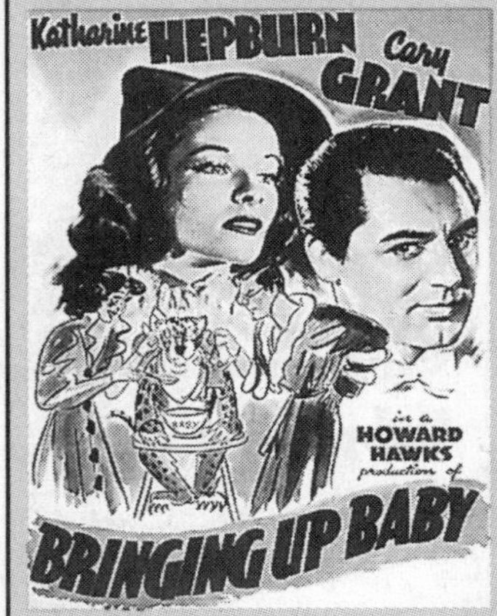

Bringing Up Baby (1938)
Howard Hawks' screwball classic stars Cary Grant as a stodgy scientist buried under a stack of dinosaur bones and Katharine Hepburn as the fun-loving society gal trying to excavate him, with some help from a leopard named Baby. With Charles Ruggles, May Robson, and Asta the dog. 102 min.
18-7114 *$19.99*

Only Angels Have Wings (1939)
Cary Grant is the no-nonsense chief of an air freight service on a treacherous Andean route, and perky Jean Arthur and vampish Rita Hayworth are the women vying to be his permanent co-pilot, in this soaring Howard Hawks adventure. 121 min.
02-1885 *$19.99*

The Howards Of Virginia (1940)
Revolutionary War drama stars Cary Grant as the Virginia woodsman whose marriage to an aristocrat's daughter is imperiled by the rising call for independence. Martha Scott, Sir Cedric Hardwicke co-star. 116 min.
02-1742 Was $69.99 *$19.99*

His Girl Friday (1940)
Cary Grant and Rosalind Russell shine in director Howard Hawks' revamping of "The Front Page." Rapid-fire dialogue and memorable supporting characters make this tale of newsmen, newswomen and escaped convicts a comedy classic. With Ralph Bellamy. 93 min.
10-2027 Was $19.99 *$14.99*

Penny Serenade (Color Version) (1941)
Melodramatic work from director George Stevens stars Cary Grant and Irene Dunne as a couple about to separate. Through flashbacks, the joys and sorrows of their life together are recounted. Beulah Bondi, Edgar Buchanan, Ann Doran give fine supporting turns in this sentimental favorite. 120 min.
63-1531 *$19.99*

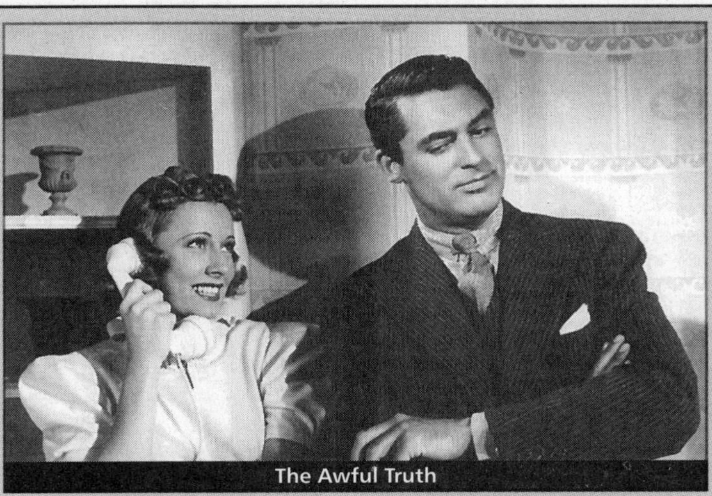
The Awful Truth

Cary Grant

The Talk Of The Town (1942)
George Stevens' acclaimed blend of screwball comedy and social satire stars Cary Grant as a fugitive anarchist who hides in the home of conservative law professor Ronald Colman. Jean Arthur, Edgar Buchanan, Rex Ingram co-star. 118 min.
02-1745 Was $69.99 *$19.99*

Once Upon A Honeymoon (1942)
Comedy-drama of an American woman in Europe who unwittingly marries a Nazi and the reporter who saves her. Laughs, danger and action with Ginger Rogers and Cary Grant. 117 min.
05-1007 *$19.99*

Mr. Lucky (1943)
The ultra-suave Cary Grant is owner of a floating casino, but just managing to keep his head above water. The answer: seduce virtuous and wealthy Laraine Day. He wins more than he bargained for in this stylish comedy. 99 min.
05-1115 *$19.99*

None But The Lonely Heart (1944)
Cary Grant's great performance as a Cockney wanderer who gets drawn into a robbery ring until he learns of his mother's terminal illness highlights this emotional drama scripted and directed by Clifford Odets. Ethel Barrymore co-stars as Grant's mother; with Jane Wyatt, Barry Fitzgerald. 113 min.
05-1336 *$14.99*

Destination Tokyo (1944)
A taut, thrilling war saga, starring Cary Grant as the skipper of an American submarine who commandeers it from San Francisco to Tokyo Bay and into battle. Exciting fighting footage and interplay between crew members John Garfield, Dane Clark and John Ridgley are two of the highlights of this classic. 135 min.
12-2076 *$19.99*

Destination Tokyo (Color Version)
Cary Grant and John Garfield don't have to look at murky waters thanks to this colorized edition.
12-2077 *$19.99*

Night And Day (1946)
The life and career of composer Cole Porter are saluted in this Movies Unlimited favorite. Cary Grant plays Porter, following him from his days at Yale, his experiences in World War I, his stormy marriage, and his amazing musical accomplishments. Alexis Smith, Monty Woolley, Jane Wyman co-star. Score includes "You're the Top," "Don't Fence Me In," more. 128 min.
12-2239 *$19.99*

The Bachelor And The Bobby-Soxer (1947)
Playboy Cary Grant gets in trouble with the law, and judge Myrna Loy orders him to date her teenage sister, played by Shirley Temple, in order to end her infatuation with him. What develops is a delightful romantic comedy. 95 min.
05-1351 Was $19.99 *$14.99*

The Bishop's Wife (1947)
Delightful comedy starring Cary Grant as a suave angel who comes to Earth to help distraught young bishop David Niven raise money for a new cathedral and soothe over his wife's neglected feelings. Also stars Loretta Young, Monty Woolley and James Gleason. 109 min.
44-1838 Was $19.99 *$14.99*

Every Girl Should Be Married (1948)
Eager husband-seeker Betsy Drake launches an elaborate campaign to land eligible doctor Cary Grant (a plot that predated their own real-life marriage) in this breezy romantic comedy. With Franchot Tone, Diana Lynn. 84 min.
18-7017 *$19.99*

Every Girl Should Be Married (Color Version)
And every girl should also be able to color co-ordinate her wardrobe, a feat now possible thanks to high-tech tinting.
18-7789 *$19.99*

Mr. Blandings Builds His Dream House (1948)
Cary Grant and Myrna Loy's third screen pairing finds them as hapless Manhattanites whose dream of an idyllic life in the suburbs of Connecticut turns into a nightmare after they pour their money into a 200-year-old "fix-'er-upper." Gag-filled rib-tickler co-stars Melvyn Douglas, Reginald Denny, Louise Beavers. Also includes the original theatrical trailer. 94 min.
18-7655 *$19.99*

I Was A Male War Bride (1949)
French Army officer Cary Grant and American WAC officer Ann Sheridan decide to get married in Europe after a stormy courtship, but the only way Cary can get into the U.S. and avoid red tape is pose as a war bride, donning a wig and WAC uniform. Hilarious cross-dressing shenanigans ensue in Howard Hawks' screwball farce. William Neff and Marion Marshall co-star. 105 min.
04-2782 □*$19.99*

People Will Talk (1951)
Sparkling comic gem with moments of great poignancy stars Cary Grant as a physician whose belief in the curative powers of the mind seems too unorthodox to his associates, while his love for a pregnant, emotionally distressed medical student (Jeanne Crain) only brings about even more disdain. Hume Cronyn and Walter Slezak co-star; Joseph L. Mankiewicz writes and directs. 110 min.
04-2783 □*$19.99*

Monkey Business (1952)
Howard Hawks' "fountain of youth" comedy stars Cary Grant as a scientist whose rejuvenation serum causes chaos for himself and everyone around him. With Ginger Rogers, Charles Coburn and Marilyn Monroe in an early role. 97 min.
04-2080 *$14.99*

Dream Wife (1953)
Male chauvinist Cary Grant wants girlfriend Deborah Kerr to quit her State Department job so she can stay home and care for him. When Kerr shuns Grant's wishes, he calls on a Middle Eastern princess he met years earlier. But after Kerr teaches the beauty some lessons about feminism, Grant's plans for happiness are disrupted. With Betta St. John; directed by Sidney Sheldon. 100 min.
12-3092 *$19.99*

An Affair To Remember (1957)
Grand remake of 1939's "Love Affair" stars Cary Grant and Deborah Kerr as the shipboard lovers who return to their separate lives in New York and promise to meet six months later atop the Empire State Building, until a tragic accident threatens to keep them apart. With Richard Denning, Neva Patterson. 115 min.
04-2298 Was $19.99 □*$14.99*

The Pride And The Passion (1957)
In Stanley Kramer's adventure saga, Cary Grant is a British naval officer who must retrieve a huge cannon abandoned by Spanish troops in order to use it against Napoleon's army. After enlisting guerrilla Frank Sinatra for the mission, Grant falls for his girlfriend (Sophia Loren). With Theodore Bikel and Jay Novello. 132 min.
12-2513 Was $19.99 *$14.99*

Houseboat (1958)
Housekeeper Sophia Loren signs on board to care for widower Cary Grant's children, but the two find themselves in a shipboard romance in this fun, frothy romantic tale. With Martha Hyer, Harry Guardino. 110 min.
06-1446 *$14.99*

Indiscreet (1958)
Classic sophisticated comedy finds rich American playboy Cary Grant and beautiful European actress Ingrid Bergman having a romantic fling with "no strings attached," then finding out they mean more to each other than they admitted. With Cecil Parker; Stanley Donen directs. 100 min.
63-1553 Letterboxed □*$14.99*

Father Goose (1964)
Beachcomber Cary Grant reluctantly agrees to monitor Japanese military activity around his Pacific island home in 1943. Things get even more hectic when schoolteacher Leslie Caron and her female charges are stranded with him. How the pair fall in love and help the war effort makes for delightful comedy. Trevor Howard also stars. 113 min.
63-1878 Letterboxed □*$14.99*

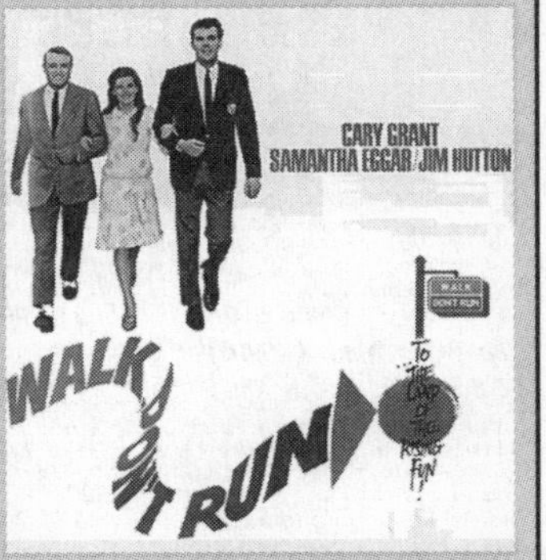

Walk, Don't Run (1966)
In his last film appearance, Cary Grant plays matchmaker to secretary Samantha Eggar and athlete Jim Hutton when over-crowding forces the trio to share an apartment during the Tokyo Olympics. Light, breezy remake of "The More the Merrier" also stars John Standing, George Takei. 114 min.
02-1817 Was $69.99 *$19.99*

Cary Grant: The Leading Man
Sterling tribute to the star whose sophisticated style served him in roles ranging from romantic comedies to suspenseful thrillers. Includes interviews with Leslie Caron, Stanley Donen, Deborah Kerr and others; narrated by Richard Kiley. 60 min.
50-6791 Was $19.99 *$14.99*

Please see our index for these other Cary Grant titles: *Arsenic And Old Lace* • *Blonde Venus* • *Charade* • *I'm No Angel* • *North By Northwest* • *Notorious* • *Operation Petticoat* • *The Philadelphia Story* • *She Done Him Wrong* • *Suspicion* • *Suzy* • *That Touch Of Mink* • *To Catch A Thief*

Up In Mabel's Room (1944)
Frothy bedroom farce, based on an earlier play and film, features Dennis O'Keefe as a newlywed who innocently gets in romantic trouble with pretty young Gail Patrick, who happens to be engaged to his boss. Marjorie Reynolds is O'Keefe's wife, whose misinterpretation of the situation leads to laughs. With Lee Bowman, Mischa Auer and Binnie Barnes. 76 min.
08-1779 *$19.99*

Getting Gertie's Garter (1945)
Based on a hit play, this wacky comedy stars Dennis O'Keefe as a professor who has given a jewel-laden garter to girlfriend Marie McDonald. But now McDonald is marrying O'Keefe's pal and she plans to keep the sexy undergarment in case the union fails. Can O'Keefe get to snag the garter before the situation gets worse? With Barry Sullivan, Sheila Ryan, Binnie Barnes. 72 min.
08-1780 *$19.99*

Fiddlers Three (1944)
Amusing time-travel comedy in which two sailors on leave attempt to find refuge from a rainstorm by ducking under an altar in Stonehenge. When the altar is zapped by lightning, they are thrust back to Ancient Rome, where they delight the empress with their predictions...but soon face death in the lions' den. Tommy Trinder and Frances Dey star in this Ealing Studios farce. 88 min.
09-5015 *$19.99*

The Facts Of Love (1945)
The calm, middle-class world of a British couple is abruptly shattered when, while on a Mediterranean holiday, their attractive daughter gets engaged and their son becomes smitten with a predatory older woman. Gordon Harker, Betty Balfour and Jimmy Hanley star. AKA: "29 Acacia Avenue." 81 min.
09-2336 Was $24.99 *$19.99*

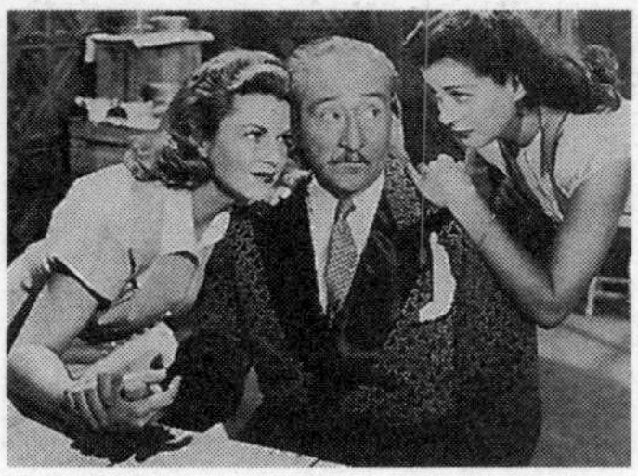

The Bachelor's Daughters (1946)
A terrific cast is featured in this funny farce about four female department store workers who take a house in Long Island and pose as wealthy women in order to snag rich husbands. They even recruit a fellow worker to pose as their father. Claire Trevor, Gail Russell, Ann Dvorak, Billie Burke, Jane Wyatt, Eugene List and Adolphe Menjou star. 88 min.
09-5149 *$19.99*

The Farmer's Daughter (1947)
Loretta Young won an Oscar for her performance as a Swedish girl who's hired on as servant to congressman Joseph Cotten and his politically powerful mother (Ethel Barrymore), and finds herself stumping for a congressional seat for a party on opposite sides of her boss's. Co-stars Charles Bickford; look for James Arness. 97 min.
04-1543 *$14.99*

Million Dollar Weekend (1948)
Heist comedy about a swindler who tries to rip off the title total from his company. While heading for Shanghai, he falls for a woman being blackmailed by a con man who makes off with his million. Gene Raymond, Stephanie Paull and Francis Lederer star. 73 min.
10-8239 Was $19.99 *$14.99*

Dreaming (1944)
The popular British comedy duo of Bud Flanagan and Ches Allen star in this farce about a soldier who is knocked unconscious and dreams of attending the races at Ascot, fighting in Africa and Germany, and visiting the Stage Door Canteen. Hazel Court and Dick Francis co-star in this Ealing Studios effort. 78 min.
09-5014 *$19.99*

The Ghosts Of Berkeley Square (1947)
A charming British comedy about two ghosts who try to aid their homeland during World War II and wind up doomed to haunt a mansion until freed by a reigning monarch of England. Robert Morley, Felix Aylmer star. 61 min.
09-1430 Was $24.99 *$19.99*

The Cardboard Cavalier (1949)
Laughs abound in this farce set in the 17th century about a peasant who gets involved in a plot to overthrow Oliver Cromwell in order to help Charles II's return to the English throne. Sid Field, Margaret Lockwood and Mary Clare star. 97 min.
09-5012 *$19.99*

The Kid Sister (1945)
A teenage girl decides she's offically "grown up"—and sets out to prove it by winning away her big sister's boyfriend—in this charming domestic comedy. Judy Clark, Constance Worth, Roger Pryor star. 56 min.
09-1239 Was $24.99 *$19.99*

The Butler's Dilemma (1943)
British farce mixes mistaken identities with jewel thieves and butlers. Hermione Gingold, Richard Hearne, Ian Fleming. 75 min.
09-1587 Was $19.99 *$14.99*

Hay Foot (1941)
William Tracy stars as a wide-eyed draftee in the peacetime army who lands in hot water every time he inadvertently upstages his hot-headed sergeant. Hal Roach-produced featurette co-stars Joe Sawyer, James Gleason and Elyse Knox. 47 min.
09-2262 *$19.99*

Machine Gun Mama (1944)
Music and laughs surround the adventures of two brash Brooklynites (Wallace Ford, El Brendel) as they try to deliver Bunny the elephant to a Mexican carnival and tangle with the evil "Joe the Gyp," who's trying to close the show. Co-stars Armida, Jack La Rue. 61 min.
09-2265 *$14.99*

Li'l Abner (1940)
It's hillbilly hilarity in the first film based on the beloved comic strip, as Li'l Abner (Granville Owen) tries his darndest to steer clear of marriage-minded Daisy Mae (Martha O'Driscoll). With Mona Ray, Chester Conklin, Edgar Kennedy and Buster Keaton as Lonesome Polecat. 72 min.
09-1000 *$19.99*

Danny Kaye

The Kid From Brooklyn (1946)
Danny Kaye scores a comedic knockout in this tale of a mild-mannered milkman who accidentally KOs a middleweight boxing champ and is turned by the champ's scheming manager into a fighter himself. Virginia Mayo, Lionel Stander, Vera-Ellen co-star in this remake of Harold Lloyd's "The Milky Way." 113 min.
44-1831 Was $19.99 *$14.99*

Wonder Man (1946)
One of Danny Kaye's finest hours, as he tackles the roles of twin brothers—one a meek nerd, the other a glib showman. When crooks rub out the flashy sibling, the other has to take his place—with riotous results. Virginia Mayo, Vera-Ellen also star. 97 min.
44-1843 Was $19.99 *$14.99*

The Secret Life Of Walter Mitty (1947)
Fine adaptation of James Thurber's short story stars Danny Kaye as the harried milquetoast who daydreams of manly prowess and heroic deeds, only to have his dreams become reality when he meets a beautiful heiress pursued by jewel thieves. With Virginia Mayo, Ann Rutherford, Boris Karloff and the Goldwyn Girls. 110 min.
44-1834 Was $19.99 *$14.99*

The Inspector General (1949)
Hysterical comedy, based on the Gogol play, stars Danny Kaye as a medicine show flunkie who's mistaken for a high-ranking government agent by the corrupt officials of a small European village. Walter Slezak, Barbara Bates, Elsa Lanchester co-star. 102 min.
12-2466 ☐*$19.99*

THE
Court Jester

The Court Jester (1956)
Laugh-filled costume farce stars Danny Kaye as a valet who impersonates a court jester to overthrow evil baron Basil Rathbone. Features the famous "I've put a pellet of poison in the vessel with the pestle" line and ace support from Glynis Johns and Angela Lansbury. 101 min.
06-1197 *$14.99*

Me And The Colonel (1958)
In Paris in 1940 during the Nazi occupation, Jewish refugee Danny Kaye teams with anti-Semitic Polish colonel Curt Jurgens to flee the city and head for Spain. Along the way, they are joined by Jurgens' assistant (Akim Tamiroff) and mistress (Nicole Maurey). Kaye eventually uses his wits to get his fellow travellers out of trouble and wins the respect of the nasty Jurgens. 110 min.
02-2851 *$19.99*

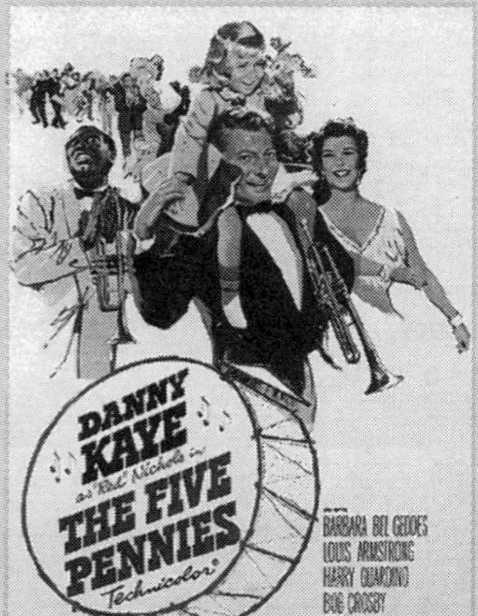

The Five Pennies (1959)
Danny Kaye stars as jazz great Red Nichols in this biopic that chronicles the stormy life of the '20s cornet wizard, including Nichols' domestic problems and musical triumphs. Barbara Bel Geddes, Tuesday Weld, Louis Armstrong, Bob Crosby co-star; tunes include "Good Night, Sleep Tight," "The Music Goes Round and Round," "The Battle Hymn of the Republic." 117 min.
06-1916 Was $19.99 *$14.99*

Please see our index for these other Danny Kaye titles: *Hans Christian Andersen • The Madwoman Of Chaillot • White Christmas*

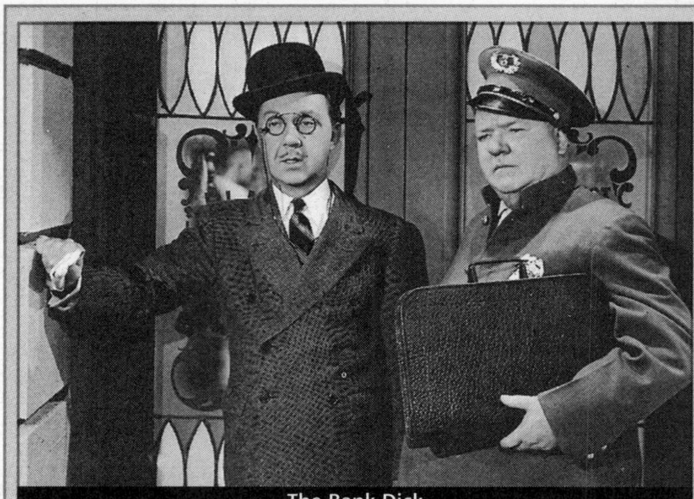
The Bank Dick

W.C. Fields

W.C. Fields: 6 Short Films
"Godfrey Daniel!" Now you can have six of the comedic master's classic two-reelers on one video. See Fields show off his billiards expertise in his first movie, the silent "Pool Sharks" (1915). The Great One next takes his shots on the links as "The Golf Specialist" (1930), gets too close to a female patient in "The Dentist" (1932), utters the immortal line "Ain't a fit night out for man nor beast" in "The Fatal Glass of Beer" (1932), dispenses drugs and laughs as "The Pharmacist" (1933), and runs a "clip joint" in "The Barber Shop" (1933). 112 min. total.
22-5882 Remastered *$19.99*

Sally Of The Sawdust (1925)
One of W.C. Fields' first film roles was as carnival juggler Eustace McGargle in this classic D.W. Griffith comedy. Fields must help his young ward Sally (Carol Dempster) find her missing grandparents, while staying one step ahead of the law. Includes color-tinted sequences. 113 min. Silent with music score.
53-8627 Remastered *$24.99*

Running Wild (1927)
Unrestrained hilarity abounds in this silent comedy starring W.C. Fields as a devout milquetoast whose life and luck are miraculously transformed through a bizarre accident with a horseshoe. Co-stars Mary Brian, Claud Buchanan. 68 min. Silent with music score.
06-1433 Was $29.99 *$14.99*

Million Dollar Legs (1932)
Surreal slapstick and satire mix in director Eddie Cline's offbeat comedy, made to coincide with (and spoof) the Los Angeles-held 1932 Olympic Games. W.C. Fields stars as the president of Klopstokia, a tiny mythical nation whose residents are all superior athletes and which intends to make a name for itself by entering the Olympics. The cast of crazies also includes Jack Oakie, Andy Clyde, Ben Turpin, Hugh Herbert and Lyda Roberti. 62 min.
07-2667 ☐*$14.99*

International House (1933)
Comedy and music galore in this wild farce set in a Chinese hotel where an eccentric scientist is demonstrating his latest invention: television! See George Burns and Gracie Allen, Bela Lugosi, Rudy Vallee, W.C. Fields in his "Spirit of South Brooklyn" and Cab Calloway singing "Reefer Man." 70 min.
07-1459 Was $29.99 *$14.99*

Six Of A Kind (1934)
A "second honeymoon" trip for bank teller Charlie Ruggles and wife Mary Boland turns into a cross-country nightmare, thanks to travelling companions George Burns and Gracie Allen, their pet Great Dane, a suitcase with $50,000 in stolen money, and crooked sheriff W.C. Fields, in this slapstick romp highlighted by Fields' classic pool-playing routine. 63 min.
07-2450 ☐*$14.99*

You're Telling Me (1934)
In a remake of his earlier silent comedy "So's Your Old Man," W.C. Fields plays an inventor out to impress the family of his daughter's suitor. He comes up with an automobile tire that can't be punctured, but fouls things up at a demonstration. By chance, a beautiful princess comes to his aid and helps him regain his confidence. Joan Marsh, Adrienne Ames and Buster Crabbe co-star. 66 min.
07-2666 ☐*$14.99*

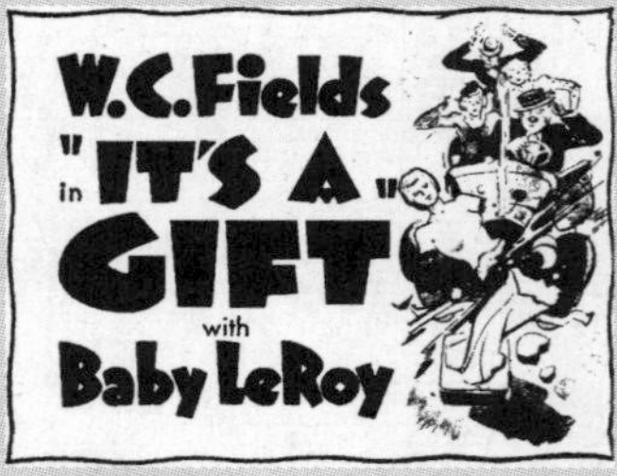

It's A Gift (1934)
W.C. Fields' hilarious look at family life, with the Great Man playing harried husband and shopkeeper Harold Bissenette. Watch as he contends with an indignant blind customer, a mischievous Baby Le Roy and an insurance salesman looking for "La-Fong...Carl LaFong," all the while dreaming of growing oranges in California. With Kathleen Howard, Charles Sellon. 68 min.
10-3058 ☐*$14.99*

The Big Broadcast Of 1938 (1937)
The final installment of the hit series stars W.C. Fields as an ocean liner owner who pits his ship against another vessel in a high-speed race. While on the journey, a host of musical and comedy stars do their acts, including Martha Raye, Dorothy Lamour, Kirsten Flagstad, and Bob Hope (his first feature), who sings his signature tune, the Oscar-winning "Thanks for the Memory." 91 min.
07-2286 ☐*$14.99*

You Can't Cheat An Honest Man (1939)
Has W.C. Fields met his match in Charlie McCarthy? Watch the fun when circus owner Larson E. Whipsnade (Fields) tries to pull the wool over everyone's eyes, including Edgar Bergen and his knotty pine pals Charlie and Mortimer Snerd. With Constance Moore, Eddie "Rochester" Anderson and Grady Sutton. Includes the original theatrical trailer. 79 min.
10-3184 ☐*$14.99*

The Bank Dick (1940)
W.C. Fields is at his best as Egbert Sousé, henpecked husband and layabout, who inadvertently foils bank robbers, becomes the new guard, and still manages to slip off to the Black Pussycat Cafe. Co-stars Grady Sutton, Franklin Pangborn and Shemp Howard. 73 min.
07-1172 Was $29.99 *$14.99*

W.C. Fields: On Stage, On Screen, On The Air
Vaudeville juggler, Hollywood comedy star, nemesis of small children and wooden puppets—W.C. Fields was all of these, but on the whole he'd rather be in Philadelphia. The varied career of the virtuoso of virtuelessness is examined, with clips from his hilarious film legacy. 60 min.
50-6303 *$19.99*

Please see our index for these other W.C. Fields titles: *David Copperfield • Follow The Boys • My Little Chickadee • Sensations Of 1945 • Tales Of Manhattan*

Ginger Rogers

The Thirteenth Guest (1932)
Thirteen years after a dinner party abruptly ended when the host was found murdered, the guests are summoned back to the scene of the crime, where someone begins bumping them off one by one. A young Ginger Rogers stars as the late host's daughter, and Lyle Talbot is a detective trying to find the killer, in this creepy thriller. 70 min.
62-1147 *$19.99*

A Shriek In The Night (1933)
Ginger Rogers and Lyle Talbot repeat their roles from "The Thirteenth Guest" in this mystery comedy of reporters on the trail of a murderer. Suspense and laughs à la "The Thin Man." 66 min.
08-8002 *$19.99*

Bachelor Mother (1939)
Priceless farce stars Ginger Rogers as a sales clerk who happens upon a little bundle of joy, with everyone believing she's the baby's unwed mother. Somewhat suggestive shenanigans (for 1939) co-stars David Niven and Charles Coburn. 82 min.
05-1347 *$19.99*

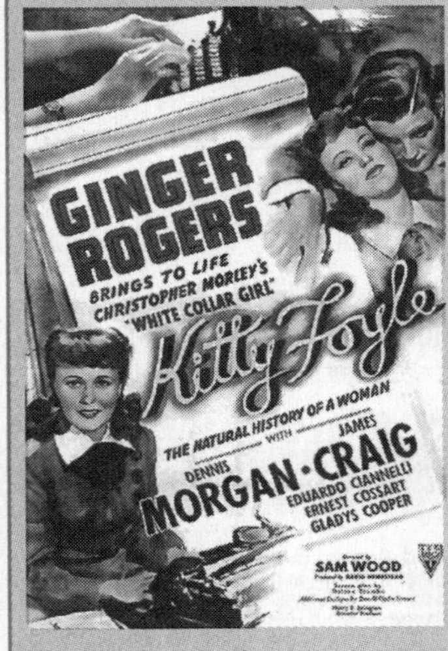

Kitty Foyle (1940)
Ginger Rogers won an Oscar (in her first dramatic role) as a Philadelphia working-class woman who marries into a well-to-do Main Line family, but seeks solace with an old flame when the marriage sours. Dennis Morgan, James Craig co-star. 107 min.
05-1343 *$14.99*

Roxie Hart (1942)
Set in Roaring '20s Chicago, this broad and breezy comedy stars Ginger Rogers in the title role of the brash dance hall girl who confesses to a murder committed by her no-good husband, in the hope of giving her show career a boost. Adolphe Menjou shines as Rogers' slick attorney; with George Montgomery, George Chandler, Phil Silvers. 74 min.
04-2927 *□$19.99*

The Major And The Minor (1942)
The Hollywood directorial debut of Billy Wilder (who also co-scripted with Charles Brackett), this classic screwball comedy stars Ginger Rogers as a woman who can only afford a child's ticket for a cross-country train ride and poses as a 12-year-old girl. Ray Milland is the Army officer who becomes Rogers' "guardian" on the train and insists she accompany him to his military academy. With Diana Lynn, Robert Benchley, and Rogers' real-life mom Lela as her mother. 101 min.
07-2627 *□$14.99*

Weekend At The Waldorf (1945)
New York's majestic Waldorf-Astoria Hotel served as the setting for this semi-remake of "Grand Hotel." Comedy and drama mix as the experiences of such guests as movie actress Ginger Rogers, war reporter Walter Pidgeon, stenographer Lana Turner, flyboy Van Johnson and tycoon Edward Arnold are recounted. With appearances by Robert Benchley and Xavier Cugat and His Orchestra. 130 min.
12-2723 *□$19.99*

Heartbeat (1946)
Ginger Rogers stars in this romantic comedy set in Paris. She plays a recent graduate of a pickpocketing "school" whose first victim is a wealthy diplomat she meets at a ritzy dance. Jean-Pierre Aumont, Adolphe Menjou and Basil Rathbone also star in this light farce. 100 min.
10-1391 *$19.99*

The Groom Wore Spurs (1951)
Jack Carson is a Hollywood cowpoke with a rough-and-tumble image onscreen, but who is a pushover in reality. After getting in trouble with gambling and gals in Las Vegas, he calls on lawyer Ginger Rogers, and sparks soon fly. Joan Davis co-stars. 81 min.
10-8250 *$19.99*

Forever Female (1953)
Aspiring playwright William Holden pens what he thinks will be a hit play, but when fading star Ginger Rogers wants the college-age leading lady role he must rework the script to accommodate her, and a pretty, younger actress is also vying for the part. Paul Douglas, Pat Crowley and George Reeves co-star in a witty comedy in the "All About Eve" vein. 93 min.
06-2045 *□$12.99*

Twist Of Fate (1954)
Ginger Rogers is a showgirl kept by a wealthy man who promises her marriage after he divorces his wife. Little does she know that her lover is also a counterfeiter. Her life changes, however, when she falls for a struggling artist (played by Rogers' then-spouse, Jacques Bergerac). With Herbert Lom. AKA: "Beautiful Stranger." 89 min.
10-8342 *$19.99*

Tight Spot (1955)
Tough, well-crafted noir outing, with Ginger Rogers as a model who is taken into police custody so she can testify against a ruthless mob boss and Edward G. Robinson as the federal attorney assigned to protect her. Brian Keith, Lorne Greene co-star. 97 min.
10-2376 Was $19.99 *$14.99*

Please see our index for these other Ginger Rogers titles: *42nd Street • The Barkleys Of Broadway • The Gay Divorcee • Monkey Business • Shall We Dance • A Song To Remember • Swing Time • Tales Of Manhattan*

Trottie True (1949)
Romantic comedy set in the early 1900s, about a successful entertainer who gave up true love for her career. She married the Lord Wellwater and is happy until she runs into her old flame again! Stars Jean Kent, James Donald and Hugh Sinclair. AKA: "Gay Lady." 98 min.
48-1090 *$19.99*

Tanks A Million (1941)
Hal Roach comic programmer starring William Tracy as a goofy genius with an incredible memory who joins the Army and quickly ascends to the rank of sergeant. All is well...until his recruits give him a tough time. James Gleason, Noah Beery, Jr. co-star. 50 min.
17-9028 Was $19.99 *$14.99*

Heading For Heaven (1947)
After a nervous realtor is given an incorrect health report stating he has three months to live, he goes into hiding, but his friends and family believe he has done himself in. In fact, they're so convinced of it, they hire a psychic to find his spirit. Stu Erwin, Glenda Farrell, George O'Hanlon, Irene Ryan star. 65 min.
17-9056 Was $19.99 *$14.99*

Her Favorite Patient (1946)
Humorous lark about a harried doctor who needs help desperately, but can't get his physician niece to stay in town. The doc's got a plot, though: have the airline pilot his niece likes fake an injury. John Carroll, Ruth Hussey, Charlie Ruggles and Ann Rutherford star. AKA: "Bedside Manner." 79 min.
53-6023 Was $29.99 *$19.99*

Scattergood Baines (1941)
Guy Kibbee plays the title role of the "cracker-barrel philosopher," who dispenses advice to the residents of the tiny New England village of Coldriver, in this first in a series of films based on the popular radio series. Here Scattergood saves his fortunes—and his town's—from some devious types. With Carol Hughes, John Archer. 69 min.
09-5340 *$19.99*

Scattergood Survives A Murder (1942)
The final entry in RKO's "Scattergood Baines" series finds small-town storekeeper Guy Kibbee turning detective to uncover the truth behind the mysterious deaths of two local spinsters who left their entire estate to their cat. With John Archer, Wallace Ford, Margaret Hayes. 69 min.
09-5341 *$19.99*

Up In The Air (1940)
A page boy who wants a comedy radio show with his pal, a black porter, gets a chance of a lifetime when the station's stars are systematically killed during their broadcasts. Frankie Darro, Marjorie Reynolds and Mantan Moreland star. 62 min.
50-1909 *$14.99*

People's Choice (1946)
Unusual comedy filmed in 16mm and telling of a small-town milquetoast who runs for mayor, then gains enough confidence to stop the local corruption he finds. Drew Kennedy, Louise Arthur, George Meeker and Fred Kelsey star in this likable fable. 65 min.
55-3057 *$19.99*

Things Happen At Night (1948)
An insurance investigator is called in (Bill Murray being busy) by a family living in a spooky old house, when strange goings-on indicate they're sharing their home with a prank-playing poltergeist, in this British ghostbusting comedy. Gordon Harker, Alfred Drayton star. 79 min.
68-8030 *$19.99*

Ghost And The Guest (1943)
Newlyweds in a honeymoon mansion believe it's haunted when gangsters begin spooking around looking for stolen loot, in this comedy of frights scripted by Morey Amsterdam. James Dunn, Florence Rice star. 59 min.
68-8032 *$19.99*

King Arthur Was A Gentleman (1942)
Interesting comic fantasy in which a British soldier in Africa uses his sword—which he believes to be King Arthur's Excalibur—to help save his friends from captivity. Arthur Askey, Evelyn Dall, Anne Shelton star. 99 min.
68-8948 *$19.99*

Vice Versa (1948)
Father and son use a magic stone to change their identities, and wacky and whimsical situations begin to occur in this delightful fantasy directed by Peter Ustinov. Roger Livesey, Kay Walsh and a young Anthony Newley star. 111 min.
68-8950 *$19.99*

Dixie Jamboree (1944)
There's comedy, romance and music on the mighty Mississippi when a gangster on the run hides out on an old-fashioned showboat making its way down the river to New Orleans. Frances Langford, Guy Kibbee, Lyle Talbot and Louise Beavers star. Songs include "Way Down Yonder in New Orleans." 69 min.
09-1274 *$19.99*

The Ghost Train (1941)
Third remake of the popular British comedy/thriller about travellers stranded at a desolate train station who are startled by an apparent ghost train, part of a very real smuggling conspiracy. Arthur Askey stars. 78 min.
68-8236 *$19.99*

A Night Of Magic (1944)
A unique wartime comic fantasy with music from England in which a man dreams he has inherited a 3,000-year-old mummy from his uncle. The mummy comes to life in the guise of an Egyptian princess, who has a great night on the town, then takes the young man back to ancient Egypt. Robert Griffith, Marian Olive and Billy "Uke" Scott star. 56 min.
68-9135 *$19.99*

One Touch Of Venus (1948)
Delightful fable about a department store statue of Venus that's brought to life by a window dresser's kiss. Ava Gardner is radiant as the goddess of romance, who returns to spread love throughout the world. Co-stars Robert Walker, Dick Haymes, Eve Arden. The Ogden Nash/Kurt Weill songs include "Speak Low," "The Trouble with Women." 81 min.
63-1027 Remastered *□$14.99*

One Touch Of Venus (Color Version)
Ava Gardner, as the goddess of love, makes all your fantasies come true in vibrant computerized color.
63-1530 *$19.99*

Shake Hands With Murder (1944)
Mystery mixes with comedy in this breezy caper flick about bailbondsmen who get involved in a murder. Iris Adrian, Frank Jenks, Douglas Fowley star. 63 min.
68-8471 Was $19.99 *$14.99*

Whisky Galore (1949)
Droll British comedy deals with Scottish islanders during World War II who must cope without alcohol...until a shipload of whiskey is stranded just off their shores and a "rescue" run is planned. Basil Radford, Catherine Lacey, Joan Greenwood star. AKA: "Tight Little Island." 81 min.
44-1072 Was $29.99 *$19.99*

Mad Little Island (1958)
Sequel to "Whisky Galore" tells of an Englishman sent to a small Scottish island to oversee construction of a missile site who faces outrage from its inhabitants. The local schoolteacher devises a plan to stop the missile base: dye a bird pink and claim it as an endangered species. Jeannie Carson, Donald Sinden star. AKA: "Rockets Galore." 94 min.
09-5154 *$19.99*

Red Skelton

Whistling In The Dark (1941)
A radio detective has to do some real sleuthing when he's kidnapped by a phony religious cult leader and his followers as part of a scheme to make off with a million-dollar inheritance. Red Skelton, in his first starring role, became a sensation as "The Fox." Conrad Veidt, Ann Rutherford and Virginia Grey also star in this humorous thriller with lots of surprises. 77 min.
12-2652 *$19.99*

Whistling In Dixie (1942)
Red Skelton's radio detective Wally "The Fox" Benton travels to the South to join his girlfriend in helping a former college friend in trouble and finds himself stuck in the middle of a search for hidden Civil War treasure. Ann Rutherford, Guy Kibbee also star. 73 min.
12-2821 *$19.99*

Whistling In Brooklyn (1943)
Red Skelton returns as wacky radio sleuth "The Fox," who goes undercover with the Brooklyn Dodgers in order to find a killer posing as a baseball player. Ann Rutherford, Jean Rogers, William Frawley also star. 87 min.
12-2651 *$19.99*

The Show-Off (1946)
Office clerk Red Skelton's lies, designed to impress girlfriend Marilyn Maxwell, lead him into all sorts of trouble in this laugh-filled farce. Eddie "Rochester" Anderson and Marjorie Main also star. 83 min.
12-2819 *$19.99*

Merton Of The Movies (1947)
Red Skelton is a theater usher whose dream of making it big in Hollywood comes true when he wins a trip to Tinseltown in a contest and is discovered by a savvy talent agent. Red performs some hilarious slapstick feats in this farce based on the play by George S. Kaufman and Marc Connelly. Virginia O'Brien, Gloria Grahame also star. 82 min.
12-2818 *□$19.99*

The Fuller Brush Man (1948)
Red Skelton is the world's most inept door-to-door salesman in this screwball comedy in which his soft-sell technique gets him involved in romance and a murder. Co-stars Janet Blair, Adele Jergens. 93 min.
02-1427 Was $19.99 *$14.99*

A Southern Yankee (1948)
Bellhop Red Skelton becomes a reluctant spy behind Confederate lines, and finds time to romance Southern belle Arlene Dahl, in this hilarious Civil War comedy. Includes the classic scene of Red walking in the midst of a battlefield with a blue-gray uniform (one of several gags supplied by an uncredited Buster Keaton). With Brian Donlevy, John Ireland. 90 min.
12-2352 *$19.99*

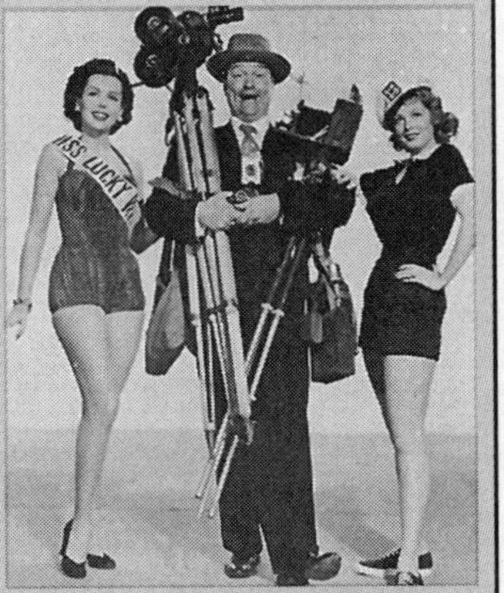

Watch The Birdie (1950)
The focus is on laughs when news cameraman Red Skelton accidentally films a construction scam while covering a building's dedication ceremony, and has to run for his life from the crooks. Slapstick shutterbug caper also stars Arlene Dahl, Ann Miller, Leon Ames, and Skelton as his own father and grandfather. 70 min.
12-2353 *$19.99*

The Yellow Cab Man (1950)
Red Skelton romps through this zany farce as a cab-driving inventor who comes up with unbreakable elastic glass and draws the attention of gangsters out to steal the formula. Walter Slezak, Gloria de Haven and Edward Arnold also star. 85 min.
12-2551 *$19.99*

The Clown (1953)
Taking a tip from "The Champ," Red Skelton portrays a down-and-out comic looking for love and acceptance from his young son in this sentimental comedy/drama. With Tim Considine, Jane Greer; look quickly for Charles Bronson. 92 min.
12-1100 *$19.99*

Please see our index for these other Red Skelton titles: *Bathing Beauty • DuBarry Was A Lady • The Fuller Brush Girl • Panama Hattie • Ship Ahoy • Texas Carnival • Those Magnificent Men In Their Flying Machines • Thousands Cheer • Three Little Words*

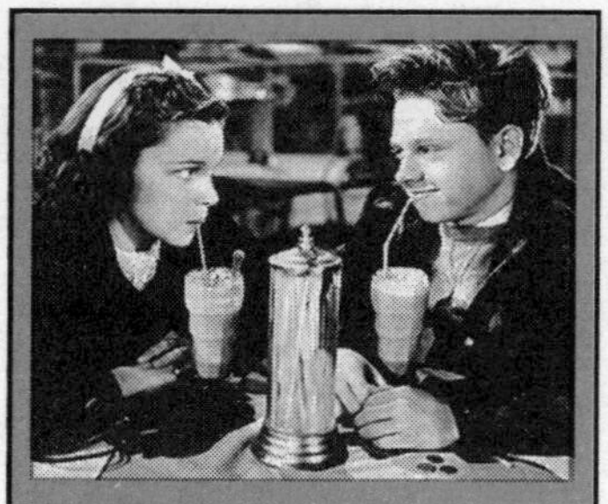

Love Finds Andy Hardy (1938)
Fourth entry in MGM's perennially popular film series has Andy (Mickey Rooney) in trouble with steady gal Ann Rutherford when he's paid to escort a buddy's date (Lana Turner). Judy Garland makes her series debut as Andy's pal Betsy; with Lewis Stone, Fay Holden. 90 min.
12-1978 *$19.99*

Andy Hardy Gets Spring Fever (1939)
While producing the school play "Adrift in Tahiti," the hot floods and electric breezes addle Andy's brain and he falls pot over palm for the drama coach. Mickey Rooney, Helen Gilbert, Ann Rutherford star. 88 min.
12-1981 *$19.99*

Andy Hardy Meets Debutante (1940)
While in New York with his father, Mickey Rooney tries to meet glamorous society gal Diana Lewis through mutual friend Judy Garland. The highlight is Judy singing "I'm Nobody's Baby." 89 min.
12-1983 *$19.99*

Life Begins For Andy Hardy (1941)
Breaking with his father over plans for college, Mickey Rooney leaves quiet Carvel for an office job in New York, but has trouble making ends meet. Judy Garland makes her final appearance as Andy's platonic confidante Betsy. 100 min.
12-1979 *$19.99*

Andy Hardy's Private Secretary (1941)
Andy's college plans are stalled when he fails his high school final, but the indulgent faculty gives him a second chance. In his autobiography, Mickey Rooney admits he tried unsuccessfully to date debuting co-star Kathryn Grayson. 101 min.
12-1982 *$19.99*

Andy Hardy's Double Life (1942)
Esther Williams was among several starlets MGM tried out for screen appeal in the Hardy series, casting her as one of two girls who simultaneously accept collegial Andy's (Mickey Rooney) marriage proposal. 91 min.
12-1980 *$19.99*

Love Laughs At Andy Hardy (1946)
The Hardy family is back in this fine family film. Andy (Mickey Rooney) returns from the Army, but finds that his home life, especially with women, is just as complicated as ever. Lewis Stone, Sara Haden co-star. 93 min.
01-1345 *$14.99*

The Ghost And Mrs. Muir (1947)
Spirited romantic comedy stars Gene Tierney as a widow who moves into a haunted seashore house and Rex Harrison as the nautical spectre who first tries scaring her away, then falls in love with her. With George Sanders, Edna Best, Natalie Wood. 104 min.
04-2300 □*$19.99*

Take It Big (1944)
When vaudevillian Jack Haley (who plays the back end of a horse on stage) inherits a run-down dude ranch, it takes some help from his show biz pals, including bandleader Ozzie Nelson and singer Harriet Hilliard (in their second film together), to keep the place going in this lively, song-filled comedy. With Mary Beth Hughes, Fuzzy Knight, Frank Forest. 75 min.
09-1638 Was $29.99 *$24.99*

Here Come The Nelsons (1952)
In between the radio and TV versions of their long-running sitcom, Ozzie and Harriet Nelson, plus sons David and Ricky, hit the big screen with this lively tale. Advertising man Ozzie (yes, folks, he really had a job) must cope with trying to develop a women's wear company's campaign while the town's centennial celebration has him and Harriet fighting over rival houseguests...and hers is Rock Hudson! Barbara Lawrence, Jim Backus also star. 76 min.
07-2583 *$14.99*

The Devil And Miss Jones (1941)
Charles Coburn is a millionaire department store owner who decides to investigate employee complaints by working as a sales clerk. Co-stars Jean Arthur, Robert Cummings, William Demarest and S.Z. "Cuddles" Sakall. 92 min.
63-1062 Was $19.99 □*$14.99*

Sitting Pretty (1948)
Clifton Webb first brought the character of haughty know-it-all Mr. Belvedere to the screen with this popular comedy. As a cover while he researches a book on suburbia, author Webb signs on as the new babysitter/nursemaid for Robert Young and Maureen O'Hara's three rambunctious sons. With Richard Haydn, Ed Begley.
04-3809 *$14.99*

Miss Tatlock's Millions (1948)
A Hollywood stunt man is hired to impersonate a young woman's brother in order to fool her wealthy—and wildly eccentric—family, but problems arise when he would-be sibling falls for his "sister" in the screwball romp. John Lund, Wanda Hendrix, Barry Fitzgerald and Monty Woolley star; directed by character actor Richard Hadyn, who appears in a cameo. NOTE: The quality of this print is below our usual standards. 96 min.
09-3031 *$19.99*

Private Snuffy Smith (1942)
The irascible comic-strip hillbilly made it to the big screen in this wartime comedy that has Snuffy signing up for Army duty and getting mixed up with enemy spies. Bud Duncan, Edgar Kennedy, Sarah Padden star. AKA: "Snuffy Smith, Yard Bird." 65 min.
09-2174 Was $29.99 *$24.99*

Hillbilly Blitzkrieg (1942)
Mountain man-turned-G.I. Snuffy Smith (Bud Duncan) and his long-suffering sergeant (Edgar Kennedy) return to more down-home wartime laughs, guarding a top-secret rocket site in the Tennessee hills from Nazi spies. Snuffy's comic-strip pal Barney Google, he of the goo-goo-googly eyes, also makes an appearance. With Cliff Nazarro, Lucien Littlefield. 63 min.
09-2971 *$19.99*

The Canterville Ghost (1944)
Delightful blend of spooky comedy and wartime adventure, based on an Oscar Wilde story, stars Charles Laughton as the spectre doomed to haunt the family castle until he proves his courage. He gets his chance when he aids a squad of American soldiers billeted there. Robert Young, Margaret O'Brien, Una O'Connor co-star. 95 min.
12-2081 □*$19.99*

The Canterville Ghost (1986)
Wonderful reworking of the spooky comedy classic stars Sir John Gielgud as the 300-year-old spectre condemned to haunt his ancestral castle until a descendant breaks the ancient curse. Ted Wass, Alyssa Milano, Andrea Marcovicci co-star. 96 min.
02-1779 Was $19.99 *$14.99*

The Canterville Ghost (1998)
Lively treatment of the Oscar Wilde story about the resident ghost of a British castle who haunts the new American residents of the property. Ian Richardson stars as Sir Simon de Canterville, and Celia Imrie, Ian McNeice and Rik Mayall co-star. 90 min.
53-6345 *$24.99*

An Ideal Husband (1948)
Paulette Goddard shines as a manipulative woman who threatens to expose a young politician for some sleazy dealings if he doesn't support a phony Argentine canal scheme in Parliament. Oscar Wilde wrote the story upon which this British comedy-drama was based. With Michael Wilding, Hugh Williams; directed by Alexander Korda. 96 min.
09-5019 *$19.99*

An Ideal Husband (1999)
Set in England in the late 1800s, this acerbic filming of Oscar Wilde's farce features Rupert Everett as the idle, witty Lord Goring, a devout bachelor whose sneaky ex-fiancée (Julianne Moore) attempts to blackmail Everett into marriage in order to save his best friend, "ideal husband" and Parliament member Jeremy Northam, from scandal. Cate Blanchett, Minnie Driver also star. 98 min.
11-2367 Was $99.99 □*$19.99*

It Happened Tomorrow (1944)
Novice reporter Dick Powell is able to get a jump on his competitors when a mysterious colleague gives him copies of the next days' newspapers, but is the future carved in stone when one headline warns of his imminent death? Linda Darnell, Jack Oakie and Edgar Kennedy also star in director René Clair's charming, comical fantasy. 84 min.
53-6322 *$24.99*

On Our Merry Way (1948)
An all-star cast is featured in this unusual comedic anthology. To prove to wife Paulette Goddard that he's his newspaper's "Inquiring Reporter," ad clerk Burgess Meredith asks people how a child has influenced their life. The respondents are jazzmen Henry Fonda and James Stewart, who tried to win a rigged small-town talent show; movie star Dorothy Lamour, who lampoons her "sarong girl" image; and would-be "kidnappers" Fred MacMurray and William Demarest. Directed by King Vidor, Leslie Fenton, and an uncredited John Huston and George Stevens. AKA: "A Miracle Can Happen." 107 min.
53-6813 *$24.99*

Three Broadway Girls (1932)
Sassy comedy of a trio of gold-digging gals (Joan Blondell, Ina Claire, Madge Evans) seeking husbands, set against a show biz background. Later remade as "How to Marry a Millionaire," this film features a quick appearance by the later movie's Betty Grable. AKA: "The Greeks Had a Word for Them." 79 min.
08-5046 *$19.99*

Humphrey Takes A Chance (1950)
This entry in the popular "Joe Palooka" series finds the boxer and his sidekick, Knobby, taking on a nefarious mayor and a shady promoter who have duped a fighter into signing a deceptive contract. Joe Kirkwood, Leon Errol and Lois Collier star. 62 min.
09-5151 *$19.99*

Easy Living (1937)
When millionaire Edward Arnold throws his wife's new fur coat out the window, it lands on office girl Jean Arthur, who gets a whole new life she never could have imagined. Believed to be the tycoon's mistress, she gets free luxuries from storeowners and falls in love with Arnold's son, Ray Milland. Preston Sturges scripted this hilarious screwball classic. 88 min.
07-2648 □*$14.99*

The Beachcomber (1938)
Delightful British comedy based on a story by Somerset Maugham. Charles Laughton is a bitter, lonely beach bum who finds his solitude shattered when missionary Elsa Lanchester decides to "reform" him. A classic by all standards. 85 min.
08-8064 *$19.99*

The Amazing Mr. Forrest (1939)
Lively comedy abounds when a special insurance investigator (Jack Buchanan) tries to wrangle a group of jewel thieves by going undercover. Edward Everett Horton, Otto Kruger and Jack LaRue also star. AKA: "The Big Steal." 77 min.
10-9696 *$19.99*

Flirting With Danger (1934)
A trio of explosives experts (Robert Armstrong, Edgar Kennedy and William Cagney) are involved in an assignment in South America when they mistake a fireworks display for a political coup. This unusual comedy effort also stars Maria Alba, Ernest Hilliard. 69 min.
68-8961 *$19.99*

Lonely Wives (1931)
The ever-timorous Edward Everett Horton shines in dual roles in this bedroom farce about a somber lawyer who becomes a wild womanizer at night and the vaudeville impersonator who wants to add him to his list of imitations. With Patsy Ruth Miller, Laura La Plante. 86 min.
09-1249 Was $29.99 *$24.99*

The Royal Bed (1930)
Mary Astor stars in a comedy-drama about the foibles of monarchy. A tiny European kingdom finds itself beset by revolutionaries, and the royal family seems more than willing to abdicate the throne. With Lowell Sherman, J. Carroll Naish. 73 min.
09-1260 Was $19.99 *$14.99*

Half Shot At Sunrise (1930)
The popular '30s comedy duo of Bert Wheeler and Robert Woolsey demonstrated their special style of comic patter in this madcap military tale featuring them as AWOL doughboys on the streets of Paris in 1918. With Enda May Oliver, Dorothy Lee; music by Max Steiner. 78 min.
09-1245 *$19.99*

Hook, Line And Sinker (1930)
More frenetic and frantic fun from Wheeler and Woolsey, as they help bail out heiress Dorothy Lee's run-down luxury hotel and end up as target practice for some gangsters looking to rob the place. With Hugh Herbert. 74 min.
09-1911 *$19.99*

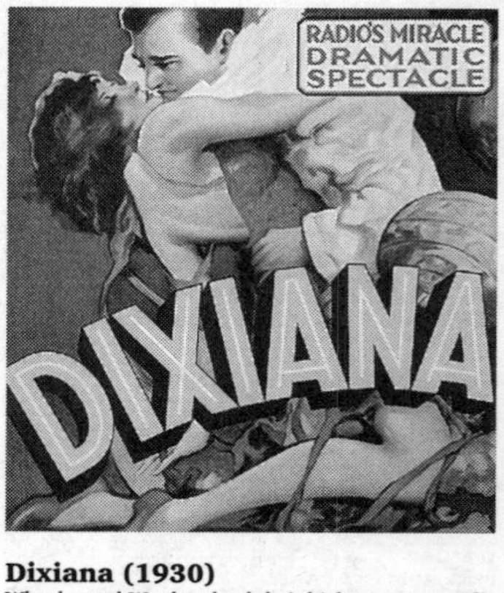

Dixiana (1930)
Wheeler and Woolsey lend their high-strung comedic talents to this musical/comedy about a circus performer (Bebe Daniels) who's sweet on a wealthy Southerner (Everett Marshall). With Bill "Bojangles" Robinson. Songs include "Guiding Star," "My One Ambition Is You." This rare print includes the Mardi Gras sequence in color. 100 min.
10-7046 Was $19.99 *$14.99*

Will Hay

Those Were The Days (1934)
Will Hay, a British music hall star, made his film debut here, playing a proper magistrate married to a woman he believes is younger than her actual age. Trouble ensues when her and her son from a previous marriage's deception is revealed at a party. Iris Hoey, Angela Baddely also star. 80 min.
09-5035 *$19.99*

Boys Will Be Boys (1936)
Crime comedy about a school headmaster who discovers that one of his students' parents is a jewel robber and tries to stop him. Will Hay, Gordon Harker and Claude Dampier star.
09-5011 *$19.99*

Windbag The Sailor (1936)
Funny British hijinks ensue when bragging sailor Will Hay is called on to command a ship by a wealthy businessman. Little does Hay realize that his assignment has something to do with an insurance scam. Moore Marriott and Graham Moffatt also star. 85 min.
09-5237 *$19.99*

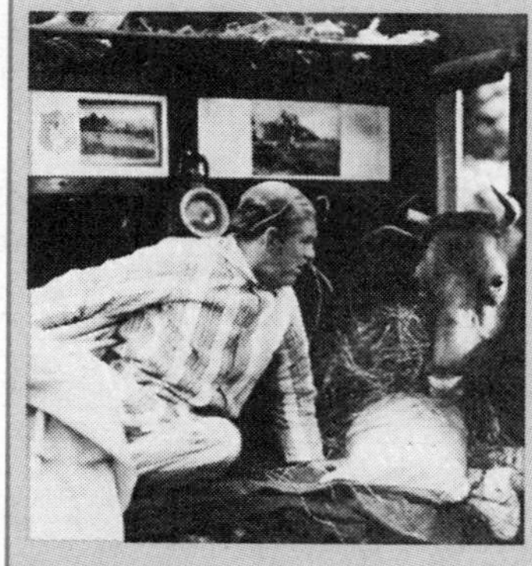

Oh, Mr. Porter! (1937)
Will Hay is the trouble-prone son of a family that arranges to get him a job as a stationmaster in a small, barely used railway stop in Ireland. His help includes an old geezer and a heavy, young porter, but Hay gets to work revitalizing the place. Eventually, a train carrying the local soccer team disappears and Hay must find it. Moore Marriott also stars. 82 min.
10-2796 *$14.99*

Old Bones Of The River (1938)
Inspired by two novels by Edgar Wallace, this comic adventure stars Will Hay as a teacher who is assigned to open a school for tribesmen in Africa. When Commissioner Sanders (of Paul Robeson's "Sanders of the River") comes down with malaria, Hays takes his place, but his tax collecting soon gets him in trouble with the natives. With Moore Marriott. 90 min.
09-5027 *$19.99*

Convict 99 (1938)
Superb British romp featuring top comic Will Hay as a shabby schoolteacher who is mistakenly named warden of a prison. Soon, he turns his new place of employment into a business and allows the convicts to run it. With Garry Marsh, Googie Withers. 91 min.
09-5231 *$19.99*

The Black Sheep Of Whitehall (1941)
Wartime comic situations ensue when a correspondence course teacher finds himself in the middle of a Nazi plot to sabotage a trade agreement between South America and Britain and dons a variety of daffy disguises to beat the Germans at their own game. With Will Hay, John Mills. 89 min.
09-5010 *$19.99*

The Ghost Of St. Michael's (1941)
A London boys' school is relocated during World War II to a supposedly haunted Scottish castle where, according to legend, the sound of bagpipes precedes a death. When two teachers are found dead, addle-pated Will Hay tries to find out the truth before he becomes the next victim. Elliott Mason, Claude Hulbert co-star in this comedy from the Ealing Studios. 82 min.
09-5016 *$19.99*

The Goose Steps Out (1942)
Fine Ealing Studios wartime farce in which comic actor Will Hay plays dual roles as a British spy and his lookalike Nazi counterpart. The British agent poses as the German in order to get into a university and steal a top-secret bomb. With Peter Ustinov, Julien Mitchell. 79 min.
09-5017 *$19.99*

My Learned Friend (1943)
British comedy favorite Will Hay plays a shyster lawyer targeted for death by an escaped convict out to even the score with the people who sent him to the nick. As people involved in the con's imprisonment are murdered, Hay becomes more and more rattled. With Claude Hurlburt. 74 min.
10-9712 *$19.99*

Joe Palooka (1936)
The famed comic-strip boxer made his feature film debut in this exciting comedy/drama charting Joe's rise to the top of the ring. Stuart Erwin has the title role, but Jimmy Durante steals the show as manager Knobby Walsh. With Lupe Velez, Thelma Todd and William Cagney (Jimmy's brother). 86 min.
08-1793 *$19.99*

Lend Me Your Husband (1935)
A slick Englishman carrying on an illicit affair with his wife's good friend decides to run off with her, only to face all sorts of marital predicaments. You'll never guess the complexities that occur in this farce that's surprisingly risqué for its time. John Stuart, Nora Swinburne star. 61 min.
09-2335 *$19.99*

Thanks For Listening (1937)
Hayseed Pinky Tomlin is roped into getting involved in a series of scams by a conwoman and her cronies in this farce that features the musical numbers "I Like to Make Music" and "In the Name of Love." With Maxine Doyle, Aileen Pringle. 60 min.
09-5034 *$19.99*

It Happened In Paris (1935)
Carol Reed's first directorial credit (he co-directed) is a story of a wealthy man who pretends that he's poor in order to win over a needy young woman. John Loder and Nancy Burne star. 68 min.
09-5021 *$19.99*

The Headless Horseman/ Will Rogers Anthology (1922)
A rare collection of silent films featuring the legendary American humorist. First Rogers plays Ichabod Crane in a hilarious 1922 rendition of the Washington Irving tale, followed by a collection of short subjects featuring Rogers' famed rope tricks. 95 min.
62-5213 Was $29.99 *$19.99*

Ambassador Bill (1931)
Frontier slapstick mixes with political satire when Oklahoma cattleman Will Rogers is appointed U.S. ambassador to the tiny European country of Sylvania and, in between revolutions, befriends the boy king. The famed Rogers wit shines in this comic tale. Tad Alexander, Marguerite Churchill, Ray Milland co-star. 68 min.
04-2394 *$19.99*

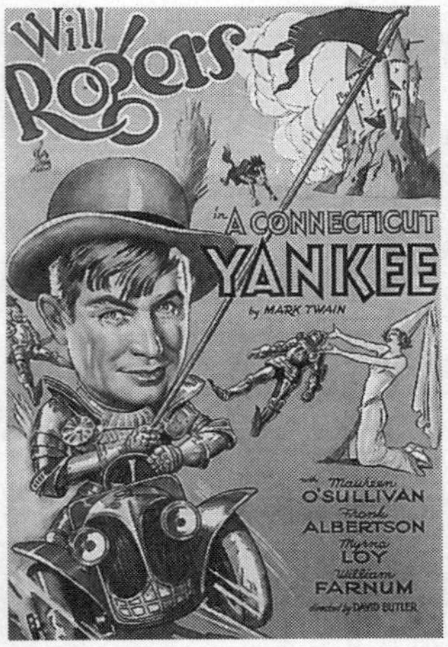

A Connecticut Yankee (1931)
Will Rogers stars as the 20th-century repairman who gets zapped on the noggin and awakens to find himself in Camelot and accused of being a wizard. The first sound filming of Mark Twain's novel is highlighted by Rogers' trademark quips and a fine supporting cast that includes Myrna Loy, Maureen O'Sullivan and Frank Albertson. 95 min.
04-2395 *$19.99*

Mr. Skitch (1933)
When the family farm is lost to the bank, Will Rogers and ZaSu Pitts pack up their brood and head off on a cross-country trip for Hollywood. Hilarious, light-hearted journey also stars Florence Desmond, Rochelle Hudson. 70 min.
04-2396 ❏*$19.99*

Judge Priest (1934)
Perhaps the best film example of the down-home wit of humorist Will Rogers was this early comedy-drama from John Ford. Rogers plays a small town judge whose unconventional but sound policies endear him to his constituents. Hattie McDaniel and Stepin Fetchit also star. 80 min.
10-4015 *$19.99*

The Story Of Will Rogers
Narrated by Bob Hope, this superb factual look at one of America's greatest humorists and entertainment personalities covers Rogers' life from his Oklahoma roots and his incredible popularity in radio and in the movies to his tragic plane crash death in Alaska. 60 min.
63-7065 *$19.99*

The Cocoanuts (1929)
The feature film debut of the Marx Brothers, taken from their hit Broadway comedy, finds the quartet in a run-down Florida hotel, where owner Groucho insults guests, woos Margaret Dumont, and vainly tries to auction off "choice" resort property. Features the infamous "Why a duck?" routine. 93 min.
07-1616 Was $19.99 *$14.99*

Animal Crackers (1930)
The Four Marx Brothers in a zany tale involving high society parties, a stolen painting, African explorers, young lovers, and a manic game of bridge. With Margaret Dumont, Lillian Roth, and the song "Hooray for Captain Spaulding." 98 min.
07-1012 Was $19.99 ❏*$14.99*

Monkey Business (1931)
It's anything but smooth sailing for the Four Marx Brothers when they stowaway on an ocean liner in this, their first comedy written expressly for the screen. Gobs, gangsters and gals galore in this gem of Marxian comedy mania. With Thelma Todd, Harry Woods. 77 min.
07-1302 Was $19.99 *$14.99*

Horse Feathers (1932)
College president Groucho, encouraged by son Zeppo to build a winning football team, signs up "star players" Chico and Harpo in time for the big game, while "college widow" Thelma Todd woos all four siblings. And remember, the password is "swordfish." 67 min.
07-1597 Was $19.99 *$14.99*

Duck Soup (1933)
The pinnacle of Marxian madness. Groucho is Rufus T. Firefly, the President of Freedonia; Chico is his trusted aide and a spy; Harpo sells peanuts and tries to chauffeur; Zeppo nods his head. Political satire and wild humor that was ahead of its time. With Margaret Dumont, Louis Calhern and Edgar Kennedy. 68 min.
07-1005 Was $19.99 ❏*$14.99*

A Night At The Opera (1935)
Considered by many to be the Marx Brothers' best film. Groucho, Harpo and Chico take on the opera world in order to reunite singers Allan Jones and Kitty Carlisle, and "Il Trovatore" will never be the same. Includes the classic stateroom scene. Margaret Dumont, Sig Rumann co-star. 92 min.
12-1014 *$19.99*

A Day At The Races (1937)
Groucho is horse doctor Hugo Z. Hackenbush, treating hypochondriac Margaret Dumont, while Harpo and Chico wreak humdinging havoc at trackside. With Maureen O'Sullivan, Allan Jones. Anyone for a tootsi-fruitsi ice cream? 111 min.
12-1068 *$19.99*

Room Service (1938)
Groucho, Harpo and Chico are Broadway producers who have a play, some hungry actors, no backers and a hotel bill that keeps rising. Their attempts to stay one step ahead of everyone will leave you in the aisle. Lucille Ball, Ann Miller, Frank Albertson co-star. 79 min.
05-1329 *$19.99*

At The Circus (1939)
More Marx Brothers mania, as the boys try to save circus owner Kenny Baker's big top from bankruptcy. The high point is Groucho's rendition of "Lydia the Tattooed Lady." With Margaret Dumont. 87 min.
12-1116 *$19.99*

Go West (1940)
It's round-up time for comedy when Groucho, Chico and Harpo head out for California in the days of the Gold Rush. Along the way they meet some modern Indians, land-grabbing villains, and the wildest train chase scene in movie history. 81 min.
12-1087 *$19.99*

The Big Store (1941)
There's laughs on every floor when the Marx Brothers run roughshod over an ultra-modern department store, saving the life of owner Tony Martin in the process. Typical Marxist hi-jinks, and a final screen pairing for Groucho and Margaret Dumont. 80 min.
12-1011 *$19.99*

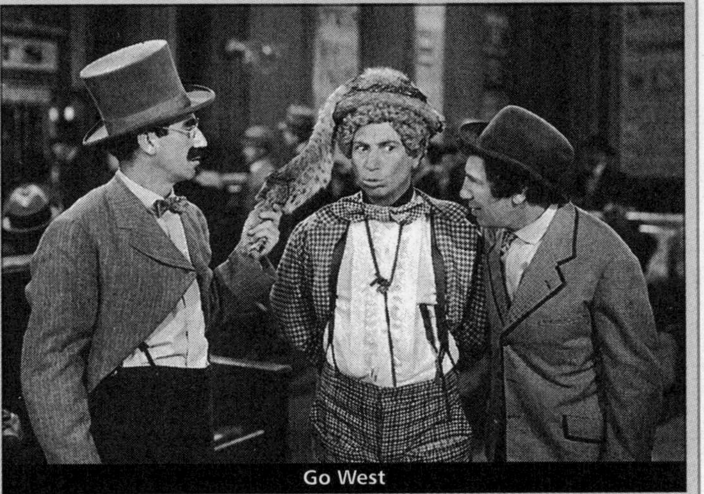
Go West

The Marx Brothers

A Night In Casablanca (1946)
Groucho, Chico and Harpo turn the North African city of mystery upside-down with laughter as they manage to get the goods on a German war fugitive. Frantic Marx Brothers fun, highlighted by a hilarious trunk-packing routine and a chase with a runaway plane, also stars Sig Rumann, Lois Collier. 85 min.
31-3024 *$14.99*

Copacabana (1947)
Groucho Marx's first film sans his brothers was this wild comedy about a booking agent who gets his top (and only) client two singing jobs at the same nightclub. Carmen Miranda plays her normal Latin role and doubles as a French chanteuse. 92 min.
63-1023 *$19.99*

Copacabana (Color Version)
How do you make a film starring Groucho Marx and Carmen Miranda even more colorful? With the aid of computers, of course!
63-1523 *$14.99*

Love Happy (1949)
The Marxes' last film as a team. Groucho is ace detective Sam Grunion, after stolen diamonds. Theatre pianist Chico inadvertently passes them on to happy wanderer Harpo. A lighthearted musical-comedy that also stars Raymond Burr, Ilona Massey and a young Marilyn Monroe. 91 min.
63-1005 *$14.99*

The Best Of Groucho
This video could be titled "The Best of Groucho on 'You Bet Your Life'," because some of Groucho's funniest moments from his hit TV series are here, like trading quips with a 90-year-old Baptist minister, sparring with Rocky Marciano's mother and even welcoming the champ himself to the show. 60 min.
10-2583 *$14.99*

You Bet Your Life
"Here he is. The one, the only...GROUCHO!!" The master funnyman charms his way through two episodes from the classic '50s game show, along with such standbys as the duck, the "secret woid" and George Fenneman. Plus, a commercial with Harpo and Chico pitching creamy Prom. 60 min.
01-1457 *$19.99*

You Bet Your Life: Boxed Set
"Say the secret word" and this seven-tape boxed set is yours: seven hours of Groucho at his funniest hosting the hit TV show "You Bet Your Life." See the brother Marx encounter everyone from pretty underwater divers and crime reporters to such celebrities as Edith Head, Ray Bradbury, Edgar and Candice Bergen, Don Drysdale and many others.
16-5045 *$49.99*

The Groucho Marx Scrapbook
Rare scenes on- and off-stage, including highlights from the pilot episode for "You Bet Your Life," and a late '50s TV interview, TV commercials with Harpo and Chico and original movie trailers for many of the Marx Brothers' films. 60 min. total.
01-5053 *$19.99*

Chico And Harpo Marx Rarities
Two members of the comedic clan make rare solo TV appearances in this collection. First, Chico is head of a boisterous Italian clan getting its first telephone in the 1950 "Silver Theatre" episode "Papa Romani," co-starring William Frawley and Margaret Hamilton. Next, Harpo plays a dramatic role—without speaking, of course—in "A Silent Panic," from 1960's "The Dupont Show," and also does a hilarious "Today Show" interview. 65 min.
10-9012 *$14.99*

The Unknown Marx Brothers
The wildest comedy team in film history is saluted through interviews with family and colleagues, vintage home movies and promo films, and rare outtakes (from Harpo appearing solo in a 1925 film to the brothers' unaired TV pilot, "Deputy Seraph"). Leslie Nielsen narrates this sidesplitting look at the public and private lives of Groucho, Chico, Harpo and Zeppo. 120 min.
08-8398 Was $19.99 *$14.99*

The Marx Bros. Collection
Spend "A Night at the Opera," "A Day at the Races" and some time "At the Circus" with Groucho, Chico and Harpo in this three-tape set of the brothers' wildest films.
12-2525 Save $10.00! *$49.99*

Please see our index for these other Marx Brothers titles: *Double Dynamite • Will Success Spoil Rock Hunter?*

Meet The Mayor (1938)
Frank Fay, a favorite on the vaudeville circuit, stars in this farce playing a small-town elevator operator who is thrust into a mayoral race. Ruth Hall, Franklin Pangborn also star. 62 min.
09-5025 *$19.99*

Always In Trouble (1938)
Stylish comic yarn starring Jane Withers as a gal whose father strikes it rich in oil, then finds her mother forcing her, her father and her siblings into acting snobby and flaunting their leap up the social ladder. Mom eventually learns a lesson after a yachting trip goes bad and smugglers cause trouble. Jean Rogers, Arthur Treacher and Eddie Collins co-star. 69 min.
09-5147 *$19.99*

The Guv'nor (1936)
First-class British comedy finds George Arliss and Gene Gerrard as bums in France who are picked up by the police. When Arliss gives his last name as "Rothschild," the deception lands them a 2,000-franc gift from the famed family, a line of credit at a local bank, and a job that lets the good-hearted con men help a woman involved with a crook. AKA: "Mister Hobo." 80 min.
09-5150 *$19.99*

Bill Cracks Down (1937)
A wastrel-like playboy has one year to shape up—or lose the family business—when his father puts him in charge of a steel mill in this comedy. Grant Withers, Ranny Weeks, Beatrice Roberts star. AKA: "Men of Steel." 53 min.
09-5328 *$19.99*

His Lordship Goes To Press (1939)
Romantic comedy stars Hugh Williams as an English aristocrat who poses as a common farmer in order to teach American reporter June Clyde a lesson. 80 min.
09-5331 *$19.99*

False Pretenses (1935)
Comedy of class conflicts about a millionaire who schemes to help a young waitress work her way into society. Irene Ware, Sidney Blackmer, Russell Hopton star. 67 min.
09-5348 *$19.99*

Forbidden Music (1936)
The princess has just banned music from the music-loving duchy of Lucco since its citizens have neglected everything else, including paying taxes. Leave it to foreign correspondent Jimmy "Schnozzle" Durante to conduct a musical uprising. 80 min.
10-1200 Was $19.99 *$14.99*

Cash (1934)
Romping romantic comedy of a young man who shuts off the electricity of delinquent bill-payers, only to find a surprise behind one door. Robert Donat, Wendy Barrie, Edmund Gwenn co-star. 73 min.
10-3006 *$19.99*

August Week-End (1936)
Funny British social comedy about a wealthy entrepreneur living a life of leisure who decides it's time for a change and gets involved in an income tax scandal. Valerie Hobson, Paul Harvey and G.J. Huntley, Jr. star. 70 min.
09-5148 *$19.99*

The Affairs Of Cappy Ricks (1937)
Walter Brennan is a salty sea dog who wrecks his ship on a deserted island in order to teach his daughters a lesson about love and making the proper choice in picking their future husbands. Mary Brian, Kyle Talbot and Frank Shields also star. 58 min.
10-1714 *$19.99*

His Double Life (1933)
Stylish comedy about an aristocrat who takes the place of his late valet and enjoys the world more as a "servant." Roland Young, Lillian Gish star. 67 min.
10-3008 *$19.99*

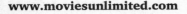

Laurel & Hardy & Friends, Vol. 1
This collection of laugh-filled shorts features silent solo turns by Stan Laurel in "Hustling for Health" (1928) and Oliver Hardy in "Along Came Auntie" (1918), followed by fellow Hal Roach Studio alumni Our Gang in "School's Out" (1930); Edgar Kennedy in "Motor Maniacs" (1946); and "When Wifey's Away" (1941), starring Leon Errol. 94 min. total.
50-8072 *$19.99*

Laurel & Hardy & Friends, Vol. 2
Stan and Ollie appear as asylum inmates who make life miserable for neighbor Max Davidson in the silent comedy "Call of the Cuckoo" (1927). Other gems in this volume include the Edgar Kennedy shorts "A Quiet Fourth" (1941) and "Hold Your Temper" (1943), plus Hal Roach's kid-detective whodunit "Who Killed Doc Robbin?" (1947). 99 min. total.
50-8073 *$19.99*

Laurel & Hardy & Friends, Vol. 3
Handyman Stan Laurel is the dupe a neglected wife uses to make her husband jealous, and Oliver Hardy plays the family butler, in "Slipping Wives" (1926). Next, Harry Langdon plays a love-starved reporter in "The Big Flash" (1932); Harold Lloyd has a cameo in the silent Our Gang short "Dogs of War" (1923); and Edgar Kennedy slowly burns in "I'll Fix That" (1941). 102 min. total.
50-8074 *$19.99*

Laurel & Hardy & Friends, Vol. 4
Although not working as a team, Stan and Ollie first appeared together in the Hal Roach comedy "Forty-Five Minutes from Hollywood" (1926), a slapstick look at California life. Laurel also stars, sans Hardy, in "Scorching Sands" (1923); Our Gang goes camping in "Bear Shooters" (1930); and James Gleason stars in the Roach "streamliner" musical "Hay Foot" (1941). 104 min. total.
50-8075 *$19.99*

Laurel & Hardy & Friends, Vol. 5
"On the Front Page" (1926), a Stan Laurel solo comedy, is followed by the thin one co-starring with Ollie in "Sailors Beware" (1927). The duo also make a cameo as hitchhikers in the Charley Chase short "On the Wrong Trek" (1936), followed by Our Gang in "Derby Day" (1923) and Edgar Kennedy in "Duck Soup" (1942). 96 min. total.
50-8076 *$19.99*

Laurel & Hardy & Friends, Vol. 6
Follow Stan Laurel into "Roughest Africa" (1923) and Oliver Hardy as "Cupid's Rival" (1923), two silent rib-ticklers from the duo's pre-team days. Next, the original Our Gang kids crash "High Society" (1924), followed by the early Technicolor featurette "Fiesta" (1941). 119 min. total.
50-8077 *$19.99*

Laurel & Hardy & Friends, Vol. 7
Stan and Ollie are just part of an all-star cast that includes Wallace Beery, Gary Cooper, Joan Crawford, Buster Keaton, Our Gang and Edward G. Robinson in the Masquers Club benefit short "The Stolen Jools" (1931). Then, Edgar Kennedy slowly burns in "The Big Beef" (1945) and "Brick-a-Brac" (1935); Our Gang answers "The Fourth Alarm" (1926); and Laurel goes solo in "Oranges and Lemons" (1923). 95 min.
87-5022 *$19.99*

Laurel & Hardy & Friends, Vol. 8
Ollie appears with Clyde Cook in the nautical comedy "Should Sailors Marry?" (1925), while Stan stars in "The Soilers" (1923), with frequent L&H foil James Finlayson. Harry Langdon has roadside troubles in "The Hitch-Hiker" (1933), followed by "Our Gang Follies of 1938" (1937) and "Rough on Rents" (1942), starring Edgar Kennedy. 91 min. total.
87-5023 *$19.99*

Laurel & Hardy & Friends, Vol. 9
The fellas are spotlighted in early solo turns, with Stan starring in "Short Kilts" (1924) and Ollie in "Bromo and Juliet" (1926). Next, Leon Errol plays opposite a young Veronica Lake in "The Wrong Room" (1939); Our Gang stars in "Good Cheer" (1926); and Edgar Kennedy learns to "Act Your Age" (1939). 102 min. total.
87-5024 *$19.99*

Laurel & Hardy & Friends, Vol. 10
"Love 'Em and Weep" (1927), which the boys later remade as "Chickens Come Home," finds candidate Ollie being blackmailed by an old flame. Hardy also appears with Charley Chase in "Fluttering Hearts" (1927), followed by Edgar Kennedy in "Radio Rampage" (1944) and "Sock Me to Sleep" (1935) and the Our Gang short "Monkey Business" (1926). 106 min. total.
87-5025 *$19.99*

Do Detectives Think? (1927)
Many of them do, but not gullible gumshoes Laurel and Hardy, who are assigned to protect judge James Finlayson from a mad killer out to get him, in one of the boys' first films as a full-fledged team. 20 min. Silent with music score.
87-5009 *$12.99*

Flying Elephants (1927)
Rival cavemen Laurel and Hardy try—badly—to show who's the best hunter in order to win the hand of a pretty cavegirl in this gem of prehistoric slapstick. 20 min. Silent with music score.
87-5010 *$12.99*

The Battle Of The Century (1927)
This long-lost comedy has been "restored" with still photos and continuity to link the missing footage. The fun starts with a boxing match pitting Stan against real-life champion weightlifter Noah Young. Later, an insurance scam leads to a wild pie fight. Look for Lou Costello at ringside of the fight. Features a Vitaphone score (from 1929) and sound effects. 28 min.
87-5017 *$19.99*

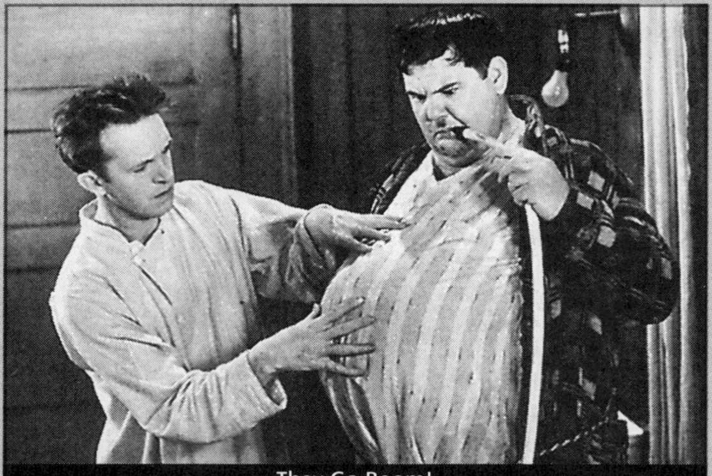
They Go Boom!

Laurel & Hardy

Duck Soup (1927)
Unearthed in Belgium(!) some six decades after its first showing, this long-lost short subject stars Laurel and Hardy as two vagrants tapped by the Forest Service to help extinguish a fire that was set by two vagrants...and the inevitable confusion sets into motion a hilarious chain of events. 18 min. Silent with a Vitaphone soundtrack.
87-5019 *$19.99*

Sugar Daddies (1927)
When oil tycoon James Finlayson wakes up from a drunken spree to learn he married a golddigger the night before, he turns to butler Ollie and lawyer Stan to help him out of his predicament. Silent L&H short features a wild amusement park chase. 20 min. Silent with music score.
87-5020 *$12.99*

You're Darn Tootin' (1928)
Laurel and Hardy are band members whose playing eventually drives the local townsfolk into a frenzy of kicking, punching and violence (and all this decades before punk rock!). Regular L&H foil Edgar Kennedy directed this wild, unpredictable outing. 20 min. Silent with music score.
87-5007 *$12.99*

Their Purple Moment (1928)
Stan and Ollie's first foray into domestic comedy finds them holding out their weekly pay from their wives—and getting caught in the act. Stan's wife substitutes his hidden loot with cigar coupons, and when the duo go out for a night of carousing sans spouses, all heck breaks loose. 21 min. Silent with music score.
87-5008 *$12.99*

Early To Bed (1928)
After inheriting a fortune and hiring Stan as his butler, Ollie turns into a bullying boss whose comeuppance comes with a hilarious frenzy of destruction by Laurel. 20 min. Silent with music score.
87-5012 *$12.99*

We Faw Down (1928)
Looking for a night away from the wives, Stan and Ollie get a lot more than they bargained for...including being caught, minus trousers, with some young ladies. 20 min. Silent with music score.
87-5014 *$12.99*

Habeas Corpus (1928)
"Everybody needs some bodies sometimes," especially Laurel and Hardy, who are hired by a mad scientist to rob a local cemetery for his experiments in this offbeat L&H tale. 20 min. Silent with music score.
87-5015 *$12.99*

The Finishing Touch (1928)
Hired to complete an under-construction house, hapless handymen Laurel and Hardy manage to build a series of slapstick incidents that leave their client with a less-than-secure home, the residents of a neighboring hospital seeking peace and quiet, and beat cop Edgar Kennedy covered in whitewash! 23 min. Silent with music score.
87-5026 *$12.99*

The Hoose-Gow (Color Version) (1929)
Laurel and Hardy, mistaken for crooks, are sent to a prison camp where they create chaos while working on a chain gang. In computerized color. 25 min.
58-5051 *$12.99*

That's My Wife (1929)
Laurel and Hardy get "dragged" into hilarious trouble when Ollie has to persuade Stan to impersonate his missing wife in order to win favor with a rich uncle. 20 min. Silent with music score.
87-5005 *$12.99*

Two Tars (1929)
Laurel and Hardy "retribution" classic in which Stan and Ollie are sailors on leave who take a pair of gals for a ride but soon encounter a wild traffic jam, dangerous gumballs littering the highway, and irate motorist Edgar Kennedy. And wait until you see the boys get revenge! 21 min. Silent with music score.
87-5001 *$12.99*

Liberty (1929)
In one of their most amazing, stunt-filled films, Laurel and Hardy are escaped prisoners who wind up wearing each other's pants and hiding out in an elevator which takes them to the top of an under-construction skyscraper...and into bigger trouble. Look for Jean Harlow in a cab. 20 min. Silent with music score.
87-5003 *$12.99*

Big Business (1929)
Stan and Ollie are Christmas tree salesmen in sunny Southern California who are having little luck hawking their wares. They decide to take orders for next year's trees from prospective customer James Finlayson, but he doesn't take kindly to their pitch, and a wild melee ensues. 20 min. Silent with music score.
87-5004 *$12.99*

Double Whoopee (1929)
Taking a job as replacements for New York hotel doormen, Stan and Ollie are soon mistaken for a Prussian prince and his associate. After ripping the skirt off of a young Jean Harlow and causing all sorts of trouble, the boys' antics leave the real prince stuck in an elevator shaft. 20 min. Silent with music score.
87-5006 *$12.99*

Double Whoopee (All-Talking Version)
Also available in a special "talkie" edition with voices by comedian/Laurel and Hardy buff Chuck McCann and a '20s danceband score.
87-5021 *$12.99*

Wrong Again (1929)
A mix-up between a horse named "Blue Boy" and the famed painting of the same name sends Laurel and Hardy on a wacky chase that winds up with the boys supporting a piano with the steed on top. 20 min. Silent with music score.
87-5013 *$12.99*

Bacon Grabbers (1929)
In one of their final silent shorts, Laurel and Hardy are process servers who'll stop at nothing to repossess a radio from debtor Edgar Kennedy, who's just as eager to keep the pair out of his house. Jean Harlow also appears as Kennedy's wife. 20 min. Silent with music score.
87-5027 *$12.99*

Angora Love (1929)
It takes a lot to get Stan and Ollie's goat...especially when the boys go to outrageous lengths to hide the stray animal from their landlord. 21 min. Silent with music score.
87-5011 *$12.99*

Berth Marks (Color Version) (1929)
In their debut talkie screen turn (shown in computerized color), Laurel and Hardy are musicians taking a cramped train ride to a vaudeville show. Paulette Goddard appears as an extra. 25 min.
58-5049 *$12.99*

Men O' War (Color Version) (1929)
A true Laurel and Hardy classic has Stan and Ollie as sailors on leave, looking for love in all the wrong places. There are memorable scenes at a soda fountain and in an "unsinkable" canoe. In computerized color. 25 min.
58-5048 *$12.99*

Unaccustomed As We Are (1929)
This Laurel and Hardy double bill features the beloved screen pair's first full sound short as well as its silent counterpart. Ollie's promise to Stan of a home-cooked meal by his wife brings forth a good deed by a blonde neighbor, the anger of her policeman husband, and an array of thrown pots and pans. 40 min. Silent version includes Vitaphone music.
87-5018 *$19.99*

A Perfect Day (Color Version) (1929)
Stan and Ollie plan a relaxing Sunday picnic for their wives, but things go awry thanks to car trouble, quarrelsome neighbors and gout-plagued uncle Edgar Kennedy. In computerized color. 25 min.
58-5050 *$12.99*

They Go Boom! (1929)
Ollie's sneezing and wheezing prompts Stan to try to figure out a way to rid his pal of a cold, but his inventive medical methods lead to disaster in this early L&H talking comedy, beautifully mastered from an original 35mm nitrate negative. 20 min.
87-5002 *$12.99*

Night Owls (Color Version) (1930)
Slapstick gem with Stan and Ollie as hoboes who agree to help out neighborhood cop Edgar Kennedy by breaking into the police chief's house and allowing Kennedy to collar them. In computerized color. 25 min.
58-5052 *$12.99*

Another Fine Mess (Color Version) (1930)
Colorized version of one of Laurel and Hardy's funniest short comedies has the boys, on the run from the police, hiding in a swank mansion whose owner is on vacation. When visitors show up, Ollie masquerades as the owner, with Stan as his maid! Thelma Todd, James Finlayson also star. 28 min.
58-5063 *$12.99*

The Devil's Brother (1933)
Stan and Ollie play bandits hired by a real robber called Fra Diablo out to bilk a king of his treasures. Superior L & H moments mix with operatic sequences for a hilarious and hummable effort. Dennis King and Thelma Todd co-star. AKA: "Fra Diavolo." 88 min.
12-2357 *$19.99*

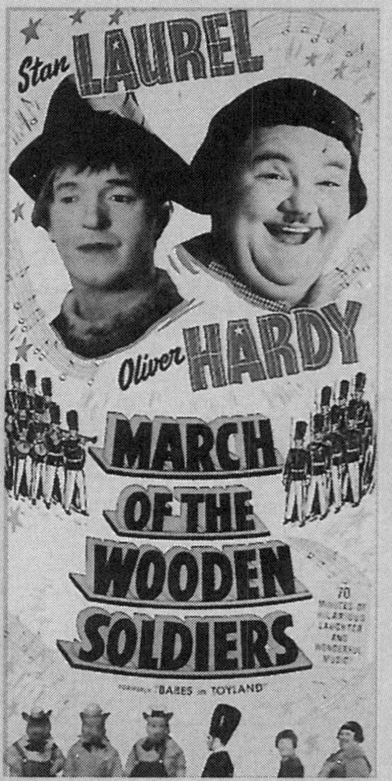

March Of The Wooden Soldiers (Restored Version) (1934)
Victor Herbert's operetta "Babes in Toyland" was adapted to fit the screen antics of Laurel and Hardy, and the result is a magical film comedy for all ages. Stan and Ollie are apprentice toymakers for Santa Claus who must save Mother Goose and other nursery rhyme characters from crooked Mr. Barnaby. This special edition includes the original "storybook" opening and musical number. 77 min.
09-5412 *$14.99*

March Of The Wooden Soldiers (Restored Color Version)
Also available in a colorized edition.
10-2343 Was $19.99 *$14.99*

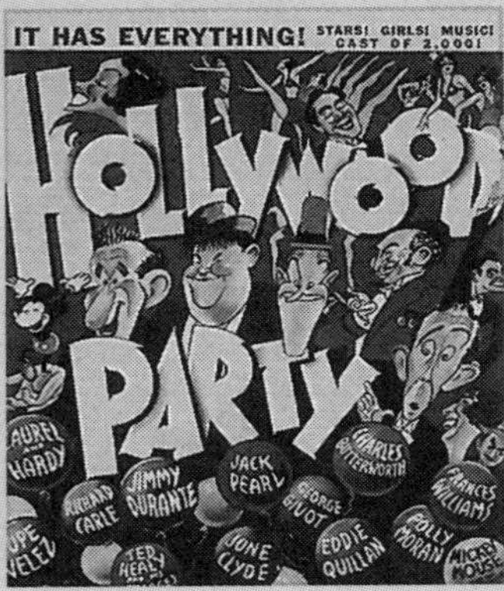

Hollywood Party (1934)
Star-studded comedy musical features Jimmy Durante as jungle film hero "Schnarzan," who throws a lavish party to impress the owner of some prize lions he'd like to use in his next movie. Among the invited (and uninvited) guests are Laurel and Hardy, Ted Healy and the Three Stooges, Lupe Velez, Jack Pearl and even Mickey Mouse (who introduces a Technicolor cartoon sequence). Songs by Rodgers and Hart include "Reincarnation" and the title song. 68 min.
12-2358 $19.99

Bonnie Scotland (1935)
Take the high road to laughter with Laurel and Hardy as they play two bumblers who are unwittingly inducted into the Scottish army and become stationed in the Indian desert. 80 min.
12-1664 $19.99

Pick A Star (1937)
A young girl from Iowa comes to Hollywood in search of fame and, after some tough times, gets a chance thanks to the efforts of a publicity man. Hal Roach's comic inside look at Tinseltown features Laurel and Hardy in hilarious cameo appearances; Jack Haley, Rosina Lawrence, Patsy Kelly and Mischa Auer co-star. AKA: "Movie Struck." 76 min.
12-2550 $19.99

The Flying Deuces (1939)
Laurel and Hardy join the Foreign Legion, but it's not as much fun as they might have thought. Sinister Charles Middleton (Ming in the Flash Gordon series) is the commander and he means business! One of the wildest airplane sequences ever filmed makes this old-time comedy a real treasure. 78 min.
10-2042 Was $19.99 $14.99

Great Guns (1941)
When Laurel and Hardy joined the army, the enemy never had it so easy. Stan and Ollie's mix-ups make for much merriment in this feature-length comedy. Dick Nelson, Sheila Ryan co-star; look for a young Alan Ladd. 74 min.
04-3036 $29.99

Air Raid Wardens (1943)
After a series of miscues in different jobs, Laurel and Hardy enlist in the service and are made air raid wardens. Their ineptitude elicits a less-than-patriotic response from the town, especially when they try to practice their first aid "skills." Edgar Kennedy, Jacqueline White also star. 67 min.
12-2549 $19.99

The Big Noise (1944)
A crackpot scientist has invented a new bomb, but when crooks try stealing it, he sets out to hire the best guards available. Unfortunately, there's a war on, so "the best guards available" turn out to be Laurel and Hardy! The boys do their part for the war effort in this comedy that also stars Doris Merrick and Little Bobby Blake. 74 min.
04-2930 $14.99

Nothing But Trouble (1944)
Laurel and Hardy excel in this humorous fable, playing a pair of servants who help an exiled boy king in trouble. After the boys are put in jail for kidnapping the ruler, he helps them find freedom. Hilarious comedy bits abound. Henry O'Neill and David Leland co-star. 69 min.
12-2547 $19.99

The Bullfighters (1945)
One of Laurel and Hardy's last films turns out to be one of their best feature comedies, as the duo head out to Mexico for a rest, only to run into gangsters who mistake Stan for a top matador. Lots of laughs, including a great closing sight gag. 61 min.
04-3035 $29.99

Utopia (Atoll K) (1951)
Laurel and Hardy's final film has the boys inheriting a South Seas island, only to discover that their paradise is rich in uranium. A funny and fond farewell to Hollywood's funniest duo. 83 min.
17-1104 Was $19.99 $14.99

Country Gentlemen (1936)
Charming comedy with the slapstick team of Olsen and Johnson, who play a pair of swindlers trying to fleece the residents of a veterans' home with phony oil wells. 54 min.
09-1244 $19.99

All Over Town (1937)
Ole Olsen and Chic Johnson are vaudeville comics who run afoul of gangsters while trying to help a woman reopen a "jinxed" theatre in this wild comedy. 62 min.
09-1874 $19.99

Mistaken Identity (Three Of A Kind) (1936)
Rollicking, fast-paced farce about a con man, a con woman, an heiress, a nice young fellow and the crazy happenings at a swanky hotel. Stars Evalyn Knapp, Chick Chandler and Billy Gilbert. 75 min.
09-1832 $19.99

Cotton Queen (1937)
Scottish comedian Will Fyffe and Stanley Holloway headline this snappy farce about cotton mill owners who are rivals and can't agree on merging their businesses. A wacky lark from Great Britain. 65 min.
09-2104 Was $29.99 $14.99

We're In The Legion Now (1937)
Fine slapstick fun with Reginald Denny and Vince Barnett as inept gangsters hiding out in Paris who are forced into signing up for the Foreign Legion when their pursuers find them. 56 min.
09-2146 Was $24.99 $14.99

Love In High Gear (1932)
A broad cast of comical characters, including a Brooklyn detective, a crusty old hotel manager and a deaf charwoman, inhabits this fun farce with Harrison Ford as a notorious playboy tangled up in a stolen jewelry case. Co-stars Alberta Vaughn, Arthur Hoyt. 61 min.
09-2261 Was $19.99 $14.99

Mr. Boggs Steps Out (1937)
Smalltown dullard Oliver Boggs (Stuart Erwin) uses his skills as a statistician to win the grand prize in a bean-counting contest, and uses his newfound wealth to enhance his boring life by opening up (of all things) a barrel factory. Co-stars Helen Chandler, Toby Wing, Milburn Stone. 68 min.
09-2264 Was $24.99 $14.99

Clancy In Wall Street (1930)
A spoof of the stock market crash starring Charles Murray as a plumber who hits the jackpot with his stock investment and bids farewell to his partner and daughter, who runs away from home, but loses it all when the market tumbles. With Lucien Littlefield. 76 min.
09-5013 $19.99

Three Legionnaires (1937)
A loony war comedy follows the bungled adventures of a pair of G.I.s holed up in a small Russian village during World War I who somehow become embroiled in the Bolshevik Uprising. Stars Robert Armstrong, Lyle Talbot, Donald Meek and Man Mountain Dean. 67 min.
09-2285 Was $19.99 $14.99

Doughnuts And Society (1936)
A pair of doughnut-making hash-slingers strike it rich in a gold investment. Can the gals adapt to their sophisticated new surroundings? Louise Fazenda, Maude Eburne, Franklin Pangborn star. 70 min.
09-1584 Was $29.99 $14.99

Swing It Sailor! (1937)
Pleasant little service farce about the misadventures of funny swabbies. Great pet store scene where dogs, cats and monkeys stage a chaotic rebellion. Wallace Ford stars. 61 min.
09-1588 Was $24.99 $14.99

When Knights Were Bold (1936)
Humorous satire finds a man inheriting his ancestral English castle and learning the ways of chivalry. Very funny stuff, featuring Jack Buchanan, Fay Wray. 55 min.
09-1639 $19.99

Make A Million (1935)
Screwball comedy of the Depression era stars Charles Starrett as a fired college professor who decides to test his ideas by making a million as a panhandler! Lively comedy co-stars Pauline Brooks. 66 min.
09-1790 Was $29.99 $14.99

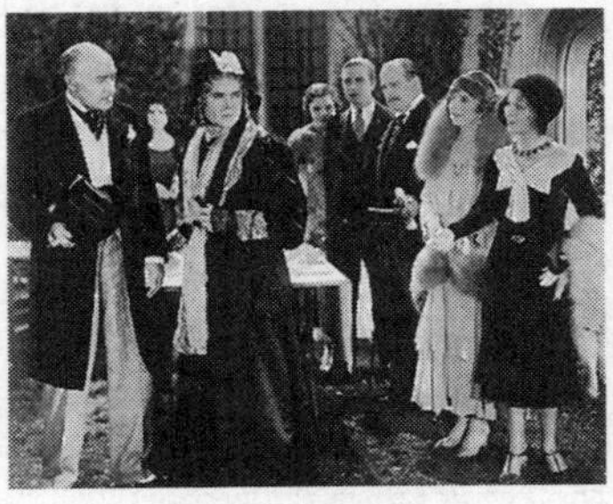

Charley's Aunt (1930)
The first talkie version of the classic 19th-century stage farce stars Charlie Ruggles as the Oxford University student who masquerades as a matronly aunt to serve as chaperone for two fellow students and their dates. Co-stars June Collyer, Hugh Williams.
10-9486 $14.99

Young Fugitives (1938)
When an elderly Civil War veteran dies, his friend tries to find the man's son, whom he promised to treat as his own. It turns out, however, that the son would rather cheat the man out of his share of the money that the two old soldiers saved. Moving comedy/drama stars Harry Davenport, Robert Wilcox. 67 min.
09-5036 $19.99

I See Ice (1938)
Wacky British comedy about a property man for an ice ballet group who invents a special camera and eventually becomes a newspaper photographer. George Formby and Kay Walsh star; look quickly for a young Roddy McDowall. 77 min.
09-5020 $19.99

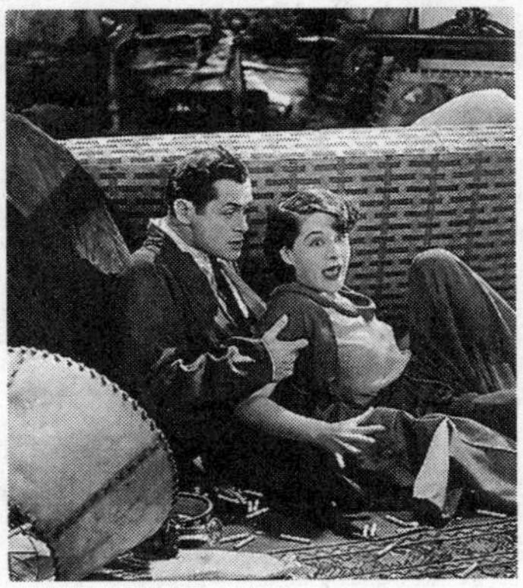

Private Lives (1931)
Noel Coward's marvelous romantic farce receives a terrific treatment with Norma Shearer and Robert Montgomery as feisty former spouses who bump into each other at a French hotel while vacationing with their current, boring "loved ones." Fights start, sparks fly and romance blooms again in this ageless charmer. With Reginald Denny, Una Merkel and Jean Hersholt. 84 min.
12-2488 $19.99

Rhythm In The Clouds (1937)
A talented but struggling songwriter is booted out of her apartment because she hasn't paid her rent. Her plan to get back on track involves writing a letter explaining that she's the niece of a famous songwriter and is moving into his fashionable apartment. Soon, she's romantically involved with a songwriter neighbor. Patricia Ellis, Warren Hull star. 53 min.
09-2332 $19.99

With Love And Kisses (1937)
Rip-roaring comedy with music about "Spec" Higgens, a country songwriter who can only compose tunes in the presence of his cow. When a New York radio crooner claims one of "Spec's" songs as his own, he must travel to the big city to put things right, and things get even zanier. Pinky Tomlin, Toby Wing, Kane Richmond star. 64 min.
09-2339 $24.99

In The Money (1933)
Richard "Skeets" Gallagher presides over the comic chaos that knocks the chocks from under the Higginbottom family when it's discovered dad's company has gone broke. Depression-era chin-lifter co-stars Lois Wilson, Louise Beavers, Warren Hymer. 63 min.
09-3084 $19.99

Two Wise Maids (1937)
A feisty schoolteacher copes with a classroom full of rowdy students, an antagonistic young principal, and a school board trying to force her to retire in this heartfelt mix of comedy and melodrama. Alison Skipworth, Polly Moran, Donald Cook star. 53 min.
09-3087 $14.99

Come On George! (1939)
George Formby brings his musical charms to the big screen with this British-made comedy-with-music. Here, he plays a racetrack ice cream vendor who is falsely accused of stealing a jockey's wallet. As he is being chased, Formby stumbles upon and forms a bond with a formerly unrideable horse named Maneater. 85 min.
09-3140 $19.99

Night Work (1930)
Nice guy department store clerk Eddie Quillan mistakenly gives a $10 tip to a nurse trying to care for an orphan boy and, after taking a liking to the woman and kid, begins working another job to help support them. Things get complicated when a wealthy man claims the kid is his grandson. With Sally Starr, Frances Upton. 94 min.
09-5026 $19.99

Joe E. Brown

Earthworm Tractors (1936)
High-pressure tractor salesman Joe E. Brown is out to land his most difficult sale yet, to timberman Guy Kibbee, and pulls out all the stops in this ground-shaking comedy. With June Travis, Dick Foran. 68 min.
10-7673 Was $19.99 $14.99

When's Your Birthday? (1937)
Joe E. Brown, Marian Marsh and Fred Keating star in this comedy about a boxer who only wins when the astrological signs are right. 76 min.
09-1248 Was $19.99 $14.99

Riding On Air (1937)
Joe E. Brown stars as a bungling smalltown newspaperman with an amazing knack for doing the wrong thing, but having it work out OK in the end! Guy Kibbee, Florence Rice co-star. 70 min.
10-3082 Was $19.99 $14.99

Fit For A King (1937)
It's high court hi-jinx when newshound Joe E. Brown, assigned to cover an elderly archduke, takes a shine to the crown princess and reveals an assassination plot. With Helen Mack and Paul Kelly. 73 min.
10-7047 Was $19.99 $14.99

The Gladiator (1938)
After ingesting a professor's experimental serum, college student and 98-pound weakling Joe E. Brown gains superhuman strength and becomes the campus's star athlete. Loosely based on Philip Wylie's sci-fi novel, this effects-filled comedy/fantasy also stars June Travis, Lucien Littlefield and wrestler Man Mountain Dean. 70 min.
10-5290 Was $19.99 $14.99

Wide Open Faces (1938)
Soda jerk Joe E. Brown has to outwit a mess of mobsters who are taking over girlfriend Jane Wyman's inn while they search for a fortune in hidden loot in this fast-paced romp. With Alison Skipworth, Lucien Littlefield, Sidney Toler. 67 min.
10-5291 Was $19.99 $14.99

Flirting With Fate (1938)
When his vaudeville troupe's South American tour flops and leaves them stranded, a guilt-stricken Joe E. Brown decides to kill himself so the performers can return home on his life insurance money. Brown's comical attempts to do himself in (which include insulting bandito Leo Carrillo) are a delight to watch. With Beverly Roberts, Steffi Duna. 70 min.
10-5292 $14.99

Beware, Spooks! (1939)
After catching some crooks and then letting them escape, bumbling cop Joe E. Brown sets out to recapture his quarry, with some help from a Coney Island funhouse. Slapstick fun with Mary Carlisle, Don Beddoe. 76 min.
53-7646 Was $19.99 $14.99

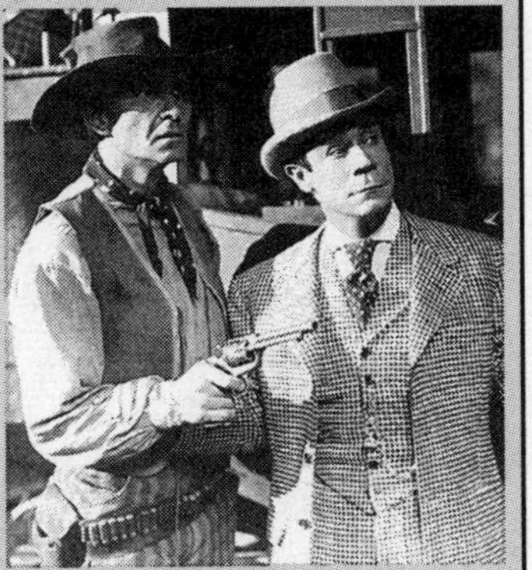

Shut My Big Mouth (1942)
Tenderfoot Joe E. Brown gets a taste of frontier life when he heads out West, gets elected marshal, and must foil a band of kidnappers. Victor Jory, Adele Mara, Fritz Feld also star. 80 min.
53-7648 Was $19.99 $14.99

The Daring Young Man (1942)
4-F reject Joe E. Brown's attempts to serve his country get him mixed up with a spy ring and a top-secret weapon (a radio-controlled bowling ball!) in this wacky wartime comedy. With Marguerite Chapman, William Wright; look for a young Lloyd Bridges. 74 min.
53-7647 Was $19.99 $14.99

The Tender Years (1947)
In a rare twist, comedian Joe E. Brown turns in a dramatic performance as a country minister faced with problems brought on by his son's friendship with a stray mongrel. Also stars Richard Lyon and Noreen Nash. 82 min.
27-6504 $14.99

Ladies Of Leisure (1930)
An early effort from Frank Capra starring Barbara Stanwyck as a gorgeous gold-digging model who gets a wealthy aspiring artist interested in her, only to have his parents shun her because of her reputation. Ralph Graves, Lowell Sherman, Marie Prevost star in this drama laced with comedy. Silent version; features music score. 85 min.
10-8367 *$19.99*

Platinum Blonde (1931)
Frank Capra's comedy tells the story of tabloid newsman Robert Williams, loved from afar by sassy reporter Loretta Young, who marries a socialite gal (Jean Harlow) planning to turn him into a proper gentleman. Bored with his upper-class lifestyle, Williams throws a party for his hard-drinking pals...much to the dismay of Harlow! 86 min.
02-2211 *$19.99*

The Miracle Woman (1931)
In Frank Capra's powerful adaptation of a Broadway play (loosely based on the life of Aimee Semple MacPherson), Barbara Stanwyck turns in a superb performance as a pastor's daughter enlisted by a con artist to pose as an evangelist. Using all sorts of tricks, Stanwyck becomes the top faith healer in America, but has second thoughts when she falls for a blind ex-pilot. With David Manners, Sam Hardy. 90 min.
02-3055 *$19.99*

American Madness (1932)
Frank Capra's heralded, little-seen drama stars Walter Huston as a bank president who gets in trouble with his board of directors for making loans to working-class depositors without sufficient collateral. When a crooked teller's antics cause a run on the bank, Huston's devoted employees and the small businessmen he's helped out come to his aid. With Kay Johnson, Pat O'Brien, Constance Cummings. 76 min.
02-3054 *$19.99*

The Bitter Tea Of General Yen (1933)
Controversial for its time, Frank Capra's lavish adventure stars Barbara Stanwyck as an American woman who travels to war-torn China to marry her missionary fiancé. Separated during a shootout, she is carried off and romanced by courtly, handsome warlord Nils Asther. With Gavin Gordon, Walter Connolly. 78 min.
02-2455 *$19.99*

Lady For A Day (1933)
Frank Capra's wonderful adaptation of Damon Runyon's story about "Apple Annie," a Times Square peddler who is transformed into a society woman by a soft-hearted gangster, stars May Robson, Warren William and Guy Kibbee. This sentimental favorite, nominated for four Academy Awards, was later remade by Capra as "Pocketful of Miracles." 96 min.
53-7458 Was $29.99 *$14.99*

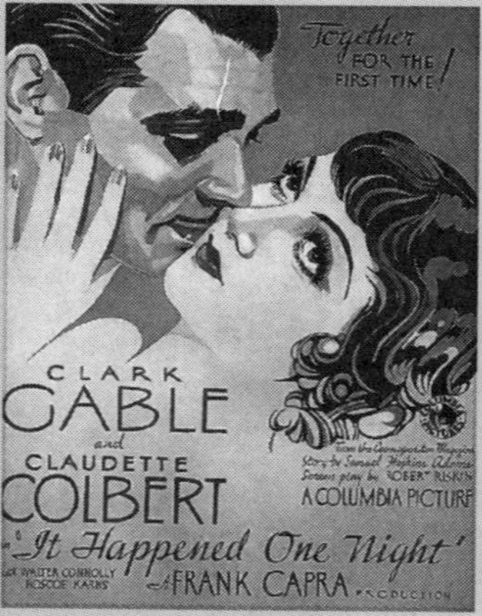

It Happened One Night (1934)
The classic screwball comedy from Frank Capra was the first film to win the five major Academy Awards, with Clark Gable as a news-hungry reporter chasing runaway rich girl Claudette Colbert from Miami to New York, falling in love in between their hilarious bickering. Co-stars Roscoe Karns, Walter Connolly. 105 min.
02-1363 □*$19.99*

Broadway Bill (1934)
In Frank Capra's classic horse story, Warner Baxter plays a businessman troubled by his dead-end job and his coying wife who purchases a racehorse named Broadway Bill. He enters the horse into a big race, but is confronted by shady gamblers, large debts and a sick pony before the finish line is in sight. Myrna Loy, Walter Connolly, Helen Vinson also star. 102 min.
06-2242 □*$19.99*

Mr. Deeds Goes To Town (1936)
Gary Cooper is the "pixilated" small-town resident who refuses to let a $20 million inheritance and a New York mansion alter his down-to-earth faith in people, in Frank Capra's delightful comedy. Jean Arthur co-stars as the cynical reporter who falls for Deeds; with Douglass Dumbrille, Lionel Stander. 115 min.
02-1953 *$19.99*

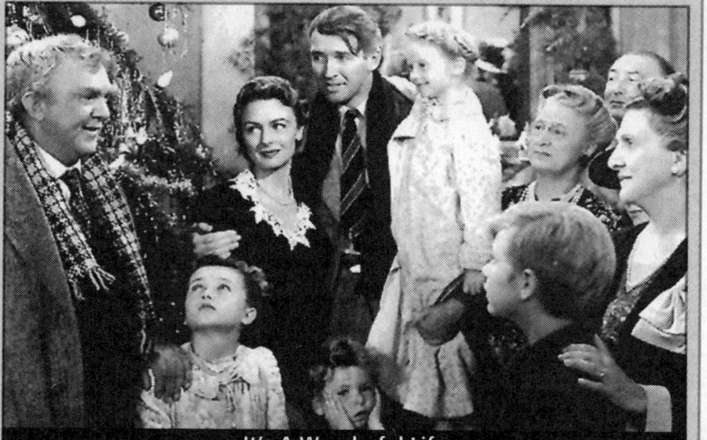

It's A Wonderful Life

Frank Capra

Lost Horizon (1937)
A group of travelers lost in the Tibetan mountains comes upon the mystical valley of Shangri-La, a Utopia detached from the rest of the world, in Frank Capra's classic adventure/romance saga. Ronald Colman, Jane Wyatt, Sam Jaffe, John Howard, H.B. Warner, Thomas Mitchell star; restored 132-minute version.
02-1726 *$19.99*

You Can't Take It With You (1938)
Winner of the 1938 Academy Awards for Best Picture and Best Director, Frank Capra's adaptation of the Kaufman/Hart play stars Lionel Barrymore as the head of an eccentric family preparing for a visit by granddaughter Jean Arthur's beau (James Stewart) and his strait-laced parents. Delightfully daffy comedy also stars Edward Arnold, Spring Byington, Ann Miller. 126 min.
02-1960 *$19.99*

Mr. Smith Goes To Washington (1939)
Frank Capra's classic comedy-drama about government and the American spirit. Jimmy Stewart is an idealistic senator who tries to stem the tide of graft he finds around him. Claude Rains is a corrupt colleague, Jean Arthur a jaded secretary who joins Stewart's crusade. 129 min.
02-1066 Remastered *$14.99*

Meet John Doe (1941)
Only filmmaker Frank Capra could carry off this tale of a naive "average American" (Gary Cooper) who is used by an unscrupulous politician (Edward Arnold) through a nationwide "goodwill drive." Barbara Stanwyck is the reporter who falls in love with Cooper and must save him when the campaign is exposed. Walter Brennan, Gene Lockhart also star. 123 min.
03-1722 *$19.99*

Arsenic And Old Lace (Color Version) (1941)
Frank Capra's filming of the Broadway black comedy about an odd Brooklyn family, and the two sweet old ladies whose basement holds a murderously funny secret, stars Cary Grant, Raymond Massey, Peter Lorre, Priscilla Lane and Josephine Hull. 116 min.
12-1883 *$19.99*

It's A Wonderful Life (1946)
Classic comedy/drama (and the quintessential Frank Capra film) stars James Stewart as a small-town banker saved from suicide one Christmas Eve by a neophyte angel who shows him what a difference his "wasted" life has made to those around him. Great cast includes Donna Reed, Lionel Barrymore, Thomas Mitchell and Henry Travers. 132 min.
63-1472 □*$14.99*

It's A Wonderful Life: 50th Anniversary Deluxe Gift Set
It's a gift any "guardian angel" would love: a collector's boxed set that features the anniversary edition of the film, a separate "making of" documentary tape, the "It's a Wonderful Life" book and Christmas album CD, special behind-the-scenes photos, and reproductions of the original theatrical poster and lobby card.
63-1778 □*$79.99*

State Of The Union (1948)
Based on a hit Broadway play, this insightful Frank Capra film stars Spencer Tracy as a would-be presidential candidate and Katharine Hepburn as his estranged wife, who agrees to pose as a loving spouse for the campaign. Hepburn comes to care again for Tracy and tries to stop him from abandoning his deals for the sake of politics. With Adolphe Menjou, Angela Lansbury, Van Johnson. 124 min.
07-1031 Was $39.99 *$19.99*

Here Comes The Groom (1951)
Happy-go-lucky musical-comedy from Frank Capra stars Bing Crosby as a journalist who has to persuade former wife Jane Wyman to remarry him in order to adopt two French orphans. Featuring Franchot Tone and Alexis Smith, cameos by Dorothy Lamour, Louis Armstrong and Phil Harris and the Academy Award-winning song "In the Cool, Cool, Cool of the Evening." 113 min.
06-1745 *$14.99*

Pocketful Of Miracles (1961)
Frank Capra's final film is a hilarious translation of a Damon Runyon tale set in 1930s New York, as gangster Glenn Ford repays street peddler Bette Davis for her "good luck" apples by passing her off as a well-to-do society lady for her visiting daughter (Ann-Margret in her film debut). Remake of Capra's 1933 "Lady for a Day" co-stars Peter Falk and Hope Lange. 136 min.
12-3198 Was $19.99 *$14.99*

Pocketful Of Miracles (Letterboxed Version)
Also available in a theatrical, widescreen format.
12-3197 Was $19.99 □*$14.99*

Frank Capra's American Dream
His unshakable belief in the basic goodness of the "common man" and the "American dream" were themes as prevalent in his own life, from his emigration from Sicily to his legendary career in Hollywood, as they were in such films as "It Happened One Night," "Mr. Smith Goes to Washington" and "It's a Wonderful Life." Film clips, rare footage, stills and interviews with Robert Altman, Martin Scorsese, Richard Dreyfuss and more, tell the story of this uniquely American filmmaker. 110 min.
02-3064 *$19.99*

Frank Capra/Jimmy Stewart Set
A couple of collaborations between Frank Capra and Jimmy Stewart, "Mr. Smith Goes to Washington" and "You Can't Take It with You," plus the documentary "Frank Capra's American Dream" are available in this money-saver.
02-3062 *$39.99*

Frank Capra/Academy Awards Set
Capra's trio of Best Director Oscar-winners, "It Happened One Night," "Mr. Deeds Goes to Town" and "You Can't Take It with You," and the documentary "Frank Capra's American Dream" are available in a money-saving set.
02-3063 *$59.99*

Frank Capra's Winning Circle Gift Set
The director's two classic horseracing films, "Broadway Bill" and its 1950 remake, "Riding High," with Bing Crosby, are available in this special collector's set.
06-2244 □*$39.99*

The Frank Capra Collection
This special boxed set includes "A Hole in the Head," "Lady for a Day" and "Pocketful of Miracles."
12-3192 *$44.99*

Please see our index for these other Frank Capra titles: *Long Pants* • *The Strong Man*

Climbing High (1939)
High-spirited British comedy from director Carol Reed about a poor model who is nearly run over by a dashing millionaire. After sparks fly between the two, the model discovers the man's real identity and shuns him before returning to save him from marrying a spoiled aristocrat. Jessie Matthews, Michael Redgrave, Alastair Sim star. 76 min.
10-9299 *$19.99*

Keep Your Seats Please (1936)
An early version of the story that was filmed by Mel Brooks as "The Twelve Chairs," this farce tells of a man and his shady attorney who try to find some priceless gems that are part of an inheritance. The tricky part is getting the jewels, which were sewn into the lining of six chairs. George Formby, Florence Desmond star. 82 min.
10-9302 *$19.99*

Boss Foreman (1939)
Ethnic comedy stars Henry Armetta as ebullient Italian papa Mike, the boss foreman at a construction company. When the mob threatens the company, Mike takes action and his life takes a hysterical turn for the worse. 58 min.
09-1817 Was $24.99 *$14.99*

Join The Marines (1937)
A New York City cop is thrown off the force and the Olympic boxing team after he's wrongly accused of drunkenness. He soon falls for the woman responsible for his problems and, in order, to impress her father, he joins the Marines. Paul Kelly, June Travis and Purnell Pratt star. 55 min.
10-9700 *$19.99*

The Lad (1935)
Lively comic tale about an ex-crook who is mistaken for a detective and hired by a wealthy family to keep their private lives private. Can a former girlfriend now working as the family's maid help him stay straight? Gordon Harker, Betty Stockfield, Jane Carr and Geraldine Fitzgerald star. 72 min.
10-9701 *$19.99*

Second Honeymoon (1931)
A married woman looking for an out to her dull life decides to get romantically entangled with her husband's best friend. But the friend proves to be more loyal than she originally believed, and when the new couple arrives at a retreat, hubby makes an appearance trying to win the woman back. Josephine Dunn, Edward Earle star. 60 min.
10-9703 *$19.99*

Third Time Lucky (1931)
British comedy that finds a shy reverend determined to overcome his timidity and come to the defense of his beautiful young ward, who is being blackmailed by an angry former lover. Bobby Howes, Gordon Parker, Dorothy Boyd star. 85 min.
10-9781 *$19.99*

Three Of A Kind (1936)
A trio of smooth-talking guys continually tries to one up each other with a variety of schemes and masquerades in this fast-paced comedy. Chick Chandler, Evalyn Knapp, Berton Churchill and Richard Carle star. 68 min.
10-9782 *$19.99*

The Guardsman (1931)
A sparkling version of Molnar's farce, starring Alfred Lunt as an actor who imagines that wife Lynn Fontaine is unfaithful. The actor's jealousy leads him to impersonate his spouse's imagined suitor—a Russian nobleman with a heavy accent. Roland Young, ZaSu Pitts and Ann Dvorak also star. 83 min.
12-2486 *$19.99*

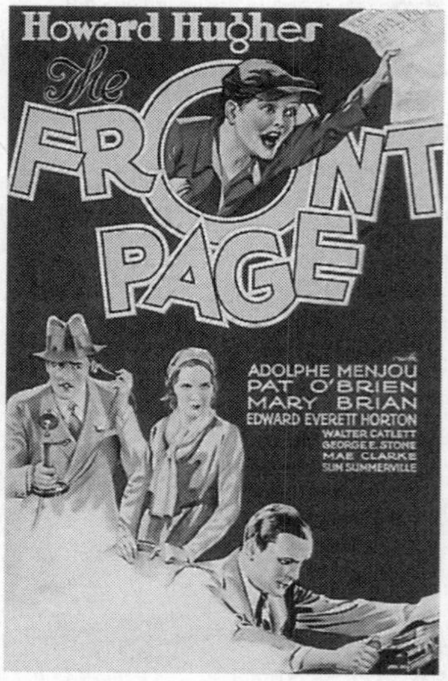

The Front Page (1931)
The original film version of the Hecht/MacArthur stage classic about the newspaper business. Adolphe Menjou, Pat O'Brien and Mae Clarke star in this fast-paced and witty tale of escaped convicts, shady politicians and cynical reporters. 101 min.
08-8067 *$19.99*

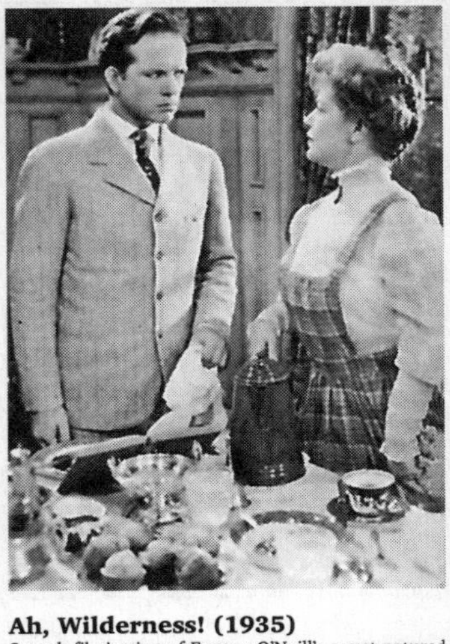

Ah, Wilderness! (1935)
Superb filmization of Eugene O'Neill's sweet-natured comedy about the funny, warm adventures that welcome a teenager (Eric Linden) to adulthood: his first romance, his senior year in high school, and his relationship with his cantankerous uncle (Wallace Beery). With Aline MacMahon, Cecilia Parker, Mickey Rooney and Lionel Barrymore. 98 min.
12-2484 □$19.99

Blessed Event (1932)
Fast-paced newspaper comedy stars Lee Tracy as a Gotham gossip columnist whose womanizing ways get him in trouble with a chorus girl. Dick Powell makes his film debut as a stage crooner; with Mary Brian, Ned Sparks. 78 min.
12-2619 $19.99

Eternally Yours (1939)
Lovely Loretta Young discovers that being a magician's wife can be tricky. She's jealous of hubby David Niven's professional status, and believes that he had more than rabbits in his hat. Directed by Tay Garnett; with Broderick Crawford, ZaSu Pitts. 95 min.
17-1048 $19.99

Red Lights Ahead (1937)
After investing in a gold mine and hitting pay dirt, Andy Clyde is one happy camper. But when things go downhill, he faces the mine's closing. Then he gets advice from his grandfather regarding how to save the business. Lucille Gleason and Paula Stone star. 70 min.
09-5157 $19.99

Young And Beautiful (1934)
Hollywood-themed comedy starring William Haines as a studio PR man who tries to make his girlfriend a star, but may lose her to a handsome actor when he starts neglecting her. With Judith Allen, Franklin Pangborn, and the 12 starlets picked as "1934 WAMPAS Baby Stars" by movie admen. 68 min.
09-5325 $19.99

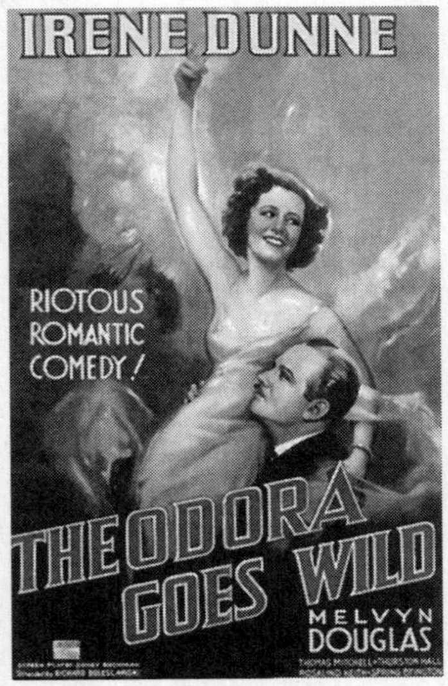

Theodora Goes Wild (1936)
Classic screwball comedy starring Irene Dunne as the writer of a steamy best-seller who uses a pen name so she doesn't rile the residents of her small town. While in Manhattan, sophisticated artist Melvyn Douglas takes a liking to her, and joins her, first at home, where he poses as a gardener, then in the Big Apple, where Dunne tries to teach Douglas to face his politician father and estranged wife. Thomas Mitchell also stars. 94 min.
02-2848 $19.99

Back Page (1933)
Lighthearted comedy about an idealistic young reporter quits her job after a high profile and very controversial story is stopped by her editor. She takes a job as an editor of a paper in California, but then discovers a plot of corruption that goes higher than she ever could have imagined. Stars Peggy Shannon, Russell Hopton, Sterling Holloway. 61 min.
10-9783 $19.99

Check And Double Check (1930)
The two white actors who played "Amos 'n' Andy" on radio, Freeman Gosden and Charles Correll, donned blackface for their only screen appearance in this slapstick comedy that features music by the Duke Ellington Orchestra. 73 min.
01-1151 $19.99

Here Comes Cookie (1935)
Flighty society gal Gracie Allen turns her father's Park Avenue mansion into a Vaudeville rooming house, and wisecracking George Burns becomes her favorite tenant, in this fast-paced comedy loaded with songs and specialty acts (including "Cal Norris and Monkey"). With Betty Furness, George Barbier. 65 min.
07-2451 □$14.99

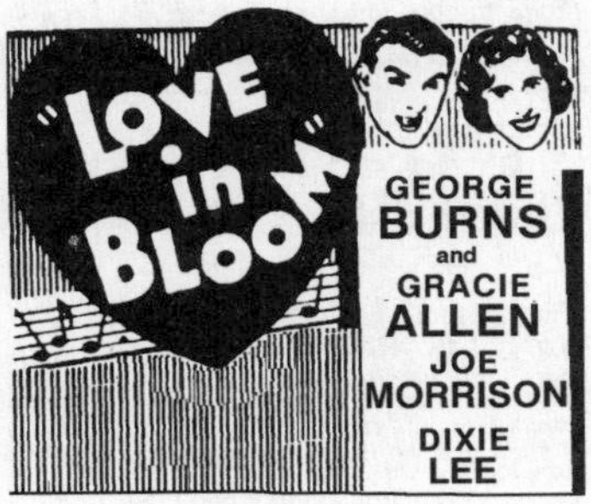

Love In Bloom (1935)
George Burns and Gracie Allen offer fine comedic supporting turns in this breezy romantic tale about a carnival owner's daughter who visits New York City and falls for a young songwriter. With Dixie Lee, Joe Morrison. 75 min.
07-2452 □$14.99

Dreaming Out Loud (1940)
Radio stars Lum and Abner's film career got off the ground with this homespun comedy that follows the Jot 'Em Down General Store proprietors in a series of misadventures, as they hang out their shingles as fundraisers, matchmakers and detectives. With Chester Lauck and Norris Goff. 81 min.
10-7048 $19.99

The Bashful Bachelor (1942)
Wacky "Lum and Abner" farce in which Lum tries to win over ZaSu Pitts by proving his bravery through a series of rescues of his partner. Chester Lauck and Norris Goff star; with Grady Sutton. 78 min.
10-8345 $19.99

Two Weeks To Live (1943)
In their fourth film outing, Lum and Abner are bequeathed a railroad but must first come up with some cash, which, through a strange twist of fate, sends Abner to Mars in a rocketship. With Chester Lauck, Norris Goff and Franklin Pangborn. 76 min.
10-7049 $19.99

So This Is Washington (1943)
Lum and Abner go to D.C. to hold council with some politicians who've agreed to lend support to the boy's new invention: synthetic rubber. With Chester Lauck, Norris Goff. 64 min.
10-7050 $19.99

Goin' To Town (1944)
What's this: Lum and Abner selling their beloved Jot 'Em Down store? It's all thanks to a slick con man who's convinced the boys that there's oil under their property and gets them to trick the locals into "investing" in his scheme. Chester Lauck, Norris Goff, Barbara Hale, Dick Elliott and Grady Sutton star. 68 min.
09-5290 $19.99

Lum And Abner Abroad (1956)
The beloved down-home duo are off on a European vacation that finds them reuniting a ballerina with her missing reporter beau, running afoul of smugglers in Paris, and breaking the bank in Monte Carlo. Chester Lauck and Norris Goff re-create their radio and screen characters in this feature culled from episodes of the rarely-seen 1949 "Lum and Abner" TV series. 72 min.
09-5291 $19.99

People Are Funny (1946)
Based on the popular radio (and later, TV) show, this music-filled comedy follows the rivalry between two radio producers to please a sponsor. Jack Haley, Philip Reed, Helen Walker, Rudy Vallee, Ozzie Nelson star, with host Art Linkletter as himself. 94 min.
09-1243 $19.99

It's A Joke, Son! (1947)
The vociferous Senator Claghorn (Kenny Delmar) from radio's "Allen's Alley" stars in his own Southern-fried comedy, facing the toughest election of his career when he runs against his wife Magnolia. With Una Merkel, Douglas Dumbrille, June Lockhart. 63 min.
18-3017 $19.99

Irish Luck (1939)
A bellhop turned amateur sleuth gets his Irish up to help exonerate a lovely lass who has been implicated in the murder of a guest at his hotel. Breezy comedy/mystery stars Frankie Darro and Dick Purcell. 58 min.
10-7172 Was $19.99 $14.99

Meet The Boy Friend (1937)
Romantic farce about a popular male crooner who is being swindled into marriage by a golddigging actress, but is really loved by the niece of an insurance executive. David Carlyle, Carol Hughes, and Oscar and Elmer star. 63 min.
17-9062 Was $19.99 $14.99

Melody Cruise (1933)
Millionaire Phil Harris and pal Charlie Ruggles end up on an ocean liner loaded with matrimony-minded females in this spry comedy laced with music. With Helen Mack, Greta Nissen and a brief appearance by Betty Grable. 75 min.
18-7194 $19.99

Goodbye Love (1933)
Rich fellow Sidney Blackmer and trusted valet Charlie Ruggles get out of prison after avoiding their alimony-paying duties and wind up in Atlantic City. Romance and comic complications ensue in the resort town, as Sid and Charlie fall for the same gold-digging gal (Verree Teasdale). 65 min.
53-6021 $29.99

Little Orphan Annie (1932)
Decades before the Broadway play and big-budget film, the comics' blank-eyed waif came to the screen in this family comedy. Mitzi Green stars as Annie, with Edgar Kennedy as Daddy Warbucks. 60 min.
62-5013 Was $19.99 $14.99

Letter Of Introduction (1938)
Sparkling comedy/drama with Adolphe Menjou as a matinee idol whose long-lost daughter arrives one day to ask her father's help in boosting her career as an actress. Co-stars Andrea Leeds, George Murphy, Eve Arden, Edgar Bergen and Charlie McCarthy. 104 min.
01-1169 Was $19.99 $14.99

The Rage Of Paris (1938)
In her American movie debut, French actress Danielle Darrieux stars as a beautiful young woman in New York City, newly arrived from France and looking for work as a model, who becomes tangled up with a conniving ex-actress and her accomplice. Stars Douglas Fairbanks, Jr. and Mischa Auer; look for Mary Martin in her film debut. 78 min.
01-1178 Was $19.99 $14.99

My Love For Yours (1939)
Dandy romantic comedy starring Fred MacMurray as a man who thinks he can get tough, career-minded Madeleine Carroll to fall in love with him. Entanglements ensue when Carroll gets cold feet after they begin dating—she heads to Nassau and MacMurray goes to Bali to marry his boss's daughter. Allan Jones, Akim Tamiroff co-star. AKA: "Honeymoon in Bali." 95 min.
10-3382 $19.99

Sin Takes A Holiday (1930)
Constance Bennett is the secretary of a suave divorce lawyer who marries her to get out of a legal predicament. The marriage pact gives her $5,000 a year and a chance to travel around the world, but while she's alone on her "honeymoon cruise," Bennett meets and is taken with one of her hubby's pals. Kenneth MacKenna, Basil Rathbone co-star. 80 min.
17-3036 $19.99

Mae West

Night After Night (1932)
The film debut of the inimitable Mae West finds her in a memorable supporting role as the sassy gal-pal of George Raft, a nightclub owner who attempts to transform his streetwise demeanor in order to help him woo a society girl. Constance Cummings, Alison Skipworth and Roscoe Karnes also star. 73 min.
07-1955 $14.99

She Done Him Wrong (1933)
In her second film, Mae West re-creates her stage role as Lady Lou, notorious saloon singer who invites Salvation Army officer Cary Grant to "come up sometime...and see me." Along the way she also tosses out some classic one-liners and sings "Frankie and Johnny" and "Easy Rider." With Noah Beery, Gilbert Roland; co-written by West. 65 min.
07-1527 Was $29.99 $14.99

I'm No Angel (1933)
Hilarious, naughty pre-Production Code farce featuring Mae West as an unscrupulous carnival entertainer who takes a turn as a lion-tamer in order to get her boyfriend and fellow con artist out of a jam. Along the way she also falls for suave millionaire Cary Grant, the cousin of an admiring playboy. Songs include "I Want You, I Need You" and "They Call Me Sister Honky Tonk." With Edward Arnold. 68 min.
07-1959 $14.99

Belle Of The Nineties (1934)
New Orleans singer Mae West heats up "The Big Easy" as Ruby Carter, "the most talked about woman in America," who juggles romances with a boxer and a millionaire while avoiding her flirtatious boss. There's lots of wild West one-liners and music by Duke Ellington and His Orchestra, including the song "My Old Flame." With Roger Pryor and Johnny Mack Brown. 73 min.
07-1954 $14.99

Goin' To Town (1935)
After inheriting an oil field from her husband, newly widowed Mae West finds it difficult, despite her newfound wealth, to land a new man, so she takes etiquette lessons in order to crash high society. West warbles such tunes as "He's a Bad, Bad Man, But He's Good Enough for Me" and excels in the "Samson and Delilah" sequence. 71 min.
07-1958 $14.99

Go West, Young Man (1936)
Movie star Mae West heads to a small town to attend the preview of her newest film and finds romantic complications among the common folk while falling for down-to-earth farmboy Randolph Scott. Mae's marvelous one-liners, satirical swipes at Hollywood, and songs like "I Was Saying to the Moon" and "On a Typical Tropical Night" are among the highlights. With Warren William, Alice Brady. 80 min.
07-1957 $14.99

Klondike Annie (1936)
After killing her lover in self-defense, Barbary Coast madam Mae West hops an Alaska-bound freighter and soon winds up impersonating an evangelist in order to elude the law. Offbeat West entry mixes comedy, drama and music; songs include "It's Better to Give Than to Receive" and "I'm an Occidental Woman in an Oriental Mood." With Victor McLaglen, Phillip Reed. 77 min.
07-1960 $14.99

Every Day's A Holiday (1937)
Mae West is a slick, turn-of-the-century con woman who poses as a sultry French singer in order to elude the law. Her efforts lead to the ousting of a corrupt police chief and the electing of a reform mayor into office. Edmund Lowe, Lloyd Nolan and Louis Armstrong also star. 79 min.
07-1956 $14.99

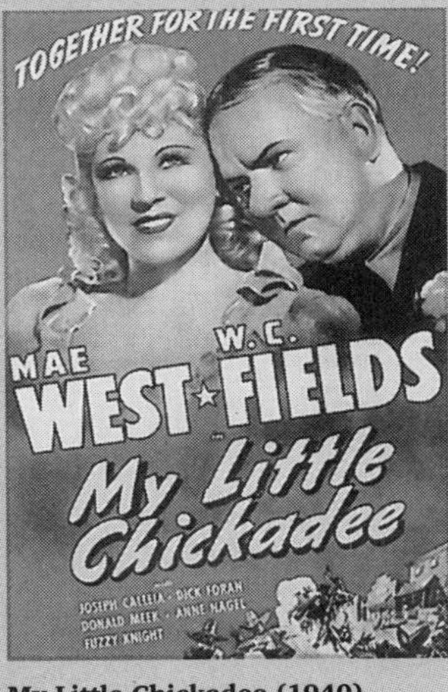

My Little Chickadee (1940)
The Wild West gets even more wild when W.C. Fields and Mae West team up in this comedy classic. He's Cuthbert Twillie, con man and "notions seller," and she's Flowerbelle Lee, the shame of her town. Together they clean up a lawless city, capture the notorious Kissing Bandit and toss off the fastest array of one-liners you ever heard. 83 min.
07-1023 $14.99

The Heat's On (1943)
Broadway star Mae West has her hands full when she becomes the prize in a rivalry between two conniving stage producers, while also being pursued by the brother of a bluenosed matron out to keep Mae's "immoral" entertainment off the Great White Way. Frenetic, song-filled comedy also stars Victor Moore, William Gaxton, Almira Sessions. 79 min.
02-2453 $19.99

Sextette (1978)
Who else but Mae West could portray a Hollywood sex symbol whose honeymoon with her sixth husband, English nobleman Timothy Dalton, is constantly interrupted by visits from the press and Mae's ex-spouses? Campy comedy that was the wild, wild West's screen farewell also stars Alice Cooper, Tony Curtis, Dom DeLuise, George Hamilton, Keith Moon, George Raft and Ringo Starr. 91 min.
03-1120 $19.99

The Three Stooges: The Early Years

Stooges fans won't want to miss this amazing three-tape collection of rarities featuring the comedy team. Larry, Moe and Curly star with ex-boss Ted Healy in the 1933-34 MGM shorts "Nertsery Rhymes," "Beer and Pretzels," "Plane Nuts" and "The Big Idea"; Curly appears with George Givot in "Roast Beef and Movies" (1934); and Shemp does solo work for Vitaphone in "Salt Water Daffy" (1933), "Corn on the Cop" (1934) and "His First Flame" (1935). Also includes "Disorder in the Court," "Brideless Groom," "Malice in the Palace" and "Sing a Song of Six Pants." 222 min. total on three tapes.

67-5030 *$39.99*

The Three Stooges: A Bird In The Head

In "A Bird in the Head" (1946), a mad scientist wants to experiment on Curly, Moe and Larry. They're "Three Sappy People" (1939) when they impersonate doctors and crash a society party. Then, the boys join the Air Corps in "Dizzy Pilots" (1943). 60 min. total.

02-1002 *$14.99*

The Three Stooges: Micro-Phonies

Join intrepid Union spies Moe, Larry and Curly in "Uncivil Warriors" (1935). Next, follow the guys on a movie shoot in darkest Africa as the "Three Missing Links" (1938). Finally, Curly has to impersonate a female singer in "Micro-Phonies" (1946). 55 min. total.

02-1067 *$14.99*

The Three Stooges: An Ache In Every Stake

The prize patient of dog doctors Larry, Curly and Moe is abducted in "Calling All Curs" (1939). The fellas also try their hand at delivering ice in "An Ache in Every Stake" (1941) and pose as art students in "Pop Goes the Easel" (1935). 55 min. total.

02-1075 *$14.99*

The Three Stooges: Woman Haters

This zany collection is highlighted by the Stooges' first Columbia short (with all the dialogue in rhyme), "Woman Haters" (1934). Next the boys demolish a golf course in "Three Little Beers" (1935); and in "Tassels in the Air" (1938), they impersonate interior decorators. 60 min. total.

02-1101 *$14.99*

The Three Stooges: Healthy, Wealthy And Dumb

You "coitenly" won't want to miss Moe, Larry and Curly testifying in a murder trial in "Disorder in the Court" (1936). "Pardon My Scotch" (1935) has them playing eccentric distillers McSniff, McSnuff and McSnort; and Curly wins a radio jingle contest in "Healthy, Wealthy and Dumb" (1938). 60 min. total.

02-1139 *$14.99*

The Three Stooges: A-Plumbing We Will Go

Hear Moe, Larry and Curly sing the famous "B-A-Bay" alphabet song in "Violent Is the Word for Curly" (1938). Next, Curly turns boxing star thanks to "Pop Goes the Weasel" in "Punch Drunks" (1934). "A-Plumbing We Will Go" (1940) has the boys opening the floodgates at a society party. 60 min. total.

02-1181 Was $29.99 *$14.99*

The Three Stooges: Movie Maniacs

Watch as Moe, Larry and Curly raise havoc as photographers in "Dutiful but Dumb" (1941), "Hollywood executives" in "Movie Maniacs" (1936), and panhandlers who strike black gold in "Oily to Bed, Oily to Rise" (1939). 60 min. total.

02-1236 Was $29.99 *$14.99*

The Three Stooges: Cash And Carry

In "Cash and Carry" (1937), Moe, Larry and Curly are treasure hunters who break into a U.S. Mint. "No Census, No Feeling" (1940) has the boys as census-takers, and "Some More of Samoa" (1941) finds them as tree doctors looking for the Puckerless Persimmon. 60 min. total.

02-1284 Was $29.99 *$14.99*

The Three Stooges: Yes, We Have No Bonanza

Moe, Larry and Curly head for Egypt and the tomb of King Rootin-Tootin in "We Want Our Mummy" (1939). In "Restless Knights" (1935), the Queen is kidnapped and her "stalwart" guards must find her. Finally, the Stooges are out West looking for gold in "Yes, We Have No Bonanza" (1939). 60 min. total.

02-1319 Was $29.99 ❑*$14.99*

The Three Stooges: If A Body Meets A Body

Spread out, so everyone can watch Moe, Larry and Curly as inept bodyguards who foil enemy spies in "Spook Louder" (1943). Next is the Stooges' Oscar-nominated hospital spoof, "Men in Black" (1934). Then Curly is heir to a fortune in "If a Body Meets a Body" (1943). 60 min. total.

02-1354 Was $29.99 ❑*$14.99*

The Three Stooges: What's The Matador?

Moe, Larry and Curly find themselves in the Army in "Boobs in Arms" (1940). Next it's a trip down to Mexico to throw the bull in "What's the Matador?" (1942), followed by "Mutts to You" (1938), with the boys as "dog wash" owners who find an abandoned baby. 55 min. total.

02-1397 Was $29.99 ❑*$14.99*

The Three Stooges: Three Little Pigskins

The boys are hired to "play" college football in "Three Little Pigskins" (1934), with a young Lucille Ball. Next a gorilla drives the Stooges ape when they're "Dizzy Detectives" (1943), and in "Sock-A-Bye Baby" (1942) an abandoned baby makes them instant fathers. 55 min. total.

02-1498 Was $29.99 ❑*$14.99*

The Three Stooges: They Stooge To Conga

The Axis powers had to fight on the European Front, the Pacific Front and the Stooge Front. Watch as repairmen Larry, Moe and Curly uncover an enemy spy nest in "They Stooge to Conga" (1941), followed by the boys' hilarious Hitler spoofs, "You Nazty Spy!" (1940) and "I'll Never Heil Again" (1940). 55 min. total.

02-1921 *$14.99*

The Three Stooges: Cookoo Cavaliers

Would you trust your hair to the Three Stooges? That's what happens when Curly, Moe and Larry buy a "beauty saloon" in "Cookoo Cavaliers" (1940). Never ones to shirk hard work, they also enter a milking contest in "Busy Buddies" (1944) and set out in a fishing boat in "Booby Dupes" (1945). 55 min. total.

02-1922 *$14.99*

The Three Stooges: Crash Goes The Hash

The Stooges try to cash in on an insurance policy by having Curly pretend to be insane (pretend?) in "From Nurse to Worse" (1940). "Crash Goes the Hash" (1944) finds the boys as newshounds out to take society photos, while the post-WWII housing shortage is spoofed in "G.I. Wanna Home" (1946). 55 min. total.

02-1923 *$14.99*

The Three Stooges: How High Is Up?

"Pygmalion" gets that special Stooge treatment with "Half-Wits' Holiday" (1947), Curly's last short with the team. Next, head out West with a hearty cry of "Moe, Larry, cheese!" in "Horse Collars" (1935), and find out "How High Is Up?" (1940) when the boys work as steeplejacks. 53 min. total.

02-1924 *$14.99*

The Three Stooges: Idiots Deluxe

Curly and Larry take Moe for a "restful" vacation in the woods in "Idiots Deluxe" (1945). Next, Curly's toothache keeps everybody in pain in "I Can Hardly Wait" (1944), while "Idle Roomers" (1944) finds the boys in a hotel with a werewolf. 55 min. total.

02-1925 *$14.99*

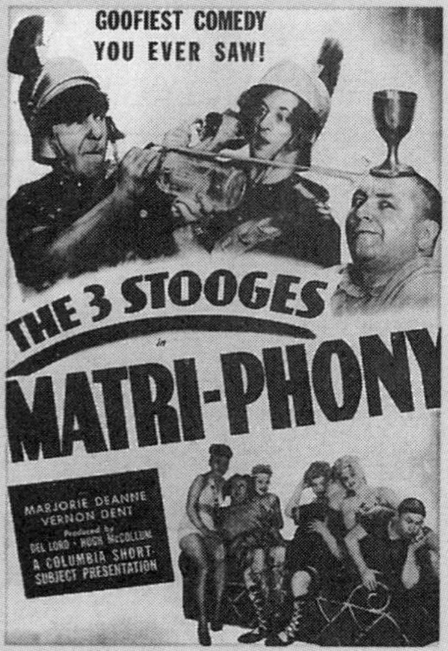

GOOFIEST COMEDY
YOU EVER SAW!
THE 3 STOOGES
in
MATRI-PHONY
MARJORIE DEANNE
VERNON DENT
Produced by
DEL LORD · HUGH McCOLLUM
A COLUMBIA SHORT SUBJECT PRESENTATION

The Three Stooges: Loco Boy Makes Good

It's "Loco Boy Makes Good" (1942) when Curly, Larry and Moe help an elderly woman keep her hotel. The Stooges are in Ancient Rome in "Matri-Phony" (1942), when a disguised Curly becomes the emperor's wife, then they're three inept salesmen in "Saved by the Belle" (1939). 55 min. total.

02-1436 Was $29.99 ❑*$14.99*

The Three Stooges: Higher Than A Kite

Who else but Larry, Moe and Curly could try to become R.A.F. pilots and wind up in a bomb dropped on General Bommel's headquarters? It happens in "Higher than a Kite" (1943), followed by the trio's encounter with escaped Japanese POWs in "The Yoke's on Me" (1944) and their masquerade as three Japanese soldiers in a Nazi spy nest in "No Dough, Boys" (1944). 55 min. total.

02-2553 *$14.99*

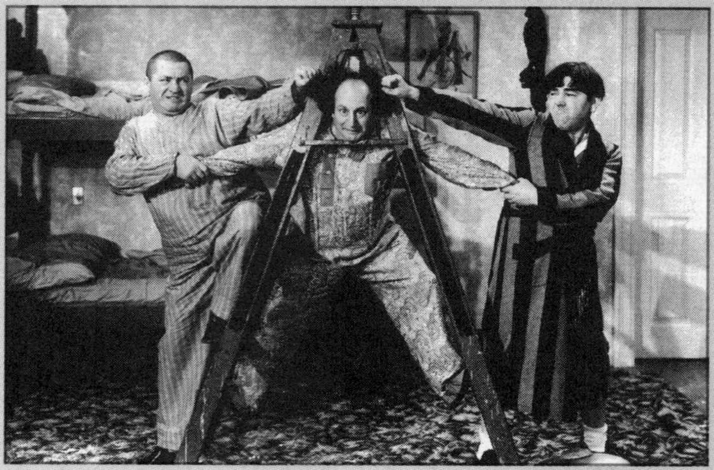

The Three Stooges

The Three Stooges: Nutty But Nice

Larry, Curly and Moe are "coitenly" "Nutty But Nice" (1940) when they help look for a little girl's missing father. Next, they're "The Sitter-Downers" (1937) when they strike to gain the right to marry three sisters, and in "Slippery Silks" (1936) they're furniture designers who inherit a dress shop. 55 min. total.

02-1926 *$14.99*

The Three Stooges: Three Little Pirates

Moe, Larry and Curly use their classic "Maha!" ("A ha!") routine to escape an evil ruler's clutches in "Three Little Pirates" (1946), help the Pilgrims settle the colonies in "Back to the Woods" (1937), and wind up on opposite sides of the war in "Uncivil War Birds" (1946). 55 min. total.

02-1980 *$14.99*

The Three Stooges: Monkey Businessmen

When their fiancées' father is framed, Larry, Moe and Curly go into jail to help him in "Three Smart Saps" (1942). The Stooges' plans to make their own beer blow up in their faces in "Beer Barrel Polecats" (1946), and a rest home visit is anything but restful in "Monkey Businessmen" (1946). 55 min. total.

02-1981 *$14.99*

The Three Stooges: All The World's A Stooge

Move over, Hulkster! Moe, Larry and Curly step into the wrestling ring in "Grips, Grunts and Groans" (1937). Next, the boys try to talk their pa (who looks just like Curly) out of marrying a golddigger in "Three Dumb Clucks" (1937), and they're "war orphans" in "All the World's a Stooge" (1941). 55 min. total.

02-1982 *$14.99*

The Three Stooges: Rhythm And Weep

Would-be vaudevillians Moe, Larry and Curly team up with three gorgeous actresses when an eccentric millionaire offers to sponsor them in a stage show in "Rhythm and Weep" (1946). The boys go "Back to the Front" (1943) as Merchant Marines who uncover a Nazi spy ring and become "The Three Troubledoers" (1946) out West to save a girl from outlaws. 55 min. total.

02-2551 *$14.99*

The Three Stooges: So Long, Mr. Chumps

The search for an honest man leads Moe, Curly and Larry to prison(!) in "So Long, Mr. Chumps" (1941). "Three Loan Wolves" (1946) finds the Stooges as pawnbrokers who wind up caring for an abandoned infant; and they become owners of Seabiscuit, the "talking" horse, in "Even as I.O.U." (1942). 55 min. total.

02-2555 *$14.99*

The Three Stooges: Hoi Polloi

Can trash haulers Moe, Larry and Curly be turned into refined gentlemen? That's the wager two educators make in "Hoi Polloi" (1936). Next, the boys play janitors who are mistaken for doctors by crooks in "A Gem of a Jam" (1943), and are ex-soldiers who mistakenly re-enlist, much to the delight of their sadistic sergeant, in "Half-Shot Shooters" (1936). 53 min. total.

02-2888 *$14.99*

The Three Stooges: False Alarms

Going to parties is more important than battling blazes to firemen Moe, Curly and Larry in "False Alarms" (1936). Also, the fellas are "Three Pests in a Mess" (1945) when some crooks think they're contest winners, and "Flat Foot Stooges" (1938) finds the boys back to fighting fires—this time in their own station! 48 min. total.

02-2889 *$14.99*

The Three Stooges: A Ducking They Did Go

After selling fake duck club memberships to the police chief and other officials, Larry, Curly and Moe have to supply their own gamebirds in "A Ducking They Did Go" (1939). A swanky party has pest problems, thanks to the boys' exterminator techniques, in "Ants in the Pantry" (1936), followed by Stooge madness under the big top in "Three Little Twerps" (1943). 55 min. total.

02-2556 *$14.99*

The Three Stooges: In The Sweet Pie And Pie

In order to collect an inheritance, three sisters marry condemned convicts Moe, Larry and Curly in "In the Sweet Pie and Pie" (1941), but the joke's on them when the boys are pardoned. "Phony Express" (1943) finds our heroes as salesmen out West who are mistaken for outlaws; while they make the leap from hashslingers to racehorse owners in "Playing the Ponies" (1937). 55 min. total.

02-2557 *$14.99*

The Three Stooges: Dizzy Doctors

Pitchmen Moe, Larry and Curly try selling their miracle product Brighto ("makes old bodies new") at Los Arms Hospital in "Dizzy Doctors" (1938). "Goofs and Saddles" (1937) finds Moe as Wild Bill Hiccup, Curly as Buffalo Billious and Larry as Just Plain Bill after cattle rustlers, and the boys are Navy laundrymen who masquerade as officers in "Three Little Sew and Sews" (1939). 51 min. total.

02-2890 *$14.99*

The Three Stooges: A Pain In The Pullman

Vaudeville performers Moe, Curly and Larry have their hands full when their pet monkey gets loose on the train in "A Pain in the Pullman" (1936). "Gents Without Cents" (1944) is highlighted by the classic "Niagara Falls" sketch," and "Termites of 1938" (1938) follows the boys as exterminators who are accidentally hired as escorts at a swanky society party. 55 min. total.

02-3023 *$14.99*

The Three Stooges: Whoops I'm An Indian

Frontier con men Moe, Larry and Curly masquerade as Indians to escape the law, then must dodge a burly trapper who's fallen for "squaw" Curly in "Whoops I'm an Indian" (1936). Next, the boys are scouts leading a group of chorus girls out West in "Rockin' Through the Rockies" (1940), while "Cactus Makes Perfect" (1942) finds them trying their hand at gold prospecting. 72 min. total.

02-3025 *$14.99*

The Three Stooges: Curly Classics 2-Pack

Why be a "victim of coicumstance"? Celebrate the most beloved Stooge of them all with this two-tape set featuring some of Curly's craziest comedies. "Cactus Makes Perfect," "Gents Without Cents," "Termites of 1938," "Rockin' Thru the Rockies" and "Whoops I'm an Indian" make up Volume 1, while Volume 2 includes "Men in Black," "Micro-Phonies," "Punch Drunks," "Three Little Pigskins" and "Woman Haters." 170 min. total. NOTE: Individual volumes available at $19.99 each.

02-3257 Save $5.00! *$34.99*

The Three Stooges: Who Done It?

Shemp, Larry and Moe are boxing managers who get into trouble with gangsters in "Fright Night" (1947), Shemp's first film with the team. The boys take a train to track down a con artist in "Hold That Lion" (1947), with a cameo from Curly, and play detective when they try to solve "Who Done It?" (1949). 55 min. total.

02-1977 *$14.99*

The Three Stooges: Wee Wee Monsieur
After spending time seeing the Paris sights, Larry, Moe and Curly accidentally join the French Foreign Legion in "Wee Wee Monsieur" (1938). Shemp takes over "third stooge" duty for "Pardon My Clutch" (1948), in which a planned camping trip never gets past the fellas' front door, and "Fiddlers Three" (1948), where the fellas help Old King Cole find his missing daughter. 50 min. total.
02-3024 *$14.99*

The Three Stooges: Fuelin' Around
Moe, Larry and Shemp meet up with "ghosts" in Glenheather Castle in "Hot Scots" (1948), develop a special "rocket fuel" in "Fuelin' Around" (1949), and teach dancing to some South Seas natives in "Hula-La-La" (1951). 55 min. total.
02-1978 *$14.99*

The Three Stooges: Shivering Sherlocks
As "Studio Stoops" (1950), publicity men Moe, Shemp and Larry plan a starlet's "kidnapping" that becomes the real thing. Jewel thieves plan an operation when Shemp swallows the Punjab Diamond in "Crime on Their Hands" (1948), while the boys have to face a brute named Angel ("He'll do a nice quiet job") in "Shivering Sherlocks" (1948). 55 min. total.
02-1979 *$14.99*

The Three Stooges: Three Arabian Nuts
Shemp, Larry and Moe never had a friend like the genie they find in an antique lamp in "Three Arabian Nuts" (1951). Next, the boys are tailors who sew up some crooks in "Sing a Song of Six Pants" (1947) and druggists who invent a "youth serum" in "All Gummed Up" (1947). 55 min. total.
02-2550 *$14.99*

The Three Stooges: Gents In A Jam
A landlady looking for rent, a wrestler looking for his wife, and a visit by rich Uncle Phineas add up to trouble for Moe, Larry and Shemp, the "Gents in a Jam" (1952). Also, some jewel thieves have a run-in with the Stooges in "A Snitch in Time" (1950); and installing a TV antenna turns into a disaster in "Goof on the Roof" (1953). 55 min. total.
02-2552 *$14.99*

The Three Stooges: I'm A Monkey's Uncle
It's "Jurassic Stooges" when cavemen Moe, Shemp and Larry get their clubs out to do some courting in "I'm a Monkey's Uncle" (1948). Next, the boys turn troubador to help a blacksmith win a princess's hand in "Squareheads of the Round Table" (1948); and "Mummy's Dummies" (1948) finds them as used-chariot salesmen in ancient Egypt. 55 min. total.
02-2554 *$14.99*

The Three Stooges: Out West
Shemp's "vein trouble" sends the fellas "Out West" (1947), where they get mixed up with outlaws and save the heroic Arizona Kid. There's more frontier frolics when the Stooges and the Kid re-team to stop gold thieves in "Punchy Cowpunchers" (1950), followed by the boys being mistaken for lawmen in "Merry Mavericks" (1951). 51 min. total.
02-2891 *$14.99*

The Three Stooges: Dopey Dicks
A scientist lacks a human brain for his headless robot man, but will private eyes Moe, Larry and Shemp have what he needs in "Dopey Dicks" (1950)? Next, ex-sanitarium patient Shemp may not be over his hallucinations, as he plans to wed his homely nurse, in "Scrambled Brains" (1951), and the boys are frontier dentists in "The Tooth Will Out" (1951). 47 min. total.
02-2892 *$14.99*

The Three Stooges: Listen, Judge
Inept repairmen Larry, Moe and Shemp fill in as kitchen "help" for a dinner party in "Listen, Judge" (1952). Next, the boys are druggists who think they've invented a youth serum in "Bubble Trouble" (1953), and unwilling stowaways on an ocean liner with a foreign spy named Bortch in "Dunked in the Deep" (1949). 51 min. total.
02-2893 *$14.99*

The Three Stooges: Corny Casanovas
The course of true love takes a daffy detour in "Corny Casanovas" (1952), as Shemp, Moe and Larry all fall for the same gold-digger. Shemp's cry of "bunyon ache!" wins him a $50,000 (before taxes) radio jackpot in "A Missed Fortune" (1952), followed by Larry scheming to woo away Moe's wife and Shemp's fiancée in "He Cooked His Goose" (1952). 48 min. total.
02-3026 *$14.99*

The Three Stooges: Heavenly Daze
Sent down from Heaven, would-be angel Shemp has to reform Larry and Moe in order to win his wings in "Heavenly Daze" (1948). "The Ghost Talks" (1949) has the boys as movers who are spooked by a haunted suit of armor (and a skeleton named Red), while the great hypnotist Svengarlic clouds their minds (more than usual) and sends them out on a skyscraper flagpole in "Hocus Pocus" (1949). 49 min. total.
02-3027 *$14.99*

Three Stooges Festival
Three of their zaniest shorts. "Disorder in the Court" (1936) has Curly, Larry and Moe as star witnesses in a murder case. "Malice in the Palace" (1949) is a Middle Eastern farce where Shemp, Larry and Moe are out to find the treasure of the tomb of King Rootin' Tootin', and the boys are tailors in "Sing a Song of Six Pants" (1947). 52 min. total.
05-1430 *$14.99*

The Three Stooges: Vagabond Loafers
"This house has sho' gone crazy" when plumbers Larry, Shemp and Moe are called in to fix a leak at a swank mansion in "Vagabond Loafers" (1949), and crash another society gathering as exterminators who supply their own pests in "The Pest Man Wins" (1951). Finally, the boys enter the political arena in the slapstick satire "Three Dark Horses" (1952). 48 min. total.
02-3028 *$14.99*

Start Cheering (1938)
All-star campus musical farce with Charles Starrett (westerns' Durango Kid) as a Hollywood matinee idol who decides to go to college in order to escape the spotlight. His managers (Walter Connolly and Jimmy Durante) try to bring him back to the studio. The Three Stooges play firemen who help the football team in a big game. With Broderick Crawford, Joan Perry, Louis Prima and His Orchestra. 80 min.
15-9025 Was $19.99 *$14.99*

Cookin' Up Trouble (1944)
In order to stop their young charge from being taken to an orphanage, Shemp Howard, Billy Gilbert and Maxie Rosenbloom go to hilarious lengths to keep the boy in this heartwarming comedy. AKA: "Three of a Kind." 67 min.
15-9022 Was $19.99 *$14.99*

Ghost Crazy (Crazy Knights) (1944)
Join Shemp Howard and Billy Gilbert as carnival performers who team with wacky chauffeur Maxie Rosenbloom in a haunted mansion, where they try to save an heiress from a murder plot, in this spooky comedy. Tim Ryan, Jayne Hazard co-star. 60 min.
15-9045 *$19.99*

Trouble Chasers (1945)
The mob tries to get into the boxing world by fixing fights, which presents trouble for Shemp Howard, Maxie Rosenbloom and Billy Gilbert and laughs for us. 60 min.
15-9021 Was $19.99 *$14.99*

The Three Stooges: Jerks Of All Trades (1949)
In 1949, Moe, Larry and Shemp made a half-hour pilot for a planned TV series. Never aired, the show features the fellas as inept interior decorators who wreck the home of clients (and big-screen foils) Emil Sitka and Symona Boniface. Also included on this video are highlights from a 1998 Three Stooges convention, with knuckleheads aplenty. 40 min. total.
08-8737 *$12.99*

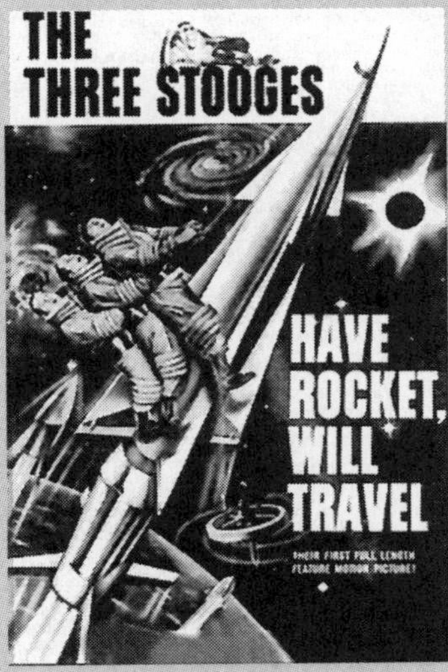

Have Rocket, Will Travel (1959)
Astro-nuts Moe, Larry and Curly Joe made their first feature together in this space spoof that has them trapped in a rocket and launched to the planet Venus, where the slapstick trio finds a talking unicorn, giant spiders and other oddities. With Jerome Cowan, Anna-Lisa, Robert Colbert. 76 min.
02-2768 *$14.99*

Stop! Look! And Laugh! (1960)
Who can help but laugh at this collection of the Three Stooges' funniest screen moments? There's clips from "Micro Phonies," "What's the Matador?," "How High Is Up?" and other shorts, sandwiched around commentary from hosts Paul Winchell, Jerry Mahoney and Knucklehead Smif. 78 min.
02-2770 *$14.99*

Snow White And The Three Stooges (1961)
Skating and slapstick mix when Snow White (Olympic skating star Carol Heiss) is protected from the evil Queen by hapless heroes Moe, Larry and Curly Joe in an exciting and funny fairy tale for the whole family. 108 min.
04-3055 *$14.99*

The Three Stooges Meet Hercules (1962)
Those lovable knuckleheads, Moe, Larry and Curly Joe, journey back to ancient Greece, where they become prisoners on a galley ship, have a run-in with a pair of Cyclopean brothers and meet the famous strongman. Co-stars Vicki Trickett, Quinn Redeker. 89 min.
02-2755 *$14.99*

The Three Stooges In Orbit (1962)
Blast off with Moe, Larry and Curly Joe, as the boys protect inventor Emil Sitka's rocket-sub-tank weapon from a pair of scheming Martians named Ogg and Zogg, in this feature-length romp. With Edson Stroll, Carol Christensen. 87 min.
02-2766 *$14.99*

The Three Stooges Go Around The World In A Daze (1963)
It's a "kook's tour" when Larry, Moe and Curly Joe help Phileas Fogg III follow in the globe-trotting footsteps of his famous great-grandfather, but can the crazy quartet make it around the world in 80 days without paying for any transportation? Feature-length farce also stars Jay Sheffield, Joan Freeman. 94 min.
02-2769 *$14.99*

The Outlaws Is Coming (1965)
A wacky western spoof that was the final film for the Three Stooges as a team. Conservation-minded Larry, Moe and Curly Joe head to the frontier to save the buffalo and wind up helping a newspaper editor (Adam West) and the famed Annie Oakley (Nancy Kovack) battle a passel of the prairie's toughest gunslingers (played by such TV kids' show hosts as Officer Joe Bolton, Bill "Icky Twerp" Camfield and Philly's own Sally Starr). Look for Henry Gibson as an Indian. 88 min.
02-2767 *$14.99*

The Three Stooges: Kook's Tour (1970)
The beloved slapstick screen trio made their final appearance together in this pilot for a proposed TV series. After retiring from show business, Moe, Larry and Curly Joe pack up their camper and, along with faithful dog Moose, set out on a "relaxing" fishing vacation that proves to be anything but. 53 min.
08-8738 *$12.99*

The Joe Palooka Festival
Featured here are "Kick Me Again" and "The Choke's on You," two "Joe Palooka" shorts from the mid-1930s with Robert Norton as the not-so-bright pugilist and Shemp Howard as manager Knobby Walsh, followed by "Turkey for Terry," from 1954's "The Joe Palooka Story" TV series, with Joe Kirkwood, Jr., Luis Van Rooten and "Slapsy" Maxie Rosenbloom. 65 min.
10-9395 *$24.99*

Shemp's Night Out
Stooge completists won't want to miss these two shorts the great Shemp did for Vitaphone before he rejoined Larry and brother Moe. Shemp co-stars with the legendary Fatty Arbuckle in "In the Dough" and "Close Relations." What a wacky night out! 40 min.
15-9018 Was $19.99 *$14.99*

Shemp Steps In
A rare find and a great package: four Vitaphone shorts featuring a solo Shemp Howard. Titles include "Why Pay Rent," "A Peach of a Pair," "I Scream," and the Joe Palooka short "The Choke's on You," with Shemp as Joe's manager, Knobby Walsh. 80 min.
15-9019 Was $19.99 *$14.99*

Mondo Shemp
The great Shempster in some rarely seen '30s shorts from his Vitaphone days. Included are "Dizzy and Daffy" (with baseball's famed Dean Brothers), "Serves You Right," "Here Comes Flossie!" and the fireman comedy "His First Flame." 80 min.
15-9020 Was $19.99 *$14.99*

Shemp And Sitka: Hi Ho Boys!
What a comedic combo! It's Shemp Howard and Stooges regular Emil Sitka in two uproarious shorts from slapstick's finest days. "Where the Pests Begin" (1945) features Shemp as an exterminator who acts like a pest to his customers. In "Hiss and Yell," Shemp and Emil are joined by comedienne Verra Vague. 40 min.
15-9026 Was $19.99 *$14.99*

Sitka's Shorts
The ever-popular Emil Sitka, known as "The Fourth Stooge," is featured in four comedy shorts from RKO. Comics Andy Clyde and Leon Errol also turn up for laughs in "Night Club Dance," "Punchy Cowpuncher," "Newlyweds Take a Chance" and "The Fresh Painter." 80 min.
15-9027 Was $19.99 *$14.99*

The Two Joe's
Some say Curly, some say Shemp. But how about the two Joes: Joe De Rita and Joe Besser? These underrated funnymen who played "Third Stooge" are featured in two shorts. Besser's in "Caught on the Bounce" (1952), while De Rita shines with Christine McIntyre in "Slappily Married" (1946). 40 min.
15-9029 Was $19.99 *$14.99*

The Three Stooges Potpourri
See Moe, Larry and Curly with Ted Healy in the 1932 MGM musical short "Hollywood on Parade." Shemp appears in a rare 1937 solo short, "Knife of the Party," and joins Moe and Larry in a live TV appearance on "The Ed Wynn Show" from 1950. With film trailers and a '60s TV commercial with Moe, Larry and Curly-Joe. 65 min.
10-2124 Was $19.99 *$14.99*

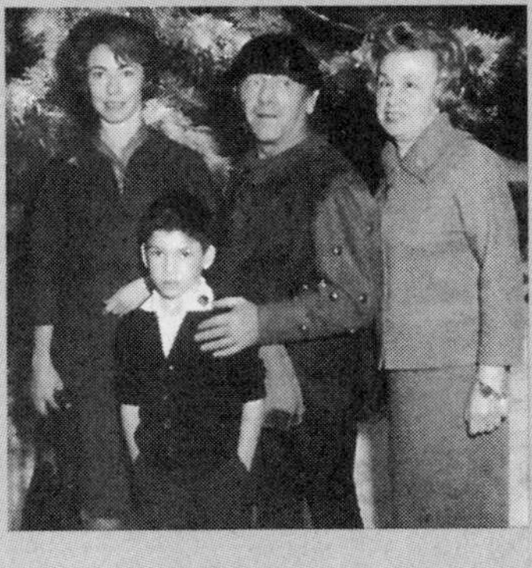

The Three Stooges Family Album
If you've ever wondered what Moe, Larry, Curly and company were like off the set, this collection of vintage home movie footage—much of it never before seen on video—gives you a rare glimpse at the Stooges' private lives. See the fellas on the road with Ted Healy, on a transatlantic cruise and touring London; watch Moe host a backyard barbecue; join Curly Joe's birthday party; see photographs and hear stories from family members; and much more. 27 min.
08-8684 *$14.99*

The Stooges Home Movies
Real rare stuff, soitain to make you laugh, including home movies of Moe, Larry and Curly appearing on stage in Chicago in the 1940s, a county fair performance with Joe DeRita in the early '60s, clowning around on the set of "The Outlaws Is Coming," a family barbecue and more. 30 min.
15-9028 Was $19.99 *$14.99*

Three Stooges Scrapbook, Vol. 4
Along with the ABC-TV pilot "Goofs of the Trade" (1949), with Shemp, Larry and Moe, this tape also features the boys in the short "Brideless Groom" (1947), followed by Moe, Larry and Curly Joe as "Star Spangled Salesmen" (1968) for U.S. Savings Bonds, in a Treasury Department film that also features Milton Berle, Carol Burnett, Tim Conway and Howard Morris.
10-7427 Was $19.99 *$14.99*

Three Stooges Scrapbook, Vol. 6
Four more eccentric two-reelers featuring pre-Stooge Shemp Howard, including "I Scream," "Serves You Right," "Here Comes Flossie!" and "Dizzy and Daffy." Ah-cheep-cheep-cheep!
10-7429 Was $19.99 *$14.99*

The Joy Of Stooge-ing
A real collector's anthology of Three Stooges finds. See an animated Curly, the young and "handsome" Shemp, Moe going solo with nightclub comics and soitainly much more. And you thought you've seen everything the boys ever appeared in!
10-7941 Was $19.99 *$14.99*

The Stooges: Lost And Found
Here's the one Stoogemaniacs have been waiting for: the rarely seen pilot episode of the Three Stooges' weekly comedy series on ABC, featuring Larry, Moe and Shemp. The boys are interior decorators who turn the house they're working on topsy-turvy. Emil Sitka and Joseph Kearns (Mr. Wilson from "Dennis the Menace" fame) also appear.
10-7942 Was $19.99 *$14.99*

The Lost Stooges
A treasure trove of Stoogeiana, featuring Moe, Larry and Curly in their first screen appearances, alongside Ted Healy. See the boys in early '30s MGM films, clowning with Gable, Crawford and Durante, plus scenes from their rare Technicolor short subjects. Leonard Maltin hosts. 68 min.
18-7213 *$14.99*

50 Years With The Three Stooges
Take a rare look into the lives and careers of Hollywood's wildest slapstick team. Scenes from films, rare footage and interviews with family, friends and co-workers trace the 50-year comedy history of Moe, Larry, Curly, Shemp, Joe and Curly Joe. A must for Stooges fans; narrated by Steve Allen. 90 min.
40-1048 *$24.99*

The Three Stooges Comedy Adventure
So you think you know everything there's to know about the Three Stooges, eh? Well, spread out, you knuckleheads, because this great tribute is jammed with more information, interviews, and rare footage than ever before revealed...and that ain't just soicumstance! 55 min.
50-6222 *$19.99*

The Three Stooges: Nyuks x 10 Giftbox
It's "stooges galore" with this 10-tape boxed set featuring 30 shorts. The volumes include "A Plumbing We Will Go," "Crash Goes the Hash," "Higher Than a Kite," "I'm a Monkey's Uncle," "Yes, We Have No Bonanza," "In the Sweet Pie and Pie," "If a Body Meets a Body," "Idiot's Deluxe," "Movie Maniacs" and "Loco Boy Makes Good," and many more.
02-2894 Save $20.00! *$129.99*

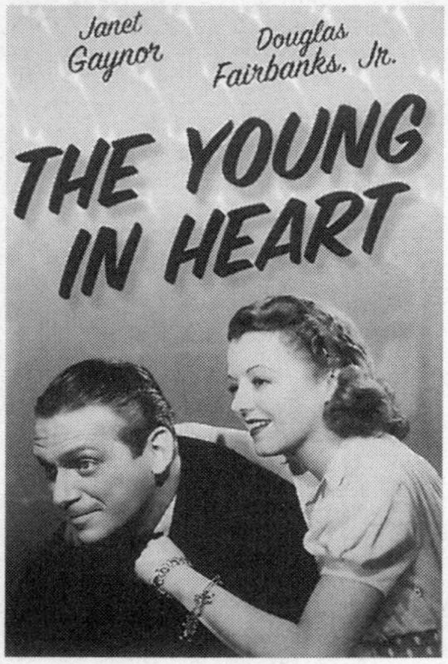

The Young In Heart (1938)
Winning and warm comedy focusing on a family of con artists who meet their match and are shown the error of their ways by a charming old woman during a European train trip. Stars Roland Young, Minnie Dupree, Janet Gaynor, Douglas Fairbanks, Jr. and Paulette Goddard. 94 min.
08-8171 *$14.99*

Three Men On A Horse (1936)
Stylish farce about a greeting card writer with a knack for choosing the winners at racetracks. A group of gamblers kidnap him and force him to pick the horses for their profit. Little do his captors know that when he attends the track, his talent is ineffective. Frank McHugh, Joan Blondell, Sam Levene, Guy Kibbee and Eddie "Rochester" Anderson lead the cast. 96 min.
12-2490 ◻*$19.99*

Lady Behave (1937)
Light-hearted romantic romp about a woman who elopes with a millionaire after drinking too much at a party. Problem is, she's already married, and her sister must impersonate her in order to save the twice-wed woman from a bigamy charge! Sally Eilers, Neil Hamilton, Patricia Farr star. 55 min.
10-8208 *$19.99*

Pygmalion (1938)
George Bernard Shaw wrote this adaptation of his play, on which the musical "My Fair Lady" was later based. Leslie Howard and Wendy Hiller star in this delightful version of Professor Henry Higgins' attempt to turn Cockney flower seller Eliza Doolittle into an elegant lady. 90 min.
22-5806 *$24.99*

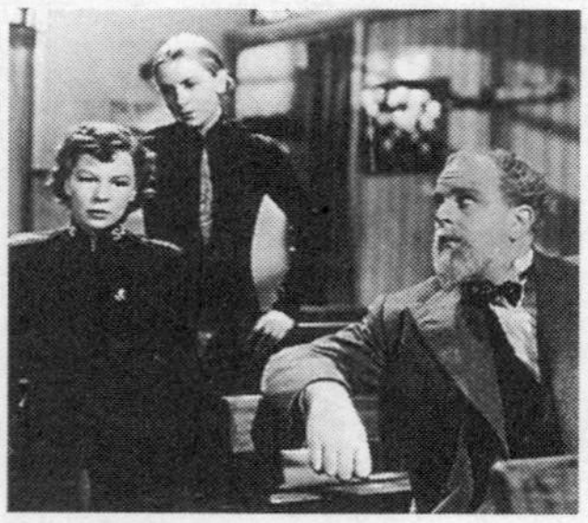

Major Barbara (1941)
George Bernard Shaw's pointed look at capitalism and social "do-gooders" features Rex Harrison as a teacher smitten with heiress-turned-Salvation Army worker Wendy Hiller. Robert Morley co-stars as Hiller's father, owner of a munitions factory and target of his daughter's anti-business crusades. With Deborah Kerr, Robert Newton. 131 min.
22-5438 Was $39.99 *$29.99*

Androcles And The Lion (1952)
Travel back to Ancient Rome in this film adaptation of George Bernard Shaw's classic fable of a stalwart slave who removes a thorn from a lion's paw and gains a friend. But will their friendship carry them through a bout at the Colosseum? Alan Young, Jean Simmons and Victor Mature star. 100 min.
22-5801 Remastered *$29.99*

George Bernard Shaw Gift Set
The master playwright's comic genius is evidenced in this collector's set featuring three Shavian films. Included are "Androcles and the Lion," "Major Barbara" and "Pygmalion."
22-5808 Save $5.00! *$79.99*

Edgar Kennedy Comedies
Edgar Kennedy's "slow-burn" antics are wonderfully displayed on this collection that offers five full-length shorts. Included are "The Hillbilly Goat" (1936), "Ears of Experience" (1937), "I'll Fix It" (1941), "Love Your Landlord" (1943) and "Mothers-in-Laws Day" (1945).
03-5020 *$24.99*

Robert Benchley And The Knights Of The Algonquin
One of the leading lights of the Algonquin Round Table, writer and humorist Robert Benchley, is featured in a selection of the short films he made for the Fox and Paramount studios. Included are "The Treasurer's Report" (1928), "The Sex Life of a Polyp" (1928), "The Trouble with Husbands" (1940), "The Witness" (1941), "Crime Control" (1941) and "The Man's Angle" (1942), along with Alexander Woollcott in "Mr. W's Little Game" (1934), and Donald Ogden Stewart in "Humorous Flights" (1929) and "Traffic Regulations" (1929). 86 min.
53-6299 *$24.99*

Cavalcade Of Comedy
In the early days of talking pictures, Paramount brought some of the top stars of Broadway and vaudeville to its Astoria studio in Queens to capture their songs and comedy routines on film. Among the talents featured in this collection are Burns and Allen in "Fit to Be Tied" (1930) and "100% Service" (1931), Jack Benny in "A Broadway Romeo" (1931), "Getting a Ticket" (1929) with Eddie Cantor, George Jessel in "It Might Be Worse" (1931), the legendary Smith & Dale in "What Price, Pants?" (1931) and others. 111 min.
53-6300 *$24.99*

Boys Will Be Girls (1937)
British comedy follows the plight of a party-loving bloke who has to give up smoking and drinking to gain a hefty inheritance. Leslie Fuller is the profligate out to make "easy money." 66 min.
17-3074 *$19.99*

Ruggles Of Red Gap (1935)
Classic comedy from director Leo McCarey stars Charles Laughton as a very proper English "gentleman's gentleman" who is lost in a poker game and becomes the butler to a rancher's family in the Old West. The great cast includes Charlie Ruggles, Mary Boland and ZaSu Pitts. 90 min.
07-1563 Was $29.99 *$14.99*

Lost In The Stratosphere (1935)
Two Air Force lieutenants who constantly play practical jokes on each other have words over the same woman, which leads to a real-life feud. William Cagney, Edward Nugent and June Collyer star. 64 min.
10-8251 *$19.99*

Ticket To Paradise (1936)
A wacky screwball farce centering on an amnesia victim who runs off with a young woman, prompting the girl's father to hire a detective to find the couple. Roger Pryor, Wendy Barrie and Claude Gillingwater star. 70 min.
10-8316 *$19.99*

Manhattan Love Song (1934)
Following their financial advisor's death, two wealthy sisters find themselves penniless. They allow their chauffeur and maid to move in with them, leading to funny situations. Robert Armstrong and Dixie Lee and Franklin Pangborn star. 72 min.
10-8338 Was $19.99 *$14.99*

A Woman's Man (1934)
John Halliday, Margueritte De La Motte and Wallace Ford star in this romantic farce about a temperamental movie star who quits her current film in order to continue a whirlwind romance with a colorful boxer. 64 min.
10-8340 Was $19.99 *$14.99*

Money Talks (1933)
Sort of a Jewish version of "Brewster's Millions," this comedy tells the story about a man who will inherit a half-million dollars from his sister if he can spend his entire bank account in 30 days. Julian Rose, Kid Berg and Gladdy Sewell star. 66 min.
10-8346 Was $19.99 *$14.99*

Strangers Of The Evening (1932)
Comedienne ZaSu Pitts heads the hilarious proceedings in this comedy chiller, as the city morgue is thrown into turmoil by a missing corpse, and a detective ferrets out a political cover-up. With Eugene Pallette, Tully Marshall. 70 min.
68-8044 *$19.99*

Slander House (1938)
The title house in question is in fact a beauty parlor whose staff and clients delight in hearing and spreading the latest gossip and rumors about their friends, from gambling to adultery, without regard to the truth or the consequences. Adrianne Ames, Esther Ralston star.
68-9096 *$19.99*

A Successful Failure (1934)
"Mr. Ed" auteur Arthur Lubin launched his directing career with this unpretentious little comedy about a hard-bitten newspaper man (William Collier, Sr.) who makes the best of his problems, including an inconsiderate family and his recent firing, to hit it big on the radio. With Lucille Gleason. 61 min.
09-2287 *$19.99*

One Rainy Afternoon (1936)
Frothy romantic comedy set in Paris, where playboy actor Frances Lederer kisses Ida Lupino in a movie theater, thinking she's his date. Lederer's subsequent arrest on morals charges becomes a national scandal, makes him a celebrity, and brings him and Lupino together. With Hugh Herbert, Roland Young. 78 min.
09-1261 *$19.99*

The Frozen Limits (1939)
Six top English music hall comics teamed up as "The Crazy Gang" to make a series of slapstick comedy films. Here the guys head off to Alaska when they read a newspaper headline about a gold strike...unaware the paper was 40 years old! 84 min.
17-3007 Was $19.99 *$14.99*

Okay For Sound (1945)
Lively British farce with the Crazy Gang as six wacky, unemployed brothers who get jobs at a Hollywood studio thanks to their page boy relative and wind up being mistaken for important movie executives. Fred Duprez, Graham Moffat, Jimmy Nervo star. 85 min.
10-9256 Was $19.99 *$14.99*

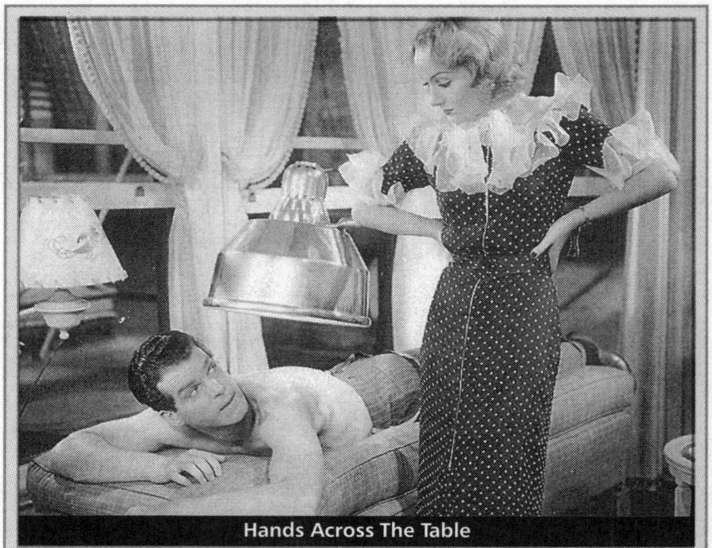
Hands Across The Table

Carole Lombard

Big News (1929)
Crackerjack newspaper tale about a tough reporter who's fired while trying to expose one of his paper's biggest advertisers. He goes out on his own and discovers that the man he's investigating is guilty of murder. Robert Armstrong, Carole Lombard and Tom Kennedy star in this drama from Gregory La Cava ("My Man Godfrey"). 75 min.
17-9044 *$19.99*

High Voltage (1929)
Early talkie feature for Carole Lombard features her as a sherrif's prisoner, one of a busload of passengers trapped in a remote mountain cabin during a snowstorm, who falls for a man staying at the cabin who's had his own problems with the law. William Boyd, Billy Bevan also star. 57 min.
62-1200 *$19.99*

The Racketeer (1929)
This trend-setting gangster film stars Carole Lombard as an attractive young woman who accepts the advances of a cocky racketeer, played by Robert Armstrong, to promote the career of her true love, a failing classical violinist. NOTE: A selection of vintage '30s cartoons precedes the film on this special video edition. 66 min.
68-8109 *$19.99*

Supernatural (1933)
Bereaved heiress Carole Lombard contacts a phony psychic in hopes of reaching the spirit of her late brother, but during a seance she is possessed by the vengeance-seeking spectre of one of the would-be seer's former victims in this occult-tinged suspense tale. With Alan Dinehart, H.B. Warner, Vivienne Osborne, Randolph Scott. 65 min.
07-2328 *$14.99*

Twentieth Century (1934)
John Barrymore's outrageous performance as tyrannical Broadway director Oscar Jaffe highlights Howard Hawks' screwball classic set on board a cross-country train. Carole Lombard co-stars as Barrymore's ex-protégé/lover, whom he tries to woo away from her fiancé and back to the stage. Witty script by Ben Hecht and Charles MacArthur. 91 min.
02-1884 *$19.99*

Lady By Choice (1934)
Carole Lombard plays a fan-dancer who is forced to clean up her act after being arrested. In lieu of a jail sentence, Lombard adopts bag lady May Robson as a "mom" to help her change her ways. Soon, Robson is pushing Lombard into acting lessons and into the arms of a wealthy lawyer. Roger Pryor, Walter Connolly co-star in this Runyonesque story. 77 min.
02-2210 *$19.99*

Hands Across The Table (1935)
Snappy screwball comedy starring Carole Lombard as a manicurist about to wed wealthy Ralph Bellamy for his fortune when penniless playboy Fred MacMurray walks into her life. Will Lombard and MacMurray, who's also about to marry for money, ditch their prospective spouses for true love? With Astrid Allwyn, Marie Prevost and William Demarest. 80 min.
07-2299 *$14.99*

The Princess Comes Across (1936)
Wacky romantic comedy showcases Carole Lombard as a wannabe actress from New York posing as a Swedish socialite while on a transatlantic cruise. After falling for bandleader Fred MacMurray (who performs "My Concertina"), Lombard and her new flame become prime suspects in a passenger's murder. William Frawley, Sig Rumann co-star. 77 min.
07-2300 *$14.99*

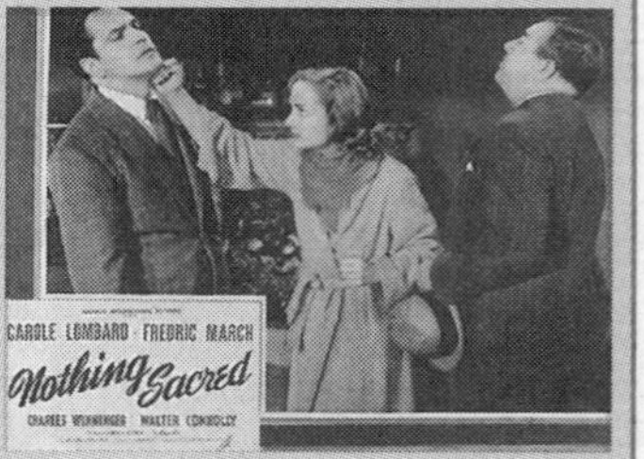

Nothing Sacred (1937)
Classic screwball comedy from director William Wellman and co-scripter Ben Hecht stars Fredric March as a scheming New York tabloid newsman who builds a story around small-town girl Carole Lombard when she's misdiagnosed with radium poisoning, bringing the "dying" Lombard to the Big Apple for a publicity tour and trying to keep other reporters from learning the truth. With Walter Connolly, Charles Winninger, Margaret Hamilton. 75 min.
01-1174 Was $19.99 *$14.99*

Swing High, Swing Low (1937)
Song-filled tale of showbiz ups and downs stars Carole Lombard as a singer who falls for trumpet player Fred MacMurray on a New York-to-Panama cruise and helps him become a star. When he's offered a gig back home, he leaves Lombard behind for the company of sultry Latin American singer Dorothy Lamour. With Anthony Quinn. 95 min.
08-8057 *$19.99*

Made For Each Other (1939)
Carole Lombard and James Stewart star in a classic comedy-drama about a young married couple who face a variety of problems ranging from financial pressures to a meddling mother and a newborn baby. With Charles Coburn, Lucile Watson. 94 min.
04-2149 Was $19.99 *$14.99*

Please see our index for these other Carole Lombard titles: *The Eagle And The Hawk • My Man Godfrey • No Man Of Her Own • Now And Forever • To Be Or Not To Be • We're Not Dressing*

Pop & Rock

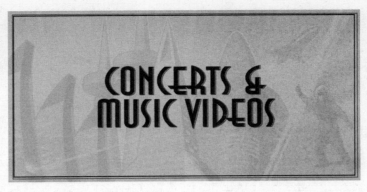

CONCERTS & MUSIC VIDEOS

Classic Albums: The Band: The Band
"Up on Cripple Creek" and "Rag Mama Rag" are among the standards featured on the folk-rock combo's eponymous 1969 album. Hear from former Band members on the creation of this, their second album and the one considered by many to be their masterpiece. 75 min.
15-5421 *$19.99*

Robbie Robertson: Going Home
Get an intimate look at Robbie Robertson, leader of The Band and master of many types of music, in this superior program. Trace Robertson's career, from 1950s rhythm-and-blues specialist to guitarist for The Hawks with Ronnie Hawkins, from Bob Dylan sideman to solo performer and movie music composer. Eric Clapton, Martin Scorsese and Barry Levinson share their insights. 70 min.
89-7023 *$14.99*

Boy Krazy: An Unauthorized Tribute To The World's Hottest Boy Bands
Backstreet Boys...98°...'NSYNC; the ever-popular boy bands are put under a microscope for this unauthorized documentary that looks into their music and members' lives. See how each group got together, how they became so popular, and how their songs have captivated millions of fans. 50 min.
50-8674 *$19.99*

Indigo Girls: Live At The Fillmore, Denver, November 20, 1999 (1999)
The Grammy Award-winning duo is back with another classic performance from the Fillmore featuring their best old and new music about the issues that are most important to them, plus exclusive interview footage. Among the songs featured are "Go," "Trouble," "Closer to Fine," "Galileo," "Sister," "Scooter Boys," "Compromise" and many others. 91 min.
04-5738 *$14.99*

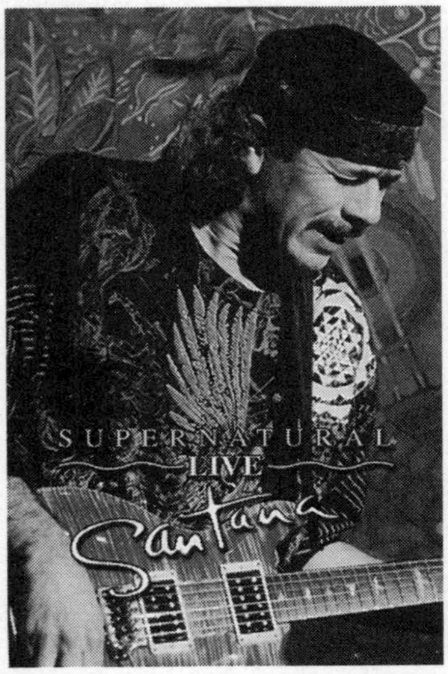

Santana: Supernatural Live (2000)
Guitar legend Carlos Santana won nine Grammy Awards for his album "Supernatural" in 1999. Now he is here with all of his collaborators performing songs from that album in this Fox TV concert. Among the featured tracks are the hits "Smooth" with Rob Thomas, "Put Your Lights On" with Everlast, "Maria Maria" with Product G&B and Wyclef Jean, plus many more. 90 min.
02-9278 *$19.99*

The Very Best Of Frankie Valli And The Four Seasons (1992)
Filmed in Atlantic City, this program features Frankie Valli and the Four Seasons at their best, performing an array of their smash hits in their incomparable style. Included are "Working My Way Back to You," "Dawn," "I've Got You Under My Skin," "Silence Is Golden," "Sherry," "Walk Like a Man," "December 1963," "Grease," "Big Girls Don't Cry" and "Can't Take My Eyes Off of You." 76 min.
89-7029 *$14.99*

British Rock Symphony (2000)
The Beatles, The Rolling Stones, The Who and Led Zeppelin are just a few of the incredible English rock bands paid tribute to in this video featuring an orchestra, gospel choir and singers such as Roger Daltrey, Alice Cooper and Paul Young performing classics like "Come Together," "Stairway To Heaven," "Start Me Up," "Who Are You" and many others. 88 min.
50-8734 *$19.99*

Jennifer Lopez: Feelin' So Good
Interviews, live performances and hot videos comprise this spectacular collection from film star-turned-singing sensation Lopez. Hear such songs as "If You Had My Love," "No Me Ames," "Waiting for Tonight," "Feelin' So Good" and more on this high-energy program. 60 min.
07-5744 *$19.99*

INXS: The Great Video Experience
Australian alternative rockers INXS are known for their special sound and amazing videos, and this program includes rare footage, music videos and more. Songs include "New Sensation," "Heaven Sent," "Not Enough Time," "The Strangest Party," "Need You Tonight" and "Mystify." 94 min.
02-8253 *$14.99*

Hall And Oates Video Collection: 7 Big Ones
Seven of Daryl and John's "blue-eyed soul" hits are featured here in music video form: "Say It Isn't So," "Adult Education," "Family Man," "Private Eyes" and more. 30 min.
02-1371 Was $19.99 *$14.99*

Come Dancing With The Kinks
One of rock's longest-lasting and best-selling groups takes the stage in a collection of live performances and music videos. Classic Kinks songs like "Lola" and "You Really Got Me" are featured, along with recent hits "Come Dancing," "Predictable" and others. 30 min.
02-1589 Was $19.99 *$14.99*

The Very Best Of Samantha Fox
From page three in England to the Top Ten worldwide, this Foxy lady is a sultry musical sensation. Now you can see her live on stage, in personal interviews, and in her hit music videos. "Touch Me," "Naughty Girls" and many more. 52 min.
02-7082 *$19.99*

Samantha Fox: Just One Night
Sexy singer Samantha Fox woos you and wows you with videos like "Just One Night," "Another Woman" and "Hurt Me, Hurt Me (But the Pants Stay On)," plus behind-the-scenes footage in New York. 32 min.
02-7439 *$14.99*

Tina Turner: Do You Want Some Action!—Live From Barcelona 1990
Tina onstage in Spain during her 1990 world tour...what more do we have to say? Among the hits performed in this red hot concert are "Steamy Windows," "Better Be Good to Me," "Private Dancer," "Proud Mary," "Be Tender with Me Baby" and many more. 100 min.
02-7261 Was $19.99 *$14.99*

Tina Turner Live In Amsterdam: Wildest Dreams Tour (1996)
Talk about your "Dutch treat"! The tantalizing Tina shines in a live concert before 150,000 fans at the Amsterdam Arena as part of her Wildest Dreams Tour. Along with such songs as "What's Love Got to Do with It?," "River Deep Mountain High," "Addicted to Love," "Goldeneye" and others, you'll also see exclusive backstage and rehearsal footage with Turner. 112 min.
53-8931 Was $24.99 *$14.99*

ABBA Gold: Greatest Hits
A look at the career of Sweden's pop superstars as told through live performances, television appearances and video clips. There are 19 hit tunes here, including "S.O.S.," "Dancing Queen," "Waterloo" and "Does Your Mother Know." 78 min.
02-7840 *$19.99*

More ABBA Gold: More ABBA Hits
Ready for a second helping of golden sounds as only ABBA can deliver? This collection of favorites from the Scandinavian superstars includes "Summer Night City," "I Do, I Do, I Do, I Do," "Head Over Heels," "Happy New Year," "That's Me" and more. 50 min.
02-8447 *$19.99*

ABBA: Thank You ABBA
"It's the total ABBA experience," a song-filled salute to Agnetha, Benny, Bjorn and Annifrid that includes concert clips, rare interviews and never-before-seen footage that traces the group's chart-topping history. Relive the sounds of the '70s with "Waterloo," "Fernando," "Dancing Queen," "Knowing Me Knowing You" and other favorites. 55 min.
02-8235 *$19.99*

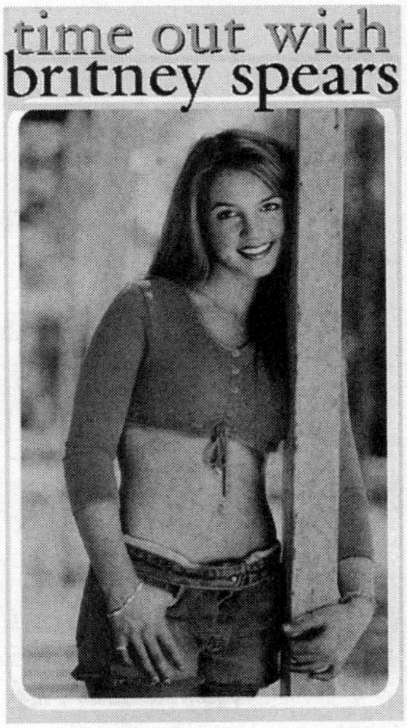

Time Out With Britney Spears
Get up-close and personal with the chart-topping teen songstress with this video program that features footage of Britney at home in Louisiana with her family, clips of her performing "Born to Make You Happy" and "From the Bottom of My Broken Heart" on her Disney Channel special, the music videos for "...Baby One More Time," "Sometimes" and "(You Drive Me) Crazy," and more. Also included is a "Jive 2K" music sampler audiocassette with answering machine message by Britney! 53 min.
02-9188 *$19.99*

Britney Spears: Star Baby Scrapbook
Trace the beginnings of teen pop sensation Britney Spears in this unauthorized program that shows how she went from child performer to the top of the charts. Archival footage, interviews and more give you a picture of Ms. Spears. 50 min.
50-8671 *$19.99*

LFO: Live From Orlando... And More! (2000)
After opening for Britney Spears, LFO gained lots of attention, and this video shows you why. See the Orlando, Fla.-based boys turn on the electricity in such live songs as "Summer Girls," "Baby Be Mine," "West Side Story" and "Can't Have You," as well as video clips for "Summer Girls" and "Girl on TV."
02-9223 *$19.99*

Kenny G: Live
For a soulful display of "sax appeal," look no further than this superlative concert video featuring the dynamic Kenny G. Among the songs featured are "Songbird," "Against Doctor's Orders," "Going Home," "Silhouette," duets with Dudley Moore ("Brogan") and Michael Bolton ("Don't Make Me Wait for Love"), and more. 80 min.
02-7084 *$19.99*

Paula Abdul: Under My Spell
Captured live during her tour of the Far East, pop songstress Paula Abdul delivers a spectacular show filled with spirited singing and dancing. Included on this program are "Spellbound," "The Way That You Love Me," "Forever Your Girl," "Opposites Attract" and "Rush Rush." 70 min.
02-7848 *$14.99*

The Cranberries: Live
Chart-topping Irish group The Cranberries perform an exciting live concert in this performance punctuated by Delores O'Riordan's vocal strength. Among the numbers here are "Pretty," "Linger," "Dreams," "Zombie" and "Not Sorry." 65 min.
02-8062 *$19.99*

Eurythmics: Greatest Hits
Music video history of Eurythmics, featuring the innovative audio and video stylings of Annie Lennox and Dave Stewart. Songs include "Sweet Dreams," "Here Comes the Rain Again," "Would I Lie to You?," "I Need a Man" and more. 95 min.
02-7315 *$19.99*

Annie Lennox: Live In Central Park
This thrilling 1995 concert from Central Park in New York features the diva performing a number of her best-loved songs, including "Who's That Girl?," "Why," "Train in Vain," "Money Can't Buy It" and "Sweet Dreams (Are Made of These)." Also featured are video clips of "A Whiter Shade of Pale" and others. 91 min.
02-8475 *$19.99*

Eurythmics: Peacetour (1999)
The excitement of the Annie Lennox-Dave Stewart reunion tour of 1999 is captured in this performance from London's Docklands Arena. Songs include such favorites as "Missionary Man," "Who's That Girl?," "Here Comes the Rain Again," "Why," "Sisters Are Doin' It for Themselves," "I Want It All" and "Sweet Dreams (Are Made of These)." 96 min.
02-9221 *$19.99*

Keep The Faith: An Evening With Bon Jovi
Filmed at the Kaufman-Astoria Studios in Queens, this rocking concert by Jersey's own Bon Jovi mixes electric numbers with acoustic versions of their big hits. Included on the program are "Love for Sale," "Lay Your Hands on Me," "Living on a Prayer" and "Blaze of Glory." 90 min.
02-7811 *$19.99*

Bon Jovi: Cross Road: The Video
An archival look at top rockers Bon Jovi featuring the group's hit videos from various stages of their career. Included are "Keep the Faith," "Blaze of Glory," "Livin' on a Prayer," "Dry County," "I'll Be There for You," "Always" and more. 80 min.
02-8167 *$19.99*

MTV Unplugged
The award-winning MTV series that features some of the top names in music in intimate acoustic concerts comes to home video with these special "best of" compilations. Each tape runs about 45 min.

MTV Unplugged: Classic Moments
Artists include The Allman Brothers Band ("Midnight Rider"), Eric Clapton ("Before You Accuse Me"), Sheryl Crow ("Leaving Las Vegas"), Chris Isaak ("Wicked Game"), Seal ("Prayer for the Dying") and others. 50 min.
04-5695 *$14.99*

MTV Unplugged: Finest Moments
Artists include Elvis Costello ("Deep Dark Truthful Mirror"), The Cure ("Just Like Heaven"), Live ("Lightning Crashes"), Oasis ("Listen Up"), 10,000 Maniacs ("These Are Days") and others. 50 min.
04-5696 *$14.99*

MTV Unplugged: Superstars
Artists include Tony Bennett ("I Left My Heart in San Francisco"), Hall and Oates ("She's Gone"), Paul McCartney ("We Can Work It Out"), Paul Simon ("Late in the Evening"), Squeeze ("Pulling Mussels from a Shell") and others. 35 min.
04-5711 *$14.99*

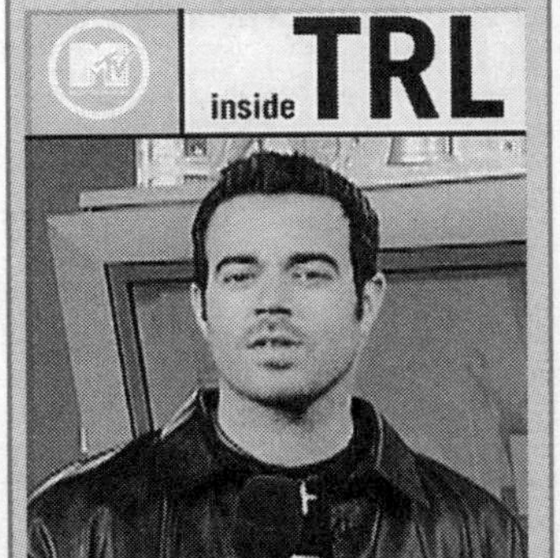

Inside TRL
MTV viewers know those letters stand for "Total Request Live," where top rock and pop stars drop by the Times Square studio for exclusive live performances. Get a behind-the-scenes look with host Carson Daly and hear songs from Christina Aguilera ("Genie in a Bottle"), Backstreet Boys ("I'll Never Break Your Heart"), Limp Bizkit ("Nookie"), 98° ("Because of You"), 'N SYNC ("Tearin' Up My Heart") and others. 46 min.
04-5734 *$14.99*

Rap's Most Wanted
Some of the most controversial rap artists, including Luther Campbell, Bushwick Bill, Ice-T and Chuck D, present their much-talked-about videos and comment on the state of their music...and their country. Songs include "Me So Horny," "The Ghetto," "New Jack Hustle" and "Do It Like G.O." 90 min.
19-3228 *$19.99*

Too $hort's Cocktales Videos: Raw, Uncut And Uncensored
They're nasty and uncensored! Finally, the Oakland Mack's wildest music videos have been collected on one program. Included are "Top Down," "I'm a Player," "Cocktales" and fellow Dangerous Crew member Goldy's "Nuthin' But a Tramp." 30 min.
02-8319 *$14.99*

Jazzy Jeff & Fresh Prince: Greatest Hits: The Videos
Before he became a TV and film star, Will Smith was one half of one of the most popular rap acts of all time. Now join "Fresh Prince" Will and partner DJ Jazzy Jeff in a video collection of their most popular songs, including "Girls Ain't Nothing But Trouble," "Parents Just Don't Understand," "Summertime," "Boom! Shake the Room" and many more. 49 min.
02-8856 *$19.99*

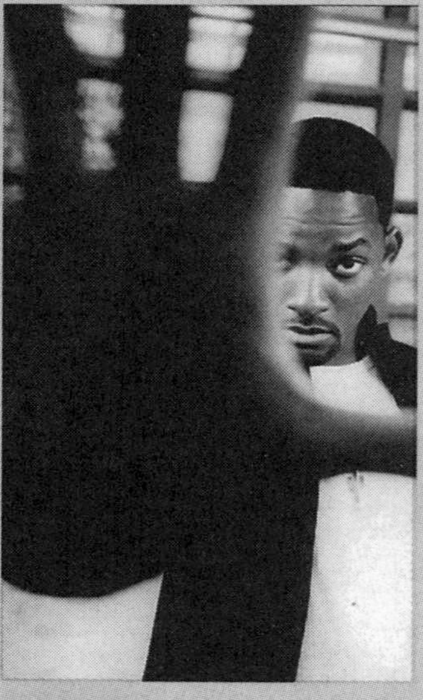

The Will Smith Music Video Collection
Seven chart-topping music videos from Philly's own "Fresh Prince," Will Smith, have been compiled in a special program that also mixes in behind-the-scenes outtakes and bloopers. Included are "Men in Black," "Just Cruisin'," "Gettin' Jiggy Wit' It," "Just the Two of Us," "Miami," "Wild Wild West" and "Will2K." 40 min.
04-5717 *$14.99*

Beastie Boys
Everybody's watching these three gruff but lovable streetboys, and now this video collection will bring out the Beastie in you. Includes "She's on It," "No Sleep 'Till Brooklyn," the haunting "Fight for Your Right (to Party)" and more. 25 min.
04-2064 *$19.99*

Beastie Boys: The Skills To Pay The Bills
A dozen hit music videos trace the evolution of the Beasties from their beginnings in 1981 to their rap-inspired success. "Hay Ladies," "Shadrach," "Looking Down the Barrel of a Gun," "Pass the Mic," "Nelly's Girl" and other songs are featured. 37 min.
44-4078 *$14.99*

Ruffhouse 10th Anniversary Special
The record label known for being in the vanguard of the hip-hip and R&B pop scene marks 10 years of hits with a collection of music videos and interview footage with Ruffhouse founders Joe Niccolo and Chris Schwartz and such artists as Cypress Hill ("Insane in the Brain"), The Fugees ("Fu-Gee-La," "Killing Me Softly with His Song"), Lauryn Hill ("Doo Wop (That Thing)"), Kriss Kross ("Jump") and others. 58 min.
04-5701 *$14.99*

Master P Presents No Limit Records Video Compilation, Vol. 1
This video compilation features Master P and the rest of the raunchy, rappin' No Limits crew, including Silk the Shocker, Mystical and Mia X. See the videos that are banned on cable and learn why Master P and pals shock and amaze their fans! 120 min.
50-8294 *$19.99*

Thug Immortal: The Tupac Shakur Story
This documentary looks at the tumultuous life of the late rap singer and actor Tupac Shakur. Using rare home movie footage and interviews with people who knew him best, the program offers a personal view of the talented but troubled star of such films as "Juice" and "Gridlock'd."
54-9781 *$24.99*

Wild Style (1983)
One of the first films to chronicle New York's nascent hip-hop scene, this funky mix of documentary and drama looks at the rap performers, breakdancers and graffiti artists of the South Bronx, including Grandmaster Flash, Fab 5 Freddy, Busy Bee and others. 82 min.
59-5038 *$14.99*

The Show (1995)
The hottest names in rap music take Philadelphia by storm in this high-energy concert film that also takes you behind the scenes. Among the performers are Dr. Dre, Naughty By Nature, Snoop Doggy Dogg, Tha Dogg Pound, Run DMC, Slick Rick and the Wu-Tang Clan. 92 min.
02-2977 Was $19.99 □*$14.99*

Rhyme & Reason (1997)
More than just a concert film, this documentary-like look at the world of rap music includes backstage and at-home footage of some of the genre's biggest names, including exclusive interviews with the late Tupak Shakur and Notorious B.I.G. Ice-T, Dr. Dre, Da Brat, Salt-N-Pepa and The Fugees are among the artists spotlighted. 93 min.
11-2199 Was $19.99 □*$14.99*

R. Kelly: 12 Play—The Hit Videos, Vol. 1
With his platinum debut album, "Born Into the 90s," R. Kelly burst onto the scene with an exhilarating blend of pop, R&B, ballads and funk. Here's a video collection from that album and "12 Play," featuring such numbers as "Sex Me (Part I)," "Sex Me (Part II)," "Your Body's Callin'" and "Bump and Grind." 30 min.
02-8080 *$14.99*

U2: Zoo TV: Live From Sydney
U2's live extravaganza from Australia features the lads performing a stunning repertoire of 23 songs old and new. High-tech gadgetry and emotional playing bring out the best in such numbers as "Zoo Station," "The Fly," "Mysterious Ways," "New Year's Day," "With or Without You," "Pride (In the Name of Love)" and more. 120 min.
02-8066 *$19.99*

U2: PopMart: Live From Mexico City
Filmed in Foro Sol Autodromo in Mexico City in December of 1997, this spectacular concert features U2 at their finest, offering a stunning musical and visual show. Among the 24 songs featured on this program are "Pop Muzik," "Last Night on Earth," "New Year's Day," "I Still Haven't Found What I'm Looking For," "Please," "With or Without You" and "Mysterious Ways." 127 min.
02-9002 *$19.99*

U2: Rattle And Hum (1988)
Dynamic musical experience follows superstar combo U2 on their 1988 American tour, a cross-country journey that takes the band to a church recital in Harlem, a visit to Graceland, a meeting with Blues great B.B. King and an impromptu San Francisco street performance. Special 90-minute video version contains nine extra songs.
06-1630 *$14.99*

TLC: The Video
The three-girl group's first two albums have earned them legions of fans, and this show captures all the excitement of TLC on video and in concert. Among the videos are "Creep," "Red Light Special" and "Waterfalls," as well as interviews and a special live treatment of "Diggin' on You."
02-8359 *$14.99*

Mark Knopfler: A Night In London
Dire Straits lead man and expert guitarist Mark Knopfler performs some of his finest songs in this performance from BBC Studios. Among the numbers presented are "Walk of Life," "Last Exit to Brooklyn," "Sultans of Swing," "Money for Nothing," "Brothers in Arms," "Romeo & Juliet" and the instrumental "Going Home (Theme from "Local Hero")." 112 min.
02-8552 *$19.99*

Sultans Of Swing: The Very Best Of Dire Straits
Celebrating the 20th anniversary of the innovative British combo, this comprehensive collection of music videos and live concert clips includes such Dire Straits faves as "Sultans of Swing," "Lady Writer," "Romeo and Juliet," "So Far Away," "Money for Nothing," "Walk of Life" and 10 more.
02-9056 *$19.99*

Dire Straits: On The Night
Thrilling live concert offers Mark Knopfler and his mates at their best, performing a host of their hits, including "Walk of Life," "Romeo and Juliet," "Calling Elvis," "Money for Nothing," and others. 90 min.
19-3418 *$24.99*

Dire Straits: The Videos
Exciting collection of videos by the chart-topping group includes "Sultans of Swing," "Tunnel of Love," "Walk of Life," "Will You Miss Me," "Going Home: Theme of 'Local Hero'," and the award-winning "Money for Nothing." 98 min.
19-3419 *$24.99*

They Might Be Giants: Direct From Brooklyn
They're quirky; they're from Hoboken; they're both named John. The offbeat rock duo takes center stage in a collection of their acclaimed music videos. Included are "Doctor Worm," "Istanbul (Not Constantinople)," "Birdhouse in Your Soul," "Ana Ng," "Don't Let's Start" and more, plus special "Tiny Toons" versions of "Istanbul" and "Particle Man."
02-9100 *$14.99*

Endless Summer: Donna Summer's Greatest Hits
Relive the '70s with the First Lady of Disco, Donna Summer, in this collection of her finest hits in music video form. Songs include "I Feel Love," "Last Dance," "MacArthur Park," "She Works Hard for the Money" and more. 60 min.
02-8177 *$19.99*

Donna Summer: Live And More—Encore
As the ad states, "There are many great voices in pop music...and then there is DONNA SUMMER." The disco diva and Oscar-winning singer is featured in a dazzling concert program in which she performs "MacArthur Park," "This Time I Know It's for Real," "On the Radio," "Last Dance" and many more, including "Someone to Watch Over Me" and four more songs not featured on TV. 90 min.
04-5669 *$19.99*

Sarah McLachlan: Fumbling Towards Ecstasy
Ethereal Canadian singer-songwriter Sarah McLachlan performs live at a concert in Montreal, turns in a separate acoustic set with her band, and is interviewed in this captivating program. Among the numbers performed are "Good Enough," "Possession," "Plenty," "Out of Shadows" and Tom Waits' "Ol' 55." 90 min.
02-8191 *$14.99*

Sarah McLachlan: Mirrorball
The atmospheric folk/rock sound that has earned Sarah McLachlan multitudes of fans is on display in this video counterpart to her "Mirrorball" album, featuring nine songs not available on the CD. Included are "Intro (Last Dance)," "Building a Mystery," "Hold On," "I Will Remember You," "Into the Fire," "Fumbling Towards Ecstasy" and more.
02-9183 *$14.99*

Nirvana: Live! Tonight! Sold Out!
Conceived by Kurt Cobain and three years in the making, the initial video effort from the groundbreaking Seattle band features over a dozen live concert clips (many from Nirvana's own video library), interviews and behind-the-scenes footage. Songs include "Aneurysm," "Dive," "Smells Like Teen Spirit," "Come As You Are," "Lithium" and more. 83 min.
07-4118 *$24.99*

Hype! (1995)
A funny, insightful look at the "grunge music" scene that blossomed in the Seattle area in the late 1980s, featuring such groups as Mudhoney, Soundgarden, The Posies, Dead Moon and Nirvana, who perform the first-ever live version of "Smells Like Teen Spirit." 84 min.
63-1888 Letterboxed □*$19.99*

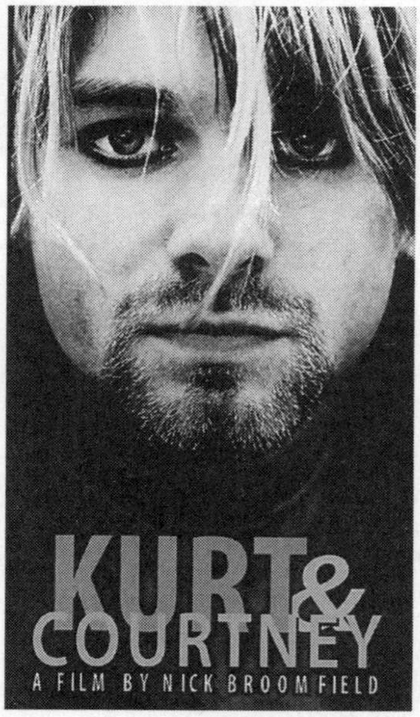

Kurt & Courtney (1998)
The film that was banned at the Sundance Film Festival because of legal problems is a probing, no-holds-barred inquiry into the 1994 death of Nirvana star Kurt Cobain and the role wife Courtney Love may have played in his demise. Director Nick Broomfield ("Heidi Fleiss: Hollywood Madam") questions relatives, Seattle musicians and all sorts of eccentric characters to explore the story behind the story. 95 min.
02-9029 Was $99.99 *$14.99*

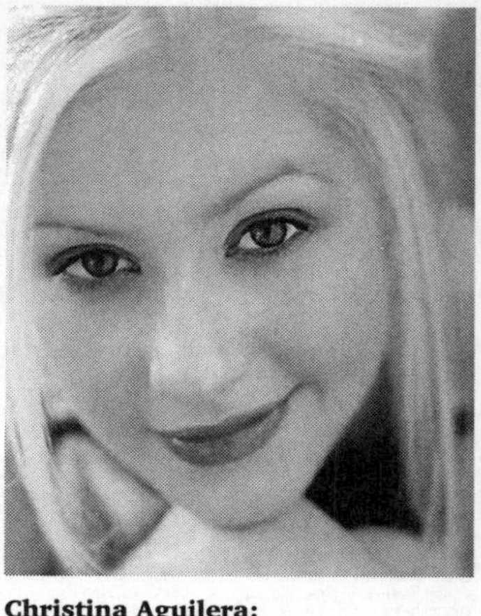

Christina Aguilera: Genie Gets Her Wish
And fans of the bubbly pop songstress will get their wish too with this special video program that features concert clips and backstage footage, music videos, and exclusive interviews with Christina. Songs include "Genie in a Bottle," "So Emotional," "Come on Over (All I Want Is You)," "At Last" and more.
02-9199 *$19.99*

Christina Aguilera: Out Of The Bottle
Teen sensation singer Christina Aguilera shows you where it all began on this video that follows her rise to fame, from childhood to success on "Star Search" and "The Mickey Mouse Club" to top pop and Latin songstress. 48 min.
50-7579 *$14.99*

The Allman Brothers Band: Brothers Of The Road, Concert 1
The prime purveyors of Southern rock reunite for this jam-filled concert from Gainesville, Florida, where Gregg Allman, Dickey Betts, Butch Trucks and company perform favorites like "Jessica," "Let Me Ride," "Statesboro Blues" and, of course, "Whippin' Post." Also includes rare hotel jam footage. 48 min.
02-8087 *$14.99*

The Allman Brothers Band: Brothers Of The Road, Concert 2
The reunited Allmans turn out a rockin' evening of Southern-fried music from the Capitol Theater with such tunes as "Melissa," "Can't Take It With You," "In Memory of Elizabeth Reed," "The Judgement," "Southbound" and "Ramblin' Man." 63 min.
02-8088 *$14.99*

The Allman Brothers Band: Live At Great Woods
Join Greg Allman and company in a rousing concert from their 1991 tour that celebrated their 20-plus years in the music business. Songs include "Jessica," "End of the Line," "Elizabeth Reed," "Whipping Post" and "Statesboro Blues." 90 min.
04-5171 *$19.99*

Earth, Wind & Fire: Live
One of the most popular bands of all time performs a dynamic concert in Japan, turning in such popular songs as "That's the Way of the World," "Shining Star," "Let's Groove," "Sing a Song," "Boogie Wonderland," "After the Love Is Gone," and 11 more. 60 min.
02-8337 *$19.99*

Earth, Wind & Fire: Live In Japan (1990)
Filmed at the Tokyo Dome during their "Heritage" tour, soulful superstars Earth, Wind & Fire offer up a dazzling concert experience that includes such chart-topping songs as "Get Away," "Shining Star," "After the Love Is Gone," "Let's Groove," "That's the Way of the World" and more. 90 min.
85-1194 *$14.99*

Wham!: The Final
Gone(?) but not forgotten, the solid gold British popsters return with a quintet of their music video hits. Includes "I'm Your Man," "Freedom," "Edge of Heaven," "Where Did Your Heart Go," "Different Corner." 25 min.
04-2022 *$19.99*

George Michael
The pop music mega-star is spotlighted in a collection of his hit music videos from Michael's Wham! days to the present, concert footage and a no-holds-barred interview. Songs include "Wake Me Up Before You Go-Go," "Careless Whisper," "Faith," "Praying for Time" and more. 60 min.
04-5064 *$19.99*

Ladies & Gentlemen, The Best Of George Michael
The name says it all: over 20 of Michael's greatest hits, in live and music video versions, have been gathered for a special retrospective. Included here are "Careless Whisper," "I Want Your Sex," "Kissing a Fool," "Outside," "Don't Let the Sun Go Down on Me" with Elton John, "I Knew You Were Waiting (For Me)" with Aretha Franklin and many more.
04-5661 *$19.99*

Elton John/
Bernie Taupin: Two Rooms
A look at the 25-year partnership of composer Elton John and lyricist Bernie Taupin, featuring anecdotes about writing such songs as "Daniel," "Someone Saved My Life Tonight" and more, plus stars like Eric Clapton, Phil Collins, Tina Turner, Sting and The Who performing John/Taupin tunes. 90 min.
02-7426 *$14.99*

Behind The Music: Blondie
One of the first bands to emerge from New York's '70s punk scene, Blondie had a string of hits before suddenly breaking up in 1982. The story of Debbie Harry, Chris Stein, Jimmy Destri and Clem Burke is told in this entry in the VH-1 series, from the group's CBGB beginnings through their triumphs, tragedies and reunion in 1999. Includes 10 minutes of footage not seen on TV. 60 min.
02-9067 *$14.99*

Blondie Live In New York (1999)
After a 17-year hiatus, the pioneering punk combo that went from CBGB to the top of the pop charts reunited. In this live concert at New York's Town Hall, Debbie Harry, Clem Burke, Jimmy Destri and Chris Stein perform "Dreaming," "Maria," "Call Me," "X Offender," "Heart of Glass," "Rapture" and other favorites.
02-9196 *$24.99*

Toni Braxton:
The Home Video Collection
After winning accolades and Grammys, what can the soulfully sexy Toni Braxton do next? Why, put out a program filled with such hit videos as "Another Sad Love Song," "Seven Whole Days," "Breathe Again," "You Mean the World to Me" and "Love Shoulda Brought You Home." 30 min.
02-8069 *$14.99*

Mariah Carey: True Visions
She burst onto the music scene with two number one singles and a multi-platinum debut album. Now take an up-close look at Mariah Carey in this special program that features music videos, live clips and interviews. Songs include "Vision of Love," "Love Takes Time," "Someday," "I Don't Wanna Cry" and more. 40 min.
04-5073 *$19.99*

Mariah Carey: Unplugged + 3
Top-selling songstress Mariah Carey is featured in her acclaimed performance on the MTV "Unplugged" series. Along with such renditions of "If It's Over," "Vision of Love" and "I'll Be There," there are music videos for "Emotions," "Can't Let Go" and "Make It Happen." 50 min.
04-5154 *$19.99*

Mariah Carey
Mariah's first network television special, shown on Thanksgiving Night, 1993, is presented in a special home video edition. Included are performances of "Someday," "Without You," "Make It Happen," "I'll Be There," plus live and music video versions of "Dreamlover." 60 min.
04-5211 *$19.99*

Fantasy: Mariah Carey At Madison Square Garden
Mariah Carey excels in this concert from New York's Madison Square Garden that also includes interviews and footage of the singer with children at the Fresh Air Fund's Camp Mariah. Among the selections sung are "Fantasy," "Make It Happen," "Dreamlover," "Hero," "One Sweet Day" with Boyz II Men, and "I'll Be There" with Wanya Morris of Boyz fame. 60 min.
04-5434 *$19.99*

Mariah Carey: Around The World
It's a non-stop global tour with the lovely Mariah, as you follow Carey to concert and promo appearances in Australia, Japan, Hawaii and Manhattan. Among the songs performed are "Fantasy," "Dreamlover," "I Still Believe," "I'll Be There" with Trey Lorenz, "Hopelessly Devoted to You" with Olivia Newton-John, "Hero" and many more. 52 min.
04-5658 *$14.99*

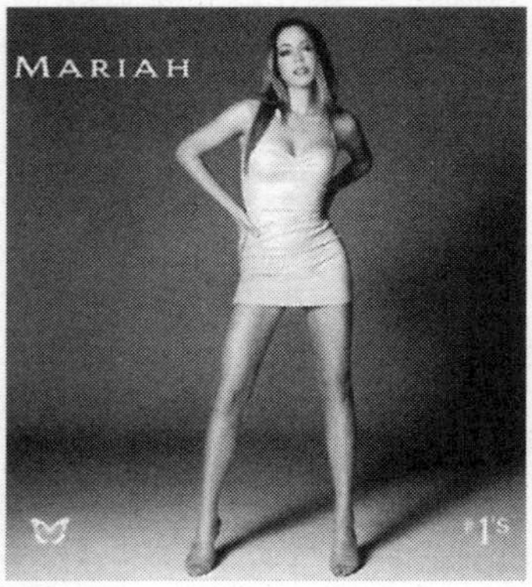

Mariah Carey: #1's
If you're looking for only the best of Mariah Carey, this collection featuring 14 of her #1 singles is sure to please. Among the songs featured are "My All," "Honey," "Vision of Love," "Dreamlover," "One Sweet Day" with Boyz II Men, "Heartbreaker" with Jay-Z and many more. 75 min.
04-5699 *$14.99*

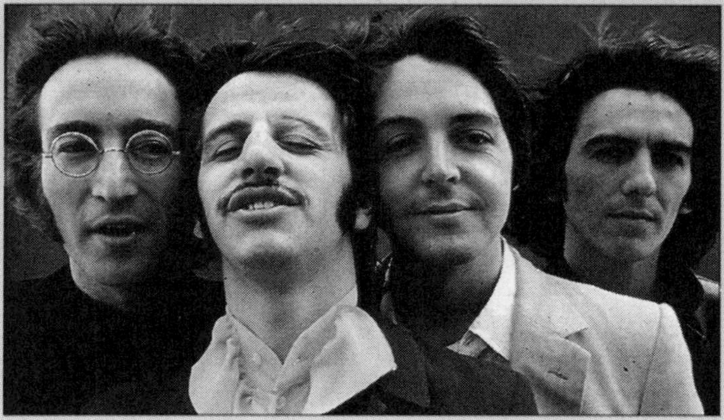

The Beatles

Help! (1965)
John, Paul, George and Ringo are back (along with director Richard Lester) in a wild romp centering around a religious cult's attempts to retrieve a priceless ceremonial ring...guess which moptop has it? With Leo McKern, Victor Spinetti; songs include "Ticket to Ride," "You're Gonna Lose That Girl" and the title tune. This remastered edition also features the original theatrical trailer, silent out-takes on the set, and radio ads and interviews with the band. 98 min. total.
50-7328 Remastered *$19.99*

Magical Mystery Tour (1967)
The Beatles take a holiday bus trip that proves to be colorful, song-filled and wild. Includes great tunes like "I Am the Walrus," "Your Mother Should Know," and more. 50 min.
50-6322 Was $29.99 *$19.99*

Yellow Submarine (1968)
When the happiness-hating Blue Meanie and his monstrous allies overrun Pepperland, it's John, Paul, George and Ringo (or, at least, their animated likenesses; actors supplied their voices) to the rescue in this psychedelic animated odyssey. Along with the previously unavailable "Hey, Bulldog," the Fab Four score includes "Lucy in the Sky with Diamonds," "When I'm 64," "Eleanor Rigby" and more; co-written by Erich Segal ("Love Story"). 90 min.
12-1711 Remastered 🗨*$19.99*

The Beatles:
The First U.S. Visit (1964)
A collector's must-have, this tape features rare footage of The Beatles' American debut, from their arrival in New York to behind-the-scenes shots of them at their hotel, dancing at nightclubs and riding the train to Washington. There's also 13 songs from The Fab Four's first three "Ed Sullivan Show" appearances and D.C. concert, including "She Loves You," "I Wanna Hold Your Hand," "Twist and Shout," "From Me to You" and more. 85 min.
50-6880 Was $89.99 *$24.99*

The Beatles Scrapbook
Truly gear rare interviews, news footage of tours and special appearances and previews of their fab films capture Beatlemania in full froth.
10-7426 Was $19.99 *$14.99*

The Beatles: A Celebration
Rare footage, interviews, photos, press conferences and insight from Eric Clapton, Brian Epstein, Pete Best, Linda McCartney, Yoko Ono and Maharishi Mahesh Yogi take you into the world of the greatest rock group in history. This magical mystery tour of sights and sounds is perfect for casual fans or real Beatles boosters. 56 min.
89-7003 *$14.99*

The Beatles Story:
Days Of Beatlemania
The Beatles and their rise from obscurity to worldwide sensation is traced in this program that features never-before-seen footage and interviews with the four mates at important times in their lives. 60 min.
22-1468 *$14.99*

You Can't Do That: The Making Of "A Hard Day's Night"
This collector's delight takes an inside look at the production of The Beatles' classic debut movie and features commentary from the film's creators, footage of the band backstage and recording at the Abbey Road Studio, a performance of "You Can't Do That" that was shot for the movie but not used, U.S. and European theatrical trailers and lots more. Phil Collins hosts. 65 min.
50-7300 *$19.99*

Give My Regards To
Broad Street (1984)
A day in the life of Paul McCartney, in which fantasy, music and a mystery plot come together. Songs include "No More Lonely Nights," "Eleanor Rigby," "Yesterday," and others. Ringo Starr, Tracey Ullman, Barbara Bach. 108 min.
04-1808 Was $19.99 🗨*$14.99*

Paul McCartney:
Movin' On (1993)
Catch Paul McCartney outside of the spotlight, rehearsing such tunes as "Penny Lane," "Drive My Car" and "Looking for Changes," performing in the videos for "C'Mon People" and "Off the Ground," and touring "The Beatles' Studio," Studio 2, Abbey Road. See what goes on in a day in the life of a legend. 60 min.
50-7105 *$19.99*

Paul McCartney: Paul Is Live—In Concert On The New World Tour
In a memorable concert, Paul McCartney rocks out in his inimitable style, performing his greatest hits from The Beatles, Wings and his illustrious solo career. The 20 selections include "Magical Mystery Tour," "Michelle," "Penny Lane," "Let Me Roll It," "Live and Let Die," "Good Rockin' Tonight," and three songs not on the album, "Yesterday," "Let It Be" and "Hey Jude." 84 min.
02-8021 *$14.99*

Ringo Starr And His All Starr Band: Live From Montreux
A "Who's Who's" of musical talent, including Joe Walsh, Burton Cummings, Todd Rundgren, Dave Edmunds, Nils Lofgren and Zak Starkey, join the one and only Ringo on stage for a must-see Montreux concert. "With a Little Help from My Friends," "The No-No Song," "Photograph," "American Woman" and "Bang on the Drum" are among the two dozen songs featured. 120 min.
50-7147 *$19.99*

Ringo Starr And
His Fourth All-Starr Band
Ringo's 1997 US concert tour arrives on home video with a blast. His band of legends includes Peter Frampton on guitar, Gary Brooker on keyboards, Jack Bruce on bass, Simon Kirke on drums, and Mark Rivera on horns. Together, they perform some of their own personal hits as well as the "Funny One's" Beatles and solo faves: "It Don't Come Easy," "Yellow Submarine," "All Right Now," "Sunshine of Your Love" and others. 135 min.
50-7470 *$19.99*

The Mike Douglas Show With John Lennon & Yoko Ono: Boxed Set (1972)
One of the most memorable events in rock TV history was when John Lennon and Yoko Ono spent a week as co-hosts of Douglas' Philly-based, nationally syndicated talk show. All five episodes, featuring John performing and welcoming such guests as Chuck Berry, George Carlin, Ralph Nader and Bobby Seale, are available in this special five-tape boxed set that also includes a photo-filled, 48-page hardcover book. 375 min. total. NOTE: Individual volumes available at $19.99 each.
15-5419 *$99.99*

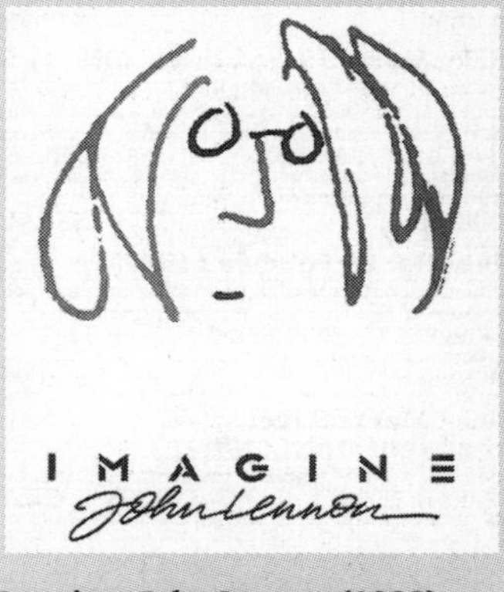

Imagine: John Lennon (1988)
From the birth of The Beatles to his untimely death, the life and music of John Lennon are featured in a remarkable documentary that contains interviews with family and friends, concert clips, TV footage and more, backed by Lennon's greatest Beatles and solo songs and "narrated" by Lennon himself. 103 min.
19-1681 🗨*$24.99*

Keppel Road: The Life And Music Of The Bee Gees
Rare home video footage, exclusive interviews, and special performances of their greatest hits are featured in this salute to Barry, Maurice and Robin Gibb that traces the brothers' boyhoods in England and Australia, their rise to pop stardom in the '60s and '70s, and the renewed interest in The Bee Gees' music. 92 min.
02-8674 *$19.99*

Bee Gees Live: One For All Tour
They've been "stayin' alive" on the pop charts for over 20 years. Now the Brothers Gibb are featured in a spectacular two-tape concert that traces their hit-laden career. "Massachusetts," "How Can You Mend a Broken Heart," "Nights on Broadway," "How Deep Is Your Love," many more. 112 min. total.
50-6496 *$29.99*

The Bee Gees:
One Night Only (1997)
Live from the MGM Grand in Las Vegas, Robin, Maurice and Barry Gibb offer up 30 years of top 40 hits in this dynamic concert video. Such Bee Gees faves as "Stayin' Alive," "Too Much Heaven," "Jive Talkin'," "How Can You Mend a Broken Heart" and many more are featured, plus a guest appearance by Celine Dion and a special "duet" with late brother Andy on "Our Love (Don't Throw It All Away)." 111 min.
50-1389 *$19.99*

Backstreet Boys: All Access Video
From the back streets of Orlando, Florida, comes the chart-topping quintet that sold over 17 million records in their first two years. Now this video program mixes live concert clips, music videos and behind-the-scenes footage to tell the Boys' story. Songs include "Everybody (Backstreet's Back)," "As Long As You Love Me," "Get Down ("You're the One for Me)," "All I Have to Give" and more. 80 min.
02-8860 *$19.99*

A Night Out With
The Backstreet Boys (1998)
Those popular pop sensations perform live in Cologne, Germany, presenting their greatest hits along with interview footage and select video clips. Songs include "Why Do You Love," "As Long as You Love Me," "10,000 Promises," "Like a Child" and lots more. 70 min.
02-9031 *$19.99*

Backstreet Boys: Homecoming: Live In Orlando (1998)
Join A.J., Brian, Howie, Kevin and Nick for a special hometown New Year's Eve concert filled with the music and dances that have made the Boys worldwide stars. Among the 17 Backstreet faves featured are "That's the Way I Like It," "Just to Be Close to You," "Quit Playing Games (With My Heart)," "All I Have to Give," "We've Got It Goin' On" and more. 60 min.
02-9092 *$19.99*

An Evening With
Christopher Cross
Oscar- and Grammy-winner Cross performs his most popular mellow rock hits in this concert. Among the favorites showcased are "Ride Like the Wind," "Sailing," "Arthur's Theme," "Never Be the Same" and "Swept Away." 90 min.
02-8878 *$19.99*

Adam Ant:
Antics In The Forbidden Zone
If other music videos have lost their taste, why not try another flavor? This hit-loaded collection of videos from Adam's career with the Ants and solo includes "Antmusic," "Stand and Deliver," "Prince Charming," "Vive le Rock," "Goody Two Shoes" and more. 42 min.
04-5063 *$19.99*

'NSYNC: 'n The Mix
Those pop favorites 'N SYNC are showcased in a rockin' video clip collection that includes "I Want You Back," "Tearin' Up My Heart," "Here We Go," "For the Girl Who Has Everything" and more. 75 min.
02-9048 *$19.99*

The Ultimate 'N SYNC Party
Go behind the scenes of music sensations 'N SYNC and discover how Chris, Lance, J.C., Justin and Joey got together and other tidbits. Also, hear why fans love the group and see never-before-seen footage of the teen and pre-teen scene faves. 45 min.
50-8279 *$14.99*

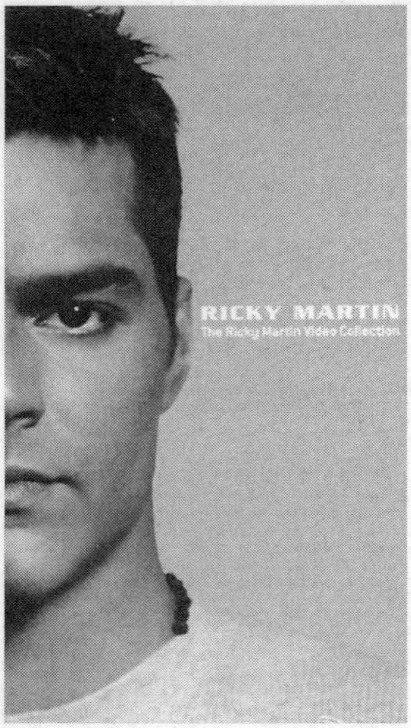

Ricky Martin: The Ricky Martin Video Collection
Former Menudo star Ricky Martin is sure to dazzle with his bouncy tunes and macho bravado in this sizzling video compilation. Included are "Livin' la Vida Loca" (both English and Spanish versions), "La Bamba," "Perdido Sin Ti" "Vuelve," "Maria" (in Spanglish)," "Bella (She's All I Ever Had)" (in Spanish) and a live Grammy performance of "The Cup of Life." 40 min.
04-5690 *$14.99*

Ricky Martin: It's A Crazy Life
The former Menudo member took America by storm with his smash "Livin' la Vida Loca" and now you can learn about his fascinating life, including his stint on a soap opera and Broadway experiences. This unauthorized video includes rare photos, behind-the-scenes footage and more. 48 min.
50-8291 *$14.99*

Menudo: La Pelicula (1983)
Exciting concert footage and rare film clips show you the story of Menudo, how the group came together and became the singing sensation of America. Spanish-language version. 84 min.
48-1052 *$29.99*

Ricky Martin Live: One Night Only! (1999)
One night is all it takes for the chart-topping Latin heartthrob to dazzle an audience at New Jersey's Liberty State Park. Ricky offers sizzling renditions of "La Copa de la Vida" and "She's All I Ever Had," plus a medley of "Light My Fire"/"Guajira"/"Oye Como Va" with guests Jose Feliciano and Carlos Santana, and even "Livin' la Vida Loca." 45 min.
04-5700 *$14.99*

Cheap Trick: Every Trick In The Book
Rick Nielsen, Bun E. Carlos and the rest of "The Trick" want you to want this collection of their greatest hits. There's "Surrender," "Way of the World," "Dream Police," "Can't Stop Fallin' in Love" and more. 65 min.
04-5050 *$19.99*

Cheap Trick: Live In Australia (1988)
Be "On Top of the World" Down Under with this spectacular concert video of Cheap Trick performing live in Sydney. "Dream Police," "I Want You to Want Me," "Just Got Back," "Surrender" and many more of the band's chart-busting tunes are featured. 73 min.
15-5406 *$19.99*

Sade: Diamond Life Video
Pronounce it "shar-day," then watch this sultry songstress from Nigeria in these soulful videos, including "Your Love Is King," "Hang On to Your Love," "When Am I Going to Make a Living?," and an extended version of "Smooth Operator." 23 min.
04-1864 *$14.99*

Sade: Life Promise Pride Love
A greatest hits compilation that features videoclips of some of the romantic singer's finest songs, including "Paradise," "Sweetest Taboo," "Smooth Operator," "Kiss of Life," "Is It a Crime" and "Your Love Is King." 68 min.
04-5196 *$19.99*

Sade: Live Concert Home Video
The sultry songstress performs her most popular tunes in a concert filmed in San Diego in 1993. Among the numbers performed are "Sweetest Taboo," "Your Love Is King," "Haunt Me," "Kiss of Life," "Pearls," "Paradise" and others. Includes 30 minutes of footage not seen during the program's PBS showing. 90 min.
04-5244 *$19.99*

Stevie Ray Vaughan & Double Trouble: Pride And Joy
The late guitar master is remembered in this collection of Vaughan's best music videos, plus rare concert footage. "Love Struck Bay," "Couldn't Stand the Weather," "I'm Leaving You," "Tick Tock" and many more songs included. 40 min.
04-5066 *$17.99*

Stevie Ray Vaughan & Double Trouble: Live From Austin, Texas
Culled from Vaughan's barn-burning 1983 and 1989 appearances on the PBS "Austin City Limits" series, this amazing video features Stevie and Double Trouble performing live such songs as "Pride and Joy," "Texas Flood," "The House Is Rockin'," "Leave My Girl Alone" and other favorites, plus a bonus music video of "Little Wing." 63 min.
04-5402 *$19.99*

Stevie Ray Vaughan & Double Trouble: Live At The El Mocambo (1983)
The legendary guitarist shines in a Toronto concert with his bandmates, bassist Tommy Shannon and drummer Chris Layton. "Testify," "Texas Flood," "Hug You Squeeze You," "Voodoo Shuffle" and other favorites are played in Vaughan's inimitable blues-rock style. 60 min.
04-5135 *$19.99*

A Tribute To Stevie Ray Vaughan (1996)
An all-star gathering that includes Eric Clapton, Robert Cray, Dr. John, Buddy Guy, B.B. King, Bonnie Raitt and Stevie's brother, Jimmie Vaughan, takes the stage for a moving concert salute to the music and memory of the guitar legend. 80 min.
04-5469 *$19.99*

The Rolling Stones: Happy Hour At The Voodoo Lounge
Feel like lounging with Mick, Keith and the boys? This video features live concert footage from The Stones' 1995 world tour (with special guests Bo Diddley and Robert Cray), music videos and more. The songlist includes "Tumbling Dice," "Start Me Up," "Satisfaction," "Not Fade Away," "The Worst," "It's All Over Now" and much more. 95 min.
02-8366 *$19.99*

The Rolling Stones: Bridges To Babylon 1998
It's 1998 and do you know where The Rolling Stones are? They're touring, of course, performing their greatest hits and more in support of their "Bridges to Babylon" album. Follow Mick, Keith and the rest of the band as they offer up "Satisfaction," "Let's Spend the Night Together," "Hip the Switch," "Sympathy for the Devil," "Out of Control" and 14 others. 120 min.
50-5992 *$19.99*

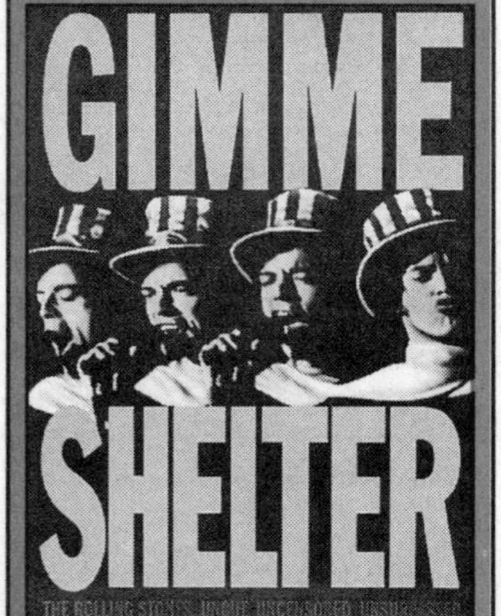

Gimme Shelter (1970)
The controversial Altamont, Cal., show that climaxed The Rolling Stones' 1969 U.S. tour and saw the murder of a concertgoer by Hell's Angels "security guards" was filmed by documentarians David and Albert Maysles. Along with stunning Stones renditions of "Jumping Jack Flash," "Brown Sugar," "Sympathy for the Devil" and more, the concert also features Tina Turner, The Jefferson Airplane and The Flying Burrito Bros. Remastered, uncensored version; 90 min.
02-1009 *$29.99*

The Rolling Stones: Live At The Max (1994)
Even if you don't have a five-story movie screen in your home, you'll still enjoy this maxed-out concert film, shot during the European leg of The Stones' 1990 Steel Wheels Tour. Jagger, Richards, Wyman, Watts and Wood cut loose with rock anthems like "Start Me Up," "Tumbling Dice," "Paint It Black," "Street Fighting Man" and 12 others. 85 min.
02-8217 *$19.99*

The Bruce Springsteen Video Anthology
Concert footage and music videos combine for an unsurpassed "greatest hits" sampler of Bruce and the E Street Band from 1978 to 1987. All your Springsteen favorites are here, including "Born to Run," "Rosalita," "Born in the USA," "Dancing in the Dark," "Tunnel of Love" and much more. 100 min.
04-5012 *$14.99*

Bruce Springsteen: Plugged (1992)
Although normally a showcase for artists to perform their music acoustically, "MTV Unplugged" allowed Bruce Springsteen and his new band to crank it out electric... But remember he's "The Boss." Songs include "57 Channels," "Darkness on the Edge of Town," "Thunder Road," "Growin' Up," and two songs never released by Bruce in any format, "Red Headed Woman" and "The Light of Day." 115 min.
04-5181 *$19.99*

Bruce Springsteen & The E Street Band: Blood Brothers (1995)
In conjunction with the release of his "Greatest Hits" album, Bruce and the boys reunited for a recording session that resulted in such new songs as "Blood Brothers," "Murder Inc." and "Secret Garden," all of which are featured in this in-the-studio documentary that also includes "Cadillac Ranch," "Hungry Heart," "This Hard Land" and other tunes, interviews and more, plus a bonus, limited-edition five-song CD. 85 min.
04-5483 *$19.99*

Billy Joel: The Video Album, Vol. 1
Long Island's living legend in a great compilation of his snappiest songs. See the video of "Piano Man," made expressly for this collection, plus "Tell Her About It," "Pressure," "Keepin' the Faith," six more. 48 min.
04-1994 *$14.99*

Billy Joel: The Video Album, Vol. 2
The "Piano Man" keeps playing, and the hits keep on coming, in a second music video compilation. Watch and hear Billy perform "Uptown Girl," "Allentown," "It's Still Rock and Roll to Me," "Baby Grand" and more. 50 min.
04-2004 *$14.99*

Billy Joel: Greatest Hits, Vol. III—The Video
He's got more greatest hit albums than many performers have albums, and in this latest compilation "Piano Man" Billy Joel offers live and music video clips for such songs as "A Matter of Trust," "We Didn't Start the Fire," "The River of Dreams" and others, including four ("Shameless," "No Man's Land," "To Make You Feel My Love" and "Hey Girl") previously unreleased. 80 min.
04-5548 *$14.99*

Billy Joel: Live At Yankee Stadium (1990)
The House That Ruth Built has been home to many barrages of hits, but none have equalled the show that Billy Joel puts on in a dazzling live performance. Songs include "Scenes from an Italian Restaurant," "Piano Man," "A Matter of Trust," "Pressure," "We Didn't Start the Fire" and more. 90 min.
04-5062 *$19.99*

Loverboy: Anyway You Look At It
Listen as the boys lay down some guitar licks that form a searing amalgamation. Includes "Turn Me Loose," "Hot Girls in Love," "Queen of the Broken Hearts," "Lovin' Every Minute of It" and more. 37 min.
04-1942 *$19.99*

David Gilmour
The driving power of Pink Floyd's David Gilmour is showcased in this video extravaganza that mixes exciting footage, music videos and an intimate look at the music maker from his solo career. 100 min.
04-1714 *$14.99*

Pink Floyd: The Delicate Sound Of Thunder
Mind-blowing light effects and state-of-the-art camera work enhance this film archive of Pink Floyd's sold-out 1988 concert tour, featuring "Shine on You Crazy Diamond," "Signs of Life," "Comfortably Numb" and other space-age anthems. 100 min.
04-5019 *$24.99*

Pink Floyd Live At Pompeii (1972)
The ruins of an ancient amphitheater are brought to life via the sound of Roger Waters, David Gilmour, Nick Mason and Richard Wright. Dazzling concert film experience includes "Saucerful of Secrets," "Careful with That Axe, Eugene," "Set the Controls for the Heart of the Sun" and more. 80 min.
02-7060 *$19.99*

Roger Waters: The Wall—Live In Berlin (1990)
On July 23, 1990, former Pink Floyd leader Roger Waters led an all-star aggregation in a performance of the rock musical "The Wall" for the reunited city. This historic concert features such stars as Van Morrison, Sinéad O'Connor, Bryan Adams, Thomas Dolby, Joni Mitchell, Cyndi Lauper and The Scorpions. 120 min.
02-7187 *$14.99*

Pink Floyd: Pulse (1994)
Recorded live at Earls Court in London, this pulse-pounding video features David Gilmour leading Pink Floyd in concert. Songs include "Another Brick in the Wall (Part Two)," "Money," "Wish You Were Here," "Tack It Back" and many more, including a complete performance of "Dark Side of the Moon." 145 min.
04-5356 *$24.99*

25 Years Of #1 Hits: Arista Record's 25th Anniversary Celebration
A rousing evening of musical entertainment is had by all in this tribute to the "House That Clive (Davis) Built." Join hosts Jay Leno, Billy Bob Thornton and Magic Johnson as they welcome performers Santana ("Smooth"), Annie Lennox ("Why"), Aretha Franklin (performing a medley of her hits with Boyz II Men), Melissa Etheridge, Whitney Houston, Patti Smith and others.
02-9220 *$19.99*

Prime Cuts, Vol. I
A compilation of the best music videos around! Cyndi Lauper ("Girls Just Want to Have Fun"), Bonnie Tyler ("Total Eclipse of the Heart"), Quiet Riot ("Cum on Feel the Noize"), Men at Work ("Down Under") and others. 38 min.
04-1191 *$19.99*

Michael Jackson: Dangerous—The Short Films
A fantastic collection of videos produced for Jackson's hit "Dangerous" album. Dance along to "Black or White," with George Wendt and Macauley Culkin; "Remember the Time," with Eddie Murphy and Magic Johnson; "JAM," featuring Michael Jordan; plus "In The Closet," "Heal the World" and more, including backstage footage. 95 min.
04-5195 *$19.99*

Michael Jackson: Video Greatest Hits—HIStory
The top music videos from the Prince of Pop's solo career have been gathered for this must-have retrospective that also features "Brace Yourself," a sampler from his "HIStory" album. Songs include "Rock with You," "Billie Jean," "Thriller," "Bad," "Black or White," "Remember the Time" and more. 75 min.
04-5355 *$19.99*

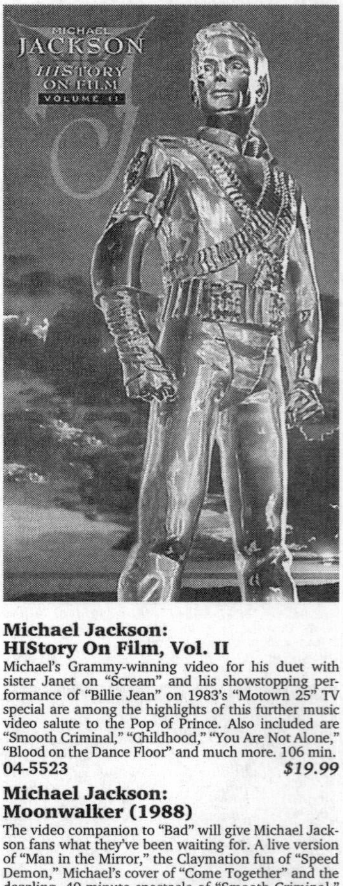

Michael Jackson: HIStory On Film, Vol. II
Michael's Grammy-winning video for his duet with sister Janet on "Scream" and his showstopping performance of "Billie Jean" on 1983's "Motown 25" TV special are among the highlights of this further music video salute to the Pop of Prince. Also included are "Smooth Criminal," "Childhood," "You Are Not Alone," "Blood on the Dance Floor" and much more. 106 min.
04-5523 *$19.99*

Michael Jackson: Moonwalker (1988)
The video companion to "Bad" will give Michael Jackson fans what they've been waiting for. A live version of "Man in the Mirror," the Claymation fun of "Speed Demon," Michael's cover of "Come Together" and the dazzling, 40-minute spectacle of "Smooth Criminal," plus many more. 94 min.
04-5009 *$24.99*

Janet Jackson: janet.
Her eponymous album sold over 10,000,000 copies worldwide, and on this special compilation Janet Jackson's hit videos for "That's the Way Love Is," "Again," "If," "Anytime, Anyplace" and other songs have been assembled, along with alternate versions and exclusive candid documentary footage.
44-4107 *$19.99*

Janet Jackson: The Velvet Rope Tour: Live In Concert (1998)
Janet brings her dazzling "Velvet Rope" stageshow to New York's famed Madison Square Garden for an unforgettable, hit-filled concert experience. Songs include "If," "Control," "Escapade," "I Get Lonely," "Black Cat," "Rhythm Nation," "Together Again" and many more. 121 min.
50-5754 *$19.99*

Luther Vandross: Live At Wembley
A crossover favorite with soul and rock audiences, Vandross' wonderful London concert features "Never Too Much," "Any Love," "Love Won't Let Me Wait," "Superstar" and other favorites. 90 min.
04-5026 *$19.99*

Luther Vandross: An Evening Of Songs (1994)
Recorded live at London's Royal Albert Hall, this wonderful concert special features Vandross performing many of his chart-topping favorites, including "Stop to Love," "Never Too Much," "Killing Me Softly," "Evergreen," "Give Me the Reason" and many more. 90 min.
04-5260 *$19.99*

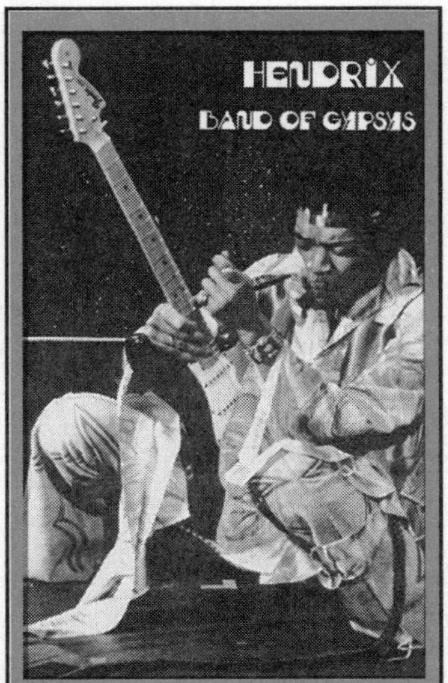

Jimi Hendrix: Band Of Gypsys
Rock history was made on New Year's Eve, 1969 when Jimi Hendrix, Billy Cox and Buddy Miles took the stage at New York's Fillmore East for a show that later was used in Hendrix' "Band of Gypsys" album. Now you can relive their groundbreaking performance, along with exclusive interview footage (including Jimi on "The Dick Cavett Show"), with this must-see video. 83 min.
07-2741 *$14.99*

Classic Albums: Jimi Hendrix: Electric Ladyland
The third album by the Jimi Hendrix Experience, 1968's "Electric Ladyland" reached number one on the Billboard charts and features such seminal Hendrix tunes as "Crosstown Traffic," "All Along the Watchtower" and "Little Miss Strange." Get the story behind the making of this psychedelic landmark and see rare performance footage of Jimi and bandmates Noel Redding and Mitch Mitchell. 60 min.
15-5423 *$19.99*

Jimi Plays Monterey (1967)
The immortal Jimi Hendrix plays (literally) the hottest guitar in rock in this film record of his ground-breaking Monterey Pop Festival performance with The Jimi Hendrix Experience. Songs include "Can You See Me," "Wild Thing," "Foxy Lady," "Like a Rolling Stone," "The Wind Cries Mary," "Purple Haze" and others. 50 min.
44-1632 Was $19.99 *$14.99*

Jimi Hendrix Live At The Isle Of Wight (1970)
Hendrix' last concert appearance, less than a month before his untimely death, was this performance in England. The guitar great offers up "Sgt. Pepper's Lonely Hearts Club Band," "Dolly Dagger," "Voodoo Chile," "Machine Gun," "God Save the Queen" and more. 56 min.
15-5344 *$19.99*

Jimi Hendrix: Rainbow Bridge (1970)
Sixties buffs, take note: Jimi's historic Hawaii concert (a film-within-a-film known as "The Rainbow Bridge Laboratory Color Sound Experiment") is finally available in its restored, uncut version. Sandwiched inside a visit to the famed "Occult Meditation Center" in Maui, Hendrix's turns on "Get My Heart Back Together," "Hear My Prayer," "Foxy Lady" and others make this a psychedelic must-see. 125 min.
44-7058 *$19.99*

Jimi Hendrix (1973)
An intimate look at the great Jimi Hendrix. Clips of Jimi and his brilliant guitar-playing in concert, interviews with family, friends and such performers as Mick Jagger, Little Richard, Lou Reed, Eric Clapton and Pete Townshend. "Red House," "Machine Gun," "Like a Rolling Stone," "Purple Haze" and more! 102 min.
19-1350 Was $19.99 *$14.99*

Meat Loaf: Hits Out Of Hell
If you've been hungry for a heaping slice of Meat Loaf, the wait is over. The rock and roll heavyweight's hit music videos, including "Bat Out of Hell," "Two Out of Three Ain't Bad," "Paradise by the Dashboard Light," "Read 'Em and Weep" and more, are collected on one smash tape. 52 min.
04-5100 *$19.99*

Meat Loaf: Bat Out Of Hell II—Picture Show
"Meat Loaf again?" You bet, and the hard-rockin' singer revs up his engine on this compilation that includes the videos for his hits "I'd Do Anything for Love," "Objects in the Rear View Mirror May Appear Closer Than They Are" and "Rock and Roll Dreams Come Through," live concert footage, and an exclusive interview with the Loaf man.
07-4117 *$19.99*

Classic Albums: Meat Loaf: Bat Out Of Hell
Since its debut in late 1977, the mix of adolescent angst and operatic rock from singer Meat Loaf and songwriter Jim Steinman has gone on to sell over 30 million copies. See how the pair's at-times stormy relationship led to one of the best-selling albums of all time through rare archival footage and performance clips. "Paradise by the Dashboard Light," "Two Out of Three Ain't Bad" and "Heaven Can Wait" are among the featured songs. 60 min.
15-5544 *$19.99*

Gloria Estefan: Don't Stop!
You're in for a non-stop look at pop diva Gloria Estefan with this collection of videos for such songs as "Oye," "Don't Stop," "You'll Be Mine (Party Time)," "Tes Deseos" and many others. Also included is footage of Estefan on a promo tour for her "gloria!" album, hosting the World Music Awards in Monaco, and more. 70 min.
04-5632 *$19.99*

Gloria Estefan & Miami Sound Machine: Homecoming Concert (1988)
The Latino-flavored pop group "lets it loose" in a live Miami concert. Songs include "Conga," "I'd Do Anything for You," "Hot Summer Nights," "Bad Boy" and more hits. 80 min.
04-5016 *$14.99*

Gloria Estefan: The Evolution Tour—Live In Miami (1996)
The "Rhythm Is Gonna Get You" as the effervescent Estefan and the Miami Sound Machine offer up a Gloria-ous evening of song, recorded live at the Miami Arena, that features such tunes as "Conga," "Don't Wanna Lose You," "Everlasting Love," "Coming Out of the Dark," "Turn the Beat Around" and more. 120 min.
04-5487 *$19.99*

Joe Satriani: The Satch Tapes
Guitar master Satriani, whose 1987 "Surfing with the Alien" album broke new ground in instrumental rock, looks back on his career with this searing amalgamation of music videos (including "Surfing with the Alien" and "Flying in a Blue Dream") concert clips, and in-the-studio and interview footage. 53 min.
04-5642 *$14.99*

Pop Up Video: '80s
Enjoy some of the biggest songs of the "Reagan Era"—and watch as fascinating and funny facts pop up on the screen—in a music video collection culled from the popular VH1 series. Featured are The Buggles ("Video Killed the Radio Star"), Donna Summer ("She Works Hard for the Money"), Sammy Hagar ("I Can't Drive 55"), Peter Gabriel ("Shock the Monkey"), Robert Palmer ("Addicted to Love") and six more. 65 min.
04-5662 *$14.99*

New Kids On The Block: Greatest Hits: The Videos
Okay, so they're not that new anymore. Danny, Donny, Joe, Jonathan and Jordan still managed to snare four Top 20 albums and nine Top 10 singles in just five years. This collection of music videos and concert clips includes all of NKOTB's biggest hits, including "Step by Step," "You Got It (The Right Stuff)," "Didn't I (Blow Your Mind)," "I'll Be Loving You (Forever)" and many (others). 55 min.
04-5668 *$14.99*

The Bangles: Greatest Hits
Susanna Hoffs and the all-girl band star in this collection of video favorites of such hits as "Manic Monday," "Walk Like an Egyptian," "Hero Takes a Fall" and six more. 40 min.
04-5044 *$19.99*

Toto: Past To Present
Here's 14 songs by the slick power popsters. You'll enjoy such tunes as "Africa" and "Roseanna" in this pleasing tribute to one of rock's most beloved groups. 75 min.
04-5059 *$19.99*

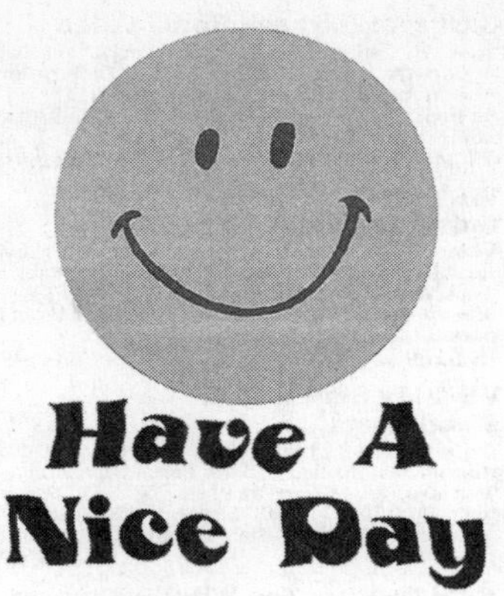

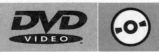

Have A Nice Day
Take a far-out trip back to the '70s and relive the good old days through some of your favorite hits from the era of Nixon, "The Godfather" and acid-washed jeans. Each volume runs about 40 min.

Have A Nice Day, Vol. 1
Artists include Hall & Oates ("Rich Girl"), Dr. Hook ("Cover of the 'Rolling Stone'"), Bonnie Tyler ("It's a Heartache"), Melanie ("Brand New Key") and more.
15-5450 *$14.99*

Have A Nice Day, Vol. 2
Artists include Alice Cooper ("Eighteen"), America ("Horse with No Name"), The Doobie Brothers ("China Groove"), The Ramones ("Blitzkrieg Bop") and more.
15-5451 *$14.99*

The Moody Blues: A Night At Red Rocks With The Colorado Symphony Orchestra
The superband from the Sixties and Seventies turns in an evening of inventive, artistic rock music, in which they perform such gems as "Tuesday Afternoon," "Lovely to See You," "Nights in White Satin," "Question" and "Ride My See-Saw." 90 min.
02-7812 *$19.99*

James Taylor In Concert
"J.T." is presented at his best here, in a wonderful concert in which the beloved singer-songwriter performs such songs as "Fire and Rain," "Smiling Face," "Shower the People," "Carolina on My Mind," "Sweet Baby James" and more. 60 min.
04-5117 *$19.99*

James Taylor: Squibnocket
James Taylor performs a selection of new songs and his greatest hits in this performance filmed in Martha's Vineyard, where the singer-songwriter lives. Tunes include "Copperline," "(I've Got to) Stop Thinkin' 'Bout That," "You've Got a Friend," "Country Road," "Mexico," "Fire & Rain" and more. 65 min.
04-5188 *$19.99*

James Taylor: Live At The Beacon Theatre
This May, 1998 concert in New York's Beacon Theater showcases J.T. at his best, performing some of his best-loved hits and numbers from his 1997 album, "Hourglass." Featured tunes include "Don't Let Me Be Lonely Tonight," "Shower the People," "You've Got a Friend," "Steamroller Blues," "Your Smiling Face," "Fire and Rain," "Another Day" and more. 104 min.
04-5623 *$19.99*

REO Speedwagon: A Video Anthology: 1978-1990
Roll with the greatest hits from one of the most popular bands of the last few decades. This program features videos from such favorites as "Roll With the Changes," "Time for Me to Fly," "Keep on Loving You," "One Lonely Night" and more. 75 min.
04-5125 *$19.99*

REO Speedwagon: Wheels Are Turnin' (1985)
The guitar licks form a searing amalgamation in this spectacular concert experience. The megahit combo gets their gears spinnin' with hits like "Don't Let 'Em Go," "I Do Wanna Know," "Take It on the Run," "Tough Guys" and much more. 80 min.
04-1934 *$29.99*

Guns N' Roses: Use Your Illusion Live, Vol. 1
It's a rock video event that's too big for one tape! Guns N' Roses take their high-voltage stageshow to Japan in one of the most explosive concerts ever, along with backstage footage, candid interviews and more. Featured songs include "Welcome to the Jungle," "Wild Horses," "Don't Cry," "Live and Let Die" and 11 others. 90 min.
07-4089 *$19.99*

Guns N' Roses: Use Your Illusion Live, Vol. 2
The G N' R assault on the Far East continues. More dynamic hard rock from Axl, Slash, Duff and crew as they perform "Sweet Child o' Mine," "Knockin' on Heaven's Door," "Rocket Queen" and eight more of their biggest hits. 90 min.
07-4090 *$19.99*

The Monkees: Heart And Soul
The one, the only, the original Monkees are here in their first original music video! Join Mickey Dolenz, Davy Jones and Peter Tork for songs from their hit album "Pool It," interviews and some of the classic Monkee madness. 40 min.
15-5059 Was $19.99 *$14.99*

The Monkees: 33 1/3 Revolutions Per Monkee (1969)
For their only broadcast TV special, Davy, Peter, Mickey and Mike were joined by such rock legends as Fats Domino, Jerry Lee Lewis and Little Richard in a wild mix of comedy and music. "I'm a Believer," "Naked Persimmon," "String for My Kite" and "Listen to the Band" are among the songs featured, plus an oldies medley that includes "At the Hop," "I'm Ready," "Tutti-Frutti" and more. 60 min.
15-5364 *$19.99*

The Monkees: Hey Hey We're The Monkees (1997)
Trace three decades of "Monkeemania" with this song-filled retrospective that includes never-before-seen interviews with Peter, Mike, Davy and Mickey; vintage clips from their '60s show and other TV appearances and the fellas' pre-Monkee days; a solo Mike Nesmith performance; and more. 110 min.
15-5401 *$19.99*

Pearl Jam: Single Video Theory
Get a raw glimpse into the intimate world of Pearl Jam as they rehearse for their upcoming tour and discuss the progress of their latest album, "Yield," as well as the evolution of Pearl Jam as a band. Shot on 16mm over three days by award-winning filmmaker Mark Pellington. Songs include "All These Yesterdays," "No Way," "MFC," "In Hiding" and others. 45 min.
04-5607 *$12.99*

Savage Garden: The Video Collection
Aussie pop stars Savage Garden are in full bloom in this sizzling compilation of videos that includes "Truly, Madly, Deeply," "I Want You," "To the Moon and Back," "Break Me Shake Me" and "Tears of Pearls." 21 min.
04-5622 *$14.99*

British Big Beat: The Invasion
Rarely seen British groups at the forefront of the early '60s pop import boom include The Hollies ("Here I Go Again"), Lulu & The Luvvers ("Shout"), The Merseybeats ("Don't Turn Around"), Millie Small ("My Boy Lollipop"), The Swinging Blue Jeans ("Don't You Worry About Me") and others. AKA: "Go Go Big Beat." 70 min.
15-5095 Was $19.99 *$14.99*

Classic Albums: Steely Dan: Aja
The sixth album from the progressive jazz-rock combo, 1977's "Aja" spent over a year in the top 40 and was Steely Dan's biggest album ever, yielding such hits as "Peg," "Deacon Blue" and the title tune. Hear from Walter Becker, Donald Fagen and company on the making of this rock landmark. 60 min.
15-5574 *$14.99*

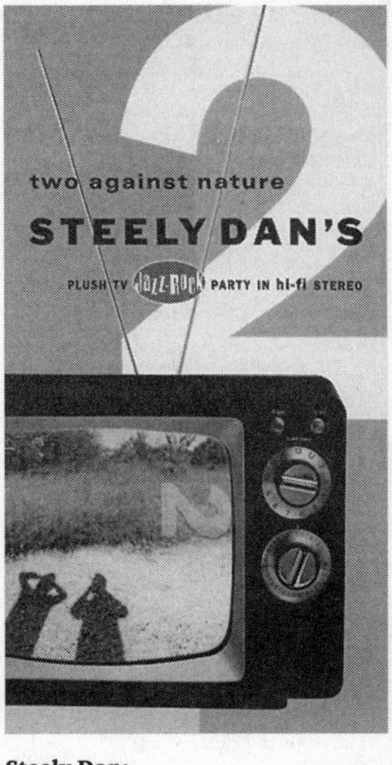

Steely Dan: Two Against Nature (2000)
After a 20-year hiatus, Walter Becker and Donald Fagen reunited in 2000 for the Steely Dan album "Two Against Nature." In this special concert, shot live at New York's Sony Studios, the duo perform a selection of favorites old ("Green Earrings," "FM," "Peg," "Pretzel Logic") and new ("Cousin Dupree," "Gaslighting Abbie," "What a Shame About Me"). 101 min.
50-8559 *$19.99*

Cyndi Lauper: Twelve Deadly Cyns
Cyndi Lauper's career is chronicled in this music video collection that features narration by Lauper herself, who tells the stories behind her songs and her life. Videos include "Money Changes Everything," "She Bop," "Girls Just Want to Have Fun," "All Through the Night" and the 1995 entries "Hey Now (Girls Just Want to Have Fun)" and "Come on Home." 80 min.
04-5365 *$19.99*

Cyndi Lauper In Paris (1987)
The lilting Ms. Lauper shines in the final show of her 1987 world tour. A full 17 of her most popular numbers are featured, including "Change of Heart," "She Bop," "Time after Time," "True Colors" and "Money Changes Everything." 90 min.
04-2083 *$24.99*

G3 Live In Concert: Joe Satriani/ Eric Johnson/Steve Vai
Talk about a searing amalgamation of guitar licks! Three of rock's premier instrumental guitarists pool their talents in a dynamic live stage show that features Vai, Johnson and Satriani performing solo and in tandem. Songs include "Cool #9," "Manhattan," "For the Love of God," "Going Down," "My Guitar Wants to Kill Your Mama" and others. 75 min.
04-5522 *$19.99*

We're All Devo
A special "greatest hits" package from the Spud Boys from Akron, Ohio. Includes the music videos for "Satisfaction," "Jocko Homo," "Whip It," "Beautiful World," "Dr. Detroit" and more. 54 min.
15-5117 Was $19.99 *$14.99*

The Turtles: Happy Together
Hip history of the popular '60s combo features interviews with Ray Manzarek, Graham Nash and ex-Turtles Flo and Eddie, TV clips from "Shindig!" and "Where the Action Is," and hits like "Happy Together," "It Ain't Me Babe," "You Showed Me" and more. 90 min.
15-5154 Was $19.99 *$14.99*

Garbage: Garbage Home Video
"Now, it's Garbage," with a video compilation that includes the band's acclaimed "Vow," "Only Happy When It Rains," "Stupid Girl" and "Queer" music videos from their hit debut album, plus live performance footage and more. 31 min.
07-2487 *$12.99*

VH-1 My Generation: Guitar Legends
A host of guitar greats are featured in all their glory. See Johnny Winter's "Johnny B. Goode," Joe Walsh's "Walk Away," Jimi Hendrix' "Hey Joe," B.B. King's "Heartbreaker," Duane Eddy's "Peter Gunn" and more. 33 min.
15-5269 *$14.99*

VH-1 My Generation: Metal Roots
The early days of heavy metal are recalled in this program that spotlights Black Sabbath performing "Iron Man," Alice Cooper's anthem "Eighteen," Mountain's "Don't Look Around," Steppenwolf's "Rock Me," Deep Purple's "Highway Star," and more. 38 min.
15-5270 *$14.99*

John Denver: The Wildlife Concert
John Denver's 1995 concert is captured in this terrific live show in which the singer-songwriter performs some of his most popular songs. Among the tunes are "Rocky Mountain High," "Annie's Song," "Calypso," "Back Home Again" and more. 113 min.
04-5364 *$19.99*

John Denver: A Portrait
Fans of John Denver won't want to miss this career retrospective of one of the most popular singer-songwriters ever. Filled with hit songs like "Calypso," "Rocky Mountain High," "Annie's Song," "Sunshine on My Shoulder" and "Leaving on a Jet Plane," the program offers Denver performing and talking about his interests, inspirations and career. 60 min.
27-6864 Was $24.99 *$19.99*

Folk

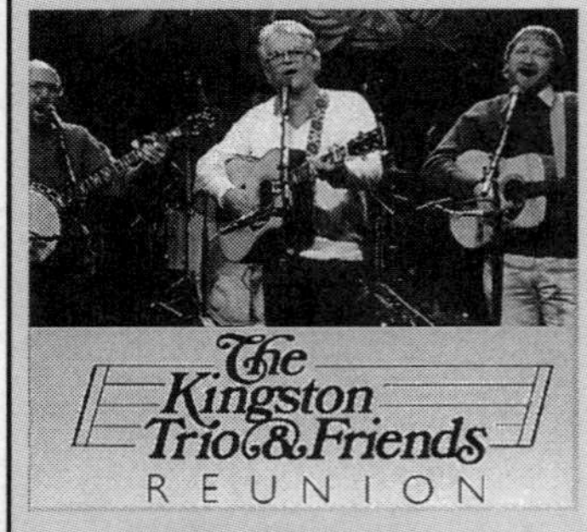

The Kingston Trio & Friends Reunion
The legendary folk-singing group performs together for the first time since 1961 in a thrilling concert of their greatest hits, including "Tom Dooley," "Scotch and Soda" and "A Worried Man." Joining them are guests Tommy Smothers, Mary Travers, Lindsey Buckingham and John Stewart. 50 min.
22-1316 *$19.99*

The Book Of Chapin
This classic 1974 concert from PBS's "Soundstage" showcases famed singer-songwriter Harry Chapin at his best, performing such beloved tunes as "The Cat's in the Cradle," "Taxi," "W.O.L.D.," "She Sings Songs Without Words" and "Mr. Tanner." 60 min.
15-5309 *$19.99*

Peter, Paul And Mary: Lifelines
Favorites old and new from the perennially popular folk-pop trio are featured in this special program that follows Peter, Paul and Mary performing with such guests as Richie Havens, John Sebastian, Tom Paxton, Odetta and others, plus special rehearsal footage and scenes of the three in their lives away from each other. Songs include "Blowin' in the Wind," "Stewball," "Freedom Medley" and more. 95 min.
19-3937 *$19.99*

Cajun Country
Take a trip to Louisiana, where you'll meet some of the world's greatest musicians performing their distinctive type of music, which has absorbed 200 years of influence yet has remained original at the same time. Featured are Queen Ida, Dewey Balfa, Wayne Toups, Boozoo Chavis and the Savoy-Doucet Band. Hosted by Aly Bain. 60 min.
63-7153 *$19.99*

Pure Pete Seeger
Get to know one of America's best-loved folk performers in this winning special hosted by Bill Moyers. Filmed on the eve of Seeger's 75th birthday at his home in New York's Hudson Valley, the program looks at the music and politics of the controversial singer/songwriter. 51 min.
80-7163 *$29.99*

Ladies And Gentlemen... Mr. Leonard Cohen (1965)
This acclaimed National Film Board of Canada profile of the Montreal-born author/songwriter features a look at Cohen shortly before the beginning of his musical career, reading his poems before enthusiastic coffeehouse and college audiences and discussing the inspirations for his work. Also included on this video are "In Short: Leonard Cohen" and videos for "I'm Your Man," "Poen," "A Kite Is a Victim" and "Angel." 78 min.
53-6595 *$19.99*

Folk City: 25th Anniversary Concert (1989)
Here's a salute to Greenwich Village's famous folk club, where many beloved musicians got their start. See and hear Suzanne Vega ("Crackin'"), The Roches ("Face Down at Folk City"), Richie Havens ("Freedom"), Peter Yarrow ("Puff, the Magic Dragon"), Eric Anderson, Tom Paxton, Joan Baez and many more. 83 min.
15-5151 Was $19.99 *$14.99*

Fairport Convention: Beyond The Ledge (1998)
One of England's longest-lived and most influential bands, folk-rock pioneers Fairport Convention are featured in a live concert appearance at the Cropredy '98 Festival. "Who Knows Where the Time Goes," "Matty Grooves" and "Meet on the Ledge" are among the favorites performed by Chris Leslie, Simon Nicol, Dave Pegg and company. 120 min.
50-8345 *$19.99*

The McGarrigle Hour (1999)
This tribute to Kate and Anna McGarrigle offers the beloved singer-songwriter siblings along with friends and other artists who have performed some of their tunes. Among the guests are Emmylou Harris, Linda Ronstadt and Loudon, Rufus and Martha Wainright, and among the selections are "Cool River," "Talk to Me of Mendocino," "Year Of the Dragon" and more.
02-9165 *$19.99*

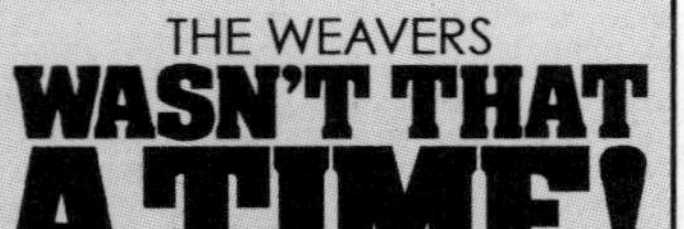

The Weavers: Wasn't That A Time (1982)
Outstanding documentary about the legendary folk group that included Pete Seeger, Lee Hays, Fred Hellerman and Ronnie Gilbert. The film chronicles The Weavers' music, lives and politics and their triumphant 1981 reunion concert at Carnegie Hall. Songs include "If I Had a Hammer," "Guantanamera," "Goodnight Irene" and more. 78 min.
19-3318 *$19.99*

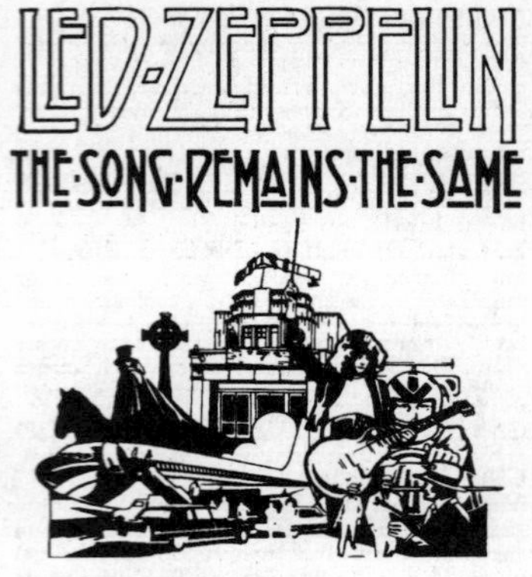

The Song Remains The Same (1976)
Led Zeppelin fans will find a stairway to heaven in this much-requested docu-fantasy. Robert Plant, John Bonham, John Paul Jones and Jimmy Page perform such tunes as "Whole Lotta Love," "Black Dog" and "Dazed and Confused." They also live out some wild, mind-boggling fantasies. 136 min.
19-1352 Was $19.99 *$14.99*

Jimmy Page & Robert Plant: No Quarter Unledded
The driving forces behind rock kings Led Zeppelin reunite for this MTV special that's highlighted by some knockout unplugged selections. Among the mix of old songs and new tunes are "Thank You," "Gallows Pole," "Kashmir," "Wah Wah," "Wonderful One" and more. And guess what? There's no "Stairway to Heaven." 93 min.
19-3709 *$29.99*

Dan Fogelberg Live: Greetings From The West
Folk rock singer-songwriter Dan Fogelberg performs his favorite tunes in this 1991 show from St. Louis. Included on the program are "Run for the Roses," "Leader of the Band," "Part of the Plan," "Same Auld Lang Syne," and more, plus an appearance with flautist Tim Weisberg on "The Power of Gold." 100 min.
04-5132 *$19.99*

The Eagles: Hell Freezes Over
For the first time in over a decade, Glenn Frey, Don Henley, Timothy B. Schmitt and Joe Walsh reunited for an album and tour, and on this video companion Eagles fans will get to see live performances of such old and new songs as "Hotel California," "Tequila Sunrise," "Get Over It," "Take It Easy," "Desperado" and many more, plus interviews and behind-the-scenes footage. 100 min.
07-4119 *$24.99*

Tom Petty And The Heartbreakers: Playback
"Play Over and Over" might be a better title, because that's what you'll do with this collection of 17 "greatest hits" videos from Tom and the boys. Included are "Refugee," "The Waiting," "Don't Come Around Here No More," "I Won't Back Down," "Mary Jane's Last Dance" and many more.
07-4126 *$19.99*

Tom Petty And The Heartbreakers: High Grass Dogs: Live From Fillmore (1999)
San Francisco's legendary Fillmore concert hall is the setting for an electrifying show by Tom Petty and The Heartbreakers, featuring more than 20 years of hits. Songs include "Runnin' Down a Dream," "Breakdown," "Mary Jane's Last Dream," "Angel Dream," "Free Girl Now," "Mona" (with special guest Bo Diddley) and many more. 90 min.
19-4065 *$19.99*

Saturday Morning Cartoons' Greatest Hits
Your favorite rock superstars pay tribute to their favorite animated kids' TV theme songs in this sugar-coated, super-charged video collection, hosted by Drew Barrymore. Performers include Matthew Sweet ("Scooby-Doo, Where Are You?"), Sublime ("Hong Kong Fooey"), The Ramones ("Spider-Man"), Juliana Hatfield and Tanya Donelly ("Josie and The Pussycats") and many more. 60 min.
07-4128 *$19.99*

No Doubt: Live In The Tragic Kingdom
"Don't Speak"; just pop this concert video in your VCR and enjoy Gwen Stefani and No Doubt as they perform their infectious brand of alternative pop live from Anaheim, California, the perfect place for their 1997 "Tragic Kingdom" tour. Songs include "Just a Girl," "Sunday Morning," "End It on This," "Move On" and more. 93 min.
07-4142 *$19.99*

Family Values Tour '98
It was one of the biggest and most controversial rock revues in recent memory, and this video chronicle of the Family Values Tour features rare backstage footage and interviews, plus dynamic live performances by KoRn ("Got the Life," "Freak on a Leash"), Rammstein ("Du Hast"), Ice Cube ("Check Ya Self"), Limp Bizkit ("Faith") and Orgy ("Blue Monday"). 86 min.
04-5648 *$19.99*

Geffen Vintage 80s, Vol. 1: The Videos
A salute to 1980s video rock featuring some of the most popular songs and music videos from the early MTV era. Included in this collection are "Dance Hall Days" by Wang Chung, Madness' "Our House," Rick Ocasek's "Emotion in Motion," "A Million Miles Away" by The Plimsouls, and more. 55 min.
07-4520 *$14.99*

Duran Duran: The Video Collection
Join Simon Le Bon, Nick Rhodes, Andy Taylor, John Taylor and Roger Taylor in a compilation of their popular videos. Included are "Rio," "Planet Earth," "Girls on Film," "Save a Prayer," "Careless Memories," "Hungry Like the Wolf" and more. 55 min.
44-1111 *$24.99*

Duran Duran: Dancing On The Valentine
New Wave faves in three of their hottest videos, seen here in uncut, uncensored form. Includes "The Reflex," "Union of the Snake" and "New Moon on Monday." 15 min.
45-5058 *$14.99*

Duran Duran: Greatest: The Videos
The great, MTV-savvy pop group of the 1980s are the stars of these pioneering videos of their biggest hits. Included are "Girls on Film" (uncensored), "Rio," "The Reflex," "Union of the Snake," "Planet Earth," "Serious," "Electric Barbarella" and many others. 101 min.
59-7112 *$24.99*

Duran Duran: Sing Blue Silver (1984)
Follow the top British band on their 1984 North American tour through concert and behind-the-scenes footage. They perform "Rio," "Girls on Film," "Reflex" and more in small halls and huge stadiums. 85 min.
44-1233 *$24.99*

Fleetwood Mac: The Early Years
Trace the beginnings of one of rock's most enduring and popular groups with this collection of vintage TV appearances, rare photos and concert clips. Original band members Mick Fleetwood, Peter Green, Danny Kirwan, John McVie and Jeremy Spencer offer up such blues-flavored early Fleetwood Mac faves as "Black Magic Woman," "Albatross," "Man of the World" and others. 55 min.
15-5353 *$14.99*

Classic Albums: Fleetwood Mac: Rumours
Go behind the scenes with the members of Fleetwood Mac to hear about the creation of what became one of rock's best-selling albums of all time. Along with interviews with the band, you'll see live versions and music videos of such songs as "Dreams," "Gold Dust Woman," "You Make Loving Fun" and more, including newly recorded versions of Christine McVie's "Songbird" and an acoustic version of "Never Going Back Again" by Lindsey Buckingham. 75 min.
15-5407 *$19.99*

Fleetwood Mac: Tango In The Night
A live concert performance at San Francisco, featuring the re-united supercombo along with guests Billy Burnette and Rick Vito. Songs include "Chain," "Dreams," "Gold Dust Woman," "Standback," "Songbird" and many more. 60 min.
19-3060 *$14.99*

Stevie: Live At Red Rocks (1987)
The ever-bewitching Stevie Nicks is featured in a dazzling concert show. Joined by special guests Peter Frampton and Mick Fleetwood, she performs "Dreams," "Stand Back," "Edge of Seventeen," "Talk to Me" and more. 60 min.
45-5396 Was $19.99 *$14.99*

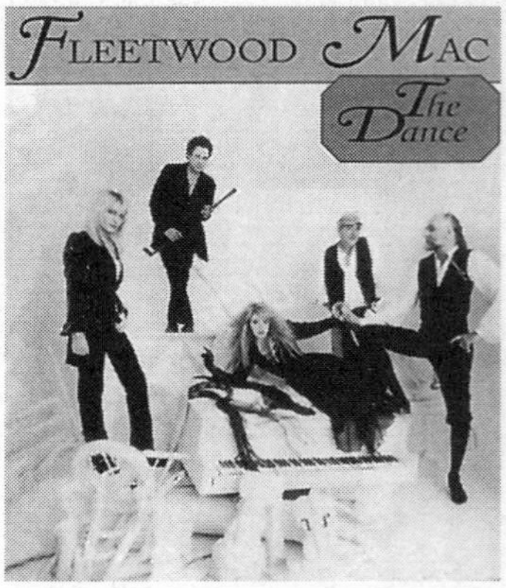

Fleetwood Mac: The Dance (1997)
For the first time in nearly 15 years, Fleetwood Mac members Lindsey Buckingham, Mick Fleetwood, Christine McVie, John McVie and Stevie Nicks re-united for a series of live performance recording sessions. Among the classic tunes featured are "Dreams," "Say That You Love Me," "Go Your Own Way," "Rhiannon," "Tusk" and many more, including four exclusive-to-video songs. 90 min.
19-3994 *$19.99*

Classic Albums: Bob Marley And The Wailers: Catch A Fire
The first album by Marley and his group to be marketed outside their native Jamaica, 1973's "Catch a Fire" helped introduce reggae music to American audiences. Performances of such songs as "Stir It Up," "Stop That Train," "Kinky Reggae" and others are featured, along with rare interview footage of Marley and fellow Wailers Peter Tosh and Bunny Livingston. 60 min.
15-5575 *$14.99*

One Love: The Bob Marley All-Star Tribute (1999)
His name has become synonymous with reggae, and in this remarkable concert such stars as Erykah Badu, Tracy Chapman, Jimmy Cliff, Chrissie Hynde, Queen Latifah and others join the Marley Family and The Wailers for a salute to the music of Bob Marley. Songs include "Jammin'," "No Woman No Cry," "Get Up Stand Up," "One Love" and 20 more. Special video version includes five songs not shown on broadcast TV.
02-9213 *$19.99*

Sly & Robbie: Drum & Bass Strip To The Bone
Unusual mix of funky, reggae-based music and softcore sex from ace musicians-producers Sly Dunbar and Robbie Shakespeare (of Tom Tom Club fame) features such tracks as "Stripped to the Bone" and "Fatigue Chic" set to exotic dancers stripping for your delight.
20-8403 *$19.99*

Lucky Dube: Live In Concert
International Reggae star Lucky Dube will thrill you with his astonishing concert performance, filmed on location in his South Africa homeland. Lucky uses a classic Reggae beat with politically insightful lyrics for an intoxicating mix. 90 min.
63-7090 *$29.99*

Heartland Reggae
Filmed in 1977 and 1978 in Jamaica, this superb concert film features Bob Marley and The Wailers in top form, joined by The I-Threes, and featuring Jacob Miller, Peter Tosh, Judy Mowatt, U-Roy, Dennis Brown, Junior Tucker and Lloyd Parks. 95 min.
84-1009 *$14.99*

Peter Gabriel: Secret World Live (1994)
Recorded during his first live tour in six years, this dazzling concert video showcases Peter Gabriel and his band performing such favorites as "In Your Eyes," "Come Talk to Me," "Sledgehammer" and many others. 103 min.
07-4113 *$24.99*

Iron Butterfly: In-A-Gadda-Da-Vida
It was the song that served as an anthem for an entire generation, and now it's available in all of its uncut glory along with other favorites by Sixties greats Iron Butterfly. Did it really mean "In the Garden of Eden"? Ponder it, man. 40 min.
15-5315 *$14.99*

Marilyn Manson: Dead To The World
Looking to spend some time with "The Beautiful People"? This raw and uncensored chronicle of the controversial "shock-rock" band's 1997 "Antichrist Superstar" tour features amazing concert footage and no-holds-barred interviews with Marilyn and company. WARNING: Contains explicit language and nudity. 60 min.
07-4143 *$19.99*

Marilyn Manson: God Is In The T.V.
Their 1999 tour packed arenas—inside with fans and outside with protesters—across America. Now witness Marilyn Manson in the comfort of your own home with this concert video that features such songs as "Coma White," "Rock Is Dead," "The Dope Show," "The Beautiful People," "Lunch Box" and more.
44-4180 *$19.99*

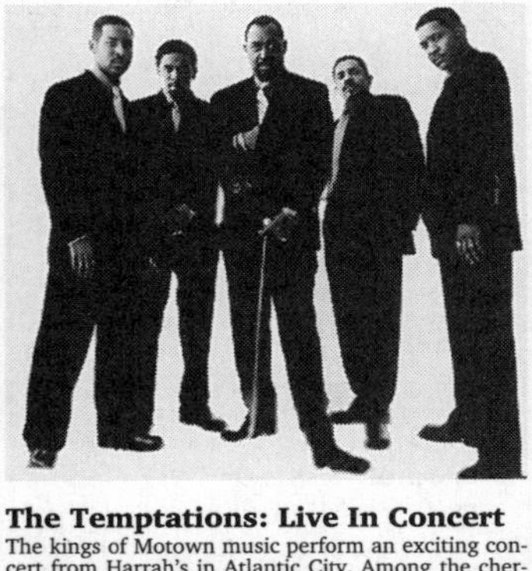

The Temptations: Live In Concert
The kings of Motown music perform an exciting concert from Harrah's in Atlantic City. Among the cherished songs are "My Girl," "I Wish It Would Rain," "Ain't Too Proud to Beg," "Can't Get Next to You," "Papa Was a Rolling Stone," "Cloud Nine," "Get Ready," "Runaway Child, Running Wild," and a dozen more. 60 min.
22-1320 *$14.99*

Ministry: Tapes Of Wrath (2000)
Ministry, the kings of the industrial music scene, have assembled a collection of videos spanning their entire career from 1985 to the present, including two songs from the group's spin-off band, The Revolting Cocks. Among the 13 featured selections are "Stigmata," "The Land of Rape and Honey," "Just One Fix," "Jesus Built My Hotrod" and "Bad Blood." 70 min.
19-4087 *$19.99*

The Doors: Live In Europe 1968
Grace Slick and Paul Kantner host a recently unearthed collection of vintage concert footage from The Doors' infamous 1968 European tour. The charismatic Jim Morrison lives on in the songs "Love Me Two Times," "Hello I Love You," "Light My Fire," "Unknown Soldier" and others. 58 min.
19-3176 *$19.99*

The Doors: The Doors Are Open (1968)
A rare find for fans of the groundbreaking '60s band, featuring footage of The Doors performing at London's Roundhouse for the BBC in a concert that drummer John Densmore called the group's "best performance on tape." Songs include "Five to One," "When the Music's Over," "The Unknown Soldier" and more. 50 min.
19-3173 *$19.99*

New Wave Hits Of The '80s: Just Can't Get Enough, Vol. 1
It's never too soon for '80s nostalgia, and with this video you can relive the "Age of Reagan" through music videos for such New Wave faves as Gary Numan ("Cars"), Bow Wow Wow ("I Want Candy"), Haircut 100 ("Love Plus One"), Duran Duran ("Girls on Film"), ABC ("Poison Arrow") and others. 35 min.
15-5305 *$14.99*

New Wave Hits Of The '80s: Just Can't Get Enough, Vol. 2
Harken back to MTV's infancy with more "modern rock" classics in music video form from such artists as M ("Pop Muzik"), A Flock of Seagulls ("I Ran"), Big Country ("In a Big Country"), The Fixx ("One Thing Leads to Another") and others. 35 min.
15-5306 *$14.99*

The Cars: Heartbeat City
Always on the cutting edge of rock music, Boston's top band, The Cars, are featured in this video collection. Included are "You Might Think," "Hello Again" "Magic," "Shake It Up" and "Panorama," and more. 60 min.
19-1336 *$14.99*

Classic Albums: The Grateful Dead: Anthem To Beauty
Trace the early recording history of one of rock music's most enduring bands with this documentary that takes you from the Dead's 1968 "Anthem of the Sun" to "American Beauty" in 1970. Live performances, rare home movies and interviews with Jerry Garcia and company are featured; songs include "Box of Rain," "Sugar Magnolia," "Truckin'" and more. 75 min.
15-5408 *$19.99*

Grateful To Garcia
This tribute to Grateful Dead leader Jerry Garcia is a Deadhead's dream: a two-tape exploration into his life and music filled with rare footage and interviews. See what made "Captain Trips" and the band enduring legends in the rock world in this salute to San Francisco psychedelia's finest. 90 min.
64-3426 *$12.99*

Grateful Dead: Downhill From Here (1989)
One of the favorite "Deadhead" tour stops, Alpine Valley Music Theater, is the setting for this energetic concert. Among the songs the band performs are "Let the Good Times Roll," "Desolation Row," "Uncle John's Band," "Gimme Some Loving" and many more, including three not available anywhere else live: "Built to Last," "Standing on the Moon" and "West L.A. Fadeaway." 150 min.
27-7038 *$29.99*

Tie-Died: Rock 'N Roll's Most Deadicated Fans (1995)
Take a fascinating, funky look at the pop culture phenomenon of the "Deadheads," the hard-core fans of The Grateful Dead who have been truckin' with their favorite group around the world for decades. Shot during one of the Dead's final tours, the film examines Deadhead etiquette, customizing vans and trucks, the truth behind those "sex and drugs" stories, life on the road for the children of Deadheads and other topics. 88 min.
02-8452 Was $19.99 *$14.99*

Grateful Dead: View From The Vault (1990)
From along the banks of the scenic Monongahela River in Pittsburgh, this vintage Dead concert features the band live at Three Rivers Stadium, performing "Touch of Grey," "Mama Tried," "Mexicali Blues," "Samson and Delilah," "Terrapin Station," "Wang Dang Doodle," "Black Peter" and many more faves. 153 min.
27-7359 *$24.99*

Grateful Dead: The Concerts Boxed Set
What a long, strange trip it'll be when you watch this boxed collector's set that includes "The Grateful Dead Movie," "The Grateful Dead: Dead Ahead" and "The Grateful Dead: Ticket to New Year's." Each volume is available separately.
27-6989 Save $10.00! *$74.99*

Classic Albums: Stevie Wonder: Songs In The Key Of Life
Three Grammy awards, including Album of the Year, went to Stevie Wonder's 1976 work that featured such favorites as "I Wish," "Isn't She Lovely" and "Sir Duke." Interviews with Motown founder Berry Gordy, producer Quincy Jones, lyricist Gary Byrd and others help tell the story behind the album's creation, and a special reunion performance of "Sir Duke" and "I Wish" is featured. 75 min.
15-5416 *$19.99*

Neil Young: Unplugged
Neil Young turns in a gripping acoustic concert for MTV's "Unplugged" program, performing such songs from his "Harvest Moon" album as "From Hank to Hendrix" and such classics as "Mr. Soul" and "Helpless." Neil's backed by such past collaborators as Nils Lofgren, Nicolette Larson and Ben Keith. 70 min.
19-3428 *$19.99*

Rust Never Sleeps (1978)
The acclaimed filmed concert from their 1978 world tour features Neil Young & Crazy Horse live in San Francisco for a raw and resonant show that includes favorite songs like "Sugar Mountain," "After the Gold Rush," "I Am a Child," "My My, Hey Hey (Out of the Blue)" and many more. 116 min.
19-3461 *$29.99*

Neil Young: The Human Highway (1983)
A surreal, rarely seen musical fantasy starring Neil Young as a goofy car mechanic whose bizarre fantasies involve nuclear meltdowns, limousines, romance and Devo. Also starring are Dean Stockwell, Sally Kirkland and Dennis Hopper; songs include "My My Hey Hey," "Ride My Llama" and "Come Back Jonee." Directed by Young (under the name "Bernard Shakey"). 83 min.
19-3730 *$19.99*

Neil Young & Crazy Horse: Weld (1991)
Neil Young and Crazy Horse turn in a thrashing evening of rock, taken from their 1991 tour. From their Woodstock tribute version of "The Star-Spangled Banner" to oldies like "Cinnamon Girl" and all-out scorchers like "Powderfinger," "Rockin' in the Free World" and "Hey, Hey (My, My)," Young and pals deliver a mesmerizing show. 120 min.
19-3260 *$29.99*

Neil Young: Silver & Gold (1999)
Recorded at the Bass Concert Hall in Austin, Texas, during Young's 1999 solo acoustic tour, this dynamic concert features Neil performing such old and new favorites as "Looking Forward," "Buffalo Springfield Again," "Philadelphia," "Long May You Run," "Harvest Moon," "Silver & Gold" and more. 62 min.
19-4079 *$19.99*

Classic Albums: Paul Simon: Graceland
Paul Simon's innovative mix of American pop and African styles and musicians garnered the 1986 Album of the Year Grammy. Go into the studio with Simon and engineer Roy Halee to see how "Graceland" was created. Live performance footage and video clips for such songs as "You Can Call Me Al," "Diamonds in the Soles of Her Shoes," "The Boy in the Bubble" and the title tune are featured. 75 min.
15-5417 *$19.99*

SIMON AND GARFUNKEL
THE CONCERT IN CENTRAL PARK

Simon And Garfunkel: The Concert In Central Park (1982)
The much-loved songwriting team regrouped on September 19, 1981 for a memorable concert in New York, performing such classics as "Mrs. Robinson," "Homeward Bound," "Feeling Groovy," "The Sounds of Silence" and "Bridge Over Troubled Water." 87 min.
04-1607 Was $19.99 *$14.99*

Paul Simon: Graceland—The African Concert (1987)
Based on his Grammy-winning album that blended rock with traditional African music, Simon is featured in his 1987 world tour, performing in Zimbabwe with renowned trumpeter Hugh Masekela and South African singers Ladysmith Black Mambazo. Songs include "You Can Call Me Al," "Homeless," "Boy in the Bubble" and the title tune. 90 min.
19-3042 *$14.99*

Paul Simon's Concert In The Park (1991)
New York's Central Park is the site of this legendary concert that drew nearly 750,000 people. Paul Simon, backed by a top-notch band, performs new tunes like "The Obvious Child" and "Born at the Right Time," along with favorites from the "Graceland" album and classics like "The Sounds of Silence," "The Boxer" and "Bridge Over Troubled Water." 140 min.
19-3258 *$29.99*

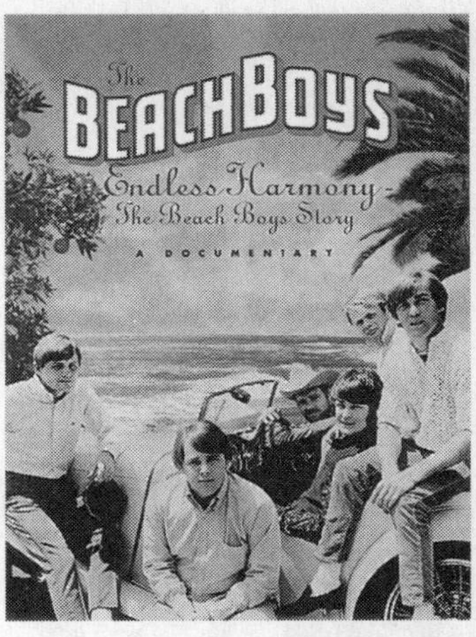

The Beach Boys: Endless Harmony
Hear the story of rock's paramount "surf band" in the members' own words in this song-filled retrospective. Rare concert and backstage footage and exclusive interviews take you through four decades of the "California sound." Songs include "Loop De Loop," "California Girls," "Fun, Fun, Fun," "Good Vibrations," "Little Deuce Coupe," "Sloop John B" and many more.
44-4188 *$19.99*

The Beach Boys: Nashville Sounds: The Making Of Stars And Stripes
The West Coast meets the South when Brian Wilson, Carl Wilson, Mike Love, Al Jardine and Bruce Johnston take the stage with some of the top stars in country music to put a new spin on classic Beach Boys tunes. Guests include Lorrie Morgan ("Don't Worry Baby"), Junior Brown ("409"), Collin Raye ("Sloop John B"), Sawyer Brown ("I Get Around") and many more. 58 min.
50-8564 *$14.99*

The Beach Boys: The Lost Concert (1964)
Originally filmed as part of a closed-circuit "mega-concert" that also featured The Beatles and Lesley Gore, this classic performance by Brian, Carl, Dennis, Mike and Al was lost for over 30 years and offers a rare look at the quintessential California band's early years. Songs include "Little Deuce Coupe," "Fun, Fun, Fun," "In My Room," "Papa Oom-Mow-Mow," "Surfin' USA" and others. 22 min.
50-8209 *$12.99*

Brian Wilson: Imagination
The video companion to Wilson's 1998 album of the same name, this program includes a candid interview with Wilson conducted by Sean Lennon and features The Beach Boys co-founder in a live concert, performing with an all-star combo that includes Christopher Cross, Bruce Johnson and Timothy B. Schmitt. "California Girls," "In My Room," "South America," "Your Imagination" and "Don't Worry Baby" are among the songs. 60 min.
19-2818 ▢*$19.99*

Depeche Mode: Some Great Videos
"Great" is the word for this video collection from the dazzling techno-pop foursome. Songs include "Blasphemous Rumours," "Somebody," "People Are People," "Love in Itself," more. 50 min.
19-3023 *$24.99*

Depeche Mode: The Videos 86-98
In the "mode" for some striking synth-pop music? This special compilation features such Depeche faves as "Strangelove," "Never Let Me Down Again," "Personal Jesus," "Walking in My Shoes," "Barrel of a Gun," "Only When I Lose Myself" and many more, plus special interviews with the band and the aptly-titled "Depeche Mode: A Short Film." 120 min.
19-4037 *$24.99*

Depeche Mode 101 (1989)
An introductory course in great rock rhythm, this documentary look at Depeche Mode's U.S. tour is a pulsing primer in new music. Acclaimed film from D.A. Pennebaker ("Dont Look Back") features the songs "Blasphemous Rumours," "Everything Counts," "Route 66," "People Are People," and many more. 117 min.
19-3085 *$19.99*

The B-52's: 1979-1989
'60s rhythms and dances mixed with New Wave nuttiness are the Athens, Ga., combo's hallmark. Great dance collection of The B-52's hits in video form includes "Rock Lobster," "Legal Tender," "Love Shack," "Channel Z" and more. 29 min.
19-3094 *$19.99*

The B-52's: 1979-1998 Time Capsule: Songs For A Future Generation
One of pop music's most unique and endearing bands is celebrated in a collection featuring two decades of their greatest music video hits. Among the songs are "Rock Lobster," "Girl from Ipanema Goes to Greenland," "Roam," "Love Shack" and "Good Stuff," as well as their new video "Debbie." 60 min.
19-4025 ▢*$19.99*

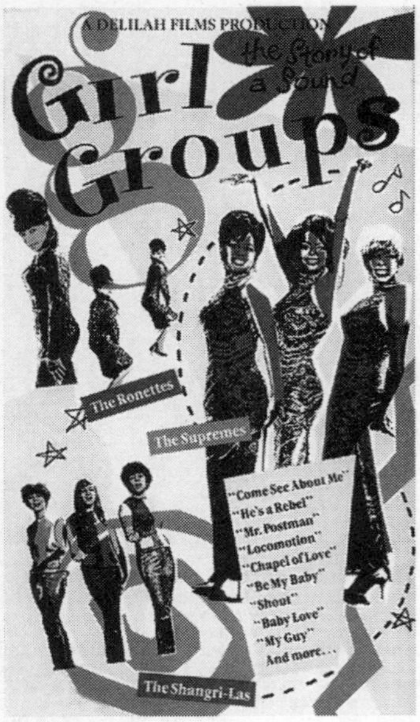

Girl Groups
A fun, music-filled look at the greatest Girl Groups. See and hear The Supremes, Ronettes, Shangri-Las and others performing such zippy tunes as "Be My Baby," "Stop in the Name of Love," "Locomotion," and over 20 other hits. 65 min.
12-1274 Was $19.99 ***$14.99***

Natalie Merchant:
Ophelia: Home Video
Produced as a video counterpart to her best-selling "Ophelia" album, these special short films feature Merchant playing a series of seven characters inspired by the album's music. Along with the title song, "Kind and Generous," "Break Your Heart," "Jealousy," "Wonder" and "Carnival" are also included. 48 min.
19-4046 ***$19.99***

10,000 Maniacs:
MTV Unplugged (1994)
In what proved to be one of their final concert appearances together, Natalie Merchant and 10,000 Maniacs wowed the MTV audience with an acoustic performance. This special video includes such hits as "These Are Days," "Like the Weather," "Because the Night" and more, including three songs with special guest David Byrne and seven not seen on TV. 113 min.
19-3647 ***$19.99***

Virtual 60's: Complete Set
In the spirit of Woodstock comes this three-tape set that mixes the sights, sounds and experience of the 1960s in a unique and mesmerizing fashion. Hosted by Dr. Timothy Leary and featuring such faves as Canned Heat, Leon Russell, Country Joe McDonald and Edgar Winter, the videos are the next best thing to dropping Windowpane at Fillmore West. 150 min. total. NOTE: Individual volumes available at $14.99.
22-1348 Save $5.00! ***$39.99***

Tori Amos: Little Earthquakes
Live clips and music videos from the lithesome singer's hit debut album are featured on this tape. "Crucify," "Silent All These Years," "China" and "Winter" are among the songs that made Amos famous. 55 min.
19-3381 ***$19.99***

Tori Amos:
The Complete Collection 1991-1998
Celebrate eight chart-topping years of edgy "waif rock" with this collection of Tori's acclaimed music videos. Included are "Silent All These Years," two alternate versions of "Cornflake Girl," "Winter," "Crucify," "Pretty Good Year" and more. 75 min.
19-4043 ***$19.99***

Linda Ronstadt:
Canciones De Mi Padre
Linda returns to her roots in this concert celebration of Mexico and its heritage. Ronstadt performs such numbers as "Dos Arbolitos," "El Gusto," "La Bamba," "Yo Soy El Corrido," and more. 70 min.
19-3291 ***$19.99***

ZZ Top: Greatest Hits
Those zany, hot-rockin' Texans turn out some of the funniest, sexiest music videos ever, and this collection boasts all of your faves. Check out "My Head's in Mississippi," "Sharp Dressed Man," "Legs," "Gimme' All Your Lovin'" and a new version of "Viva Las Vegas." 50 min.
19-3304 ***$19.99***

Classic Albums:
Phil Collins: Face Value
The longtime Genesis drummer/singer found success on his own with his 1981 debut solo album, "Face Value," which contained such hits as "In the Air Tonight," "I Missed Again" and "If Leaving Me Is Easy." Hear from Collins through rare home movies and performance footage about the creation of this landmark album. 60 min.
15-5545 ***$19.99***

Foreigner:
Feels Like The First Time
Top-selling rock-and-rollers Foreigner are saluted in this mix of high-energy concert footage, videos and an interview with band leader Mick Jones by Billy Joel. "Feels Like the First Time," "Cold as Ice," "Hot-Blooded," "I Want to Know What Love Is" and other hits are featured. 60 min.
19-3186 ***$19.99***

Chris Isaak: Wicked Game
Chris Isaak takes his moody, evocative hit single, "Wicked Game," to video with an uncensored movie clip directed by top photographer Herb Ritts. Also on the program are musicvids for "Dancin'," "Blue Hotel" and more. 20 min.
19-3189 ***$14.99***

Rod Stewart:
Storyteller 1984-1991
Rod proves once more that "Blondes Have More Fun" in this sampler of video hits. Included are "Infatuation," "Some Guys Have All the Luck," "People Get Ready," "Forever Young," "The Motown Song," "This Old Heart of Mine" and more. 60 min.
19-3259 ***$19.99***

Rod Stewart:
The Vagabond Heart Tour
Rod Stewart proves why he's been one of rock's most popular performers in this super-charged concert from his successful 1991-1992 tour. Songs include "Some Guys Have All the Luck," "Maggie May," "Every Picture Tells a Story," "The Motown Song," "Sweet Soul Music" and lots more! 90 min.
19-3317 ***$24.99***

Rod Stewart And Faces:
The Final Concert (1974)
In what proved to be one of their last performances together, "Rod the Mod" and the band Faces take the stage at London's Kilburn Theatre with special guest Keith Richards. Songs include "It's All Over Now," "Maggie May," "Twistin' the Night Away" and more. 75 min.
55-9019 Was $49.99 ***$29.99***

Dead Can Dance:
Toward The Within
They blend traditional Celtic and folk melodies with world music influences, resulting in a unique and haunting sound. Now see Dead Can Dance in a live concert at Santa Monica, plus interviews with group founders Brendan Perry and Lisa Gerrard. Songs include "Rakim," "Song of the Sibyl," "Tristan," "The Wind That Shakes the Barley" and more. 75 min.
19-3605 ***$19.99***

Huey Lewis And The News:
Four Chords & Several Years Ago—The Concert
Get to "the heart of rock and roll" with Huey Lewis and The News in a Chicago concert shown on public TV. Among the classic News hits and rock classics performed are "I Want a New Drug," "The Power of Love," "Stagger Lee," "But It's Alright," "I Thank You" (with guest Sam Moore) and many more, including three songs not seen on TV. 64 min.
19-3659 ***$19.99***

Woodstock:
The Lost Performances
From the cutting room floor to your video screen, long-thought lost film footage of Janis Joplin, Blood, Sweat and Tears, Joan Baez, Crosby, Stills and Nash, Richie Havens, Sly and the Family Stone and others that was not included in the feature film is now available and a must for rock devotees everywhere. "Don't eat the brown acid! I'm WAWNING you! Don't eat the brown acid!" 68 min.
19-1905 Was $19.99 ***□$14.99***

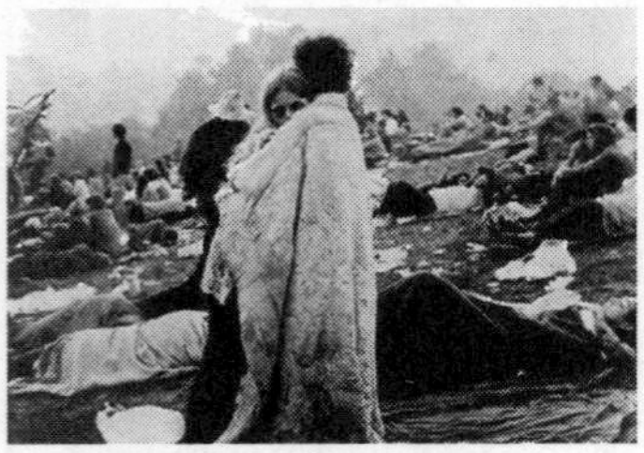

Woodstock:
The Director's Cut (1970)
To mark the 25th anniversary of the three-day rock concert that became a capstone for the Sixties, director Michael Wadleigh added over 40 minutes of never-before-seen footage to this restored print of his Oscar-winning musical chronicle. Return to Max Yasgur's farm with Canned Heat, Joe Cocker, Crosby, Stills and Nash, Jimi Hendrix, Janis Joplin, Jefferson Airplane, Santana, Sly and The Family Stone, The Who and half a million strong. 225 min.
19-2253 Letterboxed ***□$24.99***

Woodstock '94 (1994)
The legend lived on with "3 more days of peace and music" and some of the top names in pop music. This documentary of the landmark festival features, along with on-site reports and exclusive backstage footage, an all-star array of performers: Aerosmith, The Cranberries, Crosby, Stills and Nash, Peter Gabriel, Metallica, Nine Inch Nails, Red Hot Chili Peppers, Salt N' Pepa and many more. 165 min.
02-8162 ***$24.99***

Erasure: ABBA-Esque
Erasure performs the songs of ABBA in this concept video that offers such songs as "Take a Chance on Me," "S.O.S.," "Voulez-Vouz" and "Lay All Your Love on Me." 20 min.
19-3347 ***$14.99***

Erasure: Pop!—The First 20 Hits
A video companion to Andy Bell and Vince Clarke's greatest hits album, this tape features the pop-ular duo performing such songs as "Chains of Love," "Heavenly Action," "Victim of Love," "Blue Savannah," "Take a Chance on Me," "A Little Respect," and others. 76 min.
19-3396 ***$19.99***

The Pretenders: The Singles
Video offering featuring videos of Chrissie Hynde and company's greatest hits. Included are "Brass in Pocket," "Message of Love," "Talk of the Town," "Back on the Chain Gang," "2,000 Miles" and many more. 56 min.
19-3048 ***$14.99***

The Pretenders:
The Isle Of View (1995)
In a special live acoustic performance that features special guests The Duke Quartet string ensemble and Damon Albarn of Blur, The Pretenders deliver an impressive show that includes such songs as "Brass in Pocket," "2000 Miles," "Back on the Chain Gang," "I Go to Sleep," "Creep" and more. 70 min.
19-3862 ***$19.99***

Jethro Tull:
20 Years Of Jethro Tull
Entering their fourth decade as one of rock's superstar groups, Grammy winners Jethro Tull talk about their music and lives in this blend of concert footage and music videos. "Aqualung," "Living in the Past," "Lap of Luxury," and 10 other classics. 80 min.
19-3077 ***$19.99***

Spice Girls:
One Hour Of Girl Power
Their debuts in England and America were the biggest thing in pop music since The Beatles, and they're the spiciest females since Mrs. Dash! Get the inside story on Emma, Geri, Victoria, Mel B. and Mel C. through clips of the girls' first global tour, exclusive interviews and behind-the-scenes footage, and the music videos for "Wannabe," "Say You'll Be There," "2 Become 1," "Who Do You Think You Are" and more. 60 min.
19-2616 ***$14.99***

Spice Girls In America:
A Tour Story
Go on the road and across the country with Emma, Victoria, and Mels B. and C. with this video chronicle of the girls' 1998 "Spiceworld" tour. Learn how the Spices cope with tour life, catch rare backstage footage, and hear such songs as "Who Do You Think You Are?," "Say You'll Be There," "If U Can't Dance," "Trance," "2 Become 1" and many more.
44-4167 ***$19.99***

Girl Power: The Unauthorized Biography Of The Spice Girls
Get a close look at the world's sexiest singing sensations. See how these five British beauties got started and ascended to the top of the pop charts. Also, find out how these spicy ladies have changed since being greeted by such adulation throughout the world. 50 min.
50-5555 ***$14.99***

Spice Exposed: Too Hot For TV!
How spicy is Spice Girl Ginger (Gerri Halliwell)? Find out with this exposé on her colorful and provocative career, which features sizzling nude photos and a nude modelling session, shot before she was a superstar. Also, you'll hear former associates talk about how spicy this Ginger really is! 48 min.
50-5637 ***$14.99***

Spice Girls: Girl Power!
Live In Istanbul (1997)
The ancient Turkish city becomes the spiciest spot on the planet for one night, as England's chart-topping Spice Girls take the stage in their first-ever live concert. See Baby, Ginger, Posh, Scary and Sporty strut their stuff as they perform such hit tunes as "If U Can't Dance," "Who Do You Think You Are," "Say You'll Be There," "Spice Up Your Life," "Wannabe" and more. 90 min.
44-4135 ***$19.99***

Spice Girls:
Live At Wembley (1998)
To conclude their globe-hopping Spiceworld Tour, Sporty, Scary, Posh and Baby wowed their fans with a dazzling live show at London's Wembley Stadium. Among the Spicy faves featured in this concert video are "Step to Me," "2 Become 1," "Too Much," "Where Did Our Love Go?," "Wannabe," "Spice Up Your Life" and many more, plus behind-the-scenes interviews.
44-4148 ***$19.99***

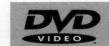

DVD VIDEO
ASK ABOUT OUR GIANT DVD CATALOG!

Rage Against The Machine: Revolution USA?
The music and causes of politically-conscious rockers Rage Against the Machine is the subject of this provocative program that includes samples of the band's edgy rap and metal music mix and interviews with members Zack de la Rocha, Tim Commerford, Brad Wilk and Tom Morello. See what makes the pro-Mumia Abu-Jamal, anti-Nazi, anti-censorship group tick! 50 min.
50-8386 ***$14.99***

Madonna:
The Immaculate Collection
Thank your "Lucky Star," all of the "Material Girl's" early music videos have been collected on this Madonna-rific tape. "Open Your Heart" and "Cherish" such songs as "Borderline," "Papa Don't Preach," "Like a Prayer," "Vogue" and many more. 60 min.
19-3147 ***$19.99***

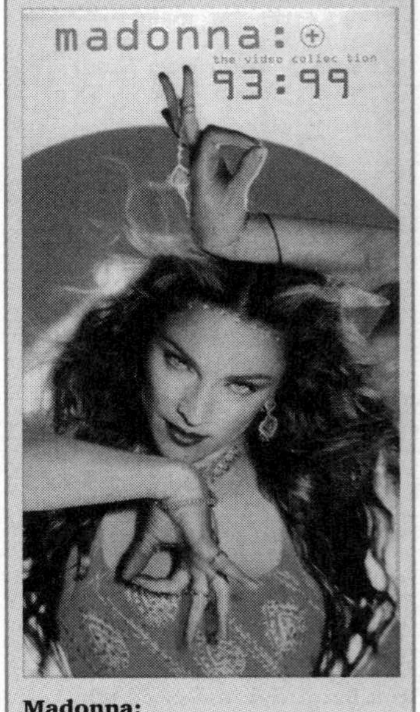

Madonna:
The Video Collection 93:99
The ongoing pop saga that is Madonna continues with this follow-up to "The Immaculate Collection" that features all her top '90s music videos in one program. "Erotica," "Bad Girl," "Rain," "Take a Bow," "Ray of Light" and "Beautiful Stranger" are just a few of the featured hits. 68 min.
19-4064 ***$19.99***

Madonna: Justify My Love
The headline-grabbing pop star, in the video that was too hot for MTV! Now you can decide for yourself, as you watch Madonna in her sultry music video for "Justify My Love," a steamy look inside a Paris hotel room that features nudity, bisexuality, cross-dressing and a touch of sadomasochism. Be a part of this uncut, uncensored video first! 5 min.
19-3153 ***$12.99***

Madonna: The Girlie Show—Live Down Under
Madonna brings her exciting 1993 "Girlie Show" tour to Australia, and it's a spectacle to behold, mate. The "Material Girl" performs such songs as "Erotica," "Fever," "Rain," "Holiday," "Like a Virgin," "In This Life" and "Express Yourself" in an incredible, provocative outing. 120 min.
19-3516 ***□$29.99***

Madonna Live:
The Virgin Tour (1986)
A smash concert in her hometown of Detroit features these highlights of Madonna's on-stage escapades: "Holiday," "Into the Groove," "Crazy for You," "Like a Virgin," "Material Girl" and many others. 50 min.
19-3010 ***$14.99***

Ciao Italia: Madonna
Live From Italy (1987)
Direct from her 1987 world tour, Madonna stars in a dazzling concert video that features over one dozen of her top hits, including "Open Your Heart," "Lucky Star," "True Blue," "Who's That Girl" and many more. 100 min.
19-3053 ***$29.99***

Madonna: Truth Or Dare (1991)
Show business sensation Madonna pulls out all the stops in this candid chronicle of her 1990 Blonde Ambition Tour. The film captures the intensity of her performances, as well as many controversial behind-the-scenes moments. Songs include "Material Girl," "Like a Prayer," "Cherish," and "Like a Virgin." Special video edition features concert footage not shown in theatres. 131 min.
27-6721 Was $89.99 ***$12.99***

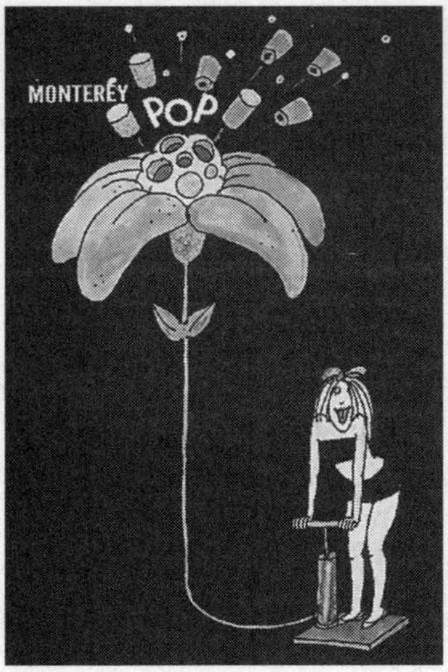

Monterey Pop (1968)
One of the first and best rock concert films ever made, director D.A. Pennebaker's chronicle of the 1967 Monterey Pop Festival features, along with the American debut of the Jimi Hendrix Experience ("Wild Thing"), classic performances from such psychedelic-era icons as The Who ("My Generation"), Simon and Garfunkel ("59th Street Bridge Song"), Otis Redding ("I've Been Loving You Too Long"), The Mamas and the Papas ("California Dreaming"), Jefferson Airplane ("Today"), Big Brother and the Holding Company "(Ball and Chain") and others. Special video edition includes nine minutes of never-before-seen footage. 98 min.
45-5133 Was $29.99 *$19.99*

Lifestyles Of The Ramones
The four lovable moptops from Queens whose music helped create the Punk movement are featured in an anthology of music videos, concert clipsand original interview footage. Join Joey, Johnny, Dee Dee and Marky (and Richie and C.J.) for "I Wanna Be Sedated," "Rock 'N' Roll High School," "Something to Believe In," "Pet Sematary" and more. 60 min.
19-3109 *$19.99*

The Smiths: The Complete Picture
One of the most compelling and innovative bands of the '80s is feted in this video salute. Morrissey, Johnny Marr, Andy Rourke and Mike Joyce are on hand for such upbeat Smiths songs as "Heaven Knows I'm Miserable Now," "The Boy with the Thorn in His Side," "Panic," "Girlfriend in a Coma" and others. 50 min.
19-3393 *$19.99*

R.E.M.: Parallel
Culled from R.E.M.'s smash "Automatic for the People" and "Monster" albums are the music videos for "Everybody Hurts," "Man on the Moon," the uncensored "Nightswimming," "What's the Frequency, Kenneth?," "Bang and Blame" and six others, plus excerpts from the short films shown during the group's 1995 tour. 70 min.
19-3762 *$19.99*

R.E.M.: The Tour (1989)
Shot during the band's 1989 "Green" tour, this film features R.E.M. in concert. Among the 17 songs performed are "Stand," "The One I Love," "Fall on Me" and "Pop Song 89." 86 min.
19-3112 *$19.99*

Chicago In Concert At The Greek Theatre
The group whose popularity has spanned decades showcases their wonderful blend of rock, jazz and classical music with this concert from L.A.'s Greek Theatre. Among the selections Lamm, Pankow and company perform are "Make Me Smile," "Searchin' So Long," "I'm a Man," "25 or 6 to 4" and others. 80 min.
19-3813 *$24.99*

Chicago: And The Band Played On (1992)
Trace 20-plus years of chart-topping songs with the perennially popular rock group in this live performance of such Chicago faves as "Saturday in the Park," "25 or 6 to 4," "Make Me Smile," "Hard Habit to Break," "Inspiration" and others are included. 60 min.
19-3391 *$19.99*

Björk: Volumen
She's the biggest thing to come out of Iceland since...ice, maybe?...and the best of Björk's innovative music videos have now been compiled into one "volumen-ous" program. Included are "Human Behaviour," "I Miss You," "It's Oh So Quiet," "Play Dead," "Violently Happy" and many more. 64 min.
19-4045 *$19.99*

Björk: Live At Shepherd's Bush Empire (1997)
The Scandinavian songstress won international acclaim both as a member of The Sugarcubes and in her solo career, and in this live concert video Björk performs such faves as "Human Behaviour," "Army of Me," "Possibly Maybe," "Anchor Song" and others.
19-4044 *$19.99*

Bryan Ferry & Roxy Music: Video Collection
A salute to one of rock's most innovative bands, this compilation of music videos spotlights Ferry's work solo and with Andy Mackay, Phil Manzanera and company. Among the songs featured are "These Foolish Things," "The Price of Love," "Angel Eyes," "Jealous Guy," "Kiss and Tell," "Mamouna" and others.
44-4154 *$19.99*

Brian Eno: Imaginary Landscapes
A stunning blend of music and visual imagery, this look at the work of the innovative rock composer/video artist focuses on Eno discussing his work and artistic goals, while selections of his most daring compositions fill the soundtrack. 40 min.
70-7103 *$19.99*

Selena: All My Hits/Todos Mis Exitos
The chart-topping Tejano singer is remembered with this collection of music videos for her most popular songs. Included are "Amor Prohibido," "Buenos Amigos," "Donde Quiera Que Estas," "Dreaming of You," "I Could Fall in Love with You" and many more.
44-4168 *$16.99*

The Tubes: Live At The Greek
Their wild brand of music and theatrics thrilled audiences for years. Now The Tubes and leader Fee Waybill bring it out live at L.A.'s Greek Theater. "Remote Control," "Don't Touch Me There" and "White Punks on Dope" are but a few of the hits performed. 60 min.
27-6034 Was $39.99 *$19.99*

Flashbacks
Take a musical trip back to the past with these fantastic tapes that feature top stars of the '60s and '70s singing the tunes that made them great. Each volume runs about 30 min.

Flashbacks: Soul Sensations
Includes The Ike & Tina Turner Revue ("She Came in Through the Bathroom Window," "Proud Mary"), Gladys Knight and The Pips ("You're All I Need to Get By"), Bo Diddley ("Hey Bo Diddley"), more.
22-7136 *$14.99*

Flashbacks: Pop Parade
Includes Sonny and Cher ("The Beat Goes On"), Jim Croce ("You Don't Mess Around with Jim"), The 5th Dimension ("Up, Up and Away"), Dionne Warwick ("Reach Out and Touch"), Lou Rawls ("It Was a Very Good Year") and others.
22-7137 *$14.99*

Flashbacks: Easy Lovin'
Includes The Carpenters ("Superstar"), Bobby Darin ("If I Were a Carpenter"), Sonny and Cher ("I Got You, Babe"), Kenny Rogers and The First Edition ("Cherish"), more.
22-7138 *$14.99*

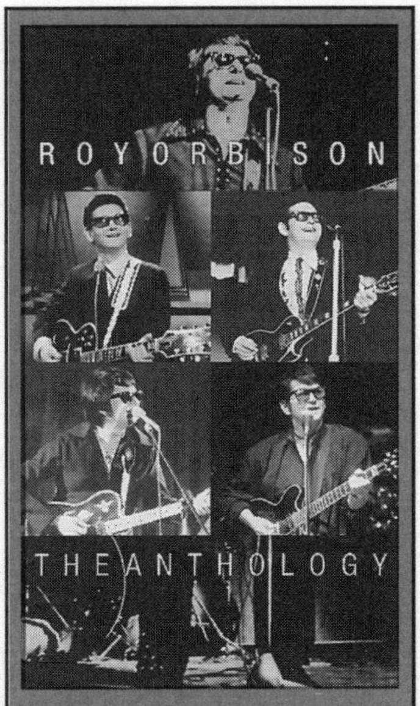

Roy Orbison: The Anthology
One of rock and roll's most distinctive voices is saluted in this special collection of concert and video clips spanning Orbison's 30-plus-year career and featuring 14 of his most memorable songs. Included are "Only the Lonely," "Running Scared," "Crying," "Oh, Pretty Woman," "In Dreams" and many more. 52 min.
22-1666 *$19.99*

Roy Orbison: In Dreams
Coming out of Sun Studios in Memphis in the mid-'50s, Roy Orbison continued to record country-flavored rock hits until his death 30 years later. Rare home movies, classic concert clips, and interviews with friends and colleagues tell the story of Roy and his music. Guest stars include Bono, Johnny Cash, Jerry Lee Lewis, Willie Nelson, Bruce Springsteen and others. 93 min.
22-1743 *$19.99*

The Righteous Brothers: 21st Anniversary Celebration
Bill Medley and Bobby Hatfield mark two decades-plus of their special brand of "blue-eyed soul" in this triumphant performance at L.A.'s Roxy Theatre. Included are hits like "Soul and Inspiration," "You've Lost That Lovin' Feeling" and "Unchained Melody." 60 min.
50-2250 *$14.99*

Bonnie Raitt: Road Tested
Bonnie Raitt belts out some of her best-loved tunes solo and with such guests as Bruce Hornsby, Jackson Browne, Bryan Adams and Kim Wilson in this live 1995 concert from Oakland's Paramount Theatre. Selections include "Thing Called Love," "Something to Talk About," "Come to Me," "I Can't Make You Love Me," "Burning Down the House" and "Rock Steady."
44-4123 *$14.99*

Radiohead: Meeting People Is Easy
Looking for an "easy" introduction to the acclaimed alternative rock band? This mix of live performance clips, exclusive interviews and footage of life on the road offers a rare look at Radiohead on-stage and off. Songs include "Palo Alto," "Paranoid Android," "Karma Police" and more. 90 min.
44-4152 *$19.99*

Jackson Browne: Going Home
Twenty-five years of chart-topping songs are featured in this acclaimed special that traces Browne's life and career and includes a concert in which such guest stars as David Crosby, Don Henley, Graham Nash, Bonnie Raitt and others join Jackson on stage. 90 min.
19-3932 *$19.99*

Alanis Morissette: jagged little pill, Live
Culled from over 200 hours of footage from her 1995-96 world tour, this dynamic video salute to the Canadian-born singer features Morissette and her band on the road and performing all of the songs from her acclaimed "jagged little pill" album, along with the new tunes "Can't Not" and "No Pressure Over Cappuccino." 90 min.
19-3989 *$19.99*

John Fogerty: Premonition
The legendary frontman of Creedence Clearwater Revival is featured in this concert video counterpart to his "Premonition" album that showcases his CCR and solo hits. Among the Fogerty faves featured are "Born on the Bayou," "Who'll Stop the Rain," "Green River," "Centerfield," "Bad Moon Rising," "Proud Mary" and more, including four songs not featured on the album: "Blueboy," "Bring It Down Jellyroll," "A Hundred and Ten in the Shade" and "Walking in a Hurricane." 80 min.
19-4024 *$19.99*

Live At Knebworth
This magnificent benefit concert was held in Knebworth, England, in 1990 and features a sterling selection of performers, including Tears For Fears, Cliff Richard, Phil Collins, Eric Clapton, Dire Straits, Elton John, and Jimmy Page and Robert Plant, who reunite for "Rock 'n' Roll." 194 min.
50-5644 *$29.99*

The Rock And Roll Collection
Dick Clark presents this incredible collection of great pop songs, sung in their entirety by their original artists. Each tape offers rock treasures, culled from Dick's vaults. Among the 55 performances are "ABC" (The Jackson 5), "Bad, Bad Leroy Brown" (Jim Croce), "Try a Little Tenderness" (Otis Redding), "Mama Told Me Not to Come" (The Three Dog Night) and "Reunited" (Peaches and Herb), and many, many more. Available in an attractive four-tape boxed set, it's a must for rock fans that clocks in at four hours.
50-6782 *$99.99*

Close To You: Remembering The Carpenters
Follow the hit-filled career and stormy personal lives of the siblings who epitomized the "mellow '70s" sound in this moving documentary. Featured are rare interviews and performance clips of Karen and Richard, tributes by Herb Alpert, Burt Bacharach, Les Paul and others, with such Carpenters classics as "For All We Know," "We've Only Just Begun," "Superstar" and many more. 75 min.
50-7442 *$19.99*

Peter Frampton: Live In Detroit
"Thank You!" Brace yourself for a searing amalgamation of talking guitar riffs, as the man who defined '70s rock takes the stage for an evening of Frampton faves old and new. Included are "Baby (Somethin's Happening)," "Show Me the Way," "You Can't Take That Away," "Do You Feel Like We Do," "I Don't Need No Doctor" and 11. 101 min.
50-8563 Letterboxed *$19.99*

James Brown: Live From The House Of Blues
"The Godfather of Soul" will blow you away with this electrifying performance from the Las Vegas House of Blues. James sings "Living in America," "Hot Pants," "Try Me," "I Feel Good," "Sex Machine," "Papa's Got a Brand New Bag" and lots more. 90 min.
50-8627 *$19.99*

James Brown: The Lost James Brown Tapes (1979)
An energized performance by "The King of Soul," who turns in electrified versions of "Try Me," "Georgia on My Mind," "Papa's Got a Brand New Bag," "I Can't Stand It," and a marathon treatment of "Sex Machine." 60 min.
19-3294 *$14.99*

Buffy Sainte Marie: Up Where We Belong
Singer-songwriter Buffy Sainte-Marie performs with aboriginal singing groups Stoney Park and Red Bull in this concert that showcases such tunes as "Universal Soldier," "Bury My Heart at Wounded Knee," "Until It's Time for You to Go" and the popular "Up Where We Belong" from "An Officer and a Gentleman." 47 min.
50-8622 *$14.99*

Lou Reed: Rock & Roll Heart
Follow the life of one of rock's most distinctive performers in this program from PBS's "American Masters" series, from Reed's youth in the New York suburbs and his years with Andy Warhol's Factory crowd as a founding member of the groundbreaking Velvet Underground to his tempestuous solo career. "Waiting for the Man," "Heroin," "Sweet Jane" and "Walk on the Wild Side" are among the classic Reed tunes featured, with comments from John Cale, Holly Woodlawn, Patti Smith, David Bowie, David Byrne and others. Special video edition includes footage not shown on TV. 75 min.
53-6227 *$19.99*

Ten Years After: At The Marquee
Guitarist Alvin Lee leads the band with his searing solo licks on such songs as "Love Like a Man," "Good Morning, Little School Girl" and that "Woodstock" favorite, "I'm Going Home." 55 min.
64-1301 *$19.99*

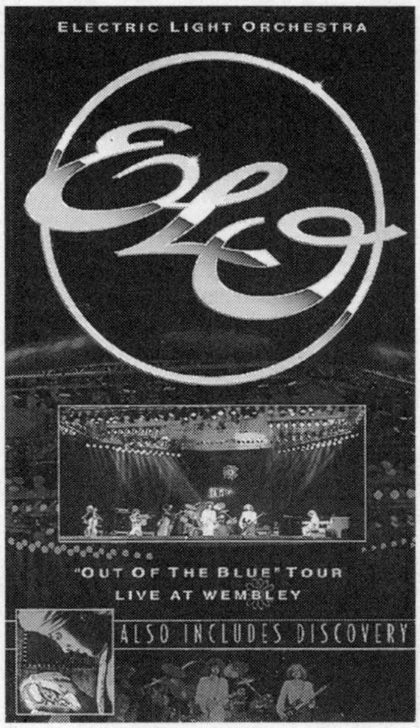

Electric Light Orchestra: Live—Discovery (1978)
Recorded live at Wembley, England, during their "Out of the Blue" tour, ELO puts on a dazzling concert spectacle of sight and sound. Among the many favorites performed by the band are "Shine a Little Love," "Confusion," "Don't Bring Me Down," "Turn to Stone," "Telephone Line" and many more. 102 min.
04-1572 *$19.99*

Nine Inch Nails: Closure
A unique two-tape set takes all you "knights who say NIN" into the heart of Trent Reznor and company. A collection of raw and uncensored live footage from the band's "Self-Destruct Tour" features performances of "Hurt," "March of the Pigs," "Wish" and more, while the second tape offers "Closer," "Happiness in Slavery," "The Perfect Drug" and other music videos, all in their uncut form.
68-1862 *$24.99*

Smokey Robinson: The Greatest Hits Live
People say he's the life of the party, just because he sings a song or two. But when Smokey sings, you don't forget it, and that's what he does in this performance of such classics as "Tears of a Clown," "Shop Around," "I Second That Emotion," "Get Ready," "Going to a Go-Go," "Since I Lost My Baby" and, of course, "Tracks of My Tears." 86 min.
89-7024 *$14.99*

Pat Benatar: Live In New Haven (1983)
The Grammy-winning rocker belts out 14 of her greatest hits, including "Fire and Ice," "You Better Run," "Heartbreaker," "Hit Me with Your Best Shot," "Hell Is for Children" and more, in this electrifying live concert video. 60 min.
15-5425 *$14.99*

Diana: Visions Of Diana Ross (1984)
The dynamic Ms. Ross shines in a collection of six music videos, including her best-selling hit "Missing You," a marvelous rendition of "Why Do Fools Fall in Love?" and her duet with Julio Iglesias on "All of You." 28 min.
02-1432 *$14.99*

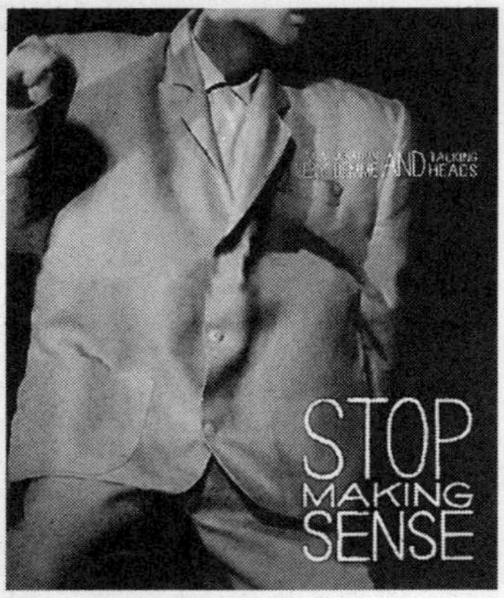

Stop Making Sense (1984)
This 15th anniversary edition of the groundbreaking concert film by innovative New Wave band Talking Heads and director Jonathan Demme features David Byrne, Chris Frantz, Jerry Harrison, Tina Weymouth and company performing at Los Angeles' Pantages Theatre. Spotlighted are such Heads classics as "Psycho Killer," "Take Me to the River," "Burning Down the House," "Girlfriend Is Better," "Cities" and many more. Includes the original theatrical trailer.
02-1489 Remastered *$19.99*

Stop Making Sense (Letterboxed Version)
Also available in a theatrical, widescreen format.
02-9150 *$19.99*

Weekend Rebellion: Grand Funk Railroad (1970)
Originally made in 1967 as a travelogue/concert film entitled "Mondo Daytona" and featuring performances by Billy Joe Royal ("Down in the Boondocks"), The Swingin' Medallions ("Double Shot of My Baby's Love") and The Tams ("What Kind of Fool"), this salute to Spring Break fun was revamped with new footage starring Grand Funk Railroad ("On Time," "Paranoid"). 85 min.
55-9020 *$29.99*

Otis Redding: Shake (1967)
Backed by Booker T. & The MG's at the famed Monterey Pop Festival, Otis performs "Shake," "Respect," "I've Been Loving You Too Long," "Satisfaction" and "Try a Little Tenderness" and other songs in one of Redding's rare live concert appearances. 19 min.
44-1634 *$12.99*

Roots Of Rhythm: Boxed Set
Hosted by Harry Belafonte, this three-tape set celebrates Latin music, tracing its roots and showcasing a number of superstars, including Gloria Estefan, Dizzy Gillespie, Celia Cruz, Ruben Blades, Desi Arnaz, King Sunny Ade and many others. Travel to New York dance floors to African jungles to Cuban carnivals to experience the music's infectious rhythms. 171 min. total.
53-8961 *$39.99*

Ladysmith Black Mambazo: In Harmony: Live At The Royal Albert Hall
London's famed Royal Albert Hall is the setting for a stirring concert featuring the African musical group whose a capella stylings have brought them worldwide acclaim. Songs include "Homeless," "Rain Beautiful Rain" and more. 75 min.
63-7174 *$19.99*

Raga: Ravi Shankar
His work with George Harrison in the '60s brought Indian music to Western audiences. Now, sitar master Ravi Shankar returns to his homeland in a video odyssey that traces his musical roots and the role of music in Indian culture. Shankar is also seen performing with Harrison, Alla Rakha, Yehudi Menuhin and others. 95 min.
70-7105 Was $29.99 *$19.99*

Kodo: Heartbeat Drummers Of Japan (1983)
Kodo, a group of young Japanese musicians and dancers who perform traditional and contemporary drumming exercises, is the focus of this documentary filmed on the remote island of Sado and at Tokyo's National Theatre. From gentle rhythms to powerful folk dances, this dynamic group amazes audiences the world over with their drumming talents. 58 min.
53-7620 *$19.99*

The Return Of Rubén Blades (1987)
The multi-faceted world of Rubén Blades—Panamanian-born salsa singer, crossover artist, lawyer and political activist—is examined in Robert Mugge's acclaimed documentary. Joining Blades and his band Seis del Solar in concert clips are guests Linda Ronstadt and Pete Hamill; songs include "Pedro Navaja," "Muevete," "Buscando America." 82 min.
45-5403 *$19.99*

The 5th Dimension Travelling Sunshine Show (1970)
It's an evening of mellow rock in this vintage TV special featuring The 5th Dimension and their special guests Dionne Warwick, Merle Haggard, The Carpenters, all performing such hits as "Light Sings All Over the World," "Someone Like You," "The Games People Play," special medleys and more. 48 min.
22-7081 Was $19.99 *$14.99*

Message To Love: The Isle Of Wight Festival: The Movie (1970)
The long-sought film of the five-day pop festival that came to be known as "Britain's Woodstock." Along with the final stage performances of Jimi Hendrix ("Foxy Lady," "Voodoo Chile") and Jim Morrison with The Doors ("The End," "When the Music's Over") and the debut of supergroup Emerson, Lake and Palmer ("Pictures at an Exhibition"), the line-up includes Joan Baez, Leonard Cohen, Joni Mitchell, The Who, Jethro Tull, and many others. 120 min.
04-5510 *$19.99*

Yessongs (1972)
Classic concert documentary features the legendary Yes line-up (Rick Wakeman, Jon Anderson, Steve Howe, Alan White, Chris Squire) performing such hits as "Roundabout," "I've Seen All Good People," "Close to the Edge" and more. 75 min.
15-1056 Was $19.99 *$14.99*

House Of Yes: Live At House Of Blues (1999)
Progressive rock giants Yes turn in a thrilling performance at the Las Vegas House of Blues in this concert video. This 1999 appearance, part of the "Ladder" tour, features Jon Anderson, Steve Howe, Chris Squire, Alan White, Igor Khorshev and Billy Sherwood delivering "Yours Is No Disgrace," "Your Move/I've Seen All Good People," "Homeworld (The Ladder)," "Roundabout" and others. 112 min.
02-9222 *$19.99*

Three Dog Night (1975)
If you're in a late '60s-early '70s musical mood, you won't want to miss this live performance from one of the era's most popular groups on the PBS "Soundstage" show. Songs include "One," "Try a Little Tenderness," "Celebrate," "Joy to the World," "An Old Fashioned Love Song" and more. 60 min.
15-5275 *$19.99*

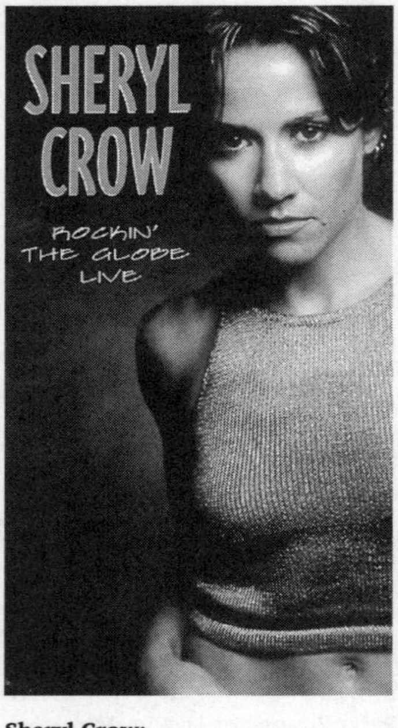

Sheryl Crow: Rockin' The Globe Live (1999)
If all you wanna do is have some fun, look no further than this live concert video featuring Sheryl from her "The Globe Sessions" tour. The Grammy-winning singer/songwriter performs "Anything But Down," "If It Makes You Happy," "Everyday Is a Winding Road," "A Change," "Home" and more. 83 min.
50-8377 *$19.99*

Marvin Gaye: Greatest Hits Live In '76 (1976)
In a rare concert appearance filmed in Holland, the legendary Motown singer performs many of his best-loved tunes, including "What's Going On," "I Heard It Through the Grapevine," "It Takes Two," "Ain't No Mountain High Enough" and many more. 53 min.
04-5080 *$19.99*

Queen: We Will Rock You (1982)
Over-the-top theatrical rock lives on with this live concert from Queen's 1982 world tour. Freddie Mercury, Roger Taylor, Brian May and John Deacon perform "Killer Queen," "Bohemian Rhapsody," "Tie Your Mother Down," "Under Pressure" and other classic hits. Long live the Queen! 90 min.
70-3169 *$14.99*

Blitzkrieg Bop (1977)
In the mid-'70s, New York's Bowery nightclub, CBGB, was the launching pad for the raw, energetic music known as "punk rock." This gritty documentary features rare, early concert footage of three of the genre's most influential bands: Blondie ("In the Flesh," "X Offender"), The Dead Boys ("Ain't Nothing to Do," "Sonic Reducer") and The Ramones ("Blitzkrieg Bop," "Sheena Is a Punk Rocker"). 52 min.
15-5343 *$29.99*

The Great Rock 'N' Roll Swindle (1980)
Get the inside story from Sex Pistols manager Malcolm McLaren on how to get rich with a band that can't play, in Julien Temple's mix of concert film, documentary and detective story that chronicles the history of the infamous punk combo that changed the face of rock. Songs include "Anarchy in the U.K.," "God Save the Queen," "My Way," "Who Killed Bambi?" and more. 104 min.
19-3388 *$19.99*

The Filth And The Fury (2000)
After filming manager Malcolm McLaren's take on the rise and fall of punk icons The Sex Pistols in 1980's "The Great Rock 'n' Roll Swindle," director Julien Temple offers the band's view on their brief, controversial time together in this acclaimed documentary. Vintage news and interview footage (including an outrageous 1978 bedside chat with Sid Vicious and Nancy Spungen) is mixed with comments from Johnny Rotten and company today, plus concert clips with such songs as "Anarchy in the U.K.," "God Save the Queen," "Holidays in the Sun" and others.
02-5234 *$99.99*

Dead Kennedys Live (1984)
The infamous punk band, fronted by lead singer and social gadfly Jello Biafra, assaults the issues of the day and the audience's senses in a driving hometown San Francisco concert. Songs include "Jock O Rama," "MTV Get Off the Air," "Do the Slag" and other uncensored faves. 63 min.
15-5156 *$19.99*

Another State Of Mind (1984)
Fascinating documentary follows hardcore punk bands Social Distortion, Youth Brigade and Minor Threat on a six-week, 10,000-mile tour across America, with driving rock music and a fascinating look at the punk community and life on the road. 90 min.
69-1079 *$19.99*

Aretha Franklin: Live At Park West (1985)
The soulful singer belts out her greatest songs in this dynamic performance that originally aired on the PBS "Soundstage" series. Among the numbers Aretha sings are "Respect," "Jump to It," "The Freeway of Love," "Rock Steady" and others. 60 min.
15-5296 *$19.99*

Celine Dion: The Colour Of My Love Concert (1993)
Filmed live in concert in her hometown of Quebec City, the chart-topping Celine Dion shines as she performs such favorites as "If You Asked Me To," "Love Can Move Mountains," "When I Fall in Love," "The Power of Love," "Beauty and the Beast" (with Peabo Bryson), "Only One Road" and more, including the title tune. 67 min.
04-5404 *$19.99*

Half Japanese: The Band That Would Be King (1993)
Called by one critic "idiot savants of rock music," the DC-based band Half Japanese, fronted by brothers Jad and David Fair, built a cult following with its raw and experimental sound. Follow the ups and downs of the Fairs and their struggle to break into the "musical mainstream" in this acclaimed documentary filled with performance clips and interviews. 90 min.
22-9035 *$19.99*

Glastonbury: The Movie (1995)
This British version of Woodstock has been staged regularly since 1970, drawing over 100,000 people for a three-day rock, blues, folk and alternative music festival. Among the bands featured here are The Lemonheads, The Filberts, The Verve and Porno for Pyros. 101 min.
50-8626 Letterboxed *$19.99*

Prince And The Revolution Live (1985)
Stop looking for the ladder and catch Rock's Purple Prince and his band in concert. This video, taped from the world tour, features 18 hits, including "1999," "Let's Go Crazy," "Little Red Corvette" and "I Would Die 4 You." 118 min.
19-3001 *$29.99*

Prince: Rave Un2 The Year 2000 (2000)
Paisley Park Studio in Minneapolis serves as the stomping ground for Prince, one of the most acclaimed musicians in pop music history, as he performs songs from his catalog including "Kiss," "1999," "Let's Go Crazy," "Get Off," "She's Always In My Hair" and others as well as performances from special guests Lenny Kravitz, Morris Day and the Time and others. 122 min.
50-8733 *$19.99*

The Industry (1998)
From "Big Baller Records and Films" comes a film that takes you where the action is. Learn all about the business of rap and sports as such stars as Jermaine Dupri, Trick Daddy, Luke, Erricht Rhett and others take you inside their worlds for an in-depth look at what they do.
64-3443 *$19.99*

Who's Better, Who's Best
For 25 years they've shaped and exceeded the expectations of rock fans. Follow the tempestuous, hit-filled career of The Who in this collection of videos and concert footage. Includes "Magic Bus," "See Me, Feel Me," "You Better You Bet" and over a dozen other tunes. 60 min.
02-7033 Was $24.99 *$14.99*

The Who: 30 Years Of Maximum R&B Live
Assembled from three decades of classic concert footage, this video features two dozen Who favorites, including "Baba O'Reilly," "Behind Blue Eyes" and others, from appearances by the group at the 1967 Monterey Pop Festival, the Isle of Wight in 1970, a 1979 concert in Chicago and much more. Also includes interviews and other exclusive clips. 150 min.
07-4112 *$29.99*

The Who: Live At The Isle Of Wight Festival 1970: Listening To You
Taking the stage at the famed British music festival at 2 a.m. on August 30, 1970, Roger Daltrey, John Entwistle, Keith Moon and Pete Townshend electrified the early-morning audience with performances of such Who faves as "I Can't Explain," "My Generation," "Magic Bus," and others, including several songs from the group's then-new rock opera, "Tommy." 85 min.
15-5459 *$19.99*

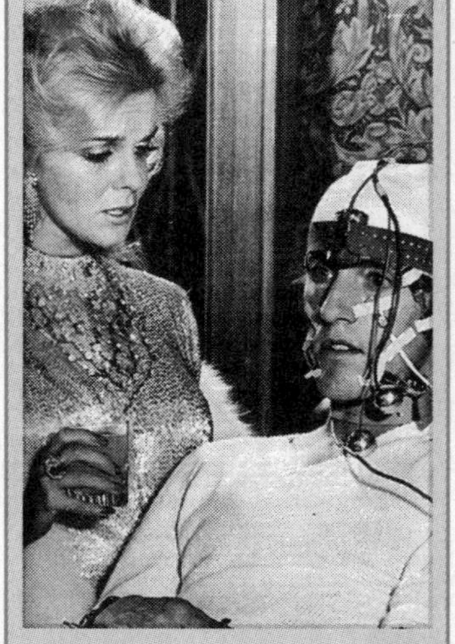

Tommy (1975)
The Who's innovative rock opera gets an electrifying, eye-popping film treatment from director Ken Russell. Roger Daltrey plays the "deaf, dumb and blind kid" whose pinball prowess makes him a global sensation; Ann-Margret, Oliver Reed, Elton John, Tina Turner, Eric Clapton and Jack Nicholson also star. Songs include "Pinball Wizard," "The Acid Queen," "See Me, Feel Me." 119 min.
02-1100 *$14.99*

The Who: Tommy Live! (1989)
As a part of their 1989 U.S. tour, the venerable British rockers were joined onstage in Los Angeles by Phil Collins, Billy Idol, Elton John, Patti LaBelle and Steve Winwood for a live performance of the classic rock opera. Add 13 more Who favorites and the result is an unforgettable night of music. 120 min.
04-5029 *$19.99*

Quadrophenia (1979)
The early 1960s: in England, the country's new music fans, the Mods, are battling with the greasy-haired Rockers. Revolution is in the air in this exciting, eye-opening film, sparked by great era music and tunes from The Who's rock opera on which it is based. Phil Daniels, Mark Wingett, Sting. 115 min.
02-1240 Was $19.99 *$14.99*

The Kids Are Alright (1979)
Explosive rockumentary look at one of pop music's greatest bands, The Who. Follow the rise of Pete Townshend, John Entwistle, Roger Daltrey and Keith Moon through concert clips, vintage TV appearances and interviews, and more. Hear "My Generation," "Won't Get Fooled Again," "Pinball Wizard," "Who Are You" and many more classic tunes, including the newly-added title song. 99 min.
44-1064 *$19.99*

Gift (1991)
A compelling mix of film narrative and music video co-created by alternative rock fave Perry Farrell (Jane's Addiction, Porno for Pyros). Around a love story of two drug addicts (Farrell and Casey Niccoli) trying to escape their self-destructive lifestyle, Jane's tunes like "Classic Girl" and "Ain't No Right" are featured, along with a duet by Farrell and Ice-T on "Don't Call Me Nigger, Whitey." 80 min.
19-3451 *$19.99*

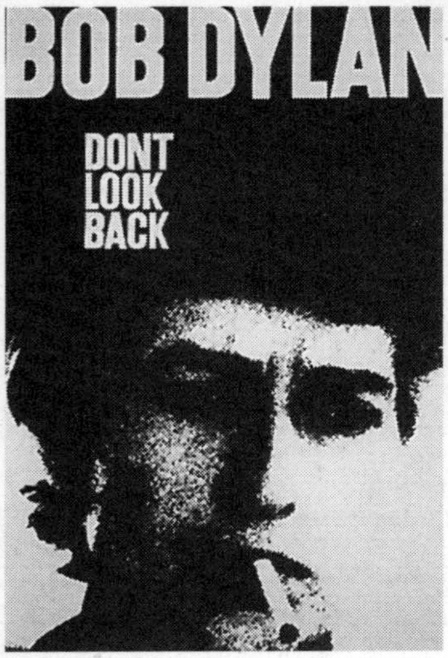
BOB DYLAN
DONT
LOOK
BACK

Dont Look Back (1967)
Bob Dylan's 1965 tour of England is the background for this seminal "rockumentary" by D.A. Pennebaker ("Monterey Pop") that looks at Dylan's music, his off-stage moments with other tour members (including Joan Baez, Donovan and Allen Ginsberg), and the philosophies that brought about the youth movements of the late '60s. 90 min.
19-3248 *$19.99*

Bob Dylan: MTV Unplugged (1994)
The one and only Robert Zimmerman's acclaimed "Unplugged" appearance features the rock legend in classic form, performing an acoustic set that includes "Knockin' on Heaven's Door," "All Along the Watchtower," "Like a Rolling Stone," "Desolation Row," the exclusive-to-video "John Brown" and many more. 73 min.
04-5401 *$19.99*

Richard Marx: Hold On To The Night (1987)
If you've yet to be indoctrinated into the joy of Marxism, this live concert will make a convert out of you. Includes hits like "Endless Summer Nights," "Should've Known Better," "Hold on to the Nights" and much more. 60 min.
50-6316 *$19.99*

Dancin' In The Street (1987)
Some of the greatest stars of the '60s and '70s "Detroit sound" take the stage in this rare concert. Featured performers include Mary Wells ("Two Lovers," "My Guy"), Temptations colleagues David Ruffin and Eddie Kendricks ("Just My Imagination," "Ain't Too Proud to Beg," "Get Ready"), and Martha Reeves ("Jimmy Mack," "Heat Wave"). 90 min.
50-8301 *$19.99*

This Is Michael Bolton (1992)
One of America's most popular singers is featured in his debut TV special, with 20 extra minutes previously unseen. Bolton belts out such favorites as "Since I Fell for You," "Georgia on My Mind" (with Kenny G), "How Can We Be Lovers," "Yesterday" and "Soul Provider." 70 min.
04-5180 *$19.99*

Curtis Mayfield: Live At Ronnie Scott's (1988)
In this rare live performance from the legendary English nightclub, Curtis Mayfield performs selections from his solo career and his years with The Impressions. Getting soulful treatments are "We Gotta Have Peace," "People Get Ready," "Pusherman," "I'm So Proud" and "Freddie's Dead." 58 min.
15-5212 Was $19.99 *$14.99*

Del Shannon: Live In Australia (1989)
In one of his final concert appearances before his untimely death the following year, Shannon shines in a show at the Castle Hill RSL. Among the favorites Del and his band perform are "Runaway," "Hats Off to Larry," "Keep Searchin'" and others. 60 min.
15-5390 *$19.99*

Nico Icon (1995)
German model/actress/chanteuse Christa Paffgen gained fame in the '60s as Nico, a member of Andy Warhol's Factory entourage and singer with the influential rock band The Velvet Underground, but drug abuse and a hedonistic lifestyle led to her death in 1986 at the age of 42. Learn about Nico's wild and tumultuous life in this compelling documentary that includes interviews with Factory colleagues Viva and Paul Morrissey, Velvet Underground members John Cale and Sterling Morrison, and others. 67 min. In English and French and German with English subtitles.
53-9884 Was $59.99 *$19.99*

Eddie Money: Shakin' With The Money Man (1997)
"Baby Hold On" for a "Shakin'" good time, as Eddie Money performs his greatest hits live. Included on the program are "She Takes My Breath Away," "Take Me Home Tonight," "Two Tickets to Paradise" and many more. 60 min.
02-8793 *$19.99*

Styx: Return To Paradise (1997)
It's "five, six, pick up a searing amalgamation of guitar licks" when the chart-topping '70s band reunites at the Rosemont in their hometown of Chicago for a rockin' show that includes "Come Sail Away," "Grand Illusion," "Lady," "Show Me the Way" and more. 108 min.
02-8792 *$19.99*

Lynyrd Skynyrd: Lyve From Steel Town (1997)
"What song is it you want to hear?" Well, how about all of Ronnie Van Zant and his group's greatest hits, including "Saturday Night Special," "What's Your Name," "That Smell," "Sweet Home Alabama" and "Free Bird." It's wild, live Southern rock at its best and baddest! 97 min.
02-8877 *$19.99*

Divas Live (1998)
The top songstresses in the pop world gather together in this wonderful musical happening that originally ran on VH-1. Mariah Carey, Celine Dion, Gloria Estefan, Aretha Franklin and Shania Twain are the talents who belt out 14 numbers, including "My All," "Make It Happen," "Turn the Beat Around," "Heaven's What I Feel," "Chain of Fools" and "My Heart Will Go On." 80 min.
04-5621 *$19.99*

Divas Live 99 (1999)
It's "Ladies' Night" once again in the second VH-1 distaff concert event, as divas supreme Brandy, Cher, Tina Turner and Whitney Houston are joined by guest divas Mary J. Blige, Faith Hill, Chaka Khan and LeAnn Rimes and honorary diva Elton John. Among the featured songs are "Simply the Best," "The Bitch Is Back," "If I Could Turn Back Time," "Have You Ever?," "I Will Always Love You," "I'm Every Woman" and many more. 59 min.
02-9200 *$19.99*

Pet Shop Boys: Somewhere (1997)
Where? How about London's Savoy Theatre, where Neil Tennant and Chris Lowe are captured live on stage, performing "Yesterday When I Was Mad," "Truck Driver and His Mate," "Go West," "It's a Sin/I Will Survive," "Left to My Own Devices" and more. 91 min.
50-8561 *$19.99*

The Earth Day Special (1990)
Here's an all-star salute to the environment, commemorating the 20th anniversary of Earth Day. Join Dan Aykroyd, Chevy Chase, Kevin Costner, Meryl Streep, Dustin Hoffman, Danny DeVito, Michael Douglas, Robin Williams, Bette Midler and the Muppets for a program of skits, songs and comedy with a message. 95 min.
19-1793 *$14.99*

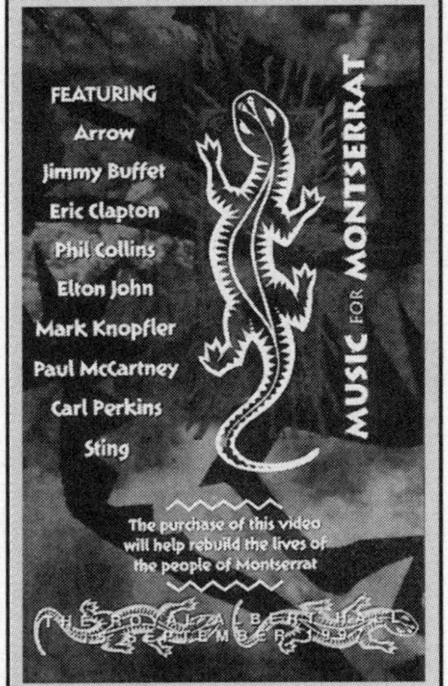
FEATURING
Arrow
Jimmy Buffet
Eric Clapton
Phil Collins
Elton John
Mark Knopfler
Paul McCartney
Carl Perkins
Sting
MUSIC FOR MONTSERRAT
The purchase of this video
will help rebuild the lives of
the people of Montserrat

Music For Montserrat (1997)
Some of the world's greatest rock stars—including Jimmy Buffet, Eric Clapton, Phil Collins, Elton John, Paul McCartney, Carl Perkins and Sting—came together at London's Royal Albert Hall in a special benefit concert for the hurricane-damaged Caribbean island of Montserrat. Among the songs performed are "Take Me Home," "Blue Suede Shoes," "Message in a Bottle," "Your Song," "Layla," "Hey Jude" and more. 120 min.
50-5921 *$19.99*

The Paris Concert For Amnesty International (1998)
Some of the top names in music lit up the City of Lights in a benefit marking the 50th anniversary of the Universal Declaration of Human Rights. Join Tracy Chapman ("New Beginning"), Peter Gabriel ("Signal to Noise"), Alanis Morissette ("Thank U"), Jimmy Page and Robert Plant ("Rock and Roll"), Radiohead ("Karma Police"), Bruce Springsteen ("Born in the USA"), Shania Twain ("You're Still the One") and others in a moving concert event. 120 min.
50-8210 *$19.99*

Joe Cocker Live: Across From Midnight Tour (1997)
Berlin's historic Waldbuhne Auditorium was a site for Joe Cocker's Across from Midnight Tour. Among the 17 songs performed by Cocker and his band in this live video are "Up Where We Belong," "When the Night Comes," "Could You Be Loved," "Summer in the City," and his tribute to Princess Diana, "You Are So Beautiful." 90 min.
53-6240 Was $24.99 *$14.99*

Carly In Concert: My Romance (1990)
Carly Simon torches it up in a lush nightclub setting, showcasing the songs of Rodgers/Hart and Rodgers/Hammerstein. Included are "My Funny Valentine," "Something Wonderful," "Bewitched" and her own "What Has She Got." Jazz pianist Harry Connick, Jr. guests to join Carly for two duets. 80 min.
02-7164 *$19.99*

Storefront Hitchcock (1998)
Director Jonathan Demme, who captured the Talking Heads on film in 1984's "Stop Making Sense," turns his camera on another cult rocker, idiosyncratic British singer/songwriter Robyn Hitchcock. Shot during a two-day period, Hitchcock and his band perform in a lower Manhattan storefront, with traffic and pedestrians glimpsing through the windows. Among the songs are "The Yip Song," "Glass Hotel," "I Don't Remember Guildford," "I'm Only You" and more.
12-3313 *$14.99*

Alice In Chains: Live Facelift
Hard-rocking band Alice in Chains shows you the stuff that's made them one of the hottest groups in the U.S. in this program of music videos and concert footage. Selections include "Man in the Box," "Real Thing," "Sea of Sorrow" and "Bleed the Freak." 45 min.
04-5118 *$17.99*

Alice In Chains: Video Bank
Coming out of Seattle's embryonic music scene in the late '80s, Alice in Chains blended hard rock with an alternative sound that won them national acclaim. Included in this video counterpart to the band's "Music Bank" retrospective are "We Die Young," "Man in the Box," "Would?," "Heaven Beside You," "Over Now" and many more. 95 min.
04-5692 *$19.99*

Joni Mitchell: Painting With Words And Music (1998)
The legendary singer-songwriter is showcased in an intimate setting, performing an eclectic mix of her jazz and folk stylings. Highlights include "Big Yellow Taxi," the haunting "Amelia," Marvin Gaye's "Trouble Man," "Woodstock," "Black Crow," "Night Ride Home," and "Facelift" and "Crazy Cries of Love" from Mitchell's recent "Taming the Tiger." 98 min.
50-5753 *$19.99*

Twentieth Century Blues: The Songs Of Noël Coward (1998)
An all-star collection of artists, including Marianne Faithfull, Elton John and Sting, offer their own unique spins on the witty music of the songwriter/actor/raconteur whose songs came to symbolize England for a generation. 60 min.
50-8211 *$19.99*

The First Waltz (1999)
Staged to benefit Chicago's Neon Street's work against teenage homelessness, this concert by The Nicholas Tremulis Band features guest appearances by Lonnie Brooks, Billy Corgan, Rick Danko, Jon Langford, Ivan Neville, Rick Nielsen and others.
02-9202 *$19.99*

Stamping Ground (1971)
Classic slice of '60s psychedelia, European style. The Holland Music Festival is the setting for dynamic performances by Pink Floyd, Jefferson Airplane, The Byrds, Canned Heat and It's a Beautiful Day. 80 min.
50-1503 *$29.99*

Sonny & Cher: Nitty Gritty Hour (1970)
"The Beat Goes On" in this TV special that predated the duo's hit TV series. Join Sonny and Cher for comedy skits and such hits as "We've Only Just Begun," "I've Got You Babe," plus a medley that includes "Alfie," "All You Need Is Love" and "Funky Broadway." 48 min.
22-7082 Was $19.99 *$14.99*

Cher: Live In Concert (1999)
Her string of Top 10 hits stretches across four decades, and in this dynamic live concert the one and only Cher performs such favorites as "Gypsies, Tramps and Thieves," "Half Breed," "If I Could Turn Back Time," "Believe" and many more, along with a roomful of costume changes. 75 min.
44-2203 *$19.99*

The Cure: Staring At The Sea—The Images
Video collection showcasing the British combo whose music ranges from early Punk to stylized Rock with a nihilistic outlook. Includes "Killing an Arab," "Boys Don't Cry," "Play for Today," "Close to Me" and more. 82 min.
19-3022 *$24.99*

Jewel: A Life Uncommon
She became one of the top rock stars to ever come from Alaska before her 25th birthday, and this video look at Jewel on and off the stage features interviews and concert footage. Songs include "Barcelona," "Deep Water," "Down" and "Love Me Just Leave Me Alone." 60 min.
19-4071 *$19.99*

Cream: Farewell Concert
The famed English blues-rock trio of Ginger Baker, Jack Bruce and Eric Clapton bade farewell to an enthusiastic crowd of Cream fans inside London's Royal Albert Hall on November 26, 1968, in what was to become a legendary concert performance. Includes rare off-stage interviews and such songs as "Sunshine of Your Love," "White Room" and "I'm So Glad." 50 min.
64-1324 Was $19.99 *$14.99*

The Cream Of Eric Clapton
The cream rises to the top, and Slowhand's been at rock's pinnacle for decades. This marvelous video collection of Clapton classics old ("Layla," "Strange Brew") and new ("Tearing Us Apart," "Forever Man") will please all generations. 75 min.
02-7092 Was $24.99 *$14.99*

Eric Clapton: 24 Nights
He's been an innovator in the rock and blues music world, and in this dynamic program, "Slowhand" Clapton turns in a powerful performance playing and singing such tunes as "White Room," "Running on Faith," "Wonderful Tonight" and "Bell Bottom Blues." He's also joined by guests like Robert Cray, Phil Collins, Albert Collins and Buddy Guy. 90 min.
19-3247 *$24.99*

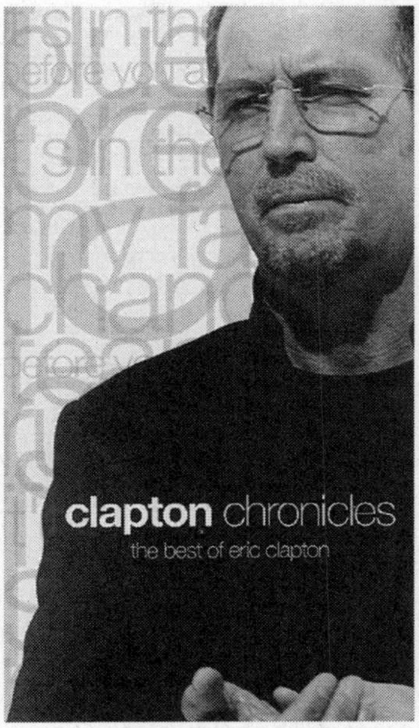
clapton chronicles
the best of eric clapton

Clapton Chronicles: The Best Of Eric Clapton 1981-1999
Follow two decades of music from one of rock's greatest stars with this collection of Clapton music videos. Among the timeless favorites from Eric are "Forever Man," "Bad Love," "Tears in Heaven," "Blue Eyes Blue" and more, including his "Unplugged" renditions of "Layla" and "Running on Faith." 109 min.
19-4063 *$19.99*

Eric Clapton: Unplugged (1992)
The legendary musician's acoustic turns on "MTV Unplugged" have been gathered on this special video. Joined by guest artists Andy Fairweather-Low, Nathan East and Ray Cooper, Clapton performs such favorites as "Tears in Heaven," "Nobody Knows You," "Layla," "San Francisco Bay Blues" and others. 60 min.
19-3337 *$19.99*

Eric Clapton: Live In Hyde Park (1996)
London's venerable Hyde Park is the setting for an unforgettable evening of rock and blues standards from the guitar legend and his band. "Layla," "I Shot the Sheriff," "Tearin' Us Apart," "Have You Ever Loved a Woman" and "White Room" are among the dozen songs performed. 90 min.
19-3706 *$19.99*

Eric Clapton & Friends: In Concert: A Benefit For The Crossroads Centre At Antigua (1999)
Recorded live at New York's famed Madison Square Garden, this all-star gathering features Clapton taking the stage with guests Bob Dylan, Mary J. Blige and Sheryl Crow. Among the songs performed are "River of Tears," "Goin' Down Slow," "My Favorite Mistake," "Tears in Heaven," "Layla," "Crossroads" and more. Special video version includes footage not shown on TV. 108 min.
19-4062 *$19.99*

Carole King In Concert
Superb concert from Carole King's 1993 "Colour of Your Dreams" tour in which the singer-songwriter delivers an energetic performance of songs like "It's Too Late," "You've Got a Friend," "I Feel the Earth Move," "Jazzman" and others. 82 min.
22-1350 *$19.99*

Alice Cooper: Prime Cuts
The greatest hits of the master of shock rock include "I'm Eighteen," "Clones," "No More Mr. Nice Guy," "Elected," "Trash," "School's Out," "Poison" and lots more. 90 min.
02-7403 *$19.99*

Alice Cooper: Welcome To My Nightmare (1975)
The king of '70s "shock rock" welcomes you to a dazzling concert video that is macabre and mesmerizing. Among the classics performed by Alice and the band in a wild stage show are "School's Out," "No More Mr. Nice Guy," "Black Widow," "Only Women Bleed" and "I'm Eighteen." 82 min.
15-5076 Was $19.99 *$14.99*

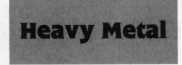

Heavy Metal

The Very Best Of Thin Lizzy: Dedication
A "very best of" video compilation, featuring music videos, rare TV performance clips and concert footage. All your Thin Lizzy faves are here, including "The Boys Are Back in Town," "Jailbreak," "Whiskey in the Jar," "Dancin' in the Moonlight," "Chinatown" and more. 55 min.
02-7277 Was $19.99 *$14.99*

Def Leppard: Visualize
"Let's Get Rocked" with this video retrospective of the Leppard lads that includes such Def hits as "Have You Ever Needed Someone So Bad," "I Wanna Touch You," "Make Love Like a Man" and more. 95 min.
02-7942 *$19.99*

Def Leppard: Video Archive
Fans of hard-rockin' music won't turn a "def" ear to this "best of" collection featuring classic Leppard videos, live concert clips, and special acoustic performance pieces. Songs include "Let's Get Rocked," "Pour Some Sugar on Me," "Two Steps Behind," "Rock of Ages," "Ziggy Stardust" and others. 108 min.
02-8365 *$19.99*

Iron Maiden & Simon Drake: Raising Hell
An amazing collaboration between heavy metal favorites Iron Maiden and horror illusionist Simon Drake, this exciting, mind-expanding program features such songs as "Trooper," "Wrathchild," "Transylvania," "Sanctuary" and 13 more. 110 min.
02-8034 *$19.99*

Iron Maiden: From There To Eternity
The greatest hits of super-duper heavy metalists Iron Maiden are presented in this smashing collection. This must-own package offers the likes of "Run to the Hills," "Wrathchild," "Tail Gunner," "The Trooper," "From Here to Eternity" and 15 more. 90 min.
04-5156 *$19.99*

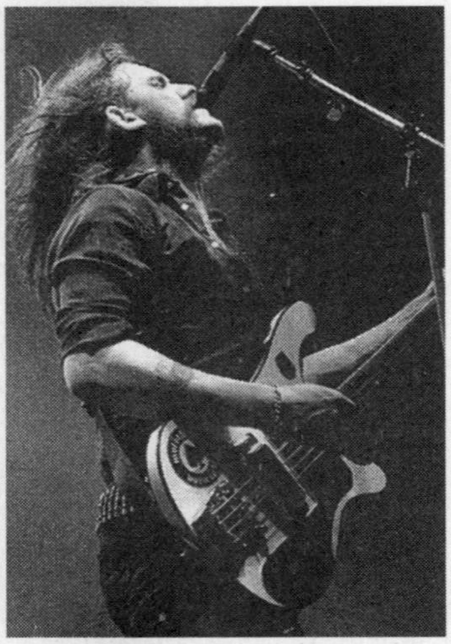

Motorhead Live: Everything Louder Than Everything Else
Clocking in at 120-plus decibels, British trash masters Motorhead rip it up in live concert footage, music videos for their hit "1916" album, and uncensored interviews. Songs include "No Voices in the Sky," "Love Me Forever," "Orgasmatron," and the tribute tune, "Ramones." 66 min.
04-5099 *$19.99*

Kiss: X-treme Close-Up
Take an "x-treme" look at 12 years of hit songs from the band that revolutionized heavy metal rock. This collection features Kiss at their finest, thrashing through such tunes as "I Want You," "Forever," "I Just Wanna," and more. 90 min.
02-7648 *$19.99*

AC/DC: Let There Be Rock (1981)
Turn up the volume and rock with those outrageous Aussies, AC/DC, in concert and in interviews with Malcolm and Angus Young and crew. Thirteen songs, including "Highway to Hell," "Live Wire," "Shot Down in Flames" and the title song. 98 min.
19-1451 Was $19.99 *$14.99*

AC/DC: Live At Donington (1991)
Two hours of high-voltage music from AC/DC, live from the Castle Donnington Festival. Angus Young and company perform songs from throughout the group's career, including "Dirty Deeds," "Highway to Hell," "Back in Black" and "Thunderstruck." 117 min.
19-3375 *$19.99*

Slayer: Live Intrusion (1995)
This one'll slay ya: a bone-crunching live concert from Phoenix that features the ever-intense quartet performing "Raining Blood," "Killing Fields," "South of Heaven," "Angel of Death" and other fun-filled favorites, plus a cover of Venom's "Witching Hour" unavailable anywhere else. 85 min.
19-3864 Was $24.99 *$14.99*

Quiet Riot: Bang Thy Head
Get ready to bang yer head against the wall when this sampling of videos from those heavy metal houseshakers hits your VCR, includes "The Wild and the Young," "Cum on Feel the Noize," "Bang Your Head (Mental Health)," and more. 27 min.
04-1993 Was $19.99 *$14.99*

Aerosmith Video Scrapbook
Get "Back in the Saddle" with Boston's masters of heavy metal rock. Concert and video footage features hits like "Dream On," "Walk This Way," "Sweet Emotion" and more, and a highlight is an all-new introduction by Steve Tyler. 55 min.
04-2107 Was $19.99 *$14.99*

Aerosmith: Live Texxas Jam '78
Over 150,000 rock fans packed Dallas' Cotton Bowl for a July 4th rock spectacle, highlighted by an on-target Aerosmith performance. "Seasons of Wither," "Dream On," "Rats in the Cellar" and other songs are included. 50 min.
04-5015 *$19.99*

Aerosmith: Things That Go Pump
Here's a hard-rockin' video collection that definitely has "What It Takes," along with "Love in an Elevator," "Janie's Got a Gun," "Young Lust" and other Aerosmith faves. 45 min.
07-4043 *$19.99*

Aerosmith: Big Ones You Can Look At
This video counterpart to Aerosmith's "Big Ones" album features Steve, Joe and the boys in concert clips and videos for such old and new hits as "Cryin'," "Amazing," "Crazy," "Eat the Rich," "Livin' on the Edge" and others. 100 min.
07-4115 *$24.99*

The Yngwie Malmsteen Collection
Sweden's guitar master performs in concerts from Tokyo and Leningrad, laying out such tunes as Jimi Hendrix' "Spanish Castle Magic," "Far Beyond the Sun," "Making Love," "Déjà Vu" and more. 66 min.
02-7598 *$19.99*

Black Sabbath: The Last Supper
Filmed during the legendary metal combo's 1999 Reunion tour, this ultra-intense concert video features Geezer Butler, Tony Iommi, Bill Ward and the inimitable Ozzy Osbourne performing such Sabbath standards as "Into the Void," "Snowblind," "Paranoid," "Iron Man," "War Pigs" and more, plus exclusive behind-the-scenes footage. 107 min.
04-5663 *$29.99*

Black Sabbath: The Black Sabbath Story, Vol. 1
One of heavy metal's greatest bands is spotlighted in this awesome amalgamation of interviews, videos and live performances. Join Ozzy Osbourne and company, as they perform "Symptom of the Universe," "It's Alright," "War Pigs" and more. 58 min.
19-3341 *$19.99*

Black Sabbath: The Black Sabbath Story, Vol. 2
The second half of Black Sabbath's history features the post-Ozzy era, with Ronnie James Dio and Ian Gillian taking the singing chores. Songs include "The Shining," "Headless Cross," "No Stranger to Love," "Trashed" and "Neon Knights." 55 min.
19-3367 *$19.99*

The Ultimate Ozzy
Cheered by metal manics and feared by chickens and bats around the world, the one and only Ozzy Osbourne stars in a white-hot video collection that no rock fan should miss. "Shot in the Dark," "Iron Man," "Lightning Strikes," "Bark at the Moon," "Paranoid" and more featured. 85 min.
04-1970 Was $19.99 *$14.99*

Ozzy Osbourne: Live & Loud
The great and powerful Ozz is captured live and at his wildest in this concert program that features such headbangers' delights as "Change the World," "I Don't Know," "No More Tears," "Bark at the Moon," "Shot in the Dark" and "Changes." 111 min.
04-5191 *$29.99*

Metallica: Cliff 'Em All
Their very name promises the best in searing amalgamations of guitar licks. Rare concert footage is mixed with interviews with original Metallica members James Hetfield, Lars Ulrich, Dave Mustaine and the late Cliff Burton. Songs include "Creeping Death," "Am I Evil?," "No Remorse," more. 90 min.
19-3045 *$19.99*

Metallica: A Year And A Half In The Life Of Metallica
Follow the metal masters for 16 months on the road, in the studio, and at home with this two-tape retrospective that features rare concert footage, music video clips and exclusive interviews. Songs include "Sad But True," "For Whom the Bell Tolls," "Enter Sandman," "Nothing Else Matters" and more. 180 min.
19-3380 *$34.99*

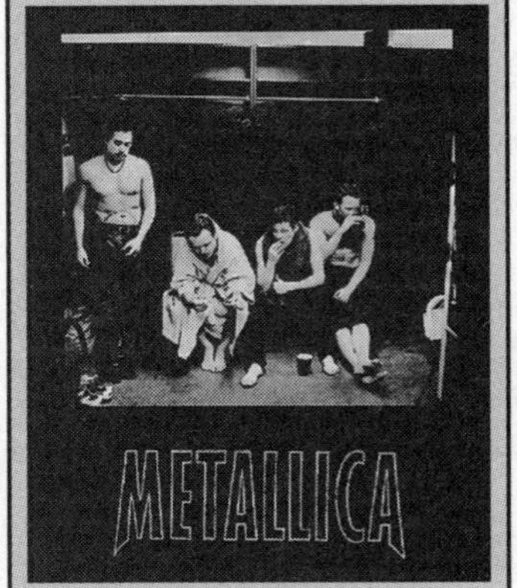

Metallica With The San Francisco Symphony
It's heavy metal with a classical touch when Metallica is joined on stage by conductor Michael Kamen and the San Francisco Symphony for a unique concert experience. Featured on this video are such songs as "The Ecstasy of Gold," "The Memory Remains," "No Leaf Clover," "For Whom the Bell Tolls," "Human," "Enter Sandman" and more.
19-4068 *$19.99*

Deep Purple In Concert With The London Symphony Orchestra (1999)
The timeless hard rock combo, once listed as "loudest rock band" in the Guinness Book of World Records, takes the stage at London's venerable Royal Albert Hall. Joined by the London Symphony Orchestra and special guests Ronnie James Dio, Sam Brown, and The Steve Morse Band, Deep Purple performs "Pictured Within," "Love Is All," "Concerto for Group and Orchestra," "Smoke on the Water" and more. 120 min.
50-8592 *$19.99*

Dokken: One Live Night
Get ready to raise the roof with a live and searing amalgamation of guitar licks from the masters of metal. Songs include "Alone Again," "I Will Remember," "Into the Fire," "It's Not Love" and more. 80 min.
02-8590 *$19.99*

Anthrax: Return Of The Killer A's
"Bring the Noise" into your TV with this collection of killer music videos featuring "thrash metal" masters Anthrax. "Ball of Confusion," "Caught in a Mosh," "I Am the Law," and "Among the Living" are among the faves included. 80 min.
02-9204 *$19.99*

Skid Row: Roadkill
Actually, "killer roadshow" is a better way to describe this mind-blowing concert video featuring Skid Row on stage in Rio, Tokyo, Iceland(!) and other exotic spots, as well as U.S. tour footage. Hear Skid Row faves like "Big Guns," "Slave to the Grind," "Delivering the Goods" and more, plus the 3-D video for "Pyscho Love" (and yes, glasses are included). 120 min.
19-3468 *$19.99*

Van Halen: Video Hits, Vol. 1
Halen, Halen, the gang's all here in this collection of the band's chart-topping music videos. Included are "Can't Stop Loving You," "Jump," "Poundcake," "Right Now" and others. 60 min.
19-3966 *$19.99*

David Lee Roth
Our high-kicking hero displays his "charisma" in exclusive interview footage and classic video clips: "California Girls," "Just a Gigolo/I Ain't Got Nobody," "Yankee Rose," "Goin' Crazy." 30 min.
19-3032 *$14.99*

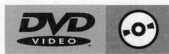

DVD VIDEO
ASK ABOUT OUR GIANT DVD CATALOG!

Uriah Heep: Live In London
Hard-rocking heavy metalists Uriah Heep display their brand of music in this concert performed in London's Camden Palace. Peter Goalby leads the group in songs like "Stealin'," "On the Other Side of Midnight," "Angel," "Easy Living" and more. 61 min.
64-1300 *$19.99*

Behind The Music: Mötley Crüe
One of the most successful heavy metal bands of the '80s, Mötley Crüe's antics on and off the stage were as wild as their music. In this VH1 special, Tommy Lee, Mick Mars, Vince Neil and Nikki Sixx talk candidly about the drugs, sex, car crashes and personal feuds that tore the Crüe apart, and the rebel spirit that kept them together. Includes 10 minutes of footage not shown on TV. 60 min.
02-9101 *$14.99*

Judas Priest: Fuel For Life
Leather up and get down with heavy metal monsters Judas Priest in a high-octane collection of music videos. Includes "Hot Rockin'," "Locked In," "You've Got Another Thing Comin'," "Breaking the Law" and many more. 40 min.
04-1949 Was $19.99 *$14.99*

Judas Priest Live (1987)
Holy head bangers! Those ministers of metal mania are back in a cacophonous concert experience that's hotter than a custom van. Includes "Locked In," "You've Got Another Thing Comin'," "Love Bites," and much more. 94 min.
04-2057 Was $19.99 *$14.99*

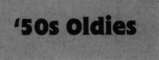

'50s Oldies

Fabulous Fifties
An honor roll of the most influential rock acts of the '50s featuring, among others, Elvis Presley ("Hound Dog"), Bill Haley and the Comets ("Rock Around the Clock"), Fats Domino ("Blue Monday"), Chuck Berry ("Sweet Little Sixteen") and Jerry Lee Lewis ("Great Balls of Fire"). 30 min.
10-2225 *$12.99*

Rock 'N' Soul Heaven
An all-star, all-dead line-up of Rock's tragic heroes with vintage performances by Elvis Presley ("Ready Teddy"), Bobby Darin ("Mack the Knife"), Buddy Holly ("That'll Be the Day"), Otis Redding ("Try a Little Tenderness"), Marvin Gaye ("Ain't No Mountain High Enough") and more. 30 min.
10-2226 *$12.99*

Pat Boone: 40 Years Of Hits
Get out your white buck shoes and listen to the squeaky-clean sound of '50s teen idol Pat Boone in this collection of performances from his "Chevy Showroom" TV series. "Ain't That a Shame," "April Love," "I Almost Lost My Mind" and "Love Letters in the Sand" are among the hits featured. 49 min.
15-5319 *$19.99*

Fats Domino And Friends
It'd be a shame if any rock and roll fan missed this all-star jam session with the legendary pianist/singer, as he's joined on stage by Ray Charles, Jerry Lee Lewis, "Late Night's" Paul Shaffer and Rolling Stone Ron Wood. 56 min.
44-1551 *$19.99*

Little Richard: Keep On Rockin' (1969)
The wildman of rock 'n' roll turns in rip-roaring performances of "Lucille," "Tutti Frutti," "Long Tall Sally," "Good Golly Miss Molly," and "Keep a Knocking." A-womp-bomp-a-looma-a-bomp-bam-boom! 30 min.
19-3296 *$14.99*

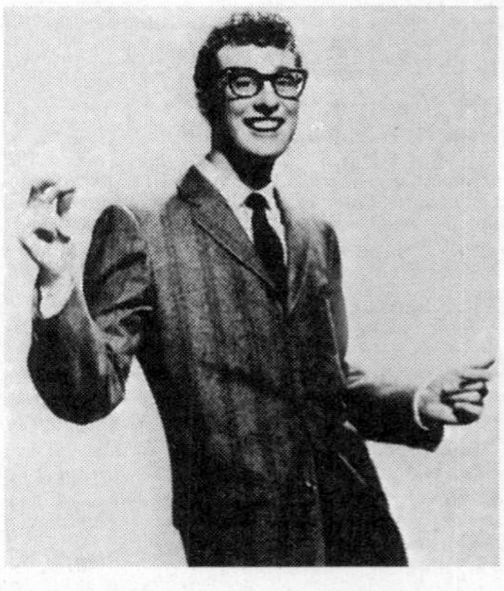

The Real Buddy Holly Story
Paul McCartney produced this film tribute to one of rock music's first and most enduring legends. Rare film clips of Holly and The Crickets performing, a duet with Jerry Lee Lewis, interviews with family and friends and a concert salute to Holly by McCartney are featured. 86 min.
45-5358 *$19.99*

Bo Diddley: 30th Anniversary All-Star Jam (1985)

In this superb stage show from California's Irvine Ampitheatre, guitar legend Bo Diddley is joined by the likes of Mick Fleetwood, John Mayall, Mitch Mitchell, Carl Wilson and Ron Wood for scorching renditions of such songs as "I'm a Man," "Bo Diddley," "Who Do You Love?" and more. 48 min.

02-7502 Was $19.99 *$14.99*

Chuck Berry With Tina Turner

Old rockers never die, they just improve with age. Mr. "Johnny B. Goode" is joined on stage in a 1982 concert at L.A.'s Roxy by the dynamic Ms. T. for a dynamic double event. Songs include "Roll Over Beethoven," "Reelin' and Rockin'" and more. 60 min.

45-7001 *$14.99*

Chuck Berry: Rock And Roll Music (1969)

Rock pioneer Chuck Berry turns in a thrilling performance, playing such greats as "Maybelline," "Sweet Little Sixteen," "Too Much Monkey Business," and, of course, "Johnny B.Goode." Directed by D.A. Pennebaker ("Dont Look Back"). 45 min.

19-3293 *$14.99*

Jerry Lee Lewis And Friends (1990)

Live from London, rock and roll's legendary "Killer" is joined on stage by such guests as Van Morrison, Brian May, John Lodge, Dave Edmunds and Dave Davies for a "greatest hits" concert that truly spans the ages. "I Am What I Am," "I Got a Woman," "High School Confidential," "Whole Lotta Shakin' Goin' On" and "Wild One" are among the songs. 61 min.

07-4044 *$19.99*

Rhythm & Blues

Muddy Waters: Got My Mojo Working (2000)

In these rare performances from 1968 to 1978, Muddy Waters, the father of the "Chicago blues sound," shows off his talent alongside his greatest sidemen in three different tours. This is some of the earliest footage available with Muddy, featuring such songs as "Country Boy," "Honey Bee," "Got My Mojo Working" "They Call Me Muddy Waters" and more. 55 min.

63-7178 *$19.99*

Bluesland: A Portrait In American Music

The complete history of the blues in America and its influence on jazz, rock and R&B includes rare footage of such greats as Muddy Waters, Sonny Boy Williamson, B.B. King and Leadbelly, as well as Dinah Washington, Son House and Roosevelt Sykes. 90 min.

02-8013 Was $29.99 *$19.99*

Jammin' With The Blues Greats

English Blues meets Chicago and Memphis Blues in this evening of incredible music, in which John Mayall's crew of Bluesbreakers, including Mick Taylor, John McVie and Colin Allen, pay homage to—and are joined by—Albert King, Etta James, Buddy Guy, Junior Wells and the 83-year-old Sippie Wallace. Songs include "The Dark Side of Midnight," "Don't Start Me Talkin'" and more. 90 min.

02-8089 *$19.99*

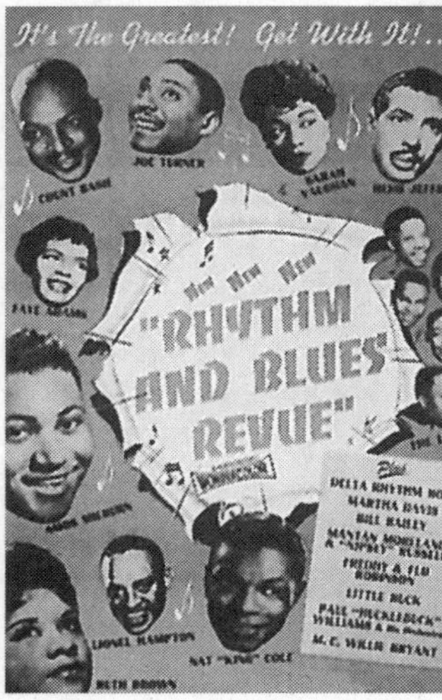

Rhythm And Blues Review (1954)

Tremendous music and comedy revue, captured live and hot onstage at the Apollo Theatre. Stars include Lionel Hampton, Herb Jeffries, Sarah Vaughan, Count Basie, Nat "King" Cole, Cab Calloway, Nipsey Russell, Mantan Moreland. 70 min.

01-1414 Was $29.99 *$14.99*

The Search For Robert Johnson

Unknown for most of his career, his seminal blues recordings helped to inspire later R&B and rock artists. Now Robert Johnson is remembered in this special tribute that takes host John Hammond, Jr. through the South to interview friends of the singer. Includes interviews with Eric Clapton, Keith Richards and Johnny Shines and scenes of important locations in Johnson's life. 72 min.

04-5138 *$19.99*

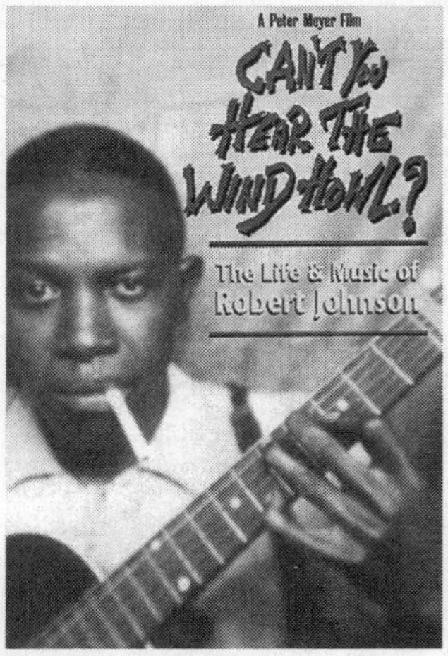

Can't You Hear The Wind Howl?: The Life & Music Of Robert Johnson (1997)

Rare photographs, documents and interviews with Robert Cray, Eric Clapton and John Hammond highlight this program on enigmatic blues great Robert Johnson. Hosted by Danny Glover and featuring musician Keb' Mo' playing Johnson, this documentary explores the life and career of one of American music's greatest artists. 76 min.

53-6326 *$24.99*

Hellhounds On My Trail: The Afterlife Of Robert Johnson (1999)

Even though he died in 1938 at age 27, Mississippi-born bluesman Robert Johnson continues to influence R&B, jazz and rock artists today. Documentarian Robert Mugge ("Deep Blues") examines his musical heritage through performance clips and interviews, including one with a childhood friend of Johnson. Among the artists featured are Joe Louis Walker, Keb' Mo', Bob Weir and Rob Wasserman, Robert Lockwood, Jr. (Johnson's stepson) and others. 95 min.

53-6684 *$19.99*

Buddy Guy: Live—The Real Deal

R&B great Buddy Guy joins forces with G.E. Smith and the Saturday Night Live Band in this concert program that really cooks. Among the songs performed by Guy and company are "Talk to Me Baby," "My Time After Awhile," "I've Got News for You," "Damn Right I've Got the Blues" and "Let Me Love You Baby." 55 min.

02-8453 *$14.99*

Blues Masters: The Essential History Of The Blues

Rare archival recordings, film clips, photographs and interviews help to trace the origins and legendary masters of this uniquely American musical genre. Each tape runs about 50 min.

Blues Masters, Vol. 1

Includes performances by Bessie Smith, Leadbelly, Big Bill Broonzy, Ethel Waters, Son House and many others.

15-5271 Was $19.99 *$14.99*

Blues Masters, Vol. 2

Billie Holiday, Muddy Waters, Big Mama Thornton, Buddy Guy and B.B. King are among the featured artists.

15-5272 Was $19.99 *$14.99*

B.B. King: Blues Summit Concert

Live from his own nightclub/restaurant on historic Beale Street in Memphis (try the Mississippi Mud Pie), the legendary B.B. King performs with a dazzling array of special guests that includes Ruth Brown ("Ain't Nobody's Business"), Robert Cray and Koko Taylor ("Playin' with My Friends"), Buddy Guy ("The Thrill Is Gone"), Joe Louis Walker ("T-Bone Shuffle") and others, plus an all-star jam on "Hey, Hey, The Blues Is Alright."

07-4125 *$19.99*

B.B. King: Live At Nick's (1983)

Live from Dallas' famous blues nightspot, the "King of the Blues" performs some of his best-loved songs, including such cheerful selections as "The Thrill Is Gone," "Inflation Blues," "Everyday I Have the Blues" and more. 50 min.

45-5163 Was $29.99 *$14.99*

Messin' With The Blues

Recorded live at the 1974 Montreux Jazz Festival, legendary musicians Muddy Waters, Buddy Guy and Junior Wells perform an unforgettable program of blues music. Songs include "Messing with the Kid," "Hoochie Coochie Man," "Mannish Boy," "Got My Mojo Working" and more. 54 min.

15-5157 Was $19.99 *$14.99*

Dr. John: New Orleans Swamp

Get ready for a real New Orleans funk party with Dr. John and The Meters in this rousing evening of Cajun, Zydeco and blues which originally aired on PBS' "Soundstage." The good doctor tickles the ivories on such tunes as "Whole Lotta Loving," "Call a Doctor," "Qualified," "Walk Right In/Shake, Rattle and Roll," "Such a Night," and more. 60 min.

15-5266 *$19.99*

Koko Taylor: The Queen Of The Blues

A biography and rousing concert performance from Koko Taylor, one of the great blues performers of all time. She recalls her life and career, then dazzles you by crooning R&B favorites, some with legends like Willie Dixon and Buddy Guy. Songs include "Wang Dang Doodle," "Let the Good Times Roll," "Hey Baby" and more. 55 min.

50-6904 *$19.99*

Harlem Swings

A rip-snortin' collection of comedy, dance, song and red-hot rhythm & blues from the '30s, '40s and '50s. It all takes place in Harlem, where jukeboxes jump and soundies swing! With Eddie Green, Artie Young and Doris Axe.

10-7937 *$19.99*

On The Road Again: Down Home Blues, Jazz, Gospel And More (1963)

Filmed in the streets, music halls, clubs and churches of Dallas, Nashville, New Orleans, San Francisco and other cities, this timeless, song-filled film features rare performance clips (in some cases the only known footage) of such artists as Black Ace, Sweet Emma Barrett, Lowell Fulsom, Lightnin' Hopkins, The Preservation Hall Jazz Band, Hop Wilson and more.

63-7175 *$19.99*

Masters Of The Blues (1966)

Originally produced for Canadian TV and unseen for decades, this rare studio gathering includes such legendary blues performers as Muddy Waters ("Got My Mojo Workin'," "You Can't Lose What You Never Had"), Otis Spann ("Blues Don't Like Nobody"), Mable Hillery ("How Long This Train Been Gone"), Sonny Terry & Brownie McGhee ("Cornbread and Peas"), Willie Dixon ("Crazy for My Baby") and others. 60 min.

15-5370 *$19.99*

Deep Blues (1991)

Journey into the heart of blues country—the hills of Northern Mississippi and Tennessee—with filmmaker Robert Mugge and music scholar Robert Palmer, as they visit porches, parlors and honky tonks to talk and listen to veteran blues artists. Roosevelt "Bubba" Barnes, R.L. Burnside, Jessie Mae Hemphill, Junior Kimbrough and Bud Spires are among the performers. 90 min.

53-6683 *$19.99*

Lightnin' Hopkins/ Roosevelt Sykes

Catch Roosevelt Sykes in a performance of great blues and boogie. And enjoy Lightnin' Hopkins and his low-down Texas blues—filmed at Texas bars for great effect. 60 min.

63-7086 *$24.99*

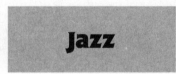

Jazz

Louis Jordan And His Tympany Five

A collection of "soundies" featuring jazz master Louis Jordan, whose jumpin' jive music inspired the Broadway hit "Five Guys Named Moe." Songs include "Shine," "Caldonia," "Fuzzy Wuzzy" and "Don't You Worry About That Mule," along with performances by Sammy Davis, Jr. and Nat King Cole. 48 min.

02-7572 *$19.99*

The World According To John Coltrane

Using rare performance footage, early recordings and interviews with Alice Coltrane, Wayne Shorter and Tommy Flanagan, this program gives you an intimate look at jazz saxophone pioneer John Coltrane. "Trane's" genius is evident in numbers like "My Favorite Things," "Alabama," "Giant Steps" and "Naima." 60 min.

02-7908 Was $29.99 *$19.99*

John Coltrane: The Coltrane Legacy

The legendary saxophone artist and jazz composer is spotlighted in this compilation of rare concert and TV performances, solo work by McCoy Tyner and Eric Dolphy and interviews with many of Coltrane's contemporaries. 60 min.

22-3040 *$29.99*

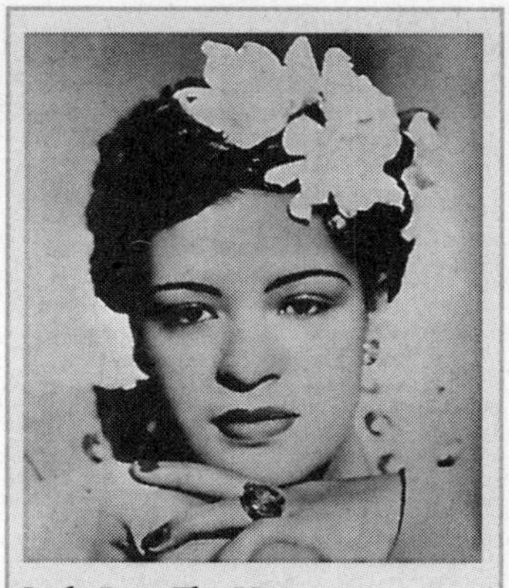

Lady Day: The Many Days Of Billie Holiday

A stunning musical portrait of Billie Holiday, chronicling her singing career and personal tragedies. Rare film clips, letters from Holiday (read by Ruby Dee) and interviews with Carmen MacRae, Mal Waldron and others help to tell the true story of the "lady who sang the blues" in songs like "Strange Fruit," "God Bless the Child" and "Lover Man." 60 min.

22-1204 Was $29.99 *$19.99*

The Ladies Sing The Blues

A once-in-a-lifetime collection of some of the legendary names in blues singing, women whose plaintive voices could melt the wax on a candle. Rare film footage of Bessie Smith and Billie Holiday, plus concert clips featuring Ethel Waters, Lena Horne, Dinah Washington, Miss Peggy Lee and others make this a music-filled must-have. 60 min.

22-7052 *$29.99*

Sarah Vaughan: The Divine One

Packed with live performances of such classics as "Misty" and "Someone to Watch Over Me," interviews and more, this loving program focuses on one of the great singers of our time. Trace Ms. Vaughan's incredible career through music and insightful commentary. 60 min.

02-7965 Was $29.99 *$19.99*

The Story Of Jazz

Celebrate the history of jazz in this insightful and exciting program that offers newly-discovered footage of a host of jazz greats, and performances and commentary from Louis Armstrong, Miles Davis, Duke Ellington, Coleman Hawkins, Charlie Parker, Lester Young, Benny Goodman, Sarah Vaughan, Count Basie and others. 90 min.

02-8014 Was $29.99 *$19.99*

The Story Of Jazz: Boxed Set

Along with "The Story of Jazz," this special collector's set also includes the musical programs "Bluesland," "Count Basie: Swingin' the Blues," "Sarah Vaughan: The Divine One," "The World According to John Coltrane" and "Thelonious Monk: American Composer."

02-8732 Save $40.00! *$79.99*

Keith Jarrett: Tokyo 1996

Keith Jarrett is joined by Gary Peacock and Jack DeJohnette in this electrifying concert from Tokyo's Orchard Hall in March, 1996. Selections performed include "It Could Happen to You," "Never Let Me Go," "Summer Night," "Mona Lisa," "Autumn Leaves" and others.

02-8985 *$19.99*

Stanley Turrentine In Concert

Tenor saxophone great Stanley Turrentine displays his incredible playing and tremendous diversity in this live performance filmed at New York's Village Gate. Selections include "My Romance," "Sugar" and "Salt Song." 60 min.

22-1205 Was $29.99 *$19.99*

Harry Connick, Jr.: Swinging Out Live

From the record charts to Broadway, everybody's just wild about Harry. This live show, featuring Connick performing with his trio, big band, and orchestra, includes such tunes as "It Had to Be You," "Hudson Bomber," "Something's Gotta Give," "It's All Right with Me" and others. 80 min.

04-5074 *$19.99*

Lullaby Of Harlem

Scores of bebop and jazz greats of yesteryear are presented in this program comprised of rare footage taken from the Cotton Club, the Apollo Theatre and the Savoy. Featured performers include Cab Calloway, Nat "King" Cole," Billy Eckstine, Billie Holiday, Louis Armstrong and many others. 60 min.

05-5102 *$14.99*

Thelonious Monk: American Composer

A true American original, Thelonious Monk drew praise and controversy with his groundbreaking experiments with bebop. This program documents his career and captures his artistry through performances of notable compositions like "Round Midnight" and "Straight, No Chaser," plus remembrances from Monk's son, Marion White, Randy Weston and Billy Taylor. 60 min.

02-7970 Was $29.99 *$19.99*

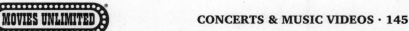

Duke Ellington:
Memories Of Duke (1968)
A tribute to the great Duke Ellington featuring interviews with musicians and vintage footage of early performances of Duke's band in action. Numbers include "Take the 'A' Train," "Satin Doll," "Don't Mean a Thing If it Ain't Got that Swing" and the previously unreleased "Mexican Suite." 85 min.
19-3159 *$19.99*

Royal Ellington
This is the 1989 debut public performance of Duke Ellington's 1957 composition "The Queen's Suite," which he wrote after a private audience with Queen Elizabeth. Performed by a 16-piece orchestra assembled by saxophonist Bob Wilber. 64 min.
22-1377 *$19.99*

Harlem Jazz Festival
Jump and swing with some of the legendary stars of the "golden age" of Harlem music on this tape. See vintage performances by Count Basie ("One O'Clock Jump"), Duke Ellington ("VIP Boogie"), Cab Calloway ("Calloway's Boogie") and Dinah Washington ("I Don't Hurt Any More"), plus Ruth Brown, Lionel Hampton and many more. 70 min.
62-1360 *$19.99*

On The Road With
Duke Ellington (1967)
Maverick documentary filmmakers Robert Drew Associates were behind this involving look at the famous jazz musician, capturing Ellington in recording studios, in hotels, in concert and behind the scenes, and off the record discussing Louis Armstrong, performing and other subjects. 58 min.
76-7439 *$39.99*

Duke Ellington's
Sacred Concerts (1998)
Among the last works created by the renowned musician/composer were three "Sacred Concerts" Ellington wrote from 1965 to 1973. Now, to mark the 100th anniversary of Duke's birth, Lugano Cathedral is the setting for an all-star recital of his moving religious music. 79 min.
50-8396 *$19.99*

George Shearing:
Lullaby Of Birdland
Legendary jazz pianist George Shearing turns in a superb performance at the Paul Masson Winery from September, 1991. Selections include "Isn't It Romantic," "Estate," "Memphis in June," "Moose the Mooch" and more. 57 min.
22-7106 *$19.99*

Joe Williams: A Song Is Born
Stylish jazz singer Joe Williams proves why he is one of the all-time greats in this excellent concert from the Paul Masson Winery in 1991. Songs include "Just Friends," "Muddy Water," "Tenderly" and more. Williams is joined by George Shearing on piano, Paul Humphrey on drums and Neil Swainson on bass. 57 min.
22-7107 *$19.99*

Oscar Peterson:
Music In The Key Of Oscar
Following his father's credo to "be the best," Oscar Peterson has won acclaim as one of the greatest jazz pianists of all time. His life and career, from playing boogie-woogie in Montreal as a teen to the present, are traced in this mix of documentary and concert footage. Interviews with Peterson, Ella Fitzgerald, Dizzy Gillespie, Quincy Jones and other stars are featured. 96 min. on two tapes.
22-7158 *$29.99*

Oscar Peterson:
The Life Of A Legend
Hear in Peterson's own words about his music, and the man behind it, in this up-close and personal documentary. Oscar talks candidly about his contemporaries in the jazz world, the problems faced by him and bandmates Ray Brown and Herb Ellis due to racism, and his family life. Also includes interview segments with Quincy Jones, Norman Granz, Ella Fitzgerald and others. 102 min. on two tapes.
22-7159 *$29.99*

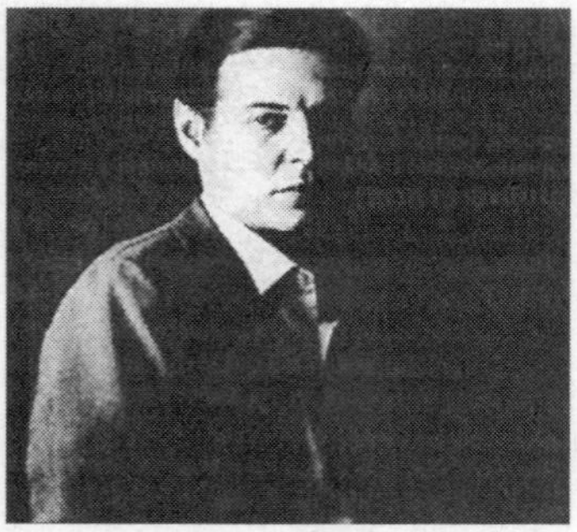

Antonio Carlos Jobim:
An All-Star Tribute
Filmed live in Brazil in a concert that proved to be his last recorded performance, composer/bossa nova cocreator Antonio Carlos Jobim is joined by Shirley Horn, Gonzalo Rubalcaba, Herbie Hancock, Gal Costa and other greats. Songs include "Once I Loved," "A Felicidade," "Girl from Ipanema" and more. 60 min.
22-7157 *$19.99*

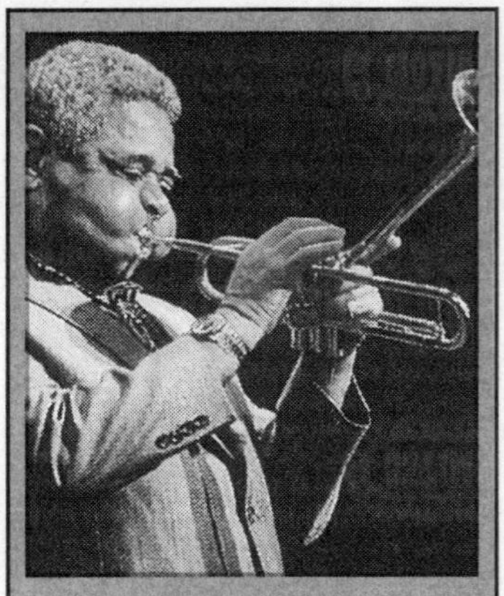

Dizzy Gillespie: Live In London
Jazz great Dizzy Gillespie is joined by James Moody, Flora Purim, Paquito D'Rivera, Slide Hampton and other stars in this incredible concert from London's Royal Festival Hall. Among the numbers in this program (its recording won a Grammy Award) are "Manteca," "A Night in Tunisia," "Moody's Mood for Love" and more. 91 min.
22-1289 Was $29.99 *$19.99*

Dizzy Gillespie:
A Night In Tunisia
The founding father of bebop is seen in rehearsal and in concert in this documentary that recounts Gillespie's life and career. Learn how Dizzy brought Afro-Cuban rhythms to the jazz world, and how he became America's Ambassador of Music. 28 min.
22-7075 Was $19.99 *$14.99*

Dizzy Gillespie:
A Night In Chicago
In a fantastic "Windy City" concert recorded live, the one and only Dizzy performs "Embraceable You," "Swing Low, Sweet Cadillac," "Nature Boy," "A Night in Tunisia" and other favorites. 53 min.
22-7121 *$19.99*

Dizzy's Dream Band (1982)
New York's Lincoln Center was the setting for a once-in-a-lifetime gathering of jazz giants, spearheaded by bebop pioneer Dizzy Gillespie. Joined by Pepper Adams, Milt Jackson, Gerry Mulligan, Max Roach and others, Gillespie offers up "Manteca," "A Night in Tunisia," "Mr. Hi Hat," "Tin Tin Deo," "Salt Peanuts (Vote Dizzy)" and more. Also included is rare footage of Dizzy performing "Hot House" with the legendary Charlie Parker. 89 min.
53-6594 *$19.99*

Celebrating Bird:
The Triumph Of Charlie Parker
His music revolutionized the world of jazz and influenced genres from rhythm and blues to rock. Rare film clips, interviews with family and colleagues, and a soulful soundtrack help legendary alto saxman Charlie Parker come alive in this documentary. Songs include "Yardbird Suite," "Ballade," "Just Friends," "Koko," many more. 58 min.
45-5351 Was $29.99 *$19.99*

Bird Now
This documentary traces the music, life and impact of Charlie "Bird" Parker, the legendary jazz artist whose work served as an inspiration to jazz and popular musicians around the world. His life included bouts of drug addiction and alcoholism, police harassment and racial segregation, which were reflected in his groundbreaking music. 90 min.
53-6379 *$19.99*

Legends Of Jazz Drumming
This history of drumming in the world of jazz spans from 1920 to 1950 and displays the greatest performers of those decades in highlights from their illustrious careers. Gene Krupa, Cozy Cole, Max Roach, "Philly" Jo Jones, Buddy Rich and Shelley Manne are among the featured artists. Check out the three-way duel between Krupa, Rich and Louie Bellson, the show's narrator. 60 min.
50-8054 *$39.99*

Buddy Rich:
Jazz Legend: Complete Set
An extraordinary look at an extraordinary talent: drumming great Buddy Rich. This two-tape set traces Rich's career from his early days as a player with such bandleaders as Tommy Dorsey, Harry James and Artie Shaw to his world-renowned solo career. Rich turns in rousing performances of "West Side Story" and "Channel One Suite," plays an amazing five-minute drum duel with Gene Krupa, and even kibitzes with Johnny Carson and the Muppets. Commentary is supplied by friends and family, narrator Mel Torme and Rich himself. 147 min. total. NOTE: Individual volumes available at $39.99 each.
50-8055 Save $20.00! *$59.99*

Chaka Khan
Recorded live in Washington as part of the "BET on Jazz" series, this dynamic concert features the soulful singer offering her own jazzy spin on such songs as "Dark Secret," "Them There Eyes," "My Funny Valentine," "I'll Be Around," "Love Me Still" and many more.
50-8570 *$19.99*

Alberta Hunter:
Jazz At The Smithsonian
The late blues singer is featured here in one of her final performances. Songs include "My Castle's Rocking," "Handy Man," "Nobody Knows You When You're Down and Out" and other jazz favorites. 60 min.
45-5076 Was $29.99 *$14.99*

Art Blakey:
Jazz At The Smithsonian
Art Blakey, a talented pianist/drummer who's worked with Billie Holiday, Charlie Parker, Billy Eckstein and other jazz and blues legends, is caught live in concert. Songs include "Little Man," "My Ship" and more. 60 min.
45-5077 Was $29.99 *$14.99*

Benny Carter:
Jazz At The Smithsonian
Concert from the alto sax master and composer who has worked with Charlie Parker, Miles Davis and other greats. Features "Misty," "Autumn Leaves," "Take the A Train" and more. 57 min.
45-5085 Was $19.99 *$14.99*

Red Norvo:
Jazz At The Smithsonian
Xylophone maestro Red Norvo shows off his mastery in this swinging show featuring guest stars Mavis Rivers and Tal Farlow. 60 min.
45-5086 Was $29.99 *$14.99*

Joe Williams:
Jazz At The Smithsonian
Smooth-as-silk singer Joe Williams performs such blues favorites as "Well Alright, OK, You Win," "Everyday I Have the Blues" and others. 60 min.
45-5097 Was $29.99 *$14.99*

Bob Wilbur:
Jazz At The Smithsonian
Wilbur, one of the best-known soprano sax players in jazz, directs the Smithsonian Jazz Repertory Ensemble and joins them for "Summertime," "Daydreams" and other songs in a tribute to sax great Sidney Bechet. 59 min.
45-5099 Was $29.99 *$14.99*

Alberta Hunter:
My Castle's Rockin'
The life of remarkable singer-songwriter Alberta Hunter is celebrated in this film that features live performances, Hunter's last recorded interview, and music by colleagues like Louis Armstrong, Fats Waller and King Oliver. Songs include "Handy Man," "I'm Having a Good Time" and more. 60 min.
22-7105 *$19.99*

Jazz Highlights
Some of the best jazz musicians from all over the world got together to pay tribute to the uniquely American art form at the acclaimed "Days of Jazz Festival" in Stuttgart, Germany. Among the talent: Mike Mainieri, Archie Shepp, Mike Stern, John Zorn, and the inimitable Sun Ra and his Arkestra. 59 min.
22-7187 *$19.99*

Blue Note:
A Story Of Modern Jazz
Trace over 50 years in the history of one of the most influential record labels in American music in this all-star documentary tribute to Blue Note, home to such famed jazz artists as Bud Powell, Thelonious Monk, Art Blakey, John Coltrane, Max Roach, Herbie Hancock and others. 90 min.
44-4133 *$19.99*

Dexter Gordon:
More Than You Know
The legendary jazz artist whose tenor sax mastery was a highlight of the 1986 film "Round Midnight" is saluted with this Danish-made documentary. Along with interviews with Gordon and such colleagues as Ben Webster, Woody Shaw and others, footage from a 1964 Copenhagen concert features Gordon performing "Fried Bananas," "More Than You Know," "King Neptune" and more. 52 min.
44-4158 *$19.99*

Gil Scott-Heron: Black Wax
Thrill to the wonderful sounds of jazz-fusion artist, poet and social satirist Gil Scott-Heron, performing live with his 10-piece Midnight Band at Washington's famed Wax Museum Nightclub. Songs include "Paint It Black," "Angel Dust," "Black History" and "Whitey on the Moon." 86 min.
45-5231 *$19.99*

Baby Laurence: Jazz Hoofer
A legacy from the career of master tap dancer Baby Laurence, whose be-bop and jazz-influenced dance style helped revitalize the form. A segment on tap history features spry footage of King Rastus Brown, Bill Robinson and John Bubbles. 28 min.
53-7226 *$19.99*

The Last Of The Blue Devils
Bruce Ricker's broad-ranging documentary looks at everything from jazz in the big-band era to the Kansas City sound and the blues influence on rock and roll. Music by Count Basie and His Orchestra, Big Joe Turner and Jay McShann is featured. 90 min.
53-7227 *$19.99*

Art Pepper:
Notes From A Jazz Survivor
A stirring mix of concert film and biographical self-portrait, this film features noted alto sax jazzman Art Pepper talking candidly about his life, from his problems with drugs to his prison terms. Pepper is also seen performing three of his works—"Red Car," "Patricia" and "Miss Who?"—in an California nightclub. 55 min.
63-7176 *$19.99*

The Newport Jazz Festival (1962)
Classic performances by the likes of the Oscar Peterson Trio, Roland Kirk, Pee Wee Russell, Duke Ellington and His Orchestra and other greats are captured in this acclaimed film. 60 min.
10-8358 *$29.99*

The Universal Mind Of
Bill Evans (1966)
One of jazz's legendary composers is examined in this film comprised of inventive and stimulating music, and an exploration of the creative process of an artist at work. Steve Allen adds commentary; songs include "Spartacus Love Theme," "How About You?," "Very Early Time" and more. 45 min.
53-7617 *$19.99*

Lionel Hampton:
One Night Stand (1971)
It's an all-star jazz jam with vibes specialist Lionel Hampton and guests Mel Torme, Zoot Sims, Gene Krupa, Buddy Rich, B.B. King, Johnny Mercer and Teddy Wilson. Songs include "Smackwater Jack," "Put Your Hand in the Hand" and more. 53 min.
22-3168 *$29.99*

Grover Washington, Jr.
In Concert (1981)
Ace saxophone artist Grover Washington, Jr. is captured live in his native Philadelphia for an exciting evening of jazz. Joining him are guest stars Steve Gadd, Richard Tee and Ralph MacDonald. Songs include "Let It Flow," "Just the Two of Us," "Mister Magic" and more. 60 min.
22-7079 *$19.99*

Imagine The Sound (1981)
The jazz world's answer to "The Last Waltz" looks at the life and careers of four '60s jazz greats: Cecil Taylor, Archie Shepp, Bill Dixon and Paul Bley. The music soars in this acclaimed film from documentarian Ron Mann ("Poetry in Motion"). 90 min.
64-7013 Was $59.99 *$19.99*

Sonny Rollins:
Saxophone Colossus (1986)
Impressive documentary look at the jazz giant from filmmaker Robert Mugge. Along with interviews and archival footage, the film features Rollins in concert performing "Don't Stop the Carnival," "G-Man," "The Bridge" and more, plus the Japanese world premiere of his "Concerto for Tenor Saxophone and Orchestra." 101 min.
45-5342 *$24.99*

Latino Session (1989)
A "magnifico" evening of Latin pop and Salsa music, featuring such great stars as Tito Puente, Pancho Sanchez and Celia Cruz, along with special guests Ruben Blades, Carlos Santana and Jerry Garcia. Songs include "Mandela," "Get Uppa," "Quimbara," "Cuentas Del Alma" and more. 60 min.
15-5258 Was $19.99 *$14.99*

Listen Up: The Lives Of
Quincy Jones (1990)
A music-filled portrait of Grammy-winning composer/producer/musician Quincy Jones. Follow his career, from his formative years with jazz greats Miles Davis, Dizzy Gillespie and Lionel Hampton to his work with Barbra Streisand, Frank Sinatra and Michael Jackson and his solo projects. Interviews with admirers and collaborators and fascinating footage highlight this jazz lover's dream film. 116 min.
19-1865 Was $19.99 *$14.99*

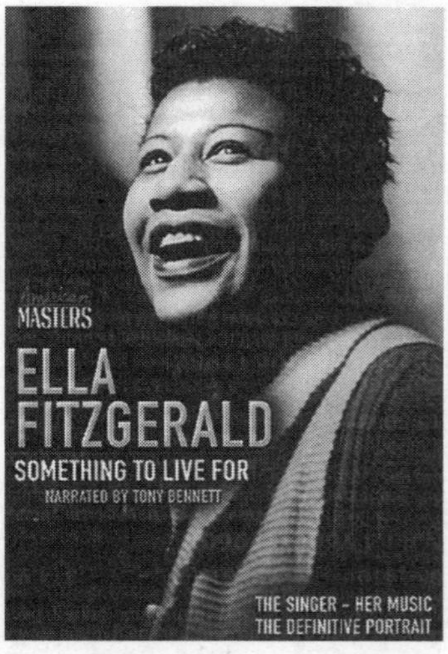

Ella Fitzgerald:
Something To Live For
America's "First Lady of Song," Ella Fitzgerald overcame an impoverished childhood in 1920s Virginia and went on to become one of the most acclaimed and influential jazz voices of all time. Tony Bennett narrates this retrospective on her life and art, with rare performance clips of Ella singing with Louis Armstrong, Bing Crosby, Nat King Cole, Frank Sinatra and others, plus interviews with Fitzgerald as well as friends and colleagues. 86 min.
53-6669 *$19.99*

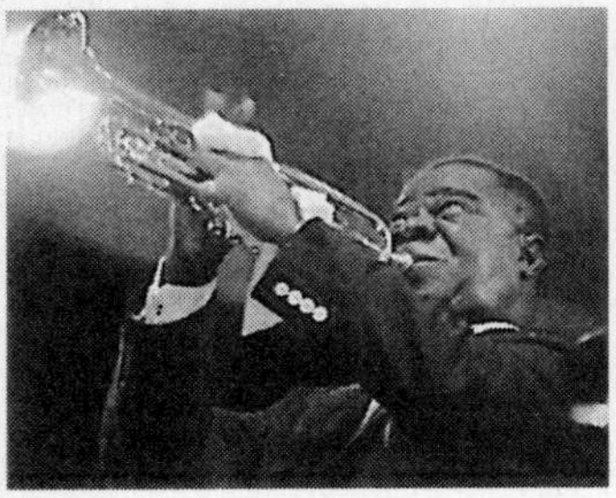

Louis Armstrong: Satchmo
His matchless trumpet playing and unmistakable voice helped bring jazz into mainstream American life. Now look back at the life and career of Louie Armstrong in a song-filled salute that features vintage performance segments, interviews and scenes from Satchmo's film appearances. 86 min.
04-5023 *$19.99*

Jazz Casual
From 1960 to 1968, noted music critic Ralph Gleason produced and hosted TV's first series devoted solely to jazz. Playing on National Education Television (PBS's precursor), "Jazz Casual" featured top artists discussing their life and music and performing in intimate settings. Each tape runs about 30 min.

Jazz Casual: Cannonball Adderly (1961)
A trio of classic Adderly tunes are presented by the music teacher-turned-sax master: "Arriving Soon," "Unit Seven" and "Scotch & Water."
15-5486 *$14.99*

Jazz Casual: Dizzy Gillespie (1961)
There's plenty of "Blues After Dark" with the pioneer of be-bop jazz, who also lets loose with "Norm's Norm," "Lorraine" and "Toccata from Gillespiana."
15-5487 *$14.99*

Jazz Casual: John Coltrane (1963)
In his only U.S. performance captured on film, the legendary saxman offers up "Afro Blue," "Alabama" and "Impressions."
15-5478 *$14.99*

Jazz Casual: Mel Tormé (1964)
The inimitable "Velvet Fog" performs "Route 66," "Quiet Night," "We've Got a World That Swings," "When Sunny Gets Blue" and others.
15-5485 *$14.99*

Jazz Casual: Count Basie (1966)
"I Don't Know," "Handful of Keys," "Squeeze Me," "Twenty Minutes After Three" and "National Educational Television Blues" are among the tunes performed by Basie and his quartet.
15-5477 *$14.99*

Jazz Casual: Carmen McRae (1968)
The popular singer is joined by the Vince Guaraldi Trio for "I'm Gonna Lock My Heart," "Trouble Is a Man," "Round Midnight," "Love for Sale" and more.
15-5479 *$14.99*

Charles Mingus: Triumph Of The Underdog (1997)
Acclaimed documentary look at the life and art of the famed jazz musician/bandleader/composer. Learning his craft with such notables as Duke Ellington and Charlie Parker, Mingus went on to create his own innovative music, weathering physical and mental health problems, until his untimely death in 1979. Rare interviews and performance footage are included. 78 min.
63-7168 *$19.99*

Jeffrey Osborne (2000)
You'll be "Back in Love Again" after watching Osborne in concert from BET's "BET on Jazz" series, taped live in Washington. Jeffrey offers up a selection of his jazz-flavored R&B hits, including "On the Wings of Love," "Stay with Me Tonight" and "You Should Be Mine (The Woo Woo Song)," along with tunes from his "That's for Sure" album. 75 min.
50-8571 *$19.99*

Soundies, Vol. 1
Journey back to the early days of jazz, when musicians made short promotional films to promote their records. This collection includes surprisingly sexy and imaginative "soundies" for "Give This Girl a Great Big Hand," "I Look at You" with Rita Rio, "I Don't Want to Walk Without You" with The Juvenile Jungle, Fats Waller performing "Ain't Misbehavin'," and others.
79-5986 *$19.99*

Soundies, Vol. 2
Dig these short jazz films, they're real gone! Jump and jive to The Whipperpools' "Hardlife Blues," "Estrelita" with Benito Moreno, "Montana Plains" by Jimmy Wakeley and His Oklahoma Cowboys & Cowgirls, "Swing Rhumba," "I May Be Wrong" with Les Elgart and His Orchestra and many more.
79-5987 *$19.99*

Soundies, Vol. 3
The sounds (and the soundies) swing wildly in this nifty compilation. Get in the groove with Gene Austin's "Melancholy Baby," "The Lazy River" by The Mills Brothers, "Lydia" with Rudy Vallee, Lena Horne crooning "Boogie Woogie Dream," "Is You Is or Is You Ain't My Baby" from Ida James and The King Cole Trio and more.
79-5988 *$19.99*

Al Hirt Live On Bourbon Street
The bearded, Grammy-winning titan of jazz trumpet performs his greatest hits in an enjoyable concert from New Orleans' Bourbon Street. Included are such numbers as "Java," "Way Down Yonder in New Orleans," "Little Rock," "Someone to Watch Over Me," "St. James Infirmary" and more. 43 min.
89-7002 *$14.99*

Great Guitars: The Jazz Guitar Supergroup
Jazz guitar geniuses Herb Ellis, Charlie Byrd and Barney Kessel are joined by bassist Joe Byrd and drummer Wayne Phillips in a super-session produced for PBS in the early 1970s. "Outer Drive," "Tangerine," "Alfie," "On Green Dolphin Street," "The Days of Wine and Roses" and "Flying Home" are among the selections. 59 min.
63-7145 *$19.99*

Hollywood Rhythm: Boxed Set
Produced between the late 1920s and early 1940s for theaters by Paramount, these short films featured such greats as Louis Armstrong, Cab Calloway, Bing Crosby, Artie Shaw, Duke Ellington, Billie Holliday, and early appearances by Cary Grant and Ginger Rogers in entertaining mini-musicals. Many of the stars' signature songs are presented, along with some elaborate set pieces. 325 min. on four tapes. NOTE: Individual volumes available at $24.99 each.
53-8948 Save $10.00! *$89.99*

Jazz Scene USA: Cannonball Adderley Sextet/ Teddy Edwards Sextet
Saxman Cannonball Adderley will blow you away on such numbers as "Jessica's Birthday," "Primitive," "Work Song" and "Jive Sambo" (called "Bossa Nova Nemo" here) with his sextet, which includes brother Nat and pianist Jow Zawinul. Also, tenor saxophonist Teddy Edwards is joined by Stan Gilbert and company, performing "Cellar Dweller," "Good Gravy" and others. 60 min.
63-7147 *$19.99*

Jazz Scene USA: Phineas Newborn, Jr. Trio/ Jimmy Smith Trio
Phineas Newborn, Jr., one of jazz's greatest pianists, is joined by Al McKibbon on bass and Kenny Dennis on drums for a superb outing featuring such numbers as "Theme for Basie," "Lush Life," "Oleo" and "New Blues." And Jimmy Smith's incredible work on the Hammond B-3 organ is highlighted, performing "Walk on the Wild Side" and "Mack the Knife" with his trio. 60 min.
63-7148 *$19.99*

Jazz Scene USA: Frank Rosalino Quartet/ Stan Kenton And His Orchestra
Trombonist par excellence Frank Rosalino and his sterling quartet offer up such melodic jazz favorites as "Mean to Me," "Lover Man," "Don't Bug Me" and Thelonious Monk's "Well, You Needn't." And Stan Kenton and His Orchestra turn in memorable performances on "Malaguena," "Maria," "All the Things You Are" and others. 60 min.
63-7149 *$19.99*

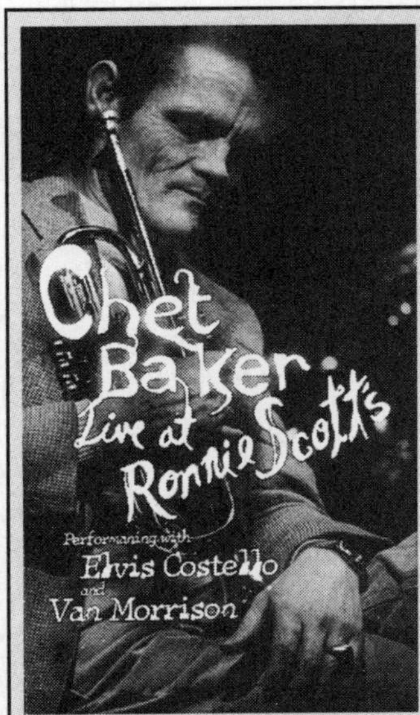

Chet Baker: Live At Ronnie Scott's (1986)
Jazz trumpet legend Chet Baker turns in a memorable set in his final filmed performance, at London's Ronnie Scott's. Along with "Ellen David," "Shifting Down," "Love for Sale" and "If I Should Lose You," he's also joined by Elvis Costello on "You Don't Know What Love Is," "I'm a Fool to Want You" and "The Very Thought of You" and Van Morrison on "Send in the Clowns." 58 min.
02-8189 Was $19.99 *$14.99*

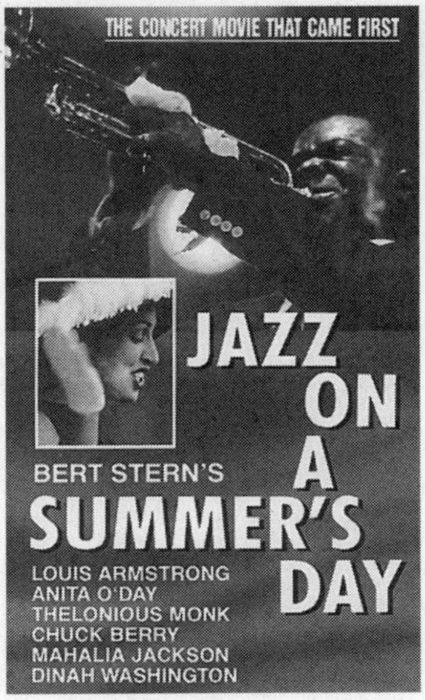

Jazz On A Summer's Day (1958)
This precursor to Woodstock is the granddaddy of all concert films, a chronicle of the Newport Jazz Fest in Rhode Island, where music greats Louis Armstrong, Thelonious Monk, Chuck Berry, Mahalia Jackson, Dinah Washington and others gave electrifying performances. Also includes the "making of" featurette "A Summer's Day with Bert Stern." 114 min. total.
53-7383 Was $59.99 *$29.99*

Monterey Jazz Festival: 40 Legendary Years
This celebration of America's premier jazz festival features highlights from its 40-year history and clips of such greats as Louis Armstrong, Billie Holiday, Thelonious Monk, Dave Brubeck, Joe Williams and others. Also featured are modern greats Joshua Redman and Patrice Rushen in a jam session with Clark Terry, Mundell Lowe, Gerald Williams and Kyle Eastwood. 80 min.
19-2775 *$19.99*

Pat Metheny Group: More Travels
Pat Metheny and group members Lyle Mays, Steve Rodby, Paul Wertico and Pedro Aznar perform a memorable concert of classic jazz fusion which includes such numbers as "Opening," "Have You Heard," "Last Train Home," "The Road to You," "First Circle" and more. 70 min.
07-4094 *$19.99*

Lionel Hampton's Jazz Circle (1971)
This companion video to Hampton's "One Night Stand" has Lionel back with all his pals for a grand all-star jam session. Among the featured players are drum greats Gene Krupa and Mel Lewis, pianist Joe Buskin, Roy Eldridge on trumpet, Zoot Simms on saxophone, Tyree Glenn on trombone and others. 30 min.
22-3235 *$19.99*

Jazz Concert, Vol. 1
Louis Armstrong and Duke Ellington are featured in two different "Goodyear Jazz Concerts" broadcast on TV in the early '60s. "Satchmo" and his "All-Stars" perform a selection of his hits, while Duke and crew do "Take the 'A' Train" and other faves. 60 min.
10-8248 Was $19.99 *$14.99*

Miles Davis: Miles In Paris
Innovative jazz trumpet legend Miles Davis pulls out all the stops in this exciting performance. Miles and his incredible band perform "Human Nature," "Amanda," "Tutu" and "Mr. Pastorious."
19-3137 *$19.99*

Miles Davis & Quincy Jones: Live At Montreux
The final performance of jazz master Miles Davis teams him with conductor Quincy Jones, who re-creates the original arrangements Miles performed with Gil Evans. Tunes include "Miles Ahead," "Summertime" and "Solea"; featured performers include Kenny Garrett and Wallace Roney. 77 min.
19-3432 *$29.99*

Modern Jazz Quartet
One of the most elegant jazz troupes around, the Modern Jazz Quartet features John Lewis, Milt Jackson, Percy Heath and Connie Kay. Here they celebrate their 35th anniversary with a performance at the Arts Festival in Freiburg, Germany. 60 min.
22-1314 *$19.99*

40 Years Of MJQ
They learned their craft as the rhythm section of Dizzy Gillespie's big band, and four decades later the members of the Modern Jazz Quartet are still going strong. In a special 40th anniversary show three of the MJQ's founding members are featured performing "Sketch," "Alexander's Fugue," "A Day in Dubrovnik" and more. 58 min.
22-7155 *$19.99*

Trumpet Kings
There's nothing wrong with these guys tooting their own horns; they're the greatest trumpeters of all time. See concert footage featuring Louis Armstrong in a duet with Dizzy Gillespie, Harry James, Miles Davis, Freddie Hubbard, and many more. 72 min.
22-3041 *$29.99*

Cobham Meets Bellson
When two living legends of jazz drumming sit down to jam, the results are not to be missed. Billy C joins Louie's Big Band for a duel of riffs that will bring you to your feet; caught live in Switzerland in 1984. 36 min.
22-7029 *$19.99*

Fela In Concert
Fela Anikulapo Kuti, the celebrated Nigerian composer/keyboardist/saxophonist, brings you a rousing performance of his distinctive "Afro-beat" sound that fuses jazz and funk with African traditional sounds. Captured live in Paris in 1981. 57 min.
22-7033 Was $29.99 *$19.99*

Bob James Live
The smooth-sounding and acclaimed pianist/composer provides a spectacular live performance at the 1985 Queen Mary Jazz Festival. The theme from "Taxi," "Zebra Man" and "Unicorn" are just a few of the best-loved selections offered here. 56 min.
22-7035 *$19.99*

Bobby Short At The Cafe Carlyle
The inimitable dean of Cafe Society is captured rendering a 25-song performance in the setting that suits him best. Porter, Gershwin, Sondheim and many others done with flair. 75 min.
22-7038 *$29.99*

Nancy Wilson At Carnegie Hall
A memorable concert from the Grammy-winning jazz/pop singer, accompanied by a full string orchestra, that is sure to delight fans of all musical tastes. Among the songs featured are "Dearly Beloved," "Guess Who I Saw Today," "Forbidden Lover," "How Glad I Am" and more. 52 min.
22-7077 *$19.99*

Herbie Hancock Trio: Hurricane! With Billy Cobham And Ron Carter
The master keyboard player performs an incredible program of jazz stylings with guest stars bassist Cobham and drummer Carter, live in Switzerland. Songs include "Eye of the Hurricane," "Willow Weep for Me," "Dolphin Dance" and more. 60 min.
22-7085 *$19.99*

Big Bands

Music Classics
Get ready to swing and sway with this hep collection of vintage "soundies": short musical films from the '40s that played on special video jukeboxes. Top artists from the big bands, jazz, be-bop and swing are featured performing some of their greatest hits. Each tape runs about 65-75 min. There are 10 volumes available, including:

Music Classics, Vol. 1
Artists include Count Basie ("This Could Be the Start of Something Big"), Harry James ("Walk on the Wild Side"), Thelma White ("Hollywood Boogie"), Cab Calloway ("Hot Cha Razz-Ma-Tazz") and others.
50-6886 *$19.99*

Music Classics, Vol. 2
Artists include Harry Levine ("Bugle Call Rag"), Bobby Hackett ("Won't You Come Home Bill Bailey"), Tommy Dorsey ("Marie"), Louis Armstrong ("Shine") and others.
50-6887 *$19.99*

Music Classics, Vol. 3
Artists include Dizzy Gillespie and Helen Humes ("Hey Baba Leba"), Duke Ellington and Herb Jeffries ("Flamingo"), Guy Lombardo ("Sleep Baby Sleep"), Lionel Hampton ("Georgia on My Mind") and others.
50-6888 *$19.99*

Music Classics, Vol. 4
Artists include Tex Beneke ("In the Mood"), Cab Calloway ("Blues in the Night"), Artie Shaw ("Jeepers Creepers"), Duke Ellington ("Jam Session—C Jam Blues") and others.
50-7544 *$19.99*

Music Classics, Vol. 5
Artists include Harry James and Buddy Rich ("Two O'Clock Jump"), Jimmy Dorsey with Helen O'Connell and Ray Eberle ("Green Eyes"), Benny Goodman ("I've Got a Heartful of Music"), Louis Armstrong ("When It's Sleepytime Down South") and others.
50-7545 *$19.99*

Music Classics, Vol. 6
Artists include Frank Sinatra and Louis Armstrong ("Birth of the Blues"), The Andrews Sisters ("Three Little Sisters"), Hoagy Carmichael ("Hong Kong Blues"), The Nat "King" Cole Trio ("I'm an Errand Boy for Rhythm") and others.
50-7546 *$19.99*

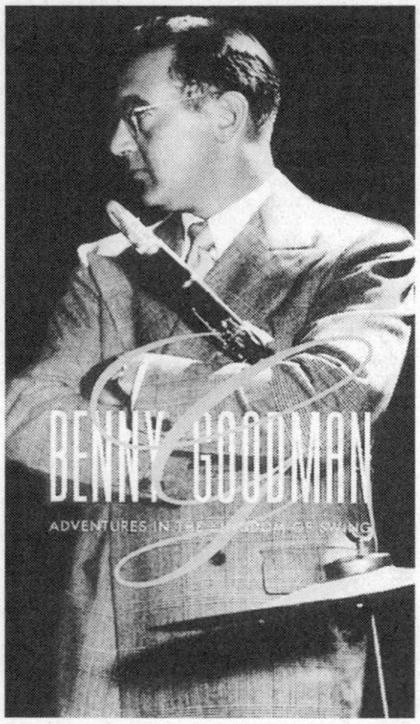

Benny Goodman: Adventures In The Kingdom Of Swing
Fantastic retrospective on clarinetist and big band leader Benny Goodman. Learn about "The King of Swing's" illustrious career through home movies, rare audio tracks, performances and stories from friends Ella Fitzgerald, Louis Armstrong, Lionel Hampton, Gene Krupa, Harry James and many others. "Let's Dance," "Tiger Rag," "Roll 'Em" and "Sing Sing Sing" are featured. 60 min.
04-5220 *$19.99*

Benny Goodman At The Tivoli
Benny Goodman and his all-star band perform a number of his Big Band classics, live from Tivoli Gardens in Copenhagen. Songs include "I Should Care," "Airmail Special Delivery," "The World Is Waiting for the Sunrise" and "Send in the Clowns." 50 min.
22-1287 Was $29.99 *$19.99*

Swing, Swing, Swing!
The Big Band Era lives on in this series that collects classic swing and jazz short subjects made by Vitaphone for Warner Bros. in the '30s and '40s.

Swing, Swing, Swing!, Vol. 1
Featured performers include Artie Shaw, Jimmy Dorsey, Red Nichols and Ozzie Nelson and their orchestras. 80 min.
12-2970 *$14.99*

Swing, Swing, Swing!, Vol. 2
Cliff Edwards and Larry Clinton, and Stan Kenton, Cab Calloway and Desi Arnaz and their orchestras are among the artists swinging away on this volume. 90 min.
12-2971 *$14.99*

The Swingin' Singin' Years
Who better than Ronald Reagan(!) to host this vintage salute to the greatest jazz and swing artists of all time? The all-star assemblage includes Dinah Washington, Louis Jordan, Stan Kenton, Woody Herman, Jo Stafford, Charlie Barnet and many more, performing their greatest hits. 60 min.
50-2305 Was $24.99 *$19.99*

Gene Krupa: Jazz Legend
Take a fascinating look at legendary drummer Gene Krupa, the man responsible for making the drums a solo instrument. Using rare photos, footage with Lionel Hampton, Benny Goodman and Red Rodney, a drumming duel with Buddy Rich and an interview with Krupa himself, this program paints a complete portrait of a jazz great. 60 min.
50-8050 *$39.99*

Middle Of The Road

The Mills Brothers Story
This is the complete story of the fabulous Mills Brothers, singing troupe extraordinaire, whose career spanned five decades. Included are such songs as "Paper Doll," "Glow Worm," "You're Nobody Till Somebody Loves You" and more. 56 min.
22-1230 Was $29.99 *$19.99*

The Lou Rawls Show (1971)
"Sweet" Lou croons a few favorites in his inimitable style and is joined by the great Duke Ellington, Freda Payne and Stanley Myron Handleman. 60 min.
22-7072 Was $19.99 *$14.99*

Hawaiian Rainbow
Filmmaker Robert Mugge's musical portrait of the Hawaiian Islands features authentic slack key guitar, gently strumming ukuleles and native a capella and falsetto singing against lush, tropical vistas. 90 min.
45-5466 *$19.99*

Michael Feinstein & Friends
Popular pianist Michael Feinstein performs the timeless music of George and Ira Gershwin, Harold Arlen, and Duke Ellington in this winning program, featuring guests like Rosemary Clooney and the Duke Ellington Orchestra. Tunes include "He Loves and She Loves," "I Can't Give You Anything But Love" and "Take Love Easy." 60 min.
22-1251 *$24.99*

Michael Crawford: A Touch Of Music In The Night
Broadway's original "Phantom" stars in his very own music video collection, showcasing the Tony Award-winner in segments featuring him in the studio and performing live on stage. Songs include "Speak Low," "Only You," "She Used to Be Mine," "Music of the Night" and more. 40 min.
19-3509 *$19.99*

Michael Crawford In Concert (1998)
Live from the Cerritos Center in Los Angeles, stage and recording star Crawford presents a selection of Broadway favorites and classic ballads, including "Music of the Night," "Gethsemane," "Before the Parade Passes By," "All I Ask of You," "On Eagle's Wings" and others. 60 min.
19-2696 *$19.99*

An Intimate Evening With Anne Murray
The Grammy-winning pop songstress takes the stage for a wonderful live concert, performing such favorites as "Just Another Woman in Love," "Shame on Me," "Danny's Song" and many more, including duets with fellow Canadians Bryan Adams ("What Would It Take"), Jann Arden ("Insensitive," "Snowbird") and Celine Dion ("When I Fall in Love"). 60 min.
53-6448 *$19.99*

Rosemary Clooney's Demi-Centennial: A Girl Singer's Golden Anniversary
Rosemary Clooney, the "symbol of good, modern American music," takes the stage in Orlando in a gala concert celebration of her great career. Along with performances of "Danny Boy," "Straighten Up and Fly Right" and "Mambo Italiano," she's joined by Lily Tomlin for "You've Got a Friend." Also includes words from nephew George Clooney and Bob Hope. 90 min.
53-8438 *$19.99*

Frank Yankovic: America's Polka King
You've seen his greatest hits albums promoted on late-night television. But did you know that Frank Yankovic is a true American icon, a master of a musical art form? This documentary looks at his amazing career, which included performing in front of millions over three generations. Songs include "Beer Barrel Polka," "Just Because," "The Blue Skirt Waltz" and more. 58 min.
22-1388 *$29.99*

Korla Pandit
The finest music from organist Korla Pandit's 1950s TV show, featuring such songs as "Pelone Telefone," "Kumar," "Song of India" and more. There's also Hindu dance numbers by Bupesh Guha. Move over Larry Ferrari, heeeeeere's Korla, a featured performer in "Ed Wood." 60 min.
50-2238 *$19.99*

Eartha Kitt: The Most Exciting Woman In The World
The dazzling star of stage, screen and television shines in this live one-woman show. Among the favorite songs made popular by Kitt and performed here are "Here's to Life," "Champagne Taste," "C'est Si Bon" and others. 60 min.
22-1322 *$24.99*

The Best Of Perry Como: Collector's Edition
Culled from Perry's long-running TV variety show and Christmas specials, this two-tape set includes "Pennies from Heaven," "Dream Along with Me," "No Other Love Than I," "Catch a Falling Star," plus such holiday tunes as "White Christmas" and "Winter Wonderland." 120 min. total.
19-3315 *$34.99*

The Patti Page Video Songbook
One of the best-selling female vocalists of all time, Patti Page charmed audiences with hits like "I Went to Your Wedding," "Doggie in the Window," "Tennessee Waltz" and more, as evidenced in this career-spanning, tune-filled tribute. 45 min.
22-7078 Was $19.99 *$14.99*

Music Of Ireland

Riverdance: The Show
This stunning stage show, offering modern interpretations of traditional Celtic song and dance, has entertained audiences on both sides of the Atlantic, and in a special live performance taped in Dublin, the Riverdance troupe will delight you with beautiful music and breathtaking dancing. Performers include Michael Flatley, Jean Butler, Maria Pagés, Davy Spillane, Moiseyev. 78 min.
02-2873 *$24.99*

Riverdance: A Journey
The Irish dance sensation that has marveled audiences the world over is traced from its origins as a seven-minute interval performance on a Dublin stage in 1994 to packed houses in London and New York just two years later. Experience all the magic and passion both on and off the stage with this video profile of the dance troupe. 73 min.
02-3058 *$19.99*

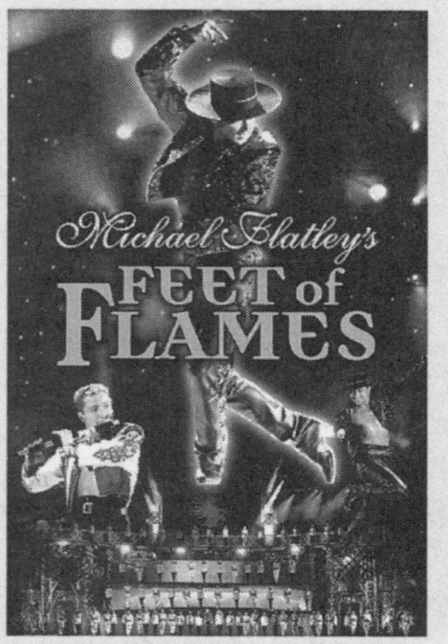

Michael Flatley's Feet Of Flames
Michael Flatley's final performance as "Lord of the Dance" was filmed in London's Hyde Park and features spectacular dance numbers boasting 100 dancers, stunning choreography, dazzling lighting and incredible costumes. 110 min.
02-9004 Was $24.99 *$19.99*

Frank Patterson: Songs Of Faith And Inspiration
Frank Patterson, "Ireland's Golden Tenor," sings songs that have inspired people for ages in this moving program that features such stunning locales as Ireland's mythic hills and the grandeur of the American West. Joined by his son Eanon on violin and the Little Gaelic Singers of New York, Patterson performs "Bless This House," "Amazing Grace," "Let There Be Peace" and more.
50-8711 *$19.99*

Paddy Reilly Live
One of the best-loved singers in all of Ireland, Paddy Reilly performs ballads old and new, including "Spancil Hill," "Carrickfergus," "Fields of Athenry," "Town I Loved So Well" and many more. 50 min.
50-1608 Was $29.99 *$14.99*

Ireland In Song
He's performed for the Pope and President Reagan, sold out Radio City Music Hall, and was featured in John Huston's "The Dead." Now renowned Irish tenor Frank Patterson takes you on a musical odyssey through his homeland, singing "Maggie," "Tipperary So Rare," "Danny Boy" and more. 60 min.
50-1643 *$24.99*

The Chieftains: The Bells Of Dublin
The popular Irish band are joined in the studio by guest performers Jackson Browne, Ricki Lee Jones, Marianne Faithfull, and Kate and Anna McGarrigle as they record their Christmas-themed "Bells of Dublin" album. This video record of the event features such songs as "O Holy Night," "I Saw Three Ships a Sailing," "The Rebel Jesus" and more. 60 min.
02-7447 *$14.99*

The Chieftains: An Irish Evening
Recorded live at the Grand Opera House in Belfast, this rich evening of favorites and surprises features Ireland's premier traditional group and guest stars Roger Daltrey and Nanci Griffith. Numbers include "Paddy's Jig," "Little Love Affair," "Any Old Iron" and "Behind Blue Eyes." 60 min.
02-7494 *$14.99*

A Feast Of Irish Set Dances
Traditional set dancing has been a living tradition in Ireland, passed on from the rural areas of centuries ago to the big cities of today. This foot-stomping tape will have you singing more than just "Three Leafed Shamrock." 56 min.
50-1936 Was $29.99 *$19.99*

Let's Have An Irish Party
Aye, a great Irish party, filled with lively songs, exciting dancing and out-and-out fun. Carmel Quinn serves as hostess and performs "The Isle of Innisfree" and "Wee Hughie," songstress Anna McGoldrick pipes "Danny Boy" and "Star Spangled Molly," while Richie O'Shea toots out "Streets of New York" and "One Day at a Time," plus dancers, jokes and more. 60 min.
50-1186 Was $19.99 *$14.99*

Carmel Quinn: Raised On Songs And Stories
The Dublin-born Irish-American songstress who entertained early TV audiences on "Arthur Godfrey and His Friends" will delight you in this special evening of music and Gaelic humor. "Galway Bay," "How Are Things in Glocca Mora" and "Roamin' in the Gloamin'" are among the favorites Quinn performs, and there's even a traditional sing-along. 55 min.
50-2922 *$29.99*

Faith Of Our Fathers: The Video
Live at Dublin's Point Theatre, some of the top names in Irish music present a unique and moving concert of classic religious anthems. Such performers as Frank Patterson, Regina Nathan, Iarla O'Lionaird, Tommy Keane, the Monks of Glenstal Abbey, and the Irish Philharmonic Orchestra and Chorus are featured. 78 min.
50-2972 *$29.99*

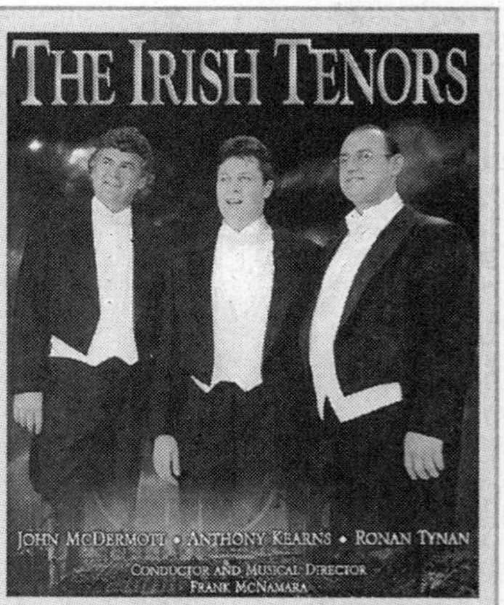

The Irish Tenors
They're three of the greatest names in Irish music—Anthony Kearns, John McDermott and Ronan Tynan—and in this moving program they take the stage along with a 60-piece orchestra in Dublin. "Believe Me," "I'll Take You Home Again Kathleen," "Toora-Loora-Looral," "Danny Boy," "Galway Bay" and "Amazing Grace" are among the favorites performed. 71 min.
53-6654 *$19.99*

The Irish Tenors: Live From Belfast (2000)
The three Gaelic giants—Anthony Kearns, John McDermott and Ronan Tynan—are back and better than ever with a tremendous selection of songs from a performance in Belfast. "Carrickfergus," "Bantry Bay," "Scorn Not His Simplicity," "Fields of Athenry," "Star of the County Down" and many others are featured.
50-8720 *$29.99*

Celtic Feet
If you liked "Riverdance," you'll love this Irish music video featuring "Riverdance" sensation Colin Dunne. See Colin demonstrate the basics of Irish dance, and be exhilarated when he and his cohorts perform incredible choreographed routines. 55 min.
50-5343 Was $19.99 *$14.99*

The Irish... And How They Got That Way
The acclaimed stage show by "Angela's Ashes" author Frank McCourt comes to home video in this production by the Irish Repertory Theatre. Songs, comedy and moving stories help relate the "Irish Experience" in Eire and America. 110 min.
50-8191 *$19.99*

The Clancy Brothers & Tommy Makem: Reunion Concert
Filmed at Ulster Hall in Belfast, this fantastic concert features the Irish faves performing "Irish Rover," "Rocky Road to Dublin," "Jug of Punch" and lots more. A toe-tapping touch of the Emerald Isle. 60 min.
63-7000 *$24.99*

The Story Of The Clancy Brothers And Tommy Makem
Get the inside story on the top Irish performers in this video history that follows their American debut in the late '50s, live and TV appearances in the '60s, and Lincoln Center reunion concert. Along with great music, there's interviews with Bob Dylan, Mary Travers and Tom Paxton. 60 min.
63-7001 *$24.99*

Frank Sinatra

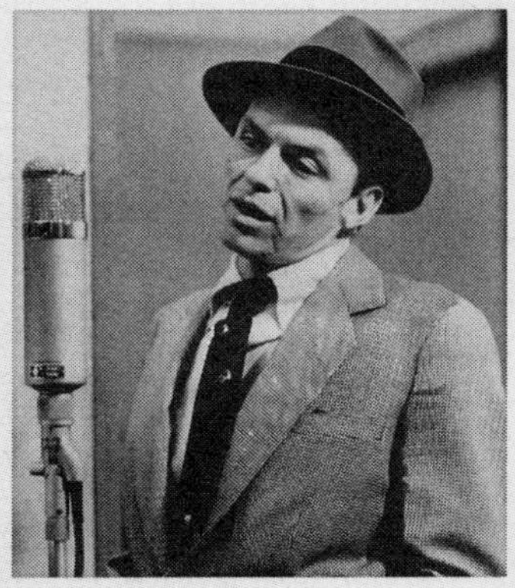

Frank Sinatra: A Man & His Music (1965)
The landmark TV special that spurred on one of Frank's many career "comebacks" features Sinatra joined by Nelson Riddle and his orchestra. Songs include "I've Got You Under My Skin," "I Get a Kick Out of You," "My Kind of Town," "Witchcraft," "Put Your Dreams Away," "Nancy" and a medley of best-loved tunes. 50 min.
19-3148 *$19.99*

Frank Sinatra: A Man & His Music, Part II (1966)
Frank mixes impromptu sessions with Nelson Riddle and his Orchestra and a special medley assembled by conductor Gordon Jenkins in this TV concert. Songs include "Fly Me to the Moon," "Luck Be a Lady," "My Kind of Town," a duet with daughter Nancy on "Yes Sir, That's My Baby," and more. 50 min.
19-3287 *$19.99*

Frank Sinatra: A Man & His Music + Ella + Jobim (1967)
The Chairman of the Board takes the stage with special guest stars Ella Fitzgerald and Antonio Carlos Jobim for a memorable evening of music. Along with medley duets with each guest, Frank performs "Get Me to the Church on Time," "Ol' Man River," "Put Your Dreams Away" and more. 50 min.
19-3149 *$19.99*

Frank Sinatra: Sinatra (1969)
It's a name synonymous with music, and the ever-pleasing song stylings of Sinatra are much in evidence in this TV special. Frank croons such tunes as "For Once in My Life," "Little Green Apples," "My Kind of Town" and "My Way," along with a film clip medley of his top movie musical moments. 50 min.
19-3162 *$19.99*

Frank Sinatra: Ol' Blue Eyes Is Back (1973)
C'mon, you knew Frank wouldn't stay retired back in the '70s. His triumphant return to television was this wonderful special that features such tunes as "You Will Be My Music," "Street of Dreams," "Send in the Clowns," and more. Guest Gene Kelly joins Frank for a special medley and a duet on "Nice and Easy." 50 min.
19-3150 *$19.99*

Frank Sinatra: Sinatra—The Main Event (1974)
A knockout performance by the Chairman, this TV concert spectacular starts out with Frank's introduction by none other than Howard Cosell. Sinatra is in fine form as he belts out favorites old ("The Lady Is a Tramp," "I Get a Kick Out of You") and new ("Let Me Try Again," "Bad, Bad Leroy Brown," "You Are the Sunshine of My Life"). 50 min.
19-3164 *$19.99*

Frank Sinatra: Sinatra: The Man & His Music With The Count Basie Orchestra (1981)
The Chairman and the Count make for an untoppable combination in this amazing show that showcases Frank's interpretation of such standards as "Pennies From Heaven," "I Get a Kick Out of You," "New York, New York," "Thanks for the Memories," and others. 50 min.
19-3288 *$19.99*

Frank Sinatra: The Reprise Collection, Vol. 2
Music fans eager for a second helping of that Sinatra magic have their wish granted with this tuneful trio: "Sinatra", "Sinatra in Concert at Royal Festival Hall", and "Sinatra: The Main Event", together in a special boxed collector's edition. 150 min. total.
19-3161 *$69.99*

Frank Sinatra: The Reprise Collection, Vol. 1
Frank-ly speaking, this deluxe boxed set that includes the specials "A Man and His Music," "A Man and His Music + Ella + Jobim" and "Ol' Blue Eyes Is Back" is a Sinatra lover's dream and a bargain hunter's delight. 150 min. total.
19-3124 *$69.99*

Sinatra: The Best Is Yet To Come
He was known simply as "the Voice," and for nearly 60 years he entertained generations of Americans. This unique retrospective look at the life and career of Frank Sinatra, authorized by his family, features highlights from the Chairman's most memorable films, stage and TV appearances, including duets with Ella Fitzgerald and Elvis Presley; full performances of "Summer Wind," "For Once in My Life," "When You're Smilin'" and more from his 75th Birthday Concert; rare "at-home" interviews; celebrity tributes and much more. 87 min.
73-1308 *□$19.99*

Liberace: World's Greatest Showman
It's a star- and sequin-filled salute to the life and career of Liberace, as you follow the beloved pianist's early radio and stage career, see clips and screen tests from his film roles, tour Lee's fabulous homes, and watch him cavort on TV with the likes of Jack Benny, Sammy Davis, Jr., Groucho Marx, Elvis Presley and Vampira. 95 min.
10-2592 Was $19.99 *$14.99*

Liberace Boxed Set
Celebrate the glitter-filled life of the entertainer known as "Mr. Showmanship" with this unique three-tape set featuring a pop-up Liberace photo card. Included are "Leapin' Lizards, It's Liberace!," a 1978 special from the Las Vegas Hilton with guest star Debbie Reynolds; "Liberace Valentine's Day," in which Lee performs on stage, hosts a tour of the Liberace Museum, and romps with Lola Falana and Sandy Duncan on board the Queen Mary; and "Liberace Live with the London Philharmonic," an elegant salute to the pianist's 40th anniversary in show business. 180 min. total.
15-5460 *$59.99*

Liberace Valentine's Day
After landing a hot-air balloon on the stage of the Las Vegas Hilton, Liberace goes right into an incredible show, performing "Night and Day," "My Funny Valentine," Chopin's "Nocturne in E Flat," a Gershwin medley and more. Lee also takes you on a tour of his home and the Liberace Museum and goes on board the Queen Mary with special guests Lola Falana and Sandy Duncan in this fun-filled Valentine's Day treat. 50 min.
15-5471 *$19.99*

Liberace And His Family (1954)
This Hollywood-style Christmas special features "Lib" performing some of his favorite songs and reminiscing about the holidays in Milwaukee and enjoying the yuletide with his mother, sister, brothers and French poodle. 30 min.
10-2132 *$12.99*

The Tapestry Series
The world's most fascinating locales take on new depth when they're accompanied by unforgettable classical and contemporary musical scores in this series from the producers of the Windham Hill videos. Each tape runs about 50 min.

Portrait Of Africa
The continent's natural vistas are featured, with music by Vangelis, Ladysmith Black Mambazo and Miriam Makeba.
06-1690 Was $29.99 *$19.99*

Portrait Of England
Visit scenic manors and gardens unchanged for centuries, and listen to Wynton Marsalis perform Pachabel, Vivaldi and Handel.
06-1691 Was $29.99 *$19.99*

Portrait Of Ireland
A spectacular tour of Eire, highlighted by the flute music of James Galway, the sensuous singing of Enya and folk music greats The Chieftains.
06-1756 Was $29.99 *$19.99*

Divine Madness

Divine Madness (1980)
Bette Midler in a thrilling, music-filled show. All the stops are pulled as Bette rock-n-raunches through "Boogie Woogie Bugle Boy," "The Rose," and other favorites. 86 min.
19-1173 Was $19.99 *$14.99*

Natalie Cole: The Unforgettable Concert
Multiple Grammy-winner Natalie Cole performs some of father Nat King Cole's best-loved tunes in this wonderful concert in which she's accompanied by a quartet, big band, and full orchestra. Songs include "Paper Moon," "Unforgettable," "Avalon" and "Nature Boy." 90 min.
19-3376 *$24.99*

Nat King Cole: Unforgettable
An array of stars, including Frank Sinatra, Mel Torme, Quincy Jones, Harry Belafonte and Natalie Cole, pays tribute to the life and career of Nat King Cole in a collection of interviews, TV clips and concert footage. "Mona Lisa," "Nature Boy," "Christmas Song" and other Cole classics are featured. 90 min.
50-6371 Was $24.99 *$19.99*

Eddie Fisher: A Singing Legend
One of the most popular crooners of the '50s, Eddie's greatest hits have been assembled for this collection of rare performances, including clips from the "Coke Time with Eddie Fisher" TV series. Among the Philly-born singer's featured tunes are "Anytime," "Wish You Were Here," "I Feel a Song Coming On," "White Christmas," "Oh My Papa" and many more. 40 min.
19-3577 *$19.99*

Julio Iglesias In Spain (1988)
Taped live from his 1988 European concert tour, this splendid performance features the one and only Julio singing favorites old and new, plus a rare backstage interview. 57 min.
04-5024 *$19.99*

Julio Iglesias: Starry Night (1990)
The modern Latin lover is seen in a romantic live concert at the Greek Theater in Los Angeles. Join Julio for old and new favorites like "Amor," "To All the Girls I've Loved Before," "Moonlight Lady," "Mona Lisa," "Me Va, Me Va" and many more. 78 min.
04-5072 *$19.99*

One Night In Eden: Sarah Brightman Live In Concert (1999)
Produced in conjunction with her smash 1999 tour to promote her "Eden" album, this video concert features Brightman performing 18 tracks, including "In Paradisum," "Eden," "Who Wants to Live Forever," "First of May," "Deliver Me," "Time to Say Goodbye" and other favorites old and new. 90 min.
44-4159 *$24.99*

Paul Anka '62 (1962)
Originally titled "Lonely Boy," this documentary on pop star Paul Anka captures all of the singer's energy and his fans' adulation, as it chronicles Anka in concert and the backstage manuevers of manager Irving Feld. Songs include "Diana," "Put Your Head on My Shoulder," "Mr. Wonderful" and "Lonely Boy." 34 min.
22-1317 *$14.99*

George Gershwin Remembered
Before his untimely death at the age of 38, George Gershwin rose from the ranks of New York's Tin Pan Alley tunesmiths to become America's best-known songwriter and composer. Follow his life and career in this fascinating documentary that features performances of classic Gershwin works by the Royal Philharmonic Orchestra, including "Rhapsody in Blue," "An American in Paris" and selections from "Porgy and Bess." 100 min.
53-8530 *$19.99*

George Gershwin 's Wonderful (1998)
To mark the 100th anniversary of the legendary composer's birth, an all-star cast of singers, dancers and musicians came together at the London Palladium for an unforgettable evening of Gershwin tunes. Among the performers are Maureen McGovern, Julia Migenes, Cliff Richard, violinist Joshua Bell, and Paul Gemignani conducting the London Gershwin Orchestra. 60 min.
90-1032 *□$19.99*

Tony Bennett: A Family Christmas
The great song stylist performs a grand collection of holiday favorites, including "The Christmas Waltz," "Winter Wonderland," "Santa Claus Is Coming to Town," "My Favorite Things" and more. Joining Tony are The Manhattan Transfer ("The Christmas Song") and members of his family. 57 min.
04-5170 *$19.99*

Johnny Mathis: Home For Christmas
Chances are you'll want to own this yuletide treat in which classy crooner Johnny Mathis performs such holiday winners as "Winter Wonderland," "The Christmas Story," "The First Nöel," "Have Yourself a Merry Little Christmas" and more. Bet you're ready for the holly and egg nog already. 55 min.
04-5056 *$19.99*

Peter, Paul & Mary: Holiday Concert
Everyone's favorite folk trio is captured live in a joyous yuletide concert. They're joined by a 40-piece orchestra and the New York Choral Society for songs like "We Wish You a Merry Christmas," "Puff, the Magic Dragon," "Blowin' in the Wind" and "Silent Night." 90 min.
15-5144 *$19.99*

The All-Star Christmas Show (1958)
Produced by the USO for the troops overseas, this must-see concert film features over 50 top names from stage, screen and TV in an evening of music and comedy. The stars include Bing Crosby, Louis Armstrong, Benny Goodman, Dinah Shore, Bob Hope, Jack Benny, George Burns, Jimmy Stewart, Milton Berle, Danny Thomas, Jane Russell and many, many more. 90 min.
08-9000 *$19.99*

John Denver: Montana Christmas Skies (1991)
The late, great John Denver performs some beloved Christmas tunes with help from country stars Clint Black, Patty Loveless and Kathy Mattea. This CBS special includes "Christmas for Cowboy," "Wild Montana Skies," "Rudolph the Red-Nosed Reindeer," "Jingle Bells," "Away in a Manger" and more. 47 min.
89-7011 *$14.99*

The Andy Williams Christmas Show
Live from Andy Williams' theatre in Branson, Missouri, comes this delightful holiday show in which the smooth singer croons such favorites as "It's the Most Wonderful Time of the Year," "Joy to the World," "The Christmas Song," "Jingle Bells" and more. His special guests include The Osmond Brothers and Lorrie Morgan. 78 min.
22-1344 *$14.99*

Judy Collins: Christmas At The Biltmore Estate (1997)
The Grammy-winning folk-rock singer invites you to join her for a special holiday concert at the famed Biltmore Estate in North Carolina. "I'll Be Home for Christmas," "Away in a Manger," "Joy to the World," "Let It Snow" and "White Christmas" are among the favorites Collins performs. 100 min.
53-6311 *$19.99*

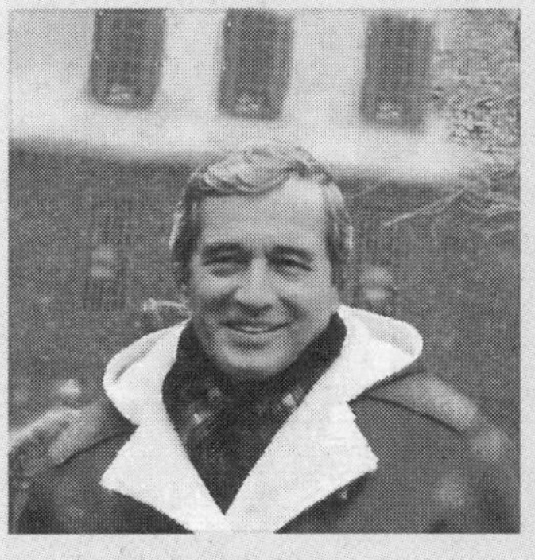

Perry Como's Christmas Concert
The beloved Como in a special holiday concert from 1993 at the Point Theatre in Dublin, Ireland. Joined by a choir, an orchestra and guest star Adele King, Como performs "We Need a Little Christmas," "Toyland," "Little Drummer Boy," "Wind Beneath My Wings" and many others. 83 min.
08-8292 Was $19.99 *$14.99*

Perry Como's Christmas Classics Gift Pack
Have yourself a "Perry" little Christmas with this two-tape boxed set of holiday TV specials. "Christmas in the Holy Land" features splendid location shots of Jerusalem, Bethlehem and Galilee, guest star Richard Chamberlain reading "The Sermon on the Mount," and Como performing "Ave Maria," "Bless This House," "Hava Nagila" and more, while Colonial Williamsburg is the setting for "Early American Christmas," with Perry welcoming John Wayne, the William and Mary Choir and the Williamsburg Fife and Drum Corps. Songs include "Deck the Halls," "Home for the Holidays," "The Little Drummer Boy" and others. 96 min. total.
86-9001 Save $5.00! *$24.99*

A Bing Crosby Christmas
Celebrate Christmas the way you used to know with this wonderful collection of Der Bingle's hit holiday TV specials from 1962 to 1977. Along with old friends Fred Astaire, Jackie Gleason, Mary Martin and many others, Crosby sings 20 of his most memorable hits, including "White Christmas." 60 min.
50-5965 Was $19.99 *$14.99*

Neil Diamond: The Special Christmas
Neil Diamond brings his trademark style to this collection of holiday tunes, singing such favorites as "Silent Night," "White Christmas," "Jingle Bell Rock," "O Holy Night," "Little Drummer Boy" and "O Come, O Come Emmanuel/We Three Kings of Orient Are." 45 min.
04-5194 *$19.99*

Anne Murray's Classic Christmas
Taped in Toronto, this joyous holiday celebration features Canada's Anne Murray performing favorite Christmas songs with such guests as Olympic skater Elvis Stojko, pop group Barenaked Ladies and international sensation Roch Voisine. Songs include "White Christmas," "Winter Wonderland," "Little Drummer Boy" and more. 48 min.
53-6325 Was $19.99 *$14.99*

Andy Williams In Concert At Branson
Andy performs some of his most popular songs in this concert from the Andy Williams Moon River Theatre in Branson, Missouri. Selections include "Moon River," "The Theme from 'The Godfather,'" "Days of Wine and Roses," a gospel medley and two medleys of hits from the 1940s and 1950s. 85 min.
22-1349 *$14.99*

The Best Of The Andy Williams Show
From 1962 to 1971, "The Andy Williams Show" featured some of the best musical performances in television history. Now Andy has selected his favorite moments and put them on one collection. Along with Williams' solo turns, there are duets with such guest stars as Julie Andrews, Tony Bennett, Bing Crosby, Sammy Davis, Jr., Judy Garland and many others. 60 min.
50-8712 *$19.99*

Barry Manilow: Live On Broadway
He's been around forever and he may have sung the very first song. Barry belts out his most beloved tunes in a sold-out Broadway show. Capture the razzle-dazzle at home! Features 30 minutes of exclusive material. 90 min.
02-7104 *$19.99*

Barry Manilow: The Greatest Hits... And Then Some (1993)
Devoted followers of The Divine Mr. M won't want to miss out on this live concert from London's Wembley Arena. Barry performs such favorites as "Ready to Take a Chance Again," "Daybreak," "Can't Smile Without You," "Stay," "I Write the Songs" and, in medley form, "Mandy," "Send in the Clowns" and "This One's for You." 95 min.
02-7980 *$19.99*

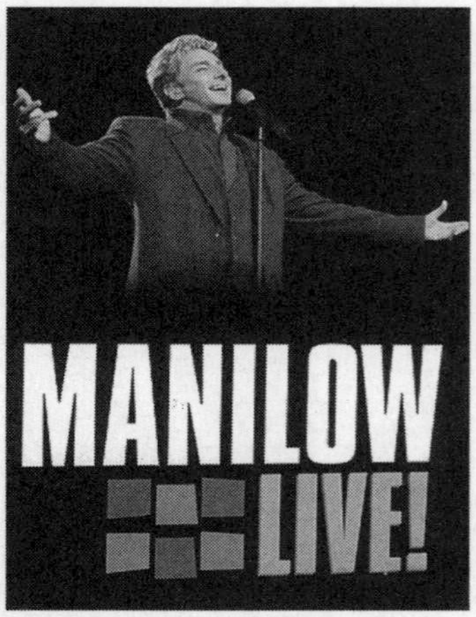

Manilow Live! (2000)
It's 24 favorite songs marking a quarter-century of topping the charts, as Barry Manilow is joined by a 30-piece band for an unforgettable live performance from Nashville. "Could It Be Magic," "Mandy," "I Write the Songs," "Weekend in New England," "I Made It Through the Rain," "Daybreak," "Even Now" and many more Manilow classics are performed. 115 min.
53-7561 Letterboxed *$19.99*

Bing Crosby Scrapbook
Der Bingle's first film efforts are collected, including "Road to Hollywood," a compilation of work done for Mack Sennett; a trailer for "Going Hollywood"; plus early short films "Crooner's Holiday" (1939) (AKA: "Dream House"), "Sing, Bing, Sing" (1933) and "Blue of the Night" (1933). 120 min.
10-7433 *$19.99*

The Magic Of Bing Crosby, Part 1
It's an evening of musical magic indeed with this wonderful collection of "Der Bingle" performing solo and with guest artists like Louis Armstrong, Dean Martin, Rosemary Clooney, Mary Martin and others. There's interviews, vintage concert footage, and such songs as "It Had to Be You," "Accentuate the Positive," "Don't Fence Me In" and, of course, "White Christmas." 55 min.
19-3243 *$19.99*

Bing Crosby Edsel Show (1957)
If consumers didn't run out to buy the 1958 Edsel, it wasn't for lack of Ford's pushing its latest model in this star-studded musical-variety special hosted by Bing Crosby. Joining Der Bingle are Frank Sinatra, Louis Armstrong, Rosemary Clooney and The 4 Preps, with a special appearance by a mystery guest (a fella who's been on the "road" with Crosby more than once). Includes original commercials. 58 min.
53-6305 *$19.99*

Bing Crosby Oldsmobile Special (1959)
It's all singing, all dancing, and all vintage Oldsmobiles in this musical-variety show in which host Bing welcomes guests Frank Sinatra, Louis Armstrong, Peggy Lee, and pianists Joe Bushkin, George Shearing and Paul Smith. This video also includes original Olds commercials featuring Florence Henderson and Bill Haley.
53-6304 *$19.99*

Liza Minnelli: Live From Radio City Music Hall
Lovely Liza turns in a classic performance from her record-setting appearances at New York's Radio City Music Hall, singing a number of favorites. Included are "Quiet Love," "Some People," "Live Alone and Like It," "Imagine," "Men's Medley," "Theme from 'New York, New York'" and more. 93 min.
04-5176 *$29.99*

Tom Jones: Live At This Moment (1989)
"Dynamic" is the only word to describe this concert featuring the Welsh-born singer who's being discovered by a new generation of fans. From classics like "It's Not Unusual" and "What's New, Pussycat?" to current faves "Kiss" and "At This Moment," this is Tom Jones! 65 min.
02-7095 *$19.99*

Pia Zadora's American Songbook (1987)
The one, the only, the inimitable Pia captured on video, rendering classic torch numbers as only she can. Among the 12 lavishly mounted performances are "It Had to Be You," "The Man that Got Away," "Come Rain or Shine" and "All of Me." 42 min.
04-2084 *$24.99*

The Quintessential Peggy Lee
Singer extraordinaire Peggy Lee performs a concert spotlighting the greatest hits from throughout her career, including "Is That All There Is?," "Fever," "It's Wonderful," "As Time Goes By," "Just One of Those Things" and others. 86 min.
22-1376 *$19.99*

Neil Diamond's Greatest Hits—Live
It's the world's hardest substance, and while you can't cook on it, this Diamond has been creating musical gems for decades. Wonderful concert features Neil performing his old and new: "Coming to America," "September Morn," "Cherry Cherry," "Hello Again," "Heartlight" and many more. 60 min.
04-5013 *$19.99*

Neil Diamond: Love At The Greek
Recorded live at Los Angeles' famed Greek Theater in 1976, the multi-faceted singer/songwriter performs the hits that made you love him. "Sweet Caroline," "Cracklin' Rosie," "I Am...I Said," "Play Me" and many more faves, sung in the Diamond manner. 52 min.
04-5143 *$14.99*

Neil Diamond: The Roof Party—Songs From The Brill Building
Neil goes back to his formative years in this concert performed in a studio re-creation of the roof of New York's famed Brill Building. Joined by guests Paul Shaffer and Neil Sedaka, Diamond performs "You've Lost That Lovin' Feeling," "Will You Still Love Me Tomorrow?," "Cherry Cherry," "Up on the Roof" and "Happy Birthday Sweet Sixteen." 35 min.
04-5215 *$14.99*

Tony Bennett's New York
The singing talents of one of the most legendary crooners of the twentieth century, Tony Bennett, are showcased in these Atlantic City performances along with New York interviews and archival footage of Tony's friends. Among the featured songs are "I Left My Heart In San Francisco," "Just In Time," "Stranger In Paradise" and many more. 90 min.
50-8731 *$19.99*

You're The Top: The Cole Porter Story (1991)
You'll get a kick out of this tribute to Cole Porter which features the great composer's songs performed by the likes of Frank Sinatra, Fred Astaire, Ethel Merman, Judy Garland, Shirley MacLaine and others. Classic renditions of "Night and Day," "You Do Something to Me," "My Heart Belongs to Daddy," "True Love" and more are featured. Bobby Short hosts. 56 min.
02-7290 *$19.99*

Bernadette Peters In Concert (1998)
In a stunning live performance at London's Royal Festival Hall, stage and screen star Bernadette Peters sings such favorites as "Broadway Baby," "Time Heals Everything," "Some People" and more, including tunes from her acclaimed "I'll Be Your Baby Tonight" album. Features footage not shown on TV. 91 min.
50-8273 *$19.99*

Tony Bennett Live: Watch What Happens
After 40 years in show business, Tony Bennett is still a master crooner. This performance from London's Prince Edward Theater showcases Bennett at his best, singing "In a Sentimental Mood," "The Shadow of Your Smile," "Fly Me to the Moon" and "I Left My Heart in San Francisco," plus more. 90 min.
04-5119 *$19.99*

Engelbert Humperdinck Live
Experience the magic of "King of Romance" in concert in this wonderful evening of love songs. Included are "Still," "The Wanderer," "Release Me," "Quando, Quando, Quando" and, yep, "Wild Thing." 80 min.
81-1021 *$14.99*

Engelbert Humperdinck: Live At The Royal Albert Hall
London's renowned recital hall is the setting for an unforgettable command performance by the one and only Engelbert. Among the Humperdinck favorites presented are "After the Lovin'," "I Walk Alone," "Help Me Make It Through the Night," "Quando Quando Quando," "Lonely Is a Man Without Love" and many more. 60 min.
50-8206 *$19.99*

Music Of Scotland With Peter Morrison
Take a song-filled stroll through the highlands with famed baritone Peter Morrison as your guide, as he shows off the historic sites, colorful towns and breathtaking scenery of his native Scotland and performs such beloved ballads as "Scotland the Brave," "Loch Lomond," "The Piper O'Dundee," "My Love Is Like a Red Red Rose," "Will Ye No Come Back Again" and others. 40 min.
81-3008 *$19.99*

Country/ Western

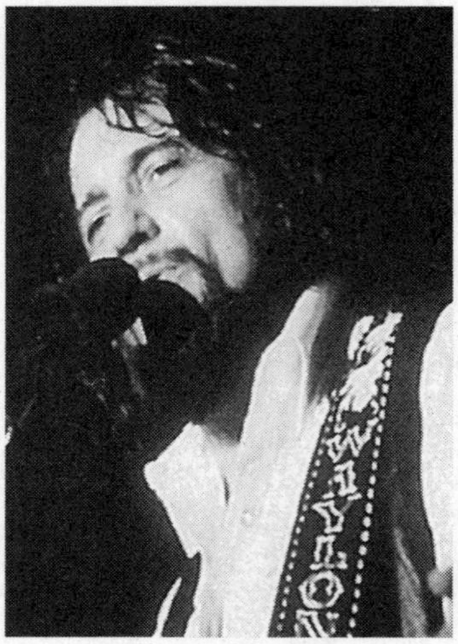

Waylon: The Lost Outlaw Performance (1978)
A legendary performance from Waylon Jennings and The Waylors took place at The Grand Ole Opry on August 12, 1978, but all recordings were locked away until now. Waylon and his band perform "Amanda," "Honky Tonk Heroes," "Mammas, Don't Let Your Babies Grow Up to Be Cowboys" and other favorites. 55 min.
44-9002 *$14.99*

Alan Jackson: Here In The Reel World
In the video counterpart to his best-selling debut album "Here in the Real World," country crooner Jackson is featured in videos for "Wanted," "Chasin' That Neon Rainbow" and more, plus live performances of "Home" and "Dog River Blues."
02-7215 *$14.99*

Alan Jackson: The Greatest Hits Video Collection
"(Who Says) You Can't Have It All?" Certainly not Alan Jackson, who offers up on this video a heaping helping of his greatest hits in music video form. Included are "Blue Blooded Woman," "Chasin' That Neon Rainbow," "Don't Rock the Jukebox," "Chattahoochee," "I Don't Even Know Your Name" and many more. 75 min.
02-8393 *$19.99*

Brooks & Dunn: The Greatest Hits Collection
They're a staple on the country music charts, and now the award-winning songs of Kix Brooks and Ronnie Dunn are gathered in a music video collection that includes "Lost and Found," "Boot Scootin' Boogie" and more, plus the all-new video for "Honky Tonk Truth." 55 min.
02-8778 *$19.99*

Alabama: For The Record: 41 Number One Hits Live, Vol. 1
In October of 1998, the phenomenally successful country combo offered an evening filled with their chart-topping tunes at the Las Vegas Hilton. In this first video program culled from the event, Alabama performs "Tennessee River," "Why Lady Why," "Old Flame," "Roll On (Eighteen Wheeler)," "She and I" and others.
02-9181 *$19.99*

Alabama: For The Record: 41 Number One Hits Live, Vol. 2
They just had too many hits to fit onto one tape! Come back to Alabama with this second concert video and enjoy such favorites as "My Home in Alabama," "Face to Face," "Song of the South," "Born Country," "In Pictures" and others.
02-9182 *$19.99*

The Charlie Daniels Band: The Saratoga Concert
The good ol' country boy plucks that fiddle and leads his band in such favorites as "The Devil Went Down to Georgia," "The South's Gonna Do It," "Saddle Tramp" and more. So hot it could melt a barn! 75 min.
04-1604 *$29.99*

The Best Of Austin City Limits
Some of the greatest names in country, folk and pop music have graced the stage of the acclaimed PBS concert series, and among the stars spotlighted in this "best of" sampler are Asleep at the Wheel, Mary Chapin Carpenter, Merle Haggard, Waylon Jennings, George Jones, The Judds, k.d. lang, Willie Nelson, Tammy Wynette and others. 60 min.
04-5478 *$19.99*

Willie, Waylon, Cash & Kris: Highwaymen Live
Four of the top names in country music (Willie Nelson, Waylon Jennings, Johnny Cash and Kris Kristofferson) combine their considerable talents for an unforgettable concert. Songs include "Ring of Fire," "Always on My Mind," "Me and Bobby McGee" and 20 more. 95 min.
04-5061 *$19.99*

The Highwaymen: On The Road Again
Shot during their first tour of Europe, country music greats Johnny Cash, Waylon Jennings, Kris Kristofferson and Willie Nelson are featured performing on stage and talking candidly about their music backstage. Songs include "Folsom Prison Blues," "Always on My Mind," "Crazy," "Help Me Make It Through the Night" and more. 60 min.
22-1312 *$14.99*

The Willie Nelson Special (1984)
Willie Nelson and his guest Ray Charles, two giants of popular music, get together for a uniquely wonderful video concert. From a duet on "Georgia on My Mind" to "I Can't Stop Loving You," "On the Road Again," "Always on My Mind" and "Whisky River," the pair are at their best. 48 min.
53-1429 Was $19.99 *$14.99*

Reba McEntire: Reba In Concert
Country-western sensation Reba McEntire performs at the University of Texas at Austin, singing such hits as "Love Will Find Its Way to You," "Somebody Should Leave," "Walk On," "Fancy" and "Cathy's Clown." 70 min.
07-4060 *$14.99*

Reba McEntire: Greatest Hits
Reba McEntire, country's reigning songstress, performs her greatest songs in this program. Included are "Take It Back," "Does He Love You," "The Heart Won't Lie" and more, plus Reba's rendition of "The Night the Lights Went Out in Georgia." 31 min.
07-4099 *$19.99*

Reba: Celebrating 20 Years
There's lots "more Reba" in this special look back at the country favorite's life and hit-filled career. McEntire performs such selections as "You're No Good," "I Won't Mention It Again," "Starting Over," "Ring on Her Finger, Time on Her Hands" and many more. 70 min.
44-4129 *$19.99*

Country Gold, Vol. 1
Get the hoedown lowdown on 50 years of country music with this foot-stompin' program that features Lynn Anderson ("I Never Promised You a Rose Garden"), Loretta Lynn ("Coal Miner's Daughter"), Merle Haggard and Ernest Tubb, Waylon Jennings, and more. Dennis Weaver hosts. 50 min.
15-5219 *$19.99*

Country Gold, Vol. 2
More of the greatest country crooners of all time, singing their most popular tunes. Included are Waylon Jennings ("Ain't Livin' Like This"), Tanya Tucker ("Delta Dawn"), Ray Price ("For the Good Times"), Tammy Wynette, Ricky Skaggs and others. 95 min.
15-5229 *$19.99*

Shania Twain Live
"Come on Over" and enjoy one of country music's hottest performers in a dazzling live concert. Shania sizzles as she sings "Man! I Feel Like a Woman!," "Honey, I'm Home," "You're Still the One," "God Bless the Child," "From This Moment On" and many more. 120 min.
02-9086 *$19.99*

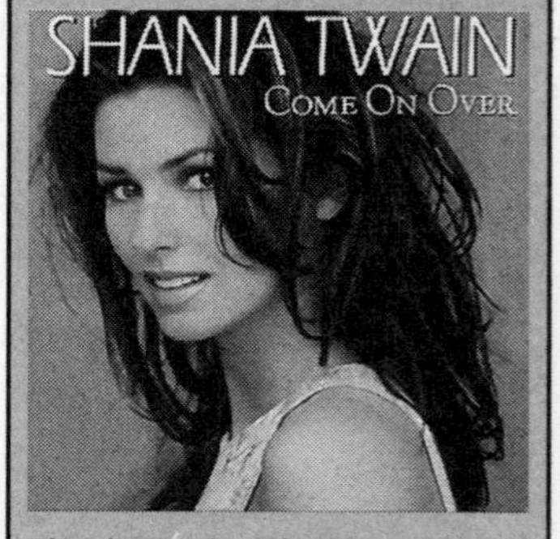

Shania Twain: The Come On Over Video Collection
The Canadian-born country singer has wowed audiences on both sides of the border, and you'll see why with this collection of Shania's music videos for such hits as "Love Gets Me Every Time," "You're Still the One," "Man! I Feel Like a Woman!," "You've Got a Way" and others. 36 min.
44-4181 *$14.99*

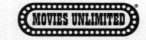

Randy Travis: Forever (And Ever)
One of country/western's premier artists performs seven of his most popular tunes, including "It's Just a Matter of Time," "Forever and Ever, Amen," "Point of Light" and more. 45 min.
19-3221 *$19.99*

Neal McCoy: You Gotta Love That!
You've had your fill of country music posers, now experience the Neal McCoy in this compilation from the popular chart-topper. Includes "Wink," "No Doubt About It," "Day-O," "The City Put the Country Back in Me," "For a Change," and more. 45 min.
19-3688 *$14.99*

Travis Tritt: The Restless Kind Of Video Collection
This video companion to the popular country performer's gold "The Restless Kind" album includes such top Travis tunes as "Worth Every Mile," "Sometimes She Forgets," the duets "Helping Me Get Over You" (with Lari White) and "Here's Your Sign" (with comic Bill Engvall), and others, plus an exclusive interview with Tritt. 50 min.
19-4008 *$14.99*

Gentleman Jim Reeves: The Story Of A Legend
This program chronicles the career of country star Jim Reeves, who tragically died in an airplane crash in 1964. Included are such songs as "Four Walls," "He'll Have to Go" and "Adios Amigo," which help tell the smooth balladeer's life story. 45 min.
22-1285 *$19.99*

Jim Reeves/ Ray Price With Ernest Tubb
Three all-time legends of country music perform some of their finest songs in this program culled from performances from 1954 to 1956. Songs include "I Wonder Why You Said Goodbye," "Dear Judge," "You Done Me Wrong" and "I'm Hurtin' Inside." 60 min.
63-7027 *$24.99*

Webb Pierce: Greatest Hits
Shortly before his death in 1991, country legend Webb Pierce compiled this collection of vintage performance pieces and provided background narration. Seventeen of Pierce's greatest hits, including "Wondering," "There Stands the Glass" and "More and More," are featured. 52 min.
22-1309 *$14.99*

George Jones: Golden Hits
Country great George Jones is the focus of this song-filled tribute that includes lots of music and interview with Jones. Selections include "White Lightning," "She Thinks I Still Care," "The Race Is On," "He Stopped Loving Her Today" and others. 50 min.
22-1341 *$19.99*

Kris Kristofferson
The music and film career of singer-songwriter-actor Kris Kristofferson is the subject of this biography that features great songs like "Me and Bobby McGee," "Help Me Make It Through the Night" and "Sunday Morning Coming Down" and interviews with the likes of Dennis Hopper, Willie Nelson, Johnny Cash and Michael Cimino. 90 min.
22-1360 *$14.99*

Louisiana Hayride: Cradle Of The Stars
From 1948 to 1958 radio audiences throughout the South were treated to live broadcasts from Shreveport's famed country music showcase. Narrated by Hank Williams, Jr., this documentary mixes film clips, photos and rare recordings to help tell the story of the show whose performers included Hank Williams, Sr., Johnny Cash and Elvis Presley. 62 min.
22-1419 *$14.99*

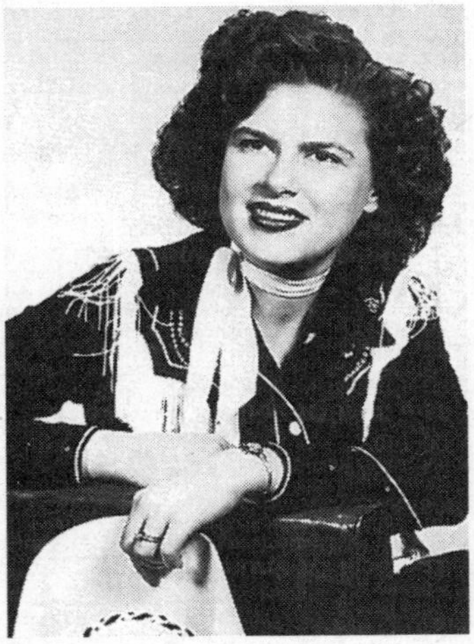

The Real Patsy Cline
A film biography helped a new generation of country singers and fans rediscover this legendary songbird. Now see an actual stage performance of the great Patsy Cline singing "Crazy," "Sweet Dreams," "I Fall to Pieces" and more, plus interviews with contemporaries like Carl Perkins, Dottie West and Loretta Lynn. 48 min.
58-5008 Was $19.99 *$14.99*

Hank Williams: The Show He Never Gave
Country great Hank Williams comes to life in this one-man show by singer "Sneezy" Waters. The film features "Williams" giving an impromptu concert in a roadside bar, where the famed star performs 25 of his greatest hits. 86 min.
22-1253 *$24.99*

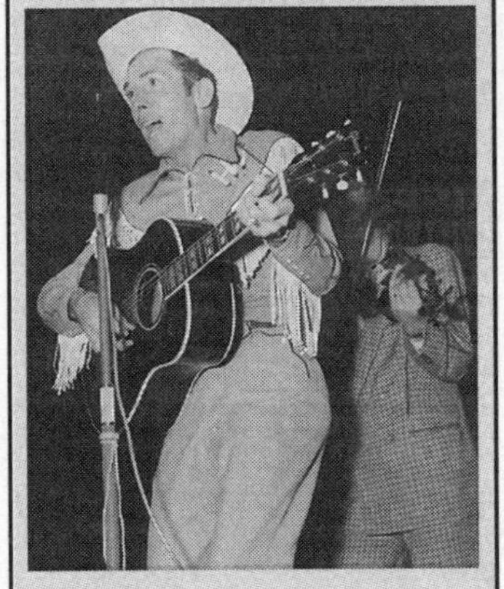

In The Hank Williams Tradition
The short, tragic life of Hank Williams is recounted in a revealing documentary that mixes rare clips, musical performances and anecdotes from country music greats Roy Acuff, Minnie Pearl and Chet Atkins. Songs featured are "Half as Much," "I'm So Lonesome," "Hey Good Lookin'" and "Your Cheatin' Heart." 60 min.
22-1295 *$19.99*

Roger Miller: King Of The Road
The incredible life story of singer-songwriter Roger Miller is chronicled in this video that includes many of his homespun favorites, such as "Dang Me," "England Swings," "Chug-a-Lug" and others. Featured are Willie Nelson, Johnny Cash and Kris Kristofferson; narrated by Waylon Jennings. 60 min.
22-1470 *$19.99*

Path To Stardom
Country's greatest stars are showcased in this series which features film clips, interviews and anecdotes from the stars, their friends and their families. Learn intimate details about the performers and their rise to fame. Each tape runs about 30 min. There are 10 volumes available, including:

Path To Stardom: Chely Wright
She's got the same heart-wrenching vocal style that has reminded country fans of Connie Smith and Loretta Lynn. Now, learn about Chely's "Wright" moves to stardom.
22-1559 *$14.99*

Path To Stardom: Aaron Tippin
Chart the growth of best-selling country star Aaron Tippin, a performer with an unmistakable voice, best known for his hit album "Read Between the Lines."
22-1563 *$14.99*

Path To Stardom: David Ball
Honky-tonker David Ball shows you why his songs keep appearing on the charts in this insightful program that's sure to delight country-western buffs.
22-1564 *$14.99*

Path To Stardom: Carlene Carter
See how Carlene Carter's family ties have played a big part in her innovative music career. With Johnny Cash as her stepfather and June Carter Cash as her mother, it's easy to see why Carlene has chosen the musical path she has.
22-1567 *$14.99*

Tennessee Ernie Ford: Amazing Grace
The beloved entertainer performs 22 of his all-time favorite hymns and songs of praise in this unique collection culled from Ford's long-running variety series. Among the tunes are "I Want to Be Ready," "Just a Closer Walk with Thee," "I Am a Pilgrim," "Old Rugged Cross," "What a Friend We Have in Jesus" and more. 55 min.
22-1638 *$19.99*

Fiddlin' Man: The Life & Times Of Bob Wills
Known as "The King of Western Swing," Wills helped popularize the blend of country/western, blues and old-time fiddle music with his band, The Texas Playboys, in the '30s and '40s. This documentary salute features interviews with Wills' friends and colleagues, rare performance clips and more. Songs include "San Antonio Rose," "Lone Star Rag," "Goodbye Liza Jane." 61 min.
22-7175 *$19.99*

Marty Robbins/Ernest Tubb
Superior collection of songs by two country singing greats. Included are Robbins classics like "I Can't Quit," "My Castle in the Sky," "Gossip" and more; Ernest Tubb's tunes include "Don't Look Now," "Tomorrow Never Comes" and "Answer the Phone." 60 min.
63-7026 *$24.99*

Chris LeDoux: Greatest Hits: The Video Collection
The rising young country star is featured in five of his finest music videos: "Life Is a Highway," "Honky Tonk World," "For Your Love," "This Cowboy's Hat" and "Five Dollar Fine" (with guest star Garth Brooks). 30 min.
44-4155 *$14.99*

The Best Of Minnie Pearl: Let Minnie Steal Your Joke
You know her as the wacky Grand Ol' Opry favorite with the flowers and a pricetag in her straw hat. Now Minnie Pearl shows why she's one of Nashville's beloved figures with her humor and priceless delivery. Ralph Emery and Roy Acuff are also featured. 60 min.
50-2807 *$19.99*

The Dixie Chicks: Chicks Rule
Pop country sensations The Dixie Chicks are the focus of this program that presents surprising details of the lives of members Natalie Maines, Martie Seidel and Emily Erwin. See what makes this sensational, award-winning group tick. 40 min.
50-8473 *$14.99*

Times Ain't Like They Used To Be
This captivating program traces early rural and popular American music from 1928 to 1935, and features an incredible array of rare footage and classic music performances. There's Jimmie Rodgers, Jack Johnson's Jazz Band, Bela Lam, Otto Gray's Oklahoma Cowboys, and Bob Wills and the Texas Playboys. 70 min.
63-7056 *$24.99*

That High Lonesome Sound
This collection features three acclaimed films by music documentarian Joe Cohen. "The High Lonesome Sound" looks at Eastern Kentucky singer-guitarist Roscoe Holcomb; Appalachian ballad singer Dillard Chandler is profiled in "The End of an Old Story"; and "Sara and Maybelle" are the focus of a film salute to two original members of The Carter Family. 70 min.
63-7152 *$19.99*

High Lonesome: The Story Of Bluegrass Music (1993)
A fascinating, critically acclaimed look at the world of bluegrass music, tracing it roots from the Kentucky hills to its modern forms. Featuring 100 songs from the likes of Bill Monroe, the Stanley Bros., Flatt & Scruggs and Jimmy Martin, the films meshes music and historical footage depicting the country's changes. 95 min.
63-7092 *$19.99*

Texas Fiddle Legends
A unique mixture of the simple and the ornate, the Texas style of fiddling is an extraordinary form of music not to be ignored. Two legends of fiddling—Dick Barrett and Benny Thomasson—are presented here with rare footage of a concert given in the early 1970s. 50 min.
63-7171 *$19.99*

Mary Chapin Carpenter: Jubilee: Live At Wolf Trap (1995)
From the PBS "Spotlight" series comes this stunning performance from one of country's greatest singer-songwriters. Included are favorites such as "Passionate Kisses," "I Feel Lucky," "The Last Word" and "He Thinks He'll Keep Her," plus duets with Shawn Colvin and Joan Baez. Also featured are three songs exclusive to this video, including "Quittin' Time." 90 min.
04-5417 *$19.99*

Garth Brooks
He's at the forefront of today's new breed of country singers, and now the award-winning Garth Brooks brings his popular sound to video. This collection includes the hits "If Tomorrow Never Comes," "The Dance" and "The Thunder Rolls," along with exclusive interview footage. 20 min.
07-4068 *$14.99*

The Garth Brooks Video Collection: Vol. II
More memorable music videos from country music's "cat in the hat," including "Standing Outside the Fire," "The Change," and the award-winners "We Shall Be Free" and "The Red Strokes," along with exclusive behind-the-scenes footage and an interview with Brooks.
44-4125 *$14.99*

Garth Brooks: His Life...From Tulsa To The Top
See how Oklahoma-born Troyal Garth Brooks went on to become one of the biggest names in country music with this unauthorized video biography. Learn about Garth's influences on his life and music, how he got his big break, what life on the road is like, and more. 45 min.
50-8214 *$14.99*

The Nashville Sound (1972)
Join in on this country-western jamboree which celebrates the 44th anniversary of the Grand Ole Opry. Featured performers include Johnny Cash ("Folsom Prison Blues"), Tex Ritter ("High Noon"), Jeannie C. Riley ("Harper Valley, PTA"), Skeeter Davis ("The End of the World") and Roy Acuff ("Wabash Cannonball"). 90 min.
55-9042 *$19.99*

DVD VIDEO
ASK ABOUT OUR GIANT DVD CATALOG!

Faith Hill: Faithfully Yours
The gorgeous and talented country sensation Faith Hill is profiled in this unauthorized program. See what makes Faith tick, from her early days as a crooner to her amazing success on the top of the charts. 50 min.
50-8672 *$19.99*

Loretta (1980)
The real "Coal Miner's Daughter," Loretta Lynn, is filmed in concert live from Las Vegas. Her hits include "Naked in the Rain," "Don't Come Home A-Drinkin'," "I Saw the Light" and a Gospel medley. 61 min.
07-1008 Was $29.99 *$14.99*

Vince Gill: I Still Believe In You
The award-winning country crooner will make you a believer with this compilation of his popular music videos. Includes the title tune, "When I Call Your Name," "Liza Jane," more. 24 min.
07-4083 *$14.99*

Tammy Wynette In Concert
Grammy-winning country star Tammy Wynette performs a dynamic concert filled with great tunes. Included are "I Don't Want to Play House," "D-I-V-O-R-C-E" and Hillary Clinton's favorite, "Stand by Your Man." 60 min.
15-5224 *$14.99*

Still Swingin'
Characterized by the likes of Bob Wills and His Texas Playboys, Red Steagall and Stonehorse, and Asleep at the Wheel, Texas Swing is a mix of country music and swinging jazz tempos from Texas and Oklahoma. This tribute features great music from the groups that popularized the musical style and includes such tunes as "Lone Star Rag," "San Antonio Rose" and "Ida Red." 57 min.
08-1529 *$19.99*

Dwight Yoakam: Just Lookin' For A Hit
They're not hard to find for this hot young country star, and even easier for you on this six-pack of music videos and concert clips. "Honky Tonk Man," "Little Sister," "Long White Cadillac" and more. 30 min.
19-3079 *$14.99*

Dwight Yoakam: Pieces Of Time
Country twanger Dwight Yoakam is the star of this video compilation that includes such hits as "You're the One," "Pocket of a Clown," "Ain't That Lonely Yet," "It Only Hurts When I Cry," the video for "Suspicious Minds" from the film "Honeymoon in Vegas" and more. 49 min.
19-3591 *$19.99*

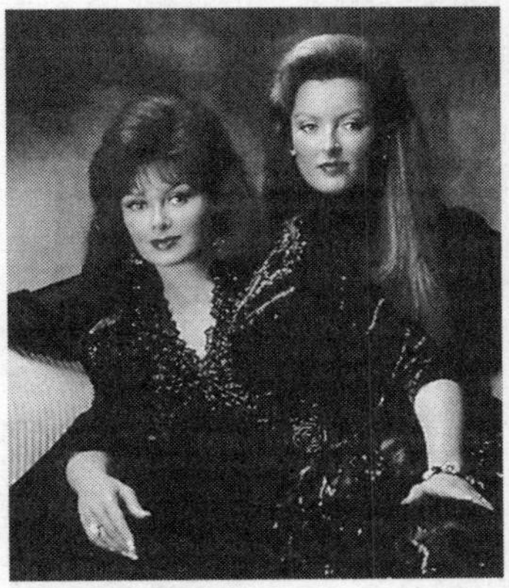

The Judds: Love Can Build A Bridge
It's Naomi and Wynonna in 3-D! That's right, this music video collection, which includes interviews, scenes from the country duo's final tour together and hits like "This Country's Rockin'," "Born to Be Blue" and "Rompin' Stompin' Blues," also features the 3-D video for the title cut (free glasses included). 60 min.
50-6631 *$19.99*

The Judds: Their Final Concert (1991)
After seven years of accolades and awards, Naomi and Wynonna made their last concert appearance as a duo in a moving live performance. The 19 favorite songs on this must-have video include "Born to Be Blue," "Why Not Me," "Guardian Angel," and many more. 104 min.
50-6926 *$19.99*

k.d. lang: Harvest Of Seven Years (Cropped And Chronicled)
k.d. lang has been one of the country music world's most popular and most interesting performers over the last few years, and a number of her best hits are on this fine collection. Includes "Hanky Panky," "Turn Me Round," "Honky Tonk Angels," "Johnny Get Angry" and a duet with Roy Orbison on "Crying." 60 min.
19-3222 *$19.99*

k.d. lang: Live In Sydney
It's the concert video music fans have been constantly craving for, as k.d. takes the stage Down Under for an electrifying show that includes "Crying," "Rose Garden," "Miss Chatelaine," "Pullin' Back the Reins," "What's New, Pussycat?" and more. There's also special backstage footage and interviews with lang. 83 min.
19-4007 *$19.99*

Gospel/ Christian Rock

Daryl Coley: Live In Oakland—Home Again
In a moving hometown concert, award-winning gospel singer Daryl Coley teams up with the group he started as a teen, The New Generation Singers, as he performs "I Will Bless Your Name," "I Will Sing Glory," "Removal of the Mask," "What He's Done for Me" and more, including a duet with Coley and his mother on "Jesus Loves Me." 86 min.
02-8783 *$19.99*

WOW Gospel 1999
It's the Super Bowl of gospel music, featuring the most inspirational of performers. Included are John B. Kee ("Strength"), CeCe Winans ("Well All Right"), Shirley Caesar ("You're Next in Line"), Yolanda Adams ("Only Believe"), Kurt Carr ("For Every Mountain"), Dr. Bobby Jones ("What a Friend") and others.
02-9068 *$19.99*

The Story Of Gospel Music
It evolved from traditional hymnals and black spiritual music, resulting in a uniquely American sound that was upbeat and uplifting. Trace gospel's history with this vibrant, song-filled program that features rare recordings and film footage of Rev. Thomas Dorsey, Mahalia Jackson, The Dixie Hummingbirds, Aretha Franklin and other stars. 90 min.
04-3824 Was $19.99 *❑$14.99*

Shirley Caesar: Live In Memphis
Grammy-winning gospel belter Shirley Caesar wows you with her singing and style, performing such favorites as "No Charge," "Yes, Lord, Yes," "His Blood" and "Never." 60 min.
04-5147 *$19.99*

Mountain Homecoming
From the historic Grove Park Inn in the heart of North Carolina's Blue Ridge Mountains, gospel stars Bill and Gloria Gaither are joined by their Homecoming Friends for a special evening of music. "It's Gonna Be a Good Day," "We'll Work 'Til Jesus Comes," "There's Something About a Mountain" and "The Love of God" are among the songs featured.
44-4160 *$19.99*

Gospel (1982)
A collection of performances that will make you throw your head back and let go. James Cleveland, Walter Hawkins, Mighty Clouds of Joy, Shirley Caesar, and the Clark Sisters are featured in this uplifting musical experience. 92 min.
27-6058 *$39.99*

The Winans: The Lost Concert (1984)
Unseen for over 13 years, this rare concert film features the famed gospel group performing in Chicago with guest artists Vanessa Bell Armstrong and The Commissioned (with their original line-up). 80 min.
54-9194 *$19.99*

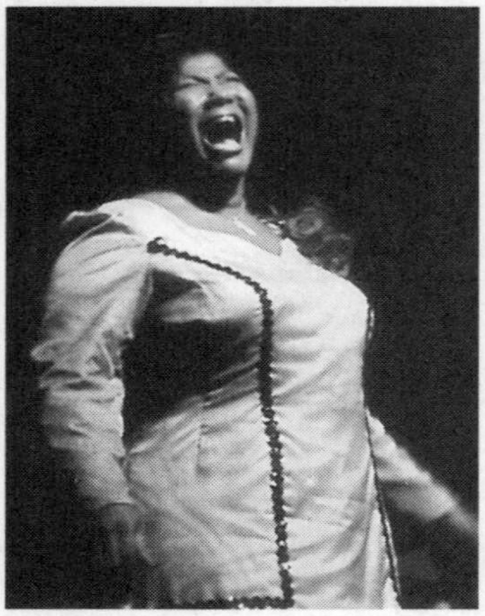

Mahalia Jackson
Gospel music's greatest voice is profiled during a European tour shortly before her death in 1972, proclaiming her faith in her signature energetic and emotional style. Included in Jackson's inspirational repertoire are "Come On, Children," "Didn't It Rain," "Down by the Riverside," "He's Got the Whole World in His Hands," "We Shall Overcome" and more. 86 min.
22-1575 *$19.99*

Mahalia Jackson: The Power And The Glory (1997)
Paul Winfield narrates a moving, song-filled look at the life and career of the legendary gospel singer who went from an impoverished childhood in Louisiana to performing on the world's great concert stages. 90 min.
54-9177 *$19.99*

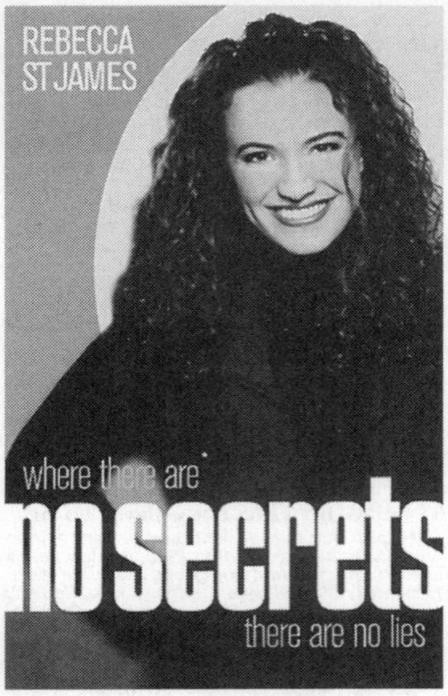

Rebecca St. James: No Secrets
Follow a "day in the life" of the popular Christian music star with this special program that features music videos, live concert footage, and footage with Rebecca, her family and friends. Songs include "God," "Go and Sin No More," "Pray" and many more.
44-4164 *$19.99*

The Gospel According To Al Green (1985)
The rhythm and blues superstar and ordained minister raises his voice to the heavens in a knockout live performance. You'll be brought to your feet as Green renders many beloved inspirational standards in his inimitable manner. 94 min.
69-1107 *$19.99*

Donnie McClurkin: Stand
Concert performances, music videos and behind-the-scenes footage showing the recording of "I Am" for the "Prince of Egypt" soundtrack offer you an up-close look at this talented young gospel singer. Included here are "Church Medley," "Tis So Sweet," "Stand" and more.
19-4077 *$19.99*

Hallelujah! The Best Of The Brooklyn Tabernacle Choir
Their music has won them fans worldwide and earned them Dove and Grammy Awards. Now see moving concert footage, TV performance clips from "The Billy Graham Crusade" and "The 700 Club," and interviews with choir leaders Jim and Carol Cymbala. Songs include "My Help (Cometh from the Lord)," "Favorite Song of All," "He's Been Faithful," "How Great Thou Art" and many more.
19-4078 *$14.99*

I'll Meet You On The Mountain
The second program from the Gaither family's "Mountain Homecoming" series, filmed live in Ashville, North Carolina, has Bill and Gloria welcoming guests Buddy Greene, Bonnie Keen, Karen Peck and others, performing such songs as "There Is a Mountain," "Jesus Is Coming Soon," "I'm Free Again," "In the Garden" and many more.
44-4170 *$19.99*

Bishop Clarence McClendon Presents The Harvest Fire Mega Mass Choir: Shout Hallelujah
Recorded during the 1999 Harvest Fire Conference in Los Angeles, this rousing mix of worship and song features Bishop McClendon and his choir performing "I Came to Magnify," "There Is a Fountain," "All Hail the Power," "May the Lord God Bless You Real Good" and more.
04-5725 *$14.99*

Brooklyn Tabernacle Choir: God Is Working...Live: The Video (2000)
The legendary Grammy- and Dove Award-winning choir is back, preaching the word of God with a host of songs recorded at the Brooklyn Tabernacle Church. Such wonderful gospel numbers as "Keep Me True," "Nothing Is Impossible," "I Found the Answer," "Holy Like You" and others are featured.
04-5743 *$19.99*

Say Amen, Somebody (1983)
An acclaimed, joy-filled celebration of gospel music, filled with performances from such great gospel performers as Willie Mae Ford Smith, Thomas A. Dorsey, The Barrett Sisters and the O'Neal Twins. 100 min.
70-5074 Was $29.99 *$19.99*

Welcome To The Freak Show: dc Talk Live In Concert (1996)
Filmed during their popular "Jesus Freak World Tour," this concert video featuring the Grammy- and Dove Award-winning Christian pop group includes such songs as "Luv Is a Verb," "Colored People," "What If I Stumble," "Jesus Freak" and others.
44-4139 *$19.99*

New Age

Winter Solstice On Ice
Among the artists featured in this special Windham Hill salute to the sights and sounds of winter are Phil Perry ("Winter"), Yanni ("Santorini"), George Winston ("Skating"), Peabo Bryson ("I Wish I Could"), Tuck and Patti ("Christmas Wish"), Hiroshima ("Silent Night") and many more.
02-9224 *$19.99*

Enya: Moonshadows
Mesmerizing videos for "Orinoco Flow," "Exile," "Storms in Africa," "Evening Falls..." and "Caribbean Blue" consist of liquid colors and impressionistic images, which help complement the mysterious music of this Irish songbird. 25 min.
19-3285 *❑$14.99*

Chasing Rain
Enjoy refreshing rain gardens, dreamy whirlpools, rushing rivers and other watery imagery in this New Age environmental video featuring music by Craig Huxley, Doug de Forest and Gary Chase. It's better than the Weather Channel—and a lot more refreshing! 50 min.
50-8487 *$14.99*

Civilization
"Mankind's journey from cave to computer" is chronicled in this effort from the group Civilization which draws on "sounds and visions from the world's enormous library." Called a "classic example of global soul," this program mixes incredible images with experimental music. 45 min.
50-8488 *$14.99*

Kitaro: World Tour: Kojiki
Taking an 8th-century Japanese fable passed down orally from generation to generation, renowned musician Kitaro transforms the tale into a haunting five-part "story in concert" that showcases his mesmerizing guitar artistry. 55 min.
85-1411 *$14.99*

Kitaro: An Enchanted Evening (1999)
The Japanese guitarist/musician whose work combines traditional Asian instruments and stylings with New Age rhythms and influences is featured in a truly enchanting concert video that proves a feast for eyes and ears alike. 84 min.
85-1328 *$14.99*

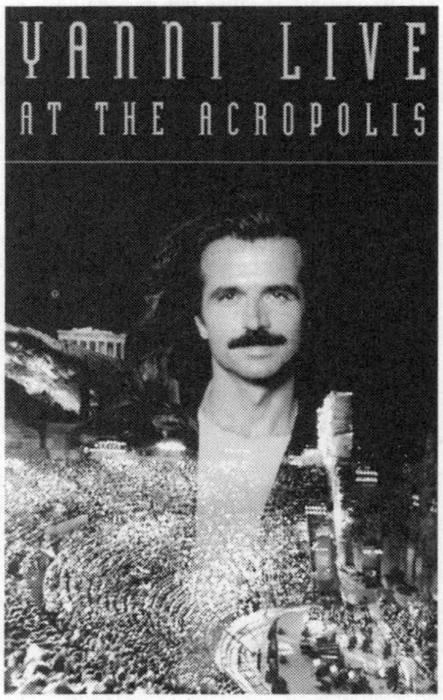

Yanni: Live At The Acropolis
The New Age sensation presents a number of his most popular songs in this hypnotic concert. Among the selections performed by Yanni and the Royal Philharmonic Concert Orchestra are "Keys to Imagination," "Nostalgia," "Reflections of Passion" and "Within Attraction." 99 min.
02-8017 *$19.99*

Yanni: Tribute (1997)
Beneath the majestic backdrops of India's Taj Mahal and the Forbidden City in Beijing, China, the one and only Yanni, backed by a full orchestra, presents a dazzling dual concert experience that includes "Deliverance," "Adagio in C Minor," "Nightingale," "Love Is All," "Niki Nana (We're One)" and more. Also included is the behind-the-scenes documentary "No Borders, No Boundaries." Christopher Plummer narrates. 142 min.
44-4134 *$24.99*

Comedy

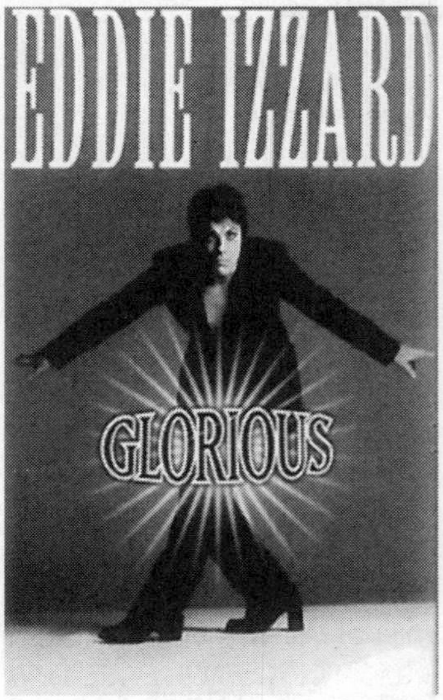

Eddie Izzard: Glorious
It's a blizzard of laughs with the British comedy wizard, as the offbeat Eddie Izzard presents a one-man show of his unique stand-up routines, complete with a gallery of wild characters and off-the-wall observations.
02-8825 *$19.99*

Jerry Seinfeld: I'm Telling You For The Last Time (1998)
Following the end of his long-running sitcom, Jerry Seinfeld returned to his stand-up roots, going on the road for a "farewell tour" of his classic comedy routines. Catch Jerry's final act, live from New York's Broadhurst Theater, with this laugh-filled special that includes footage not seen on TV. 75 min.
44-2201 *$19.99*

Out There In Hollywood
"Kids in the Hall" and "The Larry Sanders Show" regular Scott Thompson is the emcee for a gathering of gay and lesbian comedy stars. Robin Greenspan, Jason Stewart, Shelly Mars, Lea DeLaria and others are featured. 50 min.
15-5350 *$12.99*

Jackie Mason: An Equal Opportunity Offender
A salute to master comic Jackie Mason and his stormy career, featuring Mason on "The Steve Allen Show," the famous incident on "The Ed Sullivan Show" that hurt his career and clips from Jackie's popular Broadway shows. 52 min.
22-1424 *$19.99*

Jackie Mason At The National Press Club
When Jackie Mason goes to Washington, look out! Mason brings his hilarious, uncompromising insights on politics and social issues to a live show from the nation's capital and in front of some of the country's top political journalists. 52 min.
22-1459 *$19.99*

Jackie Mason On Campus
The ever-acerbic Mason travels to England's Oxford University, where a chair is to be named in his honor: "The Jackie Mason Lectureship in Contemporary Judaism." And his speech in front of students and faculty is a hilarious comic performance. 52 min.
22-1460 *$19.99*

Jackie Mason In Israel
The master of mirth goes to the Holy Land and turns in an outrageously funny evening of comedy featuring some of his greatest spiels. The "Land of Milk and Honey" becomes the "Land of Lots of Funnies" when Mason jars the audience with his wit. 56 min.
22-1461 *$19.99*

Jackie Mason: Look Who's Laughing!
You'll be counting yourself among those laughing once you watch this yock-filled concert filmed at the one and only London Palladium and featuring Jackie in his funniest and most insightful routines from his hit Broadway stage shows. 45 min.
53-9986 Was $19.99 *$14.99*

Brett Butler: The Child Ain't Right
The star of "Grace Under Fire" performs her no-holds-barred, Southern-fried brand of comedy in this hilarious comedy performance. An untamed live performance, recommended for adults only. 26 min.
06-2317 *❑$12.99*

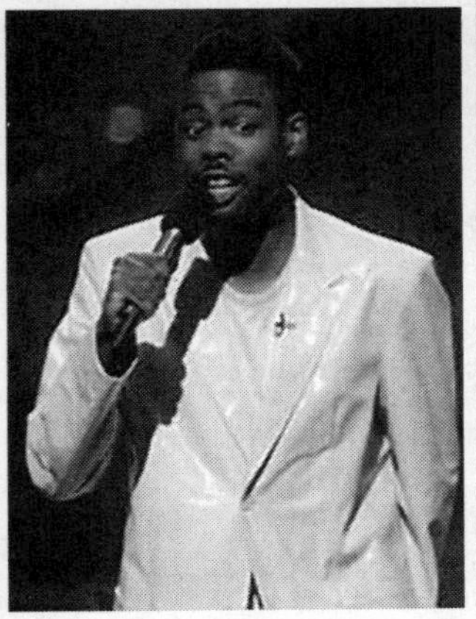

Best Of The Chris Rock Show
One of the hippest, edgiest voices in comedy brings the funniest moments from his Emmy-winning cable TV series to home video. Let Chris rock your world with Maya Angelou's poetic salute to Marion Barry, "The Rules" by Ike Turner, "Taxi Driver Confessions," "When Animals Attack in High Speed Chases II" and more. 59 min.
44-2200 $19.99

Hip Hop Comedy With Chris Rock
Chris Rock will have you rolling with laughter in this evening of urban comedy. Rock does his hilarious thing, along with top laughmakers Mario Joyner (who's opened for Jerry Seinfeld) and Charles Burnett. 60 min.
73-9305 *$14.99*

Hip-Hop Comedy Jam With Chris Rock
Chris Rock hosts this evening of hip-hop ha-ha boasting such top urban comics as Mario Joyner, Charles Barnett, Don Ware and Larry Ragland. Rock will make you roll with his wild observations in this early performance at Rascal's Comedy Club. 60 min.
73-9311 *$14.99*

Chris Rock: Bring The Pain (1996)
Former "Saturday Night Live" regular and voice of "Little Penny" Chris Rock brings hilarious insights to such topics as women, politics and racial relations in this terrific live performance. Chris holds nothing back, so be prepared for uncensored, adults-only material. 60 min.
07-2480 *$19.99*

Chris Rock: Bigger & Blacker (1999)
Live from the stage of New York's famed Apollo Theatre, the raucous Rock offers his own hilarious commentary on topics ranging from marital infidelity and racism to parents and Ricky Martin. 65 min.
44-2210 *$19.99*

Martin Lawrence: You So Crazy (1994)
The star of TV's hit sitcom "Martin" takes his unpredictable, uncensored comedy routine to the big screen in this hilarious concert performance. Lawrence takes no prisoners, offering no-holds-barred commentary on crack addicts, "Driving Miss Daisy," masturbation and other wide-ranging subjects. Lots of laughs and profanity abound in this "adults only" show. Unrated version; 85 min.
44-1968 Was $19.99 *$14.99*

Elayne Boosler: Live Nude Girls
She's made you laugh in comedy clubs around the country and in that zany deodorant commercial, and now you can see Boosler at her finest in a live show in which she tackles such subjects as men, remote controls, fitness freaks and plastic furniture covers. 59 min.
06-2319 *$12.99*

Richard Jeni: Crazy From The Heat
Richard Jeni, star of TV's "Platypus Man" and "The Mask," turns in his trademark, no-holds-barred brand of insightful humor. He takes no prisoners in this outrageous, adults-only show from Miami. 58 min.
06-2381 *$14.99*

The Jim Bailey Experience
See Jim Bailey at his best, performing his uncanny impressions of Judy Garland, Barbra Streisand, Marilyn Monroe and Madonna. He's the world's most renowned female impersonator, and included on the program are clips from TV shows, a photo layout, and more. 60 min.
73-9010 *$39.99*

Gilda Live (1980)
Live, from New York, it's Gilda Radner on Broadway. All of her great "SNL" characters are here, from Emily Litella to Candy Slice, plus a lot of things she couldn't say on TV. 90 min.
19-1035 *$14.99*

Eddie Murphy Raw (1987)
The language is raw, but the comedy is well done. Eddie Murphy shines in an outrageous concert film, taking on everyone from Michael Jackson to Bill Cosby, from feminists to bigots. Robert Townsend helms this non-stop, not-for-the-young-or-easily-offended laugh experience. 91 min.
06-1526 *$14.99*

Harry Anderson: Hello, Sucker!
The star of "Night Court" and "Dave's World" shows why he was one of the country's top magicians in this live show in which he adopts the alter ego of con man "Harry the Hat" and performs some of his funniest tricks. Taped in 1985 at the Comedy and Magic Club in Hermosa Beach, the program also features guests John Larroquette and Rich Hall.
76-7447 *$19.99*

The Lenny Bruce Performance Film/ Thank You, Masked Man (1965)
A double header of Lenny Bruce at his best. "Performance" features Lenny at his uncensored best, live, speaking about sex, religion, politics and ethnicity. And "Thank You, Masked Man" is the animated Lone Ranger spoof written by and featuring the voice of Bruce. 68 min. total.
15-5222 *$19.99*

The Paula Poundstone Show
Offbeat, on-target hilarity can be found in this HBO special showcasing Paula Poundstone, who mixes mirthful monologues and inventive routines, with guests like Pat Benatar and former astronaut Scott Carpenter. 60 min.
58-8118 *$12.99*

Paul Rodriguez Live: I Need The Couch (1989)
Off-the-cuff comedy that's oh-so-true and oh-so-raunchy. Hispanic rib-tickler Rodriguez lashes out on communism, marriage, policemen, sex and much more. Recommended for adults only. 59 min.
44-1719 Was $59.99 *$14.99*

Lily Tomlin: Appearing Nitely (1979)
Lily Tomlin's Tony-winning show is captured in all its hilarity and poignancy, appearing as a host of her most popular characters, including the suburban girl, the bratty adolescent and the bag lady. There's also some backstage footage of Lily and some famous members of the audience. 85 min.
76-2004 *$19.99*

Lily: Sold Out! (1981)
Won over by the glitziness of Las Vegas, Lily Tomlin takes her array of personae to the city's famous Strip where she plays her favorite characters, as well as lounge singer Tommy Velour. Among the guest stars are Paul Anka, Joan Rivers, Dolly Parton and Liberace. 77 min.
76-2006 *$19.99*

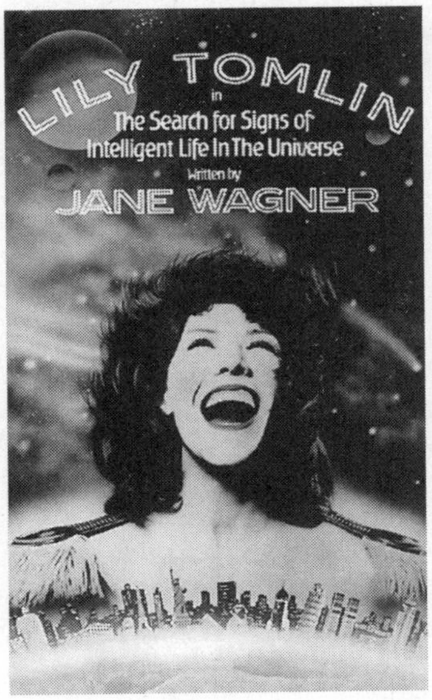

The Search For Signs Of Inteligent Life In The Universe (1991)
Lily Tomlin's Tony Award-winning performance in Jane Wagner's extraordinary play loses none of its brilliance in its transfer to the screen. Join Lily as Trudy the bag lady, taking a group of aliens thru a whirlwind tour of humankind in all its splendors and frailties. Tomlin essays many characters, including Agnes Angst and Kate, a bored socialite. 120 min.
76-2001 Was $89.99 *$29.99*

The Lily Tomlin Video Collection
This five-volume set features "Search for Signs of Intelligent Life in the Universe"; "Lily: Sold Out!," "Lily for President," "Appearing Nitely" and "Ernestine: Peak Performances," all including never-before-seen footage. 360 min.
76-2002 Save $35.00! *$69.99*

Sam Kinison Family Entertainment Hour
A live concert featuring the always-outrageous comic for whom no subject was too controversial. Joining Kinison in this performance at the Wiltern Theatre in Los Angeles by The Randy Hansen Band, a group of sexy gals and his wife-to-be, Malika. 50 min.
15-5263 Was $19.99 *$14.99*

Sam Kinison: Banned
High-decibel rock and high-decibel comedy from the outrageous and somewhat manic Sam Kinison. This unchained, uncensored program includes the videos for Sam's renditions of "Under My Thumb," "Mississippi Queen" and "Wild Thing." 60 min.
19-3151 *$19.99*

Sam Kinison: Why Did We Laugh?
His taboo-busting brand of humor and banshee-like stage presence made him a comedy superstar, and his untimely death in 1992 at the age of 38 made him a legend. Follow the meteoric career of comic Sam Kinison, and see his blistering stage persona in action, in this video tribute that also features appearances by Rodney Dangerfield, Jay Leno, Dennis Miller, Richard Pryor and others. 90 min.
53-9978 *$19.99*

Jeff Foxworthy: You Might Be A Redneck If...
The popular Southern-fried comic is a hoot-and-a-half in this hilarious performance from Georgia. Jeff reflects on dating, family life and redneck chic. 30 min.
53-8186 Was $19.99 *$14.99*

Jeff Foxworthy: Totally Committed (1998)
Commit yourself—to laughter—with the best-selling comedy album star and master of Southern-fried stand-up, as Jeff Foxworthy offers his hilarious insights into life below the Mason-Dixon Line in a live show. 60 min.
44-2161 Was $19.99 *$14.99*

Howie Mandel: Hooray For Howie Would
And hooray for this howling hullabaloo of Howie hilarity, as the ever-manic Mandel takes to the stage for a riotous evening of his crazy comedy routines and daffy observations on everyday life. 60 min.
47-2066 *$14.99*

Gallagher: Stuck In The Sixties
It's a groovy gagfest when the inimitable Mr. G. takes on the silliest fads and moments from the '60s and takes on "the decade that refuses to die." 60 min.
06-1233 *$19.99*

Gallagher: Over Your Head
That mustachioed maven of mirth and madness returns for a madcap comedy show that goes over, above and beyond anything you've ever seen, all with that special Gallagher magic. 58 min.
06-1319 *$19.99*

Dr. Demento: 20th Anniversary Collection
Celebrating two decades of radio dementia, the good Doctor hosts this collection of the greatest novelty music videos of all time. Included are artists like Cab Calloway ("Minnie the Moocher"), Spike Jones ("Cocktails for Two"), Barnes and Barnes ("Fish Heads"), "Weird Al" Yankovic ("I Lost on Jeopardy") and many more. 50 min.
15-5169 Was $19.99 *$14.99*

Milton Berle's Mad World Of Comedy
Who better than "Uncle Miltie" to host this all-star salute to the greatest yockmeisters in show biz history? Groucho Marx, Bob Hope, Flip Wilson and Albert Brooks are just some of the comedy greats featured in this laugh-a-second special. 60 min.
15-5145 Was $19.99 *$14.99*

More Milton Berle's Mad World Of Comedy
A second helping of skits, one-liners and classic comedy routines, presided over by "The Thief of Bad Gags" himself. Joining Berle are guests Mort Sahl, Dick Martin and Pat Buttram, and there are vintage clips starring Will Rogers, Abbott and Costello, Martin and Lewis, Lenny Bruce and others. 88 min.
15-5158 Was $19.99 *$14.99*

Dirty, Dirty Jokes
Andrew Dice Clay, Jackie "The Jokeman" Martling and Robert Schimmel lead the comedic troops in this assault on your senses. Redd Foxx plays host for an evening of lewd, crude and rude yucks. 58 min.
47-1308 Was $39.99 *$14.99*

George Carlin: Jammin' In New York
The ever-popular comic turns in a dynamo performance at New York's Paramount Theater, providing hilarious insight into such subjects as the Persian Gulf War, the environment, relationships and more. 59 min.
02-2508 Was $19.99 *$14.99*

George Carlin: Doin' It Again
Master comic George Carlin turns in a classic performance covering such favorite topics as politics, profanity, "life's little moments," social criticism and more. 59 min.
02-2526 Was $19.99 *$14.99*

Carlin On Campus
George Carlin takes his acute observations and rapid-fire wit to UCLA, where students roll down the aisle with laughter. Quips on everything are in store, including some classic material. 59 min.
47-1293 *$14.99*

Comedy's Dirtiest Dozen (1992)
A group of the wildest comics in the world get together to offer their funniest and raunchiest material in this no-holds-barred show. Tim Allen, Jackie "The Jokeman" Martling, Chris Rock, Bill Hicks and Thea Vidale are among the jokemeisters who let it all hang out when the spotlight goes on. For adults only. 95 min.
53-9961 *$19.99*

Kevin Pollak: Stop With The Kicking
Comic/actor Kevin Pollak ("A Few Good Men," "The Usual Suspects") turns in a rapid-fire evening of non-stop laughs in this concert that features a host of hilarious impressions of the likes of Schwarzenegger, Shatner, Nicholson and Albert Brooks. 58 min.
02-2430 Was $59.99 *$14.99*

Andy Kaufman: Tank You Vedy Much
His outrageous comedy antics often blurred the line between acting and reality. Now you can follow the life and many personalities of Andy Kaufman with this retrospective that includes interviews, exclusive family photos, and TV clips of Kaufman at work. 35 min.
10-1748 *$14.99*

Andy Kaufman: I'm From Hollywood
The comedic talents of the late, great Andy Kaufman are showcased in this retrospective of the man known as the co-star of "Taxi," a coed wrestling champ, and one of the most innovative comedians ever. Included here are interviews with "Taxi" colleagues Tony Danza and Marilu Henner. 60 min.
63-7040 Was $19.99 *$14.99*

The Andy Kaufman Special (1977)
Master impressionist, amateur wrestler and "bad boy" of comedy Andy Kaufman is featured in his own TV special, unaired for two years. Along with Andy's Elvis impersonation and "Foreign Man" character are guest stars Cindy Williams and Howdy Doody. 50 min.
05-1439 Was $29.99 *$14.99*

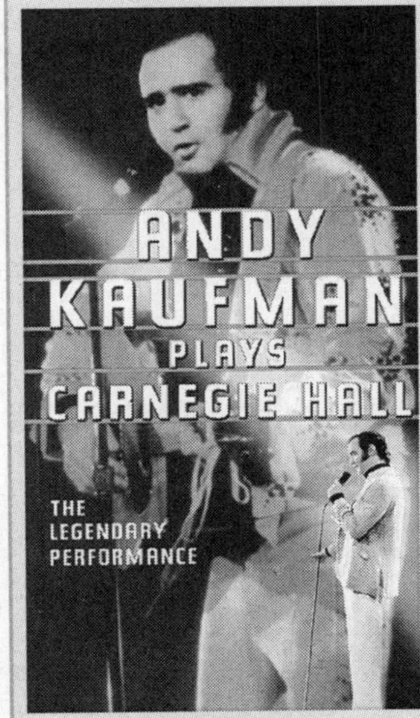

Andy Kaufman Plays Carnegie Hall (1979)
New York's famed concert hall is the setting for a unique evening of comedy with the legendary Andy Kaufman. Watch as Kaufman wows the audience with his impression of Elvis, a demonstration of inter-gender wrestling, some snappy tunes from Tony Clifton and more, including a guest appearance by Robin Williams. Sorry, milk and cookies not included. 78 min.
12-3295 *$12.99*

Andy Kaufman: The Midnight Special (1981)
Great January, 1981, episode of the rock TV series gave full reign to Kaufman's mad genius, including his Elvis impersonation, the African percussion rendition of "It's a Small World," lounge singer Tony Clifton and much more; Freddie "Boom Boom" Cannon and Slim Whitman also appear. 55 min.
04-5698 *$12.99*

Andy Kaufman: The Andy Kaufman Show (1983)
The unforgettably off-center antics of comedian Andy Kaufman take center stage in a hilarious evening of laughs; also features comedienne Elayne Boosler. 59 min.
47-3168 Was $59.99 *$14.99*

Richard Pryor: Live And Smokin' (1971)
Go back to the formative years of one of America's most inventive comic talents with this early stand-up show, recorded at New York's Improv club. Pryor pulls no punches in an "adults only" concert that includes his outrageous "Wino Preacher & Willie the Junkie" sketch. 46 min.
47-1333 Was $19.99 *$14.99*

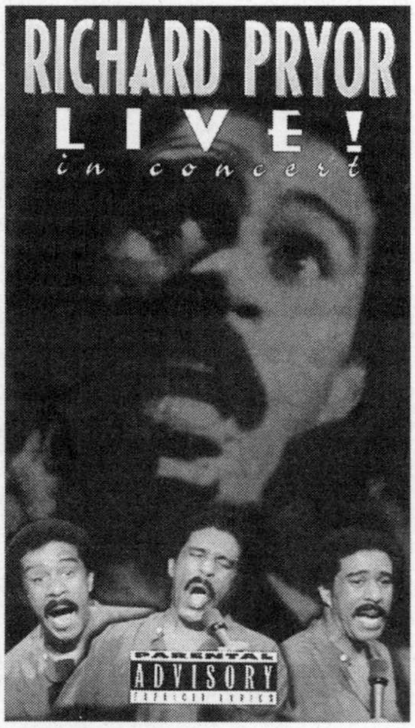

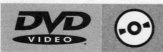

Richard Pryor: Live In Concert (1979)
This is Richard Pryor at his best...uncensored, wildly imaginative and uproariously funny. The comic's classic first concert film features Pryor discussing such topics as sex, racism, surviving a heart attack and the deaths of his beloved pet monkeys. 78 min.
47-1002 *$19.99*

Richard Pryor: Live On The Sunset Strip (1982)
Pryor's back and burning! Hysterically funny, "a rare experience, often hilarious and very moving. He is one of the great originals," wrote Vincent Canby of the New York Times. You'll be roaring and crying at the same time. 82 min.
02-1146 *$14.99*

Richard Pryor: Here And Now (1983)
Pryor is back in this uproarious concert tape. He talks about his bouts with drugs, booze and other real-life subjects, with pointed, hilarious observation. As you will find here, he's one of the world's funniest men. 94 min.
02-1281 Was $79.99 *$14.99*

One Night Stand: Damon Wayans And Bill Maher
Wayans, star of "In Living Color," "Mo' Money" and "Major Payne," brings his outrageous comedy act to the stage. Then, the always "Politically Incorrect" Bill Maher offers up his hilarious insights into politics and relationships. 60 min.
58-8116 *$12.99*

Wise Cracks (1992)
Women comics are the focus of this hilarious and insightful documentary featuring live performances, interviews and film clips. Whoopi Goldberg, Paula Poundstone, Carol Burnett, Phyllis Diller, Kim Wayans and Ellen DeGeneres are among the comediennes spotlighted in this uncensored film. 93 min.
76-9047 Was $49.99 *$19.99*

Jerry Clower Live: Vol. 1
If you're looking for some down home laughs, this live performance by country humorist Jerry Clower is just the ticket. Among his many tales shared here are "King Solomon's Words," "Marcel and the Troop Train" and "MCA Records Visits Yazoo City." 30 min.
07-4028 *$12.99*

Jerry Clower Live: Vol. 2
Ready for a second helpin' of Brother Jerry's good-natured, country-flavored comedy? Here you'll see him on stage as he talks about "Eatin' Grits in Memphis," "McDonald's Hamburgers in Russia," "George Jones and Manuel Noriega" and more. 30 min.
07-4029 *$12.99*

Tim Allen Rewires America
With toolbelt securely in place and tongue firmly in cheek, Allen expounds on "men's stuff" in this hilarious concert. Hear Tim relate stories about grunting, burping, babies and other outrageous subjects. 31 min.
06-2380 □*$14.99*

Tim Allen: Men Are Pigs (1990)
The star of "Home Improvement" and "The Santa Clause" brought his testosterone-laden brand of stand-up comedy to this hilarious live special, as Tim explains the how-to's of lawn care, shopping at the hardware section at Sears, and other manly facts of life. 30 min.
06-2288 □*$12.99*

Ernestine: Peak Experiences
"One-ringy-dingy, two ringy-dingys..." The ever-popular operator, Ernestine, appears in a collection of hilarious bits culled from "Saturday Night Live," the Emmy Awards and other sources from 1969 to 1985. Lily will leave you laughing! 30 min.
76-2003 *$14.99*

Joan Rivers: Abroad In London (1992)
"God Save the Queen...of Comedy," as Joan stars in a live comedy special from "across the pond," discussing such topics as plastic surgery mishaps and the role large diamonds play in preserving a marriage. There's also a guest appearance by the inimitable Dame Edna Everage. 57 min.
06-2290 *$12.99*

Billy Crystal: Midnight Train To Moscow
Take a trip back to comedy's original "Borscht Belt," as stage/TV/screen star Billy Crystal brings an evening of "Jokenost" to an audience of Muscovites at the famed Pushkin Theatre, and also introduces you to such little-known Soviet sites as Leninland. 72 min.
44-1712 Was $19.99 □*$14.99*

The Best Of...What's Left Of... Not Only...But Also: The Video
Reunited for the first time in years, the inimitable comedy team of Peter Cook and Dudley Moore present a rib-tickling assortment of their greatest and funniest skits, sketches and characters. 90 min.
04-2470 Was $19.99 *$14.99*

Without You, I'm Nothing (1990)
The ever-audacious Sandra Bernhard adapts her one-woman revue for this outrageous blend of comedy and music. Bernhard adopts a variety of personas while she muses on growing up Jewish at Christmastime, the Motown and disco sounds, New Age thinking and more. 94 min.
50-7062 Was $59.99 *$14.99*

Sandra Bernhard: I'm Still Here...Damn It! (1999)
Sandra's hit one-woman stage show has been captured in all of its outrageous glory in this program that features extra footage not seen in the original HBO broadcast. Bernhard sings "On the Runway," a satiric salute to supermodels, and offers insights on Lilith Fair, sex, drugs and the beautiful women of Hollywood. 90 min.
02-9194 *$19.99*

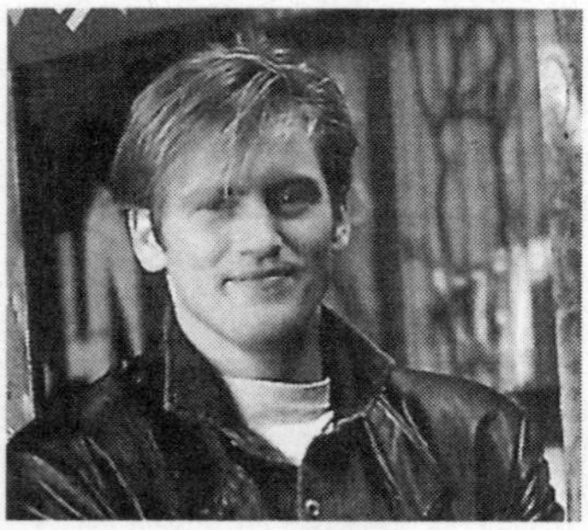

Denis Leary: No Cure For Cancer (1992)
The acerbic, chain-smoking comic's acclaimed one-man show, which ran for months in New York, brings his act to home video. Uninhibited and uncensored, Leary vents his anger at vegetarians, tobacco foes, Beatles assassins and other societal woes. 63 min.
06-2289 □*$12.99*

The Comedy Store 20th Birthday
Los Angeles' legendary comedy club has played host to some of the biggest names in show business over its two decades, and many of them return to pay tribute in an all-star special. Performing live on stage are Louie Anderson, Jim Carrey, Pauly Shore and, in a rare appearance, Richard Pryor; Arsenio Hall, David Letterman and Robin Williams share their Comedy Store memories; Andy Kaufman and Sam Kinison are seen in vintage clips; and more. 50 min.
89-5036 *$14.99*

Chonda Pierce: On Her Soapbox
Christian comic Chonda Pierce is sure to keep you laughing with her insights that mix everyday occurrences with peoples' relationship with God. Taped before a sold-out audience at Nashville's famed Ryman Auditorium, Chonda delivers a hilarious evening—on her soapbox! 97 min.
04-5687 *$14.99*

Andrew Dice Clay: No Apologies
Andrew Dice Clay takes on world politics, the sexes and nursery rhymes in a ribald concert performance at Westbury Music Fair during the summer of '93. See Dice work out before the show and get ready behind the scenes in this bold, adults-only comicfest. 65 min.
02-7926 *$29.99*

Andrew Dice Clay And His Gang: The Valentine's Day Massacre
Before he dropped the "Dice" and became a big sitcom star in the hit series "Bless This House," Andrew Clay was well-known for his no-holds-barred, adult-oriented comedy. Here he's at his most profane, rattling off his warped insights on a variety of topics. He's also joined by fellow comedy outlaws John Mulrooney and Paul Mooney. 105 min.
50-7329 *$19.99*

Dice Rules (1991)
Hickory Dickory Dock...We'll stop there and let you hear the rest of this "X-rated" nursery rhyme by watching the uncut concert film starring the notorious Andrew Dice Clay, the world's most controversial comic. See and hear the leather-clad "Diceman" at his raunchiest in a sold-out Madison Square Garden. WARNING: Graphic language; adults only. 88 min.
47-2050 Was $89.99 *$14.99*

Andrew Dice Clay: I'm Over Here Now
The ever-acerbic, always-outrageous "Diceman" delivers the type of off-color comedy you desire in this hilarious live performance from the Las Vegas Hilton. Not for the squeamish, Dice shows you why he is one of the most reviled and revered talents around. Features behind-the-scenes footage. 60 min.
50-8670 *$19.99*

Life's A Joke
Looking for a good laugh? You're bound to find dozens in these videos that feature real people from all walks of life sharing their favorite jokes before the camera. They're funny, zany and racy. "Say, did you hear the one about...?" Each tape runs about 60 min.

Life's A Joke, Vol. 1
50-8215 *$14.99*

Life's A Joke, Vol. 2
50-8216 *$14.99*

Def Comedy Jam All-Stars
This hilarious collection of HBO programs from producer Russell Simmons offers the hottest black comics in the world, performing no-holds-barred material in outrageous live shows. See lots of hot, rising comics before they became movie and TV stars. Each tape runs about 55 min.

Def Comedy Jam All-Stars, Vol. 1
Features Martin Lawrence, D.L. Hughley, Adele Givens and J. Anthony Brown.
50-8648 *$14.99*

Def Comedy Jam All-Stars, Vol. 2
Features Chris Rock, Bernie Mac, Chris Tucker and Martin Lawrence.
50-8650 *$14.99*

Def Comedy Jam All-Stars, Vol. 3
Features Bill Bellamy, Martin Lawrence, Eddie Griffin and J'vonne Pearson.
50-8651 *$14.99*

Def Comedy Jam All-Stars, Vol. 4
Features Dave Chappelle, D.L. Hughley, Bernie Mac and Steve Harvey.
50-8652 *$14.99*

Def Comedy Jam All-Stars, Vol. 5
Features Jamie Foxx, Martin Lawrence, Chris Tucker and Sheryl Underwood.
50-8653 *$14.99*

Def Comedy Jam All-Stars, Vol. 6
Features Martin Lawrence, Yvette Wilson, Arnez J. and Ellen Cleghorne.
50-8654 *$14.99*

Def Comedy Jam All-Stars, Vol. 7
Features Mark Curry, D.C. Curry, Arnez J. and Steve Harvey.
50-8655 *$14.99*

Def Comedy Jam All-Stars, Vol. 8
Features George Wallace, Cedric the Entertainer, Coco and Mike Epps.
50-8656 *$14.99*

Def Comedy Jam All-Stars, Vol. 9
Features Joe Torry, Sommore, Will E., DJ Robo and Drew Fraser.
50-8657 *$14.99*

Def Comedy Jam All-Stars, Vol. 10
Features Steve Harvey, Ricky Harris, Tracy Morgan and Chocolate.
50-8658 *$14.99*

Mambo Mouth: John Leguizamo
The acclaimed one-man stageshow from Hispanic actor-comic-writer John Leguizamo is a telling look at Latino life in America. Among the six characters he portrays are "The Crossover King," a Latino-turned-Japanese executive; "Loco Louie," a sex-obsessed teen; and "Manny the Fanny," a female prostitute. 60 min.
02-7547 *$19.99*

Allen & Rossi Comedy Special
Hello dere! The fabulous comedy team of Marty Allen and Steve "The Legend" Rossi stars in their very own comedy special, filled with classic routines like "Doctor David Dirty," "The Winetaster" and "Crazy Leggs Allen." On hand are guests Jerry Lewis, Rich Little, Don Rickles, Engelbert Humperdinck and Martin Sheen. Who needs Las Vegas? 40 min.
22-1375 *$19.99*

Rodney Dangerfield: I Can't Take It No More!
Angie Dickinson, Andy Kaufman, Harold Ramis and Donna Dixon are among the guests dropping in on Rodney Dangerfield in this riotously funny TV special from 1983. There are some great skits, lots of surprises and Rodney with some great zingers. 47 min.
10-3408 *$12.99*

Bill Cosby: Himself (1984)
Bill performs his hilarious comedy routines in this concert film. There's the Cosby Clan and sweet and funny reminiscing of the good old days in Philadelphia, as well as observations on the current state of affairs. 104 min.
04-1809 Was $29.99 □*$14.99*

The Best Of Spike Jones, Vol. 1
Long before "Dr. Demento" and "Weird Al" Yankovic, Spike Jones and his City Slickers made madcap music. These highlights from their 1950s TV show feature some of their zaniest hits. Cocktails For Two (Clink! Clink!). 51 min.
06-1409 *$19.99*

The Best Of Spike Jones, Vol. 2
More symphonic silliness that's louder than a plaid sportcoat and funnier than a night at the Met. Spike and his City Slickers rev up with "Indian Love Call," "Stranger in Paradise," and more. 53 min.
06-1438 *$19.99*

The Best Of Spike Jones, Vol. 3
The band that plays for fun makes mincemeat of the popular tunes "Bye Bye Blues," "Pop Goes the Weasel," "Cocktails for Two" and "Running Wild," and welcomes guests Howdy Doody, Buffalo Bob Smith, Clarabell and ZaSu Pitts. 54 min.
06-1615 *$19.99*

Spike Jones: A Musical Wreck-We-Um!
Spike Jones turns up the volume on his wild musicianship in this program that gives new meaning to the phrase "looney tunes." A battle of the bands, Billy Barty's imitation of Cagney singing "Yankee Doodle Dandy," George Rock crooning "All I Want for Christmas Is My Two Front Teeth" and more musical mirth are featured. 51 min.
06-1881 □*$19.99*

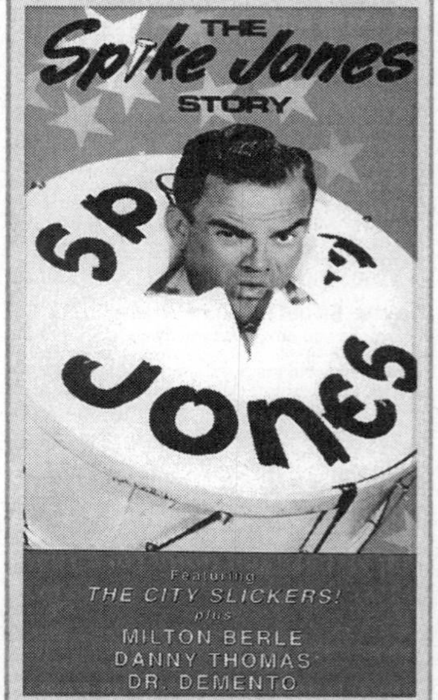

The Spike Jones Story
A look at the loony musicologist who took popular and classical tunes and turned them into something altogether wild and zany. This program recaps his life and career and includes such favorites as "Cocktails for Two," "Der Fuerher's Face" and "All I Want for Christmas Is My Two Front Teeth." 60 min.
22-1231 *$19.99*

Saturday Night Sleazies, Vol. 1
Two "classic" softcore features from the early '60s make for a campy evening of fun, drive-in style. See the pent-up passions and wild drug-filled orgies of "College Girl Confidential" and "Suburban Confidential." They don't make 'em like this anymore! 150 min. total.
15-5013 Was $29.99 *$24.99*

Saturday Night Sleazies, Vol. 2
Another classic "roadhouse" double feature, featuring two choice items of '60s softcore. Early sex queen Marsha Jordan stars in the lusty epic "Lady Godiva Meets Tom Jones," while a nerd's pin-up fantasies come to life in "Bachelor's Dream." 150 min. total.
15-5017 Was $29.99 *$24.99*

Saturday Night Sleazies, Vol. 3
Drive-in atmosphere so authentic, you'll want to climb into the back seat and neck! Check in for torrid passion at "Motel Confidential," and see how the white-collar crowd "turns on" in "Office Love-In." Vintage "adults only" '60s sexploitation! 150 min. total.
15-5036 Was $29.99 *$24.99*

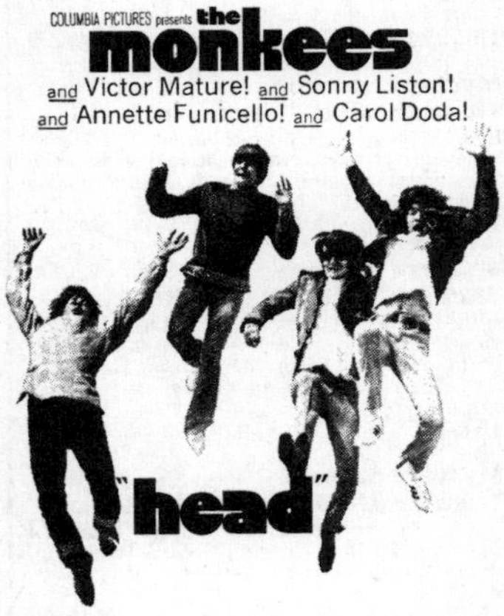
COLUMBIA PICTURES presents the
monkees
and Victor Mature! and Sonny Liston!
and Annette Funicello! and Carol Doda!
"head"

Head (1968)
The Monkees' only feature film is a riotous hodgepodge of spaced-out comedy vignettes mixed with a collage of old film clips and cameos Frank Zappa, Victor Mature, Teri Garr, Annette Funicello, Carol Doda and others. This classic culmination of Monkeemania was co-authored by Jack Nicholson and director Bob Rafelson. 86 min.
02-1636 Was $69.99 *$19.99*

True Stories (1986)
A New Wave "Our Town," courtesy of co-scripter/director/narrator David Byrne, takes us through a quirky Texas town populated by living "National Enquirer" headlines like the Laziest Woman in America, the Man who Advertises for a Wife, and others. John Goodman, Spalding Gray, Swoosie Kurtz star; music by Talking Heads. 111 min.
19-1562 Was $19.99 *$14.99*

The Psychotronic Man (1980)
Egregiously bad sci-fi shocker that has become a cult item and lent its name to an entire film genre. Producer/co-scripter Peter Spelson plays a Chicago barber with the mental ability to look at people, blink, and force them to die instantly or leap out of windows (non-tippers, beware!). Christopher Carbis, Robin Newton co-star in this psychotronic treat. 88 min.
48-1182 *$59.99*

Star Struck (1983)
"Babes in Arms" meets the New Wave in this quirky, song-filled comedy from Australia. Jo Kennedy is a teenage would-be rock star who, spurred on by her younger cousin/manager, tries to win a TV talent contest. Features hilarious musical numbers and a great soundtrack from Mental as Anything and The Swingers. Directed by Gillian Armstrong ("My Brilliant Career"). 93 min.
53-1161 *$19.99*

The Toxic Avenger (1985)
After being dumped on by his peers and dumped in chemical wastes, a 98-pound nerd becomes the disfigured defender who cleans up the town his way. Hilarious violence and gory humor highlight this wild sci-fi send-up featuring "the first superhero from New Jersey." 87 min.
47-3190 *$14.99*

The Toxic Avenger: The Director's Cut
The classic Troma effort starring the mutated superstar is available in a special, unrated director's edition that offers once-deleted scenes of gore; a head-crushing sequence; and a segment in which Toxie plays golf. 90 min.
46-8016 *$19.99*

The Toxic Avenger Part II: Director's Cut (1989)
The world's ugliest and most unusual crimefighter is back! Spawned from toxic waste, the Avenger has cleaned up Tromaville and even found romance, but sinister businessmen lure him to Tokyo with the hope of doing him in and making America safe for chemical dumping. Second outrageous "Toxi" tale stars Ron Fazio, Phoebe Legere. 96 min.
19-1720 □*$14.99*

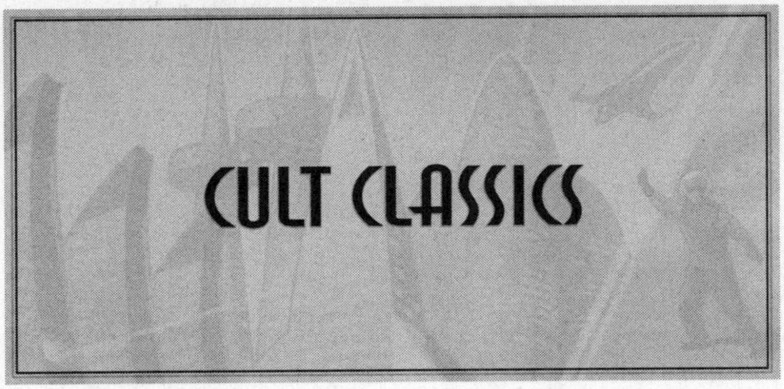
CULT CLASSICS

The Robot vs. The Aztec Mummy (1959)
Mad Dr. Krupp builds a robot with a human brain and limbs of steel to raid the treasure room in an Aztec pyramid, a trove that's guarded by a mummified warrior. Dio Mio! 65 min.
68-8215 *$19.99*

Rock 'N' Roll Wrestling Women vs. The Aztec Ape (1962)
You say you like gorgeous Mexican female wrestlers? You say you like mad scientists who create robot gorillas and artificial girl grapplers? And you say you don't care if the actors' words don't match their lips? Well, have we got a film for you! Todo el mundo se diverte! AKA: "Doctor of Doom." 75 min.
15-5037 *$14.99*

Attack Of The Mayan Mummy (1963)
A woman is hypnotized by a greedy archeologist so she can recall her past life as a princess and lead him to a fortune in buried jewels. "Raiders"-style adventure meets New Age-style channeling meets Mexican-style monsters; Richard Webb, Nina Knight star. 77 min.
68-8063 Was $19.99 *$14.99*

Rock 'N' Roll Wrestling Women vs. The Aztec Mummy (1964)
From our friends South of the Border comes this incredible tale of horror and hammer-locks. Looters of an ancient Aztec tomb release a vengeful mummy. In the other corner, Prince Fugiyata and the Oriental female wrestlers. Muy loco y extranjo! 60 min.
15-5058 *$14.99*

The Beatniks (1959)
A "hep cat" gang member with a golden throat is discovered by a recording talent scout, but the would-be singing star's "friends" aren't happy with his shot at fame and get him mixed up in murder! Totally "flipsville" teen tale directed by Paul Frees (the voice of Boris Badenov) stars Peter Breck, Tony Travis. 78 min.
79-5164 Was $24.99 *$19.99*

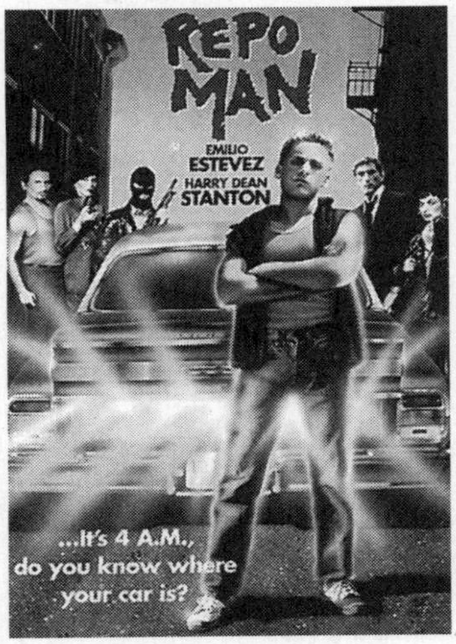
REPO MAN
EMILIO ESTEVEZ
HARRY DEAN STANTON
...It's 4 A.M., do you know where your car is?

Repo Man (1984)
Young L.A. punk Emilio Estevez gets an indoctrination into the sleazy world of car repossession by "repo man" Harry Dean Stanton in director Alex Cox's offbeat comedy/fantasy of teen rebels, government agents and missing space aliens. Great rock soundtrack includes Iggy Pop, Black Flag and The Circle Jerks. 93 min.
07-1212 Was $19.99 *$14.99*

Repo Man (Letterboxed Collector's Edition)
Also available in a theatrical, widescreen format. Includes original and video trailers.
08-8882 *$14.99*

Girl Gang (1954)
A lost female juvenile delinquent film has been unearthed and it it's something to behold! The hellcats in the title get off on marijuana and heroin, steal cars, assault boys and delve into other areas of sordidness. Joanne Arnold and Timothy Farrell star in this production from noted schlockmeister George Weiss ("Glen or Glenda").
79-5670 Was $24.99 *$19.99*

Teenage Wolfpack (1957)
Juvenile delinquency runs rampant in Germany. Gangs, robbery, violence, murder...you name it! Starring Henry Bookholt (later Horst Buchholz), billed as "the next James Dean." 90 min. Dubbed in English.
68-8451 Was $19.99 *$14.99*

Horrible Horror
"Cool Ghoul" Zacherley is in the process of cleaning out the film vault in his dungeon, and we're given the pleasure of seeing some of the spookiest and zaniest horror flicks that Hollywood had to offer. See clips from "Brainiac," "Devil Bat," "Glen or Glenda," plus rare footage of Bela, Lon, Boris and more. 110 min.
10-2112 *$12.99*

Trasharama
A ticket to exploitation thrills, featuring trailers for faves like "Teenage Crime Wave" and "The Shameless Sex," as well as zany propaganda shorts and other goodies. Trash around the clock with this tape!
10-7938 Was $19.99 *$14.99*

Sleazemania
Sick? Disgusting? Lacking in redeeming social value? Maybe, but you'll love watching these previews and clips from some of the weirdest films ever made. "Jailbait," "Scum of the Earth," "Pin Down Girls," "Flesh Merchants" and other cinema sleaze. 60 min.
15-5001 *$19.99*

Sleazemania Strikes Back
More "coming attraction" trailers from the strangest, sickest, downright sleaziest films ever made. "Thrill" to such works as "Dance Hall Racket," "Honeymoon of Terror," "Sex Slaves in Bondage" and other greats. 60 min.
15-5005 *$19.99*

Sleazemania III: The Good, The Bad, And The Sleazy
Third tasteless treasure trove of total tackiness to taint your TV! Among the priceless finds highlighted are Lenny Bruce's rare smoker "Dance Hall Racket," "Mondo Psycho," "Tijuana After Midnight," and "Smut Peddler Meets Emmanuel"! 60 min.
15-5031 *$19.99*

Sleazemania On Parade
You won't want to miss this parade filled with sleazoid appearances from the likes of Gene Autry ("The Phantom Empire"), Larry Drake ("This Stuff'll Kill Ya!") and Angie Dickinson ("Big Bad Mama"), plus trailers for such cinematic slime as "The Naked Zoo," "I Passed for White," "Dr. Silkini's Original Spook Show," "Girl in the Woods" and many more.
79-5338 Was $24.99 *$19.99*

Mondo Sleazo (Drive-In Sleaze)
Dozens of trailers from the finest drive-in films ever driven to! "Marijuana," "The Reluctant Sadist," "Girl from S.I.N.," "Glen or Glenda," "A Bucket of Blood," "Superchick" and many more! Relive those favorite backseat moments with this gem! 100 min.
62-1260 *$19.99*

Mondo Sleazo Returns
A second sleazo serving of "coming soon" trailers from the silliest, sickest, strangest movies of all time. Think you can stand "Girls for Rent," "Nazi Love Camp 27," "They Came from Within," "I, Monster," "Kung Fu Fury" and others? 100 min.
62-1361 *$19.99*

It Came From Hollywood (1982)
An outlandish look at some of the worst films ever made! Dan Aykroyd, John Candy, Cheech and Chong and Gilda Radner host this compilation film featuring awful horror movies, outrageous exploitation yarns and even a tribute to Ed Wood, the notorious director of "Plan 9 from Outer Space." 80 min.
06-1171 Was $59.99 *$14.99*

Confessions Of A Vice Baron
Hollywood's first subject for a compilation film was none other than the guard-yer-kids genre of the 1930s. Catch highlights from "Mad Youth," "Smashing the Vice Trust," and other camp classics in this "That's Entertainment" of exploitation. 70 min.
50-1506 *$19.99*

Pin Down Girls (1951)
Rock 'em, sock 'em schlock about a crooked wrestling promoter and the gritty lady grapplers who are a part of his stable. Timothy Farrell ("Glen or Glenda"), Clare Mortensen and Peaches Page star. AKA: "Blonde Pickup," "Racket Girls." 81 min.
68-8268 *$19.99*

Sgt. Kabukiman N.Y.P.D. (1997)
He's the most outrageous superhero since the Toxic Avenger, using such weapons as heat-seeking chopsticks and flying parasols to augment his martial arts abilities to combat evil. Watch as New York policeman Harry Griswold is transformed into the magical Sgt. Kabukiman in this wild action-comedy-fantasy from the fine folk at Troma. Unrated director's cut; 105 min.
46-8023 Was $59.99 *$14.99*

Vegas In Space (1995)
Life in space is a drag in this truly astonishing, gender-bending sci-fi farce in which four "male" astronauts prohibited from landing on the all-girl planet Clitoris take a special pill that turns them into women and offers them an opportunity to impersonate 20th-century Earth showgirls. And guess what? They're fabulous at it! With Ginger Quest, Doris Fish and Tippi. 85 min.
46-8009 Was $69.99 *$14.99*

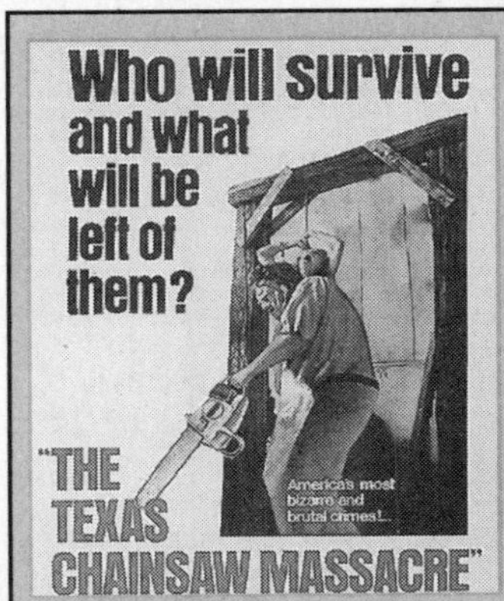
Who will survive and what will be left of them?
America's most bizarre and brutal crimes!
"THE TEXAS CHAINSAW MASSACRE"

The Texas Chainsaw Massacre (1974)
Director Tobe Hooper's modern horror classic that helped launch the "splatter" genre and was based, like "Psycho," on real-life murderer Ed Gein. A group of teens is attacked by a family of psychotic degenerates with a special barbecue recipe and a fondness for power tools. With Marilyn Burns, Ed Neal and Gunnar Hansen as Leatherface; an uncredited John Larroquette narrates. Restored, uncut version; 83 min.
50-7144 *$19.99*

The Texas Chainsaw Massacre, Part 2 (1986)
Leatherface, the Cook, Grandpa and company are back to prove that the family that slays together stays together in Tobe Hooper's follow-up to his 1974 shock classic. Dennis Hopper plays a (surprise!) deranged ex-lawman who teams with a late-night deejay to track down the killer brood as they prowl the prairie in search of fresh "meat." With Caroline Williams and Bill Johnson as Leatherface. 95 min.
03-1530 *$14.99*

Leatherface: The Texas Chainsaw Massacre III (1989)
"The saw is family" to Leatherface and his cannibalistic clan, and the desert will run red with blood once again as they pursue two college students and a gun-toting survivalist in a gore-a-thon battle to the finish. Kate Hodge, Viggo Mortensen, and R.A. Mihalioff, in the title role, star. 81 min.
02-2007 □*$14.99*

Leatherface: The Texas Chainsaw Massacre III (Uncut Letterboxed Version)
Also available in an uncut, unrated version in a theatrical, widescreen format. 85 min.
02-5102 □*$19.99*

Texas Chainsaw Massacre: The Next Generation (1994)
A car accident on the night of their senior prom leads four teens into an evening of horror when a sadistic recluse with a remote-controlled leg arrives to "help" them. Soon, the teens come face-to-face with Leatherface and the rest of the cannibalistic "Chainsaw" family. Renee Zellweger ("Jerry Maguire") and Matthew McConaughey ("Contact") star. 94 min.
02-3144 Was $99.99 □*$14.99*

The Texas Chainsaw Massacre: A Family Portrait
What really went on when Tobe Hooper filmed "The Texas Chainsaw Massacre" in 1972? Here's the inside story of the making of this horror classic, featuring interviews with Leatherface, the Hitchhiker, Grandpa and the rest of that lovable crew! 60 min.
82-5005 Was $29.99 *$19.99*

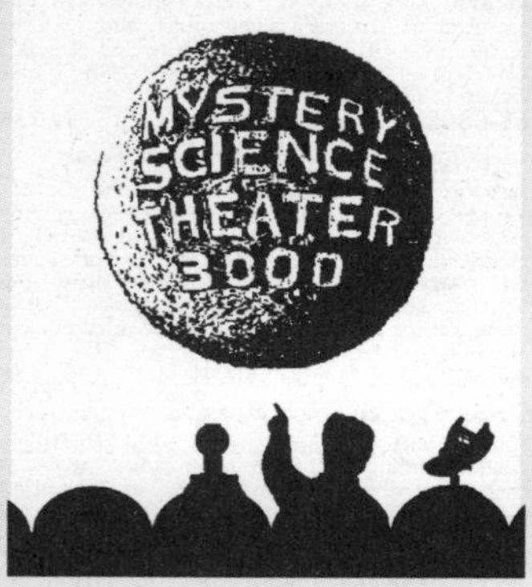

Mystery Science Theater 3000
Watching cheesy movies has never been more enjoyable than in this cult fave cable TV series. Join futuristic janitor Joel Robinson, shot into space by mad scientists Dr. Clayton Forrester and TV's Frank, as he and robot friends Crow, Gypsy and Tom Servo view (and offer a comedic running commentary on) the worst films ever made. Each volume runs about 95 min.

Mystery Science Theater 3000: The Crawling Hand
You have to hand it to Joel and the bots for sitting through this first-season stinkfest about an astronaut's severed hand that goes on a five-finger killing spree.
15-5474 *$19.99*

Mystery Science Theater 3000: Cave Dwellers
Ator the Blademaster slices his way through his foes, while Joel and the bots make some cutting quips on the proceedings.
15-5328 *$19.99*

Mystery Science Theater 3000: The Pod People
"Trumpy, you can do magic things!," exclaims the precocious youngster in this tale of fuzzy aliens, drunken hunters, and a rock band on vacation in the woods.
15-5341 *$19.99*

Mystery Science Theater 3000: The Unearthly
Will mad scientist John Carradine's outrageous operations and Tor Johnson's immortal line, "Time for go to bed!," make this the movie that sends Joel and the bots over the edge?
15-5376 *$19.99*

Mystery Science Theater 3000: Catalina Caper
It's swingin' beach babes in bikinis, a stolen antique scroll, some musical interludes by Little Richard, and love at first sight for Tom Servo, thanks to the fish-loving "creepy girl."
15-5517 *$19.99*

Mystery Science Theater 3000: The Sidehackers
Remember when all America was caught up in the wild motorcycle racing craze known as "sidehacking"? Well, neither did Joel, Tom and Crow, but they still have to watch this cinematic spinout featuring characters named J.C., Gooch and Rommel.
15-5560 *$19.99*

Mystery Science Theater 3000: Manos: The Hands Of Fate
What movie could possibly be so bad that Dr. Forrester and Frank actually *apologize* to Joel and the bots for showing it? How about this low-budget horror outing of a Satanic cult, a vacationing family, and Torgo the handyman?
15-5413 *$19.99*

Mystery Science Theater 3000: Eegah
What's scarier: a fur-clad Richard Kiel playing the lovestruck titular caveman, or Crow and Tom Servo's insidious scheme to turn Joel into the film's nominal hero, Arch Hall, Jr.?
15-5375 *$19.99*

Mystery Science Theater 3000: I Accuse My Parents
Joel and the bots are none too "happy in their work" when the Mads force them to view this sordid look at teenage delinquents.
15-5391 *$19.99*

Mystery Science Theater 3000: Gunslinger
Director Roger Corman takes dead aim at Joel, Tom Servo and Crow with a "B-Minus" western starring Beverly Garland in a frontier version of "She's the Sheriff."
15-5412 *$19.99*

Mystery Science Theater 3000: Mitchell
As the guys riff on slovenly cop Joe Don Baker's pursuit of drug dealer Martin Balsam, Gypsy and "Happy Temp" Mike Nelson try to get Joel off the ship.
15-5326 *$19.99*

Mystery Science Theater 3000: The Brain That Wouldn't Die
Dr. F and Frank have picked a real winner for Mike's first experiment, but will the sci-fi saga of "Jan in the Pan" and her mad doctor boyfriend break Mr. Nelson and the bots?
15-5342 *$19.99*

Mystery Science Theater 3000: The Atomic Brain
Demented scientists, wicked old ladies, beautiful women held captive, and killer kitties are waiting for Mike and company in this off-the-wall brain-transplant shocker!
15-5392 *$19.99*

Mystery Science Theater 3000: The Wild World Of Batwoman
Is it the guano pile of a film whose lead is a woman with a bat plastered on her chest, or the short film "Cheating," that sets Crow on the first step down the path of criminal behavior?
15-5473 *$19.99*

Mystery Science Theater 3000: The Beginning Of The End
Thrill with Mike and the bots as a stalwart Peter Graves defends the city of Chicago...okay, postcards of the city of Chicago...from giant grasshoppers on the rampage.
15-5475 *$19.99*

Mystery Science Theater 3000: Skydivers
What do you get when you mix a love triangle, a dancing Scotsman, and loads of footage of parachutists? A lot of cinematic misery, as Mike and the bots quickly learn!
15-5518 *$19.99*

Mystery Science Theater 3000: Red Zone Cuba
From the opening credits, when John Carradine(!) sings the theme song, you can tell this twisted Coleman Francis thriller will give Mike and the bots a workout!
15-5393 *$19.99*

Mystery Science Theater 3000: Angels Revenge
The '70s live on when Mike and the bots are exposed to this shameless rip-off of guess-what-hit TV show, as a group of foxy fighting females take on drug lord Peter Lawford(!). Includes the hit song "Shine Your Love."
15-5442 *$19.99*

Mystery Science Theater 3000: Bloodlust
What's more frightening than Mr. Brady stalked by a hunter in a revamping of "The Most Dangerous Game"? How about the first visit to Deep 13 by Dr. Forrester's mother?
15-5558 *$19.99*

Mystery Science Theater 3000: The Creeping Terror
If you think the scariest thing about carpet is static electricity, you've never seen this no-budget tale of man-eating rug-monsters from outer space...and that puts you one up on Mike, Crow and Servo!
15-5559 *$19.99*

Mystery Science Theater 3000: Shorts
Just because a bad movie is 20 minutes long doesn't make it any easier to sit through, as Joel, Mike and the bots learn in a special compilation. Included are "The Home Economics Story," "Junior Rodeo Daredevils" (with old-timer Billy Slater), "Cheating," "A Date with Your Family," "Why Study Industrial Arts?," and more.
15-5443 *$19.99*

Mystery Science Theater 3000: Shorts, Vol. 2
Watch and wonder as Joel, Mike, Tom and Crow make "short work" of a half-dozen mind-numbing mini-films that try—and fail hilariously—to educate, entertain and uplift the youth of America. Includes "Catching Trouble," "A Day at the Fair," "Last Clear Chance," "What to Do on a Date" and more. 80 min.
15-5519 *$19.99*

Mystery Science Theater 3000: Poopie!
Even on a high-tech wonder like the Satellite of Love, things are bound to go wrong. See some of the most hilarious flubs and outtakes from Joel, Mike and the bots in this wild blooper tape. 34 min.
15-5453 *$14.99*

Mystery Science Theater 3000 Two-Pack
Don't get caught at "movie sign" without your official MST3K boxer shorts, available only with this two-tape collector's set featuring "Angels Revenge" and "Shorts."
15-5444 *$39.99*

Mystery Science Theater 3000 3-Pack, No. 1
Think you've got what it takes to sit through bad movie after bad movie like Joel, Mike and the robots? See if you can last through this boxed collection that includes "The Atomic Brain," "I Accuse My Parents" and "Red Zone Cuba."
15-5394 Save $10.00! *$49.99*

Mystery Science Theater 3000 3-Pack, No. 2
Here's a bargain you'll never see on TV's Frank's Shopping Network: a boxed collector's set featuring "Gunslinger," "Manos: The Hands of Fate," and the "Poopie!" tape.
15-5414 *$49.99*

Mystery Science Theater 3000 3-Pack, No. 3
In the not-too-distant future, every home in America will have this three-tape boxed set that contains "Beginning of the End," "The Crawling Hand" and "The Wild World of Batwoman," but lucky you can own it now!
15-5476 Save $10.00! *$49.99*

Mystery Science Theater 3000 3-Pack, No. 4
Looking for the perfect gift to give to your own "creepy girl"? How about this boxed set that includes "Catalina Caper," "Skydivers" and "Shorts, Vol. 2"?
15-5520 Save $10.00! *$49.99*

Mystery Science Theater 3000: 3-Pack, No. 5
Just repeat to yourself "it's just a show," and just relax with a boxed collector's set that includes "Bloodlust," "The Creeping Terror" and "The Sidehackers."
15-5561 Save $10.00! *$49.99*

Mystery Science Theater 3000: The Movie (1996)
Blast off on the Satellite of Love with Mike Nelson, Tom Servo and Crow in the big-screen version of the hilarious TV series, as they wisecrack their way through Dr. Forrester's latest bad movie experiment, the 1955 sci-fi epic "This Island Earth." There's high-domed aliens, giant mutant insects, the Professor from "Gilligan's Island," and more pop references than you can shake a stick at. 74 min.
07-2434 Was $99.99 *$14.99*

Apartheid Slave Women's Justice (1998)
Ted V. Mikels ("The Corpse Grinders") mixes the experimental with exploitation in this powerful tale set in Africa. After a slave uprising, 10 black mistresses of a white landowner capture their master after he refuses to turn over his ill-gained wealth. He is then cast in chains and is subjected to a trial with shocking consequences. Jennifer Dove stars. 90 min.
50-5012 *$24.99*

Attack Of The Killer Tomatoes! (Director's Cut) (1978)
A tomato farm near a nuclear reactor grows intelligent, monster-sized vegetables (or is it fruits?) that run amok and threaten Southern California. Can anything stop the man-eating fruits (or is it vegetables?), or will San Diego drown in a sea of ketchup? Outrageous sci-fi spoof features David Miller, Jack Riley, the San Diego Chicken and the hit song "Puberty Love." This special video edition also features extra footage and an interview with an actual killer tomato. 100 min.
11-1922 *$19.99*

Killer Tomatoes Strike Back (1991)
John Astin is a mad doctor who poses as the host of a TV tabloid talk show and is set on taking over the world with his frightful fruit. An ambitious cop and gorgeous scientist team up to stop the wacky doc before his plan, er, stews to perfection. Rick Rockwell (the groom of "Who Wants to Marry a Multi-Millionaire?"), Crystal Carson co-star. 87 min.
04-2480 Was $89.99 ❑*$29.99*

Killer Tomatoes Eat France! (1991)
It's the most frightening menace to hit Paris since Jerry Lewis! Evil scientist John Astin has taken his ketchupy killers across the Atlantic in his latest scheme of conquest, and it's up to an American tourist and his girlfriend to save the day. Marc Price, Angela Visser co-star. 94 min.
04-2584 Was $89.99 *$29.99*

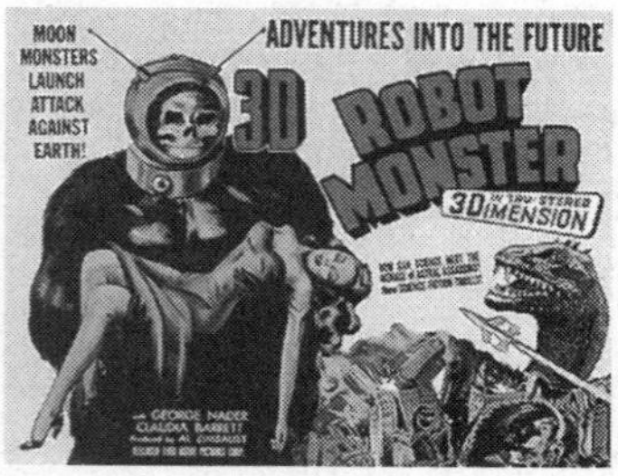

Robot Monster (Monster From Mars) (1953)
Ro-Man, the title character, is the most ludicrous monster in cinema history: a gorilla wearing a space helmet! His invasion fleet has conquered Earth, but one feisty family holds out for survival. You won't want to miss the alien equipment that blows bubbles and the score by future Oscar-winner Elmer Bernstein. With George Nader, Claudia Barrett and George Barrows as Ro-Man. Not in 3-D. 58 min.
45-5295 *$19.99*

Robot Monster (3-D Version)
Also available in a 3-D version; includes two pairs of glasses.
15-5186 *$12.99*

Broadway Jungle (1955)
Directed by Phil Tucker ("Robot Monster"), this totally incomprehensible look at life in Hollywood (see, even the title doesn't make sense) features Bruno, a mute who can't talk but sure does kill people. Music changes midway through scenes, shots are framed too low, and people talk into ringing phones. A masterwork with Diana Dors, Herbert Lom and Eddie Constantine.
79-5669 Was $24.99 *$19.99*

Surf Nazis Must Die (1987)
In the devastating wake of post-earthquake Southern California, weapon-toting gangs on surfboards have taken over the beaches. But when they murder a young black man, his elderly mother breaks out of the retirement home to eliminate the Surf Nazis once and for all. Outrageous sci-fi satire from Troma stars Barry Brenner, Bobbie Breese and Gail Neely. 94 min.
03-1592 *$19.99*

Deadbeat At Dawn (1990)
The leader of a tough street gang wants to settle down with his drug sale proceeds, but when his girlfriend is killed by a rival gang, he teams with his junkie father to plot an outrageously warped revenge. There's kung fu, knife fights and all sorts of unsettling action in this demented cult film. With Paul Harper and Jim Van Bebber. 80 min.
72-4010 *$19.99*

Mod F**k Explosion (1998)
This off-the-wall ode to teenage angst was voted "Best Feature" at the 1995 New York Underground Film Festival. Director Jon Moritsugu's twisted tale of first dates, incest, gang fights and punk fashion includes a dream sequence set in a "garden" of rotting meat. 71 min.
78-9021 *$39.99*

Zachariah (1971)
Before "Miami Vice" made him a star, Don Johnson appeared in some very offbeat film roles, including this "electric western" that combined a standard gunfight plot with '60s psychedelia. With John Rubinstein, Pat Quinn, Country Joe and the Fish; co-scripted by Firesign Theatre. 92 min.
04-3188 Letterboxed *$14.99*

Harold And Maude (1972)
Harold (Bud Cort) is a rich teenager obsessed with death; Maude (Ruth Gordon) is a wacky septuagenarian who loves life. Their bittersweet romance makes for an uproarious and touching comedy that you will want to see again and again. Harold's faked suicides, Maude's eccentricities and Cat Stevens' score make this a very special movie. 90 min.
06-1025 ❑*$14.99*

Dance With The Devil (1998)
In this extreme sex- and violence-soaked road movie from the director of "Day of the Beast" and the writer of "Wild at Heart," Rosie Perez is a prostitute who joins forces with voodoo-worshipping creep Javier Bardem to drive trucks with human fetuses to Las Vegas for a mobster. Their trip includes the kidnapping of a young couple and hot pursuit from the authorities. With James Gandolfini, Aimee Graham. Unrated version; 121 min.
83-1463 Was $99.99 *$14.99*

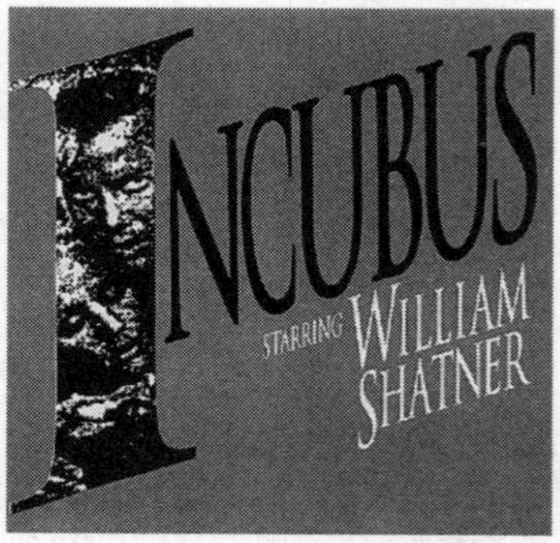

Incubus (1965)
This legendary lost film, shot in the "universal" language of Esperanto by Oscar-winning cinematographer Conrad Hall, is an eerie tale starring William Shatner as Marc, a soldier who is seduced by a beautiful demon succubus named Kia. When Kia realizes she has fallen in love with Marc, her sister summons a monster for revenge. With Allyson Ames; directed by "Outer Limits" vet Leslie Stevens. 76 min. In Esperanto with English subtitles.
50-8594 *$39.99*

The Adventures Of Priscilla, Queen Of The Desert (1994)
Outrageously campy and disco-drenched comedy follows a trio of drag show performers on a journey across the unsophisticated (and at times unfriendly) regions of the Australian Outback in a rickety bus named Priscilla. Terence Stamp offers a fine performance as the transsexual leader of the group; with Guy Pearce ("L.A. Confidential"), Hugo Weaving, Bill Hunter. 102 min.
02-8205 Was $19.99 $14.99

Hollywood Chainsaw Hookers (1987)
When a private dick takes to the Sunset Strip to look for a missing teen, he finds her in the clutches of a band of call girls who've joined a "human sacrifice" cult. Outrageous blend of gore, nudity, comedy, and social commentary stars Linnea Quigley, Jay Richardson, Gunnar Hansen ("Texas Chainsaw Massacre"). Directed by schlockmeister Fred Olen Ray; special uncut director's cut with interviews and trailer. 82 min.
72-5010 Was $39.99 $29.99

You Are What You Eat (1968)
This blast from the past is the quintessential 1960s experience, capturing swinging lifestyles and trends, including be-ins, body painting, surfing, a "Teen Fair" and the one and only Tiny Tim. Music is supplied by Harper's Bizarre, David Crosby, The Electric Flag, Frank Zappa and others. Groovy, man. 75 min.
55-9027 $29.99

Women Of The Prehistoric Planet (1966)
"Hi-keeba!" An interplanetary expedition, searching for the sole survivor of an earlier rocket crash, lands on a savage world filled with giant lizards doing dinosaur imitations and beautiful, leopard-skin clad women. Don't dare give away the surprise ending to this "so bad it's good" sci-fi saga starring Wendell Corey, John Agar, Irene Tsu and the immortal Stuart Margolin. 87 min.
58-1057 $19.99

The Beach Girls And The Monster (1965)
Sure, the title says it all, but you'll want to see this one anyway: for the seaweed-covered, pinhead creature messing up tan lines on the beaches, for a son telling his scientist father, "there's more to life than test tubes and fish," and for a scorching Frank Sinatra, Jr. bongo score. Jon Hall stars. 70 min.
68-8061 $19.99

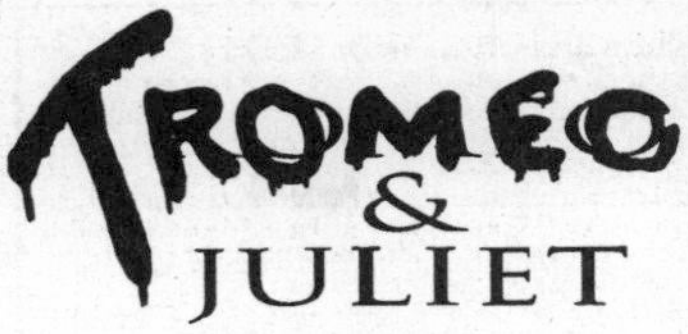

Tromeo & Juliet (1996)
"Tromeo, Tromeo...where far out thou, Tromeo?" Far, far out, according to this outrageous Troma production of the William Shakespeare classic. Can true love prevail over kinky sex, incest, blood and gore, contemporary Times Square settings, lesbianism and Lemmy from Motorhead? Will Keenan and Jane Jensen star. Unrated version; 105 min.
46-8020 Was $59.99 $14.99

Killer Condom (1998)
Proving there's just no such thing as "safe sex," this outrageous German horror-comedy is set in New York's seedy Hotel Quickie, where the male clientele is falling prey to a invasion of fanged, mutant, penis-chomping prophylactics. It's up to a gay detective and his straight partner to stop the rampaging rubbers. Based on a German comic book series, the outrageous satire stars Udo Samel, Peter Lohmeyer; condom creatures created by "Alien" artist H.R. Giger. 108 min. In German with English subtitles.
46-8037 Was $59.99 $14.99

The Brain That Wouldn't Die (1963)
A demented (but hopelessly romantic) surgeon keeps his fiancée's disembodied head alive after an auto accident while he searches for a body transplant "donor." Outrageously bad sci-fi shocker, available in its uncut version to show the full, bloody vengeance of the "pinhead in the closet." Herb (Jason) Evers, Virginia Leith star. 89 min.
68-8382 $14.99

Shopping For Fangs (1998)
Adventurous low-budget mix of horror, spoof and lesbian love with an Asian cast follows two simultaneous stories. A nerdy office worker develops a hair growth problem and thinks he's becoming a werewolf, while an unhappily married woman and a waitress begin a relationship. Radmar Jao and Jeanne Chin star in this one-of-a-kind effort. 91 min.
76-7449 Letterboxed $69.99

Cape Canaveral Monsters (1960)
Phil Tucker, the auteur of "Robot Monster," directs this sci-fi tale in which a married couple, killed in a car crash, become possessed by alien beings. Their new habitat: a cave. Their mission: to stop American's space program. Katherine Victor, Jason Johnson and Scott Peters star.
68-8366 $19.99

The Secret Adventures Of Tom Thumb (1993)
A unique blend of stop-motion animation and human "pixilation" is used for this incredible fantasy that updates the fairy tale. A tiny mutant child is kidnapped by evil government agents and taken to a lab where he's the subject of horrifying experiments, and after befriending other "creatures" in the lab, little Tom escapes with Jack the Giant Killer and searches for his father. 61 min.
02-8331 Was $29.99 $14.99

Tales From The Gimli Hospital (1988)
Truly bizarre, surrealistic film from Canada's Guy Maddin about two smallpox patients in a decrepit hospital in the early 1900s who share stories about their lives while experiencing the horrors of the building in which they are quarantined. Shadowy visuals, silent film techniques, disturbing imagery, eerie soundtrack; David Lynch, step aside. With Kyle McCulloch. 72 min.
53-7823 Was $79.99 $24.99

Careful (1992)
From Guy Maddin ("Tales from the Gimli Hospital"), Winnipeg's answer to David Lynch, comes this surreal fable about the repressed inhabitants of a small Alpine town who hide their violent, incestuous and disturbing tendencies while living in fear of an avalanche burying them. To tell this eerie tale, Maddin uses such silent movie motifs as title-cards and tinting. 96 min.
53-8480 Was $79.99 $24.99

The Wacky World Of Doctor Morgus (1962)
New Orleans TV horror host Dr. Morgus (Sid Noel) broke into film with this outlandish sci-fi comedy. The mad scientist's latest invention, a machine that can turn people into sand and back again, is sought by an agent from the country of Microvania, who wants to use it to sneak spies into America. With Dan Barton, Jeanne Teslof, and Tommy George as Morgus' executioner assistant, Chopsley. 87 min.
55-9026 $29.99

Sid And Nancy (1986)
Playing like "Romeo and Juliet" on heroin, the bizarre love story of punk rock pioneer Sid Vicious and American groupie Nancy Spungen is graphically brought to the screen by Alex Cox. Gary Oldman plays the Sex Pistols bassist, and Chloe Webb is his partner in a downward spiral of drugs, violence and, ultimately, death. Music by The Pogues and Joe Strummer. With Drew Schofield, David Hayman; look quickly for Courtney Love. 111 min.
53-1648 $14.99

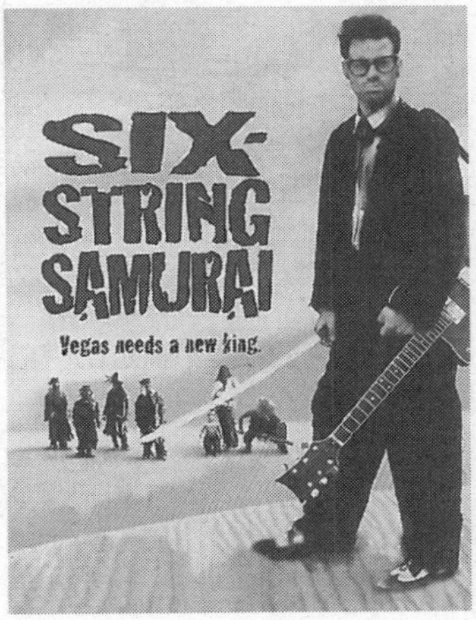

Six-String Samurai (1998)
After Russia drops a bomb on America in 1957, only Las Vegas survives and Elvis rules the new nation. Forty years later, Elvis dies and a group of warrior musicians—including a Buddy Holly-look-alike—battle for the presidency using their martial arts skills. This wild rock-and-roll/kung fu/musical/action odyssey stars Jeffrey Falcon and features music by The Red Elvises. 91 min.
02-9079 $19.99

Narcotic (1933)
From low-budget filmmaking team Dwain and Hildagarde Esper ("Maniac") comes a creaky and freaky look at the dangers of drug addiction. Follow a clean-living medical student on a downward spiral of vice-filled "light-up" parties, opium dens, bordellos, carnival sideshows and, ultimately, death. Harry Cording, Joan Dix star. 57 min.
09-1748 $19.99

Marijuana: Assassin Of Youth (1935)
In the mold of "Reefer Madness" this campy "I Told You So" exposé shows what can—and will—happen when a girl smokes weed: her life goes down the tubes! Luana Walters stars. 74 min.
62-1164 Was $19.99 $14.99

Marihuana (1936)
"Did you know that the use of marihuana is steadily increasing among the youth of the country?" Watch what happens as a teenage "pot party" leads to crime, murder, insanity, pregnancy, sloth and avarice. Don't Bogart that joint, Bro! Stars Hartley Wood. 57 min.
09-1932 Was $24.99 $19.99

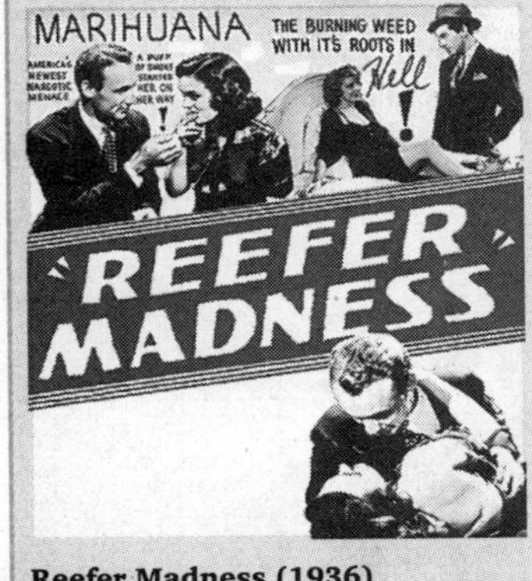

Reefer Madness (1936)
"The devil weed with its roots in Hell!" The classic anti-marijuana propaganda film that depicts innocent high school kids being "turned on" by adult pushers. See teens turn into giggling fiends after one puff, a puff that propels them down a road of vice and death. Laughable, even by '30s standards. 69 min.
10-2034 $19.99

Cocaine Fiends (1937)
It's the pause that demolishes...the white powder whose use spells death! More campy scare tactics from the '30s that have little if any foundation in reality. Drugs, sex and swing music! 58 min.
62-1092 Was $19.99 $14.99

The Devil's Harvest (1942)
High school kids sure are the wildest. Witness the ones depicted in this movie: they purchase reefer from a hot dog vendor across the street from school; they get high on booze and pot at a party; two guys square off over a girl and accidentally kill her; and one gal goes undercover as a showgirl to get the goods on racketeers. High school kids sure are the wildest. June Doyle, Leo Anthony star.
79-5881 Was $24.99 $19.99

She Shoulda Said "No"! (1948)
At the precise moment a chorus girl ends her addiction to marijuana, an exploitation filmmaker stops his addiction to weird, out-of-focus camera shots to simulate hallucinations. After being busted with Robert Mitchum on drug possession charges the year before, Lila Leeds made her public redemption with this effort. AKA: "Wild Weed."
79-5815 $19.99

The Flaming Teenage (1956)
Cheapie anti-drugs-and-drinking drama is presented in two parts: in the first half, a son learns about the effects of booze from his dad, and part two concerns a drug addict who becomes an evangelist. Noel Reyburn stars.
68-8835 $19.99

One Way Ticket To Hell (1956)
A wayward girl starts hanging out with a drug-crazed motorcycle gang and, in short order, winds up addicted to pot, pills and heroin and becomes a dealer for "Mr. Big" to support her habit. Follow her on a terrifying "cold turkey" run through Mexico in this heavy-duty JD thriller. Barbara Marks, Robert Sherry star. AKA: "Teenage Devil Dolls." 70 min.
68-9258 $19.99

The Narcotic Story (1958)
The cast: drug addicts, their pushers, policemen and narcotics investigators. The setting: the alleys of your town! The subject: dope, from hupes to maryjane to goofballs. Can the police save juvenile delinquents from a horrible fate? This is the whole story...from the first "connection" to the "hooked" addict. 75 min.
79-5165 Was $24.99 $19.99

Curfew Breakers (1958)
A dead-serious, now-camp classic that exposes the dangers of drugs and drug abuse as it follows a narcotics cop in action. There's juke joints, pool parties, cool sunglasses and more in this hilarious cheapo epic starring Sharon Strand and Darlene Hendricks and featuring a song that goes like this: "Baby, baby, baby, have yourself a time...." AKA: "Narcotics Squad."
79-5328 $19.99

Satan's Bed (1965)
A rare find, this brutal drug drama (actually two films edited together) features Yoko Ono in the fiancée of a drug pusher who wants to go straight. His supplier kidnaps Ono in order to keep him selling dope, while in an unrelated story three black-clad addicts terrorize women. With Glen Nielson, Val Avery; from the creators of "Snuff."
79-5008 Was $24.99 $19.99

Something's Happening (1967)
Filmed during 1967's "Summer of Love," this pseudo-documentary takes you to the middle of the hippie world: Haight-Ashbury, where sex and drugs and rock-and-roll rule the roost. Witness love-ins, mock weddings, discotheques, communes and more in this blast from the past that includes footage shot in Santa Barbara and Los Angeles. AKA: "The Hippie Revolt," "The World Of Acid."
79-5291 $24.99

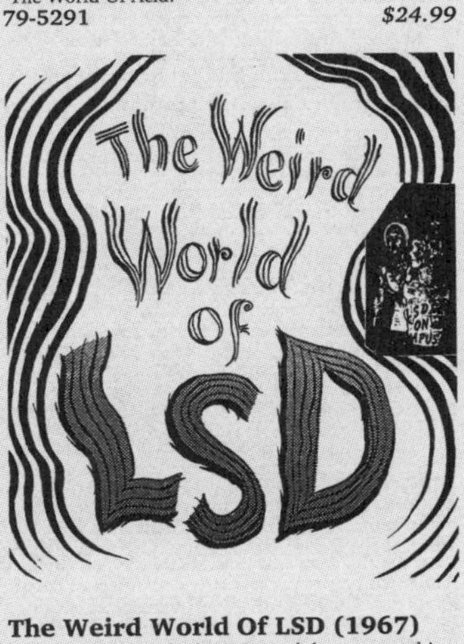

The Weird World Of LSD (1967)
A truly outrageous look at LSD and the way-out things it does to human beings. Psychedelic special effects help show what happens when acid-laced substances are taken. One subject wants to fly like a bird, another takes a "trip" on a dragster. Oh, man! With Terry Tessem, Yolanda Morino. 120 min.
79-5080 $19.99

Alice In Acidland (1968)
There's nothing "wonderful" about the sordid adventures a beautiful college student named Alice undergoes after being introduced to alcohol, pot, LSD and wild parties by her lesbian French teacher. A psychedelic drug drama drenched with nudity, jazz music and flashing colors. Groovy, man!
79-5007 $24.99

Mantis In Lace (1968)
Way-way-out murders occur after a movie starlet takes some heavy acid and commits hallucinatory homicide. Classic sicko-psychedelia from director William Rotsler, photographed by Laszlo Kovacs and starring Susan Stewart, Steve Vincent and Stuart Lancaster of Russ Meyer films fame.
79-5026 $19.99

Blonde On A Bum Trip (1968)
"Tour the hippie 'pot-holes' of New York." A shocking docudrama set in New York's East Village during the height of psychedelia. Check out the swinging scene with free-love parties, flower children, sadism and more. 65 min.
79-5244 $19.99

Pot, Parents And Police (1971)
A 13-year-old boy goes off the deep end after his dog dies and finds himself rubbing elbows with hippies, taking acid and getting into all sorts of police trouble. Phillip Pine wrote, directed, produced and stars; with Robert Mantell, Madelyn Keen.
79-5326 Was $24.99 $19.99

The Devil's Joint
An outrageous collection of clips from marijuana scare flicks of the '20s and '30s, loaded with horrific side-effects and the like. The filmmakers and the narrators can't hide their prejudices—they're pro-pot—in their documentation of classic camp films.
79-5110 $19.99

Dope Mania
Just say "yes" to this crazy collection of "enlightening" government films from the 1950s. Learn how a child's acceptance of a piece of candy inevitably leads to drug addiction and how a contact high turns straight-laced students into drug-thirsting monsters. 60 min.
15-5039 $19.99

Mindbenders, Vol. 1
Tune in! Drop out! Freak out! Do whatever you want! And dig these anti-drug flicks of the '60s and '70s, too. "The Mindbenders," "LSD: Trip or Trap?," "LSD: Trip to Nowhere" and "LSD" are included on this psychedelic compilation of classroom scare flicks.
79-5271 Was $24.99 $19.99

Hell, American Style: Teenage Dope Attack
Johnny Legend presents this compendium of weird and wacky anti-everything movies. Hear from Dr. Timothy Leary and the victim of a bad acid trip in "L.S.D.—The Trip to Where?" Witness Sonny Bono warning kids against the dangers of "Marijuana!" Be amazed as the U.S. Navy tackles drugs, unwanted pregnancy and homosexuality in "The Decision Is Yours!" Wow!
79-5510 Was $24.99 $19.99

LSD Psychedelic Freak-Out 2000
Wow, man. These movies are really groovy. Like, there's a hippie orgy, lots of acid-dropping, "white bird-riding," hippie chicks, way-out colors and lots more cool things. It's a way-so-hip compilation of the weirdest moments from drug movies, drug movie trailers and anti-dope films like "LSD Sex Cult," "Alice in Acidland," "Hippie Revolt" and others. Wow, man.
79-5572 Was $24.99 $19.99

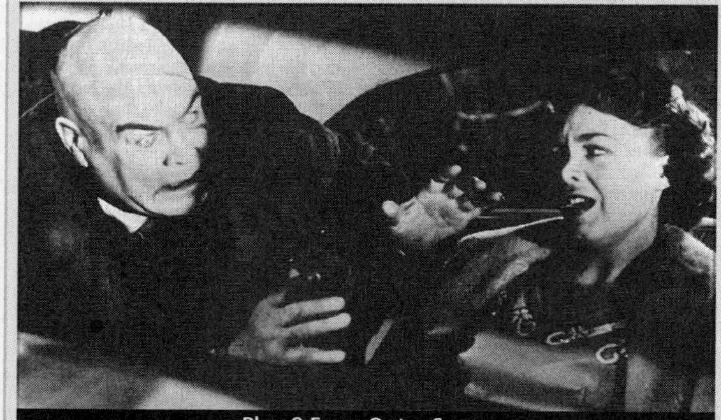
Plan 9 From Outer Space

Ed Wood

Glen Or Glenda (I Changed My Sex) (1952)
Writer/director Ed Wood pseudonymously starred in this transvestite/sex-change docudrama that was his most autobiographical film. Will Glen's fiancée let him wear her angora sweater? Hear scientist-narrator Bela Lugosi warn viewers to "bevare of the big green dragon that sits on your doorstep," see daffy dream sequences, and learn the inner turmoil of men who wear "pink satin undies." With Dolores Fuller, Lyle Talbot. AKA: "I Led Two Lives." 67 min.
09-1756 *$19.99*

Crossroad Avenger (1953)
After setting Hollywood ablaze with "Glen or Glenda," writer/director Ed Wood tried his hand at TV work with this rare color pilot for a Western series. Tom Keene stars as the Tucson Kid, a gunslinger framed for killing the sheriff by saloon owner Lyle Talbot. With Tom Tyler, Kenne Duncan, and a cameo on horseback by Wood. This tape also features trailers for other Wood films and a short of trick gunplay by Duncan. 47 min. total.
68-9041 *$19.99*

Jail Bait (1954)
A hard-as-nails gangster film, Ed Wood-style. A hood on the lam shoots his partner, then forces the guy's surgeon-father to change his face. The stars include Lyle Talbot, Dolores Fuller, Timothy Farrell and a young Steve Reeves; don't miss the "hilarious" blackface minstrel sequence! 75 min.
05-9007 *$19.99*

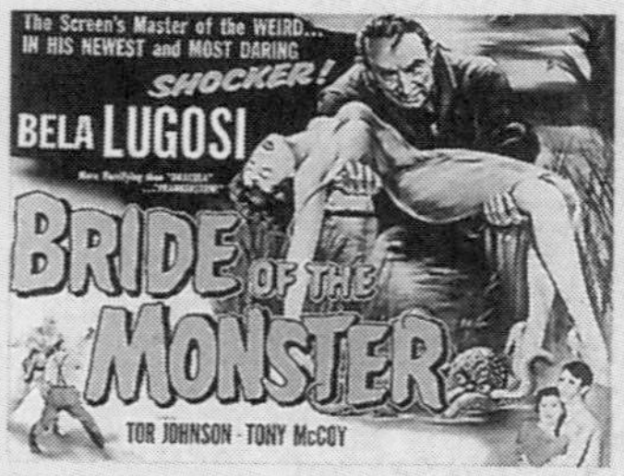
The Screen's Master of the WEIRD...
IN HIS NEWEST and MOST DARING
SHOCKER!
BELA LUGOSI
BRIDE OF THE MONSTER
TOR JOHNSON · TONY McCOY

Bride Of The Monster (1956)
Wood and Lugosi team up again in this tale of a mad scientist out to create a race of "atomic super-giants." See Tor Johnson as Lobo, Lugosi's mute lab assistant! See Bela wrestle with an obvious rubber octopus! See Tor wrestle with Bela's platform-heeled stand-in! "He tampered in God's domain!" With Tony McCoy, Loretta King. 70 min.
10-4006 *$19.99*

The Violent Years (1956)
Ed Wood was the screenwriter on this "torn from the headlines" gem about bad girls and fast cars. An all-female gang rides a crime wave of theft, vandalism, rape (!) and wantonness that leads to murder, prison and an illegitimate child. Jean Moorehead, Barbara Weeks, Timothy Farrell star. AKA: "Female." 80 min.
15-5045 *$14.99*

Plan 9 From Outer Space (1959)
Recognized on six continents as "the worst film ever made," this sci-fi travesty from Ed Wood features anti-nuclear aliens whose ships look like paper plates, Tor Johnson and Vampira as zombie slaves, Bela Lugosi in two minutes of stock footage (a stand-in with a cape took his place), and narration by famed psychic Criswell. "Can you prove it didn't happen?" 78 min.
05-1346 *$14.99*

The Ed Wood Story: The Plan 9 Companion (1992)
An amazing tribute to Wood's most infamous movie, featuring rare footage of the cross-dressing auteur in action, film clips, a tour of the sites where "Plan 9" was shot, and interviews with cast and crew, along with comments from fans like Forrest J. Ackerman and Sam Raimi. AKA: "Flying Saucers Over Hollywood." 111 min.
50-7304 *$19.99*

Night Of The Ghouls (1959)
The long-lost "sequel" to "Bride of the Monster" stars Criswell, Vampira and the ever-popular Tor Johnson in a tale of fake mediums who find themselves up against the true "walking dead." Writer/director Wood calls them "Monsters to be pitied...monsters to be despised." Who are we to argue? 77 min.
68-8315 *$19.99*

The Sinister Urge (1961)
Writer/director Ed Wood takes on the menace of pornography ("a dirty name for an ugly business"). Who is the mysterious psycho who's been killing young women, and what's his connection to a smut filmmaking ring? See a cop in drag, a very brief nude scene and a cameo by Wood. James Moore, Jean Fontaine, Dino Fantini star. 72 min.
01-1306 Was $59.99 *$19.99*

Orgy Of The Dead (1966)
Found at last! The "missing film" from the canon of "Plan 9 from Outer Space" auteur Ed Wood. Vampires, werewolves and topless go-go girls(!) cavort and creep in a tomb for horror hi-jinx that must be seen. Stars Criswell the Psychic; directed by A.C. Stephen. 90 min.
15-5002 *$14.99*

One Million AC/DC (1968)
Using the name "Akdov Telmig" (read it backwards), Ed Wood penned this nutty prehistoric sex farce that offers a smorgasbord of softcore fun, chintzy effects, sex with a gorilla, stock footage, cavemen and lines like "I'm off to see the lizard"! With Gary Kent, who gets to sing a song called "The Spear Went Over the Mountain." Wow!
79-5825 Was $24.99 *$19.99*

Love Feast (1969)
Also known as "The Photographer," this rare softcore romp features the legendary Ed Wood in one of his weirdest roles ever! He's a shutterbug with a penchant for kinkiness who lures models into his studio, then snaps photos of them after they undress. Soon, the tide is turned when one of the posers has him fitted with a dog chain and nightgown! With Linda Coplin. 63 min.
79-5134 *$19.99*

Take It Out In Trade: 7The Outtakes (1970)
A real collector's item: silent outtakes from the notorious, long-lost Wood-directed effort "Take It Out in Trade," featuring some of the late auteur's weirdest work. Check out pool table sex, an androgynous couple making out, Wood veteran Duke Moore and Ed himself, wearing a lime-green dress, blonde wig and white go-go boots as a drag queen named Alecia. Beware!
79-5622 Was $24.99 *$19.99*

Necromania (1971)
Long believed to be lost, Ed Wood, Jr.'s final film is a sexploiter involving a young couple who want to help their love life by taking part in Madam Heles' supernatural sex clinic. Filmed for $5,000 in two days, the film offers such "Woodian" trademarks as fractured dialogue, bizarre music and off-the-wall humor. With porn stalwarts Ric Lutze and Rene Bond. This is the recently discovered 43-minute version that's missing some original footage.
79-5541 Was $24.99 *$19.99*

The Class Reunion (1972)
They were guarding their reputations back in high school and sex education was just a class with icky pictures. But experience has improved these former cheerleaders and dance queens, and they're going to the class reunion as the "Girls Most Likely To." Rene Bond, Sandi Carey and Marsha Jordan star in this carnal collaboration between A.C. Stephen and co-writer Ed Wood.
03-1696 Was $24.99 *$19.99*

Drop Out Wife (1972)
Ed Wood, Jr.'s wacky script and several hot simulated sex scenes make this erotic A.C. Stephen entry a must-have. Angela Carnon is a housewife and mother who dumps family life to join the sixties swingers. While experimenting with group sex and other free love enterprises, she makes some not-so-startling revelations about the opposite sex. With Candy Samples, Terry Johnson and Sandy Dempsey.
79-6480 Was $24.99 *$19.99*

The Snow Bunnies (1973)
Four gals led by comely Marsha Jordan head to a Canadian ski resort to snag some men—and soon they not only snag 'em, they shag 'em, too. The women meet them in the bar and at the ski shop, and get it on in such heated encounters that the snow practically melts. Rene Bond and Sandi Carey co-star; Ed Wood co-scripted with director A.C. Stephen.
79-6484 Was $24.99 *$19.99*

Fugitive Girls (1974)
Wild drive-in fave finds Rene Bond leading fellow female inmates on a jail break out of a work farm and to loot tucked away in the California wilds. The group of gals—which includes a black inmate, a lesbian and a good girl—encounter hippies, a biker gang and a handicapped Vietnam vet and his Latino lady, who Rene takes a liking to. A.C. Stephen directs; Ed Wood, Jr. co-scripts.
67-1010 Was $24.99 *$19.99*

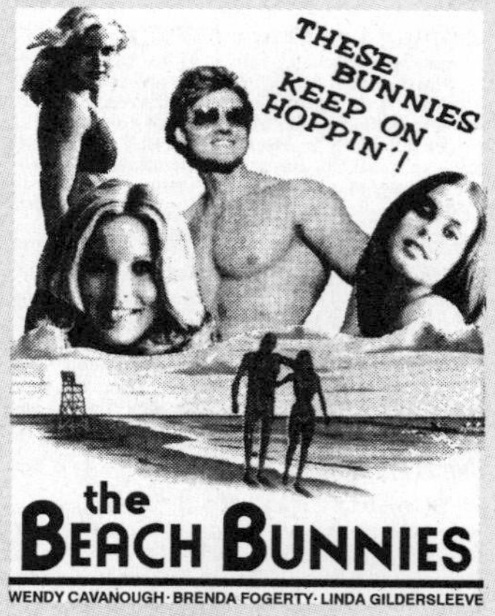
THESE BUNNIES KEEP ON HOPPIN'!
the BEACH BUNNIES
WENDY CAVANOUGH · BRENDA FOGERTY · LINDA GILDERSLEEVE

The Beach Bunnies (1976)
It's "Beach Bunny Bango" in this sex-and-sand saga co-scripted by Ed Wood, Jr. and directed by A.C. Stephen. The female editor of Blue magazine and three gorgeous staffers travel to a beach resort to get the goods on Hollywood star Rock Sanders. With its unending selection of sin and sodomy, this place makes Club Med look like Club Dead. With Brenda Fogerty and Mariwin Roberts.
79-6478 Was $24.99 *$19.99*

The Haunted World Of Edward Wood, Jr. (1995)
The life and films of Ed Wood are extensively covered in this terrific documentary that mixes rare film footage and great interviews. Among the members of Wood's entourage featured are Dolores Fuller, Bela Lugosi, Conrad Brooks, Vampira and Lyle Talbot. Find out what made the cross-dressing, sweater-addicted auteur really tick—if you dare! 110 min.
73-3002 Was $29.99 *$19.99*

On The Trail Of Ed Wood
He's been called "The Worst Filmmaker of All Time," was the director of such classics as "Plan 9 from Outer Space" and "Glen or Glenda," and really, *really* liked angora sweaters. Ed Wood's amazing life is examined through flim clips, by touring his homes, and with commentary by Conrad Brooks, one of Ed's favorite thespians. 60 min.
50-2237 *$19.99*

Ed Wood: Look Back In Angora
Writer...director...transvestite. The remarkable life and career of grade-Z filmmaker Ed Wood are profiled in this video retrospective that includes anecdotes, interviews, and scenes from such Wood efforts as "Jail Bait" and the classic "Plan 9 from Outer Space." Gary Owens hosts. 50 min.
15-5300 Was $19.99 *$14.99*

Ed Wood Deluxe Pink Angora Boxed Set
Celebrate Wood-en acting, scripting and direction with this collectible boxed set (done in imitation pink angora) that includes "Bride of the Monster," "Glen or Glenda" and "Plan 9 from Outer Space."
15-5340 Save $20.00! *$34.99*

HIGH SCHOOL *Confidential*

High School Confidential! (1958)
This teen exploitation classic stars Russ Tamblyn as an undercover cop posing as a student, out to uncover drug dealer "Mr. A." Sex kitten Mamie Van Doren and Jerry Lee Lewis are joined by Jackie Coogan and a young Michael Landon in a school that is a teacher's nightmare! Produced by B-movie mogul Albert Zugsmith. 85 min.
63-1051 Letterboxed *$14.99*

Girls Town (1959)
Perennial B-movie bad girl Mamie Van Doren plays a troubled teen who is sent to a special school, run by nuns for wayward girls, after she's falsely blamed in an accidental death. Wild "J.D." drama from producer Albert Zugsmith also stars Paul Anka a teen crooner, Mel Torme as a hot-rodder, and The Platters as themselves. AKA: "The Innocent and the Damned." 92 min.
63-1602 *$12.99*

The Sheriff Was A Lady (1964)
Talk about making a German spectacle out of itself! This European sagebrusher is unlike anything you've ever seen before, a tale of Black Bill (German Elvis-wannabe Freddie Quinn), a singing Teutonic cowpoke in search of his parents' killer, and Anita, the sexy female sheriff searching for those same creeps, who also swiped her father's gold. Mamie Van Doren is also featured. Wow!
79-6422 Was $24.99 *$19.99*

Navy vs. The Night Monsters (1966)
Campy sci-fi classic stars Mamie Van Doren, Anthony Eisley, Billy Gray, Pamela Mason and Bobby Van as inhabitants of a South Pacific naval base under attack by mobile killer trees from the Ice Age. Cheesy plant creatures and the buxom Mamie make this a must-see. AKA: "Monsters of the Night," "The Night Crawlers." 87 min.
58-1063 *$19.99*

The Bubble (1967)
When an electrical storm forces their plane to land in a remote town, three travellers find that the locals have been turned into mindless drones and the entire town is surrounded by a force field set up by aliens. Filmed in "3-D Space Vision" by fantasist Arch Oboler, this offbeat sci-fi tale stars Michael Cole, Deborah Walley, Johnny Desmond. Comes with two pair of 3-D glasses. AKA: "The Fantastic Invasion of Planet Earth," "The Zoo." 91 min.
15-5514 *$14.99*

Domo Arigato (1972)
The final film from director/3-D pioneer Arch Oboler, this visually stunning "3D Space Vision" drama follows the romance between a young soldier returning home from Vietnam and an American girl he meets in Japan. Bonnie Sher stars. Comes with two pairs of 3-D glasses. 90 min.
15-5563 *$14.99*

Peeping Tom (1960)
Director Michael Powell's disturbing and fascinating cinema experiment in fear was denounced when first released but has gone on to become a cult classic. Carl Boehm is a camera-obsessed psychopath who kills young women while capturing their deaths on 16mm film, and Anna Massey is the downstairs neighbor who attracts his eye. Moira Shearer co-stars in the classic thriller. 101 min.
22-5500 Letterboxed *$19.99*

Futz (1969)
More than just your typical "boy meets pig" romance, director Tom O'Horgan's adaptation of the off-Broadway satire of one man's "swine love"—and the scorn he meets with from the townspeople—from the La Mama troupe features more blood, pyromania, murder, incest and porcine pathos than one film should be allowed to have. 92 min.
31-3014 *$29.99*

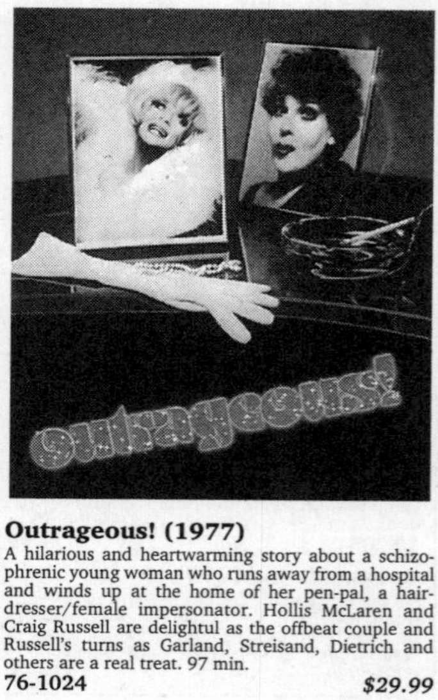
outrageous!

Outrageous! (1977)
A hilarious and heartwarming story about a schizophrenic young woman who runs away from a hospital and winds up at the home of her pen-pal, a hairdresser/female impersonator. Hollis McLaren and Craig Russell are delightful as the offbeat couple and Russell's turns as Garland, Streisand, Dietrich and others are a real treat. 97 min.
76-1024 *$29.99*

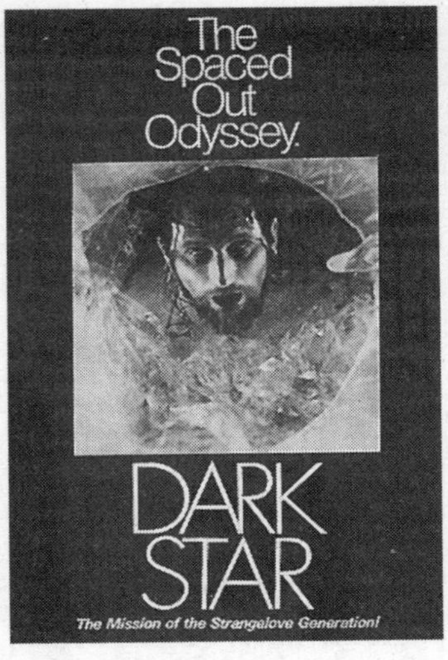
The Spaced Out Odyssey.
DARK STAR
The Mission of the Strangelove Generation!

Dark Star (1972)
This quirky tale of "Californians in Space" was the senior project for film students John Carpenter ("Halloween") and Dan O'Bannon ("Alien"). A ship equipped to blow up unstable planets with talking bombs is nearing the end of its mission, but the crew's nerves have been stretched to the limit. Stars O'Bannon, Dre Pahich. 91 min.
08-1410 Was $19.99 ***$14.99***

Naked Youth (1960)
Two teenage inmates of a desert "honor farm" break out, joining up with a murderer on the lam. Together the three search for a stash of heroin hidden in a doll. Outrageous "J.D." thriller stars Robert Arthur, Steve Rowland. 60 min.
15-5053 ***$12.99***

Basket Case: Special Edition (1982)
Duane Bradley and his little telepathic twin brother, Belial, have come to New York City looking for the doctors who operated on them years earlier. When they find the creeps, Belial pops out of his wicker basket and wreaks havoc. Frank Henonletter's novel horror film stars Kevin Vanhentenryck. This remastered special edition includes a theatrical trailer and never-before-seen outtakes.
03-1156 ***$19.99***

Liquid Sky (1983)
Way-out cult film that mixes sci-fi, hip Greenwich Village locales and sensibilities and druggy visuals. Aliens land in a New York apartment building in search of heroin, but discover that the chemicals produced in the brain during orgasms will suit them fine. Creepy lovers of bisexual model Anne Carlisle (who has a dual role) become the aliens' unexpected targets.
03-1185 Was $39.99 ***$29.99***

Where's Poppa? (1970)
Outlandish, madcap cult favorite stars George Segal as a New York City lawyer desperate to get rid of his abrasive, aged mother (Ruth Gordon), even if he has to dress up as a gorilla and scare her to death! Carl Reiner directed this wickedly funny comedy. Co-stars Trish Van Devere, Ron Leibman; look for Rob Reiner, Garrett Morris. 83 min.
12-2029 ***$19.99***

The Female Bunch (1969)
Notorious exploitationer stars Russ Tamblyn as a rugged cowpoke who sends a group of man-hating women swooning when he arrives at their ranch. Sex, violence, sordidness with Lon Chaney, Jr. as a drug pusher, direction by Al Adamson ("Dracula vs. Frankenstein") and location filming on the actual Manson Ranch. With Jenifer Bishop and Regina Carrol. 94 min.
68-8738 ***$19.99***

Freaks (1932)
Definitely a film made before its time, Tod Browning's ("Dracula") drama of circus life's minimal plot (a midget is poisoned by a "normal" trapeze artist and her lover for his money) is eclipsed by unforgettable scenes with actual Siamese twins, pinheads, armless and legless wonders and other "mistakes of nature." Banned for many years; Harry Earles, Olga Baclanova, Wallace Ford star. 64 min.
12-1600 ***$19.99***

Maniac (1934)
A gorilla impersonator eating a cat eye! All-girl hypodermic duelling! Star Bill Woods as a vaudevillian body snatcher! The original slasher movie offers all this...and less! From the folks who gave you "Marijuana, Weed with Roots in Hell." 51 min.
62-1132 ***$19.99***

Mad Youth (1939)
Exploitation film charts the agony of a middle-aged gigolo-chasing mother (Betty Compson) trying to steer her troubled daughter off the primrose path of night-club neon and that devil rhumba beat. Baby, don't dip! 64 min.
68-8204 ***$19.99***

The Clash: Rude Boy (1980)
Great concert scenes by "the only band that matters" fuel this compelling look at Punk-era England, as a burned-out London youth (Ray Gange) gets a job working as a roadie for The Clash but continues down a road of alienation and self-destruction. Among the songs performed by Jones, Strummer, Simonon and Headon are "I'm So Bored with the USA," "I Fought the Law," "White Riot" and more. 130 min.
04-5133 ***$19.99***

Breaking Glass (1980)
New Wave musical tells the rags-to-riches story of rebellious rock star Hazel O'Connor and her group, Breaking Glass. With Phil Daniels, Jonathan Pryce. 94 min.
06-1072 Was $49.99 ***$19.99***

The Man Who Fell To Earth (1976)
David Bowie makes an unforgettable acting debut as a frail alien genius who comes to Earth in search of water for his drought-stricken planet. He uses his technology to become an industrial magnate, but falls victim to American consumerism and his own desires. Rip Torn, Buck Henry, Candy Clark co-star; directed by Nicolas Roeg. Uncut, 140-minute version.
02-1876 Letterboxed ***$14.99***

A Boy And His Dog (1975)
Harlan Ellison's award-winning short story takes place on a post-nuclear future Earth where the two most valuable items are food and women. Vic (Don Johnson) and his telepathic canine companion Blood search for both in a kinky sci-fi tale of survival. With Jason Robards, Susanne Benton. 87 min.
03-1004 ***$29.99***

The Worm Eaters (1977)
You'll squirm with delight at this horror-comedy of a nerd who gets back at the townspeople who scorned him by infesting their food with worms! The locals begin turning into "wormpeople," but you can bet the worm will turn. Writer/director Herb Robins stars in this Ted V. Mikels production. 75 min.
59-5017 ***$19.99***

Please Don't Eat My Mother (1972)
A softcore horror-comedy that unabashedly rips off "Little Shop of Horrors," as mama's boy and peeping Tom Buck Kartalian begins feeding nubile young women to his carnivorous plant. But what about Mother? AKA: "Hungry Pets." 95 min.
62-1334 ***$19.99***

Roger Corman

Five Guns West (1955)
The first film directed by Roger Corman, this action-packed sagebrusher stars John Lund as a Confederate officer who joins forces with a group of outlaws in order to stop a stagecoach carrying a Confederate traitor and $30,000 in gold. In order to complete their mission, the outlaws and their leader face Indians and Union officers. With Dorothy Malone, Jonathan Haze. 78 min.
10-2722 ***$12.99***

Swamp Women (1955)
Rough and tumble bayou actioner directed by Roger Corman about an undercover policewoman tagging along with trashy escapees from a woman's prison to track down a fortune in stolen jewels. Mike "Touch" Connors, Beverly Garland and Marie Windsor star. AKA: "Swamp Diamonds." 70 min.
09-2415 ***$19.99***

Gunslinger (1956)
Unusual frontier drama directed by "B"-movie legend Roger Corman has sheriff's widow Beverly Garland taking over her husband's job. John Ireland is the outlaw who comes to town to kill her, but winds up falling for her. With Allison Hayes, William Schallert, Dick Miller. 77 min.
10-8056 Was $19.99 ***$14.99***

She Gods Of Shark Reef (1956)
Pearl-diving beauties inhabit a deserted tropical island. Two brothers, one good and one bad, disrupt their adventures in paradise. Say "aloha" for action, sensuality and sharks. Don Durant and Bill Cord star in this Roger Corman extravaganza.
68-8457 Was $19.99 ***$14.99***

Attack Of The Crab Monsters (1957)
Roger Corman's sci-fi favorite tells of a group of scientists studying the effects of atomic radiation on a Pacific island. Eventually, they encounter monstrous crustaceans with the ability to communicate using the voices of their human victims. Richard Garland, Pamela Duncan, Mel Welles, Russell Johnson and Ed Nelson star. 85 min.
10-1641 ***$19.99***

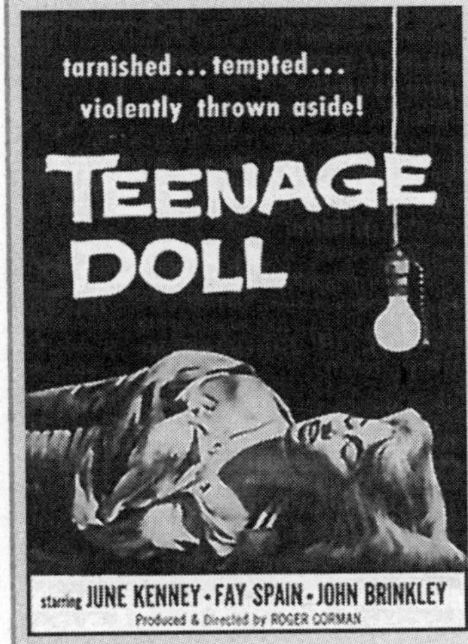
tarnished... tempted...
violently thrown aside!
TEENAGE DOLL
starring JUNE KENNEY · FAY SPAIN · JOHN BRINKLEY
Produced & Directed by ROGER CORMAN

Teenage Doll (1957)
Director Roger Corman's distaff spin on the "juvenile delinquent" drama genre stars June Kenney as a member of the Vandalettes, an all-girl gang. When a fight with the rival Black Widows ends with Kenney fatally stabbing another girl, it leads to an all-out rumble between the gangs and their boyfriends. Fay Spain, Richard Devon and Ziva Rodann as "Squirrel" also star. 68 min.
73-3003 ***$19.99***

The Undead (1957)
Early Roger Corman classic concerning a call girl who channels back to a previous existence...that of a condemned witch in the middle ages! Cleavage and cleavage abound; with Pamela Duncan, Allison Hayes, Billy Barty and the great Dick Miller. 71 min.
10-7189 ***$19.99***

Carnival Rock (1958)
Roger Corman directed this rarely-seen tale of teen rebels, gangsters, and a run-down carnival night club. Susan Cabot, Brian Hutton and the great Dick Miller star, with musical guests The Platters, The Blockbusters, and David Houston. 80 min.
15-5048 ***$12.99***

I, Mobster (1959)
A gang leader, called to testify before a Senate committee, recounts a sordid life that stretches from crime-filled slum alleys to opulent vice palaces in this bullet-riddled thriller from Roger Corman. Steve Cochran, Lita Milan, Robert Strauss star, with an appearance by legendary stripper Lili St. Cyr. 81 min.
27-6626 ***$19.99***

A Bucket Of Blood (1959)
Outrageous B-film cult classic from the Corman studio that blends beatniks, murder, and the art world. Busboy Dick Miller becomes a celebrity when he accidentally kills people, covers them with clay, and displays them in bohemian coffee-houses. With Anthony Carbone, Barboura Morris; it took them all of five days to film! 65 min.
68-8142 ***$14.99***

The Wasp Woman (1959)
Cosmetics producer Susan Cabot thinks she's discovered a new age-retarding cream, but learns that the "wasp enzymes" in the formula turn her into an insect-headed monster at night! Horrific (dare we say it?) "B"-movie from Roger Corman co-stars Michael Marks, Barboura Morris. 66 min.
68-8147 ***$14.99***

The Little Shop Of Horrors (1960)
Roger Corman's shot-on-pennies quickie horror spoof became a cult classic and inspired a stage musical. Flower shop nebbish Jonathan Haze's bloodthirsty plant makes him a celebrity, as long as he supplies it with fresh victims. With Jackie Joseph, Dick Miller, Mel Welles and a young Jack Nicholson as a masochistic dental patient. 70 min.
08-8060 Was $19.99 ***$14.99***

The Creature From The Haunted Sea (1960)
Who but director Roger Corman could offer up a slice of terror that combines fugitive American gangsters in the Caribbean, an undersea monster and a Castro-like dictator? Half-horror/half-spoof stars Antony Carbone, Besty Jones-Moreland and Beach Dickerson. 114 min.
09-1015 Was $19.99 ***$14.99***

The Fall Of The House Of Usher (1960)
The first of director Roger Corman's screen adaptations of the works of Edgar Allan Poe was this chiller. Vincent Price is a study in madness as Roderick Usher, a man set on stopping his family's heritage of insanity, even if it means burying his own sister alive! With Myrna Fahey, Mark Damon. 85 min.
19-1090 Was $59.99 ***$14.99***

The Last Woman On Earth (1960)
On a boat in the Caribbean following WWIII, a gangster and lawyer fight to decide who'll get to repopulate the planet with the titular female, the mobster's moll. Offbeat Roger Corman sci-fi drama puts screenwriter Robert Towne ("Chinatown") in front of the camera as Edward Wain. 64 min.
68-8195 ***$19.99***

Atlas (1960)
Chintzy Roger Corman classic with muscular Michael Forest as the title character who fights for an evil emperor, then battles against him for the hand of a beautiful woman. Frank Wolff (later a regular in spaghetti westerns) and Barboura Morris also star. 84 min.
68-8544 ***$19.99***

The Pit And The Pendulum (1961)
A young man's search for the truth behind his sister's death leads him into a medieval torture chamber and the demented schemes of brother-in-law Vincent Price. Chilling entry in director Roger Corman's Poe series also stars Barbara Steele, John Kerr. 80 min.
19-1089 ***$14.99***

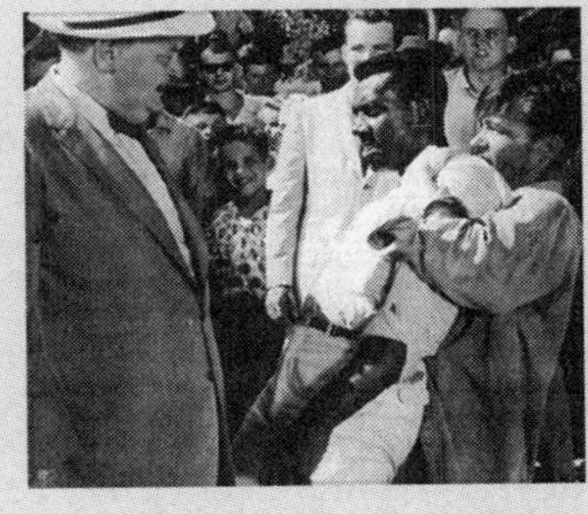

Shame (1962)
William Shatner turns in a solid performance in this dramatic portrayal of racism in the early '60s South. A member of a white supremacist group arrives in a small town provoking citizens in a calculated campaign against court-ordered school integration. Directed by Roger Corman; co-stars Frank Maxwell and Beverly Lunsford. AKA: "I Hate Your Guts," "The Intruder." 84 min.
10-7073 Was $19.99 ***$14.99***

Tales Of Terror (1962)
Three chilling short stories by Edgar Allan Poe come to the screen in grand fashion under director Roger Corman: "Morella," "The Black Cat" and "The Case of M. Valdemar." Scares are served in generous portions by stars Peter Lorre, Vincent Price and Basil Rathbone. 85 min.
73-1145 ***$14.99***

The Raven (1963)
There's little to do with Poe's poem in this classic horror spoof, written by Richard Matheson and directed by Roger Corman, about a three-way duel of wizardry between Vincent Price, Boris Karloff and half-man/half-raven Peter Lorre. Jack Nicholson and Hazel Court also star. 86 min.
19-1281 ***$14.99***

The Terror (1963)
When "The Raven" finished shooting three days early, a thrifty Roger Corman used the cast and sets for this suprisingly effective chiller. Jack Nicholson plays a lieutenant in Napoleon's army who is haunted by a mysterious woman in mad baron Boris Karloff's sinister castle. With Sandra Knight and the great Dick Miller. 81 min.
10-1076 Was $19.99 ***$14.99***

The Wild Angels (1966)
One of the first and best of the '60s biker movies, this intense drama stars Peter Fonda as Heavenly Blues, leader of a violent biker gang that destroys a hospital, takes over a church for a funeral that turns into a drunken orgy, and fights some rightfully annoyed townspeople. With Nancy Sinatra, Diane Ladd, Michael J. Pollard and "members of the Hell's Angels of Venice, California," as themselves; directed by Roger Corman. 87 min.
73-1185 Was $19.99 ***$14.99***

Von Richthofen And Brown (1971)
Roger Corman helmed this colorful look at World War I flying aces and arch-rivals Baron Manfred von Richthofen, Germany's infamous Red Baron, and Roy Brown, the Canadian who flew for the British. Thrilling aerial footage and exciting dogfights highlight Corman's last directing effort until "Frankenstein Unbound" in 1990. With John Phillip Law, Don Stroud. 96 min.
12-3087 ***❑$19.99***

Frankenstein Unbound (1990)
Roger Corman returns to directing after a 20-year absence with a unique approach to the classic horror story. John Hurt plays a brilliant scientist who, through a time warp, travels from the 21st century to Geneva in the 1800s. There he meets Mary Shelley, Dr. Victor Frankenstein, and the frightening monster invented by the not-so-good doctor. Raul Julia, Bridget Fonda and Michael Hutchence co-star. 86 min.
04-2415 Was $89.99 ***❑$14.99***

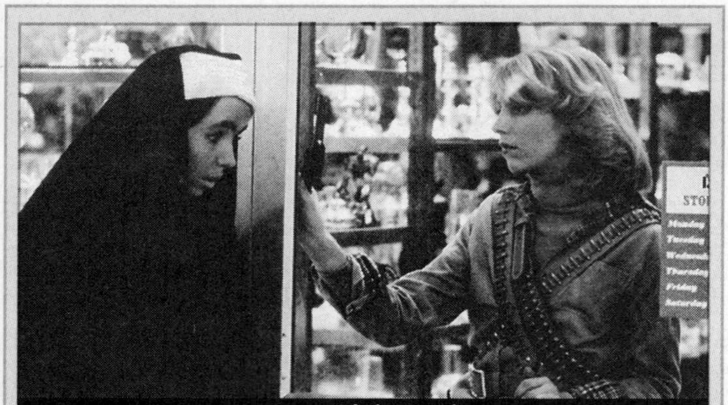

Dawn Of The Dead

George Romero

Night Of The Living Dead (1968)
The landmark shocker about a group of people trapped in an isolated farmhouse under siege by hordes of the recently deceased, returned to "life" as flesh-eating ghouls. Gruesome and groundbreaking, director/co-writer George Romero's cult classic stars Duane Jones, Judith O'Dea, Karl Hardman. 96 min.
10-2045 ***$14.99***

Night Of The Living Dead (Color Version)
The blood flows red in this newly colorized version of the modern horror classic.
18-3035 ***$19.99***

Night Of The Living Dead: Collector's Edition
This special tape features the original film with Scott Vladimir Licina's musical score, plus the theatrical trailer for the 30th Anniversary Edition. 90 min.
08-8794 ***$14.99***

Night Of The Living Dead: 30th Anniversary Edition
To mark three decades of undead chills and thrills, co-creator John A. Russo, producer/co-star Russ Streiner and "cemetery zombie" Bill Hinzman shot 15 minutes of new scenes that expand on characters and story points and added them into the original film. This special edition also includes an all-new musical score by Scott Vladimir Licina of Dark Theatre and a scene from Hinzman's film "Flesheater."
08-8795 ***$14.99***

Dawn Of The Dead (Director's Cut) (1979)
One of the all-time great fright films, George Romero's follow-up to "Night of the Living Dead" adds new dimensions of dark comedy and social satire to the original horror. The zombies are rising across America, and one small band of humans makes their last stand in a suburban shopping mall that the dead are drawn to by "instinct." David Emge, Ken Foree, Gaylen Ross star. Restored director's cut includes 11 minutes of footage not shown in theaters, plus theatrical film trailers and a Monroeville Mall commercial. 139 min.
08-8749 ***$14.99***

Day Of The Dead (1985)
George Romero's third "living dead" shocker is the most explicit and bloody yet! As the last camp of human survivors fight among themselves in an underground military base, the zombies begin to form a rudimentary intelligence as they prepare for a final assault. Richard Liberty, Lori Cardille and Terry Alexander star. 102 min.
03-1492 ***$12.99***

Day Of The Dead (Letterboxed Version)
Also available in a theatrical, widescreen format, which includes behind-the-scenes footage and the original theatrical trailer.
08-8679 ***$14.99***

Night Of The Living Dead (1990)
Original "Night" co-creator George A. Romero scripted this all-new updating of the horror classic, directed by special effects master Tom Savini. Who will survive the most terrifying night ever, as the dead come back to life to feast on the living? And the gore's in color, too! Tony Todd, Patricia Tallman star. 92 min.
02-2081 Was $19.99 ***$14.99***

Night Of The Living Dead: 25th Anniversary Documentary (1993)
A ghoulish celebration of one of the most successful horror films of all time, featuring director George A. Romero, writer John Russo and cult directors John Landis, Wes Craven and Tobe Hooper. Highlights include film clips, rare photos and fascinating insights into the making of the zombie classic. 83 min.
82-5003 Was $29.99 ***$19.99***

There's Always Vanilla (1971)
George Romero's long-lost coming-of-age drama tells of a drifter and war vet who carries on a tumultuous, sex- and drug-fueled affair with a pretty fashion model. Eventually, the two decide to go their separate ways. Featuring wild montages, keen dialogue and a cast that includes such "Night of the Living Dead" players as Judith Streiner (nee Ridley) and Bill Hinzman. AKA: "The Affair."
79-6444 Was $24.99 ***$19.99***

Season Of The Witch (Collector's Edition) (1972)
A young housewife's interest in a neighbor's occult practices draws her deeper and deeper into a witchy web of terror. Writer/director George Romero juxtaposes suburban life, feminism and black magic in this creepy tale. Jan White, Ray Laine star. AKA: "Hungry Wives," "Jack's Wife." 89 min.
67-7004 Remastered ***$14.99***

The Crazies (Collector's Edition) (1973)
A military plane crashes near a small Pennsylvania town, infecting the local water supply with an experimental virus that turns the residents into deranged killers. The government quarantines the area and sends in the army to "clean up" the situation in this chiller from director George Romero. Lane Carroll, W.G. McMillan star. AKA: "Code Name: Trixie." 103 min.
67-7001 Remastered ***$14.99***

Martin (Collector's Edition) (1976)
George Romero's twisted take on vampire films is set in Pittsburgh (where else?) and focuses on a young man who believes he is a real bloodsucker. Lacking fangs and wings, Martin must make do with drugging women and slashing their wrists with razor blades for his "nourishment." John Amplas, Lincoln Maazel, Tom Savini star. Special remastered edition includes the original theatrical trailer. 96 min.
08-8572 ***$14.99***

Knightriders (1981)
An offbeat story of a modern-day Camelot by George Romero. A touring group of motorcyclists stage medieval festivals with swordfights and cycle jousting, but personal conflicts and the commercial spotlight threaten their society. With Ed Harris, Tom Savini, Amy Ingersoll and a cameo by Stephen King. 145 min.
03-1171 Was $54.99 ***$19.99***

Monkey Shines: An Experiment In Fear (1988)
A monkey, trained to care for a quadriplegic young man, shares a bizarre mind link with her master, and starts to act out his subconscious thought of revenge. Spine-chilling shocker from George Romero stars Jason Beghe, Melanie Parker, Joyce Van Patten, Janine Turner. 115 min.
73-1025 ***$14.99***

Document Of The Dead (1989)
One of the most influential filmmakers in horror cinema history, George A. Romero, is the focus of a documentary salute that features interviews, a look at the creation of those gory special effects, and the scariest moments from "Night of the Living Dead," "Martin," "Dawn of the Dead" and other films. 83 min.
77-7002 ***$19.99***

Please see our index for these other George Romero titles: *Creepshow • Creepshow 2 • The Dark Half*

Samson vs. The Vampire Women (1961)
Mexican wrestling hero Santo was called Samson here in the States (under that mask, who could tell?). In this adventure, he battles a swarm of female vampires who keep beefcake slaves in their underground crypt. 89 min.
01-1286 ***$19.99***

Samson In The Wax Museum (1963)
Heroic Santo, the silver-masked strongman of Mexico, hikes up his leotard to wrestle a madman who turns villagers into monsters and keeps them in a wax horror tableau. AKA: "Santo in the Wax Museum." 92 min.
68-8410 ***$19.99***

The Choppers (1961)
Hot-roddin' action as you've never seen it before, as Arch Hall, Jr. leads his auto theft gang (Torch, Flip and Snooper) on a teen crime wave, but still finds time to sing "Monkey in My Hatband." Outrageous Arch Hall, Sr. production also stars former Playboy centerfold Marianne Gaba. 70 min.
15-5073 ***$19.99***

Eegah! (1963)
Richard Kiel (007 foe "Jaws") cuts a fine figure in this deliciously bad spin on the "Beauty and the Beast" theme. Kiel, in the title role, is a million-year-old caveman who kidnaps a geologist and his teenage daughter, with whom Kiel falls in love. Action, romance and rock-and-roll from the producer's son. Co-stars Marilyn Manning and Arch Halls Jr. and Sr. 92 min.
15-5006 ***$14.99***

The Sadist (1963)
When their car breaks down, three teachers find themselves in the clutches of the titular psychotic and his buxom girlfriend, and the deadly duo intend to get back for all those detention slips! Egregious "teen delinquent" film stars Arch Hall, Jr., Marilyn Manning. 95 min.
15-5069 ***$19.99***

Deadwood '76 (1965)
A whacked-out sagebrush saga with Arch Hall, Jr. as a handsome young gunslinger who arrives in a frontier town only to be mistaken for Billy the Kid and forced into defending himself...against Wild Bill Hickok! With Jack Lester, Melissa Morgan and Arch Hall, Sr., who also directed. Photography by William (Vilmos) Szigmond. 100 min.
15-5165 ***$29.99***

Times Square (1980)
Two runaway teenage girls, one shy and studious, the other a brassy free spirit, find friendship, sanctuary and adventure in the heart of New York City in this song-filled drama. Trini Alvarado, Robin Johnson and Tim Curry star; music by Gary Numan, The Pretenders and Roxy Music. 111 min.
44-1003 Was $79.99 ***$14.99***

My Dinner With Andre (1981)
One of the most acclaimed films of the '80s, the deceptively casual dinner conversation between friends Andre Gregory and Wallace Shawn covers such topics as modern theatre, modern philosophies and electric blankets and provides much food for thought. With Jean Lenauer as the waiter; Louis Malle directs. 110 min.
07-8112 ***$29.99***

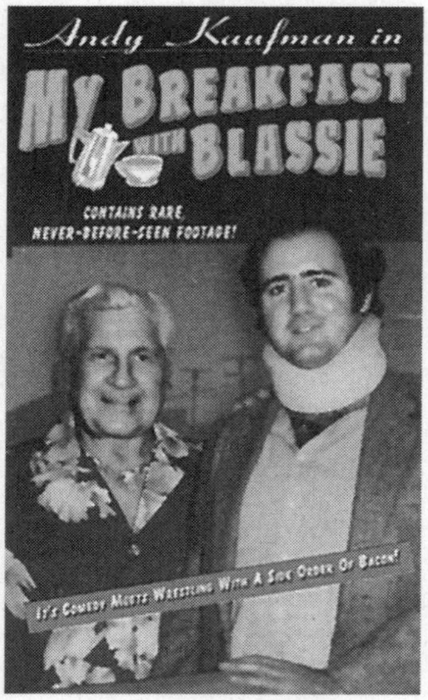

My Breakfast With Blassie (1983)
Move over, Andre (the Giant, that is)! Wrestling legend "Classy" Freddie Blassie, "The King of Men," meets comedian/champion co-ed grappler Andy Kaufman for breakfast at an L.A. Sambo's. Their engrossing conversation on such topics as pro wrestling, Japan and stardom provides much grappling for thought. 60 min.
15-5000 ***$14.99***

Moron Movies
You've seen them in New York, on "The Tonight Show," and even in Lansdowne. Now you can watch some of the most hilarious short films ever made in your own home; includes "Jello Makes a Lousy Doorstop," and more. 60 min.
50-6015 ***$19.99***

Flesh (1968)
One of the first Warhol Factory films to achieve "mainstream" recognition, this cinema vérité journey through New York's seamier streets features Joe Dallesandro as a bisexual street hustler. The graphic sexual themes still manage to shock and intrigue; with Candy Darling, Jackie Curtis, Geraldine Smith, Patti D'Arbanville. 90 min.
06-1539 ***$19.99***

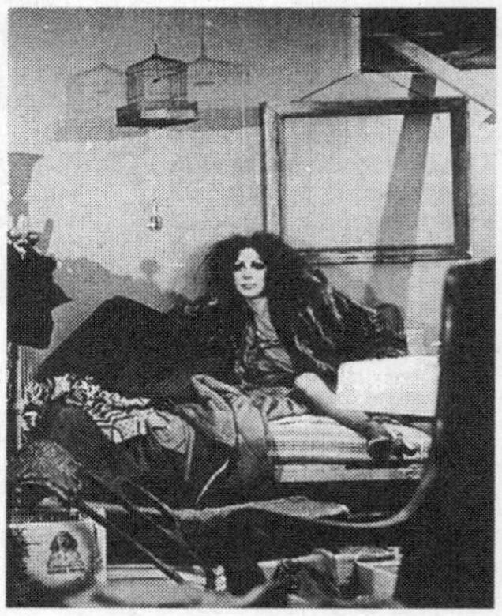

Trash (1970)
Outrageous tale of two of life's losers, courtesy of the Warhol Factory. Joe Dallesandro is a heroin-addicted male hustler whose girlfriend, Holly Woodlawn, harps on him to "better himself" so they can qualify for welfare. No sleazy detail is left out, including an infamous scene with transvestite Woodlawn and a beer bottle. Paul Morrissey directs. 103 min.
06-1540 ***$19.99***

Heat (1971)
Warhol Studio superstar Joe Dallesandro meets Sylvia Miles in Hollywood. What follows is a romance of passion and desperation that moves from palatial mansions to seedy hotels. Andy himself makes a guest appearance in this funky, funny movie that manages to capture the many moods of love and loneliness. Directed by Paul Morrissey. 101 min.
06-1541 ***$19.99***

Women In Revolt (1972)
This Andy Warhol-Paul Morrissey collaboration is a manic salute to—and savage satire of—women's liberation in the guise of a soap opera. The three female roles are played with improvisational relish by cross-dressing Factory regulars Candy Darling as a Long Island socialite, Jackie Curtis as a 21-year-old virgin who hires a lover, and Holly Woodlawn as a high-fashion model from Bayonne. 97 min.
50-5985 ***$19.99***

Andy Warhol's Frankenstein (1974)
The goriest, sexiest and funniest filming ever of the classic chiller. Udo Kier is the doctor who gleefully goes around dismembering townfolk for parts for his monsters, while his sex-starved wife and lab assistant have other things on their mind. With Joe Dallesandro, Monique Van Vooren; Paul Morrissey directs. Not in 3-D. AKA: "Flesh for Frankenstein." 96 min.
72-9001 Was $59.99 ***$19.99***

Flesh For Frankenstein (Letterboxed Version)
This is the unrated, theatrical, widescreen edition of "Andy Warhol's Frankenstein." 95 min.
50-5986 ***$19.99***

Andy Warhol's Dracula (1974)
Campy, outrageously gory vampire saga with Udo Kier as the ghoulish count seeking virgin blood in Italy. Joe Dallesandro, Vittorio de Sica also star in Paul Morrissey's perverse companion piece to "Andy Warhol's Frankenstein." AKA: "Blood for Dracula." 94 min.
72-9004 Was $79.99 ***$19.99***

Blood For Dracula (Letterboxed Version)
This is the unrated, theatrical, widescreen edition of "Andy Warhol's Dracula." 103 min.
50-5987 ***$19.99***

Andy Warhol's Bad (1977)
The classic Factory tale of murder, lust and depravity that one critic called "a movie with something to offend absolutely everybody." Carroll Baker is a New York electrolysist who also manages a female hit man syndicate. Co-stars Perry King, Susan Tyrrell, Stefania Cassini. 107 min.
53-1324 ***$29.99***

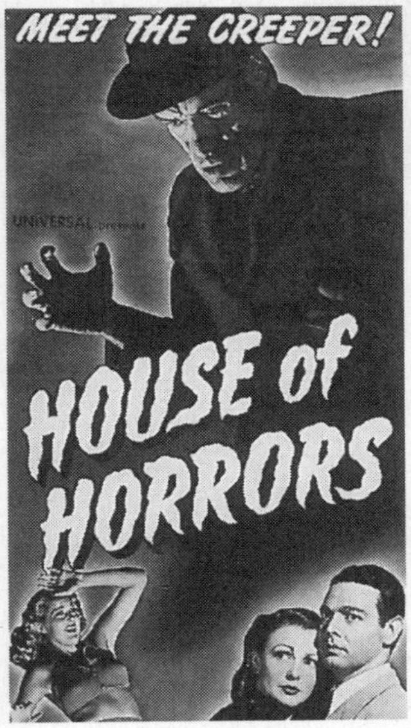
MEET THE CREEPER!
UNIVERSAL
HOUSE of HORRORS

House Of Horrors (1946)
In this eerie thriller, a Greenwich Village sculptor saves a deformed man from drowning, then uses him as a model for his work. When he receives "thumbs down" reviews from the critics, the artist sends his friend out to off the naysayers. Robert Lowery, Virginia Grey and Rondo Hatton, playing "The Creeper," star. 65 min.
07-2137 *$14.99*

The Brute Man (1946)
Rondo Hatton, the real-life victim of acromegaly who became a B-movie staple at Universal as "the Creeper," had his only starring role in this semi-autobiographical shocker. A handsome young man is disfigured in a lab experiment and seeks vengeance on his former friends. His only friend is a blind girl pianist. 60 min.
45-5367 *$14.99*

Paul Bartel's The Secret Cinema (1969)
Years before his work with Roger Corman, filmmaker Paul Bartel ("Eating Raoul") made his directorial debut with this unusual story of a young woman (Amy Vane) convinced her life is really a movie and she is controlled by its diabolical director. Also included is Bartel's short, "Naughty Nurse." 37 min.
15-5012 Was $19.99 *$12.99*

Private Parts (1972)
Wonderfully bizarre and kinky cult comedy by Paul Bartel, ignored when first released. A young girl leaves home and moves into her aunt's boarding hotel, which is populated by such characters as a "reverend" with a fetish for bodybuilders and a photographer who puts the girl's face on his water-filled love doll. Ann Ruymen, Lucille Benson, Stanley Livingston star. 87 min.
12-2253 *$14.99*

Death Race 2000 (1975)
Action-packed sci-fi satire from the Corman Studios. In the near future, the only sport left is the Trans-Continental Death Race, where points are accumulated by how many spectators are hit. David Carradine is the current champion, Sylvester Stallone and Mary Woronov are among his challengers; directed by Paul Bartel. 80 min.
19-1005 Was $19.99 *$14.99*

The Brain From Planet Arous (1958)
Earth is the battleground for two dueling aliens in this campy classic of '50s sci-fi. Second-string film legend John Agar is a scientist possessed by the evil alien, able to blow up planes with his stare. The good being, girding for a fight, takes over the body of...Agar's dog. No-holds-barred action! 71 min.
15-5066 *$19.99*

Fiend Of Dope Island (1961)
Sleaziness pervades this way-out adventure yarn featuring former screen Tarzan Bruce Bennett as the no-nonsense ruler of a Caribbean island where dope and gun-dealing are his prime concerns. All Bennett needs is a woman—and he gets one in blonde dancer Tania Velia. Whipping, savagery and some topless hoochie-coochie ensue! With future "Lassie" star Robert Bray. AKA: "Whirlpool."
79-6421 Was $24.99 *$19.99*

Let My Puppets Come (1978)
One of the most bizarre films in history, Gerard Damiano's demented fantasy mixes puppets and live actors in a sexual roundelay of raunchiness. With the mob closing in fast for cash they're owed, a group of New York businessmen decide to produce a porn film. Al Goldstein and assorted XXX performers appear in this "adults only" toy story. 74 min.
27-1144 *$29.99*

Performance (1970)
Mick Jagger and James Fox are superb in this duel of personalities. A gangster on the lam hides out in the home of a reclusive rock star, but soon finds himself a prisoner in a trap of drugs and sex. A taut psychological study and a masterpiece of suspense from Donald Cammell and Nicolas Roeg. 105 min.
19-1149 Was $59.99 *$19.99*

Comin' At Ya! (1981)
One of several '80s attempts to revive the 3-D movie craze, this "Spaghetti Western" semi-spoof follows a bank robber as he tries to rescue his girlfriend from the outlaw brothers who kidnapped her and shot him and left him for dead on their wedding day. Bullets, flaming arrows, rats, bats and a baby's bottom(!) all jump from the screen. Tony Anthony, Gene Quintano and Victoria Abril star. Includes two pairs of glasses. 91 min.
15-5501 *$14.99*

Prehistoric Women (1950)
You'll roar with delight at this camp classic about a group of amazon women who hunt for their mates when they get impatient with the male species. Laurette Luez, Joan Shawlee, and the unforgettable "Icelandic Giant" star. 74 min.
15-5004 *$14.99*

Wild Women (1953)
They filed the fangs of the fiercest beast and snared the mightiest serpent, but against the wild women of the jungle, they were mere magillas in the mist. Lewis Wilson stars as the leader of an African expedition who is captured by siren Frances Dubay and her untamed lasses. 75 min.
68-8344 *$19.99*

Wild Women Of Wongo (1959)
"Wild" indeed is the only way to describe this silly Stone Age romp, as the beautiful, alligator-worshipping Wongo women leave their Neanderthal husbands for the muscular men of a neighboring island. With Ed Fury and Adrienne Bourbeau (is this an early role for "Maude's" daughter or another actress with a strikingly similar name?). 80 min.
10-1399 *$19.99*

Fritz The Cat (1972)
R. Crumb's frisky feline comes to life in Ralph Bakshi's landmark "X-rated and animated" effort. Follow the adventures of the cool cat as he encounters 1960s culture—including sex, drugs, Hell's Angels, blacks and brutal cops (portrayed as pigs)—while turning into a full-blown radical. Skip Hinnant and Rosetta Le Noire provide the voices.
19-1214 *$39.99*

Heavy Traffic (1973)
Ralph Bakshi's heralded, adult animated social comedy (with live actors in its finale) tells of the son of a Jewish mother and adulterous Italian father who focuses his attentions on drawing cartoons. Eventually, he moves out, falls for a black woman and hangs out with Manhattan lowlifes who become the subjects of his art. 76 min.
19-1215 Was $29.99 *$14.99*

Hey, Good Lookin' (1975)
Life on the streets of Brooklyn in the '50s is graphically and humorously depicted by adult animator Ralph Bakshi in this wild and sexy cartoon version of "Mean Streets" that features voices by that film's Richard Romanus and David Proval. 77 min.
19-1236 *$19.99*

Street Fight (1975)
Maverick animator Ralph Bakshi's most controversial film, this blending of live-action and cartoon footage follows the odyssey of three rural blacks through a vice- and crime-ridden ghetto. Voices by Philip Michael Thomas, Scatman Crothers. AKA: "Coonskin." 85 min.
71-5097 *$19.99*

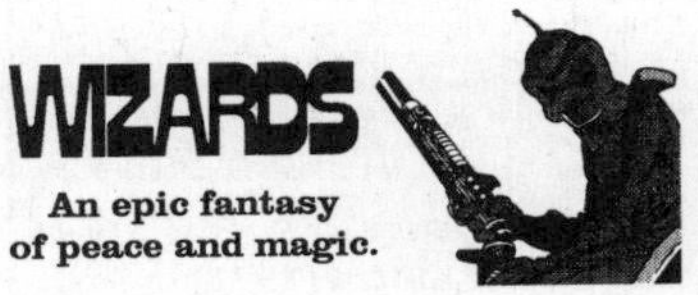
WIZARDS
An epic fantasy
of peace and magic.

Wizards (1977)
Dazzling animated fantasy epic by Ralph Bakshi, set 10 million years in the future. An evil mage conjures a demon army based on Nazi propaganda, and only his brother wizard, a fairy princess and a young warrior can save the world. Mark Hamill supplies voices. 80 min.
04-3133 Was $79.99 ❑*$19.99*

Cool World (1992)
The line between reality and fantasy is torn apart in director Ralph Bakshi's mind-blowing blend of animation and live-action. Gabriel Byrne plays an artist who is drawn into a bizarre cartoon universe where he meets the pen-and-ink girl of his dreams, Holli Would. Kim Basinger voices the animated Holli and plays her real-life persona; with Brad Pitt. 101 min.
06-2051 Was $89.99 ❑*$14.99*

The Nine Lives Of Fritz The Cat (1975)
Fritz returns in this sequel, minus the input of original director Ralph Bakshi. The cartoon cat finds himself in a catastrophic situation, on welfare and living in the slums. He turns to stoned fantasies to make things better and imagines himself on Mars, working for Henry Kissinger and involved with pornography. Voices are provided by Skip Hinnant and Reva Rose.
19-1621 *$39.99*

John Waters

Mondo Trasho (1969)
John Waters' first feature, filmed in the alleys, gutters, laundromats and dumps around Baltimore, follows a gold lamé-clad Divine through her travails. A hit and run accident, a sinister hog farm, the Infant of Prague, and a nude jogger all play a part; with Mary Vivian Pearce, David Lochary. 95 min. Silent with music score.
14-6152 *$29.99*

Multiple Maniacs (1970)
"Lady Divine's Cavalcade of Perversions" pitches its tents in Baltimore and the city will never be the same. Soon, the residents of "America's Charm City" are greeted by a freak show of transvestites, junkies, cannibalism and 15-foot lobsters. Divine, David Lochary, Mary Vivian Pearce and Edith Massey star in John Waters' notorious effort. 81 min.
14-6153 *$14.99*

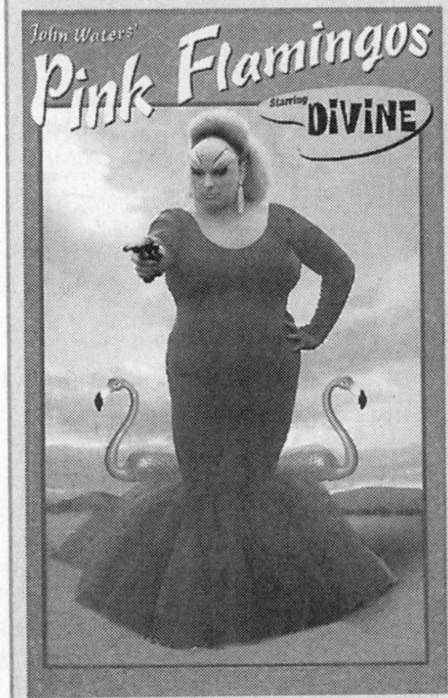
John Waters'
Pink Flamingos
Starring DIVINE

Pink Flamingos: 25th Anniversary Edition (1972)
The landmark "exercise in poor taste" from writer/director John Waters that still fascinates and repels moviegoers. From a trailer hideout near Baltimore, "filthiest person alive" Divine and her demented family defend her title from would-be usurpers David Lochary and Mink Stole, and the results include rape, incest, cannibalism, cruelty to chickens and the most famous film ending since "King Kong." With Mary Vivian Pearce, Danny Mills, and Edith Massey as Edie the Egg Lady. Special anniversary edition includes commentary by Waters, bonus unused footage, and the original theatrical trailer. 108 min.
47-1864 ❑*$19.99*

Female Trouble (1974)
Divine is Dawn Davenport: teenage delinquent, unwed mother, working girl and murderer. Follow her outrageous life of violence, and learn why "crime is beauty," in John Waters' cult comedy. With Edith Massey, David Lochary and Cookie Mueller. 95 min.
14-6046 Was $39.99 *$29.99*

Desperate Living (1977)
Described by creator John Waters as "a monstrous fairy-tale comedy for adults with the minds of 7-year-olds," this vulgar fable follows the unhappy lives of the residents of Mortville, a town inhabited by criminals, perverts and other misfits. Mink Stole, Edith Massey, Jean Hill, Susan Lowe and Liz Renay star. 90 min.
02-2382 *$19.99*

Polyester (1981)
Poor Francine Fishpaw (Divine) is living in a suburban nightmare. Surrounded by an unfaithful husband, rebellious children and an unsympathetic mother, can she find happiness with sophisticated drive-in owner Todd Tomorrow (Tab Hunter)? John Waters' off-center satire of the American Dream also stars Edith Massey, Ken King, Mink Stole and Stiv Bators. 86 min.
02-2381 *$19.99*

Hairspray (1988)
Can blacks and whites Madison their way to harmony in 1962 Baltimore? Writer/director John Waters says "yes" in his outrageously funny, surprisingly sentimental look at one girl's dreams of stardom on a TV teen dance show, and how they lead to a civil rights milestone. Stars Divine, Jerry Stiller, Sonny Bono, Debbie Harry, Michael St. Gerard and Ricki Lake. 90 min.
02-1858 ❑*$14.99*

Cry-Baby (1990)
There's music, laughs and loads of juvenile delinquent fun in John Waters' salute to '50s teen hoods. Johnny Depp stars as misunderstood rebel "Cry-Baby" Walker, whose love for a "good girl" lands him in trouble with the law; with a supporting cast that includes Ricki Lake, Iggy Pop, Susan Tyrrell, Traci Lords, Amy Locane, Patty Hearst, Polly Bergen, and Kim McGuire as "Hatchet-Face." 85 min.
07-1650 Was $19.99 ❑*$14.99*

Serial Mom (1994)
She's the perfect all-American parent: a great cook and homemaker, a devoted recycler, and a woman who'll literally kill to keep her children happy! Kathleen Turner's murderous habits turn her into a media celebrity in John Waters' sharp-edged satire on family life, tabloid TV, video store customers who don't rewind and other topics. With Sam Waterston, Ricki Lake, Mink Stole and Suzanne Somers as herself. 93 min.
44-1966 Was $19.99 ❑*$14.99*

Pecker (1998)
A funny and touching look at overnight success and its price, courtesy of trash auteur John Waters. Edward Furlong is the camera-obsessed Pecker, a Baltimore teen whose black-and-white shots of his offbeat family and friends make him the toast of New York's art world, thanks to gallery owner Lili Taylor. With Christina Ricci, Martha Plimpton, Mary Kay Place and Brendan Sexton III. 86 min.
02-5196 Was $99.99 ❑*$19.99*

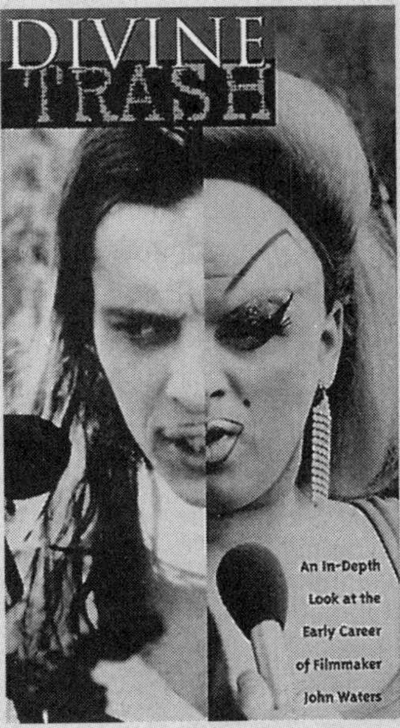
DIVINE TRASH
An In-Depth
Look at the
Early Career
of Filmmaker
John Waters

Divine Trash (1998)
Get the lowdown (and we mean low down!) on one of the most infamous films of all time—John Waters' 1972 cult classic "Pink Flamingos"—in this acclaimed documentary. Along with rare rehearsal and on-the-set footage, there are interviews with family, colleagues and cast members (including the late Divine) that reveal Waters' lifelong fascination with both "show biz" and "shock biz." 105 min.
53-6842 *$19.99*

Divine Double Feature
A tribute to the late, great Divine, "the most beautiful woman in the world" and "the filthiest person alive." First is the early John Waters short "The Diane Linkletter Story," with Divine in the title role and David Lochary and Mink Stole as her concerned parents. Next, a rare (and grainy) filming of "The Neon Woman," an outrageous cabaret drama with Divine as a strip joint owner with all manner of family problems. 110 min.
53-7507 *$39.99*

Love Letter To Edie (1973)
You loved her as "The Egg Lady" in "Pink Flamingos," as Aunt Ida in "Female Trouble," and as Queen Carlotta in "Desperate Living." Edith Massey gets her own showcase in this fictionalized account of her life and career which features director John Waters and fellow Waters regular Mink Stole. 15 min.
76-7363 *$14.99*

Herschell Gordon Lewis

The Prime Time (1960)
Herschell Gordon Lewis produced this rarely seen look at rebellious teens and beatniks. A young woman traps an older police detective into marrying her, while spurning her teenage boyfriend and a psychotic hipster called The Beard. Karen Black made her debut here, and Jo Ann LeCompte and Frank Roche also star, along with nude models. AKA: "Hell Kitten."
79-5125 Was $24.99 *$19.99*

Living Venus (1960)
One of H.G. Lewis' first films was this sexploitation melodrama about the rise and decline of a men's maagzine publisher who falls for and marries one of his models, but continues to have affairs with the beautiful women paraded before him. William Kerwin, Danica D'Hondt star; look for Harvey Korman in his film debut. 87 min.
79-5590 *$19.99*

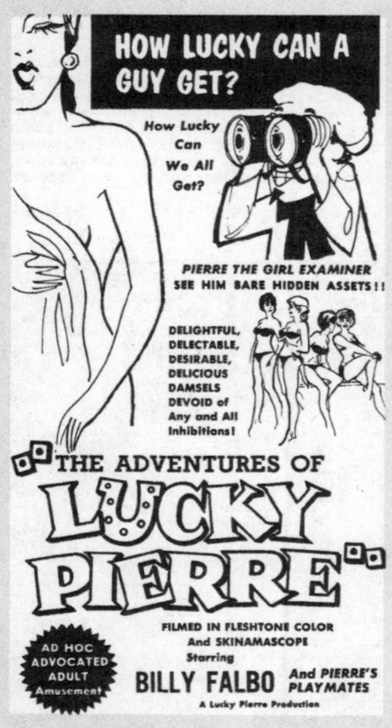

The Adventures Of Lucky Pierre (1961)
Lucky Pierre is a bumbling artist whose sexual fantasies won't stop in this nudes-a-poppin' farce from sultan of schlock Herschell Gordon Lewis. Nudity abounds in this made-in-a-week "skinemascope" masterpiece, as Pierre encounters naked gals all over the place—even in his studio and at the drive-in! Billy Falbo and William Kerwin star.
79-5006 Was $24.99 *$19.99*

Nature's Playmates (1962)
Horror Director H.G. Lewis goes the "nudie picture" route with this tale of a male-female Chicago detective team whose investigation takes them to the naturist camps of Florida. Scott Osborne, Vickie Miles and the members of the Sunny Rest Lodge Nudist Camp star. 56 min.
62-1340 *$19.99*

BOIN-N-G! (1962)
"The most protracted peeks...longest leers...and greatest guffaws yet...as two simple citizens set out to make a 'cutie' movie!" Classic shot-on-pennies sex flick from Herschell Gordon Lewis and David Friedman features "damsels by the dozen in various stages of array and disarray!" With Tommy Sweetwood, Bill Johnson and Christina Castel.
79-5005 *$19.99*

Daughter Of The Sun (1962)
Hershell Gordon Lewis and David Friedman made this nudie classic featuring Miss Rusty Allen as a teacher defending herself for appearing sans clothes in a nudist magazine. There's volleyball, showers and more naked fun in the sun; shot in beautiful Miami.
79-5028 Was $24.99 *$19.99*

Blood Feast (1963)
The first "splatter film" from gore auteur Herschell Gordon Lewis. An ancient Egyptian cult that thrived on human sacrifices is resurrected in a modern metropolis, under the guise of...a catering service! The unprecedented display of slashing, murder and dismemberment stars Mal Arnold, Connie Mason. 70 min.
70-3005 *$19.99*

Bell, Bare And Beautiful (1963)
An ultra-rare H.G. Lewis "nudie" effort about a millionaire who seeks the gal of his dreams, a burlesque queen played by stripper Virginia Bell (48-24-36). In order to nab her, he must get past her tough mob-connected agent. Shot in Spartan's Tropical Gardens of Miami, Florida. With Thomas Sweetwood. 64 min.
79-5118 *$19.99*

Scum Of The Earth (1963)
The last nudie collaboration between Herschell Gordon Lewis and David Friedman was this no-holds-barred look at the nude modeling industry and a sleazy photographer who teams with his top model to blackmail gorgeous young women to pose in uncompromising positions. Thomas Sweetwood and Sandra Sinclair star.
79-5794 *$19.99*

Goldilocks And The Three Bares (1963)
Herschell Gordon Lewis (billed as "Lewis H. Gordon") helmed this nudie gem about a nightclub singer who joins his comedian friend to track down their girlfriends during one of their secret weekend trips. They land in Sunshine Park, a Miami nudist resort, and soon get into the swing of naked things. Rex Marlow, Vickie Miles and "Former Light Heavyweight Champion of the World" Joey Maxim star.
79-6490 Was $24.99 *$19.99*

2000 Maniacs (1964)
What do you get when you mix "The Beverly Hillbillies" with "Brigadoon" and toss in oodles of blood, gore and violence? You get H.G. Lewis' tale of townsfolk massacred during the Civil War who come back to life to torture unwary Yankee tourists. Playboy centerfold Connie Mason stars. Y'all come back now, y'hear? 75 min.
14-6023 *$19.99*

Color Me Blood Red (1965)
H.G. Lewis' look at the art world follows a struggling painter who cannot complete his latest work until after killing his girlfriend and finding just the right shade of red. He becomes a hit, but must maintain a steady supply of the special pigment. "They say Gauguin was obnoxious, too!" Don Joseph stars. 78 min.
14-6031 Was $24.99 *$19.99*

Moonshine Mountain (1965)
Wild, fightin', furious, still-swiggin' hillbilly flick from H.G. Lewis centers on a successful Country and Western star who returns to his beloved Carolina hills only to be pulled into the middle of a feud between two rival clans. Chuck Scott, Adam Song and the Sweet Gum Sisters star. 90 min.
68-8750 *$19.99*

Jimmy, The Boy Wonder (1966)
A family film by noted goremeister Herschell Gordon Lewis? Yep, and it's as weird as you think. A young boy, bored with school, goes on a magical adventure to find who stopped the world's time and encounters an absent-minded astonomer, an evil character named Mr. Fig, and even discovers what awaits at World's End.
79-5066 *$19.99*

The Girl, The Body And The Pill (1967)
Lewis' cautionary tale of a hip high school instructor who teaches sex education classes, gets canned by the uncool principal and continues her lectures at home. Meanwhile, her students learn about "the pill" and play musical beds, while one punk tries to rape the teacher. Pamela Rhea, Bill Rogers and Nancy Lee Noble, "the teenie-bopper bombshell," star.
79-5004 *$19.99*

The Blast-Off Girls (1967)
H.G. Lewis presents his own version of "A Hard Day's Night" in this not-to-be-believed tale of unscrupulous rock promoter Boojie Baker, who guides a band called The Big Blast! to fame, fortune and gorgeous groupies, only to have the whole gig turn sour. Far-out flick features Dan Conway, Ray Sagar and "guest star" Col. Harland Sanders. 85 min.
79-5228 *$19.99*

A Taste Of Blood (1967)
Herschell Gordon Lewis' ambitious vampire epic centers on a man who drinks two mysterious bottles of brandy and turns into a ghastly bloodsucker. The ghoul goes to England and Europe to quench his thirst for human blood, leaving a trail of dead bodies in his wake. Bill Rogers, Elizabeth Wilkinson star. AKA: "The Secret of Dr. Alucard." 120 min.
79-5463 Was $24.99 *$19.99*

The Gruesome Twosome (1967)
Oh, well, you know what they say: "Hair today, gone tomorrow." Gory Herschell Gordon Lewis masterwork about the hair-raising happenings that go on in a college rooming house and "The Little Wig Shop," which deals in amazingly fresh hairpieces made of "100% Human Hair!" Stars Elizabeth Davis and Chris Martell.
79-5589 *$19.99*

Suburban Roulette (1967)
A wild and appropriately seedy wife-swapping epic from H.G. Lewis about the evils of suburbia, where husbands offer their spouses in lotteries and sex-lusting housewives rant and rave until they get it on. Once taboo-shattering drama, now a camp classic, starring Elizabeth Wilkinson. 91 min.
79-5592 *$19.99*

Something Weird (1968)
A man is horribly disfigured in an industrial accident that also gives him the power of E.S.P. He soon becomes involved in a bizarre mix of witchcraft, murder and psychic suspense in this psychedelic treat from H.G. Lewis. Tony McCabe, Elizabeth Lee star. 87 min.
70-3148 *$19.99*

How To Make A Doll (1968)
Herschell Gordon Lewis directed this amusing sex farce about a nerdy math professor whose intense shyness with the ladies inspires him to carry on his late mentor's work and invent android women to satisfy his sexual needs. Robert Wood and Jim Vance star.
79-5043 Was $24.99 *$19.99*

She-Devils On Wheels (1968)
"We don't owe nobody nothin,' and we don't make no deals; We're swingin' chicks on motors, we're man-eaters on wheels." From B-film legend Herschell Gordon Lewis comes this tale of a deadly female biker gang and their codes of sex and violence. Features special Lewis "gore" touches and real members of the Iron Cross cycle club. 83 min.
79-5587 *$19.99*

Just For The Hell Of It (1968)
The "teen gang" genre receives the Herschell Gordon Lewis touch in this violent tale of a group of young vandals who call themselves Destruction, Inc. and get their kicks from crashing parties, dousing cars with paint, pushing blind people into traffic and other anti-social actions. Ray Sager, Nancy Lee Noble star. 88 min.
79-5588 *$19.99*

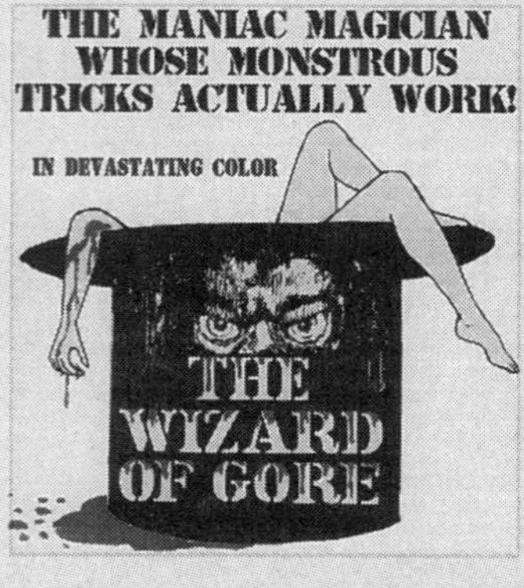

The Wizard Of Gore (1970)
Illusion defies reality (or does it?) when Montag the Magician performs his amazing tricks of mutilation on female volunteers from the audience...but will a nosy local TV personality bring the curtain down on his all-too-real act? All of the gore and horror effects that H.G. Lewis fans have come to expect, plus a wild "zen" ending. With Ray Sager.
79-5591 *$19.99*

Stick It In Your Ear (1970)
A man mysteriously awakes in a Gothic building and quickly disappears into a world of psychedelia, where he takes drugs, partakes in swinging sex and experiences flashbacks of Vietnam. After becoming a hired assassin (and having sex with his intended victim), he searches for his real identity. Guido Conte stars in this Herschell Gordon Lewis presentation.
79-5532 Was $24.99 *$19.99*

This Stuff'll Kill Ya (1971)
Wild stuff, Herschell Gordon Lewis-style, telling the story of a preacher who uses his religious musings as a cover for his moonshine ring and other seedy activities. Strange sexual happenings, shoot-outs, fights with the Feds and serial murders highlight this film that boasts "Lovin', Likker' and Lawbreakin'." With Tim Holt, Jeffrey Allen; look for Larry Drake ("L.A. Law") in his film debut. 100 min.
79-5117 *$19.99*

The Gore-Gore Girls (1972)
The final horror entry from splatter maven H.G. Lewis follows a detective's search for the fiend who has been horribly mutilating and killing beautiful young dancers. Among the suspects are a bar patron who smashes melons with his bare hands, a tough "women's libber," and nightclub owner Henny Youngman (that's right, we said Henny Youngman!). 84 min.
36-2014 *$19.99*

The Blood Trilogy Outtakes
It's a sure bet the Hays Office never would have approved of these depraved outtakes from the grossest films ever, Herschell Gordon Lewis' "Blood Feast," "2000 Maniacs" and "Color Me Blood Red." Producer David Friedman found this footage somewhere, and now they're offered to you in all their disgusting glory.
70-5826 Was $24.99 *$19.99*

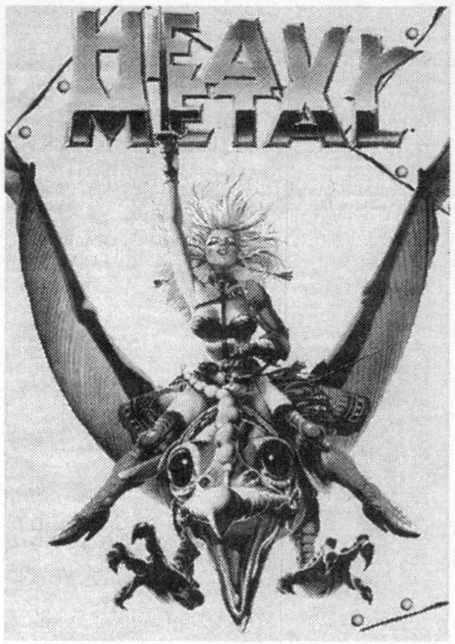

Heavy Metal (1981)
One of the most requested titles at Movies Unlimited is this cutting-edge animated adventure inspired by the popular fantasy magazine. The fantastic stories, which revolve around the powers of a mysterious jewel, include a futuristic cab driver, a sword-swinging warrior, a Pentagon secretary abducted by a UFO and a doomed B-17 pilot. John Candy and Joe Flaherty contribute their voices; music by Black Sabbath, Blue Oyster Cult, Cheap Trick and others. 90 min.
02-2880 Was $19.99 *$14.99*

Heavy Metal 2000 (1999)
Mind-blowing in-name-only sequel to the 1981 animated cult fave tells of a curvaceous futuristic warrior named Julie whose home planet, Eden, holds the key to immortality and is destroyed by Tyler, a space pirate. Tyler also kidnaps Julie's sister, whom he bleeds for an invisibility serum he needs to pursue immortality, prompting Julie to take action. Michael Ironside, Julie Strain and Billy Idol provide the voices. 88 min.
02-3471 *$99.99*

Flesh Gordon (Collector's Edition) (1972)
Outrageous and campy, this adult version of the Saturday matinee classic follows Flesh, Dale Ardor and Dr. Jerkoff into outer space to stop a strange sex ray flowing from the planet Wang towards Earth. Lots of nudity, a giant Penisaurus, Candy Samples as a lesbian space queen, and an uncredited voice-over by Craig T. Nelson. Restored version includes 10 minutes of previously unseen footage and the original theatrical trailer. 90 min.
53-6102 *$29.99*

Flesh Gordon 2: Flesh Gordon Meets The Cosmic Cheerleaders (1993)
The horny space hero returns in this outrageously sexy sci-fi spoof that finds him and girlfriend Dazzling Dale trying to save the galaxy from a libido-lobotomizing threat. Joined by the Cosmic Cheerleaders, Flesh overcomes gas-spewing "assteroids," Massive Mountains, Master Bator and other hazards to meet the challenge. With Vince Murdocco and Melissa Mounds. Unrated version; 90 min.
21-9038 Was $89.99 *$14.99*

High School Caesar (1960)
John Ashley is the teenage crime boss who "had more rackets than Al Capone" in this classic J.D. drama of high school protection rackets, hot rod races and gang rumbles. With Lowell Brown, Judy Nugent. 75 min.
15-5047 *$12.99*

Forbidden Adventure (1937)
An extremely rare exploitation item filled with phony stuff of all sorts and detailing the adventures of two explorers who travel to Cambodia in search of the hidden city of Angkor. What they find are "ape-men" (or are they men in ape suits?) after the native women travelling with them. Ferns and shrubbery are superimposed over the topless natives. Authentic, huh? With Wilfred Lucas. 80 min.
79-5497 Was $24.99 *$19.99*

BLOODSUCKING FREAKS

Bloodsucking Freaks: The Director's Cut (1977)
And "cut" is certainly an understatement when it comes to this uncensored version of the grisly shocker with a cult following! Meet Sardu, maniacal master of ceremonies at a way-off-Broadway theatre where the sadistic stage proceedings include dismemberment, human dart boards, amateur dentistry, and using a straw to (what else?) suck brains. Seamus O'Brien, Louie DeJesus, Viju Krim star. 91 min.
46-8010 *$19.99*

Street Of Forgotten Women (1925)
An egregious example of early exploitation filmmaking, this silent "docu-drama" follows the sordid exploits of prostitutes and their clients, the partners in exploitation they seek out in the public thoroughfares. The more things change...
68-8134 $19.99

This Nude World (1932)
Nudists...Uninhibited sun-worshipers or shameless perverts? Nature lovers or degenerate beasts? This campy nudist camp exposé pretends concern for these moral dilemmas while peeking over fences in France, Germany and the U.S. 55 min.
62-1319 $19.99

Damaged Lives (1933)
The horrors of venereal disease are explored in this social drama that had a tough time with censors upon its release. The story centers on a young couple whose future is endangered when the husband makes a terrible mistake. Diane Sinclair and Lyman Williams star; Edgar G. Ulmer directs. 60 min.
10-9249 Was $19.99 $14.99

Guilty Parents (1933)
A roadshow classic from the 1930s detailing a pretty blonde's descent into the world of cheap sex, and the drunken roadhouse parties, crimes, abortions, murders and strip poker games that occur when carnal education is ignored.
79-5335 Was $24.99 $19.99

Tomorrow's Children (1934)
"Is every woman entitled to motherhood?" Not according to this bizarre look at one woman's troubles. Forced by the state to submit to sterilization when it's learned her family has a history of drunkenness, insanity and idiocy, it's up to her doctor to save her. Unintentionally funny camp drama. 55 min.
09-1695 $19.99

Sex Madness (1937)
How far can a "good girl" go? See what happens to those who "go all the way" in this unintentionally hilarious anti-sex diatribe. Wild dancing and heavy petting lead to pregnancy, social diseases, drugs and even death! Racy for its time, the film contains brief semi-nude scenes. 55 min.
62-1090 $19.99

Damaged Goods (1937)
Upton Sinclair co-authored this blend of social drama and anti-VD diatribe, focusing on a marriage tarnished by venereal disease. The husband contracts it from a party girl and, ignoring the problem, infects his wife and child. Douglas Walton, Arletta Duncan star. AKA: "Forbidden Desires," "Marriage Forbidden."
79-5334 Was $24.99 $19.99

Secrets Of A High School Girl (1937)
High schooler Beth needs Mom's help in explaining the birds and the bees, but Mom's just too busy to help her. With some advice from her maid, Beth tries to avoid her newfound sexual desires, but it's not easy. Helen MacKellan and Cecelia Parker star in this story of "heedless youth speeding through life with the throttle wide open."
79-5639 Was $24.99 $19.99

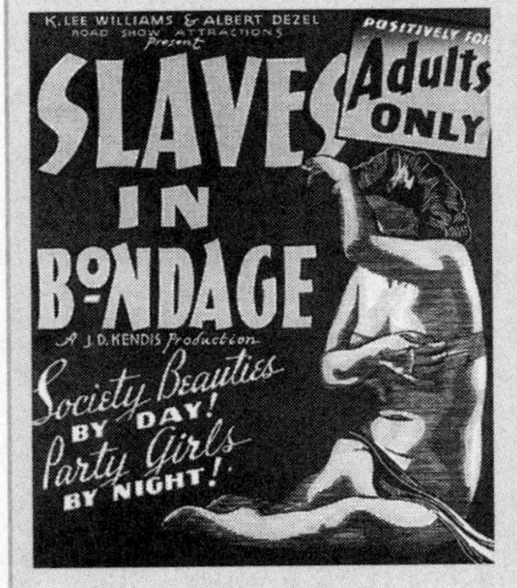

Slaves In Bondage (1937)
"Society beauties by day! Party Girls by night!" See what happens to naive young ladies who are drawn by the pleasures of the big city into a sordid life of sin, scandal and spanking (yep, spanking, too!) in this early roadshow drama. Lona Andre, Wheeler Oakman star.
68-8845 $19.99

Secrets Of A Model (1940)
A sleazeball with the hots for a carhop with a sickly mother talks the gal into modeling for an artist for cash. He takes her to a party, gets her drunk, proposes and takes advantage of her, shattering the innocent's morals. Sharon Lee, Harold Daniels star; also includes the shorts "How to Take a Bath" and "These Girls Are Fools."
79-5638 Was $24.99 $19.99

They Wear No Clothes (1941)
This wild documentary purports to be a serious sociological study of nudism and those who work in the buff, but after watching scene after scene of strippers, artist's models, naked horseback riders and white jungle goddesses(!) viewers will enjoy it as pure campy fun. Also included is the short subject, "How to Hold a Husband." 55 min.
03-1347 $19.99

Child Bride (1941)
A roadshow exploitation classic set in hillbilly territory about a schoolteacher who wants to change the region's custom of having adults marry young gals. Shirley Miles plays the nubile girl whom an ornery moonshiner wants to take down the aisle. This restored edition of the film features the infamous "skinny-dipping" scene. With Angelo Rossito and R.G. Armstrong.
79-5349 Was $24.99 $19.99

The Curse Of The Clap
The spread of sexually transmitted diseases was as real and threatening as any enemy the U.S. military ever faced, as portrayed by these two government-produced training films decrying unrestrained behavior. Features "One a Minute" (1944) and "The Miracle of Living" (1947), starring Darren McGavin. 54 min. total.
09-3086 $14.99

Mom And Dad (1947)
This camp classic by William "One Shot" Beaudine depicts a young girl whose mother fails to tell her the facts of life. Guess who gets pregnant soon after? A sequence showing an actual Caesarian delivery was added to the film, shown as an "educational feature" to sex-segregated theatres. "Uncut version" includes an opening sing-along of "The Star-Spangled Banner"! 97 min.
62-1307 $19.99

Because Of Eve: The Story Of Life (1948)
Upon their visit to the doctor's before their wedding, Sally and Bob learn of each other's past and it ain't pretty: Sally had a child out of wedlock and Bob had V.D. So Doc shows them three films: "The Story of Reproduction," "The Story of V.D." and "The Story of Birth." There's nudity, gross sores and an actual childbirth. Pure exploitation promoted as education! 72 min.
79-5502 Was $24.99 $19.99

Street Corner (1949)
Classic "hygiene film" from the 1940s in the tradition of "Mom and Dad." A high school girl finds she's pregnant, and, to make matters worse, her boyfriend dies in a car accident. A hash house waitress sends her to a neighborhood abortionist, but will she survive the operation? Includes a Cesarean and regular birth sequence (the latter shot in color in the 1960s!). With Marcia Mae Jones.
79-6166 Was $24.99 $19.99

Birthright (1951)
Produced by the "Southern Educational Film Production Service," this sex-ed epic is unusual in that its story of a chicken farmer who gives his pregnant wife venereal disease is interrupted by both nudie footage (of other performers!) and a graphic childbirth sequence. Marjory Morris, Boyce Brown and who-knows-who-else star. 50 min.
79-5875 Was $24.99 $19.99

Mated (1952)
Sex education in marriage is the topic of this info-oriented exploiter about a newly hitched couple who discover everything about their bodies, from pubic hair to menstruation, often with help from hunky beefcake photos of naked men. There's also a sequence on enlarging breasts through suction and giving birth. Wow! 62 min.
79-5878 Was $24.99 $19.99

Test Tube Babies (1953)
Sublimely sleazy sex-ed shocker that was the darling of the censorship boards. John Maitland, Monica Davis ("Rocket Attack, U.S.A.") star; from the makers of "The Flesh Merchants" and "Glen or Glenda."
10-7186 $19.99

Bad Girls Do Cry (1954)
And bad movies like this one will make you laugh. A teenage exploitation epic of young women caught up in a big-city sex-for-hire rings features nubile girls stripping down to their undies. Bill Page, Misty Ayers star; directed by "Make Room for Daddy" regular Sid Melton. 59 min.
68-8455 $19.99

Unmarried Mothers (1955)
A Swedish drama, promoted as an exploitation item for American drive-ins. Four Swedish gals "do it" before taking the vows and suffer the consequences. Eva Sliberg stars as one of the promiscuous misses.
68-8456 $19.99

Wasted Lives (1958)
French sex kitten Etchika Choureau ("Darby's Rangers") in a "Joy of Childbirth" tale that's "as daring a picture as the screen will ever get...the birth of twins told with delicacy and reverence." Twice the movie you may be expecting. 92 min. Dubbed in English.
68-8416 $19.99

You've Ruined Me, Eddie (1959)
Campy exploitation item set in a small town where the rich daughter of the hamlet's leading doctor discovers she's pregnant and battles tooth and nail over having the child with her lover, an area orphan. With double-crosses, sleazy lawyers, corrupt cops. Jeanne Rainer, Ted Marshall star. AKA: "The Touch of Flesh." 76 min.
79-5221 $19.99

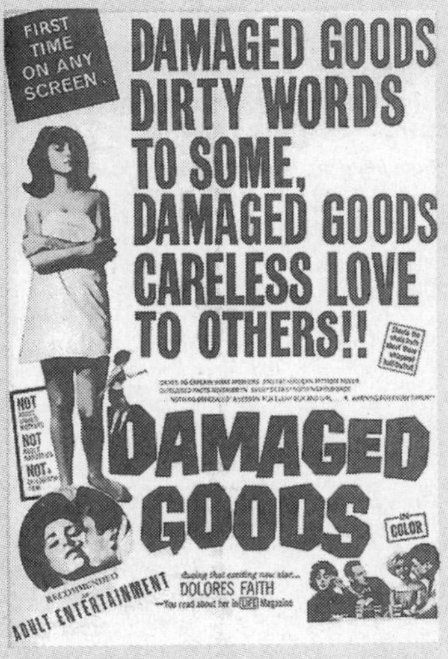

V.D.: Damaged Goods (1960)
The juvenile delinquent flick goes the sex education route in this tale of a high school track star who gets venereal disease from a floosie after he goes boozing with guys for the weekend. There's lots of other complexities in the plot, plus some disturbing footage of VD victims. Dolores Faith, Charlotte Stewart star; theme music is provided by The Ventures.
79-5888 Was $24.99 $19.99

My Baby Is Black! (1961)
This French-made drama may have a tabloid title and exploitation elements (including beatniks, nude models and such), but it's also a surprisingly serious examination of a subject rarely seen at the time on American screens. A young woman has an affair with a black student and, without his knowledge, gives birth to their child. With Francois Giret, Gordon Heath. Dubbed in English.
79-5961 Was $24.99 $19.99

Married Too Young (1962)
Harold Lloyd, Jr. and Trudy Marshall are high school kids who elope, only to find the road to marital bliss is blocked by unapproving parents, meddlesome friends and money woes. Provocative in its day, this camp drama also has hotrodding, crime in the streets, and those torrid back seat dates. 76 min.
01-1308 $19.99

The Price Of Sin (1966)
Filmed on location at the Gynecological Clinic of Zurich, this fact-based exposé was one of the last of the European "birth exploitation" cycle. Two doctors square off over the subject of abortion and, in the interim, there's loads of "candid" footage focusing on childbirth, sterilization, birth control pills and IUDs. With Tadeuss Lomnicki. AKA: "Wages of Sin." Dubbed in English.
79-5965 Was $24.99 $19.99

The Pill (1967)
Learn all about the pros and cons of birth control pills in "a startling factual study of modern married life." What happens when the pill interferes with the sacred art of mating? You'll see what's on the tip of every girl's lip in this adults only production.
79-6190 $19.99

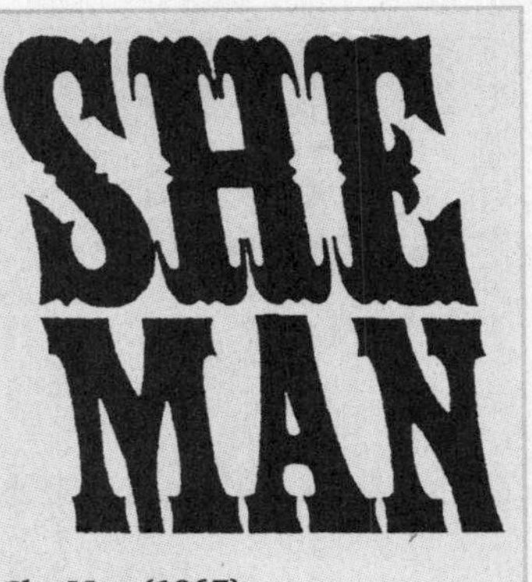

She Man (1967)
Bob Clark ("Porky's," "Children Shouldn't Play With Dead Things") directed this astonishing exploiter about an army deserter who transforms his former lieutenant into Rosie, a French maid, in order to help a dominatrix-extortionist. A psychiatrist adds insight into the perverse proceedings. Leslie Marlowe and Wendy Roberts star.
79-5671 Was $24.99 $19.99

Teenage Mother (1968)
Jerry Gross, the man behind "Girl on a Chain Gang," plays up every school board's worst sex education fears when a "nice" girl fakes pregnancy to divert her beau's interest in the new Swedish health teacher. With actual childbirth footage; stars Arlene Sue Farber, Julie Ange. 78 min.
68-8417 $19.99

Heavy Petting (1989)
Remember those trying times of adolescence: first date, first kiss, first...? All those memories will come rushing back with this campy salute to young love. Clips from "serious" dating films of the '50s and '60s, reminiscences by David Byrne, Abbie Hoffman, William Burroughs, Sandra Bernhard and Spalding Gray, and contemporary movie scenes and songs make for a nostalgic comedy that touches "all the bases." 75 min.
71-5176 $19.99

Sex And Buttered Popcorn (1991)
Outrageously funny look at Hollywood sexploitation films of the past, featuring clips from such classics as "Forbidden Daughters," "They Wear No Clothes," "Child Bride" and the inimitable "Mom and Dad." There's interviews with schlockmeisters David F. Friedman and Dan Sonney, as well as Mildred Babb, widow of master showman Kroger Babb. Narrated by Ned Beatty. 70 min.
20-7021 $29.99

U.S.S. V.D. Ship Of Shame/ Red Nightmare
These two federally funded propaganda films are unintentionally riotous fun. First, a gunship in liberty port becomes the shame of the fleet when its crew comes down with...VD! Next, Jack Webb narrates the tale of an ordinary American town and its life as a Communist satellite, with everyone becoming emotionless automatons. 82 min.
01-1040 Was $19.99 $14.99

Mystery Of Womanhood/ Painless Childbirth
Two exploitation films disguised as educationals. Learn about "the facts of life" with these not-for-the-squeamish epics. Explore the mystery of womanhood and what makes the feminine sex tick, and see the birth of babies through natural, breech and cesarean methods. It's frank! It's revealing! 30 min.
15-9005 $14.99

Teaserama
Pull the shades down, turn the lights off and leave your socks on for a steamy batch of vintage stag films including "Oh Baby," "A Fishy Story," "Evolution of a Glamour Girl," "Dark Exchange," "Cabbages & Kinks" and seven more. 55 min.
62-1320 $19.99

No Greater Sin: The Wondrous Story Of Birth
A sequel-of-sorts to Kroger Babb's infamous "Mom and Dad," presenting the birth of a baby, a Caesearian delivery and the birth of triplets, as well as the feature "The Secrets of Love and Birth." These roadshow "educational" films enlightened moviegoers while raking in millions with their sensational ad campaigns. Includes "The Wondrous Story of Birth," "Love and Birth," and more. 120 min.
79-5598 Was $24.99 $19.99

I Am Legend (1994)
Cult movie historian and Howard Hughes-lookalike (according to Russ Meyer) Johnny Legend presents this intimate portrait of, well, himself, as he appears on talk shows, in wrestling arenas, in nightclubs and at his own indoor drive-in theater. He performs such tunes as "High School Caesar" and "Pencil Neck Geck," and meets such celebs as Melissa Moore, Mary Woronov, Garrett Morris and Pia Zadora.
79-5504 Was $24.99 $19.99

Cannibal: The Musical (1994)
"In the tradition of 'Friday the 13th, Part 2' and 'Oklahoma!'" comes this riotously rancid musical horror-thon from "South Park" co-creator Trey Parker. The story is real, tracing the adventures of 1890s Mormon Alferd Packer, the only American ever convicted of cannibalism. The seven songs add a special element to the proceedings that make it a one-of-a-kind....something! 105 min.
46-8012 Was $69.99 $19.99

Spy Squad (1961)
In the tradition of "Rocket Attack, U.S.A." comes this obscure anti-communist classic about a slick American agent who attempts to capture an important satellite capsule from the Soviets, but eventually realizes that they may not have the real thing. No suspense, bad acting, weak technical credits: who could ask for anything more? With Richard (the great Dick) Miller, Dick O'Neill. AKA: "Capture That Capsule."
79-5478 Was $24.99 $19.99

Santa Sangre (1989)
A surrealistic, graphically violent descent into madness from cult director Alejandro Jodorowsky ("El Topo"). A boy spends 10 years in an asylum after seeing his father mutilate his mother before he took his own life. When he's released, a bizarre bond forms between mother and son, a relationship that turns to murder. Guy Stockwell, Blanca Guerra, Axel Jodorowsky star. 120 min.
63-1413 $19.99

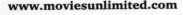

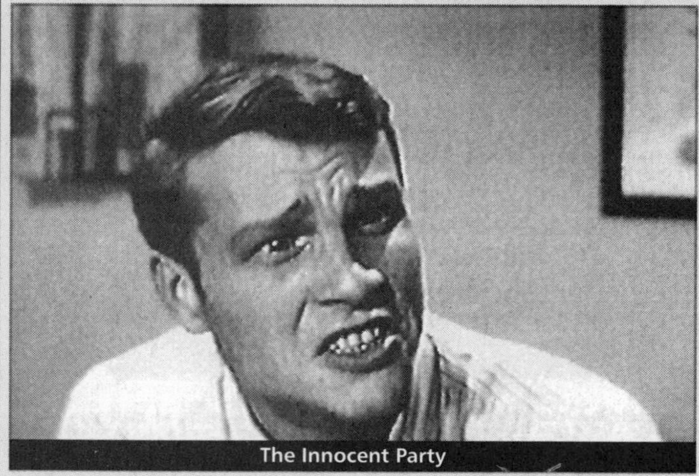

The Innocent Party

The 1950's Time Capsule
Remember those "good conduct" films they made you watch in grade school? Well, some of the best have been collected on this delightful video of vintage "ephemera." Includes "Safety on Our School Bus," "Plan for Pleasant Living," "Behind the Scenes in a Supermarket" and "Lunchroom Manners." Don't be a "Mr. Bungle!" 45 min.
01-9080 *$19.99*

Exploitation Mini Classics, Vol. 1
Hungry for exploitation, but not so starved you could swallow a full course of stereotypes and degeneracy all by yourself? This prurient pu-pu platter is just the thing, with classic short subjects like "Sally Rand's Fan Dance," "How to Undress in Front of Your Husband," "Dating Do's and Don'ts" and more!
68-8352 *$19.99*

Ellis In Freedomland
Truly unique early 1950s industrial film sponsored by Westinghouse in which an appliance huckster having trouble with sales falls asleep in a department store and, during his dream, discovers all of the mannequins have come to life. Then things get really weird when the appliances start talking to him with the voices of James Mason, Lucille Ball, Jerry Colonna and others. 85 min.
10-9252 Was $19.99 *$14.99*

Rumpus In The Classroom
Outrageous, straightforward educational shorts from the 1950s and 1960s, featuring "Joan Avoids a Cold," "Candy Is Healthy," "Dating: Do's and Don'ts" and "Fun with Speech Songs." 40 min.
15-9033 Was $19.99 *$14.99*

Highway Safety Films
Remember Driver's Ed. class? Here's two hours of campily brutal training films, including the astonishing "Signal 30," which features explicit scenes of post-accident carnage from the files of the Ohio State Police. Hear state troopers warn young drivers: "See what could happen when teens drive drunk!" 120 min.
79-5037 Was $24.99 *$19.99*

Sex Hygiene Scare Films, Vol. 1
See what shocking situations teens can get into if they don't prescribe to safe sex in these now-campy short films. Included are "Forbidden Desire" (1936), "Know For Sure" (1939), "Human Reproduction" (1947), "A Quarter Million Teenagers" (1965), "Sex Hygiene" (1942) and "VD—Damaged Goods" (1962). 110 min.
79-6173 Was $24.99 *$19.99*

Sex Hygiene Scare Films, Vol. 2
Here's more scary warnings about the dangers of mufky-fufky. Featured are "VD—Name Your Contacts"; "Sex in Today's World," with Frank Zappa and Playboy Club footage from the 1960s; the 1940s War Department epic "The Pick-Up"; and the sex-ed films "Boy to Man" and "Girl to Woman."
79-6174 Was $24.99 *$19.99*

Sex Hygiene Scare Films, Vol. 3
Looking for an edifying way to spend some time? Well, you won't find it here, watching frightening warnings about venereal disease from the 1960s and 1970s. There's "Beware Of: V.D. Every 30 Seconds," "Going Steady," "Personal Health for Girls" and more. Shoulda worn that raincoat! 110 min.
79-6175 Was $24.99 *$19.99*

Sex Hygiene Scare Films, Vol. 4
Clinically explicit films about sex and transmitted diseases can be fun—we think! Witness these gems from the '60s and '70s: "The U.S. Navy Presents Hygiene for Men," "It's Wonderful Being a Girl" and "Miracles in Birth." 110 min.
79-6176 Was $24.99 *$19.99*

Classroom Scare Films, Vol. 1
This collection of short shockers for schoolkids will astound, educate and amaze you. Shot in the '60s and '70s, they feature everything you wanted to know about the "truth" of drug addiction. Titles include "Drugs and the Nervous System," "Boozers and Users," "Keep Off the Grass" and others. 120 min.
79-5513 Was $24.99 *$19.99*

Classroom Scare Films, Vol. 2
Here's more films from the 1960s and 1970s designed to scare students into good health habits: "Smoking, It's Your Choice," "Prevention and Control of Dental Disease," "Scoliosis," "Your Mouth," "Drug Use or Abuse," "VD: Truth or Consequences" and more. 120 min.
79-5514 Was $24.99 *$19.99*

Classroom Scare Films, Vol. 3
Drugs are the main subject of these scholastic propaganda films from the 1960s and 1970s that present many campy thrills. Among the entries are "People Versus Pot," "The Trip Back," "Marijuana Driving and You," "Smoky Joe's High Ride," "No Smoking" and "Marijuana, the Hidden Danger." Cool, man.
79-6033 Was $24.99 *$19.99*

Classroom Scare Films, Vol. 4
The scary thing might be that these hilariously campy instructional films were made to be taken seriously! Become a proper adolescent by watching "Dating: Do's and Don'ts," "Junior Prom," "Getting Ready for School," "Safety for School," "Safety to School," "Traffic Rules" and "Going Steady," which is an anti-drug short despite its title.
79-6108 *$19.99*

Drivers' Ed Scare Films, Vol. 1
These unsettling shorts were created to help neophytes learn about the dangers of bad driving. Today, they remain as gross as ever and make one wonder why, with these warning films, there are still so many morons on the roads. Included are "Mechanized Death," "School Bus Fires," "Booby Traps" and "The Smith System of No Accident Driving."
79-6110 Was $24.99 *$19.99*

Drivers' Ed Scare Films, Vol. 2
Learn how to be a courteous and careful motorist—or else!—from these drivers' education films that were produced for your safety instruction in the 1960s and 1970s. There's "Signal 30," "Freeway Driving Tactics," "Fatal Meeting," "Alco Beat" and the animated "Traffic Rules."
79-6462 Was $24.99 *$19.99*

Campy Classroom Classics, Vol. 1
Camp out with "The Toy Telephone Truck," which traces the evolution of a special toy; "Kiddieland," in which two youngsters have a surreal amusement park trip; "The Story of Beef," which is about, well...beef; "Paper and I," in which a talking bag expounds upon the history of paper; "Ways to Good Habits"; "Over Night"; "Am I Trust Worthy?"; and the incredible "Riddle of the Friendly Stranger," featuring a deranged puppet dispensing wisdom about strangers. Strange!
79-6637 *$19.99*

Campy Classroom Classics, Vol. 2
Wowie compilation of "educational" oddities includes "Mental Health," in which a teacher tells his graduating class of 40 that at least two of them will have mental health problems; "Manners in Public"; "Making the Most Out of School"; "Appreciating Our Parents"; "The ABCs of Babysitting" and "The Dangerous Stranger," from scholastic scaremeister Sid Davis; "Your School Safety Patrol" and more.
79-6638 *$19.99*

Campy Classroom Classics, Vol. 3
Sit up straight at your desk and enjoy "Acts of Courtesy," from "Carnival of Souls" creator Herk Harvey, as teens learn the value of manners; "The Walk to School"; "Care of the Skin"; "On Our Own"; "Adventures on an Outboard"; "Which Way?," a geography primer; and "Getting Along with Others," an important study of compromise.
79-6639 *$19.99*

Lifestyles U.S.A., Vol. 1
You'll have faith in the American way of life after watching this campy collection of industry and promo films. Included are "To New Horizons," a filmed version of General Motors' Futurama exhibit from 1939-40 World's Fair; "Leave It to Roll-Oh" (1940), about an automated butler; the futuristic GM musical "Design for Dreaming" (1956); "American Thrift" (1962), a salute to U.S. housewives' shopping practices; the '40s scenery-blocking blockbuster "Billboards U.S.A."; "Our Community" (1952), which features a cameo by Howdy Doody; and more.
79-6642 *$19.99*

Teenage Turmoil, Vol. 1
Kids...what was the matter with kids in those days? Find out in these films that depict teenage trauma. A youth council helps kids get along in "Make Way for Youth"; "The Cool Hot Rod" is too cool for a small town; girls learn about "Making the Most of Your Face"; romance blossoms as you see "What to Do on a Date"; "The Show-Off" means trouble for his school chums; and more.
79-6646 *$19.99*

Teenage Turmoil, Vol. 2
A whirlpool of teenage angst is presented in this compendium that features "Make Your Own Decisions"; "Sharing Work at Home"; "Mike Makes His Mark," in which a hot-head turns it around; "Good Grooming for Girls"; "Mary's Menstruation Cycle"—'nuff said!; "Going Steady"; and "Dance, Little Children," a somber chronicle of a small town's VD outbreak.
79-6647 *$19.99*

G.I. Scare Films, Vol. 1
This menagerie of gross, campy and hilarious help films produced by Uncle Sam includes "First Aid for All Hands" (1958), about how to spot a wounded soldier; "Medical Defense Against Chemical Warfare: Gas Attack First-Aid" (1958); "Chemical Warfare Decontamination: Personnel" (1954); a short with George Reeves and DeForest Kelley; and others.
79-6470 Was $24.99 *$19.99*

G.I. Scare Films, Vol. 2
You don't need military experience to get scared watching "Abandon Ship" (1943), a Navy primer on how to be safe from sharks, burning oil and Japanese fighter planes; "Damage Control: Shipboard Fire Fighting, Basic" (1960); "A Physical Fitness Program for the United States Navy" and "Sex Hygiene" (1941), a film with disturbing images but a healthy George Reeves.
79-6471 Was $24.99 *$19.99*

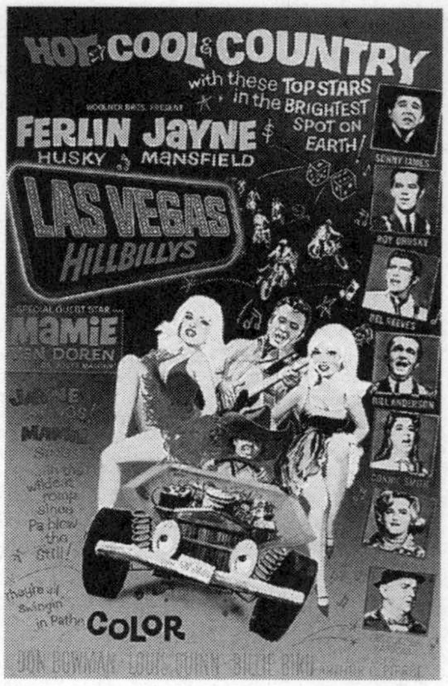

Las Vegas Hillbillys (1966)
Country bumpkin Ferlin Husky lands in Las Vegas, inherits a dilapidated casino and turns it into a moneymaker with help from Jayne Mansfield and Mamie Van Doren (what a pair!). With Sonny James, Del Reeves and Richard Kiel. Spawned the sequel "Hillbillys in a Haunted House." 90 min.
77-7030 Was $19.99 *$14.99*

Hillbillys In A Haunted House (1967)
Ghosts meet grits as two country-and-western singers stop at an abandoned mansion filled with spooks. Ferlin Husky, Joi Lansing, John Carradine, Lon Chaney, Basil Rathbone star. 88 min.
08-1147 Was $19.99 *$14.99*

Teenage Bad Girl (1957)
"She's a doll! She's a dish! She's a delinquent!" Actually, she's a spoiled British babe whose nighttime jaunts and rebelliousness drive her widowed mother to her wits' end. Sordid tale of adolescent abandon stars Sylvia Sims, Anna Neagle. 100 min.
68-8452 *$19.99*

Nation Aflame (1937)
Silly attempt at searing exposé of "The Black Legion," a Ku Klux Klan-type racist group. As the mastermind, Noel Madison does some heavy scowling, but the whole thing is about as incendiary as a Campfire Girls meeting. Lila Lee co-stars. 74 min.
68-8240 *$19.99*

The Beast Of Yucca Flats (1961)
You'll really "yuc" it up at this hilarious sci-fi turkey starring the legendary Tor Johnson as a Russian scientist who gets caught up in an A-bomb blast and becomes a cave-dwelling wildman ("Tor not like nuclear proliferation!"). With Douglas Mellor, Barbara Francis, and off-screen narration à la "The Creeping Terror." Speical video edition includes a conversation with producer Anthony Cardoza and actor Conrad Brooks. 60 min.
68-8552 *$19.99*

Jesse James Meets Frankenstein's Daughter (1965)
As often happens with films of this caliber, it's actually the infamous mad doctor's granddaughter who makes a monster out of Jesse's buddy and sends "Igor" after his gunslinger pal. John Lupton and Narda Onyx play the title roles in director William Beaudine's sublimely silly sagebrush shocker. 83 min.
53-1565 Was $19.99 *$14.99*

Billy The Kid vs. Dracula (1966)
Bloodletter meets bloodsucker in this celebrated clinker from director William "One Shot" Beaudine. Vampires walk in broad daylight, corpses move their arms, and rubber bats terrorize outlaw-turned-hero Chuck Courtney. John Carradine plays Dracula for the first time since 1945's "House of Dracula," and Virgina (Mrs. Olsen) Christine also stars. 72 min.
09-1540 Was $29.99 *$19.99*

Beat Girl (1960)
Wild British teen exploitation drama, as a young gal decides to follow in her stepmother's footsteps and become a stripper. Gillian Hills, Oliver Reed, Christopher Lee and pop singer Adam Faith star; John Barry supplied the music. AKA: "Wild for Kicks." 85 min.
68-8453 *$19.99*

The Wild World Of Batwoman (1966)
A beautiful masked crime-fighter and her squad of go-go dancers battle mad scientist Dr. Neon and the masked Ratfink for a stolen atomic-powered hearing aid. Freaked-out reunion of "Teenage Zombie" star Katherine Victor and director Jerry Warren, who lost a lawsuit over the title and never made another movie. AKA: "She Was a Hippy Vampire." 70 min.
15-5096 *$14.99*

Desperate Teenage Lovedolls (1984)
The Lovedolls are an all-girl rock group whose next gig could be their last, if their arch-rivals, the She Devils, have anything to say about it. An outrageous blend of Punk Rock, softcore sex, violent action and sharp satire, with music by Black Flag, Sin 34, Darkside and other L.A. hardcore bands. 60 min.
01-1369 Was $19.99 *$14.99*

Unspeakable (2000)
Troma presents the story of James Fhelleps, an average middle-class man who erupts into a violent rampage when a tragic accident kills his daughter and cripples his wife. With his menacing straight razor he slices his way through the corrupt city, hoping that it will bring him closer to his deceased child. With Roger Cline, Tamera Noll and Leigh Silver.
46-8066 *$49.99*

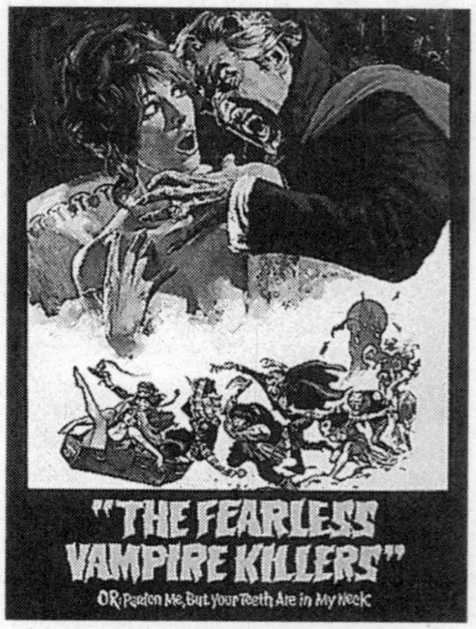

The Fearless Vampire Killers, Or: Pardon Me, But Your Teeth Are In My Neck (1967)
Director/co-writer/star Roman Polanski's biting spoof of the bloodsucker legend features an inept pair of vampire hunters' attempts to destroy the undead Count Von Krolock and his followers, rescue virginal Sharon Tate, and learn why crosses don't affect all vampires. With Jack MacGowran, Ferdy Mayne, Alfie Bass. AKA: "Dance of the Vampires." 107 min.
12-2083 *$14.99*

The Dangerous Years (1966)
Made to reach out to "troubled youth," this '60s docudrama featuring David McCallum offers actual interviews with kids and policemen on such topics as teen crime, drug abuse and more. Also included on this tape is a look at a much simpler and more wholesome adolescence, the '50s educational short "Dating Do's and Don'ts."
68-9241 *$19.99*

The Electric Chair (1977)
A regional exercise in sordidness, this Carolina-lensed shocker details the story of Rev. Sam, who, frustrated by his wife's aloofness, has an affair with a married woman. When the lovers are found shot to death, a local religious fanatic is convicted and sentenced to the "hot seat." TV horror host "Pat" Patterson directs and stars with wife Nita. 85 min.
79-5486 Was $24.99 *$19.99*

The Horror Of Party Beach (1963)
Frankie and Annette never had problems like this! Atomic waste, sea slime and dead sailors combine to form ridiculous-looking monsters (picture the Creature from the Black Lagoon with a mouthful of hot dogs) who prey on the teens at a beachside resort. Features the hit song "Zombie Stomp" by The Del-Aires; John Scott and Alice Lyon star. 72 min.
05-9004 *$19.99*

Date Bait (1960)
"Too young to know; too wild to love; too eager to say I will. At 16 a girl learns about love—one way or the other!" Two young hepcats want to get hitched, but dad and mom just say "no." With Gary Clarke and Marlo Ryan. 71 min.
10-7943 Was $19.99 *$14.99*

Invasion Of The Star Creatures (1962)
In this spectacularly goofy sci-fi enterprise, oddball soldiers Bob Ball and Frankie Ray encounter vegetable monsters under the control of two gorgeous alien invaders who have to be taught such Earth customs as smooching. With Gloria Victor and Dolores Reed; written by Jonathan Haze ("Little Shop of Horrors"). 70 min.
10-9366 *$14.99*

Voyage To The Planet Of The Prehistoric Women (1968)
Film critic Peter Bogdanovich got a crash course in filmmaking when Roger Corman let him add new scenes to a Russian sci-fi epic. Mamie Van Doren plays the queen of a group of cavewomen who greet a group of astronauts that have landed on their world. The gals wear clamshell bikinis, communicate telepathically and worship a pterodactyl! With Mary Mark and Paige Lee. 78 min.
68-8553 *$19.99*

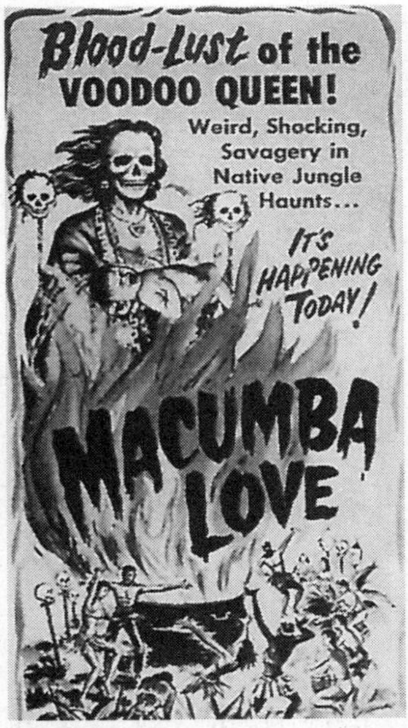

Macumba Love (1960)
Shot in Brazil, this way-out thriller follows a writer to the wilds of South America, where he hopes to learn if voodoo was involved in a series of grisly, unsolved murders. Directed by Douglas Fowley (who played Doc Holiday in the "Wyatt Earp" TV series), the film is noted for tribal dancing and, in this uncut edition, sexpot June Wilkinson's nudity. With Walter Reed.
51-1020 *$29.99*

Santa Claus Conquers The Martians (1964)
When a horde of malevolent Martians and their awesome killer robot come to Earth to kidnap St. Nick for their own children's enjoyment, the results are unintentionally hilarious. See alien guns that look like Wham-mo Air Blasters! See a fierce polar bear! See a drunken Santa Claus! And best of all, see Pia Zadora in her film debut as a Martian child! 80 min.
53-1322 *$19.99*

Mesa Of Lost Women (1953)
A feast for bad movie buffs, as Jackie (Uncle Fester) Coogan plays the mad Dr. Araña, whose experiments on a Mexican mountain result in giant tarantulas, killer dwarves, and savage "spider women." Wallopin' websnappers! Look for stars like Dolores Fuller ("Glen or Glenda"), George Barrows ("Robot Monster") and Angelo Rossitto. From Ron Ormond. 80 min.
68-8123 *$19.99*

Untamed Mistress (1957)
A gorgeous woman named Velda is joined by her fiancé when she journeys back to where she was born, in the jungle, the mighty jungle. But the lions aren't sleeping tonight—or any night—when she reunites with girl-crazy gorilla Lolowok in Ron Ormond's oddball odyssey. Gorilla her dreams? You bet! With Jacqueline Fontaine. 75 min.
82-5065 *$19.99*

Please Don't Touch Me (1959)
Ron Ormond's outrageous essay tells of a young newlywed whose sexual problems with her new husband are attributed to an unsettling incident in her past. A doctor tries to use an "Electro-Cyclometer" to help her conquer her frigidity, and even a hypnotist is called on to help. Ruth Blair and B-Western hero Lash LaRue star in this sex education opus. 66 min.
82-5067 *$19.99*

Forty Acre Feud (1965)
It's feudin' time in ol' Tennessee when the Calhouns and Culpeppers square off for a seat in the legislature. Ferlin Husky, Minnie Pearl, Del Reeves, George Jones, Loretta Lynn and The Willis Brothers make appearances on top of old Smokey...and sing, too! Directed by Ron Ormond ("Mesa of the Lost Women"). 85 min.
10-7940 *$19.99*

White Lightnin' Road (1965)
Filmed at top speedways in the South, this auto racing rouser from Ron Ormond tells of two rival drivers who battle it out on the track and slug it out off the track for the affections of Ruby, a platinum blonde bombshell. Ruby doesn't take her love to town; she's having too much fun watching the good ol' boys go against each other for it! 96 min.
82-5066 *$19.99*

Girl From Tobacco Row (1966)
A small, quiet Southern town explodes in this action-filled oddity from Ron and June Ormond. Convict "Snake" Richards seeks hidden money in a small tobacco town, and falls for the preacher's pretty daughter in the process. A rival group of gangsters give "Snake" a scare when they look for the loot. Tex Ritter, Ralph Emery and Rachel Roman star. 87 min.
64-3024 *$19.99*

The Monster And The Stripper (1968)
Classic exploiter from Ron Ormond in which a Bayou safari hunts down a hideous swamp monster and turns it into a sideshow attraction at a nightclub, trained by a backwoods boy. The loincloth-clad creature eventually falls for a singer in this incredible film that features strippers, rockabilly music and gore. With singer Sleepy LaBeef. AKA: "The Exotic Ones." 91 min.
64-3025 *$19.99*

Ormond Five-Pack
Fans of Ron and June Ormond's special brand of Southern-fried exploitation will want to own this great five-tape set. Included are "Girl from Tobacco Row," "The Monster and the Stripper," "Please Don't Touch Me," "Untamed Mistress" and "White Lightnin' Road."
82-5201 Save $25.00! ***$49.99***

Dance Hall Racket (1956)
Controversial comic genius Lenny Bruce made his only feature film appearance in this roadshow melodrama about an FBI agent who goes undercover to break up a white slavery/smuggling ring operating out of a seedy dime-a-dance joint. Bruce's future wife Honey also stars; Phil Tucker ("Robert Monster") directs.
50-1508 Was $24.99 *$19.99*

Blonde In Bondage (1957)
In this rare exploitation thriller, an American reporter uncovers sleazy show business managers in Europe keeping showgirls on drugs in order to retain their services. Mark Miller, Anita Thallaug star.
50-5918 *$19.99*

The Flaming Urge (1953)
Harold Lloyd, Jr. stars in this blistering social issue film about a town plagued by arsonists. Give the producers credit—it wasn't easy figuring out what turned decent kids into uncontrollable pyromaniacs before the rise of Rock and Roll.
68-8133 *$19.99*

Cuban Confidential (1956)
Truly unique and bizarre film that makes the works of David Lynch look like Frank Capra. Produced by softcore schlockmeister Manny Conde, this effort follows a man wandering through pre-Castro Cuba contemplating streets, cemeteries, hospitals, the carnivale and revolutionaries. Emilio G. Navarro stars in this rare...um...whatever. AKA: "Backs Turned." 57 min.
79-5885 Was $24.99 *$19.99*

Journey To Freedom (1957)
A real rarity, this wild thriller is based on the life of its writer, exploitation filmmaker and Ed Wood ally Stephen Apostolof ("Orgy of the Dead"). After his release from a Bulgarian prison, a man has a series of adventures before landing in America, where he fights the "Red Peril." Anti-communist drama features Jacques Scott, Jean Ann Lewis and Tor Johnson.
79-6541 Was $24.99 *$19.99*

Bill And Coo (1947)
The old buck and wing like it's never been done before—a romantic melodrama with an all-bird cast! This fine-feathered farce was given a special Academy Award. Could this film have been what the birds in Hitchcock's movie were so upset about? 61 min.
01-1191 *$19.99*

Delinquent Daughters (1944)
American youth is getting into trouble. The secret: the Merry-Go-Round Club, a teenage meeting place where the loot from robberies is stashed. June Carlson. 71 min.
09-1421 *$19.99*

I Accuse My Parents (1945)
Egregious exploifeature that places its finger firmly upon the cause of juvenile delinquency! Watch as a young man is driven by inattentive, tipsy parents onto a sordid trail of organized crime and murder. Features the hit song, "Are You Happy in Your Work?" Mary Beth Hughes, Robert Lowell star. 68 min.
10-7230 Was $29.99 *$19.99*

Souls In Pawn (1940)
After Lois informs her college student husband she is pregnant, he has their marriage annulled, landing her in a home for unwed mothers overseen by a quack doctor who sells babies on the side. A sassy burlesque star eventually adopts Lois' baby—for $500! Lloyd Ingraham and stripper Ginger Britton star in this odd mix of social drama and burlesque. 62 min.
79-5496 Was $24.99 *$19.99*

The Terror Of Tiny Town (1938)
While the plot of evil ranchers and cattle rustling sounds like hundreds of other B-Westerns, this one is decidedly different: everyone is a midget! You'll howl when you see these pint-sized pioneers ride Shetland ponies, walk under saloon doors, and make short work of the villains. 62 min.
01-5126 *$19.99*

Teenage Confidential
Take a look back at how Hollywood and Washington viewed the threat of juvenile delinquency in this campy collection of film trailers, newsreels of government "scare films" from the '40s and '50s. Remember, the J.D.'s of yesterday are the political and business leaders of today! 60 min.
15-5046 *$12.99*

Bambi Meets Godzilla & Other Weird Cartoons
Features the cult masterpiece "Bambi Meets Godzilla," Betty Boop in "Crazy Town," Max Fleischer's "Small Fry," and more off-the-wall animated wonders. 30 min.
15-5148 *$14.99*

Rock 'N' Roll Wrestling Music Television
What happens when a band of rock-starved pro wrestlers takes over an "easy listening" radio station and play their kind of music? Watch as Kamala the Ugandan Giant, The Moondogs, Randy "Macho Man" Savage and other grappling greats get down! 30 min.
15-5149 *$14.99*

Teenage UFO Rock N Roll Monster Show
Join Johnny Legend and pals for a teen time capsule filled with time-hopping clips from the '50s, '60s and '70s and featuring Bill Haley and the Comets, cavemen, juvenile delinquents, groupies and the shorts "Teenage Crusade" and "Twist Crusade."
79-5339 Was $24.99 *$19.99*

Blank Generation (1979)
A rare cinematic look at the final days of New York's '70s punk rock scene, this music-laced drama from director Ulli Lommel ("Cocaine Cowboys") stars Richard Hell as a struggling musician torn between his career and his relationship with journalist Carole Bouquet. Along with live concert footage of Hell and his band, The Voidoids, at the legendary CBGB, there's also an appearance by Andy Warhol. 85 min.
08-8841 Letterboxed *$14.99*

Smithereens (1983)
Director Susan Seidelman's ("Desperately Seeking Susan") first feature was this gritty look at life in the New Wave music scene of Manhattan. Wren (Susan Berman) is an ambitious, if untalented, "singer-promoter" who tries to latch onto a successful performer (Richard Hell) while sharing a van with a naive boy newly arrived from the Midwest. With Brad Rinn, Nada Despotovich. 90 min.
03-1294 *$29.99*

Man Of Steel (1965)
This classroom religious feature must be seen to be believed! At first, it's set in a steel industry town where a working class brood rallies against big business America, then shifts to the Yukon to become a "Wilderness Family"-style adventure. Next, it's back to the big city, where teens get turned on to booze and sex before finally coming to God. Whew! With Harry Elders.
79-6029 Was $24.99 *$19.99*

Christian Youth Scare Films
These collections of squeaky clean religious films depict typical difficult situations and show how seeking the help of the Lord can steer their intended audience in the right direction. Each fascinating compilation runs about 90 min.

Christian Youth Scare Films, Vol. 1
Includes "Teenage Conflict," "Teenage Witness," "Teenage Code" and a revealing look behind-the-scenes of "Teenage Conflict."
79-6012 Was $24.99 *$19.99*

Christian Youth Scare Films, Vol. 2
Includes "Teenage Choice," "Teenage Christmas," "Teenage Loyalty" and "The Right Start."
79-6013 Was $24.99 *$19.99*

Christian Youth Scare Films, Vol. 3
Includes "Teenage Testament," "Teenage Challenge," "Teenage Crusade" and "Red Trap."
79-6014 Was $24.99 *$19.99*

Christian Youth Scare Films, Vol. 4
Includes "What Happened to Jo Jo?," "God Is in the Streets" and "Yellow Slippers."
79-6469 Was $24.99 *$19.99*

Christian Youth Scare Films, Vol. 5
Includes "Teenage Diary," "Our Children: Spending Money,"."Our Children: Turn the Other Cheek," "The Big Deal" and "Crisis in Morality."
79-6634 Was $24.99 *$19.99*

Christian Youth Scare Films, Vol. 6
Includes "Unto Thyself Be True," "Teenagers Parents," "Our Child: A Clean House," "How Do I Love Thee?" and "Our Children: King of the Block" with Alan Hale, Jr.
79-6635 Was $24.99 *$19.99*

Christian Youth Scare Films, Vol. 7
Includes "Just a Stranger," "Winsome Witness," "Tokens of Love," "Our Children: A Bigger Reward" and "Painful Confession."
79-6636 Was $24.99 *$19.99*

The Harder They Come (1973)
Reggae-flavored cult drama stars Jimmy Cliff as a Jamaican youth who dreams of becoming a singing star. After some run-ins with the law, he kills a corrupt policeman, and his fugitive status makes a recording he made a hit. Rough and raw blend of action and political polemic features music by Cliff, Toots and The Maytals, Desmond Dekker. Songs include "You Can Get It If You Really Want," "Many Rivers to Cross," and the title track. 93 min.
44-1068 *$19.99*

Putney Swope (1969)
Nothing is sacred in independent filmmaker Robert Downey's acclaimed spoof of the Madison Avenue mentality, as a token black ad executive becomes head of the firm and changes it into the ultra-hip and brutally honest Truth and Soul, Inc. The "commercials" the company devises are hilarious. Arnold Johnson, Allen Garfield, Antonio Fargas star. 84 min.
02-1014 Was $59.99 *$19.99*

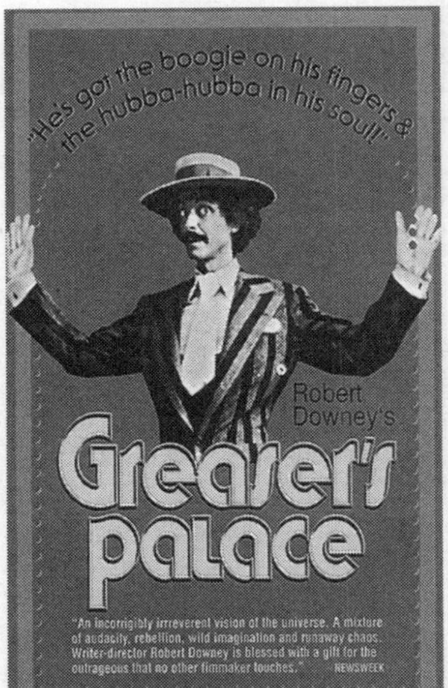

Greaser's Palace (1972)
Described by writer/director Robert Downey as "a cross between 'The Greatest Story Ever Told,' 'High Noon,' and a Las Vegas floorshow," this outrageous satire is set in a sleepy frontier town visited by Zoot Suit (Allan Arbus), a miracle-working song-and-dance man whose routine rouses the ire of saloon owner Greaser (Albert Henderson). Luana Anders, Herve Villechaize also star. 91 min.
02-1244 *$19.99*

Ray Dennis Steckler

Sinthia: Devil's Doll (1960)
Ray Dennis Steckler's salute to Ingmar Bergman features all sorts of bizarre camerawork and flash-forwards in telling the story of a 12-year-old girl who commits murder...but was she possessed? Shula Roan, Diane Webber star.
79-5024 *$19.99*

Secret File Hollywood (1961)
A private eye on the Hollywood beat who accidentally kills a bystander in a beatnik joint takes a job at a tabloid magazine edited by a beautiful, conniving woman and owned by a mysterious man with questionable motives. Made-on-pennies crime thriller was photographed by Ray Dennis Steckler, which may have something to do with all the boom microphones on view. With Robert York.
79-5023 *$19.99*

Wild Guitar (1962)
Country boy singer Arch Hall, Jr. finds the road to Hollywood stardom is paved with "dishonest DJ's," "hungry hucksters," "gold digging groupies" and other sordid types. Unintentionally funny rock drama produced by Arch Hall, Sr. and directed by Ray Dennis Steckler ("Rat Pfink and Boo-Boo"). 92 min.
15-5007 *$12.99*

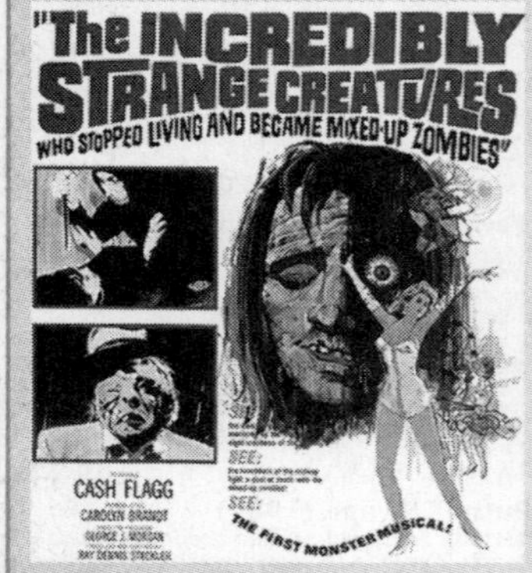

The Incredibly Strange Creatures Who Stopped Living And Became Mixed-Up Zombies (1964)
Well, what would you call a film about a carnival fortune teller who, aided by her hunchbacked assistant, hypnotizes her victims, scars their faces with acid and locks them in cages? Writer/director Ray Dennis Steckler (AKA Cash Flagg) stars in "the first monster musical," with the "Mixed Up Zombie Stomp." AKA: "Teenage Psycho Meets Bloody Mary." 81 min.
64-9001 *$19.99*

The Thrill Killers (1965)
A brutal killer named "Mad Dog" and three escaped asylum inmates add up to "Four for Gore" in writer-director-star Ray Dennis Steckler's outrageous splatterfest that was the only film to be made in "Hallucinogenic Hypno-Vision!" With ecdysiastic legend Liz Renay. AKA: "The Maniacs Are Loose." 72 min.
64-9002 *$19.99*

Rat Pfink A Boo Boo (1966)
In response to the "Batmania" craze that swept America, Ray Dennis Steckler created this super-hero send-up. Can Rat Pfink and sidekick Boo Boo rescue the girl from the evil Chain Gang and defeat Kogar the Swinging Ape! Holy Camp! Vin Saxon and Carolyn Brandt star. 72 min.
64-9003 *$19.99*

The Lemon Grove Kids Meet The Monsters (1966)
Ray Dennis Steckler's way-out salute to the Bowery Boys flicks features Steckler himself (billed as Cash Flagg) as the leader of a group of goofy guys who have a race and are met at the finish line by a gorilla, a mummy, a female vampire and a beatnik spy. With Carolyn Brandt.
64-9004 *$19.99*

Body Fever (1969)
This Ray Dennis Steckler production involves a private detective in search of a woman who has stolen a million dollars of heroin from a dangerous drug dealer. With Carolyn Brandt, Bernard Fein and Gary Kent. AKA: "Supercool." 77 min.
64-9005 *$19.99*

Blood Shack (1971)
A maniacal killer is on the loose in an eerie old house, savagely attacking victims with a sharp axe. Who is he? And how can anyone stop the terror? A Ray Dennis Steckler shocker. AKA: "The Chopper." 70 min.
64-9006 *$19.99*

The Hollywood Strangler Meets The Skid Row Slasher (1973)
There's tons of terror in Tinseltown, thanks to this perverse pair of malevolent murderers! You can bet there'll be one huge body count of models and winos racked up before they square off in a gore-soaked showdown! Pierre Agostino, Carolyn Brandt star in this Ray Dennis Steckler production. AKA: "The Model Killer." 72 min.
64-9007 *$19.99*

The Hollywood Strangler In Las Vegas (1986)
After spending seven years in prison for a killing spree, a brutal psychopath is freed on a technicality and travels to Las Vegas, where he soon returns to his old habits and slaughters beautiful young women. Based on a true story, this Ray Dennis Steckler production stars Pierre Agostino and Tara McGowan. 87 min. AKA: "The Las Vegas Serial Killer." 87 min.
64-9008 *$19.99*

Summer Fun (1997)
Ray Dennis Steckler's first family film since 1964's "The Lemon Grove Kids Meet the Monsters" is a silent movie with music starring daughter Bailey Steckler as Zoe, a youngster who keeps getting into all sorts of trouble. Herb Robins and the Las Vegas comedy team of Flip and Flop co-star. 70 min.
64-9016 *$19.99*

The Incredibly Strange Ray Dennis Steckler, Vol. 1
Cult phenom Ray Dennis Steckler is captured live at the York Theater in San Francisco, talking about his life and films. Included are clips from such gems as "The Thrill Killers" and "The Incredibly Strange Creatures Who Stopped Living and Became Mixed-Up Zombies." 60 min.
64-9009 *$14.99*

The Incredibly Strange Ray Dennis Steckler, Vol. 2: Low Budget Films At Their Best
Steckler shares his insights on producing and directing movies on a shoestring in this program that includes clips from his own "Rat Pfink and Boo-Boo," "The Lemon Grove Kids" and "Goof on the Loose," a rare short dedicated to old filmmakers. 60 min.
64-9010 *$14.99*

Steckler Interviews, Vol. 1
Film critic John Roberts interviews cult great Ray Dennis Steckler, who discusses his most popular film, "The Incredibly Strange Creatures Who Stopped Living and Became Mixed-Up Zombies," in detail. He gives you insight into the film's production, tells how to use ingenuity on a low budget and explains why the dancing girls were out of step. 60 min.
64-9013 *$14.99*

Forbidden Zone (1981)
Wild cult oddity follows teenage Frenchy Hercules through a door in her family's basement that leads to the Forbidden Zone, a whacked-out land ruled by King Fausto, who wants Frenchy for his harem, and jealous Queen Doris, who wants to torture her. Can Frenchy's Grandpa and brother Flash save her? Zoot suits, dancing frog-men and Danny Elfman's hyperkinetic score make this a must-see. Herve Villechaize, Susan Tyrrell, Marie-Pascal Elfman, the Kipper Kids and "The Mystic Knights of the Oingo Boingo" star. 75 min.
03-1236 *$29.99*

Blood Orgy Of The She-Devils (1974)
When Mara, Queen of the Black Witches, and her bevy of female followers take over a deserted castle as a place to hold their bloody sacrifices, the result is a chilling and erotic tale of occult powers, reincarnation and witch-killing. Lila Zaborin, Tom Pace, Leslie McRae star; Ted V. Mikels directs. 73 min.
59-5041 *$19.99*

Rock 'N' Roll High School (1979)
"Hey, ho, let's go" with free-spirited Vince Lombardi High student P.J. Soles as she literally blows the roof off the school and overthrows tyrannical principal Mary Woronov, with the help of "the hottest band this side of the Iron Curtain," The Ramones. See exploding lab mice, bullying hall monitors, and Johnny, Joey, Dee Dee and Marky in concert in this vibrant, song-filled romp. With Vincent Van Patten, Dey Young, Paul Bartel and the great Dick Miller. 94 min.
19-1253 *$14.99*

The Phantom Of The Paradise (1974)
Brian DePalma's bizarre blend of rock music, "Faust" and "The Phantom of the Opera," ignored when first released but now a cult favorite. William Finley is vengeful songwriter Winslow Leach, Paul Williams the mysterious star Swan, Jessica Harper the innocent singer Phoenix, and Gerrit Graham the glam rock sensation Beef; Williams supplied the score. 92 min.
04-1909 Was $19.99 *$14.99*

Attack Of The 50-Foot Woman (1958)
A suspicious wife gets the upper hand (literally) on her philandering husband when a stranded alien zaps her with a "growth ray." Allison Hayes cuts several fine figures as the beauteous behemoth in this classic sci-fi turkey. With Yvette Vickers, William Hudson. 66 min.
04-1782 ❑*$14.99*

Attack Of The 50 Ft. Woman (1994)
A contemporary and satiric reworking of the 1958 cult classic, starring Daryl Hannah as a successful businesswoman who discovers that her philandering hubby only wants her for her money. After she's transformed into a giant by an alien spaceship, she seeks revenge. Frances Fisher also stars. 90 min.
44-1970 Was $19.99 *$14.99*

Queen Of Outer Space (1958)
Camp masterpiece about a group of astronauts who land on Venus and discover a civilization populated by voluptuous women, including chief scientist Zsa Zsa Gabor. And you thought the Beverly Hills Police Department was in trouble! Eric Fleming, Paul Birch, Laurie Mitchell co-star; the script was inspired by a Ben Hecht story. 80 min.
04-2450 ❑*$14.99*

Cat Women Of The Moon (1954)
The unforgettable Sonny Tufts leads an expedition to the lunar surface. Once they get there, they find an underground civilization of futuristic feline femmes in leotards, a giant spider filled with sawdust and a threat to the planet Earth. Unintentional hilarity. AKA: "Rocket to the Moon." 64 min.
05-1215 *$19.99*

Missile To The Moon (1959)
Even-tackier-than-the-norm expedition to the planet of pretty girls in short skirts from director Richard Cunha ("Frankenstein's Daughter"). Blatant remake of "Cat Women of the Moon," right down to the same giant spider puppet! Richard Travis, Gary Clarke star. 78 min.
68-8189 *$14.99*

Teenage Devil Dolls (1952)
Cassandra, a high school hellcat from the wrong side of the tracks, falls in with a thrill-seeking gang and soon becomes a pot-smoking, pill-popping, garbage-scrounging street walker and asylum inmate. Don't laugh, kids, it could happen to you! AKA: "One-Way Ticket to Hell." 70 min.
15-5054 *$12.99*

For Your Height Only (1979)
This Philippine rarity is a secret agent spoof with a difference...the hero barely reaches James Bond's belt buckle! When an international gang steals a super-bomb and its creator, it's up to diminutive Agent 00 and his flying remote-controlled hat to save the world. Mini-Me move over; all three feet of Weng Weng is here! 88 min.
64-3439 *$14.99*

Village Of The Giants (1965)
When some teenagers drink a secret formula and become 60-foot adolescents, every adult in town learns to show them respect. Classic camp sci-fi romp with Tommy Kirk, Tisha Sterling, Beau Bridges, The Beau Brummels, Joy Harmon, and Ronny Howard as "Genius." 80 min.
53-1323 Was $59.99 *$14.99*

The Beautiful, The Bloody And The Bare (1969)
Sande N. Johnsen directs this sordid screamer in the H.G. Lewis mold about a depraved artist who enjoys killing the nude models who pose for him. Features a gruesome conclusion and a look at New York City in its cool days, circa 1969. Stars Jack Jowe, Marlene Denes, Debra Page.
79-5119 Was $24.99 *$19.99*

The Psychic (1968)
Produced with the help of H.G. Lewis, this bizarre thriller follows a man who gains ESP after an accident and uses his abilities to acquire women, wealth and power. Early softcore teaser stars Dick Genola and Robin Guest. AKA: "Copenhagen's Psychic Loves." Directed by James F. Hurley. 90 min.
79-5533 Was $24.99 *$19.99*

The Fat Black Pussycat (1964)
Three beautiful young women are murdered by a maniac with a penchant for ladies in high heels. In order to find the killer, a police detective must enter New York's beatnik scene. The best moment in the film features the cop reciting beat poetry: "Parking in a hospital zone is strictly prohibited...man." With Frank Jamus and Janet Damon. 80 min.
79-5307 Was $24.99 *$19.99*

Runaway Girl (1962)
A totally out-of-control exploitation item that begins as a story about wayward female teens picking fruit at a special detention camp and turns into a trashy titillator showcasing nude shower scenes, a Peeping Tom, naked underwater sequences, catfighting, gangsters, stripper Lili St. Cyr and Jock Mahoney.
79-5672 Was $24.99 *$19.99*

Chained For Life (1950)
The first, and almost certainly last, movie to star Siamese twins. Violet and Daisy Hilton, vaudeville performers and co-stars of "Freaks," dance and sing in this turgid tearjerker of love and betrayal. When one is accused of murder, the resultant trial is legal and movie history. 75 min.
05-9002 *$19.99*

Attack Of The Mushroom People (1963)
You'll have some fungus with this unbelievably silly Japanese sci-fi thriller about a boatload of stranded tourists who are trapped on a fog-draped island covered with tasty toadstools. After the castaways eat them, however, they begin turning into half-human, half-mushroom monsters! With a shock ending you won't believe; Akira Kubo, Kenji Sahara star. AKA: "Matango, the Fungus of Terror."
79-5923 Was $24.99 *$19.99*

High School Hellcats (1958)
"What must a good girl do to 'belong'?" For new student Yvonne Lime, it means joining up with Jana Lund's all-female gang of trouble-makers—unless handsome soda jerk Brett Halsey can talk her out of it before it's too late—in this distaff "J.D." drama. 68 min.
12-3296 *$14.99*

Fanatic (The Last Horror Film) (1984)
An about-to-retire horror movie actress is stalked by a psychotic fan at the Cannes Film Festival in this gory shocker that mixes elements of "The Fan" and "Targets." Joe Spinell's a real maniac; Caroline Munro's a real scream queen. Originally made in 1981, the film also stars Spinell's real-life mom, Mary, as his mother. 87 min.
03-1232 *$14.99*

Meet The Feebles (1989)
One-of-a-kind film from Peter Jackson ("Dead Alive," "Heavenly Creatures") that's actually an outrageous, adults-only soap opera enacted by puppets. A junkie, knife-throwing frog, a rat that makes porno films and a rabbit with VD are among the participants preparing for a live telecast of "The Feebles Variety Show." 92 min.
82-5011 *$29.99*

The Cars That Ate Paris (1974)
Nightmarish black comedy from Australia was Peter Weir's directorial debut. Why are teenaged hoods in the small town of Paris driving like maniacs? What happens to the many wrecked cars, and bodies of drivers, that dot the landscape? Bizarre satire stars Terry Camilleri, Melissa Jaffa, Bruce Spence ("Road Warrior's" gyro captain). AKA: "Cars That Eat People." 91 min.
02-1812 Was $69.99 *$19.99*

Schlock (1972)
The first film from director John Landis ("Animal House") was this low-budget sci-fi spoof in which he also plays the title role of the Schlockthropus, a prehistoric man-ape frozen during the Ice Age. Thawed out in the present, he runs amok, killing and leaving behind a trail of banana peels. Make-up by Rick Baker; with Saul Kahan, Eliza Garrett. AKA: "Banana Monster."
59-1034 Was $69.99 *$19.99*

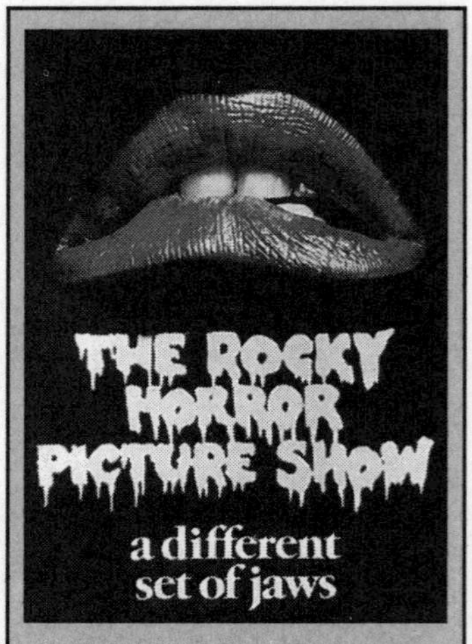

The Rocky Horror Picture Show: Special Edition (1975)
The horror-comedy-musical and quintessential cult movie follows hero Brad Majors (Barry Bostwick) and heroine Janet Weiss (Susan Sarandon) as a flat tire leads them to a bizarre castle and the "hospitality" of mad scientist Dr. Frank N. Furter (Tim Curry). Richard O'Brien (the show's author), Patricia Quinn, Little Nell and Meatloaf also star. Along with such classic tunes as "Time Warp," "Sweet Transvestite" and "Dammit Janet," this special video version also features two numbers cut from American theatrical prints, "Once in a While" and "Superheroes." 100 min.
04-2377 Was $99.99 ❑*$14.99*

Shock Treatment (1981)
The long-awaited sequel to "Rocky Horror" brings us back to downtown Denton, where Brad and Janet Majors (Cliff De Young and Jessica Harper) find themselves in a TV studio that replaces real life. "Rocky" stars Little Nell, Patricia Quinn, Charles Gray and Richard O'Brien (who also wrote the music) appear; songs include "Denton," "Little Black Dress" and the title song. 94 min.
04-1788 Was $19.99 *$14.99*

Intimate Portrait Series
Explore the public and private lives of some of the world's most famous, accomplished and inspirational women in this compelling documentary series from the Lifetime cable network. Each tape runs about 60 min. There are 62 volumes available, including:

Intimate Portrait: Audrey Hepburn
83-1292 *$14.99*

Intimate Portrait: Bette Davis
83-1293 *$14.99*

Intimate Portrait: Maya Angelou
83-1295 *$14.99*

Intimate Portrait: Mae West
83-1413 *$14.99*

Intimate Portrait: Jane Seymour
83-1422 *$14.99*

Intimate Portrait: Pam Grier
83-1498 *$14.99*

Sacred Sites: Prehistoric Monuments Of Europe
Among the remarkable archeological sites featured in this documentary are the avenue of megaliths at Carnac in Brittany, believed to have been used for star observation; the royal tomb at Gavrinis; underground burial labyrinths on the islands of Malta and Gozo; the oldest known sculptures in Europe and more. 43 min.
80-7143 Was $29.99 *$19.99*

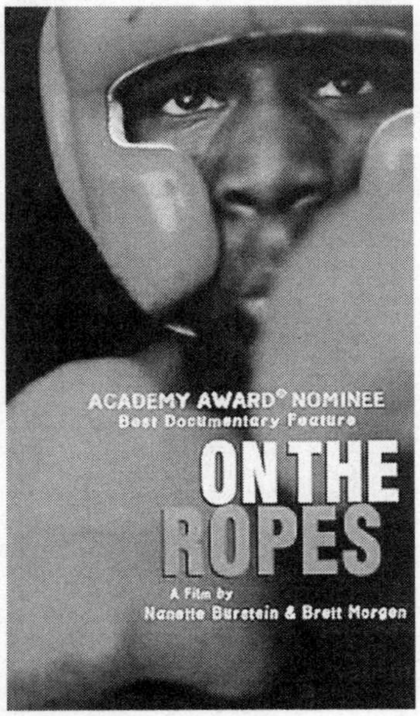

On The Ropes (1999)
Nominated for an Academy Award, this acclaimed film looks at three young boxers training for the 1997 Golden Gloves tournament. The trio—a talented but emotionally unstable Hispanic teen, a fighter offered money by a shifty promoter, and a black woman whose shot is threatened by a drug raid on her family's home—all see the ring as the best chance to escape the poverty and crime of their Brooklyn neighborhood. 90 min.
53-6759 *$19.99*

Invisible Places: Complete Set
You've got an invitation to visit some of the world's most remote and secret locales with this offbeat three-tape series. Go where ordinary people never can, as you explore tunnel systems from the Roman aqueducts to the world beneath Chicago's Sears Tower in "Subtropolis"; tour Irish crypts, Polish salt mines and the catacombs of Rome in "Underworld"; and see government sanctuaries built during the Cold War in "World of War." 150 min. total. NOTE: Individual volumes available at $14.99 each.
83-1389 Save $10.00! *$34.99*

Ends Of The Earth: Death Valley
Perhaps the most desolate spot in the United States, California's Death Valley National Park is paradoxically becoming one of the region's top tourist attractions. Follow a pair of geologists as they traverse the region, a desert waste filled with unique plants and animals, rare fossils, and an otherworldly beauty. Peter Coyote hosts; music by Ry Cooder. 52 min.
83-1340 Letterboxed *$19.99*

Ends Of The Earth: The Secret Abyss Of Movile Cave
Only recently discovered, Movile Cave in Romania contains an unusual underground lake that is home to dozens of plants and animals not found anywhere else on Earth. Take a rare look inside Movile Cave and explore a subterranean wonderland cut off from the world for millions of years. Paul McGann narrates. 52 min.
83-1352 *$19.99*

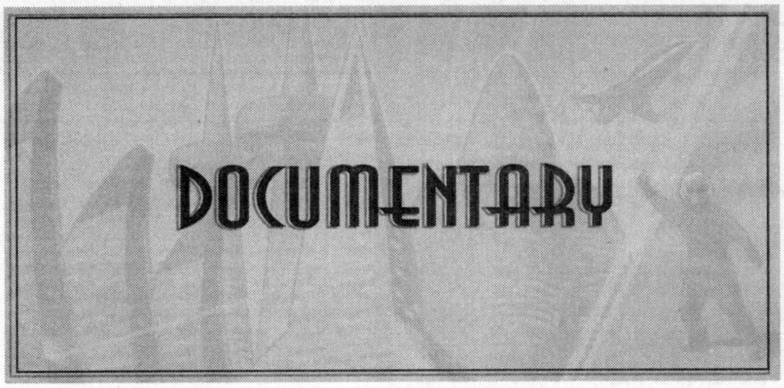

Caught In The Act!
This controversial program was banned in British video stores—and it's easy to see why! There's live-action footage taken from surveillance cameras that capture armed robberies, assaults, drug deals and intimate sex acts. Even Princess Diana is featured in a scandalous segment that was the tabloid rage of Europe. 50 min.
22-1479 *$14.99*

La Belle Epoque (1987)
"The Beautiful Era"—art nouveau, the beginnings of jazz, the last glory days of European royalty—is recalled by those who lived through the years between 1890 and 1914. Includes newsreel clips, period costumes, photographs and interviews with Erte, Jacques-Henri Lartigue and others; narrated by Douglas Fairbanks. 105 min.
22-5157 *$39.99*

Amusement Parks: The Pursuit Of Fun
Take a tour of the wildest amusement rides in the greatest recreation parks in America with this thrill-packed, fun-filled video. Among the sites you'll visit are Kennywood near Pittsburgh, home of the Kennywood Steel Phantom; Williamsburg's Busch Gardens; Cedar Point, near Lake Erie in Ohio; and Universal Studios in Los Angeles. 54 min.
76-7470 *$19.99*

America's Greatest Roller Coaster Thrills In 3-D
They terrify—and delight—millions of Americans every year, and some of them have been on the job for decades. Remarkable 3-D camerawork gives you a front-row seat for every twist and turn of such classic coasters as Coney Island's venerable Cyclone; the Thunderbolt and Steel Phantom at Kennywood Park near Pittsburgh; Cedar Point, Ohio's Magnum XL-200, Mean Streak and Raptor; Batman and Robin—the Ride in Six Flags Magic Mountain and others. Two pairs of glasses included. 60 min.
89-5068 *$19.99*

America's Greatest Roller Coaster Thrills 2 In 3-D
Pry your hands off the arms of your chair and brace yourself for a second spin around the country's most hair-raising theme park rides, all in pulse-pounding 3-D. Wildwood, New Jersey's Comet and Great Nor'Easter; the classic Jack Rabbit at Pennsylvania's Kennywood Park; Busch Gardens Williamsburg's Loch Ness Monster; and the skyscraping High Roller in downtown Las Vegas are just a part of the itinerary. Two pairs of glasses included. 60 min.
89-5069 *$19.99*

World's Greatest Roller Coaster Thrills In 3-D
Take a lightning-fast, loop-the-loop tour of amazing amusement park attractions in Europe, Asia, Canada and Mexico in this 3-D documentary. Included are stops at Blackpool, England's Pepsi Max—the Big One; Mexico City's La Montana Rusa; the Big Dipper of Sydney, Australia; the Dragon in Hong Kong and more. Two pairs of glasses included. 65 min.
89-5070 *$19.99*

Great Old Amusement Parks
Get ready for a "coaster-to-coaster" tour of some of America's most historic and best-loved amusement parks in this thrill-packed program. From Coney Island and Playland in New York to Pennsylvania's Kennywood Park, Ohio's Cedar Point and Oaks Park in Oregon to the Santa Cruz Beach Boardwalk along the California coast, you'll see classic rides and learn why fans of all ages keeping coming back. 60 min.
90-1048 □*$14.99*

Coney Island (1991)
Step right up and take a look at the fabulous history of New York City's legendary amusement spot, the place where circus sideshows, roller coasters and daredevil rides, and Nathan's hot dogs were king. This nostalgic documentary from Ric Burns offers rare film footage of Steeplechase Park, Luna Park and Dreamland and some of their wildest attractions, from the park's beginnings in the late 1800s to their decline a century later. 68 min.
76-7436 *$39.99*

Thrill Ride: The Science Of Fun (1997)
This breathtaking IMAX documentary puts you in the front of some of America's most exciting (or, sometimes, nausea-inducing) amusement park attractions. Trace the history of thrill rides, from 19th-century Parisian coasters to today's gravity-defying steel monsters and computer simulations, and learn what goes into their high-tech design and construction. 45 min.
02-3180 □*$19.99*

Music, Memories & Milestones: Complete Set
Look back over the unforgettable people, events and tunes of the 20th century with this remarkable four-tape collection of American and British newsreel footage. Volumes includes "The 1930s," "The 1940s," "The 1950s" and "The 1960s." 240 min. total. NOTE: Individual volumes available at $19.99.
22-1818 *$79.99*

What A Blast: Complete Set
What goes up comes down—loudly—in this four-tape boxed set that features amazing footage of building demolitions and offers a behind-the-scenes look at the people whose job it is to bring the steel giants down. Included in the series are "Architecture in Motion," "Demolition Artist," "Detonation Countdown" and "For Kids!" 165 min. total. NOTE: Individual volumes available at $12.99 each.
83-1437 Save $12.00! *$39.99*

Things That Aren't Here Anymore (1995)
They just don't make things like they used to. Some of Los Angeles' most nostalgia-inspiring landmarks from the past are explored in this documentary. Whether it was the rides at Pacific Ocean Park, Schwab's Pharmacy or the jazzy nightlife of Central Avenue, you'll see there are some things that are gone but can never be forgotten. Hosted by Ralph Story. 62 min.
50-5881 □*$19.99*

More Things That Aren't Here Anymore (1995)
Remember when ten bucks was a lot of money for a teenager? Even if you aren't old enough to recall that, take a trip down memory lane anyway with another look at Southern California's colorful past. Explored here are Lion Country Safari, Cubs minor-league baseball and Busch Gardens, among many others. Hosted by Ralph Story. 63 min.
50-5882 □*$19.99*

New York: The Way It Was: Complete Set
Take a nostalgic journey to the Big Apple in the good old days in this three-tape documentary set filled with fun, rare footage. "The Way It Was" offers reminiscences about Coney Island and Ebbets Field from Alan King and others; Harlem, Yorkville, Brooklyn and the Bronx are surveyed in "The Old Neighborhood"; and "Wish You Were Here" goes to the Catskills, Rockaway Beach and other vacation locales. 150 min. total. NOTE: Individual volumes available at $19.99 each.
50-2915 *$59.99*

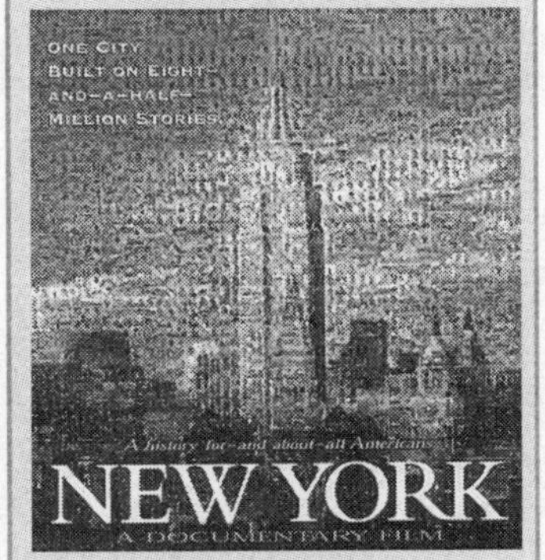

New York (1999)
Follow over 350 years of Big Apple history and lore with director Ric Burns' epic five-part documentary on America's largest city, the founding of Dutch trading post New Amsterdam in 1626 to its rise as a global leader in economics, fashion, communications and the arts. David Ogden Stiers narrates. Volumes include "The Country and the City (1609-1825)," "Order and Disorder (1825-1863)," "Sunshine and Shadow (1865-1898)," "The Power and the People (1898-1914)" and "Cosmopolis (1914-1931)." 10 hours on five tapes.
18-7876 □*$99.99*

Always Tomorrow (1941)
The history and spirit of the Coca Cola Company is explored in this portrait of an American business success story, produced by...the Coca Cola Company. Trace the soft drink bottler's journey from its invention by Georgia pharmacist Dr. John Pemberton in 1886 to its meteoric rise to an international corporation. 55 min.
10-6002 *$14.99*

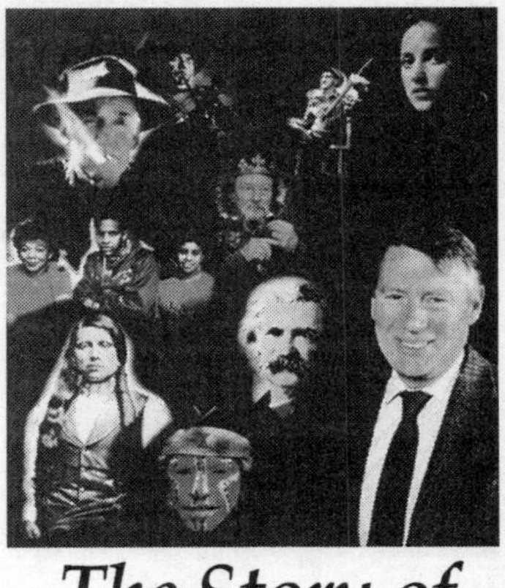

The Story of
English

The Story Of English: Complete Set
It's rapidly becoming the unofficial global language, and the multi-cultural heritage of English is reflected here in an array of regional dialects. Commentator Robert MacNeil hosts this acclaimed PBS series that traces the history, development and diversity of America's "mother tongue." 8 1/2 hrs. on five tapes. NOTE: Individual volumes available at $24.99 each.
22-5238 Save $25.00! *$99.99*

Helen Keller In Her Story (1955)
Oscar-winning documentary about the incredible true story of Helen Keller, following her tutoring by teacher Anne Sullivan, her education at Radcliffe College and her friendships with artists, musicians and leaders of state. Features interviews, newsreels and footage of Keller at home and on tour. 50 min.
53-6040 *$29.99*

The Queen (1968)
The forerunner to "Paris Is Burning," this documentary captures the 1967 Miss All-America Camp Beauty Contest in all of its cross-dressing glory. Shown are the preparations for the glittery contest by 40 contestants, including Miss Harlow, a blonde Philadelphia favorite. Andy Warhol, George Plimpton, Terry Southern and Edie Sedgwick are among the celebrity judges. 68 min.
70-5084 Was $59.99 *$29.99*

I Wanna Be A Beauty Queen (1979)
If you're tired of Miss America, you may want to see some of the most outrageous "girls" ever vie for the title of the Alternative Miss World. This funky, spacy drag queen contest features commentary by guest emcee Divine, a peek behind the scenes, and a zippy title song by Little Nell. 81 min.
44-7010 *$29.99*

Paris Is Burning (1991)
Equally outrageous, funny and touching, Jenny Livingston's acclaimed documentary looks at a very vocal segment of the gay community: the drag "houses" of Harlem that compete in elaborate fashion shows known as "balls," with contestants dressed as Vogue models, socialites, military men and other sartorial stereotypes. These inner-city groups serve as surrogate families to the gay minority youths who join them. 76 min.
71-5248 Was $19.99 *$14.99*

Wigstock: The Movie (1995)
"A celebration of life, liberty and the pursuit of big hair," New York City's annual Wigstock drag festival is the focus of this wild and exuberant documentary. See wild costumes and hairdos; celebrity guests such as supermodel RuPaul, rock group Deee-Lite and emcee the Lady Bunny; and duelling Tallulah Bankheads performing "Born to Be Wild." 82 min.
88-1034 Was $19.99 *$14.99*

All Dressed Up And No Place To Go (1996)
The world of cross-dressing—heterosexual men who enjoy wearing women's clothing—is surveyed in this acclaimed, entertaining documentary. The filmmakers spent three years chronicling four cross-dressers, including a computer consultant, a 68-year-old CEO and a former NASA engineer. Meet the men and the women in their lives.
50-5491 *$29.99*

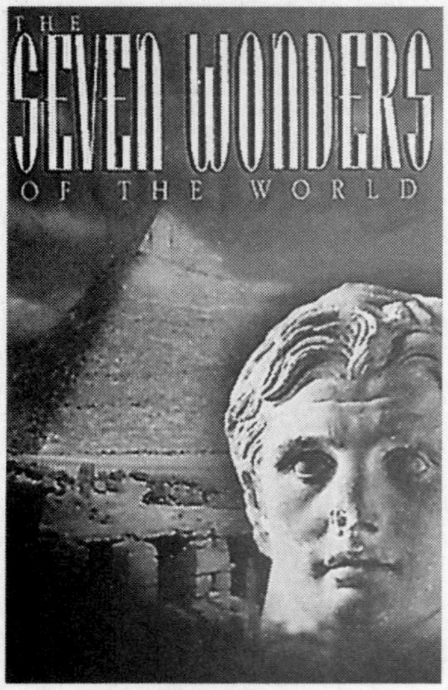
THE
SEVEN WONDERS
OF THE WORLD

The Seven Wonders Of The World: Complete Set
Noted scholar John Romer hosts this two-tape look at the history and lore of the ancient world's most memorable structures, from the giant tomb of King Mausolus of Caria that gave birth to the word "mausoleum" and the elaborate Hanging Gardens of Babylon to the 100-foot-tall Colossus of Rhodes and the sole surviving wonder, the Great Pyramid of Giza. Included are "Simply the Best/The Magic Metropolis" and "Wonders of the East/Ghosts of Wonder." 190 min. total. NOTE: Individual volumes available at $14.99 each.
27-7216 *$29.99*

The Hutterites: To Care And Not To Care (1993)
Fascinating documentary on the people who are spiritual cousins of the Amish and Mennonites and live a simple life in collective agricultural communities while shunning modern conveniences. 60 min.
63-7064 *$19.99*

The Amish: Not To Be Modern
They came to America from Europe to escape religious persecution, and for centuries have remained separate and untouched by society. This film look at the life and ways of the "plain folk" offers a rare glimpse at a culture increasingly threatened by the encroachment of modern American culture. 57 min.
50-6356 *$29.99*

Floating Palaces: Complete Set
Throughout the first half of the 20th century, magnificent ocean liners such as the Queen Mary, Normandie and Queen Elizabeth II were the final word in transatlantic luxury. Relive the Golden Age of Travel with this four-tape series that offers a stem-to-stern tour of these famed ships, memories of the people who worked and traveled on them, and rare footage of the doomed vessels Titanic,
53-8541 *$59.99*

The Great Ships: The Sailing Collection
The History Channel produced this incisive look at the world of sailing ships, presented in a three-tape set. Using 3-D computer graphics, unique simulations and in-depth research, the series takes you on board "The Whalers," "The Galleons" and "The Clippers." 150 min. total. NOTE: Individual volumes available at $19.99 each.
53-8834 Save $10.00! *$49.99*

Video Aquarium
Psychologists have found the perfect way to relax: watching this electric fish bowl, as a variety of sea creature floats by your TV screen, without the hassles of feeding and changing dirty water. 60 min.
50-1050 *$14.99*

Ocean Waves
Even if you can't get to the ocean, this tape gives you a crystal-clear view of the tranquil breaking water. Wave lovers, rejoice! With natural ocean sound. 60 min.
50-1183 *$14.99*

America The Beautiful
Take a musical tour of the country with this enchanting production from Reader's Digest that mixes sight and sound to let you visit fall in New England ("Autumn Leaves"), the bustle of the Big Apple ("New York, New York"), the Ozark Mountains ("Missouri Waltz"), the prairies of Kansas ("Over the Rainbow") and other all-American locales. 120 min.
50-1273 *$29.99*

Video Fireplace (3-Hour Version)
No logs to haul or ashes to clean! Relax as the flames crackle the wood away. Ideal way to reduce tension. 180 min.
50-8603 *$19.99*

Liquified
Take the plunge into an kaleidoscopic wonderland of undersea images. This program features an amazing array of aquatic animals, shifting, blending and morphing their shapes, as a rhythmic ambient soundtrack plays in the background, resulting in a soothing video experience unlike any you've had before. 43 min.
83-1380 *$14.99*

Underwater Realm
Want to experience the breathtaking beauty of an underwater dive, but worried about getting "the bends"? Pop this tape into your VCR and take part in an aquatic odyssey that brings you up close to colorful fish, playful sea turtles, a fish-filled shipwreck and other remarkable sights. 43 min.
83-1381 *$14.99*

High Roller's Vegas
Go inside the high-stakes world of America's gaming mecca in this Discovery Channel program. See how casinos keep a high-tech eye open to foil cheaters; how "high-rolling" customers receive lavish treatment; how volcanoes, pirate ships and risqué stageshows are all part of a typical day's entertainment; and more. Jason Robards narrates. 52 min.
27-7200 *$14.99*

The Real Las Vegas
Originally broadcast on the A&E Network, this four-tape series offers the most complete look at Las Vegas ever, covering its history from frontier days and the mob's influences to the booming casino and resort Mecca of today. Archival footage and interviews with Mirage mogul Steve Wynn, author Nicholas Pileggi, Milton Berle and Debbie Reynolds help shape this fascinating portrait. 200 min. total.
53-8723 Was $59.99 *$39.99*

Blasted In Las Vegas
It's not the original title of "Leaving Las Vegas." Rather, it's a collection of some of the most amazing blasts in "Glitter Gulch's" history, implosions of casino-hotels such as the Sands, the Dunes, the Landmark and the Hacienda. 30 min.
76-7347 *$14.99*

The Speeches Collection
These are the leaders whose words challenged, exhorted and inspired the world. This documentary series features highlights from each man's career and from their greatest addresses. Each tape runs about 60 min. There are 21 volumes available, including:

The Speeches Of Franklin D. Roosevelt
50-6244 *$19.99*

The Speeches Of Winston Churchill
50-6245 *$19.99*

The Speeches Of John F. Kennedy
50-6247 *$19.99*

The Speeches Of Martin Luther King
50-6312 *$19.99*

The Speeches Of Adolf Hitler
50-6497 *$19.99*

The Speeches Of Ronald Reagan
50-7338 *$19.99*

The Speeches Of Malcolm X
50-7419 *$19.99*

The Speeches Of Our Founding Fathers & The American Revolution
50-7422 *$19.99*

Paramedics: Complete Set
From the Learning Channel comes this intense four-tape survey of EMT and rescue workers who are on a life-and-death mission to save people in emergency situations. Follow them as they ride in ambulances and in fire and helicopter rescue units to preserve lives in the most dire of circumstances. Volumes include "Pararescumen: That Others May Live," "Paramedics: After Dark," "Paramedics: Desert Sirens" and "Paramedics: No Limits." 240 min. total. NOTE: Individual volumes available at $14.99.
27-7555 *$59.99*

Rescue 911: World's Greatest Rescues
From the hit TV series comes these remarkable real-life dramas of daring rescues from around the world. Firefighters in New Zealand race to save a girl trapped under a burning gasoline tanker; a mother makes a desperate choice to save her children in a French apartment fire; a stand-off pits Moscow police against a hostage-holding gunman; and much more. 75 min.
89-5100 *$19.99*

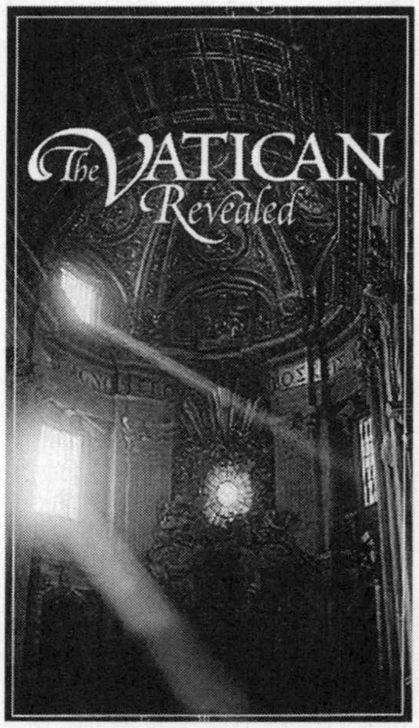
The VATICAN
Revealed

The Vatican Revealed
It's one of the smallest countries in the world, yet its influence reaches around the globe. Trace the 2,000-year story of the Vatican City, home of the Roman Catholic Church and repository of some of the world's greatest architectural and art treasures, with this interesting documentary that offers commentary from theologians and historians and rare looks at places tourists never see. 100 min. on two tapes.
53-6763 *$29.99*

Saints And Sinners: Complete Set
The 2,000-year history of the Roman Catholic Church and the Papacy, and their influence on world religion, politics, art and culture, are traced in a six-volume documentary series produced with the cooperation of the Vatican. Included are "Upon This Rock," "Between Two Empires," "Set Over Nations," "Protest and Division," "The Pope and the People" and "The Oracles of God." 310 min. total.
50-5739 Was $79.99 *$59.99*

Religions Of The World
Examine the origins, doctrines and historical significance of the world's major faiths with this remarkable six-part documentary series narrated by Ben Kingsley. Included in the set are looks at Buddhism, Catholicism, Hinduism, Islam, Judaism and Protestantism. 300 min. total.
50-8141 *$99.99*

Altars Of The World: Complete Set
Follow the practices of the world's major religions, and learn about the common patterns of faith and ritual that unite them, in this fascinating two-tape set hosted by Lew Ayres. "The Eastern Religions" examines Buddhism, Hinduism, the Jains, Sikhism and Zoroastrianism, while Christianity, Islam and Judaism are the focus of "The Western Religions." 125 min. total. NOTE: Individual volumes available at $24.99 each.
53-6459 Save $10.00! *$39.99*

Merton: A Film Biography (1984)
A profile of Thomas Merton, who spent 27 years as a Trappist monk and was censured for his outspoken books of theology and social criticism, this critically acclaimed documentary features interviews with the Dalai Lama, Joan Baez, Lawrence Ferlinghetti and other friends and colleagues of Merton. 57 min.
70-5004 Was $39.99 *$29.99*

Behind The Veil: Nuns (1984)
A look at women's roles in the Catholic Church, this acclaimed film contrasts nuns who live and work in inner cities and isolated monasteries, reviews the important contributions of women to religion throughout history, and calls for changes in the Church's current patriarchal attitudes. 130 min.
70-5029 Was $59.99 *$29.99*

The Buried Mirror: Complete Set
The Hispanic world of Europe and the Americas is explored in this five-part series hosted by author and diplomat Carlos Fuentes. Learn the history of the Hispanic people and their culture from around the globe, and understand the economic, political and cultural changes faced by the expanding Hispanic population in the U.S. Includes "The Virgin and the Bull," "Conflict of the Gods," "The Age of Gold," "The Price of Freedom" and "Unfinished Business." 300 min. total. NOTE: Individual volumes available at $29.99 each.
22-5865 Save $50.00! *$99.99*

Haiti: A Painted History
Follow 500 years of Haitian history through artwork by the Caribbean nation's top painters in this compelling documentary. Starting with Columbus' arrival in 1492 and continuing through colonial rule, the cruelties of the Duvalier regimes and the 1992 overthrow of Aristede, the paintings convey a tale of violence, sorrow and an ongoing struggle for freedom. 56 min.
22-6053 *$29.99*

Amazon: The Invisible People
Take a journey deep into the Amazon wilderness, home to groups of people who have no contact with the outside world. In the Ecuadorean rain forest, you'll discover the Tageari, a tribe whose way of life is threatened when their land is targeted by exploration teams in search of oil and other resources. 60 min.
22-9008 *$19.99*

Peru's City Of Ghosts
Explore long-hidden ruins in the Nazca Plains city of Cahuachi in Southern Peru in this Discovery Channel program. Italian archeologist Giuseppe Orefici reveal the fruits of 17 years' work: elaborate pyramids and ceremonial buildings; pottery and musical instruments; and well-preserved mummies that show evidence of ritual sacrifice. 50 min.
27-7223 *$14.99*

Tango: Our Dance (1987)
Explore the development of Argentina's national dance, the tango, and the culture that has grown around it throughout the Americas in this lively, music-filled documentary by Jorge Zanada. 70 min. In Spanish with English subtitles.
53-9592 *$59.99*

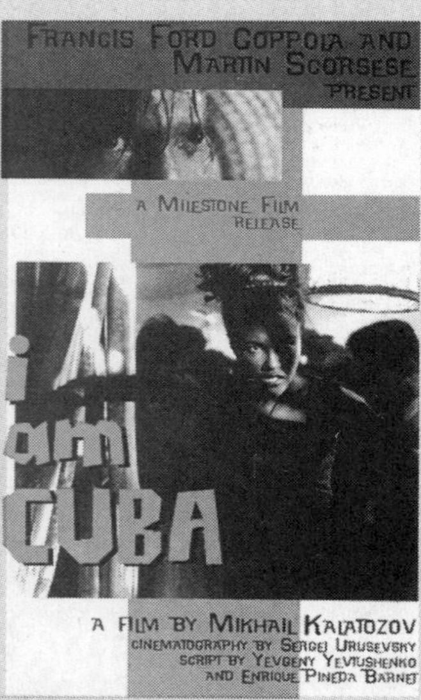
FRANCIS FORD COPPOLA AND
MARTIN SCORSESE
PRESENT
A MILESTONE FILM
RELEASE
i am
CUBA
A FILM BY MIKHAIL KALATOZOV
CINEMATOGRAPHY BY SERGEI URUSEVSKY
SCRIPT BY YEVGENY YEVTUSHENKO
AND ENRIQUE PINEDA BARNET

I Am Cuba (1964)
Unseen by the West for nearly 30 years, this unusual Cuban/Soviet co-production was meant to help train Cuban filmmakers and build support for Castro's regime. Four dramatic vignettes depict, in a visually hypnotic blend of Party propaganda and Latin American energy, the corruption of Battista's Havana, the hard life of rural farmers, and the fervor of the student revolutionaries who propelled Castro to victory. Directed by Mikhail Kalatozov ("The Cranes Are Flying"). 141 min. In Russian and Spanish with English subtitles.
80-5025 Was $79.99 *$29.99*

The Other Cuba (1983)
This fascinating documentary, filmed in secret over a period of several years, offers a sobering look at both the official history of Castro's Cuba and the reality of life within a totalitarian regime. Mixing newsreel images and raw footage, the film juxtaposes dancing children and music festivals with prison camps and executions, and features interviews with censored artists and writers. 94 min. In English and Spanish with English subtitles.
53-6354 *$29.99*

In The Shadow Of The Incas
Examine the pinnacle of the Incan civilization, the pre-Columbian city of Machu Picchu in Peru, in this documentary that explains who built it, why it was built and why it was abandoned. The program also travels back to 1500 B.C. and looks at the neighboring cultures whose people and heritages were absorbed into the Incan Empire. 43 min.
80-7142 Was $29.99 *$19.99*

The Incas Remembered (1984)
Acclaimed filmmaker Lucy Jarvis delves into the rich and mysterious history of a lost civilization: the Incas. Far more advanced than given credit for, the Incas made useful agricultural discoveries, performed highly intricate brain surgery and built such architectural wonders as Machu Picchu. 60 min.
27-6500 *$24.99*

The Panama Deception (1992)
Controversial, Academy Award-winning study of U.S. policy under the Reagan/Bush administration toward Panama, focusing on "Operation Just Cause," which involved the removal of Panamanian dictator Manuel Noriega. Directed by Barbara Trent ("Cover-Up"), the film presents a no-nonsense account of events that the mainstream media ignored. Narrated by Elizabeth Montgomery. 91 min.
15-5267 *$79.99*

El Che: Investigating A Legend (1998)
This probing program chronicles the rise and fall of one of the most talked-about leaders of the 20th century: Che Guevara. An ongoing figure of debate, Guevara led an adventurous life of revolution, guerrilla warfare and leadership as he worked under Fidel Castro, and after his death at 39 became a symbol for an entire generation. 90 min.
22-1591 *$19.99*

Paris 1900 (1950)
Wonderful period documentary that brings fin de siecle Paris to vivid life. The fads, the fashions, and the famous are captured in rare footage that spans till the dawn of World War I. The narration by Monty Woolley is a tremendous plus. 76 min.
01-1396 Was $29.99 *$24.99*

The Foreign Legion
Their exploits have been romanticized and depicted in literature and films for decades, but the French Foreign Legion continues to this day as the world's most elite mercenary army. Take a rare look at Legionnaire training and day-to-day life in this fascinating documentary. 100 min.
22-1546 *$29.99*

Ancient Greece: Complete Set
Get a fresh perspective on Ancient Greece with this two-tape set that looks at art and architecture, mining, unusual customs and myths. Includes "Art in Ancient Greece/Mining in Ancient Greece" and "Bacchus, The God of Wine/Fire Walking in Greece." 180 min. total. NOTE: Individual volumes available at $29.99 each.
22-1572 *$59.99*

The Odyssey Of Troy
Join a team of archeologists as they travel to Troy in modern-day Turkey to investigate the legends of the Trojan War, Helen of Troy and Achilles. Discover for the first time what the team found and how it differs or corresponds to the story of "The Iliad." Leonard Nimoy narrates. 50 min.
53-8195 *$14.99*

Rome And Pompeii
Through the magic of computer animation, archeologists and video artists re-create in this documentary what the cities of Rome and Pompeii looked like at the height of the Roman Empire. See the restored splendor of the Colosseum and the Forum, tour markets and taverns, and witness the terror of Nero's Rome ablaze and the eruption of Vesuvius. 60 min.
50-4835 *$29.99*

Ancient Rome: Boxed Set
Explore "the grandeur that was Rome" with this four-tape documentary series that follows the rise and fall of one of the world's great empires. See how Rome became the dominant power in Europe and the Middle East for more than 500 years, the continuing influence of Roman art, architecture and law, and how such rulers as Nero and Caligula became synonymous with corruption and decadence. 200 min. total.
50-8122 Was $59.99 *$39.99*

Rome: Power & Glory: Complete Set
Follow the rise and fall of the Roman Empire with this comprehensive six-tape series. Remarkable on-location footage, dramatic re-enactments and commentary from scholars and historians track Rome's cultural, political, military and artistic history. Programs include "The Rise," "Legions of Conquest," "Seduction of Power," "Grasp of Empire," "The Cult of Order" and "The Fall." Peter Coyote narrates. 312 min. total.
50-8349 *$99.99*

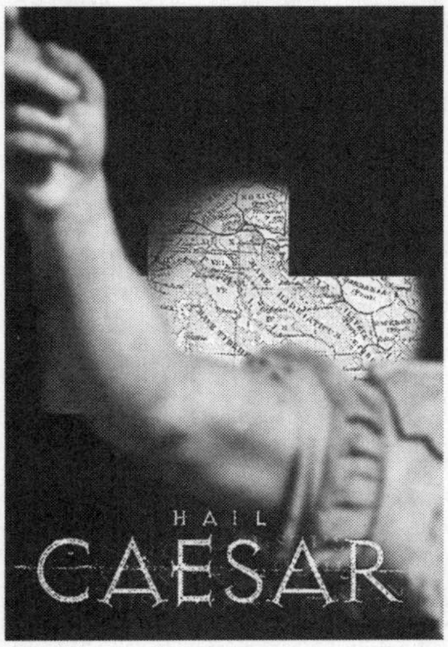

Hail Caesar: Complete Set
They were heroes and villains, warriors and madmen, and nearly 2,000 years after their reign ended the name Caesar is still synonymous with conquest and power. This six-tape boxed set traces the rise and fall of the Roman Empire through the lives of Julius, Augustus, Nero, Hadrian, Constantine, Justinian and other rulers. 300 min. total.
53-9984 Was $99.99 *$59.99*

In The Footsteps Of Alexander The Great
Before his 30th birthday, he had conquered most of the known world. This engrossing program traces Alexander's career as a military and political leader who sought to unite, by force, the Eastern and Western worlds. Hosted by Michael Wood. 240 min.
90-1003 ❑*$29.99*

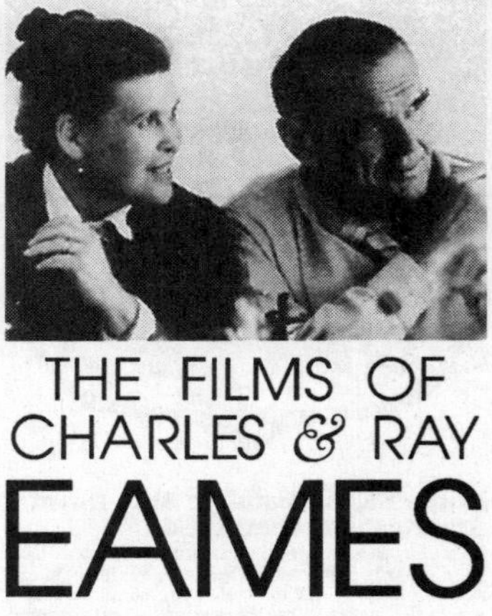

The Films Of Charles & Ray Eames, Vol. 1: Powers Of Ten
Famed architects, designers and photographers Charles and Ray Eames also made several films. "The Powers of Ten" offers an amazing look at time and space. Beginning with a close-up of a man's hand and increasing in distance every 10 seconds, the film eventually looks at the universe in a spectacular way. Gregory Peck hosts. 21 min.
50-2137 *$39.99*

Toccata For Toy Trains
The classic film by Charles and Ray Eames follows a collection of miniature trains that travel from railyard and roundhouse to a bustling station. Their journey in this delightful film is complemented by Elmer Bernstein's wonderful score. Also featured is "Parade," a colorful cinematic pageant of mechanized toys set to the music of John Philip Sousa. 22 min.
50-2509 *$19.99*

Boston: The Way It Was, Vol. 1
Celebrate the good old days of Beantown with this nostalgic program from Boston's WGBH, hosted by Thomas O'Connor of Boston College. You'll take a trip down Memory Lane with the Boston Braves, the Totem Pole Ballroom, the Old Howard, Scollay Square and more, and you'll hear from people who were there. 60 min.
50-5234 ❑*$19.99*

Boston: The Way It Was, Vol. 2
It's a treasure of memories for Bostonians who cherish their city's exciting past. Through newsreel footage, photos and expert commentary by Boston College professor Thomas O'Connor, the Boston Garden, the Bruins' "Kraut Line," the Metropolitan Theatre, and the Cocoanut Grove come alive again. 60 min.
50-5235 ❑*$19.99*

Lighthouses Of North America
The world of North America's fascinating lighthouses is explored in this video that takes you from Pemaquid Point, Maine to Point Arena, California. You'll hear stories about ghosts, shipwrecks and heroic deeds and see beautifully photographed lighthouses from around the continent. 60 min.
50-5442 *$19.99*

Gardens Of The World With Audrey Hepburn: Boxed Set
Actress and goodwill ambassador Audrey Hepburn hosts this enchanting six-part series that takes viewers on a journey to some of the world's most beautiful green spots. Join Hepburn as she visits such locales as Mt. Vernon, Versailles and Holland in "Country Gardens," "Flower Gardens," "Formal Gardens," "Public Gardens & Trees," "Roses & Rose Gardens" and "Tulips & Spring Bulbs." 180 min. total. NOTE: Individual volumes available at $19.99 each.
50-2499 Save $20.00! *$99.99*

Gardens Of The World With Audrey Hepburn: Tropical Gardens & Japanese Gardens
In this special two-tape collection, Hepburn explores lush tropical greenery in botanical gardens in the Caribbean, the South Pacific and Asia, followed by a visit to Japan, home to the Shinshin-an garden paths, the Detached Palace at Katsura and Hakusanso's teahouses. 60 min. total.
89-5018 *$29.99*

Labyrinth: The History Of The Maze
This intriguing documentary studies the lore and lure of mazes, from the famed Labyrinth of Crete to medieval mazes of England, from modern mazes to incredible garden puzzles. Maze desginer Adrian Fisher serves as your guide to this beautiful and mystical world.
80-7231 *$19.99*

Bloom: Boxed Set
Six episodes from the popular English TV series that looks at the beauty and lore of flowers have been collected in this three-tape boxed set. Join hosts Anne Swithinbank and Bill Chudziak as they tour some of Britain's loveliest homes and gardens. Included are "Irises & Foxgloves," "Orchids & Pinks" and "Roses & Rhododendrons." 180 min. total.
80-7298 *$49.99*

Glory: The Military Music Tradition
The role of music in America's military and its historical importance are traced in this documentary that captures the pageantry and patriotic display of such renowned units as the U.S. Army Drill Team, the "Old Guard" Fife and Drum Corps, and more. 50 min.
50-1465 *$19.99*

Trolley: The Cars That Built Our Cities
Watch the evolution of horse-drawn streetcars to trolley lines and elevated trains to today's rediscovered light railways in this superb program. Rare footage shows the introduction of PCC streamliner cars and some unusual publicity stunts used by trolley companies. 54 min.
50-2408 *$19.99*

Subway: The Empire Beneath New York's Streets
The history of the New York City subway system is revealed in this remarkable documentary that looks at what makes the tunnels, cars and technology tick. Learn how tycoons and corrupt politicians played parts in subway construction, how the lines were dug beneath the streets, what's being done to combat graffiti and more. 50 min.
53-8012 *$19.99*

Famous Americans Of The 20th Century
Examine the lives of 11 Americans who made a difference in our way of life in a number of different fields. With newsreel footage, speeches and interviews, this biographical series adds insight into their world. Each tape runs 55 min. There are 11 volumes available, including:

The Story Of Thomas A. Edison
50-4292 Was $29.99 *$19.99*

The Story Of Henry Ford
50-4293 Was $29.99 *$19.99*

The Story Of Franklin D. Roosevelt
50-4298 Was $29.99 *$19.99*

The Prize: The Epic Quest For Oil, Money And Power: Complete Set
Critically-acclaimed four-tape chronicle of oil and its effects on global politics and world economy features interviews with those who shaped the industry, never-before-seen archival footage and newly filmed segments. Based on the Pulitzer Prize-winning book by Daniel Yergin, who also narrates. 480 min. total. NOTE: Individual volumes available at $29.99 each.
22-5597 Save $20.00! *$99.99*

Riding The Rails
During the Great Depression, hundreds of thousands of teenagers would leave their hometowns and hop freight trains, hoping to find a better life wherever the rails would take them. Their remarkable true stories are recounted in this acclaimed documentary that mixes interviews, archival film footage, period music and letters to show the romantic and realistic aspects of "hobo life." 72 min.
50-5180 *$29.99*

Lost Treasures Of The Ancient World
They still inspire wonder and awe as they did centuries ago, and now some of the most amazing historical sites from around the world can be seen in this series. Learn each ancient marvel's story, and see through 3-D computer animation how they looked when first built. Each tape runs about 50 min.

Lost Treasures Of The Ancient World: Set #1
Included in this six-tape boxed set are "Ancient Rome," "Hadrian's Wall," "Mayans & Aztecs," "Pompeii," "The Pyramids" and "Stonehenge." 300 min. total. NOTE: Individual volumes available at $19.99 each.
22-1662 Save $20.00! *$99.99*

Lost Treasures Of The Ancient World: Set #2
Included in this six-tape boxed set are "Ancient Egypt," "Ancient Greece," "Ancient Jerusalem," "Carthage," "The Romans in North Africa" and "The Seven Wonders of the Ancient World." 300 min. total. NOTE: Individual volumes available at $19.99 each.
22-1754 Save $10.00! *$99.99*

Celtic Legends: Boxed Set
The folklore of the Celtic people continued to influence the mythology and fables of the British isles long after the region fell to the Romans. In this three-tape series you'll learn about Celtic culture as you explore "The Arthurian Legends," "Irish Legends" and "Scottish Legends." 150 min. total. NOTE: Individual volumes available at $19.99 each.
22-1742 Save $10.00! *$49.99*

The Celts: Complete Set (1998)
They were warriors and artists, poets and mystics, and today, 2,000 years after their control of Western Europe and Britain was lost to Rome, the Celtic heritage and traditions live on. This three-tape documentary series looks at the history of the Celts and their unique culture. 300 min. total.
04-3601 Was $49.99 *$39.99*

When Ireland Starved: The Great Famine
A harrowing look at the Great Potato Famine of Ireland in the mid-1840s, when the island lost over 2,000,000 people through starvation and emigration to other countries. This program delves into England's involvement in the tragedy. 120 min.
50-2601 *$29.99*

Michael Collins: The Shadow Of Béalnabláth
Award-winning look at the life of the revolutionary who was a leading figure in the 1916 Easter Uprising for Irish independence from Great Britain. Interviews with colleagues and family members, newsreel footage and dramatic re-creations tell the story of Collins' political victories and his mysterious murder in 1922. 120 min.
50-4829 *$29.99*

1641: The Curse Of Cromwell
Historical documents and accounts and location filming help bring to life England's 17th-century campaign against Irish Catholics after erroneous reports stated they had killed 300,000 Ulster Protestants. Under the direction of Oliver Cromwell, Irish towns were destroyed, the region was occupied by English troops, and thousands were forced into slavery in the New World. 58 min.
50-5279 *$19.99*

The McCourts Of Limerick
Learn the remarkable true story of the family behind the Pulitzer Prize-winning book "Angela's Ashes" with this documentary by author Frank McCourt's nephew, Conor. Travel to Ireland as you trace the McCourt clan's history through family photographs, interviews and video footage, including a McCourt brothers reunion and the actual scattering of Angela's ashes. 50 min.
53-6309 *$19.99*

Out Of Ireland
Widespread famine that plagued Ireland in the mid-19th century drove tens of thousands from their homeland to the promise of the New World. Trace the history of Irish emigration to America in this documentary that uses the letters and journals of eight immigrants, read by Gabriel Byrne, Brenda Fricker, Liam Neeson and Aidan Quinn, to bring the story into personal focus. 111 min.
63-7130 *$19.99*

Legends Of Ireland: Complete Set
Meet the heroes, heroines and fantastic figures whose stories fill the lore of the Emerald Isle with this three-tape collection. Travel from the dawn of history to the 1700s as you study "Fairies and Leprechauns," "Saint Patrick/Brendan the Navigator" and "The Warrior Queen/The Pirate Queen." 130 min. total. NOTE: Individual volumes available at $19.99 each.
50-5922 Save $30.00! *$29.99*

The Irish In America
From colonial times to the present, the people of the Emerald Isle have made contributions to all facets of American life and culture. Aidan Quinn hosts this two-tape program that features interviews, archival footage and dramatic re-creations to trace the history of the Irish experience in the New World. 100 min. total.
53-8906 *$29.99*

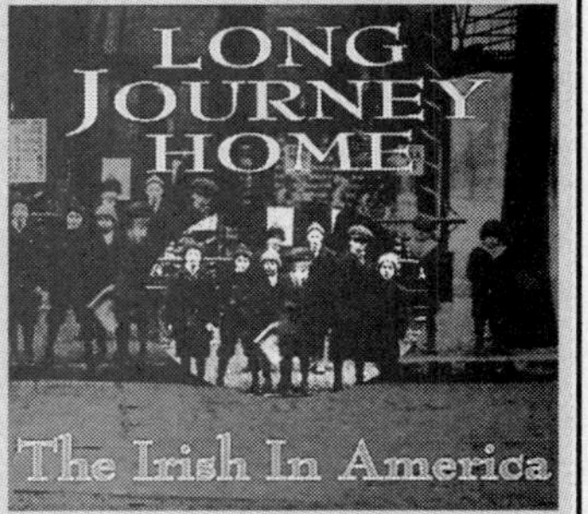

The Irish In America: Long Journey Home (1998)
Follow 150 years of Irish-American history with this four-tape collector's set of the acclaimed documentary series that aired on PBS. From the first wave of immigrants that arrived from a famine-plagued homeland in the 1840s, you'll see the roles that the Irish have played in politics, sports, the performing arts and more. Includes music by Elvis Costello, Van Morrison, The Chieftains with Paddy Moloney, and others. 6 hrs. total.
11-2212 ❑*$79.99*

Island Soldiers: The History Of The Celtic Saints
Trace nearly 2,000 years of Celtic Christianity with this compelling two-part documentary hosted by Anglican Canon Martin Shaw. Along with visits to such sites as Ireland's holy mountain of Croagh Patrick; the home of St. David, Wales' patron saint; and a Cistercian monastery on Caldy Island, Shaw looks at the connections between Celtic and Christian traditions and the men and women who have kept both alive through the centuries. 120 min. total.
80-7219 *$39.99*

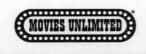

History's Turning Points: Complete Set
Some of the pivotal events in world history are examined in this superb six-part series that mixes newsreel footage with dramatizations. Included are "The Battle of Salamis/The Great Wall of China," "The Battle of Actium/The Conquest of Spain," "The Black Death/The Siege of Constantinople," "The Conquest of the Incas/The Marriage of Pocahontas," "The Battle for Canada/Zulus at War/The Battle of Tsushima" and "The Russian Revolution/The Atom Bomb."
14-9151 *$149.99*

Living Islam: Complete Set
The Muslim world is explored in great depth in this six-part series that looks at the religion's influences, traditions and followers around the globe. Some of the most evocative places in the Islamic faith are visited and many Islamic celebrations are showcased. 300 min. total. NOTE: Individual volumes available at $29.99 each.
14-9118 Save $30.00! *$149.99*

The Hidden City Of Petra
Its name comes from the Greek for "city of rock," and this ancient fortress carved from the mountains of Southwest Jordan served as the capital of the Nabataean people for over 900 years until it was taken by the Muslims in the 7th century. Learn about the vanished Nabataean people and their culture as you explore the remarkable ruins of Petra. 50 min.
53-8387 *$14.99*

The 50 Years War: Israel And The Arabs
Follow a half-century of conflict, cooperation, and a struggle for peace and independence in this compelling PBS documentary that chronicles the establishment of Israel in 1948, the Arab-Israeli wars of 1948, 1967 and 1973, the creation of the PLO, 1978's Camp David accords and the 1993 Oslo peace agreement. Among those interviewed are PLO head Yasir Arafat, Israeli prime ministers Shimon Peres, Yitzhak Shamir and Benjamin Netanyahu, King Hussein of Jordan and others. 150 min. on two tapes.
90-1021 Was $39.99 *$29.99*

People Of The Wind (1976)
The annual migration of Iran's nomadic Bakhtiari people to take their animals to summer feeding grounds—a grueling eight-week, 200-mile odyssey across the formidable Zagros Mountains—is followed in this breathtaking documentary that earned an Academy Award nomination. James Mason narrates. 110 min.
80-5037 Letterboxed *$39.99*

The Story Of Islam (1989)
A look at the origins and spread of the religion of Islam, tracing its roots from the birth of the prophet Mohammed in 600 through its current following of one billion people. 120 min.
50-6513 *$24.99*

Triumph Of The Nerds: Complete Set
This three-tape set traces the evolution of the personal computer, looking at the accomplishments and influences of "computer nerds" Bill Gates, Steve Jobs, Steve Wozniak. Hosted by author Bob Cringely, the series includes "Impressing Their Friends," which features the start of Intel, Altair 8800 and Apple II; "Riding the Bear," about the early days of Microsoft, the invasion of clones and the introduction of Windows; and "Great Artists Steal," focusing on Windows 95, satellite links, Xerox PARC and the Internet. NOTE: Individual volumes available at $19.99 each.
14-9164 Save $10.00! *$49.99*

Nerds 2.0.1.: A Brief History Of The Internet: Complete Set
"Nerds" they may have been, but these pioneers of the "information superhighway" are changing the world at the dawn of the new century. Join host Bob Cringley for a lighthearted look at the evolution of the Net and the multi-billion-dollar software industry. Included in this three-tape series are "Networking the Nerds," "Serving the Suits" and "Wiring the World."
18-7831 *$39.99*

Oratorio For Prague (1968)
At the risk of their own lives, filmmaker Jan Nemec and his crew were able to record the 1968 Soviet invasion of Czechoslovakia that crushed the anti-Communist movement there. This award-winning documentary features the first footage of the event seen in the West. 26 min. Narrated in English.
53-9143 *$19.99*

Rings Around The World (1967)
That universal institution of mirth, merriment and majesty, the circus, is highlighted in this special tape for all ages. Don Ameche hosts a look at the most amazing acts from the four corners of the globe: lions, elephants, acrobats, clowns, daredevils and much, much more. Directed by Gilbert Cates. 79 min.
02-1839 *$69.99*

Pirate Tales
Avast, me hearties, and prepare to separate fact from fiction in this two-part look at the fearless, and at times bloodthirsty, men (and women) who prowled the seven seas in search of gold and adventure. See such infamous buccaneers as Blackbeard, Captain Kidd and others come to life in dramatic re-creations; Roger Daltrey, as 17th-century pirate William Dampier, hosts. 4 1/2 hrs. total.
18-7769 □*$29.99*

Pirates
Well, shiver your timbers! The infamous buccaneers of the past come to life in this top-notch production that uses re-creations, artifacts, animation and more to tell their amazing, true stories. Sir Francis Drake, Captain Morgan, Captain Kidd, Blackbeard and Anne Bonny are among the scourges of the seas showcased here. 104 min.
80-7284 *$29.99*

KGB: The Soviet Sword And Shield Of Action: Complete Set
Take a rare look behind the shadowy world of international espionage and learn about the history and operations of the Soviet Union's spy network with this three-volume series. Includes "The Spies," "The Secrets" and "The Terrorists." 180 min. total. NOTE: Individual volumes available at $19.99 each.
10-1637 *$59.99*

Nightmare In Red
Vintage '60s TV documentary look at the early years of Communist rule in the Soviet Union and the hardships faced by the Russian people. 60 min.
10-8160 *$19.99*

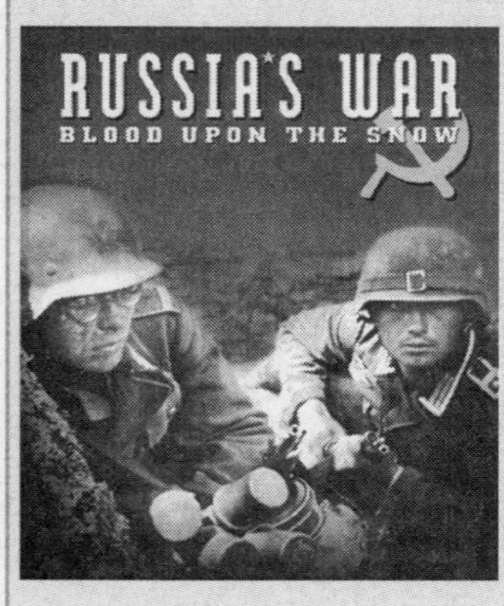
RUSSIA'S WAR
BLOOD UPON THE SNOW

Russia's War: Blood Upon The Snow: Boxed Set
For the people of the Soviet Union, the Second World War was a struggle for survival against not only the German war machine, but against the murderous rule of Joseph Stalin as well. Former Secretary of State Henry Kissinger hosts this five-tape series that recounts the key events of what Russians have come to call the Great Patriotic War. Volumes include "The Darkness Descends," "Between Life and Death," "The Fight from Within," "The Citadel" and "The Fall of the Swastika." 600 min. total.
18-7836 *$69.99*

The Face Of Russia: Complete Set
Explore Russia's past, present, and future through its wondrous culture, architectural masterpieces and sacred churches. Included in this three-volume series are "The Face on the Firewood," "The Facade of Power" and "Facing the Future." 180 min. total. NOTE: Individual volumes available at $29.99 each.
22-5974 Letterboxed *$79.99*

Nicholas & Alexandra
Filmed on location across Russia Union and Europe and using once-secret KGB documents, this program presents the real story of the last Czar and his family. Delve into the mysterious reign of the Romanovs and their violent demise in this chronicle. 100 min.
53-8189 *$29.99*

Ten Days That Shook The World (1979)
World history was forever altered in Russia during the fall of 1917. Rare historical footage, interviews with people who lived through the events, and Russian film re-creations help to put the Communist Revolution in perspective. Orson Welles narrates. 77 min.
50-6289 *$29.99*

Harvest Of Despair (1984)
Devastating study of the 1923-33 Ukrainian "terror famine" which marked the death of 7 million people. Through interviews with survivors and rare footage, this documentary shows how Stalin orchestrated the famine in order to destroy Ukrainian peasantry, who resisted collectivism. 55 min.
53-9338 *$39.99*

From Czar To Stalin (1987)
The first 20 years of the Soviet Union were among the bloodiest in any nation's history. See rare footage of Russia's turbulent past, from the 1917 Communist Revolution that overthrew the Czar to Lenin's rule and the violent purges of the Stalin era. 93 min.
50-6221 *$19.99*

Anna (1993)
Beginning when his daughter Anna was six years old in 1980, Russian director Nikita Mikhalkov ("Burnt by the Sun") would surreptitiously film a series of five questions answered by her each year till she was 18. Anna's thoughts on her fears, hopes and desires reflect not only her evolving persona, but also the momentous changes occurring in Russian society through the last days of Communism. AKA: "Anna: From Six to Eighteen." 99 min. In Russian with English subtitles.
53-6346 Letterboxed *$89.99*

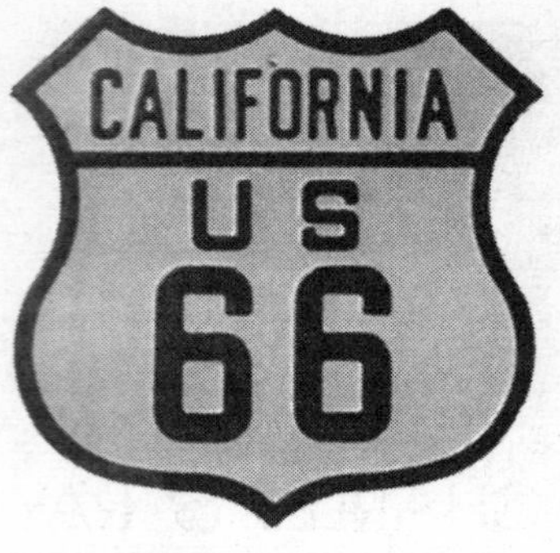
CALIFORNIA
US
66

Route 66: A Nostalgic Ride Down America's Mother Road
Its heyday as a transcontinental travel route may have gone the way of Burma-Shave signs, but fans old and new are keeping the spirit of Route 66 alive. Take a trip from Chicago to Los Angeles and go off the interstate, as you visit the people and places that still exist along the remaining stretches of "the highway that's the best." 105 min.
22-1587 *$19.99*

The Route 66 Collection
"It winds from Chicago to L.A.," and viewers can travel across 2,000 miles of the "Mother Road" with this two-tape set of freewheeling documentaries. "Route 66: An American Odyssey" traces the highway's history, from the glory days of the '30s and '40s to its current revival, while "Route 66: A Cruise Down Main Street" lets you join supermodel Hunter Reno on a cross-country road trip filled with such exotic locales as the Cozy Dog restaurant and the Wigwam Motel. 100 min. total.
89-5020 *$19.99*

Africa: Complete Set
Basil Davidson, one of the world's leading authorities on the Dark Continent, is your host for a four-tape chronicle on Africa's little-known history, its rise from colonialism, and its hopes for the future. Episodes include "Different But Equal," "Mastering a Continent," "Kings and Cities" and others. 8 hrs. total. NOTE: Individual volumes available at $29.99 each.
22-5855 Save $10.00! *$79.99*

Those Fabulous Cars Of Yesteryear (Wheels Across Africa) (1934)
Follow an amazing 4,200-mile expedition across the African continent in a caravan of the latest Dodge trucks and sedans. Among the wonderful sites on explorer Armand Denis' motor safari: natives performing traditional dances, lions and rhinos getting in their way, snake charmers, a man who eats glass, and more. 60 min.
82-1035 *$19.99*

General Idi Amin Dada (1978)
Barbet Schroeder's fascinating, chilling study of the brutal Ugandan dictator responsible for over 300,000 deaths during his eight years in power captures Amin's charismatic persona and the sadistic streak that lay beneath it. Reportedly, Amin (who even performed the film's accordion soundtrack) was unhappy with his onscreen depiction and gave Schroeder an ultimatum: edit or else! 113 min.
19-1856 Was $59.99 *$29.99*

Soldier Child (1998)
Since 1990, thousands of Ugandan boys have been taken from their families and forced to take part in a civil war in neighboring Sudan. This sobering documentary chronicles these atrocities, the abduction and brainwashing techniques of rebel leader Joseph Kony, and the rehabilitation drive of Ugandan charities to save the children. Danny Glover narrates. 55 min.
75-7219 *$14.99*

Wonders Of The African World (1999)
Lost after centuries of poverty, conflict and colonialism, the history of the African continent and its people is examined by Harvard professor Henry Louis Gates, Jr. in this three-tape series. Join Gates as he travels throughout Africa to uncover a millennia-old heritage of great cities and bloody wars, of slavery and majesty. Included are "Black Kingdoms of the Nile/The Swahili Coast," "The Slave Kingdoms/The Holy Land" and "The Road to Timbuktu/Lost Cities of the South." 6 hrs. total.
90-1045 □*$59.99*

Full Circle With Michael Palin: Boxed Set
Join Michael Palin on his wildest journey yet, as he travels the 50,000 miles of the Pacific Rim. It's a four-continent odyssey that takes him from the frozen isolation of Alaska and Siberia to the bustle of Hong Kong and the tropical splendor of the East Indies, all in a five-volume collector's set.
18-7832 *$99.99*

Michael Palin's Hemingway Adventure (1999)
Setting his sights on the well-worn footsteps of famed author/outdoorsman Ernest Hemingway, Monty Python alum Michael Palin traces "Papa's" life and travels. Hemingway's boyhood homes in Chicago; the Italy of World War I and Paris of the '20s; the plains of Kenya; Key West and Havana; and Hemingway's last home in the Idaho hills are all on Palin's itinerary. 240 min.
90-1100 □*$29.99*

Jung On Film
Rare film interview with pioneer psychologist Carl Gustav Jung, who discusses his life work, his relationship with Sigmund Freud, his use of dreams and his own life. This illuminating interview is conducted by Dr. Richard I. Evans. 77 min.
22-5423 *$29.99*

The Wisdom Of The Dream: The World Of C.G. Jung: Complete Set
Fascinating three-part series that traces the work and theories of the father of analytical psychology. Jung's schism with Freud, his major works on dreams and his discovery of the "collective subconscious" are all relived via rare footage and interviews in "A Life of Dreams," "Inheritance of Dreams" and "A World of Dreams." 180 min. total. NOTE: Individual volumes available at $24.99 each.
22-5867 Save $15.00! *$59.99*

Matter Of Heart (1985)
Fascinating film look at the life and teachings of Carl Gustav Jung, one-time colleague of Freud who broke off with him and went on to found analytical psychology. Rare home movies and interviews are woven together to provide a full portrait of one of this century's most influential thinkers. 107 min.
53-7134 Was $79.99 *$24.99*

Titanic Memories: A Video Scrapbook
Titanic devotees won't want to miss this rarity, a real collector's item filled with interesting vintage film footage. Included are interviews with survivors of the sinking, rare newsreel and nickelodeon sequences, a 1950s dramatization of the life of "Unsinkable" Molly Brown and lots more. 70 min.
10-9764 *$14.99*

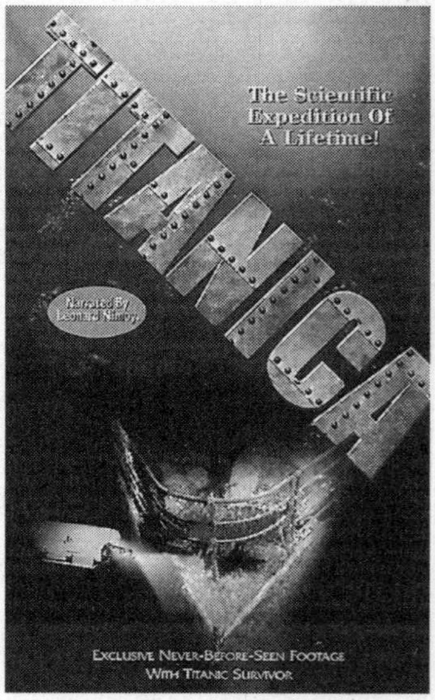
The Scientific Expedition Of A Lifetime!
TITANICA
Narrated By Leonard Nimoy
Exclusive Never-Before-Seen Footage With Titanic Survivor

Titanica (1992)
Travel to the depths of the North Atlantic and visit modern maritime history's most famous shipwreck with this spectacular IMAX documentary. High-tech subs and amazing underwater photography let you explore the remains of the "unsinkable" liner as they've sat for over 75 years, and you'll also see interviews with Titanic experts and survivors. 75 min.
11-2263 Was $19.99 □*$14.99*

Titanic (1994)
It was the world's largest ship and was said to be "unsinkable," but on April 15, 1912, the maiden voyage turned into a maritime disaster that saw the loss of over 1,500 lives. This four-tape documentary, seen on TV's A&E Network, traces the tragic history of the Titanic from its construction to the discovery of the wreckage in 1985. Includes rare historical films and photos, interviews with survivors, and much more. 200 min. total. on four tapes.
53-8078 Was $39.99 *$19.99*

The Hindenburg
This two-tape program looks at one of the most infamous disasters in history through interviews with survivors and eyewitnesses, a minute-by-minute account of the May, 1937 incident and rare footage of the airship. A must for history and aviation fans! 100 min.
53-8443 *$29.99*

Lost Ships: Boxed Set
Go on a thrilling search for some of history's most famous shipwrecks with Oxford instructor and explorer Mensun Bond in this three-tape series that mixes historical re-creations, computer animation and undersea footage to detail each wreck's story. Included are "Galley of the Gods," about a 1st-century B.C. Roman ship filled with Greek art; "Ghost of Trafalgar," following the search for Lord Nelson's first ship, the HMS Agamemnon; and "The Last Broadside," about the WWII German battleship Graf Spee. 156 min. total. NOTE: Individual volumes available at $19.99 each.
89-5190 Save $20.00! *$39.99*

The Good Heart: A Buddhist Perspective On The Teachings Of Jesus: Complete Set
In an intriguing four-tape series of talks by the Dalai Lama, passages from the Four Gospels are examined, and the similarities of thought between Christian and Buddhist philosophies are discussed. Included are "St. Matthew's Gospel," "St. Mark's Gospel," "St. Luke's Gospel" and "St. John's Gospel." 404 min. total. NOTE: Individual volumes available at $19.99 each.
50-7448 *$79.99*

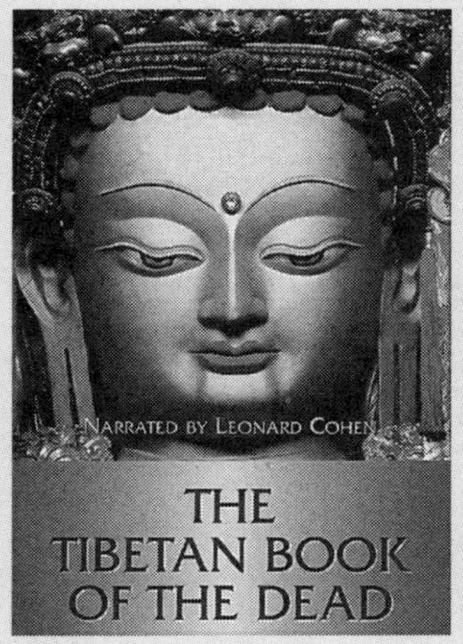

The Tibetan Book Of The Dead: Boxed Set
Learn about the doctrines, history and application of this key text to the Tibetan Buddhist tradition in an innovative two-part documentary. "A Way of Life" follows the Book of the Dead from its beginnings in Asia to modern acceptance in the West; while animated sequences depict a deceased person's odyssey into the afterlife in "The Great Liberation." Musician/Buddhist student Leonard Cohen narrates. 92 min. total. NOTE: Individual volumes available at $24.99 each.
53-6677 Save $10.00! *$39.99*

God And Buddha: A Dialogue
What are the differences—and, more importantly, the similarities—between the teachings of Buddhism and those of the Hindu Vedanta? In a special discussion held in New York, Robert Thurman and Deepak Chopra examine how these two schools of Eastern thought teach the way to freedom from suffering, the nature of shared consciousness, and other topics. 90 min.
53-6757 *$29.99*

Heart Of Tibet: An Intimate Portrait Of The 14th Dalai Lama
A revealing study of Tibetan spiritual leader and Nobel Peace Prize laureate the Dalai Lama as he visits Los Angeles, this program shows him as a simple man with an important political agenda for the people of his occupied homeland. 60 min.
70-7122 *$29.99*

Lojong: Transforming The Mind
In this five-tape series of lectures, the Dalai Lama discusses the Buddhist idea of transforming the mind ("Lojong" in Tibetan) through such disciplines as enhancing compassion, developing a balanced attitude between one's self and others, and using adverse situations to build spiritual development. 6 hrs. total.
70-7274 *$109.99*

Seven Years In Tibet (1957)
The original documentary chronicle of explorer Heinrich Harrer's seven-year sojourn in Tibet before its invasion by Chinese forces, this compelling film mixes dramatic re-creations with original footage, shot by Harrer, of Tibet's Forbidden City and the young Dalai Lama. 79 min.
53-6153 *$24.99*

H.H. The Dalai Lama On Campus (1997)
Presenting a message of hope for the new millennium, the Dalai Lama speaks on the problems facing the world and how to overcome suffering, on an individual and global basis, through compassion and a spiritual reawakening. Richard Gere introduces the Dalai Lama in this program, recorded at UCLA. 95 min.
50-7443 *$19.99*

The Lion's Roar (2000)
A rare peak into Buddhist life and philosophy is depicted in this detailed account of the Karmapa lineage. Reincarnation has long been a tradition and belief of the Tibetan Black Hat Lama beginning in the 8th century. Focusing primarily on the 16th Karmapa, this film centers on the theme of impermanence in Buddhist teachings. James Coburn narrates this enlightening documentary. 50 min.
70-7277 *$29.99*

Our Favorite Toys
The beloved playthings of childhood—which in some cases have now become prized collectibles—live on in this nostalgic documentary. Learn the stories behind the creation of such baby boomer treasures as the Slinky, Etch-a-Sketch, Matchbox cars, Barbie, G.I. Joe (why does he have that scar?) and others. 52 min.
50-5937 *$14.99*

Spies: Complete Set
Go beyond the James Bonds and Matt Helms with this 13-part series that traces the amazing real-life espionage exploits of men and women in the 20th century, from the seductive Mata Hari and the trusted Nazi agent who delivered false details of the Allied landing at Normandy to the Cold War dealings of the CIA and KGB. Episodes include "OSS Covert Action," "Wartime Espionage," "Code Breaking," "Atomic Bomb Espionage," "Sexpionage," "Spying for the KGB," "Assassination" and more. 552 min. total. NOTE: Individual volumes available at $19.99 each.
50-7473 Save $60.00! *$199.99*

Top Secret: Inside The World's Most Secret Agencies: Boxed Set
We could tell you what this series is about, but then we'd have to kill you. Three of the world's top intelligence organizations—the National Security Agency, Israel's Mossad, and Scotland Yard—offer unprecedented access to their inner workings in this compelling series that examines their everyday operations: breaking codes, fighting terrorists, and protecting their countries with a vengeance. Narrated by Johnny Depp. 150 min. total. NOTE: Individual volumes available at $19.99 each.
89-5126 Save $20.00! *$39.99*

The Secret World Of...
You're invited to a rare, behind-the-scenes look at the world's most glamorous places and fascinating businesses and professions with this documentary series that presents amazing footage, inside secrets and eye-opening interviews. Each tape runs about 48 min. There are 13 volumes available, including:

The Secret World Of... Amusement Parks
50-7527 *$14.99*

The Secret World Of... Circuses & Sideshows
50-7530 *$14.99*

The Secret World Of... Professional Wrestling
50-7535 *$14.99*

ABC News: Great TV News Stories
Relive the momentous events and memorable faces of the TV era with this collection of original ABC News broadcast footage, featuring commentary by Peter Jennings, Ted Koppel, Barbara Walters and others. Each tape runs about 60 min. There are 14 volumes available, including:

17 Days Of Terror: The Hijacking Of TWA 847
50-6430 *$24.99*

From Disaster To Discovery: The Challenger Explosion And The Space Shuttle
50-6434 *$24.99*

The Great Debates: Kennedy vs. Nixon
50-6440 *$24.99*

Images Of The '80s
Relive the people, events and memories of this tumultuous decade in this special co-production of ABC News and Time magazine. Host Peter Jennings takes you through the Age of Reagan, reacquaints you with Gorby and Ollie, Madonna and Michael, and shows such unforgettable scenes as the Challenger explosion and the Berlin Wall's dismantling. 55 min.
50-6461 *$19.99*

The 50th Barbara Walters Special
Her insightful, intimate interviews with the biggest names in sports, entertainment and world affairs are perennially popular. Now, Barbara Walters looks back at her most memorable interviews. The guest list includes Presidents Ford, Carter and Reagan, Fidel Castro, John Wayne, Bing Crosby, George Burns, Johnny Carson, Sylvester Stallone and many more. 100 min.
50-6702 *$19.99*

Nightline
The best programs from ABC's nightly news and discussion show are now available on home video. Join host Ted Koppel for a look at the people, events and controversies that have shaped modern world history. There are 47 volumes available, including:

Nightline: John Lennon Murdered
50-6639 *$14.99*

Nightline: Assassination Attempt On President Reagan
50-6641 *$14.99*

Nightline: Challenger Disaster
50-6661 *$14.99*

Nightline: Death Of Lucille Ball
50-6679 *$14.99*

The History Of Sex
Follow five thousand years of human sexuality in its many forms in this revealing five-episode History Channel series. See how religion, politics, science and societal changes have affected the evolution of love and sex in "Ancient Civilizations," "The Eastern World," "The Middle Ages," "From Don Juan to Queen Victoria" and "The 20th Century." 250 min. on four tapes.
53-6802 *$59.99*

In The Shadow Of Angkor Wat
Trace the rise and fall of Cambodia's Khmer kingdoms and the magnificent art and architecture that flourished within them for centuries in this documentary that looks at the majestic remains of temples, including legendary Angkor Wat, and examines the religious significance behind sculptures and artwork found there. 55 min.
22-5922 *$29.99*

Cleopatra's Alexandria
Founded 2,300 years ago by Alexander the Great, it was a center for science and culture and eventually served as the capital of Egypt. Learn about the history of lore of Alexandria, and follow a government archeological team as they search underwater for the sunken remains of Cleopatra's palace, in this fascinating program. 60 min.
22-1747 *$19.99*

Cleopatra: The First Woman Of Power
Her name has come down through time to become synonymous with beauty and seductive guile, but what do we really know about the life of Cleopatra? Anjelica Huston narrates this documentary that uses interviews with historians, re-enactments and location footage to tell the full story of the Queen of the Nile. 50 min.
50-8348 *$19.99*

The Great Pharaohs Of Egypt
Explore the 3,000-year history of one of mankind's first great empires in this four-volume series that traces the rise and fall of Ancient Egypt. As you visit such historic sites as Luxor and Karnak, you'll learn about the reality behind the legends of Cleopatra, Ramses and King Tut, peer into the pyramids and long-sealed royal tombs, and more. 200 min. total.
53-9817 *$59.99*

Tut: The Boy King (1977)
Orson Welles hosts this remarkable look of one of history's greatest archeological finds, the tomb of King Tutankhamen, the "boy king." From extravagant furnishings to priceless artifacts, this program reveals secrets that have been concealed for centuries. 60 min.
27-6835 *$24.99*

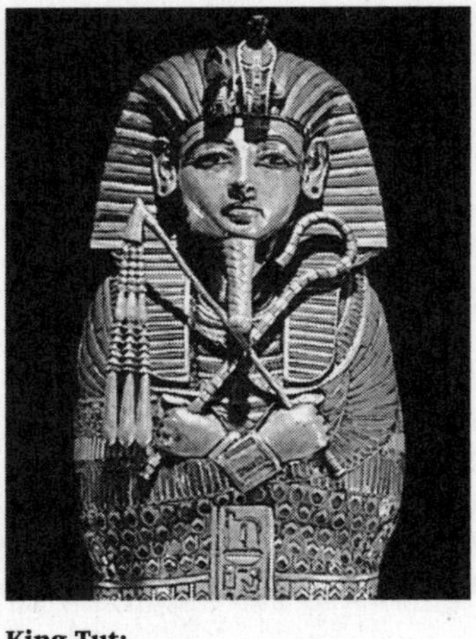

King Tut: Tomb Of Treasure (1992)
This program offers a rare glimpse into the magnificent artifacts discovered by archeologist Howard Carter in 1922, following eight years of exploration. Enter the ancient shrine of King Tut, and travel to the Cairo Museum and the New Orleans Museum of Art to see the "Boy King's" treasures. 25 min.
22-5547 *$19.99*

Great Cities Of The Ancient World: Complete Set
This three-tape series examines the amazing civilizations of "Rome and Pompeii," showcasing the Colosseum and the devastation of Vesuvius; "Athens and Ancient Greece," which looks at the Acropolis and Parthenon; and "The Pyramids and the Cities of the Pharaohs," an examination of the Great Pyramids of Giza and the Lighthouse of Alexandria. 210 min. total. NOTE: Individual volumes available at $29.99 each.
50-2817 *$79.99*

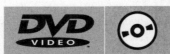

DVD VIDEO
ASK ABOUT OUR GIANT DVD CATALOG!

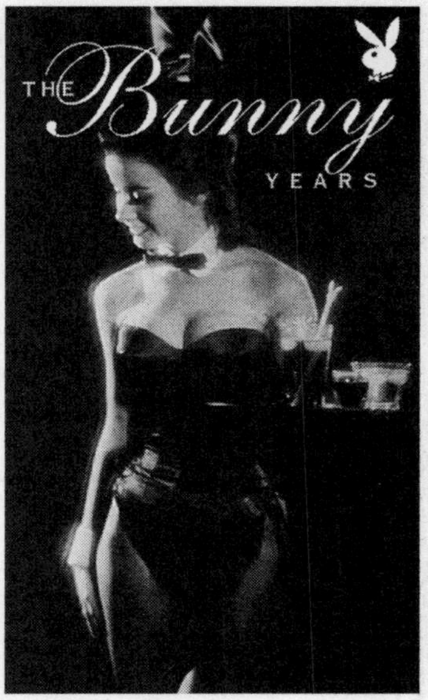

The Bunny Years
The beautiful waitresses with the cotton-tailed "Bunny suits" became a living symbol for Playboy's worldwide chain of nightclubs for over 20 years. Now go behind the scenes for a revealing look at what life "under the ears" was like, with rare photos and film from the Playboy archives, interviews with former Bunnies (including actress Lauren Hutton), and more. 100 min.
53-6731 *$19.99*

Sex For Sale: Boxed Set
"The oldest profession" has evolved over the years into a global business that rakes in over $30 billion annually. Explore the many facets of the international sex industry, from street-corner prostitutes and Hollywood call girls to the adult film business and Asian sex clubs, in this revealing and candid three-part series. Included are "Around the World," "Behind Closed Doors" and "The Extreme Experience." 135 min. total. NOTE: Individual volumes available at $14.99 each.
83-1366 Save $10.00! *$34.99*

Not Angels But Angels (1994)
A riveting, unflinching documentary on boy prostitution in Prague, in which young males attempt to supply Eastern and Western tourists with sexual activity for easy money. The hustlers' frankness will jolt you, as they reveal their sordid experiences. 80 min. In Czech with English subtitles.
01-1503 *$39.99*

Body Without Soul (1996)
Long known as one of Europe's leading cultural centers, the Czech capital of Prague has the dubious distinction of also being home to a burgeoning adult video industry. This compelling documentary from director Wictor Grodecki ("Not Angels But Angels") offers a disturbing look at the young men who arrive from throughout Europe to work as street hustlers and models, as well as an interview with a leading adult filmmaker. 103 min. In Czech with English subtitles.
01-1532 *$39.99*

Fetishes (1996)
This unflinching documentary from Nick Broomfield ("Kurt and Courtney") focuses on the dominatrixes and clientele of Pandora's Box, a New York City "adult club" specializing in sado-masochism. Broomfield captures the professionals who frequent the place to indulge in rubber garments, foot worship, infantilism and other fantasies. Unrated version; 87 min.
83-1290 Was $89.99 *$14.99*

The Unveiling (1999)
A revealing (in every sense of the word) documentary, this film offers an up-close look at the women—and men—who take to the runway and doff their duds for cash. Learn about stripper life on and off the stage, hear from '30s "ecdysiast" Dixie Evans, "the Marilyn Monroe of Burlesque," about the art of stripping, and more.
01-1565 *$29.99*

Pimps Up, Ho's Down: The Director's Cut (1999)
In this extraordinary documentary, you'll enter the world of pimps and their ladies. See how these "businessmen" dress, talk and operate and why their flashily dressed women trust them. It looks like a 1970s blaxploitation film, but this is real, uncensored, contemporary stuff! Unrated version features 20 minutes of previously unseen footage. 94 min.
82-5153 Was $59.99 *$14.99*

American Pimp (1999)
From filmmakers Allen and Albert Hughes ("Menace II Society") comes a gritty documentary about the life of a pimp. Several professional flesh peddlers describe their seamy world as they see it in a series of interviews mixed with surveillance footage and classic film clips. Their philosophies, from why prostitutes need pimps to why the sex trade is illegal, are told in bold and shocking detail. 87 min.
12-3326 ❑*$99.99*

The Royal Windsor Style
ABC News presents this lustrous look at England's Royal Family throughout the 20th century, featuring Edward VIII's abdication in 1936, Queen Elizabeth II's coronation, Princes Charles and Andrew, Princess Diana, and Sarah, the Duchess of York. 60 min.
50-6841 *$19.99*

The Windsors: A Royal Family
Trace over 80 years of British royal history with this four-part set that takes viewers behind palace walls for an intimate look at the House of Windsor. From George V's coronation in 1910 and the shocking abdication of Edward VII to the ascension of Elizabeth II and the scandals that have rocked England in recent years, the complete story is objectively presented. 228 min. total. NOTE: Individual volumes available separately at $19.99 each.
50-7262 *$79.99*

Royal Revelations
Buckingham Palace may have plenty of closets, but are there enough to hold all the Royal Family's skeletons? Rare news footage and interviews bring to light the secrets and scandals of the House of Windsor, from King George VI's private torments and Queen Elizabeth II's bisexual uncle to Her Majesty's feuds with daughters-in-law Diana and Fergie. 51 min.
50-7615 *$14.99*

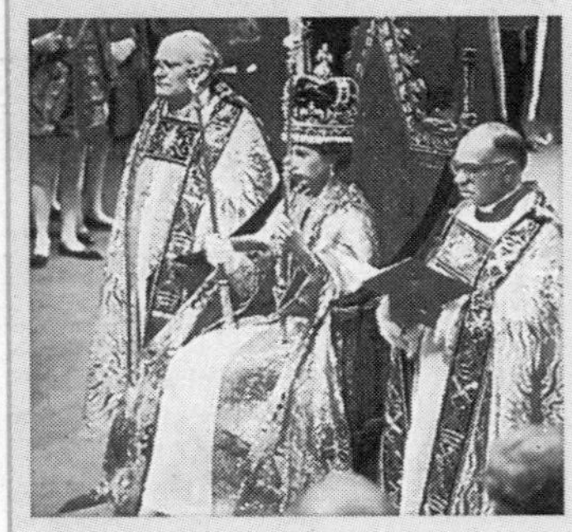

A Queen Is Crowned (1953)
The official documentary of the 1952 coronation of Queen Elizabeth II features all of the pomp and pageantry of the ceremony and the celebration that spread throughout Britain. Laurence Olivier narrates.
65-1001 *$29.99*

Queen Elizabeth II: Three Portraits
This three-tape set offers an all-encompassing look at the English monarch. In "From Princess to Queen," Elizabeth's early years, from her birth in 1926 to her unexpected succession to the throne are covered; her public and private lives are the focus of "Elizabeth R: A Year in the Life"; and the Trooping of the Color is featured in "The Queen's Birthday Party." NOTE: Individual volumes available at $19.99 each.
53-6495 Save $10.00! *$49.99*

The Victorians: Deluxe Set
This three-tape overview of the Victorian Era looks at Britain's longest-reigning monarch and the important changes that occurred during her time on the throne. Also covered in the series is how the British built a presence in Africa. Includes "Queen Victoria," "Life in Victorian England" and "The Colonial Wars." 150 min. total.
80-7278 *$59.99*

A King's Story (1967)
It was the love story to end all love stories when, in 1936, England's King Edward VIII abdicated his throne to marry American Mrs. Wallis Simpson. Orson Welles narrates this documentary look at the legendary couple, featuring contemporary newsreel footage (including color clips) and rare interviews. 102 min.
65-1031 *$29.99*

Majesty: The History Of The British Monarchy
A remarkable two-tape documentary that uses re-enactments and "eyewitness" interviews to bring to life 10 centuries of history and British royalty, from the turbulent Anglo-Saxon times through the splendor of the Elizabethan era, the overthrowing of Charles I, Victoria's 63-year reign, and the rise of the House of Windsor. 104 min.
80-7176 *$39.99*

Notes From A Small Island: Boxed Set
Based on the best-selling book by American-born author Bill Bryson, this three-tape series offers a lighthearted and affectionate look at Britain, from the customs of England, Scotland and Wales to the various lifestyles and chats with everyone from pub owners and Japanese visitors to top British comics Stephen Fry and Alexi Sayle. 180 min. total. NOTE: Individual volumes available at $14.99 each.
22-1700 Save $5.00! *$39.99*

The Aristocracy: Boxed Set
Follow the rise and fall of the British aristocracy during the last 100 years, beginning at the height of the Victorian era, when such families owned over 80% of the land, through the many changes brought about in English society in recent decades. Included in this four-tape set are "Born to Rule: 1875-1914," "Never the Same Again: 1918-1945," "Letting in the Hoi Polloi: 1945-1970" and "Survival of the Fittest: 1970-1997." 180 min. total. NOTE: Individual volumes available at $24.99 each.
22-5988 Save $20.00! *$79.99*

For God And Country
Take tours through two of England's most famous cathedrals in this two-tape set. Included is "Canterbury Cathedral," narrated by Nigel Hawthorne and tracing the church's history from the first Archbishop of Canterbury to today, and "Westminster Abbey: A House of Kings," an absorbing 900-year chronicle. 155 min. total. NOTE: Individual volumes available for $24.99 ("Canterbury Castle") and $19.99 ("Westminster Abbey").
22-6060 Save $5.00! *$39.99*

The Treasures Of Great Britain: Complete Set
Take an incredible tour of England's most lavish estates and most precious treasures with this four-tape set. Included are "Treasures of the British Crown," a look at the Royal Family's amazing art collection, and the three-volume "Treasure Houses of Britain," including "Building for Eternity," "Palaces of Reason and Delight" and "Recapturing the Past." NOTE: Individual volumes available at $19.99 each.
22-6063 Save $20.00! *$59.99*

British Military Pageantry
The ceremonies, celebrations and events that are part of Britain's great military heritage are featured in this colorful program that includes the Royal Tournament, the Tower of London's "Ceremony of the Keys" and others. 50 min.
50-2728 *$19.99*

Merlin, Arthur And The Holy Grail
England's most compelling legends come to life with these three programs. Learn about the legendary mage who was said to be the last Druid priest and to have served as tutor to the young Arthur; the ruler who wielded the sword Excalibur and oversaw the building of Camelot; and the fabled last drinking cup of Jesus that became a knight's ultimate quest. 78 min.
50-5924 Was $19.99 *$14.99*

Camelot
Are the people and places of Arthurian times merely stories, or did they exist? Separate fiction from fact in this historical documentary that takes you across England and Wales to visit Tintangel Castle, a possible site of Camelot, and King Arthur's supposed final resting place in Glastonbury. Leonard Nimoy narrates. 50 min.
53-8385 *$19.99*

Benjamin Britten
Composer Benjamin Britten collaborated with Alberto Cavalcanti and poet W.H. Auden for several inventive scores of documentaries produced by the G.P.O. Featured here are "Coal Face" (1935), "Night Mail" (1936), "Instruments of the Orchestra" (1947) and "Steps of the Ballet" (1948), all boasting Britten's music.
53-7718 *$29.99*

Wartime Homefront
Filmmaker Humphrey Jennings' touch for lyricism is prevalent in two documentaries about England's involvement in World War II: "London Can Take It" (1940) and the rarely-seen "Fires Were Started" (1943), which inspired FDR to alter his foreign policy towards England's needs.
53-7719 *$29.99*

Wartime Moments
Three superb documentaries from Humphrey Jennings studying how people on the homefront were affected during World War II are featured in this program: "Listen to Britain" (1942), "Target for Tonight" (1941) and "A Diary for Timothy" (1945).
53-7720 *$29.99*

Knights And Armor
Let this documentary take you back to the days of chivalry, as you learn the history of armored combat and knighthood with all its pomp and ceremony. Follow the true exploits of renowned medieval warrior Sir William Marshal, and tour museum armor galleries, including Austria's famed Graz collection. 100 min.
53-8140 *$29.99*

Charles And Diana: For Better Or Worse (1991)
A fascinating history of the heir to the British throne and the school teacher-turned-princess, following the ups and downs of Charles and Di's 10-year marriage. Follow the couple as they celebrate the birth of their two children, on holiday, and through successful royal tours. 60 min.
50-6839 Was $19.99 *$14.99*

Diana: Legacy Of A Princess (1997)
Her wedding to Prince Charles in 1981 captured the world's attention, and throughout the ups and downs of life in the public eye Diana, Princess of Wales, won peoples' hearts with her poise, her devotion to her sons and her commitment to social causes. This documentary tribute looks at Diana's stormy marriage, her relationship with the Royal Family, and the tragic Paris accident that claimed her life. 60 min.
50-7438 *$14.99*

Diana: A Celebration—The People's Princess Remembered
The storybook life and shocking death of Princess Diana are recounted in this official BBC commemorative video. Exclusive interview footage with Diana is mixed with segments that trace her marriage to Prince Charles, Diana's dedication to her sons and her many charitable causes, and the funeral and accompanying global outpouring of grief. 57 min.
04-3543 ❑*$14.99*

Diana, Princess Of Wales 1961-1997: The People's Princess
This official commemorative video, produced by Britain's Independent Television News network, offers a comprehensive look at the life of the woman known as the "Fairy Tale Princess," from her childhood and her marriage to Prince Charles to her charity works and the accident that claimed her life in 1997. Also included are highlights from Diana's Westminster Abbey funeral. 78 min.
19-4012 ❑*$14.99*

Diana: In Her Own Words
Celebrate the life and times of the princess who matured from a shy newlywed to a woman who charmed the world. This incredible tribute to Princess Diana includes various public appearances, inspirational statements, and exclusive interviews. 50 min.
50-7472 *$19.99*

Heroes Of Scotland: Set
This boxed set includes three factual sagas of highland heroes. "William Wallace" looks at the man who faced English oppression and was the basis for the film "Braveheart." The brave bandit who became a 17th-century Robin Hood is followed in "Rob Roy." And "The Bruce of Bannockburn" surveys the life of Robert the Bruce, the Scottish king who battled King Edward II. 150 min. total. NOTE: Individual volumes available at $19.99 each.
22-1805 Save $10.00! *$49.99*

Three Faces Of Scotland: Complete Set
Get to know Scotland intimately through its history, its beauty and its people. Included in this three-tape set are "Birth of Nation," a look at Scotland's early years and its struggle for independence; "Mountains of Majesty," which recounts struggles that have divided the land for centuries; and "Taking the High Road," a look at Scotland's artistic achievements. 180 min. total. NOTE: Individual volumes available at $29.99 each.
80-7189 Save $20.00! *$69.99*

Scotland The Brave
In a moving 200th anniversary tribute that also marked their final parade and inspection before the unit's retirement, Scotland's famed 51st Highland Division Gordon Highlanders display the precision and patriotic splendor that was a hallmark. Prince Charles oversees the Highlanders' parade and pipe and drum performance in Aberdeen, followed by a regimental band "farewell concert." 50 min.
50-2394 Was $19.99 *$14.99*

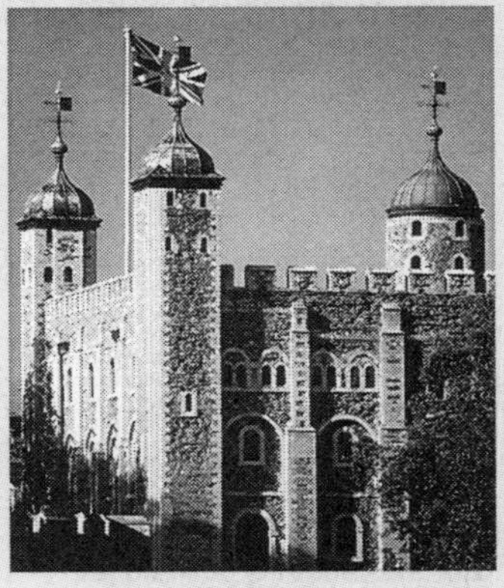

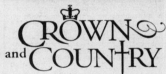

CROWN and COUNTRY

Crown And Country: Complete Set
Take a tour of some of the most historic cities and sites in the history of the English monarchy, with Prince Edward Windsor as your host, with this fascinating three-tape series. Volumes include "Windsor Castle & Portsmouth," "Cambridge & Sandringham" and "Winchester & Bury St. Edmunds." 180 min. total.
90-1011 ❑*$49.99*

Crown And Country II: Complete Set
Join host Prince Edward Windsor on a further exploration of England's majestic architectural heritage, from the historic town of St. Albans and the forbidding Tower of London to Buckingham Palace, in this three-tape set. Volumes include "The River Thames," "Royal Palaces" and "Stately Homes & Ancient Castles." 180 min. total.
90-1020 *$49.99*

The Wonderful Planet
Seven aspects of Earth are explored with awesome footage and great music. Travel through space, over mountains and volcanoes and into a rain forest, and see endangered species, beautiful flowers and more. 44 min.
02-7711 *$14.99*

Yosemite: The Fate Of Heaven
Robert Redford produced and narrates this look at one of the world's most beautiful areas. Marvel at its majesty and natural wonder and learn how people struggle to preserve it. 61 min.
27-6668 Was $19.99 *$14.99*

Searching For Lost Worlds: Complete Set
Retrace some of the greatest scientific and archeological finds of the 20th century with this five-part look at man's ongoing quest to explore his past. Included are "Atlantis: Mystery of the Minoans," "Dragon Hunters: Secrets of the Gobi Desert," "Machu Picchu: Secrets of the Incan Empire," "Skull Wars: The Missing Link" and "Tutankhamen: The Last Pharaoh." 260 min. total. NOTE: Individual volumes available at $19.99 each.
83-1445 *$99.99*

Albert Schweitzer (1957)
This Academy Award-winning documentary focuses on the life and work of the noted physician, author and humanitarian, from his early days in Austria through his medical work at his hospital in French Equatorial Africa. Narrated by Burgess Meredith and Fredric March, the film uses archival footage, still photos and dramatizations featuring Schweitzer's own son. 80 min.
08-1777 *$14.99*

Bike Week '95
Welcome to Daytona Bike Week, where Playboy model Carol Shaya hosts a gathering of the nation's bikers. There's egg wrestling, drag racing, tattooing, bike rodeo, cole slaw wrestling and more in this program. 90 min.
76-7244 *$19.99*

Hawg Wild In Sturgis (1995)
Sturgis, South Dakota, is the site of the wildest biker gathering in the world, a place where thousands of "hog" riders compare machines, chase women, drink whiskey and partake in amazing cycling events. Check out all the outrageous activities in this debauched program. 50 min.
74-3018 *$29.99*

Wurlitzer Pipe Organ Factory Tour
This rare documentary was made in the early 1920s and focuses on the Rudolph Wurlitzer Manufacturing Company in Tonawanda, New York. Witness a mighty pipe organ being built and enjoy a score provided by Ray Brubacher, a popular performer. 30 min.
10-9996 *$14.99*

Fashion Flashbacks
Take a wild walk down Memory Lane with this collection of highlights from various fashion shows from the 1950s and 1960s. For those who forgot about the first mini-skirts, metallic skirts, astro-fashions, peek-a-book dresses, go-go boots, loo-loos and granny glasses, they're all here—and lots more!
76-7213 *$29.99*

Unzipped (1995)
High-energy documentary of high-energy fashion designer Isaac Mizrahi, chronicling the evolution of his 1994 collection, which was inspired in parts by "The Mary Tyler Moore Show," "Nanook of the North" and Loretta Young in "Call of the Wild." Along with Mizrahi's witty one-liners, you'll meet his mother and models Cindy Crawford, Naomi Campbell and Linda Evangelista. 73 min.
11-1964 Was $89.99 ❑*$19.99*

Childhood: Complete Set
This in-depth, factual program looks at different phases of childhood, using scientific data and focusing on 12 families on five different continents in everyday situations. Produced by the creators of "Cosmos," the seven-tape series shows how events such as the birth of a sibling, the first day of school, and divorce affect children. 420 min. total. NOTE: Individual volumes available at $29.99 each.
14-9007 Save $60.00! *$149.99*

History Of The Federal Republic Of Germany
Trace the history of the now-reunited Germany, from the East-West division after World War II to the visits to Berlin by the Kennedys in the '60s, in this documentary filled with fascinating archival footage. 58 min.
10-9462 *$19.99*

The Fall Of The Berlin Wall (1990)
The Berlin Wall, which separated a city and signified the Cold War for almost 30 years, was finally torn down in late 1989. This program, which is taken from German television, chronicles the bloody history of the Wall, and provides fascinating footage of its end. 49 min.
19-1812 *$59.99*

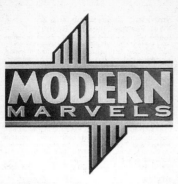

Modern Marvels
The greatest engineering and architectural efforts of the century are the focus of this fascinating documentary series, as seen on cable's A&E Network. Each tape runs about 50 min. There are 13 volumes available, including:

Empire State Building
53-7864 *$19.99*

Panama Canal
53-7865 *$19.99*

The Golden Gate Bridge
53-8149 *$19.99*

Tunnels
53-8445 *$19.99*

Human Guinea Pigs: Set
This four-tape series offers incredible, unsettling true stories about how the military used humans and animals in different types of testing, and features Air Force documentation and uncut film sequences. Included are "Nuclear Effects," "Human Bullet," "Beyond Human Tolerance" and "Human Rock." 180 min. total. NOTE: Individual volumes available at $14.99 each.
50-5836 Save $10.00! *$49.99*

Italians In America: Boxed Set
It's a connection that goes as far back as Christopher Columbus, and in this two-tape documentary you'll trace the history of Italian-American society and the contributions made in politics, the performing arts, sports and more. Profiles of such notable sons (and daughters) of Italy as Perry Como, Francis Ford Coppola, Geraldine Ferraro, Dean Martin, Frank Sinatra and others are featured. 100 min. total.
50-8125 *$29.99*

Hollywood: Wild In The Streets
Follow the trail of the paparazzi as they snap the secret world of celebrities and expose the darker sides of Hollywood's Sunset Strip. Cameron Diaz, Carmen Elektra, Anna Nicole Smith, George Clooney and Ice-T are among the stars caught in the act. WARNING: features nudity and violence; adults only. 62 min.
50-8282 *$14.99*

Blast 'Em (1992)
Fascinating study of the work of celebrity photographers focusing on young, hot-shot paparazzi Victor Malafronte, who uses his street smarts and aggressiveness to snap the rich and famous. Features appearances by Madonna, Michael J. Fox, Matt Dillon, Robert De Niro, Sean Penn, Jack Nicholson, Sophia Loren and others. 103 min.
71-5290 Was $89.99 *$19.99*

Paparazzi (1997)
This inside look at the world's most notorious sharpshooters shows how they operate and offers never-before-seen footage of Princess Diana, Princess Caroline, Liz Taylor, Cher, Elton John and many others. 60 min.
59-7041 *$29.99*

The Mighty Mississippi
Explore the legendary waterway whose spelling baffles schoolchildren to this day with this two-volume program. Flowing from the frozen north in Minnesota to the warm waters of the Gulf of Mexico, the "big river" has played an important role in America's economic, military, literary and musical development, all of which is traced here. 200 min. total.
53-6215 *$29.99*

Women And Spirituality: Boxed Set
This three-part documentary series takes viewers through thousands of years of spiritual history to examine women's unique roles in faith and belief. "Goddess Remembered" looks at the "earth goddess" cultures that predated the world's major religions; the persecution and murder of witches and female heretics in medieval Europe is the focus of "The Burning Times"; and "Full Circle" focuses on the recent revival in the women's spirituality movement. 167 min. total. NOTE: Individual volumes available at $24.99 each.
53-6674 Save $15.00! *$59.99*

Fireworks
Take an explosive tour around the world with host George Plimpton, who shares the colorful history of fireworks from their invention in ancient China to today's vibrant, computer- and hologram-enhanced displays. You'll also tour fireworks factories in Japan, India and England, and watch pyrotechnic pageantry at Walt Disney World. 100 min.
53-8141 *$29.99*

Fishing With John: Complete Set
Not since "Fishin' Musician" Gil Fisher has TV seen such an off-the-wall sports/adventure/talk show, as rock star/actor John Lurie takes a bunch of his film buddies to some of the world's most beautiful and exotic spots for fishing trips that turn into offbeat explorations of life. Included in this three-tape set are "Montauk with Jim Jarmusch/Jamaica with Tom Waits," "Costa Rica with Matt Dillon/Maine with Willem Dafoe" and the two-part "Thailand with Dennis Hopper." 202 min. total. NOTE: Individual volumes available at $14.99 each.
22-6015 Save $15.00! *$29.99*

Rat
You know them, you hate them, and you fear them, but what do you really know about these furry little survivors that, in most American cities, outnumber the two-legged inhabitants many times over. Go beneath the streets of New York to learn how rats live and thrive in the world of humans, and see how humans wage war against them, in this program by award-winning filmmaker Mark Lewis. 56 min.
22-9000 *$19.99*

Colt Firearms Legends
Follow the invention and development of the Colt handgun and learn about its impact on American life in this fascinating documentary. Mel Torme narrates. 66 min.
45-5534 Was $29.99 *$14.99*

Guns Of The Old West: 1803-1861
Fascinating look at the firearms that helped forge the nation, from Flintlock rifles and pistols of frontiersmen to the first rapid fire weapons. Footage is taken from the Remington, Colt and Buffalo Bill Historical Center collections; hosted by Hoyt Axton. 60 min.
50-4303 *$19.99*

The Story Of The Gun: The Complete History Of Firearms
An informative documentary on guns and their makers, this four-tape set shows you the story behind the development of firearms, following the efforts of such inventors as Colt, Remington, Gatling and Kalashnikov. Cliff Robertson narrates. 200 min. total.
53-8645 Was $59.99 *$39.99*

20th Century Wonders: Complete Set
The greatest architectural and engineering efforts of the 20th century are the focus of this fascinating three-tape series from ABC News and the Discovery Channel. See what went into the revolutionary designs of these structures, and how workers put their lives on the line during construction. Volumes include "The Empire State Building," "The Golden Gate Bridge" and "The Building of Hoover Dam." 150 min. total. NOTE: Individual volumes available at $19.99.
50-7619 *$59.99*

Japan
This impressive series on "The Land of the Rising Sun" looks at technology, trends and the people of the industrious country. The programs include "The Electronic Tribe," "The Sword and the Chrysanthemum," "The Legacy of the Shogun" and "A Proper Place in the World." Jane Seymour hosts. 4 hrs. total.
50-6941 *$79.99*

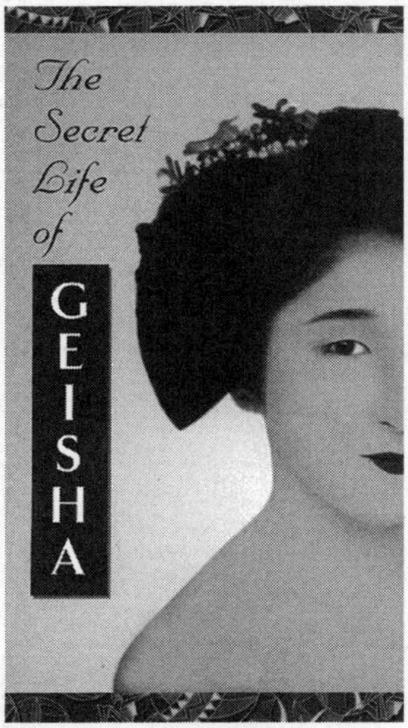

The Secret Life Of Geisha
Dismissed by Western society as little more than high-priced call girls, the Japanese women known as Geisha are part of a centuries-old tradition that made them a vital part of that country's society. See how they were trained from childhood in music, the arts, conversation and "massaging the male ego," and visit with modern-day Geisha, in this revealing program. 100 min.
53-6730 □*$19.99*

Great Quakes: San Francisco
The 1989 San Francisco Earthquake, which registered 7.1 on the Richter Scale and resulted in 62 deaths and over $6 billion in damage, is chronicled in this documentary that shows how findings from the devastation have helped scientists searching for ways to predict where and when quakes will occur. 60 min.
27-7208 *$14.99*

The San Francisco Earthquake: October 17, 1989
It was the most devastating temblor to hit the Bay Area since 1906, and the immediacy of TV news brought the stories of tragedy and heroism into everyone's home. This tape features ABC News footage of the earthquake and its aftermath, and discusses guidelines on quake safety precautions. 60 min.
50-6448 *$14.99*

Tornado Chasers
Some folks do it to collect information that will save lives; some do it just to put their lives on the line against the destructive fury of nature. Follow real-life "storm chasers," from scientists to thrill-seekers, and witness awesome footage of tornadoes and the devastation they leave behind. 60 min.
27-7209 *$14.99*

Tornadoes!!
Footage from 46 tornadoes from the last 40 years is presented in this astonishing program. Twisters of all types are featured, from mile-high to stubby, from mile-wide killers to needle-thin waterspouts. Witness nine shocking minutes with the Andover, Kansas, killer tornado. 60 min.
50-2508 Was $29.99 *$19.99*

Tornado Chasers
Travel to "Tornado Alley" in Oklahoma, where savagely beautiful storms astonish and frighten the Alley's residents at the same time. This program captures some of the most ferocious storms on Earth and the fearless thrill-seekers who rush off to witness nature's unbridled fury. 50 min.
53-8202 Was $19.99 *$14.99*

Storm Of The Century
New England was hit by one of the most violent storms in its memory in the fall of 1991, with 100-mile-per-hour winds and gigantic waves that sank the 70-foot boat Andrea Gail. See amazing footage of the storm's fury, and learn about efforts to track and predict where such systems will occur. 60 min.
27-7210 *$14.99*

Wonders Of Weather: Deadly Forces, Killer Storms, Savage Seas
From terrifying tornadoes and horrific hurricanes to fearsome floods and tscary tsunamis, this TLC special puts your in the middle of some of the most out-of-control weather conditions ever witnessed. 75 min.
27-7211 *$14.99*

Volcanos: Cauldrons Of Fury
Mother Nature blows her top, and you're there to witness all the destructive force in this documentary look at a (literally) red-hot subject. Trace famous eruptions throughout history, including Mt. Vesuvius, Krakatoa, Mt. St. Helens and Mt. Pinatubo; follow death-defying scientists down into volcanos, and much more. 55 min.
50-7424 *$19.99*

California Firestorm
A captain in the Metropolitan Fire Department of Southern California shot the incredible footage on this program that takes you into the middle of the fires that raged through the area in 1993. Witness the terror, confusion and devastation in close proximity to the fires. 60 min.
78-3023 *$14.99*

The Eruption Of Mount St. Helens (1981)
May 18, 1980: the great Washington volcano ended its 100-year plus dormancy and threatened thousands with the Earth's fury. Riveting documentary footage of the eruption and its aftermath. 30 min.
50-3463 *$24.99*

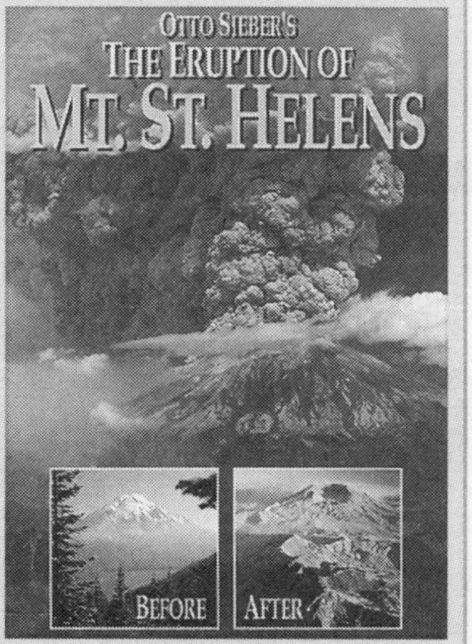

The Eruption Of Mount St. Helens (1998)
Awesome IMAX production capturing the 1980 eruption of Washington's Mount St. Helens that allows viewers to witness the first incredible explosion as well as subsequent incidents. Marvel at a force equal to 27,000 atomic bombs and ash that travels 16 miles in the air, then return to the site 10 years after it first erupted. 28 min.
50-8525 *$19.99*

Savage Seas: Complete Set
They cover seven-tenths of the Earth's surface, but their mysteries are still waiting to be fully explored. Learn about the majesty, danger and wonder of the world's seas and oceans with this compelling four-part documentary series hosted by Stacy Keach. Included are "The Deep," "Rescue," "Killer Storms" and "Killer Waves." 228 min. total. NOTE: Individual volumes available at $19.99 each.
50-7575 *$79.99*

Extreme Disaster: Nature's Deadly Force
Nature asserts itself with a vengeance in this chronicle of some of the most destructive forces this side of a trailer park. Witness terrifying twisters captured by amateur video, the devastating power of storms created by El Niño, plus footage of hurricanes, lightning strikes, earthquakes and more. 60 min.
83-1238 *$14.99*

Nature's Fury: Extreme Disasters: Boxed Set
Nature's wrath is displayed in this three-tape boxed set that includes "Nature's Deadly Force," which includes stunning footage of tornadoes, earthquakes and hurricanes; "Real Volcanoes," a gripping study of deadly volcanoes; and "Infernos of Destruction," another fascinating program on powerful volcanoes. 149 min. total. NOTE: Individual volumes available at $14.99 each.
83-1277 Save $5.00! *$39.99*

The California Reich (1978)
A chilling documentary that looks at Nazi cults in modern-day America, their recent resurgence and the people who follow their beliefs. It is an unforgettably disturbing look at people who may well be your friends or neighbors. 55 min.
06-1330 Was $29.99 *$14.99*

Blood In The Face (1991)
This powerful, critically hailed film reveals the inner workings of the Ku Klux Klan, the American Nazi Party, the Aryan Nations and David Duke. Shot partially at a white-supremacist convention in Michigan, the film gives its subjects an opportunity to talk about their beliefs in disturbing fashion. Michael Moore ("Roger and Me") conducts some of the interviews. 78 min.
70-5038 Was $59.99 *$19.99*

Calcutta (1976)
Famed director Louis Malle takes an amazing journey through India's great city and captures its people and customs. The camera finds Moslem and Hindu people living together because of poverty, a skyscraper being built without modern equipment, religious festivals, street performers and more. Narrated in English. 99 min.
53-8052 *$29.99*

Those Crazy Americans
A wacky look at the country's weirdest fads and follies from the '20s to the '60s. From bobbysoxers to go-go girls, tightrope walkers to hula hoopsters, college pranks and wacky weddings, it's a salute to America's never-ending search for fun. Narrated by George Gobel. 52 min.
50-8445 *$14.99*

Story Of A Junkie (1985)
A compelling look at the drug culture in and around New York's East Village, this gritty documentary from Lech Kowalski ("D.O.A.") follows a real-life junkie named John Spacely as he talks openly about how he came from California hoping to find success, only to fall into the fatal world of drugs (he died shortly after the film was made). AKA: "Gringo."
46-8031 *$14.99*

The Heroin Highway (2000)
This unflinching documentary journeys through the world of Asian and American druglords who are in the business of making and selling heroin. From stakeouts to shoot-outs, the police endlessly battle this devastating drug and the stigma of "heroin chic" culture across the globe. 60 min.
73-9364 *$19.99*

Streetwise (1985)
A very graphic and unforgettable look at the dilemma of runaway children. Interviews with teenagers living on the streets of Seattle paint a disturbing picture of poverty, petty theft, prostitution and drugs, and show the unique sub-society created by these "throw-aways." Music by Tom Waits. 92 min.
70-1072 Was $59.95 *$19.99*

Girltalk (1987)
Graphic look at the tribulations of three runaway teenage girls in Boston. Pinky hides in alleys and dodges truant officers; Mars is a stripper, working seedy clubs; and Martha faces teenage pregnancy. An unflinching, poignant, bittersweet document of our times. 85 min.
53-7665 Was $79.99 *$19.99*

Behind The Scenes With...: Complete Set
Take an offbeat and light-hearted look at the creative process with this acclaimed 10-volume documentary series, as hosts Penn and Teller talk with top painters, sculptors, musicians and performing arts professionals about their work and the philosophy behind it. Volumes include "David Hockney," "Julie Taymor," "Max Roach," "Carrie Mae Weems," "Wayne Thiebaud," "David Parsons," "Allen Toussaint," "Nancy Graves," "Robert Gil De Montes" and "JoAnn Falletta." 300 min. total. NOTE: Individual volumes available at $14.99.
70-5187 Save $50.00! *$99.99*

Huston Smith: The Mystic's Journey: Boxed Set
Explore spiritualism within three very different traditions from different parts of the world in this three-tape collection hosted by author Huston Smith ("The World's Religions"). Included are "India and the Infinite: The Soul of a People," "Requiem for a Faith: Tibetan Buddhism" and "Islamic Mysticism: The Sufi Way." 90 min. total. NOTE: Individual volumes available at $19.99 each.
53-9384 Save $20.00! *$39.99*

Harlan County, U.S.A. (1977)
Oscar-winning documentary covers a strike by Kentucky coal miners against a monolithic power conglomerate. Director Barbara Kopple goes beyond the usual "labor story" to focus on the 108 families affected by the dispute and their struggles. 103 min.
02-1010 *$29.99*

American Dream (1991)
Riveting, Oscar-winning documentary from Barbara Kopple ("Harlan County, U.S.A.") centering on the bitter mid-'80s strike of meatpackers for the Hormel company in Austin, Minnesota. The struggle ignited conflict between workers and management, local and parent unions, and even family members. 98 min.
44-1911 Was $89.99 ❑*$19.99*

Fallen Champ: The Untold Story Of Mike Tyson (1993)
A provocative, unauthorized look at the life, career and troubled times of former heavyweight champion Mike Tyson by acclaimed documentarian Barbara Kopple. Chronicled here in unflinching detail are Tyson's stormy marriage to Robin Givens, his relationships with promoter Don King and trainer Cus D'Amato, and his imprisonment for rape. 93 min.
02-2420 Was $19.99 ❑*$14.99*

San Francisco Pride 1999
Join in the celebration at San Francisco's annual Lesbian, Gay, Bisexual and Transgender Parade, one of the country's largest such events. See the different groups march and enjoy the pageantry of the day in this two-tape chronicle. 240 min.
76-2081 *$29.99*

Word Is Out: Stories Of Some Of Our Lives (1978)
The experience of being gay in America is captured in this acclaimed documentary that looks at 26 diverse men and women—ages 18 to 77—who recount their experiences and allows us to see them in a sensitive, real way that breaks down stereotypes. 130 min.
53-7666 Was $79.99 *$29.99*

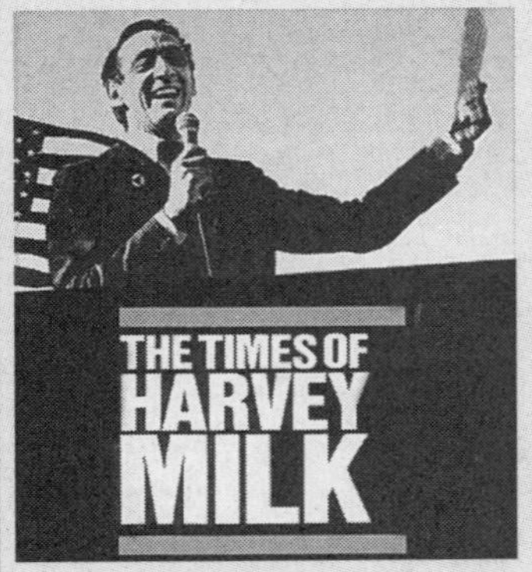

The Times Of Harvey Milk (1984)
More than a story of one man's life, this Academy Award-winning documentary traces the coming of age of the Gay Rights Movement in the late '70s. Milk, a San Francisco resident, became that city's first openly gay elected official and was a nationally-known leader until his murder in 1978. Interviews, news footage and scenes of the citywide memorial services are featured. 87 min.
07-8063 *$39.99*

Improper Conduct (1984)
The oppression and imprisonment of homosexuals in Castro's Cuba is looked at in this acclaimed documentary from renowned cinematographer Nestor Almendros. Interviews with emigrants and political leaders are combined with a history of the regime's anti-gay policies and their striking parallels with American rightist attitudes. 115 min.
50-3167 Was $79.99 *$19.99*

Before Stonewall (1984)
A groundbreaking look at the birth of the gay and lesbian movement, this award-winning documentary follows the history of the homosexual experience in America, from social experimentation of the 1920s to McCarthy-era scapegoats to the beginning of the gay rights crusade. Includes interviews with Allen Ginsberg, Audre Lorde, Barbara Gittings and others. 87 min.
50-7059 Was $29.99 *$24.99*

After Stonewall (1999)
Gay and lesbian life in America in the wake of the 1969 Stonewall riots in New York City is chronicled in this documentary follow-up to "Before Stonewall." The groundbreaking gay rights campaigns of the '70s, the devastation and call to action in the wake of AIDS, and the ongoing fight for freedom and acceptance are followed through film footage and interviews with Rita Mae Brown, Barney Frank, Armistead Maupin and others. Melissa Etheridge narrates. 88 min.
70-5158 *$29.99*

Before/After Stonewall 2-Pack
Both documentaries are also available in a money-saving set.
70-5160 Save $5.00! *$49.99*

Desire (1989)
Acclaimed documentary looks at gay life in Germany from 1910 to 1945 and chronicles the culture's acceptance in Berlin after World War I and its oppression and persecution during the rise of Nazism. Using archival footage, photos and interviews, the film offers a rare look at the society showcased in the film "Cabaret." 88 min.
01-1467 Was $39.99 *$29.99*

Tongues Untied (1989)
A provocative and controversial documentary, director Marlon Riggs' examination of black homosexuals in America mixes intimate interviews, poetry, rap pieces and performance art for a funny, touching look at the joys and trials they face in everyday life. 55 min.
78-9003 Was $39.99 *$19.99*

The Male Escorts Of San Francisco (1992)
Provocative documentary on the male escorts and prostitutes of the Bay Area, featuring intimate, revealing interviews with five men who relate anecdotes from their profession. Learn how they advertise, hear them talk frankly about their clients, and witness the pitfalls that surround such a dangerous line of work. 42 min.
53-9559 *$29.99*

Sex Is... (1993)
An acclaimed examination of sexuality in the lives of contemporary gay men featuring interviews with 15 homosexual men coming to terms with their intimacy. Erotic footage, archival clips, and funny and touching anecdotes help chronicle the state of gay sex in the 1990s. 80 min.
01-1489 Was $39.99 *$29.99*

Coming Out Under Fire (1994)
The real-life experiences of gay men and women who served in America's armed forces during and after World War II in the face of prejudice and persecution are recounted in this moving, award-winning documentary. 71 min.
53-8403 Was $29.99 *$14.99*

BloodSisters (1995)
This candid documentary on the lesbian leather and sado-masochism community of San Francisco is not for the squeamish. The focus is on nine women who represent a cross-section of the S&M environment and on different competitions held throughout the country. You'll learn about their interests and desires through extremely graphic footage. 75 min.
01-1561 *$39.99*

Dear Jesse (1997)
Gay filmmaker Tim Kirkman's "letter home" to his fellow North Carolinian, veteran U.S. senator, right-wing champion and avowed homophobe Jesse Helms, is both a humorous, sobering and revealing look at Helms' allies and detractors from across the state and a chronicle of Kirkman's coming to terms with his homosexuality. An ironic coda to this documentary is a 1996 interview with Kirkman and future Wyoming gay-bashing victim Matthew Shepard. 90 min.
53-6476 *$89.99*

The Castro (1997)
This look at San Francisco's Castro district shows how the once quiet, working-class neighborhood transformed into the world's first "gay hometown." Produced by WQED, the film uses archival material and interviews to paint a passionate, sad and funny look at one of the world's most famous urban areas, a hotbed for gay culture. 86 min.
76-2976 ❑*$29.99*

Out Of The Past (1998)
Set against the true story of 17-year-old Kelli Peterson, who ignited a nationwide controversy when she tried to start a gay and lesbian student group at her Utah high school, this award-winning documentary opens a long-neglected chapter in American history as it profiles key figures in the struggle for inclusion by homosexuals. Features the voices of Edward Norton, Stephen Spinella and Gwyneth Paltrow; Linda Hunt narrates. 70 min.
83-1261 *$24.99*

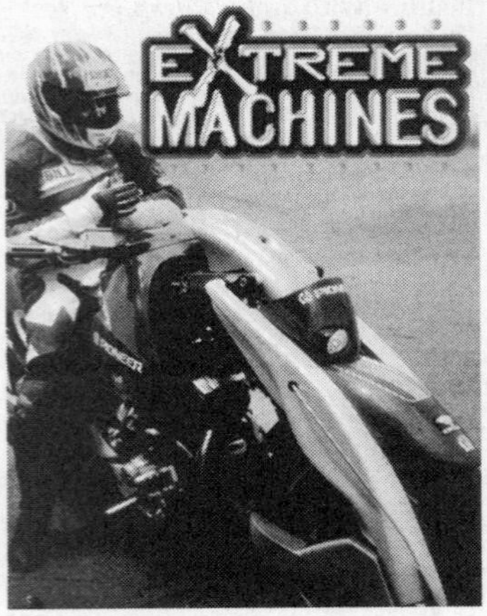

Extreme Machines: Complete Set
Get ready for an "extreme" experience as you travel across the land, on the waves, in the skies and even into outer space with this six-tape series that takes you inside the hottest vehicles and weapons. Included are "Car Crazy & 4-Wheel Force," "Flight Power & Smart Weapons," "Motorcycle & Mega Trucks," "Power Boats & Supersonic Landspeed," "Super Sight & Earth Breakers" and "Tanks & Carriers." 12 hrs. total. NOTE: Individual volumes available at $14.99 each.
83-1478 Save $30.00! *$59.99*

Essential Alan Watts: Complete Set
Millions have studied his teachings through lectures, books and radio programs. Now, in this three-volume collection, taped shortly before his death, British-born Zen mystic/philosopher Alan Watts shares his views on such topics as "Man in Nature/Work as Play," "On Meditation and Nothingness" and "Time and the More It Changes." 248 min. total. NOTE: Individual volumes available at $24.99 each.
70-7215 Save $15.00! *$59.99*

Zen: The Best Of Alan Watts
This collection of films featuring Alan Watts were produced by filmmaker Elda Hartley, from 1965 to Watts' death in 1973. One of the West's foremost interpreters of Eastern thought, Watts explores "The Mood of Zen," "Zen and Now," "Buddhism, Man and Nature" and "The Art of Meditation." 60 min.
70-9001 Was $24.99 *$19.99*

4X4 By Watts: Eastern Wisdom And Modern Life: Boxed Set
Author of "The Spirit of Zen," Alan Watts played a major role in bringing Eastern religion and philosophy to Western audiences in the '60s and '70s. This four-part collection of filmed lectures features Watts discussing the differences—and connections—between Eastern and Western thought, the nature of pain, the basic concepts of Zen, and other topics. 440 min. total. NOTE: Individual volumes available at $14.99 each.
83-1377 Save $10.00! *$49.99*

Metamorphosis
A "trialogue" discussion between scientist/philosophers Terence McKenna, Rupert Sheldrake and Ralph Abraham, in which the three discuss "chaos theory," its connection to life on Earth as a whole, and creativity and the imagination. The documentary is supplemented by stunning natural visuals and computer animation and music by Gabrielle Roth and The Mirrors. 88 min.
70-7183 *$29.99*

Apocalypse: Revelations For The New Millennium: Boxed Set
As mankind enters a new millennium, what can be learned from the world's religions and their predictions of apocalyptic change and renewal? Travel around the globe to explore the evolution of the human spirit in this five-part series that also features interviews with the Dalai Lama, Terence McKenna and others. Volumes include "A Vision of the End," "Sunset in the East," "The Great Contradiction," "The Invisible City" and "The Eye of the Heart." 300 min. total. NOTE: Individual volumes available at $24.99 each.
70-7261 Save $25.00! *$99.99*

Mysteries And Myths Of The 20th Century: Boxed Set
Learn the inside story of the century's most enigmatic stories in this 10-tape set. Included are "Mata Hari/The Red Baron," "George Patton/Rudolf Hess," "Hindenburg/Titanic," "Mummy's Tomb/Loch Ness," "Comet/Aliens," "Amelia Earhart/Lindbergh's Son," "Pearl Harbor/Atomic Bomb," "Ghosts/Madonnas," "Apollo 13/Glenn Miller" and "Korean Flight 007/Chernobyl." 600 min. NOTE: Individual volumes available for $14.99 each.
72-3031 Save $50.00! *$99.99*

Houses Of Mystery: Boxed Set
They've stood for centuries as monuments to man and god, but their origins and secrets remain a source of speculation. This two-tape documentary series features "Cathedrals," which takes you to Notre Dame, Chartres and the Duomo in Florence, and "The Pyramids," which posits that another civilization before the Egyptians built the stone behemoths. 110 min. total. NOTE: Individual volumes available at $19.99 each.
89-5186 Save $10.00! *$29.99*

Smoking: Everything You & Your Family Need To Know
Former U.S. Surgeon General C. Everett Koop offers eye-opening information about the dangers of smoking, including facts on cancer, second-hand smoke, pregnancy and tobacco, and other topics. Smokers and non-smokers present their thoughts on the subject, and there are examples of how commercials have shaped the image of smoking. 30 min.
58-8113 *$12.99*

Deadly Duels: Boxed Set
Over the centuries it evolved out of traditions of "trial by combat" and came to symbolize honor and justice. Follow the history and lore of dueling in Europe and America in this three-volume series narrated by Stacy Keach. "Duels of Chivalry," "Duels of Honor" and "Duelling in the New World" are included. 150 min. total. NOTE: Individual volumes available at $19.99 each.
53-8849 Save $20.00! *$39.99*

Rivals
From the courtroom and the silver screen to the global arena, some of the most memorable rivalries of the 20th century are recounted in this intriguing documentary series that features rare film footage and interviews. Gerald McRaney hosts. Each tape runs about 46 min. There are six volumes available, including:

Rivals: J.F.K. vs. Khrushchev
In October of 1962 the world stood poised on the brink of nuclear war, as the leaders of the U.S. and the Soviet Union played a game of brinkmanship over missiles in Cuba.
63-1901 ❑*$12.99*

Rivals: Monroe vs. Mansfield
Their names have become synonymous with Hollywood glamour and untimely deaths, and throughout the '50s Jayne Mansfield attempted to topple Marilyn Monroe as the screen's reigning sex queen.
63-1903 ❑*$12.99*

Rivals: Karloff vs. Lugosi
"Dracula vs. Frankenstein" was more than a movie title, thanks to Boris Karloff's catapulting to stardom in a role that was offered to and turned down by Bela Lugosi.
63-1904 ❑*$12.99*

Burger Town
This tasty program takes you through the legend and lore of America's favorite food, the hamburger, as it traces the history of Los Angeles drive-in restaurants and coffee shops. Along with dancing car hops, vintage fast food TV commercials, and an interview with McDonald's co-founder Richard McDonald, you'll see some of California's wildest and most nostalgic burger joints. 50 min.
89-5002 *$19.99*

A Hot Dog Program (1999)
Take a culinary cruise in the world of hot dogs and sausages in this scrumptious survey of way-out wieners. Learn their history and visit Nathan's on Coney Island; Pink's in L.A.; New Jersey's Rutt's Hut, home of the deep-fried "ripper"; and Frank's in Columbia, South Carolina, where they make "slaw dogs." You'll say "franks a lot" after watching this tasty tape. 60 min.
90-1041 Was $19.99 ❑*$14.99*

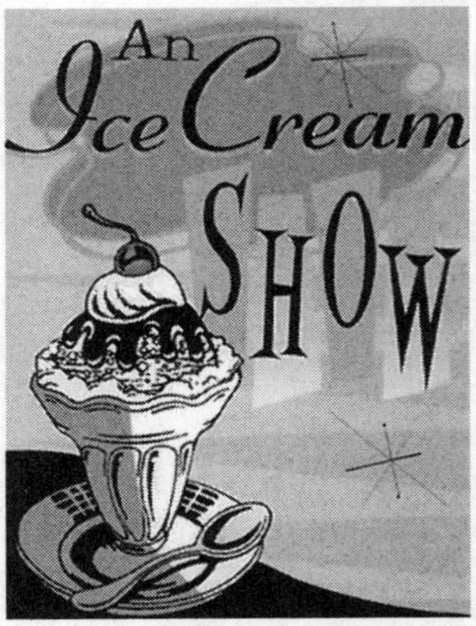

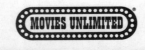

An Ice Cream Show
"I scream, you scream, we all scream" for this tasty look at America's favorite taste treat. Learn about the flavorful history of ice cream and take a tour of the country's most popular and unusual ice cream parlors. Sorry, sprinkles not included. 60 min.
90-1049 ❑*$14.99*

Dinner On The Diner: Set
Get on board this boxed four-tape set featuring a quartet of great chefs exploring different regions' people, culture and food by train. Included are "Dorinda Hafner in South Africa," "Graham Kerr in Scotland," "Martin Yan in Southeast Asia" and "Mary Ann Esposito in Spain." 240 min. total. NOTE: Individual volumes available at $19.99 each.
90-1103 Save $20.00! *$59.99*

Ring Of Fire: Complete Set
A fascinating four-volume series by filmmakers Lorne and Lawrence Blair representing their 10-year exploration of the Indonesian Archipelago, a chain of active and dormant volcanic islands that forms a curtain between the present age and mankind's primitive infancy. 232 min. total. NOTE: Individual volumes available at $24.99 each.
70-7044 Save $10.00! ❑*$89.99*

Beyond The Ring Of Fire
Eight years after he and his late brother Lorne completed their epic "Ring of Fire" documentaries, Lawrence Blair makes a return voyage to several of the Asian islands visited in that series. In an odyssey to New Guinea, Timor, Tanimbar and the Spice Islands, Blair examines the land, the wildlife, and the inhabitants of this long-unchanged area. 58 min.
70-7221 *$19.99*

Nitro Girls Swimsuit Calendar Special
The sexy dancers who, sometimes, are the most exciting thing to watch on "WCW Monday Nitro" take to the beach for a sizzling calendar photo shoot, and you've got a front row seat. Join Kimberly, Fyre, Tygress, Chae and the rest of the Nitro Girls as they romp along the shore in skimpy swimwear, and see them strut their stuff in the squared circle. 60 min.
18-7888 *$14.99*

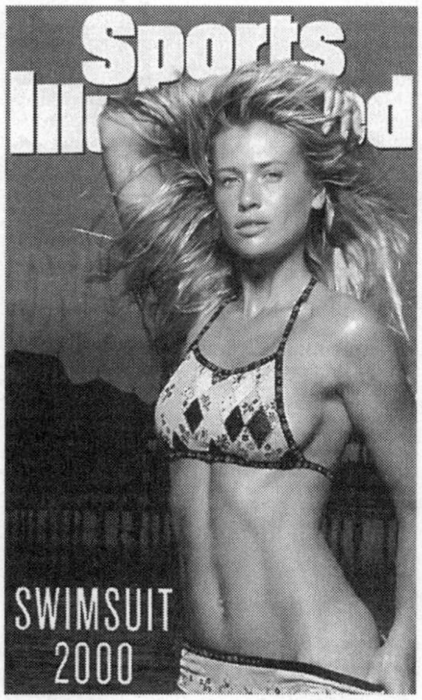
SWIMSUIT
2000

Sports Illustrated Swimsuit 2000
Next to the Forbes 500, it's the biggest annual event in magazine publishing, and this video counterpart to SI's yearly salute to skimpy swimwear and the supermodels who pose in it offers you a behind-the-scenes peek. Visit exotic seaside locales and watch Heidi Klum, Christy Hinze, Daniela Pestova and other gorgeous models show what they'll be wearing (barely) at the beach. 45 min.
50-8590 *$14.99*

Sports Illustrated Swimsuit Collection: Boxed Set
The fine folk at Sports Illustrated have assembled a spectacular five-volume boxed set of their swimsuit videos spanning the years 1995 to 1999. Each tape features a host of the sexiest models in the world, including Cheryl Tiegs, Kathy Ireland, Rebecca Romijn-Stamos, Niki Taylor and others, wearing next to nothing and cavorting in many exciting locations. 230 min. total. NOTE: Individual volumes available at $14.99 each.
50-8713 Save $35.00! *$39.99*

Beach Patrol: Boxed Set
What do you get when you cross "Baywatch" with "Cops"? You get this exciting three-tape series chock full of beautiful women in bikinis, exotic shore locales and hair-raising action and danger. Includes "International Swimsuit Spectacular," "Extreme Reality" and "Uncensored." 120 min. total. NOTE: Individual volumes available at $14.99.
83-1246 Save $10.00! *$34.99*

Supermodels In The Rainforest
A celebration of beauty, music and life, set in the verdant jungles of Costa Rica and featuring such supermodels as Tasha Moto Cunha, Tyra Banks, Frederique Van Der Wahl and Rebecca Romijin. The models pose in order to raise money for the protection of the rainforest, with music by Soul II Soul, Enigma and Duran Duran. 60 min.
84-5040 *$19.99*

The History Of The Bikini
Who better than "Baywatch" star Gena Lee Nolin to host this revealing retrospective of the skimpy swimwear that changed women's fashions around the world? See the first bikini bathing suits from the '40s, delight to screen sex kittens from the '50s and '60s modeling bikinis, and look at some of the hottest styles of today, as worn by gorgeous models. 60 min.
89-5003 *$19.99*

Apogee: Life In Motion
A stunning travelogue of man-made and natural landscapes from around the world, featuring time-lapse photography and stunning effects. Travel to Hong Kong, Tokyo, India, China, Japan, Canada and the Seychelle Islands to see sights you've never witnessed before, all set to an original soundtrack of rock, percussion and new age music. 45 min.
22-7128 Was $19.99 *$14.99*

South Sea Adventures (1932)
A rare 1932 documentary with famed Western author Zane Grey deep-sea fishing in the Pacific and encountering the natives of a remote island. 60 min.
10-8204 Was $19.99 *$14.99*

Shore Things
"By the sea, by the sea, by the beautiful sea" has been a vacation destination for Americans for over a century, and in this nostalgia-filled documentary you'll trace the love affair with the beach and take a coast-to-coast tour of some of the most popular "sand and surf" spots under the sun. 60 min.
90-1050 ❑*$14.99*

Sherman's March (1986)
It started as a retracing of the Civil War general's vandalic sweep through the South, but filmmaker Ross McElwee's acclaimed documentary became "an improbable search for love," as he introduces the viewer to a diverse and fascinating assortment of Southern women. 155 min.
70-5002 Was $59.99 *$29.99*

Time Indefinite (1993)
Ross McElwee's sequel-of-sorts to his acclaimed "Sherman's March" finds the documentary filmmaker announcing his marriage plans to his assistant at a family party, then recounting some of the most whimsical, heartfelt and tearful incidents that occurred in his life with footage he shot over the years and new events he captured while shooting this film. 117 min.
70-5063 Was $79.99 *$29.99*

Six O'Clock News (1997)
The effects of nightly depictions of natural disasters and other calamities on TV news broadcasts form a backdrop for documentarian Ross McElwee's revealing third entry in cinematic self-discovery. As he travels across America to visit the victims of various disasters seen on news reports (including Charleen from his earlier "Sherman's March"), McElwee grapples with his own mid-life crises and puts them in perspective. 102 min.
70-5134 Was $59.99 *$29.99*

Legong: Dance Of The Virgins (1930)
It's the dance of the virgins with an all-native cast performing exotic dances and religious rites, photographed on the island of Bali under the direction of Marquis de la Falaise. 50 min.
10-8205 *$19.99*

26 Bathrooms (1985)
A wacky and fascinating documentary by the ever-eccentric Peter Greenaway ("Prospero's Books") that takes an intimate look at 26 different bathrooms and the people—and animals—who inhabit them. Whether its antique porcelain or the Samuel Beckett Memorial Bathroom, this film offers a tub of unusual fun. AKA: "Inside Rooms—The Bathroom." 30 min.
80-7038 *$19.99*

A Dreamer And The Dreamtribe
Peter Coyote narrates this look at the Temair Senoi people of Malaysia, an isolated tribe whose remarkably harmonious, non-violent lifestyle is attributed to their tradition of dream-directed habits. Learn how studies of the Senoi in the 1930s helped to inspire the concept of "lucid dreaming" therapy, and see how they struggle to preserve their endangered rain forest home and their way of life. 60 min.
70-7270 *$29.99*

28 Up (1985)
The fourth entry in Michael Apted's fascinating documentary series, begun with 1964's "7 Up" for British TV, in which filmmakers captured the hopes, fears and lives of a group of 7-year-olds in England and then returned to chronicle their progress every seven years. 136 min.
53-7592 Was $79.99 *$19.99*

35 Up (1992)
The children of "7 Up" are now reaching middle age and director Michael Apted is there to capture them reflecting on their lives: the ups, the downs, and, in one case, the journey to and from madness. 123 min.
71-5281 Was $89.99 *$19.99*

42 Up (1998)
This installment in Michael Apted's acclaimed "7 Up" project looks at 11 of the original 14 subjects who participated with the filmmaker when he started the project in 1964. Among them are Tony, a cab driver who has settled into a middle-class lifestyle; Nick, a professor who moved to the U.S.; Suzy, a bereavement counselor; and Bruce, a former missionary who has found happiness after getting married. 134 min.
70-5193 *$79.99*

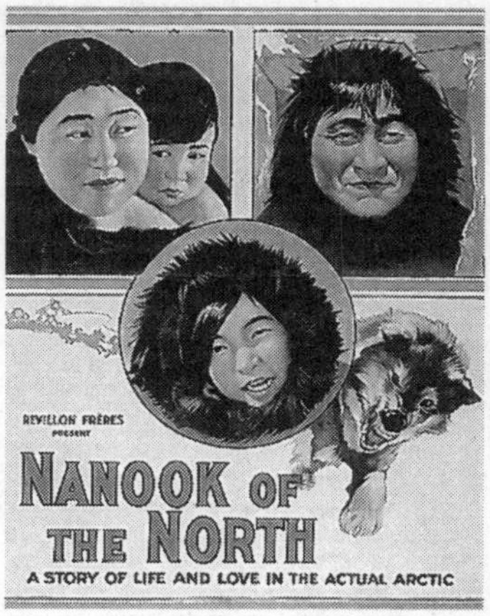
REVILLON FRÈRES
PRESENT
NANOOK OF THE NORTH
A STORY OF LIFE AND LOVE IN THE ACTUAL ARCTIC

Nanook Of The North (1922)
The groundbreaking silent film detailing the harsh existence of an Eskimo family living on the frigid shores of Canada's Hudson Bay wasn't the first documentary, but it did establish the tone of the genre for years to come. Director Robert Flaherty's breathtaking outdoor photography, especially the boating scenes, still retains its vitality. This restored, color-tinted director's cut also features an 1958 interview with Flaherty's wife, who co-edited the film. 79 min. Silent with music score.
53-6010 Restored *$24.99*

The Land (1942)/ Louisiana Story (1948)
Robert Flaherty's compassionate documentary about poor migrant farm workers of the American South and West, which originated as a Department of Agriculture study of erosion but became a stirring portrait of farm life. Then, Flaherty directs the tale of a backwoods youth and the effect a nearby oil derrick has on his family. 119 min. total.
53-7363 *$39.99*

Ken Burns

Brooklyn Bridge (1981)
An insightful look at the history of the Brooklyn Bridge and the men who helped build it from acclaimed documentarian Ken Burns ("The Civil War"). Learn how the "Great East River Bridge's" construction, begun in 1869 and completed 14 years later, was marked by puzzling problems and ingenious solutions, and how the span became a symbol of American know-how and promise. 58 min.
18-7626 ❑*$14.99*

Huey Long (1985)
From Ken Burns comes a biography of one of 20th-century America's most beloved and hated politicians, Louisiana governor and U.S. Senator Huey P. Long. This portrait of the colorful populist hero known as "The Kingfish" includes archival footage and interviews with Arthur M. Schlesinger, Jr., I.F. Stone and Robert Penn Warren, who based his novel "All the King's Men" on Long's life. 88 min.
18-7629 ❑*$14.99*

The Statue Of Liberty (1985)
The definitive portrait of "the Lady" and those she has touched and inspired over the years. Hear how France's gift to America was first met with skepticism and derision, see rare photos and film of the statue's construction and early years, and comments by Mario Cuomo, Ray Charles, Milos Forman and Jerzy Kosinski; directed by Ken Burns ("The Civil War"). 58 min.
47-1581 ❑*$14.99*

The Congress: The History And Promise Of Representative Government (1988)
In this enlightening, thoughtful look at one of America's most important and most misunderstood institutions, Ken Burns ("Baseball") uses historical photographs, newsreels and interviews to examine the issues, personalities and events that have helped shape Congress and the country for 200 years. 90 min.
18-7627 ❑*$14.99*

Thomas Hart Benton (1988)
Called "the best damned painter in America" by fellow Missourian Harry Truman, Thomas Hart Benton was known for his colorful murals of everyday American life in the 1930s. This program from director Ken Burns tells the bittersweet story of the artist's life, works and ideals. 86 min.
18-7628 ❑*$14.99*

The Shakers: Hands To Work. Hearts To God. (1989)
Ken Burns offers a fascinating portrait of the people known as Shakers, members of the United Society of Believers in Christ's Second Appearing, who are part of one of the most enduring movements in American religious history. The Shakers' beliefs (including their celibate lifestyle) and furniture-making abilities are examined through diaries and photographs. 58 min.
18-7630 ❑*$14.99*

Empire Of The Air: The Men Who Made Radio (1991)
Documentarian Ken Burns turns his camera on the history of radio, from the first experiments at the turn of the century to the golden age of the '30s and '40s. Rare newsreels, broadcast clips, and interviews with notables like Norman Corwin, Red Barber and Garrison Keillor are used to explore the medium and the men who fought for its development and its control. Jason Robards hosts. 120 min.
07-8306 ❑*$14.99*

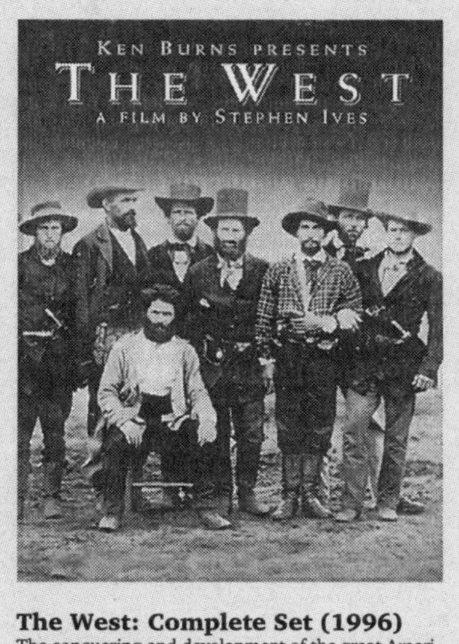
KEN BURNS PRESENTS
THE WEST
A FILM BY STEPHEN IVES

The West: Complete Set (1996)
The conquering and development of the great American frontier is the focus of this nine-part documentary from producer Ken Burns. Hear the true stories of the men and women who called the West their home, from Native Americans forced off their ancestral lands to pioneering settlers, fortune-seekers and outlaws. Included are "The People," "Empire Upon the Trails," "The Speck of the Future," "Death Runs Riot," "The Grandest Enterprise Under God," "Fight No More Forever," "The Geography of Hope," "Ghost Dance" and "One Sky Above Us." 12 hrs. total. NOTE: Individual volumes available at $19.99 each.
18-7691 Save $30.00! *$149.99*

Thomas Jefferson (1997)
From documentarian Ken Burns comes this insightful look at one of America's most remarkable and controversial statesmen. Learn about the man behind the myth, and explore Jefferson's role in the Declaration of Independence, the American and French Revolutions, the Louisiana Purchase and other historical events. Narrated by Ossie Davis, with Jefferson's writings read by Sam Waterston. 180 min. on two tapes.
18-7726 ❑*$29.99*

Lewis & Clark: The Journey Of The Corps Of Discovery (1997)
Their two-year, 8,000-mile odyssey helped to open the American West, and now documentarian Ken Burns traces the 1804-1806 expedition of Meriwether Lewis and William Clark and their party through the newly-acquired Louisiana Territory, from St. Louis, up the Missouri and Columbia Rivers, to the shores of the Pacific. 240 min.
18-7781 ❑*$29.99*

Frank Lloyd Wright (1998)
The life and work of one of the century's most innovative and influential architects are traced in this film from Ken Burns and Lynn Novick. Learn how Wright's use of "organic architecture" and his theories of function dictating form influenced the face of modern America. 178 min.
18-7827 ❑*$29.99*

Ken Burns' America: Complete Set
This seven-tape boxed set of Ken Burns' acclaimed documentaries includes "Brooklyn Bridge," "The Congress," "Empire of the Air," "Huey Long," "The Shakers," "The Statue of Liberty" and "Thomas Hart Benton."
18-7621 Save $15.00! ❑*$89.99*

The Story Of Elizabeth Cady Stanton & Susan B. Anthony: Not For Ourselves Alone (1999)
Their 50-year friendship was driven by a common passion to win equal rights for women. Now filmmakers Ken Burns and Paul Barnes chronicle the lives of 19th-century social reformers Elizabeth Cady Stanton and Susan B. Anthony, who spearheaded the suffragette movement and whose work continues to affect American society. 210 min. on two tapes.
18-7877 ❑*$29.99*

Please see our index for these other Ken Burns titles: *Baseball* • *The Civil War*

Dead Blue (1998)
It's a condition that affects over 18 million Americans, yet it remains shrouded in secrecy and shame. Three prominent people coping with clinical depression—psychologist Martha Manning, Pulitzer Prize-winning writer William Styron, and "60 Minutes" reporter Mike Wallace—talk candidly about the illness and how they've dealt with it in this HBO documentary. 55 min.
44-2208 *$24.99*

Hands On A Hard Body (1998)
The title "body" is a 1995 Nissan pickup truck at a Texas auto dealership, and 24 people are trying to win the vehicle by being the last one standing with their hands touching it. As the contest stretches into hours and days, the hopes and lives of several of the entrants—among them an impoverished farmer, a young woman who gets around by bike, and an elderly man hoping to surprise his wife—are revealed in this offbeat and surprisingly poignant slice of Americana. 97 min.
50-8303 Was $59.99 *$14.99*

Hoop Dreams (1994)
Acclaimed, one-of-a-kind documentary detailing 4 1/2 years in the lives of two Chicago teens who are counting on their basketball skills to bring them out of the inner city and into college and the NBA. Follow their triumphs and tragedies on and off the court as they cope with personal, family and academic problems while playing in pursuit of their dreams. 176 min.
02-5046 Was $89.99 ❑*$19.99*

Soul In The Hole (1997)
For some the game of basketball is still more than multi-million-dollar salaries and TV ratings. Danielle Gardner's acclaimed documentary follows Kenny's Kings, a street team from Brooklyn's Bed-Sty neighborhood, through a summer of wins, losses and community spirit as it faces opponents from across New York City in raucous, in-your-face hoops competition. 90 min.
54-9172 Was $59.99 *$14.99*

Female Misbehavior (1992)
Monika Treut ("Seduction: The Cruel Woman") directed this four-part documentary on sexual practitioners of the extraordinary kind. Among the subjects: Dr. Camille Paglia, the Philadelphia-based author of "Sexual Personae"; Annie Sprinkle, porn star and performance artist; Carole, an S&M specialist; and Max, a female-to-male transsexual. 80 min.
70-5060 Was $59.99 *$29.99*

Mother Teresa (1987)
Hailed by critics nationwide, this captivating journal of Mother Teresa's life and work among India's impoverished was years in the making and offers a remarkable portrait of one of the truly unique spirits of our time. Narrated by Richard Attenborough. 82 min.
67-5011 *$19.99*

In The Blood (1989)
Teddy Roosevelt IV retraces his great-grandfather's footsteps by taking part in a big-game safari hunt in Africa. Directed by George Butler ("Pumping Iron"), the film includes archival footage of Teddy in action and follows his descendant on the dangerous trek. 90 min.
20-7000 Was $39.99 *$19.99*

The Cruise (1998)
This revealing and captivating documentary focuses on Timothy "Speed" Levitch, an eccentric tour guide on a New York City double-decker bus who dispenses off-the-wall philosophy and poetry along with the info he offers tourists about Manhattan, its landmarks and its residents. 76 min.
27-7112 ❑*$99.99*

Baraka (1994)
In the tradition of "Koyaanisqatsi" comes this awesome, wordless look at architecture, strange rituals and topographical marvels and the contrast between natural beauty and industrial destruction. Filmed in 24 countries and on six continents, this gorgeous and disturbing epic was directed by Ron Fricke, cinematographer of "Koyaanisqatsi." 96 min.
50-7313 Was $29.99 *$19.99*

A Wall In Jerusalem (1966)
Richard Burton narrates this insightful and unforgettable analysis of the emergence of the Jewish homeland that uses newsreel and archival footage stretching from the notorious Dreyfus Affair until 1966; directed by Frederick Rossif. 91 min.
53-6004 Was $59.99 *$24.99*

West Of Hester Street (1983)
Sam Jaffe narrates this fascinating look at the frontier migration of Jewish immigrants to America over the last 100 years, focusing on a young peddler who leaves Russia to settle in Texas. 58 min.
53-9268 *$39.99*

The Yidishe Gauchos (1989)
The fascinating little-known story of the "Yidishe Gauchos" is recounted in this acclaimed documentary focusing on Jews who fled from Russian pogroms in the late 19th century to Argentina, where they became ranchers and farmers—or "Jewish Gauchos." Narrated by Eli Wallach. 28 min.
53-6848 *$29.99*

The Exiles (1990)
A compelling and inspiring documentary chronicles the experiences of Jewish artists, writers and intellectuals who fled Nazi Germany and found new lives in America. Through rare historical footage and interviews, remarkable true stories of hardship and triumph are brought to life. 116 min.
53-7782 Was $59.99 *$29.99*

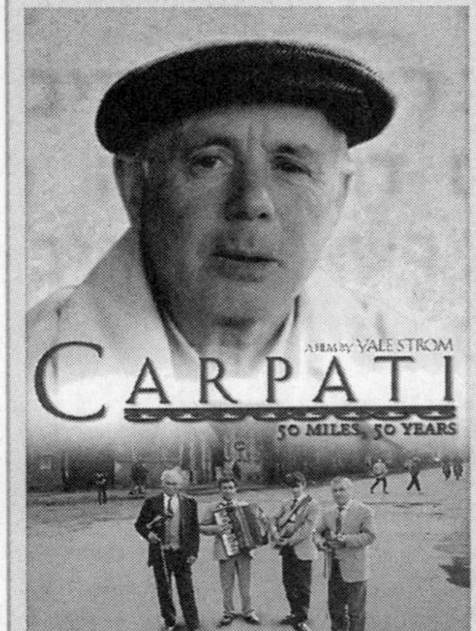

Carpati: 50 Miles, 50 Years (1996)
From the makers of "The Last Klezmer" comes this moving documentary look at the unique Jewish communities that managed to survive pogroms and the Holocaust in the Carpathian Mountains regions of Eastern Europe, but seem destined to die out in the near future. 80 min. In English, and Russian and Yiddish with English subtitles.
53-6546 Was $89.99 *$29.99*

A Tickle In The Heart (1997)
A documentary that's as warm and energetic as its subject matter, this acclaimed film follows the remarkable "comeback" of eightysomething klezmer musicians Willie, Julie and Max Epstein. First gaining fame in New York in the '20s and '30s, the Epstein brothers are seen at home and on the road, bringing their lively Jewish music to a new generation of fans. 83 min.
53-9969 *$59.99*

A Life Apart: Hasidism In America (1998)
This insightful look at Hasidism, the ultra-religious Jewish sect, takes you into their insular world. Learn about their rituals, laws, dress and language from a variety of Hasids, including Rebbes and Holocaust survivors. Narrated by Leonard Nimoy and Sarah Jessica Parker. 95 min.
70-5138 Was $59.99 *$29.99*

Arguing The World (1998)
A celebration of ideas, debate and the courage of one's convictions, this lively and thought-provoking documentary explores the heyday of New York's Jewish intellectual community, from the '30s to the '60s, through the lives of four of its most notable—and combative—members: Daniel Bell, Nathan Glazer, Irving Howe and Irving Kristol. 109 min.
70-5151 Was $39.99 *$29.99*

Israel: A Nation Is Born
Narrated by Abba Eban, this comprehensive documentary chronicles the events that led to the establishment of Israel; the subsequent conflicts, including the 1967 Six-Day War and the 1973 Yom Kippur War; the Egyptian-Israeli peace treaty; and other important events. The five-part series includes footage of such figures as Meir, Ben-Gurion, Begin and Rabin. 250 min. total.
48-5156 *$99.99*

Jerusalem
Now celebrating its 3,000th anniversary, one of the world's greatest cities is the birthplace of Christianity, the spiritual home of Judaism and the site where Mohammed visited in a dream before ascending to heaven. This comprehensive two-tape historical retrospective offers stunning aerial photography and rare film footage; hosted by historian Sir Martin Gilbert. 150 min.
53-8568 *$29.99*

Legendary Voices: Cantors Of Yesteryear
A real collector's item, this program presents some of the greatest cantorial music from some of the greatest cantors ever captured on film: David Roitman, Adolph Katchko, Moishe Oysher, Yossele Rosenblattand and others. Here's a rare opportunity to see and hear the finest cantors of their day. 45 min.
48-5096 *$59.99*

Teiman: Music Of Yemenite Jewry
With musical instruments being banned in the culture of Yemenite Jewry since the destruction of the Second Temple, the people have turned to singing, drumming, rhythm and dancing. Their music is offered in this program along with men singing poetry inspired by the 300-year-old Diwan and women performing ballads of love and family. 27 min.
48-5124 *$49.99*

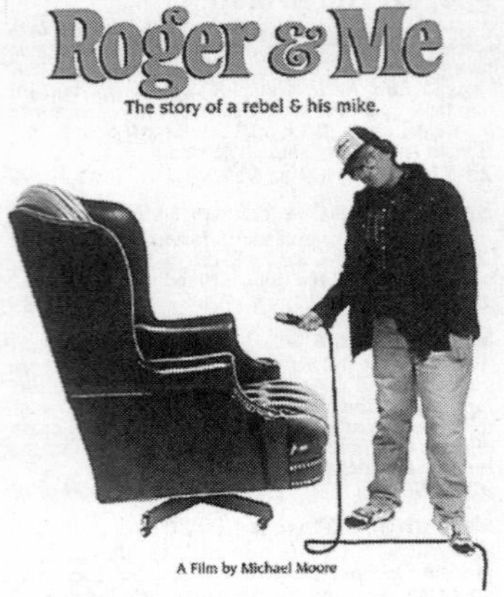

Roger & Me (1989)
Writer/director/narrator Michael Moore puts a barbed spin on the documentary genre with this acclaimed look at Moore's hometown of Flint, Michigan, and the economic devastation caused by General Motors' closing of the local auto factories. Join Moore on a search for GM chairman Roger Smith, and along the way see half-baked plans for reviving Flint and meet some unforgettable characters. 91 min.
19-1770 Was $19.99 ❑*$14.99*

The Big One (1998)
Corporate gadfly Michael Moore ("Roger and Me") is back and on the trail of more big business bigwigs to berate during the 1996 promo tour for his "Downsize This" book. Among those coming under his cross-country scrutiny are the makers of Payday candy bars, the Border's bookstore chain, and Nike shoes, whose CEO, Phil Knight, comes on camera to talk to Moore about his labor practices. 90 min.
11-2798 Was $99.99 ❑*$19.99*

Thank You And Goodnight! (1991)
A bittersweet and humorous documentary, writer/director Jan Oxenberg's look at the imminent death of her octogenarian grandmother explores such themes of familial love (and rivalry), friendship, Jewish life in New York City, life after death, and the desire for a really nice purple armchair. Tears and laughter mix in this acclaimed film. 81 min.
53-7742 *$19.99*

Jupiter's Wife (1994)
At once funny, tragic and surprising, director Michel Negroponte's award-winning documentary traces two years in the life of Maggie Cogan, a middle-aged woman who lived with her six dogs in New York's Central Park and claimed, among other things, to be actor Robert Ryan's daughter and married to the Roman god Jupiter. 78 min.
53-8612 *$24.99*

Sex, Drugs And Democracy (1995)
A provocative documentary look at Holland, where prostitution is legal, marijuana and hashish are sold openly, and the government finances abortion, euthanasia and sex education. In spite of these facts—or because of it—the country has some of the lowest rates of drug abuse, AIDS and abortion in the world. Dutch officials, police, hookers and drug dealers are among those interviewed for this eye-opening film. 87 min.
50-5663 *$24.99*

Breasts: A Documentary (1996)
Over 20 women of all ages, sizes and walks of life go before the camera (sometimes topless) and talk candidly and honestly about their breasts—from such topics as adolescence, nursing, implants and cancer to how society's ideals have influenced their image of themselves—in this acclaimed documentary. 50 min.
44-2119 Was $39.99 ❑*$14.99*

Unmade Beds (1998)
Can true love really be found through the personal ads? Filmmaker Nicholas Barker's alternately funny and sobering faux documentary follows the romantic odysseys of four New Yorkers—50ish would-be screenwriter and ladies' man Mikey, 40-year-old single mother Brenda, 5' 4" Italian-American Michael, and overweight, Kansas-born Aimee—as they set out on nerve-wracking first dates, bemoan the lack of love in their lives, and discuss their futures. 93 min.
53-6475 Was $99.99 *$29.99*

Off The Menu: The Last Days Of Chasen's (1998)
A funny and surprisingly revealing look at Chasen's, the long-standing Hollywood eatery famous for its chili, its star-studded clientele and its "Flame of Love" drink, invented for Dean Martin. The restaurant's fascinating history is celebrated, along with its crew of colorful, hard-working workers. 90 min.
53-6583 *$24.99*

The Brandon Teena Story (1998)
The heartbreaking tale of Teena Brandon, a Nebraska teenager who felt she was really a male and tried to live as one, is recounted in this acclaimed documentary that led to the 1999 drama "Boys Don't Cry." Directors Susan Muska and Greta Olafsdottir trace Brandon's childhood, her decision to live as "Brandon Teena," her romance with a girl, and how the discovery of her true gender led to her brutal rape and murder in 1993. 88 min.
53-6655 *$24.99*

Project Grizzly (1996)
One part "Grizzly Adams" and one part "Moby Dick," this offbeat Canadian documentary follows the devoted—if not obsessive—quest of bear researcher Troy Hurtubise to design a special, high-tech "grizzly-proof" outfit that will allow him to get up close to his subjects in the wild. 72 min.
70-5146 *$29.99*

Buckminster Fuller: Thinking Out Loud (1996)
R. Buckminster Fuller is the subject of this critically acclaimed documentary that uses personal papers, interviews with John Cage, Arthur Penn and Al Hirschfield and readings by Spalding Gray to present a complete portrait of the architect, poet, philosopher and inventor—a true Renaissance man. 94 min.
76-7209 *$39.99*

So Wrong They're Right (1996)
Take a 10,000-mile trek across America in search of a lost cultural artifact: the 8-track tape. Along with the editor of "8-Track Mind" magazine and a fellow "tracker," you'll explore the kitschy subculture of this defunct format's enthusiasts, who offer anecdotes, fix-it tips, sales pitches and political statements, all about the love of their life—8-tracks! 92 min.
76-7350 *$24.99*

Joseph Campbell And The Power Of Myth: Complete Set
Acclaimed six-part PBS series, with host Bill Moyers conducting some of the last interviews on film with noted author/mythologist Campbell. Tracing the common threads that bind the world's religions and cosmologies, Campbell talks about the "goddess figure," the role of storytellers and shamen, and the places myth and ritual have in modern society. 360 min. total.
70-7039 Was $149.99 *$99.99*

The Hero's Journey
The ideals that guided the life of teacher/author/mythologist Joseph Campbell are presented through interviews and classroom sessions. The teachings repeat a basic thread of Campbell's writing, that every life fulfills a mythic model and each person casts themselves as hero or pawn. 57 min.
70-7160 *$19.99*

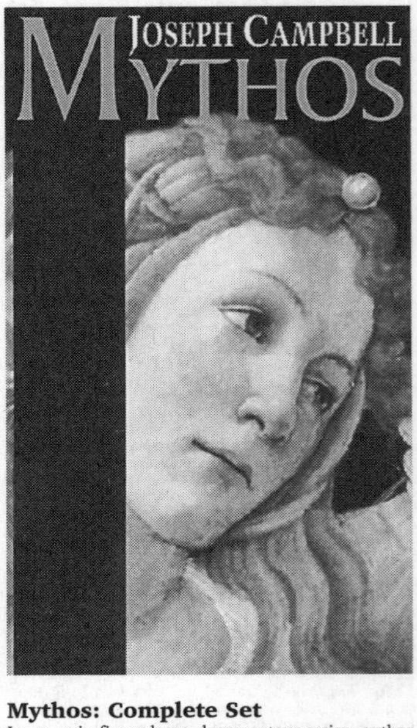

Mythos: Complete Set
In an epic five-volume documentary series, author Joseph Campbell gives an overview of the ideals and schools of thought that have shaped the world's mythologies and faiths, and, at the same time, how these myths have evolved with mankind's changing perceptions of the world around them. Included are "Psyche & Symbol," "The Spirit Land," "On Being Human," "From Goddess to God" and "The Mystical Life." Susan Sarandon hosts. 270 min. total. NOTE: Individual volumes available at $19.99 each.
70-7231 Save $10.00! *$89.99*

Mythos 2: Complete Set
Exploring the basic beliefs of Hinduism and Buddhism, Joseph Campbell looks at the differences and similarities between Eastern and Western schools of thought in this five-part continuation of his "Mythos" series. Included are "The Inward Path," "The Enlightened One," "Our Eternal Selves," "Way to Illumination" and "Experience of God." 270 min. total. NOTE: Individual volumes available at $19.99 each.
83-1194 Save $10.00! *$89.99*

Sukhavati: Place Of Bliss
The only feature film by author and mythological scholar Joseph Campbell takes viewers on a global tour of sacred and spiritual sites, including Stonehenge, Glastonbury and locales in India, Nepal and Tibet. Through images, music and sound, Campbell examines the common mythological heritage that unites all people, and how its loss affects modern society. 80 min.
70-7254 *$29.99*

Burden Of Dreams (1982)
A great film about making films, Les Blank's documentary focuses on German director Werner Herzog's struggle against all odds to complete "Fitzcarraldo" in the jungles of Peru. Mick Jagger, Jason Robards, Klaus Kinski and Herzog are featured in this incredible chronicle. 94 min.
50-3144 *$59.99*

Sans Soleil (1982)
French filmmaker Chris Marker ("La Jetée") filters his observations about cultural dislocation in Japan, Africa and Iceland through letters, quotes and the lens of a fictional, emotionless cameraman. High-tech meets low-tech in this humorous meditation of the quality of life on Earth. 100 min.
53-7774 Letterboxed *$29.99*

He Makes Me Feel Like Dancin' (1983)
Winner of a Best Documentary Feature Academy Award, this rousing film from director Emile Ardolino looks at the work of National Dance Institute founder Jacques d'Amboise to nurture creativity and a love of the dance in New York's inner city schoolchildren. 48 min.
53-6335 *$19.99*

The Family Album (1986)
Splicing together audiotapes and home movie footage from over 150 different families, documentarian Alan Berliner turns his yard sale treasure trove into a fascinating chronicle of American homelife from the '20s to the '50s, tracking the family's changing role and the universal experiences from childhood to adulthood. 60 min.
80-5033 *$29.99*

Nobody's Business (1996)
Filmmaker Alan Berliner examines the life of his father Oscar, a 79-year-old retired sportswear manufacturer, in this compelling documentary. What begins as a study of an ordinary man becomes a drama of life choices and real-life family conflicts, as son confronts father on issues about his immigrant past, time in the Navy during World War II, marriage and other events. 60 min.
80-5032 *$29.99*

Bill Moyers: Healing And The Mind: Complete Set
Explore the connection between the body and the mind in this fascinating five-part series, hosted by Bill Moyers, that looks at various Eastern and Western cultures and examines their differing approaches to healing, medicine and meditation. 320 min. total. NOTE: Individual volumes available at $29.99 each.
14-9092 Save $20.00! *$129.99*

Amazing Grace
Bill Moyers hosts this study of the history and power of "Amazing Grace," the 18th-century hymn written by an English slave ship captain. Judy Collins, Johnny Cash, Jessye Norman, and the Boys Choir of Harlem add insight and performances. 87 min.
80-7119 *$24.99*

The Wisdom Of Faith With Huston Smith: Complete Set
Religion expert Huston Smith joins Bill Moyers for this insightful series exploring the way the world worships. With help from samples of art, architecture, music and poetry, Smith allows the basic beliefs and common threads behind each faith. Included in the five-part series are "Hinduism and Buddhism," "Confucianism," "Christianity and Judaism," "Islam" and "Personal Philosophy." 275 min. total. NOTE: Individual volumes available at $29.99 each.
80-7193 Save $30.00! *$119.99*

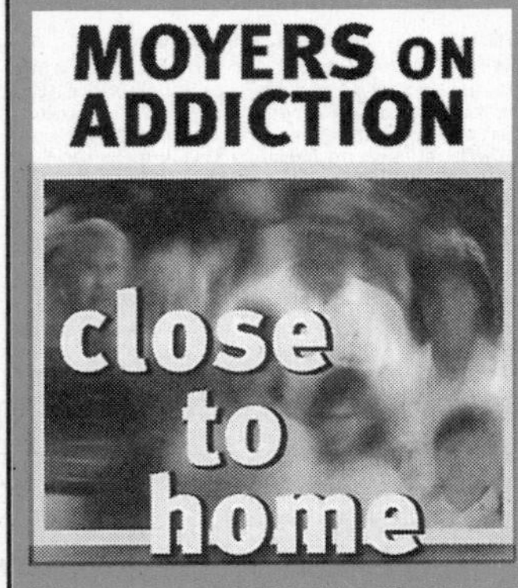

Moyers On Addiction: Close To Home Complete Set (1998)
It's a problem that crosses all walks of life across the country, and even reached into the family of host Bill Moyers. This acclaimed five-part PBS series takes a comprehensive, compassionate look at drug and alcohol abuse, their causes and effects, and how best to help the addicted. Included are "Portrait of Addiction," "The Hijacked Brain," "Changing Lives," "The Next Generation" and "The Politics of Addiction." 300 min. total. NOTE: Individual volumes available at $29.99 each.
08-7226 Save $30.00! *$119.99*

Didn't Do It For Love (1998)
Norwegian-born Eva Norvind travelled to Mexico at 20 and, with her stunning blonde good looks, became one of that country's leading film stars, until her advocacy of "free love" forced her to leave in 1966. Moving to New York, she opened a popular S&M salon and became a lecturer and talk show guest. Filmmaker Monika Truet ("The Cruel Woman") examines Norvind's many lives in this unusual and compelling documentary. 80 min.
70-5156 *$39.99*

Manufacturing Consent: Noam Chomsky And The Media (1992)
Does America's mass media contribute to a "web of deceit" that stifles dissent and maintains a status quo? Renowned author, linguist and social philosopher Noam Chomsky tackles this and other weighty issues in a two-part documentary that includes a variety of interviews while tracing Chomsky's life and controversial career. 166 min.
82-3002 Was $59.99 *$39.99*

Road Scholar (1992)
Transylvanian emigré and NPR commentator Andrei Codrescu gets behind the wheel of a '68 Cadillac convertible for a cross-country look at the American psyche in this funny, insightful documentary. Religious communities of a variety of faiths, a sausage plant, a punk rock band of Arizona retirees and the neon canyons of Las Vegas are among the sights Codrescu visits. 82 min.
88-1009 ▢*$14.99*

Silverlake Life: The View From Here (1993)
An award-winning, compassionate documentary focusing on Tom Joslin and Mark Massi, lovers since the 1970s, who decided to turn their battle against the AIDS virus into a film diary. Each man contracts the disease, but Mark is the first to die, and Tom records his companion's painstaking struggle on film. 99 min.
53-8023 *$19.99*

Grass (1925)
"King Kong" creators Merian C. Cooper and Ernest B. Schoedsack risked their lives to make this monumental documentary about the Bakhtiari people of western Persia (Iran), who each year confront harsh weather and towering mountains to bring their herds more than 200 miles to pasture. 70 min. Silent with new musical score.
80-5001 *$39.99*

Chang (1927)
A spectacular adventure from filmmakers Merian C. Cooper and Ernest B. Schoedsack, this magnificent docudrama follows an Asian native family's difficult existence as they attempt to survive against tigers, leopards and ferocious elephants, which rampage in a thrilling charge towards the film's finale. Shot on location in Siam. 67 min.
80-5005 *$39.99*

Mystic Origins Of The Martial Arts
Known only to small groups of students and followers in Asia centuries ago, today karate, judo, ninjitsu and other martial arts are practiced by millions around the world. Yet few know the history and spiritual heritage of these disciplines, which are revealed in this fascinating documentary narrated by George Takei. 100 min.
53-8854 ▢*$19.99*

The Burning Man Festival (1986)
This film chronicle of Nevada's notorious "Burning Man Festival," which attracts 15,000 participants to a five-day carnival of artistic creativity and general debauchery in the desert, presents an amazing look at what can be termed "Weirdstock." See people strut naked, race in rocket-powered cars, shoot automatic weapons and do whatever comes naturally. 30 min.
76-7453 *$19.99*

Chronos (1987)
Ron Fricke, the cinematographer of "Koyaanisqatsi," takes you on a dazzling journey through time to some of the world's most intriguing spots, including Paris, Egypt and the Vatican. Filmed in 70mm and using groundbreaking film techniques and time-lapse photography, this film offers an amazing look at the man-made world. 40 min.
02-7574 Was $19.99 *$14.99*

Heaven (1987)
Diane Keaton's directorial debut is a dazzlingly different documentary look at the question of whether there's an afterlife. Impressions from her family, friends and the "ordinary" folk of Venice Beach, California, are interspersed with Hollywood's most outrageous filmic interpretations of paradise to create a heavenly movie experience. 88 min.
07-8115 Was $19.99 *$14.99*

Broken Noses (1987)
A stark documentary on fighter Andy Minsker and his Portland, Oregon, boys' boxing club. Shot by photographer Bruce Weber ("Let's Get Lost") in black-and-white with some color sequences, this is a moody look at a former Golden Gloves champ and the hard-working fighters he treats like his sons. Featuring a jazz score by Julie London, Chet Baker and Gerry Mulligan. 75 min.
53-7681 *$29.99*

Kumu Hula: Keepers Of A Culture (1989)
Colorful documentary about the history of the Hula, Hawaii's national treasure and one of the world's favorite dances. Sway to the island rhythms and lovely scenery, captured by Robert Mugge, the award-winning chronicler of some of music's most fascinating subjects. 85 min.
53-7408 Was $29.99 *$19.99*

Biography

Biography
Trace the lives of the famous and infamous in the award-winning documentary series from cable's A&E Network. Host Peter Graves shares insights into the men and women who have shaped the modern world, combined with rare vintage footage and exclusive interviews. Except where noted, each tape runs about 50 min. There are hundreds of volumes available, including:

Biography: Ann-Margret: Sugar & Spice
53-6989 *$14.99*

Biography: Don Knotts: Nervous Laughter
53-6990 *$14.99*

Biography: Donna Reed: I'll Take The Moon
53-6991 *$14.99*

Biography: Doris Day: It's Magic
53-6992 *$14.99*

Biography: Ernie Kovacs: Please Stand By
53-6993 *$14.99*

Biography: George C. Scott: Power & Glory
53-6994 *$14.99*

Biography: Harrison Ford: The Reluctant Hero
53-6995 *$14.99*

Biography: Shirley MacLaine: This Time Around
53-6996 *$14.99*

Biography: Vincent Price: The Versatile Villain
53-6997 *$14.99*

Biography: Stone Cold Steve Austin: Lord Of The Ring
31-5239 *$14.99*

Biography: Audrey Hepburn: The Fairest Lady
53-6171 Was $19.99 *$14.99*

Biography: Anne Frank: The Life Of A Young Girl
53-6391 *$14.99*

Biography: Jackie O: In A Class Of Her Own
53-6393 *$14.99*

Biography: Kirk Douglas
53-6679 Was $19.99 *$14.99*

Biography: Elvis: Story Of A Legend
53-7846 *$14.99*

Biography: Jackie Robinson
53-7853 Was $19.99 *$14.99*

Biography: Gene Autry: America's Singing Cowboy
53-7869 Was $19.99 *$14.99*

Biography: Pope John Paul II: Statesman Of Faith
53-8107 Was $19.99 *$14.99*

Biography: Benjamin Franklin: Citizen Of The World
53-8206 Was $19.99 *$14.99*

Biography: Bette Davis: If Looks Could Kill
53-8207 *$14.99*

Biography: Sherlock Holmes: The Great Detective
53-8275 *$14.99*

Biography: The Three Stooges
53-8577 *$14.99*

Biography: Abraham Lincoln: Preserving The Union
53-8673 Was $19.99 *$14.99*

Biography: Vincent Van Gogh: A Stroke Of Genius
53-8686 Was $19.99 *$14.99*

Biography: Boris Karloff
53-8691 *$14.99*

Biography: Malcolm X: A Search For Identity
53-8743 Was $19.99 *$14.99*

Biography: Jack The Ripper: Phantom Of Death
53-8765 Was $19.99 *$14.99*

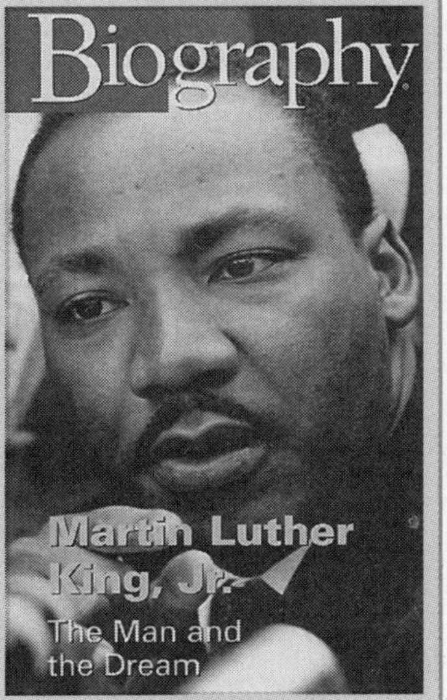

Biography: Martin Luther King, Jr.: The Man And The Dream
53-8772 Was $19.99 *$14.99*

Biography: Ted Bundy: The Mind Of A Killer
53-8804 Was $19.99 *$14.99*

Biography: William Shakespeare: A Life Of Drama
53-8810 *$14.99*

Biography Of The Millennium: 100 People 1000 Years
The most influential and important people of the last 10 centuries are the subject of this superb four-tape program from the producers of "Biography." The rich cross-section of the famous and infamous includes such luminaries as Thomas Jefferson, Gandhi, Winston Churchill and Martin Luther King, leading up to the "Biography of the Millennium." 200 min. total.
53-6582 *$39.99*

Theremin: An Electronic Odyssey (1995)
The remarkable life of the Russian-born musician/inventor, whose eponymous instrument's haunting sounds were heard on concert stages and in such films as "Spellbound" and "The Day the Earth Stood Still," is traced in this acclaimed documentary. See how Professor Leon Theremin pioneered electronic music in New York in the '20s and '30s, until he was taken back to Moscow and forced to work on espionage devices for Stalin, and follow the elderly Theremin's return visit to America in 1993. 84 min.
73-1240 Was $89.99 ▢*$14.99*

Cadillac Desert: Boxed Set (1997)
The quest to supply the Western United States with fresh water, a decades-long struggle that was marked by engineering marvels, greed and political scandal and inspired the movie "Chinatown," is traced in this four-part PBS documentary. Narrated by Alfre Woodard, the series tracks the flowering of Southern California and Arizona, as well as other parts of the world, in "Mulholland's Dream," "An American Nile," "The Mercy of Nature" and "Last Oasis." 270 min. total. NOTE: This special collector's set also includes the 1974 film "Chinatown." Individual volumes available at $29.99 each.
22-5912 Save $20.00! *$99.99*

An American Love Story (1999)
A remarkable achievement in documentary filmmaking, Jennifer Fox's acclaimed PBS series chronicles a year and a half in the lives of an interracial couple living in Queens, New York, and their two daughters. As the cameras follow Bill Sims and Karen Wilson, their 30-year saga of marriage, family life and the attendant ups and downs form a powerful real-life drama. 500 min. on five tapes.
53-6549 Was $99.99 *$59.99*

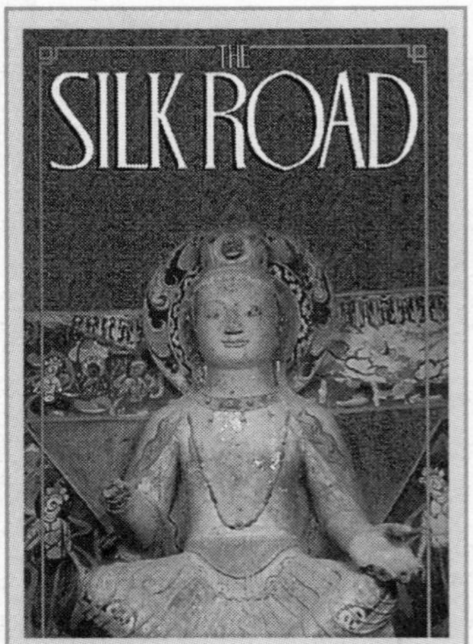

The Silk Road
An ancient world of adventure awaits you when you watch this retracing of the route travelled by Marco Polo which linked China and Europe. Through deserts, grasslands and seas used by Alexander the Great and Genghis Khan, this inaccessible region is filled with riches and treasures, featured in these stunning, beautifully filmed series.

The Silk Road: Collector's Gift Set 1
Includes volumes 1-6 of the series: "Glories of Ancient Chang-An," "A Thousand Kilometers Beyond the Yellow River," "The Art Gallery in the Desert," "The Dark Castle," "In Search of the Kingdom of Lou-Lan" and "Across the Taklamakan Desert." 300 min. total. NOTE: Individual volumes available at $29.99 each.
20-7007 Save $80.00! *$149.99*

The Silk Road: Collector's Gift Set 2
Includes volumes 7-12 of the series: "Khotan—Oasis of Silk and Jade," "A Heat Wave Called Turfan," "Through the Tian Shan Mountains by Rail," "Journey Into Music—South Through the Tian Shan Mountains," "Where Horses Fly Like the Wind" and "Two Roads to the Pamirs." 300 min. total. NOTE: Individual volumes available at $29.99 each.
20-7109 Save $80.00! *$149.99*

Riddle Of The Desert Mummies
What was the origin of the scores of preserved bodies, all of them blonde and red-haired Caucasians, that were recovered from the desert sands of Northern China's Xinjiang region? Join scientists as they study clothing samples and use the latest DNA analysis to unravel a 4,000-year-old mystery in this fascinating Discovery Channel documentary. 50 min.
27-7220 *$14.99*

Imperial Tombs Of China: The Museum Tour
These magnificent sculptures, funereal relics and personal effects from 25 centuries of Chinese imperial rule have never been seen outside of their native country, until this fascinating documentary that lets you get up close to the treasures of the emperors and their families. 60 min.
50-4732 Was $29.99 *$19.99*

China Rising: The Epic History Of 20th Century China
The 20th-century history of Asia's "sleeping giant" is told with all its joy and tragedy in this absorbing three-tape series. Follow the anti-imperialist crusade of Chiang kai-Shek in the 1920s, Japan's 1932 invasion of Manchuria, Mao Tse-Tung and the Communists' rise to power, the bloody purges of the Cultural Revolution, and the country's current role in global politics. Eileen Atkins narrates. 150 min. total.
53-8644 *$49.99*

China: A Century Of Revolution: Boxed Set
Over the course of the 20th century China went from being an imperial nation to a democracy to the world's largest Communist country, a tumultuous history that is thoughtfully examined in this three-part documentary series. Segments include "China in Revolution," "The Mao Years" and "Born Under the Red Flag." 6 hrs. total. NOTE: Individual volumes available at $19.99 each.
53-9925 Save $10.00! *$49.99*

Millennium: Complete Set
Follow a thousand years of global history with this compelling CNN series that looks at the key people, events and achievements of the last 10 centuries through vignettes set in five different locales. 10 hrs. on five tapes.
18-7881 *$99.99*

The 1900 House (1999)
Take a trip back in time with a typical English family who move into an authentically restored Victorian home for three months in this four-part PBS series. Join Paul and Joyce Bowler and their four children as they learn to cope without such modern conveniences as indoor plumbing, electric appliances, fast food and even shampoo...and with such 1900 staples as corsets, chamber pots and wood-burning stoves. 240 min. on two tapes.
90-1114 □*$29.99*

The Coming Plague
Follow the doctors and scientists who travel around the world to study and combat infectious disease outbreaks—and often put their own lives on the line in the process—in this two-part cable TV documentary based on the Pulitzer Prize-winning book. 180 min.
18-7755 □*$29.99*

The Middleton Family At The 1939 New York World's Fair (1939)
Produced by Westinghouse, this wonderful film follows a typical American family (Mom, Dad, Sis and Junior) as they visit the World's Fair and get a glimpse of "The World of Tomorrow" (although they rarely seem to leave the Westinghouse exhibit). Marvel at the robotic antics of "Elektro, The Moto-Man," an early look at television, the kitchen of the future, and more. 55 min.
82-1001 *$19.99*

The World Of Tomorrow (1984)
Superb documentary on the 1939 New York World's Fair, the wondrous exposition that offered an array of technological marvels and impressive architectural exhibits and promised visitors a glimpse of a bright future, even as the world was on the verge of war. Home movies, cartoons, newsreels and interviews bring the fair to life in all of its glory. Narrated by Jason Robards, Jr. 84 min.
76-7445 *$49.99*

New York World Fair Memories Of 1964 (1964)
A documentary double feature spotlights the 1964-65 exposition whose motto was "Peace Through Understanding." Lowell Thomas narrates "World Fair Planning," detailing the construction of the fair and showcasing the most popular exhibits. Next, follow two girls "To the Fair" and see it in all its Technicolor splendor. 60 min. total.
82-1002 *$19.99*

The 1964 World's Fair (1996)
It was the exhibition where one could see both Michelangelo's "Pieta" and Disney's "It's a Small World," and where the technological optimism of the '50s ran headlong into the social realities of the '60s. Judd Hirsch narrates this nostalgic salute to the 1964-65 New York Fair that takes you from construction to closing day with colorful film footage and reminiscences of fair workers and visitors (remember the Unisphere, Sinclair's Dinoland and those great Belgian Waffles?). 60 min.
81-3005 *$29.99*

Civilisation: Complete Set (1969)
Noted historian Sir Kenneth Clark hosts this acclaimed BBC documentary series that aired on PBS in 1971. The wonders of European thought, philosophy, architecture, art, music and literature are explored, from the final days of Ancient Rome and the Middle Ages through the Renaissance and into contemporary times. 10 hrs. on five tapes. NOTE: Individual volumes available at $24.99 each.
22-5662 Save $25.00! *$99.99*

The Thin Blue Line (1988)
Filmmaker Errol Morris ("Gates of Heaven") tackles a serious subject in this engrossing documentary that follows the 12-year struggle of Randall Adams, a Texas man who was convicted and sentenced to life in prison for killing a policeman, a crime he says he didn't commit. Interviews, filmed re-enactments, old movie clips and a Philip Glass score make for a unique real-life drama. 101 min.
44-1572 Was $89.99 *$14.99*

Fast, Cheap & Out Of Control (1997)
Maverick documentary filmmaker Errol Morris ("The Thin Blue Line") sets his cameras on four different men attempting to examine the relation between science and humanity. Among them are a scientist studying mole rats, an animal trainer, a robot expert and a gardener. This highly acclaimed film uses interviews, footage from old movies and a hypnotic score to tell their stories. 83 min.
02-3175 Was $99.99 □*$24.99*

Mr. Death: The Rise And Fall Of Fred A. Leuchter, Jr. (1999)
Continuing his fascination with the most unlikely of documentary topics, filmmaker Errol Morris turns his camera on a quiet man who made dying his life's work. Self-taught capital punishment expert Fred Leuchter became the country's leading authority on designing "humane" killing methods, until his testimony denying the Holocaust in a Canadian Neo-Nazi's 1988 trial proved to be his professional and personal downfall. 92 min.
07-2868 □*$99.99*

Party Monster (1999)
This revealing documentary focuses on Michael Alig, a young man from the Midwest who became Manhattan's premier party promoter in the 1980s, only to have his decadent life destroyed when he was arrested for killing his druggie roommate in 1996. Go behind the scenes of the circus-like New York club scene with this fascinating look at its ringmaster.
76-2071 *$29.99*

Monty Roberts: A Real Horse Whisperer (1997)
He's a former rodeo champion whose autobiography, "Monty Roberts: The Man Who Listens to Horses," was a best-seller. Learn how Roberts uses non-violent methods to tame wild horses in this fascinating documentary. 48 min.
04-3669 *$14.99*

Pop (1998)
Photographer Joel Meyerowitz's moving film chronicles the Miami-to-New York road trip he took with his 87-year-old father Hy, a man ready to face old age and the onset of Alzheimer's Disease with courage and optimism. Follow their trip back to Hy's childhood home in this emotional documentary. 80 min.
70-5162 *$29.99*

Super Structures Of The World: Complete Set (1998)
An intriguing three-part series that examines some of the most amazing architectural and engineering achievements of the 20th century. Follow, from the drawing board to completion, such modern wonders as the English Channel "Eurotunnel," the US submarine "Seawolf" and the world's tallest "Skyscrapers." 156 min. total. NOTE: Individual volumes available at $14.99 each.
83-1239 Save $5.00! *$39.99*

Sick: The Life And Death Of Bob Flanagan, Supermasochist (1998)
Unique, unflinching documentary on performance artist/poet Bob Flanagan. Struggling since birth with cystic fibrosis—an illness in which victims rarely survive their teens—Flanagan learned to cope with his condition through a mixture of dark humor, creativity, and a lifelong fascination with pain and sexual submission. Special video version includes footage not shown in theaters. 78 min.
85-5101 *$89.99*

The People Bomb
How many inhabitants can the planet support before its resources are taxed beyond their limits? This special report from CNN focuses on the global population explosion, its consequences, and the steps countries are taking to limit growth. 90 min.
18-7417 Was $19.99 *$14.99*

The Farmer's Wife (1998)
Filmmaker David Sutherland's acclaimed documentary, first seen on PBS, was shot on location over a three-year period to movingly chronicle the struggles of Juanita and Darrel Buschkoetter, a young Nebraska farm couple, to keep their family's farm and, ultimately, their marriage going. 6 1/2 hrs. on three tapes.
90-1010 □*$49.99*

Great Events Of The 20th Century: Boxed Set
This seven-tape set allows you to review history's most important incidents of the 20th century, from 1900 to 1995. Included is archival footage of various wars, inventions, world leaders, the Depression and lots more. 315 min. total.
16-5032 *$49.99*

This Great Century: Collector's Set
The triumphs, tragedies, upheavals and advances that marked the world in the 20th century are recounted in this insightful, informative five-part documentary series that traces events from "1900-1918," "1918-1939," "1939-1958," "1958-1980" and "1980-1990." 495 min. total. NOTE: Individual volumes available at $19.99 each.
20-7633 Save $10.00! *$89.99*

The 20th Century: Boxed Set
A collection of rare and famous footage and commentary is used to tell the story of the 20th century in this impressive ten-tape set. Included are "The 1900s: The Seeds of Progress," "The 1910s: The Modern Age Begins," "The 1920s: A Decade of Contradictions," "The 1930s: The Great Depression," "The 1940s: War, Recovery and Rebirth," "The 1950s: Promoting the American Dream," "The 1960s: A Global Revolution," "The 1970s: Power Plays," "The 1980s: A Decade of Decadence" and "The 1990s: America's Hard Drive." 12 1/2 hours total. NOTE: Individual volumes available at $19.99 each.
50-7592 Save $70.00! *$129.99*

TheCentury America's Time

The Century: America's Time: Boxed Set (1999)
From ABC News comes an unprecedented look back at the people, events and trends of the 20th century, and how they shaped America and the world. From Kitty Hawk to Tranquility Base, from the shooting of President McKinley to the death of Princess Diana, the defining moments of the era are presented through archival photos and film footage, some of it never before seen, in this six-tape retrospective. Peter Jennings hosts this documentary based on his book. 11 1/2 hrs. total.
19-9248 Was $99.99 □*$74.99*

CNN Millennium 2000 (2000)
It's a global event that comes along once in a thousand years, as CNN cameras follow the dawn of January 1st, 2000 around the world to chronicle the celebrations from dozens of locales. Relive the festivities with this highlight program that takes you to Sydney, Tokyo, Moscow, Berlin, Paris, London, New York, Washington, Los Angeles and more. 120 min.
18-7895 *$14.99*

American History

America In The '40s: Boxed Set
It was a decade that opened with the country still climbing out of the Depression and ended with unparalleled prosperity, and saw wars both hot and cold grip the nation. Take a "sentimental journey" through the '40s, and relive the events, fads, fashions and people that shaped them, with this three-tape collector's set.
18-7834 *$49.99*

America Goes To War: World War II
The American homefront during the Second World War is the focus of this nostalgic, four-volume documentary presentation. See how a nation still coping with the effects of the Great Depression pulled together in the wake of Pearl Harbor. Vintage newsreel footage helps bring the story to life, with narration by veteran TV journalist Eric Sevareid. 216 min.
50-5890 *$69.99*

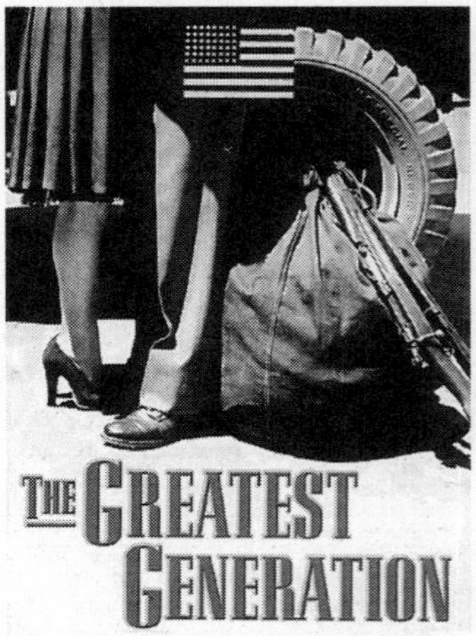

The Greatest Generation (1999)
Based on the best-selling book by NBC newsman Tom Brokaw, this compelling documentary looks at the men and women who came of age in the late '30s and early '40s, a time that saw America rise up out of the Depression and survive the struggles of World War II. Hear from military heroes and ordinary citizens as they recount the challenges that shaped their generation and the nation. 50 min.
53-6394 Was $19.99 *$14.99*

Inside The Secret Service
This incisive study of America's oldest and most elite law enforcement agency features a look at the agent who blames himself for the death of President Kennedy and a revealing look at the service's training methods in its secret Beltsville Training Center. Rare archival film and dramatic reconstructions are used. 90 min.
22-1405 *$19.99*

Inside The CIA: On Company Business: Complete Set
The story of the Central Intelligence Agency has been an active and controversial one. This three-part series explores the ideologies and operations of "the agency" from its inception after World War II to the end of the Cold War. Included are "The History," "Assassination" and "Subversion." 174 min. total. NOTE: Individual volumes available at $19.99 each.
50-6201 *$59.99*

Mind Control (1998)
Go beyond "The Manchurian Candidate" and learn the just-as-compelling true story behind government-sponsored brainwashing and mind control experiments. Interviews with medical experts, information from newly declassified CIA files, and amazing film footage of actual sessions are included. 60 min.
18-7828 *$19.99*

Secrets Of The CIA (1998)
For decades its been America's eyes and ears around the world, but the Central Intelligence Agency's inner workings have been shrouded in secrecy. Now go behind the scenes through interviews with former agents—as well as their M-15, KGB and Mossad counterparts—and news footage that chronicles the agency's controversial history and operations. 60 min.
18-7829 *$19.99*

The Prohibition Era
Learn about the 14-year experiment to keep America "on the wagon," and how Prohibition led to a social revolution across the country and helped give rise to organized crime, with this three-part documentary series. All the lawmen, gangsters, crusaders and artists of the "Jazz Age" live on in "The Dry Crusade," "The Roaring Twenties" and "The Road to Repeal." 150 min. total.
53-8076 *$39.99*

The Jazz Age
This marvelous and illuminating history of America from the end of World War I to the Great Crash of 1929 offers a look at the historical, social, music and cultural events that took place in this exciting era. Fred Allen narrates. 60 min.
63-7093 *$19.99*

California (1954)
The Bank of America celebrated its 50th anniversary with this star-studded dramatization detailing the history of the Golden State. Among those appearing are Thomas Mitchell, Jack Benny, John Carradine, Doris Day, Bonita Granville, Howard Keel and others. 55 min.
10-6001 *$14.99*

The Menace Of Communism!
Three vintage "Red Scare" documentaries from the late '50s and early '60s are featured, depicting the methods of Communist insurgents to take over a country from within: "Communist Blueprint for Conquest" (1955), "The Communist Weapon of Allure" (1956) and "Communist Target: Youth" (1962). 100 min.
09-2404 Was $49.99 *$19.99*

The Berlin Airlift
One of the first Cold War showdowns between East and West came in early 1948, as Soviet forces cut off land routes to the Allied-occupied city of Berlin. This documentary traces the year-long operation which saw American and British pilots fly over 270,000 deliveries of desperately needed food and supplies to the residents of Berlin. Paul Duke narrates. 60 min.
83-1284 *$19.99*

Point Of Order (1964)
Finally available on home video in its uncut version, underground filmmaker Emile De Antonio's groundbreaking documentary tracks the rise and fall of right-wing demagogue Joseph McCarthy, the leading force behind the "Red Scare" of the '50s, through the senator's own words and televised footage of the Army/McCarthy Hearings. 97 min.
53-6347 *$89.99*

One Week In October (1964)
In 1962 the entire world teetered on the brink of global war, as America and the Soviet Union faced a dangerous stalemate over Russian missiles in Cuba. Actual spy-plane scenes from Cuba and newsreel footage of Kennedy, Rusk and Stevenson give the viewer a behind-the-scenes look at the crisis. 29 min.
65-1007 *$19.99*

A CENTURY OF WOMEN

A Century Of Women: Complete Set
The remarkable strides and achievements made by 20th-century women in the fields of politics, civil rights, science and the arts are the focus of this three-part documentary series. Sally Field, Jodie Foster, Halle Berry, Betty Friedan, Gloria Steinem, Maya Angelou and other notables join narrator Jane Fonda to offer commentary and insight. 285 min. total. NOTE: Individual volumes available at $19.99 each.
18-7496 Save $20.00! *$39.99*

Women: First & Foremost: Complete Set
This three-part documentary series looks at women's accomplishments throughout history. Included are "Remember the Ladies," which traces women who have broken new ground, from doctors to legislators; "Touching the Clouds with Pen and Plane," which looks at writers, pilots and others; and "A Lady in the Spotlight," which follows the impact of female entertainers. 180 min. total. NOTE: Individual volumes available at $24.99 each.
27-6941 *$69.99*

The Eighteenth Century Woman (1987)
An in-depth view of the role of women in the 18th-century, using the lavish costume collection of the Metropolitan Museum of Art as a focal point. Includes interviews with museum director Philippe de Montebello, costume curator Stella Blum and fashion maven Diana Vreeland. 60 min.
22-5155 *$39.99*

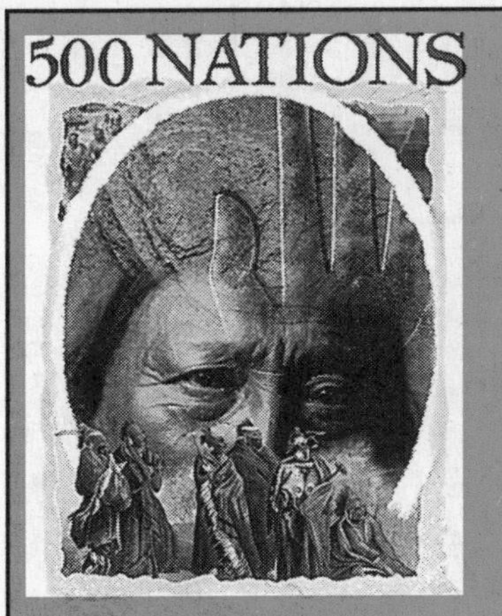

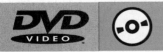

500 Nations: Complete Set
Learn the history of the North American continent from its original inhabitants in this powerful eight-part documentary series produced and hosted by Kevin Costner. Narrators such as Graham Greene, Amy Madigan, Edward James Olmos and Patrick Stewart bring to life stories of heroes and warriors, discovery and conquest. Included are "The Ancestors," "Mexico," "Roads Across the Plains," "Attack on Culture" and more. 376 min. total. NOTE: Individual volumes available at $19.99 each.
19-2339 Save $20.00! *$139.99*

Last Stand At Little Big Horn
The fateful showdown between Custer and Sitting Bull is told with fresh insight in this compelling program that aired as part of the PBS series "The American Experience." Here are accounts by whites and Native Americans from journals and oral accounts, plus archival and feature films. Native American writer Scott Momaday narrates. 60 min.
50-2653 *$19.99*

End Of The Trail
Perhaps the first honest look at the white man's treatment of Native Americans in this country was this installment of the 1960's "Project Twenty" series on NBC. Focusing on the conflicts that arose during the 19th-century Western migration, this program offers a soul-searching look into a dark side of American history. Narrated by Walter Brennan. 60 min.
63-7095 *$19.99*

Native Land: Nomads Of The Dawn
Using ritual dance, drama and storytelling, noted author Jamake Highwater looks at the nomadic Indians whose descendants became the Aztecs, Incas and other South American tribes. Witness their incredible artwork, pottery and sculpture in this program. 58 min.
83-1081 Was $19.99 *$14.99*

Primal Mind
The differences between Native American and European cultural perspectives are explored in this program featuring author Jamake Highwater. Contrasting views of art, time, architecture, medicine and dance are presented, along with how such creators as Martha Graham, Jackson Pollock and Pablo Picasso were influenced by American Indian art. 58 min.
83-1082 Was $19.99 *$14.99*

In The Land Of The War Canoes (1914)
Engrossing study of the Kwakiutl Indians of Vancouver Island, directed by premier photographer Edward S. Curtis, who spent three years living with the tribe. The film captures the customs, costumes and incredibly detailed canoes of the Kwakiutl and features an authentic score recorded in 1972. 47 min.
80-5003 *$39.99*

The Shadow Catcher: Edward S. Curtis And The North American Indian (1976)
In the early part of the 20th century, anthropologist and photographer Edward S. Curtis set out to document the vanishing lifestyle of Native Americans. His work, including rare silent film footage, is traced in this blend of documentary and drama. Donald Sutherland reads from Curtis' writings. 88 min.
70-7131 *$29.99*

Incident At Oglala (1992)
The true story that inspired the film "Thunderheart" focuses on the case of Leonard Peltier, a Native American convicted of killing two FBI agents on a South Dakota Indian reservation in 1975. Directed by Michael Apted ("35 Up") and narrated by Robert Redford, the documentary provocatively looks at both sides of the issue and raises questions about the verdict. 93 min.
27-6785 Was $89.99 *$19.99*

Ishi: The Last Yahi (1992)
This remarkable documentary centers on the lone surviving member of the Yahi tribe, who appeared in California in 1911 after living in the wilderness for four decades following the massacre of his people by the encroaching white settlers. Archival footage, recordings of Ishi, photographs and Linda Hunt's narration tell the story. 60 min.
63-7097 *$19.99*

Seeing Red (1984)
Superb documentary focusing on Americans who embraced communism from the '30s to the '50s and faced McCarthyism and blacklists, along with disillusionment with "the party" in later years. Nominated for an Academy Award, the film weaves newsreel footage with interviews with singer Pete Seeger, union organizer Rose Podmaka and others. 100 min.
76-7117 *$29.99*

The Unforgettable Fifties
The 1950s come alive again with this seven-tape series comprised of classic newsreels of the era. See the important events, the most famous leaders and the most popular entertainers in "Human Interests," "Disasters," "Inventions," "Fashions," "Royalty," "Faces of the Fifties" and "Sports Highlights." 420 min. total.
16-5023 *$49.99*

This Is America (1932)
Early Hollywood documentary, produced by Frederic Ullman, Jr., that traces America's history from the onset of our involvement in World War I to the Great Depression and gives us a rare contemporary look at the "Roaring '20s." Also included is "The American Road," a look at the development of the automobile narrated by Raymond Massey.
10-7557 *$29.99*

Millhouse: A White Comedy (1970)
It's frightening! It's shocking! It's a real-life documentary of the first years of Richard Nixon's presidency as seen by notorious underground filmmaker Emile de Antonio ("Painters Painting"). Notorious satire that predated Watergate and landed its creator on the White House "enemies list." 80 min.
50-6100 *$39.99*

Wonderland (1997)
Shortly after World War II, housing designer William Levitt revolutionized American homelife when he built the country's first planned suburb, Levittown, on Long Island. Filmmaker John O'Hagan takes a light-hearted look at 50 years of suburban life as he talks with some of the community's original residents and their offspring, and explores how $7,900 could buy a white, pre-fab slice of the American dream. 80 min.
53-6331 *$24.99*

Our Constitution (1940)
Documentary tracing the early years of America and its government. Follows the efforts of the Founding Fathers to affect a democracy, the passage of the Constitution and Bill of Rights and the creation of the Monroe Doctrine. 61 min.
09-1676 Was $24.99 *$19.99*

No Substitute For Victory (1970)
Who better than John Wayne to host this documentary look at "America's fight against Communist aggression" in Vietnam? Along with a history of Red atrocities from the Russian Revolution to Southeast Asia, Wayne talks with such notables as Martha Raye, newsman Lowell Thomas and Green Beret-turned-pop star Sgt. Barry Sadler and puts the blame for the war's dragging on squarely on the shoulders of a "hostile press." 70 min.
16-1165 *$19.99*

David Halberstam's The Fifties: Boxed Set
It was a decade of quiet suburban families and rock-and-roll rebellion, of McCarthyism and the realization of racial inequalities, and hanging over every American's head was the threat of the atomic bomb. Join best-selling author David Halberstam in a fascinating six-volume series that looks at the people, events, fads and fashions that shaped America in the '50s. 390 min. total.
53-9970 *$99.99*

America's Historic Trails: Complete Set
They were the backwoods roads and hazardous mountain trails that the pioneers of early America followed, and in this six-tape collection host Tom Bodett takes you on a history-filled tour of "The California Trail & El Camino Real," "The Great Wagon Road & The Wilderness Trail," "The Mormon Trail & California's Mission Trail," "The Old Post Road," "The River Road & The Natchez Trace" and "Yukon Gold Rush Trail." 330 min. total. NOTE: Individual volumes available at $24.99 each.
50-3461 Save $30.00! *$119.99*

The River (1937)
Produced by the U.S. Farm Security Administration, Pare Lorentz's acclaimed documentary looks at the history of the Mississippi River, the farms and industries that grew along it, and how years of misuse led to flooding and other disasters in the '30s. A moving early example of the documentary's use as social propaganda. 32 min.
09-1818 *$19.99*

Power And The Land (1940)
A special collection of four federally-sponsored documentaries that depict the hardships faced by rural America during the Great Depression. Included are Joris Ivens' "Power and the Land" (1940), "The New Frontier" (1934) by H.B. McClure, and Pare Lorentz's "The River" (1937) and "The Plow That Broke the Plains" (1936). 105 min. total.
53-7988 Was $59.99 *$29.99*

We Interrupt This Program...
The live, uninterrupted broadcasts of special news bulletins are presented in this terrific program. Re-experience the assassination of Martin Luther King, the hijacking of TWA Flight 847, the 1989 California Earthquake and more. 55 min.
50-6609 *$19.99*

1968: America Is Hard To See
Perhaps the most turbulent year of a very turbulent decade, 1968 saw riots in the streets of Harlem, a bloody protest in Chicago, a changing of the guard in Washington, and a nationwide shift in attitudes. From underground filmmaker Emile de Antonio ("Millhouse"). 88 min.
50-6314 *$59.99*

Chicago 1968
This "American Experience" installment recounts the tumult that surrounded the 1968 Democratic National Convention in Chicago, as Vietnam War protesters, civil rights activists, and members of the "Yippie" movement were met by 25,000 police called out by Mayor Daley. See network coverage of the violent confrontation, hear from people on both sides, and learn about the riots' aftermath. 60 min.
63-7151 *$19.99*

The Fabulous '60s: Complete Set
It was the decade that saw man walk on the moon, a president fall in Dallas, and a nation torn apart by war half a world away. Relive the people and moments of the tempestuous era in this 11-tape set, with one volume dedicated to each year, plus a retrospective on the decade. 660 min. total. NOTE: Individual volumes available at $19.99 each.
50-7487 Save $20.00! *$199.99*

Timothy Leary's Last Trip
The icon of the psychedelic '60s, Dr. Timothy Leary, lives on in this documentary that traces his wild life and times and concludes with Leary's final appearance at counterculture cult figure Wavy Gravy's annual "Hog Farm Picnic" with special guests Ken Kesey and the Merry Pranksters. The soundtrack includes several songs by The Grateful Dead. 60 min.
53-8939 Was $19.99 *$14.99*

Timothy Leary's Dead (1997)
Was the Harvard educator-turned-drug guru a mind-expanding pioneer or a dangerous subversive? This acclaimed film explores Leary's stranger-than-fiction story, from his '60s exploits to footage of his head being removed from his body shortly after his death in 1996 and cryogenically preserved. 85 min.
50-3380 Was $59.99 *$19.99*

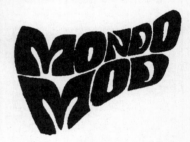

MONDO MOD

Mondo Mod (1967)
Groovy look at the psychedelic sixties that includes stops at the Sunset Strip, where the "Now Generation" shops and hangs out; the beaches of Hawaii and Southern California, where hepcats surf; the road, where motorcyclists race their bikes; and the mind, where drugs like LSD enable you to turn on. Humble Harve narrates; music by Sam the Soul and the Inspirations, and others. 89 min.
79-5406 Was $24.99 *$19.99*

It's A Revolution Mother (1968)
A truly incredible look at the sixties, chronicled by a narrator in a Jack Webb-like manner and focusing on protests, civil rights and, in particular, motorcycle gangs. The main bikers featured are the Aliens, who, along with protesters and hippies, face off against the "pigs" and politicians. Way, way out archival stuff from a turbulent decade.
79-5991 *$19.99*

Underground (1974)
Emile De Antonio's controversial documentary on the "Weathermen" radical group and their rise to infamy in the '60s. Interviews and rare news footage suppressed by the FBI are a highlight in this look at a turbulent time in American history. 88 min.
50-6095 *$29.99*

Berkeley In The Sixties (1990)
An acclaimed film of the major events of the 1960s, including the civil rights movement, free speech protests and anti-war rallies, as seen by 15 leading activists of the era. Allen Ginsberg, Todd Gitlin and Huey Newton are among those who comment on the era in this wild ride through the decade that changed America. 117 min.
07-8365 *$29.99*

Twist (1993)
Funny and fascinating look at the '60s dance sensation, the Twist. Follow its evolution and popularity through priceless archival footage and music by Hank Ballard, Chubby Checker, Smokey Robinson and The Isley Brothers as you relive those incredible memories of "American Bandstand" and the Peppermint Lounge. 78 min.
02-2512 Was $19.99 *$14.99*

THE AMERICAN PRESIDENT

Lincoln
He rose from backwoods obscurity to lead a nation torn in half by war and become one of America's greatest presidents. This four-volume documentary series looks at Abraham Lincoln's career and personal life through his writings, historical photos and papers, and narration by such stars as Ned Beatty, Glenn Close, James Earl Jones and Jason Robards. 240 min.
07-8359 Was $49.99 □*$29.99*

Abraham Lincoln: A New Birth Of Freedom
The tumultuous life and times of the 16th president are recounted through Lincoln's own speeches and letters, as well as the words of friends, opponents and colleagues. Peter Coyote and Lou Gossett, Jr. supply voices; narrated by Andrew Young. 60 min.
89-5164 *$19.99*

The Lincoln Assassination
Remaikable look at the murder of Abraham Lincoln by actor John Wilkes Booth that offers answers to many of the event's most controversial questions. Forensic experts and modern historians separate fact from fiction regarding the tragedy that shook a nation. Two-tape set; 100 min.
53-8220 *$29.99*

The Plot To Kill Lincoln
In April of 1865, a newly reunited America was shocked to learn of the first presidential assassination. Now this revealing documentary looks at the events surrounding Abraham Lincoln's murder and those involved. Was the plot hatched by members of Lincoln's cabinet? Did John Wilkes Booth escape a burning barn and leave someone else to fill his grave? The truth will amaze you. 52 min.
89-5225 *$19.99*

Theodore Roosevelt
The son of well-to-do parents, he made a crusade of battling big business; an avid big game hunter, he became a noted conservationist; a war hero, he used America's military power to preserve world peace. The many facets of America's youngest president, Theodore Roosevelt, are explored in this fascinating two-tape documentary from PBS's "The American Experience." 240 min.
90-1056 □*$29.99*

The Indomitable Teddy Roosevelt (1983)
The life and times of the 26th president, the youngest man to ever hold the office. Outdoorsman, Rough Rider, political leader, "trust buster"...rare film footage highlights this look at the man who helped set the tone for America's place in the 20th century. George C. Scott narrates. 94 min.
46-5263 Was $79.99 *$19.99*

FDR: Complete Set
Franklin Delano Roosevelt's life in and out of the White House is chronicled in this exhaustive four-part documentary series, hosted by David McCullough. "The Center of the World" looks at FDR's childhood and family background; "Fear Itself" follows his recovery from polio and journey to the presidency; the Depression years are the focus of "The Grandest Job in the World"; and "The Juggler" studies Roosevelt during World War II. 270 min. total. NOTE: Individual volumes available at $19.99 each.
63-7105 □*$69.99*

The Eleanor Roosevelt Story (1965)
This inspiring, Oscar-winning documentary takes a close-up look at the life and times of Eleanor Roosevelt: social activist, author, First Lady and U.S. representative to the United Nations. Special video edition includes an introduction by First Lady Hillary Rodham Clinton. 90 min.
08-1481 *$29.99*

Truman
The plain-talking haberdasher from Missouri had a big pair of shoes to fill after FDR's death in April of 1945, but Harry Truman led the nation to final victory in World War II and set the tone for postwar global politics in his dealings with Russia, Eastern Europe and Korea. Trace the career and legacy of the 33rd president in this two-tape "American Experience" program. 240 min.
90-1055 □*$29.99*

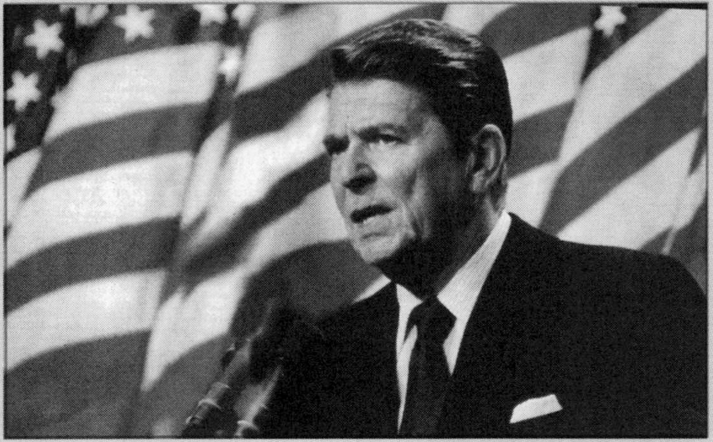

Eisenhower
The life and times of the 34th President of the United States are examined in this fascinating portrait. Using archival footage, interviews and documents, this two-part program traces Ike's military greatness during World War II in "Soldier"; and examines his two-term presidency, the Cold War and McCarthyism in "Statesman." 150 min.
63-7080 □*$39.99*

LBJ
Five years in the making, this acclaimed portrait of Lyndon Baines Johnson offers a fresh look at the 36th president. Through interviews, family photographs and news footage, you'll examine Johnson's years in Texas politics, his tragedy-tainted rise to the presidency, and the "Great Society's" record of civil rights, urban problems, and escalated American involvement in Vietnam. 240 min.
07-8292 □*$29.99*

The LBJ Tapes: Boxed Set
Take a rare look behind White House doors with this four-tape documentary series, featuring newsreel footage and photos that complement recently-discovered audiotapes made of President Lyndon B. Johnson's Oval Office conversations. See how Johnson dealt with crises ranging from the JFK assassination to the civil rights movement and Vietnam in "Hello, Mr. President," "RFK vs. LBJ," "Into Vietnam: Playing with the Truth" and "Uncivil Liberties: Hoover and King." 240 min. total. NOTE: Individual volumes available at $19.99 each.
22-1704 Save $10.00! *$69.99*

Nixon
Villain or victim; more than a quarter-century after he became the first man to resign from the presidency, the debate on Richard Nixon's legacy continues. In this two-tape program from PBS's "The American Experience," you'll explore the complex world of Nixon's stormy political career, his remarkable rise to the White House, the accomplishments of his administration, and the scandal that drove him out of office. 240 min.
90-1054 □*$29.99*

The Nixon Interviews With David Frost: Collector's Set
Television history was made when David Frost conducted a series of revealing and far-reaching talks in 1977 with former President Richard M. Nixon. Hear the only man ever to resign from the Oval Office candidly discuss "Watergate," "The World," "The War at Home and Abroad," "The Final Days" and "The Missing 18 1/2 Minutes and More" in this five-tape set. 6 hrs. total. NOTE: Individual volumes available at $19.99 each.
07-2335 Save $20.00! □*$79.99*

Reagan (1997)
The charismatic leader of the 1980s conservative revival, the Hollywood star-turned-public servant constantly amazed his critics throughout his political career. This two-part documentary from the PBS "American Experience" series traces Ronald Reagan's life in both the public and private arenas, the ups and downs of his two terms as president, and his place in history. 240 min.
18-7795 □*$29.99*

Ronald Reagan: The Great Communicator: Complete Set
Relive eight years of "the Reagan Revolution" through his own words with this special, four-tape boxed set that examines the highlights of the 40th president's administration using news footage, speeches and "off-the-record" quips. Included are "The Reagan Presidency," "The Military and the Soviet Union," "Reagan on Government and the American Dream" and "The Man." 340 min. total. NOTE: Individual volumes available at $19.99 each.
50-7560 *$79.99*

The President's Testimony: Clinton Under Oath
On August 17, 1998, President William Jefferson Clinton answered a grand jury's questions involving his relationship with Monica Lewinsky in relation to accusations of perjury. This historic video features the complete testimony and offers a revealing look into Clinton's presidency and private life, as well as his reaction to special prosecutor Kenneth Starr's tactics. 270 min.
50-5995 *$14.99*

The War Room (1993)
Entertaining and enlightening behind-the-scenes look at Bill Clinton's 1992 presidential campaign that details the dogged efforts of charismatic campaign manager James Carville and slick communications director George Stephanopoulos. Directors Chris Hegedus and D.A. Pennebaker chronicle the shaky road from the New Hampshire primary to the Little Rock victory party. 96 min.
68-1305 Was $89.99 □*$12.99*

Clinton's Angels
Go beyond the tabloid headlines and TV news bites with this revealing documentary that looks at the allegations of sexual misconduct that rocked the Clinton presidency and the three women—Gennifer Flowers, Paula Jones and Monica Lewinsky—whose statements have made them instant celebrities. Explore the origins of "Zippergate," hear from key players on both sides of the issue, and more. 40 min.
50-7460 *$14.99*

The Presidents Collection I Boxed Set
They led the country through the turmoil of the '60s, and their public and private lives were marked by triumph and tragedy. Hear the amazing life stories of "The Kennedys," "LBJ" and "Nixon" in this six-tape collection of documentaries from PBS's "The American Experience."
18-7778 □*$69.99*

The Presidents Collection II Boxed Set
Two of the 20th century's greatest presidents came from the same family, and now "The American Experience" presents "Theodore Roosevelt" and "FDR," together in a four-tape collector's set.
18-7779 □*$59.99*

The Presidents Collection III Boxed Set
This four-tape collection of episodes from "The American Experience" spotlights the chief executives whose decisions shaped the destiny of post-WWII America, "Truman" and "Ike."
18-7780 □*$59.99*

Portraits Of American Presidents
NBC News presents a fascinating look at the American presidency, from George Washington to George Bush. The three-volume series offers historical insights, rare film footage, and photos and paintings from the National Archives and other important historical societies. Included are "Presidents of a New Nation" (1789-1829), "Presidents of a National Struggle" (1829-1901), and "Presidents of a World Power" (1901-1992). 3 1/2 hrs. total.
50-4308 *$59.99*

Hail To The Chief
The 41 men who have served as the country's chief executive are profiled in this historical retrospective. Interviews with scholars and biographers, and rare archival photos and film footage help tell the story of the presidency from Washington to Clinton, examining the highs and lows of each man's administration and his role in American history.
50-4589 *$14.99*

Presidential Bloopers
It's a laugh a minute with this hilarious look at the flubs made by our fearless leaders. See rare, behind-the-scenes footage of chief executives from Nixon to Clinton as they botch speeches, make "off the record" miscues, stumble at official gatherings and more. 40 min.
50-8661 *$14.99*

The American President: Complete Set (2000)
The highs and lows of the country's highest office—and the 41 very different men who have held the position—are chronicled in this comprehensive five-volume PBS series. Rare film footage and interviews and commentary from historians and scholars trace the evolution of the presidency in "A Matter of Destiny," "Politics and the Presidency," "Executive Vision," "The Candidate" and "An Office and Its Powers." 10 hrs. total.
90-1057 □*$99.99*

Stalking The President: The History Of American Assassins
A fascinating look into the attempts on the lives of presidents Jackson, Lincoln, Garfield, McKinley, Teddy Roosevelt, FDR, Truman, Kennedy, Ford and Reagan. Little known facts are revealed, dynamic footage is presented and the tragic shootings of Martin Luther King, Robert Kennedy and George Wallace are also covered. 50 min.
22-1272 *$19.99*

Air Force One: Flight II
Remarkable look at "The Flying White Houses" that have served as a means of transportation for presidents from FDR to George Bush includes interviews with pilots, crew members and President Bush and a rare look inside Air Force One. Charlton Heston narrates. 90 min.
50-6807 Was $24.99 *$14.99*

First Ladies (1989)
Colorful and invigorating ABC News study of our fabulous First Ladies—wives of the Commanders in Chief, spouses of the Top Dogs, companions of the Head Honchos. From Martha Washington through Mary Lincoln to Barbara Bush, you'll explore the way they really were. 60 min.
50-6474 *$19.99*

The Sensational '70s: Complete Set
Take the video time machine back to the 1970s, "the Me Decade." Richard Nixon, Watergate, "Star Wars," Patty Hearst, leisure suits, "All in the Family," E.R.A., disco, hostage crises, "The Godfather," Vietnam: it was the best of times, it was the worst of times, and it's all here in this 10-tape set, with one volume dedicated to each year. 600 min. total. NOTE: Individual volumes available at $19.99 each.
50-7488 Save $20.00! *$179.99*

The History Of The 80s: Complete Set
From the archives of ABC News comes this 10-tape look at the decade that saw the rise of Reagan and Bush, the fall of the Iron Curtain, and a variety of scandals ranging from Oliver North to Jim and Tammy Baker, with one volume dedicated to each year. 600 min. total. NOTE: Individual volumes available at $19.99 each.
50-7489 Save $20.00! *$179.99*

The Story Of Washington, D.C.: The Capital Of The United States
1990 marked the 200th anniversary of our nation's capital, and in celebration this video traces Washington's history and shows the original designs for the Capitol building, the White House and other historical monuments. Presented by NBC News, this documentary features the resources of the National Archives and the Smithsonian Institute. 60 min.
50-4309 *$29.99*

American Legends: Boxed Set
This three-tape series looks at a trio of great American leaders. "George Washington" traces the soldier and statesmen's life from his early days in Virginia to wartime victories to the presidency. "Abraham Lincoln" looks at "Honest Abe's" actions during the Civil War. And "General U.S. Grant" surveys the military man's mastery as leader of the Union army. 150 min. total. NOTE: Individual volumes available at $19.99 each.
22-1794 Save $10.00! *$49.99*

The March Of Time: American Lifestyles 1939-1950 Collector's Edition
The focus here is on the changes American society faced in its family life in the '30s and '40s. Includes "The American Family: The War Years," "The American Family: The Postwar Years," "American Fashion and Leisure," "America's Youth," "Show Business: The War Years" and "Show Business: The Postwar Years." 538 min. on six tapes.
53-1659 *$99.99*

The March Of Time: War Breaks Out 1941-1945 Collector's Edition
America's involvement in World War II is traced in this boxed set. Included are the two-part "Americans Prepare," "The Battle Beyond," "The Military Prepares" and "Praying for Peace." 650 min. on six tapes.
53-1680 *$99.99*

The March Of Time: America At War 1941-1945 Collector's Edition
What was life like on the American homefront and overseas during World War II? Find out in this special set that features "On the Homefront," the three-part "Friend and Foe," and parts one and two of "American Defense." 678 min. on six tapes.
53-1712 *$99.99*

The March Of Time: The Great Depression 1930-1940 Collector's Edition
It was a time of breadlines, Hoovervilles, and a dynamic leader who promised the country a New Deal. Featured in this boxed set are the documentaries "Time Marches In 1935," "Economy Blues," "Trouble Beyond Our Shores," "War and Labor Woes," "Prosperity Ahead?" and "Reality and America's Dreams." 572 min. on six tapes.
53-1752 *$99.99*

The Untold West: Complete Set
The secrets of the American West are revealed in this three-volume series that shows you a side of life often overlooked by historians and the movies. Film clips, archival photos, interviews with descendants of frontier legends and narration help tell the stories of prairie passion in "Hot on the Trail," the truth of "Outlaws, Rebels and Rogues," and the untold tales of "The Black West." 180 min. total. NOTE: Individual volumes available at $12.99 each.
18-7478 *$19.99*

The Wild West: Complete Set
The men and women, heroes and villains who were a part of the Old West tell their stories in this five-tape collection, narrated by Jack Lemmon. Letters and journals, paintings and photographs, and the music of the period are blended to relate the tales of "Cowboys," "Settlers," "Indians," "Gunfighters," "Mythmakers" and others. Among the celebrity voice-overs are Lloyd Bridges, James Coburn, Larry Fishburne, Helen Hunt and Wes Studi. 7 1/2 hrs. total. NOTE: Individual volumes available at $19.99 each.
19-2155 *$74.99*

The Real West (1961)
One of the first programs ever produced to present the West as it really was, this documentary uses archival footage and historical accounts to depict the struggles, heroes and hardships of America in the 1800s. Gary Cooper narrates. 60 min.
63-7066 *$19.99*

The Donner Party (1992)
From director Ric Burns comes a haunting look at the ill-fated Donner Party and the shocking events that surrounded the doomed trip to California in 1849. Narrated by David McCullough, the film features the voices of Timothy Hutton, Amy Madigan, George Plimpton and Eli Wallach to tell this dark, true story. 84 min.
76-7462 *$49.99*

Ellis Island
For millions of immigrants in the 1800s and early 1900s, it was their first destination in America, and around the world Ellis Island, situated in New York harbor, came to symbolize the promise of the New World. Hear the emotional true stories of some of the nearly 20 million men, women and children who passed through its gates in this fascinating documentary. 150 min.
53-8893 *$49.99*

Mr. Sears' Catalogue
In the early 20th century two books could be found in nearly every American home: the Bible and the Sears Roebuck catalog. Trace the rise of retail legend Richard Sears, his revolutionary mail order empire, and the 1,500-page volume that allowed rural Americans to fill their homes (or even build one) and helped to epitomize a society. 60 min.
63-7157 *$19.99*

The Oregon Trail: Complete Set
Journey along the 2,000-mile-long pioneer trail that opened up the American Northwest with this two-part program that features a historical overview of the Oregon Trail, settlers' first-hand accounts and more. "Across the Plains" takes you from Independence, Missouri to Ft. Laramie in Wyoming, and the trail ends at Oregon's Ft. Hall in "Through the Rockies." 120 min. total. NOTE: Individual volumes available at $19.99 each.
80-7252 *$39.99*

America 1900
The sweeping social, technological and political changes that the United States faced at the dawn of the 20th century—changes that would be amazingly mirrored 100 years later—are followed in this documentary from PBS's "American Experience" series. 180 min.
90-1008 *$29.99*

Henry Ford's Mirror Of America
Produced by the National Archives and the Ford Motor Company, this program features intriguing footage of America from 1914 to 1945. Among the subjects photographed are New York's Coney Island and Lower East Side, Pennsylvania Avenue in Washington, Buffalo Bill's circus and soldiers preparing for World War I. 36 min.
09-1525 *$14.99*

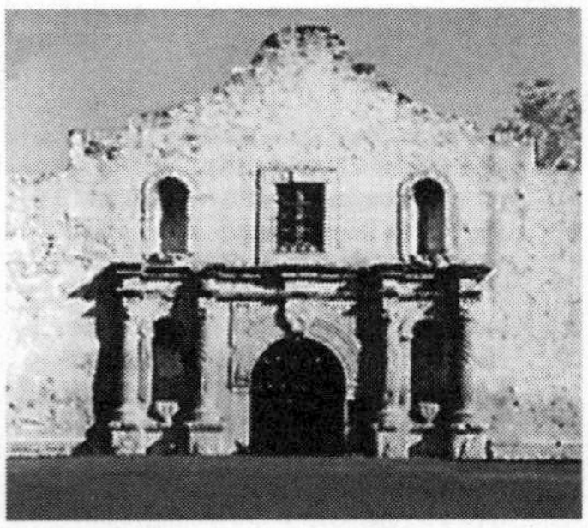

The Alamo
Using rare archival materials, eyewitness accounts and dramatic re-enactments, this program, produced by American Heritage magazine, chronicles the Texas fight for independence against Mexico in 1836. You'll meet Davy Crockett, Jim Bowie and William Travis as they battle Santa Ana's 4,000-man army during the "13 days of glory." 100 min.
53-8562 *$29.99*

Jack: The Last Kennedy Film
A revealing and personal portrait of John F. Kennedy which traces his life from his childhood, his marriage and his family life up through his political career and presidency. Rare footage and family films that were narrated by Kennedy help show a side of the man never before seen. 90 min.
04-2861 *$14.99*

JFK In Ireland
June, 1963: President John F. Kennedy travels to Ireland and is met with open arms everywhere he goes. This program chronicles JFK's visit with rare footage of the trip to his family's birthplace. 42 min.
22-1539 *$19.99*

The Many Faces Of Lee Harvey Oswald
This program delves into the personality of Lee Harvey Oswald and the conspiracy theory surrounding the assassination of John F. Kennedy. With research by photo analyst Jack White and Jim Marrs, author of "Crossfire: The Plot That Killed Kennedy," the video reveals a world of secret agents, photo forgeries and murder.
50-2961 *$19.99*

Confession Of An Assassin: The Murder Of JFK
Is it a hoax or proof of a conspiracy? You decide as you watch this chilling video interview, the result of a five-year search by private investigator Joe West, with an Illinois prison inmate who claims to have been part of a high-level assassination plot against President Kennedy that culminated in that fateful day in Dallas in November, 1963. 76 min.
50-7403 *$19.99*

Four Days In November (1964)
From fateful motorcade to horse-drawn funeral procession, the assassination of John Kennedy and his succession by Lyndon Johnson are chronicled in this vivid document of the tragic days that changed the course of American history.
12-1846 Was $29.99 *$14.99*

The Plot To Kill JFK: Rush To Judgment (1965)
Did the Warren Commission close the book too soon on Kennedy's assassination? Engrossing documentary, based on attorney Mark Lane's best-seller, sheds new light on the many theories surrounding the killing. Directed by Emile de Antonio. 98 min.
50-6160 *$19.99*

The Men Who Killed Kennedy (1988)
Startling new evidence about JFK's assassination is presented in this shattering documentary program. Did Bobby Kennedy's plan to kill Castro backfire and lead to the death of his brother? Also, a highly-decorated Army colonel talks about how he was trained to eliminate key assassination witnesses. 50 min.
53-8442 *$19.99*

The Men Who Killed Kennedy: Complete Set (1988)
This exhaustive five-part documentary series, produced in England, takes an impartial and comprehensive look at questions that have surrounded the assassination of John F. Kennedy for a quarter of a century, examining eyewitness testimony, claims of missing evidence, and the many conspiracy theories. Volumes include "The Coup D'Etat," "The Forces of Darkness," "The Cover-Up," "The Patsy"
70-1404 Was $59.99 *$29.99*

JFK: The Day The Nation Cried: November 22, 1963 (1989)
An in-depth overview chronicling the life and death of one of this country's most beloved leaders that uses never-before-seen videotape and television news footage to provide new insights into the man and the myth. 52 min.
22-7061 *$19.99*

Two Men In Dallas (1991)
A riveting documentary on the Kennedy assassination from Mark Lane, author of "Rush to Judgement" and "Plausible Denial," that focuses on former Dallas Deputy Sheriff Roger Craig, whose eyewitness account of the incident was ignored by the Warren Commission. 60 min.
76-7050 *$29.99*

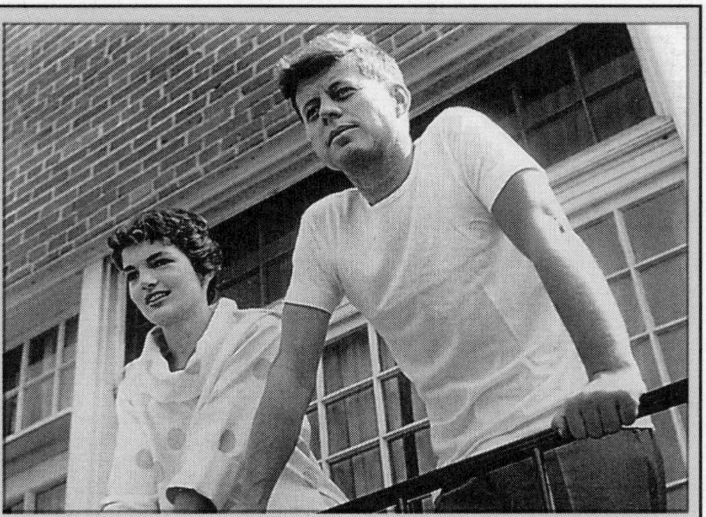

Who Killed JFK?: Facts Not Fiction (1992)
Dan Rather hosts this episode of "48 Hours" that looks at the many mysteries and conspiracy theories surrounding the assassination of President Kennedy. Among the highlights are clips from the Zapruder film, never-before-seen film footage, and interviews with such figures as Governor John Connally, Lee Harvey Oswald's widow and director Oliver Stone. 70 min.
04-2551 *$14.99*

Beyond JFK: The Question Of Conspiracy (1992)
This fascinating documentary probes many of the questions raised in the film "JFK" and presents new research on the assassination. Included are the last interview with Jim Garrison before his death; talks with witnesses and officials portrayed in the movie; a 1969 TV interview with LBJ by Walter Cronkite; and coverage of the Garrison investigation. CBS newsman Ike Pappas narrates; directed by Barbara Kopple. 90 min.
19-2028 *$19.99*

Image Of An Assassination: A New Look At The Zapruder Film (1998)
On November 22, 1963, Dallas dress manufacturer Abraham Zapruder became an accidental chronicler of one of the century's most tragic events when his 8mm home movie camera captured the shooting of President Kennedy. Now available in its entirety on home video for the first time, the controversial "Zapruder Film" has been digitally enhanced and enlarged. This special program also features interviews with Zapruder's business associates, National Archives workers and photography experts. 45 min.
50-7471 *$19.99*

Thank You, Mr. President (1983)
E.G. Marshall hosts this look at the press conferences of John F. Kennedy, the first president to truly understand the influence of television. Comments on such topics as women's rights, nuclear war, Central America and the Soviet Union seem as timely now as they were then. 45 min.
14-3053 *$12.99*

John F. Kennedy: A Celebration Of His Life And Times
The promise and the pride, the triumph and the tragedy; all are captured and relived in this unique three-tape tribute to the New Frontiersman. Return to Camelot and see "The Man Who Would Be President (1917-1956)," "The Race for the White House (1957-1960)" and "The President and the Legacy (1961-1963)." 180 min. total.
50-4067 *$69.99*

Dangerous World: The Kennedy Years
Go behind three decades of secrecy and learn about the darker side of the Kennedy White House with this ABC News special hosted by Peter Jennings. Former friends and colleagues and retired Secret Service agents discuss JFK's alleged mob ties, his extramarital affairs, and the covert war against Castro that may have led to Kennedy's assassination. 86 min.
50-7510 *$19.99*

The Kennedys: Complete Set
This acclaimed two-part series, shown on PBS' "The American Experience," takes an intimate look at one of America's most influential families, focusing on the Kennedys' rise to power, their many tragedies, and their effect on history. Included are "The Early Years" (1900-1961) and "The Later Years" (1962-1980). 240 min. total. NOTE: Individual volumes available at $19.99.
63-7039 *$39.99*

Bobby Kennedy: In His Own Words
Attorney General, U.S. senator, presidential candidate, martyr...the life and career of Robert F. Kennedy are told through home movies and archival footage in this inspiring documentary. 53 min.
44-2025 *$14.99*

Jackie Onassis: An Intimate Portrait
Her style, grace and courage made her one of America's most beloved First Ladies. Now this special documentary traces the life and times of Jacqueline Kennedy Onassis, from her storybook upbringing and the Camelot years to her final days and the 1994 funeral that made global headlines. Sharon Gless narrates. 46 min.
06-2275 *$14.99*

Jackie: Behind The Myth
The world watched and admired her through the tragedies and triumphs that marked her life, and in this moving PBS documentary you'll learn the true story behind Jackie Kennedy's public and private side through rare news and interview footage and comments from family and friends. 120 min.
90-1052 *$19.99*

The Young Kennedy Women
This salute to the distaff side of America's most famous political family offers intimate looks at the lives of Caroline Kennedy Schlossberg, Maria Shriver, Kathleen Kennedy Townsend and Kerry Kennedy Cuomo, along with Rose Kennedy, Jackie Kennedy Onassis and others. 50 min.
53-6383 *$19.99*

Hoover Dam: The Making Of A Monument
Constructed over a five-year period at the height of the Great Depression, Hoover Dam rises over 700 feet above the mighty Colorado River it was built to tame and stands as a marvel of modern engineering. Follow the project through rare newsreel footage and interviews, and learn how it changed the face of the Southwest, in this "American Experience" presentation. 60 min.
90-1014 *$19.99*

The Great Depression
Beginning with the Stock Market Crash of 1929 and for over a decade, Americans struggled to survive through the worst economic slide in the country's history. The political and social aspects of life in the Great Depression are covered in a four-volume documentary series that features photos, interviews and newsreel footage. Former New York governor Mario Cuomo hosts. 200 min. total.
53-8375 *$59.99*

Edison's Miracle Of Light
This (dare we say it?) enlightening documentary goes beyond the familiar story of Thomas Alva Edison's invention of the incandescent light, detailing how the dawn of the electric age was met with awe and, sometimes, fear, and how Edison and his General Electric Company were bogged down in a brutal business war with George Westinghouse's firm. 60 min.
63-7138 *$19.99*

Japanese Relocation/ Tale Of Two Cities
Two government-made documentaries provide insight into America's view of the Japanese during and after World War II. First is a film explaining the order that placed over 100,000 Japanese-Americans in "relocation camps," depicting people "happily complying." Next, military footage bears witness to the atomic devastation left at Hiroshima and Nagasaki. 23 min. total.
65-1024 *$29.99*

Life In The Thirties
An exhilarating look at life in the 1930s, an era rich with discovery and excitement despite the turmoil of the Great Depression. Alexander Scourby narrates this program that spans from the Crash of 1929 to 1939's New York's World Fair and includes footage of bank nights at the movies, Benny Goodman and the birth of Swing, pinball machines and bingo. 60 min.
63-7094 *$19.99*

Founding Fathers: Boxed Set (2000)
This informative four-tape set goes beyond the textbooks to explore the public and private lives of the men who founded a nation. Adams, Franklin, Jefferson, Madison: everything from their brilliance as politicians to their adulterous affairs is examined through letters and historical accounts, with readings Brian Dennehy, Burt Reynolds and James Woods. 200 min. total.
53-6998 *$39.99*

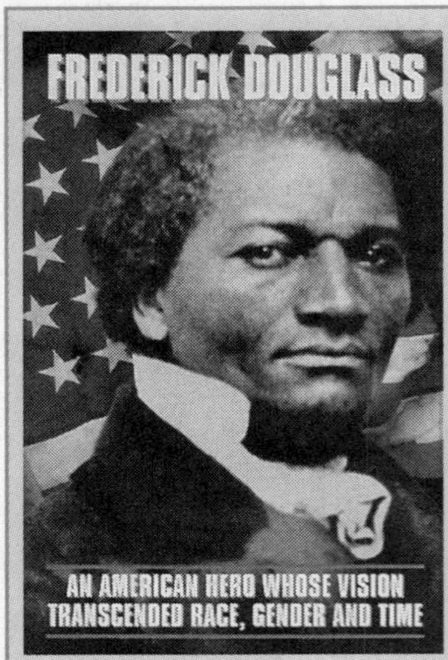
FREDERICK DOUGLASS
AN AMERICAN HERO WHOSE VISION TRANSCENDED RACE, GENDER AND TIME

Frederick Douglass: When The Lion Wrote History
He called himself a "graduate from the institution of slavery with his diploma on his back" and became a leading abolitionist speaker and spokesman for black Americans. Follow the inspiring life and career of 19th-century orator/author Frederick Douglass in this documentary narrated by Alfre Woodard and featuring Charles S. Dutton reading Douglass' words. 90 min.
18-7516 *$19.99*

Africans In America: Boxed Set
The first three centuries of the black experience in the New World—a history of servitude, suffering and an indomitable quest for freedom—are chronicled in this four-tape PBS series narrated by Angela Bassett. Volumes include "Terrible Transformation" (1562-1750), "Revolution" (1750-1805), "Brother Love" (1776-1834) and "Judgement Day" (1831-1861). 360 min. total.
50-2975 *$59.99*

Martin Luther King: I Have A Dream
Before hundreds of thousands in Washington, D.C., on August 28, 1963, Dr. Martin Luther King delivered his famous speech of brotherhood and national unity. That speech is included in this documentary that also contains scenes of the ongoing struggle for civil rights. 30 min.
50-6196 *$14.99*

Martin Luther King Commemorative Collection
His words became the fuel for a struggle that continues to this day, and he became a hero for all Americans. Dr. Martin Luther King is remembered in this special video tribute by such people as Jimmy Carter, Andrew Young, and Bill Cosby, as well as by an anthology of his most stirring speeches. 120 min.
50-6267 *$29.99*

Martin Luther King, Jr.: Legacy Of A Dream
James Earl Jones narrates this examination of the life and times of the late civil rights leader and his still-timely legacy. His insights and inspirations are brought to life in this powerful program. 30 min.
50-6861 *$14.99*

The Assassination Of Martin Luther King, Jr.
The 1968 shooting of the civil rights leader in Memphis continues to raise questions and controversy. This compelling documentary follows King's final days and his murder and looks at some of the many theories surrounding the crime. Included are interviews with King's associates and the first reporter to talk with convicted assassin James Earl Ray. 90 min.
50-7462 *$19.99*

Assassinated: The Last Days Of King And Kennedy (1998)
They were two men whose fights for justice for all Americans made them heroes in the '60s...and whose violent deaths, coming two months apart in 1968, made them martyrs. Follow the final months in the lives of Martin Luther King and Robert F. Kennedy, and see how their legacy lives on, in this compelling CNN production. 90 min.
18-7809 *$19.99*

The FBI's War On Black America
Using news footage, interviews and long-suppressed FBI documents, this powerful program uncovers J. Edgar Hoover's fear of the '60s Civil Rights movement and his plans for discrediting and defusing the "militant threat" to America. 50 min.
50-6607 *$29.99*

Malcolm X: Make It Plain
Insightful documentary on the slain African-American leader includes interviews with those who knew him intimately, including family members, politicians, members of the Nation of Islam and Mike Wallace, Maya Angelou and Alex Haley. Features rare archival footage. 136 min.
50-7303 *$29.99*

The Real Malcolm X: An Intimate Portrait Of The Man (1992)
Dan Rather hosts this look at the life and times of the charismatic, controversial civil rights leader which features never-before-seen footage of Malcolm X, excerpts from important speeches and interviews with Quincy Jones, Dick Gregory and others. 60 min.
04-2589 *$19.99*

The Voyage Of La Amistad: A Quest For Freedom
Go beyond the acclaimed Steven Spielberg movie and learn the amazing true story of a group of Africans who were sold into slavery and rebelled against their captors on the Spanish ship La Amistad in 1839. This moving documentary uses archival documents and dramatic readings by Charles Durning and Brock Peters to follow their fight to prove themselves free. Alfre Woodard narrates. 70 min.
50-7449 *$19.99*

Underground Railroad
For over 80 years tens of thousands of slaves escaped oppression in the South through a clandestine network of "stations" manned by free blacks and white abolitionists that led them North. Alfre Woodard narrates this dramatic look at the history of the Underground Railroad, and how such leaders as Frederick Douglass and Harriet Tubman risked their lives in the struggle for freedom. 100 min.
53-6419 *$19.99*

Mississippi, America (1985)
One of the most violent chapters in the story of the civil rights movement occurred during the "Freedom Summer" of 1964, when people of all colors came from across America to help Mississippi's blacks register to vote. Hear from those who took part in the campaign, often putting their lives on the line, in this compelling documentary. Narrated by Ossie Davis and Ruby Dee. 60 min.
18-7845 □*$19.99*

Flyers: In Search Of A Dream (1986)
Rare film footage and photographs and dramatic recreations are combined to tell the story of such little-known aviation pioneers as Bessie Coleman and Hubert Julian, African-American pilots who had to battle prejudice to fulfill their dreams of flight. 60 min.
18-7843 □*$19.99*

Portraits In Black (1986)
Three special programs that examine black culture and history in America are featured, including a salute to poet Paul Laurence Dunbar, 200 years of African-American art and artists, and three renowned figures: Frederick Douglass, Harriet Tubman and Denmark Vesey. 60 min.
50-3886 *$39.99*

Kennedy vs. Wallace (1989)
This updated version of the classic 1963 Robert Drew documentary "Crisis: Behind a Presidential Commitment" takes a look behind the scenes at the showdown between President John F. Kennedy and Alabama governor George Wallace over the entrance of two black students to the all-white University of Alabama. 60 min.
76-7437 *$39.99*

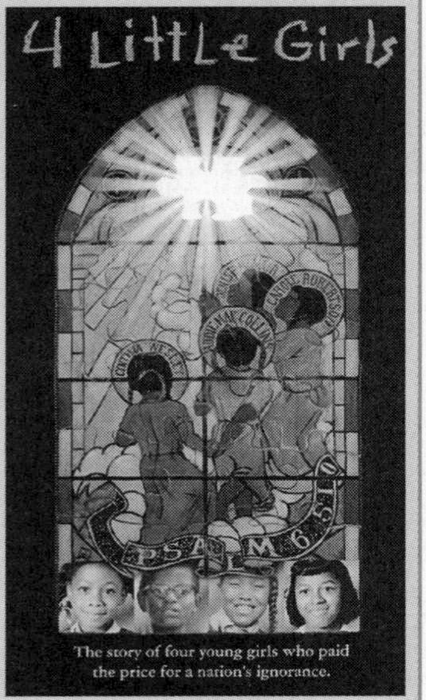
4 Little Girls
The story of four young girls who paid the price for a nation's ignorance.

4 Little Girls (1997)
Acclaimed director Spike Lee examines one of the most shocking crimes to occur in American history—the 1963 bombing of a black church in Birmingham, Alabama, that resulted in the deaths of four children attending Sunday School—in a moving documentary that earned an Academy Award nomination. Along with archival news footage, Lee talks with surviving family members and interviews Coretta Scott King, Walter Cronkite, Bill Cosby and former Alabama governor George Wallace. 102 min.
44-2170 Was $19.99 *$14.99*

Feed (1992)
The raw, unrehearsed side of presidential politics is satirically served up in a documentary by Kevin Rafferty ("The Atomic Cafe"), shot during the 1992 New Hampshire primary with extra footage from network news feeds that catches the candidates "off-camera." See George Bush reminding a TV crew he's not Dana Carvey, a shoving match between Bush and Buchanan supporters, a Gennifer Flowers press conference interrupted by Howard Stern sideman "Stuttering John" and more. 76 min.
70-5053 Was $29.99 *$19.99*

The Last Party (1993)
Filmed before the 1992 presidential election, this hip documentary relates the mood of the country's young voters as they're interviewed by Robert Downey, Jr. Also appearing are Sean Penn, Oliver Stone, Spike Lee, Mary Stuart Masterson and others. 96 min.
27-6844 Was $89.99 *$14.99*

A Perfect Candidate (1996)
The 1994 Virginia senatorial campaign that pitted incumbent Charles Robb, the object of sex and drug scandals, against Marine-turned-Iran-Contra figure Oliver North is chronicled in this acclaimed documentary from R.J. Cutler ("The War Room") and David Van Taylor, who were granted unlimited access to the candidates, their handlers and the media. 105 min.
70-5120 Was $29.99 *$19.99*

Daley: The Last Boss
Acclaimed study of Chicago mayor Richard J. Daley, who ran the city from 1955 to 1976 during some of the most difficult and controversial times in America. Using intimidation and political rewards, Daley was the last of the big city bosses, and helped to revive the national Democratic machine. Archival footage and interviews add insight into the complex man. 112 min.
22-5862 □*$19.99*

Atomic TV, Vol. I
The future is now in this technology-mad line-up of industry and informational films from the '50s and '60s. Featured are the bold predictions for a home video camera, the computerized kitchen, and a picturephone in every home by 1980. Also, the downright silly nuclear survival guide "Duck and Cover" narrated by Edward R. Murrow. 60 min.
01-9051 *$19.99*

You Can Beat The A-Bomb
Nostalgic for the "Cold War" and the constant threat of nuclear warfare? This compilation features four government-sanctioned documentaries from the '50s with hopelessly naive views on the subject. Includes the optimistic "You Can Beat the A-Bomb"; Edward R. Murrow hosting the sobering "One Plane, One Bomb"; a dramatized atomic attack in "Warning Red"; and "The House in the Middle." 60 min.
09-2170 Was $24.99 *$19.99*

Atomic Memories
Don't "duck and cover," or else you'll miss these once-sobering, now-campy films dealing with the fears of nuclear war. Along with Burt the Turtle teaching kids to hide their heads in order to survive an A-bomb explosion(!), there's "Duck and Cover," "The Effects of Atomic Bomb Explosion," "Survival under Atomic Attack," "The Atomic Dilemma: Challenge of Our Age" and "Atom Bomb Tests: Bikini." 59 min.
09-3028 *$14.99*

Atomic Scare Films
If you put only one videotape in your bomb shelter, it should be this collection of ludicrously outdated Cold War shorts dealing with nuclear war and its aftereffects. Included are "Survival Under Atomic Attack," "Duck and Cover," "American Cities Atomic Fallout Strategy," "The Atom Strikes," "You Can Beat the A-Bomb" and Civil Defense commercials.
79-6034 *$19.99*

The Doomsday Plan
How do you prepare for the unimaginable? Trace 50 years of government defense programs designed to protect America from enemy attack—whether from terrorist groups or all-out nuclear war—in this fascinating documentary that features plans ranging from the monumental to the outright silly. 45 min.
18-7810 *$19.99*

Meltdown At Three Mile Island
On March 31, 1979 central Pennsylvania's Three Mile Island generating facility was the scene of the worst nuclear mishap in the country's history, when a partial core meltdown released radioactive gas into the atmosphere. Learn how a combination of mechanical failure and human error led to the accident, and the status of the plant and nuclear power today, in this "American "Experience" presentation. 60 min.
18-7865 Was $19.99 □*$14.99*

Atomic Journeys: Welcome To Ground Zero
Think you live nowhere near a nuclear blast site? This revealing documentary takes you on a coast-to-coast tour for a look at some of the surprising places where atomic tests for "peaceful purposes" were conducted, from the Alaskan wilderness and the backwoods of Mississippi to underground gas wells in Colorado and "the most bombed place on Earth," the Nevada Test Site. William Shatner narrates. 52 min.
89-5165 *$19.99*

Atomic Attack (1950)
The typical suburban lifestyle of the Mitchell family is rudely interrupted when New York City, 50 miles away, gets bombed out of existence. The sobering, if optimistic, look at post-nuclear survival was broadcast on "The Magnavox TV Hour" and stars Phyllis Thaxter, Patty McCormack, and a young Walter Matthau as a Geiger counter-wielding doctor. 50 min.
65-1011 *$34.99*

The H-Bomb And Other Smash Hits (1951)
Five government-produced films that have taken on camp value over the years. There's "A New Look at the H-Bomb," a hilarious look at brave Americans facing radioactive fallout; "Operation Cue," about how to protect yourself from atomic blasts; "United States Civil Defense in Action" with "Duck and Cover's" Burt the Turtle; plus more. 58 min.
09-2165 Was $24.99 *$19.99*

The Unquiet Death Of Julius And Ethel Rosenberg (1974)
Award-winning, thought-provoking documentary by Alvin Goldstein probes the procedures underlying the trial of the "atomic spies" and raises serious questions as to whether the case was justly tried or colored by Cold War sentiment. 83 min.
53-9062 Was $59.99 *$29.99*

The Day After Trinity: J. Robert Oppenheimer And The Atomic Bomb (1982)
The state of the world was forever changed in the New Mexico desert on July 16, 1945. This sobering documentary look at the dawn of the Atomic Age features interviews with workers on the "Manhattan Project," rare A-bomb explosion footage, and a film discussion with Oppenheimer during his later opposition to nuclear weapons. 88 min.
50-3887 *$39.99*

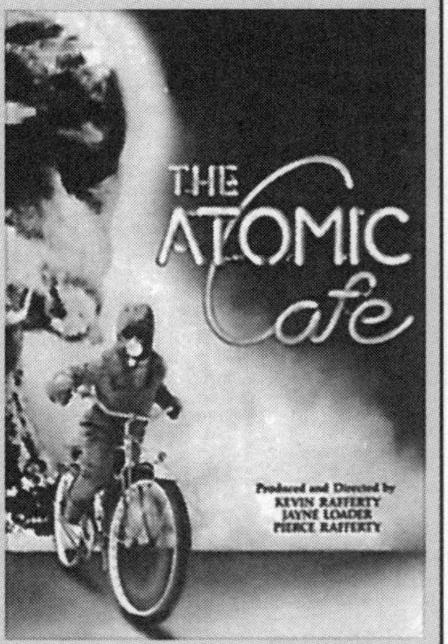
THE ATOMIC Cafe
Produced and Directed by
KEVIN RAFFERTY
JAYNE LOADER
PIERCE RAFFERTY

The Atomic Cafe (1982)
An ironic and darkly funny documentary look at the "Cold War" mentality of the '40s and '50s. U.S. government films, newsreels, contemporary songs and Hollywood clips show America's naive attitudes towards nuclear power, the A-bomb, and World War III. See children "duck and cover" to avoid fallout, tour custom-built bomb shelters, and get some sound advice from Hugh Beaumont. 88 min.
70-5052 *$29.99*

Trinity And Beyond: The Atomic Bomb Movie (1996)
Rarely-seen film footage from dozens of nuclear tests by the United States, Russia, England and China, much of it classified "top secret" for decades, was collected and restored by special effects expert Peter Kuran for this visually stunning documentary. Follow the development of the atomic bomb as you watch awe-inspiring explosions on the ground, under the seas and even in space. William Shatner narrates. 95 min.
89-5001 *$24.99*

Trinity And Beyond: The Atomic Bomb Movie (Special Director's Cut)
Also available in a special extended version that features the amazing bonus segment "Atomic Tests in 3-D" (one pair of glasses included). 120 min.
89-5216 *$24.99*

The Atomic Filmmakers: Behind The Scenes (1997)
They were the cameramen and documentarians who captured one of the most awesome sights imaginable—a nuclear explosion—on film, yet their work remained a government secret for decades. Now "Trinity and Beyond" producer Peter Kuran brings to light the story of these dedicated filmmakers and their top-secret Hollywood studio and presents amazing A-bomb footage. 50 min.
89-5056 *$19.99*

Waco:
The Rules Of Engagement (1997)
Nominated for an Academy Award for Best Documentary, this controversial feature chronicles the 1993 stand-off in Waco, Texas, between the Branch Davidian cultists led by David Koresh and federal agents from the FBI and ATF. Director William Gazecki uses interviews and footage from congressional hearings and newsreels to examine the events that led to more than 80 deaths. 136 min.
76-7402 *$29.99*

Crime

Terrorism: A World In Shadows
The dark and dangerous world of terrorism is surveyed in this fascinating and frightening seven-part series. Included are "Series Preview," a historical overview; "Ethnic Terrorism"; "Religious Terrorism"; "Ideological Terrorism"; "State-Sponsored Terrorism"; "Genocide: The Ultimate Terrorism" and "Future Terrorism and Counter Terrorism." 385 min. total.
16-5016 *$49.99*

Murder By Number:
Inside The Serial Killers
What makes a person want to kill again and again? This compelling CNN documentary examines the rise in serial murders and their impact on American society through news footage and interviews with the killers, their families and psychologists, and the relatives of their victims. 116 min.
18-7430 Was $19.99 *$14.99*

Secrets Of The Rock:
Return To Alcatraz
It opened in 1933 as an "escape-proof" prison for the country's most dangerous criminals, and Al Capone, "Machine Gun" Kelly and "Birdman" Robert Stroud at various times all called it home. Learn what life on "The Rock" was like from accounts of inmates and guards, hear about the most infamous escape attempts, and tour the island today. 60 min.
50-2940 *$19.99*

Public Enemies Of The '20s & '30s
An exciting overview of the notorious men (and women) who made the Roaring Twenties roar offers portraits of such personalities as Capone, Dillinger, Floyd, Kelly, Schultz, Bonnie and Clyde and others. Rare photographs and archival footage help detail their law-breaking legacies. AKA: "The Real Stories of Al Capone, John Dillinger and Bonnie & Clyde." 75 min.
50-2813 Was $29.99 *$19.99*

When Cops Attack (1998)
Police all over the United States have one of the toughest tasks imaginable: keeping the streets safe. Now, some of their most violent arrests have been documented on this two-tape set. From daring chases and knock-down brawls to police dog attacks, you decide whether the men and women in blue step "over the line." 90 min.
64-3442 *$12.99*

Summer Of Terror:
The Real Son Of Sam Story
He held the country's largest city in a grip of fear during a year-long killing spree before his arrest in 1977. Now hear from convicted "Son of Sam" killer David Berkowitz, as well as the detectives who captured him and the doctors who examined him, in this compelling real-life mystery. 49 min.
50-7553 *$19.99*

Dealers In Death
Broderick Crawford hosts this look at the violent and colorful history of America's gangsters. Photos and rare footage recount the lives of such infamous figures as Bonnie and Clyde, Al Capone, John Dillinger and others. 60 min.
50-6022 *$19.99*

Jack The Ripper:
The Final Solution
Using new evidence, this program examines the case of Jack the Ripper, the infamous killer who terrorized the East End of London in 1888. The conspiracy theories, the victims, the gory murders, the Royal Family...all this and more are covered, along with "Saucy Jack's" possible true identity. 50 min.
22-1406 *$19.99*

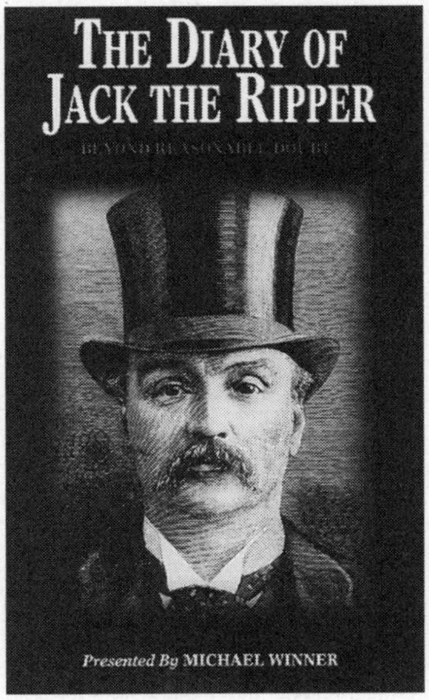

The Diary Of
Jack The Ripper (1993)
He held a city in a grip of fear in the late 1880s, and to this day who he was remains a mystery. Through historical accounts and readings from the killer's fictionalized diary, this compelling documentary chronicles Jack the Ripper's reign of terror and offers surprising theories as to his true identity. 65 min.
50-5623 *$19.99*

American Gangsters:
The Promised Land
The roots of American gangsterdom are uncovered in this look at how immigrants got involved in criminal activities after they discovered that the "American Dream" was not always fair to them. 52 min.
27-7334 *$14.99*

The Rise And
Fall Of The Mafia: Complete Set
This three-tape series offers a survey of the inner workings of the Mob. "Speak No Evil" looks at the downfall of the Mafia in the 1980s and 1990s and features segments of John Gotti's secret tapes; "Vow of Silence" follows wise guys who turned informant; and "The Pizza Connection" gets the dope on an international drug ring. 156 min. total. NOTE: Individual volumes available at $14.99 each.
27-7333 Save $5.00! *$39.99*

Lords Of The Mafia: Set
They've climbed the organized crime ladder rung by bloody rung, and now the true stories behind the world's most dangerous mobsters can be told in this six-tape series. Surveillance and expert interviews reveal how their empires of greed, violence and power were built. Included are "Britain/Sicily," "Japan/China," "Los Angeles/Vietnam," "Mexico/Colombia," "New York/New Orleans" and "Russia/Jamaica." Robert Stack hosts. 720 min. total. NOTE: Individual volumes available at $14.99 each.
50-8589 Save $15.00! *$74.99*

Mafia: An Exposé: Boxed Set
This 10-tape series uses archival footage and rare photos to trace the history of the Mob in America. Included in the boxed set are "Coming to America," "Al Capone," "Valachi-Luciano-Gallo," "Hollywood," "Vegas," "Hoffa," "The Kennedy Connection," "Gallo-Colombo-Bonnano," "Gotti" and "Resumé." 600 min. total. NOTE: Individual volumes available at $14.99 each.
72-3012 Save $50.00! *$99.99*

The American Gangster (1992)
This chronicle of the history of organized crime in America features thrilling newsreel footage and fascinating profiles of such legendary public enemies as Al Capone, Bugsy Siegel, John Dillinger, Lucky Luciano and others. Dennis Farina ("Crime Story") narrates. 45 min.
02-2215 *$14.99*

Don't Call Me Bugsy! (1992)
This is the real story of Benjamin "Bugsy" Siegel, the gangster depicted by Warren Beatty on the big screen. Using candid interviews, authentic footage and photographs, this program tells the tale of the man who went from the tough streets of New York to the mansions of Hollywood and the Flamingo Hotel in Las Vegas. 70 min.
50-6959 *$19.99*

Mafia
The History of the Mob in America

Mafia: The History Of
The Mob In America (1993)
This chronicle of the Mafia and its power in America offers inside information and rare footage to paint a harrowing picture of crime and violence. The four-part series includes "The Prohibition Years/Birth of the American Mafia," "The Kennedys and the Mob," "Unions and the Mob" and "Empire of Crime." Narrated by Bill Kurtis. 250 min. total.
53-7858 *$59.99*

Justice Factory: Boxed Set
Produced with teen audiences in mind but perfect for all ages, this 13-part series takes viewers on a comprehensive tour through the American legal system to show how each aspect of it works. Volumes include "The Assistant District Attorney/The Public Defender," "Judges/Juries and the Jury Selection Expert," "Arrest & Representation/Punishment for Teen Offenders," "Mock Trials/Environmental Law/Teens in Prison" and more. 390 min. on six tapes.
14-9170 *$119.99*

Charles Manson And The Boston
Strangler: The Untold Story
Their heinous crimes shocked America in the '60s, and their very names have become synonymous with murder and mayhem. Rare film footage highlights this look at the Tate/LaBianca slayings and Albert DeSalvo's reign of terror.
50-6363 *$14.99*

Serial Killers:
Profiling The Criminal Mind
This four-tape set includes fascinating and frightening profiles of some of the world's most notorious mass murderers. Interviews, police files and archival footage tell the stories of Charles Manson, Jeffrey Dahmer, John Wayne Gacy and criminal profilers, those who track down the killers. 200 min. total. NOTE: Individual volumes available at $14.99 each.
53-6576 *$39.99*

American Justice
Superb study of the crimes that changed the face of the American justice system in which the methods, motives and madness of murderers are revealed in terrifying, provocative fashion. Included are sequences on the Lindbergh Kidnapping, Lucky Luciano, Al Capone, the Jonestown Massacre, the Boston Strangler, Son of Sam, the Manson Family, Ted Bundy, Gary Gilmore, John Wayne Gacy, John Dillinger, the Hillside Strangler and Dr. Sam Shepherd. This four-tape set runs 420 min.
53-7874 *$99.99*

Court TV: The Nanny Murder Trial:
Massachusetts vs. Woodward
One of the biggest legal stories of 1997 was the trial of 19-year-old British au pair Louise Woodward for killing an infant left in her care. This "Court TV" special presents the highlights of the case, the jury's conviction of Woodward on second-degree murder charges, and the judge's controversial decision to lesson the charge to manslaughter and set her free. 50 min.
53-9914 *$14.99*

Miami S.W.A.T.
Forget the movies and television fiction; this documentary puts you on the frontline with Miami's Special Weapons and Tactics police unit. Watch as they use their high-tech equipment and combat-style tactics to bring down a drug dealer's heavily armed stronghold. Narrated by Andre Braugher. 52 min.
27-7203 *$14.99*

Murder Of The Century
Nearly 90 years before the O.J. Simpson trial, all of America was fascinated with the 1906 New York murder of noted architect Stanford White by Pittsburgh railroad heir Harry K. Thaw, the culmination of their rivalry over the affections of showgirl and "Gibson Girl" model Evelyn Nesbit. See how Thaw's trial and the details of the "love triangle" captivated the nation and fueled the tabloid newspaper industry. 60 min.
63-7137 *$19.99*

L.A. Gang Violence
Disturbing look at gang violence in the City of Angels, featuring gory footage of its victims unlike anything you've seen before. 82 min.
78-3010 *$14.99*

Al Capone:
The Untouchable Legend
His name has become synonymous with organized crime and the wild days of the "Roaring Twenties." Now learn the true story of Alphonse "Al" Capone, from his Brooklyn boyhood and the fight that led to his "Scarface" nickname, to his reign as the king of Chicago's mobs, to his tax evasion trial and final days. Rare film footage, interviews with family and Capone experts, and more are featured. 52 min.
81-3011 *$19.99*

Brother's Keeper (1992)
Highly praised real-life mystery focusing on the murder of Bill Ward, one of four eccentric siblings who lived together in a crumbling shack in rural New York State for 60 years. After authorities discovered Bill's death, his younger brother, Delbert, admitted to killing him in an act of mercy, but rescinded his confession not long after. 104 min.
53-7790 Was $89.99 *$19.99*

Heidi Fleiss:
Hollywood Madam (1995)
Engrossing documentary on the infamous Hollywood call girl ring operator and her bizarre group of associates, which included Ivan Nagy, a producer and ex-boyfriend; Madam Alex, her money-hustling mentor; and Victoria Sellers, a close friend and daughter of Peter Sellers. Directed by Nick Bromfield ("Aileen Wuornos: The Selling of a Serial Killer"). 106 min.
02-8461 Was $19.99 *$14.99*

No Mothers Crying,
No Babies Dying (1999)
In this powerful documentary, the impact of gang violence on mothers of the victims is explored. Real documentary footage is mixed with re-enactments of street crimes to tell the harrowing story. with Danny Trejo, Lupe Ontiveros and Mike Moroff. 90 min.
50-8447 *$39.99*

THE FARM
Life Inside
ANGOLA PRISON

The Farm:
Life Inside Angola Prison (1998)
A Sundance favorite and winner of several critics' awards, this sobering look at one of America's most notorious maximum-security penitentiaries—Louisiana's Angola Prison—tracks a year in the lives of six inmates coping with life behind bars, from a convict whose religious work helped lead to his parole to a terminally ill murderer. 100 min.
50-5629 *$24.99*

Mumia: A Case For
Reasonable Doubt? (1996)
This documentary traces one of the nation's most controversial courtroom struggles, telling the story of Philadelphia journalist and activist Mumia Abu-Jamal, who was convicted and sentenced to death in the 1981 murder of city policeman Daniel Faulkner. Questions about the shooting and alleged racism in the trial have prompted such celebrities as Paul Newman and Ed Asner to come to Abu-Jamal's defense. 74 min.
53-8896 Was $59.99 *$19.99*

Unexplained Phenomena

The Incredible Life And
Times Of Robert Ripley:
Believe It Or Not! (1994)
For decades he brought Americans the weird and fantastic in newspapers, on the radio and in the movies with his "Believe It or Not." Now Robert Ripley comes back to Earth to share with a young fan his colorful life and experiences in this entertaining mix of documentary footage and dramatization. Richard Portnow, Jason Marsden star. 95 min.
18-7492 *$12.99*

The Amazing World Of Ghosts
This in-depth documentary surveys the world of ghosts and offers startling discoveries about the spooky subject. Are they stale myths or real entities? 94 min.
08-1581 *$14.99*

True Tales Of
America's Haunted Houses
Explore some of America's most intriguing haunted houses in this incredible program. A murdered slave girl wanders Myrtles Plantation in Louisiana, a red-coat spy appears in New York's Raynham Hall, and other restless spirits are visited in Old Salem and California. 100 min.
53-8652 *$19.99*

Hauntings Across America
If you thought ghosts and haunted houses were only part of movies and TV, this video will make you a believer. Take a scary excursion to an airplane hangar in Kansas haunted by a dead pilot; travel to the South, where a mansion has been haunted by a "little girl lost" since the Civil War; and witness incredible footage and photos.
85-7000 *$19.99*

Spirits Of The Deep
The occult and the sea have been linked for ages, and this program examines the connection, following stories of witchcraft and superstition from Japan to Brazil and from Baja California to the Red Sea. 92 min.
08-1599 *$14.99*

THE UNEXPLAINED

The Unexplained
From modern-day cannibals to miraculous cures, there are occurrences out there that can't be explained...or can they? This intriguing series from A&E sheds light on the things that have been chalked up to science fiction or delusions of grandeur. Each tape runs about 50 min. There are eight volumes available, including:

The Unexplained: Cannibals
53-6241 *$14.99*

The Unexplained:
Prophets And Doom
53-6242 *$14.99*

The Unexplained:
The Vampire Myths
53-6465 *$14.99*

The Lash Of The Penitentes (1936)
A precursor to the "Mondo"-style documentary, following the religious rites of a small sect of Indians living in New Mexico. See actual floggings and self-mutilations, the burial of a live rooster, and other strange practices filmed "at the risk of the cameramen's lives." NOTE: This 35-minute version is the only print currently available of this rare find.
09-1992 $19.99

Bowanga, Bowanga (1941)
"1,000 Adventures! 10,000 Dangers!" Who knows how much fake footage? This bogus African shockumentary has it all: gals running around in leopard-skin suits, white hunters drawing the attention of jungle sirens, gorillas running rampant and native dances that look like they're in the Dallas Cowboy Cheerleaders repertoire. Only two words describe the action: "Bowanga, Bowanga."
79-5499 Was $24.99 $19.99

Wild Rapture (1950)
The original African shockumentary, shot in the Congo by 12 French scientists. Ritual hunting, elephant slicing, lion-killing and many other gory practices not intended for the faint of heart. 68 min.
62-1278 Was $29.99 $14.99

Mau Mau (1954)
Electrifying Africa explodes with naked terror in this mondo documentary on the weird customs of the "dark continent," and to make matters interesting (and more profitable), the creators added studio-shot footage. See frenzied terrorists in blood-drinking ceremonies! Witness secret killer societies! Watch naked native women! Enjoy Chet Huntley's narration! 53 min.
79-5345 Was $24.99 $19.99

Cannibal Island (1956)
Incredible documentary footage of savage Pacific island tribes that "was used by the U.S. government for valuable secret war information(!)" See man-hungry cannibals, scalp-happy headhunters, women being traded for pigs, blood, gore and more. 60 min.
39-1815 $19.99

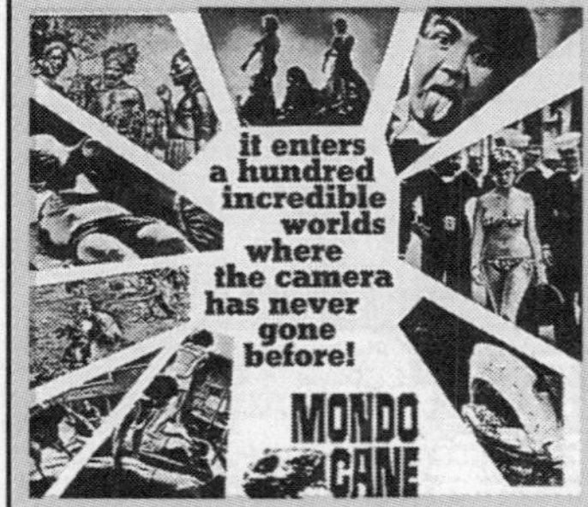

Mondo Cane (1963)
The one...the only...the original! This is an incredible documentary chronicle of the macabre and gruesome customs of the people of the world. Strange delicacies, violent rituals...you name it, it's here in this incredible movie, not recommended for the faint of heart. Includes the Academy Award-nominated hit song "More." 90 min.
50-1170 $19.99

Ecco (1963)
George Sanders narrates this "mondo" documentary that inspired the likes of "Mondo Cane." Among the subjects covered are the last performance of the Paris Grand Guignol, a man who sticks needles into his chest, people watching a couple having sex on a car in Sweden, and lots more. 98 min.
79-5305 $19.99

Mondo Pazzo (1963)
This sequel to the cult shockumentary looks at some of the world's weirdest customs with unsettling authenticity. There's human pincushions, cops in drag, bloody magazine models and more grotesque sequences. Features a theme song by "The Legend," Steve Rossi. AKA: "Mondo Cane 2." This is the complete 95-minute version.
79-5325 Was $24.99 $19.99

Slave Trade In The World Today (1964)
Raw and primitive, this film was shot secretly so the filmmakers wouldn't be sentenced to death. See sheiks' harems, girls being shipped and smuggled around the world; practices that have been banned in almost every civilized country...we thought! This is a shocker for discriminating viewers only! 88 min.
50-1171 $19.99

Mondo Balardo (1964)
Boris Karloff narrates this essential "mondo-mentary" that features transvestites, lesbian bars, native rituals, Hercules movies, Japanese bondage, a man who claims to be the reincarnation of Rudolph Valentino, and other weird, way-out subjects. 86 min.
79-5293 $19.99

Kwaheri (1965)
The ad campaign for this mondo documentary look at African wildlife and strange native customs said it all: "SEE the burning of a virgin! SEE power of witch doctor over women! SEE pygmies with fantastic Physical Endowments!!!" And, as if that weren't enough, "SEE 400 Elephants slaughtered for their 800 Tusks!" 80 min.
75-7202 $19.99

Witchdoctor In Tails (1966)
In the graphic tradition of "Mondo Cane" comes this brutal and fascinating look at strange customs from around the globe. Snake charmers, firewalkers, abattoir workers, tribal shamans and other offbeat types are seen defying death, loving death, and embracing the bizarre. Narrated by George Sanders. 96 min.
53-7510 $29.99

Mondo Bizarro (1966)
Sordid schlockumentary from schlockmeisters Lee Frost and Bob Cresse offers all sorts of outrageous "real" events. Witness people laying on beds of nails, getting whipped, being auctioned off, changing into lingerie and more! 80 min.
79-5484 $19.99

Mondo Freudo (1966)
Shocking rituals! Naked women! Incredible sights! This ultra-brutal "mondo movie" features a Japanese club where people are really clubbed, a young virgin's involvement in the Black Mass, the auction of women in a Mexican city and much, much more! AKA: "The Sensual Taboo." 75 min.
79-5133 $19.99

Malamondo (1966)
The secrets of "The Thrill Generation" are exposed in this shockumentary in the tradition of "Mondo Cane." Motorcyclists compete for women, male skiers seek more than slopes, French high-schoolers play a dangerous elevator game called "chicken," and French military cadets partake in a strange dance called "The Madison." Music by Ennio Morricone.
79-5806 $19.99

Africa Blood And Guts (1970)
Amazing documentary on the customs and brutality of Africa, the mystery continent. Scenes so bizarre, so savage that you'll cringe. For adults only! From the makers of "Mondo Cane." This film is a re-edited version of 1966's "Africa Addio." 80 min.
50-1181 $19.99

Mondo Magic (1972)
A graphic, never-before-seen look at bizarre, brutal occult practices throughout the world. From human "pin cushions" and cannibalistic feasts to grisly eye-plucking and virgin-testing ceremonies, viewers are subjected to a chilling array of real-life horrors. "WARNING: The grotesque nature of this film warrants that it be seen by mature audiences only." AKA: "Naked Magic." 90 min.
69-1064 $19.99

Shocking Asia (1975)
The mysterious East is home to strange and gory customs that no visitor may ever see, but this incredible "Mondo"-type travelogue is your ticket to these hidden worlds. See erotic tattooing practices, self-torture cults, the skinning of live bats and snakes and much more, all shocking and all real! WARNING: Not for the children or weak-hearted. 80 min.
69-1065 $29.99

That's Offensive
Welcome to the "mondo" world of this video filled with the wildest and most politically incorrect events ever captured on film. There's tots smoking cigars and drinking beer, a human dartboard, watermelon-eating and tobacco-spitting contests, human oddities, real "catfighting" and lots more insensitive material. 27 min.
73-9246 $19.99

Jaws Of The Jungle/ Beasts Of The Jungle/ Adventures In The Jungle
Wild triple-feature of jungle documentaries from the 1930s featuring topless natives, strange rituals, rampages and stock footage you've seen in countless Africa adventures.
79-5712 $19.99

Executions (1994)
A sensation in England, this no-nonsense look at capital punishment will frighten and fascinate viewers at the same time. The history of violent acts towards man—from stonings and beheadings to shootings and the electric chair—are chronicled with archival footage. Are executions humane? You decide...after watching this powerful, not-for-the-squeamish program. 55 min.
82-5008 $79.99

Strange Science: Complete Set
An "almanac of the strange and the unusual," this five-part series takes you to the frontiers of study of such offbeat topics as psychic powers, weird weather, sea monsters and more. Included are "Bizarre Phenomena," "Mysterious Skies," "Odd Sounds," "Unusual People" and "Weird Places." 300 min. total. NOTE: Individual volumes available at $19.99 each.
83-1455 $99.99

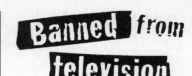

Banned from television

Banned From Television, Vol. 1 (Special Edition)
Deemed too outrageous and disturbing for TV, these real-life events are sure to shock just about everyone. But here they are, collected on a tape for your amazement. There's a great white shark attack, a public execution, a sex club bust and distressing accidents. WARNING: Not for the squeamish; adults only! 60 min.
50-5910 $24.99

Banned From Television, Vol. 2
The censors clipped them from TV, but now you can catch this compilation of wild moments captured on tape. There's an FBI drug bust gone wrong, a pit bull attack, horrifying accidents and the infamous Tonya Harding-Jeff Gillooly wedding video. WARNING: Not for the squeamish; adults only! 45 min.
50-5911 $19.99

Banned From Television, Vol. 3
There's video surveillance sharpshooters, a hostage standoff, a preacher who attempts a strip show and lots of other banned footage in store on this no-holds-barred collection of TV no-nos. WARNING: Not for the squeamish; adults only! 45 min.
50-5996 $19.99

Banned From Television: Set
Volumes 1, 2 and 3 are also available in a collector's set.
50-7582 Save $25.00! $39.99

Banned From Television: The Prison Files
This footage can't be shown elsewhere because it's so shocking. Go behind bars to see what really goes down in the slammer! Not for the squeamish, the video offers uncensored and harrowing moments you won't forget! 59 min.
50-8179 $14.99

In The Grip Of Evil (1997)
Leading experts in the field of psychology and theology lend their insights into the subjects of demonic possession and exorcism and how such beliefs relate to contemporary times. Featured is an exploration of the 1949 exorcism of a 13-year-old boy which was the basis for "The Exorcist," as well as other incidents. 50 min.
53-8913 Was $19.99 $14.99

The Vampire Interviews
Sink your teeth into this documentary look at vampirism in fact and fiction. Learn about the legends of the "living dead," follow Hollywood's fascination with vampires through film clips and rare interviews with Bela Lugosi, Christopher Lee and Peter Cushing, and even hear from "real-life" bloodsuckers as they search for acceptance and a good meal. 60 min.
15-5308 $12.99

Vampires
Frightening and factual look at vampires featuring a trip to Transylvania, "eyewitness" accounts of corpses with pulses, graves where no vegetation will grow and other unexplained phenomena. Other vampire sightings are followed in China, Greece and the U.S. 50 min.
53-7983 Was $24.99 $19.99

Vampires: Thirst For The Truth
Explore the undying (no pun intended) fascination with vampires in folklore and pop culture with this compelling documentary. Follow bloodsucker lore and their place in films and music, and hear from such experts as Bela Lugosi, Jr., Maila (Vampira) Nurmi and Lara Parker. William Marshall ("Blacula") narrates. 100 min.
83-1330 $19.99

The Legend Of Loch Ness
The wondrous history of the Loch Ness Monster is chronicled in this program that includes a search for the legendary creature. Also included is a sighting from a submarine. Arthur Franz narrates. 92 min.
08-1586 $14.99

Loch Ness Discovered
The world's most famous "lost" creature, "Nessie" has eluded hunters, scientists and the curious for centuries. Travel to Scotland as you follow researchers using the latest underwater photography and high-tech equipment to track down the aquatic enigma, and hear theories on the monster's true identity. 60 min.
27-7195 $14.99

Doomsday: Boxed Set
What lies in store for Earth at the dawn of the new millennium, and does the key to the future lie in the prophecies of centuries past? This two-tape series examines such topics as the Egyptian Pyramids, the lost continent of Atlantis, "sleeping prophet" Edgar Cayce and others, exploring predictions of imminent destruction or a new "golden age." Volumes include "Knocking at Doomsday's Door" and "Prophecy and Prediction: Threat or Warning?" 137 min. total. NOTE: Individual volumes available at $19.99.
53-6629 Save $10.00! $29.99

Incredible Mysteries Of Our Planet: Boxed Set
This three-tape collection takes you around the world in search of man-made, natural and supernatural phenomena. Learn if the wonders of an ancient civilization lie under the waves in "Atlantis: In Search of a Lost Continent"; see where ships and planes have vanished in "Bermuda Triangle: Secrets Revealed"; and examine evidence of ancient astronauts in "Chariots of the Gods: The Mysteries Continue." 140 min. total. NOTE: Individual volumes available at $19.99 each.
50-2933 Save $10.00! ❑$49.99

Death: The Ultimate Mystery
The face of death is prominent in this harrowing documentary narrated by Cameron Mitchell. Included are painstaking hospital surgery scenes, ghoulish mummies and more gruesome footage. Not for the squeamish! 97 min.
08-1490 Was $29.99 $19.99

Death: The Trip Of A Lifetime: Complete Set
"The undiscovered country" that everyone visits sooner or later is surveyed through stops at 12 countries to probe people's beliefs, customs and rituals regarding dying and the afterlife. Hosted by Greg Palmer, this compelling four-tape series examines the foreboding and often-forbidden topic with reverence and wit. 220 min. total. NOTE: Individual volumes available at $29.99 each.
14-9104 Save $20.00! $99.99

Death: The Ultimate Horror
In the tradition of the "Faces of Death" series comes this gruesome look at death featuring uncut footage of executions, bombings, assassinations and lots more. Not for the squeamish, this unsettling video takes you beyond the door of disturbing and into the realm of...well, find out for yourself! 90 min.
46-8011 $79.99

Snuff Perversions: Bizarre Cases Of Death
This cavalcade of disturbing footage includes all sorts of horrifying deaths and is certainly not for the squeamish. There are impalings, shootings, beatings and more, all collected one tape not for the timid. The footage was reportedly found in a Kentucky farmhouse (also not for the faint of heart). WARNING: adults only! 80 min.
73-9297 $19.99

The Coroner's Camera
Move over "Faces of Death"—here's a no-holds-barred bonanza of bodies from the files of coroners, pathologists and medical examiners. Their subjects are victims of murder, suicide, airplane crashes, animal attacks and car wrecks. This cavalcade of cadavers is purportedly all real and uncensrored, so, if you're not squeamish, "enjoy"! 90 min.
73-9317 $39.99

Of The Dead (1979)
See: an actual cremation! See: in vivid, bloody detail, a team of doctors working on a victim of multiple stab wounds! See: funeral and embalming practices from all over the globe! A truly terrifying look into the final terror in the gruesome tradition of "Faces of Death." WARNING: Not for the squeamish. Uncut, unrated 104-minute version. AKA: "Des Morts."
50-6055 $14.99

Bigfoot
Call it "Yeti," "Sasquatch" or just plain "Bigfoot." By any name it has intrigued scientists and others since 1884. What is the truth behind the ominous ape-like creature? Using famous and not-so famous footage of alleged sightings, computer analysis and modern technology, some of the long-time mysteries of the legend are revealed in this fascinating program. 50 min.
53-8014 Was $24.99 $19.99

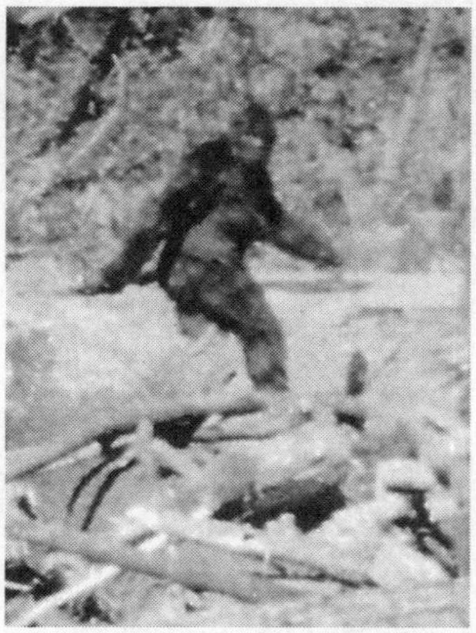

The Legend Of Bigfoot (1975)
He's out there, and he's on a rampage, eating humans for breakfast! A small town in turmoil struggles to track down the legendary beast that just won't quit. Don't go outside without a shotgun. This Sunn Classics-styled pseudo-documentary mixes nature footage and legendary film and more. AKA: "Bigfoot: Man or Beast." 92 min.
55-3024 $19.99

Life After Death: Complete Set
It's the ultimate destination, and it remains mankind's ultimate mystery. Join author and host Tom Harpur for a compelling and revealing five-volume investigation into the theories, beliefs and alleged accounts of what happens after death. Episodes include "The Near Death Experience/Contact With the Beyond," "Children and Dying/Dreams of the Dying," "Visions of Hell/Visions of Heaven," "Reincarnation/The Testimony of Science" and "Nobody's Getting Out of Here Alive/The Conclusion." 300 min. total. NOTE: Individual volumes available at $19.99 each.
53-9873　　　Save $20.00!　　　$79.99

There And Back: Interviews With Near-Death Experiences
The personal accounts of four different people who have survived near-death experiences are the focus of this powerful program. See how these people have glimpsed "the other side" following such events as near-fatal accidents at birth to car crashes. 75 min.
73-9230　　　　　　　　　　$39.99

The Secrets Of Magic & Illusion
In the interest of saving face in the professional community, a world-class magician has donned a mask to reveal to you how seven classic stage illusions are actually performed. The Chinese linking rings, the lady-tiger switch, sawing a person in half and other feats of prestidigitation will be secrets no longer. 52 min.
04-1986　　　Was $29.99　　　□$19.99

The World's Most Dangerous Magic
Forget pulling fluffy little bunnies out of hats; these are some of the scariest, most death-defying stunts ever captured on video! Watch as Roger Gallup falls 150 feet bound and gagged; Dean Gunnarson is suspended high over Hoover Dam; Steve Wyrick walks through the spinning blades of a jet turbine engine; and more. 91 min.
68-1964　　　　　　　　　　$14.99

Houdini
His name has become synonymous with magic and death-defying escapes, and this revealing program uses rare film clips and interviews with associates and historians to tell Harry Houdini's story. See segments on his greatest stunts and learn more about his mysterious life...and death. 61 min.
83-1101　　　　　　　　　　$19.99

The Art Of Magic
The illusory art of legerdemain is thoroughly explored in this PBS program which traces its history from its beginnings in ancient times to the current revival of interest in magic. Caligostro, Houdini, Blackstone, and even Siegfried and Roy are among the legendary mages spotlighted. 150 min.
90-1004　　　　　　　　　　□$29.99

Mysteries Of Magic: Boxed Set
They've been feared, worshipped and admired for centuries. Now you can trace the history of magicians and the evolution of their art with this three-tape documentary series that uncovers the secrets behind many of their most amazing—and dangerous—illusions. Volumes include "Death Defying Feats," "The Impossible Made Possible" and "Masters of Mystery." 156 min. total. NOTE: Individual volumes available at $14.99 each.
83-1371　　　Save $10.00!　　　$34.99

ASK ABOUT OUR GIANT DVD CATALOG!

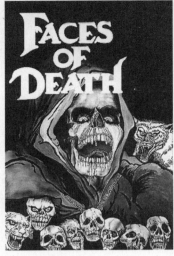

Faces Of Death
The greatest mystery of all, Death, is explored in graphic detail in these brutal and violent documentaries. Look in on autopsy rooms, prison death rows, German Autobahn casualties, wedding party massacres, daredevils who risk (and lose) their lives, and much more. WARNING: Contains graphic footage. Not recommended for the young or weak of heart!

Faces Of Death
15-9046　　　Was $29.99　　　$19.99

Faces Of Death II
15-9047　　　Was $29.99　　　$19.99

Faces Of Death III
15-9048　　　Was $29.99　　　$19.99

Faces Of Death IV
15-9049　　　Was $29.99　　　$19.99

Faces Of Death V
50-7551　　　　　　　　　　$19.99

Faces Of Death VI
50-7552　　　　　　　　　　$19.99

The Worst Of Faces Of Death
An amalgam of atrocities taken from the "Faces of Death" series. Incredible deaths, dismemberments and disgusting situations are captured for the camera and available for your pleasure. WARNING: Truly upsetting and gory, this tape is not for youngsters or faint-hearted folk. 60 min.
15-9050　　　Was $29.99　　　$19.99

Faces Of Death: Boxed Set
If you're into death and gore, this is the perfect gift: a set of the first four "Faces of Death" films plus "The Worst of Faces of Death."
15-9053　　　　　　　　　　$99.99

Faces Of Death: Collector's Set
If you're into death, gore, violence and saving money, you'll want this special collection featuring all six outrageous "Faces of Death" films.
50-7565　　　Save $20.00!　　　$99.99

Faces Of Death: Fact Or Fiction
At last...the truth about the notorious "Faces of Death" films is revealed in this real-life look into the phenomenon that shocked the world. Find out from the series' creator and director whether some of the films' most notorious scenes were simulated. Also includes a "Faces of Death" music video and shocking footage uncovered in the video company's vaults. 60 min.
50-7555　　　　　　　　　　$19.99

The Strange And The Gruesome
Producers claim that everything—and they mean EVERYTHING!—on this tape is real, and once you witness the disturbing images here, you're not likely to disagree. Surgeries, mutilations and more are offered in this collection of heinous sights culled from travelogues, medical training films and more. From the fine folks who gave you "Faces of Death." 54 min.
50-7556　　　　　　　　　　$19.99

Mummies: Frozen In Time
The faces of the past stare back at you as you watch this fascinating Discovery Channel documentary that traces the history of preserving the dead, whether by accidental (Ice Age bodies in Greenland and Europe's Bog People) or deliberate (Mexico's eerie Museo de los Momias and hi-tech cryogenic experiments) means. 50 min.
27-7221　　　　　　　　　　$14.99

Mummies: The Real Story
If you think mummies were solely a product of ancient Egypt, think again! This documentary examines the worldwide practice of mummification as a way of getting ready for the afterlife, as well as the gruesome details of preparing a body, and offers a look at some modern-day practitioners. 52 min.
27-7222　　　　　　　　　　$14.99

Secrets Of The Dead: Set
Startling new evidence regarding some of the world's biggest catastrophes is revealed in this four-tape set. Included are "Catastrophe!," about methods scientists use to look into the past; "What Happened to the Hindenburg?," featuring a new theory on the tragedy; "The Lost Vikings," which links religion to the end of the Vikings; and "Cannibalism in the Canyon," a look at the lost world of the Anasazi. 300 min. total. NOTE: Individual titles available at $19.99 each.
90-1109　　　Save $20.00!　　　$59.99

Nostradamus: His Life And Prophecies
Michel de Nostradame made some of the most frighteningly accurate predictions in history, proclaiming correctly the French Revolution and the fall of Napoleon, the assassination of JFK, the collapse of the Third Reich, and many other natural catastrophes. This program examines his many predictions, as well as what may happen during the next millennium. 60 min.
65-7001　　　　　　　　　　$19.99

The Man Who Saw Tomorrow (1981)
Orson Welles narrates this documentary looking at the life of Nostradamus, the 16th-century occultist and seer whose prophecies have astounded believers and skeptics for centuries. Did he actually foresee America's rise to power, Napoleon and Hitler, World Wars I and II and, ultimately, Armageddon? 88 min.
19-1488　　　　　　　　　　$19.99

Nazi UFOs & The Illuminati Conspiracy
Did the Nazis really develop saucer-shaped aircraft in the final days of World War II? Was there a joint German/Japanese mission to Mars? And how are these alleged events connected to the Illuminati, a clandestine, worldwide organization whose plans for world domination date back centuries? Lecturer Morris Terziski presents amazing evidence on these and other subjects. 90 min.
76-7322　　　　　　　　　　$24.99

The Philadelphia Experiment, Part I: Strange Events
Who is Al Bielek and what does he know about "The Philadelphia Experiment," the legendary Navy experiment to render warships invisible during World War II? Bielek, who claims he was sent 40 years into the future, brought back, and then brainwashed by the government in 1947, stuns an audience during this on-stage presentation of what he believes are the facts in the case. 60 min.
76-7320　　　　　　　　　　$19.99

The Philadelphia Experiment, Part II: The Workshop Of Terror
Just when you thought Al Bielek's discussion was wild, things get even wilder, as he offers illustrations and photos of locations where the incidents involving "The Philadelphia Experiment" supposedly occurred. This is truly Bielek's stock in bloom! 90 min.
76-7321　　　　　　　　　　$29.99

We Are Not Alone: Set
For everyone who wants to believe, this three-tape documentary series presents the latest facts and theories regarding the universe, extraterrestrial life and "close encounters." Included are "Alien Hunters," "Sky Watchers" and "Space Voyagers." 150 min. total. NOTE: Individual volumes available at $14.99 each.
63-1909　　　　　　　　　　□$44.99

Alien Autopsy: (Fact Or Fiction?)
Startling evidence of an alien autopsy performed after a UFO landing in Roswell, New Mexico, in 1949 is presented in this uncut version of the TV special that captivated viewers. Decide for yourself if the vintage footage is authentic or staged by hoaxers. Hosted by Jonathan Frakes. 70 min.
68-1782　　　Was $19.99　　　$14.99

CHARIOTS of the GODS

Chariots Of The Gods? (1969)
Groundbreaking documentary, based on the controversial best-seller by Erich von Daeniken, examines the theory that beings from outer space visited the Earth centuries ago and helped to create such wonders as the Pyramids. 98 min.
08-1021　　　Was $19.99　　　$14.99

In Search Of Ancient Astronauts (1973)
Based on the best-selling book by Erich von Daeniken ("Chariots of the Gods?"), this documentary looks at the theory that Earth was visited by aliens thousands of years ago and that they left hints of their presence throughout the world. Leonard Nimoy narrates. 53 min.
10-9981　　　　　　　　　　$14.99

Mysteries Of The Gods (1979)
The thought-provoking speculations of Erich von Daeniken that Earth was visited centuries ago by alien astronauts are further explored in this fascinating follow-up to "Chariots of the Gods?." William Shatner hosts. 87 min.
08-1720　　　　　　　　　　$14.99

The Outer Space Connection (1975)
Lots of film documentaries have claimed that aliens visited Earth in the past, but only this one dares to name the date when they'll return (we're not saying, but it's less than 23 years away)! Rod Serling narrates this shocking look at the case for ancient astronauts and flying saucers. 94 min.
08-1031　　　　　　　　　　$19.99

Alien Encounters (1979)
Astonishing look at several documented encounters with aliens featuring startling evidence that we are not alone. Are aliens studying our planet as we are outer space? Find out now. AKA: "UFOs Are Real." 94 min.
08-1580　　　　　　　　　　$14.99

Tunguska: The Russian Roswell (1998)
Roswell may be the most famous case of an "alien crash landing" on Earth, according to many Russian people, it wasn't the first. Thousands of witnesses claimed to have seen a mysterious object explode over the skies of Siberia in 1906 with enough force to level trees for miles. Was it a meteor, a UFO, or something else? 40 min.
71-9026　　　　　　　　　　$19.99

P.T. Barnum And His Human Oddities
The master showman who brought the world the excitement of the circus and the thrill of human "curiosities" is the focus of this program that features George S. Irving as the man who claimed "there's a sucker born every minute." Among the discoveries re-created here are Tom Thumb, "the world's smallest man"; the oldest woman in the world; and more. Richard Kiley hosts. 42 min.
58-8150 *$12.99*

Freaks Uncensored! A Human Sideshow
This look at the world's special people offers a fascinating and uncompromising study of human oddities of all shapes, sizes and characteristics, from bearded ladies to Siamese twins, multi-legged individuals to "pinheads" and lots more. You'll see the famous Johnny Eck, the Dog-Faced Boy, the Mexican monkey woman and more in this critically acclaimed documentary. 100 min.
50-8251 *$59.99*

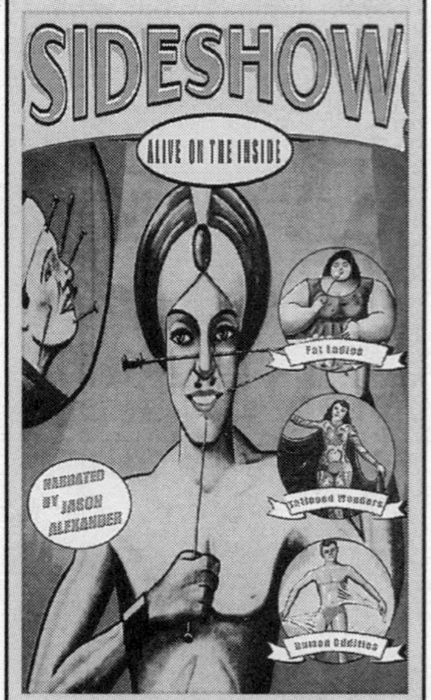

Sideshow: Alive On The Inside
Explore the colorful history of a vanishing entertainment tradition—the carnival and circus sideshow—with this fascinating documentary. You'll be shocked and amazed as you learn about classic "10 in 1" acts (sword swallowers, human pincushions) and "human oddities" (Siamese twins, pinheads, bearded ladies), hear from the performers about their lives on and off the stage, and more. Jason Alexander narrates. 105 min.
63-7172 *$19.99*

Beyond Bizarre
Truth is stranger than fiction...and you'll believe it after watching this collection of real-life oddities that ranges from bizarre natural phenomena, voodoo and tales from the dead to UFO visits, walking zombies and spontaneous human combustion. Be scared, be very scared. Hosted by Jay Robinson. Each volume runs about 47 min.

Beyond Bizarre, Episode 1
Includes "Pentecostal Serpent Handlers," "Witches of Wicca," "Rocks that Move" and more.
50-7463 *$14.99*

Beyond Bizarre, Episode 2
Includes "Self-Made Freaks," "Ghostly Visitations," "Cryptozoology" and more.
50-7464 *$14.99*

Beyond Bizarre, Episode 3
Includes "Bizarre Healing Practices," "Weird World of Pets," "Shoshone Shamanic Ritual" and more.
50-7465 *$14.99*

Beyond Bizarre, Episode 4
Includes "Weird Food," "Bizarre Houses," "Trepanning: Ancient Brain Surgery" and more.
50-7466 *$14.99*

Beyond Bizarre, Episode 5
Includes "Voodoo," "Phuket Vegetarian Festival," "Crystal Skulls" and more.
50-7467 *$14.99*

Beyond Bizarre, Episode 6
Includes "UFOs," "Spontaneous Human Combustion," "Alien Implants" and more.
50-7468 *$14.99*

Beyond Bizarre, Episode 7
Includes "Weird Anthropology," "Zombies," "Chupacabra," "Bizarre Audio Phenomena" and more.
50-7469 *$14.99*

Beyond Belief
Right before your very eyes, see a man bend metal objects with a simple touch...see a man convincingly explain his encounter of the third kind...see Picasso execute sketches from the other world via automatic drawing. Also, learn the unshakable truth behind telepathy and reincarnation. 94 min.
08-1347 *$19.99*

Mysteries Of The Pacific
On an inaccessible island in the Pacific, ancient stone temples were discovered, although no houses, tombs or any other trace of man have been found. This documentary delves into the origins of the ruins and their unknown builders. 91 min.
08-1602 *$14.99*

Rod Serling: The Master Of The Supernatural: Supernatural Double Feature
Rod Serling narrates two thought-provoking documentaries: "UFO's: It Has Begun," an examination of the history of flying saucer sightings, from ancient times to U.S. government case histories; and "Encounter with the Unknown," a dramatization of three runins with the supernatural. 185 min. total.
08-1774 *$19.99*

Secrets Of The Unknown
Journey into the realms of mystery and otherworldly phenomena with host Edward Mulhare ("The Ghost and Mrs. Muir") as he probes the great riddles of the ages. Each tape runs about 30 min. There are 26 volumes available, including:

Jack The Ripper
50-6338 *$14.99*

Pyramids
50-6341 *$14.99*

Stonehenge
50-7228 *$14.99*

Lake Monsters
50-7229 *$14.99*

Bigfoot
50-7230 *$14.99*

English Ghosts
50-7242 *$14.99*

Miracles And Visions: Fact Or Fiction?
Who better than actress Roma Downey (TV's "Touched By an Angel") to host this compelling look at miraculous phenomena around the world. From sightings of the Virgin Mary at Medjugorje and cloud images of Jesus to milk-drinking statues to sudden cures of serious diseases, you'll examine these mysteries and watch as their validity is put to the test.
68-1803 Was $19.99 *$14.99*

Technologies Of The Gods
From the creators of Atlantis Rising magazine comes a program that offers a maverick, intriguing theory on the development of civilization on Earth. Through visits to such sites as the Pyramids, Stonehenge and Macu Picchu, plus writings and research from John Anthony West, Robert Bauval, Colin Wilson, Edgar Cayce and other authorities, you'll be shocked and amazed at what this video claims. 60 min.
70-7255 *$19.99*

Satanis: The Devil's Mass (1969)
Want to see what really goes on in a satanic ritual? This documentary chronicles Anton LeVay's Satanic Church in the late 1960s. Included is footage of a ceremonial mass, interviews with followers, a church official getting whipped and women getting naked for Satan.
79-6003 *$19.99*

Divine Horsemen: The Living Gods Of Haiti (1976)
As a Voodoo initiate in the 1940s, filmmaker Maya Deren was able to record arcane rituals where devotees were "possessed" by the god-like Loa. Years later this footage was assembled to give the viewer an astounding look at the many mysteries behind the Voodoo religion. 53 min.
70-7016 *$29.99*

Monuments To Life: Complete Set (1998)
Are the keys to Earth's future hidden in the past? This two-tape program from authors Graham Hancock and Robert Bauval examines the links between the pyramids of Egypt and Central America, the real reasons for their construction, the possibility of a "lost continent" lying beneath Antarctica, and other provocative topics. 180 min. total.
71-9030 *$39.99*

Sightings
The hit TV series that takes viewers inside the world of the unexplained comes to home video with these special compilations that investigate psychic phenomena, the search for extraterrestrial life, and other topics. Tim White hosts. Each tape runs about 57 min.

Sightings: The Ghost Report
06-2427 □*$14.99*

Sightings: The UFO Report
06-2428 □*$14.99*

Sightings: The Psychic Experience
06-2429 □*$14.99*

Explorers

Great Adventurers: Complete Set
Relive amazing true stories of adventure, courage, triumph and tragedy with this boxed set of documentaries spotlighting six of the most famous explorers in history: "Christopher Columbus," "Sir Francis Drake," "David Livingstone," "Sir Walter Raleigh," "Robert Falcon Scott" and "Ernest Shackleton." 300 min. total. NOTE: Individual volumes available at $19.99 each.
22-1673 Save $20.00! *$99.99*

Into The Rising Sun: Complete Set
While Columbus and others sought a westward sea route to Asia, Portuguese explorers in the 15th and 16th centuries reached India by making their way around the African continent, launching an age of colonialism in the process. This four-part documentary series follows the quest of such adventurers as Prince Henry the Navigator and Vasco da Gama. Volumes include "The Barrier of Fear," "Beyond the Cape of Storms," "The Passage to India" and "A Liar's Tale." 208 min. total. NOTE: Individual volumes available at $19.99 each.
22-6030 Save $20.00! *$59.99*

Africa Speaks! (1930)
Renowned cinema diary of Paul L. Hoefler's 14-month trek through the depths of Equatorial Africa brings you up close to many fascinating forms of fauna, the rites and rituals of the Pygmy, Ubangi, and Massai, and much more. 58 min.
09-2092 Was $24.99 *$19.99*

Mt. Everest: The Fatal Climb
The amazing but tragic account of a man whose obsession with reaching the summit of the tallest mountain in the world was realized, but cost him his life. Contains actual footage of the climb itself, as well as eyewitness accounts. 52 min.
65-7021 *$14.99*

Into The Thin Air Of Everest: Mountain Of Dreams, Mountain Of Doom: Complete Set
Reaching up over 29,000 feet into the skies of Central Asia, Mt. Everest was revered for centuries and thought to be insurmountable. See how men and women risked (and sometimes lost) their lives to reach the summit in this three-tape documentary series that includes the 1953 Academy Award nominee "The Conquest of Everest," "Everest: The Quest" and "Tempting Fate." 170 min. total. NOTE: Individual volumes available at $19.99 each.
89-5080 *$39.99*

The Conquest Of Everest (1953)
Oscar-nominated documentary that recounts the many grueling and sometimes disastrous attempts to climb the formerly insurmountable Mt. Everest, from the earliest undertakings in the '20s up to Edmund Hillary and Tenzing Norgay's reaching of the summit in 1952. 78 min.
09-1988 Was $29.99 *$24.99*

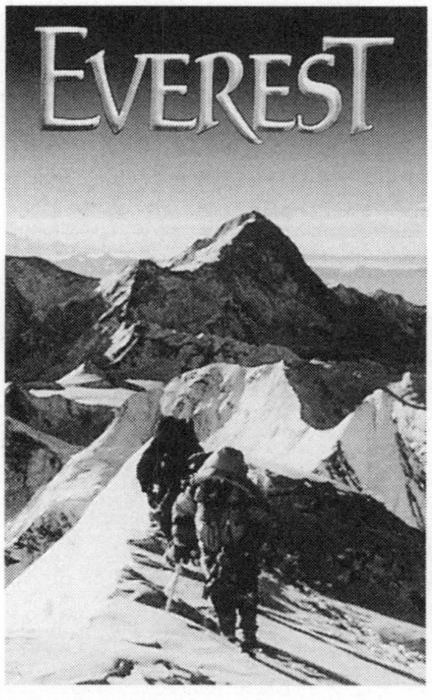

Everest (1998)
You've got an appointment at the top of the world with this spectacular IMAX documentary. Filmed in the spring of 1996, when avalanches and other disasters claimed the lives of 12 climbers from various expeditions, the film chronicles the tortuous ascent that was described in the best-selling book "Into Thin Air" and features breathtaking scenes from the summit. Liam Neeson narrates. 45 min.
11-2292 □*$19.99*

Thor Heyerdahl: Explorer & Scientist
Enigmatic but amazing, the life and times of Heyerdahl and his groundbreaking adventures are explored in this fascinating documentary. Included is his famous Kon-Tiki trip, as well as his expedition to Easter Island in 1954 and his latest find, a series of archeological digs in the pyramids of Tucume in Peru. 52 min.
81-3002 *$29.99*

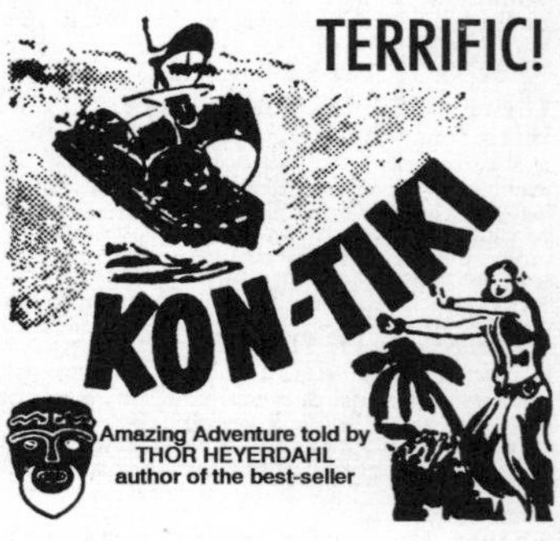

Kon-Tiki (1951)
In 1947, Norwegian explorer Thor Heyerdahl and his crew of scientists sailed over 4,300 nautical miles across the Pacific Ocean, from Peru to Polynesia, on a balsa raft similar to those built by pre-Columbian peoples to prove that the island natives could have been descended from South Americans. Their grueling, historic 101-day odyssey led to Heyerdahl's best-selling book and this film, winner of the Best Documentary Academy Award. 58 min.
81-3001 *$29.99*

Outside Television: Complete Set
Get ready for intense adventures from around the world with this three-tape video series from Outside Magazine. Travel to Mt. Kailas in Tibet, and kayak down the Karnali River in "Liquid Off the Throne of Shiva"; follow a 148-mile foot race across the Sahara Desert in "Marathon of the Sands"; and hear from Robert F. Kennedy, Jr. on the fight to preserve one of America's historic waterways in "The Hudson Riverkeepers." 144 min. total. NOTE: Individual volumes available at $19.99 each.
70-5184 Save $20.00! *$39.99*

Frozen Heart: A Film About Roald Amundsen (1999)
Through documentary footage and dramatic re-creations, this compelling film follows the life of Norwegian explorer/adventurer Roald Amundsen, who became the first man to reach the South Pole in 1911, flew over the North Pole in a dirigible in 1926, and disappeared in the Arctic while searching for a missing colleague in 1928. Bjørn Floberg portrays Amundsen. 90 min.
22-1746 *$19.99*

Heart Of Antarctica: Complete Set
Explore the awesome geography and bitter climate of the mysterious continent in this two-volume program, filmed during a 1998 expedition. Follow scientists, adventurers and mountaineers as they scale Antarctica's tallest peak, 16,000-foot Mt. Vinson, in "Journey to the Ice," and go on a meteorite hunt and retrace early polar explorers' steps in "The End of the Earth & Beyond."
50-8482 *$59.99*

South: Ernest Shackleton And The Endurance Expedition (1919)
An amazing true story of human courage and survival, this is the original filmed account of explorer Sir Ernest Shackleton and his crew's nearly two-year ordeal in the Antarctic following the destruction of their ship Endurance. Restored video version includes color-tinted scenes. 88 min. Silent with music score.
80-5036 *$29.99*

Shackleton's Boat Journey: The Story Of The James Caird (1999)
A sequel-of-sorts to "South: Sir Ernest Shackleton and the Endurance Expedition," this documentary focuses on the incredible 800-mile journey the Irish-born explorer and his men took on the 23-foot-long boat James Caird in order to save themselves. Original photos from the expedition and scholarly research enlighten this remarkable survival story. 31 min.
80-5047 *$19.99*

With Byrd At The South Pole (1930)
This Oscar-winning documentary celebrates the accomplishments of Commander Richard E. Byrd, known for his expeditions to the North Pole and Antarctica, where he established the station called Little America. The film features spectacular photography and offers an intimate look at the explorer. 82 min.
80-5007 *$39.99*

90° South (1933)
A remarkable film composed mainly of footage shot in 1913 of Captain Robert Scott's ill-fated voyage to the South Pole, a trek in which the British explorer and his entire crew perished on the trip home. Scott's friend, photographer Herbert G. Ponting, later weaved incredible shots of Antarctic terrain and wildlife with segments from Scott's diary to tell this inspiring but tragic story; narrated by Ponting. 72 min.
80-5002 *$39.99*

Travel

Civil War River Journey
Take a nostalgia-filled riverboat tour of the Mississippi, Tennessee, Ohio and other historic waterways that played a pivotal role in the War Between the States. Chattanooga, Chickamauga, Fort Donelson and Vicksburg are among the sites visited. 50 min.
50-5257 Was $19.99 *$14.99*

The American South By Rail
Sit back in your seat on the restored American Orient Express and ride the rails of the Deep South, as you see historic sites of Richmond, the restored town of Savannah, beautiful antebellum mansions, the spicy fun of New Orleans and much more. 56 min.
50-8599 □*$19.99*

Over Florida
"The Sunshine State" has never been seen quite as you'll see it in this program filmed from the perspective of a soaring bird. Travel from the Everglades to resorts and points in-between with this breathtaking video. 60 min.
14-9147 *$19.99*

Florida: Playground In The Sun
It's one of America's favorite vacation spots, with something for everyone to enjoy. From the country's first city, St. Augustine, to the Key Islands; from Disney World to Universal Studios; from the Kennedy Space Center to the Everglades, this tape is the next best thing to a trip to Florida. 56 min.
50-4529 *$24.99*

Greetings From Forgotten Florida
Before the age of the giant Florida theme parks, the Sunshine State was dotted with small, quirky roadside attractions that drew thousands of tourist families. In this nostalgic program you'll see many unique sites, some still operating: Cypress Gardens, Parrot Jungle, Weekiwachee Springs (home of performing mermaids), Panama City's Miracle Strip amusement park and others. 60 min.
80-7290 *$19.99*

New Orleans: Queen Of The Mississippi
"Have big fun on the bayou" with this travel video that shows the many wonders of the Crescent City. Take a ride on a paddlewheel boat to visit antebellum plantations, party on Bourbon Street in the French Quarter, and have a front-row seat for the annual Mardi Gras Parade. 55 min.
50-4854 *$24.99*

North Carolina: A Video Travel Guide
Travel to North Carolina, where you'll journey from the coast through the Piedmont and on to the mountains. Stop at waterfalls, lighthouses, museums, festivals, biking trails, trains and other spots in "The Tar Heel State."
76-7236 *$19.99*

Virginia's Great Plantation Homes
The stately homes of three presidents (Washington's Mount Vernon, Jefferson's Monticello, Monroe's Ash Lawn-Highland) are among the 11 Old Dominion plantations featured on this video travelogue. 56 min.
50-4983 *$24.99*

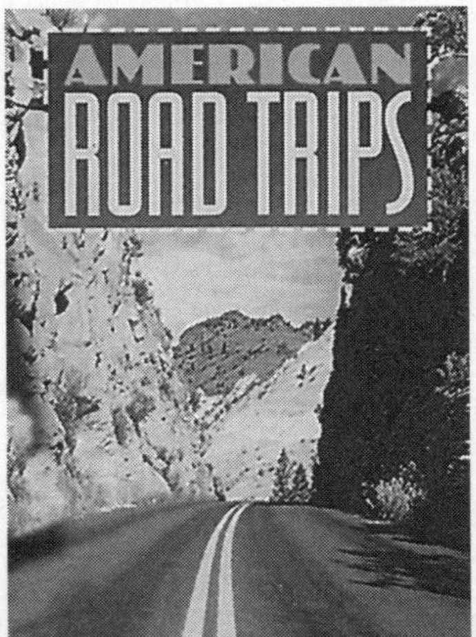

American Road Trips: Complete Set
Get ready for the ride of your life—right in your living room—with this four-tape travel series that takes you through some of the country's most scenic drives and interesting attractions. Included are "Blue Ridge/Vermont/Michigan," "California/Hawaii/Alaska," "Montana/Idaho & Wyoming/Washington" and "Red Rock Rim/Northern New Mexico/Natchez Trace." 240 min. total. NOTE: Individual volumes available at $19.99 each.
50-8321 Save $20.00! *$59.99*

Washington, D.C.
Send someone really deserving to Washington...yourself. This fact-finding mission to the seat of government includes the Smithsonian Institute, the Capitol, the Lincoln and Vietnam memorials, the White House and more. 50 min.
50-1725 *$24.99*

Washington Monuments
Robert Prosky narrates this comprehensive tour of the capital's 16 most significant structures, including the White House, Washington Monument, Lincoln Memorial, Kennedy Center, Smithsonian museums, Supreme Court, Vietnam Veterans Memorial and many others. 30 min.
50-1819 Was $19.99 *$14.99*

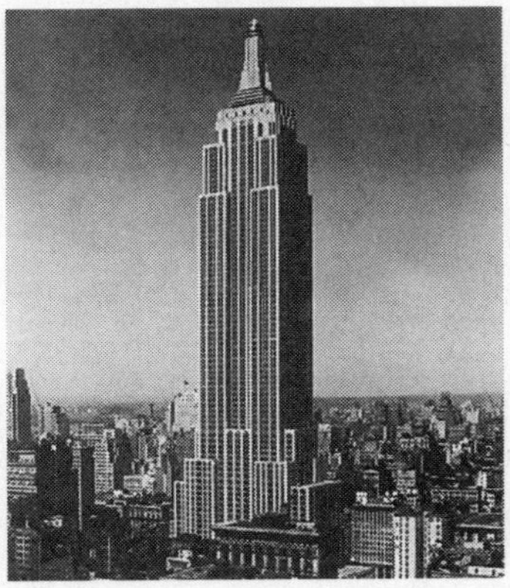

New York: First City In The World
Check out the Big Apple in a whole new way with this video tour that, along with such traditional sights as the Statue of Liberty and Rockefeller Center, focuses on the city's rich array of art museums: the Metropolitan Museum of Art, MOMA, the Frick Collection and others. 52 min.
22-7188 *$19.99*

New York: City Of Cities
It's a wonderful town, as you'll see on this video tour. Witness sights like the Statue of Liberty, Wall Street, the Empire State Building, Times Square and the Met, stroll through Greenwich Village, Chinatown, Little Italy and other neighborhoods, and sample that Big Apple nightlife. 45 min.
50-3880 *$24.99*

New York
You'll take Manhattan, and more, when you take a video tour that stretches from the Statue of Liberty, Wall Street and Little Italy to the Empire State Building, the United Nations and Broadway, among other New York hot spots. 33 min.
50-4870 *$24.99*

Niagara Falls: Raging Rapids
There's more to the legendary waterfalls than honeymooning couples, barrel-riding daredevils and vaudeville routines. This documentary looks at the geological history of Niagara Falls, showing how the river has carved its way into the earth for over 12,000 years, and offers breathtaking footage of the rapids and falls shot in HDTV format. 54 min.
81-3012 Letterboxed *$19.99*

Niagara: Miracles, Myths & Magic (1999)
In this spectacular IMAX production, the great Niagara Falls is captured in all of its magnificent splendor. Along with incredible footage of the falls, you'll learn about its fascinating history and the daredevils who tested their skills at the site. Directed by Kieth Merrill ("Windwalker") with music by Bill Conti. 52 min.
50-8532 *$19.99*

New England: America's Living Heritage
It's a region rich in the country's history, from colonial Plymouth and Salem to Minute Man National Park and the lavish estates of Newport. A tour of covered bridges, a ride on a lobster boat, and a maple tree-tapping trip are also on "tap." 55 min.
50-1255 *$24.99*

Chicago: One Magnificent City
Get to know "The Windy City" intimately, from the Art Institute and the "Miracle Mile" shops to the Shedd Aquarium and Field Museum of Natural History. Also, visit the city's ethnic neighborhoods and partake in some Chicago blues music. 55 min.
50-4364 *$24.99*

Mt. Rushmore And The Black Hills Of South Dakota
A tour of the Black Hills, stamping grounds of Wild Bill Hickok and Calamity Jane, with stops at the Badlands, Custer State Park, Wind Cave and more. Also, the inspiring story of Mt. Rushmore's famous monument. 30 min.
50-1722 *$24.99*

Explore Colorado
Catch the pioneer spirit in a whirlwind tour of Colorado's breathtaking scenic areas and fascinating historic sites, including Mesa Verde, the Million Dollar Highway, mining centers, Pikes Peak, Colorado Springs and Royal Gorge. 60 min.
50-1727 *$24.99*

Pikes Peak Country With Colorado Springs
Explore over 40 attractions and scenic marvels in the fabled Colorado Springs resort area, including museums and pioneer towns, The Garden of the Gods, Pikes Peak, Royal Gorge, the Air Force Academy and much more. 50 min.
50-1735 *$24.99*

The Rockies By Rail
Take a train journey across the heart of the American West with this thrilling video. Climb aboard the restored Pullman cars of the American Orient Express as you visit Salt Lake City, the Continental Divide, Yellowstone and Grand Teton National Parks and other Rocky Mountain sites. 55 min.
50-2453 *$19.99*

Yellowstone (1998)
This gorgeous look at the natural wonder of America's oldest national park presents fantastic sights, from incredible landscapes and half-frozen rivers to snow-capped mountains and two-ton bears. Produced by IMAX; directed by Kieth Merrill; music by Bill Conti. 32 min.
50-8533 *$19.99*

Great National Parks I: Collector's Set
Tour America's vast natural heritage in this special three-tape series of travel tapes, produced in conjunction with Reader's Digest. See the famous tour sights, plus footage of locales rarely glimpsed, along with travel tips, the history of each park, and much more. Includes "Grand Canyon: Amphitheatre of the Gods," "Yellowstone: The First National Park" and "Yosemite: A Gift of Creation." 166 min. total. NOTE: Individual volumes available at $24.99 each.
50-3868 Save $5.00! *$69.99*

Great National Parks II: Collector's Set
Includes "Bryce Canyon and Zion: Canyons of Wonder," "Grand Teton and Glacier: Land of Shining Mountains" and "Mount Rainier and Olympic: Northwest Treasures."
50-4469 Save $5.00! *$59.99*

America's National Parks: Scenic Route
Made in conjunction with the National Park Service, this breathtaking cross-country odyssey takes viewers on a 14-state tour with stops at nearly two dozen national parks and monuments. Included are visits to Big Bend, Devil's Tower, Great Smoky Mountains, Isle Royale, Petrified Forest, Shenandoah, Yosemite and many more. 360 min.
50-4590 *$19.99*

Las Vegas: Only In America
The neon canyons shine and bustle 24 hours a day, and now you can visit America's gambling mecca without leaving your home. See dazzling casinos and resorts, along with other man-made wonders like Hoover Dam and Lake Mead. 52 min.
50-4250 *$24.99*

Zion Canyon (1999)
Experience the myth, drama and magic of Zion Canyon in Utah with this beautiful IMAX production. You'll discover the canyon with Mormon pioneers and early explorers, find hidden treasures, hang from a 2,000-foot-high cliff and enjoy an astonishing view of Zion National Park.
50-8530 *$19.99*

New Mexico: Land Of Enchantment
The American Southwest is becoming one of the hottest tourist destinations, and this video vacation to New Mexico will have you visiting Indian cliff dwellings, kayaking down the Rio Grande, spelunking in Carlsbad Caverns and much more. 58 min.
50-4987 *$24.99*

Arizona: Spirit Of The Southwest
There's a lot more to see in Arizona than just the Grand Canyon, and on this video you'll visit the remarkable Anazi cliff dwellings, see Navajo rug makers and an Apache spirit dance, watch a shoot-out in famed Tombstone, and tour the booming cities of Tucson and Phoenix. 55 min.
50-4931 *$24.99*

Grand Canyon: The Hidden Secrets (1998)
This impressive trip through the Grand Canyon takes you to places you've never been before, like on a raft sweeping through dangerous rapids or flying in an ultralight craft a mile over the canyon's floor. This IMAX production offers thrills, spills and spectacular scenery. Kieth Merrill directs; Bill Conti composed the score. 50 min.
50-8534 *$19.99*

America's Greatest Caverns
Some of the country's greatest natural wonders never see the light of day...literally. Take a tour of such remarkable tourist attractions as Mammoth Cave National Park in Kentucky, Tennessee's Lost Sea, Luray Caverns in Virginia and many more, as you learn about how caves are formed, how animals adapt to life in darkness, how caves are linked to the Civil War and Jesse James, and more. 60 min.
50-8535 *$19.99*

Carlsbad Caverns And Guadalupe Mountains National Park
A visit to one of the largest cave systems in the world, an underground labyrinth whose extent is still unknown. Sights include the main caverns and surrounding park, a lanternlight tour, the New Cave and hundreds of thousands of bats in flight. 53 min.
50-1704 *$24.99*

San Simeon...Hearst's Castle
Hollywood's home movie man, Ken Murray, shares his archives of William Randolph Hearst's fabulous personal Xanadu, San Simeon. Included with rare color interior footage are candid clips of Hearst guests Cary Grant, the Marx Brothers, Charlie Chaplin, and others. 75 min.
10-1348 Was $19.99 *$14.99*

San Francisco: The Golden Gateway
As the sun slowly sets into the Pacific, you'll still have more sights to see in this video travelogue of charming Frisco. Stroll through Chinatown, see a Japanese festival and Union Square, ride a cable car and more, including a helicopter tour of the city. 55 min.
50-3997 *$24.99*

Los Angeles, Hollywood & Southern California
Take a, like, totally rad excursion from San Diego to Santa Barbara that'll fill you to the max with the scenic, cultural and tourist attractions throughout the Southern California region. Gnarly, fer sure! 50 min.
50-4984 *$24.99*

Hearst Castle: Building The Dream (1999)
Take a tour of California's incredible Hearst Castle, built by newspaper magnate William Randolph Hearst and inspired by his many trips to European castles. From the mansion's priceless furnishings to magnificent gardens, pools and walkways, this IMAX program shows you a real-life enchanted castle. Narrated by John Gavigan. 51 min.
50-8531 *$19.99*

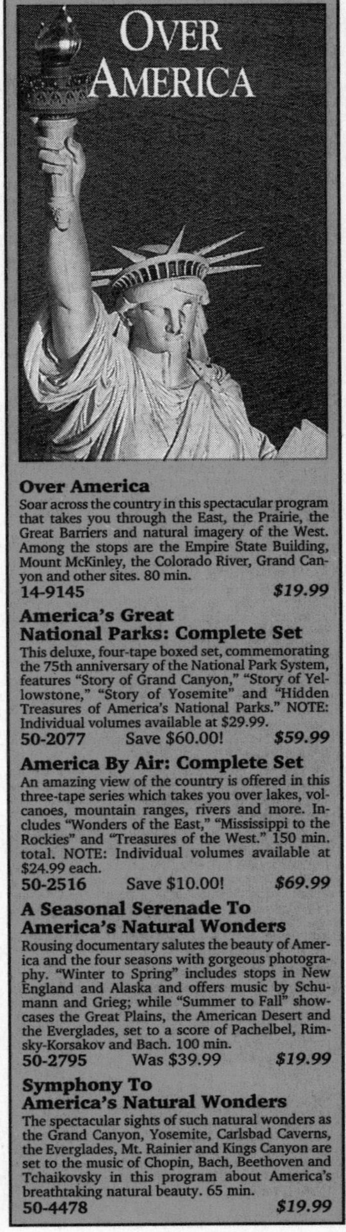

Over America
Soar across the country in this spectacular program that takes you through the East, the Prairie, the Great Barriers and natural imagery of the West. Among the stops are the Empire State Building, Mount McKinley, the Colorado River, Grand Canyon and other sites. 80 min.
14-9145 *$19.99*

America's Great National Parks: Complete Set
This deluxe, four-tape boxed set, commemorating the 75th anniversary of the National Park System, features "Story of Grand Canyon," "Story of Yellowstone," "Story of Yosemite" and "Hidden Treasures of America's National Parks." NOTE: Individual volumes available at $29.99.
50-2077 Save $60.00! *$59.99*

America By Air: Complete Set
An amazing view of the country is offered in this three-tape series which takes you over lakes, volcanoes, mountain ranges, rivers and more. Includes "Wonders of the East," "Mississippi to the Rockies" and "Treasures of the West." 150 min. total. NOTE: Individual volumes available at $24.99 each.
50-2516 Save $10.00! *$69.99*

A Seasonal Serenade To America's Natural Wonders
Rousing documentary salutes the beauty of America and the four seasons with gorgeous photography. "Winter to Spring" includes stops in New England and Alaska and offers music by Schumann and Grieg; while "Summer to Fall" showcases the Great Plains, the American Desert and the Everglades, set to a score of Pachelbel, Rimsky-Korsakov and Bach. 100 min.
50-2795 Was $39.99 *$19.99*

Symphony To America's Natural Wonders
The spectacular sights of such natural wonders as the Grand Canyon, Yosemite, Carlsbad Caverns, the Everglades, Mt. Rainier and Kings Canyon are set to the music of Chopin, Bach, Beethoven and Tchaikovsky in this program about America's breathtaking natural beauty. 65 min.
50-4478 *$19.99*

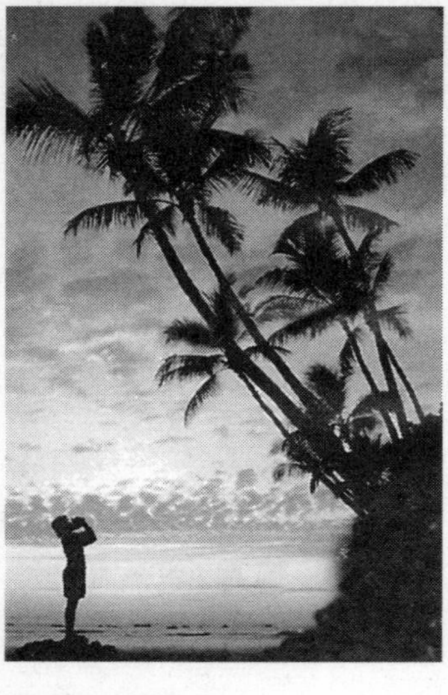

Hawaiian Paradise
More than just a travel tape, this comprehensive look at the people, environment and history of the Aloha State takes you to all six major islands. Visit with Hawaii's multi-ethnic inhabitants, learn how the islands were formed, see volcanic eruptions, native dances, daredevil surfers and hang gliders, and much more. 90 min.
50-4145 *$29.99*

Hawaii: The Pacific Paradise
The complete history of Hawaii is told in this insightful two-part program that uses historical photographs, film footage and re-enactments to trace its 1,000-year heritage, including the arrival of the Polynesians; the exploits of Captain Cook, Kamehameha the Great and Father Damien; the bombing of Pearl Harbor; and the culture and customs of the islands. 150 min.
50-4898 *$39.99*

Hidden Hawaii
Hawaii is a land of many sights and sounds, a beautiful paradise filled with something for everyone. In this IMAX production, you'll visit some of the most amazing parts of the 50th state, from fiery volcanoes to a kayak expedition along the Molokai coast, from Maui's 10,000-foot-high Haleakala Crater to the highest sea cliffs in the world. Music by Mark Isham. 35 min.
50-8528 *$19.99*

Alaska: Spirit Of The Wild (1997)
Experience the land of incredible sights in this Oscar-nominated documentary narrated by Charlton Heston. From tremendous glaciers to the awesome Aurora Borealis, from stampedes of caribou to beautiful polar bear, this IMAX production is sure to astonish you. 40 min.
50-8484 *$19.99*

Willard Scott's Taste Of Puerto Rico
The weather's always sunny as Willard takes you on a tour of America's Caribbean paradise. Explore the sights and sounds (not to mention the tastes) of the island, and join Scott as he visits historic sights and meets Puerto Rico's people. 50 min.
22-1612 *$19.99*

Staying At A Lighthouse
For years they guided mariners along America's coasts, and now their lights serve as a welcoming beacon for tourists. Take a video tour of lighthouses that do double duty as romantic vacation havens, from New England and the Great Lakes to the Pacific coast and more. 45 min.
50-8157 Was $19.99 *$14.99*

Natural Wonders Of America: Boxed Set
Some of the most breathtaking scenery the country has to offer can be viewed on this three-tape series. "Endless Journeys" includes Yosemite, Mt. Rainier and Crater Lake; such Northern sites as Yellowstone and Olympic Glacier are part of "Land of Enchantment"; and travel from the South Dakota Badlands and the Rocky Mountains to the Grand Canyon in "Natural Beauty." 210 min. total. NOTE: Individual volumes available at $14.99 each.
53-6483 Save $15.00! *$29.99*

Romantic Inns Of America: Complete Set
Looking for a unique vacation getaway? This four-tape collection, taken from the hit TV series, lets you visit some of the country's finest inns and small hotels for a look at the decor, cuisine and activities. Volumes include "California," "New England," "The South" and "The West." 350 min. total. NOTE: Individual volumes available at $14.99 each.
89-5041 Save $10.00! *$59.99*

Ireland: Isle Of Memories
If "everybody's got a little bit of Irish in them," then no one should miss this video tour of Eire. Visit the rugged Donegal coast, the picturesque Aran Islands, charming Dublin, the home of the Blarney Stone and Waterford crystal, and more. 50 min.
50-1605 Was $29.99 *$19.99*

A History Of Ireland
The rich and colorful history of Eire comes to life in this video documentary that traces Ireland's past from the Celts and Vikings through its centuries-long struggle for independence. See the people and the countryside, and watch a special section on tracing your Irish "roots." 58 min.
50-1682 *$29.99*

Wales: Heritage Of A Nation
Richard Burton narrates this visit to beautiful Wales, country of fascinating Roman relics, centuries-old abbeys and castles, the cottage home of Dylan Thomas, and those breathtaking Welsh landscapes. 27 min.
22-5188 *$14.99*

London: City Of Majesty
Take a tour of London from its historical and artistic perspective with this program that includes visits to a number of the city's museums and monuments, as well as examples of architecture and literature. 48 min.
22-7112 *$19.99*

London: Heart Of A Nation
London swings like a pendulum do, especially in this superb travelogue that stops at Trafalgar Square, Buckingham Palace, Notting Hill Carnival and St. Paul's Cathedral. 58 min.
50-4360 *$24.99*

Castles Of Scotland: Complete Set
In this three-tape boxed collector's series you'll tour some of the most magnificent and historically significant stone fortresses to be found throughout Scotland. Among the landmarks visited are Edinburgh Castle, Stirling Castle, Eileen Donan, Glamis and many more. 150 min. total. NOTE: Individual volumes available at $19.99 each.
50-1920 Save $30.00! *$29.99*

Discovering England
It's an island filled with natural beauty and historic splendor, and on this video visit to Merrie Olde England you'll see Canterbury Cathedral, mysterious Stonehenge, Stratford-upon-Avon, charming Cornwall, and even the changing of the guard at Buckingham Palace. 85 min.
50-4142 *$24.99*

Discovering Scotland
From mountain peaks to legendary lochs, this journey offers a wide-ranging look at the gorgeous land located atop the British Isles. You'll take the high road and the low road to Abbottsford, Sir William Scott's home; Ayshire, the home of poet Robert Burns; Fingel's Cave and more. 105 min.
50-4608 *$24.99*

Tower Of London: The Official Guide
It's been fortress, palace, prison, museum and tourist site for over 900 years. See the many buildings that comprise the Tower of London, including the "Bloody Tower" where Sir Walter Raleigh was imprisoned, get an up-close look at the Crown Jewels, and learn the truth about the Tower ravens. 45 min.
50-4943 *$24.99*

British Rail Journeys: Complete Set
This tourist's delight takes you on an incredible journey along Britain's most scenic railways, from steam trains to high-speed lines and on locomotives of yesteryear. The four-tape set includes "Northern England," "Central Highlands," "North Wales" and "South West." 220 min. total. NOTE: Individual volumes available at $19.99 each.
50-5181 *$79.99*

British Rail Journeys II: Complete Set
"All aboard" for a second collection of rail odysseys filled with colorful scenery, natural wonder and the rich history that is Britain. The five volumes include "Around the Lake District," "Around the Peak District," "East Anglia," "West Coast of Scotland" and "Weymouth to the Isle of Wight." 275 min. total. NOTE: Individual volumes available at $19.99 each.
50-5453 Save $10.00! *$89.99*

British Rail Journeys III: Complete Set
Board the trains for a third delightful tour of some of Great Britain's most beautiful scenery, from ancient Roman amphitheaters to quaint oceanside villages. The four-tape collection includes "The Severn Valley and the Cotswolds," "The North East," "South Wales and the Borders," and "South West Scotland." 240 min. total. NOTE: Individual volumes available at $19.99 each.
50-5864 Save $50.00! *$29.99*

Scotland...Beauty And Majesty
Get an in-depth look into the fantastical world of Scotland, from its history as a country to its timeless folklore and proud people. This video also explores the beautiful landscapes, natural wonders, and extraordinary architecture, including its numerous castles and ancient cities. 52 min.
65-7012 *$19.99*

An Irish Country Calendar: Complete Set
Travel to eight country houses located in different parts of Ireland in this four-volume series. From the misty bogs of County Sligo to the Galty mountains of Tipperary, these programs ("Spring," "Summer," "Autumn" and "Winter") offer a scenic look at the crafts, music and history of each region. 200 min. total. NOTE: Individual volumes available at $19.99 each.
50-2949 Save $40.00! *$39.99*

Discovering Ireland
You'll truly enjoy this video tour of the loveliest sights of Eire, and that's no blarney. The landmarks of Dublin, beautiful County Wicklow, the "Wellie Toss" at the Bantry Bay Regatta, the "Ring of Kerry" at Killarney, so much more. 85 min.
50-3640 *$29.99*

A Touch Of Ireland
The magical land of Ireland is truly a force of beauty to be reckoned with, with its numerous different counties (32 in total), each with their own history, legend and lore. From the moors of Donegal to the modern city of Dublin, this country is truly a window to the past. 52 min.
65-7011 *$19.99*

A Celtic Journey: Four Pack
Take a delightful journey through the British Isles with these sumptuous travel tapes featuring haunting Celtic memories and lovely photography. Included in the boxed set are "Ireland," "Scotland," "Wales" and "England." NOTE: Individual volumes available at $14.99 each.
72-3042 *$39.99*

Venice: Queen Of The Adriatic
A fabulous look at the romantic Italian city comprised of 119 islands and 160 canals. See the most amazing room in Europe, the Piazza di San Marco; the Basilica, built in 829 A.D.; and the pink marble Palace of the Doges. 30 min.
22-7101 *$19.99*

Rome: The Eternal City
Some of the astounding sights of one of the world's most fascinating cities are visited in this program that includes stops at the Colosseum and the Sistine Chapel, as well as a look at artwork by Michelangelo, Raphael and others. 45 min.
22-7130 *$19.99*

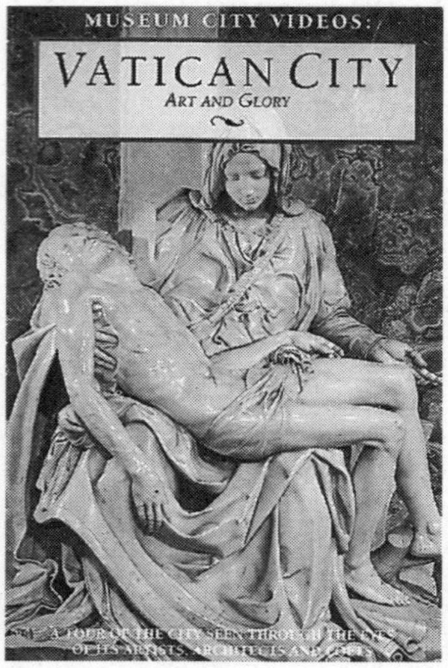

Vatican City: Art And Glory
The world's smallest country is home to some of the world's greatest art treasures, and on this video you'll see such masterpieces as the Sistine Chapel paintings, Michelangelo's "Pieta," the "School of Athens" by Raphael and many more. 45 min.
22-7142 *$19.99*

Discovering Italy
Quicker than you can say "cappicola," this video will whisk you away for a video tour of this magical country. See the isle of Capri and the wine regions of Tuscany, ride a gondola in Venice and shop in Milan, visit the fabled Roman Forum and much more. 79 min.
50-4932 *$29.99*

Touring London, Paris, Rome
Europe's great cities are explored in this video which takes you to London's Westminster Abbey, Tower Bridge and Buckingham Palace; Rome's Colosseum, Pantheon, St. Peter's and the Forum; and the Eiffel Tower, the Louvre, Moulin Rouge and Notre Dame Cathedral in Paris. 60 min.
50-4548 *$29.99*

Mediterranean
Among the stops on this tour of Mediterranean hot spots are the historic Greek Islands of Santoríni and Crete, Athens and Rome, the romantic resorts of the Côte d'Azur and the famed Sagrada Familia Cathedral in Barcelona. 52 min.
50-4963 *$24.99*

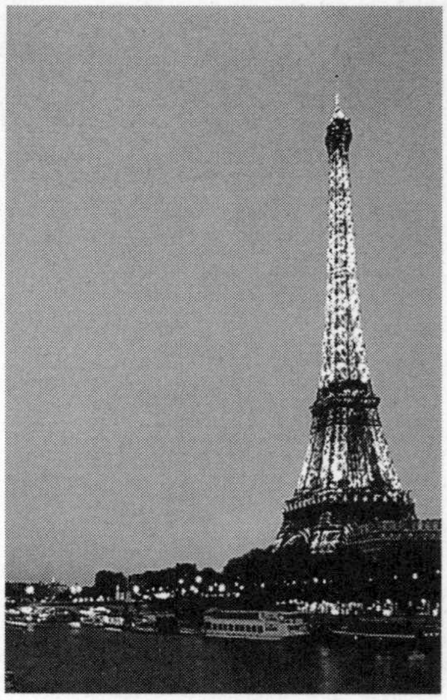

Paris: City Of Light
More than just a travel tape, this documentary takes you on a cultural tour of the French capital, focusing on Paris' legendary museums and art treasures, the architecture and monuments, and the city's literary and artistic heritage.
22-7167 *$19.99*

Touring France
In this thrilling travelogue, you'll get a great overview of the top spots to visit in France, including Nice, Cannes, Provence, Lourdes, Normandy, Verdun, and the sights of Paris, such as the Louvre, Arc de Triomphe, Sacre Coeur, Champs-Elysees and more. 60 min.
50-2827 *$29.99*

In Love With Paris
You can love Paree in the springtime, or anytime, with this wonderful compilation. The magnificent views from the Eiffel Tower and Arc De Triomphe, the treasures of the Louvre, the Notre Dame Cathedral, the boutiques of the Left Bank, many other points of interest. 50 min.
50-3616 *$24.99*

Barcelona: Archive Of Courtesy
The host city for the 1992 Olympics is seen in all its glory. Visit the museums, the historical buildings, the galleries, the artwork and much, much more. 40 min.
22-7131 *$19.99*

Spain: Everything Under The Sun
Video tour will take you to all of sun-drenched Spain's brightest spots. Visit the Prado and Plaza Mayor in Madrid, see the sword makers of Toledo hone their craft, catch rays on the Costa Del Sol, experience the Alhambra in Granada, much more. 50 min.
50-3615 *$24.99*

Portugal, Land Of Discoveries
Journey to the westernmost tip of the European continent for an unforgettable travel experience. See enchanting Moorish churches and castles, picturesque canals and beaches, lively bullfights and so much more. 60 min.
50-4251 *$24.99*

Portugal!
Take a guided tour of Portugal, a picturesque country brimming with history and great sites. Visit Lisbon, with its spacious parks and mosaic walks, along with Madeira, the Azores, a Portuguese bullfight and more. 60 min.
73-5214 *$19.99*

Great Lakes Of Europe: Complete Set
This four-tape travel series will let you tour the magnificent lakes of the Alpine regions of Austria, France, Germany, Italy and Switzerland and see awesome mountain scenery, luxurious villas and historic castles. Included are "Lake Lugano/Lake Maggiore," "Alpine Lakes/Lakes of Salzburg," "Lake Como/Lake Garda" and "Lake Geneva/Lake Constance." 240 min. total. NOTE: Individual volumes available at $19.99 each.
50-2145 Save $40.00! *$39.99*

Europe's Romantic Inns: Complete Set
See the splendor and luxury of some of the continent's most beautiful classic inns with this two-tape set that takes you to lavish castles and chateaus, historic country homes, and even a monastery designed by Michelangelo. Included are "England, Scotland & Ireland" and "Italy & France." 160 min. total. NOTE: Individual volumes available at $19.99 each.
89-5084 Save $10.00! *$29.99*

Greece, Playground Of The Gods
Great Zeus! A monumental holiday awaits you as you visit the ruins of Knossos and the Acropolis, Santorini's volcanic beaches, the charming windmills of Mykonos and much more. 50 min.
50-4249 *$24.99*

Czechoslovakia: Triumph And Tragedy
From medieval castles to architectural treasures, this country offers breathtaking sights and a fascinating history. You'll visit Prague and its historic Old Town Square, the Prague Castle and St. Vitus Cathedral. 55 min.
50-4361 *$24.99*

Discovering Germany
Sail along the Rhine and Elbe Rivers, celebrate Oktoberfest in Munich, see the art treasures of Meissen and the remnants of the Berlin Wall, and more in this video tour of reunited Germany. 90 min.
50-4362 *$24.99*

Discovering Holland, Luxembourg, Belgium
Western Europe's Benelux countries enchant tourists with their many wonders. The Netherlands features canals, the paintings of Van Gogh, the Anne Frank House, tulips, cheeses and Delft porcelain; medieval castles and vineyards mark tiny Luxembourg; and history ranging from Reubens' studio to Waterloo are among the sites of Belgium. 75 min.
50-4785 *$24.99*

Poland: A Proud Heritage
Journey to a land rich with cultural treasures and natural beauty, as you travel through historic Warsaw and the seaport of Gdansk, walk in some of Europe's last remaining virgin woodlands in the Bailowieza Forest, and make a moving visit to the grounds of Auschwitz. 55 min.
50-3996 *$24.99*

Hungary, Land Of Hospitality
Is the Danube really blue? Find out in this excursion to Budapest, where the Royal Palace stands majestically and the neo-Gothic Matthias Church inspires. Also, visit the Hungarian Riviera, Lake Balaton and the Vineyards of Eger. 55 min.
50-4154 *$24.99*

Discovering Russia
The fall of the Iron Curtain has meant a rise in tourism for the world's largest country. This enlightening travelogue takes viewers across Russia, from the Ural Mountains to the Siberian wilderness, with stops at Moscow, St. Petersburg and other sites of interest. 60 min.
50-2910 *$24.99*

Ukraine: Ancient Crossroads, Modern Dreams
"Rano!" Long known as the Soviet Union's breadbasket, the independent Ukraine has its own distinctive heritage and traditions to offer visitors. Here you'll see Kiev's splendid Cathedral of St. Sophia, the mysterious caves of the Perchersk Monastery, the seaside resorts of the Crimea, artists creating intricate embroideries and Easter eggs, and much more. "Yeem kashu!" 55 min.
50-4783 *$24.99*

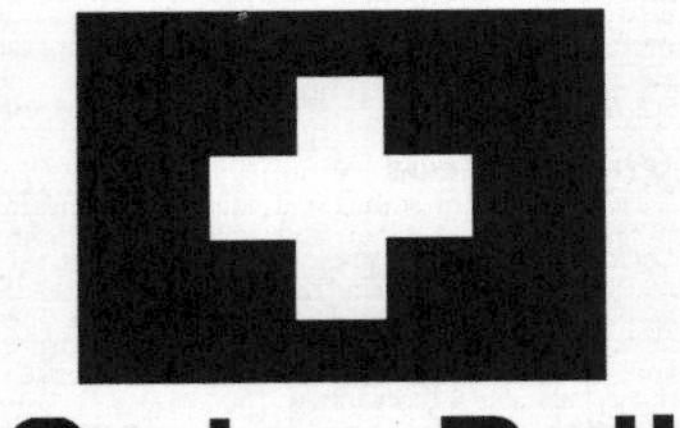

Swiss Rail Journeys

Swiss Rail Journeys
Fantastic Alpine scenery and the rich history of Switzerland are spotlighted in this exciting travel series that looks at one of the world's most fascinating rail systems and the towns, castles and other attractions that make the country one of the world's most gorgeous.

Swiss Rail Journeys I: Complete Set
Included in this special boxed set are "The Albula Line," "The Davos Line," "The Montreaux-Oberland-Bernois Railway," "The Arosa Line" and "The Bruenig Line, Vols. 1 and 2." NOTE: Individual volumes available at $19.99 each.
50-4890 Save $20.00! *$99.99*

Swiss Rail Journeys II: Complete Set
Included in this special boxed set are "The Gotthard Line, Vols. 1 and 2," "The Bern-Lotschberg-Simplon Company," "The Emmental Railways," "The Appenzell Railway" and "The Bodensee-Toggenburg Railway." NOTE: Individual volumes available at $19.99 each.
50-2738 Save $20.00! *$99.99*

Swiss Rail Journeys III: Complete Set
Included in this special boxed set are "The Bernina Express," "The Engadine Line" and "The Gruyere Railway." NOTE: Individual volumes available at $19.99 each.
50-5004 Save $30.00! *$29.99*

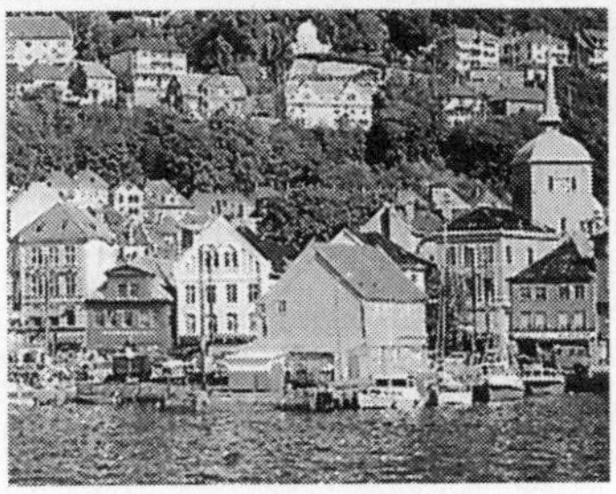

Norway: Nature's Triumph
No need to go "pinin' for the fjords" once you take a video tour of this majestic Scandinavian nation. See a medieval fortress in the capital city of Oslo, stroll the scenic Bergen waterfront, attend a National Theater rendition of an Ibsen play, and more. 53 min.
50-4524 *$24.99*

Scandinavia: Land Of The Midnight Sun
An invigorating tour through Scandinavia, including stops at Denmark's Copenhagen, Tivoli Gardens and Kronbrog Castle; cosmopolitan Stockholm in Sweden; and Oslo and the fjords of Norway. 57 min.
50-4363 *$24.99*

Finland, Fresh And Original
Here's Helsinki, a stunning city that offers Senate Square and the Temppeliaukio Church. Also, see the Alvar Aalta museum, the Lutheran Cathedral and Lapland, home of reindeer. 50 min.
50-4155 *$24.99*

Sweden: Nordic Treasure
The glacial glory of Sweden is explored in this tape that takes you from Stockholm and Gamla Stan to the world of the Laplanders. You'll say "I'll Take Sweden" after watching this program. 53 min.
50-4398 *$24.99*

The Philippines: Pearls Of The Pacific
The islands of the Philippines are home to lush rain forests and mountains covered with pine trees, to tropical beaches and cosmopolitan beaches. You'll see it all on this video travelogue that also includes a visit to a "psychic surgeon" and the caves of St. Paul's Subterranean National Park. 57 min.
50-1261 *$24.99*

New Zealand: Islands Of Adventure
Take in "God's Own Country" in this amazing travelogue to adventure. Fly over Mount Cook's peaks, visit lovely Marlborough Sounds, take in the sights of boat-haven Auckland and the capital city of Wellington. 60 min.
50-2031 *$19.99*

The Wonders Down Under
Panoramic two-volume look at the natural splendor of Australia and New Zealand includes "Touring Australia," which visits such sites as Melbourne, Sydney and Ayers Rock; and "Touring New Zealand," featuring stops at Auckland, Christchurch and some of the country's most interesting locales. 120 min. total.
50-2828 *$39.99*

Islands Of The South Pacific
Spend "some enchanted evening" in front of the TV watching this travelogue. Visit exotic locales like romantic Tahiti and the lush valleys of Samoa, see fire-walking rituals in Fiji and traditional crafts in Tonga, plus much more. 75 min.
50-4851 *$24.99*

Tahiti
The South Pacific paradise will enchant you, from grass skirt dances and pearl diving to sailing voyages to lush, unspoiled locales like Bora Bora and Huahine. 33 min.
50-4872 *$24.99*

The Great Barrier Reef (1999)
The colorful, majestic islands and sheltered seas of Australia's 1,200-mile natural phenomenon are explored in this IMAX production. You'll discover the incredible aquatic environment and astounding beauty of the reef. Narrated by Phillip Clark and Rosalind Ayres. 48 min.
50-8527 *$19.99*

Touring Egypt
A fascinating tour of Egypt, featuring a walk through Cairo, a look at the Pyramids and the Sphinx, the Nile, the Valley of the Kings and Tut's tomb. Also explore the culture of the Suez Canal, the Red Sea and the Sinai. 60 min.
50-1930 *$29.99*

Egypt: Land Of Ancient Wonders
Walk like an Egyptian to see a land where Africa meets Asia and the old meets the new. Cruise the Nile and watch ships pass through the Suez Canal, take a camel ride into the desert to view the Pyramids and the Sphinx, see Cairo and Alexandria, and more. 58 min.
50-4850 *$24.99*

Jordan: The Desert Kingdom
A visit to the Middle East wouldn't be complete without a trip to Jordan, where sites of historical and religious interest (the ancient city of Petra, Hadrian's Arch and the River Jordan) and contemporary excitement (the capital city of Amman) await. 51 min.
50-2911 *$24.99*

Kenya Safari: Essence Of Africa
Kenya safari? Sure ya ken, and ya will on this exciting video journey! See the game reserves of Amboselli, Abedare, Samburo-Isioli and Mara, the villages of the Masai, the striking land of Lamu, and all of that picturesque, remarkable wildlife. 45 min.
50-3811 *$24.99*

Southern Africa Safari
Do not fear, wildlife fans! This is a video "photo safari" of Botswana, Zambia and Zimbabwe that'll bring you up close to the animal inhabitants of Africa's largest oasis, the Okavango delta, fly you above breathtaking Victoria Falls, take you down the white water of the Zambesi River, and more. 60 min.
50-4272 *$24.99*

South Africa: A Journey Of Discovery
The new era of unity in South Africa means that the world is rediscovering this exotic vacation spot. See cosmopolitan cities that are short drives from lush game reserves, a topography that ranges from desert to forest, and a mix of European, African and Asian cultures and heritages. 55 min.
50-4852 *$24.99*

Journey Through The Bible Lands
A video visit to sites that draw thousands of pilgrims every year. Follow the journey of Moses and the Israelites through the Sinai wilderness, visit Jesus' birthplace of Bethlehem, and retrace his final walk along the Via Dolorosa, and much more. 45 min.
50-4864 *$24.99*

Morocco: A Bridge Across Time
The cultures of Europe, Arabia and Africa all blend to give Morocco its unique character, as you'll see on this travelogue that takes you to colorful markets and folklore festivals, desert oases and cosmopolitan cities, and even an exotic nightclub in Casablanca. 53 min.
50-4933 *$24.99*

Africa's Champagne Trains
Some of the world's most lavish passenger trains still running can be found in Africa, and in this two-tape set you'll experience classic rail luxury in your own home. "The Blue Train" takes you on a 1,000-mile trek between Cape Town and Pretoria, South Africa, while national parks, the Namibian desert and spectacular Victoria Falls can be glimpsed on board "The Pride of Africa—Rovos Rail." 100 min.
89-5181 *$19.99*

Experience Canada: Set
It's a country two big for one videocassette, and on this two-tape collection you'll explore the many sights of the Great White North. Learn about the people and the provinces in a "Canadian Journey," then explore the nation's natural splendor in "Touring Canada's National Parks." NOTE: Individual volumes available separately.
50-3152 Save $10.00! *$39.99*

Great Canadian Parks: Collector's Set
This three-tape set explores Canada's most amazing and beautiful parks. Included are stops at "Kluane National Park Reserve in the Yukon/Quebec's Saguenay-St. Lawrence Marine Park," "British Columbia's Ts'il-os National Park/New Brunswick's Parks of Fundy" and "Waterton Lakes in Alberta/Cypress Hills Interprovincial Park between Alberta and Saskatchewan." 145 min. total. NOTE: Individual volumes available at $14.99 each.
50-5293 *$39.99*

Jamaica, Land Of Wood And Water
The next best thing to a Caribbean vacation is to turn on this charming video stroll down the sparkling beaches and quaint streets of Jamaica. Fishing villages, open-air markets, dazzling nightspots and other sights await. 50 min.
50-4143 *$24.99*

Islands Of The Caribbean
Jamaica, Bahamas...ooo, pretty mama. Go to the real-life Kokomo, along with vacation spots like St. Thomas, Aruba, Curacao and the Cayman Islands to enjoy scuba diving, gambling, reggae and calypso music and those fabulous beaches. 53 min.
50-4166 *$19.99*

Brazil: Heart Of South America
The world's third largest country, Brazil offers sun-kissed tropical beaches, mountainous wilderness, and some of the world's last remaining rain forests. Take a video tour that stretches from the natural beauty of Iguazu Falls to lively Rio. 55 min.
50-3991 *$24.99*

Costa Rica: The Land Of Pure Life
One of Central America's most scenic countries, the sights of Costa Rica range from sunny Pacific beaches to lush tropical forests. There are also man-made wonders like colorful markets and the nightlife of San José, the capital city. 56 min.
50-4527 *$24.99*

Peru: A Golden Treasure
It was the homeland of the ancient Incas, and their heritage still influences the people of Peru. On this tape you'll see Incan ruins in Cuzco, the treasures in Lima museums, the gorgeous Pacific resort of Las Dunas, the mysterious ground drawings of Nazca, and more. 53 min.
50-4528 *$24.99*

Discovering The Amazon And The Andes
Travel the longest river in the Americas and see dolphins, jungle birds and the people who make the Amazon and its rain forests their home. Then, tour the ruins of Machu Picchu in Peru, and learn how the descendants of the Incas live. 56 min.
50-4986 *$24.99*

Song Of Ceylon
A lushly photographed, leisurely paced excursion to Ceylon (now Sri Lanka), a true tropical paradise. Directed for the Tea Marketing Board by England's Basil Wright, this award-winning film from the '30s surpasses its commercial origins with stunning beauty and artfulness. 40 min.
10-7327 Was $29.99 *$19.99*

Thailand, The Golden Kingdom
Yul Brynner may not be there anymore, but this Southeast Asian nation has much to offer tourists. Native markets and winding canals in bustling Bangkok, the magnificent Grand Palace and Emerald Buddha, sprawling rain forests, beaches and other natural wonders. 52 min.
50-4252 *$24.99*

Indonesia: The Jeweled Archipelago
The islands that make up the nation of Indonesia have an amazing array of natural and man-made wonders for travellers to experience, from the capital city of Jakarta and Balinese dancers to jungle-dwelling orangutans and giant Komodo lizards. 57 min.
50-1248 *$24.99*

Exploring The Himalayas, Nepal & Kashmir
Visit the real Shangri-La, the land written about in "Lost Horizon." Journey through incredible mountain ranges to Dal Lake, then to ancient cities on wild rivers and incredible national parks. Explore temples, celebrate ancient festivals, and climb Mt. Everest. 60 min.
50-1944 *$29.99*

India: Land Of Spirit And Mystique
For a video tour of one of the world's most exotic tour destinations, book a passage here, and see centuries-old temples, the bustling city of Bombay, a pilgrimage to the Ganges River and more. 55 min.
50-3993 *$24.99*

Destinations: Boxed Set
Journey to some of the most exotic and remote regions of India, and see how the inhabitants live lives seemingly untouched by the outside world, in this three-tape travelogue series. Included are looks at the mountainous Kashmir region, bordered by Pakistan; Rajasthan, home to Jaipur and the Great Indian Desert; and Southern India. 165 min. total.
85-7029 *$39.99*

Touring Korea
Visit the sprawling modern metropolis of Seoul, majestic Mt. Soraksan, Dragon Valley and the underwater tomb of King Moon. Gaze at the treasures of the National Museum and meet the people that comprise this 5,000-year-old country. 60 min.
50-1943 *$29.99*

Malaysia: Land Of Harmony
The jungle nation of Malaysia is a fascinating mix of primitive peoples only a generation removed from head hunting and bustling urban centers in the Oriental style. See the Batu Caves, Kota Bharu, Georgetown, and more! 45 min.
50-3906 *$24.99*

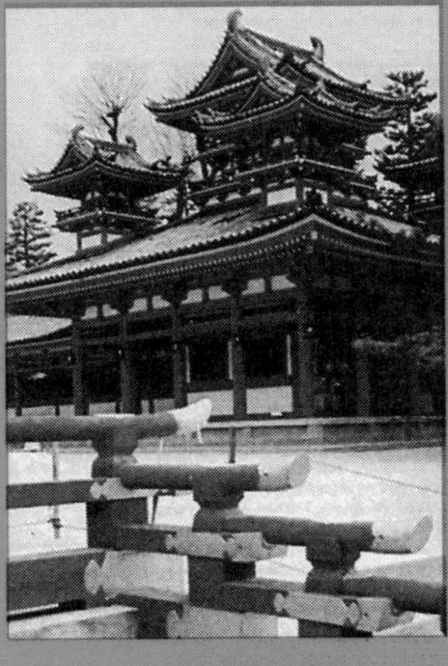

Japan: The Island Empire
Perhaps in no other nation have the old and the new blended so successfully as in Japan. Watch the spectacle of an ancient Shinto ceremony, tour 400-year-old Himeji Castle, visit modern downtown Tokyo and many other sights not to be missed. 50 min.
50-3994 *$24.99*

James A. Fitzpatrick's Traveltalks 1930-1933
For three decades filmmaker James Fitzpatrick took audiences to the far-flung corners of the world with his MGM-produced "Traveltalks" short subjects. This video program features 10 travelogues made between 1930 and 1933 that offer a vintage glimpse of the sights and people of Ireland, Italy, India, Japan, China, Dutch New Guinea and elsewhere. 91 min.
53-6155 *$24.99*

The World's Most Exotic Islands: Complete Set
"No man is an island," but there's sure to be a vacation island for every man—and woman—in this three-tape travel series hosted by model Hunter Reno. "The Caribbean" takes you to the British Virgin Islands, Belize, St. Kitts, Arbua; Canary Islands, Gotland, the Azores and Iceland are the focus of "Europe"; and "The South Pacific" spotlights Fiji, Vanuatu, Western Samoa and Nusa Tenggara. 255 min. total. NOTE: Individual volumes available at $14.99 each.
89-5238 Save $5.00! *$39.99*

The Greatest Places (1998)
This IMAX production takes you on an unforgettable journey to seven of the most amazing locations on our planet. Among the stops captured with incredible photography are Amazonia, Greenland, the Kalahari Desert, Madagascar, Tibet and Iguazu Falls. Narrated by Avery Brooks. 50 min.
50-8485 *$19.99*

Three Perfect Days
Based on the popular column in the travel magazine Hemispheres, this video travelogue series gives you all the info you need for a memorable weekend—or longer—vacation to some of the world's most exciting cities and regions. Info on tourist sites, hotels and restaurants, cultural activities and more is included. Each tape runs about 30 min. There are 12 volumes available, including:

Three Perfect Days: New Orleans
83-1320 *$14.99*

Three Perfect Days: Paris
83-1327 *$14.99*

Three Perfect Days: Honolulu
83-1346 *$14.99*

Three Perfect Days: Shanghai
83-1407 *$14.99*

Three Perfect Days: San Francisco
83-1408 *$14.99*

Travel The World By Train
Experienced travellers know that when it comes to seeing a country close-up, nothing beats a train. Now you can ride some of the world's most interesting and scenic railways with this exciting video series. Each tape runs about 60 min. There are 13 volumes available, including:

Travel The World By Train: Africa
85-1177 *$14.99*

Travel The World By Train: Asia
85-1178 *$14.99*

Travel The World By Train: Europe, Part 1
85-1181 *$14.99*

Travel The World By Train: Europe, Part 2
85-1182 *$14.99*

Travel The World By Train: South America
85-1185 *$14.99*

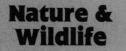

Nature & Wildlife

Sea Of Cortez
Take a stunning look at a land almost untouched by civilization: Mexico's rugged Baja California. You'll see some of the incredible sights and such creatures as killer whales, sharks and manta rays that live off its shores. 92 min.
08-1603 *$14.99*

Mysteries Of The Polar Seas
Journey to the Arctic and Antarctica, home to some of the roughest waters in the world, where temperatures can reach 85 degrees below zero. 95 min.
08-1598 *$14.99*

Monkey People
Susan Sarandon narrates this amazingly insightful look at the relationship between man and ape. Filmed in Africa, Asia and South America, this film offers amazing footage of primates in the wild.
53-7601 Was $79.99 *$19.99*

Mozu The Snow Monkey
The remarkable true story of a Japanese macaque monkey who, despite being born with deformed limbs, kept up with the other members of her troop and raised four healthy children.
63-7134 *$19.99*

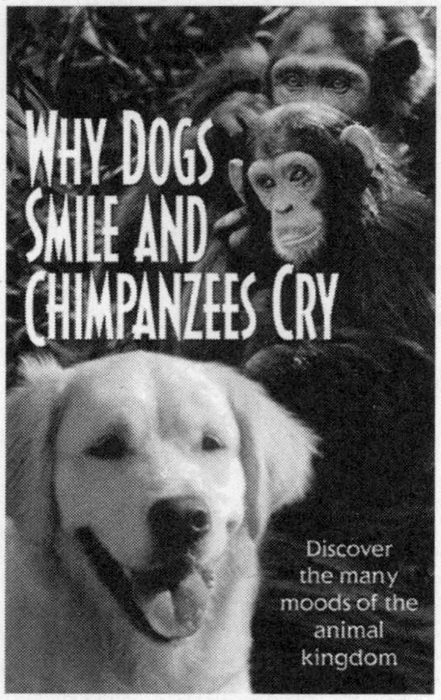

Why Dogs Smile And Chimpanzees Cry
We think of emotions as a uniquely human quality, but just what sort of feelings do animals share with us, and how do they help them grow and survive? This fascinating Discovery Channel program looks at creatures wild and domestic and shows how they may experience happiness, fear, love, anger and even grief. Sigourney Weaver narrates. 100 min.
27-7183 *$14.99*

A Little Duck Tale
In the parks surrounding the Imperial Palace in downtown Tokyo, a family of ducks deals with the flashing photography of tourists, angry swans, and the dangerous rush of a nearby highway, all the while just trying to live one day to the next.
02-8953 ❑*$14.99*

Amazon: Journey To A Thousand Rivers
Cousteau travels down the mysterious Amazon River, the New World's longest, and discovers amazing sights and creatures. 98 min.
18-7338 ❑*$19.99*

The Best Of Cousteau Boxed Set
This deluxe, seven-tape collector's set includes "Bering Sea: Twilight of the Alaskan Hunter," "Borneo: Forests Without Land," "Haiti: Waters of Sorrow," "Riders of the Wind," "Thailand: Convicts of the Sea" and "Western Australia: Out West Down Under."
18-7582 *$119.99*

Killers Of The Great Barrier Reef
Travel to Australia's Great Barrier Reef, an undersea kingdom filled with beauty and danger. Crocodiles, sea snakes, toadfish, moray eels and the deadly Box Jellyfish are among the creatures you'll see. 94 min.
08-1595 *$14.99*

The Great White Shark
Explore shark-infested waters as you get to witness how great white sharks live, kill and survive in this program from the BBC. David Attenborough serves as host to this magnificently photographed documentary. 50 min.
04-3254 ❑*$14.99*

Great White Death
Host Glenn Ford takes you for a look at sharks around the world in this stunning look at nature's most dangerous jaws. Learn the history of these "killing and feeding machines" and see the actual capture of a Great White. 88 min.
16-1115 *$19.99*

The Ultimate Guide: Sharks
This primer on the world's sharks includes incredible footage of a variety of these sea creatures and their predatory ways. You'll see first-time footage of the Greenland shark from the Arctic, plus the huge but passive whale shark, the bizarre hammerhead shark, and others. 60 min.
27-5588 *$14.99*

Search For The Great Sharks (1992)
This documentary takes an in-depth study of blue sharks, whale sharks and the great white shark as it follows the work of researchers Rodney Fox and Dr. Eugenie Clark, who have been studying the creatures since the 1950s. An IMAX production, the film offers spectacular photography and expert insight into some of the world's most misunderstood species.
50-8486 *$19.99*

The Great White Shark: Lonely Lord Of The Sea
Witness the terror and beauty of the Great White Shark in this incredible program that features never-before-seen footage of the 2,000-pound, 16-foot creature. A truly amazing Cousteau adventure. 60 min.
18-7404 ❑*$19.99*

Lifesense: Our Lives Through Animal Eyes
A remarkable, award-winning program on how animals perceive humans. Special effects re-create the actual senses of different animals—from the family dog to microscopic parasites—to see how we affect them. This two-tape set runs 179 min.
04-3255 ❑*$39.99*

Anima Mundi
Director Godfrey Reggio and composer Philip Glass, collaborators on "Koyaanisqatsi," combine for this dazzling journey through the animal kingdom. Up-close looks at creatures ranging from microscopic organisms to the largest mammals, blended with Glass' haunting music, celebrate the idea of the world as a living entity and the wide variety of life that inhabits it. 30 min.
16-7084 Letterboxed *$19.99*

Cats
"Miiidniiight, and the kitties are" the focus of this fascinating feline documentary. See how cats have been pampered, worshipped and even feared through the centuries, explore the mysteries of cat behavior, and see what's made them America's most popular pet. 49 min.
18-7491 *$14.99*

The Secret Life Of Cats
The cat is one of the most popular pets in the world. It was worshipped as a symbol of life in ancient Egypt, and in centuries past was adored by farmers and sea captains alike. However, there is a predator inside every feline, and this program will let you explore a housecat's "secret world."
19-5006 *$19.99*

How Animals Do That!
From surviving in subzero temperatures to spotting objects two miles away, the animal kingdom sports a number of amazing adaptations that man needs technology to emulate. In this documentary you'll see some of the amazing adaptations animals have made that allow them to thrive in the wild. Wendie Malick narrates. 53 min.
27-7184 *$14.99*

Wolves At Our Door
Jim and Jamie Dutcher's awe-inspiring experience of raising a pack of gray wolves in Idaho's remote Sawtooth Mountains is recounted in this remarkable program that will enchant the whole family.
02-8952 ❑*$19.99*

Wolves: A Legend Returns To Yellowstone
National Geographic chronicles the controversial government program to reintroduce wild wolves back into Yellowstone National Park. Witness the triumphs and tribulations of this beautiful beast as it deals with a new environment and conflicts with man.
19-5005 *$19.99*

World Safari
Safaris seeking adventure and such animals as Bengal tigers, Ugandan leopards and elephants near the Nile are featured in this documentary. 93 min.
08-1304 *$14.99*

Dolphins (2000)
Pierce Brosnan narrates this insightful film, originally made for IMAX theaters, on the beautiful world of dolphins from bottlenoses to duskies. From the waters off Argentina to the Bahamas where these aquatic mammals live, you'll learn about their environment, how they communicate, and even why they perform amazing acrobatic acts. Music by Sting; a "making of" featurette is included. 77 min.
50-8750 *$19.99*

Voyage Of The Great Southern Ark
Fascinating study of the Australian continent from prehistoric times to now that grants a greater perspective on the world as a whole. The striking beauty and mystery of Australia's flora and fauna make for a remarkable presentation. 138 min.
22-5311 *$39.99*

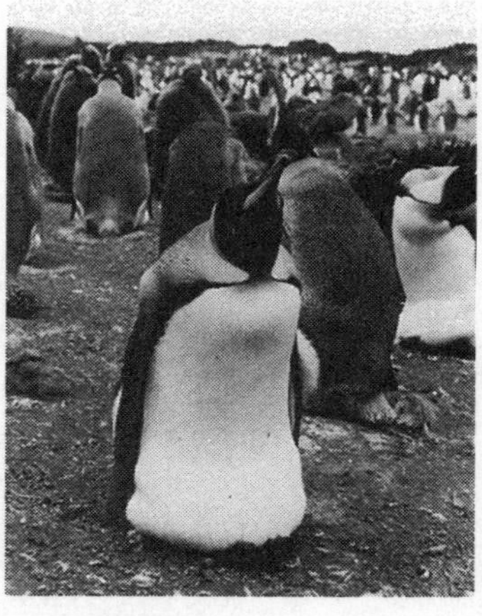

Penguin World
What's black and white and fun all over? This Smithsonian documentary takes you throughout Antarctica and the Southern Hemisphere for a close-up look at these flightless birds who have adapted to an aquatic lifestyle. 45 min.
83-1043 *$14.99*

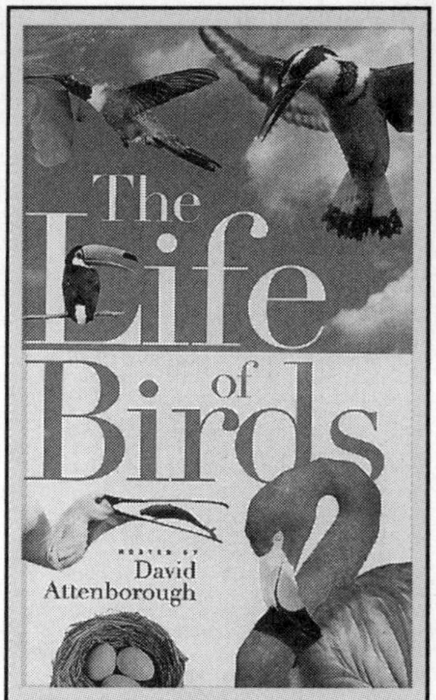

The Life Of Birds
They number over 3,000 different species and can be found on every continent on Earth. David Attenborough hosts this extensive, 10-episode look at the avian kingdom, travelling around the world to follow birds' migratory, feeding and breeding habits and study their roles in nature and man's history. 550 min. on five tapes.
04-3825 ❑*$89.99*

Life On Earth (1982)
The award-winning PBS nature series is available in a special home video version. Host David Attenborough travels to all seven continents for a fascinating look at the origins of the world's plants and animals, their interdependence, and their unique adaptations to the environment. 240 min.
19-1564 *$39.99*

Banks' Florilegium: The Flowering Of The Pacific
Joseph Banks, a botanist who accompanied Captain James Cook on an 18th-century transglobal voyage, discovered over 700 new plant species. 200 years later, his notes and drawings are being printed for the first time, a process shown in this fascinating documentary. 60 min.
22-5067 *$39.99*

Wild Indonesia
Take an inside look at the exotic wildlife of Indonesia in this three-part program from PBS. "When Worlds Collide" studies the differences in the wildlife in the many Indonesian islands; "The Mystery of Sulawski" focuses on some of the area's strangest creatures; and in "Creatures of the Island Kingdoms," you'll learn about how the changes in the archipelago has made things habitable for its animals. 150 min.
90-1038 ❑*$24.99*

Cane Toads: An Unnatural History
Legions of ugly cane toads have taken over Australia, and this fascinating, quirky documentary chronicles their story in a, um, riveting manner. With warts and all, this film chronicles how the toads were imported down under in 1935 to rid the country of beetles, but turned out to be proficient only at procreating. 48 min.
70-5033 Was $29.99 *$19.99*

Survival In The Wild
Forget heartwarming scenes of baby critters. This BBC series takes a raw and savage look at how animals, in their struggle to survive, sometimes function as both hunter and hunted. Sir Anthony Hopkins narrates; each tape runs about 50 min.

Survival In The Wild: Pack Hunters
The most powerful predators of the animal kingdom are social hunters who travel together in packs while searching for food. Among the fauna featured in this incredible program are white wolves, grizzly bears and vampire bats.
19-3494 *$14.99*

Survival In The Wild: Predators & Prey
An amazing look at predators that are on a continuous quest to kill and avoid being killed. Featured are cheetahs, sharks, leopards and other creatures.
19-3495 *$14.99*

Survival In The Wild: Deadly Illusion
Animals and their uncanny camouflage skills are the focus of this program in which slyness and nature's gift play a part in survival. Observe chameleons adapting to their surroundings, snapping turtles luring prey and other oddities.
19-3496 *$14.99*

Orca: Killers I Have Known
They're known as the deadliest predators in the sea, but the "Free Willy" films have shown the gentle side of the killer whale. Learn the truth about these amazing animals in this documentary that features awesome footage of Orcas in the wild, hunting their prey and caring for their young. 60 min.
83-1550 *$14.99*

Whales: An Unforgettable Journey (1998)
Here's a whale-of-a-tale about the world's largest mammals—the Blue Whale and its fellow seafarers like humpbacks, Orcas and right whales, as well as dolphins. Get close to these awe-inspiring creatures in this one-of-a-kind adventure that was produced for IMAX. Narrated by Patrick Stewart. 52 min.
50-8529 *$19.99*

Exploring Antarctica
It's the last remaining frontier on the planet, a long-unexplored region that contains uniquely adapted wildlife and 90 percent of the world's fresh water. Trace the history of Antarctic exploration, relive the race for the South Pole, and see penguins, seals and killer whales. 60 min.
50-2063 *$29.99*

Vanishing Wilderness (1973)
Take a look at the vast American wilderness, a land threatened with destruction, in this nature documentary from acclaimed German photographer Heinz Seilmann. Animals range from majestic buffalo and mustangs to arctic whales. Narrated by Rex Allen.
03-1533 *$14.99*

Hunters Of The Deep (1954)
This exploration of the undersea world features stunning panoramas of the ocean floor. You'll witness underwater forests along with turtles, starfish, stingrays, sea elephants and other creatures. Edited from over 25,000 feet of footage, the film is narrated by Dan O'Herlihy and features a score by George Antheil. 65 min.
09-2970 *$19.99*

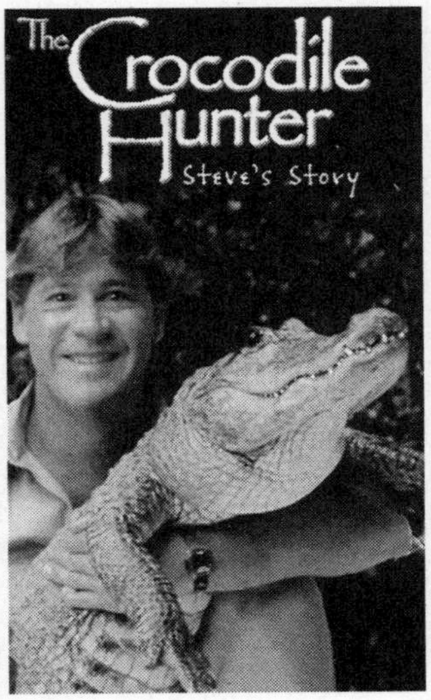

The Crocodile Hunter
He's Steve Irwin, the animal-catching wonder from Down Under who, along with wife Terri, travels the globe to get up close—sometimes *too* up close—to the world's most dangerous creatures. See the most amazing moments from their popular TV series in these thrilling videos. Each tape runs about 50 min.

The Crocodile Hunter: Steve's Story
Just what turns a nice Australian boy into a wildlife daredevil? Learn all about the life and wild times of Steve and Terri and see amazing home movies.
27-7185 *$14.99*

The Crocodile Hunter: Steve's Most Dangerous Adventures
Ever found yourself in the middle of a group of hungry tiger sharks, chased by lions and elephants, or treed by the world's largest lizard, the Komodo Dragon? Steve has, and you'll see all this and more here!
27-7186 *$14.99*

The Crocodile Hunter: Greatest Crocodile Captures
Whoever said "never smile at a crocodile" never met Steve and Terri, who you'll see tussling with their reptilian pals as they try to return them to the wild.
27-7187 *$14.99*

The Crocodile Hunter 3-Pack
All three tapes are also available in a special collector's set that won't take a bite out of your wallet.
27-7188 Save $10.00! *$34.99*

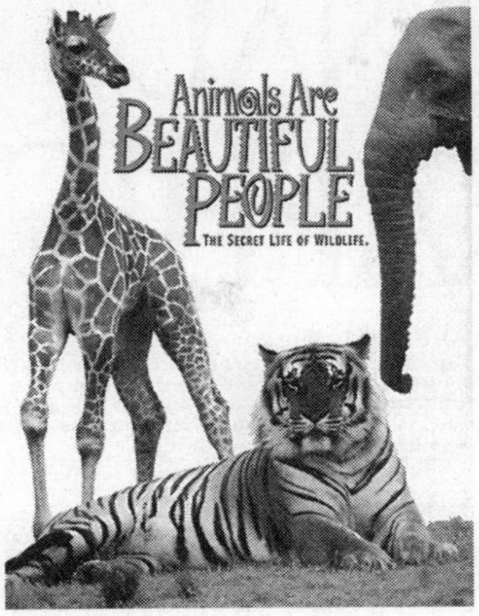

Animals Are Beautiful People (1975)
An amazing, warmhearted look at African animal life from the creators of "The Gods Must Be Crazy." Four years in the making, this documentary shows the struggle for survival and almost "human" behavior of the world's most diverse fauna. 92 min.
19-1107 Was $19.99 *$14.99*

Maneaters Of Tsavo
Explore the true account of two lions who killed nearly 200 railway workers in Africa in the 1890s, a story that inspired the 1996 film "The Ghost and the Darkness." This documentary takes you to Tsavo National Park in Southern Kenya to search for the descendants of the maneaters and features interviews with "Ghost and the Darkness" stars Michael Douglas and Val Kilmer. 50 min.
53-8844 Was $19.99 *$12.99*

The Nature Of Sex: Complete Set
Originally shown as part of "Nature" on PBS, this remarkable six-part series looks at mating rites and family life in the animal kingdom. See how courtship rituals, fights for dominance and choosing partners are a part of life, from insects to man. Includes "The Primal Instinct," "A Time and a Place," "The Sex Contract," "Sex and the Human Animal," "A Miracle in the Making" and "The Young Ones." 6 hrs. total. NOTE: Individual volumes available at $19.99 each.
63-7078 Save $20.00! *$99.99*

Crawl Into My Parlour: Complete Set
Join Professor Erik Holm as he visits the world of arthropods, studying the role these fascinating creatures play in the world. Fine photography brings you up close to a world rarely seen by the naked eye. The six-volume series includes "The Art of Killing," "Cold-Blooded Killers," "Come into My Parlour," "Itching for Ichor," "Legend of Legs" and "The Lobster Lobby." 144 min. total. NOTE: Individual volumes available at $14.99 each.
76-7290 *$89.99*

Birds Of The World: Complete Set
In this award-winning, five-part series from England you'll get an up-close look at the wondrous world of our fine, feathered friends as you watch them hunt for food, construct their nests, raise their young, and more. Includes "Eagles: The Majestic Hunters," "The Master Builders," "The Feathered Athletes," "Seabirds" and "A Little Owl's Story." 210 min. total. NOTE: Individual volumes available at $19.99 each.
80-7181 *$99.99*

Tarantulas & Their Venomous Relations
Step into these spiders' parlors and you might not ever step out! Get an up-close look at some of the world's largest—and most dangerous—spiders through remarkable micro-cinematography, see how these amazing arachnids prey on birds and mammals many times their size, and learn the truth about how deadly their bite is to humans. 53 min.
83-1326 *$14.99*

Deadly Snakes: Boxed Set
People have been both repelled and fascinated by them since the Garden of Eden, and in this three-tape collection you'll be face-to-flickering tongue with the world's most dangerous snakes. Included are "Cobra: King of Snakes," "Rattlesnakes" and "The 10 Deadliest Snakes." 156 min. total. NOTE: Individual volumes available at $14.99 each.
83-1345 *$39.99*

Body By Nature: Natural Wonders Of The Evolutionary Kind
Travel the world for a look at how different species have adapted over thousands of years to their environment, a process that continues to this very day, in this fascinating documentary. 52 min.
83-1461 *$14.99*

Natural Born Winners: Superstars Of The Wild
Their abilities on land, in the water and in the air would put any human athlete to shame. Learn about the animal kingdom's top performers in the game of survival in this exciting program. 50 min.
83-1462 *$14.99*

Bride Of The Beast (1932)
American husband-wife explorers Osa and Martin Johnson head into the dark continent in this early documentary done in a "docudrama" style a la "Trader Horn." Follow them on an African odyssey that includes ferocious animals and dangerous pygmy savages. 57 min.
62-1195 Was $19.99 *$14.99*

Baboona (1935)
Famed documentarians Martin and Osa Johnson encounter lions, charging rhinos, a baby elephant and a legion of baboons in this thrilling factual film that chronicles "the most glorious and delightful safari" they ever had. 73 min.
09-2403 *$19.99*

Borneo (1937)
The final documentary made by explorer-filmmaker Martin Johnson records a fascinating journey to Africa, Asia and the South Seas. See strange creatures, breath-taking sights and more! Lowell Thomas narrates. 76 min.
09-1604 Was $29.99 *$24.99*

Jungle Cavalcade (1941)
Great White Hunter Frank Buck ventures deep into the foreboding jungles of the Dark Continent to bag a menagerie of wildlife in this exciting compilation of his adventure documentaries from the '30s. See Buck get the upper hand on a man-eating tiger, a 30-foot python and a honeybear cub. 77 min.
09-1984 Was $29.99 *$24.99*

Marty Stouffer's Wild America
Marty Stouffer and his brothers bring you the finest in animal kingdom adventures in this series filled with astonishing wildlife footage.

Marty Stouffer's Wild America: The Man Who Loved Bears
A Grizzly cub is prepared to survive in the wild. Will Geer hosts. 60 min.
50-5772 *$14.99*

Marty Stouffer's Wild America: Set 1
Includes "Wacky Babies," "Watching Wildlife" and "Cute as a Cub." NOTE: Individual volumes available at $14.99.
50-5775 Save $15.00 *$29.99*

Marty Stouffer's Wild America: Set 2
Includes "Predators," "The Man Who Loved Bears," "Great Escapes" and a bonus tape, "Photographing Wildlife," featuring Marty's photographing techniques. NOTE: Individual volumes available at $14.99 each.
50-5776 *$44.99*

Housefly: An Everyday Monster
Get up close to one of nature's most elusive and fascinating insects: the housefly! Through the spectacular technology of Macro-Photography, this program examines the everyday life of the ordinary housefly as it hunts for food and avoids numerous enemies that either want to eat it (like spiders) or simply eliminate it (like people). 45 min.
53-6188 Was $19.99 *$14.99*

The Amazing World Of Mini Beasts
The sex, relationships, violence and turf wars that occur in the insect kingdom are revealed in this extraordinary documentary that employs incredible photographic techniques. Among the insects featured are a praying mantis, greengrocer cicadas and molting grasshoppers. 50 min.
53-6381 *$19.99*

Bitten By The Bug: Complete Set
They're icky, creepy...and fascinating! Bugs of the world are featured in this fact-filled five-tape series on the insect kingdom, from the search for food and shelter to mating techniques and the benefits and trouble they bring to humanity. Includes "Cradle Snatchers to Grave Robbers," "Hear No Evil, See No Evil," "Keepers of the Gate," "Love at First Sight" and "The Moving Story of Insects." 125 min. total. NOTE: Individual volumes available at $14.99 each.
76-7289 *$74.99*

Insects: The Little Things That Run The World
They have highly-evolved societies, they can lift many times their own weight, and they outnumber humans 1,000 to one. Learn about the short but busy lives of the insect world's varied denizens, thanks to remarkable microscopic photography. 58 min.
83-1045 *$14.99*

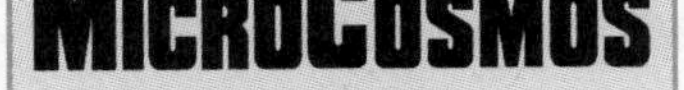

Microcosmos (1996)
It's a fascinating, dangerous and beautiful world filled with strange and savage creatures—and it's just outside your front door! Get an eerily up-close look at a day in the life of the insect kingdom in a marvelous documentary that will amaze the whole family. Narrated by Kristin Scott Thomas. 75 min.
11-2150 *$14.99*

The Barefoot Bushman
His real name is Rob Bredl, and in this three-tape collection the Australian animal expert will take you on a death-defying, up-close visit with some of the island continent's most feared (and misunderstood) creatures, as he explains their behavior and habitat. Volumes include "Kissing Crocodiles," "Playing with Snakes & Lizards" and "Dancing with Dingoes." 150 min. total.
89-5103 *$24.99*

Africa: The Serengeti (1994)
This incredible documentary offers a look at Africa's Serengeti Plains with a focus on the wildlife that lives there. Filmed in Kenya and Tanzania, the film shows how such predators as lions, crocodiles and cheetahs pursue their prey. A stunning picture of beauty and savagery, this IMAX production is narrated by James Earl Jones and features music by Hans Zimmer. 40 min.
50-8483 *$19.99*

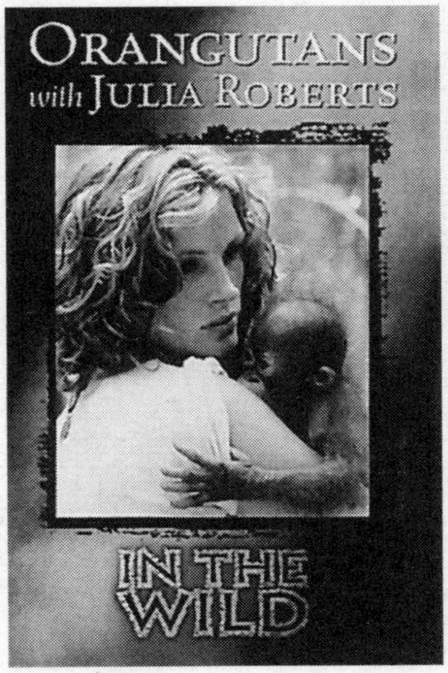

In The Wild
You'll go "wild" for these exciting episodes from the PBS nature series in which Hollywood stars travel the world for up-close encounters with endangered species. Each tape runs about 60 min.

In The Wild: Orangutans With Julia Roberts
18-7803 *$19.99*

In The Wild: Baby Animals With Whoopi Goldberg At The San Diego Zoo
18-7868 *$19.99*

In The Wild: Lemurs With John Cleese
18-7869 *$19.99*

Masters Of The Congo Jungle (1958)
Produced by Belgian documentary producer Henri Storck, this awe-inspiring film looks at the native tribes and wild animal life found in the Belgian Congo and illustrates "the wisdom and dignity of the Masters of the African jungle in their relationship to nature." Gorillas, birds in mating season, zebras, hippos and lions are featured. Orson Welles narrates. 87 min.
09-2986 *$19.99*

The Living Sea (1995)
Explore a remarkable world that covers seven-tenths of the world's surface, yet few people ever see up close, in this Academy Award-nominated short created for Imax screens. From Canada's Bay of Fundy and kelp fields off the California coast to strange creatures living thousands of feet below the surface, amazing underwater images celebrate the world's seas. Meryl Streep narrates; music by Sting. 40 min.
50-8397 *$19.99*

Wolves
The nearly extinct Northern Grey Wolf is caught in the middle of a fight in Minnesota between naturalists and farmers whose livestock is threatened. Robert Redford narrates this compelling look at the conflict over these revered predators. 60 min.
47-2098 *$14.99*

Super Predators
Spectacular wildlife footage highlights this award-winning look at such predators as lions, leopards, cheetahs, hyenas, wild dogs and crocodiles in Africa's Kruger National Park and Kenya's Masai Mara. You'll be able to observe these creatures stalking, hunting, attacking and killing their prey. 50 min.
50-2825 *$19.99*

Beavers (1999)
Get up close to the woodlands' master engineers in this acclaimed IMAX documentary. Follow a family of beavers at work and play in Canada's Rocky Mountains, and see how they build their home, avoid predators, and raise their young. 31 min.
50-8450 *$19.99*

NATIONAL GEOGRAPHIC

The National Geographic Specials
The acclaimed, award-winning documentary series from the National Geographic Society takes you to exotic lands, lets you experience thrilling journeys and brings you face to face with unusual animals. Except where noted, each tape runs approximately 60 min. There are 109 volumes available, including:

Crocodiles: Here Be Dragons
Take a dazzling journey to Africa's Grumeti River, where crocodiles infest the waters, quietly awaiting their prey.
02-2409 *$19.99*

Volcano!
Follow the daring team of Maurice and Katia Krafft (who have died since the filming of this program) as they risk their lives to film the awesome power of volcanoes.
02-2410 *$19.99*

The Lost Fleet Of Guadalcanal
Join Dr. Robert Ballard as he travels to the South Pacific to find ships that have remained unseen for 50 years. Retrace the amazing events that led to the Allied and Japanese wreckage of hidden ships, and hear recollections of Guadalcanal veterans. Features an introduction by George Bush; narrated by Stacy Keach. 106 min.
02-2438 *□$19.99*

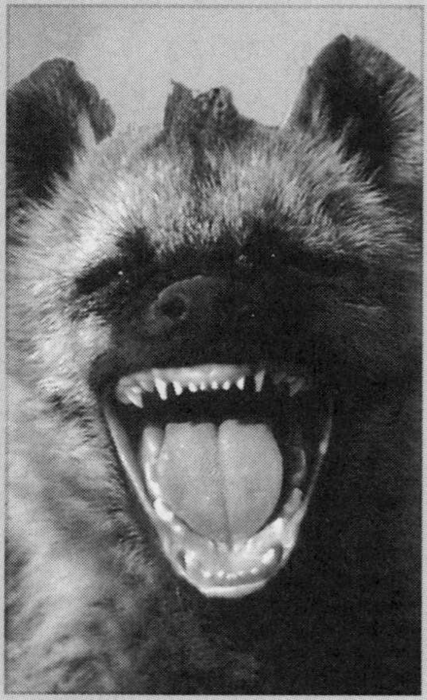

Eternal Enemies: Lions And Hyenas
In Northern Botswana, lions and hyenas clash in an intense feud where the hyena matriarch and a male lion fight to the death. One of nature's most savage conflicts is captured by incredible photography.
02-2495 *$19.99*

Killer Whales: Wolves Of The Sea
An enthralling study of killer whales and their quest for survival, hunting in packs like wolves as they search for their next meal. Brilliant photography captures these amazing mammals underwater and hurling themselves onto the beach to grab their prey.
02-2519 *□$19.99*

Season Of The Cheetah
Follow three Cheetah brothers—the fastest animals alive—as they hunt for prey in Africa's Serengeti in this program that truly chronicles survival of the fittest...and the swiftest. F. Murray Abraham narrates.
02-2584 Was $19.99 *□$14.99*

Last Voyage Of The Lusitania
What really occurred on May 7, 1915, when a German U-Boat torpedoed one of the largest luxury liners in the world, killing two-thirds of the 1,959 people aboard? Dr. Robert Ballard, the discoverer of the Titanic, investigates one of the most mysterious maritime tragedies in history. Martin Sheen narrates.
02-2618 *□$19.99*

Lions Of Darkness
Observe the wondrous world of a lion pride living on the plains of Botswana, from the arrival of three renegade males who fight and depose the clan's aging leader to the birth of new cubs, as they play, feed and train for survival.
02-2669 *□$19.99*

Giant Bears Of Kodiak Island
Travel to Alaska's Kodiak Island, where 2,700 Kodiak bears—cousins of the grizzly—reside amidst large mountains on the jagged coastline. Here you'll see the world's largest carnivores fish, search for food and teach their cubs how to survive. Richard Kiley narrates.
02-2676 *□$19.99*

Braving Alaska
The harsh world of America's 49th state is explored as you follow four families who have chosen to live in Alaska and their experiences adapting to the area and its fierce climate. These modern pioneers must hunt for food, stay warm and fend off grizzlies and other hazards. Martin Sheen narrates.
02-2677 *□$19.99*

Those Wonderful Dogs
This is an absorbing look at "man's best friend" and how canines help humans in many ways. You'll see all sorts of pooches: dogs trained as messengers in World War II, Iditarod sled-racers and even Lassie!
02-2745 *□$19.99*

Cats: Caressing The Tiger
An informative look at the wonderful world of felines, which chronicles their history, from being worshipped in ancient Egypt and persecuted in Europe to acting as comforting companions to the elderly and autistic.
02-2746 *□$19.99*

The Great Indian Railway
All aboard for a ride on the famed Great Indian Railway, as you travel through the Himalayas, along the Ganges and into Bombay. Witness the sumptuous "Palace on Wheels" and classic steam engines that are part of one of the oldest railways in the world. Linda Hunt narrates.
02-2788 *□$19.99*

Nature's Fury!
The works of man are swept, blown and carried away by the unstoppable power of natural disasters, as National Geographic takes you around the world. Earthquakes in California and Japan, hurricanes in Florida and Bangladesh, and a flood-swollen Missisippi River are all on display here.
02-2883 *□$19.99*

Cyclone!
Witness the awesome spectacle of (and the destruction wrought by) hurricanes, tornadoes and typhoons in this National Geographic documentary that puts you in the eye of the storm. Learn about the global "hot spots" for tropical storms, see amazing scenes of the damage they cause, and hear how scientists are trying to predict their creation. Peter Coyote narrates.
02-2884 *□$19.99*

Last Feast Of The Crocodiles
This program chronicles a harsh African drought that led animals to the Luvuvhu River, where they encountered hungry crocodiles face-to-face. Among the animals visiting the river are baboons, impala, elephants and lions, unaware of the dangers that awaited them there.
02-2918 *□$19.99*

Russia's Last Tsar
Follow the final days of Tsar Nicholas II, Empress Alexandra and their children through rare photos and films of the Romanovs and long-suppressed footage of Soviet authorities uncovering the family's remains. Jeremy Irons narrates.
02-2932 *□$19.99*

2000: Amazing Moments In Time
A "millennium special" from National Geographic, this eons-spanning program takes viewers from the beginnings of the universe to the possibilities of the future. You'll see how, along with plants and animals, many primitive societies are on the brink of extinction; what effects the population explosion may have on the global climate; how such sci-fi fantasies as cloning and artificial intelligence are coming true, and more. John Lithgow narrates.
18-7891 *□$19.99*

Beauty & The Beasts: A Leopard's Story
In the vast wilderness of South Africa, the lives of both predator (a leopard) and prey (a warthog) are intertwined.
19-2542 *□$19.99*

Dinosaur Hunters
Go beyond the fiction of "Jurassic Park" with a team of paleontologists as they search for remains and find, among other prizes, a fossilized oviraptor embryo.
19-2543 *□$19.99*

Secrets Of The Titanic: Collector's Edition
Perhaps the most important discovery in underwater exploration was Dr. Robert Ballard 1985 detection of the wreckage of the "unsinkable" S.S. Titanic on the Atlantic floor. Along with glimpses of the luxury liner's remains never before seen on video, this special edition of the National Geographic documentary includes an exclusive interview with Ballard. 75 min.
19-2546 *□$14.99*

Webs Of Intrigue
Step into the parlors of some of the more than 30,000 species of spiders that spin their webs throughout the world, from aquatic types that hunt their prey underwater to the giant Nephila spider, whose webs are large enough to trap birds. 45 min.
19-2556 *□$19.99*

Mysteries Underground
Get ready to see the real "wonders down under" with this documentary on caves and the people who risk their lives to explore these fascinating worlds of total darkness. Watch the first expedition in 1986 of New Mexico's Lechuguilla cave and marvel to massive stone columns, subterranean lakes and other natural wonders; and more.
19-2561 *□$19.99*

Volcano: Nature's Inferno
Mother Nature blows her top, and National Geographic is there to show you the fiery fury and thrilling footage of volcanic eruptions from around the world. Stacy Keach narrates.
19-2569 *□$19.99*

Tigers Of The Snow
Follow a Russian/American scientific team into the white wilderness of the Siberian forest to track the beautiful and endangered Siberian Tiger, the world's largest cat, in this Emmy-winning entry in the series.
19-2593 *□$19.99*

Nightmares Of Nature
From National Geographic comes a hair-raising series that takes you up close to some of the animal kingdom's strangest, rarest and most lethal denizens. Learn just how much people have to fear from these creatures, and hear about amazing real-life encounters. Each tape runs about 30 min.

Nightmares Of Nature: Deadly Reptiles
Sink your fangs into a look at rattlers, cobras and other venomous snakes, along with the world's largest lizard, the Komodo dragon.
19-2622 *□$14.99*

Nightmares Of Nature: Night Stalkers
The focus is on such nocturnal predators as bats, centipedes and spiders, all of whom have adapted to hunting in a world without sun.
19-2623 *□$14.99*

Sea Nasties
What sort of strange and dangerous creatures are waiting for you beneath the surf? Leslie Nielsen knows, and he's ready to take you on an eye-opening and fun-filled undersea enocunter with sea snakes, jellyfish, sting rays, poisonous catfish and more.
19-2628 *□$14.99*

Treasures Of The Deep
World-famous undersea explorer Robert Ballard, the discoverer of the Titanic, takes you on another exciting aquatic odyssey as he searches through fabled Roman shipwrecks of the Mediterranean.
19-2734 *$19.99*

The Greatest Flight
In a re-creation of a WWI Vickers Vimy biplane, two pilots set out in 1994 to trace an England-to-Australia flight that was made 75 years earlier. Join them on their historic voyage in this compelling program.
19-2559 *□$19.99*

Egypt: Secrets Of The Pharaohs
Travel to the golden land of mystery, intrigue, and endless deserts: Egypt. Deep down within the pyramids, hidden with the pharaohs, are mysteries that have puzzled people for centuries...until now. Watch as archeologists and researchers uncover the secrets of mummification and the construction of the pyramids.
19-2738 *$19.99*

Untold Stories Of WWII
How close was Germany to developing the atomic bomb? Did Japan plan an underwater attack on Pearl Harbor? What effect did the kamikaze pilots have on the war in the Pacific? Hidden for over 50 years, the secrets behind these and other tales of World War II are revealed in a fascinating National Geographic special.
19-2788 *□$19.99*

The Battle For Midway
It was perhaps the pivotal naval conflict of World War II, and in this National Geographic battle you'll join underwater explorer Robert Ballard on an odyssey 17,000 feet beneath the Pacific to explore sunken ships and search for the remains of the battleship U.S.S. Yorktown.
19-2841 *□$19.99*

Stock Car Fever
NASCAR and National Geographic? The globe-trotting cameramen turn their lenses on Alabama's Talladega Speedway for a look at the fast-paced world of auto racing, with appearances by champion drivers Dale Jarrett and Jeff Gordon.
19-2852 *□$14.99*

Land Of The Anaconda
Follow a husband-wife team deep into the South American jungle as they attempt to capture and study one of the world's largest (sometimes more than 20 feet) and deadliest (squeezing its prey to death) of snakes, the anaconda.
19-2863 *□$19.99*

The Noble Horse
They were among the first animals domesticated by man, and the horse has been a constant companion in war and peace for over 4,000 years. Learn about the special connection between human and animal, and see tame and wild horses from around the world, in this National Geographic special.
19-2918 *□$19.99*

Mysteries Of Egypt
Originally made for IMAX theatres, this stunning National Geographic film takes you through five millennia of splendor of one of the world's great civilizations. See how the art, architecture, religion and lore of Egypt continue to fascinate to this day. Omar Sharif narrates. Includes a "making of" documentary. 90 min.
19-2919 *□$19.99*

Beyond 2000: The New Explorers
Meet the new breed of scientists, researchers and adventurers who are facing the final frontiers of the planet head on and leading the exploration of the next millennium in this National Geographic special.
19-2920 *□$19.99*

Phantom Quest: The Search For Extra Terrestrials
Join National Geographic on a journey across the planet—and beyond—for evidence of extraterrestrial life and the ongoing efforts to contact them. 30 min.
19-2921 *□$14.99*

Surviving Everest: The Collector's Edition
This special National Geographic presentation features the 1983 documentary "Return to Everest," in which climbers Sir Edmund Hillary and Tenzing Norgay look back on their 1953 conquest of the world's highest peak; a bonus program and an exclusive interview with Hillary. 100 min.
19-2922 *□$19.99*

Hindenburg's Fiery Secret
Was it an accident or sabotage that caused the German airship Hindenburg to burst in flames during its May, 1937 landing in New Jersey, killing 33 people? Hear amazing first-hand stories from survivors and eyewitnesses, and hear new evidence of what happened on the dirigible's final flight.
19-2936 *□$19.99*

Dinosaur Giants Found
Go in the field in Afrcia with paleontologist Paul Sereno as he uncovers a newly-discovered species of dinosaur, go on a hunt for dinosaur eggs, a meet a T-Rex named Sue—well, her skeleton, anyway—in this National Geographic presentation.
19-2943 *$19.99*

The Swarm: India's Killer Bees
They're twice as big as regular bees and a menace to animals and man. Travel to mountainous regions of Northeast India to study this aggressive insect and how quickly the danger of killer bees is spreading around the world.
19-2965 *□$19.99*

Australia's Kangaroos
The living symbol of their homeland, the remarkable marsupials are the stars of this National Geographic program that looks at a year in the life of a red kangaroo family and examines the animals' habitat and their link to Australia's aborigines.
19-2972 *□$19.99*

Australia's Great Barrier Reef
Stretching for more than 1,200 miles, the world's largest coral reef lies just a few miles off the Northwest Australian coast. Explore the many wonders of this beautifully delicate ecosystem, home to such unusual creatures as damsel fish, manta rays, barracuda and others.
19-2973 *□$19.99*

Australia's Aborigines
Their ways and traditions have remained unchanged for centuries, but Australia's increasing settlement threatens the aborigines' society.
47-1999 *$19.99*

Great White Shark: The Truth About The Legend
Three people intimately associated with sharks—"Jaws" author Peter Benchley, undersea photographer David Doublet and shark attack victim-turned-preservationist Rodney Fox—separate fact from fiction as they look at this fascinating, and endangered, aquatic predator.
19-2974 *□$19.99*

Gorilla
Enter the domain of the mightiest of the apes, from rare African jungle footage to an interview with "talking gorilla" Koko.
47-1590 *$19.99*

Destination Space
Is interplanetary exploration in mankind's near future? This National Geographic program examines the possibilities for a manned mission to Mars in the next century and how the next generation of rockets may take us even farther.
19-2980 ☐*$19.99*

Submarine I-52: In Search Of WWII Gold
Does a fortune in Japanese gold lie at the bottom of the Atlantic Ocean? Join the hunt for a Japanese sub, sunk during World War II, and its $15 million cargo in this thrilling National Geographic program.
19-2987 ☐*$19.99*

Jane Goodall: My Life With The Chimpanzees
The extraordinary saga of Jane Goodall and her work with wild apes in Africa is chronicled in this fascinating program stretching from her first trip to Africa in 1960 to the present and chronicling Goodall's efforts to save the chimps' homelands. Hosted by Jack Lemmon.
02-2786 ☐*$19.99*

Land Of The Tiger
The Indian jungle is home to this beautiful and mysterious jungle cat. The Bengal tiger, both feared and revered by man for centuries, is seen in rare nature footage.
47-1543 *$14.99*

The Incredible Human Machine
Award-winning odyssey inside the body, showing the amazing interaction of various systems and the wonders of life.
47-1591 *$14.99*

Yukon Passage
Four explorers take an unforgettable trip through the Canadian and Alaskan wilderness in this odyssey, narrated by James Stewart.
47-1592 *$19.99*

Rain Forest
Explore a Central American rain forest and see how this fragile environment shelters some of the world's most unique flora and fauna.
47-1702 *$14.99*

The Invisible World
Special photography has enabled us to witness wonders previously beyond the range of human vision. Follow the path of a bullet in flight, watch flowers bloom, and see the incredible array of life within a drop of water.
47-1852 Was $19.99 *$14.99*

In The Shadow Of Vesuvius
Recent archeological digs have brought back to life the cities of Pompeii and Herculaneum, buried for centuries under volcanic debris.
47-1923 *$19.99*

The Search For The Battleship Bismarck
One of Germany's most famous WWII ships, the mighty Bismarck took 2,000 lives when it was sunk by Allied forces in the North Atlantic. Now the discoverers of the Titanic wreckage take you on a fantastic journey to witness the actual finding of the Bismarck.
47-2000 *$19.99*

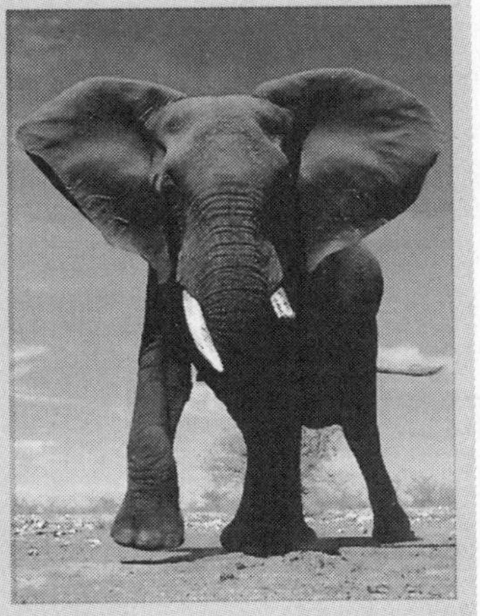

Elephant
Exciting, informative look at elephants around the world and their uncertain future. Travel to Sri Lanka and Kenya, where you'll see how the giant beasts communicate over great distances and are an object of worship and affection. Narrated by E.G. Marshall.
47-2017 Was $19.99 ☐*$14.99*

For All Mankind (1989)
Outstanding look at the Apollo moon flights, featuring actual NASA footage and narration by the astronauts themselves. Nominated for an Academy Award, Al Reinert's stunning documentary presents the wonder of spaceflight in a way that's never been shown before. 80 min.
02-2424 ☐*$19.99*

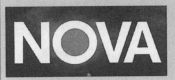

Science

Future Fantastic
A joint BBC/Learning Channel production, this compelling documentary series features interviews with leading researchers and science-fiction writers to track the possible courses of science and technology over the next century and beyond. Included in the two-tape set are "Alien," "I, Robot," "The Incredible Shrinking Planet," "Space Pioneers" and "Immortals." Gillian Anderson hosts. 240 min. total.
04-3821 ☐*$29.99*

The Miracle Of Birth
What happens in the nine short months from conception to delivery that results in the birth of a human baby? This special, culled from the BBC's "Intimate Universe" series, tracks the development from fertilized egg to embryo to fetus, with incredible photography from inside the womb. 50 min.
04-3827 ☐*$12.99*

Intimate Universe: The Human Body
It's a strange and rarely-seen universe of wonders, and it lies right under your skin! Travel inside the human body via amazing time-lapse and micro-photography with this BBC-produced documentary series. Included in the four-tape set are "Lifestory/Everyday Miracle," "First Steps/Raging Teens," "Brain Power/As Time Goes By" and "The End of Life/Making of the Human Body." 400 min. total.
04-3828 ☐*$59.99*

After The Warming
A fascinating two-part program on the "Greenhouse Effect" and its possible consequences for the Earth in the future. Join James Burke and his "Virtual Reality Chamber" to witness the year 2050, how the global warming crises of the 1990s led to worldwide catastrophes, and what can be done now to prevent them. 110 min.
14-9008 *$49.99*

Connections 2/Connections 2: The Journey Continues: Complete Set
The origins of and links between scientific discoveries throughout history are surveyed in this acclaimed series hosted by James Burke. How did the invention of bottle caps lead to the Hubble Space telescope, or Dutch pirates to ballpoint pens? Find out in this five-tape boxed set of all 20 episodes of "Connections 2" and "Connections 2: The Journey Continues." 10 hrs. total.
14-9163 *$129.99*

Connections 3: Journey On The Web: Complete Set
Host James Burke's intertwining odyssey through history and science takes him (and you) through such seemingly unconnected items as calamine lotion, electricity, Einstein's theory of relativity and the atomic bomb in this three-volume series. Included are "Feedback," "What's in a Name?" and "Drop the Apple." 180 min. total.
14-9168 *$49.99*

A. Einstein: How I See The World
Legendary genius Albert Einstein is profiled in this documentary that uses newsreel footage as well as Einstein's personal diaries and writings to look at both the public and private sides of the Nobel-winner and peace advocate. William Hurt narrates. 60 min.
18-7544 Was $24.99 *$19.99*

Creation Of The Universe
Journalist Timothy Ferris takes you on a journey from the Big Bang 15 billion years ago to today's frontiers of science. Examine subjects from quarks to quasars with help from computer graphics, special effects and commentary from experts. 90 min.
18-7545 Was $24.99 ☐*$19.99*

Antarctica
It's the most isolated place on Earth, and now, through amazing IMAX photography, you can explore the frozen wilderness of Antarctica, see the animals that live there, and hear the exploits of the courageous explorers who braved its brutal climate. 40 min.
50-5342 *$29.99*

Intimate Strangers: Unseen Life On Earth
They're the smallest and most pervasive living things on the planet, and in this four-volume documentary series you'll get an up-close look at the world of microbes and bacteria. Learn how these one-celled wonders have shaped the environment for billions of years, and how they both protect and endanger human life. 200 min. total.
53-6832 *$59.99*

The Mysterious Origins Of Man: Collector's Gift Boxed Set
Did man live alongside dinosaurs? Is the lost continent of Atlantis buried beneath ice? Did alien visitors genetically engineer the first humans? These and other thought-provoking questions regarding human evolution and development are examined in this three-tape collection. Included are "Rewriting Man's History," hosted by Charlton Heston; "Challenging New Theories" and "The Mystery of Jurassic Art." 170 min. total. NOTE: "Rewriting Man's History" is available separately at $19.99.
20-7751 *$39.99*

NOVA

Nova Video Library
The award-winning PBS science series is once again available on home video. Movies Unlimited is proud to offer these amazing journeys into the wondrous worlds around, inside and beyond us. Except where noted, each tape runs about 60 min. There are 48 volumes available, including:

The Real Jurassic Park
Could the premise of the hit Steven Spielberg movie—that scientists could re-create dinosaurs from fossilized DNA samples—really come true? Join "Jurassic" star Jeff Goldblum and author Michael Crichton to explore this fascinating question.
07-2319 ☐*$9.99*

The Bermuda Triangle
What are the bizarre secrets behind this region of the Atlantic Ocean where many planes and ships have vanished without a trace?
47-1859 Was $29.99 ☐*$19.99*

This Old Pyramid
In order to reveal the secrets of the ancient pyramids, Egyptologist Mark Lehner and master stonemason Roger Hopkins decide to construct one themselves, putting together a structure near the Great Pyramid of Giza. 90 min.
50-2652 ☐*$24.99*

Mysterious Crash Of Flight 201
An investigative report into the questions surrounding the disaster of Flight 201, which suddenly broke up while flying 9,000 feet over a jungle in Panama. Join National Travel Safety Board investigator Thomas Heueter as he pieces together a deadly puzzle.
50-2661 *$19.99*

Little Creatures Who Run The World
This remarkable look into the lives of ants shows how the highly socialized insects live in a world of rigid work details, intimate partnerships and deadly warfare (sound familiar?). With amazing photography and commentary from Harvard University's Edward Wilson.
50-2666 *$19.99*

The Universe Within
Take a tour through the human body and witness things that will astound you—things occurring in your body even as you read this! Microscopic photography and enthralling graphics help take you on a fantastic voyage.
50-2667 *$19.99*

Ebola: The Plague Fighters
The mysteries of one of the world's deadliest diseases are examined in this unflinching program that chronicles four weeks in the quarantined city of Kikwit, Zaire, where the virus killed over three-fourths of its victims.
50-5201 ☐*$19.99*

B-29 Frozen In Time
Follow the incredible mission of pilot Daryl Greenmayer and his team to revive and fly the Kee Bird, a rare B-29 bomber stranded in Greenland for almost 50 years.
50-5204 ☐*$19.99*

Nomads Of The Rainforest
Eastern Ecuador is the setting for this insightful look at the Waironi Indians and their unspoiled way of life.
50-5210 ☐*$19.99*

Titanic's Lost Sister
Join Robert Ballard, the man known for uncovering the Titanic, as he searches for the Britannic, the ship's twin. Ballard and his crew are equipped with a nuclear submarine, sonar and high-tech cameras as they look for the vessel that served as a luxury liner, then a hospital ship when the Germans sank it during World War I in the Aegean Sea. 60 min.
50-5404 ☐*$19.99*

Secrets Of Lost Empires: Boxed Set
Some of the greatest structures in the world are given a close look in a five-tape series that features experts testing different ingeniously designed archeological sites using traditional methods. Can the experts better the originals? Included are "Colosseum," "Inca," "Obelisk," "Pyramid" and "Stonehenge." 300 min. total. NOTE: Individual volumes available at $19.99 each.
50-5413 Save $30.00! ☐*$69.99*

The Science Of Crime: Set
This three-tape set includes "Hunt for the Serial Arsonist," in which a series of Los Angeles fires are traced to a single suspect; "The Bombing of America," focusing on the disturbing rise in bombing cases and the latest forensic techniques to solve them; and "Mind of a Serial Killer," about a special FBI unit that gets "into the heads" of the most dangerous and elusive of murderers. 180 min. total. NOTE: Individual volumes available at $19.99 each.
50-5419 Save $10.00! ☐*$49.99*

Einstein Revealed
What was Albert Einstein really like? This insightful installment of "Nova" answers that question, delving into the man's personal and professional life through testimony from scholars, computer animation that illustrates his theories and quotes from Einstein himself, who is played by actor Andrew Sachs ("Fawlty Towers"). 120 min.
50-5407 ☐*$19.99*

Amazing Animals: Boxed Set
You'll roar with delight and wonderment with this three-tape set of "Nova" episodes that features "All-American Bear," a look at the North American black bear; "Little Creatures Who Run the World," a remarkable documentary on ants; and "Mystery of Animal Pathfinders," which focuses on animal migration. 180 min. total. NOTE: Individual volumes available at $19.99 each.
50-5429 Save $10.00! ☐*$49.99*

Odyssey Of Life: Boxed Set
This three-tape package spotlights the work of Lennart Nilsson, the master of micro-photography behind "The Miracle of Life." Included are "The Ultimate Journey," an astounding look at life from the womb before birth; "The Photographer's Secret," in which Nilsson reveals some of his "tricks"; and "The Unknown World," featuring a close look at critters lurking at home. 180 min. total. NOTE: Individual volumes available at $19.99 each.
50-5433 Save $10.00! ☐*$49.99*

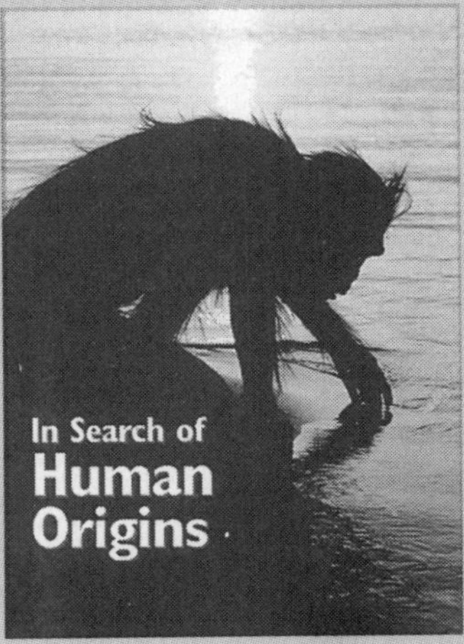

In Search Of Human Origins: Complete Set
This special three-part "Nova" presentation is hosted by anthropologist Don Johanson, who returns to the site in Ethiopia where, in 1974, he found the skeletal remains of "Lucy," the oldest known human ancestor. Learn about the latest theories on human development in "In Search of Lucy," "Surviving in Africa" and "The Creative Revolution." 180 min. total. NOTE: Individual volumes available at $19.99 each.
50-2654 *$59.99*

Nature's Fury: Complete Set
Three exciting and frightening programs allow you to join the "storm chasers" as they encounter "Flood!," featuring footage of 1993's disastrous Mississippi River floods; "Lightning!," an unforgettable look at nature's dangerous impulses; and "Hurricane!," a chronicle of Camille and Gilbert's devastation. 180 min. total. NOTE: Individual volumes available at $19.99 each.
50-5211 Save $10.00! ☐*$49.99*

Mystery Of The Senses: Complete Set
This five-part series examines the human senses through scientific research and dazzling imagery. You'll visit the world's largest perfumery, the quietest place on Earth and other "sense-ible" spots. Included are "Hearing," "Smell," "Taste," "Touch" and "Vision." 300 min. total. NOTE: Individual volumes available at $19.99 each.
50-5215 Save $30.00! ☐*$69.99*

Natural Disasters: Boxed Set
Featured in a boxed set are three films from the "Nova" series depicting nature at its most frightening. "The Day the Earth Shook" details the 1994 earthquake that devastated Southern California; a squad of "storm chasers" working on the worst day in tornado history is the focus of "Tornado!"; and "Path of the Killer Volcano" looks at the 1991 eruption of Mt. Pinatubo in the Philippines. 180 min. total. NOTE: Individual volumes available at $19.99 each.
50-5396 Save $20.00! ☐*$49.99*

The Vikings
Their brutal reputation made them a feared enemy across Europe, but they were also savvy traders and intrepid explorers who reached America centuries before Columbus and established the world's oldest surviving parliament. This "Nova" program traces the history and culture of the Norse people, separating fact from fiction and showing how they shaped the face of medieval Europe. 120 min.
90-1066 *$19.99*

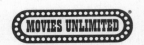

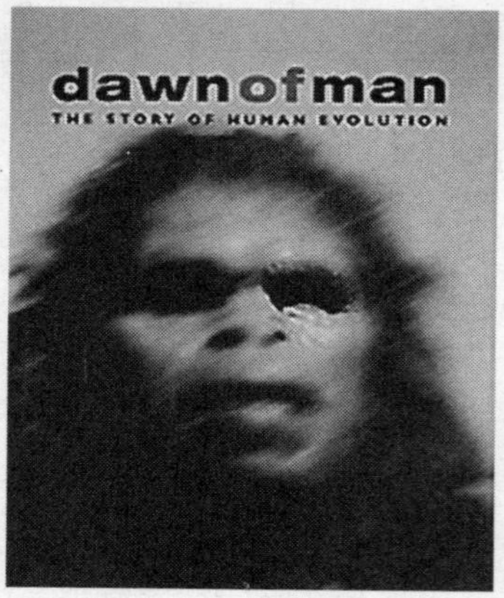

Dawn Of Man: Boxed Set (2000)
Follow more than five million years of human evolution with this compelling BBC series seen stateside on the Learning Channel. Paleoanthropologists and other experts offer a look at man's development, from the earliest ape-like hominids in Africa to the rise of Neanderthals and Cro-Magnon to the present, while computer animated re-creations vividly depict the day-to-day life of our ancestors. Special video version includes a bonus episode not seen on broadcast TV. 5 hrs. on three tapes.
19-5010 *$49.99*

The Discoverers (1993)
Acclaimed IMAX documentary, based on Dr. Daniel J. Boorstin's Pulitzer Prize-winning book, looks at man's ongoing quest to explore and understand the world around him, from Sir Isaac Newton's experiments in his 17th-century lab to contemporary researcher Dr. Louis Herman's work in dolphins in Hawaii. Also includes a special "making of" documentary. 72 min.
50-8463 *$19.99*

Ape Man: The Story Of Human Evolution
Walter Cronkite hosts this fascinating look at the ascent of man from the creators of "Dinosaur." The four-tape series includes "The Human Puzzle," focusing on the world after the Age of Reptiles; "Giant Strides," about man's ability to walk; "All in the Mind," exploring man's brain and drive for survival; and "Science and Fiction," in which evolutionists predict the future. 200 min. total.
53-8026 *$79.99*

Life By The Numbers: Complete Set
Explore the world of mathematics, and how its principles play a role in everything from microscopic life to the motion of planets, in this seven-part series hosted by Danny Glover. Included are "Seeing Is Believing: Special Effects," "The Numbers Game: Sports," "Patterns of Nature: Biology," "Chances of a Lifetime: Probability," "Shape of the World: Exploration," "A New Age: Information Age" and "Making a Difference: Education." 420 min. total. NOTE: Individual volumes available at $19.99 each.
27-7135 Save $20.00! *$119.99*

A Glorious Accident
Some of the greatest minds of the day discuss, separately and in a group, their thoughts on man's place in the cosmos in this compelling seven-part documentary series. Included are "Daniel C. Dennett: Consciousness Explained," "Freeman Dyson: Disturbing the Universe," "Stephan Jay Gould: Strange Life," "Oliver Sacks: Awakenings," "Daniel C. Sheldrake: A New Science of Life," "Stephen Toulmin: Wittgenstein's Vienna" and the two-part "A Clash of Minds." 16 hrs. on eight tapes. NOTE: Individual volumes available at $29.99 each.
80-7048 Save $60.00! *$179.99*

Fractals: The Colors Of Infinity
First developed by Polish-born French mathematician Benoit Mandelbrot in the 1970s, fractals are geometric figures created by running a simple pattern through a series of rules, resulting in designs that artists and scientists alike can appreciate. Arthur C. Clarke narrates this easy-to-follow exploration into the world of fractal geometry, with interviews with Mandelbrot and other experts and a dazzling array of images. 52 min.
80-7251 *$29.99*

Planet Earth: Complete Set
Learn about the origins, development, and ever-changing face of the fragile world mankind calls home in this Emmy-winning seven-tape documentary series. Volumes include "The Living Machine," "The Blue Planet," "The Climate Puzzle," "Tales from Other Worlds," "The Solar Sea," "Gifts from the Earth" and "The Fate of the Earth." 403 min. total. NOTE: Individual volumes available at $19.99 each.
83-1070 Save $40.00! *$99.99*

Science Of The Impossible: Boxed Set
Explore the frontiers of medicine, astronomy, cybernetics and other fields of study, and watch science fiction become science fact, with this fascinating five-tape series. Included are "Aliens: Where Are They?," "Can We Reach the Stars?," "Facing Doomsday," "Future Body" and "Invisible Forces." 250 min. total. NOTE: Individual volumes available at $14.99 each.
83-1318 Save $15.00! *$59.99*

Stephen Hawking's Universe: Complete Set
The renowned physicist, teacher, and author of "A Brief History of Time" explores the nature of the universe, its probable beginning and its ultimate end in this fascinating six-part documentary series. Included are "Seeing Is Believing," "The Big Bang," "Cosmic Alchemy," "On the Dark Side," "Black Holes and Beyond" and "An Answer to Everything." 6 hrs. total.
18-7782 *$59.99*

A Brief History Of Time (1992)
An acclaimed look at the fascinating world of Stephen Hawking, the brilliant ALS-stricken physicist and author whose work has revolutionized science. Directed by Errol Morris, the film juxtaposes Hawking's own life story with inventive illustrations of his writings and theories, examining such topics as the universe's origin, the nature of time, and which came first, the chicken or the egg. Music by Philip Glass. 84 min.
06-2083 Was $89.99 *$19.99*

Beyond T-Rex
Barney, take a seat; the real Tyrannosaurus Rex was the baddest, toughest dinosaur to ever walk the Earth...or was he? This new program from the Discovery Channel uncovers new evidence that suggests that perhaps there were two other prehistoric creatures that could take T. Rex on in a Battle Royal any day. Decide for yourself. 50 min.
02-8887 *$19.99*

T-Rex: The Real World
It was the largest predator that ever walked the Earth, and now you can explore the prehistoric world of Tyrannosaurus Rex in this fascinating documentary. Visit the sites where several T-Rex skeletons have been found, as well as South Dakota's Black Hills Institute of Geological Research, the world's largest fossil preparation lab. 35 min.
20-7752 *$19.99*

Walking With Dinosaurs
Get ready to go back 65 million years and come face to face with the largest creatures ever to roam the landscape with this BBC documentary series. Amazing computer graphics and the latest scientific data tell the story of how the dinosaurs lived, thrived and ultimately perished. Kenneth Branagh narrates. 180 min. on two tapes.
04-3938 *$24.99*

The Dinosaurs!: Complete Set
They've been extinct for millions of years, but dinosaurs are possibly more prevalent now than ever before. This four-part series from PBS looks back on their prehistoric world, the first fossil discoveries, and the latest theories on how they lived in "The Monsters Emerge," "Flesh on the Bones," "The Nature of the Beast" and "The Death of the Dinosaur." 240 min. total. NOTE: Individual volumes available at $14.99 each.
07-8386 Save $20.00! *$39.99*

Dinosaur!: Complete Set
Join host Walter Cronkite for an examination of the remarkable creatures who ruled the Earth for millions of years. This acclaimed four-volume series includes "The First Clue: Tale of a Tooth," "The Fossil Rush: Tale of a Bone," "Birth of a Legend: Tale of an Egg" and "Giant Birds of the Air: Tale of a Feather." 200 min. total. NOTE: Individual volumes available at $19.99 each.
53-7607 Save $20.00! *$59.99*

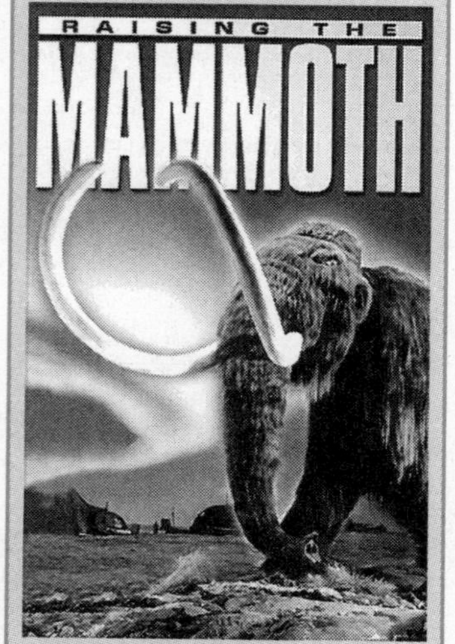

Raising The Mammoth (2000)
One of the most popular programs in the history of the Discovery Channel, this remarkable documentary chronicles the attempt to retrieve a perfectly preserved, frozen woolly mammoth from its 20,000-plus-year home in the Arctic wilderness of Siberia. Learn how these vanished giants lived, and hear how scientists may one day use cloning to bring the mammoth back to life. Narrated by Jeff Bridges. 120 min.
27-7207 *$14.99*

Aurora: Rivers Of Light In The Sky
The natural beauty of Aurora Borealis—the "Northern Lights"—has fascinated and bewildered people for centuries. Now take an even closer look at this natural phenomenon through its myths and legends, the actual science behind the auroral display, and gorgeous photography of the lights themselves. 40 min.
89-5124 *$19.99*

The Miracle Of Life (1982)
Acclaimed documentary, seen on the PBS series "Nova," takes the viewer inside the human body to witness human growth and development from conception to birth. Microscopic photography makes this a fascinating, unforgettable viewing experience; produced for Swedish Television and photographed by Lennart Nilsson. 60 min.
50-3757 *$19.99*

Fine Arts

George Grosz In America
Born in Berlin in 1893, expressionist painter/illustrator George Grosz was one of the first artists to criticize the Nazi regime and fled to America in 1932. This documentary from the Museum of Modern Art examines his life, influence and work in the New World. 90 min.
22-1624 *$19.99*

Works By Women: From The Heart
Produced by the Museum of Modern Art, this documentary explores the work of nine 20th-century women artists, all of whom are represented in the noted Gihon art collection. 60 min.
22-1634 *$19.99*

Discovery Of Art: Boxed Set
This unique six-tape series offers viewers an up-close look at some of the Western world's most memorable artists and their works and offers insights into art history. Included in the set are "Anne of Brittany: The Great Book of Hours," "Books and Kings," "Botticelli: The Humanist Trilogy," "Pablo Picasso's Guernica," "Paintings in Books" and "Vermeer: The Magical Light." 270 min. total. NOTE: Individual volumes available at $19.99 each.
22-1681 Save $20.00! *$99.99*

Masters Of Sea And Sail
Works by such masters as Rembrandt, Vermeer, Vroom, Porcellis and others help tell the story of the Dutch marine artists of the 16th and 17th centuries, some of whom sailed on board naval ships to authentically capture scenes of maritime combat. 45 min.
22-1714 *$19.99*

The Great Artists: The Impressionists: Boxed Set
In the mid-19th century a school of French artists rejected the prevailing styles of painting and gave rise to a new term: impressionism. Learn about the men and their work in this six-tape series that highlights some of the greatest names in art: Degas, Manet, Monet, Pissarro, Renoir and Seurat. 300 min. total. NOTE: Individual volumes available at $19.99 each.
22-1734 Save $20.00! *$99.99*

The Great Artists: The Dutch Masters: Boxed Set
With works ranging from landscapes and depictions of peasant life to elegant portraits and bizarre fantasy images, the painters of 15th- to 17th-century Holland were as diverse as their subjects. This six-tape series gives insight into the world and art of Bosch, Bruegel, Rembrandt, Rubens, Van Dyck and Vermeer. 300 min. total. NOTE: Individual volumes available at $19.99 each.
22-1786 Save $20.00! *$99.99*

Edvard Munch
The Norwegian painter used the traumas of his childhood and the lifelong grief that followed to shape his art, and in so doing helped to develop the expressionist style. Follow Edvard Munch's story, and learn about the man behind such memorable works as "The Scream." 52 min.
22-1777 *$19.99*

Magritte
A leading exponent of the "magic realism" school of Surrealist artists, Belgian-born René Magritte challenged sensibilities with his depiction of commonplace items in his paintings. Get insight into the man and his work in this fascinating program. 55 min.
22-1778 *$19.99*

Monsieur René Magritte
He was the first Surrealist to shift focus from personal reflection to the exterior world...and he created a fascinating world where everyday objects would shed their familiarity. An absorbing and compelling chronicle. 60 min.
22-5101 Was $39.99 *$29.99*

The Great Masters: Boxed Set
This illuminating eight-tape series casts light on some of Europe's most renowned artists, their works and their world. Included are "Caravaggio," "Fra Angelico," "Francesca," "Michelangelo," "Raphael," "Strozzi," "Tintoretto" and "Van Dyck." 6 hrs. total. NOTE: Individual volumes available at $19.99 each.
22-1809 Save $60.00! *$99.99*

Georgia O'Keeffe
The only documentary interview with the woman whose landscapes of the American Southwest earned her immortality in the realm of fine art. O'Keeffe discusses her life and work with candor and wit in this PBS production. 59 min.
22-5002 *$39.99*

Mary Cassat: Impressionist From Philadelphia
She left Main Line society for Paris, studied with Degas, and is recognized today as ranking with the foremost American painters of the 1800s. Her story and works are given reverent presentation in this PBS production. 30 min.
22-5003 *$29.99*

Louise Nevelson In Process
The camera follows the celebrated environmental sculptress in action as she renders two new works in her inimitable manner. Her beginnings, spent creating masterworks from street junk, are also discussed. 29 min.
22-5004 *$29.99*

Paul Cadmus: Enfant Terrible At 80
His satirical renderings caused uproar in the '30s and '40s, and time had not mellowed him. Cadmus reminisces about his past while creating works in egg yolk tempera for the camera in this David Sutherland film. 57 min.
22-5005 *$39.99*

Salvador Dali: A Soft Self-Portrait
A video portrait as unique and fascinating as its subject. Orson Welles narrates this look at the Spanish surrealist whose works, lifestyle and moustache have made him a legend in 20th century art; co-produced by Dali. 60 min.
07-8090 *$29.99*

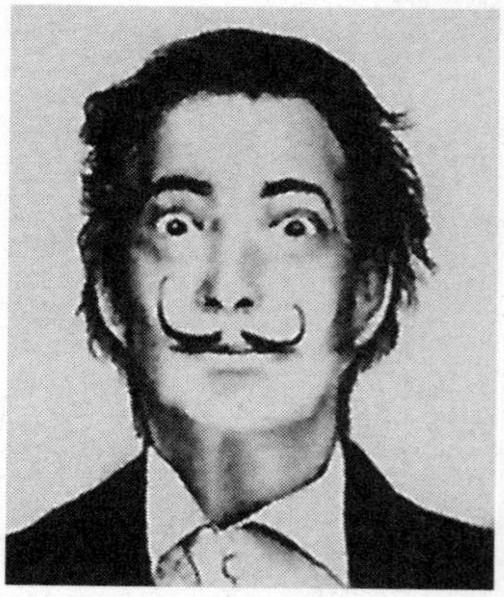

The Definitive Dali: A Lifetime Retrospective
His influence in painting, sculpture, writing and cinema cannot be overstated. Now the life and work of Salvador Dali are featured in a documentary that combines interviews with friends and associates of Dali, rare studio footage, film clips and looks at some of his most famous creations. 75 min.
22-1093 Was $29.99 *$19.99*

El Greco
The life and contributions of the 16th-century artist, whose works include "View Of Toledo," are depicted in this documentary that also examines the Counter-Reformation, El Greco's inspiration for his religious works. 30 min.
22-5037 *$29.99*

Suleyman The Magnificent
Produced to coincide with the recent international exhibit, this collection of rare art treasures and relics from the 16th-century Ottoman emperor's reign gives a rare insight into the culture and heritage of the Renaissance Middle East. 57 min.
22-5071 *$39.99*

Marcel Duchamp: In His Own Words
One of the guiding figures in modern art history, French-born painter/sculptor Marcel Duchamp discusses his early works in what would come to be known as the Cubist and Dada schools of art in this Museum of Modern Art presentation. 35 min.
22-1615 *$19.99*

Marcel Duchamp: The Secret Of Marcel Duchamp
This fascinating study of the man who turned the art establishment on its head by turning everyday subjects into works of art, focuses on the French artist's final creation, the Etant Donnés, discovered years after his death in 1968. Also chronicled is Duchamp's affair with Maria Martins, and the effect this had on his artwork. 50 min.
22-6070 *$29.99*

Marcel Duchamp: A Game Of Chess
A portrait of groundbreaking artist Marcel Duchamp, one of the leading forces in Dada, surrealism, futurism and kinetic/conceptional art. His incredible life is traced from his years in France to his move to America in 1915. 56 min.
22-5480 Was $39.99 *$29.99*

Sister Wendy's Story Of Painting: Complete Set

She's the British nun who's made the world of art history her "habit," and now Sister Wendy's witty and insightful BBC series is available in a five-volume collection. Filmed on location around the world, Sister Wendy shares her thoughts on the great masters as she guides you through "Early Art," "The Renaissance," "Baroque to Romanticism," "The Age of Revolution" and "Modernism." 300 min. total.
04-3509   *$99.99*

Sister Wendy's Grand Tour

For decades her world was confined to the convent that was her home, as she devoted herself to the study of art. Now you can follow Sister Wendy Beckett on a tour of Europe's finest museums and historical sites, as she witnesses first-hand the masterworks she previously had only seen in books. 100 min.
04-3753   *$19.99*

Germany: Dada

The Dada movement, which rejected Western influence on European culture, later spawned pop art and surrealism. The works of Dadaists like Hans Richter and Richard Huelsenbeck are chronicled in this fascinating collage of 20th-century art, music and poetry. 55 min.
10-3202   *$19.99*

Van Gogh: A Museum For Vincent

Tour Amsterdam's popular Van Gogh Museum, which features a world-famous collection of the painter's works. Also, learn about Van Gogh's stormy personal life through his paintings, and then visit France, the Netherlands and Belgium. 32 min.
22-1226   *$29.99*

In A Brilliant Light: Van Gogh In Arles

The 444 days in which the Dutch Master sequestered himself in the South of France resulted in some of his most memorable efforts. This compelling study of that work casts fresh light on the man, as well. 57 min.
22-5096   Was $39.99   *$29.99*

Van Gogh's Van Goghs

Produced to commemorate the 1998-99 American exhibition of 70 Van Gogh paintings on loan from Amsterdam's Van Gogh Museum, this program traces the painter's career through three distinct phases: Van Gogh's early work in Holland, the influence of Impressionists on his paintings, and his years in the South of France. Jacqueline Bisset narrates. 57 min.
22-6033   *$29.99*

Vincent: The Life And Death Of Vincent Van Gogh (1987)

Australia's Paul Cox ("My First Wife") directed this widely acclaimed look at the life, art and soul of painter Vincent Van Gogh. The film uses letters and never-before-seen drawings to help illustrate Van Gogh's world. A fascinating film, with John Hurt providing the voice of the tormented artist. 99 min.
53-7511   *$89.99*

Jackson Pollock: Love And Death In Long Island

His colorful, chaotic canvases earned him the nickname "Jack the Dripper," but Wyoming-born painter Jackson Pollock became a vanguard in modern American art before his 1956 death in a car accident. This BBC documentary features rare film footage of Pollock at work in his Long Island studio; interviews with his wife, artist Lee Krasner, and actor Ed Harris; and more. 46 min.
22-6089   *$29.99*

Varga Girl: The Esquire Pin-Up Girl

Alberto Varga's paintings of gorgeous women graced Esquire magazine's pages for decades. This documentary retrospective features 60 classic beauties, plus calendar artwork and personal photos and letters. 55 min.
22-1431   *$19.99*

Thomas Eakins: A Motion Portrait

Recognized as a master of 19th-century American art, Philadelphia-born Eakins was criticized at the time for his nude paintings. Kevin Conway plays Eakins in this unique documentary that uses photos of his work and interviews with contemporaries to provide insights into the artist's world. Sam Waterston narrates. 60 min.
22-5073   *$39.99*

Art Of The Western World: Complete Set

A stunning historical and visual account of the world of art, from Ancient Greece to Post-Modernism, is presented in this four-tape collection. Host Michael Wood is joined by a team of international art experts to offer insight into over 2,000 years of the creative process. 450 min. total. NOTE: Individual volumes available at $29.99 each.
22-1336   Save $20.00!   *$99.99*

Edward Hopper: The Silent Witness

Regarded as one of the finest artists of the 20th-century American Realism style, Hopper's life and *oeuvre* are studied in this documentary that goes to Cape Cod to look for sites that served as inspirations for his stark, moody paintings. 43 min.
22-1415   *$19.99*

Jasper Johns: Take An Object

Making art out of everyday objects—and objects out of his paintings—placed Jasper Johns in the forefront of 20th century American painters. This Museum of Modern Art presentation features footage of Johns in his studio and a retrospective of his innovative works. 30 min.
22-1613   *$19.99*

Matisse Centennial At The Grand Palais

The renowned 1969 exhibition of early 20th-century French painter Henri Matisse's works at Paris' Grand Palais museum is chronicled in this documentary by the Museum of Modern Art. 55 min.
22-1616   *$19.99*

Pissaro: At The Heart Of Impressionism/Jackson Pollock/ Willem de Kooning: The Painter

Produced by New York's Museum of Modern Art, this trio of short subjects examines the evolution and work of three of the most influential painters of the last 150 years: French impressionist Camille Pissaro, American abstract icon Jackson Pollock, and Dutch-born Willem de Kooning. 45 min.
22-1617   *$19.99*

Alexander Calder: Calder's Universe

The Philadelphia-born artist, best known as the creator of mobile sculpture, is seen in his studio working on an array of spinning mobiles, rotating spheres and prints. 30 min.
22-1618   *$19.99*

Alexander Calder

A third-generation sculptor, his revolutionary "mobile" and "stabile" works ranged from matchbox-sized miniatures to seven-story wonders. The life and art of Alexander Calder is discussed in this fascinating retrospective, first seen on PBS's "American Masters" series. 60 min.
53-6479   *$19.99*

Brancusi Retrospective At The Guggenheim Museum

A colleague of Rodin and the Impressionists, Romanian-born sculptor Constantin Brancusi went on to revolutionize the artform with his simplified styles and organic shapes. Along with a tour of the Guggenheim's exhibition of his works, this Museum of Modern Art program also takes a look inside Brancusi's Paris studio. 25 min.
22-1621   *$19.99*

Treasures Of The Holy Land: Ancient Art From The Israel Museum

In 1986 museums across America displayed rare artifacts from the Holy Land. This documentary, produced in conjunction with the Metropolitan Museum of Art, features a sampling of the artworks, jewelry, household objects and other finds, including two of the famed Dead Sea Scrolls. 30 min.
22-5089   Was $29.99   *$19.99*

Louvre 200: Complete Set

Follow the history of the famed Paris museum, built in the 15th century as a royal palace and now home to a startling array of over 360,000 works of art and host to nearly 5 million visitors each year, in this special three-volume series made to mark the Louvre's bicentennial. 180 min. total. NOTE: Individual volumes available at $19.99 each.
22-5666   Save $10.00!   *$49.99*

The Louvre (1978)

Join host Charles Boyer for a tour of one of the world's great museums, Paris' Louvre. Great works of art such as the Mona Lisa, Winged Victory and Venus De Milo are seen, along with a history of the Louvre itself. 53 min.
19-1373   *$24.99*

Art Ache: Complete Set

A comprehensive three-part look at the world of modern art: the philosophies and creative processes of today's top artists; the promotion games of agents, galleries and museums; and the business side that turns art into a multi-million-dollar commodity. 150 min. total. NOTE: Individual volumes available at $39.99 each.
22-5690   Save $20.00!   *$99.99*

Montparnasse Revisited: Complete Set

Between the years 1900-1940, the Montparnasse district of Paris became a haven for artists, musicians, writers and "bohemians" from throughout France and the world. This 10-volume collection mixes period music and art, rare film footage, and interviews with the men and women involved to bring the era to vibrant life. 550 min. total. NOTE: Individual volumes available at $29.99 each.
22-5756   Save $100.00!   *$199.99*

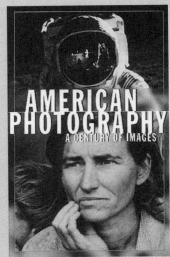

The History Of The Comics: Complete Set
A centenary salute to an indigenous American art form, this four-volume series looks at the four-color characters who have entertained readers of all ages for generations. From early strips such as "The Katzenjammer Kids" and "Krazy Kat" and the debuts of Superman and Batman to today's more sophisticated comics, the history is traced through rare art and interviews. 6 hrs. total. NOTE: Individual volumes available at $19.99 each.
22-1249 $79.99

The Masters Of Comic Book Art
Comics aren't just for kids anymore, as this tape proves. Interviews with such renowned creators as Will Eisner, Jack Kirby, Steve Ditko, Neal Adams, Berni Wrightson, Frank Miller, Moebius and others are highlighted with samples of their work. Author Harlan Ellison hosts this enlightening look at a uniquely American art form. 60 min.
50-1571 Was $19.99 $14.99

The Confessions Of Robert Crumb (1987)
His art fueled the "underground comix" movement of the '60s and made him the cartoon chronicler of the era's zeitgeist. Learn about the stormy private life and controversial career of Robert Crumb in this BBC-produced documentary. 60 min.
22-6085 $19.99

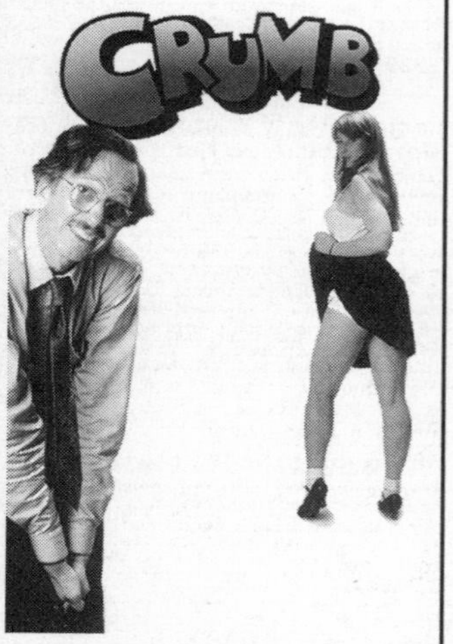

Crumb (1994)
Intimate and disturbing look at the life of Robert Crumb, the underground comix artist responsible for "Fritz the Cat," "Mr. Natural" and the ubiquitous "Keep on Truckin'" cartoon. The film surveys Crumb's controversial work, his well-documented sexual fantasies, his troubled family life, and his relationship with reclusive brother Charles. Filmed over the course of six years by director Terry Zwigoff. 119 min.
02-2817 Was $89.99 □$19.99

Comic Book Confidential (1989)
A nostalgia-filled look at the history of comic books in America and the artists and writers who gave the characters life. See Superman's debut in 1938, the '50s scare over horror titles, the birth of Marvel Comics and '60s undergrounds, the recognition of comics as an art form for all ages, and more. Includes interviews with Jack Kirby, Stan Lee, Will Eisner, Harvey Kurtzman, Robert Crumb and others. 85 min.
07-8369 $19.99

Making Masterpieces: Complete Set
Join host Neil MacGregor for a behind-the-scenes tour of London's famed National Gallery with this three-tape series that explores the museum's impressive art collection, the stories behind some of the most notable works, and the latest in art study and restoration. Included are "Pictures as Things/The Materials of Faith," "The Conquest of Light/From Illusion to Emotion" and "Old Tricks and New Pigments/Loss and Recovery." 180 min. total. NOTE: Individual volumes available at $29.99 each.
22-5958 Save $10.00! $79.99

Edouard Manet: Les Silences De Manet
All-inclusive look at the career and oeuvre of the influential Impressionist whose work outraged 1860s Paris. Masterful documentary is highlighted by footage from Manet exhibitions in Paris and New York. 60 min.
22-5284 $39.99

Masters Of Illusion
The importance of artistic and scientific principles discovered by Renaissance masters such as da Vinci, Botticelli, Michelangelo and Raphael are examined in this program. Learn how such techniques are still being utilized today. 30 min.
22-5476 $29.99

Toulouse-Lautrec
Study of the French painter/lithographer/illustrator whose post-impressionistic works chronicling Parisian nightlife broke new ground in the art and graphic worlds. Produced in conjunction with an exhibit at London's Royal Academy, this program features many of his works and sheds new light on Toulouse-Lautrec's life. 60 min.
22-5418 Was $39.99 $29.99

Velazquez: The Painter Of Painters
Along with Goya and El Greco, Diego Rodriguez de Silva y Velazquez ranks as one of the greatest of Spanish artists. Shot during an exhibition of his major works at the Prado in Madrid, this film looks at Velazquez' years in the royal courts of 17-century Spain and the naturalistic style that marked his painting. 56 min.
22-5539 $39.99

Balthus
A rare interview with Count Balthazar Klossowski de Rola, the Polish-Swiss painter better known as Balthus, is featured in this retrospective look at his life and art. Balthus discusses his relationships with Picasso, Giacometti and other artists and candidly talks about his portraits of adolescent girls. 51 min.
22-5963 $39.99

Chuck Close: A Portrait In Progress
Truly a miracle of modern art, Chuck Close's paintings have bewildered and amazed the public since 1969. This intriguing program follows the artist's personal journey from his first series of large, black-and-white portraits to his recovery from a debilitating spinal condition that is nothing short of incredible. Music by Philip Glass. 57 min.
22-5973 □$29.99

The Much Loved Friend: A Portrait Of The National Gallery
You're invited to take an exclusive, behind-the-scenes tour of one of the world's finest art collections, London's National Gallery, with this program that features interviews with such notables as Prince Charles, Monty Python alumnus/film director Terry Gilliam, and art historian Sister Wendy Beckett. 47 min.
22-6017 $19.99

Chihuly Over Venice
The design, creation and installation of a series of fanciful chandeliers throughout the canals and alleys of Venice, Italy, by noted decorative glass artist Dale Chihuly and his aides is the focus of this fascinating documentary. 90 min.
22-6024 $29.99

Siqueiros: Artist And Warrior
A colleague of Rivera and Kahlo, David Alfaro Siqueiros was a leader of the Mexican muralist school in the mid-20th century and a devoted follower of left-wing political causes. Ricardo Montalban narrates this compelling look at how his art and his politics shaped one another. 59 min.
22-6045 $29.99

Painting The World
Neil MacGregor, the director of London's National Gallery, offers witty commentary on key paintings from different countries and centuries in this two-tape series. Artworks showcased include "The Donne Triptych" by Hans Memlinc; Paolo Veronese's "The Family of Darius Before Alexandra"; Peter Paul Rubens' "An Autumn Landscape with a View of Het Steen"; and "Experiment on a Bird in the Air Pump" by John Wright of Derby. 120 min.
22-6054 $39.99

Portraits By Ingres
When he died in 1867, Jean-Auguste-Dominique Ingres was probably the most famous artist in the world. This program traces his life and career, which spanned six decades and included the support of early patron Napoleon Bonaparte. See Ingres' incredible allegorical, historical and religious works, as well as his acclaimed nudes. 25 min.
22-6068 $19.99

Georges De La Tour: Genius Lost And Found
Seventeenth-century artist Georges de la Tour was forgotten for 300 years, until critics and patrons recognized his genius. A painter for the King of France and the Dukes of Lorraine, de la Tour's unique works, which included card cheats, gamblers and religious subjects, are featured in this program from art historian Edwin Mullins. 59 min.
22-6069 $29.99

Bernard Buffet: From Here To Eternity
Boasting recently discovered archival footage, this program paints a stunning portrait of artist Bernard Buffet, who specializes in large canvasses and focusing on a single subject. See the reclusive Buffet's paitings on Paris, the circus and the life of Joan of Arc and find out more about this mysterious, acclaimed artist. 56 min.
22-6071 $29.99

Paul Delvaux: The Sleepwalker Of Saint-Idesbald
After studying at the Royal Academy of Arts in his native Belgium, Paul Delvaux was influenced by meetings with Dali and Magritte and began adapting his expressionistic art style to a more surrealist view. Hear in Delvaux's own words about his life and work in this compelling look at one of the overlooked geniuses of 20th-century art. 59 min.
22-6075 $29.99

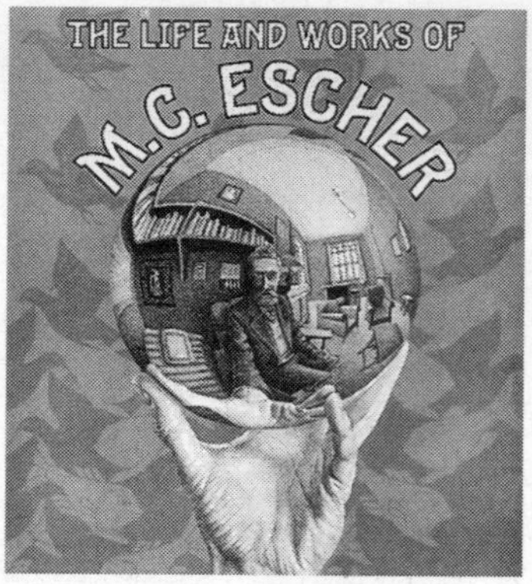

The Life And Works Of M.C. Escher
There's probably not a college dorm room in America that hasn't had an Escher poster on its walls at one time or another, and in this fascinating documentary you'll learn about the Dutch-born artist's intricate work and the cult following it inspired. A rare filmed interview with Escher himself is included. 60 min.
50-8208 Was $19.99 $14.99

The Fantastic World Of M.C. Escher
This program delves into the life and art of M.C. Escher, the Dutch graphic artist whose works distorted space and perspective and remain as popular as ever today. What inspired Escher and what mathematical principles are at work in his paintings and sketches? 50 min.
50-2577 Was $19.99 $14.99

Charles Rennie Mackintosh: A Modern Man
Rejecting the ornate stylings of his Victorian contemporaries, Scottish architect and designer Charles Rennie Mackintosh's sparse, geometric work gained him a global following and had a profound influence on 20th-century architecture. This documentary offers a retrospective of Mackintosh's work and a rare look at his stormy personal life. 45 min.
40-3005 $29.99

Tiffany: The Mark Of Excellence
Just as his father did with the family jewelry business, Louis Comfort Tiffany made his name a household world with his decorative stained glass lamps, vases and art objects. Take a fascinating look at the colorful world of Tiffany glass, and see dazzling examples of his work, as you hear from art historians and Tiffany family members. 50 min.
53-6403 $19.99

Robert Rauschenberg: Inventive Genius
A major figure in 20th-century American painting, Robert Rauschenberg spearheaded the shift from abstract expressionism to pop art. In this "American Masters" program, Rauschenberg's colorful life and his role as guru to the modern art world are examined. Dennis Hopper narrates. 60 min.
53-6478 $19.99

Art Treasures Of Spain: Hieronymus Bosch
His paintings expressed Christian beliefs and themes through bizarre, almost surreal scenes that featured allegorical images and creatures. Follow the life of this 16th-century Flemish artist who, living at the height of the Renaissance, maintained a medieval style of work. 30 min.
80-7141 Was $24.99 $19.99

Chihuly
This six-tape series looks at legendary glass artist Dale Chihuly and follows him in the studio and around the world as he works on amazing, bueatiful creations. The programs include "Chihuly Niijma Floats," "Chihuly in Action," "Chihuly River of Glass," "Chihuly Working with Lino Tagliapietra," "Chihuly Atlantis" and "Chihuly Working with Pino Signoretto." 177 min. total.
22-6102 $99.99

The Popes And Their Art: The Vatican Collections
James Mason narrates this dazzling look at the artwork of the Vatican, which includes works by such masters as Michelangelo, Raphael and Leonardo da Vinci. Paintings, sculptures, precious jewels and original manuscripts are just part of the priceless collection. 60 min.
27-6836 $24.99

Inside The Vatican: Complete Set
Oscar-winner Peter Ustinov hosts this four-tape set that explores the magnificent art and rich history of the Vatican. Filmed on location across Europe, the programs include "Upon This Rock," "The Flight from Rome," "The Renaissance" and "The Third Millennium." 200 min. total.
53-8204 Was $59.99 $39.99

The Architecture Of Frank Lloyd Wright
Actress Anne Baxter, Wright's granddaughter, hosts this documentary that traces the life and work of America's most famous architect. See Wright's influence on urban life, as evidenced by the Guggenheim Museum, Johnson Wax corporate headquarters and more, including the striking Fallingwater. 75 min.
22-5197 $49.99

The Homes Of Frank Lloyd Wright
Perhaps the freest expression of noted architect Wright's art and theories can be seen in the three houses he designed and built for himself. This program takes you on a rare behind-the-scenes look at the bold and innovative Frank Lloyd Wright Home and Studio in suburban Chicago, Taliesin in Wisconsin, and Arizona's Taliesin West. 50 min.
53-7794 $19.99

Frank Lloyd Wright: Fallingwater
This incisive study of the famous Frank Lloyd Wright-designed Fallingwater house in Mill Run, Pennsylvania, features home movies of Wright and owner Edgar Kaufman, an interview with Kaufman's son, and other fascinating info on the home that was designed and built between 1934 and 1937. 56 min.
76-7433 $39.99

Soleri's Cities: Architecture For Planet Earth And Beyond
Fascinating look at the ideas of architect Paolo Soleri, a former student of Frank Lloyd Wright, who believed cities should be built in accordance with nature. Soleri's prototype of such a city—called the Arcology—is examined. 30 min.
22-5717 $19.99

America's Castles: The Grand Tour: Boxed Set
This six-tape boxed set looks at some of the country's most extraordinary estates. Included in this series are "Newport Mansions," "Florida's Grand Estates," "Gold Coast Estates," "Hudson River Valley Estates," "Grand Plantations" and "Adirondack Camps." 300 min. total.
53-8501 $99.99

Bob Vila's Guide To Historic Homes: Complete Set
Join host Bob Vila as he tours some of the most impressive and glorious homes in the country, including Thomas Jefferson's Monticello, Frank Lloyd Wright's Fallingwater and others. The three-tape set includes "The Northeast," "The South" and "The Midwest & West." 300 min total. NOTE: Individual volumes available at $19.99 each.
53-8507 $59.99

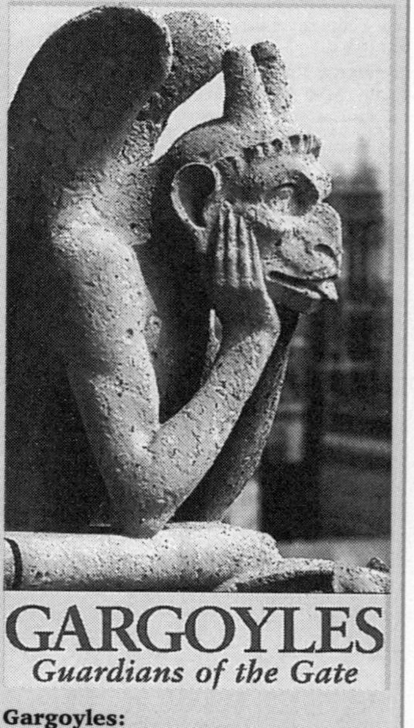

Gargoyles: Guardians Of The Gate
The mysterious stone beasts that guard some of the world's greatest examples of architecture are examined in this fascinating program. Trace the origins of gargoyles and learn why sculptors and painters have been fascinated with them for centuries. Also, journey to Notre Dame, New York and some of the great universities to see examples of the creatures. 56 min.
80-7230 $19.99

Antonio Gaudi (1984)
From Japanese director Hiroshi Teshigahara ("Woman in the Dunes") comes a documentary look at the unique and haunting work of 19th-century Spanish architect Antonio Gaudi, whose organic blending of Gothic and Art Nouveau predated the surrealists and influenced the art of Picasso, Miró and Dali. 72 min. In Japanese with English subtitles.
80-5028 Was $89.99 $29.99

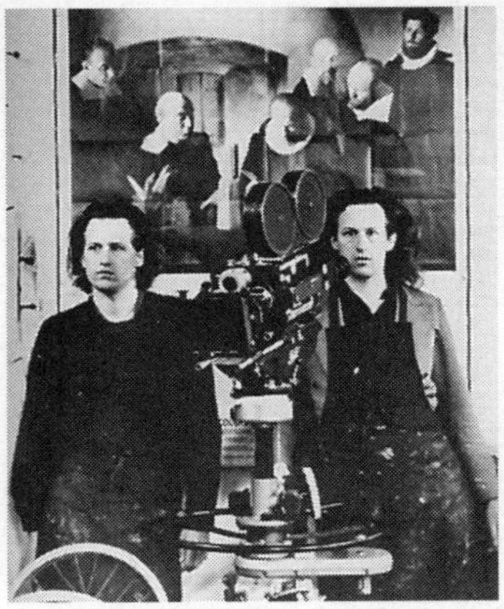

ART ON FILM FILM ON ART

Art On Film, Film On Art: Complete Set (1991)
What influence have the fields of fine art and cinema had on one another, and how has each medium regarded the other? This unique five-volume series features discussions between noted art experts and historians, along with a variety of short documentary films from around the world. Included are "Balance: Film/Art," "Film Sense/Art Sense," "Film Form/Art Form," "Film Voice/Art Voice" and "Film/Art Subject and Expert." 322 min. total. NOTE: Individual volumes available at $39.99 each.
22-5879 *$199.99*

A Day On The Grand Canal With The Emperor Of China (1988)
A collaboration of painter David Hockney and filmmaker Philip Haas, this thought-provoking film focuses on a 72-foot-long Chinese scroll from the late 1690s depicting the Emperor Kangxi's tour of his domain. Hockney uses the scroll's paintings to bring 17th-century China to life and tells how this unique work was created. 48 min.
80-5004 *$39.99*

American Visions: Complete Set (1997)
The evolution of America's art and architecture, and how their development has been influenced by the "melting pot" of popular culture, is lovingly and somewhat irreverently discussed by acclaimed critic Robert Hughes in this eight-volume PBS documentary series. 8 hrs. total.
18-7745 *$149.99*

Man Ray: Prophet Of The Avant-Garde (1997)
Born in Philadelphia as Emanuel Radensky, he was a leader in the abstract and Dada art movements in America and France. Explore the many worlds—painter, sculptor, photographer, filmmaker and teacher—of Man Ray in this "American Masters" presentation that features drawings from his student years, rare movie footage and a long-lost interview found in a Rotterdam museum. 60 min.
53-6693 *$19.99*

Masterpiece Or Forgery?: The Story Of Elmyr De Hory (1997)
Over his lifetime he created over 1,000 fake paintings, enough false Van Goghs, Matisses and others to fill several museums...and in fact, many institutions around the world display his work without knowing it! Learn about the jet set life, and 1976 disappearance and supposed death, of master art forger Elmyr de Hory in this fascinating documentary. 52 min.
81-3010 *$24.99*

Hogarth's Progress
His paintings and engravings depicted the lighter aspects of everyday English life in the 18th century, and many of William Hogarth's satirical works are on display in this retrospective of his life and art. 50 min.
22-5956 *$39.99*

Hogarth's Marriage A-La-Mode
Considered William Hogarth's masterpiece, Marriage A-La-Mode has been called one of the greatest and most original creations in British 18th-century art. This program, narrated by playwright Alan Bennett, follows the tragic and comic drama of the six paintings through analysis and focusing on their great detail. 40 min.
22-6055 *$19.99*

John Singer Sargent: Outside The Frame
Considered the premier American portrait painter of the late 19th and early 20th century, John Singer Sargent was noted for his naturalistic depictions of the era's wealthy and elite. Many of the finest examples of these works, along with the murals and landscapes he preferred to create, are featured in this documentary retrospective. Jacqueline Bisset narrates. 57 min.
22-6084 *$29.99*

Norman Rockwell: An American Portrait
His paintings and illustrations captured the heart and spirit of small-town America for over half a century, as depicted in this documentary salute to Norman Rockwell featuring over 300 of the artist's Saturday Evening Post covers. Hosted by Mason Adams, Erma Bombeck and Robert Cole. 60 min.
22-7135 Was $29.99 *$19.99*

Norman Rockwell: Painting America
This "American Masters" production centers on the life and work of the artist whose memorable covers for the Saturday Evening Post brought him incredible popularity. Archival and TV footage and sketches from the Norman Rockwell Museum in Stockbridge, Massachusetts, are presented along with interviews with critics, historians and family members. 86 min.
53-6622 *$19.99*

Norman Rockwell's World: An American Dream (1972)
Perhaps modern America's best-known and most popular artist, Rockwell himself narrates this Oscar-winning look at his life and work. Included are looks at many of his famous magazine cover illustrations. 30 min.
22-5063 Was $29.99 *$19.99*

Monet: Legacy Of Light
Dynamic look at the work of Claude Monet, the French impressionist painter who used light and stylization to bring out the color and realism of his work. Includes many of his most famous paintings. 27 min.
22-5353 Was $29.99 *$19.99*

The Landscapes Of Frederic Edwin Church
Enthralling documentary on the famous member of the Hudson River School, best known for landscapes of the Hudson River Valley and South American and European locales. 29 min.
22-5354 *$29.99*

Paul Gauguin: The Savage Dream
The National Gallery of Art explores the latter work of the bank clerk whose obsessive search for unfettered ways of living and seeing led him to the South Seas and the creation of monumental works of Post-Impressionist painting. 45 min.
22-5191 Was $39.99 *$29.99*

The Hermitage: A Russian Odyssey: Deluxe Boxed Set
Noted commentator Rod MacLeish hosts a journey to the Hermitage Museum in St. Petersburg, Russia, which houses one of the world's great art collections. The museum was once a palace for the Czars, and many of their treasures are featured in the three-volume documentary. 180 min. total. NOTE: Individual volumes available at $29.99 each.
22-5763 Save $10.00! *$79.99*

Hermitage Masterpieces: Boxed Set
Built in the mid-18th century by Catherine the Great to be the seat of the Russian Empire, St. Petersburg's Hermitage Palaces are home to nearly 3 million exhibits and considered to be one of the finest art museums in the world. This six-tape series takes you on a comprehensive tour of the Hermitage galleries, tracing the history of art as it reveals the colorful (and violent) past of the buildings.NOTE: Individual volumes available at $19.99 each.
89-5017 *$119.99*

The Impressionists: Boxed Set
Begun as a response to the formalized classicism of early 19th-century painting, the Impressionist movement shocked the art community and provided a new way of looking at the world. This four-tape series, hosted by art critic/editor Tim Marlow, tours some of the world's finest museums as it examines the work of eight Impressionist masters: Cezanne, Degas, Gauguin, Manet, Monet, Renoir, Toulouse-Lautrec and Van Gogh. 240 min. total.
80-7282 *$49.99*

Degas: Beyond Impressionism
While he was a contemporary of the French Impressionists, Edgar Degas' work, especially in his later years, eschewed their use of natural subjects and lighting. This National Gallery production examines how Degas' mature works influenced generations of artists to come. 30 min.
22-5998 *$19.99*

The Hudson River And Its Painters
In the mid-1800s the natural splendor of New York's Hudson River Valley inspired a group of artists who became the country's first native school of landscape painters. Take a look at the works of Cole, Durand, Church, Gifford and others, plus prints of the period and a view of the region today. 57 min.
22-5165 *$39.99*

Andy Warhol
Painter, graphic artist, filmmaker, professional celebrity: he was the most renowned and controversial figure in modern art. Interviews with Andy Warhol, his family, and members of the Factory crew are blended with a look at his most famous works to provide an overview of the enigmatic Andy. 78 min.
22-5201 *$39.99*

Picasso
Produced to coincide with the opening of Paris's Musee Picasso, this film looks at the private collection amassed by Picasso over the years, paintings and sketches that were among his personal favorites, and follows the diverse artistic styles that marked his career. 81 min.
22-5242 Was $39.99 *$29.99*

Picasso: The Man And His Work
A unique documentary tribute, featuring intimate looks at Picasso at work and at home during the final two decades of his life. Rare footage, interviews and still photos, including shots of works never seen by the public, trace the life, influences and career of this legendary creator. 90 min.
22-7001 Was $79.99 *$59.99*

Ginevra's Story
Painted in the mid 1470s by a twentysomething Leonardo da Vinci, "Ginevra de Benci" is the artist's first known portrait work and the only da Vinci on permanent display in America. Questions surrounding the painting and its mysterious subject are explored in this National Gallery of Art production, narrated by Meryl Streep. 57 min.
22-6087 *$29.99*

Pierre-Auguste Renoir
A leading figure in the Impressionist school of 19th-century France, Pierre-Auguste Renoir gained fame for his brilliant, colorful works, which included the controversial nude figure studies known as "The Bathers." The painter's life and art are examined in this documentary program. 26 min.
22-6091 *$19.99*

Botero: Four Seasons
His corpulent creations have made him a world leader in contemporary art, and in this program you'll follow sculptor/painter Fernando Botero in his studio and visiting his old haunts in his native Colombia, at a Paris exhibition of his statues along the Champs Elysees, and more. 53 min.
22-6097 *$29.99*

Painters Painting (1972)
Emile de Antonio's landmark documentary listens in on some of the classic artists of our time (Andy Warhol, Willem de Kooning, Barnett Newman, Jasper Johns and others) frankly discussing their work, their lives and the creative process. Also includes comments from critics and curators. 116 min.
70-7096 *$29.99*

Homage To Chagall (1977)
For over three-quarters of a century, Russian-born Marc Chagall set new standards for modern art with his colorful, heartfelt paintings, murals and stained glass works. In rare filmed interviews and looks at his creations Chagall's devotion to his Jewish heritage and his love of humanity is shown. 90 min.
53-7131 *$39.99*

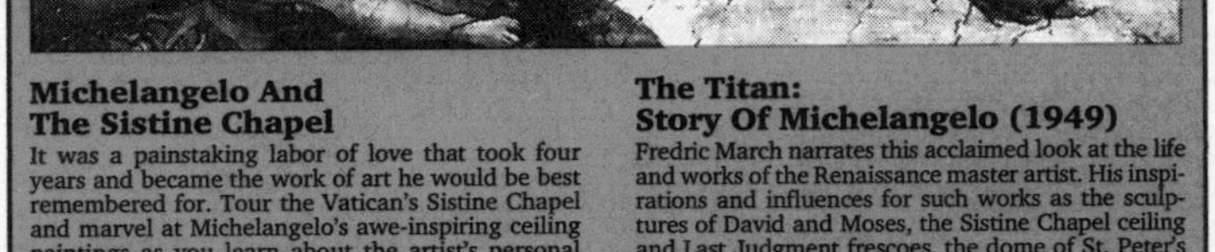

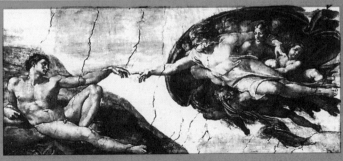

Michelangelo And The Sistine Chapel
It was a painstaking labor of love that took four years and became the work of art he would be best remembered for. Tour the Vatican's Sistine Chapel and marvel at Michelangelo's awe-inspiring ceiling paintings as you learn about the artist's personal vision that inspired them and the meanings behind them. 35 min.
22-7171 *$19.99*

The Titan: Story Of Michelangelo (1949)
Fredric March narrates this acclaimed look at the life and works of the Renaissance master artist. His inspirations and influences for such works as the sculptures of David and Moses, the Sistine Chapel ceiling and Last Judgment frescoes, the dome of St. Peter's Cathedral and others are recounted and many of Michelangelo's masterpieces are examined. 67 min.
53-7452 Was $59.99 *$29.99*

Writers

Aldous Huxley: The Gravity Of Light
While best known for his 1932 dystopian novel "Brave New World," British-born author Aldous Huxley wrote insightful and prophetic essays on such topics as sex, religion and technological growth. His ideas and writings are brought to life in this unusual mix of documentary footage and computer animation. 70 min.
01-1567 *$29.99*

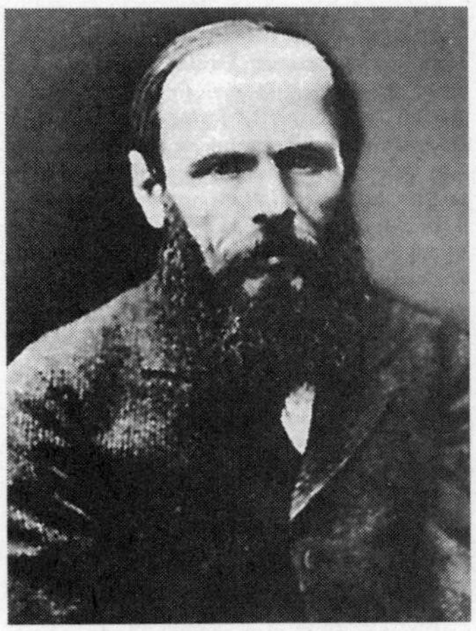

Great Russian Writers: Complete Set
From a vast land rich in tradition, but torn by war and political oppression, has come some of the literary world's greatest names. Through readings, photos and rare film footage, this eight-volume documentary series recounts the lives and times of "Alexander Blok," "Anton Chekhov," "Fyodor Dostoevsky," "Maxim Gorky," "Vladimir Mayakovsky," "Boris Pasternak," "Alexander Pushkin" and "Leo Tolstoy." 240 min. total. NOTE: Individual volumes available at $19.99 each.
22-1696 *$159.99*

The Poetry Anthology: Boxed Set
A unique overview of English poetry, this three-tape series examines many of the most renowned writers of the last 300 years and offers insight into their lives and work. Included in the set are "The Augustan Poets," "The Romantic Poets" and "The Victorian Poets." 150 min. total. NOTE: Individual volumes available at $19.99 each.
22-1738 Save $10.00! *$49.99*

Dante: The Divine Comedy
A masterpiece of medieval literature, the allegorical odyssey through Hell, Purgatory and Paradise by Dante Alighieri has influenced not only Western poets, but our view of the afterlife, for centuries. Explore the themes and meaning of the 14th-century writer's epic, through interviews and analysis with Dante scholars and on-location footage in Florence. 50 min.
22-1755 *$19.99*

Chester Himes: A Writer's Turbulent Journey
Explore the writings and world of the noted African-American author who revolutionized the crime fiction genre through such works as "Cotton Comes to Harlem," "If He Hollers Let Him Go" and "The Crazy Kill." 30 min.
22-1756 *$19.99*

Balzac
Plagued throughout his life by doomed romances, ill health and debt, 19th-century French writer Honore de Balzac broke new ground with his "suprarealistic" depictions of everyday life and his monumental series of novels "The Human Comedy." Learn about his art and his stormy private life in this compelling program. 50 min.
22-1757 *$19.99*

Stratis Tsirkas
Creator of the "Drifting Cities" trilogy, Stratis Tsirkas has emerged as one the leading literary lights of post-WWII Greece. This documentary follows the author and his work through letters and diaries as well as his acclaimed writings. 50 min.
22-1758 *$19.99*

Gabríel Gárcia Marquez: Tales Beyond Solitude
This award-winning documentary features a rare interview with the acclaimed Colombian author of "Life in the Time of Cholera" discussing his life and the films based on his works. The film includes interviews with directors Ruy Guerra and Fernando Birri. 59 min.
22-5617 *$19.99*

Jack Kerouac's Road
This acclaimed program, produced by the National Film Board of Canada, traces the background of the beat icon and author of "On the Road." Using dramatized excerpts, period footage and candid interviews, Kerouac's French-Canadian roots, and how they fueled his writing, are explored. 54 min.
50-2150 Was $59.99 ***$19.99***

The Beat Box Set
You'll "howl" for this special collection that includes "The Coney Island of Lawrence Ferlinghetti," "Fried Shoes, Cooked Diamonds," "Kerouac," "Love Lion" and "William S. Burroughs: Commissioner of Sewers" in a boxed set perfect for taking "on the road."
53-6405 Save $60.00! ***$89.99***

The Third Mind
A video montage of words of music, chronicling the artistic joint venture of Beat poet/playwright Michael McClure and Doors keyboardist Ray Manzarek. The "third mind" (as described by Beat guru William Burroughs) that evolves from their collaboration is seen from conception to performance and features comments from Jim Carroll, Lawrence Ferlinghetti, Allen Ginsberg and others. 58 min.
53-6685 ***$24.99***

Kerouac (1985)
His writings spoke to a generation, and by the time he died at the age of 49, Jack Kerouac had become a major figure in 20th-century American literature. This acclaimed documentary mixes dramatic re-creations, rare TV appearances, and interviews with many of Kerouac's friends and contemporaries to trace his life story. Peter Coyote narrates. 73 min.
70-7201 ***$29.99***

What Happened To Kerouac? (1986)
Incisive, absorbing documentary look at the messiah of the Beat Generation. Anecdotes and recollections from Neal Cassady, Allen Ginsberg, William Burroughs, Lawrence Ferlinghetti and others combine with rare TV interviews with Steve Allen and William F. Buckley for a distinctive film portrait. 96 min.
68-1072 Was $69.99 ***$19.99***

William S. Burroughs: Commissioner Of Sewers (1986)
The controversial writer whose works include "Naked Lunch" and "Junky" is profiled by German filmmaker Klaus Maeck in a documentary that combines footage from some of Burroughs' public readings with rare film appearances, shots of his paintings, and discourses on the use of language as a weapon. 60 min.
70-7133 ***$29.99***

Beat Generation: An American Dream (1987)
They were the poets, painters and musicians who, in the quiet and conservative atmosphere of post-WWII America, created a cultural revolution. Steve Allen narrates this look at the men and women who became known as "beatniks" and whose artwork came to represent rebellion. 86 min.
53-6247 ***$19.99***

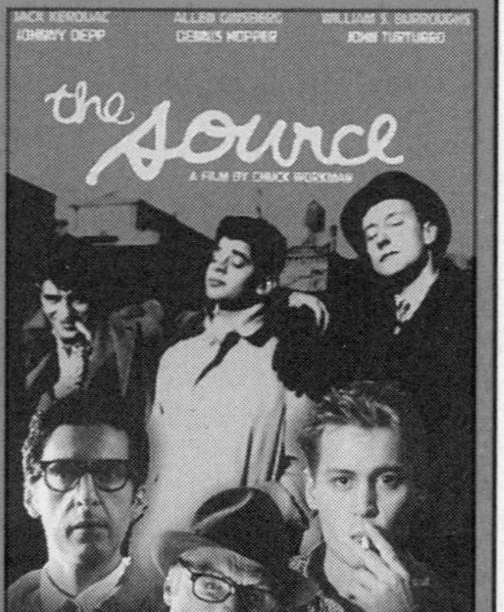

The Source (1999)
Acclaimed documentarian Chuck Workman chronicles the 50-year history of the Beat Generation and its lasting effects on American literature, music, art and society. Rare film and TV footage, interviews, and dramatic readings by Johnny Depp (as Jack Kerouac), Dennis Hopper (as William Burroughs) and John Turturro (as Allen Ginsberg) tell the story of the rebels who laid the groundwork for the social upheaval of the '60s and '70s. 89 min.
53-6791 ***$19.99***

Voices & Visions
Originally shown on PBS, this series takes in-depth looks at the world of some of America's greatest poets through their work, commentary by experts and rare footage. Seven years in the making, the series allows the poets' words to come to life in stirring fashion. Each tape runs about 60 min. There are 13 volumes available, including:

Voices & Visions: Walt Whitman
70-7165 ***$19.99***

Voices & Visions: Emily Dickinson
70-7169 ***$19.99***

Voices & Visions: Sylvia Plath
70-7172 ***$19.99***

Voices & Visions: Langston Hughes
70-7176 ***$19.99***

Profile Of A Writer
This made-for-British TV series delves into the rich imaginations of the following authors and playwrights, detailing the creative background behind their more famous works. There are 6 volumes available, including:

Jorge Luis Borges: Borges And I
22-5110 Was $39.99 ***$19.99***

Jean Cocteau: Autobiography Of An Unknown
22-5198 Was $39.99 ***$19.99***

Toni Morrison
22-5199 Was $39.99 ***$19.99***

Agatha Christie: How Did She Do It?
22-5200 Was $39.99 ***$19.99***

Emily Dickinson: A Certain Slant Of Light
Julie Harris hosts this look at one of America's greatest writers, which includes her years at Amherst Academy and Mount Holyoke Female Seminary. Experimenting with form and rhyming schemes, Dickinson wrote some of the world's most compelling poetry. 30 min.
27-6937 ***$24.99***

An Evening With Emily Dickinson
This special two-tape boxed set includes Julie Harris as the author in "Emily Dickinson: A Certain Slant of Light," plus "The World of Emily Dickinson," starring Clair Bloom, from "The Master Poets Collection." 60 min. total.
27-7167 ***$39.99***

The Master Poets Collections
Their names rank among the immortals of English literature, and you'll learn about these men and women and their works in these wonderful documentary programs. Each boxed collector's set features four tapes and runs about 120 min. NOTE: Individual volumes available at $24.99 each.

The Master Poets Collection I
Special boxed set includes "Robert Frost: New England in Autumn," "Spoon River Anthology/Edgar Lee Masters: A Poetic Portrait Gallery," "William Shakespeare: A Poet for All Time" and "The World of Emily Dickinson."
27-7054 Save $10.00! ***$89.99***

The Master Poets Collection II
Special boxed set includes "The Brontës of Haworth," "Robert and Elizabeth Browning," "Scott, Tennyson and Kipling: The Heroic Tradition" and "Wordsworth and Coleridge: The Lake Poets."
27-7080 Save $10.00! ***$89.99***

The Master Poets Collection III
Special boxed set includes "e.e. cummings: An American Original," "Sylvia Plath: Growth of a Poet," "Walt Whitman and the Civil War" and "So That's Where It's From!," a collection of famous lines from obscure poems.
27-7161 Save $10.00! ***$89.99***

The Master Poets Collection IV
Special boxed set includes "D.H. Lawrence: A Restless Spirit," "The Poetical Art of William Blake," "Thomas Hardy's Wessex" and "William Butler Yeats: The Heart of Ireland."
27-7166 Save $10.00! ***$89.99***

The War Within: A Portrait Of Virginia Woolf
An acclaimed documentary on Virginia Woolf, this film uses archival footage, period paintings, family photos and interviews with relatives to paint an indelible portrait of the writer. A fine look at the life and times of the author who penned such classics as "To the Lighthouse" and "Jacob's Room" before committing suicide at the age of 59. 52 min.
48-7025 ***$59.99***

Dashiell Hammett. Detective. Writer.
The guiding light behind the "hard-boiled" school of American crime fiction, private eye-turned-author Dashiell Hammett, is the focus of this "American Masters" program. Follow the controversy-filled life and career of the man behind "The Maltese Falcon" and "The Thin Man," from his stormy relationship with Lillian Hellman to his run-in with HUAC in the '50s. 60 min.
53-6593 ***$19.99***

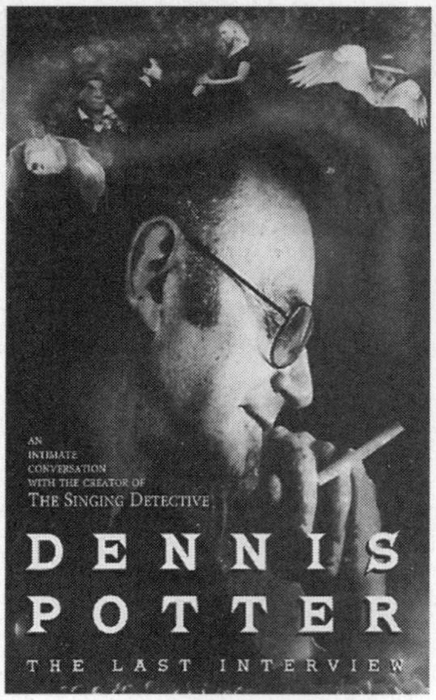

Dennis Potter: The Last Interview
The controversial, highly acclaimed British author of "The Singing Detective" and "Pennies from Heaven" discusses his life and work in this penetrating interview which took place in April, 1994, after Potter was diagnosed with terminal cancer. 70 min.
53-8199 ***$19.99***

Colette
Fascinating documentary look at the legendary writer as she discusses her life and work and is joined by Jean Cocteau for an intimate chat. In French with English subtitles. This program also includes "La Chevre De Monsieur Seguin," an adaptation of the Alphonse Daudet story, recited by Fernandel. In French with no subtitles. 49 min. total.
53-7030 Was $29.99 ***$14.99***

The Jane Austen Collection
Travel back to early 19th-century England and learn how a country rector's daughter went on to become one of the world's best-loved authors before she died at the age of 42, in this three-tape series. Volumes include "Jane Austen's Life," "Jane Austen's Works" and "Jane Austen's Society." 180 min. total.
65-7002 ***$39.99***

The Henry Miller Odyssey
The legendary author of such ground-breaking books as "Tropic of Capricorn," "Sexus" and "Nexus" serves as host for a voyage from Brooklyn to Paris, in which he visits friends and reminisces about his life and writing. 90 min.
70-7069 ***$29.99***

Herman Hesse's Long Summer
His pacifist policies shaken by the First World War, German-born author Herman Hesse left his wife and children in 1919 and moved to Switzerland, where he wrote some of his greatest works and spent the rest of his life. Explore the man behind such novels as "Siddhartha," "Steppenwolf" and "The Glass Bead Game" in this compelling program. 60 min.
70-7243 ***$29.99***

Mark Twain's America
An enlightening study of great American writer, humorist and adventurer Mark Twain, the author of classics like "Tom Sawyer" and "A Connecticut Yankee in King Arthur's Court." This program spans Twain's life and compares it to the country's growth from frontier days to world power. 60 min.
73-6067 ***$19.99***

Beatrix Potter: A Private World
Filmed in England's picturesque Lake District that was both Potter's home and the setting of her books, this documentary follows the life and work of the mild-mannered woman whose words and pictures brought to life such beloved children's characters as Peter Rabbit, Squirrel Nutkin and Jemima Puddle-Duck. 42 min.
89-5182 ***$24.99***

Gertrude Stein: When This You See, Remember Me (1970)
She became as famous for the artists and authors who frequented her Paris home and for her openly gay lifestyle as she was for her own work as a novelist, poet and lyricist. Rare interviews, photos and film footage, and selections from Stein's and Virgil Thomson's opera "Four Saints in Three Acts" help tell Stein's amazing story and bring to life the world of 1920s Europe. 89 min.
53-8358 Was $39.99 ***$29.99***

Isaac Bashevis Singer: Isaac In America (1986)
This Academy Award-nominated documentary looks at the Polish-born writer and Nobel Prize-winner who penned such memorable tales as "The Family Moskat," "The Manor" and many others. Judd Hirsch narrates. 60 min.
27-6917 ***$24.99***

Where The Heart Roams (1988)
A funny, acclaimed look at romance writers and their dogged fans. Barbara Cartland, Janet Dailey, Jude Devereaux and Rebecca Brandewyne are interviewed, as they discuss how much sex to put in their books and the secrets of writing about kissing. 81 min.
07-8169 Was $24.99 ***$19.99***

Looking For Langston (1989)
The world and works of black poet Langston Hughes are examined in this docudrama that focuses on his gay lifestyle, using footage from the Cotton Club and '30s Harlem, dramatic re-creations of events in Hughes' life, and the controversial photos of Robert Mapplethorpe. Directed by Isaac Julien ("Young Soul Rebels"). 45 min.
01-1469 Was $39.99 ***$29.99***

Resident Alien (1991)
This look at Quentin Crisp offers an intimate glimpse of the flamboyant author of "The Naked Civil Servant" in and around his Manhattan apartment, talking to friends, and lecturing on his colorful life and what it's like to be a gay Englishman in New York. Among the acquaintances featured in this film are John Hurt, Sting, Michael Musto and Fran Lebowitz. 85 min.
53-8158 Was $79.99 ***$19.99***

James Ellroy: Demon Dog Of American Crime Fiction (1993)
Fascinating, two-fisted documentary on crime novelist James Ellroy, author of "L.A. Confidential," "The Big Nowhere" and "American Tabloid." Ellroy, a former golf caddy and shoplifter and recovering alcoholic, takes viewers on a whirlwind tour of L.A. spotlighting different crime sites, including the alleyway where his mother was killed. Directed by Reinhard Jud. 90 min.
70-5142 Was $59.99 ***$29.99***

Anne Rice: Birth Of The Vampire (1994)
The modern mistress of literary horror, Anne Rice's tales of vampires, witches and other creatures have earned her legions of fans. Now this special documentary looks at her writings and private life, mixing a talk with Rice and quotes from her "Interview with the Vampire" for a unique self-portrait. 50 min.
04-2886 ***$14.99***

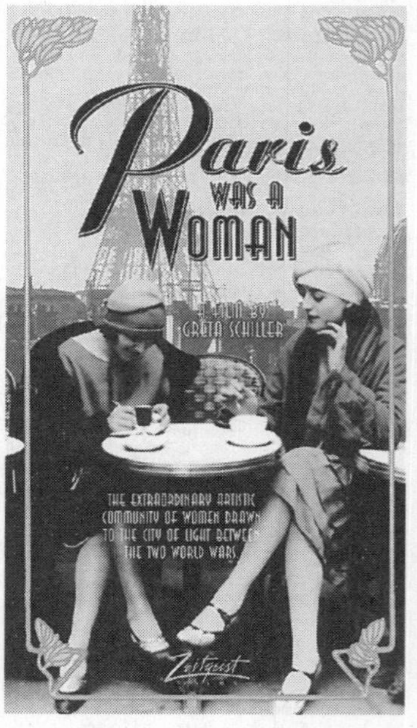

Paris Was A Woman (1996)
The women artists who resided on the Left Bank of Paris in the 1920s are the focus of this acclaimed documentary by Greta Schiller ("Before Stonewall"). Through archival footage and interviews, you'll meet Gertrude Stein, Colette, Romaine Brooks and others who found acceptance and camaraderie in the City of Lights between the wars. 75 min.
82-3003 ***$59.99***

Paul Monette: The Brink Of Summer's End (1997)
Award-winning biographical documentary chronicles the life and work of poet, writer and gay rights activist Paul Monette. The author of "Borrowed Time: An AIDS Memoir" and "Becoming a Man: Half a Life Story" is seen talking about his art and his struggle against discrimination before his own death from AIDS in 1995. Narrated by Linda Hunt. 90 min.
70-5148 Was $39.99 ***$24.99***

Ayn Rand: A Sense Of Life (1998)
The incredible, often controversial life of the writer and objectivism champion is surveyed in this documentary that traces Rand's life, from her early days in Russia to her career as novelist of such works as "The Fountainhead" and "Atlas Shrugged," with looks at her Hollywood screenwriting tenure and her philosophical beliefs. 145 min.
78-9024 Was $79.99 ***$19.99***

Hemingway:
Winner Take Nothing (1998)
Before her 1996 suicide, actress Margaux Hemingway began a film in which she followed the European travels of her grandfather, famed author/adventurer Ernest Hemingway. Completed by Margaux's husband, director Bernard Foucher, this riveting documentary juxtaposes location shots in Paris, Venice, Pamplona and Idaho and interviews with Ernest's friends and colleagues with the story of Margaux's own downward spiral of depression and addiction that eventually claimed her life. 86 min.
50-7517   *$19.99*

Great Themes Of Literature
This rarity is hosted by Orson Welles and focuses on the themes of authority and rebellion in fiction, examining both Herman Wouk's novel "The Caine Mutiny," as well as the 1954 film version starring Humphrey Bogart, Jose Ferrer and Van Johnson. 33 min.
10-6005   *$14.99*

Sam Shepard: Stalking Himself
This study of Pulitzer Prize-winning playwright-actor Sam Shepard examines his distinctly American work along with his family life and personal experiences. Ethan Hawke, Gary Sinise, John Malkovich and Ed Harris are among the associates of Shepard who add their own insights into the creator of "True West" and "Fool for Love." 60 min.
53-6380   *$19.99*

The Famous Authors Series
The lives and works of some of the world's greatest men and women of letters are detailed in this informative and entertaining documentary series. Commentary, writings, and archival pictures and film footage offer fascinating insights into these literary giants. There are 28 volumes available, including:

Famous Authors: William Faulkner
22-1496   *$19.99*

Famous Authors:
F. Scott Fitzgerald
22-1497   *$19.99*

Famous Authors: James Joyce
22-1502   *$19.99*

Famous Authors: George Orwell
22-1507   *$19.99*

Famous Authors: Edgar Allan Poe
22-1508   *$19.99*

Famous Authors:
William Shakespeare
22-1510   *$19.99*

Famous Authors: John Steinbeck
22-1513   *$19.99*

Music

Jacques Brel
A look at the life of French composer-singer Jacques Brel, whose lyrics achingly chronicled the joys and heartaches of life and love. 60 min.
80-7003   *$29.99*

Buena Vista Social Club (1999)
German filmmaker Wim Wenders' documentary counterpart to the Grammy-winning album follows guitarist/musicologist Ry Cooder on a trip to Havana and an encounter with some of Cuba's greatest musicians and singers, many of whom are found living in obscurity, and culminates with the "Club's" aging members giving a triumphant concert at New York's Carnegie Hall. 105 min.
27-7148   Was $22.99   *$14.99*

The Famous Composers Series
The lives and works of some of the world's greatest masters of music are detailed in this informative and entertaining documentary series. Commentary, archival pictures and film footage offer fascinating insight into each composer, while excerpts of their most famous pieces are performed by the Elysian Ensemble. There are 11 volumes available, including:

Famous Composers:
Johann Sebastian Bach
22-1526   *$19.99*

Famous Composers:
Ludwig Van Beethoven
22-1527   *$19.99*

Famous Composers:
Wolfgang Amadeus Mozart
22-1530   *$19.99*

Famous Composers:
Richard Wagner
22-1537   *$19.99*

Beats Of The Heart
This documentary series takes viewers on an around-the-world tour to experience the many facets of music and its role in society. Noted English filmmaker Jeremy Marre shot the street-level look at the lives of musicians and songwriters across the globe. Each tape runs 60 min. There are 15 volumes available, including:

Roots, Rock, Reggae
63-7029   *$24.99*

The Spirit Of Samba
63-7031   *$24.99*

Salsa
63-7034   *$24.99*

Great Russian Composers: Complete Set
Their music, steeped in the heritage of their homeland, won them international acclaim. Learn about "Modest Mussorgsky," "Sergei Rachmaninov," "Nikolay Rimsky-Korsakov," "Alexander Scriabin" and "Peter Tchaikovsky" in this five-tape series that features biographical information, photos and rare film footage, and selections from their greatest works. 150 min. total. NOTE: Individual volumes available at $19.99 each.
22-1687   *$99.99*

Whole Notes: Stories Behind The Classics: Complete Set
Learn about some of the greatest classical composers in history—and the music they're remembered by—in this fascinating six-tape series hosted by noted pianist Jon Kimura Parker. Biographical information, interviews with top musicians, and performances by the National Arts Centre Orchestra of Canada bring to life such titans as Bach, Beethoven, Mozart, Rachmaninoff, Ravel and Tchaikovsky. 180 min. total. NOTE: Individual volumes available at $14.99 each.
22-1725   Save $10.00!   *$79.99*

Latcho Drom (1996)
An acclaimed, song-filled documentary that traces the mystery-shrouded origins, global diversity, and shared joy of Gypsy music, showing indigenous performers in such locales as India, Egypt, Turkey, Romania, Spain and France. 103 min. In French with English subtitles.
53-8650   Letterboxed   *$89.99*

The Lives And Works Of Bach, Mozart, Beethoven And Bruckner: Complete Set
Noted filmmaker Hans Conrad Fischer combines scores by top European orchestras—including the Berlin Philharmonic, Leipzig Gewandhaus, Vienna Philharmonic and others—with on-location footage and readings of original letters and documents to tell the stories of four giants of the musical world: Johann Sebastian Bach, Ludwig Van Beethoven, Anton Bruckner and Wolfgang Amadeus Mozart. 485 min. total. NOTE: Individual volumes available at $29.99 each.
22-1793   Save $20.00!   *$99.99*

Guitarra!:
A Musical Journey Through Spain
The Spanish guitar has long been one of the most easily identified musical styles, from its earliest beginnings to the present day. Shot in Spain and featuring guitarist Julian Bream, this two-tape documentary series traces the 500-year history of Spanish guitar music and features incredible performance pieces. 210 min. total.
22-5869   *$29.99*

The Mississippi:
River Of Song: Boxed Set
From an Indian powwow in Northern Minnesota to New Orleans jazz clubs, the mighty Mississippi has given birth to a wide array of musical styles and lore. Singer/songwriter Ani DiFranco narrates this four-part look at the people who live along the river and their music: R&B, soul, gospel, jazz, zydeco, rock and more. Volumes include "Americans Old and New," "Midwestern Crossroads," "Southern Fusion" and "Louisiana, Where Music Is King." 240 min. total. NOTE: Individual volumes available at $19.99 each.
50-8163   Save $40.00!   *$39.99*

Yours For A Song:
The Women Of Tin Pan Alley
Few know of the women songwriters who toiled on Tin Pan Alley, but this "American Masters" show offers an introduction to such musical greats as Dorothy Fields, Kay Swift and Anne Ronell. Featuring performances from Michael Feinstein, Nora Michaels and host Betty Buckley, the show includes such songs as "A Fine Romance," "Can't We Be Friends?," "Yours for a Song" and more. 55 min.
53-6624   *$19.99*

Harold Arlen:
Somewhere Over The Rainbow
While such songs as "Over the Rainbow," "Stormy Weather," "Get Happy" and "Ac-cent-tchu-ate the Positive" live on, composer Harold Arlen is virtually unknown to the public. This salute to the great music man shows why his style and talent were ahead of its time. Tony Bennett, Frank Sinatra, Mel Tormé, Cab Calloway and others are featured in the special program. 70 min.
53-6540   *$19.99*

Genghis Blues (1999)
This captivating, Oscar-nominated effort centers on blind San Francisco blues musician Paul Pena, who taught himself the unusual art of "throat singing" after hearing a broadcast on a Russian radio station years earlier. Acting upon an invite to take part in a singing contest in the Siberian region of Tuva, Pena travels there and befriends the country's throat singing champion. 80 min.
53-6943   *$24.99*

Entertainment

Hollywood Behind The Scenes, Part One
In the first of several rare short subjects, Gig Young tours Warners Studio and checks out a giant water tank used in the filming of "Sea Haawk." Next, John Wayne shows home movies, and John Ford and James Dean are visited on location. A Universal tour from 1925 features stars from "The Phantom of the Opera" and "The Hunchback of Notre Dame." 50 min.
01-9043   *$19.99*

Rare Hollywood Shorts
Public service messages include testimonials for the Will Rogers Foundation from Bette Davis, Judy Garland, Edgar Bergen and Kay Kyser; John Wayne supports the Red Cross; Abbott and Costello stump for Christmas Seals; Ralph Bellamy speaks for literacy. Also, Jack Benny in "Taxi Tangles." 45 min.
01-9045   *$19.99*

Oscar's
Greatest Moments 1971-1991
A wonderful tribute to two decades of the Academy Awards, featuring clips of winning films, musical numbers, and fondly-remembered appearances. See Charlie Chaplin's touching return, Marlon Brando's "stand-in," the infamous "streaker" incident, plus stars like Jane Fonda, Sally Field, Paul Newman, Kevin Costner and others. Karl Malden hosts this nostalgia-filled collector's item. 110 min.
02-2161   Was $19.99   *$14.99*

The Academy
Award Winners: Complete Set
Go Oscar wild with this star-studded 10-volume collection of the Academy Awards' first half-century, from 1927 to 1977, featuring footage of winning and losing actors, actresses and films. Go behind the scenes of the awards and learn fascinating facts about Hollywood's greatest moments. 8 1/2 hrs. total.
70-3310   *$79.99*

The 27th Annual
Academy Awards (1955)
Celebrate the '54 Oscars in this show featuring Humphrey Bogart (nominee for "The Caine Mutiny") Grace Kelly (a winner "The Country Girl"), Marlon Brando (who won the Best Actor statue for "On the Waterfront"), Bing Crosby, Bette Davis, Martin and Lewis and more. Hosted by Bob Hope. 95 min.
09-1216   *$14.99*

American Cinema: Complete Set
Featuring clips from over 200 films and comments from Clint Eastwood, Spike Lee, Julia Roberts, Steven Spielberg and others, this exhaustive British-made look at Hollywood covers such topics as "The Star," "The Studio System," "Romantic Comedy," "The Film School Generation" and more. 10 hrs. total on five tapes. NOTE: Individual volumes available at $29.99 each.
04-2938   Save $25.00!   *$124.99*

The Classic Western Newsreels
This treat for sagebrush fans includes William S. Hart's 1939 farewell to movies, a documentary of a Roy Rogers toy giveaway in South America, highlights of the California Parade of Stars with Gene Autry, Buck Jones and others, TV bloopers from "Rawhide" and "Gunsmoke," and much more. 55 min.
01-9050   *$19.99*

Meanwhile, Back At The Ranch
A rousing tribute to the cowboy stars of old, featuring clips of the likes of Roy Rogers, Gene Autry, Hopalong Cassidy, Gabby Hayes and many others in action. Narrated by Pat Buttram. 80 min.
10-9124   Was $19.99   *$14.99*

The American West Of John Ford (1971)
This look at the legendary filmmaker behind "Stagecoach," "The Searchers," "Fort Apache" and "The Man Who Shot Liberty Valance" is a rarely seen but essential documentary that features Ford at the age of 77, a few years before his death. Along with clips from his classic westerns, frequent collaborators John Wayne, Henry Fonda and James Stewart are interviewed. 60 min.
10-6008   *$14.99*

A Century Of Science-Fiction
Christopher Lee hosts this tribute to classic science-fiction films which traces the genre from Lumiere's "A Trip to the Moon" to such 1950s gems as "The Day the Earth Stood Still" and recent winners like "The Terminator." Included are interviews with sci-fi staples and more! 120 min.
05-5085   *$19.99*

The Stars Of Star Wars
They put the "Star" in "Star Wars." Take a look and listen to the different performers who have helped make "Star Wars" so popular. From original cast members Harrison Ford, Carrie Fisher and Mark Hamill to recent recruits Liam Neeson, Jake Lloyd and Natalie Portman, the actors offer insight into "the Force." Plus, others tell what impact the films have had on their lives. 60 min.
05-5112   *$19.99*

The Unauthorized
Star Wars Story
This celebration of "Star Wars" and its sequels (and prequels) offers commentary from Harrison Ford, Carrie Fisher and other cast members, along with creator George Lucas and others. The impact of the film is looked at, as well as behind-the-scenes stories, gossip and facts surrounding the beloved film. 62 min.
50-8246   *$14.99*

TV Guide
Looks At Science Fiction
William Shatner and Robby the Robot host this exciting survey of the sci-fi, fantasy and horror genres on TV, tracing its roots from the early kids' shows of the '50s, through such '60s faves as "Lost in Space" and "Star Trek," to "The X-Files" and other contemporary hits. 60 min.
50-5574   *$14.99*

The Sci-Fi Files: Complete Set
This four-tape program follows the out-of-this-world artform known as science fiction from the earliest Jules Verne tales to "The X-Files" and examines how, through novels, comics, film and TV, the genre has become both a barometer and a predictor of technological, social and political trends. Volumes include "Children of Frankenstein," "Living in the Future," "March of the Machines" and "Spaceships and Aliens." 200 min. total. NOTE: Individual volumes available at $19.99 each.
53-6248   Save $20.00!   *$59.99*

Myrna Loy: So Nice To Come Home To
Known in '30s Hollywood as the "Queen" to Clark Gable's "King," Myrna Loy excelled in roles ranging from screwball comedy to heartfelt drama. Kathleen Turner hosts this tribute to the beloved star that includes clips from "The Thin Man," "Love Crazy," "The Best Years of Our Lives," "Mr. Blandings Builds His Dream House" and other films. 46 min.
18-7331 Was $19.99 *$14.99*

Kisses
This romantic program salutes 100 years of fabulous film smooches, featuring scenes from such movies as "Jezebel," "The Postman Always Rings Twice," "Casablanca," "Gone with the Wind" and more. It's passion personified as Gable and Leigh, Tracy and Hepburn, and Bogie and the program's host, Lauren Bacall, practice puckering on the big screen. 47 min.
18-7354 *$14.99*

Jack L. Warner: The Last Mogul
Fascinating inside look at the man who ran Warner Bros. Studios from his grandson, award-winning director Gregory Orr. Using rare footage, home movies, interviews and film clips, the glory days of the studio where "Casablanca," "The Adventures of Robin Hood," "The Maltese Falcon" and "Yankee Doodle Dandy" were produced. Narrated by Efrem Zimbalist, Jr. 104 min.
22-1428 *$19.99*

Here's Looking At You, Warner Bros. (1991)
It was the studio that brought sound to the screen, filled the '30s with gangsters and tap dancers, and made stars ranging from Bette and Bogart to Bugs and Batman. Trace the history of Warner Bros. in this nostalgia-filled tribute featuring clips from such films as "The Jazz Singer," "42nd Street," "Casablanca," and many more. Hosted by Barbra Streisand, Clint Eastwood, Steven Spielberg and others. 108 min.
19-2069 *$19.99*

Warner Bros.: 75 Years Of Award Winners (1998)
Follow over seven decades of screen greatness with this documentary salute to the Warner studio and its legacy of award-winning films. Included are clips from such classic movies as "Casablanca," "Yankee Doodle Dandy," "Chariots of Fire," "Driving Miss Daisy," "Unforgiven" and many more. 50 min.
19-2684 ☐*$19.99*

Warner Bros.: 75 Years Of Superstars (1998)
Some of the greatest names in Hollywood history have appeared in films bearing the "WB" shield, and in this nostalgia-filled retrospective you'll see movie clips with such unforgettable stars as Bette Davis, James Cagney, Humphrey Bogart, John Wayne, Elizabeth Taylor, Barbra Streisand, Clint Eastwood, Mel Gibson, Kevin Costner and others. 50 min.
19-2697 *$19.99*

Rock 'N' Roll Invaders: The AM Radio DJ's
They were the flamboyant, rules-flaunting showmen who sent the revolutionary sound of rock and roll over the airwaves in the '50s and '60s, often becoming stars in their own right. Learn about the people behind the voices—and how their antics changed the face of pop music—in this song-filled documentary. Includes interviews and film clips of Alan Freed, Wolfman Jack, Cousin Brucie Morrow, Dick Clark and many more. 90 min.
53-6406 *$19.99*

After Sunset: The Life And Times Of The Drive-In Theater (1996)
Wonderful look at that All-American icon known as the drive-in movie theater, as seen by filmmaker Jon Bokenkamp and a few of his friends, who take a cross-country trip to some of the country's remaining ozoners. Among the stops are a theater motel and a Texas spot that specializes in a snack bar specialty called Chihuahuas. With interviews with John Carpenter, Joe Bob Briggs and Samuel Z. Arkoff. 45 min.
50-5492 *$29.99*

Lumiére & Company (1996)
To mark the centenary of France's Lumiére Brothers' first motion pictures, 40 of the world's top directors were given an original Lumiére camera and asked to make a one-minute film. The result: this intriguing collection that includes works by John Boorman, Spike Lee, Claude Lelouch, David Lynch, Wim Wenders and Zhang Yimou. 88 min. In English and French with English subtitles.
53-8656 Was $59.99 *$19.99*

The Universal Story
The studio behind such classics as "All Quiet on the Western Front," "Dracula," "Frankenstein," "The Sting," "E.T." and "Waterworld" is saluted in this clip-filled program narrated by Richard Dreyfuss. Go behind the scenes and learn the history of Carl Laemmle's creation with archival footage and great cinematic sequences. 119 min.
07-2386 ☐*$12.99*

Hollywood's Leading Men: Boxed Set
In this seven-tape set, you'll get the inside scoop on the lives and careers of Hollywood favorites Sean Connery, Kirk Douglas, Cary Grant, Paul Newman, Robert Redford, James Stewart, and John Wayne. 210 min. total.
16-5017 *$49.99*

Hollywood's Leading Ladies: Boxed Set
Get to know Hollywood's most talented and beautiful women intimately with this seven-tape series. Included are programs on Lauren Bacall, Ingrid Bergman, Bette Davis, Audrey Hepburn, Katharine Hepburn and Marilyn Monroe. 210 min. total.
16-5018 *$49.99*

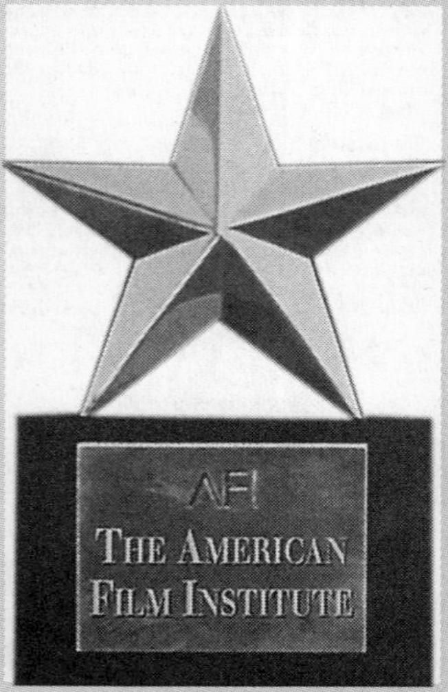

The American Film Institute Life Achievement Awards
The greatest actors, actresses and directors in cinema history are honored by the AFI in these wonderful all-star salutes, featuring rare footage from each recipient's work and tributes from their co-workers. Each tape runs about 90 min.

American Film Institute: Frank Capra
14-3227 *$14.99*

American Film Institute: Henry Fonda
14-3229 *$14.99*

American Film Institute: John Ford
14-3230 *$14.99*

American Film Institute: Lillian Gish
14-3231 *$14.99*

American Film Institute: Alfred Hitchcock
14-3232 *$14.99*

American Film Institute: Jack Lemmon
14-3235 *$14.99*

American Film Institute: Jimmy Stewart
14-3236 *$14.99*

American Film Institute: Orson Welles
14-3237 *$14.99*

American Film Institute: Billy Wilder
14-3238 *$14.99*

American Film Institute: Clint Eastwood
14-3437 *$14.99*

American Film Institute: Steven Spielberg
14-3439 *$14.99*

AFI's 100 Years, 100 Movies: Boxed Set (1999)
This 10-part series from the American Film Institute offers a cavalcade of star and film clips in a centennial celebration of America's top 100 movies of all time. "Citizen Kane," "Casablanca," "Gone With the Wind," "Star Wars"...all the greats are here. James Woods narrates; Jodie Foster, Richard Gere and Sally Field host. 460 min. on five tapes.
50-8619 *$79.99*

AFI's 100 Years, AFI's 100 Stars: America's Greatest Screen Legends (1999)
The greatest stars in film history are saluted by the American Film Institute in this special program hosted by Shirley Temple Black. James Caan, Clint Eastwood, Goldie Hawn, Jack Lemmon, Julia Roberts and many others add commentary, with clips showcasing such classic favorites as Humphrey Bogart, Marilyn Monroe, Cary Grant and more. 136 min.
50-8621 *$19.99*

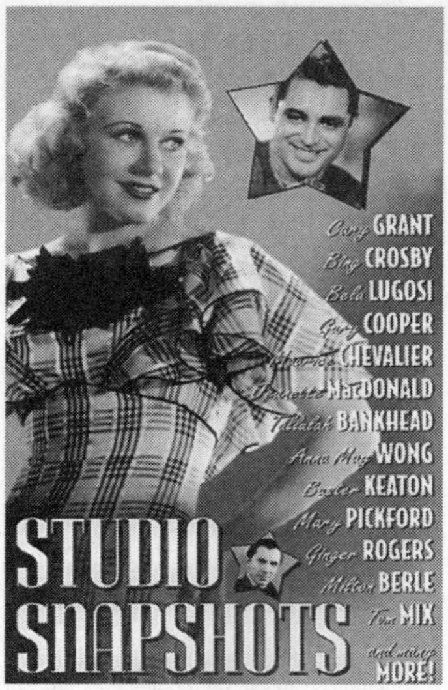

Studio Snapshots
During the early '30s, Paramount's "Hollywood on Parade" shorts treated audiences to lively songs and comical skits with many of the screen's biggest names. This compilation features such stars as Fredric March, Ginger Rogers (performing in male drag), Burns and Allen, Gary Cooper, Buster Keaton (driving his famous "land yacht"), Kate Smith, and even Helen Kane as Betty Boop meeting Bela Lugosi's Dracula. Also includes the musical shorts "Sing, Sing, Sing!" (1933), with Bing Crosby, and "Poppin' the Cork" (1933), starring Milton Berle. 101 min.
53-6301 *$24.99*

Hollywood Haunts
Is the movie capital of the world also the ghost capital of the world? Find out in this Discovery Channel documentary, as you follow paranormal experts and investigators as they search the Queen Mary, the Playboy Mansion, the Paramount studio and the former homes of such vanished(?) stars as Charlie Chaplin, Carole Lombard, Jim Morrison and others. 50 min.
27-7224 *$14.99*

Hollywood Scandals And Tragedies
Talent made them stars, but scandal made them legends. Get the lowdown Hollywood dirt on James Dean, Vivien Leigh, Sharon Tate, Rock Hudson, Sal Mineo, Jayne Mansfield and many others. 90 min.
50-6317 Was $79.99 *$19.99*

101 Dead Legends
The resting places, corpses, caskets and even coroner's sketches of some of the world's most famous people are shown in this creepy documentary. Rare photos and newsreel footage show Marilyn Monroe, Humphrey Bogart, Gary Cooper, Babe Ruth, Al Capone and others in their final state. Features a stirring montage of grave photos of 90 stars. 80 min.
75-6012 Was $59.99 *$14.99*

The Search For Haunted Hollywood (1989)
John Davidson hosts this tour of Tinseltown's most terrifying sites, from Tom Mix's haunted house and Mary Pickford's creepy dressing room to the Roosevelt Hotel, where the ghosts of Marilyn Monroe and Montgomery Clift have been spotted. Jack Carter, Norm Crosby, ghost hunter Richard Senate, paranormal expert Hans Holzer and magician Harry Blackstone are featured. 92 min.
08-1505 *$14.99*

George Stevens: A Filmmaker's Journey
A special look at the life and career of one of Hollywood's most revered directors, put together by his son. Interviews with friends and colleagues, clips from such movies as "Alice Adams," "Gunga Din," "A Place in the Sun," "Shane" and "Giant," and never-before-shown WWII footage shot by Stevens with the Army Signal Corps are featured in this remarkable documentary. 110 min.
22-5550 Was $29.99 *$14.99*

MGM: When The Lion Roars Complete Set
This acclaimed three-part documentary traces the colorful history of the studio that boasted "more stars than there are in heaven," Metro-Goldwyn-Mayer. See MGM's beginnings in the silent era, the golden age of the '30s and '40s, and the decline and eventual demise of the studio through memorable film clips, behind-the-scenes footage and interviews. Patrick Stewart hosts. This special boxed set includes a 12-page commemorative booklet. NOTE: Individual volumes available at $19.99 each.
12-2451 *$59.99*

Minnelli On Minnelli
Daughter Liza Minnelli talks about life with her father, Vincente, the director of such classic MGM musicals as "An American in Paris," "Kismet," "The Band Wagon" and "The Pirate." A poignant look at a Hollywood great! 84 min.
12-2825 *$19.99*

Hollywood Without Makeup
Join Ken Murray, "Mr. Hollywood Home Movies," for an incredible collection of stars at work, home and play: Cary Grant, Mae West, Clark Gable, Dick Powell, Marilyn Monroe, and others. Includes behind-the-scenes looks at the shooting of 1939's "Gunga Din" and a tour of William Randolph Hearst's estate, San Simeon. 50 min.
01-5129 *$19.99*

Neorealism
A film style born out of wartime hardship and economic necessity, Italy's Neorealism movement of the '40s and '50s had a profound influence on world cinema. This three-part series, produced by the Museum of Modern Art, traces the key movies and such directors as Rossellini, De Sica, Lizzani, Fellini and others. Each tape runs about 60 min. and is in Italian with English subtitles.

Neorealism Up To 1945
22-1627 *$19.99*

Neorealism Up To 1950
22-1628 *$19.99*

Neorealism Up To 1954
22-1629 *$19.99*

First Works, Vol. 1
A number of today's top filmmakers discuss their experiences directing their first films and the beginnings of their career in this program that also features footage from the auteurs' earliest efforts. See Oliver Stone's Vietnam-themed student film, the project that got Steven Spielberg interested in Robert Zemeckis, plus Spike Lee, Roger Corman and others. 122 min.
15-5313 *$39.99*

First Works, Vol. 2
More interviews and footage from Hollywood's top talents are offered in this look at their early works. John Carpenter, Ron Howard, Martin Scorsese, John Milius, Susan Seidelman and Richard Donner are featured. 120 min.
15-5314 *$39.99*

Catastrophe!: Hollywood Disaster Movies
Disaster in the movies means more than Kevin Costner in "The Postman," as evidenced in this salute to the world of the cinema of calamity. "Earthquake," "Meteor," "The Poseidon Adventure," "San Francisco," "The Towering Inferno" and "Krakatoa, East of Java" are among the disaster epics highlighted. 90 min.
05-5110 *$14.99*

Masters Of Disaster
This nifty compilation of "making of" shorts details the production of classic disaster films, including "The Poseidon Adventure," "The Cassandra Crossing," "The Towering Inferno" and "The Swarm." 88 min.
10-9950 *$14.99*

Going Hollywood: The War Years
Van Johnson hosts this nostalgia-filled look at the films and stars of the '40s and how the war looked on the silver screen. Clips from "Bataan," "Crash Dive," "Pride of the Marines," "The More the Merrier," "Cover Girl" and other movies, newsreel highlights (including color footage of Pearl Harbor) and interviews with stars are featured. 76 min.
19-1647 Was $19.99 *$14.99*

Cartoons Go To War
During World War II, many of America's favorite animated stars were "drafted" into drumming up support on the homefront, and top cartoon studios such as Disney and Warner Bros. worked with the government to produce films for the men overseas, with such original characters as Private Snafu and Mr. Hook. See clips from the best of these wartime toons, and hear from the folks who made them, in this nostalgia-filled documentary. 50 min.
53-8401 *$19.99*

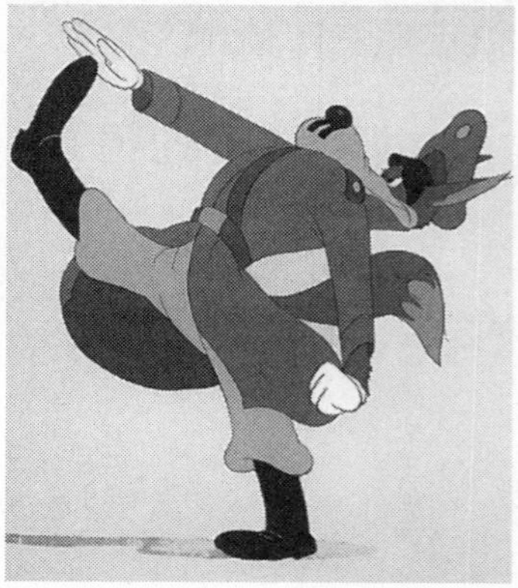

Toons At War!
Hollywood's animators (and their creations) did their part for the war effort in the '40s, and this "V for Victory" compilation features the best of these gung-ho gigglers. See Bugs Bunny, Porky Pig and Elmer Fudd shilling war bonds, Superman tackling "Japoteurs," "Bugs Bunny Nips the Nips," "The Ducktators," "Tokio Jokio," "Blitz Wolf," Donald Duck in "The Spirit of '43" and more. 88 min.
65-5020 Was $29.99 *$19.99*

Hollywood Musicals Of The 50's
The classic movie musicals of the 1950s are feted in this toe-tapping tape that includes clips from "Singin' in the Rain," "An American in Paris," "Showboat," "Seven Brides for Seven Brothers," "Damn Yankees," "Oklahoma!" and others. Also featured are interviews with Shirley Jones, Debbie Reynolds and Ann Miller. 60 min.
05-5078 *$19.99*

Hollywood Musicals Of The 40's
"The Golden Age of Hollywood Musicals" is feted in this entertaining collection of film clips, recollections and classic sequences. Among the films highlighted are "Thank Your Lucky Stars," "Yankee Doodle Dandy," "Moon Over Miami," "Holiday Inn," "Easter Parade" and "Cabin in the Sky." Mickey Rooney, Judy Garland and others put on a show! 120 min.
05-5107 *$19.99*

Hollywood Musicals Of The 60's
The best and worst of times for Hollywood musicals can be found in the 1960s, and this video offers evidence of the high and low points. Segments from "Mary Poppins," "The Music Man," "My Fair Lady," "Bells Are Ringing," "Gypsy" and "Oliver!" are featured, along with such stars as Julie Andrews, Shirley Jones, Dean Martin and others. 120 min.
05-5108 *$19.99*

Hollywood Rocks 'N' Rolls In The 50's
You'll shake, rattle and roll when watching this tribute to the great rock films of the 1950s, including "Jailhouse Rock," "Rock Around the Clock," "Jamboree" and "Rock! Rock! Rock!" Famous disc jockey Alan Freed returns by way of early clips to introduce some classic groups of the era. 60 min.
05-5090 *$14.99*

Small Steps, Big Strides: The Black Experience In Hollywood
Follow the struggles and triumphs of African-American actors and actresses on the silver screen from the silent era to 1970 in this fascinating and moving documentary that includes rare film clips, interviews with top stars and more. 56 min.
04-3566 *$19.99*

Midnight Ramble: The Story Of The Black Film Industry
The remarkable history of the black cinema is told in this insightful documentary that looks at an industry which flourished between 1910 and World War II, far from the Hollywood spotlight. Rare film clips and interviews with actors and directors of the era are featured, along with a look at pioneering filmmaker Oscar Micheaux; James Avery narrates. 60 min.
63-7110 □*$19.99*

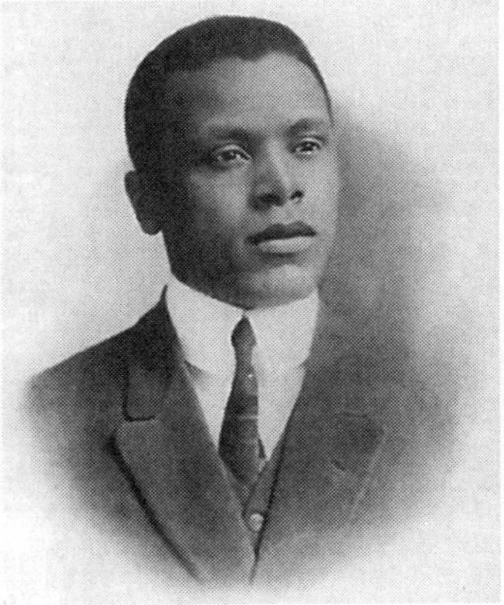

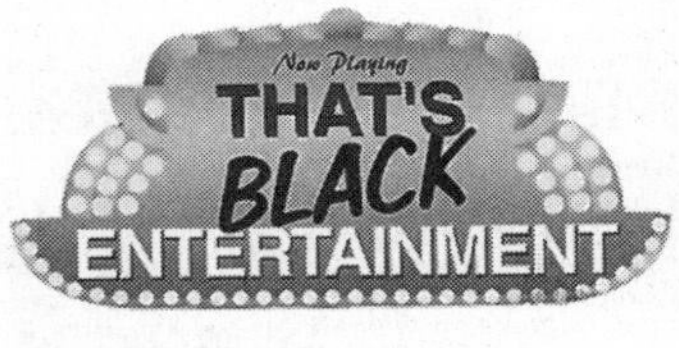

That's Black Entertainment
Explore the long-neglected works of African-American stars and filmmakers with this two-tape collection. Included are "Race Movies: The Early History of Black Cinema," a look at pioneering all-black studios that also features the vintage short films "St. Louis Blues" starring Bessie Smith, "Hi-De-Ho" with Cab Calloway and "Boogie-Woogie Dream" with Lena Horne, plus "The Soundies Era: Black Music Videos from the 1940s," a sampler of 16 shorts with such artists as Count Basie, Nat "King" Cole, Lionel Hampton and others. 106 min. total.
89-5019 *$29.99*

Classified X (1998)
Filmmaker Melvin Van Peebles takes an intriguing look at the treatment of African-American characters throughout the history of Hollywood. With his trademark candor and wit, he exposes how Tinseltown has encouraged the institutionalization of racism from its earliest incarnations on the big screen. 50 min.
53-6191 Was $24.99 *$19.99*

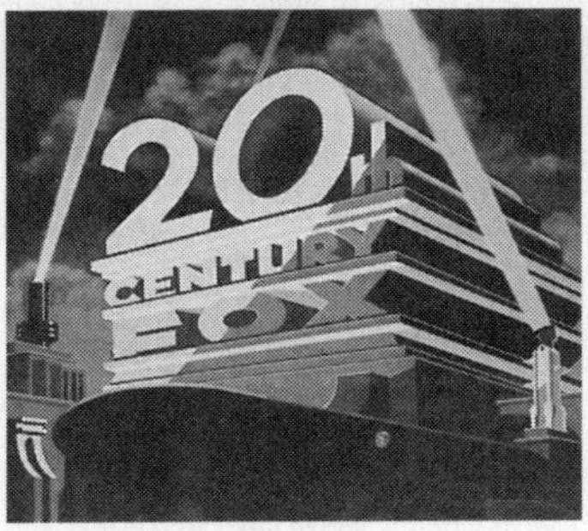

20th Century Fox: The First 50 Years
When Joe Schenck and Darryl F. Zanuck merged their Twentieth Century Pictures with William Fox's Fox Films in 1935, they created a Hollywood legend. This star-studded retrospective of the studio's first half-century, hosted by James Coburn, offers interviews with Alice Faye, Roddy McDowall, Debbie Reynolds, Julie Andrews and other Fox alumni, along with clips from such films as "Poor Little Rich Girl," "The Grapes of Wrath," "Laura," "Oklahoma!," "The Longest Day," "Cleopatra," "The Sound of Music" and more. 129 min.
04-3588 *$19.99*

The World Of Darryl F. Zanuck
Legendary movie mogul and 20th Century Fox top dog Darryl F. Zanuck is the subject of this absorbing documentary. Learn of Zanuck's passionate approach to producing such films as "All About Eve," "Gentlemen's Agreement" and "Viva Zapata!" and see exactly how the no-nonsense Hollywood king operates—from new York! 60 min.
10-9924 *$14.99*

Music For The Movies: Bernard Herrmann
The master composer of scores for such films as Orson Welles' "Citizen Kane," Martin Scorsese's "Taxi Driver" and Alfred Hitchcock's "Psycho" and "North By Northwest" is the focus of this Oscar-nominated documentary that mixes film footage and commentary from noted directors and Herrmann's contemporaries. 58 min.
04-5397 *$24.99*

Music For The Movies: The Hollywood Sound
Hollywood's Golden Age, the 1930s, saw the rise of such brilliant composers as Erich Korngold, Alfred Newman, Max Steiner and Franz Waxman, who are profiled in this documentary featuring interviews and film clips. Also includes the BBC National Orchestra of Wales performing selections from "The Adventures of Robin Hood," "Gone with the Wind," "Laura" and others. 86 min.
04-5410 *$24.99*

100 Years Of Comedy
This salute to cinematic silliness ranges from the earliest days of movies to contemporary times, presenting film clips of scores of stars, including Laurel and Hardy, the Marx Brothers, the Three Stooges, and Jerry Lewis, and scenes from such classics as "His Girl Friday," "It Happened One Night," "The Naked Gun" and more. 120 min.
05-5084 *$19.99*

Legends Of Comedy: Complete Set
The best-loved laughmakers from stage, screen and television, from Chaplin, Keaton and Fields to Burns and Allen, Jackie Gleason and Sid Caesar, are brought together in one unforgettable three-tape collection featuring their funniest routines. Includes "The Golden Age of Comedy," "Great Stars of Film and Radio" and "TV Comedy Classics." 165 min. total. NOTE: Individual volumes available at $24.99 each.
50-4845 Save $15.00! *$59.99*

MGM's Big Parade Of Comedy (1964)
This collection of classic comic moments from the early years of MGM features clips of Laurel and Hardy, the Marx Brothers, Clark Gable, Robert Benchley, Marion Davies and others. Compiled by Robert Youngson. 100 min.
12-2554 *$19.99*

The Best Of British Film Comedy (To See Such Fun) (1981)
Who says the English have no sense of humor? Dozens of Britain's balmiest comic actors are featured in clips from their funniest films. Peter Sellers, Alec Guinness, Marty Feldman, Eric Idle, Benny Hill, Spike Milligan and Margaret Rutherford are among the jovial jokesters on hand. 91 min. on two tapes.
50-5283 Was $29.99 *$19.99*

The Art Of Illusion: 100 Years Of Hollywood Special Effects
Throughout film history, effects artists have put the impossible on the silver screen. Follow a century of cinema magic with this behind-the-scenes documentary that features clips from "A Trip to the Moon," "King Kong," "Ben-Hur," "Ghostbusters," "Die Hard," "Apollo 13" and many others. Adrienne Barbeau narrates. 50 min.
83-1046 *$14.99*

Titanic: The Premiere
You'll be first in line for the American premiere of "Titanic," James Cameron's epic movie. You'll see Leonardo DiCaprio, Gloria Stuart and James "King of the World" Cameron as they arrive at Mann's Chinese Theatre in Hollywood for this star-studded event. Among the guests are Linda Hamilton, Celine Dion, Dustin Hoffman and Ray Liotta. 60 min.
05-5073 *$14.99*

Hollywood Hookers
Prostitutes have been in no short supply in the movies, and this video offers glimpses of some of filmdom's most famous—and sexiest—hookers. Included are clips from "Taxi Driver," "The Happy Hooker," "Crimes of Passion," "Sweet Charity," "American Gigolo" and "Klute." 60 min.
05-5082 *$14.99*

Women Who Made The Movies
A fascinating study of female directors from the 1890s to the present, focusing on Ida Lupino, Leni Riefenstahl, Lois Weber and Cleo Madison. See how they braved prejudice to make important films. 56 min.
08-1479 *$19.99*

Great Hollywood Chase Scenes
Have a smashing good time with this behind-the-scenes look at how those daredevil stunts and death-defying auto chases are created for the screen. Scenes from "The French Connection," "Smokey and the Bandit," "Lethal Weapon 2" and other "smash" hits are included. 37 min.
10-2320 *$12.99*

The World's Greatest Stunts!
Christopher Reeve hosts this action-packed salute to Hollywood's unsung heroes, the brave stuntmen who risk their lives for the movies. Mel Gibson, Arnold Schwarzenegger and Tom Selleck guest star in this wild program featuring some of cinema's best stunts. 60 min.
50-6541 *$19.99*

Shoot To Thrill (1998)
This exciting program shows how some of Hollywood's most dangerous aerial stunts are performed. Aerial stunt coordinator Marc Wolff explains how he makes the impossible seem real in such films as "Cliffhanger" and "Tomorrow Never Dies," and how he manages to bring his crews back alive every time. 50 min.
53-6192 Was $19.99 *$14.99*

Hispanic Hollywood
This salute to Latin Americans in film and TV features interviews with leading Hispanic performers and clips from movies about the Latin experience. "West Side Story," "The Ballad of Gregorio Cortez," "Stand and Deliver" and "Neptune's Daughter" are among the films showcased, while Jimmy Smits, Antonio Banderas, Sonia Braga and others offer insight. 120 min.
05-5106 *$19.99*

Batman Two-Pack
Biff! Bam! Sock-o! Included in this two-tape set are "Batman and Robin and Other Super Heroes," with Adam West and Burt Ward, "The Green Hornet's" Van Williams and Bruce Lee, and other heroes; and "Batman and Robin vs. the Super Villains," which includes such Dynamic Duo dastardlies as the Joker, the Penguin, the Riddler, Catwoman and others. 100 min.
05-5109 *$14.99*

Great Hollywood Memories, Vol. 1
Gene Kelly hosts this nostalgia-filled look at the early days of movie-making, from Thomas Edison's short films to the advent of sound. Silent stars like Pickford, Chaplin, Fairbanks, Garbo, Chaney and others are seen at work and in rare behind-the-scenes footage, along with tours of the first Hollywood studios, clips from "Ben-Hur," "Wings," "The Jazz Singer" and more. 60 min.
10-8157 Was $19.99 *$14.99*

Great Hollywood Memories, Vol. 2
Tinseltown's "Golden Age," from the late '20s to the '50s, is recounted in this wonderful salute hosted by Henry Fonda. There's rare clips of stars at parties, premieres and in front of the famed Chinese Theatre, salutes to Busby Berkeley musicals, gangster films and other genres, and much more. Grant, Davis, Gable, Temple, Wayne, Garland, Monroe, Brando...they're all here! 60 min.
10-8158 Was $19.99 *$14.99*

Great Hollywood Memories, Vol. 3
"The Great Stars" are spotlighted in this dazzling display of Tinseltown greats from silent days to the early '60s. Pickford, Fairbanks, Cagney, Crawford, Davis, Bogart, Wayne, Taylor, Monroe and many more are featured, along with Gable at the premiere of "Gone with the Wind," Khrushchev on the set of "Can Can," and Chaplin clowning for Churchill. Henry Fonda hosts. 60 min.
10-8326 Was $19.99 *$14.99*

100 Years Of Horror
Hammer Studios great Christopher Lee hosts this look at horror movie history, from "Frankenstein" and "Dracula" to recent shockers. Featured are clips, trailers, interviews and lost footage. 120 min.
05-5087 *$19.99*

100 Years Of Horror: Collector's Set
This 13-tape salute to classic shockers, from the earliest days to contemporary times, is hosted by Christopher Lee and features clips, archival footage and interviews with some of the genre's best. Included are segments on "Aliens & Sorcerers," "The Walking Dead," "Frankenstein," "Double Demons," "Witches & Demons," "Giants & Dinosaurs," "Scream Queens & Girl Ghouls," "Mad Scientists & Mad Monsters," "Gruesome Twosome" and "Ghosts & Phantoms." 700 min. total.
05-5091 *$129.99*

The Mummy
Trace the history of horror cinema's bandaged bad guys in this documentary featuring film clips with Karloff and other scary "wrap"-pers from 1932's "The Mummy," plus "The Mummy's Hand," "Curse of the Mummy" and more. Hosted by Christopher Lee, who played the character for Hammer Studios. 60 min.
05-5105 *$14.99*

Frankenstein: A Cinematic Scrapbook
A tribute to everyone's favorite screen monster, filled with clips; segments on actors who played the role, like Boris Karloff, Lon Chaney, Jr., Bela Lugosi and others; and lots of great trivia. Ohhhh, Frankie! 60 min.
15-5178 *$14.99*

The True Story Of Frankenstein
Mary Shelley created a monster in 1818, and writers, actors and filmmakers haven't been able to get enough of it ever since. The history of the creature on and off the screen includes clips from Thomas Edison's 1910 filmization to Kenneth Branagh's 1994 treatment, plus interviews with Robert De Niro, Mel Brooks, Roger Corman and others. Hosted by Roger Moore; narrated by Eli Wallach. 100 min.
53-8163 *$19.99*

Dracula: A Cinematic Scrapbook
Get the inside track on Drac in this documentary on film's Princes of Darkness. Clips of Bela Lugosi, Christopher Lee, Lon Chaney, Jr. and other cinematic bloodsuckers help make this bit of Transylvanian "ghoulash" a must-have item. 60 min.
15-5179 *$14.99*

Wolfman: A Cinematic Scrapbook
No, it's not the deejay from "American Graffiti"! It's a scary, hairy look at the legendary lycanthropes of the silver screen, with such gruesome greats as Lon Chaney, Jr., Bela Lugosi, Michael Landon, Oliver Reed and others transforming from man to beast before your very eyes. Rare film and TV clips, interviews, much more. 57 min.
15-5192 *$14.99*

The Horror Of It All
Welcome to the Cinema Ghoul School, where Hollywood horror reigns supreme. This look at the history of terror in film features Boris Karloff, Bela Lugosi, Vincent Price and others, plus clips from classics like "Nosferatu," "The Horror of Dracula" and more. 60 min.
50-6796 Was $19.99 *$14.99*

Halloween: The Happy Haunting Of America
Get the lowdown on the scariest people, places and things in America with this terrifying travelogue hosted by actor Daniel Roebuck ("The Late Shift") and make-up expert Bob Burns. Go behind the scenes at mask-maker Don Post Studios, see scary haunted houses and meet horror film notables Robert Englund, Tom Savini and Angus Scrimm. Boo! 50 min.
76-7354 *$19.99*

Coming Soon (1983)
Join hostess Jamie Lee Curtis for this fascinating, frightening look at over 50 films from the vaults of Universal Pictures. "Dracula," "The Mummy," "The Wolf Man," "The Creature from the Black Lagoon," "The Phantom of the Opera," "Psycho," "Jaws"...they're all here! A must for film buffs; directed by John Landis. 55 min.
07-1173 *$14.99*

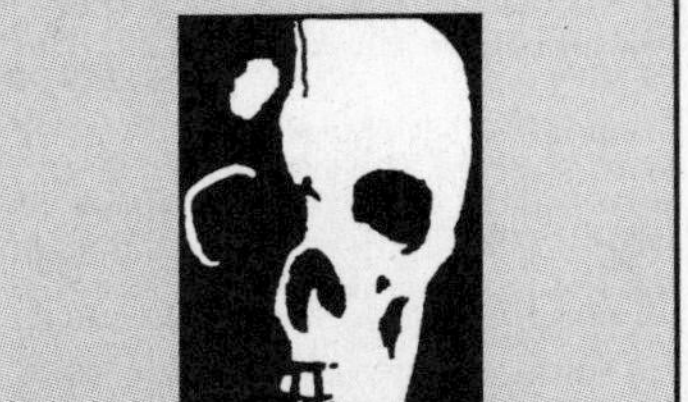

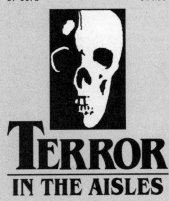

Terror In The Aisles (1984)
Spend 84 horrifying minutes with the scariest moments in screen history. This compilation includes clips from "Halloween," "Poltergeist," "When a Stranger Calls," "Texas Chainsaw Massacre," Hitchcock favorites and more! Donald Pleasence and Nancy Allen host the shocking array of gore, scares and screams. 84 min.
07-1268 Was $19.99 *$14.99*

Anatomy Of A Filmmaker: Otto Preminger's Life In Film
The acclaimed, controversial director whose movies included "Laura," "The Moon Is Blue," "The Man with the Golden Arm" and "Exodus" is spotlighted in this documentary that looks at Preminger's work and tempestuous career. Includes interviews with Frank Sinatra, Vincent Price, James Stewart, Michael Caine and others; Burgess Meredith hosts. 119 min.
19-2214 *$19.99*

Hollywood's Golden Era: Leading Ladies
Relive the memorable careers of such glamorous screen immortals as Bette Davis, Carole Lombard, Barbara Stanwyck and Joan Crawford in this salute that features film clips, interviews and much more. 55 min.
50-6279 *$19.99*

Hollywood's Golden Era: Leading Men
They're the sturdy, larger-than-life legends we've loved for decades. Now see a special salute to the lives and careers of stars Cary Grant, Errol Flynn, Gary Cooper and Jimmy Stewart. 55 min.
50-6280 *$19.99*

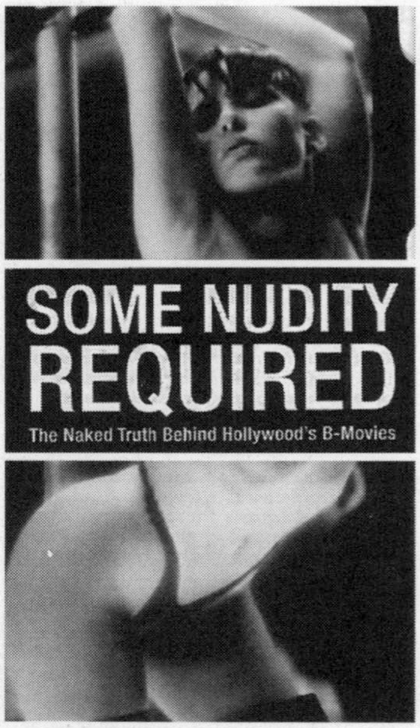

Some Nudity Required (1998)
Odette Springer, a music executive for Roger Corman's Concorde Pictures, decides to turn the cameras on her own industry in this survey of the world of exploitation movies. Springer talks to Corman, directors Fred Olen Ray, Jim Wynorski and Andy Sidaris, and starlets Julie Strain and Maria Ford, all of whom offer insight into the world of big breasts and big explosions. 74 min.
53-6474 Was $59.99 *$19.99*

Hollywood On Trial
One of the most frightening real-life stories to come from Hollywood happened in the '40s and '50s, when the "Red Scare" and its resultant blacklists destroyed friendships, careers, and sometimes lives. John Huston narrates this look at McCarthy-era movieland, with interviews from some of the victimized actors, writers and directors. 90 min.
50-6374 *$29.99*

Scandalize My Name: Stories From The Blacklist
At the height of the anti-Communist hysteria that gripped Hollywood in the '50s, some of the hardest hit people were African-American performers and celebrities who were already victims of racial prejudice. In this insightful program you'll learn how the blacklist affected such people as Harry Belafonte, Ossie Davis, Paul Robeson, Jackie Robinson, Hazel Scott and others. Morgan Freeman narrates. 60 min.
83-1499 *$19.99*

Michael Caine: Breaking The Mold
The actor reflects on his life and films in this invigorating documentary that offers an intimate look at one of the world's most popular performers. Clips from "Educating Rita," "Alfie," "Sleuth" and "Hannah and Her Sisters" are showcased, along with recollections from Dyan Cannon, Roger Moore, Julie Waters and others. 60 min.
50-7174 Was $19.99 *$14.99*

Fred MacMurray: The Guy Next Door
While Baby Boomers know him primarily as a Disney film star and the pipe-smoking dad on "My Three Sons," Fred MacMurray was a versatile actor who went from song-and-dance man to dramatic lead. Clips from such films as "Double Indemnity," "The Caine Mutiny" and "The Apartment" and interviews with Jack Lemmon, Billy Wilder and Beverly Garland are featured in this video tribute narrated by daughter Kate MacMurray. 50 min.
50-7607 *$14.99*

The Pin-Ups
A ravishing salute to the sexiest women in the world, featuring revealing looks at beauties throughout the ages, from 19th-century Can-Can dancers to today's supermodels, with the likes of Sophia Loren, Brigitte Bardot, Marilyn Monroe and Betty Grable in between. 60 min.
53-8203 *$19.99*

The Hollywood Censorship Wars
The history of cinematic censorship is covered in this program that traces the battle of art versus regulation from the earliest days of movies to today. See how the Hollywood Production Code dictated the rules in Hollywood and learn about other controversial censorship struggles from critics, performers and filmmakers. 50 min.
53-8294 *$19.99*

Howard Hawks: American Artist
Unlike his contemporaries such as John Ford and Alfred Hitchcock, who specialized in one genre, director Howard Hawks' body of work ranged from comedies ("Bringing Up Baby, "His Girl Friday") and westerns ("Red River") to crime dramas ("The Big Sleep," "Scarface") and musicals ("Gentlemen Prefer Blondes"). Follow his half-century in Hollywood through film clips and interviews with such stars as Lauren Bacall, Peter Bogdanovich, James Caan, Angie Dickinson and others. 57 min.
53-9480 Was $19.99 *$14.99*

Hollywood Bloopers
Classic originals from the greats of Hollywood. Watch as stars like James Cagney, Bette Davis, Errol Flynn, Humphrey Bogart, Jimmy Stewart, Kirk Douglas and others flub, curse and laugh their way through classic films of the '30s and '40s; even Porky Pig gets hot under the collar! 75 min.
62-1009 *$19.99*

Hidden Hollywood: Behind The Scenes
A true mondo delight of film rarities, oddities and nostalgia items: Christmas with Joan Crawford and her kids, James Dean on driving safety, the 1939 Academy Awards, Bogie and Bacall in a screen test for an unmade movie. Previously seen as "Hollywood Outtakes," this tape also includes new footage featuring The Beatles, Marilyn Monroe, Elvis and others. 100 min.
62-1333 *$19.99*

Hedda Hopper's Hollywood
A filmed version of Hopper's influential gossip column featuring some of the arch-snooper's biggest scoops from the years 1940-1959, with star-targets Lucille Ball, Gary Cooper, Gloria Swanson, Liza Minnelli and many others. 60 min.
63-1322 *$19.99*

The World Of Jim Henson
One of America's most creative and beloved entertainers is spotlighted in this terrific program from the "Great Performances" series. Witness Henson's beginnings on local TV, his success with "Sesame Street," the creation of his greatest characters, and his work in feature films. 85 min.
80-7165 Was $29.99 *$19.99*

Star Power: The Creation Of United Artists
One industry wag said, "So the lunatics have taken charge of the asylum" when Charlie Chaplin, Douglas Fairbanks, D.W. Griffith and Mary Pickford announced in 1919 that they were forming their own studio. In this program, you'll see how these four pioneers rose to the top of Hollywood, and how their company put the art back in the hands of the artists. Narrated by Roddy McDowall. 54 min.
83-1249 *$19.99*

Hollywood On Parade (1932)
Fredric March hosts this amazing collection of five short subjects filled with Hollywood stars mugging for the camera. Among the spotlighted performers are Jack Oakie, Jimmy Durante, Tom Mix, Ken Maynard, Jeanette MacDonald, Bela Lugosi, Helen Kane, Jean Harlow, Mary Pickford and many others. 59 min.
09-1220 *$19.99*

The House That Shadows Built (1932)
Produced to mark Paramount Pictures' "Twentieth Birthday Jubilee," this fascinating documentary takes you behind the gates of one of Hollywood's great studios. See how Hungarian-born penny aracde owner Adolph Zukor teamed up with Jesse Lasky's Famous Players company to form Paramount. Sarah Bernhardt, George M. Cohan, Mary Pickford, Lon Chaney, Maurice Chevalier and the Marx Brothers are among the stars spotlighted. 60 min.
10-9228 *$19.99*

The Film Parade (1933)
A rare early history of cinema lovingly assembled by Edison collaborator J. Stuart Blackton and Vitagraph director William P.S. Earle, with original film clips from "The Big Parade," "Steamboat Willie" and others, and remarkable re-creations of such landmark moments as Edison's 1890's short "The Sneeze." 65 min.
10-7559 Was $29.99 *$19.99*

The Epic That Never Was (1965)
A revealing documentary that chronicles the 1937 production of Robert Graves' "I, Claudius," which was aborted after only a few weeks of shooting. The potential masterpiece, which had Josef von Sternberg behind the helm, Alexander Korda as producer and Merle Oberon and Charles Laughton starring, featured what many consider to be Laughton's finest hour as an actor. Hosted by Dirk Bogarde. 74 min.
09-1987 *$19.99*

Hollywood's Children
Incisive documentary about child actors, from Shirley Temple and Jackie Cooper to Jodie Foster and Brooke Shields. What drives them to success? What role do their parents play? And how do they handle sudden fame? Roddy McDowall narrates. 60 min.
50-6795 Was $19.99 *$14.99*

Grace Kelly: The American Princess
She came from a wealthy Philadelphia family, moved on to Hollywood to become a leading screen star in "High Noon" and "Dial M for Murder," then gave up her career for royalty, as Princess Grace of Monaco. Jimmy Stewart, Alec Guinness and Louis Jourdan add insight into Grace's storybook life. 60 min.
50-6799 Was $19.99 *$14.99*

Hollywood Chronicles
This fascinating series looks at the real Hollywood, uncovering the stories behind the screen. You'll meet legendary stars of long ago, witness Tinseltown's greatest scandals, and see what made Hollywood's greatest films so great with help from clips, interviews and narration from Jackie Cooper. Each tape runs about 50 min. There are 13 volumes available, including:

Hollywood Chronicles: Scandal!/Mysteries & Secrets
50-6825 *$19.99*

Hollywood Chronicles: Censorship—The Unseen Cinema/Sex In The Movies
50-6829 *$19.99*

Hollywood Chronicles: Stereotypes & Minorities/ Familiar Faces, Unknown Names
50-6833 *$19.99*

Stella Adler: Awake And Dream!
One of the most influential acting teachers of all time is profiled in this program. A leading exponent of Stanislavsky's techniques, Adler is shown with such students as Warren Beatty, Marlon Brando and Robert De Niro, and her work is recalled by colleagues and students. 57 min.
22-5651 *$39.99*

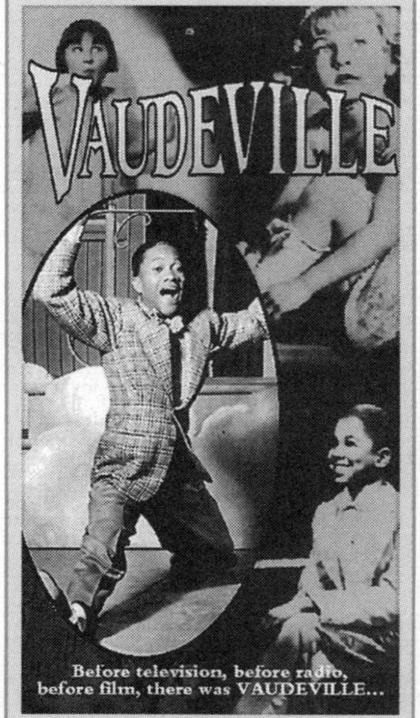

Vaudeville (1997)
From the late 19th century to the first half of the 20th, America's most popular form of entertainment was the touring variety shows whose acts ranged from Burns and Allen, W.C. Fields and Bert Williams to jugglers, unicyclists and Swain's Rats and Cats. Follow the rise and fall of vaudeville in this "American Masters" program that features rare photos and performance footage, plus interviews with such stage veterans as Billy Barty, Rose Marie, Bobby Short and The Nicholas Brothers. 112 min.
53-6670 *$19.99*

Moon Over Broadway (1997)
Renowned filmmaker D.A. Pennebaker ("Dont Look Back") proves there's as much drama behind the scenes as on the boards of a Broadway show in this revealing look at the making of the 1997 comedy "Moon Over Buffalo." Backstage bickering between stars Carol Burnett and Philip Bosco, director Tom Moore and writer Ken Ludwig is replaced by "show must go on" camaraderie as the production goes from rehearsal to opening night. 98 min.
53-6836 *$24.99*

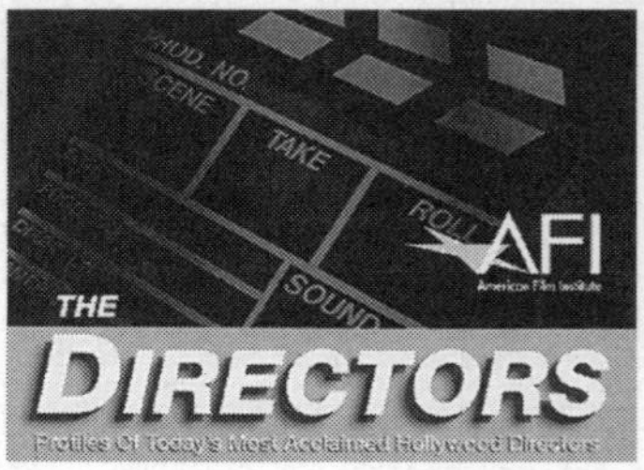

The Directors
Originally run on American Movie Classics, this incisive series offers in-depth interviews with Hollywood's top directors, who discuss their craft, relate behind-the-scenes stories about their films and offer tips to aspiring filmmakers. Each tape runs about 50 min. There are 22 volumes available, including:

The Directors: Ron Howard
53-6621 *$14.99*

The Directors: William Friedkin
53-6793 *$14.99*

The Directors: Steven Spielberg
53-6871 *$14.99*

The Directors: Milos Forman
53-6873 *$14.99*

The Directors: Robert Altman
53-6875 *$14.99*

The Directors: Martin Scorsese
53-6877 *$14.99*

Roger Moore: A Matter Of Class
The son of a London policeman, Roger Moore would go on to symbolize sophisticated British crimefighters, first on TV as the Saint, then through seven big-screen outings as James Bond. See how he worked to avoid being "just another handsome face" in this video biography that features comments from Michael Caine, Gregory Peck and Maud Adams and clips from Moore's TV and film work. 52 min.
50-7609 *$14.99*

Celebrities Caught On Camera, Vol. 1
Go behind the headlines and see celebrities caught with their guard down at bars, clubs and movie premieres. Among the stars snagged by the video paparazzi are Heather Locklear, Charlie Sheen, Leonardo DiCaprio, Tommy Lee, Julia Roberts, Sylvester Stallone and Matthew Perry. 53 min.
50-8134 *$19.99*

The Best Of British Cinema
Celebrate 50 years of England's top films, filmmakers and stars with this comprehensive retrospective that presents clips from such movies as "The Private Life of Henry VIII," "The Scarlet Pimpernel," "The Thief of Bagdad," "The Four Feathers" and many more. Vivien Leigh, Charles Laughton, Laurence Olivier and Merle Oberon are among the stars featured. Sir John Mills narrates. 120 min.
50-8339 *$19.99*

Grace Kelly
This story of the Philadelphia-born actress who became a queen offers home movies and rare photos to tell its enchanting story. Follow Grace's career, including such films as "High Noon" and "Rear Window" and her Oscar-winning turn in "The Country Girl," along with her marriage to Prince Rainier of Monaco. 60 min.
53-6384 *$19.99*

Behind Your Radio Dial And Westinghouse Presents (1948)
NBC produced this documentary look behind the scenes of how radio programs are produced and transmitted. Includes a tour of Radio City and the first NBC television station, WNBT in New York. With Fred Allen, Toscanini and Fibber McGee and Molly. 45 min.
09-1386 Was $24.99 *$19.99*

Brother, Can You Spare A Dime? (1975)
Remember those "good old days" of the Great Depression? This documentary mixes newsreel footage of American life in the '30s with film clips of such contemporary Hollywood favorites as James Cagney, Humphrey Bogart, King Kong and the Marx Brothers for an offbeat and compelling look back in time. 103 min.
08-1042 *$19.99*

Film Before Film (1986)
A fascinating, often humorous look at the "prehistory" of cinema, featuring shadow plays, peep shows, flip books, magic lanterns, early animation and pornographic images. A celebration of invention from German filmmaker Werner Nekes. 83 min.
53-7613 *$29.99*

Keepers Of The Frame
More than half of all movies ever made—including 90 percent of all silent films—have been lost forever. Follow the ongoing struggle to restore and preserve America's cinematic heritage with this documentary. Film archivists and historians, along with such notables as Alan Alda, Leonard Maltin and Roddy McDowall, discuss the effort to save "lost" films, several examples of which are featured. 70 min.
53-6751 *$19.99*

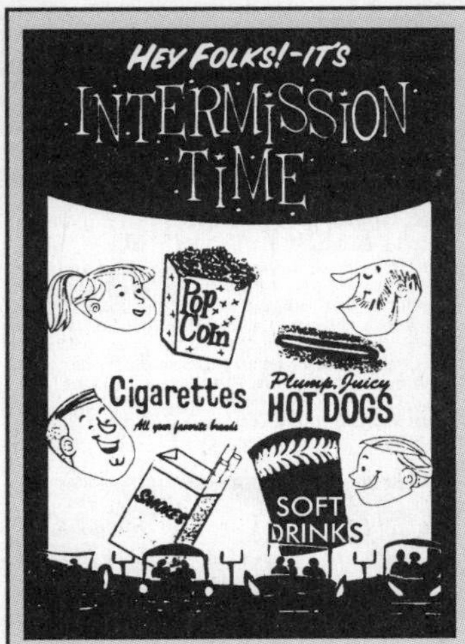

Movie Trailers

Hey Folks, It's Intermission Time!, Vol. 1
An amazing collection of drive-in movie ads from the 1940s, '50s and '60s are presented in this one-of-a-kind program. Witness chintzy animated countdowns ("9 Minutes 'Til Showtime"); shills for scrumptious egg rolls, Castleberry beef sandwiches and dancing hot dogs; the introduction of movie ratings like "GMRX," and lots more goodies. A real blast from the past. 90 min.
79-5120 *$19.99*

Hey Folks, It's Intermission Time!, Vol. 2
More memorable ads for movie theaters, including come-ons for Christmas, Halloween and Mother's Day shows, cartoon carnivals, Milkshake candy bars, a Spike Jones live performance and films like "Cinderfella." Also, see Rosemary Clooney's happy holiday greeting, Virginia Mayo promoting Christmas Seals and an anti-Pay-TV announcement. 90 min.
79-5292 *$19.99*

Hey Folks, It's Intermission Time!, Vol. 3
It's another collection of intermission specialties that are sure to get you all nostalgic, this time with the accent on "spook show" come-ons from Southern ghoul master Donn Davison and a nifty group of celebrity endorsements with John Wayne, Tyrone Power, Cary Grant, Gary Cooper and others. And let's not forget the yummy pitches for those scrumptious snacks!
79-5967 *$19.99*

Hey Folks, It's Intermission Time!, Vol. 4
Take a nostalgic trip back to the classic days of movie-going with another amusing sampler of promotional shorts shown in theaters and drive-ins. There's WWII propaganda, family holiday advertising, fright fest promos and psychedelic shills for snacks.
79-6011 *$19.99*

Hey Folks, It's Intermission Time!, Vol. 5
Relive the golden days of the drive-in theater, when life was simpler, hamburgers were greener and mosquitoes were bigger. This selection of short promos includes cool chroma-key graphics; animation and photo montages; along with ads for Toddy, the chocolate drink, Marty's Toasted Almond Bar, tons of popcorn, movies in Cinerama, and lots more. 110 min.
79-6103 *$19.99*

Hey Folks, It's Intermission Time!, Vol. 6
Just when you thought it was safe to go back to the snack bar, here come some wild intermission memories to make you laugh. There's some, um, scrumptious promos for Smithfield Barbeque, Peter Max-styled Pepsi commercials, a cavalcade of "Five Minutes 'Til Showtime" countdowns, an offer of a $50 reward for drive-in speaker swipers, James Coburn for Easter Seals and a promo with Richard Burton. 90 min.
79-6172 *$19.99*

Monsterama Sci-Fi Late Night Creature Feature Show
You saw them on "Dr. Shock," "Zacherle" and "Ghoulardi" when you were young. Now you can relive the experience by catching the coming attractions of classic monster movies. See creepy come-ons for "Ghost of Frankenstein," "Tarantula," "The Mad Magician," "The Giant Mantis," "Invaders from Mars," "War of the Worlds" and more. 120 min.
79-5971 *$19.99*

Dusk-To-Dawn Trash-O-Rama Show, Vol. 1
Enjoy all the trailers of the drive-ins of the past...without the trouble of sneaking friends in through the trunk or eating green pizza. Witness must-see come-ons for "Switchblade Sisters," "Superchick," "Women in Cages," "The Glory Stompers," "The Wild Riders," "Sugar Hill," "Flesh Gordon," "Black Belt Jones," "Night of the Lepus" and more. 120 min.
79-5896 *$19.99*

Dusk-To-Dawn Drive-In Trash-O-Rama, Vol. 2
Relive the glory days of ozoners in this awesome compilation of drive-in trailer delights. Whether you want to see coming attractions for biker films, kiddie flicks, shockers or sexploitation, they're here, including come-ons for "Suspiria," "Mandingo," "Kansas City Bomber," "The Deathmaster," "Slumber Party Massacre," "Galaxina," "Fearless Fighters" and more.
79-5968 *$19.99*

The Incredibly Strange Filmworks Video Sampler
One of the wildest collections of trailers ever, this compilation includes previews for such favorites as "The Wasp Woman," "The World of Batwoman," "Goliath and the Dragons," "The Terror," "Hercules Against the Moon Men" and many more. It's two hours of total weirdness.
53-9724 *$19.99*

Classic Horror Trailers, Vol. 1
Over two dozen scary previews, including "The Tingler," "Zotz," "Horrors of the Black Museum," "13 Ghosts" and the original "Little Shop of Horrors."
68-8251 *$19.99*

Classic Horror Trailers, Vol. 2
Includes bloodcurling trailers from "Fearless Vampire Killers," "Psycho," "The Birds," Roger Corman's Poe series, "The Oblong Box," and dozens more!
68-8252 *$19.99*

House Of Hammer Trailers, Vol. 1
Horrific trailers culled from the house terror fans love. Included are "Horror of Dracula," "Brides of Dracula," "Five Million Years to Earth," "The Horror of Frankenstein," "The Vampire Lovers," "One Million Years, B.C.," plus more.
68-8699 *$19.99*

Universal Horror Trailers, Vol. 1
Relive the classic days of Universal horror by watching trailers for "Dracula," "Frankenstein," "The Mummy," "Abbott & Costello Meet Frankenstein," "The Black Cat" and many more.
68-8702 *$19.99*

Universal Horror Trailers, Vol. 2
More movie previews from the house that Karloff, Lugosi and Chaney built. "The Invisible Woman," "Man of a Thousand Faces," "The Mummy's Ghost" and more are offered.
68-8703 *$19.99*

Super Horrorama Shriek Show, Vol. 1
Get a fistful of fright with this mind-boggling bonanza of blood, gore and more. Check out the creepy coming attractions for such horror as "The Werewolf," "Curse of the Demon," "Circus of Horrors," "The Incredible Melting Man," "The Car," "Rabid," "It's Alive," "Abby," "The Texas Chainsaw Massacre," "Tales from the Crypt" and many others. 120 min.
79-5895 *$19.99*

Blood-O-Rama Shock Show
Guts, blood, horror, general depravity. This collection has all the essentials to give you the willies: two hours of trailers from the sickest films ever on celluloid. Included are come-ons for "Tender Flesh," "Deranged," "Meatcleaver Massacre," "I Dismember Mama," "Carnival of Blood," "Orgy of the Living Dead" and more.
79-5573 *$19.99*

Martial Arts Mayhem, Vol. 1
Everybody's kung-fu fighting in this compilation of the greatest chop-sockey spectacles of the Seventies. There's smashing trailers for "Enter the Dragon," "Five Fingers of Death," "The Streetfighter," "Slaughter in San Francisco," "Deadly China Doll," "Shogun Assassin" and lots more. 120 min.
79-6085 *$19.99*

Martial Arts Mayhem, Vol. 2
There's more kung-foolery in store for martial arts mavens who can't get enough of the karate stuff in this collection of trailers from the Far East and beyond. Included are coming attractions for "Super Fist," "The Japanese Connection," "Temple of Death," "Ten Tigers of Shaolin," "Single Fighter" and more.
79-6226 *$19.99*

Classic Sci-Fi Trailers, Vol. 1
Includes preview clips from "The Thing," "The Werewolf," "First Men in the Moon," "Giant Gila Monster," "Godzilla, King of the Monsters," and 20 more!
68-8256 *$19.99*

Classic Sci-Fi Trailers, Vol. 2
More than 24 science fiction previews include "Invaders from Mars," "Robot Monster," "Colossus of New York," "Brain That Wouldn't Die," and others.
68-8257 *$19.99*

Juvenile Schlock Trailers, Vol. 1
Get hip to the scene with cool coming attractions for "Reform School," "Senior Prom," "Blackboard Jungle," "Beatniks," "Beach Party," "The Cry Baby Killer," "Unwed Mother" and more.
68-8687 *$19.99*

Juvenile Schlock Trailers, Vol. 2
Rock all over the room with trailers for "Dragstrip Girl," "Hot Rod Gang," "Winter a-Go-Go," "Riot on the Sunset Strip," "The Love-Ins," "Let It Be," "Woodstock" and more.
68-8688 *$19.99*

Kung Fu Classics, Vol. 1
Here are trailers from the greatest martial arts movies ever made: "Fists of Fury," "The Chinese Connection," "Shogun Assassin," "The Black Dragon," "Deadly China Doll" and much more. Hiii-ya!
68-8691 *$19.99*

Jungle Thrillers, Vol. 1
Get stranded in the jungle with previews for movies like "White Gorilla," "The Naked Jungle," "Wild Women of Wongo," "Tarzan the Magnificent," "King of the Congo," plus lots more.
68-8696 *$19.99*

Spy Thrillers, Vol. 1
Go underground and uncover trailers for these super spy films: "The Liquidator," "Scorpio," "Agent 8 3/4," "The Manchurian Candidate," "Rocket Attack, USA," "Murderers' Row" and more. 60 min.
68-8776 *$19.99*

Rock 'N' Roll Scrapbook
There's a whole lotta shakin' goin' on in this way out collection of studio production trailers from rock and roll epics like "Rock, Rock, Rock," "Celebration at Big Sur," "The T.A.M.I. Show," "Woodstock" and many more.
10-7432 *$19.99*

Early Silent Movie Prevues
This nifty compilation offers trailers from the teens and '20s and features the likes of W.C. Fields, Clara Bow, Gary Cooper, Lon Chaney, Buster Keaton and others. Includes previews for "Wings," "Lilac Time" and more. 60 min.
10-9085 *$19.99*

Drive-In Saturday Night
A collection of rare drive-in promotional shorts and vintage movie trailers, this video will make you feel that you're back at the ozoner again, adjusting the tinny sound on the speakers and fighting the mosquitoes. Trailers include "The Patsy," "A Night at the Opera," Mummy movies and more. 120 min.
10-9251 *$19.99*

Exploitation Classics, Vol. 1
Grab your popcorn and take a gander at these great coming attractions from a line-up of cult and exploitation classics. There's "Freaks," "Maniac," "Glen or Glenda," "I Passed for White," "Myra Breckinridge," "Supervixens" and lots more.
68-8692 *$19.99*

Super Atomic Sci-Fi Thrill-O-Rama Show, Vol. 1
Sci-fi fans won't want to miss this out-of-this-world collection of weird, wacky and classic film trailers of the '50s, '60s and '70s. Included are come-ons for "Creature from the Black Lagoon," "Rodan," "The Time Machine," "The Mole People," "Five Million Miles to Earth," "Message from Space," "The Time Machine" and lots more. 120 min.
79-5897 *$19.99*

Sword & Sandal Classics, Vol. 1
Think sitting through a dozen gladiator films would be a Herculean labor? Then sit back and enjoy this collection of trailers featuring plenty of action and no drawn-out plots. Included are "Atlas," "Goliath and the Vampires," "The Giant of Metropolis," "Jason and the Argonauts," "The Golden Voyage of Sinbad," more. 60 min.
68-8802 *$19.99*

The Laughing, Leering, Lampooning Lures Of David F. Friedman
This astonishing collection features trailers for the softcore sextravaganzas of producer David F. Friedman, noted for his outrageous showmanship. Included are provocative previews for "The Defilers," "Trader Hornee," "Masterpiece," "The Long Swift Sword of Siegfried," "Love Camp 7," "The Ramrodder," "Headmistress" and more. 120 min.
79-5020 *$24.99*

Afros, Macks & Zodiacs
If you want some action that'll put you in traction, get your satisfaction with these black exploitation coming attractions! "Dolemite" star Rudy Ray Moore hosts this tribute to the good old days of African-American actioners with trailers for "The Mack," "Monkey Hustle," "Black Caesar," "Sheba Baby," "Black Belt Jones," "Shaft," "Disco Godfather" and many others.
79-5816 *$19.99*

Crime Wave U.S.A. Gangsterama Show, Vol. 1
A unique collection of trailers for *film noir* and no-nonsense pseudo-documentaries from the 1940s and 1950s. Included are coming attractions for "Nightmare Alley," "Postmark for Danger," "Calling Homicide," "House of Numbers," "The Naked City," "This Man Is Dangerous" and many more. 120 min.
79-5898 *$19.99*

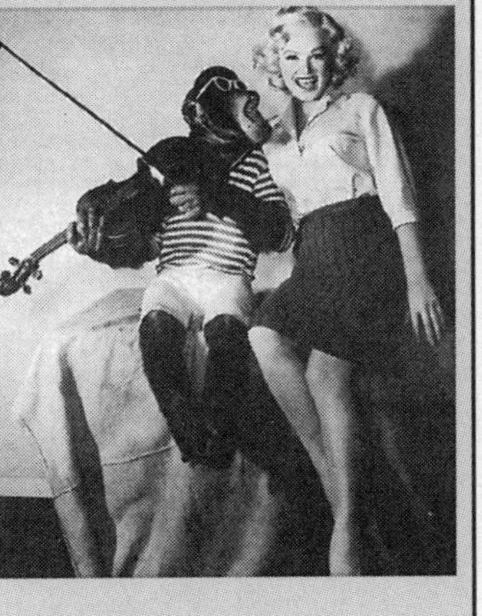

Sex Kitten Classics, Vol. 1
Meeeowww, sir, this enticing trailer compilation features three of the screen's sexiest starlets—Mamie Van Doren, Jayne Mansfield and Brigitte Bardot—in "coming attractions" clips from such racy favorites as "Girls Town," "Sex Kittens Go to College," "It Happened in Athens," "Will Success Spoil Rock Hunter?," "Primitive Love," "School for Love," and others. 60 min.
68-8771 *$19.99*

Muscles, Maidens And Monsters
"Johnny, do you like movies about gladiators?" Then you'll love this compilation of trailers from the greatest German, Italian, Mexican, Yugoslavian and international cast spectacles of all time. Muscle in on previews for "Terror of Rome," "Seven Slaves Against the World," "Revenge of the Gladiators," "Goliath and the Dragons," "The Giant of Metropolis" and more.
79-6007 *$19.99*

From The Journals Of Jean Seberg (1995)
From director Mark Rappaport ("Rock Hudson's Home Movies") comes this offbeat documentary look at actress Jean Seberg, who went from college student to film star in 1957's "Saint Joan," gained fame in such movies as "Breathless" and "Lilith," and became a target of the press and the FBI due to her support of radical political causes until her suicide in 1979. Mary Beth Hurt (who, like Seberg, was born in Marshalltown, Iowa) portrays Seberg, while film clips offer insight into her career. 97 min.
01-1525 Was $59.99 *$29.99*

Carmen Miranda: Bananas Is My Business (1995)
The flamboyant singer-dancer known as the "Brazilian Bombshell" and noted for her fanciful costumes and headwear is the focus of this fascinating documentary that mixes vintage film clips, interviews and dramatic re-creations. Miranda's life story is followed, from her childhood in Rio de Janeiro (where her father ran, of all things, a fruit business) to her success in Hollywood musicals and an image that both defined and confined her. 90 min. In English and Portuguese with English subtitles.
53-8494 Was $89.99 *$19.99*

Wild Bill: Hollywood Maverick (1996)
His exploits as a WWI flying hero were nearly as legendary as his clashes with actors and studio bosses, and now the turbulent life of director William Wellman is recounted in a fascinating documentary. Clips from Wellman's most memorable films, including "Wings," "Public Enemy," "A Star Is Born," "Beau Geste," "The Ox-Bow Incident" and "The High and the Mighty," are featured along with interviews with Clint Eastwood, Robert Mitchum, Gregory Peck, Martin Scorsese and others. Alec Baldwin narrates. 93 min.
53-8867 *$24.99*

Elia Kazan: A Director's Journey (1995)
The Academy Award-winning director of such films as "Gentleman's Agreement," "A Streetcar Named Desire," "On the Waterfront" and "East of Eden" is the focus of a revealing documentary that traces Kazan's life and career. His innovative work on Broadway, his stormy Hollywood career, and his controversial appearance before the House Un-American Activities Committee in the '50s are followed through interviews, film clips and more. 75 min.
70-5135 Was $29.99 *$19.99*

Yul Brynner:
The Man Who Was King
The man who made bald heads sexy to movie audiences in the '50s and '60s, Yul Brynner played everything from cowboys to Biblical characters, but will always be remembered as the King of Siam. Learn about his mysterious youth and acclaimed career in this tribute. Clips from "The Ten Commandments," "The Magnificent Seven" and "Westworld" and interviews with family and friends are included. 59 min.
50-7612 *$14.99*

John Huston: The Man, The Movies, The Maverick (1989)
Award-winning, affectionate look back at the life and films of one of Hollywood's most accomplished directors and unforgettable characters. Robert Mitchum hosts this unique tribute and is joined by Anjelica Huston, Paul Newman, Lauren Bacall and Michael Caine.
18-7157 Was $19.99 *$14.99*

The Republic Pictures Story (1991)
This tribute to one of Hollywood's most prolific studios features clips from thrilling cliffhanger serials, John Wayne epics, exciting Westerns starring the likes of Roy Rogers and Gene Autry, and classic films with Orson Welles, Myrna Loy, Robert Mitchum and Joan Crawford. 114 min.
63-1512 *$19.99*

Visions Of Light: The Art Of Cinematography (1993)
Marvelous study of cinematography chronicling the importance of the cameraman in filmmaking from the early days of movies to today. Included are interviews with Allen Daviau ("E.T."), Michael Chapman ("Raging Bull"), Conrad Hall ("In Cold Blood") and Vittorio Storaro ("The Last Emperor"); and clips from "The Godfather," "Citizen Kane" and others. 95 min.
04-2789 Was $89.99 ❑*$29.99*

East Side Story (1997)
What's that? You've never heard of such vintage movie musicals as "Tractor Drivers," "Volga Volga" and "I Don't Want to Marry?" That's probably because they're among the socialist propaganda films made by the Soviet Union and Eastern European nations—replete with singing pig farmers, overall-clad chorus girls and heaping helpings of Marxist ideology—featured in this wildly entertaining documentary look at Communism's campier side. 77 min. Subtitled in English.
53-9968 Was $59.99 *$24.99*

Hollywood: An Empire Of Their Own (1998)
The incredible story of the Eastern European Jewish immigrants who started America's film industry is covered in this program based on Neal Gabler's best-selling book. Through the biographies of Adolph Zukor, Louis B. Mayer, Carl Laemmle, the Warner Brothers and other moguls who used film to depict their vision of the American dream, the origins of Hollywood take on new meaning. 100 min.
53-6213 *$19.99*

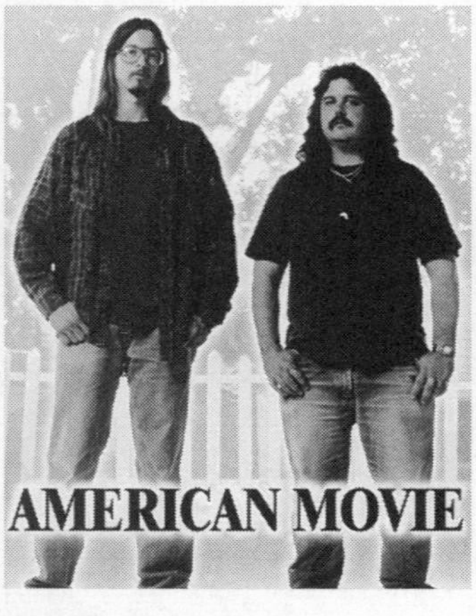

American Movie (1999)
Funny, acclaimed documentary focuses on Wisconsin filmmaker Mark Borchardt, a Hollywood wannabe who will do anything to finish his latest no-budget horror short, "Coven," in order to move on to a more serious project. Helping the manic, cash-strapped Borchardt is his elderly uncle, who supplies much of the financing, and his eclectic, ever-helpful family and friends, who serve as cast and crew. 104 min.
02-3425 ❑*$99.99*

Get Bruce! (1999)
One of the best-known "secrets" in Hollywood, comedy writer Bruce Vilanch has crafted one-liners and "off-the-cuff" remarks for such stars as Billy Crystal, Whoopi Goldberg, Bette Midler, Roseanne, Robin Williams and others. Hear these and other celebrities talk with and about Bruce, and see how he went from would-be comedian to in-demand collaborator, in this laugh-filled documentary. 72 min.
11-2392 ❑*$99.99*

Automobiles

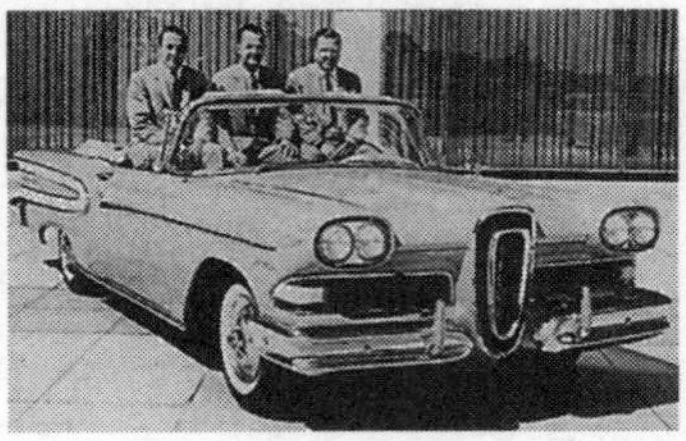

Ford Motor's Cars Of The 50's
The classic cars of the Ford Motor Company are featured in this blast from the past. Included are TV commercials, footage of test drives and promo material for such gems as Ford Fairlanes, Edsels, Thunderbirds, early Mercurys, Crown Victorias, Skyliner Retractables and more. 50 min.
22-1568 *$19.99*

Ford Mustang
See the car that Joe drives in this superior salute to one of the most popular autos of all time. Classic commercials, rare footage of prototypes and the 25th anniversary celebration are showcased. 50 min.
22-1570 *$19.99*

Bikers, Blondes & Blood!
This tape was born to be wild! There's bikers, babes, stars like John Ashley, Jayne Mansfield and Jack Nicholson and clips from 30 years of action-packed action flicks. Also features the U.S. military training short "Blondes Prefer Gentlemen." 92 min.
79-5340 Was $24.99 *$19.99*

Dream Cars Of The 50's And 60's, Vol. 1
Roll back the top and cruise through this groovy grouping of classic car commercials from the '50s and '60s. See TV ads for the '57 Chevy, '50 Mercury, the little Henry J, 'Vettes, GTOs, Thunderbirds and more. 60 min.
10-2111 *$12.99*

Dream Cars Of The 50's And 60's, Vol. 2
Fast-paced follow-up to the classic car commercial series is a sportster buff's delight. Your favorite Chevys, Fords and other vehicles from the days of racy lines and cheap gasoline are here in rare promo films and TV spots. 60 min.
10-2240 *$12.99*

America's Favorite Sportscars
Relive the country's love affair with the automobile in this sporty, high-powered look at some of the greatest models of the '50s and '60s. There are Thunderbirds, Corvettes, Mustangs and others, plus interviews, footage of the 1963 test drive of the first Stingray, and much more. 60 min.
02-2244 Was $19.99 *$14.99*

Romancing The Classics
Classic autos and classic rock music combine for this unique look at the 1950s car culture, featuring disc jockey Big Daddy, songs like "At the Hop," "Peggy Sue" and "Calendar Girl," and legendary wheels like Edsels, Hudsons, Studebakers, Packards and others. 40 min.
22-1391 *$14.99*

The History Of The Volkswagen
The beloved Volkswagen Beetle and its history are the focus of this documentary that traces the "bug's" beginnings in '30s Germany (some early design sketches were made by Hitler!) to its popularity as a '60s "anti-establishment" car and Disney screen hero. 30 min.
22-1392 *$14.99*

Corvette: America's First Sportscar
This tribute to the coolest car on the road includes rare promo footage from 1953, as well as segments on the Stingray, the Mako Shark and the contemporary C5 Corvette. See rare footage of road tests, restored classics and lots more. 50 min.
22-1569 *$19.99*

Trucks: Masters Of The Open Road
Climb into the cab for a hard-driving look at the history of American trucking. You'll see some unusual trucks, tour the Mack Brothers Motor Company factory, hear about the "romance of the open road," and more. 50 min.
53-8384 *$19.99*

Merrily We Roll Along: The Early Days Of The Automobile
Groucho Marx narrates this fascinating program that looks at the transition from horse-and-buggy to horseless carriages. Priceless footage of the earliest automobiles—some successes and some not—highlight this entertaining blast from the past. 60 min.
63-7068 *$19.99*

Car And Driver: Ten Top Exotic Cars
If you've ever dreamed of owning a Corvette ZR-1, Lamborghini Countach, Porsche 911 Turbo, Ferrari Testarossa or any other ultra-fast, ultra-expensive dream machine...well, here's the next best thing. See sleek, stylish autos from around the world up close, plus Car and Driver's exclusive statistical comparisons of each car. 44 min.
64-1234 *$19.99*

One Second From Eternity: The History Of The Land Speed Record
This thrilling documentary chronicles the history of the people who attempted to conquer the world land speed record. Beginning in 1898 in France, when the first record is set, the program includes sequences on Sir Malcolm Campbell, John Cobb, Capt. George Eyston and other prominent speedsters. 88 min.
71-9019 *$24.99*

Wheels: Complete Set
This six-tape series looks at some of the greatest developments in the history of the automobile and their impact on American culture. Featured are "The Enduring Crown and Crest," about Cadillacs; "Reflections of Stylemakers," focusing on Corvettes; a look at jeeps in "The Unstoppable Soldier"; the Volkswagen's story in "The Lovable Beetle"; "Tail Fins and Drive-Ins," about classic '50s cars; and "Dreams of Steel," a study of futuristic-looking vehicles. 330 min. total. NOTE: Individual volumes available at $14.99 each.
83-1103 Save $40.00! *$49.99*

Chrysler Comparisons (1958)
Check out the latest models from Chrysler with Mechanix Illustrated auto writer Tom McCahill, as he goes to the foot of the High Sierras to pit them against Buicks, Lincolns and Cadillacs in "McCahill Tests the 1958 Chrysler and the 1958 Imperial." Next, "You're on the Test Track" at the Chrysler proving grounds. Non-stop action and fender-benders abound as Chrysler Windsors, Saratogas and New Yorkers go through their paces. 55 min.
82-1033 *$19.99*

Dodge Rebellion Memories
"Join the Dodge Rebellion" with the dealer announcement promo film "The 1967 Dodge Rebellion Theater," featuring the company's complete car and truck line and the comical song stylings of the inimitable Tom Lehrer. You'll also see 11 classic commercials for 1965-68 Dodge autos. 60 min.
82-1034 *$19.99*

Enzo Ferrari: The Man, The Legend
Learn about the Italian-born designer and tycoon whose name became synonymous worldwide with automotive excellence with this fascinating documentary that features interviews with family, friends and colleagues and racing footage with classic Ferrari cars. 70 min.
22-1698 *$19.99*

Railroads

All Aboard! The Pennsylvania Railroad
The only place it's seen these days is on the Monopoly board, but you can take a nostalgic ride on the "Pennsy" with four short films from the mid-'50s. Learn about the latest advances in "Progress on the Rails"; get a detailed look at locomotives in "Wheels of Steel"; trace a century of cross-country freight shipping in "Opening a New Frontier"; and steam, diesel and electric engines are the focus of "Clear Track Ahead." 69 min. total.
09-3038 *$19.99*

America's Railroads: The Steam Train Legacy
Terrific vintage footage lets you trace the history of America's railroads and their legacy, from the earliest steam engines and the importance of trains in the growth of America to the innovations that have been made over the years. This seven-tape series runs 420 min.
16-5006 *$49.99*

Great American Railroads: Complete Set
Trace the history of rail travel in America in this seven-tape set that uses official Association of American Railroads footage to tell its moving story. Included in the series are "The Golden Spike," about the first transcontinental railroad, the Union Pacific and Central Pacific; "The Nickel Plate Story"; "the Big Train"; "Operation Reading"; "Easy Does It"; "End of an Era" and "Train Wrecks & Stories." 360 min. total.
16-5025 *$49.99*

The Great Train Stations Of America
In the days when everyone travelled by rail, these "temples of transportation" were lavish urban landmarks that captured the public's imagination. This video tour of classic train stations takes you to New York's Grand Central Station and old and new Penn Station, Reading Terminal and 30th Street Station in Philadelphia, the Union Stations of Washington, St. Louis and Los Angeles, and more. 50 min.
50-5171 ❑*$19.99*

Colorado's Narrow Gauge Railroads
Visit four famous railroad lines that serviced Colorado's booming mining towns before the 1880s, when America adopted the standard rail gauge. Ride the Durango & Silverton, Chambres & Toltec, Cripple Creek & Victor and the Georgetown Loop and see the Colorado Train Museum. 55 min.
50-1738 *$24.99*

The Great Trans-American Train Ride
Take a coast-to-coast tour of the United States on board three of the country's most famous passenger trains. Starting in New York, the now-defunct Broadway Limited winds through Philadelphia, the Pennsylvania Dutch Country and Pittsburgh on the way to Chicago. The California Zephyr makes its way across prairies and mountains to Denver and Salt Lake City, and the Desert Wind takes passengers (and you) from Utah to Las Vegas and, ultimately, Los Angeles. 85 min.
50-4550 *$29.99*

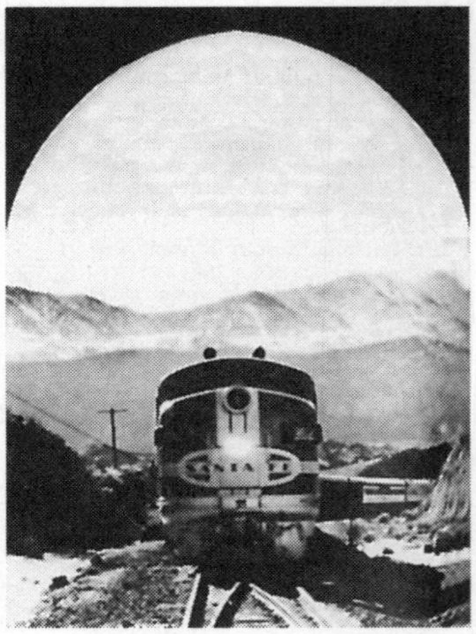

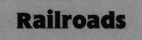

Super Santa Fe Selections
Three wonderful short films from the legendary rail line. A cocky young train worker gets a lesson in safety (mounting engines, braking, riding on top, etc.) from a wise old timer in "Play It Safe" (1953); follow the story of bread, from wheatfield to bakery to store, all via train, in "Wheat" (1956); and take a ride from Chicago to California on the one and only "Super-chief" (1948). 55 min. total.
82-1006 *$24.99*

Train Rides, Vols. I & II
Relive the days of steam engines as you take 30 favorite locomotive rides from across the United States. Spectacular scenery and small towns from the Rocky Mountains to California are featured in this exciting two-tape program. 120 min. total.
50-2820 *$29.99*

World Class Trains: Boxed Set
The Golden Age of Rail Travel lives on with a thrilling six-tape series that spans the globe to take you on some of the world's most exotic and luxurious trains. Included in the set are "The Eastern and Oriental Express," "The Great South Pacific Express," "The Imperial Express," "The Palace on Wheels," "Rovos Rail" and "The Royal Scotsman." 330 min. total.
50-8567 *$79.99*

Trains Unlimited: The Story Of America's Railroads
This comprehensive four-volume set covers the history of the Iron Horse that linked the nation and opened the frontier. Starting from the steam trains that dominated the rails for over a century and ending with the modern wonder of New York's Grand Central Station, the series is a must-see for railroad buffs. 250 min. total.
53-6216 *$39.99*

Union Pacific Memories
"Last of the Giants" (1960) is a wonderful look at the last days of the giant steam engines, with rail, yard and roundhouse footage of trains, including the gargantuan "Big Boy." Next, "The Human Side" is a humorous look at UP workers from the mid-'50s that looks at the daily routines of clerks, conductors, porters and station agents. 50 min. total.
82-1007 *$24.99*

American Railroad Memories
Three nostalgia-filled documentaries take viewers back to the 1950s, when the steam engines still ruled the rails and the train was the way to travel. Included are "Big Trains Rolling," "Mainline USA," and "The Passenger Train," set aboard the Santa Fe Chief. 55 min. total.
82-1009 *$24.99*

Railroad Journeys Around The World: Complete Set
All aboard for a ride along some of the world's most scenic and breathtaking rail lines. With this four-tape boxed collection, you'll see the sights—along with some up-close train footage—of "France," "Ireland," "Scotland" and "United States." 220 min. total. NOTE: Individual volumes available at $19.99 each.
50-8520 *$59.99*

Great American Ghost Trains Of The Old West: Complete Set

Take a trip back in time as you ride the classic railroad lines and engines of the American frontier in this two-tape set. See meticulously restored trains from the Santa Fe, Union Pacific and others as they chug along breathtaking scenery. Volume One looks at the Nevada Northern #40, Durango & Silverton and more; Volume Two tracks the Southern Pacific #1, the Sierra Railroad, and others. 120 min. total. NOTE: Individual volumes available at $19.99 each.
27-7029 *$39.99*

Meeting The Challenge (1946)

The first rail line to offer passenger service, in 1830, the Baltimore and Ohio Railroad had come a long way by 1946, with the introduction of stewardess-nurses and radio-telephones on board, as well as "courteous service, good food and on-time dependability." Whether it was the transporting of coal to Pittsburgh or passengers to New York, it was "B&O...the way to go!" 28 min.
09-3095 *$14.99*

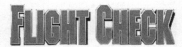

Aviation

The Age Of Flight

Off you go into the wild blue yonder with this fascinating series about the history of air travel. Follow the patterns of flight from the Wright Brothers to the space age with thrilling archival and aerial footage. Each tape runs about 55 min. There are 12 volumes available, including:

The Age Of Flight: Kitty Hawk

50-6705 *$19.99*

The Age Of Flight: Bombers

50-6706 *$19.99*

The Age Of Flight: Choppers

50-6712 *$19.99*

B-17: Flying Fortress

With fascinating archival footage, this program traces the history of the B-17, the massive bomber whose missions in World War II helped to inaugurate the concept of "total war." 55 min.
22-1254 *$19.99*

The Fighting Lady

World War II naval airmen engage the enemy in savage dogfights in Truk, Kwajalein, Tinian, Saipan, and the Marianas Turkey Shoot from the decks of our carrier fleet. Narrated by Robert Taylor. 56 min.
52-7079 *$24.99*

The Blue Angels: Around The World At The Speed Of Sound

An astonishing look at the legendary Blue Angels filmed by the first civilian crew to ever travel with the aerial team. Along with great flight footage, this program shows the first time the Angels appear in Russia, Russian MiGs welcoming the squadron, and more. Hosted by Dennis Quaid; music by Los Lobos, Tony Bennett and others. 100 min.
53-7981 Was $29.99 *$19.99*

America's Flying Aces: Blue Angels 50th Anniversary Edition

Celebrate the golden anniversary of the country's elite flight exhibition team with this high-flying program that features thrilling airshow stunts, inside-the-cockpit footage, and interviews with "the Blues." John Travolta (not a bad pilot in his own right) hosts. 44 min.
83-1162 *$19.99*

The Thunderbirds

Thrill to the high-flying maneuvers and precision flying of the Air Force's Thunderbirds as they dazzle audiences during their "Thunder Over the Pacific" tour, and hear from members of the original 1953 team, in this exciting documentary salute. Hosted by Candice Bergen. 100 min.
53-8253 *$19.99*

Air Disasters: The Facts

This gripping video shows you some of the most astonishing crashes in aviation history, as you learn about the latest attempt to make air travel safer. 50 min.
53-8912 *$14.99*

FLIGHT CHECK

Flightcheck: Combat Missions: Boxed Set

The training films compiled on this seven-tape boxed set were required viewing for future combat pilots of World War II. They teach how to fly combat missions and different tactics for pilots of such aircraft as the P-39 Airacobra, B-25 Mitchell, P-47 Thunderbolt, B-24 Liberator, B-17 Flying Fortress, P-61 Black Widow, P-40 Warhawk, B-26 Marauder, B-29 Superfortress and P-38 Lightning. 420 min. total.
16-5036 *$49.99*

The Red Baron

Compelling documentary look at Manfred von Richtofen and his legend contains interviews with the surviving aces who flew with and against him, actual WWI aerial footage, the tale of his last flight and the unsettled questions surrounding his death. 60 min.
62-5218 *$19.99*

Amelia Earhart: The Price Of Courage

The real-life drama and mystery surrounding the first woman to fly solo across the Atlantic are covered in this insightful biography. The early life of Earhart is depicted, as well as her publicity-oriented plane trips across the country and her attempt to encircle the equator in 1936 that led to her eerie disappearance. Kathy Bates narrates. 60 min.
63-7081 ❑*$19.99*

Going Boeing

The gradual development of the passenger jet is traced through these four color promo films by Boeing. "An Airport" (1960) looks at the Pan Am 707, while the jumbo jet 747 is followed from design to test flight in 1969's "Welcome Aboard—747" and "A New Dimension," and "Putting the Pieces Together" (1972) shows what goes into the 707, 727 and 737. 60 min. total.
82-1037 *$19.99*

The B-24 Trilogy Boxed Set

Thrill to the WWII exploits of "the Victory Bombers" and the men who flew them in this three-tape collection that features rare combat footage that puts you inside the cockpit. Included are "The B-24: Bombers Over Normandy," "The B-24: Target Nazi Europe" and "The B-24: Target Japan." 180 min. total. NOTE: Individual volumes available at $14.99 each.
89-5007 *$39.99*

Birth Of The Bomber: The Story Of The B-24 Liberator

Amazing combat footage and vintage government film clips help tell the story of the remarkable B-24 bomber plane and the important role it played for the Allied effort in World War II. See how the Ford Motor Company's retooled Willow Run plant turned out a plane every 53 minutes, and hear from the men who flew the Liberators to victory. 60 min.
89-5050 *$19.99*

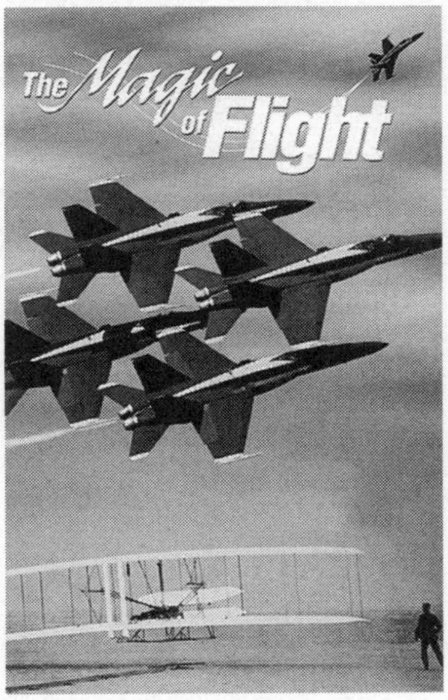

The Magic Of Flight (1997)

Beginning with a re-creation of the Wright Brothers' historic 1903 flight, this breathtaking Imax documentary takes you high into the skies with amazing aerial footage, including a look at the U.S. Navy's Blue Angels precision flying team and scenes of jets taking off and landing from aircraft carriers. Also includes a special "making of" documentary. Tom Selleck narrates. 82 min.
50-8398 *$19.99*

Test Flights: Beyond The Limits: Boxed Set

They're the pilots who put their lives on the line as they test the boundaries of aeronautic science, and you'll see them in action in this three-part series that takes you behind the scenes at NASA's Dryden Flight Research Center in California. Follow experimental craft from the designer's table to the runway in "Flights of Discovery," "The Need for Speed" and "The New Frontier." 150 min. total. NOTE: Individual volumes available at $19.99 each.
89-5242 Save $20.00! *$39.99*

Lindbergh (1990)

From the acclaimed PBS series "The American Experience" comes this superior documentary on the turbulent life of America's "Lone Eagle." Narrated by Stacy Keach, the program covers Lindbergh's historic 1927 New York-to-Paris flight, the tragedy of his son's abduction and murder, and the controversies that clouded his personal life, with rare film footage and interviews with surviving family members. 60 min.
63-7164 *$19.99*

The Last Great Adventure

Spectacular documentary chronicling the epic race to be the first hot air balloon team to circumnavigate the Earth. Follow the incredible competition with gorgeous footage, interviews with the three top challengers (including Virgin's Richard Branson) and amazing challenges. 156 min. on three tapes.
53-6952 *$39.99*

Space

Apollo 11: The Eagle Has Landed

The dramatic saga of man's first walk on the moon is chronicled in this program filled with stunning archival footage. Astronauts Armstrong, Aldrin and Collins offer their insights on the flight that is chronicled here from lift-off to splashdown. 79 min.
58-8189 *$14.99*

Moon Shot

Mercury 7 astronauts Alan Shepard and Deke Slayton host this inside look at Project Apollo. Along with amazing footage of the lunar landings, this eye-opening documentary reveals how, while America raced to be the first to the moon, the competition between the astronauts themselves was just as fierce. 189 min.
18-7486 *$19.99*

From Here To Infinity

"Star Trek: The Next Generation's" Patrick Stewart hosts this exciting excursion into the cosmos in which computer graphics and audio technology allow you to visit planets, witness a supernova, journey through a black hole and encounter other wonders of the galaxy. 43 min.
06-2348 ❑*$14.99*

The Astronomers: Complete Set

Over five years in the making, this acclaimed six-part PBS series, hosted by Richard Chamberlain, takes an amazing look at the wonders of the night sky and the men and women who explore the mysteries of the universe. Included are "Prospecting for Planets," "Searching for Black Holes," "Stardust," "Waves of the Future," "Where Is the Rest of the Universe?" and "A Window to Creation." 342 min. total. NOTE: Individual volumes available at $14.99 each.
07-8202 Save $10.00! *$79.99*

Space Mysteries: Boxed Set

This seven-tape set looks at the universe through stunning photography and fascinating facts, and features programs with Orson Welles, Carl Sagan and others. Included are "A Man's Reach Should Exceed His Grasp/Universe," "Who's Out There?/View of the Sky," "A New View of Mars/Planet Mars," "Jupiter Odyssey/The Moon: An Emerging Planet," "The Cloud of Venus/Mercury: Exploration of a Planet," "Pathfinders from the Stars" and "Skylab and the Sun/Space Shuttle: A Remarkable Flying Machine." 360 min. total.
16-5029 *$49.99*

Fire From The Sky

To many scientists, it's not a question of "if" an asteroid will one day hit the Earth, but "when." Hear from noted astronomers and physicists about the effects that could be expected from such a collision, the theory that an asteroid led to the extinction of the dinosaur, and more. 45 min.
18-7753 ❑*$19.99*

Meteorites

They've shaped the face of the moon and planets, and have been considered divine omens and lucky charms throughout history. Now learn the latest scientific facts on meteors, and hear about how meteorites may have been responsible for the extinction of the dinosaurs and guided the Three Wise Men to Bethlehem, in this two-part program. 84 min.
50-4903 *$29.99*

The Planets

This eight-volume series produced by the BBC offers a startling glimpse into the solar system through seldom-seen NASA footage, computer graphics, special effects and imagery from the Hubble telescope. The set includes "Different Worlds," "Terra Firma," "Giants," "Moon," "Star," "Atmosphere," "Life Beyond the Sun" and "Destiny." 400 min. total.
53-6616 *$99.99*

Apollo 13: To The Edge And Back

Launched in April of 1970, the crew of Apollo 13 faced disaster as an explosion forced them to abandon a planned lunar landing and implement a return to Earth in a damaged craft. This fascinating documentary mixes news footage, computer animation and interviews with astronauts Jim Lovell and Fred Haise, their families, and NASA officials. 86 min.
50-2670 ❑*$9.99*

Apollo 13: For The Record

In his own words, Apollo 13 mission commander James Lovell describes how he and his crewmates faced their terrifying ordeal in space, and how they managed their courageous return to Earth, in this compelling documentary which features official NASA photos and film footage. 45 min.
67-5041 *$14.99*

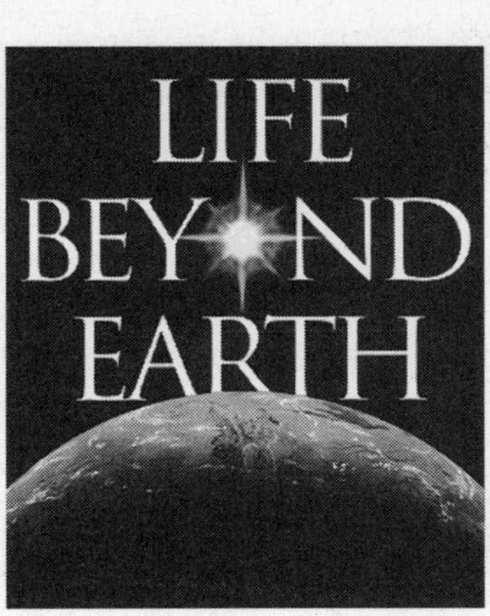

Life Beyond Earth

Does intelligent life exist elsewhere in the universe, and can man make contact with it? This two-part documentary, hosted by teacher/author Timothy Ferris, examines the ongoing search for the secrets to life on Earth and beyond in "Are We Alone?" and "Is Anyone Listening?" 120 min.
90-1044 ❑*$19.99*

The Infinity Series: Complete Set

NASA film footage and stunning animation are combined in this four-tape series to depict the wonder and mysteries of our solar system and the universe. "The Solar System" looks at Earth's neighboring planets, the Sun and comets; "Deep Space" examines the birth and death of stars, quasars and galaxies; "The Light Beyond Light & Life" looks at infrared and ultraviolet light, X-rays and gamma rays; and "The Crystal Space/Time Ship" is "the ultimate music video," using New Age music in an exploration of our universe. 225 min. total. NOTE: Individual volumes available at $19.99 each.
08-1556 *$79.99*

Spaceflight: Complete Set

Martin Sheen narrates this superb four-part chronicle of the manned exploration of space, featuring film footage and interviews that traces the U.S./Soviet space race, the Apollo lunar landings, the development of the space shuttle and much more. Volumes include "Thunder in the Skies," "The Wings of Mercury," "One Giant Leap" and "The Territory Ahead." 240 min. total.
07-8318 Was $79.99 ❑*$59.99*

3 Minutes To Impact

Millions of years ago, experts say, an asteroid hit the Earth, and the result was the death of the dinosaurs. Could a similar fate be in store for Man? Hear from astronomers and other scientists about the possibility of such a cosmic collision occurring, and what the planetary consequences would be. 104 min.
83-1551 *$14.99*

Footsteps On The Moon

NASA's secret files are revealed in this documentary that features footage never seen before by the public. Watch spellbound as fiction turns to fact in America's great space odyssey. Narrated by rocket pioneer Werner von Braun. 92 min.
08-1584 *$14.99*

The Race For Space

Produced in 1959 by David Wolper but never broadcast because of "disinterest," this documentary on the space program features incredible footage from both US and USSR archives. Entertaining and informative, the program examines man's reaching for the stars from the dawn of history. Mike Wallace narrates; score by Elmer Bernstein. 60 min.
10-9951 *$19.99*

Blast Off!: True Stories From The Final Frontier

The wonders—and dangers—of space exploration are chronicled in this compelling program that looks at the perilous voyage of Apollo 13, the tragedies of the 1967 Apollo 1 fire and the 1986 Challenger explosion, Russia's struggle to keep the Mir space station in orbit, and more. Ed Harris narrates. 104 min.
27-7196 *$14.99*

In Search Of Liberty Bell 7

America's second manned spaceflight nearly ended tragically in July of 1961, when the hatch of Gus Grissom's Mercury capsule blew open prematurely and Liberty Bell 7 sank 300 miles off the Florida coast. Now join the hunt for a piece of history, and learn what really happened, as undersea explorers locate the long-missing capsule beneath three miles of ocean. 100 min.
27-7198 *$14.99*

John Glenn: American Hero

At an age when many Americans are settled into retirement, 77-year-old Mercury astronaut-turned-U.S. senator John Glenn rode the space shuttle Discovery back into the history books in 1998. Glenn looks back on his military, aerospace and political milestones, and ahead to the future of space exploration, in this PBS-produced documentary that features footage not shown on TV. 90 min.
90-1015 ❑*$19.99*

Mysteries Of Deep Space: Set
Recent developments in astronomy and space exploration have given mankind new insights into the creation and workings of the cosmos, yet many unanswered questions remain. This remarkable three-part PBS series lets you investigate these mysteries in "To the Edge of the Universe," "Exploring Stars and Black Holes" and "The Search for Alien Worlds." 180 min. total.
18-7756 *$49.99*

Destination Cosmos: Boxed Set
Explore the wonders of the universe, and how they affect life on Earth, with this three-tape collection. Programs include "Distant Worlds," a look at the planets of the solar system; "Reaching Out," which follows the search for extraterrestrial life; and "Secrets of the Stars," with the focus on stars, comets and asteroids.
80-7289 *$49.99*

War

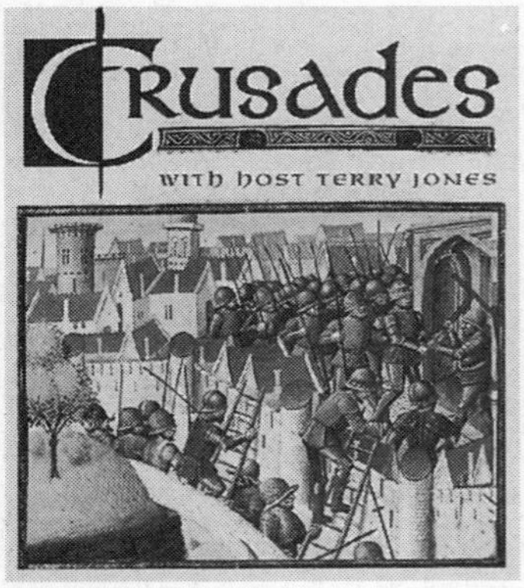

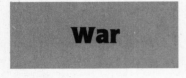

Crusades
For 200 years the armies of Europe battled Muslim forces for control of the Holy Land (and its riches). Now the full story is told in exciting fashion in a four-tape set hosted by Terry Jones of "Monty Python" fame. Re-enactments, computer graphics and animation help bring these incredible adventures of kings and knights, pilgrims and mercenaries, to life. 200 min. total.
53-8156 *$59.99*

The Campaigns Of Napoleon: Boxed Set
Napoleon's military genius is revealed in this three-tape series: "The Battle of Austerlitz," in which he led his armies against Austro-Russian forces in 1805; "Napoleon's Road to Moscow," about Napoleon's failed invasion of Russia; and "The Battle of Waterloo," a look at Napoleon's final battle in 1815. 165 min. total. NOTE: Individual volumes available at $19.99 each.
22-1651 *$59.99*

The Campaigns Of Napoleon, Vol. 2: Boxed Set
Relive the triumphs and defeats of the man who conquered most of Europe with this three-tape collection. Included are "The Battle of Trafalgar," in which Lord Nelson bested the French fleet, at the cost of his own life; "The Battle of Borodino," the 1812 conflict that led to Napoleon's defeat in Russia; and the 16-year-long "Napoleonic Wars." 165 min. total. NOTE: Individual volumes available at $19.99 each.
22-1712 *$59.99*

Fight For Freedom
A unique look at the battle that forged a nation, this program follows over 2,000 Revolutionary War enthusiasts as they take part in a re-creation of 18th-century combat on the Daniel Boone Homestead in Pennsylvania. 50 min.
80-7291 *$19.99*

The American Revolution: Complete Set (1994)
The War for Independence is brought to life in this acclaimed series that uses battle re-enactments, rare documents and the voices of Kelsey Grammer, Cliff Robertson and others to trace the history of the conflict. The set includes six programs: "The Conflict Ignites," "1776," "Washington and Arnold," "The World at War," "England's Last Chance" and "Birth of the Republic." 300 min. total.
53-8112 Was $99.99 *$59.99*

Liberty! The American Revolution: Boxed Set (1998)
The acclaimed PBS series that traced the events leading up to Colonial America's severing its ties with England, the people and battles that marked the Revolutionary War, and the turmoil of the new nation's early days is available in a three-tape collection. Dramatic readings by Philip Bosco, Roger Rees, Campbell Scott and others bring the words of the men and women on both sides of the conflict to life. 6 hrs. total.
18-7794 *$59.99*

Secret Weapons: Boxed Set
Learn about the evolution of military hardware and technology in the 20th century through this 13-part, six-tape documentary series hosted by John Palmer. Rare archival footage and combat films highlight the weapons that have won wars and preserved peace. Included are "The Jet Revolution/The Fabulous Flops," "The Fighting Elite/The Foot Soldier/Hide and Seek," "Waves of Steel/The Shark Hunters," "The Nuclear Hammer/The Expendables," "Rapid Fire/The Armor Busters" and "The Sharpshooters/Firestorm." 329 min. total. NOTE: Individual volumes available at $14.99 each.
50-7416 Save $10.00! *$79.99*

Great Battles Of War: Complete Set
A remarkable mix of documentary footage and eyewitness accounts puts you in the middle of some of the pivotal combat campaigns of the 20th century, as seen in this six-part series. Includes "The German Invasion of the Soviet Union," "Battle of the Bulge," "The Battle for Warsaw," "The Battle for Cassino," "The Battle of Burma" and "The Battle for Dien Bien Phu." 300 min. total. NOTE: Individual volumes available at $19.99 each.
64-1372 *$119.99*

Wars And Warriors
This superb series focuses on great commanders and the key battle in each of their military careers. Rare archival material helps tell the stirring stories behind the subjects in two-tape sets. Each set runs about 110 min.

Wars And Warriors: Oliver Cromwell/ The Battle Of Marston Moor
80-7279 *$39.99*

Wars And Warriors: Robert E. Lee/ The Battle Of Gettysburg
80-7280 *$39.99*

Wars And Warriors: George Armstrong Custer/ The Battle Of The Little Big Horn
80-7281 *$39.99*

Crucible Of Empire: The Spanish-American War
It lasted less than eight months in 1898, and when it was over the United States entered the ranks of world powers. Learn how economic pressures and a burgeoning news media helped fuel the country's "war fever," how the drives for Cuban and Filipino independence were influenced by America, and relive the key events and battles in this often overlooked conflict. Edward James Olmos narrates. 120 min.
90-1046 *$19.99*

The Splendid Little War (1992)
A thrilling document of the Spanish-American War of 1898, featuring rare film clips of Teddy Roosevelt and his Rough Riders, the campaign for Santiago, an interview with the last survivor of the Battle for San Juan Hill, and much more. 55 min.
50-2324 *$29.99*

The Spanish Earth (1937)
Masterful documentary from Joris Ivens on the Spanish Civil War which chronicles Fascist cruelties with incredibly powerful footage. Ernest Hemingway wrote and read the narration for the film; proceeds went to the Loyalist cause. 54 min.
10-8212 *$29.99*

The Will Of A People (1946)
Dramatic documentary look at the Spanish Revolution and Generalissimo Francisco Franco's brutal rise to power. Rare Spanish archival footage, long suppressed by the Fascist regime, was smuggled out, and English narration was added to provide a rare glimpse of the war. 55 min.
09-1382 Was $24.99 *$19.99*

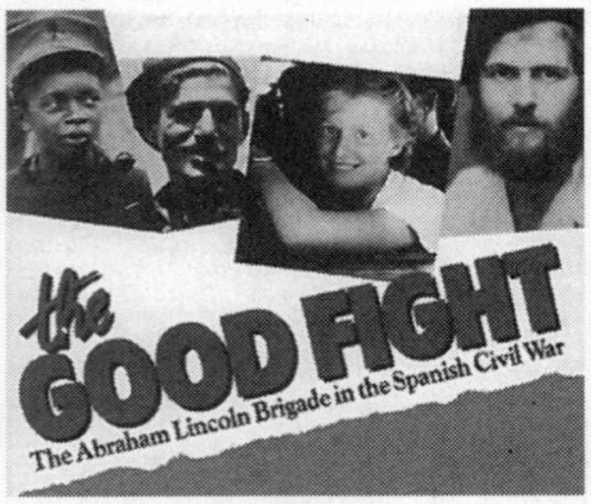

The Good Fight (1984)
This acclaimed documentary details the exploits of the nearly 3,000 Americans who went to Spain in 1936 to fight alongside the Republic's army in its doomed defense against Franco's Fascist forces. An extraordinary, stirring look at a neglected part of recent American history. 98 min.
53-7387 Was $69.99 *$29.99*

The Spanish Civil War (1987)
From 1936 to 1939 the world's attention was drawn to the struggle between Spanish loyalists and General Franco's Fascist rebels. While America stayed neutral, thousands of Americans went to fight in a bloody campaign that saw over three million dead. Rare newsreel footage and long-suppressed interviews bring to life the war and its aftermath. 360 min.
50-6236 *$59.99*

The Civil War

The Divided Union: The Story Of The American Civil War 1861-1865: Complete Set
A thorough five-volume history of America's most devastating conflict, using written eyewitness accounts, authentic photographs, interviews with writers and historians, and thrilling battlefield re-enactments to bring to life the causes, events and heroes of the war. 260 min. total. NOTE: Individual volumes available at $24.99 each.
22-5727 Was $149.99 *$99.99*

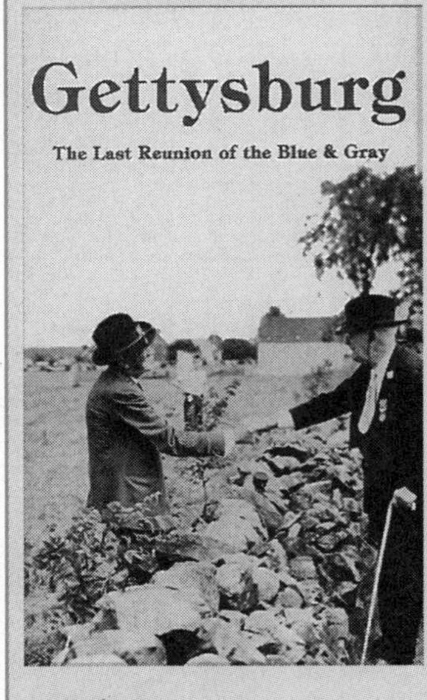

Gettysburg 75th Anniversary 1863-1938
Using newsreel and radio broadcasts recorded at the 75th commemoration of the Battle of Gettysburg in 1938, this program features 2,000 veterans from Union and Confederate forces recalling their experiences in the pivotal Civil War battle. 55 min.
50-2446 *$29.99*

Guns Of The Civil War: Complete Set
The War Between the States featured the development of several new and important types of weaponry, and the fascinating stories behind the guns and the men who used them are told in this three-volume series, hosted by Charles Martin Smith. 180 min. total. NOTE: Individual volumes available at $24.99 each.
27-6840 Save $5.00! *$69.99*

Gettysburg Battlefield Tour
Views of the countryside, monuments and noble statuary of the Pennsylvania battlefield illustrate an exciting account of the Civil War's most famous confrontation. 35 min.
50-1745 *$24.99*

Ironclads: The Monitor And The Merrimac
Edwin Newman narrates this compelling look at the history of these revolutionary Civil War battleships, from their design and building to the four-hour standoff off the Virginia coast. Intriguing footage includes shots of the Monitor on the ocean floor. 30 min.
50-1821 Was $19.99 *$14.99*

Robert E. Lee
Comprehensive video portrait of the leader of the Confederate forces and master strategist features noted historian's analysis of his complex character, the landmarks of his life as visited today, rare photographs and paintings, much more.
50-1834 Was $19.99 *$14.99*

Stonewall Jackson
Evocative video capsule of the life and times of the Confederacy's idiosyncratic military genius. Contemporary visits to the places of his youth, training, and greatest battles, historians' perspectives on the man himself, rare photographs, much more.
50-1835 Was $19.99 *$14.99*

Twilight Of The Blue And Gray
Recollections from an eyewitness to the attack on Fort Sumter, a reunion of Gettysburg veterans, and an interview with one of Robert E. Lee's body-servants highlight this collection of rare film clips. 30 min.
50-2325 *$21.99*

Echoes Of The Blue And Gray, Vol. 1
Rare archival film footage dating back to the 1890s comprises this engrossing and painstakingly rendered testimonial to the spirit and courage of the Civil War veteran, as they were recorded years later recounting their days in battle. 60 min.
50-1900 *$29.99*

Echoes Of The Blue And Gray, Vol. 2
Second volume of vintage films dealing with the War Between the States. Included are such items as a Grand Review 50th Anniversary march from the 1910s, the final reunions of Confederate and Union veterans, and more. 55 min.
50-2002 *$29.99*

Touring Civil War Battlefields
An action-packed survey of the men who fought in the War Between the States. Four battles are depicted: Manassas, Antietam, Fredericksburg and Gettysburg. Relive the battles and the important moments in history. 60 min.
50-1931 *$29.99*

America's Civil War: Gift Set
The conflict that pitted American against American is vividly brought to life, through re-created battle scenes, maps and expert narration, in this 10-volume collection. Includes "1st Manassas," "Shiloh," "Antietam," "Chancelorsville," "Gettysburg," "Vicksburg," "Spotsylvania," "Atlanta," "Franklin" and "Appomattox." 7 1/2 hrs. total. NOTE: Individual volumes available at $14.99 each.
50-2518 Save $20.00! *$129.99*

Great Campaigns Of The Civil War
The 14 greatest battles of the Civil War come to life in this two-tape set that features 10,000 re-enactors in authentic gear and uniforms. Among the campaigns brought to life are Fort Sumter, Manassas, Ft. Donelson, Shiloh, New Orleans, Gettysburg, Atlanta and Appomattox. Narrated by James Whitmore and Barbara Harris. 150 min. total.
50-2814 *$39.99*

The Irish Brigade In The American Civil War
Learn about a little-known chapter in Irish-American history with this look at one of the Civil War's most renowned units. Comprised of recently-arrived immigrants, the Irish Brigade, under the command of Gen. Thomas F. Meagher, fought not only to preserve the Union, but as a prelude to an anticipated war for Irish independence. 30 min.
50-8140 *$19.99*

Civil War Combat
This four-tape series looks at the War Between the States' fiercest battles with emphasis on tactical information, the political consequences of the alteration, and the military strategy on the field of battle. The boxed set includes "The Wheatfield at Gettysburg," "The Bloody Lane at Antietam," "The Hornets' Nest at Shiloh" and "The Tragedy at Cold Harbor." 200 min. total.
53-6900 *$39.99*

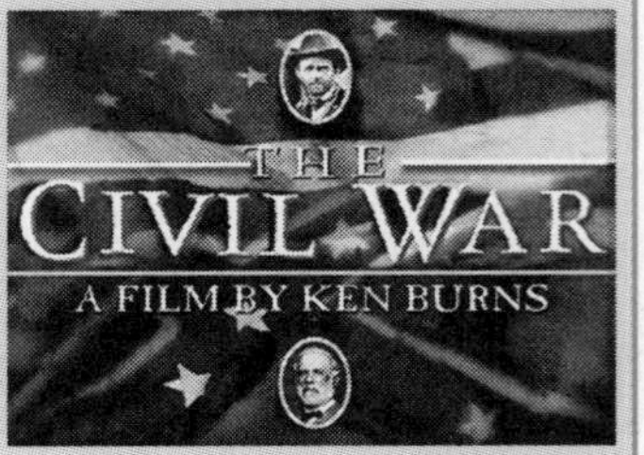

The Civil War: Collectors' Set (1990)
Producer Ken Burns' nine-episode opus, the Emmy Award-winning PBS documentary that brought to life the most turbulent chapter in American history. Maps, drawings, vintage photographs and narration featuring the words of those who went to war (and those who were left behind) are blended to recount the causes, conflicts and resolution of the War Between the States. 680 min. total. NOTE: Individual volumes available at $19.99 each.
07-8194 Save $30.00! *$149.99*

Songs Of The Civil War (1991)
A companion piece to the PBS series "The Civil War," this video compilation features some of today's top stars in pop, country and folk performing 24 popular songs from the era. Kathy Mattea, Waylon Jennings, Judy Collins, Richie Havens, Sweet Honey in the Rock, John Hartford and others appear. 60 min.
04-5104 *$19.99*

World War I

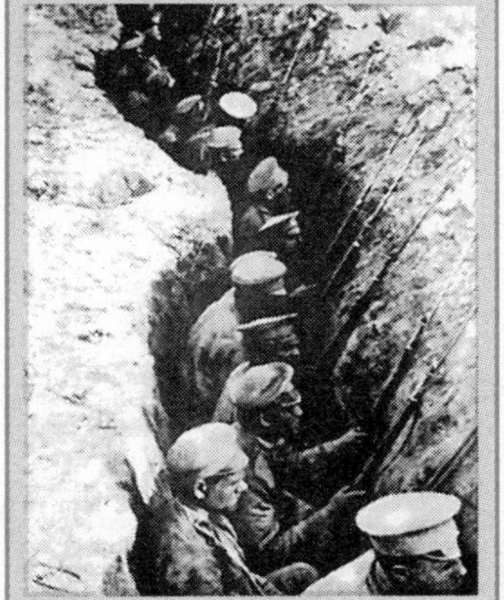

The Great War And The Shaping Of The 20th Century: Boxed Set
This Emmy-winning PBS documentary series traces the origins, battles and consequences of World War I, and shows how this "Great War" dictated global events for decades to come. The four-tape collection includes "Explosion/Stalemate," "Total War/Slaughter," "Mutiny/Collapse" and "Hunger/War Without End."
18-7833 □*$99.99*

Aces: A Story Of The First Air War
They battled in the skies over Europe, at first shooting at each other with pistols and rifles, and their dangerous exploits changed the face of warfare forever. Learn about the pilots of World War I in this exciting documentary that features rare film footage from both sides of the conflict. 93 min.
50-5231 *$19.99*

America Over There: The United States In World War I 1917-1918
This exciting, informative film looks at America's part in "the war to end all wars" and features incredible footage shot by the U.S. Army Signal Corp. Segments focus on President Wilson signing the declaration of war, General Pershing, and combat footage from Selleau Wood, St. Mihiel and the Argonne. Produced in 1927, the program has been remastered and features new narration. 72 min.
50-5336 *$29.99*

The Battle Of Verdun
World War I footage from the Allied and German sides helps tell the story of the 1916 battle, in which the French held German troops back against insurmountable odds and nearly 700,000 men died. 50 min.
80-7084 *$19.99*

The Guns Of August (1964)
A compelling look at World War I, using stunning photos, rare footage and fascinating graphics to chronicle the period between the funeral in 1910 of Edward VII to Armistice Day in 1918. Narrated by Fritz Weaver; based on the Pulitzer Prize-winning book by Barbara W. Tuchman. 100 min.
07-1921 *$19.99*

Over There: 1914-1918 (1964)
Compiled in France, this documentary features newsreel and government film from World War I, focusing on the foot soldier in combat. 90 min.
10-8227 Was $29.99 *$19.99*

Mutiny On The Western Front
One of the untold stories of World War I involved the 300,000-member Anzac unit. These volunteers from Australia and New Zealand suffered significantly more casualties than other forces and eventually rebelled against the Allied officers who commanded them. 60 min.
52-1021 Was $64.99 *$39.99*

The Doughboys: Heroes Of World War I
Rare film footage found in government archives comprises this stirring look at World War I, from the 1914 assassination of Archduke Ferdinand to the momentous 1918 American victory celebration in New York led by General Pershing. 41 min.
76-7335 *$19.99*

Combat At Sea
Trace the history of naval warfare from World War II to the massive supercarriers of Operation Desert Storm. With vintage combat films and rare behind-the-scenes footage, you'll ride above, below and on the seas with the sailors and pilots on their most dangerous missions; presented by U.S. News & World Report. Each tape runs about 50 min. There are 13 volumes available, including:

Combat At Sea: The Battleships
02-2570 *$19.99*

Combat At Sea: Submarines
02-2576 *$19.99*

World War II: Campaigns In The Pacific
This seven-tape collection features stunning footage of the Pacific Theatre in World War II, chronicling everything from Japanese aggression in the late '30s to the Allied counterattacks and the atomic bombing of Hiroshima. 600 min. total.
16-5003 *$49.99*

Submarine Warfare (Now It Can Be Told)
Gene Kelly narrates part of this fascinating documentary, produced by the Department of Defense. Great action scenes, including the USS Guadalcanal with the Naval Task Force trying to capture a German sub in 1944. Also a look at the Silent Service subs. 53 min.
10-1136 *$14.99*

Achtung Panzer!: German Tanks At War
Spectacular wartime footage and insightful commentary from experts highlight this six-episode series presented on three tapes. Featured are "Steel Tigers," which includes "Steel Tigers" and "Michael Wittmann—Tiger Ace"; "Sturmgeschutze and Panzerjaeger," which offers "Assault Guns and Tank Hunters" and "Into Battle"; and "Sturmartillerie," which has "Sturmartillerie" and "Anvil of Victory: The Story of Blitzkrieg." 300 min. total.
80-7271 *$49.99*

George Stevens: D-Day To Berlin
Stirring, personal look at the final year of World War II featuring frontline footage shot by noted Hollywood director George Stevens ("Shane") and his colleagues like William Saroyan and Irwin Shaw, who were known as "The Stevens' Irregulars." Compiled by George Stevens, Jr., the program includes color footage of D-Day, the fall of Berlin and more. 50 min.
02-5068 □*$19.99*

Great Battles Of World War II: Complete Set
This seven-tape collection offers stunning footage of legendary WWII conflicts. Included are "The Battle of North Africa"; "The Battle of St. Vith"; "Tried by Fire," which looks at the 84th Infantry Division and the Battle of the Bulge; "Beachhead Anzio/Battle for San Pietro"; "Bridge at Remagan"; "The Battle of Manila/Fortress in the Sea"; and "The Battle for New Guinea/Battle for Midway." 390 min. total.
16-5027 *$49.99*

To The Shores Of Iwo Jima (1945)/Guadalcanal
Stirring account of the Marines' attack on Iwo Jima and the intense fighting, which lasted over 25 days. Also included is a history of the battle at Guadalcanal, among the bloodiest battles fought. 41 min.
10-1138 *$19.99*

Return To Iwo Jima
Forty years after one of World War II's final and bloodiest Pacific battles, American and Japanese veterans meet in an emotional and solemn reunion that serves as a memorial to their fallen comrades. Ed McMahon narrates. 58 min.
22-5086 *$19.99*

The Normandy Invasion
June 6, 1944: The largest sea invasion ever staged takes place on the French shores of Normandy. Relive the real-life drama of D-Day in this collection of rare documentary footage.
10-1166 Was $19.99 *$14.99*

Turning Point At Normandy: The Soldiers' Story
Relive the events of June 6, 1944, when Allied forces initiated the largest sea invasion of all time against the Germans on the shores of Normandy, France, in this ABC News special hosted by Peter Jennings. Amazing frontline footage and interviews with men from both sides of the conflict are featured. 70 min.
50-7499 *$19.99*

D-Day: The Total Story
Relive the drama, heartbreak and heroism that marked the Allied landing on the shores of Normandy on June 6, 1944, with this special three-tape documentary series from the History Channel. Rare film footage from Allied and Axis sources, interviews with the men who fought there, and expert commentary bring the D-Day story alive in "D Minus 1," "H-Hour" and "Breakout." 150 min. total.
53-6491 *$29.99*

D-Day Remembered (1994)
This stirring film looks at the invasion of Europe at Normandy on June 6, 1944 by the Allied forces. With help from incredible German, American and British film archives, this pivotal point in history is presented in an inspiring but unromanticized account of the event. Narrated by David McCullough. 53 min.
76-7435 *$39.99*

Pearl Harbor: Two Hours That Changed The World
A fascinating look at Pearl Harbor is presented by ABC News and Japan's oldest network. Filled with never-before-seen archival footage and historic newsreels, this program sheds new light on "the day that will live in infamy." 100 min.
50-6892 Was $29.99 *$19.99*

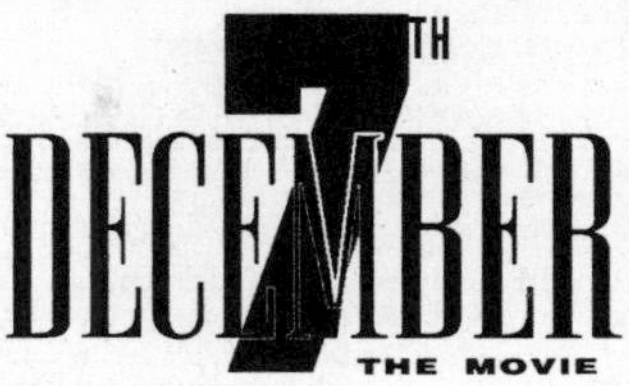

December 7th: The Movie (1943)
Director John Ford's controversial, previously banned docudrama about the Japanese attack on Pearl Harbor was seized by the military (who felt the film portrayed them as being unprepared) and never shown in its complete form. Walter Huston stars as a complacent Uncle Sam who is prodded by his conscience into readying for war. An edited version of the film won the Best Documentary Short Subject Oscar. Uncut version runs 85 min.
20-7035 *$19.99*

World War II: A Personal Journey 1941-1945: Complete Set
This four-volume collection stands as a tribute to all those involved in World War II. Newsreel footage and movie clips are included, while President Gerald Ford, Senator Daniel Inouye, Bill Mauldin, Mike Wallace and others discuss their first-hand experiences. Hosted by Glenn Ford. 180 min. total. NOTE: Individual volumes available at $24.99 each.
50-4597 Save $25.00! *$79.99*

Great Fighting Machines Of World War II: Allied Fighters
This three-tape set tells the story of the Allies' airpower during World War II through rare footage from both U.S. and British sources. "Allied Fighters" looks at Spitfires, Mustangs, Lightnings and Corsairs; "Allied Bombers" focuses on Flying Fortresses, Lancasters and Liberators; and "Allied Armor" includes footage of Shermans, Lee/Grants, Churchills and T-34s. 180 min. total. NOTE: Individual volumes available at $14.99 each.
50-4759 Save $10.00! *$34.99*

Great Fighting Machines Of World War II: Axis Fighters
The planes of the Nazi and Japanese air fleets of World War II are presented in this three-program set. "Axis Fighters" includes film of early operational jets, as well as the ME-109, FW-190 and Zero; "Axis Bombers" looks at the craft used in blitzkriegs, like Stukas, HG-IIIs and Vals; and Panzers, Tigers and lesser-known planes are showcased in "Axis Armor." 180 min. total. NOTE: Individual volumes available at $14.99 each.
50-4760 Save $10.00! *$34.99*

V For Victory: Collector's Set
Follow the history of World War II from its earliest days to the surrender of Germany and Japan in this fascinating 10-tape set hosted by Eric Sevareid and Edwin Newman. Among the programs are "Pearl Harbor to Midway," "Guadalcanal and the Pacific Counterattack" and "The Eagle Triumphant." 450 min. total. NOTE: Individual volumes available at $14.99 each.
50-2740 Save $80.00! *$69.99*

The Fight For The Sky: Complete Set
A four-part look at the airborne battles of World War II, with rare film clips from British and Eastern European archives. Includes "History of the Luftwaffe," "The Battle of Britain," "Fighter Aces" and "Elite Forces." 240 min. total. NOTE: Individual volumes available at $29.99 each.
22-1170 Save $10.00! *$109.99*

War On Land And Sea: Complete Set
World War II's greatest campaigns and leaders are examined in this four-tape set featuring footage from Eastern European countries and Britain never seen before. Includes "Churchill's War," "Dunkirk," "Waffen-SS" and "D-Day." 240 min. total. NOTE: Individual volumes available at $29.99 each.
22-1165 Save $10.00! *$109.99*

From D-Day To Victory In Europe
Actual frontline footage recalls the last year of the European campaign in World War II, from the Normandy landings and the Battle of the Bulge to the Reich's last days. 112 min.
50-6039 *$39.99*

The Road To War
Rare combat footage and vintage newsreels show the world on the brink of disaster in this look at the beginnings of World War II. Follow the rise of Hitler and Mussolini, the Japanese invasion of China and the first battles in Europe. 75 min.
50-6076 *$39.99*

World War II Battle Force: Complete Set #1
Learn about the weapons and craft used by German forces in World War II in this three-tape documentary series that features rare frontline footage to tell the stories of "Panzer," "Stuka" and "U-Boat." 180 min. total. NOTE: Individual volumes available at $14.99 each.
19-2846 □*$44.99*

World War II Battle Force: Complete Set #2
Learn about the weapons and craft used by Allied and German forces in World War II in this six-tape documentary series that uses rare frontline footage and high-tech computer graphics and animation. Included are "Airborne," "Amphibious," "Carrier," "Panzer," "Stuka" and "U-Boat." 360 min. total. NOTE: Individual volumes available at $19.99 each.
90-1028 Save $30.00! □*$89.99*

Nostalgia World War II, Vol. 1
Three films sponsored by the U.S. Government. "Battle Wreckage" looks at the steel industry's involvement in WWII, and features incredible shots of ruined supplies, artillery, tanks. "War Speeds Up" is narrated by Jose Ferrer and includes thrilling combat footage. "It Can't Last" is a look at a soldier hoping to get rescued after a battle. 46 min. total.
09-1552 Was $24.99 *$14.99*

Nostalgia World War II, Vol. 2
An interesting compilation of vintage wartime newsreels and U.S. Government films made for the folks on the home front. Includes scenes of jungle warfare in New Guinea, bombing raids over Germany, the rigors of army laundry detail(!) and a message for female factory workers by Veronica Lake on the dangers of long hair on the assembly line. 51 min.
09-1619 Was $24.99 *$14.99*

Nostalgia World War II, Vol. 3
More government propaganda and rare newsreel footage from the '40s. Features actual aerial combat scenes, a look at the liberation of Naples and Rome, and a recently-discovered film about an all-black combat troop. Also included is a Coast Guard documentary about the luxury liner Manhattan and its rebirth as a cargo transport ship. 61 min.
09-1620 Was $24.99 *$14.99*

Nostalgia World War II, Vol. 4
A rousing collection of government and Hollywood films produced during WWII. "The Caissons Go Rolling Along" and "The Marines' Hymn" are sung; Bing Crosby sings about U.S. bonds; and Lt. Ronald Reagan and Lt. Burgess Meredith star in the heroic short, "The Rear Gunner." 61 min. total.
09-1642 Was $24.99 *$14.99*

September 1939
Documentary account of the German invasion of Poland that launched the Second World War. Rare battlefield footage and newsreels from both sides show the incredibly swift Nazi strikes that fragmented the nation and the heroic defense of the citizens of Warsaw. 60 min.
09-1875 Was $24.99 *$19.99*

Marines At Tarawa (1944)/ Return To Guam (1945)
Two films produced by the Office of War. First is an Academy Award-winning look at the brutal, bloody carnage of the Pacific campaign as it happened on Tarawa. Then, see the Marines take Guam back from the Japanese after 31 months of occupation. 41 min.
10-1135 *$19.99*

Famous Marine Battles: Tarawa
Because it was so fiercely defended from Japan's desperate kamikaze fighters by determined Marines, the islands along this 22-mile reef are forever known as "Bloody Tarawa." Exciting documentary footage tells the story of this brutal WWII confrontation. 55 min.
50-6309 *$19.99*

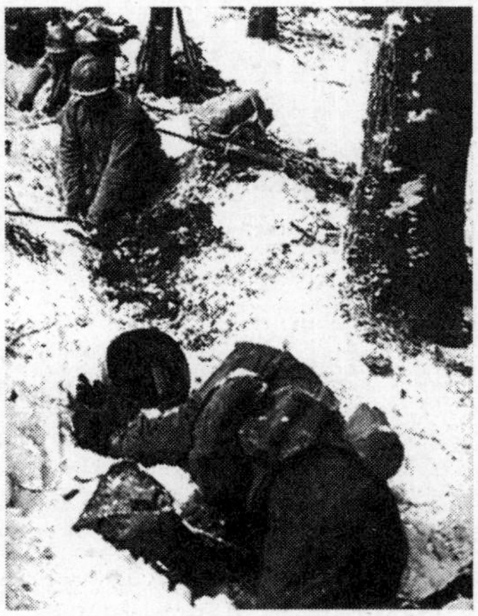

The Battle Of The Bulge
Stirring documentary on one of World War II's most devastating battles, as Hitler's troops drove through American lines, leading to 80,000 soldiers being killed, maimed or captured. Incredible footage shows the psychological and physical conditions faced by the brave Allied forces. David McCullough narrates. 90 min.
63-7112 □*$19.99*

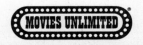

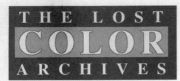

THE LOST COLOR ARCHIVES

WWII: The Lost Color Archives
This three-tape set features recently discovered color footage from World War II. Presented in the form of diaries and first-person accounts, the films—which chronicle such events as the London Blitz, D-Day and Hiroshima—offer a new perspective on the struggle faced by soldiers and civilians alike. Included are "A New World Order," "Total War" and "Triumph and Despair." 150 min. total.
53-6899 *$29.99*

WWII In Color
Recently declassified and newly restored, this collection of remarkable color film footage presents the tragedy and heroism of World War II as never seen before. Among the highlights are scenes of the D-Day Landing and Allied march towards Paris; a B-17 bombing raid shot by William Wyler; John Ford's footage of the Battle of Midway; the bloody aftermath of Tarawa, Iwo Jima and Okinawa; Hitler and Eva Braun at their Eagle's Nest retreat; and more. 105 min.
89-5132 *$29.99*

How Hitler Lost The War
New insights on Hitler's defeat in World War II are presented by former Reich officers in this documentary that looks at the Führer's costliest mistakes. Animated maps and startling documentary footage help relate how delays in attacks on Britain and Russia, and the development of jet aircraft were detrimental to Germany. 67 min.
22-1273 *$29.99*

Submarine: Steel Boats—Iron Men
The bravery of men who serve on submarines is the focus of this insightful program, which includes a visit to a "sub school," interviews with commanders and the development of submarines in World Wars I and II. Author Tom Clancy makes a special appearance. 59 min.
22-1281 *$29.99*

Taking Off With Jimmy Stewart And Clark Gable (1942)
Lt. James Stewart hosts the Army Air Force recruitment film "Winning Your Wings," telling would-be pilots, "Consider the effect these shining wings have on the gals." Next, "Wings Up" is a look at the rigorous AAF officer training school in Miami is narrated by and features flyboy Clark Gable. 36 min. total.
65-1023 Was $19.99 *$14.99*

The Battle Of Midway (1942)/Global War (1943)
Two documentary looks at World War II, featuring rarely-seen Army footage. First relive the pivotal Pacific conflict in incredible color scenes, then see an Army newsreel detailing the Allied war effort in both theatres during 1943. 46 min. total.
10-2146 *$12.99*

Ronald Reagan: For God And Country (1943)/Jap Zero (1943)
Two vintage War Department shorts made during WWII, both starring the 40th President of the United States. First Reagan plays a newly-assigned Catholic chaplain who explains the war to his charges; next he's a pilot who must learn the differences between our P-40 plane and a Zero. 62 min. total.
10-2147 *$12.99*

Report From The Aleutians (1943)
John Huston directed this acclaimed Army Signal Corps documentary that looked at one of the least known fields of battle in WWII's Pacific Theater, Alaska's isolated Aleutian Islands. 47 min.
10-7949 *$19.99*

The Battle Of Russia (1943)
Hitler's forces are victorious in Moscow and Leningrad but, like Napoleon's troops, are thoroughly defeated at the Battle of Stalingrad; Academy Award nominee. 83 min.
50-6216 *$14.99*

The Eye Of Vichy (1993)
Director Claude Chabrol fashions a devastating documentary about France and its involvement with the Nazis during World War II. Using newsreels and propaganda films designed to turn the French people against the Allied Forces and the Jews, Chabrol explores how media manipulation nearly changed history. 110 min. In English and French with English subtitles.
70-5091 Was $59.99 *$29.99*

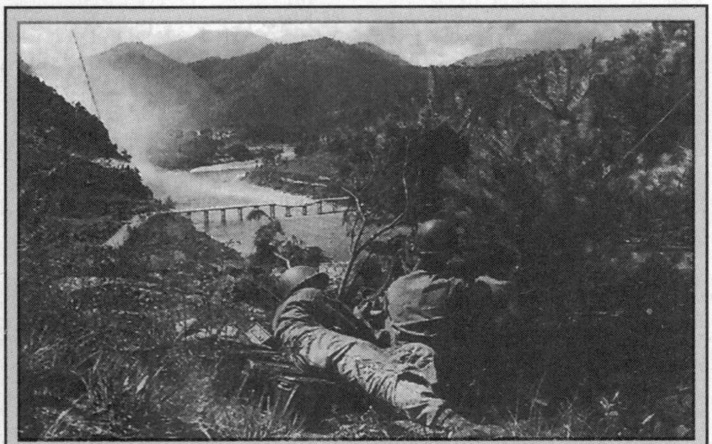

The Korean War

The Korean War: Complete Set
A remarkable five-volume documentary on "America's Forgotten War," featuring never-before-seen footage of the conflict that started in the aftermath of World War II, cost over 33,000 Americans their lives, and continues to affect Asian politics today. James Whitmore narrates. 10 hrs. total. NOTE: Individual volumes available at $19.99 each.
22-1269 Save $20.00! *$99.99*

Korean War
Produced for the History Channel, this comprehensive four-tape set explores the origins, conduct, military strategies and political implications of the Korean War through rare newsreels, eyewitness accounts and frontline footage. One of the least examined conflicts in U.S. history is finally looked at in remarkable style. 200 min. total.
53-6617 *$59.99*

With The Marines: Chosen To Hungnam/Carrier Action Off Korea
Fighting off a Chinese surprise attack, US Marines staged a "strategic withdrawal" to the Hungnam shore that caught the enemy off-guard. Relive the harrowing action with actual frontline footage, followed by a look at life on board an aircraft carrier stationed off the Korean coast. 43 min. total.
65-1010 *$29.99*

This Is Korea (1951)/December 7th (1943)
Two amazing propaganda films directed by John Ford. "December 7th" (in B&W) depicts in detail the sneak attack on Pearl Harbor. Both actual footage and studio trickery are employed. "This Is Korea" (in color) employs a gung-ho attitude to try and sell the unpopular war to the American public. 85 min. total.
62-1024 *$19.99*

The Motion Picture History Of The Korean War (1958)
Actual combat footage and newsreel interviews are mixed to give a comprehensive contemporary overview of America's involvement in Korea from 1950 to the 1953 armistice. 58 min.
65-1014 Was $34.99 *$19.99*

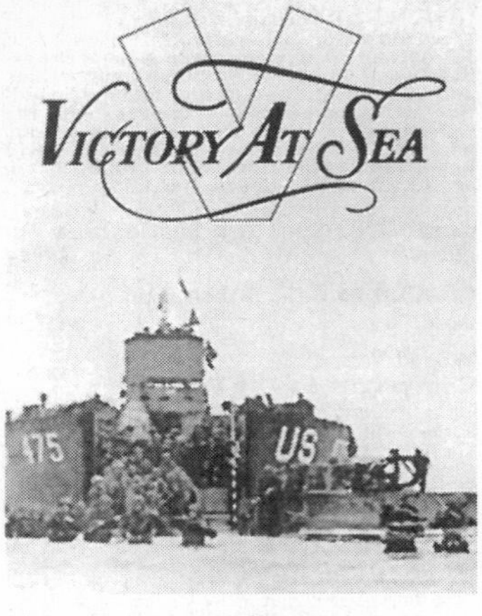

Victory At Sea: Collector's Set
Winner of 12 major awards, this stirring documentary series, chronicling WWII naval operations in the Atlantic and Pacific campaigns and featuring action footage obtained from Allied and Axis government film vaults, aired on NBC in 1952-53. Richard Rodgers supplied the original music score; Leonard Graves narrates. 11 hrs. on six tapes. NOTE: Individual volumes available at $19.99 each.
53-1540 Save $20.00! *$99.99*

Blood & Iron: The Story Of The German War Machine: Boxed Set
This engrossing three-tape boxed set explores the secrets of 100 years of the German industrial and military machine. "The Great War Comes" focuses on the country's use of technology in World War I; "Fatal Alliances" surveys Germany before and during World War II; and "From Nuremberg to NATO" chronicles post-WWII Germany and the war crime trials. 180 min. total.
50-7361 *$79.99*

Secrets Of War: Spy Games Of World War II: Boxed Set
Special four-tape set includes "D-Day Deceptions," about the strategy behind the massive 1944 invasion; "German Intelligence in WWII," about Third Reich spies; "Rommel's Enigma," which tracks the defeat of German forces in North Africa; and "Tools of Deception," a look at decoys and fakery. 207 min. total.
50-8174 *$39.99*

Marines In Combat: Complete Set
A remarkable documentary series on the Marines fighting in the Pacific during WWII offers stunning newsreel footage and stirring narration by Lt. General Holland M. Smith. Included in this five-tape set are "Guam/Midway/Bougainville," "New Britain/Tarawa/Saipan/Tinian," "Pelileu/Iwo Jima/Okinawa," "A-Bomb/Pusan/Pusan Perimeter" and "Inchon/Chinese Attack/Helicopters." 600 min. NOTE: Individual volumes available for $19.99 each.
50-5773 Save $20.00 *$79.99*

Heroes And Tyrants Of The Twentieth Century: Complete Set
Six well-researched programs explore some of the greatest and most despised leaders in modern history: "Churchill," "Gandhi," "Hitler," "Lenin," "Mussolini" and "Roosevelt." Archival footage and scholars' commentary help give viewers the inside scoop on how these men rose to (and in some cases were toppled from) power. 240 min. total. NOTE: Individual volumes available at $19.99 each.
50-6206 *$119.99*

The War Years: Britain In World War II: Complete Set
This thrilling five-part series documents the history of World War II and its effects on England's civilian population, as the constant threat of German bombers loomed overhead. Included are "The Phony War," "The Battle of Britain," "The Blitz," "The Tide Turns" and "The Final Chapter." 300 min. total. NOTE: Individual volumes available at $29.99 each.
80-7266 Save $50.00! *$99.99*

The West Point Story: Fortress Of Freedom
Trace almost 200 years of the history and pride that is "the Long Gray Line" with this comprehensive documentary look at the United States Military Academy at West Point, New York. Learn about the academy's founding and such notable alumni as Grant, Lee, MacArthur and Eisenhower; hear from graduates Buzz Aldrin, Alexander Haig and H. Norman Schwarzkopf; and see what life is like for the men and women who study there. 110 min.
89-5034 *$24.99*

West Point: Songs Of Inspiration
A key part of life at "the Point" since its 1802 founding, the United States Military Academy Mixed Glee Club is spotlighted in this moving program that traces its history and features interviews with such West Point alumni as astronaut Frank Borman and Gen. Norman Schwarzkopf. The 40-voice choir is also seen performing "America the Beautiful," "Battle Hymn of the Republic," "Onward Christian Soldiers" and other favorites. 55 min.
89-5167 *$19.99*

Target For Tonight (1941)
Winner of a Special Academy Award, this thrilling sketch of the planning and execution of the Royal Air Force's bombing mission to destroy an oil storage depot focuses on the bomber "F For Freddie" and the brave men and women who saved England from annihilation. 50 min.
09-1380 Was $24.99 *$19.99*

Desert Victory (1943)/ Cameramen At War (1943)
Featured on this program are "Desert Victory," an Academy Award-winning account from Captain Ray Boulting of the battle between British troops and Rommel's Afrika Korps, and "Cameramen at War," which examines the filmmakers' danger-filled job.
53-9811 *$19.99*

Desert Victory (1943)
The British 8th Army's taking of Occupied Africa in 1943, from the trouncing of Tobruk to the triumph at Tripoli, can be relived once more with this superlative film. The footage of the 8th Army's cameramen, combined with captured German war film, create an indelible portrait. 65 min.
62-5219 *$14.99*

Appointment In Tokyo (1945)
Produced by the Army Signal Corps, and featuring remarkable footage taken from seized enemy newsreels, this compelling documentary chronicles the 1942 Japanese assault on the Philippine island of Corregidor. Forced to evacuate, General MacArthur vows to return and retake the island, a promise he keeps in May of 1945. 55 min.
09-3142 *$14.99*

The Big Battles: Complete Set
Spanning the years 1939 to 1945, this superb 15-volume documentary series uses newsreel and combat footage and interviews with military personnel to tell of the greatest square-offs of World War II. Among the episodes are "France," "Britain," "Atlantic," "Pacific," "Europe," "Moscow," "Stalingrad," "Normandy," "Italy," "Germany," "Berlin" and "The Pacific." 675 min. total.
58-8199 *$99.99*

Famous Third Army (1950)
Intense look at General George S. Patton's 281-day drive through Europe to defeat the German forces. See why this maverick leader was considered by the Germans to be the only American general equal to their best Panzer generals. 22 min.
65-1063 *$19.99*

The Silent Service (1946)
An account of the U.S. Navy's submarine campaign during World War II against the Japanese that, due to security issues, was dubbed "the Silent Service." Several battles are re-created in combination with actual combat footage in this gritty wartime chronicle. 37 min.
65-1073 *$19.99*

Red Bull Division: 34th Infantry Division (1953)
Unlike the fictional worlds of soldiers, the real life of an infantryman is one of bitter cold, extreme heat, death, and utter hardship. This gripping documentary depicts the misery of soldiers in North Africa and Italy during World War II. 29 min.
65-1069 *$19.99*

Warrior (1975)
What happens inside the mind of a soldier in the heat of combat? This intense program, from the creators of "The World at War," puts you on the frontline through the first-hand accounts of men who fought in World War II and rare archival footage, giving you an unforgettable look at what makes a man a warrior. 50 min.
44-2260 *$14.99*

The Propaganda Wars: Japan And The U.S. And The Battle For Hearts And Minds
Documentary units from Japan and the United States combined to produce this incredible examination of how each country used propaganda during World War II to gain support of their citizens. Newsreels, training films and clips from features show "evil, maniacal Japanese" and "ruthless, barbaric Americans." 50 min.
53-8297 *$19.99*

GREAT BLUNDERS OF WWII

Great Blunders Of WWII
This four-tape set focuses on the amazing miscues that occurred during World War II. Archival footage and expert research bring you the inside word on "The Great German Blunder at Dunkirk/Hitler's Declaration of War on the U.S.," "The Pilot Who Bombed London/Hitler's Flying Blunders," "Japan's Mistakes at Midway/The Failure of the Kamikaze" and "Death at Stalingrad/Operation Sea Lion." 208 min. total.
53-6823 *$39.99*

Adolf Hitler
An inside look at the life and times of Adolf Hitler, using home movies, newsreel footage and more to show the rise and fall of history's most prolific killer. 101 min.
08-1487 Was $19.99 ***$14.99***

Holocaust: World War II: The Nuremberg Trials
A stunning documentary that covers the rise of the Third Reich and ends with the International Military Tribunal of 1945-1946 in which Rudolf Hess, Albert Speer, Herman Göering and other architects of the Holocaust were brought to justice. With stunning footage from Nazi archives and film from the Nuremberg Trials, this program paints a horrifying picture. 78 min.
10-2548 ***$12.99***

Traitors To Hitler
This British documentary tells of the plot to assassinate Hitler formulated by some of his generals in 1944. Rare footage of the famous trial is featured, along with footage of the anti-Nazi officials. 65 min.
10-9461 ***$19.99***

Hitler: The Final Chapter
The shocking details of the last days of Adolph Hitler are chronicled in this shocking program that explores the myths and reality surrounding the Nazi leader's demise. 51 min.
20-7407 ***$29.99***

Führer! Rise Of A Madman
His bizarre rise to power and evil machinations forever changed the world; witness in this special documentary film the life and twisted vision of Adolf Hitler, from "Mein Kampf" to the final days in the bunker. 108 min.
50-6074 ***$39.99***

Hitler's Henchmen
The shattering reality of the horrors of the Nazi death camp are on view in this horrifying documentary. A piece of propaganda that stands a telling statement on the nature of the human condition. 60 min.
50-6089 ***$39.99***

Nazi War Crimes: Babi-Yar
An unforgettable document of the area in the Ukraine which Nazis occupied in 1941 and used for genocidal experiments. 50 min.
50-6591 ***$19.99***

The Nazis
Produced by the BBC, this stunning and informative six-tape series traces the history of the Third Reich, from its rise under Hitler's leadership and its campaign of hate to the conflict that engulfed the world and its bloody demise. Several fallacies that have been accepted as truth for decades are exploded thanks to first-hand interviews, meticulous research and archival footage. 300 min. total.
53-6581 ***$79.99***

Nazi Propaganda
Three films documenting the Third Reich's rise to power. Leni Riefenstahl's "Day of Freedom" (1935) chronicles German army maneuvers, while the 1939 invasion of Poland is "justified" in "Baptism of Fire." Finally, vintage Nazi newsreels show the fall of Belgium and Paris, Hitler visiting troops and other subjects. 72 min. total.
53-7457 ***$29.99***

The Rise And Fall Of Adolf Hitler: Boxed Set
One of the first German-produced series to examine Hitler's reign of terror, this six-part collection offers an in-depth profile of the man, his twisted beliefs, and how he led a nation to the brink of annihilation. Rare newsreel footage, much of it never before seen in America, interviews and documents shed light on this darkest period in human history. 300 min. total.
53-8110 Was $99.99 ***$59.99***

Assorted Nazi Political Films: 1932-1943
Rare German films of Nazi rally speeches provide a historical overview of Hitler's rise to power. Orations by Hitler from 1932, and 1938 victory speech after Austria's annexation, and a 1943 newsreel of Goebbels' "total war" Berlin address are included. 31 min. total. In German with English subtitles.
65-1004 ***$39.99***

Pre-War German Featurettes
Four Reich-produced documentaries from the mid-'30s are featured. "Yesterday and Today," "Three Years of Adolf Hitler" and "Honor of Work" compare National Socialism to the Weimar Republic, while "Becoming an Army" depicts the Rhineland campaign. 60 min. total. In German with English subtitles.
65-1006 ***$49.99***

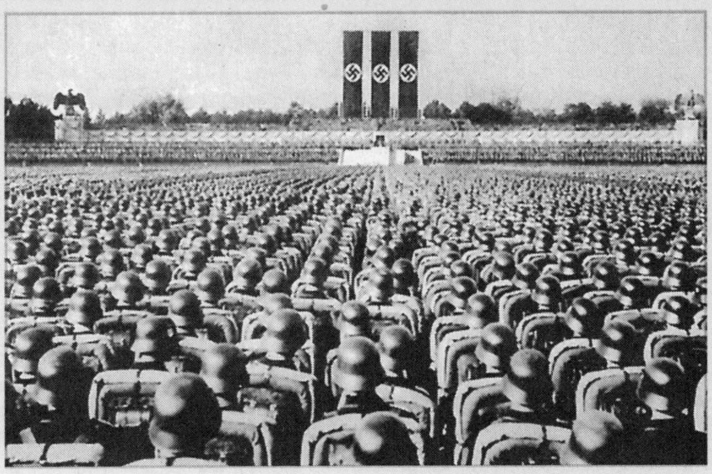

The Third Reich

The Rise And Fall Of Adolf Hitler
An exhaustive biography of Adolf Hitler, tracing his megalomaniacal rise to power and looking at the psychological, economic and political forces that played a part in his powerful reign. What really went into Hitler's theories on slave labor, genocide and propaganda? 150 min.
80-7085 ***$29.99***

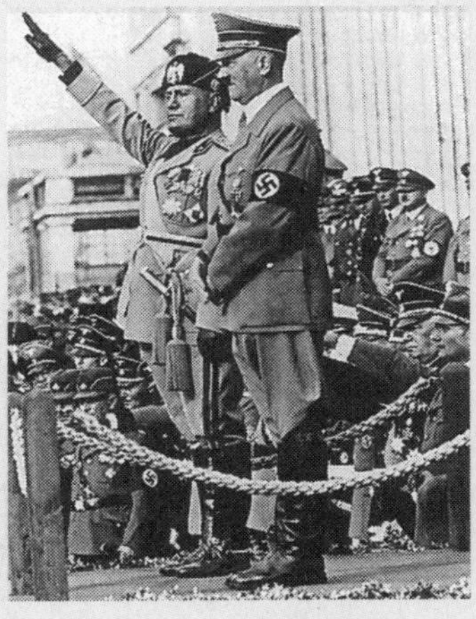

Mussolini Visits Hitler (1937)
The official Nazi film record of Il Duce's 1937 trip to Berlin and his fateful meeting with the Führer includes scenes of Army and Luftwaffe field maneuvers, a spectacular nighttime military parade, and speeches by the two dictators to a crowd that numbered over 1,000,000. 31 min. In German with English subtitles.
65-1022 ***$39.99***

Germany Celebrates Hitler's Birthday (1939)
Rare German documentary depicting the nationwide festivities for the Führer's 50th birthday, climaxing with a massive rally and military demonstration and some rather nervous-looking European diplomats. 21 min. In German with English subtitles.
65-1003 ***$34.99***

German Invasion Of Poland: 1939 (1939)
Produced by Nazi filmmakers to depict Polish aggression against border towns (and thus justify Germany's incursion) this rare documentary includes footage of the assault on Dazig, German and Russian troops joining forces, and scenes of Hitler near the front lines. In German with English subtitles.
65-1005 ***$39.99***

The Private Film Collection Of Eva Braun (1939)
Unseen for many years, this incredible find features footage taken at Hitler's Alpine retreat from 1936 to 1943 and includes unique glimpses of the dictator meeting with officials and diplomats, conferring with his generals, and relaxing with visitors and children. Commentary in English. 60 min.
65-1026 ***$39.99***

Campaign In Poland (1940)
Nazi-produced propaganda film that seeks to justify the German invasion of Poland on the grounds that the Poles needed to be "liberated." Directed by Fritz Hippler, who was also responsible for the highly disturbing "The Eternal Jew." Program also includes several Nazi newsreels. 68 min. total. In German with English subtitles.
10-7359 Was $29.99 ***$19.99***

March With The Führer (1941)
A masterpiece of propaganda looks at the role of the Hitler Youth in building the Third Reich, with emphasis on the activities at the 1938 party rally. 60 min. In German; no English subtitles.
53-7073 Was $29.99 ***$19.99***

Sieg Im Westen (Victory In The West) (1941)
One of the rarest and most comprehensive war documentaries to come out of Hitler's Germany, chronicling the 1940 Nazi military campaigns against France, Belgium and the Netherlands. Amazing combat footage takes the viewer inside the Panzer tanks and Heinkel bombers, follows a triumphant Hitler into a defeated France, and offers a rare glimpse of the German soldier's personal life. 120 min. In German with English subtitles.
65-1018 ***$49.99***

Nazi War Crime Trials (1945)
A brutal compilation of documentary footage, graphically depicting the trials and executions of German and Japanese war criminals. Five newsreels, a theatrical trailer and a Russian-made film documentary are included. WARNING: Actual scenes of hangings and firing squads are not for the squeamish. 67 min.
09-1200 ***$19.99***

The Nuremberg Trials (1946)
In 1946, 22 German military and political leaders faced an international court to stand trial for the unprecedented crimes against humanity committed by Hitler's Third Reich. This Russian-made documentary, narrated in English, offers rare footage of Nazi atrocities, postwar Germany and the trial itself. 65 min.
10-7442 Was $19.99 ***$14.99***

Love Life Of Adolph Hitler (1948)
Exploitation documentary that mixes footage of Hitler, Eva Braun and Mussolini along with sequences of Nazi atrocities and Nazi bathing beauties(!). Reportedly, Dwain Esper ("Maniac") was involved in this production. AKA: "Conform or Die."
68-9121 ***$19.99***

The Life Of Adolf Hitler (1961)
Rare footage of the Nazis' rise to power and eventual fall is featured in this German-made documentary that traces Hitler's bloody reign from the wreckage of post-WWI Germany to the last days in the Berlin bunker. 101 min.
09-1199 ***$19.99***

Black Fox: The Rise And Fall Of Adolf Hitler (1962)
Winner of the 1962 Academy Award for Best Documentary Feature, this unique biographical sketch of history's most feared and fanatical leader explores Hitler's bitter youth in Austria, his frustrated ambitions to be a successful artist, his years as a soldier in World War I and his stranglehold over the people of Germany; narrated by Marlene Dietrich. 89 min.
22-1175 ***$29.99***

The Rise And Fall Of The Third Reich (1968)
This definitive pictorial record of Nazi power, based on William Shire's book, features interviews with Hitler's closest associates and disturbing footage of the sadistic cruelties of the elite SS Corps. 120 min.
12-1268 ***$59.99***

Germany Awake (1968)
Compilation documentary on the use of film propaganda by the Third Reich. Includes clips from "March with the Führer," "Victory in the West," and others. 90 min. In German with English commentary.
53-7071 Was $29.99 ***$19.99***

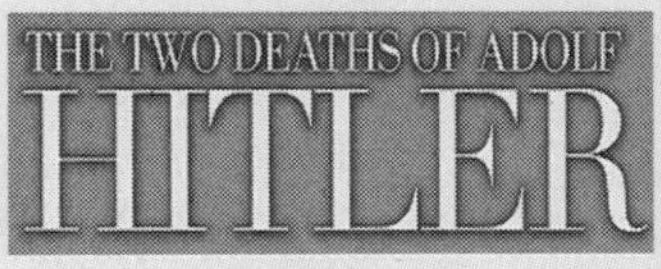

The Two Deaths Of Adolf Hitler (1975)
How did the infamous dictator meet his end in a Berlin bunker in 1945: gunshot or poison? In this British TV documentary, you'll hear eyewitness accounts by Hitler's personal secretary and valet, along with members of the Russian medical team that examined his corpse, to recount Hitler's final days. 52 min.
44-2259 ***$14.99***

The Architecture Of Doom (1993)
Critically acclaimed study of the inner workings of the Third Reich and the Nazi aesthetic of art, popular culture and architecture. Tracing Hitler's rise from failed artist to terrifying dictator to his death, the film uses rare footage and music by Richard Wagner to delve into a world of horror and kitsch. 119 min.
70-5083 Was $59.99 ***$29.99***

The Eye Of The Third Reich (1994)
Walter Frentz, the subject of this intriguing and insightful look into the films of Nazi Germany, served as cameraman for "Triumph of the Will" and was a personal cameraman for Adolf Hitler. Samples of his work are woven together with excerpts and interviews with a man who felt no guilt because he "only reproduced, never produced" what he saw. 61 min.
65-1071 ***$29.99***

The Trial Of Adolf Eichmann (1997)
The capture of Nazi official Adolf Eichmann, living in exile in Argentina since the end of World War II, in 1960 and his subsequent trial and execution in Israel made headlines around the world. David Brinkley hosts this compelling chronicle of the trial of the man who implemented and oversaw Hitler's "Final Solution" and sent thousands of Jews to their deaths. 120 min.
18-7744 ***$19.99***

In The Shadow Of The Reich: Nazi Medicine (1997)
As shocking as the deaths of millions in Nazi concentration camps during World War II were, the most terrifying stories to come from this time may have been those of German doctors' experiments on inmates. Rare and shocking government footage is featured in this compelling documentary look at what atrocities were committed under the guise of science. 54 min.
70-5124 ***$29.99***

The War Chronicles: World War II: Set
Through amazing archival footage and powerful interviews, you'll get the inside story on some of the greatest battles of World War II. Included in this two-tape set are "The War in Europe," which features the Battle of the Bulge and D-Day; and "The War in the Pacific," which offers a look at the Asian theater. 300 min. total. NOTE: Individual volumes available at $14.99 each.
53-8817 ***$29.99***

Battleship Scharnhorst: Complete Set
One of the first large battleships to be built by Germany since 1918, the "speed battleship" Scharnhorst and her sister ship Gneisenau ushered in a new era in nautical combat. Follow the craft from its first designs in the late '20s to its sinking in 1943 in this two-part documentary. Included are "Part 1: The Early Years" and "Part 2: 1943—The Final Year." 131 min. total. NOTE: Individual volumes available at $29.99 each.
65-1075 Save $10.00! ***$49.99***

The Great Commanders: Complete Set
Filmed on location throughout the world, this sensational six-volume series looks at legendary military leaders and the key battles of their careers, using special 3-D computer animation. Learn about what drove Alexander the Great, Julius Caesar, Napoleon, Lord Nelson, Ulysses S. Grant and Georgi Zhukov to greatness. 270 min. total. NOTE: Individual volumes available at $24.99 each.
14-9111 Save $30.00! ***$119.99***

Unsolved Mysteries Of World War II: Boxed Set
This six tape set looks at the mysteries of WWII and what effect these enigmas had in reshaping the world. Included are "Peoples & Plots," which includes "The Riddle of Rudolph Hess" and "Hitler's Secret War"; "Battle Mysteries," featuring "Pearl Harbor" and "Decision at Dunkirk"; and "Occult & Secrets," including "Himmler's Castle" and "The Last Days of Hitler."
72-3026 ***$59.99***

Preserving The Past To Ensure The Future
Acclaimed look at some of the most tragic victims of the Holocaust, the one-and-a-half million children whose only "crime" was to have been born Jewish. The reactions of visitors to Jerusalem's Yad Vashem Museum tell the horrifying story, as well as poetry and artwork created in the death camps and contemporary footage of racist violence. Nominated for an Academy Award for Best Short Subject Documentary. 15 min.
53-7493 *$39.99*

Opening The Gates Of Hell: American Liberators Of The Nazi Concentration Camps
American WWII veterans share their recollections of the role they played in freeing the survivors of Hitler's death camps, detailing the brutality of Nazi oppression in unflinching detail. Warning: this tape contains graphic archival footage. 45 min.
48-5119 *$39.99*

Bach In Auschwitz
This moving film documents the 50th anniversary reunion of 11 women who survived the horrors of the Holocaust and were members of the all-female orchestra assembled at the Auschwitz concentration camp in Poland. Hear how through their music and their friendship they managed to come through an unimaginable ordeal. 105 min.
53-6752 *$19.99*

America And The Holocaust: Deceit And Indifference
This incisive documentary takes a penetrating look at American anti-Semitism during World War II and how the country delayed action, suppressed information and blocked efforts that could have saved thousands of lives. Hal Linden narrates this program, which aired on PBS as part of "The American Experience." 60 min.
63-7096 *$19.99*

The Last Seven Months Of Anne Frank
A powerful document that begins where Anne Frank's diary ended, following the accounts of the final nights and days of Anne's life from eight women who knew the family in concentration camps in Westerbork, Auschwitz-Birkenau and Bergen-Belsen. 75 min.
48-5138 *$59.99*

Anne Frank Remembered (1995)
This Academy Award-winning documentary is a compelling look at the real Anne Frank which uses eyewitness accounts from those who knew her and her family to trace her life, from her childhood in Germany to the two years of hiding in an Amsterdam attic and her death at Bergen-Belsen at age 16 in 1944. Narrated by Kenneth Branagh and Glenn Close. 117 min.
02-2973 Was $89.99 ❑*$19.99*

Anne Frank: The Missing Chapter (1998)
Suppressed by the Frank family for over 50 years, several never-before-seen portions of Anne Frank's diary were made public in 1998. In this program, you'll hear Anne's thoughts regarding her parents' relationship and her hopes for the diary's publication, along with comments from friends of the Frank family and an audio interview with Otto Frank. 43 min.
22-6079 *$29.99*

Night And Fog (1956)/ Le Retour (1945)
Two brilliant and disturbing French documentaries dealing with the Holocaust. First is Alain Resnais' look at the concentration camps that uses actual footage taken inside the camps, followed by an emotional filming of the Allies' liberation of several camps in 1945; directed by Henri Cartier-Bresson. 65 min. total.
10-7588 Was $24.99 *$19.99*

Warsaw Ghetto (1969)
Exceptional British documentary that retraces the 10-day resistance of 500,000 Jews trapped within a half-mile radius of the city by the occupying Nazi military. A powerful and compelling piece of filmmaking. 51 min.
01-1380 Was $19.99 *$14.99*

Who Shall Live And Who Shall Die? (1982)
A scathing investigation of the policy adopted by the Roosevelt administration and American Jewish leaders in response to evidence of the Holocaust in Europe, a course of inaction that may have cost millions of lives. Contains previously classified materials and rare film. 90 min.
53-7291 Was $79.99 *$29.99*

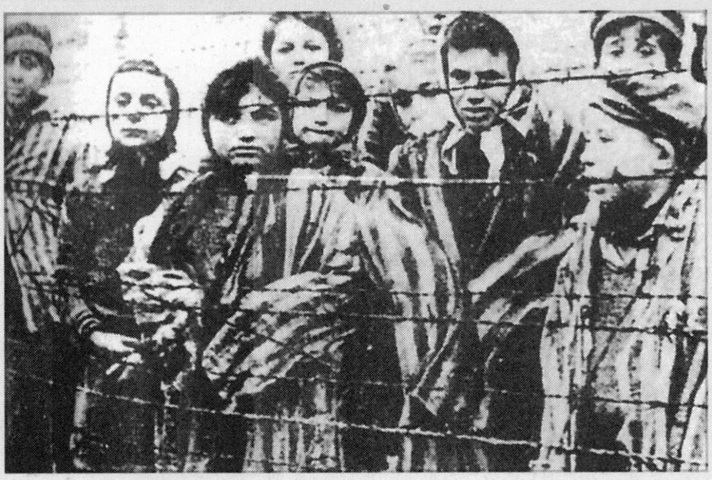

The Holocaust

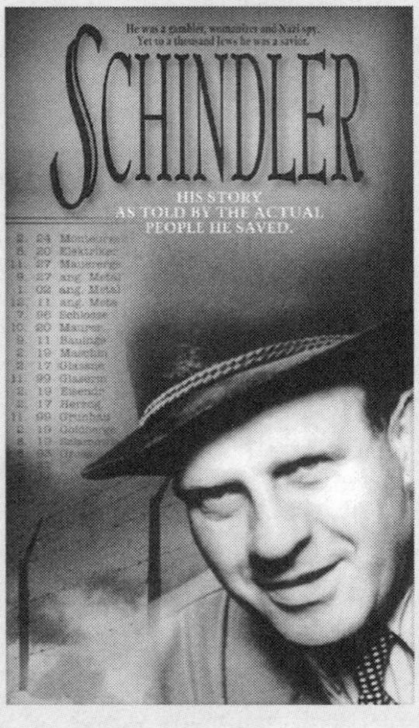

Schindler (1983)
In this powerful and revealing documentary, the life of Oskar Schindler—the subject of "Schindler's List—is chronicled. With archival footage and interviews with the businessman's widow, his driver, the mistress of Amon Goeth (aka "The Butcher of Plaszow") and others, an unforgettable portrait of the man who saved 1,100 Jews from death is painted. 82 min.
44-1963 Was $49.99 *$14.99*

Raoul Wallenberg: Between The Lines (1984)
Acclaimed documentary on Raoul Wallenberg, the Swedish diplomat who defended the Jewish population of Budapest from the Nazis, only to be imprisoned after the war by the Russians. Could he still be alive? Interviews with colleagues and Holocaust survivors and rare newsreel footage help tell this fascinating true story. 85 min.
15-5164 *$29.99*

Shoah (1985)
Director Claude Lanzmann's epic 9-1/2-hour Holocaust documentary eschews previously seen film footage for interviews with death camp survivors, workers and former Nazi officials, all witnesses to the horror, contrasted with glimpses of the camps today. "Shoah" (Hebrew for "annihilation") is a remarkable, insightful look at the unthinkable and unforgettable. 563 min. total. In English and other languages with English subtitles.
06-1355 *$299.99*

Partisans Of Vilna (1986)
Passionate, inspiring World War II documentary that recounts the story of the brave men and women who inhabited the predominantly Jewish Lithuanian town and their determined efforts to undermine the Nazi juggernaut. A fascinating profile in courage. 130 min.
75-1002 *$69.99*

Survivors Of The Holocaust (1986)
The almost unimaginable tragedy of the Holocaust is brought into achingly personal focus, as survivors recount to their families and the viewers what they witnessed before, during and after the Nazi atrocities. Archival film footage adds to the emotional power of this remarkable documentary presented by Steven Spielberg, who is featured in a special discussion. 54 min.
18-7611 ❑*$19.99*

Hotel Terminus: The Life And Times Of Klaus Barbie (1988)
Winner of both the Best Documentary Academy Award and the Cannes International Critics Prize, Marcel Ophuls' riveting film details the heinous crimes committed by the S. S. "Butcher of Lyon," his escape after the war and the subsequent global search, and his capture in 1983. 267 min. on two tapes.
74-1066 Was $29.99 *$19.99*

Weapons Of The Spirit (1989)
Enlightening documentary focusing on the inhabitants of the French town of Le Chambonsur-Lignon, who helped save 5,000 Jews from the Nazis. Directed by Pierre Sauvage, this acclaimed film offers fascinating interviews and archival footage. 90 min.
48-7020 *$59.99*

The Cross And The Star: Jews, Christians And The Holocaust (1992)
Where were foreign governments, organized religion and Christian neighbors when the Nazi atrocities were happening? This thought-provoking documentary by John J. Michalczyk, a Jesuit priest, examines this and other questions regarding anti-Semitism throughout history by using archival footage of Nazi Germany, propaganda films and interviews with Holocaust survivors and clergy members. 55 min.
70-5044 Was $59.99 *$29.99*

Good Evening, Mr. Wallenberg (1993)
A compassionate account of Raoul Wallenberg, the businessman who saved the lives of thousands of Jews in the Budapest ghetto with help from the Swedish Embassy. This documentary explores the man and his triumphant achievement in rescuing others from death. 115 min. In Swedish with English subtitles.
53-7944 Was $89.99 *$19.99*

The Eighty-First Blow (1974)
An Academy Award nominee for Best Documentary that uses film footage shot by the Nazis and testimony by witnesses in the Eichmann trial to tell the horrifying story of the Jewish ghettos. 115 min.
48-5040 *$79.99*

One Survivor Remembers (1995)
Home Box Office and the United States Holocaust Memorial Museum teamed to produce this Academy Award-winning look at Holocaust survivor Gerda Weissmann Klein and her memories of the horrors she faced during world War II. Interviews, photographs and haunting footage help tell her haunting true story. 39 min.
76-7440 *$39.99*

Varian Fry: The Artist's Schindler (1997)
Chagall, Duchamp, Ernst...these were but a few of the over 2,000 people, including dozens of noted artists, writers and intellectuals, who escaped Nazi persecution thanks to the efforts of American teacher/journalist Varian Fry. Learn about his dangerous missions inside occupied Europe in this amazing real-life tale of heroism and intrigue. 50 min.
22-6078 *$29.99*

The Last Transfer (1997)
Compelling factual study looks at the Holocaust survivors living in the psycho-geriatric ward of Abarnel Hospital in Bat-Yam, Israel, who face the horrors they encountered years ago on a daily basis. The film questions whether their lengthy hospitalization is the result of trauma, the war or the neglect of Israeli society. 55 min.
53-6849 *$29.99*

The Lost Children Of Berlin (1997)
Fifty Holocaust survivors, students of the last Jewish school in Berlin before the Gestapo closed it in 1942, returned to the reopened school in 1996 to share their accounts of what Jewish life was like before, during and after the brutal reign of the Third Reich. Anthony Hopkins hosts this emotional program. 50 min.
53-9818 *$19.99*

The Long Way Home (1997)
Germany's fall and the liberation of Nazi death camps by Allied forces in 1945 didn't end the suffering of Europe's Jews, as chronicled in director Mark Jonathan Harris' Academy Award-winning documentary. Archival film footage and interviews detail how the treatment Holocaust survivors faced (which sometimes included placement in overcrowded "displaced person" camps) led to massive immigration drives to Palestine and the push for the establishment of a Jewish homeland. 120 min.
82-9011 *$19.99*

The Last Days (1998)
The winner of the Academy Award for Best Documentary Feature, this unforgettable film details the incredible stories of five people who survived the Holocaust in WWII Hungary. A grandmother, a teacher, a businessman, an artist and a U.S. Congressman recount their horrific pasts and return to Hungary to relive their experiences. Directed by James Moll and produced by Steven Spielberg. 87 min.
02-9107 Was $99.99 *$14.99*

Kovno Ghetto: A Buried History (1998)
Learn the incredible true story of the courageous people of the Kovno Ghetto during World War II. Before Hitler came to power, almost 35,000 Jews lived in Kovno, Lithuania. Few escaped the Holocaust, but now, thanks to the photography of survivor Zvi Kadushin, as well as interviews with 18 other survivors, their story will never be forgotten. Narrated by historian Sir Martin Gilbert. 100 min.
53-6214 *$19.99*

There Once Was A Town (1999)
Acclaimed documentary surveys the remarkable journey of four survivors of Eishyshok, Poland, where, in 1941, the Germans murdered nearly all of its 3,500 Jewish residents. Narrated by Edward Asner, a descendant of an Eishyshok family. 90 min.
22-6101 *$29.99*

Kamikaze: Death From The Sky
The true story of the Japanese pilots who flew suicide missions into U.S. ships during World War II, including graphic footage from the final 10 months of the war in the Pacific—the most intense period of Kamikaze activity. 60 min.
50-6876 Was $29.99 *$14.99*

The Horrors Of War
A chilling look at war atrocities in the 20th century, this graphic documentary was censored for many years. Scenes from Nazi concentration camps and other shocking WWII are featured. 60 min.
10-1185 *$19.99*

The Unknown Soldier
Jason Robards narrates this tribute to the thousands of fighting men and women declared "missing in action" in America's wars, and looks at the history of Arlington National Cemetery's Tomb of the Unknowns, heroes "known but to God." 58 min.
22-5085 *$19.99*

Thunderbolt (1945)
Thrilling color photography of the Allied invasions of Italy and France highlights this WWII documentary, produced under the auspices of William Wyler and John Sturges. 45 min.
10-1164 *$14.99*

Empire Of The Rising Sun, Vol. 1
This program looks at Japan's involvement in World War II, tracing the events that led to their decision to attack Pearl Harbor and draw the United States into the war; features rare newsreel footage. 59 min.
10-1288 *$19.99*

Empire Of The Rising Sun, Vol. 2
Japan's role in World War II, from "the day that will live in infamy" to their eventual surrender to America, is chronicled in this program that uses vintage newsreel clips. 59 min.
10-1289 *$19.99*

Let There Be Light (1944)
A powerful look at the human cost of war, director John Huston's acclaimed (and long-suppressed) documentary chronicles the lives of shell-shocked WWII veterans in an Army hospitals and the efforts to return them to society. Walter Huston narrates. 58 min.
01-1279 *$19.99*

Combat America! (1943)
Tremendous WWII documentary, produced by the U.S. Army and narrated by Army Air Force officer Clark Gable, that follows a B-17 crew from their training to their missions over the skies of Europe. 61 min.
65-5027 Was $29.99 *$19.99*

Mein Krieg (My Private War) (1993)
This unusual and powerful look at World War II features footage taken by the home movie cameras of six young German infantrymen. The cameras capture training, combat and the day-to-day workings of the Nazi war machine as it moves towards Russia in 1942. 90 min. In German with English subtitles.
53-8866 Was $79.99 ***$24.99***

Vlasov: General For Two Devils (1995)
One of the most controversial figures of World War II, Soviet General Andrei Vlasov was captured by German forces in 1942 and eventually agreed to lead a Russian Liberation Army to attempt to overthrow Stalin. This compelling documentary looks at Vlasov's ill-fated choices and examines whether he was a traitor or a patriot. 59 min.
65-1076 ***$29.99***

Fire Storm Over Dresden (1997)
The 1945 Allied bombing of Dresden is still a source of debate today. The horror of what it was like to be in the town during the bombing is recounted through witnesses's first-hand accounts and a 1990 memorial service. 77 min.
65-1064 ***$29.99***

Hans-Joachim Marseille: The Star Of Africa (1997)
One of history's greatest WWII fighting aces is spotlighted this intriguing program from Germany. Exclusive interviews with Marseille's commanding officer and surviving squadron mates are intercut with previously unavailable footage of his incredible aerial feats. 47 min.
65-1067 ***$29.99***

Fire On The Mountain (1997)
Superior documentary chronicling the story of the U.S. Army's 10th Mountain Division, an amalgamation of world-class skiers, mountaineers and climbers who participated in mountain and winter warfare in World War II. Astonishing footage and remembrances of its members—many of whom went on to great post-war success—help bring this little-known piece of history to life. 72 min.
70-5104 Was $29.99 ***$19.99***

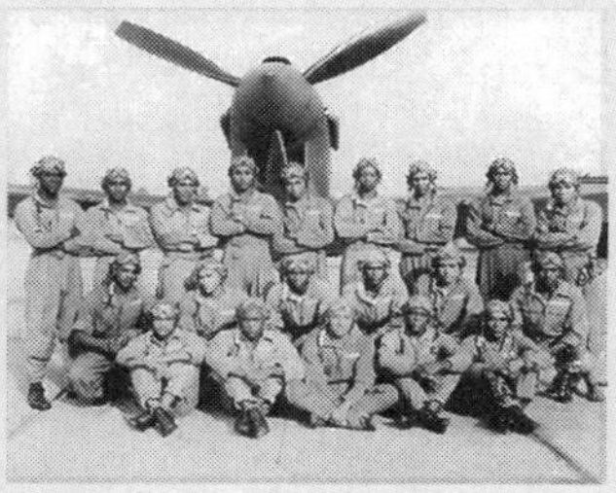

African-American Heroes Of World War II
Terrific collection of wartime documentaries focusing on the African-American experience during World War II. "From These Beginnings" looks at the Army Air Corps training program at Tuskegee Institute for flyers; "Jubilee: Strictly G.I." tells of the hip black radio show popular with black soldiers, and features performances by Lena Horne and Eddie "Rochester" Anderson; and "Tuskegee Airmen" delves into the triumphs of the heroic pilots. 46 min.
76-7336 ***$19.99***

Liberators: Fighting On Two Fronts In World War II
This powerful film looks at the efforts of African-American battalions in World War II, focusing on the work of the 761st Tank Battalion, which spearheaded General Patton's Third Army and liberated the Dachau, Lambach and Buchenwald concentration camps. Witness how these soldiers braved discrimination both at home and while fighting overseas. 90 min.
76-7438 ***$39.99***

African Americans In WWII: A Legacy Of Patriotism And Valor
Though they faced prejudice at home, they bravely fought for freedom in Europe and the Pacific. This documentary tribute to the contributions of African-American men and women in World War II uses interviews and rare film footage to tell the story of the Tuskegee Airmen, the Red Ball Express, the 92nd Infantry Division, and other notable military heroes. 60 min.
89-5076 ***$19.99***

Tuskegee Airmen: American Heroes!
Fighting racial prejudice and opening up doors for many to come, the 332nd Fighter Group and the 99th Fighter Squadron—the Tuskegee Airmen—are saluted in this extraordinary program that chronicles their days of combat and escort duty during World War II. Using archival footage and never-before-seen interviews, this is an experience not be missed. Narrated by Ossie Davis. 50 min.
89-5105 ***$19.99***

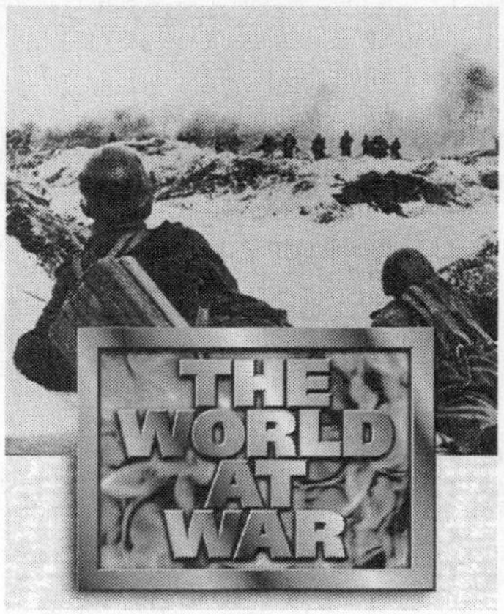

The World At War: Complete Set (1974)
The much-lauded documentary series chronicles the events of World War II through the experiences of the men and women—soldiers, military leaders, historians and innocent victims—on both sides of the most momentous conflict in world history. Along with the original 26 episodes, this nine-tape boxed set includes two bonus programs: "Secretary to Hitler" and "From War to Peace." Narrated by Laurence Olivier. 26 hrs. total.
44-2014 Was $469.99 ***$99.99***

Hiroshima: Why The Bomb Was Dropped
What convinced the Truman Administration to use the atomic bomb on Japan? Were non-civilian areas originally targeted? Was the Japanese government willing to surrender before the bombing? Host Peter Jennings examines these and other questions in an ABC News special that features incredible footage of Hiroshima after the bomb was dropped and the human toll. 67 min.
50-7500 ***$19.99***

Suicide Missions: Dangerous Tours Of Duty: Boxed Set
Amazing frontline footage highlights this intense four-tape series that puts you in the middle of some of the most dangerous combat situations imaginable. Watch as fighting men put their lives on the line in "Ball Turret Gunners," "Combat Medics," "Snipers" and "Wild Weasels." 200 min. total.
53-6664 ***$39.99***

Attila '74: The Rape Of Cyprus (1974)
Compelling and highly personal record from Cyprus-born filmmaker Michael Cacoyannis ("Zorba the Greek") of the Turkish invasion of his homeland. Cacoyannis journeyed to the heart of the conflict with only a cameraman and soundman, and the end result is a devastating portrait of a land in turmoil. 101 min. In Greek with English subtitles.
53-9041 Was $59.99 ***$19.99***

The Mercenary Game (1981)
A fascinating look at real-life Rambos, this documentary looks at "soldiers of fortune" who travel the world, gun in hand, to fight wherever the money's good. Controversial film includes an actual commando raid being filmed. 60 min.
50-6096 ***$19.99***

Battle For The Falklands (1984)
After 150 years of uninterrupted British rule, peace on the Falkland Islands was broken by the invasion of Argentinean forces, and you can be witness to the events and battles that captured the world's attention. 110 min.
50-6352 ***$39.99***

Fly Girls
The brave women who served in the skies during World War II are the focus of this stirring documentary, originally broadcast on PBS's "The American Experience." See how mothers, wives, working women and others joined the Women Airforce Service Pilots and made an important contribution, test-piloting aircraft, ferrying planes and logging millions of miles of airtime. 60 min.
90-1042 ***$19.99***

The Big Picture: General Patton/World War II Battlefields Revisited
Produced in the mid-'60s by the U.S. Army, this documentary double feature includes a look at the life of the maverick WWII general known as "Old Blood and Guts", narrated by Ronald Reagan, followed by a moving visit to such battle sites as Normandy, Cherbourg, Saint-Lo, Aachen and Bastogne. 56 min. total.
09-3106 ***$14.99***

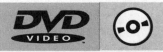

The U.S.-Mexican War: 1846-1848 (1998)
It was a conflict between neighbors for freedom as well as greed, and while it officially only lasted for two years, the origins stretched back for decades. This two-part PBS special chronicles the war's history, from Texas' battle for independence from Mexico to the battles that ended with the United States gaining not only Texas, but also California and the Southwest. 240 min.
90-1009 ***$29.99***

Follow Me: The Story Of The Six-Day War
The world held its breath for one tense week in 1967, as Arab nations went to war against Israel. Rarely seen frontline footage highlights this documentary look at the conflict that changed the map of, and balance of power in, the Middle East. 95 min.
17-5012 ***$39.99***

The Yom Kippur War
An unflinching look at the October, 1973 war, when Egypt joined Syria to attack Israel on Yom Kippur, Judaism's holiest day. The war is viewed on the frontline, along with the reaction to the fighting by the people of Israel. 30 min.
17-5021 ***$39.99***

Battle For Survival: The Arab-Israeli Six Day War
This amazing documentary was filmed by a Canadian TV crew, the only such unit allowed behind the lines in the aftermath of the 1967 conflict that saw Israel launch an attack and, despite overwhelming odds, defeat the armies of Egypt, Jordan and Syria. Included in the program is the rare film "Strike Zion!," presented for the first time on home video. NOTE: Some sound and picture imperfections exist. 60 min.
89-5106 ***$19.99***

Frontline: The Gulf War
Some stunning revelations about Operation Desert Storm and its aftermath are made in this acclaimed program that offers spectacular footage and interviews with Generals Schwarzkopf and Powell, as well as with such world leaders as Margaret Thatcher and Mikhail Gorbachev. 240 min.
50-5232 ***$39.99***

Schwarzkopf: How The War Was Won (1991)
Get the full story on Operation Desert Storm from America's newest military hero, General "Stormin' Norman" Schwarzkopf. News footage and press conferences with "The Bear" detail the Allied campaign against Iraq, from the early days of Desert Shield to the awesome air campaign and ground battles against Saddam Hussein's forces, and the final victory. 70 min.
50-6733 ***$19.99***

MacArthur
As admired as he was criticized, General Douglas MacArthur took on not only the armies of Japan and North Korea, but even his own commander-in-chief. This "American Experience" program takes you through the public and personal sides of one of the country's great military leaders. 240 min.
19-2842 ***$29.99***

The True Glory (1945)
General Dwight D. Eisenhower's Oscar-winning documentary shows how Allied forces smashed Hitler's war machine. The battle footage utilizes the voice of real men, women, nurses and townspeople who were there! 86 min.
09-1809 ***$14.99***

Patton: Old Blood And Guts
Remarkable, comprehensive biography of one of WWII's most successful and controversial generals, tracing from his childhood to his most impressive battlefield victories. Narration provided by Ronald Reagan. 25 min.
50-6226 ***$14.99***

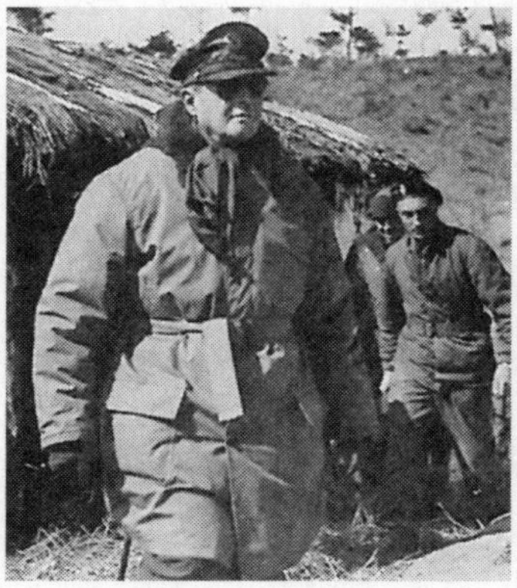

American Caesar: Boxed Set
Military genius, national hero, figure of controversy...General Douglas MacArthur was all of these things and more. Follow the life and career of the man who led America to victory in the Pacific in World War II, and who went head-to-head with Truman over the Korean War, in this four-tape documentary series based on William Manchester's best-selling biography. John Huston hosts. 240 min.
82-9042 Was $69.99 ***$49.99***

Triumph Of The Will (1934)
The most famous propaganda film of all time! Leni Riefenstahl's documentary, commissioned personally by Hitler, is a masterpiece of cinematography and a spellbinding look at the early days of Nazism as depicted during the 1934 Nuremberg rallies. 122 min. In German with English subtitles.
53-1798 ***$29.99***

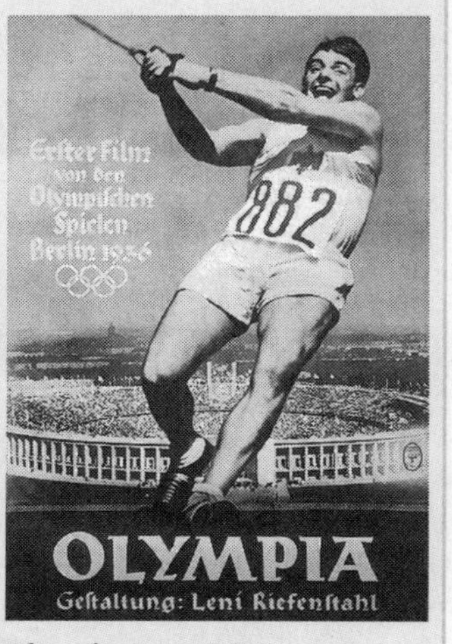

Olympia, Parts I & II: Complete Set (1938)
Commissioned by the Nazi government to film the 1936 Berlin Olympic Games, documentarian Leni Riefenstahl fashioned a mesmerizing tribute to athletic grace and beauty, while juxtaposing the Olympian spirit of Ancient Greece to "the ideals of National Socialism." Part one features the opening ceremonies, marathon, high-dive and more. Part two covers events around the stadium and Olympic village, as well as swimming, equestrian, the Pentathlon, the Decathlon and more. 215 min. total. NOTE: Individual volumes available at $29.99.
22-5899 Save $10.00! ***$49.99***

The Wonderful, Horrible Life Of Leni Riefenstahl (1993)
Despite her fame as an actress and director in the '20s and '30s, German filmmaker Leni Riefenstahl will best be remembered as the creator of the modern propaganda film with "Triumph of the Will" and "Olympia." In this acclaimed documentary, the 90-year-old Riefenstahl talks candidly about her work under the Nazi regime, her alleged personal relationships with Hitler and Goebbels, and how her artistic drive blinded her to the realities of the Third Reich. 186 min. In German with English subtitles.
53-8127 Was $89.99 ***$39.99***

Archives Of War: Boxed Set
Trace the evolution of 20th-century warfare in this special six-part series that uses combat and documentary footage from around the world to depict the defining conflicts of the era. Included are "World War I and the Interwar Years" (which features the U.S. premiere of the classic 1925 film short "The Battle of Ypres"), "World War II—The Leaders," "World War II—The Battles," "The Cold War," "Korea" and "Vietnam." 570 min. total. NOTE: Vols. 1-4 are available at $19.99 each; Vols. 5 and 6 are $14.99 each.
50-7622 Save $10.00! ***$99.99***

Making Marines
"All right, you mewling mama's boys, listen up! Do you have what it takes to watch this intense look at a group of Marine Corps recruits undergoing the grueling 12-week basic training course at Parris Island, South Carolina? Can you survive the rigorous exercises, culminating in 54 hours of simulated combat known as 'the Crucible'? If not, drop and give me 20!" 52 min.
27-7201 ***$14.99***

Enola Gay And The Atomic Bombing Of Japan
World history was forever changed on the morning of August 6, 1945 over the skies of the Japanese city of Hiroshima. This compelling documentary features interviews with the men who took part in the bombing run of the Enola Gay, as well as rare, never-before-seen film footage taken by the Army Air Corps. 75 min.
53-8343 ***$19.99***

Weapons Of War
Get an up-close look at the hardware of warfare with this fascinating documentary series that examines planes, tanks and bombs that have changed the course of military history. Each tape runs about 50 min. There are five volumes available, including:

Weapons Of War: The Hydrogen Bomb
64-1228 ***$19.99***

Weapons Of War: The Atomic Bomb
64-1229 ***$19.99***

Beyond Barbed Wire
This stirring and inspiring documentary tells of the American-born Japanese who fought in World War II for the U.S. in order to prove their loyalty, even as their families were held in internment camps. The "Nisei" who comprised the 442nd Infantry eventually become the most decorated unit in American military history. Noriyuki "Pat" Morita narrates this acclaimed film.
53-6449 *$29.99*

Robot Warriors
Is the frontline soldier about to go the way of the town crier, iceman and blacksmith? See how remote-controlled weapons, from 116-foot-wide Global Hawk aircraft to dragonfly-sized robotic warriors, promise to change the face of military conflict. 52 min.
27-7202 *$14.99*

The Battle Of San Pietro (1945)/ The Marines Have Landed
Two acclaimed WWII documentaries. John Huston's "San Pietro" is a stirring look at an Italian farming community that was turned into a battlefield; "Marines" salutes the fighting men in action with thrilling newsreel footage. 60 min.
10-7948 Was $19.99 *$14.99*

Yankee Samurai: The Little Iron Men
Provocative examination of the 100-442nd regiment of the United States Army, which consisted of 4,800 Japanese-American combat soldiers who battled bravely against the enemy in Europe and against prejudice and discrimination at home. 50 min.
50-6353 *$29.99*

They Drew Fire: Combat Artists Of World War II (1999)
With pencils, pens and paintbrushes they captured the heroism, horror, tragedy and triumph of warfare. In this moving program you'll learn the little-known story of the more than 100 servicemen and civilians whose job it was to tell the story of World War II through their art. 57 min.
22-6086 *□$19.99*

Warbirds Of World War II
This seven-tape collection looks at the major military planes of World War II, including the B-17 "Flying Fortress," P-47 "Thunderbolts," P-51 "Mustangs," B-14 "Liberators," P-40 "Warhawks," the P-38 "Lightning" and the B-29 "Superfortress." 300 min. total.
16-5024 *$49.99*

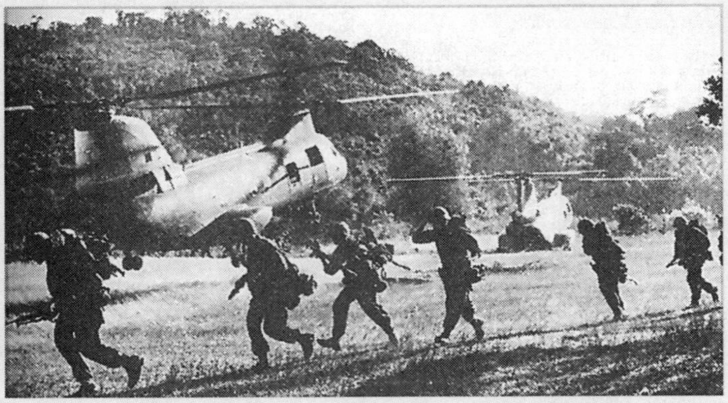

Vietnam: In The Year Of The Pig (1968)
Emile de Antonio's award-winning documentary (Grand prize at Cannes, Academy Award nominee) is a harrowing, thought-provoking look at the drama and bloodshed of the war in Southeast Asia. It is a controversial excursion through the horror of the Vietnam experience. 103 min.
50-6059 *$39.99*

Vietnam: Remember (1968)
Two 1968 documentaries on the men and missions of America's longest war. First is the story of The Battle of Khe Sanh, where U.S. forces suffered a devastating blow. Next, follow a jungle incursion squad on a mission into enemy territory, where ambush is a constant fear. 60 min.
50-6187 *$39.99*

Vietnam: A Television History: Complete Set (1985)
The Emmy-winning, 13-episode PBS series, presented here in a seven-volume set, takes an exhaustive look at America's longest and most controversial conflict. Included are "Roots of a War/The First Vietnam War," "America's Mandarin/LBJ Goes to War," "America Takes Charge/America's Enemy," "Tet 1968/Vietnamizing the War," "Cambodia and Laos/Peace Is at Hand," "Homefront USA/The End of the Tunnel" and "Legacies." 780 min. total. NOTE: Volumes 1-6 available separately at $29.99 each; Volume 7 available at $19.99.
45-5280 Save $100.00! *□$99.99*

The Vietnam War

Vietnam Experience
Archival film footage depicting the American soldier in combat in Vietnam is interspersed with the music of the decade to bring you a truly enduring musical and visual experience. Features songs from Country Joe McDonald. 30 min.
50-6223 *$19.99*

Situation Critical: The USS Forrestal
In July of 1967 a fire broke out on the deck of the aircraft carrier USS Forrestal, stationed off the coast of North Vietnam, that burned for four days and was responsible for over 100 deaths. See amazing footage from on-board TV cameras of the tragic accident, and hear amazing rescue stories from surviving crew members. 50 min.
53-9921 Was $19.99 *$14.99*

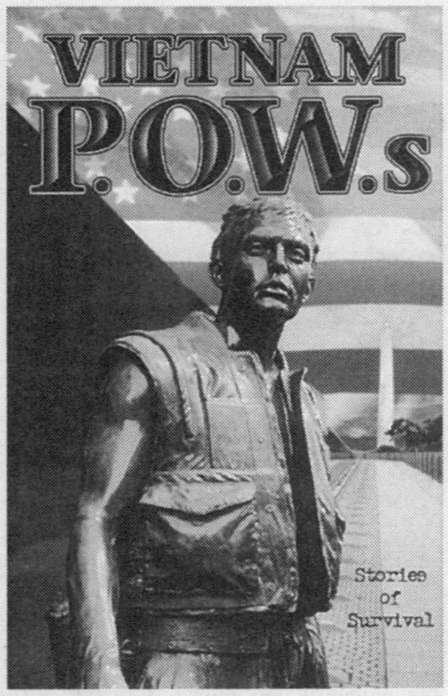

Vietnam P.O.W.s: Stories Of Survival
Hear the harrowing, heroic true stories of Vietnam War veterans, including Senator John McCain, who survived the ordeal of captivity by North Vietnamese forces. Remarkable film footage taken from inside the "Hanoi Hilton" and other prison camps helps bring their tales of torture, determination and courage to life. 52 min.
83-1507 *$14.99*

The Battle Of Khe Sanh/ Screaming Eagles In Vietnam
Superlative frontline footage highlights these Vietnam documentaries. First American forces secure a Viet Cong-held region below the DMZ in one of the war's most significant battles, followed by a look at the Air Force's 101st Battalion, charged with clearing territory for ground forces. 60 min. total.
10-2129 *$12.99*

Vietnam: The Soldiers' Story
Remarkable combat footage from ABC News and never-before-seen North Vietnamese film, along with emotional first-hand accounts by the men who fought the battles, let this three-tape series show you the real stories behind the Vietnam War. Volumes include "Ambush!: The Battle of Ia Drang/Under Siege at Khe Sanh," "Tet: The Battle for Hearts and Minds/War in the Skies" and "Secret Wars, Secret Men/Last Chopper Out: The Fall of Saigon." Vietnam vet and ABC News correspondent Jack Smith hosts. 312 min. total.
19-9247 *□$59.99*

Choosing Sides: I Remember Vietnam: Complete Set
Whether they supported or opposed it, few Americans in the '60s and '70s were neutral on the Vietnam War. This two-part series takes a personal look at the conflict through interviews with people on both sides of the issue, from senator and former POW John McCain to West Point graduate-turned-anti-war advocate Jan Barry, along with combat footage and period music. Episodes include "Fields of Fire" and "The War at Home." 96 min. total. NOTE: Individual volumes available at $19.99 each.
53-8860 Save $10.00! *$29.99*

Vietnam Newsreel Review: 1967
Eighteen newsclips taken by the Air Force's 600th Photo Squadron give the viewer a rare look into military activity and everyday life at the height of the Indochina conflict. Bomber and fighter raids on enemy targets, airlift and reconnaissance missions, Armed Forces broadcasts and other "you are there" footage is included. 50 min.
65-1020 *$34.99*

The Anderson Platoon (1967)
One of the first documentaries made about the Vietnam War, this Oscar-winning French production follows the day-to-day maneuvers of a group of American soldiers deep in the Southeast Asian jungle. Directed by French Vietnam veteran Pierre Schoendoerffer. 64 min.
22-5087 *$19.99*

A Face Of War (1967)
For 97 days director Eugene Jones and a three-man crew trekked through the Vietnam jungle with the "point squad" of a Marine platoon. The resulting documentary is an unflinching look at war up close, from jungle patrols and twilight Viet Cong attacks to a child's birth in a village and a danger-filled mission that results in more than one death (the filmmakers themselves were wounded several times). 77 min.
65-1021 *$39.99*

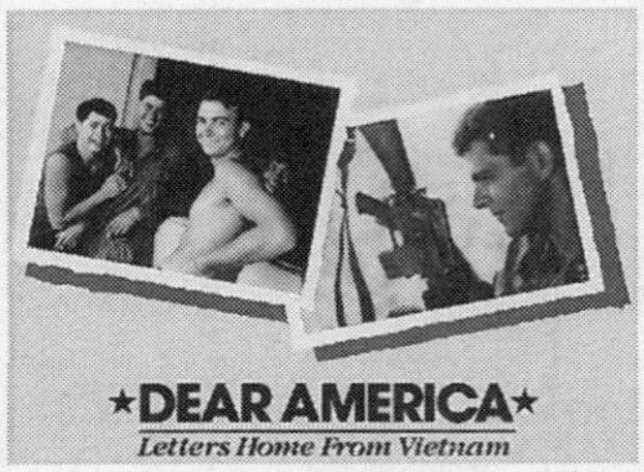

Dear America: Letters Home From Vietnam (1987)
This is the real story of the Vietnam War, captured in the words and images of the men and women who served, fought, and all too often died there. Soldiers' letters to their loved ones are read by stars like Robert De Niro, Willem Dafoe, Sean Penn, Michael J. Fox and Kathleen Turner, accompanied by combat newsreel footage and "home movies" from the frontlines. Music by Jimi Hendrix, Bruce Springsteen, and The Doors. 84 min.
44-1586 Was $89.99 *□$19.99*

Starting Place (1993)
Twenty-five years after touring Vietnam in his controversial documentary "People's War," filmmaker Robert Kramer returns to Southeast Asia and revisits some of the subjects of his earlier effort. His experiences in the country today are moving, bittersweet and stimulating. 80 min. In English and Vietnamese with English subtitles.
53-8505 *$39.99*

Maya Lin: A Strong Clear Vision (1994)
Winner of the Academy Award for Best Documentary Feature, this stirring film looks at the moving story of the 20-year-old Asian-American student whose winning design for Washington's Vietnam Veterans Memorial ignited a nationwide controversy. See how the simple black wall weathered protests to become one of the capital's most visited sites, and follow Lin's subsequent career and such later works as Montgomery, Alabama's Civil Rights Monument. 98 min.
76-7312 *$69.99*

Regret To Inform (1998)
A unique perspective on the Vietnam War—as seen by women on both sides of the conflict who lost their husbands and families—is offered in this award-winning documentary. On the 20th anniversary of her first husband's death, filmmaker Barbara Sonneborn travels to Southeast Asia to retrace his final days and talks to American and Vietnamese war widows. Their remembrances make for a heart-wrenching and unforgettable experience. 78 min.
53-6707 *$24.99*

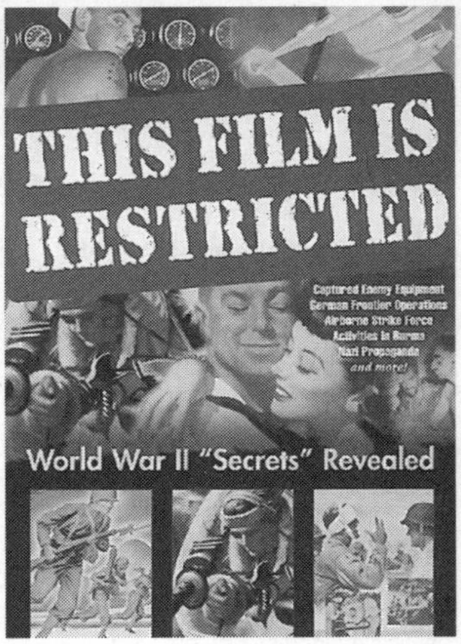

This Film Is Restricted: Complete Set
Inside secrets of World War II are revealed in this seven-tape series filled with formally classified United States Armed Forces films from the 1940s. Among the segments featured are "Embarkation to Anzio," "Invasion of Southern France," "Battle for Lorraine," "British Take Antwerp," "The Holland Front," "European Front" and "Advance in Burma." 390 min. total.
16-5026 *$49.99*

U.S.S. Intrepid: The Story Of The "Fighting I"
She saw her baptism of fire in the Battle of Leyte Gulf, and for many years thereafter the U.S.S. Intrepid served America in wartime (from World War II to Vietnam) and in peace (recovering returning astronauts). Along with exciting combat footage of the "Fighting I" and her crew in action, this documentary looks at the ship's new life as a floating museum in New York City. 50 min.
53-8412 *$19.99*

Conspiracy Of War: Boxed Set
This three-tape set offers an incisive peek into the world of classified military weaponry and restricted information. Episodes include "The Killing Machines," a look at the history and future of advanced weapons; "Down in Flames," a study of aerial tragedies; and "Silent and Deadly," involving spy planes and stealth technology. 103 min. total. NOTE: Individual volumes available at $14.99 each.
83-1273 Save $15.00! *$29.99*

The Hidden Army: Women In World War II
The vital roles played by women on the homefront and in the battle theater are examined in three wartime documentaries. "The Hidden Army" and "Women in Defense," which was written by Eleanor Roosevelt and narrated by Katharine Hepburn, look at the efforts of the 18 million females who joined the lines of America's factories and defense plants, while "Army and Navy Nurse P.O.W.s in WWII: They All Came Home" uses interviews and archival footage to tell the story of Allied nurses taken prisoner by the Japanese in the Pacific. 57 min.
76-7334 *$19.99*

Die Kriegsmarine
Long sought by collectors and war buffs, this double feature offers two rare German-made documentaries on WWII naval warfare. See life on board the German battle cruiser Scharnhorst, then watch as merchant ships are transformed into deadly "Q-boats." 45 min. total.
65-1030 *$49.99*

The Stilwell Road (1945)
U.S. Government documentary narrated by Ronald Reagan. A look at the Chinese-Burmese-Indian conflict, told with incredible footage. 46 min.
01-5083 *$14.99*

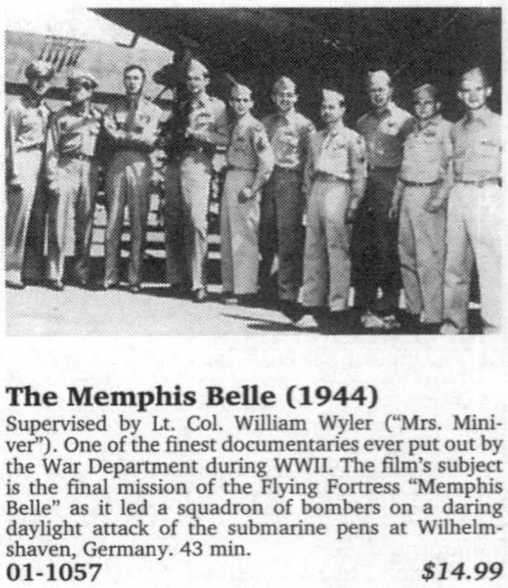

The Memphis Belle (1944)
Supervised by Lt. Col. William Wyler ("Mrs. Miniver"). One of the finest documentaries ever put out by the War Department during WWII. The film's subject is the final mission of the Flying Fortress "Memphis Belle" as it led a squadron of bombers on a daring daylight attack of the submarine pens at Wilhelmshaven, Germany. 43 min.
01-1057 *$14.99*

The Audrey Hepburn Story (2000)
She overcame a childhood of hardship and abandonment to become one of the world's best-loved screen heroines. Jennifer Love Hewitt stars as Audrey Hepburn in this lavish biodrama that follows her life from her early days in war-torn Europe to the stage and film roles that won her international acclaim. Eric McCormack, Frances Fisher, Gabriel Macht also star. 133 min.
02-3444 ❑*$19.99*

Girl (2000)
In this coming-of-age tale, Dominique Swain ("Lolita") plays a high school senior with good grades who seeks some spark in her life as she's about to enter college. Hoping to "become a woman," Swain searches for excitement in the seedier part of town, where she falls for a singer in a rock band and ditches her straightforward lifestyle. With Sean Patrick Flanery, Selma Blair. 99 min.
02-3455 ❑*$99.99*

Black And White (2000)
Controversial study of race, class and music by James Toback ("Two Girls and a Guy") looks at a group of New Yorkers taking on different identities, including wealthy white teens who adopt the hip-hop lifestyle and rap musicians trying to cross over to a white market. Brooke Shields, Robert Downey, Jr., Ben Stiller, Allan Houston, Claudia Schiffer, Elijah Wood and Mike Tyson star. 99 min.
02-3460 ❑*$99.99*

Center Stage (2000)
This exhilarating dance drama follows the trials and tribulations of three students attending the esteemed American Ballet Academy in New York. Maureen is a hard-working talent with issues with her mother; good-looking Jody struggles with her dancing dynamics; and Eva's anti-authority feelings hamper her potential. Susan May Pratt, Amanda Schull and Zoe Saldana star. 116 min.
02-3472 ❑*$99.99*

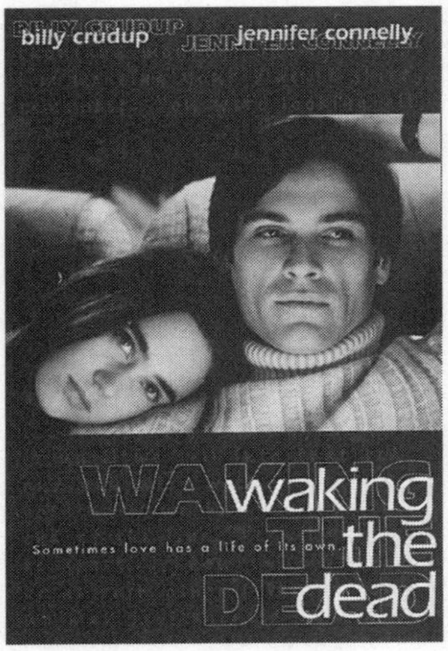

Waking The Dead (2000)
A haunting and romantic drama, with Billy Crudup as a Coast Guard officer and rising lawyer in the early 1970s whose relationship with social activist Jennifer Connelly is strained over their political differences. Ten years later, after Connelly is killed in a car bombing, congressional candidate Crudup begins having visions of her and starts to question her death and his sanity. Molly Parker, Janet McTeer and Hal Holbrook also star in this time-hopping tale from Keith Gordon ("A Midnight Clear"). 106 min.
02-9273 ❑*$99.99*

The Price Of Glory (2000)
In this compelling drama, Jimmy Smits is a failed Mexican-American boxer living in a small Arizona town who is raising his three sons to be fighters. But Smits' attempts to control the lives of his children begin to interfere with their dreams, leading to family tension. Jon Seda, Clifton Collins, Jr., Ernesto Hernandez and Ron Perlman also star.
02-5236 ❑*$99.99*

Love & Basketball (2000)
Thrilling and sensitive story traces the lives of two hoops-loving teens and next-door neighbors—Monica (Sanna Lathan), who wants to be the first female NBA player, and Quincy (Omar Epps), who dreams of becoming a pro court star like his dad—from high school and college into adulthood, showing how their dedication to the game brings them together and keeps them apart. Alfre Woodard and Dennis Haysbert also star; produced by Spike Lee. 127 min.
02-5238 ❑*$99.99*

The Bumblebee Flies Anyway (2000)
This compelling drama stars Elijah Wood as an amnesia victim trying to piece his life together after a car accident. After receiving help from doctor Janeane Garofalo at a center for terminally ill youngsters, Wood befriends a group of patients and becomes romantically involved with one teen's sister, played by Rachael Leigh Cook. With Joseph Perrino, Roger Rees. 95 min.
02-9210 Was $99.99 *$14.99*

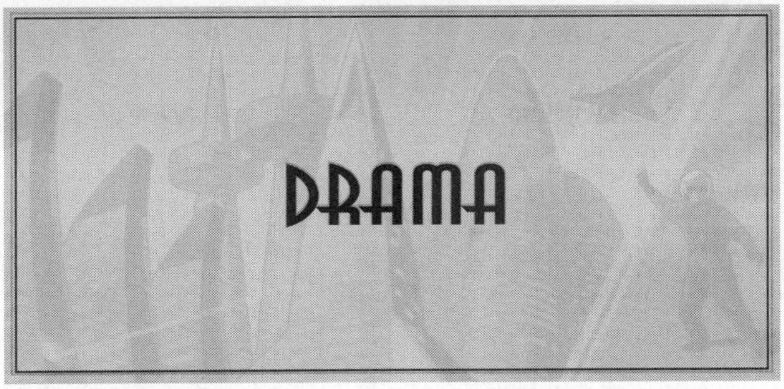

A Good Baby (2000)
Set in the backwoods of South Carolina, this acclaimed drama tells of Raymond (Henry Thomas), a recluse who tries to pawn off a baby he has found to different local women. When he has no takers, Raymond keeps the infant girl and soon grows attached to her. When the child's real father appears, Raymond must find a way to protect her. With David Strathairn. 88 min.
53-6980 *$59.99*

The Firing Squad (2000)
Compelling look at vigilante justice in the mean streets of the inner city, as a young woman's abuse by her gangster boyfriend drives the woman's best friend to try and take matters into her own hands, with deadly results. Kevin Mambo, Megahn Perry, Regina Williams star.
54-9196 *$24.99*

Madame Bovary (2000)
One of the most infamous novels of all time comes to life in this lush BBC production. Frances O'Connor stars in the title role of the 19th-century French woman whose desire to leave her loveless marriage and find happiness with another sows the seeds of her own destruction. With Greg Wise, Hugh Bonneville. 150 min.
04-3940 *$19.99*

The Next Best Thing (2000)
Madonna, a single woman approaching her forties, accidentally becomes impregnated by her best friend, gay gardener Rupert Everett, during an evening of drunkenness. Madonna decides to have the baby and raise the child with Everett, but when Madonna falls for Benjamin Bratt, a bitter custody battle ensues. With Michael Vartan, Josef Sommer and Lynn Redgrave. 108 min.
06-3007 Was $99.99 ❑*$14.99*

A House Divided (2000)
Fair-skinned Jennifer Beals, the product of a relationship between her plantation owner father and a slave, grows up believing herself to be white, only to learn the truth after her father dies and his will is disputed in court. Sam Waterston and Tim Daly also star in this antebellum drama based on historical events. 99 min.
06-3033 ❑*$49.99*

Starry Night (2000)
In this whimsical fantasy, Vincent van Gogh lands in Los Angeles 100 years after his death and is astounded to learn that his paintings—only one of which he was able to sell in his lifetime—now go for millions of dollars. The artist attempts to reclaim his works and cash in and winds up falling for a pretty art student. Abbott Alexander, Lisa Waltz, Sally Kirkland, Lou Wagner star. 98 min.
07-2920 ❑*$99.99*

Blood And Tears (2000)
Sir Dyno has just been released from San Quentin after nine years behind bars and is looking forward to spending time with his family and getting a clean start. But when a family member is killed by a local street hood, Sir Dyno is torn between seeking revenge or putting his criminal life behind him. This tense drama also features Angel Aviles, Cesar Herrera.
82-5212 *$49.99*

Hitman's Journal (2000)
Vincent (Danny Aiello) is looking to retire from his life as a hit man for mob boss Don Cucci. But that has to wait when the boss is sentenced to life after information is leaked to the feds and Vincent, fingered as the traitor, must work to clear his name. Also featuring William Forsythe, Polly Draper, Vincent Pastore and Aida Turturro. 95 min.
82-5217 *$89.99*

Kiss Of Fire (2000)
Christina Applegate will wow you as a young woman who shuns her wealthy family and takes a job as a laundress on an island off the coast of Georgia and also strips at a local club at night. Her life becomes even more complicated when she becomes involved with a young Italian drifter. Stefano Dionisi co-stars in this scorching, erotic drama. AKA: "Claudine's Return." 92 min.
11-2442 ❑*$99.99*

Deadlocked (2000)
When Charles S. Dutton's son is convicted of murder and sentenced to death, an enraged Dutton, convinced of the boy's innocence, holds the jury hostage. D.A. David Caruso must uncover evidence that will overturn the verdict in order to save the jurors' lives in this gripping thriller. Jo D. Linz, Jonn Finn also star. 90 min.
19-5002 ❑*$99.99*

Joe Gould's Secret (2000)
Director Stanley Tucci plays New Yorker writer Joe Mitchell, who formed a unique and at times antagonistic relationship with Joe Gould (Ian Holm), a charismatic homeless man who mooches off the artists and poets of '40s Greenwich Village while "working" on his monumental oral history of the world. After penning an article on Gould, Mitchell can't seem to shake his new, lonely pal. With Hope Davis, Steve Martin and Susan Sarandon.
02-9275 *$99.99*

Up At The Villa (2000)
Set in Florence in 1938 and based on a Somerset Maugham novella, this beautifully realized film stars Kristin Scott Thomas as a British widow who is put on the spot when British diplomat James Fox proposes marriage. A meeting with dashing American adventurer Sean Penn makes Thomas reconsider her decision and enlist Penn to thwart her wedding plans. Jeremy Davies, Anne Bancroft also star.
02-9276 *$99.99*

Here On Earth (2000)
Chris Klein is a snotty senior at a boys' prep school whose recklessness leads to a car crash and the destruction of a diner. Part of his probation involves rebuilding the eatery with townie rival John Hartnett, who was also involved in the crash. During the construction, Klein meets and falls in love with Leelee Sobieski, daughter of the diner's owners and Hartnett's girlfriend. Michael Rooker, Annie Corley and Annette O'Toole also star. 96 min.
04-3981 ❑*$99.99*

Timecode (2000)
Shot in real time on digital video and unfolding on four different sections of the screen, this experimental effort by Mike Figgis ("Leaving Las Vegas") presents a quartet of interconnected stories set in the Los Angeles moviemaking community. The first scene opens as Saffron Burrows tells her problems to therapist Glenne Headly, while actress Salma Hayek has an affair with lover Jeanne Tripplehorn's studio exec husband. Meanwhile, a group of producers discusses upcoming projects, and the casting for a film continues. With Holly Hunter, Kyle MacLachlan, Stellan Skarsgard, Steven Weber. 97 min.
02-3464 ❑*$99.99*

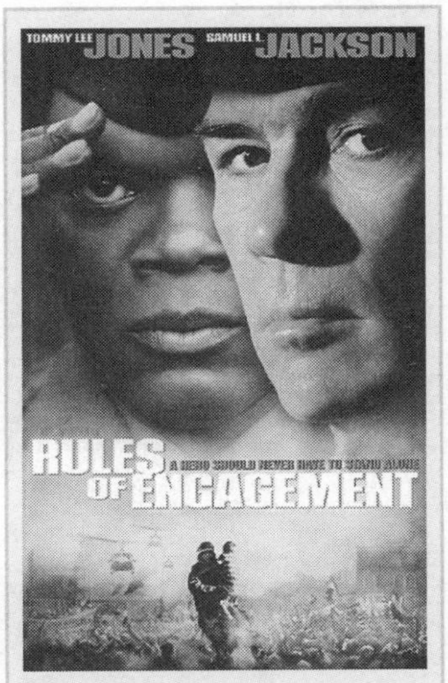

Rules Of Engagement (2000)
Samuel L. Jackson and Tommy Lee Jones are lifelong friends who served in Vietnam together. Twenty-eight years later, Jones, now a Marine lawyer, must defend Jackson in a court martial case after he's accused of instructing his troops to fire on supposedly unarmed protesters outside the U.S. embassy in Yemen. Guy Pearce and Ben Kingsley also star in this tense military courtroom drama from director William Friedkin. 127 min.
06-3029 ❑*$99.99*

River Of Love (2000)
This film focuses on Mata Amritanandamayi Devi, the beloved "Ammachi" (mother) and revered teacher of millions who counsels people from all walks of life. Her life, mission and work are presented through dramatic re-creations in a rich and incredible journey from her Southwestern Indian homeland and beyond. 87 min.
53-6979 *$29.99*

Dirty Pictures (2000)
The events surrounding the 1990 obscenity trial of Cincinnati museum curator Dennis Barrie, who launched a nationwide controversy when his arts center exhibited sexually graphic photography of Robert Mapplethorpe, are brought to life in this compelling docudrama. James Woods stars as Barrie, whose prosecution came to symbolize the fight for freedom of expression. Craig T. Nelson, Diana Scarwid also star. 104 min.
12-3340 ❑*$49.99*

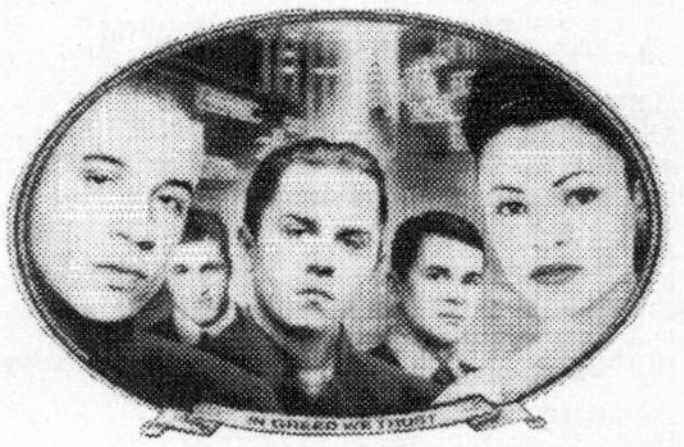

BOILER ROOM

Boiler Room (2000)
Intense, high-energy account of a New York college student named Seth who runs an illegal casino out of his apartment. After promising his father, a judge, to go legit, Seth joins a Long Island brokerage specializing in selling naive buyers questionable stocks. Soon, Seth's making a killing in the chop shop, but will it catch up with him? Giovanni Ribisi, Vin Diesel, Nia Long and Ben Affleck star. 120 min.
02-5231 Was $99.99 ❑*$14.99*

Gossip (2000)
James Marsden, Lena Headey and Norman Reedus are college roommates who, for their final project in "Communication Studies," decide to start and track a rumor about a couple of classmates to see how far it will go. But their plan backfires and takes a dangerous turn, threatening to destroy the lives of those involved. Kate Hudson, Joshua Jackson, Edward James Olmos star. 90 min.
19-5001 ❑*$99.99*

Freedom Song (2000)
Set in the fictional town of Quinlan, Miss., in 1961, this powerful drama stars Danny Glover as a gas station owner who opposes his teenage son's involvement in a student movement to end segregation. Glover's reminders of his own battles against racism prove futile, and his son soon finds himself in serious trouble. With Vondie Curtis-Hall, Vicellous Reon Shannon and Loretta Devine. 117 min.
19-2977 Was $99.99 ❑*$14.99*

Don Quixote (2000)
In this fanciful version of Cervantes' classic story, John Lithgow is the middle-aged Spaniard who retreats into a world of fantasy while searching for adventure, giants and romance with rusty armor, an old horse and peasant Sancho Panza (Bob Hoskins) as his squire. Isabella Rossellini and Vanessa L. Williams also star; directed by Peter Yates ("Breaking Away"). 120 min.
19-2997 ❑*$99.99*

Just One Night (2000)
In this romantic drama, Timothy Hutton is a physics professor about to be married in New York who sees gorgeous Maria Grazia Cucinotta ("Il Postino") at the San Francisco airport and immediately becomes infatuated with her. A series of strange circumstances and a taxi accident bring them together...and bring Hutton to a tough decision about his future. With Natalie Shaw, Seymour Cassel and Udo Kier. 90 min.
83-5014 *$99.99*

The Virgin Suicides (2000)
A man reminisces about the tragic end of five young sisters during the '70s in an upper class Michigan suburb. When the strict and overprotective nature of their parents along with several other events inevitably lead to one tragedy after another, the seemingly all-American family eventually succumbs to ruination. James Woods, Kathleen Turner, Kirsten Dunst and Scott Glenn star. 97 min.
06-3049 ❑*$99.99*

Spent (2000)
Jason London is a compulsive gambler from a privileged Hollywood background whose life is on the verge of being destroyed by his habit. His unconventional bets and his alcoholic girlfriend conspire to ruin him, unless he can learn to deal with his problems and turn his life around, in this stark drama. Charlie Spradling, Richmond Arquette and Rain Phoenix also star. 90 min.
85-1512 *$59.99*

Rated X (2000)
The bizarre, tragic story of the porno mavens known as the Mitchell Brothers is chronicled in this film directed by Emilio Estevez. Estevez plays Jim Mitchell and real-life brother Charlie Sheen plays Artie Mitchell, San Francisco-based siblings who open the popular O'Farrell Theater, introduce moviegoers to Marilyn Chambers and eventually slide into a world of cocaine addiction that leads to a nasty rivalry and murder. With Tracy Hutson, Rafer Weigel, Peter Bogdanovich. Unrated version.
67-9029 *$19.99*

Longitude (2000)
A contest in early 18th-century England to devise a means for sailors and merchants to determine longitude at sea provides a backdrop for this compelling drama that follows two stories: 1700s clockmaker Michael Gambon's efforts to build a timekeeping device that would earn him the £20,000 prize, and the quest 200 years later of naval officer Jeremy Irons to recover and restore Gambon's inventions. Ian Hart, Gemma Jones also star. 200 min. on four tapes.
53-6913 *$59.99*

Agnes Browne (2000)
Anjelica Huston directs and plays the title role in this warm, anecdotal story of a widowed mother in 1967 Dublin struggling to care for her daughter and six sons. The film follows Agnes' life as she sells fruit at an outdoor market, goes on a date with a French baker, deals with her friend's sickness and gets a chance to meet her idol, singer Tom Jones. Marion O'Dwyer, Ray Winstone also star. 92 min.
02-9225 *$79.99*

Around The Fire (2000)
Devon Sawa enters a rehab program when he's barely out of high school and reflects on the events that led him into such a desperate situation. A father who remarried quickly after his mother's death and a group of slacker friends who faithfully follow a Grateful Dead-like group are among the factors to Sawa's predicament. Tara Reid and Eric Mabius also star. 96 min.
83-1557 *$99.99*

Colorz Of Rage (2000)
When an interracial couple moves to the Big Apple, tensions throw their lives into turmoil. Tony is harassed by a local militant thug, and Debbie is pressured to be "true" to her black culture. Amid violence and chaos, the two lovers must struggle in order to stay together. Redman, Cheryl "Pepsii" Riley, Nikki Richards and writer/director Dale Resteghini star. 91 min.
83-1562 *$99.99*

Night Runs Red (2000)
Eve, a lusty woman with an ex-lover just out of jail and a new drug-dealing boyfriend, gets involved in a risky double-cross that threatens everyone's lives in this gritty New York-based drama. With Dell Maara, Elaine Del Valle and Seth Emers. 80 min.
83-5195 *$49.99*

The Savage Woman (1991)
A woman abandons her violent homelife and wanders in the Canadian wilderness. Near death, she's saved by an engineer who nurses her to health and soon discovers there is a horrible secret she is hiding. A steamy romance ensues between the two, but when it's learned that the woman is being pursued by police, a difficult choice must be made. Patricia Tulasne stars. 100 min. In French with English subtitles.
01-1474 Was $79.99 *$39.99*

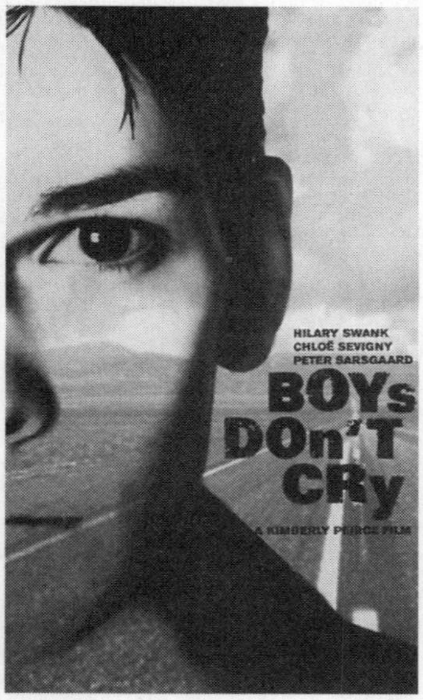

Boys Don't Cry (1999)
Powerful true story of the amazing life and shocking murder of Teena Brandon, a young woman in rural Nebraska who, for several years, lived as male "Brandon Teena" while waiting to undergo a sex-change operation. The superb cast includes Hilary Swank, in an Academy Award-winning performance as the doomed Brandon, and Chloe Sevigny as the factory worker with whom she's romantically involved. 116 min.
04-3931 Was $99.99 *□$14.99*

Art For Teachers Of Children (1995)
A frank and controversial look at a taboo subject, writer/director Jennifer Montgomery's semiautobiographical film chronicles a teenage student's affair with her adult dorm counselor, who also likes to take nude pictures of his charges. Caitlin Grace McDonnell, Ducan Hannah star; introduction by Film Society of Lincoln Center program director Richard Peña. 82 min.
01-1337 Was $59.99 *$29.99*

Twisted (1996)
This dark revamping of "Oliver Twist," set in modern-day New York, stars William Hickey as the evil owner of a brothel of young boys who sets his greedy sights on Andre, a 10-year-old orphan boy. Andre's only hope for salvation lies in Angel, a former hustler and drug dealer who comes to his aid. 100 min.
01-1547 *$39.99*

100 Proof (1996)
This impressive first film from writer-director Jeremy Horton focuses on small-time hustlers Rae and Carla, who turn tricks to continue their drug and alcohol habits. After facing abuse by her degenerate father, Rae joins Carla in an act of shocking brutality. Based on a true story; Pamela Stewart, Tara Bellando and Jim Varney star. 94 min.
01-1558 *$29.99*

Barriers (1998)
Tori, an affluent black student from Manhattan's West Side, befriends Snake, a streetwise kid from Harlem, much to his mother's disapproval. When Tori's mother's credit card is missing, Snake becomes the suspect, but Tori learns Snake's older, troubled brother Keith may be responsible. Annie Golden, Jamaul Roots and Quentin Crisp star. 90 min.
01-1568 *$29.99*

Side Out (1990)
What "Long Shot" did for foosball and "Dreamer" did for bowling, this action-packed film does for volleyball! C. Thomas Howell and Peter Horton star as two of California's volleyball masters who meet their match on and off the beach. Courtney Thorne-Smith and Harley Jane Kozak also star. 103 min.
02-2043 Was $89.99 *□$14.99*

Uncaged (1991)
A gritty drama set on the mean Sunset Strip, where a beautiful prostitute goes on the defense to protect herself and her hooker friends from a psychotic pimp. Leslie Bega, Jeffrey Dean Morgan star. 78 min.
02-2139 *$79.99*

Rich Girl (1991)
A young woman whose wealthy family has a posh Bel Air mansion attempts to make it on her own as a member of a rock group. She falls for a handsome, working-class band member, but her jealous ex-boyfriend and possessive father try to persuade her to return to the life she wants to forget. Jill Schoelen, Don Michael Paul and Willie Dixon star. 96 min.
02-2141 *$89.99*

Boyz N The Hood (1991)
A graphic and powerful look at black life in South-Central Los Angeles, as three young men attempt through different means to escape the violence-filled life of the streets. Writer/director John Singleton's acclaimed debut feature stars Cuba Gooding, Jr., Morris Chestnut, Larry Fishburne and rapper Ice Cube. 112 min.
02-2165 Was $19.99 *□$14.99*

Boyz N The Hood (Letterboxed Version)
Also available in a theatrical, widescreen format.
02-3314 *□$19.99*

Men Of Respect (1991)
Shakespeare's "Macbeth" goes gangster in this drama depicting the rise (and eventual fall) of a psychopathic soldier in the New York Mafia who will stop at nothing to become "head of the family." Violence-filled story stars John Turturro, Katherine Borowitz, Peter Boyle, Rod Steiger and Dennis Farina. 107 min.
02-2092 Was $19.99 *□$14.99*

Big Night (1996)
Deliciously passionate look at two Italian brothers who immigrate to New Jersey, where they open a small restaurant. But chef Primo and businessman Secondo's enterprise verges on disaster, until a rival restaurateur promises singer Louis Prima and his band will stop in for dinner. Stanley Tucci (who also co-scripted and co-directed), Tony Shalhoub, Minnie Driver and Isabella Rossellini star. 109 min.
02-3038 Was $99.99 *□$19.99*

Big Night (Letterboxed Version)
Also available in a theatrical, widescreen format.
02-3203 *□$19.99*

Life Of Sin (1990)
A passion-filled drama about a beautiful young woman who rises from the poverty of her Caribbean homeland to become a wealthy and glamorous madame, only to face an equally steep fall from power. Miriam Colon, Raul Julia, Jose Ferrer star. 112 min.
02-2347 *$89.99*

Strapless (1990)
Powerful romantic drama depicting the love lives of two American sisters living in England. Blair Brown plays a middle-aged, sexually repressed physician who confronts her own jealousy over free-spirited younger sister Bridget Fonda's announcement that she's pregnant. Bruno Ganz also stars. 102 min.
02-2044 Was $79.99 *$14.99*

Strapless (Letterboxed Version)
Also available in a theatrical, widescreen format.
08-8883 *$14.99*

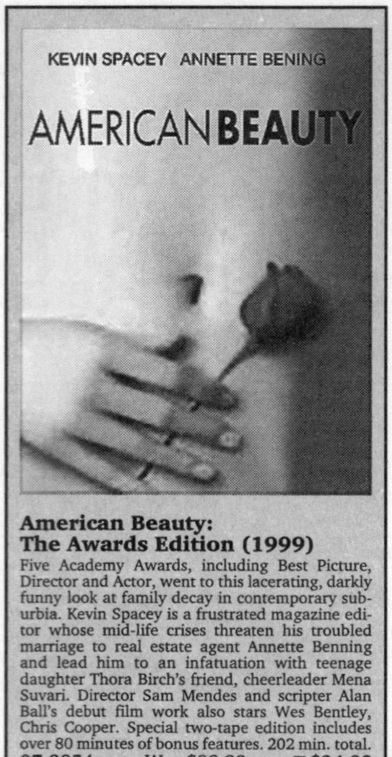

American Beauty: The Awards Edition (1999)
Five Academy Awards, including Best Picture, Director and Actor, went to this lacerating, darkly funny look at family decay in contemporary suburbia. Kevin Spacey is a frustrated magazine editor whose mid-life crises threaten his troubled marriage to real estate agent Annette Benning and lead him to an infatuation with teenage daughter Thora Birch's friend, cheerleader Mena Suvari. Director Sam Mendes and scripter Alan Ball's debut film work also stars Wes Bentley, Chris Cooper. Special two-tape edition includes over 80 minutes of bonus features. 202 min. total.
07-2854 Was $99.99 *□$24.99*

Delusion (1991)
An offbeat and suspenseful drama about a computer whiz who embezzles money from his company and sets out to start a new life elsewhere. While in the Nevada desert, however, he picks up two hitchhikers who involve the white-collar criminal in some murderous business. Jim Metzler, Kyle Secor, Jennifer Rubin and Jerry Orbach star. 100 min.
02-2126 *$89.99*

Wind (1992)
Set sail for rousing action and romance in this drama starring Matthew Modine and Jennifer Grey as former lovers who reunite to lead the U.S. squad in the America's Cup sailing race and reclaim the trophy from the Australian team. Thrilling nautical sequences add to the excitement. With Cliff Robertson, Jack Thompson. 126 min.
02-2352 Was $19.99 *□$14.99*

Family Prayers (1993)
A sensitive coming-of-age story set in Los Angeles in 1969, focusing on a young Jewish boy entering adulthood who struggles with problems within his family due to his father's gambling addiction. The boy turns to his iconoclastic Bar Mitzvah tutor for guidance. Joe Mantegna, Anne Archer, Paul Reiser, Patti LuPone and David Margulies star. 109 min.
02-2423 Was $89.99 *$19.99*

Zebrahead (1992)
Gritty urban romantic drama about the relationship between two teenagers, a Jewish rapper and the pretty African-American cousin of his best friend. Set on the streets of Detroit, this acclaimed drama looks at the hurdles they face among friends, families and themselves. Michael Rapaport and DeShonne Castle star; produced by Oliver Stone. 102 min.
02-2441 Was $19.99 *□$14.99*

Fathers And Sons (1993)
Recognizing the danger of living in New York City, a movie director moves his family to a small seaside town in New Jersey. But he and his family soon discover that the town is being terrorized by a serial killer, while a mysterious prophet's predictions begin to come true. Jeff Goldblum, Rosanna Arquette, John C. McGinley and Joie Lee star. 100 min.
02-2469 Was $89.99 *$14.99*

The Killing Beach (1992)
A defiant investigative journalist (Greta Scacchi) and a Saigon prostitute (Joan Chen) find themselves in terrible turmoil when they attempt to save a group of Vietnam refugees from a massacre. A powerful drama, based on the best-selling book "Turtle Beach." With Jack Thompson and Art Malik. 88 min.
02-2474 Was $89.99 *□$19.99*

Mac (1993)
Actor-director John Turturro's powerful and poignant account of three Italian brothers who start a carpentry business in Queens, New York, in the 1950s and discover that despite the inspiration from their late father, their explosive tempers keep getting in their way. Carl Capotorto, Katherine Borowitz, Michael Badalucco and Ellen Barkin co-star. 118 min.
02-2476 Was $89.99 *□$19.99*

Alan & Naomi (1992)
Sensitive and powerful story, set during World War II, of a young Jewish boy living in New York who befriends a refugee girl traumatized by her father's death by the Nazis. The boy uses his skills at ventriloquism to bring the girl out of her shell and into the real world. Lukas Haas, Vanessa Zaoui and Michael Gross star. 95 min.
02-2248 Was $89.99 *$14.99*

Better Than Ever (1997)
Two elderly veterans with opposite dispositions decide to leave their nursing home and end their life with dignity. They head to a wooded area by cab, but their plans are disrupted by a kidnapper who has taken a young boy hostage, launching an effort by the pair to save the youngster. Coming-of-old-age tale stars William Hickey, Carl Gordon, Joey Buttafuoco and Frank Gorshin. 85 min.
01-1569 *$29.99*

The Krays (1990)
Tough, true-life account of British twin brothers who ruled London's underworld in the 1960s with a steel fist...and a sharp sword. Follow their rise from street thugs to powerful crime barons, and witness the strange influence their strong-willed mother played in her sons' "careers." With Gary and Martin Kemp (of the rock group Spandau Ballet) and Billie Whitelaw. 119 min.
02-2085 Was $19.99 *$14.99*

Alone In The Neon Jungle (1991)
Gritty police story starring Danny Aiello as the police chief of a city riddled with crime, drug-dealing and cops on the take. He enlists the help of a female police captain (Suzanne Pleshette) who soon discovers some unsettling facts while investigating a fellow cop's death. Joe Morton and Georg Stanford Brown co-star. 90 min.
02-2171 Was $79.99 *$14.99*

Radio Flyer (1992)
After moving to a new city in California with their mother, two young brothers band together to overcome their fear of their abusive stepfather. They relate fantastic tales about talking animals, monsters in the closet and a red wagon that flies in order to escape the reality of day-to-day life. Elijah Wood, Joseph Mazello, Lorraine Bracco star in this sensitive film, narrated by Tom Hanks. 114 min.
02-2257 Was $19.99 *□$14.99*

Falling From Grace (1992)
John Mellencamp directed and stars in this powerful drama about a country singer who finds that the appropriate time to change his successful but staid life is during a visit to his Indiana hometown. Mariel Hemingway plays his wife, Kay Lenz his former flame, and Claude Akins his father. Written by Larry McMurtry ("Lonesome Dove"). 100 min.
02-2268 Was $19.99 *□$14.99*

Over The Hill (1993)
A 60-year-old widow from Bar Harbor, Maine, decides to visit her daughter living in Sydney, Australia, but feels uncomfortable when she arrives. After borrowing her granddaughter's '59 Chevy, the woman sets off for Melbourne and has some exciting and romantic adventures in the Australian Outback. Olympia Dukakis, Bill Kerr and Sigrid Thornton star. 97 min.
02-2442 *□$14.99*

Gas Food Lodging (1992)
A compassionate, sharply observed drama set in a remote New Mexico town where a mother and her two teenage daughters face an uphill battle to survive against difficult odds. Younger daughter Fairuza Balk attempts to find a man for waitress mom Brooke Adams, while promiscuous older sibling Ione Skye discovers that she is pregnant. Robert Knepper and James Brolin also star. 101 min.
02-2370 Was $89.99 *$19.99*

Gladiator (1992)
Savage boxing story focusing on a tough teen who brings his skill at defending himself on the streets of Chicago into the ring. Aside from battling a score of brutal opponents, he also goes up against a shady promoter, his gambler father and, finally, a friend whom he meets head-on in a ferocious match. James Marshall, Cuba Gooding, Jr., Brian Dennehy and Ossie Davis star. 102 min.
02-2280 Was $19.99 *□$14.99*

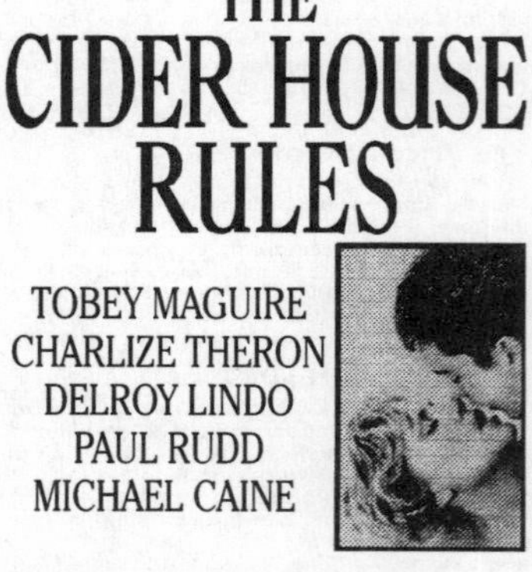

The Cider House Rules (1999)
Writer John Irving's adaptation of his novel set in '40s New England earned him an Academy Award. Young Tobey Maguire leaves the only home he's known, a Maine orphanage run by physician mentor Michael Caine (who took home the Best Supporting Actor Oscar), to find his place in the world. While working on the apple farm of a friend who's gone off to war, Maguire falls for the man's girlfriend (Charlize Theron) and befriends a father/daughter pair of black migrant workers (Delroy Lindo and singer Erykah Badu) who are hiding a dark secret. Lasse Hallstrom directs. 125 min.
11-2448 Was $99.99 *□$19.99*

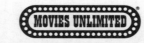

Age Old Friends (1990)
Whimsical and warm tale starring Hume Cronyn as a feisty senior citizen living in a retirement home who must make a difficult decision: should he live with his daughter and her family or help his ill old pal, played by Vincent Gardenia? Tandy Cronyn and Esther Rolle also star. 89 min.
44-1736 □*$79.99*

Torrents Of Spring (1990)
Timothy Hutton, Nastassja Kinski and Valeria Golino star in this lavish tale of betrayal, passion and romance. Hutton plays a Russian aristocrat who falls in love with a beautiful, young German woman. When another, free-spirited woman attracts his attention, he is forced to make a difficult decision. Directed by Jerzy Skolimowski ("Moonlighting"). 101 min.
44-1743 *$14.99*

The Fourth War (1990)
A maverick American army officer (Roy Scheider) stationed along the West German/Czech border begins a rivalry with his Russian counterpart (Jurgen Prochnow) on the other side, a rivalry that escalates into a vicious personal war with dangerous consequences. John Frankenheimer directed this hard-hitting, post-Cold War drama; with Harry Dean Stanton, Tim Reid. 91 min.
44-1761 Was $89.99 *$14.99*

Chattahoochee (1990)
A stirring true drama about a troubled Korean War hero who is sentenced to a Florida mental institution with horrible conditions. After suffering many nightmarish experiences, he enlists other patients to help start a reform movement. Gary Oldman, Dennis Hopper, Frances McDormand and M. Emmet Walsh star. 98 min.
44-1764 Was $19.99 □*$14.99*

Women And Men: Stories Of Seduction (1990)
A trilogy of stories of romance and passion, written by Mary McCarthy, Dorothy Parker and Ernest Hemingway, and starring Melanie Griffith, James Woods, Beau Bridges, Elizabeth McGovern, Molly Ringwald and Peter Weller. A woman gets involved with a quick-talking travelling salesman; a lothario with an ever-ringing phone seduces a jealous woman; and a train station is the site of revelations for two lovers. 90 min.
44-1769 Was $89.99 □*$14.99*

Women And Men 2 (1991)
Three more stories exploring love by three great authors. Irwin Shaw's "Return to Kansas City" features Matt Dillon as a boxer and Kyra Sedgwick as his wife; Carson McCullers' "A Domestic Dilemma" explores a difficult marriage between Ray Liotta and Andie MacDowell; and Scott Glenn, as writer Henry Miller, becomes involved with prostitute Juliette Binoche in Miller's "Mara." 90 min.
44-1854 Was $89.99 □*$14.99*

Criminal Justice (1990)
The victim in a vicious robbery and knifing identifies a man as her attacker, but as the legal wheels start turning, questions are raised about his guilt and the chances for a plea bargain. Thought-provoking drama stars Forest Whitaker, Rosie Perez, Jennifer Grey, Anthony La Paglia. 92 min.
44-1775 Was $89.99 *$19.99*

Judgment (1990)
Shocking, based-on-fact drama starring Keith Carradine and Blythe Danner as parents of a young son who discover that he has been molested, along with eight other children, by a parish priest. The other families accept a financial settlement in the case, but Carradine and Danner decide to fight for justice in court. David Strathairn, Jack Warden co-star. 89 min.
44-1787 *$89.99*

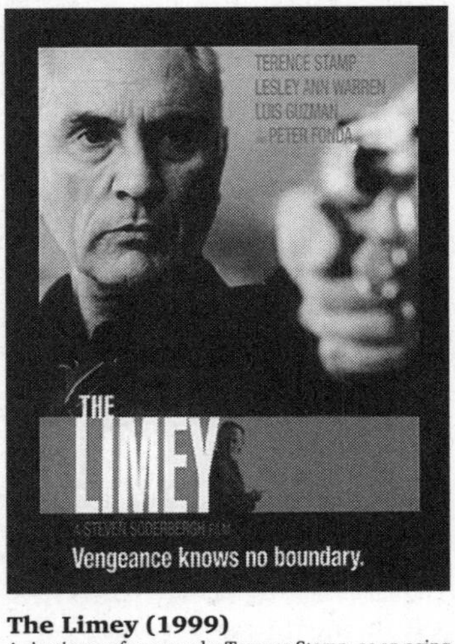
TERENCE STAMP
LESLEY ANN WARREN
LUIS GUZMAN
and PETER FONDA
THE LIMEY
A STEVEN SODERBERGH FILM
Vengeance knows no boundary.

The Limey (1999)
A riveting performance by Terence Stamp, as an aging British crook newly released from prison who comes to Los Angeles looking for revenge on the record producer responsible for his daughter's death, drives this hard-edged, stylish thriller from director Steven Soderbergh ("Out of Sight"). Peter Fonda, Luis Guzman, Barry Newman and Lesley Ann Warren also star. 89 min.
27-7180 Was $99.99 □*$14.99*

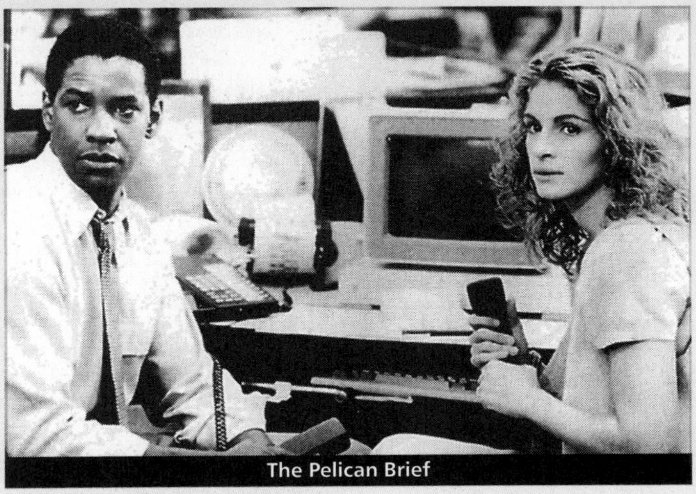
The Pelican Brief

Julia Roberts

Baja Oklahoma (1987)
Rip-roarin' comedy, based on Dan Jenkins' ("Semi-Tough") novel. Lesley Ann Warren is the Fort Worth barmaid with dreams of being a country singer. Also stars Swoosie Kurtz, Peter Coyote, Julia Roberts and musical guests Willie Nelson and Emmylou Harris. 100 min.
40-1390 Was $89.99 *$19.99*

Satisfaction (1988)
An all-girl band heads to the shore for the rockingest summer of their lives in a song-filled comedy that features Justine Bateman in her starring film debut. Co-stars Trini Alvarado, Liam Neeson, Scott Coffey and Julia Roberts. 92 min.
04-1100 □*$19.99*

Steel Magnolias (1989)
Humor mixes with tragedy in this star-studded adaptation of the hit play. A beauty parlor in a small Louisiana town is where the area's women meet to discuss the sweet and sad experiences of their lives. Dolly Parton, Shirley MacLaine, Daryl Hannah, Sally Field, Olympia Dukakis and Julia Roberts star; Herbert Ross directs. 118 min.
02-2020 Was $89.99 □*$14.99*

Blood Red (1989)
The land feud between an immigrant vineyard owner and a cattle baron in 19th-century California erupts into a violent range war. Compelling drama stars Dennis Hopper, Giancarlo Giannini, Burt Young, and siblings Eric and Julia Roberts. 91 min.
53-1780 Was $19.99 *$14.99*

Pretty Woman: 10th Anniversary Edition (1990)
The modern-day "Pygmalion" comedy that became a smash hit stars Julia Roberts as a hooker hired by corporate raider Richard Gere to pose as his girlfriend for a week. Their "strictly business" relationship, however, soon blossoms into romance. Laura San Giacomo, Hector Elizondo, Jason Alexander, Ralph Bellamy co-star; Garry Marshall directs. Special director's cut includes bonus footage and behind-the-scenes interviews. 124 min. total.
11-1504 Was $19.99 □*$14.99*

Flatliners (1990)
Five medical students stretch the border between life and death by conducting dangerous experiments on each other. But as each experiences clinical death, what they face on "the other side" returns to haunt them. Suspenseful and fantastic thriller stars Julia Roberts, Kevin Bacon, Kiefer Sutherland, William Baldwin, Oliver Platt. 111 min.
02-2067 Was $19.99 □*$14.99*

Sleeping With The Enemy (1991)
Upon discovering that her once-kind husband has turned into an abusive monster, young wife Julia Roberts fakes her own death and begins a new life in a small town with a new identity. There she meets and falls for a college professor, but her obsessive husband is not far behind. Patrick Bergin and Kevin Anderson co-star in this hit thriller. 99 min.
04-2445 Was $19.99 □*$14.99*

Dying Young (1991)
In this three-hankie weepie, Julia Roberts shines as a beautiful but unkempt and uneducated woman hired to help nurse a wealthy, 28-year-old leukemia victim (Campbell Scott). Their antagonistic relationship soon blossoms into love, but the shadow of death hangs over their romance. With Vincent D'Onofrio, Colleen Dewhurst and David Selby. 111 min.
04-2476 Was $19.99 □*$14.99*

The Pelican Brief (1993)
Riveting thriller based on John Grisham's best-seller stars Julia Roberts as a New Orleans law student who writes a paper exposing the conspiracy surrounding the deaths of two Supreme Court justices and Denzel Washington as the investigative reporter who helps her dodge the assassins and special agents on her trail. Sam Shepard, John Heard and Hume Cronyn co-star. 141 min.
19-2228 Was $19.99 □*$14.99*

I Love Trouble (1994)
Rookie reporter Julia Roberts and veteran newspaperman Nick Nolte find themselves competing to crack the mystery surrounding a train accident while trying to avoid falling in love in this crackling good mix of action, romance and comedy. With Saul Rubinek. 123 min.
11-1845 Was $19.99 □*$14.99*

Something To Talk About (1995)
When affluent, neurotic Southern woman Grace (Julia Roberts) learns husband Eddie (Dennis Quaid) is having an affair, she's forced into making some tough decisions about her and her daughter's future. Grace may get little help from her horse-breeder father (Robert Duvall), but her feisty little sister (Kyra Sedgwick) has advice to offer. Comedy-drama co-stars Gena Rowlands. 105 min.
19-2411 Was $19.99 □*$14.99*

Mary Reilly (1996)
This unique treatment of Robert Louis Stevenson's chilling story stars Julia Roberts as the dedicated Irish servant to Edinburgh physician Dr. Jekyll who eventually realizes that she is in love with both him and his horrific alter ego, Mr. Hyde. John Malkovich, Glenn Close, George Cole and Michael Gambon also star; directed by Stephen Frears ("The Grifters"). 108 min.
02-2921 Was $19.99 □*$14.99*

My Best Friend's Wedding (1997)
Julia Roberts is back in fine comedic form, playing a food critic who anticipates turning down ex-lover-turned-best buddy Dermot Mulroney's marriage proposal...and is shocked to learn he's going to wed someone else. Convinced they should be together, Roberts has four days to halt Mulroney and fiancée Cameron Diaz's nuptials and win him back. Rupert Everett, a delight as Roberts' gay confidante, also stars in this hit romance. 105 min.
02-3103 Was $19.99 □*$14.99*

Stepmom (1998)
Wonderfully moving melodrama stars Julia Roberts as a New York fashion photographer who moves in with divorced boyfriend Ed Harris and finds herself in competition for the attention of his two children with their mother, Susan Sarandon. The two women must come to terms with their place in the modern-day extended family when Sarandon is diagnosed with a terminal illness. Jena Malone, Liam Aiken also star; directed by Chris Columbus ("Mrs. Doubtfire"). 125 min.
02-3310 Was $19.99 □*$14.99*

Notting Hill (1999)
In this audience-pleasing charmer, Hugh Grant is the divorced owner of a travel book store who lives in London's Notting Hill suburb with scruffy roommate Rhys Ifans. A chance meeting with customer Julia Roberts, a superstar film actress, leads to romantic sparks, but her celebrity lifestyle soon gets in the way of their relationship. With Emma Chambers and unbilled cameos by Alec Baldwin and Matthew Modine. 124 min.
07-2797 Was $99.99 □*$19.99*

Runaway Bride (1999)
The "Pretty Woman" duo reteams again for a witty romantic romp featuring Julia Roberts as a Maryland hardware store clerk with a habit of leaving prospective grooms stranded at the altar. An article criticizing her actions by newspaper columnist Richard Gere prompts an angry response and leads him to investigate further in her hometown, where the mismatched pair eventually fall in love. With Joan Cusack, Rita Wilson; directed by Garry Marshall. 116 min.
06-2914 Was $99.99 □*$19.99*

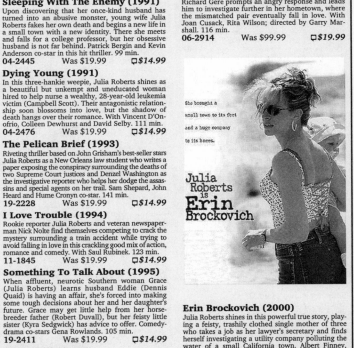

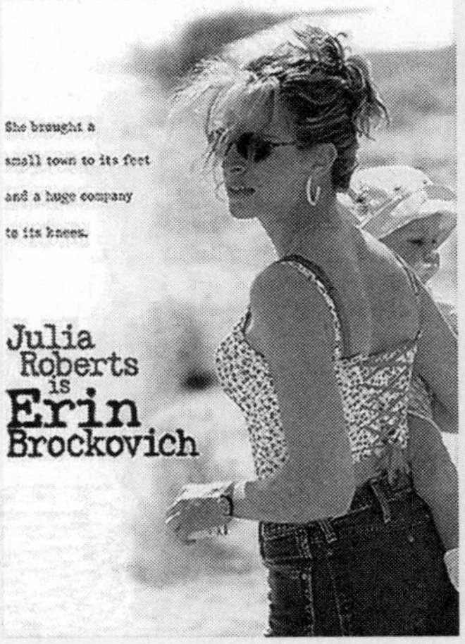
She brought a
small town to its feet
and a huge company
to its knees.
Julia
Roberts
is
Erin
Brockovich

Erin Brockovich (2000)
Julia Roberts shines in this powerful true story, playing a feisty, trashily clothed single mother of three who takes a job as her lawyer's secretary and finds herself investigating a utility company polluting the water of a small California town. Albert Finney, Aaron Eckhart and Marg Helgenberger also star in this acclaimed effort by Steven Soderbergh ("Out of Sight"). 132 min.
07-2887 □*$19.99*

Please see our index for these other Julia Roberts titles: *Conspiracy Theory • Everyone Says I Love You • Hook • Michael Collins • Ready To Wear*

Straight Out Of Brooklyn (1991)
Gritty, acclaimed first film from 19-year-old writer/director/co-star Matty Rich focuses on the exploits of a young black man who joins two friends in robbing a drug dealer in order to get money to leave their horrific New York neighborhood. With George T. Odom, Ann D. Sanders and Lawrence Gilliard, Jr. 83 min.
44-1848 Was $19.99 □*$14.99*

Without Warning: The James Brady Story (1991)
In this powerful true-life story, Beau Bridges plays press secretary James Brady, who finds his life tragically altered when he catches a bullet fired by John Hinckley, intended for President Reagan. The film chronicles Brady's difficult recovery and his transformation into a crusader for gun control. Joan Allen, David Strathairn co-star. 120 min.
44-1849 *$89.99*

Just Another Girl On The I.R.T. (1993)
A critically acclaimed first feature from writer-director Leslie Harris focusing on an African-American teenager from Brooklyn who seeks a way out of the projects by going to college and becoming a doctor. Ariyan Johnson, Kevin Thigpen and Ebony Jerido star. 96 min.
27-6832 Was $89.99 *$14.99*

The Playboys (1992)
An enchanting tale set in a small Irish village where a beautiful, young unmarried mother's involvement with an actor in a travelling theater group sets off sparks with the townspeople and the local constable, who has been courting her for years. Robin Wright, Aidan Quinn, Albert Finney and Milo O'Shea star in this exhilarating seriocomedy from the writer of "My Left Foot." 110 min.
44-1904 Was $89.99 □*$14.99*

Bonanno: A Godfather's Story (1999)
One of the longest-reigning kingpins in the American Mafia tells his own real-life crime story in this riveting drama. Martin Landau stars as Joseph Bonanno, who left his native Italy and rose through the ranks of organized crime to become the youngest Mafia boss ever. With Robert Loggia, Edward James Olmos, Costas Mandylor and Tony Nardi as the young Bonanno. 139 min.
27-7173 Was $29.99 □*$14.99*

Animal Room (1995)
A disturbingly timely film, this drama stars Neil Patrick Harris as a drug-using high schooler placed in an experimental program that isolates troubled and trouble-causing teens in an orderless environment where only survival matters. Matthew Lillard, Brian Vincent also star. 98 min.
22-9031 *$79.99*

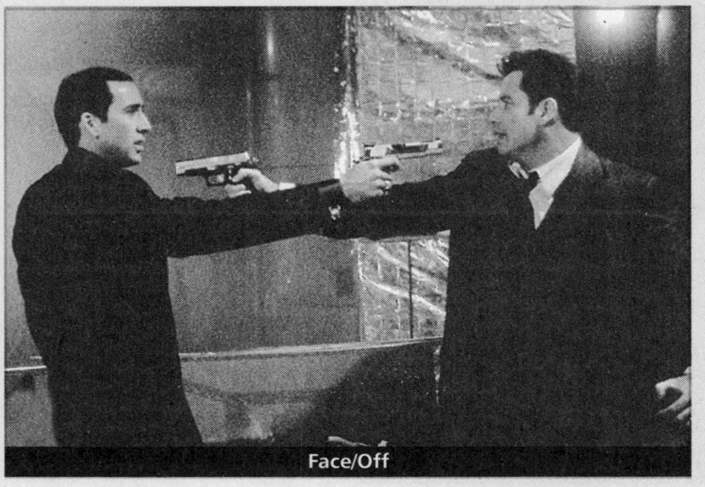

Face/Off

John Travolta

The Devil's Rain (1975)
Chilling horror story about a Satan-worshipping cult that takes over a small town in the Southwest. Your flesh will crawl as the coven's flesh melts during the title torrent! Ernest Borgnine, Tom Skerritt, William Shatner, Ida Lupino, Eddie Albert and John Travolta (barely recognizable under heavy make-up in his film debut) star. 85 min.
08-1005 Was $19.99 ***$14.99***

The Devil's Rain (Letterboxed Version)
Also available in a theatrical, widescreen format.
08-1725 ***$19.99***

The Boy In The Plastic Bubble (1976)
John Travolta's first starring role was in this drama of a young man whose life is one of total isolation. Lack of biological immunities forces him to live inside a sterile plastic room, but when he falls for the girl next door, he must choose between his life and love. Glynnis O'Connor, Robert Reed co-star. 96 min.
46-5046 Was $49.99 ***$14.99***

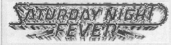

Saturday Night Fever

Saturday Night Fever (1977)
The electrifying film that sent millions to the disco and redefined Hollywood's definition of musicals. John Travolta is dynamic as a Brooklyn youth who only lives for his weekends on the dance floor. Karen Lynn Gorney, Barry Miller also star; music by The Bee Gees, Yvonne Elliman, others. Uncut, 119-minute version.
06-1052 ***$14.99***

Staying Alive (1983)
John Travolta reprises his powerhouse role of "Saturday Night Fever's" Tony Manero. Now he's trying out for a big Broadway musical, testing all his dazzling dancing skills. Directed by Sylvester Stallone. With Cynthia Rhodes, Finola Hughes; music by The Bee Gees. 96 min.
06-1199 ***❑$14.99***

Urban Cowboy (1981)
Moving from his rural Texas home to take an oil refinery job near Houston, young hardhat John Travolta begins hanging out at famed honky tonk nightclub Gilley's. In this world of country music, "weekend cowboys" and fast women, Travolta falls for feisty Debra Winger, but their romance has more bumps than a ride on the mechanical bull. Scott Glenn, Madolyn Smith co-star, with appearances by The Charlie Daniels Band, Bonnie Raitt and others. 135 min.
06-1075 ***❑$14.99***

Blow Out (1981)
Brian DePalma's suspenseful take on the film "Blow-Up" features John Travolta as a movie sound effects expert who inadvertently records an important clue in an accident involving a prominent politician. With Nancy Allen, John Lithgow, Dennis Franz; filmed in Philadelphia. 108 min.
19-1180 ***$14.99***

Two Of A Kind (1983)
John Travolta and Olivia Newton-John are back together in this exhilarating, music-filled romantic comedy. Since God sees Earth going down the drain, he chooses them to make eternal sacrifices for each other. If they do, the world is saved. Oliver Reed, Charles Durning, Scatman Crothers. 87 min.
04-1689 Was $19.99 ***❑$14.99***

Perfect (1985)
Enter today's world of exercise and health, where men and women strain and sweat to reach "perfection." John Travolta stars as the reporter looking for the "inside story" on the fitness craze, while falling for aerobics instructor Jamie Lee Curtis. Co-stars Laraine Newman and Jann Wenner. 120 min.
02-1490 Was $79.99 ***❑$14.99***

The Experts (1989)
The KGB spirits New York hipsters John Travolta and Arye Gross to a prefabricated town on the Russian prairie, where they unknowingly teach modern American behavior to a class of Soviet agents-in-training. East-West comedy summit co-stars Charles Martin Smith and Kelly Preston. 94 min.
06-1642 Was $19.99 ***❑$14.99***

Chains Of Gold (1992)
A concerned social worker befriends a 13-year-old boy trying to escape the clutches of a crack-dealing gang, but when the gang decides to kill the teen rather than let him leave, a desperate fight to save one young life ensues. Tense and timely thriller stars John Travolta, Joey Lawrence, Hector Elizondo, Marilu Henner. 95 min.
71-5259 ***❑$14.99***

Get Shorty (1995)
John Travolta is a slick loan shark from Miami whose search for a dry cleaner who took $300,000 in mob money leads him to Hollywood and debt-ridden "B" movie producer Gene Hackman. The two try to make a movie together while battling crooks, creeps and arrogant actors. Rene Russo, Danny DeVito, Dennis Farina, Delroy Lindo and Bette Midler co-star in this terrific Elmore Leonard story. 105 min.
12-3049 Was $19.99 ***❑$14.99***

Get Shorty (Letterboxed Version)
Also available in a theatrical, widescreen format.
12-3211 ***❑$14.99***

White Man's Burden (1995)
Race relations are turned on their head in this thought-provoking, speculative drama set in an America where the privileged black majority controls all levels of society and a white minority is confined to low-paying jobs and run-down neighborhoods. John Travolta plays an unjustly-fired factory worker who, after losing his home and family, kidnaps ex-boss Harry Belafonte in order to plead his case. With Kelly Lynch, Carrie Snodgress. 89 min.
44-2034 Was $19.99 ***$14.99***

Broken Arrow (1996)
Slam-bang actioner starring John Travolta as a renegade Stealth Bomber pilot who hijacks two nuclear warheads during a test flight over the Utah desert, intending to blackmail the U.S. government, and Christian Slater as his ex-partner, who joins with feisty park ranger Samantha Mathis to stop Travolta's plan. With Frank Whaley, Delroy Lindo and Howie Long; directed by John Woo. 110 min.
04-3341 Was $19.99 ***❑$14.99***

Broken Arrow (Letterboxed Version)
Also available in a theatrical, widescreen format.
04-3407 ***$19.99***

Phenomenon (1996)
Winning mixture of drama, romance and fantasy stars John Travolta as an easygoing small-town mechanic who, after a late-night encounter with a mysterious light in the sky, acquires a genius-level mentality and amazing telekinetic abilities. This touching story also features Kyra Sedgwick, Robert Duvall and Forest Whitaker. 123 min.
11-2074 Was $99.99 ***❑$19.99***

Michael (1996)
A pair of Chicago-based tabloid reporters and a beautiful "angel expert" travel to a small Iowa town to investigate a woman's claim that the archangel Michael is living in her house, but the skeptical trio aren't prepared for what they find: a grungy, beer-drinking woman-chaser with wings on his back. John Travolta shines as the slightly shabby seraph in director/co-writer Nora Ephron's heartfelt comic fantasy. William Hurt, Andie MacDowell, Robert Pastorelli and Jean Stapleton also star. 106 min.
19-2533 Was $19.99 ***❑$14.99***

Face/Off (1997)
"Losing face" takes on new meaning in director John Woo's hyper-kinetic actioner. FBI agent John Travolta, in order to learn where in Los Angeles a nerve gas bomb was hidden by his arch-enemy, terrorist assassin Nicolas Cage, undergoes an experimental operation to give him the voice and appearance of his foe. The procedure works—until Cage manages to assume Travolta's face and identity and leave him behind bars. Joan Allen, Gina Gershon, Alessandro Nivola also star. 140 min.
06-2640 Was $99.99 ***❑$14.99***

Face/Off (Letterboxed Version)
Also available in a theatrical, widescreen format.
06-2703 ***❑$14.99***

She's So Lovely (1997)
Director Nick Cassavetes, working from a script written by father John years earlier, creates a gritty "romantic fable." Sean Penn plays a hot-headed, working-class alcoholic whose rampage after learning wife Robin Wright Penn was assaulted by a friend lands him in an asylum. Ten years later, Penn returns home to find his wife now wed to wealthy John Travolta and raising Penn's daughter, as well as their own kids. With Harry Dean Stanton, Debi Mazar, Gena Rowlands. 96 min.
11-2220 Was $19.99 ***❑$14.99***

Primary Colors (1998)
John Travolta stars as Jack Stanton, a Clinton-esque, unknown Southern governor whose White House run could be detoured by ethical questions and sexual scandals, in director Mike Nichols and scripter Elaine May's bitingly funny satire, based on the "anonymous" roman a clef novel. Emma Thompson plays the governor's long-suffering wife, and Adrian Lester is an idealistic campaign aide. With Kathy Bates, Billy Bob Thornton and Maura Tierney. 144 min.
07-2660 Was $99.99 ***❑$14.99***

A Civil Action (1998)
Knockout true-life courtroom drama starring John Travolta as accident lawyer Jan Schlictmann, who takes on the owners of a tannery he believes are responsible for the leukemia deaths of several children. Because the tannery is owned by a large corporation, the case threatens to bankrupt Travolta's law firm. With Robert Duvall, William H. Macy, Kathleen Quinlan and John Lithgow. 115 min.
11-2327 Was $19.99 ***❑$14.99***

The General's Daughter: Special Edition (1999)
When a female Army captain is found brutally raped and murdered on a military base, warrant officer John Travolta is called in to investigate. Partnered on the case with former lover Madeline Stowe, Travolta soon finds his search for the killer stonewalled by the victim's father, an influential general with political ambitions. Compelling drama also stars James Cromwell, James Woods. Special edition includes a behind-the-scenes featurette, four deleted scenes, and an unused alternate ending. 117 min.
06-2915 Was $99.99 ***❑$19.99***

BATTLEFIELD EARTH

Battlefield Earth (2000)
John Travolta's dream project—an adaptation of Scientology founder L. Ron Hubbard's sci-fi novel—is set in the year 3000 and features Travolta as a leader of the Psychlos, an alien race that conquered Earth and reduced mankind to savage slaves. When Travolta makes cave-dwelling youth Barry Pepper part of his gold-mining operation, Pepper uses it as a chance to launch a rebellion. Forrest Whitaker, Kim Coates also star; look for Kelly Preston as a Psychlo with a large tongue.
19-5020 Available 1/01 ***❑$99.99***

The Travolta Collection
"What?" Three of John Travolta's most popular films: "Grease," "Saturday Night Fever" and "Urban Cowboy." "Where?" Right here in a boxed collector's set.
06-2962 ***$44.99***

Please see our index for these other John Travolta titles: *Carrie • Grease • Look Who's Talking • Look Who's Talking Now • Look Who's Talking Too • Mad City • Pulp Fiction • The Thin Red Line*

Cradle Will Rock (1999)
In Depression-era New York, the forces of artistic and social change challenged the political and business establishment, and a controversial play called "The Cradle Will Rock" literally became the stage for confrontation. Writer/director Tim Robbins deftly blends real and fictional characters in his account of the "leftist" drama's stormy production. Ensemble cast includes Hank Azaria, Bill Murray, Susan Sarandon, Emily Watson, John Cusack as Nelson Rockefeller, and Angus MacFadyen as Orson Welles. 135 min.
11-2424 Was $99.99 ***❑$14.99***

Guinevere (1999)
Written and directed by "The Truth About Cats and Dogs" scripter Audrey Wells, this poignant and emotional coming-of-age drama stars Sarah Polley as an insecure young woman who falls under the sway of an older man, charismatic photographer Stephen Rea. Foregoing college, Polley becomes Rea's apprentice, but soon learns she is the latest in a string of protégé/lovers. Gina Gershon, Jean Smart also star. 104 min.
11-2403 ***❑$99.99***

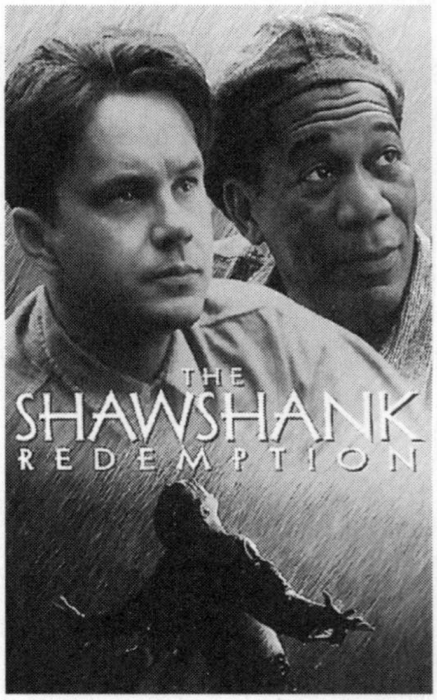

The Shawshank Redemption (1994)
A powerful look at men fighting to maintain hope in the most hopeless of circumstances, this adaptation of a Stephen King story stars Tim Robbins as a convicted murderer who is tutored in the brutal realities of life in New England's Shawshank Prison by hardened fellow inmate Morgan Freeman. James Whitmore, William Sadler co-star. 142 min.
02-2752 Was $19.99 ***❑$14.99***

The Shawshank Redemption (Letterboxed Version)
Also available in a theatrical, widescreen format.
19-2724 ***❑$19.99***

B. Monkey (1999)
Romantic drama and suspenseful action are in ample supply in this thriller starring Asia Argento as B., an expert thief who tires of her life of crime and looks for normalcy with teacher/jazz D.J. Jared Harris. It isn't long, however, before B.'s need for danger—and her former partners in plunder—threaten her new life. Rupert Everett, Jonathan Rhys Meyers co-star. 92 min.
11-2404 Was $99.99 ***❑$19.99***

Down In The Delta (1998)
The acclaimed directing debut of poet Maya Angelou focuses on Alfre Woodard, a drug- and alcohol-addicted Chicago woman sent with her two neglected children by her mother to live with her aunt and uncle on a Mississippi farm. While there, Woodard inherits a family heirloom and begins to straighten out her life. With Mary Alice, Al Freeman, Jr., Esther Rolle and Wesley Snipes. 111 min.
11-2330 Was $99.99 ***❑$19.99***

The Mighty (1998)
Sensitive family saga tells of the friendship between two young outcasts: Maxwell (Eldon Henson), a large, good-natured 13-year-old who lacks courage and smarts, and Kevin (Kieran Culkin), a small, intelligent boy suffering from a congenital disease. The two bond through a school assignment and use Arthurian legends to guide them through real and fantasy worlds. With Sharon Stone, Gillian Anderson, Gena Rowlands. 100 min.
11-2325 Was $99.99 ***❑$19.99***

A Walk On The Moon (1999)
This bittersweet film takes place in a Jewish Catskill bungalow in 1969, where Diane Lane, the wife of TV repairman Liev Shreiber, is vacationing with rebellious teenage daughter Anna Paquin. Both mother and daughter face revelations about their sexuality during the summer of Woodstock and the moon landing. With Viggo Mortensen; directed by Tony Goldwyn. 107 min.
11-2351 Was $99.99 ***❑$19.99***

ARTISAN ENTERTAINMENT

BRINGING YOU THE BEST IN INDEPENDENT FILMS...

Available For Just...

$14.99 EACH ON VHS
$19.99 EACH ON DVD

BUENA VISTA SOCIAL CLUB (1999)

German filmmaker Wim Wenders' documentary counterpart to the Grammy-winning album follows guitarist/musicologist Ry Cooder on a trip to Havana and an encounter with some of Cuba's greatest musicians and singers, many of whom are found living in obscurity, and culminates with the "Club's" aging members giving a triumphant concert at New York's Carnegie Hall. 105 min.

27-7148 VHS **$14.99**

Also available on DVD:
Standard; Soundtrack: Spanish 5.1; Subtitles: English; musician information; production notes; additional scenes; theatrical trailer; scene access.

D1-6025 DVD **$19.99**

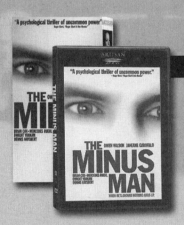

FELICIA'S JOURNEY (1999)

Felicia (Elaine Cassidy), a young Irish woman in search of her soldier boyfriend in the British Midlands, is befriended by Joseph Hilditch (Bob Hoskins), a caterer with a strange affection for his late mother. Little does Felicia realize that Joseph is, in fact, a deranged serial killer...and she's targeted as his next victim. Atom Egoyan ("Exotica") directed this disturbing tale. 111 min.

27-7192 VHS **$14.99**

Also available on DVD:
Widescreen; Soundtrack: English 5.1; Subtitles: English; audio commentary; biographies; featurette; additional footage; recipes; production notes; TV spots; theatrical trailers; scene access.

D1-7129 DVD **$19.99**

THE MINUS MAN (1999)

In this eerie suspenser directed by "Blade Runner" scripter Hampton Fancher, Owen Wilson is a serial killer who settles in a small Pacific Northwest town where he rents a room from troubled couple Mercedes Ruehl and Brian Cox, who helps him get a job at the post office. But even while holding a job and dating workmate Janeane Garofalo, Wilson can't stop killing people. With Sheryl Crow. 114 min.

27-7191 VHS **$14.99**

Also available on DVD:
Widescreen; Soundtrack: English 5.1; serial killer information; production notes; scene access.

D1-6817 DVD **$19.99**

ILLUMINATA (1999)

Set in early 1900s New York, this witty comedy features John Turturro (who also directed) as the leader of a theatrical company who's eager to put on a new play he's written to impress leading lady Katherine Borowitz (Turturro's real-life wife). The on-stage romance pales next to the many backstage trysts and misunderstandings that surround the troupe. Susan Sarandon, Ben Gazzara, Christopher Walken, Bill Irwin and Beverly D'Angelo also star. 120 min.

27-7147 VHS **$14.99**

Also available on DVD:
Widescreen; Soundtracks: English 2.0; Subtitles: English; audio commentaries; cast and crew information; additional scene; production notes; theatrical trailer; scene access.

D1-6111 DVD **$19.99**

ARTISAN
HOME ENTERTAINMENT™

Shooting The Past (1999)
Unusual and compelling tale from maverick director Stephen Poliakoff ("Century") stars Liam Cunningham as an American businessman with plans to renovate a London office building. Instead of finding the building cleared upon his arrival, Cunningham finds an incredible photograph collection and a staff of librarians who'll do anything to preserve them. With Timothy Spall, Lindsay Duncan. 180 min. on two tapes.
08-8831 □*$29.99*

Far Harbor (1996)
A young couple, struggling with the sudden death of their newborn daughter, finds the strength to cope during an emotional weekend retreat with friends on a Long Island shore town. Moving drama stars Jennifer Connelly, Dan Futterman, Marcia Gay Harden, George Newbern and Jim True. AKA: "Mr. Spielberg's Boat." 99 min.
08-8739 *$19.99*

Unhook The Stars (1996)
Middle-aged widow Gena Rowlands, looking for meaning in her life since her grown children moved away, finds it in an unexpected place when she agrees to look after neighbor Marisa Tomei's young son and strikes up a friendship with the boy and his divorced mother. Sensitive drama from first-time director Nick Cassavetes (son of Rowlands and John Cassavetes) also stars Gerard Depardieu, Moira Kelly. 105 min.
11-2119 Was $99.99 □*$19.99*

The Substance Of Fire (1996)
Jon Robin Baitz adapts his own acclaimed play into this commanding drama centering on a New York publisher, haunted by his childhood experiences during the Holocaust, whose decision to only produce political books leaves the future of both his company and family threatened. Ron Rifkin, Tony Goldwyn, Timothy Hutton and Sarah Jessica Parker star. 101 min.
11-2128 Was $19.99 □*$14.99*

Jodie Foster

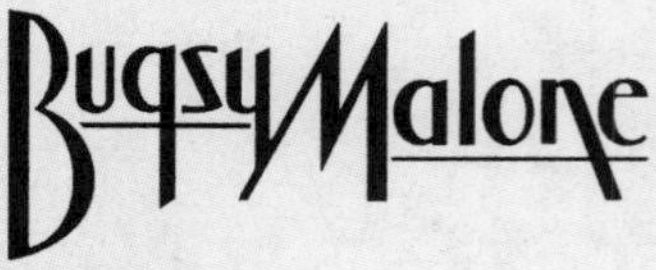

Bugsy Malone (1976)
One of the most original film musicals ever is a tale of gangsters in New York during the "Roaring Twenties." The catch is that the cast are all kids—led by Jodie Foster and Scott Baio. Music by Paul Williams; Alan Parker ("Fame") directs. 94 min.
06-1112 Was $24.99 *$14.99*

Foxes (1980)
On the glittery streets of L.A. four teenage girls are on the prowl, looking for fun, for kicks, for love. Jodie Foster, Scott Baio, Sally Kellerman and Cherie Currie star in this sizzling look at the dark side of "Val Girl" life; directed by Adrian Lyne ("Fatal Attraction"). 106 min.
12-2608 *$14.99*

Carny (1980)
Overlooked drama of everyday life in a travelling carnival, filled with wonderful moments and offbeat characters. Teenage runaway Jodie Foster joins the show and becomes involved with clown Gary Busey and carny boss Robbie Robertson. Meg Foster, Kenneth McMillan co-star. 106 min.
19-1758 *$19.99*

Shocked (1985)
Gripping drama stars Jodie Foster as the teenage bride of trader John Lithgow in 19th-century New Zealand. His abusive attitude towards her drives her to devise a bizarre murder scheme. AKA: "Mesmerized." 84 min.
75-7032 Was $19.99 *$14.99*

Siesta (1987)
It takes place during the hottest part of the day, when the mind can play tricks on a person. Stuntwoman Ellen Barkin soon finds her involvement with lover Gabriel Byrne taking a violent twist in this sensual, suspenseful drama. Also stars Jodie Foster, Isabella Rossellini, Julian Sands, Martin Sheen. 97 min.
40-1392 Was $19.99 □*$14.99*

The Accused (1988)
Three men commit a brutal gang rape in a crowded bar, but because their victim has a reputation as a "party girl" the district attorney (Kelly McGillis) can only pursue minor charges against them. Jodie Foster earned an Academy Award for her role as a woman denied justice in this gripping, fact-based drama. 110 min.
06-1641 □*$14.99*

Five Corners (1988)
Two very different stories are featured in this slice of Bronx life, circa 1964, from writer John Patrick Shanley ("Moonstruck"). Two lovable nitwits take their dates on a hilarious "night on the town," while nearby a young woman is confronted by the ex-con who tried to rape her years earlier. Jodie Foster, Tim Robbins and John Turturro star. 92 min.
12-2659 *$14.99*

Stealing Home (1988)
Mark Harmon stars in this wistful comedy-drama as a pro ballplayer who, while returning to his hometown after the suicide of the babysitter who was his guide and confidant (Jodie Foster), flashes back on their times together. Harold Ramis co-stars as Harmon's best friend; filmed in Philadelphia. 98 min.
19-1688 Was $19.99 □*$14.99*

The Silence Of The Lambs (1991)
The third film in Oscar history to win five top awards, director Jonathan Demme's harrowing cinematic thriller stars Jodie Foster as an FBI trainee who engages in a mental duel with jailed serial killer Hannibal "The Cannibal" Lecter (the understatedly sinister Anthony Hopkins) to gain information needed to track down another murderer. With Scott Glenn, Ted Levine. 118 min.
73-1105 □*$14.99*

Little Man Tate (1991)
Jodie Foster's directing debut is a sensitive story about a troubled 7-year-old genius (Adam Hann-Byrd) and the battle for his heart and mind between his working-class mother (Foster) and a child psychologist (Dianne Wiest) who runs a school for gifted youngsters. Harry Connick, Jr. co-stars. 99 min.
73-1116 Was $19.99 □*$14.99*

Sommersby (1993)
Based on the 1982 French film "The Return of Martin Guerre," this beautifully filmed romantic drama stars Richard Gere as a Confederate soldier who returns home to wife Jodie Foster after a six-year absence. So changed is Gere's behavior that Foster and the townsfolk begin to think he may be an impostor. James Earl Jones, Bill Pullman star. 114 min.
19-2098 Was $19.99 □*$14.99*

Nell (1994)
Jodie Foster was nominated for an Oscar for her portrayal of a young woman who developed a language all her own while living alone with her disabled mother in the Smokey Mountains. After the mother dies, Foster is faced with institutionalization, but doctor Liam Neeson attempts to communicate with her and help her assimilate into society. Natasha Richardson co-stars. 113 min.
04-2951 Was $19.99 □*$14.99*

Contact (1997)
Radio astronomer Jodie Foster receives signals from outer space which, when decoded, offer plans for building a ship that could help her reach the star Vega, the source of the signals. Standing in the way of realizing her lifelong dream are former boss Tom Skerritt and government agent James Woods. Matthew McConaughey co-stars as a spiritual advisor/author. Robert Zemeckis directs; based on Carl Sagan's best-seller. 150 min.
19-2598 Was $19.99 □*$14.99*

Contact (Letterboxed Version)
Also available in a theatrical, widescreen format.
19-2711 □*$19.99*

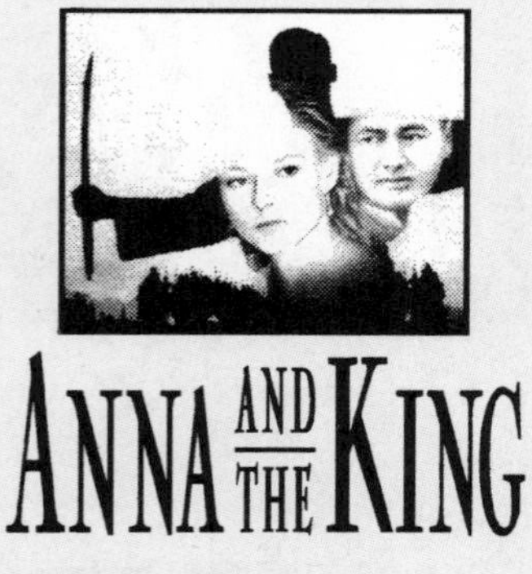

Anna And The King (1999)
One of history's most unusual love stories receives a fresh translation in this lush drama. Jodie Foster stars as the widowed English schoolteacher who moves with her young son to Siam in the mid-19th century, and Chow Yun Fat is the willful monarch whose children she's hired to educate. Amid the turmoil of a nation in the throes of change, their battle of wills grows into a special relationship. Bai Ling, Syed Alwi also star. 147 min.
04-3962 Was $99.99 □*$14.99*

Please see our index for these other Jodie Foster titles: *Alice Doesn't Live Here Anymore • Candleshoe • Maverick • Napoleon And Samantha • One Little Indian • Smile, Jenny, You're Dead • Taxi Driver • Tom Sawyer*

Cider With Rosie (1998)
Based on the popular autobiographical tale by Laurie Lee, this elegantly understated drama follows a young man's coming of age in England's Gloustershire countryside during the summer of 1918. Joe Roberts, Juliet Stevenson, David Troughton and Dashiell Reece star. 120 min.
08-8741 □*$19.99*

Keys (1994)
Former forensic pathologist Marg Helgenberger, haunted by her young son's disappearance years earlier, runs a helicopter business in the Florida Keys. When an old mentor draws her back into a case, Helgenberger becomes convinced there's a connection to her missing child. Compelling drama also stars Gary Dourdan, Ralph Waite. 93 min.
08-8752 *$14.99*

Goodnight Mister Tom (1998)
Based on the acclaimed Michelle Magorian novel, this moving "Masterpiece Theatre" presentation stars John Thaw as gruff Englishman Tom Oakley, who forms an unexpected friendship with a young boy sent to live with him in his quiet village during the London Blitz. Nick Robinson, Annabelle Apsion also star. 90 min.
08-8776 □*$19.99*

A Rather English Marriage (1998)
Superior treatment of Angela Lambert's novel stars Albert Finney as a former fighter pilot and Tom Courtenay as a milkman who move in together after their wives' deaths and try to put their lives back together. Finney tries to forge a relationship with a local woman, while Courtenay attempts to get closer to his estranged son. Joanna Lumley also stars. 120 min.
08-8810 □*$19.99*

The Boxer (1997)
Turning his attention again to the ongoing turmoil in Northern Ireland, director/co-writer Jim Sheridan ("In the Name of the Father") reteams with star Daniel Day-Lewis for this compelling story of an amateur fighter and ex-IRA member who returns to his Belfast home after 14 years in prison. Looking to resume his ring career—and his romance with married ex-lover Emily Watson—Day-Lewis' plans to reopen the local gym as a boxing club for Catholic and Protestant boys rouses the anger of IRA hardliners. Brian Cox, Gerard McSorley also star. 114 min.
07-2639 Was $99.99 □*$14.99*

Welcome To Sarajevo (1997)
Based on the actual experiences of news correspondents covering the civil war in the former Yugoslavia, this compelling drama follows an international group of veteran reporters during the 1992 siege of the Bosnian capital of Sarajevo. The journalists' objectivity is tested when the conflict threatens the residents of a local orphanage. Stephen Dillane, Woody Harrelson, Emily Lloyd and Marisa Tomei star. 102 min.
11-2255 Was $99.99 □*$19.99*

Rounders (1998)
Stylish gambling drama starring Matt Damon as a poker-playing law student who reteams with ex-con pal Ed Norton to partake in a series on underground card games in the New York area. When trouble-making Norton gets into trouble with some thugs, Damon must battle Russian mobster John Malkovich in a high-stakes showdown. With Gretchen Mol, Martin Landau and John Turturro as Knish; directed by John Dahl. 121 min.
11-2295 Was $19.99 □*$14.99*

Seeing Red (1999)
This affecting true story stars Sarah Lancashire as Coral Atkins, a party girl of the '70s who starred on stage and screen. While appearing at a charity event, Adkins sees a distressed child in foster care which makes such an impression on her that she dedicates her life to helping foster children. Ann Aris, Tim Barker also star. 120 min.
08-8870 □*$19.99*

Monsignor Renard (1999)
John Thaw of "Inspector Morse" fame plays a humble priest whose ideals are seriously tested during World War II, when he must choose between the peaceful Christian doctrine and the violent necessity of the emerging Resistance movement. Cheryl Campbell, Dominic Monaghan and Des McAleer also star. 360 min.
08-8872 □*$29.99*

The Unknown Soldier (1998)
During the First World War, a wounded, amnesiac soldier is rescued from the battlefield and cared for by a beautiful nurse who falls in love with her mysterious patient. What will happen to them once the questions surrounding the soldier's past are answered? Passionate drama stars Gary Mavers, Juliet Aubrey, Aislin McGuckin. 180 min.
08-8703 □*$29.99*

54 (1998)
It was the celebrity-filled New York nightclub that came to symbolize everything good—and bad—about the Disco era. Go behind the scenes at Studio 54 in this glittery, song-filled drama that examines the lives of a group of club workers who saw it as a chance to fulfill their dreams. Neve Campbell, Salma Hayek, Ryan Phillippe, and Mike Meyers as 54's colorful co-creator, Steve Rubell star. 92 min.
11-2285 Was $19.99 □*$14.99*

The War At Home (1996)
A Vietnam veteran who cannot forget the horrors of what he saw a year after his return to his family's Texas home leads his parents and sister into an emotional confrontation one Thanksgiving in this powerful and moving adaptation of James Duff's stage drama "Homefront." Emilio Estevez (who also directed), Kathy Bates, Martin Sheen and Kimberly Williams star. 123 min.
11-2167 Was $19.99 □*$14.99*

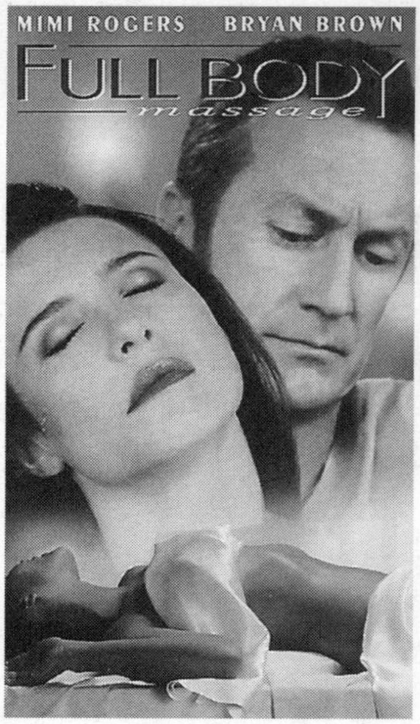

Full Body Massage (1995)
From director Nicolas Roeg ("Don't Look Now") comes this sensually charged drama starring Mimi Rogers and Bryan Brown in a tale of a lonely California art gallery owner and the masseur who comes into her life, and the steamy relationship that grows between them. 93 min.
06-2440 Was $89.99 □*$14.99*

Shades Of Fear (1993)
Set shortly after the end of World War II, this intriguing character drama from writer Jeanette Winterson ("Oranges Are Not the Only Fruit") explores the relationships that develop—and the secrets that are revealed—among the passengers of a transatlantic cruise to London. Rakie Ayola, John Hurt, Jonathan Pryce and Vanessa Redgrave star. AKA: "Great Moments in Aviation." 93 min.
11-2197 Was $99.99 □*$19.99*

The Night And The Moment (1994)
In 18th-century France, a writer and notorious playboy, at the request of a noblewoman he wishes to seduce, recounts the story of a romance he once had in jail, exchanging letters with an unknown woman in the adjoining cell. Lavish and erotic costume drama stars Willem Dafoe, Lena Olin, Miranda Richardson and Jean Claude Carrière. 89 min.
11-2226 Was $99.99 □*$19.99*

Squeeze (1997)
Three 14-year-olds struggling to survive in Boston's crime- and poverty-plagued Dorchester Fields neighborhood are helped by a local youth leader, but must fend for themselves when they're threatened by a street gang. Rookie writer/director Robert Patton-Spruill's acclaimed urban drama features a cast of local kids from the Dorchester Youth Collective. 105 min.
11-2224 Was $99.99 □*$14.99*

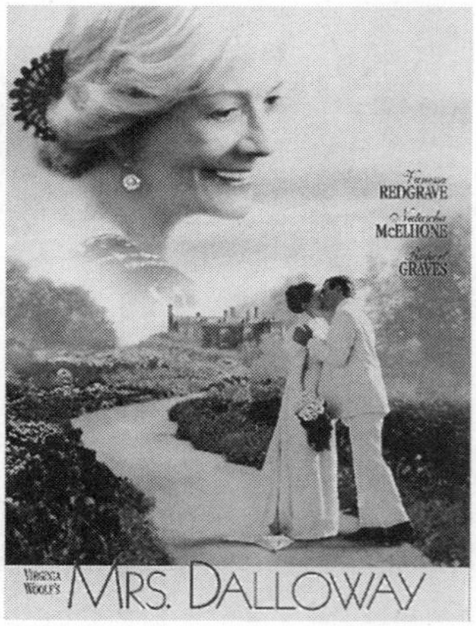

Mrs. Dalloway (1998)
Virginia Woolf's beloved tale of romance and regret is brought to life in this critically acclaimed drama from director Marleen Gorris. Vanessa Redgrave stars as Clarissa Dalloway, a "perfect hostess" in her fifties who reflects on her past and reconsiders old decisions. Natascha McElhone plays the younger Clarissa; Rupert Graves, Michael Kitchen and Sarah Bedel also star. 97 min.
02-8965 Was $99.99 *$19.99*

218 · DRAMA MOVIES UNLIMITED CALL · 1-800-4-MOVIES

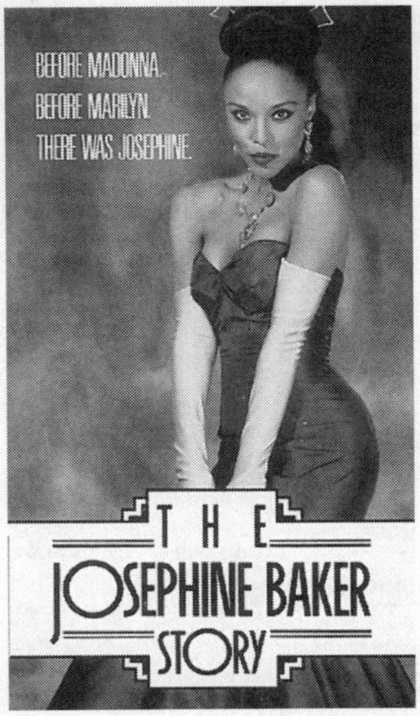
BEFORE MADONNA.
BEFORE MARILYN.
THERE WAS JOSEPHINE.
THE
JOSEPHINE BAKER
STORY

The Josephine Baker Story (1991)
Fascinating true story of the woman who started singing at Harlem nightspots, then made a name for herself in '20s Paris with exotic semi-nude dance numbers and went on to star in movies. All the triumphs, glamour and tragedies of Baker's life are captured in this acclaimed film starring Lynn Whitfield, Ruben Blades, David Dukes and Louis Gossett, Jr. 129 min.
44-1814 Was $19.99 □*$14.99*

Descending Angel (1991)
Powerful drama starring George C. Scott as a former Nazi collaborator whose past is discovered when his daughter decides to get married. The daughter and her husband-to-be take on father and his henchmen in this gripping tale. Diane Lane, Eric Roberts also star. 98 min.
44-1795 Was $89.99 *$19.99*

Bad Lieutenant (1992)
An explosive, audacious melodrama featuring the electrifying Harvey Keitel as a depraved, sex-, gambling- and drug-addicted New York police detective who uses his badge as a passport to partake in crime, rather than enforce it. When a young nun is raped, the case leads Keitel, a lapsed Catholic, to question his tormented soul. Directed by Abel Ferrara. Uncut NC-17 version; 96 min.
27-6822 Was $19.99 □*$14.99*

House Of Cards (1992)
Compelling, challenging drama starring Kathleen Turner as a recently widowed architect so self-absorbed in her own problems that she doesn't notice that her 6-year-old daughter is slipping into a state of autism. Tommy Lee Jones plays the state-appointed psychiatrist called in to help the young girl. Asha Menina and Esther Rolle also star. 109 min.
27-6846 Was $19.99 □*$14.99*

Killing Zoe (1994)
American safecracker Eric Stoltz travels to Paris to help an old friend execute a daring Bastille Day bank robbery, but the heist is threatened when the two get involved in a love triangle with French art student/hooker Julie Delpy. Roger Avary, who worked on the scripts of "True Romance" and "Pulp Fiction," wrote and directed this steamy, fast-paced crime drama. 96 min.
27-6903 Was $19.99 □*$14.99*

The Winner (1997)
In this noirish drama from director Alex Cox ("Sid and Nancy"), a gullible loser (Vincent D'Onofrio) on a gambling winning streak in Las Vegas becomes the target of a manipulative lounge singer (Rebecca DeMornay) and her partner (Billy Bob Thornton). Stakes are raised when hit men and the loser's brother arrive on the scene. With Frank Whaley, Michael Madsen, Delroy Lindo. 89 min.
27-7039 Was $99.99 □*$19.99*

A Brooklyn State Of Mind (1999)
Vincent Spano is a Brooklyn native who works for local mobster Danny Aiello. When filmmaker Maria Grazia Cucinotta appears in the neighborhood, Spano shows interest both in her and her documentary on Brooklyn. But when he discovers the filmmaker is trying to expose Aiello's dark side, he's torn between his allegiance and the truth. With Abe Vigoda, Jennifer Esposito and Tony Danza. 90 min.
27-7120 Was $99.99 □*$14.99*

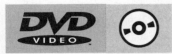

DVD VIDEO
ASK ABOUT OUR GIANT DVD CATALOG!

Niagara, Niagara (1998)
Robin Tunney and Henry Thomas star as two misfits who fall in love and head out on the road in search of a rare doll. Tunney is affected with Tourette's Syndrome and drinks heavily in lieu of taking medicine, while Thomas is a longtime victim of child abuse. Michael Parks also stars in this unusual and emotional drama. 93 min.
27-7075 Was $89.99 □*$14.99*

Tracked (1997)
In the dog unit of a maximum security prison, prisoner Dean Cain runs for his life from the vicious canines tracking him. But why has the district attorney really set the dogs on him? And what connection does it all have to a brutal slaying behind bars? Bryan Brown and Tia Carrere also star in Ken Russell's intense prison drama. AKA: "Dog Boys." 92 min.
27-7091 □*$89.99*

Laurel Avenue (1993)
Highly-acclaimed, insightful look at the Arnetts, an African-American family from St. Paul, Minnesota, over the course of a weekend. Members of the family include twin sisters, one a cop, the other a struggling single mother with a drug problem. Mary Alice and Juanita Jennings star; directed by Carl Franklin ("One False Move"). 156 min.
44-1953 Was $69.99 □*$49.99*

Sticks And Stones (1998)
Tired of a neighborhood bully's aggression, a group of three adolescent boys decide between themselves to exact a violent revenge for his tormenting them in this compelling, disturbing drama. Chauncey Leopardi, Max Goldblatt, Jordan Brower, Gary Busey and Kirstie Alley star. 96 min.
27-7096 □*$89.99*

The Maker (1997)
Dark coming-of-age film that concerns an orphaned 18-year-old who is taught the ways of drug dealing and crime by his smooth-talking con man older brother. With Matthew Modine, Michael Madsen, Mary-Louise Parker, Fairuza Balk and Jonathan Rhys-Myers. 90 min.
27-7074 □*$89.99*

The Infiltrator (1995)
Riveting true story starring Oliver Platt as an American journalist in Germany who goes undercover to uncover a link between the young neo-Nazis responsible for attacking immigrants and surviving soldiers and members of Hitler's Third Reich. Arliss Howard, Peter Riegert and Alan King co-star. 102 min.
44-2015 Was $19.99 *$14.99*

The Affair (1995)
A black American soldier stationed in England during World War II becomes romantically involved with a British woman whose husband is serving overseas. When the husband returns and finds out about the affair, a violent confrontation follows that has the American G.I. on trial for his life. Powerful drama stars Courtney B. Vance, Kerry Fox, Ned Beatty. 104 min.
44-2027 Was $19.99 □*$14.99*

Sugartime (1995)
The controversial love affair between Las Vegas mobster Sam Giancanna and popular singer Phyllis McGuire, a romance that rocked America and made the couple the targets of FBI spies, forms the basis of this compelling drama. John Turturro, Mary-Louise Parker, Maury Chaykin star. 110 min.
44-2045 Was $99.99 □*$14.99*

Don't Look Back (1996)
When he accidentally comes into possession of a suitcase full of drug money, L.A. musician and drug addict Eric Stoltz tries to change his life by returning to his boyhood home of Galveston, Texas, and the friends he left behind, but the crooks whose cash he took will stop at nothing to get it back. Powerful thriller also stars John Corbett, Annabeth Gish, Josh Hamilton. 90 min.
44-2064 Was $19.99 □*$14.99*

Dangerous Passion (1995)
The bitter rivalry between urban crime bosses Carl Weathers and Billy Dee Williams gets even hotter when the two compete for the attentions of the same woman in this intense, action-filled drama. With Lonette McKee. 94 min.
27-6960 □*$89.99*

The Only Thrill (1997)
Diane Keaton and Sam Shepard star as co-workers whose decades-long friendship hides a mutual love they're afraid to express. Will Keaton's husband's death and Shepard's wife's serious illness bring them together? With Diane Lane, Robert Patrick. 108 min.
27-7097 □*$89.99*

No Way Home (1997)
In this gripping and action-filled crime drama, ex-con Tim Roth tries to follow the straight and narrow path to a new life, only to be drawn into a dangerous drug-dealing scheme by his brother. James Russo, Deborah Kara Unger also star. 101 min.
27-7044 □*$99.99*

Strapped (1993)
When his pregnant girlfriend is jailed on drug charges, a young black man has three ways to free her: turn police informer, raise the bail money by joining in a black market gun ring, or play both sides against each other and pray he doesn't get caught! Top-notch urban drama, directed by Forest Whitaker, stars Bokeem Woodbine, Michael Biehn. 102 min.
44-1954 Was $19.99 □*$14.99*

Hot Boyz (1999)
With his girlfriend falsely accused in a cop's murder, young rapper Silkk the Shocker is given a chance by detective Gary Busey to clear her name by infiltrating a drug-selling ring. When he learns that the police are using him and his girlfriend was killed in jail, Silkk teams with pals Snoop Dogg and C-Murder to form his own death-dealing gang in this intense urban drama, written and directed by co-star Master P. 98 min.
27-7181 Was $99.99 □*$14.99*

Against The Wall (1994)
An intense story set against the 1971 Attica prison riots and focusing on two disaffected prisoners who start the turmoil in order to obtain better conditions within the New York penitentiary and a young guard caught in the middle of the explosive situation. Kyle MacLachlan, Samuel L. Jackson, Clarence Williams III, Harry Dean Stanton star; John Frankenheimer directs. Unrated version; 111 min.
44-1969 Was $19.99 *$14.99*

Russell Crowe

Hammers Over The Anvil (1991)
Simple and moving drama set in early 1900s Australia, as a young crippled boy develops a friendship with a local horse trainer, only to find the relationship strained when the man has an affair with a married Englishwoman. Russell Crowe, Alexander Outhred and Charlotte Rampling star. 101 min.
53-7570 *$19.99*

Proof (1992)
A provocative Australian drama laced with black humor, as an embittered blind man obsessed with photography, a manipulative woman who cleans his house and a cafe worker are involved in a complex triangle that leads to surprising revelations. Jocelyn Moorhouse's acclaimed film stars Hugo Weaving, Genevieve Picot and Russell Crowe. 90 min.
02-5010 Was $89.99 □*$19.99*

The Crossing (1992)
Powerful romantic drama from Australia about a woman who decides to stay with her family when her artist boyfriend leaves their small-town home to pursue his career. She falls in love with his best friend, but when he returns home, a nasty rivalry ensues. Russell Crowe, Danielle Spencer star. 92 min.
63-1579 Was $89.99 □*$14.99*

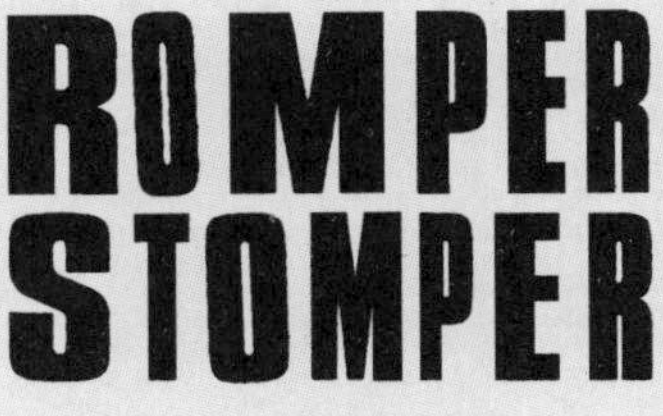
ROMPER
STOMPER

Romper Stomper (1992)
A powerful look at the global problem of neo-Nazi gang violence, writer/director Geoffrey Wright's debut feature follows a group of teenage skinheads in Melbourne, Australia. Amid their attacks on immigrants and internal squabbling, the film paints a three-dimensional, at times poignant, look at young people for whom hatred is a way of life. Russell Crowe, Jacqueline McKenzie star. Unrated version; 88 min.
71-5296 *$19.99*

For The Moment (1996)
A bittersweet romantic drama about an egocentric Canadian airman training for combat duty during World War II who falls for a local married woman. The two carry on a passionate affair that is soon threatened by his military obligations. Russell Crowe and Christianne Hurt star. 120 min.
04-3367 Was $29.99 □*$14.99*

No Way Back (1997)
Smashing action yarn starring Russell Crowe as an FBI agent who finds himself a pawn in a powerful mobster's game of revenge after an assignment goes awry. The mob leader kidnaps Crowe's son in order to force him to assassinate the Japanese hood responsible for the mobster's son's death. Helen Slater, Michael Lerner also star. 92 min.
02-3067 Was $19.99 □*$14.99*

Rough Magic (1997)
When her mentor is accidentally killed by her conniving would-be politician fiancé, magician's assistant Bridget Fonda flees and hides out in a small Mexican town. Hired to locate Fonda, rumpled reporter Russell Crowe winds up falling for her and joins her on a quest for a magical Indian potion. Winning blend of romance, mystery and mysticism also stars Jim Broadbent, Paul Rodriguez, Kenneth Mars. 104 min.
02-3126 Was $99.99 *$19.99*

L.A. Confidential (1997)
Smashing translation of James Ellroy's celebrated pulp novel of life in the L.A. police department in the 1950s. Russell Crowe, Guy Pearce and Kevin Spacey are three cops who must put aside their differences in order to crack the brutal Nite Owl Massacre, wending through a maze of police corruption, organized crime, high-priced call girls and sleazy journalists. With James Cromwell, Danny DeVito and Best Supporting Actress Oscar-winner Kim Basinger; Curtis Hanson directs. Special video edition also includes a 19-minute "making of" documentary, "Off The Record." 156 min. total.
19-2680 Was $19.99 □*$14.99*

L.A. Confidential (Letterboxed Version)
Also available in a theatrical, widescreen format.
19-2737 □*$19.99*

Breaking Up (1997)
For everyone who's tired of romantic comedies detailing the beginnings of a relationship comes this funny and biting look at a couple's long, ragged road to break-up. Russell Crowe and Salma Hayek, the film's only characters, play the lovers whose conflicts, partings and reunitings are tellingly depicted in a variety of situations and vignettes. 89 min.
19-2682 Was $99.99 □*$19.99*

Heaven's Burning (1997)
A Japanese newlywed abandons her husband on their Australian honeymoon and becomes a hostage in an aborted bank robbery. She's rescued by the getaway driver and joins him in a wild cross-country run from both the law and her estranged husband. Offbeat, action-filled road drama stars Russell Crowe ("L.A. Confidential") and Youki Kudoh. 99 min.
68-1873 Was $99.99 □*$14.99*

The Insider (1999)
This riveting true-life story centers on Jeffrey Wigand (Russell Crowe), a scientist with a major tobacco company who reveals potentially damaging, top-secret industry information to "60 Minutes" producer Lowell Bergman (Al Pacino) and reporter Mike Wallace (Christopher Plummer), only to have his career and life threatened. Diane Venora, Philip Baker Hall and Lindsay Crouse also star in director Michael Mann's ("Heat") powerful drama. 158 min.
11-2409 Letterboxed □*$19.99*

Mystery, Alaska (1999)
A change of pace from director Jay Roach (the "Austin Powers" films) and co-scripter David E. Kelley ("Ally McBeal"), this rousing mix of sports drama and small-town comedy follows a Sports Illustrated writer who returns to his Alaska hometown with a challenge for the local pond hockey team: a televised exhibition game with the New York Rangers. Russell Crowe is the veteran player/sheriff, Burt Reynolds the local judge and team's coach, and Hank Azaria the transplanted writer; with Mary McCormack, Colm Meaney and a cameo by Mike Myers. 119 min.
11-2423 Was $99.99 □*$14.99*

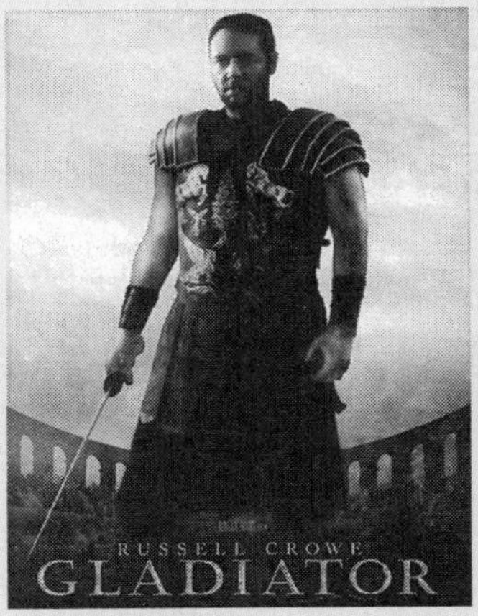
RUSSELL CROWE
GLADIATOR

Gladiator (2000)
Stirring "sword and sandal" spectacle from director Ridley Scott stars Russell Crowe as Maximus, a Roman general whose battlefield heroics make him a favorite of ailing emperor Richard Harris, who picks Crowe as his successor. But when Joaquin Phoenix, Harris' duplicitous son, learns of these plans, he orders Crowe and his family killed. Left for dead and sold into slavery, Crowe emerges as the empire's greatest gladiator, leading to a deadly showdown in the Colosseum and a chance for vengeance. With Oliver Reed, Connie Nielsen, Djimon Hounsou and Derek Jacobi. 155 min.
07-2952 □*$99.99*

Please see our index for these other Russell Crowe titles: *Brides Of Christ • The Efficiency Expert • The Quick And The Dead • The Silver Stallion: King Of The Wild Brumbies • Virtuosity*

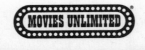

Leonardo DiCaprio

This Boy's Life (1993)
The acclaimed coming-of-age memoir by Tobias Wolff is turned into a powerful and poignant drama set in the 1950s. Ellen Barkin portrays a single mother who marries a seemingly wonderful man (Robert De Niro) in the hopes that he'll be a perfect father for her son (Leonardo DiCaprio), but her new husband turns out to be a hot-headed authoritarian against whom her boy stages a brutal rebellion. 115 min.
19-2141 Was $19.99 ❑*$14.99*

Total Eclipse (1995)
The relationship between 19th-century French poets Arthur Rimbaud and Paul Verlaine is explored in this erotic drama from director Agnieszka Holland ("Europa Europa"). The rebellious, egocentric Rimbaud's stay with Verlaine and his pregnant wife in Paris leads to a kinky, mysterious affair between the two men. Leonardo DiCaprio, David Thewlis, Romane Bohringer star. 110 min.
02-5091 Was $99.99 ❑*$19.99*

The Basketball Diaries (1995)
Jim Carroll's autobiographical cult favorite is the basis for this gritty film starring Leonardo DiCaprio as Carroll, a basketball star at a Catholic prep school whose promising future comes tumbling down when he gets addicted, first to glue-sniffing, then heroin. Mark Wahlberg, Lorraine Bracco and Bruno Kirby also star in this harrowing slice-of-New York-life. 102 min.
02-8318 ❑*$14.99*

TITANIC

Titanic (1997)
The highest grossing film of all time, winner of a record-tying 11 Academy Awards (including Best Picture and Best Director), is now an unforgettable home video event. As an undersea expedition explores the remains of the RMS Titanic, a 100-year-old survivor of the doomed ship relates her account of the 1912 voyage, when, as a young socialite, she had a life-changing romance with a handsome steerage passenger. Their tragic love affair is set amid spectacular scenes of the liner's collision with an iceberg and sinking. Leonardo DiCaprio, Kate Winslet, Billy Zane, Gloria Stuart and Bill Paxton star; James Cameron directs. 194 min.
06-2746 ❑*$24.99*

Titanic (Letterboxed Version)
Also available in a theatrical, widescreen format.
06-2747 ❑*$24.99*

Titanic: Collector's Edition
Near...far...wherever they are, "Titanic" fans will want this limited edition boxed set that, along with the movie, includes an exclusive, 24-page photo book and a special framed filmstrip.
06-2863 Ltd. Quantities ❑*$39.99*

Titanic: Collector's Edition (Letterboxed Version)
Also available in a theatrical, widescreen format.
06-2864 Ltd. Quantities ❑*$39.99*

The Man In The Iron Mask (1998)
Leonardo DiCaprio plays both the ruthless King Louis XIV of France and the monarch's masked and imprisoned twin brother in this lush, action-filled rendition of the Dumas novel. With the country on the verge of collapse, the legendary Musketeers (Gabriel Byrne, Gerard Depardieu, Jeremy Irons, John Malkovich) reunite and launch a daring plan to switch the nasty Leo with his jailed double. 131 min.
12-3253 Was $19.99 ❑*$14.99*

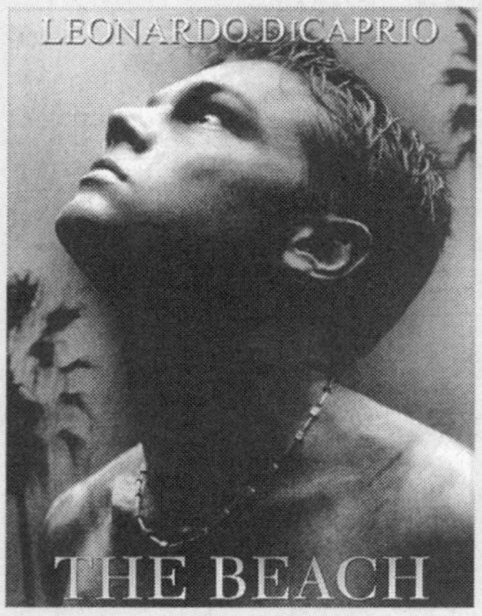

The Beach (2000)
The discovery of a hidden island paradise off the Thai coast leads to a sensual idyll for American tourist Leonardo DiCaprio and French fellow travellers Virginie Ledoyen and Guillaume Canet, but their seaside Shangri-La hides a dark secret that threatens their lives. Lushly filmed adventure from director Danny Boyle and scripter John Hodge ("Trainspotting") also stars Tilda Swinton, Robert Carlyle. 119 min.
04-3965 ❑*$99.99*

Leonardo DiCaprio: In His Own Words
The star of "Titanic" talks about his role in the epic film, as well as his parts in such other works as "Marvin's Room," "William Shakespeare's Romeo + Juliet" and "The Basketball Diaries." Leo reveals his likes, dislikes, his approach to acting and lots more.
05-5072 *$19.99*

Portrait Of Leonardo: The Kid Who Took Hollywood
With his starring role in "Titanic," Leonardo DiCaprio took the world by storm. This video chronicles his life and career through film clips, interviews and special footage of where Leo has lived and where he can be found in Los Angeles and New York. There's also footage of the never-released "Don's Plum" and "The Foot-Shooting Party." 60 min.
05-5074 *$19.99*

Leo Mania
At the ripe old age of 23, Leonardo DiCaprio has become one of the biggest names in Hollywood. This intimate, unauthorized biography takes you through the life and career of the "Titanic" star. Included are interviews with friends, fans, and former mentors, as well as footage from Leo's early TV and film appearances. 60 min.
10-2803 *$14.99*

Leonardo DiCaprio: 3 Tape Collector's Set
This three-tape special collection features two hours of Leo, Leo and more Leo! There's "Titanic: The Premiere," a look at the film's opening at Mann's Chinese Theatre in Hollywood, plus two tapes filled with interviews with DiCaprio and such co-stars as Robert De Niro, Johnny Depp, Sharon Stone and director James Cameron. It's a Leo fan's dream!
05-5083 *$24.99*

Please see our index for these other Leonardo DiCaprio titles: *Celebrity • Critters 3 • Marvin's Room • Poison Ivy • The Quick And The Dead • What's Eating Gilbert Grape • William Shakespeare's Romeo + Juliet*

Halfmoon (1995)
Three typically offbeat short stories from the pen of Paul Bowles come to the screen in this anthology from directors Frieder Schlaich and Irene von Alberti. Two young Moroccan men's friendship is threatened when they both fall for the same woman in "Merkala Beach"; a honeymoon voyage along the Amazon reveals surprises to a British couple in "Call at Corazon"; and "Allal" follows a young snake charmer's becoming one with his pet. Bowles himself serves as narrator. 90 min. In English and Arabic with English subtitles.
70-5098 Was $59.99 *$29.99*

Reversal Of Fortune (1990)
Jeremy Irons won a much-deserved Academy Award for his icy portrayal of Claus von Bulow, the social-climbing playboy accused of trying to kill wealthy wife Sunny and putting her into a coma. Glenn Close is the drug-addicted spouse and Ron Silver is hard-working defense attorney Alan Dershowitz in this fascinating drama laced with acid humor and moral ambiguity. Barbet Schroeder directs. 112 min.
19-1860 Was $19.99 ❑*$14.99*

Someone To Die For (1995)
Seduced and framed for murder, a man fights to clear his name and bring the beautiful killer to justice in this powerful, action-packed drama starring Corbin Bernsen, Ally Walker. 98 min.
19-3879 *$89.99*

One More Chance (1990)
An unusual friendship ensues when an ex-con, just out of the slammer, calls on the help of a frightened young woman to help him find his young son. Kirstie Alley and John LaMotta star in this riveting drama. 102 min.
19-7074 *$59.99*

Broken Trust (1995)
Municipal judge Tom Selleck is recruited by federal agents to help in a sting operation designed to catch shady judges. But Selleck's involvement soon brings him into conflict with family and colleagues. Elizabeth McGovern, William Atherton and Marsha Mason star. 96 min.
18-7576 Was $89.99 *$14.99*

The Passion Of Darkly Noon (1996)
A hauntingly beautiful woman turns a shy young man's desires into reality, before letting those passions lead him down a road of jealousy and madness, in this suspenseful and erotic drama starring Ashley Judd, Brendan Fraser, Viggo Mortensen and Loren Dean. 146 min.
18-7720 Was $99.99 ❑*$14.99*

Hope (1997)
In a small Southern town in 1962, a young girl struggles with a dark family secret that, if revealed, holds the key to the violent racial tensions tearing her community apart. Jena Malone, Christine Lahti, Catherine O'Hara and Jeffrey D. Sams star in this compelling and compassionate directorial debut for Goldie Hawn. 95 min.
18-7792 Was $79.99 ❑*$14.99*

The Railway Station Man (1992)
Julie Christie and Donald Sutherland reunite for the first time since "Don't Look Now" in this powerful drama set in modern-day Ireland. Christie plays a widow who moves with her young son from the turmoil of Northern Ireland and settles in a small village where she meets and falls in love with American visitor Sutherland, but their romance is threatened by a secret in his past. 93 min.
18-7421 Was $89.99 ❑*$14.99*

Percy And Thunder (1992)
Exciting boxing yarn stars James Earl Jones as an old-school trainer who thinks he's found a new champion in a young middleweight fighter. Problems ensue, however, when powerful impresario Billy Dee Williams wants the boxer working for him. Zakes Mokae, Gloria Reuben, Robert Wuhl and Courtney B. Vance co-star. 90 min.
18-7533 ❑*$49.99*

The Water Engine (1992)
David Mamet wrote this suspense-filled drama set during the Depression and focusing on a machine shop worker who builds an automobile engine that runs on water, but finds business interests are intent on keeping his invention out of the public's hands. William H. Macy, Joe Mantegna, Treat Williams and John Mahoney star. 88 min.
18-7540 ❑*$49.99*

The Habitation Of Dragons (1992)
Powerful drama from Horton Foote ("Tender Mercies") set in a small Texas town where lawyer brothers George and Leonard Tollivar find that their success and failures in their careers have gotten in the way of their personal relationship. Brad Davis, Hallie Foote, Frederic Forrest and Joanna Miles star. 94 min.
18-7541 ❑*$49.99*

That Night (1993)
Flavorful coming-of-age story set in a New York suburb in 1961 where a young girl (Eliza Dushku) is obsessed with a teenage neighbor (Juliette Lewis), whose sexy relationship with her boyfriend (C. Thomas Howell) sparks controversy with the parents on the block. When the teenager becomes pregnant and is sent away to a special home, her young friend joins the boyfriend to find her. 90 min.
19-2175 Was $19.99 ❑*$14.99*

M. Butterfly (1993)
The incredible true story of a French diplomat who had a long love affair with a male Chinese opera star whom he believed was a woman has been turned into a provocative movie by maverick director David Cronenberg. Jeremy Irons plays the obsessed politician, and John Lone is the focus of his affections. David Henry Hwang adapted his own acclaimed play for the screen. 101 min.
19-2209 Was $19.99 ❑*$14.99*

The Saint Of Fort Washington (1993)
Compelling social drama set around a Manhattan homeless shelter and focusing on a Vietnam veteran (Danny Glover) who befriends an emotionally troubled man (Matt Dillon) just released from a mental hospital and forced to live on the streets. Tim Hunter ("River's Edge") directs this powerfully acted story. 104 min.
19-2210 Was $89.99 ❑*$19.99*

Heaven And Earth (1993)
The final film in Oliver Stone's "Vietnam Trilogy" (which includes "Platoon" and "Born on the Fourth of July") tells the amazing true story of Le Ly Haslip, a Vietnamese woman whose experiences are traced throughout the war to her new life in the West, married to a troubled American soldier. Hiep Thi Le, Tommy Lee Jones, Joan Chen and Haing S. Ngor star. 142 min.
19-2230 Was $89.99 ❑*$19.99*

With Honors (1994)
When a homeless man living on the campus of Harvard University finds the thesis paper of a political science student, he strikes a deal: the student must perform a good deed for every page of the thesis he gets back. The two men eventually form an unlikely friendship in this touching comedy-drama that stars Joe Pesci, Brendan Fraser, Moira Kelly and Gore Vidal. 101 min.
19-2255 Was $19.99 ❑*$14.99*

The Girl In The Cadillac (1995)
Erika Eleniak is a 17-year-old Texas girl who leaves her small town and takes to the road in search of her real father. Along the way, she meets handsome crook William McNamara and joins him in a bank heist. With Michael Lerner, Bud Cort and Valerie Perrine. Inspired by James M. Cain's "The Enchanted Isle." 89 min.
18-7573 *$99.99*

Houdini (1998)
His name has become synonymous with magic and death-defying escapes, but much of his private life was shrouded in mystery. Johnathon Schaech stars as showman extraordinaire Harry Houdini in this compelling drama that depicts his life, his amazing stunts, and his crusade to debunk spiritualists and mediums. With Stacy Edwards, Paul Sorvino, George Segal. 94 min.
18-7855 Was $89.99 ❑*$14.99*

The Mambo Kings (1992)
An exhilarating, music-filled drama based on the Pulitzer Prize-winning novel about two musical Cuban brothers who arrive in 1950s America with hopes of making it big in the world of Mambo music. Armand Assante, Antonio Banderas, Cathy Moriarty, Maruschka Detmers and Talisa Soto star in this seductive film that also features appearances by Celia Cruz, Tito Puente and Desi Arnaz, Jr. 104 min.
19-1995 Was $19.99 ❑*$14.99*

The Power Of One (1992)
Powerful, action-packed drama set in South Africa chronicles the struggles of an orphaned boy who becomes a hero to the repressed black population when he scores as a champion boxer. Stephen Dorff, Morgan Freeman, Armin Mueller-Stahl and John Gielgud star in this compelling story, directed by John G. Avildsen ("The Karate Kid"). 127 min.
19-2008 Was $19.99 ❑*$14.99*

South Central (1992)
Produced by Oliver Stone, this hard-hitting drama focuses on an ex-L.A. gang member who is released from a 10-year prison stint for manslaughter and soon realizes that his son may be heading down the same hellish path. In order to stop his son's involvement in the criminal world, he must stand up to his old gang. Glenn Plummer and Carl Lumbly star. 99 min.
19-2030 Was $19.99 ❑*$14.99*

Double Edge (1992)
Newspaper reporter Faye Dunaway is on a three-week stint as a correspondent in Israel. She becomes an eyewitness to the harrowing events surrounding the ongoing Israeli-Palestinian struggle and is forced into playing a part in the disturbing drama that is unfolding in front of her. Amos Kollek co-stars and directed this riveting, true-to-life drama. 85 min.
19-2031 Was $89.99 *$19.99*

Murder In The First (1995)
Explosive true story stars Kevin Bacon as Henri Young, a teenager incarcerated in Alcatraz in the 1930s for stealing $5 from a gas station. Following regular beatings by an official, Young kills a fellow inmate after an escape attempt and joins forces with young public defender Christian Slater to battle the prison system. Gary Oldman also stars. 123 min.
19-2352 Was $19.99 ❑*$14.99*

Pure Country (1992)
Grammy-winning country-western star George Strait makes his film debut as a successful singer who leaves the glitz of his concert career in order to get back to his roots. Much to his agent's dismay, he returns to his hometown, where he meets and falls for a feisty local woman. Lesley Ann Warren and Isabel Glasser also star. 113 min.
19-2042 Was $89.99 ❑*$14.99*

The Trials Of Oscar Wilde (1960)
The true story of Oscar Wilde's trial for sodomy is dramatized in this acclaimed film that stars Peter Finch as the notorious playwright, who brings a libel suit against the Marquis of Queensbury after he accuses Wilde of seducing his son. Lionel Jeffries, John Fraser and James Mason also star. AKA: "The Man With the Green Carnation." 123 min.
09-5084 Was $19.99 *$14.99*

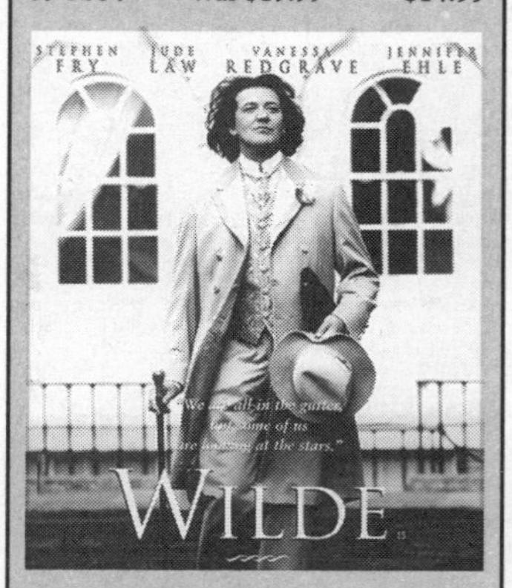

Wilde (1998)
Stephen Fry delivers a tour-de-force performance as Oscar Wilde, the Irish-born writer who delighted Victorian England with his witty insights and flamboyant lifestyle, and whose 1895 trial on sodomy charges ended in prison and disgrace. Wilde's life, the realization of his homosexuality, and the events leading to his downfall are chronicled in this acclaimed production. With Jude Law, Jennifer Ehle and Vanessa Redgrave. 116 min.
02-3230 Was $99.99 ❑*$22.99*

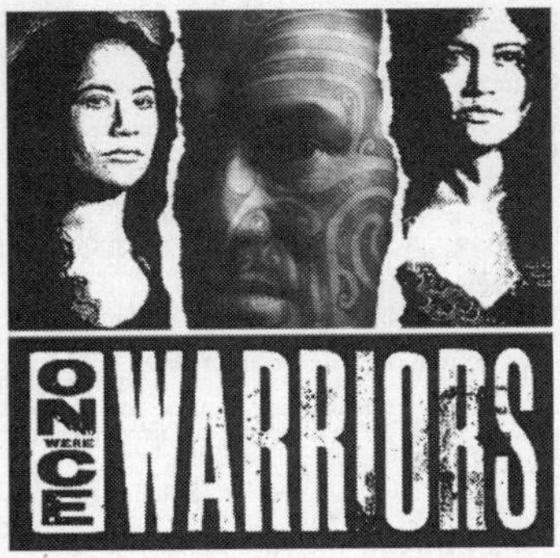

Once Were Warriors (1995)
Powerful drama from New Zealand depicting a Maori woman's struggle against the domestic violence inflicted upon her by her alcoholic husband. How his behavior affects her and their children is the focus of this acclaimed film that takes an intimate look at Maori ghetto life. With Rena Owen and Temuera Morrison. 102 min.
02-5062 Was $89.99 ❑*$19.99*

Lush Life (1994)
A powerful and music-filled tale about a black jazz trumpeter who befriends an adulterous white sax player. When the trumpet player tells the saxman he only has six months to live, the two live life to its fullest, delving into wine, women and long jam sessions. Forest Whitaker, Jeff Goldblum and Kathy Baker star. 96 min.
02-2667 Was $89.99 ❑*$19.99*

A Man Of No Importance (1994)
Set in Dublin in 1961, this touching slice-of-life story features a fine performance by Albert Finney as a homosexual bus conductor obsessed with reading Oscar Wilde to his passengers and putting on amateur theatre productions. A planned staging of "Salome" is the catalyst that forces Finney and the play's leading lady to re-evaluate their lives. Tara Fitzgerald, Brenda Fricker co-star. 98 min.
02-2800 Was $89.99 ❑*$19.99*

Poetic Justice (1993)
Writer-director John Singleton follows "Boyz N the Hood" with this perceptive drama starring Janet Jackson as a hairdresser and aspiring poetess from South Central L.A. who finds herself falling in love with a postal worker (rapper Tupac Shakur) she once detested after sharing a car trip to Oakland. Maya Angelou wrote the poetry and makes a cameo appearance. 109 min.
02-2523 Was $19.99 ❑*$14.99*

Amongst Friends (1993)
Gritty look at deceit, friendship and violence among young, Jewish gangsters in Long Island, centering on the streetwise pal of two hoods who serves prison time after being caught in a drug deal. When he's released from prison, he finds that one of his chums has taken up with his girlfriend, which leads to a series of explosive altercations. With Joseph Lindsey. 88 min.
02-2527 Was $19.99 ❑*$14.99*

Above The Rim (1994)
Enthralling sports drama involving a highly-touted high school basketball player attempting to get a scholarship to Georgetown. He finds himself caught between two brothers who want to look after him, a gangster and a former athlete with a tragic background. Exciting hoops footage and powerful performances from Duane Martin, Tupac Shakur and Leon are the highlights. 97 min.
02-2651 Was $19.99 ❑*$14.99*

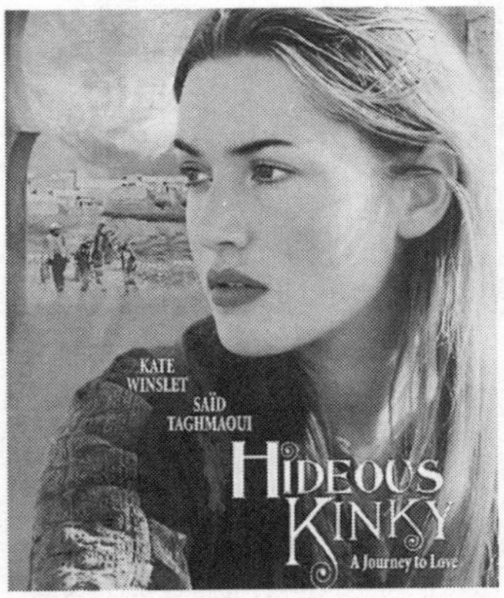

Hideous Kinky (1999)
Set in 1972, this sensual drama stars Kate Winslet as a single parent of two daughters who has moved to Marrakesh to get away from her stifling life in England. The girls introduce their mother to a Moroccan acrobat and the two start a sexually charged relationship before Winslet moves to Algiers to study Eastern philosophy. Sira Stampe, Said Taghmaoui co-star. 99 min.
02-3377 Was $99.99 ❑*$14.99*

Pump Up The Volume (1990)
For his fellow high school students, he's the voice of rebellion. Christian Slater stars as a shy teen who lives a double life as the owner of a pirate radio station, where he speaks out against a corrupt principal. Samantha Mathis co-stars; great rock soundtrack. 100 min.
02-2068 Was $19.99 *$14.99*

Higher Learning (1995)
Controversial, explosive social drama from John Singleton set at a fictitious California college where a group of freshmen face such dilemmas as racism, sexism, date rape and campus unrest. Kristy Swanson, Omar Epps, Jennifer Connelly, Michael Rapaport, Ice Cube and Laurence Fishburne star. 126 min.
02-2780 Was $19.99 ❑*$14.99*

Julian Po (1997)
An isolated small town's peaceful way of life is abruptly shaken with the arrival of mysterious stranger Christian Slater, and the residents' attempts to learn the reason behind his presence lead to some surprising revelations. Robin Tunney also stars in this offbeat drama. 82 min.
02-5167 Was $99.99 ❑*$19.99*

Bed Of Roses (1996)
Romance blooms in this tender drama starring Mary Stuart Masterson as an investment banker whose successful career is matched by an unfulfilling personal life, until florist Christian Slater enters it, bearing roses and baring his soul. With Pamela Segall, Josh Brolin. 88 min.
02-5094 Was $99.99 ❑*$14.99*

Waterland (1992)
Powerful, inventive study of a disillusioned high school history teacher (Jeremy Irons) who comes to understand his tragic life by relating stories from his past to his students. Sinead Cusack, Ethan Hawke and John Heard also star. 94 min.
02-5028 Was $89.99 ❑*$19.99*

The Long Day Closes (1992)
Set in the mid-1950s, this lovingly filmed remembrance centers on an 11-year-old boy's experiences going to the movies and listening to the radio while growing up in working-class England. Leigh McCormack and Marjorie Yates star in director Terence Davies' ("Distant Voices, Still Lives") gentle, nostalgic saga. 84 min.
02-2561 Was $89.99 ❑*$19.99*

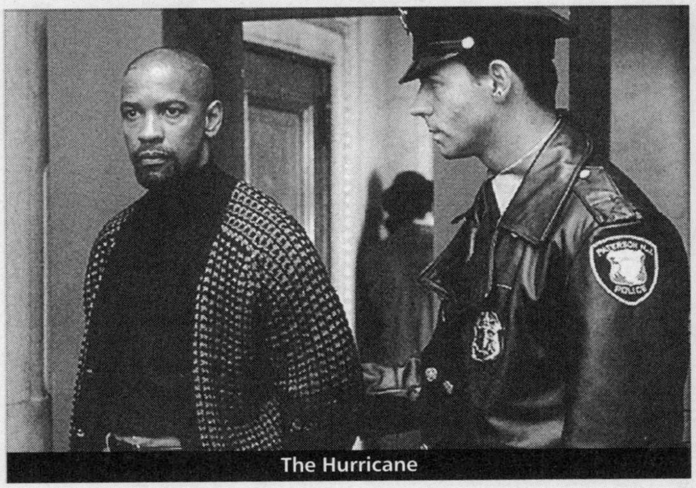
The Hurricane

Denzel Washington

A Soldier's Story (1984)
The murder of an unpopular black sergeant at a Southern army base in 1944 fans feelings of anger and disharmony in this riveting drama. Howard E. Rollins, Jr. is the military attorney sent to investigate, and Adolph Caesar is the sergeant. Denzel Washington, Larry Riley, Patti LaBelle co-star in this adaptation of Charles Fuller's play; Norman Jewison directs. 102 min.
02-1445 ❑*$14.99*

The George McKenna Story (1986)
An inspiring true story starring Denzel Washington as a principal who turns things around at a drug-ridden high school in South Los Angeles. Lynn Whitfield, Akousa Busia and Richard Masur also star. 95 min.
46-5563 Was $89.99 *$14.99*

Cry Freedom (1987)
Stirring epic drama by Richard Attenborough ("Gandhi") that follows the friendship between white South African journalist Donald Woods (Kevin Kline) and black activist Stephen Biko (Denzel Washington) through the violent struggle against their country's racist regime. 157 min.
07-1618 Was $19.99 *$14.99*

Glory (1989)
Stirring Civil War drama recounts the inspiring true story of the Union's 54th Regiment, comprised of black soldiers who had to fight prejudice and neglect to win the chance to prove themselves in battle. Matthew Broderick, as the 54th's white commander, stars along with Morgan Freeman and Denzel Washington, who earned a Best Supporting Actor Oscar. 122 min.
02-2040 Was $19.99 ❑*$14.99*

Glory (Letterboxed Version)
Also available in a theatrical, widescreen format.
02-2042 Was $19.99 ❑*$14.99*

Glory: Gift Set
A beautiful deluxe boxed set, this collector's dream includes the Academy Award-winning drama, plus the documentary "The True Story of Glory Continues."
02-2090 Save $5.00! *$24.99*

Glory: Gift Set (Letterboxed Version)
The collector's set is also available with the film in a theatrical, widescreen format.
02-2412 ❑*$24.99*

The True Story Of Glory Continues (1990)
Morgan Freeman hosts this documentary look at the acclaimed Civil War drama and the real-life heroes that inspired it, the soldiers of the all-black 54th Massachusetts Regiment. Period photographs and accounts bring the men of the 54th to life, plus there's never-before-seen footage from "Glory." 45 min.
02-2089 *$14.99*

The Mighty Quinn (1989)
Denzel Washington is Quinn, police chief of a small Caribbean island and a man caught between a rock and a hard place when the prime suspect in a murder case is a local hero and boyhood friend. Reggae-flavored thriller also stars M. Emmet Walsh, Robert Townsend, Sheryl Lee Ralph and Mimi Rogers. 98 min.
12-2776 Was $19.99 ❑*$14.99*

Heart Condition (1990)
Bob Hoskins is a bigoted L.A. cop who inherits the heart of one of his toughest enemies, a freshly-murdered black lawyer, played by Denzel Washington. The lawyer's ghost teams with the cop to find his own killer in this wild action-comedy. With Chloe Webb. 100 min.
02-2015 ❑*$14.99*

Mississippi Masala (1991)
A culture clash comedy/drama that's as spicy as the Indian dish it's named for, director Mira Nair's film stars Denzel Washington as a black American businessman in the South who falls in love with East Indian immigrant Sarita Choudhury. The pair face pressure from both sides to break off their romance. Charles Dutton, Roshan Seth co-star. 117 min.
02-2259 Was $19.99 ❑*$14.99*

Ricochet (1991)
An explosive actioner starring Denzel Washington as a cop applauded for his capture of psycho killer John Lithgow. But when Lithgow escapes and vows vengeance, Washington must call on boyhood friend Ice-T, now a drug dealer, for help. 104 min.
44-1866 Was $19.99 ❑*$14.99*

Devil In A Blue Dress (1995)
An unemployed ex-G.I. in 1948 Los Angeles is hired to locate a missing woman with ties to a mayoral candidate, but the search lands him in a deadly web of political corruption and forbidden passions. Denzel Washington shines as reluctant PI "Easy" Rawlins in this atmospheric mystery based on Walter Mosley's novel, features fine supporting turns by Jennifer Beals, Tom Sizemore, and Don Cheadle as Washington's trigger-happy sidekick, Mouse. 101 min.
02-2859 Was $19.99 ❑*$14.99*

Virtuosity (1995)
Futuristic cyber-thriller starring Denzel Washington as a former cop in prison for killing the murderer of his wife and daughter. When a computer-generated police training villain made up of over 180 different serial killers—among them Washington's nemesis—escapes into the real world, the ex-officer is the only one who can catch him. With Russell Crowe, Kelly Lynch. 107 min.
06-2413 Was $89.99 ❑*$14.99*

Crimson Tide (1995)
As renegade forces seize control of nuclear weapons in Russia, the submarine USS Alabama sails into dangerous waters. When communications with the Pentagon are lost, the situation gets even more tense, prompting a riveting face-off between egomaniacal captain Gene Hackman and officer Denzel Washington over whether the Alabama should launch its missiles against Russia. 116 min.
11-1940 Was $19.99 ❑*$14.99*

Courage Under Fire (1996)
Forceful military drama from director Edward Zwick ("Glory") stars Denzel Washington as a guilt-ridden Army officer investigating Medavac pilot Meg Ryan, a candidate for a posthumous Medal of Honor for her heroism during the Persian Gulf War. Washington uncovers a series of troubling incidents which led to Ryan's death while interviewing members of her platoon. Lou Diamond Phillips, Matt Damon also star. 116 min.
04-3403 Was $99.99 ❑*$14.99*

Courage Under Fire (Letterboxed Version)
Also available in a theatrical, widescreen format.
04-3673 ❑*$19.99*

The Preacher's Wife (1996)
Vibrant fantasy/comedy, based on 1947's "The Bishop's Wife," features Denzel Washington as an angel sent to Earth to help Whitney Houston and her minister husband save their failing New York neighborhood church. But will the romantic feelings that Houston and Washington begin to have for each other endanger his mission? Director Penny Marshall's warm and winning film also stars Courtney B. Vance, Gregory Hines. 123 min.
11-2109 Was $19.99 ❑*$14.99*

The Siege (1998)
As New York reels from a series of terrorist bombings, FBI agent Denzel Washington and CIA agent Annette Bening search for the militant Arab group responsible. Their hunt takes on new urgency when the government imposes martial law on the city, with tanks patrolling the streets and Arab-American men detained in prison camps, under the command of zealous general Bruce Willis. Intense and thoughtful actioner from director Edward Zwick ("Glory") also stars Tony Shaloub. 116 min.
04-3830 Was $99.99 ❑*$14.99*

Fallen (1998)
Homicide detective Denzel Washington must try to track down a serial killer he caught once before—and who was already put to death. Washington follows a deadly trail of ancient evil, as the murderous spirit passes from one human host to another, in this eerie supernatural suspenser that was filmed in and around Philadelphia. John Goodman, Donald Sutherland, Embeth Davidtz and Elias Koteas also star. 124 min.
19-2699 Was $19.99 ❑*$14.99*

Fallen (Letterboxed Version)
Also available in a theatrical, widescreen format.
19-2745 ❑*$19.99*

The Bone Collector (1999)
Intense thriller starring Denzel Washington as a quadriplegic NYPD forensics expert called on to help investigate the brutal slaying of a prominent businessman. With policewoman Angelina Jolie serving as Washington's crime-scene "eyes," the duo uncover a series of bizarre murders and race to find the killer. Michael Rooker, Queen Latifah and Luis Guzman also star. 118 min.
07-2845 Was $99.99 ❑*$19.99*

The Hurricane (1999)
Denzel Washington turns in a ferocious, multi-layered performance as Rubin "Hurricane" Carter, the promising boxer wrongly convicted of murdering three men in his hometown of Paterson, New Jersey. His two-decade fight for freedom, as seen through the eyes of a teenage boy and his Canadian foster family who befriend Carter, becomes a worldwide crusade. With Vicellous Reon Shannon, Liev Schreiber and Dan Hedaya; directed by Norman Jewison. 144 min.
07-2882 ❑*$99.99*

Please see our index for these other Denzel Washington titles: *He Got Game • Malcolm X • Mo' Better Blues • Much Ado About Nothing • The Pelican Brief • Philadelphia • Power*

www.moviesunlimited.com MOVIES UNLIMITED DRAMA · 221

Johnny Depp

Private Resort (1985)
What do you get when you mix a luxurious resort hotel, two sex-crazed teenage boys, some gorgeous female guests, a snoopy house dick and a cunning jewel thief? You guessed it: zany, racy, titillating fun. Johnny Depp, Rob Morrow, Andrew Dice Clay, Karyn O'Bryan star. 82 min.
02-1503 *$14.99*

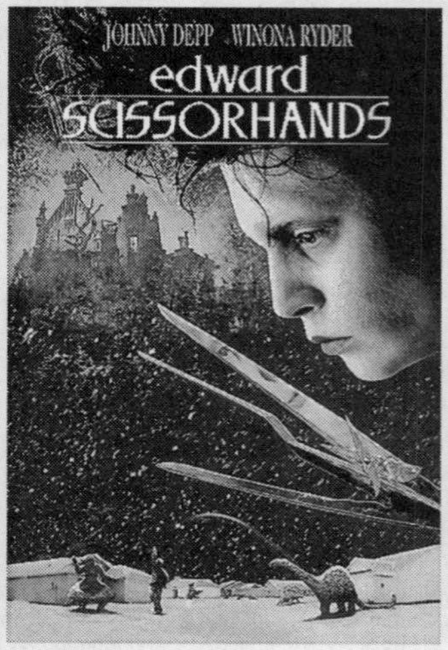

Edward Scissorhands (1990)
He's got a sad, white face, a wild haircut, and shears at the ends of his arms. He's Edward Scissorhands (Johnny Depp), creation of a mad scientist, who leaves his castle home and becomes the hit of suburbia with his proficiency at hair- and tree-clipping and falls in love with the local Avon lady's daughter. Winona Ryder, Dianne Wiest and Vincent Price co-star in Tim Burton's bittersweet fantasy. 98 min.
04-2426 Was $19.99 ❏*$14.99*

Arizona Dream (1991)
In this quirky comic fable, Johnny Depp plays a New York game warden who travels to Arizona to act as best man at uncle Jerry Lewis' wedding. After deciding to stay in town to work at his relative's Cadillac dealership, Depp soon finds himself involved with widow Faye Dunaway and heiress stepdaughter Lili Taylor. AKA: "The Arrowtooth Waltz." 119 min.
19-2303 Was $89.99 ❏*$19.99*

What's Eating Gilbert Grape (1993)
Quirky dramedy from Lasse Hallström ("My Life as a Dog") about a small-town Iowa grocery store clerk (Johnny Depp) with dreams of getting away from his family, which includes a retarded younger brother (Leonardo DiCaprio) and a 500-pound mother (Darlene Cates). Will Becky (Juliette Lewis), the young woman who just arrived in town, help him realize his dreams? Mary Steenburgen also stars. 118 min.
06-2219 Was $19.99 ❏*$14.99*

Benny & Joon (1993)
Whimsical fable about an auto mechanic (Aidan Quinn) who finds that caring for his emotionally disturbed sister (Mary Stuart Masterson) has gotten in the way of his own life. Making matters even more complicated is the arrival of a bizarre, free-spirited young man (Johnny Depp) who has taken a liking to the sister. Julianne Moore and Dan Hedaya also star. 98 min.
12-2742 Was $19.99 ❏*$14.99*

Don Juan DeMarco (1995)
A delightful romantic fable featuring Johnny Depp as a young man who believes he's legendary lover Don Juan. After being spurned by his one true love, a suicidal Depp is saved by psychiatrist Marlon Brando. During therapy sessions with Depp, Brando realizes the passion he's lost at life and love, and attempts to rekindle his relationship with wife Faye Dunaway. 92 min.
02-5063 Was $19.99 ❏*$14.99*

Nick Of Time (1995)
Accountant Johnny Depp must become a hit man when crooks kidnap his daughter, using her to force Depp to assassinate the governor of California during a public appearance, in this compelling thriller where on-screen events occur in "real time." Christopher Walken co-stars as the head of the villains; with Charles S. Dutton, Roma Maffia, Marsha Mason. 89 min.
06-2441 Was $99.99 ❏*$14.99*

Donnie Brasco (1997)
Based on a true case, this dramatic tale of honor and betrayal within the Mafia stars Johnny Depp as an undercover FBI agent who works his way into the mob's inner circle and Al Pacino as the small-time hood who becomes Depp's mentor and friend. With Anne Heche, Bruno Kirby, Michael Madsen. 127 min.
02-3078 Was $19.99 ❏*$14.99*

Donnie Brasco (Letterboxed Version)
Also available in a theatrical, widescreen format.
02-3316 ❏*$19.99*

Fear And Loathing In Las Vegas (1998)
Johnny Depp stars in director Terry Gilliam's psychedelic film adaptation of Hunter S. Thompson's semi-autobiography. Join wigged-out journalist Raoul Duke (Depp) and his partner in haze, lawyer Dr. Gonzo (Benicio Del Toro) as they head from L.A. to Vegas in a drug-induced odyssey of trashed hotel rooms, reptilian hallucinations and "bad craziness." With Gary Busey, Cameron Diaz, Christina Ricci. 118 min.
07-2669 Was $99.99 ❏*$14.99*

Fear And Loathing In Las Vegas (Letterboxed Version)
Also available in a theatrical, widescreen format.
07-2694 Was $99.99 ❏*$14.99*

The Astronaut's Wife (1999)
Returning to Earth after a mysterious incident during a spacewalk, astronaut Johnny Depp seems unaffected at first. Charlize Theron's fears that something is wrong with her husband are multiplied when she learns she's pregnant, leading to a terrifying discovery not of this world, in this gripping sci-fi suspense tale. Joe Morton, Nick Cassavetes, Clea DuVall also star. 110 min.
19-2938 Was $99.99 ❏*$14.99*

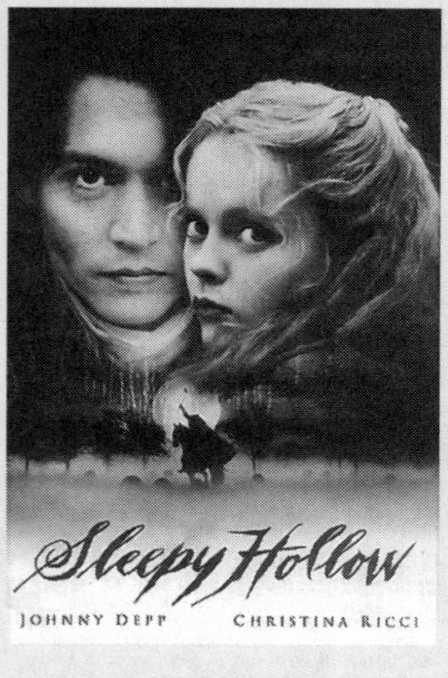

Sleepy Hollow (1999)
Washington Irving's timeless tale of an 18th-century New York village terrorized by a noggin-stealing spectre is given a suspenseful screen translation by director Tim Burton. Johnny Depp is foppish, "scientifically-minded" constable Ichabod Crane, sent to Sleepy Hollow to investigate a series of bizarre killings that the locals attribute to the vengeful Headless Horseman. Christina Ricci plays Depp's love interest; with Michael Gambon, Miranda Richardson, Casper Van Dien and Christopher Lee. 105 min.
06-2975 Was $99.99 ❏*$14.99*

The Ninth Gate (2000)
In Roman Polanski's haunting thriller, Johnny Depp is a rare book dealer hired by wealthy collector Frank Langella, owner of a strange 17th-century occult tome whose engravings were said to be done by Satan, to track down the other two existing copies. Depp's worldwide search has him facing threats on his life, two mysterious women, and a demonic conspiracy. With Lena Olin, Emmanuelle Seigner, Barbara Jefford. 133 min.
27-7215 ❏*$99.99*

Please see our index for these other Johnny Depp titles: *Cry-Baby • Dead Man • A Nightmare On Elm Street • Platoon • The Source*

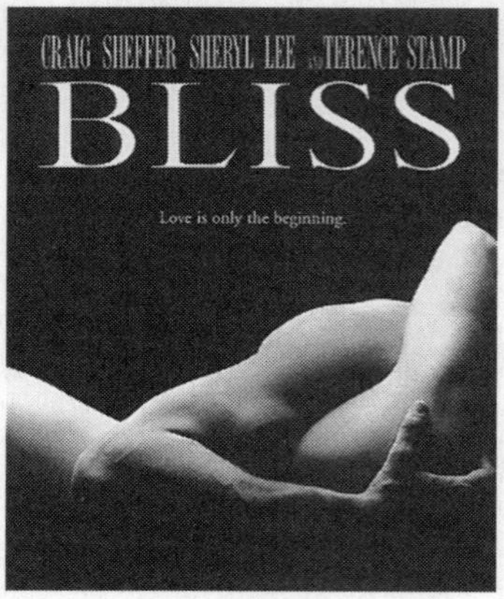

Bliss (1997)
A frankly honest, beautifully erotic drama that follows a couple's exploration of their sexuality and the secrets that lie beneath it. Eager to help her troubled six-month marriage to architect Craig Sheffer, wife Sheryl Lee seeks guidance from unconventional sex therapist Terence Stamp, who makes love to Lee before shepherding the spouses into new areas of eroticism. 103 min.
02-3130 Was $99.99 ❏*$19.99*

Sunset Park (1996)
Plucky Rhea Perlman is a Brooklyn high school teacher who takes on the job of coaching her school's basketball team. Applying her feisty personality and positive attitude to her students on and off the court, Perlman eventually gains their confidence. Fredro Starr, Carol Kane and James Harris also star in this rap music-propelled film. 99 min.
02-2938 Was $19.99 ❏*$14.99*

Safe (1995)
Thought-provoking tale of modern-day alienation from filmmaker Todd Haynes ("Poison") stars Julianne Moore as an upper-class L.A. housewife who develops allergic reactions to common chemicals and substances. Her growing intolerance to her environment forces Moore to leave her home and move to an experimental New Mexico clinic for treatment. With Xander Berkeley, Peter Friedman. 119 min.
02-2831 Was $89.99 ❏*$19.99*

Love And Human Remains (1995)
Provocative look at love and sex in the '90s from Canadian director Denys Arcand ("Jesus of Montreal") centering on a group of friends that includes a gay waiter; a book reviewer considering a lesbian liaison with a teacher; and a mysterious bartender. While these characters contemplate past and new relationships, a killer runs amuck nearby. With Mia Kirshner, Thomas Gibson. 95 min.
02-2836 ❏*$19.99*

Beyond Rangoon (1995)
American doctor Patricia Arquette, attempting to cope with the deaths of her husband and son, travels to the Southeast Asian nation of Burma and witnesses brutal government crackdowns on pro-democracy demonstrators. She later befriends an ex-professor and makes an eye-opening and dangerous odyssey into the countryside. Director John Boorman's powerful, fact-based drama also stars Frances McDormand, U Aung Ko, Spalding Gray. 100 min.
02-2841 Was $89.99 ❏*$19.99*

The Run Of The Country (1995)
This sensitive drama from director Peter Yates ("Breaking Away") is set in Ireland, where a teenage boy leaves home after his mother's death. After his wealthy girlfriend becomes pregnant and tragedy strikes an irascible friend, the youth returns home and tries to reconcile with his tough policeman father. Albert Finney, Matt Keeslar and Victoria Smurfit star. 110 min.
02-2852 Was $89.99 ❏*$19.99*

Manny & Lo (1996)
Captivating indy road movie about two parentless young sisters who flee separate foster homes and take off in their dead mother's rickety station wagon for an incredible odyssey. When 16-year-old Lo learns she's pregnant, she and 11-year-old Manny decide to get help by kidnapping a maternity-store clerk, whom they eventually befriend. With Aleksa Palladino, Scarlett Johansson and Mary Kay Place. 89 min.
02-2992 Was $99.99 ❏*$24.99*

The Spitfire Grill (1996)
A young woman, released from jail after serving time for manslaughter, moves to a small town in Maine in an attempt to start a new life and gets a job in a local cafe. The special friendship that forms between her and the restaurant's owner is the focus of this moving drama. Alison Elliott, Ellen Burstyn, Marcia Gay Harden and Will Patton star. 117 min.
02-3037 ❏*$19.99*

Heavy (1996)
An overweight and lonely pizza chef at his family's restaurant gets a new lease on life with the arrival of a new waitress, a beautiful but troubled college dropout, in this sensitive drama. Liv Tyler, Pruitt Taylor Vince, Shelley Winters, Deborah Harry and Evan Dando star. 104 min.
02-3057 Was $99.99 ❏*$19.99*

Where Angels Fear To Tread (1992)
Sumptuous adaptation of E.M. Forster's novel focuses on the events that occur when a widowed Englishwoman (Helen Mirren) travels to Italy with her friend (Helena Bonham Carter) and decides to marry a native man half her age. This angers her late husband's family, who travel to Italy in hopes of "straightening her out." Rupert Graves, Judy Davis co-star. 112 min.
02-2339 Was $89.99 ❏*$19.99*

Switched At Birth (1992)
What if the child you've raised as your own for years turned out to belong to another family? Based on a true story, this compelling drama follows the controversial courtroom trial that followed one such discovery, and the emotional pain that the two families involved faced. Bonnie Bedelia, Brian Kerwin, Ed Asner star. 192 min.
02-2346 *$79.99*

The Last Days Of Chez Nous (1993)
A compassionate look at a problem-torn Sydney family from Australian director Gillian Armstrong ("Little Women") focusing on the troubling relationships between mother, father, daughter, grandfather and aunt. Lisa Harrow, Bruno Ganz and Bill Hunter star in this knockout drama. 96 min.
02-2507 Was $89.99 ❏*$19.99*

Equinox (1993)
Alan Rudolph's eerie, darkly comic mystery tells of two siblings—one a gangster, the other a shy mechanic—who are separated at birth, but find themselves squaring off against each other when they learn of a secret that can change their lives. Matthew Modine, Marisa Tomei, Fred Ward, Lara Flynn Boyle and M. Emmet Walsh star. 110 min.
02-2510 Was $89.99 ❏*$19.99*

Wide Sargasso Sea (1993)
Exotic, erotic account of a West Indian sugar heiress whose open sensuality confounds the proper Englishman chosen to be her husband by her parents. In hopes of keeping her new paramour happy, the heiress asks her mystic housekeeper for guidance, but the maid's involvement in voodoo leads to tragic results. Karina Lombard, Nathaniel Parker, Michael York and Rachel Ward star in this steamy adaptation of Jean Rhys' prequel to "Jane Eyre." Unrated version features scenes not shown in theaters; 100 min.
02-2516 Was $89.99 ❏*$19.99*

The Music Of Chance (1993)
A moody, darkly humorous tale of fate concerning two small-time gamblers who find themselves in a high-stakes poker game with a pair of wealthy eccentrics trained by a famous card shark. Duped out of their money, the drifters are forced to work off their debt by assuming the roles of servants. James Spader, Mandy Patinkin, Charles Durning and Joel Grey star. 98 min.
02-2521 Was $89.99 ❏*$19.99*

Vanya On 42nd Street (1994)
Exhilarating and unusual filming of Anton Chekhov's "Uncle Vanya" as scripted by David Mamet and directed by Louis Malle. A group of actors who once performed in "Vanya" together meet in a vacant Times Square theater and re-enact the play under the guidance of director Andre Gregory. Wallace Shawn, Julianne Moore, Brooke Smith and Larry Pines lead the stellar cast. 119 min.
02-2779 Was $89.99 ❏*$19.99*

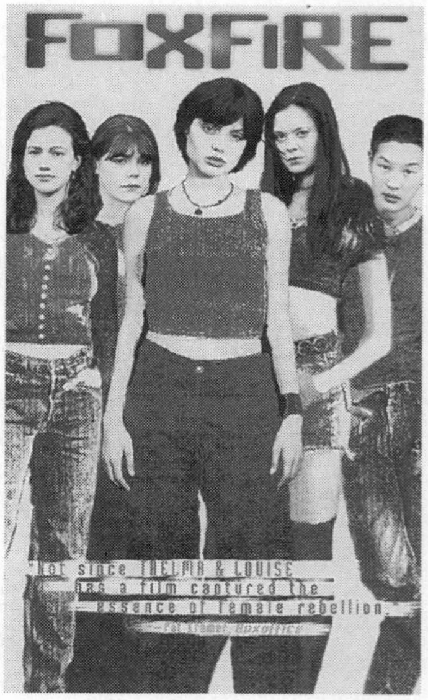

Foxfire (1996)
The Joyce Carol Oates story is turned into a provocative film centered on four affluent but troubled teenage girls who are liberated by Legs Sadovsky, a pretty drifter with feminist terrorism on her agenda. Angelina Jolie, Hedy Burress and Jenny Lewis star. 102 min.
02-3019 Was $99.99 ❏*$14.99*

Basquiat (1996)
Revealing biography of avant-garde painter Jean-Michel Basquiat, graffiti writer-turned-Andy Warhol protegé who took the New York art world by storm but met an untimely death at 27 from a drug overdose in 1988. The first effort directed by artist Julian Schnabel, the film features Jeffrey Wright as Basquiat and David Bowie as Warhol; with Christopher Walken, Michael Wincott, Dennis Hopper, Claire Forlani. 110 min.
11-2083 Was $99.99 ❑*$19.99*

Mother Teresa: In The Name Of God's Poor (1997)
Geraldine Chaplin stars as the Albanian-born nun whose half-century of tireless care and devotion to the neglected, ill and dying of Calcutta's slums earned her a Nobel Peace Prize and the world's admiration, in this moving biographical drama of the woman who was called "a living saint." David Byrd also stars. 93 min.
88-1162 ❑*$19.99*

Mama Flora's Family (1998)
Cicely Tyson stars in the title role of the aging matriarch of a black family whose life of struggle, tragedy and perseverance is chronicled in this moving drama based on a story by Alex Haley. Blair Underwood, Mario Van Peebles and Queen Latifah also star. 140 min.
88-1184 Was $19.99 ❑*$14.99*

The Destiny Of Marty Fine (1998)
When an ex-middleweight boxer witnesses a mob hit, he is given a choice; work for the mob and commit a murder, or be killed himself. However, an attack of conscience forces him to make a decision and prove that he is still a man in control of his own fate. Alan Gelfant, Norman Fell, Michael Ironside, James LeGros and Katherine Keener star. 85 min.
88-7012 *$59.99*

Annie O (1995)
A teenage girl tries out for and makes her school's varsity male basketball squad, but as the team pushes towards the state championship Annie faces resentment and anger from her teammates, other students, and even her own family. Moving family drama stars Coco Yares, Chad Willet. 93 min.
88-1046 Was $89.99 ❑*$14.99*

Wild Side (1995)
A beautiful bank executive who spends her nights as a high-priced call girl is drawn into the seductive world of an enigmatic millionaire and his wife, only to find herself caught in kinky erotic encounters with the wife and involved in a money-laundering ring, in this provocative drama. Anne Heche, Christopher Walken and Joan Chen star. Uncut, unrated version; 96 min.
88-1052 Was $89.99 ❑*$14.99*

Playing God (1997)
When drug-addicted ex-surgeon David Duchovny saves the life of a shooting victim, he's offered a chance by the man's boss, crime ring head Timothy Hutton, to work as his "personal physician." With the lure of money (and Hutton's beautiful girlfriend, Angelina Jolie) on one side and the FBI pursuing him on the other, which way will Duchovny go in this stylish, noir-flavored crime thriller? 94 min.
11-2241 Was $19.99 ❑*$14.99*

Breaking The Waves (1996)
A powerful film debut by Emily Watson fuels writer/director Lars von Trier's unusual, passionate drama. Watson, a naive and pious girl from a remote Scottish village, is happy after marrying a virile oil rig worker, but when an accident leaves him paralyzed, he tells her she can "aid his recovery" by having sexual encounters with strangers and describing them to him. With Stellan Skarsgård. 152 min.
88-1134 Was $99.99 ❑*$14.99*

Breaking The Waves (Letterboxed Version)
Also available in a theatrical, widescreen format.
88-1135 Was $99.99 ❑*$14.99*

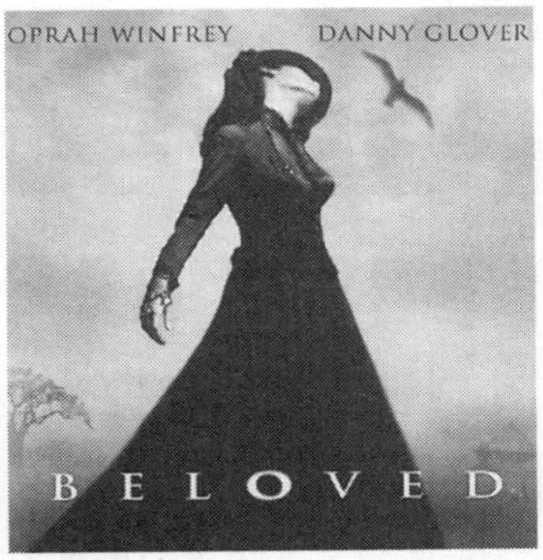

Beloved (1998)
Toni Morrison's Pulitzer Prize-winning novel about the physical and emotional anguish of slavery and its aftermath is movingly brought to the screen by director Jonathan Demme. Set in 1870s Ohio, the film stars Oprah Winfrey as a woman trying to provide for herself and teenage daughter Kimberly Elise. The ghosts of the past come back—in every sense of the word—with the arrival of fellow former slave Danny Glover and Thandie Newton, a mysterious young woman known as Beloved whose own past is shrouded in mystery. 172 min.
11-2310 Was $99.99 ❑*$19.99*

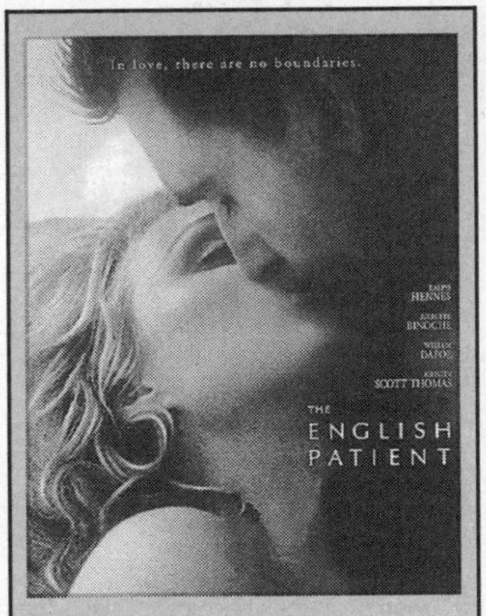

The English Patient (1996)
In a ruined Italian monastery-turned-Allied hospital in World War II, a mysterious amnesiac patient, severely burned from a plane crash, is cared for by a devoted young nurse. Through flashbacks, the story of the man's past, a tale of wartime intrigue and forbidden love in the sands of North Africa, unfolds. Ralph Fiennes, Juliette Binoche, Kristin Scott Thomas and Willem Dafoe star in director/scripter Anthony Minghella's lush, romantic adaptation of the Michael Ondaatje novel; winner of seven Academy Awards, including Best Picture, Director and Supporting Actress. 162 min.
11-2158 Was $19.99 ❑*$14.99*

The English Patient (Letterboxed Version)
Also available in a theatrical, widescreen format.
11-2165 Was $19.99 ❑*$14.99*

The English Patient: Deluxe Collector's Set
This special limited boxed set includes the letterboxed version of the Academy Award-winning drama; a second video featuring voice-over commentary by director Anthony Minghella, producer Saul Zaentz and author Michael Ondaatje; and a copy of the original novel.
11-2213 ❑*$34.99*

The Cape (1996)
The lives, loves and ambitions of the men and women who work at the Kennedy Space Center are the focus of this absorbing drama, the pilot to the hit TV series. Among them: a former astronaut now in charge of spaceflight training; a Marine who wants his own space mission; a female Navy pilot; and others. With Corbin Bernsen, Adam Baldwin, Tyra Ferrell and Cameron Bancroft. 120 min.
10-2744 *$14.99*

Firelight (1997)
In order to pay off her father's debts, a young woman in 1830s England agrees to bear a child for a wealthy landowner whose wife lies in a coma. Unable to forget her child, and without the father's knowledge, the woman returns seven years later and takes a job as the girl's governess. Sophie Marceau, Stephen Dillane and Kevin Anderson star in this lush, passionate melodrama. 104 min.
11-2307 Was $99.99 ❑*$19.99*

Fabio: A Time For Romance (1993)
Fabio, the fabulous hunk of romance novel covers, calendars and TV's "Acapulco H.E.A.T.," stars in these three steamy love stories that are sure to make you swoon. In "Conquest of the Viking," he's a Nordic he-man; in "The Pirate Rogue," he's a dashing swashbuckler; in "Dream Lover," he's a fantasy count. And, of course, in each of the stories, Fabio gets the sexy heroine. 40 min.
10-2433 *$19.99*

Deadly Bet (1991)
He's been playing against the odds all his life, but this time the game could cost him his life, as a Vegas gambler must save himself and his girl from a vicious gangster. Jeff Wincott, Charlene Tilton star. 93 min.
86-1058 Was $29.99 *$14.99*

The Battlers (1998)
Based upon the popular novel by Kylie Tennant, this dramatic mini-series shows the economic hardship endured by an itinerant worker who, after his marriage falls apart, sets out on the road to find his fortune, as well as himself. His journeys bring out both the worst and the best in him. Stars Gary Sweet, Peter Stoneham, Richard Piper, Amanda Cross. 240 min.
10-2799 *$24.99*

Lakota Woman: Siege At Wounded Knee (1994)
This passionate, true story is set against the backdrop of the 1973 Wounded Knee, South Dakota, uprising, where members and supporters of the American Indian Movement held off federal officers in a bloody 70-day siege, and one woman found her own voice in her people's struggles. Irene Bedard, Tantoo Cardinal and August Schellenberg star. 113 min.
18-7524 Was $89.99 ❑*$14.99*

Set Me Free (1999)
Growing up in 1963 Montreal isn't an easy task for 13-year-old Hanna, whose stressed homelife has her feeling confused and suicidal. Her only outlet is the movies, where she finds a kindred spirit in actress Anna Karina's character in "My Life to Live." Along with the help of her teacher, brother and best friend, Hanna struggles to make sense of her life in Canadian director Lea Pool's sensitive coming of age tale. Karine Vanasse, Nancy Huston star. 95 min. In French with English subtitles.
22-6104 Letterboxed *$29.99*

The Butcher Boy (1998)
Set in Ireland in the early 1960s, this moody, darkly humorous autobiographical story from Neil Jordan ("The Crying Game") focuses on Francie, a 12-year-old bully who remains a terror to those who surround him. Francie's behavior, however, can be traced to his dysfunctional family, including his troubled mother and alcoholic father. With Eamonn Owens, Stephen Rea and Fiona Shaw. 110 min.
19-2752 Was $99.99 ❑*$14.99*

Traveller (1997)
This fascinating look at the Travellers, a group of Irish grifters operating in the Southern U.S., features Bill Paxton as a slick con artist who takes young swindler Mark Wahlberg under his wing. Together the two pull off a number of scams and team with a rival thief to out-scheme Romany Gypsies. With Julianna Margulies, James Gammon. 101 min.
88-1158 Was $99.99 ❑*$14.99*

Losing Chase (1996)
In his directorial debut, Kevin Bacon tells a sensitive story starring Helen Mirren as a woman with emotional problems who, after a long absence, joins husband Beau Bridges in Martha's Vineyard for a summer vacation. Bridges hires psychology student Kyra Sedgwick to help with the kids, and she soon shares secrets with Mirren. 94 min.
88-1130 Was $99.99 ❑*$14.99*

The Funeral (1996)
An explosive gangster drama from renegade director Abel Ferrara ("Bad Lieutenant") set in 1930s New York, where criminal siblings Christopher Walken and Christopher Penn try to figure out who killed kid brother Vincent Gallo. As the investigation unfolds, the brothers' brutal lifestyle and interest in labor matters are revealed. With Annabella Sciorra. 101 min.
88-1131 Was $99.99 ❑*$14.99*

Grand Canyon (1991)
The lives, crises and needs of a group of '90s Los Angeles residents intersect in Lawrence Kasdan's seriocomic exploration of the problems of contemporary urban life. Among the characters examined are an immigration lawyer (Kevin Kline) and his wife (Mary McDonnell); a tow-truck driver (Danny Glover); and an egomaniacal film producer (Steve Martin). With Mary-Louise Parker, Alfre Woodard. 134 min.
04-2508 Was $19.99 ❑*$14.99*

Avalon (1990)
Fifty years and three generations in the life of an immigrant family's quest of the American Dream are eloquently recounted by writer/director Barry Levinson. This seriocomic capstone to the "Baltimore Trilogy" that began with "Diner" and "Tin Men" stars Armin Mueller-Stahl, Aidan Quinn, Elizabeth Perkins, Joan Plowright and Kevin Pollack. 126 min.
02-2071 Was $19.99 ❑*$14.99*

Restoration (1995)
Lavish mix of history and fiction, set in 1663 London, in which a young, naive doctor is appointed personal physician to Charles II and begins a series of tragic, comic and erotic adventures that help turn him into a man. Robert Downey, Jr., Meg Ryan, Sam Neill, David Thewlis, Ian McKellen and Hugh Grant star in this Oscar-winning film. 118 min.
11-2037 Was $99.99 ❑*$19.99*

Grand Isle (1991)
Set in Louisiana in the late 19th century, this tender, romantic drama stars Kelly McGillis as a 28-year-old mother and wife whose passionate relationship with a handsome, young Creole man awakens her emotions and sends her on a journey of self-discovery. Julian Sands, Adrian Pasdar, Glenne Headly and Ellen Burstyn star; based on a novel by Kate Chopin. 94 min.
18-7407 Was $89.99 ❑*$14.99*

The Sheltering Sky (1990)
Bernardo Bertolucci directs Debra Winger and John Malkovich in an erotic, hypnotic adaptation of the acclaimed novel by Paul Bowles. Set just after World War II, the beautifully photographed epic follows a trio of disaffected Americans on a soul-searching journey across the North African desert. Campbell Scott, Jill Bennett also star. 138 min.
19-1843 ❑*$19.99*

Dogfight (1991)
Set in early '60s San Francisco, this bittersweet drama stars River Phoenix as a young Vietnam-bound Marine who partakes in a cruel game with his fellow leathernecks. He must find the ugliest girl to take to a party, but his choice (Lili Taylor) turns out to be a lot more than he expected. Richard Panebianco, Brendan Fraser and Holly Near co-star; directed by Nancy Savoca ("True Love"). 92 min.
19-1915 Was $89.99 ❑*$19.99*

Getting Out (1994)
In this powerful drama, Rebecca DeMornay is a young parolee who tries to change her life after serving an eight-year stint behind bars. She attempts to regain custody of the son she gave birth to while in jail, but finds the struggle just as difficult as surviving prison. Ellen Burstyn, Robert Knepper also star. 92 min.
88-1004 Was $89.99 ❑*$12.99*

Wait Until Spring, Bandini (1990)
The tale of an Italian immigrant family struggling in 1920s Colorado, this bittersweet story features Joe Mantegna as the clan's father, an unemployed bricklayer involved with a wealthy widow, who leaves his wife and two sons to fend for themselves. Faye Dunaway, Ornella Muti and Burt Young also star in this lyrical comedy-drama. 104 min.
19-1887 Was $89.99 *$19.99*

School Ties (1992)
Compelling drama set in a New England prep school in the late 1950s, where a working-class Jewish teenager and football star is admitted on the condition that he not reveal his race. When his classmates learn the truth, he must stand up to their prejudice and scorn. Brendan Fraser, Chris O'Donnell, Matt Damon, Ben Affleck and Amy Locane star. 110 min.
06-2078 Was $19.99 ❑*$14.99*

Saturday Night Special (1994)
A gorgeous, deceitful woman in a small town carries on a heated affair with a mysterious roadhouse singer that leads to danger and murderous schemes. Steamy drama with lots of country music stars Maria Ford and former Fleetwood Mac-member-turned-country crooner Billy Burnette. Uncut, unrated version; 97 min.
21-9054 Was $89.99 *$14.99*

Little Boy Blue (1998)
Gritty drama featuring John Savage as a Vietnam veteran who runs a bar down South with wife Nastassja Kinski during the day, but turns terrifying at night, threatening Kinski, their three sons and others while drunk. When local police investigate the death of a detective in Savage's tavern, stunning revelations about him are revealed. Ryan Phillipe also stars. 104 min.
19-2756 Was $99.99 ❑*$14.99*

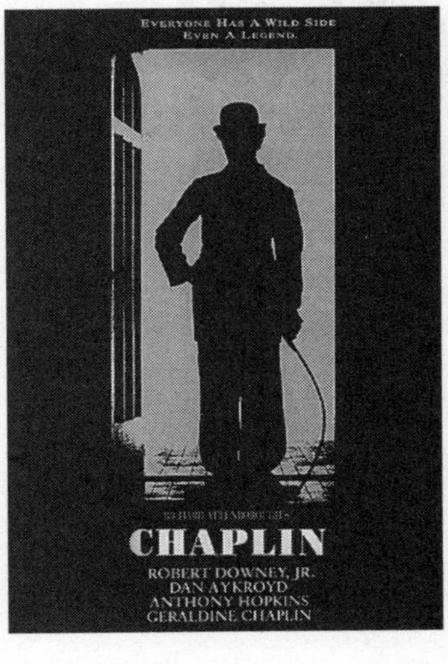

Chaplin (1992)
Robert Downey, Jr. turns in a tour-de-force performance as the celebrated comic genius in Richard Attenborough's sprawling biography. The film covers Charlie Chaplin's amazing life, from his early, poverty-stricken years and his pioneering cinematic endeavors to his troubled romantic life and his political problems. Kevin Kline, Dan Aykroyd, Anthony Hopkins and Diane Lane co-star. 135 min.
27-6805 Was $19.99 ❑*$14.99*

Chaplin (Letterboxed Version)
Also available in a theatrical, widescreen format.
27-7061 ❑*$14.99*

Angels & Insects (1996)
Haunting, erotically charged drama set in Victorian England, where a poor anthropologist decides to take residence with a wealthy family after a disastrous trip to the Amazon. The young man falls in love with the family's beautiful daughter and they marry, but he soon uncovers startling secrets about her past. Patsy Kensit, Mark Rylance, Kristin Scott Thomas star. 118 min.
88-1078 Was $19.99 ❑*$14.99*

Permanent Midnight (1998)
This harrowing true-life story stars Ben Stiller as Jerry Stahl, a successful TV writer whose marriage is destroyed and life threatened by a heroin habit that grows to $5,000 a week. Elizabeth Hurley, Maria Bello, Janeane Garofalo and Owen Wilson co-star in this daring and sometimes darkly comic look at the sordid side of Hollywood. 88 min.
27-7104 Was $99.99 ❑*$14.99*

Belly (1998)
The friendship between Queens gangsta buddies Sincere and Tommy (rap stars Nasir "Nas" Jones and "Earl "DMX" Simmons) is tested when Sincere tries to leave their lethal, drug-dealing lifestyle behind in this powerful urban drama from acclaimed music video director Hype Williams. Taral Hicks and Wu Tang Clan alumnus Clifford "Method Man" Smith also star. 95 min.
27-7109 Was $99.99 ❑*$14.99*

Swoon (1992)
Acclaimed independent dramatization of the infamous Leopold-Loeb murder case of the 1920s, in which two intelligent, well-respected teenagers senselessly murdered a 13-year-old boy from their upper-class Hyde Park neighborhood. Director Tom Kalin explores the killers' homosexual lifestyles, as well as other controversial aspects of the incident. Daniel Schlachet and Craig Chester star. 95 min.
02-5017 Was $89.99 □$19.99

Nil By Mouth (1997)
The directorial debut of actor Gary Oldman is a harrowing study of four generations of a working class family struggling with drugs, alcohol, poverty, physical and emotional abuse and themselves in South London. Members of the clan include the alcoholic petty thief father, his long-suffering wife and her junkie brother. With Ray Winstone and Kathy Burke. 128 min.
02-3193 □$99.99

The Whole Wide World (1996)
The moving true story of the romance that developed in rural '30s Texas between schoolteacher Novalyne Price and pulp writer Robert E. Howard, an enigmatic and repressed man best known as the creator of Conan the Barbarian, is told in this sensitive, acclaimed drama. Vincent D'Onofrio, Renee Zellweger, Ann Wedgeworth and Harve Presnell star. 111 min.
02-3110 Was $99.99 □$24.99

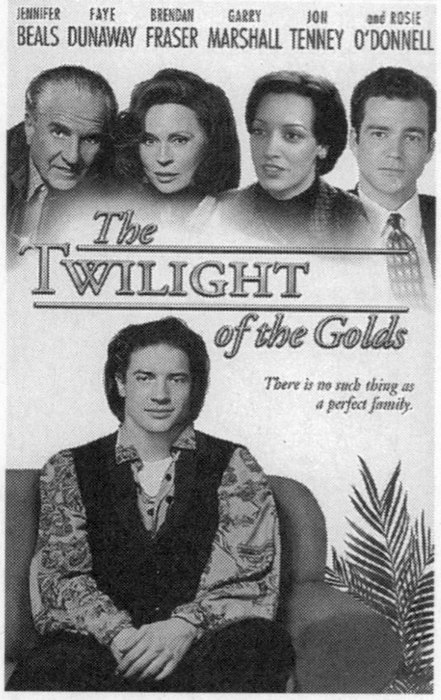

The Twilight Of The Golds (1997)
How far should parents go to have a "perfect child?" When an expectant couple learns through genetic testing that their unborn son will probably be gay, they debate whether or not to abort the pregnancy with the wife's family, including her gay brother. The compelling play is turned into a top-notch film with Brendan Fraser, Jennifer Beals, Faye Dunaway, Garry Marshall and Jon Tenney. 90 min.
02-8813 Was $99.99 $14.99

Dancer, Texas Pop. 81 (1998)
Touching coming-of-age drama about four childhood pals living in a small Texas town who made a vow that they would all move to Los Angeles after they graduate from high school. During their final weekend in town, they review their past and confront their uncertain future. Breckin Meyer, Ethan Embry, Peter Facinelli and Eddie Mills star. 97 min.
02-3224 Was $99.99 □$14.99

The Third Miracle (1999)
Ed Harris is a Catholic priest investigating whether a recently deceased woman should be recommended for sainthood. During his inquiry, the skeptical Harris questions his own faith while looking into the woman's supposed miracles and gets involved with his subject's daughter (Anne Heche). With Armin Mueller-Stahl; directed by Agnieszka Holland ("The Secret Garden"). 118 min.
02-3435 □$99.99

New Blood (1999)
In this offbeat crime drama, a botched kidnapping scheme leaves petty crook Nick Moran mortally wounded. With no one else to turn to, he visits estranged father John Hurt and makes a bizarre bargain: in exchange for Moran donating his heart to save his terminally ill sister, Hurt will pose as the abducted businessman Moran and his pals accidentally killed. Carrie-Anne Moss, Shawn Wayans, Joe Pantoliano also star. 92 min.
02-3429 □$99.99

The Governess (1998)
In early Victorian London, a young Jewish woman's family is in dire financial straits when her father dies. Disguising her identity, she takes a job caring for a girl whose family lives on an isolated Scottish island, but soon finds herself drawn to her charge's photographer father. Minnie Driver shines in the title role in writer/director Sandra Goldbacher's lush, romantic drama; with Tom Wilkinson, Harriet Walter. 114 min.
02-3275 Was $99.99 □$19.99

Somebody Is Waiting (1998)
After their mother is killed during a bank robbery, a group of youngsters is reunited with their estranged alcoholic dad. Soon, however, the father's abusive ways lead to a violent confrontation with his 18-year-old son that ends with the man's accidental death, sedning the teen on the run from the law and his siblings searching for him. Gabriel Byrne, Nastassja Kinski, Johnny Whitworth star. 90 min.
02-3282 □$99.99

Shadow Of Doubt (1999)
High-profile L.A. defense attorney Melanie Griffith tackles a murder case with a young boy as a suspect that pits her against former lover, assistant district attorney Tom Berenger. While desperately trying to find evidence to prove the boy's innocence, Griffith finds herself threatened by both a wealthy and powerful family and the threat of a rapist. With Craig Sheffer and Huey Lewis. 103 min.
02-3327 Was $99.99 □$19.99

Outside Ozona (1998)
The title location is the string of lonely Southwest highways near Ozona, Texas, and it's on these roads that the lives of three carloads of strangers are about to collide, thanks to the search for a serial killer and the on-air philosophizing of a DJ each car is tuned in to. Offbeat drama features a fine ensemble cast that includes Sherilyn Fenn, Robert Forster, Meat Loaf, Taj Mahal, David Paymer and Kevin Pollak. 105 min.
02-3344 Was $99.99 □$19.99

The General (1998)
Gritty examination of the life and crimes of Martin Cahill, the legendary Irish crook who was killed by an IRA agent in 1994. Director John Boorman traces Cahill's incredible experiences, from his poverty-stricken youth to his sly robbery schemes to his duels with policeman (and ex-friend) Ned Kenny. With Brendan Gleason, Jon Voight, Adrian Dunbar and Maria Doyle Kennedy. 124 min.
02-3349 Was $99.99 □$21.99

Finding Graceland (1999)
Haunted by the accident that took his wife's life, Jonathan Schaech's aimless cross-country drive takes a strange detour when he meets Memphis-bound hitchhiker Harvey Keitel, who claims to be Elvis Presley. Schaech becomes caught up in Keitel's "fantasy" and joins him on an emotional road trip in this compelling comedy/drama. With Bridget Fonda as a Marilyn Monroe impersonator. 97 min.
02-3357 Was $99.99 □$19.99

Go (1999)
In this slacker piece of pulp fiction directed by Doug Liman ("Swingers"), impoverished Los Angeles supermarket clerk Sarah Polley's attempt to make some money by getting in the middle of a drug deal sets into motion a series of wild, dangerous and hilariously unpredictable events involving her friends and acquaintances. With Jay Mohr, Katie Holmes and Taye Diggs. 103 min.
02-3359 Was $99.99 □$14.99

This Is My Father (1999)
Touching tale stars James Caan as an Illinois teacher who travels to Ireland's County Galway with his nephew to trace his family's roots. Through a flashback to the late '30s, the story of the doomed romance between Caan's parents, and the roles religion and class played in their relationship, is revealed. With Aidan Quinn, Stephen Rea and Moya Farrelly; directed and photographed by Quinn's brothers Paul and Declan. 120 min.
02-3366 Was $99.99 □$14.99

The Loss Of Sexual Innocence (1999)
This haunting, autobiographical meditation on love, loss and sex from filmmaker Mike Figgis ("Leaving Las Vegas") centers on the life of a British director who reflects on his life as he is about to start a new project in Tunisia. His memories include being raised in Kenya and engaging in varied sexual experiences. With Julian Sands, Saffron Burrows and Hanne Klinton. 107 min.
02-3382 Was $99.99 □$14.99

The Big Brass Ring (1999)
Based on an unproduced screenplay by Orson Welles, this compelling and still-timely political drama stars William Hurt as a Missouri gubernatorial candidate. For Hurt, the governor's mansion looks to be an easy stepping stone to the White House, until a scandal from his past threatens to explode. Nigel Hawthorne, Iréne Jacob, Miranda Richardson also star. 104 min.
02-3395 Was $99.99 □$14.99

Twin Falls Idaho (1999)
Taking the "love triangle drama" to new heights, filmmaking siblings Mark and Michael Polish play conjoined twins waiting in a rundown hotel room for one brother's failing health to eventually do them both in. The arrival of their "birthday gift"—beautiful young hooker Michelle Hicks—leads healthy twin Mark to fall for her and consider life as a separate individual. Patrick Bauchau, Garrett Morris and Lesley Ann Warren also star in this offbeat, darkly funny tale. 110 min.
02-3400 Was $99.99 □$21.99

Normal Life (1996)
In this disturbing look at the struggles of contemporary life, Luke Perry plays a policeman in a small Illinois town whose desire for happiness and financial security is sidetracked when wife Ashley Judd begins having emotional problems. After losing his job and failing at his own business, Perry turns to robbing banks, but his smooth criminal operation is soon threatened by Judd's unpredictable behavior. 108 min.
02-5121 Was $99.99 □$19.99

Eat A Bowl Of Tea (1989)
Evocative and enjoyable comedy from director Wayne Wang set in New York's Chinatown in the 1940s and concerning a young Chinese-American man whose happy (albeit arranged) marriage is jeopardized by the onset of stress-induced impotence. Gently funny charmer stars Russell Wong, Cora Miao, Victor Wong. 102 min.
02-1975 Was $89.99 $19.99

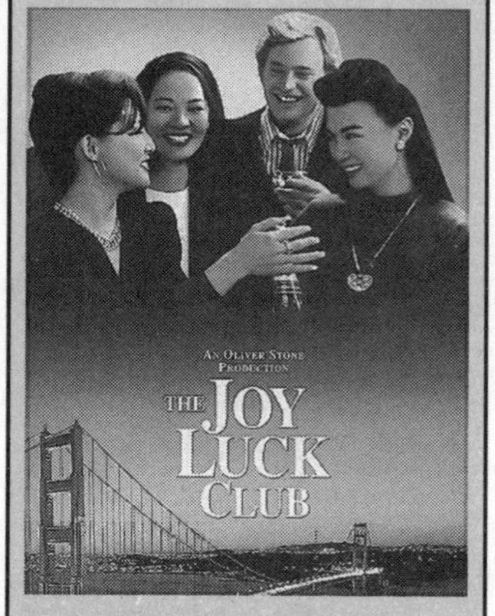

The Joy Luck Club (1993)
A powerful, heartfelt treatment of Amy Tan's acclaimed novel looks at the lives of four Chinese women and their daughters, and the tragedies and joys they share both decades ago in China and in contemporary America. A superlative ensemble cast, including Kieu Chinh, France Nuyen and Tamlyn Tomita excels, under Wayne Wang's sensitive direction. 139 min.
11-1772 Was $19.99 □$14.99

Smoke (1995)
A neighborhood cigar shop in Brooklyn is the setting for this engaging, multi-character film from writer Paul Auster ("The Music of Chance") and director Wayne Wang ("The Joy Luck Club"). Harvey Keitel is the store's streetwise manager who welcomes depressed writer William Hurt, former flame Stockard Channing and many others to his establishment. 96 min.
11-1945 Was $ 89.99 □$19.99

Blue In The Face (1995)
Filmed in just three days, this improvised "companion piece" to "Smoke" chronicles the further exploits at the Brooklyn cigar shop that serves as a neighborhood meeting place where such weighty topics as love, fidelity, the "Brooklyn attitude," Belgian waffles and Jackie Robinson are discussed. Harvey Keitel, Roseanne, Michael J. Fox, Jim Jarmusch, Madonna, Lou Reed and Lily Tomlin are featured. 84 min.
11-2015 □$19.99

Chinese Box (1998)
Hong Kong's 1997 return to China sets the stage for this romantic drama starring Jeremy Irons as a British journalist living in Hong Kong who falls in love with Vivian (Gong Li), a waitress with a rich boyfriend. When her beau refuses to marry her, Li and Irons start an intense and passionate affair. With Maggie Cheung, Ruben Blades; directed by Wayne Wang ("The Joy Luck Club"). 99 min.
68-1889 Was $99.99 □$14.99

Chinese Box (Letterboxed Version)
Also available in a theatrical, widescreen format.
68-1891 Was $99.99 □$14.99

Absence Of The Good (1999)
Haunted by the shooting death of his son, veteran detective Stephen Baldwin tries to lose himself in the search for a serial killer stalking the streets of Salt Lake City in this gripping crime thriller. Rob Knepper, Allen Garfield, Tyne Daly also star. 99 min.
02-3402 Was $99.99 □$21.99

Voices From A Locked Room (1995)
This true story is set in London in 1930, where music critic Philip Heseltine shows his intense dislike for composer Peter Warlock in a series of scathing reviews. While trying to figure out the reasons behind Heseltine's disdain, his girlfriend, a cabaret singer, uncovers a startling secret. Jeremy Northam, Tushka Bergen and Allan Corduner star. AKA: "Voices." 92 min.
02-3417 Was $99.99 $21.99

Death And The Maiden (1994)
Roman Polanski's intense film of Ariel Dorfman's play stars Sigourney Weaver as a South American woman who believes that her lawyer husband's associate is the man who tortured and raped her years earlier. Against her husband's wishes, Weaver takes justice into her own hands, holding the man captive in order to force him to confess. Ben Kingsley and Stuart Wilson also star. 103 min.
02-5053 Was $89.99 □$19.99

My Family (1995)
Engrossing multigenerational account of the Mexican-American Sanchez family from director Gregory Nava ("El Norte"). The film begins in the 1920s, when one of the family members attempts to walk from his Mexican village to Los Angeles. What follows is a tale involving immigration woes, gangs, joy and tragedy. With Jimmy Smits, Esai Morales and Edward James Olmos. 126 min.
02-5065 Was $19.99 □$14.99

An Awfully Big Adventure (1995)
Set in Liverpool after World War II, this drama focuses on a ragtag theatrical troupe which includes a cruel, effete director (Hugh Grant) and an enigmatic, motorcycle-riding lead actor (Alan Rickman). An orphan girl gets involved in the unpredictable backstage world and experiences the joys and pain of first love. With Georgina Cates. 113 min.
02-5072 Was $89.99 □$19.99

Frankie Starlight (1995)
Whimsical and charming fable following the lives of Bernadette, a French woman who immigrates to Ireland after World War II, and Frank, her son, a talented but put-upon dwarf fascinated with the stars and the universe. Anne Parillaud, Matt Dillon, Gabriel Byrne and Corban Walker star in this one-of-a-kind movie adapted from the novel "The Dork of Cork." 100 min.
02-5090 Was $99.99 □$19.99

Tollbooth (1996)
Intriguing comedy-drama set around a tollbooth near the Florida Keys where tolltaker Lenny Von Dohlen waits impatiently to marry gas station attendant-girlfriend Fairuza Balk. But Balk won't say "yes" until her long-lost cabby father returns home. Dad's surprise visit to Von Dohlen one night leads to a series of strange occurrences. With Louise Fletcher, Seymour Cassel. 108 min.
02-5098 Was $99.99 □$19.99

House Made Of Dawn (1996)
Based on the Pulitzer Prize-winning novel by Scott Momaday, this mystical and thought-provoking drama follows a young Native American named Abel who experiences ancestral visions that put him in conflict with the white man's world and lead him to an encounter with a charismatic Indian preacher. Larry Littlebird and John Saxon star. 77 min.
02-5105 $14.99

Across The Sea Of Time (1995)
Produced for IMAX theaters, this spellbinding film tells of an 11-year-old Russian boy who comes to New York in search of his relatives. Using old letters and a special viewer to guide him, the boy goes to Coney Island, where he rides a roller-coaster, travels on a subway and imagines himself flying over Manhattan. With Peter Reznik. Not in 3-D. 50 min.
02-3088 $19.99

Carried Away (1996)
Respected small-town high school teacher Dennis Hopper puts his career and his long-standing relationship with fellow instructor Amy Irving in jeopardy when he becomes romantically involved with a beautiful student. Emotional and sensual drama also stars Amy Locane, Gary Busey, Hal Holbrook. 108 min.
02-5107 Was $99.99 □$19.99

Crash (1996)
Taking the phrase "auto-eroticism" to new levels, writer/director David Cronenberg's explicit, controversial adaptation of the J.G. Ballard novel stars James Spader and Holly Hunter as strangers who literally meet by accident, in a highway collision, and subsequently begin an affair that draws them into a sexual subculture of car crash enthusiasts, a world where man and machine, pain and pleasure, and even life and death come together. With Elias Koteas, Rosanna Arquette, Deborah Kara Unger. Uncut, NC-17 version; 100 min.
02-5145 Was $99.99 □$19.99

Crash (R-Rated Version)
Also available in a less graphic, edited edition.
02-5146 Was $99.99 □$19.99

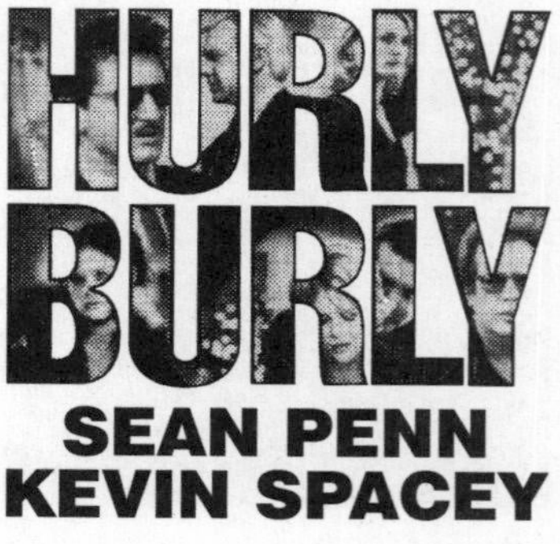

Hurlyburly (1998)
High up in the Hollywood hills, the lives of four friends—casting director Sean Penn, associate/housemate Kevin Spacey, would-be actor Chazz Palminteri and producer Garry Shandling—are a swirling maelstrom filled with drugs, sex, misogyny, self-loathing and a desperate search for meaning. Writer David Rabe's adaptation of his searing Broadway drama also stars Robin Wright Penn, Meg Ryan and Anna Paquin as the women caught up in the guys' personal crises. 126 min.
02-5211 Was $99.99 □$19.99

Shine (1996)
In his masterful, Academy Award-winning performance, Geoffrey Rush shines as David Helfgott, the real-life Australian concert pianist who suffers an emotional breakdown just as his musical career is about to take off. This passionate film looks at the musician's relationship with his demanding father and his triumphant recovery. With Armin Mueller-Stahl, Noah Taylor and Sir John Gielgud. 120 min.
02-5133 Was $99.99 ❑*$19.99*

Shine (Letterboxed Version)
Also available in a theatrical, widescreen format.
02-5157 ❑*$19.99*

love jones (1997)
Set amidst the trendy jazz clubs and coffeehouses of Chicago, this bright and contemporary look at romance in middle-class black culture follows the blossoming relationship between author Larenz Tate and photographer Nia Long, a romance fraught with a variety of pitfalls. Isaiah Washington, Bill Bellamy also star. 110 min.
02-5147 Was $19.99 ❑*$14.99*

Gummo (1997)
Harmony Korine, scripter of the controversial "Kids," does double duty behind the camera for this off-the-wall drama. Set in a small Ohio town left devastated by a tornado years earlier, the film follows the jobless, aimless adult and teen residents as they go through the motions of living. Nick Sutton, Chloe Sevigny, Max Perlich, Linda Manz star. 95 min.
02-5170 Was $99.99 ❑*$19.99*

Romeo Is Bleeding (1993)
A darkly funny and over-the-top crime drama starring Gary Oldman as a crooked New York cop whose already complicated professional and personal lives get worse when the mob orders him to rub out Russian-born hit woman Lena Olin, a seductive, amoral killer with a love for murder and sexy lingerie. Steamy thriller loaded with double-crosses also stars Annabella Sciorra, Juliette Lewis, Roy Scheider. 110 min.
02-8068 ❑*$19.99*

Roseanne: An Unauthorized Biography (1994)
The outrageous, always unpredictable life of Roseanne (Barr, Arnold, whatever) is recounted in this TV movie that traces her troubled early years, her rise to stardom as a comedienne, her relationship with fellow comic Tom Arnold and the trials and tribulations surrounding her family and hit TV series. Denny Dillon and David Graff star. 90 min.
02-8193 Was $49.99 ❑*$14.99*

Panther (1995)
An arresting look at the controversial '60s Black Panther movement headed by Huey Newton and Bobby Seale traces their rise through a fictional character, a Vietnam veteran double-agent, working for the Feds and the Panthers. Directed by Mario Van Peebles, this explosive effort stars Kadeem Hardison, Courtney Vance, Marcus Chong and Richard Dysart. 123 min.
02-8327 Was $89.99 ❑*$14.99*

Drunks (1996)
A meeting of a New York Alcoholics Anonymous group is the setting for brutal honesty and emotional self-revelations in this powerful drama with an ensemble cast that includes Faye Dunaway, Spalding Gray, Richard Lewis, Parker Posey, Howard Rollins and Dianne Wiest. 90 min.
02-8654 Was $99.99 ❑*$14.99*

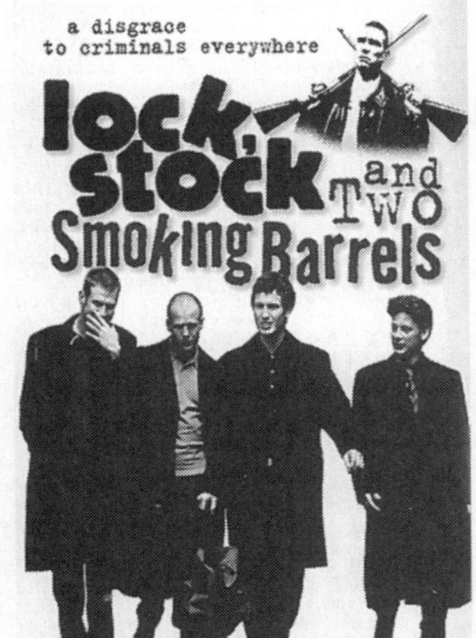
a disgrace
to criminals everywhere
lock, stock and two
Smoking Barrels

Lock, Stock And Two Smoking Barrels (1998)
In-your-face, serio-comic crime caper set in London's East End and focusing on four pals looking to make a big score in a card game. When the plan goes awry and they're left owing big money to a local crime boss, they hatch a desperate scheme to rip off a group of crooks who rob a marijuana-growing operation. Nick Moran, Jason Flemyng and soccer star Vinnie Jones star. 108 min.
02-9108 Was $99.99 *$14.99*

Michelle Pfeiffer

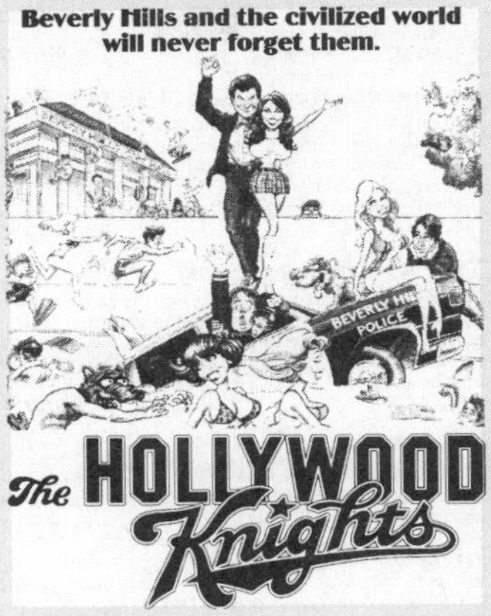
Beverly Hills and the civilized world
will never forget them.
BEVERLY HILLS POLICE
The HOLLYWOOD
Knights

The Hollywood Knights (1980)
One of the most-asked for titles in Movies Unlimited history, this nostalgic comedy filled with songs and bellylaughs is set in Beverly Hills in 1965. Faced with the imminent closing of their drive-in restaurant hangout, a gang of hot rod-loving teens sets out on a wild spree of "protest pranks" and mayhem. Along with the screen debuts of Tony Danza, Michelle Pfeiffer and Robert Wuhl, the cast also includes Fran Drescher, Leigh French and Gailard Sartain. 91 min.
02-3423 Was $89.99 ❑*$14.99*

Falling In Love Again (1980)
First-time director Steven Paul also produced and co-wrote this warm-hearted look at a man's mid-life crisis on the way to his high school reunion. Susannah York and Michelle Pfeiffer (her film debut) play Elliott Gould's wife in the present and in his recollections, respectively. 99 min.
83-1123 Was $19.99 *$14.99*

Callie And Son (1981)
Effective drama of a poverty-stricken Texas girl forced to give up her illegitimate son, and her search to find him decades later after her rise to the top of Dallas society. Memorable turns by Lindsay Wagner, Jameson Parker, Dabney Coleman, Michelle Pfeiffer. 97 min.
40-1182 Was $19.99 *$14.99*

Ladyhawke (1985)
Delightful fantasy-adventure set in the Middle Ages with Matthew Broderick as a sneak thief who aids a knight and his lady love (Rutger Hauer, Michelle Pfeiffer) in breaking a curse put on them by a malevolent wizard. Action, romance and comedy all come together; directed by Richard Donner. 124 min.
19-1454 Was $19.99 ❑*$14.99*

Sweet Liberty (1986)
A Hollywood film crew invades the small Southern town of the author whose Revolutionary War novel they've turned into a racy teen comedy, much to his consternation. Alan Alda wrote, directed and stars in this lively farce, supported by Michael Caine, Michelle Pfeiffer, Bob Hoskins and Lillian Gish. 107 min.
07-1452 Was $19.99 ❑*$14.99*

Power, Passion & Murder (1987)
The lust for success, fame and love burns white hot in this drama set against the glamour of Hollywood, with Michelle Pfeiffer, Darren McGavin and Stella Stevens. 104 min.
68-1118 Was $19.99 *$14.99*

Dangerous Liaisons (1988)
Stephen Frears' gorgeous costumer set in 18th-century France follows a carnal wager proposed by aristocratic seducers Glenn Close and John Malkovich. Among the victims of this sexual gamesmanship are Michelle Pfeiffer and Uma Thurman as a virtuous wife and wife-to-be targeted for corruption by Malkovich, and Keanu Reeves as Close's lover. 120 min.
19-1703 Was $19.99 ❑*$14.99*

The Fabulous Baker Boys (1989)
Acclaimed seriocomic look at two lounge-singing brothers whose waning careers are rescued when a sexy female crooner joins the act. Jeff Bridges, Beau Bridges and Michelle Pfeiffer star in this sultry tale, highlighted by bluesy numbers and Pfeiffer's radiant sensuality. 113 min.
27-6665 Was $89.99 ❑*$14.99*

Frankie & Johnny (1991)
Winning romantic comedy-drama stars Michelle Pfeiffer as a lonely New York luncheonette waitress who begrudgingly falls for Al Pacino, a raucous short-order cook with a criminal past. There's humor, pathos and fine performances in Garry Marshall's winning adaptation of Terrence McNalley's off-Broadway hit; with Hector Elizondo and Kate Nelligan. 117 min.
06-1921 Was $19.99 ❑*$14.99*

Love Field (1992)
Michelle Pfeiffer turns in a strong performance as an early '60s housewife who idolizes Jackie Kennedy and is devastated by the shooting of JFK. She decides to take a bus trip to Washington to attend the president's funeral and, during the trip, befriends a black man and his daughter and learns first-hand about racism. Dennis Haysbert, Brian Kerwin and Stephanie McFadden also star. 104 min.
73-1128 Was $19.99 ❑*$14.99*

Dangerous Minds (1995)
A compelling true story starring Michelle Pfeiffer as Louanne Johnson, a hard-nosed ex-Marine who takes a job teaching English to smart but under-achieving kids in an inner-city school. Pfeiffer draws on her background to educate the kids on topics ranging from martial arts to the poetry of Dylan Thomas while battling gang members and a strict principal. With George Dzundza. 99 min.
11-1961 Was $19.99 ❑*$14.99*

To Gillian On Her 37th Birthday (1996)
Even though she died two years earlier in a boating accident, Peter Gallagher still speaks to wife Michelle Pfeiffer each day. But the grief has affected his relationship with his teenage daughter and, after a family reunion on Nantucket Island, he decides it may be best to let go of the past. Claire Danes, Kathy Baker and Wendy Crewson also star in this sensitive drama. 92 min.
02-3039 Was $99.99 ❑*$14.99*

One Fine Day (1996)
It's "boy-with-daughter meets girl-with-son" in this engaging romantic comedy starring George Clooney and Michelle Pfeiffer as career-driven New York divorced parents who spend a hectic day together trying to juggle their respective careers, looking after each other's kindergarten-age kids, and discovering a mutual attraction. With Charles Durning, Amanda Peet. 108 min.
04-3441 Was $99.99 ❑*$14.99*

Up Close And Personal (1996)
Loosely based on the life of late TV news anchorwoman Jessica Savitch, this romantic drama stars Michelle Pfeiffer as an ambitious journalist who, with skill, determination and help from boss and lover Robert Redford, becomes a star TV reporter in Miami and Philadelphia. With Stockard Channing, Joe Mantegna and Kate Nelligan. 124 min.
11-2042 Was $19.99 ❑*$14.99*

The Deep End Of The Ocean (1999)
In this emotional drama based on the best-selling novel, Michelle Pfeiffer and Treat Williams are parents whose lives are torn apart when their 3-year-old son is abducted during a visit to Chicago. Nine years later, they discover that the boy is living just blocks away from their new home, with a new name and a man he calls "Dad." Whoopi Goldberg, Jonathan Jackson co-star. 109 min.
02-3356 Was $99.99 ❑*$14.99*

The Story Of Us (1999)
Follow the ups and downs of 15 years in the lives of Bruce Willis and Michelle Pfeiffer, a couple facing the possible end of their marriage, in director Rob Reiner's funny and moving seriocomic look at modern romance and the give and take of relationships. Fine supporting cast includes Julie Hagerty, Tim Matheson, Paul Reiser, Rita Wilson. 96 min.
07-2827 Was $99.99 ❑*$14.99*

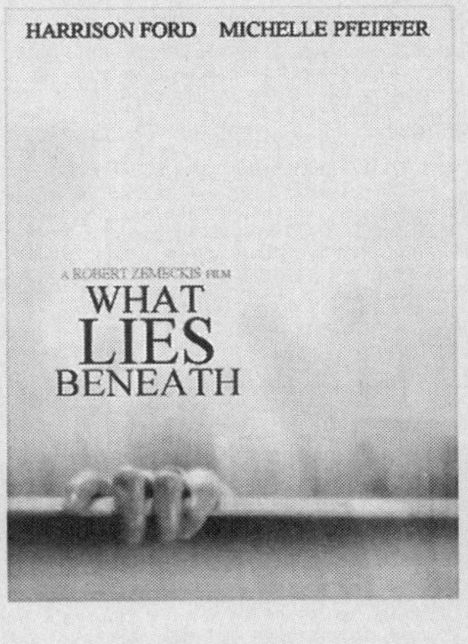
HARRISON FORD MICHELLE PFEIFFER
A ROBERT ZEMECKIS FILM
WHAT
LIES
BENEATH

What Lies Beneath (2000)
Creepy suspenser from Robert Zemeckis ("Contact") stars Michelle Pfeiffer and Harrison Ford as a married couple who live in a large house near a Vermont lake. While Ford, a university research scientist, works on an important project, Pfeiffer sees the image of a young woman in water and believes her mysterious neighbors have something to do with the eerie sight. After other bizarre incidents and a visit to a psychiatrist, Pfeiffer becomes convinced her house is haunted. With Diana Scarwid.
07-2951 ❑*$99.99*

Please see our index for these other Michelle Pfeiffer titles: *The Age Of Innocence • Amazon Women On The Moon • Batman Returns • Grease 2 • The Prince Of Egypt • The Russia House • Scarface • Tequila Sunrise • A Thousand Acres • William Shakespeare's A Midsummer Night's Dream • The Witches Of Eastwick • Wolf*

Return To Paradise (1998)
Intense drama in the tradition of "Midnight Express" centers on Americans Joaquin Phoenix, Vince Vaughn and David Conrad, who enjoy a raucous vacation in Malaysia. Two years later, lawyer Anne Heche informs Vaughn and Conrad that Phoenix will be hanged on a drug charge if they don't return to the country, admit their involvement in the crime and serve time in prison. 112 min.
02-9051 Was $99.99 *$14.99*

Hilary And Jackie (1998)
They were sisters united by their shared passion for music, but torn apart by their love of the same man. The amazing true story of virtuoso siblings Hilary (Rachel Griffiths) and Jacqueline du Pré (Emily Watson) is recounted in this acclaimed biodrama that focuses on Jackie's meteoric rise to international fame, her stormy marriage to conductor Daniel Barenboim, and how her career was cut short by a fatal illness. Charles Dance, James Frain also star. 124 min.
02-9105 Was $99.99 ❑*$14.99*

Nostromo (1996)
Set in a war-torn South American nation in the late 1800s, this sprawling BBC drama, based on the Joseph Conrad novel, chronicles the turmoil in and around the remote city of Sulaco as an English silver mine head, his wealthy American backer, and the workers' leader, a man known as "Nostromo," all fall prey to corruption and the lust for wealth and power. Joaquim De Almeida, Brian Dennehy, Albert Finney, Colin Firth, Serena Scott Thomas star. 180 min. on three tapes.
04-3426 ❑*$59.99*

Light It Up (1999)
A protest over a popular teacher's suspension at a run-down Queens high school erupts into chaos when a security guard is accidentally shot. Six students hole up in the library with the wounded guard as their "hostage," using the resulting stand-off with police as a chance to demand better conditions. Compelling urban drama stars Usher Raymond, Rosario Dawson, Robert Ri'chard, Sara Gilbert, Forest Whitaker and Judd Nelson.
04-3924 ❑*$99.99*

Star Maps (1997)
Unusual and provocative drama that juxtaposes the glamour of Hollywood with the poverty and desperation of Los Angeles' Latino neighborhoods. A young Hispanic man returns to his family after two years in Mexico with dreams of film stardom, only to wind up working for his pimp father in a prostitution ring that uses "maps to the stars' homes" salesmen as a front. Written and directed by Miguel Arteta; Douglas Spain, Efrain Figueroa, Kandeyce Jorden star. 90 min.
04-3558 ❑*$99.99*

Dreaming Of Joseph Lees (1999)
Outwardly a wallflower, shy English sawmill worker Samantha Morton longs to experience real-life passion, which to her means dreaming of distant cousin Rupert Graves. But loneliness drives Morton to become involved with lusty pig farmer Lee Ross. One day, the disabled Graves appears, forming up a love triangle based on obsession and desire—with tragic results. 114 min.
04-3958 ❑*$99.99*

Oscar And Lucinda (1997)
They were unconventional people in an era ruled by convention. Drawn to one another by their common love of gambling while on a sea voyage from England to Australia in the late 1800s, charismatic clergyman Ralph Fiennes and independent businesswoman Cate Blanchett share a romance and a quest—to deliver a glass church to an Outback community—in this offbeat drama from director Gillian Armstrong ("Little Women"). 130 min.
04-3659 Was $99.99 ❑*$29.99*

Manhattan Merengue (1995)
Miguel, an aspiring dancer from the Dominican Republic, enters the U.S. illegally and takes a job as a janitor at a small dance school, where his talents draw the attention and affection of the lead instructor. Soon, Miguel becomes the teacher of a Latin dance group, but a series of events soon change his life and threaten his future in America. George Perez, Lumi Cavazos star; directed by Joseph Vasquez ("Hangin' with the Homeboys"). 94 min.
02-8666 Was $99.99 *$14.99*

Brokedown Palace (1999)
Intense drama in the tradition of "Midnight Express" centers on American teens Claire Danes and Kate Beckinsale, who enjoy a post-high school vacation in exotic Thailand. An encounter with an handsome Australian leads to the girls' being arrested at the Bangkok airport for heroin possession. Sent to a hellish women's prison, they must try to prove their innocence. Bill Pullman, Lou Diamond Phillips also star. 82 min.
04-3919 Was $99.99 ❑*$14.99*

Vital Signs (1990)
A group of third-year medical students confronts complicated romances, jealousy and difficult studies in this powerfully acted drama. Adrian Pasdar, Diane Lane and Jack Gwaltney are the students trying to survive the painful year; Jimmy Smits is their understanding teacher. 102 min.
04-2378   Was $89.99   ☐ $14.99

The Quarrel (1991)
Acclaimed drama from Canada set in Montreal in 1946, where a meeting between two Holocaust survivors leads to an examination of the effect the experience has had on their lives. One has become a rabbi who seeks solace in prayer, while the other, a writer, has turned his back on religion. Saul Rubinek and R.H. Thomsen star. 90 min.
02-8480   Was $19.99   ☐ $14.99

My Antonia (1994)
This sensitive drama, based on Willa Cather's celebrated story, tells of an orphaned farm boy who travels to the wilderness to live with his grandparents. There he meets an immigrant girl, and the two share a special, poignant relationship. Jason Robards, Eva Marie Saint, Neil Patrick Harris and Elina Löwensohn star. 92 min.
06-2314   Was $89.99   ☐ $19.99

Bloodhounds (1996)
A tough cop forms an uneasy alliance with a best-selling writer to track down an escaped killer in this offbeat and romantic crime drama. Corbin Bernsen, Christine Harnos star. 86 min.
06-2564   Was $99.99   ☐ $14.99

Bloodhounds 2 (1997)
Corbin Bernsen returns as best-selling author Harry Coyle, who hires a pretty, street-smart detective when he discovers his top fan is a psychotic killer. Nia Peebles also stars. 89 min.
06-2621   Was $99.99   ☐ $14.99

Last Exit To Brooklyn (1990)
Set in '50s Brooklyn, this searing film, based on Hubert Selby Jr.'s celebrated underground novel, focuses on the lives and loves of local residents. Among the characters are a cynical, abused hooker (Jennifer Jason Leigh), a homosexual union boss (Stephen Lang) and a factory worker (Burt Young) up in arms over his daughter's shotgun wedding. Peter Dobson, Jerry Orbach, Ricki Lake also star. 103 min.
02-2052   Was $89.99 $19.99

Critical Choices (1997)
The ongoing debate over abortion is brought into focus in this compelling and timely drama about a women's clinic that is targeted for an evangelist's demonstrations, and what happens when the protests on both sides lead to violence. Betty Buckley, Pamela Reed, Diana Scarwid and Brian Kerwin star. 88 min.
06-2657   Was $99.99   ☐ $99.99

The Wood (1998)
Stricken with wedding-day jitters, would-be bridegroom Taye Diggs gets support from best friends Omar Epps and Richard T. Jones, who share stories of the trio's experiences growing up a decade earlier in L.A.'s mostly black suburb of Inglewood, in this funny and moving coming-of-age tale. Sean Nelson, Duane Finley and Trent Cameron co-star as the guys' younger selves. 106 min.
06-2931   Was $99.99   ☐ $14.99

Varsity Blues (1999)
The back-up quarterback for a Texas high school team is reluctantly thrust into the spotlight when he's called on to replace the starting QB and finds the hopes of his school—and the entire community—resting on his shoulders. Seriocomic look at small-town sports heroism and teen angst stars James Van Der Beek, Paul Walker, Scott Caan and Jon Voight as the driven coach. Special edition includes a behind-the-scenes featurette and two music videos. 105 min.
06-2853   Was $99.99   ☐ $14.99

The Adventures Of Sebastian Cole (1998)
What's a teen to do when his father is a cold and distant architect, his mother is an alcoholic who wants to move back to England, and the stepfather he's close to announces he's going to become a woman? For Sebastian Cole (Adrian Grenier), it's just the start of a series of life-changing experiences in this funny and touching "coming of age" tale from rookie writer/director Tod Williams. Margaret Colin, Clark Gregg, Aleksa Palladino also star. 100 min.
06-2948   Was $99.99   ☐ $14.99

Desperate Remedies (1995)
Set in an imaginary town in the late 19th century, this lush, romantic drama from New Zealand chronicles a young woman's attempt to save her sister from a doomed love and her family from ruin. Jennifer Ward-Lealand, Kevin Smith, Lisa Chappell star. 92 min.
06-2467   ☐ $89.99

The Wharf Rat (1995)
When his policeman brother is murdered by crooked colleagues, a waterfront con man teams up with an investigative reporter to set a trap for the killers in this elaborate crime drama. Lou Diamond Phillips, Judge Reinhold, Rachel Ticotin, Rita Moreno star. 88 min.
06-2430   ☐ $89.99

Naked City: Justice With A Bullet (1998)
Loosely based on the classic '50s TV show, this gritty urban drama stars Scott Glenn and Courtney B. Vance as New York City cops investigating the robbery of two young, female tourists by a limo driver. While the women are soon embroiled in dangerous situations, Vance becomes a target for a hit man. With Robin Tunney, Kathryn Erbe, Giancarlo Esposito. 107 min.
06-2862   ☐ $99.99

Naked City: A Killer Christmas (1998)
It'll be anything but a merry Christmas for Sgt. Scott Muldoon (Scott Glenn) and Officer James Halloran (Courtney B. Vance) when a TV journalist's reports of a serial killer stalking the streets send New York into a panic. Laura Leighton, Nigel Bennett also star; directed by Peter Bogdanovich. 92 min.
06-2929   ☐ $79.99

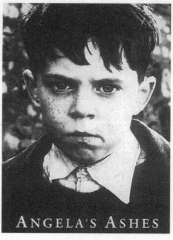

ANGELA'S ASHES

Angela's Ashes (1999)
Director Alan Parker expertly brings Frank McCourt's acclaimed recollection of life in 1930s Limerick, Ireland, to the screen in this touching and emotional drama. Returning to Europe after living for years in New York, the McCourt family copes with poverty, prejudice and unemployed father Robert Carlyle's alcoholism, while mother Emily Watson struggles to provide for her sons and Frank (played at various ages by Joe Breen, Ciaran Owens and Michael Legge) dreams of returning to America. 146 min.
06-2988   Was $99.99   ☐ $14.99

Rescuers: Stories Of Courage: Two Women (1997)
The remarkable true stories of two women who put their lives on the line to aid Jews fleeing from the terrors of the Holocaust are movingly depicted in this drama from director Peter Bogdanovich. Elizabeth Perkins plays a nanny protecting the son of a friend in "Mamusha," while "Woman on a Bicycle" stars Sela Ward as a French woman who helps the local bishop hide refugees. 107 min.
06-2711   Was $79.99   ☐ $14.99

Rescuers: Stories Of Courage: Two Couples (1998)
Amid the horrors of the Holocaust, the real-life people shown here risked everything—even their lives—to save others. "Aarte and Johte Vos" are a newlywed couple (played by Martin Donovan and Dana Delany) who turn their country house into a hideaway for refugees. In "Madame Tacquet," Linda Hamilton and Alfred Molina hide Jewish boys in their Catholic school. 109 min.
06-2785   Was $79.99   ☐ $14.99

Rescuers: Stories Of Courage: Two Families (1998)
Robin Tunney stars as teenage hero "Malka Csizmadia," who, along with her family, risked capture to help Jewish escapees from a prison camp behind their home, and carnival performers Daryl Hannah and Tim Matheson hide a Jewish family within their travelling show in "We Are Circus," in this moving double feature of true Holocaust survival stories. 105 min.
06-2825   Was $69.99   ☐ $14.99

A Face To Kill For (1999)
Framed by her scheming husband for embezzlement and sent to prison, Crystal Bernard is attacked and her face horribly scarred. When surgery gives her a new appearance and she's released, Bernard hatches a scheme of her own to clear her name, regain her family's ranch and get revenge on her dastardly spouse. Doug Savant, Billy Dean also star. 91 min.
06-2886   ☐ $69.99

Where's The Money, Noreen? (1996)
In this high-energy crime drama, Julianne Phillips plays the title character, a woman whose involvement in a $3 million bank heist lands her behind bars for 25 years. After her release from the state penitentiary, she attempts to rebuild her life, but the past—and the still-missing loot—still haunt her. With A Martinez, Nigel Bennett. 93 min.
06-2501   ☐ $99.99

Flipping (1997)
Tough-as-nails crime drama set in Los Angeles, where a group of four white hoods are ordered by their black leader to knock off a rival crime boss. This order causes friction between the crooks, who may now want to whack their own boss. David Amos, David Proval, Mike Starr and Keith David star in this unusual tale that includes a gay subplot involving a con artist and a cop. 102 min.
06-2606   Was $99.99   ☐ $14.99

The Con (1998)
Seductive scam artist Rebecca De Mornay, on the run from mobsters after losing their money in a failed scheme, hides out in a small town. Rumors that local mechanic William H. Macy is about to inherit a fortune hatch a new con in De Mornay's head—to woo, wed and then dump him—but nothing is what it seems to be in this stylish thriller. With Mike Nussbaum, Frances Sternhagen. 92 min.
06-2753   ☐ $69.99

Winona Ryder

Lucas (1986)
Delightful comedy/drama about a shy, bright 14-year-old high school student whose friendship with an older girl develops into a crush and is threatened when she's courted by the school football captain. Touching, heartfelt tale stars Corey Haim, Kerri Green, Charlie Sheen, Winona Ryder. 100 min.
04-1997   Was $79.99   ☐ $14.99

WINONA RYDER
CHRISTIAN SLATER
Heathers

Heathers (1989)
"The Breakfast Club" meets "Blue Velvet" in an outrageously dark comedy of high school cliques and teen angst. Winona Ryder is the reluctant member of a popular quartet of girls who, with the help of outsider Christian Slater, accidentally kills the lead "Heather," setting off a rash of suicides by status-conscious teens looking for posthumous popularity. Co-stars Shannen Doherty. 102 min.
70-1266   Was $89.99 $14.99

Heathers (Letterboxed Collector's Edition)
Special remastered collector's edition includes the original theatrical trailer and a "making of" featurette. 119 min. total.
08-8556   Letterboxed $14.99

Great Balls Of Fire! (1989)
Dennis Quaid sizzles as Jerry Lee Lewis in a frenetic biopic that traces "the Killer's" rise to rock and roll stardom in the '50s and the marriage to his teenage cousin that nearly ended it. Winona Ryder co-stars as Lewis' child bride, along with Alec Baldwin, Trey Wilson, John Doe. 108 min.
73-1056   Was $19.99   ☐ $14.99

Welcome Home, Roxy Carmichael (1990)
A small Midwest town is reluctantly preparing for a visit from a local woman who left years ago and became a national celebrity. Teen outcast Winona Ryder is excited, too, because she's convinced Roxy is really her mother. Offbeat comedy/drama also stars Jeff Daniels, Laila Robins. 98 min.
06-1827   Was $89.99 $14.99

Mermaids (1990)
A film for everyone whose mother ever drove them crazy, this comedy/drama stars Cher as the free-spirited head of a family in a small 1963 New England town, Winona Ryder as the daughter she's increasingly at odds with, and Bob Hoskins as the shoe salesman who'd like to become part of the family. Michael Schoefling, Christina Ricci co-star. 110 min.
73-1102   ☐ $14.99

Little Women (1994)
Lovingly realized treatment of Louisa May Alcott's classic tale stars Winona Ryder, Kirsten Dunst, Claire Danes and Trini Alvarado as Connecticut siblings who experience the joys and sorrows of impending womanhood while being raised by their mother during the Civil War. Susan Sarandon, Gabriel Byrne, Christian Bale, Eric Stoltz and Samantha Mathis also star. 118 min.
02-2773   Was $19.99   ☐ $14.99

Reality Bites (1994)
Snappy romantic comedy centering on the relationships, dreams and disappointments of a group of twentysomethings. Living together are aspiring filmmaker Winona Ryder, Gap manager Janeane Garofalo, sexually confused Steve Zahn and grunge rocker Ethan Hawke. When yuppie TV executive Ben Stiller (who also directed) falls for Ryder, friendships are threatened. 99 min.
07-2131   Was $19.99   ☐ $14.99

How To Make An American Quilt (1995)
Winona Ryder is 26-year-old Finn Dodd, a young woman working on her thesis on handicraft, who travels to her North California hometown while considering her boyfriend's marriage proposal. She meets a group of women working on a wedding quilt who relate stories of love in their lives. Kate Nelligan, Jean Simmons, Alfre Woodard and Anne Bancroft co-star. 117 min.
07-2409   Was $19.99   ☐ $14.99

The Crucible (1996)
Arthur Miller wrote the screenplay for director Nicholas Hytner's acclaimed adaptation of his allegorical drama set during the Salem Witch Trials in 17th-century Massachusetts. A young girl's spurning by her married lover leads to accusations of witchcraft, and soon an entire village is gripped in a fever of hysteria, bigotry and fear. Daniel Day-Lewis, Winona Ryder, Joan Allen and Paul Scofield star. 123 min.
04-3468   Was $99.99   ☐ $14.99

The Crucible (Letterboxed Version)
Also available in a theatrical, widescreen format.
04-3739 $14.99

WINONA RYDER   ANGELINA JOLIE
GIRL, INTERRUPTED

Girl, Interrupted (1999)
Based on Susanna Kaysen's best-selling memoir of her two-year stay in a New England psychiatric hospital in the late '60s, this acclaimed drama stars Winona Ryder as a troubled teen who commits herself after a suicide attempt. The friendship of a rebellious fellow inmate (Best Supporting Actress Oscar-winner Angelina Jolie) and a no-nonsense nurse (Whoopi Goldberg) helps Ryder come to terms with her life and fight to reclaim her freedom. With Vanessa Redgrave, Jared Leto. 127 min.
02-3430   Was $99.99   ☐ $19.99

Please see our index for these other Winona Ryder titles: *The Age Of Innocence* • *Alien Resurrection* • *Autumn In New York* • *Beetlejuice* • *Bram Stoker's Dracula* • *Edward Scissorhands* • *The House Of The Spirits* • *Looking For Richard*

Taps (1981)
Timothy Hutton, Sean Penn and Tom Cruise are cadets defending their Pennsylvania military school when they discover it's about to be torn down. Intense, exciting drama, filmed in Valley Forge, Pa., featuring George C. Scott as the gruff veteran commander of the school. 126 min.
04-1446 Was $59.99 *$14.99*

Risky Business

Risky Business (1983)
A teenage boy's parents leave their house and Porsche to their son when they go on vacation. After taking a hint from a friend, he "cuts loose," getting involved with prostitutes, killer pimps and into all sorts of trouble. Sharp, erotic, funny comedy/drama stars Tom Cruise, Rebecca De Mornay. 99 min.
19-1296 *$14.99*

All The Right Moves (1983)
A dynamic performance by Tom Cruise fuels this drama of a high school football star who sees a college scholarship as his only chance of leaving the impoverished steelmill town he calls home. With Lea Thompson, Chris Penn, Craig T. Nelson (playing, of all things, Cruise's coach). 90 min.
04-1673 Was $19.99 ❑*$14.99*

Top Gun (1986)
Tom Cruise is Maverick; ace Navy fighter pilot, member of elite "Top Gun" school; goes against the rules and riles boss Tom Skerritt and fellow pilots Val Kilmer and Anthony Edwards; falls for teacher Kelly McGillis; wants to fly his way; exciting dogfight finale; blazing jets; lots of rock and roll. 109 min.
06-1421 ❑*$14.99*

Top Gun (Letterboxed Version)
Also available in a theatrical, widescreen format.
06-2506 ❑*$14.99*

Legend (1986)
A dazzling fantasy/adventure set in a mystical world where the forces of good and evil fight the ultimate battle for domination. Tom Cruise is the guardian of Nature, Mia Sara his true love, and Tim Curry is the Prince of Darkness; Ridley Scott directs. 89 min.
07-1447 ❑*$14.99*

Cocktail (1988)
It's risky business behind the taps and bottles of New York's bar scene, but cocky outsider Tom Cruise has dreams the color of money and all the right moves to become a libation legend and a top gun bartender. Can Elisabeth Shue's endless love change him, or does he risk losin' it all? Hit drama co-stars Bryan Brown as Cruise's mixological mentor. 104 min.
11-1467 Was $19.99 ❑*$14.99*

Born On The Fourth Of July (1989)
The gut-wrenching true story of Ron Kovic, a Vietnam vet who was left paralyzed by a sniper's bullet in battle and returned home to eventually become an outspoken opponent of the war, is fueled by a knockout performance by Tom Cruise as Kovic and Oscar-winning direction from Oliver Stone. Willem Dafoe, Kyra Sedgwick and Tom Berenger co-star. 144 min.
07-1648 Was $19.99 ❑*$14.99*

Born On The Fourth Of July (Letterboxed Version)
Also available in a theatrical, widescreen format.
07-2674 Was $19.99 ❑*$14.99*

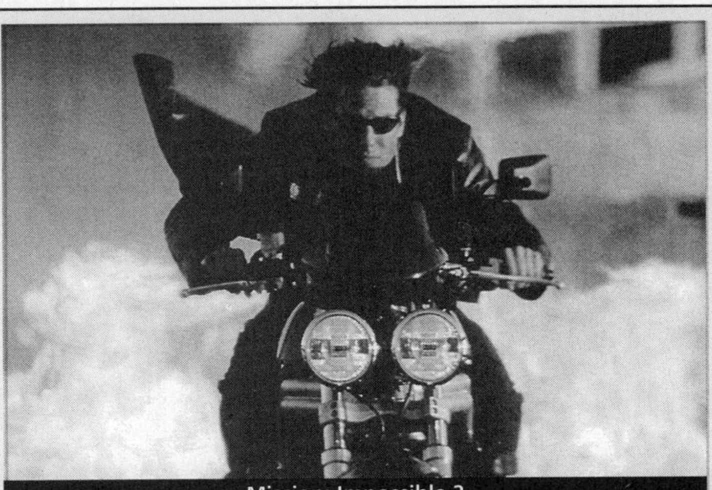

Mission: Impossible 2

Tom Cruise

Days Of Thunder (1990)
His vehicle may be land-based here, but Tom Cruise is still the fastest guy around in this thrilling drama set against the danger-filled world of auto racing. Exciting racing footage fuels the action. Robert Duvall, Nicole Kidman, Randy Quaid co-star. 107 min.
06-1928 ❑*$14.99*

A Few Good Men (1992)
Powerful courtroom drama starring Tom Cruise as a cocky Navy lawyer given the assignment of defending two young Marines accused of murdering one of their bunk-mates. Joined by a pesky attorney (Demi Moore), Cruise finds his investigation pointing to the actions of a tough-as-nails colonel (Jack Nicholson). With Kevin Pollak and Kiefer Sutherland; directed by Rob Reiner. 135 min.
02-5015 Was $19.99 ❑*$14.99*

A Few Good Men (Letterboxed Version)
Also available in a theatrical, widescreen format.
02-5029 ❑*$14.99*

Far And Away (1992)
Ron Howard's epic romantic drama stars Tom Cruise as a 19th-century Irish farmer who is joined on his pursuit for land and freedom in America by the daughter of a wealthy land baron (Nicole Kidman). The couple encounters a series of adventures and hardships en route to claim territory during the Oklahoma Land Rush. Robert Prosky and Thomas Gibson co-star. 140 min.
07-1865 Was $19.99 ❑*$14.99*

Far And Away (Letterboxed Version)
Also available in a theatrical, widescreen format.
07-1964 Was $19.99 ❑*$14.99*

The Firm (1993)
Riveting filmization of John Grisham's best-seller stars Tom Cruise as an ambitious young lawyer recruited by a posh Memphis law firm. Soon, Cruise and wife Jeanne Tripplehorn suspect shady maneuvers by his employers and uncover blackmail and ties to organized crime. With Gene Hackman, Holly Hunter, Gary Busey and Ed Harris; directed by Sydney Pollack. 154 min.
06-2160 Was $19.99 ❑*$14.99*

Interview With The Vampire: Special Edition (1994)
This creepy adaptation of Anne Rice's popular novel stars Tom Cruise as Lestat, the stylish, ages-old vampire who recruits 18th-century plantation owner Louis (Brad Pitt) into his nocturnal family to join him in the endless search for blood. Kirsten Dunst, Stephen Rea, Antonio Banderas and Christian Slater also star; Neil Jordan directs Rice's script. Special edition includes an introduction by Rice and Jordan, a "making of" documentary, and the theatrical trailer. 158 min. total.
19-2967 ❑*$19.99*

Jerry Maguire (1996)
Writer/director Cameron Crowe's hit seriocomic look at the high-pressure business side of pro sports stars Tom Cruise as a top athletic agent who speaks out against greed in sports...and is promptly fired. With only a flamboyant NFL player (Best Supporting Actor Oscar-winner Cuba Gooding, Jr.) left as a client, Cruise tries to rebuild his career while at the same time falling for pretty assistant Renee Zellweger. With Kelly Preston, Bonnie Hunt. 139 min.
02-3022 Was $19.99 ❑*$14.99*

Jerry Maguire (Letterboxed Version)
Also available in a theatrical, widescreen format.
02-3317 ❑*$19.99*

Mission: Impossible (1996)
The hit TV series is turned into a suspenseful, explosive feature starring Tom Cruise as Ethan Hunt, a special agent with the top-secret "Impossible Mission Force" who encounters mysterious arms-dealers, dangerous computer files and duplicitous government agents on his globe-trotting adventure. With Jon Voight, Ving Rhames and Emmanuelle Béart; directed by Brian De Palma. 110 min.
06-2512 Was $19.99 ❑*$14.99*

Mission: Impossible (Letterboxed Version)
Also available in a theatrical, widescreen format.
06-2537 Was $19.99 ❑*$14.99*

Mission: Impossible 2 (2000)
Tom Cruise's Ethan Hunt is back, this time assigned to Australia, where he must track down former compatriot Sean Ambrose (Dougray Scott), who has swiped an antidote for a deadly, genetically-altered flu bug from a bio-tech firm. Hunt recruits gorgeous Nyah Hall (Thandie Newton), a thief and former lover of Ambrose's, to help him stop Ambrose and save the world. John Woo's high-adrenaline action-thriller also stars Anthony Hopkins and Ving Rhames; scripted by Robert Towne. Includes two "making of" documentaries. 124 min.
06-3036 ❑*$99.99*

tom cruise

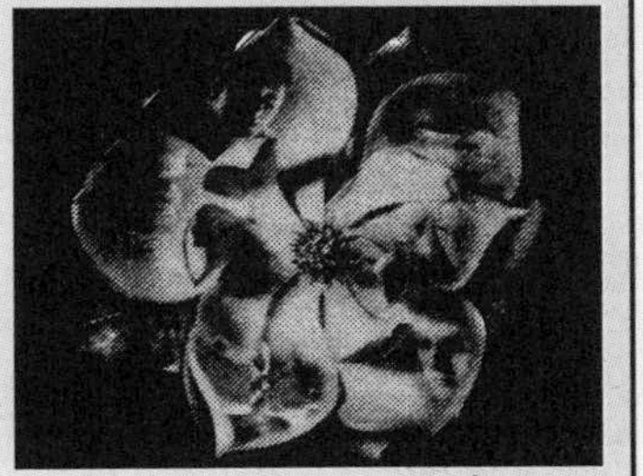

magnolia

Magnolia (1999)
Paul Thomas Anderson followed his acclaimed "Boogie Nights" with this bold study of a group of disparate—and desperate—characters in Los Angeles' San Fernando Valley. At the center of the story is dying TV producer Jason Robards, distraught wife Julianne Moore and estranged son Tom Cruise, who stars in "Seduce and Destroy" infomercials. With Philip Seymour Hoffman, William H. Macy, Philip Baker Hall and John C. Reilly. 188 min.
02-5232 Was $99.99 ❑*$19.99*

The Tom Cruise Collection
In the skies, on the fast track, or working on his briefs, Cruise will thrill and entertain you in this boxed set that includes "Top Gun," "Days of Thunder" and "The Firm."
06-2468 *$44.99*

Please see our index for these other Tom Cruise titles: *The Color Of Money • Eyes Wide Shut • The Outsiders*

Best Laid Plans (1999)
A meeting at a bar between two old high school friends leads to a twisted tale of seduction, kidnapping and betrayal in this "Gen-X"-flavored noir thriller. Josh Brolin, Alessandro Nivola and Reese Witherspoon star. 92 min.
04-3920 Was $99.99 ❑*$14.99*

A Show Of Force (1990)
Riveting, factual thriller starring Amy Irving as an American-born journalist who uncovers the government-sanctioned murders of two young protesters in Puerto Rico. Andy Garcia, Lou Diamond Phillips and Robert Duvall also star in the gripper in the mold of "Missing" and "Salvador." 93 min.
06-1771 Was $89.99 ❑*$14.99*

The Land Girls (1998)
During World War II, three women work as volunteers for the Women's Land Army, living on a farm on the English countryside and tending to chores to address Great Britain's food shortage. The women—played by Catherine McCormack, Rachel Weisz and Anna Friel—eventually become romantically involved with different men and learn important lessons about life. 111 min.
02-9011 Was $89.99 *$19.99*

Photographing Fairies (1998)
Based on a true incident that occurred in a small English village after World War I, this intriguing film tells of a photographer investigating two young girls who claim to have taken pictures of flying fairies. The photographer's obsession leads him to a series of tragic occurrences and an amazing discovery. With Toby Stephens, Ben Kingsley and Emily Woof. 107 min.
02-9012 Was $99.99 *$19.99*

After The Shock (1990)
Stunning true-life account of the 1989 San Francisco earthquake and its frightening aftermath. Yaphet Kotto, Rue McClanahan, Jack Scalia and Scott Valentine star in this intense, documentary-like film about the courageous people who faced death after the world shook. 92 min.
06-1831 ❑*$79.99*

Talent For The Game (1991)
Sensitive drama stars Edward James Olmos as a veteran baseball scout who finds his job on the line when the team's new owner decides to eliminate the scouting program. Can he find a hot diamond talent to save the struggling franchise? Lorraine Bracco, Jeff Corbett and Jamey Sheridan also star. 91 min.
06-1898 Was $89.99 ❑*$14.99*

Original Intent (1991)
A young, idealistic lawyer is asked by an old college friend to help save a homeless shelter and finds himself embroiled in a fierce battle against the city's most powerful power broker. Kris Kristofferson, Jay Richardson, Candy Clark and Martin Sheen star. 97 min.
06-1947 ❑*$89.99*

Digging To China (1998)
The directorial debut of Timothy Hutton is a compassionate drama detailing the relationship between Harriet, a lonely young girl who dreams of leaving her small Pennsylvania town, and Ricky, an older, retarded man who is about to be institutionalized. The two form a strong friendship and eventually take to the road. With Kevin Bacon, Evan Rachel Wood and Mary Stuart Masterson. 103 min.
02-9030 Was $99.99 *$14.99*

Hunting (1992)
John Savage plays a ruthless businessman who lives for the thrill of seducing women. He draws an alluring married woman in his sensuous game of desire, and she finds herself caught in a dangerous affair. With Kerry Armstrong, Guy Pearce. 97 min.
06-1955 ❑*$19.99*

Go Now (1995)
Robert Carlyle ("The Full Monty") turns in a terrific performance as Nick, a Scottish craftsman and soccer player whose life is suddenly thrown into disarray when he discovers he is suffering from multiple sclerosis. His illness soon tests the boundaries of his relationship with his girlfriend and others around him. With Juliet Aubrey. 87 min.
02-9046 Was $19.99 *$14.99*

All Over Me (1997)
Set amid the "riot grrrl" music scene in New York, sisters Alex and Sylvia Sichel's acclaimed independent drama stars Alison Forland and Tara Subkoff as two teenage best friends who begin to grow apart and must face the disintegration of their relationship. Music by Babes in Toyland, Ani DiFranco and Patti Smith. 95 min.
02-5152 Was $99.99 ❑*$19.99*

Lewis & Clark & George (1995)
A pair of escaped convicts named Lewis and Clark already have their hands full with a wild cross-country run from the law, but things really get complicated when they're joined by a beautiful mute woman named George. Rose McGowan, Dan Gunther and Salvator Xuereb star in this offbeat road drama. 90 min.
02-8872 Was $69.99 *$14.99*

Shameless (1996)
Powerful drama starring Elizabeth Hurley as a drug addict who uses new friend C. Thomas Howell to obtain drugs for her. After the two fall in love following a night of passion, he battles the odds to help her kick her deadly habit. Joss Ackland and Claire Bloom also star. 99 min.
02-8580 Was $99.99 *$14.99*

Infinity (1996)
Matthew Broderick directed and stars in this fascinating portrayal of a young Richard Feynman, the Nobel Prize-winning physicist renowned for his work on the Manhattan Project. The film focuses on Feynman's relationship with his wife, as well as his accomplishments in the field of science and math. With Patricia Arquette and Peter Riegert. 120 min.
02-8596 Was $19.99 *$14.99*

Eden (1998)
Set during the mid-1960s, this sensitive, spiritual drama stars Joanna Going as a housewife stricken with multiple sclerosis who seeks help with her illness and her frustrated married life by experimenting with astral projection. Dylan Walsh and Sean Patrick Flanery also star in this unusual tale. 106 min.
02-8986 Was $99.99 *$19.99*

Gravesend (1997)
What starts out as just another Saturday evening of hanging out in a pal's basement for a bunch of teens in the Brooklyn Italian-American neighborhood of Gravesend turns into a harrowing and—for one of them—fatal series of scrapes, thanks to an accidental shooting. Unusual and gripping urban drama stars Mackey Aquilino, Michael Parducci, Tony Tucci. 85 min.
02-8810 Was $99.99 *$19.99*

Silent Shakespeare
The lack of dialogue didn't deter the first filmmakers from bringing the Bard's plays to the screen, often with top stage actors. This collection of seven short films includes British versions of "King John" (1899) with Herbert Beerbohm Tree, "The Tempest" (1908) and "Richard III" (1911); "A Midsummer Night's Dream" (1909) and "Twelfth Night" (1910) from the U.S.; and Italian productions of "King Lear" (1910) and "The Merchant of Venice" (1910) with Francesca Bertini. 88 min. Silent with music score.
80-5040 *$29.99*

Othello (1922)
A silent filming of a Shakespeare play? Yes, and this German-made production, a faithful translation, is fueled by Emil Jannings' performance in the title role of the jealous Moor of Venice. With Werner Krauss, Lya de Putti. 81 min. Silent with music score.
09-5391 *$19.99*

Othello (1995)
Electrifying version of Shakespeare's play features Laurence Fishburne as the warrior Moor who faces fierce prejudice when he marries Desdemona (Irene Jacob), a white Venetian noblewoman. Their all-consuming love leads to tragedy when Othello's jealous aide, Iago (Kenneth Branagh), tells him untrue stories of his wife's infidelity. 124 min.
02-2915 Was $99.99 ❑*$19.99*

A Midsummer Night's Dream (1935)
An all-star cast is featured in this Hollywood re-creation of Shakespeare's timeless comedy. James Cagney, Dick Powell, Olivia de Havilland and Jean Muir are the star-crossed lovers; Mickey Rooney is the mischievous Puck, and Hugh Herbert, Joe E. Brown and Victor Jory are also featured. Max Reinhardt directs. 150 min.
12-2724 *$19.99*

A Midsummer Night's Dream (1968)
Diana Rigg, David Warner, Ian Richardson, Judi Dench and Ian Holm star in Shakespeare's farce, presented by the Royal Shakespeare Company. Mismatched lovers, supernatural beings and some hearty bellylaughs make up this classic tale. 124 min.
01-1479 *$24.99*

A Midsummer Night's Dream (1996)
Originally produced for British TV, this lush and lyrical rendition of the Bard's romantic fantasy features fine performances by a Royal Shakespeare Company cast that includes Lindsay Duncan as Hippolyta and Titiana, Alex Jennings as Theseus and Oberon, Desmond Barrit as Bottom, and Barry Lynch as Puck. 103 min.
11-2338 Was $99.99 ❑*$19.99*

A Midsummer Night's Dream (1998)
A quartet of quarrelsome lovers in Ancient Athens come to a magical forest whose inhabitants have their own romantic problems, thanks to a mischievous sprite named Puck, in this colorful telling of the Bard's most popular comedy. Skunk T'weed, Maureen Freehill, Liza McCarthy, Bristol Pomeroy star.
46-8045 Was $59.99 *$14.99*

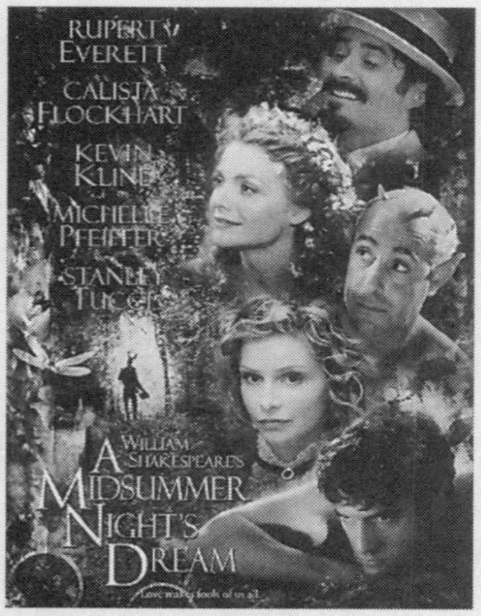

William Shakespeare's A Midsummer Night's Dream (1999)
Lovely, wonderfully performed version of the Bard's enchanted comedy is now set in Tuscany in the 1800s, where nymphs, satyrs and fairies cohabit the world of star-crossed lovers, kings and weavers with donkey ears. The sublime cast includes Kevin Kline as Nick Bottom, Michelle Pfeiffer as Titana, Stanley Tucci as Puck, Rupert Everett as Oberon and Calista Flockhart as Helena. 115 min.
04-3868 Was $99.99 ❑*$14.99*

As You Like It (1936)
Shakespeare's lighthearted portrayal of the comical side of love stars Laurence Olivier as the very proper Orlando, who becomes the target of affection for the lovelorn Rosalind (Elisabeth Bergner), who resorts to posing as a boy to be near her beloved. 90 min.
62-5194 *$14.99*

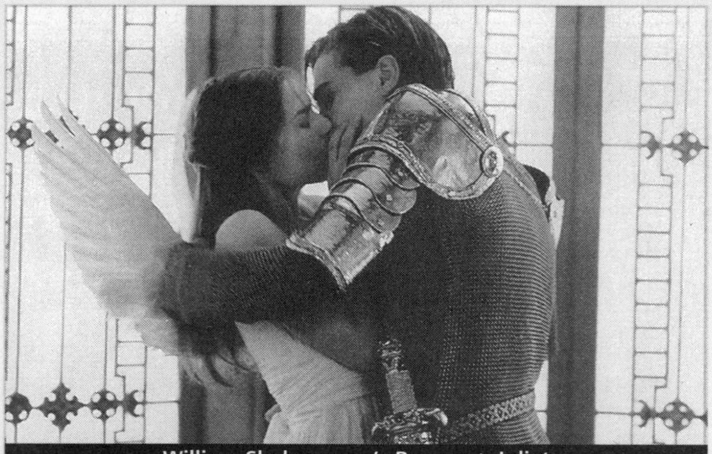

William Shakespeare's Romeo + Juliet

Shakespeare

Romeo And Juliet (1936)
The overage, but nonetheless convincing, duo of Leslie Howard and Norma Shearer star as Shakespeare's doomed lovers in this lush Irving Thalberg-George Cukor filming of the famed tragedy. Able support comes from a cast that includes John Barrymore, Basil Rathbone, Edna May Oliver and C. Aubrey Smith. 126 min.
12-2383 *$19.99*

Romeo And Juliet (1954)
The love story to end all love stories, this lavish rendition of the Shakespeare drama stars Laurence Harvey and Susan Shentall in the title roles, with support from Flora Robson, Sebastian Cabot and Mervyn Johns. 142 min.
15-1184 Was $19.99 *$14.99*

Romeo And Juliet (1968)
Director Franco Zeffirelli's exceptional version of Shakespeare's immortal tale casts young unknowns Olivia Hussey and Leonard Whiting as the teenage lovers crossed by the stars and doomed by their families' hatred. Co-stars Michael York, Milo O'Shea; narrated by Laurence Olivier. 138 min.
06-1051 Was $19.99 *$14.99*

Romeo And Juliet (1968) (Letterboxed Version)
Also available in a theatrical, widescreen format.
06-2504 ❑*$14.99*

Romeo And Juliet (1994)
Passion-filled British adaptation of the timeless Shakespeare drama of two young people whose love for each other is tested by their families' bitter feud. Jonathan Firth, Geraldine Somerville, John Woodvine and Jenny Agutter star. 81 min.
44-2046 *$19.99*

William Shakespeare's Romeo + Juliet (1996)
Director Baz Luhrmann's audacious, stylized updating of the Bard's timeless romance shifts the setting to modern-day Verona Beach, where two brutal crime families, the Montagues and the Capulets, vie for power. Amid the violence, teenagers Leonardo DiCaprio and Claire Danes meet and fall in love, but their parents' bitter rivalry leads to tragedy all around. Brian Dennehy, John Leguizamo, Pete Postlethwaite and Paul Sorvino also star. 121 min.
04-3433 Was $99.99 *$14.99*

William Shakespeare's Romeo + Juliet (Letterboxed Version)
Also available in a theatrical, widescreen format.
04-3675 ❑*$19.99*

Hamlet (1948)
Five Oscars, including Best Actor and Picture, went to Laurence Olivier's turn as the Melancholy Dane. Stunning locations and black-and-white photography add to the timeless drama. Basil Sydney, Jean Simmons, Felix Aylmer, Norman Wooland head the impressive supporting cast; look quickly for Peter Cushing and Christopher Lee. 147 min.
06-1529 Was $19.99 ❑*$14.99*

Hamlet (1969)
Star Nicol Williamson and director Tony Richardson bring their successful stage version of the world's most famous play to the screen, with striking results. Along with Williamson as Hamlet are Anthony Hopkins as Claudius, Judy Parfitt as Gertrude, and rock chanteuse Marianne Faithfull as Ophelia; look for Anjelica Huston as a lady of court. 114 min.
02-1844 *$19.99*

Hamlet (1976)
Experimental treatment of Shakespeare's tragedy offers two actors (twins, in fact) as the schizophrenic Hamlet, a focus on an incestuous relationship between Hamlet and his mother, and many homosexual overtones. Dubbed "the naked 'Hamlet'" upon its release, the film stars David Meyer, Anthony Meyer, Helen Mirren and Quentin Crisp. 65 min.
59-7101 *$29.99*

Hamlet (1990)
Mel Gibson turns in a tour de force performance as Shakespeare's Danish prince in this dazzling Franco Zeffirelli epic. Glenn Close, Alan Bates, Paul Scofield, Helena Bonham Carter and Ian Holm also appear in this lushly photographed film that works as both a fine adaptation of the play and an exciting adventure. 135 min.
19-1867 Was $19.99 ❑*$14.99*

Discovering Hamlet (1990)
It's considered the greatest role in the English-speaking theatre, and in this unique documentary you'll watch acclaimed actor Kenneth Branagh as he prepares to play Shakespeare's Melancholy Dane, under the direction of former Hamlet Derek Jacobi, at England's Birmingham Repertory Theater. Follow the play's production from rehearsal to opening night. Patrick Stewart narrates. 53 min.
90-1018 *$19.99*

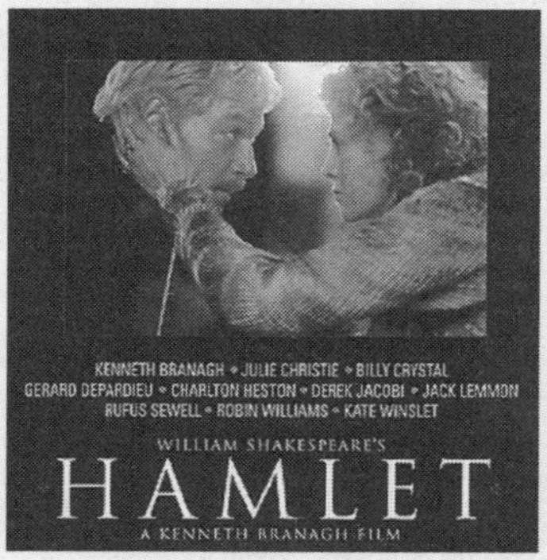

Hamlet (1996)
Magnificent, lushly filmed, star-studded version of Shakespeare's tragedy about the Prince of Denmark stars adapter/director Kenneth Branagh in the title role. The film, which includes the entire text of the play, also features Julie Christie, Billy Crystal, Gerard Depardieu, Charlton Heston, Derek Jacobi, Jack Lemmon, Robin Williams and Kate Winslet. 242 min.
02-3076 Was $99.99 ❑*$24.99*

Hamlet (Letterboxed Version)
Also available in a theatrical, widescreen format.
02-3411 ❑*$24.99*

Hamlet (2000)
Shakespeare's tragedy is turned into a modern morality tale with Ethan Hawke as the title character, now an angry film student suspicious of widowed mother Diane Venora's quick marriage to his creepy uncle, new CEO of the Denmark Corporation Kyle MacLachlan. Director Michael Almereyda ("Nadja") sets his film in a high-tech Manhattan and even places the "To be or not to be" soliloquy in the "action" section of a seedy video store. Julia Styles, Bill Murray and Liev Schreiber also star. 123 min.
11-2481 ❑*$99.99*

Macbeth (1948)
Orson Welles directed and stars in this classic treatment of Shakespeare's play about a Scottish nobleman undone by his lust for power. Jeanette Nolan, Dan O'Herlihy, Roddy McDowall, Erskine Sanford also star. Newly restored version features 21 minutes not seen since the film's initial release. 112 min.
63-1035 *$19.99*

Macbeth (1954)
One of the finest achievements of television's Golden Age, this version of Shakespeare's tragedy from "Hallmark Hall of Fame" stars Maurice Evans in the title role, Judith Anderson as Lady Macbeth, and a distinguished supporting cast. Imaginative sets and costumes enhance this live presentation. 103 min.
09-1626 *$19.99*

Macbeth (1971)
Roman Polanski's violent retelling of Shakespeare's story of the Scottish war hero, prompted by supernatural prophecy and his own ambitions, who kills a king and wears his crown. Jon Finch, Martin Shaw and Francesca Annis star. 139 min.
02-1595 Was $59.99 *$19.99*

Macbeth (1988)
Elaborate Thames TV production of the gripping drama of ambition and destiny by Shakespeare features an acclaimed cast that includes Michael Jayston, Barbara Lee Hunt, Richard Warner. 110 min.
44-1762 Was $39.99 *$19.99*

Macbeth (1997)
Lively and well-acted treatment of the Shakespeare tragedy features a fine performance by Jason Connery as the doomed king and Helen Baxendale as Lady Macbeth. The superb cast also includes Graham McTavish and Kenneth Bryans. 150 min.
80-7267 *$24.99*

Macbeth (1998)
Inventive translation of Shakespeare's tragedy features Greta Scacchi as Lady Macbeth and Sean Pertwee in the title role. This TV production from Britain's Channel 4 uses the original text in a contemporary setting. With Lesley Joseph and Denise Black. 98 min.
22-6100 Letterboxed *$19.99*

The Taming Of The Shrew (1950)
Tremendous production of Shakespeare's comedy has several features of note: a young Charlton Heston is featured as Petruchio; and the play is presented in modern dress. Lisa Kirk co-stars in this wonderful find from "Westinghouse Studio One." 60 min.
09-2047 Was $24.99 *$14.99*

The Taming Of The Shrew (1967)
What better screen couple than Richard Burton and Elizabeth Taylor to play Shakespeare's battling couple Petruchio and Kate? Franco Zeffirelli's rollicking screen adaptation of the classic "battle of the sexes" comedy also stars Michael Hordern, Natasha Pyne, Michael York. 122 min.
02-1056 *$19.99*

Coriolanus (1951)
Shakespeare's tragedy is given a fascinating modern dress treatment which shifts the setting from the Roman Empire to Il Duce's Fascist Italy. A literate "Westinghouse Studio One" presentation with Richard Greene, Judith Evelyn, and Tom Poston. 60 min.
09-1864 Was $24.99 *$14.99*

King Lear (1953)
Rarely-seen filming of Peter Brook's production of the Shakespeare tragedy, with Orson Welles essaying the role of the monarch blinded by anger and jealousy to the treachery that surrounds him. 75 min.
01-1443 Was $29.99 *$14.99*

King Lear (1983)
In a memorable capstone to his Shakespearean career, Sir Laurence Olivier stars as the Bard's elderly monarch, driven to madness by his scheming daughters. The distinguished cast in this stage production includes Diana Rigg, John Hurt, Anna Calder-Marshall and Leo McKern. 158 min.
22-1136 Was $29.99 *$24.99*

King Lear (1998)
Shakespeare's classic drama of a ruler who sows the seeds of his own downfall in his power-hungry children is magnificently staged by England's Royal National Theatre company. Ian Holm stars in the title role; with Barbara Flynn, Amanda Redman, David Lyon and Victoria Hamilton. 150 min. on two tapes.
08-8696 ❑*$29.99*

Julius Caesar (1953)
Heralded rendition of Shakespeare's historical play tracking the conspiracy that laid the Roman emperor low boasts a superlative cast headed by Marlon Brando's revealing Marc Antony. James Mason, Louis Calhern, John Gielgud, Edmond O'Brien, Greer Garson, and Deborah Kerr co-star under the direction of Joseph L. Mankiewicz. 120 min.
12-1927 *$19.99*

Julius Caesar (1970)
John Gielgud as Caesar, Charlton Heston as Antony and Jason Robards as Brutus, along with Diana Rigg, Richard Chamberlain and Robert Vaughn, are featured in Shakespeare's tale of murder and political intrigue in Ancient Rome. 116 min.
63-1146 *$19.99*

Richard III (1955)
Laurence Olivier is unforgettable as the scheming, twisted monarch of England in this elaborate adaptation of Shakespeare's drama. The superlative cast includes Ralph Richardson, John Gielgud, Cedric Hardwicke and Claire Bloom. Restored 158-minute version.
22-5646 Letterboxed *$24.99*

Richard III (1995)
Smashing treatment of Shakespeare's famed play brings the drama to Europe in the 1930s as it traces the rise of fascism through the persona of a power-obsessed dictator, played by Ian McKellen, who also scripted. Annette Bening, Robert Downey, Jr., Maggie Smith and Jim Broadbent also star in this audacious effort. 104 min.
12-3053 ❑*$14.99*

Looking For Richard (1996)
A unique combination of drama and documentary, director/star Al Pacino's labor of Shakespearean love follows him and a group of actors (including Alec Baldwin, Aidan Quinn, Winona Ryder and Kevin Spacey) through rehearsals and filmed scenes for a production of "Richard III." Interspersed with these sequences are segments in which the cast discusses how to present Shakespeare to modern audiences, talks with such famed Shakespearean actors as John Gielgud and Kenneth Branagh, and a visit by Pacino to the Bard's home in Stratford-Upon-Avon, England. 113 min.
04-3434 Was $99.99 *$29.99*

The Merchant Of Venice (1973)
Laurence Olivier excels in this superb film of Shakespeare's tale about the money-lender Shylock and his attempt to get revenge for a life of persecution. Joan Plowright is his daughter, Portia, and Jeremy Brett plays Bassanio. 131 min.
27-6826 Was $19.99 *$14.99*

Antony & Cleopatra (1974)
The Bard's romantic tragedy is given a splendid treatment by the Royal Shakespeare Company in this cinematic adaptation, highlighted by powerful acting from Richard Johnson as the soldier-turned-ruler of Ancient Rome and Janet Suzman as the sensuous Queen of the Nile; with Patrick Stewart, Corin Redgrave. 161 min.
27-6827 Was $19.99 *$14.99*

Henry V (1989)
Following in Olivier's footsteps, scripter/director/star Kenneth Branagh brings a stunning adaptation of the Shakespeare drama to the screen. Branagh's headstrong 15th-century British ruler, who leads his woefully outnumbered troops into battle against the French, earned him an Oscar nomination. Superlative cast includes Paul Scofield, Ian Holm, Emma Thompson. 138 min.
04-2365 Was $89.99 ❑*$14.99*

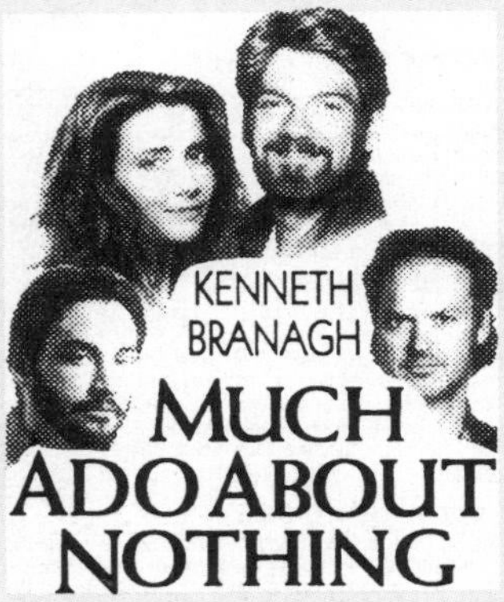
KENNETH
BRANAGH
MUCH
ADO ABOUT
NOTHING

Much Ado About Nothing (1993)
The perfect answer to anyone who thinks Shakespeare means dark, stodgy dramas, this sunny and buoyant romp from Kenneth Branagh is loaded with mismatched lovers, squabbling brothers, comic constables and bawdy humor. Emma Thompson, Denzel Washington, Keanu Reeves, Robert Sean Leonard, Kate Beckinsale and Michael Keaton co-star with Branagh. 111 min.
02-2534 Was $19.99 ❑*$14.99*

Twelfth Night (1996)
Writer/director Trevor Nunn skillfully updates Shakespeare's comical tale of star-crossed—and cross-dressed—lovers. Imogen Stubbs is a young woman who masquerades as a boy and is asked by wealthy duke Toby Stephens to help him woo Helena Bonham Carter, who was in love with Stubbs' presumed-dead brother. Complications arise when Carter falls for Stubbs, who falls for Stephens, and Stubbs' sibling shows up alive and well. With Richard E. Grant, Nigel Hawthorne, Ben Kingsley. 133 min.
02-5131 Was $99.99 ❑*$19.99*

Shakespeare's Women & Claire Bloom (1998)
Renowned for her stage and screen portrayals of the Bard's heroines, British actress Claire Bloom offers her own insights into Shakespeare. Along with dramatic readings by Bloom, this fascinating program features film and TV clips of her as Lady Anne in Laurence Olivier's "Richard III"; in "Hamlet" with Derek Jacobi, as Ophelia; and more. 54 min.
70-5172 *$29.99*

Titus (1999)
"Titus Andronicus," Shakespeare's first tragedy, is given a striking treatment by director Julie Taymor (Broadway's "The Lion King"), who melds ancient settings with modern accoutrements. Anthony Hopkins is the Roman commander who becomes the target of treacherous Tamora (Jessica Lange) after she marries Saturnius (Alan Cumming), an emperor Titus has backed. Laura Fraser, Colm Feore, James Frain and Harry J. Lennix also star. 168 min.
04-3980 ❑*$99.99*

Urban Menace (1999)
Driven over the edge by the burning of his neighborhood church and the murder of his family by a crime ring, ghetto preacher Snoop Dogg eschews turning the other cheek and launches a violent campaign of unholy vengeance. Fellow rap stars Ice-T, Fat Joe the Gangster and Big Punisher join the Snoopster in this intense, action-filled drama. Includes behind-the-scenes footage and a music video. 95 min.
64-9047 *$99.99*

B.U.S.T.E.D. (1999)
Contemporary British gangster yarn tells of ex-con Ray, recently out of the slammer, who tries to pursue his dream of becoming a musician while his hot-headed cousin Terry attempts to keep him in the family underworld business. As friction between the two gets intense, Terry's sexual desires for his cousin become more evident. Writer/director Andrew Goth stars alongside Goldie and David Bowie. AKA: "Everybody Loves Sunshine." 100 min.
64-9055 *$89.99*

Two Small Bodies (1994)
In this sexually-charged two-character drama directed by underground filmmaker Beth B, Fred Ward plays a gruff detective who questions single mother and strip club hostess Suzy Amis about the two children she has reported missing. The interrogation leads both people to face their feelings about sex, death, feminism and fantasy. 85 min.
53-8022 Was $19.99 *$14.99*

Crush (1993)
Filmed in Australia, this creepy, darkly comic tale stars Marcia Gay Harden as a woman whose reckless driving and ensuing car accident triggers a number of strange incidents involving a friend who was injured in the crash, a novelist with whom she has an affair, and the novelist's teenage daughter. William Zappa also stars. 97 min.
53-8025 Was $19.99 *$14.99*

The Neon Bible (1995)
Rural Georgia in the 1940s is the setting of the first American effort of British director Terence Davies ("The Long Day Closes"), a chronicle of the adventures of David, a poor teenage boy whose life is changed when his aunt, a former showgirl, comes to live with his family. Gena Rowlands, Jacob Tierney, Diana Scarwid and Denis Leary star in this stunning film. 92 min.
53-8620 Was $89.99 *$19.99*

...and the earth did not swallow him (1994)
Moving adaptation of the groundbreaking novel by Tomás Rivera follows the many hardships faced by a family of Mexican-American migrant farm workers in the 1950s as seen through the eyes of a 12-year-old boy. Jose Alcalá, Rose Portillo star. 99 min.
53-8811 Was $79.99 *$24.99*

Falling For A Dancer (1998)
Set in Ireland in the 1930s and 1940s, this sprawling romantic tale centers on the exploits of Elizabeth Sullivan, a headstrong beauty who becomes pregnant by an actor at the age of 19, but is forced to marry a widower with a large family by her parents. After moving away to a remote town, she deals with her loveless marriage and, later, a life-changing flirtation. With Elisabeth Dermot-Walsh, Liam Cunningham. 200 min.
53-6651 *$59.99*

Savage Play (1995)
In this saga, Pony, the athletic son of a Maori leader, travels from his native New Zealand to the United Kingdom to find his long-lost father. While searching in Scotland, Pony meets and falls in love with Charlotte, the daughter of an earl, but the couple's social differences soon play a part in their relationship. Ian Richardson, Liza Walker and Gavin Richards star. 140 min.
53-6652 *$59.99*

Always Afternoon (1999)
Romantic period piece by the team that produced and directed "A Town Like Alice," examining the love affair between a young Australian girl and an interned German violinist during World War I. As German-Australians are rounded up and imprisoned, neighbors find themselves divided, and fear and bigotry test the strength of the couple's new love. Lisa Harrow, Jochen Horst star. 210 min.
53-6781 *$39.99*

Golden Fiddles (1990)
The troubles of a struggling Australian family appear to be over when they receive an unexpected inheritance during the worst days of the Depression. But they soon discover that the money is a mixed blessing, threatening the bonds that once held the loving family together. A heartwarming tale of decency and values, starring Kate Nelligan and John Bach. 190 min.
53-6782 *$39.99*

The War Zone (1999)
A dramatic and emotionally raw look at a working-class family in England's Devon countryside being torn apart by incest, actor Tim Roth's directorial debut follows the teenage son's turmoil when he confronts his father and older sister about their relationship. Ray Winstone, Tilda Swinton, Freddie Cunliffe and Lara Belmont star in this acclaimed film. Uncut, unrated version; 99 min.
53-6867 *$99.99*

Knockout (1999)
Fifteen years after her father retired from the ring, 24-year-old Isabelle uses the skills she learned from him and tries to become a top fighter in a violent world dominated by men. Tony Plana, Paul Winfield, Maria Conchita Alonso and Sophia-Adella Hernandez star in this gritty drama set in and around the mean streets of East Los Angeles. 90 min.
65-9000 *$99.99*

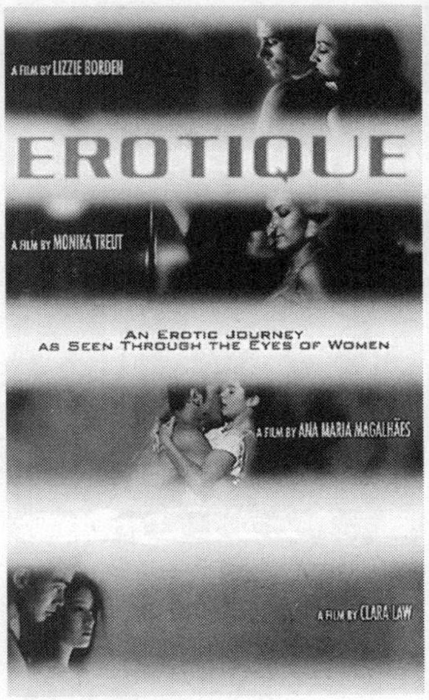
A FILM BY LIZZIE BORDEN
EROTIQUE
A FILM BY MONIKA TREUT
AN EROTIC JOURNEY
AS SEEN THROUGH THE EYES OF WOMEN
A FILM BY ANA MARIA MAGALHÃES
A FILM BY CLARA LAW

Erotique (1994)
Four top woman directors explore the world of female sexuality in this frank and revealing anthology. A phone-sex operator (Kamala Lopez-Dawson) becomes attracted to a client in Lizzie Borden's "Let's Talk About Sex"; an American woman (Priscilla Barnes) in Germany joins her lesbian lover in a search for a one-time "fling" with a man in "Taboo Parlor" by Monika Treut; Ana Maria Magalhães' "Final Call" follows a teacher's memorable train ride; and a Chinese couple try to overcome cultural differences in Clara Law's "Wonton Soup." Uncut, unrated version; 120 min.
53-8835 Was $89.99 *$19.99*

The Book Of Stars (1999)
An emotional and lushly photographed tale of two sisters linked by love, tragedy and hope, this independent drama stars Jena Malone as a teenager struggling to cope with cystic fibrosis and Mary Stuart Masterson as her older sister and caretaker, who sells herself nightly on the streets to support them. Karl Geary, Delroy Lindo, D.B. Sweeney are the men who affect their lives. 98 min.
53-6893 *$89.99*

Onegin (1999)
In this lush adaptation of the novel by Pushkin, Ralph Fiennes plays caddish St. Petersburg aristocrat Eugene Onegin, whose callous dismissal of neighbor Liv Tyler's love leads to a duel with her sister's husband. Years later, a desolate Fiennes returns to find Tyler wed to a handsome prince and the romantic tables turned. Lena Headey, Toby Stephens also star; directed by Fiennes' sister, Martha. 100 min.
64-9063 *$99.99*

Strangers (1991)
A steamy trilogy of tales about three people for whom travel means new sights, new sounds, and new erotic experiences. Linda Fiorentino plays a wife in Paris looking for an affair—with her husband's help; an auto accident leads Joan Chen to a fateful encounter at a friend's apartment; and exchange student Timothy Hutton becomes entranced by a gorgeous neighbor. 85 min.
46-5549 *$14.99*

The Hours And Times (1992)
A speculative drama that probes the question: Did John Lennon and Beatles manager Brian Epstein have a weekend love affair in Barcelona in 1963? David Angus and Ian Hart star in this provocative, much-heralded film from Christopher Münch that focuses on the relationship between the ultra-civilized Epstein and rebellious artist Lennon. 54 min.
53-7778 Was $69.99 *$19.99*

The Trial (1993)
Franz Kafka's celebrated novel is turned into a gripping, stylish film centering on the plight of Josef K., a man who is arrested for unknown reasons on his 30th birthday, then faces an unending series of bureaucratic obstacles while he awaits trial. Kyle MacLachlan, Anthony Hopkins, Jason Robards and Polly Walker star; Harold Pinter scripted. 120 min.
53-7992 Was $89.99 *$19.99*

December Bride (1995)
This unconventional story set in an Irish village at the turn of the century tells of strong-willed, independent Sarah, who is at odds with the people around her when she decides to take two lovers: Hamilton and his younger brother, Frank. Saskia Reeves, Donal McCann and Ciaran Hinds star in this compassionate film. 90 min.
53-8315 Was $89.99 *$19.99*

Killing In A Small Town (1990)
Barbara Hershey turns in a powerful performance as a repressed Texas housewife who becomes involved with a married man. When the man's wife confronts her, Hershey brutally kills her with an axe. Brian Dennehy and Hal Holbrook also star in this riveting true-life story. 95 min.
68-1235 ❑*$89.99*

The Keeper (1996)
An unusual and thought-provoking look at life inside the Brooklyn House of Corrections for both the inmates and their guards, prison psychiatrist-turned-filmmaker Joe Brewster's drama stars Giancarlo Esposito as a guard who befriends a Haitian immigrant charged with a rape he says he didn't commit. Esposito goes so far as to post the man's bail and move him, over his wife's objections, into their home. Isaach De Bankole, Regina Taylor also star. 89 min.
53-9204 Was $79.99 *$24.99*

The Natural History Of Parking Lots (1990)
Remarkable independent film set in Los Angeles and focusing on the relationship between a rebellious teenager who gets his kicks stealing 1950s cars and his estranged older brother, who's been paid by his father to watch his sibling. Charlie Bean, b. Wyatt and Charles Taylor star. 92 min.
53-9588 *$49.99*

Bix (1991)
A powerful chronicle of cornetist Bix Beiderbecke, who helped change the role of jazz musician from dance band accompanist to inventive artist, and who died at the age of 28 in 1931. The story of the rebellious and sensitive "Bix" unfolds in flashbacks as a former partner recalls his life. Included are such songs as "In a Mist (Bixology)" and "Riverboat Shuffle." With Brant Weeks. 100 min.
53-7994 Was $59.99 *$19.99*

The House Of Eliott (1991)
Set in London during the Roaring '20s, this acclaimed BBC production concerns Beatrice and Evangeline Eliott, two sisters born into a wealthy family who find themselves suddenly penniless and struggling to regain their fortunes with pioneering fashion ideas. Stella Gonet and Louise Lombard star; Jean Marsh hosts. Six-tape boxed set includes the first 12 episodes of the series. 600 min. total.
53-8097 Was $129.99 *$99.99*

Lipstick On Your Collar (1993)
From the pen of Dennis Potter ("The Singing Detective") comes this provocative look at two young British Army clerks working in the War Office during the fading days of the Suez Crisis in the mid-1950s. Bored with their jobs, the clerks discover that rock-and-roll can lead them to women—at least in their fantasies. Peter Jeffrey and Louise Germaine star. 390 min. on three tapes.
53-8200 *$59.99*

Margaret's Museum (1997)
Poignant drama starring Helena Bonham Carter as a woman in a 1940s Nova Scotia mining community who is determined not to marry—and be widow to—a local coal miner like other women in her family. Margaret weds a drifter, but their happiness is threatened when he loses his restaurant job and must get work in the mines. With Kate Nelligan, Clive Russell. 118 min.
58-5253 Was $99.99 ❑*$14.99*

Last Light (1993)
Powerful prison drama starring Kiefer Sutherland (who also directed) as a career criminal on death row who forms a surprising and moving friendship with tough prison guard Forrest Whitaker. This no-holds-barred look at life behind bars also stars Kathleen Quinlan and Amanda Plummer. 104 min.
68-1290 Was $89.99 ❑*$14.99*

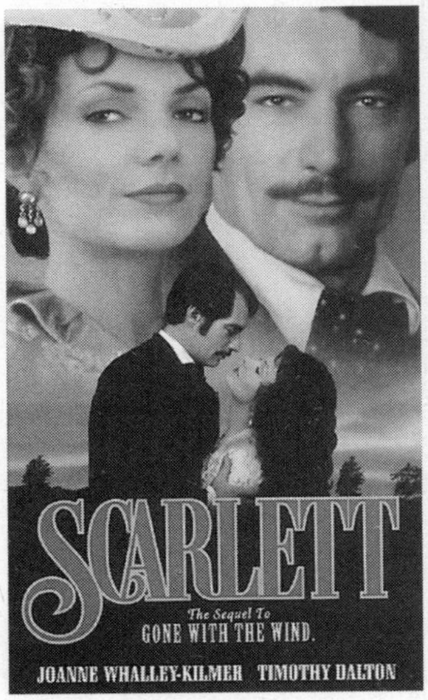
SCARLETT
The Sequel To
GONE WITH THE WIND.
JOANNE WHALLEY-KILMER TIMOTHY DALTON

Scarlett (1994)
The most famous love story in film history continues in the hit mini-series adaptation of the sequel to "Gone with the Wind." Follow Scarlett O'Hara (Joanne Whalley-Kilmer) as she travels to her family's Irish homeland to forget Rhett Butler (Timothy Dalton) and finds the journey filled with romance, tragedy and adventure. Ann-Margret, John Gielgud, Stephen Collins and Annabeth Gish also star. 360 min.
58-5173 Was $24.99 ❑*$14.99*

Terminal Bliss (1991)
Luke Perry, star of "Beverly Hills, 90210," makes his feature film debut in a drama of two teens whose strong friendship is tested when they compete for the beautiful new girl in town. Timothy Owen and Estee Chandler are also featured in this insightful, sexy look at today's youth. 94 min.
19-7088 Was $89.99 □*$19.99*

One Night Stand (1995)
Feeling alone and yearning after a recent divorce, a woman has a steamy one-night romance with a stranger who could be the man of her dreams, but who's covering up a secret that could make her worst nightmares come true. Intense and erotic drama stars Ally Sheedy, A Martinez, Frederic Forrest, Jodi Thelen; Talia Shire directs. 95 min.
21-9107 Was $89.99 *$14.99*

Skin (1991)
The 1986 Howard Beach tragedy, in which a black man in a mostly white Queens neighborhood was chased by a racist mob into highway traffic, where he was struck by a car and killed, is traced in this powerful drama that depicts the citywide turmoil that erupted during the official investigation. Daniel J. Travanti, Joe Morton, William Daniels and Regina Taylor star. 85 min.
21-9108 *$89.99*

Machine Gun Blues (1995)
The taboo love affair that develops between a young white gangster and a beautiful black jazz chanteuse threatens to not only destroy their lives, but throw all of Prohibition-era New York into a violent mob war, in this action-filled drama. Nick Cassavetes, Cynda Williams, Joe Viterelli and Garrett Morris. AKA: "Black Rose of Harlem." 73 min.
21-9110 Was $89.99 *$14.99*

187 (1997)
A year after he was stabbed by a student in a New York high school, idealistic teacher Samuel L. Jackson moves to Los Angeles and takes a job at a violence-plagued school in a mostly Latino neighborhood. A battle of wills between Jackson and a gang leader leads to the teen's murder, but was a rival gang responsible...or has Jackson snapped? Powerful urban drama also stars Kelly Rowan, Clifton Gonzalez Gonzalez. 119 min.
19-2619 Was $19.99 □*$14.99*

Some Mother's Son (1996)
Based on the true story of Northern Irish prisoners who went on a hunger strike against their English captors in 1981, this powerful drama from director/co-scripters Terry George and Jim Sheridan ("In the Name of the Father") stars Helen Mirren as a widow whose son is among the striking inmates and who fights for their rights with other mothers. Aidan Gillen, Fionnula Flanagan also star. 111 min.
19-2580 Was $99.99 □*$19.99*

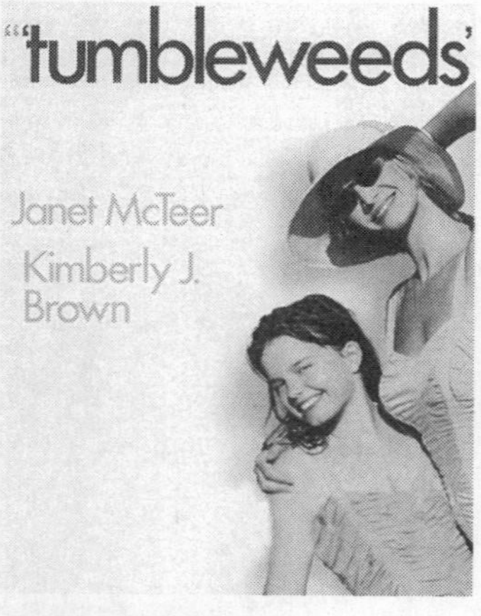

Tumbleweeds (1999)
In the aftermath of another ill-fated relationship, free-spirited Southern sexpot Janet McTeer shepherds 12-year-old daughter Kimberly Brown into their car and sets off on a cross-country search for a new life in this heartfelt comedy-drama from director/co-scripter Gavin O'Connor, who also stars as a truck driver trying to woo McTeer. With Michael J. Pollard, Jay O. Sanders. 100 min.
19-2964 Was $99.99 □*$19.99*

Midnight In The Garden Of Good And Evil (1997)
New York magazine writer John Cusack is sent to picturesque Savannah, Georgia, to cover a lavish Christmas party hosted by local antiques merchant Kevin Spacey, but he gets more of a story than he imagined when Spacey is charged with shooting his male lover and the subsequent trial exposes the private lives of many of the quirky town's citizens. Director Clint Eastwood's adaptation of the John Berendt best-seller also stars Jack Thompson, Jude Law, Alison Eastwood, and local drag queen Lady Chablis as herself. 150 min.
19-2681 Was $19.99 □*$14.99*

Midnight In The Garden Of Good And Evil (Letterboxed Version)
Also available in a theatrical, widescreen format.
19-2744 □*$19.99*

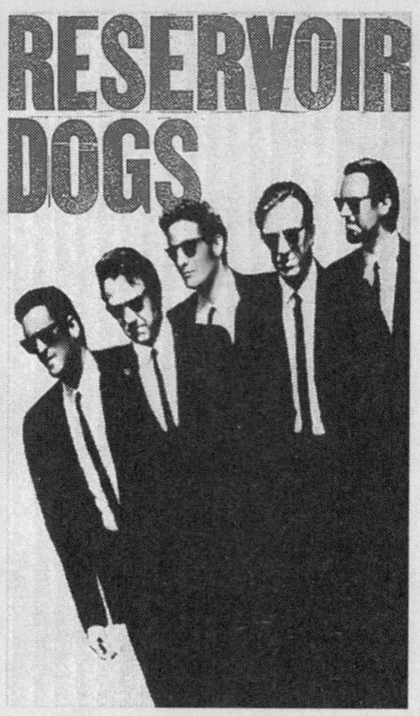

Reservoir Dogs (1992)
A (literally) gut-wrenching look at an aborted diamond heist and its bloody aftermath, rookie writer/director Quentin Tarantino's powerful crime drama mixes dark comedy with ferocious violence as the caper's survivors gather at a hideout to uncover the informer among them. Harvey Keitel, Tim Roth, Michael Madsen, Steve Buscemi, Chris Penn and Lawrence Tierney star. 100 min.
27-6803 Was $19.99 □*$14.99*

Reservoir Dogs (Letterboxed Version)
Also available in a theatrical, widescreen format.
27-7018 □*$14.99*

Pulp Fiction: Special Collector's Edition (1994)
Writer/director Quentin Tarantino's Oscar-winning salute to old-time crime novels flips back and forth in time to interweave tales of temptation, violence and redemption involving an ensemble cast that includes hit man odd couple John Travolta and Samuel L. Jackson, coke-sniffing mobster's wife Uma Thurman, and crooked boxer Bruce Willis. With Harvey Keitel, Ving Rhames, Tim Roth, Amanda Plummer. This special collector's video features footage not shown in theatres and a behind-the-scenes exclusive hosted by Tarantino. 164 min. total.
11-1892 Was $19.99 □*$14.99*

Pulp Fiction: Special Collector's Edition (Letterboxed Edition)
Also available in a theatrical, widescreen format.
11-1950 Was $89.99 □*$19.99*

Four Rooms (1995)
The rooms of the title are in an antiquated L.A. hotel where new bellhop Tim Roth can't avoid getting involved with such zany guests as a coven of witches seeking special sperm to complete a potion, a sadistic hubby and his game-playing wife, a gangster's mischievous kids, and a group of party-goers who make a macabre wager. With Antonio Banderas, Jennifer Beals, Madonna, Marisa Tomei, Bruce Willis; directed by Allison Anders, Robert Rodriguez, Alexandre Rockwell and Quentin Tarantino. 98 min.
11-2025 Was $99.99 □*$19.99*

Jackie Brown (1997)
Quentin Tarantino brings his wit and humor back to the big screen with his action-packed adaptation of Elmore Leonard's "Rum Punch." Pam Grier stars as Jackie, the charismatic, street-smart stewardess blackmailed by the FBI to assist in a sting operation to bring down her other employer, gunrunner Samuel L. Jackson. With the help of bail bondsman Robert Forster, though, Jackie has plans of her own. Robert De Niro, Bridget Fonda, Michael Keaton also star. 154 min.
11-2770 Was $19.99 □*$14.99*

Jackie Brown (Letterboxed Version)
Also available in a theatrical, widescreen format.
11-2294 □*$19.99*

Everything That Rises (1998)
A Montana family headed by rancher Dennis Quaid faces an emotional challenge when an accident leaves Quaid's son paralyzed. Moving drama, directed by Quaid, also stars Mare Winningham, Harve Presnell, Meat Loaf and Ryan Merriman. 94 min.
19-2785 Was $79.99 □*$14.99*

Pirates Of Silicon Valley (1999)
The dawn of the computer revolution is deftly dramatized in this look at the true saga of America's most successful cybernerds. Noah Wyle and Joey Slotnick play Steve Jobs and Steve Wozniak, the hippie students-turned-feuding founders of Apple Computer, and Anthony Michael Hall is Microsoft creator Bill Gates, who was Apple's main competitor and eventual savior. 95 min.
19-2905 Was $99.99 □*$14.99*

Kleptomania (1995)
Rich and beautiful Amy Irving befriends poor and beautiful Patsy Kensit, and the two get involved in their favorite pastime of thievery, partaking in petty heists across New York. When Irving is thrown in prison, she asks Kensit to bail her out, but first they make an agreement to find out who murdered Kensit's lover. Victor Garber co-stars. Unrated version; 90 min.
19-3720 *$89.99*

The Liars' Club (1993)
A group of high school football stars discovers that their friendship and futures are on the line when one of them is accused of a heinous sex crime. Will the jocks tell the truth and risk their loyalty? Or will they lie to protect the accused? Wil Wheaton, Brian Krause, Soleil Moon Frye and Bruce Weitz star. 91 min.
21-9039 Was $89.99 *$14.99*

Woman With A Past (1994)
A woman with a reputation as a devoted wife and mother and model citizen turns out to have a secret past that includes a criminal record. Pamela Reed, Dwight Shultz and Paul LeMat star in this explosive drama of a woman who went against the law to protect her family. 95 min.
21-9056 *$89.99*

Till Murder Do Us Part (1992)
This powerful true story stars Meredith Baxter as California housewife Betty Broderick, whose happy life is shattered when she discovers that her husband is involved with another woman...and her humiliation and rage lead her to murder. Stephen Collins, Michelle Johnson also star. AKA: "A Woman Scorned: The Betty Broderick Story." 95 min.
21-9077 Was $89.99 *$14.99*

Midnight Murders (1991)
A team of federal marshals, sent to arrest the leader of an ultra-right-wing revolutionary movement, is caught in a violent gunfight that leaves several government agents dead and the target at large. One FBI agent must infiltrate a racist underground network and bring him to justice. Rod Steiger, Michael Gross and Gary Basaraba star. 87 min.
21-9083 Was $89.99 *$14.99*

Lilian's Story (1996)
Released from the mental hospital where she was confined for 40 years, an Australian woman winds up living on the streets, reciting long passages from her beloved Shakespeare, befriending fellow outcasts, and recalling the abusive father responsible for her institutionalization. Based on a true story, this moving drama stars Toni Collette and Ruth Cracknell as the young and elderly Lilian, respectively; with Barry Otto. 94 min.
22-9045 *$79.99*

The Height Of The Sky (1999)
On a remote Southern farm during the Great Depression, the news that a sharecropper has come down with tuberculosis forces his family to make a difficult decision and threatens to reveal a long-held secret. Directed and co-written by Lyn Clinton (a cousin of the president) and based on a Clinton family story, this compelling independent drama stars Jennifer Weedon, Jackie Stewart, Grant Moninger. 116 min.
22-9046 *$79.99*

Bellyfruit (1999)
The lives of three young urban girls are interwoven in this stark drama about teenage pregnancy which is based on real-life stories. Shanika has been abandoned and is living in a shelter when she becomes pregnant; Aracely and her boyfriend must deal with life on their own when she is kicked out; and Christina is following in the footsteps of her wild mother. Featuring a bright young cast. 95 min.
22-9050 *$79.99*

Entertaining Angels: The Dorothy Day Story (1997)
The inspirational true story of the early 20th-century journalist who went on to found the Catholic Worker movement and fight for the rights of the poor and downtrodden in the Great Depression is told in this moving drama. Moira Kelly, Brian Keith, Martin Sheen star. 112 min.
19-2577 Was $99.99 □*$19.99*

Because Of You (1995)
"Tokyo Decadence" director Ryu Murakami offers a change of pace with this tender story of a young Japanese woman (Saki Takaoka) who comes to New York to see the ex-GI who taught her Latin dance when he was stationed overseas years earlier. Upon discovering the man (Carlos Osorio) is dying of AIDS and unable to remember her, Takaoka agrees to help Osorio get to Miami to see his family. AKA: "Kyoko." 85 min.
21-9211 *$69.99*

Black Rock (1998)
Edgy drama from Australia about some teens in a coastal town who hold a "welcome home" party for one of their surfing pals. The party is a successful affair, but the next morning, a 15-year-old girl is found raped and murdered. Amidst tremendous media attention, one youth remains silent. Will he reveal what he knows about the incident? Simon Lyndon and Linda Cropper star. 102 min.
22-9182 Was $79.99 *$29.99*

Franz Kafka's It's A Wonderful Life...And Other Strange Tales
Leading off this collection of acclaimed short films is the 1995 Academy Award-winner "Franz Kafka's It's a Wonderful Life," starring Richard E. Grant as the Czech-born writer, struggling with the opening lines of his short story "Metamorphosis." Also includes "Seven Gates," about a memorable Christmas family gathering; the big-business satire "The Deal"; and a story about a '60s Southern man's prized possession, "Mr.McAllister's Cigarette Holder." 84 min. total.
22-9183 *$29.99*

Ivory Tower (1998)
Politics in the corporate world is the focus of this tale of a young marketing executive who finds himself at odds with his interfering boss while trying to launch a new computer product. Michael Ironside, Kari Wuhrer, James Wilder and Patrick Van Horn also star. 107 min.
22-9184 Was $79.99 *$29.99*

The Field (1990)
Richard Harris was nominated for a Best Actor Academy Award for his towering performance as an elderly eccentric who refuses to give up his cherished field to an American land developer. Set against the beautiful backdrop of Ireland, this stirring drama from director Jim Sheridan ("My Left Foot") also stars Tom Berenger, John Hurt and Brenda Fricker. 110 min.
27-6719 Was $19.99 *$14.99*

Iron & Silk (1991)
Autobiographical account of an English teacher's journey to China and his obsession with, and eventual assimilation into, Chinese culture. Mark Salzman essentially plays himself, a martial arts fan who becomes a master at self-defense and begins a relationship with a doctor once punished for reading Western books. Affectionate and lovingly filmed; with Pan Qingfu, Vivian Wu. 94 min. In English and Mandarin with English subtitles.
27-6726 Was $79.99 *$19.99*

Proudheart (1994)
Country music sensation Lorrie Morgan makes her dramatic debut in this story of a single mother who returns to her childhood home of Proudheart, Tennessee, with her daughter after her father's death. There, she tries to smooth things over with her mother, saves the family gas station and becomes romantically involved with a local fellow. 60 min.
22-1418 *$19.99*

The Next Step (1995)
Broadway dancer Nick has to scramble to get another job when his show closes. While trying to land a job, Nick faces problems with his two girlfriends and struggles to make a living as a maitre' d. Filled with energized dance sequences and erotic bedroom scenes, this drama offers a revealing look at a side of show biz rarely seen. With Rick Negron, Kristin Moreu. 97 min.
22-9005 Letterboxed *$29.99*

Angel Blue (1997)
This Latino "Lolita" tells of a California banker who befriends a newcomer to his small town. The banker soon forms a bond with the newcomer's beautiful teenage daughter and gets her babysitting jobs. Soon, the relationship blossoms into a torrid affair that shocks the community. Sam Bottoms, Lisa Eichhorn and Yeniffer Behrens star. Director's cut; 91 min.
22-9010 Was $79.99 *$29.99*

Desert Winds (1995)
Mystical drama starring Heather Graham as a woman who lives with her mother on the outskirts of a New Mexico town. Graham discovers that, by using a wind tunnel, she can communicate with a man who lives in Arizona, 500 miles away. After sharing secrets and thoughts, the two try to talk to each other again, years later. Michael A. Nickles and Grace Zabriskie also star. 97 min.
22-9016 Was $79.99 *$29.99*

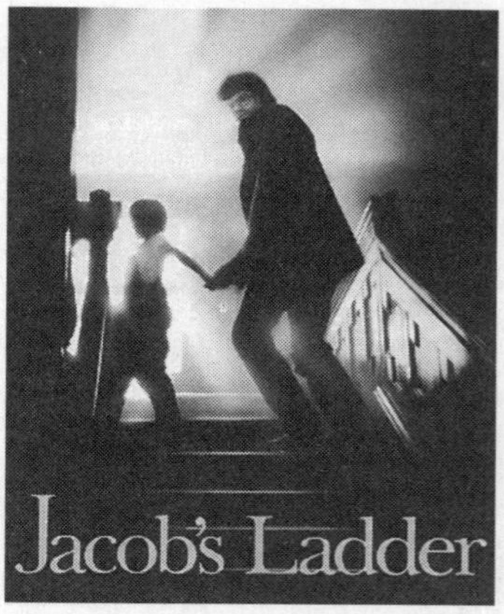

Jacob's Ladder (1990)
Audacious, much-talked-about psychological thriller about a postal worker and Vietnam veteran who begins to see strange hallucinations and disturbing wartime images. He discovers his war pals are having similar visions and soon uncovers a complex conspiracy...or does he? Gripping, disturbing film stars Tim Robbins, Elizabeth Peña, Danny Aiello, Macaulay Culkin; directed by Adrian Lyne ("Fatal Attraction"). 113 min.
27-6706 Was $89.99 □*$12.99*

Goodbye, Norma Jean (1976)
The troubled adolescence and stormy early film career of screen goddess Marilyn Monroe are amazingly portrayed in this biodrama by Larry Buchanan ("Beyond the Doors"). Misty Rowe stars as Marilyn; with Patch Mackenzie, Terence Locke. 95 min.
44-1039 Was $19.99 ***$14.99***

Norma Jean And Marilyn (1996)
The tragic life of Marilyn Monroe is depicted in innovative and compelling fashion in this fascinating film. Ashley Judd plays Norma Jean Daugherty in the actress's earlier years and Mira Sorvino is Marilyn after plastic surgery and during her reign as Hollywood sex queen. Josh Charles, Ron Rifkin, Peter Dobson and David Dukes also star. 129 min.
44-2060 Was $19.99 ***$14.99***

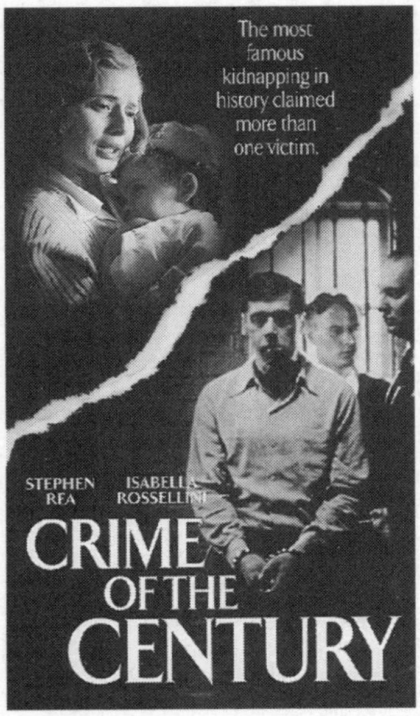

Crime Of The Century (1996)
The kidnapping and murder of national hero Charles Lindbergh's infant son in 1932 shocked America, and the subsequent trial, conviction and execution of German immigrant Bruno Hauptmann remains controversial to this day. Was Hauptmann a killer or a scapegoat? Compelling dramatization of the case stars Stephen Rea, Isabella Rossellini, J.T. Walsh and David Paymer. 116 min.
44-2077 Was $19.99 ❑***$14.99***

Saints And Sinners (1995)
A drug dealer named "Big Boy" welcomes his old friend "Pooch" back to their old turf in Vail, Colorado. But unbeknownst to "Big Boy," his pal is now a cop. And when both fall for the sexy Eva, trouble begins. Damian Chapa, Scott Plank and Jennifer Rubin star. 99 min.
27-6961 ***$89.99***

Mi Vida Loca: My Crazy Life (1994)
An explosive cinematic essay on East L.A.'s Hispanic Echo Park gangs centers on Sad Girl and Mousie, best friends at odds over their desire for Ernesto, a drug dealer who has impregnated both of them. When he is killed by a rival gang member, the men of Echo Park seek revenge, while the women band together to survive. Angel Aviles, Seidy Lopez, Salma Hayek and Panchito Gomez star. 94 min.
44-1980 Was $89.99 ❑***$19.99***

The Burning Season (1994)
In this acclaimed true-life drama, Raul Julia plays peasant activist Chico Mendes, whose efforts to stop the destruction of the Amazon rain forest led to his mysterious death. Edward James Olmos, Esai Morales and Sonia Braga co-star in this powerful tale; expert direction by John Frankenheimer ("The Manchurian Candidate"). 123 min.
44-1984 Was $79.99 ❑***$19.99***

Citizen X (1995)
Shocking true story of the search for one of history's most prolific serial killers stars Stephen Rea as a forensics expert investigating horrific murders in the Soviet Union during the 1980s. Helped by superior Donald Sutherland and psychiatrist Max Von Sydow and hindered by government bureaucracy, Rea eventually discerns the identity of the killer and discovers scores of bodies. Jeffrey DeMunn co-stars. 102 min.
44-1994 Was $19.99 ***$14.99***

Indictment: The McMartin Trial (1995)
One of the most sensational trials in history is dramatized in this powerful film about the 1983 California case in which a mother accused teachers at her son's pre-school of sexually abusing him. The accusations begin a rash of charges against the school's staff and owners, a national scandal on tabloid TV shows, and a six-year search for the truth. James Woods, Mercedes Ruehl, Henry Thomas, Sada Thompson star. 133 min.
44-2000 Was $19.99 ❑***$14.99***

Restraining Order (1999)
Lawyer Eric Roberts is caught in a crisis of conscience when he witnesses a client commit murder, but his plan to help a friend in the D.A.'s office convict the killer backfires. Now Roberts' friend is dead, his wife is framed for the crime, and he must take the law into his own hands to see that justice is done. Gripping thriller also stars Hannes Jaenicke, Dean Stockwell. 95 min.
27-7219 ❑***$99.99***

And The Band Played On (1993)
A powerful and compelling adaptation of author Randy Shilts' chronicle of the evolution of the AIDS crisis, this acclaimed drama follows the battles of doctors and scientists against an uncaring bureaucracy to identify the virus, while the stories of AIDS patients from all walks of life and those close to them bring the problem into a deeply personal focus. Matthew Modine, Glenne Headly, Charles Martin Smith, Lily Tomlin star. 140 min.
44-1952 Was $19.99 ❑***$14.99***

Shot Through The Heart (1998)
Based on a true story, this powerful drama is set in the war-ravaged city of Sarajevo, Yugoslavia. Vincent Perez and Linus Roache star as former childhood friends who grew up to become Olympic marksmen, only to find themselves on opposite sides of the conflict tearing their homeland apart. With Lothaire Bluteau. 115 min.
44-2178 Was $89.99 ❑***$14.99***

2 Days In The Valley (1996)
Hit men Danny Aiello and James Spader are hired to kill the adulterous former husband of Olympic athlete Teri Hatcher. But after the ex is offed, the situation takes several dangerous (and darkly comical) turns as vice cops, a suicidal movie director and an abused secretary enter the picture. Smashing Southern California crime caper also stars Charlize Theron, Eric Stoltz, Paul Mazursky. 105 min.
44-2076 Was $19.99 ❑***$14.99***

2 Days In The Valley (Letterboxed Version)
Also available in a theatrical, widescreen format.
44-2153 Was $19.99 ❑***$14.99***

Mistrial (1996)
When an accused cop-killer is acquitted and the detective who shot two bystanders while attempting to catch him finds his professional and personal worlds about to collapse, he takes the law into his own hands by holding the courtroom hostage and demanding the trial start again under his rules. Gripping drama stars Bill Pullman, Robert Loggia, Blair Underwood. 89 min.
44-2078 Was $19.99 ***$14.99***

Grand Avenue (1996)
After her husband's death, a Native American woman and her three children leave their reservation home to start a new life with relatives in a Northern California city, but clashes of culture and the pressures of urban life will test their bonds. Powerful drama of modern Native American life stars A Martinez, Irene Bedard, Rachel Pfeffer. 167 min.
44-2088 ❑***$19.99***

Dead Silence (1996)
A trio of killers takes a busload of schoolchildren and their adult guardians hostage, and special agent James Garner must deal with not only the criminals but also antagonism from local law enforcement officials to end the standoff without bloodshed. Marlee Matlin, Charles Martin Smith and Lolita Davidovich also star in this tense drama. 99 min.
44-2108 Was $99.99 ❑***$14.99***

Miss Evers' Boys (1997)
One of the more shameful chapters in American history, the "Tuskegee Experiment" of the 1930s, in which Southern black men were left untreated for syphilis so that the effects of the disease could be studied by the federal government, forms the basis for this moving drama. Alfre Woodard, Laurence Fishburne, Craig Sheffer, Joe Morton and Ossie Davis star. 118 min.
44-2109 Was $19.99 ❑***$14.99***

Subway Stories (1997)
Take a dramatic and surprising ride underneath the streets of New York City, as 10 top directors (including Julie Dash, Jonathan Demme, Ted Demme, Abel Ferrara and Craig McKay) present a collection of short films dealing with life on the subway. Lovers meet and separate; music draws strangers together; and beggars and businessmen share their dreams. The cast includes Anne Heche, Gregory Hines, Bonnie Hunt, Bill Irwin, Christine Lahti, Denis Leary, Rosie Perez, Jerry Stiller and Lili Taylor. 81 min.
44-2150 Was $99.99 ❑***$19.99***

A Lesson Before Dying (1999)
Based on the acclaimed novel by Ernest J. Gaines, this powerhouse drama stars Don Cheadle as a teacher who returns to his hometown in the segregated South. When he's called on to counsel Mekhi Phifer, a young man wrongly convicted of killing a white store owner and sentenced to die, each undergoes a life-changing experience and a lesson in dignity. Irma P. Hall, Cicely Tyson also star. 101 min.
44-2202 Was $99.99 ***$14.99***

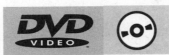

In The Gloaming (1996)
For his directorial debut, Christopher Reeve has fashioned a compassionate drama about a young man with AIDS who returns home to die, but finds that tensions rise within his family while he seeks comfort. Glenn Close, Bridget Fonda, Whoopi Goldberg, Robert Sean Leonard and David Strathairn head up the dynamic cast. 67 min.
44-2114 Was $19.99 ❑***$14.99***

Dark Harbor (1999)
Atmospheric, sensual thriller featuring Alan Rickman and Polly Walker as a bickering couple on their way to their New England island vacation home. After offering help to an injured young man they find along the road, he joins them at their isolated home, and soon strange sexual games begin. Norman Reedus co-stars. 89 min.
27-7189 ❑***$99.99***

The Perfect Husband (1992)
Tim Roth stars as a 19th-century opera singer whose specialties are music and women, for whom he has survived 29 duels with irate husbands. But Roth's free-wheeling world is disrupted when Peter Firth, an old friend whose wife once had an affair with Roth, enters his life again, plotting his revenge. 90 min.
53-6815 ***$29.99***

Don King: Only In America (1997)
The flamboyant showman who made millions promoting fights—and himself—and whose name is synonymous with controversy is vividly portrayed in an award-winning performance by Ving Rhames. Follow King's life from the streets to the top of the sports world in this acclaimed drama. Vondie Curtis-Hall, Jeremy Piven, Loretta Devine also star. 112 min.
44-2158 Was $79.99 ❑***$14.99***

Next Of Kin (1984)
An intriguing comedy/drama about family relations from Canada's Atom Egoyan. A young man, while undergoing experimental video therapy in order to resolve problems with his tyrannical parents, sees a tape about a couple who gave their child up for adoption decades earlier. He then sets out to become their long-lost son. Patrick Tierney, Berge Fazlian star. 72 min.
53-7578 ***$29.99***

Calendar (1993)
Atom Egoyan's seductive drama features the director as a photographer who reviews the shots of churches he took while on a trip to his Armenian hometown, and through the photos, traces the disintegration of his relationship with his then-wife. With Arsinee Khanjian. 73 min.
53-8324 Was $79.99 ***$24.99***

Exotica (1995)
This eerie, erotic meditation on sex, lies and voyeurism from Canada's Atom Egoyan is set in and around a strip club frequented by a docile tax auditor. As the taxman is drawn into a fantasy world created by a pretty teenage dancer and the club's creepy DJ, his obsessions and mysterious past are revealed. Mia Kirshner, Bruce Greenwood and Elias Koteas star. 104 min.
11-1936 Was $89.99 ❑***$19.99***

The Sweet Hereafter (1997)
As the residents of a remote Canadian town try to cope with the aftermath of a school bus crash that injured dozens and left 14 children dead, they are divided by the arrival of a lawyer who, driven by a tragedy in his own past, encourages them to sue for damages. Director Atom Egoyan's acclaimed drama, based on the novel by Russell Banks, stars Ian Holm, Sarah Polley, Bruce Greenwood and Gabrielle Rose. 112 min.
02-5175 Was $99.99 ❑***$19.99***

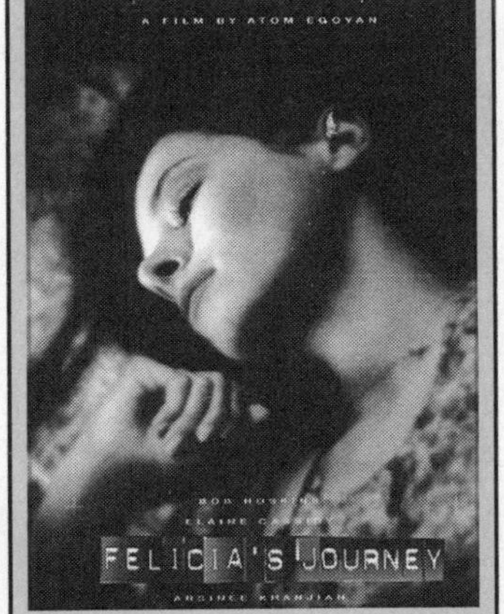

Felicia's Journey (1999)
Felicia (Elaine Cassidy), a young Irish woman in search of her soldier boyfriend in the British Midlands, is befriended by Joseph Hilditch (Bob Hoskins), a caterer with a strange affection for his late mother. Little does Felicia realize that Joseph is, in fact, a deranged serial killer...and she's targeted as his next victim. Atom Egoyan ("Exotica") directed this disturbing tale. 111 min.
27-7192 Was $99.99 ❑***$14.99***

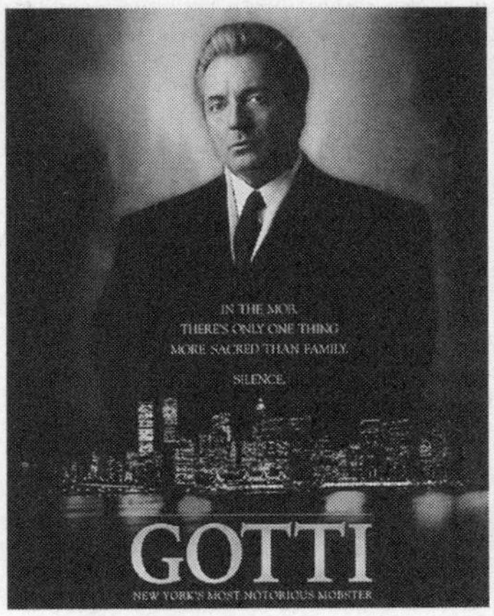

Gotti (1996)
The life and crimes of New York's "Teflon Don" are vividly brought to life in this explosive production. Armand Assante plays the smooth and streetwise John Gotti, leader of the Gambino crime family whose recklessness led to his downfall. William Forsythe, Anthony Quinn and Frank Vincent also star. 117 min.
44-2073 Was $19.99 ***$14.99***

Witness To The Mob (1998)
Riveting true-life gang story chronicles mobster Sammy "the Bull" Gravano's decision to turn in state's evidence against his boss, New York's long-reigning crimelord, John Gotti. Nicholas Turturro is Gravano and Tom Sizemore plays Gotti in this film, co-produced by Robert De Niro. With Debi Mazar, Abe Vigoda and Philip Baker Hall. 172 min.
68-1955 ❑***$79.99***

Ambushed (1998)
When a black cop is the main suspect in the murder of a KKK leader, he's forced to team up with the only witness to the crime—the victim's racist son—to find out the truth behind the killing before they're both eliminated. Suspenseful drama stars Courtney B. Vance, Jeremy Lelliott, Virginia Madsen and Robert Patrick. 99 min.
44-2181 Was $89.99 ❑***$14.99***

Winchell (1998)
For decades he was the most influential media figure in America, and a word from him could make or break an actor or a politician. Stanley Tucci is sensational as newspaper/radio columnist Walter Winchell, whose staccato delivery and drive to "scoop" the competition made him as big a news story as the celebrities whose lives he investigated. Glenne Headly, Paul Giamatti, Christopher Plummer also star. 108 min.
44-2183 ❑***$99.99***

Excellent Cadavers (1999)
Based on the harrowing true stories of Italian law enforcement officials who put their lives on the line battling the Mafia, this intense drama stars Chazz Palminteri and Andy Luotto as government operatives in Palermo, Sicily, who attempt to bring down a powerful crime boss without becoming "excellent cadavers." F. Murray Abraham, Anna Galiena also star. 86 min.
44-2217 ❑***$99.99***

RKO 281 (1999)
Learn how the greatest movie of all time was nearly never made in this acclaimed look at the creation of "Citizen Kane." Liev Schreiber stars as mercurial theatrical "boy wonder" Orson Welles, whose attempt to film his and co-writer Herman Mankiewicz's (John Malkovich) thinly-veiled look at the life of publisher William Randolph Hearst (James Cromwell) and his mistress, actress Marion Davies (Melanie Griffith), brought down the wrath of the aging magnate.
44-2218 ❑***$99.99***

Witness Protection (1999)
When his bosses put a price on his head, mob member Tom Sizemore has no choice but enter himself and his family in the federal witness protection program. U.S. marshal Forest Whitaker guides Sizemore, wife Mary Elizabeth Mastrantonio and their children through the harrowing experience of having every facet of their lives stripped away and replaced in this compelling fact-based drama. 101 min.
44-2221 ***$99.99***

Selling Hitler (1991)
In 1981, a West German shopkeeper managed to fool some of Europe's top newsmen and historians with what he claimed were the handwritten World War II diaries of Adolf Hitler. See how the quest for a scoop led to one of the biggest forgery scandals in history in this outrageous and often funny docudrama. Jonathan Pryce, Alexi Sayle, Alan Bennett and Alison Doody star. 204 min.
44-2261 ***$29.99***

To Sleep With Anger (1990)
In this mystical seriocomic fable, Danny Glover plays a charismatic drifter from the South whose visit to a black Los Angeles family disrupts their lives and makes them question their relationships. An audacious, spirited tale highlighted by Glover's magnetic performance, fine support by Mary Alice, Richard Brooks and Carl Lumbly, and Charles Burnett's inventive direction. 102 min.
45-5496 Was $19.99 ❑***$14.99***

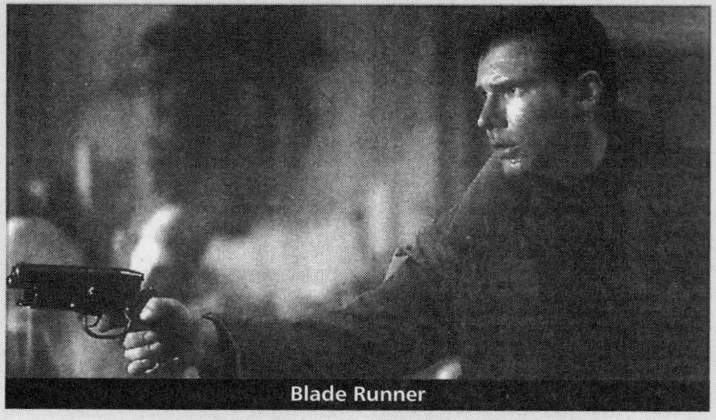
Blade Runner

Harrison Ford

The Possessed (1977)
Satanic chiller about a supernatural force that has taken over a girls' school, and the defrocked priest who risks his life to exorcise the evil. James Farentino, Joan Hackett, Ann Dusenberry, Diana Scarwid and, in an early role, Harrison Ford star. 78 min.
48-1173 *$59.99*

Force 10 From Navarone (1978)
Robert Shaw, Harrison Ford, Franco Nero, Carl Weathers and Edward Fox are the force, and a vital supply route bridge in Nazi-held Yugoslavia is their target. But will the traitor in their midst end their mission before it starts? All-star follow-up to "The Guns of Navarone" also features Barbara Bach, Richard Kiel. 118 min.
73-1168 ❑*$14.99*

Hanover Street (1979)
Lush, romantic suspense/drama about a love affair between ace WWII bomber pilot and a beautiful military aide. Harrison Ford, Lesley-Anne Down, Christopher Plummer. Great John Barry score. 109 min.
02-1143 *$14.99*

The Frisco Kid (1979)
Gene Wilder is a Polish rabbi picked to lead a congregation in 1850s San Francisco, who gets off the boat in Philadelphia. What follows is a hilarious cross-country trek where he meets up with and befriends outlaw Harrison Ford. 119 min.
19-1183 *$14.99*

Blade Runner:
The Director's Cut (1982)
Ridley Scott's reconstructed version of the science-fiction favorite, starring Harrison Ford as a detective tracking down artificial humans called "replicants" in Los Angeles circa 2019, differs from the original release by the addition of an important dream sequence and the omission of Ford's voice-over narration. Rutger Hauer, Sean Young and Daryl Hannah co-star. 117 min.
19-2070 Letterboxed ❑*$14.99*

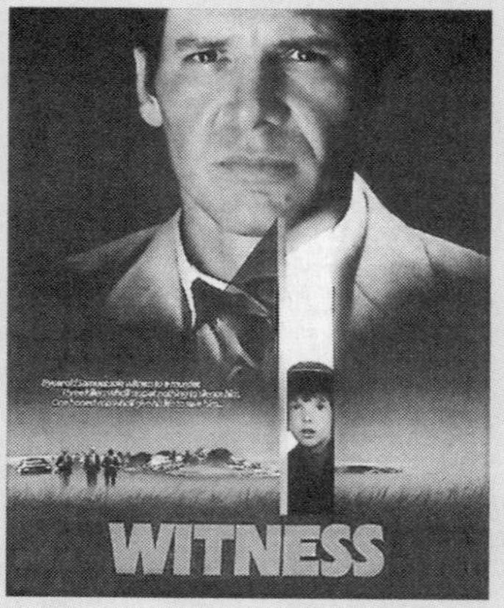

Witness (1985)
Philadelphia detective Harrison Ford must protect the sole witness to a murder, a 10-year-old Amish boy, when the crime is linked to police corruption, forcing Ford to hide on the boy's family's rural farm. Peter Weir's compelling, visually eloquent drama also stars Kelly McGillis, Lukas Haas, Josef Sommer, Danny Glover. 112 min.
06-1335 ❑*$14.99*

Witness (Letterboxed Version)
Also available in a theatrical, widescreen format.
06-2710 ❑*$14.99*

The Mosquito Coast (1986)
Harrison Ford gives his most electric performance as an eccentric, obsessive inventor who uproots his family and moves to the remotest part of Central America. His terrifying tunnelvision leads to tragedy in this mesmerizing adventure that co-stars Helen Mirren, River Phoenix, and Andre Gregory; Peter Weir ("Witness") directs. 119 min.
19-1568 Was $19.99 ❑*$14.99*

Working Girl (1988)
A distaff Horatio Alger tale for the '80s, starring Melanie Griffith as a plucky Manhattan secretary who steps in when her boss is hospitalized and puts together her own deal. Sigourney Weaver, Harrison Ford and Joan Cusack co-star in Mike Nichols' comedic ode to climbing the corporate ladder. 115 min.
04-2243 Was $19.99 ❑*$14.99*

Frantic (1988)
A trip to Paris becomes a rollercoaster ride of danger and suspense for doctor Harrison Ford when his wife is kidnapped by criminals after a mysterious item in a thriller from shockmaster Roman Polanski. Emmanuelle Seigner co-stars as the sultry smuggler who aids Ford in his search. 120 min.
19-1645 Was $19.99 ❑*$14.99*

Presumed Innocent (1990)
A riveting murder mystery, based on the best-selling novel, stars Harrison Ford as a deputy prosecutor who investigates the death of a colleague with whom he had an affair. While attempting to hide their relationship, he becomes a prime suspect in the killing and a pawn in a political game. Bonnie Bedelia, Brian Dennehy, Raul Julia, Greta Scacchi co-star. 127 min.
19-1820 ❑*$14.99*

Regarding Henry (1991)
In this heartfelt drama, Harrison Ford plays a sleazy legal eagle who is shot in the head by a robber and sent into a coma. When he awakes, he has amnesia and, aided by his wife and daughter, must learn his life over. Annette Bening, Bill Nunn and Mikki Allen co-star; Mike Nichols directs. 85 min.
06-1910 Was $89.99 ❑*$14.99*

Patriot Games (1992)
Tom Clancy's best-selling novel is turned into an intense action thriller with Harrison Ford playing Jack Ryan, the former CIA advisor who finds his and his family's lives threatened by a group of Irish terrorists after he kills one of them during a trip to London. Anne Archer, Patrick Bergin, Samuel L. Jackson and Richard Harris also star. 117 min.
06-2011 Was $89.99 ❑*$14.99*

Patriot Games
(Letterboxed Version)
Also available in a theatrical, widescreen format.
06-2509 ❑*$14.99*

Clear And
Present Danger (1994)
In this intense treatment of the hit Tom Clancy novel, Harrison Ford's Jack Ryan is called on to take over ailing superior James Earl Jones' CIA post. Ford unravels an elaborate scandal involving warring South American drug cartels and stretching from the Colombian jungle to the Oval Office. Willem Dafoe, Donald Moffat and Anne Archer also star. 141 min.
06-2285 Was $89.99 ❑*$14.99*

Clear And Present Danger
(Letterboxed Version)
Also available in a theatrical, widescreen format.
06-2510 ❑*$14.99*

The Jack Ryan Collection
A triple play of espionage action and suspense, courtesy of author Tom Clancy, features Ryan as played by Alec Baldwin in "The Hunt for Red October" and Harrison Ford in "Patriot Games" and "Clear and Present Danger."
06-2375 *$44.99*

The Fugitive (1993)
Inspired by the classic TV series, this intense chase thriller stars Harrison Ford as Richard Kimble, a Chicago surgeon wrongly convicted of murdering his wife. On the way to prison, Ford escapes and sets out to find the real killer, but hot on his trail is obsessive Deputy U.S. Marshal Gerard (Academy Award-winner Tommy Lee Jones). Sela Ward, Julianne Moore co-star. 131 min.
19-2195 Was $24.99 ❑*$19.99*

The Fugitive
(Letterboxed Version)
Also available in a theatrical, widescreen format.
19-2512 ❑*$19.99*

Sabrina (1995)
Sparkling reworking of the 1954 favorite, featuring Julia Ormond as the beautiful chauffeur's daughter in love with Greg Kinnear, the irresponsible, engaged member of a wealthy family. When Ormond returns from Paris, Harrison Ford, Kinnear's workaholic sibling, tries to woo her for business reasons, only to wind up falling for her himself. Sydney Pollack directs. 127 min.
06-2464 Was $99.99 ❑*$14.99*

Air Force One (1997)
When fanatical Russian nationalists seize control of the U.S. presidential airplane in mid-flight and threaten to kill everyone on board unless their group's leader is released from jail, Vietnam vet/chief executive Harrison Ford escapes from his captors and proceeds to veto their scheme. Director Wolfgang Petersen's hit actioner also stars Gary Oldman, Glenn Close, Wendy Crewson, William H. Macy. 124 min.
02-3128 Was $19.99 ❑*$14.99*

Air Force One
(Letterboxed Version)
Also available in a theatrical, widescreen format.
02-3129 ❑*$19.99*

Six Days, Seven Nights (1998)
Frothy, picture postcard-pretty comedy/adventure featuring Anne Heche as a magazine editor, on a South Pacific vacation with boyfriend David Schwimmer, who hires local pilot Harrison Ford to fly her to Tahiti for a last-minute photo session. After the plane crashes on a remote island, Heche and Ford's danger-filled odyssey of survival soon leads to romance. Directed by Ivan Reitman; 102 min.
11-2807 Was $19.99 ❑*$14.99*

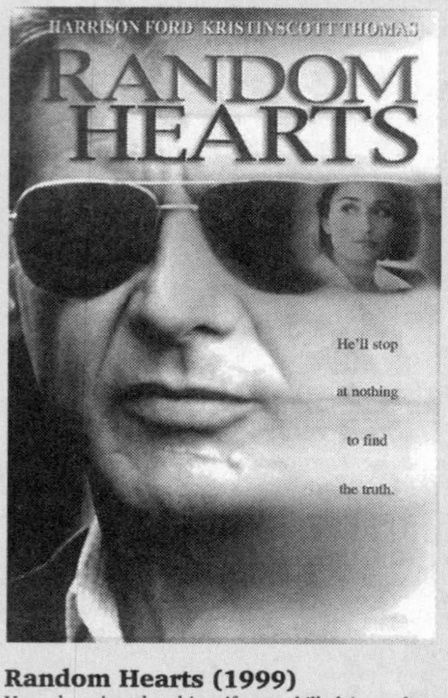

Random Hearts (1999)
Upon learning that his wife was killed in a plane crash—while travelling with another man—Washington, D.C. cop Harrison Ford seeks out the dead man's wife, congresswoman Kristin Scott Thomas, as he tries to learn the truth behind the affair. Ford's quest leads him and Thomas into each other's arms in this intriguing and emotional drama from director Sydney Pollack. Charles S. Dutton, Bonnie Hunt also star. 133 min.
02-3410 Was $99.99 ❑*$14.99*

Harrison Ford Gift Set
There's more than one Ford in your future when you purchase this boxed collector's set with four fantastic Harrison hits: "Clear and Present Danger," "Patriot Games," "Sabrina" and "Witness."
06-2539 *$59.99*

Please see our index for these other Harrison Ford titles: *American Graffiti • The Conversation • Dead Heat On A Merry-Go-Round • The Devil's Own • Getting Straight • Heroes • Indiana Jones trilogy • Luv • What Lies Beneath*

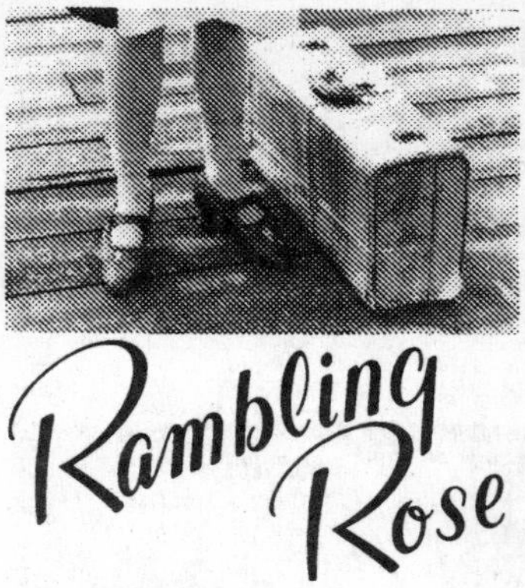

Rambling Rose (1991)
Bittersweet, sexy and wonderfully acted tale starring Laura Dern as an orphaned young woman who takes a job as a maid for a Southern family during the Depression. Soon, her sexually precocious ways rattle her staid surrogate family and the small town they live in. Robert Duvall, Diane Ladd and Lukas Haas co-star in this tenderly filmed story. 115 min.
27-6756 Was $19.99 ❑*$14.99*

Hourglass (1995)
High-powered fashion industry executive C. Thomas Howell is lured into a seductive trap of temptation and betrayal by beautiful designer Sofia Shinas in this glossy, suspenseful drama. With Ed Begley, Jr., Tim Bottoms. 91 min.
27-6959 ❑*$89.99*

Love Crimes (1992)
Director Lizzie Borden's sexually-charged thriller stars Sean Young as an assistant D.A. who offers herself as bait to trap photographer Patrick Bergin, who specializes in erotic photos and has a history of humiliating and beating his models. This unrated "director's cut" features eight minutes of steamy footage not shown in theaters. 90 min.
44-1873 Was $19.99 ❑*$14.99*

One Man's War (1991)
In this powerful true story, Anthony Hopkins plays Dr. Joel Filartiga, who runs a free health clinic in strife-torn Paraguay. An outspoken critic of the dictatorship government, the physician's son is tortured and killed by the police, and he teams with a crusading lawyer to battle the government-sanctioned murder. With Norma Aleandro and Ruben Blades. 91 min.
44-1816 ❑*$89.99*

Afterburn (1992)
After a top fighter pilot dies in a plane crash in Korea, his wife is informed by the Air Force that his death was due to "pilot error." Along with her lawyer, she investigates the incident and discovers that the instruments may have been at fault and the Air Force is involved in a cover-up. Laura Dern, Vincent Spano and Robert Loggia star in this true story. 103 min.
44-1905 Was $89.99 ❑*$19.99*

A Private Matter (1992)
Based on a true story, this timely and compelling drama stars Sissy Spacek as the hostess of a kid's TV show in 1960s Arizona who took Thalidomide during pregnancy and, fearing the chances of birth defects, chooses with her husband to have an abortion. Their decision costs Spacek her job and unleashes a firestorm of controversy. Aidan Quinn, Estelle Parsons also star. 89 min.
44-1909 ❑*$89.99*

Teamster Boss (1992)
Forceful true story starring Brian Dennehy as Jackie Presser, another in a line of controversial Teamsters union chiefs, who associated with members of organized crime, played informant for the FBI and was indicted on racketeering charges in 1986. Maria Conchita Alonso, Jeff Daniels, Eli Wallach also star. 111 min.
44-1913 Was $89.99 ❑*$14.99*

The Last Way Out (1996)
Modern film noir about a man who has been hiding from his criminal past for the last two years. When an unavoidable turn of events puts him back together with his former partners, he is forced to make a deadly decision: make one last heist, or get out for good. Kurt Johnson, Kevin Reed star. 88 min.
22-9001 *$24.99*

The Climb (1997)
Bob Swaim ("La Balance") directed this touching drama in the tradition of "Stand by Me." In Baltimore in 1959, 12-year-old Danny, who is bent on proving his bravery by scaling a huge radio tower, befriends Langer, a cranky, dying engineer. The two form a strong relationship, and Langer tries to help him complete his mission. John Hurt, Gregory Smith, David Strathairn star. 94 min.
22-9028 *$79.99*

Timeless (1996)
A haunting look at two New York teens trying to escape a dead-end existence on the streets, this acclaimed independent drama follows 18-year-old grifter Terry and his hooker girlfriend Lyrica as they try to find a better life in a remote Long Island community, but find the past catching up to them. Peter Byrne, Melissa Duge star. 90 min.
22-9032 *$29.99*

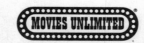

At Play In The Fields Of The Lord (1991)
This stunning adaptation of Peter Matthiessen's acclaimed novel tells the story of the collision of cultures in the South American rain forests. A pair of mercenary pilots are hired to drive an Indian tribe out of their forest home, but change their minds when they meet the natives and confront two teams of missionaries working to "save" the Indians. Tom Berenger, Aidan Quinn, Kathy Bates, John Lithgow, Daryl Hannah and Tom Waits star. 186 min.
07-1804 ❑$19.99

The Defenders: Payback (1997)
The groundbreaking TV legal series of the 1960s is reworked for contemporary times, as veteran attorney Lawrence Preston (E.G. Marshall) is joined by nephew Don (Beau Bridges) and granddaughter M.J. (Martha Plimpton) on a case involving a man who has confessed to committing a vengeful act. Yaphet Kotto, John Larroquette also star. 96 min.
06-2784 ❑$69.99

The Defenders: Choice Of Evils (1998)
When a noted black journalist whose investigations have earned him the enmity of the police is wrongly convicted of murder and attempts to escape, his only hope for proving his innocence lies with the Preston family. E.G. Marshall, Beau Bridges and Martha Plimpton return as the crusading three-generation lawyers in this powerful drama. With James McDaniel. 96 min.
06-2824 ❑$69.99

The Defenders: Taking The First (1998)
The family of a man beaten to death by followers of a racist hate group file a wrongful death suit against the group's leader, and lawyers Beau Bridges and Martha Plimpton find themselves arguing against freedom of speech as they seek to stop a message of violent intolerance in this compelling "Defenders" drama. Jeremy London, Philip Casnoff also star. 98 min.
06-2887 ❑$69.99

American Me (1992)
An exciting, ultra-realistic account of the rise and fall of the Hispanic leader of an East L.A. gang. Edward James Olmos directs and stars as Santana, the tough crime kingpin who starts his gang while a young man serving a term in Folsom Prison, and who uses his power to control the barrio upon his release. With William Forsythe, Pepe Serna and Evelina Fernandez. 125 min.
07-1849 Was $19.99 ❑$14.99

White Lie (1991)
When a black press secretary discovers that his father was the victim of a lynching years earlier, he sets out to further investigate the incident by returning to his Southern birthplace. Along with the help of a white doctor with whom he becomes romantically involved, he uncovers the truth behind the disturbing mystery. Gregory Hines, Annette O'Toole and Bill Nunn star. 93 min.
07-1851 Was $89.99 ❑$14.99

In The Name Of The Father (1993)
Intense, true-life account of Gerry Conlon (Daniel Day-Lewis), a rebellious young Belfast native who, along with several members of his family, is wrongly convicted for the 1974 IRA bombing of an English pub. Conlon spends 15 difficult years in prison—many in a cell with his estranged father (Pete Postlethwaite)—before a crusading lawyer (Emma Thompson) has his case reviewed in court. Directed and co-scripted by Jim Sheridan ("My Left Foot"). 133 min.
07-2120 Was $19.99 ❑$14.99

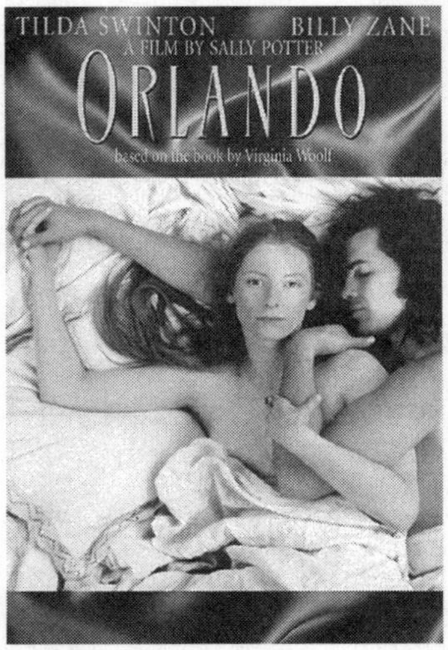

Orlando (1993)
Sally Potter's mysterious gender-bending excursion, adapted from Virginia Woolf's book, follows the incredible journey of the title character, a nobleman in the court of Queen Elizabeth I who, 200 years later and unchanged in age, has transformed into a woman. Tilda Swinton stars as the sexually ambiguous Orlando; with Quentin Crisp, Billy Zane. 93 min.
02-2592 Was $89.99 ❑$19.99

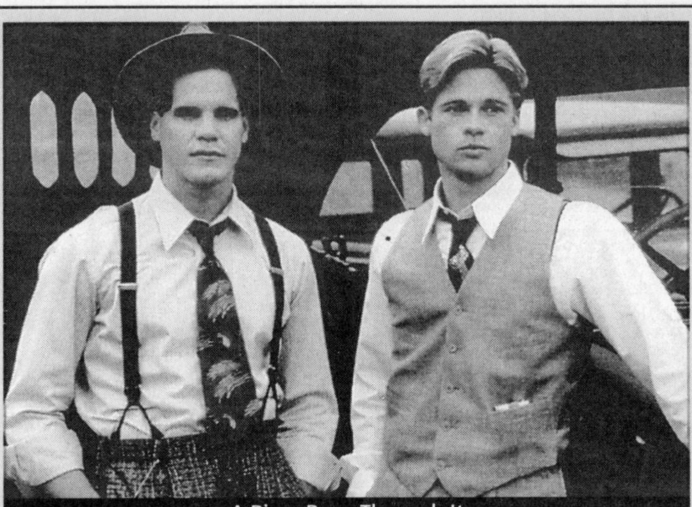

A River Runs Through It

Brad Pitt

The Dark Side Of The Sun (1988)
The drama that marked Brad Pitt's film debut, lost for years before being recovered and completed in 1997. Pitt shines as a terminally ill young man whose worldwide search for a cure unexpectedly brings him a life-changing romance. Cheryl Pollack, Guy Boyd also star. 107 min.
04-3776 ❑$69.99

Too Young To Die (1990)
Teenager Juliette Lewis, abandoned by her parents and forced to fend for herself on the city streets, takes up with hustler Brad Pitt and winds up on trial for murder. Compelling drama also stars Michael Tucker, Michael O'Keefe. 92 min.
63-1741 Was $89.99 ❑$12.99

Across The Tracks (1991)
An emotionally-charged story of two brothers caught in fierce competition between each other. One is a well-behaved, athletic young man hoping to get a track scholarship; the other is an angry teenager whose rivalry with his brother reaches explosive heights. Rick Schroder, Brad Pitt, Carrie Snodgress star. 100 min.
71-5216 $89.99

A River Runs Through It (1992)
Robert Redford directed this sensitive film of Norman Maclean's acclaimed story about a minister father who uses fly-fishing to relate to his two sons, one of whom is drawn to literature and the other a reckless type heading for danger. Tom Skerritt, Craig Sheffer, Brad Pitt and Emily Lloyd star in this lyrical drama. 123 min.
02-2401 Was $19.99 ❑$14.99

Johnny Suede (1992)
He's a cool dude from Brooklyn who plays guitar, idolizes Ricky Nelson, and has the world's wildest and highest pompadour. But Johnny has some romantic problems, torn between Miss Right and Miss Wrong. What's a fashion-plate in suede shoes to do? Tom DiCillo's ultra-hip comedy stars Brad Pitt, Catherine Keener, Nick Cave and Tina Louise. 97 min.
06-2095 ❑$89.99

Kalifornia (1993)
A writer working on a book about serial killers and his photographer girlfriend hire a white-trash couple to drive them from Pittsburgh to California for a cross-country tour of famous murder sites, unaware that they're taking a dangerous ride with a parole-jumping murderer and his lover. Juliette Lewis, Brad Pitt, David Duchovny and Michelle Forbes star in this disturbing road movie.
12-3328 $14.99

Legends Of The Fall (1994)
Set in Montana in the early 1900s, this sprawling drama stars Brad Pitt, Aidan Quinn and Henry Thomas as three disparate brothers raised by their father, free-spirited former cavalry officer Anthony Hopkins. Familial strife ignites with the outbreak of World War I and the arrival of the youngest brother's fiancée, beautiful Easterner Julia Ormond, for whom all three share an affection. 133 min.
02-2772 Was $19.99 ❑$14.99

Legends Of The Fall (Letterboxed Version)
Also available in a theatrical, widescreen format.
02-3049 Was $19.99 ❑$14.99

The Favor (1994)
Sophisticated romantic story starring Harley Jane Kozak as a happily married woman who enlists friend Elizabeth McGovern to check out former high school sweetheart Ken Wahl while on a trip to Denver. When Wahl and McGovern have a steamy one-nighter, all sorts of comedic complications ensue. Bill Pullman, Brad Pitt also star. 97 min.
73-1175 Was $89.99 ❑$14.99

Seven (1995)
Intense shocker starring Morgan Freeman as a veteran big city detective who teams with young partner Brad Pitt to find a diabolically clever serial killer responsible for a series of grotesque murders inspired by the seven deadly sins. Gwyneth Paltrow, Kevin Spacey and John C. McGinley also star. 127 min.
02-5085 Was $19.99 ❑$14.99

Seven (Director's Letterboxed Edition)
Also available in a special edition, featuring a behind-the-scenes featurette and star interviews, in a theatrical, widescreen format. 136 min.
02-5100 ❑$19.99

Sleepers (1996)
Writer/director Barry Levinson's adaptation of the best-selling book follows four young boys from New York's Hell's Kitchen in the '60s, when they're sent to a brutal reform school and assaulted by a sadistic guard. Two decades later, the four—now grown up as a pair of criminals, a writer and an assistant D.A.—launch an elaborate plan of revenge. Powerful drama is fueled by an ensemble cast that includes Kevin Bacon, Robert De Niro, Ron Eldard, Vittorio Gassman, Dustin Hoffman, Jason Patric and Brad Pitt. 148 min.
19-2497 Was $19.99 ❑$14.99

Sleepers (Letterboxed Version)
Also available in a theatrical, widescreen format.
19-2589 ❑$19.99

The Devil's Own (1997)
IRA assassin Brad Pitt escapes British surveillance and makes his way to America in order to obtain Stinger missiles from an illegal arms dealer. Staying in the home of New York cop Harrison Ford and his family, Pitt befriends his hosts, until his violent past catches up to him and puts Pitt and Ford in a deadly confrontation. Director Alan J. Pakula's action-filled drama also stars Treat Williams, Margaret Colin, Ruben Blades. 111 min.
02-3087 Was $19.99 ❑$14.99

Seven Years In Tibet (1997)
Brad Pitt stars in the remarkable true story of Austrian adventurer and mountaineer Heinrich Harrer, who was a British POW in Asia during World War II and later became a confidante of the young Dalai Lama shortly before the Chinese takeover of Tibet, in this sweeping drama of one man's physical and spiritual odyssey from director Jean-Jacques Anaud. David Thewlis, B.D. Wong, Mako, and Jamyang Jamtsho Wangchuk as the Dalai Lama star. 131 min.
02-3156 Was $19.99 ❑$14.99

Seven Years In Tibet (Letterboxed Version)
Also available in a theatrical, widescreen format.
02-3157 Was $99.99 ❑$19.99

Meet Joe Black (1998)
Would you mind dying if the Grim Reaper looked like Brad Pitt? In director Martin Brest's loose remake of the 1934 fantasy "Death Takes a Holiday," Pitt plays the spirit of Death, incarnated in the body of a car crash victim, who puts off claiming communications magnate Anthony Hopkins for a few days so that Pitt can learn from him the joys and pains of mortal existence. Things get complicated when Pitt falls for Hopkins' youngest daughter, physician Claire Forlani. With Marcia Gay Harden, Jake Weber. Special edition includes a "making of" documentary with interviews with the cast. 180 min.
07-2731 Was $19.99 ❑$14.99

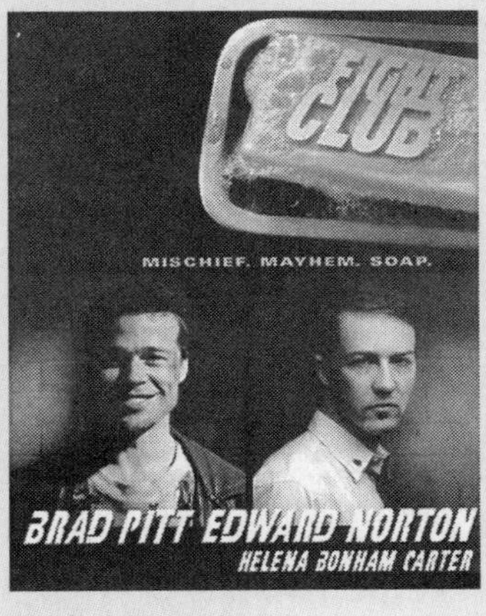

Fight Club (1999)
One part "Raging Bull" and one part Susan Faludi essay, "Seven" director David Fincher's controversial drama stars Edward Norton as a burned-out insurance worker who seeks out connections by attending support group meetings. A chance encounter with off-the-wall soap salesman Brad Pitt leads the two to form Fight Club, an underground group where men bond and find catharsis through beating each other to a pulp. Norton isn't prepared for the consequences when Pitt moves the violence outside the ring. Helena Bonham Carter, Meat Loaf Aday also star. 139 min.
04-3922 Was $99.99 ❑$14.99

Brad Pitt: Hollywood Hunk
Hunk he may be, but it's Brad Pitt's acting ability, along with his good looks, that have made him an international film star. In this documentary you'll learn about Pitt's Oklahoma boyhood, his early days in Hollywood (which included a stint in a fast food chicken costume), and his TV and movie breakthroughs. Interviews with friends, colleagues and Pitt himself are included. 60 min.
05-5103 $14.99

Please see our index for these other Brad Pitt titles: *Cool World • Interview With The Vampire • True Romance • 12 Monkeys*

End Of Summer (1998)
The elite and exclusive world of the upper class is turned upside-down when two people who shouldn't have ever met start an affair that ends up spinning a web of scandal and sexual intrigue in this turn-of-the-century drama. Stars Jacqueline Bisset, Peter Weller and Julian Sands. 95 min.
06-2750 Was $89.99 ❑$14.99

A Dangerous Woman (1993)
In this moody and erotic drama, Debra Winger plays a brutally honest, childlike woman named Martha who lives on a ranch with Frances, her wealthy aunt (Barbara Hershey). Martha's relationship with a handyman (Gabriel Byrne), who also carries on an affair with Frances, leads to disastrous consequences. With David Strathairn, Chloe Webb. 93 min.
07-2088 Was $19.99 ❑$14.99

Sin And Redemption (1994)
A young rape victim seeks help from her boyfriend after he offers her his love and his hand in marriage. But as soon as she begins rebuilding her life, she discovers that her new husband has a dark secret that's unsettling. Richard Grieco and Cynthia Gibb star. 94 min.
06-2787 $69.99

This Is The Sea (1997)
Amid the ongoing turmoil and suspicion of Northern Ireland, the blossoming romance between a sheltered Protestant girl and a young Catholic man whose brother is involved with the IRA faces pressure from all sides in this powerful drama. Samantha Morton, Ross McDade, Gabriel Byrne and Richard Harris star. 104 min.
06-2820 ❑$69.99

Foreign Student (1994)
This sensitive coming of-age tale, set in a Southern college in the '50s, focuses on a European exchange student who falls in love with a black teacher from across town. In order for the romance to continue, both must face tremendous hurdles. Robin Givens, Marco Hofschneider and Charles Dutton star. 96 min.
07-2214 Was $89.99 ❑$14.99

The Perfect Daughter (1996)
A drug-addicted runaway who has spent two years on the city streets is involved in a hit-and-run accident that leaves her with amnesia—and no idea where she hid $100,000 in drug money. When she rejoins her family, the drug dealers pursue her for the cash, putting her family in jeopardy. Tracey Gold, Bess Armstrong and Michael Schulman star. 92 min.
07-2490 ❑$89.99

Federal Hill (1994)
Striking gangster saga about five Italian-American friends attempting to survive their tough Federal Hill neighborhood in Providence, Rhode Island. Nicholas Turturro is explosive as Ralph, a petty crook who finds his friendship with best friend Nicky (Anthony De Sando) under fire when a pretty student comes between them. Black-and-white theatrical version. 100 min.
68-1366 □*$89.99*

Federal Hill (Color Version)
Witness Providence, Rhode Island, in all its splendor in this colorized version of the acclaimed independent drama.
68-1367 □*$89.99*

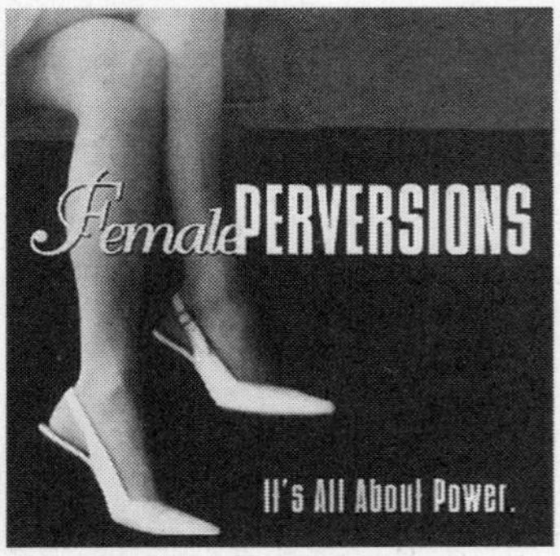
Female PERVERSIONS
It's All About Power.

Female Perversions (1996)
Based on a non-fiction book of the same title, this compelling and erotic drama stars Tilda Swinton ("Orlando") as a beautiful and successful attorney who is up for a judicial appointment, but whose businesslike facade hides a private life of dark dreams and sexual fantasies. Amy Madigan, Clancy Brown, Karen Sillas and Frances Fisher also star. 114 min.
68-1868 Was $99.99 □*$14.99*

Kids (1995)
Controversial, groundbreaking documentary-style drama from director Larry Clark chronicles 24 hours in the lives of teens in Manhattan. The unflinching film centers on an HIV-positive boy whose joys in life are skateboarding and deflowering virgins. When one of his conquests discovers she has contracted HIV, she mounts a search to find him. Rosario Dawson, Leo Fitzpatrick, Justin Pierce, Chloe Sevigny star. Uncut, unrated version; 102 min.
68-1789 Was $19.99 □*$14.99*

Circle Of Passion (1996)
A successful and happily married London banker is transferred to Paris, where he meets and falls in love with a beautiful, free-spirited woman. Forced to choose between his passion and his responsibility, which way will he go? Charles Finch, Jane March and Sandrine Bonnaire star in this powerful drama. 94 min.
68-1860 □*$99.99*

Eve's Bayou (1997)
Highly acclaimed directorial debut from actress Kasi Lemmons is a richly-textured gothic family drama set in Louisiana in 1962. Samuel L. Jackson is a loving but philandering doctor whose adulterous ways lead Eve, his youngest daughter, to seek help from a local voodoo queen. The film's superior cast also includes Lynn Whitfield, Diahann Carroll and Jurnee Smollett as Eve. 108 min.
68-1869 Was $99.99 □*$14.99*

First Love, Last Rites (1998)
Set in Louisiana's bayou country, this steamy and romantic drama stars Natasha Gregson Wagner and Giovanni Ribisi as the young couple whose first serious relationship comes complete with passion, devotion...and a choice that threatens to tear them apart. Robert John Burke also stars as Wagner's eel fisherman dad; directed by Lemonheads alumnus Jesse Peretz. 94 min.
68-1904 □*$99.99*

Slam (1998)
This acclaimed drama tells of Ray Joshua, an aspiring rapper from Washington, D.C. who lands in jail on a drug charge. While behind bars, Joshua finds himself through his poetry and rapping talent, and with the help of Lauren, a beautiful writing teacher. Saul Williams and Sonja Sohn star. 103 min.
68-1908 Was $99.99 □*$14.99*

Trading Favors (1997)
A group of college boys out for a good time thinks they've hit the jackpot when a seductive older woman joins them. They do...but a stolen car, a convenience store hold-up and a jealous boyfriend are among the "prizes" waiting for them in this wild mix of "Risky Business" and "Something Wild" from director Sondra Locke. Rosanna Arquette, Devon Summerall, Peter Greene and Cuba Gooding, Jr. star. AKA: "Do Me a Favor." 103 min.
68-1872 □*$99.99*

Phoenix (1998)
Tough-as-nails crime yarn focusing on a Phoenix detective whose gambling problem has him in deep to loan sharks and bookies. Desperate, he decides to pull off a heist at a mobster's club in order to settle his debts. Ray Liotta, Anthony LaPaglia, Anjelica Huston, Daniel Baldwin and Kari Wuhrer star. 107 min.
68-1896 Was $99.99 □*$14.99*

Ground Control (1998)
Still haunted by the crash that cost him his job and everything he held dear, former air traffic controller Kiefer Sutherland is the only person who can save hundreds of passengers when a storm knocks out navigation systems at Phoenix and dozens of planes need to land. Gripping and suspenseful drama also stars Michael Gross, Robert Sean Leonard, Kelly McGillis, Kristy Swanson. 97 min.
68-1914 □*$99.99*

The Break (1995)
A teenager dreams of stardom as a pro tennis player, but his controlling father hires a former player-turned-coach to try and dissuade him. The boy's determination inspires both teacher and pupil to reach for their goals in this moving drama. Vincent Van Patten, Ben Jorgensen, Martin Sheen, Rae Dawn Chong star. 104 min.
68-1786 □*$89.99*

Another Day In Paradise (1998)
This sordid, energetic drama from director Larry Clark ("Kids") tells of young runaway Vincent Kartheiser and girlfriend Natasha Gregson Wagner, who are taken under the wing of junkies James Woods and Melanie Griffith. The four form a highly volatile union of low-lifes involved in criminal acts while searching for a big score. 101 min.
68-1918 Was $99.99 □*$14.99*

Raising The Heights (1999)
Set in Brooklyn's racially-divided Crown Heights neighborhood, this powerful drama focuses on two people caught in the turmoil: Michael, a black teenager with dreams of success, and Judy, a reporter who has denied her Jewish heritage. When a drug deal in the area leads to violence, both must put aside their fears and work together. Gilbert Brown, Jr., Fia Perera star. 88 min.
68-1935 □*$99.99*

The Blood Oranges (1998)
Director/co-scripter Philip Haas ("Angels & Insects") turns the acclaimed John Hawkes novel into a sultry tale of erotic explorations. Sheryl Lee and Charles Dance play a hedonistic couple exploring the freedom of their "open marriage" in a European village in the '70s. The arrival of tourists Colin Lane and Laila Robins leads to a series of sexual encounters with far-reaching consequences. 94 min.
68-1958 □*$69.99*

The Tempest (1998)
The Shakespeare fantasy of magic and romance is transferred to the Mississippi bayou country during the Civil War in this imaginative rendition. Peter Fonda stars as sorcerer Gideon Prosper, who uses his spells to confound Union and Confederate forces and find true love for his daughter Miranda. Katherine Heigl, John Glover, Eddie Mills also star. 88 min.
68-1960 □*$69.99*

Joe The King (1999)
Actor Frank Whaley's debut as writer/director is a compelling and unsentimental look at adolescence as seen through the eyes of Joe (Noah Fleiss), a troubled 14-year-old whose problems include an alcoholic and debt-riddled father (Val Kilmer), a lack of friends at school, and an older brother (Max Ligosh) who's begun to ignore him. The moving, semi-autobiographical tale also stars Karen Young, Ethan Hawke, Camryn Manheim. 100 min.
68-1971 □*$79.99*

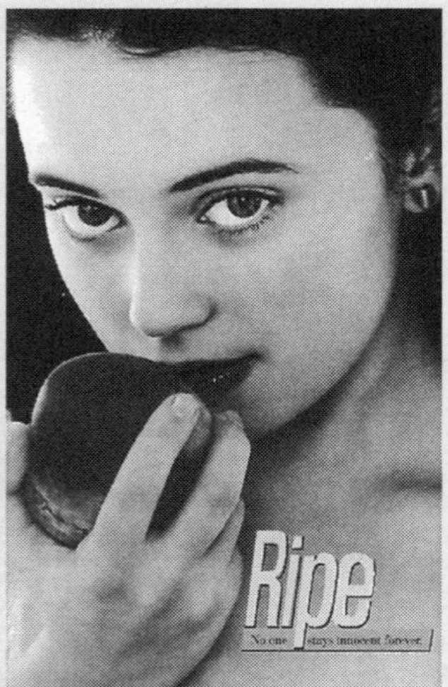
Ripe
No one stays innocent forever.

Ripe (1997)
Rose and Violet are teenage twins who flee the car accident that kills their parents and head to Kentucky, hoping to find a better life. Instead, they land on a military base, where they are taken in by a janitor and become accepted by the residents. But Violet's sexuality and Rosie's affection for guns leads to trouble. Provocative story stars Monica Keena, Daisy Eagan. 93 min
68-1850 Was $99.99 □*$12.99*

BELLA MAFIA

Bella Mafia (1997)
When the head of a powerful Sicilian crime family and his sons are murdered by a rival clan, their widows band together for a vendetta against the brutal killings. Sweeping TV drama of love, loyalty and vengeance stars Vanessa Redgrave, Jennifer Tilly, Nastassja Kinski, Illeana Douglas, Dennis Farina and Franco Nero. Special feature-length version; 117 min.
68-1875 Was $99.99 □*$14.99*

Bella Mafia: The Complete Mini-Series
The complete mini-series, featuring additional footage never before seen, is also available in a two-tape set. 179 min.
68-1902 □*$24.99*

Tail Lights Fade (1999)
Looking for a comedy filled with drugs, sex and fast cars? In this offbeat romp from Canada, a young woman gets a call from her brother, who's been arrested for dealing pot. Now she, her boyfriend, and another couple are on a wild 2,500-mile race from Toronto to Vancouver to destroy the brother's "harvest" before it's discovered by the cops or his competitors. Tanya Allen, Jake Busey, Breckin Meyer and Denise Richards star. 88 min.
68-1972 □*$69.99*

Blue Juice (1995)
When one thinks of surfing hotbeds, the Cornwall coast of England doesn't immediately spring to mind, but the waveriders in this unusual comedy/drama are dedicated to their sport. Sean Pertwee stars as a local surfing "legend," faced with having to grow up as he hits 30, Catherine Zeta-Jones plays his waitress girlfriend, and Ewan McGregor is a zonked-out compadre. 93 min.
68-1977 □*$69.99*

Prince Of Central Park (1999)
A young boy runs away from a negligent foster home to find his birth mother, only to encounter the cold, brutal world of the New York City streets. As he proceeds to get into trouble with some local criminals, he's befriended by a caring social worker and an eccentric man who lives in Central Park. Intriguing family drama stars Kathleen Turner, Harvey Keitel, Cathy Moriarty and Frankie Nasso. 110 min.
68-2030 □*$69.99*

The Bloody Child (1996)
A U.S. Marine, newly returned from the Persian Gulf, is found digging a grave in the Mojave Desert, his wife's body in the back seat of their car. His arrest for her murder and the effect that the crime has on the arresting Marine officer, forms the basis for this haunting drama, based on a true incident, from independent filmmaker Nina Menkes. Tinka Menkes, Russ Little star. 85 min.
70-3473 *$79.99*

Committed (1990)
This striking biographical drama of the troubled life of actress Frances Farmer, who went from Hollywood sensation to resident of a state mental hospital 10 years later. Directed by and starring Sheila McLaughlin, this independent production delves into areas ignored in the 1982 Jessica Lange film. 75 min.
70-5027 Was $59.99 *$29.99*

Utz (1992)
An intense, complex drama from director George Sluizer ("The Vanishing") about a wealthy Czech who collects porcelain figures and mysteriously disappears one day along with his coveted collection. When an art dealer tries to find him, he unravels a fascinating mystery. Armin Mueller-Stahl, Peter Riegert, Paul Scofield, Brenda Fricker star. 95 min.
70-5059 Was $29.99 *$19.99*

Butterfly Kiss (1996)
Amanda Plummer is Eunice, a mysterious serial killer roaming North England in search of another woman named Judith. Instead, she meets Miriam (Saskia Reeves), a gas station attendant, who is quickly drawn to her. After a night of lovemaking, Miriam comes under Eunice's spell, and the two embark on a murder spree. Directed by Michael Winterbottom ("Welcome to Sarajevo"). 90 min.
70-5121 Was $79.99 *$29.99*

Begotten (1990)
Experimental filmmaker Edmund Elias Merhige's acclaimed first feature is a provocative creation story in which a godlike "thing" dies while giving birth to "Mother Earth," who will be sacrificed, along with her own child, by savage tribesmen. Filmed with visceral and haunting images, this mix of "Eraserhead" and "The Bible" is performed without dialogue. 78 min.
70-3398 Was $39.99 *$24.99*

The Sex Of The Stars (1994)
Sensitively told drama from Canada about a 12-year-old girl who longs for the loss of her transsexual father. When her father—now a woman named Marie-Pierre—finally returns, the girl goes against her mother's wishes and tries to get to know her better. 100 min. In French with English subtitles.
70-5081 *$59.99*

Friends (1994)
A stirring drama focusing on three female roommates—a white political activist, a black teacher and an Afrikaner archeologist—in a Johannesburg suburb. When the activist accidentally kills two people with a bomb, the women's friendship is tested. Kerry Fox ("An Angel at My Table") stars. 109 min.
70-5087 Was $59.99 *$29.99*

Secret Games 3 (1994)
In this pulse-pounding installment in the titillating thriller series, the sexually frustrated wife of a physician joins an exclusive club where she and other women can live out their wildest fantasies. When she gets involved with a criminal, her marriage—and her husband's life—are threatened. Rochelle Swanson, Woody Brown and May Karasun star. Unrated version; 87 min.
71-5316 Was $89.99 *$14.99*

Till Death Us Do Part (1991)
A suspenseful and sensual real-life drama, based on the best-seller by Los Angeles D.A. Vincent Bugliosi. Treat Williams stars as a scheming, psychopathic excop who marries women and murders them for their insurance money, and Arliss Howard plays Bugliosi, who becomes obsessed with bringing Williams to justice. 93 min.
72-9005 *$14.99*

Laws Of Gravity (1992)
A raw and powerful slice of Brooklyn street life from rookie writer/director Nick Gomez, chronicling the misadventures of two small-time toughs who get involved in a stolen gun scam and find themselves way over their heads. Acclaimed independent feature stars Adam Trese as a hot-headed hood, Peter Greene as his more even-tempered partner, and Arabella Field as Trese's put-upon girlfriend. 100 min.
72-9014 Was $89.99 *$14.99*

Carolina Skeletons (1992)
A Green Beret (Lou Gossett, Jr.) sets out to clear his brother's name in a double murder committed decades earlier, but comes across a series of disturbing secrets in the small Southern town where they grew up. Bruce Dern and G.D. Spradlin also star in this riveting story. 94 min.
72-9017 Was $89.99 *$14.99*

JEREMY IRONS · DOMINIQUE SWAIN

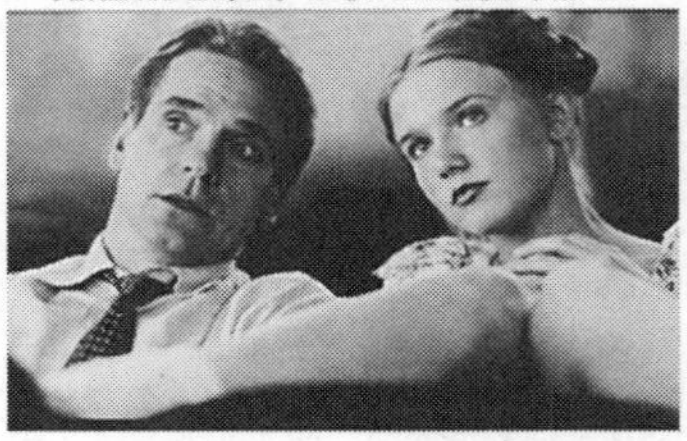

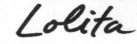

Lolita

Lolita (1997)
The movie that was too controversial for American studios is now on home video. Director Adrian Lyne's ("Fatal Attraction") lush, sardonic rendition of the Nabokov novel is driven by Jeremy Irons' gripping performance as Humbert Humbert, the teacher whose obsession with seductive nymphet Dominique Swain leads to tragedy. Frank Langella, Melanie Griffith also star. 137 min.
68-1936 *$14.99*

Only The Brave (1994)
A startling drama from Australia set in the seedy outskirts of Melbourne, where two teenage girls attempt to overcome the hardships of school and home by smoking dope, setting fires and hanging out at abandoned houses. While desperately searching for affection, one of the girls has a sexual relationship with her female teacher. Elena Mandalis, Dora Kaskanis star. 62 min.
70-5088 Was $29.99 *$19.99*

Brothers In Trouble (1996)
The delicately balanced lives of a group of illegal Pakistani immigrants living in a house in 1960s England are thrown into disarray when one of the men moves his pregnant British girlfriend in with them. Director Udayan Prasad's moving mix of laughter and pathos stars Om Puri, Pavan Malhotra, Angeline Ball. 104 min.
70-5128 Was $79.99 *$24.99*

Common Bonds (1991)
A wheelchair-bound patient and a violent criminal are teamed up in an experimental program where they must work together to fight a psychotic out to destroy them. Dynamic drama stars Brad Dourif, Michael Ironside and Rae Dawn Chong. AKA: "Chaindance." 109 min.
71-5242 *$12.99*

Voyager (1991)
A sexy and haunting film starring Sam Shepard as a globe-trotting engineer who falls in love with a dazzling, young European woman during one of his many sojourns. As their romance grows, he realizes that a past affair may have something to do with his current infatuation. Julie Delpy and Barbara Sukowa also star; directed by Volker Schlöndorff. 113 min.
71-5245 Was $19.99 *$14.99*

Chameleon Street (1992)
The incredible true story of William Douglas Street, who impersonated a surgeon, a lawyer, a reporter and a Yale student, is told in this remarkable, highly acclaimed film. Street's daring tale also served as the basis for the hit play "Six Degrees of Separation." Written and directed by star Wendell B. Harris. 95 min.
71-5254 *$19.99*

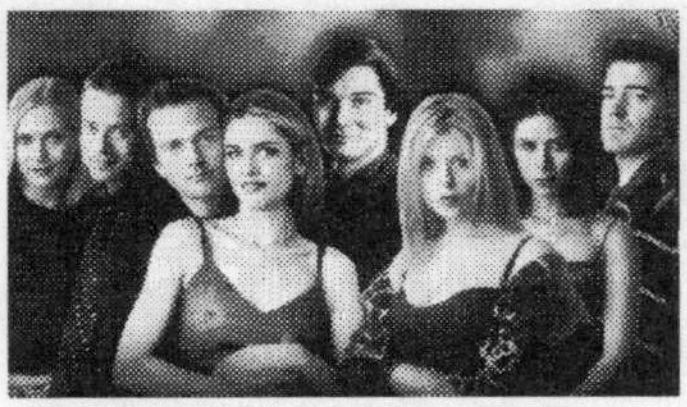

BODY SHOTS

Body Shots (1999)
A scorching and controversial look at sex at the turn of the millennium, focusing on a group of eight twentysomethings who meet and pair off at a trendy club. Their alcohol-fueled search for meaningful contact turns dark when one woman accuses her date of raping her. Tara Reid, Jerry O'Connell, Sean Patrick Flanery, Amanda Peet and Brad Rowe star. Unrated version includes footage not shown in theatres; 106 min.
02-5277 Was $99.99 ❑*$14.99*

The St. Tammany Miracle (1994)
An inspiring story in the tradition of "Hoosiers" and "Rudy" about how a young, unpredictable coach turns a losing girl's basketball team into state champions. Mark-Paul Gosselaar, Soleil Moon Frye and Jamie Luner star. 90 min.
08-1537 *$14.99*

Breaking The Code (1995)
Derek Jacobi gives a stunning performance in this biographical drama based on the life of Alan Turing, a British mathematical wizard who designed the computer that cracked Germany's Enigma Code in World War II, but suffered official and personal persecution because of his admitted homosexuality. 90 min.
08-8541 ❑*$19.99*

Broken Glass (1996)
Based on Arthur Miller's play, this compelling drama is set in 1938 Brooklyn, where a young Jewish housewife is suddenly stricken with inexplicable paralysis in her legs. The doctor trying to help her must look for a cause in unusual places, from her husband's hatred of his own Jewish heritage to the rise of anti-Semitism in Nazi Germany. Mandy Patinkin, Margot Leicester and Henry Goodman star. 100 min.
08-8542 ❑*$19.99*

Reckless (1997)
A handsome young English doctor moves to Manchester to care for his elderly father and becomes romantically involved with a beautiful older woman he meets there, unaware she's the wife of his new boss, in this seductive drama. Robson Green, Francesca Annis, Michael Kitchen star. 312 min. on three tapes.
08-8640 ❑*$39.99*

Reckless, The Sequel (1998)
The forbidden romance between married Anna (Francesca Annis) and her younger lover, Owen (Robson Green), takes on new dimensions when Anna divorces her husband Richard (Michael Kitchen) and moves in with Owen. The couple quickly make plans to marry while Richard is out of the country. Will he return in time to stop the wedding, or does Anna have her own misgivings? 102 min.
08-8766 ❑*$19.99*

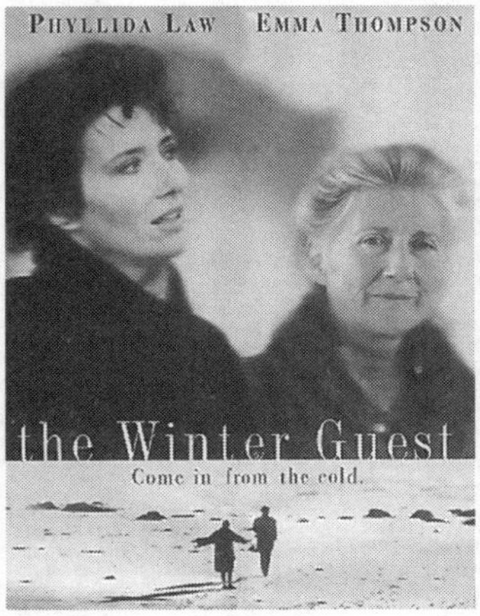

The Winter Guest (1997)
The arrival of an elderly woman to visit her recently widowed daughter in a remote Scottish coast town one bitterly cold day leads to a confrontational and cathartic odyssey for both women. Real-life mother-daughter duo Phyllida Law and Emma Thompson star in this emotional drama, based on the stageplay by director/co-writer Alan Rickman. 110 min.
02-5179 Was $99.99 ❑*$19.99*

Monument Ave. (1998)
Set in Boston's working-class Irish neighborhood of Charlestown, this gritty, Gaelic spin on "Mean Streets" stars Denis Leary as a thirtysomething, leather-jacketed hood who, like his pals, spends his days stealing cars, drinking and doing cocaine. When boss Colm Meaney has Leary's cousin killed for snitching in prison, Leary must reconsider his life, or the lack of it. Famke Janssen, Billy Crudup and Martin Sheen also star. 93 min.
11-2304 Was $99.99 ❑*$14.99*

Tom & Viv (1994)
The stormy relationship between poet T.S. Eliot and British aristocrat Vivien Haigh-Wood is the subject of this brilliantly acted film. Beginning with their meeting as college students in 1914, the film recounts her mysterious medical ailments, his rise to literary acceptance and her eventual stay in a mental hospital. Willem Dafoe, Miranda Richardson and Rosemary Harris star. 115 min.
11-1929 Was $89.99 ❑*$19.99*

Vibrations (1995)
Christina Applegate plays a young woman who becomes the driving force behind a would-be rock musician faced with a devastating handicap in this energized story of love, courage and salvation. James Marshall also stars. 104 min.
11-1930 Was $89.99 ❑*$14.99*

Ethan Frome (1993)
Sumptuous, expertly acted adaptation of Edith Wharton's classic novel stars Liam Neeson as the title character, a sad young man who falls in love with the beautiful cousin of his sickly wife. Joan Allen and Patricia Arquette also star. 99 min.
11-1714 Was $89.99 ❑*$19.99*

Dead Presidents (1995)
The second feature from the Hughes Brothers ("Menace II Society") is an explosive drama focusing on Anthony, an 18-year-old black man from the Bronx who enlists in the Marines in 1968, sees fierce action in Vietnam and returns from battle to face scorn from others. Along with some high school friends, Anthony gets involved in pulling off a dangerous heist. Larenz Tate, Chris Tucker star. 119 min.
11-2009 Was $19.99 ❑*$14.99*

Quiz Show (1994)
Director Robert Redford's acclaimed look at the scandal that rocked America during the Golden Age of Television, the revelation that popular game shows like "Twenty-One" and "The $64,000 Question" were rigged and champions were fed answers for the sake of ratings, features a superlative cast that includes Ralph Fiennes, Rob Morrow, John Turturro, David Paymer and Paul Scofield. 133 min.
11-1874 ❑*$14.99*

Divided By Hate (1996)
Tom Skerritt directed and stars in this intense drama about a farmer trying to save his family and community from a charismatic cult leader who has taken hold of their lives. Dylan Walsh and Andrea Roth also star. 92 min.
07-2507 ❑*$99.99*

Dad Savage (1998)
Engaging, change-of-pace crime drama stars Patrick Stewart as a tulip-growing country-and-western fan who also happens to be involved in criminal activities. When his son's friends discover where Stewart keeps his money, they decide to use the son to help them steal the loot. This taut crime drama from England also features Jake Wood, Joe McFadden and Helen McCrory. 104 min.
02-8980 Was $99.99 ❑*$14.99*

When A Man Loves A Woman (1994)
Powerful drama starring Meg Ryan as a high school guidance counselor whose painstaking struggle against alcoholism threatens her seemingly happy marriage to airline pilot Andy Garcia. While attempting to solve Ryan's drinking addiction, they discover that their marriage wasn't as perfect as they once believed. With Lauren Tom, Ellen Burstyn. 126 min.
11-1816 Was $19.99 ❑*$14.99*

Priest (1995)
Controversial British film focuses on Father Greg, a young priest who arrives at a small parish only to face a series of moral dilemmas that challenge his faith. Questions regarding another priest's sexual liaisons with a housekeeper, a young parishioner abused by her father and his own homosexuality are among the crises with which the cleric struggles. Linus Roache stars. 98 min.
11-1938 Was $89.99 ❑*$19.99*

The Glass Shield
Riveting drama about a young, idealistic black cop who gets a rude awakening about the force when he encounters racism and other forms of hatred in his Los Angeles precinct. He teams with a bitter white policewoman to expose the hatred and corruption around them. Michael Boatman, Lori Petty and Ice Cube star in this forceful film from Charles Burnett ("To Sleep with Anger"). 110 min.
11-1944 Was $19.99 ❑*$14.99*

Picture Bride (1995)
Set in Hawaii in the early 1900s, this compassionate drama tells of a Japanese woman who moves there to marry a sugarcane worker she knows only through letters and a photo, only to find a much older man than she expected, along with horrible living conditions. The woman is then forced into making a difficult decision about her future. Youki Kudoh, Akira Takayama, Tomlyn Tomita and Toshiro Mifune star. 95 min.
11-1951 Was $89.99 ❑*$19.99*

Simon Birch (1998)
In a small New England town in the 1960s, Simon Birch is an abnormally small but wise-beyond-his-years lad, convinced that God has a special purpose in life awaiting him. His friendship with another "outcast," a fatherless boy named Joe, and how the relationship affects both their lives, is movingly depicted in this drama based on John Irving's novel "A Prayer for Owen Meaney." Ian Michael Smith plays the title role; with Joseph Mazzello, Ashley Judd, Oliver Platt, and Jim Carrey as the adult Joe. 114 min.
11-2302 Was $99.99 ❑*$19.99*

Velvet Goldmine (1998)
The glittery, sex- and drug-filled world of England's early '70s glam rock scene is the setting for director Todd Haynes' trippy tribute to the era of Ziggy (Stardust) and Iggy (Pop). Christian Bale plays a reporter in 1984 England investigating the whereabouts of glam superstar Brian Slade (Jonathan Rhys Meyers), who vanished years earlier after a fake assassination attempt. Ewan McGregor co-stars as Slade's colleague, Kurt Wild; with Toni Collette, Eddie Izzard. 119 min.
11-2317 Was $99.99 ❑*$19.99*

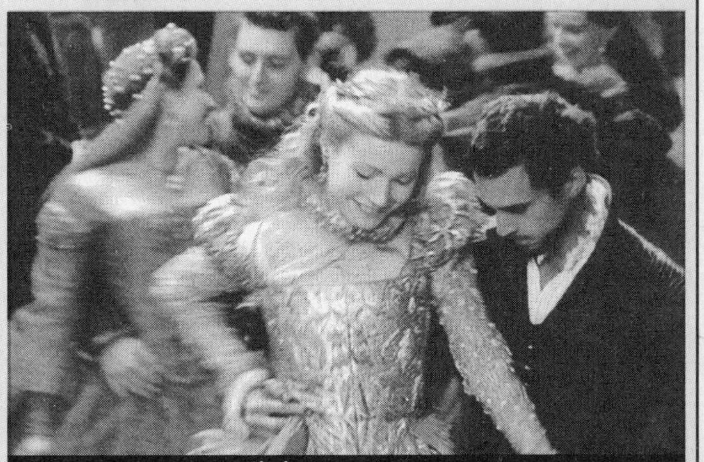

Shakespeare In Love

Gwyneth Paltrow

Flesh And Bone (1993)
Moody, atmospheric drama starring Dennis Quaid as a Texas vending machine worker haunted by memories of a murder committed years earlier by his scam artist father (James Caan). After falling for a married, alcoholic dancer (Meg Ryan), Quaid's brief happiness is interrupted when Caan suddenly steps back into his life. Gwyneth Paltrow also stars. 127 min.
06-2199 Was $89.99 ❑*$19.99*

Moonlight And Valentino (1995)
Following the death of her husband, college professor Elizabeth Perkins finds comfort, friendship and a renewed interest in life from the company of younger sister Gwyneth Paltrow, ex-stepmother Kathleen Turner and neighbor Whoopi Goldberg. Winning "female bonding" seriocomedy also stars rocker Jon Bon Jovi as a sexy housepainter. 104 min.
02-8370 Was $19.99 ❑*$14.99*

Hard Eight (1996)
Intense drama about a veteran gambler who takes a down-on-his-luck young man under his wing and shows him how to gamble in Las Vegas. The two new friends take their act to Reno, where the young man falls for a beautiful hooker who eventually leads him into trouble. Philip Baker Hall, John C. Reilly, Gwyneth Paltrow and Samuel L. Jackson star; directed by Paul Thomas Anderson ("Boogie Nights"). 100 min.
02-3098 Was $99.99 ❑*$19.99*

The Pallbearer (1996)
"Friends" co-star David Schwimmer graduates to features in this comedy, playing an unemployed young New Yorker who gets a call to deliver a eulogy at the funeral of a high school chum he can't remember. After the funeral, Schwimmer pursues a former classmate he once had a crush on—much to the dismay of the deceased's mother. Gwyneth Paltrow, Barbara Hershey also star. 98 min.
11-2058 Was $19.99 ❑*$14.99*

Emma (1996)
The course of true love runs hilariously askew once would-be Cupid Emma Woodhouse (Gwyneth Paltrow) gets her hands on it in director/scripter Douglas McGrath's adaptation of the Jane Austen novel. While Emma tries to fix up others, will her own true love slip through her fingers? Fine cast also features Toni Collette, Ewan McGregor, Greta Scacchi. 121 min.
11-2102 Was $99.99 ❑*$19.99*

Great Expectations (1998)
The classic story of love and devotion from Charles Dickens is given a lavish modern-dress revamping by director Alfonso Cuaron ("A Little Princess"). Ethan Hawke is a struggling young New York painter whose childhood sweetheart and artistic inspiration, Gwyneth Paltrow, suddenly re-enters his life—only to leave him again. Robert De Niro, Anne Bancroft and Hank Azaria also star. 122 min.
04-3676 Was $99.99 ❑*$14.99*

Sliding Doors (1998)
How much difference can a seemingly trivial decision and a few minutes make in a person's life? That question is the basis for this romantic tale featuring Gwyneth Paltrow as a Londoner taking the subway home after being fired from her public relations job. As the film's parallel scenarios show, whether Paltrow catches or misses a train determines her relationship with two-timing boyfriend John Lynch...and a possible new romance with stranger John Hannah. Jeanne Tripplehorn also stars. 99 min.
06-2765 Was $99.99 ❑*$14.99*

Shakespeare In Love (1998)
Witty, romantic, sexy—and fictional—account of the Bard's early days stars Joseph Fiennes as the young playwright, struggling with a work he's planning to call "Romeo and Ethel, The Pirate's Daughter." Inspiration and love come in the form of nobleman's daughter Gwyneth Paltrow, who, unknown to Shakespeare, is also appearing in male drag in his upcoming production. Geoffrey Rush and Dame Judi Dench also star in this lively farce, which won seven Oscars, including Best Picture, Best Actress and Best Supporting Actress. 123 min.
11-2335 Was $19.99 ❑*$14.99*

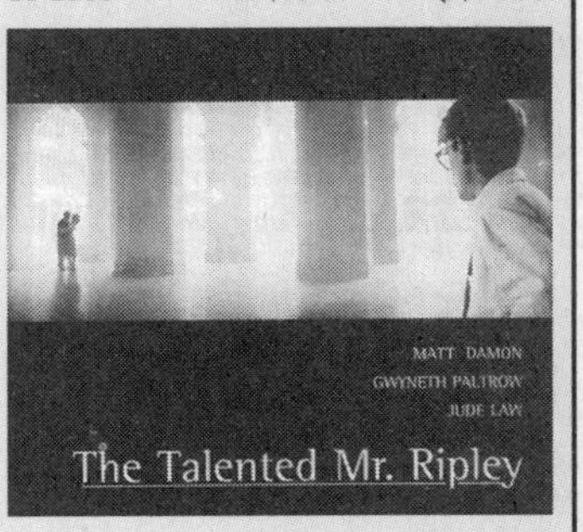

The Talented Mr. Ripley (1999)
Lush, involving thriller based on Patricia Highsmith's novel stars Matt Damon as Tom Ripley, a young New Yorker hired by a tycoon to persuade wastrel son Jude Law to leave his Italian villa and return to America. After befriending Law and girlfriend Gwyneth Paltrow, Damon's devious nature—and his knack for forgery and imitation—come into play. With Cate Blanchett, Philip Seymour Hoffman; directed by Anthony Minghella ("The English Patient"). 139 min.
06-2984 Was $99.99 ❑*$14.99*

Please see our index for these other Gwyneth Paltrow titles: *Hook • Jefferson In Paris • Malice • Mrs. Parker And The Vicious Circle • A Perfect Murder • Seven*

Jane Campion

Two Friends (1986)
The directorial debut from Australia's Jane Campion is a heartfelt look at two teenage girls that uses a series of sequences, in reverse chronological order, to trace how these close friends drifted apart and, ultimately, what brought them together. Emma Coles, Kris Bidenko, Kris McQuade star. 76 min.
53-9859 Letterboxed *$89.99*

AN ANGEL AT MY TABLE

Angel At My Table (1991)
Originally made as an Australian TV mini-series, director Jane Campion's award-winning drama vividly depicts the troubled life of New Zealand writer Janet Frame, from her impoverished family life and the drowning death of her sisters to her school years and stays in a mental hospital. Kerry Fox stars as Frame. 157 min.
02-2164 *$19.99*

The Piano (1993)
Holly Hunter stars as a non-speaking mail-order bride who travels with her 6-year-old daughter (Anna Paquin) from 1850s Scotland to the New Zealand wilderness to join her landowner (Sam Neill). When her prized possession, a piano, is sold to a coarse settler (Harvey Keitel), she strikes a sexual deal with Keitel to get it back. Jane Campion's compelling, erotic drama won Academy Awards for Best Actress, Supporting Actress and Screenplay. 121 min.
27-6859 Was $19.99 □*$14.99*

The Piano (Letterboxed Version)
Also available in a theatrical, widescreen format.
27-7060 □*$14.99*

The Portrait Of A Lady (1996)
Henry James' classic novel is stirringly brought to the screen by director Jane Campion ("The Piano"), with Nicole Kidman as an American woman of independent means living in Europe in the late 1800s. Refusing to wed until she finds a suitable mate, Kidman becomes a pawn in scheming friend Barbara Hershey's games and marries duplicitous artist John Malkovich. With Mary-Louise Parker, Martin Donovan, Shelley Winters, John Gielgud. 144 min.
02-8650 Was $19.99 *$14.99*

The Portrait Of A Lady (Letterboxed Version)
Also available in a theatrical, widescreen format.
02-8651 Was $19.99 *$14.99*

Holy Smoke! (1999)
On vacation in India, Australian Kate Winslet winds up joining the followers of a Hindu guru. Her panic-stricken family tricks Winslet into returning home so that cult expert Harvey Keitel can deprogram her, but their battle of wills takes a bizarre sexual turn (and believe us, Keitel wandering the desert in a dress and lipstick is rather bizarre!) in this quirky, satirical comedy/drama from director Jane Campion ("The Piano"). With Sophie Lee, Pam Grier.
11-2449 □*$99.99*

Eden Valley (1994)
From England's acclaimed Amber Production Team comes this drama about a troubled inner-city youth given a second chance by his father, who abandoned him 10 years earlier. The boy is taken to his father's horse farm, where he develops respect for him and realizes his own potential. The cast, which mixes amateurs and professionals, includes Brian Hogg and Mike Elliott. 95 min.
53-6111 Was $59.99 *$24.99*

Dash And Lilly (1999)
Sam Shepard and Judy Davis star as mystery writer Dashiell Hammett and playwright Lillian Hellman in this wonderful biographical drama that follows their tempestuous romance from the glitter of 1930s Hollywood to the turmoil of the McCarthy era. With Bebe Neuwirth, David Paymer; directed by Kathy Bates. 100 min.
53-6464 □*$19.99*

Dog Years (1998)
Innovative independent effort about Wally, a rebellious kid who is attacked by a group of drug dealers and has his dog dognapped. When Wally fights back, he is thrown in prison, but he must find a way out in order to clear his name and find his pooch. R. Michael Caincross stars.
46-8032 Was $59.99 *$14.99*

The Silent Touch (1992)
Poland's Krzystof Zanussi directed this gripping drama featuring Max Von Sydow as a retired classical composer and Holocaust survivor who is coaxed back into the world of music by a young musicologist. In order to help him, the musicologist enlists the aid of an attractive young secretary, which does not sit well with Von Sydow's long-suffering wife. With Lothaire Bluteau, Sarah Miles. 92 min.
50-5719 *$99.99*

Deacon Brodie (1996)
In Edinburgh, Scotland, in 1788, cabinet maker and town official William Deacon Brodie is accused of stealing money from the city's Customs and Exise offices. During the trial, Brodie's secret life is revealed and he's sentenced to die on the gallows he designed. Billy Connolly ("Mrs. Brown"), Catherine McCormack and Patrick Malahide star. 90 min.
53-6136 *$24.99*

Millions (1991)
Intense drama of passion and betrayal in the ranks of the filthy rich, as a scheming young socialite begins affairs with his sister-in-law and cousin in order to gain control of the family fortune. Billy Zane, Lauren Hutton, Alexandra Paul and supermodel Carol Alt star. 118 min.
46-5521 Was $19.99 *$14.99*

Learning Curve (1991)
This true, inspirational story traces Don Castro's rise to prominence as a flat track motorcycle rider. Young Don has a learning disability, and his father purchases a motorcycle for him as an incentive for doing well in school. Later, when Don becomes a champion rider, his father serves as his mechanic. Roger Guiterrez and Enrique Esparza star. 90 min.
50-5168 Was $29.99 *$14.99*

Shadowlands (1985)
Acclaimed BBC production about the life of Christian author and fantasist C.S. Lewis and the transformation of his life through the love and death of his American poetess wife, Joy Gresham. Claire Bloom and Joss Ackland star. 73 min.
50-2439 *$19.99*

Shadowlands (1993)
A poignant, superbly acted account of the romance of British writer-theologian C.S. Lewis (Anthony Hopkins), an academic who keeps his feelings hidden, and Joy Gresham (Debra Winger), a feisty American divorcée who awakens Lewis to his true emotions. Richard Attenborough directs this moving film that evokes laughter and tears. 133 min.
44-1964 Was $19.99 □*$14.99*

The Ride (1997)
In this inspirational drama, Smokey Banks, a world champion bull rider, is assigned to work at a ranch for orphaned boys after his drinking problems lead to stealing a truck. Smokey befriends a 14-year-old named Danny who helps him see the error of his ways. Michael Biehn, Brock Pierce and Jennifer O'Neill star. 98 min.
50-8261 *$24.99*

Finding Love...Again (1997)
A down-on-his-luck man who lives on the streets tries to overcome his tragic past by finding a reason to live again after a terrible accident dramatically alters his life. Jeff Nicholson and Juniper Purinton star. 82 min.
50-8470 *$19.99*

Horton Foote's Alone (1997)
From award-winning writer Horton Foote comes this moving drama starring Hume Cronyn as a recent widower who is offered a nice sum by a Texas oil man for the mineral rights to his land. The proposal ignites debate within his family over the prospect of easy money. James Earl Jones, Shelley Duvall, Frederic Forrest, Piper Laurie and Ed Begley, Jr. also star. 107 min.
53-6302 Was $89.99 *$19.99*

Berkeley Square (1998)
Follow the compelling lives of three young women working as nannies in London's Berkeley Square around 1900. The women include Matty, a streetwise East Ender who climbs up the domestic ladder of society families; Hannah, who has fled to the city with child after a disastrous affair; and naive farm girl Lydia. Clare Wilkie, Victoria Smurfit and Tabitha Wady star. 510 min.
53-6344 *$89.99*

Carla's Song (1996)
Insightful and emotional Ken Loach film that blends romance with social drama. Robert Carlyle ("The Full Monty") plays a Glasgow bus driver taken with an impoverished Nicaraguan woman on his route. After helping her find a place to live and caring for her, Carlyle agrees to accompany the woman back to her war-ravaged homeland to search for her missing boyfriend, presumed killed by the Contras. Oyanka Cabezas and Scott Glenn also star. 127 min. In English and Spanish with English subtitles.
53-6364 Was $89.99 *$19.99*

Lily Was Here (1991)
A pregnant 17-year-old leaves her parents' home to fend for herself and soon drifts into the world of prostitution and crime. She pulls off a series of petty thefts which escalates into a crime spree and must eventually choose between motherhood and freedom. Marion Van Thijn, Thom Hoffman and Monique van de Ven star. 110 min.
45-5529 *$79.99*

Illicit Behavior (1992)
Action and eroticism mix in this story of a troubled, brutal cop who finds himself the subject of an internal affairs investigation. Soon, he takes his anger out on his gorgeous wife, and when she seeks revenge, a game of deadly seduction ensues. Jack Scalia, Joan Severance, Robert Davi and Jenilee Harrison star. Uncut, unrated version; 104 min.
46-5532 *$14.99*

Forever (1992)
A director of music videos gets involved in a very unusual love triangle when he moves into a haunted house and is pursued by both his agent and a gorgeous ghost. Offbeat supernatural drama stars Keith Coogan, Sean Young, Sally Kirkland, Diane Ladd and Steve Railsback. 90 min.
46-5580 *$89.99*

Ninth Street (1999)
This sensitive drama is set in Junction City, Kansas, in 1968, where inhabitants talk about the old days, when their neighborhood was filled with popular jazz clubs that have been replaced by seedy strip joints frequented by GIs stationed nearby. Among the locals are taxi dispatcher Isaac Hayes, bar owner Queen Bey, WWII vet and wino Don Washington and minister Martin Sheen. 95 min.
50-8305 Was $59.99 *$14.99*

Resolution (1999)
After a New Year's celebration, a group of friends finds themselves in trouble when an unwelcome stranger holds them at gunpoint. One of them is soon dead while the others reveal some startling secrets. It's up to one person, who has been hiding undetected by the gunman, to save his pals. Rob Steinberg, Stephen Polk star.
50-8421 *$39.99*

Bitter Harvest (1993)
Sensual drama set in a small Southwestern town where a farmworker finds himself in the middle of a scorching sex triangle with an aspiring actress and a promiscuous realtor. Their affair turns dangerous when the women become involved in a bank robbery. Patsy Kensit, Stephen Baldwin, Jennifer Rubin and M. Emmet Walsh star. 98 min.
46-5576 *$14.99*

Eminent Domain (1990)
Intense drama stars Donald Sutherland as a member of the Polish Politburo who finds his life of privilege turned upside-down when the Communist government steps in and takes everything away from him and his family. Anne Archer, Paul Freeman also star. 102 min.
45-5507 Was $89.99 □*$19.99*

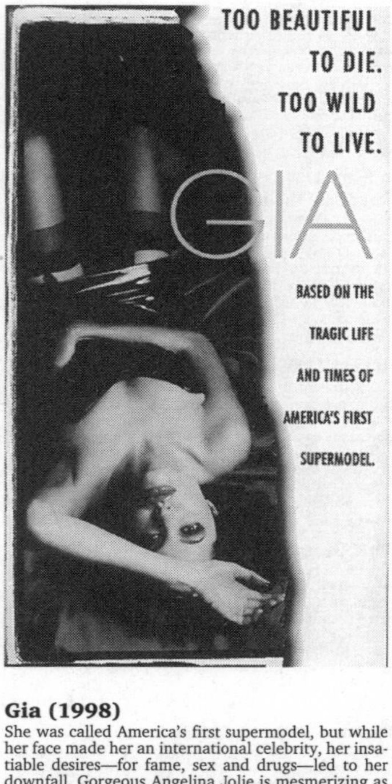

Gia (1998)
She was called America's first supermodel, but while her face made her an international celebrity, her insatiable desires—for fame, sex and drugs—led to her downfall. Gorgeous Angelina Jolie is mesmerizing as Philadelphia-born cover girl Gia Carangi, whose meteoric career led to her death in 1986 at the age of 26, in this compelling and provocative biodrama. Faye Dunaway, Elizabeth Mitchell and Mercedes Ruehl also star. Unrated video version includes footage not shown on TV. 126 min.
44-2165 Was $99.99 □*$19.99*

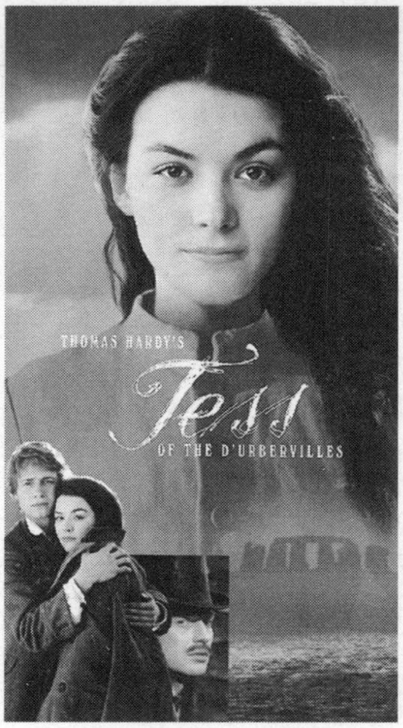

Tess Of The D'Urbervilles (1998)
One of literature's most beloved and unforgettable heroines comes to life in this lavish adaptation of Thomas Hardy's classic novel. Justine Waddell stars as Tess Durbyfield, a woman on a search for true love whose refusal to remain a victim leads her to tragic consequences. 180 min.
53-6203 *$29.99*

Locked In Silence (1999)
This bizarre true story tells of a 9-year-old boy named Steven who conspires with his older brother to keep a disturbing secret to himself. Steven adopts a new mute personality, but when the time comes for the secret to finally be revealed, he has lost the ability to speak. Bonnie Bedelia, Bruce Davison and Dan Hedaya star. 94 min.
67-9024 □*$14.99*

In A Class Of His Own (1999)
This compelling true story features Lou Diamond Phillips as a school custodian and friend to the students who must pass his high school equivalency exam in order to hold onto the job he's worked at for 10 years. Joan Chen and Cara Buono also star. 94 min.
67-9025 □*$14.99*

Priceless Beauty (1990)
Real-life husband and wife Christopher Lambert and Diane Lane star in this erotic romance laced with fantasy. Lambert is a rock star depressed over the accidental death of his brother. One day he finds an antidote to his sad state when a beautiful genie washes up on a nearby shore. 94 min.
63-1404 Was $89.99 *$14.99*

Denial (1991)
Robin Wright, Jason Patric and Rae Dawn Chong star in this tale of three friends whose intertwined lives lead to desire, anger and obsession. A beautiful, free-spirited woman develops a dangerous attraction to a tempestuous young artist. 103 min.
63-1459 Was $89.99 □*$14.99*

Cadence (1991)
Charlie Sheen plays a lonely soldier who goes into a drunken rage after hearing that his father has died and winds up in a stockade with five black men. Taunted by a tyrannical sergeant (Martin Sheen), the men band together to confront racism and show their bravery against the officer. Larry Fishburne, F. Murray Abraham also star. 97 min.
63-1466 □*$12.99*

Brides Of Christ (1991)
Acclaimed three-part British drama set during the turbulent 1960s and focusing on the members of a Catholic convent and the local community, and detailing the changes in the lives and their faith during this unpredictable era. The cast includes Brenda Fricker, Sandy Gore, Lisa Hensley, Naomi Watts, Philip Quast; look for a young Russell Crowe. 300 min.
53-8027 *$59.99*

Hedd Wyn (1993)
Nominated for a Best Foreign Film Academy Award, this acclaimed drama from Wales tells the tragic true story of the talented young poet who met an untimely death on the battlefield of World War I. Huw Garmon stars in the title role; with Sue Roderick, Judith Humphreys. 123 min. In Welsh with English subtitles.
53-8561 Was $89.99 *$19.99*

Two Deaths (1996)
Nicolas Roeg directed this psychological drama set in Romania in 1989, where, amidst a falling Communist regime, a wealthy physician hosts a reunion party at a mansion attended by only three guests. A photo of the doctor's beautiful housekeeper ignites the curiosity of his guests, who soon play a part in the revelations that unfold. Michael Gambon, Sonia Braga star. 102 min.
53-8619 Was $89.99 *$19.99*

A World Of Great Video Entertainment!

from KULTUR & WHITE STAR

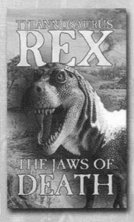

Mark Twain Tonight! (1967)
Hal Holbrook won an Emmy Award for this broadcast of his acclaimed one-man stageshow based on the life and works of 19th-century author, humorist and iconoclast Samuel L. Clemens. 90 min.

| 22-1655 | VHS | $24.99 |
| D1-7020 | DVD | $29.99 |

**So You Want
To Be An Actor?**
For everyone who's dreamed of a Broadway career, this program offers practical advice on everything from casting calls and getting an agent to financial survival in New York. Jerry Stiller and Anne Meara host. 75 min.

| 22-1699 | VHS | $19.99 |

**Tyrannosaurus Rex:
The Jaws Of Death**
The life and behavior of prehistory's most famous predator are examined in a computer-animated documentary. Thrill to this exciting adventure that offers a look at how T-Rex may have stalked and attacked and raised its young. 50 min.

| 22-1835 | VHS | $19.99 |

WHITE ★ STAR

Great Moments In Opera
This collection of rare performance clips from "The Ed Sullivan Show" features such notables as Maria Callas, Marilyn Horne, Robert Merrill, Lily Pons, Leontyne Price, Beverly Sills, and Joan Sutherland. 95 min.

| 22-3190 | VHS | $29.99 |
| D1-9856 | DVD | $29.99 |

© Kultur International Films Ltd., Inc

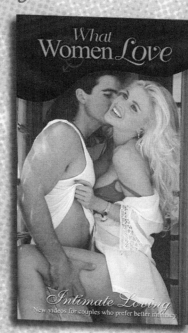

Memphis (1992)
A dose of Southern hospitality isn't exactly what Cybill Shepherd gets when she arrives in Memphis with her boyfriend and his pal. They want to pull off a simple kidnapping, but plans go awry. Now they're in deep trouble...and there's no way out! John Laughlin, Moses Gunn co-star. 92 min.
18-7375 □*$89.99*

Jane Eyre (1934)
The first sound filming of the timeless Charlotte Brontë romance. Virginia Bruce essays the title role, with Colin Clive as the mysterious Rochester, whose stern facade hides a dark secret that Jane must uncover. With Beryl Mercer, Jameson Thomas. 62 min.
17-3089 *$19.99*

Jane Eyre (1971)
An acclaimed turn by George C. Scott as Mr. Rochester and moody English scenery highlight this made-for-TV rendition of the original Gothic romance tale that also stars Susannah York as Charlotte Brontë's hard-life heroine. With Ian Bannen, Jack Hawkins, Jean Marsh. 110 min.
10-1676 *$14.99*

Jane Eyre (1983)
Vivid realization of the Brontë classic stars Zelah Clarke as the determined governess whose willfulness brings her under the eye of the brooding, fascinating Mr. Rochester. Timothy Dalton co-stars in this exceptional presentation. 239 min.
04-2068 Was $29.99 □*$24.99*

Jane Eyre (1997)
Charlotte Brontë's put-upon orphan girl who grows up to become governess of Thornfield Hall and finds herself falling under the spell of her employer, the mysterious Rochester, is wonderfully played by Samantha Morton in this stunning production. Ciaran Hinds co-stars as Rochester. 108 min.
53-9816 Was $19.99 □*$14.99*

Wuthering Heights (1970)
One of the all-time great love stories, Emily Brontë's timeless story features Timothy Dalton and Anna Calder-Marshall as tragic lovers Catherine and Heathcliff. Superb drama highlighted by lush atmosphere and fine performances co-stars Harry Andrews and Hugh Griffith. 105 min.
44-1417 Was $79.99 *$19.99*

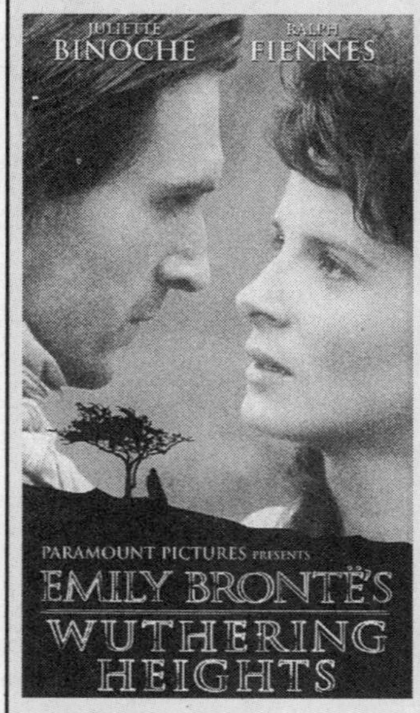

Emily Brontë's Wuthering Heights (1992)
The haunting Gothic tale of love, loss and redemption on the windswept English moors becomes a stirring drama featuring Ralph Fiennes as the brooding Heathcliff and Juliette Binoche as both the love of his life, Catherine, and her daughter. Janet McTeer, Simon Shepherd, Sophie Ward also star. 107 min.
06-2638 Was $99.99 □*$14.99*

Wuthering Heights (1998)
From British TV and "Masterpiece Theatre" comes this stirring adaptation of Emily Brontë's classic novel. Robert Cavanah plays the mysterious, tormented Heathcliff, and Orla Brady is the wild, doomed Cathy. With Ian Shaw, Crispin Bonham-Carter. 112 min.
08-8695 □*$19.99*

The Tenant Of Wildfell Hall (1996)
Anne Brontë's second novel, whose depiction of an alcoholic's degeneration shocked Victorian England, receives a lush translation starring Tara Fitzgerald as Helen Graham, the beleaguered wife who receives redemption through the triumph of love. Co-stars Rupert Graves, Toby Stephens. 117 min.
04-3541 *$29.99*

Civil War Diary (1990)
A courageous young man braves harsh winters and difficult farmwork while searching for the murderer of his sister during the Civil War. Based on the award-winning novel "Across Five Aprils." Todd Duffey, Miriam Byrd-Nethery, Holis McCarthy star. 82 min.
15-5197 Was $79.99 *$19.99*

Showgirls (1995)
One of the most controversial studio films ever made, with "Basic Instinct" director Paul Verhoeven and scripter Joe Eszterhas re-teaming for a graphic and unflinching drama set amid the world of Las Vegas dancers. A young woman arrives on the Strip dreaming of stardom, but first must work at a sleazy strip joint as a "pole dancer" while befriending a top showgirl and seducing her hotel bigshot boyfriend. Elizabeth Berkley, Gina Gershon, Kyle MacLachlan star. Uncut, NC-17 version; 131 min.
12-3022 Was $19.99 □*$14.99*

Hurricane Streets (1997)
Affecting, award-winning drama focuses on the life of Marcus, a young petty thief being raised by his grandmother while his mother serves a prison sentence. Marcus terrorizes pedestrians while riding his bike with his tough friends through New York, but finally gets an opportunity to change his life when he meets Melena, a Latino girl. Brandan Sexton III, Isidira Vega, Jared Harris star. 86 min.
12-3264 □*$99.99*

Rogue Trader (1999)
The collapse of London's famed Barings Bank is the focus of this intense drama starring Ewan McGregor as Nick Leeson, the son of a plasterer, who becomes a merchant banking hot-shot in Singapore. When Leeson begins playing with the company's books and illegally moving funds around, his actions lead to his—and his company's—undoing. With Anna Friel, Nigel Lindsey. 97 min.
11-2363 Was $19.99 □*$14.99*

Of Mice And Men (1992)
A powerful, majestically acted version of John Steinbeck's classic about the relationship between the strong but feeble-minded Lennie (John Malkovich) and his protector, George (Gary Sinise), migrant laborers who toil in the California fields during the Depression. Ray Walston, Sherilyn Fenn and Casey Siemaszko also star; Sinise also directed from Horton Foote's script. 110 min.
12-2627 Was $89.99 □*$19.99*

The Lover (1992)
This scorching, stylishly filmed story is set in Saigon in the 1920s and centers on a French schoolgirl who has an intense sexual affair with a wealthy, older Chinese man. Hailed as an erotic masterpiece, Jean-Jacques Annaud's adaptation of Marguerite Duras' novel is presented in the uncut, unrated version that was a sensation in Europe. Jane March and Tony Leung star. Unrated version; 115 min.
12-2640 Was $19.99 □*$14.99*

Convict Cowboy (1995)
Jon Voight plays Ry Weston, a former rodeo champ serving a life sentence for murder, who befriends a younger inmate serving a two-year stretch for public drunkenness. The two become friends and attempt to get Weston prepared for the big prison rodeo. This action-packed drama also stars Kyle Chandler, Marcia Gay Harden. 98 min.
12-3012 Was $89.99 □*$19.99*

Tea With Mussolini (1999)
This poignant autobiographical tale from director Franco Zeffirelli is set in Florence, Italy, and covers the years 1935 to 1945 in the life of a boy named Luca who is sent by his father to live with Englishwoman Joan Plowright. As Mussolini rises to power, Luca encounters Plowright's eccentric acquaintances Maggie Smith, Cher and Lily Tomlin. With Charlie Lucas. 117 min.
12-3286 Was $99.99 □*$14.99*

That Championship Season (1999)
This powerful version of Jason Miller's award-winning play details the dramatic events that occur at the 20th reunion of a Scranton, Pa., high school basketball team that won the state championship. Paul Sorvino (who also directed) plays the team's coach while his former players include alcoholic Gary Sinise, mayor Tony Shalhoub and sleazy businessman Vincent D'Onofrio. 126 min.
12-3287 Was $49.99 □*$14.99*

Jason's Lyric (1994)
Gritty and sensual drama of two brothers from a tough Houston neighborhood. Both haunted by their father's death, the pair are heading in very different directions: Jason's (Allen Payne) relationship with waitress Lyric (Jada Pinkett) inspires him to improve his life, while Josh (Bokeem Woodbine) falls into drugs and theft. With Forest Whitaker, Treach.
12-3289 *$14.99*

Molly (1999)
Elisabeth Shue is Molly, a 28-year-old autistic woman left in the care of older brother Aaron Eckhart. Unable to cope with her needs, Eckhart talks Shue into signing up for an experimental medical procedure that could cure her, but is Molly's chance for a "normal" life worth the risk...and the loss of her self? Jill Hennessy, Thomas Jane co-star in this moving drama. 87 min.
12-3301 □*$99.99*

Kiss The Sky (1998)
In this smart, sexy, sophisticated drama, two old buddies (William Petersen, Gary Cole) have become bitter about their boring, workaday lives. They decide to dump wives, families and responsibilities to live in an island paradise. But mutual love for a beautiful woman tears the friends apart. Sheryl Lee, Patricia Charbonneau and Terence Stamp also star. 105 min.
12-3308 Was $99.99 *$14.99*

Miss Julie (1999)
The interplay between sex, money and power keeps August Strindberg's drama as relevant as ever. This latest version, by "Leaving Las Vegas" director Mike Figgis, pulls no punches in its adaptation of the battle of wills between beautiful, aristocratic Miss Julie (Saffron Burrows) and footservant Jean (Peter Mullan). 101 min.
12-3309 *$99.99*

Runaway Father (1991)
When the father of three young children leaves his family and then mysteriously dies, his wife finds herself with nowhere to turn. When she discovers her husband has staged his own death, she hires an investigator to look into his disappearance. Jack Scalia, Donna Mills and Chris Mulkey star in this gripping story. 94 min.
14-3410 □*$89.99*

Checkered Flag (1990)
A top-notch, action-filled drama follows two drivers on a racing team whose love of the same woman threatens their success. William Campbell ("The Rocketeer"), Amanda Wyss, Pernell Roberts, Robert Forster and Carrie Hamilton star. 95 min.
15-5206 *$79.99*

Orpheus Descending (1990)
The triumphant staging of Tennessee Williams' classic drama of unbridled lust, Southern style, is brought to video in all its steamy glory. Vanessa Redgrave is the woman who lives an unfulfilled life in a Southern town. Her marriage to a tyrant in failing health stifles her...until a young stranger ignites her with passion. Kevin Anderson and Brad Sullivan also star. 117 min.
18-7251 □*$79.99*

Heat Wave (1990)
Powerful, fact-based drama set against the backdrop of the Watts riots of 1965. Blair Underwood plays aspiring journalist Bob Richardson, who works as a messenger for the Los Angeles Times. After tensions flair in Watts, violence breaks out and Richardson gets a shot at the big time, reporting on the events. Cicely Tyson, James Earl Jones and Sally Kirkland also star. 94 min.
18-7254 Was $79.99 □*$14.99*

Forgotten Prisoners (1990)
A harrowing look at actual stories of imprisonment and torture of political prisoners, taken from the case files of Amnesty International. Set in Turkey, the drama follows the efforts of a teacher and a human rights lawyer to obtain the release of several captives. Ron Silver, Hector Elizondo, Roger Daltrey star. 92 min.
18-7279 □*$79.99*

Ivory Hunters (1990)
Sent to Africa to catch a murderer, a man becomes involved with a beautiful biologist and her struggle to save elephant herds from poachers. John Lithgow, Isabella Rossellini and James Earl Jones star in this thrilling drama laced with romance and adventure. 94 min.
18-7284 □*$79.99*

Which Way Home (1991)
Thrilling drama stars Cybill Shepherd as a Red Cross nurse trying to save a group of refugee Cambodian children from the terror of the Khmer Rouge revolution. Her only ally is Australian smuggler John Waters, and the unlikely allies undertake a dangerous boat ride. 141 min.
18-7285 □*$79.99*

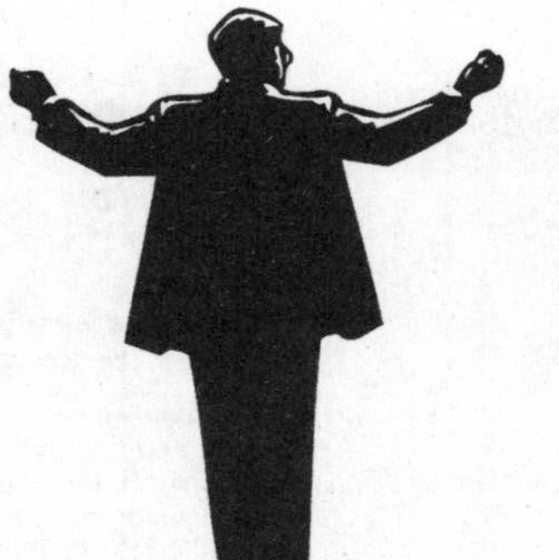

Mr. Holland's Opus (1995)
Oscar-nominated Richard Dreyfuss is Glenn Holland, a man whose ambitions to compose a symphony are superseded by financial obligations that lead him to a job as a high school music teacher. He stays on the job for three decades, facing budget crises, at times unappreciative students and a strained relationship with his wife and hearing-impaired son. With Gleanne Headly, Jay Thomas, Jean Louisa Kelly. 143 min.
11-2029 Was $19.99 □*$14.99*

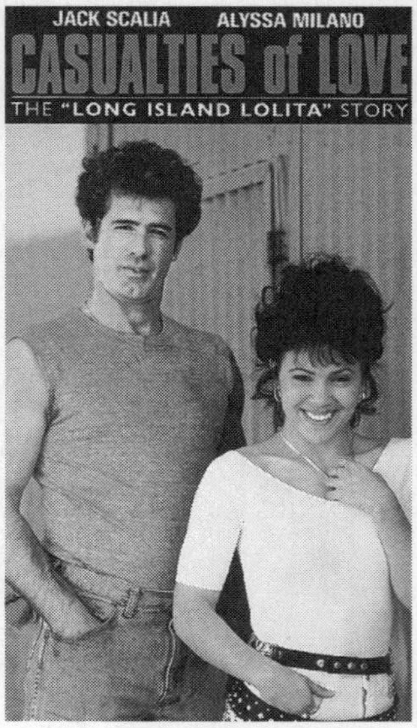

Casualties Of Love: The "Long Island Lolita" Story (1993)
The crime made headlines across America, and now Joey and Mary Jo Buttafuoco tell their side of the story. See how teenager Amy Fisher's obsession with Joey drove her to try to kill his wife. Alyssa Milano, Jack Scalia and Leo Rossi star in this true-life drama. 96 min.
02-2406 Was $59.99 *$14.99*

The Amy Fisher Story (1993)
The sensational "Long Island Lolita" story is recounted in this steamy drama starring Drew Barrymore as the teenager who shot the wife of a middle-aged man with whom she allegedly had a love affair. Anthony John Denison and Harley Jane Kozak also star in this special video version featuring scenes too hot for TV. 96 min.
19-9001 Was $29.99 *$14.99*

Body Moves (1991)
Forget "Lambada," "Flashdance" and "Dirty Dancing." Here's the latest sexy dance sensation, as rival gangs battle for love, turf and dance contests in this scorching story that has all the right moves. Diane Granger and Kirk Rivera star. 98 min.
46-5512 *$79.99*

Never Forget (1991)
Powerful true story starring Leonard Nimoy as Mel Mermelstein, a survivor of Auschwitz who accepts a challenge from a historical revisionist group to prove in court that the horrors of the Holocaust actually took place...a challenge which will fulfill a promise he made to his dying father to be "a witness to the world." Co-stars Dabney Coleman and Blythe Danner. 94 min.
18-7335 □*$89.99*

Final Verdict (1991)
Gripping drama stars Treat Williams as a lawyer faced with a tremendous conflict when he defends two men accused of murder. Should he remain honest like his minister father (Glenn Ford) taught him, or "bend" justice to help his clients? 93 min.
18-7355 □*$89.99*

Miracle In The Wilderness (1991)
Spirited adventure stars Kris Kristofferson as a former gunslinger who is taken hostage by an Indian tribe along with his wife and child. The Indian chief seeks revenge for the death of his son, whom Kristofferson killed in self-defense, and it's up to the former gunman's wife to dissuade the Indians by telling them the story of Christmas. Kim Cattrall co-stars. 88 min.
18-7374 Was $89.99 □*$14.99*

Duel Of Hearts (1992)
An epic of romance, love and murder based on a novel by Barbara Cartland, this is the story of Lady Caroline Faye, who attempts to save a handsome nobleman accused of murder and discovers his wealthy family is filled with strange secrets. Michael York, Geraldine Chaplin, Alison Doody and Billie Whitelaw star. 95 min.
18-7386 Was $89.99 □*$14.99*

Power Of Attorney (1995)
Facing federal indictment on charges of extortion and murder, mob kingpin Danny Aiello uses money, sexual blackmail and political influence in order to intimidate U.S. attorney Elias Koteas. Nina Siemaszko, Rae Dawn Chong co-star. 97 min.
18-7562 *$89.99*

Better Off Dead (1995)
A female thief, forger and prostitute is charged with killing a cop and finds help in her case from an attorney who once prosecuted her. Mare Winningham, Tyra Ferrell and Kevin Tighe star. Executive produced by Gloria Steinem. 91 min.
18-7563 *$89.99*

Captives (1993)
Compassionate and erotic true-life tale stars Julia Ormond as a prison dentist who carries on a scorching affair with convict Tim Roth. When other prisoners discover the romance, they blackmail Ormond into getting involved in their drug-dealing operation. 96 min.
11-2070 Was $99.99 ❑*$19.99*

Radio Inside (1994)
A young man, upset over his father's recent death, moves in with his older brother. A friendship is formed with his brother's neglected girlfriend and threatens to grow into something more in this compelling, revealing drama. Dylan Walsh, Elisabeth Shue, William McNamara star. 91 min.
12-2976 Was $89.99 ❑*$19.99*

Of Love And Shadows (1996)
Set against the political turmoil of Chile in the late 1970s, this romantic drama stars Antonio Banderas as a daring photographer hired by magazine writer Jennifer Connelly to work on an important story. When they stumble on a dangerous secret, they have to elude government forces. At the same time, they fall in love. 110 min.
11-2072 Was $99.99 ❑*$19.99*

A Price Above Rubies (1998)
Renee Zellweger stars as a young woman chafing from the constraints of life in Brooklyn's Hasidic Jewish community. After trying to fulfill her expected role as wife and mother with an arranged marriage to a Talmudic scholar, Zellweger's quest for personal freedom leads her to a job in her brother-in-law's jewelry store and an illicit affair with him. With Christopher Eccleston and Julianna Margulies. 120 min.
11-2787 Was $99.99 ❑*$19.99*

Basil (1998)
Passion and betrayal are the order of the day in turn-of-the-century England, as a handsome young aristocrat's quest for happiness puts him at odds with his demanding father and the self-absorbed woman he loves. Christian Slater, Jared Leto, Claire Forlani and Derek Jacobi star in this lavish adaptation of the Wilkie Collins novel. 102 min.
11-2311 Was $99.99 ❑*$19.99*

Crooked Hearts (1991)
Powerful drama focuses on the problems in a family sparked by the tenuous relationship between the father (Peter Coyote) and his rebellious 26-year-old son (Vincent D'Onofrio). When the young man discovers that his father was involved with a woman he liked, he sets the home on fire and flees. Jennifer Jason Leigh, Pete Berg and Juliette Lewis also star. 113 min.
12-2334 Was $19.99 ❑*$14.99*

I Love You, I Love You Not (1997)
What happens when the boy you've had a crush on for what seems like the longest time, and who you never thought would ever notice you, actually starts to feel the same way? That is the problem facing Claire Danes, who faces a crisis of romance as well as identity, in this heartwarming drama that also stars Jeanne Moreau. 92 min.
11-2773 Was $99.99 ❑*$19.99*

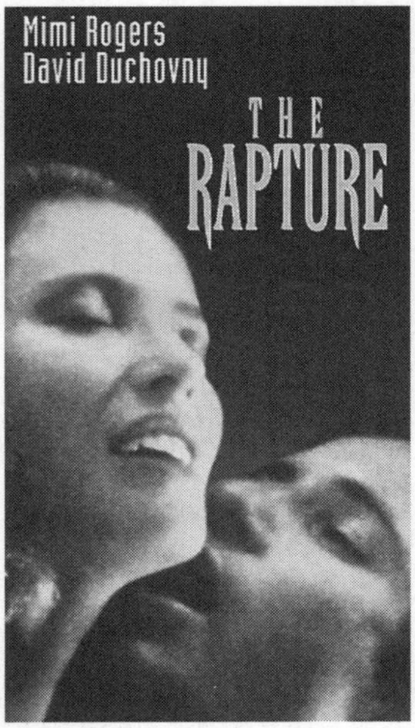

The Rapture (1991)
An audacious, thought-provoking film, with Mimi Rogers as a world-weary and sexually promiscuous telephone operator whose life takes a dramatic shift when she becomes involved with a fundamentalist cult that believes the end of the world and second coming of Jesus are near. David Duchovny, Patrick Bauchau co-star in this controversial effort. 102 min.
02-2177 Was $19.99 ❑*$14.99*

The Rapture (Letterboxed Version)
Also available in a theatrical, widescreen format.
02-5149 ❑*$19.99*

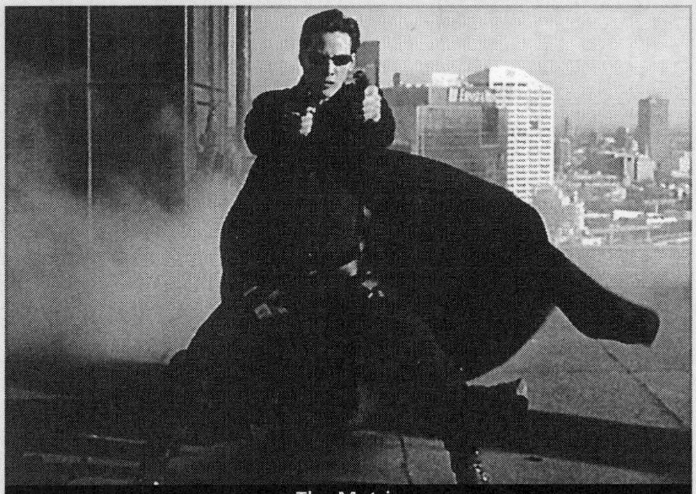

The Matrix

Keanu Reeves

Dream To Believe (1985)
In the tradition of "Rocky" and "Ice Castles" comes this hard-hitting drama starring Olivia D'Abo as a determined teenage gymnast who, with the support of her boyfriend (Keanu Reeves, in an early role), overcomes troubles at home to make the championship trials. With Rita Tushingham, Sean McCann. AKA: "Teenage Dream." 96 min.
14-6141 Was $19.99 *$14.99*

Brotherhood Of Justice (1986)
A group of teen vigilantes set out to clean up the crime-ridden streets of their town, but their campaign (and the violence) escalates to deadly proportions in this timely drama. Keanu Reeves, Kiefer Sutherland, Billy Zane, Lori Loughlin star. 97 min.
08-8433 *$14.99*

River's Edge (1987)
Chilling drama, based on a true incident, about a gang of teens in a small town who swear to silence when one of them kills his girlfriend, and the group's lack of emotion over the crime. Powerful, disturbing vision of adolescence stars Crispin Glover, Daniel Roebuck, Keanu Reeves, Roxana Zal, Dennis Hopper. 99 min.
53-1703 Was $19.99 *$14.99*

The Prince Of Pennsylvania (1988)
Quirky and captivating comedy-drama casts Keanu Reeves as an aimless young man who wants more from life than his coal town existence can give...and concocts a bizarre plan for busting out. Fractured, fetching sample of Americana with fine turns by Amy Madigan, Fred Ward, Bonnie Bedelia. 93 min.
02-1933 Was $19.99 *$14.99*

Permanent Record (1988)
A compelling and timely drama that depicts the reactions of a popular high school student's friends and family after he takes his own life, and how they cope with the loss. Keanu Reeves, Michael Meyrink and Alan Boyce star. 91 min.
06-1606 Was $89.99 *$14.99*

The Night Before (1988)
Must have been a rough night for young Winston, since besides his memory he lost his wallet, his dad's car, his prom date, and his virginity (guess he found a receipt). Keanu Reeves and Lori Loughlin star in a zany comedy. 90 min.
44-1561 Was $79.99 *$14.99*

Tune In Tomorrow... (1990)
A hilarious and multi-layered comedy set in a New Orleans radio station in the '50s. Keanu Reeves is a young newswriter who falls for worldly aunt Barbara Hershey, while eccentric soap opera scripter Peter Falk uses his art to advance their romance...and vice versa. Based on a Mario Vargas Llosa novel, this farcical tale features "film-within-a-film" cameos by John Larroquette, Elizabeth McGovern and Hope Lange. 90 min.
44-1790 Was $19.99 *$14.99*

My Own Private Idaho (1991)
A disturbing, stylish and affecting story of two male hustlers (River Phoenix and Keanu Reeves) who travel from Portland to Idaho to Italy in order to find Phoenix's long-lost mother. Their relationship and the people they meet—including a German cabaret performer, a beautiful Italian girl and a band of thieves—help make this another triumph from director Gus Van Sant ("Drugstore Cowboy"). With William Richert, Udo Kier. 105 min.
02-2186 Was $89.99 ❑*$19.99*

Point Break (1991)
Energized, action-packed story about a young FBI agent (Keanu Reeves) investigating a series of Southern California bank robberies. In order to get more info on the suspects, Reeves joins a group of surfers and soon gets indoctrinated into their thrill-seeking lifestyle by their philosophical leader (Patrick Swayze). Lori Petty, Gary Busey co-star. 117 min.
04-2485 Was $19.99 ❑*$14.99*

Bill And Ted's Bogus Journey (1991)
Oh, no, dudes! Bill and Ted have to go to incredible lengths to win an important band contest. It's, like, into Heaven and Hell they go, encountering some look-alike robots and challenging the Grim Reaper to a game of Battleship. Totally awesome, outrageous comic adventure stars Keanu Reeves, Alex Winter, William Sadler and George Carlin. 98 min.
73-1107 Was $89.99 ❑*$14.99*

Johnny Mnemonic (1995)
Wild filming of cyberpunk author William Gibson's story stars Keanu Reeves as a courier who has the ability to store information on a computer implant in his brain. When a mysterious corporation sends out thugs to retrieve important data Reeves has downloaded, he teams with a pretty security guard to stop them. Dina Meyer, Dolph Lundgren and Ice-T also star. 96 min.
02-2805 Was $19.99 ❑*$14.99*

Johnny Mnemonic (Letterboxed Version)
Also available in a theatrical, widescreen format.
02-3238 ❑*$19.99*

A Walk In The Clouds (1995)
From director Alfonso Arau ("Like Water for Chocolate") comes this lush, romantic drama. Keanu Reeves stars as a newly-returned WWII soldier who agrees to help a woman he befriends on a bus by posing as her husband and meeting her family at their Napa Valley vineyard. As the ruse continues, Reeves falls in love with his "wife" and sets out to prove his worth to her father. Aitana Sanchez-Gijon, Giancarlo Giannini, Anthony Quinn co-star. 102 min.
04-3285 Was $89.99 ❑*$14.99*

Feeling Minnesota (1996)
Hip and quirky film starring Keanu Reeves as a drifter who returns to "the Gopher State" in order to attend his older brother's wedding and resolve family problems. But when Reeves has a sexual liaison with his sibling's new wife, those old problems hit new heights of comic disaster. Cameron Diaz, Vincent D'Onofrio, Tuesday Weld and Dan Aykroyd also star. 95 min.
02-5119 Was $99.99 ❑*$14.99*

Chain Reaction (1996)
High-octane thriller stars Keanu Reeves as a member of a Chicago university scientific team that's developed a cheap, pollution-free energy source. When the lab is attacked and Reeves framed for the murder of project head Morgan Freeman, he and fellow researcher Rachel Wiecz must flee from federal agents as they try to break the sinister conspiracy trying to obtain their invention. 107 min.
04-3392 Was $99.99 ❑*$14.99*

The Last Time I Committed Suicide (1997)
Based on the groundbreaking autobiographical writings of early "Beat Generation" writer Neal Cassady, this acclaimed independent drama stars Thomas Jane as the young Cassady, living in post-WWII Denver and looking for a direction in life, when he falls under the influence of pool hall mentor Keanu Reeves. With Claire Forlani, Marg Helgenberger. 92 min.
07-2538 Was $99.99 *$14.99*

The Matrix: Collector's Edition (1999)
Slam-bang sci-fi actioner stars Keanu Reeves as a computer hacker told by rebels Laurence Fishburne and Carrie-Anne Moss that the world, as he knows it, is actually a form of virtual reality. Reeves is enlisted to use his intelligence and strength to topple the oppressive computer-fueled powers that control the world. With Joe Pantoliano and Hugo Weaving. Special collector's edition features 26 minutes of bonus footage, including two "making of" documentaries. 162 min. total.
19-2901 ❑*$22.99*

The Matrix: Collector's Edition (Letterboxed Version)
Also available in a theatrical, widescreen format.
19-2902 ❑*$22.99*

The Matrix: Collector's Set
This special collector's set of the Keanu Reeves smash includes a set of lobby cards; a framed Senitype graphic from the film; a CD soundtrack; a one-sheet movie poster; and a special letterboxed edition of the film that includes the making-of documentaries "What Is Bullet Time?" and "What Is the Concept?"
50-8477 Letterboxed ❑*$79.99*

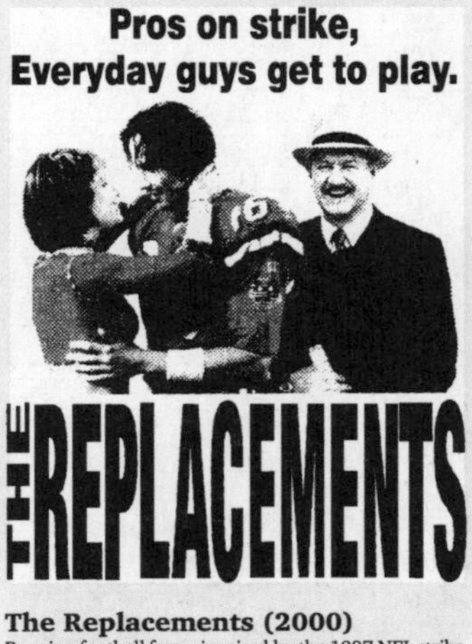

The Replacements (2000)
Rousing football farce, inspired by the 1987 NFL strike, in which washed-up coach Gene Hackman recruits a colorful assortment of has-been and never-were players to take to the gridiron for the pro Washington Sentinels during a labor walk-out. Keanu Reeves is the quarterback prone to losing the big game; Brooke Langton the cheerleader he falls for; and Jon Favreau, Orlando Jones and Rhys Ifans are among the players. With Pat Summerall, John Madden.
19-5019 ❑*$99.99*

Please see our index for these other Keanu Reeves titles: *Bram Stoker's Dracula • The Devil's Advocate • Even Cowgirls Get The Blues • I Love You To Death • Much Ado About Nothing • Parenthood • Speed • Youngblood*

Little Voice (1998)
Jane Horrocks re-creates her acclaimed stage role in this unusual musical-dramedy as LV, a withdrawn young woman who spends her days listening to her late father's records and singing in uncanny impersonations of Judy Garland, Marlene Dietrich, Shirley Bassey and others. After hearing her, small-time agent Michael Caine plots with LV's mother, brassy Brenda Blethyn, to cash in on her talents. With Ewan McGregor. 96 min.
11-2322 Was $99.99 ❑*$19.99*

My Son The Fanatic (1998)
From "My Beautiful Laundrette" scripter Hanif Kureishi comes a thoughtful and emotional drama. A Pakistani native (Om Puri) who's spent 25 years driving a cab in a grimy town in Northern England feels cut off from those around him—including his wife and newly conservative Muslim son—and finds unexpected solace with a prostitute (Rachel Griffiths) he shuttles to her clients. With Akbar Kurtha; directed by Udayan Prasad. 87 min.
11-2380 Was $99.99 ❑*$19.99*

Trainspotting (1996)
Controversy and acclaim have followed this British drama across the Atlantic. A gritty, graphically painful and, at times, blackly funny look at a group of heroin addicts in Edinburgh, Scotland, director Danny Boyle's ("Shallow Grave") adaptation of the Irvine Welsh novel follows one young man as he repeatedly tries to kick his drug habit, only to be lured back. The fine ensemble cast includes Ewan McGregor, Robert Carlyle, Kelly Macdonald, Jonny Lee Miller. 94 min.
11-2079 Was $99.99 ❑*$19.99*

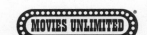

Stacy's Knights (1983)
In this early effort, Kevin Costner plays a gambling expert whose killing by casino henchmen provokes his female student to set up a plan to "break the bank." Andra Millian also stars. 95 min.
47-1213 Was $19.99 ***$14.99***

Fandango (1984)
Five college buddies take off for a weekend "road trip" across the Texas badlands in this funny and moving "coming of age" serio-comedy. Judd Nelson, Kevin Costner, Sam Robards, Suzy Amis star. 91 min.
19-1423 Was $19.99 ***$14.99***

Silverado: Collector's Edition (1985)
Director/co-scripter Lawrence Kasdan's rollicking salute to the Hollywood westerns of yesteryear stars Kevin Costner, Scott Glenn, Danny Glover and Kevin Kline as the good guys, out to free the wild town of Silverado from crooked sheriff Brian Dennehy and his cohorts. Rosanna Arquette, John Cleese, Linda Hunt also star. Special edition includes a "making of" featurette with interviews with the cast and crew. 132 min.
02-3326 Remastered ❑***$14.99***

Silverado: Collector's Edition (Letterboxed Version)
Also available in a theatrical, widescreen format.
02-3320 ❑***$19.99***

American Flyers (1985)
Two brothers, separated since their father's death, put their differences aside to compete in a grueling team cycling competition in this inspiring drama. Kevin Costner, David Grant, Rae Dawn Chong, Alexandra Paul star. 114 min.
19-1485 Was $19.99 ❑***$14.99***

Sizzle Beach, U.S.A. (1986)
An aspiring actress, an aerobics instructor and a pop singer share a beach house in Malibu while cultivating business contacts and knockout tans. Bouncy beach comedy, filmed in 1974, features Terry Cognie, Leslie Brander, and the screen debut of Kevin Costner. 93 min.
68-1125 Was $79.99 ***$14.99***

No Way Out (1987)
Naval officer Kevin Costner has a brief affair with beautiful, mysterious Sean Young, but when she is murdered he learns that she was the mistress of Defense Secretary Gene Hackman. What's more, Costner must investigate the death, knowing that "evidence" will make him the main suspect. Hit suspense film highlighted by a memorable limousine ride. 114 min.
44-1508 Was $19.99 ❑***$14.99***

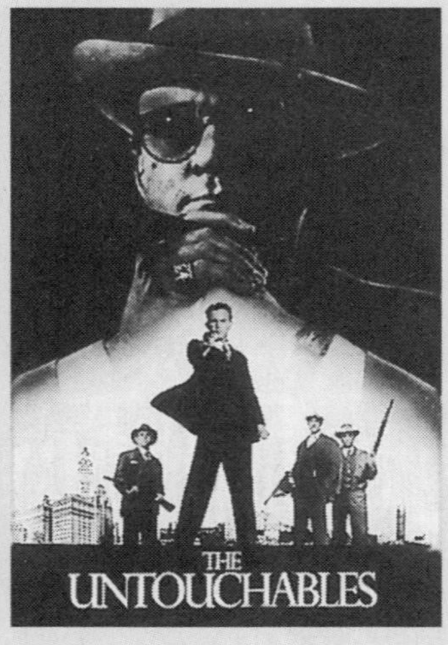

The Untouchables (1987)
The saga of the battle of Eliot Ness (Kevin Costner) and his incorruptible T-men to wrest prohibition-era Chicago from the grasp of Al Capone (Robert De Niro) is brought to blazing life by director Brian De Palma. Sean Connery, Charles Martin Smith, Andy Garcia co-star. 119 min.
06-1524 ❑***$14.99***

The Untouchables (Letterboxed Version)
Also available in a theatrical, widescreen format.
06-2709 ❑***$14.99***

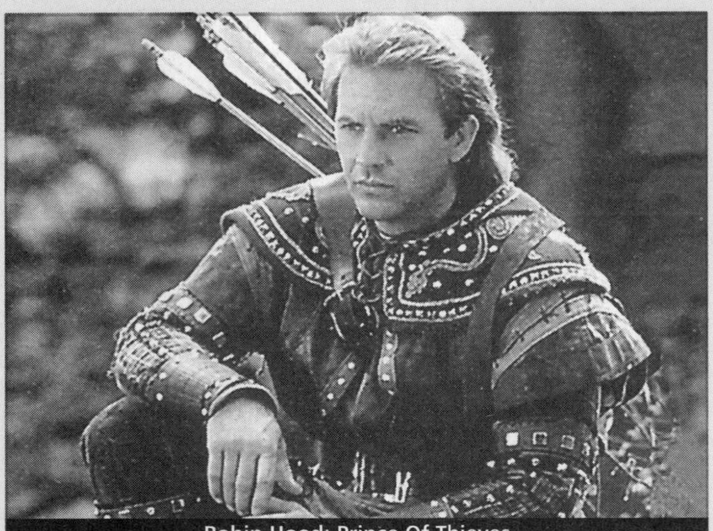
Robin Hood: Prince Of Thieves

Kevin Costner

Bull Durham (1988)
Major league comedic hit follows a minor league baseball team in North Carolina, focusing on the off-beat love triangle between veteran catcher Kevin Costner, cocky pitching phenom Tim Robbins, and baseball devotee/groupie Susan Sarandon. With Trey Wilson, Robert Wuhl, and the legendary Max Patkin. 108 min.
73-1023 Was $19.99 ❑***$14.99***

Field Of Dreams (1989)
Iowa farmer Kevin Costner, heeding a voice only he hears, plows under his crops to build a baseball diamond that will become the "home field" to an all-star team of long-gone players. Part sports drama, part fantasy and part father-son story, this beautifully filmed adaptation of W.P. Kinsella's novel "Shoeless Joe" also stars Amy Madigan, James Earl Jones, Burt Lancaster and Ray Liotta. 106 min.
07-1630 ❑***$14.99***

Field Of Dreams (Letterboxed Version)
Also available in a theatrical, widescreen format.
07-2785 ❑***$14.99***

Revenge (1990)
An ex-Navy pilot befriends a powerful tycoon living in Mexico, but when he gets involved with the businessman's beautiful young wife a deadly battle of wills and retribution ensues. Kevin Costner, Anthony Quinn and Madeleine Stowe star in this powerful drama of greed, passion and vengeance. 124 min.
02-2032 Was $19.99 ***$14.99***

Dances With Wolves (1990)
Winner of seven Academy Awards, including Best Picture, this stirring, visually enthralling Western epic is set on the Dakota plains of the 1860s. Director/star Kevin Costner is an Army officer who is assigned to a remote post where he befriends a tribe of Sioux Indians, whom he discovers are more civilized than his own people. Mary McDonnell, Graham Greene, Rodney A. Grant also star. 181 min.
73-1104 Was $99.99 ❑***$14.99***

Robin Hood: Prince Of Thieves (1991)
In this large-scale swashbuckler, Kevin Costner plays the legendary archer hero who romances Maid Marian (Mary Elizabeth Mastrantonio) and, with help from his Moor sidekick (Morgan Freeman), leads his Merrie Men against the villainous Sheriff of Nottingham (Alan Rickman). Christian Slater and Nick Brimble also star. 144 min.
19-1879 Was $24.99 ❑***$19.99***

Robin Hood: Prince Of Thieves (Letterboxed Version)
Also available in a theatrical, widescreen format.
19-2511 ❑***$19.99***

JFK: Director's Cut (1991)
Oliver Stone's controversial account of the Kennedy assassination and its aftermath stars Kevin Costner as New Orleans D.A. Jim Garrison, who charged a local businessman with involvement in a highly-placed conspiracy behind the president's death. This special video version features 17 minutes of restored footage shedding new light on Stone's theories. Tommy Lee Jones, Joe Pesci, Sissy Spacek co-star. 206 min.
19-2027 ❑***$24.99***

JFK: Director's Cut (Letterboxed Version)
Also available in a theatrical, widescreen format.
19-2821 ❑***$24.99***

The Bodyguard (1992)
Smash hit starring Whitney Houston as a world-famous singer-actress who hires former Secret Service agent Kevin Costner as her personal protector after she receives threatening letters from a disturbed fan. While trying to adjust to life in the public eye, the bodyguard falls in love with his beautiful client. Songs include "I Have Nothing" and "I Will Always Love You." 129 min.
19-2097 Was $19.99 ❑***$14.99***

The Bodyguard (Letterboxed Version)
Also available in a theatrical, widescreen format.
19-2510 ❑***$19.99***

The War (1994)
From "Fried Green Tomatoes" director Jon Avnet comes this heartfelt drama set in Mississippi in 1970, where 11-year-old twins build a treehouse, then join their friends in defending it from neighborhood toughies. Meanwhile, father Kevin Costner returns home from Vietnam, devastated by his own combat experiences. Elijah Wood, Mare Winningham also star. 126 min.
07-2268 Was $19.99 ❑***$14.99***

Wyatt Earp (1994)
The oft-filmed tale of the gunfight at the O.K. Corral gets a dramatic modernist spin from co-writer/director Lawrence Kasdan and star Kevin Costner. As farmer-turned-outlaw-turned-marshal, Costner's Earp comes to the frontier town of Tombstone and teams with his brothers and ally Doc Holliday in the fateful shootout with the Clanton gang. Dennis Quaid co-stars as Holliday; with Gene Hackman, Jeff Fahey, Michael Madsen. 191 min.
19-2281 Was $89.99 ❑***$24.99***

Wyatt Earp: The Director's Cut
This special expanded version of the Western epic offers 20 minutes of footage not shown in theatres, including scenes of Earp's teen years, first romance, early days as a lawman and his friendship with the Mastersons. 212 min.
19-2345 ❑***$29.99***

Waterworld (1995)
Exciting, exhilarating (and expensive) sci-fi saga, set on an ecologically ravaged future Earth covered by water. Kevin Costner, as a solitary wanderer known as the Mariner, helps the inhabitants of a man-made floating island defend themselves from pirate Dennis Hopper and his band of jet-ski-riding freebooters, and helps decipher clues that may lead to the location of the mythical "Dryland." With Jeanne Tripplehorn, Tina Majorino. 136 min.
07-2366 Was $19.99 ❑***$14.99***

Waterworld (Letterboxed Version)
Also available in a theatrical, widescreen format.
07-2421 ❑***$19.99***

Tin Cup (1996)
Amateur golfer Kevin Costner falls in love with pretty psychologist Rene Russo, but in order to draw her attention from PGA touring pro boyfriend Don Johnson, he must battle him in the U.S. Open. Cheech Marin and Linda Hart also star in this comedy-drama from Ron Shelton ("Bull Durham"). 133 min.
19-2472 Was $19.99 ❑***$14.99***

Tin Cup (Letterboxed Version)
Also available in a theatrical, widescreen format.
19-2552 ❑***$19.99***

The Postman (1997)
In the post-apocalyptic future of 2013, America has become a patchwork quilt of isolated communities preyed upon by roving gangs and militias. Into this wasteland comes mail-toting drifter Kevin Costner, whose claim to represent a restored United States government revives the survivors' hope and makes him a reluctant leader. Will Patton, Olivia Williams and Laurenz Tate also star in this sweeping science-fiction drama directed by Costner. 178 min.
19-2700 Was $99.99 ❑***$19.99***

The Postman (Letterboxed Version)
Also available in a theatrical, widescreen format.
19-2746 ❑***$19.99***

Message In A Bottle (1999)
Sensitive romantic story adapted from the popular novel stars Robin Wright Penn as a divorced Chicago newspaper researcher who finds a bottle containing a moving love letter on a Cape Cod beach. She tracks it to Kevin Costner, a lonely North Carolina boat mender and widower and the two eventually begin a tentative relationship. Paul Newman co-stars as Costner's cantankerous father. 131 min.
19-2878 Was $99.99 ❑***$19.99***

Message In A Bottle (Letterboxed Version)
Also available in a theatrical, widescreen format.
19-2930 ❑***$19.99***

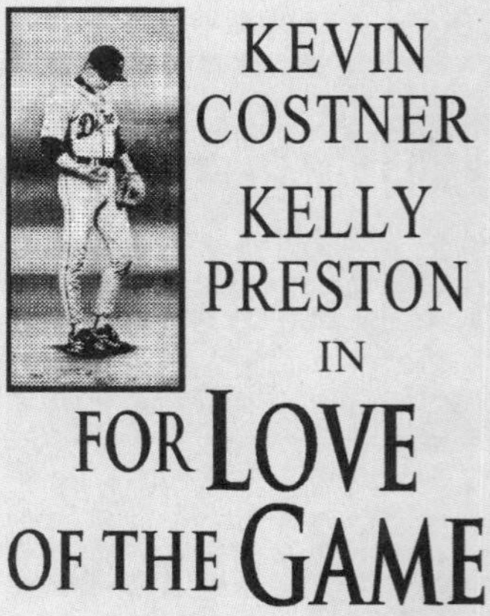

For Love Of The Game (1999)
Kevin Costner steps into the cleats once again, playing a 40-year-old Detroit Tigers pitcher wrestling with the imminent end of his career and his latest relationship—all while trying to complete a perfect game on the season finale in Yankee Stadium. Kelly Preston is Costner's girlfriend, about to leave him for a job in England, and John C. Reilly is his catcher. Sam Raimi ("A Simple Plan") directs. 138 min.
07-2846 Was $99.99 ❑***$14.99***

Please see our index for these other Kevin Costner titles: *A Perfect World* • *Testament*

Map Of The Human Heart (1993)
A stirring romantic saga involving an Eskimo boy and a half-breed girl who fall in love when they are youngsters and, after years of separation, reunite during World War II. He's now a bombardier for the Canadian Air Force; she's a photo analyst for the military. But they both must overcome one huge obstacle: she's married to the man who saved his life when he was a child. Jason Scott Lee, Anne Parillaud and Patrick Bergin star. 109 min.
44-1941 Was $19.99 ❑***$14.99***

Little Odessa (1994)
Set amid the Russian-American community of Brooklyn's Brighton Beach, this compelling crime drama from rookie writer/director James Gray stars Tim Roth as a mob hit man who, in order to fulfill a contract, returns to his old neighborhood, where he must face his disapproving father and dying mother, a younger brother who looks up to him, and an old flame. Edward Furlong, Maximilian Schell, Vanessa Redgrave, Moira Kelly also star. 98 min.
27-6934 Was $99.99 ❑***$14.99***

The Temptations (1998)
"Get Ready" for the remarkable true story of the legendary Motown group with this acclaimed bio-drama that follows the soulful singers' rise up the charts and the personal crises that tore them apart and brought them back together. Soundtrack includes such original Temps hits as "My Girl," "Ain't Too Proud to Beg," "Just My Imagination" and "Ball of Confusion." Charles Malik Whitfield, Terron Brooks, DB Woodside and Leon star. 150 min.
27-7108 Was $19.99 ***$14.99***

America's Dream (1996)
This wonderful drama tells three different stories of African-Americans and their struggles from 1938 to 1958. In "Long Black Song," Danny Glover is an Alabama farmer who discovers his wife has had an affair with a white salesman; Wesley Snipes is a school principal who must make a difficult decision about "The Boy Who Painted Christ Black"; and Lorraine Toussaint is a jazz pianist who faces a childhood nemesis in "The Reunion." 86 min.
44-2051 Was $19.99 ***$14.99***

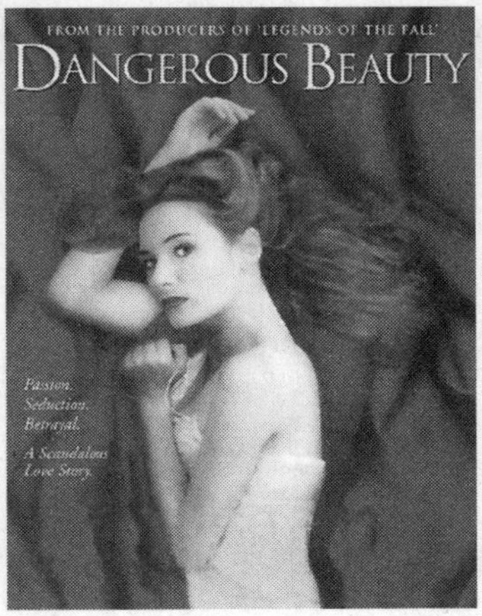
FROM THE PRODUCERS OF 'LEGENDS OF THE FALL'
DANGEROUS BEAUTY
Passion.
Seduction.
Betrayal.
A Scandalous
Love Story.

Dangerous Beauty (1997)
Catherine McCormack ("Braveheart") stars in this lavish and sensual drama based on the real-life story of Veronica Franco, who used her looks and body to become part of society in Renaissance Venice. With Rufus Sewell, Oliver Platt, Moira Kelly and Fred Ward. 112 min.
19-2743 Was $99.99 □*$14.99*

Doublecrossed (1992)
Dennis Hopper turns in a riveting performance as Barry Seal, a former drug smuggler-turned-DEA operative who worked to smash the Central American drug cartels by using his contacts from his dealing days. Riveting real-life story also features Robert Carradine and Adrienne Barbeau. 111 min.
19-1968 Was $79.99 □*$19.99*

Rapa Nui (1994)
Set in the 1600s on fabled Easter Island in the South Pacific, this drama of romance, rivalry and bigotry stars Jason Scott Lee as a member of the island's elite Long Ear people who falls in love with a woman from the Short Ear tribe and must compete for her against his best friend. With Esai Morales, Sandrine Holt. 107 min.
19-2295 Was $89.99 □*$19.99*

Second Best (1994)
Set in Wales, this touching drama stars William Hurt as a lonely, middle-aged postal worker who adopts the 11-year-old son of a convict in hopes of creating the family he never had. Wonderful acting and beautiful photography highlight this poignant tale. With John Hurt, Chris Cleary Miles. 105 min.
19-2305 Was $89.99 □*$19.99*

Silent Fall (1994)
A 9-year-old autistic boy is the only witness to a brutal double murder, and a child psychologist with a tragedy in his own past is the only person able to break through the boy's silence and learn the truth. Richard Dreyfuss, Liv Tyler, Linda Hamilton, John Lithgow and Ben Faulkner star in this powerful drama by director Bruce Beresford. 101 min.
19-2325 Was $19.99 □*$14.99*

The Stars Fell On Henrietta (1995)
Offbeat and affecting drama set in the Depression-era Southwest and starring Robert Duvall as an elderly "wildcatter" whose constant search for oil takes him to the struggling farm of Adain Quinn and Frances Fisher, who are desperate for any chance to save their land. Brian Dennehy also stars. 110 min.
19-2426 Was $89.99 □*$14.99*

Sweet Nothing (1996)
A middle-class New York husband and father falls into an ever-increasing downward spiral when a friend introduces him to crack cocaine and he becomes an addict. Based on a true story, this grittily powerful drama stars Michael Imperioli and Mira Sorvino. 89 min.
19-2496 Was $99.99 □*$19.99*

The Proprietor (1996)
A wistful and haunting romantic drama from director Ismail Merchant stars Jeanne Moreau as an aging French author living in New York. When the Paris apartment she grew up in during World War II, before her mother was taken away by the Gestapo, is put up for sale, Moreau returns to France to buy it. With Sean Young, Sam Waterston, Nell Carter. 114 min.
19-2500 Was $99.99 □*$19.99*

Sunchaser (1996)
Desperate to reach a lake that a Navajo medicine man says has mystical healing properties, a teenage killer with a terminal illness kidnaps a doctor and forces him to drive there. The bond that develops between the pair forms the basis of director Michael Cimino's offbeat "road" drama. Woody Harrelson, Jon Seda, Anne Bancroft and Talisa Soto star. 123 min.
19-2502 Was $99.99 □*$19.99*

36 Hours To Die (1999)
Brewery owner Treat Williams is against the wall when a local mobster tries to extort money from him and ruin his business. Williams enlists the help of his wife for her expertise at finances and uncle for his brawn to beat the hood at his own game. Kim Cattrall, Saul Rubinek and Carroll O'Connor also star. 94 min.
19-2906 Was $99.99 □*$14.99*

Stripteaser (1995)
Erotic dancer Christina Martin confronts terror during a gig at Zipper's Clown Palace. As she's bumping and grinding for the patrons, a blind man comes into the bar and holds Christina at gunpoint. It's the stripper and the psycho in a sexy, unpredictable standoff. Maria Ford and Rick Dean star. 82 min.
21-9088 Was $89.99 *$14.99*

Stripteaser 2 (1997)
A street-savvy cab driver's search for his lost kid sister leads him to the strip clubs of L.A.'s Sunset Strip, where he discovers a dark and kinky world filled with deception, power struggles and beautiful women. Can he find his sister before it's too late? Stacey Leigh Mobley, Rick Jordan and Kim Dawson star in this in-name-only sequel. 78 min.
21-9141 *$59.99*

Long Road Home (1991)
Acclaimed drama about the head (Mark Harmon) of a migrant farm worker family struggling to survive in the '30s and the conflict that arises when his son joins with labor organizers, forcing Harmon to choose between job security and his own beliefs. With Lee Purcell, Morgan Weisser. 95 min.
21-9105 *$89.99*

Children Of Fury (1992)
Based on a true incident, this taut drama follows the FBI showdown with an Utah family responsible for the bombing of a Mormon church building who then barricaded themselves with their children in their weapons-laden home. Dennis Franz, Ed Begley, Jr., Tess Harper, Kyle Secor star. 85 min.
21-9111 *$89.99*

The Prodigy (1998)
Twelve years old and illiterate, Nathan Jones decides to run away from his abusive home and take residence in a college fraternity. The frat members have no luck getting rid of Nathan, so they concoct a weird plan, posing him as a child prodigy and enrolling him in classes.
22-9018 Was $79.99 *$29.99*

Without Air (1997)
This edgy, slice-of-life story tells of Shay, a Memphis stripper and aspiring blues singer living a depressing life filled with desperation and addiction. She attempts to change her life and reach her potential as a singer with help from a veteran blues musician. Lauri Cook, Jack May and Nookie Taylor star.
22-9020 *$89.99*

Shopping (1996)
High-energy British crime drama about a group of young toughs who get their kicks driving stolen cars through department store windows, then robbing the stores. The adrenaline rises and the stakes get higher as their "shopping" sprees become more risky. Sadie Frost, Jude Law, Sean Pertwee and Jonathan Pryce star. 87 min.
21-9121 *$99.99*

Overdrive (1998)
Race car driver Steve Guttenberg hits the skids after losing his family in an accident and becomes more reckless racing his Porsche. He thinks he turns his life aorund when he meets pretty Kaela Dobkin, but she comes with her own problems—like killers hot on her trail. Robert Wagner and Stephen Meadows also star.
21-9174 *$59.99*

Where Evil Lies (1995)
Steamy sensuality permeates this tale of two exotic dancers who shake their impressive bodies in the hottest strip joint around. Then they learn that they're slated to be forced into a white slavery operation. Nikki Fritz, Melissa Park star. Unrated version; 90 min.
21-9091 Was $89.99 *$14.99*

The Raggedy Rawney (1990)
An army deserter, traumatized into silence and wandering the countryside in women's clothing, is taken in by a band of Gypsy-like refugees who believe him to be a mystical figure. Offbeat, engrossing drama, directed by co-star Bob Hoskins, features Dexter Fletcher, Zoe Wanamaker. 103 min.
19-7080 *$89.99*

Born Bad (1999)
Six teenagers attempting a robbery take everyone at a bank hostage, leading to a tense standoff with the town sheriff and an FBI agent. The teens begin to feel the heat and turn against each other over whether they should surrender to authorities. James Remar, Ryan Francis, Justin Walker and Corey Feldman star. 84 min.
21-9193 *$59.99*

The Last Best Year (1990)
Bernadette Peters and Mary Tyler Moore star in this compelling and emotional drama about a terminally ill woman who sees a therapist to help her cope with her condition. A friendship develops between the two women that allows them both to come to terms with their pasts and face the future. Dorothy McGuire, Brian Bedford co-star. 88 min.
21-9101 □*$89.99*

Demi Moore

Choices (1981)
A high school football star and violin prodigy must come to grips with changes in his life when he suffers a hearing impairment. Victor French, Val Avery, Demi Moore and Paul Carafotes star. 90 min.
23-5033 Was $19.99 *$14.99*

Blame It On Rio (1983)
Michael Caine and Joseph Bologna are best friends who journey to beautiful Rio de Janeiro for a vacation with teenage daughters Demi Moore and Michelle Johnson. Reluctant to join Bologna in sampling the wild Rio nightlife, Caine is shocked to find his pal's daughter, the luscious Johnson, trying to seduce him in this racy comedy. 110 min.
47-1243 □*$14.99*

No Small Affair (1984)
Lighthearted comedy stars Jon Cryer as a teenage photography buff who becomes romantically obsessed with would-be singing star Demi Moore after taking her picture and sets out to help her achieve fame. With George Wendt, Tim Robbins, Jennifer Tilly. 102 min.
02-1408 Was $19.99 □*$14.99*

St. Elmo's Fire (1985)
"Big Chill"-style serio-comedy about the lives, loves and challenges faced by a group of friends as they leave college and enter "the real world." Emilio Estevez, Rob Lowe, Andrew McCarthy, Demi Moore, Judd Nelson, Ally Sheedy and Mare Winningham star. 108 min.
10-2614 □*$14.99*

About Last Night... (1986)
Rob Lowe and Demi Moore are the "bar-crossed lovers" out to prove that romance lives, even in the singles-crazed world of the '80s, in this witty comedy. Fine support from Jim Belushi and Elizabeth Perkins; based on David Mamet's play "Sexual Perversity in Chicago." 113 min.
02-1697 Was $19.99 *$14.99*

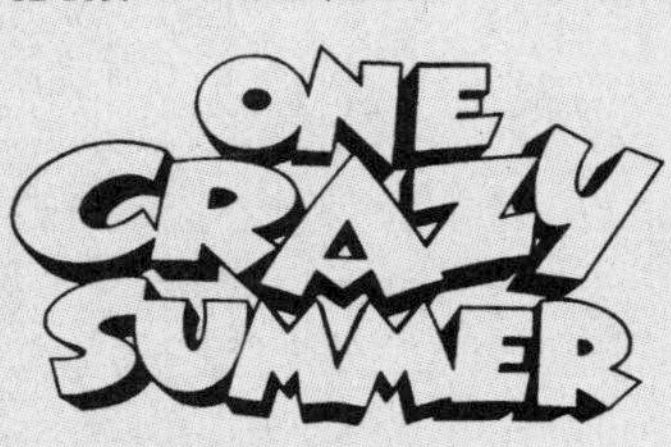
ONE
CRAZY
SUMMER

One Crazy Summer (1986)
It certainly is for John Cusack, Demi Moore, Tom Villard and Bobcat Goldthwait in this zany comedy about some "misfit" teens who team up to save a Nantucket retirement home from developers. 93 min.
19-1559 Was $19.99 □*$14.99*

Wisdom (1987)
Emilio Estevez directs, scripts and stars as a chronically unemployable young ex-con who sets himself up as a modern-day Robin Hood, knocking over banks to destroy mortgages and help the poor. Riveting drama co-stars Demi Moore, Tom Skerritt, Veronica Cartwright. 109 min.
19-1582 □*$14.99*

The Seventh Sign (1988)
Deserts frozen in ice...rivers running red with blood. What ancient prophecies do these strange occurrences fulfill? Why does a stranger haunt a young woman? And what role is her unborn child fated to play? Spine-tingling tale of Biblical catastrophe stars Demi Moore, Jurgen Prochnow, Michael Biehn. 97 min.
02-1873 Was $19.99 □*$14.99*

Mortal Thoughts (1991)
Intriguing thriller about a beautician who enlists the help of her housewife best friend to kill her brutal, good-for-nothing husband. Demi Moore, Glenne Headly, Bruce Willis and Harvey Keitel star in this gripping, stylishly presented psychological tale from director Alan Rudolph. 104 min.
02-2120 Was $19.99 □*$14.99*

The Butcher's Wife (1991)
Enchanting comedy starring Demi Moore as the new Southern wife of a Greenwich Village butcher whose clairvoyant abilities turn her neighborhood upside-down. Her powers attract the attention of psychiatrist Jeff Daniels, who is eventually drawn to the mysterious, beautiful woman. With Mary Steenburgen, George Dzundza, Frances McDormand. 107 min.
06-1922 Was $19.99 □*$14.99*

Indecent Proposal (1993)
Architect Woody Harrelson and realtor wife Demi Moore are in deep financial trouble. In hopes of getting out of debt, Moore agrees to spend an evening on a yacht with handsome billionaire Robert Redford for $1 million. Can the couple overcome the deal they made, which has led to the dissolution of their marriage? Seymour Cassel and Rip Taylor also star in this provocative hit drama. 119 min.
06-2145 Was $19.99 □*$14.99*

Now And Then (1995)
Melanie Griffith, Demi Moore, Rosie O'Donnell and Rita Wilson are former childhood friends who reunite and reminisce on the summer of 1970, when they played with a Ouija board, had their first experiences with the opposite sex and learned memorable lessons about life. Thora Birch, Gaby Hoffman, Christina Ricci and Ashleigh Aston Moore play the women as youngsters. 102 min.
02-5089 Was $19.99 □*$14.99*

The Scarlet Letter (1995)
"Freely adapted" from the Nathaniel Hawthorne novel of forbidden passion in 17th-century America, director Roland Joffe's sensual drama stars Demi Moore as Hester Prynne, an independent-minded colonist who, after her husband is presumed killed in an Indian attack, has an affair with a local minister and bears his child, bringing down the wrath of the townspeople. With Robert Duvall, Joan Plowright. 135 min.
11-1994 Was $19.99 □*$14.99*

The Juror (1996)
Artist Demi Moore becomes a juror in a mobster's murder trial and soon finds herself the target of hit man Alec Baldwin, who threatens to kill her teenage son if she doesn't vote "not guilty" for boss Tony LoBianco. James Gandolfini and Anne Heche also star in this first-rate suspense yarn. 118 min.
02-2909 Was $19.99 □*$14.99*

Striptease (1996)
Demi Moore takes it all off in this raucous and daring comedy in which she plays a woman who takes a job stripping at a Florida club in order to regain custody of her daughter from her con artist ex-husband. Burt Reynolds is a slimy politico who has the hots for her; Armand Assante an understanding detective; and Ving Rhames the club's no-nonsense bouncer. Uncut, unrated version includes footage not shown in theaters. 115 min.
02-2974 □*$19.99*

Striptease (Letterboxed Version)
Also available in a theatrical, widescreen format.
02-3319 □*$19.99*

If These Walls Could Talk (1996)
Three different stories of women faced with unwanted pregnancies are the focus of this powerful film. In 1952, Demi Moore is a recently widowed nurse impregnated by her brother-in-law. Sissy Spacek is the mother of four who discovers a baby is on the way after she returns to college in 1974. And in 1996, Anne Heche, pregnant from an affair with a married man, must choose whether to have the child or not. With Cher (who also directed the final segment). 97 min.
44-2074 Was $99.99 □*$14.99*

G.I. Jane (1997)
She's an officer and a gentlewoman, but can Navy lieutenant Demi Moore, the first woman candidate for the elite Navy SEALs unit, survive both the rigorous training and relentless verbal and emotional abuse from her superiors and male counterparts? Gritty and gung-ho military drama also stars Viggo Mortensen, Anne Bancroft. 125 min.
11-2217 Was $19.99 □*$14.99*

G.I. Jane (Letterboxed Version)
Also available in a theatrical, widescreen format.
11-2777 □*$19.99*

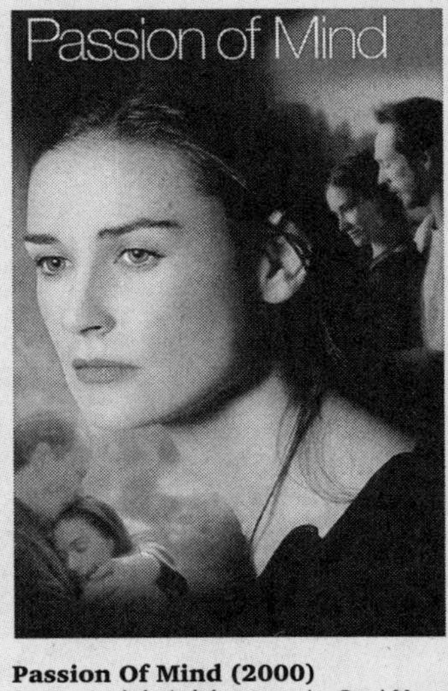
Passion of Mind

Passion Of Mind (2000)
Dreamy psychological drama starring Demi Moore in two roles, playing book reviewer Marie, who lives in a French chateau with her two daughters, and Marty, a single literary agent looking for love in Manhattan. Which life is real and which is pure fantasy? And what part do the men she's involved with (Stellan Skarsgard and William Fichtner) play? 105 min.
06-3010 □*$99.99*

Please see our index for these other Demi Moore titles: *Deconstructing Harry • Disclosure • A Few Good Men • Ghost • The Hunchback Of Notre Dame • Nothing But Trouble • We're No Angels • Young Doctors In Love*

Truth Or Consequences, N.M. (1997)
A botched robbery and a wounded undercover cop send a quartet of would-be thieves and their two hostages on the run from both the police and—thanks to a drug-filled suitcase—mobsters in this gripping crime drama directed by co-star Kiefer Sutherland. With Kim Dickens, Vincent Gallo, Kevin Pollak, Mykelti Williamson, Martin Sheen and Rod Steiger. 101 min.
02-3123 Was $19.99 ❑*$14.99*

Dream With The Fishes (1997)
Quirky road movie featuring David Arquette as a suicidal voyeur befriended by Brad Hunt, a streetwise young man with a terminal disease. The two decide to visit Hunt's estranged father on a wild road trip that includes nude bowling, armed robbery and fascinating revelations about both men. With Kathryn Erbe, Cathy Moriarty. 96 min.
02-3134 Was $99.99 ❑*$19.99*

Dream With The Fishes (Letterboxed Version)
Also available in a theatrical, widescreen format.
02-3240 ❑*$19.99*

Cafe Society (1997)
This true-life drama is set in 1950s New York, where Oleo margarine heir Mickey Jelke (Frank Whaley) lives the high life, carousing with women and hanging out in nightclubs. An undercover cop (Peter Gallagher) befriends Jelke and, with help from Jelke's hooker girlfriend, tries to put him away on prostitution charges. Lara Flynn Boyle and John Spencer also star in the jazzy tale. 104 min.
02-3137 Was $99.99 ❑*$24.99*

Hollow Reed (1997)
The battle between a gay doctor and his ex-wife for custody of their young son takes on a chilling new dimension when he begins to suspect the woman's new boyfriend has been beating the child in this emotional British drama. Martin Donovan, Joely Richardson, Ian Hart and Jason Flemyng star. 105 min.
02-3141 Was $99.99 ❑*$19.99*

Shadrach (1998)
Susan Styron directs father William's powerful story set in Depression-era Virginia and focusing on the experiences of a boy cared for by the lower-class Dabney family because of his parents' problems. The boy witnesses the arrival of an elderly ex-slave who wishes to be buried with his family on the site of his former plantation, now the Dabney property. Harvey Keitel, Andie MacDowell and John Franklin Sawyer star. 88 min.
02-3277 ❑*$99.99*

Whatever (1998)
This gritty coming-of-age film is set in a small New Jersey town in the early 1980s and tells of the experiences of Anna, a shy high school student with aspirations of becoming an artist, who faces issues about sex, morals and drugs while trying to fit in with a popular crowd. Liza Weil, Chad Morgan and Frederic Forrest star in director Susan Skoog's impressive first feature. 113 min.
02-3269 Was $99.99 ❑*$19.99*

Heaven Or Vegas (1998)
Yasmine Bleeth is a high-priced call girl who falls for male prostitute Richard Grieco. The two decide to leave the glitzy streets of Las Vegas for Montana, but during a stop at Bleeth's old home along the way, Grieco falls for her younger sister, prompting Bleeth to join a group of mysterious drifters passing through town. Andy Romano and Monica Potter also star. 110 min.
02-3273 Was $99.99 ❑*$19.99*

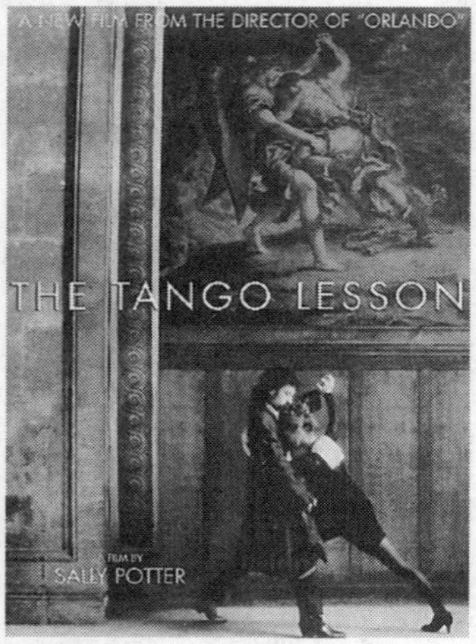

The Tango Lesson (1997)
Writer/director Sally Potter ("Orlando") mixes reality with fiction as she plays a filmmaker who, while coping with creative differences on her latest project in Paris, receives instruction in the tango from handsome young Argentinean dancer Pablo Veron. How their partnership blossoms—on and off the dance floor—is elegantly traced in this acclaimed drama. 101 min.
02-3174 Was $99.99 *$24.99*

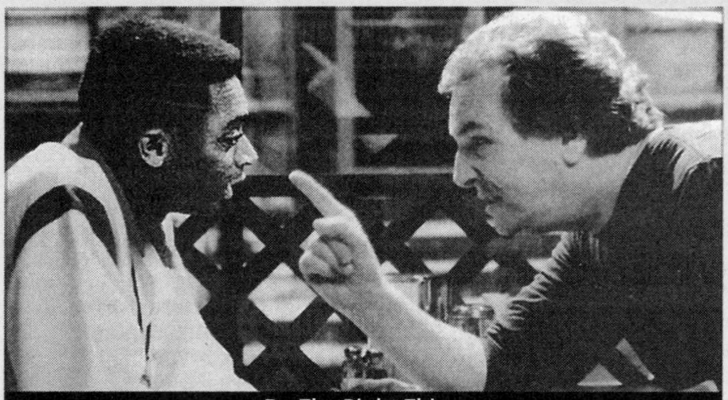

Do The Right Thing

Spike Lee

School Daze (1988)
Writer/director Spike Lee blends comedy, drama and music to depict life at a Southern all-black college, taking potshots at black frat life, student activism, and the encroachment of white culture. Larry Fishburne, Tisha Campbell, Giancarlo Esposito, Kyme, and Lee (as would-be frat brother Half-Pint) star. 114 min.
02-1864 *$14.99*

Do The Right Thing (1989)
Tempers flare, emotions run high, and a white-run pizza parlor in a black Brooklyn neighborhood becomes the center of a violent conflict on a hot summer day in filmmaker/star Spike Lee's acclaimed, controversial look at race relations. With Danny Aiello, Giancarlo Esposito and John Turturro. 120 min.
07-1633 Was $19.99 ❑*$14.99*

Mo' Better Blues (1990)
Spike Lee's enthralling, beautifully photographed look at the jazz world stars Denzel Washington as a talented, driven trumpet player who puts his career above the two women in his life and loyalty to ineffectual manager Lee above his combo's success. Cynda Williams, Joie Lee, Wesley Snipes and Giancarlo Esposito co-star; lively jazz score by Bill Lee, Branford Marsalis and others. 127 min.
07-1667 Was $19.99 ❑*$14.99*

Jungle Fever (1991)
Romance blooms between a black Harlem architect and his secretary, an Italian-American from Bensonhurst, but relatives and friends on both sides have strong reactions to their steamy, stormy relationship in Spike Lee's controversial comedy-drama. Wesley Snipes, Annabella Sciorra, Ossie Davis, Ruby Dee, Samuel L. Jackson, John Turturro and Lee star; Stevie Wonder performs his own score. 132 min.
07-1716 Was $19.99 ❑*$14.99*

Malcolm X (1992)
Spike Lee's epic biography features Denzel Washington in a dynamic performance as the black revolutionary leader. The film follows Malcolm's early days as a Harlem hepcat, his time in prison and conversion there to Islam, his family life, and his crusades to further the black race. Angela Bassett, Al Freeman, Jr., Albert Hall and Lee co-star. 201 min.
19-2065 Was $89.99 ❑*$24.99*

Crooklyn (1994)
Spike Lee's compassionate, free-spirited film looks at the joys, sorrows and struggles of a black family living in Brooklyn in the early 1970s. Schoolteacher Alfre Woodard and unemployed jazz musician Delroy Lindo are confronted by domestic and financial crises as they courageously try to raise their four boys and one girl. Zelda Harris and Lee co-star. 114 min.
07-2194 Was $19.99 ❑*$14.99*

Clockers (1995)
Spike Lee's forceful adaptation of Richard Price's acclaimed novel focuses on a young drug dealer named Strike who is asked by his boss to commit a murder. When Strike's law-abiding brother confesses to the crime, a police detective doesn't believe him—and searches for the truth in the case. Harvey Keitel, Delroy Lindo, John Turturro and Mekhi Phifer star. 129 min.
07-2384 Was $19.99 ❑*$14.99*

Get On The Bus (1996)
A cross-country bus journey becomes a ride of self-discovery, conflict and reconciliation for a diverse group of African-American men on their way to Washington for the October, 1995 Million Man March in director/co-scripter Spike Lee's inspirational slice-of-life drama. The superb ensemble cast includes Andre Braugher, Gabriel Casseus, Ossie Davis, Charles Dutton, Isaiah Washington. 122 min.
02-3046 Was $19.99 ❑*$14.99*

Girl 6 (1996)
A struggling African-American actress gets a job moonlighting as a phone sex operator and begins to get drawn into the fantasy lives of her callers—and the power she holds over them—in this funny and insightful tale from director Spike Lee. Theresa Randle stars in the title role, with special appearances by Richard Belzer, Halle Berry, Madonna, Quentin Tarantino and Lee; music by the Squiggle Formerly Known as Prince. 108 min.
04-3350 Was $99.99 ❑*$29.99*

He Got Game (1998)
Denzel Washington stars in Spike Lee's acclaimed drama as Jake, a recently paroled convict who has a week to convince his son, Jesus, who is the most sought-after high school basketball player in the country, to attend the governor's alma mater. The problem is that Jake was convicted of murdering his son's mother and Jesus wants nothing to do with him. With NBA star Ray Allen, Milla Jovovich and Ned Beatty. 137 min.
11-2791 Was $19.99 ❑*$14.99*

Summer Of Sam (1999)
Spike Lee's absorbing, audacious inner-city saga shows how the 1977 "Son of Sam" killings affect the people living in an Italian neighborhood of the Bronx. Among the residents are married couple Mira Sorvino and John Leguizamo, fake punker Adrien Brody, aspiring performance artist Jennifer Esposito, crime boss Ben Gazzara and detective Anthony LaPaglia. Adding commentary on the proceedings is famed New York columnist Jimmy Breslin. 142 min.
11-2360 Was $99.99 ❑*$14.99*

Please see our index for the Spike Lee title: *4 Little Girls*

The People vs. Larry Flynt (1996)
Is the infamous Hustler Magazine founder a First Amendment hero or a misogynistic pornographer? Both, according to director Milos Forman's acclaimed biodrama starring Woody Harrelson as the prurient publisher and tracing Flynt's professional ups and downs, his marriage to ex-stripper Althea (Courtney Love), his brief "born again" phase and crippling from a sniper's bullet, and the landmark libel suit brought by Jerry Falwell that reached the Supreme Court. With Edward Norton, James Cromwell. 130 min.
02-3061 Was $19.99 ❑*$14.99*

Ghosts Of Mississippi (1996)
Director Rob Reiner's powerful real-life drama stars Alec Baldwin as the Mississippi assistant district attorney who, in 1989, reopened the case against racist Byron de La Beckwith (James Woods), who was tried twice before in the 1963 shooting of civil rights activist Medgar Evers. Whoopi Goldberg (as Evers' widow), Craig T. Nelson and William H. Macy also star. 131 min.
02-3075 Was $99.99 ❑*$19.99*

Broken English (1997)
A beautiful young Croatian woman flees her war-torn homeland with her family and settles in Aukland, New Zealand's largest city. Her romance with a native Maori co-worker at a local restaurant angers the woman's father and leads to violent confrontations in director/co-writer Gregor Nicholas' compelling and erotically charged drama. Aleksandra Vujcic, Julian Arahanga, Rade Serbedzua star. Uncut, NC-17 version; 92 min.
02-3138 Was $99.99 *$19.99*

The Disappearance Of Garcia Lorca (1997)
A Spanish-born journalist living in Puerto Rico and obsessed with the life and controversial death of his homeland's greatest modern poet, Federico Garcia Lorca, who was murdered during Franco's rise to power, returns to Spain to uncover the truth in this gripping political thriller. Esai Morales, Edward James Olmos, Jeroen Krabbe and Andy Garcia, as Garcia Lorca, star. 114 min.
02-3140 Was $99.99 ❑*$24.99*

One Tough Cop (1998)
Stephen Baldwin stars as real-life New York cop Bo Dietl, whose loyalty to an alcoholic partner and a childhood friend who's now a high-ranking mob member put his integrity and his career on the line, in this gritty drama based on Dietl's autobiography. Chris Penn, Michael McGlone, Gina Gershon and Paul Guilfoyle also star; directed by Bruno Barreto. 94 min.
02-3305 Was $19.99 ❑*$14.99*

Savior (1998)
Embittered after the killing of his family by terrorists, American mercenary Dennis Quaid loses himself in his murderous work, until a mission in Bosnia throws him together with a young woman and her infant child and forces him to care again. Based on a true story, this compelling drama also stars Natasha Ninkovic, Nastassja Kinski. 104 min.
02-3306 Was $19.99 ❑*$14.99*

Bodies, Rest & Motion (1992)
This dramatic study of the restlessness experienced by "Generation X"ers involves a disaffected young couple (Tim Roth and Bridget Fonda) who move to a small Arizona town to settle and find that their troubled lives are disrupted by a handsome, philosophical house painter (Eric Stoltz). Phoebe Cates also stars. 94 min.
02-5037 Was $19.99 ❑*$14.99*

Swept From The Sea (1997)
Based on a Joseph Conrad story, this lush drama stars Rachel Weisz as a simple young woman shunned by the other residents of her English town in the 1800s. Following a fierce storm, she falls in love with Vincent Perez, the Ukrainian survivor of a shipwreck. Their romance leads to marriage and, eventually, tragedy. Ian McKellen and Kathy Bates also star. 114 min.
02-3191 Was $99.99 ❑*$14.99*

Gloria (1999)
In the title role of this action-filled remake of the 1980 John Cassavetes drama, Sharon Stone plays a tough-as-nails woman fresh out of jail and on the run from her gangster ex-boyfriend. Stone takes under her wing a 7-year-old boy whose parents were killed by the boyfriend and who has on him an incriminating computer disk. Jean-Luke Figueroa, Jeremy Northam also star; directed by Sidney Lumet. 108 min.
02-3321 Was $99.99 ❑*$14.99*

Nevada (1998)
The arrival of a beautiful and mysterious stranger in a remote Nevada town where everyone seems to have a skeleton or two in their closet threatens to destroy the local women's conspiracy of silence. Offbeat and compelling drama stars Amy Brenneman, Kirstie Alley, Gabrielle Anwar, Saffron Burrows, Kathy Najimy and James Wilder. 109 min.
02-3242 Was $99.99 ❑*$19.99*

Shadow Of China (1991)
A tycoon with a mysterious past attempts to seize control of Hong Kong and hide his background from the people around him. John Lone, Sammi Davis, Vivian Wu star in this intriguing, action-packed political drama. 100 min.
02-5004 Was $89.99 *$14.99*

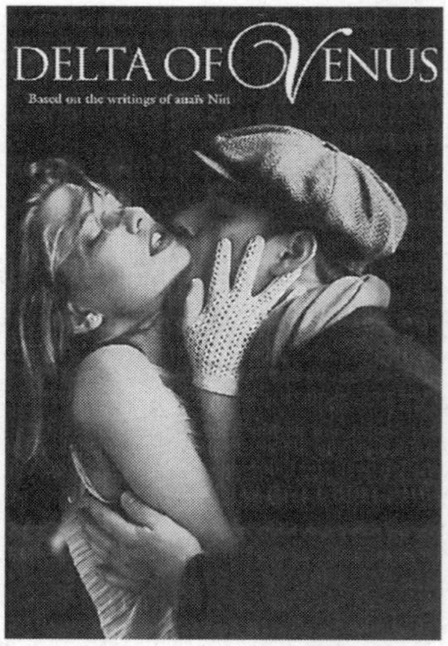

Delta Of Venus (1995)
Based on the infamous best-seller by Anaïs Nin, this steamy and erotic outing from softcore auteur Zalman King ("Red Shoe Diaries") follows a young American writer living in Paris on the eve of World War II on a series of sexual adventures with a French author, streetwalkers, a Nazi sympathizer and other eccentrics. Audie England, Costas Mandylor star. Uncut, unrated version; 101 min.
02-5087 Was $89.99 ❑*$19.99*

Damage (1992)
Louis Malle's steamy, provocative drama stars Jeremy Irons as a middle-aged member of the British Parliament obsessed with his son's gorgeous girlfriend. The two carry on a kinky sexual affair, which leads to disturbing repercussions. Miranda Richardson, Rupert Everett and Juliette Binoche also star in this erotic story presented in this uncut, unrated version. 112 min.
02-5016 Was $89.99 ❑*$19.99*

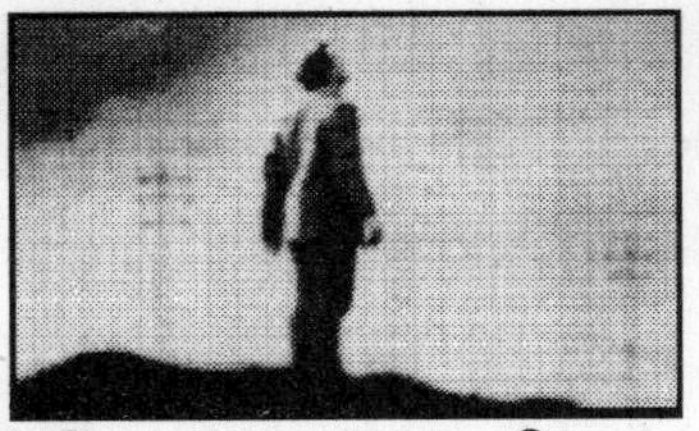

OCTOBER SKY

BASED ON AN EXTRAORDINARY TRUE STORY

October Sky (1999)
Set in the 1950s, this real-life story tells of Homer Hickam, Jr., a West Virginia teenager whose obsession with Russia's launch of Sputnik I causes friction with his coal miner father and prompts him to construct and attempt to launch a rocket with his three friends. Jake Gyllenhaal, Chris Cooper and Laura Dern star in this superior family saga from director Joe Johnston ("The Rocketeer"). 108 min.
07-2759 Was $99.99 ❑*$14.99*

Matters Of The Heart (1990)
A young man who dreams of becoming a concert pianist finds help from a beautiful composer. As their admiration for each other's talent gets more intense, so does their romantic interest. Jane Seymour, Christopher Gartin, James Stacy star. 94 min.
07-1738 Was $89.99 ❑*$14.99*

The Last Prostitute (1991)
A sensitive coming-of-age story about two teenage boys in search of a prostitute elevated to legendary status by a late uncle's tales. They finally find the talked-about woman but discover she has retired and now raises horses. Still, she will play a part in helping the teens become men. Sonia Braga, Wil Wheaton and David Smith star. 93 min.
07-1800 *$89.99*

Sins Of The Mind (1997)
A beautiful young woman escapes death in a car accident, but the resultant trauma leaves her unable to keep her erotic desires under control and leads her into a series of increasingly wild affairs. Can her parents and friends help her before it's too late? Missy Crider, Jill Clayburgh, Mike Farrell and Louise Fletcher star. 92 min.
06-2713 ❑*$59.99*

The Garden Of Redemption (1996)
In a small village in German-occupied Italy in World War II, local priest Anthony La Paglia finds his courage tested when a resistance group asks for his help, even as his love for a beautiful woman tests his vows. Powerful drama also stars Embeth Davidtz, Dan Hedaya, Peter Firth. 99 min.
06-2654 Was $89.99 ❑*$14.99*

Melanie Darrow (1997)
Compelling courtroom drama stars Delta Burke as a lawyer facing her toughest case yet when a client claims they've been framed for murder. Brian Bloom, Jonathan Banks also star. 88 min.
06-2714 Was $59.99 ❑*$14.99*

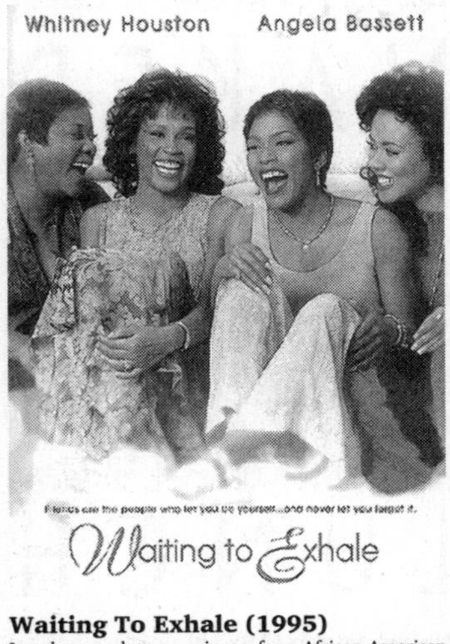

Waiting To Exhale (1995)
Laughter and tears mix as four African-American women share their experiences on the rocky road to true romance, and the men who were "detours" along the way, in this engaging hit comedy/drama based on Terry McMillan's novel. Angela Bassett, Whitney Houston, Loretta Devine and Lela Rochon star as the quartet of friends; with Gregory Hines, Dennis Haysbert, Wesley Snipes. 123 min.
04-3312 Was $19.99 ❑*$14.99*

Hollywood Confidential (1996)
The seamy underside of Tinseltown life provides a comfortable living for L.A. cop-turned-private eye Edward James Olmos and his team of operatives, but his latest case, involving a top director's illicit love affair, could be more costly than anyone imagined. Suspenseful drama also stars Ricky Aiello, Brendan Kelly and Charlize Theron. 92 min.
06-2716 Was $69.99 ❑*$14.99*

Tricks (1997)
Gift shop clerk by day, Las Vegas hooker by night! That's what Mimi Rogers is. But trouble ensues when a customer beats Rogers and she has trouble getting work. Even a veteran gangster can't help her. How's a gift shop clerk by day, Las Vegas hooker by night going to take care of this problem? Tackle the culprit herself! Tyne Daley and Ray Walston also star. 96 min.
06-2719 ❑*$99.99*

A Soldier's Sweetheart (1998)
Unusual drama set during the Vietnam War in which Army field medic Skeet Ulrich arranges to bring girlfriend Georgina Cates over from America. Her presence, however, has a disturbing effect on the other soldiers, even as the horrors of war Cates witnesses profoundly change her. Kiefer Sutherland also stars. 111 min.
06-2849 ❑*$69.99*

My Very Best Friend (1996)
Jaclyn Smith is a beautiful ex-model about to settle down with a wealthy tycoon. When secrets are revealed that end the relationship, Smith turns to best friend Jill Eikenberry for help. Soon, Smith's ruthless ambition threatens her long-lasting friendship with Eikenberry. Tom Irwin, Mary Kay Place also star. 97 min.
06-2720 ❑*$99.99*

Leaving Normal (1992)
Two disgruntled women set out to change their less-than-thrilling lives, with Wyoming housewife Meg Tilly leaving her abusive husband and joining cocktail waitress Christine Lahti on a road trip to Alaska filled with wacky characters, romance and personal reflection, in this "dramedy" directed by Edward Zwick ("Glory"). 110 min.
07-1857 Was $19.99 ❑*$14.99*

A Taste For Killing (1992)
Two best friends from well-to-do families take a job on an offshore oil-drilling rig in Texas. Their boss learns of their background and makes their lives miserable, but they are eventually befriended by a fellow rig worker who is in reality a dangerous con artist. Michael Biehn, Jason Bateman and Henry Thomas star. 87 min.
07-1912 ❑*$89.99*

Coma (1978)
A renowned medical center is the setting for director Michael Crichton's suspense-filled adaptation of the Robin Cook thriller. Doctor Genevieve Bujold risks her life to discover why patients are mysteriously lapsing into comas following surgery and then vanishing. Michael Douglas, Richard Widmark co-star; look for Tom Selleck as a corpse (!). 113 min.
12-1005 Was $59.99 ❑*$14.99*

Coma (Letterboxed Version)
Also available in a theatrical, widescreen format.
12-3166 ❑*$14.99*

It's My Turn (1980)
Urbane and sophisticated romantic comedy stars Jill Clayburgh as a happily-married woman who becomes attracted to ballplayer Michael Douglas, the father of her son's fiancée. With Charles Grodin, Steven Hill; look for Daniel Stern and Dianne Wiest. 91 min.
02-1071 Was $64.99 *$19.99*

The Star Chamber (1983)
Criminals released by the justice system on technicalities are being "executed" by a panel of vigilante judges, and Michael Douglas is the judge who discovers the murders in this pulse-pounding suspense thriller. Yaphet Kotto, Hal Holbrook co-star. 109 min.
04-1657 Was $19.99 *$14.99*

Romancing The Stone (1984)
Novelist Kathleen Turner teams up with wisecracking soldier-of-fortune Michael Douglas in the Colombian jungle to search for her missing sister. Rousing blend of action, wit and romance also stars Danny DeVito, Zack Norman. 105 min.
04-1706 ❑*$14.99*

The Jewel Of The Nile (1985)
More thrilling comedy and hilarious adventure in "Romancing the Stone"s" hit sequel. Here Kathleen Turner, Michael Douglas and Danny DeVito find themselves in the middle of an Arabian revolution and must locate the mysterious "jewel." Chases, laughs, romance and danger galore. 106 min.
04-1954 ❑*$14.99*

Wall Street (1987)
Writer/director Oliver Stone takes aim at corporate America, with devastating results. Michael Douglas earned an Oscar as the Machiavellian magnate who shows young broker Charlie Sheen the underside of the business world. Terence Stamp, Daryl Hannah, Sean Young and Martin Sheen also star. 124 min.
04-2163 ❑*$14.99*

Fatal Attraction (1987)
The hit thriller that scared the pants back on adulterers stars Michael Douglas as a married attorney who has a weekend tryst with editor Glenn Close. The affair soon becomes an obsession to the unbalanced Close, who harasses Douglas' family and eventually threatens their lives. Anne Archer co-stars. 120 min.
06-1525 ❑*$14.99*

Fatal Attraction (Directors' Series)
Now, U.S. audiences can see the original excised ending of this controversial hit. Also, director Adrian Lyne discusses his thoughts on the making of the film and shows clips of stars Michael Douglas and Glenn Close in rehearsal. 159 min. total.
06-1923 Letterboxed ❑*$19.99*

The War Of The Roses (1989)
A magnificent home becomes a battlefield for the increasingly bitter divorce feud waged by Michael Douglas and Kathleen Turner, while seedy attorney (and director) Danny DeVito adds commentary on the proceedings, in this hilariously nasty account of every couple's worst nightmares. 116 min.
04-2342 ❑*$14.99*

Black Rain (1989)
Stylish suspenser stars Michael Douglas as a New York detective who loses the extradited Yakuza hit man he escorted back to Japan and is thrust into a mob war on the Osaka streets. Andy Garcia, Ken Takakura, Yusaku Matsuda co-star; Ridley Scott directs. 126 min.
06-1714 ❑*$14.99*

Shining Through (1992)
Sweeping World War II romance-thriller stars Melanie Griffith as a secretary who falls in love with her mysterious new boss (Michael Douglas), who she soon discovers is an American intelligence agent who enlists her for some dangerous undercover work behind enemy lines. Sir John Gielgud and Liam Neeson also star. 133 min.
04-2535 Was $19.99 ❑*$14.99*

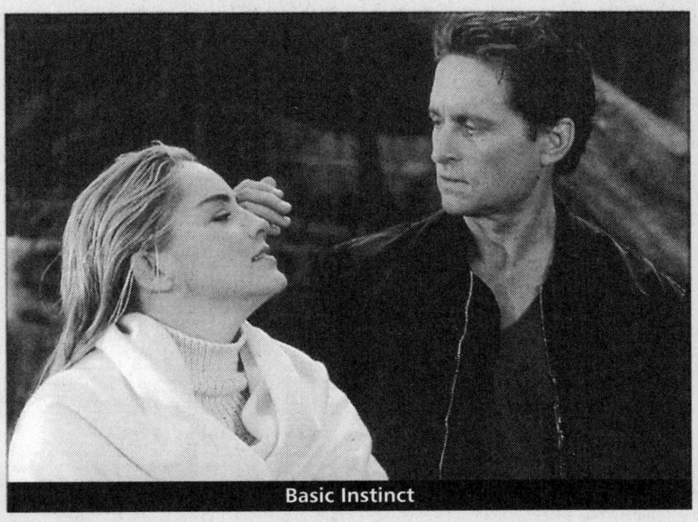

Basic Instinct

Michael Douglas

Basic Instinct (1992)
Controversial, sexually-charged suspenser stars Michael Douglas as a burned-out San Francisco police detective investigating a brutal ice-pick murder who carries on a torrid affair with one of the case's suspects, seductive bisexual writer Sharon Stone. Jeanne Tripplehorn and George Dzundza co-star; Paul Verhoeven directs. 123 min.
27-6787 Was $19.99 ❑*$14.99*

Basic Instinct: The Original Director's Cut
This special edition of the boxoffice smash features ultra-steamy scenes cut from the film's original release, interviews with director Paul Verhoeven and stars Michael Douglas and Sharon Stone, and a trailer too hot to be shown in theatres. 150 min. total.
27-6801 Was $24.99 ❑*$14.99*

Basic Instinct: The Original Director's Cut (Letterboxed Version)
The special edition is also available in a theatrical, widescreen format.
27-6881 ❑*$24.99*

Falling Down (1993)
Unsettling study of an unemployed, divorced Los Angeles defense worker (Michael Douglas) who loses his cool one day and sets off on a violent cross-town rampage, railing against societal problems, towards a reunion with his ex-wife and young daughter. Robert Duvall is a veteran cop trying to stop the emotionally distressed urban anti-hero; Barbara Hershey, Tuesday Weld co-star. 112 min.
19-2099 Was $19.99 ❑*$14.99*

Disclosure (1994)
Exciting, expertly crafted thriller based on Michael Crichton's best-seller stars Michael Douglas as a Seattle computer executive accused by new boss and former girlfriend Demi Moore of sexual harassment. With his marriage and career threatened, Douglas calls on high-tech help to clear him of the false charges. With Donald Sutherland; directed by Barry Levinson. 129 min.
19-2351 Was $19.99 ❑*$14.99*

The American President (1995)
Politics makes strange bedfellows, as well as a blizzard of media attention, when widower U.S. president Michael Douglas begins courting environmental lobbyist Annette Bening in this winning mix of romantic comedy and political intrigue from director Rob Reiner. With Richard Dreyfuss, Michael J. Fox, Samantha Mathis and Martin Sheen. 114 min.
02-2878 Was $19.99 ❑*$14.99*

The Ghost And The Darkness (1996)
Intense adventure drama, set in 1890s East Africa, stars Val Kilmer as an Irish engineer sent by British railroad officials to oversee construction of a vital bridge. When the worksite is terrorized by a pair of man-eating lions, Kilmer teams up with famed American hunter Michael Douglas to bring down the savage, seemingly supernatural beasts. 110 min.
06-2566 Was $99.99 ❑*$14.99*

The Ghost And The Darkness (Letterboxed Version)
Also available in a theatrical, widescreen format.
06-2613 ❑*$14.99*

The Game (1997)
Successful but detached investment banker Michael Douglas receives a most unusual 48th birthday present from younger brother Sean Penn: membership to a mysterious service called "the Game" that promises to add whatever is missing in one's life. For control-freak Douglas, that means a series of increasingly dangerous incidents that threaten his job, his way of life and his very identity. Gripping suspense tale from director David Fincher ("Seven") also stars Deborah Kara Unger, James Rebhorn. 128 min.
02-8807 Was $19.99 ❑*$14.99*

The Game (Letterboxed Version)
Also available in a theatrical, widescreen format.
02-8960 Was $19.99 ❑*$14.99*

A Perfect Murder: Collector's Edition (1998)
Sleek reworking of Hitchcock's "Dial 'M' for Murder" stars Michael Douglas as a wealthy commodities trader married to beautiful but unfaithful U.N. translator Gwyneth Paltrow. With Paltrow set to land a $100 million inheritance, Douglas hatches a plot to have her killed and blackmails her lover, ex-con Viggo Mortensen, into committing the crime. Directed by Andrew Davis ("The Fugitive"). Special video version includes an unused alternate ending and commentary by Davis. 108 min.
19-2749 Was $99.99 ❑*$19.99*

A Perfect Murder (Letterboxed Version)
Also available in a theatrical, widescreen format.
19-2858 ❑*$19.99*

Please see our index for these other Michael Douglas titles: *The China Syndrome • A Chorus Line: The Movie • Napoleon And Samantha*

Mickey Rourke

Act Of Love (1980)
True-life drama stars Ron Howard as the brother of Mickey Rourke, whose life is shattered when he's paralyzed after a motorcycle accident. Howard shoots Rourke as an act of mercy, then gives himself up to authorities in hopes of calling attention to euthanasia. With Robert Foxworth, Mary Kay Place and Jacqueline Brookes. 100 min.
10-9947 *$14.99*

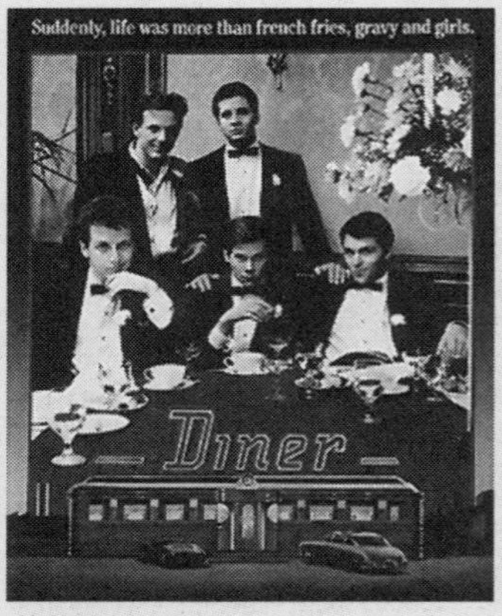
Suddenly, life was more than french fries, gravy and girls.
Diner

Diner: Special Edition (1982)
Director Barry Levinson's warm, heartfelt comedy about life in '50s Baltimore, centering around a group of young men, their favorite eatery hangout, and the choices they face as they enter adulthood. The talented ensemble cast includes Steve Guttenberg, Mickey Rourke, Daniel Stern, Kevin Bacon, Timothy Daly, Paul Reiser and Ellen Barkin. Includes an introduction by Levinson and a "making of" documentary. 145 min. total.
19-2946 *$19.99*

The Pope Of Greenwich Village (1984)
Gritty urban drama, laced with humor and reminiscent of "Mean Streets," with Mickey Rourke and Eric Roberts as two street toughs who wind up crossing with the Mafia. Co-stars Daryl Hannah, Kenneth McMillan. 120 min.
12-1388 Was $19.99 *$14.99*

Year Of The Dragon (1985)
"This is not Brooklyn. This is not the Bronx. This is not even New York...this is Chinatown."...And all Hell's breaking loose, as police captain Mickey Rourke sets out on his own private war against ganglord John Lone's drug-dealing organization. Scripted by Oliver Stone; Michael Cimino directs. 136 min.
12-1517 Was $19.99 □*$14.99*

9 1/2 Weeks (Unrated Version) (1986)
Director Adrian Lyne's erotically charged, controversial drama stars Kim Basinger and Mickey Rourke as a young New York couple whose relationship, based on sexual attraction, develops into a kinky, sadomasochistic obsession that draws them in and refuses to let go. Unrated, European version features scorching scenes too hot for American audiences. 118 min.
12-2726 *$19.99*

9 1/2 Weeks (R-Rated Version)
Also available in a less-explicit, theatrical edition. 114 min.
12-1606 *$14.99*

Another 9 1/2 Weeks (1997)
Just when you thought it was safe to put away the leather straps and close the refrigerator door, along comes Mickey Rourke, depressed over the end of his affair with Kim Basinger. He travels to Paris, where he intends to buy some of her paintings, and soon meets her best friend. The two have a torrid affair that leads to obsession. Angie Everhart, Agathe De La Fontaine co-star. 104 min.
68-1848 Was $99.99 □*$14.99*

Barfly (1987)
L.A.'s dark underbelly is the setting for this mesmerizing journey through the seedy existence of a brilliant, but dissipated, alcoholic poet. Mickey Rourke and Faye Dunaway are superb as the bitter artist and his equally dissolute lover in this drama based on the writings of Charles Bukowski. 110 min.
19-1634 □*$19.99*

Angel Heart (1987)
Atmospheric, highly controversial mystery by Alan Parker stars Mickey Rourke as a '50s private eye on a manhunt through the voodoo-shrouded streets of New Orleans. The scorching sex scenes between Rourke and Lisa Bonet that earned the film an "X" rating have been restored in this uncut version. Co-stars Charlotte Rampling and Robert De Niro as Rourke's mysterious client. 113 min.
27-6530 *$14.99*

Johnny Handsome (1989)
A disfigured small-time crook is set-up by his partners and sent to jail. While there, surgery gives him a new face and he develops a new identity, but when he's released he's ready to settle an old score. Gripping crime thriller from Walter Hill stars Mickey Rourke, Ellen Barkin, Elizabeth McGovern, Morgan Freeman, Forest Whitaker. 95 min.
27-6664 Was $89.99 □*$14.99*

Desperate Hours (1990)
Escaped killer Mickey Rourke terrorizes a suburban family while hiding from the law in their home in this gripping updating of the suspense classic. Anthony Hopkins, Mimi Rogers, Kelly Lynch also star; Michael Cimino ("Year of the Dragon") directs. 105 min.
12-2165 Was $89.99 □*$14.99*

Harley Davidson And The Marlboro Man (1991)
Set in the year 1996, this rip-snorting action yarn stars Mickey Rourke and Don Johnson as cycle-riding rebels who plot a daring armored car robbery in order to save their beloved bar. When the dynamic duo's plans go awry, they find themselves going head-to-head with a group of nasty hit men. Chelsea Field, Vanessa Williams and Tom Sizemore co-star. 98 min.
12-2381 Was $89.99 □*$14.99*

White Sands (1992)
Arresting thriller starring Willem Dafoe as a New Mexico sheriff who encounters stolen cash, arms dealers, a beautiful woman and duplicitous CIA agents when he tries to uncover the mystery of a corpse found in his territory. Mickey Rourke, Mary Elizabeth Mastrantonio, Samuel L. Jackson and Mimi Rogers also star. 101 min.
19-2007 Was $19.99 □*$14.99*

The Last Outlaw (1994)
In this pistol-packing adventure, Mickey Rourke plays Graff, the leader of a gang of ex-Confederate soldiers who rob Yankee banks after the Civil War. After being threatened by Graff, his right-hand man (Dermot Mulroney) recognizes his mentor's mean streak and a vicious fight ensues between two former friends. With John C. McGinley, Steve Buscemi and Keith David. 90 min.
44-1959 Was $89.99 □*$14.99*

Fall Time (1995)
As a prank, three teens plan a "shooting" in front of a small-town bank, but they stage their hoax just as a pair of crooks are launching their own robbery scheme, and the youths find themselves in a deadly confrontation. Intense thriller stars Mickey Rourke, Stephen Baldwin, David Arquette, Sheryl Lee. 88 min.
27-6953 Was $19.99 □*$14.99*

The Last Ride (1995)
Mickey Rourke is an angry rodeo renegade who falls for a girl dodging her past in this action-crammed tale packed with eroticism, spectacular stuntwork and incredible scenery of the West. Lori Singer, Peter Berg, Brion James and Aaron Neville also star. 102 min.
88-1008 Was $89.99 □*$14.99*

Bullet (1996)
On the mean streets of the city, you've got to fight for your survival every day, because it only takes one bullet to take it away. Mickey Rourke and Tupac Shakur star in this gritty urban action tale. With Ted Levine. 96 min.
02-5117 Was $19.99 □*$14.99*

Exit In Red (1997)
Mickey Rourke stars as a Beverly Hills psychiatrist whose bedside manner has gotten him accused of contributing to the suicide of a beautiful patient. While starting over in Palm Springs, he meets another gorgeous woman and soon becomes a prime suspect in her husband's murder. Annabel Schofield, Anthony Michael Hall and Carré Otis also star. 96 min.
06-2620 Was $99.99 □*$14.99*

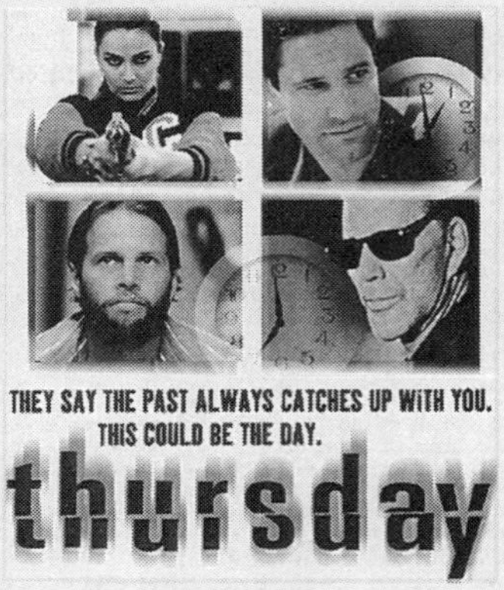
THEY SAY THE PAST ALWAYS CATCHES UP WITH YOU.
THIS COULD BE THE DAY.
thursday

Thursday (1998)
Scorching crime thriller about a former L.A. con artist and drug dealer who now lives respectably as an architect in a suburban house with a beautiful wife. When his former partner re-enters the scene with a case filled with heroin, the architect's quiet life is threatened. Thomas Jane, Aaron Eckhart, Paulina Porizkova and Mickey Rourke star. Unrated version; 87 min.
02-9045 Was $99.99 *$19.99*

Thicker Than Blood (1998)
Inspired by true-life events, this powerful drama tells of an Ivy League graduate who postpones entering law school to teach at an inner-city mission school. In this violent, depressed world he finds a talented student who becomes his major focus, bringing the teacher into conflict with the school's headmaster, a priest. Dan Futterman, Mickey Rourke and Carlo Alban star. 95 min.
19-2825 Was $99.99 □*$14.99*

Point Blank (1998)
When a group of the most deadly criminals in Texas goes on a crime spree, a maverick cop must bring them in—even though his brother is among their number. Extreme action tale stars Mickey Rourke, Frederic Forrest, Danny Trejo, Kevin Gage. 111 min.
64-9027 *$99.99*

Out In Fifty (1999)
Just out of prison, ex-con Balthazar Getty looks forward to reclaiming his life and the woman he loves. A sinister detective, however, has his own plans for Getty's future, and they involve being framed for murder! Mickey Rourke and Christina Applegate co-star in this intense actioner. 95 min.
82-5173 *$89.99*

Please see our index for these other Mickey Rourke titles: *1941 • Body Heat • Buffalo '66 • Double Team • Heaven's Gate • The Rainmaker • Rumble Fish*

Jerry And Tom (1998)
Surprise-filled directing debut by actor Saul Rubinek centers on Chicago car dealer Joe Mantegna, who takes dim bulb Sam Rockwell as a partner in his side business as a hit man. But after 10 years of killing people, the differences between the two emerge, especially when Rockwell becomes more and more ruthless. With William H. Macy, Ted Danson, Charles Durning. 92 min.
11-2454 □*$99.99*

The Cutting Edge (1992)
Can a rebellious small-town hockey player with dreams of the pros find success on and off the ice with a beautiful but temperamental figure skater? Highlighted by thrilling skating sequences, this winning romance stars D.B. Sweeney, Moira Kelly, Roy Dotrice and Terry O'Quinn. 101 min.
12-2537 Was $19.99 □*$14.99*

Woman Wanted (1999)
Emotional drama stars Holly Hunter as a woman hired as a housekeeper by widower Michael Moriarty and son Kiefer Sutherland. Both men fall in love with her, a situation that becomes more complex when Hunter announces she's pregnant. Sutherland also directed this tale of an unusual love triangle. 116 min.
11-2381 □*$99.99*

Miracle At Midnight (1999)
In this stirring, true story set in 1943 Denmark, Sam Waterston is a Copenhagen surgeon who joins forces with wife Mia Farrow and neighbors to hide Jews targeted for death by Nazi forces at midnight on Rosh Hashanah, then send them to safety in Sweden. With Justin Whalin and Nicola Mycroft. 89 min.
11-2434 □*$99.99*

Fires Within (1991)
Jimmy Smits, Greta Scacchi and Vincent D'Onofrio star in this exciting, smoldering tale about a political prisoner of Castro's Cuba who heads to Miami after his release after eight years in prison and discovers his wife has fallen in love with another man. Gillian Armstrong ("My Brilliant Career") directs. 90 min.
12-2347 Was $19.99 □*$14.99*

Silver Strand (1995)
Action and passion mix in this drama starring Nicollette Sheridan as the bored, base-bound wife of a tough Navy SEALs commander who begins a steamy affair with a cocky young recruit. With Gil Bellows; written by Douglas Day Stewart ("An Officer and a Gentleman"). 104 min.
12-3041 Was $89.99 □*$59.99*

Lost For Words (1998)
Based on the autobiographical writings of Deric Longden, this moving drama follows Longden (Pete Postlethwaite) and new wife Aileen (Penny Downie) coming to terms with the realization that his ailing mother, left mute after suffering a stroke, can no longer be left on her own. Thora Hird also stars.
08-8828 *$19.99*

Untamed Heart (1993)
A sensitive drama starring Christian Slater as a sheltered, monosyllabic young man infatuated with pretty waitress Marisa Tomei, who works with him at a Minneapolis diner. When Slater saves Tomei from being raped late one night, a romance develops between them. Rosie Perez also stars in this engaging film. 104 min.
12-2741 Was $19.99 □*$14.99*

Moondance (1997)
Two Irish adolescent brothers find the bonds of their friendship stretched to the limit when they both fall for a cute new neighbor girl in this warm and entertaining coming-of-age tale. Ruaidhri Conroy, Ian Shaw, Julia Brendler and Marianne Faithfull star; Van Morrison supplies songs. 96 min.
11-2229 Was $99.99 □*$19.99*

The Man In The Moon (1991)
This bittersweet, powerful drama tells the story of two sisters' coming-of-age experiences in a small Southern town in the 1950s. Seventeen-year-old Maureen and 14-year-old Dani find their friendship tested when they both fall for a handsome new neighbor boy. Sam Waterston, Tess Harper, Emily Warfield and Reese Witherspoon star. 99 min.
12-2445 Was $19.99 □*$14.99*

The Man In The Moon (Letterboxed Version)
Also available in a theatrical, widescreen format.
12-3135 □*$14.99*

Rush (1991)
Compelling and timely drama stars Jason Patric and Jennifer Jason Leigh as two narcotics officers who team up to go undercover and bring down a local drug lord, only to become addicted to their seductive new lifestyle and its pleasures. Rock star Greg Allman offers fine support as the cops' dealer target, and Eric Clapton supplies the music. 120 min.
12-2452 Was $19.99 □*$14.99*

A Family Thing (1996)
Touching drama with comedic moments starring Robert Duvall as a Southern good ol' boy who discovers through an old letter that his mother was black and he has an African-American half-brother. Duvall travels to Chicago to find his sibling, who turns out to be policeman James Earl Jones. But will they accept each other? With Irma P. Hall. 109 min.
12-3106 Was $19.99 □*$14.99*

A Family Thing (Letterboxed Version)
Also available in a theatrical, widescreen format.
12-3235 □*$14.99*

Talk Of Angels (1997)
Set amid the turmoil of the Spanish Civil War, this seductive melodrama stars Polly Walker as an Irish woman who serves as governess to aristocratic doctor Franco Nero's household. Problems arise when Walker falls for Nero's married son, anti-Franco government official Vincent Perez. With Marisa Paredes, Frances McDormand, Penélope Cruz. 97 min.
11-2316 Was $99.99 □*$19.99*

Rosewood (1997)
Drawing on a dark and little-known chapter in American history, director John Singleton ("Boyz N the Hood") recounts the destruction of Rosewood, a thriving all-black town in rural Florida, in 1923 by an angry white mob from nearby communities after a white woman falsely claimed she was assaulted by a black man. Ving Rhames, Jon Voight, Don Cheadle, Michael Rooker and Esther Rolle star. 142 min.
19-2563 Was $19.99 □*$14.99*

Rosewood (Letterboxed Version)
Also available in a theatrical, widescreen format.
19-2662 □*$19.99*

The Indian Runner (1991)
Sean Penn's directorial debut, inspired by Bruce Springsteen's song "Highway Patrolman," takes an unsparing look at the volatile relationship between two brothers in 1968 Nebraska, policeman David Morse and troubled Vietnam veteran Viggo Mortensen. Charles Bronson, Sandy Dennis, Dennis Hopper and Valeria Golino also star. 127 min.
12-2435 □*$14.99*

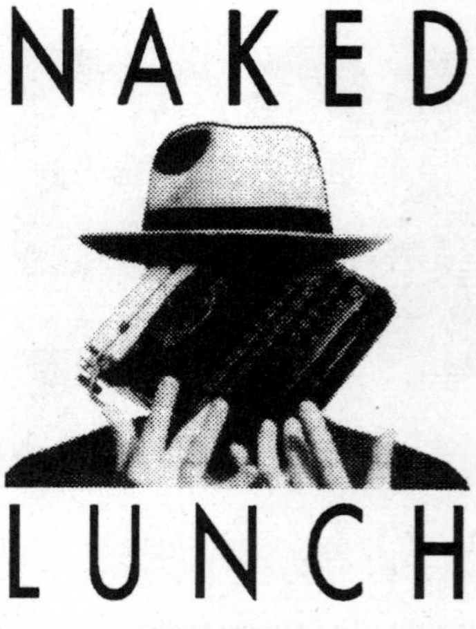
NAKED
LUNCH

Naked Lunch (1991)
David Cronenberg's creepy, darkly funny adaptation of the writings of William Burroughs focuses on the adventures of a drug-addicted exterminator/author (Peter Weller) who, after accidentally shooting his wife, journeys to a surrealistic Mediterranean country in hopes of unleashing his creative impulses. Judy Davis, Ian Holm and Roy Scheider co-star. 115 min.
04-2509 Was $89.99 □*$29.99*

CARRINGTON

EMMA THOMPSON
JONATHAN PRYCE

She had many lovers but only one love.

Carrington (1995)
Exquisitely acted and filmed study of the turn-of-the-century relationship between gay English writer Lytton Strachey (Jonathan Pryce) and painter Dora Carrington (Emma Thompson). While the two fell in love and lived together, they had various lovers (and, in Carrington's case, a husband) over the years—a revolutionary idea for its time. 122 min.
02-8442   Was $19.99   *$14.99*

Perfect Harmony (1991)
Set in the South, this sensitive drama tells of a group of boys' adventures in the school choir and how they deal with prejudice. Mr. Sanders, the new choir leader, tries to reduce some of the tension among the students by getting Zeke, the grandson of the school's caretaker, involved with the choir. Cleavon Little, Peter Scolari, Catherine Mary Stewart and Darren McGavin star.
11-1704 $19.99

Blood In...Blood Out: Bound By Honor (1993)
Rugged, powerful gang epic from Taylor Hackford ("An Officer and a Gentleman") detailing the lives of two Hispanic brothers and their half-Anglo cousin as they struggle for survival in the violence-filled barrios of East L.A. Drug addiction, gunplay, family rivalry and broken dreams are the elements explored in this forceful drama. With Jesse Borrego. AKA: "Bound by Honor." 180 min.
11-1747   Was $19.99 $14.99

The Program (1993)
James Caan is the tough football coach of Eastern State University who is put under the gun by school officials to get his team into bowl competition. His players grapple with important issues involving school, romance, alcohol, family and steroids while trying to win the big one for their coach. With Omar Epps, Craig Sheffer, Halle Berry and Kristy Swanson. 112 min.
11-1758   Was $19.99 $14.99

Not In This Town (1997)
Based on a true incident, this powerful drama stars Kathy Baker as a woman in Billings, Montana, who takes a courageous stand when racist hate groups attempt to take over her town. Adam Arkin, Ed Begley, Jr. also star. 95 min.
07-2632 $99.99

An Unexpected Family (1996)
Moving drama for all ages stars Stockard Channing as a driven career woman who unexpectedly becomes a "mother" when her sister leaves her children in her care. With Stephen Collins, Christine Ebersole. 93 min.
07-2496   Was $89.99 $14.99

Inventing The Abbotts (1997)
Set in a small mid-'50s Illinois town, this moving coming-of-age drama follows two working-class brothers (Billy Crudup, Joaquin Phoenix) who, for love and other reasons, become involved with the well-to-do and beautiful Abbott sisters (Jennifer Connelly, Joanna Going, Liv Tyler). Kathy Baker also stars. 116 min.
04-3498   Was $99.99 $29.99

The Wedding Gift (1994)
Julie Walters gives a moving performance in this bittersweet drama laced with laughs, playing a devoted wife and mother who learns she is terminally ill and sets out to make sure her husband finds someone to be with after she's gone. Jim Broadbent, Diana Longden co-star. 87 min.
11-1844   Was $89.99 $19.99

Fresh (1994)
Fresh, a 12 year-old motherless boy living in poverty in Brooklyn, serves as a lookout and runner for the local drug dealers while his vagrant father plays chess in the park. When a friend is killed, Fresh takes matters into his own hands, plotting an elaborate scheme to dupe the ruthless drug lords. Sean Nelson and Samuel L. Jackson star in this explosive urban story. 114 min.
11-1861   Was $89.99 $14.99

Georgia (1995)
Intense personal drama starring Jennifer Jason Leigh as a substance-addicted grunge rocker who lives in the shadow of folk-rock star sister Mare Winningham. When Leigh joins Winningham and her family in her Washington State home after a gig that falters, fireworks ignite between the sisters. Ted Levine co-star; written by Barbara Turner (Leigh's mother). 117 min.
11-2028 $19.99

Camilla (1994)
Sensitive road movie starring Jessica Tandy as a feisty, elderly musician who joins young aspiring singer Bridget Fonda on a cross-country road trip from Savannah to Canada. Along the way the pair encounter a good-natured traveller (Graham Greene) and Tandy's old flame, played by real-life husband Hume Cronyn. 91 min.
11-1883   Was $89.99 $19.99

Dog Day Afternoon

Al Pacino

Serpico (1973)
Al Pacino, in a dynamic performance, is Frank Serpico, the undercover cop who goes against the system and finds both crooks and fellow cops after him. Riveting, action-packed real-life drama, based on the Peter Maas book, co-stars John Randolph, M. Emmet Walsh. 129 min.
06-1102 $14.99

Scarecrow (1973)
Gene Hackman and Al Pacino play two eccentric drifters whose idea of success is owning a car wash in Pittsburgh. Their relationship forms the core of this bittersweet serio-comedy. Ann Wedgeworth, Eileen Brennan co-star. 112 min.
19-1153   Was $19.99 $14.99

Dog Day Afternoon (1975)
A tour-de-force for Al Pacino as a confused criminal who holds hostages in a Brooklyn bank in exchange for money to pay for his lover's sex-change operation and becomes a media hero. With John Cazale, Charles Durning and Chris Sarandon; based on a true case. 125 min.
19-1027 $19.99

Bobby Deerfield (1977)
Al Pacino is dynamic as a Grand Prix racing champion involved in an affair with aristocrat Marthe Keller, who, unknown to him, is suffering from a terminal illness. Exciting race scenes and tender romance combine to make this a winner. 124 min.
19-1111 $14.99

...And Justice For All. (1979)
Criminals go free, justice proves to be not-so blind, and lawyers and judges make deals...except for one young idealistic lawyer (Al Pacino) who bucks the system while representing a ruthless judge (John Forsythe) accused of a brutal rape. Co-stars Christine Lahti, Jack Warden and Lee Strasberg; directed by Norman Jewison, and written by Barry Levinson and Valerie Curtin. 117 min.
02-1069 $14.99

Cruising (1981)
Engrossing, controversial drama stars Al Pacino as a cop who goes undercover in New York's gay community to catch a serial killer of homosexuals. Graphic and violent, with Karen Allen, Paul Sorvino, Richard Cox. 105 min.
19-1751   Was $19.99 $14.99

Author! Author! (1982)
Playwright Al Pacino has his hands full when, in the middle of trying to finish his latest work, wife Tuesday Weld leaves home to find herself. Can Pacino handle their kids, his own writer's block, and an offbeat leading lady at the same time? Insightful comedy also stars Dyan Cannon, Alan King. 108 min.
04-1486   Was $59.99 $14.99

Scarface (1983)
Al Pacino is riveting in the title role of this ultra-violent, controversial updating of the '30s gangster classic. He's a Cuban hood out to become the "Cocaine King" of Florida—and the world. With Steven Bauer, Michelle Pfeiffer. Directed by Brian DePalma; written by Oliver Stone. 169 min.
07-1206   Was $19.99 $14.99

Scarface (Letterboxed Version)
Also available in a theatrical, widescreen format.
07-2675   Was $19.99 $14.99

Revolution (1985)
A dramatic look at "the world turn'd upside down," the world of the American Revolution. Al Pacino stars as a Scottish immigrant who fights the British to rescue his kidnapped son and falls for rebel Nastassja Kinski. Epic story from Hugh Hudson ("Chariots of Fire") also stars Donald Sutherland. 123 min.
19-1499 $14.99

Sea Of Love (1989)
The murders of several men who answered newspaper personal ads send detective Al Pacino out as a decoy, but when he becomes attracted to sexy suspect Ellen Barkin, will he pay with his life? Steamy suspenser also features John Goodman. 113 min.
07-1638   Was $19.99 $14.99

Scent Of A Woman (1992)
Al Pacino turns in an Oscar-winning performance as a bitter, blind, retired lieutenant colonel who enlists the help of a young prep school student (Chris O'Donnell) to join him on a whirlwind journey to New York. While there, the feisty Pacino offers his companion a surprise-filled initiation into manhood. Gabrielle Anwar also stars in this powerful and bittersweet story. 157 min.
07-1923   Was $19.99 $14.99

Scent Of A Woman (Letterboxed Version)
Also available in a theatrical, widescreen format.
07-2716   Was $19.99 $14.99

Carlito's Way (1993)
Knockout gangster yarn from Brian DePalma starring Al Pacino as Hispanic drug dealer Carlito Brigante, who runs into all sorts of trouble when he's released from prison and tries to go straight, operating a disco club in New York in the 1970s. Sean Penn is his coked-out lawyer compadre and Penelope Ann Miller is the exotic dancer he loves. 144 min.
07-2073   Was $19.99 $14.99

Carlito's Way (Letterboxed Version)
Also available in a theatrical, widescreen format.
07-2603   Was $19.99 $14.99

Drop Squad (1994)
A controversial and thought-provoking drama about an underground African-American organization that kidnaps blacks who, in its view, are denying or exploiting their ethnic heritage in order to "deprogram" them. But are the squad's methods betraying its goals? Produced by Spike Lee; Eriq LaSalle, Vondie Curtis-Hall, Ving Rhames star. 88 min.
07-2249   Was $19.99 $14.99

Cry, The Beloved Country (1995)
Stirring drama based on Alan Paton's acclaimed novel (first filmed in 1951) and starring James Earl Jones as a rural South African priest who befriends Richard Harris, a man whose activist son has been murdered in Johannesburg. New experiences and disturbing revelations occur when Jones travels to the city for the first time in his life. With Charles S. Dutton. 120 min.
11-2026   Was $99.99 $19.99

Two Bits (1995)
Nostalgic drama set in South Philadelphia during the Depression and featuring Al Pacino as an elderly man who promises his 12-year-old grandchild a quarter if he runs an important errand so he can go to the local movie theater. While doing the errand, the youngster learns an important lesson about life. Mary Elizabeth Mastrantonio, Jerry Barone co-star; Alec Baldwin narrates. 84 min.
11-2027 $19.99

City Hall (1996)
Gripping drama of big city politics starring Al Pacino as a charismatic, deal-making New York mayor whose power and allegiances are questioned by idealistic aide John Cusack after an African-American boy and a policeman are killed. Bridget Fonda, Danny Aiello, Martin Landau and Anthony Franciosa co-star. 112 min.
02-2914   Was $19.99 $14.99

The Devil's Advocate (1997)
One part "The Firm" and one part "Rosemary's Baby," this supernatural suspenser features a rousing turn by Al Pacino as the charismatic head of a powerful New York law firm that lures hot young attorney Keanu Reeves away from his small Southern town with promises of fame and success. But will Reeves discover his boss's diabolical origins before the job costs him his soul? Charlize Theron, Craig T. Nelson also star. 144 min.
19-2629   Was $19.99 $14.99

The Devil's Advocate (Letterboxed Version)
Also available in a theatrical, widescreen format.
19-2717 $19.99

The Al Pacino Collection
Al's on both sides of the law—and even plays the ultimate in villains—in this three-film boxed set that includes "The Devil's Advocate," "Dog Day Afternoon" and "Heat."
19-2793 $54.99

Any Given Sunday: Special Edition Director's Cut (1999)
Oliver Stone's no-holds-barred, multi-character gridiron drama looks at the on- and off-the-field struggles of the Miami Sharks, a once-mighty team in turmoil. While struggling to get a playoff spot, veteran quarterback Dennis Quaid finds his spot threatened by flashy backup Jamie Foxx, while fiery coach Al Pacino's style is at odds with offensive coordinator's Aaron Eckhart's tactics. Cameron Diaz, LL Cool J, Lauren Holly, James Woods, Ann-Margret and Charlton Heston also star. Special edition director's cut; 157 min.
19-2995   Was $99.99 $19.99

Please see our index for these other Al Pacino titles: *Dick Tracy • Donnie Brasco • Frankie & Johnny • The Godfather trilogy • Heat • The Insider • Looking For Richard*

Sports Biodramas

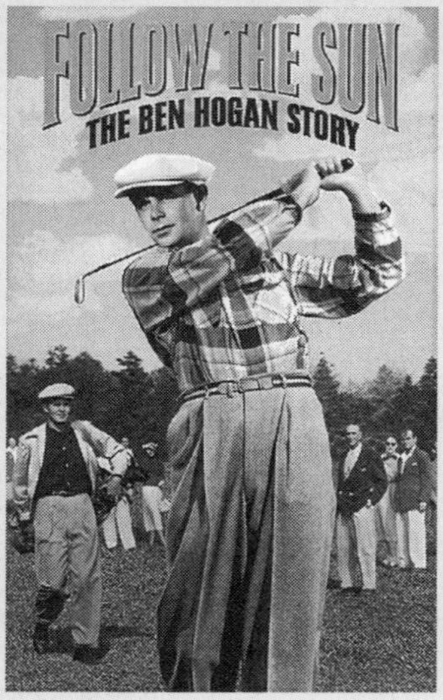

Follow The Sun (1951)
The courageous true-life story of champion golfer Ben Hogan and his triumphant return to the pro circuit after being involved in a debilitating car accident. Glenn Ford, Anne Baxter, Dennis O'Keefe and Sam Snead star in this fine sports drama. 93 min.
04-2828 Was $19.99 ❑*$14.99*

The Tiger Woods Story (1998)
He was playing golf before he could walk, and at the age of 21 he amazed the sports world by becoming the youngest Masters champion in history. Follow the remarkable true story of golf prodigy Tiger Woods in this moving and inspiring biodrama. Keith David, Khalil Kain, Freda Foh Shen star. 103 min.
06-2834 ❑*$69.99*

Spirit Of Youth (1938)
The only feature the "Brown Bomber," boxing great Joe Louis, ever made. A classic tale of a poor boy making good, with some fine boxing sequences. Plus a Louis sports short from the 1940s. Edna Mae Harris, Clarence Muse. 68 min.
17-1109 Was $29.99 *$24.99*

The Joe Louis Story (1950)
Coley Wallace stars as the "Brown Bomber," overcoming poverty and prejudice to become the world heavyweight boxing champion. Paul Stewart and Hilda Simms co-star; features actual footage of Louis' greatest fights. 88 min.
08-5030 *$14.99*

The Greatest (1977)
The fascinating life of boxing great Muhammad Ali gets a knockout screen treatment—with Ali playing himself! Follow the Champ from his childhood in Kentucky to his triumphs in boxing around the world. Excellent fight sequences, support by Ernest Borgnine, Robert Duvall and James Earl Jones. 101 min.
02-1357 *$14.99*

Heart Of A Champion: The Ray Mancini Story (1985)
Robert Blake plays '40s boxer Lenny Mancini, whose shot at the lightweight title was denied due to World War II, while Doug McKeon plays son Ray, who years later followed his father into the ring and won the belt. Two-fisted drama includes fight sequences arranged by Sylvester Stallone. 94 min.
04-2212 Was $59.99 ❑*$29.99*

Rocky Marciano (1998)
In this knockout biography, Jon Favreau plays famed heavyweight boxing champion Rocky Marciano. The film follows Rocky's formative years in blue-collar Brockton, Mass., and his relationship with his shoemaker father, as well as his most memorable bouts, including one with idol Joe Louis. George C. Scott, Penelope Ann Miller, Judd Hirsch and Tony Lo Bianco also star. 100 min.
12-3285 Was $49.99 ❑*$14.99*

Tyson (1995)
An electrifying account of the life of Mike Tyson encompassing his early years in and out of detention centers, the discovery of his boxing abilities by trainer Cus D'Amato, his rise to World Heavyweight Champion, his relationship with promoter Don King, his failed marriage to Robin Givens, and his jail sentence for rape. Michael Jai White, George C. Scott and Paul Winfield star. 110 min.
44-1993 Was $19.99 *$14.99*

Chariots Of Fire (1981)
The winner of 1981's Best Picture Oscar is an exciting human study of two competing runners in the 1924 Olympics. An exhilarating experience with stellar acting from Ben Cross, Ian Charleson, Ian Holm; directed by Hugh Hudson. Music by Vangelis. 124 min.
19-1227 Was $19.99 ❑*$14.99*

The First Olympics— Athens 1896 (1984)
Exciting film depiction of the events that led to the creation of the modern Olympic Games, and how a hastily-formed American team shocked the sports world with their success. David Ogden Stiers, Alex Hyde-White, Jason Connery star. 280 min.
02-1883 *$29.99*

The Jesse Owens Story (1984)
Inspiring, true story of the triumphs and tragedies of Jesse Owens, the legendary track star who won four gold medals over Hitler's supermen and captured America's hearts. Dorian Harewood, Debbi Morgan, Ben Vereen, LeVar Burton. 180 min.
06-1219 Was $69.99 *$24.99*

Run For The Dream: The Gail Devers Story (1996)
The compelling true story of Olympic gold medalist Gail Devers is brought to life in this inspiring film that chronicles her fight to overcome Graves' Disease and become the fastest sprinter in the world. With Charlayne Woodard and Lou Gossett, Jr. as coach Bob Kersee and cameos from track stars Florence Griffith Joyner and Willie Gault. 99 min.
88-1114 Was $99.99 *$14.99*

Without Limits (1998)
Before his untimely death at the age of 24, he became the leading distance runner in sports and set every American record for 2,000 to 10,000-meter events. Billy Crudup is superb as Steve Prefontaine in this moving look at his life and drive to reach the top. Monica Potter and Donald Sutherland also star; directed and co-written by Robert Towne. 118 min.
19-2816 Was $99.99 ❑*$14.99*

Endurance (1999)
Mixing actual race footage with dramatic re-creations, documentarian Leslie Woodhead and Olympic chronicler Bud Greenspan tell the story of champion distance runner Haile Gebrselassie. Growing up in a rural Ethiopian village, Haile left his family farm for years of intense training before shattering world track records and bringing home the gold for the 10,000-meter race at the 1996 games. Gebrselassie and his family play themselves. 83 min.
11-2406 Was $99.99 ❑*$19.99*

The Jackie Robinson Story (1950)
Jackie himself starred in this autobiographical account of his groundbreaking entry into baseball's major leagues. In the face of pressure and prejudice, Robinson proved he had the necessities to be a winner. Ruby Dee, Louise Beavers and Minor Watson also star. 76 min.
12-2823 Was $19.99 *$14.99*

The Court-Martial Of Jackie Robinson (1990)
Stirring drama about a little-known chapter in the life of the legendary sports hero. Andre Braugher ("Glory") stars as Robinson, who, as a WWII recruit, was tried for insubordination when he refused to ride in the back of a bus. Bruce Dern, Ruby Dee, Daniel Stern also star. 93 min.
18-7264 Was $79.99 ❑*$14.99*

The Pride Of St. Louis (1952)
Appealing baseball biodrama of Hall of Fame pitcher Jay Hanna "Dizzy" Dean stars Dan Dailey as the '30s hurler who backed up his on-the-field stunts with matchless skills. With Joanne Dru and Richard Crenna as teammate/sibling "Daffy" Dean. 93 min.
04-2321 ❑*$19.99*

Fear Strikes Out (1957)
Anthony Perkins portrays '50s baseball star Jimmy Piersall, who fought back from a mental breakdown to return to the majors, in a compelling diamond biodrama. Karl Malden, Norma Moore also star. 100 min.
06-1706 *$14.99*

It's Good To Be Alive (1974)
Paul Winfield stars as baseball legend Roy Campanella in this moving biodrama of the Dodger star's life after the 1958 auto accident that left him a quadriplegic, but couldn't put out his courage and will to live. Ruby Dee, Lou Gossett, Jr. AKA: "The Fight." 100 min.
75-7050 *$14.99*

A Love Affair: The Eleanor And Lou Gehrig Story (1977)
The tragic, inspiring story of the baseball legend and the woman who loved him is told in this drama, as seen from Mrs. Gehrig's view. Blythe Danner, Edward Herrmann, Patricia Neal star. 96 min.
14-3061 *$19.99*

Don't Look Back: The Story Of LeRoy "Satchel" Paige (1981)
Inspirational true story of baseball pitching great "Satchel" Paige, tracing his career from his barnstorming adventures in the 1920s to his great years in the Negro Leagues and a major league career, which began at the age of 43 with the Cleveland Indians. Lou Gossett, Jr., Beverly Todd, Cleavon Little and the real Paige star. 96 min.
19-2241 Was $79.99 *$14.99*

A Winner Never Quits (1986)
Sensitive true-life story of 1940s pro baseball player Pete Gray, who made it to the majors despite missing one arm and whose courage inspires a young handicapped fan. Keith Carradine, Mare Winningham, Dennis Weaver and Dana Delaney star. 96 min.
02-2447 *$59.99*

The Babe (1992)
John Goodman puts on the pinstripes to play baseball legend Babe Ruth in this exciting account of "The Sultan of Swat's" colorful life. The film follows "The Bambino" from his early years at a boy's school in Baltimore to his glory days with the Yankees and his sad final season with the Boston Braves. Kelly McGillis, Bruce Boxleitner and Trini Alvarado also star. 115 min.
07-1858 Was $19.99 ❑*$14.99*

Cobb (1994)
Tommy Lee Jones turns in a galvanizing performance as Ty Cobb, the baseball legend idolized by fans and hated by opponents and teammates alike. Hired to co-author Cobb's autobiography, writer Robert Wuhl soon realizes that everything he's heard about the drunken, bigoted septuagenarian is true—and then some! Lolita Davidovich also stars; directed by Ron Shelton ("Bull Durham"). 129 min.
19-2353 Was $19.99 ❑*$14.99*

Soul Of The Game (1996)
Fact-based biodrama, set in the days of segregated baseball, looks at the three Negro League players—troubled slugger Josh Gibson (Mykelti Williamson), colorful pitcher Satchel Paige (Delroy Lindo) and rookie infielder Jackie Robinson (Blair Underwood)—who were finalists in Brooklyn Dodger president Branch Rickey's search for a man to break the majors' racial barrier. 94 min.
44-2057 Was $19.99 ❑*$14.99*

The Pistol (1991)
Inspiring true story of "Pistol" Pete Maravich, focusing on the basketball hall of famer's teenage years and the support given him by his father, Press Maravich. A wonderful, family-oriented sports drama, in the tradition of "Hoosiers." Adam Guier, Nick Benedict, Millie Perkins star. 104 min.
45-5505 Was $19.99 ❑*$14.99*

Rebound (1996)
He was one of the greatest basketball talents to ever come from the sidewalk courts of Harlem, but Earl "The Goat" Manigault's abilities couldn't save him from the brutal realities of life on the streets that kept him reaching the pros. Gritty sports drama, based on a true story, stars Don Cheadle, James Earl Jones, Loretta Devine, Forest Whitaker and Eriq La Salle, who also directed. 111 min.
44-2087 Was $19.99 ❑*$14.99*

Passing Glory (1999)
Set in 1965 New Orleans, this inspiring true drama stars Andre Braugher as priest and high-school basketball coach Joseph Verrett, who struck a blow for racial equality when he led his all-black team in a groundbreaking game against the region's top all-white squad. Rip Torn, Ruby Dee, Bill Nunn also star; directed by Steve James ("Hoop Dreams"). 94 min.
18-7867 Was $79.99 ❑*$14.99*

Michael Jordan: An American Hero (1999)
The fascinating life and spectacular career of NBA superstar Michael Jordan is the subject of this made-for-cable feature. Follow Jordan's relationship with his father; his early years playing basketball; his college days at North Carolina; his incredible career with the Chicago Bulls; his retirement; and his triumphant comeback. Michael Jace, Debbie Allen star. 93 min.
82-5125 *$49.99*

Harmon Of Michigan (1941)
Michigan football star Tom Harmon (father of actor Mark Harmon) plays himself in this exciting biography. Following an illustrious collegiate career, Harmon plays pro ball, marries his girlfriend and eventually joins the coaching staff at his alma mater. Anita Louise and Oscar O'Shea also star. 65 min.
10-9063 Was $19.99 *$14.99*

The Great Dan Patch (1949)
Exciting true drama of the champion trotting horse in the early 20th century and the family that owned and loved him. Dennis O'Keefe, Gail Russell and Ruth Warrick star. 92 min.
59-5018 *$19.99*

Brian's Song (1970)
One of the most popular made-for-television movies of all time depicts the true story of the inseparable friendship between fellow Chicago Bears running backs Gale Sayers and Brian Piccolo, and the tragedy they faced together. Co-stars James Caan, Billy Dee Williams, Shelley Fabares and Jack Warden. 73 min.
02-1029 Was $19.99 ❑*$14.99*

Grambling's White Tiger (1981)
Olympic medalist Bruce Jenner stars in this true story about Jim Gregory, the first white person ever to play on Grambling University's football team. Hard-hitting, emotional drama, which combines timely insights along with a first-rate sports story, co-stars LeVar Burton and Harry Belafonte. 98 min.
07-1330 *$39.99*

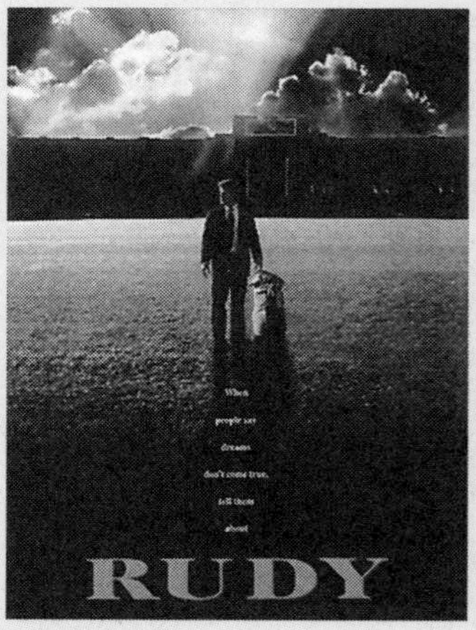

Rudy (1993)
Stirring, true-life tale of Daniel "Rudy" Ruettiger, a teenager from a working-class family with the impossible dream of playing football for his beloved Notre Dame. After going to great lengths to gain admission to the school and making the team, Rudy is relegated to benchwarmer status before he wins the respect of his teammates and coach Ara Parseghian. Sean Astin, Ned Beatty, Charles Dutton star. 114 min.
02-2599 Was $19.99 ❑*$14.99*

8 Seconds (1994)
Luke Perry saddles up for the ride of his life when he stars as bull-riding champion Lane Frost, who met with a quick rise to stardom before his untimely death, in this rousing rodeo drama from director John Avildsen ("Rocky"). With Stephen Baldwin, Cynthia Geary. 104 min.
02-2664 Was $19.99 ❑*$14.99*

Breaking The Surface: The Greg Louganis Story (1996)
Based on the best-selling autobiography by Olympic gold medal-winning diver Greg Louganis, this compelling drama depicts the adopted Louganis' difficult relationship with his parents, his closeted homosexual lifestyle, his athletic triumphs and the revelation that he is HIV-positive. With Mario Lopez, Michael Murphy. Special unedited video version; 95 min.
73-9182 Was $49.99 *$29.99*

The Jesse Ventura Story (1999)
Trace the incredible true story of the man who rose from the ranks of pro wrestling to national political prominence as the outspoken governor of Minnesota. Jesse's life is surveyed, from his days as a Navy SEAL and his colorful careers as bouncer, disc jockey and wrestler to his stunning gubernatorial win. Nils Allen Stewart plays Ventura, and ring stars Goldberg, Raven and Chris Kanyon also appear. 95 min.
74-3045 *$39.99*

Until The End Of The World (1992)
Wim Wenders' dazzling globetrotting adventure is set in 1999, where the world waits for a runaway nuclear satellite to fall from the sky. William Hurt is a fugitive gathering images for his inventor father's creation, which enables blind people to see. In Europe, Hurt encounters a beautiful woman (Solveig Dommartin) carrying stolen cash, and soon she becomes involved in his mesmerizing quest. Max von Sydow, Sam Neill and Jeanne Moreau also star. 158 min.
19-1977 Was $89.99 ❑*$19.99*

The End Of Violence (1997)
Two seemingly unconnected stories—a slick Hollywood action film producer who goes into seclusion after an abduction and attempt on his life, and a surveillance expert who's dotted the city of Los Angeles with hundreds of hidden cameras—dovetail together in director Wim Wenders' thoughtful examination of crime, security and the media in modern society. Bill Pullman, Gabriel Byrne, Andie MacDowell, Traci Lind star. 123 min.
12-3221 Was $99.99 ❑*$14.99*

At First Sight (1999)
Science gave him the gift of sight, but will opening his eyes force him to close his heart? Val Kilmer stars as a masseur, blind since childhood, who falls for client Mira Sorvino and, at her urging, undergoes an experimental operation that restores his vision. Will Kilmer's struggle to adjust to the sighted world tear their romance apart? Based on a true story by Dr. Oliver Sacks ("Awakenings"), this moving romantic drama also stars Kelly McGillis, Bruce Davison, Nathan Lane. 126 min.
12-3274 Was $99.99 ❑*$14.99*

Meeting Venus (1991)
Glenn Close is a temperamental opera diva set to star in a globally broadcast production of Wagner's "Tannhäuser." She begins a love affair with the opera's Hungarian conductor, but he's got other problems to worry about: union woes, management squabbles, and protesters picketing the theatre. Niels Arestrup co-stars in this engaging backstage comedy/drama by Istvan Szabo ("Mephisto"); soprano Kiri Te Kanawa supplies Close's singing voice. 121 min.
19-1959 Was $89.99 ❑*$19.99*

Fried Green Tomatoes (Special Edition) (1991)
Wonderfully acted comedy/drama, based on the best-selling novel by Fannie Flagg, about a frustrated housewife (Kathy Bates) who is transfixed by the tales spun by an elderly nursing home resident (Jessica Tandy). The stories involve two independent women (Mary Stuart Masterson and Mary-Louise Parker) who ran a popular cafe in 1930s Alabama and whose friendship survived a number of incredible events. With Cicely Tyson, Chris O'Donnell. Special video version includes six minutes of extra footage and interviews with Masterson, Parker and director Jon Avnet. 130 min.
07-2744 ❏*$14.99*

Fried Green Tomatoes (Letterboxed Version)
Also available in a theatrical, widescreen format.
07-2745 Was $19.99 ❏*$14.99*

Reach The Rock (1999)
Former teen scene specialist John Hughes ("Pretty in Pink") penned this story of rebellious 21-year-old Alessandro Nivola and his relationship with police sergeant William Sadler. After he's thrown into prison for breaking a storefront window, Nivola tries to get the best of the lawman and his deputy. Karen Sillas and Bruce Norris also star. 100 min.
07-2760 Was $99.99 ❏*$19.99*

Last Night (1999)
With the world about to come to an end at midnight on January 1, 2000, a group of people in Toronto contemplate how to deal with the event in this provocative, irony-filled drama from Canadian actor-screenwriter-director Don McKellar. Sandra Oh, David Cronenberg, Sarah Polley, Genevieve Bujold and McKellar star in the intriguing independent effort. 95 min.
07-2844 Was $99.99 ❏*$19.99*

All The Little Animals (1999)
Emotional drama stars Christian Bale as a mentally-impaired young man threatened with institutionalization if he doesn't turn over control of his family's store to scheming stepfather Daniel Benzali. Running away to England's Cornwall countryside, Bale is taken in by mysterious recluse John Hurt, who spends his days caring for wounded and dead animals along the roadside. 114 min.
07-2856 Was $99.99 ❏*$19.99*

Snow Falling On Cedars (1999)
In 1950s Washington state, Japanese-American Rick Yune stands accused of killing a white fisherman. As the trial threatens to stir up old prejudices, local newspaperman Ethan Hawke must deal with his feelings for the accused's wife (Youki Kudoh), with whom he had a teenage romance that ended with Pearl Harbor and her family's internment in a prison camp. Based on David Guterson's best-selling novel, this lushly photographed drama also stars Max Von Sydow, Sam Shepard. 128 min.
07-2867 ❏*$99.99*

A Call To Remember (1997)
Joe Mantegna and Blythe Danner star in this moving story about a couple with two teenage sons who are struggling to build a new life together in America after escaping the Nazi horrors of World War II. However, an unexpected phone call throws them into a turmoil that threatens their future. With David Lascher. 111 min.
07-2664 ❏*$99.99*

Metroland (1999)
Acclaimed drama is set in the 1970s and features Christian Bale as a man who has settled into a middle-class existence with his wife and toddler in the London suburbs. After one of Bale's bachelor drinking pals pays him a visit, he longs for the good old days, and soon wonders if they're worth returning to. Emily Watson and Lee Ross also star. 102 min.
07-2793 Was $99.99 ❏*$19.99*

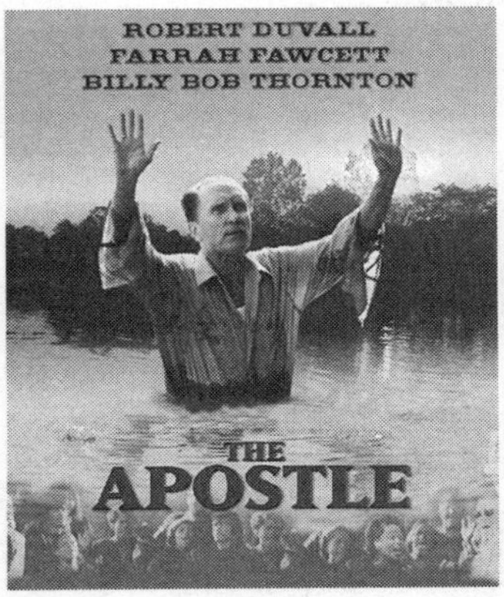

The Apostle (1997)
Robert Duvall gives the performance of his career as a preacher searching for redemption in this acclaimed drama he also wrote and directed. After his wife leaves him for another man, Duvall assumes a new identity in a new town with nothing but his will to do the right thing and to spread the word of God. Also stars Farrah Fawcett, Billy Bob Thornton and Miranda Richardson. 134 min.
07-2654 Was $99.99 ❏*$14.99*

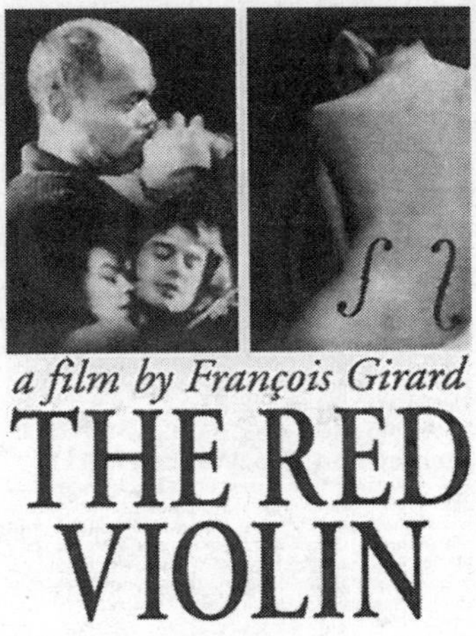

The Red Violin (1999)
This acclaimed film from Quebec helmer Francois Girard traces the history of a violin, from its crafting in 17th-century Italy, and the fates of its various owners through the years. Among those who share in its beauty, joy and tragedy are novelist Greta Scacchi; her lover, violin virtuoso Jason Flemyng; and instrument expert Samuel L. Jackson. In English and French, German, Italian and Mandarin with English subtitles. 132 min.
07-2799 Was $99.99 ❏*$19.99*

The Color Of Courage (1999)
Set in 1944, this powerful true story features Lynn Whitfield as Minnie McGhee, an African-American woman welcomed to her new Detroit home by white neighbor Anna Sipes (Linda Hamilton). But McGhee and her family's welcome is short-lived when they discover community members are out to have them evicted because of their skin color. Sipes is appalled and tries to stop the action. With Bruce Greenwood. 92 min.
07-2794 ❏*$99.99*

TwentyFourSeven (1998)
Bob Hoskins stars in this moving British drama about a man who returns to his hometown to find it a desolate post-industrial wasteland with frequent breakouts of petty violence. He starts up a boxing club to bring the local youths together, giving redemption to them as well as himself in the process. Frank Harper, Pamela Cundell, Danny Nussbaum co-star. 96 min.
07-2670 Was $99.99 ❏*$14.99*

Commandments (1997)
After losing his wife, home and job through a series of catastrophes that includes being struck by lightning, a forlorn Aidan Quinn decides to challenge God by breaking each of the Ten Commandments in this offbeat allegorical drama laced with dark humor. Anthony LaPaglia, Courteney Cox also star. 88 min.
07-2540 Was $99.99 ❏*$14.99*

Any Place But Home (1997)
A woman's sister and her conniving brother-in-law abduct the son of a wealthy businessman. After the woman snatches the boy from her unscrupulous relatives, she learns that he's hiding a dark secret. Joe Lando, Dale Midkiff and Mary Page Keller star. 92 min.
07-2557 ❏*$99.99*

Our Mother's Murder (1997)
A wealthy widow falls for the charms of a younger man, but after they're married, her suspicions about his true nature are chillingly and violently confirmed, and she is forced into a desperate fight for her life. Based on the true story of newspaper heiress Anne Scripps Douglas, this gripping drama stars Roxanne Hart, James Wilder. 92 min.
07-2631 ❏*$99.99*

Jumpin At The Boneyard (1992)
Two brothers, one a jobless wanderer and the other a drug addict, attempt to help each other find meaning in their lives and set things right during a one-day trip through the New York City neighborhoods where they grew up. Gritty slice-of-life drama from rookie writer/director Jeff Stanzler stars Tim Roth, Alexis Arquette, Danitra Vance. 107 min.
04-2624 Was $89.99 *$29.99*

Stealing Beauty (1996)
Bernardo Bertolucci's sensuous, beautifully filmed drama stars Liv Tyler as a 19-year-old woman who travels to Italy to renew a relationship with an old friend and discern the secret of her late mother's diary. While staying with a sculptor and his wife, she learns about love, sex, life and herself. Jeremy Irons, Jean Marais and Sinead Cusack also star. 118 min.
04-3393 Was $99.99 ❏*$14.99*

Paradise Road (1997)
A group of British and American women fleeing the Japanese invasion of Singapore in 1942 is captured by enemy forces and sent to a prison camp in Sumatra. The only relief they get from the horrible conditions and tortures inflicted by their captors is through singing in a choir with other inmates. Stirring, true-life story stars Glenn Close, Frances McDormand, Juliana Margulies, Pauline Collins. 120 min.
04-3532 ❏*$99.99*

My Husband's Secret Life (1998)
As she searches for the truth behind her policeman husband's death, Anne Archer must battle not only the infamous "blue wall of silence," but also a citywide conspiracy that reaches deep into City Hall, in this powerful drama. James Russo, Maria Conchita Alonso also star. 93 min.
07-2698 ❏*$99.99*

Opposite Corners (1998)
A young man striving to win the famous Golden Gloves boxing competition must battle inside and outside the ring when he learns disturbing facts about his father's Mafia connections. Powerful drama stars Billy Warlock, Cathy Moriarty, Frankie Valli. 106 min.
06-2840 ❏*$69.99*

Backdraft (1991)
Astonishing special effects and fabulous stunts highlight this powerful story from director Ron Howard centering on the rivalry between a career fireman (Kurt Russell) and his younger brother (William Baldwin), a fire inspector investigating a series of mysterious blazes. Scott Glenn, Robert De Niro, Rebecca De Mornay and Donald Sutherland also star. 135 min.
07-1714 ❏*$14.99*

Backdraft (Letterboxed Version)
Also available in a theatrical, widescreen format.
07-1839 Was $19.99 *$14.99*

An Unexpected Life (1997)
The story of artist Stockard Channing and the two children entrusted to her continues in this warm and touching sequel to "An Unexpected Family," as the makeshift brood moves from the city to the country and finds new challenges and surprises. Stephen Collins, Christine Ebersole and RuPaul also star. 92 min.
07-2733 ❏*$89.99*

Strawberry Fields (1997)
Powerful tale set in the 1970s and focusing on Irene, a young Japanese-American woman. Troubled by the death of her sister, she begins a journey of self-discovery after she discovers that members of her family died in an internment camp during World War II and travels out West to see the site where her family was sent. With Susie Nakamura. 86 min.
22-9223 *$79.99*

The Old Man And The Sea (1990)
Ernest Hemingway's celebrated story receives a stirring translation as Anthony Quinn takes the role of Santiago, the luckless Cuban fisherman. Facing difficult times, Santiago goes to sea and reels in a tremendous marlin, but soon finds marauding sharks seeking his catch. Alexis Cruz, Patricia Clarkson also star. 95 min.
53-9600 Was $24.99 *$19.99*

The Cure (1995)
Sensitively filmed drama about a young Minnesota boy who contracts the HIV virus from a blood transfusion. Shunned by children and parents alike, he is eventually befriended by another boy who has recently moved to the area from the South. Together, the two set out on a search for a cure for the disease. Joseph Mazzello, Brad Renfro, Annabella Sciorra star. 99 min.
07-2340 Was $89.99 ❏*$19.99*

Lily In Winter (1995)
Compassionate drama about friendship stars singer Natalie Cole as a Manhattan housekeeper who takes a trip to the small Alabama town of her youth and is surprised to find her employers' young son has joined her on the journey. While the two realize their similarities and differences, Cole learns about the family she left behind. With Brian Bonsall. 94 min.
07-2358 Was $89.99 ❏*$14.99*

A Mother's Prayer (1995)
After learning she is HIV-positive, single mother Linda Hamilton must confront her own impending death while trying to find a family to raise her 8-year-old son after she's gone. Powerful drama also stars Noah Fleiss, Bruce Dern, Kate Nelligan, RuPaul. 94 min.
07-2365 Was $89.99 ❏*$14.99*

Grace Of My Heart (1996)
Set against the backdrop of the music industry in the '50s and '60s, this tune-filled story stars Illeana Douglas as an aspiring singer who, with help from manager John Turturro, becomes a top pop songwriter. Director Allison Anders ("Gas Food Lodging") traces Douglas' ever-evolving work and the men in her life who influence it. With Matt Dillon, Eric Stoltz; music by Elvis Costello, Burt Bacharach, Joni Mitchell and others. 114 min.
07-2482 Was $99.99 ❏*$14.99*

David Lynch

The Elephant Man (1980)
The emotional true story of John Merrick, whose hideous deformities cast him as a freak in Victorian London. John Hurt is "the Elephant Man," and Anthony Hopkins is the compassionate doctor who shows him the first kindness in his life. Director David Lynch's striking black-and-white drama also stars Anne Bancroft. 124 min.
06-1082 *$14.99*

Dune (1984)
Frank Herbert's classic sci-fi story is faithfully brought to the screen by director David Lynch. In the distant future, two rival interplanetary clans find their ultimate battlefield on the desert planet called Dune, where one young man must face his mystical destiny. Kyle MacLachlan, Francesca Annis, Jurgen Prochnow, Jose Ferrer, Patrick Stewart, Sting and Sean Young star. 137 min.
07-1288 ❏*$14.99*

Dune (Letterboxed Version)
Also available in a theatrical, widescreen format.
07-2508 ❏*$14.99*

Blue Velvet (1986)
David Lynch's unsettling drama of violent and erotic surrender in a small town. A young man's investigation of a grisly discovery draws him into affairs with an innocent teenage girl and a masochistic singer involved with a sadistic psychopath. Stars Kyle MacLachlan, Isabella Rossellini, Laura Dern and Dennis Hopper. 120 min.
40-1269 ❏*$14.99*

Twin Peaks: Fire Walk With Me (1992)
You may know "who killed Laura Palmer," but how did she spend the last week of her life? Going back before the events shown in his cult fave TV series, director/co-writer David Lynch returns to the quirky Northwest town where nothing is what it seems and an evil spirit has found a place to dwell. "Peaks" regulars Sheryl Lee, Ray Wise and Kyle MacLachlan star, along with Chris Isaak, Moira Kelly. 134 min.
02-5011 Was $89.99 ❏*$14.99*

Lost Highway (1997)
Let director David Lynch chauffeur you down a dark and twisted road of passion, madness and murder, as the seemingly unconnected stories of musician Bill Pullman and wife Patricia Arquette, who learn someone is videotaping them inside their home, and mechanic Balthazar Getty, who has an affair with mob boss Robert Loggia's mistress (Arquette again), are brought together, thanks to the machinations of white-faced mystery man Robert Blake. With Gary Busey, Richard Pryor, Jack Nance. 135 min.
02-8688 Was $99.99 ❏*$19.99*

Lost Highway (Letterboxed Version)
Also available in a theatrical, widescreen format.
02-8689 Was $99.99 ❏*$19.99*

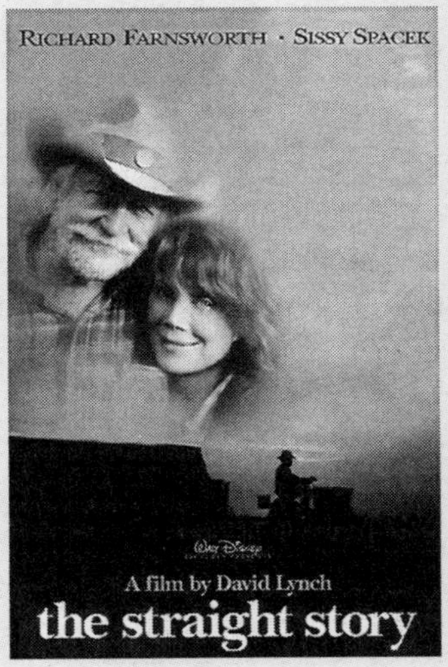

The Straight Story (1999)
In a gentle, G-rated change of pace that still features his trademark fascination with rural American quirkiness, director David Lynch recounts the true story of 73-year-old Iowa retiree Alvin Straight (Richard Farnsworth). Upon learning his estranged brother has suffered a stroke, and unable to drive a car, Straight loaded up his riding mower and set out on a 300-mile trek to Wisconsin to see his sibling and make amends. Sissy Spacek, Everett McGill, Harry Dean Stanton also star. 112 min.
11-2425 Was $99.99 ❏*$19.99*

Pretty As A Picture: The Art Of David Lynch (1997)
Explore the singularly twisted oeuvre of the filmmaker behind such works as "Eraserhead," "Blue Velvet" and "Twin Peaks" with this documentary, produced during the shooting of Lynch's "Lost Highway," in which Lynch talks candidly about his life, his art and the creative process. Film clips and interviews with Robert Blake, Jack Nance, Bill Pullman, Dean Stockwell and others are also included. 85 min.
53-8956 *$19.99*

The Fifteen Streets (1989)
Acclaimed drama, based on a Catherine Cookson novel, about two hard-working, brawling brothers who work on the shipyard docks. When the eldest brother falls in love with the daughter of a local ship magnate, he faces danger and bigotry. Sean Bean, Owen Teale and Clare Holman star. 108 min.
53-9609   *$24.99*

The Man Who Cried (1993)
This compelling tale of love and loss centers on an unhappily married man who goes to great lengths to make a happy life for his son. After his married lover is murdered, the man leaves his spiteful wife and, along with his son, searches for a fresh start. But an affair with a widow and her younger sister complicates things even further. Ciaran Hinds stars. 156 min.
53-9598   Was $49.99   *$29.99*

The Cinder Path (1994)
A man attempts to overcome his tumultuous childhood, which included terrible beatings and continuous taunting from his father, in this powerful drama taken from Catherine Cookson's novel. Lloyd Owen, Catherine Zeta Jones and Maria Miles star. 145 min.
53-9612   Was $29.99   *$19.99*

The Dwelling Place (1995)
Following the death of her parents, a 16-year-old girl tries to keep her family together, turning a cave into a home and caring for her younger siblings. Her life takes several strange turns after she is raped and impregnated by a drunken aristocrat. Tracy Whitwell and James Fox star in this stirring adaptation of the Catherine Cookson story. 145 min.
53-9611   *$29.99*

The Glass Virgin (1995)
Catherine Cookson's story focuses on Annabella Lagrange, a young woman who has lived a life of luxury, unaware that her reclusive father is a spendthrift and womanizer. At the age of 17, she discovers a shocking secret about her birth and takes to the road to start a new life. 150 min.
53-9713   *$34.99*

The Gambling Man (1995)
Epic drama from Catherine Cookson focusing on Rory O'Connor, an entrepreneur and gambler whose vices may lead to a tough prison sentence. When his wife is lost at sea, O'Connor finds solace with his female boss, whom he eventually marries. But the past returns one day to haunt him. Robson Green stars. 150 min.
53-9714   *$34.99*

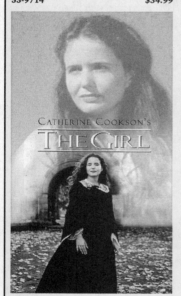

CATHERINE COOKSON'S
THE GIRL

The Girl (1996)
A beautiful young woman, born out of wedlock and raised in the home of her father and his resentful wife, finds herself trapped in a loveless marriage as part of her "stepmother's" schemes in this drama based on the Catherine Cookson novel. Siobhan Flynn, Jonathan Cake, Jill Baker star. 156 min.
08-8587   *$29.99*

The Rag Nymph (1997)
The "Rag Nymph" of the title is an abandoned child from a bad part of town who is taken in by Aggie Winkowski. The two form a special relationship that helps Aggie find meaning in her life and molds the young woman's destiny. Claire Skinner, Anne Reid star in an adaptation of Catherine Cookson's story. 150 min.
53-9908   *$34.99*

The Moth (1997)
Set in 1913, this Catherine Cookson tale tells of Robert Bradley, a talented carpenter who leaves the shipyards where he works for his uncle's furniture business in the countryside. But when he finds himself at odds with his relatives, Bradley gets employment with a troubled family and soon falls for the woman of the house. Jack Davenport, Juliet Abrey star. 150 min.
53-9909   *$34.99*

Catherine Cookson's
The Wingless Bird

The Wingless Bird (1997)
The title "bird" in this Catherine Cookson story is Agnes Conway, a young woman dismayed at spending another Christmas season in her family's candy shop and unsure about her future. Her fortunes change when a series of encounters link Agnes to a well-to-do local family and another clan with a shady reputation. Claire Skinner, Edward Atterton, Anne Reid star. 156 min.
08-8655   □*$29.99*

The Round Tower (1998)
Set in post-war Britain, Catherine Cookson's epic drama focuses on Vanessa Ratcliffe, the teenage daughter of a wealthy, socially-conscious family, and Angus Cotton, a streetwise engineer for Vanessa's father. When Angus is blamed for Vanessa's pregnancy, a series of unusual complications ensue. With Emilia Fox, Keith Barron. 150 min.
53-6368   *$29.99*

Colour Blind (1998)
Set shortly after World War I, this Catherine Cookson story tells of Bridgette McQueen, a young woman who returns to her large family with a black husband and their baby daughter in tow. Their appearance sends shockwaves throughout the clan that are felt throughout the community as the mixed-race child grows up. Niamh Cusack, Carman Ejago star. 150 min.
53-6369   *$29.99*

Tilly Trotter (1999)
Catherine Cookson's popular tale is set in 1836 and concerns a beautiful young woman accused of witchcraft who is rescued by a local, married farmer. After causing marital problems while taking refuge in his house, the woman goes to work for a mine-owner, and must eventually choose between him and the farmer. Carli Norris, Simon Shepherd and Gavin Abbott star. 220 min.
53-6649   *$29.99*

The Secret (2000)
Author Catherine Cookson's thriller concerns Freddie Musgrave, a runner for criminals in 19th-century England who receives a chance at a legitimate job from Maggie Hewitt, a woman he was once drawn to years earlier. Freddie's new life is threatened by a mysterious diamond, a murder scheme and a dangerous charmer after Maggie's foster daughter. With Elizabeth Carling. 156 min.
53-6951   *$29.99*

The Catherine Cookson Collection, Vol. 1
"The Cinder Path," "The Dwelling Place," "Fifteen Streets" and "The Man Who Cried" are also available in a collector's set.
53-9613   Save $10.00!   *$89.99*

The Catherine Cookson Collection, Vol. 2
"The Gambling Man" and "The Glass Virgin" are also available in a boxed set.
53-9712   *$69.99*

The Catherine Cookson Collection, Vol. 3
"The Moth" and "The Rag Nymph" are also available in a boxed set.
53-9894   *$69.99*

The Catherine Cookson Collection, Vol. 4
"Colour Blind" and "The Round Tower" are also available in a boxed set.
53-6370   *$59.99*

The Man Who Made Husbands Jealous (1997)
Jilly Cooper's sizzling novel becomes a sizzling drama detailing the adventures of Lysander Hawkley, a handsome 23-year-old who makes women's hearts melt. When Hawkley is lured into a scheme to punish some of his female acquaintances' adulterous hubbies, deceit, lust and trouble ensue. Stephen Billington and Rhona Mitra star. 150 min.
53-6342   *$29.99*

Visas And Virtue (1997)
Winner of the 1997 Academy Award for Best Live-Action Short Film, this compelling effort details the real-life story of Consul General Chiune Suihara, a Japanese diplomat stationed in Lithuania during World War II. Suihara is faced with making a difficult decision involving the saving of Jewish refugees, a decision which could cost him his career. Chris Tashima stars. 26 min.
53-6450   *$19.99*

Stanley And The Women (1991)
Based on an acclaimed novel by Kingsley Amis, this epic British drama features John Thaw as a man whose life is shaken when his son is diagnosed with schizophrenia. Thaw attempts to cope with his son's illness, but finds a number of women—including his wife, his ex-wife, an ex-lover and a psychiatrist—continue to harass him. Geraldine James and Sheila Gish co-star. 240 min.
53-6135   *$79.99*

Bleeding Vegas (1997)
A film director's trip to Las Vegas leads him to a beautiful exotic dancer who has some troubling secrets in her past. The filmmaker attempts to help her, but when she is threatened by some of her clients, they're both put in danger. David Carradine, Dave Alvin and Vanessa Preziosi star. 82 min.
50-5847   *$49.99*

Conceiving Ada (1997)
High-tech science-fiction and Victorian melodrama mesh in this offbeat film. Emmy (Francesca Faridany), an expert in computers and genetic memory, devises a way to contact her heroine, 19th-century English feminist, mathematician and proto-computer programmer Ada Byron King (Tilda Swinton). The lives of these two similar women become linked in a surprising fashion. Featuring unique "virtual sets" for its 19th-century scenes, the film also stars Karen Black and Timothy Leary as Emmy's mentor. 85 min.
53-6681   Was $89.99   *$19.99*

Windhorse (1998)
Clandestinely filmed on location in Chinese-ruled Tibet (several actors and crew members had their names withheld for fear of reprisal), documentarian Paul Wagner's compelling drama follows three young Tibetans faced with moral dilemmas: a rising pop star asked by her Chinese official boyfriend to sing pro-government songs; her brother, an embittered drunk; and their cousin, a Buddhist nun savagely beaten after shouting anti-Chinese slogans. Dadon, Jampa Kelsang star. 97 min. In English, Mandarin and Tibetan with English subtitles.
53-6712   Letterboxed   *$89.99*

P.T. Barnum (1999)
In this exciting biodrama, Beau Bridges plays P.T. Barnum, master showman and the creator of the modern-day circus. Learn how Barnum made (and lost) more than one fortune as he introduced the world to such unique acts as General Tom Thumb, Jumbo the elephant, and "Swedish Nightingale" Jenny Lind. With Jordan Bridges, Henry Czerny and George Hamilton. 200 min.
53-6575   *$29.99*

P.T. Barnum (Feature Version)
Also available in a feature-length edition. 138 min.
88-1209   □*$19.99*

THE CEMENT GARDEN

The Cement Garden (1992)
Psychosexual drama focuses on a family of four children who, fearing separation after their mother dies, fail to notify the authorities and seal her body in cement in the basement. As the siblings begin retreating into their own world, the oldest girl tries to serve as a surrogate mother, while her teenage brother begins to develop incestuous feelings towards her. Charlotte Gainsbourg, Andrew Robertson star. 105 min.
53-8661   Was $89.99   *$29.99*

halle BERRY

RIGHT WOMAN
RIGHT PLACE
WRONG TIME

INTRODUCING
DOROTHY DANDRIDGE

Introducing Dorothy Dandridge (1999)
One of the first black women to achieve Hollywood stardom, singer/actress Dorothy Dandridge fell victim to the prejudices of her time as well as tragedies in her private life. Halle Berry stars as the '50s screen beauty who fought to overcome the racial barriers that surrounded her, and paid a heavy price, in this compelling biographical drama. Klaus Maria Brandauer, Loretta Devine, Brent Spiner also star. 115 min.
44-2213   Was $99.99   □*$14.99*

Joseph's Gift (1999)
Family trust and betrayal are the themes for this powerful story about the youngest member of a family successful in the garment industry in Los Angeles. Joseph, a young son favored by his father over his other brothers, becomes the brunt of a practical joke which leads to years of estrangement. With Freddy Rodriguez, Brion James, John Saxon and Marcel Marceau star.
50-8422   *$39.99*

First Time Felon (1997)
A street-hardened gang member from Chicago is convicted of drug dealing and given a choice: a five-year prison sentence or four months in a special boot camp that stresses discipline. Can he survive the harsh, Marines-style treatment, and will what he learns save him from returning to a life of crime? Powerful urban drama stars Omar Epps, Delroy Lindo, William Forsythe. 106 min.
44-2157   Was $99.99   □*$19.99*

Twenty-One (1991)
Patsy Kensit turns in a sexy, commanding performance as a young, free-spirited British woman who recounts her experiences with men in New York and London. Among her paramours are a black singer, a married lawyer and a drug addict she falls in love with. Jack Shepherd and Patrick Ryecart co-star. 101 min.
45-5514   *$89.99*

Homicide (1991)
Writer/director David Mamet's riveting drama stars Joe Mantegna as a respected Jewish Baltimore detective who, while investigating the murder of an elderly shopkeeper, is drawn into allegations of an anti-Semitic conspiracy that lead him to reconsider his work, life and faith. W.H. Macy and Natalija Nogulich co-star. 100 min.
45-5520   Was $19.99   □*$14.99*

December (1991)
Compelling look at five New England prep school students who are forced into confronting themselves and making important decisions about their lives on the day the Japanese bombed Pearl Harbor. Wil Wheaton, Chris Young, Balthazar Getty and Brian Krause star. 92 min.
45-5531   *$89.99*

Back Road Diner (1998)
A group of four African-American friends from New York set out on a cross-country drive, but a confrontation with bigoted locals at a roadside restaurant leads to violent attacks and a shocking conclusion. Powerful and thought-provoking drama features a bright young cast and a hit-filled soundtrack with Afrika Bambaataa, Kingsize and more. 93 min.
46-8041   Was $59.99   *$14.99*

Mister Johnson (1991)
Set in Nigeria in 1923, this fascinating drama from Bruce Beresford ("Driving Miss Daisy") focuses on a black clerk working for British officials who fantasizes about having a more cultured (i.e., white) lifestyle. Soon, he begins stealing from his employer, a Civil Service Officer, which leads to a series of unfortunate complications. Pierce Brosnan, Edward Woodward and Maynard Eziashi star. 102 min.
47-2058   *$14.99*

Challenge The Wind (1991)
In this inspirational drama, a teen haunted by his father's death in Vietnam finds great difficulty when he moves to his grandparents' farm. Soon, however, he discovers a gift for running, and with the help of his grandfather, he competes against his school's best athlete. With Mark Whittington, Katy Dickson and Jay Jones. 85 min.
48-1181   *$29.99*

Foxfire (1987)
In this sensitive drama, Jessica Tandy turns in an Emmy-winning performance as a widow who has spent her entire life in an isolated home in the Blue Ridge Mountains. When her singer son (John Denver) tries to persuade her to move, a clash occurs between traditional and modern values. With Hume Cronyn. 118 min.
63-1514 ❑$14.99

Caroline? (1990)
Suspenseful tale, originally presented on the "Hallmark Hall of Fame." A young woman, believed by her family to have died 15 years earlier, reappears to collect money from an inheritance...but is she the real Caroline? Stephanie Zimbalist, Pamela Reed, Patricia Neal and George Grizzard star. 100 min.
63-1539 Was $89.99 ❑$14.99

Decoration Day (1990)
Highly acclaimed drama stars James Garner as a retired judge who attempts to help his childhood friend receive a Congressional Medal of Honor for his bravery during World War II. Judith Ivey, Ruby Dee, Larry Fishburne and Bill Cobbs co-star in this "Hallmark Hall of Fame" production. 99 min.
63-1580 Was $89.99 ❑$14.99

One Against The Wind (1991)
Astonishing true story from "The Hallmark Hall of Fame" stars Judy Davis as an English-born socialite who, during World War II, operated the most successful escape route for downed Allied airmen in France during the Nazi occupation. Sam Neill also stars in this magnificently acted tale of courage. 96 min.
63-1587 Was $89.99 ❑$14.99

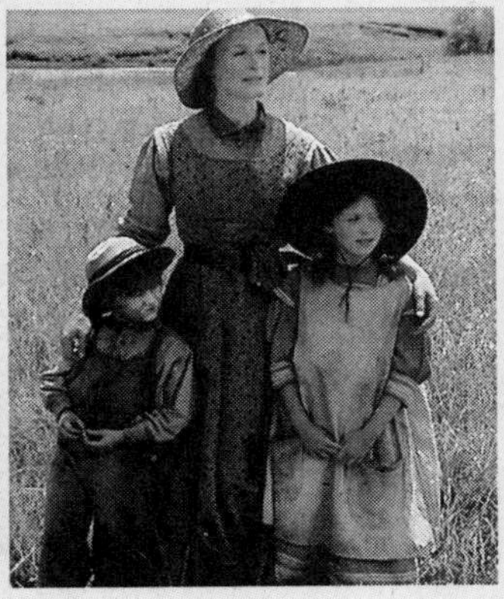

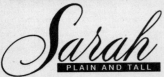

Sarah
PLAIN AND TALL

Sarah, Plain And Tall (1991)
Glenn Close and Christopher Walken star in this acclaimed "Hallmark Hall of Fame" adaptation of Patricia MacLachlan's award-winning family drama. Set in New England in 1910, it details the emotional effect a strong-willed woman has on a lonely widower and his two children. 98 min.
63-1489 ❑$14.99

Skylark (1993)
The further adventures of Maine mail-order bride Sarah and farmer Jacob Whitting are recounted in this sensitive sequel to "Sarah, Plain and Tall." The story follows their lives on the Kansas prairie, where they encounter natural disasters and a decision that could separate them. Glenn Close and Christopher Walken star. 98 min.
63-1614 Was $89.99 ❑$14.99

Sarah, Plain And Tall: Winter's End (1999)
The arrival of Jacob's estranged father to the Whitting farm brings old quarrels and bitterness to the surface in this third installment of the moving family saga. Glenn Close, Christopher Walken and Jack Palance star. 99 min.
27-7143 ❑$14.99

The Sarah, Plain And Tall Trilogy Boxed Set
All three features are also available in a money-saving boxed set.
27-7144 Save $5.00! $39.99

Miss Rose White (1992)
Powerful drama about a young woman who flees Poland during World War II and becomes a career girl, working for a prominent New York department store. Her happy life is upset, however, when her lost sister arrives in America, bringing secrets of the past. Kyra Sedgwick, Amanda Plummer and Maximilian Schell star; based on the play "A Shayna Maidel." 95 min.
63-1605 Was $89.99 ❑$14.99

Blind Spot (1993)
Powerful "Hallmark Hall of Fame" drama stars Joanne Woodward as a mother and U.S. congresswoman whose run for the Senate is put in jeopardy when a secret is revealed that also threatens to tear apart her family. With Laura Linney, Fritz Weaver. 99 min.
63-1647 Was $89.99 ❑$14.99

An American Story (1993)
Six soldiers return from World War II and find government corruption on all levels in their hometown. In order to fight the deception, the veterans organize their own political party to unseat the local government. Brad Johnson and Kathleen Quinlan star in this "Hallmark Hall of Fame" production. 97 min.
63-1654 Was $89.99 ❑$14.99

The Shell Seekers (1993)
In this compassionate drama, Angela Lansbury plays a widow who attempts to recapture her happy past after suffering a heart attack and struggles with her three grown children. She travels back to the beach she loved when she was younger in hopes of restoring peace to her life. Irene Worth and Sam Wanamaker also star in this "Hallmark Hall of Fame" presentation. 94 min.
63-1664 Was $89.99 ❑$14.99

To Dance With The White Dog (1993)
Shortly after their 50th wedding anniversary, Cora Peek passes away, leaving her husband Sam alone, battling his own medical problems and under the scrutiny of his overprotective children. But Sam is given a new lease on life when he befriends a mysterious white dog. Hume Cronyn and Jessica Tandy star in this touching drama. 98 min.
63-1688 ❑$14.99

Breathing Lessons (1994)
The acclaimed novel by Anne Tyler ("The Accidental Tourist") is the basis for this film that stars James Garner and Joanne Woodward as a long-married couple whose road trip to a neighboring town is filled with adventure, unusual occurrences and an opportunity to renew their marriage. With Kathryn Erbe, Paul Winfield. 98 min.
63-1725 Was $89.99 ❑$14.99

A Place For Annie (1994)
A head nurse at a pediatric ward is touched by an orphaned baby girl with a terminal illness and decides to adopt the child. With help from a no-nonsense nanny, the woman constructs a world for the girl—a world shattered when her birth mother returns to claim her. Sissy Spacek, Mary-Louise Parker and Joan Plowright star. 98 min.
63-1737 Was $89.99 ❑$14.99

The Return Of The Native (1994)
Thomas Hardy's romantic classic receives a distinguished rendering in this lavish production. A young woman is stifled living with her grandfather in the country and uses her seductive beauty to charm a handsome suitor. But when a localite returns from Paris with dreams of marrying the woman, she finds herself torn between the two. With Catherine Zeta Jones, Ray Stevenson, Joan Plowright. 99 min.
63-1758 Was $89.99 ❑$14.99

Redwood Curtain (1995)
From Lanford Wilson's acclaimed play comes this compassionate story of an 18-year-old Asian-American girl who looks for her real parents after living happily for years with her wealthy, adoptive family. Her search takes her to Northern California, where she meets a hostile Vietnam veteran who may be her father. With Jeff Daniels, Lea Salonga, John Lithgow. 99 min.
63-1795 Was $89.99 ❑$14.99

Harvest Of Fire (1996)
When an arsonist disrupts a peaceful Amish community, FBI agent Lolita Davidovich begins investigating the crimes, but gets the cold shoulder from the reclusive sect. Amish woman Patty Duke, curious about the outside world, earns the agent's trust and jeopardizes her way of life to help her solve the case. With Jean Louisa Kelly, Craig Wasson. 99 min.
88-1102 Was $99.99 ❑$14.99

Calm At Sunset (1996)
Powerful drama stars Michael Moriarty as a commercial fisherman who tries to dissuade his son from following in his footsteps. With Kevin Conway, Kate Nelligan and Peter Facinelli. 98 min.
88-1137 Was $99.99 ❑$14.99

The Summer Of Ben Tyler (1996)
James Woods stars as a struggling lawyer in a small Southern town during World War II who causes a sensation when he and wife Elizabeth McGovern allow their late black housekeeper's teenage son to move into their home. The tension increases when Woods is asked to defend the son of the town's chief justice on a murder charge. Len Cariou, Kevin Isola also star. 134 min.
88-1139 Was $99.99 ❑$14.99

Rose Hill (1996)
A group of orphans and the abandoned baby they save must become a makeshift family and survive in the American frontier of the 19th century in this compelling "Hallmark Hall of Fame" drama. Jennifer Garner, Jeffrey Sams, Zak Orth and Casey Siemaszko star. 99 min.
88-1185 ❑$14.99

Old Man (1997)
Horton Foote ("Tender Mercies") adapted William Faulkner's story set in rural Mississippi about a prisoner who was dispatched to save a pregnant woman hanging from a tree during the great flood of 1927 and returns to befriend her and her newborn son. Arliss Howard and Jeanne Tripplehorn star. 94 min.
88-1146 Was $99.99 ❑$14.99

Ellen Foster (1997)
Jena Malone stars as Ellen, a troubled adolescent girl who overcomes a series of personal crises as she learns about the true meaning of "family," in this Hallmark Hall of Fame production. With Ted Levine, Glynnis O'Connor and Julie Harris. 97 min.
88-1198 ❑$14.99

The Love Letter (1998)
Campbell Scott discovers a letter written by a woman during the Civil War era in an antique desk he bought and, mailing a reply, begins a correspondence with Jennifer Jason Leigh, who now lives in the home of the woman who wrote the letter. The two form a relationship that jeopardizes their impending weddings. With Estelle Parsons and David Dukes. 99 min.
88-1179 ❑$14.99

What The Deaf Man Heard (1998)
Funny and touching drama about a young boy, mute since his mother's murder, who arrives in a small Georgia town in 1945. He is taken in by the bus depot manager and cafe owner and eventually becomes the town's handyman. As an adult, the boy learns some secrets that may hold a key to his past. Matthew Modine, James Earl Jones, Claire Bloom star. 107 min.
88-1180 ❑$14.99

Saint Maybe (1998)
Anne Tyler's touching story is set in Baltimore in the mid-1960s and focuses on Ian Bedloe, a young man riddled with guilt after his older brother dies. Looking for help, Bedloe turns to the Church of Second Chance, a storefront ministry. Eventually, the man finds peace by adopting his brother's children. Blythe Danner, Edward Herrmann, Thomas McCarthy and Mary-Louise Parker star. 98 min.
88-1181 ❑$14.99

Grace & Glorie (1998)
Grace (Gena Rowlands), a feisty independent woman recovering from a broken hip meets Glorie (Diane Lane), a hospice worker, and the two form a bond. As Glorie helps Grace with her physical problems, Grace helps Glorie come to terms with the loss of her young son in this touching, superbly acted drama. 98 min.
88-1182 ❑$14.99

Night Ride Home (1998)
Faced with an overwhelming tragedy, a family pulls together to overcome it, but soon discovers that coping comes with an unexpected price. Moving "Hallmark Hall of Fame" presentation stars Keith Carradine, Rebecca De Mornay, Ellen Burstyn and Thora Birch. 94 min.
88-1186 ❑$14.99

The Echo Of Thunder (1998)
When her mother dies, a teenage girl is sent to live with her tree farmer father and his new family in the Australian wilderness, but has trouble adjusting to the tumultuous changes in her life. Judy Davis, Jamey Sheridan and Lauren Hewett star in this warm and emotional "Hallmark Hall of Fame" drama. 98 min.
88-1196 ❑$14.99

Durango (1999)
Stirring, romantic tale set in the Irish coutnryside on the eve of World War II. A young farmer attempts to court the daughter of the town's most powerful man. In order to prove his worth, he enlists the help of his resourceful aunt to pull off a complex cattle drive. Matt Kesslar, Brenda Fricker, Nancy St. Alban and Patrick Bergin star. 108 min.
27-7118 ❑$14.99

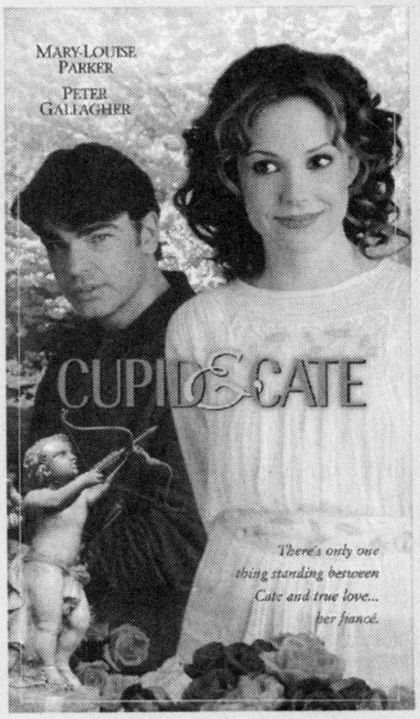

Cupid & Cate (2000)
In this "Hallmark Hall of Fame" production, Mary-Louise Parker is Cate, a young woman about to marry her boring fiancé, but whose life is changed when her sister introduces her to witty, wise and endearing Harry (Peter Gallagher). They hit it off, but soon they face several hurdles, including Cate's tough father (Philip Bosco) and disease. With Bebe Neuwirth and Brenda Fricker. 98 min.
27-5594 $14.99

Missing Pieces (2000)
James Coburn and Paul Kersey are a father and son torn apart by Kersey's involvement in an auto accident years earlier that claimed his mother's life. When his son is murdered, Coburn must overcome years of bitterness as he seeks to bring the killer to justice in this compelling "Hallmark Hall of Fame" tale. Lisa Zane co-stars. 99 min.
88-1208 ❑$14.99

Human Cargo (1998)
Intense true tale stars Treat Williams as an American businessman working in Saudi Arabia who is kidnapped from his hotel room and imprisoned. While in jail, Williams battles against horrific conditions to save his life. With Stephen Lang, Sasson Gabai. 108 min.
67-9002 ❑$14.99

Color Of Justice (1997)
Intense, provocative drama studies the media's power and effect on a controversial trial of five black youths who are accused of killing a white woman. F. Murray Abraham, Judd Hirsch, Bruce Davison and Gregory Hines star. 91 min.
67-9009 ❑$14.99

Final Appeal (1994)
A woman accused of killing her abusive husband tries to convince her attorney brother to take her case. Making it difficult to prove her self-defense claim is the crime's only witness, the husband's lover, who believes he was murdered. Brian Dennehy and JoBeth Williams star in this gripping story. 94 min.
63-1745 ❑$89.99

Buddy's Song (1992)
Emotional drama laced with a driving rock score, with ex-Who member Roger Daltrey starring as a singer who dreams of having his son follow in his performing footsteps. Chesney Hawkes, Sharon Duce also star. 106 min.
68-1240 $89.99

The King's Whore (1990)
A dazzling tale filled with swashbuckling action, historical drama and aristocratic romance, as a young woman finds herself wronged and turned over to the monarch who covets her. Can she use her body to win the revenge she craves? Timothy Dalton, Valeria Golino, Stephane Freiss star. 113 min.
68-1254 Was $89.99 ❑$12.99

Dark Tide (1993)
Suspense and eroticism mix as a sexy female deep sea diver and her boyfriend battle sea snakes, as well as a handsome boat captain with whom she had a scorching affair. Richard Tyson, Brigitte Bako and Chris Sarandon star. Uncut, unrated version; 94 min.
68-1287 Was $89.99 ❑$12.99

The Tigress (1993)
In the jungle it's the female that's the deadliest of the species, and it's no different in the glamorous world of the rich and powerful that this sensual seductress prowls. Steamy tale of passion and deception stars Valentina Vargas, James Remar and George Peppard. Uncut, unrated version; 89 min.
68-1260 ❑$89.99

Mirrors (1992)
Timothy Daly is a reporter whose story on beautiful dancer Marguerite Hickey helps her career skyrocket. The two start a romance, but she leaves town for New York, where she auditions for Broadway. Will he win her back? Keenan Wynn co-stars. 99 min.
68-1229 ❑$89.99

Southie (1999)
After fighting to escape his South Boston neighborhood, Donnie Wahlberg must return there to save his family and finds himself caught in the middle of a violent gang war. Tough urban drama also stars Rose McGowan, Lawrence Tierney. 105 min.
64-9048 $69.99

Dangerous Relations (1993)
Gritty drama about a convict about to end his 15-year prison term who discovers that the new kid on his block is the son he deserted years earlier. Lou Gossett, Jr., Blair Underwood and Rae Dawn Chong star in this powerhouse story. 93 min.
71-5287 $12.99

The Bachelor (1993)
An erotic period drama concerning a shy physician who adjusts to life after a family tragedy and discovers he has a knack for attracting women of all sorts. Keith Carradine, Miranda Richardson, Kristin Scott-Thomas and Max Von Sydow star. 105 min.
72-9018 Was $89.99 $14.99

Corrupt (1999)
In this gritty inner-city gang drama, a young man (Silkk the Shocker) sees a fragile truce behind two long-time rival gangs as his last chance to escape a life, and death, in the streets. But can he get out before his arch-enemy Corrupt (Ice-T) gets him? With Miss Jones, Ernie Hudson, Jr. 72 min.
64-9052 $99.99

Patrick Swayze

Red Dawn (1984)
Exciting action hit set against a Soviet invasion of the United States. A small band of plucky high school students turns freedom fighters and fights for their survival. Patrick Swayze, Charlie Sheen, Jennifer Grey and Ron O'Neal star. 100 min.
12-1389 Was $19.99 *$14.99*

Youngblood (1986)
Fans of "Rocky" and "The Mighty Ducks" will enjoy this hard-hitting tale starring Rob Lowe as a naive farm boy learning about manhood on the hockey rink. Cynthia Gibb, Patrick Swayze co-star; look for Keanu Reeves in his big-screen debut. 111 min.
12-1576 *$14.99*

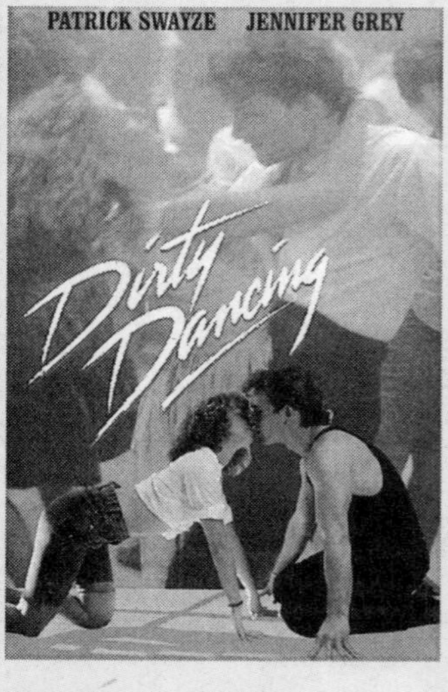

Dirty Dancing (1987)
A teenage girl on vacation with her parents in a Catskills resort in 1963 learns about love in the hands of a handsome dance instructor in this sensual, music-filled drama. Jennifer Grey is the sheltered teen, Patrick Swayze the stud with the moves; with Cynthia Rhodes, Jerry Orbach. 100 min.
47-1819 *$14.99*

Dirty Dancing (Letterboxed Version)
Also available in a theatrical, widescreen format.
27-7021 Remastered *$19.99*

Dirty Dancing: Collector's Twin Pack
Have the time of your life with this two-tape set featuring the movie and the original production "Dirty Dancing: Live in Concert."
27-7036 Save $15.00! *$24.99*

Steel Dawn (1987)
Patrick Swayze trades his dancing shoes for a broadsword in this futuristic action epic, playing an itinerant warrior who comes to the aid of farmers besieged by a cruel warlord. Incredible fantasy thriller also stars Lisa Niemi, Anthony Zerbe. 102 min.
47-1851 *$12.99*

Tiger Warsaw (1988)
Patrick Swayze shines in this compelling drama, as a wayward son returns to the home he left 15 years earlier to try and reunite with his family. Piper Laurie, Lee Richardson, Barbara Williams and Kaye Ballard also star. 93 min.
45-5448 *$14.99*

Road House (1989)
Patrick Swayze goes from dancing across Catskill ballroom floors to dancing on the faces of Texas tough guys in this roughhouse action hit about a bar bouncer who pits his fighting skill against the local town "boss." With Ben Gazzara, Sam Elliott, Kelly Preston, Terry Funk. 110 min.
12-1939 Was $19.99 ❑*$14.99*

Next Of Kin (1989)
Patrick Swayze is at his two-fisted best as a tough Chicago cop who teams with his hillbilly kinfolk when a younger brother is brutally murdered by mobsters. Lots of action in store as Mr. "Dirty Dancing" tackles a dirty "Don." Liam Neeson, Adam Baldwin co-star. 108 min.
19-1750 Was $19.99 ❑*$14.99*

Ghost (1990)
The surprise hit blend of suspense, romance and fantasy stars Patrick Swayze as a New York yuppie who is killed during a mugging and returns to Earth with a mission: find his murderer and save fiancée Demi Moore from the same fate. Warm and winning drama also features an Oscar-winning turn by Whoopi Goldberg as a medium who can communicate with Swayze. 121 min.
06-1829 Was $89.99 ❑*$14.99*

Ghost (Letterboxed Version)
Also available in a theatrical, widescreen format.
06-2779 ❑*$14.99*

City Of Joy (1992)
Director Roland Joffe's epic drama stars Patrick Swayze as a disillusioned American doctor who moves to India in order to find a new life for himself. He takes up residence in an impoverished and crime-ridden Calcutta ghetto and falls in love with a British woman trying to start a hospital for the poor. Pauline Collins, Om Puri also star. 135 min.
02-2295 Was $19.99 *$14.99*

Father Hood (1993)
Patrick Swayze stars as a small-time crook whose cross-country journey to pull off the biggest caper of his career hits two small snags: his children, whom he rescues from the foster home they were placed in after their mother's death. Exciting blend of action and comedy also stars Halle Berry, Michael Ironside, Sabrina Lloyd. 95 min.
11-1774 ❑*$14.99*

To Wong Foo, Thanks For Everything! Julie Newmar (1995)
Patrick Swayze, Wesley Snipes and John Leguizamo kick up their (high) heels as a trio of New York drag queens whose cross-country road trip to an L.A. pageant takes a surprise detour when their car breaks down in a sleepy Midwest town whose residents are crying for a "makeover." Alternately outrageous and touching hit comedy also stars Stockard Channing, Blythe Danner, Chris Penn. 109 min.
07-2376 Was $19.99 ❑*$14.99*

Three Wishes (1995)
Heartfelt and moving fantasy-drama, set in mid-'50s suburbia, stars Patrick Swayze as a mysterious drifter who is injured in an accident and taken home to recuperate by single mom Mary Elizabeth Mastrantonio. While there, Swayze becomes a mentor to the woman's two young sons, while teaching them all a magical lesson in the value of families. Joseph Mazzello, Seth Mumy also star. 115 min.
44-2042 Was $19.99 ❑*$14.99*

Black Dog (1998)
Action-packed truck demolition derby with Patrick Swayze playing an ex-convict who is tricked into hauling a shipment of illegal firearms in his big rig. Once a caravan full of machine gun-toting maniacs attacks him on the road, he decides to take matters into his own hands and do a little hard driving to save his life. Randy Travis and Meat Loaf co-star. 89 min.
07-2668 Was $99.99 ❑*$14.99*

Letters From A Killer (1998)
Wrongly convicted and jailed for his wife's murder, Patrick Swayze begins romantic correspondences with three women. When he's finally freed from prison, Swayze tries to put his past behind him, but one of his spurned pen-time pen pals is killing people and framing him for the crimes. Can Swayze find out who's responsible? Gia Carides, Kim Myers, Roger E. Mosley co-star. 103 min.
64-9054 *$99.99*

Patrick Swayze 3-Pack
Go "cwayze" for Swayze with this three-tape boxed collection that features Patrick packing a punch in "Red Dawn," "Road House" and "Youngblood."
12-3333 Save $20.00! *$24.99*

Please see our index for these other Patrick Swayze titles: *The Outsiders • Tall Tale: The Unbelievable Adventure • Uncommon Valor*

I'll Remember April (1999)
Shortly after the bombing of Pearl Harbor, four 10-year-old boys discover an injured Japanese sailor on the beach and make him a "prisoner of war" in their clubhouse, unsure of what to do next. Their decision becomes even harder when a life-saving incident sparks a friendship between the boys and their supposed enemy. Haley Joel Osment, Trevor Morgan, Pat Morita and Yuki Okumoto star. 90 min.
85-1514 *$39.99*

Walls Of Sand (1999)
Shirin Etessam is a young, isolated Iranian girl struggling to acquire a green card so she can make a life for herself in America. She takes a job taking care of an agorophobic's (Jan Carly Marsh) son and the two women form an unlikely bond through the child until circumstances beyond their control threaten to destroy their friendship and change their lives forever. 115 min.
73-9372 *$39.99*

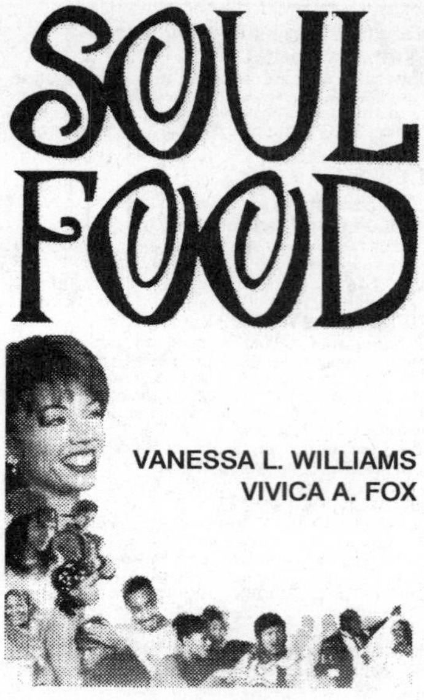

Soul Food (1997)
One of the surprise hits of the year, writer/director George Tillman, Jr.'s warm and emotional comedy/drama tracks the career and romantic travails of the members of a close-knit African-American brood, particularly sisters Vivica A. Fox, Nia Long and Vanessa L. Williams, over the course of several months' worth of voluminous Sunday family dinners. Michael Beach, Irma P. Hall, Mekhi Phifer also star. 114 min.
04-3561 Was $19.99 ❑*$14.99*

The American Angels: Baptism Of Blood (1990)
A beautiful young woman sets out to make it in the wild world of women's wrestling in this action-packed drama that features some of America's sexiest gal grapplers. Jan MacKenzie, Tray Loren and the Magnificent Mimi star. 99 min.
06-1757 Was $89.99 ❑*$14.99*

A Brother's Kiss (1997)
Two brothers from the streets of East Harlem grow up and attempt to escape the problems and temptations of their past—one as a pro basketball player, the other as a cop—but find the going tougher than they could have imagined in this compelling urban drama, adapted by director Seth Zvi Rosenfeld from his stageplay. Nick Chinlund, Justin Pierce, Rosie Perez, Michael Rapaport, John Leguizamo and Marisa Tomei star. 93 min.
02-8944 Was $99.99 *$14.99*

Jude (1996)
Sumptuously filmed version of Thomas Hardy's "Jude the Obscure" details the life of Jude Fawley, a stonemason with intellectual aspirations in late 19th-century England. After a failed marriage, Jude enrolls in college and there meets his cousin Sue, with whom he falls in love. Their relationship leads to exile and tragedy. Christopher Eccleston and Kate Winslet star. 122 min.
02-8621 Was $19.99 ❑*$14.99*

Boston Kickout (1995)
Gritty British drama about alienated youth focusing on recent high school grad Phil and his three pals, who find themselves rebelling against society by getting involved with drugs, violence and crime. As Phil's life takes a downward spiral, he meets a young woman named Shona who tries to help him find the right path to happiness. John Simm, Emer McCourt star. 107 min.
02-8667 Was $99.99 *$14.99*

A Cool, Dry Place (1999)
This domestic drama features Vince Vaughn as a Chicago lawyer whose life unravels when he loses his job and his wife abandons him and their young son. Hoping to start anew, Vaughn relocates to Kansas, where he falls for earthy local Joey Lauren Adams. Eventually, he's forced into making some tough decisions when his wife comes back into the picture. With Monica Potter. 120 min.
04-3882 ❑*$99.99*

The Proposition (1997)
Drama, romance and suspense are mixed in a compelling tale set in 1930s Boston. When they're unable to conceive a child, successful attorney William Hurt hires a young law clerk to impregnate his wife, author Madeleine Stowe. Fears that the purely businesslike relationship is turning into romance leads to murder and a series of explosive revelations. Kenneth Branagh, Neil Patrick Harris, Robert Loggia also star. 115 min.
02-8863 Was $19.99 ❑*$14.99*

The Leading Man (1997)
Up-and-coming actor Jon Bon Jovi gives a wickedly seductive performance in this compelling drama as an American stage actor in London who is asked by an English playwright to woo his wife, so that the writer can continue an affair of his own. Lambert Wilson, Thandie Newton and Anna Galiena also star. 99 min.
02-8956 Was $99.99 *$14.99*

A Map Of The World (1999)
Gripping drama, based on Jane Hamilton's novel, stars Sigourney Weaver as a school nurse who lives on a Wisconsin farm. While watching a group of children, her friend's toddler walks away and drowns in a nearby pond. The town turns against Weaver, who is accused of child abuse, and she faces a difficult trial where her sense of self-righteousness works against her cause. With Julianne Moore, David Strathairn and Chloe Sevigny. 127 min.
02-9226 *$79.99*

My Heroes Have Always Been Cowboys (1991)
This heartfelt family drama featuring thrilling rodeo sequences stars Scott Glenn as a veteran bull-rider who returns home to find his father in an old-age home, romantic interest from his widowed childhood sweetheart, and a strong urge to get back to the rodeo circuit. Kate Capshaw, Ben Johnson, Gary Busey, Tess Harper and Balthazar Getty also star. 106 min.
03-1785 Was $19.99 ❑*$12.99*

American History X (1998)
Released from prison after serving three years for the shooting of two black youths, former skinhead Edward Norton tries to shed his past and neo-Nazi friends while working to keep younger brother Edward Furlong from following in his footsteps. Director Tony Kaye's powerful and chilling look at America's racist underground also stars Fairuza Balk, Avery Brooks, Beverly D'Angelo and Stacy Keach. 119 min.
02-5202 Was $99.99 ❑*$19.99*

The Theory of Flight (1998)
An unusual and moving tale of the special bond that forms between two outcasts: wheelchair-bound ALS patient Helena Bonham Carter, who communicates through a voice synthesizer and wants to experience sex, and eccentric Kenneth Branagh, whose attempts to build his own flying machine landed him in court and a community service term as Carter's caretaker. Gemma Jones, Holly Aird co-star. 98 min.
02-5205 Was $99.99 ❑*$19.99*

Besieged (1999)
A lush Roman villa is the setting for this erotic and emotional love story from "Last Tango in Paris" director Bernardo Bertolucci. A reclusive British musician (David Thewlis) is irresistibly drawn to the African medical student (Thandie Newton) who works as his housekeeper, but what she asks of him to prove his love for her could mean the end of their future together. 95 min.
02-5218 Was $99.99 ❑*$19.99*

Face (1997)
The title is British slang for a gangster, and in director Antonia Bird's gripping crime drama a group of hoods from London's East End launch a raid on a securities firm which they hope will set them up for life. The heist seemingly goes off as planned, but a warehouse rendezvous turns up less money than expected and convinces the gang one of them is a traitor. Robert Carlyle, Ray Winstone, Damon Albarn star. 107 min.
02-5226 Was $99.99 ❑*$19.99*

The Buddha Of Suburbia (1995)
From Hanif Kureishi, writer of "My Beautiful Laundrette" and "Sammy and Rosie Get Laid," comes a culture clash tale set in '70s England, as a teenage boy of Indian descent finds his family life turned upside-down when his father becomes a guru for Zen Buddhism devotees. Naveen Andrews, Roshan Seth, Brenda Blethyn star; includes original music by David Bowie. 220 min.
04-3465 ❑*$29.99*

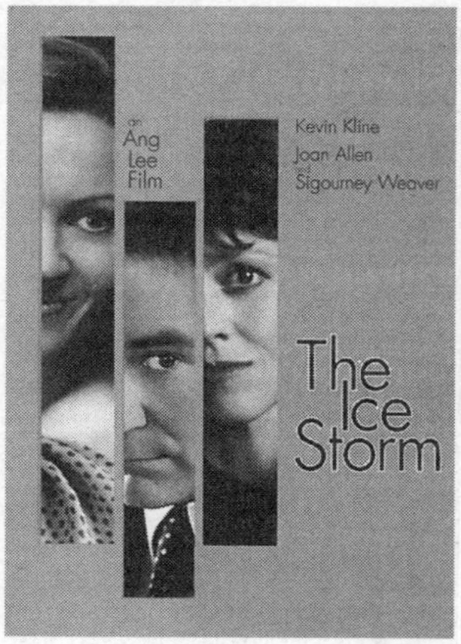

The Ice Storm (1997)
Set in a suburban Connecticut community in 1973, director Ang Lee's stark, ironic look at familial and sexual detachment stars Kevin Kline and Joan Allen as a married couple for whom the upcoming Thanksgiving weekend could provide a chance to reach out to each other and teenage children Christina Ricci and Tobey Maguire. However, Kline is busy having an affair with neighbor Sigourney Weaver, the teens are pursuing their own romantic targets, and a bitter winter storm that hits the region brings all these human dramas to a surprising climax. 110 min.
04-3607 Was $99.99 ❑*$14.99*

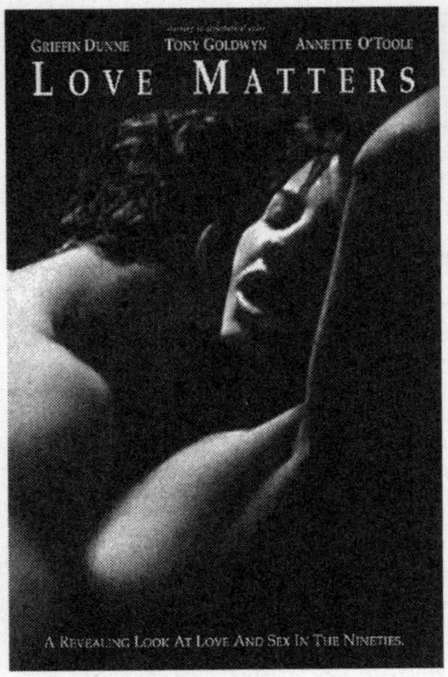

Love Matters (1993)
A provocative look at love, lust and jealousy, as a couple whose marriage is in trouble allows a married friend and his sexy girlfriend to spend the night at their house. What follows is a sensual roundelay that threatens to tear more than one relationship apart. Griffin Dunne, Annette O'Toole, Tony Goldwyn, Gina Gershon star. Uncut, unrated version; 103 min.
63-1639 Was $89.99 ❑$14.99

Bad Behavior (1993)
Director Les Blair's improvised comedy-drama stars Stephen Rea and Sinead Cusack as an Irish couple living in North London whose marriage is having its problems. She's restless in her role as a housewife and mother; he's disillusioned with his job; and their house is falling apart. Can they change their direction before it's too late? 103 min.
68-1289 ❑$89.99

Girls' Night (1998)
Brenda Blethyn and Julie Waters are best friends and sisters-in-law who work at a Northern England computer factory. After Blethyn discovers she has a fatal disease, she hits big in a bingo game and splits the cash with Waters. The women decide to head to Las Vegas, where they meet sexy cowboy Kris Kristofferson. 105 min.
67-9003 ❑$14.99

Boca (1994)
From "9 1/2 Weeks" producer Zalman King comes this exotic political drama starring Rae Dawn Chong as an American TV reporter who joins her photographer ex-lover in Rio de Janeiro, where they question government authorities about the murder of the city's street kids. Martin Kemp, Martin Sheen also star. 91 min.
63-1760 Was $89.99 ❑$14.99

Love, Lies & Murder (1992)
A riveting account of a 1985 murder case involving a man who conceives a bizarre plot to murder his wife. His stepdaughter confesses to the incident, but when she discovers her father is living with his teenage sister-in-law, the truth behind the crime is revealed. Clancy Brown, Sheryl Lee and Moira Kelly star. 190 min.
63-1585 ❑$89.99

Daughters Of The Dust (1991)
Set in 1902, this acclaimed drama follows a black family, the descendants of slaves, who live in communities on islands off the Carolina coast. As they prepare to move to the North, the various members who've returned for a reunion look back on their lives and heritage. Cora Lee Day and Alva Rogers star in Julie Dash's lushly photographed story. 114 min.
53-7683 Was $79.99 $24.99

Clean, Shaven (1993)
After his release from a mental institution, a schizophrenic patient haunted by hallucinations searches for his daughter, who was put up for adoption. At the same time, he is pursued by a detective convinced he's responsible for a rash of child killings. Harrowing and compelling psychological drama stars Peter Greene, Robert Albert, Jennifer MacDonald. 80 min.
53-8366 Letterboxed $19.99

Black & White (1991)
Acclaimed independent drama from Russian-born filmmaker Boris Frumin follows the friendship that develops between a Russian woman studying medicine in Manhattan and an African-American building superintendent, and how an unlikely romance blossoms. With Elena Shevchenko, Gilbert Giles. 96 min.
53-9647 $59.99

Small Time (1991)
In the tradition of "Menace II Society" comes this gritty, streetwise drama about a punk in Harlem whose daily activities include robbing stores, snatching purses and hustling homosexuals. Will he be able to survive this life of crime, his parasitic mother or his fiery relationship with his girlfriend? With Richard Barboza. 88 min.
54-9111 $69.99

China Cry (1991)
An acclaimed, inspirational drama about two people whose love endures the oppressive forces in China during the 1950s. The story focuses on the plight of Sung Neng Yee, who escaped from Communist China to Hong Kong, while battling against a state-appointed tormentor. Julia Nickson Soul, Russell Wong, James Shigeta and France Nuyen star. 103 min.
55-1313 $19.99

A Great American Tragedy (1998)
A brilliant aerospace engineer suddenly finds that his well-paying job has been taken away from him. As a result, his marriage goes on the skids, his employment prospects become fewer and fewer, and his life begins a downward spiral that he may not be able to get out of. With George Kennedy, Vera Miles and William Windom. 75 min.
55-3017 $19.99

When Saturday Comes (1995)
Sean Bean, a resident of a town in Northern England, has two opportunities for employment: to work in a pit or in a factory. His dream is to play soccer professionally. A local talent scout tries to help him achieve that dream, but first Bean must overcome an unsupportive father, hard-drinking friends and his own problems. With Peter Postlethwaite and Emily Lloyd. 94 min.
59-7029 $99.99

Assault At West Point (1994)
This riveting true story details the 1880 trial of Johnson Whittaker, one of the first African-American cadets admitted to West Point, who faced a court-martial when it was believed he staged his own assault to avoid taking a test. Defending him are a racist lawyer and a black Harvard-educated attorney. Sam Waterston, Samuel L. Jackson and Seth Gilliam star. 98 min.
63-1394 Was $89.99 ❑$14.99

I Posed For Playboy (1992)
A college co-ed out to defy her father, a rising young stockbroker and a 37-year-old mother decide to shatter everybody's image of them by posing for Playboy. See what really goes on behind the scenes of a centerfold shoot with Amanda Peterson, Michele Greene, Lynda Carter and real Playboy centerfold Brittany York. Features steamy scenes added for video! AKA: "Posing." 98 min.
63-1558 ❑$89.99

A Woman, Her Men And Her Futon (1992)
Following the end of her marriage, a beautiful woman tries to find her identity by losing her inhibitions and becoming involved in a series of "no strings" sexual relationships. Jennifer Rubin, Lance Edwards and Grant Show star in this look at passion, eroticism and the search for self-freedom. 90 min.
63-1565 ❑$89.99

In The Line Of Duty: Ambush In Waco (1993)
Timothy Daly turns in a powerful performance as David Koresh, the self-proclaimed messiah who joined his legion of feverish followers in an intense standoff and bloody siege in Waco, Texas, in the early part of 1993. Capt. Bob Blanchard (Dan Lauria) leads the government forces against the heavily-armed, unpredictable Koresh and his Branch Davidian devotees. 93 min.
63-1658 ❑$89.99

Ruby In Paradise (1993)
A sensitive depiction of a young woman trying to start a new life on her own, writer/director Victor Nunez' acclaimed drama stars Ashley Judd as Ruby, who leaves her Tennessee home for the "Redneck Riviera" beach town of Panama City, Florida, gets a job in a souvenir shop and winds up in romances with two very different suitors. Todd Field, Bentley Mitchum, Dorothy Lyman co-star. 115 min.
63-1668 Was $89.99 ❑$14.99

Zooman (1995)
After a young Brooklyn girl is killed by a random act of violence, her distraught father explodes with rage and begins a campaign for justice in the neighborhood. His efforts eventually draw the killer out of hiding and lead him to a dangerous confrontation. Lou Gossett, Jr., Charles Dutton and CCH Pounder star in this intense drama, written by Charles Fuller ("A Soldier's Story"). 95 min.
63-1769 Was $89.99 ❑$14.99

Soul Survivor (1995)
A young man of Jamaican heritage, living in the Afro-Caribbean neighborhood of Toronto and working in a mental salon job, thinks he's found the key to a better life when he becomes a debt collector for a local gangster in this powerful urban drama. Peter Williams, George Harris, Judith Scott and Clark Johnson star. 87 min.
54-9156 $79.99

Tar (1997)
In this urban drama, a crook carjacks the car of a lady cop and soon discovers that she's his old high school sweetheart. Their love affair gets hot again as they face a series of wild and dangerous experiences, which include uncovering a group of black nationalists who tar white businessmen they kidnap. With Kevin Thigpen and Nicole Prescott. 90 min.
54-9174 $79.99

Messenger (1995)
In this powerful contemporary updating of Vittorio De Sica's "The Bicycle Thief," a black New Yorker tries to put his life of petty crime behind him and takes a job as a courier. But when his bicycle, purchased by pawning his wife's wedding ring, is stolen by a local hood, the man puts his marriage, job and future on the line to recover it. Richard Barboza stars. 80 min.
54-9119 $79.99

The Last Don: The Complete Mini-Series (1997)
Explosive treatment of Mario Puzo's novel stars Danny Aiello as Don Clericuzio, a mob leader whose empire is thrust into a bloody war after daughter Kirstie Alley marries the son of a rival Mafioso. Meanwhile, Aiello's hit man son gets involved with the family business, leading to a startling revelation. Joe Mantegna, Jason Gedrick, Daryl Hannah also star. This special boxed set also features behind-the-scenes footage and interviews with the stars and Puzo. 259 min. on three tapes.
68-1864 ❑$29.99

The Last Don (Feature-Length Version)
Also available in a special featurized edition, containing nudity and violent scenes not shown on broadcast TV. 148 min.
68-1845 Was $99.99 ❑$14.99

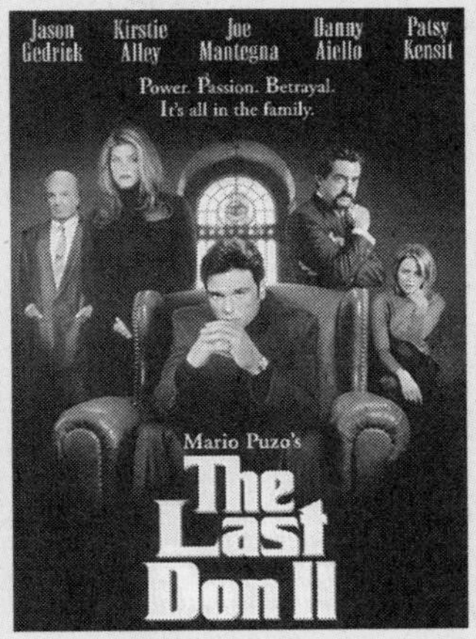

The Last Don II: The Complete Mini-Series (1998)
The compelling final chapter in Mario Puzo's acclaimed crime saga hits with brute force as Don Domenico Clericuzio, on his deathbed, begs his nephew Cross to take over the family. Cross' return to the fold ignites an internal war from which only one man can emerge victorious. Jason Gedrick, Danny Aiello, Joe Mantegna, Kirstie Alley and Patsy Kensit star. 178 min.
68-1917 ❑$24.99

The Last Don II (Feature-Length Version)
Also available in a special featurized edition. 127 min.
68-1888 Was $99.99 ❑$14.99

A Woman's Guide To Adultery (1995)
After disapproving of her girlfriends' affairs, a woman is torn between her head and her heart when she falls in love with a married university lecturer in this emotional drama. Sean Bean, Amanda Donohoe, Adrian Dunbar and Theresa Russell star. 145 min.
53-9670 $24.99

Race To Freedom: The Story Of The Underground Railroad (1993)
Follow a group of black slaves as they escape captivity in the South and begin a dangerous trek along the "underground railroad" towards freedom in Canada in this exciting historical drama. Tim Reid, Alfre Woodard, Glynn Turman, Dawnn Lewis star. 90 min.
54-9116 $29.99

Dangerous Evidence: The Lori Jackson Story (1998)
Powerful true-life drama stars Lynn Whitfield as Lori Jackson, a civil rights activist who tackles the U.S. Marine Corps by defending an African-American corporal accused of raping a white officer's wife. Richard Lineback and Jeff Clarke also star in this gripping story. 90 min.
54-9192 $59.99

America's Deadliest Home Video (1991)
If you only know Danny Bonaduce from his talk show or "The Partridge Family," you'll be surprised to see him in this gonzo excursion into the underbelly of society. He plays a video-obsessed guy who uses his camcorder to chronicle a gang of convenience store killers and robbers during their frightening reign of terror. Mick Wyhoff, Melora Walters also star. 90 min.
59-8012 $29.99

The Last Days Of Frankie The Fly (1997)
Dennis Hopper is Frankie, a small-time mobster who's tired of his life as an errand boy for boss Michael Madsen. With the help of porno filmmaker Kiefer Sutherland and ex-drug addict Daryl Hannah, Hopper hatches a scheme that could make them all rich—if they live through it—in this offbeat crime drama. 96 min.
58-5262 Was $99.99 ❑$14.99

Cafe Romeo (1992)
Catherine Mary Stewart plays a cafe waitress who is trapped in a dead-end marriage to a small-time hood. When she gets an opportunity to realize her lifelong dream of a fashion career in New York City, she must make some important decisions about her life. Jonathan Crombie co-stars. 93 min.
63-1532 ❑$14.99

The Boys Of St. Vincent (1992)
At once both harrowing and compelling, this acclaimed drama, originally made for Canadian television, chronicles a sexual abuse scandal at a Catholic-run boy's orphanage. When the mistreatment by a priest is brought to light, Church and local officials attempt to keep it a secret, but years later the now-grown victims continue to search for justice. Henry Czerny, Johnny Morina star. 186 min.
53-8426 $89.99

On My Own (1992)
Penetrating study of a 15-year-old boy attending a private boarding school who learns from his estranged father that his mother is being treated for emotional problems at a mental hospital. After the boy has his first sexual experience, his mother pays him a surprise visit and teaches him lessons about life and herself. Judy Davis, Matthew Ferguson and Jan Rubes star. 130 min.
53-8532 $79.99

Desolation Angels (1996)
After learning that his girlfriend was sexually assaulted by his best friend, a New York truck driver becomes consumed with anger and a desire for revenge that blinds him to his lover's need for understanding. Emotionally gripping drama from first-time writer/director Tim McCann stars Michael Rodrick, Jennifer Thomas. 90 min.
53-8874 Was $89.99 $19.99

Grind (1996)
Edgy independent effort starring Billy Crudup as a young man recently released from prison who looks for help from his older brother and his wife. When Crudup takes a night job, he begins spending time with his sister-in-law, and their relationship soon leads to a shattering confrontation between family members. Adrienne Shelly, Paul Schulze also star. 96 min.
53-8934 Was $89.99 $19.99

The Piano Lesson (1995)
This stunning production of August Wilson's Pulitzer Prize-winning play stars Charles S. Dutton as a ne'er-do-well from Mississippi who travels to Pittsburgh in 1936 to persuade his sister to let him sell a family heirloom—a piano—in order to buy land his slave ancestors once lived on. Alfre Woodard, Carl Gordon and Courtney B. Vance also star. 120 min.
63-1779 Was $89.99 ❑$14.99

Running Wild (1999)
In this adventure saga, Gregory Harrison plays a retired Air Force lieutenant who travels to Zimbabwe with his young son and daughter and takes a job protecting that country's endangered elephant population from ruthless poachers. Brooke Nevin, Simon MacCorkindale also star. 92 min.
67-9027 ❑$14.99

Killer: A Journal Of Murder (1996)
Set in the 1920s, this powerful true story centers on Jewish Leavenworth prison guard Henry Lewis, who attempts to befriend convicted killer Carl Panzram and soon uncovers the secrets of his life, including his theft of $40,000 from President Taft and his killing of 21 people. James Woods, Robert Sean Leonard, Steve Forrest and Ellen Greene star. 91 min.
63-1861 Was $99.99 ❑$14.99

Killer: A Journal Of Murder (Letterboxed Version)
Also available in a theatrical, widescreen format.
63-1876 ❑$14.99

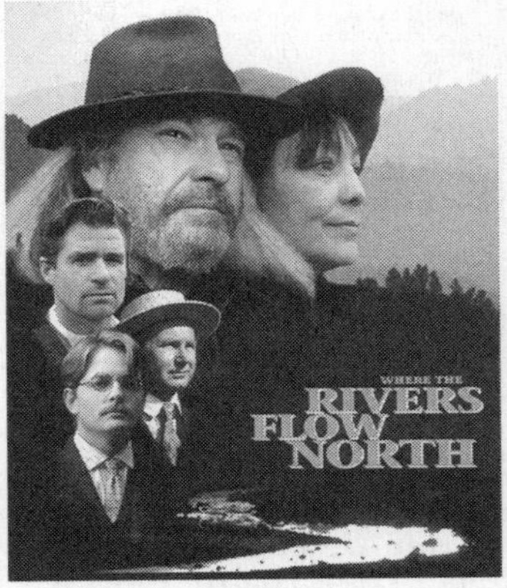

Where The Rivers Flow North (1994)
Set in 1927 Vermont, this beautifully filmed drama focuses on a legendary logger whose defiance of a power company owner leads him and his American Indian mate to be pushed off their land. The logger and executive square off in a battle of wits that's filled with thrills, humor and surprises. Rip Torn, Michael J. Fox, Treat Williams and Tantoo Cardinal star. 105 min.
83-1018 Was $89.99 $14.99

Madonna: Innocence Lost (1994)
The "Material Girl's" early years as a struggling dancer/actress/singer in New York City are dramatically depicted in this music-filled biopic. Terumi Mathews stars as the pre-fame Madonna; with Dean Stockwell, Jeff Yagher, Wendie Malick. 90 min.
04-2995 Was $79.99 ❑$29.99

Three Seasons (1999)
This haunting drama from director Tony Bui is the first American film shot in Vietnam since the war and was a top winner at the Sundance Film Festival. the stories of a variety of people struggling with the past and present in Ho Chi Minh City are followed. Among them: an ex-marine, a cyclo driver, a prostitute and a flower girl. With Harvey Keitel, Don Duong. 113 min. In Vietnamese with English subtitles.
02-9146 Was $99.99 $14.99

Detour (1999)
Edgy crime opus in which Jeff Fahey joins friend James Russo in a scheme to rob $1.2 million from a warehouse owned by mobsters. When the hoods interrupt the heist, the men take refuge at a dairy farm once run by Fahey's parents and plot to rob a nearby logging company. A family secret soon complicates Fahey's criminal plans. With Michael Madsen and Gary Busey. 93 min.
02-9148 Was $99.99 $14.99

Thicker Than Water (1999)
A pair of rival urban gang leaders who share a common goal of musical stardom form an uneasy truce in order to further their dream in this gritty drama laced with a hot rap score. The cast of top rap artists includes Mack 10, Fat Joe, Ice Cube. 90 min.
02-9189 $19.99

The Quiet Room (1997)
As her parents' marriage begins to disintegrate, a bright 7-year-old girl retreats into a world of silence, all the while trying to keep her family together, in this moving drama from Australia. Chloe Ferguson, Celine O'Leary, Paul Blackwell star. 95 min.
02-5158 Was $99.99 ❑$19.99

Digger (1994)
A warm family drama about a pre-teen boy who travels to his relatives' Pacific Northwest island home while his parents try to solve some marital problems. There, he befriends a man trying to woo his grandmother and a new pal who shares his experiences with family, loyalty, friendship and loss. Olympia Dukakis, Leslie Nielsen, Adam Hann-Byrd stars. 92 min.
06-2305 Was $89.99 ❑$14.99

A Boy Called Hate (1995)
In his film debut, Scott Caan (son of James Caan) turns in a powerful performance as a troubled teen who rescues a woman from a rapist. Believing the attacker was killed, Caan and the woman flee, but soon find themselves followed by the police and the rapist, who turns out to be an assistant DA out to frame the pair. With Missy Crider, Elliott Gould and James Caan. 98 min.
06-2466 ❑$89.99

I Want You (1999)
A stunning, erotically-charged performance by Rachel Weisz ("The Mummy") highlights this compelling drama from director Michael Winterbottom ("Welcome to Sarajevo"). A hairdresser living in an English coastal town becomes involved with a group of men including her disc jockey boyfriend, a mute teenager who tapes peoples' conversations and a lover from her past. With Alessandro Nivola and Carmen Ejogo. 87 min.
02-9169 Was $99.99 $14.99

Your Friends & Neighbors (1998)
From "In the Company of Men" creator Neil LaBute comes this disturbing study of the relationships between the sexes. Drama professor Ben Stiller, executive Aaron Eckhart, gynecologist Jason Patric, writer Amy Brenneman, copywriter Catherine Keener and art gallery curator Nastassja Kinski are the friends and lovers whose lives dangerously intersect in the bedroom. 100 min.
02-9052 Was $99.99 $14.99

Bastard Out Of Carolina (1996)
Following in her father John's footsteps, Anjelica Huston made her directorial debut with this powerful, controversial drama based on the Dorothy Allison best-seller. A 13-year-old girl in the rural South tries to protect her younger sister from the violent abuse she herself endures from her stepfather. Jennifer Jason Leigh, Ron Eldard, Glenne Headly and Jena Malone star. 101 min.
02-8642 Was $99.99 ❑$14.99

True Colors (1991)
James Spader and John Cusack are two law school friends who choose different paths in life: Spader takes a position in the Justice Department, while Cusack enters politics after aligning himself with a contractor with underworld ties. Eventually, Spader is put in the hot seat when he's forced to expose his friend's crooked ally. Imogen Stubbs, Mandy Patinkin and Richard Widmark also star. 111 min.
06-1883 Was $19.99 ❑$14.99

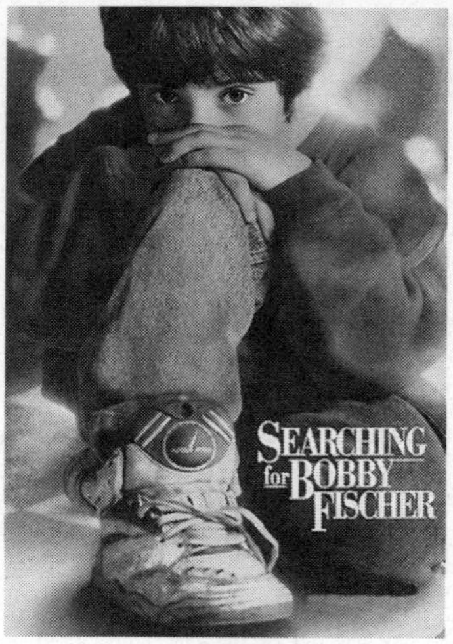

Searching For Bobby Fischer (1993)
Absorbing, true-life drama about Josh Waitzkin, a 7-year-old chess prodigy whose incredible abilities cause problems for his parents struggling to decide what's best for their son. With hopes of winning a championship, Josh seeks help from two mentors, a former world-class player and a streetwise speed-chess wizard. With Joe Mantegna, Max Pomeranc, Laurence Fishburne, Ben Kingsley. 111 min.
06-2209 Was $19.99 ❑$14.99

The Secret Passion Of Robert Clayton (1992)
A powerful courtroom story about two attorneys—a father and his son—who square off against each other in a lurid murder trial. The stakes become exceedingly high when the trial leads them to expose their lust for the same woman. John Mahoney, Eve Gordon and Scott Valentine star. 92 min.
06-2080 ❑$89.99

Lorna Doone (1993)
A stylish telling of R.D. Blackmore's classic romantic drama about a young man whose attempts at avenging the death of his parents by the predatory Doone family are quelled when he falls in love with Lorna, the Doones' beautiful daughter. Polly Walker, Sean Bean and Clive Owen star. 90 min.
06-2193 ❑$89.99

Bopha! (1993)
Stirring drama set against the political turmoil of South Africa in 1980 starring Danny Glover as a policeman who witnesses his family tearing apart after his son joins the anti-apartheid movement. Alfre Woodard, Malcolm McDowell and Marius Weyers also star in this dynamic story which marks Morgan Freeman's film directing debut. 120 min.
06-2194 Was $89.99 ❑$19.99

Telling Lies In America (1997)
In early '60s Cleveland, a teenage Hungarian immigrant's attempts at fitting in receive a boost when he's taken under the wing of a popular radio DJ, but he soon learns that entry into the "in crowd" comes at a high cost. Brad Renfro, Kevin Bacon, Calista Flockhart and Maximilian Schell star in scripter Joe Eszterhas' semi-autobiographical drama. 101 min.
02-8842 Was $99.99 $14.99

Gridlock'd (1997)
Harrowing and darkly funny look at two Detroit drug addicts (Tupac Shakur and Tim Roth) who decide to go into detox after their friend overdoses and her life remains in danger. Little do Shakur and Roth know that the road to sobriety is paved with red tape, lots of waiting and a drug dealer to tangle with. Thandie Newton also stars. 91 min.
02-8668 Was $19.99 $14.99

Ten Benny (1996)
New Jersey shoe salesman Adrien Brody borrows $10,000 from a loan shark and puts it on a "sure thing" horse race bet that will allow him to wed his waitress girlfriend, but Brody's best laid schemes land him in dutch with his fiancée and friends and on the run from mobsters. Well-done, low-budget drama in the style of "Mean Streets" also stars James E. Moriarty, Sybil Temchen. 98 min.
02-9066 Was $99.99 $19.99

Passion In The Desert (1998)
Based on the 19th-century novel by Balzac, this exotic film tells of Augustin, an officer in Napoleon's army during a 1798 Egyptian campaign, who gets lost from his troops in the desert. Threatened by a sandstorm and a Bedouin who's chasing him, Augustin finds help from a wild leopard. Soon, man and beast bond in a most unusual way. Ben Daniels stars. 91 min.
02-5192 Was $99.99 ❑$19.99

Mindwalk (1992)
An unusual and thought-provoking film, this drama follows three travellers who meet at the French island-abbey of Mont St. Michel and engage in a passionate, all-encompassing discussion of issues ranging from the environment to self-expression. Sam Waterston, Liv Ullmann, John Heard and Ione Skye star. 110 min.
06-2069 Was $89.99 $19.99

Jack The Bear (1993)
Compassionate drama starring Danny DeVito as an unstable Oakland widower who hosts a local horror TV show and struggles to raise his two boys. DeVito's unpredictable ways and a menacing neighbor present threats to the children as they try to cope with the death of their mother. With Robert J. Steinmiller, Jr., Miko Hughes, Gary Sinise and Julia Louis-Dreyfus. 99 min.
04-2708 Was $19.99 ❑$14.99

Come See The Paradise (1990)
Powerful, haunting drama from writer/director Alan Parker ("Mississippi Burning"). Dennis Quaid stars as a movie projectionist in late '30s L.A. who meets and marries a Japanese-American woman. Their love is put to the test when, while he's jailed for union activities, she and their daughter are sent to an internment camp following Pearl Harbor. Tamlyn Tomita co-stars. 135 min.
04-2427 Was $89.99 ❑$19.99

Middlemarch (1994)
The epic 19th-century novel by George Eliot receives an acclaimed treatment which originally ran on "Masterpiece Theatre." Set in England during the 1800s, the drama tells of intrigue, blackmail and passion surrounding the idealistic Dorothea Brooke and her husbands. With Juliet Aubrey, Patrick Malahide and Rufus Sewell. 360 min. on three tapes.
04-3253 ❑$59.99

Juice (1992)
A powerful look at contemporary life in Harlem, focusing on an aspiring disc jockey and his teenage friends who have to make a difficult decision: walk the straight and narrow or lead a life of crime. Eventually, they decide to rob a liquor store in response to an acquaintance's death. Omar Epps, Khalil Kain, Tupac Shakur star; Ernest R. Dickerson, Spike Lee's cinematographer, directs. 95 min.
06-1981 Was $89.99 ❑$14.99

Enchanted April (1992)
A charming and dreamlike comedy-drama set in 1920s England, as four London women with little in common travel to Italy together and spend a month in a remote castle. Once there the quartet shares their feelings about their lives, and a magical friendship blossoms. Josie Lawrence, Miranda Richardson, Polly Walker and Joan Plowright star. 93 min.
06-2052 Was $89.99 ❑$19.99

Private Lessons: Another Story (1994)
In this in-name-only sequel to the hit teenage sex comedy, a gorgeous fashion photographer travels to Miami, where she meets a young Cuban chauffeur and observes a beautiful woman seducing a date on a rooftop. Soon, her fantasies involving these two people become a reality. Mariana Morgan and Theresa Morris star in this erotic tale. 86 min.
06-2272 Was $89.99 ❑$19.99

Pontiac Moon (1994)
A whimsical drama set in 1969 and centering on eccentric teacher Ted Danson, who takes his son on a cross-country road trip in an antique Pontiac, hoping to reach Spires of the Moon National Park when Apollo 11 lands on the lunar surface and the car's mileage equals the distance between the Earth and the moon. Mary Steenburgen, Ryan Todd, Cathy Moriarty co-star. 107 min.
06-2313 Was $89.99 ❑$19.99

The Road To Galveston (1996)
Compelling story starring Cicely Tyson as Jordan Roosevelt, a woman left broke and months behind on her mortgage after her husband dies. In order to make ends meet, she decides to use her house as a caring center for three Alzheimer's patients. Outside demands eventually force her to take her patients on an incredible, life-affirming trip. Tess Harper co-stars. 93 min.
06-2476 Was $79.99 ❑$19.99

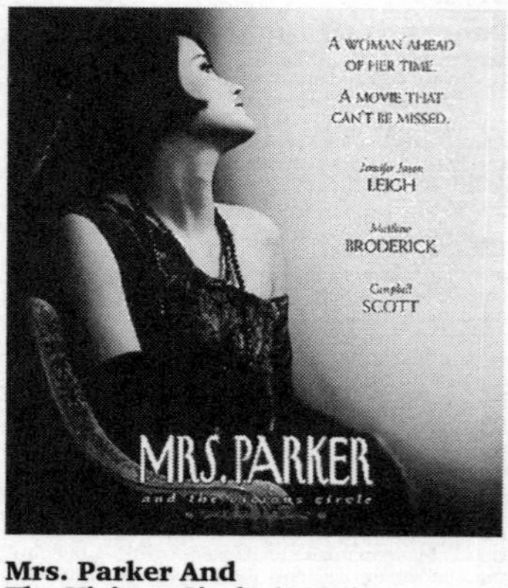

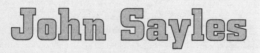

Mrs. Parker And The Vicious Circle (1994)
Director/co-writer Alan Rudolph's acclaimed look at the life of writer Dorothy Parker and her colorful colleagues at New York's famed Algonquin Round Table. Jennifer Jason Leigh shines in the title role, portraying Parker over the course of three decades and through her failed marriages, literary successes, struggles in Hollywood, and her lifelong relationship with fellow author Robert Benchley. Campbell Scott, Matthew Broderick, Peter Gallagher, Jennifer Beals and Wallace Shawn also star. 124 min.
02-5047 Was $89.99 ❑$19.99

John Sayles

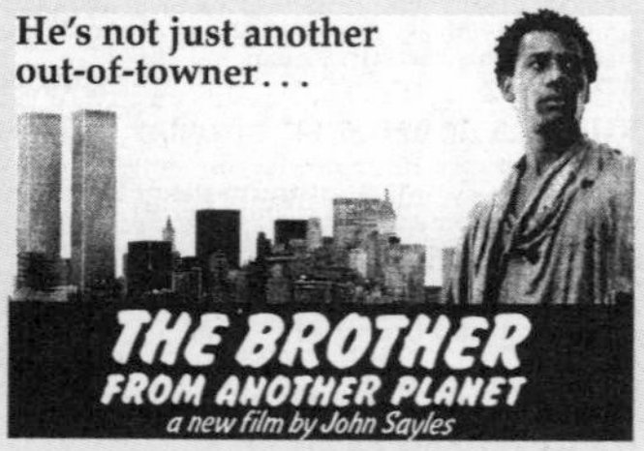

The Brother From Another Planet (1984)
A delightful sci-fi tale from John Sayles about a mute black alien (Joe Morton) who winds up in Harlem, befriended by the neighborhood and on the run from two sinister white aliens. Funny, touching and rich in character and flavor, the film also stars Joe Morton, Darryl Edwards and Sayles himself.
04-1832 $14.99

Matewan (1987)
The brutal confrontations between mine operators and striking workers in West Virginia's coal fields during the 1920s are re-created by writer/director John Sayles in this stunning drama of diverse people united by a common goal. James Earl Jones, Chris Cooper, Will Oldham star. 142 min.
40-1362 Was $19.99 $14.99

Eight Men Out (1988)
Baseball's most infamous scandal, the 1919 Chicago "Black Sox" who arranged with gamblers to throw the World Series, is brought to life by writer/director John Sayles. Rich period drama stars Charlie Sheen, D.B. Sweeney, John Cusack, Christopher Lloyd. 120 min.
73-1034 ❑$14.99

City Of Hope (1991)
Maverick filmmaker John Sayles captures the effect personal and political corruption has on the lives of 38 people (among them a building developer and his troubled son, a black city councilman, a college professor and a homeless man) in a large, decaying East Coast city in this gritty, powerful look at contemporary America. With Joe Morton, Tony Lo Bianco, Vincent Spano, Barbara Williams. 130 min.
02-2196 Was $89.99 ❑$19.99

Passion Fish (1992)
A soap opera actress left paralyzed after a car accident retreats to her family home in Louisiana and shuts herself off from the outside world. When she hires a nurse with personal problems of her own to care for her, the two women form a special friendship and learn to value life. Mary McDonnell, Alfre Woodard, David Strathairn star in writer/director John Sayles' acclaimed drama. 136 min.
02-2402 Was $19.99 ❑$14.99

The Secret Of Roan Inish (1995)
Lovingly filmed Irish fantasy from director John Sayles about a 10-year-old girl sent by her father to live with her grandparents in a coastal village after World War II. There, she and her teenage cousin investigate stories they've heard about their family's ancestral island home, a mythical creature known as the Selkie, and her brother, who drifted out to sea when he was an infant. Mick Lally, Eileen Colgan star. 102 min.
02-2809 Was $19.99 ❑$14.99

Lone Star (1996)
Set in a Texas border town, John Sayles' powerful cross-cultural saga focuses on a sheriff trying to find the truth behind the murder of a racist lawman four decades earlier. His investigation leads him to the town's mayor, its Hispanic and black residents and even to his own late father, a much-liked ex-sheriff. Chris Cooper, Kris Kristofferson, Matthew McConaughey, Elizabeth Peña star. 137 min.
02-2976 ❑$19.99

Men With Guns (1998)
From writer/director John Sayles comes this sobering and politically awakening film about a recently widowed doctor who returns to an unnamed Latin American country in order to pay a visit to some of his former students, whom he dispatched to work in the country's poorest regions. Shocked to learn that several of his protégés have been murdered, he begins to suspect that the supposedly benevolent government, the "men with guns," may be responsible. Federico Luppi, Damian Alcazar and Mandy Patinkin star. 128 min. In Spanish with English subtitles.
02-3197 $99.99

Limbo (1999)
John Sayles' surprising, intricate drama stars Mary Elizabeth Mastrantonio as a singer living with her teenage daughter in Juneau, Alaska, who starts a relationship with David Strathairn, a former fisherman. When Strathairn takes his hustler brother on a business trip on his boat, a series of bizarre occurrences lead him, Mastrantonio and her daughter into danger. Casey Siemaszko and Kris Kristofferson also star. 127 min.
02-3383 Was $99.99 ❑$19.99

Down Came A Blackbird (1995)
A reporter investigating political prisoners in a third world country must confront her own experiences as a tortured captive in this powerful drama. Laura Dern, Vanessa Redgrave and Raul Julia star. 112 min.
63-1810 Was $89.99 □*$14.99*

Mrs. Munck (1996)
A recently widowed woman moves in with her elderly invalid father-in-law to care for him, but her real intentions, springing from a deep secret in their past, come out in a malevolent game of psychological abuse with deadly consequences. Diane Ladd, Bruce Dern and Kelly Preston star in this dramatic thriller in the tradition of "Misery." 99 min.
63-1814 □*$89.99*

The Right To Remain Silent (1995)
Fetching Lea Thompson stars as a rookie policewoman assigned to process suspects at the station who encounters a number of harrowing, wrenching, hilarious and disturbing incidents. Robert Loggia, LL Cool J, Laura San Giacomo and Christopher Lloyd also star. 96 min.
63-1817 Was $99.99 □*$14.99*

Once Upon A Time... When We Were Colored (1996)
Marvelous drama chronicling the African-American experience in the deep South throughout the 1940s, '50s and '60s. The film focuses on a young man who is born in a Mississippi cotton field, is shown the horror of prejudice from his grandfather and taught about literature from an understanding, liberal woman. With Al Freeman, Jr., Phylicia Rashad, Leon; Tim Reid directs. 113 min.
63-1834 Was $99.99 □*$14.99*

Angel Baby (1996)
Highly acclaimed drama from Australia about a recovering mental patient who believes he's found the right woman in a fellow patient. They fall in love, move in together, stop taking their medication and have a baby, whom the mother believes is really an angel and communicates to her through TV's "Wheel of Fortune." John Lynch, Jacqueline McKenzie star. 101 min.
63-1874 Was $99.99 □*$14.99*

Night Falls On Manhattan (1997)
Gritty police drama from director Sidney Lumet showcasing Andy Garcia as a New York cop-turned-district attorney whose loyalty and moral values are tested when he learns that his father, a veteran policeman, may have been involved in a major scandal. Richard Dreyfuss, Lena Olin, Ron Leibman and Ian Holm also star in this powerful effort. 114 min.
63-1890 Was $99.99 □*$14.99*

Ed McBain's 87th Precinct (1995)
Ed McBain's popular book series is the basis for this exciting crime story set in one of the city's toughest police districts. Randy Quaid is Steve Cardella, a veteran detective of the precinct, who must find a serial killer wreaking terror in the area. Alex McArthur and Ving Rhames also star. AKA: "Ed McBain's 87th Precinct: Lightning." 96 min.
64-3422 *$14.99*

The First 9 1/2 Weeks (1998)
In this exotic, erotic drama, a New York currency trader falls for a billionaire client's wife while on a business trip in New Orleans. When the billionaire learns of the illicit affair, he hatches a devious, seductive plot to exact revenge. Paul Mercurio, Malcolm McDowell and Clara Bellar star.
64-9025 *$89.99*

Money Kings (1998)
Peter Falk is a Korean War vet and bar owner who's been running an illegal gambling operation out of his pub for 30 years. When the local mob starts muscling in on his action, they send a high-ranking mobster's nephew to check out his books. The situation presents danger for Falk, his friends and family. With Freddie Prinze, Jr., Lauren Holly, Timothy Hutton. 111 min.
64-9040 *$99.99*

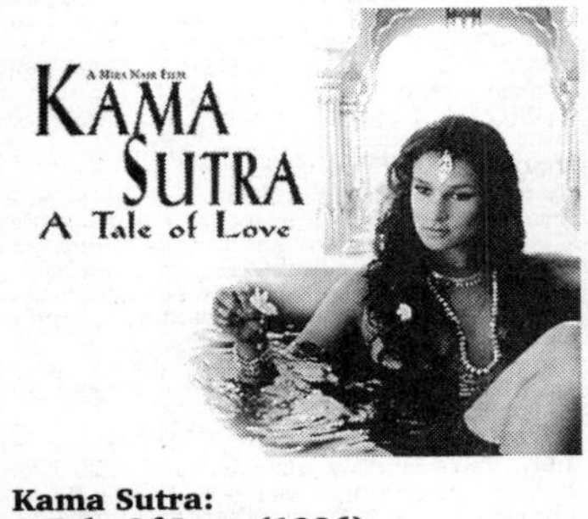
A Mira Nair Film
KAMA SUTRA
A Tale of Love

Kama Sutra: A Tale Of Love (1996)
Director Mira Nair's ("Mississippi Masala") lush and erotic drama, set in pre-colonial India, follows a princess's beautiful serving girl who is trained in the ways of lovemaking and becomes courtesan to the prince's husband, a powerful ruler, until her forbidden affair with a sculptor leads to disaster. Indira Varma, Naveen Andrews, Ramon Tikaram star. Uncut, unrated version; 114 min.
68-1841 Was $99.99 □*$14.99*

Kama Sutra: A Tale Of Love (Letterboxed Version)
Also available in a theatrical, widescreen format.
68-1863 *$14.99*

The '60s (1999)
This explosive mini-series focuses on two families—one white, the other black—and the struggles they face through modern America's most turbulent decade. The war in Vietnam, the Watts riot, the civil rights and anti-war movements, drugs and Woodstock are among the key events faced by the family members. With Charles S. Dutton, Josh Hamilton, Jerry O'Connell, Leonard Roberts and Julia Stiles. 180 min.
68-1923 Was $19.99 □*$14.99*

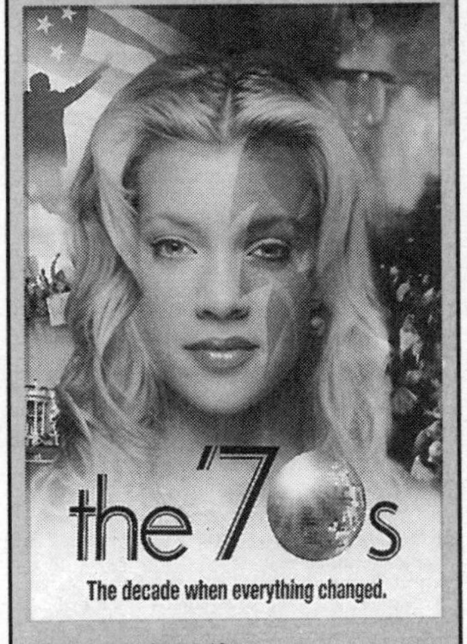
the '70s
The decade when everything changed.

The '70s (2000)
Relive the era of Vietnam, Watergate, "women's lib," disco and other pop culture milestones with this mini-series follow-up to "The '60s." Four Kent State students are followed as they go from the deadly turmoil of campus protests to the adult world and an America in the midst of change. Brad Rowe, Amy Smart, Guy Torry and Vinessa Shaw star. 170 min.
68-2005 *$69.99*

Boogie Boy (1998)
Fresh out of prison, Jesse Page wants to make a new life for himself. But when he gets involved with an old friend, he's tied to a drug deal that goes sour. With drug dealers hot on his trail, Jesse has to get to Detroit in order to be a free man. From "Pulp Fiction" co-writer Roger Avary comes this slam-bang crime drama with Mark Dacascos, Jaimz Woolvett, Emily Lloyd and Traci Lords. 104 min.
64-9026 *$89.99*

Gunshy (1998)
When writer William Petersen meets a muscleman for the mob, he finds himself drawn to his dangerous world. Soon, Petersen becomes partners with the hood in a loan shark operation and falls in love with his girlfriend. He must eventually decide between double-crossing the mob or writing an article exposing them. With Diane Lane, Michael Wincott, Meat Loaf. 101 min.
64-9038 *$69.99*

Prisoner Of Love (1998)
For this prisoner of love, there are no blue skies above. That's because she's a beautiful African-American witness to a mob hit who's being held captive in a warehouse by a creepy hood. When her captor thinks he's fallen in love with her, will she have to surrender to his desires? Naomi Campbell and Eric Thal star. 85 min.
64-9044 *$69.99*

Blind Faith (1998)
Director Ernest Dickerson's ("Juice") powerful tale of race and justice is set in New York in the '50s. Courtney B. Vance plays a small-time Bronx attorney who faces an uphill battle when his honors student nephew stands accused of killing a white teenager. Charles S. Dutton co-stars as Vance's brother, a veteran policeman; with Kadeem Hardison, Lonette McKee. 121 min.
67-9012 □*$14.99*

The Wall (1998)
Three stories linked by tokens found at Washington's Vietnam Veterans' Memorial are presented in this stirring production. Edward James Olmos is an unappreciative father who learns a lesson after his son's sacrifice for another man; Savion Glover plays a soldier who has a special bond with grandmother Ruby Dee; and soldier Michael DeLorenzo must choose between his men and his music. 94 min.
67-9020 □*$14.99*

My Own Country (1998)
Compelling true story of Dr. Abraham Verghese, a physician from India specializing in infectious diseases. Verghese settles in Johnson City, Tennessee, in 1985, when AIDS is starting to be detected in rural areas. His expertise in treating the disease brings him patients from neighboring states, but leads to problems in his marriage. With Naveen Andrews, Marisa Tomei, Glenne Headly, Hal Holbrook and Swoosie Kurtz. 106 min.
67-9021 □*$14.99*

Free Of Eden (1999)
Real-life father and daughter Sidney Poitier and Sydney Tamiia Poitier star in this moving drama. Two seemingly different people—an ex-teacher-turned-businessman who's lost touch with his past and a teenage high school dropout with no apparent future—are drawn together by tragedy and begin a series of tutoring sessions that change both their lives. With Phylicia Rashad. 98 min.
67-9023 □*$14.99*

Restless Spirits (1999)
Spirited mix of family drama and supernatural story involving a girl who stays with her grandmother in Newfoundland while trying to deal with her pilot father's death. When the girl meets the ghosts of two aviators whose plane crashed there years earlier, she helps them rebuild their plane so that they can escape their earthly captivity. Juliana Wimbles, Marsha Mason, Lothaire Bluteau star. 95 min.
67-9026 □*$14.99*

Backstreet Dreams (1990)
Brooke Shields turns in an impressive performance as a child psychologist who tries to help an autistic young boy. The boy's father, a New Jersey gangster, also attempts to improve the child's condition, and eventually he and Shields are romantically involved. A powerful drama, co-starring Jason O'Mally, Sherilyn Fenn, Burt Young and Anthony Franciosa. 104 min.
68-1171 *$89.99*

A Family Matter (1991)
A woman who saw her father gunned down by mobsters years earlier is protected by a Mafia don in Sicily. She falls in love with an American working for the mob boss, but discovers a shocking secret in his past that leads to an explosive confrontation. Eric Roberts, Carol Alt, Eli Wallach and Burt Young star. 100 min.
68-1208 *$89.99*

The Great Los Angeles Earthquake (1990)
A massive earthquake hits Southern California in this gripping drama, as survivors amid the wreckage of L.A. attempt to save themselves. Great special effects. Ed Begley, Jr., Joanna Kerns, Dan Lauria and Richard Masur star. AKA: "The Big One." 106 min.
68-1223 Was $89.99 *$12.99*

In The Hands Of The Enemy (1992)
An international terrorist is accused of killing five Americans in Barcelona and is extradited to the U.S. for trial, but his claim that his political beliefs make him a "prisoner of war" forms the basis of this timely, thought-provoking drama. Sam Waterston, Robert Davi and Ron Leibman star. 100 min.
68-1308 *$89.99*

The Road To Freedom: The Vernon Johns Story (1994)
James Earl Jones turns in a towering performance as one of the pioneers of the American Civil Rights Movement. After racial violence results in a young woman's rape and the murder of a fellow church deacon, Johns leads his family and his congregation in a courageous fight against prejudice. Mary Alice, Cissy Houston also star. 91 min.
68-1313 Was $89.99 *$14.99*

Whore 2 (1994)
This scorching sequel centers on a writer working on a book on prostitution who investigates his subject by taking a room at a seedy Manhattan hotel. When one of the hookers he has befriended is murdered, the writer comes face to face with the dangerous side of the lifestyle. Marla Sucharetza, Mari Nelson, Amos Kollek star. 85 min.
68-1328 □*$89.99*

The Substitute Wife (1994)
Unusual and emotional drama, set on the 19th-century American prairie, about a seriously ill farm wife who selects another woman to care for her husband and children after she dies. The strong-willed "substitute" wins over her new family, but problems arise when the first wife recovers and seeks to return to her brood. Farrah Fawcett, Lea Thompson, Peter Weller star. 92 min.
68-1337 *$14.99*

Witness To The Execution (1994)
In the near future, will televised executions top the ratings charts? This controversial drama stars Sean Young as an ambitious programming executive who sees death row as a pay-per-view bonanza and Timothy Daly as a convicted killer who agrees to walk the last mile on live TV. With Len Cariou, Dee Wallace Stone. 92 min.
68-1341 □*$89.99*

Love And A .45 (1994)
Energetic outlaws-on-the-run opus detailing the reckless trek taken across Texas towards the Mexican border by an expert convenience store robber and his sexy girlfriend as they try to elude the law, hit men, and a psychotic former partner after a hold-up attempt goes wrong. With Gil Bellows, Renee Zellweger, Rory Cochrane, Peter Fonda, Anne Wedgeworth. 102 min.
68-1347 Was $89.99 □*$14.99*

Curse Of The Starving Class (1994)
Producer Bruce Beresford scripted this adaptation of Sam Shepard's play, an off-centered look at the Tates, a troubled ranching clan headed by alcoholic father James Woods, who lost his family's cash in a bad deal, and mother Kathy Bates, who dreams of moving her family to France in order to escape their white trash existence. Henry Thomas, Randy Quaid, Louis Gossett, Jr. also star. 102 min.
68-1356 Was $89.99 □*$14.99*

The Road Home (1995)
A sensitive drama about two orphaned brothers who, in order to avoid being separated, set out on a perilous journey from New York to Nebraska to find Father Flanagan, the founder of Boys' Town. Their danger-filled trip brings them into contact with unusual people and makes headlines across America. Will Estes, Keegan Macintosh, Danny Aiello and Mickey Rooney star. 90 min.
63-1818 Was $99.99 □*$14.99*

Sorrento Beach (1995)
An Australian woman living in London writes a best-selling novel about her family experiences. After her father dies, she is reunited with her two sisters, who are uneasy about the book, and together they face painful emotions and memories from their past while struggling to become a family once again. Caroline Goodall, Joan Plowright star. AKA: "Hotel Sorrento." 112 min.
68-1374 □*$14.99*

The Last Word (1995)
After writing a story about a mysterious stripper he's falling in love with, a journalist learns that his pal has sold the tale to a Hollywood studio. But when the studio wants to know more about the dancer's past, the writer is put on the spot: should he sell out to get the movie done? Timothy Hutton, Chazz Palminteri, Cybill Shepherd, Joe Pantoliano and Michelle Burke star. 94 min.
68-1779 □*$89.99*

A Reason To Believe (1995)
Intense drama about a beautiful college coed who attends a party at her boyfriend's fraternity and is sexually assaulted by one of the members. Rejected by both her sorority sisters and her boyfriend, the woman decides to take legal action and seeks help from a campus support group. Jay Underwood, Allison Smith and Keith Coogan star. 108 min.
68-1797 □*$89.99*

Underworld (1997)
Gangster Denis Leary, fresh out of prison, kidnaps fellow mobster Joe Mantegna and sets out on a bullet-riddled crusade to find out who shot his father in this offbeat and sardonically funny crime drama scripted by "Trigger Happy" auteur Larry Bishop. With Annabella Sciorra, Traci Lords and Abe Vigoda. 95 min.
68-1838 Was $99.99 □*$14.99*

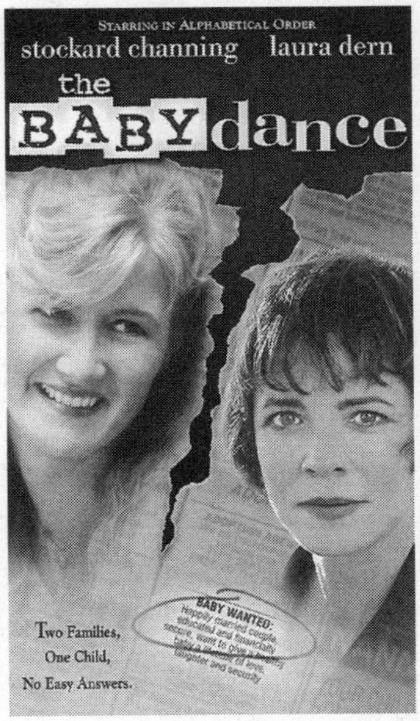
Starring in Alphabetical Order
stockard channing laura dern
the BABY dance
Two Families,
One Child,
No Easy Answers.
BABY WANTED:

The Baby Dance (1998)
Unable to have a child of their own, a successful married couple arrange to adopt the unborn baby of a mother of four struggling with her husband to care for their family. Complications arise when the child is born, leading to unexpected and emotional decisions. Stockard Channing, Laura Dern, Richard Lineback and Peter Riegert star in a moving and timely drama. 91 min.
67-9008 □*$14.99*

Vicious Circles (1997)
In order to save her brother when he's caught trying to smuggle drugs into France, a beautiful young woman joins the ranks of a high-level and high-tech call girl ring. Follow her into a world of erotic surrender and decadence in this sensual and suspenseful drama. Carolyn Lowery, Paul Hipp and Ben Gazzara star. Uncut, unrated version; 90 min.
68-1839 □*$99.99*

Nothing Personal (1997)
Set in Belfast of 1975, this stirring look at the "troubles" in Northern Ireland focuses on the aftermath of the bombing of a Belfast bar usually inhabited by Protestants. Kenny, a gang leader, seeks revenge, but when he and his men kidnap a suspected IRA member, both his loyalty and humanity are tested. James Frain, Ian Hart and John Lynch star. 85 min.
68-1843 □*$99.99*

Mutiny (1999)
Compelling docudrama tells the story of one of the U.S. military's most shameful practices: the use of black sailors with little training to load dangerous munitions onto Victory ships in World War II. After an explosion at a California base in July, 1944, killed over 300 men, 50 enlisted men who refused to go back to work were charged with mutiny. The trial's aftermath rocked naval history. Joe Morton, Michael Jai White, Duane Martin star. 90 min.
68-1986 ❑*$69.99*

The Last September (1999)
Set in County Cork, Ireland, in 1920, this filming of Elizabeth Bowen's acclaimed novel takes place at the estate of Anglo-Irish aristocrats Michael Gambon and Maggie Smith. As the battle for Irish independence wages on around them and threatens their way of life, one of their guests, 19-year-old niece Keeley Hawes, finds herself torn between a British army officer who loves her and a rebellious Irish freedom fighter. With Jane Birkin, Fiona Shaw and Lambert Wilson. 104 min.
68-2017 ❑*$69.99*

Ordinary Magic (1993)
An American teenager raised in India returns to live with his aunt when his parents are killed. Faced with life in a new town and ridicule from the local kids, he finds a special kind of inner strength to prove himself in this family-oriented drama. Ryan Reynolds, Glenne Headly star. 96 min.
72-9028 Was $89.99 *$14.99*

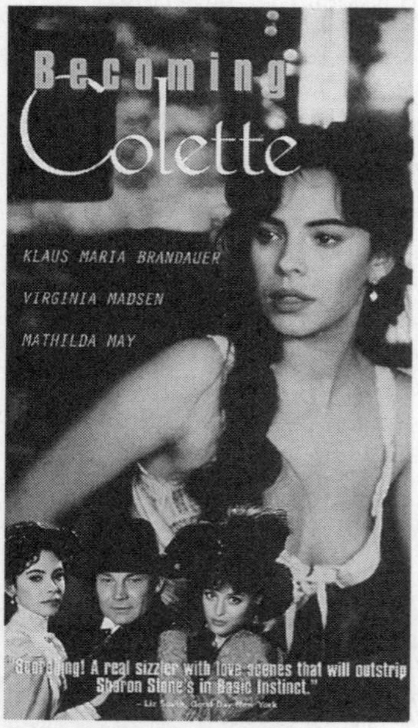

Becoming Colette (1993)
The erotic life and sensual times of French writer Gabrielle Colette are depicted in this sizzling drama starring Mathilda May as a woman whose interest in writing is sparked by her experiences in decadent turn-of-the-century Paris. Virginia Madsen and Klaus-Maria Brandauer also star in this saucy true-life story. 97 min.
71-5274 Was $89.99 ❑*$19.99*

Harmony Cats (1994)
When a classical violinist loses his orchestra gig, he takes a job with a touring country-western band called The Harmony Cats. With help from members of the band, he sheds his shy image and learns how to live. Hoyt Axton, Lisa Brokop and Kim Coates star in this music-filled film. 104 min.
72-9032 Was $79.99 *$14.99*

The Fence (1994)
After spending nearly half his life behind bars, a young man is looking forward to starting a new life on the outside with his girl, but a corrupt parole officer frames him and lands him in a dangerous fight for survival. Billy Wirth, Paul Benjamin, Erica Gimpel star. 90 min.
72-9045 Was $89.99 *$14.99*

Nowhere Fast (1998)
The hardscrabble lives of several Brooklyn residents—a man who breaks out of a psychiatric hospital to see his son; the boy's mother; her new husband, a drug-addicted Wall Streeter; and a carjacker who stumbles on a cache of cocaine—come together over the course of one day in this powerful urban drama from director/co-star Cinque Lee (Spike's brother). 96 min.
72-9280 *$59.99*

The Hot Spot (1990)
Kinky, contemporary film noir, directed by Dennis Hopper, featuring Don Johnson as a drifter who exercises his questionable morals when he takes a job as a used car dealer in a small Texas town. Soon, he's hopping in bed with the boss's hot-blooded wife, romancing a 19-year-old girl with a dark secret and planning a bank robbery. Virginia Madsen, Jennifer Connelly, Charles Martin Smith co-star. 130 min.
73-1093 Was $89.99 ❑*$14.99*

Flynn (1994)
The swashbuckling he-men portrayed by screen legend Errol Flynn pale in comparison to the real-life exploits of this wicked, wicked star. This ambitious film, starring "L.A. Confidential's" Guy Pearce, explores the actor's early years in Australia—from his protean sexual exploits to his wild and woolly adventures in the jungles of New Guinea. 96 min.
22-9040 *$79.99*

The Final Goal (1994)
A young soccer star with dreams of bringing his country a world championship finds his goal blocked by a corrupt ex-player who heads an international sports cartel that wants his team to lose...or else. High-kicking drama stars Steven Nijjar, Dean Butler and Erik Estrada. 85 min.
74-3014 *$49.99*

A Matter Of Honor (1994)
A college professor and rugby coach must confront the demons of his past when an old adversary challenges the teacher's team to a match against his professional squad, and a student athlete is killed during the game. Moving drama stars Jackson Bostwick, Allen Arkus, Rebecca Gray. 95 min.
74-3021 *$49.99*

Playtime (1995)
Super-kinky account of two women who join their husbands on a vacation in Palm Springs and soon allow their voyeuristic games to journey into the realm of taboo fantasies. Monique Parent, Jennifer Burton and Craig Stepp star in this steamy excursion. Unrated version; 95 min.
72-9050 Was $89.99 *$14.99*

Friend Of The Family (1995)
Scorching erotic drama in which a free-spirited woman is welcomed into a family's home during a cross-country backpacking trip and is drawn into the sexual lives of the parents and their two grown offspring. Shauna O'Brien, Annelyn Griffin Drew star. Uncut, unrated version; 98 min.
72-9051 *$89.99*

Friend Of The Family 2 (1996)
In this super-steamy sequel, Shauna O'Brien returns as a seductive but unstable woman who has a one-night stand with a married businessman. When the man tells her he's not interested in continuing the affair, she seeks revenge while posing as a nanny with his family. With Paul Michael Robinson, Jenna Bodner. Uncut, unrated version; 90 min.
72-9076 *$49.99*

Lap Dancing (1995)
A young girl moves to Hollywood dreaming of a job as a movie actress, but after months of failure she reluctantly becomes an exotic dancer at a nightclub. As her exposure to the hitherto unknown world of sex and seduction grows, so do erotic desires within her. Steamy drama star Lorissa McComass, Tane McClure. Uncut, unedited version; 93 min.
72-9060 Was $89.99 *$14.99*

Watch Me (1996)
A kinky drama about a gorgeous voyeuse who moves into an apartment owned by a photographer. As she witnesses the photographer's girlfriend having an affair with his friend and agrees to pose for erotic photos, the woman's sensual, mysterious past is revealed. Jennifer Burton stars. Uncut version; 90 min.
72-9068 Was $89.99 *$14.99*

Article 99 (1992)
A group of doctors in a Kansas City veterans' hospital become outlaws when the hospital's administration ignores the needs of both the patients and the staff. This forceful, sometimes darkly humorous film features a terrific ensemble cast that includes Ray Liotta, Kiefer Sutherland, Lea Thompson, Forest Whitaker and John Mahoney. 99 min.
73-1122 Was $89.99 ❑*$14.99*

There Goes My Baby (1994)
A group of high school seniors in 1965 Southern California faces a variety of personal, scholastic and romantic crises on the eve of graduation in this sensitive "coming of age" comedy/drama. The talented young cast includes Dermot Mulroney, Rick Schroder, Jill Schoelen, Kristin Minter. 98 min.
73-1188 Was $89.99 ❑*$14.99*

Gang Related (1997)
Impressive urban drama stars Tupac Shakur (in his final film role) and James Belushi as crooked cops who set up drug dealers, kill them and keep their money. But when one of their targets turns out to be an undercover DEA agent, their attempt to pin the murder on a street gang could escalate into a citywide war. Lela Rochon, James Earl Jones, Dennis Quaid also star. 106 min.
73-1278 Was $99.99 ❑*$14.99*

Ulee's Gold (1997)
Peter Fonda gives a standout performance as a middle-aged Florida beekeeper who cares for his imprisoned son's daughters. Fonda reluctantly agrees to help save the girls' drug addict mother from some hoods who are holding her hostage in exchange for money his son owes them. Writer/director Victor Nunez's sensitive drama also stars Patricia Richardson, Christine Dunford. 113 min.
73-1280 Was $99.99 ❑*$14.99*

The Hanging Garden (1998)
The ghosts of the past are an ever-present reminder, as a gay man's return to his family's Nova Scotia home for his sister's wedding leads to a series of disturbing revelations, in this offbeat drama that jumps back and forth in time to present the family's history. Chris Leavins, Kerry Fox, Peter MacNeill, Troy Veinotte and Sarah Polley star. 91 min.
73-1311 Was $99.99 ❑*$14.99*

Day At The Beach (1997)
Edgy drama with comic elements focuses on a group of friends working on an independent film who head for a quick vacation in the Hamptons when one of them accidentally kills a fisherman. Their trip proves less than relaxing when they confront their pasta factory boss—who happens to also be a mobster. Nick Veronis, Jane Adams and Catherine Kellner star. 92 min.
73-3044 *$59.99*

Under The Skin (1997)
In this intense, critically acclaimed drama, Samantha Morton and Claire Rushbrook are sisters affected in different ways by the death of mother Rita Tushingham. Rushbrook grieves, then continues with her life, but the repressed Morton begins a series of bizarre sexual adventures that lead to self-destruction. With Stuart Townsend, Christine Tremarco. 85 min.
73-3045 *$59.99*

Darkest Soul (1995)
Dark and disturbing drama involving two friends who find themselves on a wild, nightmarish adventure filled with sex, drugs and alcohol. Tommy, an angry, young man, and Mark, his shy pal, travel from place to place and job to job, until Tommy's girlfriend gets caught in the crossfire of their tumultuous relationship. Al Darago and Jeff White star. 65 min.
73-9106 Was $29.99 *$19.99*

Bang (1996)
Four policemen are captured and held hostage in an abandoned garage where they are tortured. Each hour, another one is killed, and each recalls what got them into the predicament while awaiting their meeting with destiny. An explosive mixture of action, drama and offbeat humor starring King Jeff and Gorio. 85 min.
73-9189 *$59.99*

Childhood's End (1996)
A suburban Minneapolis town is the setting for this study of the sexual coming-of-age of three recent high school graduates: Greg, an aspiring journalist who has an affair with the older Evelyn; Chloe, a model wannabe and Greg's sister; and Rebecca, a shy girl who has a lesbian relationship with Denise, Evelyn's daughter. Cameron Foord, Heather Gottlieb star. 115 min.
73-9264 *$39.99*

Free Floaters (1999)
Jess and Marc decide to spread their message across America by breaking into video stores and taping their own counter-culture film onto hundreds of popular videos (kids, don't try this at home!). Their mission is disrupted when they encounter menacing people on their cross-country journey who threaten their lives. Marc Forget, Gia Buonaguro star. 95 min.
73-9313 *$59.99*

Intimate Betrayal (1996)
A scorching erotic drama in which two friends reunite in hopes of putting their past sins behind them. What ensues, however, is an evening of sex and betrayal with a woman coming between them and some startling double-crosses. Dwier Brown, Richard Edson, Jessica Hecht and Cristi Conaway star. 90 min.
74-3037 *$89.99*

Some Folks Call It A Sling Blade (1995)
The award-winning short film that was a prequel-of-sorts to 1996's "Sling Blade" follows a reporter who arrives at a Northern California mental hospital to interview a retarded man about to be released after committing a shocking crime 25 years earlier. Molly Ringwald and J.T. Walsh co-star alongside scripter Billy Bob Thornton. Also includes a "making of" featurette. 42 min. total.
76-7316 Was $24.99 *$14.99*

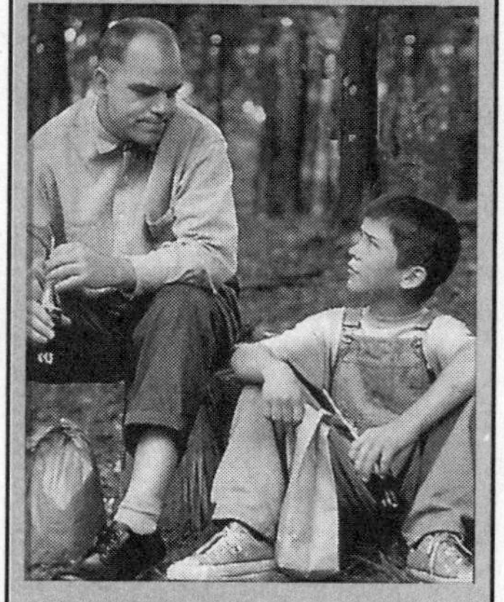

Sling Blade (1996)
Billy Bob Thornton wrote, directed and stars in this quietly powerful character study of Karl Childers, a mildly retarded man who returns to his hometown after serving 25 years in an institution for killing his mother and her lover. Childers moves in with a woman and her young son, whom he has befriended, but soon faces adversity from the woman's redneck boyfriend. Lucas Black, Dwight Yoakam, John Ritter co-star. 135 min.
11-2127 Was $19.99 ❑*$14.99*

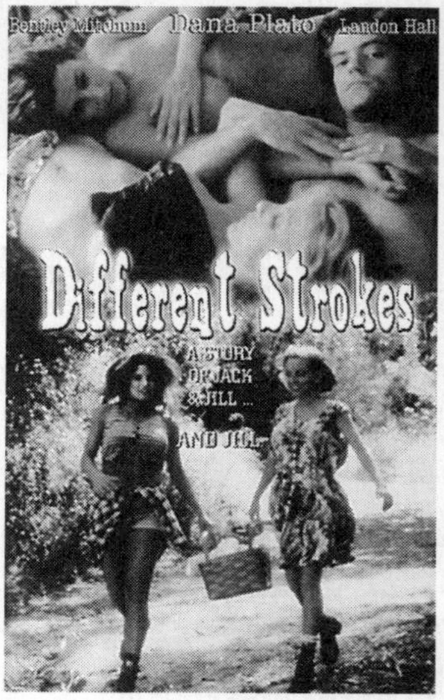

Different Strokes: The Story Of Jack, Jill And...Jill (1996)
In a role which will surprise you, Dana Plato (of TV's "Diff'rent Strokes") plays an art director involved in a romantic threesome with a male fashion photographer and his beautiful model girlfriend, who has a sizzling lesbian lovemaking scene with Plato. Landon Hall, Bentley Mitchum co-star. Uncut, unrated version; 85 min.
73-9188 *$49.99*

Farmer & Chase (1996)
After his longtime partner is killed during a robbery, a veteran criminal looking to pull that "one big job" before retiring turns to his son, an inept petty thief, for help. Old hatreds and new rivalries threaten to kill their partnership before it starts in this offbeat crime drama. Ben Gazzara, Todd Field, Lara Flynn Boyle star. 90 min.
74-3039 *$89.99*

Dirty Cop No Donut (1999)
Follow a cop who takes the law into his own hands and goes on a wild spree during his 10-hour graveyard shift. Witness him mutilating rapists, annihilating drunk drivers, stealing a local drug dealer's stash and propositioning hookers. Is this real or an incredible piece of fiction? You decide. Welcome, America! 80 min.
73-9367 *$39.99*

Where The Air Is Cool And Dark (1998)
Upon returning clean and sober to his Pacific Northwest hometown, Emmett LeClere plans to shoot a film about the region he left. But he starts watching his pal's marijuana crop and socializing with an ex-lover, which leads to him indulging in booze and drugs. Until a friendship with a recovering alcoholic woman, however, gets him on the right track. Emmanuel Malcolm Martinez stars. 95 min.
73-9299 *$59.99*

In The Kingdom Of The Blind The Man With One Eye Is King (1995)
Intense crime drama about a New York police detective who gets a call alerting him that his estranged brother and two associates are responsible for the death of a powerful mobster's brother. The gangsters want the detective to bring his brother in, but he must make a decision: should he save his wayward sibling? With William Petersen, Michael Biehn, Leo Rossi, Paul Winfield. 99 min.
74-3023 *$89.99*

Homage (1996)
Playwright Mark Medoff ("Children of a Lesser God") penned this disturbing psychosexual drama about a failed TV sitcom star who returns to the farmhouse home of her reclusive mother, only to find a handsome, eccentric hired hand living with her. A ménage a trois ensues, leading to a series of startling complications. Blythe Danner, Sheryl Lee, Frank Whaley and Bruce Davison star. 100 min.
74-3036 *$89.99*

I Shot A Man In Vegas (1997)
Gritty, "Rashomon"-like crime drama in which John Stockwell plays a man who kills his best friend. Janeane Garofalo is Stockwell's girlfriend, who decides to tell the police of the incident before they flee into the Nevada desert along with the dead man's friend and his fiancée. With Noelle Lippman. 90 min.
74-3041 *$99.99*

2 Seconds (1998)
Laurie, a mountain bike rider, pauses two seconds before the beginning of a race, and the act costs her a spot on the team. While trying to re-evaluate her life, Laurie takes a job as a bike messenger and meets an elderly Italian man who runs a bike shop and has his own story about "two seconds" to relate. Charlotte Laurier and Dino Tavarone star in this Canadian production. 100 min. In French with English subtitles.
76-2105 *$39.99*

What About Me (1996)

New York City is the setting for this gritty underground drama from writer/director/star Rachel Amodeo about a young woman forced into homelessness after the aunt she was staying with dies. Among the people she encounters on the streets are a shell-shocked Vietnam vet, a crack-addicted East Villager and other societal outcasts. With Richard Edson, Nick Zedd, Richard Hell and Johnny Thunders, who also supplied music. 87 min.

76-7317 — $29.99

Dead Homiez (1996)

Shot in and around South Central Los Angeles and featuring actual members of the Crips and Bloods street gangs, this explosive film tells of Little Cartoon, a Crip out to avenge the drive-by shooting of his brother. Poobear, a young member of the Bloods, is killed out of revenge, and his mother has to try to stop the violence before it affects the rest of the family. Shannon Luckey stars. 105 min.

76-7318 — $49.99

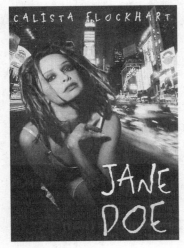

CALISTA FLOCKHART
JANE DOE

Jane Doe (1997)

"Ally McBeal" star Calista Flockhart is Jane, a troubled young woman who moves in with a struggling New York writer and becomes his friend and inspiration, until drug addiction and her self-destructive ways threaten to destroy them both. Christopher Peditto, Elina Lowensöhn also star. 93 min.

83-1392 — Was $99.99 — $14.99

The Versace Murder (1998)

The sensational real-life story of the 1997 murder of fashion designer Gianni Versace is recounted in this film, directed by Menahem Golan. Follow FBI Special Agent John Jacoby's attempts to find primary suspect Andrew Cunanan, the homosexual playboy whose killing spree grabbed the nation's attention. Franco Nero, Steven Bauer, Shane Perdue star.

76-7397 — $79.99

Kin Folks (1997)

In the tradition of "Soul Food" comes this drama laced with comedy about a South Central L.A. family as seen through the eyes of the youngest son, an aspiring rapper. The son is embarrassed to invite his girlfriend to his house during the holidays because of their feisty, unpredictable nature. Maia Campbell, Casey Lee and Stacey Jae Johnson star. 98 min.

76-7401 — $69.99

Magenta (1998)

A forbidden night of passion sparks a deadly game of sex and deception in this shocking thriller about a successful businessman who has a brief but intense affair with the seductive younger sister of his beautiful wife. Julian McMahon, Alison Storry and Crystal Atkins star.

76-7416 — $69.99

Headless Body In Topless Bar

Inspired by the infamous 1983 New York Post headline, this tense hostage drama is set in a Big Apple dive where a gunman takes a group of people captive. Among the bar's denizens held at gunpoint by the unstable former con are a topless dancer, a kinky lawyer, two partying teens and a wheelchair-bound man. Raymond J. Barry, Jennifer McDonald and David Selby star. 101 min.

76-7426 — $39.99

Madam Hollywood (1999)

A beautiful reporter infiltrates a famous Hollywood call girl ring and soon finds herself getting involved with all the decadence and perversion that surrounds her. Trouble ensues when her boyfriend leaves her because of her new, kinky ways and when her clients' desires turn violent. Sonny Landham, Joe Estevez, Brittany McKrenna stars. 90 min.

76-7471 — $79.99

Kill Crazy (1999)

Gripping crime drama tells of Jonesy, a struggling musician lost in the world of sex, drugs and rock and roll. When Jonsey's mounting debts land him in dutch with crooks, he trades in his guitar for a gun and tries to shoot his way out of trouble. Peter Fernandez, Natalie Jovaanovic also star. 90 min.

76-7479 — $79.99

Bye Bye Blues (1991)

Acclaimed story from Canada focusing on a young woman who receives a chance to pursue her lifelong dream of becoming a jazz singer after her soldier husband is reported missing overseas during World War II. Rebecca Jenkins, Michael Ontkean, Stuart Margolin star. 110 min.

76-9027 — Was $89.99 — $14.99

Father (1992)

Powerful drama stars Max Von Sydow as a kind man and father who is accused of Nazi war crimes. His disbelieving daughter can't believe the charges and must decide whether to stick by her father when the truth emerges. Carol Drinkwater, Julia Blake also star. 106 min.

76-9037 — $19.99

Giant Steps (1993)

A young trumpet player is inspired by the career of a veteran jazz master in this music-filled drama that stars Billy Dee Williams. 94 min.

76-9042 — Was $19.99 — $14.99

Cadillac Girls (1993)

In this provocative tale of seduction and betrayal, a single mother and her headstrong teenage daughter experience life on a wild road trip in their yellow Caddy, but the trip takes a strange detour when they both fall for the same man. Gregory Harrison, Jennifer Dale, Mia Kirshner star. 99 min.

76-9054 — Was $19.99 — $14.99

Season Of Change (1995)

Compelling family drama set in Montana after World War II where young Sally Mae deals with her parents' marriage problems and, along with her best friend, Fay, is introduced to the world of sex by spying into a neighbor's bedroom. Michael Madsen, Kira Endsley and Hoyt Axton star. 93 min.

76-9073 — Was $89.99 — $14.99

Stand Off (1996)

Intense drama in which an ex-con seizes control of the Bahamian Consul's office in hopes of getting his former cellmate sprung from the slammer and having the city open a homeless shelter. A battle of wills ensues between the man and the authorities. With Stephen Shellen, David Strathairn and Gordon Clapp. 95 min.

76-9086 — Was $19.99 — $14.99

Bang (1997)

Acclaimed independent film about a struggling Los Angeles woman (Darling Narita) who, after being accosted by a film producer during an audition and being terrorized by a policeman, swipes the cop's uniform and motorcycle and tests her powerful new identity on a wild ride across the city. Peter Greene co-stars in this provocative story spiked with action and a feminist perspective. 98 min.

76-9099 — Was $99.99 — $14.99

where desire
breaks all
the rules.

married people
single sex

Married People, Single Sex (1993)

Scorching, erotic look at how the problems in contemporary marriage can lead to the ultimate in sexual satisfaction. The film focuses on three couples: a bored wife who seeks love outside her home; a man who gets more than he expected when he starts making kinky phone calls; and a proposed break-up that doesn't go as planned. Chase Masterson, Josef Pilato star. Uncut, unrated version; 110 min.

72-9025 — Was $19.99 — $14.99

Married People, Single Sex 2: ...For Better Or Worse (1994)

The grass may be greener on the other side of the fence, but are the erotic pleasures greater in another couple's bed? Three couples bored with their love lives set out to find out for themselves in this super-steamy sequel. Kathy Shower, Monique Parent star. Uncut, unrated version; 93 min.

72-9043 — Was $89.99 — $14.99

Too Fast, Too Young (1996)

Wild crime story in which petty thief Chase Parish is talked into participating in an armored car robbery by his murderous cousin Dalton. Little does Chase realize that his relative has duped him, snagging his part of the take and squealing on Chase's whereabouts to the cops. Michael Ironside, James Wellington and Patrick Tiller star. 92 min.

76-9088 — Was $19.99 — $14.99

The Prince (1995)

A new executive at a toy company seeks advice from a man who espouses the Machiavellian philosophy. The man becomes the executive's mentor and shows him how to seize control of the company by using ruthless tactics that eventually lead to murder. Michael Riley, Billy Dee Williams, Henry Silva and Edie McClurg also star. 89 min.

76-9107 — Was $19.99 — $14.99

Possums (1999)

Frustrated by a 25-year losing streak, Nowata High School cancels its football program. Desperate announcer Mac Davis breaks into the radio station and broadcasts an imaginary game in which the team wins. The town's enthusiasm leads Davis to continue the practice, but when the real state champs challenge the Possums to a showdown, Davis has to recruit a team—pronto! With Andrew Prine. 97 min.

76-9117 — $89.99

The Florentine (1999)

A neighborhood tavern in a run-down Pennsylvania steel town, and the hard-luck regulars who frequent it, are the focus of this compelling slice-of-life drama. As bar owner Michael Madsen prepares for sister Virginia Madsen's wedding, groom-to-be Luke Perry loses the money for the event to con man James Belushi. Mary Stuart Masterson, Chris Penn, Tom Sizemore also star. 104 min.

76-9118 — $99.99

Wildflowers (1999)

Clea DuVall is the daughter of 1960s hippies trying to adjust to life in Northern California in the 1980s. DuVall is drawn to older, exotic runaway Daryl Hannah, but as the two get closer, DuVall learns more of Hannah's mysterious past—and how it will affect her. Eric Roberts, Tomas Arana also star; music by Santana, Blues Traveler, Jane's Addiction and others. 98 min.

76-9125 — $59.99

Eclipse (1995)

From the producer of "Exotica" comes this erotic Canadian production about how a solar eclipse affects the loves and desires of a group of 10 people, all of whom seek intimacy and sexual relations as the sky darkens. Von Flores, John Gilbert star in this unique film festival favorite. 96 min.

78-9012 — Was $39.99 — $19.99

River Of Grass (1995)

Playing like a "Generation X" road movie, this acclaimed independent film looks at a couple who have ambitions of becoming a '90s Bonnie and Clyde, yet never manage to hit the road, commit a crime, or even fall in love. Lisa Bowman, Larry Fessenden and Michael Buscemi star in writer/director Kelly Reichardt's offbeat comedy/drama. 77 min.

78-9013 — $39.99

Rhythm Thief (1994)

Shot in two weeks for about $11,000, director/co-writer Matthew Harrison's acclaimed drama stars Jason Andrews as a Manhattan slacker who makes a living by selling bootleg concert tapes of local bands on the street. Problems arise when an old flame from his hometown arrives in New York just as a "riot grrrl" punk band angry at Harrison's "business" comes looking for him. Kevin Corrigan, Kimberly Flynn also star. 88 min.

78-9019 — Was $39.99 — $19.99

Love Is The Devil (1998)

Based on the life on noted British "artist of decay" Francis Bacon, this raw and compelling drama stars Derek Jacobi as the rage- and alcohol-driven painter. Holding court with his own artistic clique in '60s London, Bacon is seen seducing would-be burglar Daniel Craig and drawing the man into his world of creativity and debauchery. Tilda Swinton co-stars. 88 min.

78-9039 — $79.99

Moon Over Paradise (1994)

The old-fashioned Paradise Bar in Honolulu is transformed into a slick nightclub, but its manager, clientele and neighborhood residents are not quite ready for the new style. Interesting look at Hawaii's changing culture stars Pat Morita, Joe Moore, James Hong and Megan Ward. 101 min.

81-9010 — $89.99

Naked Ambition (1997)

Gorgeous blonde Gail seeks a career in Hollywood, so she decides to pose nude for a men's magazine. Her provocative layout draws the attention of Tinseltown's power players and her career seems ready to take off, but Gail soon discovers a darker side awaits her in the land of fame and fortune. Sizzling adult drama with Gabriella Hall, Cheryl Bartel. Unrated version.

81-9032 — $14.99

James Dean: Live Fast, Die Young (1998)

The life and meteoric career of James Dean is chronicled in this film that follows the actor's rise in Hollywood through starring roles in "Rebel Without a Cause," "East of Eden" and "Giant," his tumultuous personal relationships, and his tragic death at the age of 24 in a car accident. Casper Van Dien, Dianne Ladd and Robert Mitchum (as director George Stevens) star. 90 min.

81-9074 — $89.99

MASSEUSE
Have you ever been rubbed the right way?

Masseuse (1995)

In this seductive drama, a beautiful young woman, shocked after learning of her fiancé's infidelity, seeks revenge by turning her home into a massage parlor and rubbing her male clients the right way. Griffin Drew, Monique Parent, Tim Abell star. Steamy, unedited version; 90 min.

72-9064 — Was $89.99 — $14.99

Illicit Confessions (1998)

Stripper Blake Pickett resorts to hooking while trying to battle the legal system for custody of her daughter. See how far she'll go in this sex-packed drama that also stars James Patrick Keefe, Lisa Comshaw. AKA: "Confessions of a Lapdancer." Unrated version; 90 min.

81-9043 — $89.99

Stalked (1998)

Aleksander escapes the atrocities of the Bosnian Civil War and travels to America in hopes of pursuing his dream of freedom and happiness. His new life begins with a romance with his American friend's sister, but soon is threatened when his town's mayor frames him for murder. Jorgo Ognenovski, Nick Hill star. 93 min.

81-9063 — $99.99

An American Affair (1998)

Corbin Bernsen is a district attorney trying to win a Senate seat whose future is threatened when he becomes romantically involved with best friends Maryam D'Abo and Jayne Heitmeyer. His relationship leads to deception, blackmail and intrigue. With Robert Vaughn. 95 min.

81-9073 — $89.99

Fifth Ward (1998)

After his brother is killed during a botched drug deal, a young black man seeks a way off the violence-filled streets of his inner city neighborhood. Will the love of his Asian employer's daughter be enough, or will their cross-culture romance doom them both? Moving drama stars Kory Washington, Donna Wilkerson, Thomas Miles star. 95 min.

81-9100 — $59.99

A State Of Mind (1997)

Sage, Cookie and Moira are three street-smart young women who've banded together for support. But their friendship—and their lives—are in danger after a random act of violence sets an unforeseeable chain of events in motion. A gritty urban drama about choices that change lives forever. 80 min.

81-9102 — $59.99

Stripshow (1995)

Gorgeous takeoff artist Tane McClure has inherited $2 million from her sugar daddy, and, along with her cowboy ex-lover, she finds herself in a heated triangle with new-stripper-on-the-block Monique Parent. With Steve Tietsort.

82-5015 — $89.99

Stripshow 2 (1997)

This sequel to the sexy sizzler focuses on a scam artist who is mistaken for a hired killer by the madam of a small-town bordello. The man soon falls in love with a beautiful prostitute, but the situation is further complicated when the real hit man arrives on the scene...and his target is the hustler's new girl. Tane McClure and Monique Parent star. 89 min.

82-5035 — $89.99

Absent Without Leave (1996)

Set in New Zealand during World War II, this drama tells of a young soldier who marries his pregnant 16-year-old girlfriend. When his company is suddenly called up, he faces a court-martial when he goes AWOL in order to see his new wife safely back to their home, leading to a soul-searching journey across the countryside. Craig McLachlan, Katrina Hobbs star. 104 min.

82-5020 — $89.99

Risk (1995)
Karen Sillas (TV's "Under Suspicion") stars as Maya, a frustrated painter who makes her living as a nude model in New York City. A drifter persuades Maya to leave the city for the country, where she slowly reveals her mysterious past to the drifter and his family. Acclaimed drama with erotic moments also stars David Ilku, Molly Price. 85 min.
82-5010 *$69.99*

Bleeding Hearts (1997)
An interracial couple have their work cut out for them as they face prejudice from all sides. When the woman gets pregnant, the couple finds their situation even more difficult and battle the odds to make their relationship work. Mark Evan Jacobs and Karen Kirkland star.
81-9038 Was $89.99 *$14.99*

Dingo (1990)
Jazz great Miles Davis plays Billy Cross, a legendary musician whose performances ignite a young music fan's passion for trumpet playing. But does the fan want to give up everything in order to become like his idol? In order to find out, he must travel to Paris. Colin Friels and Helen Buday co-star in this free-form drama with superb music by Davis and Michel Legrand. 108 min.
82-5022 Was $89.99 *$19.99*

Blessing (1994)
Beautifully filmed drama set in the America heartland and focusing on Randi, a woman who desperately wants off her family's Wisconsin dairy farm. Lyle, a young man in a Winnebago, seduces her, but she must eventually choose between him and his fantastic dreams or her family. Melora Griffiths and Carlin Glynn star. 94 min.
82-5032 *$59.99*

Fun (1995)
Much-talked-about Sundance Film Fest entry about two troubled teenage girls from Southern California who try to kill an elderly woman just for kicks. Their heinous crime lands them in a juvenile detention center, where they try to explain their actions. Alicia Witt, Renee Humphrey, Leslie Hope and William R. Moses star. 100 min.
82-5037 *$99.99*

Detention (1998)
"The Breakfast Club" goes to the 'hood when a high school teacher requests that five "trouble" students stay for an afternoon detention at their inner-city school. Soon, their mistrust, fears and struggles are exposed in powerful form. Charisse Brown and John Hall star. 85 min.
82-5136 *$89.99*

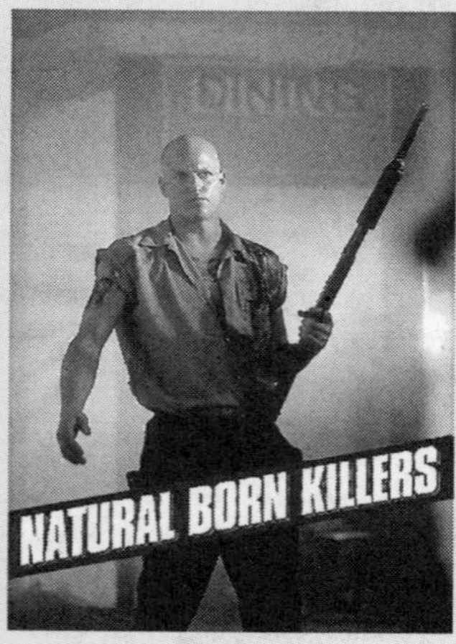
NATURAL BORN KILLERS

Natural Born Killers (1994)
A pointed and darkly humorous look at the American public's fascination with violence, director Oliver Stone's gonzo road movie stars Woody Harrelson and Juliette Lewis as Mickey and Mallory, two lovers whose bloody cross-country crime spree lands them in prison and makes them media-hyped celebrities. With Robert Downey, Jr. as the host of a tabloid TV show, Tommy Lee Jones as a crazed warden, and Rodney Dangerfield as Mallory's abusive father; from a story by Quentin Tarantino. 119 min.
19-2294 Was $89.99 *□$19.99*

Natural Born Killers: Unrated Director's Cut
Look out, Bob Dole! This deluxe edition of Oliver Stone's controversial drama features three minutes of graphic footage cut before the film's release in order to receive an R rating, plus 28 minutes of intense outtake scenes narrated by Stone, the Nine Inch Nails video for "Burn," and exclusive interviews with Stone and the cast. 182 min. total.
19-2368 Was $29.99 *□$19.99*

Natural Born Killers: The Director's Cut (Letterboxed Version)
Also available in a theatrical, widescreen format.
68-1806 Was $29.99 *□$19.99*

The Money Game (1997)
Five friends decide to spend counterfeit cash they created for a student film on a week-long buying lark. But things get dangerous when extra fake cash the printer produces becomes part of a bad drug deal and a seductive woman involves them in a scheme to switch their funny money with mob loot. Filmed in Philadelphia and its suburbs, the film stars Marc Gorman and Margaret Lamonica.
82-5058 *$59.99*

Drinking Games (1998)
After the funeral of one of their number, a group of twentysomething friends get together for a night of "festive" drinking and sobering revelations. Christian Leveler, Diana Left, Geoffrey L. Smith star in this poignant comedy/drama filmed in Portland, Oregon. 94 min.
82-5069 *$99.99*

Wicked City (1998)
An idealistic young girl enters the big city of New York with big dreams and a will to achieve them. However, after the reality of the world catches up to her and she is forced to live on the street, she meets a young musician who may or may not be the answer to her prayers. Victoria Spiro stars; Richie Vetter directs. 90 min.
82-5081 *$69.99*

Black White & Red All Over (1996)
Six young African-American men get together in a house in their violence-stricken inner-city neighborhood to get high, have fun, and ignore the problems of their lives. However, as their home fills up with gangsters, drug dealers and murderers, they are forced to deal with the frightening reality that to continue in their ways will leave them with no future. 100 min.
82-5084 *$99.99*

Wildly Available (1998)
Joe, a seemingly straightforward art gallery owner with a wife, a daughter and a rather normal life, has a kinky affair with a beautiful dominatrix. Joe hopes that this walk on the wild side will better his low-keyed life, but he soon finds himself addicted to the pains and pleasures of the flesh. Kristoffer Tabori and Jennifer Sommerfield star. Unrated version; 98 min.
82-5098 *$89.99*

17 And Under (1998)
Thanks to a recently-passed law mandating that convicted juvenile offenders spend time with the families of violent crime victims, a young gang member named Juan Sanchez is assigned to live with the Romeros, who lost a son to gang violence. Juan soon learns some important lessons about his lifestyle and his "family" in this powerful independent drama. 107 min.
82-5106 *$89.99*

Down For The Barrio (1998)
A sobering and action-filled look at Hispanic-American street life. A man newly released from prison seeks to mend his ways and keep his young son from following in his criminal footsteps, but his efforts with an activist clergyman earn him the enmity of the local gang leader, who launches a violent street war. Tony Plana, Cesar Alejandro star. 87 min.
82-5107 *$99.99*

Dance Of Desire (1998)
An aspiring film director working on a music video has a dispute with his producer which leads him to restage Salome's "Dance of the Seven Veils." The filmmaker soon has a steamy romance with a beautiful, young dancer. Now, the staging of the video's grand finale finds him putting more on the line than his project. Stars Monique Parent, Brian Cooper and Jennifer Barlow.
82-5109 *$89.99*

Goodbye America (1998)
In the tradition of "A Few Good Men" comes this intense drama in which two Navy SEALs stationed in the Philippines try to cover for a fellow SEAL who murdered a local man. When he's failed to be extricated, the accused SEAL turns into an armed fugitive whose emotions have gone haywire. Corin Nemec, Rae Dawn Chong, Alexis Arquette, John Haymes Newton and James Brolin star. 115 min.
82-5111 *$89.99*

Streetwise (1998)
Gritty urban drama focusing on two Washington, D.C., brothers who become crack cocaine dealers when they can't overcome the poverty they encounter each day in their neighborhood. When one of the siblings hatches a plan to take over the local druglord's market, all hell breaks loose. With DJ Kool, Big Tony Fisher. 115 min.
82-5112 *$89.99*

The Girl Next Door (1998)
When a married doctor with a pregnant wife agrees to watch his neighbor's 18-year-old daughter, things get out of control and they have a sizzling sexual interlude. When the girl is found murdered, the physician becomes a prime suspect—especially after incriminating videotape is discovered. Who really killed her? Henry Czerny, Polly Shannon and Gary Busey star. 100 min.
82-5121 *$99.99*

True Friends (1999)
Three young friends witness the murder of a man by a local mobster in their Bronx neighborhood. They make a pact to keep the incident a secret, but years later the crime haunts them in unpredictable ways. James Quattrochi, Loreto Mauro, Rodrigo Botero, Dan Lauria, Mackenzie Phillips and Peter Onorati star in this intense and touching true story. 98 min.
82-5124 *$99.99*

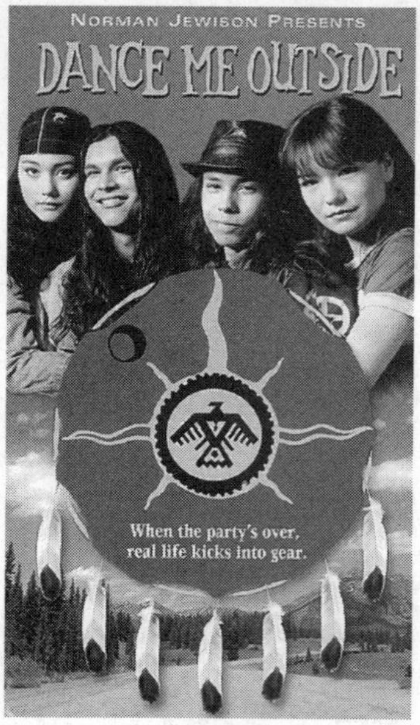
Norman Jewison Presents
DANCE ME OUTSIDE
When the party's over, real life kicks into gear.

Dance Me Outside (1995)
This quirky look at contemporary Indian life is set on a reservation in Northern Ontario where the rape and murder of one of the residents affects four teenagers and their friendships in different ways. Based on a story by W.P. Kinsella, the film stars Ryan Black, Adam Beach and Sandrine Holt. 91 min.
83-1040 Was $89.99 *$14.99*

Me & Will (1998)
In this offbeat road movie, Sherrie Rose and Melissa Behr are motorcycle-riding drug users who meet at a clinic and become friends. When one of their friends dies, they decide to take to the highway on an unusual quest to find the legendary chopper ridden by Peter Fonda in "Easy Rider." The trip is filled with all sorts of unusual experiences. With Seymour Cassell, Traci Lords.
82-5133 *$89.99*

Luscious (1999)
In this sexual odyssey, an artist having trouble with both his career and lovelife finds new inspiration when he and his girlfriend discover a unique style of painting—smearing their bodies with paint and making love on the canvas. The resulting works become a hit with the in-crowd, leading to great success...and, eventually, troubles. Kari Wuhrer, Stephen Shellen star. AKA: "Vivid." Unrated version; 95 min.
82-5142 *$89.99*

White Lies (1998)
Sarah Polley stars as an alienated teenager who begins airing her problems on an Internet chat site. Through the net, she gets involved with the National Identity Movement, a group consisting of other disaffected youths, and soon becomes a poster child for their causes. Little does she know how far their white supremacist beliefs go. Inspired by a true story, the film also stars Lynn Redgrave and Jonathan Scarfe.
82-5162 *$89.99*

Naked Acts (1996)
Cicely, a twentysomething black woman and aspiring actress, dreams of landing more substantial roles than her blaxploitation film star mother got. When her ex-boyfriend offers her a part in a movie he's directing, however, Cicely's dismayed to learn it includes a nude scene that she's desperate to avoid doing. Writer/director Bridgett M. Davis' thoughtful look at women's self-images stars Jake-Ann Jones, Ron C. Jones.
82-5163 *$89.99*

Divided We Stand (1999)
A young African-American woman on a Midwest college campus joins a black political action group, but gets a disturbing surprise when she claims she was assaulted by a fellow member. When the woman's story surfaces, one of the group's leaders must decide whether he should reveal secrets about the organization. J.R. Jarrod and Crayton Robey star. 90 min.
82-5187 *$89.99*

Dream Rider (1996)
Moving true story of Bruce Jennings, a young man who loses his leg in a motorcycle accident. Through determination and help from his mentor, Jennings faces the most challenging ride of his life on a cross-country bike race. Leigh Taylor-Young, E.J. Peaker and Matthew Geriak star. 90 min.
82-5203 *$29.99*

Johnny B. (1999)
After his older brother is murdered, angry African-American Johnny B. quits college and becomes a street hustler. When he discovers that his former girlfriend and mother of his young daughter is getting married to a lawyer, he goes ballistic in a dangerous battle that leads to City Hall. With Richard Brooks, Richard E. Gant and Vonetta McGee. AKA: "Johnny B. Good." 98 min.
82-5194 *$99.99*

Across The Line (1999)
Intense tale about a young Mexican woman who witnesses the execution of a young couple by drug smugglers in a Texas border town. Her desire to tell the truth is eventually endangered, and, while trying to help her, a sheriff uncovers some nasty skeletons in the town's closet. Brad Johnson, Sigal Erez and Adrienne Barbeau star. 97 min.
82-5207 *$99.99*

Sleepover (1995)
A trio of close teenage pals are planning to spend a night on the streets looking for girls after telling their parents they'll be sleeping over a friend's house. However, the night soon takes a dangerous turn and each boy must learn to face his own issues in this look at adolescent suburban life. Michael Albanese, Karl Giant, Ken Miles star. 88 min.
82-5220 *$59.99*

Notes From Underground (1995)
Moody updating of the Dostoevsky novella stars Henry Czerny as the Underground Man. Lonely and spiteful, yet honorable, Czerny tries to figure out his life by making a video diary where he recounts his worst moments, including a party with college classmates and an encounter with a prostitute. Sheryl Lee, Jon Favreau also star in this existential drama. 90 min.
82-5221 *$59.99*

Tales Of The Kama Sutra: The Perfumed Garden (1998)
This exotic, erotic tale tells of an American couple who go to India in hopes of rekindling their sex life. The husband begins working on ancient erotic scriptures, while a beautiful Indian woman instructs the couple in the ancient Kama Sutra. At the same time, another tale of passion that took place 1,000 years earlier is recounted. Ivan Baccarat, Amy Lindsay, Pravesh Kumar star. AKA: "The Perfumed Garden."
82-5224 *$99.99*

Seduce Me: Pamela Principle 2 (1994)
This sequel to the dramatic sizzler stars Playboy Playmate India Allen as a charmer who ignites the passions of a married photographer. When his wife discovers the affair, she begins having a tryst of her own—with a younger man. Alina Thompson and Nick Rafter also star. 96 min.
83-1015 *$14.99*

A Man In Uniform (1994)
An actor preparing to play a policeman on a TV cop show wears his "uniform" out on the streets and begins interacting with real-life police and criminals, but as he becomes more and more obsessed with the role the line between fiction and reality becomes fainter. Powerful and eerily compelling, this acclaimed independent drama stars Tom McCamus, Kevin Tighe, Brigitte Bako. 99 min.
83-1019 Was $89.99 *$14.99*

Paris, France (1994)
Intensely sexual account of a beautiful Canadian writer, bored with her marriage, who counts on a young and adventurous lover to unleash her wildest erotic desires. Filled with kinky encounters of the straight and gay variety, this stylish sensual odyssey stars Leslie Hope, Peter Outerbridge. NC-17 version; 96 min.
83-1025 Was $19.99 *$14.99*

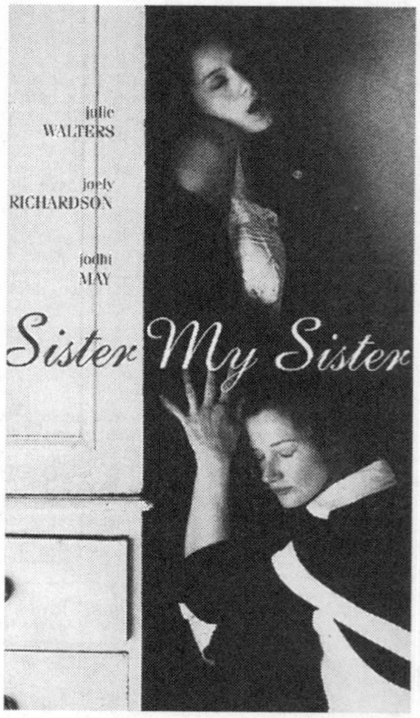
julie WALTERS
joely RICHARDSON
jodhi MAY
Sister My Sister

Sister My Sister (1995)
Sensational true events that occurred in a French town in the 1930s are the basis for this sizzling, unsettling look at incest, lesbianism and murder. Joely Richardson and Jodhi May are siblings involved in a forbidden relationship who murder their stern employer and her daughter. With Julie Walters. 98 min.
83-1041 Was $89.99 *$14.99*

Menace II Society

Menace II Society (1993)
Set in L.A.'s South Central 'hood, this explosive drama centers on a troubled youth so deeply involved with his friends in the lifestyle of robbery, drug dealing and murder that he can't get out. When he finally finds hope with a level-headed girlfriend who wants to help him, tragedy ensues. Tyrin Turner stars in this electrifying first effort from the Hughes Brothers. 104 min.
02-2517 Was $19.99 ❑*$14.99*

Pastime (1991)
Winning baseball drama set in the minor leagues of 1957, where a former big-league pitcher sees his interest in the game and life revitalized when he helps his team's newest player, a talented 17-year-old hurler. William Russ, Glenn Plummer and Noble Willingham star in this atmospheric, bittersweet story. 95 min.
02-2189 Was $89.99 *$14.99*

Let Him Have It (1991)
An explosive true-life drama about a controversial British case from the 1950s, involving a simple-minded teenager who falls in with a group of young gangsters and is sentenced to death for the murder of a policeman. Christopher Eccleston, Paul Reynolds and Tom Courtenay star; Peter Medak ("The Krays") directs. 115 min.
02-2212 Was $19.99 *$14.99*

Cold Justice (1992)
A hard-drinking priest inspires a down-and-out prize-fighter to get back into the ring and change his life. Soon, however, it's discovered that money that was to be used for charity is missing, and the priest is the prime suspect. Roger Daltrey, Dennis Waterman star in this gritty tale. 106 min.
02-2213 Was $89.99 *$19.99*

Heaven Is A Playground (1991)
The mean streets of Chicago's South Side serve as the backdrop for this thrilling and inspiring tale of an inner-city coach and an idealistic lawyer who team up to oversee a basketball team comprised of troubled schoolyard hoop players. D.B. Sweeney, Michael Warren and Richard Jordan star; NBA stars Bo Kimble and Hakeem Olajuwon also make appearances. 104 min.
02-2176 Was $19.99 ❑*$14.99*

Late For Dinner (1991)
Whimsical fantasy/drama about a Santa Fe milkman and his slow-witted brother-in-law who get into trouble with the law and are cryogenically frozen by a California scientist in 1962. They awake in modern-day Los Angeles, discover how much the world has changed and travel back to New Mexico to see their family. Brian Wimmer, Peter Berg, Marcia Gay Harden star. 92 min.
02-2188 Was $19.99 ❑*$14.99*

Roadside Prophets (1992)
Called an "'Easy Rider' for the '90s," this road adventure features rockers John Doe (from the group X) and Adam Horovitz (one of the Beastie Boys) as two pals who bike from L.A. to Nevada with the ashes of a fellow cyclist. Along the way, they meet all sorts of eccentric characters, played by Timothy Leary, David Carradine, Arlo Guthrie and John Cusack. 95 min.
02-2296 Was $19.99 *$14.99*

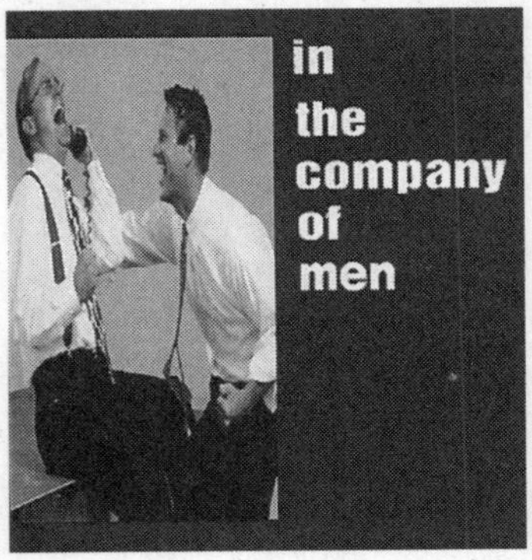

In The Company Of Men (1997)
If there was ever an antithesis of the "first date movie," filmmaker Neil LaBute's bitterly caustic look at male-female mind games is it. Two frustrated junior executives on a temporary reassignment, tired of their stalled careers and dead-end relationships with women, decide to "strike back" by dating and then callously dumping a trusting, deaf secretary in their office, just to show they can. Aaron Eckhart, Matt Malloy, Stacy Edwards star. 97 min.
02-3146 Was $99.99 ❑*$24.99*

Me & Veronica (1993)
While on her way to jail, Veronica (Patricia Wettig), a wisecracking welfare cheat, visits Fanny (Elizabeth McGovern), her estranged sister. The two share a raucous, hard-drinking good time and recall the darker sides of their past before Veronica leaves Fanny a special parting gift. Michael O'Keefe co-stars. 97 min.
02-2530 Was $89.99 *$14.99*

Chantilly Lace (1993)
A superb ensemble cast of actresses is featured in this comedy-drama about seven friends who get together at a mountain cabin and share their innermost secrets about love, sex and the relationships in their lives. Lindsay Crouse, Helen Slater, Talia Shire, Jill Eikenberry, JoBeth Williams, Ally Sheedy and Martha Plimpton star. 102 min.
02-2544 Was $89.99 *$14.99*

Red Hot (1993)
A group of '50s Soviet teens defy their oppressive society and form a band to play "subversive" American rock and roll music in this unusual and emotional drama that features a great oldies score. Balthazar Getty, Carla Cugino, Armin Mueller-Stahl and Donald Sutherland star. 95 min.
02-2782 *$89.99*

Twogether (1995)
Sensual love story set in Venice, California, dissecting the heated relationship between struggling artist Nick Cassavetes and environmentalist Brenda Bakke. Their passionate one-nighter leads to a Las Vegas wedding and a quick divorce, but they decide to give it a go once more—with surprising consequences. With Jeremy Piven. Uncut, unrated version; 122 min.
02-2827 ❑*$89.99*

Fly By Night (1994)
A gritty chronicle of two rappers who join forces to get into the music industry and face violence, criminals and tragedy as their popularity grows. Jeffrey Sams, Ron Brice and MC Lyte star in this powerful, music-filled hip-hop saga. 93 min.
02-2666 Was $89.99 *$19.99*

Bitter Moon (1994)
Roman Polanski's ultra-kinky drama centers on the bizarre interaction of four passengers on an ocean liner bound for India. A repressed British couple (Hugh Grant, Kristin Scott-Thomas) meet a mysterious woman (Emmanuelle Seigner) and her handicapped writer husband (Peter Coyote), who titillate and frighten them with stories of their sadomasochistic relationship. 139 min.
02-2650 Was $89.99 ❑*$19.99*

Birdy (1984)
William Wharton's allegorical WWII novel is updated to the Vietnam War, with Nicolas Cage as a wounded stateside soldier who visits boyhood friend Birdy (Matthew Modine), who's had a lifelong obsession with birds and flight, in a military hospital and works to bring him out of his catatonic stupor; directed by Alan Parker. 120 min.
02-1435 Was $19.99 ❑*$14.99*

Racing With The Moon (1984)
A funny and touching drama that takes place in Northern California shortly after Pearl Harbor. Sean Penn and Nicolas Cage are two teens waiting to be drafted and facing an uncertain future. Elizabeth McGovern is the "society girl" who enters Penn's life. 108 min.
06-1220 Was $59.99 ❑*$14.99*

The Boy In Blue (1986)
Nicolas Cage is 19th-century Canadian rowing champion Ned Hanlan. Hanlan, a former Ontario bootlegger, meets with success at the Philadelphia Centennial Regatta and failure after being banned from American competition. Also stars Christopher Plummer and David Naughton. 97 min.
04-2025 Was $79.99 ❑*$29.99*

Moonstruck (1987)
Three Academy Awards, including Best Actress and Supporting Actress, went to this wonderful romantic comedy featuring Cher as an Italian-American widow whose plans to remarry hit a snag when her fiancé's brother falls in love with her. Nicolas Cage, Danny Aiello, Vincent Gardenia and Olympia Dukakis also star; Norman Jewison directs. 103 min.
12-1784 Was $19.99 ❑*$14.99*

Fire Birds (1990)
Nicolas Cage is a tough pilot chosen to fly a special high-powered military helicopter into action against South American drug dealers in this action-packed excursion that also stars Tommy Lee Jones and Sean Young. 85 min.
11-1531 ❑*$14.99*

Time To Kill (1990)
Powerful, action-filled drama starring Nicolas Cage as a young soldier in Africa whose life is turned upside-down when he accidentally kills the woman he loves. Giancarlo Giannini, Robert Liensol co-star. 103 min.
63-1416 Was $19.99 ❑*$12.99*

Honeymoon In Vegas (1992)
Quirky, romantic farce about a private detective (Nicolas Cage) who heads to Las Vegas to marry his girlfriend (Sarah Jessica Parker). While there he gets into a card game with gambler James Caan and loses his fiancée on a bet. Now he must go through all sorts of hurdles to get her back, including parachuting with the "Flying Elvises." With Pat Morita and Jerry Tarkanian. 94 min.
02-2337 Was $19.99 ❑*$14.99*

Amos & Andrew (1992)
Noted black scholar and writer Samuel L. Jackson rents a New England summer house in an upscale white neighborhood, but the neighbors and police chief Dabney Coleman assume he's a crook. After having his men open fire on the house, Coleman realizes his mistake and hires real thief Nicolas Cage to hold Jackson hostage. Satiric look at race relations also stars Michael Lerner. 96 min.
02-5027 Was $19.99 ❑*$14.99*

Deadfall (1993)
Erotic, atmospheric noir thriller starring Michael Biehn as a con man who teams with criminal uncle James Coburn and seedy right-hand man Nicolas Cage for a scam involving $2 million in diamonds. When Biehn falls for Cage's sexy but calculating girlfriend, desire leads to danger and murder. Sarah Trigger, Charlie Sheen and Peter Fonda co-star. 99 min.
68-1294 Was $89.99 ❑*$14.99*

It Could Happen To You (1994)
Zesty, based-on-a-true-story romantic comedy stars Nicolas Cage as an amiable New York City cop who doesn't have the cash to leave luckless waitress Bridget Fonda a tip, so he shares a lottery ticket with her. When the ticket hits for a multi-million-dollar jackpot, Cage makes good on his pact, against selfish wife Rosie Perez's wishes. With Isaac Hayes, Seymour Cassel. 101 min.
02-2727 Was $19.99 ❑*$14.99*

Trapped In Paradise (1994)
A trio of bumbling criminal brothers pulls off a daring Christmas Eve bank robbery in the tiny town of Paradise, Pennsylvania, but making a getaway turns into a life sentence, thanks to the crooks' own ineptitude and the locals' well-meaning kindness. Slapstick comic treat stars Nicolas Cage, Jon Lovitz, Dana Carvey and Mädchen Amick. 111 min.
04-2943 Was $89.99 ❑*$14.99*

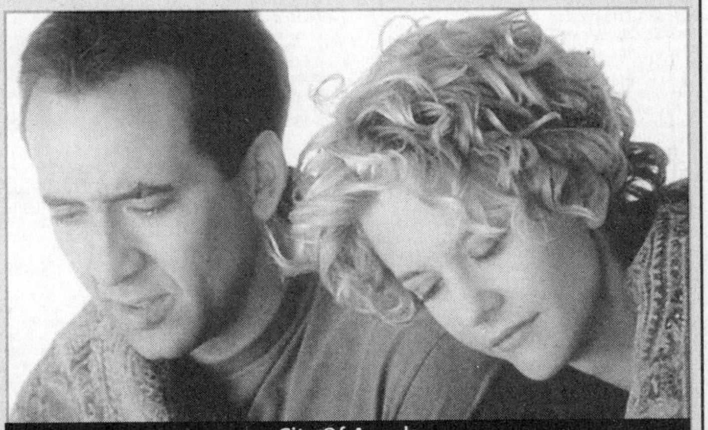
City Of Angels

Nicolas Cage

Kiss Of Death (1995)
The classic crime drama gets a stylish and gritty updating. David Caruso stars as an ex-con trying to go straight who lands back in jail, cut off from his family and caught in the middle of a deadly tug of war between the law (hard-edged cop Samuel L. Jackson) and the mob (deranged crime boss Nicolas Cage). With Michael Rapaport, Kathryn Erbe, Helen Hunt; Barbet Schroeder directs. 101 min.
04-2994 Was $89.99 ❑*$14.99*

Leaving Las Vegas (1995)
Powerful, critically acclaimed study of the depths of alcoholism with Nicolas Cage in an Oscar-winning role as a boozing, out-of-control Hollywood executive who leaves his job and heads for Las Vegas, where he plans to drink himself to death. He meets abused hooker Elisabeth Shue and the two become romantically involved, but is it too late for Cage to be saved? Mike Figgis ("Internal Affairs") directs. 112 min.
12-3051 Was $19.99 ❑*$14.99*

Leaving Las Vegas (Letterboxed Version)
Also available in a theatrical, widescreen format.
12-3134 ❑*$14.99*

The Rock (1996)
In this smashing action opus, deranged military man Ed Harris and his followers take over Alcatraz Island and threaten to launch rockets loaded with deadly nerve gas on San Francisco. FBI biochemical expert Nicolas Cage teams with federal prisoner Sean Connery, the only man to ever escape from "the Rock," to break into the impenetrable prison and stop Harris. Michael Biehn, William Forsythe also star. 136 min.
11-2059 Was $19.99 ❑*$14.99*

The Rock (Letterboxed Version)
Also available in a theatrical, widescreen format.
11-2073 ❑*$19.99*

Con Air (1997)
Fly some very unfriendly skies with former Army ranger Nicolas Cage, newly parolled and ready to be reunited with his family, when the special prison transport plane he's travelling home on is taken over by a rogue's gallery of murderers, rapists and assorted scum, all led by psychotic mastermind John Malkovich. John Cusack, Steve Buscemi and Ving Rhames also star in this high-altitude, high-testosterone actioner. 115 min.
11-2183 Was $19.99 ❑*$14.99*

Con Air (Letterboxed Version)
Also available in a theatrical, widescreen format.
11-2200 Was $99.99 ❑*$19.99*

Snake Eyes (1998)
When a championship boxing match in an Atlantic City resort ends with the fatal shooting of the secretary of defense at ringside, local detective Nicolas Cage teams with his friend, Navy commander Gary Sinise, to locate the sniper. What Cage finds, however, is a far-reaching conspiracy in director Brian DePalma's taut suspense thriller. With Carla Gugino, John Heard. 98 min.
06-2818 Was $99.99 ❑*$14.99*

Snake Eyes (Letterboxed Version)
Also available in a theatrical, widescreen format.
06-2854 ❑*$14.99*

City Of Angels (1998)
Is true love worth giving up immortality? That's the choice facing angel Nicolas Cage in this heartwarming fantasy-drama based on the 1989 German film "Wings of Desire." After seeing surgeon Meg Ryan try to revive a patient whose soul he's come to escort, Cage falls for her and considers "falling" and becoming mortal to be with her. Andre Braugher, Dennis Franz also star. 113 min.
19-2740 Was $99.99 ❑*$19.99*

City Of Angels (Letterboxed Version)
Also available in a theatrical, widescreen format.
19-2789 ❑*$19.99*

8MM (1999)
In Joel Schumacher's dark, disturbing thriller, Nicolas Cage is a Pennsylvania surveillance expert called on by a wealthy widow to find out the identity of a teenage girl whose murder was captured on an 8mm movie found in the widow's husband's safe. The case leads Cage down the dark, dangerous corridors of Los Angeles' underground porn world. With Joaquin Phoenix, James Gandolfini, Catherine Keener. 123 min.
02-3350 Was $19.99 ❑*$14.99*

Gone In Sixty Seconds (2000)
This reworking of the 1974 drive-in fave features Nicolas Cage as a legendary car thief who returns to Southern California after calling it quits to save brother Giovanni Ribisi, who will be bumped off by a British crimelord he ran afoul of. Cage's job: steal 50 hard-to-find cars in three days. Angelina Jolie, Robert Duvall, Delroy Lindo and Will Patton also star in this flashy Jerry Bruckheimer production.
11-2487 ❑*$99.99*

Please see our index for these other Nicolas Cage titles: *Bringing Out The Dead • Face/Off • Fast Times At Ridgemont High • Guarding Tess • Peggy Sue Got Married • Raising Arizona • Red Rock West • Rumble Fish*

West New York (1998)
Tom, a former policeman, plans to sell off small amounts of corporate bonds he has stolen from the New Jersey bank he supervises. When a local mob boss discovers that he hasn't been cut in on the scam, he has hit men out looking for the mastermind. Frank Vincent and Vincent Pastore star in this gritty crime effort. 90 min.
82-5161 *$89.99*

Body Strokes (1995)
The producers of "Secret Games" and "Animal Instincts" present their most scorching effort yet. A painter seeks inspiration from two young, gorgeous models. When the modeling sessions lead into sexual liaisons, the artist's wife decides to leave him. Will she return and become part of her husband's hottest work ever? With Dixie Beck, Kristin Knittle. Unrated version; 85 min.
83-1055 Was $89.99 *$14.99*

Animal Instincts: The Seductress (1995)
Her erotic fantasies are fueled by an audience; his, by watching others "in the act." When these two meet and enter into a bizarre and intense sexual relationship, the result is a white-hot drama of human passion and animal instincts. Wendy Schumacher, James Matthew, John Bates star. Uncut, unrated version; 92 min.
83-1059 Was $89.99 *$14.99*

Bad Love (1995)
In the tradition of "True Romance" and "Gun Crazy" comes this violent, hard-hitting drama featuring Tom Sizemore as a gas station attendant who falls for Pamela Gidley, a beautiful woman with a dark side. Seeking an opportunity to start a better life, the two stage a dangerous robbery. Debi Mazar, Richard Edson, Seymour Cassel and Joe Dallesandro co-star. 93 min.
83-1071 Was $89.99 *$14.99*

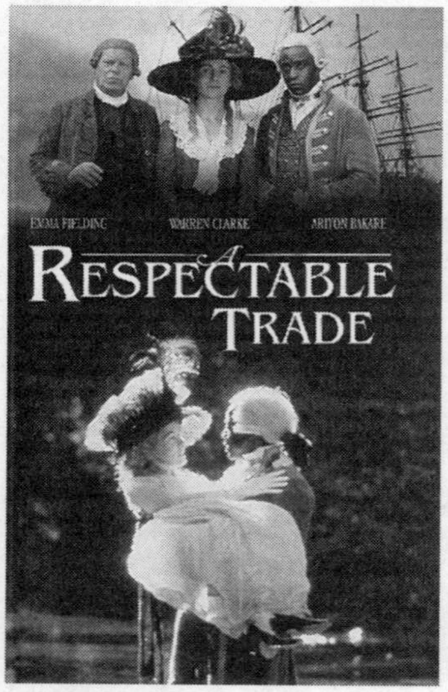

A Respectable Trade (1998)
Near destitute after her father's death, a young woman in 18th-century England weds a coarse shipbuilder who seeks to build his fortune by importing slaves from Africa. The relationship that develops between the woman and a handsome, learned African man drives this compelling drama, based on the novel by Philippa Gregory. Emma Fielding, Warren Clarke, Ariyon Bakare star. 240 min.
08-8704 *❑$29.99*

Dark Secrets (1995)
A beautiful woman is drawn into the seductive world of Southern California's wealthiest citizens, a world where the wildest sexual desires can be fulfilled, and every pleasure and every body has its price, in this steamy drama. Julie Strain, Monique Parent, Justine Carroll star. Uncut, unrated version; 90 min.
83-1072 Was $89.99 *$14.99*

The Proposition (1996)
To save her family from attackers, a pioneer woman must give up her honor to a gun-toting wanderer who comes to their aid. Powerful frontier drama stars Theresa Russell, Patrick Bergin, Richard Lynch. 99 min.
83-1125 Was $99.99 *$14.99*

Good Luck (1997)
Refusing to let his wheelchair be an obstacle, Gregory Hines sets out with pal Vincent D'Onofrio, a blind former football star, to win a whitewater rafting competition in this rousing and inspiring drama. James Earl Jones, Max Gail also star. 95 min.
83-1151 Was $99.99 *$14.99*

Love To Kill (1997)
A gun-running gangster is happy with his job's financial rewards, but finds his lifestyle is hampering any chances for a lasting romance with a new girlfriend, in this offbeat mix of action, comedy and crime drama. Tony Danza, Michael Madsen, Elizabeth Barondes and Amy Locane star. AKA: "The Girl Gets Moe." 102 min.
83-1199 Was $99.99 *$14.99*

Rude (1995)
Stylish urban drama set on the mean streets of Toronto, where a sensuous disc jockey serves as your host to three fascinating stories. You'll meet "The General," a gang member just out of prison who's trying to decide on his future; a boxer involved in a gay-bashing incident; and a woman troubled by her decision to have an abortion. With Maurice Dean Wint, Clark Johnson. 90 min.
83-1099 Was $99.99 *$14.99*

Men (1998)
Compelling drama starring Sean Young as a sexually promiscuous woman who leaves her alcoholic boyfriend in New York and seeks a new life for herself, attempting to start a career as a chef. Eventually she meets a young photographer with whom she has her first true romance. Dylan Walsh and Richard Hillman also star. 93 min.
83-1286 Was $99.99 *$14.99*

Junior's Groove (1997)
Offbeat drama from Canadian filmmaker Clement Virgo ("Rude") about a sensitive but hugely obese teenager whose passion for classical piano draws him into an elaborate fantasy world. Martin Villafana, Lynn Whitfield, Margot Kidder, Sarah Polley star. AKA: "The Planet of Junior Brown." 91 min.
83-1362 Was $99.99 *$14.99*

Lies & Whispers (1997)
While attending a conference in Prague, American psychologist Gina Gershon meets and falls in love with former dissident writer Rade Serbedzija. Their relationship, however, is tested when Gershon learns shocking facts about war crimes committed by her Czech-born grandfather during World War II in this moving drama. AKA: "Prague Duet." 95 min.
83-1383 Was $99.99 *$14.99*

In The Shadows (1998)
A young woman hired to serve as caretaker and companion to a wealthy, terminally ill woman hatches a scheme with her slacker boyfriend in which he'll seduce her employer and inherit her fortune. Things take an unexpected turn in this dramatic and suspenseful tale of an unusual love triangle. Joely Richardson, Molly Parker, Aden Young star. 115 min.
83-1384 Was $99.99 *$14.99*

Race (1997)
The contest between a veteran black politician and a Latino house painter-turned-candidate for a vacant Los Angeles city council seat turns into a bitter, racially divisive battle in this compelling drama. Paul Rodriguez, CCH Pounder and Cliff Robertson star. 100 min.
83-1391 Was $99.99 *$14.99*

A Stranger In The Kingdom (1999)
Remote Kingdom County in Vermont seems to a peaceful place, but the killing of a Canadian mail-order bride and the arrest of a local minister who tried to help her leads to shocking revelations. Compelling, suspenseful drama stars Ernie Hudson, Martin Sheen, David Lansbury and Jean Louisa Kelly. 111 min.
83-1394 Was $99.99 *$14.99*

Broken Vessels (1999)
A college graduate newly arrived in Los Angeles takes a job as an assistant paramedic, but nothing prepares him for the daily dose of death and violence their patients provide...or the opportunities for casual sex and drug abuse their job offers. Emotionally jolting drama stars Todd Field, Jason London. 91 min.
83-1431 Was $99.99 *$14.99*

Forever Together (1999)
In this heartwarming romantic fantasy, a shy high schooler gets advice on winning the heart of his dream girl from a quirky jazz musician, who has a secret romance of his own to pursue, that he meets in a cemetery. Bryan Burke, Michelle Trachtenberg, Ralph Macchio and Rachel Ticotin star. AKA: "Can't Be Heaven." 91 min.
83-1554 *$49.99*

Sunday (1998)
Moody and moving romantic drama starring David Suchet as a homeless man living in a New York shelter who carries on a relationship with a struggling actress who believes Suchet is actually a famous director with whom she once worked. Lisa Harrow and Jared Harris also star in this acclaimed effort. 93 min.
85-5099 *$89.99*

Forbidden Games (1995)
A former Justice Department operative is hired to find the person responsible for the murder of a prominent model agency honcho. His search leads him into the mysterious and sexy world of supermodels, where seduction and danger lie at every turn. Jeff Griggs, Lesli Kay Sterling and Gail Harris star. Uncut, unrated version; 89 min.
86-1092 Was $89.99 *❑$14.99*

The Boys (1997)
Newly released from jail, a violent young hood returns to his Sydney home and begins a bitter fight for supremacy with his two younger bothers, one of whom is following in his sib's criminal footsteps, the other trying with his wife's encouragement to break away from the ultra-dysfunctional situation. Intense Aussie drama stars David Wenham, Anthony Hayes, Toni Collette. 85 min.
83-1555 *$69.99*

Drowning On Dry Land (1999)
A New York woman's hectic life is threatening to drive her over the edge. When it finally becomes too much to bear, she hops in a cab and tells the driver to head for the desert. The two of them eventually fall in love as they journey from the East Coast to the heart of Arizona in this heartwarming tale featuring Barbara Hershey and Naveen Andrews. 101 min.
83-1559 *$99.99*

Sinatra (1992)
On the stage, on the screen, and in his private life, he did it "his way." The acclaimed TV mini-series, authorized by Frank Sinatra, traces the ups and downs of "The Chairman of the Board's" record-setting career and his homelife. Featured Sinatra songs (performed by Frank himself) include "That Old Black Magic," "Come Fly with Me," "That's Life" and many more. Philip Casnoff, Marcia Gay Harden, Olympia Dukakis and Rod Steiger star. 239 min.
19-2014 *❑$29.99*

The Rat Pack (1998)
The glory days when Frank Sinatra and pals ruled Las Vegas and Palm Springs and wielded heavy political influence come to life in this exhilarating feature that takes you backstage and allows you to see the inner workings of "the Chairman," his pack and the Kennedys. With Ray Liotta as Sinatra, Joe Mantegna as Dean Martin, Don Cheadle as Sammy Davis, Jr., Angus MacFadyen as Peter Lawford, Bobby Slayton as Joey Bishop, and William Petersen as John F. Kennedy. 120 min.
44-2175 Was $79.99 *❑$14.99*

Stand-Ins (1997)
Set during the course of an evening in Hollywood in 1937, this effort details the exploits of a group of women who serve as stand-ins for Tinseltown's biggest stars. Among the women who congregate at a bar and discuss their hopes and dreams are subs for Greta Garbo, Bette Davis, Marlene Dietrich, Rita Hayworth and Mae West. Missy Crider, Katherine Heigl, Daphne Zuniga star. 88 min.
83-5006 *$89.99*

Let The Devil Wear Black (1999)
Contemporary Los Angeles stands in for medieval Denmark in this stylish, noir-flavored thriller based on "Hamlet." A college student returns home after his wealthy father's death and begins to suspect his uncle and mother, who are planning to marry, may have been responsible. Jonathan Penner, Jacqueline Bisset, Mary-Louise Parker and Jamey Sheridan star; directed by Stacy Title ("The Last Supper"). 90 min.
83-1553 *$99.99*

Alegria (1998)
This lovely romantic fantasy from "Cirque de Soleil" artistic director Franco Dragone is about Frac, a disgruntled street mime who saves the life of Momo, an 11-year-old boy, when he's almost run over by a train carrying travelling circus performers. Frac meets and falls for Giuletta, a circus singer, but must first deal with her disapproving father. René Bazinet, Julie Cox and Frank Langella star. 93 min.
83-5007 Was $79.99 *$14.99*

Mesmer (1994)
This intriguing film looks at Dr. Franz Anton Mesmer, the 18th-century Austrian physician who drew controversy and an incredible following with his use of hypnotism and magnetism for healing. Alan Rickman turns in a tour-de-force performance as Mesmer; Amanda Ooms and Jan Rubes co-star. Scripted by Dennis Potter ("The Singing Detective"). Director's cut; 107 min.
83-5011 *$24.99*

The Life Before This (1999)
After a random shooting in a downtown Toronto coffee shop leads to the death of several customers and employees, this unusual drama flashes back to reveal the victims' lives before the fatal incident. There's a man accused of a phony sexual harassment charge, a lawyer facing embezzlement charges, a single woman readying for a date and more. With Catherine O'Hara, Stephen Rea, Sarah Polley. 93 min.
83-5013 *$99.99*

A Merry War (1998)
Can a struggling neophyte poet in 1930s London ever find creative and financial independence while his day job has him turning out such prose as "New Hope for the Ruptured"? That's the crisis of conscience facing advertising copywriter Richard E. Grant and his girlfriend and co-worker, graphic artist Helena Bonham Carter, in this winning comedy/drama, based on George Orwell's novel "Keep the Aspidistra Flying." With Harriet Walter, Jim Carter. 101 min.
83-1288 Was $99.99 *$14.99*

Quiet Days In Hollywood (1997)
The lives of a variety of Los Angeles residents—among them hooker Hilary Swank, thief Daryl "Chill" Mitchell, waitress Meta Golding, duplicitous lawyer Chad Lowe and closeted gay actor Peter Dobson—intersect in dramatic, erotic and violent ways in this compelling character study of Tinseltown life. AKA: "The Way We Are." 95 min.
83-5012 *$89.99*

Godmoney (1997)
A streetwise New Yorker with a background in drug-dealing decides to change his life radically by moving to the San Fernando Valley near Los Angeles. His hopes to stay out of trouble are soon dashed when his roommate's financial troubles play a part in his own cash flow problems, causing him to do business with a local dope seller. Rick Rodney and Bobby Field star. 98 min.
83-5008 Was $19.99 *$14.99*

The Designated Mourner (1997)
In David Hare's adaptation of Wallace Shawn's three-character stageplay, Mike Nichols plays a journalist who relates a story of his past involving ex-wife Miranda Richardson and her father, author and liberal activist David de Keyser, whose political beliefs get him in trouble with the totalitarian government of their unnamed homeland. 95 min.
83-5009 *$79.99*

Mr. And Mrs. Loving (1996)
Compelling true story set in the early 1960s and starring Timothy Hutton and Lela Rochon as an interracial couple whose marriage prompts a bigoted Southern judge to exile them from the state of Virginia. An idealistic lawyer eventually takes their case to the Supreme Court at the dawn of the civil rights movement. Isaiah Washington, Ruby Dee also star. 96 min.
88-1081 Was $99.99 *$14.99*

Journey (1996)
Touching drama stars Jason Robards and Brenda Fricker as the grandparents of an 11-year-old boy who is crushed when his mother deserts him, his sister and their family farm. Using photography to reveal the boy's past, Robards helps his grandson understand the intricacies of families. With Max Pomeranc, Meg Tilly, Eliza Dushku. 99 min.
88-1082 Was $89.99 *❑$14.99*

I Shot Andy Warhol (1996)
Independent film fave Lili Taylor turns in a tour-de-force performance as disturbed hardcore feminist Valerie Solanis, a hanger-on of Andy Warhol's Factory crowd, whose paranoia drove her to shoot the famed pop artist in his New York studio in 1968. Jared Harris as Warhol, Martha Plimpton and Stephen Dorff also star in this edgy, acclaimed effort. 104 min.
88-1096 Was $19.99 *❑$14.99*

Homecoming (1996)
Stirring drama about a quartet of children, forced to fend for themselves when their emotionally troubled mother leaves them, who travel cross-country to find the reclusive grandmother they've never known. Although the lonely, embittered woman at first wants nothing to do with them, the kids attempt to forge a relationship. Anne Bancroft and Kimberlee Peterson star. 105 min.
88-1103 Was $99.99 *❑$14.99*

Girls Town (1996)
Acclaimed independent drama focusing on a trio of female high school seniors who face their fears and goals after one of their friends, a beautiful Ivy League-bound girl, kills herself. Among the young women are a slacker who wants to be a car mechanic (Lili Taylor); an angry poet (Bruklin Harris); and a wallflower who wants to bloom (Anna Grace). 90 min.
88-1112 Was $19.99 *$14.99*

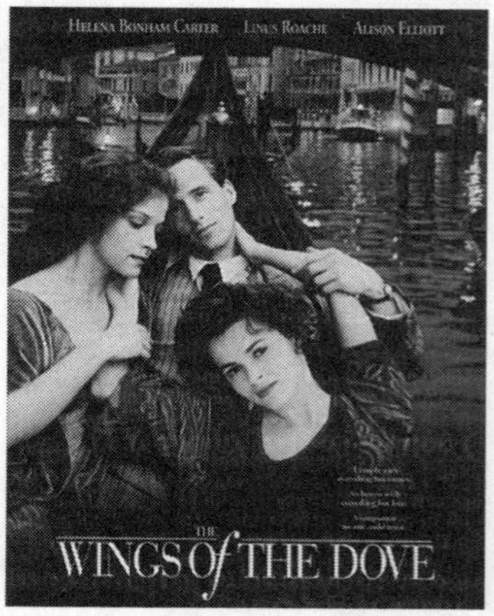

The Wings Of The Dove (1997)
Helena Bonham Carter shines as a young woman in late 19th-century English society who finds herself torn between her duty to her impoverished father and her love for an honest but poor journalist. A chance meeting with an ailing American heiress leads Carter to devise a daring plot to make her dreams a reality in this lush adaptation of Henry James' novel. Linus Roache, Alison Elliott and Charlotte Rampling also star. 102 min.
11-2254 Was $99.99 *❑$19.99*

I Like To Play Games (1995)
Super-steamy, sensual drama in which a man in search of a partner to satisfy his kinky needs finally gets more than he could have imagined in a gorgeous, open-minded woman who takes a job at his office. Soon, they're indulging in wild sexual games that eventually turn dangerous. Playboy model Lisa Boyle and Ken Steadman star. Uncut, unrated version; 95 min.
83-1038 Was $89.99 *$14.99*

I Like To Play Games, Too (1998)
Suzanne loves playing teasing games with men, but she meets her match in Dominic, a master of titillation and manipulation. The two carry on together seductively, but things eventually lead into the realm of danger, blackmail and possibly murder. Maria Ford, Kim Dawson star. Unrated version; 96 min.
07-2767 *$39.99*

Chanel Solitaire (1981)
Marie-France Pisier stars as Coco Chanel, the feisty Parisian woman who overcame her impoverished background to rise to the top of the fashion world. International cast also features Timothy Dalton, Karen Black, Rutger Hauer. 120 min.
03-1259 Was $59.99 *$19.99*

A Question Of Honor (1982)
Gritty drama stars Ben Gazzara as an honest New York cop set up by the government and used as a pawn in a corruption probe. With Paul Sorvino, Robert Vaughn, Tony Roberts, Danny Aiello. 135 min.
03-1464 *$14.99*

Tell Me A Riddle (1980)
An elderly woman suffering from a terminal illness visits with her grown granddaughter in San Francisco, a visit that adds a new dimension to both their lives. Moving drama, based on a story by Tillie Olsen, stars Lila Kedrova, Brooke Adams, Melvyn Douglas. 94 min.
03-1510 Was $79.99 *$14.99*

Variety (1983)
A young woman starts working as a ticket seller at a seedy Times Square adult theatre and becomes increasingly interested in the world of pornography and the theater's patrons. Compelling and unsettling, independent filmmaker Bette Gordon's feminist-themed drama stars Sandy McLeod, Will Patton and Richard Davidson; score by John Lurie. 97 min.
03-1535 *$24.99*

Tough Guys Don't Dance (1987)
A gritty drama written and directed by author Norman Mailer. Ryan O'Neal is a down-and-out loafer who awakens from an alcoholic stupor to find himself accused of murder, sought by a drug kingpin, and reunited with the two women in his life. With Isabella Rossellini, Wings Hauser, Debra Sandlund. 108 min.
03-1586 *$14.99*

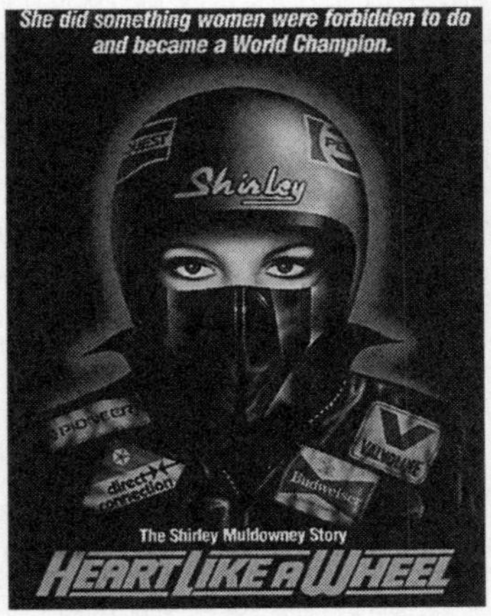
She did something women were forbidden to do and became a World Champion.
Shirley
The Shirley Muldowney Story
HEART LIKE A WHEEL

Heart Like A Wheel (1983)
Bonnie Bedelia won critical acclaim for her portrayal of race car driver Shirley Muldowney in this touching and inspiring true life story, co-starring Beau Bridges, Anthony Edwards, Hoyt Axton and Leo Rossi. 113 min.
04-1661 *$14.99*

Monsignor (1982)
A provocative and controversial story about an ambitious American priest (Christopher Reeve) who becomes involved with smuggling and falls in love with a nun. Co-stars Genevieve Bujold, Fernando Rey. 121 min.
04-1505 Was $59.99 *$29.99*

Without A Trace (1983)
Emotional powerhouse about a woman, played dynamically by Kate Nelligan, who searches for her missing son with the help of a determined police detective (Judd Hirsch). Based on a true story. 118 min.
04-1620 Was $59.99 *$29.99*

Tough Enough (1983)
He took it on the chin as a country/western singer, but good ole boy Dennis Quaid straps on the leather to fight in one "Tough Man" competition after another to help support his wife and son. Co-stars Warren Oates, Stan Shaw, Carlene Watkins, Pam Grier. 107 min.
04-1629 Was $59.99 *$29.99*

Jane Austen

Persuasion (1971)
Sumptuous, wonderfully acted BBC presentation of Jane Austen's last novel focuses on Anne Elliott, a woman who listens to her affluent family's suggestion that she shouldn't wed Captain Wentworth. Years later, Anne and Wentworth meet again, but fortunes have shifted and the captain is about to marry another. 225 min.
04-3344 Was $29.99 *$24.99*

Persuasion (1995)
An aristocratic young woman in 1800s England, at the behest of her class-conscious parents and friends, breaks off her engagement to a poor but earnest naval officer. Seven years later, the now-successful captain returns to find the woman's family in dire financial straits. Amanda Root, Ciaran Hinds and Corin Redgrave star in this lavish drama, based on Jane Austen's final novel. 104 min.
02-2860 Was $89.99 *$19.99*

Emma (1972)
Superb BBC production of Jane Austen's 1816 novel focuses on Emma Woodhouse, a well-intentioned but self-serving woman who tries to "improve" the romantic and personal lives of those around her. A difficult lesson is in store when her latest "protégé," the orphaned Harriet Smith, decides to marry a man Emma secretly loves. Doran Godwin, John Carson, Debbie Bowen, Mollie Sugden star. 257 min. on two tapes.
04-3343 Was $29.99 *$24.99*

Emma (1996)
Kate Beckinsale stars in the title role of Jane Austen's feisty heroine, determined to play matchmaker for her friends and acquaintances in 19th-century England, in this stylish and enchanting comedy of manners. With Prunella Scales, Samantha Bond. 107 min.
53-8672 Was $19.99 *$14.99*

Pride And Prejudice (1985)
Lavish adaptation of Jane Austen's novel concerning the struggles of five well-to-do sisters in 19th-century England as they seek to choose their own husbands, against their mother's machinations. Elizabeth Garvie, David Rintoul star. 226 min.
04-2096 Was $29.99 *$24.99*

Pride And Prejudice (1995)
The countryside of early 1800s England is the setting for laughter, tears and romance in this superb drama based on the Jane Austen novel, as five sisters are "gently" pushed by their parents into finding suitable husbands and thus preserving the family estate. The fine cast includes Colin Firth, Alison Steadman, Jennifer Ehle, Susannah Harker. 300 min. on six tapes.
53-8411 Was $99.99 *$59.99*

Mansfield Park (1986)
Jane Austen's timeless romance is retold in this striking BBC-made drama. A destitute young woman's determination wins the respect of her wealthy, haughty relatives and the love of her devoted cousin. Sylvestra Le Touzel, Bernard Hepton, Nicholas Farrell star. 261 min.
04-2097 Was $29.99 *$24.99*

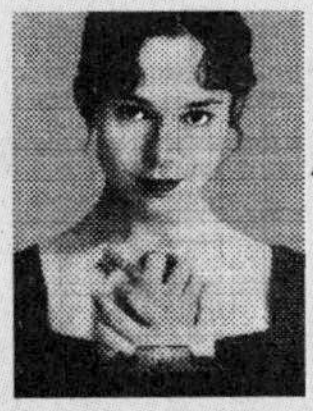

JANE AUSTEN'S
WICKED
COMEDY

MANSFIELD PARK

Mansfield Park (1999)
Jane Austen's classic novel is the basis for this controversial and acclaimed adaptation from Canada's Patrice Rozema. Frances O'Connor is Fanny Price, a poor woman raised on her aunt and uncle's estate during the 18th century. She establishes a strong bond with her male cousin, but relationships change when a brother and sister seeking spouses arrive at the estate from London. Jonny Lee Miller, Embeth Davidtz, Alessandro Nivola and Harold Pinter also star. 113 min.
11-2443 *$99.99*

Sense And Sensibility (1986)
Wonderful story of two dissimilar sisters whose attempts to find husbands run afoul of the prevailing morality of 1700s English society. Sumptuous adaptation of Jane Austen's first novel stars Irene Richard and Tracey Childs. 174 min.
04-2098 Was $29.99 *$24.99*

Sense And Sensibility (1995)
Marvelous adaptation of Jane Austen's novel is set in rural England in the late 18th century, where the Dashwood sisters, Elinor (Emma Thompson), Marianne (Kate Winslet) and Margaret (Emile Francois), experience the joys and hardships of love while living in a cottage owned by their cousins. Alan Rickman, Hugh Grant also star. Thompson's script won an Oscar; Ang Lee directs. 136 min.
02-2901 Was $19.99 *$14.99*

Sense And Sensibility (Letterboxed Version)
Also available in a theatrical, widescreen format.
02-3053 *$19.99*

Northanger Abbey (1986)
Jane Austen's tale of intrigue and romance is set against the decadence of 18th-century Bath, where suspense unfolds when Catherine Morland arrives for a romantic liaison with Henry Tilney in his ancestral home of Northanger Abbey. Peter Firth, Googie Withers and Robert Hardy star. 90 min.
53-9508 Was $29.99 *$19.99*

Mommie Dearest (1981)
The story of legendary movie star Joan Crawford, as she struggles to further her career while battling the inner demons of her private life stars Faye Dunaway in an uncannily effective portrait of the troubled actress. Based on her daughter's controversial best-selling book. Co-stars Diana Scarwid, Steve Forrest. 129 min.
06-1117 *$14.99*

I'm Dancing As Fast As I Can (1982)
Jill Clayburgh is a successful career woman coping with an addiction to Valium in this all-too-real drama. With Nicol Williamson, Daniel Stern, Joe Pesci, John Lithgow. 107 min.
06-1128 Was $59.99 *$14.99*

The Lords Of Discipline (1982)
Riveting tale of suspense as a young cadet at a Southern military academy in 1964 must protect the first black recruit. But "the Ten," a secret society within the school, wants them both...dead. David Keith, Robert Prosky, Judge Reinhold, Bill Paxton co-star. 103 min.
06-1176 Was $39.99 *$14.99*

Daniel (1983)
Timothy Hutton is a young man trying to clear his family name years after his parents are executed for conspiracy. Taken from the best-selling novel by E.L. Doctorow and based on the story of Julius and Ethel Rosenberg. Mandy Patinkin, Lindsay Crouse, Amanda Plummer. Sidney Lumet directs. 130 min.
06-1204 Was $59.99 *$14.99*

Threshold (1982)
Knockout drama involves the mystery, emotional conflicts and problems revolving around a breakthrough heart transplant. Donald Sutherland, Jeff Goldblum and Mare Winningham turn in exceptional performances in this sleeper. 97 min.
04-1671 Was $59.99 *$29.99*

Hotel Du Lac (1980)
Wonderful rendition of the Anita Brookner novel regarding the observations about British leisure-class life that are noted by a celebrated author during her self-imposed exile at a seaside resort. Touching presentation stars Anna Massey. 75 min.
04-2067 *$19.99*

Less Than Zero (1987)
The controversial, best-selling novel of the seamy underside of L.A. yuppie life becomes a stylish, riveting film. Andrew McCarthy, Jami Gertz and Robert Downey, Jr. are the three high school friends who find an adult world of drugs, sex, and shallow thrills that threatens to engulf them. With James Spader, Nicholas Pryor. 98 min.
04-2126 Was $19.99 *$14.99*

The Stone Boy (1984)
A rural family's love is tested when the youngest son kills his brother in a hunting accident in this poignant drama. Robert Duvall and Glenn Close are the parents, Jason Presson the traumatized child. With Frederic Forrest, Wilford Brimley. 93 min.
04-1828 Was $59.99 *$29.99*

Turk 182 (1985)
Timothy Hutton is a young man fighting the system in this rousing drama. When his fireman brother (Robert Urich) is denied a pension after being wounded, Hutton starts a one-man graffiti campaign against the city bureaucracy. Kim Cattrall, Robert Culp co-star. 96 min.
04-1865 Was $79.99 *$29.99*

The Burning Bed (1985)
The critically-acclaimed drama, based on a true story, stars Farrah Fawcett as an abused wife driven by her husband (Paul LeMat) to protect herself and her children at any costs. A shattering look at a nationwide concern. 95 min.
04-1947 Was $79.99 *$14.99*

Codename Icarus (1985)
A young math genius is sent to a school for gifted students, but soon learns that the program is actually a front for a sinister military secret. Stars Barry Angel, Jack Galloway. 106 min.
04-2049 *$19.99*

Silas Marner (1985)
Ben Kingsley is nothing short of superb in his portrayal of George Eliot's wronged, reclusive weaver who learns to love and trust again from the waif he brings into his home. Jenny Agutter, Freddie Jones, and Angela Pleasence co-star. 92 min.
04-2066 *$29.99*

Dogs In Space (1987)
Take an unflinching look into the anarchic, dissolute lifestyle of a clique of New Wave rockers in late '70s Australia in this rock-filled drama that features a tremendous star turn for INXS singer Michael Hutchence. With Tony Helou, Saski Post. 105 min.
04-2154 Was $79.99 *$29.99*

Tomorrow's Child (1982)
A childless couple turns to medical science in order to have the baby of their dreams, but the resultant publicity over the "test tube birth" threatens their marriage. Timely drama stars Stephanie Zimbalist, William Atherton, Ed Flanders. 95 min.
04-2182 Was $59.99 *$29.99*

Middle Age Crazy (1980)
An often funny drama charting the mid-life crisis of builder Bruce Dern, who celebrates turning 40 by trading his business suit for hip threads, his sensible car for a Porsche, and wife Ann-Margret for a Dallas Cowboys cheerleader. 89 min.
04-2233 Was $59.99 *$29.99*

Christabel (1989)
Harrowing tale, based on the true story of an Englishwoman's attempts to save her German husband from the horror of Hitler's death camps. Elizabeth Hurley, Stephen Dillon, Geoffrey Palmer star; Dennis Potter ("The Singing Detective") scripts. 148 min.
04-2261 Was $39.99 *$19.99*

When The Whales Came (1989)
A lyrical drama that will delight nature fans. A school of narwhal whales washes up on the shore of a British island, prompting an enigmatic sculptor to believe the island will be cursed. Paul Scofield, Helen Mirren and Max Rennie star. 100 min.
04-2336 Was $89.99 *$14.99*

Willie And Phil (1980)
Paul Mazursky's salute to François Truffaut's "Jules and Jim" is a bittersweet account of the "menage a trois" that develops between best friends Ray Sharkey and Michael Ontkean and free spirit Margot Kidder. Jan Miner, Larry Fishburne and Natalie Wood co-star. 116 min.
04-2478 Was $59.99 *$29.99*

Fortunes Of War (1987)
An epic drama set at the onset of World War II focuses on the lives of an English college professor and his wife (Kenneth Branagh and Emma Thompson) who become involved with anti-fascist politics and British Secret Service members when they move to Romania in 1939. 335 min.
04-2536 *$29.99*

Secret Places (1985)
Moving family drama set in a private girls' school in 1941 England, and the difficulties faced there by a teenage German refugee and her only friend, a shy English girl. Marie-Theres Relin, Tara MacGowran star. 98 min.
04-3093 Was $79.99 *$29.99*

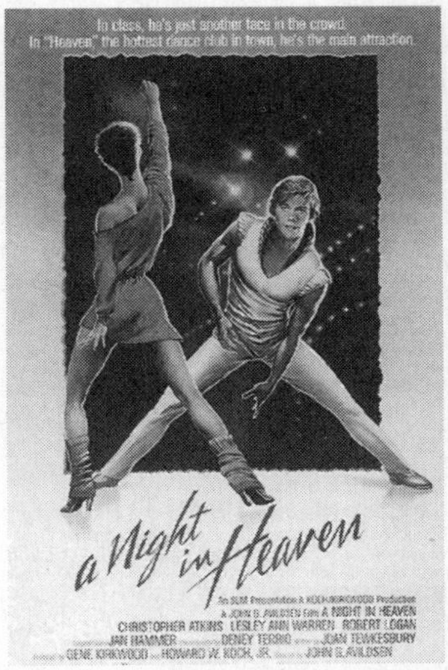
In class, he's just another face in the crowd.
In "Heaven," the hottest dance club in town, he's the main attraction.
a Night in Heaven
CHRISTOPHER ATKINS LESLEY ANN WARREN ROBERT LOGAN

A Night In Heaven (1983)
This torrid tale focuses on the steamy relationship between a beautiful young schoolteacher and one of her students—a sexy male stripper. Lovely Lesley Ann Warren and hunky Christopher Atkins star as the obsessive lovers. 85 min.
04-1696 Was $59.99 *$29.99*

Meryl Streep

The Seduction Of Joe Tynan (1979)
Provocative drama written by and starring Alan Alda as an idealistic young senator who faces ethical and personal dilemmas in his rise to Washington power. Meryl Streep, Barbara Harris, Rip Torn and Melvyn Douglas co-star. 107 min.
07-1028 Was $69.99 ***$14.99***

The French Lieutenant's Woman (1981)
A film-within-a-film structure was applied to John Fowles' romantic novel, with Meryl Streep and Jeremy Irons playing both the woman of dubious reputation and her refined gentleman lover in Victorian England and the actress and actor portraying the pair in a contemporary film production. Karel Reisz directs Harold Pinter's script. 123 min.
12-1152 Was $19.99 ***$14.99***

Still Of The Night (1982)
Stylish murder mystery in the Hitchcock tradition from scripter/director Robert Benton. Psychiatrist Roy Scheider is suspected by the police of killing patient Meryl Streep's husband. Did he? Did she? We're not telling. Jessica Tandy co-stars. 97 min.
12-1798 ***$14.99***

Sophie's Choice (1982)
Meryl Streep earned her second Academy Award for her masterful performance as a Nazi death camp survivor who moves to America, but cannot escape the dark secret from her past that haunts her. Kevin Kline and Peter MacNicol give able support as the men in her life. Alan J. Pakula directs this moving adaptation of the William Styron novel. 150 min.
27-6771 ***$14.99***

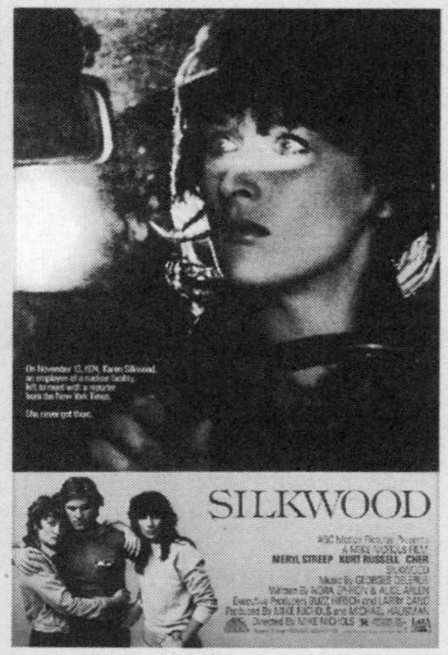

Silkwood (1983)
Acclaimed biodrama of Karen Silkwood, who died in a mysterious accident in 1974 after threatening to expose unsafe conditions at the Oklahoma nuclear supply plant where she worked. Meryl Streep shines in the title role, supported by Kurt Russell, Cher, Craig T. Nelson, Fred Ward and Ron Silver, in this gripping Mike Nichols film. 131 min.
53-1159 ***$14.99***

Silkwood (Letterboxed Version)
Also available in a theatrical, widescreen format.
08-8682 ***$14.99***

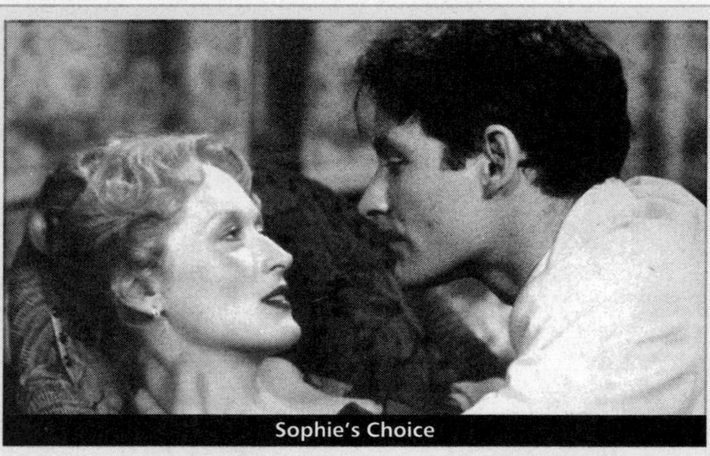

Sophie's Choice

Falling In Love (1984)
Robert De Niro and Meryl Streep are reunited for the first time since "The Deer Hunter" in this tender drama of two married people whose accidental encounter leads to friendship and, finally, a forbidden romance. Harvey Keitel, Jane Kaczmarek also star. 107 min.
06-1258 Was $19.99 ***$14.99***

Out Of Africa (1985)
Spectacular, beautiful filming of author Isak Dinesen's accounts of her life in 1910s Africa won seven Academy Awards, including Best Picture and Director. Meryl Streep stars as the Danish woman who reluctantly goes to Africa with husband Klaus Maria Brandauer to run a coffee plantation, but slowly comes to fall in love with the untamed land and with hunter Robert Redford; directed by Sydney Pollack. 161 min.
07-1427 Was $19.99 ***$14.99***

Out Of Africa (Letterboxed Version)
Also available in a theatrical, widescreen format.
07-2555 ***$19.99***

Heartburn (1986)
Nora Ephron's novel, based on her stormy marriage to reporter Carl Bernstein, is brought to the screen by director Mike Nichols. Meryl Streep and Jack Nicholson star as the ill-fated lovers, struggling with new responsibilities (home, family) and old problems (infidelity). Able support from Jeff Daniels, Stockard Channing, Catherine O'Hara, Milos Forman. 108 min.
06-1413 Was $19.99 ***$14.99***

A Cry In The Dark (1988)
Meryl Streep's Oscar-nominated performance fuels this harrowing drama based on a real-life murder case in Australia. Streep is the mother accused, due to circumstantial evidence and her own seeming indifference, with the killing of her daughter. Sam Neill co-stars; directed by Fred Schepisi. 121 min.
19-1694 Was $19.99 ***$14.99***

She-Devil (1989)
Revenge was never sweeter, or funnier, than when spurned housefrau Roseanne Barr launches a vendetta against husband-stealing romance novelist Meryl Streep and wayward spouse Ed Begley, Jr. Susan Seidelman directs this catty comedy, based on Fay Weldon's novel. 99 min.
73-1077 ***$14.99***

Postcards From The Edge (1990)
Based on the best-selling roman a clef novel by Carrie Fisher (who also wrote the screenplay), this wickedly funny seriocomedy stars Meryl Streep as an actress on the rebound from drug addiction and forced by her studio to be "supervised" by her antagonistic, boozy mother (Shirley MacLaine). Dennis Quaid, Gene Hackman also star. 101 min.
02-2070 Was $19.99 ***$14.99***

The River Wild (1994)
In her first action role, Meryl Streep plays a Boston woman who joins her architect husband and 10-year-old son on a rafting trip in the Western area where she was raised. Their journey takes a dangerous turn when two fishermen they've helped turn out to be gun-toting fugitives counting on Streep to lead them to freedom through treacherous waters. Kevin Bacon, David Strathairn co-star. 112 min.
07-2248 Was $19.99 ***$14.99***

The River Wild (Letterboxed Version)
Also available in a theatrical, widescreen format.
07-2717 Was $19.99 ***$14.99***

The House Of The Spirits (1994)
An epic adaptation of Isabel Allende's acclaimed novel follows the romantic and political turmoil faced by a South American family over a 50-year period. Jeremy Irons is the rancher patriarch of the clan; Meryl Streep is his daughter; and Winona Ryder is her daughter, who falls in love with revolutionary Antonio Banderas. With Glenn Close, Armin Mueller-Stahl and Vanessa Redgrave. 109 min.
27-6872 Was $19.99 ***$14.99***

Before And After (1996)
When their teenage son is accused of killing his girlfriend, disbelieving parents Meryl Streep and Liam Neeson fight to save him. But when they tamper with evidence that might have connected him to the crime, they are forced to take another look at his claims of innocence. Gripping drama also stars Edward Furlong, Alfred Molina, Julia Weldon; directed by Barbet Schroeder. 108 min.
11-2045 Was $19.99 ***$14.99***

Marvin's Room (1996)
In this powerful drama laced with humor, Diane Keaton, a Florida woman who has cared for bedridden father Hume Cronyn for years, discovers she has leukemia. In order to survive, Keaton calls on estranged sister Meryl Streep to help her by supplying bone marrow for a transplant, leading to an emotional reunion. Robert De Niro, Leonardo DiCaprio and Gwen Verdon also star. 98 min.
11-2121 Was $19.99 ***$14.99***

...First Do No Harm (1997)
Making her first dramatic TV appearance in nearly 20 years, Meryl Streep plays a devoted mother who goes up against the medical establishment as she searches for a cure for her epileptic son and starts him on a controversial treatment. Fred Ward, Seth Adkins also star. 94 min.
11-2177 Was $99.99 ***$19.99***

Dancing At Lughnasa (1998)
Brian Friel's Tony-winning play has been transformed into a haunting and powerful film featuring Meryl Streep as Kate Mundy, a school teacher and the eldest of five sisters living in rural Ireland in the 1930s. Kate's routine life is changed by the appearance of two men: her eldest brother, from missionary work in Africa, and Gerry, Streep's ex-lover. With Catherine McCormack, Sophie Thompson and Michael Gambon. 95 min.
02-3339 Was $99.99 ***$21.99***

One True Thing (1998)
Based on the best-selling novel by Anna Quindlen, this cathartically emotional drama stars Renee Zellwegger as a young New York magazine writer who reluctantly agrees to return to her upstate hometown to help look after her ailing mother, cancer patient Meryl Streep. Long-standing conflicts between the independent Zellwegger, seemingly simplistic homemaker Streep, and patriarch William Hurt are brought to the surface as Streep's condition worsens. Directed by Carl Franklin ("One False Move"). 128 min.
07-2724 Was $99.99 ***$14.99***

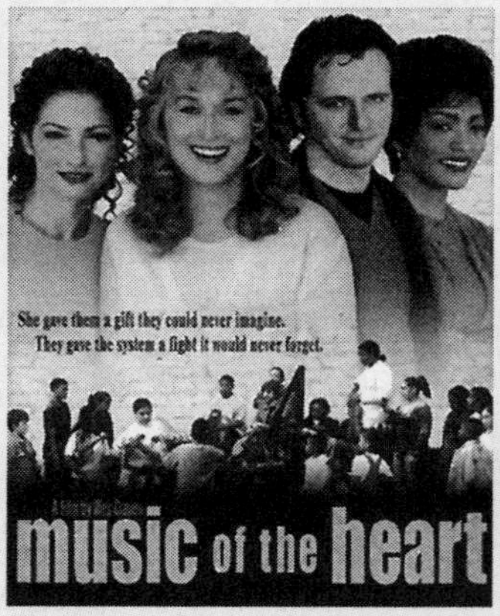

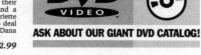

Music Of The Heart (1999)
This sensitive true-life drama stars Meryl Streep as Roberta Guaspari, a single mother of two asked by a friend to teach music at an impoverished East Harlem high school. After convincing the school's disbelieving principal of her abilities, Guaspari instructs a group of students in violin and soon affects their lives through the music. Aidan Quinn, Gloria Estefan and Angela Bassett also star in Wes Craven's film. 123 min.
11-2410 Was $99.99 ***$14.99***

Please see our index for these other Meryl Streep titles: *The Bridges Of Madison County • Death Becomes Her • The Deer Hunter • Defending Your Life • Julia • Kramer vs. Kramer • Manhattan*

Jesus Of Montreal (1989)
Acclaimed Canadian comedy-drama that takes savage swipes at modern religious hypocrisy and greed. An unemployed actor is hired by a Montreal priest to run a local Passion Play, but his attempts to re-create the Easter story place him in some antagonistic situations that strangely parallel the play's scenes. Writer/director Denys Arcand's moving satire stars Lothaire Bluteau, Remy Girard. 119 min. In French with English subtitles.
73-1094 Was $79.99 ***$19.99***

The Falcon And The Snowman (1985)
The chilling true story of two American youths (Timothy Hutton, Sean Penn) who become involved in selling intelligence secrets to Soviet spies, only to find themselves over their heads in deception and danger. With Lori Singer, David Suchet. 131 min.
73-1167 ***$14.99***

Summer Lovers (1982)
Beautiful Greek locales and beautiful young bodies enmesh in this fun-filled, romantic tale of two American students' Mediterranean vacation and the young French woman who joins them in their sensual odyssey. Daryl Hannah, Peter Gallagher, Valerie Quennessen star; Randal Kleiser ("The Blue Lagoon") directs. 98 min.
73-1173 ***$14.99***

Desperate For Love (1989)
A teenage love triangle in a small Southern town turns deadly, and a young man stands accused of killing his best friend, in this powerful drama based on a true incident. Christian Slater, Tammy Lauren, Brian Bloom and Veronica Cartwright star. 96 min.
75-7173 Was $19.99 ***$14.99***

Termini Station (1989)
The different but connected dreams of a mother and daughter living in a sleepy little town form the basis for this compelling, human drama. Colleen Dewhurst, Megan Follows ("Anne of Green Gables"), Gordon Clapp star. 105 min.
76-9032 Was $79.99 ***$19.99***

A Time To Remember (1988)
Heartfelt family drama of a man in search of fulfilling his lifelong dream, and his effect on those around him, stars Donald O'Connor, Morganna King, Ruben Gomez and Tommy Makem. 80 min.
77-7007 ***$14.99***

Silence Of The Heart (1984)
Powerful study of how a family is affected by their teenage son's suicide. Strong performances and a compelling script highlight this film starring Mariette Hartley as the boy's mother, valiantly trying to deal with the tragedy. Charlie Sheen, Chad Lowe, Dana Hill and Howard Hesseman also star. 90 min.
78-1056 ***$12.99***

The Unbearable Lightness Of Being (1988)
Director Philip Kaufman uses the 1968 Soviet invasion of Czechoslovakia as the setting for a highly erotic and sensitive adaptation of Milan Kundera's novel. Daniel Day-Lewis plays a brash Prague surgeon who divides his romantic attention between two women—photographer/wife Juliette Binoche and lover Lena Olin—until fate and politics throw their lives into turmoil. With Derek de Lint. 171 min.
73-1022 Was $19.99 ***$14.99***

Into Thin Air (1985)
Timely drama stars Ellen Burstyn as a mother searching for her missing teenage son, who vanished while travelling from his Canadian home to school in Colorado. Based on a true story, the film co-stars Robert Prosky and Sam Robards. 97 min.
74-5006 ***$39.99***

DVD VIDEO
ASK ABOUT OUR GIANT DVD CATALOG!

The Pride Of Jesse Hallam (1980)
Johnny Cash gives a heart-warming performance as an unemployed man who must swallow his pride by admitting the secret he's been keeping: he never learned to read or write. Brenda Vaccaro and Eli Wallach co-star. 105 min.
04-3108 ***$19.99***

Straight For The Heart (1988)
A photojournalist involved in a ménage a trois with a woman and another man returns home after a long absence to find his two partners have fallen in love with each other. The experience leads him on a quest to discover himself in his home city of Montreal. 92 min. In French with English subtitles.
01-1475 Was $79.99 ***$39.99***

Cloud Waltzing (1986)
A lovely American journalist, in search of the big story, wangles an interview with a reclusive French millionaire...and discovers fulfillment in his arms. Stars Kathleen Beller and Francois-Eric Gerndon. 100 min.
06-1452 ***$19.99***

Sweet Lorraine (1987)
A young girl spends the summer working at her grandmother's Catskill resort, a once-proud hotel on the brink of closing, and learns a lesson about growing up in this tender comedy/drama. Maureen Stapleton, Trini Alvarado star. 91 min.
06-1505 Was $59.99 ***$14.99***

THE SEA HAS A SECRET
THE BIG BLUE

The Big Blue: Director's Cut (1988)
Luc Besson's hypnotic deep-sea drama tells of a rivalry between divers Jean-Marc Barr and Jean Reno, childhood friends who challenge the ocean depths in a dangerous diving competition. Rosanna Arquette is the American woman involved with Barr, whose obsessions eventually take their toll on the relationship. This director's cut restores 34 minutes of footage and Eric Serra's original score; 132 min. In English and French with English subtitles.
02-3445   *$14.99*

Miracle Of The Heart: A Boys Town Story (1986)
Art Carney stars as a Boys' Town priest who's facing retirement, but wants to help his final charge, a troubled inner city youth, before he leaves. Moving drama co-stars Casey Siemaszko, Jack Bannon. 96 min.
02-1801   Was $69.99   *$19.99*

Tex (1982)
In this moving adaptation of the novel by S.E. Hinton ("The Outsiders"), Matt Dillon shines as Tex McCormick, a teenager living on an Oklahoma farm who encounters growing pains after his father deserts him and his mother dies. Attempting to help him face the problems of young adulthood is his troubled brother, played by Jim Metzler. With Emilio Estevez, Meg Tilly. 102 min.
11-1061   *$14.99*

Tex (Letterboxed Version)
Also available in a theatrical, widescreen format.
08-8803   *$14.99*

Souvenir (1988)
Haunted by the memory of a beautiful French girl and a love that ended with World War II, a former German soldier who has been living 40 years in New York makes a nostalgic journey to Europe with his rebellious daughter. Christopher Plummer and Catherine Hicks star. 93 min.
06-1663   *$14.99*

Hawks (1989)
Two terminally ill patients, an English lawyer and an American football player, decide to sneak out of their hospital rooms and live to the max. It's off to Amsterdam they go, in search of the good life and good brothels. A poignant, life-affirming film starring Timothy Dalton and Anthony Edwards. 105 min.
06-1715   Was $59.99   *$19.99*

Under The Volcano (1984)
Engrossing drama dealing with an alcoholic ex-British official living in Mexico, his estranged wife and her former lover, the man's own brother. Albert Finney, Jacqueline Bisset and Anthony Andrews all shine in this lyrical, "stream of consciousness" tale, from the classic novel by Malcolm Lowry; John Huston directs. 112 min.
07-1279   *$79.99*

Distant Thunder (1988)
A troubled Vietnam vet living in seclusion in a Washington rain forest defends himself from emotional and physical assaults during a reunion with his son. A moving drama of exile and reconciliation starring John Lithgow and Ralph Macchio. 114 min.
06-1643   *$14.99*

ANNE BANCROFT
ANTHONY HOPKINS
84 CHARING CROSS ROAD

84 Charing Cross Road (1987)
Endearing, acclaimed drama that traces the true-life 20-year friendship that blossomed via correspondence between a New York copywriter (Anne Bancroft) and a British bookstore clerk (Anthony Hopkins). 97 min.
02-1790   Was $79.99   *$19.99*

Gorillas In The Mist (1988)
Sigourney Weaver stars in this biography of Dian Fossey, the American naturalist who lived amongst the mountain gorillas of Central Africa, and whose unflagging crusade for their preservation may have cost her her life. Lush and lovingly rendered film co-stars Bryan Brown, Julie Harris; directed by Michael Apted. 130 min.
07-1604   Was $19.99   *$14.99*

Talk Radio (1988)
A mega-watt performance by Eric Bogosian sparks Oliver Stone's "shock radio" drama about an abrasive Dallas broadcaster set to take his frank talk, fanatic listeners and stacks of hate mail into national syndication. Adapted from Bogosian's stage play, with Alec Baldwin and Ellen Greene. 110 min.
07-1615   Was $19.99   *$14.99*

Taken Away (1989)
Single mother Valerie Bertinelli struggles to raise her daughter and make ends meet. But when her daughter has an emergency and calls for help while she's home alone, Bertinelli is charged with child neglect and is faced with the authorities taking custody of her child. With Kevin Dunn, Juliet Sorcey. 94 min.
07-2000   ▢*$89.99*

Tai-Pan (1986)
James Clavell's sprawling romantic adventure about the foreign traders who established the port of Hong Kong in the early 19th century is drama on a grand scale. Bryan Brown stars as the "Tai-Pan" (tycoon) who dreams of a trading empire in the Pacific. With Joan Chen, John Stanton; filmed on location in China. 127 min.
08-8431   *$14.99*

Ordinary People (1980)
Robert Redford's directorial debut, the moving story of a seemingly perfect family torn apart by tension, lack of communication and guilt, won Oscars for Best Picture, Director, Screenplay and Supporting Actor. Mary Tyler Moore, Donald Sutherland, Timothy Hutton, Judd Hirsch and Elizabeth McGovern star. 124 min.
06-1081   *$14.99*

Merchant & Ivory

The Householder (1962)
The first collaboration from filmmakers Ismail Merchant and James Ivory focuses on a young couple from India whose arranged marriage turns out to be troublesome, as they are too young and inexperienced to adjust to one another. The husband's mother gets involved in their marital problems, but her domineering presence becomes more than they can bear. Shashi Kapoor, Leela Naidu star. 101 min.
53-7702   Was $79.99   *$29.99*

Bombay Talkie (1970)
Entrancing drama follows middle-aged British "junk novelist" Jennifer Kendall as she sojourns to India in an attempt to turn back the clock, and how her tempestuous affair with younger Indian film actor Sashi Kapoor leads to tragedy. Zia Moyheddin co-stars. 105 min.
53-1690   Letterboxed   *$19.99*

Savages (1972)
A Merchant/Ivory production that takes a satirical look at society and its manners, as a group of natives enter a deserted mansion and begin to dress and behave like their "civilized" counterparts. Sam Waterston, Lewis J. Stadlen, Susan Blakely, Kathleen Widdoes star. 105 min.
47-3002   Was $59.99   *$29.99*

Autobiography Of A Princess (1975)
A divorced Indian princess, now living in self-imposed exile in London, has her family's former tutor over for a tea party which becomes a wistful look back at India's imperial past. Moving character study from the team of Ismail Merchant and James Ivory stars James Mason, Madhur Jaffrey. 59 min.
53-7659   *$29.99*

Roseland (1977)
The famed New York City ballroom serves as the setting for a dramatic trio of stories from the Merchant/Ivory team: A lonely widow learns to love again; a sly gigolo gets his comeuppance; and a German charwoman treats herself to a night on the town. Teresa Wright, Lou Jacobi, Christopher Walken, Geraldine Chaplin and Lilia Skala star. 100 min.
47-1081   Was $89.99   *$29.99*

The Europeans (1979)
The Henry James novel about the contrasts between a 19th-century New England family and their European-raised cousins is expertly translated to the screen by the Merchant-Ivory team. Lee Remick, Lisa Eichhorn, Wesley Addy star. 90 min.
47-1039   Was $59.99   *$19.99*

Quartet (1981)
A young woman in 1920s Paris is taken in by an older English couple when her husband has a brush with the law and lands in jail, but soon finds herself caught up in decadent games of seduction and betrayal. Moody drama from director James Ivory stars Isabelle Adjani, Alan Bates, Maggie Smith. 101 min.
19-1260   Was $69.99   *$19.99*

A Streetcar Named Desire (1984)
Dramatic fireworks occur in this explosive version of Tennessee Williams' play featuring Treat Williams as brutish Stanley Kowalski, Beverly D'Angelo as long-suffering wife Stella, and Ann-Margret as Blanche DuBois. Randy Quaid also stars. 96 min.
14-3401   *$12.99*

Return To Eden (1983)
Expansive saga of romance, betrayal and revenge concerning an Australian socialite left to die in the crocodile-infested swamps by her philandering husband...but who survives to adopt a new identity and wreak a terrible vengeance! Rebecca Gilling, James Reyne, Wendy Hughes star. 259 min.
14-3158   *$69.99*

Stone Fox (1987)
Lovely, family-themed drama set in 1905 about a 12-year-old boy, his grandfather and their pet dog as they experience hardships on their Wyoming ranch during a rough winter. In order to save the ranch, the boy must enter a dog race with a purse of $500. Buddy Ebsen, Joey Cramer and Belinda Montgomery star. 96 min.
14-3244   *$12.99*

South Bronx Heroes (1986)
Gritty drama about two young runaways who leave their foster father and try to survive on the streets. They eventually seek shelter in a South Bronx apartment building where they meet another pair of siblings who use their schoolteacher sister for financial support. Mario Van Peebles, Megan Van Peebles, Brendan Ward and Melissa Esposito star.
14-6124   *$14.99*

The Idolmaker (1980)
Rousing drama about an aggressive music promoter in the '50s (based on Philadelphia's own Bob Marcucci, the mentor of Frankie Avalon and Fabian) who molds two teenage singers into pop sensations. Ray Sharkey turns in a dynamic performance in the title role; with Tovah Feldshuh, Peter Gallagher, Paul Land. 119 min.
12-1328   *$14.99*

The Bostonians (1984)
Henry James' epic of life in 19th-century New England gets a splendid screen treatment. Feminism, jealousy and sexual needs are examined in a tale involving a lawyer (Christopher Reeve), a spinster (Vanessa Redgrave) and a charismatic teenage girl (Madeleine Potter). With Jessica Tandy and Wallace Shawn; directed by James Ivory. 120 min.
47-1356   Was $19.99   *$14.99*

A Room With A View (1986)
A delightful tale of Victorian romance and British conceit, concerning the interwoven lives and loves of a group of English tourists on holiday in Italy and their reunion back home. Helena Bonham Carter, Maggie Smith, Denholm Elliott, Julian Sands and Daniel Day-Lewis star. Oscar-winning adaptation of E.M. Forster's novel from Ismail Merchant and James Ivory. 117 min.
04-2041   Was $19.99   ▢*$14.99*

Slaves Of New York (1989)
Tama Janowitz' best-selling tale of the young and trendy artistes populating New York's Lower East Side stars Bernadette Peters as the would-be designer struggling to make her mark. Mary Beth Hurt, Adam Coleman Howard co-stars. 121 min.
02-1955   *$89.99*

The Ballad Of The Sad Cafe (1991)
Provocative adaptation of Carson McCullers' story about a plain, lonely woman (Vanessa Redgrave) in a small Southern town and the battle of wills she faces with her ex-con husband (Keith Carradine). Rod Steiger, Austin Pendleton co-star in this Merchant-Ivory production; directed by Simon Callow. 100 min.
45-5530   Was $89.99   *$19.99*

Howards End (1992)
This magnificent adaptation of E.M. Forster's novel from producer Ismail Merchant and director James Ivory concerns the loves and class struggles of two families in England in 1910. Academy Award-winner Emma Thompson and Helena Bonham Carter are middle-class sisters whose lives become entwined with an aristocratic clan headed by Anthony Hopkins and Vanessa Redgrave. 143 min.
02-2400   Was $89.99   ▢*$19.99*

The Remains Of The Day (1993)
Magnificently acted, beautifully realized Merchant/Ivory production about a repressed English butler (Anthony Hopkins), his 20 years of service to his employer, Lord Darlington (James Fox), and his lost chance at love with the estate's housekeeper (Emma Thompson). With Christopher Reeve, Hugh Grant; adapted from Kazuo Ishiguro's acclaimed novel. 134 min.
02-2588   Was $89.99   ▢*$19.99*

Howards End/ Remains Of The Day: Letterboxed Collector's Set
Both acclaimed Merchant-Ivory dramas are available in their theatrical widescreen format in this special boxed set.
02-2815   Save $5.00!   *$34.99*

Race Against The Harvest (1987)
Wayne Rogers and Earl Holliman star in this story of a Kansas farmer's feud with his former brother-in-law, a rivalry that starts with the machines Rogers needs to gather his crops before the onset of storm season and escalates into a bitter race against time. AKA: "American Harvest."
14-3251   *$12.99*

Bellman And True (1988)
Absorbing and intelligent drama catapulted by unrelenting action and a solid performance from Bernard Hill, as a brilliant computer systems engineer who is coerced into cracking a bank's sophisticated alarm system by hoods holding his stepson captive. Co-stars Richard Hope, Kieran O'Brien; from the makers of "Mona Lisa." 112 min.
12-2654   *$14.99*

Captive Hearts (1987)
Wartime drama of two American soldiers held prisoner in a Japanese village during World War II and the conflicts that arise when one falls in love with the daughter-in-law of the village's leader. Chris Makepeace, Michael Sarrazin and Pat Morita star. 97 min.
12-2656   *$14.99*

Hands Of A Stranger (1987)
Armand Assante, Beverly D'Angelo, Blair Brown and Michael Lerner star in this intense thriller, based on the novel by Robert Daley ("Prince of the City"), about a police detective obsessed with finding the man who raped his wife. 179 min.
14-3252   Was $89.99   *$14.99*

Dreamchild (1985)
Enchanting, haunting drama flashes back and forth through the life of 80-year-old Alice Hargreaves, who as a child served as Lewis Carroll's inspiration for "Alice in Wonderland." The film depicts her memories of the sexually repressed writer and fantasy adventures with the Wonderland characters, with special effects supplied by Jim Henson. Peter Gallagher, Ian Holm, Nicola Cowper star. 90 min.
12-2657   *$14.99*

Feast Of July (1995)
Handsome and sensual Merchant-Ivory production set in England in 1883, where a single woman who recently suffered a miscarriage is taken in by a kind lamplighter and his family. She soon becomes the object of affection of the man's three sons: a womanizer, a shoemaker and a troubled ne'er-do-well. Which one will she fall in love with? Embeth Davidtz, Ben Chaplin and Gemma Jones star. 116 min.
11-2008   Was $99.99   ▢*$19.99*

NICK NOLTE
GRETA SCACCHI
Jefferson in Paris

Jefferson In Paris (1995)
Nick Nolte plays Thomas Jefferson in this stunning Merchant-Ivory production. The focus is on Jefferson's romantic life while he served as Ambassador to France in the late 1780s, at the start of the French Revolution. Among the women said to be involved with the widowed statesman are an Italian socialite and Sally Hemmings, one of his slaves. Greta Scacchi, Gwyneth Paltrow, Thandie Newton co-star. 139 min.
11-1933   Was $89.99   ▢*$19.99*

Surviving Picasso (1996)
The private side of the 20th century's most renowned and influential painter is memorably brought to life by star Anthony Hopkins in this stirring Merchant-Ivory biodrama. Set in France in the '40s and '50s, the film follows the middle-aged Picasso's stormy relationship with one of his several mistresses, aspiring artist Natascha McElhone. With Julianne Moore and Joss Ackland as Henri Matisse. 126 min.
19-2499   Was $99.99   ▢*$19.99*

A Soldier's Daughter Never Cries (1998)
Based on the semi-autobiographical novel by Kaylie Jones, daughter of "From Here to Eternity" author James Jones, this moving coming-of-age drama from Ismail Merchant and James Ivory stars Leelee Sobieski as a teenage girl living in Paris in the late '60s with her expatriate American parents, Barbara Hershey and writer Kris Kristofferson, and her adopted French brother. 128 min.
07-2732   Was $99.99   ▢*$14.99*

Sally Field

Maybe I'll Come Home In The Spring (1971)
Sally Field stars in this acclaimed drama, playing a young woman who leaves her suburban middle-class family for a drug-filled life at a hippie commune, but finds difficulty dealing with her parents when she returns home. Eleanor Parker, Jackie Cooper and David Carradine also star; featuring songs by Linda Ronstadt. AKA: "Deadly Desires." 90 min.
58-8168 $14.99

HENRY WINKLER SALLY FIELD

Finding the one you love... is finding yourself.

HEROES

Heroes (1977)
Two mismatched people, a troubled Vietnam vet (Henry Winkler) and a young woman (Sally Field) unsure about her impending marriage, are brought together in a frantic, emotional cross-country bus trip. Delightful comedy/drama co-stars Harrison Ford. 97 min.
07-1419   Was $59.99 $14.99

Norma Rae (1979)
Sally Field copped a Best Actress Oscar for her performance as a Southern textile worker who joins with a labor organizer to unionize her mill. Ron Leibman, Beau Bridges add able support to this heartfelt drama. Martin Ritt directs. 114 min.
04-1119   Was $19.99 $14.99

Kiss Me Goodbye (1982)
Sally Field is about to marry fiancé Jeff Bridges...that is, until James Caan, her dead husband, shows up to throw a monkey wrench into the marital proceedings, in this lighthearted American retelling of "Dona Flor and Her Two Husbands." 101 min.
04-1530   Was $59.99 $29.99

Gauguin The Savage (1980)
David Carradine plays Paul Gauguin, the Paris stockbroker who abandoned his job, wife and children to live as an artist in Tahiti, and whose paintings depicting life in the South Seas became world famous. Bernard Fox, Michael Hordern, Ian Richardson and Lynn Redgrave star. 120 min.
10-9516 $14.99

Goodbye, Miss 4th Of July (1988)
Compelling true-life drama of teenager Niki Janus, who flees persecution in Greece and settles in West Virginia with her family. Niki befriends a black handyman, but she soon learns of new horrors that await her in her new home: the Ku Klux Klan and a flu epidemic. Louis Gossett, Jr., Chris Sarandon and Roxana Zal star. 89 min.
11-1706   ☐$19.99

Rowing With The Wind (1987)
Early turns by Hugh Grant and Elizabeth Hurley highlight this lush melodrama that looks at the stormy romance of literary legends Percy Shelley (Valentine Pelka) and Mary Godwin (Lizzy McInnerny) and the infamous 1816 Swiss vacation that led to Mary's writing of "Frankenstein." 95 min.
11-2318   Was $99.99   ☐$19.99

Goldeneye (1989)
Before he brought James Bond to life, his own life proved to be as exciting and dangerous as his fictional hero. Charles Dance stars as British author Ian Fleming in this biodrama that follows Fleming's WWII career as an undercover Naval Intelligence operative, his life-changing romance with a married woman, and his creation of the legendary superspy. Phyllis Logan, David Quilter also star. AKA: "Spymaster: The Secret Life of Ian Fleming." 103 min.
08-8833 $14.99

Murphy's Romance (1985)
Charming "love triangle" comedy stars Sally Field as a ranch owner in a small Arizona town whose relationship with a local "town character" (James Garner) is threatened by the arrival of her shiftless ex-husband (Brian Kerwin). 107 min.
02-1604   ☐$14.99

Surrender (1987)
Sally Field and Michael Caine play a "gun shy" couple who soon find themselves doing the last thing in the world they expected...falling in love. Whimsical romantic comedy also stars Steve Guttenberg and Peter Boyle. 95 min.
19-1625   ☐$14.99

Punchline (1988)
Tom Hanks is the brash stand-up comic who takes housewife and would-be performer Sally Field under his wing in writer/director David Seltzer's comic look at the very serious quest for stardom. With John Goodman, Mark Rydell. 128 min.
02-1908   Was $19.99   ☐$14.99

Soapdish (1991)
Riotous all-star satire about the dirt behind a fictitious soap opera, featuring Sally Field as the darling of daytime TV who finds her life falling to pieces, thanks to the return of ex-lover and co-star Kevin Kline and a devious plan hatched by a jealous actress. Wildly hilarious complications ensue; with Whoopi Goldberg, Robert Downey, Jr., Teri Hatcher, Cathy Moriarty. 97 min.
06-1885   Was $19.99   ☐$14.99

Not Without My Daughter (1991)
The harrowing true story of an American wife who returns with her husband and daughter to his Iranian homeland during the Khomeini regime, then finds herself bound by Islamic laws that keep her from leaving with the child. Sally Field is excellent as the woman risking her life for her daughter's and her own freedom. Alfred Molina, Roshan Seth co-star. 107 min.
12-2205   Was $19.99 $14.99

Eye For An Eye (1996)
Intense drama starring Sally Field as a Los Angeles businesswoman whose teenage daughter is viciously raped and murdered. When the chief suspect, deliveryman Kiefer Sutherland, avoids prosecution because of a legal loophole, Field goes on the offensive, taking justice into her own hands. Ed Harris and Joe Mantegna also star; directed by John Schlesinger. 102 min.
06-2469   Was $99.99   ☐$14.99

A Cooler Climate (1999)
After having trouble finding work following her divorce, Sally Field takes a job housekeeping for wealthy Judy Davis. Initially the pair don't get along, but when Davis' marriage fails, the two women form a life-saving bond in this moving drama written by Marsha Norman (""Night Mother"). 100 min.
06-3034   ☐$49.99

Please see our index for these other Sally Field titles: *Absence Of Malice • Beyond The Poseidon Adventure • The End • Forrest Gump • Homeward Bound I & II • Hooper • Mrs. Doubtfire • Smokey And The Bandit I & II • Steel Magnolias • The Way West • Where The Heart Is*

Until September (1984)
American tourist Karen Allen falls for a French banker in this erotic romance. The beautiful sights of Paris and the steamy relationship make this ideal entertainment. Thierry Lhermitte. 95 min.
12-1402   Was $79.99   ☐$14.99

The Aviator (1985)
Christopher Reeve is flying again in this turn-of-the-century drama, but he's doing it with an airplane. He's a rugged barnstormer whose plane crashes in the wilderness with a spirited young passenger aboard (Rosanna Arquette). Together they struggle to stay alive, falling in love in the process. 98 min.
12-1433 $14.99

We Are The Children (1987)
Romance blossoms in civil war-torn Ethiopia between a brash TV reporter and a nurse who works in a famine-ravaged village. Ted Danson, Ally Sheedy and Judith Ivey star. 92 min.
46-5511 $79.99

Marie: A True Story (1985)
Sissy Spacek stars as a Tennessee criminal justice head who uncovers a massive conspiracy of graft and corruption that reaches the state capital, and her battle against the odds to expose it. Thrilling real-life story of one woman's fight against the system also stars Jeff Daniels, Morgan Freeman. 112 min.
12-1567 $79.99

The Berlin Affair (1985)
A haunting, erotic drama by director Liliana Cavani ("The Night Porter"), set in 1938 Germany, that follows a Japanese ambassador's daughter as she seduces a series of men in order to achieve her own ends. Mio Takaki, Kevin McNally star. 97 min.
12-1651 $79.99

The Getting Of Wisdom (1980)
Director Bruce Beresford's lush coming-of-age tale follows a 13-year-old girl who leaves her home in the Australian Outback to attend a Melbourne boarding school in 1910. Based on Ethel Richardson's autobiographical novel, the sensitive drama stars Susannah Fowle, Barry Humphries, Julia Blake and John Waters. 100 min.
12-1042 $19.99

The Dresser (1983)
An acting tour-de-force about the relationship between an aging actor-manager of a Shakespearean troupe and his dresser in wartime England. Albert Finney is the drunken, cynical "Sir," Tom Courtenay his loyal, pampering manservant. Peter Yates directs. 118 min.
02-1331 $14.99

Touched By Love (1980)
Diane Lane is a girl with cerebral palsy and Deborah Raffin a dedicated teacher in this emotional drama of personal triumph. The teacher eventually draws the girl out of her shell, and she corresponds with a new pen-pal—Elvis Presley. Michael Learned also stars. 95 min.
02-1343 $59.99

To Kill A Priest (1989)
An intense true-to-life drama about a young priest who battled the Communist government and the Church's policy of compromise in order to support Poland's outlawed Solidarity union. The top international cast includes Christopher Lambert, Ed Harris and Joanne Whalley. 117 min.
02-2001   ☐$89.99

Immediate Family (1989)
Glenn Close and James Woods are an upper middle-class couple with one thing missing from their lives: a baby. They decide to adopt the child of a young working class woman, but when she comes to visit them, problems arise. Mary Stuart Masterson and Kevin Dillon co-star in this sensitive dramedy. 99 min.
02-2006   Was $89.99   ☐$14.99

Cast The First Stone (1989)
Controversial, true story starring Jill Eikenberry as a schoolteacher who is raped, becomes pregnant and decides to keep the baby. When she is looked down upon by her community and loses her job, she wages a courageous battle to win back her job and dignity. With Richard Masur, Joe Spano and Charles Kimbrough. 96 min.
02-2214 $14.99

A Test Of Love (1984)
Tender drama from Australia, based on the true story of a disabled teenager who was mistakenly confined to a home for the retarded since infancy, and the therapist who fights authorities for her release. Angela Punch McGregor, Tina Arhondis star. 93 min.
07-1397 $69.99

Naked Lie (1989)
The steamy clandestine affair between D.A. Victoria Principal and judge James Farentino turns complicated when she's assigned to a blackmail case he's prosecuting...and deadly when new evidence makes him a suspect. Riveting drama also stars Glenn Withrow. 100 min.
10-2345 $12.99

Whose Life Is It Anyway? (1981)
Richard Dreyfuss is phenomenal as an artist who is left a quadriplegic after an accident and must face what life has come to offer him. Christine Lahti and John Cassavetes co-star in director John Badham's filmization of Brian Clark's popular play. 119 min.
12-1210 $69.99

TENNESSEE WILLIAMS

THE GLASS MENAGERIE

JOANNE WOODWARD JOHN MALKOVICH
KAREN ALLEN JAMES NAUGHTON

The Glass Menagerie (1987)
Tennessee Williams' classic drama of a family caught between reality and dreams receives moving screen treatment, courtesy of director Paul Newman. Joanne Woodward is the possessive matriarch, John Malkovich her restless son, Karen Allen the withdrawn daughter, and James Naughton the "gentleman caller" whose presence forever alters their world. 134 min.
07-1581   Was $79.99 $19.99

She was married at 13. She had four kids by the time she was 20. She'd been hungry and poor. She'd been loved and cheated on. She became a singer because it was the only thing she could do. She became a star because it was the only way she could do it.

COAL MINER'S DAUGHTER

SISSY SPACEK TOMMY LEE JONES "COAL MINER'S DAUGHTER"
also starring BEVERLY D'ANGELO, LEVON HELM Directed by MICHAEL APTED

Coal Miner's Daughter (1980)
Sissy Spacek took home the Academy Award for her honest portrayal of singer Loretta Lynn, from her dirt poor childhood in Butcher Hollow, Kentucky, to her rise to the pinnacle of success in the country/western world. Co-stars Tommy Lee Jones, Levon Helm and Beverly D'Angelo as Patsy Cline; directed by Michael Apted. 124 min.
07-1003 $14.99

Sam's Son (1984)
Michael Landon co-wrote and directed this family drama of a small-town boy who finds acceptance and a chance for a new life on his high school track team. Eli Wallach, Anne Jackson, Timothy Patrick Murphy star. 107 min.
14-3085 $12.99

Stranger In My Bed (1986)
Lindsay Wagner stars as a teacher and happy mother of two whose life is turned inside-out when a car accident leaves her with complete amnesia and forces her to struggle to start her life from scratch. Armand Assante, Douglas Sheehan also star. 100 min.
14-3268 $12.99

A Deadly Business (1986)
Tough, true-life story stars Alan Arkin as a con-turned-informant infiltrating the world of mobster Armand Assante, who has made a fortune dumping toxic waste illegally. Michael Learned and Jon Polito also star in this contemporary gangster chronicle. 96 min.
14-3277 $12.99

God Bless The Child (1988)
Compassionate story of a woman who is abandoned by her husband and forced onto the city streets with her young daughter. Can she fight against insurmountable odds to save herself and her child? Mare Winningham, Dorian Harewood and Grace Johnston star. 93 min.
14-3336   ☐$12.99

Shoot The Moon (1982)
Emotional drama from director Alan Parker stars Diane Keaton and Albert Finney as a well-off couple whose 15-year marriage is falling apart. With Karen Allen, Peter Weller, Dana Hill, Tina Yothers. 123 min.
12-1217 $14.99

Brimstone And Treacle (1982)
An eerie psychological drama about a manipulative and mesmerizing young man (Sting) who worms his way into the home and lives of a middle class couple, claiming to be the ex-boyfriend of their comatose daughter. With Denholm Elliott and Joan Plowright. 85 min.
12-1269 $14.99

Cold Sassy Tree (1989)
Sensitive drama set in a small Georgia town stars Faye Dunaway and Richard Widmark as May/December lovers whose marriage shocks their fellow townspeople. 97 min.
18-7198 $14.99

The Nightmare Years (1989)
The thrilling true story of William Shirer, an American journalist who risked his life to expose Hitler and Nazism during the 1930s and went on to write "The Rise and Fall of the Third Reich." Sam Waterston and Marthe Keller star in this tale of courage and intrigue. 237 min.
18-7202 $89.99

Stranger On My Land (1988)
Tommy Lee Jones turns in a riveting performance as a Vietnam vet who returns from action in Southeast Asia only to find his Montana ranch has been seized by government officials who want to turn it into a missile base. He joins with his father and an understanding nurse to fight the government. Dee Wallace Stone and Ben Johnson also star. 100 min.
14-3224 $14.99

Challenge Of A Lifetime (1985)
Penny Marshall stars as a recently divorced, former college athlete who overcomes her depression by training for a grueling triathlon competition in Hawaii. Bart Conner, Cathy Rigby McCoy and Mark Spitz also star in this exciting drama. 95 min.
18-7227   Was $59.99 $14.99

Joe (1970)
One of the milestone films of its era, this satirical drama stars Peter Boyle as a bigoted, beer-swilling hardhat who helps a strait-laced advertising executive search for his young daughter, who has taken up the hippie lifestyle. Their journey includes a stop at a Greenwich Village "org-gy." Dennis Patrick and Susan Sarandon (in her screen debut) also star. 107 min.
12-2666 **$14.99**

Lovin' Molly (1974)
Playing like a Panhandle "Jules and Jim," Sidney Lumet's offbeat romance stars Blythe Danner, Beau Bridges and Anthony Perkins as three residents of a small Texas town whose menage a trois relationship is tracked over a 40-year period. Susan Sarandon, Conrad Fowkes also star; based on Larry McMurtry's novel "Leaving Cheyenne." AKA: "The Wild and the Sweet."
68-1913 ❑**$12.99**

F. Scott Fitzgerald And The Last Of The Belles (1974)
Richard Chamberlain stars as F. Scott Fitzgerald in this acclaimed biopic that mixes glimpses of the writer's life with wife Zelda in the early '20s with dramatized scenes from his short story "The Last of the Belles," a fictionalized account of the couple's courtship. Blythe Danner, Susan Sarandon, David Huffman also star. AKA: "The Last of the Belles." 100 min.
75-7103 Was $19.99 **$14.99**

The Other Side Of Midnight (1977)
Sensuous, steamy story of one young woman who uses her wits and her body to become a film star, only to later learn the price she must pay. Marie-France Pisier, Susan Sarandon, John Beck star; based on the best-seller by Sidney Sheldon. 160 min.
04-1834 Was $59.99 **$29.99**

King Of The Gypsies (1978)
Fascinating essay on Gypsy society in modern America stars Eric Roberts as the unwilling heir to the leadership of his people who must fight his father for the title. Susan Sarandon, Judd Hirsch, Sterling Hayden, Brooke Shields, Shelley Winters also star. 112 min.
06-1030 **$14.99**

Pretty BABY

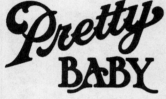

Pretty Baby (1978)
Louis Malle's stunning and controversial look at 1910's New Orleans' famed Storyville red light district, as seen through the eyes of photographer Keith Carradine, and at Carradine's obsession with 12-year-old Brooke Shields, the daughter of prostitute Susan Sarandon. 109 min.
06-1049 Was $69.99 **$14.99**

Tempest (1982)
Paul Mazursky's beguiling, offbeat comedy about an architect facing a mid-life crisis who decides to leave his wife and move to Greece along with his mistress and teenage daughter. John Cassavetes, Gena Rowlands, Susan Sarandon, Raul Julia, Molly Ringwald star in this quirky take on Shakespeare's play. 140 min.
02-1189 **$14.99**

Who Am I This Time? (1982)
Susan Sarandon and Christopher Walken star as two painfully shy amateur actors whose passions come alive only when they're on stage. Jonathan Demme directs this romantic, witty adaptation of a Kurt Vonnegut, Jr. story. 60 min.
03-1415 **$24.99**

The Buddy System (1983)
Richard Dreyfuss and Susan Sarandon make an attractive and funny romantic pair in this amiable, winning comedy. He's an eccentric writer picked by her son to be his next daddy. Nancy Allen, Jean Stapleton, Wil Wheaton co-star. 110 min.
04-1685 Was $59.99 ❑**$29.99**

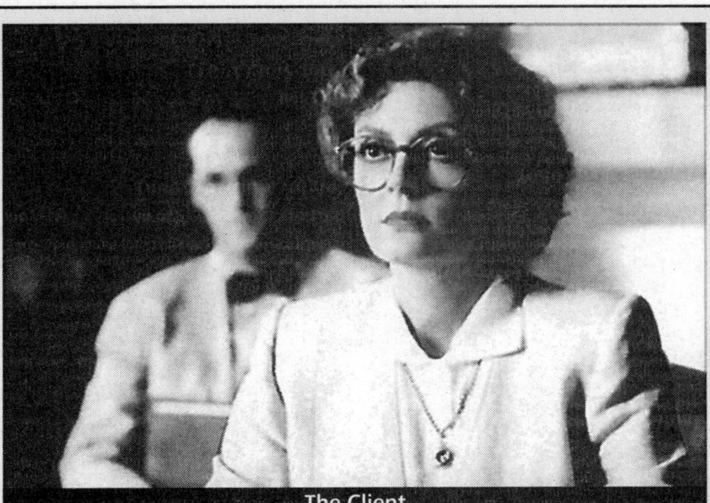
The Client

Susan Sarandon

The Hunger (1983)
Catherine Deneuve and David Bowie star as ages-old vampires looking for new blood and companionship...and find it in the form of Susan Sarandon. Stylish, frightening chiller with some hot erotic moments, including a controversial love-making scene with Deneuve and Sarandon, from director Tony Scott. 97 min.
12-1292 Was $19.99 ❑**$14.99**

The Hunger (Letterboxed Version)
Also available in a theatrical, widescreen format.
12-3176 ❑**$14.99**

Compromising Positions (1985)
The murder of a suburban ladies' man dentist prods one of his patients to tackle the mystery herself in this outrageous, slightly kinky comedy/thriller. Susan Sarandon, Raul Julia, Judith Ivey, Edward Herrmann, Mary Beth Hurt star. 98 min.
06-1328 Was $19.99 ❑**$14.99**

Women Of Valor (1986)
Susan Sarandon and Kristy McNichol star in this harrowing WWII drama based on the real-life exploits of U.S. Army nurses who were taken prisoner and tortured by the Japanese in the Philippines. 95 min.
46-5419 **$79.99**

Sweet Hearts Dance (1988)
Warm and funny country reel centering around two couples in a small New England town. Don Johnson and Susan Sarandon are the high school sweethearts whose marriage is on the rocks, while Jeff Daniels yearns to wed Elizabeth Perkins. Scripted by Ernest Thompson ("On Golden Pond"). 101 min.
02-1918 Was $19.99 ❑**$14.99**

Thelma & Louise (1991)
Controversial "female road movie" stars Susan Sarandon as a bored waitress and Geena Davis as a put-upon housewife who decide to take a trip to a friend's cabin for some R&R. While stopping at a bar, a man attempts to rape Davis and Sarandon shoots him dead, sending the pair on the run from the police and on a wild and woolly drive across the Southwest. Harvey Keitel, Brad Pitt also star; Ridley Scott directs. 130 min.
12-2285 Was $19.99 ❑**$14.99**

Thelma & Louise (Letterboxed Version)
Also available in its theatrical widescreen format.
12-2455 ❑**$14.99**

Lorenzo's Oil (1992)
How far would parents go to save their child's life? Susan Sarandon and Nick Nolte star in this moving, based-on-fact drama as a couple whose pre-schooler son is stricken with a rare nerve disease that leaves him unable to move or communicate. Told by doctors that nothing can be done, the two refuse to give up and begin a daunting and relentless search for a cure. With Peter Ustinov, Zack O'Malley Greenburg. 135 min.
07-1924 Was $19.99 **$14.99**

Light Sleeper (1992)
Paul Schrader's powerful, haunting story focuses on a delivery man (Willem Dafoe) for a classy New York drug dealer (Susan Sarandon) who realizes that time is passing on and he must change his job and his life. When he meets his old girlfriend and becomes a suspect in a criminal investigation, he takes drastic steps to turn things around. Dana Delany and David Clennon co-star. 103 min.
27-6794 Was $19.99 ❑**$14.99**

Safe Passage (1994)
Susan Sarandon turns in a powerful performance as Mag Singer, an estranged wife and mother of seven who re-examines her life and principles when she learns that one of her sons may have been killed in a bomb attack in the Middle East. Sam Shepard, Robert Sean Leonard and Nick Stahl also star in this compassionate effort. 98 min.
02-5052 Was $19.99 ❑**$14.99**

The Client (1994)
A young boy who witnesses the suicide of a lawyer with mob ties is caught in a tug-of-war between an ambitious prosecutor who wants him to testify and a woman lawyer who takes the boy's case, and is marked for death by the mobsters to ensure his silence. Tommy Lee Jones and Susan Sarandon star in this gripping adaptation of John Grisham's novel; with Brad Renfro, Mary-Louise Parker. 121 min.
19-2282 Was $19.99 ❑**$14.99**

Dead Man Walking (1995)
Forceful, true-life drama starring Oscar-winner Susan Sarandon as Sister Helen Prejean, a progressive Louisiana nun who decides to serve as spiritual advisor to convicted racist murderer Matthew Poncelet (Sean Penn) before he's executed by lethal injection. Robert Prosky, Raymond J. Barry also star. Directed by Tim Robbins; features a title song by Bruce Springsteen. 122 min.
02-8460 Was $19.99 ❑**$14.99**

Dead Man Walking Collector's Set
This two-tape boxed set includes a letterboxed version of the Oscar-winning drama and a second edition featuring running commentary and details on the film's making from director Tim Robbins.
02-8634 **$19.99**

Illuminata (1999)
Set in early 1900s New York, this witty comedy features John Turturro (who also directed) as the leader of a theatrical company who's eager to put on a new play he's written to impress leading lady Katherine Borowitz (Turturro's real-life wife). The on-stage romance pales next to the many backstage trysts and misunderstandings that surround the troupe. Susan Sarandon, Ben Gazzara, Christopher Walken, Bill Irwin and Beverly D'Angelo also star. 120 min.
27-7147 Was $99.99 ❑**$14.99**

Earthly Possessions (1999)
Housewife Susan Sarandon is about to leave her minister hubby when she becomes a willing accomplice to young criminal Stephen Dorff in a bank robbery. While on the lam, the two develop a relationship, but Sarandon eventually learns that Dorff decided to pull off the robbery to help his pregnant girlfriend. With Jay O. Sanders; based on Anne Tyler's book. 103 min.
44-2199 Was $99.99 ❑**$14.99**

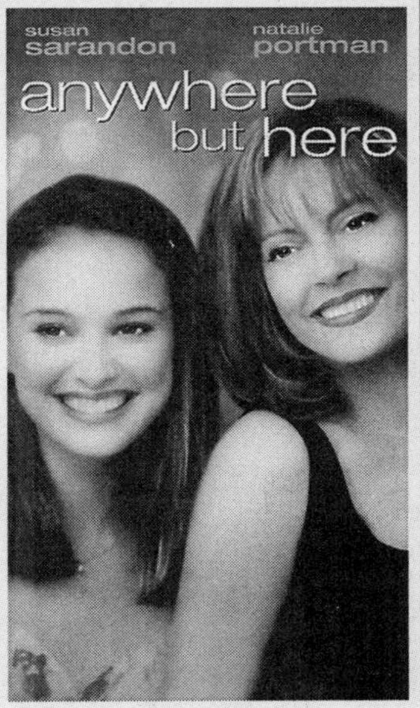

Anywhere But Here (1999)
Eager to build a better life for herself and teenage daughter Natalie Portman, Wisconsin mom Susan Sarandon packs up the car and, without telling Portman in advance, relocates them to a "working class" section of Beverly Hills. The pressures of the new environment and Sarandon's plans for Portman to become an actress test their already-strained relationship in this moving tale from director Wayne Wang ("The Joy Luck Club"). With Corbin Allred, Shawn Hatosy. 114 min.
04-3923 Was $99.99 ❑**$14.99**

Please see our index for these other Susan Sarandon titles: *Atlantic City • Bob Roberts • Bull Durham • Cradle Will Rock • James And The Giant Peach • The January Man • Joe Gould's Secret • Loving Couples • Our Friend, Martin • The Rocky Horror Picture Show • Stepmom • Twilight • The Witches Of Eastwick*

Fallen Angel (1981)
Riveting drama about the sensitive subject of "kiddie porn." A local softball coach is actually involved in a ring that lures children into the world of child pornography. Melinda Dillon, Ronny Cox, Richard Masur, Dana Hill star. 100 min.
02-1260 **$59.99**

The Principal (1987)
A "bottom of the barrel" inner city high school has finally met its match when Jim Belushi is assigned as the new principal. With the help of security guard Louis Gossett, Jr. and a Louisville Slugger in hand, he tries to run the drug dealers out of the halls. Also stars Rae Dawn Chong, Esai Morales. 112 min.
02-1833 **$14.99**

Fresh Horses (1988)
Finding love from across opposite sides of the tracks are "Pretty in Pink" co-stars Molly Ringwald and Andrew McCarthy, but pressure from friends threatens to pull them apart. Rocky romantic drama co-stars Patti D'Arbanville, Ben Stiller. 105 min.
02-1919 Was $89.99 ❑**$14.99**

Where Are The Children? (1985)
Jill Clayburgh stars as a happily married woman with a dark secret whose past makes her the leading suspect in the kidnapping of her two children. Co-stars Frederic Forrest, Max Gail and Barnard Hughes. Based on the bestseller by Mary Higgins Clark. 92 min.
02-1650 ❑**$79.99**

Violets Are Blue (1986)
Bittersweet drama stars Sissy Spacek and Kevin Kline as former lovers who are reunited after many years and rekindle their romance. One catch: he's now married. Moving story of love's endurance features Bonnie Bedelia as Kline's wife. 86 min.
02-1661 **$79.99**

Desert Bloom (1986)
JoBeth Williams and Jon Voight are the heads of a troubled 1950s Nevada family in this insightful, low-key drama that juxtaposes the eldest daughter's entry into adolescence, a visit from a free-spirited aunt and the community's "celebration" of an A-Bomb test. With Ellen Barkin, Annabeth Gish, Allen Garfield. 104 min.
02-1681 **$14.99**

Out Of Bounds (1986)
Anthony Michael Hall makes his dramatic debut as a young man from the Midwest whose first trip to L.A. has him accused of murder and on the run from both the police and drug pushers. Exciting drama also stars Jenny Wright, Jeff Kober. 93 min.
02-1687 ❑**$79.99**

Beulah Land (1985)
Epic drama of the collapse of the Old South as seen through the eyes of one aristocratic family and those around them. Lesley Ann Warren, Michael Sarrazin, Jenny Agutter, Hope Lange, Eddie Albert and Don Johnson star. 267 min.
02-1699 **$29.99**

Arch Of Triumph (1985)
Anthony Hopkins and Lesley-Anne Down star in this remake of the classic melodrama set in Paris at the dawn of World War II. Hopkins is a refugee doctor with a secret in his past who falls for Down, but clouding their love affair is the growing threat of war. With Donald Pleasence, Frank Finlay. 95 min.
78-1115 **$12.99**

We Of The Never Never (1983)
Life on the Australian frontier, circa 1902, as told through the eyes of the first white woman to visit the aboriginal wilderness, is the focus for a haunting drama. Angela Punch McGregor, Tony Barry star. 132 min.
02-1221 **$59.99**

Quicksilver (1986)
Kevin Bacon is a Wall Street wunderkind fired after losing his golden touch. Reduced to working as a bicycle messenger, he learns lessons in humility and concern for others, especially his fellow gofers, who are threatened by merciless pushers. 106 min.
02-1625 Was $79.99 ❑**$14.99**

Zelly And Me (1988)
Haunting drama about a young girl who copes with the death of her parents by fixating on the life of Joan of Arc, and the French governess she comes to equate with the heroine. Isabella Rossellini and David Lynch, the co-star and director of "Blue Velvet," star with Alexandra Johnes. 87 min.
02-1871 **$79.99**

The Wedding Party (1967)
Originally shot in 1963 by graduate student Brian DePalma, this offbeat comedy about a young man whose wedding jitters multiply during a visit to his fiancée's family's island estate also marks the film debuts of Jill Clayburgh and Robert De Niro. With Charles Pfluger, Jennifer Salt. 88 min.
15-1038 *$14.99*

Greetings (1968)
An early effort for both writer/director Brian DePalma and star Robert De Niro, this underground-style comedy of three New York buddies exploring a world of free sex, political conspiracy and an omnipresent draft board is steeped in '60s philosophy. With Gerrit Graham, Allen Garfield, Jonathan Warden. 88 min.
68-1130 *$79.99*

Hi, Mom! (1970)
Brian DePalma's scathing and hilarious sequel to "Greetings" follows unemployed Vietnam veteran and novice porno filmmaker Robert De Niro throughout Manhattan as he records a number of eccentric New Yorkers with his Super 8mm camera. The film includes a segment in an off-Broadway theater, where the play "Be Black, Baby" is staged. With Allen Garfield, Jennifer Salt, Gerrit Graham, Charles Durning and Lara Parker. 87 min.
55-1258 Was $19.99 *$14.99*

The Swap (1969)
Early Robert De Niro effort casts him as a New York film editor working on a documentary about Richard Nixon who meets a group of shallow people during a weekend in Long Island. Viva and Jennifer Warren also star. AKA: "Sam's Song." 92 min.
12-2677 *$14.99*

The Gang That Couldn't Shoot Straight (1971)
Funny Mafia farce based on Jimmy Breslin's book looks at the antics of a group of inept mobsters trying to execute a powerful gang leader. Jerry Orbach, Leigh Taylor-Young, Lionel Stander, Jo Van Fleet and a young Robert De Niro star. 96 min.
12-3073 ❑*$19.99*

Born To Win (1971)
Engrossing, enervating look into the drug culture stars George Segal as a trendy Manhattan hairdresser whose $100-a-day heroin habit knocks him off the fast track and into the abyss. Director Ivan Passer's ("Cutter's Way") powerful drama also stars Robert De Niro, Karen Black, Paula Prentiss. AKA: "The Addict." 90 min.
75-7097 *$19.99*

Bang The Drum Slowly (1973)
A moving, powerfully acted baseball film about the on- and off-field friendship that develops between a major league pitcher and his teammate, a catcher suffering from a terminal illness. Robert De Niro, Michael Moriarty, Vincent Gardenia star; look for Danny Aiello in his film debut. 98 min.
06-1121 *$14.99*

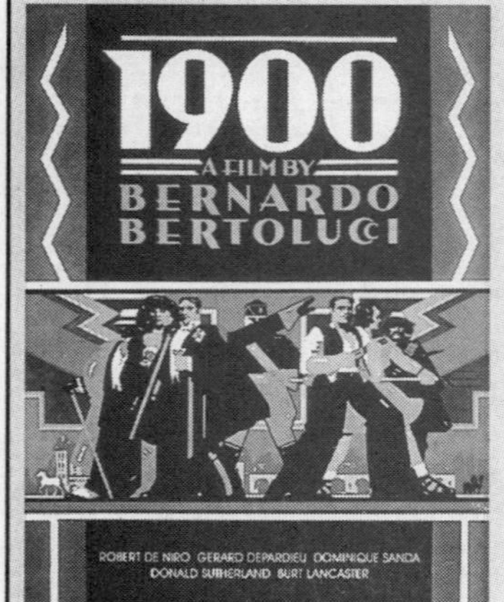

1900 (1976)
Bernardo Bertolucci's sweeping epic of early 20th-century Italy stars Robert De Niro as a weak-willed landowner who becomes a pawn of the Fascists and Gerard Depardieu as a Marxist insurgent farm worker. Grand drama also stars Burt Lancaster, Dominique Sanda, Donald Sutherland, Stefania Sandrelli. 255 min.
06-1555 ❑*$24.99*

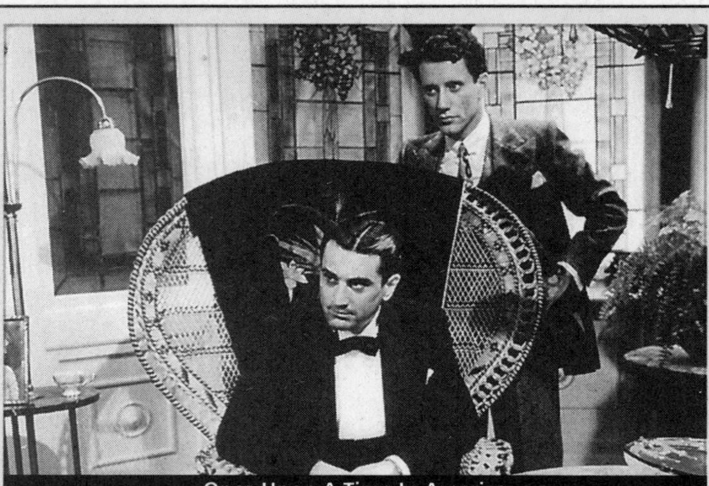

Once Upon A Time In America

Robert De Niro

The Last Tycoon (1976)
Robert De Niro stars as F. Scott Fitzgerald's enigmatic, power-driven 1930s movie mogul (a character based on MGM "boy wonder" Irving Thalberg) in this excellent drama from director Elia Kazan. The stellar cast also includes Robert Mitchum, Tony Curtis, Jeanne Moreau and Jack Nicholson; screenplay by Harold Pinter. 125 min.
06-1302 Was $19.99 *$14.99*

The Deer Hunter (1978)
Winner of five Oscars, this harrowing indictment of war from director Michael Cimino stars Robert De Niro, Christopher Walken and John Savage as three Pennsylvania steeltown friends whose lives are forever changed by their experiences together in Vietnam. Co-stars Meryl Streep, John Cazale. 183 min.
07-1015 Was $19.99 *$14.99*

The Deer Hunter (Letterboxed Version)
Also available in a theatrical, widescreen format.
07-2556 Was $19.99 *$14.99*

True Confessions (1981)
The brutal murder of a prostitute in 1948 Los Angeles brings the seemingly unconnected worlds of two brothers—hardened homicide detective Robert Duvall and corrupt monsignor Robert De Niro—together. A well-written, superbly acted crime drama, with support from Charles Durning, Ed Flanders, Burgess Meredith. 108 min.
12-1215 Was $19.99 *$14.99*

True Confessions (Letterboxed Version)
Also available in a theatrical, widescreen format.
12-3238 ❑*$14.99*

Once Upon A Time In America (1984)
Sprawling gangster opus from Sergio Leone follows the rise to power of New York hoods Robert De Niro and James Woods, showing them at various times of their lives from the '20s to the '60s. Violent, controversial and engrossing; with Treat Williams, Elizabeth McGovern, Burt Young, Tuesday Weld, Joe Pesci and Jennifer Connelly (her film debut). Director's cut; 226 min.
19-1392 ❑*$29.99*

The Mission (1986)
South America, the 1700s: a pacifistic priest (Jeremy Irons) and a reformed slaver (Robert De Niro) join to convert the native Indians. The two men are thrust into conflict when corruption within Church and state threaten to violently destroy all that they have built. Acclaimed drama by director Roland Joffe ("The Killing Fields"). 126 min.
19-1588 Was $19.99 ❑*$14.99*

Midnight Run (1988)
Robert De Niro as an irritable bounty hunter whose supposedly easy retrieval of a passive mob accountant turns into a gauntlet of hit men, FBI agents, and rival bail bondsmen. Charles Grodin is at his best as the nagging and glum $100,000 prize with an eerie talent for self-preservation. 122 min.
07-1596 Was $19.99 *$14.99*

We're No Angels (1989)
Robert De Niro and Sean Penn team up for a reworking of the 1955 Humphrey Bogart comedy. They're escaped cons who pose as priests and set up shop in a small town near the Canadian border. Demi Moore, Wallace Shawn and Hoyt Axton co-star. 115 min.
06-1721 ❑*$14.99*

Jacknife (1989)
A reunion between Vietnam War buddies is the catalyst that ignites old anger and new passions in a compelling story of two men coping with the violence in their past. Robert De Niro, Ed Harris and Kathy Baker star in a gripping drama. 102 min.
44-1660 Was $19.99 ❑*$14.99*

Guilty By Suspicion (1991)
Powerful study of the Hollywood blacklist of the 1950s starring Robert De Niro as a successful director who is given a choice by the House Un-American Activities Committee: name names of colleagues who are "Reds" or remain silent and risk his career. Annette Bening, George Wendt and Patricia Wettig also star in this compelling drama. 105 min.
19-1874 Was $19.99 ❑*$14.99*

Night And The City (1992)
Robert De Niro turns in an electrifying performance as a sleazy accident lawyer, desperate to make a big score. Along with bar owner's wife Jessica Lange, he begins promoting boxing matches, but the scheme eventually leads to trouble with gangsters. Alan King, Cliff Gorman and Jack Warden also star in this powerful reworking of the 1950 film noir favorite. 104 min.
04-2630 Was $19.99 ❑*$14.99*

Mistress (1992)
A wickedly funny satire on the business side of Hollywood, with Robert Wuhl as a would-be filmmaker who cajoles three businessmen into investing in his latest project. The catch: each backer wants his own girlfriend to have the lead role, and two men unknowingly share the same mistress. Martin Landau, Danny Aiello, Eli Wallach, Robert De Niro, Laurie Metcalf, Sheryl Lee Ralph co-star. 112 min. Please note: Title is available only as a manufacturer's cut-out; though product is new, box has a minor cut on the upper flap.
27-6799 Was $19.99 *$14.99*

A Bronx Tale (1993)
Robert De Niro's directing debut is an acclaimed coming-of-age story set in an Italian neighborhood in the Bronx in the early 1960s, where the son of a bus driver is torn between his devotion to his father and the gangster he idolizes. Chazz Palminteri (who adapted his play for the screen), Francis Capra, Lillo Brancato, Joe Pesci and De Niro star in this forceful film. 122 min.
44-1957 Was $19.99 ❑*$14.99*

A Bronx Tale (Letterboxed Version)
Also available in a theatrical, widescreen format.
44-2154 Was $19.99 ❑*$14.99*

Mary Shelley's Frankenstein (1994)
Kenneth Branagh's sensitive, wildly stylized take on the classic horror story stars Branagh as Victor Frankenstein, the obsessive scientist who creates a creature from body parts. Robert De Niro turns in a startling performance as the monster; Tom Hulce, Aidan Quinn and Helena Bonham Carter also star. Produced by Francis Ford Coppola. 123 min.
02-2758 Was $19.99 ❑*$14.99*

Mary Shelley's Frankenstein (Letterboxed Version)
Also available in a theatrical, widescreen format.
02-3089 ❑*$19.99*

Heat (1995)
Michael Mann's intense police story showcases Al Pacino as a frazzled Los Angeles detective out to stop a group of thieves headed by mastermind Robert De Niro, who's looking for one last score, and Val Kilmer, a demolitions ace. The stakes rise as Pacino and De Niro get entangled in a cat-and-mouse game with explosive results. Ashley Judd, Jon Voight co-star. 171 min.
19-2443 Was $19.99 ❑*$14.99*

Heat (Letterboxed Version)
Also available in a theatrical, widescreen format.
19-2482 Was $24.99 *$19.99*

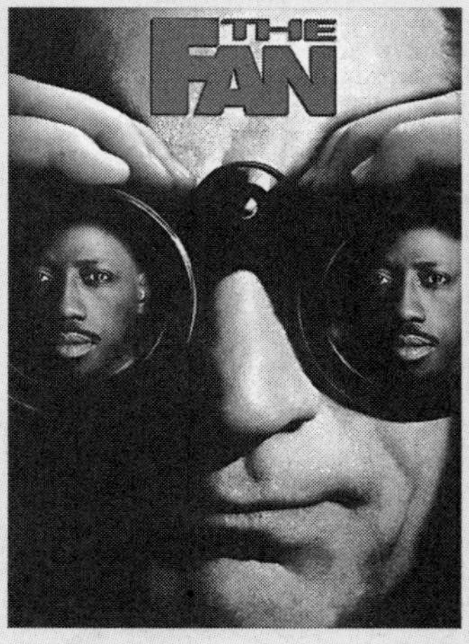

The Fan (1996)
Spoiled baseball superstar Wesley Snipes signs a big contract with the San Francisco Giants and, after a terrible slump, becomes the target of obsessive fan and former knife salesman Robert De Niro's rage. John Leguizamo, Ellen Barkin and Benicio Del Toro also star in this gripping thriller from Tony Scott ("Crimson Tide"). 116 min.
02-2994 Was $19.99 ❑*$14.99*

Ronin (1998)
In John Frankenheimer's taut, exciting thriller, Robert De Niro is a freelance secret agent hired along with other international spies by an Irish terrorist to retrieve a mysterious briefcase. The search for the case leads to intense gunplay, wild car chases and suspicions among the operatives on the job. Jean Reno, Natascha McElhone, Sean Bean and Jonathan Pryce co-star. 121 min.
12-3270 Was $99.99 ❑*$14.99*

Ronin (Letterboxed Version)
Also available in a theatrical, widescreen format.
12-3278 ❑*$14.99*

Flawless (1999)
After a stroke suffered while trying to halt a robbery leaves him partially paralyzed, New York security guard Robert De Niro gets speech therapy through singing lessons from an unlikely teacher: his upstairs neighbor, brash drag queen Philip Seymour Hoffman. The grudging friendship that builds between the mismatched pair fuels this heartfelt tale from writer/director Joel Schumacher. Wanda De Jesus, Barry Miller co-star. 105 min.
12-3300 Was $99.99 ❑*$14.99*

Please see our index for these other Robert De Niro titles: *The Adventures Of Rocky And Bullwinkle • Analyze This • Angel Heart • Awakenings • Backdraft • Brazil • Cape Fear • Casino • Cop Land • Falling In Love • The Godfather Part II • Goodfellas • Great Expectations • Jackie Brown • The King Of Comedy • Marvin's Room • Mean Streets • New York, New York • Raging Bull • Sleepers • Stanley & Iris • Taxi Driver • This Boy's Life • The Untouchables • Wag The Dog*

Corrupt (1983)
Violent psychological drama with a cult following stars Harvey Keitel as a crooked New York cop who kidnaps street hood and possible cop-killer John Lydon (of Sex Pistols fame) and chains him up in Keitel's apartment, hoping to gain information. The battle of wills between captor and captive escalates into a deadly final confrontation. Sylvia Sydney co-stars. AKA: "Cop Killer," "Order of Death." 98 min.
78-1121 Was $19.99 *$14.99*

Out Of The Blue (1980)
Powerful drama featuring a great performance by Linda Manz as a troubled, punk rock-loving teen. Isolated in her small-town home and unable to talk to her drug-addicted mother, Manz hopes for a better life with the pending release of her alcoholic father (Dennis Hopper, who also directed) from jail, but things soon spiral out of control. With Sharon Farrell, Raymond Burr. AKA: "No Looking Back." 93 min.
08-8763 Letterboxed *$14.99*

Hide In Plain Sight (1980)
Gripping true drama directed by and starring James Caan as a divorced working-class husband and father who stages a desperate search for his missing ex-wife and children. Caan discovers that his ex's new husband is involved in organized crime, and he and Caan's family have been given new identities and a new home. Jill Eikenberry, Kenneth McMillan and Danny Aiello also star. 96 min.
12-1051 *$19.99*

Driving Miss Daisy (1989)
The winner of four Academy Awards, including Best Picture and Best Actress, tells the poignant story of the decades-long relationship between an elderly stubborn Jewish woman living in the '40s South and her benevolent black chauffeur. Jessica Tandy, Morgan Freeman and Dan Aykroyd star in this touching comedy-drama, adapted from Alfred Uhry's Pulitzer-winning play. 99 min.
19-1772 Was $19.99 ❑*$14.99*

The Competition (1980)
Competition among prize piano students is fierce, but the rewards are great...or are they? A winning romantic drama with Richard Dreyfuss, Amy Irving, Lee Remick. Great classical score. 123 min.
02-1084 Was $69.99 ***$14.99***

Passion And Valor (1983)
Amazing true story stars Michael Landon as Australian journalist John Evingham, who attempts to rescue a Laotian girl left behind in Pathet Lao during the Vietnam War years earlier. Jurgen Prochnow, Priscilla Presley and Moira Chen (alias Laura Gemser of "Emmanuelle" movie fame) also star. AKA: "Love Is Forever." 77 min.
75-7040 ***$14.99***

Dreams Lost, Dreams Found (1987)
A young woman visiting Scotland is strangely drawn to an ancient castle, and not-so-strangely drawn to the handsome young Laird. But will an ancestral curse keep them apart? Romantic drama stars Kathleen Quinlan. 102 min.
06-1579 ***$19.99***

Collector's Item (1989)
A man is reunited with a lover from his past, but what starts as a rekindling of old passions quickly turns into a bizarre and dangerous game of sexual obsession and erotic entrapment. Tony Musante and luscious Laura Antonelli star are featured in this provocative drama showcasing Antonelli at her most sensuous. AKA: "Dead Fright." 99 min.
74-5032 Was $79.99 ***$29.99***

The Dressmaker (1988)
Compelling drama set in WWII Liverpool, where a young girl's romance with a visiting American soldier puts her at odds with the two spinster aunts who raised her. Joan Plowright, Billie Whitelaw, Jane Horrocks and Tim Ransom star in this emotionally gripping tale. 89 min.
75-1007 ***$79.99***

Intimate Agony (1983)
A fashionable vacation community is the scene of a herpes outbreak that a dedicated doctor tries to control, over the objections of the resort's publicity-fearing owner. Compelling drama stars Anthony Geary, Judith Light, Robert Vaughn, Mark Harmon. AKA: "Doctor in Distress." 90 min.
78-1135 ***$19.99***

The River Rat (1984)
High adventure and touching drama mix in this tale of a 12-year-old girl and her ex-con Dad's journey up the Mississippi. Tommy Lee Jones, Brian Dennehy, Martha Plimpton co-star. 93 min.
06-1251 Was $79.99 ❑***$14.99***

First Born (1984)
A first-rate look at the problems of contemporary relationships. Teri Garr is a divorcée whose new boyfriend (Peter Weller) is at odds with her two sons. A bitter struggle ensues, resulting in a most honest account of family life, circa 1980s. 100 min.
06-1256 ❑***$14.99***

The Blue Lagoon (1980)
Two children are shipwrecked on a tropical island and grow up to discover the facts of life together. Brooke Shields and Christopher Atkins star in the beautifully photographed tale of sexual awakening; directed by Randal Kleiser. 102 min.
02-1082 ***$14.99***

Return To The Blue Lagoon (1991)
Lush sequel to the smash 1980 film focuses on the relationship between the handsome son of the original couple and a beautiful castaway girl. Their involvement on a South Pacific island sets the stage for adventure, romance and intrigue. Milla Jovovich and Brian Krause star. 102 min.
02-2156 Was $19.99 ❑***$14.99***

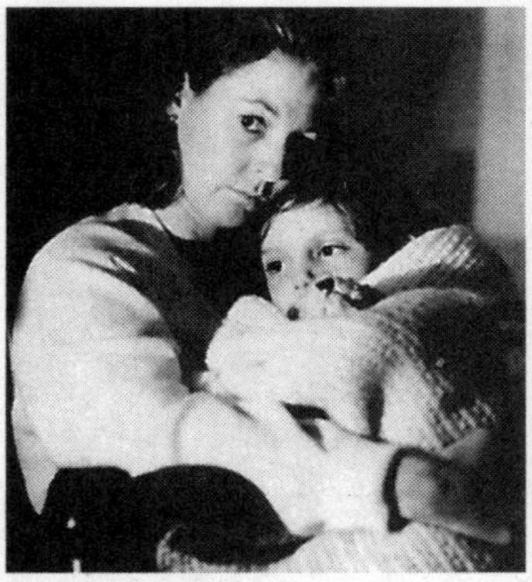

Testament (1983)
The global horror that would be World War III is brought into heartbreakingly intimate detail in this drama of one family's struggle. A small California community is cut off from the world after the bombs fall, while one woman fights to keep her family and neighbors going. Jane Alexander, William Devane, Roxana Zal, Lukas Haas star; look for early appearances by Kevin Costner, Rebecca De Mornay. 90 min.
06-1214 ❑***$14.99***

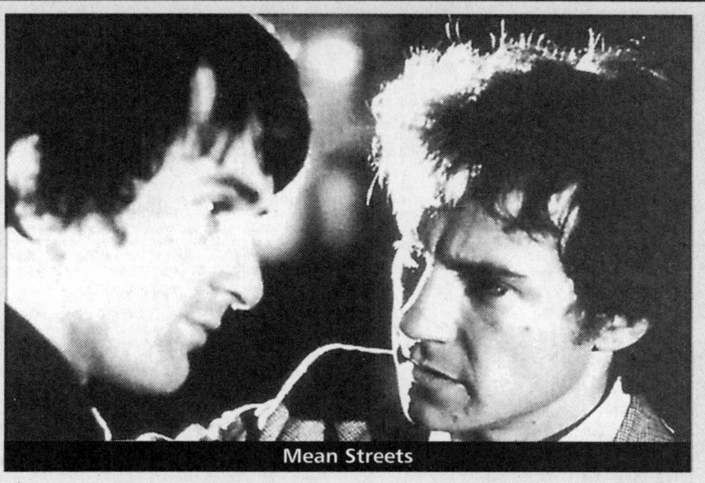
Mean Streets

Martin Scorsese

Who's That Knocking At My Door? (1968)
Martin Scorsese's first feature film stars Harvey Keitel as a native of New York's Little Italy whose Catholic upbringing gets in the way of his romance with a beautiful, independent art student. Zina Bethune and Lennard Kuras also star in this gritty drama, a reworking of a student film Scorsese directed at NYU. AKA: "J.R." 90 min.
19-1862 Was $59.99 ***$19.99***

Mean Streets (1973)
Violent drama from director Martin Scorsese has become a modern-day classic of ultra-realistic filmmaking. Robert De Niro is a two-bit hood in New York's Little Italy involved with a loan shark and Harvey Keitel his friend, trying to keep him out of trouble. With Amy Robinson and Richard Romanus. 110 min.
19-1395 ***$19.99***

Alice Doesn't Live Here Anymore (1974)
Ellen Burstyn won a well-deserved Best Actress Oscar for her wonderful portrayal of a widow and mother of a young son who struggles to overcome one hurdle after another in an effort to make it on her own. The story later became the hit TV series "Alice." Kris Kristofferson, Harvey Keitel, Diane Ladd co-star. Directed by Martin Scorsese. 113 min.
19-1063 Was $19.99 ❑***$14.99***

TAXI DRIVER

Taxi Driver: Collector's Edition (1976)
A disturbingly brutal depiction of a lonely, unstable New York City cab driver (Robert De Niro) who stalks a presidential candidate, then turns his violent obsessions towards the ruthless pimp of a 12-year-old prostitute (Jodie Foster), with whom he has struck up an unlikely friendship. Co-stars Cybill Shepherd, Harvey Keitel, Peter Boyle, Albert Brooks. Martin Scorsese directs Paul Schrader's script. Special video edition includes a never-before-seen "making of" documentary. 128 min. total.
02-3323 Remastered ❑***$14.99***

Taxi Driver (Letterboxed Version)
Also available in a theatrical, widescreen format.
02-3318 ❑***$19.99***

New York, New York (1977)
Robert De Niro joins Liza Minnelli in this extravagant musical-drama. De Niro is a jazz musician who falls for Liza during a V-J day celebration. Martin Scorsese directs. Complete, uncut version; 164 min.
12-1888 Was $24.99 ❑***$14.99***

Raging Bull (1980)
Robert De Niro gives the performance of a lifetime as Jake LaMotta, a man as furious outside the ring as he is inside. Superb boxing scenes, great performances and poetic direction highlight this riveting drama. Co-stars Joe Pesci, Cathy Moriarty. Directed by Martin Scorsese. 127 min.
12-1768 Was $19.99 ***$14.99***

The King Of Comedy (1982)
Talk-show host Jerry Lewis is abducted by obsessive fan Robert De Niro, a would-be comic desperate for fame, in Martin Scorsese's offbeat, funny look at celebrity's dark side. With Sandra Bernhard, Diahnne Abbott; scripted by Paul Zimmerman. 109 min.
02-1225 ***$19.99***

After Hours (1985)
Urban paranoia to the *nth* degree in a dark comedy by Martin Scorsese. Griffin Dunne stars as a bored yuppie whose chance encounter with a girl leads him through a harrowing night of mistaken identity, accidental death and bloodthirsty mobs. Also stars Rosanna Arquette, John Heard, Linda Fiorentino, Teri Garr, and the great Dick Miller. 97 min.
19-1498 ❑***$19.99***

The Last Temptation Of Christ (1988)
Controversy aside, Martin Scorsese's screen version of Nikos Kazantzakis' novel is a dramatic interpretation of the passion of Christ with a miraculous performance by Willem Dafoe as a self-doubting Savior. Scripted by Paul Schrader, with Harvey Keitel as Judas, Barbara Hershey as Mary Magdalene and David Bowie as Pilate. 164 min.
07-1614 ***$19.99***

Goodfellas (1990)
Martin Scorsese's electrifying gangster saga chronicles three decades in the Mafia with Irish-Sicilian mobster Henry Hill (Ray Liotta) and his "wiseguy" accomplices (played by Robert De Niro and Academy Award-winner Joe Pesci). Based on Nicholas Pileggi's novel, this violent, darkly funny epic also stars Paul Sorvino and Lorraine Bracco. 146 min.
19-1853 Was $89.99 ❑***$19.99***

Goodfellas (Letterboxed Version)
Also available in a theatrical, widescreen format.
19-2549 ❑***$19.99***

Cape Fear (1991)
Martin Scorsese's suspenseful reworking of the 1962 thriller stars Robert De Niro as a psychotic ex-con seeking vengeance against Nick Nolte, the attorney who represented him in a rape case. De Niro terrorizes Nolte, wife Jessica Lange and daughter Juliette Lewis, using the law to his own ends and forcing a violent final confrontation. With Joe Don Baker and the original's Robert Mitchum and Gregory Peck. 128 min.
07-1806 Was $19.99 ❑***$14.99***

Cape Fear (Letterboxed Version)
Also available in a theatrical, widescreen format.
07-2604 Was $19.99 ***$14.99***

The Age Of Innocence (1993)
Set against the backdrop of New York society of the 1870s, Martin Scorsese's lavish filming of Edith Wharton's classic novel stars Daniel Day-Lewis as an aristocrat lawyer who questions his wedding plans when he falls for fiancée Winona Ryder's cousin, the Countess Olenska (Michelle Pfeiffer), an American fleeing her disastrous marriage to a European nobleman. 138 min.
02-2563 Was $19.99 ❑***$14.99***

Casino (1995)
Martin Scorsese's sprawling Las Vegas saga stars Robert De Niro as a mob-appointed casino honcho whose comfortable lifestyle is threatened when quick-tempered pal Joe Pesci begins pushing people around and hustler wife Sharon Stone's cocaine and alcohol abuse gets out of hand. James Woods, Alan King, Don Rickles, Kevin Pollak and L.Q. Jones also star. 179 min.
07-2413 Was $99.99 ❑***$19.99***

Casino (Letterboxed Version)
Also available in a theatrical, widescreen format.
07-2474 ***$19.99***

Kundun (1997)
The powerful true story of the 14th Dalai Lama is brought to the screen by director Martin Scorsese in this critically acclaimed biodrama. Identified at age 2 to be the latest reincarnation of the Buddha, the Tibetan political and spiritual leader is forced to flee his homeland after the 1950 Chinese takeover. Tenzin Thuthob Tsarong, as the adult Dalai Lama, heads the non-professional cast; music by Philip Glass. 135 min.
11-2774 Was $99.99 ❑***$19.99***

Kundun (Letterboxed Version)
Also available in a theatrical, widescreen format.
11-2290 ❑***$19.99***

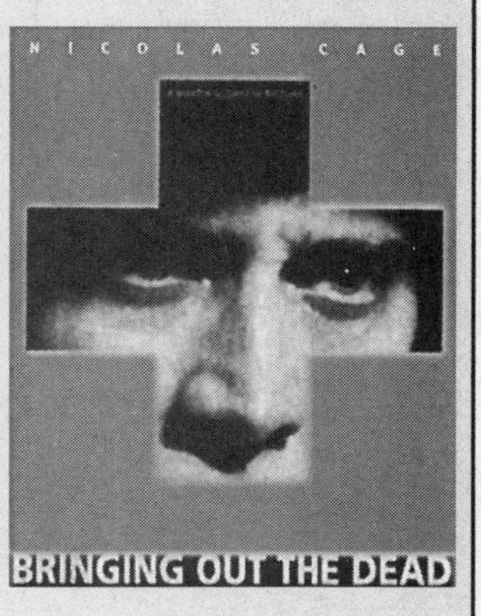

Bringing Out The Dead (1999)
Returning to the ominous New York streets they first explored in "Taxi Driver," director Martin Scorsese and scripter Paul Schrader offer a compelling, emotionally wrenching look at the life-and-death dealings of an ambulance crew. Nicolas Cage is a burned-out veteran paramedic, haunted by several recent cases he failed to save, who seeks solace with Patricia Arquette, daughter of a heart attack patient. John Goodman, Ving Rhames and Tom Sizemore also star. 121 min.
06-2950 Was $99.99 ❑***$14.99***

Bringing Out The Dead (Letterboxed Version)
Also available in a theatrical, widescreen format.
06-3023 ❑***$14.99***

A Personal Journey With Martin Scorsese Through American Movies (1998)
The acclaimed director serves as host for a look through 50 years of Hollywood history, examining the films that inspired and influenced his life and art, in this three-volume documentary series. Hundreds of clips from such movies as "Bigger than Life," "Duel in the Sun," "Lust for Life" and others are featured as Scorsese examines the films and the people who made them. 226 min. total.
11-2228 Was $59.99 ❑***$34.99***

Please see our index for these other Martin Scorsese titles: *The Color Of Money • New York Stories*

Love And Money (1982)
Investment banker Ray Sharkey falls in love with Ornella Muti, the beautiful wife of international financier Klaus Kinski, and soon gets caught in a web of intrigue involving Kinski's plans to take control of silver mines from a South American dictator. James Toback's stylish film also features Armand Assante, Susan Heldfond, King Vidor and Sonny Gibson. 90 min.
19-2354 ***$19.99***

Four Friends (1981)
Study of the turbulent decade of the '60s, seen through the lives of a quartet of friends from high school to adulthood. Craig Wasson is the college-bound son of an immigrant steelworker; Jim Metzler is an all-American jock who goes to Vietnam; Michael Huddleston is an overweight mamma's boy; and Jodi Thelen is the woman eventually involved with all of them. Arthur Penn directs.
19-1226 Was $99.99 ***$14.99***

sex, lies, & videotape (1989)
Witty, revealing, masterfully acted look at the sexual games people play. A philandering husband, his frigid wife and his sultry mistress confront their sexual problems and proclivities when hubby's college chum, an emotionally distressed drifter, arrives in town. Andie McDowell, James Spader, Laura San Giacomo and Peter Gallagher star; directed by Steven Soderbergh. 110 min.
02-2000 Was $19.99 ❑***$14.99***

Nick Nolte

Death Sentence (1974)
A man is on trial for murdering his wife, but as the evidence is presented in court, one of the jurors begins to believe that her own husband is really the killer! Nick Nolte, Cloris Leachman and Laurence Luckinbill star in this courtroom thriller. AKA: "Murder One." 74 min.
46-5160 Was $19.99 *$14.99*

Return To Macon County (1975)
Cross back over the Macon County Line with Nick Nolte (in his film debut) and Don Johnson in this rip-snorting actioner loaded with pretty women and rib-shaking violence. Co-stars Robin Mattson, Robert Viharo. 90 min.
47-1078 *$14.99*

The Deep (1978)
Two lovers on a Caribbean vacation discover a sunken wreck laden with treasure while diving, a find that makes them a target for smugglers and killers, in this underwater thriller based on Peter Benchley's novel. Nick Nolte, Jacqueline Bisset, Robert Shaw and Lou Gossett star. 125 min.
02-2540 *$14.99*

Who'll Stop The Rain (1978)
Intense, powerful tale of heroin smuggling from Vietnam to America, starring Nick Nolte and Michael Moriarty as war veterans involved in the dangerous proceedings. Based on the best-selling book "Dog Soldiers." Co-stars Tuesday Weld, Ray Sharkey. 126 min.
12-1795 *$14.99*

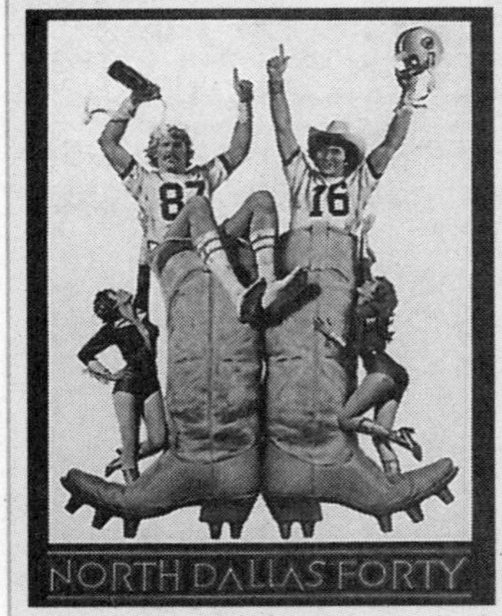

North Dallas Forty (1979)
The goings-on behind the locker room doors of the NFL are revealed in this hilarious sports comedy. Brutality, wild parties, drugs, labor relations, training camps...wait 'til you see the weird parts! Nick Nolte, Mac Davis and Charles Durning star. 119 min.
06-1044 *$14.99*

HeartBeat (1980)
The relentless, free-spirit of "On the Road" and the Beat Generation is lovingly captured in this overlooked gem. John Heard, Nick Nolte and Sissy Spacek play the parts of Jack Kerouac, Neal Cassady and Carolyn Cassady, and the film is strong in evoking a rich period flavor. Ray Sharkey co-stars. 109 min.
19-1076 Was $59.99 *$19.99*

Cannery Row (1982)
Amusing screen adaptation of John Steinbeck's twin novellas stars Nick Nolte as a has-been baseball star mixed up with flighty hooker Debra Winger along Monterey's waterfront. Co-stars Frank McRae and Audra Lindley. 120 min.
12-1212 Was $79.99 *$19.99*

Under Fire (1983)
Nick Nolte, Gene Hackman and Joanna Cassidy are three American journalists in war-ravaged Nicaragua in 1979, struggling to maintain their objectivity amidst political upheaval. Based-on-fact drama co-stars Ed Harris, Jean-Louis Trintignant. 123 min.
47-1204 *$14.99*

Teachers (1984)
Nick Nolte is a weary high school instructor trying to make sense of an educational system gone haywire in this seriocomic look at a modern "blackboard jungle." The great cast includes JoBeth Williams, Richard Mulligan, Ralph Macchio, Judd Hirsch, and early roles for Laura Dern and Morgan Freeman. 106 min.
12-2588 Was $19.99 □*$14.99*

Extreme Prejudice (1987)
A determined Texas Ranger out to stop drug smuggling across the border...his childhood friend, now a notorious cokerunner...a paramilitary force on a mysterious mission...they're on an explosive collision course in this all-out actioner from director Walter Hill. Nick Nolte, Powers Boothe, Maria Conchita Alonso, Rip Torn star. 104 min.
27-6544 *$12.99*

Farewell To The King (1989)
Nick Nolte is a WWII deserter in Borneo's jungles who becomes king of an aboriginal tribe, only to lead them against the advancing Japanese in the same cause he once rejected. John Milius ("Conan the Barbarian") directs. 114 min.
73-1045 *$19.99*

Everybody Wins (1990)
Nick Nolte and Debra Winger star in this mystery set in a New England town. While investigating a murder case that has sent an innocent man to jail, a down-and-out detective falls in love with the unstable woman who has hired him for the case. With Judith Ivey and Jack Warden; written by Arthur Miller and directed by Karel Reisz ("Who'll Stop the Rain"). 97 min.
73-1079 Was $89.99 □*$14.99*

Q & A (1990)
An assistant New York D.A., called in for a routine investigation of the shooting of a drug dealer by police, uncovers evidence of police corruption and political conspiracy. Sidney Lumet's ferociously powerful drama, loaded with violence, graphic street language and bizarre sexual situations, stars Nick Nolte, Timothy Hutton, Armand Assante and Patrick O' Neal. 132 min.
44-1759 Was $19.99 □*$14.99*

I'll Do Anything (1994)
In James L. Brooks' charming, romantic used-to-be-a-musical comedy, Nick Nolte is a formerly-hot actor whose attempts at making a comeback conflict with his unpredictable romantic life, his job as a chauffeur to a powerful producer and his irascible 6-year-old daughter. Joely Richardson, Albert Brooks, Julie Kavner, Whittni Wright and Tracey Ullman also star. 116 min.
02-2635 Was $89.99 □*$14.99*

Blue Chips (1994)
Nick Nolte stars as the high-profile, no-nonsense, tantrum-throwing coach of Western University who faces a losing season after winning two national championships. Feeling the heat from the athletic director and a sleazy school alumnus, Nolte resorts to illegal recruiting methods to get star players. Mary McDonnell, Ed O'Neill, Shaquille O'Neal and Anfernee Hardaway co-star; directed by Ron Shelton. 108 min.
06-2235 Was $19.99 □*$14.99*

Mother Night (1996)
Based on the Kurt Vonnegut classic, this moody and darkly ironic drama stars Nick Nolte as Howard Campbell, an American playwright living in Nazi Germany who is recruited by Allied agents to make pro-German propaganda speeches that contain coded information. After the war's end, Nolte returns home to a country that hates him and neo-Nazis that look upon him as a hero. With Sheryl Lee, Alan Arkin and John Goodman. 113 min.
02-5126 Was $99.99 □*$19.99*

Mulholland Falls (1996)
Set in Los Angeles in the early 1950s, this stylish crime thriller stars Nick Nolte, Chazz Palminteri, Michael Madsen and Chris Penn as members of "The Hat Squad," an elite police squad investigating the death of a pretty party girl—and Nolte's ex-lover. Their search leads them to an important scientist and a government conspiracy. With Melanie Griffith, John Malkovich, Jennifer Connelly. 108 min.
12-3101 Was $99.99 □*$14.99*

Afterglow (1997)
The stories of two troubled marriages (philandering contractor Nick Nolte and former actress Julie Christie, and job-obsessed Johnny Lee Miller and wife Lara Flynn Boyle, who wants to start a family) come together when Nolte seduces Boyle and Christie and Miller, unaware of their "connection," have an affair on their own in director Alan Rudolph's romantic comedy/drama. 114 min.
02-3173 Was $99.99 □*$24.99*

U-Turn (1997)
Small-time hustler Sean Penn is driving to Las Vegas to pay off a gambling debt, but a broken radiator hose strands him in a remote Arizona desert town whose off-the-wall residents include grimy auto mechanic Billy Bob Thornton, crooked sheriff Powers Boothe, and wealthy realtor Nick Nolte and seductive wife Jennifer Lopez, each of whom offer Penn money to bump off their spouse. Director Oliver Stone's noir thriller also stars Joaquin Phoenix, Jon Voight. 125 min.
02-3149 Was $99.99 □*$19.99*

Nightwatch (1998)
Creepy horror-thriller featuring Ewan McGregor as a law student who takes a custodial job in a local morgue. When a series of area prostitutes turn up dead, McGregor finds himself in danger, and not only is he under suspicion by police detective Nick Nolte for the murders, but the real killer intends to make him the next victim. Patricia Arquette and Josh Brolin co-star in Danish director Ole Bornedal's remake of his earlier "Nattevagten"; co-scripted by Steven Soderbergh. 99 min.
11-2789 Was $19.99 □*$14.99*

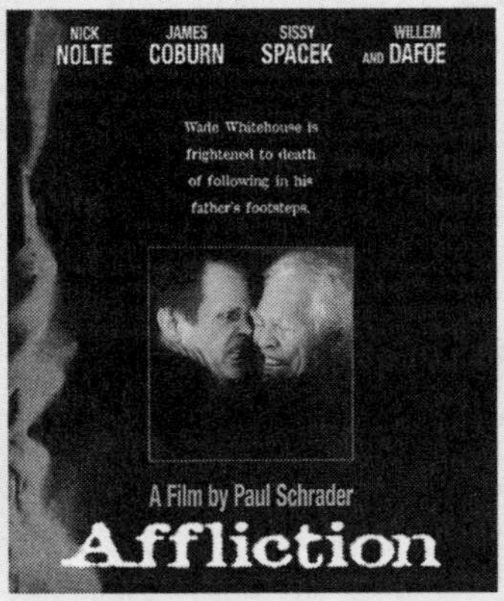

Affliction (1998)
Writer/director Paul Schrader's absorbing drama stars Nick Nolte as an emotionally scarred and embittered sheriff, the only law in a small New Hampshire town, who sees his investigation of a wealthy man's death during a hunting trip as a chance to prove himself to his family and community. James Coburn won a Best Supporting Actor Academy Award as Nolte's drunken, abusive father; with Sissy Spacek, Willem Dafoe, Mary Beth Hurt.
07-2749 Was $99.99 □*$14.99*

Please see our index for these other Nick Nolte titles: *48 Hrs.* • *Another 48 Hrs.* • *Breakfast Of Champions* • *Cape Fear* • *Down And Out In Beverly Hills* • *I Love Trouble* • *Jefferson In Paris* • *Lorenzo's Oil* • *New York Stories* • *The Prince Of Tides* • *Simpatico* • *The Thin Red Line*

Raggedy Man (1981)
This atmospheric drama stars Oscar-winner Sissy Spacek as a telephone operator in a small Texas town during the 1940s. Her life is changed when sailor Eric Roberts arrives in town. Superb acting highlights this provocative film. 94 min.
07-1083 Was $79.99 *$14.99*

Silence Of The North (1981)
This true-life story is set in the Canadian wilderness in 1919 and centers on Ellen Burstyn, an independent woman attempting to survive and raise her three children after fur-trapper hubby Tom Skerritt dies. Stirring and gorgeously photographed, the film also stars Gordon Pinsent and Jennifer McKinney. 94 min.
07-1095 Was $79.99 *$14.99*

Now And Forever (1983)
Contemporary love story stars Cheryl Ladd and Robert Coleby as a married couple who decide to divorce. Their traumas are explored, while their true love surfaces through the obstacles of time and distance. 93 min.
07-1181 *$59.99*

Hanna K. (1983)
Gripping drama from director Costa-Gavras ("Z") stars Jill Clayburgh as an American lawyer living in Israel who is called on to represent a Palestinian suing the government for the right to live on his ancestral homeland. With Gabriel Byrne. 111 min.
07-1200 *$59.99*

The Red Light Sting (1984)
Farrah Fawcett and Beau Bridges star in this tale of a call girl and Justice Department rookie who team up to catch an underworld kingpin, even if it means putting themselves in danger. 100 min.
07-1331 *$39.99*

Mask (1985)
Winning real-life drama tells the story of Rocky Dennis, a young boy whose disfigured face separates him from the world but cannot extinguish his spirit. Eric Stoltz shines as Dennis, with Cher as his biker mom, Sam Elliott and Laura Dern; directed by Peter Bogdanovich. 120 min.
07-1371 Was $19.99 □*$14.99*

Sylvester (1985)
Three orphaned youngsters are taken in by a horse trainer, helping him tame a wild horse named Sylvester in this family drama. Melissa Gilbert, Richard Farnsworth and Michael Schoeffling star. 101 min.
02-1461 □*$19.99*

Alamo Bay (1985)
A small Texas Gulf Coast town becomes engulfed in a war of hatred and prejudice when local fishermen feel their jobs are endangered by Vietnamese immigrants. Ed Harris, Amy Madigan, Ho Nguyen, Donald Moffat star; Louis Malle directs. 98 min.
02-1514 □*$79.99*

The Last Winter (1984)
Dramatic story set in Israel during the 1973 Yom Kippur War, centering on two women who both think a shadowy figure seen in newsreel footage of an Egyptian POW camp is their husband. Kathleen Quinlan, Stephen Macht and Yona Elian star in this timely, wrenching drama. 92 min.
02-1579 *$79.99*

Listen To Me (1989)
A heartfelt drama of today's youth, with Kirk Cameron and Jami Gertz as collegiate debate team members who fall in love while preparing for a national competition. Roy Scheider co-stars. 107 min.
02-1968 □*$14.99*

Fatso

Fatso (1980)
Dom DeLuise stars as the good-natured, albeit overweight, guy who tries to reduce after an obese relative's death. Funny and touching, the film co-stars Anne Bancroft (who also wrote and directed), Ron Carey and Candice Azzara. 94 min.
04-3180 Was $79.99 □*$14.99*

Kent State (1981)
Graphic and honest depiction of the events surrounding the fateful day in May of 1970, when university students protesting the Vietnam War were fired upon by National Guardsmen. When the smoke cleared, four students were dead and nine wounded. Talia Balsam, Ellen Barkin, John Getz star. 120 min.
07-1464 *$39.99*

Bullies (1986)
A newly arrived family in a rural Canadian town must fight for their lives against a deranged backwoods clan in this unbelievable, action-packed drama. Jonathan Crombie, Olivia D'Abo, Stephen Hunter. 96 min.
07-1480 □*$79.99*

Busted Up (1986)
Two-bit hoods and corrupt developers have knocked a Round Ring boxer down, but not out, in this gritty drama about the seedier side of the pugilistic world. Stars Irene Cara, Paul Coufos and Tony Rosato. 93 min.
07-1487 Was $79.99 *$14.99*

'night, Mother (1986)
Sissy Spacek and Anne Bancroft are unforgettable in this film adaptation of Marsha Norman's award-winning play, as a despondent woman plans to commit suicide and must convince her mother not to interfere. 97 min.
07-1498 Was $79.99 □*$14.99*

Zoot Suit (1981)
Powerful filmization of Luis Valdez' hit play, based on a 1942 incident in Los Angeles where a gang of Hispanics were sent to San Quentin prison on trumped-up murder charges. Daniel Valdez, Edward James Olmos, Tyne Daly, Charles Aidman star. 103 min.
07-1696 *$19.99*

Prison For Children (1986)
A teenage boy loses his parents in a tragic accident and is sent to a reform school. This the future seems bleak, as he becomes a victim of brutality and corruption until he's helped by an understanding supervisor and a caring teacher. Raphael Sbarge, Josh Brolin, Betty Thomas and John Ritter star. 96 min.
07-1969 □*$89.99*

The Night The City Screamed (1980)
A power blackout turns a modern American metropolis into a battlezone as rioters and looters run rampant, and the police and city officials are powerless to stop them. Gripping drama stars Raymond Burr, Robert Culp, Don Meredith, Georg Stanford Brown, Clifton Davis and Linda Purl. 96 min.
02-2395 *$59.99*

THE LONG HOT SUMMER

The Long Hot Summer (1985)
Don Johnson and Cybill Shepherd sizzle in this steamy remake of William Faulkner's drama, as the arrival of a drifter brings hatred, desire and rage to a small Southern town. Excellent cast includes Jason Robards, Ava Gardner, Judith Ivey, Wings Hauser. 192 min.
04-2140 Was $79.99 *$29.99*

The Grace Kelly Story (1983)
The fairy tale life of Grace Kelly, the Philadelphia-born beauty who became an Oscar-winning actress and later married Monaco's Prince Rainier, is chronicled in this compassionate biography. Cheryl Ladd turns in a fine performance in the lead, and Lloyd Bridges, Diane Ladd and Christina Applegate (as the young Grace) co-star. 104 min.
02-2771 *$19.99*

Fire And Rain (1989)
The true story of Flight 191, which crashed during its trip cross-country near Dallas/Fort Worth, turning into a burned-out shell of an aircraft. How rescue workers, volunteers and surviving passengers united to help is the focus of this study of courage. Angie Dickinson, Charles Haid, David Hasselhoff and Robert Guillaume star. 89 min.
06-1740 *$89.99*

Stones For Ibarra (1988)
Glenn Close and Keith Carradine star in this compelling, acclaimed story about an American couple who head to Mexico in order to run a copper mine they've inherited, but husband Carradine contracts leukemia and their dreams for the future are shattered. Alfonso Arau co-stars in this touching drama. 96 min.
14-3246 *$12.99*

Uncommon Valor (1983)
In this powerful, suspenseful drama, the fire chief of Salt Lake City attempts to save the lives of the patients of a hospital set ablaze by an arsonist. Mitchell Ryan, Barbara Parkins, Ben Murphy star. 120 min.
14-3265 *$12.99*

Side By Side: The True Story Of The Osmond Family (1982)
Sensitive study of the ever-popular Osmond clan, tracing the life of mother Olive (Marie Osmond) and father George (Joseph Bottoms), who struggle to raise nine children, two of whom were born hearing-impaired. Their sons form a barbershop quartet and the rest, as shown here, is history. 120 min.
14-3267 *$12.99*

Death Of A Centerfold: The Dorothy Stratten Story (1981)
Jamie Lee Curtis plays Dorothy Stratten, the Playboy centerfold killed by her disturbed husband (Bruce Weitz). The film follows Dorothy's life from a teenager in Canada to her fame as a Playboy Playmate to her horrifying death. 95 min.
12-1344 *$59.99*

Star 80 (1983)
Bob Fosse's glossy recounting of the Dorothy Stratten story focuses more on the fatal obsessions of the starlet's estranged husband, Paul Snider (chillingly played by Eric Roberts). Mariel Hemingway stars as the smalltown girl-turned-centerfold celebrity, and Cliff Robertson plays Hugh Hefner. 104 min.
19-1309 Was $19.99 *$14.99*

Prince Of The City (1981)
A knock-out drama about an honest cop called to testify about drug dealings involving his friends. An unflinching look at corruption, city life, and the compromises we must make. Treat Williams, Jerry Orbach star; Sidney Lumet directs. 167 min.
19-1176 Was $29.99 *$24.99*

The Tenth Man (1988)
Anthony Hopkins turns in a compelling performance as a French attorney who is taken hostage by the Nazis during World War II. In order to save his life, Hopkins makes a deal with another man willing to swap lives with him for his fortune. When Hopkins is released, however, a disturbing mystery unfolds. Derek Jacobi also stars in this adaptation of Graham Greene's novella. 89 min.
12-2698 Was $79.99 ❑*$19.99*

Broken Angel (1988)
This forceful story tells of a girl who seems to have it all: good looks, good grades...and a membership in one of Los Angeles' deadliest gangs. After her best friend is murdered, the girl disappears, and her father tries to find her on the city's meanest streets. William Shatner, Susan Blakely and Erika Eleniak star. 94 min.
12-2699 ❑*$14.99*

Independence Day (1983)
A touching romantic drama about a small town photographer who has big-city dreams. Kathleen Quinlan, David Keith, Dianne Wiest star. 110 min.
19-1269 *$19.99*

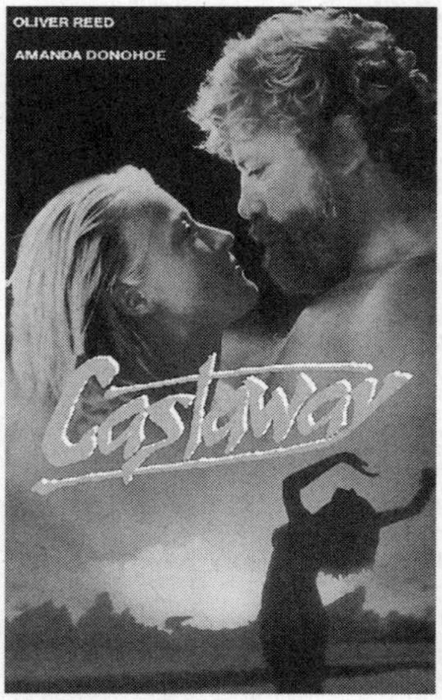

Castaway (1987)
A writer wishing to spend a year on a deserted tropical island with a "female Friday" isn't prepared for the strong-willed young woman who answers his ad in this incredible adventure/drama based on real events. Oliver Reed and Amanda Donohoe are the couple; Nicolas Roeg directs. 118 min.
19-1616 ❑*$19.99*

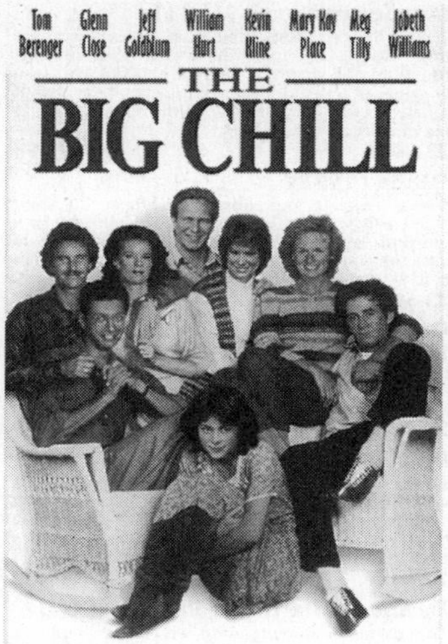

The Big Chill: 15th Anniversary Collector's Edition (1983)
Writer/director Lawrence Kasdan's acclaimed, evocative comedy/drama about a group of '60s college friends who reunite years later, after one of their circle commits suicide, and spend a weekend re-examining their lives and what brought them together in the past. Filled with memorable dialogue and a quintessential oldies score, the film stars Tom Berenger, Glenn Close, Jeff Goldblum, William Hurt, Kevin Kline, Mary Kay Place, Meg Tilly and JoBeth Williams. This remastered edition also includes a 15-minute "making of" featurette and nine minutes of deleted scenes. 103 min.
02-3250 ❑*$14.99*

The Big Chill: 15th Anniversary Collector's Edition (Letterboxed Version)
Also available in a theatrical, widescreen format.
02-3251 ❑*$14.99*

Round Midnight (1986)
Drama set in 1950s France, where a friendship develops between an aging black American jazz musician (Dexter Gordon) and a young Parisian artist (Francois Cluzet). Co-written and directed by French filmmaker Bertrand Tavernier, the movie also stars Lonette McKee, Gabrielle Haker and Herbie Hancock. 130 min.
19-1579 ❑*$19.99*

Ratboy (1986)
Pathos and comedy are blended in this tale of a window dresser (Sondra Locke, in her directorial debut) who finds a half-human, half-rodent freak in the L.A. trash dumps...and exploits both him and his affections in her quest for fame and fortune. Co-stars Christopher Hewett, Robert Townsend, Gerrit Graham and Sharon Baird as the Ratboy. 104 min.
19-1609 ❑*$19.99*

Shy People (1988)
Two very different women find they have very common feelings in this critically acclaimed drama. Big city writer Jill Clayburgh goes with her teenage daughter to the Louisiana bayou to visit relatives, an isolated backwoods brood headed by matriarch Barbara Hershey. Compelling tale also stars Mare Winningham, Martha Plimpton, Merritt Butrick. 116 min.
19-1644 ❑*$19.99*

Promise Of Love (1980)
A teenage bride who witnesses the death of her Marine Corps husband in Vietnam attempts to put her life back together with the help of a civilian recreation worker based at a military training camp. Sensitive drama stars Valerie Bertinelli, Jameson Parker, Joanna Miles and Craig T. Nelson. 96 min.
14-2003 *$19.99*

Reckless (1984)
Dramatic "Rebel Without a Cause" updating stars Aidan Quinn as the cycle-riding "hard case" who falls for cheerleader Daryl Hannah, only to find their love meets opposition from both sides. Gritty, fast-paced tale features sizzling love scenes and fine supporting turns by Kenneth McMillan and Cliff DeYoung. 93 min.
12-1347 Was $79.99 *$14.99*

Mishima: A Life In Four Chapters (1985)
The life and works of controversial 20th-century Japanese novelist Yukio Mishima are brilliantly brought to the screen by writer/director Paul Schrader. Unique stylized sets and a pulsating Philip Glass score help detail Mishima's complex philosophies and the final culmination of his art and life, his ritualistic suicide. Narration by Roy Scheider. 121 min. In Japanese with English subtitles.
19-1486 ❑*$69.99*

Duet For One (1986)
Julie Andrews is a renowned classical violinist whose world is shattered when she learns she is afflicted with multiple sclerosis. Stirring story of tragedy and triumph co-stars Alan Bates, Max Von Sydow, Rupert Everett. 107 min.
12-1694 Was $79.99 *$14.99*

Betrayed (1988)
FBI agent Debra Winger is assigned to infiltrate a white supremacist group operating in the Midwest, but enters into a dangerous relationship with farmer Tom Berenger, one of the group's leaders. Director Costa-Gavras takes a harrowing look at racism in middle America in a suspenseful drama. John Heard co-stars. 123 min.
12-1872 Was $19.99 *$14.99*

Martin's Day (1985)
Richard Harris stars as Martin, a loner looking to return to his childhood home. He kidnaps a young boy, also named Martin, and the pair discover friendship and humanity through each other. Action and human drama combine in this touching story; with Justin Henry, Lindsay Wagner, James Coburn and Karen Black. 99 min.
12-2602 *$14.99*

Track 29 (1988)
A woman (Theresa Russell) trapped in a loveless marriage receives a strange visitor, a man (Gary Oldman) who claims to be the son she abandoned years before. Is he her child, is he a liar, or is he an illusion? Bizarre, darkly funny tale of romantic obsession from Nicolas Roeg also stars Christopher Lloyd, Sandra Bernhard. 90 min.
12-2679 *$14.99*

Beyond Obsession (1982)
The exotic North African city of Marrakesh is the setting for romance, drama and intrigue in this steamy tale of a love triangle whose members are being consumed by their passions. Tom Berenger, Marcello Mastroianni, Eleonora Giorgi star. 110 min.
15-1080 Was $19.99 *$14.99*

The Kitchen Toto (1988)
Critically acclaimed drama set in British-ruled Kenya during the bloody Mau Mau rebellions of the late '50s, as an orphaned black boy is taken in by a white police chief's family as a servant and finds himself caught between sides. Edwin Mahinda, Bob Peck star. 95 min.
19-1684 Was $79.99 ❑*$19.99*

Running On Empty (1988)
Acclaimed drama of a family on the run from the law stars Judd Hirsch and Christine Lahti as '60s radicals wanted for a protest bombing that wounded an innocent victim and River Phoenix as their eldest son, who would welcome a chance at a "normal" life and the music scholarship he can't accept. Compelling story, directed by Sidney Lumet, also stars Martha Plimpton. 116 min.
19-1687 Was $19.99 ❑*$14.99*

Business As Usual (1988)
Working class drama set in Liverpool, England. When boutique manager Glenda Jackson is fired after commenting on an executive's sexual harassment of another employee, she is thrust to the forefront of a union demonstration against the store. Co-stars Cathy Tyson, John Thaw. 89 min.
19-1689 Was $79.99 ❑*$19.99*

Dancers (1987)
Take a look backstage in this dazzling, romantic ballet drama that stars Mikhail Baryshnikov as the leader of a dance troupe working on a film in Italy. Dance sequences by Lynn Seymour, Alessandra Ferri, and the members of Baryshnikov's American Ballet Theatre; with Leslie Browne, Mariangelo Melato. 99 min.
19-1630 Was $19.99 *$14.99*

Jessica Lange

Cat On A Hot Tin Roof (1983)
A stunning version of Tennessee Williams' classic tale of family conflicts and backbiting. Rip Torn is dying patriarch Big Daddy; Tommy Lee Jones his alcoholic son, Brick; and Jessica Lange the sultry Maggie the Cat. 144 min.
47-1386 *$19.99*

Sweet Dreams (1985)
Jessica Lange stars as country singer Patsy Cline, whose rise to the top ended with her death in a plane crash in 1963, in this unforgettable biodrama that traces Cline's career and her stormy marriage. Ed Harris, Ann Wedgeworth, David Clennon, John Goodman also star. 115 min.
44-1353 Was $19.99 *$14.99*

Everybody's All-American (1988)
What does a football hero do when the cheering stops? For collegiate all-star Dennis Quaid, a chance at the pros is part of the rocky road through adulthood he travels with sweetheart/wife Jessica Lange. Rousing drama from Taylor Hackford ("An Officer and a Gentleman") also stars Timothy Hutton. 127 min.
19-1693 Was $19.99 ❑*$14.99*

Far North (1988)
Author Sam Shepard makes his directorial debut with this comical allegory. Jessica Lange is a prodigal farm daughter saddled with her hospitalized father's request...shoot the horse that put him there! Charles Durning, Tess Harper, Donald Moffat. 88 min.
53-1775 *$14.99*

Men Don't Leave (1989)
In this revealing, bittersweet drama, Jessica Lange plays a woman forced to uproot her family after her husband dies. Her new life and surroundings bring promise and pain for her and her two sons, and she turns to an understanding musician for help. Joan Cusack, Arliss Howard and Chris O'Donnell co-star. 114 min.
19-1776 *$19.99*

Music Box (1989)
When an elderly Hungarian emigre is charged with being a Nazi criminal, he chooses his lawyer daughter to defend him in court. As the trial proceeds, horrifying secrets from his past are revealed. Oscar-nominated Jessica Lange, Armin-Mueller Stahl and Frederic Forrest star in this smashing drama, directed by Costa-Gavras ("Missing"). 126 min.
27-6670 Was $89.99 ❑*$14.99*

O' Pioneers! (1992)
In this "Hallmark Hall of Fame" production, Jessica Lange plays a woman who has turned her inherited farm into a successful business for herself and her family. Still, she yearns for an adventurer she recalls from her past, and when he returns to visit, feelings of desire and conflict arise. David Strathairn, Heather Graham and Reed Diamond also star. 100 min.
63-1567 ❑*$14.99*

Blue Sky (1994)
The final film by director Tony Richardson ("Tom Jones"), this emotional drama features an Academy Award-winning turn by Jessica Lange as the manic, love-starved wife of Army officer Tommy Lee Jones, who needs her help when he's caught in the middle of a military cover-up. With Powers Boothe, Carrie Snodgress, Chris O'Donnell. 101 min.
73-1191 Was $89.99 ❑*$14.99*

Losing Isaiah (1995)
Compassionate drama starring Jessica Lange as a social worker who, along with husband David Strathairn, has adopted an African-American "crack baby." When Halle Berry, the baby's destitute mother, learns that the child she left in a trash bin is still alive, she stages a painful custody battle. With Samuel L. Jackson, Cuba Gooding, Jr. and La Tanya Richardson. 108 min.
06-2369 Was $19.99 ❑*$14.99*

A Thousand Acres (1997)
"King Lear" is transplanted to the American heartland in this powerful drama starring Jason Robards as a hard-hearted farmer whose plans to divide his spread between daughters Jessica Lange, Michelle Pfeiffer and Jennifer Jason Leigh lead to jealousy, conspiracy and the digging-up of some long-buried family skeletons. Based on Jane Smiley's Pulitzer Prize-winning novel. 105 min.
11-2221 Was $19.99 ❑*$14.99*

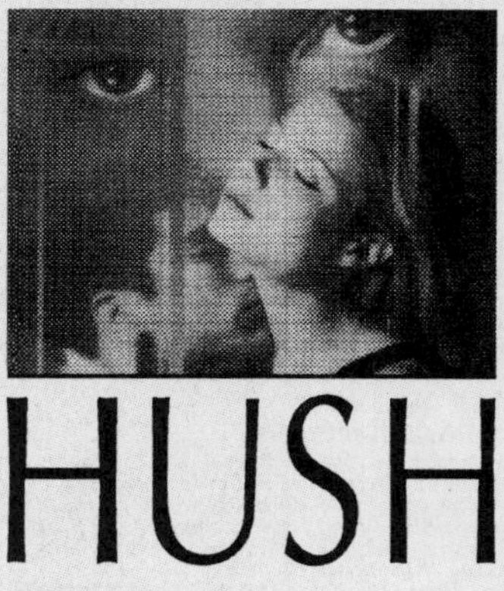

Hush (1998)
Pregnant newlywed Gwyneth Paltrow may not mind moving to husband Johnathon Schaech's family's horse farm in Kentucky at first, but manipulative mother-in-law Jessica Lange's growing obsession with Paltrow and her baby will soon have her changing her mind...and fearing for her life. Scary suspenser also stars Nina Foch, Hal Holbrook. 96 min.
02-3209 Was $99.99 ❑*$14.99*

Cousin Bette (1998)
Darkly comic translation of Balzac's novel showcases Jessica Lange as the 19th-century French spinster who exacts revenge against her insensitive relatives by using three outsiders in a cunning human chess game. Elisabeth Shue, Bob Hoskins, Hugh Laurie and Geraldine Chaplin also star in this witty period story, which marks the film debut of theatrical director Des McAnuff ("Tommy"). 110 min.
04-3732 ❑*$99.99*

Please see our index for these other Jessica Lange titles: *Cape Fear • King Kong • Night And The City • The Postman Always Rings Twice • Rob Roy • Titus*

Cal (1984)
Violence-torn Northern Ireland is the setting for this romance between a shy Catholic teenager and an older Protestant woman, the widow of a policeman the youth unwillingly helped murder. Helen Mirren, John Lynch star. 102 min.
19-1407 *$19.99*

Someone Around
A high school student with a troubled past discovers that the school's sports hero has his own problems, which she tries to help him overcome, in this timely and dramatic look at teen suicide. India Hammer, Andrew Tucker star. 38 min.
15-5225 *$19.99*

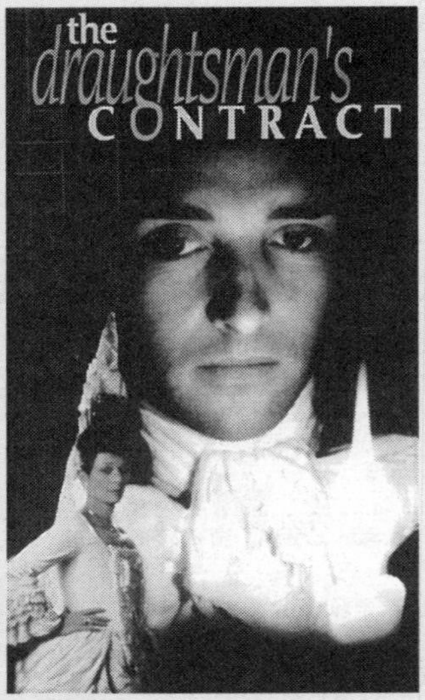

The Draughtsman's Contract (1983)
In his feature directorial debut, Peter Greenaway crafts an elegant tale of sexual gamesmanship and murder in 17th-century England. An arrogant artist is hired by an aristocrat's wife to do sketches as a gift for her husband. The draughtsman uses his position to seduce members of the household, but before long the tables are turned. Anthony Higgins, Janet Suzman star. 103 min.
12-2263 Letterboxed *$29.99*

A Zed And Two Noughts (1985)
A haunting drama about twin brothers whose wives were killed in an accident and who enter into an affair with the same woman, and how their mutual attraction and despair are affected by the twins' work in the city zoo. Brian and Eric Deacon, Andrea Ferreol star; written and directed by Peter Greenaway. AKA: "Zoo—A Zed and Two Noughts." 115 min.
07-8135 Letterboxed *$29.99*

Drowning By Numbers (1987)
In this intriguing drama with dark comedic moments from director Peter Greenaway ("Prospero's Books"), a wife named Cissie drowns her philandering husband, which sets into motion a cinematic game of sex, murder and hidden numbers involving two other women also named Cissie. Joan Plowright, Juliet Stevenson, Joely Richardson star. 121 min.
27-6754 Was $19.99 *$14.99*

The Belly Of An Architect (1987)
Compelling, stylish drama from Peter Greenaway stars Brian Dennehy as an American architect in charge of a Rome exhibition whose obsession with the show and his recurring stomach pains drive his wife into a rival's arms. Lambert Wilson, Chloe Webb co-star. 120 min.
80-1004 Was $89.99 *$14.99*

The Pillow Book (1997)
Once again blurring the line between the physical and the sensual, writer/director Peter Greenaway creates a memorable and erotic drama. A Japanese author, obsessed with both the diary kept by her namesake centuries earlier and her calligrapher father's painting of birthday blessings on her face, combines the two by taking lovers who write elaborate messages on her body. Vivian Wu, Ken Ogata and Ewan McGregor star. Unrated version; 126 min. In English and Japanese and Mandarin with English subtitles.
02-3136 Was $99.99 □*$24.99*

8 1/2 Women (2000)
The always-adventurous Peter Greenaway offers this sensual salute to "8 1/2," focusing on a British man and his adult son who become inspired by the Fellini film and decide to begin a harem with 8 1/2 women. Among their ladies are Toni Collette, a wannabe nun; the pig-and-horse-obsessed Amanda Plummer; sexual adventurer Polly Walker; and legless Manna Fujiwara. With John Standing, Matthew Delamere and Vivian Wu. 122 min.
07-2923 □*$99.99*

Love Child (1982)
The true tale of Terry Jean Moore, a convicted robber who fights for the right to keep her baby while imprisoned. Amy Madigan, Mackenzie Phillips, Beau Bridges, Rhea Pearlman star. 96 min.
19-1248 Was $19.99 *$14.99*

Double Exposure: The Story Of Margaret Bourke-White (1989)
Farrah Fawcett stars in a globe-trotting biography of the maverick photojournalist, co-starring Frederic Forrest. Famous for her portraits of the poor, men-at-arms and world leaders, she becomes notorious for a torrid affair with writer Erskine Caldwell, but shutters away her greatest passion for her work. 94 min.
18-7133 *$14.99*

Claudia (1989)
The lavish lifestyles of the English countryside provide the backdrop for a drama of love, deception, violence and murder, as a jealous husband's rage has a fatal price. Searing tale stars Deborah Raffin, Nicholas Ball, John Moulder-Brown. 88 min.
18-7191 *$69.99*

Vision Quest (1985)
Rousing drama that combines action, comedy and romance. Matthew Modine is a high school wrestler whose drive to become state champion gets sidetracked when he falls for beautiful, older houseguest Linda Fiorentino. Features a top rock score and concert footage featuring Madonna. 108 min.
19-1463 Was $19.99 □*$14.99*

Bird (1988)
His soaring saxophone and revolutionary music changed the face of jazz, but his personal life was one of addiction and sadness that ended in an untimely death. The legendary Charlie Parker is adroitly played by Forest Whitaker in a song-filled biodrama from director Clint Eastwood. With Diane Venora, Michael Zelniker. 160 min.
19-1696 □*$19.99*

Lean On Me (1989)
High school principal Joe Clark's one-man crusade to rid his school of drug pushers and gang members while instilling a sense of pride in the students is a story so improbable it had to be real. Morgan Freeman is brilliant as the dedicated, megalomaniacal Clark, supported by Robert Guillaume, Alan North. John Avildsen ("Rocky") directs. 109 min.
19-1711 □*$14.99*

Dress Gray (1986)
Superb drama starring Alec Baldwin as a military academy cadet who starts a relentless investigation into the mysterious death of a homosexual classman. Set during the Vietnam War era, this film also stars Hal Holbrook, Lloyd Bridges, Eddie Albert and Alexis Smith; script by Gore Vidal. 192 min.
19-2103 Was $79.99 □*$24.99*

Of Pure Blood (1986)
German-born businesswoman Lee Remick investigates the mysterious murder of her son in her homeland and uncovers a devious plot involving breeding farms run by Nazis, which may have a link to his death. Patrick McGoohan and Richard Munch also star in this film based on true events. 93 min.
19-2238 Was $79.99 *$19.99*

My Name Is Bill W. (1989)
Set in Akron, Ohio, in the 1930s, this powerful look at the founding of Alcoholics Anonymous stars James Woods as heavy-drinking stockbroker Bill Wilson, who helps another drinker, surgeon Robert Smith (James Garner), stay sober and launch an organization to help others. JoBeth Williams, Fritz Weaver also star. 100 min.
19-2240 Was $89.99 □*$19.99*

Crisis At Central High (1980)
Docudrama based on the landmark integration of a Little Rock, Arkansas, high school in 1957, and how one woman struggled to combat racism and keep the peace. Joanne Woodward stars as the strong-willed vice-principal; with Charles Durning, William Russ. 125 min.
19-2299 Was $19.99 *$14.99*

The Lonely Passion Of Judith Hearne (1987)
A well-acted story featuring Maggie Smith as a spinster in a dreary Dublin boarding house, a lifelong doormat for others, who rashly accepts the attentions of fortune-hunting cad Bob Hoskins. Wendy Hiller also stars. 116 min.
19-7006 Was $79.99 *$14.99*

Hot Blood (1989)
The passionate rivalry between Latin brothers fuels a bloodbath when one of the men joins with a psychotic drifter to lay siege to a rural Spanish bank, and the second sibling learns his fiancée (Sylvia Kristel of "Emmanuelle") is among the hostages. 89 min.
19-7038 *$19.99*

Berlin Blues (1989)
A chic nightclub in Berlin is the setting for this stormy romantic drama about a mesmerizing singer pursued by both a talented young pianist and a moody orchestra director. Stars Julia Migenes ("Carmen") and Keith Baxter. 104 min.
19-7065 *$79.99*

The Rose Garden (1989)
Liv Ullmann turns in a gripping performance as a lawyer who defends a Polish Jew for assailing an elderly German at an airport. Eventually she discovers the German is a former S.S. officer who was responsible for killing the accused man's sister. Intense courtroom drama co-stars Maximilian Schell, Peter Fonda. 112 min.
19-7072 *$19.99*

Murder In Texas (1981)
Farrah Fawcett, Katharine Ross, Sam Elliott and Andy Griffith star in a true drama of events surrounding the death of Joan Robinson Hill, the daughter of a wealthy Texas oil man and the wife of a noted plastic surgeon, who is the main suspect in her murder. 200 min.
23-5025 *$29.99*

Olivia (1983)
Sexual revenge and murder highlight this story about a woman who is forced to moonlight as a prostitute after being abused by her husband. Stars Susanna Love, Robert Walker. Directed by Ulli Lommel. 87 min.
23-5027 *$29.99*

Only Once In A Lifetime (1983)
Tender drama about the romance that develops between a recently widowed Hispanic painter and a school teacher. Stars Miguel Robelo, Estrellita Lopez and Sheree North. 90 min.
23-5037 *$29.99*

Prime Suspect (1981)
An ordinary man finds himself under suspicion for a series of brutal assaults on young girls, thanks to an overzealous reporter and circumstantial evidence, in this engrossing tale. Mike Farrell, Teri Garr, Veronica Cartwright star. 96 min.
27-6172 *$14.99*

Damien: The Leper Priest (1980)
True drama of a young priest who dared to go to a leper colony in 19th-century Hawaii and risk his life to help the unfortunates who lived there. Ken Howard, Mike Farrell and Wilfrid Hyde-White star in a tale of faith and human courage. 96 min.
27-6257 *$24.99*

Molokai: The Story Of Father Damien (2000)
David Wenham plays the canonized Father Damien, a dedicated priest who sacrificed his own life in order to bring dignity and hope to the inhabitants of a leper colony on the Hawaiian island of Molokai in the 1870s. Director Paul Cox's moving biodrama also stars Derek Jacobi, Sam Neill, Kris Kristofferson and Peter O'Toole. 120 min.
83-1560 *$99.99*

The Wild And The Free (1980)
Exciting, tender drama from the director of "Born Free" stars Linda Gray and Granville Van Dusen as scientists who get more than they bargained for when they raise chimpanzees as a zoology experiment. 96 min.
27-6295 *$14.99*

A Small Killing (1981)
Ed Asner and Jean Simmons star as a detective and a sociology professor who go undercover together as a wino and bag lady in order to catch a killer preying on street people. Co-stars Sylvia Sidney, J. Pat O'Malley. 100 min.
27-6307 *$12.99*

Two Of A Kind (1982)
George Burns and Robby Benson star in this heartwarming drama of an elderly man whose concern for his retarded grandson renews his interest in living. Life-affirming story also stars Cliff Robertson, Barbara Bates. 100 min.
27-6345 *$14.99*

The Choice (1981)
A touching and thoughtful portrait of an unwed, pregnant young girl (Jennifer Warren) who, with emotional support from her mother (Susan Clark), contemplates having an abortion. 96 min.
27-6513 *$12.99*

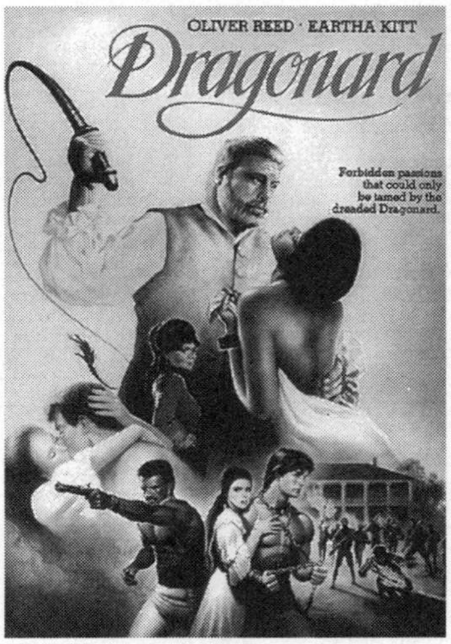

Dragonard (1987)
Temperatures and passions run high on an 18th-century Caribbean island where whip-wielding colonial officer Oliver Reed holds sway over the slaves, and where bordello owner Eartha Kitt controls him. Lavish costume drama, in the manner of "Mandingo," also stars Claudia Udy, Annabel Schofield. 93 min.
19-1691 Was $79.99 *$19.99*

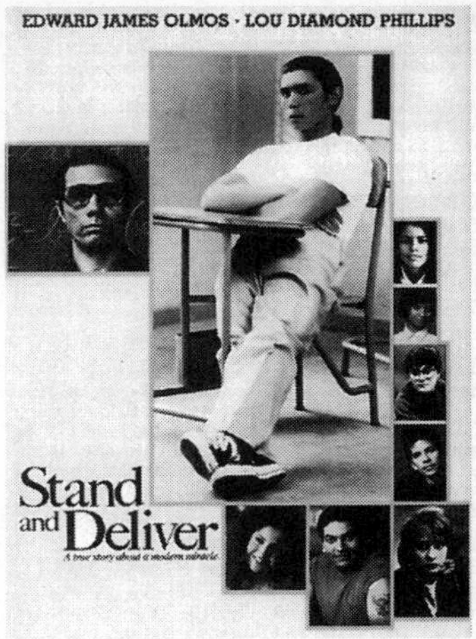

Stand And Deliver (1988)
Edward James Olmos delivers a bravura performance in the true story of Jamie Escalante, a Colombian-born engineer who left the business world to teach the youth of L.A.'s barrio slums and uses unorthodox methods to inspire them to learn. Winning drama co-stars Lou Diamond Phillips, Andy Garcia. 105 min.
19-1656 □*$14.99*

The Penitent (1987)
Raul Julia portrays a deeply religious man whose child bride (Rona Freed), becomes the wedge between his faith and his life. Also tormented by the girl is her husband's lifelong friend, romancer Armand Assante, for whom betrayal is a matter not of faith, but of broken honor between men. 94 min.
27-6589 *$12.99*

The Gold And The Glory (1989)
A footrace with a golden purse becomes the deciding test in this intense rivalry between two brothers, an athlete and a musician in love with the same girl. Thoughtful Australian drama stars Joss McWilliams and Colin Friels ("Malcolm"). 100 min.
27-6635 *$14.99*

Drugstore Cowboy (1989)
A sometimes blackly funny, but always graphic and harrowing, look at the troubled lives of a close-knit group of drug addicts in the early '70s, this powerful drama features a strong turn by Matt Dillon as the leader who tries to get straight. With Kelly Lynch and maverick writer William S. Burroughs. 104 min.
27-6667 *$14.99*

Go Tell It On The Mountain (1984)
Acclaimed "American Playhouse" production of James Baldwin's semiautobiographical novel focusing on the explosive relationship between a young African-American boy and his tough stepfather. Paul Winfield, James Bond III, Alfre Woodard and Olivia Cole star in this masterful dramatization. 100 min.
27-6914 Was $69.99 *$39.99*

To Be Young, Gifted And Black (1981)
The life and writings of noted author/poet Lorraine Hansberry, who won acclaim with her play "A Raisin in the Sun" and died at the age of 35 in 1965, are recounted in this mix of documentary footage and biographical drama. Ruby Dee, Blythe Danner star. 90 min.
27-7004 *$24.99*

The Cafeteria (1984)
Based on a short story by Isaac Bashevis Singer, this compelling character study is set in a New York eatery in the '60s and follows the unusual relationship that grows between a European-born writer and a fellow refugee, a woman who survived the horrors of the Holocaust. Bob Dishy, Zohra Lampert, Howard Da Silva star.
27-7227 *$19.99*

Nickel Mountain (1985)
Sensitive drama about a pregnant teenage girl who's abandoned by her college-bound boyfriend. Her employer offers to marry her, but complications arise when her lover returns. Michael Cole, Heather Langenkamp, Patrick Cassidy and Ed Lauter star. 88 min.
40-1069 Was $59.99 *$19.99*

The Man Who Broke 1000 Chains (1987)
Val Kilmer stars in the true, shocking story of a convicted felon and his capture 41 years after a hair-raising escape from a brutal Southern chain gang. Searing indictment of the penal system co-stars Sonia Braga, Charles Durning, Kyra Sedgwick. 113 min.
40-1361 Was $19.99 *$14.99*

Made In Heaven (1987)
Celestial lovers Timothy Hutton and Kelly McGillis are separated when she is sent back to Earth, so Hutton follows her back. Can the heavenly pair find each other amid four billion people? Divine romantic fantasy from director Alan Rudolph; with Maureen Stapleton, Ellen Barkin, and unusual cameos by Neil Young, Tom Petty and Debra Winger. 103 min.
40-1372 □*$14.99*

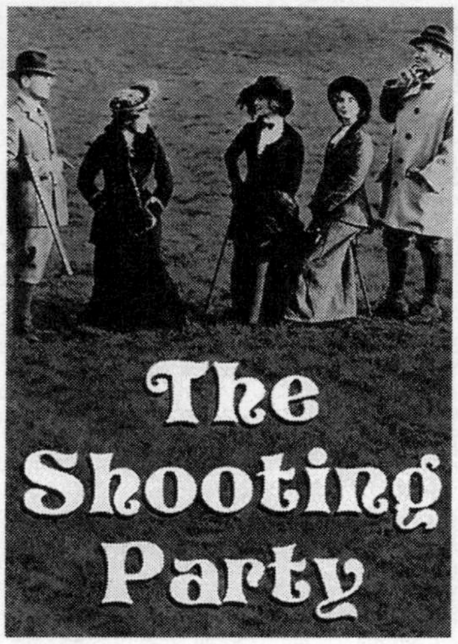
The Shooting Party

The Shooting Party (1984)
Fascinating serio-comic look at upper class life in Edwardian England, a world where those with money and influence were allowed to create their own morality. The superlative cast features Sir John Gielgud, Dorothy Tutin, Edward Fox and, in his last film, James Mason. 97 min.
44-1319 $29.99

Coward Of The County (1981)
A young pacifist in the 1940s South is branded a coward for refusing to join the Army, but when his girlfriend is raped he must choose whether or not to fight. Drama based on the hit song stars Kenny Rogers, Frederic Lehne, Ana Alicia. 100 min.
40-1138 Was $59.99 $19.99

The Beniker Gang (1984)
Great adventure tale of five young kids who make a break from their orphanage and carve themselves a new life on the run. Their survival hinges upon their pulling together as a team. With Andrew McCarthy, Danny Pintauro. 87 min.
40-1195 $14.99

American Anthem (1986)
A gifted young gymnast is torn between family responsibility and going for the gold. Stirring and riveting salute to the American spirit with Olympian Mitch Gaylord, Michelle Phillips; featuring a stellar rock score. 100 min.
40-1204 Was $19.99 $14.99

On Valentine's Day (1986)
A young woman in 1917 Texas goes against her parents' wishes by running away to marry, and her actions put a wall of silence between the family members in this emotional drama by writer Horton Foote. Hallie Foote (Horton's daughter), William Converse-Roberts and Matthew Broderick star. 106 min.
40-1237 Was $79.99 $14.99

Living Proof: The Hank Williams Jr. Story (1983)
Richard Thomas plays the title role in this song-filled biodrama depicting the country music great's early struggles, which included battles with alcoholism and a near-fatal accident, as Williams tried to cope with his father's legacy. Liane Langland, Lenora May, Clu Gulager also star; look quickly for Naomi Judd in a cameo. 97 min.
40-1262 Was $69.99 $19.99

Signal 7 (1983)
Two middle-aged San Francisco cab drivers are followed on their late night shift, an evening's drive that takes them to a play audition, encounters with the opposite sex, and the death of a fellow cabby. Acclaimed independent drama, with dialogue improvised by the actors, stars Bill Ackridge, Dan Leegant. 92 min.
40-1289 $79.99

The Lion Of Africa (1987)
A professional and romantic tug-of-war between a medical missionary and a tough diamond trader highlights this sprawling adventure, shot on location in Kenya. Stars Brooke Adams and Brian Dennehy. 110 min.
40-1360 Was $19.99 $14.99

The Long Good Friday (1982)
One of the most acclaimed gangster movies ever made, this hard-hitting British drama stars Bob Hoskins as a mob boss whose chance to go "legit" with an American-backed real estate deal is threatened by a series of violent attacks. Who is behind his associates' murders and the bombing of his clubs? With Helen Mirren, Eddie Constantine; look for Pierce Brosnan. 118 min.
44-1067 Was $19.99 $14.99

Shoot It: Black, Shoot It: Blue (1983)
Michael Moriarty is Rucker, an ultraconfident, ultraviolent, ultracist cop who guns down a black purse-snatcher in cold blood. Only when he learns of the incident's filming does he begin to sweat about the consequences. Paul Sorvino also stars. 93 min.
44-1107 Was $59.99 $14.99

Hearts Of Fire (1987)
A gritty backstage look at rock stardom, with Bob Dylan as an aging musician who takes a young would-be singer (Fiona) under his wing. Rupert Everett ("Another Country") and rock legends Richie Havens and Ron Wood also star. 95 min.
40-1379 Was $19.99 $14.99

Into The Homeland (1987)
An ex-cop searching for his missing daughter tracks her down to a right-wing paramilitary camp where she's being held against her will by her boyfriend's father, a white supremacist leader. Gripping drama stars Powers Boothe, C. Thomas Howell, Paul LeMat, Cindy Pickett. 116 min.
40-1391 Was $79.99 $19.99

End Of The Line (1988)
Two railroad men hijack a locomotive in an attempt to save their jobs and keep their small town alive in this acclaimed comedy/drama that tugs at the heartstrings. Wilford Brimley, Levon Helm, Holly Hunter, Mary Steenburgen and Kevin Bacon star. 104 min.
40-1395 $12.99

Heartland (1981)
Magnificently moving portrait of frontier life, drawn from the letters and books of Elinore Randall Stewart, stars Conchata Ferrell as a widow who moves to 1910s Wyoming with her young daughter and is befriended by gruff, reclusive farmer Rip Torn. Barry Primus, Megan Folsom also star. 96 min.
44-1022 Was $79.99 $24.99

Fake Out (1982)
The one, the only, Pia Zadora gives her all in this tale of a beautiful young nightclub singer who gets caught between her job and the police. Telly Savalas and Desi Arnaz, Jr. co-star in this exciting drama, and yes, Pia sings. 96 min.
44-1207 Was $19.99 $14.99

Cease Fire (1985)
Don Johnson stars in this emotional drama as an unemployed Vietnam vet unable to cope with his memories of the war, yet fighting to maintain his sanity and his family. With Lisa Blount, Robert F. Lyons. 97 min.
44-1365 $14.99

The Fortress (1985)
Rachel Ward stars as a schoolteacher who is abducted, terrorized and abandoned in the wild, along with her entire class. They quickly learn that their survival is in their own hands in this tense and terrifying story. 90 min.
44-1382 $14.99

Just Between Friends (1986)
The friendship of two women is put to the ultimate test when one has an affair with a man she doesn't know is the other's husband. Contemporary drama stars Mary Tyler Moore, Christine Lahti, Ted Danson and Sam Waterston. 110 min.
44-1425 Was $89.99 $14.99

All The Rivers Run (1987)
Sweeping saga set in 1800s Australia that follows the struggles of a determined woman (Sigrid Thornton) to fend for herself in a male-dominated culture and a hostile frontier that are both equally unforgiving. John Waters co-stars. 274 min.
44-1487 $79.99

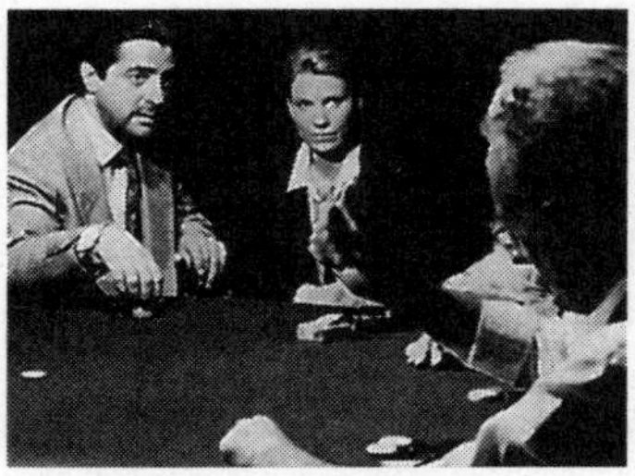

House Of Games (1987)
Striking film directorial debut for author David Mamet ("The Untouchables"), about a pop psychologist (Lindsay Crouse) who sets out to confront the charismatic con artist (Joe Mantegna) who fleeced one of her patients...and gets drawn into a web of deceit and death. J.T. Walsh, Ricky Jay co-star. 102 min.
44-1525 Was $19.99 $14.99

The Inquiry (1987)
Compelling speculative drama, set in the Roman Empire three years after Christ's crucifixion. An Imperial investigation into the claims of followers that Jesus rose from the dead leads to some surprising results. Keith Carradine, Harvey Keitel star. 110 min.
44-1567 Was $79.99 $19.99

Steal The Sky (1988)
Exciting espionage thriller, based on a true story, stars Mariel Hemingway as an American-born Israeli spy who seduces an Iraqi pilot in an attempt to hijack a Soviet fighter plane. Ben Cross ("Chariots of Fire") co-stars. 110 min.
44-1587 Was $89.99 $14.99

Dakota (1988)
Lou Diamond Phillips is John Dakota, an angry teen on the run from his past and himself. Finding work on a small family ranch in Texas, he finds an outlet for his youthful passion by aiding a disabled boy and falling in love with the boy's sister. 96 min.
44-1591 Was $19.99 $14.99

The Karate Kid (1984)
An old Oriental martial arts master teaches a high school kid how to defend himself against local bullies. Ralph Macchio and Pat Morita star in this delightful and inspiring tale from director John Avildsen ("Rocky"). Co-stars Martin Kove and Elisabeth Shue. 126 min.
02-1423 Was $19.99 $14.99

The Karate Kid Part II (1986)
Smash hit sequel continues the adventures of Daniel (Ralph Macchio) and his Oriental mentor Miyagi (Pat Morita), as the duo journey to Japan and each must face a challenge of honor. Warm, funny and touching, this is an enjoyable family drama that's on a par with its predecessor. 113 min.
02-1679 Was $19.99 $14.99

The Karate Kid Part III (1989)
In the rousing finale of the underdog saga starring Ralph Macchio and Noriyuki "Pat" Morita, an unprincipled karate instructor (Thomas Ian Griffith) undermines the friendship of Mr. Miyagi and Daniel and lures the Kid into a deadly, rigged match. 111 min.
02-1973 Was $19.99 $14.99

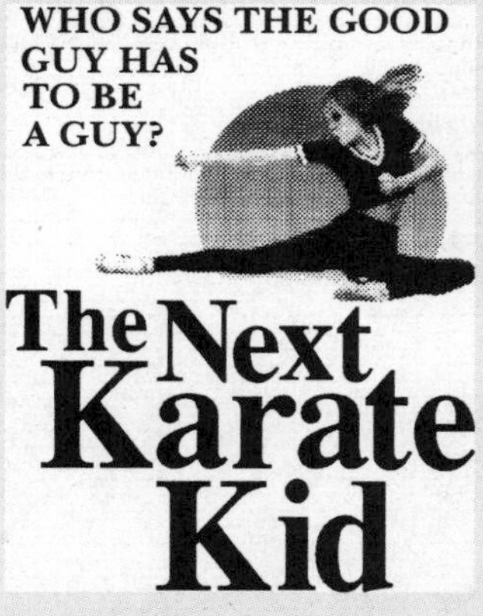
WHO SAYS THE GOOD GUY HAS TO BE A GUY?
The Next Karate Kid

The Next Karate Kid (1994)
Mr. Miyagi's back and this time he has a new student, a pretty teenager named Julie, troubled by her parents' death and at school by a gang of tough guys. When Julie's grandmother goes on vacation, Miyagi cares for her and soon teaches her how to use karate to solve some of her problems. Pat Morita, Hilary Swank and Michael Ironside star. 107 min.
02-2726 Was $19.99 $14.99

Sophia Loren: Her Own Story (1980)
The beautiful Sophia plays both her own mother and herself as an adult in this acclaimed biodrama that follows Loren's life from her impoverished childhood in war-torn Italy to her rise as an international screen sex symbol. Armand Assante, John Gavin, Rip Torn and Theresa Saldana also star. 145 min.
44-1006 $14.99

The Boost (1988)
A searing drama about the destructive fall that follows the high of drugs, starring James Woods as an aggressive L.A. real estate agent who turns to cocaine for a "boost" when business falters and Sean Young as his wife, who joins the addicted slide from Hollywood Hills to rock bottom. 95 min.
44-1635 $14.99

Combat Shock (1986)
A troubled, drug-addicted Vietnam vet, haunted by flashbacks of the war, is driven to the breaking point on the crime-filled streets of New York. Ricky Giovinazzo stars in filmmaker brother Buddy's violent and sordid tale of urban alienation and a man on the edge of sanity.
46-5290 Was $79.99 $14.99

A Killing Affair (1985)
Bizarre drama set in 1940s Appalachia, with Peter Weller as a stranger who kills a man he says murdered his family and is taken in by the man's widow. Will she be his next victim, or will he be hers? With Kathy Baker, John Glover. 100 min.
46-5407 Was $19.99 $14.99

A Bunny's Tale (1985)
Kirstie Alley plays Gloria Steinem in this drama based on the feminist author's 1963 undercover stint as a bunny at New York's newly-opened Playboy Club in order to write an investigative magazine article. Delta Burke, Joanna Kerns, Mary Woronov also star. 97 min.
46-5548 Was $59.99 $12.99

Liar's Moon (1981)
Matt Dillon is a local boy who woos and weds the town's wealthiest young lady, only to be trapped in family intrigue. With Cindy Fisher, Christopher Connelly, Broderick Crawford and Yvonne De-Carlo. 106 min.
47-1111 $14.99

Suburbia (1984)
An intense look at teenage alienation, as a gang of runaways and punk misfits called the T.R.s (Total Rejects) moves into an abandoned house and faces violent opposition from those around them. Directed by Penelope Spheeris ("The Decline of Western Civilization"); with Chris Pederson, Jennifer Clay. 99 min.
47-1288 $14.99

Saigon: Year Of The Cat (1985)
Director Stephen Frears ("Dangerous Liaisons") and writer David Hare ("Plenty") create a vivid drama set in the final days before the fall of Saigon in 1975, with Frederic Forrest as an American official trying to convince his superiors of an imminent invasion. With E.G. Marshall, Judi Dench, Wallace Shawn. 106 min.
44-1676 Was $89.99 $14.99

My Left Foot (1989)
The acclaimed true story of Christy Brown, an Irish artist and writer who refused to let the cerebral palsy that crippled him since birth make him a prisoner of his own body. Daniel Day-Lewis earned an Academy Award as Brown, as did co-star Brenda Fricker. With Ray McAnally, Hugh O'Connor. 103 min.
44-1726 Was $19.99 $14.99

The Image (1989)
Albert Finney turns in a dynamic performance as a leading TV newsman whose investigation of a bank scandal drives a wrongly accused executive to suicide and forces him to make important decisions about his life and career. The other side of "Broadcast News," co-starring John Mahoney, Kathy Baker and Marsha Mason. 91 min.
44-1732 Was $89.99 $19.99

Malarek (1989)
Years ago he escaped the city streets and became a top-flight reporter, but an investigation into conditions at a youth detention center hits close to home, and drives him to get at the truth. Gripping drama, based on a true story, stars Elias Koteas, Al Waxman, Michael Sarrazin. 105 min.
45-5477 $14.99

An Unremarkable Life (1989)
Patricia Neal and Shelley Winters play spinster sisters who must make difficult decisions about their lives when one falls for a charming widower. A bittersweet drama in the tradition of "On Golden Pond." Mako co-stars. 97 min.
45-5487 $14.99

The Bengali Night (1988)
Compelling romantic drama set in Calcutta, where British engineer Hugh Grant falls in love with the beautiful 16-year-old daughter of his employer. Their forbidden love causes all sorts of complex problems for them both, as well as the girl's family. With Suprya Pathak and John Hurt. 119 min.
45-8084 $79.99

The Manions Of America (1981)
Epic drama, created by daytime TV guru Agnes Nixon, traces 40 years in the lives of an Irish immigrant family and how their passions and dreams are fulfilled in 19th-century America. Pierce Brosnan, Kate Mulgrew, David Soul, Linda Purl and Anthony Quayle star. 284 min.
46-5157 $12.99

The Christmas Wife (1988)
A warm and emotional drama, with Jason Robards as a lonely widower looking for company for Christmas Day and Julie Harris as the woman he meets at an "introduction agency" who joins him for a memorable holiday. 73 min.
44-1681 Was $79.99 $19.99

Shag: The Movie (1989)
In the summer of '63, four young women travel to South Carolina for one last time of fun in the sun and "shag" dancing before they go their separate ways. Fast-paced, nostalgic romp stars Phoebe Cates, Bridget Fonda, Annabeth Gish, Page Hannah, Scott Coffey and Tyrone Power, Jr. 96 min.
44-1687 Was $89.99 $14.99

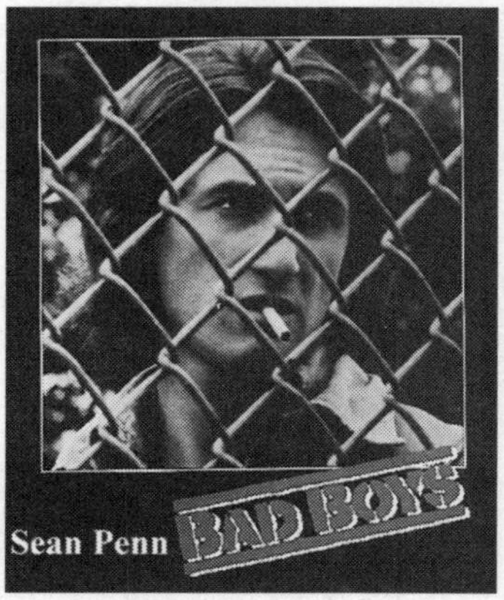
Sean Penn
BAD BOYS

Bad Boys (1983)
Sean Penn is dynamic as a juvenile delinquent sent to Chicago's toughest detention hall. He soon becomes his dorm's leader, but violence flares when a rival gang leader enters the facility. Gritty drama also stars Esai Morales, Ally Sheedy. 104 min.
44-1126 $14.99

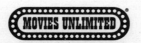

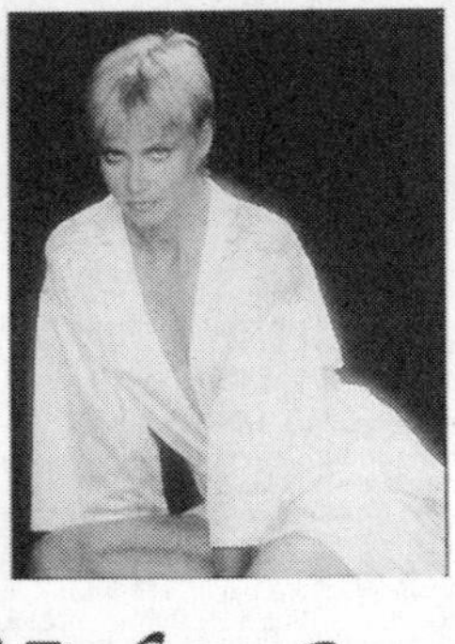

Night Games

Night Games (1980)
From Roger Vadim ("And God Created Woman") comes a sizzling erotic drama starring Cindy Pickett as a Beverly Hills housewife who attempts to get over a harrowing sexual experience in her past through a series of elaborate and kinky sensual encounters. Joanna Cassidy and Barry Primus also star in this psychological scorcher.
53-1084 *$29.99*

Blue Heaven (1987)
A happy couple, a perfect marriage, an ugly secret. A husband who truly loves his wife cannot control the rages inside of him which cause him to hurt her, even to the point where her life is threatened. Sensitive and honest portrayal of domestic violence stars James Eckhouse and Leslie Denniston. 103 min.
47-1546 *$69.99*

Queen Of The Road (1984)
After Rosy Costello inherits her father's 22-wheel tractor trailer, she quits her teaching job and heads out on the highway, tackling repossessors and the Mob. Joanne Samuel stars. 96 min.
47-1554 *$69.99*

At Close Range (1986)
Powerful drama about two brothers in a small Pennsylvania town whose father, a shiftless hood, comes back after many years. The boys emulate their dad's violent, crooked ways, but soon realize the danger they're in. Christopher Walken, and Sean and Christopher Penn star. 115 min.
47-1648 Was $19.99 *$14.99*

Guilty Conscience (1985)
A talented but philandering attorney schemes to kill his greedy wife, but a dangerous battle of wits ensues when she devises her own plans for eliminating him. Expert psychological drama stars Anthony Hopkins, Swoosie Kurtz and Blythe Danner. 100 min.
55-1402 Was $19.99 *$14.99*

Anatomy Of An Illness (1984)
A story of courage and triumph over adversity, starring Ed Asner as a man who, after being diagnosed with a degenerative spinal illness, refuses to accept his fate. Through his healthy sense of humor and the love and support of his wife, he is able to endure in ways that no one could have imagined. With Lelia Goldoni and Eli Wallach. 100 min.
55-3001 *$19.99*

Born To Be Sold (1981)
Lynda Carter stars as a well-meaning social worker who begins to suspect that an adoption agency has more to hide than it seems. After someone makes an attempt on her life, she realizes that she is on the right track, and races to prevent more "black market babies" from being sold. With Harold Gould and Dean Stockwell. 100 min.
55-3006 *$19.99*

An Innocent Love (1982)
This intimate and touching romantic drama centers around a 14-year-old math genius who goes to college and falls for the older volleyball player he tutors. With Melissa Sue Anderson, Doug McKeon, Rocky Bauer. 100 min.
55-3021 *$19.99*

Hellfire (1984)
A rightist TV evangelist wages war against all whose lifestyles and views differ from his. What follows is a compelling meeting with God, through which the preacher learns about true Christian spirit. Fascinating fantasy-drama stars David Rasche. 30 min.
50-6258 *$19.99*

Deadly Observation (1988)
A violence-prone patient in a mental hospital wins his release in a legal battle and commits a brutal murder, threatening the career of the psychiatrist who treated him. Kevin Conroy, Melissa Gilbert, Woody Harrelson and Lane Smith star. AKA: "Killer Instinct."
50-8443 *$14.99*

Paradise (1982)
A sensitive story of two teenagers who first experience sex in an isolated desert oasis. They discover each other...and so will you. Phoebe Cates, Willie Aames star. 96 min.
53-1032 Was $69.99 *$14.99*

Eddie And The Cruisers (1983)
They were a rock band on the verge of stardom in the '60s when the lead singer was killed in an auto accident...or was he? Popular, song-filled drama about the search for the truth about Eddie stars Michael Pare, Tom Berenger, Ellen Barkin. 110 min.
53-1122 ❑*$14.99*

The Trip To Bountiful (1985)
A masterful, Oscar-winning performance by Geraldine Page highlights this drama about an elderly woman who wants to escape her unhappy home life and return to her childhood home once more before she dies. Wistful, moving tale by Horton Foote also stars John Heard and Rebecca De Mornay. 106 min.
53-1587 ❑*$59.99*

The Old Forest (1985)
An acclaimed adaptation of Peter Taylor's story of life in the Depression-era South, as a Memphis man looks back on the car crash that occurred just before his wedding in 1937, and how it impacted on his life and those around him. 60 min.
50-2246 *$29.99*

In The King Of Prussia (1982)
Engrossing docudrama based on the trial of "Plowshares Eight," anti-nuclear protesters who tried to sabotage a factory in Pennsylvania that manufactured warhead nose cones. Martin Sheen and Father Daniel Berrigan star, directed by Emile de Antonio ("Millhouse"). 92 min.
50-6107 *$59.99*

Pulsebeat (1985)
Sparks fly when hard bodies, hot music, sizzling aerobics and romance combine at the most dazzling health club in America. Pumped-up drama stars Daniel Greene, Lee Taylor Allan and Peter Lupus. 92 min.
47-3110 *$69.99*

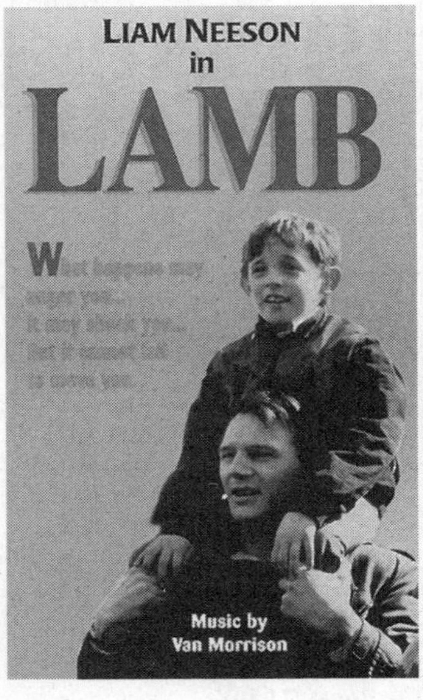

Lamb (1989)
Little-seen drama starring Liam Neeson as a teacher at a Catholic-run Irish institution for troubled boys. Neeson takes an interest in the school's most unruly pupil, a 10-year-old boy who is punished regularly by the school's headmaster. When Neeson's father dies, he takes the boy to London, where they both await their uncertain fate. With Hugh O'Connor; music by Van Morrison. 110 min.
75-1010 Was $39.99 *$14.99*

When Angels Fly (1982)
A young nurse starts work at an orthopedic rehab facility with an ulterior motive: to uncover the mystery surrounding her handicapped sister's death there. Robin Ward, Jennifer Dale star. 96 min.
48-1053 *$29.99*

American Dream (1981)
Heartfelt, very human drama about a family that moves from the upper-class suburbs to an inner-city Chicago neighborhood, facing troubles with neighbors and peers. Stephen Macht, Karen Carlson and Hans Conried star. 74 min.
48-1055 *$29.99*

To Race The Wind (1980)
Based on the autobiography of blind law student Harold Krents, whose story inspired the hit film "Butterflies Are Free." Steve Guttenberg plays the free-spirited, girl-chasing Krents as he attempts to achieve normalcy in a sighted world. 104 min.
48-1057 *$39.99*

Uptown Angel (1989)
She's an angel, all right! A beautiful black woman with a gorgeous face, street smarts and a body that didn't quit. But she was stuck in the toughest part of the city and willing to do anything...ANYTHING!...to get out. This sexy, realistic thriller stars Caron Tate, Cliff McMullen and Gloria Davis Hill. 90 min.
54-9016 *$19.99*

Slow Moves (1984)
Jon Jost's intriguing story of two wanderers who meet on the Golden Gate Bridge, become lovers, and start travelling the country committing hold-ups for support. Roxanne Rogers, Marshall Gaddis star. 93 min.
53-9078 *$69.99*

All The Vermeers In New York (1992)
Acclaimed comedy of manners from independent filmmaker Jon Jost tells the story of a Wall Street stockbroker who thinks he's found the answer to his stressed-out life when he falls in love with a French actress at the Metropolitan Museum of Art. Soon, he discovers there's more to her romantic interests than he suspected. Stephen Lack, Emanuelle Chaulet star. 87 min.
70-3194 Letterboxed *$24.99*

Sure Fire (1993)
Maverick independent filmmaker Jon Jost wrote and directed this stunning drama about Wes, an egocentric entrepreneur who has become rich wheeling and dealing in real estate while those around him suffer economically and emotionally. During a hunting trip with his son, he realizes he has lost his perspective on life, and reacts violently. Tom Blair, Kristi Hager star. 86 min.
70-3289 Was $89.99 *$24.99*

The Bed You Sleep In (1993)
Gripping melodrama about a couple who receive a letter from their college-bound daughter accusing the father of shocking sexual abuse. As the terrible rumors echo throughout their small Oregon lumber town, they find that their lives are slowly falling apart. Tom Blair, Ellen McLaughlin, Kathryn Sannella star; written and directed by Jon Jost. 117 min.
22-9002 Letterboxed *$29.99*

A Rose For Emily (1982)
William Faulkner's short story about a Southern belle driven mad by isolation and her ties to the past receives an excellent treatment, featuring Anjelica Huston in the title role. John Houseman narrates. 27 min.
50-2179 *$29.99*

A Winter Tan (1988)
Based on the outrageous sexual memoirs of author Maryse Holder that were published after her murder as "Give Sorrow Words," this compelling and frank Canadian drama stars Jackie Burroughs (who also scripted and co-directed) as Holder, a New York teacher whose Mexican vacation turned into an erotic odyssey as she sought out younger men to seduce and new pleasures to experience. With Erando Gonzales, Anita Olanick. 90 min.
53-6059 *$24.99*

Riders (1988)
From British novelist Jilly Cooper comes this passionate epic set against the backdrop of equestrian riding. Two childhood rivals—aristocratic Rupert Cambell-Black and half-Gypsy Jake Lovell—find themselves competing against each other as they get older for showjumping glory and the love of Rupert's wife. 210 min.
53-6343 *$29.99*

Vigil (1984)
From Vincent Ward ("The Navigator") comes this beautifully filmed drama set on a New Zealand sheep farm where the wife and daughter of a rancher toil following his death. Also living on the farm are a senile grandfather and a hunter who stays on to help out and is drawn to the mother, much to the daughter's dismay. Penelope Stewart, Frank Whitten, Fiona Kay star. 90 min.
53-8581 *$19.99*

Coming Through (1985)
The life and art of D.H. Lawrence is examined in this powerful two-part film starring Kenneth Branagh as Lawrence. In the first part of the drama, a biography is offered of the author's fascinating life and early days in a British village. The second tale involves a young man who uses Lawrence's words to seduce a college student. With Helen Mirren, Alison Steadman. 80 min.
53-9511 *$39.99*

The Country Diary Of An Edwardian Lady (1988)
A sumptuous filming of Edith Holden's best-selling book essays the author's life, telling of her birth in 1877, her girlhood, her adventures in Scotland and London, her teaching, and her marriage at the age of 39, and her eventual, tragic death. Pippa Guard stars. 90 min.
53-9512 *$29.99*

Sweet Perfection (1989)
When a promoter organizes a "perfect model contest," he gets more than he bargained for...in terms of trouble and in terms of beautiful black models. This is a sizzling, soulful story starring Stoney Jackson of TV's "227," Tatiana Tumbtzen and basketball star Reggie Theus. AKA: "Perfect Model." 90 min.
54-9014 *$19.99*

Mark, I Love You (1980)
Heart-wrenching drama that concerns a widowed man so distraught over the loss of his wife that he hands over custody of his son to his in-laws. However, they refuse to give him back his son when he recovers, resulting in an emotional court battle. Stars Kevin Dobson, Justin Dana, Cassie Yates and James Whitmore. 96 min.
55-3026 *$19.99*

Great Sadness Of Zohara (1983)
Stirring effort by Nina Menkes tells the tale of a young Jewish woman spurred to take a journey that requires her venturing into Arab territories...even at the risk of condemnation by the Orthodox community of Israel. 40 min.
53-9035 *$39.99*

Angel City (1980)
Unflinching account of West Virginia migrant laborers working under deplorable conditions in a Florida labor camp. Paul Winfield, Ralph Waite, Mitchell Ryan and Jennifer Jason Leigh star in this ultra-realistic drama about the human spirit succeeding against all odds. 96 min.
54-9026 *$12.99*

Solomon Northrup's Odyssey: Half Slave, Half Free, Part 1 (1984)
A freeborn black fiddler and carpenter is kidnapped and sold into slavery for 14 years and learns how to survive against horrible conditions. Avery Brooks, Petronia Paley and John Saxon star in this powerful true account of racial injustice. 113 min.
54-9032 *$24.99*

Charlotte Forten's Mission: Half Slave, Half Free, Part 2 (1985)
Compelling true-life look at the 21-year-old black woman who taught freed slaves during the Civil War on a Southern island. Melba Moore, Mary Alice, Ned Beatty and Moses Gunn star. 120 min.
54-9033 *$24.99*

Children Of The Night (1985)
The dramatic true story of student Lois Lee, whose research into the homeless children and young prostitutes of Hollywood leads her to open a halfway house and into a confrontation with a ruthless pimp. Karen Quinlan and Mario Van Peebles star. 100 min.
55-1390 Was $19.99 *$14.99*

Family Sins (1987)
Disturbing drama of a family torn apart by a "sibling rivalry" pushed too far stars Jill Eikenberry ("L.A. Law"), James Farentino, Mimi Kuzyk, Brent Spiner. 93 min.
63-1349 *$79.99*

Jesse (1988)
Powerful true story of Jesse Maloney, a caring nurse who is put on trial for practicing medicine without a license after acting as a physician in a small California community that lacks a town doctor. Stars Lee Remick, Scott Wilson and Albert Salmi. 94 min.
63-1460 ❑*$79.99*

When The Time Comes (1987)
In this powerful story, Bonnie Bedelia plays a 34-year-old woman who discovers she has cancer. When her husband refuses to accept her condition, she ponders suicide and enlists the help of a close friend. Brad Davis, Terry O'Quinn and Karen Austin also star. 94 min.
63-1480 ❑*$79.99*

Preacherman (1983)
This guy's a smooth-talkin', law-breakin' pastor disaster. Preacherman uses his gift of gab to get rich while manipulating the masses and bedding down an array of farmers' daughters. Will he ever see the light? Not if there's another family to rip off or another young woman to seduce. Amos Huxley and Ilene Kirsten star. 90 min.
58-1073 *$14.99*

Between Two Brothers (1982)
A successful lawyer attempts to come to terms with his brother, who runs the family business and feels guilty for their father's death. Michael Brandon, Pat Harrington and Helen Shaver star in this strong drama. 104 min.
58-8128 *$12.99*

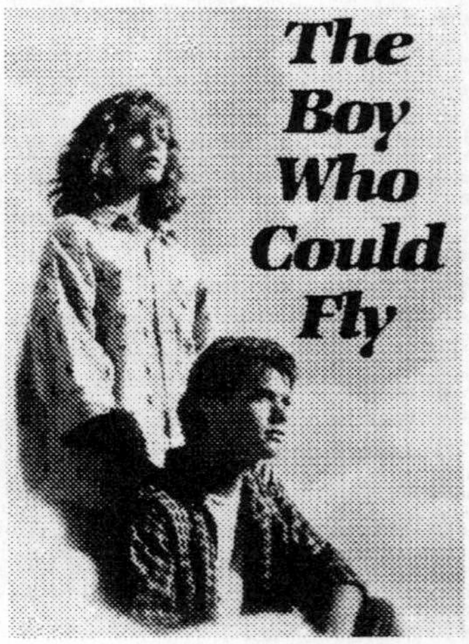

The Boy Who Could Fly (1986)
A teenage girl finds herself mysteriously drawn to an autistic boy who chooses not to speak. As she tries to bring him out of his silence, a love develops between them and an amazing secret is shared. Poignant family drama stars Jay Underwood, Lucy Deakins, Bonnie Bedelia and Fred Savage. 116 min.
40-1259 ❑*$14.99*

MOVIES UNLIMITED

Strike Force (1975)
In one of his first screen roles, Richard Gere stars in a "French Connection"-like thriller, as a New York detective, a state trooper and a federal agent team up to bust a narcotics ring. With Joe Spinell, Cliff Gorman. AKA: "Crack." 74 min.
78-1182 *$14.99*

Looking For Mr. Goodbar (1977)
Diane Keaton stars as the sexually adventurous teacher who escapes the disharmony in her personal life by retreating into the sordid and vacuous world of New York City's singles bars. Director Richard Brooks adapted the screenplay from Judith Rossner's best-seller. Co-stars Richard Gere, Tuesday Weld, William Atherton and Tom Berenger. 135 min.
06-1036 Was $39.99 *$14.99*

Days Of Heaven (1978)
Considered to be one of the most beautifully photographed films ever made, this majestic film focuses on the relationships among Texas farmworkers during the early part of the 20th century. Richard Gere, Brooke Adams, Sam Shepard and Linda Manz are the principals enhanced by Nestor Alemandros and Haskell Wexler's acclaimed cinematography; directed by Terrence Malick. 95 min.
06-1010 ❑*$14.99*

Days Of Heaven (Letterboxed Version)
Also available in a theatrical, widescreen format.
06-2706 ❑*$14.99*

Bloodbrothers (1978)
A searing drama about the adventures of an Italian family in a tough New York neighborhood. Explosive cast includes Richard Gere and Tony LoBianco. 116 min.
19-1066 *$19.99*

Yanks (1979)
Richard Gere heads the cast of this compelling drama about American GIs stationed in England during WWII and their involvement with British women from small towns. William Devane, Vanessa Redgrave, Lisa Eichhorn and Rachel Roberts also star in this sprawling story directed by John Schlesinger. 139 min.
07-1708 Was $79.99 ❑*$14.99*

American Gigolo (1980)
Is giving pleasure a crime? Not to Beverly Hills Casanova Richard Gere, who lives a life of luxury as he services wealthy women...until he finds himself the prime suspect in a murder case. Paul Schrader's steamy drama also stars Lauren Hutton, Hector Elizondo. 117 min.
06-1001 ❑*$14.99*

AN OFFICER AND A GENTLEMAN

An Officer And A Gentleman (1982)
This romantic blockbuster will "lift you up where you belong." The story of a loner who desires to be a Navy pilot, his trials in a rigorous training session with a tough drill instructor, and his love affair with a local girl. Richard Gere, Debra Winger, Louis Gossett, Jr. 126 min.
06-1156 *$14.99*

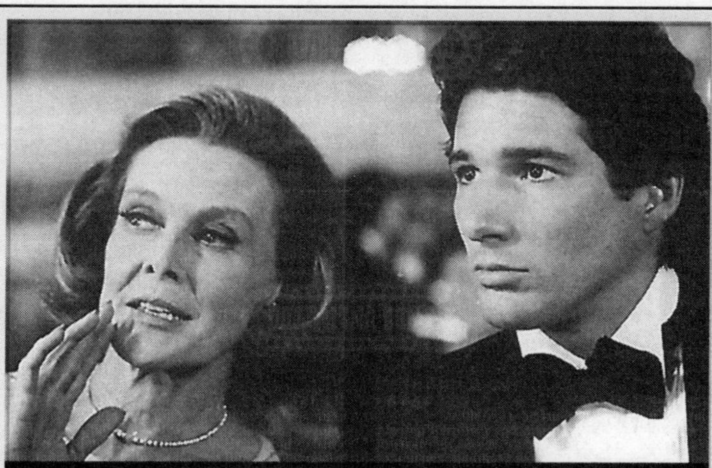
American Gigolo

Richard Gere

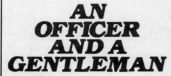

Beyond The Limit (1983)
Film version of Graham Greene's novel, "The Honorary Consul." Richard Gere is a doctor involved with ambassador Michael Caine in a dangerous love triangle in South America. Bob Hoskins. 103 min.
06-1201 Was $59.99 *$19.99*

Breathless (1983)
In this Americanized updating of the 1958 French thriller, Richard Gere stars as a small-time hood who gets deeper and deeper into a violent crime spree and gorgeous Valerie Kaprisky as a foreign student who joins hot-rodding Gere on the run from the law. With Art Metrano, John P. Ryan. 100 min.
73-1165 ❑*$14.99*

King David (1985)
Richard Gere is the King of Israel in this lavish, visually stunning historical adventure from director Bruce Beresford. See David's boyhood as a shepherd, the slaying of Goliath, his rise to power and all-consuming love for Bathsheba. 114 min.
06-1284 Was $79.99 ❑*$14.99*

No Mercy (1986)
Blazing actioner stars Richard Gere as a Chicago cop gone AWOL to the Louisiana Bayou to seek revenge upon the Cajun crimelord (Jeroen Krabbe) who had his partner killed. Kim Basinger is sultry as the kingpin's mistress. 105 min.
02-1759 Was $19.99 *$14.99*

Power (1986)
Richard Gere is the brash young political consultant who can get it for you...for a price. Director Sidney Lumet takes a dramatic look at the high-stakes world of D.C. wheeling and dealing, where the greatest passion is Power. Gene Hackman, Julie Christie, Denzel Washington and Kate Capshaw co-star. 111 min.
40-1130 Was $19.99 ❑*$14.99*

Miles From Home (1988)
Taut and topical drama starring Richard Gere and Kevin Anderson as two rural brothers who'd sooner destroy the family farm than lose it to foreclosure...and gain nationwide notoriety for their fugitive escapades. Standout supporting performances by John Malkovich, Brian Dennehy, Judith Ivey and Helen Hunt. 108 min.
19-1690 Was $19.99 ❑*$14.99*

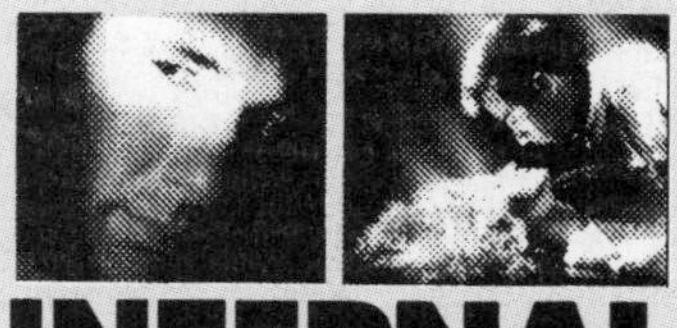

INTERNAL AFFAIRS

Internal Affairs (1990)
Richard Gere and Andy Garcia star in this cop thriller that really packs a wallop. An investigator in the L.A.P.D.'s Internal Affairs division trails a respected officer, only to find he's involved with drugs and a money-laundering operation. With Nancy Travis and Laurie Metcalf. 117 min.
06-1738 Was $19.99 ❑*$14.99*

Final Analysis (1992)
Steamy thriller about a psychiatrist (Richard Gere) who falls for the sister of one of his clients, a gorgeous but neurotic woman (Kim Basinger) unhappily married to a mobster. After the hood turns up dead, Gere helps to clear Basinger of a murder rap, but is he really a pawn in an intricate, deadly game? Uma Thurman and Eric Roberts also star. 125 min.
19-1979 Was $19.99 ❑*$14.99*

Mr. Jones (1994)
Richard Gere plays a free-spirited manic-depressive who attempts to jump off a high rise construction site and is taken to a mental hospital. He begins therapy sessions with beautiful but troubled psychiatrist Lena Olin, and the two eventually become romantically involved. Anne Bancroft also stars in this drama spiked with romance and dark comedy. 114 min.
02-2578 Was $19.99 ❑*$14.99*

Intersection (1994)
Successful architect Richard Gere faces a dilemma when he must choose between frigid, no-nonsense wife Sharon Stone and his mistress, a fiery redhead journalist played by Lolita Davidovich. After struggling over his decision, he's put on the spot when he faces a crucial moment in his life. Based on the French film "Les Choses de la Vie." 98 min.
06-2232 Was $19.99 ❑*$14.99*

Primal Fear (1996)
In this arresting thriller, Richard Gere is a slick Chicago attorney defending a shy, stuttering altar boy accused of killing a prominent Catholic leader. While he faces off in court against opposing lawyer and former lover Laura Linney, Gere unravels the unsettling mystery tied to his client and the case. With Edward Norton, Andre Braugher, Frances McDormand. 130 min.
06-2513 Was $99.99 ❑*$14.99*

Red Corner (1997)
For American attorney Richard Gere, a business trip to Beijing takes a terrifying turn when a woman is found murdered in his hotel room. Accused of killing her, Gere must endure the harsh brutalities of the Chinese legal system, without any aid from his own government, before he gets a chance to prove his innocence in this gripping drama. Bai Ling also stars as Gere's defense attorney. 122 min.
12-3229 Was $99.99 ❑*$19.99*

Red Corner (Letterboxed Version)
Also available in a theatrical, widescreen format.
12-3258 ❑*$19.99*

Autumn In New York (2000)
Old-fashioned romantic weepie stars Richard Gere as a womanizing, middle-aged restaurant owner who gets involved with Winona Ryder, a young designer he meets at his eatery. As the attraction grows stronger, Gere's fear of commitment grows apparent, but things get more complicated when Ryder discloses she has a disease that could be fatal. With Anthony LaPaglia, Elaine Stritch; directed by Joan Chen.
12-3334 Available 1/01 ❑*$99.99*

Please see our index for these other Richard Gere titles: *The Cotton Club • First Knight • The Jackal • Pretty Woman • Rhapsody In August • Runaway Bride • Sommersby*

Tales Of Ordinary Madness (1981)
Ben Gazzara stars as an alcoholic "beat" poet drawn from the writings of Charles Bukowski, whose life also inspired 1987's "Barfly." His descent into a harrowing and outrageous world makes for disturbing, often hilarious and compelling viewing. Ornella Muti and Susan Tyrrell co-star; directed by Marco Ferreri ("La Grande Bouffe"). 103 min.
47-1292 *$19.99*

Welcome Home (1989)
After being declared missing in action in Vietnam in 1970, Air Force pilot Kris Kristofferson is found living in Cambodia with a native family. Returning to America, he attempts to reconcile with his remarried wife and now-grown son. Sensitive drama also stars JoBeth Williams, Sam Waterston. 87 min.
47-2026 Was $89.99 *$14.99*

The Father Clements Story (1987)
A true story about a black Chicago priest who tries to adopt a difficult teenage boy after his parishioners show apathy over caring for the boy. Opposed by the Cardinal, the priest takes his request directly to the Vatican. Louis Gossett, Jr., Carroll O'Connor and Malcolm Jamal-Warner star. 98 min.
47-2107 Was $19.99 *$14.99*

The Far Pavilions (1983)
The complete version of one the most popular miniseries ever is a lavish epic set in British-ruled India in the late 19th century and stars Ben Cross as an English soldier in love with Indian princess Amy Irving, his childhood friend, who is engaged to another. With Rossano Brazzi, Omar Sharif, Christopher Lee. 320 min. on four tapes.
50-5190 Was $89.99 *$39.99*

And God Created Woman (1988)
Roger Vadim, director of the original erotic drama with Brigitte Bardot 30 years earlier, returns with one of today's sultriest stars, Rebecca De Mornay, as a would-be singer who uses her feminine wiles to get what she wants from men on her rise to the top. Steamy tale also stars Vincent Spano, Frank Langella. Uncensored version; 98 min.
47-1875 *$12.99*

Native Son (1987)
Depression-era Chicago: an embittered black man (Victor Love) finds employment as a servant to a wealthy white family. The patronizing attentions of the family's daughter (Elizabeth McGovern) sets the stage for tragedy. Great adaptation of Richard Wright's novel co-stars Matt Dillon and Oprah Winfrey. 112 min.
47-1770 Was $79.99 *$29.99*

Promised Land (1988)
For three high school friends, a Christmas homecoming in their small Idaho town becomes a bittersweet time that ultimately leads to a violent confrontation. Kiefer Sutherland, Jason Gedrick, Meg Ryan and Tracey Pollan star in this moving drama based on a true story. 110 min.
47-1871 Was $89.99 *$14.99*

Dance With A Stranger (1985)
Gripping true story of convicted murderer Ruth Ellis, the last woman hanged in Britain. Miranda Richardson stars as a nightclub hostess in late '40s London whose love affair with a smooth-talking, abusive upper class man is one of passion, jealousy and obsession. Rupert Everett and Ian Holm also star. 101 min.
47-1574 Was $59.99 ❑*$14.99*

Notes From A Lady At A Dinner Party (1980)
A powerful adaptation of Bernard Malamud's acclaimed story focuses on an affair between the wife of a renowned architect and her husband's partner that takes place during the course of a dinner party. Features members of Chicago's Goodman Theatre troupe. 25 min.
50-4449 *$29.99*

My Brother Tom (1986)
Set in a small town in Great Britain during World War II, this epic drama based on the best-selling novel by James Aldridge focuses on the effect the war has on the town and how the romance between two people of different faiths leads to conflict. Gordon Jackson, Keith Mitchell and Catherine McClements star. 200 min. on three tapes.
53-6372 *$59.99*

Reckless Disregard (1985)
An ambitious reporter (Leslie Nielsen) exhibits a "reckless disregard" of the truth in a reputation-destroying exposé on an innocent doctor. Tess Harper is the lawyer determined to clear her client and teach the accuser a lesson. 92 min.
47-1696 *$69.99*

Heat And Sunlight (1988)
An audacious American independent film from Rob Nilsson ("Northern Lights") that examines the final hours of a failing relationship. Nilsson plays a photojournalist desperately trying to understand why his dancer girlfriend has left him for another man. During the course of the film, he's visited by friends, visits a strip club and confronts his former lover. With Consuelo Faust and Ernie Fosselius. 98 min.
53-7437 *$29.99*

The Ballad Of Gregorio Cortez (1983)
Compelling true story of Gregorio Cortez, a Mexican who accidentally killed a Texas sheriff in self-defense in 1901. Hunted by Texans as a killer, hailed by Mexicans as a hero, Cortez was the target of a ferocious manhunt. Edward James Olmos, James Gammon, Bruce McGill star; directed by Robert Young ("Short Eyes"). 99 min.
53-1176 *$14.99*

The Far Country (1986)
Based on Nevil Shute's best-selling novel, this drama tells of a former Nazi officer, hoping to make a new life for himself in Australia, who falls in love with a beautiful doctor's daughter. Romance blossoms...until the young woman discovers there's more to her lover's past than she knows. Michael York, Sigrid Thornton and Don Barker star. 200 min.
53-6373 *$59.99*

Beyond The Doors (1989)
Jim Morrison, Janis Joplin, Jimi Hendrix...three of the biggest rock stars of the late '60s, their sudden deaths remain shrouded in controversy. This revealing docudrama depicts each performer's rise to fame and their final moments in an attempt to show that what are believed to have been suicides or accidental deaths were in fact murders. AKA: "Down on Us." 117 min.
48-1166 *$79.99*

The Heist (1989)
Released from jail for a crime he didn't commit, racetrack security expert Pierce Brosnan is ready to implement his plan for revenge on the man who framed him. Thrilling caper drama also stars Tom Skerritt, Wendy Hughes. 97 min.
44-1688 Was $19.99 ❑*$14.99*

True Believer (1988)
A Greenwich Village lawyer who once worked for the ACLU but has become a defender of rich dope dealers is the subject of another intense performance by James Woods. Roused from his cynicism by an idealistic colleague (Robert Downey, Jr.), Woods takes the case of an Asian accused in a gang slaying, attracting the ire of white racists and crooked pols. 100 min.
02-1943　　　　　　　　　　□$14.99

Stand By Me (1986)
Low-key sleeper hit, directed by Rob Reiner and based on a Stephen King story. Four young boys in 1959 Oregon set out on a camping trip in order to see a dead body one of them accidentally found. Along the way they take some hesitant steps on the road to maturity. River Phoenix, Corey Feldman, Wil Weaton star; Richard Dreyfuss is the narrator. 89 min.
02-1715　　　　　　　　　　□$14.99

Judgment In Berlin (1988)
Compelling drama based on a true incident. An East German man tries to escape to the West by hijacking an airliner to a U.S. Air Force base. Once arrested, American authorities set up a politically explosive trial. Martin Sheen, Sam Wanamaker, Heinz Hoenig star, with a special appearance by Sean Penn; Leo Penn (Sean's father) directs. 92 min.
02-1086　　　Was $29.99　　　$19.99

PIA ZADORA in HAROLD ROBBINS'
THE LONELY LADY

Jeff Bridges

The Yin And Yang Of Mr. Go (1971)
Bizarre James Bond-like action film that also spoofs many of the genre's conventions. James Mason is evil power broker Mr. Go, and only hero Jeff Bridges can stop his plans for global domination. With Broderick Crawford and Burgess Meredith (who also wrote and directed). 89 min.
64-3009　　　　　　　　　　　$14.99

In Search Of America (1971)
A college student returns home to convince his family to take a closer look at their lives and go on a trek across America to find themselves and their country. Jeff Bridges, Carl Betz, Vera Miles, Ruth McDevitt and Sal Mineo star. 72 min.
75-7046　　　　　　　　　　　$14.99

THE LAST PICTURE SHOW
PETER BOGDANOVICH

The Last Picture Show: Special Edition Director's Cut (1971)
Peter Bogdanovich's masterfully rendered, critically acclaimed drama follows the loves, dreams and fates of the denizens of a small Texas town in the early '50s. The stellar cast includes Jeff Bridges, Timothy Bottoms, Cloris Leachman, Cybill Shepherd and Ben Johnson. Nominated for eight Oscars, the film is based on the novel by Larry McMurtry. Special edition features a re-edited transfer and a 12-minute documentary. 126 min. total.
02-2069　　　Was $19.99　　　$14.99

Texasville (1990)
Director Peter Bogdanovich returns to Anarene, Texas, the site of his classic "The Last Picture Show," for a look at what the characters have been up to over the last 20 years. Original cast members Jeff Bridges, Timothy Bottoms, Cybill Shepherd, Cloris Leachman and Randy Quaid are on hand, along with Annie Potts. A feisty, bittersweet saga, adapted from Larry McMurtry's hit novel. 123 min.
53-1793　　　Was $19.99　　　□$14.99

Picture This: The Times Of Peter Bogdanovich In Archer City, Texas (1991)
This revealing documentary looks at director Peter Bogdanovich's return to Archer City, Texas, to film 1990's "Texasville," a sequel to his classic "The Last Picture Show." Bogdanovich, Cybill Shepherd, Jeff Bridges, Ben Johnson and Larry McMurtry are among those who recall their experiences filming the original and its follow-up.
76-7458　　　　　　　　　　　$19.99

Fat City (1972)
Director John Huston's downbeat boxing drama is an overlooked gem, as down-and-out fighter Stacy Keach tries to overcome alcoholism and get back into the ring with help from protégé Jeff Bridges. Susan Tyrrell, Candy Clark, Nicholas Colasanto. 100 min.
02-1814　　　　　　　　　　　$19.99

Bad Company (1972)
Terrifically entertaining tale of two mismatched young drifters (Jeff Bridges, Barry Brown) ducking in and out of trouble as they steal and connive their way across the Civil War-era West. An early gem from director Robert Benton ("Kramer vs. Kramer"). 93 min.
06-1371　　　　　　　　　　　$12.99

The Last American Hero (1973)
Jeff Bridges stars as Junior Jackson, a young backwoods moonshiner/stock car racer going up on his own against the Establishment. With Valerie Perrine, Gary Busey and Ned Beatty. AKA: "Hard Driver." 93 min.
04-1910　　　　　　　　　　　$59.99

Hearts Of The West (1975)
Hollywood, the 1930s: an aspiring writer (Jeff Bridges) in search of work gets corralled into a career as a B-movie cowboy. Funny look at the "Saturday Matinee" heroes also stars Andy Griffith, Alan Arkin and Blythe Danner. 102 min.
12-1699　　　　　　　　　　　$19.99

Rancho Deluxe (1975)
Hilarious, offbeat comedy about a pair of oddball cattle rustlers who attempt to pull off a big heist by stealing prime cattle from a wealthy landowner. Jeff Bridges and Sam Waterston are the wiseguys who find themselves battling a private detective, as well as the tycoon's wife and daughter. With Elizabeth Ashley, Slim Pickens, Harry Dean Stanton; music by Jimmy Buffett. 93 min.
12-2509　　　　　　　　　　　$14.99

Stay Hungry (1976)
Quirky seriocomedy stars Jeff Bridges as a spoiled Southerner who gets into a real estate deal that hinges on the sale of a bodybuilding gym, but has second thoughts after he gets to know the people who frequent the gym. Arnold Schwarzenegger, Sally Field and Robert Englund co-star in Bob Rafelson's perceptive film. 102 min.
12-2676　　　　　　　　　　　$14.99

Cutter's Way (1981)
An offbeat, emotionally walloping mystery about a crippled Vietnam vet and his two friends who become caught in a strange web of intrigue involving the head of a large corporation. Fine performances by John Heard, Jeff Bridges, Lisa Eichhorn. AKA: "Cutter and Bone." 105 min.
12-1220　　　　　　　　　　　$69.99

Against All Odds (1984)
Pro football star Jeff Bridges travels to Mexico to find Rachel Ward, the missing lover of bookie pal James Woods, but the two wind up falling in love and caught in a complex and deadly business scheme in this steamy thriller based on 1947's "Out of the Past." With Richard Widmark and Jane Greer (who starred in the original). 122 min.
10-2606　　　　　　　　　　　$14.99

Starman (1984)
John Carpenter's sci-fi romance stars Jeff Bridges as an alien who lands on Earth and assumes the form of a dead man, only to fall in love with "his" wife (Karen Allen). Together the two must elude the Army and government officials in order to return Bridges to his people. With Richard Jaeckel, Charles Martin Smith. 115 min.
10-2615　　　　　　　　　　　$14.99

Jagged Edge (1985)
Gripping mystery thriller stars Glenn Close as a lawyer defending client Jeff Bridges against a murder charge, only to realize after falling in love with him that he may actually be guilty...and she may be the next victim. Nerve-tingling drama also stars Robert Loggia, Peter Coyote. 108 min.
02-1570　　　　　　　　　　　□$14.99

Eight Million Ways To Die (1986)
Taut and terrific crime thriller stars Jeff Bridges as a boozing ex-cop out to avenge the murdered hooker he failed to safeguard. Unforgettable climactic shootout with diabolical drugrunners. Rosanna Arquette, Randy Brooks, Andy Garcia also star; co-scripted by Oliver Stone. 115 min.
04-1982　　　　　　　　　　　□$19.99

See You In The Morning (1989)
A realistic, dramatic look at today's splintered family situations, with newly-divorced Jeff Bridges and widowed Alice Krige marrying and facing problems ranging from their children's resentment to Bridges' ex-wife, well-played by Farrah Fawcett. Also stars Lukas Haas, Drew Barrymore, Frances Sternhagen. 115 min.
19-1717　　　Was $19.99　　　□$14.99

The Vanishing (1993)
In this reworking of the 1988 Dutch thriller, Kiefer Sutherland plays a young man obsessed with finding his girlfriend, who disappeared years earlier at a highway rest area. A mild-mannered chemistry teacher (Jeff Bridges) who claims to have kidnapped her may hold the answers, but learning them could cost Sutherland his life. With Nancy Travis, Sandra Bullock. 110 min.
04-2675　　　Was $19.99　　　□$14.99

Fearless (1993)
Peter Weir's compassionate drama stars Jeff Bridges as a survivor of a horrifying air crash who has emerged from the ordeal in an emotional shell and wanting to test the boundaries of his fearlessness. Feeling a need to help other people who have lived through terrifying experiences, he befriends a woman (Rosie Perez) who lost her baby in the same crash. Isabella Rossellini and John Turturro co-star. 122 min.
19-2208　　　Was $19.99　　　□$14.99

American Heart (1993)
Jeff Bridges turns in a powerhouse performance as an ex-convict experiencing trouble while trying to settle into everyday life in Seattle. He takes a job as a window washer and gets involved with a waitress while trying to relate to his teenage son (Edward Furlong), who's on the road to delinquency. Martin Bell ("Streetwise") directed this gritty drama. 114 min.
27-6845　　　Was $19.99　　　□$14.99

Blown Away (1994)
Boston police bomb squad member Jeff Bridges and former IRA munitions expert Tommy Lee Jones, two men connected by a secret in their past, are the players in a deadly cat-and-mouse game that puts Bridges' and his family's in danger in this (literally) explosive suspense drama. With Lloyd Bridges, Suzy Amis, Forest Whitaker. 120 min.
12-2969　　　Was $19.99　　　□$14.99

Wild Bill (1995)
The life and times of legendary frontier hero Wild Bill Hickok are brought to the screen with style and a sense of pathos by director Walter Hill. Jeff Bridges plays Hickok, who, during his last days, recalls his glory years as a gunslinger and his work with Buffalo Bill Cody in a theatrical revue. With Ellen Barkin as Calamity Jane, John Hurt, Diane Lane, Bruce Dern. 98 min.
12-3050　　　Was $99.99　　　□$14.99

Wild Bill (Letterboxed Version)
Also available in a theatrical, widescreen format.
12-3138　　　　　　　　　　　$14.99

White Squall (1996)
A true adventure set in 1960 about a group of troubled prep school students' Caribbean sailing journey that turns deadly when they face a rare turbulent storm known as a "white squall." After the survivors are rescued, captain Jeff Bridges goes on trial for his role in the doomed voyage. With John Savage, Caroline Goodall, Scott Wolf and Balthazar Getty; directed by Ridley Scott. 120 min.
11-2036　　　Was $19.99　　　□$14.99

Arlington Road (1999)
Intense thriller starring Jeff Bridges as a college professor living in Virginia with his young son and his girlfriend while trying to get over the death of his FBI agent wife. Bridges is befriended by strait-laced new neighbor Tim Robbins and his family, but soon suspects Robbins may be involved in terrorist activities. Joan Cusack and Hope Davis also star. 117 min.
02-3378　　　Was $99.99　　　□$14.99

LOVE　BETRAYAL　MONEY
NICK NOLTE
JEFF BRIDGES
SHARON STONE
SIMPATICO

Simpatico (1999)
In this powerful adaptation of Sam Shepard's play, Jeff Bridges is a millionaire whose success from breeding and training horses has brought him a Kentucky estate and beautiful wife Sharon Stone. Bridges' world is threatened when old friend Nick Nolte, who holds incriminating evidence on a past scam, seeks his help. With Albert Finney and Catherine Keener. 106 min.
02-5233　　　　　　　　　　　□$99.99

Please see our index for these other Jeff Bridges titles: *The Big Lebowski • The Fabulous Baker Boys • The Fisher King • Heaven's Gate • King Kong • Kiss Me Goodbye • The Mirror Has Two Faces • The Morning After • The Muse • Thunderbolt And Lightfoot • Tucker: The Man And His Dream*

The Lonely Lady (1983)
Pia Zadora stars as a sex-kitten out to prove to herself and her lovers that she can be a top Hollywood screenwriter. But the road to fame and fortune is rocky and includes double crosses, nude encounters, sleazy producers and other vile things. From the Harold Robbins book. 92 min.
07-1194　　　Was $59.99　　　$14.99

Gaby: A True Story (1987)
An inspiring drama in the manner of "The Miracle Worker," about a woman whose body, left practically useless due to cerebral palsy, couldn't contain her will to live and be accepted. Rachel Lewin is unforgettable as the silent Gaby, with Norma Aleandro as her devoted teacher and companion; with Liv Ullmann, Robert Loggia. 114 min.
02-1850　　　Was $79.99　　　$14.99

Coming Out Of The Ice (1982)
John Savage stars in the harrowing true story of Victor Herman, an American living in Russia in the '30s who was imprisoned and exiled for nearly 40 years on false espionage charges. Also stars Ben Cross, Willie Nelson. 97 min.
04-3132　　　　　　　　　　　$12.99

That Was Then... This Is Now (1985)
Turbulent teen drama based on S.E. Hinton's ("The Outsiders") novel stars Emilio Estevez and Craig Sheffer as two boys, raised as brothers since childhood, who find their lives drifting further and further apart. With Frank Howard, Jill Schoelen. 102 min.
06-1360　　　　　　　　　　　□$79.99

Blue City (1986)
Judd Nelson and Ally Sheedy star in this action-filled drama of a young man who returns to his hometown and searches for his father's killer. With Paul Winfield, Anita Morris. 83 min.
06-1396　　　Was $19.99　　　$14.99

Fire With Fire (1986)
Two young lovers, a repressed girl from a private school and a boy from a nearby reformatory, meet and fall in love, but soon find themselves on the run from the law when he escapes to be with her. Virginia Madsen, Craig Sheffer, Kate Reid star. 103 min.
06-1398　　　　　　　　　　　$79.99

Love With A Perfect Stranger (1986)
A beautiful American woman vacationing abroad discovers romance with a dashing Englishman. Should she throw everything away and stay with the man she loves or return to her burgeoning career? Stars Marilu Henner, Daniel Massey. 98 min.
06-1415　　　　　　　　　　　$19.99

The Last Song (1980)
Lynda Carter stars in this gripping drama as a woman whose husband is murdered by the owners of a chemical company when he learns of their responsibility for deaths caused by toxic wastes. With Ronny Cox, Nicholas Pryor. 96 min.
04-3170　　　　　　　　　　　$19.99

Call To Glory (1984)
The critics applauded this TV drama of a U.S. Army family at the dawn of the '60s, and here is the pilot film, set against the tension of the Cuban Missile Crisis. Craig T. Nelson, Keenan Wynn, Cindy Pickett, Elisabeth Shue star. 96 min.
06-1274　　　　　　　　　　　$14.99

Children Of A Lesser God (1986)
William Hurt stars as an unconventional teacher of the deaf who falls in love with a withdrawn school worker (Best Actress Oscar-winner Marlee Matlin) in this acclaimed drama based on the hit play. Hurt's attempts to teach Matlin lip-reading and his imposing of his ideas on her life threaten to tear the couple apart. Piper Laurie co-stars. 119 min.
06-1426　　　　　　　　　　　□$14.99

MOVIES UNLIMITED

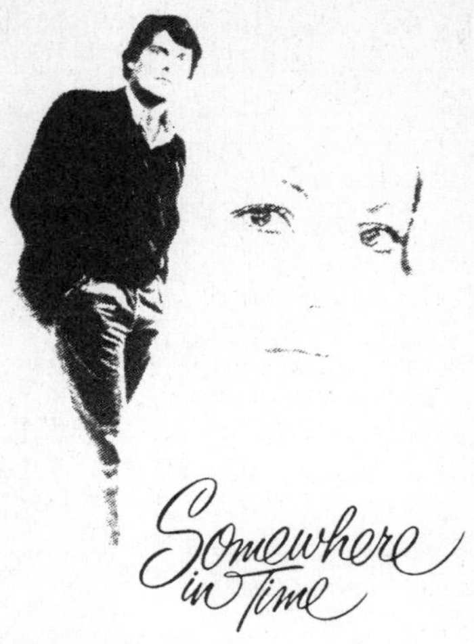

Somewhere In Time: Special Edition
Christopher Reeve stars in this lush romantic fantasy about a present-day artist, obsessed with a beautiful Victorian woman's portrait, who inexplicably finds himself transported back in time. Gorgeous scenery and Jane Seymour as the enigmatic lover make this Richard Matheson story sparkle. Also includes a documentary on the making of the film. 103 min.
07-2914 ❑*$19.99*

Thief Of Hearts (1984)
An erotic, fast-paced look at lust in the fast lane. After a burglar makes off with a married woman's secret diaries, he seduces her, using her own fantasies to become her "dream lover." Steven Bauer, Barbara Williams, John Getz, George Wendt star. 101 min.
06-1257 Was $79.99 ❑*$14.99*

Songwriter (1984)
Willie Nelson and Kris Kristofferson combine in this bittersweet drama of two country musicians who must deal with professional and personal problems, including a love affair with the same woman. Melinda Dillon, Lesley Ann Warren and Rip Torn co-star. Alan Rudolph directs. 94 min.
02-1424 *$14.99*

Crossroads (1986)
Warm-hearted drama, laced with elements of fantasy, stars Ralph Macchio as a spoiled young classical guitarist whose interest in blues music takes him on the road with an elderly sideman. Joe Seneca, Jami Gertz co-star; score by Ry Cooder. 96 min.
02-1633 ❑*$19.99*

Nijinsky (1980)
Lavish biodrama of the revolutionary and controversial 20th-century dancer, his affairs with women and men, and his slow descent into madness. Director Herbert Ross blends emotional drama and spectacular dancing sequences; George De La Pena, Alan Bates, Leslie Browne, Alan Badel. 125 min.
06-1635 Was $59.99 ❑*$14.99*

A Town Like Alice (1980)
The award-winning Australian drama, first seen on PBS, is a sweeping story that opens in WWII Malaya, where internees Bryan Brown and Helen Morse meet and fall in love in a Japanese POW settlement. Separated by their captors, the two are reunited years later on the rugged Australian frontier. With Yuki Shimoda, Gordon Jackson. 301 min.
08-8574 *$39.99*

A Town Like Alice
This fascinating look at Alice Springs, the place that inspired "A Town Like Alice," uses archival footage to tell the history of the small community in Australia's desert heartland that Neil Shute popularized. Discover what Alice Springs was really like when Jean Pagett, Joe Harmon and the book's other characters would have lived there. 60 min.
53-6378 *$19.99*

The Guyana Tragedy: The Story Of Jim Jones (1980)
Powers Boothe stars in his Emmy-winning role as the controversial cult figure who led over 900 followers to the South American jungles and, ultimately, to their deaths. Acclaimed drama also stars James Earl Jones, Ned Beatty and Brad Dourif. 192 min.
23-5021 Was $29.99 *$19.99*

Scruples (1980)
Judith Krantz's best-selling novel about the glitzy and seductive world of fashion is turned into a tale of temptation, ambition and treachery in this hit mini-series. Lindsay Wagner, Barry Bostwick, Kim Cattrall, Connie Stevens, Marie-France Pisier and Gene Tierney star. 278 min.
19-1969 ❑*$29.99*

A Man In Love (1987)
Diane Kurys' ("Entre Nous") first English-language film stars Peter Coyote as a married American film star who has a passionate affair with co-star Greta Scacchi while on location in Italy. Erotic tale of forbidden love and devotion also stars Jamie Lee Curtis, Claudia Cardinale. 110 min.
53-1725 *$14.99*

Aurora (1984)
Touching comedy-drama stars Sophia Loren as a single mother who, in order to obtain money for her son's eye operation, tracks down several former lovers and tells each that they're the boy's father. Daniel J. Travanti and Edoardo Ponti (Loren's real-life son) co-star. 91 min.
64-1377 *$14.99*

Tender Mercies (1983)
Robert Duvall won an Academy Award for his brilliant performance as a down-and-out country singer who is weaned off the bottle and finds happiness while staying with a widow and her young son. Director Bruce Beresford's poignant character study also stars Tess Harper, Wilford Brimley, Ellen Barkin, Betty Buckley. 88 min.
63-1672 Was $19.99 *$14.99*

Rockabye (1986)
When her 2-year-old son is abducted out of her arms on the streets of New York and the police are unable to help, single mother Valerie Bertinelli teams with a reporter investigating a black market child snatching ring in order to find the boy before it's too late. Gripping drama co-stars Rachel Ticotin, Jason Alexander; look for Jimmy Smits as a cop. 95 min.
64-1378 *$14.99*

Knee Dancing (1980)
A compelling, true-life drama about one woman's struggle to cope with the sexual abuse she suffered as a child. Writer/director Doreen Ross also plays the lead role in this acclaimed independent film. 97 min.
67-1003 *$19.99*

The Trial Of Bernhard Goetz (1988)
Based on actual court testimony, the headline-making trial of "subway vigilante" Goetz is re-created in this unique docudrama. Alan Feinstein, Andrew Robinson, and Peter Crombie as Goetz star. 175 min.
67-5022 *$29.99*

Vengeance (1986)
When his parents are brutally murdered during a robbery, a young man vows to get even and arranges for a hit man to fulfill his pledge. Taut drama stars Brad Davis, William Conrad, Brad Dourif. 90 min.
68-1144 *$79.99*

Romero (1989)
Raul Julia gives a stirring performance as Archbishop Oscar Romero, whose struggle for human rights in El Salvador led to his assassination in 1980, in this moving and timely biodrama. Richard Jordan also stars. 105 min.
68-1145 Was $29.99 *$12.99*

The Flight (1988)
Lindsay Wagner stars as German airline stewardess Uli Derickson, who courageously put her life on the line when Mideast terrorists hijacked a 1985 flight, in this gripping real-life drama. AKA: "The Taking of Flight 847." 96 min.
68-1151 *$79.99*

The Opponent (1989)
A blistering boxing saga about a young palooka who gets a shot at the big time when he rescues a seedy promoter's girlfriend. But he runs into a whirlwind of violence when he falls in love with her. Daniel Greene, Ernest Borgnine star. 102 min.
68-1152 *$89.99*

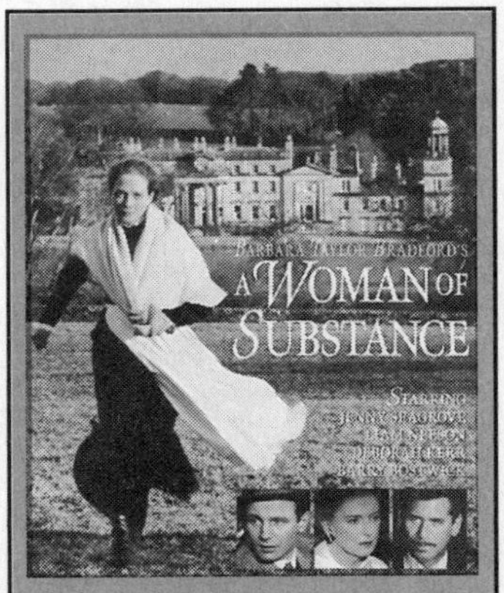

A Woman Of Substance (1984)
Barbara Taylor Bradford's sweeping best-seller of ambition, love and deception comes to life in this acclaimed mini-series. Jenny Seagrove stars as Emma Harte, an impoverished servant girl whose dreams of a better life lead her to become a successful businesswoman, but whose plans for retribution against those she feels wronged her could mean her downfall. With Deborah Kerr, Barry Bostwick, Liam Neeson. 313 min. on three tapes.
47-3128 *$39.99*

Hold The Dream (1986)
The dramatic sequel to "A Woman of Substance" continues the story of Emma Harte's struggle to maintain her business empire, and her desire to pass it along to her granddaughter. Jenny Seagrove, Stephen Collins, Liam Neeson, Deborah Kerr star. 200 min. on three tapes.
18-3037 *$39.99*

High Stakes (1989)
Thrilling, passionate drama stars Sally Kirkland and Robert Lupone as a call girl and a stockbroker who are thrown together by circumstances into a flight for their lives. 86 min.
68-1140 *$89.99*

Anna Karenina (1985)
Jacqueline Bisset and Christopher Reeve star in this lavish version of Tolstoy's classic of forbidden love in Czarist Russia. Reeve is the dashing count smitten with the beautiful Bisset, wife of dispassionate husband Paul Scofield. 96 min.
68-1160 Was $89.99 *$12.99*

Leo Tolstoy's Anna Karenina (1997)
A lavish treatment of Tolstoy's classic story from director Bernard Rose ("Immortal Beloved") stars Sophie Marceau as the 19th-century Russian wife of a wealthy, older man. Anna eventually falls in love with Count Vronsky, a dashing, younger man, but their romance leads to tragedy. With Sean Bean, Mia Kirshner and Alfred Molina. 108 min.
19-2582 Was $99.99 ❑*$19.99*

Noble House (1988)
The high-stakes world of international finance forms the backdrop for this dramatic TV mini-series based on the best-seller by James Clavell ("Shogun"). Pierce Brosnan stars as the head of a powerful Hong Kong trading firm who must deal with rivals out to bring his empire down...at any price. Deborah Raffin, John Rhys-Davies, Ben Masters, John Houseman also star. 355 min. on three tapes.
70-1380 *$39.99*

Coach Of The Year (1980)
Fine drama starring Robert Conrad as a former pro football player who returns home from Vietnam in a wheelchair. He attempts to put his life back together by serving as coach for his former team, but when they turn him down, he takes a job with a juvenile reformatory. Erin Gray, Red West co-star.
78-3013 *$14.99*

One For The Road
Cecil Moe, an alcoholic who sells his wife's car for $150 to pay off a bar tab and spends his last five dollars on booze instead of medicine for his kid, realizes he's hit rock bottom when his wife decides to leave him for good. With nowhere else to turn, he seeks salvation with the help of a preacher. Michael Madsen and Maureen McCarthy star. 90 min.
78-3029 *$14.99*

Thousand Pieces Of Gold (1989)
Powerful drama based on the true story of a young Chinese woman taken from her homeland and sent to a mining town on the American frontier, where she is forced to work in a bordello. Rosalind Chao, Dennis Dun, Chris Cooper star. 105 min.
80-1025 Was $89.99 *$14.99*

American Taboo (1982)
A shy photographer finds comfort in his work rather than in dealing with relationships. But his interest is sparked when a teenage girl moves in next door and becomes involved in his life. Jay Horenstein, Nicole Harrison star.
82-5172 *$79.99*

Sinners (1989)
Joey Travolta stars in this smashing mix of "Moonstruck" and "Death Wish." Romance is in the air in an Italian neighborhood in New York, but murder is, too, as an unfaithful husband discovers that some of his relatives carry shotguns and like to detonate cars. With Joe Palese and Sabrina Ferrand. 90 min.
86-1039 Was $29.99 *$14.99*

Resurrection (1980)
Compelling drama about a woman whose "clinical death" after a car crash leaves her with the power to cure injuries and disease with her touch. Before long, the gift becomes a curse. Ellen Burstyn shines as the unaffected "savior"; with Sam Shepard, Eva LeGallienne, Richard Farnsworth. 102 min.
07-1522 Was $59.99 *$14.99*

Kangaroo (1986)
Stirring Australian production based on D.H. Lawrence's autobiographical novel. A British author (Colin Friels) and his wife (Judy Davis) flee an unpopular political climate in Britain, only to become embroiled in violent class struggle down under. 105 min.
07-1532 *$79.99*

All My Sons (1986)
Early triumph for playwright Arthur Miller is given a stirring rendition in this production. A family's anguish over the mother's inability to accept the loss of one son to war and the dark secret in the father's past is brilliantly depicted by James Whitmore, Michael Learned, Aidan Quinn, Joan Allen. 122 min.
07-1533 *$39.99*

North Shore (1987)
A teenager from Arizona dreams of the Hawaiian surf and the thrill of riding the big waves and sets out in search of his goal, in this rousing drama that features breathtaking surfing footage. Matt Adler, Nia Peeples, Gregory Harrison star. 96 min.
07-1553 Was $79.99 *$14.99*

White Nights (1985)
We have a film, we have an awesome film. Mikhail Baryshnikov stars as a defected Soviet ballet star who is recaptured when his plane crashes in Russia. Eager to escape to the West, he plans a daring escape with an American dancer (Gregory Hines) living in Russia. Co-stars Jerzy Skolimowski, Helen Mirren. 135 min.
02-1592 Was $19.99 ❑*$14.99*

Isabel's Choice (1981)
After her boss decides to take an early retirement, a widowed executive secretary must decide which offer to accept: a new job opportunity or a marriage proposal. Jean Stapleton, Richard Kiley, Peter Coyote and Betsy Palmer star. 104 min.
58-8129 *$12.99*

Candy Mountain (1988)
A would-be recording star tries to ingratiate himself with a company exec by promising to locate a reclusive master guitar-maker. His search across the backwaters of America is the theme for a funny, insightful comedy/drama. Kevin J. O'Connor stars, with appearances from Tom Waits, Leon Redbone, Dr. John, David Johansen and Joe Strummer. 90 min.
63-1306 *$14.99*

Starlight Hotel (1988)
A young girl in 1930s New Zealand, searching for the father who left her to look for work, is joined on her cross-country journey by a man whose attempts to help poor families keep their homes and belongings has made him a fugitive from justice. Greer Robson, Peter Phelps star. 91 min.
63-1311 *$14.99*

Shame II: The Secret (1998)
Amanda Donohoe returns as former L.A. district attorney Diana Cadell, who here fights to save a mentally ill convicted murderer from execution. The crusade pits her against both the client's mother and the prosecuting attorney—who is Donohoe's lover. With Kay Lenz, Geoffrey Blake, David Andrews and George Wendt. 91 min.
06-2823 ❑*$69.99*

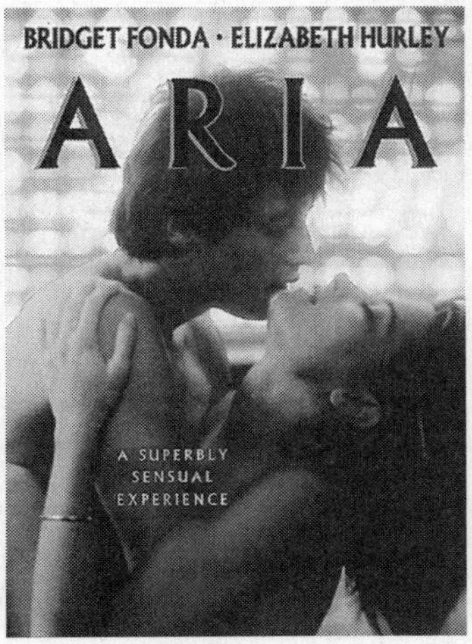

Aria (1988)
Ten top directors, including Nicolas Roeg, Jean-Luc Godard, Julien Temple, Bruce Beresford, Robert Altman, Ken Russell and Derek Jarman, offer up short films set to favorite operatic music by Verdi, Wagner, Puccini and other composers. The result is an eclectic, fascinating blend of sight and sound, with stories ranging from extramarital roundelays to a tale of doomed love in Las Vegas. Stars include John Hurt, Theresa Russell, Buck Henry, Beverly D'Angelo, Anita Morris and Bridget Fonda (her film debut). 90 min.
71-5129 *$14.99*

A Soldier's Tale (1988)
Penetrating and romantic WWII drama stars Gabriel Byrne as a British soldier stationed in France who falls for a beautiful woman (Marianne Basler) accused of being a collaborator. When an American G.I. (Judge Reinhold) with his own plans for the woman appears, Byrne is forced to make some difficult decisions. 96 min.
63-1509 *$14.99*

Eye On The Sparrow (1987)
Powerful and heart-warming true-life story starring Keith Carradine and Mare Winningham as a blind couple determined to start a family even though, under state law, they are deemed ineligible to adopt. Now, the pair must stage a brave fight against the bureaucracy. Conchata Ferrell co-stars. 94 min.
63-1511 ❑*$89.99*

Promised A Miracle (1988)
A powerful, true-life drama starring Judge Reinhold and Rosanna Arquette as a religious couple who chose faith over science in healing their diabetic son and faced manslaughter charges after his death. 94 min.
63-1582 ❑*$89.99*

Fulfillment (1989)
A woman happily married to a country farmer is driven by uncontrollable desires when her husband's handsome brother arrives at their residence. Cheryl Ladd, Ted Levine and Lewis Smith star in this passionate drama. AKA: "The Fulfillment of Mary Gray." 96 min.
63-1607 ❑*$89.99*

American Roulette (1988)
Andy Garcia is the head of a Latin American government-in-exile headquartered in London. While his country is caught in the grip of revolution, he faces death threats from both sides and can trust no one...not even the woman he loves. 102 min.
68-1111 *$12.99*

Tea And Sympathy (1956)
Controversial filming of Robert Anderson's drama, understating the play's homosexual theme, about the forbidden affair between a troubled schoolboy and a faculty member's wife. Deborah Kerr, John Kerr, Leif Erickson star under Vincente Minnelli's direction; look for Dean Jones and Tom Laughlin among the students. 122 min.
12-2097 □*$19.99*

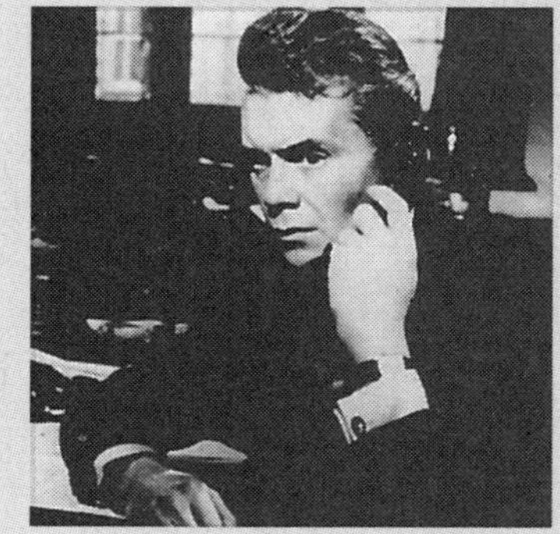

Victim (1961)
Dirk Bogarde stars as a married British lawyer whose latest case, involving a blackmail ring that targets homosexuals, threatens to reveal his own secret life. A landmark in the depiction of gays in cinema, Basil Dearden's drama also stars Dennis Price, Sylvia Sims. 100 min.
53-1672 Letterboxed *$29.99*

The Killing Of Sister George (1968)
Groundbreaking drama stars Beryl Reid as a popular British TV soap opera star whose life takes a downward turn when she loses her job and her younger lesbian lover. Coral Browne and Susannah York also star in this compelling film that features powerful performances and a no-holds-barred approach to the subject from director Robert Aldrich ("What Ever Happened to Baby Jane?"). 140 min.
04-1187 Letterboxed *$14.99*

Sticks And Stones (1970)
Excavated from obscurity, this extremely non-PC feature tells of a party at Fire Island given by Peter and Buddy for all of their gay friends. The guest list includes "leather queen" George; "The Lavender Queen," a babbling hippie; bike boy Fernando; and a pretty lesbian played by adult regular Kim Pope. Nudity, sex and squabbles galore can be found in this rare find. With Craig Dudley.
79-6494 Was $24.99 *$19.99*

Fortune And Men's Eyes (1971)
After being arrested for possession of marijuana, a young man finds life in a tough prison a harrowing experience. He must submit to an admirer who wants to protect him, or risk the chance of being raped. A gritty, no-holds-barred look at prison life, based on the controversial play by John Herbert. With Michael Greer, Wendell Burton and Zooey Hall. 102 min.
12-2493 *$19.99*

Pink Narcissus (1971)
A legendary erotic gay film detailing the surreal sexual fantasies of a young man, played by Bobby Kendall. He imagines himself as a Roman slave, a famous matador and as a harem boy involved in debauchery in a sheik's tent. Somewhere between an art film and an adult movie, this outing has been popular at film festivals over the years and was anonymously directed. 70 min.
53-9683 Was $39.99 *$19.99*

A Very Natural Thing (1973)
A breakthrough gay film focusing on a man in his twenties who leaves the priesthood to move to New York City in hopes of finding a good relationship. After getting a job as a teacher, he falls in love with a young advertising executive, and both men come to discover the passion that was missing from their lives. Robert Joel, Curt Gareth star. 85 min.
01-1512 *$39.99*

A Bigger Splash (1974)
One of the most acclaimed and controversial figures in 20th-century British art, painter David Hockney, stars as himself in this compelling mix of documentary and drama. Chronicling Hockney's break-up with lover Peter Schlesinger, the film offers a unique look at the '70s art scene and the final days of the "Swinging London" crowd. 105 min.
22-6035 Letterboxed *$29.99*

The Naked Civil Servant (1975)
John Hurt is masterful in the title role of this biography of Quentin Crisp, the British author and wit who was one of the first crusaders for gay rights. Based on Crisp's best-selling memoirs of one man's struggle to live his life as he chooses. 80 min.
44-1025 *$19.99*

Making Love (1982)
Compassionate, controversial account of a married couple who appear happily married—until the husband takes on a male lover. Kate Jackson, Michael Ontkean, Harry Hamlin. 113 min.
04-1468 Was $69.99 *$29.99*

Personal Best (1982)
Screenwriter Robert Towne's ("Chinatown") directorial debut sensitively explores the lesbian relationship between two athletes (Mariel Hemingway, Patrice Donnelly) training for the 1980 Olympics. Scott Glenn co-stars as their manipulative coach. 129 min.
19-1219 Was $69.99 *$14.99*

Abuse (1983)
From Arthur J. Bressan, Jr. ("Buddies") comes a shattering yet sensitive study of an abused 14-year-old boy who is befriended by a documentary filmmaker working on his thesis film. Their friendship leads to a love affair which makes both boy and man question their lives. Richard Ryder and Raphael Sbarge star in this controversial, acclaimed film. 93 min.
53-8531 Was $79.99 *$39.99*

An Early Frost (1985)
A family must cope with the sudden revelation that not only is their son a homosexual, but he is also suffering from AIDS. This powerful and emotional drama, with fine performances throughout from Aidan Quinn, Gena Rowlands and Ben Gazzara, won four Emmy Awards. 97 min.
02-1718 *$19.99*

Desert Hearts (1986)
The repressed wife of a teacher moves to Nevada for solitude and to consider divorce, but finds herself becoming attracted to her landlord's openly lesbian daughter. A moving and eye-opening drama set in the '50s, the film stars Helen Shaver, Patricia Charbonneau and Audra Lindley. 91 min.
47-1663 Was $29.99 *$14.99*

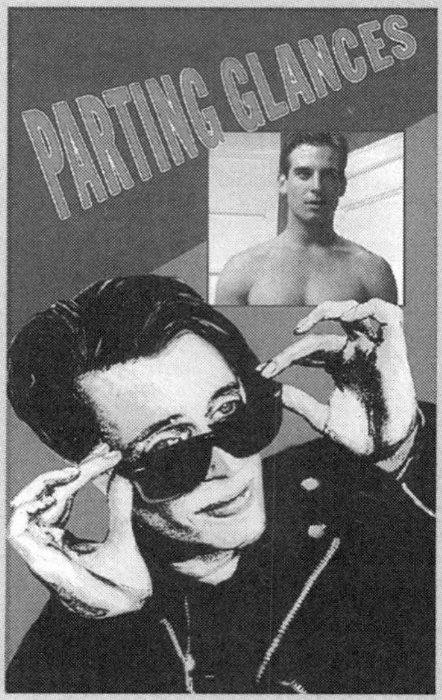

Parting Glances (1986)
A gay couple in New York, faced with an imminent separation, comes to grips with their disintegrating relationship in this acclaimed independent drama that features an honest and moving portrayal of '80s gay life. John Bolger, Richard Ganoung, Steve Buscemi star; written and directed by Bill Sherwood. 90 min.
70-5054 Was $59.99 *$29.99*

The Two Of Us (1987)
Compelling drama about Matthew, a handsome and athletic young man who believes he's gay, who manages to retain a friendship with Phil, a school friend. The relationship between the two becomes more intense, and they soon find themselves at odds with classmates and family over their sexual preferences. Jason Rush and Lee Whitlock star in this controversial drama. 60 min.
59-7038 *$79.99*

She Must Be Seeing Things (1987)
A thought-provoking lesbian love story exploring the dynamics of sexuality. The discovery of a diary makes a lawyer suspicious of her filmmaker lover. Directed by Sheila McLaughlin. 95 min.
70-5006 Was $59.99 *$29.99*

Prick Up Your Ears (1987)
Blackly funny biographical look at the relationship between Joe Orton (Gary Oldman), the homosexual British satirical playwright of the '60s, and Kenneth Halliwell (Alfred Molina), the failed actor who was his lover and, ultimately, his murderer. Vanessa Redgrave, Wallace Shawn co-star; Stephen Frears ("The Crying Game") directs. 111 min.
74-1018 *$14.99*

Maurice (1987)
Moving drama set in Edwardian England, where the love that develops between two Cambridge students earns them the scorn of those around them. E.M. Forster's long-suppressed novel of homosexual love becomes a superb film, with a brilliant cast that includes James Wilby, Hugh Grant, Rupert Graves, Denholm Elliott and Ben Kingsley. 135 min.
88-1110 *$14.99*

Fun Down There (1988)
A gay comedy in every sense of the word, this acclaimed independent film follows a young man from his quiet home in upstate New York to his first taste of Greenwich Village life, a life filled with a new job, romance, and an introduction to modern gay life. Funny and touching, with Michael Waite, Nickolas Nagurney. 89 min.
01-1459 Was $39.99 *$29.99*

Urinal (1988)
Inventively jolting look at gay life unites such dead homosexual artists as Sergei Eisenstein, Yukio Mishima, Langston Hughes and Frido Kahlo with two dead sculptors in a Toronto rest room, where they observe the arrest of men accused of soliciting sex. Each "ghost" then lectures on some aspect of what they have witnessed. 100 min.
01-1463 Was $39.99 *$29.99*

Zero Patience (1993)
At once campily outrageous and bitterly sardonic, writer/director John Greyson's "movie musical about AIDS" features 19th-century British explorer Sir Richard Burton, alive and well in modern-day Toronto, preparing a museum exhibit on AIDS and "Patient Zero," the Canadian airline worker alleged to have brought the virus to North America. Bathhouses become the setting for hilarious (and graphic) musical numbers dealing with gay life, love and loss in the '90s. John Robinson, Normand Fauteux star. 100 min.
53-8061 Was $79.99 *$39.99*

Clay Farmers/My First Suit (1988)
"Clay Farmers" focuses on a handsome drifter who takes a job on a California farm and forms a loving relationship with a farmhand. But when an abusive neighbor causes trouble after seeing the two men skinny-dipping, they learn the true meaning of intimacy. And in "My First Suit," a New Zealand teen's fitting for a suit leads to fantasies involving older, desirable men. 89 min. total.
78-5046 *$69.99*

Salut Victor (1989)
Set at a retirement home, this compassionate drama tells of a relationship between two older gay men. Fearful of his health problems, loner Philippe is helped out of his depression by Victor, a feisty man who recently lost his lover in a plane crash. This Canadian production was a film festival favorite. 83 min. In French with English subtitles.
78-9009 *$39.99*

Men In Love (1990)
An acclaimed, "New Age" gay drama detailing the sexual and emotional awakening of a young San Francisco man. After his lover dies of AIDS, Steven flies to Hawaii, where he becomes romantically involved with a native Hawaiian gardener who changes his outlook on life. Steaminess and sensitivity mix in this provocative odyssey starring Doug Self and Joe Tolbe. 87 min.
01-1460 Was $39.99 *$29.99*

Sacred Passion (1990)
A celebration of male love, this sequel to "Men in Love" depicts exotic rituals, sensual massage, rhythmic breathing and group intimacy. The lush paradise of Maui provides the setting for a journey where erotic man-to-man experiences come to life. With Gavin Geoffrey Dillard, Joe Tolbe. 60 min.
01-1462 Was $39.99 *$29.99*

No Skin Off My Ass (1990)
An engaging gay-oriented comedy from Canada about a hairdresser obsessed with a skinhead who has an eccentric lesbian sister. As he's pursued by the hairdresser, the skinhead takes advice from his sibling, who urges him to explore gay sex. G.B. Jones and Klaus Von Brucker star in this wild film by Bruce LaBruce which features explicit sex scenes. 85 min.
53-9597 *$49.99*

Super 8 1/2 (1995)
Bruce LaBruce ("No Skin Off My Ass") wrote, directed and stars in this wild satire in which he plays a former gay porn actor/helmer recounting the highlights and lowlights of his career for a documentary film. There's anecdotes from co-workers and former lovers, raw sex footage and clips from "I Am a Fugitive from a Gang Bang" and other efforts. 106 min.
53-9644 Was $39.99 *$19.99*

Hustler White (1997)
From the creators of "Super 8 1/2" comes this outrageous adult comedy featuring director Bruce LaBruce as a German journalist tracking down and falling in love with a male hustler named Montgomery Ward while working on a story on gay lifestyles. Using a no-holds-barred, often raunchy approach, this kinky film spoofs gay culture. With Tony Ward. 81 min.
78-9016 Was $59.99 *$19.99*

Hearing Voices (1990)
Provocative drama about a beautiful model involved in an abusive relationship who finds love and acceptance with a gay man who happens to be her doctor's lover. With Erika Nagy and Stephen Gatta. 87 min.
70-3279 *$79.99*

My Father Is Coming (1990)
Kinky sex farce from filmmaker Monika Treut ("Seduction: The Cruel Woman") about a frustrated German actress in New York City whose world is turned upside-down when her father decides to pay her a visit. She soon begins affairs with lesbians and transsexuals, while her father becomes involved with Annie Sprinkles, the former porno star. With Shelly Kastner, David Bronstein. 82 min.
70-5056 Was $19.99 *$14.99*

An Empty Bed (1990)
Powerful study of a gay man in his sixties looking back on his life and questioning the decisions he has made. Flashbacks depict his past relationships and explain why he couldn't commit himself to another man. John Wylie stars. 60 min.
70-5028 Was $59.99 *$29.99*

Poison (1991)
Controversial, audacious film trilogy from director Todd Haynes that's definitely for the open-minded. In "Hero," a woman recounts the murder of her husband by her young son. "Horror" is a modern-day monster movie in which a scientist drinks a strange chemical and turns into a leper sex killer, and "Homo" details a brutal homosexual romance between two convicts. James Lyons, Scott Renderer star. 85 min.
53-7656 Was $89.99 *$19.99*

Together Alone (1991)
Two men go home together and have unprotected sex, and then carry on an all-night discussion in which they reveal their inner secrets, question their attraction to men, recount college stories and discuss AIDS. Hailed as an honest and revealing look at gay relationships, this film from P.J. Castellaneta ("Relax...It's Just Sex") stars Terry Curry and Todd Stites. 85 min.
76-2056 Was $39.99 *$19.99*

Time Expired (1991)
After his release from prison, a man responsible for robbing over 1,000 parking meters finds himself in another predicament: should he choose to share his new life with his wife or with his former lover in jail, a flamboyant Hispanic transvestite? John Leguizamo, Edie Falco star in this offbeat farce. 30 min.
76-7116 *$14.99*

Smoke (1992)
An erotic, artistically filmed account of three days in the life of Michael, an alienated young man obsessed with relations with older men. As he wanders from one lover to the next, he seeks his former family priest and the father who left him during adolescence. Follow Michael at work as a men's room attendant, cruising parks and taking candle-lit baths. Mark D'Aruia directs. 90 min.
01-1485 Was $39.99 *$29.99*

The Lost Language Of Cranes (1992)
This searing drama, based on David Leavitt's acclaimed book, centers on a young man whose decision to "come out" and discuss his homosexuality candidly inspires his father to question his own sexuality. Corey Parker, Angus McFadyen, Brian Cox, Rene Auberjonois, John Schlesinger and Eileen Atkins star. 90 min.
04-2660 Was $89.99 *$19.99*

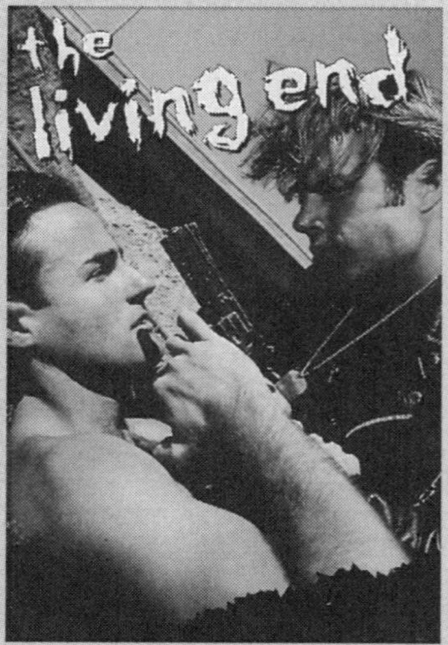

The Living End (1992)
Called "a queer 'Thelma & Louise'" by critics, this startling drama sets two HIV-positive homosexual men—one a sensitive writer, the other a strapping drifter—on an aimless road trip packed with thrills, danger and romance. Acclaimed for its starkness and politically incorrect attitude, Gregg Araki's powerful odyssey stars Craig Gilmore, Mike Dytri and Mary Woronov. 85 min.
71-5283 *$29.99*

Being At Home With Claude (1992)
A male prostitute murders his lover in brutal fashion. What prompted him to commit a disturbing act of extreme violence? The police interrogate the suspect and discover the motive in this intense Canadian drama starring Roy Dupuis and Jacques Godin. 86 min. In French with English subtitles.
71-5291 *$19.99*

Shades Of Black (1993)
A twentysomething female photographer in a small town begins a passionate affair with an older woman, an artist from New York, but her suspicions that her new lover is cheating on her lead to disturbing revelations in this chilling, gay-themed psychological drama. 115 min.
01-1539 *$39.99*

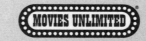

Rock Hudson's Home Movies (1993)
Intriguing look at the gay life and films of Rock Hudson, as narrated by Hudson "himself" from beyond the grave. By looking at clips from the actor's most popular films like "Pillow Talk" and tracing his career from contract player to legend, this biography reveals secrets of Hudson's life which may have been on the screen all along. Eric Farr stars; Mark Rappaport directs. 63 min.
01-1488　　Was $39.99　　　*$29.99*

My Summer Vacation (1993)
This funny and poignant story focuses on Joe, a man who suddenly finds himself alone during the "final summer of his youth." Joe takes to the streets with a movie camera in search of a replacement for his last boyfriend. He finds his perfect mate in Chris, but there's one problem: Chris is straight! With Caroline Gillis, Daniel MacIvor and Sky Gilbert, who also directed. 90 min.
01-1574　　　　　　　　　　　*$39.99*

Claire of the Moon

One woman's journey into her sexual identity.

Claire Of The Moon (1993)
A sensual lesbian drama focusing on a loving relationship that develops between a satirist and a psychologist who share a cabin—and their intimate desires—while attending a writer's conference in the Northwest. This provocative, adult film features nudity and mature themes. With Trisha Todd and Karen Trumbo. 102 min.
53-7802　　Was $89.99　　　*$29.99*

Moments: The Making Of "Claire Of The Moon" (1993)
An intimate look at what went on behind the scenes of "Claire of the Moon," the acclaimed lesbian drama. Included here are the main characters' first kiss, rehearsals, bloopers, steamy love scenes, the world premiere and more. 75 min.
76-2028　　Was $39.99　　　*$19.99*

March In April (1993)
Set against the background of a massive Washington, D.C., gay rights march, this provocative film mixes comedy and drama as it tells the stories of several of the participants, focusing on one man who debates coming out to his ill mother. Stephen Kinsella's acclaimed independent movie features cameos by Barney Frank, Keith Meinhold, Pat Schroeder and others. 60 min.
70-5075　　Was $29.99　　　*$19.99*

Salmonberries (1993)
In her acclaimed film debut, singer k.d. lang plays a young, androgynous Eskimo woman living in Alaska who falls in love with a librarian from East Berlin. Rosel Zech and Chuck Connors also star in this unusual romance, in which lang sings "Barefoot." Directed by Percy Adlon ("Bagdad Cafe"). 94 min.
76-2031　　Was $79.99　　　*$29.99*

The Boys Of Cellblock Q (1993)
An action-packed, seriocomic tale set in a corrupt correctional facility for boys, this outrageous adaptation of the hit play details the misadventures of a young convict assigned to the "Jock" farm, where he gets a lesson in prison etiquette and hierarchy. There's wild shower tussles, homoerotic fantasies and more, along with nudity and strong language. 85 min.
78-5041　　Was $39.99　　　*$29.99*

Apart From Hugh (1994)
A sensitive drama set in the Pacific Northwest centering on Collin and Hugh, two lovers celebrating their first year together. While Hugh has planned a party for the occasion, Collin has been having second thoughts about their relationship. 87 min.
01-1509　　　　　　　　　　　*$39.99*

Trevor (1994)
Winner of the Academy Award for Best Live-Action Short, this poignant story centers on Trevor, a 13-year-old boy struggling with his homosexuality. Trevor falls for Pinky, a classmate, but when his feelings are made public by other students, Trevor runs away from home and eventually considers suicide. With Brett Barksy and Jonah Rooney; introduction by Ellen DeGeneres. 23 min.
01-1549　　　　　　　　　　　*$14.99*

Serving In Silence: The Margarethe Cammermeyer Story (1994)
Emmy-winning true story of Col. Margarethe Cammermeyer, the Army nurse with over 20 years of service whose fight to remain in the service, after admitting she was a lesbian, threatened her career and family life and threw her into the national media spotlight. Glenn Close, Judy Davis, Jan Rubes star; Barbra Streisand produced. 92 min.
02-3283　　Was $99.99　　　⊡*$19.99*

I'll Love You Forever...Tonight (1994)
Acclaimed drama about gay Los Angeles residents focusing on Ethan, a photographer who joins his bartender lover on a vacation in Palm Springs where other gay acquaintances join them, including Ethan's former boyfriend. The volatile dynamics turn what was supposed to be a peaceful holiday into a series of cruel sexual interludes. Paul Marius and Jason Adams star. 80 min.
53-8169　　　　　　　　　　　*$39.99*

Grief (1994)
A stinging, funny, heartfelt look at the people behind the scenes of a tacky TV game show called "The Love Judge," including a man trying to overcome his lover's recent death from AIDS, a sexy secretary, an androgynous punker and a handsome gay writer. Alexis Arquette, Craig Chester, Illeana Douglas, Paul Bartel and Mary Woronov star. 87 min.
71-5313　　Was $59.99　　　*$19.99*

Thin Ice (1994)
Steffi, a pair skater in the Gay Games, has a big problem when her partner backs out of competition. After little success in finding a replacement, she meets Natalie, a supposedly straight woman. The two become close friends and partners and, eventually, lovers. Charlott Avery, Sabra Williams, James Dreyfuss and Ian McKellen star in this romantic comedy. 88 min.
76-2060　　Was $49.99　　　*$19.99*

Under Heat (1995)
Intense drama featuring Lee Grant, set during a family reunion in which mother Grant learns that her 36-year-old gay son has contracted AIDS. Following the revelation, Grant and other family members face their past and future fears. With Robert Knepper and Eric Swanson. 92 min.
50-8185　　Was $69.99　　　*$39.99*

Fanci's Persuasion (1995)
A hit at film festivals around the world, this innovative lesbian fairy tale is set in San Francisco, where Fanci is about to marry her gorgeous girlfriend, Loretta. A power outage occurs the night before the wedding, catapulting Fanci, friends and family into a bizarre dreamworld where anything can—and does—happen. 80 min.
01-1518　　　　　　　　　　　*$39.99*

Black Sheep Boy/ Decodings (1995)
This video features two highly acclaimed shorts, gay-themed films by filmmaker Michael Wallin. "Black Sheep Boy" is a lyrical examination of homosexuals' fascination with young men, while "Decodings" uses found footage from the 1940s and 1950s to explore director Wallin's fantasies and desires. 52 min.
01-1523　　　　　　　　　　　*$39.99*

Ladyboys (1995)
Two teenage boys living in rural Thailand leave their impoverished families and head to the bustling city of Pattaya, where they seek money and security as performers in the local transvestite cabarets. Their story, as well as their future gender-bending dancers', are followed in this frank and revealing drama. 52 min.
01-1526　　　　　　　　　　　*$39.99*

The Incredibly True Adventure Of 2 Girls In Love (1995)
Sensitive, funny and sensual comedy of a lesbian love affair involving two high school students. Randy, a defiant tomboy working at a gas station, shares a mutual attraction to Evie, an affluent African-American girl confused about her sexuality. Laurel Holloman and Nicole Parker star. 94 min.
02-5076　　Was $89.99　　　⊡*$19.99*

Derek Jarman

Sebastiane (1976)
Derek Jarman's controversial depiction of the life of St. Sebastian, one of the most enigmatic figures in the Catholic Church. Filled with homoerotic imagery, the film is a unique, often shocking attempt to interpret legend through aesthetics. With Neil Kennedy, Richard Warwick. 86 min. In Latin with English subtitles.
01-1391　　Was $79.99　　　*$39.99*

The Tempest (1979)
Shakespeare's comical fantasy of magic and vengeance on a remote island is transformed by filmmaker Derek Jarman into a colorful mix of gothic atmosphere, campy humor, elaborate musical numbers and the director's trademark gay imagery. Heathcote Williams, Karl Johnson, Peter Bull and Toyah Wilcox star. 95 min.
53-6414　　Was $79.99　　　*$24.99*

The Angelic Conversation (1985)
Fourteen sonnets by William Shakespeare are turned into a celebration of homoerotic love, courtesy of director Derek Jarman ("Sebastiane"). A series of dramatic, abstract vignettes featuring two onscreen actors depict the powerful passions and emotions in the Bard's works, as each sonnet is read by an unseen narrator. With Paul Reynolds, Philip Williamson, Judi Dench. 78 min.
70-7080　　　　　　　　　　　*$29.99*

Caravaggio (1986)
The life of Italian Renaissance painter Michelangelo Caravaggio is director Derek Jarman's springboard for a striking, quirky drama that blends 16th-century life with modern props, a traditional love story with a homosexual romance, and aristocratic corruption with artistic integrity. Nigel Terry, Tilda Swinton, Sean Bean star. 97 min.
53-7193　　　　　　　　　　　*$79.99*

The Last Of England (1987)
A subversive attack on repression, greed and environmental rape in the modern state from poet and director Derek Jarman ("Caravaggio") that combines feverish images of political violence, gay erotica and desecrated landscapes in a wrenching rock video style. With Tilda Swinton, Spencer Leigh. 87 min.
70-7050　　　　　　　　　　　*$29.99*

The Garden (1991)
Controversial director Derek Jarman's stunning examination of organized religion and its role in the oppression of homosexuals depicts the arrest and torture of two male lovers, conveying the irony between the teachings of the Gospels and the Church's history of oppression. Tilda Swinton, Johnny Mills and Kevin Collins star. 90 min.
53-7805　　Was $89.99　　　*$19.99*

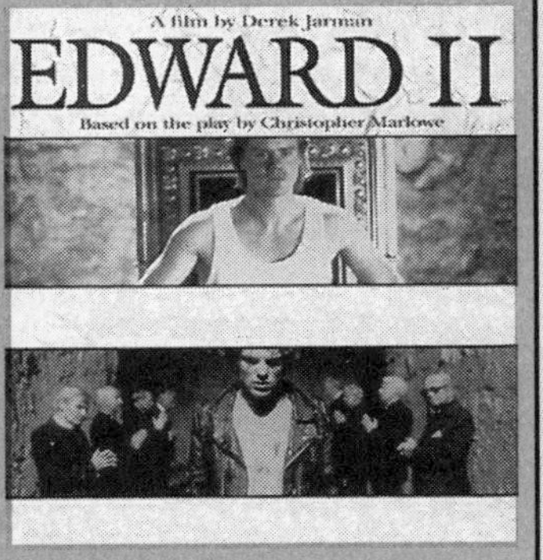

A film by Derek Jarman
EDWARD II
Based on the play by Christopher Marlowe

Edward II (1992)
Derek Jarman uses Christopher Marlowe's classic play about the 14th-century English monarch for this daring cinematic treatise on gay love and its place in the historic and modern world, focusing on Edward's stormy reign and his homosexual and heterosexual relationships, as well as his tragic end. With Steve Waddington, Kevin Collins and Tilda Swinton. 91 min.
02-2314　　　　　　　　　　　*$19.99*

Blue (1993)
A unique and haunting meditation on life and art, director Derek Jarman's final film before his death consists of a solid blue screen, music by Simon Fisher Turner, and readings from Jarman's journals in which he discusses his life, art and sexuality, as well as coming to terms with AIDS and his growing loss of sight. Narrated by John Quentin, Tilda Swinton, Nigel Terry and Jarman. 76 min.
53-8355　　　　　　　　　　　*$24.99*

Wittgenstein (1993)
Continuing his biodrama series on gay historical figures, Derek Jarman's visually stylized and campily funny look at the quirky, Austrian-born philosopher follows Ludwig Wittgenstein from his days as a child prodigy in the early 1900s to his life as a Cambridge don. Karl Johnson, Tilda Swinton, Michael Gough and Clancey Chassay star. 75 min.
53-8356　　Was $79.99　　　*$24.99*

Please see our index for the Derek Jarman title: *War Requiem*

Heaven's A Drag (1995)
When Mark, his quick-witted drag performer lover dies of AIDS, TV repairman Simon enters the world of London's gay swingers. But Simon soon finds his one-night stands disrupted by the ghostly appearance of Mark, who decides not to enter Heaven until Simon comes to terms with his grief and his love. Thomas Arklie and Ian Williams star in this darkly humorous tale. 96 min.
70-5090　　Was $59.99　　　*$29.99*

Bar Girls (1995)
A Los Angeles lesbian bar is at the center of the action in a refreshingly honest look at alternative relationships in the 1990s. Cartoonist Loretta meets Rachael, an unhappily married actress, at the Girl Bar, but soon finds that their developing relationship is complicated by jealousy, ex-lovers and other bar patrons. Nancy Allison Wolfe, Liza D'Agostino star. 95 min.
73-1221　　Was $19.99　　　⊡*$14.99*

Jeffrey (1995)
Paul Rudnick scripted this screen adaptation of his hit off-Broadway comedy that takes a sardonically funny look at gay love in the age of AIDS. Steven Weber stars as Jeffrey, a New Yorker whose vow of celibacy is put to the test when he meets the man of his dreams—who turns out to be HIV-positive. Great cast includes Michael T. Weiss, Patrick Stewart, Bryan Batt, Nathan Lane. 92 min.
73-1232　　Was $89.99　　　⊡*$14.99*

Lie Down With Dogs (1995)
A young gay man looking for a change of pace from his hectic New York lifestyle seeks new adventures on the beaches of Provincetown, Massachusetts. There, he encounters mysterious employers, a Latin ne'er-do-well and a man who could be his "Mr. Right." Wally White, Randy Brecker, Darren Dryden and James Sexton star in this frothy comedy. 84 min.
11-1963　　　　　　　　　　　⊡*$19.99*

No Ordinary Love (1995)
Lively sex romp focusing on the relationships of a group of people living in a large house. Included are a punk rock singer, a Cambodian cross-dresser, a bisexual erotic dancer, a homophobic young man who may, in fact, be gay and a bank teller with cash secretly stashed in the house's basement. Smith Forté, Erika Klein and Robert Pecora star. 104 min.
50-8184　　Was $69.99　　　*$39.99*

Devotion (1995)
Funny, critically acclaimed account of a 35-year-old lesbian comedian who gets a chance to star in a TV sitcom, but runs into trouble when she discovers that the show's producer is a now-married former friend she once tried to seduce. After ignoring her career and the producer, she decides to handle the situation in a most unusual way. Jan Derbyshire and Kate Twa star. 123 min.
76-2047　　　　　　　　　　　*$69.99*

Go Fish (1995)
Acclaimed, honest and funny comedy about a lesbian professor who attempts to play matchmaker for her young slacker roommate and a shy, older woman. As these two opposites attract, the teacher and her other friends examine their own lives and their sexuality. With Guinevere Turner, V.S. Brodie and Wendy McMillan. 83 min.
88-1024　　Was $19.99　　　⊡*$14.99*

The Art Of Cruising Men (1995)
One of England's best-selling videotapes, this amusing and extremely sexy offering studies the incredible lengths men will go to meet other men. Follow the route from first eye contact to orgasm, from prehistoric times through the forbidden worlds of bathrooms and the clubs and bars of the 1990s. Explicit nudity is featured. 70 min.
01-1517　　Was $39.99　　　*$29.99*

Man Of The Year (1995)
Fascinating mock documentary scripted and directed by star Dirk Shafer, Playgirl Magazine's 1992 Man of the Year. You'll see the events that occur during his reign as the magazine's top macho model and learn about his real, homosexual life in this poignant and funny film. With Vivian Paxton and Claudette Sutherland. 74 min.
53-8580　　Was $19.99　　　*$14.99*

The Midwife's Tale (1995)
Acclaimed lesbian fable set in medieval times. When Lady Eleanor, a noblewoman, discovers she's pregnant, she receives help from a beautiful, mysterious midwife, and the women begin a loving relationship. But the midwife is soon accused of witchcraft and Lady Eleanor's husband banishes her to the tower. Stacey Havener, Gayle Cohen star. 34 min.
73-9210　　　　　　　　　　　*$59.99*

M.U.F.F. Match (1995)
What starts out as a field hockey match between two teams of English schoolgirls (all played by adults) turns into a wild and slapstick series of sexual encounters in this lesbian comedy that's one part Sappho and one part Benny Hill. 50 min.
05-1535 *$39.99*

Madagascar Skin (1995)
Can a straight man and a gay man find love and happiness together? This question is answered in a delightful story about two misfits, a shy gay man and a shady heterosexual, who are drawn to each other because of their differences. John Hannah and Bernard Hill star. 97 min.
53-8986 *$79.99*

Raising Heroes (1996)
Called "the first openly gay action-adventure story," this independent film follows a successful gay couple whose plans to adopt a child hit a snag when one man witnesses a mob killing. Can the couple protect themselves from hit men out to silence them and still make the adoption hearing? Henry White, Troy Sistillio star. 85 min.
01-1531 *$39.99*

Never Met Picasso (1996)
A comically quirky look at Gay Bohemia with Alexis Arquette as a troubled artist working on an avant-garde theater production with actress mother Margot Kidder. Things may change for Arquette after he befriends student Don McKellar at the play's opening night party. Meanwhile, Kidder makes close friends with her son's lesbian sculptor pal, played by comic Georgia Ringsdale. 97 min.
01-1566 *$39.99*

Beautiful Thing (1996)
Set in a working-class London neighborhood, this frank and sensitive drama follows a teenager coming to terms with his attraction to a male classmate who lives next door, a situation that gets more complicated when the neighbor moves in with the boy and his mother in order to avoid his abusive father. Glenn Berry, Scott Neal, Linda Henry star. 90 min.
02-3056 Was $99.99 *$19.99*

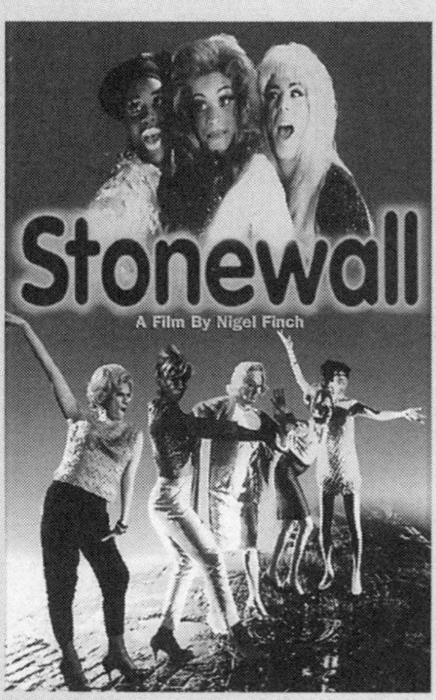

Stonewall (1996)
The 1969 riots over police harassment at a Greenwich Village homosexual bar that sparked the gay rights movement in America form the backdrop for this moving and vibrant drama that looks at the diversity of the nascent gay subculture, from the conservative suit-and-tie members of the Mattachine Society to flamboyant drag queens. With Guillermo Diaz, Frederick Weller. 99 min.
02-8652 Was $19.99 *$14.99*

Oranges Are Not The Only Fruit (1996)
Award-winning British drama about a 16-year-old girl, the product of a strict religious upbringing, who feels romantic stirrings towards another girl. Her evangelist mother tries to force her to turn away from her "sin," which leads to bitter conflict. Geraldine McEwan, Charlotte Coleman star. 165 min.
04-3466 *$29.99*

World And Time Enough (1996)
The struggle to maintain a monogamous relationship by a garbageman trying to locate his natural parents and his lover, an HIV-positive artist, is the focus of this funny, insightful and life-affirming tale from writer/director Eric Mueller. Matt Guidry, Gregory G. Giles, Kraig Swartz star. 92 min.
53-9740 Was $39.99 *$19.99*

johns (1996)
David Arquette and Lukas Haas portray L.A. street hustlers with big dreams—to spend his birthday in a posh hotel and to leave California for a Branson, Missouri, theme park, respectively—in this critically acclaimed indie drama, the debut feature from writer/director Scott Silver. Elliott Gould, Alanna Ubach, Arliss Howard and Keith David also star. 96 min.
53-6246 Was $89.99 *$19.99*

Skin Deep (1996)
Lesbian filmmaker Alex is joined by her assistant-lover Montana in making a movie about tattooing and body art. In order to learn about the subject, Alex hooks up with Chris, an androgynous young woman, who serves as a tour guide into this unusual world and with whom Alex evetnually bedcomes romantically involved. Natsuko Ohama, Keram Malicki-Sanchez also star. 82 min.
01-1560 *$39.99*

It's My Party (1996)
Eric Roberts is a man expected to die of an AIDS-related illness in the next few days who decides to throw an all-day party for his family and friends, including his former lover, before taking his own life. Darkly humorous film from director Randal Kleiser ("Grease") also stars Lee Grant, Gregory Harrison, Marlee Matlin, Olivia Newton-John, George Segal. 109 min.
12-3098 Was $19.99 *$14.99*

It's My Party (Letterboxed Version)
Also available in a theatrical, widescreen format.
12-3237 *$14.99*

L'Escorte (1996)
A penetrating study of contemporary gay relationships from Canada's Denis Langlois looks at long-term lovers Jean-Marc and Philipe, who face struggling times with the restaurant they own. A wild party joke brings Steve, a hunky escort, to their household, and both men try to win over their new guest. Eric Cabana stars. 91 min. In French with English subtitles.
53-8984 *$79.99*

Frisk (1996)
Based on the controversial Dennis Cooper novel, this acclaimed independent film explores, in graphic detail, the sadomasochistic relationship between two gay lovers and how one man's increasing attraction to violent pornographic images puts their relationship at risk. Michael Gunther, Craig Chester, Alexis Arquette and Parker Posey star. 84 min.
53-9739 Was $59.99 *$19.99*

Girlfriends (1996)
Lesbian life and love in the '90s are the focus of the four short films featured in this compelling anthology. "Watching Her Sleep" follows a fantasy romance that blooms while waiting in a supermarket checkout line; a 12-year-old girl puts up with riding in the car with her sisters in "Little Women in Transit"; a woman attempts to come out to her parents in "Playing the Part"; and "Carmelita Tropicana: Your Kunst Is Your Waffen" chronicles the adventures of a New York building super/performance artist. 80 min.
70-5099 *$29.99*

Siren (1996)
A young woman, fascinated with an infamous female writer of erotic fiction, travels to the author's country home, and what follows is a seductive and sensual story of lesbian romance. 45 min.
76-2036 Was $29.99 *$19.99*

Cynara: Poetry In Motion (1996)
Two women meet by chance along the Northwest coast in the 1880s and are drawn into an emotional and passion-filled romance in this sweeping drama described as "a lush, textured lesbian 'Wuthering Heights'." 34 min.
76-2050 *$29.99*

Green Plaid Shirt (1996)
Film journalist Richard Natale wrote and directed this compelling chronicle of the 10-year relationship between lovers Guy and Philip. Jumping back and forth through time, the film examines their story from 1978, when the pair meet at a yard sale, to Guy's death of AIDS in 1988 and focuses on different facets of their day-to-day lives. Gregory Phelan, Kevin Spirtas and Richard Israel star. 87 min.
76-2057 Was $39.99 *$29.99*

The Toilers And The Wayfarers (1996)
Two gay teenagers who are best friends are torn apart by their inability to express their feelings for each other, for fear of incurring their Minnesota community's wrath, until the arrival of a handsome German stranger changes their lives, in this emotional independent drama. Matt Klemp, Andrew Woodhouse star. 75 min. In English and German with English subtitles.
78-5087 *$59.99*

Some Prefer Cake (1997)
Snappy comedy set in San Francisco and detailing the friendship of Kira, a lesbian comic, and her restaurant critic pal Sydney. Romance, drama, comedy and women's desire for food and sex are among the topics touched on. Tara Howley and Kathleen Fontaine star. 95 min.
76-2059 Was $39.99 *$29.99*

Naked Highway (1997)
The search for the former lover who left him for dreams of Hollywood success leads a young southern man into a variety of erotic encounters—and a stint in California's gay sex industry—in this compelling and steamy gay-themed "road movie." 75 min.
76-2064 *$29.99*

Goodbye Emma Jo (1997)
Erotic love and passion are at the center of this sensual drama in which Alex laments the loss of her love, Emma, on their anniversary. Alex gets even more depressed when her car breaks down, but when an attractive woman named Haley offers help, it leads to a night neither of them will ever forget. 40 min.
76-2072 *$29.99*

Next Year In Jerusalem (1997)
Charlie is a gay man living in the West Village who hides from his Orthodox Jewish heritage, even though he is set to marry a daughter of a rabbi. At a family Passover seder dinner, Charlie meets Manny, and they form a relationship that leads to important but painful transitions for both of them. This sensitive story features former adult actress Georgina Spelvin as Charlie's mother. 103 min.
01-1557 *$39.99*

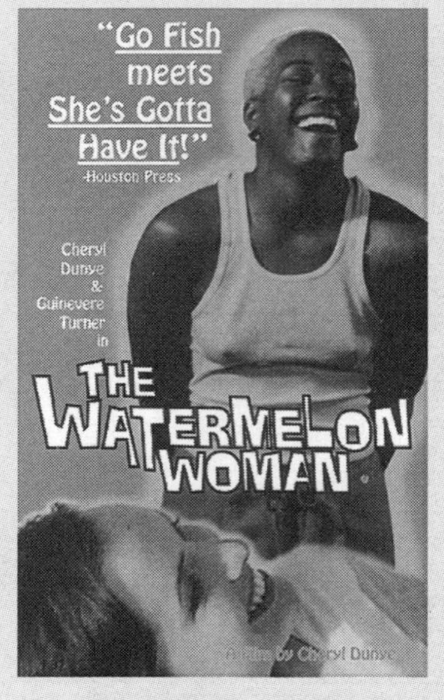

The Watermelon Woman (1997)
An offbeat comedy-drama from lesbian African-American filmmaker Cheryl Duyne in which she plays, of all things, a lesbian African-American video store clerk and aspiring filmmaker who becomes obsessed with learning the life story of a little-known black actress from the '30s who was known as "the Watermelon Woman" and was part of Hollywood's underground lesbian subculture. Guinevere Turner, Valarie Walker also star. 85 min.
70-5130 Was $79.99 *$29.99*

David Searching (1997)
In this offbeat, engaging independent comedy, gay documentary filmmaker Anthony Rapp becomes roommates with feisty, overweight waitress Camryn Manheim in an East Village apartment. Rapp searches for the right guy, while Mannheim realizes the right guy for her may be her ex-husband. With Stephen Spinella and cameos from a host of theater performers and writers. 103 min.
01-1564 *$39.99*

Chocolate Babies (1997)
This explosive "what-if" story details what happens when a group of radical, HIV-positive gay African- and Asian-Americans go ballistic and start staging surprise attacks on conservative politicians in New York. Jon Lee, claude e. sloan and Suzanne Gregg Ferguson star in this audacious effort spiked with a witty, nasty streak. 83 min.
01-1570 *$39.99*

Love! Valour! Compassion! (1997)
A series of three holiday weekends at a lakeside house in upstate New York provides a group of gay friends with opportunities for laughter, confrontation, romance and renewal. Based on the Tony Award-winning play by Terrence McNally, this witty comedy/drama features a superb ensemble cast that includes Jason Alexander, Randy Becker, John Glover (as twin brothers) and Stephen Spinella. 120 min.
02-5161 Was $99.99 *$19.99*

Boyfriends (1997)
A trio of gay male couples spends Easter weekend at a home in the English countryside, a weekend that provides each pair with a variety of insights into the nature of their relationship, in this funny and moving "Big Chill"-like seriocomedy. James Dreyfus, Michael Unwin, David Coffey star. 82 min.
70-5127 Was $79.99 *$29.99*

Leather Jacket Love Story (1997)
Called "the perfect erotic romance for the 1990s," this gay-themed comedy tells of 18-year-old Valley boy Kyle, who falls for a rough carpenter named Mike who gets his kicks through S&M. Their relationship leads both men into a decadent L.A. world of musclemen, leather studs and poolside cocktails. With Sean Tataryn, Christopher Bradley, Mink Stole and several steamy sex scenes.
73-9252 *$59.99*

Everything Relative (1997)
Called "a lesbian 'Big Chill'," this acclaimed independent film follows a group of women, gay and straight, who were friends in college in the late '70s. Reunited two decades later for a weekend in the country, the women explore the changes in their lives and loves and the bonds that still unite them. Ellen McLaughlin, Olivia Negron star, with a special appearance by Harvey Fierstein. 105 min.
76-2054 Was $99.99 *$19.99*

Bent (1997)
Stirring film rendition of the acclaimed Broadway drama dealing with the persecution of homosexuals in Nazi Germany. Clive Owen plays a gay Jewish man who betrays his lover in order to receive less harsh treatment in a concentration camp. In this brutal environment Owen forms a bond with fellow inmate Lothaire Bluteau that, although the men cannot so much as touch one another, gives them the strength to survive. With Brian Webber, Ian McKellen, and Mick Jagger as a cross-dressing cabaret owner. 104 min.
73-1312 *$14.99*

I'll Always Be Anthony (1997)
This sensitively realized comedy-drama centers on the relationship between a young gay man and a straight male friend with whom he falls in love. This independent production is inventive both in its treatment of gay lifestyles and its stylish approach to the material. With Kerry Muir. 80 min.
73-9185 *$59.99*

Butch Camp (1997)
Hilarious and wise look at sexual stereotypes centered on Matt, a sensitive gay man, unlucky at love. He decides to enlist in an assertiveness-training course at Butch Camp, where a brash dominatrix tries to teach her subjects a thing or two about sex. Paul Denniston and Judy Tenuta star in this wild satire. 103 min.
73-9265 *$49.99*

In The Flesh (1997)
Dane Ritter is a troubled male prostitute who forms an unlikely friendship with an undercover policeman working the gay nightlife in Atlanta to investigate a drug case. Their bond is threatened when Ritter becomes a murder suspect and the officer is the only one who may—or may not—be able to help him. Ed Corbin, Adrian Roberts also star. 105 min.
76-2108 *$39.99*

Fresh Kill (1997)
A lesbian couple must cope not only with the mysterious disappearance of their infant daughter but also with a contaminated sushi scare, a barge loaded with nuclear waste, strange snowfalls and the global corporation that somehow ties everything together. Bizarre gay cyberpunk drama stars Sarita Choudhury, Erin McMurtry, José Zuniga. 80 min.
78-9019 *$39.99*

Late Bloomers (1997)
As wacky as it is winsome, this acclaimed independent comedy from sisters Gretchen and Julia Dyer follows the offbeat romance that blossoms between a female high school teacher and girl's basketball coach and a married mother of two who also works at the school, and the effect the relationship has on their small Texas community. Connie Nelson, Dee Hennigan star. 104 min.
78-9020 *$59.99*

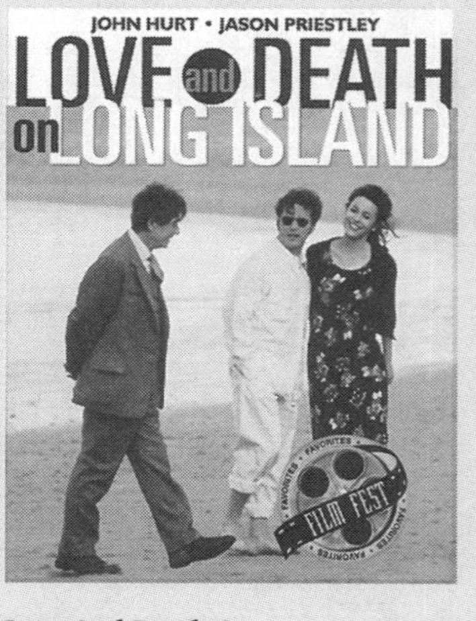

Love And Death On Long Island (1997)
Wonderfully funny and heartfelt comedy stars John Hurt as a gay English writer who becomes obsessed with American actor Jason Priestley after seeing him in a low-budget teen film comedy. His romantic fixation leads to an emotional encounter between the two on a Long Island beach. 93 min.
07-2701 Was $99.99 *$19.99*

Alive & Kicking (1997)
In this superior drama, an AIDS-infected ballet star falls for a portly therapist who has taken to the bottle in order to numb the pain of the HIV-positive patients he sees regularly. Written by Martin Sherman ("Bent"), the film received great acclaim for its treatment of gay romance in the age of AIDS. With Jason Flemyng, Antony Sher and Anthony Higgins. AKA: "Indian Summer." 100 min.
83-5004 *$59.99*

Slaves To The Underground (1997)
Incisive and smart look at the Seattle music scene focusing on the relationship of Molly Gross and Marisa Ryan, members of the all-girl punk band the No Exits, who have become lovers. When Gross considers getting back with ex-boyfriend Jason Bortz, impoverished publisher of a political newsletter, the band's future is threatened. 94 min.
83-5005 *$59.99*

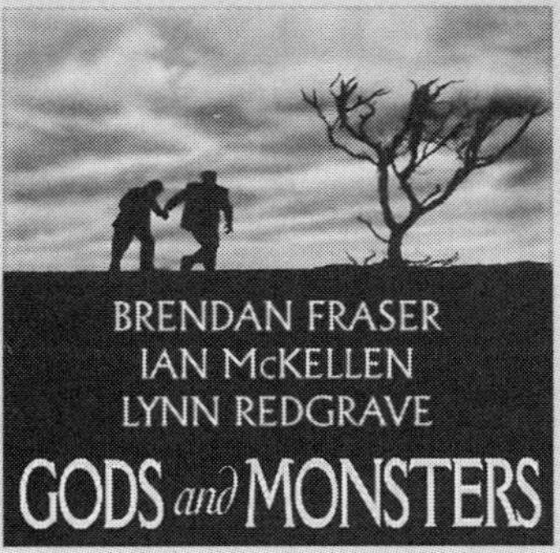
BRENDAN FRASER
IAN McKELLEN
LYNN REDGRAVE
GODS and MONSTERS

Gods And Monsters (1998)
A stunning performance by Ian McKellen drives this compelling "speculative biodrama" about the later years of British-born filmmaker James Whale, the director of "Frankenstein" and "Bride of Frankenstein" who dazzled '30s Hollywood with his talent and scandalized it with his openly gay lifestyle. Brendan Fraser is a gardener who becomes the older man's art model and confidante, and Lynn Redgrave plays Whale's devoted housekeeper. 106 min.
07-2748 Was $99.99 □*$14.99*

High Art (1998)
A disenchanted assistant editor at a posh New York fashion magazine is drawn into the dysfunctional world of her neighbor, burned-out photographer Ally Sheedy, and experiments with drugs and lesbianism, much to the dismay of her boyfriend. Writer/director Lisa Cholodenko's intriguing "bohemian" drama also stars Radha Mitchell, Patricia Clarkson. 101 min.
07-2672 Was $99.99 □*$14.99*

Like It Is (1998)
Opposites attract, but can they stay together, in this compelling and gritty gay drama about a working-class bare-knuckles fighter who begins a relationship with a handsome London record producer and faces disapproval from his yuppie circle. Steve Bell (a boxer in real life) and Ian Rose star, with support from Who alumnus Roger Daltrey as Rose's boss. 95 min.
70-5165 Was $79.99 *$29.99*

Lilies (1998)
From John Greyson ("Zero Patience") comes an award-winning tale of betrayal, revenge and forbidden love. In 1952, a Roman Catholic bishop visiting an ill prisoner is taken hostage and forced to watch dramatizations of tumultuous events that took place earlier in both men's lives, when they were at school together. Brent Carver, Matthew Ferguson and Jason Cadieux star. 95 min.
76-2055 Was $89.99 *$29.99*

Billy's Hollywood Screen Kiss (1998)
Billy is an L.A. photographer whose latest project has him re-creating famous cinematic kisses with male models. When a handsome and sexually ambiguous coffeehouse waiter begins posing for him, Billy becomes attracted to him but afraid to declare his infatuation. Sean P. Hayes, Brad Rowe, Richard Ganoung and Paul Bartel star in writer/director Tommy O'Haver's winning romantic comedy. 103 min.
68-1899 Was $99.99 □*$14.99*

It's In The Water (1998)
This lesbian romantic comedy is set in a snobby Texas town where Alex, a straight woman in a miserable marriage, takes a job at an AIDS hospice. There she reacquaints herself with Grace, a nurse and old friend who has come out of the closet following a divorce. The two begin a love affair amidst the town's homophobia. Keri Jo Chapman and Teresa Garrett star. 100 min.
76-2061 Was $39.99 *$29.99*

Finding North (1998)
After stopping a naked man, despondent over his male lover's death, from jumping off the Brooklyn Bridge, a sheltered young woman tries to break away from her protective family by joining the man on a road trip to his late lover's Texas hometown. Offbeat and touching "buddy comedy" stars Wendy Makkena, John Benjamin Hickey, Anne Bobby. 93 min.
76-2066 *$59.99*

Hey Sailor, Hey Sister (1998)
If you like a hot tale of lesbian love and women in uniform, you've selected the right title! A naval officer arrives in port in search of adventure—and gets it, big time, when she meets a gorgeous, mysterious women who may or may not be a prostitute. A fast pickup and safe, scorching sex ensue. "McHale's Navy" it ain't. 23 min.
76-2073 *$19.99*

Such A Crime (1998)
A group of lesbian "eco-terrorists" find their cause threatened when one of their members lets her libido get in the way of their mission. While suspicions and mistrust abound, so do sexual urges and desires, and suddenly some things seem more important than political causes. 46 min.
76-2074 *$29.99*

Latin Boys Go To Hell (1998)
Straight off the gay film festival circuit comes this hot and sexy send-up of male Latino "tela novellas." Director Ela Troyano takes inspiration from the New York City club scene to create wickedly tender moments of gay Latino life. Irwin Ossa, John Bryant Davila star. 71 min.
78-9022 *$59.99*

Broadway Damage (1998)
A pair of gay twentysomethings—struggling actor Michael Shawn Lucas and would-be songwriter Aaron Williams—find their dreams of success on Broadway and romantic happiness don't quite mesh with the reality of life in New York in this breezy comedy. Mara Hobel also stars as Lucas' best friend/roommate. 110 min.
76-2063 *$59.99*

The Delta (1998)
A wealthy teenager who keeps his homosexuality a secret finds solace in all-night gay movie houses and peep shows. He meets and falls in love with the Vietnamese son of a black GI, and together they head down the Mississippi River in the teen's father's cabin cruiser, with tragic consequences. Shayne Gray and Thang Chang star in this offbeat take on "Huckleberry Finn." 85 min.
78-9023 Was $59.99 *$19.99*

I Think I Do (1998)
This "Big Chill" with a gay angle concerns six college friends at George Washington University whose reunion for a wedding leads to all sorts of comic and poignant situations. Alexis Arquette is a soap opera writer who attends the wedding with his dim-witted actor lover while pining for sexually ambiguous Christian Maelen. With Lauren Velez, Marni Nixon. 90 min.
78-9027 *$59.99*

Out Of Season (1999)
This compelling lesbian drama tells of a disgruntled photographer from New York who stops by to see her ailing uncle at his Cape May, New Jersey, home. There she begins an uneasy friendship with her uncle's close friend, but the two women's differences eventually lead to romantic attraction. Carol Monda and Joy Kelly star. 98 min.
76-2070 *$29.99*

Defying Gravity (1999)
This drama centers on a popular college student named Griff, whose attraction to Peter, a frat brother, forces him to live a double life. It also leads to Pete coming under attack in a vicious gay-bashing incident. How both men deal with their sexuality and their emotions is the focus of this daring effort that stars Daniel Chilson and Niklaus Lange. 92 min.
76-2083 *$39.99*

Rites Of Passage (1999)
Powerful story tells of a lawyer who discovers that his father is having an affair. He and his younger brother join their father for a mountain retreat, but the brother's homosexual desires are brought to the surface when a group of escaped cons holds the family hostage. Dean Stockwell, James Remar, Jason Behr and Jaimz Woolvett star. 95 min.
76-2084 *$29.99*

A Luv Tale (1999)
This all-black lesbian romantic comedy tells of an overworked magazine editor who feels unfulfilled in her long-term relationship with her boss/boyfriend. Her search for happiness takes a surprising turn when she meets a beautiful freelance photographer, but the blossoming romance elicits strong opinions from their friends. Michele Lamar-Richards, Gina Rivera star. 45 min.
76-2085 *$29.99*

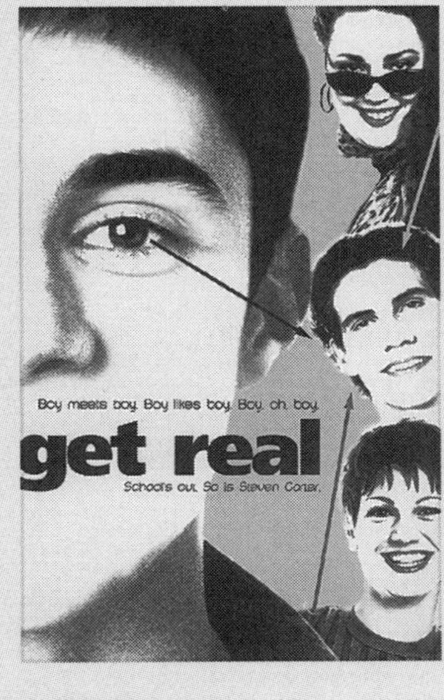
Boy meets boy. Boy likes boy. Boy, oh, boy.
get real
School's out. So is Steven Carter.

Get Real (1999)
British teen Ben Silverstone, struggling with his homosexuality and the need to keep it a secret, is surprised when, while waiting at a local park to meet older men, he encounters popular schoolmate and star athlete Brad Gorton. Their tentative relationship, and the violence Silverstone meets with when he comes out in a magazine article, are movingly depicted in this emotional comedy/drama based on Patrick Wilde's play "What's Wrong with Angry?" Charlotte Brittain, Stacey Hart also star. 111 min.
06-2946 Was $19.99 □*$14.99*

Better Than Chocolate (1999)
Lusty lesbian story concerning Maggie and Kim, two same-sex lovers in Vancouver who decide to move into an apartment together. Soon, Maggie's divorced mother and brother move in with them and eventually discover the nature of their heated relationship and meet some of the couple's eccentric friends. With Karyn Dwyer, Christina Cox, Wendy Crewson. Unrated version; 102 min.
68-1956 □*$79.99*

Parallel Sons (1999)
Compelling tale of romantic involvement between Seth, a young white man obsessed with black culture who lives in a small town in the Adirondacks, and Knowledge, an African-American escapee from a nearby prison. The unlikely meeting between the two during a hold-up at the cafe where Seth works leads to an intimate relationship. With Gabriel Mick, Laurence Mason. 93 min.
78-9037 *$59.99*

Edge Of Seventeen (1999)
Sensitive and sexy gay coming-of-age tale set in Ohio in 1985 and focusing on Eric, a young summer worker at an amusement park cafeteria who falls for Rod, a 21-year-old man who seduces him. When Rod leaves for college, Eric, struggling, dresses "New Wave" and delves into the gay culture. Chris Stafford, Tina Holmes and Anderson Gabrych star. 100 min.
78-9041 *$79.99*

Head On (1999)
Ari is a 19-year-old Greek who is constantly fighting to keep his homosexuality a secret from his homophobic family whom he depends on, as well as the close-minded Australian community they moved to when he was young. Ari must somehow learn to reconcile the gap between himself and old traditions before his negative feelings destroy him in this powerful drama. Alex Dimitriades, Paul Capsis star. 104 min.
78-9044 Letterboxed *$79.99*

Trick (1999)
Manhattan office worker/would-be musical comedy writer Christian Campbell's hunt for "Mr. Right" picks up when he catches the eye of handsome go-go dancer John Paul Pitoc on the subway. Their search for a place to have a "romantic interlude" turns into a comical quest filled with annoying roommates, snippy drag queens and interruptions from Campbell's friend, aspiring actress Tori Spelling, in this witty independent film. 90 min.
02-5223 Was $99.99 □*$19.99*

Bedrooms And Hallways (1999)
Witty, pansexual romantic romp from director Rose Troche ("Go Fish") stars Kevin McKidd as a thirtysomething man looking for meaning in his life who joins a "New Age" men's group. McKidd announces his attraction to fellow member James Purefoy and the two begin a hesitant affair, one that's complicated by Purefoy's ongoing relationship with co-worker Jennifer Ehle, who was McKidd's high school sweetheart! Simon Callow, Hugo Weaving also star. 96 min.
70-5188 Was $79.99 *$19.99*

If These Walls Could Talk 2 (2000)
The lives of three lesbian couples are explored in stories set in the same house over three different decades. First, Vanessa Redgrave must deal with discrimination and the loss of her longtime companion in 1961. 1972 finds Michelle Williams and Chloe Sevigny searching for acceptance and love in feminist and gay rights groups. Finally, Ellen DeGeneres and Sharon Stone try to have a baby together amid adversity in the year 2000. 96 min.
44-2262 □*$99.99*

Dear Diary (2000)
In this lesbian-themed romantic drama, rock singer Kate thinks she's found true love with her computer teacher Bonnie while recovering from a bad break-up, but her diary chronicles the emotional roller coaster Kate rides with her new lover, her protective manager, and her male roommate. Jo-Ann Barton, Mary De Michele star. 85 min.
73-9369 *$29.99*

Around The World The Lesbian Way
Sultry selection of lesbian-themed short films featuring "The Marching Girl Thing," with "Muriel's Wedding's" Toni Collette as a baton-twirler who develops a relationship with another girl; "Dancing," in which an older woman has fond memories after hearing a special song; "A Day in the Life of a Bull Dyke," about the life of a butcher; "Go Girl"; and "Casting." 80 min.
76-7428 *$29.99*

Two In Twenty: Complete Set
The first lesbian soap opera concerns the trials and tribulations of the members of two gay households. Humor and suspense play equal parts in this series that addresses such issues as child custody, lesbian parenting, AIDS, racism, lust, therapy, sex and more. Also includes funny commercials for fictitious products. Three-tape set includes five episodes and outtakes. 252 min. total.
76-2011 Was $59.99 *$39.99*

Dyke Drama
Some of the many sides of lesbian life are examined in this collection of award-winning short films. Include are "Ifé," about a woman's renouncement of love; "Maya," a tale of a dance student and her teacher; the roller-skating-in-New York romp "Things We Said Today"; and "A Certain Grace," in which a photographer must choose between her boyfriend and a female subject. 89 min.
76-2051 Was $29.99 *$19.99*

I Became A Lesbian And Others
Four lesbian-themed short films are presented in this collection: "Just" a Little Crush," detailing an affair between a mousy pet store clerk and a woman in red; "Cat Nip," which explores the connection between lesbians and cats; "Le Poisson D'amour," a look at the pleasures and pitfalls of lesbian life; and "I Became a Lesbian," a comedic infomercial. 52 min.
73-9209 *$39.99*

Amazing World
Tabloid stories go lesbian as crusading "queer reporters" Bing and Nico encounter pyromaniacs, UFO abductees, psychics and mutual lust. Filled with music by such Seattle groups as Los Hornets, Shugg and Cowboy Coffee, this off-the-wall tale stars Jennifer Burton and Shanda Russell. 91 min.
76-7429 *$29.99*

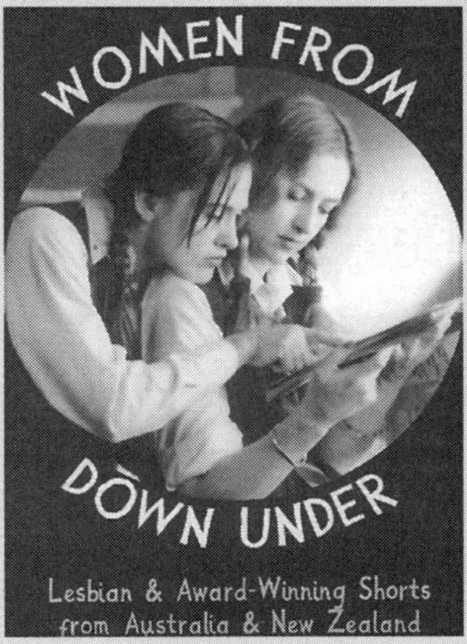
WOMEN FROM
DOWN UNDER
Lesbian & Award-Winning Shorts
from Australia & New Zealand

Women From Down Under
This collection of lesbian shorts from Australia and New Zealand includes "Peach," the story of a sexy truck driver attracted to a Maori woman, starring a pre-"Xena" Lucy Lawless; "Just Desserts," which relates a teenager's sexual awakening to Italian food; "Excursion to the Bridge of Friendship," about a Bulgarian folk singer; and "Jumpin' the Gun," a look at the morning after a hot lesbian one-night stand. 52 min.
70-5092 Was $29.99 *$19.99*

Peach And A Bitter Song
A pair of unusual short films featuring Lucy Lawless in early starring turns before she became an international star in "Xena: Warrior Princess." "Peach" is the erotic lesbian love story of a truck driver and a Maori woman in New Zealand, while "A Bitter Song" finds Lawless as a nurse who cares for a troubled young girl. 40 min. total.
70-5157 *$19.99*

Loads Of McDowell
San Francisco underground gay filmmaker Curt McDowell blazed new trails with his erotic films, and this collection spotlights several of the shorts he made from 1970 to 1980. Included are "Loads," "Confessions," "Ronnie," "Visit to Indiana," "Boggy Depot" and "Naughty Words." WARNING: Contains adult material. 80 min.
73-9266 *$39.99*

Companions
Celebrate the friendship, romance and special relationship between women with this collection of seven funny, touching and erotic short films. Included are "Breakfast with Gus," "Traveling Companion," "Peppermills," "The Dinner Party" (by "High Art" director Lisa Cholodenko) and others. 80 min. total.
76-2065 Was $39.99 *$19.99*

Thundercrack (1975)
Groundbreaking erotic film from director Curt McDowell and writer George Kuchar begins as an "Old Dark House"-styled thriller, in which a group of strangers finds themselves stranded in an old mansion. Before long, the guests partake in a series of wild and varied encounters that are sure to titillate and amaze you. WARNING: This film includes explicit material; ADULTS ONLY. 150 min.
73-9267 *$39.99*

Teasers
Four tales of lesbian eroticism and love are presented in this collection that includes "Top of the World," in which completely opposite women attract in spite of outside interference; "Why I'll Never Trust You (In 200 Words or Less)," a passionate look at a relationshiop based on touch; "Regarde-Moi," a fantasy about a French woman; and "Double Entente," about an after-work meeting with surprises. 60 min.
76-2078 Was $29.99 *$19.99*

Short Shorts
This collection of award-winning lesbian-themed short films includes "Maid of Honor," about a lesbian's decision to serve as maid of honor for a former lovers' straight wedding; "Cache," involving four women who hold up a bank; "Two Girls and a Baby," about a lesbian couple's decision regarding having a child; and the animated "Go Dyke Go," a Dr. Seuss spoof. 135 min.
76-2106 *$39.99*

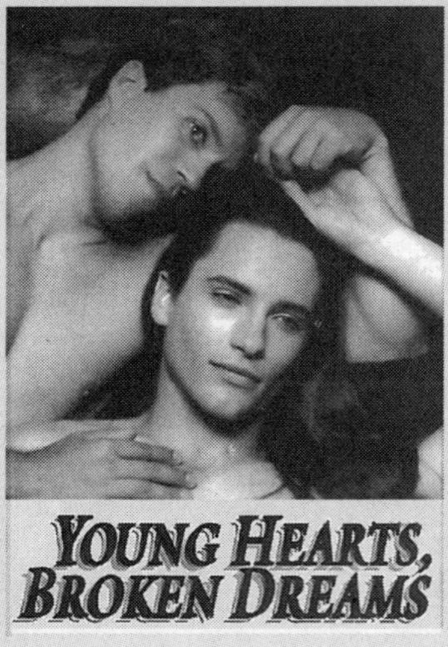

Young Hearts, Broken Dreams, Episode 1: The Delivery Boy
Making a delivery to the home of popular actor Scottie Edwards, starstruck fan Adam Harrington, hoping to befriend his idol, joins Scottie and his pals for a quick dip in the pool. Adam soon finds himself caught up in a world of dark passions and darker secrets. Extensive frontal nudity highlights this sizzling all-male soft core soaper starring Eddie Starr, Brett Winters and Marc Cannon. 45 min.
78-5023 *$39.99*

Young Hearts, Broken Dreams, Episode 2: The Search
In the wake of movie star Scottie's murder, his brother Matthew arrives in Hollywood to learn the truth behind his death and Adam's subsequent suicide. As Matthew and his friend Noah look for clues alongside a handsome detective, the three confront their own feelings and desires. This second part of the acclaimed gay-themed soap opera features moving love scenes and extensive frontal nudity. Michael Habusch, Robert Spiewak star. 83 min.
78-5077 *$49.99*

Young Hearts, Broken Dreams, Episode 3: He Loves Me, He Loves Me Not
The unique male softcore melodrama concludes with this steamy chapter that ties up all the loose ends surrounding the murder of Scottie Edwards, Matthew and Noah's feelings for each other, and the handsome detective who's looking to get his man. All this, and an earthquake, too! Michael Habusch, Kurt Schwoebel, Matthew Rector. 84 min.
78-5085 *$49.99*

Dangerous When Wet
This collection offers erotic, provocative and award-winning shorts with lesbian themes. Included are "Badass Supermama" (1996), an unusual look at blaxploitation queen Pam Grier; "Blue Diary" (1997), about a lesbian's night with a straight woman; "Sleep Come Free Me" (1998), centering on an office worker's fantasies; "Adam" (1996), a claymation story regarding mistaken gender identity; and more. 60 min.
01-1571 *$39.99*

Men In Shorts
Nine provocative shorts depicting gay life are offered on this collection that includes "Nick Dixon, Private Eye," a spoof of 1940s detective movies; "Easy Money," a look at gay hustlers and drug addicts in Hollywood; "Auto Biography," a look at being gay in a small town in Canada; "Kiss," an erotic short from 1969; music videos from "Zero Patience"; plus four other items. 70 min.
76-7176 *$19.99*

Mondo Rocco
A retrospective featuring several short films from Pat Rocco, the first openly gay American filmmaker to create gay-themed films for gay audiences. Shot from 1965 to the mid-1970s, the collection includes "A Night at Joanie's" with Jim Bailey; "The Room," a sexual romp"; and "Screen Test," a voyeuristic peek at masculinity. AKA: "It's a Gay World." 124 min.
76-7357 *$39.99*

Third Sex Cinema, Vol. 1
This collection of rare, gay-themed short features from the 1960s features Andy Milligan's notorious "The Vapors," a look at a man's first visit to a New York City bathhouse; "Shoot It Buddy," a sex loop offering two guys gallivanting around in G-strings; and "The Drag Queen's Ball," a wild transsexual romp in which guys impersonate famous gals at a Memphis Holiday Inn Dinner Theatre.
79-5331 Was $24.99 *$19.99*

Third Sex Cinema, Vol. 2: Song Of The Loon (1970)
This important, critically acclaimed gay film, based on Richard Amory's noted novel, is set in the 1870s and takes a sensitive look at the homoerotic relationship between a trapper and a young man coming to terms with his desires. Jon Iverson and Morgan Royce star. Also featured on the tape are gay-themed shorts "The Coronation" (1960) and "Lot in Sodom," a silent from 1933.
79-5623 Was $24.99 *$19.99*

Third Sex Cinema, Vol. 3: The Meat Rack (1970)
This is a seminal gay-themed film that takes a look at the seamy world of bisexual San Francisco hustler J.C.. After servicing clients like an adulterous housewife, a fat drag queen and male moviegoers during a showing of "Attack of the Crab Monsters," he saves his new love from a lecherous photographer and encounters murderous transvestites. David Calder, Donna Troy star.
79-5624 Was $24.99 *$19.99*

Third Sex Cinema, Vol. 4: Sins Of Rachel (1972)
A perverse piece of cinematic erotica in which a nightclub performer is found murdered, and the investigation leads to her disturbed adolescent son. It's learned that junior is confused about his homosexual feelings and the fact that his mother liked to sleep with him. Shot in Texturetone. With Ann Noble and Bruce Campbell.
79-5847 Was $24.99 *$19.99*

Third Sex Cinema, Vol. 5: Consenting Adults
Here's a collection of shorts from the '60s and '70s focusing on the world of gays. Homosexual lifestyle in England in the 1960s is surveyed in "Consenting Adults: A Study of Homosexuality"; two men entertain themselves in "The Male Nudists"; "Gay-In III" offers documentary footage of a gay pride happening; and two guys fool others with their drag dressing in the early '70s short "Caught in the Can."
79-6083 Was $24.99 *$19.99*

Third Sex Cinema, Vol. 6: Inside A.M.G. (1970)
This documentary takes you inside the "Athletic Model Guild," the production company responsible for the popular series of muscle-bound gay movies in the 1960s. Go behind the scenes and meet the men who starred in the films, the filmmakers who produced them and the films themselves. With Rick Cassidy and other hunks! 90 min.
79-6203 Was $24.99 *$19.99*

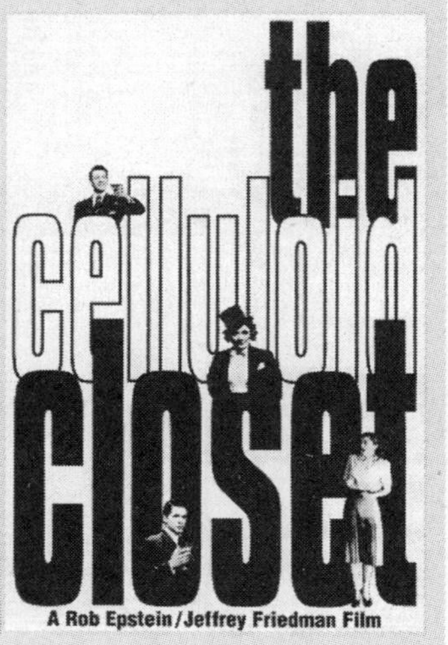

The Celluloid Closet (1996)
This entertaining and often hilarious look at homosexuality in the cinema features film clips, interviews and fascinating revelations. Among the films featured are "Spartacus," "The Boys in the Band," "The Children's Hour," "Philadelphia," "Tea and Sympathy" and many others. Lily Tomlin narrates, while Harvey Fierstein, Tom Hanks, Susan Sarandon, Gore Vidal and others comment on the films. 101 min.
02-2978 Was $99.99 □*$24.99*

Lavender Limelight: Lesbians In Film (1997)
Some of the most intriguing voices to come from the independent cinema of the '80s and '90s have been those of lesbian filmmakers. This documentary features interviews with such noted directors as Cheryl Dunye ("The Watermelon Woman"), Jennie Livingston ("Paris Is Burning"), Monika Treut ("Erotique"), Rose Troche ("Go Fish") and others, talking candidly about their art, their lives, and love and sex both on the screen and off. 57 min.
70-5132 Was $29.99 *$19.99*

The Silver Screen: Color Me Lavender (1998)
From Mark Rappaport, creator of "Rock Hudson's Home Movies," comes this cinematic treatise on gay and lesbian imagery in Hollywood films from the 1930s to the 1960s. Among the subjects Rappaport focuses on are the Hope-Crosby "Road" movies; Walter Brennan's "playing" to the leading man; and the reel and real lives of Danny Kaye, Clifton Webb and others. Narrated by "Frasier" co-star Dan Butler. 100 min.
01-1556 *$39.99*

Blood And Sand (1989)
Sizzling Sharon Stone plays a seductive woman who lures a successful matador away from his loving wife and down a downward spiral in this updating of the classic drama, marked by great bullfighting sequences and steamy sex scenes. With Chris Rydell, Ana Torent. 96 min.
68-1198 *$12.99*

Guilty Of Innocence (1987)
Powerful true drama of Lenell Geter, a black engineer from Dallas who was convicted and given life for an armed robbery he didn't commit. Dorian Harewood stars as Geter, and Dabney Coleman is the attorney who must battle the legal system to prove his client's innocence. With Paul Winfield, Hoyt Axton. 95 min.
68-1218 *$89.99*

Shattered Spirits (1986)
A husband's alcoholism and abusive behavior threaten to destroy his family in this powerful and contemporary drama. Martin Sheen, Melinda Dillon, Lukas Haas and Roxana Zal star. 93 min.
68-1224 *$89.99*

The Diamond Trap (1988)
Word of a major jewel heist taking place at a ritzy New York gallery pits two detectives and a gallery worker against a team of international thieves who'll stop at nothing in this gripping crime drama. Howard Hesseman, Ed Marinaro, Brooke Shields star. 93 min.
68-1250 □*$89.99*

Flash Fire (1981)
Tom Skerritt stars as a man who discovers that his partner plans to torch their mountain resort project and decides to hire insurance investigator James Mason to stop the deadly scheme. Wendy Hughes co-stars in this thrilling tale of greed gone awry. AKA: "A Dangerous Summer."
68-3008 Was $49.99 *$14.99*

The Weather In The Streets (1983)
Tale of forbidden romance in 1920s England, as a man trapped in an unhappy marriage reunites with his first true love. Michael York, Joanna Lumley, Lisa Eichhorn star. 110 min.
69-1013 *$24.99*

To The Lighthouse (1983)
Acclaimed drama based on Virginia Woolf's novel, as an upper-class British family on holiday at the dawn of World War I is torn apart from within and without. Rosemary Harris, Michael Gough star; look for an early appearance by Kenneth Branagh. 115 min.
69-1021 *$19.99*

After Darkness (1985)
John Hurt and Julian Sands star as two brothers, one an institutionalized schizophrenic, the other the keeper of a dark family secret that holds the key to his sibling's insanity, in this compelling drama. 104 min.
69-5062 Was $79.99 *$19.99*

A Matter Of Principle (1983)
Alan Arkin turns in a truly remarkable performance as the impoverished, cantankerous father of a large brood of children who, because of his "principles," would just as soon forget Christmas ever existed. Co-stars Virginia Madsen, Barbara Dana. 60 min.
71-5070 *$19.99*

Dealers (1989)
High-stakes drama à la "Wall Street" in this tale of London stock dealers and their actions on the floor and in the bedroom. Rebecca De Mornay, Paul McGann, Derrick O'Connor star. 92 min.
71-5182 *$12.99*

Bluegrass (1988)
Lavish made-for-TV tale starring Cheryl Ladd as the owner of a Kentucky horse farm helped by faithful farm manager Brian Kerwin while being threatened by neighbor Wayne Rogers. Anthony Andrews, Mickey Rooney, Diane Ladd and Shawnee Smith also star. 182 min.
72-3024 *$12.99*

The Best Little Girl In The World (1981)
Provocative TV movie stars Jennifer Jason Leigh as an overachieving high school student encountering emotional problems and anorexia. Melanie Mayron, Jason Miller, Eva Marie Saint and Ally Sheedy also star. 96 min.
72-3025 *$12.99*

Disaster At Silo 7 (1988)
Intense true-life story starring Michael O'Keefe as an officer in the Air Force who attempts to stop a potential disaster in a nuclear missile silo. Patricia Charbonneau, Perry King, Joe Spano, Dennis Weaver and Peter Boyle co-star. 92 min.
72-9023 Was $89.99 *$14.99*

When He's Not A Stranger (1989)
A naive college freshman is the victim of a "date rape" after a party and faces pressure from family, friends and the school when she presses charges against the assailant, a star quarterback. Timely, emotional drama stars Annabeth Gish, John Terlesky, Kevin Dillon and Paul Dooley. 90 min.
72-9009 Was $89.99 *$14.99*

Colors (1988)
A graphically realistic and compelling look at L.A.'s street gangs, focusing on the divergent methods that veteran cop Robert Duvall and headstrong rookie Sean Penn take in dealing with the young toughs who are turning the city into a battleground. With Maria Conchita Alonso; Dennis Hopper directs. 120 min.
73-1021 Was $19.99 □*$14.99*

Odd Birds (1985)
Compassionate tale of a Chinese-American teenage girl dissuaded from pursuing her dreams of starring on Broadway by her mother, who wants her to study nursing. The girl becomes involved with an unorthodox parochial school teacher who offers her encouragement and understanding. Michael Moriarty, Donna Lai Ming Lew star. 87 min.
70-3282 Was $79.99 *$19.99*

Target: Favorite Son (1988)
A charismatic senator is wounded in an assassination attempt that turns him into an instant celebrity, and a Contra leader is killed by a hit man. Two FBI agents' investigations uncover a link to the crimes and a scandal of sex and political corruption that reaches to the White House. Intriguing thriller stars Harry Hamlin, Linda Kozlowski, Robert Loggia, Lance Guest. AKA: "Favorite Son." 115 min.
68-1225 *$89.99*

Dominick And Eugene (1988)
Tom Hulce and Ray Liotta star in this drama of a young medical student preparing to leave home for college and his older, mentally handicapped brother, who must face being on his own for the first time. Warm and emotional tale also features Jamie Lee Curtis. 113 min.
73-1035 Was $19.99 □*$14.99*

Beverly Hills Madam (1986)
Businesswoman Faye Dunaway becomes love broker to the rich and famous with a stable of dazzling doxies that includes Donna Dixon, Robin Givens and Melody Anderson. Can Dunaway preserve her immoral empire when the girls begin to regret the life of a metered fun pal? 97 min.
73-1047 *$19.99*

Winter People (1988)
Touching period piece, set during the Depression, stars Kurt Russell as an itinerant clockmaker who gets waylaid in the Appalachians and embroiled in a tussle for the affections of mountain girl Kelly McGillis. Lloyd Bridges, Mitchell Ryan co-star. 110 min.
73-1051 □*$14.99*

Nightsongs (1984)
Stirring look at a Chinese-Vietnamese woman who travels to the U.S. to live with her cousins in New York's Chinatown. While writing about the family she was forced to leave behind in a refugee camp, she witnesses a relative's involvement with gangs and works in a garment industry sweatshop. Written and directed by Iranian filmmaker Marva Nabili. 116 min. In English, Mandarin and Cantonese with English subtitles.
70-3463 Was $79.99 *$29.99*

The Killing Floor (1985)
Effective and often brutal tale of the birth of the labor movement as told through the eyes of a black sharecropper who becomes a union activist in the slaughterhouses of WWI Chicago. Damien Leake, Alfre Woodard, Moses Gunn star. 118 min.
73-1053 Was $79.99 *$24.99*

Valmont (1989)
Milos Forman's lush, beautifully photographed version of the "Dangerous Liaisons" story, detailing sexual games and role-playing in 18th-century France. Annette Bening, Meg Tilly and Colin Firth star. 138 min.
73-1078 Was $89.99 □*$14.99*

Cruel Intentions (1999)
"Dangerous Liaisons" goes to prep school in this stylish and seductive drama. Spoiled rich step-siblings Ryan Phillippe and Sarah Michelle Gellar amuse themselves with wagers on their various sexual conquests, but has Phillippe finally met his match with Reese Witherspoon, the headmaster's virginal daughter? Selma Blair, Swoosie Kurtz also star. 97 min.
02-3352 Was $19.99 □*$14.99*

Two Moon Junction (1988)
Her mother warned her about this kind of boy...but she couldn't warn her about the feelings he'd inspire. Heartfelt erotic drama about two teen lovers from opposite sides of the tracks stars Sherilyn Fenn, Louise Fletcher, Kristy McNichol, Burl Ives and Richard Tyson. Featuring some super-charged sex scenes. 104 min.
02-1147 Was $19.99 *$14.99*

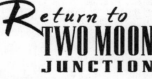

Return to
TWO MOON
JUNCTION

Return To Two Moon Junction (1994)
Sizzling sequel to the Zalman King scorcher focuses on an overworked supermodel who heads to the Southern estate of her grandmother for some relaxation after she finds her lover involved with her best friend. At the estate, she falls for a sculptor and begins a complex, erotic new romance. Melinda Clarke, John Clayton Schafer and Louise Fletcher star. 96 min.
68-1302 Was $89.99 □*$14.99*

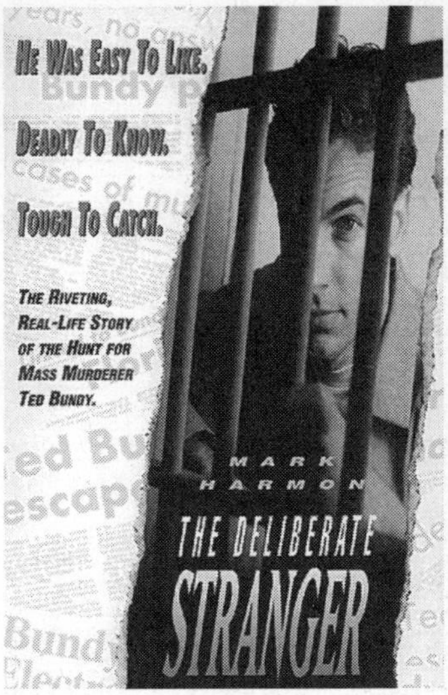
He Was Easy To Like.
Deadly To Know.
Tough To Catch.
The Riveting, Real-Life Story of the Hunt for Mass Murderer Ted Bundy.
MARK HARMON
THE DELIBERATE STRANGER

The Deliberate Stranger (1986)
Mark Harmon turns in a frightening performance as serial killer Ted Bundy, a charming law student who was convicted and charged with killing three people in Florida and suspected of killing at least 25 women in six states. This riveting film follows the desperate manhunt that led to his arrest and 1989 execution. With Frederic Forrest and M. Emmet Walsh. 188 min.
19-2037 Was $69.99 ***$24.99***

Honeysuckle Rose (1980)
Willie Nelson, Amy Irving and Dyan Cannon star in the story of a country music star who is torn between his wife and his female singing partner. 120 min.
19-1008 Was $19.99 ***$14.99***

Purple Hearts (1984)
Cheryl Ladd is a dedicated nurse, Ken Wahl a navy doctor involved in a stormy romance set against the backdrop of the Vietnam War. A look at real people involved in the turbulent conflict. 115 min.
19-1334 Was $19.99 ***$14.99***

Love Letters (1983)
This highly-charged, erotic drama features Jamie Lee Curtis in some of the hottest mainstream love scenes ever captured on film. She's a beautiful deejay who falls for an older, married artist (James Keach), until their relationship turns to emotional obsession. Bud Cort, Amy Madigan and Sally Kirkland co-star. AKA: "Passion Play." 95 min.
47-1289 ***$14.99***

Ice Castles (1979)
A young figure skater who dreams of the Olympics becomes blinded by an accident but her boyfriend encourages her to continue. Robby Benson, Lynn-Holly Johnson co-star. 109 min.
02-1044 Was $69.99 ***$14.99***

The New Centurions (1972)
George C. Scott plays a veteran L.A. beat cop terrified of his impending retirement, and Stacy Keach is his new partner, a rookie officer studying to be a lawyer in this gripping look at police life. Based on Joseph Wambaugh's book; with Jane Alexander, Erik Estrada. 103 min.
02-1052 ***$14.99***

Family Life (1971)
Moving tale, shot in documentary style, about an emotionally disturbed young British woman who struggles to break free from the grip of her domineering parents. Early work from noted director Ken Loach stars Sandy Ratcliff, Bill Dean, Grace Cave. AKA: "Wednesday's Child." 108 min.
02-1114 Was $79.99 ***$19.99***

QB VII (1974)
An epic drama from Leon Uris' best-seller tells of a libel suit involving a Polish doctor and an American writer. But the powerful story also deals with the Middle East crisis, the Holocaust, and the ethics of journalism. Ben Gazzara, Anthony Hopkins, Lee Remick. 6 hours on three tapes.
02-1122 ***$139.99***

The Liberation Of L.B. Jones (1970)
Powerhouse drama takes a searing look at racism in the South. A black man decides to divorce his wife after he finds her involved in a romance with a white cop. Roscoe Lee Browne, Lola Falana, Lee J. Cobb; director William Wyler's last film. 102 min.
02-1364 ***$59.99***

Bless The Beasts And Children (1972)
Sensitively crafted tale of six young misfit boys at summer camp, and how their efforts to save a herd of buffalo headed for slaughter represents a search for growth and meaning in their own lives. Bill Mumy, Barry Robins star; directed by Stanley Kramer. The music by Barry De Vorzon and Perry Botkin was later used as the theme for TV's "The Young and the Restless." 109 min.
02-1448 ***$14.99***

You Light Up My Life (1977)
An aspiring singer/songwriter about to give up on her dreams finds new purpose thanks to a handsome director and a hit song. With Didi Conn, Joe Silver, and that memorable title tune. 90 min.
02-1057 Was $59.99 ***$14.99***

Hardcore (1979)
George C. Scott searches for his missing daughter in the dark, bizarre world of the pornography industry. Peter Boyle, Season Hubley co-star; written and directed by Paul Schrader. 108 min.
02-1109 ***$14.99***

Hijack! (1973)
David Janssen and Keenan Wynn are truckers driving a mysterious cargo from Los Angeles to Houston who find themselves facing all sorts of hazards while trying to complete their mission. Jeanette Nolan, Lee Purcell and William Schallert also star.
50-8121 ***$19.99***

Summer Wishes, Winter Dreams (1973)
Joanne Woodward and Martin Balsam star in this tender drama as a married couple who find themselves haunted by memories of the past and desperately clinging to one another for strength. Co-stars Sylvia Sidney, Dori Brenner. 93 min.
02-1516 Was $59.99 ***$14.99***

R.P.M. (1970)
Anthony Quinn is a liberal college professor who is appointed to the school's presidency during violent campus protests and must work to defuse tensions. Evocative drama from Stanley Kramer also stars Ann-Margret, Gary Lockwood, Paul Winfield. Written by Erich Segal. 90 min.
02-1525 Was $59.99 ***$14.99***

Shattered (1975)
Peter Finch stars in this bizarre drama as a weak-willed British bureaucrat whose life takes some surprising twists when he takes in a pregnant babysitter after his wife (Shelley Winters) leaves him. Co-stars Colin Blakely and Linda Hayden. AKA: "Something to Hide." 100 min.
03-1211 ***$12.99***

The Helter Skelter Murders (1971)
Shocking dramatization of the Manson cult's reign of terror that culminated in the savage Tate-LaBianca slayings graphically depicts their depraved life of sex, drugs and violence. Features songs written and performed (if that's the correct word) by Manson himself; Brian Klinkett, Debbie Duff star. AKA: "Other Side of Madness." 83 min.
03-1698 Was $59.99 ***$19.99***

10 Rillington Place (1971)
True drama of a sensational British murder case that led to the abolition of the death penalty. John Hurt is a man sentenced to die for the murder of his family, a crime he didn't commit. Richard Attenborough, Judy Geeson co-star. 111 min.
02-1562 Was $59.99 ***$19.99***

The Go-Between (1971)
One of the most requested titles at Movies Unlimited, this sumptuously filmed story from director Joseph Losey and writer Harold Pinter is set in England in 1900 and stars Julie Christie as a woman engaged to aristocrat Edward Fox. But her heart belongs to farmer Alan Bates, and she uses a boy infatuated with her to act as a courier for her love letters. With Dominic Guard. 118 min.
02-2847 ***$19.99***

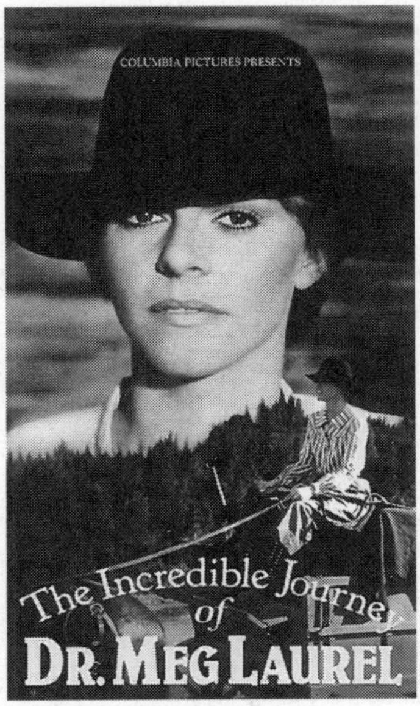
COLUMBIA PICTURES PRESENTS
The Incredible Journey of
DR. MEG LAUREL

The Incredible Journey Of Dr. Meg Laurel (1979)
Lindsay Wagner stars in this inspiring, true story about a city doctor who begins practicing in rural Appalachia in order to help the poor there. Jane Wyman co-stars in this moving drama. 150 min.
02-1379 Was $59.99 ***$19.99***

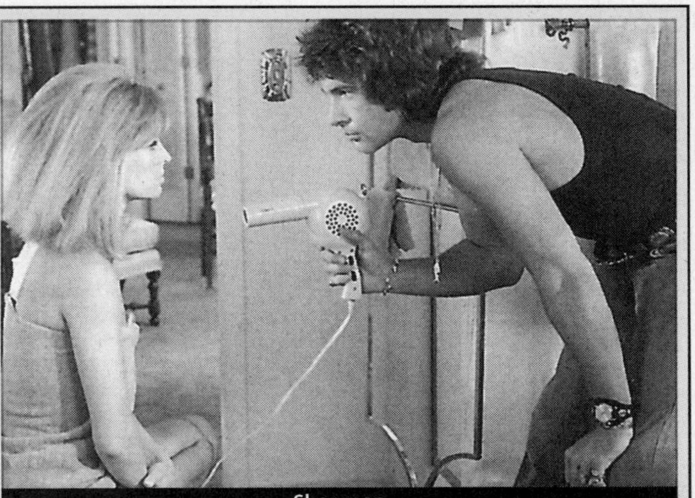
Shampoo

Warren Beatty

All Fall Down (1962)
A callous, free-spirited young man (Warren Beatty), who is idolized by his younger brother (Brandon de Wilde), seduces the older woman (Eva Marie Saint) who has come to visit his parents' home. When their relationship results in tragedy, the once-adoring brother seeks revenge for the wrongs committed by his older sibling. With Angela Lansbury, Karl Malden; scripted by William Inge. 110 min.
12-2411 ***$19.99***

Lilith (1964)
Haunting psychological drama, adapted from J.R. Salamanca's controversial novel, about a young therapist (Warren Beatty) whose love for a beautiful schizophrenic (Jean Seberg) endangers his work and, ultimately, his life. Co-stars Kim Hunter, Gene Hackman, Jessica Walter and Peter Fonda. Director Robert Rossen's ("The Hustler") final film. 115 min.
02-1414 Was $59.99 ***$19.99***

Promise Her Anything (1966)
Romantic farce stars Warren Beatty as a Greenwich Village girlie filmmaker who falls for widow Leslie Caron, the mother of an 18-month-old baby. But she's attracted to her kid-hating child psychologist boss (Robert Cummings). Hermione Gingold, Lionel Stander co-star; Arthur Hiller directs. 98 min.
06-1944 □***$14.99***

Kaleidoscope (1966)
Jet-setting playboy/gambler Warren Beatty breaks into a Geneva card factory and marks printing plates, allowing him to clean up at European casinos. When girlfriend Susannah York's Scotland Yard inspector father learns of this, he "persuades" Beatty to help the police nab a notorious drug dealer. Light-hearted mix of crime drama and romantic comedy also stars Clive Revill, Eric Porter. 103 min.
19-2416 ***$19.99***

Bonnie And Clyde (1967)
"They're young, they're in love, they rob banks!" Arthur Penn's dramatic (if not totally accurate) depiction of the famed '30s criminal pair ushered in a new era in screen realism. Warren Beatty, Faye Dunaway, Michael J. Pollard, Gene Hackman and Best Supporting Actress Oscar-winner Estelle Parsons star; look for Gene Wilder. Includes original trailer; 111 min.
19-1020 □***$19.99***

The Parallax View (1974)
Stylish, arresting thriller from Alan J. Pakula, with Warren Beatty as a determined reporter investigating an unfolding political conspiracy involving a covert organization and the mysterious deaths of witnesses to a senator's assassination three years earlier. Hume Cronyn, William Daniels, Paula Prentiss co-star. 102 min.
06-1142 ***$14.99***

Shampoo (1975)
Warren Beatty stars as the Beverly Hills hairdresser who gives his lovely customers very personal service in this sexy, Oscar-winning comedy. Hilarious look at upper class amorality in the late '60s also stars Julie Christie, Goldie Hawn, Lee Grant, Jack Warden and Carrie Fisher; Hal Ashby directs. 112 min.
02-1500 ***$14.99***

The Fortune (1975)
Director Mike Nichols' comical "love" triangle stars Warren Beatty and Jack Nicholson as a pair of slick '20s con men who become rivals for the affections—and considerable inheritance—of heiress Stockard Channing. When an elaborate marriage scheme fails, the crooks join forces to bump off Channing and share in the money. With Florence Stanley, Scatman Crothers. 88 min.
02-3167 Was $19.99 ***$14.99***

Heaven Can Wait (1978)
A magical fantasy comedy starring Warren Beatty as a deceased football player who returns to Earth as a wealthy playboy. Based on "Here Comes Mr. Jordan," this warm, likable lark co-stars Julie Christie, Dyan Cannon, Charles Grodin, Jack Warden. 100 min.
06-1026 ***$14.99***

Reds (1981)
Warren Beatty starred in, directed and wrote this epic drama about American journalist John Reed, who ventured to Russia and recorded the 1917 Revolution in his book "Ten Days That Shook the World." Exciting, romantic, with superb acting from Diane Keaton, Maureen Stapleton, Jack Nicholson. 200 min.
06-1158 Was $29.99 □***$24.99***

Dick Tracy (1990)
Director/star Warren Beatty is Chester Gould's comic-strip detective, fighting an array of grotesque villains in order to free the city from crime boss Al Pacino's grip. Madonna co-stars as singer Breathless Mahoney, who may or may not be Tracy's ally. Fantastic sets and make-up and jazzy Stephen Sondheim songs help bring the funny-page favorite to colorful life. Glenne Headly, Bill Forsythe, R.G. Armstrong and Dustin Hoffman co-star. 105 min.
11-1511 □***$14.99***

Bugsy (1991)
A lavish, romantic and entertaining account of the life and crimes of Benjamin "Bugsy" Siegel. Warren Beatty stars as the dangerous gangster who ran the Los Angeles rackets, was romantically involved with actress Virginia Hill and launched the gambling mecca of Las Vegas by building the Flamingo Hotel. Annette Bening, Ben Kingsley, Harvey Keitel, Elliott Gould co-star; directed by Barry Levinson. 135 min.
02-2208 Was $19.99 □***$14.99***

Love Affair (1994)
The third filming of the classic cinematic romance (fourth, if you count "Sleepless in Seattle") stars Warren Beatty and Annette Bening as two people who meet by chance while vacationing and fall in love. Unsure of what to do next, they separate and vow to meet in three months' time...an appointment that one will have trouble keeping. With Pierce Brosnan, Garry Shandling, and a memorable supporting turn by Katharine Hepburn as Beatty's aunt. 108 min.
19-2313 Was $19.99 □***$14.99***

Bulworth (1998)
Is the American public ready for a politician who tells the truth? In the final days of his re-election campaign, burned-out U.S. senator Warren Beatty takes out a contract on his own life and, with nothing to lose, begins speaking candidly about race relations, corruption and media politics to his astonished constituents. Halle Berry, Oliver Platt and Don Cheadle co-star in this bitingly sharp satire directed and co-scripted by Beatty. 108 min.
04-3804 Was $99.99 □***$14.99***

Bulworth (Letterboxed Version)
Also available in a theatrical, widescreen format.
04-3805 □***$14.99***

Please see our index for these other Warren Beatty titles: *$ (Dollars) • Ishtar • McCabe And Mrs. Miller • The Roman Spring Of Mrs. Stone • Splendor In The Grass*

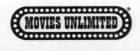

Velocity (The Wild Ride) (1958)
An early Jack Nicholson vehicle that helped establish his screen persona. Here he's a hot-rodding punk who enjoys running motorcycle cops off the road and tries to steal his ex-partner's girlfriend. Robert Bean co-stars. 59 min.
09-1311 Was $19.99 **$14.99**

Ride In The Whirlwind (1967)
Three wandering cowboys in the Old West are falsely accused of being outlaws and hunted in this action-packed film starring and co-written by Jack Nicholson. With Cameron Mitchell, Millie Perkins, and an early appearance by Harry Dean Stanton. Directed by Monte Hellman ("The Shooting"). 82 min.
14-6022 **$14.99**

Ride In The Whirlwind (Letterboxed Version)
Also available in a theatrical, widescreen format.
08-1832 **$14.99**

The Shooting (1967)
A young woman sets out with two hired guns on a mission of vengeance in this offbeat and suspenseful Western, directed by Monte Hellman. Millie Perkins, Will Hutchins, Warren Oates and Jack Nicholson star in this mystical companion piece to "Ride in the Whirlwind." 82 min.
15-1167 Was $19.99 **$14.99**

The Shooting (Letterboxed Version)
Also available in a theatrical, widescreen format.
08-1833 **$14.99**

Hell's Angels On Wheels (1967)
When the notorious Hell's Angels ride into town, gas station attendant Jack Nicholson leaves his boring life behind and joins up with them for a world of bikes, babes, booze and brawling. Things get heavy, though, when Nicholson falls for leader Adam Roarke's girl. Classic cycle thriller from director Richard Rush also stars Sabrina Scharf, Jana Taylor. 100 min.
27-6133 **$12.99**

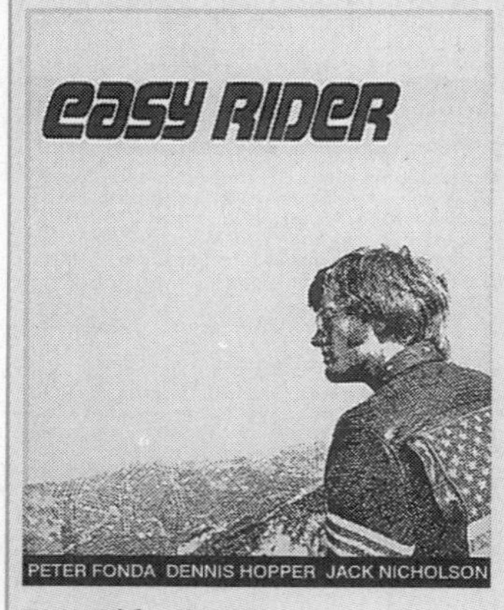

Easy Rider (1969)
Drugged-out motorcyclists Peter Fonda and Dennis Hopper "head out on the highway" on a search for America in the landmark drama that spoke to a generation. Joining them on their "trip" is spaced-out lawyer Jack Nicholson. Co-scripted and directed by the stars, the film also features Karen Black, Phil Spector, and music by Jimi Hendrix, The Byrds and others. 94 min.
02-1072 Was $19.99 **$14.99**

Easy Rider (Letterboxed Version)
Also available in a theatrical, widescreen format.
02-3152 **$19.99**

Rebel Rousers (1970)
Filmed in 1967 and not released until three years later, after the success of "Easy Rider," this revved-up motorcycle drama stars Bruce Dern and Jack Nicholson as bikers whose feud with architect Cameron Mitchell leads to a race. The prize: Mitchell's girlfriend! With Diane Ladd, Harry Dean Stanton. 77 min.
03-1061 **$12.99**

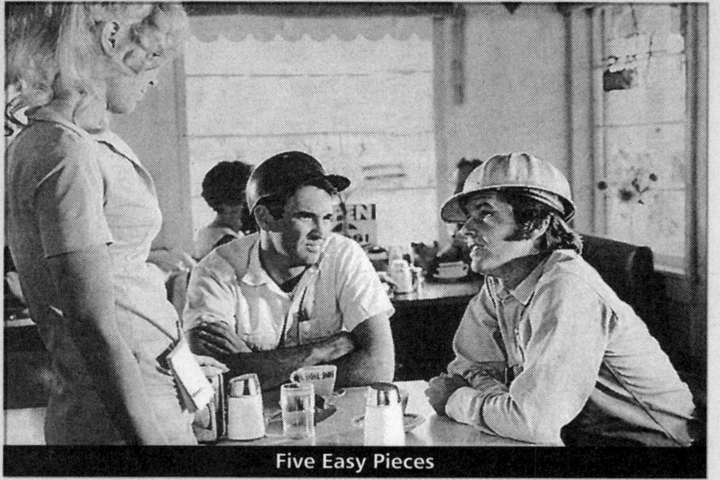
Five Easy Pieces

Jack Nicholson

Five Easy Pieces (1970)
Bob Rafelson's acclaimed drama, steeped in '60s Zeitgeist, stars Jack Nicholson as an oil rig worker who returns to the family he left behind years earlier to visit his dying father. Karen Black garnered an Oscar as Nicholson's girlfriend; with Susan Anspach, Ralph Waite, William Challee, Sally Struthers and Lorna Thayer as the "no substitutions" waitress. 96 min.
02-1889 **$14.99**

Carnal Knowledge (1971)
Potent, cynical study of the sex lives of two friends (Jack Nicholson and Art Garfunkel) which follows their initiation into sex during college to their burnt-out lives in the late '60s. Script by Jules Feiffer, directed by Mike Nichols. Candice Bergen, Ann-Margret co-star. 96 min.
53-1073 **$14.99**

The King Of Marvin Gardens (1972)
An incisive, moody study of a Philadelphia disc jockey (Jack Nicholson) who visits his crooked, beloved brother (Bruce Dern) in Atlantic City and finds that he has plans to rip off a mobster and use the loot to buy a tropical island. Ellen Burstyn and Scatman Crothers also star in Bob Rafelson's powerful, somber drama. 104 min.
02-2428 Was $79.99 **$19.99**

The Last Detail (1973)
Two Shore Patrol officers are assigned to escort a young sailor convicted of theft to a naval prison, but along the way give him a raucous "going away party." Often funny and always off-color look at life, Navy-style stars Jack Nicholson in an Oscar-nominated role, Otis Young and Randy Quaid. 104 min.
02-1118 **$14.99**

Chinatown: 25th Anniversary Edition (1974)
Roman Polanski's marvelous blend of '40s "noir" mystery and modern sexual tensions stars Jack Nicholson as Jake Gittes, the L.A. gumshoe involved in a case of shady business dealings and corrupt politics who sticks his nose where it doesn't belong one time too many. Faye Dunaway, John Huston, John Hillerman co-star. Special anniversary edition includes interviews with Polanski, producer Robert Evans and writer Robert Towne. 131 min.
06-2923 ❑**$14.99**

Chinatown: 25th Anniversary Edition (Letterboxed Version)
Also available in a theatrical, widescreen format.
06-2924 ❑**$14.99**

The Two Jakes (1990)
Jack Nicholson returns as private eye Jake Gittes in the long-awaited sequel to "Chinatown." Set in 1948 Los Angeles, this riveting mystery has Gittes investigating a case of adultery and murder, only to find a web of land fraud, scheming oil barons, and a mysterious link to the past. Harvey Keitel, Meg Tilly, Reuben Blades co-star; directed by Nicholson and written by "Chinatown" scripter Robert Towne. 137 min.
06-1790 Was $89.99 **$19.99**

One Flew Over The Cuckoo's Nest (1975)
The first film in over 40 years to win five major Academy Awards (Best Picture, Director, Actor, Actress and Screenplay), Milos Forman's emotional adaptation of the Ken Kesey novel stars Jack Nicholson as a rebellious mental ward inmate whose anti-authority ways inspire his fellow patients and pit him against dictatorial nurse Louise Fletcher. With Will Sampson, Danny DeVito, Christopher Lloyd. 129 min.
63-1612 ❑**$19.99**

Goin' South (1978)
Director-star Jack Nicholson is a nomadic cad in 1870s Kansas, spared from the hangman's noose by marrying spinster Mary Steenburgen. A love-hate relationship blossoms as they defend her ranchland; Christopher Lloyd and John Belushi co-star in this raucous romance. 109 min.
06-1022 **$14.99**

The Postman Always Rings Twice (1981)
Jessica Lange and Jack Nicholson are the people involved in a torrid love affair that leads to a murder plot. Intense, erotic reworking of the John Garfield-Lana Turner classic. Bob Rafelson directs from James M. Cain's novel. 123 min.
19-1782 Was $19.99 **$14.99**

The Border (1982)
Jack Nicholson turns in a powerful performance as a border patrolman pushed over the edge. Adult action-packed drama. Harvey Keitel, Valerie Perrine, Warren Oates. 107 min.
07-1107 Was $39.99 **$14.99**

Prizzi's Honor (1985)
Jack Nicholson and Kathleen Turner are a married couple in the same line of work; they're both contract hit men! What happens when their next assignments turn out to be each other makes for an exciting adventure tinged with dark humor. John Huston directs; with Robert Loggia, William Hickey and Best Supporting Actress Academy Award-winner Anjelica Huston. 129 min.
47-1501 Was $29.99 **$14.99**

Prizzi's Honor (Letterboxed Version)
Also available in a theatrical, widescreen format.
08-8680 **$14.99**

The Witches Of Eastwick (1987)
Devilish stranger Jack Nicholson enters a New England village and sets about seducing townswomen Cher, Michelle Pfeiffer and Susan Sarandon, releasing in each woman supernatural powers, in this stylish and darkly funny fantasy/drama. George Miller directs; adapted from the John Updike novel. 120 min.
19-1632 ❑**$14.99**

Man Trouble (1992)
After a break-in at her home and some threatening calls, opera singer Ellen Barkin decides to get a guard dog. What she winds up with is a pair of undisciplined curs: her new dog and scruffy trainer Jack Nicholson. Light-hearted romantic comedy that reunites Nicholson with "Five Easy Pieces" director and screenwriter Bob Rafelson and Carole Eastman also stars Beverly D'Angelo, Harry Dean Stanton. 100 min.
04-2594 Was $19.99 ❑**$14.99**

Hoffa (1992)
Jack Nicholson turns in a galvanizing performance as legendary labor leader Jimmy Hoffa, whose strong-arm tactics helped organize the Teamsters. The film follows Hoffa's rise to power, his feuds with organized crime figures and the government, and mysterious disappearance. Danny DeVito, who also directed, co-stars; with Armand Assante and J.T. Walsh. 140 min.
04-2632 Was $19.99 ❑**$14.99**

Wolf (1994)
After he's bitten by a wolf in the New England wilderness, world-weary New York book editor Jack Nicholson discovers that his senses have intensified and he's taking on lupine characteristics. The animal in him soon takes over as he ferociously battles enemies and has a torrid affair with his boss's daughter. Michelle Pfeiffer, James Spader and Kate Nelligan co-star; directed by Mike Nichols. 125 min.
02-2662 Was $19.99 ❑**$14.99**

Wolf (Letterboxed Version)
Also available in a theatrical, widescreen format.
02-3241 ❑**$19.99**

The Crossing Guard (1995)
Written and directed by Sean Penn, this powerful drama stars Jack Nicholson as a man whose life was shattered six years earlier when his young daughter was killed by a drunk driver. Now divorced and obsessed with revenge, Nicholson confronts the driver after his release from jail, as both men must come to terms with what the incident has cost them. David Morse, Anjelica Huston, Robin Wright co-star. 111 min.
11-2017 Was $19.99 ❑**$14.99**

As Good As It Gets (1997)
Best Actor and Actress Academy Awards went to Jack Nicholson as a curmudgeonly, psychologically obsessed New York author and Helen Hunt as the caring waitress and single mother who helps draw him out of his successful but isolated existence in writer/director James L. Brooks' acclaimed seriocomedy. With Greg Kinnear as Nicholson's gay neighbor, Shirley Knight and Cuba Gooding, Jr. 139 min.
02-3164 Was $19.99 ❑**$14.99**

As Good As It Gets (Letterboxed Version)
Also available in a theatrical, widescreen format.
02-3172 ❑**$19.99**

Blood & Wine (1997)
Jack Nicholson and director Bob Rafelson ("Five Easy Pieces") reunite for a gripping crime drama that features Nicholson as a high-living Miami wine merchant who teams with safecracker Michael Caine to rob his well-to-do clientele, until problems from Nicholson's wife (Judy Davis), mistress (Jennifer Lopez) and stepson (Stephen Dorff) threaten their proverbial "one last job." 101 min.
04-3462 Was $99.99 ❑**$14.99**

Please see our index for these other Jack Nicholson titles: *Batman • Broadcast News • Ensign Pulver • The Evening Star • A Few Good Men • The Fortune • Heartburn • The Last Tycoon • Little Shop Of Horrors • Mars Attacks! • The Missouri Breaks • On A Clear Day You Can See Forever • Reds • The Raven • The Shining • The St. Valentine's Day Massacre • Terms Of Endearment • The Terror • Tommy*

Islands In The Stream (1977)
Adaptation of Hemingway's novel about an island-dwelling sculptor (George C. Scott) and his three sons. Beautifully done in the Bahamas. 110 min.
06-1028 Was $19.99 **$14.99**

Message To My Daughter (1973)
Bonnie Bedelia, Martin Sheen and Kitty Winn turn in powerhouse performances in this drama concerning a troubled teenager who finds much-needed help for her emotional problems when she listens to tapes recorded years earlier by her now-deceased mother. 76 min.
10-1594 Was $19.99 **$14.99**

Miles To Go Before I Sleep (1975)
Martin Balsam portrays a man who is given a new lease in life when he becomes the foster father of an orphaned 14-year-old girl. MacKenzie Phillips and James Keach also star. 78 min.
08-1792 **$19.99**

Badge 373 (1973)
Gripping, controversial crime drama stars Robert Duvall as a determined NYC cop out to bring a vicious crime syndicate to its knees. Verna Bloom and Eddie Egan, the real "Popeye Doyle," star in this actioner. 116 min.
06-1372 **$14.99**

Red Alert (1977)
Trouble strikes a nuclear power plant in this timely and disturbing drama that addresses the risks of atomic energy. William Devane, Ralph Waite, Adrienne Barbeau, M. Emmet Walsh star. 100 min.
06-1520 **$19.99**

First Love (1970)
Maximilian Schell directed and stars in this wonderful love story about a 16-year-old boy who becomes infatuated with a princess. Sensual, beautifully told. Dominique Sanda, John Moulder-Brown. 90 min.
08-1174 Was $29.99 **$19.99**

Hustling (1975)
A reporter, doing an article on streetwalking, uncovers more than she bargained for. Hard-hitting, gritty, superbly acted. Lee Remick, Jill Clayburgh, Burt Young. 96 min.
14-3033 **$19.99**

The River Niger (1976)
Powerhouse look at black family trying to come to terms with themselves and the tough world they live in. James Earl Jones, Cicely Tyson, Lou Gossett, Jr. 103 min.
14-6013 **$19.99**

Ginger In The Morning (1973)
Sissy Spacek is Ginger, a free-spirited young girl whose involvement with a conservative, middle-aged divorced man (Monte Markham) leads to troubles both touching and funny. Susan Oliver also stars. 90 min.
14-6026 Was $19.99 **$14.99**

Rivals (1979)
After moving to L.A. from Wyoming with his mother and siblings, a teenager must struggle to prove himself against a group of bullies in this family drama. Stewart Petersen, Dana Kimell star. star. 100 min.
10-1376 Was $49.99 **$14.99**

Ode To Billy Joe (1979)
Why did Billy Joe McAllister jump off the Tallahatchee Bridge? Find out in this poignant study about a confused love affair. Robby Benson, Glynnis O'Connor. 100 min.
19-1198 **$14.99**

Punch And Jody (1974)
Glenn Ford turns in a sensitive performance as a travelling circus performer whose life takes an unexpected turn when his teenage daughter comes back into his life. Pam Griffin, Ruth Roman, Billy Barty and Pat Morita star. 78 min.
10-1596 Was $19.99 **$14.99**

If Ever I See You Again (1978)
Joe Brooks, the writer of the hit song "You Light Up My Life," stars as a composer out to win back the heart of the girl who rejected him years ago in this tender drama. Co-stars Jimmy Breslin and, in her first leading role, Shelley Hack. 105 min.
02-1663 *$69.99*

The Pursuit Of Happiness (1971)
A young man is tried for accidentally killing someone while driving, but while his lawyer father fights for his release, his own rebellious attitude lands him in jail. Riveting drama stars E.G. Marshall, Michael Sarrazin, Arthur Hill and Barbara Hershey. 85 min.
02-1683 *$69.99*

The Love Machine (1971)
Jacqueline Susann's torrid tale of the handsome young TV network exec (John Phillip Law) whose desire for women was only outstripped by his lust for power is brought to vivid life. Dyan Cannon, Robert Ryan, Jackie Cooper, David Hemmings co-star. 108 min.
02-1768 Was $69.99 *$19.99*

The Paper Chase (1973)
Drama about a Harvard Law School student (Timothy Bottoms) and his battle with his tough professor (John Houseman) in the classroom as well as at home, when he falls in love with the prof's daughter (Lindsay Wagner). 111 min.
04-1109 Was $19.99 *$14.99*

An Unmarried Woman (1978)
In a tour-de-force performance, Jill Clayburgh plays a New York art gallery worker trying to cope with life after her husband walks out on her following a 15 year marriage. After seeing a therapist and exploring the singles scene, Clayburgh finally finds happiness with artist Alan Bates. Sensitively written and directed by Paul Mazursky, the film also stars Michael Murphy, Lisa Lucas. 124 min.
04-1171 Was $69.99 *$29.99*

Jenny (1970)
In order to avoid the draft and going to Vietnam, aspiring filmmaker Alan Alda agrees to a marriage of convenience with unwed mother-to-be Marlo Thomas. Things take an unexpected turn when the couple fall in love in this offbeat romantic drama. Elizabeth Wilson, Vincent Gardenia also star. 90 min.
04-1294 *$14.99*

End Of The Road (1970)
Powerful, shocking drama full of '60s symbolism and sensibilities. Stacy Keach stars as an unstable college professor who, while being advised to "do his own thing," takes another teacher's wife as his lover. Co-stars James Earl Jones, Dorothy Tristan. Based on a John Barth novel; originally rated "X" for its extreme frankness. 110 min.
04-1903 Was $59.99 ❑*$14.99*

The Runner Stumbles (1979)
Dick Van Dyke and Kathleen Quinlan star in this disturbing film, based on a true incident, about the unusual secret relationship between a priest and a young nun. But when the nun is murdered, and the priest is suspect, the truth must be revealed! Absorbing drama co-stars Maureen Stapleton and Beau Bridges. 99 min.
04-1912 Was $59.99 ❑*$29.99*

Conrack (1974)
True drama stars Jon Voight as a teacher whose unconventional methods endear him to an impoverished island community in South Carolina and bring him up against a staid school superintendent. Paul Winfield, Hume Cronyn also star. 111 min.
04-3056 Was $59.99 ❑*$29.99*

War And Peace (1972)
Set against the tumult of 19th-century Russia at the height of the Napoleonic Wars, this lavish (and lengthy) BBC adaptation of Leo Tolstoy's timeless (and lengthy) novel stars Anthony Hopkins in an acclaimed early performance as the idealistic Pierre and Morag Hood as Natasha, his true love. With Alan Dobie, Rupert Davies, Fiona Gaunt and David Swift as Napoleon. 12 1/2 hrs. on six tapes.
04-3389 Was $149.99 ❑*$99.99*

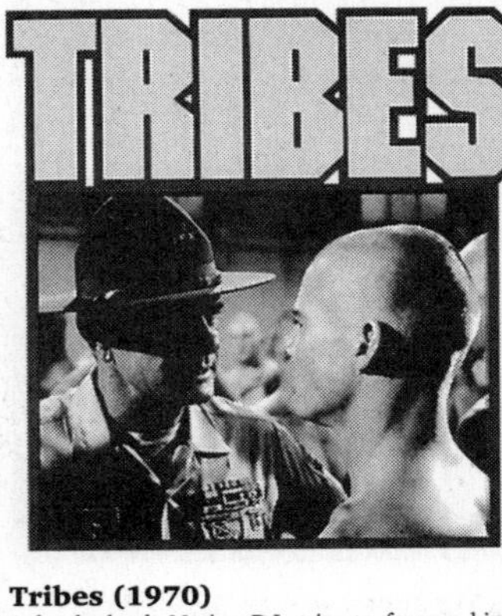

Tribes (1970)
A by-the-book Marine D.I. tries to force a hippie draftee to toe the line, but his unconventional attitude begins affecting those around him, and the battle of wills builds to a shattering climax. Incisive Emmy Award-winning drama stars Darren McGavin, Jan-Michael Vincent, Earl Holliman. 89 min.
04-2178 Was $59.99 *$29.99*

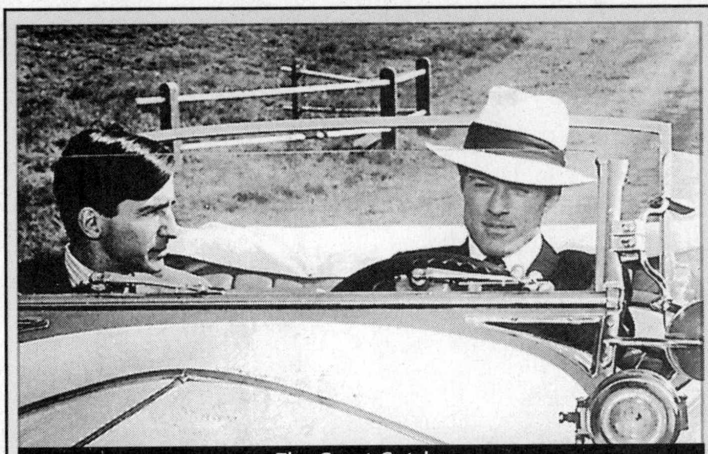

The Great Gatsby

Robert Redford

Downhill Racer (1969)
Dazzling ski scenes spark this compelling character study of an egotistical small town skier (Robert Redford) who receives a chance for fame in the Olympics, only to discover the glory to be all too fleeting. Co-stars Gene Hackman, Camilla Sparv; Michael Ritchie's directorial debut. 102 min.
06-1013 *$14.99*

The Candidate (1972)
Robert Redford plays an idealistic, young politician running for a Senate seat against an old-line incumbent. This sharp satire on politics and media features a keen supporting cast, with Peter Boyle and Allen Garfield. Michael Ritchie directs. 110 min.
19-1023 *$19.99*

Jeremiah Johnson (1972)
Exquisitely photographed in Utah, this western adventure from Sydney Pollack stars Robert Redford as a rugged mountain man in the 1830s Rockies who shuns civilization and learns to subsist in the wilderness, then hunts down the Crow Indians who were responsible for the deaths of his common-law wife and adopted son. Co-stars Will Geer. 116 min.
19-1136 Was $19.99 *$14.99*

Jeremiah Johnson (Letterboxed Version)
Also available in a theatrical, widescreen format.
19-2591 ❑*$19.99*

The Way We Were: 25th Anniversary Edition (1973)
One of the finest screen romances ever teams Robert Redford and Barbra Streisand as two philosophically different types whose love affair stretches from their '30s college days to marriage and the turmoil of '50s Hollywood. Bradford Dillman, Viveca Lindfors co-star; fine Marvin Hamlisch score. 118 min.
02-1165 Remastered ❑*$14.99*

The Great Gatsby (1974)
Robert Redford essays the title role of F. Scott Fitzgerald's gangster-turned-golden boy of '20s society in this lavishly photographed film adaptation of the classic novel. Mia Farrow co-stars as Gatsby's true love, Daisy; with Bruce Dern, Karen Black, Sam Waterston and Patsy Kensit (in her film debut). Scripted by Francis Ford Coppola. 144 min.
06-1101 Was $19.99 ❑*$14.99*

Three Days Of The Condor (1975)
Intricate thriller from director Sydney Pollack stars Robert Redford as a spy novel reader for the CIA (who looked for potential ploys in the books' plots) who sets out to discover who is responsible for the murders of his co-workers and uncovers a network of illegal activity within "The Company." Co-stars Faye Dunaway, Cliff Robertson, Max von Sydow. 117 min.
06-1066 *$14.99*

The Electric Horseman (1979)
Robert Redford and Jane Fonda team up. A man steals a valuable thoroughbred and heads for the hills with a reporter looking for a scoop, but instead they find romance. 120 min.
07-1017 Was $19.99 *$14.99*

Brubaker (1980)
An idealistic, uncompromising warden (Robert Redford) tries to implement reforms and uncovers a shocking scandal. A vivid look at prison life based on a true story. 131 min.
04-1297 Was $19.99 *$14.99*

The Natural (1984)
Robert Redford hits a grand slam as a mysterious rookie baseball player whose out-of-this-world slugging abilities bring the lowly New York Knights out of the cellar. An old-fashioned, all-American tale, based on Bernard Malamud's classic novel. Robert Duvall, Glenn Close, Kim Basinger. 138 min.
02-1362 Was $19.99 ❑*$14.99*

Legal Eagles (1986)
Robert Redford, Debra Winger and Daryl Hannah star in this comedy/drama that jabs at the worlds of art and jurisprudence, as two lawyers from opposite sides of the courtroom come to the aid of a young woman charged with stealing one of her father's paintings and become involved in a crime ring. 114 min.
07-1481 ❑*$14.99*

Havana (1990)
In Sydney Pollack's lavish romantic epic, Robert Redford plays a professional card shark looking for a big score in 1958 Cuba, a country on the verge of revolution. His involvement with the beautiful wife of a revolutionary leader leads him into a world of danger and espionage. Lena Olin, Alan Arkin and Raul Julia also star. 145 min.
07-1683 Was $19.99 ❑*$14.99*

Sneakers (1992)
A riveting, entertaining thriller starring Robert Redford as a computer wizard who has been living underground since the '60s and leads a group of other "hackers" in hi-tech security work. Some shady government agents involve them in a scheme to break national security codes. Sidney Poitier, Dan Aykroyd, Mary McDonnell, River Phoenix, Ben Kingsley also star. 125 min.
07-1906 Was $19.99 ❑*$14.99*

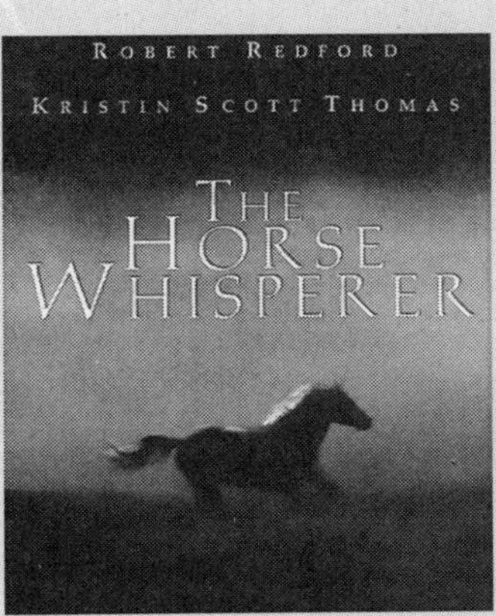

The Horse Whisperer (1998)
Robert Redford directed and stars in this poignant treatment of Nicholas Evans' hit novel. He's a Montana horse expert called on by New York magazine editor Kristin Scott Thomas to tame her horse, that's been troubled by a recent fall. Redford also lends emotional support to Thomas' handicapped daughter (Scarlett Johansson), while becoming romantically involved with Thomas. With Sam Neill. 169 min.
11-2803 Was $19.99 ❑*$14.99*

The Horse Whisperer (Letterboxed Version)
Also available in a theatrical, widescreen format.
11-2804 Was $99.99 ❑*$19.99*

Please see our index for these other Robert Redford titles: *All The President's Men • Barefoot In The Park • A Bridge Too Far • Butch Cassidy And The Sundance Kid • Indecent Proposal • Inside Daisy Clover • Out Of Africa • The Sting • This Property Is Condemned • Up Close And Personal*

A Separate Peace (1972)
John Knowles' sensitive novel depicting the adult traumas young students at an East Coast prep school must face in the early '40s, including the possibility of their participation in World War II, is faithfully translated to the screen with this drama starring John Heyl, Parker Stevenson and William Roerick. 104 min.
06-1143 Was $44.99 *$19.99*

Jonathan Livingston Seagull (1973)
Based on the popular book by Richard Bach, this warm and exhilarating film traces the life of a flock of seagulls, and of one bird in particular who learns "to fly farther, higher and faster than ever before." Includes an award-winning score composed and sung by Neil Diamond. 99 min.
06-1153 Was $29.99 *$14.99*

The Day Of The Locust (1975)
Nathanael West's novel, an unflinching decrial of 1930s Hollywood, is magnificently rendered to the screen by director John Schlesinger, with William Atherton as a high-minded art director who surrounds himself with strange characters, among them flighty, shallow actress Karen Black, her has-been vaudevillian father Burgess Meredith and her caring but oafish lover Donald Sutherland. 144 min.
06-1181 Was $49.99 *$14.99*

Mary White (1977)
This poignant film is based on the true-life story of Mary White, a girl who gave up the pampered, privileged life she led in order to seek out her own identity. Only when she dies in a tragic accident does her family realize her true value and humanity. Ed Flanders, Kathleen Beller star. 102 min.
06-1283 Was $29.99 *$14.99*

The Education Of Sonny Carson (1974)
If you were a young black man in inner-city '50s Brooklyn, you wouldn't find what you had to know to survive in any book. Acclaimed autobiographical drama of life in the mean streets stars Rony Clanton, Don Gordon, Joyce Walker. 105 min.
05-1366 *$19.99*

Mandingo (1975)
It's a hot time in the old South tonight, as plantation owner James Mason delights in buying and breeding slaves, and his newest acquisition—a towering black man played by boxer Ken Norton—captures the fancy of daughter-in-law Susan George. Filled with torture, nudity and torrid interracial sexual encounters, this steamy drama also stars Perry King and Brenda Sykes. 126 min.
06-1039 *$14.99*

The Gambler (1974)
James Caan is a gambling-obsessed college professor who tries to elude bookies on his trail with a big win in Las Vegas. But Caan takes his winnings and places them on sports bets that get him into deeper trouble. Lauren Hutton, Paul Sorvino and James Woods also star in this moody drama. 111 min.
06-1124 Was $69.99 *$14.99*

The Adventurers (1970)
Lavish drama from the popular Harold Robbins novel details the escapades (and sexcapades) of the playboy son of a Latin America ambassador who returns to his country to even the score with the dictator who raped and murdered his mother. With Bekim Fehmiu, Candice Bergen, Ernest Borgnine, Charles Aznavour, Olivia de Havilland and Jaclyn Smith. 177 min.
06-1906 ❑*$24.99*

The Dove (1974)
A 16-year-old boy sets out on a solo round-the-world boat trip, a five-year odyssey that sees him overcoming many obstacles and growing into manhood, in this exciting family drama that's based on a true story. Joseph Bottoms, Deborah Raffin, Dabney Coleman star. 105 min.
06-1929 ❑*$14.99*

Lipstick (1976)
Controversial account of the rape of a high-fashion model and her violent revenge. Margaux Hemingway shines as the model and Mariel Hemingway is her frightened sister. Chris Sarandon, Anne Bancroft co-star. 89 min.
06-1032 *$59.99*

Players (1979)
A tennis love story where Dean Paul Martin must choose between Ali MacGraw or the glory of Wimbledon. 120 min.
06-1047 Was $49.99 *$14.99*

Mahogany (1975)
Diana Ross is radiant as a world-famous fashion designer who finds success comes at the cost of her personal happiness. Moving love story also features Billy Dee Williams, Anthony Perkins. 109 min.
06-1119 Was $69.99 *$14.99*

First Love (1977)
Remember the "first time"? Well, if you do, you'll enjoy this look at all the warmth, humor and pangs of excitement of lovers falling in love. Susan Dey and William Katt play the couple, and Miss Dey has revealing, sensitive scenes in the nude. John Heard, Beverly D'Angelo. 92 min.
06-1018 Was $49.99 *$19.99*

Dementia 13 (1963)
Early directorial effort by Francis Ford Coppola is an eerie, bizarre story of madness, as a series of brutal axe murders occur on a Scottish island. Luana Anders, William Campbell, Patrick Magee star. 75 min.
10-1122 Was $19.99 ***$14.99***

Dementia 13 (Letterboxed Version)
Also available in a theatrical, widescreen format.
08-1726 ***$19.99***

You're A Big Boy Now (1966)
An early effort from director Francis Ford Coppola, this very 1960s farce follows a young man who yearns to move away from his overprotective parents and takes up with a liberal actress. Peter Kastner, Elizabeth Hartman, Geraldine Page star. 96 min.
19-1275 Was $19.99 ***$14.99***

The Rain People (1969)
Touching drama from director Francis Ford Coppola about a woman who leaves her husband and takes to the road with a former football player. Fine performances are offered by stars Shirley Knight, James Caan, Robert Duvall. 102 min.
19-1276 Was $59.99 ***$19.99***

The Godfather (1972)
Mario Puzo's brutal novel of Mafia life was brilliantly brought to the screen by director Francis Ford Coppola in this landmark drama that redefined the gangster film genre and earned Academy Awards for Best Picture, Screenplay and an (unaccepted) Best Actor Oscar for Marlon Brando as aging mob boss Don Vito Corleone. James Caan, John Cazale, Al Pacino and Robert Duvall co-star as Brando's sons, who try to keep the family "business" going in the midst of a mob war; with Diane Keaton, Talia Shire. 175 min.
06-2580 Remastered ***$24.99***

The Godfather (Letterboxed Version)
Also available in a theatrical, widescreen format.
06-2581 Remastered ***$24.99***

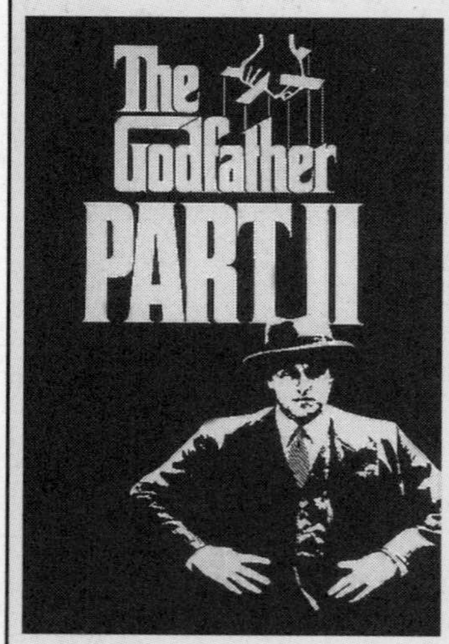
The Godfather
PART II

The Godfather, Part II (1975)
The story of the Corleone clan continues, as new boss Al Pacino launches a violent campaign to extend his family's power, while flashbacks with Robert De Niro as the young Vito Corleone show his rise to Mafia prominence, in the superb second "Godfather" film that earned six Oscars, including Best Picture, Director and Supporting Actor. With Robert Duvall, Michael V. Gazzo, Diane Keaton, Lee Strasberg. 200 min.
06-2582 Remastered ***$24.99***

The Godfather, Part II (Letterboxed Version)
Also available in a theatrical, widescreen format.
06-2583 Remastered ***$24.99***

The Godfather, Part III (1990)
The stunning third installment in Francis Ford Coppola's crime saga finds a weary Don Michael Corleone (Al Pacino) attempting to go straight for his family's sake and to finalize a complex business deal with the Vatican. However, as Pacino tries to get out, "they pull [him] back in," with tragic consequences. Diane Keaton, Andy Garcia, Talia Shire, Sofia Coppola co-star. Video version contains scenes not shown in theatres; 170 min.
06-2584 Remastered ***$24.99***

The Godfather, Part III (Letterboxed Version)
Also available in a theatrical, widescreen format.
06-2585 Remastered ***$24.99***

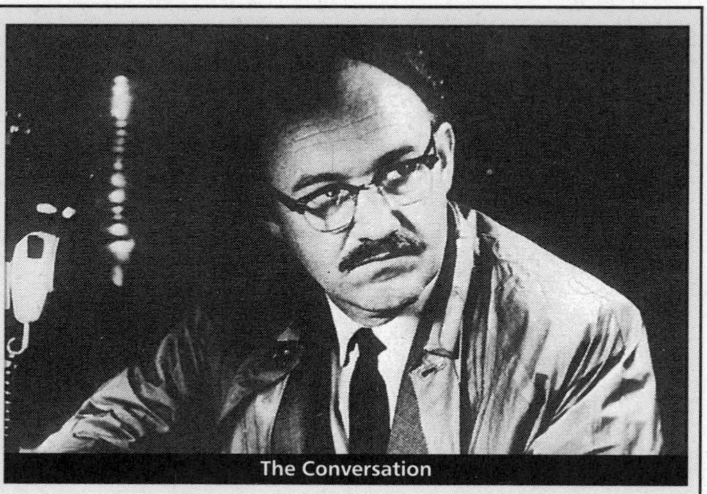
The Conversation

Francis Ford Coppola

The Godfather Collection
Here's an offer that...we think will be to your liking: all three remastered "Godfather" movies in a money-saving boxed set.
06-2586 Save $10.00! ***$64.99***

The Godfather Collection (Letterboxed Version)
Also available in a theatrical, widescreen format.
06-2587 Save $10.00! ***$64.99***

The Conversation (1974)
Francis Ford Coppola's intense study of Harry Caul (Gene Hackman), a surveillance expert who tapes a conversation shared by a young couple in San Francisco's Union Square. As Caul comes to believe the recording he made may lead to their deaths, he begins to question his profession and his own sense of privacy. John Cazale, Allen Garfield, Frederic Forrest, Cindy Williams, Teri Garr, Harrison Ford and Robert Duvall star in this stunning Watergate Era effort. Includes an 8-minute "Close-Up on 'The Conversation'" featurette.
06-1107 ***$14.99***

Apocalypse Now (1979)
Francis Ford Coppola's masterful Vietnam War-updating of Joseph Conrad's "Heart of Darkness" follows Army officer Martin Sheen on a harrowing mission to "terminate" renegade colonel Marlon Brando in his jungle fortress. Unforgettable battle sequences and sterling supporting performances from Robert Duvall, Frederic Forrest and Dennis Hopper mark this Academy Award-winning war drama. 153 min.
06-1106 Was $29.99 ***□$24.99***

Apocalypse Now (Letterboxed Version)
Also available in a theatrical, widescreen format.
06-1950 Was $29.99 ***□$24.99***

Rumble Fish (1983)
Matt Dillon is a troubled youth whose life changes when his legendary punk brother returns home. A unique look at teenage alienation, taken from S.E. Hinton's popular novel, directed by Francis Coppola. Mickey Rourke, Dennis Hopper, Tom Waits. Strikingly filmed in black and white. 94 min.
07-1198 Was $59.99 ***□$14.99***

The Outsiders (1983)
Beautiful and exciting adaptation of S.E. Hinton's classic tale of gangs and growing up in Oklahoma. Matt Dillon, Tom Cruise, Rob Lowe, Diane Lane, Patrick Swayze, Ralph Macchio, C. Thomas Howell and Emilio Estevez head the dynamic cast of rising stars; with Leif Garrett, Sofia Coppola. Francis Coppola directs. 91 min.
19-1278 ***$14.99***

The Cotton Club (1984)
The Golden Age of Harlem lives on in director Francis Ford Coppola's stunning drama, a mix of jazz music, romance and gangsters. Richard Gere stars as a musician working at the famed '30s nightclub who gets mixed up with the mob, and Diane Lane is the boss's girl he falls for; with Gregory and Maurice Hines, Bob Hoskins and Fred Gwynne.
53-1321 ***□$14.99***

Peggy Sue Got Married (1986)
A woman attending her high school reunion suddenly finds herself back 25 years in time and able to rethink the choices she made in her life. Francis Ford Coppola's comedy/drama of "second chances" stars Kathleen Turner, Nicolas Cage and Barry Miller. 104 min.
04-2034 ***□$14.99***

Gardens Of Stone (1987)
Francis Ford Coppola's stirring look at stateside soldiers during Vietnam stars James Caan and James Earl Jones as officers in charge of military burials at Arlington who try to dissuade a young recruit from requesting frontline duty. With D.B. Sweeney, Mary Stuart Masterson, Anjelica Huston. 111 min.
04-2104 Was $89.99 ***□$14.99***

Tucker: The Man And His Dream (1988)
He was the visionary '40s automaker whose ideas and independence threatened Detroit's "Big Three," and whose courage wouldn't let his dream die. Jeff Bridges stars as Preston Tucker in director Francis Ford Coppola's masterful biodrama. Lloyd Bridges, Frederic Forrest, Joan Allen also star. 111 min.
06-1626 ***□$14.99***

Bram Stoker's Dracula (1992)
Francis Ford Coppola's lush retelling of "the strangest passion the world has ever known" stars Gary Oldman as the undying Count searching for his long-lost love, Winona Ryder as a young woman who falls under Dracula's spell, and Anthony Hopkins as vampire-hunting Van Helsing. Lavish sets and special effects propel this genuinely haunting horror film; with Keanu Reeves, Sadie Frost. 128 min.
02-2403 Was $19.99 ***□$14.99***

Bram Stoker's Dracula (Letterboxed Version)
Also available in a theatrical, widescreen format.
02-3091 ***□$19.99***

Jack (1996)
Big laughs and bittersweet moments highlight this story showcasing Robin Williams as the title character, a 10-year-old with a disease that ages him at four times the normal rate who becomes both an oddity and a hero when he attends a regular school for the first time. With Diane Lane, Fran Drescher, Jennifer Lopez and Bill Cosby; directed by Francis Ford Coppola. 113 min.
11-2077 Was $99.99 ***□$19.99***

The Rainmaker (1997)
In Francis Ford Coppola's filmization of the John Grisham best-seller, Matt Damon plays a young Memphis lawyer who helps a man stricken with leukemia battle a powerful insurance company that has rejected his claims. Danny DeVito is Damon's resourceful mentor, Claire Danes a battered young wife he helps. With Jon Voight, Mickey Rourke, Mary Kay Place and Danny Glover. 134 min.
06-2717 Was $99.99 ***□$14.99***

Please see our index for these other Francis Ford Coppola titles: *Finian's Rainbow • New York Stories • Supernova*

Larry (1974)
Acclaimed TV drama about a man, mistakenly diagnosed as being mentally handicapped and institutionalized as a child, who is released into the outside world at age 26 and struggles to adjust. Frederic Forrest plays the title role in this amazing true-life story; with Tyne Daly, Robert Walden, Katherine Helmond. 78 min.
08-1822 ***$19.99***

May Morning (1970)
A steamy and violent tale set in "Swingin' Sixties" Oxford University, director Ugo Liberatore's stylish Euro-thriller stars Jane Birkin, John Steiner and Rosella Falk and features a rock soundtrack by The Tremeloes. AKA: "Alba Pagana—Delitto a Oxford." 95 min.
08-1823 Letterboxed ***$19.99***

A Sensitive, Passionate Man (1977)
Aerospace engineer David Janssen loses his job and tries to drown his sorrows with alcohol, which soon threatens his happy marriage to Angie Dickinson, in this stirring drama with fine performances. 98 min.
10-9528 ***$14.99***

Winner Take All (1975)
Shirley Jones hopes to have a happy second marriage, but her gambling habit eventually gets in the way. Asked to withdraw $30,000 from the bank by husband Laurence Luckinbill, Jones goes on a gambling spree that threatens her marriage and herself. With Sam Groom, Joyce Van Patten. 97 min.
10-9775 ***$14.99***

If Tomorrow Comes (1971)
Compelling made-for-TV film starring Patty Duke as a California girl who faces racism when she marries her Japanese-American boyfriend just before the bombing of Pearl Harbor in 1941. Frank Michael Liu, Anne Baxter and James Whitmore also star. 73 min.
10-9852 ***$19.99***

The Strawberry Statement (1970)
The shadow of the political upheaval of the 1960s is cast over this passionate drama about a disinterested college student (Bruce Davison) who becomes swept up in campus radicalism by a strong-willed girl (Kim Darby). Co-stars Bud Cort, Bob Balaban. 109 min.
12-1404 ***$69.99***

Bound For Glory (1976)
David Carradine stars as folk balladeer Woody Guthrie in the Oscar-winning biodrama by Hal Ashby. Leaving his home and family in 1930s Texas to travel America, Guthrie sees firsthand the Depression's effects on the poor and uses his music to bring their plight to the public's attention. Ronny Cox, Melinda Dillon and Randy Quaid also star. 149 min.
12-1568 Was $19.99 ***$14.99***

Lifeguard (1976)
After attending his high-school reunion, a 30-year-old lifeguard questions his aimless lifestyle and casual lovelife. Emotional drama about the hero of every woman's summer dreams stars Sam Elliott, Anne Archer, Kathleen Quinlan and Parker Stevenson. 96 min.
06-1322 Was $59.99 ***$14.99***

A Hero Ain't Nothin' But A Sandwich (1978)
Powerful, gritty film centers on a disillusioned boy who befriends a drug dealer and soon sinks into the world of drug addiction. The stars (Cicely Tyson, Paul Winfield, Kevin Hooks) and producer of "Sounder" reunited for this meaningful story, co-starring Larry B. Scott, Glynn Turman. 107 min.
06-1861 ***$14.99***

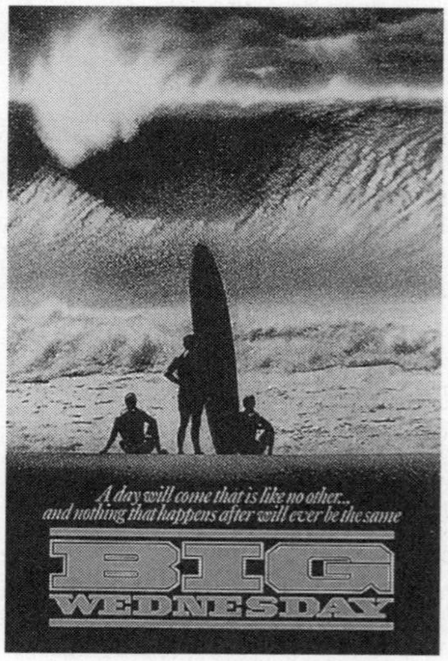
A day will come that is like no other...
and nothing that happens after will ever be the same
BIG WEDNESDAY

Big Wednesday (1978)
Gary Busey, Jan-Michael Vincent and William Katt star as three surfing buddies who are kings of the beach in '60s California, only to find themselves 10 years later in an adult world they don't understand. Fine, underrated surfer drama from John Milius ("Red Dawn") with great sports footage. 120 min.
19-1424 ***$19.99***

I Love You, Goodbye (1974)
Hope Lange is an unsatisfied housewife and mother who shocks her family when she decides to leave home for a new career and life on her own. She soon learns the hard realities of living alone, then a new love interest steps in. Michael Murphy, Patricia Smith and Earl Holliman co-star. 78 min.
08-1790 ***$19.99***

Terror Storm (1977)
In this intense drama, a powerful hurricane causes destruction on several fronts, stranding a tour boat at sea and forcing a plane to crash into the shark-infested ocean. What can the survivors of the storm do to survive? Carroll Baker, Arthur Kennedy and Lionel Stander star. AKA: "Cyclone." 100 min.
10-9776 ***$19.99***

Daisy Miller (1974)
Cybill Shepherd stars as Henry James' strong-willed 19th-century heroine in this Peter Bogdanovich adaptation of the classic drama. Follow Daisy and her family as they scandalize Victorian Europe's upper class; co-stars Cloris Leachman, Barry Brown and Eileen Brennan. 93 min.
06-1354 Was $69.99 ***$14.99***

Wife-Swapping Italian Style (1973)
Senta Berger, sensuous star of "When Women Had Tails," is featured in this story of a married couple who find an opportunity for sexy fun and adventure when they meet two swinging teenagers. Christopher Hodge also stars. AKA: "Lonely Hearts." 105 min.
09-5246   *$19.99*

The Mad Bomber (1972)
A madman takes the law into his own hands with the help of some homemade explosives. Chuck Connors is the batty bombardier; Vince Edwards the cop who must catch him. 89 min.
10-1102   *$12.99*

Summer Of '42 (1971)
"In everyone's life there's a 'Summer of '42'." For Hermie, it was the discovery of love and sex by meeting a beautiful older woman. His experiences, along with his two pals, are hilarious, touching, unforgettable. Gary Grimes, Jennifer O'Neill, Jerry Houser. 105 min.
19-1047   Was $19.99   *$14.99*

Class Of '44 (1973)
Join the "Summer Of '42" gang in another hilarious, heartfelt adventure. They're older now, involved in romance, and attending college—with surprises galore! Stars Gary Grimes, Jerry Houser, Deborah Winter. 95 min.
19-1332   *$14.99*

The Great Santini (1979)
Robert Duvall won well-deserved acclaim for his unforgettable portrayal of "Bull" Meechum, a rowdy, hard-drinking military man, whose rigid ways affect his son's well-being. Blythe Danner, Stan Shaw, Michael O'Keefe co-star. AKA: "The Ace." 115 min.
19-1073   Was $19.99   *$14.99*

Girlfriends (1978)
Refreshingly perceptive look at one young woman's response to new-found independence in New York City after her girlfriend moves out of the apartment they share to get married. Stars Melanie Mayron, Eli Wallach, Bob Balaban and Christopher Guest. 88 min.
19-1128   Was $59.99   *$19.99*

Promises In The Dark (1979)
Emotionally charged story of young cancer patient and understanding doctor. Marsha Mason, Kathleen Beller. 115 min.
19-1075   *$19.99*

Mikey And Nicky (1976)
Critically acclaimed drama from writer/director Elaine May stars John Cassavetes as a Philadelphia street hood who thinks a contract on his life has been taken out and seeks help from childhood friend and fellow mobster Peter Falk. The pair spend the night roaming their own neighborhoods, but is Falk merely setting his buddy up? With Ned Beatty, William Hickey. 106 min.
19-1464   *$14.99*

The Todd Killings (1971)
Disturbing social drama about a deranged youth (Robert Lyons) whose hold over a gang of teens in a small California town produces tragic consequences. Co-stars Richard Thomas, Ed Asner, Barbara Bel Geddes and Gloria Grahame. 93 min.
19-1671   Was $59.99   *$19.99*

Our Time (1974)
Set in a New England boarding school in 1955, this sensitive drama stars Pamela Sue Martin and Betty Slade as two young, virginal students who discover the joys and consequences of pre-marital sex. Parker Stevenson, George O'Hanlan, Jr. and Robert Walden also star. 91 min.
19-2161   Was $29.99   *$19.99*

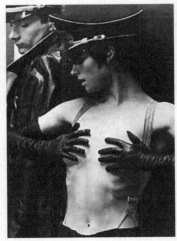

The Night Porter (1973)
A controversial, bizarrely erotic psychodrama from Italian filmmaker Liliana Cavani. Ex-Nazi prison camp officer Dirk Bogarde, living incognito as a hotel clerk in '50s Vienna, encounters former inmate Charlotte Rampling and renews their sado-masochistic love affair. Not for the squeamish! 118 min.
22-5953   Letterboxed   *$19.99*

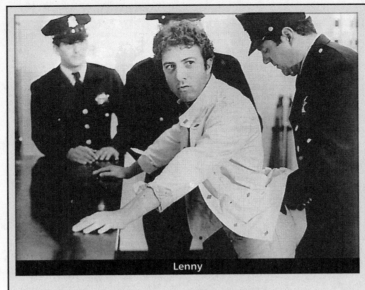

Lenny

Dustin Hoffman

Madigan's Million (1967)
Before "The Graduate," Dustin Hoffman starred in this crazy caper film about a bungling Treasury agent trying to outrun the Mob in Italy and recover stolen loot hidden by a recently murdered gangster. With Cesar Romero, Elsa Martinelli. 97 min.
59-5093   *$14.99*

The Graduate (1967)
The Oscar-winning coming-of-age comedy that launched star Dustin Hoffman's career and spoke to a generation. Follow aimless college grad Hoffman as he is seduced by the glamorous Mrs. Robinson (Anne Bancroft), only to fall in love with her daughter (Katharine Ross). Music by Simon and Garfunkel; Mike Nichols directs. 106 min.
53-1313   *$14.99*

The Graduate (Letterboxed Version)
Also available in a theatrical, widescreen format.
02-8879   *$19.99*

Midnight Cowboy (1969)
Rated "X" when first released (making it the only such film to win the Best Picture Academy Award), director John Schlesinger's gritty drama stars Jon Voight as a Texas-born stud who heads to New York with dreams of life as a high-paid hustler and Dustin Hoffman as his friend, sleazy street bum "Ratzo" Rizzo. With Sylvia Miles, John McGiver, Brenda Vaccaro. 113 min.
12-1253   Was $19.99   *$14.99*

Midnight Cowboy (Letterboxed Version)
Also available in a theatrical, widescreen format.
12-3224   *$14.99*

Straw Dogs (1971)
Director Sam Peckinpah's masterful, controversial drama stars Dustin Hoffman as a pacifistic American math teacher who moves with wife Susan George to her home village on England's Cornish countryside. A campaign of harassment against the couple by local hooligans escalates into a violent showdown, as Hoffman fends off attackers in his farmhouse. With Peter Vaughan and an uncredited David Warner. 117 min.
08-8651   Letterboxed   *$14.99*

Alfredo, Alfredo (1972)
Wry Italian farce starring Dustin Hoffman as a bank clerk who marries and impregnates gorgeous Stefania Sandrelli, but quickly gets bored of her. He soon meets another pretty Italian woman, but, because of Italy's strict laws, he is unable to divorce Sandrelli. Pietro Germi ("Divorce—Italian Style") directs. Dubbed in English.
10-1287   *$19.99*

Lenny (1974)
Dustin Hoffman gives an electrifying performance as the controversial comic genius Lenny Bruce. Bob Fosse directed this fascinating, insightful look into the life of the man who truly changed America's comic sensibilities. Fine supporting work from Valerie Perrine as Bruce's wife. 112 min.
12-1154   Was $19.99   *$14.99*

Marathon Man (1976)
Dustin Hoffman stars as a grad student who finds himself trapped in an international plot of Nazis, stolen jewels and a murderous crime cadre. Laurence Olivier is chilling as an arch-villain in this tense thriller. 125 min.
06-1041   *$14.99*

All The President's Men (1976)
Director Alan J. Pakula rendered Woodward and Bernstein's account of the unraveling of the Watergate scandal and created one of the most suspenseful political thrillers of the '70s. Robert Redford and Dustin Hoffman are the resolute Washington Post reporters, with Jason Robards as gruff editor Ben Bradlee; co-stars Jane Alexander and Hal Holbrook. 138 min.
19-1018   *$19.99*

Straight Time (1978)
Dustin Hoffman plays Max Dembo, an ex-con trying to make a life for himself outside the slammer. His struggle for a normal life is filled with shady parole officers, seedy crooks and a heist that "can't miss." Theresa Russell, Gary Busey, Harry Dean Stanton. 114 min.
19-1155   Was $19.99   *$14.99*

Kramer vs. Kramer (1979)
A moving, sensitive story about contemporary relationships and values. Dustin Hoffman is a man who finds himself starting anew when his wife walks out on him and their young son. Winner of Best Picture, Best Actor and three other Oscars. Meryl Streep, Justin Henry, Jane Alexander also star. 105 min.
02-1090   Was $19.99   *$14.99*

Death Of A Salesman (1985)
Dustin Hoffman offers a memorable turn as Willy Loman, the world-weary drummer trying to cope with family crises and the end of his career, in director Volker Schlöndorff's acclaimed version of Arthur Miller's Pulitzer Prize-winning play. With Kate Reid as Hoffman's wife, Linda, and John Malkovich and Stephen Lang as their sons. This two-tape set also includes the behind-the-scenes documentary, "Private Conversations on the Set of 'Death of a Salesman'." 218 min. total.
08-8605   *$29.99*

Ishtar (1987)
Infamous comedy epic teams Warren Beatty and Dustin Hoffman as two woefully untalented entertainers who get a booking in North Africa...and quickly fall into a tug-of-war between the CIA and local revolutionaries! Elaine May scripts and directs; Isabelle Adjani, Charles Grodin, Jack Weston co-star. 107 min.
02-1777   *$14.99*

Rain Man (1988)
Tom Cruise and Dustin Hoffman made a box-office splash in this "road" drama about a crass hustler who forms a bond with the autistic-savant brother he never knew he had during a cross-country car trip. Hoffman won a Best Actor Academy Award for his uncanny portrayal of the behaviorally disordered human abacus, as did the film, screenplay and Barry Levinson's sensitive direction. 133 min.
12-1900   *$14.99*

Rain Man (Letterboxed Version)
Also available in a theatrical, widescreen format.
12-3144   *$14.99*

Family Business (1989)
Sean Connery, Dustin Hoffman and Matthew Broderick star as three generations of a New York family of thieves who want to swipe a secret formula from a high-tech lab. Suspense and emotional conflicts ride high in this exceptionally acted caper story that mixes comedy and drama. 113 min.
02-2026   Was $19.99   *$14.99*

Billy Bathgate (1991)
A handsomely-mounted adaptation of E.L. Doctorow's award-winning novel about a teenage boy's obsession with hoodlums and his adventures with the unpredictable Dutch Schultz and his gang. Loren Dean, Dustin Hoffman, Nicole Kidman, Bruce Willis and Steven Hill star in this classy crime saga. 107 min.
11-1614   *$19.99*

Hero (1992)
Weaselly two-bit crook Dustin Hoffman anonymously aids a group of plane crash victims, but when newscaster Geena Davis, one of the survivors, announces a million dollar reward for the rescuer, handsome homeless man Andy Garcia takes it, along with nationwide fame and the romantic interest of Davis. Director Stephen Frears' poignant social comedy also stars Joan Cusack and Chevy Chase. 112 min.
02-2373   Was $19.99   *$14.99*

Outbreak (1995)
Dustin Hoffman is an Army medical expert who discovers that the virus that destroyed a small California town is the same one he found earlier in Africa. With help from physician ex-wife Rene Russo and helicopter flyer Cuba Gooding, Jr., Hoffman races against time and sinister military men to stop the threat before it's too late. With Morgan Freeman, Donald Sutherland. 128 min.
19-2365   Was $19.99   *$14.99*

American Buffalo (1996)
In this stirring adaptation of David Mamet's acclaimed play, Dennis Franz is a junk-store dealer plotting with his teenage assistant to steal a rare buffalo nickel he once possessed, but sold for a mere $90. Dustin Hoffman, Franz's seedy friend, wants to cut himself in on the deal—and the teen out of it. With Sean Nelson. 87 min.
88-1119   Was $99.99   *$14.99*

DUSTIN HOFFMAN   ROBERT DE NIRO

A comedy about truth, justice and other special effects.

WAG THE DOG

Wag The Dog (1997)
Hollywood fiction and Washington reality eerily dovetailed in director Barry Levinson's wickedly funny satire of modern politics and media manipulation. When the president is accused of sexually accosting a teenage girl in the Oval Office weeks before Election Night, top advisor Anne Heche and political troubleshooter Robert De Niro contact Hollywood producer Dustin Hoffman. Their plan: to create a fictitious military incident with Albania to divert the news media and take the heat off the White House. Woody Harrelson, Denis Leary co-star. 96 min.
02-5677   Was $99.99   *$19.99*

Mad City (1997)
TV reporter Dustin Hoffman, whose sensation-seeking style has cast him out of favor and landed him in a small California town, finds a chance for redemption when recently fired museum guard John Travolta's attempt to get his job back leads to a shooting and a hostage situation that becomes a media sideshow. Director Costa-Gavras ("Missing") deftly blends drama, suspense and satire; Alan Alda, Blythe Danner, Mia Kirshner also star. 115 min.
19-2630   Was $19.99   *$14.99*

Sphere: Collector's Edition (1998)
Deep in the Pacific, a gigantic spacecraft that apparently crashed 300 years earlier is discovered, but as a team of scientists (including psychologist Dustin Hoffman, biologist Sharon Stone, mathematician Samuel L. Jackson and astrophysicist Liev Schreiber) investigate the ship, strange and deadly events are set into motion. Barry Levinson directs this gripping adaptation of Michael Crichton's novel. Special edition includes a behind-the-scenes documentary, "Shaping the Sphere." 149 min. total.
19-2728   Was $19.99   *$14.99*

Sphere (Letterboxed Version)
Also available in a theatrical, widescreen format.
19-2784   *$19.99*

Please see our index for these other Dustin Hoffman titles: *Agatha • Dick Tracy • Hook • The Messenger: The Story Of Joan Of Arc • Sleepers*

Stigma (1972)
"Miami Vice's" Philip Michael Thomas stars as a physician in a small New England town who runs into a blockade by community officials when he tries to diminish the spread of a social disease before it reaches epidemic proportions. 93 min.
16-3018 Was $19.99 *$14.99*

Fingers (1978)
Harvey Keitel shines as a would-be concert pianist trying to escape the violent world of his gangster father, for whom Keitel works as a "debt collector," in writer/director James Toback's gritty, fascinating character study of a man torn between two worlds. Michael V. Gazzo, Tisa Farrow, Jim Brown, Danny Aiello also star. 91 min.
18-7469 *$29.99*

Rage (1972)
George C. Scott makes a shattering directorial debut and stars as a rancher poisoned by an accidental nerve gas spill on his land. When his son dies and the government turns a deaf ear to his plight, Scott cuts a bloody swath through the red tape; Martin Sheen, Richard Basehart, Barnard Hughes co-star. 100 min.
19-1523 Was $19.99 *$14.99*

Boulevard Nights (1979)
Filmed on location in the barrios of Los Angeles, this explosive drama of the Hispanic street gangs follows two brothers who find themselves on opposite sides of the struggle to escape. An interesting precursor to "Colors"; stars Richard Yniguez, Marta Du Bois. 102 min.
19-1638 Was $59.99 *$19.99*

Black Market Baby (1977)
A beautiful college girl becomes pregnant, but discovers that the father-to-be was hired by a black market baby agency to impregnate her, then sell the child for $50,000. Upon giving birth, the mother battles to keep her baby. Linda Purl, Desi Arnaz, Jr., Annie Potts and Bill Bixby star. 96 min.
14-3275 *$12.99*

The Grasshopper (1970)
A young Jacqueline Bisset stars as a small town girl who sets out to join her fiancé in L.A., but along the way is seduced by the bright lights of Las Vegas and later returns to work as a showgirl. With Joseph Cotten, Jim Brown, Corbett Monica, Tim O'Kelly, Stefanianna Christopherson. AKA: "Passions." 95 min.
19-1669 *$19.99*

In Praise Of Older Women (1978)
In this sexy and whimsical romantic drama, Tom Berenger plays a young Hungarian man whose childhood experiences after World War II include pimping to make ends meet. His obsession with older women leads to a series of robust relationships with Karen Black, Susan Strasberg and Helen Shaver, among others.
04-1079 *$29.99*

The Visitors (1972)
Elia Kazan's low-budget independent drama stars James Woods in his film debut, as a liberal Vietnam veteran living a peaceful life on a farm in Connecticut with his girlfriend and infant son. When two vets responsible for the rape of a Vietnamese woman are released from prison, they pay the family a terrifying visit. Patricia Joyce, Steve Railsback co-star. 88 min.
19-2204 *$19.99*

The Baby Maker (1970)
Robert Wise produced James Bridges' ("The China Syndrome") first film as director, this moving drama about a childless couple who hire a young hippie girl (Barbara Hershey) to give birth to the husband's child...but the relationship between father and surrogate mother grows deeper than either expected. Co-stars Sam Groom and Jeannie Berlin. 109 min.
19-1666 Was $59.99 *$19.99*

The Man Without A Country (1973)
The classic tale is brought to life by Cliff Robertson's superb performance in the title role as a man who renounces his homeland, and is then condemned to a lifetime exile at sea. Beau Bridges, Peter Strauss, Robert Ryan also star. 90 min.
14-3264 *$12.99*

Sugar Cookies (1977)
A strange, erotic horror story of beautiful people playing a terrifying game of love and death. In this shocking and suspenseful tale, a dead girl's friend wreaks havoc on those who drove her to her death. Highly-charged eroticism and lesbian lovers plays a part in the effort that stars Warhol Factory regulars Mary Woronov, Ondine and Monique Van Vooren, plus Lynn Lowry and Jennifer Welles.
15-1018 *$14.99*

The Second Coming Of Suzanne (1971)
Dazzling, surrealistic "film within a film" about a Manson-like filmmaker whose latest discovery, a 1960s flower child, is to star in his bizarre retelling of the life of Christ. Sondra Locke, Jared Martin, Richard Dreyfuss star; theme song performed by Leonard Cohen. AKA: "Suzanne." 90 min.
16-1018 Was $19.99 *$14.99*

Cat Ballou

Jane Fonda

Tall Story (1960)
Jane Fonda's screen debut finds her playing a man-seeking coed who woos college basketball phenom Anthony Perkins. Complications arise when the basketball team goes against a Russian squad, and gamblers want to get in on the action. High-spirited farce also stars Ray Walston, Anne Jackson and Van Williams. 91 min.
19-1942 Was $19.99 *$14.99*

Period Of Adjustment (1962)
Tennessee Williams penned the play that inspired this seriocomedy about two couples whose marriages are undergoing problems. Nurse Jane Fonda and Korean War veteran Jim Hutton find their recent nuptials have invited money and sexual dilemmas, while Tony Franciosa thinks wife Lois Nettleton's parents are meddling in their affairs. 112 min.
12-2487 *$19.99*

Sunday In New York (1963)
Small-town girl Jane Fonda comes to Manhattan to get advice from older brother Cliff Robertson when her fiancé tries to "go too far" before their wedding, but when Fonda learns of her sibling's playboy ways, she decides to follow in his footsteps. Breezy romantic comedy also stars Rod Taylor, Robert Culp; theme sung by Mel Torme. 105 min.
12-3028 □*$19.99*

Cat Ballou (1965)
Rip-roarin' Western comedy with Jane Fonda as the shy schoolmarm-turned-outlaw who avenges her father's death with the aid of drunken ex-gunslinger Lee Marvin. With Dwayne Hickman, Michael Callan, and the musical narration of Nat King Cole and Stubby Kaye. 97 min.
02-1060 Was $19.99 *$14.99*

Joy House (1965)
Con man Alain Delon, on the run from the mob, hides out in the home of wealthy widow Lola Albright, but becomes ensnared in a love triangle with Albright and sexy niece Jane Fonda that puts his life in greater jeopardy. Sizzling, erotic suspense tale from French filmmaker René Clément also stars Andre Oumansky. AKA: "Les Felins," "The Love Cage." 91 min.
27-6210 *$29.99*

Any Wednesday (1966)
Spry romantic farce of marital infidelity and its consequences stars Jason Robards as a philandering hubby and Jane Fonda as his once-a-week girlfriend. Based on the Broadway play, the comedy also stars Dean Jones, Rosemary Murphy. 109 min.
19-1626 *$19.99*

Barbarella (1968)
Welcome to the 41st century, where Barbarella, sexy queen of space, battles monsters and robots and handles men as handily as she wrestles with nasty intergalactic villains. Jane Fonda turns in a revealing performance as the heroine in this outrageous adventure based on the famed French comic strip. David Hemmings, Milo O'Shea, John Phillip Law. 98 min.
06-1003 Remastered *$14.99*

They Shoot Horses, Don't They? (1969)
A grueling dance marathon in 1930s Chicago is the setting for this acerbic and compelling drama that follows with increasing desperation the struggles of the contestants to keep going. Jane Fonda, Michael Sarrazin, Susannah York, Bonnie Bedelia, Bruce Dern and Red Buttons are among the dancers, with Best Supporting Actor Oscar-winner Gig Young as the contest's smarmy emcee; Sydney Pollack directs. 120 min.
08-8802 *$14.99*

They Shoot Horses, Don't They? (Letterboxed Collector's Edition)
Also available in a theatrical, widescreen format. Includes a "making of" featurette and the original theatrical trailer.
08-8791 *$14.99*

Klute (1971)
A small-town detective, a missing husband, an embittered call girl, and a sadistic killer; these are the main elements in Alan J. Pakula's tense thriller, set in New York City. Jane Fonda, in an Oscar-winning role, and Donald Sutherland star; with Roy Scheider. Includes the documentary featurette "Klute in New York: A Background for Suspense" and the original theatrical trailer. 125 min. total.
19-2780 *$19.99*

Klute (Letterboxed Version)
Also available in a theatrical, widescreen format.
19-2765 *$19.99*

A Doll's House (1972)
Jane Fonda stars as Ibsen's provocative 19th-century "liberated wife" in this film adaptation of the revolutionary stage drama. The strong supporting cast includes David Warner as Fonda's husband, Trevor Howard, Delphine Seyrig, Edward Fox. 103 min.
46-5008 *$19.99*

Steelyard Blues (1973)
A band of anti-establishment misfits try to build their own airplane in this comedy rich in '60s flavor. Jane Fonda, Donald Sutherland, Peter Boyle and Howard Hesseman star. 93 min.
19-1438 Was $59.99 *$19.99*

Fun With Dick And Jane (1977)
Jane Fonda and George Segal are a middle-class couple who take to robbing stores to make ends meet in this timely comedy. With Ed McMahon. 99 min.
02-1039 *$14.99*

Julia (1977)
Jane Fonda and Vanessa Redgrave star in this dramatic true story taken from author Lillian Hellman's memoirs, centering around her involvement with Germany's anti-Nazi movement in the '30s on behalf of her friend Julia. The film gained Oscars for Redgrave and Jason Robards (as Hellman's lover, Dashiell Hammett); look for Meryl Streep in her film debut. 118 min.
04-1082 Was $69.99 *$19.99*

Comes A Horseman (1978)
Set in Montana shortly after World War II, director Alan Pakula's lavishly photographed drama of the "new West" stars Jane Fonda as a rancher who joins with veteran James Caan to fend off a takeover of her spread by land baron Jason Robards. With Richard Farnsworth, Jim Davis.
04-1398 □*$14.99*

Comes A Horseman (Letterboxed Version)
Also available in a theatrical, widescreen format.
12-3139 *$14.99*

Coming Home (1978)
One of the first and best films made to deal with the Vietnam War, Hal Ashby's moving drama of the growing relationship between paraplegic veteran Jon Voight and volunteer worker Jane Fonda garnered Oscars for Best Actress, Actor and Screenplay. Bruce Dern also stars as Fonda's Marine officer husband; with Robert Carradine, Penelope Milford. 127 min.
12-1972 Was $19.99 □*$14.99*

The China Syndrome (1979)
A dogged TV reporter and cynical cameraman are present at a nuclear facility when the walls begin to shake...and their quest to uncover the truth about this allegedly "minor incident" leads down a path of killers and deception. Jane Fonda, Michael Douglas and Jack Lemmon star. 123 min.
02-2689 *$14.99*

The China Syndrome (Letterboxed Version)
Also available in a theatrical, widescreen format.
02-3315 □*$19.99*

Nine To Five (1980)
Jane Fonda, Dolly Parton and Lily Tomlin are three overworked and underpaid secretaries who get their chance for revenge against chauvinistic boss Dabney Coleman in this comedic salute to all "pink collar" workers. 110 min.
04-1192 *$14.99*

Rollover (1981)
Intrigue and danger in the world of high finance takes you behind the scenes of New York banking and looks at the elite people who control our economic empires. Jane Fonda, Kris Kristofferson. 116 min.
19-1220 Was $19.99 *$14.99*

Agnes Of God (1985)
The body of an infant is found in a convent, and a disturbed young nun, who claims the child was from God, is charged with murder. Dramatic film version of the hit Broadway play stars Jane Fonda as a court psychiatrist trying to solve the mystery, Anne Bancroft as the headstrong Mother Superior and Meg Tilly as the withdrawn Agnes. 99 min.
02-1557 *$14.99*

The Morning After (1986)
Engrossing murder mystery highlighted by Jane Fonda's performance as an aging, alcoholic actress who wakens one morning with something much worse than a hangover: a bloodied corpse in her bed. Has she been set up...or is she truly responsible? Jeff Bridges, Raul Julia co-star. 103 min.
40-1288 Was $19.99 □*$14.99*

Stanley And Iris (1990)
Jane Fonda and Robert De Niro star in this tender, moving drama directed by Martin Ritt ("Norma Rae"). A widowed bakery worker blows the whistle on a co-worker's illiteracy, and is then asked to teach him how to read. Eventually, a romance develops between the two. Swoosie Kurtz, Martha Plimpton co-star. 104 min.
12-2089 Was $19.99 □*$14.99*

Please see our index for these other Jane Fonda titles: *Barefoot In The Park • California Suite • The Electric Horseman • Old Gringo • On Golden Pond • Spirits Of The Dead • Walk On The Wild Side*

Get Carter (1971)
Two-fisted crime thriller from England stars Michael Caine as a small-time London tough who arrives in the grimy industrial town of Newcastle to find out who's responsible for his brother's murder. As Caine runs afoul of local mobsters, he gets in the middle of a dangerous web of blackmail, betrayal and death. Ian Hendry, Britt Ekland, John Osborne also star. 111 min.
12-3032 □*$19.99*

284 · DRAMA MOVIES UNLIMITED CALL · 1-800-4-MOVIES

A Dream For Christmas (1973)
A poor black family moves from rural Arkansas to a run-down section of L.A. when the father, a minister, is appointed to run a small church. Family drama by Earl Hamner ("The Waltons") stars Hari Rhodes, Beah Richards. 96 min.
19-2131 Was $19.99 ***$14.99***

Last Of The Mobile Hot Shots (1970)
Tennessee Williams' play "The Seven Descents of Myrtle" is turned into a controversial movie (rated "X" upon its release) starring James Coburn as an ailing Southern man who wants to acquire an heir. He chooses a TV actress floozy to bear his child, but things get complicated when she falls for his black half-brother. Lynn Redgrave, Robert Hooks co-star. 108 min.
19-2202 ***$19.99***

Joe Panther (1976)
Sensitive drama for the whole family about a Seminole Indian boy growing up in modern-day Florida who faces prejudice and conflict as he looks for a job in white society. Ray Tracey, Brian Keith, Ricardo Montalban star. 110 min.
19-2301 Was $19.99 ***$14.99***

Brothers (1977)
Powerful prison drama, based on the true story of black San Quentin inmate George Jackson's fight for freedom and his friendship with activist Angela Davis, features an impressive cast that includes Bernie Casey, Vonetta McGee, Ron O'Neal and Stu Gilliam. 104 min.
19-2413 ***$19.99***

The All-American Boy (1973)
Jon Voight stars as an abrasive young fighter who tries to use his ring abilities to reach the Olympics in this emotional drama about the drive for success. Anne Archer, Gene Borkan also star. 119 min.
19-2433 ***$19.99***

Hunter (1976)
James Franciscus stars as a man falsely imprisoned by a mysterious enemy. Eight years later, his life shattered, he is released and starts a vengeance hunt. Linda Evans, Broderick Crawford co-star in an exciting drama. 60 min.
40-1068 Was $59.99 ***$14.99***

A Tattered Web (1971)
A dedicated cop commits murder, then pins the crime on a homeless man, but will his conscience let him live with his deeds? Gripping drama stars Lloyd Bridges, Frank Converse and Broderick Crawford. 73 min.
40-1085 ***$19.99***

Badlands (1973)
Disturbingly poetic depiction of two young lovers (Martin Sheen and Sissy Spacek) who set out on a murder spree across the Midwest in the 1950s. Director Terrence Malick's acclaimed fictionalized account of the Starkweather-Fugate crimes co-stars Warren Oates, Alan Vint. Includes the original theatrical trailer. 94 min.
19-2861 Remastered ❑***$19.99***

Badlands (Letterboxed Version)
Also available in a theatrical, widescreen format.
19-2819 ❑***$19.99***

The Magician Of Lublin (1979)
Alan Arkin stars as a down-and-out mage/escape artist who tries to escape his squalid life through fantasies. Funny and touching tale, based on Isaac Bashevis Singer's novel, also stars Louise Fletcher, Shelley Winters and Lou Jacobi. 105 min.
19-7019 ***$19.99***

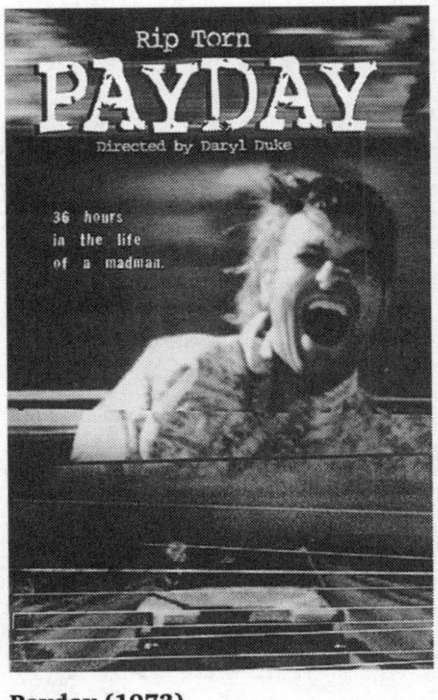

Payday (1973)
A fine road drama, this sobering look at the stormy life, on and off the stage, of a struggling country music performer features a fine performance by Rip Torn as the singer. Ahna Capri, Cliff Emmich also star. 103 min.
44-1057 Was $59.99 ***$14.99***

Corn's A Poppin' (1957)
A real rarity! Robert Altman wrote this low-budgeted comedy about a popcorn company sponsoring a country-western music TV program where everything goes wrong. Filmed in Altman's hometown of Kansas City, the film stars Richard Wallace. 65 min.
53-6050 ***$29.99***

Countdown (1968)
Before "The Right Stuff," there was this underrated gem about a planned moon shot and its effects on the astronauts and their wives. Robert Duvall, James Caan, Barbara Baxley and Ted Knight star in an early effort from director Robert Altman. 102 min.
19-1298 ***$19.99***

That Cold Day In The Park (1969)
Robert Altman's offbeat, moody tale stars Sandy Dennis as a lonely, frustrated single woman whose encounter with a mysterious young man sitting in the rain could spell tragedy for both of them. Co-stars Michael Burns and Susanne Benton. 110 min.
63-1032 ***$14.99***

M*A*S*H (1970)
Elliott Gould, Donald Sutherland, Sally Kellerman, Tom Skerritt and Robert Duvall star in director Robert Altman's innovative dark comedy about the everyday escapades of an Army medical unit during the Korean War; Ring Lardner, Jr. won an Oscar for his adaptation of Richard Hooker's novel. 116 min.
04-1099 ❑***$14.99***

Brewster McCloud (1970)
Look, up in the sky! It's a bird! It's a plane! It's...Brewster McCloud (Bud Cort), a shy young man who lives inside the Astrodome and dreams of flying with homemade wings. Robert Altman's kooky cult comedy also stars Shelley Duvall, Sally Kellerman, Michael Murphy and Margaret Hamilton. 101 min.
12-1366 Was $69.99 ***$19.99***

McCabe And Mrs. Miller (1971)
Director Robert Altman's mood piece Western about a small-time hustler (Warren Beatty) who teams with a madame (Julie Christie) to open a bordello in the remote Northwest. Co-stars John Schuck, Keith Carradine and William Devane; based on a song by Leonard Cohen. 121 min.
19-1204 ❑***$14.99***

The Long Goodbye (1973)
Robert Altman's quirky, semi-satiric updating of Raymond Chandler stars Elliott Gould as laid-back gumshoe Philip Marlowe, investigating the murder of his friend's wife and getting involved with gangsters, alcoholic writers and deceptive women. With Sterling Hayden, Nina van Pallandt, Jim Bouton, Henry Gibson; look for a young Arnold Schwarzenegger. 113 min.
12-2188 ❑***$19.99***

Thieves Like Us (1974)
Atmospheric crime drama from director Robert Altman, based on the same novel that inspired Nicholas Ray's "They Live by Night," tells the story of three crooks who terrorize the American South during the Depression by pulling off daring bank robberies. Keith Carradine, Shelley Duvall, John Schuck, Bert Remsen, Louise Fletcher and Tom Skerritt star. 123 min.
12-2860 Was $19.99 ***$14.99***

Nashville (1975)
One of the 1970s' most acclaimed films is an audacious, moving and hilarious look at 24 characters involved in a political rally in the music capital of the world. Robert Altman brilliantly directs an amazing ensemble cast of Lily Tomlin, Keith Carradine, Ronee Blakley, Karen Black, Shelley Duvall, Henry Gibson, Scott Glenn and more. 159 min.
06-1043 ***$24.99***

Buffalo Bill And The Indians, Or Sitting Bull's History Lesson (1976)
More than one myth about the "winning of the West" is deflated in director Robert Altman's satiric historical drama that stars Paul Newman as the flamboyant Buffalo Bill Cody, frontier marksman-turned-"Wild West Show" pitchman. With Joel Grey, Harvey Keitel, Burt Lancaster, and Geraldine Chaplin as Annie Oakley; scripted by Alan Rudolph. 123 min.
04-1683 Was $19.99 ❑***$14.99***

A Wedding (1978)
Two families come together to be joined in matrimony, but instead are joined in one odd predicament after another, in Robert Altman's satiric look at the American way of marriage. The wedding party includes Carol Burnett, Paul Dooley, Mia Farrow, Lauren Hutton, Lillian Gish, Howard Duff and Pam Dawber. 125 min.
04-1968 Was $59.99 ***$29.99***

Quintet (1979)
Robert Altman's masterful vision of an apocalyptic "ice city" where the remnants of mankind play a game with stakes of life and death. Paul Newman, Bibi Andersson, Nina Van Pallandt star in this stark, fascinating look at survival. 119 min.
04-1872 ***$19.99***

Streamers (1983)
David Rabe's electrifying play, dynamically transferred to the screen by Robert Altman, centers on a group of army recruits awaiting assignment in a deserted barracks at the outbreak of the Vietnam War. Matthew Modine, Michael Wright, George Dzundza and David Alan Grier star. 118 min.
03-1238 ***$12.99***

The Player

Robert Altman

Fool For Love (1985)
Robert Altman and Sam Shepard team up to bring to the screen Shepard's insightful, many-layered drama of obsessive love. Kim Basinger and Shepard renew their fiery love-hate relationship at a rundown desert hotel; Harry Dean Stanton is the ethereal wanderer who holds the key to their secret past. 107 min.
12-1599 ***$14.99***

Beyond Therapy (1987)
Amusingly off-center comedy concerning a neurotic couple (Jeff Goldblum, Julie Hagerty) who are determined to have a happy relationship...in spite of their even crazier therapists (Glenda Jackson, Tom Conti)! Robert Altman directs. 93 min.
70-1173 ❑***$12.99***

The Caine Mutiny Court-Martial (1988)
Expert filmization of Herman Wouk's novel features Brad Davis as the troubled Captain Queeg, whose growing paranoias force his officers to seize control of the ship during a typhoon. Jeff Daniels, Eric Bogosian and Peter Gallagher also star; scripted by Wouk and directed by Robert Altman. 100 min.
68-1231 Was $89.99 ***$12.99***

Vincent & Theo (1990)
Robert Altman's audacious portrait of the tortured life of painter Vincent Van Gogh, his relationship with his troubled brother, Theo, and his struggle with painter Paul Gauguin. A highly personal biography, with Tim Roth's Van Gogh a different portrayal than Kirk Douglas' in "Lust for Life." With Paul Rhys, Jean-Pierre Cassel. 138 min.
80-1003 ***$14.99***

The Player (1992)
Scathing satire of contemporary Hollywood, scripted by Michael Tolkin from his novel and directed by Robert Altman, stars Tim Robbins as a hot shot studio executive attempting to find an angry screenwriter who has been sending him death threats. His search leads him into a world of romance, murder and "high-concept vehicles" for Julia Roberts and Bruce Willis. With Greta Scacchi, Whoopi Goldberg, Cynthia Stevenson, Lyle Lovett, Fred Ward and dozens of cameos. 123 min.
02-5013 Was $19.99 ***$14.99***

The Player (Letterboxed Version)
Also available in a theatrical, widescreen format.
02-5143 ❑***$19.99***

Short Cuts (1993)
Inspired by the writings of Raymond Carver, Robert Altman's magnificent mosaic of Southern California life interweaves the funny, touching and dramatic stories of 22 characters. The ensemble cast includes Bruce Davison, Jennifer Jason Leigh, Andie MacDowell, Matthew Modine, Julianne Moore, Chris Penn, Tim Robbins, Madeleine Stowe, Lily Tomlin, Tom Waits and Jack Lemmon. 189 min.
02-2602 Was $89.99 ❑***$19.99***

Short Cuts (Letterboxed Version)
Also available in a theatrical, widescreen format.
02-5135 ❑***$19.99***

Luck, Trust & Ketchup: The Making Of Short Cuts
Follow director Robert Altman and the cast of the acclaimed drama from rehearsals to the filmmaker's trademark staging and dialogue techniques in this behind-the-scenes documentary. 94 min.
02-2632 ❑***$19.99***

Ready To Wear (Pret-A-Porter) (1994)
Robert Altman's mega-character satire is set in and around a major Paris fashion show and follows the politics, business maneuvers and romances of designers, models, reporters and fashion industry movers and shakers. Tim Robbins, Julia Roberts, Tracey Ullman, Marcello Mastroianni, Sophia Loren, Kim Basinger, Sally Kellerman, Stephen Rea and Danny Aiello head the cast. 133 min.
11-1885 ❑***$14.99***

A ROBERT ALTMAN FILM
KANSAS CITY

Kansas City (1996)
Set in the jazz clubs and gambling dens of 1930's K.C., Robert Altman's offbeat crime drama stars Jennifer Jason Leigh as a criminal's wife who kidnaps a government official's wife as part of her elaborate plan to free her husband from the clutches of a black mob boss. With Miranda Richardson, Dermot Mulroney, Steve Buscemi and Harry Belafonte. 115 min.
02-5118 Was $99.99 ❑***$19.99***

Kansas City (Letterboxed Version)
Also available in a theatrical, widescreen format.
02-5134 ❑***$19.99***

The Gingerbread Man (1997)
John Grisham's eerie thriller features Kenneth Branagh as a slick Savannah attorney who helps waitress Embeth Davidtz when she's harassed by her emotionally troubled father (Robert Duvall). After engaging in a steamy affair, lawyer and client face danger as surprises about Davidtz's past are revealed. Robert Downey, Jr., Daryl Hannah co-star; Robert Altman directs. 114 min.
02-8861 Was $19.99 ***$14.99***

Gun (1997)
Included in this collection are two installments of Robert Altman's cable TV anthology series. Housewife Rosanna Arquette gets involved with neighbor Peter Horton, unbeknownst to gun-toting hubby James Gandolfini, in "Columbus Day." And in "All the President's Women," which Altman directed, womanizing golf club president Randy Quaid can't keep track of his many romances, among them Daryl Hannah, Sally Kellerman, Sean Young and Jennifer Tilly. 90 min.
75-5088 ***$89.99***

Cookie's Fortune (1999)
Robert Altman's homespun comedy-mystery is set in sleepy Holly Springs, Mississippi, where the suicide of wealthy, eccentric Cookie (Patricia Neal) brings out the wild eccentricities of Cookie's family and the town's denizens. Among them are nieces Julianne Moore and Glenn Close, caretaker Charles S. Dutton, grand-niece Liv Tyler, sheriff Ned Beatty and deputy Chris O'Donnell. 118 min.
02-9145 Was $99.99 ***$14.99***

Please see our index for these other Robert Altman titles: *Aria* • *The James Dean Story* • *Popeye*

The Hurried Man (1977)
An international art smuggler (Alain Delon) likes to live life on the edge. His passion for sex and success could either lead him into the arms of the woman he loves or to destruction. 91 min.
48-1117 $59.99

A Home Of Our Own (1975)
True drama based on the life of Father Wasson, an American priest who founded an orphanage in Mexico, taking children off the streets and giving them a chance to build new lives. Jason Miller stars. 100 min.
14-3148 $49.99

Orphan Train (1979)
A social worker in 1850s New York must overcome many obstacles as she tries to move a group of orphan children to the West by train. Moving family drama stars Jill Eikenberry, Kevin Dobson and Linda Manz; look for an early turn by Glenn Close. 138 min.
46-5194 $14.99

The Legend Of Valentino (1975)
Franco Nero plays the famed Latin lover in this made-for-TV biography. Lesley Ann Warren, Yvette Mimieux and Milton Berle give able support in this look at a Hollywood legend.
46-5030 $19.99

Casino (1979)
There's plenty of drama, romance and adventure on board a luxurious gambling boat making its maiden voyage in the Caribbean in this action-filled tale. Mike Connors, Linda Day George, Bo Hopkins, Gary Burghoff star. 96 min.
46-5366 $12.99

Aaron Loves Angela (1975)
A romance between a black boy (Kevin Hooks) and a Puerto Rican girl (Irene Cara) is tested by the harsh realities of urban life in a gritty drama directed by Gordon Parks, Jr. 99 min.
02-1456   Was $59.99 $14.99

Return To Fantasy Island (1977)
"De plane" is landing once more on Mr. Roarke's tropical paradise, bringing a bevy of guests eager to live out their fantasies. Ricardo Montalban, Herve Villechaize, Joseph Cotten, Adrienne Barbeau star. 100 min.
46-5417 $14.99

Take Down (1979)
Edward Herrmann is a high school English teacher cornered into coaching the hapless wrestling team and recruiting an uninterested student (Lorenzo Lamas) for the squad. Lighthearted drama co-stars Kathleen Lloyd, Stephen Furst and Kevin Hooks. 86 min.
48-1058 $29.99

Last Cry For Help (1979)
A teenager attempts suicide. Only the determination of a devoted psychiatrist can save her. Linda Purl, Shirley Jones, Tony LoBianco star. 97 min.
48-1050 $29.99

"SOUNDER"
CICELY TYSON   PAUL WINFIELD
KEVIN HOOKS

Gene Hackman

First To Fight (1967)
Filmed at the height of the Vietnam War, this action-filled World War II drama stars Chad Everett as the tough, decorated Marine whose plans to settle down with his wife are derailed when he gets a patriotic urge and returns to the service. Fighting in the Pacific under tough sergeant Gene Hackman, Everett gets an opportunity to prove his heroism. With Dean Jagger. 98 min.
19-2343 $19.99

GREGORY PECK · GENE HACKMAN
MAROONED

Marooned (1969)
Science-fiction drama about a three-man team of American astronauts who are stranded in orbit 200 miles above the Earth when their ship's engines fail, and the desperate global race to rescue them. Gregory Peck, Gene Hackman, David Janssen and James Franciscus star. 134 min.
02-2702 $14.99

Riot (1969)
A prison uprising and hostage-taking incident serves as camouflage for a daring escape plan in this gripping "big house" thriller from producer William Castle. Gene Hackman plays the mastermind of the siege, and Jim Brown is an inmate reluctantly drawn into the breakout. 97 min.
06-2075 $14.99

I Never Sang For My Father (1970)
Acclaimed film version of Robert Anderson's drama stars Gene Hackman as a man returning home to help care for dying father Melvyn Douglas, whose cold manner has kept them apart for many years. Moving story also stars Estelle Parsons, Dorothy Stickney. 90 min.
02-1791   Was $69.99 $19.99

The French Connection (1971)
Five Academy Awards, including Best Picture, Director and Actor, were copped by William Friedkin's fast-moving, fact-based cop drama. Gene Hackman and Roy Scheider are the New York detectives who reluctantly work with federal agents to crack a multi-million-dollar heroin ring. The harrowing car chase scene is a film classic. With Fernando Rey, Tony Lo Bianco. 104 min.
04-1060 $19.99

The French Connection II (1975)
Gene Hackman is back as tough-as-nails New York cop "Popeye" Doyle, heading to France to track down the heroin dealer whose syndicate he busted in America. Co-stars Fernando Rey. 119 min.
04-1843   Was $59.99 $19.99

Zandy's Bride (1974)
A domestic drama in Western guise, this gorgeously photographed film is set in California's Big Sur Mountains, where cold-hearted rancher Gene Hackman sends for mail-order wife Liv Ullmann from Sweden and treats her like a servant, until she rebels. Eileen Heckart and Harry Dean Stanton also star; directed by Jan Troell ("The Emigrants"). 97 min. AKA: "For Better, For Worse."
19-2074   Was $19.99 $14.99

Bite The Bullet (1975)
Rousing Western adventure about a grueling 600-mile horse race at the turn of the century. Colorful performances by Gene Hackman, Jan-Michael Vincent, Candice Bergen and Ben Johnson and non-stop action highlight this sagebrush saga. 131 min.
02-1292   Was $59.99 $14.99

Night Moves (1975)
Gene Hackman is a football player-turned-detective, hired to locate a teenage runaway, who uncovers a bizarre web of smuggling, deception, and murder. Intriguing thriller by Arthur Penn also features Jennifer Warren, Susan Clark, and early appearances by Melanie Griffith and James Woods. 100 min.
19-1192 $19.99

Uncommon Valor (1983)
Gene Hackman, Robert Stack, Patrick Swayze and boxing star Randal "Tex" Cobb star in this action-packed drama about a special team sent to post-war Vietnam to rescue U.S. soldiers declared Missing in Action. 105 min.
06-1212 $14.99

Misunderstood (1984)
A first-class tearjerker starring Gene Hackman as a father trying to come to terms with his young sons after his wife's death. Henry Thomas and Huckleberry Fox co-star. 91 min.
12-1357 $79.99

Hoosiers (1986)
An eloquently understated drama starring Gene Hackman as a former top college basketball coach who finds redemption when he takes over the reins of a small Indiana high school team. The talented supporting cast includes Barbara Hershey as a teacher, and Dennis Hopper as a "town drunk" who assists Hackman. 114 min.
27-5444 $14.99

Bat 21 (1988)
Vietnam, 1972: A hard-nosed Air Force strategist (Gene Hackman) gets his first taste of real carnage when he is shot down in Cong-infested territory. His only chance for survival lies with a light aircraft pilot (Danny Glover) who must guide him to safety from the sky. Spellbinding wartime suspense. 106 min.
03-1675 $14.99

Split Decisions (1988)
Three generations of boxers and trainers in the McGuinn family rally around their youngest, an undefeated amateur with Olympic ambitions, when the Mob tries to manipulate his career. Gene Hackman tops this gritty action drama, co-starring Craig Sheffer, Jeff Fahey and Jennifer Beals. 95 min.
19-1706 $12.99

Mississippi Burning (1988)
Controversy and acclaim surrounded Alan Parker's fact-based look at the turbulent American South of the early '60s. The murder of three civil rights workers in a small Mississippi town brings disparate FBI agents Gene Hackman and Willem Dafoe to investigate, but the bigotry-spawned violence continues. Frances McDormand, Brad Dourif also star. 127 min.
73-1039   Was $19.99 $14.99

The Package (1989)
A tightly wrapped bundle of red herrings and baffling guises, starring Gene Hackman as an American security expert called on to stop an assassination at an international disarmament conference. Intricate thriller co-stars Joanna Cassidy, Tommy Lee Jones and John Heard. 107 min.
73-1067   Was $19.99 $14.99

Loose Cannons (1990)
As if detective Gene Hackman didn't have enough problems with a case that involves gangland murders, European politics and a pornographic film starring Adolf Hitler, his unbalanced new partner, forensics expert Dan Aykroyd, keeps changing from one TV/movie character to another. Wild action-comedy from Bob Clark ("Porky's") co-stars Ronny Cox, Dom DeLuise. 93 min.
02-2045 $14.99

Company Business (1991)
First-rate end-of-the-Cold War espionage yarn with Gene Hackman as a former CIA agent who is called back to action to escort former Soviet operative Mikhail Baryshnikov and $2 million to Berlin for a spy swap. Little do they know, they're both targets for assassination by the KGB and the CIA. Written and directed by Nicholas Meyer ("Star Trek VI"). 99 min.
12-2434   Was $19.99 $14.99

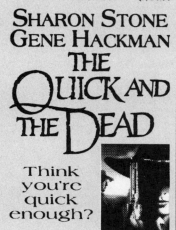

SHARON STONE
GENE HACKMAN
THE QUICK AND THE DEAD

Think you're quick enough?

The Quick And The Dead (1995)
Director Sam Raimi's off-the-wall, darkly funny sagebrush drama stars Sharon Stone as a lovely and lethal gunslinger who enters a frontier town's deadly quick-draw competition. Gene Hackman shines as the villain who controls both the contest and town and may have ties to Stone's past. With Leonardo DiCaprio, Lance Henriksen, Gary Sinise and Russell Crowe. 105 min.
02-2781   Was $19.99 $14.99

Extreme Measures (1996)
The death and subsequent disappearance of a homeless man from a New York hospital emergency room sends physician Hugh Grant on a search for the truth that will lead him into a far-reaching clandestine program whose discovery could cost him his life. Gripping suspense film also stars Gene Hackman, Sarah Jessica Parker, David Morse. 119 min.
02-3036 $19.99

The Chamber (1996)
Young lawyer Chris O'Donnell, interested in learning the secrets of his family's tragic past as much as serving the cause of justice, takes up the case of his grandfather, death row inmate Gene Hackman, who was convicted in a racist bombing decades earlier. As Hackman's date with "the chamber" draws nearer, O'Donnell fights to uncover the truth behind the crime in this suspenseful adaptation of the John Grisham novel. With Faye Dunaway, Lela Rochon. 113 min.
07-2495   Was $99.99 $14.99

Please see our index for these other Gene Hackman titles: *Absolute Power • Antz • The Birdcage • Bonnie And Clyde • A Bridge Too Far • The Conversation • Crimson Tide • Downhill Racer • Enemy Of The State • The Firm • Geronimo: An American Legend • Get Shorty • Hawaii • Lilith • The Poseidon Adventure • Postcards From The Edge • Power • Reds • The Replacements • Superman I, II & IV • Twilight • Unforgiven • Wyatt Earp • Young Frankenstein*

Sounder (1972)
The award-winning, sensitive story of a black sharecropper family in the 1930s. Cicely Tyson and Paul Winfield excel as the parents struggling to hold their family together. With Kevin Hooks as the oldest son. Directed by Martin Ritt. 105 min.
06-1213 $14.99

The Foreigner (1978)
Underground filmmaker Amos Poe ("Blank Generation") wrote and directed this punk-flavored thriller about a terrorist agent whose mission in New York exposes him to constant danger and a bizarre array of friends and enemies. Eric Mitchell, Patti Astor star, with appearances by The Cramps and Debbie Harry. 90 min.
50-3171 $69.99

Nightmare At 43 Hillcrest (1974)
Take a happy suburban family. Add a corrupt police commissioner eager to create a scandal for his own advantage. Stir in large quantities of heroin planted in the innocent family's home. Couldn't happen? It did...and this engrossing true drama will shock you. Jim Hutton, Mariette Hartley, John Karlen star. 66 min.
50-7050   Was $29.99 $14.99

The Golden Bowl (1972)
Based on the novel by Henry James, this stunning "Masterpiece Theatre" mini-series follows a wealthy widower and his grown daughter through their romance with—and stormy marriage to—a pair of former lovers. Cyril Cusack, Kathleen Byron, Gayle Hunnicutt, Barry Morse and Jill Townsend star. 180 min. on three tapes.
50-8138   Was $59.99 $39.99

Road Movie (1974)
Gritty independent drama from director Joseph Strick features Barry Bostwick and Robert Drivas as truck drivers on a cross-country odyssey and Regina Baff as the hooker who offers them sex in exchange for a ride. After she's used and rejected by the duo, Baff sets out to make them pay and leads them down a highway to destruction. 88 min.
50-8744 $19.99

Footsteps (1972)
Richard Crenna is a college football coach who attempts to relive his pro gridiron glory days with his no-nonsense approach to the game. Crenna has a chance to redeem himself when he tangles with gamblers looking to fix some important games. Clu Gulager, Joanna Pettet and Forrest Tucker co-star. 70 min.
10-9514 $14.99

Saint Jack (1979)
Ben Gazzara turns in a masterful performance as an American pimp in '70s Singapore who furnishes prostitutes to foreigners. When he discovers that his prosperous service is being stepped on by local businessmen, Gazzara winds up involved in a blackmail scheme with an American mobster. Atmospheric character study directed by Peter Bogdanovich also stars Denholm Elliott, Joss Ackland. 112 min.
47-1191 $14.99

Eliza's Horoscope (1970)
Highly original and life-enriching drama that combines sensuality and surrealism to tell the tale of a lonely, frail Canadian woman who dabbles in astrology to help her find her one true love. Stars Elizabeth Moorman, Tommy Lee Jones and Lila Kedrova. 120 min.
44-7074   Was $19.99 $14.99

Nicky's World (1974)
A family of Greek immigrants is shocked when their bakery shop is burned to the ground by arsonists. However, Nicky loves his family more than anything and wants to see them prosper in America, so he sets out to bring the guilty parties to justice. Olympia Dukakis, Mark Shera and James Broderick star. 78 min.
08-1789 $19.99

DVD VIDEO
ASK ABOUT OUR GIANT DVD CATALOG!

John Cassavetes

Shadows (1961)
This first directorial effort from John Cassavetes, based on a series of improvisations created by Cassavetes' acting group, spearheaded a movement in American independent cinema. Lelia Goldoni stars as a light-skinned black woman who, after trying to pass as white, faces the reality of racism when the man she loves discovers her true heritage. With Hugh Hurd, Ben Carruthers. 87 min.
53-8420 *$19.99*

Faces (1968)
Cassavetes' return to independent filmmaking after directing two movies for major studios is a personal study of a crumbling marriage, with John Marley as the salesman who finds comfort in the arms of prostitute Gena Rowlands, while Lynn Carlin, his wife, has a tryst with aging hipster Seymour Cassel that plunges her into depression. 129 min.
53-8425 *$19.99*

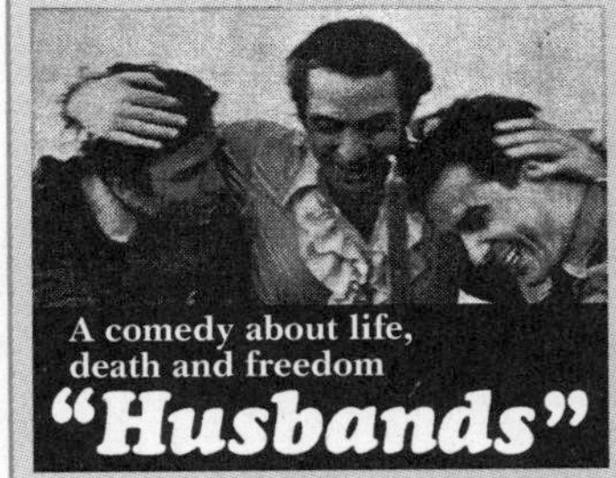

Husbands (1970)
John Cassavetes' male-bonding epic stars Peter Falk, Ben Gazzara and Cassavetes as three boyhood friends who group together after another pal dies. They soon forget wives and families and go on a carefree spree that includes drinking, playing hoops and taking a trip to London, where they consider extra-marital affairs. With Jenny Runacre, Noelle Kao. 140 min.
02-3247 ❏*$19.99*

Minnie And Moskowitz (1971)
A simple and heartfelt comedy/drama from John Cassavetes, with Gena Rowlands as a museum curator about to turn 40 who is dumped by her married lover (played by real-life husband Cassavetes) and, while on a blind date with another man, catches the eye of oddball parking lot attendant Seymour Cassel. With Val Avery, Elsie Ames and Cassavetes' mother Katherine as Cassel's mom. 105 min.
08-8786 Letterboxed *$14.99*

A Woman Under The Influence (1974)
John Cassavetes directed this acclaimed, superbly acted drama starring Gena Rowlands as a housewife whose erratic behavior prompts construction worker husband Peter Falk to have her placed in a mental institution. The film takes place before and after her six-month stay at the facility, and is filled with the sort of wild, manic and unpredictable moments that are Cassavetes trademarks. 147 min.
11-1640 Letterboxed ❏*$14.99*

The Killing Of A Chinese Bookie (1976)
John Cassavetes wrote and directed this moody study of a Los Angeles strip club owner (Ben Gazzara) who agrees to kill an Asian bookmaker to pay off his gambling and business debts. Little does he know the bookie is actually a powerful mobster, and the hit will be anything but easy. Timothy Carey and Seymour Cassel also star. 109 min.
11-1712 Letterboxed ❏*$14.99*

Opening Night (1977)
Gena Rowlands is an anxiety-ridden actress who re-examines her own life when one of her biggest fans dies in an accident on the opening night of her new Broadway play. Joan Blondell, Ben Gazzara and Zohra Lampert also star in this intimate, penetrating drama from director John Cassavetes. 144 min.
11-1690 Letterboxed ❏*$14.99*

Gloria (1980)
Gena Rowlands is marvelous as an ex-gun moll protecting a kid whose parents have been rubbed out by the Mob in this powerful, tension-filled story with humor and excitement. Written and directed by John Cassavetes. With Buck Henry, Juan Adames. 121 min.
02-1068 Was $69.99 *$14.99*

John Cassavetes: To Risk Everything To Express It All
An acclaimed stage and screen actor, John Cassavetes skipped the Hollywood studio system in the early '60s and spearheaded the independent filmmaking movement with such self-financed movies as "Faces," "Husbands" and "A Woman Under the Influence." The man and his art are examined in this comprehensive retrospective. 50 min.
22-1697 *$19.99*

The Cassavetes Boxed Set
This special five-tape collector's set includes "The Killing of a Chinese Bookie," "Mikey and Nicky," "Minnie and Moskowitz," "Opening Night" and "A Woman Under the Influence."
08-8787 Save $5.00! *$69.99*

Class Of '63 (1973)
A college reunion is the setting for this drama that looks at lost loves, lost lives, success and desperation, as old friends come to grips with their futures. James Brolin, Joan Hackett. 74 min.
40-1077 *$19.99*

The Savage Is Loose (1974)
George C. Scott directs and stars in this tale of a family stranded on a remote island and the forbidden relationship that develops between mother and son over the course of their long struggle. Co-stars Trish Van Devere, John David Carson, Lee H. Montgomery. 114 min.
23-5001 *$14.99*

Catholics (1973)
Provocative, award-winning drama set in the near future, where a young priest is sent by the Vatican to a small Irish town in order to "bring in line" a monastery whose members still practice traditional Latin masses. Martin Sheen, Trevor Howard, Cyril Cusack star. 74 min.
27-6049 Was $19.99 *$14.99*

I Know Why The Caged Bird Sings (1979)
A young black girl growing up in 1930s Arkansas learns some bittersweet lessons about prejudice in this drama based on the best-selling book by Maya Angelou. Tender, life-affirming story stars Diahann Carroll, Ruby Dee, Constance Good. 96 min.
27-6364 Was $19.99 *$14.99*

Roll Of Thunder, Hear My Cry (1978)
A warm and moving drama, depicting the struggles of a poor black family in '30s Mississippi as seen through the eyes of an 11-year-old daughter. Claudia McNeil, Lark Ruffin, Robert Christian star; look for Morgan Freeman in an early role. 95 min.
27-6691 *$14.99*

Too Far To Go (1979)
The bitter disintegration and final break-up of a 20-year marriage is traced in this compelling and emotional drama based on short stories by John Updike. Michael Moriarty and Blythe Danner shine as the caring but doomed couple; with Glenn Close, Ken Kercheval. 98 min.
27-6967 Was $89.99 *$29.99*

Go Ask Alice (1973)
The unforgettable true story of a shy high school girl who, desperate for attention, takes up with a crowd of drug users and is drawn into a world of narcotics, alcohol and prostitution. Filmed in a gritty, cinema verité style, this acclaimed TV drama based on the diary of Alice, stars Jamie Smith-Jackson, Julie Adams, William Shatner and Andy Griffith. 74 min.
55-3015 *$14.99*

Come Together (1972)
This erotic blast from the past stars "spaghetti western" star Tony Anthony as an American stuntman working in Italy who gets partnered in a kinky threesome involving swinging tourists Luciana Paluzzi and Rosemary Dexter. The three visit Pompeii, get hot in bed and wear hip threads as Anthony waxes philosophically as the narrator of this sensuous meditation on free love.
79-6492 Was $24.99 *$19.99*

The Onion Field (1979)
This riveting true story from Joseph Wambaugh is set in Los Angeles in 1963 and stars John Savage as a detective determined to see thugs James Woods and Franklyn Seales convicted for the killing of partner Ted Danson. Because of the flaws in the state's justice system, the trial takes years. Woods' role as the edgy killer brought him great attention; with Ronny Cox. 129 min.
53-1075 *$14.99*

Meetings With Remarkable Men (1979)
A young man training for the priesthood finds a philosophical gap in his life, and begins a years-long Asian quest for the answers to his questions. Visually stunning, director Peter Brooks' adaptation of the best-selling memoir by G.I. Gurdjieff stars Terence Stamp, Athol Fugard, Dragan Maksimovic. 108 min.
53-7173 *$69.99*

Mon Oncle Antoine (1971)
A sensitive coming-of-age drama, focusing on a young boy's growing up in a small French-Canadian mining town. Claude Jutra's praised film follows the boy's adventures helping his aunt and uncle in their general store, moving his late father's casket and getting involved in first love. Jean Duceppe and Oliviette Thibault star. 110 min. In French with English subtitles.
22-5394 Was $39.99 *$29.99*

Cornbread, Earl And Me (1975)
A black high school student, heading out of the ghetto on a basketball scholarship, is accidentally shot by the police in this moving drama of life in the streets. Bernie Casey, Moses Gunn, Rosalind Cash, Tierre Turner and Larry Fishburne (his film debut) star. 95 min.
44-1379 Was $59.99 ❏*$14.99*

Cockfighter (1974)
Warren Oates turns in a riveting performance in this moody and powerful study of a loner who trains cocks to fight in Georgia. Monte Hellman directed this beguiling Roger Corman production with an eye for detail and nuance. With Harry Dean Stanton. AKA: "Born to Kill." 84 min.
53-1177 *$19.99*

The Fourth Wish (1975)
Heartwarming tale of a father who must fight the system in order to help his dying son's last wishes come true. John Meillon, Robyn Nevin star. 120 min.
53-1330 *$14.99*

The Tamarind Seed (1974)
A Caribbean vacation becomes the setting for romance and intrigue when a lonely British widow (Julie Andrews) meets a suspected Soviet agent (Omar Sharif). Exciting thriller from Blake Edwards co-stars Anthony Quayle, Sylvia Syms. 87 min.
53-1436 *$12.99*

The Three Sisters (1977)
Anton Chekhov's drama of a family being torn apart in turn-of-the-century Russia is stunningly presented in this filming of the Actor's Studio 1965 stage production. Sandy Dennis, Geraldine Page, Kim Stanley, Shelley Winters, Luther Adler and Kevin McCarthy head the impressive cast. 168 min.
53-6034 *$59.99*

What? (1973)
Roman Polanski's risqué farce stars Sydne Rome as a gorgeous hitchhiker whose arrival at an eccentric, homosexual millionaire's mansion prompts all sorts of sexual complications and revelations. Marcello Mastroianni, Romolo Valli, Hugh Griffith and Polanski star. AKA: "Diary of Forbidden Dreams." Uncut version; 110 min.
53-6064 Letterboxed *$29.99*

Bone (1972)
Yaphet Kotto is an angry time bomb about to explode. Joyce Van Patten is the perfect Beverly Hills housewife on the outside, but inside is teeming with pent-up frustrations and angers. When these two volatile forces come together, they start down a trail of passion and desire that leads to murder. Explosive directorial debut from Larry Cohen also stars Andrew Duggan. AKA: "Housewife." 91 min.
53-6626 *$29.99*

Bartleby (1972)
At once funny, dramatic, ironic, and perplexing, Herman Melville's short story of an office clerk who slowly and inexorably shuts himself off from his job, his society, and ultimately his own life stars John McEnery and Paul Scofield. 73 min.
53-7185 *$29.99*

The Wild Little Bunch (1972)
Gripping British melodrama, based on a true incident, stars Jack Wild ("Oliver!") as the eldest of 11 children who tries to keep his family together when their mother passes away. David Hemmings directs. 95 min.
53-7324 *$49.99*

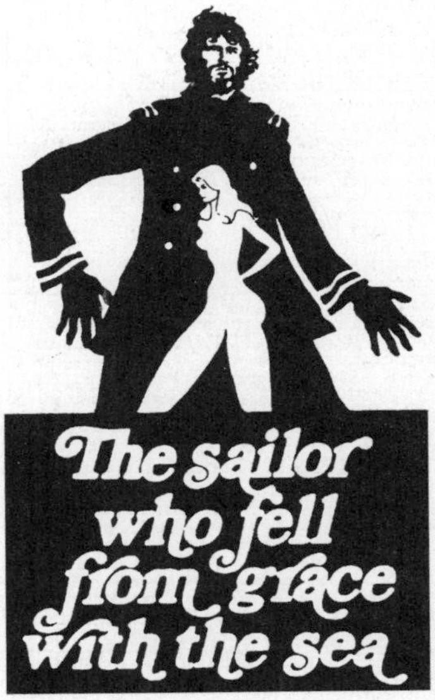

The Sailor Who Fell From Grace With The Sea (1976)
An intensely erotic romance between sailor Kris Kristofferson and lonely widow Sarah Miles and the effect their affair has on Miles' son propel this stirring drama, based on a Yukio Mishima novel. Electrifying love-making scenes and a shocking finale propel this drama. 104 min.
53-1299 Letterboxed *$14.99*

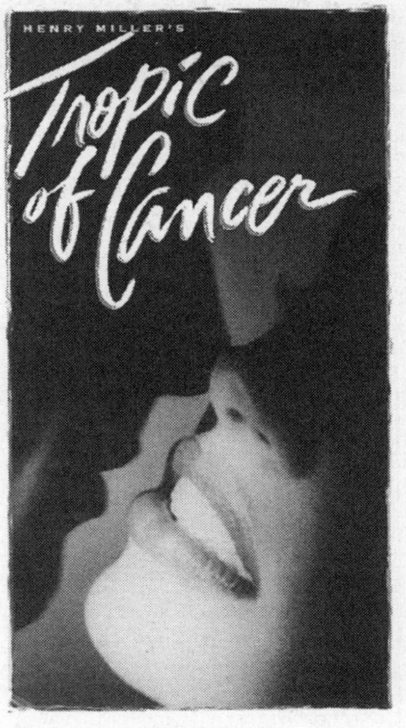

Tropic Of Cancer (1970)
Henry Miller's once-banned novel based on his sexual escapades among the denizens of 1930s Paris is boldly brought to the screen by director Joseph Strick ("Ulysses"). Rip Torn plays the writer whose chronicles in eroticism and sexual obsession blazed new trails in literature. With James Callahan and Ellen Burstyn. Uncut version, originally rated X; 87 min.
06-2138 *$19.99*

Henry & June (1990)
The steamy and sensual film that helped revamp Hollywood's ratings system, Philip Kaufman's biodrama looks at the artistic and romantic triangle that developed between "Tropic of Cancer" author Henry Miller, his wife June, and French writer Anaïs Nin in '30s Paris. Fred Ward, Uma Thurman, Maria de Madeiros star. Uncut, NC-17 version; 136 min.
07-1673 Was $19.99 ❏*$14.99*

Quiet Days In Clichy (1990)
Set in the red light district of Paris in the 1930s, Claude Chabrol's titillating adaptation of Henry Miller's erotic novel features Nigel Havers as Alfred, the womanizing photographer who takes up residence with Joe (Andrew McCarthy), an impoverished writer. They hang out at Club Melody, an establishment frequented by prostitutes, where they have ribald adventures. 100 min.
59-7015 *$99.99*

El Super (1979)
Ten years after he was exiled from his homeland, a homesick Cuban (Raymundo Hidalgo-Gato) reminisces about his life as a Manhattan apartment house super. Bittersweet tale was the first Spanish-language film made in New York City. 90 min. In Spanish with English subtitles.
53-7352 Was $89.99 *$19.99*

The Murder Of A Moderate Man (1976)
After a political leader is assassinated, an Interpol agent investigates the subsequent rash of murders that occur and tracks suspects across Europe and into the Italian Alps, where he learns a deadly secret. Denis Quilley and Susan Fleetwood star. 165 min.
53-9364 *$29.99*

Miss Melody Jones (1973)
Dramatic look at the life of a young black woman who comes to Los Angeles with those all-too-common dreams of stardom, but instead is forced into the sordid life of a stripper. Philomena Nowlin, Ronald Warren star. 86 min.
54-9002 *$19.99*

Firehouse (1972)
Richard Roundtree, Vince Edwards, Andrew Duggan and Richard Jaeckel star in this gritty look at the dangerous life of the firemen of Engine Co. 23. Roundtree is the new guy in the house, a probational recruit who struggles to prove himself. Pilot to the hit TV series. 80 min.
54-9027 Was $19.99 *$14.99*

The Suicide's Wife (1979)
After her college professor husband kills himself, a woman must try to rebuild her life and her family. She encounters feelings of guilt and responsibility and calls on her inner strength to overcome the devastating situation. Angie Dickinson, Gordon Pinsent star. 96 min.
55-1346 *$19.99*

Against All Hope (1978)
A man is driven further towards oblivion as memories of abuse from his childhood continue to resurface and add to his depression and alcoholism. With Michael Madsen and Maureen McCarthy. 89 min.
55-3000 *$19.99*

Friends (1971)
A 15-year-old English boy, neglected by his family, falls in love with a 14-year-old French orphan girl, but their idyllic life in a secluded cottage is interrupted by the surprises of life, including the arrival of a baby. This moving film, which contains controversial nude scenes, features Elton John's hit title song and stars Anicee Alvina and Sean Bury. 101 min.
06-2046 *$14.99*

Paul And Michelle (1974)
The continuing story of the teenage couple from "Friends" finds them older and confronted with new problems, from Paul's graduating prep school and their young daughter to Michelle taking a lover. With Anicee Alvina, Sean Bury and Keir Dullea. 102 min.
06-2047 *$14.99*

September 30, 1955 (1978)
A compelling look at the effect of screen hero James Dean's death on an alienated college student, played by Richard Thomas. Stunned by the news of his idol's death in a fatal car crash, Thomas assembles his friends for a ceremony honoring Dean, but tragedy soon follows. Dennis Quaid, Tom Hulce and Lisa Blount co-star. 107 min.
07-1864 Was $79.99 ❑*$14.99*

Wise Blood (1979)
John Huston translates Flannery O'Connor's first novel with an equally satirical tone. A religious zealot recruits a ragtag band of followers for his Church Without Christ. Brad Dourif, Ned Beatty and Harry Dean Stanton star. 106 min.
07-1317 *$59.99*

Ken Russell

Isadora Duncan (1966)
Produced as a BBC television film, Ken Russell's stylized biodrama combines interviews, vintage performance footage and staged re-creations to portray the life of infamous dancer and free spirit Isadora Duncan. Vivian Pickles stars in the title role; Leni Reifenstahl contributed to the photography. AKA: "Isadora Duncan, The Biggest Dancer in the World." 65 min.
10-7447 Was $29.99 *$19.99*

Women In Love (1969)
A masterful version of D.H. Lawrence's novel about the love affairs of two couples. Lusty, sensual, brilliantly acted by Oscar-winner Glenda Jackson, Alan Bates and Oliver Reed. Directed by Ken Russell. 129 min.
12-1977 Was $19.99 *$14.99*

The Boy Friend (1971)
Director Ken Russell's dazzling, heartfelt salute to '30s Hollywood musicals stars Twiggy as the understudy who fills in for ailing star Glenda Jackson in a stage revue and (wouldn't you know it?) becomes an overnight star. But can she win her co-star's heart? With Christopher Gable, Tommy Tune, and a great selection of classic show tunes. Restored, 135-min. version.
12-2023 *$19.99*

The Music Lovers (1971)
Richard Chamberlain stars as famed 19th-century composer Peter Ilich Tchaikovsky in director Ken Russell's lavish, controversial biodrama that unflinchingly depicts Tchaikovsky's tempestuous marriage, his many homosexual affairs, and his patronage by a wealthy widow. Glenda Jackson, Max Adrian also star; music by Andre Previn and the London Symphony Orchestra. 122 min.
12-2267 *$19.99*

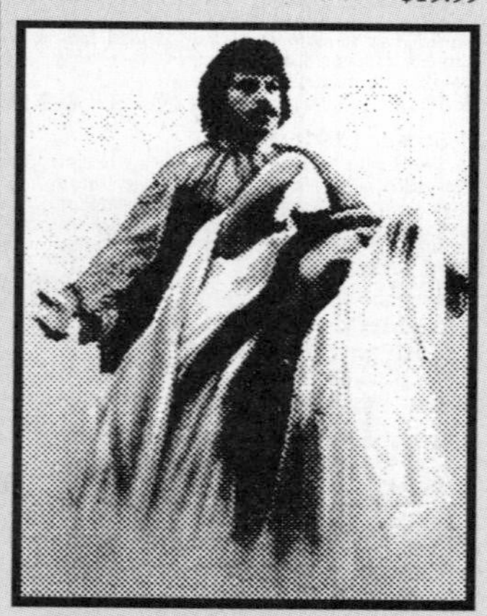

VANESSA REDGRAVE · OLIVER REED

IN

KEN RUSSELL'S FILM
THE DEVILS

The Devils (1971)
A truly epic horror film from writer/director Ken Russell. Disturbing, graphic and astonishing, it deals with sexual hysteria and bizarre religious rites in a town in 17th-century France. Vanessa Redgrave, Oliver Reed star. 103 min.
19-1086 *$19.99*

Mahler (1974)
Robert Powell stars as the turn-of-the-century Austrian composer in this visually compelling film biography from director Ken Russell that mixes stunning musical sequences with scenes from Mahler's tortured life (his troubled youth, stormy love affairs, and the growing anti-Semitism that drove him to renounce his Jewish heritage). Georgina Hale, Antonia Ellis also star. 115 min.
44-1258 *$19.99*

Lisztomania (1975)
And mania it is! Ken Russell concocted this wild and woolly biography of composer Franz Liszt, who is played by The Who's Roger Daltrey. Eye-popping visuals, electrifying score (by Rick Wakeman), way-way out costumes and colors. With Ringo Starr and Paul Nicholas. 105 min.
19-1098 Was $19.99 *$14.99*

Valentino (1977)
Ken Russell's flamboyant biography of the famed "Latin Lover" (Rudolf Nureyev) highlights the silent screen star's early years as a dance instructor, his success in films like "The Sheik," his stormy romances, and his untimely death before his 31st birthday. Leslie Caron, Michelle Phillips and Huntz Hall (as movie mogul Jesse Lasky!) also star. 127 min.
12-2861 *$19.99*

Altered States (1980)
A mind-blowing science-fiction/fantasy experience by pseudonymous writer Paddy Chayefsky and director Ken Russell. Scientists using drugs and deprivation tanks to study human consciousness and race memory unleash incredible powers that run the gamut of the evolutionary chain. William Hurt, Blair Brown, Charles Haid star; look for Drew Barrymore in her film debut. 103 min.
19-1170 ❑*$14.99*

Crimes Of Passion (Collector's Edition) (1984)
A highly charged erotic thriller from Ken Russell that features some of the hottest love scenes ever for a Hollywood film. Kathleen Turner is an enigmatic hooker named China Blue, Anthony Perkins a disheveled preacher obsessed by her, and John Laughlin is the "john" who learns her secrets. Uncut, unrated version; 107 min.
08-8592 *$19.99*

Gothic (1987)
A spellbinding account of the 1816 meeting between poets Lord Byron and Percy Shelley and writer Mary Godwin that inspired her to write "Frankenstein." Ken Russell's incredible blend of occult fantasy, drug-induced dementia and hidden desires, set against a stormy night in an isolated villa, stars Gabriel Byrne, Julian Sands and Natasha Richardson. 87 min.
47-1784 *$14.99*

Lair Of The White Worm (1988)
Terror ensnares a British countryside when a hapless archeologist uncovers a sacred relic that is sought by the centuries-old sect of a sinister serpent god. The staggering, dreamlike stylings of director Ken Russell bring bizarre life to this classic from Bram Stoker ("Dracula"); Catherine Oxenberg, Amanda Donohoe, Hugh Grant star. 94 min.
47-1943 *$14.99*

Prisoner Of Honor (1991)
The 1894 court-martial of French Army officer Alfred Dreyfus, a case that shocked the world, is recounted in this stirring historical drama by director Ken Russell. Richard Dreyfuss (no relation) stars as the counter-intelligence head who uncovers evidence that the government has sent an innocent man to prison, then fights to reopen the case. With Oliver Reed, Peter Firth. 88 min.
44-1864 ❑*$89.99*

Whore (1991)
Ultra-kinky, ultra-realistic account of the life of prostitutes in Los Angeles, featuring Theresa Russell as a woman who prefers streetwalking to working for minimum wage. She comes into contact with pimps, other women of the night and clients into S & M in this no-holds-barred story from Ken Russell ("Crimes of Passion"). With Benjamin Mouton, Antonio Fargas. Uncut, unrated version with seven minutes not shown in theatres. 92 min.
68-1217 Was $89.99 ❑*$14.99*

Lady Chatterley (1995)
Ken Russell directs this epic adaptation of D.H. Lawrence's classic novel focusing on the heated relationship between an aristocratic woman and her handicapped husband's gamekeeper, who fulfills her sexual desires. Joely Richardson, Sean Bean, Shirley Ann Field and James Wilby star. 210 min.
59-7013 *$99.99*

Please see our index for the Ken Russell title: *Aria • Tommy*

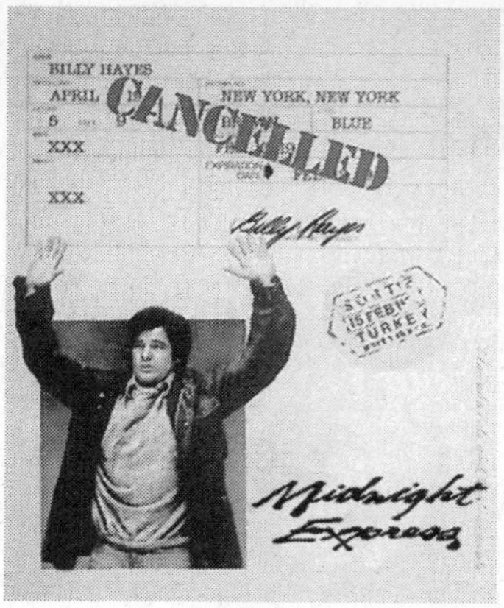

Midnight Express: 20th Anniversary Edition (1978)
Sensational, sordid, savage and true tale of American Billy Hayes' incarceration in a hellish Turkish prison for drug smuggling stars Brad Davis, Randy Quaid, John Hurt and Paul L. Smith. Scripted by Oliver Stone and directed by Alan Parker. This remastered 20th Anniversary Edition includes a "making of" featurette with the real Hayes. 122 min.
02-3220 ❑*$19.99*

Midnight Express: 20th Anniversary Edition (Letterboxed Version)
Also available in a theatrical, widescreen format.
02-3221 ❑*$19.99*

The Other Side Of The Mountain (1975)
Inspiring, life-affirming drama based on the life of Jill Kinmont (Marilyn Hassett), champion skier who was paralyzed in an Olympic tryout yet never gave up on herself. Beau Bridges co-stars as the man who gave her the courage. With Dabney Coleman, Belinda J. Montgomery. 102 min.
07-1375 Was5 $59.99 *$14.99*

The Other Side Of The Mountain, Part 2 (1978)
The story of Jill Kinmont continues in this uplifting tale of human courage. Marilyn Hassett is the disabled ex-skier; Timothy Bottoms the man who brings love back into her life. 99 min.
07-1376 Was $59.99 *$14.99*

My Sweet Charlie (1970)
Bittersweet, moving story, starring Patty Duke (in an Emmy-winning role) and Al Freeman, Jr. She's a pregnant, unmarried Southern woman; he's a black lawyer wanted for killing a white man. When Fate brings them together they learn to trust each other. 97 min.
07-1403 *$39.99*

Day Of The Wolves (1973)
Knockout crime drama in which seven mysterious bearded men arrive in a small town and proceed to sever all lines of communications. The town's former sheriff eventually arrives on the scene to stop their criminal scheme. Richard Egan, Rick Jason, Martha Hyer and Jan Murray star. 95 min.
10-9508 *$14.99*

Out Of Season (1975)
Moody and atmospheric drama concerning a stranger who has journeyed to the resort where he had an affair 20 years past...and who encounters his former lover and her grown, attractive daughter. Vanessa Redgrave, Cliff Robertson, Susan George star. AKA: "Winter Rates." 90 min.
08-1402 *$19.99*

One Russian Summer (1973)
Riveting drama set in the waning days of czarist Russia concerning an iron-fisted landowner (Oliver Reed) and a crippled young man (John McEnery) with vengeance on his mind. Claudia Cardinale co-stars. AKA: "Days of Fury." 112 min.
08-1403 Was $59.99 *$14.99*

Things In Their Season (1974)
Moving melodrama about a Wisconsin farm wife who learns she is dying and leukemia and dedicates the remaining time in her life to making her family happy and aware of what they have to live for. Patricia Neal, Marc Singer, Ed Flanders and Meg Foster star. 75 min.
08-1786 *$19.99*

Tell Me Where It Hurts (1974)
Maureen Stapleton stars in this moving drama about a woman who, after 26 years as an ordinary housewife, is moved to reconsider her place in the household—and society—when she joins a neighborhood discussion group. Paul Sorvino, Doris Dowling and Fay Kanin (who also scripted) co-star. 78 min.
08-1787 *$19.99*

The Abduction (1975)
A radical left-wing group kidnaps a wealthy college student in this dramatic thriller that eerily parallels the Patty Hearst ordeal, but was based on a novel written years earlier. Dorothy Malone, Gregory Rozakis star. 100 min.
03-1210 *$19.99*

The Promise (1978)
Two young lovers find their lives tragically altered by a horrible car accident, which leaves one person (Stephen Collins) comatose and the other (Kathleen Quinlan) disfigured. The man's mother pays for the woman's plastic surgery with the provision she never sees her son again. Years later, the former lovers meet, unaware of each other's identity. Stylish soaper co-stars Beatrice Straight. 97 min.
07-1953 *$89.99*

To All My Friends On Shore (1971)
Bill Cosby, in a rare early dramatic role, stars as a hard-working family man whose dreams of a better life are dashed when his son contracts a fatal disease. Moving tale of devotion and courage, co-written by Cosby, also stars Gloria Foster, Dennis Hines. 75 min.
08-8096 Was $19.99 *$14.99*

The 300 Year Weekend (1971)
Based on actual incidents, this unusual drama follows the members of an encounter group and their psychologist through a marathon session. Among the participants: a drug-addicted housewife, a closeted gay attorney, a farmer in a loveless marriage, and a beautiful model who's sleeping with the doctor. Michael Tolan, Sharon Laughlin, William Devane (who also co-scripted) star. 123 min.
08-8821 *$14.99*

Captains And The Kings (1976)
Taylor Caldwell's sprawling story concerns an Irish immigrant family's adventures in America from the mid-1850s through the early 1900s. Richard Jordan is the patriarch who becomes a powerful businessman who desires son Perry King to become the first Catholic president of the United States. Patty Duke Astin, Henry Fonda, Ray Bolger and Jane Seymour also star. Available in a five-tape set.
07-2911 *$44.99*

Voices (1979)
Touching romantic drama starring Michael Ontkean as a truck driver seeking a job in the music industry who falls in love with Amy Irving, a hearing-impaired woman who dreams of becoming a ballerina. Alex Rocco, Viveca Lindfors and Barry Miller also star.
12-3089 *$19.99*

The Angel Levine (1970)
Harry Belafonte plays Levine, the Heaven-sent intermediary who must show elderly Jewish tailor Zero Mostel that, despite business setbacks and an ailing wife, life is worth living, in this touching mix of laughter and tears. Based on a story by Bernard Malamud, Czech director Ján Kadár's ("The Shop on Main Street") American debut also stars Milo O'Shea, Ida Kaminska.
12-3316 *$14.99*

Louis Armstrong—Chicago Style (1976)
The dynamic Ben Vereen stars as the legendary jazz figure in this tale of the Windy City during the '20s. The young "Satchmo" finds himself in a world of guns, bathtub gin and wild women. Red Buttons, Margaret Avery co-star. 78 min.
14-3051 Was $19.99 *$14.99*

Pioneer Woman (1973)
Authentically re-created drama of homesteaders in the Wyoming Territory of the 1860s, as seen through the eyes of the women who fought to keep their families and their land. Joanna Pettet, William Shatner, Helen Hunt, David Janssen star. 78 min.
14-3074 *$14.99*

Freedom Road (1979)
Exciting drama of black America's rise after the Civil War stars Muhammad Ali as a former slave who becomes a spokesman for his people and is elected to the U.S. Senate. Co-stars Kris Kristofferson, Edward Herrmann, Ron O'Neal. 186 min.
14-3098 Was $29.99 ❑*$14.99*

Ali MacGraw Ryan O'Neal

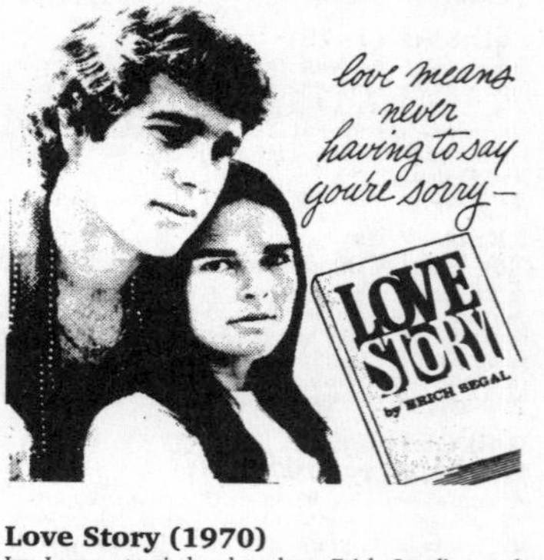

Love Story (1970)
Ivy League tearjerker based on Erich Segal's novel stars Ali MacGraw and Ryan O'Neal, two lovers who are ultimately struck by tragedy. With Ray Milland and Tommy Lee Jones (in his film debut). 99 min.
06-1037 Was $19.99 *$14.99*

Oliver's Story (1978)
Sequel to the classic film "Love Story" stars Ryan O'Neal as the bereaved Oliver and Candice Bergen as the heiress who wants to love him, if he can forget the past. Co-stars Ray Milland, Nicola Pagett. 93 min.
06-1261 Was $19.99 *$14.99*

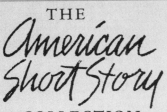

THE American Short Story COLLECTION

The Hitch-Hikers
Richard Hatch and Patty Duke star in Eudora Welty's tale of intrigue that occurs in a sleepy Southern town when a hitch-hiker is murdered. 30 min.
27-6915 *$24.99*

The Man And The Snake/ The Return
Two suspense classics by Ambrose Bierce, short story writer whose macabre wit rivaled Poe and O. Henry, are dramatically presented here in a stunning style. 60 min.
27-9051 *$24.99*

The Tell-Tale Heart
Edgar Allan Poe's classic tale of terror (boom boom!) is given a stunning treatment (boom boom!), as Sam Jaffe stars in this short drama (boom boom!) about a murderer haunted by his victim's beating heart (boom boom!). 30 min.
27-9113 □*$24.99*

The Horse Dealer's Daughter
D.H. Lawrence's story of a young woman's quest for her own identity after her father's death is given a haunting treatment. 30 min.
27-9114 □*$24.99*

The Open Window/Child's Play
Two short stories by Saki are dramatized. "The Open Window" looks at how a young girl's evocative language draws a listener's attention; and, in "Child's Play," a young boy struggles for identity and independence from his repressive guardian. 38 min.
27-9115 □*$24.99*

D.P. (1980)
While serving in post-WWII Germany, a black American soldier forms a growing attachment to a young black boy who considers the soldier his "father." Kurt Vonnegut, Jr.'s moving story stars Stan Shaw, Rosemary Leach. 51 min.
27-6552 *$24.99*

Noon Wine (1980)
A Swedish immigrant travels to America with hopes of a new life, but finds new problems in a small Texas town. Fred Ward and Lise Hilboldt star in this Katherine Anne Porter story. 50 min.
27-6553 *$24.99*

The Migrants (1974)
The hard life and conditions faced by modern-day migratory farm workers, as seen through the eyes of one family, are vividly brought to the screen in this acclaimed drama, written by Lanford Wilson from a Tennessee Williams story. Cloris Leachman, Ron Howard, Sissy Spacek and Cindy Williams star. 83 min.
27-6867 Was $89.99 *$29.99*

The Hollow Boy
Set in New York in 1936, this sensitive examination of a friendship between a young German immigrant and his Jewish neighbor was based on Hortense Calisher's acclaimed story. Alexis Arquette, Jerry Stiller and Kathleen Widdoes star. 60 min.
27-6913 *$24.99*

An Outpost Of Progress
Joseph Conrad, the author of "Heart of Darkness" and "Lord Jim," wrote this exotic tale set in a West African outpost in the late 19th century where a man fights his own isolation and morality while in search of personal honor. With Simon MacCorkindale.
27-6940 *$24.99*

The Jilting Of Granny Weatherall (1976)
Haunting story of love lost from Katherine Anne Porter stars Geraldine Fitzgerald as a dying woman tormented by the memory of a long-gone suitor. 57 min.
27-6272 *$24.99*

Soldier's Home (1976)
A soldier returns home after World War I, only to find that he no longer fits, in a study of alienation from Ernest Hemingway. Stars Richard Backus and Nancy Marchand. 41 min.
27-6403 *$24.99*

The Displaced Person (1977)
A powerful and shocking story about the turmoil released in a small Georgia town by the arrival of a Polish immigrant after World War II. The screenplay is by Horton Foote from the Flannery O'Connor short story. John Houseman and Irene Worth star. 58 min.
27-6398 *$24.99*

Almos' A Man (1977)
A black teenage boy in the Deep South of the '30s looking to be accepted as a man, thinks he's found a way when he gets a gun in this dramatic tale from the pen of Richard Wright ("Native Son"); LeVar Burton stars. 51 min.
27-6413 *$24.99*

The Blue Hotel (1977)
Stephen Crane's timeless story about a Swedish immigrant whose Wild West fantasies put him at odds with the residents of a frontier Nebraska hotel, and the tragedy that follows. David Warner and James Keach star. 55 min.
27-6440 *$24.99*

The Jolly Corner (1977)
Henry James' classic tale of a mysterious house and the unhappy man who enters it, finding ghostly visions of what his life could have been, is movingly rendered in this fine production. With Fritz Weaver, Salome Jens. 43 min.
27-6443 *$24.99*

The Music School/Parker Adderson, Philosopher (1977)
John Updike's tale of a music teacher unable to conduct his life and Ambrose Bierce's ironic diatribe about a soldier cut down in the Civil War are dramatized. 69 min.
27-6444 *$24.99*

The Man That Corrupted Hadleyburg (1978)
Robert Preston stars as a mysterious stranger with a plan to teach the hypocritical citizens of a small town a lesson in greed in this cynical slice of Americana by Mark Twain. 40 min.
27-6274 *$24.99*

Paul's Case (1978)
Eric Roberts stars as the young working-class man who finds himself at odds with a cold, materialistic society in Willa Cather's moving tale. 52 min.
27-6315 *$24.99*

I'm A Fool (1978)
Star-crossed lovers are able to overcome any problems, as poor boy Ron Howard learns when he falls for society girl Amy Irving in Sherwood Anderson's light-hearted romance. 38 min.
27-6316 *$24.99*

Bernice Bobs Her Hair (1979)
A Jazz Age "plain Jane" is transformed by her worldly cousin into a gorgeous flapper, but soon becomes the center of attention, much to her "mentor's" regret, in F. Scott Fitzgerald's classic short story. Shelley Duvall, Bud Cort star. 49 min.
27-6313 *$24.99*

The Sky Is Gray (1979)
A poor black child's trip to the dentist becomes a learning experience about life, poverty, racism and each person's right to respect themselves in a moving drama by Ernest J. Gaines. James Bond III, Olivia Cole star. 46 min.
27-6314 *$24.99*

Rappaccini's Daughter (1980)
Offbeat tale of fantasy and suspense from Nathaniel Hawthorne about a doctor whose lovely daughter kills anything she touches stars Kristoffer Tabori, Kathleen Beller. 57 min.
27-6273 *$24.99*

Barn Burning (1980)
William Faulkner's tale of alienation and bitterness between an aloof tenant farmer and his son stars Tommy Lee Jones and Diane Kagan. 40 min.
27-6275 *$24.99*

The Greatest Man In The World (1980)
Brad Davis stars as a 1920s aviator hero whose private image is nothing like his "boy next door" public facade, in this adaptation of James Thurber's satiric short story. Co-stars Carol Kane, Howard DaSilva. 51 min.
27-6369 *$24.99*

Pigeon Feathers (1988)
Celebrated author John Updike ("Witches of Eastwick") penned this story about a mother and son finding the essential tension between life and death after returning to a country home. Christopher Collet and Caroline McWilliams star. 45 min.
27-9025 *$24.99*

Honky (1971)
Tender drama of the friendship between a white man and black woman that leads to romance and conflict. John Nielson, Brenda Sykes, William Marshall and Marion Ross star. 92 min.
48-1071 *$29.99*

Watership Down (1978)
Animated drama based on Richard Adams' best-selling novel. A herd of rabbits undertakes a dangerous journey to find a new home. John Hurt, Zero Mostel and Ralph Richardson supply the voices. 92 min.
19-1105 *$14.99*

Honor Thy Father (1973)
Gay Talese's controversial best-seller is brought to the screen in brutally realistic fashion. The focus is on the Mafia Wars involving Joe Bonanno and his Family, fought on mean city streets. Raf Vallone, Joseph Bologna, Brenda Vaccaro, Richard Castellano. 97 min.
46-5024 *$14.99*

Rush It (1977)
Tom Berenger ("The Big Chill") stars in this warm tale of a romance between a 17-year-old girl and a bike messenger. Co-stars Jill Eikenberry. 78 min.
48-1051 *$29.99*

Rolling Thunder (1977)
An action-packed, knock-out drama, written by Paul Schrader ("Taxi Driver"). William Devane plays a Vietnam P.O.W. who comes home to find things have changed since he left: his family has been murdered, and he's out to find who did it. Tommy Lee Jones, Linda Haynes. 99 min.
47-1065 *$14.99*

Steel Arena (1973)
Fasten your seat belts and get ready for the ride of your life in this lightning-fast docu-drama of a young man training to be a stunt driver. Real-life auto daredevils risk life and limb in amazing feats that make freeway driving look safe by comparison. Drivers Dusty Russell, Gene Drew and Buddy Love play themselves. 99 min.
47-1531 Was $69.99 *$19.99*

Little Ladies Of The Night (1977)
A teenage runaway on the streets of Los Angeles is drawn into the world of prostitution, and a tough ex-pimp-turned-cop tries to save her in this gritty and shocking drama. David Soul, Linda Purl, Lou Gossett, Jr., Kathleen Quinlan star.
46-5039 *$14.99*

The Autobiography Of Miss Jane Pittman (1973)
Award-winning story of a black woman's life, from her childhood as a slave in the South of the 1860s to the Civil Rights movements of the 1960s. Cicely Tyson stars in her most-remembered role. 110 min.
46-5090 *$14.99*

Cinderella Liberty (1973)
A sailor on extended leave in Seattle plays pappy to a ready-made family—a reckless prostitute and her 11-year-old mulatto son. Director Mark Rydell's unconventional love story stars James Caan and Marsha Mason; with Eli Wallach and Burt Young. 117 min.
04-2232 Was $59.99 *$29.99*

In This House Of Brede (1975)
Diana Rigg was nominated for an Emmy for her dynamic performance as a sophisticated London widow who denounces her lifestyle and career as an executive in order to become a cloistered Benedictine nun in Brede Abbey. With Judy Bowker, Gwen Watford. 100 min.
08-1782 *$19.99*

The McCullochs (1975)
What if Jethro Bodine had directed "Dallas"? The result would be this sprawling drama set in 1949 Texas and starring Forrest Tucker as self-made millionaire J.J. McCulloch. Tucker's attempts to control his rebellious teenage children (Don Grady, Chip Hand, Janice Heiden, Dennis Redfield) lead to resentment and conflict. Julie Adams, William Demarest and Max Baer, Jr. (who also scripted) co-star. AKA: "The Wild McCullochs." 93 min.
08-8825 *$14.99*

The McCullochs (Letterboxed Collector's Edition)
Special edition includes a letterboxed version of the film, cast bios and the original theatrical trailer.
08-8826 *$14.99*

Sunday, Bloody Sunday (1971)
Provocative drama from director John Schlesinger ("Midnight Cowboy") in which the relationship between Jewish physician Peter Finch and wealthy divorcee Glenda Jackson is threatened when they both fall in love with a young, free-spirited sculptor, played by Murray Head. 110 min.
12-2991 □*$19.99*

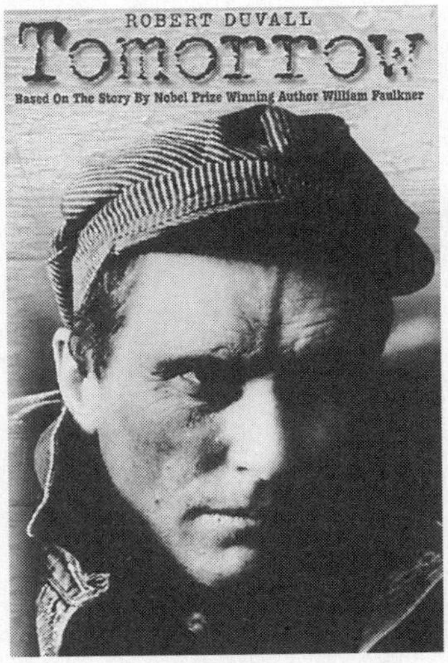

Tomorrow (1972)
Robert Duvall shines as a lonely Mississippi backwoods farmer who finds an abandoned pregnant woman (Olga Bellin) and takes her under his care. Tender, understated drama, based on a William Faulkner short story and scripted by Horton Foote. With Sudie Bond, Peter Masterson, Richard McConnell. 102 min.
27-6066 Was $29.99 *$14.99*

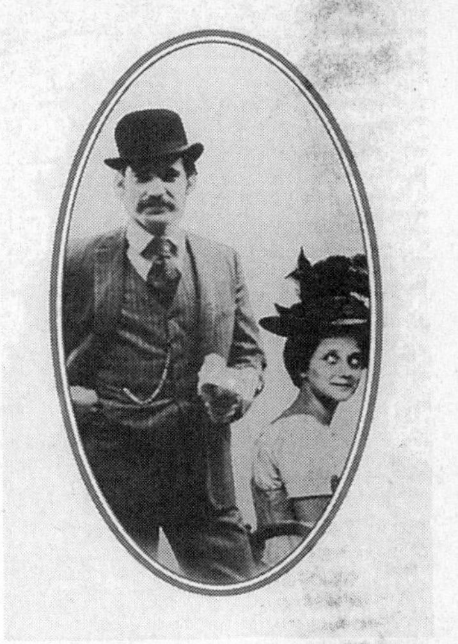

Hester Street

Hester Street (1975)
An acclaimed look at Jewish immigrants living in New York around the turn of the century. Steven Keats and Oscar-nominated Carol Kane star in this heartwarming, sensitively told look at strangers in a new land. Much of the dialogue is in Yiddish with English subtitles. 89 min.
70-5041 Was $59.99 *$29.99*

The Glass House (1972)
Vivid, brutally powerful account by Truman Capote of the experiences of inmates in a Utah prison. Alan Alda plays a college professor awaiting his manslaughter trial, while Vic Morrow is the leader of a ruthless prison faction; with Billy Dee Williams, Clu Gulager. Restored, uncut version; 91 min.
58-1118 *$19.99*

First You Cry (1978)
This is the dramatic true story of NBC news correspondent Betty Rollin and how her life changed following a mastectomy. Based on Rollin's book, the film stars Mary Tyler Moore, Anthony Perkins, Richard Crenna, Jennifer Warren, Richard Dysart and Don Johnson. 100 min.
58-8132 *$12.99*

The Hard Road (1970)
An exploitation drama steeped in counterculture accouterments about a teenager who gets pregnant, gives up her baby and gets drawn into the fast lane of sex, drugs and rock-and-roll when she takes a job as secretary for a record producer. John Alderman co-stars; Gary Graver, who served as cameraman for Orson Welles, directs. 85 min.
79-5437 Was $24.99 *$19.99*

Queen Of The Stardust Ballroom (1975)
Simple and touching made-for-TV drama that won three Emmy Awards stars Maureen Stapleton as a widow who finds romance and a new lease on life when she meets married mailman Charles Durning at a '40s-style dance hall. With Charlotte Rae, Michael Brandon. 95 min.
46-5017 *$19.99*

I Heard The Owl Call My Name (1973)
Tom Courtenay stars in this award-winning drama set in the Canadian Northwest. A young Anglican priest is assigned to an isolated church to aid an older bishop. While there, he learns gentle lessons about life, love, devotion and death from the native Indians. Dean Jagger and Marianne Jones co-star. 74 min.
46-5010 *$19.99*

Over The Edge (1979)
Fascinating, overlooked drama of teens in a planned suburban community who, out of sheer boredom, begin a series of pranks that escalate into a deadly game of violence. Matt Dillon makes his film debut as the leader; co-stars Vincent Spano, Ellen Geer. Top rock score; Jonathan Kaplan directs. 95 min.
19-1074 Was $59.99 *$14.99*

The Wanderers (1979)
Early 1960s...The Wanderers, a gang of neighborhood kids, fight their rivals and each other while growing up. Comedy, drama, bone-crunching violence and great songs from the era. Ken Wahl, Karen Allen, Olympia Dukakis. 113 min.
19-1082 Was $59.99 *$19.99*

One On One (1978)
Robby Benson in a warm and winning story of a college basketball recruit who must fight against school corruption and a sneaky coach to win. With Annette O'Toole, G.D. Spradlin; look for Melanie Griffith as a hitchhiker. 105 min.
19-1190 Was $39.99 *$14.99*

The Silver Chalice (1954)
In his film debut, Paul Newman portrays Basil the Defender, a Greek artisan who creates the cup used at the Last Supper. Sprawling costume epic centered around the birth of Christianity also stars Jack Palance, Pier Angeli, Virginia Mayo and E.G. Marshall. 144 min.
19-1573 Was $19.99 *$14.99*

Playwrights '56: The Battler (1956)
A young Paul Newman stars in this exceptional drama, directed by Arthur Penn and based on a story by Ernest Hemingway, about a young man who goes "on the bum," encountering a number of strange characters, including a crooked truck driver, a cruel cafe owner and a crazed boxer. With Phyllis Kirk, Dewey Martin. 60 min.
09-1235 Was $24.99 *$19.99*

Somebody Up There Likes Me (1956)
Robert Wise's biodrama of middleweight boxing champ Rocky Graziano won two Oscars. In his third film role (and the one that made him a star), Paul Newman plays the New York street kid who escapes a life of petty crime to become a sports legend. With Pier Angeli, Everett Sloane, Sal Mineo and Steve McQueen (in his film debut). 113 min.
12-1830 Was $29.99 □*$19.99*

Bang The Drum Slowly (1956)
A touching ballpark drama starring Paul Newman, Albert Salmi and George Peppard about the friendship between a catcher dying of Hodgkin's disease and his team's star pitcher. "The U.S. Steel Hour" aired this teleplay of Mark Harris' novel two decades before it became a movie with Robert De Niro. 60 min.
73-5046 *$14.99*

Until They Sail (1957)
Emotional drama set in WWII New Zealand follows the lives of four sisters whose men have gone to war. Jean Simmons, Joan Fontaine, Piper Laurie and Sandra Dee are the women dealing with loneliness, death and American soldiers (played by Paul Newman, Charles Drake and Wally Cassell). Directed by Robert Wise. 95 min.
12-2510 *$19.99*

The Long, Hot Summer (1958)
Paul Newman and Joanne Woodward first met while making this adaptation of several William Faulkner stories. Newman is the wanderer who takes a job on patriarch Orson Welles' spread and attracts the attention of Welles' daughter, Woodward. Sprawling drama of love in the Deep South also stars Anthony Franciosa, Angela Lansbury, Lee Remick. 116 min.
04-2305 Was $19.99 *$14.99*

The Left-Handed Gun (1958)
Director Arthur Penn's first feature is a compelling and unflinching look at the life of Billy the Kid. Paul Newman portrays the notorious outlaw as an uneducated misfit who finds himself trapped in his role. With Hurd Hatfield, Lita Milan. 102 min.
19-1572 *$14.99*

The Young Philadelphians (1959)
Ambitious lawyer Paul Newman schemes his way up the ladder, seducing his boss's wife along the way, but when he tries to defend a war buddy accused of murder his own dark past comes back to haunt him. Finely staged melodrama also stars Barbara Rush, Robert Vaughn, Alexis Smith. 136 min.
19-1243 Was $19.99 *$14.99*

The Helen Morgan Story (1959)
The colorful life of sultry singer Helen Morgan is depicted in this splashy biography featuring Ann Blyth in the title role and Paul Newman as a bootlegging promoter who helps Morgan's career. The film follows the songstress's rise to stardom, as well as her romantic and drinking problems. Richard Carlson, Alan King and Gene Evans co-star. 118 min.
19-2327 *$19.99*

From The Terrace (1960)
Superb adaptation of John O'Hara's novel stars Paul Newman as a young businessman whose relentless pursuit of corporate and social success forces him to remain in a loveless marriage, despite his love for another woman. Co-stars Joanne Woodward, Ina Balin, Myrna Loy and George Grizzard. 144 min.
04-2304 Was $19.99 *$14.99*

Exodus (1960)
Director Otto Preminger's sprawling saga about the 1947 Palestinian war for Israel's independence features an all-star cast that includes Paul Newman as a fiery resistance leader, Eva Marie Saint as an army nurse, Ralph Richardson and Peter Lawford as British officers and Sal Mineo as a radical freedom fighter. With John Derek, Lee J. Cobb; scripted by Dalton Trumbo from Leon Uris' novel. 208 min.
12-2444 Was $29.99 □*$24.99*

Exodus (Letterboxed Version)
Also available in a theatrical, widescreen format.
12-3038 □*$24.99*

The Hustler (1961)
Director Robert Rossen's brilliant character study features Paul Newman's passionate portrayal of "Fast Eddie" Felson, a hustling pool shark who drifts across the country playing in seedy pool halls and whose obsession to dethrone table legend "Minnesota Fats" (Jackie Gleason) could bring about his own downfall. Co-stars Piper Laurie, George C. Scott, Myron McCormick. 139 min.
04-1077 *$19.99*

The Color Of Money (1986)
In his Oscar-winning performance, Paul Newman returns as pool hall hustler "Fast Eddie" Felson, lured back to the table when he serves as mentor to cocky young cue whiz Tom Cruise. Captivating film for all ages, directed by Martin Scorsese, co-stars Mary Elizabeth Mastrantonio. 119 min.
11-1415 Was $19.99 □*$14.99*

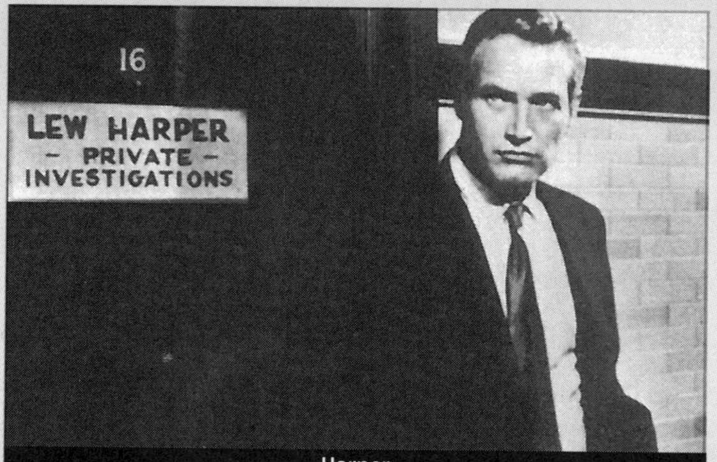

Harper

Paul Newman

Sweet Bird Of Youth (1962)
Powerful rendering of the Tennessee Williams classic stars Paul Newman as a young wastrel returning to a hometown where he isn't wanted with fading screen star Geraldine Page in tow. Fine supporting turns from Rip Torn, Shirley Knight and Oscar-winner Ed Begley under Richard Brooks' direction. 120 min.
12-1944 *$19.99*

Hud (1963)
A powerful, emotionally charged drama with Paul Newman as the ill-disposed and irresponsible son of Texas rancher Melvyn Douglas, caught between the traditional ideals of his father and the lack of principles in the New West. Oscars went to Douglas, Patricia Neal and cinematographer James Wong Howe; directed by Martin Ritt. 112 min.
06-1122 *$14.99*

A New Kind Of Love (1963)
Lavish romantic yarn with Paul Newman as an American reporter covering a Paris fashion show who meets and falls in love with a frumpy fashion buyer (Joanne Woodward) who's looking for a romantic fling. Maurice Chevalier, Thelma Ritter, Eva Gabor also star in the frothy proceedings. 110 min.
06-1917 Remastered *$14.99*

The Prize (1963)
While in Sweden to accept the Nobel Peace Prize, an alcoholic writer (Paul Newman) learns of a plot involving the kidnapping of a physicist by Russian intelligence. The writer soon discovers that an impostor has taken the physicist's place, and he must fend off Communist agents to find the real man. Edward G. Robinson, Elke Sommer and Diane Baker also star. 136 min.
12-2407 *$19.99*

The Outrage (1964)
Based on Akira Kurosawa's "Rashomon," this western drama stars Paul Newman as a Mexican outlaw waiting to die for killing a man and raping his wife. Three witnesses to the crime—con artist Edward G. Robinson, preacher William Shatner and prospector Howard Da Silva—tell different versions of what happened, but who can be believed? Laurence Harvey co-stars. 97 min.
12-3072 □*$19.99*

Lady L (1965)
Victorian era comedy starring Sophia Loren as a laundress desired by British lord David Niven while married to chauffeur Paul Newman. Sexy Loren becomes Niven's mistress while husband Newman, a closet anarchist, spends his time planning a revolution. Peter Ustinov directs. 107 min.
12-2802 *$19.99*

Harper (1966)
Paul Newman plays Ross MacDonald's cool private eye Lew Harper (renamed from the books' Lew Archer because of Newman's success with "H"-titled films), hired to locate wealthy Lauren Bacall's missing husband and finding a complex and deadly string of suspects. Shelley Winters, Julie Harris, Arthur Hill and Pamela Tiffin also star. 121 min.
19-1274 Was $19.99 *$14.99*

The Drowning Pool (1975)
Returning to the role of private detective Lew Harper, Paul Newman is called to New Orleans to find out who's been blackmailing an ex-girlfriend, wealthy oil heiress Joanne Woodward. Fast-paced thriller also stars Tony Franciosa, Murray Hamilton. 108 min.
19-1327 Was $19.99 *$14.99*

Hombre (1967)
A trip by stagecoach across Arizona brings together a disparate group of passengers, including a corrupt Indian agent (Fredric March), his wife (Barbara Rush), a working girl (Diane Cilento) and a white man (Paul Newman) raised by Apaches, who reluctantly saves them from a band of outlaws. With Richard Boone, Martin Balsam; directed by Martin Ritt. 111 min.
04-1073 Was $19.99 *$14.99*

Cool Hand Luke (1967)
Paul Newman is Lucas Jackson, a man sentenced to serve hard time in a tough chain gang in the South. What he finds there are sadistic wardens, egg-eating contests and a definite "failure to communicate." George Kennedy (in his Oscar-winning role), Strother Martin, Harry Dean Stanton, Dennis Hopper co-star. 126 min.
19-1118 *$19.99*

Cool Hand Luke (Letterboxed Version)
Also available in a theatrical, widescreen format.
19-2625 *$19.99*

The Secret War Of Harry Frigg (1968)
Paul Newman stars as an irresponsible private sent to help four generals escape from an enemy Italian villa. Funny and winning. Sylva Koscina, Tom Bosley. 123 min.
07-1148 Was $49.99 *$14.99*

Sometimes A Great Notion (1971)
Tale of Oregon-based loggers going up against nature, strikes and family. Based on Ken Kesey's novel; directed by and starring Paul Newman. Henry Fonda, Lee Remick. 115 min.
07-1126 Was $59.99 *$14.99*

The Life And Times Of Judge Roy Bean (1972)
John Huston's flavorful western stars Paul Newman as the legendary, self-appointed "Law West of the Pecos," a one-time wanted man who arrives in the town of Vinegaroon, Texas, takes over as its judge and dispenses his own brand of justice. The great supporting cast Jacqueline Bisset, Victoria Principal, Stacy Keach, Anthony Perkins, and Ava Gardner as Lily Langtry. 123 min.
19-1271 *$14.99*

Pocket Money (1972)
In order to get out of debt, easy-going cowpoke Paul Newman and hard-drinking pardner Lee Marvin tackle the job of moving 200 steer from Mexico to the U.S. for a nasty businessman. Their odyssey includes a visit to jail, swindling and a clash with their employer. Strother Martin, Wayne Rogers and Hector Elizondo co-star in this modern-day western. 100 min.
19-1829 *$14.99*

The Sting: Special Edition (1973)
Paul Newman is a con artist in '30s Chicago who teams with young swindler Robert Redford to dupe big-time crook Robert Shaw in an elaborate fake betting parlor scheme. Charismatic star turns, Scott Joplin's ragtime music, and a twist ending make this winner of seven Academy Awards, including Best Picture, a classic! Co-stars Harold Gould, Charles Durning, Ray Walston, Eileen Brennan; directed by George Roy Hill. 129 min.
07-2691 Was $19.99 □*$14.99*

The Sting: Special Edition (Letterboxed Version)
Also available in a theatrical, widescreen format.
07-2690 Was $19.99 □*$14.99*

The Mackintosh Man (1973)
Thrilling espionage yarn stars Paul Newman as a British agent sent to expose a Communist infiltrator. Double agents, action and crafty direction from John Huston. James Mason, Dominique Sanda. 98 min.
19-1398 Was $19.99 *$14.99*

Slap Shot (1977)
The Charlestown Chiefs are a minor league hockey team going nowhere in the standings and with the fans, until a trio of psychotic brothers joins them and transforms them into the Wild Bunch on ice. Paul Newman and Michael Ontkean star in this ribald and uproarious film. 122 min.
07-1029 Was $19.99 □*$14.99*

Absence Of Malice (1981)
Timely, powerful drama questions the power of the contemporary press. A businessman unknowingly becomes the subject of a criminal investigation thanks to a story written by a feisty reporter. Fine acting by Paul Newman, Sally Field, Melinda Dillon. 116 min.
02-1117 *$14.99*

Fort Apache, The Bronx (1981)
A controversial, grittily realistic depiction of life among cops in one of New York's toughest precincts, with Paul Newman as a beat cop who must buck the system when he learns that a fellow officer has killed an innocent street kid. Ed Asner, Danny Aiello, Ken Wahl, Pam Grier also star. 125 min.
44-1857 Was $19.99 *$14.99*

The Verdict (1982)
Paul Newman turns in a powerful performance as a broken-down, bottle-hitting attorney who prosecutes a formidable foe in order to vindicate himself. Able support from James Mason, Charlotte Rampling, Jack Warden. 128 min.
04-1535 Was $19.99 *$14.99*

Harry And Son (1984)
Paul Newman wrote, directed, and stars in this heart-tugging tale filled with comedy, warmth and drama. He's an aging construction worker coming to terms with his easy-going son, played by Robby Benson. With Ellen Barkin, Joanne Woodward. 117 min.
47-1247 □*$14.99*

Come Along With Me (1988)
An elderly widow finds new life as a spiritualist when her husband contacts her from beyond in Shirley Jackson's unfinished tale. Joanne Woodward directs Estelle Parsons, Sylvia Sydney and Paul Newman (as the pseudonymously credited voice of the deceased Hughie). 60 min.
27-9023 *$24.99*

Fat Man And Little Boy (1989)
A stirring historical drama starring Paul Newman as General Leslie R. Groves, the man who oversaw the building of the world's first atomic bomb in New Mexico in 1942. Dwight Schultz, John Cusack, Laura Dern and Bonnie Bedelia co-star; directed by Roland Joffe ("The Killing Fields"). 126 min.
06-1713 □*$14.99*

Mr. And Mrs. Bridge (1990)
Set in Kansas City in the late 1930s, this acclaimed drama stars Paul Newman and Joanne Woodward as an upper-crust couple who begin questioning their stodgy lifestyle after their friends and children introduce them to new ways of thinking. Kyra Sedgwick, Robert Sean Leonard and Blythe Danner also star in James Ivory's affecting, exquisitely-rendered tale. 127 min.
44-1799 Was $19.99 □*$14.99*

Nobody's Fool (1994)
Wonderfully realized drama of life in a small New York town features Paul Newman as Sully, a feisty ex-construction worker and village ne'er-do-well who is forced to confront the emptiness of his life during a visit from his estranged son. Jessica Tandy, Melanie Griffith, Dylan Walsh, Gene Saks and an unbilled Bruce Willis also star. 110 min.
06-2331 Was $89.99 □*$14.99*

Twilight (1998)
Retired private investigator Paul Newman reluctantly agrees to assist his two movie star friends Susan Sarandon and Gene Hackman when they are blackmailed by someone from their past. However, as he gets entangled in a complicated and lethal murder plot, Newman's own past may come back to haunt him. Director Robert Benton's moody whodunit also stars James Garner, Reese Witherspoon. 96 min.
06-2756 Was $99.99 □*$14.99*

Where The Money Is (2000)
Paul Newman is an aging bank robber who checks into a nursing home after having a stroke. Nurse Linda Fiorentino doesn't buy his claim, believing Newman is faking his condition to get out of prison. Wise to his ways, Fiorentino enlists him to show her the tricks of his trade, then join her and husband Dermot Mulroney in a daring robbery. 89 min.
02-9281 *$99.99*

Please see our index for these other Paul Newman titles: *Buffalo Bill And The Indians • Butch Cassidy And The Sundance Kid • Cat On A Hot Tin Roof • The Hudsucker Proxy • Message In A Bottle • Paris Blues • Quintet • Torn Curtain • The Towering Inferno • When Time Ran Out*

Eva (1962)
A self-absorbed, expatriate Welsh writer (Stanley Baker) living in Italy meets his cynical match when he falls for a manipulative prostitute named Eve (Jeanne Moreau) in this lush romantic melodrama from director Joseph Losey. Virna Lisi co-stars as Baker's fiancée. AKA: "Eva, The Devil's Woman," "Eve." 103 min. Dubbed in English.
53-6912 Letterboxed *$24.99*

David Holzman's Diary (1968)
Groundbreaking independent effort from Jim McBride ("The Big Easy") details the adventures of a young New York filmmaker who sets out to capture his life on film but soon gets into trouble with friends, the police and his girlfriend. L.M. Kit Carson, Eileen Dietz and Louise Levine star. 74 min.
53-7781 Was $79.99 *$19.99*

The Incident (1967)
A harrowing and (unfortunately) still timely drama dealing with urban violence, as two street punks (Martin Sheen, Tony Musante) terrorize the passengers of a New York City subway train. Beau Bridges, Jack Gilford, Thelma Ritter, Brock Peters, Ruby Dee and Ed McMahon also star. 99 min.
04-2291 Was $59.99 *$29.99*

The Mark (1961)
A gripping and controversial drama with Stuart Whitman as a jailed child molester whose obsessions are brought under control with the aid of psychiatrist Rod Steiger. But can he cope with his release into the outside world? Maria Schell, Donald Houston. 127 min.
08-8110 *$19.99*

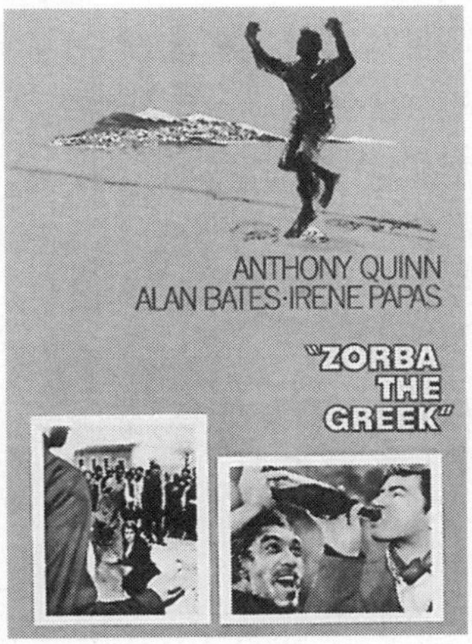

Zorba The Greek (1964)
Anthony Quinn's much-beloved performance as a lusty Greek residing on the island of Crete highlights this Oscar-winning film about living life to its fullest. Quinn's Zorba becomes mentor to a young English writer (Alan Bates), and the two find themselves involved in difficult romances, bad business schemes and tragic events. With Lila Kedrova and Irene Papas. 142 min.
04-1285 *$19.99*

The Birthday Party (1968)
An early directorial effort by William Friedkin, this moody and darkly funny adaptation of the Harold Pinter play stars Robert Shaw as a piano player whose shady past comes back to haunt him when two hoods pay a visit to the boarding house he calls home. With Dandy Nichols, Patrick Magee. 126 min.
08-8820 *$14.99*

A Public Affair (1962)
An unusual expositive drama that examines the practices of unscrupulous collection agencies and the struggles of a state senator to get laws passed to protect consumers. Edward Binns, Harry Carey, Jr., Myron McCormick, Grace Lee Whitney star. 71 min.
09-2195 Was $29.99 *$14.99*

Cervantes (1967)
Sprawling biography of the 16th-century Spanish author of "Don Quixote," tracing his early years that saw him fight with the Pope's forces against the Moors in Spain, fall in love with a courtesan, take part in a dangerous sea battle and fall captive to pirates. Horst Buchholz, Gina Lollobrigida, Jose Ferrer star. AKA: "The Young Rebel." 111 min.
09-5049 *$19.99*

Time Bomb (1961)
Seafaring drama starring Curt Jurgens as a man who helps plot the explosion of a ship for insurance purposes after the family that owns it enters into financial difficulty...but Jurgens' involvement leads to danger. Mylene Demongeot co-stars. 92 min.
09-5075 *$19.99*

The Wind Of Change (1961)
Gripping British crime drama about a rebellious teenager who is part of a street gang that beat a black man to death and who reconsiders his involvement when his sister is knifed by a gang member. Donald Pleasence, Johnny Briggs and a young David Hemmings star. 64 min.
09-5078 *$19.99*

No Time To Kill (1963)
Freed from jail after being falsely convicted of arson and serving eight years, John Ireland heads to Sweden and the man he thinks framed him. Confronting the man's wife, Ireland begins an affair with her, but his vengeance campaign has a surprising finish. Compelling drama also stars Ellen Schwiers, Frank Sundstrom. AKA: "Med Mord I Bagaget." 70 min.
09-5339 *$19.99*

Dog Eat Dog (1963)
Jayne Mansfield, Cameron Mitchell and Werner Peters star in this Albert Zugsmith production, playing bank robbers who encounter murder and heated passion while on the lam in the Mediterranean following a robbery. 84 min.
10-8141 *$19.99*

Sellers Of Girls (1967)
After facing a series of difficult situations in Paris, a young woman gets involved with a white slavery/drug racket. While en route to South America, she becomes engaged to a crewman on board her ship, then tackles the syndicate head-on. Georges Marschal, Agnes Laurent and Daniela Rocca star in this seedy melodrama.
79-6202 *$19.99*

Jacktown (1962)
A juvenile delinquent caught on a dark street with a teenage girl is sent to prison for statutory rape. While living behind bars is no picnic, he falls in love with the warden's daughter, much to the warden's dismay. And when a riot breaks out, he attempts to flee with help from his girlfriend. Gritty "JD" drama stars Patty McCormack ("The Bad Seed"), Richard Meade.
79-6208 *$19.99*

The Hi-Jackers (1963)
A woman on the run from her husband gets help from a trucker who takes her on the road. Adventure begins when the truck is hijacked and she must stop the man responsible for the deed. Jacqueline Ellis and Anthony Booth star. 69 min.
09-5057 *$19.99*

Thunder In Dixie (1965)
A racer obsessed with his girlfriend's death at the hands of a rival driver decides to even the score in a big race. But his plans go awry and he lands in the hospital with horrible injuries. While recuperating, he decides to make peace with his rival. Set at Atlanta's Dixie 400, this action-packed film stars Harry Milland, Judy Lewis and features Richard Petty.
79-6210 *$19.99*

Games Of Desire (1967)
When her ambassador husband is discovered to have more interest in his new male secretary than her, beautiful Ingrid Thulin decides to become a hooker, servicing dock workers. When she falls in love with a poor worker named Nikos, unusual complications ensue. Paul Huschmid, Nikos Kourkoulos and Claudine Auger ("Thunderball") star.
79-6450 Was $24.99 *$19.99*

The Moving Finger (1963)
Unusual "cinema vérité"-styled crime drama set in Greenwich Village. A bank robber, wounded from a job and carrying $90,000 in loot, hides out in the basement of a coffeehouse and soon discovers that the cops and local beatniks are after the cash. Lionel Stander, Barbara London and Barry Newman star; features music by Shel Silverstein. 81 min.
83-3008 Was $24.99 *$19.99*

The Happy Ending (1969)
Suburban housewife Jean Simmons, tired of her stale 16-year marriage to John Forsythe, takes off on an odyssey of hedonistic discovery that includes drugs, alcohol and a Bahamas tryst with gigolo Robert (Bobby) Darin. Dramatic look at contemporary life also stars Lloyd Bridges, Dick Shawn, Nanette Fabray. 113 min.
12-3042 □*$19.99*

The Last Voyage (1960)
An exciting precursor to "The Poseidon Adventure," this drama stars Robert Stack and Dorothy Malone as a married couple who encounter an unending series of disasters when explosions rock the ocean liner they're on. George Sanders, Edmond O' Brien and Woody Strode co-star. 87 min.
12-2502 *$19.99*

The Hoodlum Priest (1961)
Gritty true-life drama about Reverend Charles Clark (Don Murray), the St. Louis priest who helped rehabilitate former convicts after their release from prison. The film's focus is on Clark's friendship with a young thief (Keir Dullea) whose robbery and murder of his former employer lands him on Death Row. 101 min.
12-2801 Was $19.99 □*$14.99*

The Subject Was Roses (1968)
Frank Gilroy's Pulitzer Prize-winning play is triumphantly transferred to the screen with Martin Sheen as the young WWII vet who returns home to find parents Jack Albertson and Patricia Neal living in a bitter, hostile marriage. Sheen attempts to help them reconcile, but the plan goes awry, leading Sheen to question his own life. 107 min.
12-2997 □*$19.99*

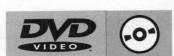

DVD VIDEO
ASK ABOUT OUR GIANT DVD CATALOG!

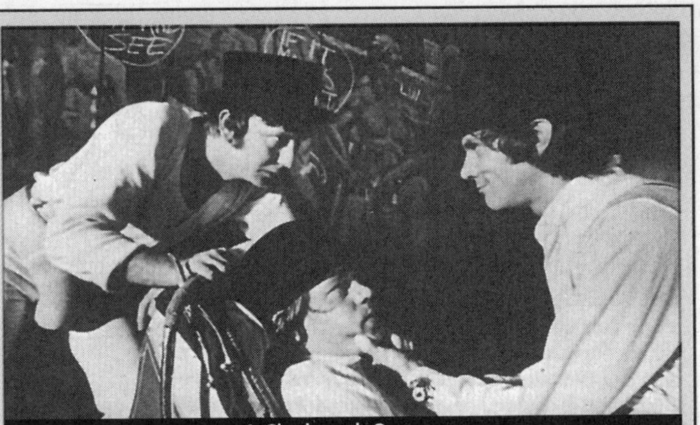

A Clockwork Orange

Stanley Kubrick

Killer's Kiss (1955)
Writer/director Stanley Kubrick's gritty, atmospheric story about a boxer trying to save the dancer he loves from a sadistic nightclub owner, who sends his thugs after the boxer while he holds the woman hostage. The film, which stars Frank Silvera, Jamie Smith and Irene Kane, was also the inspiration for 1983's "Strangers Kiss." 67 min.
12-2249 *$19.99*

The Killing (1956)
Classic caper drama that established director Stanley Kubrick has Sterling Hayden assembling a motley crew to knock off a racetrack. Kubrick's tight, claustrophobic camera work (done in part to hide the film's shoestring budget) and fine supporting turns by Elisha Cook Jr., Ted de Corsia, Marie Windsor and Timothy Carey make this a film noir favorite. 83 min.
12-1928 Was $19.99 *$14.99*

Paths Of Glory (1957)
Stanley Kubrick's gut-wrenching anti-war drama stars Kirk Douglas as an individualistic World War I officer defending three men tried for cowardice when an ill-advised "suicide mission" fails. George Macready, Adolphe Menjou, Ralph Meeker and Wayne Morris also star. 86 min.
12-1965 Was $19.99 □*$14.99*

Spartacus (1960)
Stanley Kubrick's epic adventure, presented in a restored edition, stars Kirk Douglas as the heroic slave who fights to lead his people to freedom from Roman rule. Included in this new version is the infamous bathing scene between Roman general Laurence Olivier and poet-slave Tony Curtis. With Jean Simmons, Peter Ustinov, Charles Laughton and John Gavin. 196 min.
07-1720 Restored □*$14.99*

Spartacus (Letterboxed Version)
The restored version is also available in a theatrical, widescreen format.
07-1721 Was $19.99 □*$14.99*

Lolita (1962)
Stanley Kubrick's wild version of the Vladimir Nabokov classic about a teenage temptress and the hold she has over an obsessed, middle-aged professor (James Mason). Sue Lyon, Peter Sellers, Shelley Winters co-star. 152 min.
12-1061 *$19.99*

Dr. Strangelove Or: How I Learned To Stop Worrying And Love The Bomb (1964)
Director Stanley Kubrick's "Doomsday" comedy of the absurd about a paranoid, Commie-hating Air Force general (Sterling Hayden) who launches an air attack on the Soviet Union, with nuclear annihilation the final consequence, co-stars Peter Sellers in three roles, George C. Scott, Slim Pickens. Co-scripted by Kubrick, Terry Southern and Peter George from George's novel "Red Alert." 93 min.
02-1164 *$19.99*

2001: A Space Odyssey (1968)
The senses-shattering tale of life and "afterlife" in outer space from writer Arthur C. Clarke and director Stanley Kubrick that revolutionized science-fiction films. Lunar explorers uncover an obelisk of alien origin, but who put it there, and why? Keir Dullea, Gary Lockwood and Hal 9000 the Computer star. 139 min.
12-2250 □*$19.99*

2001: A Space Odyssey (Letterboxed Version)
Also available in a theatrical, widescreen format.
12-1022 □*$19.99*

A Clockwork Orange (1971)
Stanley Kubrick's dark, dazzling, ironic tale of an ultra-violent future filled with marauding gangs, decaying cities and bizarre technologies. Follow "Little Alex" on a road to ruin you'll not forget. Malcolm McDowell, Patrick Magee. Score includes Beethoven, "Singin' in the Rain," and electronic music by Wendy Carlos. 137 min.
19-1024 □*$19.99*

Barry Lyndon (1975)
Stanley Kubrick's exquisite costume drama meticulously details the rise and fall of Redmond Barry Lyndon (Ryan O'Neal), an Irish rogue with dreams of grandeur and glory. In the tradition of "Tom Jones," highlighted by superb photography and period music. Marisa Berenson, Patrick Magee. 184 min.
19-1267 □*$24.99*

The Shining (1980)
Writer Stephen King and director Stanley Kubrick combine to bring you a classic tale of madness and terror, as a family overseeing a deserted resort hotel confronts the ghosts of a shocking and bloody past. Jack Nicholson, Shelley Duvall and Scatman Crothers star. Includes a "making of" documentary. 143 min.
19-1172 □*$19.99*

Full Metal Jacket (1987)
Stanley Kubrick's compelling look at Vietnam, marked by the director's characteristic black humor and heightened realism. Cocky Marine recruit Mathew Modine learns the horrors of war firsthand, as the film follows him from the dehumanizing rituals of boot camp to a sniper assault in a bombed-out city. With Adam Baldwin, Vincent D'Onofrio, and Lee Ermey as the sadistic D.I. 116 min.
19-1602 □*$19.99*

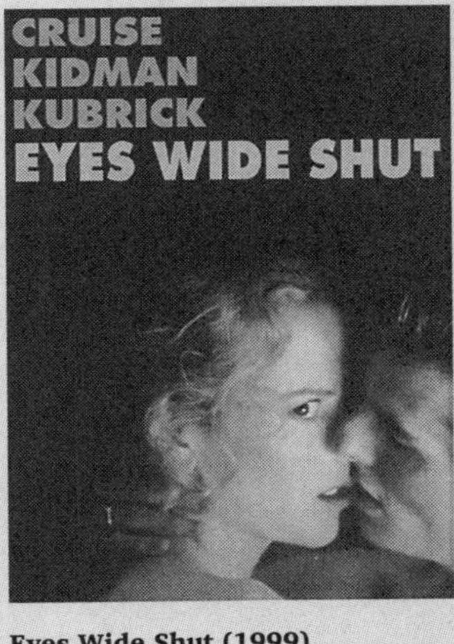

Eyes Wide Shut (1999)
The final film from master director Stanley Kubrick is an eerily detached exploration of erotic desire and obsession. An argument on fidelity with wife Nicole Kidman sends doctor Tom Cruise wandering into the Manhattan streets and into a variety of sexually-charged situations, culminating in a visit to a secret, upper-class orgy that could have dangerous consequences for Cruise and his family. Sydney Pollack, Todd Field, Marie Richardson, Alan Cumming also star. Special edition includes interviews with Cruise, Kidman and Steven Spielberg, and the theatrical trailer. 159 min.
19-2959 Was $99.99 □*$19.99*

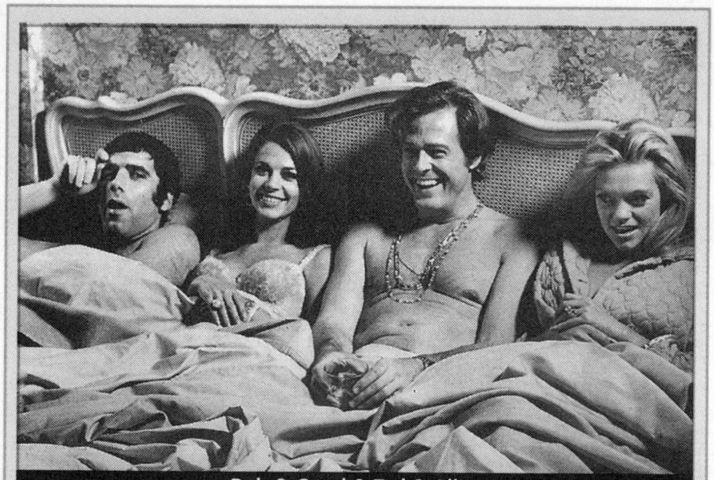

Bob & Carol & Ted & Alice

Natalie Wood

Driftwood (1947)
A 9-year-old Natalie Wood plays an charming little orphan who is adopted by pharmacist Walter Brennan. She ends up having an effect on the entire town, which is being plagued by an epidemic of spotted fever. Dean Jagger plays a doctor fighting the fever; Ruth Warrick, Charlotte Greenwood and Jerome Cowan also star. 88 min.
63-1950 *$14.99*

Green Promise (1949)
Walter Brennan and Natalie Wood star in this heartfelt tale of an "old fashioned" farmer trying to eke out a living on the family farm, until his child introduces him to "new-fangled" methods. 100 min.
08-8018 *$19.99*

The Rose Bowl Story (1952)
Pasadena's famed stadium is the setting for this gridiron drama about a star quarterback who falls for a woman he spies wearing an expensive fur coat in the stands. Trouble arises when their romance affects his performance on the field. Stars Marshall Thompson, Vera Miles, and Natalie Wood as Miles' younger sister. 73 min.
63-1951 *$14.99*

The Burning Hills (1956)
Western author Louis L'Amour penned this thrilling sagebrush epic about a young rancher (Tab Hunter) seeking revenge against the crooked cattle baron who had his brother murdered. Natalie Wood plays the beautiful half-breed woman who helps Hunter. Eduard Franz, Earl Holliman also star. 92 min.
19-2199 Was $29.99 *$19.99*

Marjorie Morningstar (1958)
Natalie Wood turns in a captivating performance as Herman Wouk's heroine in this faithful adaptation of his novel. An aspiring actress with stars in her eyes discovers only rejection and heartbreak along the road to fame and fortune. Co-stars Gene Kelly, Claire Trevor and Martin Balsam. 123 min.
63-1266 Was $19.99 *$14.99*

Cash McCall (1960)
James Garner stars as a slick corporate raider specializing in taking over ailing companies and using their losses as tax write-offs for his own successful firm. Natalie Wood and Nina Foch are the women in his life; Dean Jagger, E.G. Marshall also star. 102 min.
19-2160 Was $29.99 *$19.99*

Splendor In The Grass (1961)
Warren Beatty (in his film debut) and Natalie Wood portray young lovers in the 1920s Midwest, whose inner struggles to retain a pure and virtuous love for one another lead them only to destructive ends. Written for the screen by William Inge (who can be seen as the town minister), the popular drama costars Pat Hingle, Audrey Christie; directed by Elia Kazan. 124 min.
19-1197 ❑*$19.99*

Love With The Proper Stranger (1963)
Natalie Wood stars as the "good Italian girl" who finds herself pregnant after a one-night stand with Steve McQueen. How each comes to grips with the consequences of their affair makes for a touching comedy/drama; Edie Adams, Tom Bosley, Penny Santon, Herschel Bernardi also star. 100 min.
06-1620 Was $19.99 *$14.99*

Sex And The Single Girl (1964)
Hip, very '60s comedy (with no relation to Helen Gurley Brown's book) stars Tony Curtis as a tabloid editor who romances pop psychologist Natalie Wood in order to get the goods on her feminist group. Complications ensue when Curtis uses the name of pal Henry Fonda, who is having marital problems with wife Lauren Bacall. Mel Ferrer, Larry Storch and Stubby Kaye also star. 110 min.
19-1943 *$19.99*

Inside Daisy Clover (1965)
Acerbic look inside Hollywood focuses on the career of a teenage girl (Natalie Wood) whose meteoric rise to the top of the show business ladder brings with it a stormy personal life. Robert Redford is her narcissistic, homosexual husband; Ruth Gordon her troubled mother; and Christopher Plummer the movie mogul who helps her get a start. 128 min.
19-1949 Was $29.99 ❑*$19.99*

This Property Is Condemned (1966)
Classic melodrama based on Tennessee Williams' play stars Natalie Wood as a fanciful dreamer bored with life in a small Southern town who falls madly in love with the handsome stranger (Robert Redford) from New Orleans staying at her domineering mother's boardinghouse. Co-stars Kate Reid, Charles Bronson, Robert Blake. Co-written by Francis Coppola; directed by Sydney Pollack. 110 min.
06-1321 *$19.99*

Bob & Carol & Ted & Alice (1969)
Paul Mazursky made his directing debut with this landmark Swingin' Sixties satire, about a "sexually liberated" couple (Robert Culp and Natalie Wood) who are the envy of their more conventional friends (Elliott Gould and Dyan Cannon), and the foursome's efforts to keep the sexual revolution from passing them by. 104 min.
02-2687 *$14.99*

The Affair (1973)
Excellent romantic drama starring Natalie Wood as a songwriter with polio who has her first experience with the opposite sex when she dates an attorney (Robert Wagner). With Pat Harrington, Bruce Davison. 74 min.
14-6017 Was $39.99 *$14.99*

The Last Married Couple In America (1980)
George Segal and Natalie Wood wonder if they may soon find themselves in the title condition, as they watch the marriages of their friends crumble before them and begin to question their own relationship. Co-stars Dom DeLuise, Valerie Harper and Richard Benjamin. 103 min.
07-1110 *$69.99*

Brainstorm (1983)
An astonishing new device allows people to feel other's emotions, but the government wants the instrument as a weapon. A spectacular journey filled with dazzling special effects, starring Natalie Wood in her last role, Christopher Walken, Cliff Robertson and Louise Fletcher; Douglas Trumbull directs. 106 min.
12-1303 Was $19.99 *$14.99*

Please see our index for these other Natalie Wood titles: *Father Was A Fullback • From Here To Eternity • The Ghost And Mrs. Muir • The Great Race • Gypsy • The Jackpot • Kings Go Forth • Meteor • Miracle On 34th Street • Rebel Without A Cause • The Searchers • The Silver Chalice • The Star • Tomorrow Is Forever • West Side Story*

Portrait Of A Lady (1967)
Richard Chamberlain stars in this romantic drama about a spirited American girl brought to England by her aunt in order to search for truth in her life. She uses her freedom to make difficult—and sometimes wrong—decisions; based on the novel by Henry James. 240 min.
53-9456 Was $59.99 *$39.99*

The Ballad Of Andy Crocker (1969)
Vietnam veteran Lee Majors returns home to find his life in disarray, with his motorcycle repair business close to bankruptcy and his girl married to another man, in this powerful made-for-TV drama, the first to deal with the subject. Joey Heatherton, Pat Hingle, Marvin Gaye and Jimmy Dean also star. 80 min.
55-3004 *$19.99*

Girl In Gold Boots (1969)
It's the old familiar story: a beautiful young girl looking for stardom in the city becomes a go-go dancer, only to discover that the price of success may be higher than she thought. Stars Jody Daniel, Tom Pace ("Blood Orgy of the She-Devils"). 94 min.
59-5042 *$19.99*

Repulsion (1965)
Classic psychological drama that was director Roman Polanski's first big international success. A young woman with an abnormal fear of men is left alone by her sister in their apartment for a week, and her descent into madness is chillingly portrayed. Catherine Deneuve, Ian Hendry star. 105 min. Filmed in English.
62-1005 Was $29.99 *$19.99*

Door-To-Door Maniac (1961)
Who's that knocking at the door? "Hello, I'm Johnny Cash." The "man in black" is a psychopath teaming up with Vic Tayback for a kidnapping/bank robbery caper in this taut crime drama that also features Ronny Howard, Pamela Mason, and two songs by Cash. AKA: "Five Minutes to Live." 90 min.
62-1331 *$19.99*

The Pawnbroker (1965)
Rod Steiger turns in a brilliant performance as a Holocaust survivor whose heart was hardened by the loss of his family in the camps and who lives an isolated existence in a Harlem pawnshop. Sidney Lumet's groundbreaking drama also stars Geraldine Fitzgerald, Brock Peters. 116 min.
63-1012 ❑*$14.99*

The Fool Killer (1965)
An offbeat tale set in the 1870s South, as a 12-year-old runaway is warned by a hobo of an ax-wielding murderer roaming the countryside and later fears that a travelling companion he meets may be the "fool killer." Anthony Perkins, Edward Albert, Henry Hull, Dana Elcar star. AKA: "Violent Journey." 100 min.
63-1334 *$19.99*

This Is Not A Test (1962)
A policeman manning an isolated roadblock tries to confirm rumors of an impending atom bomb attack from increasingly panicked motorists. A rarely seen contemplation on nuclear doom, starring Seamon Glass and Mary Morlass. 72 min.
68-8148 *$19.99*

The Girl In Lover's Lane (1960)
When a young girl is found murdered in a small town, drifter Brett Halsey is thrown in jail to await trial...if the irate townsfolk don't hang him first. Drive-in youth drama also stars Jack Elam, Joyce Meadows. 78 min.
68-8371 *$19.99*

Girl On A Chain Gang (1965)
Very loosely based on the real-life case that inspired "Mississippi Burning," this low-budget civil rights drama/drive-in crime thriller follows one woman through the hell of a Southern prison when she and two other activists are arrested. Julie Ange, William Watson star. 96 min.
68-8372 *$19.99*

Night Of Evil (1962)
Egregious drive-in drama about a young girl who is raped and sent to a girl's home, wins the Miss Colorado contest (but gets drummed out of the Miss America pageant when her marriage to an ex-con is revealed), becomes a stripper, holds up a drugstore and is sent to jail. Lisa Gaye, William Campbell star. 88 min.
68-8378 *$19.99*

Uncle Tom's Cabin (1969)
The classic 19th-century novel of slavery and plantation life that fanned the flames of the anti-slavery movement becomes a powerful film drama. International cast includes Herbert Lom as the cruel overseer, Simon Legree; with John Kitzmiller, Rhet Kirby, Gertraud Mittermayr. 118 min.
76-5006 *$19.99*

Uncle Tom's Cabin (1987)
Harriet Beecher Stowe's classic about slavery set in the pre-Civil War South receives a stirring and powerful treatment. Features a knockout cast that includes Phylicia Rashad, Avery Brooks, Bruce Dern and Edward Woodward. 108 min.
14-3249 *$12.99*

The Four Horsemen Of The Apocalypse (1962)
Searing drama, set in WWII Paris, tells the story of a wealthy family whose loyalties are split by the political happenings around them. Love, honor, passion, and familial ties are intertwined in this epic tale. Stars Glenn Ford, Ingrid Thulin, Lee J. Cobb and Yvette Mimieux. 154 min.
12-1459 Was $24.99 *$19.99*

It Happened Here (1966)
Shot over an eight-year period on a shoestring budget by British film historian Kevin Brownlow and colleague Andrew Mollo, this acclaimed, harrowing speculative drama is set in a '40s England under Nazi occupation. As soldiers goosestep through London and pro-German collaborators battle resistance fighters, a nurse must decide where she stands when she learns of government atrocities. The mostly amateur cast includes Pauline Murray, Sebastian Shaw. Uncut version; 96 min.
68-8401 *$29.99*

The Singing Nun (1966)
The true story of Belgian-born Sister Ann Sourire, a guitar-playing nun who wrote the song "Dominique" for a motherless young boy. With help from a compassionate priest and a record producer, the song hits the charts and lands Sister Ann a spot on "The Ed Sullivan Show" before she must reconsider her newfound fame. Debbie Reynolds, Ricardo Montalban, Greer Garson, Katharine Ross star. 97 min.
12-2467 *$19.99*

Doctor Zhivago: 30th Anniversary Edition (1965)
David Lean's epic screen adaptation of the Boris Pasternak novel stars Omar Sharif as the Russian doctor and writer branded an enemy of the state after the 1917 Revolution. Winner of five Academy Awards, the sweeping blend of drama and romance also stars Julie Christie, Alec Guinness, Rod Steiger and Geraldine Chaplin. This special anniversary edition includes an introduction by Sharif and a 60-minute "making of" documentary with interviews, behind-the-scenes footage and more. 187 min. total.
12-3003 ❑*$24.99*

Doctor Zhivago: 30th Anniversary Edition (Letterboxed Version)
Also available in a theatrical, widescreen format.
12-3004 ❑*$24.99*

The Heart Is A Lonely Hunter (1968)
Carson McCullers' acclaimed tale of a deaf-mute in a small Southern town is sensitively brought to the screen. Alan Arkin received an Oscar nomination as the outcast befriended by a young woman (Sondra Locke). Stacy Keach, Cicely Tyson co-star. 125 min.
19-1405 Was $59.99 ❑*$19.99*

Rachel, Rachel (1968)
Joanne Woodward stars as a shy schoolteacher yearning to break out of her shell as she reaches middle age in this acclaimed drama, directed by Paul Newman. Nominated for three Academy Awards; Estelle Parsons, Donald Moffat also star. 102 min.
19-1406 *$19.99*

Hotel (1967)
Check into excitement, intrigue and romance at New Orleans' posh St. Gregory Hotel in Arthur Hailey's drama. The cast includes Rod Taylor, Karl Malden, Melvyn Douglas, Merle Oberon and Kevin McCarthy. 125 min.
19-1550 Was $19.99 *$14.99*

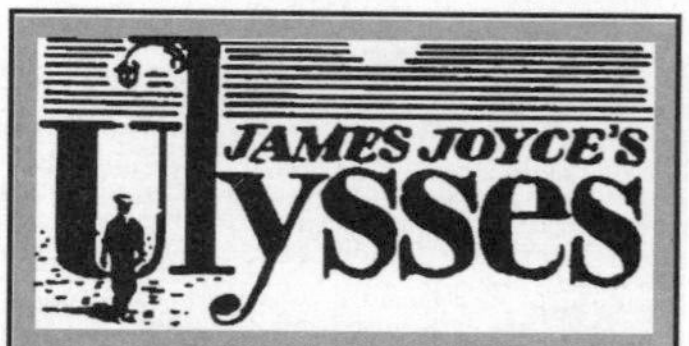

Ulysses (1967)
A daring screen version of James Joyce's stylistic masterwork tracing a day in the life of Dublin Jew Leopold Bloom (Milo O'Shea) and his spiritual heir, Stephen Daedalus (Maurice Roeves). Features readings from some of the book's more unfilmable prose, including the famous soliloquy by Molly Bloom (Barbara Jefford). 140 min.
70-7046 Was $29.99 *$19.99*

A Portrait Of The Artist As A Young Man (1979)
A thoughtful adaptation of James Joyce's autobiographical novel about the youth and homelife of Stephen Daedalus, a student coming to terms with his strict Catholic upbringing; beautifully filmed in Ireland with excellent performances by Bosco Hogan, T.P. McKenna and Sir John Gielgud. 93 min.
70-7045 Was $29.99 *$19.99*

James Joyce's Women (1983)
Fionnula Flanagan shines in a bravura performance, first as Joyce's widow Nora, then as five women the author knew in real life, or created in his mind. From Molly Bloom to Harriet Shaw Weaver (the philanthropist who supported Joyce), Flanagan gives insight into the rich, erotic currents that ran deep through Joyce's work. Chris O'Neill stars as Joyce. 89 min.
07-1401 *$69.99*

The Dead (1987)
The final film from director John Huston, based on a story by James Joyce, depicts a Yuletide society party in 1904 Ireland, a party that stirs memories among the living of lost loves and bygone days. Anjelica Huston and Donal McCann star as a couple faced with a dissolving marriage; script by Tony Huston. 83 min.
47-1876 Was $89.99 *$14.99*

No Way Out (1950)
Sidney Poitier made a memorable Hollywood debut in writer/director Joseph L. Mankiewicz' gripping social drama set in a slum neighborhood hospital. Richard Widmark plays a psychotic, bigoted hoodlum who blames intern Poitier for his brother's death and instigates a race riot to get his revenge. Linda Darnell, Harry Bellaver, Ruby Dee also star. 106 min.
04-3565 *$14.99*

Red Ball Express (1952)
The true story of the Army Transportation Corps, whose job it was to truck fuel and ammo to frontline combat units during World War II, served as the basis for this unusual war drama starring Jeff Chandler as the lieutenant in charge of supplying Patton's tank corps during their push to Paris and a young Sidney Poitier as a soldier coping with prejudice. With Alex Nicol. 84 min.
07-2394 ☐*$14.99*

Cry, The Beloved Country (1952)
One of the first film depictions of black life in South Africa, Zoltan Korda's adaptation of the Alan Paton novel stars Canada Lee as a black preacher who leaves his rural home to travel to Johannesburg in search of his son, who is charged with killing a white rancher's son. Charles Carson, Lionel Ngakane, and a young Sidney Poitier co-star. 100 min.
27-6747 Was $69.99 *$39.99*

The Mark Of The Hawk (1957)
A topical, engrossing drama set in turbulent Africa, with Sidney Poitier as a newly elected politician torn between his long-standing stance against violence and his insurgent brother's attempts to drag him into rebellion. 84 min.
10-1180 Was $19.99 *$14.99*

A Raisin In The Sun (1961)
Groundbreaking film adaptation of Lorraine Hansberry's stage drama follows a black Chicago family's attempt to get out of the slums and build a better life for themselves. Stars Sidney Poitier, Ruby Dee, Claudia McNeil, Diana Sands; look for a young Louis Gossett. 128 min.
02-1128 Was $19.99 *$14.99*

Paris Blues (1961)
The jazz scene in Paris after World War II is the setting for Martin Ritt's drama starring Paul Newman and Sidney Poitier as Americans living abroad for different reasons. Newman has immersed himself in music, while Poitier has fled the prejudices of the U.S. When two women enter their lives (Joanne Woodward, Diahann Carroll), they have to make some tough decisions. Louis Armstrong also stars. 98 min.
12-2804 Was $19.99 *$14.99*

Pressure Point (1962)
Riveting drama stars Sidney Poitier as a WWII government psychiatrist whose new patient (Bobby Darin) has been put in jail because of his neurotic behavior and his pro-Nazi sympathies. Through several intense flashbacks and analysis sessions, Poitier unearths the deep-rooted reasons for Darin's emotional troubles. Peter Falk co-stars. 87 min.
12-2508 *$19.99*

Lilies Of The Field (1963)
Sidney Poitier won an Academy Award as amiable wanderer Homer Smith, "coerced" by an order of nuns to build a chapel for them in the Arizona desert. Fine, understated drama co-stars Lilia Skala, Lisa Mann. 93 min.
12-2150 Was $19.99 ☐*$14.99*

The Long Ships (1964)
Thrilling seafaring saga in which Viking warrior Richard Widmark and Moorish chieftain Sidney Poitier race to find a fabled treasure known as the Golden Bell. With Russ Tamblyn, Oscar Homolka, Lionel Jeffries. 126 min.
02-2983 *$19.99*

The Bedford Incident (1965)
Intriguing "Cold War" drama stars Richard Widmark as a Navy captain whose destroyer, on patrol in the North Atlantic, encounters a Russian submarine, thus beginning a tense "cat and mouse" game. Sidney Poitier, Martin Balsam, James MacArthur, Wally Cox co-star. 102 min.
02-1024 Was $19.99 *$14.99*

The Slender Thread (1965)
Sydney Pollack made his film directorial debut with this compelling drama. When a distraught Anne Bancroft takes an overdose of sleeping pills and calls a crisis hotline, volunteer worker Sidney Poitier must try to keep her on the phone while a race against the clock to locate her begins. With Telly Savalas, Steven Hill, Ed Asner. 98 min.
06-1932 ☐*$14.99*

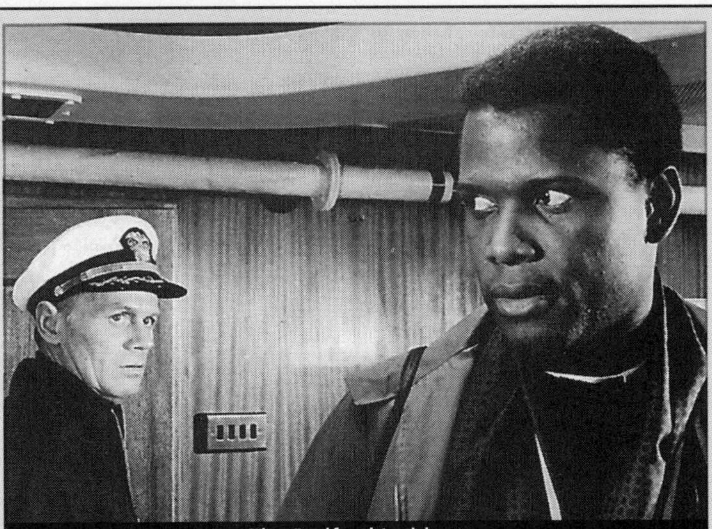
The Bedford Incident

Sidney Poitier

A Patch Of Blue (1965)
A tender drama starring Elizabeth Hartman as an 18-year-old blind girl who falls for a black man (Sidney Poitier). Their relationship is resented by Hartman's floozy-of-a-mother, played by Shelley Winters, who won a Best Supporting Actress Oscar for her memorable performance. 105 min.
12-2067 *$19.99*

A Patch Of Blue (Letterboxed Version)
Also available in a theatrical, widescreen format.
12-3123 *$19.99*

Duel At Diablo (1966)
Tempers flare and hatreds boil over among the members of an Army caravan making their way through treacherous Apache territory in this graphically violent and thoughtful Western drama. Sidney Poitier, James Garner, Dennis Weaver, Bibi Andersson and Bill Travers star. 105 min.
12-2707 ☐*$19.99*

To Sir, With Love (1967)
Sentimental heart-tugger stars Sidney Poitier as a first-year teacher at a rundown East End London high school who bucks the traditional educational system, allowing his unruly students to learn through experience and acquire a sense of responsibility. Co-stars Judy Geeson, Christian Roberts and Lulu (who sings the title tune); written, produced and directed by novelist James Clavell ("Shogun"). 105 min.
02-1158 Was $19.99 *$14.99*

In The Heat Of The Night (1967)
Oscar-winning account of a black Philadelphia detective investigating a murder in Mississippi and matching wits with a redneck sheriff. Rod Steiger, Sidney Poitier, Warren Oates, Lee Grant. Norman Jewison directs. Ray Charles sings the title tune. 109 min.
12-1765 Was $19.99 *$14.99*

They Call Me MISTER Tibbs! (1970)
Exciting sequel to "In the Heat of the Night" has Sidney Poitier heading for San Francisco to seek the murderer of a prostitute, but finding his friend is a prime suspect. Ed Asner, Martin Landau co-star; music by Quincy Jones. 108 min.
12-2678 *$14.99*

The Organization (1971)
The third outing for Sidney Poitier's Mr. Tibbs character finds the Philadelphia detective getting involved with a group of young street vigilantes in order to break a heroin-smuggling ring. Sheree North, Raul Julia and Barbara McNair also star. 105 min.
12-2669 *$14.99*

For Love Of Ivy (1968)
Director Daniel Mann ("Come Back, Little Sheba") draws touching performances from Sidney Poitier and Abbey Lincoln in this heartfelt romance. A family lures an agreeable Poitier into wooing their black maid so she'll stay on at her job rather than enter a secretarial school. Co-stars Carroll O'Connor, Beau Bridges. 100 min.
04-1343 *$14.99*

For Love Of Ivy (Letterboxed Version)
Also available in a theatrical, widescreen format.
08-8683 *$14.99*

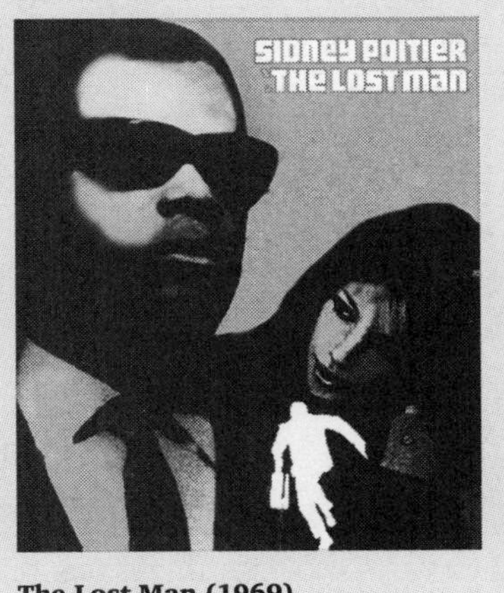

The Lost Man (1969)
North Philadelphia replaces Ireland in this dynamic reworking of "Odd Man Out" starring Sidney Poitier as a militant leader who helps families of jailed dissidents by robbing banks. As police presence grows, Poitier seeks help in distributing the cash from white social worker Joanna Shimkus. Al Freeman, Jr., Richard Dysart also star; music by Quincy Jones.
07-2820 *$14.99*

Brother John (1972)
Many years after he left his hometown, wanderer Sidney Poitier returns to be at his sister's deathbed. His arrival incites racial violence, which leads to a shocking revelation in this offbeat, emotional drama. With Will Geer, Bradford Dillman. 94 min.
02-1825 Was $19.99 *$14.99*

A Warm December (1973)
Tender romance directed by and starring Sidney Poitier as an American doctor practicing in England who falls in love with an African ambassador's niece, unaware she's suffering from a fatal illness. With Esther Anderson, George Baker. 100 min.
19-2418 *$19.99*

Uptown Saturday Night (1974)
Two pals try to regain a stolen lottery ticket and get involved with a mob kingpin. Bill Cosby, Sidney Poitier, Richard Pryor, Flip Wilson and Harry Belafonte star in this rollicking comedy. 104 min.
19-1096 Was $19.99 *$14.99*

Let's Do It Again (1975)
Hilarious story about two improbable fund-raisers who learn how to fix fights. Sidney Poitier, Bill Cosby, Jimmy Walker. Music by the Staple Singers. 112 min.
19-1097 Was $19.99 *$14.99*

The Wilby Conspiracy (1975)
South African activist Sidney Poitier must flee from the law while chained to engineer Michael Caine in this taut drama that blends the antagonism of "The Defiant Ones" with an unflinching look at apartheid. With Nicol Williamson, Persis Khambatta. 101 min.
12-1743 Was $19.99 *$14.99*

A Piece Of The Action (1977)
Bill Cosby and Sidney Poitier team up again for laughs as two con artists who are given a choice: go to jail or help a social worker at a beleaguered community center. James Earl Jones, Denise Nicholas co-star; music by Curtis Mayfield. 135 min.
19-1411 Was $19.99 *$14.99*

Little Nikita (1988)
What would you do if you found out your parents were in reality spies...for the Soviet Union! River Phoenix is faced with that problem, and when a Russian double agent marks them for death the only person he can turn to is FBI man Sidney Poitier. Great suspense thriller, directed by Richard Benjamin. 98 min.
02-1001 Was $19.99 ☐*$14.99*

Separate But Equal (1991)
Powerful, Emmy Award-winning true-life story, set in 1950s South Carolina, stars Sidney Poitier as NAACP lawyer Thurgood Marshall, who takes a tense and potentially groundbreaking segregation case from a small town to the Supreme Court. Co-stars Burt Lancaster as the opposing attorney and Richard Kiley as Chief Justice Earl Warren. 194 min.
63-1442 ☐*$14.99*

A Good Day To Die (1995)
Fine western epic starring Sidney Poitier as a famous bounty hunter who saves a young Cheyenne brave from a massacre and brings him to live with white settlers. Trouble occurs on two fronts as the settler's daughter becomes involved with the brave and Poitier faces the Ku Klux Klan when he becomes marshal of a black settlement. With Billy Wirth, Farrah Fawcett. 120 min.
68-1780 Was $89.99 ☐*$14.99*

Mandela And de Klerk (1997)
In a country torn apart by racial hatred, two men—one, a political prisoner, the other a president—courageously worked to unite their people. Sidney Poitier, as jailed African National Congress leader Nelson Mandela, and Michael Caine, as president F.W. de Klerk, star in this moving true story of the end of apartheid in South Africa. 114 min.
88-1144 Was $99.99 ☐*$14.99*

The Simple Life Of Noah Dearborn (1999)
Powerful drama starring Sidney Poitier as a quiet, reclusive farmer and craftsman in a small Georgia town whose sheltered life is thrown into turmoil when a real estate developer attempts to have him evicted from his land. Dianne Wiest, Mary-Louise Parker, George Newbern also star. 87 min.
68-1952 ☐*$69.99*

Sidney Poitier: One Bright Light
His rise to stardom signaled a new chapter in Hollywood history and changed the movies' perception of black actors. Follow the career of Sidney Poitier, the first African-American to win a Best Actor Academy Award, in this "American Masters" program that features film clips, interviews with James Earl Jones, Quincy Jones and Denzel Washington, and more. 60 min.
53-6692 *$19.99*

Please see our index for these other Sidney Poitier titles: *Band Of Angels • Blackboard Jungle • The Defiant Ones • Good-Bye, My Lady • The Jackal • Sneakers*

Sin You Sinners (1963)
A stripper finds an amulet with magical powers, but a sleazy club owner and her daughter have plans to steal it. A New York-filmed exploitation drama, starring June Culbourne and Dian Lloyd. 73 min.
68-8811 *$19.99*

Stakeout (1962)
Gritty crime drama about a crook whose shady past continually prevents him from making a better life for himself. Along with his 10-year-old son, he travels from job to job, but is forced back onto the wrong side of the law. Bing Russell, Jack Harris star. 81 min.
68-8839 *$19.99*

Feet Of Clay (1960)
While investigating a drug-smuggling ring, a lawyer learns that a probation officer is the person behind the operation in this crime drama. Vincent Ball, Robert Cawdron and Angela Douglas star. 55 min.
10-9707 *$19.99*

Serena (1962)
Honor Blackman of "Goldfinger" fame stars in this British suspenser about a police detective who discovers that an artist's wife has been murdered and one of the artist's models has assumed her identity. With Patrick Holt, Emrys Jones. 62 min.
10-9734 *$19.99*

Stark Fear (1962)
Creepy drama starring Beverly Garland as a put-upon woman whose unemployed husband physically and emotionally tortures her until she leaves him for her boss. Skip Homeier, Kenneth Tobey also star. 84 min.
68-8880 *$19.99*

Ivy League Killers (1962)
Not the true story of Penn's Mask and Wig Club, but a little-seen juvenile delinquent gem involving a group of rich teens who come into conflict with some ruthless motorcyclist creeps who sell stolen cars on the side. Don Borisenko, Barbara Bricker star.
68-9060 *$19.99*

Panic In The City (1968)
A federal investigator uncovers a plot by two Communist scientists who have built a nuclear bomb, which they plan to explode in L.A., triggering World War III. Howard Duff, Nehemiah Persoff, Linda Cristal and Dennis Hopper star in this "Cold War" thriller. 96 min.
17-9065 Was $19.99 *$14.99*

The Promise (1969)
During the siege of Leningrad, two Soviet soldiers are befriended by a beautiful homeless woman and soon become parts of a dangerous love triangle. John Castle, Ian MacKellen and Susan Macready star. 98 min.
17-9066 *$19.99*

Richard Burton

The Last Days Of Dolwyn (1949)
A Welsh man (writer/director/star Emlyn Williams) returns to the hometown that scorned him years earlier, hoping to buy out the village and destroy it, for a water project as well as his own vengeance. Richard Burton made his screen debut as the son of town dowager Dame Edith Evans in this fine drama. 95 min.
53-6017 Was $29.99 ***$19.99***

Green Grow The Rushes (1951)
In the style of "Whisky Galore" comes this lively British comedy about a group of coastal brandy smugglers who are able to operate due to an old glitch in the law. When the authorities try to clamp down, the hilarity begins. Richard Burton, Roger Livesey and Honor Blackman star. AKA: "Brandy Ashore." 78 min.
22-5864 Remastered ***$29.99***

Waterfront (1952)
Uncompromising look at the sailor's life with Robert Newton as an alcoholic seaman who cannot deal with the family he barely knows. Gritty film also stars Susan Shaw, Kathleen Harrison and a young Richard Burton. AKA: "Waterfront Women." 74 min.
10-7578 Was $19.99 ***$14.99***

Alexander The Great (1956)
Epic historical drama of the ancient Macedonian military leader who conquered most of the known world before he was 30. Richard Burton gives a fine performance as the restless genius; co-stars Fredric March, Claire Bloom. 141 min.
12-1420 Was $19.99 ***$14.99***

Alexander The Great (Letterboxed Version)
Also available in a theatrical, widescreen format.
12-2905 ***$19.99***

Look Back In Anger (1958)
Richard Burton excels as Jimmy Porter, an angry young Brit whose college degree can't help him get a job, other than as a clerk at a candy store. After wife Mary Ure leaves him because of his abusiveness, Burton becomes involved with her friend (Claire Bloom). Powerful adaptation of John Osbourne's play is directed by Tony Richardson ("Tom Jones"). 99 min.
53-1260 Was $59.99 ***$14.99***

Ice Palace (1960)
Sprawling drama based on Edna Ferber's novel is set against the splendor of Alaska and follows the decades-long rivalry between former friends, cannery tycoon Richard Burton and fishing boat skipper Robert Ryan. Martha Hyer, Carolyn Jones and Jim Backus co-star. 143 min.
19-1613 Was $19.99 ***$14.99***

The Bramble Bush (1960)
Top-notch melodrama featuring Richard Burton as a New England doctor embroiled in a steamy love affair with his dying friend's wife (Barbara Rush). When Burton performs a mercy killing on his pal, the local authorities accuse him of murder, which elicits a series of sordid revelations and a controversial trial. Jack Carson, Angie Dickinson also star. 104 min.
19-2163 Was $29.99 ***$19.99***

The Night Of The Iguana (1964)
Tennessee Williams' gripping drama involves a former preacher's affairs with three women—a nymph, a worldly woman, and an old flame. John Huston directs Richard Burton, Ava Gardner, Deborah Kerr, Sue Lyon, Grayson Hall. 119 min.
12-1079 ***$19.99***

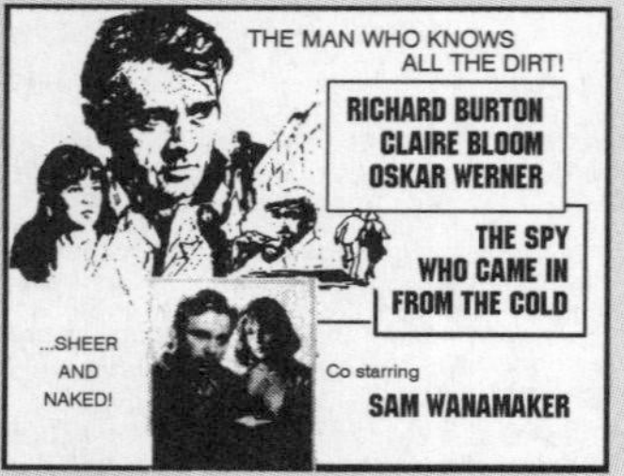
THE MAN WHO KNOWS
ALL THE DIRT!
RICHARD BURTON
CLAIRE BLOOM
OSKAR WERNER
THE SPY
WHO CAME IN
FROM THE COLD
...SHEER
AND
NAKED!
Co starring
SAM WANAMAKER

The Spy Who Came In From The Cold (1965)
Richard Burton earned an Academy Award nomination for his role as a burned-out spy who becomes a pawn in a convoluted scheme to protect a British double agent. An unglamorized, nuts-and-bolts view of intelligence work, based on the John Le Carré novel and co-starring Claire Bloom. 112 min.
06-1590 ***$19.99***

Doctor Faustus (1968)
Richard Burton and Elizabeth Taylor star in this arresting rendition of the classic drama of an aging scholar who bargains away his soul for youth regained and love discovered. Burton co-directs; Andreas Teuber, Ian Marter also star. 93 min.
02-1771 Was $69.99 ***$19.99***

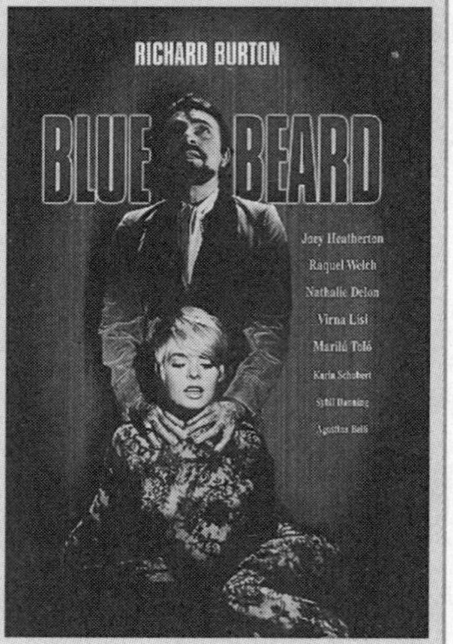
RICHARD BURTON
BLUE BEARD
Joey Heatherton
Raquel Welch
Nathalie Delon
Virna Lisi
Marilù Tolo

Bluebeard (1972)
Richard Burton is a German war hero who marries some of the world's most beautiful women—then kills them in the most unsettling ways. Among the women he encounters are Raquel Welch, Marilù Tolo, Virna Lisi, Nathalie Delon, Karin Schubert, Sybil Danning and, featured in a much-talked-about nude scene, Joey Heatherton; directed by Edward Dmytryk. Includes the original theatrical trailer. 124 min.
27-6061 Letterboxed ***$14.99***

The Klansman (1974)
When a young black man is arrested for the rape of a white woman, tensions in a small Southern town go past the boiling point, and a showdown between the law and the Klan is inevitable. Controversial drama stars Lee Marvin, Richard Burton, Linda Evans, O.J. Simpson. AKA: "The Burning Cross." 112 min.
06-1833 ❑***$14.99***

Equus (1977)
Peter Shaffer's award-winning play is a stunning drama about the human psyche and the power of the mind. A psychiatrist (Richard Burton) must discover the reasons why a disturbed stable boy (Peter Firth) blinded several horses. Shattering, emotion-packed story co-stars Joan Plowright, Colin Blakely. 138 min.
12-1465 Was $69.99 ***$14.99***

Breakthrough (1978)
An action-packed follow-up to "Cross of Iron" focuses on a German army plot to assassinate Hitler. Richard Burton plays a leader of the conspirators and Robert Mitchum is a U.S. colonel involved in the mission. With Rod Steiger, Curt Jurgens. 88 min.
14-3036 ***$12.99***

Circle Of Two (1980)
A teenage girl (Tatum O'Neal) falls in love with a 60-year-old artist (Richard Burton) who wants no part of her. What develops is a relationship that changes both their lives. Engrossing romantic drama also stars Kate Reid, Robin Gammell; Jules Dassin directs. AKA: "Obsession." 105 min.
47-1220 ***$19.99***

Wagner (1983)
Historical dazzler stars Richard Burton as the notorious composer, philosopher and scoundrel Richard Wagner. His exploits were the talk of Europe; his music inspired both Nietzsche and Hitler. Vanessa Redgrave, John Gielgud, Ralph Richardson, Laurence Olivier, Joan Plowright co-star. Unedited version runs nine hours on four tapes.
22-1052 Was $124.99 ***$79.99***

Absolution (1988)
Richard Burton turns in a powerful performance as a priest who teaches at a boy's school and finds one of his favorite students is playing a nasty practical joke on him. Dominic Guard and Billy Connolly also star in this drama filmed in 1978. 91 min.
20-5227 Was $19.99 ***$14.99***

Please see our index for these other Richard Burton titles: *Anne Of The Thousand Days • Becket • Boom! • Cleopatra • The Desert Rats • Exorcist II: The Heretic • The Longest Day • The Robe • The Sandpiper • The Taming Of The Shrew • The V.I.P.s • Who's Afraid Of Virginia Woolf?*

One Man's Way (1964)
An inspiring biography of Norman Vincent Peale (Don Murray), the son of an abusive Ohio clergyman, whose faith in God and unorthodox religious beliefs led to his writing of the best-seller "The Power of Positive Thinking." Diana Hyland, William Windom and Virginia Christine also star. 105 min.
12-2771 ***$19.99***

Toys In The Attic (1963)
After his business fails, drifter Dean Martin returns to his New Orleans family home with new bride Yvette Mimieux, but must face the obsessive jealousy of his spinster sisters (Geraldine Page, Wendy Hiller). A compelling and controversial film adaptation of the play by Lillian Hellman. 90 min.
12-2491 ***$19.99***

Harlow (1965)
The strong-willed woman who became one of Hollywood's first sex symbols and whose private life was marked by tragedy is the focus of this lavish biographical drama. Carroll Baker stars as Jean Harlow, and the superlative cast includes Martin Balsam, Angela Lansbury and Red Buttons. 125 min.
06-1363 Was $59.99 ***$14.99***

Summer And Smoke (1961)
Based on the Tennessee Williams play, this moving drama stars Geraldine Page as a minister's repressed daughter whose unrequited love for doctor Laurence Harvey leads to tragedy. With Rita Moreno, John McIntire, Pamela Tiffin. 118 min.
06-1825 Was $19.99 ❑***$14.99***

A Breath Of Scandal (1960)
Lavish romance stars Sophia Loren as a European princess who disagrees with a marriage arranged for her by her family and instead becomes involved with handsome American mining expert John Gavin. Maurice Chevalier, Angela Lansbury co-star; Michael Curtiz directs. 97 min.
06-2041 ❑***$12.99***

Negatives (1968)
Glenda Jackson, in one of her first starring roles, is featured in this adult drama of an unmarried couple and the woman who changes their love life together, entering a strange world of deceptions. 99 min.
14-6036 ***$19.99***

The Leather Boys (1963)
A moving dramatic study of the ill-fated marriage between a beautiful teenage girl (Rita Tushingham)—who wishes primarily to rebel against her parents—and a motorcyclist mechanic (Colin Campbell), and their unhappy life together. Co-stars Dudley Sutton; Sidney Furie ("The Ipcress File") directs. 105 min.
15-1131 ***$24.99***

Time Out For Love (1963)
Jean Seberg is an American woman living in Paris who leaves her live-in boyfriend for a race car driver, but eventually realizes the error of her ways. Micheline Presle and Maurice Ronet star. 91 min.
17-9080 Was $19.99 ***$14.99***

Fanny (1961)
Marcel Pagnol's "Marseilles Trilogy" is the basis for this heartwarming drama about the denizens of the French waterfront, and how two lovers are at last reunited. Leslie Caron, Maurice Chevalier, Horst Buchholz, Charles Boyer star. 129 min.
19-1245 Was $19.99 ***$14.99***

Sweetbeat (1962)
The Mello-Kings and Fred Parris and The Satins (later known as The Five Satins) are among the early British R&B bands showcased in this rare musical. A pretty would-be singer wins a trip to London and a possible record deal, but finds trouble when a slick American producer tries to ply her away from her fiancé. With Julie Amber, Billy Myles. AKA: "The Amorous Sex." 56 min.
50-1306 Was $19.99 ***$14.99***

Time Of Indifference (1964)
Set in Italy in the 1920s, this drama stars Rod Steiger as a schemer who woos a wealthy woman (Paulette Goddard) while romancing her daughter (Claudia Cardinale). Based on Alberto Moravia's story, this stylish production comments on the disintegration of the aristocracy. Shelley Winters also stars. 84 min.
53-6062 ***$29.99***

Grand Prix (1966)
Incredible racing sequences highlight this lightning-fast drama about the on- and off-track rivalries of the Grand Prix drivers. James Garner, Yves Montand, Eva Marie Saint, Toshiro Mifune star; John Frankenheimer directs. 171 min.
12-1703 Was $29.99 ❑***$24.99***

Grand Prix (Letterboxed Version)
Also available in a theatrical, widescreen format.
12-3132 ***$24.99***

Zabriskie Point (1969)
It's the height of 1960s significance, as Italian director Michelangelo Antonioni chronicles the plight of a radical student, fleeing from society and the authorities after he's suspected of killing a policeman. Music by The Grateful Dead, The Rolling Stones and The Youngbloods. Mark Frechette, Daria Halprin, Rod Taylor star; look for Harrison Ford. 112 min.
12-1334 ***$19.99***

Five Miles To Midnight (1963)
Unhappily married Sophia Loren is shocked to hear that her husband, American businessman Anthony Perkins, was killed in a plane crash...and even more shocked when Perkins shows up alive and needing her help for an insurance fraud scheme against the airline. Compelling drama also stars Gig Young, Jean-Pierre Aumont. 108 min.
12-3016 ❑***$19.99***

Black Like Me (1964)
Amazing true drama about a white writer who chemically altered his skin color in order to travel through the '50s South and experience firsthand the discrimination and bigotry faced by blacks. James Whitmore, Roscoe Lee Browne star. 110 min.
14-6032 Was $19.99 ***$14.99***

The Whisperers (1967)
Atmospheric British drama featuring an acclaimed performance by Edith Evans as an elderly woman living alone in a rundown apartment. While experiencing emotional problems, she is forced to deal with her estranged husband, crooked son and a shady neighbor. Stark, well-acted story also stars Eric Portman, Nanette Newman. 106 min.
12-3094 ***$19.99***

The Doomsday Flight (1966)
A madman threatens to blow up an airplane in midair unless his demands are met, and officials begin a desperate race against time to find the bomb. Taut thriller by Rod Serling stars Edmond O'Brien, Jack Lord, John Saxon and Van Johnson. 100 min.
07-1393 ***$39.99***

The Chalk Garden (1964)
Moving drama stars Deborah Kerr as a governess who tries to reunite three generations of an upper class British family. Dame Edith Evans shines as the matriarchal grandmother; also with John Mills, Hayley Mills and Elizabeth Sellars. 106 min.
07-1530 ***$19.99***

Single Room Furnished (1968)
Jayne Mansfield shines in her final screen appearance as a full-bodied teenager, left abandoned and pregnant by her loutish husband, who must streetwalk in order to survive. 93 min.
08-1325 ***$19.99***

Alfie (1966)
Michael Caine, in the role that made him a star, shines as the Cockney playboy who sits back and ponders his philandering existence. Delightful serio-comedy also stars Millicent Martin, Shelley Winters, Denholm Elliott. 114 min.
06-1323 Was $59.99 ***$14.99***

Of Human Bondage (1964)
Kim Novak and Laurence Harvey star in a dramatic retelling of the Somerset Maugham novel. A doctor's obsessive love for a frowzy waitress leads to heartbreak for all involved. With Robert Morley, Siobhan McKenna. 98 min.
12-1487 ***$24.99***

Up The Down Staircase (1967)
Set in an inner city high school, this acclaimed drama stars Sandy Dennis as a naive but determined neophyte teacher who deals with uncaring students and apathetic faculty colleagues in an attempt to get through to her charges. With Patrick Bedford, Eileen Heckart, Ellen O'Mara, Jean Stapleton. 124 min.
19-2244 Was $29.99 ❑***$19.99***

The Miracle Worker (1962)
The remarkable story of deaf, blind and mute Helen Keller and how she learned to communicate through the efforts of teacher Anne Sullivan. Anne Bancroft and Patty Duke both won Oscars for their work in this inspiring family classic. Co-stars Victor Jory, Andrew Prine; Arthur Penn directs. 107 min.
12-1520 Was $19.99 ***$14.99***

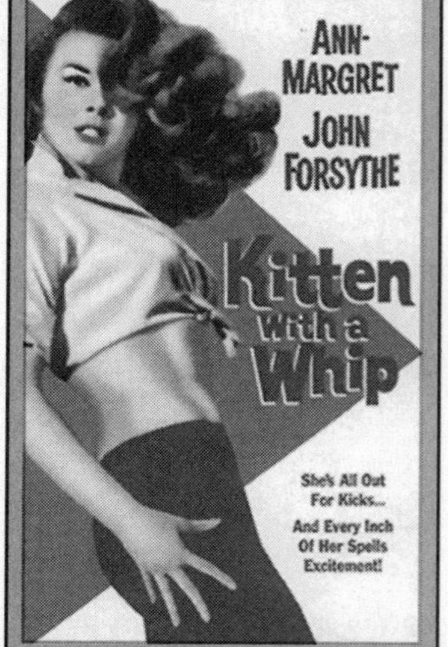
ANN-MARGRET
JOHN FORSYTHE
Kitten with a Whip
She's All Out For Kicks...
And Every Inch Of Her Spells Excitement!

Kitten With A Whip (1964)
Wild and sordid story starring Ann-Margret as a sexy escapee from a girls' juvenile home who forces politician John Forsythe into using his house as a refuge for her convict pals. The criminals' wild party turns violent, leading Ann to join Forsythe as they try to get away from her troublesome pals. Peter Brown and Richard Anderson also star. 83 min.
77-7021 ❑***$14.99***

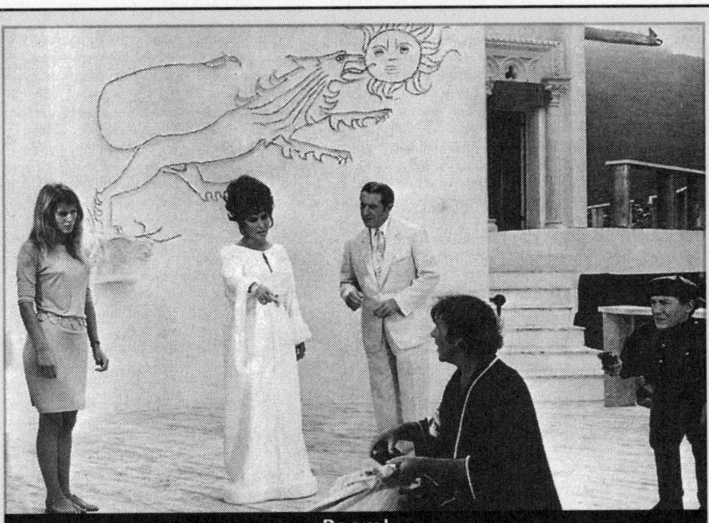
Boom!

Elizabeth Taylor

National Velvet (1944)
Classic family film about a girl named Velvet (Elizabeth Taylor), her beloved horse, and her determination to win the Grand National Steeplechase race. With Mickey Rooney, Donald Crisp, Angela Lansbury and Best Supporting Actress Oscar-winner Anne Revere. 124 min.
12-1457 Was $19.99 ❑$14.99

Julia Misbehaves (1948)
Witty sophisticated comedy starring Greer Garson as a penniless showgirl who finds adventure and romance while on a boat ride to France, where daughter Elizabeth Taylor is scheduled to get married. Upon arriving in Paris, Garson reunites with ex-husband Walter Pidgeon, which leads to humorous complications. With Peter Lawford, Cesar Romero and Reginald Owen. 99 min.
12-2714 $19.99

Little Women (1949)
The four March sisters are played by Elizabeth Taylor, June Allyson, Margaret O'Brien and Janet Leigh in Mervyn LeRoy's glossy filming of the classic Alcott novel of Civil War-era Massachusetts. Stellar cast includes Mary Astor, Peter Lawford. 121 min.
12-1827 Was $19.99 ❑$14.99

Conspirator (1949)
Suspenseful, romantic thriller starring Robert Taylor as a British army officer working for the Russians who wants to resign from his spy work, but is told that he must first kill his beautiful young wife (Elizabeth Taylor). With Robert Flemyng and Honor Blackman. 85 min.
12-2693 $19.99

The Big Hangover (1950)
Offbeat comedy/drama starring Van Johnson as an attorney suffering from a hypersensitivity to alcohol who falls for his boss's gorgeous daughter (Elizabeth Taylor) and must decide between helping the impoverished or the rich in his work. Leon Ames, Fay Holden and Percy Warran co-star. 82 min.
12-2691 $19.99

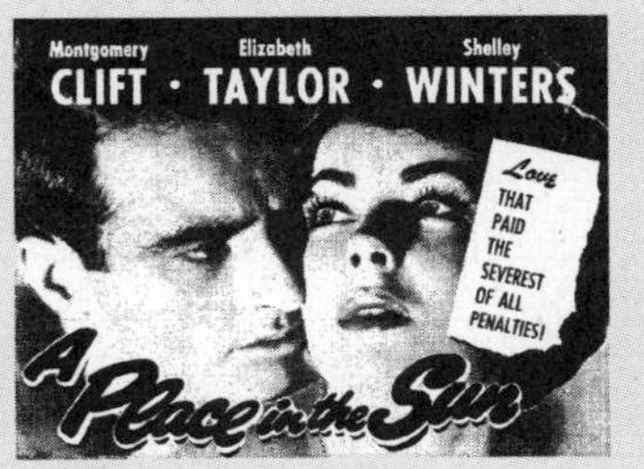

A Place In The Sun (1951)
Montgomery Clift stars as a schemer having affairs with two women (Shelley Winters and Elizabeth Taylor) in producer/director George Stevens' classic adaptation of Theodore Dreiser's "An American Tragedy." 120 min.
06-1089 Was $19.99 $14.99

Love Is Better Than Ever (1952)
A romantic comedy with Elizabeth Taylor as a small-town dancing instructor who travels to New York for a convention, where she falls in love with successful talent agent Larry Parks. This was Parks' last film before he was blacklisted. With Josephine Hutchinson, Tom Tully and Gene Kelly in a cameo; directed by Stanley Donen. 81 min.
12-2695 $19.99

The Girl Who Had Everything (1953)
Elizabeth Taylor is the title character, the spoiled daughter of a wealthy criminal attorney who falls in love with one of his clients, a gangster with interests in the gambling business. Fernando Lamas, William Powell, Gig Young and James Whitmore also star in this reworking of 1931's "A Free Soul." 69 min.
12-2694 $19.99

Elephant Walk (1954)
Exciting romantic drama starring Elizabeth Taylor as the ravishing bride of plantation owner Peter Finch who battles the elements and her love for American overseer Dana Andrews in the jungles of Ceylon. Noted for its thrilling elephant stampede and impressive location work. With Abner Biberman and Abraham Sofaer. 103 min.
06-1846 $14.99

The Last Time I Saw Paris (1954)
Elizabeth Taylor and Van Johnson star in F. Scott Fitzgerald's classic romance. Post-WWII Europe is the setting for this tearjerking human drama of love and obsession. Donna Reed, Walter Pidgeon and Eva Gabor co-star. 116 min.
12-2308 $19.99

Beau Brummel (1954)
Historical romancer starring Stewart Granger as the famous suave advisor to the Prince of Wales in 19th-century England who falls in love with blue-blood beauty Elizabeth Taylor and eventually has a falling out with the Prince, who becomes King George IV. Peter Ustinov, Robert Morley and James Donald also star in this lush MGM production. 113 min.
12-2690 ❑$19.99

Rhapsody (1954)
Love and jealousy bloom in the world of classical music. Elizabeth Taylor stars as a young, rich woman in love with talented violinist Vittorio Gassman, who decides that his music is more important than their relationship. Although she marries pianist John Ericson, her love for Gassman proves to be undying. Louis Calhern, Stuart Whitman also star. 115 min.
12-2696 ❑$19.99

Raintree County (1957)
Epic Civil War drama stars Elizabeth Taylor as a woman who stops at nothing to get what she wants, including Montgomery Clift, only to find her world coming apart. Eva Marie Saint, Lee Marvin, Agnes Moorehead. 168 min.
12-1562 Was $29.99 $24.99

Raintree County (Letterboxed Version)
Also available in a theatrical, widescreen format.
12-2910 Was $29.99 $24.99

Cat On A Hot Tin Roof (1958)
Tennessee Williams' scorching tale of heated tempers and eroticism in the deep South. Burl Ives is Big Daddy, Paul Newman is his boozing son, and Elizabeth Taylor is Maggie the Cat, whose bed she no longer shares with her husband. 108 min.
12-1056 Was $19.99 ❑$14.99

Suddenly, Last Summer (1959)
Acclaimed Tennessee Williams drama features Elizabeth Taylor as a disturbed young woman who accompanied her homosexual cousin on trips to Europe. Katharine Hepburn is her eccentric aunt who knows the bizarre secrets of her past, Montgomery Clift a sympathetic doctor who decides to help Liz. Scripted by Gore Vidal; directed by Joseph Mankiewicz. 114 min.
02-1282 Was $59.99 $19.99

Butterfield 8 (1960)
Elizabeth Taylor garnered her first Academy Award for her portrayal of a model/call girl who wants to escape her sordid life in this lush melodrama. Laurence Harvey also stars as the married socialite who falls for her; with Dina Merrill, Mildred Dunnock, Eddie Fisher. 110 min.
12-1126 Was $19.99 $14.99

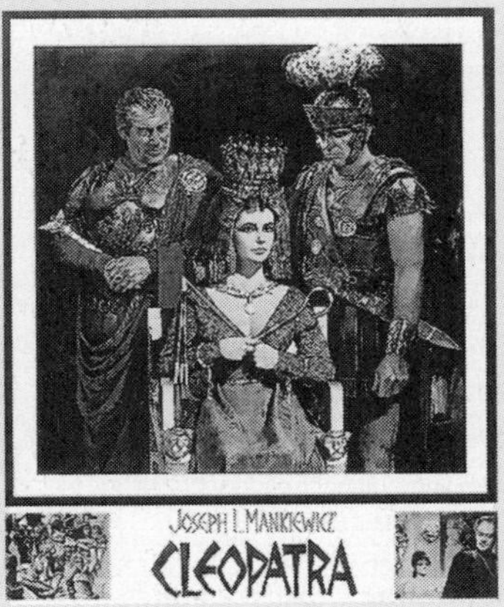

Cleopatra (1963)
Possibly the most expensive film ever made, the story of the beautiful Queen of the Nile is vividly captured. Elizabeth Taylor is breathtaking in the title role. Richard Burton and Rex Harrison are her suitors. A truly grand epic of war and romance. 243 min.
04-1471 ❑$29.99

The V.I.P.s (1963)
This multi-character drama looks at the lives and loves of a group of beautiful people who are waiting at a London airport for a number of reasons. Elizabeth Taylor is caught between the husband she has recently fled (Richard Burton) and a suave Lothario (Louis Jourdan); Orson Welles is a filmmaker; Rod Taylor an Australian businessman; and Oscar-winning Margaret Rutherford a dotty duchess. 119 min.
12-2697 ❑$19.99

The Sandpiper (1965)
Vincente Minnelli directs Elizabeth Taylor and Richard Burton, as a liberated artist begins a torrid romance with a conservative (and married) minister. Contains Oscar-winning theme "The Shadow of Your Smile." 116 min.
12-1403 $19.99

Who's Afraid Of Virginia Woolf? (1966)
An evening with George and Martha (Elizabeth Taylor and Richard Burton) becomes a searing event of vicious verbal backbiting, disclosed secrets, alcoholic indulgence and bizarre fantasies in this faithful adaptation of Edward Albee's Broadway play. Winner of five Oscars, including Best Actress and Supporting Actress, this was Mike Nichols' directorial debut. Co-stars George Segal, Sandy Dennis. Includes the original theatrical trailer. 133 min.
19-1158 $19.99

Boom! (1968)
Infamous screen treatment of Tennessee Williams' "The Milk Train Doesn't Stop Here Anymore" showcases Elizabeth Taylor as a dying millionairess whose life is changed when mystical poet Richard Burton arrives at her island estate. The two exchange philosophies about life, death, religion and other topics while Burton checks out Taylor's booze and jewelry. With Michael Dunn, Joanna Shimkus and Noel Coward as the "Witch of Capri"; directed by Joseph Losey. 113 min.
07-2908 ❑$14.99

Secret Ceremony (1968)
Believing stranger Mia Farrow is her deceased daughter, aging prostitute Elizabeth Taylor invites her to live with her in a decrepit London house. After Farrow moves in, the two develop a close relationship, but Farrow comes to realize that she is, in fact, Taylor's niece. The bizarre plot thickens when Robert Mitchum, Farrow's creepy stepfather, enters the scene. With Peggy Ashcroft, Pamela Brown; directed by Joseph Losey. 110 min.
10-3186 ❑$14.99

X,Y, And Zee (1972)
Highly charged and erotic, this controversial melodrama of a married couple who find they're both attracted to a mysterious "other woman" stars Elizabeth Taylor, Susannah York and Michael Caine. 110 min.
02-1736 Was $69.99 $19.99

Divorce His, Divorce Hers (1972)
Explore the many feelings and passions that envelop a couple in the throes of breaking up in this acclaimed drama, starring Richard Burton and Elizabeth Taylor as the troubled husband and wife. 148 min.
03-1374 Was $19.99 $14.99

Ash Wednesday (1973)
Elizabeth Taylor and Henry Fonda star in this glossy drama about a middle-aged woman who undergoes extensive plastic surgery in order to make herself look more attractive to her lawyer husband. In Italy, following her surgery, she has a fling with a younger man (Helmut Berger). 99 min.
06-1843 ❑$14.99

The Driver's Seat (1973)
Potent, emotional look at a woman who searches for a man she wants completely. When she finally finds him, she discovers he might be a murderer. Elizabeth Taylor, Mona Washbourne, Ian Bannen, Andy Warhol co-star. 90 min.
53-1113 $19.99

Sweet Bird Of Youth (1989)
Elizabeth Taylor and Mark Harmon star in director Nicolas Roeg's sizzling adaptation of the Tennessee Williams drama, as a fading film queen's affair with a handsome younger man sets a small Southern town ablaze with old passions. With Valerie Perrine, Rip Torn. 95 min.
72-9027 Was $89.99 $14.99

The Elizabeth Taylor Collection
Love Liz? Then check out this special boxed set of three of her most popular films: "Butterfield 8," "Cat on a Hot Tin Roof" and "Father of the Bride."
12-3191 $44.99

Please see our index for these other Elizabeth Taylor titles: *Courage Of Lassie • Doctor Faustus • Father Of The Bride • Father's Little Dividend • The Flintstones • Giant • Ivanhoe • Lassie Come Home • Life With Father • The Mirror Crack'd • Reflections In A Golden Eye • The Taming Of The Shrew • Victory At Entebbe*

Violated Love (1966)
Set in Buenos Aires, this seedy sex-and-crime story concerns a man who goes undercover to find out who murdered his brother. Soon, the man hooks up with a blonde nightclub entertainer with ties to the local syndicate. Libertad Leblanc and José Maria Langlais star. 72 min.
79-5210 $19.99

Five Minutes To Love (1963)
A crooked junkyard owner frames a man for auto theft in order to keep his own operation from being discovered. Sordid crime drama stars Paul Leder, Will Gregory, Gail Gordon and Rue McClanahan as "Poochie, the girl from the shack." AKA: "The Rotten Apple." 85 min.
68-8847 $19.99

Sex And The College Girl (1964)
Two free-spirited co-eds with very different views on romance and sex take off for a vacation in Puerto Rico, but both receive big surprises in their search for "Mr. Right." Now-campy dramatic look at the then-nascent "free love" movement marked the screen debuts of Charles Grodin and Julie Sommars.
70-3151 Was $24.99 $19.99

The Balcony (1963)
Fascinating version of Jean Genet's psycho-erotic play about an accommodating brothel where visitors act out elaborate fantasies of power and desire. Shelley Winters is the madam, with Peter Falk as her police chief lover and Leonard Nimoy as his political opposite, the leader of a local revolution. 87 min.
70-7048 Was $29.99 $19.99

Ordered To Love (1963)
Astounding World War II drama focusing on a woman forced to participate in a diabolical Nazi program in which she is supposed to be impregnated by German officers in order to breed the master race. Maria Perschy, Joachim Hansen star in this demented tale. 82 min.
68-8944 $19.99

Girl With An Itch (1960)
A slutty, big-breasted blonde hitchhiker enters the life of a lonely fruit rancher, but she's not as altruistic as she appears to be. She's soon sleeping with the rancher's farmhand and causing all sorts of trouble with her curves and cold demeanor. Robert Armstrong, Kathy Marlowe and Robert Clarke star.
79-5498 Was $24.99 $19.99

Force Of Impulse (1961)
"Kids in trouble" drama about two high schoolers from opposite sides of the tracks who fall in love, over the objections of the girl's father. Robert Alda, Tony Anthony, Teri Hope, Jody McCrea and J. Carroll Naish star; look for Christina Crawford ("Mommie Dearest" author). 84 min.
68-8851 $19.99

As Long As You Live (1967)
Gripping war drama about a young woman who struggles to get her town's children to safety before it's overrun by the enemy. Along the way she helps a young pilot who has injured his leg and, after hiding him in a cave, is captured and put to work at the town's hospital. Marianne Koch, Karin Dor star.
79-6145 Was $24.99 $19.99

The Miracle Of The Bells (1948)
Frank Sinatra, in an unusual role as a priest, helps press agent Fred MacMurray learn about a beautiful young actress after her untimely death. Also stars Valli and Lee J. Cobb. Anniversary package includes a reproduction of the theatrical lobby card. 120 min.
63-1037 ❑*$14.99*

The Miracle Of The Bells (Color Version)
"That inspiring small-town drama with Frank Sinatra as a priest is now also available in color? It's a miracle!"
63-1304 Was $19.99 *$19.99*

Double Dynamite (1951)
It's money, money everywhere and not a dime to spend for Frank Sinatra and Jane Russell, two lovebirds in a bank teller's cage who are suspected of embezzlement when Frank's big racing bet pays off. Groucho Marx has some great moments as the couple's pal, a greasy spoon waiter, in this light comedy. 80 min.
18-7115 *$19.99*

Suddenly (1954)
In one of his best (and most unheralded) performances, Frank Sinatra plays a pro assassin who joins other killers in the small town of Suddenly, Ca., where he plans to murder the president of the United States. Sinatra and his associates pose as federal agents in order to take a family hostage and use their house as the base for their operations. With Sterling Hayden, James Gleason. 75 min.
10-1073 *$14.99*

The Tender Trap (1955)
Quintessential Fifties romantic comedy features Frank Sinatra as a hip bachelor whose ways with the women impress his pal from Indiana, played by David Wayne. Sinatra's lifestyle is put to the test when he meets Debbie Reynolds, an ingénue who insists he drop his other girlfriends and hopes to marry him. Celeste Holm, Lola Albright and Carolyn Jones also star. 111 min.
12-2571 *$19.99*

The Man With The Golden Arm (1955)
Frank Sinatra is unforgettable as a musician trying to break his heroin addiction in this groundbreaking drama from Otto Preminger. The supporting cast includes Eleanor Parker, Kim Novak, Darren McGavin and Arnold Stang; Elmer Bernstein provides the memorable jazz score. 119 min.
19-2216 *$19.99*

Some Came Running (1958)
Would-be writer Frank Sinatra returns to his Indiana home town and finds that the idealized surface of the community covers a multitude of deceptions and lies in Vincente Minnelli's filming of the James Jones novel. Shirley MacLaine, as the bimbo hooked on Sinatra, and Dean Martin, as the local card shark, co-star. Arthur Kennedy, Martha Hyer. 137 min.
12-1829 Was $29.99 *$19.99*

Kings Go Forth (1958)
Highly entertaining blend of WWII action and human drama, featuring Frank Sinatra and Tony Curtis as soldiers stationed in France and Natalie Wood as a half-black American living overseas with whom both men fall in love. 110 min.
12-2272 *$19.99*

Never So Few (1959)
Intrigue, adventure and romance are well-blended in this WWII drama about Allied guerrilla forces in Southern Asia. American captain Frank Sinatra must lead his men against not only the Japanese, but also a traitorous Chinese warlord. The cast includes Peter Lawford, Gina Lollobrigida, Paul Henreid and Brian Donlevy, with early supporting turns by Steve McQueen and Charles Bronson. 125 min.
12-1863 *$19.99*

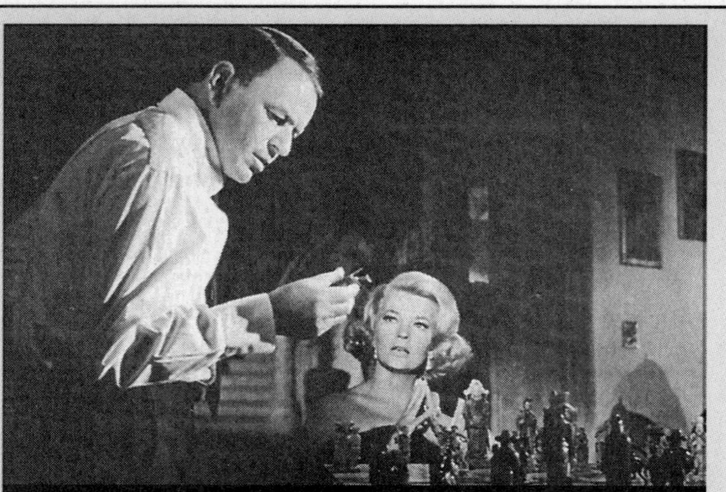
Tony Rome

Frank Sinatra

OCEAN'S 11

Ocean's 11 (1960)
The "Rat Pack"—Frank Sinatra, Dean Martin, Sammy Davis, Jr., Peter Lawford, Joey Bishop—in a masterful heist flick about Army buddies who plan to rip off five Vegas casinos in one night, faster than you can say, "Bingo, Dingo"! Look for cameos by Red Skelton, George Raft, Shirley MacLaine. 127 min.
19-1214 Was $19.99 *$14.99*

The Manchurian Candidate (1962)
One of the finest political thrillers ever made. John Frankenheimer's blend of Cold War paranoia and sly satire stars Laurence Harvey as a Korean War "hero" who has been brainwashed by the Soviets. Frank Sinatra is the war buddy who learns of the plot and must stop him; with Angela Lansbury, Janet Leigh, James Gregory, Henry Silva. 126 min.
12-1759 Was $19.99 ❑*$14.99*

4 For Texas (1963)
Frank Sinatra, Dean Martin and Charles Bronson battle for control of 1870 Galveston in this entertaining western adventure that mixes action, cowboy thrills and humor. Robert Aldrich directs; Anita Ekberg, Ursula Andress, Victor Buono and The Three Stooges are also featured. 115 min.
19-1827 Was $19.99 ❑*$14.99*

Von Ryan's Express (1965)
A POW colonel leads a daring escape, then steals an entire train to take men behind Allied lines. Frank Sinatra and Trevor Howard co-star in this suspense-filled WWII saga. 117 min.
04-1175 *$19.99*

None But The Brave (1965)
Frank Sinatra's directorial debut casts him as a Marine medic who finds himself and his crew stranded on a South Pacific island during World War II. They soon discover that the island is populated by Japanese forces, and a fragile truce is agreed upon when Sinatra saves a Japanese soldier's life. Clint Walker, Tommy Sands, Tony Bill and Tatsuya Mihashi co-star. 106 min.
19-1840 Was $19.99 ❑*$14.99*

Marriage On The Rocks (1965)
Love, romance and marital status get complicated in this romp starring Frank Sinatra and Deborah Kerr as a long-married couple who go to Mexico to enliven their relationship. When Sinatra is called back home for business, he enlists the help of swinging pal Dean Martin to care for Kerr. Little does he know that they're former lovers. Cesar Romero, Tony Bill co-star. 109 min.
19-2328 *$19.99*

Assault On A Queen (1966)
Frank Sinatra teams up with beautiful Virna Lisi to pull off the biggest heist on the high seas—using a restored U-boat to rob the Queen Mary—in this elaborate caper flick. Tony Franciosa, Richard Conte, Alf Kjellin co-star; script by Rod Serling. 105 min.
06-1931 *$14.99*

Tony Rome (1967)
Frank Sinatra's ultra-cool, Miami-based private investigator gets mixed up with murder, mayhem, stolen diamonds and a beautiful, troubled young girl in this slick detective yarn. With Jill St. John, Sue Lyon, Richard Conte and Gena Rowlands. 110 min.
04-2354 Was $59.99 *$29.99*

Lady In Cement (1968)
Wise-guy private eye Tony Rome (Frank Sinatra) is back in this intriguing mystery. The trail to catch the murderer of a woman found on the ocean floor leads Rome into a world of high-priced double-crosses, killings-for-hire and the rackets game. With Raquel Welch, Richard Conte and Lainie Kazan. 93 min.
04-2355 Was $59.99 *$29.99*

The Naked Runner (1967)
Furniture designer and expert marksman Frank Sinatra meets one of his wartime pals, now an agent for the British Intelligence Agency, who tries to get Sinatra to shoot an agent defecting to Russia. Sinatra decides to only deliver a letter for his friend, but after the assignment, he discovers that his son has been mysteriously kidnapped. Peter Vaughan co-stars in this espionage yarn. 104 min.
19-2329 Was $19.99 *$14.99*

Dirty Dingus Magee (1970)
Slapstick sagebrusher starring Frank Sinatra as a rascally outlaw in all sorts of trouble in 1880s New Mexico. After robbing George Kennedy, Sinatra finds himself in jail, involved with an Indian maiden and pursued by female sheriff Anne Jackson and a tribe of Indians. With Lois Nettleton, Jack Elam; co-written by Joseph Heller ("Catch-22"). 91 min.
12-3071 ❑*$19.99*

The First Deadly Sin (1980)
In his final starring film role, Frank Sinatra excels as a veteran New York homicide detective who must cope with two crises on the eve of his retirement: a case involving a series of violent random murders and his ailing wife's hospitalization. With Faye Dunaway, Brenda Vaccaro; look quickly for Bruce Willis in his screen debut. 112 min.
19-1329 Was $19.99 *$14.99*

Frank Sinatra: They Were Very Good Years
This five-part tape offers a compelling and fun-filled overview of the career of the "Chairman of the Board." Included are "The Bobby Sox Years," "The Hollywood Years," "Hollywood: The Second Time Around," "The Swinging Years" and "The Vintage Years." It's all presented with clips, interviews with such pals as Sammy Davis, Jr. and others, and archival footage. 300 min. total.
05-5088 *$69.99*

Frank Sinatra Memorial
It's a Sinatra celebration with this special tribute program that features Frank in vintage concert clips and rare TV interview footage, along with scenes from his film career and remembrances by such friends and colleagues as Tony Bennett, Joey Bishop, Ernest Borgnine, Quincy Jones, Debbie Reynolds and many more. 60 min.
05-5104 *$14.99*

Sinatra: A Passionate Life
Whether it was on the concert stage, the big screen or television, Frank Sinatra hit the heights of show business success and became an entertainment legend. This nostalgic, music-filled documentary lets you relive the Sinatra magic through rare photographs, film clips, interviews with friends and colleagues and more. 50 min.
89-5102 *$19.99*

The Rat Pack
This four-tape look at the famous Rat Pack includes rare footage, home movies and live performances of the coolest cats in show biz history. See how Sinatra, Martin, Davis, Lawford, Bishop and their cronies turned Las Vegas into their playground and learn what made them tick from such pals as Janet Leigh, Milton Berle and Jerry Lewis. It's money, baby! 200 min. total.
53-6580 *$39.99*

The Rat Pack Collection
Join Frank, Dean, Sammy and the rest of the crew in "Ocean's 11," "Robin and the 7 Hoods" and "4 for Texas," all slickly packaged in this set.
19-2396 *$44.99*

Please see our index for these other Frank Sinatra titles: *Anchors Aweigh • Cast A Giant Shadow • Come Blow Your Horn • The Devil At 4 O'Clock • From Here To Eternity • High Society • It Happened In Brooklyn • Not As A Stranger • On The Town • The Pride And The Passion • Robin And The Seven Hoods • A Song To Remember • Take Me Out To The Ball Game • Young At Heart*

Sweet Love, Bitter (1966)
Based on the last years of Charlie Parker, this rarely seen film stars comic Dick Gregory as a jazz saxophonist whose fervent need for drugs and alcohol is matched only by his love of music. His friends try to help him, but his self-destructive ways get in the way. Don Murray and Robert Hooks co-star; music by Mal Waldron and sax playing by Charles MacPhearson. AKA: "It Won't Rub Off, Baby!" 92 min.
53-7655 *$29.99*

Nothing But A Man (1964)
Powerful, ground-breaking look at black life in Birmingham, Alabama, in the early 1960s, focusing on a railroad worker who marries the schoolteacher daughter of a preacher and battles racism in order to make a better life for his family. Ivan Dixon, Abbey Lincoln and Julius Harris star in this compassionate tale from Michael Roemer and Robert Young. 92 min.
53-7845 Was $39.99 *$19.99*

Chappaqua (1966)
A hypnotic mix of psychedelic wonder and semi-autobiographical drama, this famed underground film from writer/director/star Conrad Rooks follows a young, well-to-do drug addict from his hometown in upstate New York to his search for a cure in Europe, as withdrawal leads him into a bizarre hallucinogenic world. With Allen Ginsberg, Jean-Louis Barrault, Ravi Shankar, and William S. Burroughs as "Opium Jones." 82 min.
53-8875 Was $59.99 *$19.99*

Sweet Ecstasy (1962)
See Elke Sommer as you've never seen her before in this sensual European drama in which she plays a jet-setter on the French Riviera who begins to have strong feelings towards a young man. This interest sparks a rivalry between him and an older man, which is to be resolved in a most unsettling way. 80 min.
83-3031 *$29.99*

The Girl-Getters (1966)
Set in a seaside resort town, director Michael Winner's "British Beat" drama stars Oliver Reed as a smooth-talking photographer who uses his camera to woo women and meets his match when he falls for a gorgeous London fashion model. Jane Merrow, Harry Andrews, David Hemmings also star. Nicolas Roeg served as cinematographer; music by The Searchers. AKA: "The System." 79 min.
53-6425 *$24.99*

Marat/Sade (1967)
The Royal Shakespeare Company's film version of Peter Weiss' acclaimed play is a dramatic, sometimes lurid "story within a story," as the infamous Marquis de Sade and his fellow inmates stage a violent play that takes on an all-too-real life of its own. The cast includes Patrick Magee, Ian Richardson, and Glenda Jackson in her film debut. AKA: "The Persecution and Assassination of Jean-Paul Marat as Performed by the Inmates of the Asylum of Charenton Under the Direction of the Marquis de Sade." 115 min.
01-1430 Was $29.99 ❑*$14.99*

Cop-Out (1967)
Based on a novel by Georges Simenon, this unusual mix of courtroom thriller and "generation gap" drama stars James Mason as a lawyer whose career and marriage were derailed by alcoholism. When estranged daughter Geraldine Chaplin's boyfriend is accused of murder, Mason explores their "mod" world into order to save him. Bobby Darin, Ian Ogilvy also star. AKA: "Stranger in the House." 95 min.
08-8839 *$14.99*

Love Play (1963)
In this sensuous drama, Jean Seberg plays a pretty American student living in Versailles who falls in love with a young sculptor kept by a wealthy, older woman. While the man introduces Seberg into womanhood, a tragedy plays a part in all the characters' lives. Christian Marquand, Francoise Prévost co-star; Seberg's then-husband, Francois Moreil, directs. AKA: "Playtime." 87 min.
83-3027 *$29.99*

The Luck Of Ginger Coffey (1964)
Out of a job and out of luck, Irish dreamer Robert Shaw moves his family to Montreal in search of a better life. His wife and daughter want to go back to Ireland, but Shaw has run out of money and struggles to keep his family together in their new home. Mary Ure (Shaw's real-life wife) and Libby McClintock co-star; Irvin Kershner directs. 100 min.
08-1784 *$19.99*

The Group (1966)
Eight friends at a prestigious women's college in the 1930s graduate and enter the adult world, where success and happiness await for some, disappointment for others. Shirley Knight, Elizabeth Hartman, Joan Hackett and Candice Bergen (in her film debut as the "Sapphic" Lakey) head the ensemble cast in this dramatic adaptation of Mary McCarthy's novel; with Hal Holbrook, Larry Hagman. 150 min.
12-2985 ❑*$19.99*

Mayerling (1969)
This remake of the 1937 French favorite stars Omar Sharif as the Prince of Hapsburg, who defies his father by leaving his royal lifestyle and joining in student protests during the Hungarian Revolution. When he falls in love with the young and wealthy Catherine Deneuve, their plans of marriage are thwarted by the king, which leads to tragedy. With James Mason, Ava Gardner. 127 min.
12-2992 ❑*$19.99*

The Angry Breed (1968)
A Vietnam veteran has trouble selling a screenplay he wrote until he saves a Hollywood producer's daughter from a gang of murderous motorcyclists. The producer gets the vet an agent, but then decides to use the motorcycle gang's leader as the movie's lead. There's LSD, a bizarre Halloween party and Jan Murray, Melody Patterson, James MacArthur, Jan Sterling, William Windom and Murray McLeod. 89 min.
17-9031 Was $19.99 *$14.99*

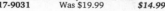

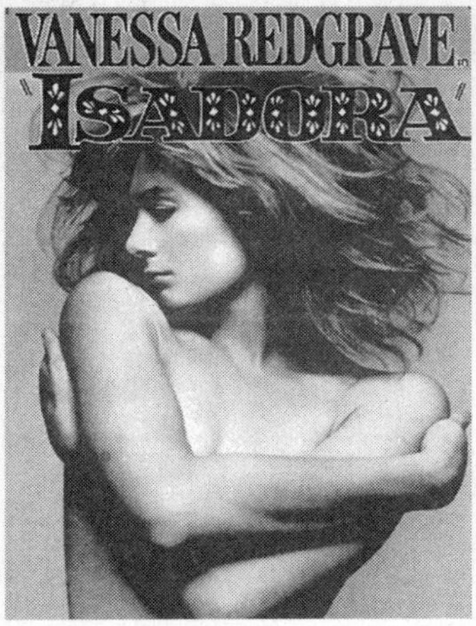
VANESSA REDGRAVE
ISADORA

Isadora (1968)
The tempestuous life of dancer Isadora Duncan is interpreted by Vanessa Redgrave. As Isadora modernized and scandalized dance by combining the classical with the animal, so has Karel Reisz created this divided film, part high drama and part earthy debauch. Also stars Jason Robards and Edward Fox. AKA: "The Loves of Isadora." 153-minute special director's version.
07-1578 Was $29.99 *$14.99*

Hollywood After Dark (1961)
Years before her "Golden Girls" success, Rue McClanahan starred in roadhouse melodramas like this one, in which she plays a would-be starlet who'll "do anything" to get into movies. She falls for a young man involved with crooks planning a waterfront heist. With Anthony Vorno, Paul Bruce. AKA: "Walk the Angry Beach." 74 min.
68-8849 *$19.99*

The Checkered Flag (1963)
Strange racing drama in which the wife of a racing champ persuades a young driver to kill her wealthy hubby on the track. The planned murder takes on even more tragic results, as the husband dies and the wife becomes horribly disfigured from rescuing the young driver (who loses his legs) in the crash. Features actual footage from Sebring; with Joe Morrison, Evelyn King. 110 min.
68-8890 *$19.99*

Stop Train 349 (1963)
Exciting Cold War drama about an American train to Frankfurt from Berlin carrying an East German stowaway. The Communists insist that the train be stopped, but commanding officer Sean Flynn (Errol's son) has other designs. Jose Ferrer, Nicole Courcel also star. 95 min.
68-8926 *$19.99*

Never Take Candy From A Stranger (1960)
Controversial social drama from Hammer Studios centers on the subject of child molestation, as an English family living in a small town in Canada discovers that their young daughter and her friend have been given candy by an elderly man in exchange for their dancing naked. Gwen Watford, Patrick Allen star. 81 min.
68-8930 Letterboxed *$19.99*

Sofi (1967)
Based on the play "Diary of a Madman," which adapted a short story by Gogol, this compelling psychological tale stars Tom Troupe as a 19th-century Russian clerk whose obsession with his superior's daughter draws him deeper into a well of hallucinations, delusions and madness. AKA: "Diary of a Madman."
68-9224 *$19.99*

Panic (1963)
London jewelry exchange worker Janine Gray is caught in a nightmare when her criminal lover and his gang launch a failed heist, killing the owner and leaving Gray knocked unconscious. Waking up with no memory, Gray wanders the city streets until she runs into a retired boxer who offers to help her solve the crime for which she's now blamed. Dyson Lovell, Glyn Houston also star. 69 min.
68-9270 *$19.99*

Free, White And 21 (1963)
Fascinating courtroom tale from Larry Buchanan ("Mars Needs Women"). Told in flashback, the fact-based film concerns a black hotel owner accused of raping a Swedish-born civil rights activist. After the accused tells his story, there's a three-minute break to let "you, the jury" decide the case. Fred O'Neal and Annalena Lund star.
71-1042 Was $24.99 *$19.99*

Louisiana Hussy (1960)
Considered one of the best "swamp trash" films of its era, this seedy drama tells of a hot-to-trot bayou gal who causes trouble for everyone she encounters. Using sex as her calling card, the "ragin' Cajun" destroys marriages and families until she gets into trouble because of her wicked ways. Nan Peterson and Betty Lynn (Thelma Lou of "The Andy Griffith Show") star.
73-3010 *$19.99*

Murder In Mississippi (1965)
The "untold truth behind the South's struggle for equality" tells the story of a civil rights activist who helps register voters in Mississippi. When she witnesses murders committed by the town's sheriff, she is taken hostage and held for ransom. Sam Stewart and Sheila Britton star. 84 min.
79-5206 *$19.99*

Gang Rape: The Shame Of Patty Smith (1961)
After she's gang raped on the beach while her boyfriend stands idly nearby, a teenager learns she is pregnant and must make a decision regarding an abortion. This tabloid drama remains particularly timely today, even with a cast that includes Merry Anders and Bruno Ve Sota ("Attack of the Giant Leeches"). 93 min.
79-5472 Was $24.99 *$19.99*

Invitation To Ruin (1968)
Disturbing, out-of-control crime drama about a white slavery ring in which the women procured by a "talent scout" are made subservient by torture and drugs administered by mean, mute Mama Lupo. Originally released in 1968, then re-edited and retitled "The Invitation" for a 1975 release. With Jim Gentry. 60 min.
79-5487 Was $24.99 *$19.99*

The Love Blackmailer (1966)
Seedy Canadian drama about a photographer who makes his living snapping shots of cheating wives, then blackmailing them for sex. Little does he know that taking pictures of a woman having an affair with her physician would put him in the middle of the couple and the woman's husband. Jean Christopher, Bruce Gray star.
79-5852 Was $24.99 *$19.99*

The Black Rebels (1965)
Outrageous "relevancy drama" in which black, white and Mexican teens square off, prompting the authorities to go undercover in high school to stop drug pushers and wild parties. Meanwhile, Rita Moreno has an interracial love affair with half-Mexican/half-black Mark Damon. Also with Dyan Cannon, Gerald Mohr, Al Freeman. The ads promised: "Switchblade Fights and Civil Rights!" AKA: "This Rebel Breed."
79-5887 Was $24.99 *$19.99*

Fall Guy (1962)
Stylishly realized crime tale about a teenager (Sonny Martin) who witnesses a mobster's murder, then goes to the police to tell them what he knows. After discovering that the police chief is a mob member, he flees from a hit man and tries to get the chief's daughter to believe what he's seen. With George Andre, Madeline Frances.
79-5889 Was $24.99 *$19.99*

The Girl Game (1962)
Set in Rio de Janeiro, this film looks at the rash of crime that occurs during Carnival time, as thieves dupe the wealthy patrons of the Copacabana Palace. Two con artists enlist a local guy with a parrot to help them with their criminal activities, while a group of stewardesses search for romance. Sylva Koscina stars. AKA: "The Saga of the Flying Hostesses."
79-5891 Was $24.99 *$19.99*

Young, Willing & Eager (1962)
A young, attractive woman tries to escape her impoverished life working at her father's diner. After she's almost raped, she decides to go to London, where, after dating older men, she meets a rock-and-roller, gets married and finds herself in trouble after her involvement in a robbery. Jess Conrad, Hermione Baddeley and Patrick Magee star in this gritty British drama.
79-6026 Was $24.99 *$19.99*

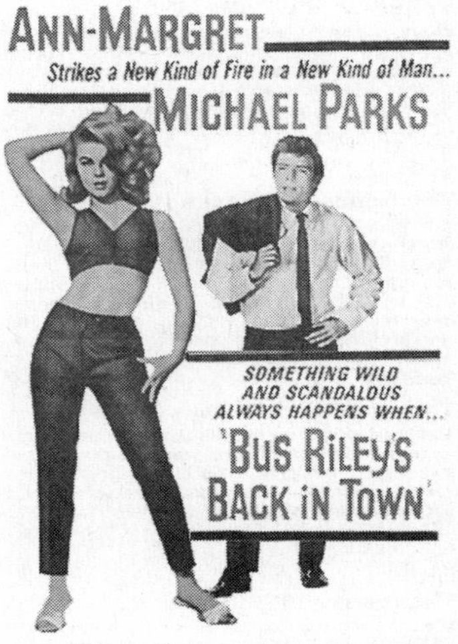
ANN-MARGRET
Strikes a New Kind of Fire in a New Kind of Man...
MICHAEL PARKS
SOMETHING WILD
AND SCANDALOUS
ALWAYS HAPPENS WHEN...
BUS RILEY'S
BACK IN TOWN

Bus Riley's Back In Town (1965)
Returning to his small-town home after serving in the military, a moody and restless Michael Parks is torn between the love of "good girl" Janet Margolin and his attraction for wealthy "bad girl" Ann-Margret. Based on a William Inge story, this steamy drama also stars Brad Dexter, Kim Darby and the inimitable Larry Storch. 93 min.
07-2840 ❑*$14.99*

Shirley MacLaine

The Matchmaker (1958)
Shirley Booth takes the title role in this delightful comedy that was the basis for "Hello, Dolly!" New York marriage broker Booth is hired by shopkeeper Paul Ford to find him a bride, but she has plans of her own for him. Shirley MacLaine, Robert Morse, Anthony Perkins also star. 110 min.
06-1822 Was $19.99 ❑*$14.99*

Career (1959)
Powerful, forcefully acted drama stars Anthony Franciosa as a struggling actor who will do just about anything to make it on Broadway. Among the people who filter through his life are his alcoholic wife (Shirley MacLaine), a successful director (Dean Martin) and a lonely agent (Carolyn Jones). 105 min.
06-1970 ❑*$12.99*

Ask Any Girl (1959)
Witty farce with Shirley MacLaine as a woman from a small town who relocates to Manhattan in hopes of finding a husband and finds work as a researcher for a motivational company run by brothers David Niven and Gig Young. Romance blossoms between Shirley and Gig...then David, too! With Rod Taylor and Jim Backus. 101 min.
12-2570 ❑*$19.99*

My Geisha (1962)
Shirley MacLaine is the actress wife of director Yves Montand who disguises herself as a geisha in order to get the role of Madame Butterfly in his new film. Lively comedy-drama also stars Edward G. Robinson, Robert Cummings and Yoko Tani. 120 min.
06-1859 *$14.99*

Irma La Douce (1963)
Billy Wilder/I.A.L. Diamond farce stars Jack Lemmon as a bumbling Paris gendarme who is fired for raiding the red light district (where his chief is a customer) and becomes an equally bumbling pimp for streetwalker Shirley MacLaine. Co-stars Lou Jacobi; Oscar-winning music by Andre Previn. 144 min.
12-2002 Was $19.99 ❑*$14.99*

Irma La Douce (Letterboxed Version)
Also available in a theatrical, widescreen format.
12-3174 Was $19.99 ❑*$14.99*

Gambit (1966)
Michael Caine and Shirley MacLaine star in this fast-paced, witty thriller as a suave British cat burglar and a wacky Eurasian dancer team up to rob a Middle Eastern tycoon of a priceless sculpture. With Herbert Lom, Roger C. Carmel. 109 min.
07-1485 Was $59.99 *$19.99*

The Bliss Of Mrs. Blossom (1968)
A very offbeat romantic comedy, this bedroom (and attic) farce stars Shirley MacLaine as the neglected wife of bra manufacturer Richard Attenborough. When a repairman shows up at her house, she sets him up in the attic and the two begin a five-year affair. With James Booth, Freddie Jones; look for John Cleese. 93 min.
06-1927 *$14.99*

The Possession Of Joel Delaney (1972)
Supernatural thriller featuring Shirley MacLaine as a rich divorcee who discovers that her brother's recent irrational behavior is attributed to his possession by the spirit of a murderous Puerto Rican teenager. Perry King, Michael Hordern co-star in this creepy Manhattan-based suspenser. 105 min.
06-1908 ❑*$19.99*

The Turning Point (1977)
Beautifully-filmed drama about two longtime friends—ballet star Anne Bancroft and ex-dancer and wife and mother Shirley MacLaine—who are forced to reconsider the choices each made when MacLaine's daughter seeks to pursue a ballet career of her own. Leslie Browne, Mikhail Baryshnikov, Tom Skerritt also star; directed by Herbert Ross. 119 min.
04-1167 Was $19.99 *$14.99*

A Change Of Seasons (1980)
A sophisticated, "romantic triangle" comedy starring Bo Derek (in a hot tub, no less), Anthony Hopkins and Shirley MacLaine. 102 min.
04-1308 Was $59.99 *$29.99*

Loving Couples (1980)
A witty and comical look at marriage on the rocks in Southern California, as two bored couples decide that a switch or two might put the excitement back in their lives. Shirley MacLaine, James Coburn, Susan Sarandon and Stephen Collins star. 97 min.
47-1010 *$14.99*

Terms Of Endearment (1983)
Follow the lives and loves of a mother and daughter over the years, and the special bond they share, in this poignant comedy-drama that garnered five Oscars, including Best Picture, Director, Actress and Supporting Actor. Shirley MacLaine is the feisty mom; Debra Winger, her independent daughter; Jack Nicholson, a womanizing ex-astronaut who lives next door. With John Lithgow, Jeff Daniels, Danny DeVito. 130 min.
06-1217 ❑*$14.99*

The Evening Star (1996)
The heartwarming story begun in "Terms of Endearment" continues, as strong-willed Aurora Greenway (Shirley MacLaine) tries to cope with raising her three grandchildren, whose problems range from lazy boyfriends to out-of-wedlock children to drug arrests. With Bill Paxton, Juliette Lewis, Marion Ross, George Newbern, and a special appearance by Jack Nicholson. 129 min.
06-2573 Was $99.99 ❑*$14.99*

Madame Sousatzka (1988)
Shirley MacLaine brings her considerable charisma to bear as she portrays a stuffy, intractable piano teacher in London who finds herself at odds with her most promising disciple, a teenage Indian boy. Dame Peggy Ashcroft, Twiggy co-star under the direction of John Schlesinger. 121 min.
07-1609 Was $19.99 *$14.99*

Used People (1992)
In this quirky seriocomic romance set in New York in 1969, Shirley MacLaine plays a widow who is courted on the day of her husband's funeral by Marcello Mastroianni, an Italian admirer obsessed with her for decades. As their awkward new relationship starts, MacLaine must deal with problems presented by her grown daughters (Marcia Gay Harden and Kathy Bates). With Jessica Tandy. 116 min.
04-2634 Was $89.99 ❑*$19.99*

Wrestling Ernest Hemingway (1993)
Two Florida retirees—a shy Cuban barber (Robert Duvall) and a craggy Irish sea captain (Richard Harris)—share secrets and swap colorful stories as they become unlikely friends in this sweet-natured comedy about life's golden years. Shirley MacLaine is Harris' landlady, who has a fondness for her tenant. 123 min.
19-2233 Was $89.99 ❑*$14.99*

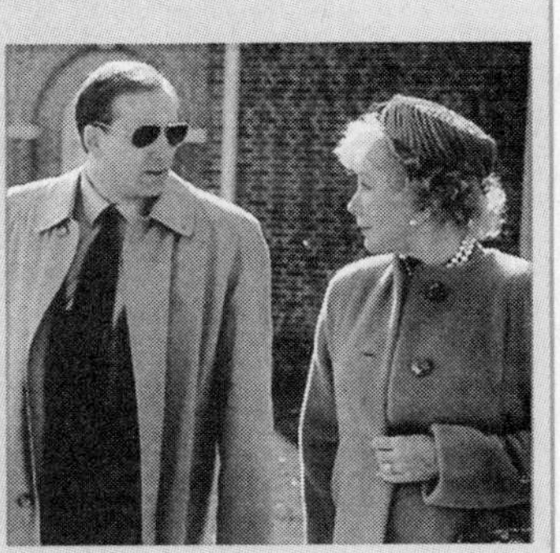

Guarding Tess (1994)
Quirky comedy starring Shirley MacLaine as a cantankerous former First Lady whose eccentricities cause all sorts of problems for the man in charge of guarding her, a by-the-book Secret Service agent played by Nicolas Cage. The agent is looking forward to a new assignment after his three-year stint, but MacLaine's stubbornness and a kidnapping attempt keep him on the job. 99 min.
02-2653 Was $19.99 ❑*$14.99*

Mrs. Winterbourne (1996)
Rescued from a train crash, pregnant and destitute Ricki Lake is mistaken for a member of the wealthy Winterbourne clan's new bride and soon assimilates herself into the household of matriarch Shirley MacLaine and Lake's "dead husband's" twin brother, Brendan Frasier. Funny and poignant moments ensue as working-class Lake jolts the family out of their stuffy old world values. 106 min.
02-2937 Was $19.99 ❑*$14.99*

Shirley MacLaine: Kicking Up Her Heels
A fill-in Broadway performance in "The Pajama Game" led to her discovery by producer Hal Wallis and a stellar Hollywood career that included a 1983 Best Actress Academy Award for "Terms of Endearment." Shirley herself narrates this look at her life (lives?), writings and movies. Clips from "Some Came Running," "The Apartment" and other films are featured, with comments from Nicolas Cage, Anthony Hopkins and Jack Lemmon. 53 min.
50-7606 *$14.99*

Please see our index for these other Shirley MacLaine titles: *The Apartment • Around The World In 80 Days • Artists And Models • Being There • The Children's Hour • Joan Of Arc • Postcards From The Edge • A Smile Like Yours • Some Came Running • Steel Magnolias • Sweet Charity • The Trouble With Harry • Two For The Seesaw • Two Mules For Sister Sara*

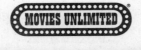

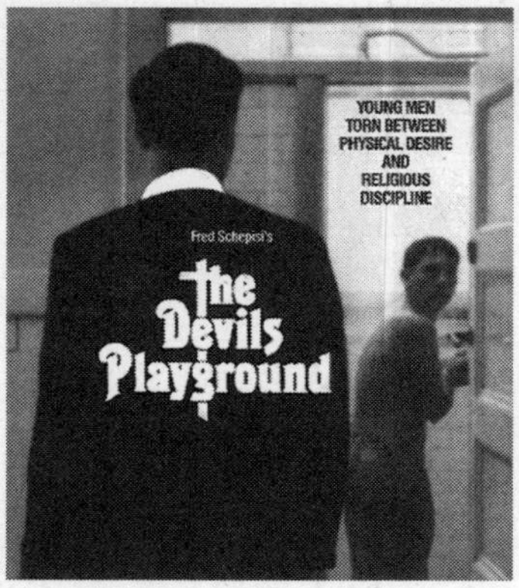
YOUNG MEN
TORN BETWEEN
PHYSICAL DESIRE
AND
RELIGIOUS
DISCIPLINE
Fred Schepisi's
the Devils Playground

The Devil's Playground (1976)
Award-winning Australian drama set in a Catholic boys' boarding school where the students' awakening sexual interests and the thwarted feelings of the priests who run the school threaten to explode. Written and directed by Fred Schepisi ("Barbarosa"); Arthur Dignam, Nick Tate, Simon Burke star. 107 min.
67-5020 *$29.99*

Blood (1975)
Alexis Krasilovsky's ironic and darkly amusing look at white, middle-class kids trying to attune to the seamy streets of New York has been hailed as "the first punk film." 21 min.
53-9028 *$29.99*

The Last Train (1974)
Romy Schneider and Jean-Louis Trintignant star in this poignant story of a doomed love affair in Nazi-occupied France. 101 min.
59-5071 *$14.99*

Billy Boy (1979)
Prize fighter Duane Bobick stars in this thrilling boxing film. A championship fight becomes a grudge match in this story of brawn and guts. Fight fans, enjoy!
64-1030 *$29.99*

The Death Of Richie (1977)
Thought-provoking made-for-TV melodrama about a 16-year-old whose basically normal life takes a turn for the worse when he becomes addicted to drugs. His father, partially responsible for his son's actions due to his distant nature, is forced to take drastic steps to protect himself and the rest of his family. With Robbie Benson, Ben Gazzara, Eileen Brennan. 97 min.
55-3011 *$19.99*

Incident On A Dark Street (1973)
Two recent law school graduates land positions in the U.S. Attorney's office in Manhattan and work to bring down a citywide crime syndicate. James Olson, David Canary, Richard Castellano, William Shatner and Gilbert Roland star in this gripping crime drama. 75 min.
55-3020 *$19.99*

Letters From Three Lovers (1973)
What happens when three letters, missing for a year, are finally delivered? June Allyson, Ken Berry, Juliet Mills, Belinda J. Montgomery, Martin Sheen and Barry Sullivan are among those who find their lives altered by the long-delayed missives, in this Aaron Spelling-produced drama. 75 min.
55-3025 *$14.99*

Moonfire (1970)
Truck driver Charles Napier gets driven into a sinister crime operation working along the Mexican border and run by an ex-Nazi in this pedal-to-the-metal tale filled with cool action and cool trucks. With Richard Egan, Joaquin Martinez and Sonny Liston as "the Farmer." 107 min.
55-3029 *$19.99*

James Dean (1976)
The tumultuous life and death of "America's teenager" is chronicled in this drama, from Dean's UCLA acting days until his tragic accident. Stephen McHattie turns in an uncanny performance as the '50s film idol; based on the book by Dean's college roommate. Also stars Michael Brandon and Candy Clark. 99 min.
70-1133 *$19.99*

Sandcastles (1972)
Romance and fantasy mix on an exotic beach where a down-on-her-luck musician meets and falls in love with a mysterious stranger. When the man is killed in an auto accident, he returns to Earth to make amends for crimes he committed when he was alive. With Jan-Michael Vincent, Bonnie Bedelia, Mariette Hartley, Herschel Bernardi star. 74 min.
55-3033 *$14.99*

Second Chance (1972)
An eccentric Wall Street player decides to purchase a deserted town in rural Nevada to create a place for people who haven't given up on life yet and want another crack at it. Brian Keith, Elizabeth Ashley, Kenneth Mars and William Windom star. 73 min.
55-3034 *$19.99*

Teenage Graffiti (1977)
Coming-of-age drama focuses on a young man's experiences of love with his girlfriend and an older woman during the summer following his high school graduation. Michael R. Driscoll, Jeanetta Arnette star. AKA: "Country Dreamin'." 90 min.
67-5027 *$19.99*

The Boxer (1971)
Exciting drama stars Robert Blake as a boxer accused of killing his corrupt manager and forced to run from police detective Ernest Borgnine while trying to prove his innocence. With Catherine Spaak. AKA: "Murder in the Ring," "Ripped Off."
75-7064 *$14.99*

Riding Tall (1971)
A modern-day rodeo cowboy travels from town to town, barely managing to make a living, and finds his life changed when he falls for a woman from New York City. Interesting country-flavored drama stars Andrew Prine, Gilmer McCormick, Robert Baston. AKA: "Honky Tonk Cowboy," "Squares." 90 min.
75-7141 Was $19.99 *$14.99*

Where The Eagle Flies (1972)
Three misfits—a burned-out rock singer, a free-spirited college girl and a warm-hearted hobo—find adventure together on the road in this offbeat "counterculture drama." Martin Sheen, Lesley Ann Warren, Jack Albertson star. AKA: "Pickup on 101." 93 min.
76-7009 *$19.99*

A Doll's House (1973)
Claire Bloom, Anthony Hopkins and Denholm Elliott head a stellar cast in this riveting screen adaptation of Henrik Ibsen's classic drama. An independent woman tries to help her financially plagued husband but suffers terribly for her actions. Screenplay by Christopher Hampton ("Dangerous Liaisons"). 96 min.
77-1018 *$14.99*

The Trial Of Chaplain Jensen (1975)
A married U.S. Navy chaplain faces a court-martial when the wives of two Navy men accuse him of adultery in this compelling film, based on a true story. With James Franciscus, Joanna Miles, Lynda Day George and Charles Durning. 72 min.
55-3039 *$19.99*

Black Jesus (1971)
Based in part on the true story of Zairian military leader-turned-dictator Mobutu Sese Seko, director Valerio Zurlini's compelling drama stars Woody Strode as an anti-colonial leader in a strife-torn African nation who is betrayed by a power-hungry follower. With Franco Citti, Jean Servais. 90 min.
55-9025 *$29.99*

Savage Abduction (1979)
Dear Mom: Our vacation to L.A. is getting off on the wrong foot! We've been kidnapped by some brutal bikers and held captive by an obsessed eccentric! He's into fantasy and murder Help!!! Signed, Your Daughter. Tom Drake, Stephen Oliver, Amy Thomson star. 90 min.
58-1081 *$14.99*

Cooley High (1975)
Fine comedy/drama in the style of "American Graffiti" and "Breaking Away" stars Lawrence-Hilton Jacobs and Glynn Turman as high schoolers facing all manners of problems in the inner city. Heartfelt urban tale, which was the basis for the TV series "What's Happening!," also stars Garrett Morris, Cynthia Davis. 107 min.
73-1098 Was $79.99 ❑*$14.99*

Conduct Unbecoming (1975)
First-rate courtroom drama set in a remote outpost in India in 1890, involving a British officer accused of molesting the widow of another officer and his defense by a fellow soldier in a secret trial run by his superiors. Michael York, Trevor Howard, Richard Attenborough, Stacy Keach and Susannah York star in this gripping film. 107 min.
67-5029 *$19.99*

The Lawrenceville Stories
Acclaimed adaptation of Owen Johnson's award-winning stories, which originally ran in the Saturday Evening Post, centers on the mischievous student body of the famed Lawrenceville Prep School, circa 1905. Nostalgic fun and genteel schoolboy drama stars Zach Galligan, Edward Herrmann, Nicholas Rowe and Robert Joy. Each tape runs 60 min.

The Lawrenceville Stories: The Prodigious Hickey
A group of students with nicknames like "Gutter Pup" and "The Triumphant Egghead" performs wacky pranks at Lawrenceville Prep under the leadership of "The Prodigious Hickey," who has devised a scheme for his undistinguished roommate to make a name for himself.
27-6775 *$24.99*

The Lawrenceville Stories: The Return Of Hickey
Following a suspension from school, Hickey returns to Lawrenceville to find that his role as school hot-shot has been challenged by a new student, "The Tennessee Shad."
27-6777 *$24.99*

The Lawrenceville Stories: The Beginning Of The Firm
Hickey finds himself stuck with a new roommate he dislikes and joins forces with arch-rival "The Tennessee Shad" to concoct a plot to squelch the new arrival.
27-6778 *$24.99*

The Lawrenceville Stories: The Complete Set
All three programs in "The Lawrenceville Stories" are presented in this money-saving boxed set.
27-6779 Save $10.00 *$64.99*

The Anonymous Venetian (1971)
Set in Venice, this romantic drama stars Tony Musante as a man dying from a brain tumor who reunites with his ex-wife to explore what led to the disintegration of their relationship. With Florinda Bolkan. 94 min.
67-5037 *$14.99*

Dirty Money (1972)
Top-notch crime drama from Quentin Tarantino fave Jean-Pierre Melville ("Bob le Flambeur") stars Alain Delon as a cop who travels to a seaside town seeking the principals in a drug-smuggling operation. While searching for the criminals, he falls for lovely Catherine Deneuve, who happens to be the mistress of gang leader Richard Crenna. AKA: "Un Flic."
67-5038 *$14.99*

One Man (1979)
A TV news reporter uncovers evidence of industrial pollution that threatens a slum, but pressure is put on him from all sides to sit on the story. Compelling social drama stars Len Cariou, Barry Morse, Jayne Eastwood. 87 min.
76-7012 *$59.99*

The Naked Flame (1970)
Filmed in 1963 and unreleased for seven years, this bizarre blend of crime thriller, religious drama and nudie exploitationer stars Dennis O'Keefe as the latest arrival in a town populated by a strange Christian sect, whose membership includes nude worshippers. When a string of violent assaults occurs, O'Keefe becomes the main suspect. 90 min.
68-8848 *$19.99*

Hurricane (1979)
Lavish and romantic South Seas adventure with an all-star cast caught in the middle of a devastating hurricane. Stars Mia Farrow, Jason Robards, Max Von Sydow, Trevor Howard and Timothy Bottoms. 119 min.
06-1151 Was $49.99 *$14.99*

For Your Love Only (1977)
Early Nastassja Kinski film stars the gorgeous actress as a teenage student who has a steamy affair with her married teacher. But a fellow student is enamored with her as well, and when he tries to force himself upon Kinski in the forest, she kills him with a rock. The teacher soon becomes the prime suspect in the murder. Wolfgang Petersen ("Air Force One") directs.
58-1060 *$14.99*

Katherine (1975)
An absorbing drama fueled by a stand-out performance from Sissy Spacek as a spoiled little rich girl, who, through her fight against social injustice, turns to radicalism and, eventually, political terrorism. Also stars Art Carney, Henry Winkler and Jane Wyatt. 98 min.
70-1132 *$14.99*

Cry Of The Penguins (1971)
John Hurt is a young, womanizing biologist who goes to Antarctica in order to study penguins and to win over Hayley Mills, a student. His observations about the birds' difficult lives inspire him to reconsider the choices he's made in his own life. Features incredible nature photography by Arne Sucksdorff. AKA: "Mr. Forbush and the Penguins." 105 min.
78-3014 *$14.99*

Territorial Men (1976)
A young, independent schoolteacher in the Colorado Territory towards the end of the 19th century finds her involvement with a cattle ranch operator is complicated by two of her students. Brenda Vacarro and Sam Groom star in this feature-length frontier drama culled from the hit TV series "Sara." 98 min.
78-3017 *$14.99*

Valley Of The Dolls (1967)
Classic melodrama based on Jacqueline Susann's best-selling novel about three aspiring actresses (Patty Duke, Barbara Parkins and Sharon Tate) who find the route to show business fame paved with drug addiction and tragedy. Susan Hayward, Paul Burke and Lee Grant also star; Dionne Warwick sings the theme song. 123 min.
04-1172 Was $19.99 *$14.99*

The Genesis Children (1972)
A long-lost classic, this film has been hailed a masterpiece by fans of the youthful male form. Stunningly filmed by nature photographer Billy Byars, this drama focuses on a group of students' trip to Italy and their surreal coming-of-age adventures away from civilization. Peter Glawson, Greg Hill star. WARNING: Contains extensive nudity. Uncut, uncensored version; 84 min.
78-5025 *$79.99*

Target Of An Assassin (1978)
Thrill-packed story set in South Africa, where a hospital worker (Anthony Quinn), faced with a fatal illness and desperate to provide for his family, kidnaps a visiting dignitary and must dodge the police and a political assassin. With Ken Gampu, John Phillip Law. AKA: "African Rage," "Fatal Assassin," "Tigers Don't Cry." 102 min.
81-1096 *$14.99*

The Interns (1962)
Life-and-death tensions run high for the young staff at a big city hospital in this dramatic sudser starring Telly Savalas, Cliff Robertson, Stefanie Powers, Buddy Ebsen and Michael Callan. 120 min.
02-1438 *$59.99*

The Virgin Soldiers (1969)
Comedy/drama about British recruits stationed in 1950s Singapore, as inexperienced in matters of romance as they are in army life. Lynn Redgrave, Hywel Bennett, Nigel Davenport star. 96 min.
02-1702 *$69.99*

The War Game (1965)
Engrossing "docudrama" about the aftermath of a nuclear war, centering on the devastation in England, that won a Best Documentary Oscar. Produced for the BBC, who later banned it, Peter Watkins' moving look at the folly of global warfare is unforgettable. 48 min.
01-1277 *$19.99*

Culloden (1964)/ The War Game (1965)
Two compelling documentary-style dramas made for the BBC by independent filmmaker Peter Watkins. "Culloden" is a "You Are There"-like re-enactment of Bonnie Prince Charlie's last battle in 18th-century Scotland, followed by Watkins' Academy Award-winning and controversial look at the aftermath of a nuclear war on England. 123 min. total.
53-7634 *$59.99*

In Cold Blood (1967)
Powerful, highly-charged account of two petty crooks who attacked and slaughtered a Kansas family in their farmhouse and were eventually caught and put to death. Based on Truman Capote's novelization of a true story, scripter/director Richard Brooks' drama stars Robert Blake, Scott Wilson and John Forsythe. 134 min.
02-1099 *$19.99*

In Cold Blood (1997)
Intense filmization of the classic Truman Capote "non-fiction novel" about the bloody slaughter in 1959 of a Kansas family by ex-cons Dick Hickock and Perry Smith. Trying doggedly to solve the case as the killers attempt to flee to Mexico is Detective Alvin Dewey. Anthony Edwards, Eric Roberts and Sam Neill star; directed by Jonathan Kaplan ("The Accused"). 140 min.
58-5237 Was $69.99 ❑*$14.99*

David And Lisa (1962)
Keir Dullea and Janet Margolin are two mentally troubled teenagers who come to terms with the world around them through a friendship that blossoms into love. Based on a true story, director Frank Perry's touching drama also stars Howard Da Silva, Neva Patterson. 94 min.
02-1739 *$29.99*

The Pumpkin Eater (1964)
Harold Pinter scripted this powerful drama starring Anne Bancroft as the mother of seven children who goes through a series of emotional problems after she discovers third husband Peter Finch is having an affair with another woman. James Mason, Janine Gray and Richard Johnson also star. 118 min.
02-2796 *$19.99*

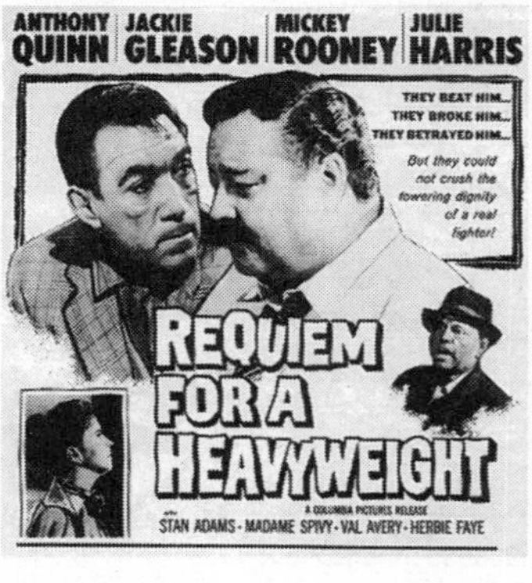
ANTHONY QUINN
JACKIE GLEASON
MICKEY ROONEY
JULIE HARRIS
THEY BEAT HIM...
THEY BROKE HIM...
THEY BETRAYED HIM...
But they could not crush the towering dignity of a real fighter!
REQUIEM FOR A HEAVYWEIGHT
A COLUMBIA PICTURES RELEASE
STAN ADAMS · MADAME SPIVY · VAL AVERY · HERBIE FAYE

Requiem For A Heavyweight (1962)
Seven years after the original version on TV's "Playhouse 90," the moving drama by writer Rod Serling came to the big screen with all of its impact intact. Anthony Quinn stars as faded boxer Mountain Rivera, faced with the end of his career in the ring and a trusted manager who bet against him and now needs his help. Jackie Gleason, Mickey Rooney, Julie Harris and Cassius Clay (Muhammad Ali), as Quinn's last ring opponent, also star. 86 min.
02-3153 *$19.99*

Charly (1968)
Cliff Robertson netted an Academy Award for his role as a retarded bakery worker who is transformed into a genius by experimental brain surgery. Scripted by Sterling Silliphant from the book "Flowers for Algernon"; with Claire Bloom, Leon Janney and Dick Van Patten. 103 min.
04-1315 Was $19.99 *$14.99*

Justine (1969)
Lush romantic drama, based on Lawrence Durell's famed novel, stars Anouk Aimee as the lustful wife of an Egyptian banker who uses her affairs to help a group fighting for pre-WWII Israel's independence. Co-stars Dirk Bogarde, Michael York. 116 min.
04-2035 Was $59.99 ❑*$29.99*

Medium Cool (1969)
Cinematographer Haskell Wexler's critically acclaimed directorial debut follows TV cameraman Robert Forster as he struggles to remain detached from the political and social upheaval that surrounds him during the 1968 Democratic Convention in Chicago. The unique, ultra-realistic drama, which was actually shot during the riots, co-stars Peter Bonerz, Verna Bloom. 110 min.
06-1182 Was $59.99 ❑*$14.99*

298 · DRAMA MOVIES UNLIMITED CALL · 1-800-4-MOVIES

The Prime Of Miss Jean Brodie (1969)
Maggie Smith earned an Academy Award for her portrayal of the eccentric, charismatic teacher at a '30s Edinburgh girls' school whose hopeless love for a married teacher and involvement in her "girls" lives leads to tragedy. Robert Stephens, Celia Johnson, Pamela Franklin co-star. 116 min.
04-2251 Was $79.99 ❑$19.99

The Learning Tree (1969)
Renowned photographer Gordon Parks wrote and directed this autobiographical tale of a black youth growing up in 1920s rural Kansas. Beautifully filmed and dramatically understated, the film stars Kyle Johnson, Alex Clarke, Dana Elcar. 107 min.
19-1581 Was $19.99 $14.99

A Dream Of Kings (1969)
Moving drama starring Anthony Quinn as a charismatic Greek immigrant in Chicago who tries to scrape together the funds needed to take his ailing son back to Greece. Irene Papas plays Quinn's shrewish wife, and Inger Stevens is a widow who falls for him. 111 min.
19-1668 $59.99

The Cardinal (1963)
Epic drama directed by Otto Preminger focuses on an Irish-American priest whose dedication carries him through the ranks to one of the highest seats of power within the Church. Fine performances from Tom Tryon, Romy Schneider, John Huston, Dorothy Gish, Burgess Meredith. 176 min.
19-2215 Letterboxed $29.99

Lord Of The Flies (1963)
Stranded without adults on a remote Pacific island when their plane crashes, a group of British schoolboys establish their own tribal "society," only to slide into hostility and savagery. Stunning film adaptation of William Golding's chilling book; directed by Peter Brook. 90 min.
22-5647 $29.99

Lord Of The Flies (1990)
This stirring new film version of William Golding's classic novel focuses on 24 military school students whose plane crashes on a deserted island. Left alone, the students fight for survival, against the elements and among themselves. Balthazar Getty and Chris Furrh star in this exciting, thought-provoking tale. 90 min.
53-1790 Was $89.99 ❑$14.99

Dutchman (1967)
Groundbreaking look at race relations based on the heralded play by LeRoi Jones. On a New York subway, a middle-class African-American man carries on a discussion with a white woman that eventually leads to a heated debate about race and rights and eventually turns violent. Al Freeman, Jr. and Shirley Knight star; directed by Anthony Harvey ("The Lion in Winter"). 55 min.
50-5290 Was $59.99 $19.99

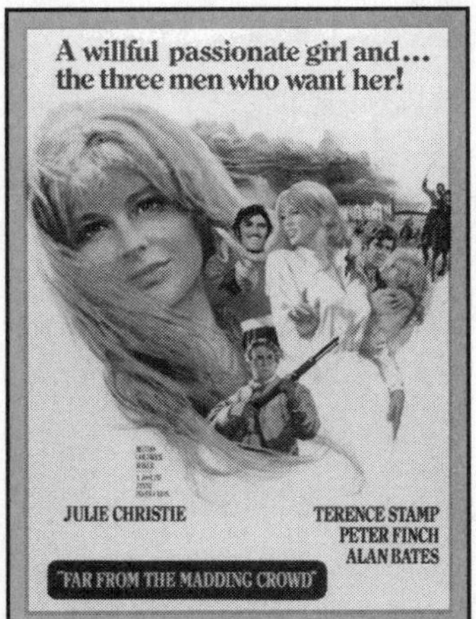

Far From The Madding Crowd (1967)
Thomas Hardy's novel about a young British farmgirl and her effect on the men who fall in love with her is wonderfully brought to the screen by director John Schlesinger. Julie Christie, Terence Stamp, Peter Finch, Alan Bates star; Nicolas Roeg served as cinematographer. 169 min.
12-1969 Was $29.99 $24.99

Far From The Madding Crowd (Letterboxed Version)
Also available in a theatrical, widescreen format.
12-3183 $24.99

Far From The Madding Crowd (1998)
A tragic tale of love and destruction set in 19th-century England, this adaptation of Thomas Hardy's famous novel concerns three men who pursue the same woman, with tragic consequences. With Paloma Baeza, Nigel Terry, Jonathan Firth. 208 min.
08-8660 ❑$29.99

The Loneliness Of The Long-Distance Runner (1962)
Classic "angry young man" movie from director Tony Richardson chronicles rebellious British teenager Tom Courtenay's experiences in a reformatory, where he finds long-distance running an outlet for his anger and defiance. Michael Redgrave, Avis Bunnage and Peter Madden co-star. 104 min.
19-1952 Was $19.99 $14.99

Girl On A Motorcycle: Collector's Edition (1968)
This erotic favorite features Marianne Faithfull as Rebecca, a housewife whose bored lifestyle prompts her to don a leather outfit, hop on a motorcycle and ride across Europe to boyfriend Alain Delon's house. During the journey, she recalls her scorching experiences with Delon. This is the complete, uncensored European version, which had been originally rated X in America until it was edited and released under the title "Naked Under Leather." 91 min.
27-6349 Letterboxed $14.99

The Servant (1963)
Dirk Bogarde is superb as a scheming valet who is hired by a weak-willed playboy to oversee his house, but begins to take over his employer's life for his own gain. James Fox, Sarah Miles co-star in this compelling drama from director Joseph Losey and scripter Harold Pinter (who appears in a cameo). 112 min.
44-1062 $14.99

Darling (1965)
Julie Christie won the Academy Award for Best Actress for her portrayal of Diana, a stunning model who climbs the social ladder by using her looks and jumping from bed to bed. Cynical, insightful film which captures a mood distinctly '60s. Co-stars Dirk Bogarde and Laurence Harvey. 122 min.
53-1513 $19.99

The Christine Keeler Affair (1964)
Before 1988's "Scandal" came this look at the events that rocked Britain, which was filmed in Denmark and banned in England. The film chronicles party girl Christine Keeler's involvement with a Russian emissary and the British minister of war. John Drew Barrymore, Yvonne Buckingham and Alicia Brandet star. AKA: "The Keeler Affair," "Scandal '64."
50-5135 Was $24.99 $19.99

Scandal (1989)
The infamous Profumo Affair, a 1963 governmental sex scandal that rocked Britain, is brought to the screen in an erotic, controversial drama. Joanne Whalley-Kilmer and Bridget Fonda are the teenagers who become party girls for Cabinet ministers and Parliamentarians; with Ian McKellen, Jeroen Krabbe, John Hurt and Britt Ekland. Unrated version; 114 min.
44-1661 Letterboxed $14.99

Rome Adventure (1962)
Romance and lush locales highlight this story of love set against the picturesque splendor of Rome. Suzanne Pleshette plays the American librarian who travels to the Eternal City to find romance and, after a relationship with a distinguished native (Rossano Brazzi), falls for American art student Troy Donahue. With Angie Dickinson, Constance Ford and Al Hirt. 119 min.
19-1844 Was $19.99 ❑$14.99

The Magnificent Matador (1955)
Compelling drama set in the world of bullfighting, with Anthony Quinn starring as a renowned matador who mysteriously "turns yellow" in the ring after introducing his young protégé. With the aid of American admirer Maureen O'Hara, Quinn faces his fears and a dark secret in his past. Budd Boetticher directs. 94 min.
23-5011 $19.99

Coming Apart (1969)
A time capsule of '60s sexuality as well as early independent cinema, Milton Moses Ginsberg's offbeat drama stars Rip Torn as a successful, adulterous New York psychiatrist. Setting up a hidden camera (by which most of the film is viewed) in a mirrored apartment, Torn coldly chronicles a series of sexual encounters with various women—among them former patient Sally Kirkland and ex-mistress Viveca Lindfors—and, eventually, his own mental breakdown. 111 min.
53-6077 Letterboxed $79.99

Crackshot (1968)
Exciting crime drama with a pre-"Hawaii Five-O" Jack Lord starring as a treasury agent who goes undercover to break a "funny money" ring. With Mercedes McCambridge, Jack Weston, Shirley Knight and Joseph Wiseman. AKA: "Counterfeit Killer." 95 min.
76-7008 $19.99

Bonjour Tristesse (1958)
Otto Preminger's compelling drama stars David Niven and Jean Seberg as a father-daughter pair of fun-seeking sybarites living on the Riviera, with Deborah Kerr as the lonely widow whose relationship with Niven ultimately leads to tragedy. 94 min.
02-1843 Was $19.99 $14.99

The Member Of The Wedding (1952)
Moving film adaptation of Carson McCullers' play. Julie Harris (25 when the movie was made) shines as an awkward 12-year-old girl who tries to grow up too quickly during her brother's impending marriage. Fine support from Brandon De Wilde, Arthur Franz, Nancy Gates and Ethel Waters. 91 min.
02-1845 Was $69.99 $19.99

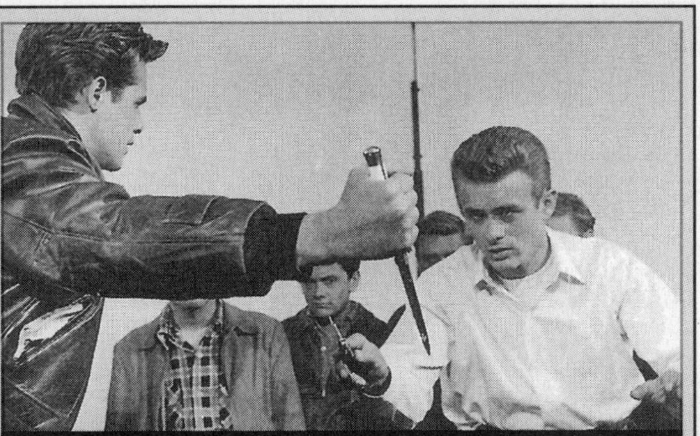
Rebel Without A Cause

James Dean

Hill Number One (1951)
Here's a truly rare find: James Dean in an early TV appearance, playing John the Baptist! This inspirational drama is about a platoon commander who uses a Biblical allegory to get his troops to take a hill. Leif Erickson, Gene Lockhart, Roddy McDowall also star. 53 min.
10-7947 $14.99

Abraham Lincoln (1952)
Robert Pastene stars as Lincoln in this TV biodrama from "Westinghouse Studio One" covering the years from his election in 1860 to his assassination five years later. The highlight, though, is a scene featuring 21-year-old James Dean as a soldier sentenced to die for dereliction of duty. 60 min.
09-1894 Was $24.99 $14.99

James Dean's Lost TV Appearance: The Trouble With Father (1952)
Here's a rare find no James Dean fan should miss: an early role for the film icon in the popular '50s Stu Erwin sitcom. On screen for a brief scene, Dean and a young Martin Milner play teenagers discussing the difficulties in getting a date(!). This print includes original commercials. 30 min.
82-1052 $14.99

A Long Time Till Dawn (1953)
Originally broadcast on "Kraft TV Theatre," this drama features James Dean in a story of an ex-con who tries to turn his life around now that he's out of prison. With Robert Simon, Naomi Riordan. 53 min.
10-9323 $14.99

Harvest (1953)
The time of the harvest also marks the time of a restless young man's search for his place in the world in this moving episode from "Robert Montgomery Presents" featuring a pre-film star James Dean, along with Dorothy Gish, Ed Begley and John Dennis. 53 min.
10-9326 $14.99

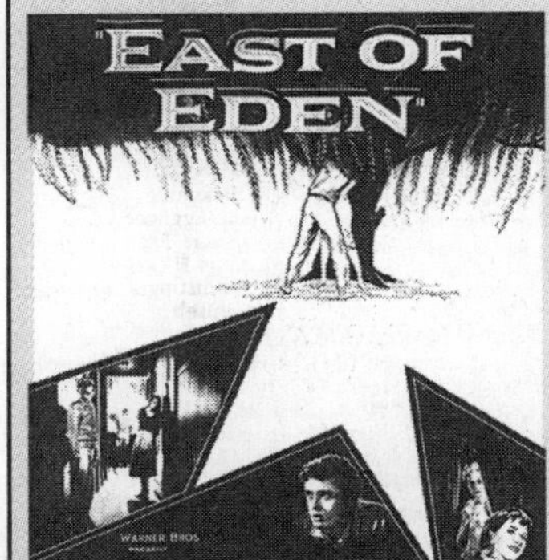

East Of Eden (1955)
In one of the most memorable starring debuts in Hollywood history, James Dean plays a troubled teen in California's Salinas Valley embroiled in a bitter rivalry with twin brother Richard Davalos for the attention of their farmer father (Raymond Massey) and the love of a neighbor (Julie Harris). With Jo Van Fleet, Burl Ives; Elia Kazan directs. 115 min.
19-1028 ❑$24.99

Rebel Without A Cause (1955)
James Dean became a national symbol for '50s teen angst with this powerful character study of an alienated young man who deals with rejection at school and inattentiveness from his parents by finding friendship with fellow outcasts Sal Mineo and Natalie Wood. With Jim Backus, Dennis Hopper; Nicholas Ray directs. Special edition includes the theatrical trailer, rare screen tests, and interviews from the "Warner Bros. Presents" TV series. 140 min. total.
19-2445 $19.99

Rebel Without A Cause (Letterboxed Version)
Also available in a theatrical, widescreen format.
19-2505 ❑$19.99

Giant (1956)
Sprawling drama of two generations in a wealthy Texas cattle clan, with Rock Hudson as the headstrong family head, Elizabeth Taylor as his wife, and James Dean (in his final film) as the ranch hand in love with Taylor. Carroll Baker, Dennis Hopper, Sal Mineo also star; George Stevens directs. Restored home video version includes newsreel footage of the movie's premieres and a special introduction by George Stevens, Jr. 201 min.
19-2480 Letterboxed ❑$24.99

Giant (Collector's Special Edition)
This limited-edition boxed set features the restored, letterboxed version of the film, the acclaimed documentary "George Stevens: A Filmmaker's Journey" and a book on the making of "Giant."
19-2481 Limited Quantities! ❑$49.99

The James Dean Story (1957)
Robert Altman's documentary on the life of James Dean. Rare photos, footage, interviews and home movies are utilized in this fascinating account on the life of this enigmatic star. 80 min.
07-8006 $14.99

Forever James Dean (1988)
Here's the definitive look at the late screen icon, which features rare TV commercials, screen tests and interviews with friends and associates, plus theatrical trailers for "East of Eden," "Rebel Without a Cause" and "Giant." 69 min.
19-1786 Was $29.99 ❑$14.99

James Dean: A Portrait
This informative and fascinating look at one of Hollywood's most revered icons features rarely seen photos, film footage from early TV dramas and Dean's own home movies. Also showcased are screen and wardrobe tests for "Giant" and other films, plus anecdotes from cohorts Dennis Hopper, Rod Steiger, Sal Mineo and Eli Wallach. 55 min.
22-1538 $19.99

James Dean And Me
The life and career of the brooding screen idol who went on, after his death at the age of 24, to become an icon for a generation are traced through rare film clips, photographs from the James Dean estate, and recollections from Dennis Hopper, Eartha Kitt, Rod Steiger and others. 50 min.
22-1556 $19.99

James Dean At High Speed
They were his driving passion and, ironically, wound up costing Hollywood legend James Dean his life. Trace the film star's lifelong love affair with sports cars and racing in this revved-up documentary that features never-before-seen footage of Dean's racing career and interviews with friends and fellow drivers, and lets you get behind the wheel of a replica of Dean's Porsche Spyder. 50 min.
22-1557 $19.99

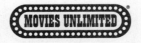

Rock Hudson

The Lawless Breed (1952)
In his first starring role, Rock Hudson plays famed frontier badman John Wesley Hardin. Director Raoul Walsh's well-crafted western biodrama follows Hardin's descent into outlaw status after killing a man in self-defense, the woman who tried to get him to change his life, and the son whom Hardin sought to stop from following in his footsteps. Julia Adams, John McIntyre and Lee Van Cleef also star. 83 min.
07-2633 □*$14.99*

Gun Fury (1953)
Fine Raoul Walsh Western thriller about a Civil War vet who must search the Arizona wilderness when his fiancée is kidnapped by outlaws. Rock Hudson, Donna Reed, Phil Carey and Lee Marvin star. 83 min.
02-1684 *$14.99*

Magnificent Obsession (1954)
Classic "three-hanky" melodrama from producer Ross Hunter, starring Rock Hudson as a playboy whose drunken ways lead to Jane Wyman's losing her husband and her sight. A repentant Hudson becomes a surgeon in order to restore Wyman's vision and falls in love with her, concealing his identity, along the way. With Barbara Rush, Otto Kruger; Douglas Sirk directs. 108 min.
07-1292 Was $59.99 *$14.99*

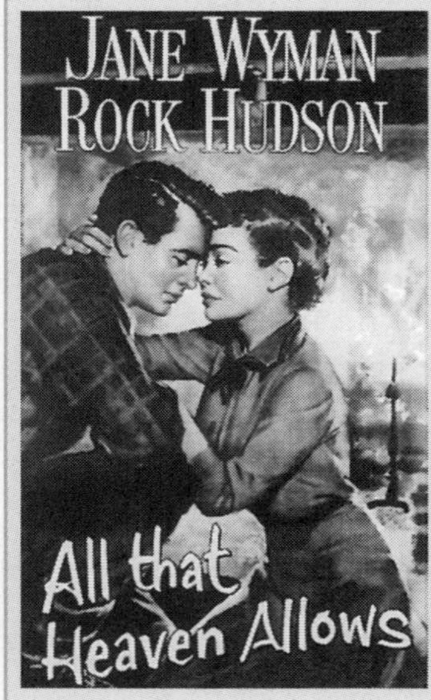

All That Heaven Allows (1955)
Producer Ross Hunter reunited "Magnificent Obsession" stars Rock Hudson and Jane Wyman and director Douglas Sirk for this lush romance in which small-town widow Wyman is drawn to handsome gardener Hudson, a man 15 years her junior, and faces scandal and scorn from her friends and family. With Agnes Moorehead, Gloria Talbot, Conrad Nagel. 89 min.
07-2525 □*$14.99*

Written On The Wind (1956)
Sweeping Douglas Sirk melodrama traces the lives, loves, and tragedies of a Texas oil family. Rock Hudson stars as the "adopted son" whose attraction to Lauren Bacall, the wife of spoiled scion Robert Stack, leads to a violent confrontation. Dorothy Malone also stars in an Oscar-winning turn as a drunken, promiscuous daughter, along with Robert Keith, Grant Williams. 97 min.
07-1582 *$14.99*

A Farewell To Arms (1957)
Hollywood legend David O. Selznick's final film as producer was this lush retelling of Ernest Hemingway's story of love and loss in World War I. Jennifer Jones (Selznick's wife) plays the British nurse who falls for wounded American ambulance driver Rock Hudson. With Vittorio De Sica, Mercedes McCambridge, Oscar Homolka.
04-1357 *$14.99*

Battle Hymn (1957)
Based on a true story, director Douglas Sirk's moving drama stars Rock Hudson as Dean Hess, an American WWII pilot who became a minister after the war and, during the Korean conflict, went to Asia to care for orphaned children. With Martha Hyer, Dan Duryea, Don DeFore. 109 min.
07-2393 □*$14.99*

The Tarnished Angels (1958)
William Faulkner's novel "Pylon" was the basis for this glossy and atmospheric Douglas Sirk drama starring Robert Stack and Dorothy Malone as barnstorming airplane daredevils in the 1930s South and Rock Hudson as a cynical reporter who becomes their ally. With Jack Carson, Robert Middleton. 91 min.
07-2396 □*$14.99*

Come September (1961)
Colorful romantic comedy stars Rock Hudson as an American businessman who arrives early for his annual September stay at his Italian villa and is shocked to find that the caretaker has been renting it out to vacationers, among them sexy Gina Lollobrigida. With Sandra Dee, Bobby Darin, Walter Slezak; look for a young Joel Grey. 114 min.
07-2391 *$14.99*

Man's Favorite Sport? (1963)
A renowned fishing "expert" (Rock Hudson) who's never had a rod and reel in hand finds himself in deep water when an attractive PR woman he's hooked on asks him to enter a major fishing tournament. Screwball comedy from Howard Hawks also stars Paula Prentiss, John McGiver and Regis Toomey. 121 min.
07-1490 Was $59.99 *$14.99*

A Gathering Of Eagles (1963)
Rock Hudson gives a bravura performance as a Strategic Air Force commander whose dedication to his duty puts a strain on his relationship with wife Mary Peach. Rod Taylor, Barry Sullivan co-star. 115 min.
07-2524 *$14.99*

Strange Bedfellows (1965)
When the tempestuous marriage of London-based American oil executive Rock Hudson and wife Gina Lollobrigida threatens his landing an important promotion, Hudson hires PR man Gig Young to smooth things over in this saucy comedy. With Terry-Thomas, Nancy Kulp. 99 min.
07-2392 *$14.99*

Seconds (1966)
Considered a cult classic, director John Frankenheimer's innovative, sci-fi-flavored drama follows bored, middle-aged New York businessman John Randolph as he meets with a mysterious company that offers him a new life in a younger body. "Reborn" as handsome artist Rock Hudson, he soon begins having second thoughts about the arrangement, but finds there may be no going back. With Will Geer, Salome Jens, and eerie cinematography by James Wong Howe. Foreign theatrical version; 107 min.
06-2574 □*$89.99*

Ice Station Zebra (1968)
Epic espionage adventure about a real Cold War at the North Pole, as a U.S. crew on a nuclear submarine confronts Soviet seamen in a search for a Russian satellite lodged in an ice cap. Rock Hudson, Patrick McGoohan, Jim Brown and Ernest Borgnine star in this adaptation of Alistair MacLean's novel. (Said to be the favorite film of Howard Hughes.) 148 min.
12-1859 *$29.99*

Hornets' Nest (1970)
World War II adventure starring Rock Hudson as an Army officer who enlists the help of young Italian Resistance fighters to blow up an important dam controlled by the Nazis. Sylva Koscina and Sergio Fantoni also star in this rugged military tale. 110 min.
12-2830 *$79.99*

Pretty Maids All In A Row (1971)
Written by "Star Trek's" Gene Roddenberry and directed by Roger Vadim, this dark, acerbic comedy stars Rock Hudson as a football coach/counselor adept at seducing his high school's cheerleaders. Hudson begins showing a student his techniques, but when his conquests turn up dead, he becomes a suspect. With Angie Dickinson, Telly Savalas, John David Carson and James Doohan. 93 min.
12-2995 □*$19.99*

Showdown (1973)
Rock Hudson and Dean Martin are old friends who split up when Hudson marries Martin's former girlfriend. Later, the two confront each other, as Rock, now a sheriff, hunts down criminal Dean after a train robbery. Susan Clark and Donald Moffat also star in this surefire western adventure. 99 min.
07-2035 □*$14.99*

Embryo (1976)
Rock Hudson is a brilliant scientist experimenting with genetics in this frightening sci-fi yarn. Gorgeous Barbara Carrera is the female newborn he produces, a superwoman who must be taught about the world. AKA: "Created to Kill." 103 min.
27-6112 *$19.99*

Please see our index for these other Rock Hudson titles: *Bend Of The River • Giant • Here Come The Nelsons • Lover Come Back • The Mirror Crack'd • Pillow Talk • Send Me No Flowers • Tomahawk • The Undefeated • Winchester '73*

Beneath The 12-Mile Reef (1953)
It's "Romeo and Juliet" among the risk-taking sponge divers of the Florida coast, with Robert Wagner and Terry Moore as the young lovers who come from rival diving families. Thrilling underwater scenes, including a battle with an octopus, highlight this drama. Gilbert Roland, Richard Boone, Peter Graves also star. 101 min.
10-1120 Was $19.99 *$14.99*

Beneath The 12-Mile Reef (Letterboxed Version)
Also available in a theatrical, widescreen format.
65-3005 *$19.99*

The Browning Version (1951)
Powerful drama about a downtrodden language teacher at an English public school who is forced for health reasons to step down from his position prematurely. Compounding his pain are the actions of his wife, who carries on an affair with one of the school's younger teachers. Superior performances from stars Michael Redgrave, Jean Kent and Wilfrid Hyde-White. 90 min.
22-5534 Was $39.99 *$19.99*

The Browning Version (1994)
This acclaimed version of Terence Rattigan's classic play stars Albert Finney as a classics professor, both respected and hated by his peers, confronted by major changes in his life when he faces retirement and with the fact that his wife has fallen in love with one of his young colleagues. Greta Scacchi, Matthew Modine and Julian Sands also star. 97 min.
06-2299 Was $89.99 □*$19.99*

Time Lock (1957)
It's Friday afternoon and a young boy becomes trapped in an airtight bank vault which won't open until Monday morning. With Robert Beatty, Betty McDowell and, in a small role, Sean Connery. 73 min.
27-6414 *$19.99*

Love Of Three Queens (1954)
Fascinating curio stars Hedy Lamarr in four roles, as a woman going to a costume party imagines herself as Helen of Troy, Empress Josephine and Genevieve de Brabant. Her sensual portrayals show us each woman's differences and similarities. With Massimo Serato; directed by Marc Allegret ("Lady Chatterley's Lover") with assist from Edgar G. Ulmer. In black-and-white. 90 min.
62-1341 *$19.99*

Four In A Jeep (1953)
A beautiful European refugee in post-WWII Vienna, whose husband escaped from a Russian prison camp, becomes involved with four M.P.s who are part of the multinational peace-keeping force. Viveca Lindfors, Ralph Meeker star. 95 min.
45-5155 *$24.99*

The Blue Lamp (1950)
Tense British crime drama about the killing of a Scotland Yard policeman in the course of duty and the manhunt that follows. Dirk Bogarde, in an early role, is truly frightening as the killer on the run. Jack Warner, Patrick Doonan co-star. 82 min.
53-6014 *$29.99*

Yellowneck (1954)
A group of Civil War deserters seek freedom, but first must survive the rugged Florida Everglades. Lin McCarty and Stephen Courtleigh star. 83 min.
53-6028 *$29.99*

A Cry From The Street (1959)
Heart-tugging tale of two welfare workers who help a group of homeless kids. Max Bygraves, Barbara Murray and Colin Peterson star in this sensitive drama, directed by Lewis Gilbert ("Educating Rita"). 100 min.
53-6030 Was $29.99 *$19.99*

Mambo (1955)
Silvana Mangano turns in a scorching, emotion-packed performance as a beautiful, poor woman caught between kindly, terminally ill nobleman Michael Rennie and seedy older businessman Vittorio Gassman. Mangano is magnificent at the mambo, and Shelley Winters plays the instructor who turns her into a dance star. Robert Rossen ("The Hustler") directs. 93 min.
53-6036 *$19.99*

Woman In A Dressing Gown (1957)
Superior acting highlights this domestic drama about a middle-aged housewife whose attempts at making life more comfortable for her distraught husband fail, leading him to have an affair with a young secretary. Anthony Quayle, Yvonne Mitchell and Sylvia Sims star; directed by J. Lee Thompson ("The Guns of Navarone"). 93 min.
53-6265 *$29.99*

The Bigamist (1953)
Deceit and adultery highlight this drama, directed by and featuring Ida Lupino. A travelling salesman marries and impregnates a lonely cook, while his wife has hopes of adopting her own child. Edmond O'Brien, Joan Fontaine and Edmund Gwenn comprise the stellar cast. 79 min.
53-7361 *$19.99*

Pandora And The Flying Dutchman (1951)
Strikingly photographed romantic fantasy starring Ava Gardner as an icy woman whose affections are desired by three different men: her current fiancé, a race car driver; her former lover, a matador; and the ghostly Dutch captain of a ship, condemned to sail the seven seas. James Mason, Nigel Patrick and Harold Warrender also star. 122 min.
53-8334 *$19.99*

The Bermuda Affair (1956)
Two Korean War buddies-turned-airline partners discuss their lives and reveal some intimate secrets and indiscretions when they find themselves in a failing plane with only one parachute. Gary Merrill, Ron Randell, Zena Marshall, Kim Hunter star. 88 min.
63-6077 Was $29.99 *$19.99*

A Dangerous Age (1957)
A juvenile flees boarding school to sample the trials of adulthood with her sullen-but-sexy lover. Director Sidney Furie outlasted this dangerous age in his career to make "The Ipcress File." Stars Anne Pearson, Ben Piazza. 70 min.
68-8408 Was $19.99 *$14.99*

Suspended Alibi (1957)
Hard-hitting study from England about a man who gets more than he bargained for when he breaks off his affair with a beautiful woman. When he asks a friend to help him with an alibi, strange things begin to take place. Patrick Holt and Honor Blackman star. 64 min.
68-8429 *$19.99*

Norman Conquest (1953)
A detective, after being drugged and framed for murder, soon discovers that the beautiful femme fatale behind the deed is involved in a gem smuggling ring with a former Nazi. Tom Conway, Eva Bartok, Anton Diffring and Ian Fleming star. 75 min.
68-8758 *$19.99*

One Too Many (1950)
A high-budget social drama by legendary B-movie producer Kroger Babb, with Ruth Warrick starring as a concert pianist and mother who suffers from alcoholism and watches her need for drink destroy her health, her career and her family. With Richard Travis, Ginger Price, Onslow Stevens. AKA: "Killer with a Label." 110 min.
68-8846 *$19.99*

Men Of Two Worlds (1952)
Unusual British-made drama about an African-born musician who returns to his home village to help colonial authorities free his people from a witch doctor's grip of fear and superstition. Robert Adams, Eric Portman, Phyllis Calvert star. AKA: "Kisenga, Man of Africa." 90 min.
68-8853 *$19.99*

The Sleeping Tiger (1954)
Leaving America during the McCarthy era, director Joseph Losey helmed this British thriller that starred Dirk Bogarde as a petty crook who is sheltered by a psychiatrist planning to use him as a "guinea pig," until Bogarde seduces his wife. Intriguing psychological drama also stars Alexander Knox, Alexis Smith. 89 min.
53-7189 Was $19.99 *$14.99*

The Sun Shines Bright (1953)
John Ford directed this reworking of his 1934 classic "Judge Priest." A respected Kentucky judge with a love of the old South must overcome prejudice and political scandal in order to defeat a Yankee carpetbagger in an upcoming election. Charles Winninger, Arleen Whelan, John Russell and Stepin Fetchit star. 100 min.
63-1376 *$19.99*

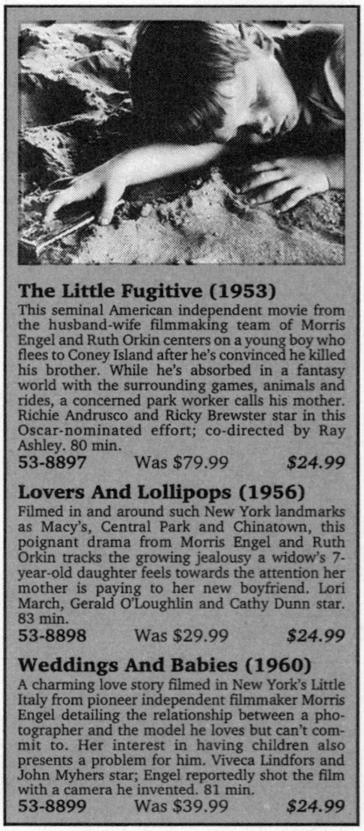

The Little Fugitive (1953)
This seminal American independent movie from the husband-wife filmmaking team of Morris Engel and Ruth Orkin centers on a young boy who flees to Coney Island after he's convinced he killed his brother. While he's absorbed in a fantasy world with the surrounding games, animals and rides, a concerned park worker calls his mother. Richie Andrusco and Ricky Brewster star in this Oscar-nominated effort; co-directed by Ray Ashley. 80 min.
53-8897 Was $79.99 *$24.99*

Lovers And Lollipops (1956)
Filmed in and around such New York landmarks as Macy's, Central Park and Chinatown, this poignant drama from Morris Engel and Ruth Orkin tracks the growing jealousy a widow's 7-year-old daughter feels towards the attention her mother is paying to her new boyfriend. Lori March, Gerald O'Loughlin and Cathy Dunn star. 83 min.
53-8898 Was $29.99 *$24.99*

Weddings And Babies (1960)
A charming love story filmed in New York's Little Italy from pioneer independent filmmaker Morris Engel detailing the relationship between a photographer and the model he loves but can't commit to. Her interest in having children also presents a problem for him. Viveca Lindfors and John Myhers star; Engel reportedly shot the film with a camera he invented. 81 min.
53-8899 Was $39.99 *$24.99*

Blackboard Jungle (1955)
Richard Brooks' gritty look at life inside the inner-city high school stars Glenn Ford as the earnest teacher determined to reach his hood students. Great support from Sidney Poitier, Anne Francis, Vic Morrow, Louis Calhern; soundtrack includes historic film debut of "Rock Around the Clock." 110 min.
12-1943   ☐$19.99

The Savage Eye (1959)
Documentary-styled drama centering on a recently divorced middle-aged woman who struggles for her independence and to make a new life for herself in Los Angeles after her marriage dissolves. Barbara Baxley, Gary Merrill and Herschel Bernardi star; co-directed by Joseph Strick and partly photographed by Haskell Wexler. 64 min.
53-6061 $29.99

Three Crooked Men (1958)
A trio of crooks looking to rob a bank by breaking into it from an adjoining store get more than they bargained for when the store's owner, then a passing stranger, show up, forcing the robbers to take both men hostage. British crime drama stars Gordon Jackson, Warren Mitchell. 73 min.
10-9792 $19.99

The Next Voice You Hear (1950)
The voice claims to be that of God, and a simultaneous worldwide radio broadcast would lend credence to the assertion. James Whitmore and Nancy Davis (Reagan) are the average American couple whose response to the voice's message is the focus of this unusual drama. 82 min.
12-2082 $19.99

The Strange One (1958)
The cadets of a Southern military school are kept under the thumb of a sadistic older student (Ben Gazzara, in his film debut) who uses fear and intimidation to get his way in this powerful filming of Calder Willingham's play "End as a Man." With George Peppard, Pat Hingle, Larry Gates. 100 min.
02-3101 $19.99

Island In The Sun (1957)
Political dealings, forbidden romances and racial tension threaten to explode on a peaceful West Indies island in this steamy drama based on Alec Waugh's novel. The stellar cast includes Harry Belafonte, Joan Collins, Dorothy Dandridge, Joan Fontaine, James Mason and Michael Rennie. 119 min.
04-3564 $14.99

The Search For Bridey Murphy (1956)
Based on the factual best-selling book, this thriller stars Teresa Wright as a housewife who, under hypnosis, discovers she lived a previous life in 19th-century Ireland. Louis Hayward, Nancy Gates and Kenneth Tobey also star. 84 min.
06-1862   ☐$14.99

The Atomic City (1952)
Nuclear-themed crime thriller with Gene Barry as a government scientist whose son is abducted by terrorists demanding a top-secret formula as ransom. Barry teams with the FBI to try to track down the culprits. Lydia Clarke, Michael Moore, Nancy Gates co-star. 85 min.
06-2040   ☐$12.99

Three Coins In The Fountain (1954)
Fine performances, gorgeous location shots of Rome and Venice, and the Oscar-winning title tune (sung by an unbilled Frank Sinatra) mark this romantic favorite that follows three American women (Dorothy McGuire, Maggie McNamara, Jean Peters) living in Italy on their search for true love. With Rossano Brazzi, Louis Jourdan, Clifton Webb.
04-2284 $19.99

MGM's DRAMA AFLAME WITH LOVE AND REVOLT!

BHOWANI JUNCTION
The famed novel filmed in Pakistan
3 years in Production Cast of thousands

AVA GARDNER   STEWART GRANGER

Bhowani Junction (1956)
One of Ava Gardner's finest outings, this romantic adventure features the actress as a young Anglo-Indian woman who finds romance and political strife as she returns to India during the British evacuation. Stewart Granger, Bill Travers and Abraham Sofaer also star; George Cukor directs. 110 min.
12-2307 $19.99

Champion

Kirk Douglas

My Dear Secretary (1948)
Romantic comedy about author Kirk Douglas, an easy-going man who meets his match in Laraine Day, a secretary whose first book becomes a bestseller. Co-stars Rudy Vallee, Keenan Wynn. 86 min.
10-1064   Was $19.99 $14.99

Champion (1949)
Powerful drama based on a story by Ring Lardner and set amid the world of pro boxing. In a breakthrough performance, Kirk Douglas plays a young man who reluctantly enters the ring and quickly rises to the top, while using the people who help him and falling under the Mob's influence. With Marilyn Maxwell, Arthur Kennedy. 100 min.
63-1729   ☐$14.99

Champion (Color Version)
Boxer Kirk Douglas scores a colorful knockout in this special techno-tinted version of the ring classic.
63-1414 $14.99

Young Man With A Horn (1950)
Classic melodrama stars Kirk Douglas as a driven trumpet player who devotes his life to music, to the exclusion of almost everything else. Doris Day and Lauren Bacall are the women in his life; Harry James performed Douglas' tunes. 112 min.
19-1575 $19.99

Along The Great Divide (1951)
Gripping frontier drama stars Kirk Douglas as a taciturn lawman who must get his man, in order to save an innocent man from the gallows. Stars John Agar, Walter Brennan, Virginia Mayo; spectacular outdoor scenes highlight this Raoul Walsh saga. 88 min.
19-1569 $14.99

The Big Trees (1952)
Kirk Douglas stars in this rousing adventure saga that takes place in a lumberjack community. Action, romance, excitement. Eve Miller, Edgar Buchanan. 89 min.
10-1081   Was $19.99 $14.99

The Bad And The Beautiful (1952)
Kirk Douglas is a tyrannical, ruthless producer whose climb up the ladder is recalled by three associates: starlet Lana Turner, director Barry Sullivan, and writer Dick Powell. Vincente Minnelli's barbed look at the Golden Age of Hollywood also features Gloria Grahame, Walter Pidgeon, Gilbert Roland. 118 min.
12-1025   Was $29.99   ☐$19.99

The Racers (1955)
Rookie race car driver Kirk Douglas attempts to break into the European racing circuit, but his success is threatened when his "win at all costs" attitude alienates those around him. Compelling drama, featuring exciting racing footage, also stars Bella Darvi, Lee J. Cobb, Gilbert Roland. 112 min.
04-2393   ☐$39.99

Man Without A Star (1955)
Kirk Douglas stars as a range-roaming cowboy who hires on as a hand on greedy rancher Jeanne Crain's spread, but faces an inner struggle when she asks to take part in a range war to increase her herd. Co-stars Richard Boone, Claire Trevor; directed by King Vidor. 89 min.
07-1265 $14.99

Ulysses (1955)
It's high adventure, Homer-style, with Kirk Douglas as the brave adventurer who battles the one-eyed Cyclops, encounters sorceress Circe (who turns his crew into pigs), and ignores the sounds of the Sirens before he returns home to win back the hand of wife Penelope. Anthony Quinn and Silvana Mangano also star; Ben Hecht and Irwin Shaw worked on the script. 110 min.
19-1470 $19.99

Lust For Life (1956)
Masterfully rendered filming of the biography of Vincent Van Gogh, with Kirk Douglas offering one of his finest performances as the tortured artistic genius. Vincente Minnelli directs; with Oscar-winning support by Anthony Quinn as Gauguin. 122 min.
12-1929 $19.99

The Devil's Disciple (1959)
George Bernard Shaw's barbed play is transformed into a sparkling satire of British colonialism set in New Hampshire in 1777. Kirk Douglas is a rowdy revolutionary who seeks help from local pastor Burt Lancaster in getting revenge for the death of his father by the leader of the British forces (Laurence Olivier). With Janette Scott and Eva La Galliene. 82 min.
12-2503 $19.99

Town Without Pity (1961)
In a small German town after World War II, four American soldiers stationed there are charged with raping a local teenage girl. Army attorney Kirk Douglas, brought in to defend the GIs in court, tries to save them from execution by attacking the victim's character in this controversial courtroom drama. With E.G. Marshall, Christine Kaufmann, Robert Blake, Frank Sutton; Gene Pitney sings the hit title song. 103 min.
12-3017   ☐$19.99

Lonely Are The Brave (1962)
Kirk Douglas plays a middle-aged cowboy who is thrown in jail when trying to help a friend and an exciting chase ensues upon his escape. Classic "new style" Western stars Gena Rowlands, Walter Matthau. 107 min.
07-1266 $19.99

The Heroes Of Telemark (1965)
In Nazi-occupied Norway, Resistance fighter Richard Harris and scientist Kirk Douglas are supposed to help British commandos take out a German factory involved in heavy water production for atomic weapon research, but are forced to try and destroy the facility themselves, in Anthony Mann's gripping WWII actioner. With Michael Redgrave, Anton Diffring. 130 min.
02-2988 $19.99

Cast A Giant Shadow (1966)
Exciting, star-studded epic focusing on the life of Mickey Marcus, the American war hero recruited by Israel to help strengthen their army against warring Arabs after the country gained its independence in 1948. Kirk Douglas turns in a steely, charismatic performance as Marcus, supported by John Wayne, Frank Sinatra, Angie Dickinson, Yul Brynner and Senta Berger. 142 min.
12-2797 $19.99

The Way West (1967)
A sprawling Western about pioneers on the Oregon Trail starring Kirk Douglas as a widowed senator and Robert Mitchum as a scout who oversees the wagon train and faces problems involving Indians and passengers aboard the train. Richard Widmark, Lola Albright and Sally Field (in her screen debut) also star. 122 min.
12-2680 $14.99

The Brotherhood (1968)
A gripping, pre-"Godfather" look at Mafia life, with Kirk Douglas as a middle-aged hood whose loyalty to the "old ways" pits him against ambitious younger brother Alex Cord and puts them in a bitter feud. With Irene Papas, Luther Adler. 96 min.
06-1518   Was $19.99 $14.99

The Arrangement (1969)
Elia Kazan's look at the amoral practices of Madison Avenue stars Kirk Douglas as an ad man who re-evaluates his life, family and job. Deborah Kerr, Faye Dunaway, Richard Boone co-star. 126 min.
19-1433   Was $59.99 $19.99

A Gunfight (1971)
Kirk Douglas and Johnny Cash are two legendary gunfighters who meet for the first time near the end of their careers, and decide to stage and promote a showdown between them, with paying spectators. Fine supporting performances by Keith Carradine, Karen Black and Jane Alexander. 95 min.
67-5018 $19.99

The Master Touch (1972)
Kirk Douglas stars as a safecracking expert just released from jail who undertakes a "foolproof" plan to rob a bank of a million dollars in this cracking crime thriller. 95 min.
46-5087 $14.99

Jacqueline Susann's Once Is Not Enough (1975)
Ultra-trashy fun based on Susann's novel about the doings, deceptions and degradations of the jet-set. Deborah Raffin stars as a young girl with a father fetish; also stars Kirk Douglas, David Janssen and Brenda Vaccaro. 121 min.
06-1303   Was $59.99 $14.99

Posse (1975)
Kirk Douglas produced, directed and stars in this political Western about a sly sheriff who goes after a notorious outlaw in order to win favor with the townsfolk. Then he discovers that the outlaw is more ornery than he thought...and the townsfolk are on the bad guy's side. Bruce Dern, Bo Hopkins and James Stacy co-star. 92 min.
06-1720   ☐$12.99

Victory At Entebbe (1976)
Exciting re-creation of the July 4, 1976 Israeli commando raid on the Ugandan airport where hijacked hostages were being held by Palestinian terrorists. Kirk Douglas, Richard Dreyfuss, Linda Blair, Elizabeth Taylor, Anthony Hopkins, Burt Lancaster, Theodore Bikel and Helen Hayes are featured in this all-star account of the rescue. 119 min.
19-2235   Was $19.99 $14.99

A BRIAN DePALMA FILM

The Fury

The Fury (1978)
Mind-blowing masterpiece about two young people's deadly gift of telekinesis—and an evil government agency that tries to control them. Brian DePalma directs Kirk Douglas, Amy Irving, Andrew Stevens, John Cassavetes. 118 min.
04-1061   Was $19.99 $14.99

The Man From Snowy River (1982)
From Australia comes this big, beautiful epic of a young man who sets out to tame a bunch of wild horses on a trek through the Australian wilderness. Kirk Douglas is on hand for two roles. Jack Thompson. 104 min.
04-1566   Was $19.99 $14.99

Diamonds (1999)
Making a bravura return to the screen, Kirk Douglas plays an aging ex-boxer (like Douglas, recovering from a stroke) who tires of living with his son's family in Canada. A visit from another son, sportswriter Dan Aykroyd, leads Douglas to talk him and grandson Corbin Allred into joining him in a trip to Nevada to look for a hidden fortune in gems that will allow Douglas to live independently. Lauren Bacall and Jenny McCarthy also star in this funny and tender road movie. 90 min.
11-2447   ☐$99.99

Please see our index for these other Kirk Douglas titles: 20,000 Leagues Under The Sea • Greedy • Gunfight At The O.K. Corral • In Harm's Way • Is Paris Burning? • A Letter To Three Wives • The List Of Adrian Messenger • Paths Of Glory • Spartacus • The Strange Love Of Martha Ivers • There Was A Crooked Man... • The Villain • The War Wagon

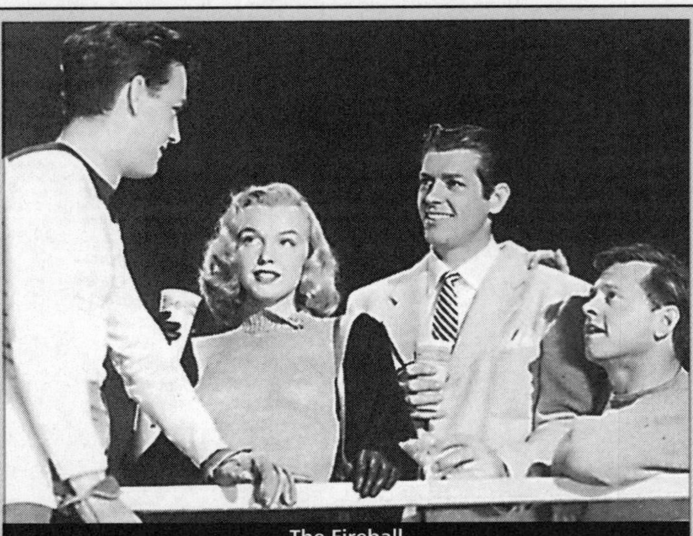

The Fireball

Marilyn Monroe

Ladies Of The Chorus (1948)
In her second film, Marilyn Monroe plays a burlesque showgirl who is wooed by a wealthy bachelor. But her dancer mother (Adele Jergens) is against the romance because it reminds her of a situation that she was in years earlier. With Rand Brooks, Nana Bryant; songs include "Anyone Can Tell I Love You." 61 min.
02-2209 *$19.99*

The Asphalt Jungle (1950)
A gang of small-time crooks plans and executes the "perfect crime" in this gritty, trend-setting drama co-written and directed by John Huston. Sterling Hayden, Sam Jaffe, Jean Hagen and (in one of her first major roles) Marilyn Monroe star. 111 min.
12-1513 *$19.99*

The Fireball (1950)
The nationwide interest, thanks to TV, in roller derby during the late '40s and '50s led to this offbeat sports drama starring Mickey Rooney as a feisty orphan who becomes a top skater, with an ego to match, until he's stricken with polio. In an early film role, Marilyn Monroe co-stars as a derby groupie who's attracted to Rooney, and Pat O'Brien plays, of all things, a caring priest. 84 min.
19-2434 *$19.99*

As Young As You Feel (1951)
Lively social comedy starring Monty Woolley as an elderly man who loses his job at a printing company, then poses as the president of the outfit to get it back. David Wayne, Thelma Ritter, Albert Dekker and a young Marilyn Monroe (as a secretary) co-star in this winner based on a Paddy Chayefsky story. 77 min.
04-2531 *$14.99*

Let's Make It Legal (1951)
Mirthful marital farce about a woman who divorces her husband of 25 years, much to the chagrin of their daughter. When the woman's former boyfriend enters the picture, the daughter tries to keep them apart. Claudette Colbert, Macdonald Carey, Barbara Bates, Robert Wagner and Marilyn Monroe star. 77 min.
04-2532 *$14.99*

Love Nest (1951)
A soldier returns to civilian life to discover his dreams of becoming a writer are shattered when he and his wife buy an apartment building and see their time occupied by servicing tenants' needs. Among the renters are a shady Casanova, and a sexy young woman and her husband. William Lundigan, June Haver, Marilyn Monroe, Jack Paar and Frank Fay star in this domestic farce. 77 min.
04-2534 *$14.99*

Home Town Story (1951)
Defeated politician Jeffrey Lynn tries to prove that corrupt "big business" has taken over City Hall, only to have a change of heart, in a drama produced with the cooperation of General Motors. With Donald Crisp, Alan Hale, Jr. and an early appearance by Marilyn Monroe. 61 min.
10-7549 *$19.99*

Don't Bother To Knock (1952)
Taut psychological thriller that benefits by the offbeat casting of Marilyn Monroe as an emotionally disturbed woman hired to babysit at a hotel. Richard Widmark is a hotel guest whose chance encounter with Monroe leads to a desperate fight to save a child's life. With Lurene Tuttle, Jim Backus and Anne Bancroft (her film debut). 76 min.
04-2527 *❑$14.99*

We're Not Married (1952)
Comic anthology about an elderly judge who discovers some of the marriage ceremonies he performed were not valid. Among the couples involved: new parents David Wayne and beauty queen Marilyn Monroe; bickering radio stars Ginger Rogers and Fred Allen; millionaire Louis Calhern and sneaky wife Zsa Zsa Gabor; soldier Eddie Bracken and pregnant spouse Mitzi Gaynor; and Eve Arden and Paul Douglas, who's considering adultery. 85 min.
04-2533 *❑$14.99*

Gentlemen Prefer Blondes (1953)
Showgirls Marilyn Monroe and Jane Russell set sail for Paris on an ocean liner with the goal of landing some eligible millionaires in the lively musical/comedy based on Anita Loos' play. With Charles Coburn, Tommy Noonan, and Monroe's legendary "Diamonds Are a Girl's Best Friend" number. 91 min.
04-1064 *$14.99*

How To Marry A Millionaire (1953)
Delicious comedy about three man-crazed women searching for eligible (and wealthy) bachelors. Marilyn Monroe, Lauren Bacall, Betty Grable and William Powell star. 95 min.
04-1401 *$14.99*

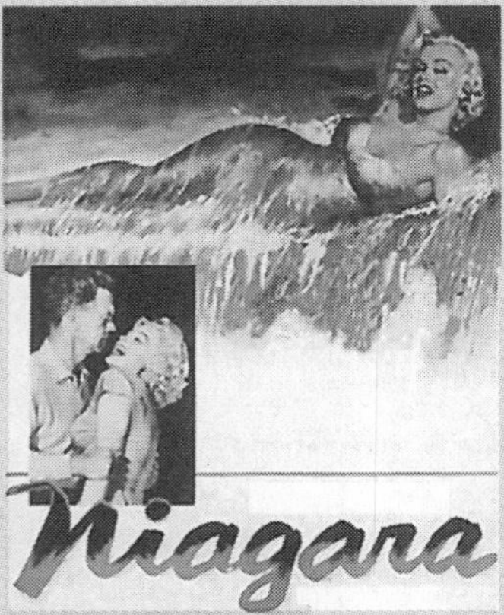

Niagara (1953)
Taut tale of romance, deception and murder, with Marilyn Monroe in a rare unsympathetic role as a scheming wife who plots her husband's death with her lover...but her plan backfires, with tragic results. With Joseph Cotten, Richard Allen and Jean Peters. 89 min.
04-2079 *$14.99*

There's No Business Like Show Business (1954)
And there's no musical like this grand salute to the songs of Irving Berlin. Classic Berlin tunes like the title song, "A Pretty Girl Is Like a Melody" and "You'd Be Surprised" are woven around the story of a close-knit vaudeville family. Ethel Merman, Dan Dailey, Donald O'Connor, Mitzi Gaynor and Marilyn Monroe star. 117 min.
04-1160 *❑$19.99*

River Of No Return (1954)
Gripping Gold Rush saga stars Marilyn Monroe as a saloon singer searching for her runaway husband with the aid of widowed trailhand Robert Mitchum. Spectacular rafting action sequences are not to be missed. Rory Calhoun, Tommy Rettig co-star under Otto Preminger's direction. 91 min.
04-2081 *$14.99*

The Seven Year Itch (1955)
Billy Wilder's delightful comedy about (imagined) adultery stars Tom Ewell as the happily married man who finds himself tempted by upstairs neighbor Marilyn Monroe while his wife is on vacation. Marilyn's famous "standing on the subway grate" scene is a highlight; with Evelyn Keyes, Sonny Tufts. 105 min.
04-1141 *$14.99*

The Prince And The Showgirl (1957)
Laurence Olivier and Marilyn Monroe essay the title roles in this period romantic comedy set in 1910 England. Olivier also directed the film, based on a play by Terence Rattigan. 117 min.
19-1209 Was $19.99 *$14.99*

Some Like It Hot (1959)
Jack Lemmon and Tony Curtis are two musicians who witness a mob hit, then escape by disguising themselves as women and joining an all-female band. You'll roar with delight at the twosome's antics, and savor Curtis' attempts to woo the gorgeous Marilyn Monroe. Billy Wilder's classic co-stars George Raft, Pat O'Brien and Joe E. Brown. 120 min.
12-3199 Was $19.99 *$14.99*

Let's Make Love (1960)
Engaging comedy concerning a millionaire (Yves Montand) who's determined to shut down a stage show that's burlesquing him...until he falls for cast member Marilyn Monroe! Tony Randall, Wilfrid Hyde-White co-star under George Cukor's direction; cameos by Bing Crosby, Gene Kelly. 118 min.
04-2082 *$14.99*

The Misfits (1961)
Engrossing drama that follows an aging cowboy and a runaway divorcee trying to rediscover a sense of purpose in the New West. Clark Gable and Marilyn Monroe star in their screen farewells; Montgomery Clift, Thelma Ritter, Eli Wallach co-star. John Huston directs Arthur Miller's screenplay. 124 min.
12-1117 Was $19.99 *❑$14.99*

Say Goodbye To The President: Marilyn And The Kennedys (1985)
The controversial BBC documentary that American networks refused to run. Was Marilyn Monroe's death linked to a Hollywood scandal? To the Mob? To the President of the United States? Never-before-seen interviews and evidence bring the screen goddess' last days into focus. 71 min.
55-1156 Was $19.99 *$14.99*

We Remember Marilyn
Marilyn Monroe's life and career are feted in this documentary that uses clips and rare footage to tell the story of the Hollywood sex siren. Along with footage from "The Misfits," "Some Like It Hot" and others, there's rare photos, the original screen test for "The Asphalt Jungle" and more. 120 min.
05-5092 *$19.99*

Marilyn: The Last Word
Produced by the people behind "Hard Copy" and hosted by Terry Murphy and Barry Noonan, this program looks at the life and death of America's greatest sex symbol. Explored are the lurid events surrounding her demise and the fatal link between Monroe, the Kennedys and mobster Sam Giancana. 57 min.
06-2271 *❑$19.99*

Marilyn Monroe Scrapbook
A revealing glimpse of the screen's unsurpassed sex symbol through rare interviews and news footage, a screen test, and original trailers for many of her classic films. 60 min.
10-7425 *$19.99*

Marilyn Monroe: Beyond The Legend
A revealing look at Marilyn Monroe's incredible, short-lived career and her troubled life, boasting home movies, film clips and commentary from Robert Mitchum, Shelley Winters, Susan Strasberg and others. Richard Widmark narrates. 60 min.
50-6792 Was $24.99 *$14.99*

Marilyn Monroe: The Early Years
Witness the transformation of a young actress named Norma Jean into a phenomenom known as Marilyn Monroe, one of Hollywood's most popular and most tragic stars. Friends like Robert Mitchum and Jane Russell recount their memories of her, while rare photos and personal letters help tell her story. 50 min.
50-4394 *$14.99*

Marilyn Monroe 3-Pack
Gentlemen may prefer blondes, but everyone prefers saving money, and that's just what you'll do with this special collector's set featuring "Gentlemen Prefer Blondes," "The Seven Year Itch" and "Let's Make Love."
04-3016 *$39.99*

Please see our index for these other Marilyn Monroe titles: *All About Eve • Clash By Night • Love Happy • Monkey Business*

Life At Stake (1955)
In this atmospheric drama, a builder is hired to construct a house for a pretty blonde woman and her husband, who's putting out the cash in the deal. The builder doesn't trust the husband, especially after he's asked to take out an insurance policy while he works. Angela Lansbury, Keith Andes and Douglas Dumbrille star in this noirish tale. 78 min.
10-9355 *$19.99*

The Big Chase (1954)
Glenn Langan, the star of "The Amazing Colossal Man," plays a neophyte cop on the juvenile beat, wary of getting a promotion because of his wife's fears and the imminent birth of his first child. But Langan soon finds himself in trouble anyway when he tries to capture a payroll thief in Mexico. Adele Jergens, Lon Chaney, Jr. also star. 60 min.
10-9458 *$14.99*

The Fearmakers (1958)
Korean War veteran Dana Andrews returns home after a harrowing experience being brainwashed as a POW and returns to his job at a Washington, D.C., public relations firm. He soon discovers that his partner has been mysteriously murdered and the company taken over by Communists. Intriguing Cold War tale features Marilee Earle, Dick Foran and Mel Tormé; directed by Jacques Torneur ("Cat People"). 83 min.
10-9780 *$14.99*

Peyton Place (1957)
One of the all-time favorite Hollywood melodramas, based on Grace Metalious' best-selling novel, takes a steamy look at the romantic secrets lurking behind the closed doors of a seemingly staid and quiet New England town in the '40s. The all-star cast includes Lana Turner, Lee Philips, Russ Tamblyn, Diane Varsi, Hope Lange, Arthur Kennedy. 157 min.
04-2422 Was $19.99 *❑$14.99*

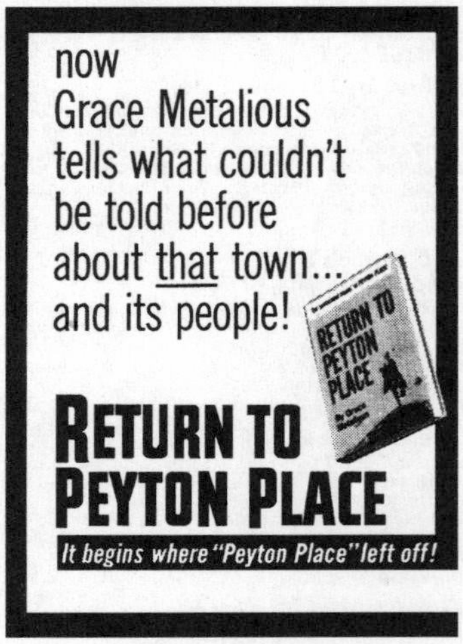

Return To Peyton Place (1961)
Writer Carol Lynley visits the hometown whose residents served as the basis for her novel, only to find that her brutally realistic depictions have turned all of Peyton Place against her and her father. Glossy sequel to the hit soaper, laced with romantic subplots, also stars Mary Astor, Robert Sterling, Tuesday Weld, Jeff Chandler, Eleanor Parker. 123 min.
04-2423 *❑$39.99*

Lonelyhearts (1958)
Montgomery Clift is the newspaper reporter whose temporary transfer to the "advice to the lovelorn" column begins to take over his personal life in this dramatic adaptation of the Nathanael West story. Myrna Loy, Maureen Stapleton, Robert Ryan co-star. 104 min.
12-1656 Was $24.99 *$19.99*

September Affair (1950)
Joan Fontaine and Joseph Cotten star in a classic soaper of two people who meet and fall in love on a New York-Rome flight. When they're mistakenly listed as victims of a plane crash, they decide to start new lives together. Melodrama also stars Jessica Tandy, Francoise Rosay. 104 min.
06-1622 Was $19.99 *$14.99*

The Young Caruso (1951)
A musical biography of singer Enrico Caruso made in Italy starring Ermanno Randi and Gina Lollobrigida. 77 min.
09-1195 Was $29.99 *$24.99*

The Black Tower (1950)
The story of a down-and-out medical student who kills and robs in order to get cash. Peter Cookson. 54 min.
09-1641 Was $19.99 *$14.99*

Johnny One-Eye (1950)
Damon Runyon's story inspired this crime drama about an amiable gangster who sets out to find a former partner who fingered him for a five-year-old murder. During his search, the gangster is helped by a young woman, whom he falls in love with, and her trusted dog. Pat O'Brien, Wayne Morris and Gayle Reed star. 74 min.
53-6054 Was $19.99 *$14.99*

Burt Lancaster

The Killers (1946)
Ernest Hemingway's short story served as the basis for this tough crime saga of a down-and-out boxer (played by the debuting Burt Lancaster) who is executed by two small-time criminals. Insurance investigator Edmond O'Brien looks into the pug's policy and uncovers his involvement with crooks and beautiful, double-crossing Ava Gardner. Directed by Robert Siodmak; remade in 1964. 103 min.
07-2610 □$14.99

Brute Force (1947)
Director Jules Dassin's powerful, noir-flavored prison drama stars Burt Lancaster as an embittered inmate who launches a desperate breakout scheme with his cellblockmates and Hume Cronyn as a power-crazed guard who revels in brutalizing the prisoners. Script by Richard Brooks; with Charles Bickford, Sam Levene, Ann Blyth, Howard Duff (his film debut). 95 min.
53-6334 $24.99

Criss Cross (1949)
Memorable "noir" thriller stars Burt Lancaster as an armored car driver whose affair with ex-wife Yvonne De Carlo forces him to help her husband, gangster Dan Duryea, in a heist. Slickly staged by director Robert Siodmak, the film also features Tony Curtis in his film debut, playing a gigolo. 98 min.
07-1558 Was $59.99 □$14.99

The Flame And The Arrow (1950)
Rousing adventure saga set in medieval Italy stars a swashbuckling Burt Lancaster as the leader of a rebel army; with Virginia Mayo, Robert Douglas. 88 min.
19-1571 Was $19.99 $14.99

Vengeance Valley (1951)
Offbeat sagebrusher in which Burt Lancaster becomes embroiled in a nasty feud with bad boy half-brother Robert Walker when he's accused of fathering an illegitimate child. Hoping to control Lancaster's stake in the family ranch, Walker joins forces with the woman's brothers to track down his sibling. Joanne Dru, John Ireland also star. 83 min.
12-2894 $19.99

Jim Thorpe—All-American (1951)
Superb biographical drama of the Native American super-athlete who won both the pentathlon and decathlon in the 1912 Olympics in Stockholm. Burt Lancaster delivers a fine performance as Thorpe, who battled alcoholism, fought prejudice and saw his medals taken away from him when the Olympic Committee discovered he played semi-pro sports. Charles Bickford, Phyllis Thaxter co-star. 107 min.
19-1936 $19.99

Come Back, Little Sheba (1952)
Moving melodrama, based on William Inge's play, stars Shirley Booth in an Academy Award-winning role as the frumpy, neglected wife of alcoholic doctor Burt Lancaster. Terry Moore is the boarder whose presence brings the couple to a dramatic change in their unhappy lives. 99 min.
06-1820 Was $19.99 $14.99

The Crimson Pirate (1952)
One of the all-time great buccaneer sagas, loaded with spectacular stunts, derring-do and good-natured fun. Burt Lancaster and Nick Cravat are the rugged privateers caught between two different sides in a struggle between islands in the Mediterranean. Eva Bartok, Torin Thatcher co-star. 104 min.
19-1570 Was $19.99 $14.99

From Here To Eternity (1953)
Classic drama of the men and women at a Pearl Harbor Army base shortly before the Japanese attack won eight Oscars, including Best Picture, Director and both supporting roles. Montgomery Clift is the rebellious officer, Burt Lancaster and Deborah Kerr the surf-swept lovers. With Donna Reed, Frank Sinatra, and Ernest Borgnine; directed by Fred Zinnemann. 118 min.
02-1724 $19.99

His Majesty O'Keefe (1953)
A colorful adventure starring Burt Lancaster as an American who helps the natives of a South Seas island modernize their technology and is soon considered a god by the tribe. After assimilating into the new environment, he marries a beautiful native girl and finds his new home threatened by white traders. Joan Rice and Andre Morell co-star. 92 min.
19-1974 Was $19.99 $14.99

Apache (1954)
One of the first Western films to show life from the Indians' point of view, with Burt Lancaster starring as an Apache warrior who continues to fight the Army for his peoples' rights after Geronimo's defeat. Jean Peters, John McIntire and Charles Buchinsky (Bronson) also star; Robert Aldrich directs. 91 min.
12-2167 Was $19.99 $14.99

The Rose Tattoo (1955)
Anna Magnani won an Oscar for her portrayal of a Sicilian-born widow in a small Louisiana fishing town whose faithfulness to her late husband is tested by the attentions of truck driver Burt Lancaster. With Ben Cooper, Marisa Pavan. 117 min.
06-1824 Was $19.99 □$14.99

The Kentuckian (1955)
Spirited adventure saga set in the 1820s, with Burt Lancaster (who also directed) as a widower who takes his young son with him on a journey from his native Kentucky to Texas. Along the way he visits his well-meaning relatives, frees and befriends a female bond-slave and is confronted by a nasty saloon owner. Donald MacDonald, Diana Lynn and Walter Matthau (in his film debut) co-star. 103 min.
12-2512 Was $19.99 $14.99

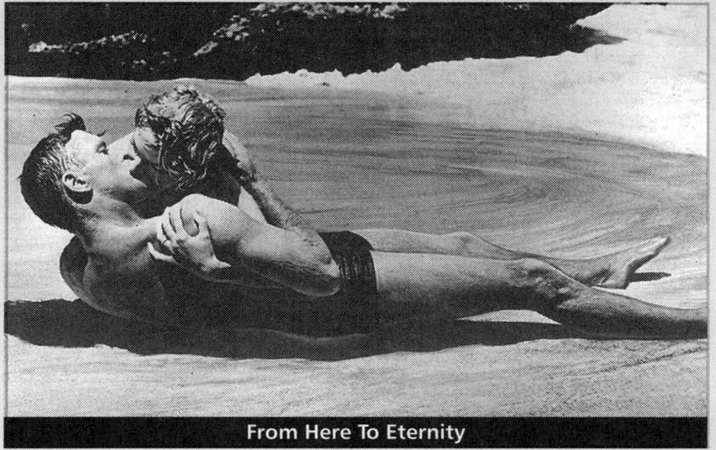

From Here To Eternity

Trapeze (1956)
Thrills and romance abound in this dazzling circus drama with Burt Lancaster as a former ace trapeze artist who becomes a mentor to would-be star Tony Curtis. Gina Lollobrigida plays the scheming tumbler for whom Tony falls, but who really loves Burt. Spectacular aerial stunt photography, expert performances and a real circus ambiance make this one soar. 105 min.
12-2514 $19.99

Gunfight At The O.K. Corral (1957)
Superbly mounted, landmark western that authentically depicts the famous showdown between Wyatt Earp and "Doc" Holliday and the Clanton Gang, while exploring the friendship between the rugged marshal (Burt Lancaster) and the dentist turned gunfighter (Kirk Douglas). Co-stars Rhonda Fleming, John Ireland; directed by John Sturges and written by Leon Uris. 122 min.
06-1024 □$14.99

Separate Tables (1958)
Exceptional version of the Terence Rattigan plays dealing with the hopes and heartbreaks of the occupants of a British seaside resort. Tremendous performances from Burt Lancaster, Rita Hayworth, Deborah Kerr and Oscar-winners David Niven and Wendy Hiller. 98 min.
12-2151 Was $19.99 $14.99

Elmer Gantry (1960)
A potent melodrama whose theme became ironically more timely as the years passed, Richard Brooks' adaptation of the Sinclair Lewis story stars Burt Lancaster as the silver-tongued salesman who joins evangelist Jean Simmons' entourage as a preacher, until his own vices doom him. Academy Awards went to Brooks, Lancaster, and Shirley Jones as Gantry's call girl ex-lover. 146 min.
12-1973 Was $19.99 $14.99

The Young Savages (1961)
Powerful drama from director John Frankenheimer ("The Manchurian Candidate") in which New York assistant D.A. Burt Lancaster is assigned to prosecute three teenage gang members for the stabbing death of a blind Puerto Rican youth. As Lancaster digs deeper into the case, he confronts political opportunism, racial prejudice and his own marital problems. Dina Merrill, Shelley Winters, Edward Andrews also star.
12-3090 $19.99

Birdman Of Alcatraz (1962)
Fascinating true story of Robert Stroud, the convict who spent his years in prison becoming a renowned authority on bird life. Burt Lancaster is superlative in the title role, and able support is given by Edmond O'Brien, Karl Malden, Thelma Ritter and Telly Savalas. Directed by John Frankenheimer. 143 min.
12-2233 Was $19.99 □$14.99

Seven Days In May (1964)
Sensational political thriller about a noble but weak president (Fredric March) whose nuclear disarmament treaty with the Soviets motivates a right-wing general (Burt Lancaster) to plot to overthrow the government. Kirk Douglas plays Lancaster's assistant, who accidentally learns of the coup and must stop it. With Ava Gardner, Edmond O'Brien. John Frankenheimer directs Rod Serling's script. 118 min.
19-2078 □$19.99

The Hallelujah Trail (1965)
Outrageous western satire about a Cavalry-guarded wagon train that must battle temperance union women, sandstorms and Indians to get its precious cargo, 40 wagons of whiskey, to Denver before the onset of winter. All-star cast includes Burt Lancaster, Lee Remick, Jim Hutton, Brian Keith, Pamela Tiffin. 155 min.
12-2203 Was $24.99 $14.99

The Train (1965)
In this riveting World War II tale, Burt Lancaster plays a railway engineer who enlists the help of members of the French Resistance to stop a train filled with art treasures that's being routed to Germany by the Nazis. Paul Scofield, Jeanne Moreau and Michel Simon also star in John Frankenheimer's exciting wartime thriller. 133 min.
12-2415 Was $19.99 □$14.99

The Professionals (1966)
Lusty, rousing tale about four soldiers of fortune (Burt Lancaster, Lee Marvin, Robert Ryan, Woody Strode) in the 1917 West hired by a cattle baron to rescue his kidnapped wife from a Mexican bandit. With Jack Palance, Claudia Cardinale, Ralph Bellamy. 117 min.
10-2613 $14.99

The Swimmer (1968)
Burt Lancaster stars as a middle-class exec who decides one afternoon to "swim" home through his neighbors' pools, encountering several truths about his life and some women from his past along the way. Unusual and emotional drama, based on John Cheever's short story, also features Kim Hunter, Janice Rule, Janet Landgard and Joan Rivers. 94 min.
02-2708 $14.99

The Scalphunters (1968)
Rousing Western adventure with Burt Lancaster as a not-too-bright fur trapper who teams with a runaway slave, played by Ossie Davis, to find the gang that swiped a batch of valuable pelts. Telly Savalas and Shelley Winters also star in this action-packed tale that features a brutal brawl in the mud. 103 min.
12-2069 $19.99

Castle Keep (1969)
Unusual WWII story from Sydney Pollack starring Burt Lancaster as a one-eyed U.S. Army major who leads a squad of misfit soldiers to an art-filled Belgian castle for some rest and relaxation. But the Americans are soon forced into helping the castle's owner, a count, when the Nazis attack. Peter Falk, Jean-Pierre Aumont, Al Freeman, Jr. and Bruce Dern also star.
02-3060 $19.99

Lawman (1971)
Provocative Western drama starring Burt Lancaster as a marshal who discovers that those responsible for hiring him to capture a group of murderous ranchers have turned against him. Robert Ryan, Lee J. Cobb, Sheree North and Robert Duvall also star. 95 min.
12-2709 Was $19.99 □$14.99

Lawman (Letterboxed Version)
Also available in a theatrical, widescreen format.
12-3232 $14.99

Valdez Is Coming (1971)
Rugged, guns-a-blazin' Western tale, adapted from an Elmore Leonard story, starring Burt Lancaster as a Mexican-American sheriff who kidnaps the wife of a wealthy rancher who has disgraced him. Susan Clark, Richard Jordan and Hector Elizondo also star. 90 min.
12-2712 Was $19.99 □$14.99

Scorpio (1973)
Expert globe-trotting espionage story stars Alain Delon as a hired assassin who is told that his associate, super CIA operative Burt Lancaster, is a double agent. A cat-and-mouse game around the world ensues, involving other agents and pitting crafty veteran Lancaster against young, slick Delon. Paul Scofield, John Colicos and Gayle Hunnicutt also star. 114 min.
12-2672 $14.99

Executive Action (1973)
Before Oliver Stone's "JFK," there was this underrated drama, based on the writings of Mark Lane, that explores the conspiracy theories behind the Kennedy assassination. Burt Lancaster, Robert Ryan, Will Geer star. 91 min.
19-1031 Was $19.99 $14.99

The Cassandra Crossing (1977)
Sophia Loren, Ava Gardner, Richard Harris and Burt Lancaster are four members of an all-star passenger list on board a trans-European train that has been contaminated with an infectious plague by terrorists. Co-stars Martin Sheen and O.J. Simpson as Father Haley. 132 min.
04-1027 $12.99

The Island Of Dr. Moreau (1977)
Burt Lancaster stars in the title role as H.G. Wells' deranged scientist, who uses his remote island as a base for experiments in creating half-human, half-animal monstrosities. Michael York is a shipwrecked sailor caught in Moreau's mad schemes, and Barbara Carrera is one of his subjects. 104 min.
19-1092 $14.99

Go Tell The Spartans (1978)
Powerful, overlooked Vietnam War drama set in 1964 during the early days of U.S. involvement. Burt Lancaster plays a cynical military advisor commanding a group of combat experts and recruits who disagrees with his higher-ups regarding the approach to stop the Viet Cong. Craig Wasson, Marc Singer and Evan Kim also star. 114 min.
44-1869 Was $19.99 $14.99

Atlantic City (1981)
Burt Lancaster is an aging gangster who finds excitement and love against the background of the changing resort town. Susan Sarandon is his lemon-freshened love interest. Louis ("Pretty Baby") Malle directs this offbeat thriller. 104 min.
06-1096 Was $79.99 □$14.99

Little Treasure (1985)
A dying man's last words send some unlikely treasure hunters on a search for a hidden fortune in this action- and laugh-filled comedy/adventure. Ted Danson, Burt Lancaster and Margot Kidder star in this wild and fun-filled romp. 95 min.
02-1518 Was $79.99 $19.99

Scandal Sheet (1985)
Cynical look at the seedy world of tabloid newspapers with Burt Lancaster as the publisher of a popular supermarket tab and Pamela Reed as the legit reporter who gets a rude indoctrination into sleazy journalism. With Lauren Hutton, Robert Urich. 120 min.
75-7035 Was $19.99 $14.99

On Wings Of Eagles (1986)
Riveting real-life story of billionaire H. Ross Perot's plan to hire a retired U.S. Army colonel to help rescue two of his employees, held in an Iranian prison shortly after the 1979 revolution. Burt Lancaster, Paul LeMat, Richard Crenna, Esai Morales star; based on Ken Follett's best-seller. 221 min.
14-3253 Was $24.99 $14.99

Control (1986)
What begins as a psychological experiment involving a group of people put in a fallout shelter turns into an all-too-real struggle to survive in this gripping drama. Burt Lancaster, Kate Nelligan, Ben Gazzara star. 83 min.
44-1521 Was $79.99 $14.99

Rocket Gibraltar (1988)
Heartfelt drama of an elderly man (Burt Lancaster) who, faced with imminent death, uses his birthday party as a chance to reunite his family and, with his grandchildren's help, to fulfill his dream of being set out to sea in a Viking ritual funeral boat. With John Glover, Suzy Amis, Patricia Clarkson, Macaulay Culkin. 100 min.
02-1911 Was $19.99 □$14.99

Burt Lancaster: Daring To Reach
A one-time circus acrobat who went on to become one of Hollywood's most beloved actors, Burt Lancaster was also one of the first stars to buck the studio system and form his own production company. Hear from friends and colleagues, including Sydney Pollack, Rhonda Fleming and Earl Holliman, and see clips from such Lancaster classics as "From Here to Eternity," "Elmer Gantry," "Atlantic City" and others. 62 min.
50-7597 $14.99

Please see our index for these other Burt Lancaster titles: *All My Sons • Buffalo Bill And The Indians • A Child Is Waiting • Field Of Dreams • Judgment At Nuremberg • Local Hero • Moses • The Rainmaker • Run Silent, Run Deep • Separate But Equal • Sorry, Wrong Number • Sweet Smell Of Success • Vera Cruz • Victory At Entebbe*

Ronald Reagan

Brother Rat (1938)
A trio of fun-loving cadets (Ronald Reagan, Wayne Morris, Eddie Albert) at the Virginia Military Institute must shape up in order to graduate with the rest of their class, but things get complicated when the secretly-married Albert learns his wife is expecting. Frenzied "buddy comedy" also stars Priscilla Lane, Jane Wyman. 89 min.
12-3025 □*$19.99*

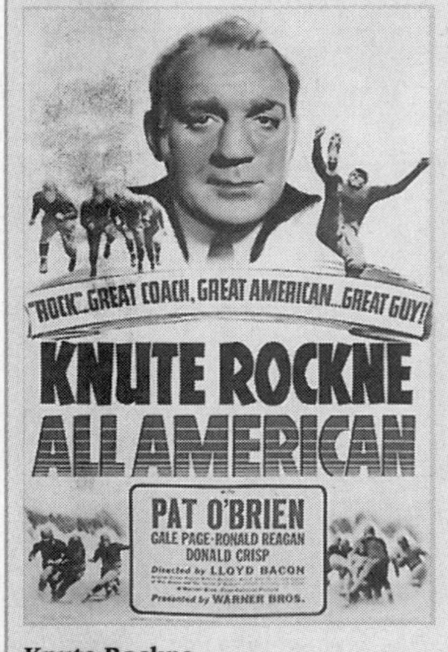

Knute Rockne— All American (1940)
Pat O'Brien's most famous role, the legendary Notre Dame football coach who revolutionized the game, makes this screen biography stand out. The cast includes Gale Page, Donald Crisp, several famous college and pro grid stars and, as "the Gipper," Ronald Reagan. 84 min.
12-1440 *$19.99*

Kings Row (1942)
A grand soap opera and one of the most-requested films at Movies Unlimited. Ronald Reagan (screaming "Where's the rest of me?" in his best screen role), Robert Cummings, Ann Sheridan, Betty Field, Claude Rains and a host of superb supporting players are involved in friendship, romance and tragedy in a small American town at the turn of the century. 127 min.
12-2375 □*$19.99*

The Hasty Heart (1949)
A sensitive WWII drama about an egocentric Scottish soldier (Richard Todd) unknowingly dying of a terminal disease while recuperating from a war injury in a Burmese hospital. American G.I. Ronald Reagan and nurse Patricia Neal attempt to befriend him, but his difficult manner keeps them at a distance. 101 min.
19-2225 *$19.99*

Cavalry Charge (The Last Outpost) (1951)
Two brothers find themselves on opposite sides in the frontier during the Civil War but join forces to save a Union fort from an Apache attack, in this well-mounted Western drama. Ronald Reagan, Bruce Bennett, Rhonda Fleming and Noah Beery, Jr. star. 88 min.
55-9011 Was $29.99 *$19.99*

The Winning Team (1952)
Ronald Reagan is Phillies and Cardinals pitching great Grover Cleveland Alexander in this powerful biography which traces his Hall of Fame career and his problems with alcoholism and epilepsy. Doris Day plays his long-suffering wife; Frank Lovejoy, Eve Miller and Rusty Tamblyn co-star. 98 min.
19-1945 Was $19.99 *$14.99*

Law And Order (1953)
Western drama stars Ronald Reagan as a marshal looking to retire with lady love Dorothy Malone, but forced to strap on his six-irons one last time to free a frontier town from the grip of outlaw leader Preston Foster, the man responsible for Reagan's brother's death. 80 min.
07-2397 □*$14.99*

Hellcats Of The Navy (1957)
Ronald Reagan and Nancy Davis (Reagan) made their only film appearance together in this WWII drama about a Pacific-based submarine and how a romantic triangle threatens its mission. With Arthur Franz. 82 min.
02-2697 *$14.99*

The Killers (1964)
After killing teacher John Cassavetes, curious hit man Lee Marvin delves into his target's past and uncovers a story of an armored car robbery, a dangerous love triangle and a fatal showdown. Director Don Siegel's adaptation of the Ernest Hemingway story, originally made for TV, also stars Angie Dickinson and, in his final film and only villainous role, Ronald Reagan. 95 min.
07-1040 Was $39.99 *$14.99*

Please see our index for these other Ronald Reagan titles: *Dark Victory • Desperate Journey • Santa Fe Trail • This Is The Army*

Captain Black Jack (1952)
Crime story stars Agnes Moorehead as a woman who poses as a socialite while supervising a drug-running operation from the Riviera. Other characters, like Herbert Marshall as a doctor, are up to more than you're led to believe. George Sanders also stars. 90 min.
17-9046 *$19.99*

Moulin Rouge (1952)
The colorful, tragic story of painter Toulouse-Lautrec and the residents of Paris' notorious Montmartre district whom he immortalized on canvas is masterfully told by director John Huston. Jose Ferrer stars as the deformed artist, with Zsa Zsa Gabor, Colette Marchand and Suzanne Flon as the women who filled his art and his life. 123 min.
12-1951 *$19.99*

Crowded Paradise (1956)
Gritty drama about a young Puerto Rican man who arrives in New York hoping to make it in America. After succeeding at landing a job and finding a fiancée, he faces adversity in the guise of his unpredictable, bigoted landlord. Hume Cronyn, Nancy Kelly and Mario Alcalde star in this effort, reminiscent of "On the Waterfront." 94 min.
08-5009 *$29.99*

The Torch (1950)
A romantic drama with some comic moments about a Mexican town controlled by a revolutionary who is both adored and disliked by the townspeople. The revolutionary falls in love with the daughter of the town's most prominent member and must prove his love to her. Paulette Goddard, Gilbert Roland and Pedro Armendariz star. 90 min.
08-5050 Was $19.99 *$14.99*

The Young Lovers (1950)
Ida Lupino made her directorial debut with this fascinating look at a dancer who tries to get her life back to normal after being stricken with a debilitating disease. While fighting depression and grueling physical therapy treatments, she becomes friendly with a fellow patient. Sally Forrest, Keefe Brasselle and Hugh O'Brian star in this powerful drama. AKA: "Never Fear." 81 min.
09-2966 *$19.99*

Castle In The Air (1952)
An earl whose fortune has diminished so much he must take in boarders is about to see his family castle turned into a youth hostel when a millionaire divorcée comes into his life with plans to marry him and buy the castle. Things get even more complex when one of the boarders wants to prove that the earl is the heir to the Scottish throne. David Tomlinson stars. 89 min.
09-5180 *$19.99*

If This Be Sin (1950)
Set on the Isle of Capri, this romantic drama stars Myrna Loy as a workaholic's wife whose flirtations attract an attractive younger man. Word of the relationship reaches Loy's husband and daughter, but she proves faithful by helping her husband when he falls ill. Peggy Cummins, Roger Livesey and Richard Greene also star. AKA: "That Dangerous Age." 70 min.
10-6003 *$14.99*

The Hoodlum (1951)
Tough guy Lawrence Tierney is a habitual criminal causing problems for all who come in contact with him and grief for his family members. But even Tierney crosses the line when he seduces his brother's girlfriend, then plots a robbery of the bank next to his sib's gas station. With Allene Roberts and Edward Tierney (Lawrence's real-life brother). 60 min.
10-6021 *$14.99*

The Bachelor Party (1957)
Paddy Chayefsky wrote this powerful drama, set in New York over the course of one night when a group of friends get together to celebrate one of their number's impending marriage with a bachelor party. Instead of fun, however, the guys ponder the mistakes they've made with women and in their lives. Don Murray, E.G. Marshall, Jack Warden, Larry Blydon star; Delbert Mann ("Marty") directs.
12-3095 *$19.99*

To Have And To Hold (1951)
Unusual melodrama from Hammer Films about a man handicapped in a fall from a horse who devotes his life to caring for his wife and daughter and actually persuades his spouse to seek affection from another man. Avis Scott, Patrick Barr and Robert Ayres star. 63 min.
10-1713 *$19.99*

Patterns (1956)
Incisive social drama from the pen of Rod Serling about ethics and big business stars Ed Begley as an aging executive, Van Heflin as his soon-to-be replacement and Everett Sloane as the company's ruthless head. 83 min.
10-2133 *$19.99*

Charade (1953)
Fascinating trilogy of tales about love and death performed, penned and produced by James and Pamela Mason. A lady artist falls for her mysterious subject; an Austrian officer is trapped in an unwinnable duel for a lady; and a maid enraptures a bored businessman who has abandoned his wealth. 83 min.
10-7215 Was $29.99 *$14.99*

Indiscretion Of An American Wife (1954)
American housewife Jennifer Jones engages in a brief encounter with her Italian lover (Montgomery Clift) on board a train and are detained by authorities in this melodrama from Vittorio De Sica; writers Carson McCullers, Alberto Moravia, Paul Gallico (each uncredited) and Truman Capote all had a hand in the script. 63 min.
08-8058 *$14.99*

The Basketball Fix (1951)
Sports drama details a basketball scandal centering on a hoop star whose involvement with seedy gamblers forces him to shave points on a big game. John Ireland, Marshall Thompson, Vanessa Brown star. 65 min.
17-9043 Was $19.99 *$14.99*

Devil On Horseback (1954)
British horsetrack drama detailing the adventures of a cocky English lad who rises from a street urchin on London's boondocks to a class jockey, only to fall because of his arrogance. Googy Withers and John McCallum star. 88 min.
09-2121 Was $29.99 *$14.99*

Outcasts Of The City (1958)
An American pilot whose plane is shot down during a bombing raid over Germany is sheltered by a war-weary woman. Their dangerous relationship leads to romance, but when her former lover arrives on the scene, trouble ensues. Osa Massen, Robert Horton star. 62 min.
09-2347 *$19.99*

Tall Timber (1950)
"Doc" Wheeler (Roddy McDowall) is a young tree surgeon, fresh out of school and yearning to get a job in the great outdoors. He joins a logging camp, but finds himself in trouble with veteran lumberjacks who think he's trying to take their jobs. With Jeff Donnell, Gordon Jones and Lyle Talbot. AKA: "Big Timber." 73 min.
09-2943 *$14.99*

Police Dog (1955)
Crime drama featuring Tim Turner as a policeman who is given a new partner after his is killed—an Alsatian dog. The cop and the canine team to find his old partner's killer. With Joan Rice and Jimmy Gilbert. 68 min.
09-5260 *$19.99*

The Devil's Pass (1957)
Popular character actor John Slater ("Passport to Pimlico") received a chance to star in this British drama, playing the stowaway on a fishing boat who helps the elderly skipper battle some nasty wreckers. Mervyn Jones also stars. 56 min.
09-5052 *$19.99*

The Winslow Boy (1950)
Top-notch British courtroom drama about a popular lawyer defending a young boy charged with stealing in school. Bristling dialogue and superior performances from Robert Donat, Cedric Hardwicke and Margaret Leighton mark this rendition of the play by Terence Rattigan; Anthony Asquith directs. 117 min.
08-5063 *$19.99*

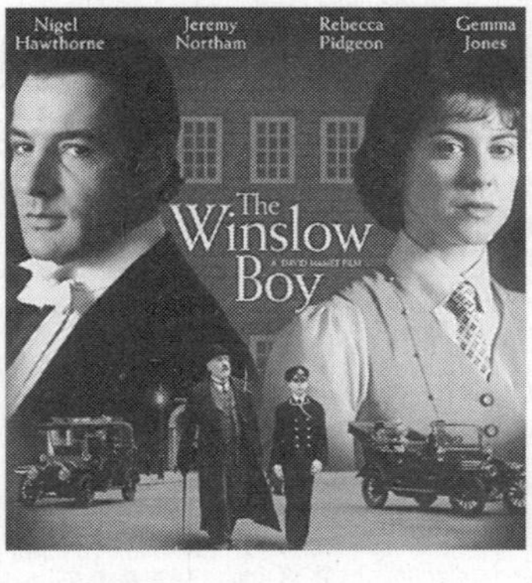

The Winslow Boy (1999)
Writer/director David Mamet's acclaimed adaptation of the Terence Rattigan play follows the true story of a 1910s English family whose teenage son is accused of theft and expelled from the Royal Naval Academy. Patriarch Nigel Hawthorne, convinced of his son's innocence, hires noted attorney Jeremy Northam to clear the boy's name, but the trial is overshadowed by the effect events have on the household...including a romance between Northam and Hawthorne's daughter, suffragette Rebecca Pidgeon. Gemma Jones, Guy Edwards also star. 110 min.
02-3403 Was $99.99 □*$21.99*

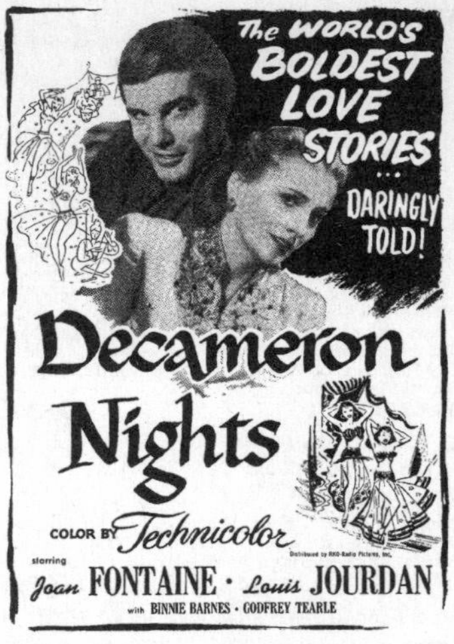

Decameron Nights (1953)
Louis Jourdan and Joan Fontaine star in three tales based on Boccaccio's legendary bawdy portrayals of medieval romance. A neglected wife is happy to be abducted by a lusty pirate, a husband wagers on his spouse's faithfulness, and a woman doctor plans to wed a king's courtier, against his protests. With Joan Collins, Binnie Barnes. 75 min.
10-1082 Was $19.99 *$14.99*

The Blue Peter (1959)
After being wounded in combat, an embittered man gets a job as athletic director at a boy's camp and finds a new purpose for living from working with the youngsters. Moving family drama stars Kieron Moore, Greta Gynt, Mervyn Johns and Anthony Newley as "Sparrow." AKA: "Navy Heroes." 93 min.
09-5008 *$19.99*

The Well (1951)
Intense "B"-drama look at prejudice in a small Texas town. A white man is jailed and charged with kidnapping a black girl, but racial tensions turn to mutual support when the girl is found alive, trapped in a well. Henry (later Harry) Morgan, Richard Rober star; score by Dimitri Tiomkin. 85 min.
08-1447 *$19.99*

The Miracle (1959)
When a Spanish nun decides to leave the convent to pursue the handsome soldier she has fallen in love with during the Napoleonic Wars, a statue of the Virgin Mary comes miraculously to life to take her place. Carroll Baker, Roger Moore, Walter Slezak, Vittorio Gassman star in this lavish, controversial drama. 120 min.
19-2133 *$19.99*

Bombers B-52 (1957)
Stunning aerial footage mixes with powerful family drama in this story of a veteran ground-crew chief and former Air Force flyer torn between his decision to retire and his love for his work. Karl Malden, Natalie Wood and Efrem Zimbalist, Jr. star. 106 min.
19-2219 Was $29.99 *$19.99*

-30- (1959)
Gritty newspaper drama with some strong similarities to "The Paper" stars Jack Webb as the managing editor of a big city daily who experiences personal and professional obstacles during the course of a day. While grappling with his wife about adopting a child, Webb covers stories about a missing girl and disappearing pilots. William Conrad, David Nelson co-star; Webb also directs. 96 min.
19-2262 *$19.99*

God's Little Acre (1958)
Erskine Caldwell's best-selling novel about the loves and lives of Georgia farmers receives a lusty adaptation with a superb cast: Robert Ryan, Tina Louise, Aldo Ray, Jack Lord, Michael Landon and Buddy Hackett; directed by Anthony Mann. 110 min.
10-1100 Was $19.99 *$14.99*

A Tale Of Five Women (1951)
An amnesiac British soldier is sent to America, where officials believe he belongs. But the New York family he's living with realizes he's from England and takes him to Europe to locate women from his past. Lana Morris, Barbara Kelly and Gina Lollobrigida star. AKA: "A Tale of Five Cities." 86 min.
17-9078 Was $19.99 *$14.99*

Two Dollar Bettor (1951)
Story about a young man's addiction to gambling, and how the innocent placing of small bets eventually leads to excessive wagering and the ruin of his life. John Litel, Marie Windsor, Steve Brodie, Carl "Alfalfa" Switzer and Barbara Billingsley star. 73 min.
17-9085 Was $19.99 *$14.99*

Train Of Events (1952)
Omnibus tale of the survivors of a British train wreck and how the event affects their lives. A driver contemplates his promotion, an actor heads for Canada with the body of his murdered wife, an orphan helps a German POW escape and a composer has a spat with his lover in this drama from Ealing Films featuring Peter Finch, Valerie Hobson and a slew of great English performers. 88 min.
53-6029 *$29.99*

Carnival Story (1954)
An American carnival on tour in Europe is the setting for this high-flying drama starring Anne Baxter as a German pickpocket who joins the show and is soon fought over by two workers. With Steve Cochran, Lyle Bettger. 95 min.
16-1084 *$19.99*

The Break In The Circle (1957)
Forrest Tucker stars as an American adventurer who gets more than he bargained for when he smuggles a Polish scientist to Hamburg on his boat. Eva Bartok, Marius Goring and Guy Middleton also star. 89 min.
17-9006 *$19.99*

The Capture (1950)
Set-in-Mexico drama starring Lew Ayres as an American oil company supervisor who shoots a man he suspects robbed the company's payroll, but discovers he's innocent. Complicating matters is the deceased man's widow (Teresa Wright), with whom Ayres has fallen in love. Victor Jory and Jacqueline White co-star. 81 min.
17-9009 Was $19.99 *$14.99*

Hollywood Thrillmakers (1953)
Inside scoop on Hollywood stuntmen focusing on a stunt expert who quits his dangerous job at his wife's insistence, then tackles a dangerous assignment so his friend's widow can collect $5,000 in insurance money. James Gleason, Bill Henry and Thelia Derin star. AKA: "Movie Stuntmen." 56 min.
17-9018 Was $19.99 *$14.99*

The Angel With A Trumpet (1950)
Sobering tale of a woman who marries the man her family has chosen for her, then discovers that her real lover has killed himself. Later, as the Gestapo is about to question her about her Jewish religion, she must make a decision about her life. Eileen Herlie, Basil Sydney, Maria Schell. 98 min.
17-9041 Was $19.99 *$14.99*

Woman's World (1954)
Corporate politics, as seen through the eyes of the wives of three auto executives brought to New York to vie for a sales manager position, is the theme of this glossy melodrama. The all-star cast includes Clifton Webb, Lauren Bacall, Fred MacMurray, June Allyson, Cornel Wilde, Arlene Dahl and Van Heflin; theme song performed by Philadelphia's own Four Aces. 94 min.
04-2922 □*$19.99*

Dance Little Lady (1955)
Tearjerker dance drama featuring Mai Zetterling as a prima ballerina who, after discovering about her husband's infidelities, has a near-fatal accident which finishes her career. The husband leaves Zetterling, but her daughter becomes a dance prodigy, hoping to follow in her mother's footsteps. Terence Morgan, Mandy Miller co-star. 87 min.
08-1753 *$14.99*

Emergency Call (1952)
Gripping drama about a young girl in desperate need of a transfusion of rare blood. The only possible providers are a black sailor about to embark on a trip to the Orient, a boxer in trouble for not fixing a big fight and a murderer who has been on the lam for years. Jack Warner, Anthony Steel star. AKA: "Hundred Hour Hunt." 92 min.
09-5245 *$19.99*

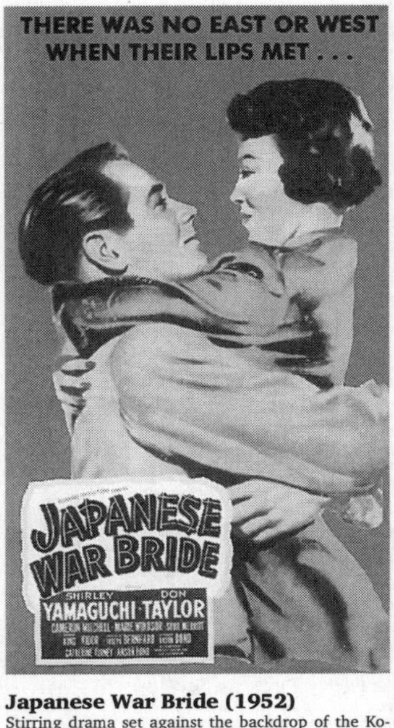
THERE WAS NO EAST OR WEST
WHEN THEIR LIPS MET . . .
JAPANESE WAR BRIDE
SHIRLEY YAMAGUCHI
DON TAYLOR

Japanese War Bride (1952)
Stirring drama set against the backdrop of the Korean War and focusing on Army officer Don Taylor, who's nursed back to health by young Japanese woman Shirley Yamaguchi. They fall in love and head to America, but soon find adversity from Taylor's relatives—particularly his scheming sister-in-law. Cameron Mitchell co-stars; directed by King Vidor. 90 min.
09-5270 *$19.99*

The Men (1950)
Marlon Brando's film debut is a riveting performance as an ex-WWII GI readjusting to life after becoming paralyzed in a wartime injury. Teresa Wright, Jack Webb. 85 min.
63-1026 □*$14.99*

A Streetcar Named Desire: The Director's Cut (1951)
Winner of four Oscars, Tennessee Williams' drama of lust and madness in New Orleans stars Marlon Brando as brutish Stanley Kowalski and Vivien Leigh as his sister-in-law, neurotic Southern belle Blanche DuBois. With Kim Hunter, Karl Malden. This newly restored edition features a digital soundtrack and four minutes of material which was cut by censors against director Elia Kazan's wishes. 125 min.
19-2203 Was $39.99 □*$19.99*

The Wild One (1954)
Marlon Brando wears leather and sneers like no one else can in the original biker drama, as a motorcycle gang terrorizes a small town until their violence turns member against member. "What are you rebelling against?" "What have you got?" Lee Marvin, Mary Murphy, Robert Keith co-star. 79 min.
02-1590 □*$19.99*

On The Waterfront (1954)
Winner of eight Academy Awards, this powerful, brilliantly performed saga focuses on the dreams, despair and corruption of New York City longshoremen. Marlon Brando, Rod Steiger, Lee J. Cobb, Karl Malden, Eva Marie Saint star under Elia Kazan's potent direction. 108 min.
02-1329 □*$19.99*

Desiree (1954)
Sumptuous costume drama stars Marlon Brando as a young Napoleon Bonaparte, just starting his rise to political power, and Jean Simmons as the wealthy merchant's daughter whom he is haunted by throughout his turbulent life. With Michael Rennie, Merle Oberon. 110 min.
04-2119 □*$19.99*

The Teahouse Of The August Moon (1956)
Whimsical, poignant adaptation of the hit Broadway play about an American G.I.'s experiences in Okinawa in 1944. Marlon Brando plays the slick native interpreter with a way of getting what he wants. Glenn Ford, Paul Ford, Eddie Albert and Machiko Kyo offer memorable supporting turns. 123 min.
12-2068 *$19.99*

Sayonara (1957)
Moving tale of race relations and romance stars Marlon Brando as an Army officer, stationed in Japan during the Korean War, who falls for theatrical performer Mikko Taka, only to face prejudice from both sides. James Garner, Ricardo Montalban, and supporting Oscar winners Red Buttons and Miyoshi Umeki also star; based on the James Michener novel. 148 min.
04-1613 *$14.99*

The Young Lions (1958)
A powerhouse performance from Marlon Brando as a disenchanted Nazi officer highlights this exceptional WWII character study from director Edward Dmytryk. Co-stars Montgomery Clift, Dean Martin and Maximilian Schell. 167 min.
04-1182 *$19.99*

The Fugitive Kind (1960)
Emotional drama, based on Tennessee Williams' "Orpheus Descending," stars Marlon Brando as a guitar-toting wanderer who disrupts the staid life of a small Mississippi town, romancing both unhappily-married Italian émigré Anna Magnani and town nympho Joanne Woodward. With Maureen Stapleton, Victor Jory; Sidney Lumet directs. 122 min.
12-2413 *$19.99*

One Eyed Jacks (1961)
Marlon Brando directs (after taking over the helm from Stanley Kubrick) and stars as a ruthless outlaw who escapes from a sadistic prison to exact vengeance upon his one-time partner, who is now the sheriff of a small town. Offbeat psychological Western co-stars Karl Malden, Ben Johnson and Katy Jurado. 141 min.
06-1104 *$14.99*

One Eyed Jacks (Letterboxed Version)
Also available in a theatrical, widescreen format.
08-1687 *$19.99*

Mutiny On The Bounty (1962)
Lavish, spectacular version of the seafaring classic stars Marlon Brando as the obsessed Mr. Christian, leading the revolt against Trevor Howard's maniacal Captain Bligh. Breathtaking Tahitian locales and powerhouse acting turns enhance this visually lush production directed by Lewis Milestone. With Richard Harris, Hugh Griffith. 179 min.
12-1032 Was $29.99 *$24.99*

Mutiny On The Bounty (Letterboxed Version)
Also available in a theatrical, widescreen format.
12-3185 *$24.99*

The Ugly American (1963)
Brando is magnificent as the American ambassador whose presence in a Southeast Asian nation stirs up conflict between democratic and communist forces...and who strives to defuse the dangerously volatile situation. Sandra Church, Pat Hingle, Eiji Okada, Arthur Hill co-star. 120 min.
07-1518 *$19.99*

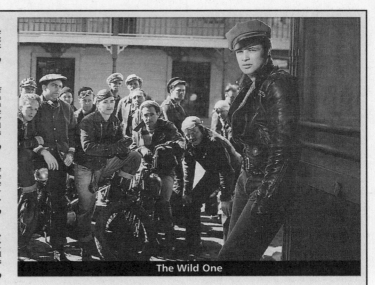

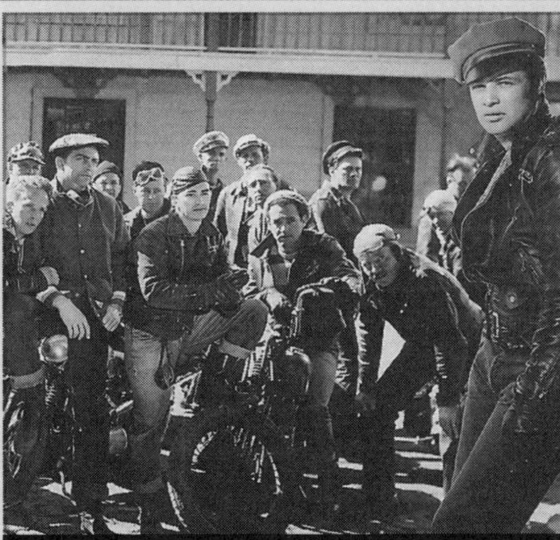
The Wild One

Marlon Brando

Bedtime Story (1964)
Light-hearted larceny comedy, later remade as "Dirty Rotten Scoundrels," stars Marlon Brando and David Niven as competing con artists who join forces to romance and plunder "soap queen" Shirley Jones. This sophisticated romp was co-scripted by "Beverly Hillbillies" creator Paul Henning. 99 min.
07-1629 Was $59.99 *$14.99*

Morituri (1965)
Exciting WWII thriller stars Yul Brynner as a German officer on a cargo ship sailing from Japan to occupied France and Marlon Brando as an undercover agent for the British posing as an SS official, charged with stopping the ship at any cost. With Trevor Howard, Martin Benrath, Janet Margolin, Wally Cox. AKA: "Saboteur: Code Name Morituri." 128 min.
04-2120 □*$19.99*

The Chase (1966)
Tense, powerful drama by Arthur Penn ("Bonnie and Clyde") set in a small Texas town. Robert Redford is the prison escapee whom sheriff Marlon Brando wants to bring back alive, but the other townsfolk aren't as fussy. Jane Fonda, E.G. Marshall, Angie Dickinson and Robert Duvall also star; script by Lillian Hellman. 135 min.
02-1580 *$14.99*

The Appaloosa (1966)
When his prize Appaloosa stallion is stolen by Mexican bandits, Marlon Brando follows the crooks to their hideout, and a desperate battle ensues. Tense frontier thriller also stars John Saxon, Anjanette Comer. 99 min.
10-3185 □*$14.99*

Reflections In A Golden Eye (1967)
Controversial, action-packed tale starring Marlon Brando as a homosexual army officer based in Georgia. Adapted from Carson McCullers' explosive novel; directed by John Huston. Elizabeth Taylor, Brian Keith and Julie Harris star. 108 min.
19-1363 Was $59.99 *$19.99*

The Night Of The Following Day (1969)
A compelling and complex crime drama starring Marlon Brando as a chauffeur who joins a gang of crooks in a kidnapping plot as they abduct a wealthy man's daughter. Before their scheme comes off, though, bickering and jealousies within the gang threaten to destroy all involved. With Richard Boone, Rita Moreno, Diane Franklin. 93 min.
07-2041 □*$89.99*

Burn! (1970)
Engrossing drama, laced with political allegory and based on a true incident, stars Marlon Brando as a British agent sent to a 19th-century Caribbean island to instigate a revolt by sugar cane workers against their Portuguese overseers. Directed by Gillo Pontecorvo ("The Battle of Algiers"). 112 min.
12-2262 *$19.99*

Last Tango In Paris (1973)
One of the most controversial films ever made, with Marlon Brando in an electrifying performance as a distraught American who plunges into a wild sexual relationship with a young French girl. Bernardo Bertolucci's mesmerizing drama also stars Maria Schneider, Jean-Pierre Leaud. Original uncut version runs 129 min.
12-1963 Was $29.99 *$14.99*

Last Tango In Paris (Letterboxed Version)
Also available in a theatrical, widescreen format.
12-3213 *$14.99*

The Missouri Breaks (1976)
Violent, offbeat western with Marlon Brando as a bizarre hired gunslinger who employs any means necessary to quash a band of horse thieves terrorizing a rancher. Along the way he tangles with the rustlers's former leader (Jack Nicholson), who has given up his life of crime for the rancher's daughter. Co-stars Randy Quaid, Frederic Forrest, Harry Dean Stanton; Arthur Penn directs. 126 min.
12-2996 Was $19.99 □*$14.99*

The Missouri Breaks (Letterboxed Version)
Also available in a theatrical, widescreen format.
12-3205 *$14.99*

The Formula (1980)
While investigating a friend's murder, detective George C. Scott learns the dead man possessed a world-shaking secret from the last days of the Third Reich: a plan for creating cheap, pollution-free synthetic fuel. His race to locate the killers and the valuable formula drives this compelling drama that also stars Marlon Brando as an oil magnate. With Marthe Keller, John Gielgud. 117 min.
12-1038 *$19.99*

The Freshman (1990)
A priceless parody by Marlon Brando of his "Godfather" character highlights this winning comedy about a naive collegian (Matthew Broderick) whose first days in New York find him working for "export magnate" Brando, schlepping a Komodo dragon across New Jersey, and engaged to Brando's daughter. All this, and Bert Parks singing "Maggie's Farm"! With Bruno Kirby, Penelope Ann Miller. 102 min.
02-2063 Was $19.99 □*$14.99*

The Island Of Dr. Moreau (1996)
In this creepy version of the classic H.G. Wells story, Marlon Brando plays the not-so-good doctor, whose experiments with genetics on a Pacific island have resulted in horrific half-human, half-animal creations. Shipwreck survivor David Thewlis gets an unsettling indoctrination into the work of Brando and equally demented colleague Val Kilmer. Fairuza Balk also stars. 96 min.
02-5114 Was $99.99 □*$14.99*

The Island Of Dr. Moreau (Letterboxed Version)
Also available in a theatrical, widescreen format.
02-5138 □*$19.99*

Free Money (1998)
Charles Sheen and Thomas Haden Church are about to marry the daughters of Marlon Brando, a powerful, small-town prison warden known as "the Swede." In order to get away from him, Sheen and Church plot to rob a money train carrying millions in unmarked bills that are about to be destroyed—and is being guarded by Brando! With Mira Sorvino and Donald Sutherland. 94 min.
64-9050 *$99.99*

Please see our index for these other Marlon Brando titles: *Apocalypse Now • Christopher Columbus: The Discovery • A Countess From Hong Kong • Don Juan DeMarco • The Godfather • Julius Caesar • Superman: The Movie*

The Keys Of The Kingdom (1944)
In his second film, Gregory Peck earned an Academy Award nomination for this sweeping religious-themed drama, tracing the career of a Catholic missionary in China. Excellent cast includes Vincent Price, Thomas Mitchell, Edmund Gwenn, and Roddy McDowall as the boyhood Peck. 137 min.
04-2307 □*$19.99*

The Valley Of Decision (1945)
Sprawling drama of romance, labor strife and class differences, set against the backdrop of the Pittsburgh steel industry of the late 1800s. Greer Garson is the daughter of a former steelworker hired as a maid at the estate of the tycoon responsible for her father's handicap. The tycoon's son (Gregory Peck) falls for her, but familial conflict and strikes disrupt their union. Donald Crisp, Preston Foster and Lionel Barrymore also star. 111 min.
12-2935 □*$19.99*

Duel In The Sun (1946)
Seven years after "Gone with the Wind," producer David O. Selznick released this equally grandiose epic set in the Old West, as a Texas land baron's feuding sons (Joseph Cotten and Gregory Peck) vie for the love of a half-breed Indian girl (Jennifer Jones). Lionel Barrymore, Lillian Gish and Walter Huston also star; directed by King Vidor. 128 min.
08-8674 *$14.99*

Gentleman's Agreement (1947)
The Oscar-winning Best Film of 1947 stars Gregory Peck as a magazine writer who researches an article on anti-Semitism and learns first-hand about prejudice when he poses as a Jew. Elia Kazan directed this controversial story; with Dorothy McGuire, John Garfield, Celeste Holm, Dean Stockwell and Jane Wyatt. 118 min.
04-1063 Was $19.99 □*$14.99*

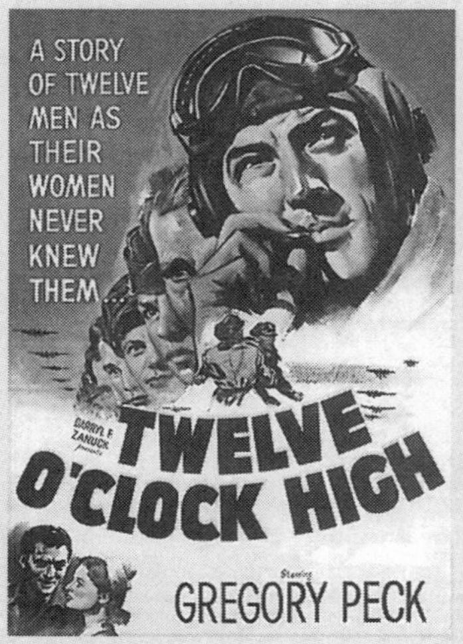
A STORY OF TWELVE MEN AS THEIR WOMEN NEVER KNEW THEM...
TWELVE O'CLOCK HIGH
GREGORY PECK

Twelve O'Clock High (1949)
Actual combat footage and a dramatic look at the burdens of command highlight this classic WWII tale set at an Allied air base in England. Gregory Peck stars as the hard-nosed general who turns the men into a crack flying unit, ably supported by Hugh Marlowe, Gary Merrill and, in an Oscar-winning performance, Dean Jagger. 132 min.
04-1168 Was $19.99 *$14.99*

The Gunfighter (1950)
One of the first of the '50s "adult Westerns," with Gregory Peck as a weary gunslinger trying to visit his estranged wife and son, but finding from town to town that he can't escape his reputation as "fastest draw in the land." Impressively staged drama also stars Karl Malden, Helen Westcott, Millard Mitchell. 84 min.
04-3182 Was $19.99 *$14.99*

David And Bathsheba (1951)
The Biblical tale of forbidden love and betrayal is given Hollywood's epic treatment, with an all-star cast that includes Gregory Peck as the troubled King of Israel and Susan Hayward the soldier's wife who becomes the object of his passions. Raymond Massey, Jayne Meadows, Kieron Moore. 116 min.
04-2245 □*$19.99*

Captain Horatio Hornblower (1951)
Thrilling adventure saga starring Gregory Peck as a British naval officer caught in the crossfire between the Spanish, the French and a Central American dictator during the Napoleonic Wars. Virginia Mayo plays an aristocrat whom Peck rescues in this lavish, action-filled adaptation of C.S. Forester's novel. With Robert Beatty. 117 min.
19-1975 Was $59.99 *$19.99*

Only The Valiant (1951)
Gregory Peck stars as a rigid, unpopular Cavalry officer who further alienates his men by ordering his second on a suicide mission. He must deal with both the Apache and his disaffected soldiers if he is to regain face. Gig Young, Ward Bond, Lon Chaney, Jr., Neville Brand co-star. 105 min.
63-1262 *$14.99*

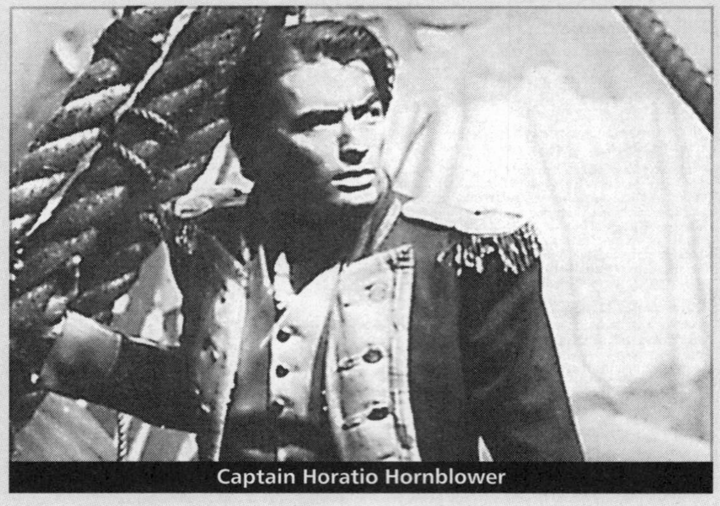

Captain Horatio Hornblower

Gregory Peck

The World In His Arms (1952)
Rousing adventure starring Gregory Peck as a seal hunter who is enlisted by Russian countess Ann Blyth to take her to Alaska so she can flee her upcoming marriage to a Russian diplomat. When Blyth is kidnapped before the journey begins, Peck and rival Anthony Quinn race to save her, betting their bounty and their ships on the outcome. Sig Rumann, John McIntire co-star. 105 min.
07-2441 □*$14.99*

The Snows Of Kilimanjaro (1952)
Gregory Peck stars as a famed adventure writer examining his life while on a safari in the African mountains in this classic action film. Co-stars Ava Gardner, Susan Hayward and Leo G. Carroll; based on a story by Ernest Hemingway. 114 min.
08-8000 Was $19.99 *$14.99*

The Man In The Gray Flannel Suit (1956)
Gregory Peck plays a Madison Avenue executive who questions the future of his marriage, his integrity and his past as a soldier in Europe during World War II. Jennifer Jones, Fredric March, Lee J. Cobb, Keenan Wynn and Marisa Pavan also star in this classic look at middle-class life in the 1950s. 152 min.
04-2357 Was $39.99 □*$19.99*

Moby Dick (1956)
Herman Melville's classic tale of Captain Ahab's relentless pursuit of the Great White Whale gets an electrifying treatment. Gregory Peck is Ahab; Orson Welles, Leo Genn, Richard Basehart also star. John Huston directs Ray Bradbury's screenplay. 116 min.
12-2033 Was $19.99 □*$14.99*

Designing Woman (1957)
Spry romantic farce stars Gregory Peck as a sportswriter and Lauren Bacall as a dress designer whose new marriage is strained because of their varied interests. Things get even more tense when their former beaus enter the scene. Vincente Minnelli directs; with Dolores Gray, Sam Levene, Chuck Connors. 117 min.
12-2316 *$19.99*

The Bravados (1958)
Powerful drama of frontier justice stars Gregory Peck as the man out to catch four outlaws he believes were responsible for assaulting and killing his wife, only to learn that his vigilante actions come at a terrible cost. Thoughtful Western co-stars Stephen Boyd, Joan Collins; look for Lee Van Cleef and "Curly Joe" De Rita as a hangman. 99 min.
04-2267 Was $39.99 □*$14.99*

The Big Country (1958)
A sea captain retires to what he thinks will be a quiet life on the frontier and a happy marriage, only to find himself in the middle of a range war in this Western classic. Gregory Peck, Charlton Heston, Jean Simmons and, in an Oscar-winning role, Burl Ives star; William Wyler directs. 168 min.
12-1549 Was $24.99 *$14.99*

Beloved Infidel (1959)
The doomed love affair between British-born writer Sheilah Graham and alcoholic author F. Scott Fitzgerald, begun when both were working in Hollywood in the late '30s, is recounted in this glossy melodrama starring Gregory Peck as Fitzgerald and Deborah Kerr as Graham. With Eddie Albert, Philip Ober. 123 min.
04-3276 *$19.99*

Pork Chop Hill (1959)
In the final days of the Korean War, an American battalion fights to maintain a strategic position. Compelling war drama by Lewis Milestone ("All Quiet on the Western Front") stars Gregory Peck, Rip Torn, Woody Strode, George Peppard and Robert Blake. 97 min.
12-1741 Was $29.99 *$14.99*

On The Beach (1959)
Classic doomsday story from director Stanley Kramer set in Melbourne, Australia, in 1964, where five people contemplate their fate after a nuclear war. Gregory Peck, Fred Astaire, Ava Gardner, Anthony Perkins and Donna Anderson star in this chilling tale. 135 min.
12-2237 Was $19.99 □*$14.99*

The Guns Of Navarone (1961)
Action-packed suspense film of a band of Allied commandos sent on a "suicide mission" to disable a German gun outpost on a remote island. Based on Alistair MacLean's novel; Gregory Peck, Anthony Quinn, David Niven, Anthony Quayle star. 157 min.
02-1061 Remastered *$14.99*

The Guns Of Navarone (Letterboxed Version)
Also available in a theatrical, widescreen format.
02-2458 *$19.99*

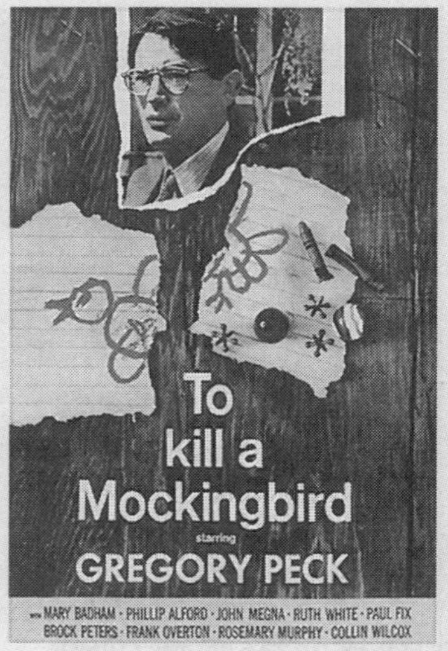
To kill a Mockingbird
starring
GREGORY PECK
with MARY BADHAM · PHILLIP ALFORD · JOHN MEGNA · RUTH WHITE · PAUL FIX
BROCK PETERS · FRANK OVERTON · ROSEMARY MURPHY · COLLIN WILCOX

To Kill A Mockingbird (35th Anniversary Edition) (1962)
Three Oscars, including a Best Actor award for Gregory Peck, went to this dramatic look at life in the '30s South, as seen through the eyes of two children whose father defends a black man charged with raping a white woman. Mary Badham, Phillip Alford, Brock Peters and Robert Duvall also star; based on Harper Lee's award-winning novel. Special anniversary version includes behind-the-scenes footage and interviews withPeck and Badham and producer Alan Pakula. 129 min.
07-2595 Letterboxed □*$19.99*

Captain Newman, M.D. (1963)
Gregory Peck stars in this acclaimed comedy-drama as a WWII military psychiatrist administering needed help to the battle fatigued. Stellar support from Tony Curtis, Angie Dickinson, Robert Duvall, Eddie Albert, Bobby Darin, and Larry Storch. 126 min.
07-1466 Was $19.99 *$14.99*

Behold A Pale Horse (1964)
Fascinating drama starring Gregory Peck as a commander for the Loyalists during the Spanish Civil War who encounters his old nemesis, diabolical police chief Anthony Quinn, while attempting to visit his mother in the hospital. Omar Sharif and Mildred Dunnock also star; directed by Fred Zinnemann. 118 min.
02-2684 *$19.99*

Arabesque (1966)
Gregory Peck and Sophia Loren star in this James Bondian adventure as a language professor, hired to decipher a secret code, must outwit hired gunmen and cut-throats in an attempt to save the life of an Arab prime minister. 105 min.
07-1420 *$14.99*

Mackenna's Gold (1969)
Sprawling frontier adventure with Gregory Peck as a sheriff who is given a map, said to show the location of a large cache of gold hidden in a valley, and soon finds he's the target of every fortune hunter in the West. The star-laden cast also includes Omar Sharif, Telly Savalas, Julie Newmar, Lee J. Cobb, Edward G. Robinson. 128 min.
02-2609 *$14.99*

The Stalking Moon (1969)
Gregory Peck stars as a retired frontier scout who agrees to help Eva Marie Saint and her half-breed son escape from their Apache captors in this taut Western drama. With Robert Forster, Frank Silvera. 108 min.
19-1659 *$14.99*

Billy Two Hats (1973)
Veteran Scottish-born outlaw Gregory Peck teams up with half-breed Desi Arnaz, Jr. for a bank robbery that backfires and soon has them on the run from the law. Offbeat western drama also stars Jack Warden, Sian Barbara Allen.
12-3143 □*$14.99*

MacArthur (1977)
An impressive, action-packed account of one of the most controversial public figures of the century. Gregory Peck is superb as the general who defied the enemy in World War II and Korea and the White House at home. With Ed Flanders. 130 min.
07-1077 Was $19.99 *$14.99*

The Sea Wolves (1980)
An edge-of-your-seat WWII caper film, with Roger Moore, Gregory Peck and David Niven as the leaders of a British volunteer regiment in India trying to blow up German ships docked there. With Trevor Howard, Patrick Macnee. 120 min.
19-1794 □*$14.99*

The Blue And The Gray (1982)
The war that shattered the nation is brought to the screen in grandiose fashion with a stellar cast and magnificent battle sequences. Gregory Peck, Geraldine Page, Stacy Keach and Colleen Dewhurst head a cast of thousands in this Civil War drama from historian Bruce Catton's novel. 295 min.
02-1652 *$29.99*

The Blue And The Gray (Uncut Version)
Also available in its original, complete version. 378 min.
02-2590 *$34.99*

The Scarlet And The Black (1983)
Exciting WWII drama based on a true story. Gregory Peck stars as a Vatican official who hides escaped POWs and refugees from the Gestapo under the eyes of German officer Christopher Plummer. With Sir John Gielgud, Edmund Purdom. 156 min.
27-6811 Was $19.99 *$14.99*

Old Gringo (1989)
An epic historical romance featuring Jane Fonda as an American schoolteacher who finds herself inadvertently thrown into the middle of the Mexican Revolution during the early 1900s. Jimmy Smits, as a rugged general in Pancho Villa's army, and Gregory Peck, as aging writer Ambrose Bierce, are the men who vie for her affections. 119 min.
02-2012 Was $19.99 □*$14.99*

The Portrait (1993)
An acclaimed family drama starring Gregory Peck and Lauren Bacall as the feuding parents of an aspiring painter (Cecilia Peck) about to get her first gallery show in Manhattan. In order to complete a portrait of her parents for the show, the artist returns home and soon realizes how troubled her family's relationships are. 89 min.
18-7437 Was $89.99 □*$14.99*

Gregory Peck: His Own Man
Gregory Peck himself tells the story of what it was like to be one of Hollywood's sturdiest leading men. His recollections are peppered with interviews featuring Audrey Hepburn, Liza Minnelli, Anthony Quinn and others, plus clips from classics like "Spellbound" and "The Guns of Navarone." 60 min.
50-6793 Was $24.99 *$14.99*

Gregory Peck Collection
You'll be up to your neck in Peck with this boxed collector's set that includes "Cape Fear," "MacArthur" and "The World in His Arms."
07-2497 Save $20.00! *$24.99*

Please see our index for these other Gregory Peck titles: *Cape Fear • How The West Was Won • Marooned • The Omen • Other People's Money • The Paradine Case • Roman Holiday • Spellbound • The Yearling*

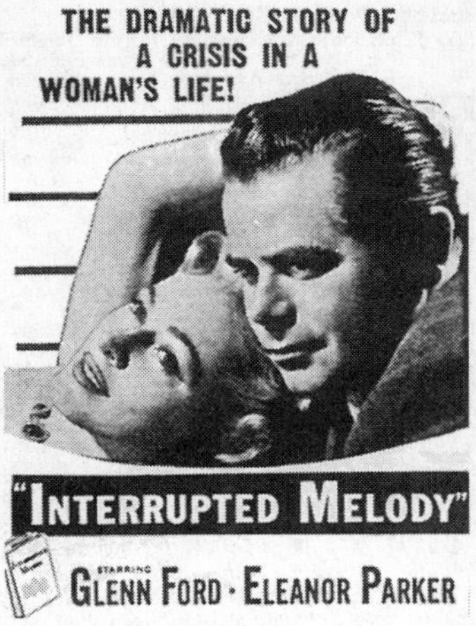
THE DRAMATIC STORY OF
A CRISIS IN A
WOMAN'S LIFE!
"INTERRUPTED MELODY"
STARRING
GLENN FORD · ELEANOR PARKER

Interrupted Melody (1955)
Sensitive biography of Australian opera singer Marjorie Lawrence, who made a courageous comeback after polio struck her at the height of her career. The cast includes Oscar-nominated Eleanor Parker as Lawrence and Glenn Ford as the physician who helps and later marries her. Eileen Farrell dubbed Parker's voice for the opera sequences; Roger Moore co-stars. 106 min.
12-2932 *$19.99*

Navajo (1952)
Unusual documentary-like film shot on a Navajo Indian Reservation and telling the story of a Navajo boy, separated from his family, who joins a friend in running from his instructors of government-mandated courses. Featuring a predominately all-Native American cast, the film co-stars Hall Bartlett (later the director of "Jonathon Livingston Seagull"), who also produced. With Sammy Ogg.
55-3954 *$19.99*

The Bullfighter And The Lady (1951)
An American sports champion travels to Spain to learn the secrets of bullfighting from a famous matador, but romance and, ultimately, tragedy are in store. Fine action sequences highlight this drama, with Gilbert Roland, Robert Stack and Joy Page. Budd Boetticher directs; restored 125 min. version.
63-1113 Was $39.99 *$19.99*

Dino (1957)
Sal Mineo stars as a troubled young teen just released from reform school who must choose between starting a new life with his girlfriend or resuming his criminal ways. Brian Keith, Susan Kohner co-star. 96 min.
63-1126 Was $39.99 *$14.99*

Try And Get Me (1950)
A family man joins a small-time crook for a series of robberies, but when their kidnapping attempt forces them to kill their victim they become the prey in this hard-hitting crime drama. Frank Lovejoy, Lloyd Bridges, Kathleen Ryan star. AKA: "Sound of Fury." 91 min.
63-1291 *$19.99*

Three Secrets (1950)
A young boy, the sole survivor of a plane crash, attracts the attention of three women, each of whom believes him to be the child they gave up for adoption years earlier, in this heartfelt melodrama. Eleanor Parker, Patricia Neal, Ruth Roman, Frank Lovejoy star; Robert Wise directs. 98 min.
63-1293 *$19.99*

The Twinkle In God's Eye (1955)
Mickey Rooney gives a spirited performance as a priest just out of seminary who comes to a western town to help rebuild a church destroyed in an Indian raid. Despite severe opposition, he wins the support of the townspeople and triumphs in the end. With Hugh O'Brian, Coleen Gray and Mike "Touch" Connors in an early role. 73 min.
63-1948 *$12.99*

Dangerous Youth (1958)
A Liverpool rock singer and street gang leader is drafted into the military, which changes his life radically. When he returns home, he marries his group's lead singer and settles down. Songs in this "alienated youth" drama include "Isn't It a Lovely Evening?" and "These Dangerous Years." With Frankie Vaughan, Carole Lesley. 82 min.
68-8909 *$19.99*

The Flying Scot (1957)
Three crooks conceive an elaborate plan to rob "The Flying Scot," an express train. The scheme goes smoothly...except for one small detail that leads the cops to them. First-rate British caper film stars Lee Patterson, Kay Collard. AKA: "The Mailbag Robbery." 70 min.
68-8964 *$19.99*

The Sun Sets At Dawn (1950)
A youth is convicted of murder and sentenced to die in the electric chair. A reporter pieces together the true story and determines he's innocent, but can the real killer be found and the young man saved before his execution? Walter Reed and Sally Parr star. 71 min.
68-9127 *$19.99*

A Face In The Crowd (1957)
Andy Griffith plays a Southern singer catapulted to fame, with dehumanizing effects, in this early look at "television celebrity" from director Elia Kazan. Patricia Neal, Walter Matthau and Lee Remick co-star; screenplay by Budd Schulberg. 125 min.
19-1431 *$19.99*

Sincerely Yours (1955)
In his starring film debut, the one and only Liberace plays a concert pianist stricken with a disease that robs him of his hearing. Song-filled drama, written by Irving Wallace, co-stars Dorothy Malone, Joanne Dru, and gruff but lovable William Demarest. 115 min.
19-1574 Was $19.99 *$14.99*

The D.I. (1957)
Trading in his flat feet for a leather neck, Jack Webb plays a no-nonsense Marine drill sergeant charged with whipping new recruits into shape and finding one soldier a particular challenge. Gritty drama, directed and co-written by Webb, co-stars Don Dubbins, Monica Lewis. 106 min.
19-1576 Was $19.99 *$14.99*

Pete Kelly's Blues (1955)
Jack Webb stars as a young trumpet player looking for a break in this song-filled drama set in the jazz world of the Roaring '20s. The cast includes Lee Marvin, Janet Leigh, Edmond O'Brien, Ella Fitzgerald (who sings two songs) and Peggy Lee; look quickly for Jayne Mansfield. 95 min.
19-1577 Was $19.99 *$14.99*

The Spanish Gardener (1957)
When his young son befriends a newly hired servant, a jealous British diplomat in Spain plans to sabotage their friendship by framing the gardener for theft. Memorable drama stars Dirk Bogarde, Michael Hordern, Jon Whitley. 95 min.
10-1390 *$19.99*

The Golden Salamander (1951)
Archeologist Trevor Howard is sent to Tunisia by the British Museum to search for lost artifacts. Soon, he finds himself involved with a beautiful Frenchwoman and at odds with treacherous gunrunners. Anouk Aimee, Herbert Lom co-star. 96 min.
10-8225 Was $29.99 *$14.99*

The Big Lift (1950)
Tense drama of G.I. pilots in Germany during the Berlin Airlift who must cope with mounting tensions and romance. Montgomery Clift, Paul Douglas star. 120 min.
08-8024 *$19.99*

Borderline (1950)
Fred MacMurray and Claire Trevor are drug agents fighting smugglers at the Mexican border, yet each unsure they can trust the other, in this drama. Co-stars Raymond Burr, Roy Roberts. 105 min.
08-8032 Was $19.99 *$14.99*

Affair In Monte Carlo (1953)
Lavishly filmed on location in Monte Carlo, this soap opera stars Merle Oberon as a wealthy woman who tries to reform a troubled gambler, played by Richard Todd. Leo Genn, Stephen Murray also star. 90 min.
09-5161 *$29.99*

Animal Farm (1955)
George Orwell's allegorical examination of totalitarianism and revolutionary thought is transformed into animated form to tell the tale of the beleaguered barnyard animals who rebel against their cruel master, only to face an equally menacing leader, Napoleon the pig. Voices by Maurice Denham. 73 min.
47-1865 Was $19.99 *$14.99*

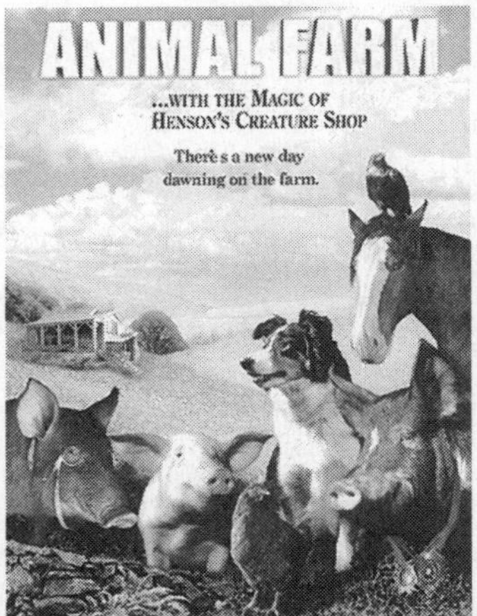
ANIMAL FARM
...WITH THE MAGIC OF
HENSON'S CREATURE SHOP
There's a new day
dawning on the farm.

Animal Farm (1999)
Wonderful effects by Jim Henson's Creature Shop bring to life the barnyard rebels of George Orwell's classic cautionary fable. Rallying to be free of human owner Pete Postlethwaite, the denizens of Manor Farm establish their own system of government, but soon learn that power comes with a price. Kelsey Grammer, Julia Louis-Dreyfus, Julia Ormond, Patrick Stewart and Peter Ustinov are among the stellar voice talents. 91 min.
88-1201 *$14.99*

Susan Hayward

The Jack London Story (1943)
This biography of the famed adventure writer features Michael O'Shea in the title role, Susan Hayward and Virginia Mayo. The life of London, from his travels in Canada, the Pacific and Japan to his success with stories like "Call of the Wild," is told with detail and excitement. 94 min.
08-8040 *$19.99*

Change Of Heart (1943)
A lively entry in the "Hit Parade" movie series (and originally called "Your Hit Parade of 1943"), this musical comedy stars John Carroll as a down-and-out tunesmith who hires songwriter Susan Hayward as a ghostwriter after he swipes a number from her. Romance ensues and so do such numbers as "Who Took Me Home Last Night," "Take a Chance" and the title track. With Gail Patrick, Eve Arden.
64-3057 *$14.99*

The Hairy Ape (1944)
Masterful adaptation of the O'Neill classic stars William Bendix as the brutish boiler room attendant seduced and suckered by vacationing vamp Susan Hayward. Superlative performances throughout; John Loder, Alan Napier, Dorothy Comingore. 90 min.
08-8094 *$19.99*

Canyon Passage (1946)
The Oregon Territory of the 1850s is the setting for a bitter rivalry between scout-turned-general store owner Dana Andrews and crooked banker Brian Donlevy—a rivalry that intensifies when beautiful Susan Hayward comes between them—in this frontier drama from director Jacques Tourneur. Ward Bond, Andy Devine and Hoagy Carmichael, who supplies two songs, also star. 92 min.
07-2634 *$14.99*

Smash-Up: The Story Of A Woman (1947)
Susan Hayward is great as a broken woman who turns to the bottle thanks in part to the irresponsibility of her successful singer husband. Reportedly based on real Hollywood situations, this film is unflinching in its depiction of alcoholism. Eddie Albert, Lee Bowman. 103 min.
59-5047 Was $19.99 *$14.99*

The Lost Moment (1947)
A publisher looking for rare papers in Europe meets and falls for a neurotic young girl who claims to have them in this compelling drama, based on a story by Henry James. Robert Cummings and Susan Hayward star. 89 min.
63-1127 Was $19.99 *$14.99*

Tulsa (1949)
Susan Hayward is a domineering woman who fights alone in a brutal war for an oil empire after the death of her father. With Robert Preston. 96 min.
10-1060 Was $19.99 *$14.99*

I'd Climb The Highest Mountain (1951)
Heartwarming drama stars Susan Hayward as a city gal who marries rural circuit preacher William Lundigan and helps him establish a church in a backwoods Georgia community. With Rory Calhoun, Barbara Bates, Alexander Knox. 88 min.
04-2905 *$19.99*

I'll Cry Tomorrow (1955)
One of the finest Hollywood biopics ever made, an unflinching look at the life of singer/actress Lillian Roth and her struggle with alcoholism. Susan Hayward earned an Oscar nomination for her portrayal of Roth and also did her own singing. With Jo Van Fleet, Richard Conte, Don Taylor. 119 min.
12-1128 *$19.99*

I Want To Live! (1958)
Susan Hayward's Oscar-winning turn is a highlight of this gripping drama, based on the true story of Barbara Graham, who was (according to the film, wrongfully) convicted of murder and sentenced to die in the gas chamber. With Theodore Bikel, Simon Oakland and Virginia Vincent. 122 min.
12-1521 Was $19.99 *$14.99*

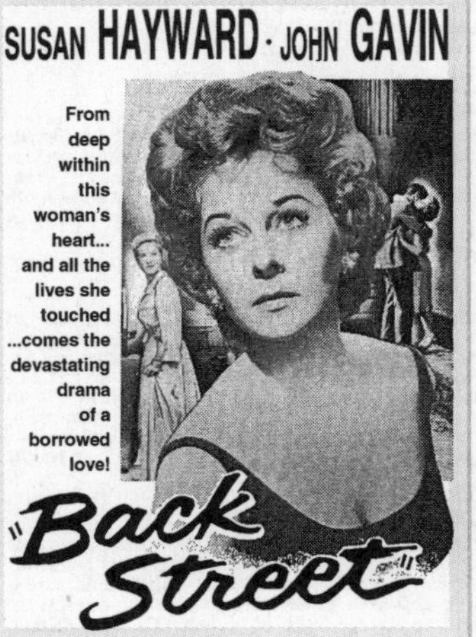
SUSAN HAYWARD · JOHN GAVIN
From deep within this woman's heart... and all the lives she touched ...comes the devastating drama of a borrowed love!
"Back Street"

Back Street (1961)
Susan Hayward created one of her most memorable roles in this sultry drama of a woman in love with a married man, who yearns to be more than a mistress, but must remain in the shadows. John Gavin, Vera Miles, Virginia Grey co-star. 107 min.
07-1293 *$14.99*

The Stolen Hours (1963)
Four-handkerchief reworking of "Dark Victory" starring Susan Hayward as the wealthy socialite with a terminal illness and given little time to live by medical authorities. She eventually finds romance with her brain surgeon, who helps her live life to its fullest in her final months. Michael Craig, Diane Baker and Edward Judd also star. 100 min.
12-2814 *$19.99*

Heat Of Anger (1972)
Nail-biting courtroom drama about a female attorney and her young partner who defend a wealthy contractor accused of killing an iron worker, who happened to be having an affair with his teenage daughter. Susan Hayward, James Stacy, Lee J. Cobb and Tyne Daly star. 75 min.
10-1593 Was $19.99 *$14.99*

Please see our index for these other Susan Hayward titles: *Adam Had Four Sons • Beau Geste • Demetrius And The Gladiators • The Fighting Seabees • The Honey Pot • House Of Strangers • I Married A Witch • Rawhide • Reap The Wild Wind • The Snows Of Kilimanjaro • Where Love Has Gone*

The Glass Mountain (1953)
Unusual drama with classical music about a young composer who finds inspiration in writing an opera from a dead girl whose spirit lies in a mountain. Valentina Cortese, Tito Gobbi and Michael Dennison star. 94 min.
08-1755 *$14.99*

Rough And Smooth (1959)
From Robert Siodmak ("Criss Cross") comes this dark drama starring Nadja Tiller as a calculating German nympho who seduces, blackmails and deceives three men in her lives, including her newest lover, an engaged archeologist. Tony Britton, William Bendix and Donald Wolfit star. 96 min.
08-1762 *$14.99*

Strange Affection (1957)
Fine British drama in which a young boy seeks help from an understanding teacher after he has been accused of murdering his abusive, alcoholic father. Richard Attenborough, Colin Petersen and Jill Adams star. AKA: "The Scamp." 92 min.
08-1805 *$19.99*

Wetbacks (1956)
Lloyd Bridges is a fishing boat skipper who tries to crack an outfit specializing in smuggling illegal aliens out of Mexico. But Bridges doesn't realize that he's being monitored by the U.S. immigration service. John Hoyt, Nancy Gates, Robert Keys star. 89 min.
08-1825 *$14.99*

A Man Called Peter (1955)
Wonderful biodrama of Peter Marshall, the Scottish immigrant who entered the clergy and went on to become U.S. Senate Chaplain and the unofficial "conscience" of Washington. Richard Todd, Jean Peters, Les Tremayne star. 117 min.
04-2308 *$19.99*

Desire Under The Elms (1958)
Sophia Loren, Burl Ives and Anthony Perkins star in this adaptation of Eugene O'Neill's play about an 1800s New England farm family torn by their greed for the land and jealousy towards each other. 115 min.
06-1821 *$19.99*

The Brothers Karamazov (1958)
Writer/Director Richard Brooks turns Dostoyevsky's literary classic into an effective and engrossing family drama. Lee J. Cobb is the domineering father whose house is divided by greed, lust and murder. Yul Brynner, William Shatner, Richard Basehart and Albert Salmi play the title roles. 146 min.
12-1584 *$24.99*

Marty (1955)
Classic drama, written by Paddy Chayefsky, about a lonely, unattractive Bronx butcher who finally meets the girl of his dreams. Star Ernest Borgnine won Best Actor Oscar, as did the film for Best Picture. Betsy Blair, Esther Minciotti co-star. 91 min.
12-1840 Was $19.99 *$14.99*

Nevada (1927)
When cattle rustlers begin to cause trouble, Nevada (Gary Cooper) comes to the rescue and falls for the daughter of the rancher having all the trouble. Thelma Todd and William Powell also star. 65 min. Silent with musical score.
10-9219 Was $19.99 *$14.99*

Fighting Caravans (1931)
Based on a classic Western by Zane Grey, this early starring role for Gary Cooper has Coop as a wagon scout charged with delivering his people to California. Complications include a band of renegade Indians and a romance with a French girl. 80 min.
09-1072 Was $19.99 *$14.99*

A Farewell To Arms (1932)
Gary Cooper, Helen Hayes, Adolphe Menjou star in the classic film version of Hemingway's masterpiece about the bittersweet romance between a soldier and a nurse during World War I. 77 min.
10-2006 Was $19.99 *$14.99*

The Lives Of A Bengal Lancer (1935)
Majestic in its scope, this superlative adventure details the camaraderie between British soldiers on the Northwest frontier of India. Gary Cooper and Franchot Tone star as veteran soldiers teaching the ropes to a colonel's inexperienced son. Nominated for three Academy Awards. 110 min.
07-1461 Was $29.99 *$14.99*

The Wedding Night (1935)
Disillusioned novelist Gary Cooper meets a Polish girl while at his Connecticut farm and, drawn to her naïveté, decides to write a book based on her and her family. Cooper recognizes his love for the girl, but when he pursues her after learning that she's soon to wed a loutish neighbor, tragedy follows. Anna Sten, Ralph Bellamy co-star; King Vidor directs. 83 min.
44-1977 Was $19.99 *$14.99*

The General Died At Dawn (1936)
Soldier of fortune Gary Cooper agrees to smuggle gold across China in order to finance a "peasants' rebellion" against warlord Akim Tamiroff in this grand adventure saga from writer Clifford Odets and director Lewis Milestone. With Madeleine Carroll, William Frawley. 97 min.
07-1602 Was $29.99 *$14.99*

The Plainsman (1937)
Epic C.B. DeMille production (what other kind was there?) of the opening of the West stars Gary Cooper as Wild Bill Hickok and Jean Arthur as Calamity Jane. The rip-roarin' pair fall in love while trying to put down an Indian uprising and ruthless gunrunners. With James Ellison, Charles Bickford, Gabby Hayes; look for Anthony Quinn as an Indian. 113 min.
07-1529 Was $29.99 *$14.99*

Souls At Sea (1937)
Compelling seafaring drama showcasing Gary Cooper as first mate on an 1800s slave ship who takes command of the vessel and frees its captives after the captain is killed during a rebellion. Following his exoneration on mutiny charges, Cooper and shipmate George Raft are recruited for a clandestine mission, and romance and adventure ensue. With Frances Dee, Henry Wilcoxon. 93 min.
07-2440 ❏*$14.99*

Bluebeard's Eighth Wife (1938)
Lively Ernst Lubitsch comedy with Gary Cooper as a pampered millionaire who's gone through seven marriages and is eager to make poor French shopgirl Claudette Colbert his next bride. Coaxed by her father, Colbert accepts Cooper's proposal, then sets out to change his ways. With David Niven, Edward Everett Horton; scripted by Billy Wilder and Charles Brackett. 86 min.
07-2242 ❏*$14.99*

Beau Geste (1939)
A Movies Unlimited favorite. Gary Cooper, Ray Milland and Robert Preston are three brothers who join the French Foreign Legion to escape a scandal. Once there they face danger from marauding desert tribes and sadistic sergeant Brian Donlevy. One of the greatest adventure epics ever. With J. Carrol Naish, Susan Hayward; William Wellman directed. 114 min.
07-1560 Was $29.99 *$14.99*

The Westerner (1940)
Classic tale of range wars in the late 1800s, with Gary Cooper as the wanderer who finds himself in the middle. Walter Brennan won his third Oscar as Judge Roy Bean, "The Law West of the Pecos"; Dana Andrews, Chill Wills and Fred Stone co-star. William Wyler directs. 100 min.
44-1845 Was $19.99 *$14.99*

Sergeant York (1941)
In his Academy Award-winning role, Gary Cooper portrays the quiet, pacifistic Tennessee farmer who went on to become a hero on the battlefields of World War I. Stirring tale of true heroism also stars Walter Brennan, Ward Bond, Joan Leslie; Howard Hawks directs. 134 min.
12-1975 *$19.99*

For Whom The Bell Tolls (1943)
Lavish treatment of Ernest Hemingway's classic novel stars Gary Cooper as an American teacher who journeys to Spain to join the Loyalist forces in their civil war against the Fascists and falls in love with fellow freedom fighter Ingrid Bergman. With Akim Tamiroff, Joseph Calleia and Best Supporting Actress Oscar-winner Katina Paxinou. This restored video version includes footage unseen since the film's premiere, along with a montage of rare production stills featured during the intermission music. 166 min.
07-2301 Was $19.99 *$14.99*

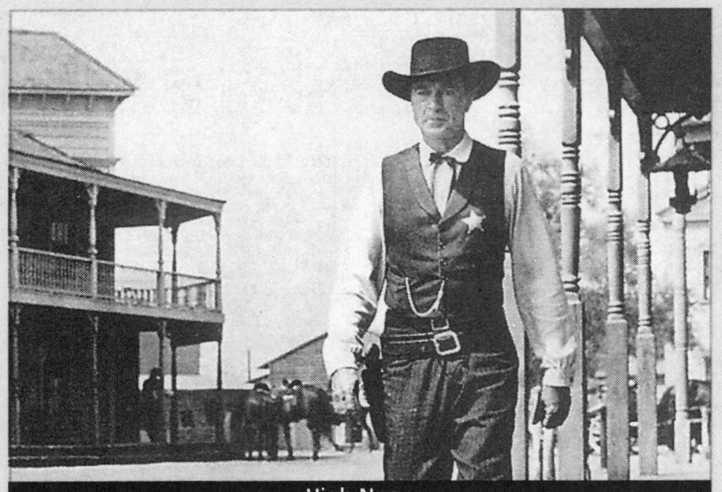
High Noon

Gary Cooper

The Story Of Dr. Wassell (1944)
Cecil B. DeMille directed this rousing slice of real-life WWII heroism, with Gary Cooper starring as the dedicated Navy doctor who risked his life to transport a group of wounded soldiers by train across the Japanese-held island of Java. Laraine Day, Dennis O'Keefe, Doodles Weaver also star. 137 min.
07-2395 ❏*$14.99*

Casanova Brown (1944)
Rollicking, warm-hearted farce featuring Gary Cooper as a college English professor whose planned second marriage is halted upon the news that his first wife has given birth to a baby girl. Upset over her plans to put the child up for adoption, Coop takes the baby back to his home to raise on his own. Teresa Wright, Anita Louise, Frank Morgan and Mary Treen also star. 94 min.
12-2778 *$19.99*

Along Came Jones (1945)
Upon entering a Western town, mild-mannered cowpoke Gary Cooper is mistaken for an ornery outlaw and quickly wins the respect of the townsfolk—until the real black hat arrives on the scene, looking to get rid of the impostor. Dan Duryea, Loretta Young and William Demarest also star in this funny sagebrusher. 90 min.
12-2777 Was $19.99 *$14.99*

Cloak And Dagger (1946)
Taut espionage thriller from Fritz Lang stars Gary Cooper as an American professor who is dropped behind enemy lines to procure valuable Nazi military secrets and becomes involved with mysterious Lilli Palmer. 106 min.
63-1254 Was $19.99 *$14.99*

Unconquered (1947)
On the American frontier of the mid-1700s, Virginia militia leader Gary Cooper has his hands full defending Fort Pitt from marauding Indians (led by chief Boris Karloff and supplied with guns by villainous trader Howard da Silva) while also romancing pretty colonist Paulette Goddard in this thrilling costume saga from Cecil B. DeMille. 147 min.
07-2246 ❏*$14.99*

Good Sam (1948)
An incurable do-gooder (Gary Cooper) finds out the hard way that some of his good deeds can land him in hot water, especially after getting his pockets picked of the employees' benefit fund while helping an old lady. Co-stars Ann Sheridan. 116 min.
63-1034 *$14.99*

The Fountainhead (1949)
Ayn Rand's classic novel is vibrantly brought to life with a screenplay by the author. Brilliant, uncompromising architect (Gary Cooper) must fight to maintain his personal integrity when critics attempt to coerce him to change his ideas for the "betterment of Society." Patricia Neal and Raymond Massey also star. 114 min.
12-1961 Was $29.99 *$19.99*

Task Force (1949)
An exciting, fictional account of the evolution of the use of aircraft carriers during World War II as seen through the eyes of determined Navy officer Gary Cooper, who convinces the government of the vessel's viability and is given command of his own ship after the attack on Pearl Harbor. Jane Wyatt and Walter Brennan also star. 116 min.
12-2782 *$19.99*

Dallas (1950)
Former Confederate officer Gary Cooper poses as a U.S. marshal sent to the rough-and-tumble Texas town and proceeds to bring the outlaw brothers running the place to justice and settle an old grudge. Two-fisted Western actioner also stars Ruth Roman, Raymond Massey, Steve Cochran. 94 min.
19-2438 *$19.99*

Distant Drums (1951)
Raoul Walsh was at the helm for this blazing adventure about swamp fighter Gary Cooper storming the Florida Everglades to suppress an attack of insurgent Seminole Indians and rescue a young girl held captive. 101 min.
63-1256 *$19.99*

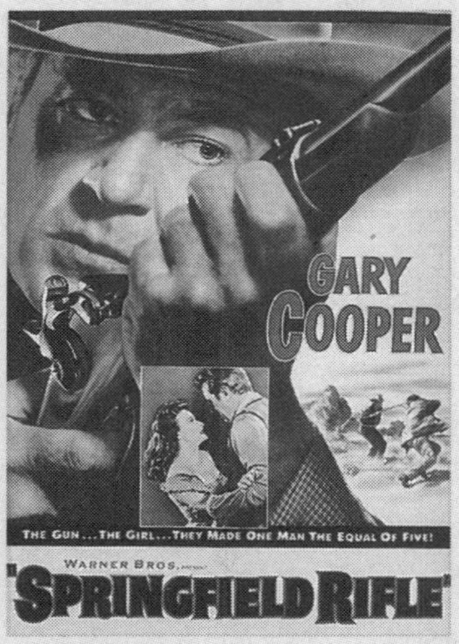

Springfield Rifle (1952)
First-rate Western adventure involving a renegade Union officer (Gary Cooper) posing as a Confederate rustler in order to discover who is supplying thieves with top-secret information about shipments of Union horses to the East. Phyllis Thaxter, Paul Kelly and Lon Chaney, Jr. co-star. 93 min.
19-2198 Was $29.99 *$19.99*

High Noon (1952)
Four Academy Awards, including Gary Cooper's second Best Actor Oscar, went to director Fred Zinnemann's landmark Western drama. Cooper shines as retiring frontier marshal Will Kane, who must stand alone when a vengeance-seeking outlaw comes to town. Grace Kelly co-stars as Kane's new Quaker wife; with Lloyd Bridges, Katy Jurado, Ian MacDonald, Thomas Mitchell. 85 min.
63-1018 Remastered ❏*$14.99*

High Noon: 40th Anniversary Deluxe Edition
Your darling may feel forsaken if you don't get them this special boxed set that features the remastered anniversary print of the Gary Cooper classic, a special "making of" documentary tape hosted by Leonard Maltin, the "Complete Films of Gary Cooper" book, and reproductions of the original theatrical poster and lobby cards.
63-1569 *$69.99*

Return To Paradise (1953)
Shot on location in Western Samoa, this exotic drama features Gary Cooper as an amiable adventurer who comes across a dictatorial missionary on a Polynesian island and soon falls in love with a native woman. Following an uprising, Cooper leaves the island, only to return years later during World War II and discover he has a grown daughter living there. With Roberta Haynes and Barry Jones. 100 min.
12-2781 *$19.99*

Blowing Wild (1953)
A well-crafted romantic thriller, with wildcatter Gary Cooper being swept up in a whirlwind of murder and intrigue after falling in love with Barbara Stanwyck, the power-hungry wife of oil tycoon Anthony Quinn in Mexico. 92 min.
63-1255 Was $19.99 *$14.99*

Vera Cruz (1954)
Exciting frontier saga stars Gary Cooper and Burt Lancaster as rival gunfighters involved in a plot to overthrow the Emperor of Mexico in the 1860s. Co-stars Cesar Romero, Denise Darcel and Charles Bronson; Robert Aldrich directs. 94 min.
12-2171 Was $19.99 *$14.99*

Vera Cruz (Letterboxed Version)
Also available in a theatrical, widescreen format.
12-3204 *$14.99*

The Court-Martial Of Billy Mitchell (1955)
Gary Cooper is in top form as the popular American general who raised the ire of the military brass by publicly condemning the lack of U.S. preparedness for aerial invasion...less than 20 years before Pearl Harbor. Co-stars Rod Steiger and Ralph Bellamy; directed by Otto Preminger. 100 min.
63-1267 *$19.99*

Friendly Persuasion (1956)
A Quaker family's faith and love is put to the test during the Civil War when the eldest son feels he must join the army in order to prove his manhood. William Wyler sensitive adaptation of the Jessamyn West novel stars Gary Cooper, Dorothy McGuire, Marjorie Main and Anthony Perkins. Restored video edition also includes outtakes, screen tests and the original theatrical trailer. 140 min.
04-1920 Was $59.99 ❏*$19.99*

Man Of The West (1958)
Compelling Western drama from director Anthony Mann stars Gary Cooper as a former outlaw forced by circumstances to reunite with his old gang, led by his sadistic uncle (Lee J. Cobb), in order to protect those around him. Brutal and stark tale also stars Julie London, John Dehner, Jack Lord. 100 min.
12-2170 ❏*$19.99*

They Came To Cordura (1959)
Tough frontier drama that looks at the nature of heroism stars Gary Cooper as a soldier accused of cowardice in 1916, charged with finding five Medal of Honor candidates and bringing them to a military outpost. With Rita Hayworth, Van Heflin, Tab Hunter. 123 min.
02-1185 Was $19.99 *$14.99*

The Wreck Of The Mary Deare (1959)
Charlton Heston and Gary Cooper star in this thrilling story about a ship salvager who helps the lone remaining crew member of a mysterious grounded boat when he is investigated for his part in destroying the vessel. During the inquisition, the truth about the Mary Deare is revealed. Michael Redgrave and Alexander Knox also star. 110 min.
12-2511 *$19.99*

Gary Cooper: American Life, American Legend
Who better than Clint Eastwood to host this salute to the taciturn leading man and Hollywood Western hero? Clips from Coop's most memorable screen moments, including "Mr. Deeds Goes to Town," "The Plainsman," his Oscar-winning turn as "Sergeant York," "High Noon" and many more are featured. 47 min.
18-7334 Was $19.99 *$14.99*

Gary Cooper: The Face Of A Hero
Hollywood's "man of few words," lanky Gary Cooper was at home playing cowboys, war heroes and baseball legends. Hear from "Coop's" family and friends, including Jane Greer, Charlton Heston, Patricia Neal and George C. Scott, in this moving tribute that includes clips from such films as "Sergeant York," "Pride of the Yankees" and "For Whom the Bell Tolls." 60 min.
50-7613 *$14.99*

Hollywood Stars: Gary Cooper Gift Pack
You mean three of Gary Cooper's greatest movies, "High Noon," "The Court-Martial of Billy Mitchell" and "Distant Drums," are available in a special collector's gift set? Yup.
63-1339 *$59.99*

Please see our index for these other Gary Cooper titles: *Ball Of Fire • Desire • It • Love In The Afternoon • Meet John Doe • Mr. Deeds Goes To Town • Now And Forever • Saratoga Trunk • Wings*

Cyrano De Bergerac (1950)
Jose Ferrer won an Academy Award for his stunning portrayal of the fabled 17th-century swordsman and wit, forced to hide his love for the beautiful Roxanne, in this stirring filming of Edmond Rostand's play. Mala Powers, William Prince co-star. 112 min.
63-1516 Was $19.99 ***$14.99***

Cyrano De Bergerac (Color Version)
Cyrano knows swordplay, Cyrano knows wordplay, Cyrano knows noses, and in this edition, Cyrano knows colorization.
63-1524 ***$19.99***

The Goddess (1958)
A young actress, desperate for fame, sleeps her way to Hollywood stardom but finds it a hollow victory in this Paddy Chayefsky drama, loosely based on the life of Marilyn Monroe. Kim Stanley stars, with Lloyd Bridges, Steven Hill and Patty Duke. 105 min.
02-1690 ***$69.99***

Woman On The Run (1950)
Top-notch crime story about an artist who goes into hiding after witnessing a mob murder. His uncaring wife discovers that he has a potentially life-threatening heart condition and decides to help police and an admiring journalist to find her spouse. Ann Sheridan, Dennis O'Keefe and Robert Keith star. 77 min.
10-8256 Was $19.99 ***$14.99***

The Second Face (1950)
A dress designer with a grotesque face decides to have plastic surgery and turns into a post-operation beauty, who soon draws the attention of her employer. Ella Raines, Bruce Bennett, Jane Darwell and Rita Johnson star. 77 min.
10-8385 Was $19.99 ***$14.99***

Adam And Evalyn (1956)
Gambler Stewart Granger becomes guardian to homeless woman Jean Simmons and tells her he's a stockbroker and she's the daughter of one of his friends. While Granger lavishes Simmons with gifts, gowns and a glitzy lifestyle, his jealous brother becomes enamored of her. Edwin Styles, Raymond Young also star. 69 min.
10-9054 ***$19.99***

The Birthday Present (1957)
A young British businessman, attempting to smuggle a watch he purchased as a gift for his wife into the country, is arrested by customs officials and sent to prison. Fine drama stars Tony Britton, Sylvia Syms, Jack Watling. 100 min.
10-9320 ***$19.99***

High Jump (1959)
Gritty British crime drama about a trapeze artist recruited for his acrobatic prowess to help a crooked dame in a jewel heist that goes sour and results in the deaths of two innocent people. Richard Wyler, Lisa Daniely and Leigh Madison star. 66 min.
10-9329 ***$19.99***

Kid Monk Baroni (1952)
Rarely seen boxing drama featuring Leonard Nimoy as a Bowery street thug who is taught how to fight by a local priest. Nimoy's disfigured face lands him the nickname "Monk," but plastic surgery and further lessons from a pro lead him to the top of the ring world...until a woman milks him of his earnings. Richard Rober, Bruce Cabot co-star. AKA: "Young Paul Baroni." 80 min.
10-9339 ***$19.99***

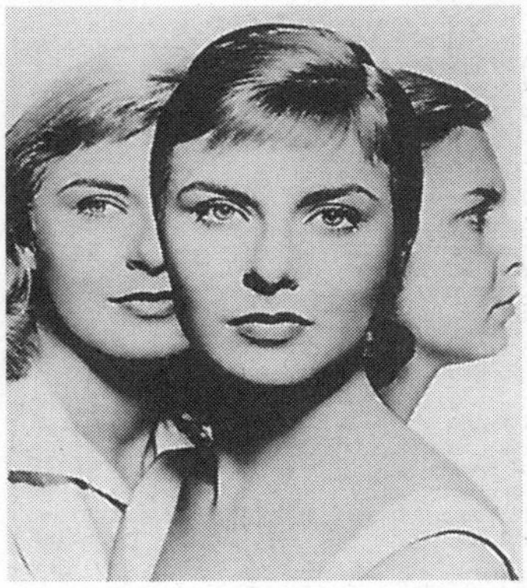

The Three Faces of Eve

The Three Faces Of Eve (1957)
Joanne Woodward won a Best Actress Academy Award for her triumphant portrayal of a shy Georgia housewife whose mind is inhabited by two other personalities, a well-balanced sophisticate and a sexually aggressive woman. Psychiatrist Lee J. Cobb delves into her past in an attempt to find what incidents triggered her condition. David Wayne, Vince Edwards also star. 91 min.
04-2288 ***$19.99***

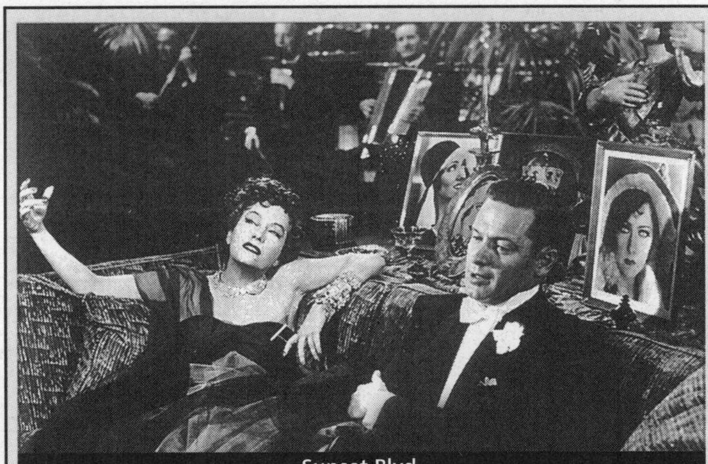

Sunset Blvd.

William Holden

Golden Boy (1939)
Clifford Odets' play becomes a moving screen drama, with William Holden (in his film debut) as a would-be violinist persuaded by girlfriend Barbara Stanwyck to forsake his musical career for the boxing ring. With Adolphe Menjou, Lee J. Cobb. 99 min.
02-2541 ***$19.99***

Arizona (1940)
Sprawling sagebrush saga set in 1860 and starring Jean Arthur as the first female resident of the city of Tucson, a no-nonsense woman who backs down from no man. She falls for drifter William Holden, who offers his help when some black hats try to destroy the freight line she's trying to start. Warren William, Porter Hall co-star. 121 min.
02-2596 ***$14.99***

Our Town (1940)
Touching film version of Thorton Wilder's Pulitzer Prize-winning play that explores the love, humor and pain of life in the typical American small town, Grovers Corners, before World War II. Marvelous cast includes William Holden, Frank Craven, Martha Scott and Thomas Mitchell. 86 min.
10-2011 Was $19.99 ***$14.99***

Texas (1941)
Slam-bang, laugh-packed classic Hollywood Western focuses on the rivalry between William Holden and Glenn Ford for the attention of Claire Trevor and a stake in the growing Lone Star State. George Marshall directs, and George Bancroft and Edgar Buchanan are along as well. 94 min.
02-1631 ***$14.99***

The Dark Past (1948)
When a gang of escaped criminals takes the occupants of an isolated resort cabin hostage, a deadly test of wills begins between manic gang leader William Holden and soft-spoken psychiatrist Lee J. Cobb. With Nina Foch, Adele Jergens. 75 min.
02-1813 Was $69.99 ***$19.99***

The Man From Colorado (1948)
Glenn Ford gives a stormy performance as a Colorado judge transformed by the Civil War into a raving sadist, and William Holden is an army friend trying to protect the town from his violence. Ellen Drew and Edgar Buchanan co-star. 98 min.
02-1916 ***$14.99***

Born Yesterday (1950)
Judy Holliday won an Academy Award for repeating her Broadway role as the streetwise but uncultured girl of junk magnate Broderick Crawford, who hires writer William Holden to give her some "class." George Cukor directed this "Pygmalion"-like comedy. 103 min.
02-1027 ***$19.99***

Sunset Blvd. (1950)
Classic Hollywood drama about a reclusive former silent movie queen who takes on a young writer as her lover. Billy Wilder directed this fascinating tale, filled with crackerjack dialogue, seediness and a special "film noir" feel. Gloria Swanson, William Holden, Erich Von Stroheim, Jack Webb, Cecil B. DeMille. 110 min.
06-1064 ***$14.99***

Force Of Arms (1951)
After he falls in love with a beautiful WAC during the fierce Battle of San Pietro, sergeant William Holden rejoins his unit and sees his friends die in battle. Feeling responsible for the tragedy, Holden must make a difficult decision: settle down or return to fight. Nancy Olson, Frank Lovejoy and Gene Evans co-star in this compelling drama helmed by Michael Curtiz. 99 min.
19-2224 ***$19.99***

Stalag 17 (1953)
Billy Wilder's acerbic, harrowing blend of comedy and drama, depicting the life of Allied POWs in a German prison camp. William Holden, Otto Preminger, Robert Strauss, Peter Graves and Harvey Lembeck star. 120 min.
06-1055 ***$14.99***

Escape From Fort Bravo (1953)
Arresting Western saga starring William Holden as a Union officer who oversees a stockade for Confederate prisoners in Arizona during the Civil War. When a beautiful visitor (Eleanor Parker) arrives at the fort, Holden falls in love with her, not knowing that she's a spy for the South. John Forsythe also stars. 98 min.
12-2800 ***$19.99***

The Moon Is Blue (1953)
The film that caused a ruckus by using words like "mistress," "seduce" and "virgin" in its dialogue is a lively farce that stars William Holden as a New York architect whose attempts at romancing "professional virgin" Maggie McNamara are thwarted by the arrival of his ex-fiancée and her lecherous father. David Niven, Dawn Addams also star; Otto Preminger directs. 95 min.
19-2217 Was $19.99 ***$14.99***

The Country Girl (1954)
Grace Kelly won an Oscar for her heartfelt performance as the strong-willed wife of an alcoholic stage actor (Bing Crosby) who's trying to launch a comeback under the guidance of a devoted director (William Holden). Director George Seaton also won an Academy Award for his adaptation of Clifford Odets' play. Anthony Ross, Gene Reynolds co-star. 104 min.
06-1172 ***$14.99***

The Bridges At Toko-Ri (1954)
Breathtaking, Oscar-winning aerial footage highlights this dramatic adaptation of James Michener's Korean War thriller. William Holden is a WWII pilot called back into service and charged with leading a dangerous bomber mission to destroy key North Korean-held bridges. Also stars Fredric March, Grace Kelly, Mickey Rooney. 103 min.
06-1517 ***$14.99***

Picnic (1955)
Superb adaptation of William Inge's play stars William Holden as a drifter who visits college friend Cliff Robertson in a small Kansas town and becomes involved with his fiancée (Kim Novak). Academy Award-winning drama also stars Rosalind Russell, Arthur O'Connell, Susan Strasberg. 115 min.
02-1996 Letterboxed ***$19.99***

Love Is A Many-Splendored Thing (1955)
A four-handkerchief weepie classic starring William Holden as a married American newspaperman in Hong Kong who falls wildly in love with Eurasian physician Jennifer Jones. The two find problems as Holden attempts to get a divorce from his wife and Jones faces prejudice from her family and co-workers. Will love conquer all? Features Thorin Thatcher and an unforgettable theme song. 102 min.
04-2283 Was $19.99 ***$14.99***

The Bridge On The River Kwai (1957)
David Lean's Oscar-winning wartime adventure epic stars Alec Guinness as a British officer in a Japanese POW camp, charged by his captors with overseeing the prisoners' construction of a railroad bridge, but escaped soldier William Holden returns to blow it up. With Sessue Hayakawa, Jack Hawkins and "The Colonel Bogey March." 162 min.
02-1058 Was $19.99 ***$14.99***

The Bridge On The River Kwai (Letterboxed Version)
Also available in a theatrical, widescreen format.
02-2443 ***$19.99***

The Key (1958)
During World War II, a long line of tugboat captains with invariably fatal duties in the English Channel are consoled by a voluptuous refugee (Sophia Loren) whose apartment key is passed from one doomed skipper to the other. Carol Reed's melancholy tale stars William Holden, Trevor Howard, Oscar Homolka. 125 min.
02-1942 Was $69.99 ***$19.99***

The World Of Suzie Wong (1960)
Exotic Hong Kong is the setting for this classic melodrama of the love affair between American painter William Holden and bar girl Nancy Kwan. Co-stars Michael Wilding, Sylvia Syms, Laurence Naismith. 129 min.
06-1621 ***$19.99***

The Counterfeit Traitor (1962)
Classic spy thriller stars William Holden as a Swedish oil trader who conducts business with the Nazis during World War II, which places him on the Allied enemies list. But he's given a chance to redeem himself after he spies on German refineries for British Intelligence. Lilli Palmer, Hugh Griffith co-star in this intense, true story. 140 min.
06-1915 ***$24.99***

The Seventh Dawn (1964)
An adventure story with political intrigue showcasing William Holden as a former guerrilla leader living in Malaysia, where he's caught in the middle of a struggle between British authorities and a former associate attempting to convert the country to Communism. Susannah York, Capucine and Tetsuro Tamba star. 123 min.
12-3000 ***$19.99***

Alvarez Kelly (1966)
A climactic stampede sequence sparks this Civil War western with William Holden as a mercenary adventurer hired to drive cattle from Mexico to Union forces in Virginia, only to be waylaid en route by sadistic Confederate officer Richard Widmark. With Patrick O'Neal, Janice Rule. 109 min.
02-2589 ***$14.99***

The Devil's Brigade (1968)
William Holden is a tough, level-headed lieutenant colonel assigned to form a crack unit of fighting men out of a band of misfit American soldiers and a well-trained Canadian unit before they are to face the Nazis on the European battlefield. Action-packed war epic based on fact co-stars Carroll O'Connor, Vince Edwards, Cliff Robertson. 130 min.
12-2314 ***$19.99***

Wild Rovers (1971)
William Holden turns in one of the most sterling performances of his career as an aging cowpoke who teams with Ryan O'Neal to knock over a bank. Will they succeed in their break for the border? Karl Malden, Rachel Roberts, Tom Skerritt, Joe Don Baker co-star; Blake Edwards directs. 109 min.
12-1700 ***$19.99***

Network (1976)
Scathing satire of the business of television mixes emotional drama with a far-out peek at future programming. Peter Finch won an Oscar as prophet-like figure Howard Beale; other Oscars went to writer Paddy Chayefsky, Beatrice Straight and Faye Dunaway. William Holden, Robert Duvall co-star. 120 min.
12-1013 Was $19.99 ***$14.99***

S.O.B.

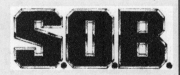

S.O.B. (1981)
Blake Edwards' hilarious lampoon of the Hollywood studio stars Richard Mulligan as a beleaguered director whose latest film, a $30 million flop, has a chance of being saved if he can turn it into a soft-core teaser and convince the film's star (Julie Andrews) to bare her breasts. Co-stars William Holden, Robert Loggia and Robert Preston. 121 min.
19-1774 Was $19.99 ***$14.99***

William Holden: The Golden Boy
William Holden's movie career and personal life were marked by his unpredictability and by the need to top himself whenever he could. The star of "Golden Boy," "Stalag 17," "The Bridge on the River Kwai" and "The Wild Bunch" is feted through clips and comments from Robert Wagner, Stefanie Powers and Sidney Lumet. 60 min.
50-6797 Was $24.99 ***$14.99***

Please see our index for these other William Holden titles: *The Country Girl • Damien: Omen II • The Earthling • Executive Suite • Forever Female • The Horse Soldiers • Miss Grant Takes Richmond • Paris—When It Sizzles • Sabrina • The Towering Inferno • When Time Ran Out • The Wild Bunch*

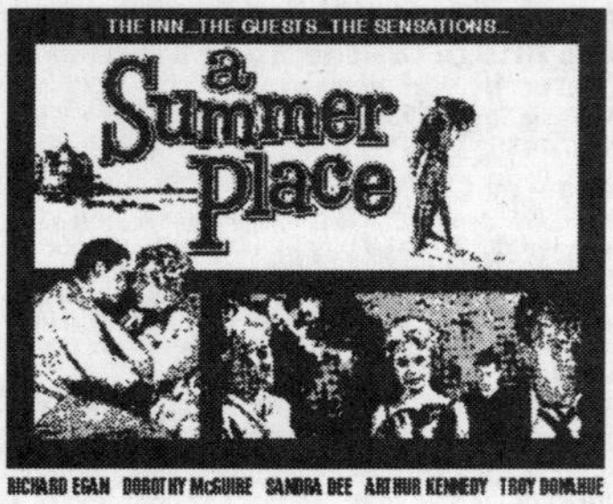

A Summer Place (1959)
Classic soap opera set in a scenic New England town where teenagers and adults discover love and its many entanglements. Richard Egan and Dorothy McGuire are the former lovers who carry on an affair behind their spouses' backs, while Sandra Dee and Troy Donahue play their respective children, engaged in their own romance. With Arthur Kennedy, Constance Ford and that ever-hummable theme song. 130 min.
19-1779 Was $19.99 *$14.99*

Man Of Conflict (1953)
A wealthy young man returns home to oversee the family business, but he soon discovers that his father has become corrupted by his wealth. Things get even more complicated when the son falls in love with the daughter of one of his company's impoverished workers. John Agar, Edward Arnold, Susan Morrow star.
68-9128 *$19.99*

Fame And The Devil (1950)
Would a man sell his soul to the devil for the love of a beautiful woman? That's the question posed in this romantic fantasy in which a diplomat, a singer and a boxer make a pact in order to experience the love of a beautiful woman. Mischa Auer, Marilyn Buford and boxing champ Marcel Cerden star.
68-9136 *$19.99*

The Bloody Brood (1959)
In one of his earliest roles, Peter Falk plays the psychotic leader of a beatnik gang who enjoys torturing people. How psychotic is he? Enough to force a man to eat a hamburger made with broken glass! Outrageous made-in-Canada crime drama also stars Ronald Hartman, Jack Betts. 69 min.
79-5161 Was $24.99 *$19.99*

Room At The Top (1959)
Landmark British "kitchen sink" drama stars Laurence Harvey as a dissatisfied war veteran who'll stop at nothing to rise from his lowly accountant job, even if it means scheming to marry a factory owner's daughter (Heather Sears) while having an affair with an older married woman (Simone Signoret, who won a Best Actress Academy Award). 118 min.
79-8006 *$19.99*

Lost, Lonely And Vicious (1959)
Anything in this drive-in drama that resembles the life of James Dean is probably intentional! A moody young actor, obsessed with fast cars, flirtatious women and death, tries to make it in Hollywood, but meets an untimely death in a sports car accident. Ken Clayton, Barbara Wilson, Richard Gilden star. 73 min.
79-5348 Was $19.99 *$14.99*

Paris Vice Squad (1958)
Lurid based-on-fact crime drama follows a runaway girl whose parents call on the police to help find her. After being discovered working at a restaurant, Denise leaps into a river to her death. An investigation shows that she was taking a dangerous new drug linked to several other mysterious deaths. Raymond Souplex, Jean Debucourt star.
79-5882 Was $24.99 *$19.99*

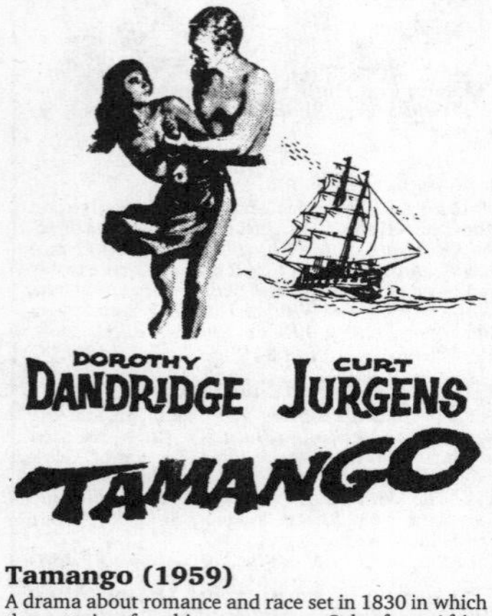

Tamango (1959)
A drama about romance and race set in 1830 in which the captain of a ship en route to Cuba from Africa purchases a group of enslaved natives. The captain takes a beautiful slave as a lover, but she eventually sides with the tribe's leader in a revolt against their captors. Dorothy Dandridge, Curt Jurgens and Alex Cressan star in this forceful tale that was once banned in France. 98 min.
55-9009 Was $29.99 *$19.99*

Las Vegas Shakedown (1955)
Joe Barnes runs the show at El Rancho Casino, but finds out that a mobster he helped put behind bars is out to get him. While the hood prepares to take him out, Joe deals with the different casino patrons, but eventually has to face his old nemesis and his men. Dennis O'Keefe, Coleen Gray, Thomas Gomez and Robert Armstrong star in this crime meller.
79-6507 *$19.99*

A Virgin In Hollywood (1953)
This pseudo-documentary takes a no-holds-barred look at young women's experiences in Tinseltown. A young lady named Darla takes a detour through "The Sidestreets of Hollywood" and viewers get a first-hand, behind-the-scenes study of the city's seamy side. With Dorothy Abbott and Thad Swift.
79-5718 Was $24.99 *$19.99*

Dark Odyssey (1957)
Co-directed by Radley Metzger ("Score"), this intense drama focuses on a young Greek sailor who jumps ship when his freighter docks in New York and sets out to kill a man who disgraced his sister years before. He soon meets a young Greek woman who tries to persuade him to avoid the confrontation. With Jeanne Jerrems and Athan Karras. AKA: "Passionate Sunday." 82 min.
83-3028 *$29.99*

The Devil's Sleep (1951)
Sordid little crime drama about a sleazy drug dealer who pushes pills at a health spa, then tries to blackmail a female juvenile judge on his trail by threatening to sell nude photos of her teenage daughter. Lita Grey Chaplin, Timothy Farrell star; produced by George Weiss ("Glen or Glenda").
79-5717 Was $24.99 *$19.99*

Personal Affair (1954)
A small English town is torn apart by gossip and suspicion when a teenage girl known to have a crush on her handsome teacher disappears and is feared dead. Leo Genn, Gene Tierney, Glynis Johns star. 119 min.
88-1073 *$19.99*

Room 43 (1958)
Shocking tale of prostitution, drugs and degradation as a cab driver discovers a white-slave operation and the very naughty Diana Dors. Herbert Lom and Eddie Constantine star. 85 min.
62-1254 *$19.99*

The Ring (1952)
Gripping "B" boxing drama that also features a frank (for its time) look at racial prejudice. A young Mexican-American must fight in and out of the squared circle as he struggles to become a contender. Gerald Mohr, Rita Moreno, Jack Elam star. 79 min.
50-1554 Was $19.99 *$14.99*

Salt Of The Earth (1954)
Controversial independent production (many of the cast and crew were blacklisted in Hollywood) tells the true story of a New Mexico miners' strike that was won when the wives took over for the mostly Mexican-American workers, who were prohibited from striking. With Will Geer, Rosoura Revueltas. 94 min.
50-6228 *$19.99*

Party Girl (1958)
Superior crime drama by director Nicholas Ray stars Robert Taylor as an attorney in Roaring '20s Chicago who tries, with the love and support of showgirl Cyd Charisse, to escape from under the thumb of mob boss Lee J. Cobb. With John Ireland, Kent Smith, Claire Kelly. 99 min.
12-2380 *$19.99*

The Magnificent Yankee (1950)
Louis Calhern re-creates his acclaimed stage role as legendary Supreme Court justice Oliver Wendell Holmes, Jr., known as "The Great Dissenter." This superb biodrama focuses on the wit and insight behind the groundbreaking decisions made by one of America's finest legal minds. With Ann Harding, Eduard Franz and Philip Ober. 80 min.
12-2770 *$19.99*

Green Fire (1955)
Romance and danger ensue when emerald miner Stewart Granger carries on a fiery affair with coffee plantation owner Grace Kelly in Colombia. Paul Douglas and John Ericson also star in this drama punctuated by such hair-raising scenes of natural disasters as landslides and tropical storms. 100 min.
12-2930 *$19.99*

The End Of The Affair (1955)
The original film version of Graham Greene's novel stars Deborah Kerr and Van Johnson as the star-crossed lovers in WWII London whose romance is punctuated by tragedy and a heartbreaking decision. John Mills, Peter Cushing also star; directed by Edward Dmytryk. 105 min.
02-3412 ❑*$14.99*

The End Of The Affair (1999)
In London shortly after World War II, author Ralph Fiennes is asked by civil servant friend Stephen Rea for help in determining whether wife Julianne Moore is seeing another man. What Rea doesn't know is that Fiennes and Moore had a passionate affair years earlier that she abruptly broke off, and now an obsessed Fiennes seeks to learn why she left him. Writer/director Neil Jordan's ("The Crying Game") rain- and emotion-soaked translation of the Graham Greene tale also stars Ian Hart. 109 min.
02-3422 Was $99.99 ❑*$19.99*

Kipps (1941)
H.G. Wells' slyly satirical novel of Victorian caste and snobbery with a brilliant Michael Redgrave stumbling and fumbling through human foibles. 95 min.
01-1212 Was $19.99 *$14.99*

A Tree Grows In Brooklyn (1945)
Academy Award-winning adaptation of the classic story of a young girl growing up in the crowded tenements of New York. Her closest relationship is with her charming, but alcoholic father and while she resents her mother, tragic developments lead the girl to discover her parents' true worth. Stars Peggy Ann Garner, James Dunn and Joan Blondell; Elia Kazan's Hollywood directorial debut. 128 min.
04-3167 ❑*$14.99*

Pinky (1949)
Groundbreaking look at race relations from director Elia Kazan focuses on a light-skinned black woman (Jeanne Crain) who, after studying nursing in New England, returns to her Southern hometown to help her grandmother (Ethel Waters) care for a wealthy woman (Ethel Barrymore). When the woman dies, the nurse's stake in her will is contested because of her race. 101 min.
04-2744 ❑*$19.99*

Portrait Of Jennie (1948)
Classic tale of a romance that transcends time stars Joseph Cotten as a struggling painter in Depression-era New York who becomes inspired by—and obsessed with—otherworldly beauty Jennifer Jones after a series of chance meetings. David O. Selznick's haunting production also stars Ethel Barrymore, Cecil Kellaway, David Wayne. 86 min.
04-2339 *$14.99*

Stairway To Heaven (1946)
Michael Powell and Emeric Pressburger's classic fantasy/romance stars David Niven as a WWII British pilot who miraculously survives a crash and goes on to fall for American WAC Kim Hunter. When a brain injury suffered in the accident leaves Niven near death, his spirit is summoned before a heavenly court where he pleads to be allowed to return to Earth. With Roger Livesey, Raymond Massey. AKA: "A Matter of Life and Death." 104 min.
02-3100 *$19.99*

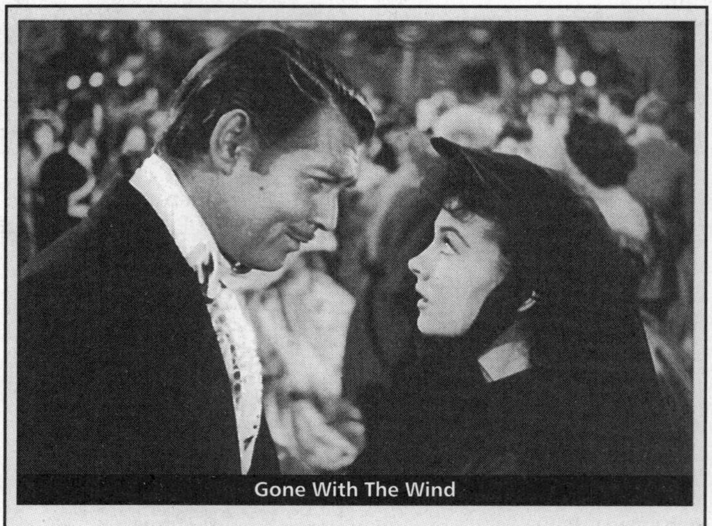
Gone With The Wind

Vivien Leigh

Dark Journey (1937)
A pre-Scarlett Vivien Leigh stars in this adventure saga of British and German spies meeting and falling in love in WWI Sweden. Conrad Veidt co-stars. 76 min.
10-3030 *$19.99*

Storm In A Teacup (1938)
Whimsical romantic comedy starring Rex Harrison as a reporter who takes a job at a paper in a small Scottish village and gets caught up in a story about a poor woman who can't pay for the license for her dog, while falling for the beautiful daughter of the town's strict legal eagle. Vivien Leigh, Sara Allgood and Cecil Parker also star. 88 min.
10-3081 *$19.99*

21 Days (1938)
That's the length of time Laurence Olivier has to spend with lover Vivien Leigh before he comes forward and admits to killing her estranged husband in self-defense. Waiting to be tried for the crime is the wrong suspect, a mentally troubled man. Olivier must come clean, even though his brother, a judge, tells him to keep the secret to himself. With Leslie Banks. 72 min.
53-6063 *$29.99*

Gone With The Wind (1939)
Vivien Leigh is coquettish Southern belle Scarlett O'Hara, Clark Gable is gambler-rogue Rhett Butler, in one of the best-loved films of all time. Olivia de Havilland, Leslie Howard and Hattie McDaniel co-star in this epic of love and loyalty in the Civil War South. Winner of 10 Academy Awards, including Best Picture, Best Actress and Best Supporting Actress. 233 min.
12-1381 Remastered ❑*$24.99*

Sidewalks Of London (1940)
First released in England in 1938, this touching drama stars Charles Laughton as a London street performer who takes homeless waif Vivien Leigh under his wing and helps her become a famous entertainer. Rex Harrison, Larry Adler also star. AKA: "St. Martin's Lane." 86 min.
10-4029 *$19.99*

Waterloo Bridge (1940)
The timeless wartime romance that is an often-requested film at Movies Unlimited. Soldier Robert Taylor and dancer Vivien Leigh meet in war-torn London and fall in love. Lucile Watson, C. Aubrey Smith and Maria Ouspenskaya are featured. 103 min.
12-1446 ❑*$19.99*

Caesar And Cleopatra (1945)
Claude Rains is the stalwart Roman commander and Vivien Leigh the seductive Queen of the Nile in this epic adaptation of George Bernard Shaw's witty look at life, politics and romance in ancient Egypt. With Flora Robson, Stewart Granger, Ernest Thesiger; co-scripted by Shaw. 129 min.
47-1301 Was $29.99 *$14.99*

Anna Karenina (1948)
The lovely Vivien Leigh is magnetic in this Korda-rendered adaptation of the Tolstoy classic, and Ralph Richardson is equally fine as the stodgy husband whose neglect drives her away. Lavish production co-stars Sally Ann Howes, Michael Gough. 98 min.
17-3057 Was $19.99 *$14.99*

The Roman Spring Of Mrs. Stone (1961)
Vivien Leigh stars as a middle-aged actress whose vacation in Italy takes an unexpected turn when she falls for a young gigolo (Warren Beatty). Touching romantic drama, based on a story by Tennessee Williams; Jill St. John, Lotte Lenya also star. 104 min.
19-1396 Was $19.99 *$14.99*

Ship Of Fools (1965)
Oscar-winning drama set on a luxury liner bound for Germany in the early '30s and detailing the lives, loves, and fears of the passengers and crew. The all-star cast includes Vivien Leigh (her last film), Lee Marvin, Oskar Werner, Simone Signoret, Jose Ferrer and Michael Dunn; Stanley Kramer directs. 149 min.
02-1523 Was $59.99 ❑*$19.99*

Vivien Leigh: Scarlett And Beyond
Forever remembered by film fans as Scarlett O'Hara, Vivien Leigh is the focus of this documentary that traces the screen beauty's tumultuous life and work. Includes reminiscences by John Gielgud, Douglas Fairbanks, Jr., Claire Bloom and other stars, clips from such movies as "Fire Over England," "Waterloo Bridge," and, of course, "Gone with the Wind," and more. Jessica Lange hosts. 46 min.
18-7333 Was $19.99 *$14.99*

Vivien Leigh 3-Pack
Three of the Academy Award-winning actress's earliest British films are available in a special collection: "Dark Journey," "Fire Over England" and "Storm in a Teacup."
22-5955 Save $10.00! *$49.99*

Please see our index for these other Vivien Leigh titles: *Fire Over England • A Streetcar Named Desire*

The Trail Of The Lonesome Pine (1936)
An ongoing feud between clans in the hill country of Kentucky forms the backdrop for this early Technicolor drama starring Sylvia Sidney as the daughter of one family who falls for visiting railroad man Fred MacMurray, much to the consternation of Sidney's brother, Henry Fonda. Beulah Bondi, Fuzzy Knight and Spanky McFarland also star. 100 min.
07-2564 *$14.99*

Wings Of The Morning (1937)
The first British film shot in Technicolor, this lush romantic drama also offered Henry Fonda in one his first starring roles, as a Canadian horse trainer who journeys to England to take part in the Epsom Downs Derby and falls for Gypsy beauty Annabella, who plans to compete incognito in the race. With Leslie Banks, Irene Vanbrugh, and famed singer John McCormack. 89 min.
53-8666 *$24.99*

Spawn Of The North (1938)
The rugged and hazardous life of Alaskan salmon fishermen was vividly brought to life in this drama starring Henry Fonda and George Raft as former friends caught on opposite sides of a conflict with Russian pirates who pillage other fishermen's nets. Dorothy Lamour, Akim Tamiroff, John Barrymore and "Slicker the Seal," as himself, co-star. 110 min.
07-2609 *$14.99*

Young Mr. Lincoln (1939)
A wonderful slice of pioneer Americana, John Ford's screen treatment of Lincoln's early life stars Henry Fonda as the inexperienced backwoods lawyer who uses common sense to defend two brothers accused of murder. Alice Brady, Donald Meek, Pauline Moore and Ward Bond co-star. 100 min.
04-2150 *$19.99*

Drums Along The Mohawk (1939)
Elements of rich period detail and high adventure are masterfully blended with humor and romance in this staggering historical drama from John Ford. Henry Fonda and Claudette Colbert are newlywed homesteaders in upstate New York during the American Revolution, fending off marauding Indians and the British. Co-stars Edna May Oliver, John Carradine. 103 min.
04-2152 *$19.99*

The Story Of Alexander Graham Bell (1939)
Don Ameche's best-known screen role cast him as the Scottish-born teacher of the deaf who, along with partner Henry Fonda, sought a way to transmit the human voice telegraphically and invented the telephone. With Loretta Young, Charles Coburn, Gene Lockhart. 97 min.
04-3274 *$19.99*

Jesse James (1939)
A slightly fictionalized (and romanticized) retelling of the lives of outlaw brothers Jesse (Tyrone Power) and Frank (Henry Fonda) James, the circumstances that drove them to crime and the violent end to Jesse's life. Classic Western entertainment; co-stars Randolph Scott, Nancy Kelly. 105 min.
04-3087 Was $19.99 *$14.99*

The Return Of Frank James (1940)
Henry Fonda returns as former outlaw Frank James, out to avenge his brother Jesse's murder in this standout "Western Noir" directed by Fritz Lang. The top-notch supporting cast includes Gene Tierney (her film debut), John Carradine, Jackie Cooper and Henry Hull. 92 min.
04-3088 Was $19.99 *$14.99*

The Grapes Of Wrath (1940)
John Ford's classic social commentary on the plight of the tenant farmer stars Henry Fonda as the eldest son of the Joads, a poor family from the dust bowl of Oklahoma who struggle to maintain their dignity while on a grueling trek to California during the Great Depression. Co-stars Oscar-winner Jane Darwell, John Carradine, Charley Grapewin; adapted from John Steinbeck's novel. 128 min.
04-1400 Was $19.99 *$14.99*

The Male Animal (1942)
Crackerjack romantic comedy with Henry Fonda as a liberal college professor whose job is threatened when he plans to read a controversial letter to his students. At the same time, wife Olivia de Havilland's former boyfriend (Jack Carson) pays her a visit, and Fonda suspects he wants to rekindle their relationship. Joan Leslie, Herbert Anderson co-star. 101 min.
12-2994 *$19.99*

The Ox-Bow Incident (1943)
Director William Wellman draws solid performances from an all-star cast (Henry Fonda, Dana Andrews, Anthony Quinn and Jane Darwell) in his brooding, chilling study of the dangers and irony of the lynch mob mentality. Truly an American classic, based on the novel by Walter Van Tilburg Clark. 75 min.
04-2151 Was $19.99 *$14.99*

The Immortal Sergeant (1943)
A stand-out performance from Henry Fonda distinguishes this wartime drama about a corporal in the British army, hesitant to lead his men into battle in North Africa, who's spurred into action by his dying sergeant (Thomas Mitchell). 90 min.
04-2153 *$19.99*

My Darling Clementine (1946)
Masterful Western from John Ford about Wyatt Earp's arrival in Tombstone and his blood feud with the Clantons, culminating in a fateful meeting at the O.K. Corral. Henry Fonda is Earp, Walter Brennan is Pa Clanton and Victor Mature is Doc Holliday, Earp's ally. 97 min.
04-3092 Was $19.99 *$14.99*

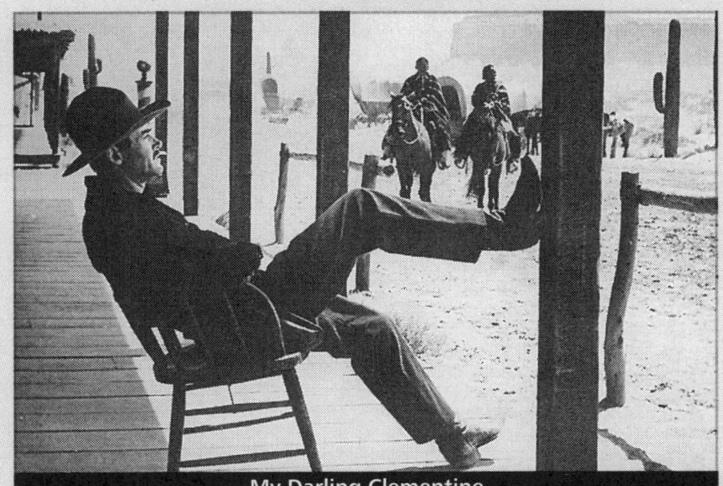
My Darling Clementine

Henry Fonda

The Long Night (1947)
Dynamite remake of Marcel Carne's "Le Jour Se Leve" features Henry Fonda as a WWII vet and factory worker who kills magician Vincent Price, then barricades himself in his apartment from the police. In flashbacks, Fonda relives the desperate situation—which involved himself, girlfriend Barbara Bel Geddes, Price and stage assistant Ann Dvorak—that drove him to kill. Anatole Litvak ("Sorry, Wrong Number") directs. 101 min.
53-6886 *$24.99*

Mister Roberts (1955)
Henry Fonda re-created his Broadway stage role in this classic comedy/drama about the dehumanizing aspects of war. On board a WWII supply ship in the Pacific, cargo officer Fonda longs for combat duty, but in the meantime serves as a buffer between the men and tyrannical captain James Cagney. With William Powell as the ship's doctor and Best Supporting Actor Oscar-winner Jack Lemmon as Ensign Pulver. This special video edition also includes outtakes and interviews with Lemmon and other cast members, a clip from a 1955 "Toast of the Town" salute with Ed Sullivan, the original theatrical trailer and more. 140 min. total.
19-2759 *$19.99*

Mister Roberts (Letterboxed Version)
Also available in a theatrical, widescreen format.
19-2760 *$19.99*

War And Peace (1956)
Spectacular mounting of Tolstoy's classic novel set in Russia during the Napoleonic Wars. Henry Fonda, Mel Ferrer, Audrey Hepburn, Herbert Lom and Anita Ekberg head the all-star cast in this epic of love, conflict and duty. Directed by King Vidor. 208 min.
06-1254 Was $29.99 *$24.99*

The Tin Star (1957)
Top-notch Western story stars Anthony Perkins as a young sheriff who joins an apathetic former lawman (Henry Fonda) to battle a nasty gunslinger. Focus is placed equally on characterization and action in this film co-starring Neville Brand and Betsy Palmer; directed by Anthony Mann. 93 min.
06-1946 *$14.99*

12 Angry Men (1957)
Landmark courtroom drama of a murder trial jury whose rush to a guilty verdict is stopped by one member's doubts stars Henry Fonda as the lone dissenter, with Lee J. Cobb, Ed Begley, E.G. Marshall, Jack Klugman, Martin Balsam and John Fiedler among the other antagonistic jurors. Sidney Lumet's first film was scripted by Reginald Rose from his TV play. 92 min.
12-1966 Was $29.99 *$14.99*

Warlock (1959)
A small frontier town hires two gunfighters to get rid of the outlaws that have been terrorizing them, but learns that the cure may be worse than the disease in this classic example of the "later" Hollywood Western. Henry Fonda, Anthony Quinn, Richard Widmark and Dorothy Malone star. 122 min.
04-3094 *$19.99*

Advise And Consent (1962)
Gripping, classic Washington drama dealing with the power plays that erupt when a controversial politician is nominated for Secretary of State. Director Otto Preminger elicits superb performances from an all-star cast that includes Henry Fonda, Charles Laughton, Burgess Meredith, Gene Tierney and Peter Lawford. 139 min.
19-2213 Letterboxed *$19.99*

Spencer's Mountain (1963)
Compassionate drama based on a novel by "Waltons" creator Earl Hamner, Jr. that also served as the basis for that series. Henry Fonda and Maureen O'Hara are the heads of a struggling Wyoming family who must choose between building a new house and sending their oldest son to college. Donald Crisp, James MacArthur, Mimsy Farmer and Wally Cox also star. 118 min.
19-2134 Was $29.99 *$19.99*

Fail-Safe (1964)
Tense Cold War drama about a squad of American bombers accidentally sent to deliver a nuclear payload on the Soviet Union and unable to be called back, while president Henry Fonda and his advisors try to stop the attack from starting World War III. With Walter Matthau, Fritz Weaver, Dan O'Herlihy. 111 min.
10-2610 *$14.99*

The Best Man (1964)
Gore Vidal adapted his play of backroom politics for this compelling Washington drama. Henry Fonda and Cliff Robertson star as competing candidates for their party's presidential nomination, a quest that tests each man's convictions. With Lee Tracy, Edie Adams, Margaret Leighton. 102 min.
12-1960 Was $29.99 *$19.99*

The Rounders (1965)
Modern-day sagebrush comedy teams Henry Fonda and Glenn Ford as Arizona cowhands who dream of making millions and living the easy life. But first they have to deal with their current state of employment—breaking horses for a cheapskate rancher. And there's one nag that's giving them lots of trouble! Sue Ann Langdon and Chill Wills also star. 85 min.
12-2710 *$19.99*

Battle Of The Bulge (1965)
Spectacular battle sequences highlight this all-star WWII epic. It's the Allied troops vs. the Nazi Panzers in the Ardennes. Some of the greatest action scenes ever presented! Henry Fonda, Robert Shaw, Telly Savalas, Charles Bronson. 156 min.
19-1333 *$19.99*

A Big Hand For The Little Lady (1966)
Breezy Western story starring Henry Fonda and Joanne Woodward as farmers who pool their savings to play in a high-stakes poker game against some local hot-shots. When Henry gets ill, Joanne takes over and rides a hot streak. Jason Robards, Kevin McCarthy, Burgess Meredith and Charles Bickford co-star. 95 min.
19-1828 *$19.99*

The Dirty Game (1966)
Rarely seen European spy thriller, featuring three tales of international espionage related by American general Robert Ryan. Undercover agent Vittorio Gassman is hired by the Soviets to kidnap an Italian rocket scientist; a series of attacks on American submarines is halted; and defecting agent Henry Fonda hides out from Iron Curtain assassins.
68-9084 *$19.99*

Madigan (1968)
First-rate police thriller from director Don Siegel concerning the trials and tribulations between a hard-bitten NYC cop (Richard Widmark) and his harried commissioner (Henry Fonda) as they attempt to stop a psychopathic murderer. Knockout supporting cast includes Harry Guardino, James Whitmore, Susan Clark, Inger Stevens and Michael Dunn. 101 min.
07-1431 Was $59.99 *$14.99*

Once Upon A Time In The West (1969)
Henry Fonda, Charles Bronson, Claudia Cardinale and Jason Robards star in this epic Western of landowners at odds with a railroad, with Fonda in a chilling role as a hired killer. Co-written and directed by Sergio Leone; great score by Ennio Morricone. Complete, uncut version; 165 min.
06-1237 Remastered *$24.99*

Too Late The Hero (1970)
Cliff Robertson and Michael Caine are "volunteered" into a suicide mission in the WWII Pacific Theater. Henry Fonda and Denholm Elliott also star in this taut wartime thriller that turns into a battle of wits between the duo and a Japanese officer. 133 min.
04-1426 Was $19.99 *$14.99*

There Was A Crooked Man... (1970)
Henry Fonda is a reform-minded prison warden in the 1880s West and Kirk Douglas is an escape-obsessed inmate in this action film that combines suspense, action and comedy. Hume Cronyn, Burgess Meredith, Warren Oates co-star. 125 min.
19-1466 *$14.99*

My Name Is Nobody (1974)
An aging gunfighter (Henry Fonda) wants to hang up his holster, but must contend with a younger man who idolizes him (Terence Hill). Easygoing Western comedy/drama also stars Leo Gordon, R.G. Armstrong. AKA: "Lonesome Gun," "Gunfire." 115 min.
10-3182 *$24.99*

Clarence Darrow (1974)
Stirring one-man stage performance stars Henry Fonda as the century's most famous lawyer, recounting his involvement with such controversial cases as the Leopold/Loeb murder trial and the Scopes "monkey trial," and Darrow's passionate belief in the rights of the individual. 81 min.
67-5014 Was $29.99 *$24.99*

Gideon's Trumpet (1980)
Henry Fonda stars in the true story of a drifter who is arrested in Florida and convicted without benefit of council. While in prison, he studies law and eventually takes his landmark appeal to the Supreme Court. Jose Ferrer, John Houseman, Fay Wray also star. 105 min.
14-3016 *$49.99*

The Oldest Living Graduate (1980)
Henry Fonda's last stage appearance was as a cantankerous World War I vet in this made-for-television drama. Fonda finds himself at odds with his family over his wish to donate valuable land to the military academy honoring him as its oldest living graduate. Timothy Hutton, David Ogden Stiers and John Lithgow co-star in this gripping story. 75 min.
23-5029 *$29.99*

On Golden Pond (1981)
Academy Awards went to Henry Fonda (his first) and Katharine Hepburn (her fourth) for this moving drama about an aging couple whose annual trip to their lakeside New England summer cottage offers Fonda a chance to reconcile his relationship with his grown daughter (Jane Fonda) and form a new friendship with her boyfriend's son. With Doug McKeon, Dabney Coleman. 109 min.
27-5414 *$14.99*

On Golden Pond (Letterboxed Version)
Also available in a theatrical, widescreen format.
27-7062 *$14.99*

The Deputy
Henry Fonda played the title character in this NBC western that ran from 1959-1961. He's a lawman in 1880s Arizona Territory who called on Alan Case, a pacifist storekeeper, to help him keep the peace. Fonda is taken hostage by an outlaw in "The Hard Decision" and Case tries to find missing loot before it's discovered upon "The Return of Widow Brown." 50 min.
09-5355 *$14.99*

Henry Fonda: The Man And His Movies
An affectionate and informative look at one of Hollywood's most honored and beloved actors, featuring film clips and interviews to follow a film career spanning from "Young Mr. Lincoln," "The Grapes of Wrath," and "My Darling Clementine" to "On Golden Pond." Arthur Hill narrates. 60 min.
18-7026 *$19.99*

Fonda On Fonda
Who better than daughter Jane to host this up-close and personal look at Henry Fonda, one of America's best-loved actors? Follow his career on stage and screen with interviews and clips from Fonda's greatest films, from "The Grapes of Wrath" and "Mister Roberts" to his final, Academy Award-winning role in "On Golden Pond." 46 min.
18-7471 *$14.99*

Henry Fonda Westerns Gift Pack
Frontier fans will be awfully "fonda" this boxed collection featuring four of Fonda's finest sagebrush sagas: "Jesse James," "My Darling Clementine," "The Ox-Bow Incident" and "The Return of Frank James."
04-3831 *$34.99*

Please see our index for these other Henry Fonda titles: *Ash Wednesday • Captains And The Kings • The Cheyenne Social Club • Firecreek • How The West Was Won • In Harm's Way • Jezebel • The Lady Eve • The Longest Day • Meteor • Midway • On Our Merry Way • Sex And The Single Girl • Sometimes A Great Notion • The Swarm • Tales Of Manhattan • Tentacles • That Certain Woman • The Wrong Man • Yours, Mine And Ours*

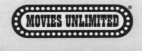

A Bill Of Divorcement (1932)
John Barrymore, Katharine Hepburn (in her film debut) and Billie Barnes excel in this touching story of a man who escapes from a mental hospital in order to join his much-surprised family. George Cukor directs this classic. 70 min.
04-2338 Was $39.99 ❑*$14.99*

Little Women (1933)
Louisa May Alcott's beloved story, focusing on the joys and sorrows of four sisters growing up in New England during the Civil War, is given a grand Hollywood treatment. Katharine Hepburn, Joan Bennett, Paul Lukas. 116 min.
12-1088 *$19.99*

Alice Adams (1935)
Katharine Hepburn is Booth Tarkington's irrepressible Alice Adams, a middle-class girl whose pretense of coming from wealth is forever being shattered by her family's graceless behavior. Fred MacMurray co-stars as her affluent intended; with Grady Sutton, Hattie McDaniel. George Stevens directs. 99 min.
05-1012 *$19.99*

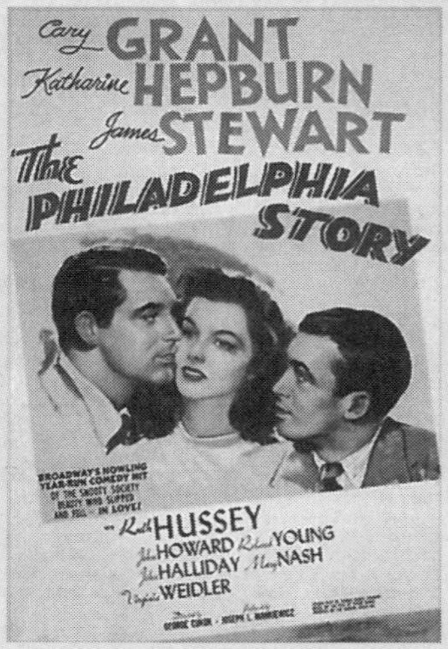

The Philadelphia Story: Special Edition (1940)
A gem of sophisticated comedy set in Philadelphia's ritzy Main Line suburbs, with Katharine Hepburn re-creating her stage role as society girl Tracy Lord, whose upcoming marriage is imperiled by the attentions of reporter James Stewart and ex-husband Cary Grant. John Howard, Ruth Hussey, Virginia Weidler co-star; directed by George Cukor. Includes the hour-long documentary "Katharine Hepburn: All About Me." 176 min. total.
19-2945 *$19.99*

Woman Of The Year (1942)
One of Hollywood's most famous on- and off-screen pairings got its start in this crackerjack comedy. Spencer Tracy plays the gruff New York sports reporter who falls for international affairs writer Katharine Hepburn, but after they wed their competing careers threaten the marriage. With Reginald Owen, William Bendix; George Stevens directs. 114 min.
12-1092 Was $19.99 ❑*$14.99*

Keeper Of The Flame (1942)
Spencer Tracy and Katharine Hepburn star in this gripping melodrama about a newspaper reporter set to write about the life of a war hero killed in an auto accident. During his investigation, Tracy interviews the hero's widow, a recluse who knows some unsavory secrets about her late, lamented husband. Richard Whorf, Margaret Wycherly and Forrest Tucker also star; George Cukor directs. 100 min.
12-2287 Was $19.99 *$14.99*

Dragon Seed (1944)
In this lavish production, based on a novel by Pearl S. Buck, an idealistic Chinese patriot leads the people of her town to resist invading Japanese forces. Captivating drama of human courage stars Katharine Hepburn, Walter Huston, Turhan Bey and Agnes Moorehead. 149 min.
12-1460 Was $19.99 *$14.99*

Without Love (1945)
The unavoidable romantic sparks fly when widow Katharine Hepburn rents a room in her Washington, D.C., home to scientist-inventor Spencer Tracy, but only after they agree to a platonic marriage for appearance sake. Keenan Wynn and Lucille Ball also star. 103 min.
12-2292 Was $19.99 *$14.99*

Undercurrent (1946)
In this suspenseful film noir directed by Vincente Minnelli, Katharine Hepburn plays a woman who discovers her new husband, an airplane manufacturer, has been lying about his past and may have framed his brother on a robbery charge. Robert Taylor, Robert Mitchum, Edmund Gwenn also star. 126 min.
12-2291 Was $19.99 *$14.99*

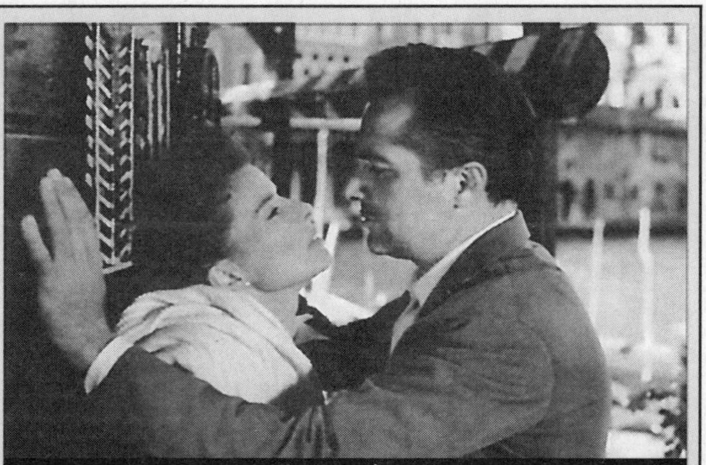
Summertime

Katharine Hepburn

The Sea Of Grass (1947)
Sprawling Western melodrama with Spencer Tracy as a ruthless cattle baron who uses both legal and illegal means to keep homesteaders off of his New Mexico land, while driving wife Katharine Hepburn into the arms of his courtroom rival, crusading attorney Melvyn Douglas. Co-stars Robert Walker and Edgar Buchanan; Elia Kazan directs. 123 min.
12-2288 Was $19.99 *$14.99*

Song Of Love (1947)
Classical-themed biodrama stars Katharine Hepburn as Clara Wieck Schumann, a pianist who devotes her life to popularizing the music of her late, emotionally troubled husband, composer Robert Schumann (Paul Henreid). With Robert Walker as Johannes Brahms, Henry Daniell as Franz Liszt, and Artur Rubinstein ghosting the stars' musical performances. 119 min.
12-2290 *$19.99*

Adam's Rib (1949)
Husband-and-wife lawyers Spencer Tracy and Katharine Hepburn face the biggest case of their professional lives when they take opposite sides in the trial of a woman accused of trying to shoot her philandering husband. Witty "battle of the sexes" comedy from Ruth Gordon and Garson Kanin also stars Judy Holliday, Tom Ewell, David Wayne. 101 min.
12-1000 Was $19.99 *$14.99*

Adam's Rib (Color Version)
Why did Tracy and Hepburn call each other "Pinky"? Find out in the computer-hued rendition of this classic comedy.
12-1802 *$19.99*

Pat And Mike (1952)
Crisp direction from George Cukor and "cherce" Ruth Gordon/Garson Kanin dialogue highlight this comedy about shady sports promoter Spencer Tracy and his latest find, college gym teacher Katharine Hepburn. With William Ching, Aldo Ray, and early appearances by Charles Bronson and Chuck Connors. 95 min.
12-1129 Was $19.99 *$14.99*

Summertime (1955)
Director David Lean's classic romantic drama of a middle-aged American woman (Katharine Hepburn) who, while on vacation in Venice, has a doomed love affair with a handsome Italian man (Rossano Brazzi), whom she eventually learns is married. 98 min.
22-5670 Remastered *$24.99*

The Rainmaker (1956)
A charismatic con man blows into a drought-stricken town and transforms it and the local spinster, more with audacity and idealism than from his unproved weather-changing powers. Katharine Hepburn and Burt Lancaster star. 121 min.
06-1591 *$14.99*

Desk Set (1957)
Spry romantic comedy with an office setting, as research department leader Katharine Hepburn pits her workers' wits against the electronic brain being brought in by efficiency expert Spencer Tracy. With Joan Blondell, Gig Young. 103 min.
04-2299 Was $19.99 ❑*$14.99*

Long Day's Journey Into Night (1962)
Eugene O'Neill's explosive autobiographical drama about homelife populated by a drug-addicted mother, a drunken father and an emotionally unstable brother. Dynamic performances by Katharine Hepburn, Jason Robards, Ralph Richardson. Directed by Sidney Lumet. 179 min.
63-1047 *$19.99*

Guess Who's Coming To Dinner (1967)
A fashionably liberal couple (Spencer Tracy and Katharine Hepburn, in their last film together) are shocked when daughter Katharine Houghton announces her engagement to a black man (Sidney Poitier). Stanley Kramer's drama features an Oscar-winning screenplay. 108 min.
02-1539 ❑*$14.99*

The Lion In Winter (1968)
Katharine Hepburn won her third Oscar as strong-willed Queen Eleanor of Aquitaine, fighting a battle of wills for England's future against Peter O'Toole's King Henry II in this classic historical drama. Co-stars Anthony Hopkins, Jane Merrow; Anthony Harvey directs. 134 min.
53-1453 *$14.99*

The Madwoman Of Chaillot (1969)
Giraudoux's farce is updated to Paris in the 1960s, where wacky Katharine Hepburn and her three friends who frequent a sidewalk cafe discover that businessmen plan to destroy the City of Lights by drilling for oil. All-star cast includes Danny Kaye, Richard Chamberlain, Charles Boyer, Yul Brynner and Margaret Leighton. 132 min.
19-1951 Was $29.99 *$19.99*

Olly Olly Oxen Free (1978)
Delightful adventure film for the whole family stars Katharine Hepburn as an eccentric junkyard owner who helps two youngsters as they repair their grandfather's hot-air balloon and take an exciting journey over Southern California. With Kevin McKenzie, Dennis Dimster. AKA: "The Great Balloon Adventure." 83 min.
19-2491 *$14.99*

The Corn Is Green (1979)
In this moving remake of the 1945 Bette Davis film, Katharine Hepburn plays a British spinster teacher who attempts to educate a group of miners in turn-of-the-century North Wales. One of the young miners shows signs of true brilliance, and Hepburn persuades him to continue his education. Ian Saynor, Bill Fraser and Anna Massey co-star; George Cukor directs. 93 min.
19-1946 Was $29.99 *$14.99*

This Can't Be Love (1994)
In this bittersweet comedy, Katharine Hepburn plays a retired actress who has led a lonely life of guarded privacy. When old flame Anthony Quinn returns to her, Hepburn is caught off-guard as sparks fly between the ex-lovers. Jamie Gertz and Jason Bateman also star; Anthony Harvey ("The Lion in Winter") directs. 94 min.
77-3002 *$99.99*

One Christmas (1995)
Truman Capote's story is set in 1930, where 8-year-old Buddy leaves his cousin's Alabama home to visit his scheming, estranged father in New Orleans for the holidays. Buddy soon realizes his dreams of snow and a visit from Santa may not occur—especially if he and his father don't reach an accord by Christmas Day. Henry Winkler, Katharine Hepburn, Swoosie Kurtz star. 96 min.
58-5216 ❑*$14.99*

Please see our index for these other Katharine Hepburn titles: *The African Queen • Bringing Up Baby • Holiday • Love Affair • On Golden Pond • Rooster Cogburn • Stagedoor Canteen • State Of The Union • Suddenly, Last Summer*

Fame Is The Spur (1947)
Revealing look at a politician's rise from poverty to national prominence in this British drama. Distinguished cast includes Michael Redgrave, Bernard John and Rosamund John; directed by England's famed Boulting Brothers. 116 min.
08-5018 Was $19.99 *$14.99*

Elizabeth Of Ladymead (1948)
A fascinating and charming tale from the husband-wife team of director Herbert Wilcox and actress Anna Neagle, who plays four generations of British wives (from 1854 to 1946) seeing their husbands off to various wars. Hugh Williams, Bernard Lee also star. 97 min.
08-5017 *$19.99*

The Southerner (1945)
Superlative rural drama by French filmmaker Jean Renoir during his '40s Hollywood period. Patriarch Zachary Scott and his family try to make a go of a small, rundown farm despite illness, floods and spiteful neighbors. Betty Field, Beulah Bondi, J. Carrol Naish co-star. 81 min.
08-8069 Was $19.99 *$14.99*

Underground (1941)
One of the first Hollywood films to take a serious look at life in Hitler's Germany, this sobering drama follows brothers Jeffrey Lynn and Philip Dorn as they follow very different paths: Lynn as a dedicated soldier, Dorn as a member of the Resistance movement. With Martin Kosleck, Kaaren Verne. 95 min.
08-1817 *$14.99*

Danny Boy (1941)
Flag-waving heart-tugger with Ann Todd as a British expatriate who does her part for the war effort by returning to Merry Olde after a successful career on Broadway. There she launches a search for her down-and-out ex-husband and the son she hasn't seen in years. With David Farrar, Wilfrid Lawson. 67 min.
09-1025 Was $19.99 *$14.99*

Wrecking Crew (1942)
Exciting drama of two demolition experts whose friendship is threatened when they fall in love with the same woman. Their differences take a back seat when both are stranded atop a structure about to collapse. Richard Arlen, Evelyn Brent and Alec Craig star. 72 min.
08-1696 *$14.99*

The Underdog (1943)
A farm family chased from their land by drought makes a difficult adjustment to city ways during WWII. Bobby Larson is the son, a target of street toughs along with his faithful dog Hobo, and Barton MacLane is his dad, a watchman at a factory infiltrated by fifth columnists. 65 min.
09-2065 *$19.99*

Identity Unknown (1945)
Heartbreaking anti-war story in the mold of "The Best Years of Our Lives." A vet returning home after World War II can't find his true home because of a case of shellshock. He travels around the country, meeting a diverse group of people whose lives he affects. Richard Arlen, Cheryl Walker and Bobby Driscoll star. 70 min.
09-2122 Was $29.99 *$19.99*

Detour To Danger (1945)
A camp curiosity, directed by Richard Talmadge (best known as Douglas Fairbanks' stunt double). Two pals (one a handsome athlete, the other old and ugly) set out on a fishing vacation and are confronted by a bevy of babes and bandits. 56 min.
09-2124 Was $24.99 *$19.99*

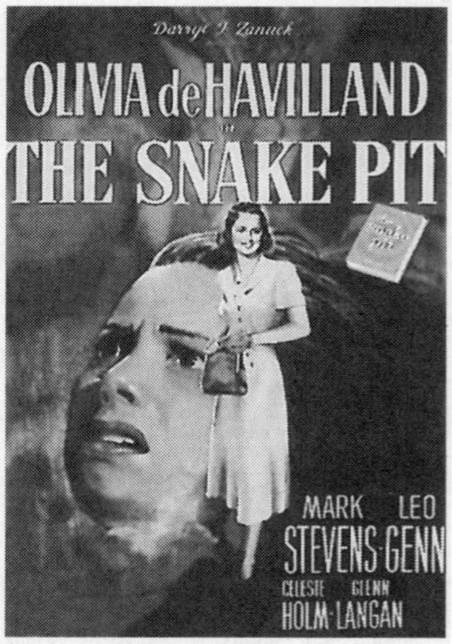

The Snake Pit (1948)
A devastating descent into the world of mental illness starring Olivia de Havilland as a disturbed young woman whose husband places her in a mental institution following an emotional lapse. There she witnesses the horrid treatment of other patients, while receiving help from an understanding psychiatrist. Mark Stevens, Leo Genn and Celeste Holm also star. 108 min.
04-2623 *$19.99*

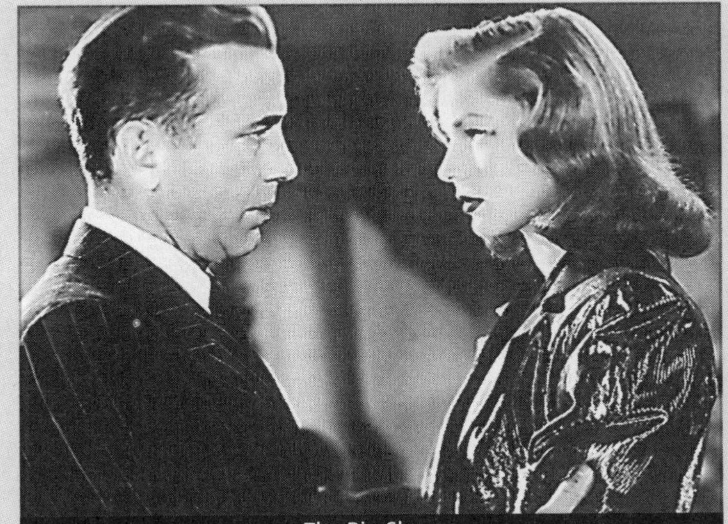

The Big Sleep

Humphrey Bogart

Call It Murder (1934)
One of Humphrey Bogart's first featured roles was as a gangster in this story of a man who must help his daughter when she is accused of murder. Henry Hull, O.P. Heggie, Sidney Fox also star. AKA: "Midnight." 80 min.
10-1071 *$19.99*

The Petrified Forest (1936)
Classic gangster drama that made Humphrey Bogart a star. Based on Robert Sherwood's play about fugitive mobsters holding the residents of an isolated Arizona cafe hostage, the film also stars Bette Davis as a dreamy waitress and Leslie Howard as a bored drifter. 83 min.
12-2000 □*$19.99*

Black Legion (1937)
A groundbreaking look at racial hatred, this Warners social drama stars Humphrey Bogart as an auto plant worker embittered when an immigrant co-worker is promoted over him. Recruited by a black-clad "Pro-American" group, Bogart gladly takes part in their increasingly violent activities, until he's forced to choose between his loyalty to the Legion and his best friend's life. Dick Foran, Erin O'Brien-Moore, Ann Sheridan also star. 83 min.
19-2940 *$19.99*

Dead End (1937)
Landmark drama of life in the crime-ridden slums of Depression-era New York stars Humphrey Bogart as a hoodlum who returns to his old neighborhood and is idolized by the local youths (the Dead End Kids, in their film debut). William Wyler's classic crime tale, scripted by Lillian Hellman, also stars Joel McCrea, Sylvia Sidney, Wendy Barrie. 92 min.
44-1876 Was $19.99 *$14.99*

They Drive By Night (1940)
Gritty and compelling road drama stars George Raft and Humphrey Bogart as truck-driving brothers who take on corrupt businessmen when they try to set up their own company. Ann Sheridan, Ida Lupino, Alan Hale co-star; Raoul Walsh directs. 93 min.
12-2247 *$19.99*

High Sierra (1941)
Humphrey Bogart is world-weary gangster "Mad Dog" Earle, on the run when his "final job" backfires and hiding in California's Sierra Mountains, in this classic crime drama. With Ida Lupino, Alan Curtis, Joan Leslie. 100 min.
12-2031 *$19.99*

The Maltese Falcon: Special Edition (1941)
One of the finest detective films ever, with Bogie as private eye Sam Spade, up to his trench coat in greed, deception and murder. Joining him in the search for the priceless "black bird" are Mary Astor, Sydney Greenstreet, Peter Lorre, Elisha Cook, Jr. and Lee Patrick. John Huston's directorial debut. Special restored version includes the documentary "Becoming Attractions: Humphrey Bogart," and a new digital transfer. 149 min. total.
12-1146 □*$19.99*

The Wagons Roll At Night (1941)
The basic plot of 1937's "Kid Galahad" was moved from a boxing ring to a big top ring for this drama starring Humphrey Bogart as the owner of a travelling carnival. When new lion tamer Eddie Albert falls for Bogart's convent-schooled sister (Joan Leslie), an overly protective Bogey plans for Albert to be "accidentally" killed by the big cats. With Sylvia Sidney, Sig Rumann. 84 min.
19-2941 *$19.99*

Casablanca (Special Edition) (1942)
As time goes by, it remains one of the best-loved films ever made. Humphrey Bogart is café owner Rick, Ingrid Bergman lost love Ilsa, Paul Henreid resistance leader Victor. Their lives and passions come together in exotic Casablanca. Winner of three Academy Awards, including Best Picture. With Claude Rains, Conrad Veidt, Dooley Wilson, Peter Lorre, Sidney Greenstreet; Michael Curtiz directs. This special video version includes an introduction by Lauren Bacall and the documentary "You Must Remember This," with newly-found outtakes and screen tests. 145 min. total.
12-1853 Was $24.99 □*$19.99*

Casablanca (50th Anniversary Deluxe Collector's Edition)
Of all the boxed sets in all the video catalogs in all the world, film fans won't want to miss this one. Along with a newly remastered edition of "Casablanca," there's a separate documentary on the making of the movie, hosted by Lauren Bacall; the coffee-table book "You Must Remember This"; a copy of the shooting script; publicity stills and more.
12-2454 □*$99.99*

Across The Pacific (1942)
Director John Huston reunites with "Maltese Falcon" principals Humphrey Bogart, Mary Astor and Sydney Greenstreet in this riveting WWII spy story. Bogie goes undercover for the U.S. and takes to a ship headed to the Pacific via the Panama Canal. Intrigue ensues with double crosses, Japanese agents and dangerous liaisons. 97 min.
12-2228 *$19.99*

All Through The Night (1942)
Dapper New York gambler Humphrey Bogart's search for the missing baker who prepares his favorite cheesecake leads him and his cronies into battle with Nazi spies in this slam-bang wartime actioner laced with comedy. The great supporting cast includes Conrad Veidt, Peter Lorre, Kaaren Verne, William Demarest, Jane Darwell and a young Jackie Gleason. 107 min.
12-2391 *$19.99*

Sahara (1943)
Humphrey Bogart excels as a world-weary commander of a huge American tank named Lulu Belle which he must move across the Sahara desert during World War II in order to rejoin the British Eighth Army. Bogey and crew face enemy forces, a diverse group of passengers and a desperate need for water while trying to reach their destination. With Bruce Bennett, Lloyd Bridges. 98 min.
02-1095 *$19.99*

Action In The North Atlantic (1943)
A hearty salute to the unsung heroics of the Merchant Marines during World War II. Tough first mate Humphrey Bogart and noble captain Raymond Massey battle U-boats and against all odds on the way to Russia with important wartime supplies. With Alan Hale, Julie Bishop, Ruth Gordon. 129 min.
12-2229 *$19.99*

To Have And Have Not (1944)
Bogart and Bacall (in her film debut) set the screen ablaze in this wartime adventure/romance, based on Ernest Hemingway's novel. A boat captain in Martinique joins the French Resistance and gets involved with a young woman. Classic Howard Hawks drama co-stars Walter Brennan, Hoagy Carmichael, Sheldon Leonard, Dan Seymour. 100 min.
12-1507 □*$19.99*

Passage To Marseille (1944)
Epic WWII drama stars Humphrey Bogart, Claude Rains, Peter Lorre, Sydney Greenstreet and Michele Morgan in a story of Devil's Island escapees who join up with Free French sailors on a ship bound for Nazi-occupied France. Michael Curtiz directs. 109 min.
12-2273 *$19.99*

Conflict (1945)
Unhappily-married architect Humphrey Bogart falls in love with his sister-in-law and plots his spouse's demise. But after he commits his "perfect" crime, Bogart is haunted by her presence in this gripping psychological mystery. Rose Hobart, Alexis Smith, Sydney Greenstreet co-star. 86 min.
12-2394 *$19.99*

The Big Sleep (1946)
Raymond Chandler's witty and convoluted whodunit comes to life under director Howard Hawks. Humphrey Bogart is private eye Philip Marlowe, investigating a wealthy family's dark secrets, and Lauren Bacall is the sharp-tongued rich girl ensnared with him in a murderous web of deceit, blackmail and murder. With Martha Vickers, John Ridgely, Elisha Cook, Jr., Dorothy Malone. This is the theatrical release version; 114 min.
12-1142 *$19.99*

The Big Sleep (Restored Pre-release Version)
Shown overseas to military audiences in 1945 and then shelved, this recently found print of the Bogart-Bacall thriller features 18 minutes of footage reshot or unused in the theatrical edition. Also included is a documentary comparing the differences between the two versions of the film. 115 min. Features nearly 20 minutes of scenes reshot or unused in the theatrical version.
12-3269 *$19.99*

Dead Reckoning (1947)
When a war buddy is found murdered, ex-G.I. Humphrey Bogart investigates the killing and is soon ensnared in a dangerous web of desire, crime, and deception. Taut "film noir" thriller also stars Lizabeth Scott, Morris Carnovsky, Marvin Miller. 100 min.
02-1826 Was $69.99 *$19.99*

Dark Passage (1947)
Escaping from prison after being framed for his wife's murder, Humphrey Bogart hides out with Lauren Bacall and undergoes plastic surgery in an attempt to find the real killer. Offbeat mystery, fueled by the Bogey/Bacall magic, also stars Agnes Moorehead, Tom D'Andrea. 106 min.
12-2030 □*$19.99*

The Two Mrs. Carrolls (1947)
Humphrey Bogart was cast against type in this effective nail-biting thriller about a psychotic artist who paints his wife as an "Angel of Death" and then kills her in order to marry Barbara Stanwyck. When another woman catches his eye, however, he attempts to repeat the crime. With Alexis Smith, Ann Carter, Nigel Bruce. 99 min.
12-2395 *$19.99*

"KEY LARGO"

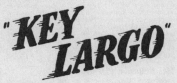

Key Largo (1948)
Gangster Edward G. Robinson takes the inhabitants of a Florida coast hotel hostage as a storm sweeps in, and engages in a battle of wills with world-weary veteran Humphrey Bogart, in John Huston's classic drama. With Lauren Bacall, Lionel Barrymore and Oscar-winner Claire Trevor; look for Jay Silverheels as an escaped con. 101 min.
12-1144 *$19.99*

The Treasure Of The Sierra Madre (1948)
Writer/director John Huston's masterful study of greed stars Humphrey Bogart and Tim Holt as American vagrants in Mexico who team up with grizzled prospector Walter Huston in a search for gold that gets them far more than they ever imagined. Winner of three Academy Awards, the film also features Bruce Bennett, Bobby Blake, and Alfonso Bedoya as the bandit who "ain't got no badges." 126 min.
12-1151 *$19.99*

Knock On Any Door (1949)
Humphrey Bogart, John Derek, Susan Perry. In the slums you can find a Nick Romano if you "knock on any door." Nicholas Ray directed this tense courtroom drama. 100 min.
02-1045 *$19.99*

Tokyo Joe (1949)
Believing his wife died in a Japanese concentration camp and ignorant of the daughter she bore, Air Corps hero Humphrey Bogart finds both in a post-war Tokyo, hostages of master spy Sessue Hayakawa, and is forced to fly war criminals out of the country to protect them. 88 min.
02-1949 Was $69.99 *$19.99*

In A Lonely Place (1950)
Potent and brooding film noir from Nicholas Ray, with Humphrey Bogart as a short-fused screenwriter, exonerated in the murder of a hat-check girl through the alibi of neighbor Gloria Grahame. But as the romance between Bogart and Grahame grows, doubts to his innocence begin to arise. Co-stars Frank Lovejoy and Carl Benton Reid. 92 min.
02-1915 Was $69.99 *$19.99*

Chain Lightning (1950)
WWII pilot Humphrey Bogart is hired after the war by aircraft factory owner Raymond Massey to fly a new, experimental jet plane from Alaska to Washington, D.C., in this fast-paced drama that features great aerial footage. Eleanor Parker, James Brown co-star. 94 min.
12-2393 *$19.99*

Sirocco (1951)
Humphrey Bogart is a gun-runner in 1920s Syria in this action-filled drama of war, exotic action and romance. Co-stars Lee J. Cobb, Marta Toren and Zero Mostel. 98 min.
02-1563 *$19.99*

The Enforcer (1951)
Bogart is captured in front-line as a crusading D.A. out to break the back of a vicious murder-for-hire ring. He must win a race against time to uncover the killer of his star witness. Everett Sloane, Zero Mostel, Ted de Corsia co-star. 87 min.
63-1257 Was $19.99 *$14.99*

Battle Circus (1953)
Nearly 20 years before "M*A*S*H," Humphrey Bogart played an Army doctor stationed at a mobile surgical hospital in the Korean War. His bitter, hard-drinking manner changes when nurse June Allyson joins the unit. With Keenan Wynn, Robert Keith. 90 min.
12-2392 *$19.99*

The Caine Mutiny (1954)
Electrifying performances by Humphrey Bogart, Jose Ferrer, Van Johnson and Fred MacMurray highlight this drama of naval officers who mutiny against a psychotic captain and are placed on trial. Based on the award-winning novel by Herman Wouk; nominated for four Academy Awards. 125 min.
02-1395 *$19.99*

The Caine Mutiny (Letterboxed Version)
Also available in a theatrical, widescreen format.
02-3239 □*$19.99*

Beat The Devil (1954)
Offbeat is the only way to describe this John Huston/Truman Capote collaboration about a ragtag group of con men out to swindle each other while on a Mediterranean cruise. Wild action spoof stars Humphrey Bogart, Jennifer Jones, Robert Morley, Peter Lorre and Gina Lollobrigida. 89 min.
02-1555 *$19.99*

The Barefoot Contessa (1954)
Ava Gardner and Humphrey Bogart star in a sardonic tale of Hollywood machinations, as a Spanish singer is groomed for stardom by an older, down-on-his-luck director. Edmond O'Brien won an Oscar for his role as a cynical press agent. 128 min.
12-1118 Was $19.99 □*$14.99*

The Left Hand Of God (1955)
Humphrey Bogart, in one of his last films, stars as an American pilot in post-WWII China who masquerades as a priest and finds himself embroiled in conflict with renegade warlord Lee J. Cobb. Gene Tierney, Agnes Moorehead and Benson Fong co-star. 87 min.
04-1730 *$19.99*

We're No Angels (1955)
Classic offbeat comedy focuses on three escaped convicts from Devil's Island—played by Humphrey Bogart, Aldo Ray and Peter Ustinov—who take to a French house for refuge. Lots of funny gags and performances here. Joan Bennett, Basil Rathbone; Michael Curtiz directs. 106 min.
06-1198 *$14.99*

The Desperate Hours (1955)
A trio of escaped prisoners terrorize a suburban family while hiding out in their house in William Wyler's gripping drama. Humphrey Bogart plays the lead con, and Fredric March is the father trying to protect his family. Arthur Kennedy, Martha Scott co-star. 112 min.
06-1667 Was $19.99 *$14.99*

The Harder They Fall (1956)
Sportswriter-turned-press agent Humphrey Bogart is hired by a crooked boxing promoter and learns first-hand how fighters are manipulated and used in this powerful social drama that was Bogart's last film. With Rod Steiger, Jan Sterling, and ring greats Max Baer and Jersey Joe Walcott. 109 min.
02-1041 Was $59.99 *$19.99*

Bogart & Bacall Collection
Their on- and off-screen romance was the stuff of Hollywood legend, and in this special boxed set you'll experience the Bogey/Bacall chemistry with "The Big Sleep" (the theatrical release version), "Dark Passage," "Key Largo" and "To Have and Have Not," plus the bonus documentary "Bacall on Bogart."
19-2942 *$59.99*

Please see our index for these other Humphrey Bogart titles: *The Amazing Dr. Clitterhouse • Angels With Dirty Faces • Brother Orchid • Bullets Or Ballots • Dark Victory • Marked Woman • The Oklahoma Kid • The Roaring Twenties • Three On A Match • Virginia City*

Citizen Kane (1941)
Director/co-writer/star Orson Welles' landmark debut film, a sweeping chronicle of the rise and fall of fictitious newspaper tycoon Charles Foster Kane and the mystery surrounding his dying word, is recognized as one of the greatest and most innovative movies of all time. The "Mercury Players" cast includes Dorothy Comingore, Joseph Cotten, Everett Sloane and Ruth Warrick. Special video release includes the original theatrical trailer and a documentary on the making of the film. 119 min.
05-1317 Remastered *$19.99*

The Battle Over Citizen Kane (1996)
How close did the most acclaimed film of all time come to being tossed in the fire alongside "Rosebud"? This acclaimed documentary looks at the showdown between 25-year-old wunderkind Orson Welles and publishing plutocrat William Randolph Hearst over Welles and co-writer Herman Mankiewicz's thinly-veiled screen biography. See how Hearst's life differed from "Kane's" fiction, watch rare footage of Welles' New York theatre and radio days, and hear from people involved on both sides of the battle. 120 min.
90-1101 ❑*$19.99*

The Magnificent Ambersons (1942)
Orson Welles' second film is a daring study of the decline of a wealthy family in the late 19th-century Midwest and the relationship between the arrogant son and his family's matriarch. Initially ill-received by its studio, the film has come to be considered a dramatic masterpiece. The translation of Booth Tarkington's novel stars Joseph Cotten, Tim Holt, Dolores Costello. Also includes the original theatrical trailer. 88 min.
18-7654 *$19.99*

Jane Eyre (1944)
This darkly romantic film of Charlotte Brontë's classic novel is set in Victorian England and stars Joan Fontaine as a spinsterish governess who takes a position on a remote estate in the Yorkshire moors and falls in love with the manor's brooding master (Orson Welles). Features an unforgettable Bernard Herrmann score and eerie photography. With Margaret O'Brien and Peggy Ann Garner; look for a young Elizabeth Taylor. 96 min.
04-2289 *$19.99*

Tomorrow Is Forever (1946)
Scarred and disabled in battle in World War I, American soldier Orson Welles goes into hiding in Austria while wife Claudette Colbert, assuming her husband is dead, remarries factory owner George Brent. Eventually, Welles is hired by Brent and returns to America to find his wife and the son he never knew. Moving melodrama also stars Richard Long and Natalie Wood (her film debut). 105 min.
12-2410 *$19.99*

The Stranger (1946)
Suspenseful cat-and-mouse thriller features director/star Orson Welles as an escaped Nazi war criminal living as a teacher in a small Connecticut college town, with Edward G. Robinson as a federal agent tracking him down. The final chase scene in an old clock tower is a classic; with Loretta Young. 94 min.
18-7371 Was $19.99 *$14.99*

The Lady From Shanghai (1948)
Orson Welles and then-wife Rita Hayworth combine for a classic "film noir" tale of a roguish sailor who signs on for a Mexican cruise with a crippled businessman, his maniacal partner and his unfaithful wife. Along the way is romance, treachery, murder and a memorable climax in a hall of mirrors. Written and directed by Welles; with Everett Sloane, Ted de Corsia. 87 min.
02-1426 *$19.99*

The Third Man (1949)
Striking visuals, a tireless chase through the Viennese sewer system, impeccable performances from Joseph Cotten, Orson Welles and Alida Valli, and a haunting zither score unite to forge one of the finest entries in British film history. Carol Reed directs Graham Greene's script about an American pulp novelist who arrives in postwar Vienna to see an old friend, the enigmatic Harry Lime, and is startled to learn of his puzzling death. This is the complete British version of the film with opening introduction by Reed. 104 min.
10-2058 *$14.99*

The Third Man (Restored Director's Cut)
Also available in a special edition that includes the original theatrical and 50th anniversary re-release trailers. 104 min.
22-5826 *$29.99*

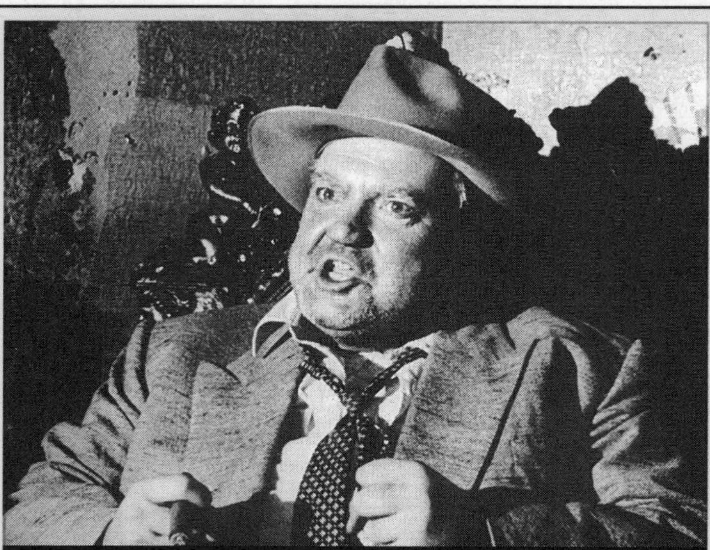
Touch Of Evil

Orson Welles

Trouble In The Glen (1954)
Orson Welles stars as a Scottish-American returned to his ancestral home in time to find himself embroiled in a fight between the villagers and the town Laird. To make matters worse, he falls for the Laird's daughter. Victor McLaglen, Margaret Lockwood co-star in this rousing drama. 91 min.
63-1117 Was $19.99 *$14.99*

Three Cases Of Murder (1955)
First-rate British omnibus that offers three thrillers in one. An art museum guide finds himself in a familiar painting in "In the Picture"; a young woman admired by two school friends is murdered by one of them in "You Killed Elizabeth"; and Orson Welles plays "Lord Mountdrago," a Parliament member who destroys the life of an associate. With Alan Badel, John Gregson. 99 min.
22-5824 Was $39.99 *$29.99*

Around The World With Orson Welles (1955)
Originally made for British television, these rarely-seen travelogues featured the noted filmmaker/raconteur on a tour of popular and out-of-the-way sights around Europe. Welles pays a visit to Jean Cocteau and Juliette Greco in Paris' "St. Germain des Pres" neighborhood; meets "Chelsea Pensioners" in London; attends a "Madrid Bullfight"; and tours Spain's Basque region in "Pays Basque I & II." 133 min. total.
50-8395 *$19.99*

Mr. Arkadin (1955)
Rarely-seen classic, directed by and starring Orson Welles, reminiscent of "Citizen Kane." A rich man's life is reviewed by the people who knew him, loved him and hated him. Great cast includes Michael Redgrave, Akim Tamiroff, Mischa Auer and Patricia Medina. AKA: "Confidential Report." Restored, uncut version; 99 min.
62-1152 *$19.99*

Man In The Shadow (1957)
The death of an immigrant laborer on the property of Texas rancher Orson Welles brings the wealthy and powerful landowner into conflict with newly appointed sheriff Jeff Chandler, who is convinced Welles and his henchmen were responsible for the killing, in this contemporary western drama. Colleen Miller, Ben Alexander and James Gleason also star. AKA: "Pay the Devil." 81 min.
07-2636 ❑*$14.99*

Touch Of Evil (1958)
Orson Welles' twisting cinematic masterpiece of style and suspense features Welles as a corrupt cane-wielding official in a seedy Mexican border town at odds with a newly married narcotics cop (Charlton Heston). Embroiled in the murder mystery are Janet Leigh, Akim Tamiroff, Joseph Cotten, Marlene Dietrich and Joseph Calleia. Original 108 min.-version.
07-1460 *$14.99*

Touch Of Evil: Special Edition
Reissued in theaters in 1998, this restored edition of Orson Welles' masterful film noir features the editing and musical alterations the director/star suggested in a 58-page memo to the studio.
07-2909 *$14.99*

COMPULSION

Compulsion (1959)
A graphic and emotionally gripping courtroom drama, based on the Leopold-Loeb murder case of the 1920s. Orson Welles stars as the Clarence Darrow-like attorney charged with defending well-to-do New York youths Bradford Dillman and Dean Stockwell in a senseless "thrill killing." With E.G. Marshall, Diane Varsi. 105 min.
04-2924 ❑*$19.99*

Ferry To Hong Kong (1959)
Classic sea adventure stars Curt Jurgens as an embittered, alcoholic "man without a country" whose only home is a Hong Kong-Macao ferry, and Orson Welles as the ship's captain, his bitter enemy. With Sylvia Syms. 108 min.
53-1016 *$19.99*

David And Goliath (1961)
Colorful and exciting Biblical adventure about the legend of David and his fierce fight with the giant Philistine Goliath. Orson Welles turns in a magnetic performance as King Saul, who awards the hand of his daughter, Merab, to David after he kills the giant. With Ivo Payer and Edward Hilton. 92 min.
68-8917 *$19.99*

The Trial (1962)
Director/writer Orson Welles took what was once considered an unfilmable novel by Franz Kafka and created a nightmarish vision of a simple clerk (Anthony Perkins) who is inexplicably abducted and charged with an unknown crime by a labyrinthine bureaucracy. Welles co-stars as Perkins' defense advocate; with Jeanne Moreau, Romy Schneider. Special edition includes the original "pin-screen" opening sequence and the film's trailer. 119 min.
08-8055 *$14.99*

The Trial (Letterboxed Version)
Also available in a theatrical, widescreen format.
53-6239 *$29.99*

Chimes At Midnight (1966)
Considered Orson Welles' final masterpiece, this powerful and poignant epic was inspired by Shakespeare's plays "Henry IV," "Henry V," "The Merry Wives of Windsor" and "Richard II." Welles stars as Falstaff, the surrogate father of Prince Hal, who shuns Falstaff's friendship when he ascends to the throne of his real father, Henry IV. With Jeanne Moreau, John Gielgud. AKA: "Falstaff." 115 min.
48-7001 *$59.99*

I'll Never Forget What's 'is Name (1967)
Wicked satire of corporate politics and advertising stars Oliver Reed as a dissatisfied director of TV commercials who quits his job and leaves his unhappy marriage to return to the small literary magazine he once wrote for. Orson Welles plays Reed's former boss, who stops at nothing to get him back behind the camera. Carol White, Frank Finlay and Marianne Faithfull also star. Includes the original theatrical trailer. 99 min.
08-8829 Letterboxed *$14.99*

The Immortal Story (1967)
Produced for French television, this dark drama, based on an Isak Dinesen novel, was directed by and stars Orson Welles as a wealthy, cantankerous merchant living on the island of Macao in the late 19th century. His abhorrence of myth and fiction leads Welles to re-create a local legend in order to make it true. Jeanne Moreau, Fernando Rey co-star. 57 min. Dubbed in English.
09-3058 *$19.99*

Ten Days' Wonder (1972)
Intriguing blending of an Ellery Queen story and the moody direction of French suspense master Claude Chabrol. Orson Welles is the patriarch of a wealthy clan with several skeletons in its closet, many of which belong to son Anthony Perkins. With Marlene Jobert. 101 min.
01-1424 *$19.99*

F For Fake (1973)
Orson Welles used discarded documentary footage to put together a delightful look at deception of all sorts. The question of "what is real?" is posed to a panel of experts, while famous fakers such as Howard Hughes "biographer" Clifford Irving and art forger Elmyr de Hory are profiled, and Welles himself offers commentary on the subject. 85 min.
22-5825 Was $39.99 *$29.99*

It's All True (1942/1993)
After being lost for over 50 years, an hour of Orson Welles' legendary unfinished film "Four Men on a Raft" was resurrected and put together here with a documentary on the ill-fated project. Intended as part of a multi-part study of Brazil called "It's All True," "Raft" chronicles the two-month raft journey taken by four fishermen from Brazil's Northeast coast to Rio, where they pleaded for social benefits for their people. 85 min.
06-2233 Was $89.99 ❑*$19.99*

Working With Orson Welles (1995)
The genius of Orson Welles is the focus of this superior documentary on the man who was both revered and shunned by Hollywood. John Huston, Peter Bogdanovich, Susan Strasberg and others talk about Welles' attempts to launch his long-dreamed-of project, "The Other Side of the Wind," and offer insight into the performer, the filmmaker and the man. 96 min.
50-5636 *$19.99*

Orson Welles 2-Pack
This special money-saving set includes Welles' "F for Fake" and "Mr. Arkadin (Confidential Report)."
22-5983 Save $10.00! *$49.99*

Please see our index for these other Orson Welles titles: *The Battle Of Austerlitz • Catch-22 • Follow The Boys • Get To Know Your Rabbit • Is Paris Burning? • King Lear • Lafayette • The Long, Hot Summer • Macbeth • A Man For All Seasons • Moby Dick • Napoleon • Scene Of The Crime • Someone To Love • Treasure Island*

It Always Rains On Sunday (1949)
Grim tale of a convicted felon who escapes from incarceration and returns home to London's working-class East End, where he is sheltered from the police by a former girlfriend who is now married with three grown children. John McCallum, Susan Shaw, Edward Chapman and Googie Withers star. 92 min.
10-9784 *$19.99*

Secret Evidence (1941)
A newly released ex-con is shot to death by a former "associate." His old girlfriend—who, up until his incarceration, didn't know he was a crook—must convince her assistant D.A. husband that her younger brother, accused of the crime, is innocent. Marjorie Reynolds, Charles Quigley, Ward McTaggart, and Bob White as Sniffy star. 68 min.
10-9787 *$19.99*

The Men Of San Quentin (1942)
Big house drama about a no-nonsense guard who becomes warden at San Quentin prison, where he tries to start reforms and eventually is put to the test when he must stop an escape attempt. With J. Anthony Hughes, Eleanor Stewart and Charles Middleton. 80 min.
09-5056 *$19.99*

Klondike Fury (1942)
A rugged dramatic story starring Edmund Lowe as a surgeon who attempts to forget his botching of an operation by learning how to fly. When he crashes the plane during a storm in the Klondike, he's nursed back to health by a woman at a trading post. Little does he know that the trading post owner needs the same type of operation. Lucille Fairbanks co-stars. 68 min.
09-5059 Was $19.99 *$14.99*

Esther Waters (1948)
Fine British drama about a maid working at an estate who is impregnated by a footman working with her. After planning to marry her, the man abandons her for another woman. Years later, when he is a successful bookie, they reunite and live a happy life until he gets ill and places their life savings on a horse race. Kathleen Ryan, Dirk Bogarde star. 108 min.
09-5242 *$19.99*

Big Town After Dark (1947)
Crusading journalist Philip Reed is pitted against some mobsters whose citywide gaming operation specializes in preying on college students. When Reed turns on the heat, the bad guys resort to kidnapping and blackmail. With Hillary Brooke, Anne Gillis. AKA: "Underworld After Dark." 70 min.
68-8136 *$19.99*

Jigsaw (Gun Moll) (1949)
Buoyed by Franchot Tone's solid performance as a crusading assistant prosecutor out to bring a murderous "hate group" to its knees, this low-key yet effective crime drama is also laced with cameo appearances by Henry Fonda, Marlene Dietrich, Burgess Meredith and John Garfield. 72 min.
10-7161 *$19.99*

The Ramparts We Watch (1940)
Intriguing docudrama, combining footage from the "March of Time" newsreels with performances by non-professional New England natives, that tells the stories of regular Americans whose lives were altered forever by WWI...in the hopes that the USA not ignore the gathering storm in Europe. Stars John Adair, Julia Kent, John Summers. 90 min.
10-7216 Was $29.99 *$14.99*

Love On The Dole (1941)
An unusual love story with political overtones from England. A family struggles to stay together when the father loses his job, but the labor activist son is killed in riots and the daughter becomes involved with underworld figures. Deborah Kerr. 89 min.
09-1632 Was $19.99 ***$14.99***

I Remember Mama (1948)
Sentimental family drama about a Norwegian-American brood living in turn-of-the-century San Francisco. Sentimental favorite stars Irene Dunne, Barbara Bel Geddes, Philip Dorn and Oscar Homolka; directed by George Stevens. 130 min.
05-1316 ***$19.99***

Gun Cargo (1949)
An unscrupulous shipowner fires his crew after they ask for shore leave, replacing them with a band of thugs, a neophyte captain and a girl in disguise. Seafaring drama stars Rex Lease, William Farnum, Smith Ballew. 49 min.
09-2143 Was $24.99 ***$14.99***

Dangerous Passage (1944)
A fortune-seeking adventurer in the South American jungle inherits $200,000. He books passage on a boat for America, only to find his fellow passengers include a sultry cabaret singer, a seedy lawyer, and other assorted riff-raff. Robert Lowery, Phyllis Brooks star. 60 min.
09-2161 Was $29.99 ***$14.99***

Sons Of The Sea (1941)
Michael Redgrave and Griffith Jones star in this historical drama as two brothers working to build the first transatlantic steamship in 1837. Valerie Hobson, Hartley Power also star; co-scripted by Emeric Pressburger. AKA: "Atlantic Ferry." 92 min.
09-2187 Was $29.99 ***$14.99***

Doctor Jim (1947)
A sentimental slice of Americana featuring Stuart Erwin as a kind country physician who reflects on his life during a surprise testimonial dinner in his honor. William Schallert, Barbara Wooddell and William Wright star. 48 min.
09-2219 Was $24.99 ***$14.99***

Rolling Home (1947)
Life in smalltown America is lovingly portrayed in this warm-hearted drama about an unconventional preacher (Russell Hayden) who can save his beleaguered church if he'll marry a wealthy snob he doesn't love. With Jean Parker, Harry Carey, Jr., Elmo Lincoln. 67 min.
09-2288 Was $19.99 ***$14.99***

The Contender (1944)
Widowed truck driver Buster Crabbe laces up the leather gloves to earn money as a prizefighter so he can send his beloved son to a swanky military academy. But will a series of pitfalls, including a gold-digging girlfriend and an addiction to the bottle, sway him from his lofty mission? Co-stars Arline Judge, Julie Gibson; directed by Sam Newfield ("The Terror of Tiny Town"). 65 min.
09-2289 Was $24.99 ***$14.99***

Underworld Scandal (1948)
Social drama about a group of wayward kids facing tough terms for a heist at a sporting goods store. A crusading reporter reveals the problems they face in reform school and gets her managing editor to help find them jobs and construct a recreation center. Philip Reed, Hilary Brooke, Darryl Hickman and Carl "Alfalfa" Schweitzer star. AKA: "Big Town Scandal." 59 min.
09-2942 ***$14.99***

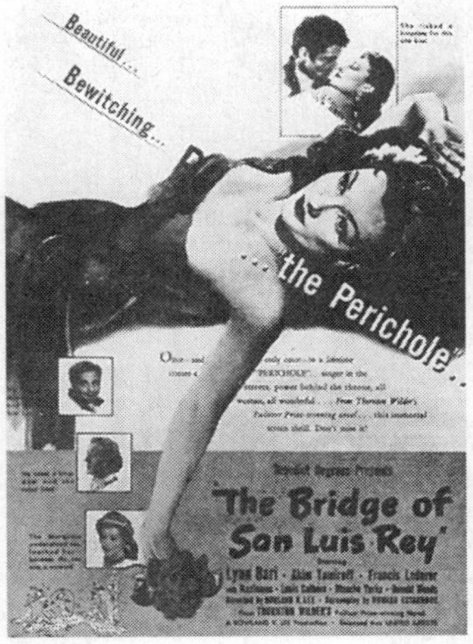

The Bridge Of San Luis Rey (1944)
A bridge near a South American village, after decades of use, suddenly breaks, killing five people. The local priest conducts his own investigation into the accident, trying to find out why God, or Fate, put those people there. Dramatic rendition of the Thorton Wilder story stars Louis Calhern, Akim Tamiroff, Lynn Bari. 89 min.
70-1053 ***$19.99***

Lloyd's Of London (1936)
The famed British insurance firm provides the background for this sweeping (albeit loosely based on fact) historical saga starring Tyrone Power as a young man in early 19th-century England who becomes a leading Lloyd's employee and helps save the company during the Napoleonic Wars. With Madeleine Carroll, George Sanders, C. Aubrey Smith, Freddie Bartholomew.
04-3279 ***□$19.99***

In Old Chicago (1938)
A sprawling epic that mixes fiction and fact to tell the story of life in 19th-century Chicago. The focus is on the O'Leary family: roguish son Tyrone Power, attorney brother Don Ameche and laundress mother Alice Brady, whose cow starts the devastating fire of 1871. Alice Faye co-stars, along with some of the most spectacular fire footage ever filmed. 95 min.
04-2740 ***□$19.99***

Marie Antoinette (1938)
Sumptuous costume drama about the last French queen, her palace intrigues, tragic love and execution by the Paris mob. Norma Shearer stars, with Tyrone Power as Count Axel de Fersen, John Barrymore and Robert Morley as Louis XV and XVI, and Gladys George as Madame Du Barry. 160 min.
12-2004 ***$19.99***

The Rains Came (1939)
Indian aristocrat Tyrone Power returns to his home province after studying medicine in America to help the needy and sick, and becomes romantically involved with married English socialite Myrna Loy. The couple finds their love and courage tested when an earthquake and flood devastate the area and a subsequent malaria epidemic threatens all. George Brent, Nigel Bruce co-star. 103 min.
04-2742 ***□$19.99***

Johnny Apollo (1940)
When his banker father is jailed for embezzlement, embittered Tyrone Power leaves his old life behind him to start a new existence as gangster Johnny Apollo. Taut crime melodrama, directed by Henry Hathaway, also stars Dorothy Lamour, Lloyd Nolan, Edward Arnold. 93 min.
04-2406 ***$14.99***

The Mark Of Zorro (1940)
The classic romantic swashbuckler stars dashing Tyrone Power as the son of a powerful nobleman in 1820s California who returns home from Europe to find his father has been replaced by evil despots. In order to defeat them, Power dons the black-masked disguise of Zorro and takes on his enemies in a series of rousing swordfights. Linda Darnell, Eugene Pallette and Basil Rathbone also star. 93 min.
04-2622 ***□$19.99***

Brigham Young—Frontiersman (1940)
A fascinating mix of historical and inspirational drama, depicting the hardships faced by Mormon settlers as they left their Illinois home in the 1840s and set out across the prairie to Utah's Great Salt Lake Basin. Dean Jagger stars as church leader Young, with Mary Astor as his wife, Vincent Price as Mormon founder Joseph Smith, and Tyrone Power and Linda Darnell as a pioneer couple. 113 min.
04-2903 ***□$19.99***

Blood And Sand (1941)
Tyrone Power inherits the role made famous by Rudolph Valentino, playing the son of a famous matador who finds fame, fortune and happiness following in his father's footsteps, only to have it taken away when a society girl averts his attention from the ring and his longtime sweetheart. Rita Hayworth, Linda Darnell, Anthony Quinn and Laird Cregar also star. 124 min.
04-1012 ***□$19.99***

A Yank In The RAF (1941)
Wartime flag-waving excitement with Tyrone Power as a brash American pilot who joins the British Royal Air Force. While romancing nightclub entertainer Betty Grable, he uses his aerial skills and all-American enthusiasm to battle the Nazis in the skies over France. With Reginald Gardiner, John Sutton, and some authentic WWII film footage. 98 min.
04-2438 ***$19.99***

Son Of Fury (1942)
An exciting swashbuckler set in the early 19th century and starring Tyrone Power as the illegitimate son of a British nobleman who is forced into servitude by his mean uncle. Power escapes to a Polynesian island where he finds fame and love with a native girl, and eventually returns to England to claim his inheritance. Gene Tierney, George Sanders and Frances Farmer also star. 98 min.
04-2741 ***□$19.99***

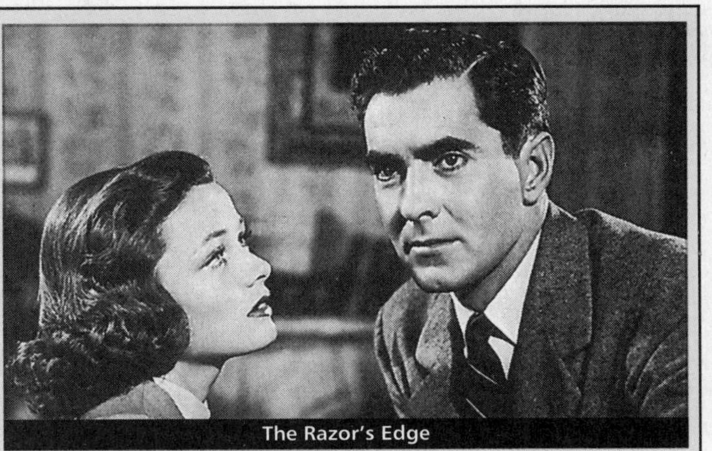

The Razor's Edge

Tyrone Power

The Black Swan (1942)
Grand seafaring saga stars Tyrone Power as a pirate who, along with his captain, Henry Morgan (Laird Cregar), reforms and moves to Jamaica in order to free the island from attacks by fellow freebooters George Sanders and Anthony Quinn. Maureen O'Hara is Power's love interest in this Oscar-winning swashbuckler. 85 min.
04-3265 ***□$19.99***

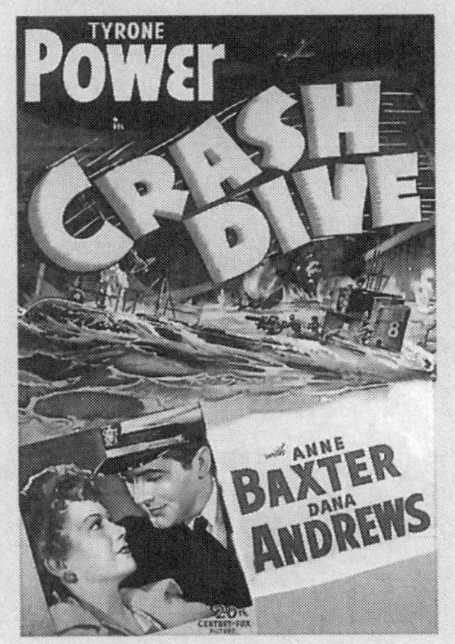

Crash Dive (1943)
Rah-rah, action-packed war drama featuring Tyrone Power as an ace PT boat skipper during World War II whose assignment to a submarine commanded by Dana Andrews leads to gutsy victories against the Nazis in the North Atlantic and romance with Andrews' schoolteacher fiancée (Anne Baxter). With James Gleason and Henry Morgan. 105 min.
04-2743 ***□$19.99***

The Razor's Edge (1946)
The first film version of Somerset Maugham's novel features Tyrone Power as the WWI veteran who turns his back on his materialistic, upper-class friends and embarks on a global search for the meaning of life. Gene Tierney, Clifton Webb, Best Supporting Actress Oscar-winner Anne Baxter, and Herbert Marshall as Maugham co-star. 146 min.
04-1857 Was $59.99 ***□$19.99***

Captain From Castile (1947)
The Spanish conquest of the Aztec Empire is the backdrop for this lush costume drama starring Tyrone Power as a 16th-century Castilian nobleman who helps his family escape persecution by the Inquisition and then joins Cortez's army on its journey to Mexico. With Jean Peters, John Sutton, Lee J. Cobb and Cesar Romero as Cortez.
04-3391 ***$19.99***

Rawhide (1951)
The 1935 gangster film "Show Them No Mercy" was transformed into a Western setting for this suspenseful tale of four people at a stagecoach station who are taken hostage by a gang of robbers. Tyrone Power, Susan Hayward, Hugh Marlowe, Dean Jagger, and Edgar Buchanan star. 86 min.
04-3184 ***$19.99***

Pony Soldier (1952)
Heroic Mountie Tyrone Power is charged with persuading a renegade band of Cree Indians who left the reservation and raided a wagon train to return to Canada. Complicating matters are determined chief Cameron Mitchell and the two hostages taken from the raid: pretty Penny Edwards and shifty ex-con Robert Horton. 82 min.
04-2928 ***$14.99***

The Long Gray Line (1955)
John Ford helmed this moving true-life story that plays like a West Point-flavored "Goodbye, Mr. Chips." Tyrone Power stars as Marty Maher, an Irish immigrant who comes to the Point as a kitchen worker and becomes an athletic director and father figure to 50 years of cadets. Maureen O'Hara plays Power's wife; with Ward Bond, Donald Crisp, Robert Francis. 138 min.
02-2183 ***$19.99***

The Eddy Duchin Story (1956)
Tyrone Power stars as the pianist/bandleader who was the talk of '30s New York cafe society but whose personal life was marred by tragedy. Glossy, song-filled biodrama also features Kim Novak, James Whitmore, and the keyboard work of Carmen Cavallaro. Songs include "What Is This Thing Called Love?," "Till We Meet Again." 123 min.
02-2179 ***$19.99***

Abandon Ship! (1957)
Set adrift after their ocean liner sinks, the occupants of a dangerously overcrowded lifeboat soon realize they may not survive unless some people sacrifice themselves, and it falls on de facto leader Tyrone Power to decide who will live and who will die. Powerful adventure film also stars Mai Zetterling, Lloyd Nolan, Stephen Boyd. AKA: "Seven Waves Away." 97 min.
02-2986 ***$19.99***

Please see our index for these other Tyrone Power titles: *Alexander's Ragtime Band • Jesse James • Rose Of Washington Square • Second Fiddle • Thin Ice • Witness For The Prosecution*

Law Of The Timber (1941)
When her logger father dies, Marjorie Reynolds takes over his company and is soon met with a number of hurdles, including sabotage and a huge order from the U.S. government. Monte Blue, J. Farrell MacDonald also star. 61 min.
10-9337 ***$19.99***

Tornado (1943)
Decades before "Twister," there was this drama about an Illinois coal miner who weds a showgirl and tries to set up his own company to mine land she inherited. Bored with the marriage, the woman begins having an affair with her husband's business rival, but a horrific tornado soon threatens all their lives. With Chester Morris, Nancy Kelly and Bill Henry. 60 min.
10-9364 ***$14.99***

Miracle Kid (1942)
A young man decides he prefers the boxing ring over his wedding ring when he leaves his wife to make a name for himself as a fighter. Will he go back with her after he learns of the rigors of the palooka world? Tom Neal ("Detour") stars with Carol Hughes; directed by William "One Shot" Beaudine. 65 min.
10-9368 ***$14.99***

Skip Tracer (1940)
A repo man for an insurance company is given the assignment of recovering a radio whose owners have fallen behind in their payments. After retrieving the item, gangsters begin to follow him, their sights set on stolen jewels hidden inside it. James Dunn, Frances Gifford star. 60 min.
10-9369 ***$14.99***

Freckles Comes Home (1942)
"Freckles" is the name of the college boy who returns home, hoping to make it an important spot on the map. But in order to get his plans going, he must get rid of a gang of robbers out to nab money from his girlfriend's father's bank. Johnny Downs, Mantan Moreland and Gale Storm, in her first role, star. 63 min.
10-9710 ***$19.99***

Queen Of Broadway (1942)
Sentimental drama about a female gambler whose attempts to adopt an orphaned little boy are stymied because of her reputation. Eventually, she gets a chance to prove her worthiness in order to get the child. With Rochelle Hudson, Buster Crabbe and Jack Mulhall. 64 min.
10-9714 ***$19.99***

Bette Davis

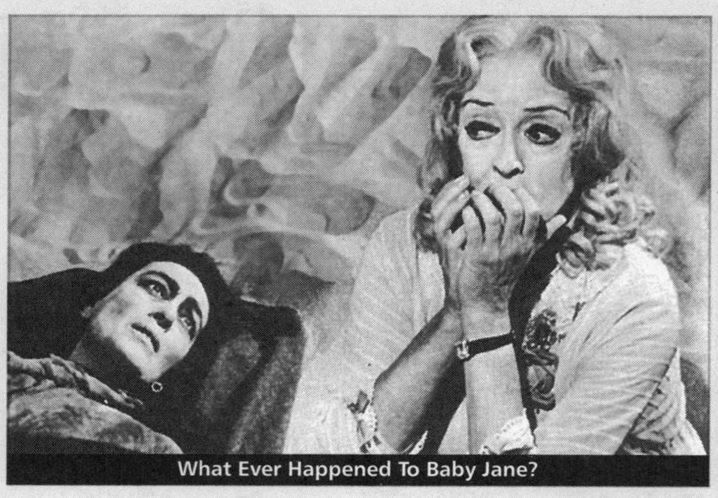
What Ever Happened To Baby Jane?

Hell's House (1932)
Bootlegger Pat O'Brien lets teenage assistant Junior Durkin take the rap during a police raid and get sent to a brutal reform school in this two-fisted Prohibition drama that features an early appearance by Bette Davis as Durkin's girlfriend. 72 min.
10-2020 Was $19.99 *$14.99*

Three On A Match (1932)
A trio of childhood girlfriends meet years later and find that their lives are intertwined in a web of love triangles, mobsters, alcohol and drugs. Compelling Mervyn LeRoy melodrama stars Bette Davis, Joan Blondell and Ann Dvorak, with support from Warren William, Lyle Talbot and Humphrey Bogart (in his first gangster role). 64 min.
12-2175 Was $29.99 *$19.99*

Cabin In The Cotton (1932)
An early starring role for Bette Davis, this Michael Curtiz melodrama casts her as the rich Southern belle daughter of an unscrupulous storekeeper who is cheating the local farmers. Enter sharecropper's son Richard Barthelmess, a man caught between his own people and their wealthy employer, and between Davis and his childhood sweetheart. Dorothy Jordan, Berton Churchill also star. 79 min.
12-2476 *$19.99*

Bureau Of Missing Persons (1933)
Gritty, often humorous thriller with gruff cop Pat O'Brien looking for a change of pace with a transfer to the force's missing persons department, but finding a strict superior (Lewis Stone) and a mysterious woman (Bette Davis) searching for her lost husband. With Glenda Farrell, Allen Jenkins. 73 min.
12-2477 *$19.99*

Ex-Lady (1933)
Advertising copywriter Gene Raymond wants to marry modern-minded woman Bette Davis, who doesn't believe in matrimony and suggests that they live together instead. They do, starting their own ad agency as well, but business problems and jealousy eventually get in the way of the liberated relationship. Frank McHugh and Monroe Owsley co-star. 67 min.
12-2478 *$19.99*

Of Human Bondage (1934)
Somerset Maugham's classic story of the ill-fated romance between a wealthy doctor (Leslie Howard) and a vulgar lower-class waitress (Bette Davis). Kay Johnson, Reginald Denny co-star. 83 min.
10-2007 Was $19.99 *$14.99*

Fashions Of 1934 (1934)
Con artist William Powell and dress designer Bette Davis cavort around the Parisian world of fashion. Busby Berkeley's classic "Spin a Little Web of Dreams" production number is a standout; songs include "Broken Melody." Reginald Owen, Frank McHugh co-star. 78 min.
62-1017 *$19.99*

Dangerous (1935)
Bette Davis garnered her first Academy Award for her portrayal of a faded stage actress-turned-alcoholic who manipulates the architect who takes her in for her own purposes. Tear-jerking drama co-stars Franchot Tone, Margaret Lindsay, John Eldredge. 78 min.
12-1954 *$19.99*

Satan Met A Lady (1936)
The second film adaptation of "The Maltese Falcon" (Bogart's was still five years away) features Bette Davis as the woman of mystery who draws detective Warren William into a deadly search for a fabulous jeweled ram's horn. Alison Skipworth plays the sinister "Fat Woman"(!); with Arthur Treacher. 75 min.
12-2141 *$19.99*

Marked Woman (1937)
When call girl Bette Davis threatens to testify in court against the city's gang boss, her sister is murdered and her own face slashed. Gritty Warner Bros. crime drama, based in part on the trial of Lucky Luciano, also stars Humphrey Bogart as a crusading D.A. With Eduardo Ciannelli, Jane Bryan, Mayo Methot (the third Mrs. Bogart). 97 min.
12-1761 *$19.99*

Jezebel (1938)
Bette Davis may have been looked over for the role of Scarlett in "Gone With the Wind," but she won her second Oscar for this drama of a manipulative Southern belle who strings along fiancé Henry Fonda. The cast includes George Brent and Best Supporting Actress winner Fay Bainter. 103 min.
12-1782 Was $19.99 *$14.99*

The Sisters (1938)
Set during a four-year period at the turn of the century, this compelling drama focuses on the joys and hardships of the lives of three sisters in a small Montana town. Expertly chronicled are the romances, marriages and relationships encountered by the trio (Bette Davis, Anita Louise and Jane Bryan). With Errol Flynn, Beulah Bondi and Alan Hale. 98 min.
12-2481 *$19.99*

That Certain Woman (1938)
A soap opera favorite starring Bette Davis as the widow of a gangster who tries to turn her life around by taking a job as secretary for an attorney. His playboy son (Henry Fonda) falls in love with her and, against his father's wishes, they get married. But a child, class, cash and a car crash play parts in the ensuing tragic events. Ian Hunter, Anita Louise and Donald Crisp also star. 96 min.
12-2482 *$19.99*

Dark Victory (1939)
The height of Hollywood soap opera with Bette Davis discovering she has a brain tumor, and George Brent as her surgeon, who falls in love with her. Co-stars Humphrey Bogart, Geraldine Fitzgerald, Ronald Reagan. 106 min.
12-1781 Was $19.99 *$14.99*

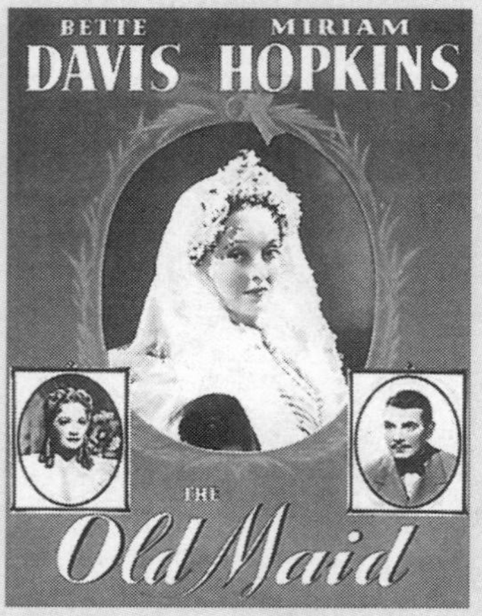

The Old Maid (1939)
Classic Civil War tearjerker that gained fame for its stars' on-screen and off-screen rivalries. Bette Davis and Miriam Hopkins are cousins in love with George Brent. Davis has Brent's daughter, but when he's killed she must raise the child as a charge in her orphanage, and can say nothing when Hopkins adopts her. Co-stars Jane Bryan, Jerome Cowan. 95 min.
12-1763 *$19.99*

All This, And Heaven Too (1940)
Lush romantic melodrama set in 19th-century France, with Charles Boyer and Bette Davis as the forbidden lovers whose affair leads to murder and scandal. Also stars Barbara O'Neil, Walter Hampden. 143 min.
12-1508 *$19.99*

The Letter (1940)
A classic suspense film directed by William Wyler, this drama stars Bette Davis as a woman accused of murder. She says it was self-defense, but will a mystery letter save her or condemn her? Herbert Marshall and Gale Sondergaard also star in this taut thriller, based on a story by Somerset Maugham. 95 min.
12-1783 Was $19.99 *$14.99*

The Great Lie (1941)
The romantic triangle between pilot George Brent, socialite Bette Davis and pianist Mary Astor takes a tragic turn when he is lost on a mission in South America, leaving Davis and a pregnant Astor behind. Classic "three-hankie" tale of love and devotion earned Astor an Academy Award; with Grant Mitchell, Hattie McDaniel. 107 min.
12-1956 *$19.99*

The Little Foxes (1941)
Bette Davis is unforgettable in this filming of Lillian Hellman's caustic drama, as the matriarch of a down-and-out Southern family drives her loved ones unmercifully in her quest for wealth and status. Herbert Marshall, Teresa Wright co-star; William Wyler directs. 116 min.
44-1885 Was $19.99 *$14.99*

Now, Voyager (1942)
One of the all-time-great melodramas, with spinster Bette Davis finding support from psychiatrist Claude Rains and romance with sophisticated Paul Henreid. Features a lush Max Steiner score, classic dialogue ("Why ask for the moon when we have the stars?"), and tips on multiple cigarette lighting. 117 min.
12-1779 Was $19.99 *$14.99*

In This Our Life (1942)
Scheming sibling Bette Davis plots to steal sister Olivia de Havilland's fiancé not once but twice in this grand soap opera-style drama from director John Huston. The cast includes George Brent, Charles Coburn, Dennis Morgan, Hattie McDaniel; look for Humphrey Bogart and the cast of "The Maltese Falcon" as customers in a bar scene. 97 min.
12-1957 *$19.99*

The Man Who Came To Dinner (1942)
Wonderful film adaptation of the Kaufman/Hart stage comedy stars Monty Woolley as acerbic New York critic Sheridan Whiteside, who manages to take over the small town household where he's convalescing after an accident. Bette Davis co-stars as Woolley's long-suffering secretary; with Richard Travis, Ann Sheridan, Billie Burke, Jimmy Durante. 112 min.
12-1958 *$19.99*

Watch On The Rhine (1943)
Paul Lukas won an Academy Award for his portrayal of a German underground leader chased by the Nazis from his homeland to America. Bette Davis co-stars as his wife in the riveting drama, adapted from Lillian Hellman's play by Dashiell Hammett. 114 min.
12-2142 *$19.99*

Mr. Skeffington (1944)
Grand romantic drama stars Bette Davis as a scheming New York socialite who marries banker Claude Rains in order to save her thieving brother. It is a loveless marriage that ends soon after their daughter's birth, but years later tragedy brings them together. Also stars Marjorie Riordan, Richard Waring. 147 min.
12-1762 *$19.99*

The Corn Is Green (1945)
Moving drama set in a 1900s Welsh mining town, with Bette Davis as a recently arrived teacher who meets opposition when she tries to establish a school for the locals. John Dall is Davis' prize pupil, and Nigel Bruce is an antagonistic landowner. With Joan Lorring, Mildred Dunnock; based on Emlyn Williams' play. 114 min.
12-1760 *$19.99*

Deception (1946)
First-class melodrama starring Bette Davis as a music teacher and kept woman of famous composer Claude Rains who falls in love with cello virtuoso Paul Henreid. When the jealous Rains learns of their involvement, he plans to ridicule Henreid before and during a big concert with his own orchestra. Bad plan, Claude. 112 min.
12-1955 *$19.99*

A Stolen Life (1946)
Bette Davis co-stars with Bette Davis in this classic drama of twin sisters (one virtuous, the other deceitful) in love with the same man, and how a tragic accident leads to a desperate impersonation. With Glenn Ford, Dane Clark, Walter Brennan. 107 min.
12-1959 *$19.99*

June Bride (1948)
A stylish farce starring Bette Davis as an editor on a leading woman's magazine who finds that her former fiancée, chauvinistic foreign correspondent Robert Montgomery, is now her new assistant. The pair are assigned to cover a "typical" wedding in Indiana, but once there, nothing turns out the way it was planned. With Fay Bainter, Betty Lynn. 97 min.
12-2479 *$19.99*

Winter Meeting (1948)
This teary drama finds Bette Davis playing a lonely spinster and aspiring poetess who falls for a World War II naval hero at a party. Romance follows, but so does his calling to the priesthood and her emotional reunion with her bed-ridden mother. James Davis, Janis Paige and John Hoyt also star. 104 min.
12-2483 *$19.99*

Beyond The Forest (1949)
Gripping melodrama of a small-town doctor's bored wife (Bette Davis) and her attentions towards a handsome neighbor also features fine supporting turns by Joseph Cotten, David Brian and Ruth Roman, the direction of King Vidor, and Davis' oft-imitated line, "What a dump!" 95 min.
12-2137 *$19.99*

All About Eve (1950)
The 1950 Oscar for Best Picture went to Joseph L. Mankiewicz' sardonic look at show business glamour and the empty lives behind it. Bette Davis is veteran actress Margo Channing; Anne Baxter is Eve, her understudy desperate for stardom. With Hugh Marlowe, George Sanders, Thelma Ritter and a brief appearance by a young Marilyn Monroe. 138 min.
04-1004 Was $19.99 *$14.99*

Another Man's Poison (1951)
Mystery writer Bette Davis' quiet life on the Yorkshire moors—that is, if you ignore her plan to steal her secretary's fiancé away—is interrupted by the arrival of her escaped convict husband. After killing him during a struggle, Davis must cope with blackmail by her spouse's fellow escapee (Gary Merrill) in this convoluted crime melodrama. With Emlyn Williams, Anthony Steel. 90 min.
50-8244 *$19.99*

Phone Call From A Stranger (1952)
A sensitive human drama, told in episodic fashion. Four strangers on a transcontinental flight share their life stories. After the plane crashes, the sole survivor takes it upon himself to break the news to the victims' families. Gary Merrill, Shelley Winters, Michael Rennie, Keenan Wynn and Bette Davis star. 96 min.
04-2121 *$19.99*

The Star (1952)
Penetrating study of Hollywood starring Bette Davis as an aging actress who has problems with work, booze, family and money, years after she won an Academy Award. After attempting to make a career comeback, she considers settling down with an admiring former actor (Sterling Hayden). Natalie Wood, Warner Anderson co-star. 91 min.
19-1953 Was $29.99 *$19.99*

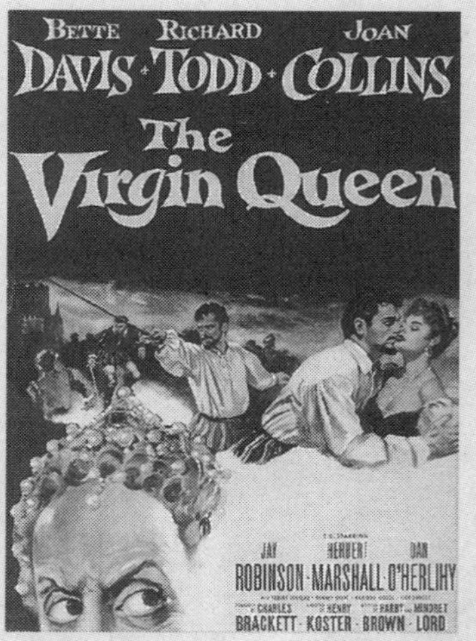

The Virgin Queen (1955)
Returning to the role she played two decades earlier, Bette Davis stars as England's Elizabeth I. Richard Todd is roguish Sir Walter Raleigh, who uses the aging monarch's interest in him for his own gains, and Joan Collins is the lady-in-waiting who comes between them. Lavish costume drama also stars Herbert Marshall, Dan O'Herlihy. 92 min.
04-2122 *$19.99*

The Catered Affair (1956)
Paddy Chayefsky's TV play was adapted by Gore Vidal for this big-screen drama. Bette Davis stars as the working-class Bronx housewife whose dreams of a grandiose wedding for daughter Debbie Reynolds begin to outgrow what cabbie husband Ernest Borgnine can afford. Understated tale also stars Rod Taylor, Barry Fitzgerald. 92 min.
12-2139 *$19.99*

What Ever Happened To Baby Jane? (1962)
Gothic psychological chiller from director Robert Aldrich stars Bette Davis as a former child star driven by jealousy and dementia to unmercifully torment sister Joan Crawford, a one-time respected actress who's now confined to a wheelchair, in their dilapidated West Hollywood mansion. Co-stars Victor Buono. 134 min.
19-1284 *$19.99*

MOVIES UNLIMITED

Where Love Has Gone (1964)
After the teenage daughter (Joey Heatherton) of a party girl/sculptor (Susan Hayward) is accused of killing her mother's newest boyfriend, the stage is set for a superior soap opera, adapted from the novel by Harold Robbins. Mike Connors is Heatherton's father, who seeks custody of his daughter; Bette Davis is the grandmother with a secret agenda. With DeForest Kelley. 114 min.
06-2139 ❑*$14.99*

Dead Ringer (1964)
In this psychological thriller, Bette Davis plays twin sisters involved in a complex web of deceit, suspense and blackmail. The story concerns one sister's love for her now-deceased brother-in-law and what occurs after she discovers the truth behind his death. Karl Malden, Peter Lawford and Philip Carey co-star; directed by Paul Henreid. 115 min.
19-1947 Was $19.99 *$14.99*

Hush...Hush, Sweet Charlotte (1965)
Director Robert Aldrich ("What Ever Happened to Baby Jane?") revisited the genre of macabre horror with this all-star suspense shocker about a family with several skeletons in its closet...and other parts of the house, too. Bette Davis, Olivia de Havilland, Joseph Cotten, Victor Buono and Mary Astor star. 133 min.
04-1880 ❑*$19.99*

The Nanny (1965)
The creepy childminder played by Bette Davis in this suspenseful tale is a long way from Mary Poppins and Fran Fine, and her young charge is certain she was responsible for his sister's drowning, for which he was blamed, years earlier. Is the boy telling the truth, and will anyone believe him before Davis puts him to rest...for good? With William Dix, Pamela Franklin. 95 min.
04-3310 *$19.99*

The Anniversary (1968)
Bitterly funny black comedy stars Bette Davis as an eyepatch-wearing widow who uses a dinner marking her wedding anniversary as a chance to tighten her control on her three grown sons' lives, despite their attempts to loosen her domineering grip. Jack Hedley, James Cossins, Christian Roberts also star. 95 min.
04-3311 *$19.99*

Burnt Offerings (1976)
Dan Curtis ("Dark Shadows") directed this spooky horror yarn about a mysterious house where inexplicable, horrific deaths occur. Karen Black, Oliver Reed, Bette Davis and Burgess Meredith star. 115 min.
12-1355 Was $19.99 *$14.99*

The Dark Secret Of Harvest Home (1978)
A New York family moves to an isolated New England farming village where modern technology is shunned and the community is run by occult practitioners. Moody, chilling horror tale based on Tom Tryon's novel stars Bette Davis, Joanna Miles, David Ackroyd, Rosanna Arquette; Donald Pleasence narrates. 118 min.
07-1440 *$59.99*

Family Reunion (1981)
Superb drama stars Bette Davis as a feisty New England teacher who sets out to see America by bus after retiring following 50 years of service. Soon, however, she discovers that her town is the target for greedy shopping mall developers, and she plans to do something to stop them. With J. Ashley Hyman (Bette's grandson), David Huddleston. 195 min.
02-2175 *$19.99*

A Piano For Mrs. Cimino (1982)
Bette Davis stars as a 72-year-old widow declared mentally incompetent by her children and doctor who, with the help of her granddaughter and a young lawyer, fights to retain control of her life. Timely, moving drama also stars Keenan Wynn, Penny Fuller, Christopher Guest. 92 min.
16-1144 Was $59.99 *$14.99*

Wicked Stepmother (1989)
A bewitching black comedy, famous for the off-screen feud between director Larry Cohen and star Bette Davis (who walked before the film's completion). Davis and Barbara Carrera are a sinister mother-daughter duo who use black magic to lure men into their clutches. With Colleen Camp, Tom Bosley, David Rasche, Richard Moll. 90 min.
12-1949 Was $79.99 *$14.99*

Starring Bette Davis: The TV Years
This collection of rare TV appearances starring the legendary Bette Davis includes "The Decorator," a TV pilot from 1965 with Bette as an interior decorator who gets involved with her clients' lives; "A Little Talk," in which Davis gets the last laugh on a magazine publisher; and "Broadway Bound," about a theatrical agent trying to manage a troubled young actor. 85 min.
62-1366 *$19.99*

Please see our index for these other Bette Davis titles: *The Bride Came C.O.D. • John Paul Jones • Juarez • Kid Galahad • The Petrified Forest • Pocketful Of Miracles • Thank Your Lucky Stars*

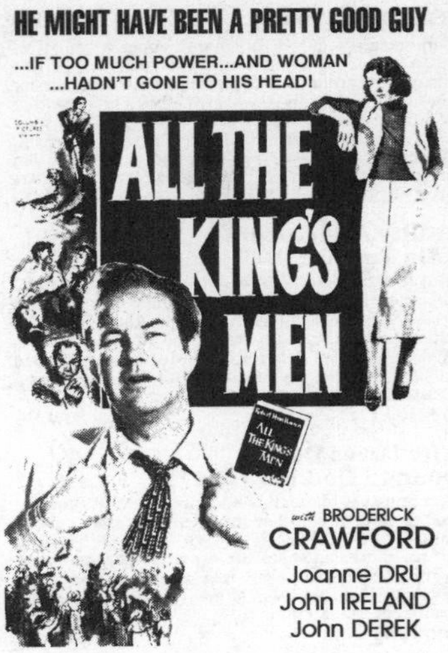
HE MIGHT HAVE BEEN A PRETTY GOOD GUY
...IF TOO MUCH POWER...AND WOMAN
...HADN'T GONE TO HIS HEAD!
ALL THE KING'S MEN
with BRODERICK
CRAWFORD
Joanne DRU
John IRELAND
John DEREK

All The King's Men (1949)
Three Oscars (Picture, Actor, Supporting Actress) went to this drama of a backwoods Southern lawyer who deals his way into the governor's mansion, but cannot control his lust for power. Broderick Crawford stars as the Huey Long-inspired kingpin. Mercedes McCambridge, John Ireland and Joanne Dru; based on the novel by Robert Penn Warren. 109 min.
02-1560 *$19.99*

Tom Brown's School Days (1940)
Classic story of life among boys at a boarding school in Victorian England stars Cedric Hardwicke and Freddie Bartholomew. 81 min.
01-1078 Was $19.99 *$14.99*

Tom Brown's Schooldays (1951)
A young boy's experiences in a Victorian English boarding school, from incurring the wrath of the class bully to gaining the understanding of the school's new headmaster, are recounted in this timeless drama. Robert Newton, John Howard Davies star. 93 min.
08-1459 *$19.99*

Beyond Tomorrow (1940)
Three well-to-do elderly men without families of their own invite a rodeo performer and a kindergarten teacher to a holiday dinner. The young couple fall in love, but when the trio of beneficiaries die in a plane crash, their spirits return to help the romance along in this charming fantasy. Richard Carlson, Jean Parker, Charles Winninger, C. Aubrey Smith star. 82 min.
01-1146 *$19.99*

Mine Own Executioner (1948)
Burgess Meredith is a disturbed psychiatrist treating a patient with homicidal tendencies and begins to assume part of his patient's guilt. 103 min.
01-1217 *$19.99*

How Green Was My Valley (1941)
John Ford's powerful winner of the Best Picture Academy Award is set in Wales at the turn of the century, and tells the story of a family of miners, looked over by a loving but stern patriarch, whose lives are filled with danger and repression. Director Ford and actor Donald Crisp also won Oscars; with Maureen O'Hara, Walter Pidgeon, Sara Allgood and Roddy McDowall. 118 min.
04-2280 Was $19.99 ❑*$14.99*

Road House (1948)
Bar owners Richard Widmark and Cornel Wilde vie for the affections of singer Ida Lupino, but when she chooses Wilde, the jealous Widmark frames his ex-friend for robbery and has Wilde paroled in his custody. Dark and moody melodrama of envy and vengeance also stars Celeste Holm. 95 min.
04-2409 *$19.99*

Anna And The King Of Siam (1946)
An English governess travels to Siam in 1862 to help the country's stern king with raising his 67 children and educating his harem of wives. This lavishly filmed drama, based on the real-life story that also inspired "The King and I," features magnificent performances from Irene Dunne, Rex Harrison, Linda Darnell, Lee J. Cobb and Gale Sondergaard. 128 min.
04-2737 Was $19.99 ❑*$14.99*

Leave Her To Heaven (1945)
A glossy and film noir-flavored melodrama fueled by Gene Tierney's performance as a calculating woman whose pathological jealousy drives her to cause her own miscarriage and even murder in order to have husband Cornel Wilde all to herself. With Jeanne Crain, Vincent Price, Darryl Hickman. 110 min.
04-2900 *$19.99*

The Lost Weekend (1945)
Billy Wilder's Oscar-winning social drama stars Ray Milland as an alcoholic writer who falls into a maelstrom of delusion and dementia and winds up in a psychiatric ward during a three-day bender. Groundbreaking look into the dangers of alcoholism that was almost not released co-stars Jane Wyman, Howard Da Silva and Frank Faylen. 101 min.
07-1573 Was $19.99 *$14.99*

My Dog Shep (1946)
Heartwarming tale of an elderly man, a young orphan, and an abandoned German Shepherd thrown together by fate who come to depend on and love one another. Fine family drama stars William Farnum, Tom Neal, Grady Sutton. 70 min.
09-1918 Was $29.99 *$19.99*

Shep Comes Home (1949)
This sequel to "My Dog Shep" tells of an orphaned young boy who takes to the wilderness with his dog Shep, and wind up helping a sheriff by stopping some bankrobbers. With Robert Lowery, Margia Dean and Billy Kimbley. 60 min.
09-5070 *$19.99*

The Old Swimmin' Hole (1940)
Family drama about a young man who must choose between staying with his widowed mother in a small town or living with his rich, miserly grandfather. Jackie Moran, Marcia Mae Jones star. 78 min.
09-1661 Was $29.99 *$19.99*

Courageous Mr. Penn (1941)
The story of William Penn, the 17th-century nobleman's son who gave up his aristocratic background to join the Quakers and move to America, where he founded Philadelphia, "City of Brotherly Love." Clifford Evans, Deborah Kerr star. 88 min.
09-1827 *$19.99*

Frieda (1947)
An RAF pilot makes a war bride of the German woman who helped him escape the POW camps, only to encounter bigotry and contempt when he brings her home. Glynis Johns, David Farrar, Flora Robson, Mai Zetterling. 98 min.
09-1899 Was $29.99 *$24.99*

My Son, My Son (1940)
Stirring drama set in England from the late Victorian era to World War I and focusing on writer Brian Aherne's stormy relationship with son Louis Hayward, whose unseemly behavior continually causes trouble for his father and his friends. Madeleine Carroll, Laraine Day and Henry Hull also star. 115 min.
08-1778 *$19.99*

Friendly Enemies (1942)
World War II erupts and severs the close friendship between two German businessmen who take opposite sides of the conflict. Trouble ensues when the Nazi sympathizer is conned into funding German sabotage missions. James Craig, Nancy Kelley and Charles Ruggles star. 95 min.
08-1788 *$19.99*

A Gentleman After Dark (1942)
Brian Donlevy stars in this noir-flavored crime drama as a convict whose daughter was raised by the judge who sent him to jail. When Donlevy learns his wife is blackmailing the judge and threatening the marriage of their now-grown child, he breaks out of jail to silence her...for good. Miriam Hopkins, Preston Foster also star. 78 min.
08-1816 *$19.99*

Love Letters (1945)
Lush romantic melodrama (scripted, surprisingly, by "The Fountainhead" author Ayn Rand) stars Jennifer Jones as a woman who loses her memory after being hit by her abusive ex-soldier husband, who in turn is killed by Jones' stepmother, and Joseph Cotten as the dead man's war buddy, who wrote love letters to Jones for his friend and falls for her. With Ann Richards, Anita Louise. 102 min.
07-2526 ❑*$14.99*

Claudette Colbert

The Sign Of The Cross (1932)
Ancient Rome is the setting for this C.B. DeMille epic that stars Fredric March as the Roman prefect in love with Christian martyr Elissa Landi, Charles Laughton in a flamboyant turn as depraved emperor Nero, and Claudette Colbert as his scheming wife, Poppea. Among the highlights are the burning of Rome, the final conflict in the arena, and Colbert's milk bath. 125 min.
07-2244 ❑*$14.99*

I Cover The Waterfront (1933)
An intrepid, relentless reporter (Ben Lyon) becomes romantically involved with the daughter (Claudette Colbert) of a ship captain in order to expose his smuggling of Chinese immigrants inside sharks' hides. Daring in its day, the film co-stars Ernest Torrence and Hobart Cavanaugh. 70 min.
01-1209 Was $19.99 *$14.99*

Cleopatra (1934)
Sumptuous Cecil B. DeMille production loaded with spectacular Roman sets, armies of soldiers and half-naked dancing girls, and a sultry turn by Claudette Colbert as the scheming, seductive Queen of the Nile. Henry Wilcoxon co-stars as Marc Antony, with Warren William as Julius Caesar. 101 min.
07-2240 ❑*$14.99*

Imitation Of Life (1934)
Lower the lights and grab a hankie for this classic tearjerker based on the Fannie Hurst novel and scripted by an uncredited Preston Sturges. Widow Claudette Colbert opens a pancake restaurant with maid and friend Louise Beavers, but both women have success (in the business world) and heartache (with their grown daughters) awaiting them. With Warren William, Rochelle Hudson. 111 min.
07-2649 ❑*$14.99*

Midnight (1939)
In order to keep a gigolo from his wife, Parisian aristocrat John Barrymore hires showgirl Claudette Colbert to impersonate a baroness and distract the would-be Romeo in this fast-paced romantic farce scripted by Billy Wilder and Charles Brackett. With Don Ameche, Mary Astor, Monty Woolley. 94 min.
07-2243 ❑*$14.99*

So Proudly We Hail! (1943)
A trio of Army nurses (Claudette Colbert, Paulette Goddard, Veronica Lake) are followed from Pearl Harbor to Bataan and the Pacific Front in this unusual, moving WWII flagwaver that mixes action and pathos with comedy and romance. George Reeves, Walter Abel and Sonny Tufts (in his film debut) also star. 126 min.
07-2241 ❑*$14.99*

Since You Went Away (1944)
Powerhouse tearjerker about a homefront family coping with hardship and tragedy during World War II, written and produced by David O. Selznick. Exceptional cast includes Claudette Colbert, Jennifer Jones, Shirley Temple, Joseph Cotten, Monty Woolley and Lionel Barrymore. 180 min.
04-2337 Was $39.99 *$29.99*

Guest Wife (1945)
A screwball outing with Don Ameche as a newspaper reporter forced to adopt a wife in order to save his job by impressing his boss. Claudette Colbert is the woman recruited for the task, much to the chagrin of banker hubby Richard Foran. 88 min.
63-1378 Was $19.99 ❑*$14.99*

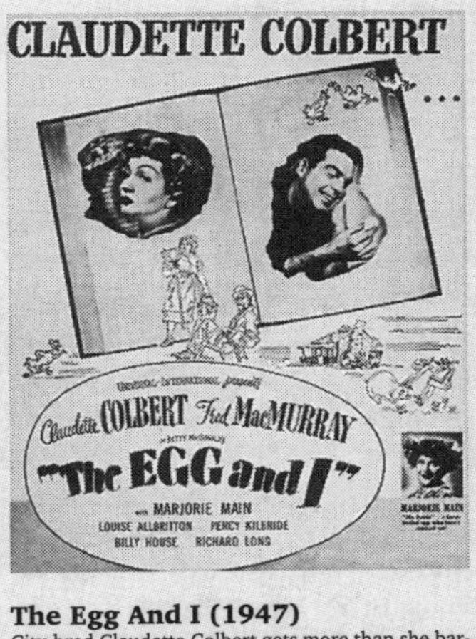
CLAUDETTE COLBERT
Claudette COLBERT Fred MacMURRAY
"The EGG and I"
with MARJORIE MAIN
LOUISE ALLBRITTON PERCY KILBRIDE
BILLY HOUSE RICHARD LONG

The Egg And I (1947)
City-bred Claudette Colbert gets more than she bargains for when she marries chicken farmer Fred MacMurray and moves to the country. All-time favorite barnyard comedy, based on Betty McDonald's book, also introduced Ma and Pa Kettle, played by Marjorie Main and Percy Kilbride. 108 min.
07-2112 Was $19.99 ❑*$14.99*

Three Came Home (1950)
Claudette Colbert stars as American author Agnes Newton Keith, who, along with her British husband, was arrested and held in a Japanese prison camp during World War II. Powerful true account of her harrowing experiences co-stars Patric Knowles and Sessue Hayakawa as the camp commander. 106 min.
10-1388 *$19.99*

Texas Lady (1956)
Claudette Colbert stars as a newspaper owner who uses her beauty, wit and journalistic skill to free the town from two feuding cattle barons. With Barry Sullivan, Gregory Walcott. 86 min.
63-1129 *$14.99*

Parrish (1961)
Romantic entanglements and family strife are the elements of this epic soaper starring fashion-plate Troy Donahue as a young man frustrated with his attempts to fit in with New England's rich tobacco growers. When his mother marries one of them, he gets his chance to join the crowd, but his mean-spirited stepfather intervenes. Connie Stevens and Diane McBain are among the women in his life; Claudette Colbert and Karl Malden also star. 138 min.
19-2162 Was $29.99 *$19.99*

Please see our index for these other Claudette Colbert titles: *Bluebeard's Eighth Wife • Drums Along The Mohawk • It Happened One Night • Let's Make It Legal • The Palm Beach Story • Tomorrow Is Forever*

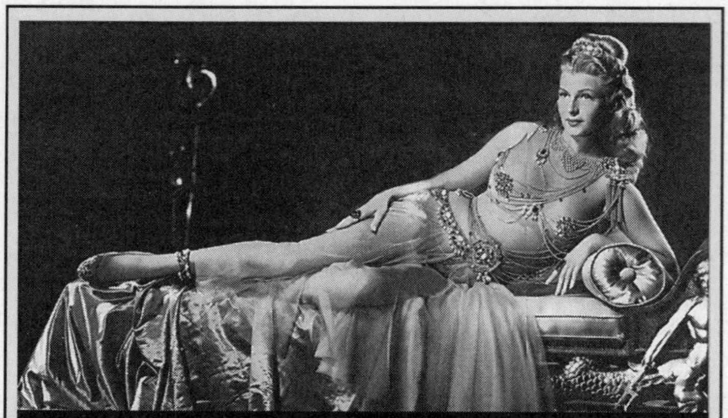
Salome

Rita Hayworth

Rebellion (1938)
Before she was "Rita Hayworth," Rita Cansino co-starred in this "B" western, playing a Mexican woman whose father is murdered by ruthless outlaws out to nab the family land in California. Presidential aide Tom Keene rescues lovely Rita, falls in love with her and becomes governor of the state. With Duncan Renaldo. 60 min.
09-5129 Was $19.99 *$14.99*

Old Louisiana (1938)
Screen cowboy Tom Keene leaves the late 1800s West for the early 1800s South in this adventure drama, playing an American representative to the Spanish colony of Louisiana. When the governor halts all trade along the river, Keene sets out to report to President Jefferson in Washington—but the Spanish have plans to stop him. A young Rita Hayworth (billed as Rita Cansino) plays the governor's daughter. AKA: "Louisiana Gal." 63 min.
10-9796 *$19.99*

Angels Over Broadway (1940)
Offbeat and sardonic comedy, written and directed by Ben Hecht, about the odd denizens of a Broadway cafe who come to the aid of a suicidal embezzler. Douglas Fairbanks, Jr., Rita Hayworth, Thomas Mitchell and John Qualen star. 75 min.
02-1654 *$19.99*

The Lady In Question (1940)
In the first pairing of magnetic screen couple Rita Hayworth and Glenn Ford, the red-haired beauty is a worker in a Paris shop with a tainted past known only to store-keeper Brian Aherne. When she falls for his son (Ford), Papa tries to scuttle the romance by revealing her secret. 78 min.
02-1947 *$19.99*

Music In My Heart (1940)
Crooner Tony Martin, facing imminent deportation, runs into singer Rita Hayworth, about to marry a dull-as-dishwater millionaire. Before long, they're singing and romancing together in this tuneful comedy that also features Alan Mowbray and Andre Kostelanetz and His Orchestra. Songs include "It's a Blue World," "Oh, What a Lovely Dream." 69 min.
02-2144 *$19.99*

Cover Girl (1944)
When nightclub singer Rita Hayworth becomes a magazine sensation, will she leave Gene Kelly's Brooklyn stage for the bright lights of Broadway? Musical comedy favorite features supporting turns by Phil Silvers and Eve Arden and songs by George Gershwin and Jerome Kern; look for a young Shelley Winters. 107 min.
02-1986 *$19.99*

Tonight And Every Night (1945)
A British theatrical troupe continues to perform during the London blitz in this sprightly, song-filled drama that features Rita Hayworth as an American singer who falls for an RAF pilot. With Leslie Brooks, Janet Blair. 92 min.
02-1789 *$19.99*

Gilda (1946)
Rita Hayworth's unforgettable allure—as evidenced in the torrid "Put the Blame on Mame" number—is on view in this classic drama. She's part of a problematical love triangle involving husband George Macready and his partner, Glenn Ford, set against a South American gambling casino. 110 min.
02-1040 Was $29.99 *$19.99*

Down To Earth (1947)
Fantasy-musical stars Rita Hayworth as Terpsichore, the Greek muse of dance, who comes to New York to stop Broadway producer Larry Parks from putting on a jazz play that mocks the gods of myth. Before long, goddess and mortal fall in love. James Gleason and Roland Culver also star in this whimsical tale that features characters from "Here Comes Mr. Jordan" and was later remade as "Xanadu." 101 min.
02-2143 *$19.99*

The Loves Of Carmen (1948)
Adding to her repertoire of legendary seductresses, Rita Hayworth stars as the fiery Gypsy dancer who tempts soldier Glenn Ford with her charms and then abandons him, with fatal consequences. Ron Randell, Luther Adler also star. 99 min.
02-1786 *$19.99*

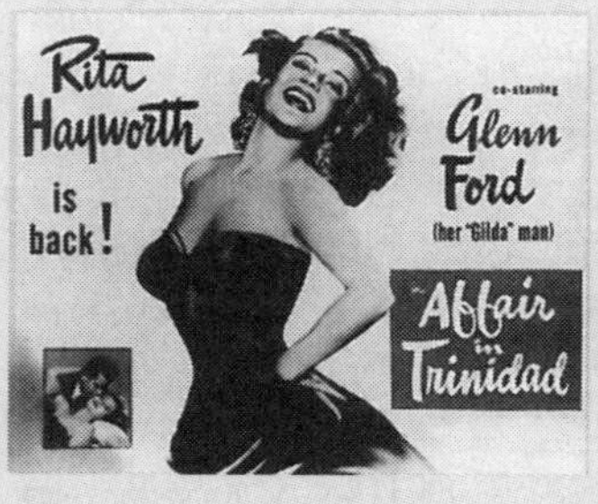

Affair In Trinidad (1952)
"Gilda" co-stars Glenn Ford and Rita Hayworth reteam in a romantic thriller about a Caribbean nightclub performer compelled by police to snuggle up with the international thief who killed her husband. Rita bumps and grinds her way through two numbers, "Trinidad Lady" and "I've Been Kissed Before." 98 min.
02-1941 *$19.99*

Miss Sadie Thompson (1953)
Rita Hayworth stars as a bawdy playgirl on a Pacific island after WWII whose encounters with a hypocritical minister (Jose Ferrer) lead to violence in this musical remake of "Rain." Songs include "The Heat Is on," "Hear No Evil, See No Evil" and "Blue Pacific Skies." 91 min.
02-1048 *$19.99*

Salome (1953)
A "revisionist" retelling of the Biblical story, starring Rita Hayworth as the princess who performs the seductive Dance of the Seven Veils in an effort to save the life of John the Baptist. With Charles Laughton as Herod, Dame Judith Anderson, Stewart Granger. 103 min.
02-1788 *$19.99*

The Rover (1967)
Based on a Joseph Conrad novel, this colorful costume drama stars Anthony Quinn as a pirate in Napoleonic France whose liberty is threatened when he falls for the niece of boarding-house owner Rita Hayworth, whose other guest is French naval officer Richard Johnson. Rosanna Schiaffino also stars. AKA: "The Adventurer." 103 min.
08-8808 *$19.99*

Champagne Safari (1952)
One part celebrity documentary and one part travelogue, this rarely-seen film chronicles Hollywood star Rita Hayworth's tour of colonial Africa with her third husband, globetrotting playboy Prince Aly Khan. Intended to be a diplomatic visit and "second honeymoon," the lavish trip proved to be one of the couple's final public appearances together. 60 min.
53-6154 *$24.99*

Please see our index for these other Rita Hayworth titles: *Blondie On A Budget • Blood And Sand • Circus World • Fire Down Below • Hit The Saddle • The Lady From Shanghai • Only Angels Have Wings • Pal Joey • The Poppy Is Also A Flower • Separate Tables • A Song To Remember • The Strawberry Blonde • Susan And God • Tales Of Manhattan • They Came To Cordura • Trouble In Texas • You Were Never Lovelier • You'll Never Get Rich*

Turf Boy (1942)
Sentimental family horse drama about a young orphan whose kindly veterinarian uncle brings him along on his rounds of the local racetracks to care for thoroughbreds. This provokes the boy's grandmother to start legal proceedings to retain custody. With Buzzy Henry, James Seay, silent film stars Francis X. Bushman and Clara Kimbal Young, and boxer Jim Jeffries. AKA: "Mr. Celebrity." 68 min.
09-2963 *$19.99*

Guilty Assignment (Big Town) (1947)
The first of three films based on the popular radio program "Big Town," this exciting newspaper drama stars Philip Reed as the new managing editor of a big-city tabloid losing a circulation war to its livelier rival, which uses a series of controversial anti-crime pieces to boost readership. With Hillary Brooke, Robert Lowery. 57 min.
09-3011 *$14.99*

The Loves Of Joanna Godden (1947)
Sumptuously photographed British tale in which a young woman who has inherited her father's sheep farm decides to run it on her own. She sends her sister off to school and shuns the expected marriage plans with her next-door neighbor in order to succeed independently, on her own terms. Googie Withers and Jean Kent star. 89 min.
09-5063 *$19.99*

Adventure In Blackmail (1943)
A playwright sued for breach of promise by a woman decides to marry her in order to avoid a lengthy trial. Following a short period of romance, resentment sets in, but after ironing out of their difficulties, a rekindling of emotions is stirred up. Clive Brook and Judy Campbell star in this British production. AKA: "Breach of Promise." 70 min.
09-5160 *$19.99*

Desirable Lady (1944)
An exotic dancer is jailed for doing an erotic dance in public, but later discovers that her boss has arranged the arrest for publicity. Jan Wiley, Phil Warren and Betty Blythe star. 75 min.
09-5179 *$19.99*

Duke Of The Navy (1942)
Complications arise when two sailors on leave find themselves in the expensive hotel suite of a wealthy woman, and a con artist, believing one of the swabbies is the woman's son, attempts to steal her savings. Ralph Byrd, Veda Ann Borg and Stubby Krugar star. 63 min.
09-5054 *$19.99*

Born To Speed (1947)
Midget auto racing provides the unique backdrop for this tale of the son of a deceased driver who teams with a mechanic to restore his father's car and race it against his rival in a big competition. Johnny Sands, Terry Austin and Don Castle star. 60 min.
10-9769 *$14.99*

The Human Comedy (1943)
Saroyan's sentimental, life-affirming drama looks at life in a small California town during World War II. Mickey Rooney, Frank Morgan, Donna Reed, Ray Collins and Van Johnson star; look for Robert Mitchum as a soldier. 118 min.
12-1485 *$24.99*

Johnny Belinda (1948)
Jane Wyman, in her Oscar-winning role, is a deaf-mute girl in a small town who learns to communicate with the help of a dedicated teacher, but later is raped by a local villager. Moving drama of human emotions also stars Lew Ayres, Agnes Moorehead and Charles Bickford. 103 min.
12-1519 Was $24.99 *$19.99*

When The Lights Go On Again (1944)
In the tradition of "The Best Years of Our Lives" comes this sobering drama about a marine returning to his hometown after being hospitalized with shellshock. Still coping with the horrors of war, the young man finds help from a local newspaper reporter in reconnecting with his happy past. James Lydon, Regis Toomey and Barbara Belden star. 75 min.
09-2342 *$24.99*

The Last Alarm (1940)
An arsonist terrorizing the area is the target of a retired fireman who has joined forces with an insurance investigator. J. Farrell MacDonald and Polly Ann Young star. 61 min.
09-5060 *$19.99*

The Mozart Story (1937)
First seen in America in 1948, this early film biopic of the legendary prodigy and composer features performances by the Vienna Philharmonic and Vienna State Opera. Hans Holt stars as Mozart, with Winnie Markus, Curt Jurgens, and Wilton Graff as Salieri. 95 min.
09-1028 Was $29.99 *$24.99*

Amadeus (1984)
Winner of eight Academy Awards, including Best Picture, Actor and Director, this soaring, engrossing story of genius, jealousy and passion stars Tom Hulce as the gifted but childish prodigy Mozart and F. Murray Abraham as bitter rival Salieri. Brilliant musical sequences are set against the opulence of 18th-century Vienna; Milos Forman directs. 158 min.
63-1611 Was $19.99 ❑*$14.99*

Amadeus (Letterboxed Version)
Also available in a theatrical, widescreen format.
19-2660 ❑*$19.99*

The Great Waltz (1938)
Lavish biography of Johann Strauss detailing "The Waltz King's" rise from an orchestra leader to a renowned composer, as well as his romantic involvements with a banker's daughter and an opera singer. Fernand Gravat, Luise Rainer and Miliza Korjus star in this beautifully photographed, music-filled film. 102 min.
12-2240 *$19.99*

The Eternal Waltz (1959)
Lively biography about famed composer Johann Strauss, known as The Waltz King. Lavish sets, beautiful music and fine performances highlight this effort from Germany, starring Bernhard Wicki, Hilde Krahl and Annemarie Dueringer. 97 min. Dubbed in English.
17-9013 *$19.99*

The Strauss Family (1972)
Follow the joys, heartaches, rivalries and genius that marked 19th-century Europe's "First Family of Music" with this acclaimed mini-series based on the lives of Johann Strauss Sr. and Jr., the "Waltz Kings" of Vienna. Eric Woolfe, Stuart Wilson, Derek Jacobi, Anne Stallybrass, Barbara Ferris and Jane Seymour star; music by the London Symphony Orchestra. 390 min. on four tapes.
82-9043 *$79.99*

The Melody Master (1941)
Biography of composer Franz Schubert, who left Austria to avoid the military and found love in a woman who helped him return to his homeland and pursue his musical dreams. Stars Alan Curtis, Ilona Massey, Binnie Barnes, Billy Gilbert and Albert Basserman. AKA: "New Wine," "The Great Awakening." 80 min.
09-1012 Was $29.99 *$19.99*

A Song To Remember (1945)
Classic Hollywood biodrama about the life and work of 19th-century composer Frederic Chopin. Cornel Wilde stars as Chopin, Paul Muni plays his mentor, and Merle Oberon is the love of Chopin's life, writer George Sand. 113 min.
02-1571 *$19.99*

Song Of My Heart (1947)
The life of Russian composer Peter Ilich Tchaikovsky is portrayed in this biography that focuses on Tchaikovsky's affair with his sponsor's beautiful daughter, a princess forbidden to marry him. Frank Sundstrom, Audrey Long and Sir Cedric Hardwicke star; selections from "Romeo and Juliet" and Tchaikovsky's 4th, 5th and 6th Symphonies are featured. 85 min.
10-9241 Was $19.99 *$14.99*

Song Without End (1960)
Dirk Bogarde stars as 19th-century Hungarian musician/composer Franz Liszt, a man torn between his desire to perform his original works and the demands of the two women in his life, in this lavish biopic that earned a Best Musical Score Academy Award. With Genevieve Page, Capucine, Lou Jacobi; directed by Charles Vidor (who died during filming) and George Cukor. 141 min.
02-2184 *$19.99*

Spring Symphony (1984)
Lyrical biographical drama recounts the real-life romance of 19th-century German musician-turned-composer Robert Schumann (Herbert Gronemeyer) and Clara Wieck (Nastassja Kinski), his mentor's daughter and a renowned pianist in her own right. Rolf Hoppe co-stars. 102 min.
47-3142 Was $79.99 *$19.99*

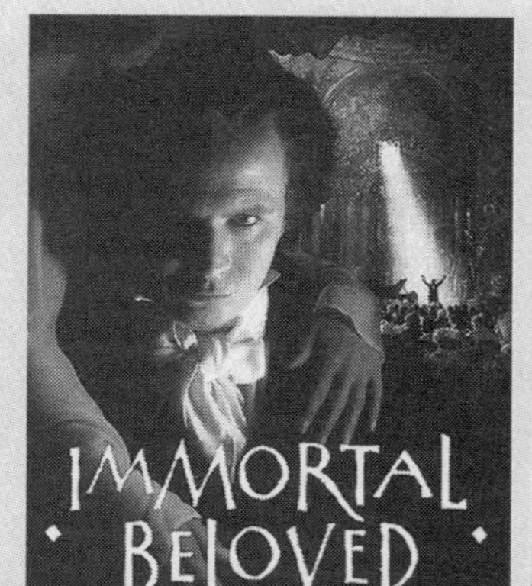

Immortal Beloved (1994)
The mysterious personal life of Ludwig von Beethoven is explored in this compassionate biography which stars Gary Oldman as the troubled genius composer. Anton Schindler, his loyal associate, attempts to find the maestro's secret lover after his death and uncovers a slew of secrets from his past. Jeroen Krabbe, Valeria Golino and Isabella Rossellini co-star. 121 min.
02-2775 Was $19.99 ❑*$14.99*

The Guinea Pig (1949)
Richard Attenborough turns in a fine performance as an English teacher from the country who is placed into a high school with higher class pupils as part of an experiment, and soon sees his values clash against those around him. Sheila Sim and Bernard Miles also star; a Boulting Brothers production. AKA: "The Outsider." 97 min.
10-1607 *$19.99*

Salome, Where She Danced (1945)
Exotic tale of intrigue and drama stars Yvonne DeCarlo as a dancer in 19th-century Berlin who is recurited by American reporter Rod Cameron to use her seductive charms as a spy between warring Prussia and Austria. With Walter Slezak, Albert Dekker. 90 min.
10-3051 *$19.99*

Speed To Spare (1948)
Richard Arlen is a daredevil race car driver who leaves his dangerous profession to start a trucking business with partner Richard Travis. The enterprise turns out to be as dangerous as racing when Arlen goes up against rival truckers. Ian McDonald, Roscoe Karns and Jean Rogers star. 57 min.
10-6011 *$14.99*

Timber Queen (1944)
Richard Arlen is a former pilot who returns home after a discharge from the Army and befriends Mary Beth Hughes, the widow of an service pal. After she inherits a financially troubled timber camp, Arlen is put on the spot to help her, using his flying expertise. Jimmy Ames, June Havoc and Sheldon Leonard also star. 65 min.
10-6017 *$14.99*

The Great Flamarion (1945)
Erich von Stroheim had one of his best roles as a misogynous circus marksman who catches the eye of his lovely assistant (Mary Beth Hughes), whose husband turns up mysteriously murdered. Directed by Anthony Mann. 78 min.
10-7070 Was $19.99 *$14.99*

The Big Wheel (1949)
Mickey Rooney tears up the tarmac as a young man whose obsessive determination to follow in his racer dad's tracks leads to tragedy and hard lessons learned. High-torque drama co-stars Mary Hatcher, Thomas Mitchell, Spring Byington, Hattie McDaniel. 92 min.
10-7229 *$19.99*

Dark Mountain (1944)
Thrilling crime drama about a forest ranger (Robert Lowery) who furnishes his childhood sweetheart (Ellen Drew) with temporary quarters in a mountain cabin, unaware that her dashing racketeer husband, on the lam from the coppers, plans to use the retreat as a hideaway. Co-stars Regis Toomey, Elisha Cook, Jr. star. 56 min.
10-8206 *$19.99*

Gambler's Choice (1944)
Set in New York in 1910, this exciting crime drama focuses on a police lieutenant who falls in love with a nightclub singer while raiding gambling joints in the Bronx. Also trying to win over the singer is a gambler who happens to be the cop's old friend. Chester Morris, Nancy Kelly, Russell Hayden and Sheldon Leonard star. 65 min.
10-8446 Was $19.99 *$14.99*

Captain Moonlight (1940)
Dashing period drama set in 1815 England, where a young country woman is forced into marriage with a conniving gambler. A soldier who is infatuated with the woman tries to stop their involvement when he learns of the gambler's unsavory background. John Garrick, Winifred Shotter star. 60 min.
10-8452 Was $19.99 *$14.99*

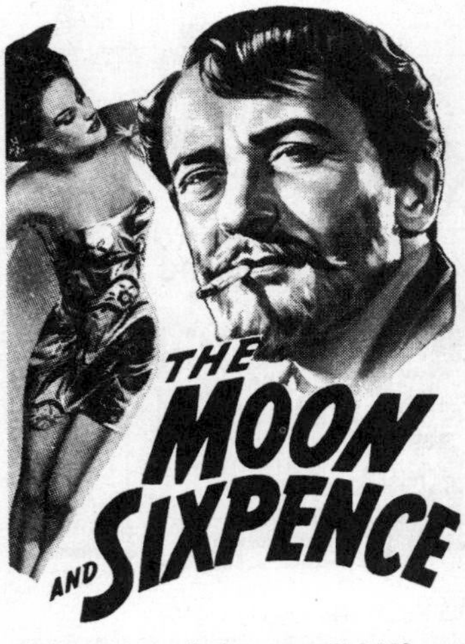

The Moon And Sixpence (1942)
Based on the W. Somerset Maugham roman a clef about Paul Gauguin, this superior film chronicles the life and work of a brilliant, difficult painter who moves to Tahiti to fulfill his lifelong ambition and success. George Sanders, Herbert Marshall, Steve Geray star in this lavishly produced tale. 89 min.
55-9003 *$29.99*

I Stand Condemned (1935)
Two Russian army officers fall in love with the same woman, but then one finds a way to frame his rival for treason. A young Laurence Olivier stars, with Harry Baur, Penelope Dudley Ward. 75 min.
10-4014 Was $19.99 *$14.99*

Fire Over England (1937)
Superb historical drama stars Laurence Olivier as a 16th-century English naval officer who undertakes a dangerous mission at the behest of Queen Elizabeth I, infiltrating the court of Spain's King Philip to learn of plans for the Spanish Armada's invasion of England. Vivien Leigh co-stars with her future husband as a lady-in-waiting; with Flora Robson, Raymond Massey. 89 min.
22-5954 *$19.99*

The Divorce Of Lady X (1938)
British comedy stars Laurence Olivier as a barrister who shares his hotel suite with a young woman (Merle Oberon), then fears his chivalry may involve him in a divorce suit. Ralph Richardson, Binnie Barnes. 90 min.
10-1123 *$19.99*

Wuthering Heights (1939)
Emily Brontë's classic novel of doomed love in 19th-century England is brought to the screen in a stunning production. Laurence Olivier is the brooding Heathcliff, and Merle Oberon is Catherine. With David Niven, Geraldine Fitzgerald; William Wyler directs. 103 min.
44-1844 Was $19.99 *$14.99*

Pride And Prejudice (1940)
Lavish period piece, based on the Jane Austen classic, depicts the trials of a woman trying to find husbands for her five daughters in 18th-century England. Greer Garson, Maureen O'Sullivan, Laurence Olivier, Ann Rutherford and Edmund Gwenn head the superlative cast. 118 min.
12-1108 □*$19.99*

The 49th Parallel (1941)
Taut British war thriller about a German U-Boat that runs aground in Canada's Hudson Bay and the manhunt that follows. Laurence Olivier, Leslie Howard and Raymond Massey star; Academy Award-winner for Best Story. AKA: "The Invaders." 105 min.
15-1134 Was $19.99 *$14.99*

The Demi-Paradise (1943)
Wartime England as seen through foreign eyes is the theme of this barbed British satire, with Laurence Olivier as a Russian scientist who finds his new country to be inhospitable, until he discovers love with a beautiful, young woman. Co-stars Penelope Dudley Ward, Margaret Rutherford, Felix Aylmer. AKA: "Adventure for Two." 103 min.
62-1197 Was $19.99 *$14.99*

Carrie (1952)
Fine screen adaptation of Theodore Dreiser's "Sister Carrie" stars Jennifer Jones as the small town girl who moves to the big city with dreams of fame and wealth and Laurence Olivier as the man who sacrifices all for her. With Eddie Albert, Miriam Hopkins. 118 min.
06-1819 *$19.99*

The Entertainer (1960)
Laurence Olivier created one of his most memorable roles as Archie Rice, an egotistical third-rate music hall performer who browbeats his family until his world collapses around him, in Tony Richardson's compelling drama. Alan Bates, Albert Finney, Joan Plowright co-star. 97 min.
01-1434 Was $19.99 *$14.99*

Khartoum (1966)
Sweeping historical epic set in Africa during the 1880s, focusing on the rivalry between enigmatic British general Charles "Chinese" Gordon (Charlton Heston) and the fierce Moslem leader known as "the Mahdi" (Laurence Olivier). Large-scale battle scenes and superlative acting highlight this intelligent, exciting saga. With Sir Ralph Richardson and Richard Johnson. 134 min.
12-2071 *$19.99*

The Shoes Of The Fisherman (1968)
Anthony Quinn is the former Russian political prisoner who becomes a cardinal and eventually assumes the Papacy in this engrossing, inspiring drama based on Morris West's best-seller. With Laurence Olivier, David Janssen, Oskar Werner. 157 min.
12-1646 Was $29.99 *$19.99*

The Shoes Of The Fisherman (Letterboxed Version)
Also available in a theatrical, widescreen format.
12-3129 *$19.99*

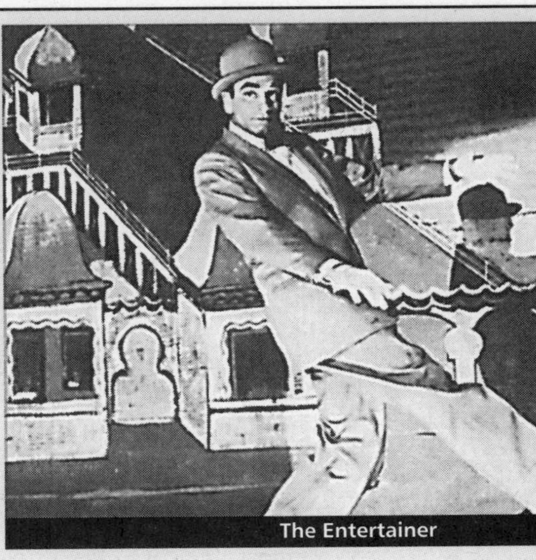

The Entertainer

Laurence Olivier

Battle Of Britain (1969)
A stellar cast that includes Michael Caine, Trevor Howard, Christopher Plummer, Susannah York, Curt Jurgens and Laurence Olivier, coupled with amazing aerial combat sequences, makes this salute to the gallant fliers who defended England against Hitler's Luftwaffe forces a landmark war drama. 133 min.
12-1864 Was $19.99 *$14.99*

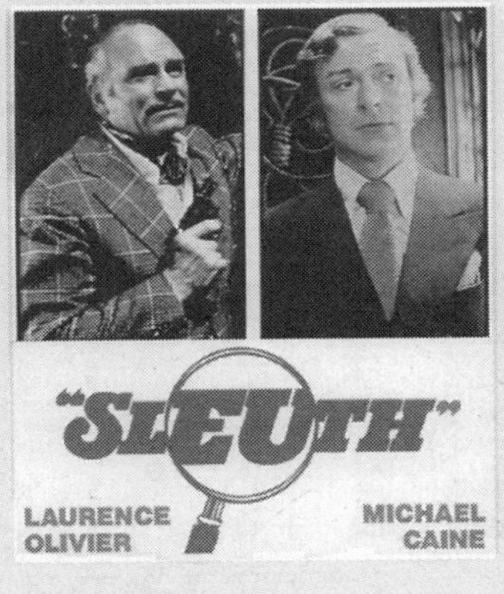

Sleuth (1972)
Intricately composed mystery from screenwriter Anthony Shaffer, who adapted his Tony-winning stageplay. Laurence Olivier is a renowned detective novelist who arranges a meeting with Michael Caine, his wife's lover, at Olivier's ornate home, a meeting that becomes a battle of wits and wills and involves robbery, faked deaths, disguises and revenge. Joseph L. Mankiewicz directs. 139 min.
08-8635 Letterboxed *$14.99*

Uncle Vanya (1977)
Triumphant production of Anton Chekhov's heralded play, directed by and starring Laurence Olivier as Dr. Astrov, the devoted country physician who falls in love with an unattainable woman. This filmization of the 1962 Chichester Drama Festival presentation stars Michael Redgrave, Joan Plowright and Rosemary Harris. 110 min.
48-7002 *$79.99*

The Betsy (1978)
Harold Robbins' sensational look at the sexual and financial intrigue in a family who made their fortune in the auto industry. Laurence Olivier is the patriarch of the clan that has created a car that appears so perfect it threatens to put the other manufacturers out of business. Robert Duvall, Tommy Lee Jones, Lesley-Anne Down and Katharine Ross star. 125 min.
19-2263 Was $19.99 *$14.99*

A Little Romance (1979)
A real charmer about two lonely, gifted children who find romance and adventure on a trek through Europe. Whimsical and winning—excellent for the entire family. Laurence Olivier, Sally Kellerman, Diane Lane. George Roy Hill directs. 110 min.
19-1041 *$14.99*

A Voyage Round My Father (1982)
Excellent adaptation of John Mortimer's autobiographical stage play concerning his relationship with his father, a crusty, blind barrister who needs his son now more than he's willing to admit. Laurence Olivier, Alan Bates, Jane Asher star. 85 min.
44-1665 Was $89.99 *$19.99*

The Wild Geese II (1985)
The world's most lethally efficient attack squad for hire is back, enlisted by a TV network to snatch Nazi war criminal Rudolf Hess from his German prison for an exclusive broadcast (don't get any ideas, Geraldo!). Scott Glenn, Edward Fox, Barbara Carrera and Laurence Olivier star. 124 min.
12-2596 *$14.99*

Laurence Olivier: A Life (1986)
A fascinating study of the life of the century's master actor. Included are interviews with Sir John Gielgud, Sir Ralph Richardson, Douglas Fairbanks, Jr., Dame Peggy Ashcroft and Olivier's wife, Joan Plowright. Winner of the British Academy Award for Best Documentary. 159 min.
22-5532 *$29.99*

Please see our index for these other Laurence Olivier titles: *As You Like It • The Bounty • A Bridge Too Far • Clash Of The Titans • David Copperfield • The Devil's Disciple • Dracula • Hamlet • King Lear • Marathon Man • Nicholas And Alexandra • The Prince And The Showgirl • Rebecca • Richard III • The Seven Percent Solution • Spartacus • 21 Days • Wagner*

Behind Green Lights (1946)
Tough crime drama that takes place during one night in a police station and focuses on a lieutenant who gets romantically involved with a woman accused of murder. The cop discovers new evidence that points to the medical examiner and his political interests. Carole Landis, William Gargan and Richard Crane star. 64 min.
10-8457 Was $19.99 *$14.99*

Blossoms In The Dust (1941)
Moving true drama stars Greer Garson as Edna Gladney, who devoted her life to founding an orphanage and working for children's aid in early 20th-century Texas. Walter Pidgeon, Marsha Hunt, Fay Holden also star. 100 min.
12-2080 □*$19.99*

Intruder In The Dust (1949)
Powerful drama about racial prejudices, based on William Faulkner's novel and set in Mississippi, where a black man accused of murder and about to be lynched is helped by a lawyer and a young boy. David Brian, Claude Jarman, Jr., Juano Hernandez and Will Geer lead the impressive cast. 87 min.
12-2632 *$19.99*

Mrs. Parkington (1944)
Glossy melodrama chronicling the life of a woman who faces many struggles on her rise from boarding house maid to wife of a wealthy (and unfaithful) mine owner and matriarch of a family faced with financial crisis. Greer Garson, Walter Pidgeon, Edward Arnold, Frances Rafferty and Agnes Moorehead star. 124 min.
12-2733 □*$19.99*

City Without Men (1943)
Emotional melodrama set in a boardinghouse next to a prison, where the inmates' wives and lovers await their release. Linda Darnell, Glenda Farrell, Margaret Hamilton, Sheldon Leonard and Edgar Buchanan star. 75 min.
17-3090 Was $19.99 *$14.99*

Journey For Margaret (1942)
Sensitive true-life drama with American journalist Robert Young faced with a horrible tragedy when his pregnant wife is injured in a London air raid. Then their dream of raising a family seems impossible, until he brings two orphans back home to the States. Laraine Day, Fay Bainter and Margaret O'Brien also star in this classic weepie. 81 min.
12-2465 *$19.99*

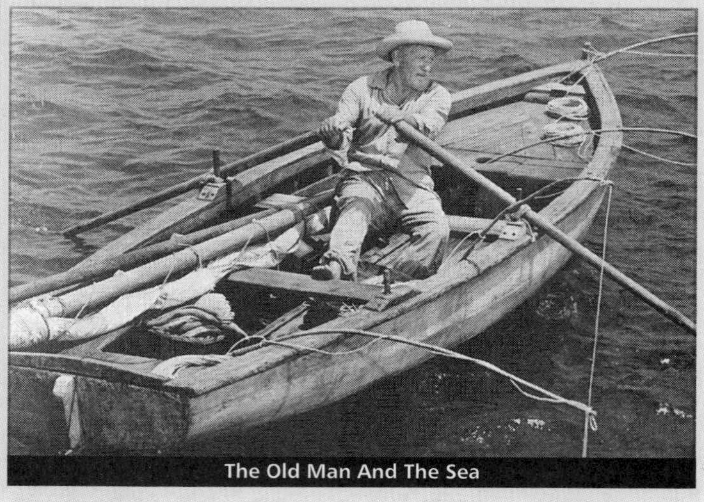

The Old Man And The Sea

Spencer Tracy

Libeled Lady (1936)
An uproarious farce with Spencer Tracy as a scheming newspaper editor whose erroneous story about temperamental heiress Myrna Loy leads her to file a multi-million dollar suit against the paper. Tracy comes up with an elaborate plot involving fiancée Jean Harlow and former co-worker William Powell to frame Loy into dropping the suit, only to have screwball complications arise. 98 min.
12-1601 *$19.99*

Fury (1936)
After being falsely accused of kidnapping, Spencer Tracy is put in a small town jail and becomes the focus of a vigilante mob set on lynching him. Striking drama from director Fritz Lang (his American debut) criticizes mob mentality and features superior performances from Tracy, Sylvia Sidney, Walter Abel and Walter Brennan. 89 min.
12-2345 *$19.99*

Captains Courageous (1937)
Rudyard Kipling's novel receives a classic screen translation, with Oscar-winner Spencer Tracy as a Portuguese fisherman who teaches human values to a millionaire's spoiled young son. With Mickey Rooney, Melvyn Douglas and Lionel Barrymore. 118 min.
12-1066 *$19.99*

Boys Town (1938)
Spencer Tracy garnered his second consecutive Academy Award for his portrayal of Father Flanagan, founder of the famed home for delinquent and underprivileged youth, in this classic MGM melodrama. Mickey Rooney shines as one of the father's more recalcitrant charges; with Henry Hull, Bobs Watson. 96 min.
12-1953 ☐*$19.99*

Men Of Boys Town (1941)
Follow-up to the successful 1938 drama has Spencer Tracy returning as Boys Town founder Father Flanagan. Along with the usual problems presented by his delinquent charges, Tracy is faced with financial hardships and the challenge of an embittered handicapped youth. Mickey Rooney, Lee J. Cobb, Larry Nunn also star. 106 min.
12-2255 *$19.99*

Stanley & Livingstone (1939)
An epic, true-to-life adventure starring Spencer Tracy as the 19th-century journalist who travels to the mysterious jungles of Africa to find the famed Scottish missionary (Sir Cedric Hardwicke). With Nancy Kelly, Richard Greene and Walter Brennan. 101 min.
04-2359 ☐*$39.99*

Northwest Passage (1940)
Rousing adventure saga based on the exploits of colonial American frontiersman Robert Rogers and his men. Spencer Tracy stars as Rogers, leading a squad that includes raw recruits Robert Young and Walter Brennan on a treacherous mission into Indian territory. 125 min.
12-1964 *$19.99*

Edison, The Man (1940)
Wonderful biodrama follow-up to "Young Tom Edison" stars Spencer Tracy as the genius whose inspiration and perspiration gave the world the light bulb, the phonograph and the Dictaphone. The film looks back on Edison's achievements through an interview conducted by reporters on the 50th anniversary of his invention of the incandescent bulb. With Rita Johnson, Charles Coburn, Gene Lockhart. 107 min.
12-2286 *$19.99*

Tortilla Flat (1942)
The colorful inhabitants of John Steinbeck's central California fishing towns are brought to life in this seriocomic tale of friendship and romance. Spencer Tracy, John Garfield, Hedy Lamarr, Akim Tamiroff and Frank Morgan star, under Victor Fleming's direction. 100 min.
12-2370 ☐*$19.99*

A Guy Named Joe (1943)
Downed fighter pilot Spencer Tracy returns to Earth to serve as a "guardian angel" in this beloved fantasy/romance, remade by Steven Spielberg as "Always." With Irene Dunne, Van Johnson, Barry Nelson, Lionel Barrymore. 120 min.
12-1017 *$19.99*

Thirty Seconds Over Tokyo (1944)
Spencer Tracy portrays war hero Jimmy Doolittle in this Grade A World War II film about the first attack on Japan by the U.S. Army Air Force. Van Johnson, Robert Walker and Robert Mitchum co-star. 132 min.
12-1582 *$19.99*

The Seventh Cross (1944)
Moving drama with Spencer Tracy as an embittered Nazi concentration camp prisoner who escapes with six other men shortly before the outbreak of World War II. While in flight to neutral Holland, the cynical escapee regains hope for mankind as stranger after stranger helps him elude the pursuing Gestapo. First major film directed by Fred Zinnemann co-stars Hume Cronyn, Jessica Tandy. 112 min.
12-2289 *$19.99*

Cass Timberlane (1947)
Spencer Tracy is a respectable Minnesota judge who marries sexpot Lana Turner and tries to keep up with his young wife while she has trouble mixing with his snobby, middle-aged friends. A move to New York rocks the marriage even further in this melodrama based on a Sinclair Lewis novel. With Zachary Scott, Mary Astor. 119 min.
12-2715 ☐*$19.99*

Father Of The Bride (1950)
Light-hearted comedy stars Spencer Tracy as the titular papa, coping with one emergency after another as daughter Elizabeth Taylor prepares to walk down the aisle. Sentimental gem, directed by Vincente Minnelli, also stars Joan Bennett, Don Taylor, Russ Tamblyn, Billie Burke. 92 min.
12-1016 Was $19.99 *$14.99*

Father Of The Bride (Color Version)
You know the bride was dressed in white. Now check out Dad and the rest of the party in this techno-tinted tale.
12-1801 Was $19.99 *$14.99*

Father's Little Dividend (1951)
Spencer Tracy, Elizabeth Taylor, Don Taylor and Joan Bennett reprise their roles in this delightful sequel to "Father of the Bride," with the imminent arrival of a grandchild making Tracy much more nervous than mother-to-be Taylor! Vincente Minnelli directs. 83 min.
12-2346 *$19.99*

Malaya (1950)
Former reporter James Stewart teams with paroled crook Spencer Tracy to tackle a dangerous mission during World War II: smuggle 150,000 tons of rubber past Japanese enemy lines and onto American ships. Inspired by true events, this rousing wartime adventure co-stars Sydney Greenstreet, Valentina Cortese. 98 min.
12-2925 ☐*$19.99*

Plymouth Adventure (1952)
Thrilling historical adventure starring Spencer Tracy as Christopher Jones, the no-nonsense captain of the Mayflower's 1620 journey from England to America. With 102 Pilgrim passengers, Jones leads the ship through treacherous weather and rough waters to the New World. Gene Tierney, Van Johnson, Leo Genn and Dawn Adams also star. 105 min.
12-2954 ☐*$19.99*

Broken Lance (1954)
Frontier cattle ranch patriarch Spencer Tracy's harsh, unemotional upbringing of his four sons leads to violent confrontation between siblings in this emotional Western drama that is part "King Lear" and part "Bonanza." Robert Wagner, Richard Widmark, Hugh O'Brian and Earl Holliman are the brothers; with Katy Jurado, Jean Peters. 96 min.
04-2268 Was $39.99 ☐*$14.99*

Bad Day At Black Rock (1955)
The quiet of a small Southwest town shortly after WWII is shattered by the arrival of a one-armed stranger (Spencer Tracy), whose presence threatens to unearth a dark secret. Compelling drama with a prejudice theme also stars Lee Marvin, Ernest Borgnine, Robert Ryan, Walter Brennan. 81 min.
12-1828 Was $29.99 ☐*$19.99*

The Mountain (1956)
Exciting mountaineering action tops this morality play about two brothers in a poor Alpine village and their vastly different reactions to the crash of a luxury airliner on a nearby peak. Spencer Tracy and Robert Wagner are the siblings, joined by Claire Trevor and William Demarest. 104 min.
06-1592 Was $19.99 ☐*$14.99*

The Last Hurrah (1958)
John Ford directed this dramatic look at political cronyism in a large Eastern city. Spencer Tracy stars as a popular mayor who finds himself at odds with the powerful machine as he runs for re-election. Great supporting cast includes Pat O'Brien, John Carradine, Donald Crisp and Jeffrey Hunter. 121 min.
02-1836 *$19.99*

The Old Man And The Sea (1958)
Ernest Hemingway's classic story of man versus nature is strikingly transferred to the screen, with Spencer Tracy starring as the elderly Cuban fisherman who hooks the catch of a lifetime and is determined to bring his prize marlin in. With Felipe Pazos, Harry Bellaver. 95 min.
19-2422 ☐*$19.99*

Inherit The Wind (1960)
Explosive courtroom drama, based on the famed Scopes "Monkey Trial" of the '20s that pitted Creationists against Evolutionists and Clarence Darrow against William Jennings Bryan. The magnificent cast, directed by Stanley Kramer, includes Spencer Tracy, Fredric March, Gene Kelly, Dick York, Donna Anderson and Claude Akins. 127 min.
12-2235 Was $19.99 ☐*$14.99*

The Devil At 4 O'Clock (1961)
Cleric Spencer Tracy asks the governor of an exotic South Seas island if he can use a trio of convicts (Frank Sinatra, Gregoire Aslan and Bernie Hamilton) to help construct a chapel for a children's hospital. When a volcano erupts, the cons help rescue the hospital's young patients. Kerwin Matthews and Alexander Scourby also star in this mix of adventure and sentiment. 126 min.
02-2692 *$14.99*

Judgment At Nuremberg (1961)
Stanley Kramer's masterful, emotional depiction of the Nazi War Trials in Nuremberg is highlighted by Abby Mann's Academy Award-winning script and a stellar cast that includes Spencer Tracy, Marlene Dietrich, Burt Lancaster, Maximilian Schell, Richard Widmark, Montgomery Clift and Judy Garland. 186 min.
12-1887 Was $29.99 ☐*$24.99*

Judgment At Nuremberg (Letterboxed Version)
Also available in a theatrical, widescreen format.
12-3036 *$24.99*

It's A Mad Mad Mad Mad World (1963)
A veritable "Who's Who" of film comedy was assembled by director Stanley Kramer for this slapstick extravaganza. A group of strangers learns about $350,000 in hidden loot from a dying gangster and sets off on a madcap cross-country race to find it. Spencer Tracy, Milton Berle, Sid Caesar, Buddy Hackett, Ethel Merman, Mickey Rooney, Dick Shawn, Phil Silvers and Jonathan Winters star, with dozens of cameos ranging from Jack Benny to the Three Stooges. Restored vesion contains scenes not shown since the film's premiere. 182 min.
12-2204 Letterboxed *$24.99*

The Spencer Tracy Legacy
Katharine Hepburn speaks frankly about her friend Spencer Tracy in this loving tribute to one of the screen's greatest teams and one of the world's finest actors. There's bittersweet and funny anecdotes, as well as film clips from Tracy's finest cinematic achievements, with and without Kate. 88 min.
12-2294 *$19.99*

Please see our index for these other Spencer Tracy titles: *Adam's Rib • Boom Town • Desk Set • Dr. Jekyll And Mr. Hyde • Keeper Of The Flame • Mannequin • Pat And Mike • Riffraff • San Francisco • Sea Of Grass • State Of The Union • Test Pilot • Without Love • Woman Of The Year*

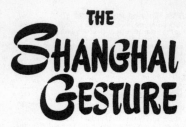

THE SHANGHAI GESTURE

The Shanghai Gesture (1941)
Faced with censor problems from day one, Joseph Von Sternberg's filming of the John Colton play depicts the battle of wills between British magnate Walter Huston and vice den owner Ona Munson. Gene Tierney, Huston's daughter, becomes a pawn in the deadly game. Hypnotic, decadent drama also stars Victor Mature, Maria Ouspenskaya. 94 min.
70-7032 Was $29.99 *$19.99*

Lady Gangster (1942)
Gritty crime drama starring Faye Emerson as a nononsense gun moll whose criminal ways are reformed with help from an understanding district attorney. With Julie Bishop, Frank Wilcox and, in one of his first films, Jackie Gleason. 62 min.
09-5241 Was $19.99 *$14.99*

Loyal Heart (1946)
The rivalry between two English farmers turns ugly when, after one is rebuffed in his efforts to buy the other's faithful sheepdog, he accuses the man of stealing sheep. Percy Marmont, Harry Welchman and Fleet the Dog star. 80 min.
09-5342 *$19.99*

Alimony (1949)
That's all scheming homewrecker Martha Vickers is after in this melodrama, playing a predatory woman who seduces rich men, weds them and then just as quickly divorces them so she can receive large alimony payments. With John Beal, Hillary Brooke, Leonid Kinskey. 71 min.
09-5344 *$19.99*

The Amazing Mr. X (1948)
Suspenseful melodrama about a man who fakes his own death and teams up with a phony spiritualist in order to bilk his rich "widow." Donald Curtis, Lynn Bari, Turhan Bey star. AKA: "The Spiritualist." 78 min.
10-1191 *$19.99*

The Overlanders (1946)
A beautiful, true-to-life adventure set in Australia during World War II. With the threat of a Japanese invasion hanging over their heads, a group of brave people lead 500,000 head of cattle cross-country to safety. Featuring gorgeous scenery and a stirring score, the film stars Chips Rafferty and John Nugent Hayward. 91 min.
10-1389 Was $19.99 *$14.99*

The Bad Lord Byron (1949)
As Lord Byron lies on his deathbed in Greece, he begins to wonder if he will enter heaven, which helps bring back memories of his colorful life and its many eventful moments. Dennis Price, Mai Zetterling, Joan Greenwood and Linden Travers star in this lavish production. 95 min.
10-1603 *$14.99*

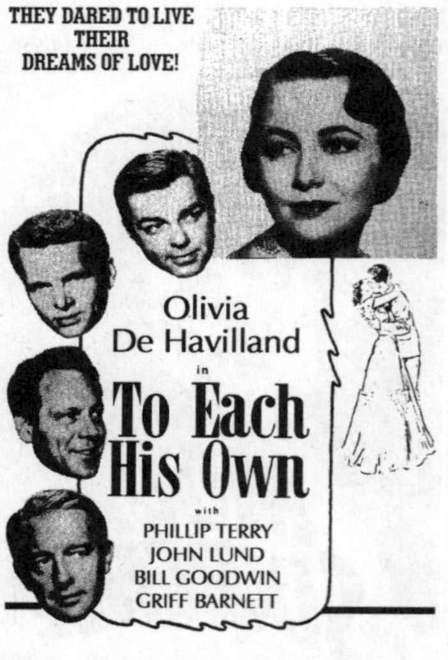
THEY DARED TO LIVE THEIR DREAMS OF LOVE!
Olivia De Havilland
in
To Each His Own
with
PHILLIP TERRY
JOHN LUND
BILL GOODWIN
GRIFF BARNETT

To Each His Own (1946)
Olivia de Havilland took home an Academy Award for her performance as a small-town unwed mother who gives her child up to another family and is later reunited with the now-grown son during World War II in London, where de Havilland moved to and found success in the cosmetics business. Classic "three-hankie" tale also stars John Lund, Roland Culver. 122 min.
07-2527 ☐*$14.99*

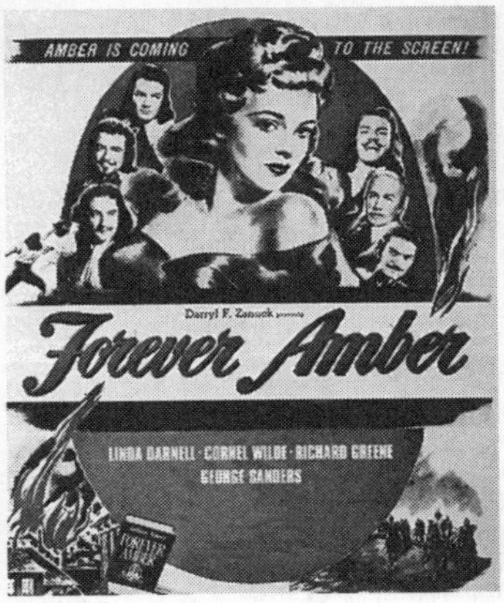

Forever Amber (1947)
Lusty, lavish account of Amber St. Clair (Linda Darnell), the poor English girl in love with a dashing soldier (Cornel Wilde) who takes on many lovers, including King Charles II (George Sanders), after he leaves her and goes to America with their child. Richard Greene and Jessica Tandy also star in Otto Preminger's impressive costume drama. 140 min.
04-2784 □*$19.99*

The Gang's All Here (1941)
Intrigue in the trucking world as sabotage and robbery is running a trucking company into trouble. Could its competitors be behind the problems? With Frankie Darro, Marcia Mae Jones, Keye Luke and Mantan Moreland. 60 min.
17-9051 Was $19.99 *$14.99*

The Treasure Of Monte Cristo (1949)
A modern version of the classic tale focusing on the descendant of the original Count who goes against a crooked lawyer for an incredible treasure. Glenn Langan, Adele Jurgens, Steve Brodie star. 76 min.
17-9082 Was $19.99 *$14.99*

The Best Years Of Our Lives (1946)
Three WWII veterans returning home must fight their own personal battles for acceptance and adjustment in this Oscar-winning William Wyler drama. Fredric March, Dana Andrews and real-life amputee Harold Russell star, along with Hoagy Carmichael, Myrna Loy and Teresa Wright. 172 min.
44-1837 Was $19.99 *$14.99*

Forever And A Day (1943)
A unique all-star cast fuels this wartime salute to English morale, tracing the lives of the residents of a London manor house from Napoleonic times to the Blitz. C. Aubrey Smith, Charles Laughton, Buster Keaton, Merle Oberon, Ray Milland, Ida Lupino, Cedric Hardwicke and many other greats appear. Rene Clair, Frank Lloyd and Edmund Goulding, among others, directed. 104 min.
53-6007 *$19.99*

Fanny By Gaslight (1948)
Lavish costume melodrama, likened to a Victorian "Peyton Place," stars Phyllis Calvert as the illegitimate child of a well-to-do British politician. Her arrival at his estate causes jealousy, forbidden loves, and more than one death. With James Mason, Stewart Granger. AKA: "Man of Evil." 90 min.
53-6015 Was $29.99 *$19.99*

The Lovable Cheat (1949)
Charlie Ruggles, Peggy Ann Garner, Alan Mowbray and Buster Keaton star in this filming of a Balzac story about a likable Parisian con artist who tries to swindle his friends in order to arrange his daughter's marriage to an elderly count. 75 min.
53-6033 *$29.99*

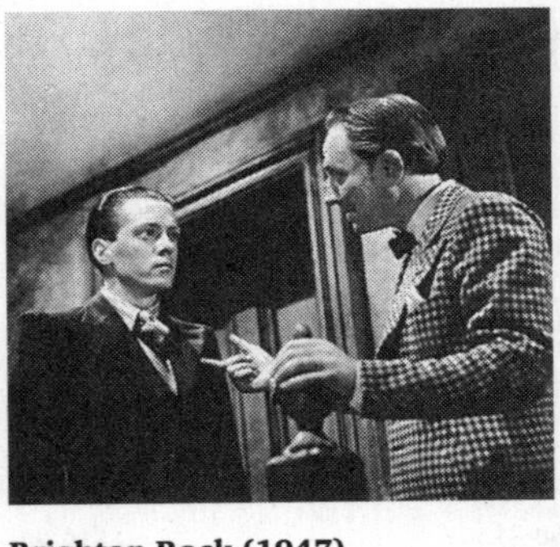

Brighton Rock (1947)
Top-notch crime drama featuring Richard Attenborough in a tour-de-force performance as a leader of a racetrack gang who marries a pretty waitress he needs for a murder alibi, then plans to get her to kill herself. Carol Marsh and Hermione Baddeley also star in Graham Greene's tale. AKA: "Young Scarface." 90 min.
10-9254 Was $19.99 *$14.99*

The Forgotten Village (1941)
John Steinbeck wrote the script for this realistic drama about a young boy and his family who live in a Mexican mountain village. The film looks at their lives, customs and interests in the supernatural. "Flight," a short written by Steinbeck about a youth who commits murder and flees to the mountains of California's Big Sur region, is also included. Narrated by Burgess Meredith. 100 min. total.
53-7453 Was $59.99 *$14.99*

The Small Back Room (1949)
Small but moving Michael Powell/Emeric Pressburger drama stars David Farrar as a lame scientist in WWII Britain. Frustrated by his handicap and embittered to those around him, he gets a chance at heroism when an unexploded German bomb threatens the town. Jack Hawkins, Leslie Banks, Robert Morley co-star. AKA: "Hour of Glory." 106 min.
53-7533 Was $39.99 *$24.99*

The Years Between (1946)
Years after he is thought killed in the war, a member of Parliament returns to find out that his wife has not only taken his seat, but is about to marry a local farmer. Daphne Du Maurier penned the play on which this drama is based; Michael Redgrave, Valerie Hobson and James McKechnie star. 98 min.
53-6066 *$29.99*

A Scandal In Paris (1946)
The real-life exploits of 19th-century criminal-turned-detective François Eugene Vidocq formed the basis for this intriguing, romantic period drama from director Douglas Sirk. George Sanders stars as Vidocq, who conned his way into the office of Paris police chief as part of an elaborate scheme, until official's daughter Signe Hasso convinces him to go straight. Carole Landis, Akim Tamiroff also star. AKA: "Thieves' Holiday." 100 min.
53-6812 *$24.99*

Hungry Hill (1947)
Daphne du Maurier's story is the basis for this drama about a 50-year feud involving two Irish families. The film starts in 1840, when the Donovan clan patriarch rebels against the Brodericks, who own a copper factory on land that previously belonged to the Donovans, prompting decades of turmoil between the families. Margaret Lockwood, Dennis Price star. 100 min.
53-6085 *$29.99*

The Strange Woman (1946)
Hedy Lamarr is at her most beautiful and mysterious in this historical drama set in New England in the early 1800s. A young woman who marries a wealthy, older businessman finds herself attracted to a number of other men, including her stepson and her husband's right-hand man. George Sanders, Louis Hayward and Gene Lockhart also star; directed by Edgar G. Ulmer. 89 min.
53-6027 Was $19.99 *$14.99*

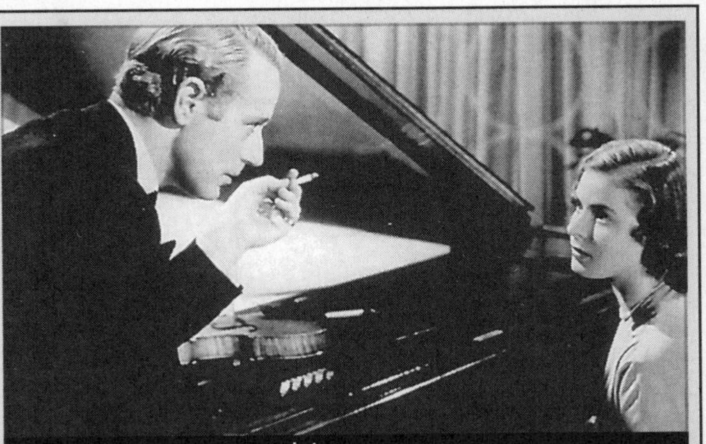

Intermezzo

Ingrid Bergman

The Count Of The Old Town (1934)
Ingrid Bergman's debut film is set in Stockholm, where a group of friends travel from tavern to tavern drinking while eluding the cops on their trail. Valdemar Dahlquist, Sigurd Wallen also star. AKA: "The Count of the Monk's Bridge." 84 min. In Swedish with English subtitles.
54-7049 Was $29.99 *$19.99*

Swedenhielms (1935)
An early screen appearance by Ingrid Bergman marks this Swedish drama of a scientist trying to keep his family together when the threat of a scandal threatens his eldest son and his own chance for a Nobel prize. Gosta Ekman, Bjorn Berglund also star. 92 min. In Swedish with English subtitles.
54-7031 Was $29.99 *$19.99*

Intermezzo (1936)
The original Swedish version of this classic cinema romance, and the film that brought Ingrid Bergman to American producers' attentions. Music teacher and family man Gosta Eckman falls in love with pianist Bergman, and the two begin a doomed affair. 91 min. In Swedish with English subtitles.
54-7033 *$29.99*

Intermezzo (1939)
One of the great romance movies, and the film that marked Ingrid Bergman's American debut, this classic melodrama stars Bergman as a young pianist who attracts the eye of married concert violinist Leslie Howard. The two run off together, but the pull of family draws Howard back. Edna Best, John Halliday also star. 70 min.
04-1612 Was $19.99 □*$14.99*

Dollar (1938)
Ingrid Bergman stars in this frothy romantic comedy as the actress wife of a wealthy businessman who bails him out of his gambling debts, then has suspicions about his faithfulness. Georg Rydeberg and Elsa Burnett also star. 74 min. In Swedish with English subtitles.
54-7042 Was $29.99 *$19.99*

A Woman's Face (1939)
Ingrid Bergman is superb as the beauty who has been horribly scarred in an accident. After plastic surgery, her life follows a different course when she gets involved with a wealthy businessman, who she discovers has plans to use her in a deadly scheme. Anders Henrikson and Karin Carlsson-Kavil also star. 104 min. In Swedish with English subtitles.
54-7050 Was $29.99 *$19.99*

June Night (1940)
After her American film debut in "Intermezzo," Ingrid Bergman returned to Sweden to star in this romantic melodrama about a young woman who attempts to end her relationship with a sailor and is accidentally shot by the suicidal lover. Per Lindberg directs. AKA: "Juniatten." 86 min. In Swedish with English subtitles.
54-7030 *$29.99*

Adam Had Four Sons (1941)
Ingrid Bergman's fine performance highlights this intense drama about a French governess who comes to the aid of a widower trying to adjust to his wife's death. Susan Hayward, Warner Baxter and Fay Wray co-star. 81 min.
02-1271 Was $59.99 *$19.99*

Walpurgis Night (1941)
Controversial drama with Ingrid Bergman as a secretary involved with her married boss. When his wife becomes pregnant and has the baby aborted, the incident becomes a scandal of blackmail and murder. Laes Hanson, Karin Carlsson also star. 82 min. In Swedish with English subtitles.
54-7051 Was $29.99 *$19.99*

Only One Night (1942)
In one of her last Swedish films, Ingrid Bergman plays a woman who falls in love with a former circus worker and discovers he's related to a wealthy aristocrat. The romance has humorous and bittersweet moments before the couple must make a decision about their future. Alno Taube and Edvin Adolphson co-star. 89 min. In Swedish with English subtitles.
54-7043 Was $29.99 *$19.99*

Gaslight (1944)
Suspense classic with Charles Boyer as a scheming husband who plots to make wife Ingrid Bergman think she's going insane. Dame May Whitty and Angela Lansbury co-star in this lush Victorian production; directed by George Cukor. 114 min.
12-1384 *$19.99*

Saratoga Trunk (1945)
Stellar "meller" from the Edna Ferber novel, starring Ingrid Bergman as the Creole beauty out to destroy the family of her adulterous father in turn-of-the-century New Orleans. She woos Texas gambler and millionaire Gary Cooper, but when he travels east on business involving a railroad, she gets involved with one of his wealthy associates. Flora Robson, John Warburton co-star. 135 min.
12-3064 □*$19.99*

Arch Of Triumph (1948)
Pre-WWII France is the setting for this romantic drama based on the novel by Erich Maria Remarque. Charles Boyer, a doctor living in Paris illegally, saves drifter Ingrid Bergman from killing herself and the two fall in love, but his past threatens their relationship. Charles Laughton, Louis Calhern also star. 120 min.
63-1011 □*$19.99*

Anastasia (1956)
In her first American film in eight years, Ingrid Bergman won an Academy Award for her portrayal of the amnesiac found on the streets of Paris by ex-Russian general Yul Brynner and coached by him to impersonate the youngest daughter of Czar Nicholas. But could this impostor actually be the real Anastasia? With Helen Hayes, Ivan Desny. 105 min.
04-2287 Was $19.99 □*$14.99*

The Inn Of The Sixth Happiness (1958)
Inspirational, large-scale drama starring Ingrid Bergman as a British domestic who travels to China shortly before World War II to help a missionary care for the locals and convert them to Christianity. She eventually falls in love with an army officer (Curt Jurgens) and courageously leads a group of children to safety during a Japanese invasion. Robert Donat also stars. 157 min.
04-1524 *$19.99*

Goodbye Again (1961)
Tired of her lover's continuous affairs with younger women, a Parisian interior decorator carries on an affair with the young son of a wealthy client. The designer must make a difficult decision when her former lover returns after a trip and discovers she's living with the young man. Ingrid Bergman, Yves Montand and Anthony Perkins star. 120 min.
12-2809 □*$19.99*

A Walk In The Spring Rain (1970)
Ingrid Bergman is the withdrawn wife of a professor, Anthony Quinn an earthy mountaineer/handyman. The two meet and fall in love, only to face an uncertain future, in this romantic drama. Fritz Weaver, Katherine Crawford co-star. 98 min.
02-1596 Was $59.99 *$14.99*

The Hideaways (1973)
Heartwarming fun and heart-stopping suspense are blended in this delightful and exciting adventure for the entire family. Two runaway children hide out in New York's Metropolitan Museum of Art, where they are helped by an elderly recluse (Ingrid Bergman). With Sally Prager, Richard Mulligan. AKA: "From the Mixed-Up Files of Mrs. Basil E. Frankweiler." 105 min.
40-1415 Was $19.99 *$14.99*

A Woman Called Golda (1982)
Ingrid Bergman won a posthumous Emmy Award for her final performance as Israeli Prime Minister Golda Meir, one of this century's most extraordinary women, from her early life in America to her 1977 meeting with Anwar Sadat. Co-stars Judy Davis as the young Meir, Leonard Nimoy and Ned Beatty. 192 min.
06-1155 *$69.99*

Ingrid Bergman: Portrait Of A Star
Documentary look at the woman...the actress...the legend that was Ingrid Bergman, from her greatest film roles to her stormy and controversial private life. John Gielgud narrates. 70 min.
50-6120 Was $19.99 *$14.99*

Ingrid Bergman: Remembered
Hosted by two of Bergman's daughters, Pia Lindstrom and Isabella Rossellini, this moving tribute to the legendary actress features clips from some of Ingrid's best-loved films—including "Intermezzo," "Casablanca," "Gaslight," "Joan of Arc" and "Anastasia"—as well as rare home movies that show her private side. 53 min.
50-7611 *$14.99*

The Ingrid Bergman Collection
Celebrate the Oscar-winning actress's pre-Hollywood career with this special collection featuring six of her Swedish films: "Dollar," the 1936 "Intermezzo," "June Night," "Only One Night," "Walpurgis Night" and "A Woman's Face."
53-6367 Save $20.00! *$119.99*

The Ingrid Bergman Collection
Three of the legendary screen beauty's finest films are presented in a handsome boxed set: "Arch of Triumph," "The Bells of St. Mary's" and "Indiscreet."
63-1621 Save $5.00! *$39.99*

Please see our index for these other Ingrid Bergman titles: *Autumn Sonata* • *The Bells Of St. Mary's* • *Cactus Flower* • *Casablanca* • *Dr. Jekyll And Mr. Hyde* • *Fear* • *For Whom The Bell Tolls* • *Indiscreet* • *Murder On The Orient Express* • *Notorious* • *Spellbound* • *Stromboli* • *Voyage In Italy (Strangers)*

Caught (1949)
A young girl tries to escape from her philandering millionaire husband and finds love with another man, but her husband's interference could lead to murder. Taut "film noir" drama stars James Mason, Barbara Bel Geddes, Robert Ryan. 88 min.
63-1125   Was $19.99 $14.99

Half A Sinner (1940)
While trying to escape the attention of an unwanted suitor, a schoolteacher steals a rich man's car and takes off. Little does she know that a gangster is stuffed in the back seat of the car and she's headed for big trouble. Heather Angel, Clem Bevans and Henry Brandon star. 55 min.
55-3048 $19.99

I've Always Loved You (1946)
Romantic drama set in the world of classical music, featuring Philip Dorn as an orchestra conductor who attempts to destroy a female pupil's career. Catherine McLeod, Maria Ouspenskaya co-star, along with the superlative playing of Artur Rubinstein. 117 min.
63-1448 $19.99

Lonesome Women (1948)
In the mountains above Brazil's diamond country, a group of ruthless men rule over innocent families and women who once sought to get rich but now serve as slaves. When a diamond is stolen, a young man is accused and all hell breaks loose when a woman tries to help him. Herbert Souto and Leonard Picchi star.
79-5641   Was $24.99 $19.99

Lana Turner

Johnny Eager (1942)
First-class gangster story starring Robert Taylor as a suave but ruthless gangster involved in racketeering and gambling who falls for sociology student Lana Turner, the daughter of a prominent attorney. Van Heflin won an Academy Award for Best Supporting Actor for his portrayal of Taylor's alcoholic sidekick. With Edward Arnold, Robert Sterling. 107 min.
12-2718 $19.99

The Postman Always Rings Twice (1946)
The original Hollywood version of James M. Cain's steamy tale of love, deception and murder stars John Garfield as a drifter who finds work in a roadside cafe and romance in the arms of sultry Lana Turner, the boss's wife. With Cecil Kellaway, Hume Cronyn, and Leon Ames. 113 min.
12-1130   Was $29.99 $19.99

The Postman Always Rings Twice (Color Version)
Neither rain, nor snow, nor gloom of "film noir" shadows stopped the computer from the swift completion of colorizing this suspense classic.
12-1131   Was $29.99 $19.99

Green Dolphin Street (1947)
Classic melodrama set in 1800s New Zealand, with Lana Turner and Donna Reed as sisters vying for the attentions of sailor Richard Hart. Van Heflin, Frank Morgan, Edmund Gwenn co-star. 141 min.
12-1499 $19.99

A Life Of Her Own (1950)
The New York fashion scene serves as the backdrop for this glossy drama about a young woman (Lana Turner) attempting to make it as a top model who finds excitement, tragedy and romance with a married man while climbing the ladder of fame. Ray Milland, Tom Ewell, Louis Calhern and Ann Dvorak also star. 108 min.
12-2720 $19.99

A Story of Lost Love...

LANA TURNER
DEBBIE REYNOLDS
EZIO PINZA
BARRY SULLIVAN

MR. IMPERIUM

Mr. Imperium (1951)
Lush romantic tale starring Ezio Pinza as a charismatic prince who falls for aspiring nightclub singer Lana Turner. When Pinza becomes king of his country, their love is lost...until he meets her years later after she has become a Hollywood star. Marjorie Main, Debbie Reynolds and Sir Cedric Hardwicke also star; songs by Harold Arlen and Dorothy Fields. 87 min.
17-9033   Was $19.99 $14.99

Latin Lovers (1953)
Wealthy heiress Lana Turner follows her millionaire boyfriend to Brazil, where she's swept off her feet by Latin lover Ricardo Montalban. This colorful musical-comedy offers Turner at her most fetching, songs like "Night and You" and "I Had to Kiss You" and a supporting cast that includes John Lund, Louis Calhern and Jean Hagen. 104 min.
12-2719 $19.99

Diane (1955)
Lavish costume drama set in 16th-century France in which Lana Turner plays Diane de Poitiers, the prostitute who served as Prince Henry II's tutor (and later mistress) and whose influence nearly destroyed Queen Catherine De Medici's power. Pedro Armendariz, Roger Moore and Marisa Pavan also star in this historical romance. 110 min.
12-2716 $19.99

The Prodigal (1955)
The New Testament parable was elaborated upon for this lavish costume drama. Edmund Purdom plays the Hebrew man who leaves home for the bright lights of Damascus and falls for seductive pagan priestess Lana Turner. Before long he is broke and sold into slavery, where he leads a revolt against Turner and her cohorts. Louis Calhern, Audrey Dalton, James Mitchell also star. 114 min.
12-2721 $19.99

Another Time, Another Place (1958)
Sentimental melodrama set in WWII London, where reporter Lana Turner meets and falls in love with fellow correspondent Sean Connery, unaware of his dark secret and of a greater shock that awaits them. With Glynis John, Barry Sullivan. 95 min.
06-1770   Was $39.99 $19.99

Imitation Of Life (1959)
Producer Ross Hunter's lush remake of the 1934 meolodrama stars Lana Turner as an actress who puts her career ahead of daughter Sandra Dee. Juanita Moore plays Turner's black housekeeper, whose light-skinned daughter (Susan Kohner) leaves home to try and pass herself off as white. John Gavin, Robert Alda also star; Douglas Sirk directs. 124 min.
07-1325   Was $59.99 $14.99

Portrait In Black (1960)
Ross Hunter produced this stylish thriller featuring Lana Turner as a beauty married to shipping mogul Lloyd Nolan but in love with doctor Anthony Quinn. After the lovers kill Nolan, they receive a letter mentioning the murder and set out to find the writer at any cost. Sandra Dee, John Saxon, Richard Basehart and Anna May Wong co-star. 113 min.
07-2439 $14.99

By Love Possessed (1961)
Shocking in its day, this soaper stars Lana Turner as the boozy wife of a crippled lawyer (Jason Robards, Jr.) who fools around with her husband's business partner (Efrem Zimbalist, Jr.). Fine supporting cast includes Barbara Bel Geddes, George Hamilton, Everett Sloane and Yvonne Craig; known to trivia buffs as the first regularly scheduled in-flight airline movie. 115 min.
12-2655 $14.99

Who's Got The Action? (1962)
When attorney Dean Martin keeps blowing his pay on the ponies, wife Lana Turner arranges to become his bookie in order to save their household. Comic trouble arises when Dino wins big and she can't pay off his and his friends' wagers. Fast-paced comedy also stars Eddie Albert, Walter Matthau. 93 min.
06-2105 $14.99

Madame X (1966)
Lana Turner stars as a woman accused of murder, defended by a lawyer who doesn't realize his connection to her. Lush, highly polished remake of classic story co-stars John Forsythe, Ricardo Montalben, Burgess Meredith and Constance Bennett. 100 min.
07-1290   Was $59.99 $14.99

Please see our index for these other Lana Turner titles: *Bachelor In Paradise • The Bad And The Beautiful • Cass Timberlane • Dr. Jekyll And Mr. Hyde • Homecoming • Honky Tonk • Love Finds Andy Hardy • The Merry Widow • Peyton Place • The Sea Chase • The Three Musketeers • Weekend At The Waldorf*

THE TRUE STORY OF A FAMILY WHO LIVED A LIE FOR TWENTY YEARS!

LOUIS DE ROCHEMONT production
"LOST BOUNDARIES"
...with BEATRICE PEARSON
MEL FERRER
Sentés Douglas ... CANADA LEE and RICHARD HYLTON
Screenplay by ALFRED L. WERKER
A DRAMA OF REAL LIFE FROM "THE READER'S DIGEST"

Lost Boundaries (1949)
Groundbreaking look at prejudice in America, based on a true story, stars Mel Ferrer as a light-skinned black doctor who, along with his family, passes for white in a small New Hampshire town. With Beatrice Pearson, Canada Lee; produced by "March of Time" creator Louis de Rochemont. 99 min.
19-2419 $19.99

Girls In Chains (1943)
When she is fired for being related to a known mobster, a teacher takes a tough job in a violent girls' reformatory to gather information that will send the crook to prison. Stars Arline Judge. 72 min.
68-8284   Was $19.99 $14.99

So Ends Our Night (1941)
Powerful tale stars Fredric March as a German man who speaks out against Hitler, but is forced to flee and leave his wife behind. He meets a young Jewish couple whom he accompanies across Europe, but when March learns that his wife is gravely ill, he risks his life to see her again. Margaret Sullavan, Glenn Ford, Frances Dee and Erich von Stroheim also star. 117 min.
55-9007 $29.99

Son Of The Navy (1940)
Amiable family drama about a little kid who adopts a sailor as his dad, despite the navy man's continuous efforts to shake him. With James Dunn, Jean Parker and Martin Spellman. 72 min.
17-9074   Was $19.99 $14.99

Not Wanted (1949)
Co-produced and co-scripted by Ida Lupino, this intriguing "B" social drama stars Sally Forrest as a young girl who is left an unwed mother after an affair with musician Leo Penn and later is consoled by handicapped veteran Keefe Brasselle. AKA: "Streets of Sin." 94 min.
53-8981 $19.99

The Naked City (1948)
This masterful, gritty crime drama, shot on location in New York City, details the investigation of a murdered woman by two policemen, a crafty veteran (Barry Fitzgerald) and his brash young assistant (Don Taylor). After numerous dead ends, the clues lead to a surprising suspect. Jules Dassin directs in slam-bang realistic fashion; with Howard Duff and Dorothy Hart. 96 min.
55-9010 $24.99

Body And Soul (1947)
Classic boxing drama stars John Garfield as a champion fighter who, on the eve of a match he's scheduled to throw for the mob, looks back on his rise to the top and the people he used to get there. With Lilli Palmer, Anne Revere, William Conrad, Canada Lee. 104 min.
63-1003   Was $19.99 $14.99

Body And Soul (1981)
Leon Isaac Kennedy scripted and stars in this knockout remake of the 1947 ring drama, playing an up-and-coming boxer who runs afoul of mobsters while falling for a gorgeous reporter (played by then-wife Jayne Kennedy). With Peter Lawford, Michael Gazzo, and Muhammad Ali as himself. 109 min.
12-1272   Was $79.99 $14.99

Body And Soul (1998)
In this reworking of the John Garfield classic, Ray "Boom Boom" Mancini plays ambitious young boxer Charlie Davis, who, with help from his friend Tiny, climbs to the top of the ring game. During his rise to stardom, however, he forgets the people who helped him get there. With Michael Chiklis, Jennifer Beals, Rod Steiger and Joe Mantegna. 95 min.
12-3303 $49.99

Force Of Evil (1949)
John Garfield stars in this dark drama of an attorney working for an underworld kingpin who must choose between his security and helping his brother fight the gangsters. Thomas Gomez, Roy Roberts, Marie Windsor co-star. Newly restored version includes an introduction by Martin Scorsese. 82 min. total.
63-1114 $14.99

The Dark Mirror (1946)
Olivia de Havilland turns in a pair of riveting performances as twin sisters—one good, the other evil—who undergo examinations from psychologist Lew Ayres (who becomes the object of both women's affections) to determine who may have been responsible for the murder of a prominent physician; directed by Robert Siodmak ("The Spiral Staircase"). 85 min.
63-1121   Was $19.99 $14.99

Diary Of A Chambermaid (1946)
A desirable serving girl (Paulette Goddard) in a monarchist French household of the 1880s has her choice of suitors offering either wealth, position or romance. Perhaps the best of Jean Renoir's Hollywood films; with Hurd Hatfield, Burgess Meredith and Irene Ryan. 81 min.
63-1323   Was $19.99 $14.99

Moonrise (1948)
The son of a hanged criminal is so haunted by the specter of bad blood in his family he accepts guilt for a murder committed in self-defense. A grim drama with sensitive performances by stars Dane Clark and Ethel Barrymore. 90 min.
63-1324 $19.99

My Girl Tisa (1948)
Touching look at immigrants during the early 1900s, focusing on a young lawyer helping a woman bring her father to America. Sam Wanamaker, Lilli Palmer, Akim Tamiroff and Alan Hale star in this insightful, bittersweet tale. 95 min.
63-1377 $19.99

The Private Affairs Of Bel Ami (1947)
Paris in the late 1890s serves as the backdrop for this lush film based on Guy de Maupassant's story about a charming rogue (George Sanders) who uses beautiful women to climb the social ladder, while avoiding the genuine love of Angela Lansbury. Co-stars Frances Dee and John Carradine. 112 min.
63-1447   Was $19.99 $14.99

Joan FONTAINE
Louis JOURDAN

Letter from an Unknown Woman

MARCEL JOURNET • ART SMITH • CAROL YORKE
Screenplay by Howard Koch • From the Story by Stefan Zweig

Letter From An Unknown Woman (1948)
Classic tearjerker, directed by Max Ophuls, stars Joan Fontaine as a lonely woman who is seduced and abandoned by pianist Louis Jourdan. She marries another, but learns she's carrying Jourdan's child. With Mady Christians, Marcel Journet. 86 min.
63-1292 $14.99

Boss Of Big Town (1943)
A trade official breaks up a scheme by mobsters to muscle into the milk business. Crime programmer stars John Litel and H.B. Warner. 65 min.
68-8285 $19.99

I'll Sell My Life (1941)
Sentimental story about a young woman who sacrifices everything to save the life of her brother proves blood is thicker than water (and tears fill more movie seats than buttered popcorn). Rose Hobart and Michael Whalen star. 73 min.
68-8346 $19.99

Robot Pilot (1942)
When test pilot Forrest Tucker looks for the cause of the crash that ruined his robot-guided plane, spoiled rich girl Carol Hughes tries to get her romance with the flyboy off the runway. AKA: "Emergency Landing." 67 min.
68-8347   Was $19.99 $14.99

MOVIES UNLIMITED®

Barbara Stanwyck

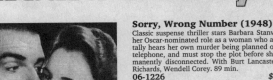

Illicit (1931)
Barbara Stanwyck's first film for Warner Bros. casts her as a woman who decides to overlook her own fears about walking down the aisle and marries the handsome boyfriend she's been living with on weekends. After two years of unhappiness, the two seek companionship with others and question the future of their marriage. James Rennie, Ricardo Cortez and Natalie Moorhead also star. 81 min.
12-2883 *$19.99*

The Purchase Price (1932)
Former torch singer Barbara Stanwyck becomes the mail-order bride of farmer George Brent. After much difficulty, she adapts to country life, but financial problems and the appearance of Stanwyck's former gangster boyfriend threaten their union. Lyle Talbot and David Landau co-star. 68 min.
12-2884 *$19.99*

Baby Face (1933)
Daring for its time, this romantic drama stars Barbara Stanwyck as an amoral, greedy gal who literally sleeps her way up the corporate ladder in a New York bank, not caring who gets hurt. George Brent, Donald Cook, Henry Kolker and a young John Wayne co-star as some of Stanwyck's conquests. 72 min.
12-2172 *$19.99*

Night Nurse (1933)
Barbara Stanwyck stars as a nurse who cares for two fatherless children and uncovers a plot to kill them for their inheritance money hatched by their drunken mother and her chauffeur lover (Clark Gable). Risqué drama also stars Joan Blondell, Ben Lyon and Charles Winninger. 72 min.
12-2297 *$19.99*

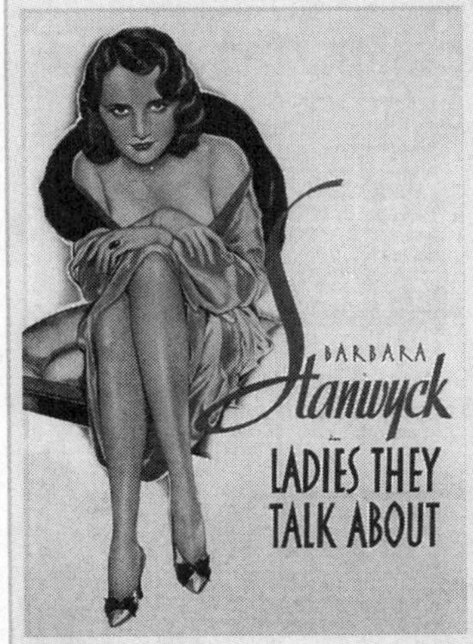

Ladies They Talk About (1933)
One of the first and best of Hollywood's "women in jail" films stars Barbara Stanwyck as a tough gun-toting moll who's sent up the river by the D.A., who happens to be her ex-boyfriend. Guess who'll be looking for revenge once she gets out? With Preston Foster, Lillian Roth, Lyle Talbot. AKA: "Women in Prison." 69 min.
12-2625 *$19.99*

Her Uncle Sam (1935)
Anti-communist comedy starring Barbara Stanwyck as the daughter of a decorated general who falls in love with a radical student. Hoping to break up the romance, dad sends Stanwyck on a vacation to Mexico, where she links up with AWOL American soldier Robert Young and helps him return to the U.S. in a stolen car. With Cliff Edwards, Hardie Albright. AKA: "Her Enlisted Man," "Red Salute," "Runaway Daughter." 78 min.
09-5018 *$19.99*

Internes Can't Take Money (1937)
The first film production to feature Dr. Kildare stars Joel McCrea as the dynamic young intern, who helps former convict Barbara Stanwyck find her missing 3-year-old daughter after she's kidnapped by a notorious gangster. Lloyd Nolan, Stanley Ridges also star. 79 min.
07-2296 ❑*$14.99*

Stella Dallas (1937)
One of Hollywood's classic tearjerkers stars Barbara Stanwyck as a working-class woman who sacrifices all for her daughter's well-being, only to be rejected by her years later. Anne Shirley, John Boles, Alan Hale and Marjorie Main co-star; King Vidor directs. 110 min.
44-1889 Was $19.99 *$14.99*

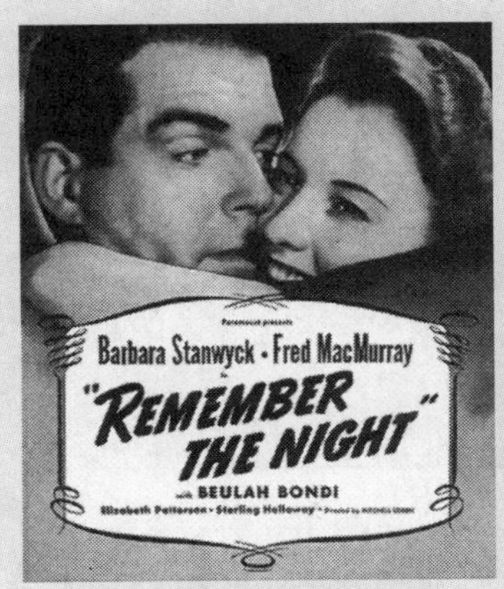

Remember The Night (1940)
Breezy mix of comedy, drama and romance stars Barbara Stanwyck as a woman picked up in New York for shoplifting right before Christmas. No-nonsense D.A. Fred MacMurray agrees to have fellow Hoosier Stanwyck released in his custody so they can go home to Indiana for the holidays, and love blooms along the way. With Beulah Bondi, Willard Robertson; scripted by Preston Sturges. 94 min.
07-2327 ❑*$14.99*

Ball Of Fire (1941)
"Snow White" meets the Jazz Age when a showgirl is hired by seven bookish professors working on an encyclopedia entry on slang, only to find romance and a jealous gangster ex-beau waiting in the wings. Madcap farce from director Howard Hawks and co-scripter Billy Wilder stars Barbara Stanwyck, Gary Cooper, Dana Andrews, S.Z. Sakall. 111 min.
44-1874 Was $19.99 *$14.99*

The Great Man's Lady (1942)
Barbara Stanwyck is an elderly woman who reminisces about her life to reporters at the funeral of a beloved senator. She tells of her love affair with the politician, their adventures in the old West, their struggles concerning the arrival of the railroad and the other man in her life. Joel McCrea, Brian Donlevy and Katherine Stevens co-star. 91 min.
07-2297 ❑*$14.99*

Lady Of Burlesque (1943)
A mystery novel by stripper Gypsy Rose Lee served as the basis for this entertaining whodunit, with Barbara Stanwyck as the star of a burlesque house who teams with a comic (Michael O'Shea) to determine the murderer of a young woman strangled by a G-string. With Iris Adrian, Pinky Lee. 91 min.
08-8063 Was $19.99 *$14.99*

Double Indemnity (1944)
A masterpiece of film noir cinema from director Billy Wilder, who also co-scripted with Raymond Chandler. Barbara Stanwyck is the definitive femme fatale who lures insurance salesman Fred MacMurray into a twisting plot of murder. Edward G. Robinson co-stars. 107 min.
07-1494 Was $19.99 ❑*$14.99*

Christmas In Connecticut (1945)
Wonderful holiday farce stars Barbara Stanwyck as a journalist out to make points with editor Sydney Greenstreet by inviting a war hero (Dennis Morgan) home for a family Christmas dinner. Now all she's gotta do is cobble together a family! Reginald Gardiner, S.Z. Sakall, Una O'Connor co-star. 101 min.
12-1720 Was $19.99 *$14.99*

The Strange Love Of Martha Ivers (1946)
Barbara Stanwyck is superb as a wealthy woman suddenly faced with memories of murder in her past. Kirk Douglas (in his first role), Lizabeth Scott, Van Heflin and Judith Anderson star. 115 min.
10-4031 Was $19.99 *$14.99*

Cry Wolf (1947)
Offbeat and intriguing mystery starring Barbara Stanwyck as a recently widowed woman who travels to her husband's family estate and learns that patriarch Errol Flynn is keeping more than a few skeletons in the clan's closet. With Richard Basehart, Jerome Cowan, Geraldine Brooks. 83 min.
12-2944 ❑*$19.99*

Sorry, Wrong Number (1948)
Classic suspense thriller stars Barbara Stanwyck in her Oscar-nominated role as a woman who accidentally hears her own murder being planned over the telephone, and must stop the plot before she's permanently disconnected. With Burt Lancaster, Ann Richards, Wendell Corey. 89 min.
06-1226 *$14.99*

East Side, West Side (1949)
Glossy tale of the trials and tribulations of New York socialites, featuring Ava Gardner as a model who returns home to rock the boat of married couple Barbara Stanwyck and James Mason, with the boat getting even shakier when Stanwyck falls for war hero Van Heflin. Cyd Charisse, Gale Sondergaard and Nancy Davis also star in this superior soaper. 108 min.
12-2304 *$19.99*

Clash By Night (1952)
Fine melodrama from director Fritz Lang stars Barbara Stanwyck as an unhappy woman who returns to her coastal California hometown and marries local fisherman Paul Douglas, only to find herself attracted to his best friend, sullen Robert Ryan. Their affair leads to trouble in this adaptation of a Clifford Odets play; with Marilyn Monroe, Keith Andes. 105 min.
08-1044 *$19.99*

All I Desire (1953)
In this Douglas Sirk-Ross Hunter production, Barbara Stanwyck attempts to return to her school principal husband and two daughters after a period of estrangement in which she pursued a career in the theater and had an adulterous affair. Richard Carlson, Maureen O'Sullivan, Marcia Henderson and Lori Nelson also star in this affecting drama. 80 min.
07-2294 ❑*$14.99*

Executive Suite (1954)
The ruthless power struggle that erupts when a major manufacturing firm's president dies is the focus of this gripping boardroom drama. Barbara Stanwyck is the company's chief shareholder, and Fredric March, William Holden, Walter Pidgeon, Paul Douglas and Louis Calhern are the executives jockeying for position. With Shelley Winters, June Allyson, Nina Foch. 104 min.
12-1024 Was $29.99 ❑*$19.99*

The Maverick Queen (1955)
Barbara Stanwyck is a hotel owner in the West who becomes mixed up with Cassidy and the Sundance Kid (portrayed here in a more realistic criminal light than the '69 film) and the Wild Bunch Gang, only to fall for a Pinkerton agent posing as Cole Younger. Co-stars Barry Sullivan, Scott Brady, Howard Petrie. 92 min.
63-1070 *$14.99*

Crime Of Passion (1957)
Overambition leads to murder in this film noir spotlighting Barbara Stanwyck as a former newspaper columnist who uses seduction and deception to help policeman husband Sterling Hayden become a top cop. When a superior reneges on a promise to promote hubby, Stanwyck takes matters into her own hands. Fay Wray, Raymond Burr also star. 84 min.
12-2808 *$19.99*

Walk On The Wild Side (1962)
New Orleans' infamous "Storyville" brothel district in the 1930s is the setting for this steamy drama. Laurence Harvey is the stranger in search of lost love Capucine, now working for madame Barbara Stanwyck. Jane Fonda's second film role, as a sympathetic hooker, and the implied lesbianism of Stanwyck's character are points of interest. 114 min.
02-1857 Was $69.99 *$19.99*

Barbara Stanwyck: Straight Down The Line
Orphaned at the age of four, she became a "Ziegfeld Girl" while a teen and moved on to the stage and Hollywood, where her charm and no-nonsense acting style made her a durable crowd favorite for decades. Along with clips from "Annie Oakley," "Double Indemnity," "Sorry, Wrong Number" and "The Thorn Birds," this tribute to Stanwyck's life and work includes interviews with Roddy McDowall, Ricardo Montalban, Robert Stack and others. 54 min.
50-7610 *$14.99*

Please see our index for these other Barbara Stanwyck titles: *The Bitter Tea Of General Yen • Blowing Wild • Ladies Of Leisure • The Lady Eve • Meet John Doe • The Miracle Woman • The Night Walker • Roustabout • Titanic • To Please A Lady • The Two Mrs. Carrolls • Union Pacific*

Thursday's Child (1943)
A family torn apart is the subject of this incisive drama about a little girl's rise to film stardom and its detrimental effects upon those around her. Stars Sally Ann Howes, Wilfrid Lawson and Stewart Granger. 81 min.
10-7064 Was $19.99 *$14.99*

The Adventures Of Mark Twain (1944)
The exciting, larger-than-life story of author and wit Mark Twain is told in this enjoyable biography. Fredric March is Samuel L. Clemens who learns how to navigate a ship down the Mississippi as a youngster, and has adventures during the California Gold Rush, as a participant in a frog-jumping contest and as a successful writer. Alexis Smith, Donald Crisp, Alan Hale also star. 130 min.
12-2768 ❑*$19.99*

Tomboy (1940)
Unabashed Hollywood hearts and flowers about city girl Marcia Mae Jones, who falls like a sack of potatoes for farm boy Jackie Moran. Grant Withers is the lad's crabby uncle who objects to the sprouting of true love. 70 min.
17-3076 Was $19.99 *$14.99*

The Courtneys Of Curzon Street (1947)
Acclaimed British look at romance and class differences focusing on an aristocrat marrying his mother's Irish maid in the early 1900s. Ostracized by society types, the woman goes back to her homeland, pregnant. Years later, their romance is rekindled. Anna Neagle, Michael Wilding and Gladys Young star. AKA: "The Courtney Affair." 112 min.
17-9010 *$19.99*

That Brennan Girl (1946)
Mona Freeman plays a woman whose thoughtless mother raised her to be disrespectful and selfish, an outlook that proves to be unhealthy when she realizes that material gain does not equal happiness in life or romance. James Dunn, William Marshall and Frank Jenks co-star. 95 min.
17-9029 Was $19.99 *$14.99*

Alaska Highway (1943)
Romantic drama set in the wilds of Alaska tells the story of two brothers' experiences in the Army Corps of Engineers and their love for the same girl. Richard Arlen, Jean Parker and Ralph Sanford star. 66 min.
17-9040 Was $19.99 *$14.99*

Mr. Ace (1946)
George Raft stars in this taut, political suspense story as Mr. Ace, the kingpin of a political machine. When a woman runs for governor without his support, he tries to force her out by blackmail, but their growing love for each other could prove to be both their undoings. Sylvia Sidney, Stanley Ridges star. 83 min.
45-5116 *$14.99*

Black Narcissus (1946)
A striking drama focuses on the emotional and sexual struggles of a group of nuns in a remote Himalayan convent. An Oscar-winner for its ravishing color cinematography, the Michael Powell/Emeric Pressburger classic is a one-of-a-kind experience. Deborah Kerr, Flora Robson, Jean Simmons, Sabu. 101 min.
47-1284 Was $19.99 *$14.99*

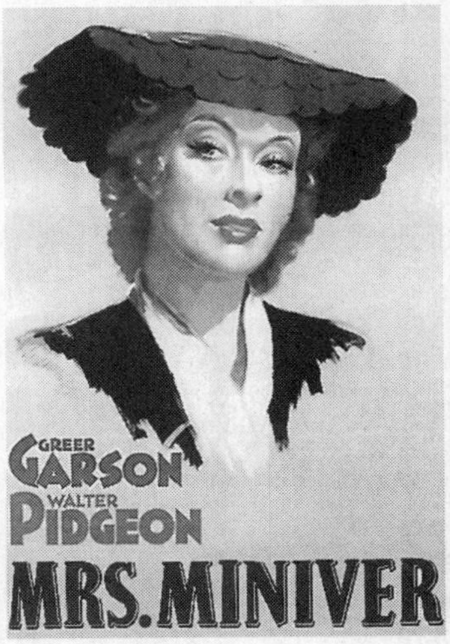

Mrs. Miniver (1942)
A grand wartime soap opera that garnered six Oscars, including Best Picture, Director and Actress. Greer Garson and Walter Pidgeon are the heads of an average British family who must keep their brood together during the German Blitz. With Teresa Wright, Richard Ney, Helmut Dantine; William Wyler directed. 134 min.
12-1841 ❑*$19.99*

The Miniver Story (1950)
This sequel to the Oscar-winning "Mrs. Miniver" is set after World War II, with matriarch Greer Garson bravely battling a life-threatening disease while trying to straighten out her family's problems and romantic entanglements. Walter Pidgeon, John Hodiak, Leo Genn, Cathy O'Donnell and Peter Finch also star. 104 min.
12-2732 ❑*$19.99*

Young Tom Edison (1940)
The early days of inventor Thomas Alva Edison are the focus of this biography starring Mickey Rooney as the future "Wizard of Menlo Park." Irascible young Tom gets into all sorts of trouble with his wacky experiments, but when his mother needs surgery, he comes to the rescue with a medical innovation. With Fay Bainter, George Bancroft. 82 min.
12-2773 *$19.99*

The Man I Love (1946)
First-rate melodrama spiked with great music about a singer (Ida Lupino) caught between a tough gangster (Robert Alda) and a piano player (Bruce Bennett). Andrea King, Martha Vickers and Alan Hale also star in this atmospheric story, said to be an inspiration for Martin Scorsese's "New York, New York." Songs include "The Man I Love" and "Body and Soul." 96 min.
12-2811 ❑*$19.99*

Saraband (1949)
Grand romantic liaisons in old England with Joan Greenwood as a woman forced into marrying a young Prince, although she desires a dashing Swedish count (Stewart Granger). Francoise Rosay, Flora Robson and Anthony Quayle co-star in this striking drama from the famed Ealing Studios. AKA: "Saraband for Dead Lovers." 96 min.
17-9024 *$19.99*

The Painted Desert (1931)
Very loosely based on "Romeo and Juliet," this story of feuding families in the Arizona wilderness stars William Boyd, Helen Twelvetrees and, in his first talking film, Clark Gable as the villain. 83 min.
10-2013 Was $19.99 ***$14.99***

A Free Soul (1931)
In one of his first major screen roles, Clark Gable plays a slyly charming criminal who escapes a murder charge with the help of alcoholic attorney Lionel Barrymore, only to seduce Barrymore's pleasure-seeking daughter, Norma Shearer. Melodramatic tale that earned Barrymore an Academy Award also stars Leslie Howard. 91 min.
12-2149 ***$19.99***

No Man Of Her Own (1932)
In order to elude detectives, New York gambler Clark Gable takes refuge in a small town upstate where he meets and marries librarian Carole Lombard. Returning to the Big Apple, Gable reverts to his gambling ways and meets an old flame who threatens to turn him over to the law. Dorothy Mackaill, Grant Mitchell co-star in this snappy farce; Gable and Lombard's only film together. 81 min.
07-2298 ***$14.99***

Red Dust (1932)
Romance and intrigue in Southeast Asia, with Clark Gable as a rubber plantation manager who has an affair with prostitute Jean Harlow, then becomes attracted to Mary Astor, the wife of one of his workers. Later remade as "Mogambo," also with Gable. 83 min.
12-1441 ***$19.99***

Strange Interlude (1932)
Superbly acted film treatment of Eugene O'Neill's tragedy stars Norma Shearer as a young woman who sees her boyfriend die during World War I and looks to overcome her grief by working at a hospital. There she meets handsome doctor Clark Gable, but marries another, an emotionally troubled man. Alexander Kirkland, May Robson, Ralph Morgan and Robert Young co-star. 110 min.
12-2489 □***$19.99***

Manhattan Melodrama (1934)
The film John Dillinger had just seen before being gunned down, this compelling crime drama stars Clark Gable and William Powell as boyhood friends from the New York streets who grow up to follow different paths, one as a gangster, the other as a crusading D.A. Co-star Myrna Loy and Mickey Rooney. 93 min.
12-2332 ***$19.99***

China Seas (1935)
Stellar cast, including Clark Gable, Jean Harlow, Wallace Beery, Rosalind Russell, Robert Benchley and Hattie McDaniel, in a tale of love, surprise and mystery aboard a cruise in the South Pacific. 90 min.
12-1436 ***$19.99***

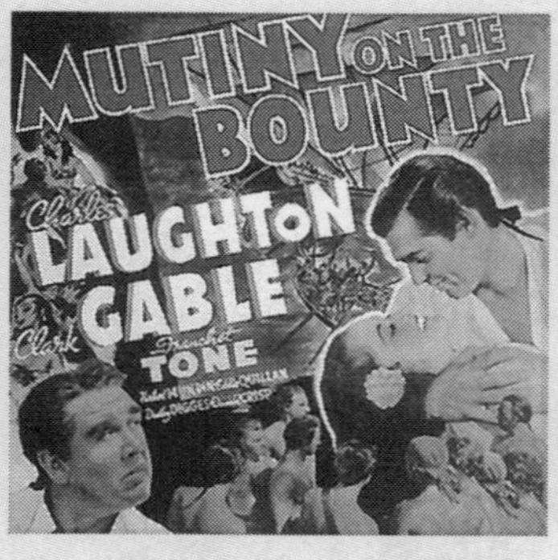

Mutiny On The Bounty (1935)
First mate Fletcher Christian (Clark Gable) leads a revolt against his sadistic commander, Captain Bligh (Charles Laughton), in this classic seafaring adventure, based on Nordoff and Hall's novelization of the real-life 1788 mutiny. Winner of the 1935 Best Picture Academy Award; with Franchot Tone, Donald Crisp. 132 min.
12-3273 ***$19.99***

San Francisco (1936)
Adventure, romance and drama set amidst the colorful background of Old San Francisco at the turn of the century. Clark Gable, Spencer Tracy, Jeanette MacDonald and Ted Healy star; spectacular earthquake climax. 115 min.
12-1444 ***$19.99***

San Francisco (Color Version)
Clark Gable, Jeanette MacDonald and Spencer Tracy discover that the Golden Gate is just that in this colorized version of the MGM classic.
12-2100 ***$19.99***

Wife vs. Secretary (1936)
Clark Gable plays a magazine publisher, beloved by his wife (Myrna Loy), who hires a sexy secretary (Jean Harlow) to help him with his hectic schedule. But his mother becomes suspicious of her son's new hire and provokes his wife to question his motives. Exceptional soap opera features May Robson, Hobart Cavanaugh. 88 min.
12-2301 ***$19.99***

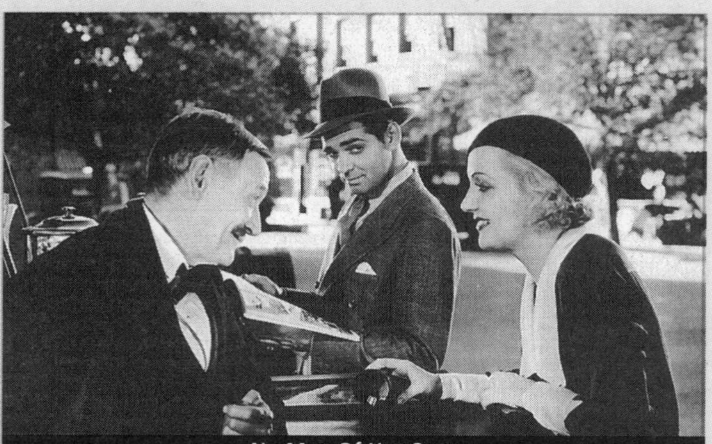
No Man Of Her Own

Clark Gable

Love On The Run (1936)
Rollicking comedy with Clark Gable as an American journalist in Europe sent to cover the marriage of flighty heiress Joan Crawford and the arrival of a renowned aviator. But Gable woos Crawford away from the wedding, and the two take off on a madcap tour of the continent in an airplane they steal from the flying ace. Franchot Tone and Reginald Owen also star. 80 min.
12-2731 □***$19.99***

Too Hot To Handle (1938)
Rousing MGM adventure saga starring Clark Gable and Walter Pidgeon as photojournalists who travel to Brazil to find the missing brother of aviatrix Myrna Loy. Their trek takes them into a jungle village where the inhabitants practice voodoo. Walter Connolly and Leo Carrillo also star. 105 min.
12-2098 □***$19.99***

Test Pilot (1938)
High-flying adventure yarn stars Clark Gable as a hotshot pilot, Spencer Tracy as his mechanic and friend, and Myrna Loy as Gable's wife, who can't accept his need to put his life on the line daily. Great aerial sequences highlight this Victor Fleming drama; with Lionel Barrymore, Marjorie Main. 118 min.
12-2333 ***$19.99***

Boom Town (1940)
Clark Gable and Spencer Tracy star in this masterful drama, playing two friends who strike it rich in the Texas oil fields, then experience rivalry over wealth and romance. Claudette Colbert, Hedy Lamarr, Frank Morgan, Lionel Atwill and Marion Martin also star in this expert epic gushing with entertainment and thrills. 117 min.
12-2070 ***$19.99***

Comrade X (1940)
In the tradition of "Ninotchka," this farce stars Hedy Lamarr as a streetcar conductor whose father talks American newspaper reporter Clark Gable into smuggling her out of Russia because of her political beliefs. Of course, not everything is as it appears to be, leading to romance, blackmail and a wacky tank chase. Oscar Homolka and Eve Arden also star; directed by King Vidor. 90 min.
12-2798 ***$19.99***

Honky Tonk (1941)
Con artist Clark Gable rides into a frontier town and marries judge's daughter Lana Turner (their first film together) as part of his scheme in this glossy romantic drama. Great supporting cast includes Frank Morgan, Claire Trevor, Chill Wills, Marjorie Main. 105 min.
12-2330 ***$19.99***

They Met In Bombay (1941)
Globetrotting adventure-comedy with Clark Gable and Rosalind Russell as rival jewel thieves after the same priceless diamond necklace. The two decide to team up and, after nabbing the piece, escape on a plane piloted by sleazy Peter Lorre, who alerts the authorities to their crime. Reginald Owen, Jessie Ralph and Alan Ladd also star. 93 min.
12-2873 ***$19.99***

Somewhere I'll Find You (1942)
Brothers Clark Gable and Robert Sterling are newspapermen vying for good Samaritan and former reporter Lana Turner on the homefront and in Indochina at the outbreak of World War II. Reginald Owen and Lee Patrick also star in this romantic drama. 117 min.
12-2722 ***$19.99***

Adventure (1945)
"Gable's back and Garson's got him!" Freewheeling seaman Clark Gable falls in love with sweet San Francisco librarian Greer Garson, but he leaves in search of thrills in another port. Gable returns to find her pregnant and tries to settle down, but will his desire for adventure prove greater than the call of family? Thomas Mitchell, Joan Blondell co-star. 125 min.
12-2870 ***$19.99***

The Hucksters (1947)
A scathing look at Madison Avenue and its foibles, featuring Clark Gable as an ad executive discovering the ruthlessness of his profession after returning from a stint in the military. Top-notch supporting cast includes Deborah Kerr, Sydney Greenstreet, Adolphe Menjou and Ava Gardner. 115 min.
12-2099 □***$19.99***

Command Decision (1948)
First-rate war saga with Clark Gable as an England-based officer who commands the Allied forces against Germany in World War II. Filmed with thrilling aerial scenes and excellent support from Walter Pidgeon, Van Johnson, Brian Donlevy and Charles Bickford. 111 min.
12-2115 ***$19.99***

Homecoming (1948)
Wartime romantic drama stars Clark Gable as an uncaring New York doctor whose life changes dramatically when he joins the Medical Corps during World War II and gets involved with his young assistant (Lana Turner). With Anne Baxter, John Hodiak and Ray Collins. 113 min.
12-2717 ***$19.99***

Any Number Can Play (1949)
Clark Gable is the gambling-loving casino owner, estranged from his wife and son, who wins new respect from his family after going head-on against a tough high-roller in a dice game and stopping some crooks from robbing his establishment. Alexis Smith, Wendell Corey, Frank Morgan and Darryl Hickman co-star. 112 min.
12-2796 ***$19.99***

To Please A Lady (1950)
Crackerjack columnist Barbara Stanwyck criticizes arrogant race car driver Clark Gable in an article, forcing him to hit the stunt car circuit. Later, she conducts an interview with him while on the comeback trail, and sparks fly between the two. Adolphe Menjou and Will Geer also star in this drama highlighted by thrilling racing segments. 91 min.
12-2815 ***$19.99***

Key To The City (1950)
Lively romantic farce with Clark Gable and Loretta Young as small-town mayors who meet at a convention in San Francisco and, through a series of comical misunderstandings, face scandal and jailtime. The two beat the rap, fall in love, and team to take on an unscrupulous politician trying to unseat Gable. With Frank Morgan, James Gleason and Raymond Burr. 101 min.
12-2871 ***$19.99***

Across The Wide Missouri (1951)
Rousing frontier saga stars Clark Gable as a trapper in the 19th-century Midwest who marries an Indian chief's daughter in order to gain access to their territories. With John Hodiak, Ricardo Montalban, Maria Elena Marques. 78 min.
12-2327 ***$19.99***

Lone Star (1952)
Epic saga set against the backdrop of the struggle for Texas' independence after the battle of the Alamo. Cattle tycoon Clark Gable is asked by President Andrew Jackson to persuade Sam Houston to bring Texas into the Union. Gable clashes with influential politician Broderick Crawford, while romancing his newspaper editor girlfriend (Ava Gardner). 94 min.
12-2872 ***$19.99***

Never Let Me Go (1953)
Stirring adventure story starring Clark Gable as a U.S. newsman who marries beautiful Russian ballerina Gene Tierney in Moscow. They plan to head back to the States, but authorities force her to stay behind. Gable then takes action by joining forces with a British man whose wife is also being held in the USSR. Richard Haydn, Kenneth More also star. 94 min.
12-2803 ***$19.99***

Mogambo (1953)
A safari in the heart of Africa offers not only danger for veteran hunter Clark Gable but also romance, courtesy of fellow travellers Grace Kelly and Ava Gardner, in director John Ford's thrilling adventure, based on Gable's 1932 "Red Dust." 116 min.
12-1050 ***$19.99***

Soldier Of Fortune (1955)
Clark Gable is the rugged title character, an American running a smuggling operation in China who is enlisted by beautiful Susan Hayward to find her missing photographer husband. Michael Rennie and Gene Barry also star in this top-notch adventure saga. 95 min.
04-2358 □***$39.99***

The Tall Men (1955)
Two ex-Confederate soldiers (Clark Gable, Robert Ryan) sign on as cowhands on a hazard-filled run from Texas to Montana in a gritty frontier drama from director Raoul Walsh. Jane Russell co-stars as the woman both men desire. 122 min.
04-3146 ***$19.99***

The King And Four Queens (1956)
Offbeat Western comedy/drama with Clark Gable as a wandering cowboy con man who cozies up to the four wives of outlaw brothers, thinking he'll find out where their husbands have hidden $100,000 in stolen gold. Eleanor Parker, Barbara Nichols, Jo Van Fleet also star. 83 min.
12-2331 ***$19.99***

Band Of Angels (1957)
After she learns she is of African lineage, the penniless daughter of a once-prosperous Kentucky family (Yvonne De Carlo) is sold as a slave to New Orleans millionaire Clark Gable and soon becomes his mistress. When the Civil War erupts, Gable is threatened by former slave Sidney Poitier. With Rex Reason, Efrem Zimbalist, Jr.; Raoul Walsh directs. 127 min.
19-2171 Was $29.99 ***$19.99***

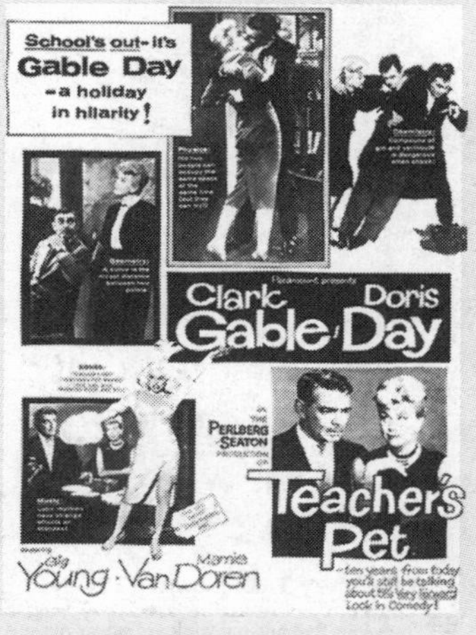

Teacher's Pet (1958)
Newspaper editor Clark Gable poses as a student and learns about writing and love from college journalism professor Doris Day in this spry romantic comedy that also features fine support from Gig Young, Mamie Van Doren and Nick Adams. 120 min.
06-1905 ***$14.99***

Run Silent, Run Deep (1958)
Exciting, expert submarine epic, starring Clark Gable and Burt Lancaster as feuding Naval officers who find themselves going head-on against a Japanese submarine during World War II. This precursor to "The Hunt for Red October" is a tense thriller, co-starring Jack Warden and Don Rickles. 93 min.
12-2114 Was $19.99 □***$14.99***

But Not For Me (1959)
Romantic comedy featuring Clark Gable as an aging theatrical producer whose life and new play are rejuvenated when a young secretary (Carroll Baker) enters his life. She inspires him to change the play, come to terms with his age and fall in love. Lilli Palmer, Lee J. Cobb and Thomas Gomez co-star. 105 min.
06-1845 ***$14.99***

It Started In Naples (1960)
American lawyer Clark Gable travels to Italy to arrange his late brother's estate and finds two surprises waiting for him: his brother's 10-year-old son from a common-law marriage, and the boy's beautiful aunt, stripper Sophia Loren. Romantic melodrama features beautiful Neapolitan locales. 100 min.
06-1857 ***$14.99***

Dear Mr. Gable (1968)
Wonderful look at the career of "the King," one of Hollywood's greatest stars, including interviews with Gable's friends and co-stars and clips from a number of his classic films. Burgess Meredith narrates. 52 min.
12-2326 ***$19.99***

Please see our index for these other Clark Gable titles: *Dance, Fools, Dance • Dancing Lady • Gone With The Wind • Hold Your Man • It Happened One Night • The Misfits • Night Nurse • Possessed • Saratoga • Strange Cargo • Susan Lenox: Her Fall And Rise*

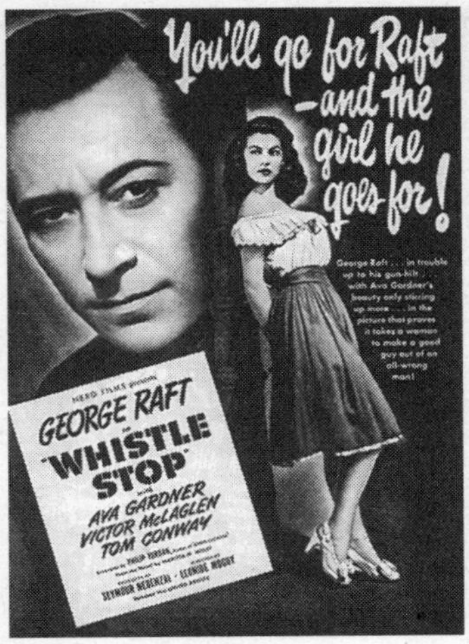
You'll go for Raft — and the girl he goes for!
GEORGE RAFT
WHISTLE STOP
AVA GARDNER
VICTOR McLAGLEN
TOM CONWAY

Whistle Stop (1946)
Melodrama at its best, as sultry Ava Gardner gets involved with playboy George Raft and night-club jockey Victor McLaglen. Tom Conway, Florence Bates and Charles Drake co-star. 84 min.
08-5055 Was $19.99 *$14.99*

Open Secret (1948)
Powerful film exploring the roots of anti-Semitism focuses on a police officer who is joined by a victimized photographer in busting a gang of racist thugs who have been attacking Jewish citizens. John Ireland, Jane Randolph and Sheldon Leonard star. 70 min.
68-8756 *$19.99*

Hoodlum Girls (1959)/ Teenage Jungle (1944)
This double-feature depicts teenage youth running wild! In "Hoodlum Girls," the juvenile delinquency problem is portrayed in realistic fashion. Joy Reese and Kay Morley star. AKA: "Youth Aflame." And it's a "Teenage Jungle" out there, as a former con tries to help his troublesome son who's on his way to life of crime. Joy Reynolds stars. AKA: "Teenage."
79-5562 Was $24.99 *$19.99*

Swamp Virgin (1947)
A strange tease-and-sleaze tale of backwoods passion, gator-hunting and other weirdness set to a "Tobacco Road"-style story. With Gaylord Pendleton, Mary Conwell and E.G. Marshall. AKA: "Untamed Fury." 65 min.
79-5674 Was $24.99 *$19.99*

Escort Girl (1941)
As evidenced in this exposé from the 1940s, escort services have been around for years, and here you'll see how businessmen who pay $25 for the companionship of pretty young gals often risk their lives facing unexpected problems.
79-5719 Was $24.99 *$19.99*

The Heiress (1949)
Olivia de Havilland won an Oscar for her portrayal of the plain spinster who is romanced by fortune hunter Montgomery Clift. Fine cast also includes Ralph Richardson, Miriam Hopkins; directed by William Wyler. Based on Henry James' novel "Washington Square." 115 min.
07-1291 Was $59.99 *$14.99*

Washington Square (1997)
Henry James' classic story, first filmed as 1949's "The Heiress," is elegantly brought to the screen by director Agnieszka Holland ("Europa, Europa"). Jennifer Jason Leigh stars as the shy and insecure Victorian woman whose search for love leads her into the arms of wastrel Ben Chaplin. Albert Finney, Maggie Smith also star. 115 min.
11-2242 Was $99.99 *$19.99*

Cheers For Miss Bishop (1941)
In the tradition of "Goodbye, Mr. Chips," this moving drama tracks the 50-plus-year career of English teacher Martha Scott on the eve of her retirement, a career filled with personal triumph and romantic heartbreak. William Gargan, Edmund Gwenn also star. 95 min.
10-4008 Was $19.99 *$14.99*

White Cargo (1942)
Scorching African drama highlighted by Hedy Lamarr's sultry performance as jungle queen Tondelayo, whose sensuous, manipulative manner wins her a marriage with a white worker on a rubber plant. Suspicious of Tondelayo's ways, the worker's boss learns of the siren's plan to kill her husband. Walter Pidgeon and Frank Morgan also star. 90 min.
12-2817 *$19.99*

You And Me (1938)
Unusual social drama with comic moments from director Fritz Lang stars George Raft as an ex-con who lands a job in a department store and woos and weds fellow employee (and, unknown to him, fellow parolee) Sylvia Sidney. When Raft learns the truth and that their marriage may be invalidated, he becomes tempted into returning to a life of crime. Harry Carey, Robert Cummings co-star; includes songs written by Kurt Weill. 94 min.
07-2614 *$14.99*

Dangerous Holiday (1937)
A young violin prodigy runs away from his greedy relatives to just be a boy with his new friends—a gang of kidnappers. Hedda Hopper stars. 54 min.
09-1318 Was $24.99 *$19.99*

Fire Alarm (1932)
Western star Johnny Mack Brown trades in his lariat for a firehose in this action-filled drama about a fireman who pauses between deadly blazes to fan the flames of love with an independent young career girl. 68 min.
09-2014 Was $19.99 *$14.99*

The Lady Refuses (1931)
A down-on-her-luck young woman is recruited by a wealthy socialite to try and woo his son away from a golddigging vamp. British melodrama stars Betty Compson, John Darrow. 72 min.
09-2189 Was $29.99 *$14.99*

Police Patrol (1935)
Tough gangster drama focuses on two police partners who have the hots for the same dame, a classy babe who happens to be employed by a mob kingpin. Pat O'Mally and James Flavin star. 61 min.
09-2220 Was $24.99 *$14.99*

Greek Street (1930)
Early English talkie, centering in London's Italian quarter, follows the rising fortunes of a young girl who was saved from starvation in the streets by a restaurant owner. Sari Maritza and Arthur Hambling star in this story of romance and violence. 53 min.
09-1795 Was $24.99 *$14.99*

False Faces (1932)
Drama of an unscrupulous surgeon whose dark past eventually confronts him. Lowell Sherman, Peggy Shannon. 80 min.
09-1721 Was $29.99 *$14.99*

All-Black Dramas

Within Our Gates (1919)
A shocker when first released, this groundbreaking Oscar Micheaux film is the earliest surviving feature directed by an African-American. The story concerns a black woman who attempts to finance a school for kids in the South by getting money in the North. The film's depictions of lynchings and rape are still disturbing today. Evelyn Preer stars. 78 min. Silent with music score.
09-2981 *$19.99*

Scar Of Shame (1927)
Milestone silent look at black relations focusing on the ill-conceived marriage of a middle-class pianist and a poor woman, whom he keeps away from his class-conscious mother. After the marriage falls apart, the pianist falls for a more socially acceptable woman. Produced by Philadelphia's Colored Players Film Company. With Harry Henderson and Lucia Lynn Moses.
10-8429 *$19.99*

Birmingham Black Bottom (1929)
Direct from the archives of film producer Al Christie comes this collection of rare talking comedy shorts from the first series made with an all-black cast. Based on Octavus Roy Cohen's popular "Darktown Birmingham" stories, the films include "Music Hath Harms," "The Melancholy Dame," "Framing of the Shrew" and "Oft in the Silly Night." With Spencer Williams, Evelyn Preer. 75 min.
63-7165 *$19.99*

Ten Minutes To Live (1932)
A pair of early all-black suspense stories that deal with trouble and treachery in the twilight world of Harlem after dark. "The Faker" and "The Killer" star Laurence Chenault, A.B. Comathiere; directed by Oscar Micheaux. 63 min.
01-1418 Was $19.99 *$14.99*

Veiled Aristocrats (1932)
A lost movie produced by black filmmaker Oscar Micheaux, this historically significant and moving social drama stars Lorenzo Tucker—known as "the black Valentino"—as a lawyer who managed to pass for white and become successful and now returns to his hometown for a reunion with his mother and sister. 45 min.
10-9093 *$19.99*

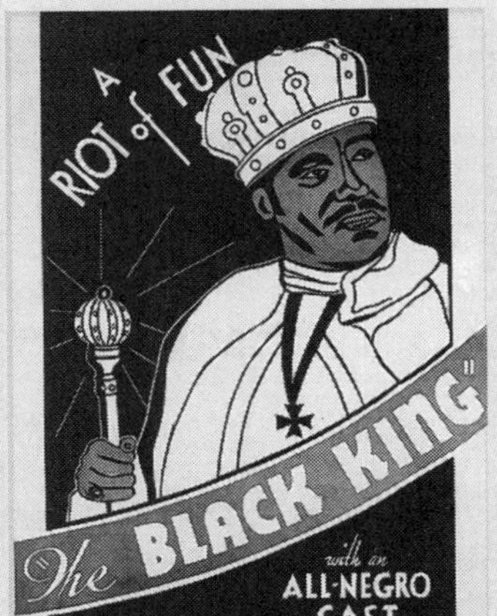
A RIOT of FUN
The BLACK KING
with an
ALL-NEGRO CAST

The Black King (1932)
Intriguing early all-black film concerns a clever con artist, loosely based on Marcus Garvey, who disguises himself as a preacher and begins a phony "back-to-Africa" movement. A.B. Comathiere, Vivian Baker star. 72 min.
01-1402 *$19.99*

Murder In Harlem (1935)
Terrific black-oriented drama from film pioneer Oscar Micheaux focusing on a night watchman at a chemical factory accused of killing a white woman found in the factory's basement. Clarence Brooks, Laura Bowman star.
10-9092 *$19.99*

The Green Pastures (1936)
Stories from the Old Testament are retold from a black perspective in this Warner Bros. adaptation of the Broadway play that, although now dated, still shines with reverence and joy. Rex Ingram stars as "De Lawd," along with Oscar Polk, Eddie Anderson and Myrtle Anderson. 90 min.
12-2630 *$19.99*

Underworld (1937)
Pioneer African-American filmmaker Oscar Micheaux directed this landmark gangster drama about a college graduate whose involvement with Chicago mobsters leads him into underworld activities. Sol Johnson, Bee Freeman and Oscar Polk star in this gritty all-black story. 65 min.
10-2802 *$14.99*

God's Stepchildren (1938)
All-black adaptation of "Naomi, Negress" that sent sparks of controversy flying in its day. The story follows a light-skinned woman whose ever-increasing resentment of her heritage leads to tragedy for herself and everyone she touches. Alice B. Russell, Jacqueline Lewis star; Oscar Micheaux directs. 65 min.
01-1407 Was $19.99 *$14.99*

Double Deal (1939)
Effective all-black drama concerning a shifty hood who's got a scheme for getting rid of his rival for a lovely lady's affections...he pulls off a jewelry store heist and sets his rival up as the culprit! Monte Hawley, Jeni Le Gon, Edward Thompson star. 60 min.
01-1405 *$19.99*

Lying Lips (1939)
Excellent all-black murder mystery concerning a nightclub chanteuse who's been set up for the crime and jailed...and it's up to her devoted boyfriend to uncover the real killer. Edna Mae Harris, Earl Jones (father of James Earl) star. 60 min.
01-1411 *$19.99*

Moon Over Harlem (1939)
Exciting, black-produced drama set against the smoky nightclub scene uptown. A young woman is alienated from her mother and set up on a murder charge by her evil stepfather. Great vintage production stars Bud Harris, Cora Green, Mercedes Gilbert, Sidney Bechet and his Swinging Band. 75 min.
01-1412 *$19.99*

The Devil's Daughter (1939)
Nina Mae McKinney, "the black Greta Garbo," essays the title role of a phony voodoo high priestess in Haiti who clashes with her innocent half-sister over their late father's banana plantation. All-black drama co-stars Ida James, Jack Carter and comic relief Hamtree Harrington. 52 min.
09-1322 *$19.99*

Keep Punching (1939)
All-out powerhouse fight saga that never gives up, about a gutsy pug and his championship mission. Great-hearted black cast features Henry Armstrong, Willie Bryant, Mae Johnson and "Casablanca" ivory-tickler Arthur "Dooley" Wilson.
10-7402 *$19.99*

The Girl From Chicago (1939)
After a numbers runner is murdered in New York, Secret Service agent Carl Mahon tries to track down the killer. Starr Calloway is his love interest, a schoolteacher. Legendary black director Oscar Micheaux produced this all-star, all-black thriller that co-stars Grace Smith.
10-8418 *$19.99*

Midnight Shadow (1939)
A travelling con artist sets a plan in motion to marry the daughter of a well-to-do landowner in this all-black melodrama from director/producer George Randol. John Criner, Frances Redd star. 63 min.
54-9108 *$19.99*

Sunday Sinners (1940)
Wonderful all-black drama concerning a minister's son who wants to clean up the mean streets of the city. When the hoods who want him out of the way frame him for murder, though, Pop's congregation shows some righteous indignation! Mamie Smith, Frank Wilson, Edna Mae Harris star. 65 min.
01-1416 *$19.99*

Gang War (1940)
A knockout all-black crime thriller, starring Ralph Cooper and Gladys Snyder. A war rages between mobsters over the profits from jukeboxes in New York.
17-1110 *$19.99*

Son Of Ingagi (1940)
Rarely seen all-black horror film concerns the efforts of a hulking ape-man to satisfy his desire for a mate. Spencer Williams (TV's "Amos 'n' Andy") scripted and stars; Zack Williams, Laura Bowman co-star. 70 min.
17-3049 *$19.99*

Murder On Lennox Avenue (1941)
After the corrupt leader of the Harlem Better Business League is ousted from office, he swears deadly vengeance against the reformer who replaced him. All this, and a love quadrangle, too, in this classic all-black melodrama. Alberta Perkins, Sidney Easton, Alec Lovejoy star. 60 min.
01-1413 *$19.99*

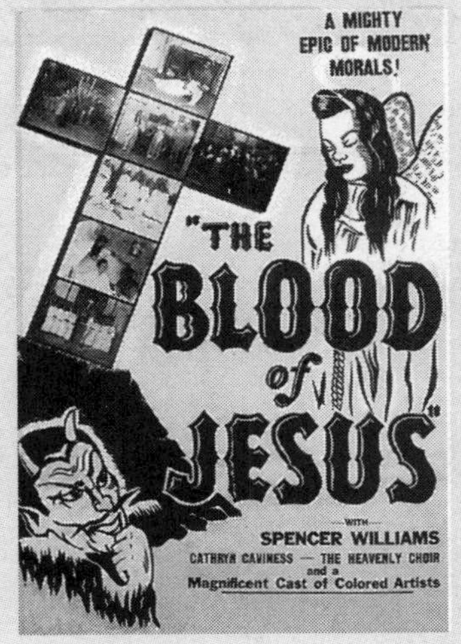
A MIGHTY EPIC OF MODERN MORALS!
"THE BLOOD of JESUS"
WITH
SPENCER WILLIAMS
CATHRYN CAVINESS — THE HEAVENLY CHOIR
and a
Magnificent Cast of Colored Artists

Blood Of Jesus (1941)
Unusual, all-black inspirational drama about a small town's turmoil when a newly-baptized woman is accidentally shot by her sinful husband...and the miracle that follows. Spencer Williams wrote, directed and stars. 50 min.
17-9004 *$19.99*

Mistaken Identity (1941)
All-black thriller about a murder that occurs in a nightclub and the possible connection to a singer's relationship with an escaped convict. Nelle Hill, George Oliver star; music provided by Skippy Williams and His Jazz Band. 60 min.
10-8419 *$19.99*

Lucky Ghost (1941)
Comic Mantan Moreland teams with F.E. Miller for a fun-filled supernatural comedy filled with pratfalls and wacky situations. This all-black production was co-produced by Tedd Toddy.
10-8430 *$19.99*

Marching On (Where's My Man Tonight) (1943)
An all-black wartime drama about a man who has no intentions of joining the Army and following in the footsteps of other family members. He is finally drafted, is sent to basic training, discovers his long-lost father and catches Japanese spies. Georgia Kelly, Hugo Martin and Emmet Jackson. 83 min.
10-9090 *$19.99*

Go Down Death (1944)
Intriguing all-black morality tale concerning a minister caught in a moral dilemma that leaves him literally on the brink between Heaven and Hell (the scenes of afterlife torment come from turn-of-the-century silent films!). Samuel J. Jones, Myra D. Hemmings star. 50 min.
01-1406 *$19.99*

Girl In Room 20 (1946)
A would-be singer heads to New York City with dreams of stardom, only to discover that success carries a high price, in this all-black cast drama laced with music. Geraldine Brock and July Jones (Robert Orr) star, along with director Spencer Williams. 63 min.
54-9109 *$19.99*

The Quiet One (1948)
A documentary-styled look at delinquency focusing on a quiet Harlem youth who drifts into a world of crime before he is rehabilitated by the Wiltwyck School for Boys. Written by James Agee ("The African Queen") and shot in 16mm. With Donald Thompson, Sadie Stockton. 65 min.
10-8420 *$19.99*

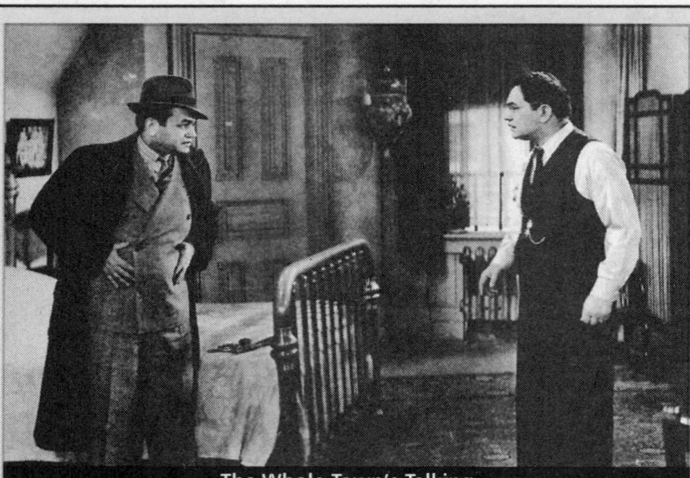

The Whole Town's Talking

Edward G. Robinson

Little Caesar (1930)
Masterful crime drama starring Edward G. Robinson as the Al Capone-inspired Italian hood who moves from petty thief to mob kingpin, blasting his machine gun all the way. Mervyn LeRoy's film hailed a new era in screen realism, made a star out of Robinson and gave us the line "Mother of mercy, is this the end of Rico?" With Douglas Fairbanks, Jr. and Glenda Farrell. 80 min.
12-2236 ❑*$19.99*

The Whole Town's Talking (1935)
Director John Ford's fast-paced crime comedy stars Edward G. Robinson in a dual role as a meek hardware company clerk who is the spitting image of a notorious mob boss. Arrested and then exonerated by the authorities, Robinson the clerk is forced to let Robinson the gangster pose as him while he pulls a string of robberies. Jean Arthur, Arthur Byron, Donald Meek co-star; look for a young Lucille Ball. 92 min.
02-3154 *$19.99*

Bullets Or Ballots (1936)
After he's thrown off the force for hitting his superior, ex-cop Edward G. Robinson is hired as an "advisor" by city crime boss Barton MacLane, but gunsel Humphrey Bogart doesn't trust him. Top-notch Warner Bros. crime drama also stars Joan Blondell, Joseph King. 81 min.
12-2377 *$19.99*

Thunder In The City (1937)
Edward G. Robinson is an American promoter who hypes a new mineral he discovers while visiting England. Crackerjack farce! Nigel Bruce, Ralph Richardson. 88 min.
10-1066 Was $19.99 *$14.99*

Kid Galahad (1937)
Top-notch boxing effort has honest promoter Edward G. Robinson getting duped by crooked rival Humphrey Bogart. He sees a chance to return to the top with a feisty young bellhop who turns out to be unbeatable in the ring, but Robinson worries when his protégé attracts the eye of his girlfriend (Bette Davis). Wayne Morris, Jane Bryan co-star; Michael Curtiz directs. AKA: "Battling Bellhop." 94 min.
12-2480 *$19.99*

I Am The Law (1938)
The corrupt old boys at City Hall name kindly law professor Edward G. Robinson special prosecutor and smirk behind their hands; but when the teacher proves as good in action as with classroom theories, they see who gets the last laugh. Crime classic co-stars John Beal. 83 min.
02-1948 *$69.99*

The Amazing Dr. Clitterhouse (1938)
Warners took aim at its popular gangster films with this satirical crime tale starring Edward G. Robinson as a noted psychiatrist/author whose research into the criminal mind leads him to commit a series of jewel robberies and become leader of a gang of crooks. Humphrey Bogart co-stars as Robinson's scheming second-in-command; with Claire Trevor, Donald Crisp. 87 min.
19-2939 *$19.99*

Brother Orchid (1940)
Offbeat gangster drama stars Edward G. Robinson as an ex-mob boss who is double-crossed by former lieutenant Humphrey Bogart. Wounded while escaping, Robinson is taken in by the members of a remote monastery and finds the peace he sought in the outside world, until circumstances force him to confront Bogart one last time. Ann Sothern, Ralph Bellamy, Donald Crisp also star. 87 min.
12-2376 *$19.99*

Dr. Ehrlich's Magic Bullet (1940)
Superb Warner Bros. biodrama starring Edward G. Robinson as Dr. Paul Ehrlich, the German physician who developed Salvarsan, the first treatment for syphilis. The film traces Ehrlich's fascinating life from his work detecting blood diseases and the problems in finding funding for research to his personal crises. With Ruth Gordon, Otto Kruger, Donald Crisp and Maria Ouspenskaya.
12-3091 *$19.99*

The Sea Wolf (1941)
Wonderful adaptation of Jack London's tale of coldly manipulative ship captain Wolf Larsen (Edward G. Robinson), who matches wits with a bookish writer he saves off the California coast. John Garfield, Alexander Knox, Ida Lupino and Gene Lockhart also star; Michael Curtiz directs. 90 min.
12-2635 *$19.99*

Mr. Winkle Goes To War (1944)
Edward G. Robinson goes against type in this delightful comedy as a mild-mannered fix-it man who is drafted and becomes a war hero under the most unusual of circumstances. Co-stars Robert Armstrong, Ruth Warrick. 80 min.
02-1501 Was $59.99 *$19.99*

Scarlet Street (1945)
Edward G. Robinson, Joan Bennett star in director Fritz Lang's compelling drama concerning a lonely middle-aged bank cashier whose life is tragically changed when he becomes involved with a predatory, manipulating woman. 103 min.
10-2015 Was $19.99 *$14.99*

Our Vines Have Tender Grapes (1945)
A tender look at life in a small Wisconsin community, with Edward G. Robinson as a widowed Norwegian-born farmer who is stern but loving with young daughter Margaret O'Brien. The film covers the tragedies and triumphs in their town and in their lives with a special bittersweet quality. James Craig and Agnes Moorehead also star. 105 min.
12-2633 *$19.99*

The Woman In The Window (1945)
Dazzling film noir from director Fritz Lang showcasing Edward G. Robinson as an amiable professor invited to join beautiful model Joan Bennett in her apartment when his wife and children are on vacation. His fantasies turn to terror when he kills her tough boyfriend and finds himself in the middle of a deadly blackmail plot. Raymond Massey, Dan Duryea, Bobby Blake and Spanky McFarland also star. 99 min.
12-3065 Was $19.99 ❑*$14.99*

The Red House (1947)
A chilling tale of suspense about a strange, abandoned house and farmer Edward G. Robinson's attempts to uncover the unknown secrets. Rory Calhoun, Judith Anderson. 100 min.
10-2032 Was $19.99 *$14.99*

All My Sons (1948)
Powerful performances by Edward G. Robinson and Burt Lancaster drive this screen adaptation of the Arthur Miller drama. Robinson is a successful arms manufacturer who may have been responsible for sending defective parts to the military during World War II, and surviving son Lancaster, whose brother was killed in combat, sets out to find the truth. Louisa Horton, Mady Christians also star. 94 min.
07-2623 ❑*$14.99*

House Of Strangers (1949)
Compelling drama stars Edward G. Robinson as a heartless banker whose ruthlessness turns three of his sons against him and leads the one loyal child to try to help him at the cost of his own freedom. Richard Conte, Luther Adler, Efrem Zimbalist, Jr. and Paul Valentine are the sons; Susan Hayward, Debra Paget co-star. 101 min.
04-2385 ❑*$39.99*

Actors And Sin (1952)
Comedy-drama contains two stories in one. "Actor's Blood" follows a has-been actor and his daughter's stage debut; "Woman of Sin" deals with a literary agent whose biggest client is a child. Edward G. Robinson, Marsha Hunt, Eddie Albert star. 82 min.
45-5316 *$19.99*

The Violent Men (1955)
Frontier drama stars Glenn Ford as a Civil War veteran who renounces violence and turns to ranching, but finds his ideals tested when grasping landowner Edward G. Robinson starts a bloody campaign for control of his spread. Barbara Stanwyck is superb as Robinson's ambitious wife; with Dianne Foster, Brian Keith. 96 min.
02-2253 *$19.99*

A Bullet For Joey (1955)
Royal Canadian Police inspector Edward G. Robinson believes an important nuclear physicist is the key to a series of killings and soon finds himself battling gangster George Raft, hired by the head of a Communist spy ring to kidnap the scientist and "convince" him to help their plan for world domination. George Dolenz, Peter Van Eyck co-star.
12-3096 *$19.99*

Seven Thieves (1960)
Suspenseful, stylish "perfect crime" thriller stars Edward G. Robinson as a professor who, before he dies, wants to pull the ultimate heist at Monte Carlo's casino. Rod Steiger is the old friend who helps him assemble a gang. Joan Collins, Eli Wallach, Michael Dante, Sebastian Cabot co-star. 102 min.
04-2388 ❑*$39.99*

Please see our index for these other Edward G. Robinson titles: *Barbary Coast • The Biggest Bundle Of Them All • Cheyenne Autumn • The Cincinnati Kid • Double Indemnity • Good Neighbor Sam • Journey Together • Key Largo • Mackenna's Gold • My Geisha • The Outrage • Song Of Norway • A Song To Remember • Soylent Green • The Stranger • Tales Of Manhattan • The Ten Commandments • Tight Spot*

Defenders Of The Law (1931)
Master gangster Big Joe Velet arrives in a large California city and proceeds to take criminal matters into his own hands. A star cop engaged to the local police chief's daughter attempts to thwart the hood and the struggle leads to a gang-battle finale. Edmund Breese, Mae Busch star. 64 min.
09-2402 *$19.99*

Symphony Of Living (1935)
Tearful melodrama about an aging concert violinist ignored by his grown children who becomes a music teacher. His most promising student, with whom he intends to make a comeback, turns out to be his own grandson! Stars Evelyn Brent, Richard Tucker and vaudeville star Al Shean. 73 min.
09-1633 Was $29.99 *$14.99*

Valley Of Wanted Men (1935)
Gritty jailbreak drama about three convicts (a dangerous killer, a small-time crook, and a falsely imprisoned bank clerk) who escape, and how the clerk's young friend fights to prove his innocence. Frankie Darro, Grant Withers, LeRoy Mason star. 56 min.
09-2160 Was $24.99 *$14.99*

Fighting To Live (1934)
Intense drama about a police dog who attempts to help a pregnant woman battle her brutish boss, then finds itself fighting for its life along with her in the desert. Marion Shilling, Gaylord Pendleton star. 50 min.
09-5055 Was $19.99 *$14.99*

Illegal Wives (1939)
An exploitation drama about Mormons? You be the judge! Bishop Miller has a revelation from the Lord and starts a community of polygamists in Arizona. Soon, however, he's on the outs with some of the members of his faction, and his daughter wants to marry a non-believer. Charles Maurice and Ann Marien star in this incredible film. AKA: "Child Marriage." 54 min.
79-5495 Was $24.99 *$19.99*

Main Street Girls (1936)
Gritty crime exploiter about "Slicker" Nixon and his thugs, who are released from prison only to start a criminal reign of terror, offering "protection" for local businesses. When a woman witnesses the murder of her father, she joins forces with a rival gangster to stop "Slicker" and his cronies. Jean Carmen, Richard Adams star. AKA: "Paroled from the Big House."
79-6212 Was $24.99 *$19.99*

Crime And Punishment (1935)
The classic Dostoyevsky novel is given a stellar American treatment with Peter Lorre as the guilt-ridden college student who kills a pawnbroker and faces off against a sly police inspector (Edward Arnold) assigned to the case. Marian Marsh and Tala Birell also star in Josef von Sternberg's striking production. 88 min.
02-2433 *$19.99*

Crime And Punishment (1998)
Patrick Dempsey stars as Raskolnikov, the arrogant student who sees himself as above the law, and Ben Kingsley is Inspector Porfiry, who plays a cat-and-mouse game with Dempsey over the brutal murder of a pawnbroker and her sister, in this compelling adaptation of the novel by Dostoevsky. Julie Delpy, Lili Horvath also star. 89 min.
68-1978 ❑*$69.99*

Speed Devils (1935)
This drama features Hollywood bad boy Paul Kelly and Russell Hardee as race drivers who decide to open their own garage after they survive a major crash. Politicians soon want to use their new place in a devious scheme, but a local reporter who likes Kelly helps put a stop to their plan. With Marguerite Churchill.
79-6021 Was $24.99 *$19.99*

Moonlight Sonata (1937)
Legendary Polish pianist/composer Ignace Jan Paderewski (who also served as his country's prime minister!) stars in this unusual, music-filled drama. A planeload of passengers, including Paderewski, lands near a remote castle in Sweden, and the maestro not only performs works by Beethoven, Chopin and Liszt, but also plays matchmaker for a young couple. Charles Farrell, Marie Tempest also star. 86 min.
09-1337 *$19.99*

The Abe Lincoln Of Ninth Avenue (1939)
Jackie Cooper plays the title character, a newsboy-by-day/law student-by-night who puts his foot down when mobsters want a piece of the action. He enlists help from his handicapped pal to clear the streets of these undesirables. With Martin Spellman and Dick Purcell. AKA: "Streets of New York." 68 min.
09-2162 Was $29.99 *$24.99*

Nana (1934)
Producer Samuel Goldwyn launched his new discovery, Russian actress Anna Sten, with this liberal adaptation of Emile Zola's novel about an unrefined Parisian street girl who becomes the toast of high society through her relationship with a famous impresario, only to be caught up in a tragic love affair. Co-stars Phillips Holmes, Lionel Atwill; look closely for Lucille Ball as a chorus girl. Dorothy Arzner directs. AKA: "Lady of the Boulevards." 83 min.
09-3104 *$19.99*

The Eleventh Commandment (1933)
A millionaire spinster dies, and a group of schemers set out to claim her fortune for themselves in this elaborately plotted drama. Marian Marsh, Alan Hale, Sr., Theodore Von Eltz, Marie Prevost star. 69 min.
09-2190 Was $19.99 *$14.99*

The Little Red Schoolhouse (1936)
A school-hating orphan who lives with his kid brother and schoolteacher sister runs away from home with his dog and rides the rails destined for New York. How will he react to the crude and manipulative people on his journey? Frankie Coughlan, Jr., Lloyd Hughes and Dickie Moore star in this social drama. 65 min.
09-2373 *$19.99*

The Port Of Missing Girls (1938)
When a San Francisco nightclub singer is implicated in a murder, she stows away on a freighter and comes in contact with a woman-hating captain, an understanding radio operator and, when the ship arrives in port, pirates, smugglers and barmaids. Harry Carey, Sr., Judith Allen and Milburn Stone of "Gunsmoke" fame star. 56 min.
09-2155 Was $24.99 *$14.99*

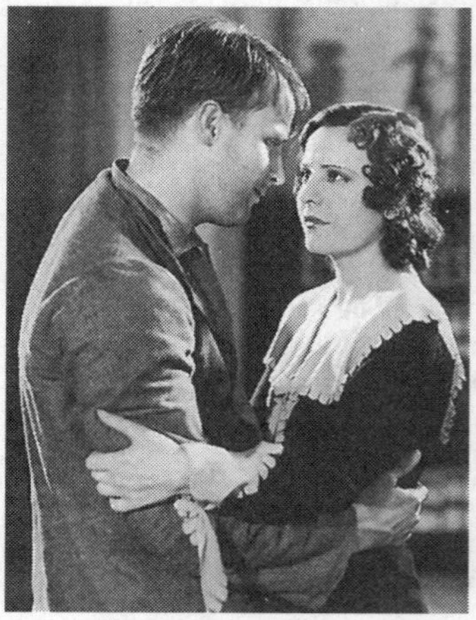

The Criminal Code (1930)
A young man, recently released from prison following a crime he didn't commit, falls in love with the daughter of the D.A. who sent him to jail in this early Howard Hawks drama. Walter Huston, Phillips Holmes, Constance Cummings, Boris Karloff star. 78 min.
02-1349 Was $59.99 *$19.99*

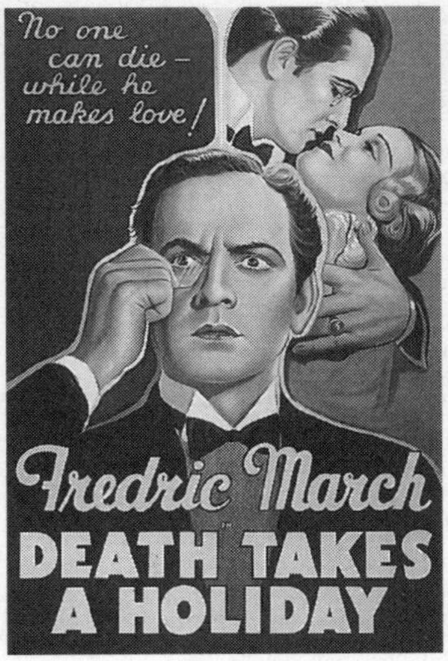
No one can die – while he makes love!
Fredric March
DEATH TAKES A HOLIDAY

Death Takes A Holiday (1934)
In this offbeat fantasy-romance, the basis for 1998's "Meet Joe Black," the Grim Reaper grows tired of his "job" and comes down to Earth, taking the form of a handsome prince, to learn why humans fear him. Complications arise when "Prince Sirki" falls in love with one of his fellow guests at an Italian villa. Fredric March is mesmerizing in the title role; with Evelyn Venable, Sir Guy Standing. 79 min.
07-2521 *$14.99*

Officer 13 (1933)
Gritty story of a thrill-seeking woman who gets in lots of trouble after she takes to hiding out with a gang of hoods. Monte Blue, Lila Lee and Seena Owen star. 62 min.
09-5065 *$19.99*

Officer O'Brien (1930)
William Boyd is an earnest young cop who has to deal with the shame of having a hood for a father...as well as save his girl's brother from being erased before he testifies against the mob. Ernest Torrence, Dorothy Sebastian co-star. 73 min.
09-2035 Was $29.99 *$14.99*

Born To Fight (1938)
A boxing trainer on the run from a crooked promoter he injured finds an up-and-coming fighter whom he manages to a title bout in this drama starring Kane Richmond, Frankie Darro, Jack LaRue. 64 min.
09-5007 *$19.99*

In His Steps (1936)
Two families feud while their children plan to marry. The kids decide to get away from the troubled parents, but the girl's family accuses the would-be groom of kidnapping her. Eric Linden, Cecilia Parker star. 78 min.
09-5058 *$19.99*

The Last Journey (1936)
When an elderly railroad worker is forced against his will to retire, he becomes angry and decides to take his train on one last ride—into a concrete wall! Can a psychiatrist talk him out of his plans? Godfrey Tearle and Hugh Williams star. 55 min.
09-5061 *$19.99*

The Marines Are Here (1938)
After a gang of crooks creates havoc, it's up to some Marines to band together and set things right in this rousing drama that stars Gordon Oliver, Guinn "Big Boy" Williams, and June Travis. 61 min.
09-5064 *$19.99*

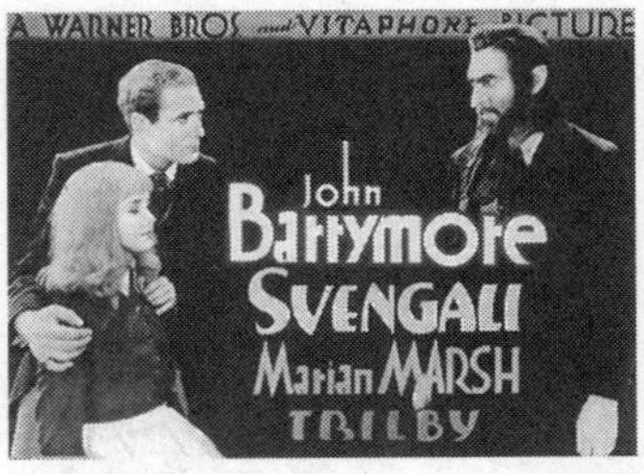
A WARNER BROS. —VITAPHONE PICTURE
John
Barrymore
SVENGALI
Marian MARSH
TRILBY

Svengali (1931)
John Barrymore stars as the mysterious music teacher whose hypnotic hold over a young model (Marian Marsh) propels her singing career, until their bizarre relationship culminates in a deadly confrontation. Co-stars Bramwell Fletcher, Donald Crisp. Based on the classic 19th-century novel "Trilby" by George du Maurier. 82 min.
01-1362 *$19.99*

Svengali (1955)
The first color version of the mesmerizing drama, this British-made effort stars Donald Wolfit as the music teacher who puts singing student Hildegarde Neff under his sinister spell. 82 min.
08-1471 *$19.99*

Lena Rivers (1932)
Melodrama about a girl who moves in with her wealthy aunt following the death of her fisherman grandfather. Her real father lives next door, and eventually she falls in love with his ward. Charlotte Henry, Beryl Mercer and James Kirkwood star. 60 min.
09-5062 *$19.99*

Java Head (1934)
Romantic melodrama about hypocrisy and prejudice in a prosperous 19th-century British port, starring Anna May Wong as the exotic Manchu princess sailor John Loder brings home to meet his rigid family. With Edmund Gwenn, Ralph Richardson. 82 min.
09-2066 Was $29.99 *$14.99*

Shop Angel (1932)
A scandal results when an ambitious dress designer at a big department store goes out with her middle-aged, skirt-chasing boss and their car crashes. Well-acted tale of blackmail and lust stars Marion Shilling and Holmes Herbert. 66 min.
09-2074 Was $29.99 *$14.99*

I Conquer The Sea (1936)
Footage of an actual whale hunt and lots of authentic whaling songs (they're the best!) add flavor to this sea-faring Newfoundland romance about a proud harpooner (Dennis Morgan) and his stormy romance with a willful Portuguese (Steffi Duna). 67 min.
09-2076 Was $29.99 *$14.99*

Action For Slander (1938)
A tight-lipped British officer shrugs off a false accusation that he cheated at cards until the mark on his character becomes the talk of London, then seeks restitution at a sensational trial. Stars Clive Brook, Ann Todd and Francis Sullivan. 83 min.
09-2077 Was $29.99 *$14.99*

London Melody (1937)
British film great Anna Neagle stars in this drama set against the glitter of London nightlife. She plays an energetic Cockney gal who romances a wealthy diplomat only to fall in love with his womanizing colleague. Italian silent star Tullio Carminati co-stars. 71 min.
09-2120 Was $29.99 *$14.99*

Kentucky Blue Streak (1935)
A young jockey, framed for murder while riding at an illegal racetrack, escapes from jail in order to ride in the Kentucky Derby and use the winnings to save the family horse ranch. Thrilling race drama stars Eddie Nugent, Patricia Scott. 61 min.
09-1297 Was $19.99 *$14.99*

White Legion (1936)
As an epidemic of yellow fever threatens the lives of those working on the Panama Canal, one strong-willed doctor (Ian Keith) investigates the dreaded disease's cause and faces scandal with a senator's daughter. Co-stars Tala Birell, Rollo Lloyd, Jason Robards, Sr. 81 min.
09-1640 Was $29.99 *$14.99*

Ten Nights In A Bar-Room (1931)
A screen version of the 19th-century temperance classic about the brutal effects of demon alcohol on family life. Melodramatic by any standards, this film is nevertheless a powerful depiction of the nightmare of alcoholism and features a riveting performance by William Farnum as the hapless Joe. 60 min.
09-1816 Was $24.99 *$19.99*

I'd Give My Life (1936)
Unusual soaper with classic elements of murder, blackmail, courage and sacrifice! A young man works for a gangster, not knowing it's his father, but when the man uses his son to blackmail his ex-wife (the boy's mother, but she doesn't know)... Sir Guy Standing, Frances Drake, Tom Brown star. 73 min.
09-1858 Was $19.99 *$14.99*

Roaring Speedboats (1937)
Zzzzzzzoooom! That's handsome William Blackwell as the All-American boy who finds himself in heated supercharger boat competition with a suave but cheating European count. A whiz-bang drama with exciting water races, romance and thrills! With Arletta Duncan and Duncan Renaldo. 62 min.
09-2145 Was $24.99 *$14.99*

The Girl From Calgary (1932)
Fifi D'Orsay stars in the title role, a gorgeous rodeo-ridin' gal who can bust a bronco and sing a song with the best of them. A promoter brings her to New York for a shot at Broadway stardom in this offbeat drama. With Paul Kelly. 60 min.
09-2197 Was $24.99 *$14.99*

Confidential (1935)
Tightly paced crime drama about a government agent who goes undercover to break open a big city crime ring and bring its leader to justice for the murder of the G-man's friend. Donald Cook, Evalyn Knapp, J. Carrol Naish star. 67 min.
09-2199 Was $24.99 *$19.99*

On Your Guard (1931)
Richard Talmadge plays the Frisco Kid, a bank robber who gets out of prison and plans to get back to a life of crime, but changes his mind, though, when he meets a backwoods gal and her siblings. With Dorothy Burgess, Edmund Breese. 59 min.
09-2215 Was $24.99 *$19.99*

Sins Of The Children (1930)
A businessman on the verge of becoming rich takes his sickly son away on a two-year stay in a drier climate. The man's partner deems him a failure, but he learns that his family is more important than finance. Louis Mann, Robert Montgomery, Elliott Nugent star; directed by Sam Wood ("The Pride of the Yankees"). 86 min.
09-5248 *$19.99*

Big City Interlude (1931)
Provocative for its day, this melodrama stars Bessie Love as a naive small-town girl who becomes the "kept woman" of a lecherous New York businessman. A chance meeting with a childhood sweetheart sends Love back home to try and change her life, but when her brother needs $1000 to stay out of jail, will she be forced to return to the "big city"? With Emma Dunn, Conway Tearle. AKA: "Morals for Women." 55 min.
09-1023 *$14.99*

Amateur Crook (1937)
This gritty crime drama from noted "B" movie producer Sam Katzman ("Rock Around the Clock") stars Bruce Bennett (aka former Tarzan Herman Brix) as an artist trying to help a woman who has stolen a diamond that belonged to her father. The diamond was supposed to pay off loan sharks, but when the crooks come looking for it, Bennett finds himself in trouble. With Joan Barclay. 60 min.
10-9982 *$14.99*

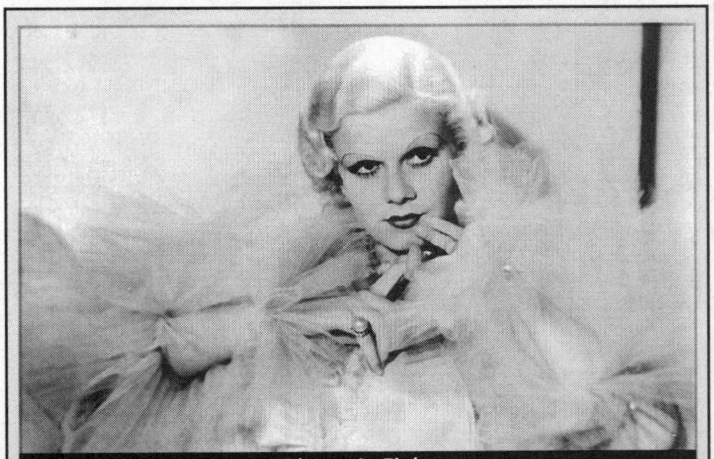
Dinner At Eight

Jean Harlow

Hell's Angels (1930)
A lavish and painstakingly authentic WWI drama that was, at the time, the most expensive movie ever made. Ben Lyon and James Hall are brothers at Oxford who join the British Air Corps when war breaks out, and Jean Harlow, in her starring debut, is the temptress who comes between them. Spectacular flying sequences (including one featuring stunt work by producer/co-scripter/co-director Howard Hughes) highlight the film. 127 min.
07-1840 Was $19.99 *$14.99*

Red Headed Woman (1932)
A saucy, pre-Production Code drama that helped cement Jean Harlow's sultry screen persona. Here Harlow plays a golddigging secretary who hooks the company's married boss, while carrying on with chauffeur Charles Boyer. With Lewis Stone, Chester Morris. 81 min.
12-2174 Was $29.99 *$19.99*

Dinner At Eight (1933)
A feast for lovers of Hollywood's Golden Age, this classic comedy/drama, centered around a formal dinner party and the private (and public) lives of the guests, stars John Barrymore, Marie Dressler, Wallace Beery, Jean Harlow, Billie Burke and Lionel Barrymore. Black tie optional. 113 min.
12-1396 *$19.99*

Bombshell (1933)
A hilarious Hollywood satire with sexy Jean Harlow as the title beauty who gets involved with wacky showbiz characters. She's got an aggressive press agent (Lee Tracy), an irascible director (Pat O'Brien) and a snobby blueblood (Franchot Tone) looking after her. With Frank Morgan, Ted Healy and Louise Beavers. AKA: "Blonde Bombshell." 90 min.
12-2110 *$19.99*

Hold Your Man (1933)
Fleeing crook Clark Gable uses Jean Harlow's apartment as a hideout, and the pair wind up falling in love. But his womanizing ways inspire Harlow to concoct an affair of her own, and Gable's jealousy results in the "lover's" death and Harlow's being sent to jail for the crime! Glossy blend of romance and crime/prison drama also stars Stuart Erwin and Dorothy Burgess. 88 min.
12-2516 *$19.99*

The Girl From Missouri (1934)
Lively comedy starring Jean Harlow as the daughter of a small-town innkeeper who joins friend Patsy Kelly in New York to search for romance...with a millionaire. Harlow thinks she's found Mr. Right when she meets tycoon Lionel Barrymore, but then falls for his handsome son while on a trip to Florida. Franchot Tone, Lewis Stone co-star. 72 min.
12-2515 *$19.99*

Riffraff (1936)
Compelling drama starring Jean Harlow as the daughter of a seaman who falls in love with fisherman Spencer Tracy. After Tracy leads his fellow workers in a rigged strike and loses his job, he disappears. Harlow's search for him leads her to the creep responsible for his firing, before justice prevails. Joseph Calleia, Una Merkel and Mickey Rooney co-star. 94 min.
12-2518 *$19.99*

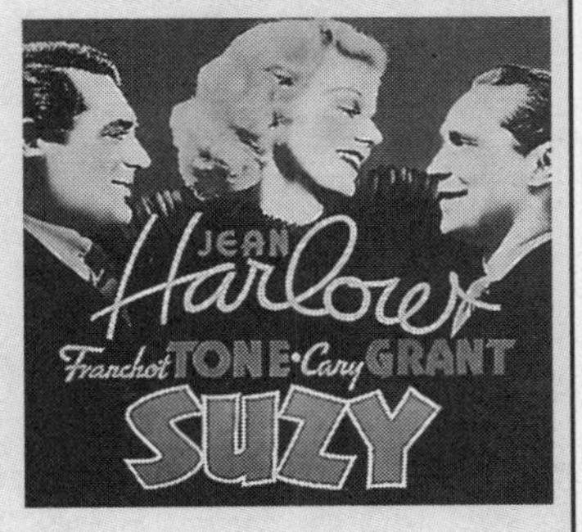
JEAN
Harlow
Franchot TONE · Cary GRANT
SUZY

Suzy (1936)
Jean Harlow plays the title character, a showgirl working in London in 1914 whose inventor husband is shot by German spies. Thinking him dead, she leaves for Paris, where she meets and weds roguish French pilot Cary Grant. But through fate (and plot twists), husband #1 builds a special plane that husband #2 is chosen to fly! Franchot Tone, Benita Hume also star. 93 min.
12-2520 *$19.99*

Personal Property (1937)
Jean Harlow is a bankrupt American widow living in England who eventually falls in love with rebellious playboy Robert Taylor, hired by creditors to keep an eye on Harlow. Reginald Owen, Una O'Connor and E.E. Clive co-star in this sexy romp. 85 min.
12-2517 *$19.99*

Saratoga (1937)
Bittersweet comedy with Jean Harlow in her final role, playing the daughter of a debt-ridden horse breeder whose property has been forfeited to his former partner, slick gambler Clark Gable. The tension between the two leads to jealousy, intrigue and, eventually, romance, set against the backdrop of the racetrack. Walter Pidgeon, Lionel Barrymore, Frank Morgan also star. 92 min.
12-2519 *$19.99*

Harlow: The Blonde Bombshell
Nineties Hollywood sex symbol Sharon Stone is the host for this intimate look at one of the first screen sirens, Jean Harlow. Before her untimely death at age 26, the "Platinum Blonde" thrilled audiences in both comedies and dramas, and is saluted here in clips from her best-loved roles. 47 min.
18-7472 *$14.99*

Please see our index for these other Jean Harlow titles: *Bacon Grabbers • China Seas • Double Whoopee • Libeled Lady • Platinum Blonde • The Public Enemy • Reckless • Red Dust • Wife vs. Secretary*

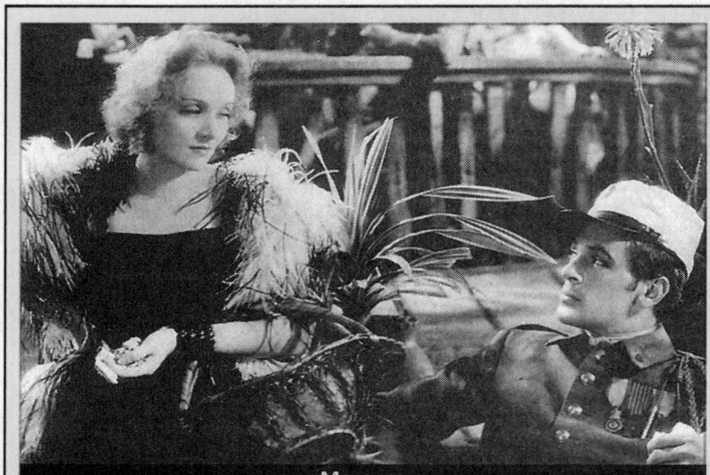

Morocco

Marlene Dietrich

The Ship Of Lost Men (1929)
Before becoming an international sensation, Marlene Dietrich ruled the German cinema with her luminous star power. In this powerful drama, Dietrich joins a boatload of refugees who are abused by the ship's cruel captain. With Fritz Kortner. 121 min. Silent with music score.
09-3129 *$19.99*

The Blue Angel (1930)
Marlene Dietrich's classic performance as a nightclub entertainer who seduces and destroys middle-aged professor Emil Jannings made her an instant star. Josef von Sternberg directs this classic drama. 98 min. In German with English subtitles.
08-8070 *$19.99*

The Blue Angel (English-Language Version)
Recently found and restored, this is the rarely-seen, filmed-in-English edition of the Von Sternberg classic, filmed simultaneously with the German version. 94 min.
50-3225 *$19.99*

Morocco (1930)
In her first American feature (and second collaboration with director Josef Von Sternberg), Marlene Dietrich shines as a Parisian cafe singer who falls for legionnaire Gary Cooper and eventually follows him to the desert. Moody, romantic drama also stars Adolphe Menjou. 92 min.
07-1990 □*$14.99*

Dishonored (1931)
Marlene Dietrich is a streetwalker in Vienna recruited by a secret agent to spy on Austria during World War I. She discovers evidence on a general selling secrets to the Russians and uncovers a Russian agent posing as an officer in the Austrian army. Victor McLaglen, Warner Oland and Gustaav von Seyffertitz star in this Josef Von Sternberg production. 91 min.
07-1992 *$14.99*

Blonde Venus (1932)
Exotic Josef Von Sternberg/Marlene Dietrich drama, about a woman's mounting struggles with a dying husband (Herbert Marshall), her son (Dickie Moore) and a rich playboy (Cary Grant). Highlight is Dietrich's seductive striptease in a gorilla suit while belting out "Hot Voodoo." 89 min.
07-1458 Was $29.99 *$14.99*

Shanghai Express (1932)
All aboard the Peking Railroad's great train, inhabited by a host of fascinating characters: Shanghai Lily (Marlene Dietrich), a strong-willed woman with a questionable reputation; Lily's former lover, a British doctor (Clive Brook); a Chinese prostitute (Anna May Wong); and a devious rebel leader (Warner Oland). An exotic Dietrich classic, directed by Josef Von Sternberg. 82 min.
07-1987 *$14.99*

The Song Of Songs (1933)
After the death of her father, country girl Marlene Dietrich moves to the big city of Berlin to work in her aunt's bookstore. A customer asks Dietrich to model for a statue he is creating called "Song of Solomon" and she finds both the statue's sculptor and a wealthy arts patron falling in love with her. Brian Aherne, Lionel Atwill co-star. 90 min.
07-2312 *$14.99*

The Scarlet Empress (1934)
The glamorous Marlene Dietrich and a dazzling celebration of style can be found in director Josef Von Sternberg's stunning biography of Catherine the Great of Russia. Dietrich's Catherine—married to the cowardly Grand Duke Peter, adulterous nephew of the cruel Empress Elizabeth—realizes that in order for her and Russia to survive, a coup d'état is necessary. With Sam Jaffe. 105 min.
07-1991 *$14.99*

The Devil Is A Woman (1935)
Marlene Dietrich is at her best as a conniving woman in 1890s Seville who gets her jollys making men lavish gifts and attention upon her, then destroying their lives. Cesar Romero is the young suitor warned by former lover Lionel Atwill that Dietrich's charms can only lead to disaster. Directed by Joseph von Sternberg, the film inspired Luis Buñuel's "That Obscure Object of Desire." 80 min.
07-2313 *$14.99*

The Garden Of Allah (1936)
Lush locales and Oscar-winning early Technicolor camerawork fuel this romantic adventure. After her father's death, socialite Marlene Dietrich seeks solace in the Algerian desert and finds it in the arms of handsome stranger Charles Boyer, who, unbeknownst to her, is a monk who left his monastery home. With Basil Rathbone, Joseph Schildkraut, Alan Marshall. 85 min.
04-1384 Was $19.99 *$14.99*

Desire (1936)
Jewel thief Marlene Dietrich uses American car designer Gary Cooper to carry the pearls she lifted in Paris past Spanish customs agents. Romance ensues between the two strangers, leading to Marlene going straight and a life happily ever after in Detroit. This sparkling tale was produced by Ernst Lubitsch and co-stars John Halliday, William Frawley and Ernest Cossart. 96 min.
07-2177 □*$14.99*

Angel (1937)
A lavish tale of marital strife and desire from Ernst Lubitsch starring Marlene Dietrich as the bored wife of a British nobleman who meets a handsome American in Paris. Sparks fly between the two, but they're shocked to discover that Dietrich's husband and the American were friends during World War I. Herbert Marshall, Melvyn Douglas and Edward Everett Horton also star. 91 min.
07-2178 □*$14.99*

The Flame Of New Orleans (1941)
In order to nab a wealthy husband, French golddigger Marlene Dietrich lands in 1840s New Orleans and fakes an illness at the opera. Her act draws the attention of a rich businessman, whom she plans to marry, but a rugged sea captain who falls for her and some old acquaintances from Europe may threaten the scheme. Roland Young, Bruce Cabot co-star; directed by René Clair. 80 min.
07-2314 *$14.99*

The Lady Is Willing (1942)
Daring (for its time) comedy starring Marlene Dietrich as a famed stage actress who finds an abandoned baby and applies to adopt it. Turned down due to her single status, she arranges an "in name only" marriage to pediatrician Fred MacMurray. With Aline MacMahon, Sterling Holloway. 91 min.
02-2454 *$19.99*

Golden Earrings (1947)
Unruly Gypsy woman Marlene Dietrich finds romance with British officer Ray Milland, whom she helps through the Black Forest on a mission to stop a Nazi plan to use poison gas during World War II. Exciting (and, now, often campy) wartime story offers the divine Marlene decked out in sultry Gypsy garb and dark make-up; with Murvyn Vye, Dennis Hoey. 95 min.
07-1989 *$14.99*

A Foreign Affair (1948)
Caustic comedy from Billy Wilder set in post-World War II Berlin, where dignified congresswoman Jean Arthur's investigation into black market influence on occupying GIs brings her in close contact with John Lund, a handsome captain. The problem is that Lund is involved with Marlene Dietrich, a nightclub singer whom Arthur learns has ties to former Nazi officials. 116 min.
07-2311 *$14.99*

An Evening With Marlene Dietrich (1972)
The timelessly beautiful model of European seduction is captured in a memorable live performance at England's London Theatre. Songs include "I Wish You Love," "Lily Marlene," "My Blue Heaven" and "Falling in Love Again." 50 min.
50-6297 *$29.99*

Marlene (1986)
Using film and concert clips and newsreel footage, director Maximilian Schell has created a stunning portrait of Marlene Dietrich: the woman, the star, and the legend. An audio interview runs through the documentary (Dietrich refused to appear in the film, saying "I've been photographed to death"). 96 min.
53-1681 *$19.99*

Marlene Dietrich Collection
You'll be "falling in love again" with marvelous Marlene after watching this boxed collector's set that features "Golden Earrings," "Pittsburgh" and "Seven Sinners."
07-2498 Save $20.00! *$24.99*

Please see our index for these other Marlene Dietrich titles: *Destry Rides Again • Follow The Boys • Judgment At Nuremberg • Kismet • No Highway In The Sky • Pittsburgh • Seven Sinners • The Spoilers • Stage Fright • Touch Of Evil • Witness For The Prosecution*

Long Shot (1939)
A race horse owner tries to snap a streak of bad luck by taking his prize steed to Arizona, but when he gets there he must team up with a young trainer to help keep his college student niece out of the clutches of a sleazy track owner. Gordon Jones, Marsha Hunt star. 69 min.
09-2405 *$19.99*

Flying Fists (1937)
Herman Brix stars as a lumberjack-turned-boxer who falls for a woman whose father was a fighter before injuries forced him to retire, leaving her with a hatred of the sport, in this ring drama. With Jeanne Martel, Fuzzy Knight, Guinn Williams. 58 min.
09-3117 *$14.99*

Prison Without Bars (1939)
A teenage girl in reform school has a crush on the establishment's doctor, but must compete for his attention with the free-thinking woman in charge of the school. An adult-minded prison drama that's actually a remake of a French film. With Corrine Luchaire, Edna Best and Barry K. Barnes. 80 min.
09-5068 *$19.99*

Broken Blossoms (1936)
A reworking of the classic D.W. Griffith drama about a girl who flees her drunken, abusive father and is befriended by a Chinese boy who disguises her as an Asian in order to elude him. Dolly Haas, Emlyn Williams and Arthur Margetson star. 75 min.
09-5240 *$19.99*

I Am A Criminal (1939)
Faced with a murder trial, a gangster adopts an orphaned newsboy in hopes of swaying the jury with sentiment. The youngster helps the gangster reconsider his criminal life, and when the gangster's girlfriend tries to rip him off, the boy steps in to save the day. John Carroll, Kay Linaker and Craig Reynolds star. 74 min.
09-5244 *$19.99*

She Had To Choose (1934)
In this drama, Buster Crabbe plays a man targeted by two women for love: a poor, orphaned girl and a wealthy debutante. The plot thickens when the deb's brother marries the orphan and Crabbe kills the brother. Isabel Jewell, Sally Blane also star. 65 min.
09-5247 *$19.99*

His Guiding Destiny (1933)
In this tough-as-nails crime melodrama, a young man gets out of the slammer after a seven-year stint with thoughts of exacting revenge on the person who sent him there on false charges. But will revenge take a back seat to his romance with the creep's gal? William Collier, Jr. stars. 60 min.
09-2316 *$14.99*

The Duke Comes Back (1937)
A self-confident boxer known as "The Harvard Hurricane" retires to settle down with his wife after winning the championship. But when his father-in-law loses a fortune in the stock market and faces a prison term, the boxer must re-don the gloves and head back into the ring. Allan Lane, Heather Angel star. 54 min.
09-2247 Was $24.99 *$19.99*

The Lure Of Hollywood (1936)
Thanks to an ad scandal, a young woman who comes to Hollywood finds herself becoming an overnight sensation, but soon learns that what goes up must come down, in this glossy melodrama of fame and its price. Marion Nixon and Kane Richmond star. 69 min.
09-5350 *$19.99*

A Parisian Romance (1932)
A rakish, womanizing world-traveller (Lew Cody) casts his cynicism towards love and women aside when he meets the woman of his dreams (Marion Schilling) in Paris, but must contend with the young beauty's fiancé. Co-stars Gilbert Roland, Joyce Compton. 77 min.
09-2283 Was $19.99 *$14.99*

Cavalcade (1933)
This winner of the 1933 Academy Award for Best Picture, based on Noel Coward's hit play, traces 30 years in a British family's lives, beginning with the Boer War and the end of the Victorian Era through World War I and the Jazz Age. Superb cast includes Diana Wynyard, Una O'Connor and Clive Brook. 110 min.
04-1197 *$19.99*

Racing Blood (1936)
A young man in love with horseracing ignores his medical career and buys a colt. He puts tremendous time and energy into training the horse, but runs into trouble when he tries to help his jockey brother, who's involved with racketeers. Frankie Darro, Kane Richmond star. 63 min.
09-2355 *$24.99*

Little Pal (1935)
A heartwarming Depression-era story starring Ralph Bellamy as a kindly physician who performs miraculous medical feats at his country spa. He becomes the focus of two women: his aide, who has left New York to work for him, and a wealthy temptress. Mickey Rooney is the youngster with polio the doctor tries to help. AKA: "The Healer." 68 min.
09-2357 *$19.99*

There Ain't No Justice (1939)
Gritty boxing drama about an auto mechanic who realizes he can be a talented fighter and decides to take to the ring to get some cash for his upcoming marriage. Trouble erupts after he becomes involved with a crooked promoter. Jimmy Hanley, Edward Rigby star. 83 min.
09-5072 *$19.99*

Illegal (1932)
This British drama stars Isobel Elsom as a woman who kicks her hubby out of her house after blowing all of his money. In order to raise cash, the woman and her friend open a sleazy club with plans to use its earnings for her daughters' schooling. When the husband comes back into the picture, dangerous situations arise. With D.A. Clarke-Smith. 64 min.
08-1824 *$14.99*

Late Extra (1935)
In his movie debut, James Mason portrays a young reporter looking to make his mark by flushing out a murderous bank thief. Absorbing crime story co-stars Alastair Sim, Cyril Cusack, Virginia Cherill, Michael Wilding. 69 min.
68-8188 Was $19.99 *$14.99*

Human Wreckage (1938)
A civic reformer who has made a name for himself by stopping crime isn't very willing to address the problems in his own life, including booze, burlesque broads and venereal disease, to his friends and family. Vivian McGill, Rose Tapley star.
79-5883 Was $24.99 *$19.99*

A Star Is Born (1937)
Marvelous William Wellman classic about the early days of the Hollywood star system. Fredric March stars as a down-and-out actor who marries movie hopeful Janet Gaynor, then makes her into Tinseltown's biggest star. One of the first films in Technicolor. Andy Devine, Adolphe Menjou, Lionel Stander; look for Lana Turner in her first film role. 111 min.
10-2009 Was $19.99 *$14.99*

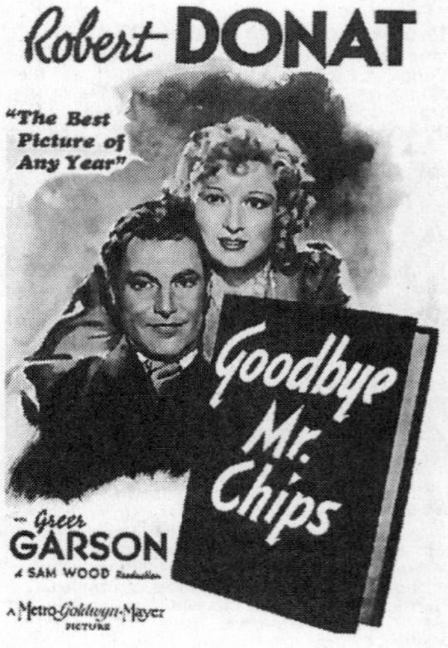

Goodbye, Mr. Chips (1939)
Robert Donat won an Oscar for his portrayal of the archetypal British boys' school teacher: stern and aloof, yet devoted to his charges. Greer Garson, Paul Henreid and John Mills co-star in this touching drama. 114 min.
12-1439 Was $24.99 □*$19.99*

James Cagney

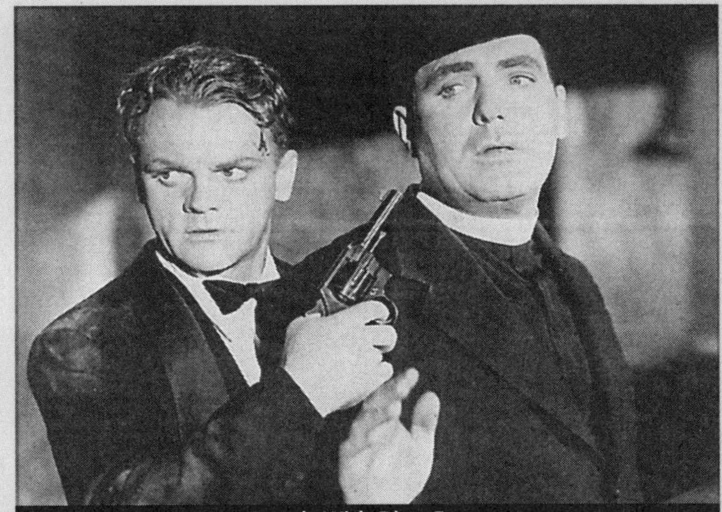

Angels With Dirty Faces

The Public Enemy (1931)
James Cagney in the role that made him a star! He's a small-time hood who gets involved with a Prohibition racket in a big way. Mae Clarke co-stars (in the classic grapefruit-in-the-face scene), along with Jean Harlow, Eddie Woods, Joan Blondell and Donald Cook. 84 min.
12-1148 *$19.99*

Blonde Crazy (1931)
James Cagney is a con man bellhop who teams with hotel worker girlfriend Joan Blondell for a big score in New York. After Cagney loses Blondell's cash in a scam, she leaves him for another man, but Cagney puts his life on the line to recoup the loss. Louis Calhern, Ray Milland also star in this fast-paced crime film spiked with romance. 78 min.
12-2298 *$19.99*

Lady Killer (1933)
Madcap Hollywood satire with James Cagney as a movie theater usher-turned-con man who gives up his life of crime and becomes a film star, until his old gang shows up to bring him back into the fold. Includes the classic scene where Cagney forces a critic to literally "eat his words." Mae Clarke, Leslie Fenton, Margaret Lindsay also star. 76 min.
12-2296 *$19.99*

"G" Men (1935)
Streetwise lawyer James Cagney joins the FBI in order to avenge the gangland murder of an agent who was his friend in this exciting crime drama that also stars Robert Armstrong, Barton MacLane, Margaret Lindsay and Ann Dvorak. 85 min.
12-2379 *$19.99*

Ceiling Zero (1935)
James Cagney turns in a dynamic performance as a cocky aviator whose rule-breaking way of doing things proves problematical for ground commander Pat O'Brien. Cagney learns his lesson when tragedy strikes because of his antics, and he attempts to redeem himself by undertaking a dangerous test flight. With June Travis and Stuart Erwin; Howard Hawks directs. 95 min.
12-2702 *$19.99*

Devil Dogs Of The Air (1935)
Wealthy and arrogant Brooklyn boy James Cagney joins the Marine Flying Corps and quickly proves his fearlessness and flying abilities in the sky, while making an enemy out of pal Pat O'Brien when they fall for the same woman. Superior action scenes and Cagney's colorful performance highlight this exciting film; with Margaret Lindsay, Frank McHugh. 96 min.
12-2703 *$19.99*

The Great Guy (1936)
Prizefighter-turned-government inspector James Cagney deals a knockout blow to racketeers and corruption in the food and meat-packing business. With James Burke, Edward Brophy and Cagney's "Public Enemy" co-star, Mae Clarke. 72 min.
10-1061 *$19.99*

Something To Sing About (1937)
Jimmy Cagney's at his foot-tappin' best as a New York bandleader who is offered a movie contract in this song-filled comedy that includes a few jabs at the Hollywood studio system. With Evelyn Daw, William Frawley. AKA: "Battling Hoofer." 84 min.
10-4002 *$14.99*

Angels With Dirty Faces (1938)
Classic Warner Bros. "urban crime drama" of two kids from the wrong side of the tracks; one becomes a priest (Pat O'Brien), the other a gangster (James Cagney). The cast also includes Humphrey Bogart, Ann Sheridan and the Dead End Kids as local youths who look up to Cagney; Michael Curtiz directs. 97 min.
12-1140 *$19.99*

Boy Meets Girl (1938)
Screwball satire of Hollywood starring James Cagney and Pat O'Brien as screenwriters who create outrageously plotted scripts as an answer to the studio head and his obnoxious cowboy star, who request material different than their typical "boy meets girl" stories. Ralph Bellamy, Marie Wilson and Dick Foran star in this witty spoof. 86 min.
12-2700 *$19.99*

Each Dawn I Die (1939)
When crusading reporter James Cagney is framed for manslaughter and sent to jail, he forms a strange friendship with crime boss George Raft and helps him in a daring escape. Top-notch "big house" drama that was a Warners specialty also stars George Bancroft, Jane Bryan. 92 min.
12-1143 *$19.99*

The Roaring Twenties (1939)
Three army buddies take different roads when World War I ends, but find they share a common destiny in Prohibition-era America. James Cagney, Humphrey Bogart and Jeffrey Lynn star in this classic gangster drama, along with Gladys George and Frank McHugh. Directed by Raoul Walsh. 106 min.
12-1149 *$19.99*

The Oklahoma Kid (1939)
Cagney climbs into the saddle and evens sings in this Western drama, playing a notorious outlaw who teams up with his marshal brother for revenge against the men who lynched his father in order to keep their grip on a frontier town. Humphrey Bogart heads up the baddies; with Rosemary Lane, Harvey Stephens, Donald Crisp. 85 min.
12-1556 *$19.99*

The Fighting 69th (1940)
Rousing World War I drama stars James Cagney as a scrappy Brooklyn boy who is recruited into the all-Irish 69th New York Regiment by Father Duffy (Pat O'Brien). While in combat in France, Cagney's reckless ways lead to the deaths of American soldiers, and it's only as he's awaiting court-martial that he's given a chance to prove his bravery in battle against German forces. George Brent co-stars. 90 min.
12-2704 *$19.99*

The Strawberry Blonde (1941)
Classic melodrama set in 1890s New York stars James Cagney as a man in love with a "good girl" (Olivia de Havilland), but obsessed with a "bad girl" (Rita Hayworth). Lively and charming period piece also stars Alan Hale, Jack Carson and Una O'Connor; look for George Reeves (TV's Superman). 97 min.
12-1557 *$19.99*

The Bride Came C.O.D. (1941)
The unusual comedy pairing of James Cagney and Bette Davis makes for lively romantic sparks. Cagney is the pilot hired by tycoon Eugene Pallette to bring wayward daughter Davis home, but complications mount when they're forced to land in a desert ghost town. Jack Carson, Stuart Erwin co-star. 90 min.
12-2138 *$19.99*

City For Conquest (1941)
Gritty "big city" melodrama features James Cagney as an aspiring prizefighter who meets with disaster after he is blinded in the ring, then devotes himself to fostering the musical career of brother Arthur Kennedy. Co-stars Ann Sheridan as Cagney's dancer ex-girlfriend, Anthony Quinn and Elia Kazan in an early acting role. 101 min.
12-2378 *$19.99*

Yankee Doodle Dandy (1942)
James Cagney is a bundle of energy in his Oscar-winning portrayal of Broadway legend George M. Cohan, from his vaudeville days with his family to fame as the writer of "Over There," "Give My Regards to Broadway," and countless other classic songs. Rosemary DeCamp and Walter Huston co-star in one of Hollywood's liveliest and best-loved musicals. 126 min.
12-1882 Was $19.99 *$14.99*

Captains Of The Clouds (1942)
First-class war yarn with James Cagney as a rebellious flyer for the Royal Canadian Air Force who leaves the military for the independence of a civilian pilot. He gets a chance to prove his patriotism, however, when he stops a German squadron while ferrying a bomber to England. Co-stars Dennis Morgan, Brenda Marshall and Alan Hale; Michael Curtiz directs. 113 min.
12-2701 *$19.99*

Johnny Come Lately (1943)
Arrested for vagrancy when passing through a small town ruled by corrupt politicos, ex-newspaperman James Cagney teams up with the local editor to expose the shady goings-on in this fast-paced comedy/drama. Grace George, Edward McNamara, Hattie McDaniel co-star. 97 min.
63-1386 *$14.99*

Blood On The Sun (1945)
Hard-hitting newspaperman James Cagney, stationed in 1930s Japan, finds himself caught in an espionage plot when he tries to warn American officials about the growing threat of war. Terrific action-drama co-stars Sylvia Sidney, Robert Armstrong. 98 min.
10-2019 Was $19.99 *$14.99*

Blood On The Sun (Color Version)
The blood is red, the sun is yellow, and Cagney is white hot in this newly-hued version of the war thriller.
63-1522 Was $19.99 *$14.99*

13 Rue Madeleine (1946)
Crack wartime espionage story stars James Cagney as an O.S.S. agent sent to WWII France to uncover the site of a German missile silo. Told in a documentary style; with Annabella, Richard Conte, Frank Latimore. 95 min.
04-1977 *$19.99*

The Time Of Your Life (1948)
James Cagney, Broderick Crawford, Wayne Morris and William Bendix star in this spectacular adaptation of the William Saroyan stage play about the people who frequent a small saloon. 109 min.
10-1093 Was $19.99 *$14.99*

White Heat (1949)
The quintessential gangster film contained James Cagney's most frightening role, that of psychopathic, mother-obsessed gunman Cody Jarrett. Raoul Walsh's riveting crime drama co-stars Virginia Mayo, Edmond O'Brien, and Margaret Wycherly as Ma Jarrett. 114 min.
12-1881 □*$19.99*

The West Point Story (1950)
Brassy musical stars James Cagney as a down-on-his-luck stage director who is hired to put on a show at West Point. Frustrated by the production's complications, Cagney strikes a cadet, and, in order to continue working, must become a cadet himself. Co-stars Virginia Mayo, Doris Day and Gordon MacRae. Songs include "You Love Me," "Long Before I Knew You" and "Military Polka." 113 min.
19-2062 Was $19.99 *$14.99*

Kiss Tomorrow Goodbye (1950)
Jimmy Cagney is in fine fettle as a ruthless hood who breaks out of prison and lets nobody on either side of the law get in his way. Slam-bang gangster thriller also stars Ward Bond, Barbara Payton, William Frawley; look for Cagney's brother William as his screen sibling. 102 min.
63-1264 *$19.99*

What Price Glory? (1952)
James Cagney and Dan Dailey star as two hard-drinking soldiers stationed in France during WWII who fall for the same French girl. Fine performances from the stars, as well as from Corinne Calvert and Robert Wagner. 111 min.
04-1976 *$19.99*

A Lion Is In The Streets (1953)
James Cagney turns in an electrifying performance as a slick Deep South politician who uses his poor sharecropping constituents to further his own career. Eventually he runs for governor, but along the way is infected with the corruption that permeates the state. Barbara Hale, Anne Francis and Lon Chaney, Jr. co-star. 88 min.
19-1961 Was $19.99 *$14.99*

Love Me Or Leave Me (1955)
Doris Day and James Cagney star in this song-filled biodrama of '20s singer Ruth Etting, focusing on her relationship with gangster Martin "the Gimp" Snyder. The glossy MGM musical treatment is mixed with a gritty story and a great soundtrack. With Cameron Mitchell, Robert Keith. 122 min.
12-1009 Was $19.99 *$14.99*

Tribute To A Bad Man (1956)
James Cagney is the title character, a no-nonsense rancher in the Colorado territory during the 1870s who uses a ruthless style of justice to punish a group of helpers he finds stealing. His frightening demeanor eventually scares his mistress into the arms of a newly hired ranch worker. Irene Pappas, Don Dubbins, Vic Morrow also star; Robert Wise directs. 95 min.
12-2893 *$19.99*

Man Of A Thousand Faces (1957)
The career and stormy private life of silent film legend Lon Chaney is effectively (if not always accurately) brought to the screen in this biodrama. James Cagney stars as the son of deaf-mute parents who thrilled audiences with his make-up and portrayals of the Phantom of the Opera, the Hunchback of Notre Dame and other grotesqueries. With Jane Greer, Dorothy Malone, Jim Backus, Roger Smith. 122 min.
07-1821 *$14.99*

Never Steal Anything Small (1959)
James Cagney stars as a larcenous longshoreman with a heart of gold in this song-filled comedy-drama look at union politics. Between trying to win the election for union president, and trying to win the heart of his lawyer's wife (Shirley Jones), Cagney will sing and dance his way into your heart. Also stars Roger Smith, Jack Albertson and Nehemiah Persoff. 94 min.
07-1400 *$59.99*

Shake Hands With The Devil (1959)
Powerful political drama features James Cagney as a college medical professor in 1920s Dublin who helps lead the Irish Republican Army in its bloody struggle against the British Black and Tan forces. Don Murray, Dana Wynter and Glynis Johns also star in this tale of Ireland's strife. 110 min.
12-2705 *$19.99*

The Gallant Hours (1960)
James Cagney plays Admiral William F. Halsey, the World War II hero known for his strategic brilliance and his victories over the Japanese on the Marshall islands and Guadalcanal. Dennis Weaver, Richard Jaeckel and Ward Costello also star in this stirring biography, directed by Robert Montgomery. 111 min.
12-2409 *$19.99*

One, Two, Three (1961)
Billy Wilder's hilarious jab at American big business and Cold War politics is highlighted by James Cagney's rapid-fire performance. He's a Coca-Cola exec in West Berlin whose future is in jeopardy when the boss' visiting daughter secretly marries a Communist East Berliner. The supporting cast includes Arlene Francis, Horst Buchholz, Pamela Tiffin. 108 min.
12-1555 Was $59.99 *$19.99*

Ragtime (1981)
Director Milos Foreman spun E.L. Doctorow's semifictional novel of 1900s Americana into a richly detailed period piece with a multifaceted plot and an exceptional cast, including the return of James Cagney after a 20-year hiatus. Co-stars Howard Rollins, Brad Dourif and Elizabeth McGovern. 156 min.
06-1126 Remastered *$24.99*

James Cagney: That Yankee Doodle Dandy
From tough guy and gangster to hoofer and comedian, Jimmy Cagney electrified movie audiences for six decades. This documentary looks at the life and career of a film original, featuring scenes from such movies as "Public Enemy," "Yankee Doodle Dandy," "White Heat" and "Ragtime," plus interviews with Pat O'Brien, Donald O'Connor and other stars. 73 min.
12-1554 Was $29.99 *$14.99*

James Cagney: Top Of The World
Whether he was a "Public Enemy" or a "Yankee Doodle Dandy," James Cagney personified the toughness of the New York streets where he grew up. Michael J. Fox hosts this tribute to Cagney's Oscar-winning film work, featuring his most memorable scenes, interviews with friends and co-stars, and much more. 60 min.
18-7470 *$14.99*

James Cagney Scrapbook
Whether merciless thug or ambitious mug, the stamp of any Cagney role was his credibility with the audience, as demonstrated in this review of crowd-pleasing highlights from his long career. Included are clips from such films as "Blood on the Sun" and "Time of Your Life." 60 min.
50-6300 *$19.99*

The James Cagney Collection
Film fans will feel on "top of the world" with this special boxed set that features Cagney in "The Public Enemy," "White Heat" and his Oscar-winning role in "Yankee Doodle Dandy."
12-2529 Save $10.00! *$49.99*

James Cagney Gift Pack
Cagney's at his toughest in "Blood on the Sun," "Johnny Come Lately" and "Kiss Tomorrow Goodbye," all gathered here in a deluxe collectors' set.
63-1400 *$59.99*

Please see our index for these other James Cagney titles: *Footlight Parade • A Midsummer's Night Dream • Mister Roberts*

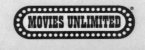

Ronald Colman

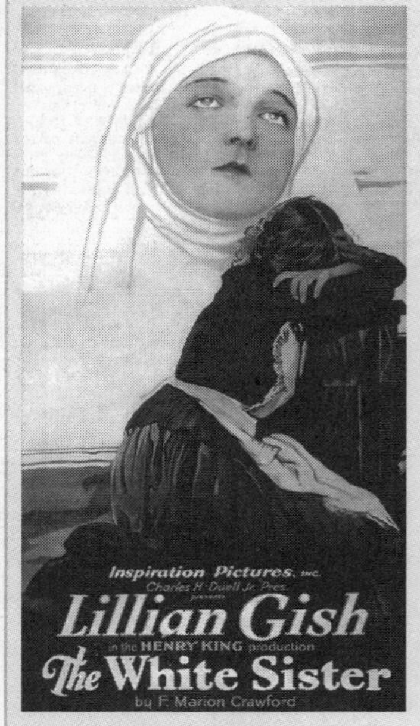

The White Sister (1923)
Lillian Gish excels as an Italian aristocrat who is driven from her estate and has her inheritance taken away by her ruthless sister after her father's death. After her boyfriend dies during the war, Gish decides to become a nun. Ronald Colman and Gail Kane also star in this silent drama directed by Henry King. 65 min.
10-1605 Was $29.99 ***$19.99***

Arrowsmith (1931)
Ronald Colman stars as Sinclair Lewis' idealistic young doctor, who leaves his small town home to work in the West Indies, in director John Ford's dramatic story of personal and professional sacrifice. Helen Hayes and Myrna Loy co-star as the women in Arrowsmith's life. 95 min.
44-1890 Was $19.99 ***$14.99***

The Prisoner Of Zenda (1937)
Greatest rendition of the adventure classic stars Ronald Colman in the dual role of a stricken prince and the look-alike commoner who replaces him at coronation, to the consternation of conspirators Raymond Massey and Douglas Fairbanks, Jr. Madeleine Carroll, David Niven, Mary Astor co-star in David O. Selznick's lavish production. 101 min.
12-1923 ***$19.99***

If I Were King (1938)
Ronald Colman shines as French poet François Villon, champion of the poor in 15th-century Paris. When he murders an oppressive official, Villon is given a week by King Louis XI (Basil Rathbone) to improve the conditions he has condemned...or else he'll lose his head. With Frances Dee, Ellen Drew; written by Preston Sturges. 102 min.
07-2650 ***$14.99***

Random Harvest (1942)
An implausible and yet sublimely compelling romantic drama, with Ronald Colman as an amnesiac WWI soldier who leaves the hospital and begins a new life with music hall dancer Greer Garson. The two are soon married and Colman becomes a writer, but a twist of fate returns him to his prior life, with no memory of Garson. Susan Peters, Edmund Gwenn. 128 min.
12-1132 Was $29.99 ***$19.99***

Kismet (1944)
Lavish costume drama set in old Baghdad and starring Ronald Colman as a wily beggar who poses as a visiting ruler in order to wed his daughter, against her wishes, to a powerful but corrupt vizier. Marlene Dietrich, as the vizier's sexy wife, performs a memorable dance covered in gold body paint; with Edward Arnold, Joy Ann Page, James Craig. 100 min.
12-3029 ***$19.99***

A Double Life (1947)
Classic psychological drama about a suave but emotionally unstable actor who begins living the role of the murderous Othello on and off the stage. Star Ronald Colman won an Oscar for his performance; with Signe Hasso, Shelley Winters, Edmond O'Brien. Newly restored version includes an introduction by Martin Scorsese. 107 min. total.
63-1009 ***$14.99***

Champagne For Caesar (1950)
Riotously funny fable about a genius, played by Ronald Colman, who goes on a radio quiz program and takes them for everything they've got. Vincent Price is the show's neurotic sponsor, who hires beautiful Celeste Holm to distract Colman. With Art Linkletter, Barbara Britton. 99 min.
08-1175 ***$19.99***

Please see our index for these other Ronald Colman titles: *Bulldog Drummond • Lady Windemere's Fan • Romola • A Tale Of Two Cities • The Talk Of The Town*

Framed (1930)
Mobster's daughter Evelyn Brent is out for revenge when her father is killed during a robbery. Years later, while in the nightclub she owns, Brent falls in love with a customer who turns out to be the son of the cop who killed her father. Regis Toomey, Maurice Black also star. AKA: "Trapped." 62 min.
10-9709 ***$19.99***

Black Eyes (1939)
Set in Moscow, this drama focuses on a waiter who uses stock tips and conversations he hears about business to help him finance a nice nest egg for his daughter. But he keeps his real occupation a secret from her—at least, until she discovers it while dining with a wealthy banker. Otto Kruger, Mary Maguire star. 70 min.
10-9376 ***$14.99***

The Common Law (1931)
Fine social drama stars Constance Bennett as a woman whose meeting with a struggling Parisian artist leads her to abandon her life as a mistress of a wealthy man and seek the artist's hand in marriage. But his bohemian ways and her former lover's attempts of sabotage keep getting in the way. Joel McCrea and Hedda Hopper also star. 72 min.
10-9706 ***$19.99***

Sensation Hunters (1934)
A woman working in a Panama beauty salon takes a young woman under her wing and acts as her mentor. When the older woman becomes ill, her young associate decides to sell herself to help her. Gritty drama stars Arline Judge, Preston Foster and Marion Burns. 73 min.
10-9718 ***$19.99***

Women Must Dress (1935)
Tiring of her adulterous husband's ways, a woman takes her daughter and begins a new life for herself as a dress designer. Her success is soon threatened by some of the sordid types she hangs around with. Will she regain her confidence and return to her happy new life? Will she continue her skid? Or will she get back to her husband? Minna Gombell, Gavin Gordon star. 76 min.
10-9720 ***$14.99***

Go Get 'Em Haines (1935)
In this exciting crime drama, a newspaper man investigates a securities fraud and finds himself in lots of trouble. William Boyd and Sheila Terry star. 65 min.
10-9372 ***$14.99***

The Sea Ghost (1931)
An American captain discovers a German submarine officer is alive after World war I. After he lets him live, the captain learns that the officer may have something to do with his wife's death on a ship. Laura La Plante, Alan Hale and Clarence Wilson star. 73 min.
10-9722 ***$19.99***

Fighting Thoroughbreds (1939)
Ralph Byrd stars in this interesting drama with a horse-racing background about the colt of a Kentucky Derby winner that becomes the centerpiece of a struggle between its owners and its mother's owners. Mary Carlisle, Robert Allen also star. 60 min.
10-9767 ***$14.99***

Love Takes Flight (1937)
When an airline pilot abandons his job for a film career, his stewardess girlfriend, in a desperate attempt to win him back, commandeers an aircraft to make a solo flight, despite never having flown a plane before. Bruce Cabot and Beatrice Roberts star in this high-flying romantic drama, the only film directed by actor Conrad Nagel. 70 min.
10-9785 ***$19.99***

Ring Around The Moon (1936)
Adaptation of Vera Hobart's novel that intertwines the very different love lives of two women: a working-class girl's romance, and the torrid affair of a beautiful upper-class society woman. Stars Erin O'Brien-Moore, Ann Doran and Donald Cook. 65 min.
10-9786 ***$19.99***

Anthony Adverse (1936)
Classic Mervyn LeRoy drama laced with adventure and laughter, as young Anthony gains maturity and wisdom through his journeys in 18th-century America. Fredric March, Olivia de Havilland, Claude Rains, Donald Woods and Gale Sondergaard (in an Oscar-winning role) star. 141 min.
12-1484 ***$19.99***

The Night Hawk (1938)
In this fast-paced crime drama, Robert Livingston is a newspaper reporter who goes after mobsters after they kill his custom agent pals. Livingston befriends a former hit man out to nab the same creeps for swiping his kid's iron lung and tackles other criminal activities in this wild tale. With Robert Armstrong, June Travis, Paul Fix and Dwight Frye. 60 min.
10-9945 ***$14.99***

Min And Bill (1930)
Early talkie with Oscar-winner Marie Dressler and Wallace Beery as waterfront dwellers who try to keep Dressler's daughter from being taken away and put in a "proper" home. Also stars Dorothy Jordan and Marjorie Rambeau. 70 min.
12-1466 Was $24.99 ***$19.99***

The Citadel (1938)
Fine acting from Robert Donat, Rosalind Russell and Rex Harrison in this superior drama about a Scottish doctor who gives up his dreams of ministering to the poor for a comfortable life of pandering to rich hypochondriacs; directed by King Vidor. 112 min.
12-1661 ***$24.99***

The Champ (1931)
The original version of the father-son tearjerker still packs a potent punch. Wallace Beery earned an Oscar as the gin-soaked boxer whose confidence is restored by the adoration of son Jackie Cooper, until the boy's mother separates the duo. King Vidor directs. 85 min.
12-2147 ***$19.99***

The Sin Of Madelon Claudet (1931)
Earning an Academy Award for this, her first sound film role, Helen Hayes plays a woman who loses her love, faces prison and degradation, and then sacrifices everything for her son. Classic melodrama, scripted by Hayes' husband, Charles MacArthur, also stars Jean Hersholt, Robert Young, Lewis Stone. 73 min.
12-2152 Was $29.99 ***$19.99***

The Hoosier Schoolmaster (1935)
This post-Civil War story tells of an ex-Union soldier who becomes the school teacher in an Indiana town and soon faces treacherous politicians and war veterans claiming that they are the rightful owners of nearby territory. Norman Foster, Charlotte Henry and Sarah Padden star. 69 min.
10-1602 ***$19.99***

The Big Chance (1933)
Gritty boxing drama about a young fighter who goes up against a veteran boxer after being instructed by a rugged trainer. John Darrow, Mickey Rooney, Mema Kennedy and J. Carroll Naish star. 60 min.
10-3379 ***$19.99***

Hearts Of Humanity (1932)
Sensitive drama starring Jean Hersholt as a Jewish antiques dealer who adopts the son of an Irish cop after he's accidentally shot. Jacki Searl and Charles Delaney also star. 66 min.
10-3380 ***$19.99***

World Gone Mad (1933)
Tough-as-nails reporter Pat O'Brien discovers the city's former district attorney was part of a murderous plot, and the current D.A. may be the next one corrupted, unless he can do something about it. Neil Hamilton, Evelyn Brent and Louis Calhern also star. 60 min.
10-3383 ***$19.99***

Indiscreet (1931)
Gloria Swanson stars in this romantic melodrama as a socialite who tries to hide a dark secret in her past from the man she loves. Ben Lyon, Barbara Kent. 92 min.
10-4012 ***$19.99***

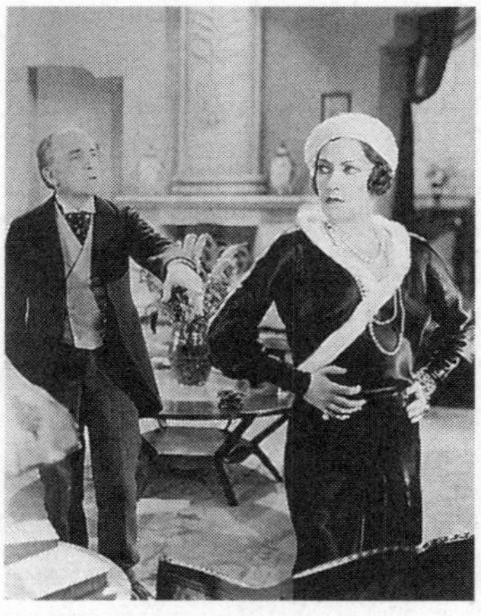

Tonight Or Never (1931)
Gloria Swanson is an opera singer on holiday in Venice with her teacher/lover who is intrigued by handsome Melvyn Douglas, whom she believes to be a gigolo. After spending an evening with him, though, Swanson not only falls for him but learns to sing with the passion she lacked before. Ferdinand Gottschalk, Boris Karloff also star; directed by Mervyn LeRoy ("Little Caesar") and photographed by Gregg Toland ("Citizen Kane"). 80 min.
80-5046 ***$29.99***

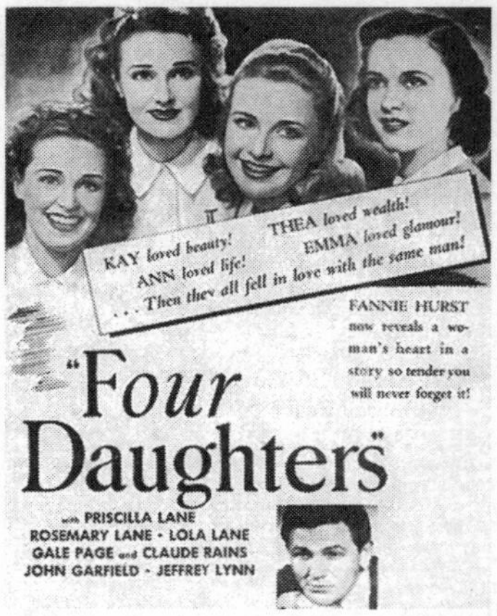

Four Daughters (1938)
Heartfelt melodrama of four small-town sisters' search for true love that spawned two sequels. Claude Rains stars as the widowed family patriarch, with Priscilla, Lola and Rosemary Lane, and Gale Page as his daughters, and Jeffrey Lynn and John Garfield (his film debut) as two would-be suitors. Later remade as "Young at Heart." 90 min.
12-2371 ***$19.99***

Big Town Czar (1939)
The younger brother of a mobster gets into lots of trouble when he tries to help him out after being falsely accused of murder. Barton MacLane, Tom Brown, Eve Arden and future TV host Ed Sullivan star in this really big crime show. 65 min.
10-9949 ***$14.99***

Hara-Kiri (The Battle) (1934)
Archetypal film Frenchman Charles Boyer plays an ambitious Japanese nobleman in charge of a huge naval fleet who goes so far as to push wife Merle Oberon into having an affair with a British navy officer in order to get secret information. John Loder, Miles Mander also star. AKA: "Thunder in the East." 65 min
10-6019 ***$14.99***

Wives Under Suspicion (1938)
James Whale ("Frankenstein"), in a remake of his own "The Kiss Before the Mirror," directed this disconcerting drama about a hardened DA (Warren William) who reconsiders his harsh stance toward a wife killer after imagining his own wife involved with another man. Co-stars Gail Patrick. 75 min.
10-7071 Was $19.99 ***$14.99***

The Barretts Of Wimpole Street (1934)
The enduring romance between 19th-century poets Elizabeth Barrett and Robert Browning served as the basis for this lavish period drama that features sterling performances from Norma Shearer and Fredric March as the literary lovers and Charles Laughton as Barrett's father. With Maureen O'Sullivan, Ian Wolfe, Una O'Connor. 110 min.
12-2382 ***$19.99***

Anything For A Thrill (1937)
A young brother-and-sister team of would-be newsreel photographers save a cameraman's job by getting the scoop on a camera-shy heiress, then louse up a plot by thieves to steal a few of her millions. Stars Frankie Darro and Kane Richmond. 58 min.
10-7164 ***$19.99***

One Third Of A Nation (1939)
Still an effective social commentary on the state of New York City slum life, this Depression-era drama focuses on the plight of Sylvia Sidney and her family and the wealthy heir (Leif Erickson) who takes a romantic interest in her. Co-stars a young Sidney Lumet in his only film appearance. 75 min.
10-7167 Was $19.99 ***$14.99***

Laughing At Life (1933)
Victor McLaglen stars as a soldier of fortune who abandons his family for a life of danger. The years lead him to the dictatorship of a banana republic...and an encounter with a defiant engineer who holds a shattering secret. William "Stage" Boyd, Regis Toomey co-star. 72 min.
10-7185 Was $19.99 ***$14.99***

The World Accuses (1935)
Fine period melodrama that tracks the tragic story of a woman who loses custody of her son after her husband's death...and can only watch from a distance as a worker in the child's nursery. Well-done weepie stars Dickie Moore, Vivian Tobin. 62 min.
10-7188 Was $19.99 ***$14.99***

Algiers (1938)
Charles Boyer, Hedy Lamarr. Mysterious adventure abounds as spoiled aristocratic girl falls under romantic spell of infamous Pepe Le Moko, the Casbah's most notorious figure. 96 min.
10-2047 Was $19.99 ***$14.99***

Backdoor To Heaven (1939)
Powerful, incisive social drama traces a criminal's sorry life back to his lower-class, deprived childhood. Wallace Ford, Aline McMahon, Stuart Erwin star. 81 min.
10-7159 Was $19.99 ***$14.99***

Joan Crawford

Our Dancing Daughters (1928)
Silent "Roaring '20s" melodrama that established Joan Crawford as the archetypal Hollywood flapper. Amid the "flaming youth," "bathtub gin" and "jazz parties," there's a romantic triangle between rebellious Joan, "good girl" Anita Page and millionaire Johnny Mack Brown. 98 min. Silent with musical score.
12-2222 Was $29.99 *$19.99*

Our Modern Maidens (1929)
For her final silent film role, Joan Crawford starred in this follow-up to "Our Dancing Daughters." Both Joan and pal Anita Page are both in love with dashing Douglas Fairbanks, Jr. The problem: Crawford's engaged to him, and Page is carrying his child! 75 min.
12-2623 *$19.99*

Dance, Fools, Dance (1931)
Joan Crawford and Clark Gable made their first screen appearance together in this racy melodrama about reporter Crawford trying to get the goods on Gable's bootlegging ring, never guessing that her brother's a gang member! The "underwear swim party" scene raised a furor in 1931! 81 min.
12-2173 *$19.99*

Laughing Sinners (1931)
Joan Crawford is a nightclub entertainer who decides to take her own life after being rejected by her businessman boyfriend. She is saved after she plunges into the river by Salvation Army worker Clark Gable, who then attempts to help her change her life. Neil Hamilton and Guy Kibbee also star. 71 min.
12-2730 *$19.99*

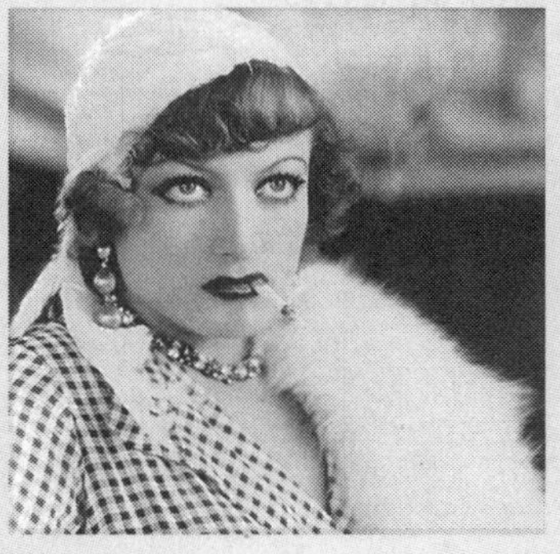

Rain (1932)
Lavish treatment of the stage play based on W. Somerset Maugham's novel set on a remote Samoan island, where career girl Joan Crawford incites the religious zeal, and eventual lust, of reform-minded pulpiteer Walter Huston. Directed by Lewis Milestone. 92 min.
10-2014 Was $19.99 *$14.99*

Today We Live (1933)
A World War I romantic drama showcasing Joan Crawford as a British party girl who falls for dashing American flyer Gary Cooper. After Cooper is reported killed in combat, Crawford returns to her former flame, Navy man Robert Young. Cooper later turns up alive to complicate the love triangle and team with Young on a dangerous mission. Franchot Tone also stars; Howard Hawks directs. 113 min.
12-2783 *$19.99*

Sadie McKee (1934)
Tearful melodrama stars Joan Crawford as a maid caught up with three men in her life: wealthy employer Franchot Tone, rakish wastrel Gene Raymond, and alcoholic millionaire Edward Arnold. With Esther Ralston, Leo G. Carroll. 90 min.
12-2131 *$19.99*

Forsaking All Others (1935)
Returning from a trip, Clark Gable is shocked to find long-time best friend Joan Crawford about to marry caddish Robert Montgomery. Complications ensue when, after being abandoned at the altar, Crawford is comforted by Gable and he realizes he's in love with her. Billie Burke, Charles Butterworth, Rosalind Russell also star. 84 min.
12-2418 *$19.99*

I Live My Life (1935)
Stylish seriocomedy with Joan Crawford as a flighty New York socialite who flirts with earthy archeologist Brian Aherne while vacationing in Greece. He follows her back to the States and attempts to woo her over the objections of her snooty friends. Frank Morgan, Arthur Treacher, Eric Blore co-star. 97 min.
12-2425 *$19.99*

The Gorgeous Hussy (1936)
Set in Washington, D.C., during the 1830s, this historical drama stars Joan Crawford as a free-spirited innkeeper's daughter who becomes involved with important politicians and, eventually, married President Andrew Jackson. Robert Taylor, Lionel Barrymore, Melvyn Douglas and James Stewart co-star. 102 min.
12-2424 *$19.99*

The Bride Wore Red (1937)
Cabaret singer Joan Crawford is whisked off to a snooty Alpine resort by millionaire George Zucco, who wants her to impersonate a society gal as a prank. Soon, she's involved with wealthy Robert Young and postman Franchot Tone. Reginald Owen and Billie Burke co-star in director Dorothy Arzner's lavish feminist fable. 103 min.
12-2416 *$19.99*

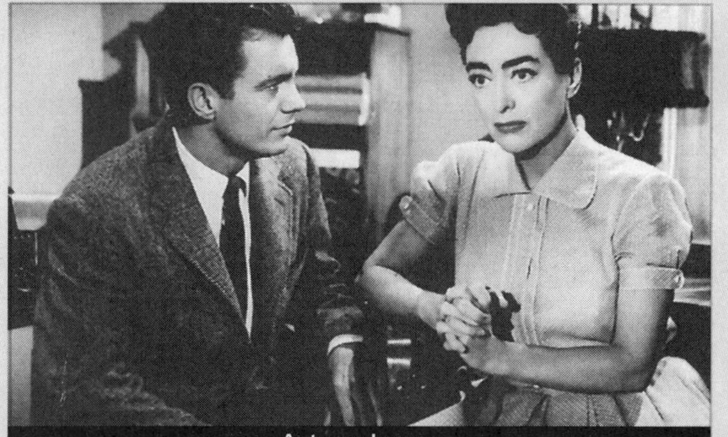

Autumn Leaves

The Last Of Mrs. Cheyney (1937)
Jewel thief Joan Crawford plies her trade at society parties along with her partner, phony butler William Powell, but they get more than they bargained for at a country mansion whose aristocratic guests have more than a few skeletons in their closets. Witty drawing room comedy also stars Robert Montgomery, Frank Morgan, Benita Hume. 95 min.
12-2419 *$19.99*

Mannequin (1937)
Joan Crawford plays a woman from New York's Lower East Side who marries a small-time con artist. She leaves him, becomes a fashion model, and remarries shipping tycoon Spencer Tracy, but Crawford's former husband returns with a scheme to blackmail the happy couple. Moving romantic melodrama co-stars Alan Curtis, Ralph Morgan and Leo Gorcey. 95 min.
12-2420 *$19.99*

The Shining Hour (1938)
Top-notch romantic drama with Joan Crawford as a vivacious New York City dancer who marries rich, conservative businessman Melvyn Douglas and joins him on the family farm. Crawford draws the attention of her married brother-in-law and the animosity of her strait-laced sister-in-law, leading to dramatic consequences. With Margaret Sullavan, Robert Young, Fay Bainter. 77 min.
12-2421 *$19.99*

The Women (1939)
Clare Booth Luce's celebrated play receives a sterling treatment from director George Cukor and an all-star cast. Soap opera and screwball comedy collide when Norma Shearer finds her marriage in trouble when Joan Crawford gets friendly with her man, while scandal maven Rosalind Russell spreads the word. Features a fashion show sequence shot in color. With Joan Fontaine, Mary Boland. 132 min.
12-1397 Was $24.99 *$19.99*

Strange Cargo (1940)
Clark Gable and Joan Crawford's eighth film together is an unusual religious allegory (banned in Rhode Island!) about a group of Devil's Island escapees who fall under the influence of a Christ-like fellow convict. With Peter Lorre, Ian Hunter and Paul Lukas. 105 min.
12-2008 *$19.99*

Susan And God (1940)
Socialite Joan Crawford returns home from Europe with a new religious fervor which eventually threatens to tear her away from her alcoholic husband, her young daughter and her friends. Fredric March, Ruth Hussey, John Carroll and Rita Hayworth also star. 117 min.
12-2422 *$19.99*

A Woman's Face (1941)
A taut, emotional drama from director George Cukor, with Joan Crawford as an embittered woman whose personality changes after she undergoes plastic surgery. Also stars Melvyn Douglas, Conrad Veidt and Osa Massen. 105 min.
12-1662 Was $24.99 *$19.99*

When Ladies Meet (1941)
Women's-rights novelist Joan Crawford is in love with married publisher Herbert Marshall but pursued by Robert Taylor. In an attempt to resolve the problem, Taylor arranges a meeting between Crawford and the publisher's wife. Greer Garson, Spring Byington also star in this comedy that mixes romance and social issues. 105 min.
12-2423 *$19.99*

They All Kissed The Bride (1942)
Joan Crawford's tough-minded career woman image was played for laughs in this romantic comedy that finds her taking over her family's trucking company and running it with an iron fist, until reporter Melvyn Douglas tries to woo her into softening her grip. Lively romp also stars Billie Burke, Roland Young. 87 min.
02-2982 *$19.99*

Above Suspicion (1943)
Crackerjack spy thriller with Joan Crawford and Fred MacMurray as British agents posing as a honeymooning couple in 1939 Europe who stay one step ahead of the Gestapo while trying to locate plans for a secret Nazi mine. Reginald Owen, Conrad Veidt and Basil Rathbone also star. 90 min.
12-2303 *$19.99*

Mildred Pierce (1945)
Fine Hollywood tearjerker with Joan Crawford (in her Oscar-winning role) as the waitress-turned-businesswoman who struggles to provide a good life for her children, only to have older daughter Ann Blyth repay her by having an affair with her stepfather. Michael Curtiz directs; with Zachary Scott, Jack Carson, Eve Arden. 109 min.
12-1974 *$19.99*

Humoresque (1946)
Classic tale has Joan Crawford as a married, promiscuous arts patron who is obsessed with talented young violinist John Garfield. She becomes his manager and sees him rise to the top of the music world while he shuns her desires. Oscar Levant, J. Carroll Naish and Robert Blake, as the young Garfield, co-star. 123 min.
12-2112 *$19.99*

Possessed (1947)
After starring in a similarly titled film in 1931, Joan Crawford earned an Academy Award nomination for this melodrama about an emotionally troubled nurse smitten with a handsome engineer. Her uncontrollable jealousy ignites disastrous problems. Van Heflin, Raymond Massey, Nana Bryant co-star. 108 min.
12-2299 *$19.99*

Flamingo Road (1949)
A soap-opera classic starring Joan Crawford as a one-time carnival dancer who lands a job as a waitress in a small town and finds romance (with politicos Zachary Scott and David Brian), and trouble (from corrupt sheriff Sydney Greenstreet). Gladys George and Fred Clark co-star in this Michael Curtiz drama. 94 min.
12-2417 *$19.99*

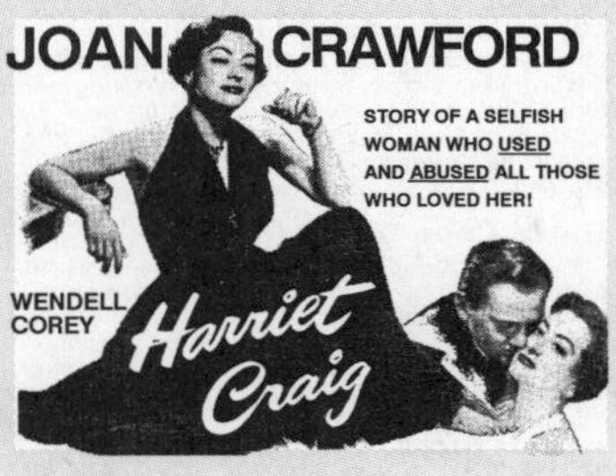

Harriet Craig (1950)
Joan Crawford turns in a powerhouse performance as the title character, a neurotic perfectionist whose need for neatness and control in her stately mansion borders on the psychotic. When husband Wendell Corey is about to be promoted, she sabotages his chances, forcing him to admit that her selfishness and torment have gotten way out of control. 94 min.
02-2850 *$19.99*

Sudden Fear (1952)
Playwright and wealthy San Francisco heiress Joan Crawford becomes romantically involved with actor Jack Palance, but Palance decides he has special plans for their relationship, as he schemes to get Crawford's hefty inheritance with help from deceptive ex-girlfriend Gloria Grahame. Will Joan stop their murderous plot in time? With Touch (Mike) Connors in his film debut. 111 min.
53-8335 *$19.99*

Torch Song (1953)
Sophisticated backstage love story with Joan Crawford as an icy Broadway star who forsakes romance for her career until a blind pianist (Michael Wilding) melts his way into her heart. Musical romance co-stars Gig Young, Harry Morgan and Michael Wilding. Songs include "Tenderly," "You Won't Forget Me" and "Blue Moon." 90 min.
12-2006 *$19.99*

Johnny Guitar (1954)
A thick-skinned ex-dancehall girl (Joan Crawford) opens up her own saloon in a Western small town and must contend with the wrath of righteous do-gooder Mercedes McCambridge and her band of zealots. Embraced by a cult following, Nicholas Ray's Western melodrama has been deciphered as both an exercise in Freudianism and an allegory for McCarthyism. Co-stars Sterling Hayden. Newly restored version includes the original trailer and an introduction by Martin Scorsese. 116 min. total.
63-1015 Was $19.99 *$14.99*

Queen Bee (1955)
Expert tale of deceit and manipulation, Southern style, with Joan Crawford as the rotten Georgia peach married to mill tycoon Barry Sullivan. When a pretty cousin from New York arrives at their home, backstabbing, illicit love and jealousy follow, with Joan's controlling ways getting the better of everyone—and herself. John Ireland, Betsy Palmer and Lucy Marlow co-star. 95 min.
02-2797 *$19.99*

Autumn Leaves (1956)
Joan Crawford stars as a lonely, middle-aged spinster who finds the love she always longed for with a handsome younger man, unaware of the dark secrets in his past, in Robert Aldrich's classic melodrama. With Cliff Robertson, Vera Miles, Lorne Greene. 108 min.
02-2537 *$19.99*

The Story Of Esther Costello (1957)
While on vacation in Ireland to forget her failed marriage, wealthy American socialite Joan Crawford takes an interest in the plight of a young girl left blind, deaf and mute since a childhood trauma and brings her back to the States to try and help cure her. Movingly acted melodrama also stars Rossano Brazzi, Lee Patterson, and Heather Sears as Esther. 102 min.
02-2984 *$19.99*

The Best Of Everything (1959)
Follow the tumultuous affairs of a group of women trying to juggle romantic fulfillment with a career in New York's publishing industry in this glossy, soap-styled drama. Diane Baker, Martha Hyer, Hope Lange and Suzy Parker are the ladies; Stephen Boyd, Robert Evans and Louis Jourdan are among the men in their lives; and Joan Crawford plays the no-nonsense boss. 121 min.
04-2926 *$19.99*

The Caretakers (1963)
Unusual medical drama with Robert Stack as a concerned doctor at a West Coast mental hospital trying to help new patient Polly Bergen, wracked with guilt over her child's accidental death. Joan Crawford is memorable as the judo-tossing head nurse who dominates her charges. With Diane McBain, Van Williams, Janis Paige, Robert Vaughn. 97 min.
12-2982 *$19.99*

Berserk! (1967)
Circus owner Joan Crawford sees her sales receipts soar after a series of sadistic murders of her performers. See the tightrope walker fall to his death into a bed of bayonets! See Joan's partner with a spike through his head! See Diana Dors sawed in half! Also stars Judy Geeson. 96 min.
02-1720 Was $69.99 *$19.99*

Trog (1970)
TROG! Missing link between man and beast! TROG! Found living in a cave by anthropologist Joan Crawford (her final film role)! TROG! Caught and caged, he escapes to wreak havoc on the English countryside! TROG! Ain't no stoppin' him now! TROG! Mark this flick in your horror film log! With Michael Gough, Bernard Kay, and Joe Cornelius as Trog. 91 min.
19-2250 Was $19.99 *$14.99*

Joan Crawford: Always A Star
Her struggle to overcome an impoverished childhood and her rise to Hollywood fame mirrored many of her still-popular movies. Learn the true story behind Joan Crawford's tempestuous career and stormy family life in this documentary. Clips from "Grand Hotel," "Rain," "The Women" and "What Ever Happened to Baby Jane?" and other films, plus interviews with Diane Baker, Cliff Robertson and daughter Cindy, are featured. 57 min.
50-7614 *$14.99*

The Joan Crawford Collection
Put-upon heroine or unstable manipulator? You decide with this boxed set of three of Joan's classic films: "Humoresque," "Mildred Pierce" and the 1947 drama "Possessed."
12-2527 Save $10.00! *$49.99*

Please see our index for these other Joan Crawford titles: *Dancing Lady • Grand Hotel • I Saw What You Did • Reunion In France • Strait-Jacket • Tramp, Tramp, Tramp • What Ever Happened To Baby Jane?*

Tomorrow's Youth (1935)
Dickie Moore is the young child trying to face the trauma of divorce when his parents go their own separate ways in this teary drama. John Miljan and Franklin Pangborn co-star. 63 min.
09-5076 *$19.99*

The Barefoot Boy (1938)
A wholesome youngster tries to teach a spoiled newcomer to the neighborhood a lesson before he and his pals accept him into his group in this drama. Jackie Moran, Marcia Mae Jones star. 60 min.
09-5164 *$19.99*

Circus Girl (1937)
The big top is the setting for this drama in which performers Bob Livingston and Donald Cook compete for the love of June Travis. Features terrific aerial routines performed by the Escalante family. With Betty Compson. 64 min.
09-5169 *$19.99*

Easy Money (1936)
A gangster is murdered for trying to abandon his life of crime, and his insurance investigator brother attempts to find those responsible. His search leads to a group of gangsters and their sleazy attorney. Onslow Stevens, Kay Linaker and Noel Madison star in this strong crime drama. 70 min.
09-5172 *$19.99*

Killers Of The Sea (1937)
Documentary-like account of a ship captain who has won acclaim for finishing off such "killers of the sea" as sharks, swordfish and octopi. Lowell Thomas narrates; Wallace Caswell, Bruce Stilwell and Hubert Dykes star. 48 min.
09-5177 *$19.99*

The Challenge (1938)
Early mountain climbing drama set against the majesty of the Matterhorn and the Swiss Alps. Luis Trenker, Robert Douglas star; spectacular photography. 77 min.
09-1301 *$19.99*

The Fighting Rookie (1934)
Crackerjack police yarn with usual bad guy Jack LaRue playing a cop who's set up and has to go undercover to prove his innocence. 65 min.
09-2132 Was $29.99 *$14.99*

Owd Bob (1938)
Affecting drama about an elderly Scottish farmer who finds his life complicated when his new, young neighbor enters his sheepdog in competition against the farmer's pooch. At the same time, his daughter takes a liking to the neighbor. Will Fyfe, Margaret Lockwood and John Loder star. AKA: "To the Victor." 78 min.
09-5066 *$19.99*

Law Of The Sea (1932)
A castaway family is rescued by a sadistic skipper who blinds the father in a fight and assaults his wife, who later kills herself. Years later, the chance for revenge occurs. William Farnum, Rex Bell, Priscilla Dean star. 60 min.
09-2144 Was $24.99 *$14.99*

Small Town Boy (1937)
A nobody finds a $1,000 bill and lots of sudden attention from the local townspeople. Overnight, he transforms from humble sap to ruthless businessman. Broadway-based character study stars Stuart Erwin and Joyce Compton. 61 min.
09-2256 Was $24.99 *$14.99*

Ladies Crave Excitement (1935)
The world of movie newsreels was the setting for this unusual drama about two rival news companies who fight to be "first on the scene." Norman Foster, Evelyn Knapp star. 57 min.
10-1352 *$19.99*

Show Them No Mercy (1935)
A young couple and their child are taken hostage by kidnappers hiding out from the law in this suspenseful thriller, later remade as the 1951 western "Rawhide." Bruce Cabot, Edward Norris, Rochelle Hudson and Cesar Romero star. 76 min.
04-2410 *$19.99*

Charles Dickens

Oliver Twist (1933)
Dickie Moore and William Boyd star in Dickens' classic of the escapades of orphan boy. Well-mounted re-creation of Dickens' London is perfect for those who enjoy a tear or two. 70 min.
10-1078 *$14.99*

Oliver Twist (1948)
The first British sound filming of the Dickens novel, David Lean's classic drama is highlighted by Alec Guinness' portrayal of the sinister Fagin. Robert Newton is menacing Bill Sikes, a young Anthony Newley is the Artful Dodger, and John Howard Davies is little Oliver. 111 min.
06-1531 Was $19.99 *$14.99*

Oliver Twist (1985)
Exceptional version from the BBC of Dickens' timeless tale of the plucky urchin pitted against the pitfalls of the London streets. First-rate production stars Eric Porter, Frank Middlemass, and Ben Rodska as Oliver. 333 min.
04-1112 *$29.99*

Great Expectations (1934)
The first sound filming of the Charles Dickens novel follows the lifelong quest of diligent young orphan Pip (Phillips Holmes) to win the heart of true love Estella (Jane Wyatt). With Henry Hull, Alan Hale and Florence Reed as the demented Miss Havisham. 102 min.
07-2621 *❏$14.99*

Great Expectations (1974)
A lush telling of the Charles Dickens tale of Pip, an orphan who escapes his lower-class life after meeting an escaped convict and the deranged Miss Havisham. Michael York, Sarah Miles, James Mason and Robert Morley star. 124 min.
27-6825 Was $19.99 *$14.99*

Great Expectations (1981)
Sumptuous rendition of Dickens' masterpiece regarding the life and times of Pip, a penurious boy who's vaulted to wealth by a unknown benefactor. Epic version from the BBC stars Gerry Sundquist, Strafford Johns, Joan Hickson. 300 min.
04-1111 *$29.99*

Great Expectations (1989)
A distinguished cast, including Anthony Hopkins, Jean Simmons and John Rhys-Davies, heads up this grand three-tape adaptation of the perennially popular Dickens tale of young Pip and his adventures in Victorian London. 310 min.
11-1538 *❏$49.99*

Great Expectations (1999)
In 19th-century England, a tenacious orphan named Pip is saved from a life of squalor by a mysterious benefactor and sets out to win the hand of the woman he grew up with in this "Masterpiece Theatre" adaptation of Dickens' novel. Ioan Gruffudd ("Horatio Hornblower") stars as Pip; with Justine Waddell, Bernard Hill, and Charlotte Rampling as Miss Havisham. 180 min. on two tapes.
08-8756 *❏$29.99*

The Mystery Of Edwin Drood (1935)
The famous unfinished last work of Charles Dickens served as the basis for this moody and suspenseful Universal thriller. Claude Rains stars as a respected choirmaster whose secret life includes opium addiction and unrequited love for the fiancée of his nephew Edwin, an obsession that leads to murder. With Heather Angel, David Manners. 86 min.
07-2428 *$14.99*

A Tale Of Two Cities (1935)
The fifth filmization (and first sound version) of Charles Dickens' masterpiece, set against the turmoil of the French Revolution, boasts an all-star cast that includes Ronald Colman, Basil Rathbone, Reginald Owen, Edna May Oliver and Elizabeth Allan. 120 min.
12-1076 *$19.99*

A Tale Of Two Cities (1980)
"It is a far, far better thing" that Chris Sarandon does in this sweeping rendition of Charles Dickens' timeless tale, as the lives and loves of several people are forever changed by the turmoil of the French Revolution. The stellar cast includes Peter Cushing, Alice Krige, Barry Morse, Billie Whitelaw. 158 min.
27-6809 Was $19.99 *$14.99*

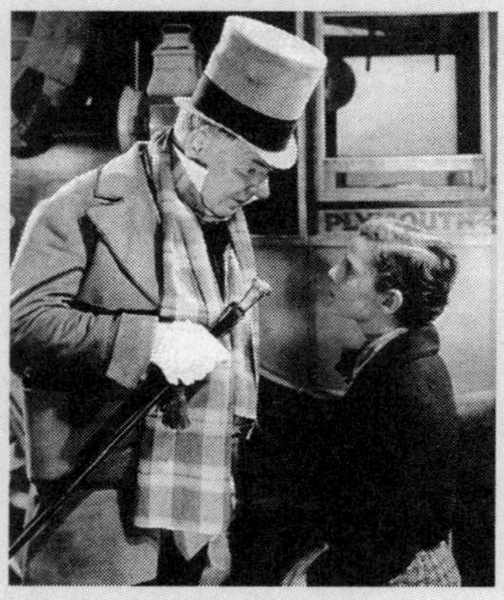

David Copperfield (1935)
Charles Dickens' plucky boy hero is well-served in this lavish production, featuring the best casting ever for a Hollywood "literary film." Basil Rathbone, W.C. Fields, Edna May Oliver and Roland Young star, with Freddie Bartholomew as David. 130 min.
12-1437 *$19.99*

David Copperfield (1970)
This lavish British production of the Charles Dickens classic is told in flashback from the 28-year-old David Copperfield's point of view. He recalls his incredible experiences with his mean stepfather, days at a boarding school, romances, and encounter with the swindler Uriah Heep. Richard Attenborough, Robin Phillips, Laurence Olivier, Ron Moody and Susan Hampshire star. 118 min.
10-1592 Was $19.99 *$14.99*

David Copperfield (1999)
This epic "Masterpiece Theatre" version of Charles Dickens' classic tells of a young fatherless boy's adventures in 19th-century England and the extraordinary experiences he has. Bob Hoskins plays forever-in-debt guardian Micawber, Maggie Smith eccentric Aunt Betsey Trotwood, Ian McKellen abusive headmaster Mr. Creakle, and Daniel Radcliffe is David. 210 min.
08-8871 *❏$29.99*

The Old Curiosity Shop (1935)
A superb adaptation of the Charles Dickens novel. A shopowner with a penchant for gambling and his granddaughter face a life on the London streets if they are evicted from their home by their landlord, the grotesque Mr. Quilp. Ben Webster, Elaine Benson and Hay Petrie star. 92 min.
63-1646 Was $19.99 *$14.99*

The Old Curiosity Shop (1994)
Peter Ustinov is the kindly shopkeeper, Sally Walsh his granddaughter, Little Nell, and Tom Courtenay the conniving Mr. Quilp in this filming of the beloved Charles Dickens story. 190 min.
88-1012 Was $19.99 *❏$14.99*

Nicholas Nickleby (1947)
Charles Dickens' immortal novel is brought to the screen by a top-notch British cast. A poor young man encounters every extreme of Victorian society in his attempts to better his family. Derek Bond, Cedric Hardwicke, Sally Ann Howes. 106 min.
08-8044 Was $19.99 *$14.99*

The Life And Adventures Of Nicholas Nickleby: Complete Boxed Set (1982)
A stunning adaptation of Charles Dickens' classic story of a young boy's adventures in not-so merry old England, where he overcomes his horrible experiences at school and his uncle's nefarious schemes to find happiness in a theatrical troupe. Roger Rees and the Royal Shakespeare Company star in this award-winning stage production. 540 min. total on nine tapes.
53-8152 Was $149.99 *$99.99*

The Pickwick Papers (1952)
The timeless adventures of Charles Dickens' Pickwick Club come to life in this lively adaptation, featuring a cast of renowned British actors. James Hayter stars as Pickwick, with Hermione Baddeley, Nigel Patrick, Donald Wolfit and Kathleen Harrison. 109 min.
08-1413 Was $19.99 *$14.99*

Bleak House (1985)
Stellar BBC adaptation of the Dickens classic concerning the heartbreaking revelations a young man uncovers when he investigates the lawsuit that nearly ruined his mentor years before. Denholm Elliott, Diana Rigg. 391 min.
04-1113 *$39.99*

Little Dorrit: Nobody's Fault (1988)
The first part of the acclaimed adaptation of Dickens' satiric novel of changing fortunes focuses on middle-aged Arthur Clennam, a directionless Londoner who becomes fascinated with a girl from debtor's prison working at his mother's house, young Amy Dorrit. Joan Greenwood, Sarah Pickering, Roshan Seth and Alec Guinness star. 176 min.
19-7056 Was $29.99 *$24.99*

Little Dorrit: Little Dorrit's Story (1988)
Amy Dorrit and her family are the subject of the conclusion of this ambitious epic: their decades in the poorhouse where Amy was born; the windfall that changes the status of patriarch William (Alec Guinness); and the clan's difficult adjustment to sudden affluence. With Cyril Cusack, Sarah Pickering, Robert Morley and Derek Jacobi. 184 min.
19-7057 Was $29.99 *$24.99*

Martin Chuzzlewit (1996)
Social comedy and serious drama blend in this BBC adaptation of Charles Dickens' tale. Greed turns the family and friends of Martin Chuzzlewit, a wealthy but embittered old man, against one another as they scheme to inherit his fortune. The cast includes Paul Scofield, John Mills, Tom Wilkinson and Julia Sawalha. 288 min. on three tapes.
04-3419 Was $59.99 *$39.99*

Our Mutual Friend (1998)
Based on Charles Dickens' novel, this lavish "Masterpiece Theatre" production is set in 1860s London and concerns two converging love affairs, one involving a millionaire's son who fakes his own death in order to avoid a loveless marriage, the other focusing on the daughter of the boatman suspected in the son's "murder." Paul McGann, Keely Hawkes, Anna Friel star. 339 min.
04-3801 *$39.99*

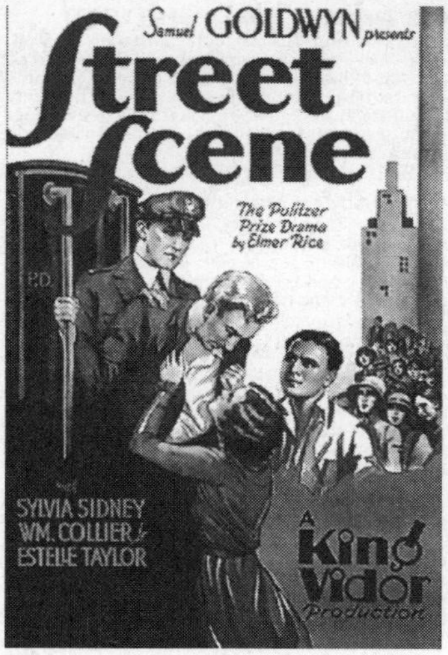

Street Scene (1931)
The dispirited and static lives of the residents of New York City's tenements in the '30s are realistically portrayed in Elmer Rice's adaptation of his Pulitzer Prize-winning play about a love triangle that boils over into violence; features a classic score by Alfred Newman. Sylvia Sidney, David Landau, Estelle Taylor star; King Vidor directs. 80 min.
10-4032 *$19.99*

The Duke Of West Point (1938)
Louis Hayward stars in this rah-rah drama, playing a Cambridge graduate who goes to West Point and becomes a football and hockey star while romancing Joan Fontaine, a pretty young woman popular with the plebes. Richard Carlson, Tom Brown and Alan Curtis co-star. 107 min.
08-1781 *$19.99*

The Mill On The Floss (1939)
George Eliot's classic Victorian drama of two people whose romance is threatened by their different stations in life is exquisitely brought to the screen. James Mason and Geraldine Fitzgerald head an impressive cast. 80 min.
08-8009 Was $19.99 *$14.99*

The Mill On The Floss (1997)
Emily Watson stars as headstrong heroine Maggie Tulliver, whose romance with the son of her family's bitter enemy is threatened from all sides, in this stirring British TV adaptation of the George Eliot novel. Cheryl Campbell, James Frain, Bernard Hill also star. 120 min.
08-8610 *❏$19.99*

Craig's Wife (1936)
Rosalind Russell stars in this intense drama of an unloving woman who marries for money, but soon learns that her obsessive ways brought her nothing but loneliness. John Boles, Billie Burke co-star. 75 min.
02-1609 Was $59.99 *$19.99*

Bird Of Paradise (1932)
Lavish Hawaiian location shots and great special effects highlight this early South Seas drama, with Joel McCrea as a Western playboy who falls for native beauty Dolores Del Rio. John Halliday, Lon Chaney, Jr. and an erupting volcano star; King Vidor directs. 82 min. X
08-8036 Was $19.99 *$14.99*

The Devil's Party (1938)
Victor McLaglen stars in this drama about a grown-up band of "Hell's Kitchen" boys whose yearly reunion is marred when one is killed. William Gargan, Paul Kelly, Beatrice Roberts star. 65 min.
10-1140 Was $19.99 *$14.99*

Social Error (1935)
Wild college student David Sharpe gets into one scrape after another—fighting with a bully in a cafe and fleeing the police in a stolen car—and is threatened with expulsion. Can he turn his life around by rescuing a kidnapped heiress? With Gertrude Messinger, Monte Blue, Fred "Snowflake" Toones.
68-9240 *$19.99*

Two Minutes To Play (1936)
Following in their fathers' footsteps, college football heroes Herman Brix and Eddie Nugents are rivals on the field and for the hand of a pretty coed in this gridiron drama. Betty Compson, Jeanne Martel, Duncan Renaldo also star. 74 min.
68-9253 *$19.99*

Female Fugitive (1938)
Evelyn Venable is forced to go on the run from the law when she's unfairly implicated in her husband's truck-hijacking operation. She falls for artist Reed Hadley, but the past—and her conniving spouse—catch up to her in this crime drama. Craig Reynolds, John Kelly also star. 60 min.
68-9267 *$19.99*

The Scarlet Letter (1934)
Hawthorne's classic drama of 17th-century Puritan life and one woman whose love secret caused her to wear the letter of shame. Colleen Moore, William Farnum star. 69 min.
10-3011 *$19.99*

Probation (1932)
Betty Grable makes one of her first appearances in this programmer about a judge who sentences a playboy to serve as his daughter's chauffeur. Sally Blane and Eddie Phillips star. 60 min.
68-8354 *$19.99*

The Strange Love Of Molly Louvain (1932)
Ann Dvorak is the title character, a hotel worker whose affair with a playboy leaves her pregnant. After he abandons her, she finds company with a criminal, a bellhop and a newspaper reporter, all of whom lead her into various types of trouble. Lee Tracy, Leslie Fenton and Richard Cromwell also star in this steamy (for its time) social drama; directed by Michael Curtiz. 72 min.
12-2886 *$19.99*

The Big House (1930)
Pioneering, Oscar-winning prison drama follows three convicts and their life in and out of "the big house." Forger Chester Morris escapes and vows to go straight after finding love, while tough killer Wallace Beery's plans for a big breakout are thwarted when young con Robert Montgomery turns stoolie. Lewis Stone, Leila Hyams also star. 86 min.
12-2922 *$19.99*

Our Daily Bread (1934)
Directed by King Vidor, who saw the film as a rural counterpart to his earlier "The Crowd," this powerful social drama follows a couple who inherit a run-down farm. Taking on unemployed men and organizing the farm into a collective, they struggle to survive a withering drought, but a visiting vamp from the city tempts the husband. Tom Keene, Karen Morley, Barbara Pepper star. 71 min.
17-1107 *$19.99*

Love Affair (1939)
Irene Dunne and Charles Boyer are magnificent as the couple whose ocean liner romance before their respective marriages blossoms into more than either had counted on, and whose love overcomes hardship. The first version of the oft-filmed tear-jerker also features Maria Ouspenskaya, Lee Bowman. Original, theatrical version; 87 min.
17-3001 Was $19.99 *$14.99*

Gangster's Boy (1938)
Child star Jackie Cooper branched out into older roles with this crime drama about a high schooler haunted by his father's ex-convict past. In order to make amends, he takes a murder rap for a well-to-do friend. Lucy Gilman, Robert Warwick co-star. 80 min.
17-9052 Was $19.99 *$14.99*

Les Miserables (1935)
Magnificently staged version of the classic Victor Hugo tale of justice and the law. Fredric March is Jean Valjean, a petty thief in 18th-century France who escapes jail and begins a new life, and Charles Laughton is the unfeeling detective obsessed with his capture. Also stars Cedric Hardwicke, Rochelle Hudson. 104 min.
04-1029 Was $29.99 *$14.99*

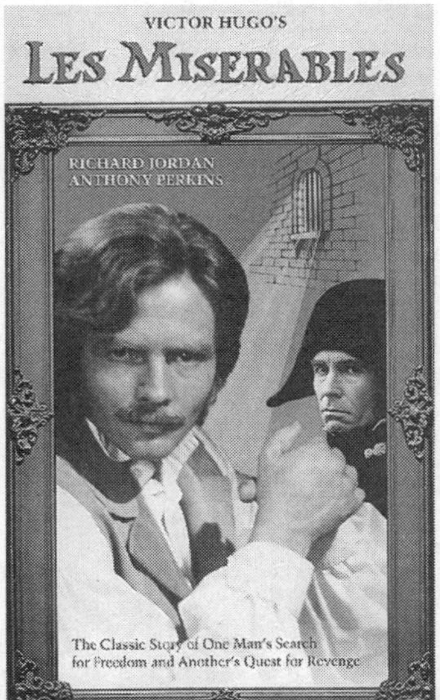

Les Miserables (1978)
Richard Jordan is escaped convict Jean Valjean and Anthony Perkins relentless pursuer Inspector Javert in this literate rendition of Victor Hugo's novel. With Sir John Gielgud, Ian Holm and Cyril Cusack. 123 min.
27-6824 Was $19.99 *$14.99*

Les Miserables (1998)
Lavish, superbly acted adaptation of Victor Hugo's classic stars Liam Neeson as Jean Valjean, the fugitive who has become a mayor in France during the 1820s. Tragically, Valjean's past haunts him in the form of tenacious Inspector Javert (Geoffrey Rush), a former guard at the prison from which Valjean escaped. Uma Thurman and Claire Danes also star; Bille August directs. 134 min.
02-3228 Was $99.99 *$14.99*

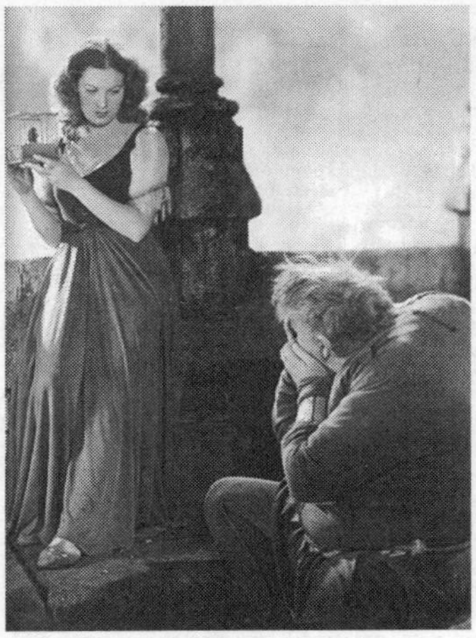

The Hunchback Of Notre Dame (1939)
Charles Laughton gives a stunning and touching performance as Quasimodo, the deformed bellringer in 15th-century Paris who is befriended by Gypsy girl Maureen O'Hara. Cedric Hardwicke and Edmond O'Brien also star in this classic period drama, the first sound rendition of Victor Hugo's novel. Special video release includes the original trailer, a "making of" documentary, and an interview with O'Hara. 115 min.
05-1328 *$19.99*

The Hunchback Of Notre Dame (1957)
Colorful filming of the Victor Hugo story stars Anthony Quinn as misshapen bellringer Quasimodo, who defies both Church and crown to save Gypsy dancer Gina Lollobrigida from death. With Jean Danet, Alain Cuny. 104 min.
11-2106 Was $99.99 *$19.99*

Hunchback (1982)
Anthony Hopkins shines in the title role of Quasimodo in this stirring adaptation of Victor Hugo's "The Hunchback of Notre Dame." Leslie-Anne Down is the beautiful Esmerelda, who steals the hunchback's heart, and Derek Jacobi and Sir John Gielgud also star. 102 min.
68-1178 Was $89.99 *$12.99*

The Hunchback (1997)
This superb adaptation of Victor Hugo's classic story features Mandy Patinkin as Quasimodo, the tortured bell-ringer of the Notre Dame cathedral; Salma Hayek as the beautiful Gypsy woman, Esmerelda; and Richard Harris as Frollo, the man of God driven by lust to murder. 100 min.
19-2583 Was $99.99 *$19.99*

Hotel Continental (1932)
Made and released shortly before the premiere of "Grand Hotel," this crime drama involves a former jewel thief who returns to the title hotel searching for the gems he stashed there years before, but is forced to wait after discovering the room where the loot is hidden is occupied. With Theodore Von Eltz, Peggy Shannon, Alan Mowbray. 55 min.
17-3005 *$19.99*

Boy Of The Streets (1937)
Striking social drama stars Jackie Cooper as a troubled teenager from the Bowery who commands a rebellious gang of youths, but performs a complete turnaround when he becomes the target of a gangster's bullet. With Maureen O'Connor, Marjorie Main. 74 min.
17-3016 *$24.99*

Clipped Wings (1936)
Two decades after his aviator half-brother is reported missing in action during the Great War, flyboy William Jannings sets out to nab a gang of racketeers with the help of a G-man, whose striking resemblance to his missing relative proves to be more than a coincidence. Co-stars Lloyd Hughes, Rosalind Keith, Jason Robards, Sr. 61 min.
17-3020 *$19.99*

Convention Girl (1935)
Forget the plot of this ol' programmer, and just drink in those nostalgic, amazing location shots of Atlantic City! The diving horse at Steel Pier, the rolling chairs, the big beaches, the gambling (in the back room, of course)...All this, and Shemp Howard, too? What are you waiting for? 66 min.
17-3021 Was $19.99 *$14.99*

By Appointment Only (1933)
Lew Cody, Aileen Pringle and Sally O'Neill star in this melodrama about a doctor who becomes the guardian of a patient whose mother has recently died. Although he's engaged, he begins to have feelings for the new woman in his life. 66 min.
17-9008 Was $19.99 *$14.99*

Bank Alarm (1937)
Crime programmer with Conrad Nagel as a tough G-man who puts the life of his girlfriend (Eleanor Hunt) in jeopardy while on the trail of ruthless bank robbers. Co-stars Vince Barnett, Frank Milan and Wheeler Oakman. 64 min.
17-9042 *$19.99*

Gorilla Ship (1932)
While on a trip on his yacht, a wealthy businessman suspects his best friend is flirting with his wife. Ralph Ince, Vera Reynolds and Reed Howes star. 60 min.
17-9054 Was $19.99 *$14.99*

South Riding (1938)
Acclaimed British drama set in an area of Yorkshire and focusing on a number of its residents, including a squire and his emotionally troubled wife, teenage daughter and girlfriend, and a headmistress, a preacher, and a socialist. Ralph Richardson, Ann Todd, Glynis Johns and Edmund Gwenn star. 84 min.
17-9076 *$14.99*

Dodsworth (1936)
Upon reaching success, an American businessman finds he is in danger of losing his wife and the secure life he built for himself in this dramatic adaptation of Sinclair Lewis' novel. Walter Huston stars in the title role; David Niven, Mary Astor co-star. William Wyler directs. 101 min.
44-1839 Was $19.99 *$14.99*

Rembrandt (1936)
Charles Laughton paints an unforgettable film portrait in this biodrama of the 17th-century Dutch artist, focusing on his later years and the depression he suffered after the death of his wife. Elsa Lanchester, Gertrude Lawrence also star in this Alexander Korda production. 84 min.
44-1892 Was $19.99 *$14.99*

The Edge Of The World (1937)
Director Michael Powell's first major success is an engrossing account of life on Foula, a Shetland Island off the coast of Scotland, where a young man must choose between staying on the dying island with his pregnant girlfriend or leaving for the mainland. Finlay Currie, Niall MacGinnis and Grant Sutherland star in this striking drama. 80 min.
53-6052 Was $29.99 *$19.99*

The Struggle (1931)
Pioneering director D.W. Griffith's final film, the melodramatic story of a mill worker who drinks tainted "bathtub gin" that sends him on a downward spiral of alcoholic despair, was seen as both a temperance picture and a condemnation of Prohibition, and was re-released years later as a comedy! Hal Skelly, Zita Johann, Edna Hagan star; co-scripted by Anita Loos. 77 min.
53-8628 Remastered *$24.99*

Turn Of The Tide (1935)
Dramatic look at a family in a Yorkshire fishing village, and the rivalry between the family and a new group of people who move there. John Garrick, Geraldine Fitzgerald and Sam Livesey star. 80 min.
17-9083 Was $19.99 *$14.99*

Exiled To Shanghai (1937)
Fascinating drama with a journalism background stars Wallace Ford as a cameraman fired by editor Dean Jagger for photographing the wrong general during the Spanish Civil War. After establishing a television newsreel service(!), Ford is hired as an editor for his former news agency and finds himself battling Jagger over the hand of June Travis. 60 min.
55-3047 *$19.99*

Port Of Lost Dreams (1935)
Gritty, romantic crime drama involving a gun moll who hides out on a fishing ship where she eventually falls for the vessel's captain. Unfortunately, her life of crime gets in the way of the couple's happiness and she's arrested by the authorities, forcing the skipper to take extreme measures. Lola Lane, Morgan Rock star. 70 min.
55-3059 *$19.99*

Reckless Way (1936)
A blue-collar woman becomes a Hollywood star, but finds that success has a way of interfering with her love life, in this melodrama. Inez Courtney, Harry Harvey and Arthur Howard star. 70 min.
55-3060 *$19.99*

Murder In The Night (1939)
Snappy crime drama from England centering on a Chicago gangster situated in London who operates a nightclub as a cover for his illicit activities. When he guns down one of his associates, the man's wife pretends to fall for the hood in order to implicate him in the crime. Jack LaRue, Sandra Storme, Bernard Lee and Googie Winters star. AKA: "Murder in Soho." 70 min.
68-9126 *$19.99*

The Flying Irishman (1939)
Legendary aviator Douglas "Wrong Way" Corrigan, who made headlines in 1938 when his planned New York-to-California flight landed him in Ireland (which some say was his goal all along), stars as himself in this high-flying drama based on his exploits. With Paul Kelly, Robert Armstrong, Gene Reynolds. 70 min.
65-3007 *$19.99*

Paul Robeson

Body And Soul (1925)
The legendary Paul Robeson made his film debut in this rare all-black silent feature, playing a scheming escaped convict who masquerades as a preacher in a small Southern town where he gives free rein to his vices. Julia T. Russell, Mercedes Gilbert co-star; directed by pioneering African-American filmmaker Oscar Micheaux. 102 min. Silent with music score.
53-9943 *$24.99*

The Emperor Jones (1933)
Early film adaptation of the Eugene O'Neill play, with Paul Robeson giving an unforgettable performance as the Pullman porter sentenced to prison for an accidental killing who escapes to a Caribbean island, where he becomes a feared ruler. With Dudley Digges, Frank Wilson. BONUS: Also includes a half-hour documentary on Paul Robeson narrated by Sidney Poitier. 101 min. total.
22-5531 *$19.99*

Sanders Of The River (1935)
A dated but intriguing adventure drama, set in British colonial Africa and based on an Edgar Wallace story. Leslie Banks is Sanders, the government official charged with keeping the peace, and Paul Robeson is a loyal native assistant. AKA: "Coast of Skeletons." 98 min.
10-3027 *$19.99*

Song Of Freedom (1936)
A stevedore-turned-opera singer (Paul Robeson) leaves England for Africa in an effort to trace his royal ancestry. While there he helps rid a village of disease and the tyrannical influence of a local witch doctor. Co-stars Elizabeth Welch, George Mozart. 80 min.
53-9944 *$24.99*

Big Fella (1937)
Marseilles dockworker Paul Robeson finds a missing boy who ran away from his uncaring family on an ocean liner, but when the child says he'll accuse Robeson of kidnapping if he tries to return him, the only option is to hide him and, with a local cafe songstress, serve as substitute parents. Warm, song-filled tale also stars Elisabeth Welch, Eldon Grant. 73 min.
53-9274 *$24.99*

Jericho (Dark Sands) (1937)
Court-martialed and sentenced to die for the accidental death of his sergeant, Army corporal Paul Robeson escapes and flees into the deserts of North Africa. There he goes on to become ruler of a sheikdom, but the officer who let Robeson get away vows to track him down. Robeson sings "Golden River," "Silent Night" and other songs in this compelling drama that also stars Henry Wilcoxon. 75 min.
53-9942 *$24.99*

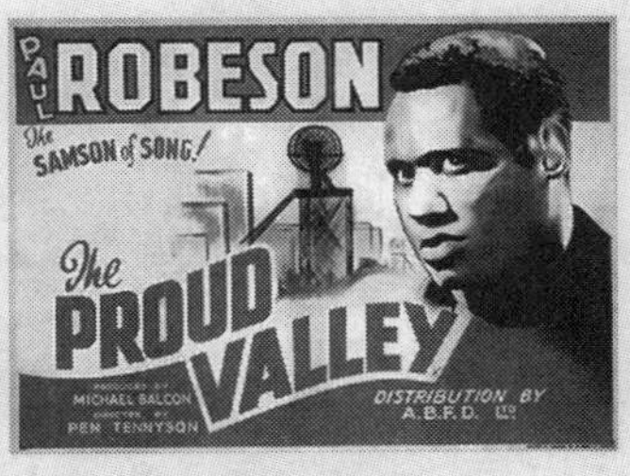

The Proud Valley (1941)
Paul Robeson excels as a stoker in a Welsh coal town whose marvelous singing voice brings attention from the townspeople who want him to sing in their choir. When an accident kills the man responsible for getting Robeson the job, he puts his life on the line to save the mine. Edward Chapman and Simon Lack co-star in this Ealing Studios production. 77 min.
10-1589 *$19.99*

Native Land (1942)
A powerful blend of wartime film propaganda and political activism, this independent film depicts through a series of vignettes assaults on the basic rights of all Americans and calls for a renewed spirit of patriotism. The cast includes Fred Johnson, Mary George, Howard da Silva; Paul Robeson narrates. 88 min.
53-7985 Was $59.99 *$29.99*

Paul Robeson: The Tallest Tree In Our Forest (1977)
A fine documentary on the life of actor, activist and singer Paul Robeson, this study looks at Robeson's controversial politics and their influence on African-American society today.
10-9096 *$19.99*

Paul Robeson: Here I Stand (1998)
Produced for the "American Masters" series, this superior look at the life of Paul Robeson delves into the man's many talents, as well as the actions that made him a controversial figure in his own country. Along with interviews with Harry Belafonte and Pete Seeger, this program includes rare photos, footage and a performance of "Ol' Man River." Ossie Davis narrates. 117 min.
53-6535 *$19.99*

Please see our index for these other Paul Robeson titles: *King Solomon's Mines • Show Boat • Tales Of Manhattan*

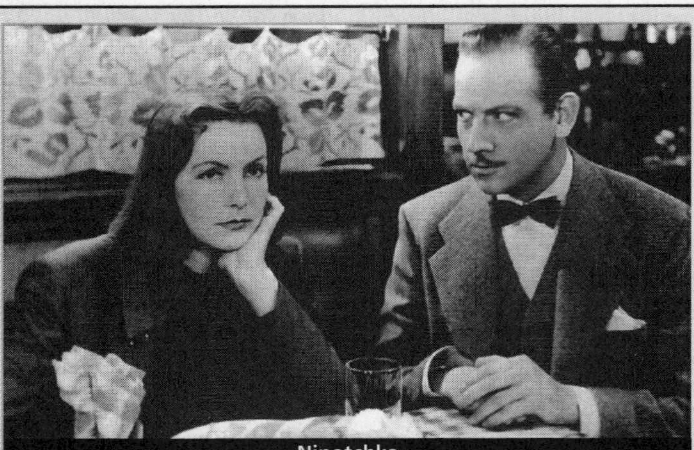
Ninotchka

Greta Garbo

Gösta Berling's Saga (1924)
In her second film role, Greta Garbo plays a young married woman who becomes the object of a defrocked priest's attentions. Moving Swedish drama of lost love and redemption, directed by Garbo's mentor, Mauritz Stiller, also stars Lars Hanson. AKA: "Atonement of Gösta Berling," "The Saga of Gösta Berling." 93 min. Silent with music score.
09-5383 *$19.99*

Joyless Street (1925)
Greta Garbo turns in an alluring performance in this acclaimed silent drama detailing the plight of two young women in post-WWI Vienna. Also stars Asta Nielsen, Werner Krauss; directed by G.W. Pabst. 96 min.
53-7465 *$24.99*

Flesh And The Devil (1926)
Sumptuous silent melodrama stars Greta Garbo as a seductive wife who leads military man John Gilbert down a path of temptation that culminates on the "field of honor." First screen pairing for the duo, who became off-screen lovers as well. 113 min. Silent with music score.
12-1135 *$29.99*

A Woman Of Affairs (1928)
Lavish silent melodrama stars Greta Garbo and John Gilbert as lovers whose marriage plans are shattered by Gilbert's father. Afterwards, Garbo embarks on a series of romantic escapades that end in tragedy. With Lewis Stone, Douglas Fairbanks, Jr. 108 min. Silent with music score.
12-2146 *$29.99*

The Mysterious Lady (1928)
Russian spy Greta Garbo tries to seduce Austrian officer Conrad Nagel, only to fall for him and be forced to choose between love and country, in this lush silent costume drama. 99 min. Silent with musical score.
12-2224 *$29.99*

Wild Orchids (1929)
In this romantic silent drama set in Java, Greta Garbo shines as a woman who must choose between neglectful husband Lewis Stone and handsome native prince Nils Asther. 119 min. Silent with musical score.
12-1392 *$29.99*

The Single Standard (1929)
Glossy silent melodrama stars Greta Garbo as a free-spirited woman who, refusing to be tied down to one man, spurns a handsome millionaire's proposal to embark on a series of doomed affairs before learning her lesson. Nils Asther and B-western star John Mack Brown co-star. 73 min. Silent with musical score.
12-2221 *$29.99*

The Kiss (1929)
In her last silent film, Greta Garbo plays a woman on trial for allegedly killing her husband to protect a young man he suspected her of having an affair with. In court she is defended by her true love, attorney Conrad Nagel. Lew Ayres co-stars. 62 min. Silent with music score.
12-2220 *$29.99*

Anna Christie (1930)
Greta Garbo proves her greatness as an enigmatic screen presence in this romance, her first talkie. Eugene O'Neill wrote the story, about a relationship between Garbo and sailor Charles Bickford. 90 min.
12-1391 *$19.99*

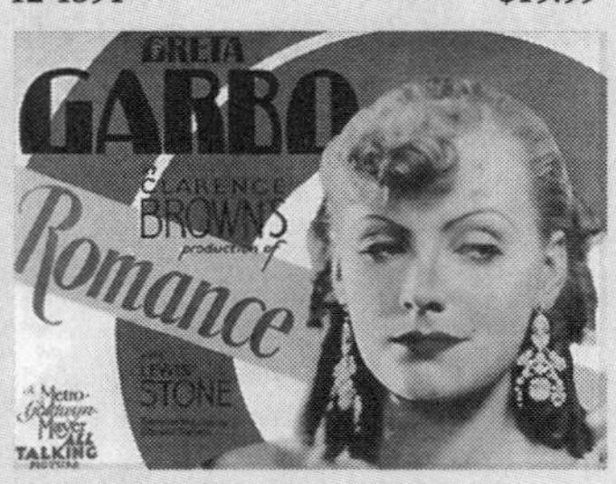

Romance (1930)
Fine romantic drama about an elderly bishop who warns his grandson about marrying an actress by relating the story of his infatuation with an Italian opera singer years before. Greta Garbo is alluring and mysterious as the diva; with Lewis Stone, Gavin Gordon, Elliott Nugent. 76 min.
12-2305 *$19.99*

Inspiration (1930)
Greta Garbo brings her special brand of sensuality to this tale of a Parisian model with a lurid background whose love affair with a French bureaucrat endures years of struggle. Robert Montgomery, Lewis Stone, Karen Morley also star in this romantic tale based on the novel "Sappho." 73 min.
12-2306 *$19.99*

Mata Hari (1931)
The famed spy who used her seductive charms for the Germans in World War I is vividly portrayed by Greta Garbo in this thrilling, if somewhat fictionalized, biodrama. Lionel Barrymore and Ramon Novarro co-star as two of Garbo's many conquests. 90 min.
12-2103 *□$19.99*

Susan Lenox: Her Fall And Rise (1931)
Greta Garbo and Clark Gable meet on screen for the only time in this sprawling romantic drama offering lots of sparks between the two performers. She's the daughter of a poor farmer who seems to run from man to man and country to country in search of her destiny. He's the successful architect whose life turns sour when she leaves him. With Jean Hersholt and Alan Hale. 74 min.
12-2102 *$19.99*

Grand Hotel (1932)
Welcome to Grand Hotel—a beautiful Berlin hotel filled with palatial splendor and occupied by a galaxy of MGM's greatest stars. Comedy and drama are mixed in 1932's Best Picture Oscar-winner. John and Lionel Barrymore, Greta Garbo, Joan Crawford, Wallace Beery, Lewis Stone and Jean Hersholt head the stellar cast. 113 min.
12-1411 *□$19.99*

As You Desire Me (1932)
Intriguing drama stars the ever-mysterious Greta Garbo as an amnesiac countess led by her Svengali-like lover to a life as a nightclub singer, until she is returned to her real husband. Erich von Stroheim, Melvyn Douglas, Hedda Hopper also star. 71 min.
12-2101 *$19.99*

Queen Christina (1933)
Overruling Louis Mayer himself, Greta Garbo got former lover John Gilbert to co-star and with director Rouben Mamoulian forged a romantic classic, about a fierce-willed Swedish monarch who shuns a political marriage to pursue ideal love. 97 min.
12-2009 *$19.99*

The Painted Veil (1934)
The wife of a Western physician treating a cholera epidemic in China enters into an affair with a suave politician in this romantic drama based on a W. Somerset Maugham novel. Greta Garbo shines as the woman caught between love and duty; Herbert Marshall, George Brent, Warner Oland co-star. 83 min.
12-2104 *$19.99*

Anna Karenina (1935)
After starring in a contemporary silent adaptation in 1927, Greta Garbo gave one of her greatest performances as Tolstoy's tragic heroine in this lavish costume drama. Fredric March is the officer who steals her heart and Basil Rathbone is her husband. With Maureen O'Sullivan, May Robson, Freddie Bartholomew. 95 min.
12-1655 *$19.99*

Camille (1937)
Greta Garbo shines as a courtesan who relinquishes her love for a young man in order to keep him from learning of her impending death. Faithful adaptation of the novel by Alexandre Dumas *fils* co-stars Robert Taylor, Lionel Barrymore, Elizabeth Allan. 108 min.
12-1590 *$19.99*

Conquest (1937)
Epic historical drama starring Charles Boyer as Napoleon and Greta Garbo as a Polish countess who has an affair with the French general. Lavishly produced and filled with superb performances, the film also stars Reginald Owen, Alan Marshall. 155 min.
12-2121 *$19.99*

Ninotchka (1939)
A sparkling comic treat filled with witty dialogue (supplied by Billy Wilder), expert direction ("that Lubitsch touch") and shining performances. Greta Garbo is a stone-faced Russian agent who falls for suave playboy Melvyn Douglas in Paris. Sig Ruman, Bela Lugosi co-star. 110 min.
12-1390 *$19.99*

Two-Faced Woman (1941)
Greta Garbo's last film is a frothy comedy about a ski instructor who tests the fidelity of her playboy husband by posing as her own twin and seducing him. Melvyn Douglas reteams with his "Ninotchka" co-star; George Cukor is an uncredited director. 94 min.
12-2005 *$19.99*

The Divine Garbo
Glenn Close hosts this salute to one of the most beautiful and mysterious of stars. Follow Greta Garbo's life and career from her screen debut in her native Sweden and rise to fame in such films as "Flesh and the Devil," "Anna Christie," "Grand Hotel," "Camille" and "Ninotchka" to her abrupt farewell to Hollywood in 1941 and virtual solitude. 47 min.
18-7332 Was $19.99 *$14.99*

East Meets West (1934)
George Arliss excels as the Sultan of Rungay, the sly chief of a small Asian country with a harbor coveted by both England and Japan. Using his wits, Arliss plays both countries against each other and reap great rewards. At the same time, his son has a relationship with a crooked British official's wife. Lucie Mannheim, Godfrey Tearle also star. 74 min.
10-9300 *$19.99*

Speed Reporter (1936)
Set against the exciting world of the newspaper business, this gritty drama stars Richard Talmadge as a crusading reporter investigating a corrupt reform league. Luana Walters, Richard Cramer also star. 60 min.
10-9035 Was $19.99 *$14.99*

Danger Ahead (1935)
Action-packed tale of a crusading reporter out to find who stole $40,000 from a sea captain. Wearing dark suits and sporting mustaches, the crooks cause a reign of terror that must be stopped—and the reporter is out to stop them! Laurence Gay, Sheila Mannors and Fuzzy Knight star. 58 min.
09-2302 *$14.99*

The Return Of Casey Jones (1933)
The legendary Casey Jones helps a young engineer in need of a role model in this exciting look at the famed locomotive man. With Western star Charles Starrett, Ruth Hall, Robert Elliott and Gabby Hayes. 65 min.
10-9114 Was $19.99 *$14.99*

Money Means Nothing (1934)
A shy tire clerk falls in love with a wealthy young woman, but her family wants no parts of him. When the rubber salesman turns out to be hero in a situation involving a tire hijacking, the family changes their mind. Interesting mix of romance, mystery and drama starring Wallace Ford, Gloria Shea and Edgar Kennedy. 70 min.
10-9120 *$19.99*

The Villiers Diamond (1938)
Fine crime caper drama in which a former crook gets a hold of the famous Villiers Diamond, but finds that the person he got it from and his penniless daughter are after him for cash. Edward Ashley, Evelyn Ankers and Frank Birch star. 60 min.
10-9229 Was $19.99 *$14.99*

Men Are Not Gods (1937)
A terrific cast highlights this Alexander Korda production about a critic's secretary who is fired after she alters her boss's negative review of "Othello" to a positive one. She becomes involved with the play's lead actor, but reveals their romance in a unique, dramatic fashion. Miriam Hopkins, Rex Harrison, Gertrude Lawrence and A.E. Matthews star. 80 min.
10-9235 Was $19.99 *$14.99*

What Price Crime? (1935)
Cowboy favorite Charles Starrett tries a change of pace, playing an undercover FBI agent who poses as a prizefighter in order to get the goods on crooks swiping weapons from the government. Noel Madison, Virginia Cherrill co-star. 65 min.
10-9248 Was $19.99 *$14.99*

Missouri Nightingale (1935)
A college football player with a desire to play in the pros finds himself in the middle of trouble when he faces corruption and double-dealing. Jeannette Loff, Johnny Mack Brown and Earl Foxe star. 68 min.
10-9442 *$19.99*

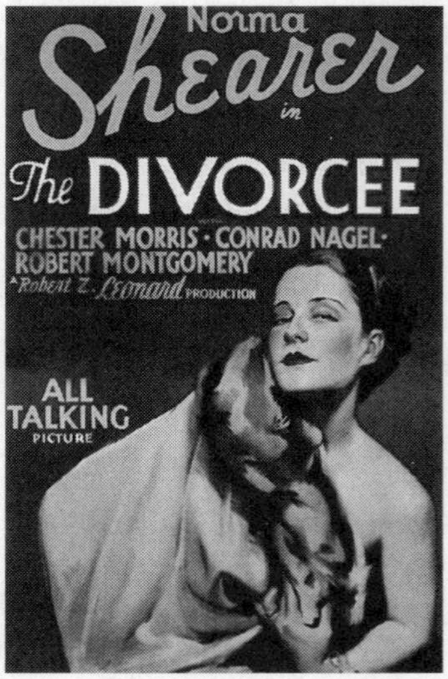

The Divorcee (1930)
Norma Shearer, in her Academy Award-winning role, plays the newspaperman's wife whose acceptance of her husband's extra-marital affairs reaches the breaking point. She divorces him and embarks on her own series of encounters (a racy theme for its time). Chester Morris, Conrad Nagel, Robert Montgomery also star. 83 min.
12-2148 Was $29.99 *$19.99*

Suicide Squad (1935)
Taxi driver Norman Foster joins the fire department's Suicide Squad, which is run by his girlfriend's father, but soon gets in trouble because he never seems to be at the right place at the right time. After being rejected by his boss and his girl, he has an opportunity to get back in everyone's good graces with a daring rescue. Joyce Compton, Robert Homans co-star. 60 min.
09-5178 *$19.99*

Park Avenue Logger (1937)
The patriarch of a blue-blood family doesn't think his son is becoming a rugged enough man, so he sends him to a logging camp. The young man's wrestling abilities reach fruition at the camp and, known as "The Masked Marvel," he smashes some crooks and helps a young woman's logger father when he gets in trouble. George O'Brien, Ward Bond and Beatrice Roberts star. 65 min.
10-9052 Was $19.99 *$14.99*

Riptide (1934)
When her wealthy English husband is away on business, American socialite Norma Shearer attends a swanky party where she meets playboy and former lover Robert Montgomery. An accident sends them to the hospital, alerting the press and Shearer's husband of a supposed scandalous affair, and prompting the couple's divorce. Herbert Marshall also stars in this classy MGM soap opera. 90 min.
12-2867 *$29.99*

Big Business Girl (1931)
Controversial at the time of its initial release, this drama stars Loretta Young as a woman who decides to enter the world of advertising when her bandleader husband leaves to tour Europe. During his absence, she becomes romantically involved with her boss, who tries to break up the couple's marriage. With Frank Albertson, Ricardo Cortez. 75 min.
12-2882 *$19.99*

Scarlet Dawn (1932)
Lavish and surprisingly decadent period drama starring Douglas Fairbanks, Jr. as a Russian diplomat who lands in Turkey after the revolution with his maid (Nancy Carroll). The two marry and attempt to settle into a working-class lifestyle, but Fairbanks' aristocratic ways lead him into an affair, and even an orgy. Earle Fox, Lilyan Tashman also star. 76 min.
12-2885 *$19.99*

Stormy (1935)
Sensitive drama about a young man who is thrown from a train carrying a race horse and its colt. He befriends the young colt and soon discovers himself caught between two brothers—one who wants to save the colt and other wild horses, the other who wants to use the animal for financial gain. Noah Beery, Jr., Jean Rogers and J. Farrell McDonald star. 70 min.
10-9250 Was $19.99 *$14.99*

Danger Lights (1930)
This striking railroad drama benefits from solid performances from Jean Arthur and Robert Armstrong as lovers who decide to elope, leaving loyal but dull fiancée Louis Wolheim in the lurch, as well as some great footage of classic trains in action. 87 min.
10-3039 *$19.99*

Uptown New York (1932)
Jack Oakie stars as Eddie Doyle, a bubble-gum machine mechanic in love with a girl who loves someone else. But when the girl's guy gets going, she goes after Eddie! Teary melodrama at its wettest; also stars Shirley Grey and Leon Waycoff. 76 min.
10-3086 Was $19.99 *$14.99*

Nurse Edith Cavell (1939)
Stirring true story of the nurse who, along with three other civilians, risked her life to aid Allied forces in Belgium during WWI. Anna Neagle, Edna Mae Oliver, ZaSu Pitts and George Sanders star. 96 min.
10-3087 Was $19.99 *$14.99*

The Stars Look Down (1939)
Michael Redgrave and Margaret Lockwood star in this powerful social drama about a small British town's dependency on an unsafe mine. 96 min.
10-4030 *$19.99*

The Face On The Barroom Floor (1932)
Taking its cue from the famous poem, this vaudeville drama weaves a prohibition-era parable about a bank clerk whose desire for drink leads him down the path to ruin. Bramwell Fletcher, Dulcie Cooper star. 65 min.
10-7224 Was $29.99 *$19.99*

Hoosier Schoolboy (1937)
A young Mickey Rooney stars as an impoverished small town lad who must fight for his self-respect because of his shell-shocked, alcoholic father. Co-stars Anna Neagle, Frank Shields. 62 min.
10-7232 *$19.99*

Pleasure (1931)
Intriguing drama concerning an author who, regardless of the impact on his marriage, enters an affair with a model...not realizing that the other man in her life is his own brother. Conway Tearle, Francis Dade, Roscoe Karns star. 51 min.
10-7233 Was $29.99 *$14.99*

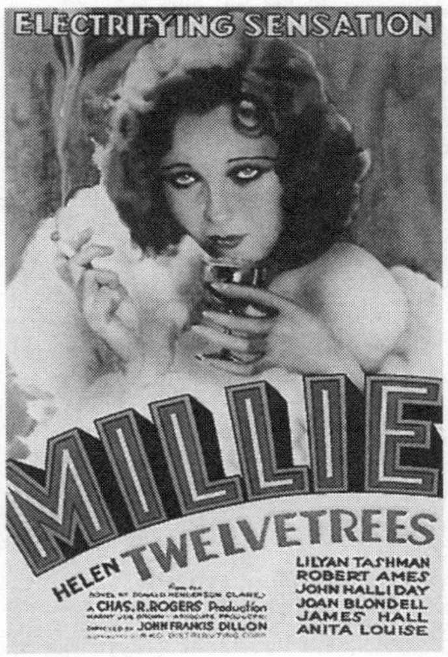
ELECTRIFYING SENSATION
MILLIE
HELEN TWELVETREES
LILYAN TASHMAN
ROBERT AMES
JOHN HALLIDAY
JOAN BLONDELL
JAMES HALL
ANITA LOUISE
A CHAS. R. ROGERS' Production
JOHN FRANCIS DILLON

Millie (1931)
Helen Twelvetrees stars as a woman who bounces from man to man after her first love affair goes sour. She longs for a romantic relationship with a suave socialite, but discovers that he's already involved...with her own 16-year-old daughter. Lilyan Tashman, Joan Blondell, John Halliday co-star in this superior soaper. 80 min.
17-9021 Was $19.99 *$14.99*

Sons Of Steel (1935)
Effective and affecting drama concerning two brothers partnered in the smelting business. One dreams and schemes to raise himself on the social scale, the other humbly and dutifully plugs away at work. Loretta Young (billed as "Polly Ann"), Charles Starrett star. 65 min.
10-7242 Was $19.99 *$14.99*

Corsair (1931)
Chester Morris stars in this tale of rum-runners and modern piracy as a mug who impresses a swindler's daughter by being an even bigger crook than her old man. The unrepentant cast includes Alison Loyd (soon to be Thelma Todd), Fred Kohler, and sparkling Ned Sparks. 75 min.
10-7346 Was $19.99 *$14.99*

A Woman Of Experience (1931)
An assignment from Austrian intelligence to romance a German spy gives a woman with a shady past a last chance at respectability. WWI soaper stars Helen Twelvetrees, H.B. Warner, ZaSu Pitts, Franklin Pangborn. 65 min.
10-7383 Was $19.99 *$14.99*

Young Bride (1932)
Daydreamer Helen Twelvetrees falls for a street-wise sharpie and they wed, but his penchant for poolhall hustles and dime-a-dance chippies soon sours the match. Tenement melodrama also stars Eric Linden. AKA: "Love Starved." 80 min.
10-7384 Was $19.99 *$14.99*

Kept Husbands (1931)
When steelworker Joel McCrea saves two people in a factory accident, the boss's daughter falls for him, vowing to make a society husband of blue collar Joel within a month. 76 min.
10-7385 *$19.99*

Behind Office Doors (1931)
RKO "woman's film" stars Mary Astor as a super-efficient secretary who holds the real power in her office, while holding a torch for an unappreciative executive. Robert Ames co-stars. 82 min.
10-7386 Was $19.99 *$14.99*

The Animal Kingdom (1932)
David O. Selznick produced this story of passion, romance and a mismatched marriage. Leslie Howard plays a handsome publisher who opts to marry the sophisticated Myrna Loy over free-spirited artist Ann Harding. William Gargan and Neil Hamilton co-star. 90 min.
10-8085 *$19.99*

Honeymoon Limited (1936)
Neil Hamilton, who later played Commissioner Gordon on TV's "Batman," stars as a writer in need of cash who takes to the road in search of a story. His New York-to-San Francisco trek soon finds him involved with a group of runaway sisters and gangsters. With Irene Hervey, Lloyd Hughes. 73 min.
10-8244 Was $19.99 *$14.99*

Great God Gold (1935)
A hotel owner's daughter teams with a financial reporter to get the goods on a banker who's drawn into a crooked operation. Regis Toomey, Sidney Blackmer and Martha Sleeper star. 71 min.
10-8253 Was $19.99 *$14.99*

Siren Of The South Seas (1937)
This romantic drama shot in Samoa tells the story of a blind painter who seeks an operation to restore his sight and falls in love with a native girl during his travels. Movita, Warren Hull and George Pilita star. AKA: "Paradise Isle." 73 min.
10-8335 Was $19.99 *$14.99*

Telephone Operator (1937)
A devastating flood traps a pair of telephone operators with two linemen. Will their romance reach higher ground before their lives are disconnected? Tense drama stars Judith Allen, Grant Withers. 62 min.
10-8337 Was $19.99 *$14.99*

Under The Big Top (1938)
Effective drama set at the circus, where the future of a trapeze trio is threatened when two men fall for the same female troupe member. Anne Nagel, Grant Richmond and Jack LaRue star. 63 min.
10-8339 Was $19.99 *$14.99*

Blazing Barriers (1937)
This film trumpeted President Franklin Roosevelt's Civilian Conservation Corps by telling the story of two young boys who cause lots of trouble but learn their lesson after they spend time at a C.C.C. camp. Frank Coughlan, Jr., Florine McKinney, Edward Arnold, Jr. star. 65 min.
10-8344 Was $19.99 *$14.99*

Boys' Reformatory (1939)
Lively crime melodrama about an orphaned boy who takes the rap for his step-brother and lands in prison. After receiving rough treatment behind bars, he plots an escape and revenge against the crooks who set up his brother. Frankie Darro, Grant Withers star.
10-8369 Was $19.99 *$14.99*

Hell-Ship Morgan (1936)
The title character is a salty fishing boat captain (George Bancroft) who decides to make the ultimate sacrifice when he learns his new wife (Ann Sothern) has fallen in love with his handsome, clean-cut first-mate (Victor Jory). Romance, adventure and drama are on deck in this one!
10-8379 Was $19.99 *$14.99*

Ten Laps To Go (1938)
An exciting yarn set in the world of auto racing, where a top driver gets into an accident and finds that strange occurrences point to his being responsible. He must find the real perpetrator of the events and get his girl back, who has fallen for a rival driver. Rex Lease, Muriel Evans, Duncan Renaldo and Marie Prevost (in her last film) star.
10-8380 *$19.99*

Skyway (1933)
After taking a job at a bank, a former pilot is accused of stealing cash from his employers and sets out to find the real culprit and clear his name. Kathryn Crawford, Ray Walker, Gabby Hayes star.
10-8449 Was $19.99 *$14.99*

Department Store (1935)
In this interesting crime drama, an ex-convict is mistaken for the heir of a department store owner by the store's dishonest manager. Garry Marsh, Eve Gray and Sebastian Shaw star.
10-8450 Was $19.99 *$14.99*

History Is Made At Night (1937)
Drama of an embittered wife who leaves her husband for another man, only to unleash a vengeance that leads to death. Charles Boyer, Jean Arthur, Colin Clive star. 98 min.
19-1823 *$19.99*

Meet Dr. Christian (1939)
Inaugural entry in the heartwarming Dr. Christian series about the small town doctor in Rivers End, Minnesota, struggling to pay bills. Stars Jean Hersholt, Dorothy Lovett, Robert Baldwin. 70 min.
09-1026 Was $19.99 *$14.99*

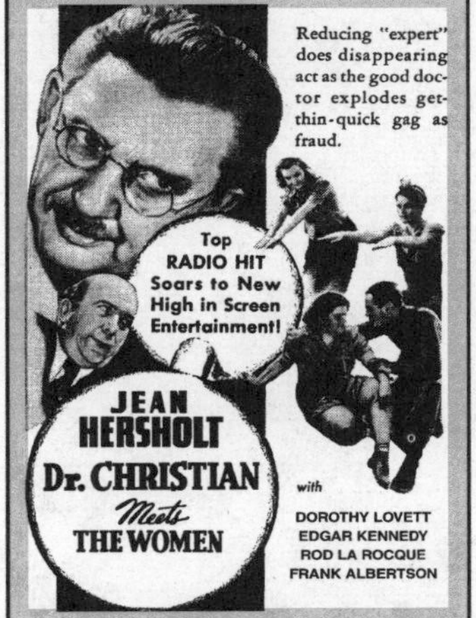
Reducing "expert" does disappearing act as the good doctor explodes get-thin-quick gag as fraud.
Top RADIO HIT Soars to New High in Screen Entertainment!
JEAN HERSHOLT
Dr. CHRISTIAN
Meets
THE WOMEN
with
DOROTHY LOVETT
EDGAR KENNEDY
ROD LA ROCQUE
FRANK ALBERTSON

Dr. Christian Meets The Women (1940)
The dedicated Dr. Christian has his hands full in this drama, dealing with a quack medic who has come to town and played up to the ladyfolk. Jean Hersholt, Edgar Kennedy, Dorothy Lovett star. 69 min.
08-8003 Was $19.99 *$14.99*

The Courageous Dr. Christian (1940)
A courageous doctor tries to upgrade a poor community, but an epidemic of spinal meningitis breaks out. With Jean Hersholt. 66 min.
09-1298 Was $19.99 *$14.99*

Remedy For Riches (1940)
In this, the fourth outing for Dr. Christian (Jean Hersholt), the good doc has his hands full with a charlatan who claims to have discovered oil in town. With Edgar Kennedy. 66 min.
09-1990 Was $29.99 *$14.99*

Melody For Three (1941)
Jean Hersholt stars as the kindly Dr. Christian, who here must help a young violin prodigy and bring the boy's feuding parents back together. Fay Wray, Walter Woolf King co-star. 76 min.
08-8012 Was $19.99 *$14.99*

They Meet Again (1941)
When a young man is accused of embezzlement, it's up to kindly Dr. Christian to clear his name. Jean Hersholt, Neil Hamilton, Dorothy Lovett star. 68 min.
10-3012 Was $19.99 *$14.99*

My Old Kentucky Home (1938)
After going blind when a rival throws acid in his face, a concert singer leaves New York for his grandmother's home in Kentucky. Little does he know that his girlfriend has staged a special celebration to help him regain his confidence. Evelyn Venable and J. Farrel MacDonald star, along with the Hall Johnson Choir. 70 min.
10-8456 Was $19.99 *$14.99*

Waterfront Lady (1935)
A houseboat in a fishing colony is the locale where much of this exciting crime drama takes place. A man takes the rap for his partner, who's been accused of killing a lookout on a gambling ship during a raid. Ann Rutherford, Frank Albertson and J. Farrell MacDonald star.
10-8941 *$19.99*

The Outer Gate (1936)
Interesting crime drama starring Ralph Morgan as a bookkeeper who falls in love with his boss's daughter, only to find himself wrongly accused of theft and sent to prison. When Morgan gets out of jail, he seeks revenge. With Kay Linaker, Eddie Acuff. 60 min.
10-8980 *$19.99*

Tango (1936)
A chorus girl struggles to find success and to win over the family of the man she loves. When things get tough, she takes jobs waitressing and modeling, and calls on a close friend for career and personal advice. Marian Nixon, Chick Chandler, Marie Prevost star. 65 min.
10-8984 *$19.99*

Heroes For Sale (1933)
An audacious social drama from Warner Brothers starring Richard Barthelmess as a soldier who returns home from World War I and confronts morphine addiction, the Depression and, after he becomes wealthy, labor strikes. Aline McMahon and Loretta Young also star in this unflinching story directed by William Wellman. 71 min.
12-2295 *$19.99*

Employee's Entrance (1933)
A swanky department store is the setting for this glossy (and somewhat risqué) melodrama featuring Warren William as the store's tyrannical manager and Loretta Young as an employee's wife who becomes the unwilling recipient of his romantic attentions. With Wallace Ford, Alice White. 75 min.
12-2620 *$19.99*

Female (1933)
Intriguing drama starring Ruth Chatterton as a woman in charge of an automobile factory. Her tough, no-nonsense business attitude is matched by the way she conducts her love life, but her outlook changes when she meets new executive George Brent. With Phillip Reed, Johnny Mack Brown; Michael Curtiz directs. 60 min.
12-2621 *$19.99*

Gabriel Over The White House (1933)
A remarkable satire of politics starring Walter Huston as an irresponsible president who sees a heavenly vision while recuperating from a serious auto accident. Soon, he changes his life and becomes a man of the people. But his newfound style is not appreciated by all, including his former cohorts. Karen Morley, Franchot Tone and Arthur Byron also star. 87 min.
12-2629 *$19.99*

Three Comrades (1938)
Set against the backdrop of post-WWI Germany, this superb film stars Robert Taylor, Franchot Tone and Robert Young as three wartime friends who fall in love with the same woman (Margaret Sullavan). Lionel Atwill and Guy Kibbee also star in this stylish drama, co-written by F. Scott Fitzgerald and based on Erich Maria Remarque's book. 99 min.
12-2636 *$19.99*

Smilin' Through (1932)
The second version of the first-rate weepie stars Norma Shearer in dual roles as a bride who is mistakenly shot by a jealous suitor (Fredric March) on her wedding day and as the bride's niece who, years later, falls in love with the suitor's son (also played by March). Leslie Howard and Ralph Forbes also star in this romantic fantasy. 100 min.
12-2813 *$19.99*

Madame X (1937)
Classic soap opera stars Gladys George as the bored wife of a diplomat whose amorous affair with a dashing playboy leads to the destruction of her privileged lifestyle and her descent into prostitution, blackmail and murder. Warren William, John Beal and Reginald Owen also star. 71 min.
12-2864 *$29.99*

They Call It Sin (1932)
Kansas-raised country girl Loretta Young arrives in New York with hopes of making it in the music world. Soon, she's being wooed by a dashing playboy (David Manners) and adored by a theatrical producer (Louis Calhern). But instead of choosing between the two, she opts for the hand of a physician (George Brent). 75 min.
12-2887 *$19.99*

Heroes In Blue (1939)
Crime yarn about brothers on the force who become sworn enemies when one of them takes up with gangsters and a racetrack murder scheme. Dick Purcell stars. 60 min.
68-8263 *$19.99*

Prison Break (1938)
A convict struggles to cope with parole while trying to flush out the killers who sent him to the big house on a bum murder rap. Barton MacLane and Glenda Farrell star in this melodrama. 68 min.
68-8271 Was $19.99 *$14.99*

Tough Kid (1939)
Gangsters call all the shots in the boxing career of a street-toughened kid until his smarter brother steps in to set things square. Bare-knuckled urban melodrama stars Frankie Darro and Dick Purcell. 61 min.
68-8350 *$19.99*

Panama Patrol (1939)
Experts in codes and intelligence, they deciphered their hearts and found "love" was the secret word. Army spies (and sweethearts) Leon Ames and Charlotte Wynters crack a Chinese espionage ring in the Canal Zone. 67 min.
68-8351 *$19.99*

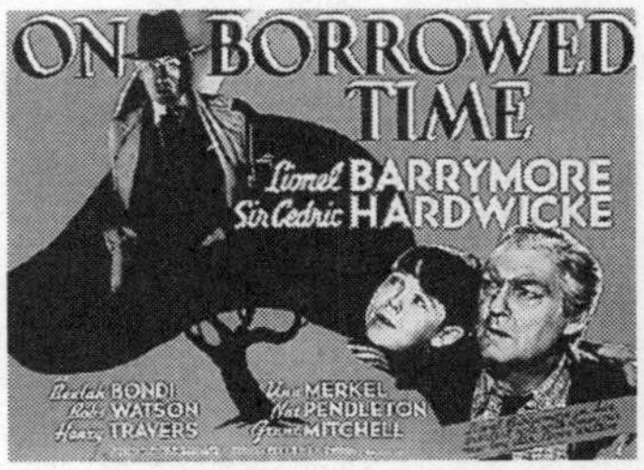
ON BORROWED TIME
Lionel BARRYMORE
Sir Cedric HARDWICKE
Beulah BONDI
Bobs WATSON
Henry TRAVERS
Una MERKEL
Nat PENDLETON
Grant MITCHELL

On Borrowed Time (1939)
An old man caring for his orphaned grandson is confronted by Death, come to Earth in human form. Unwilling to follow, the cagey codger manages to trick the Grim Reaper into climbing an apple tree and traps him there. Lionel Barrymore, Sir Cedric Hardwicke, Una Merkel, Beulah Bondi and Bobs Watson star in this whimsical fantasy. 99 min.
12-2494 *$19.99*

I Can't Escape (1934)
A criminal finds civilian life is not as peachy as it seemed from behind bars...especially since he can't get a job with his past record. Attitudes change, however, after he exposes a stock fraud. Lila Lee and Onslow Stevens star. 60 min.
68-8537 *$14.99*

Prison Shadows (1936)
An exciting blend of sports action and underworld drama, as a fighter just out of prison for killing an opponent knocks off another boxer in the ring. He soon discovers that a gambling ring is behind the incident and he sets out to stop their crooked dealings. Eddie Nugent and Lucille Lund star. 67 min.
68-8893 *$19.99*

Delinquent Parents (1938)
Early screen attempt to depict the problem of juvenile delinquency. A teen mother, her marriage annulled by the boy's upper-class parents, gives up her baby for adoption. Years later, when the young woman has grown up to become a juvenile court judge, who should come before her but her own adolescent daughter! Helen MacKeller, Doris Weston star.
68-9097 *$19.99*

Port Of Hate (1939)
The discovery of a black pearl bed near a remote Pacific island leads to a bitter rivalry between two American adventurers. When one of them is found shot dead, a young woman is accused of the crime. Unusual South Seas drama stars Polly Ann Young (Loretta's sister), Kenneth Harlan.
68-9099 *$19.99*

Chloe (1934)
Rarely seen, ultra-atmospheric drama in which the daughter of a black voodoo mistress from the Everglades discovers she may really be the daughter of the white plantation owner. Taboo in its time for its depiction of interracial romance; with Olive Borden, Reed Howes and Molly O'Day. AKA: "Chloe: Love Is Calling You."
68-9116 *$19.99*

Sixteen Fathoms Deep (1933)
Lon Chaney, Jr. stars as a deep-sea sponge fisherman who is involved with a series of intrigues after borrowing capital from a villainous rival boat captain. Striking underwater photography and Catalina Island locations highlight this salty tale. 57 min.
68-8011 Was $19.99 *$14.99*

Seven Sinners (1936)
Innovative British-made crime drama with Americans Edmund Lowe and Constance Cummings starring in a story about a detective from the States who travels across the Atlantic to end the trail of terror imposed by train-wrecking gunrunners. Co-stars Thomy Bourdelle, Henry Oscar. AKA: "Doomed Cargo." 70 min.
68-8095 *$19.99*

Buried Alive (1939)
A man sent to prison on phony charges fights for parole and discovers why he's being held behind bars. Only the prison nurse trusts his word. Beverly Roberts and Robert Wilcox star in this tense drama.
68-8534 *$19.99*

The Mystery Man (1935)
A top Chicago crime reporter runs afoul of his boss and winds up out of a job. Not one to let grass grow under his feet, he moves to St. Louis and promptly offers to uncover the city's most notorious murder case, involving a killer known as "the Eel." Offbeat crime drama stars Robert Armstrong. 62 min.
68-8100 Was $19.99 *$14.99*

The Informer (1929)
An earlier version of the story that John Ford filmed in 1935, Lars Hansen stars as Gypo Nolan, the beleaguered man who takes money from authorities to squeal on his friend, an IRA member. Lya de Putti and Warwick Ward also star. 83 min.
10-9226 Was $19.99 *$14.99*

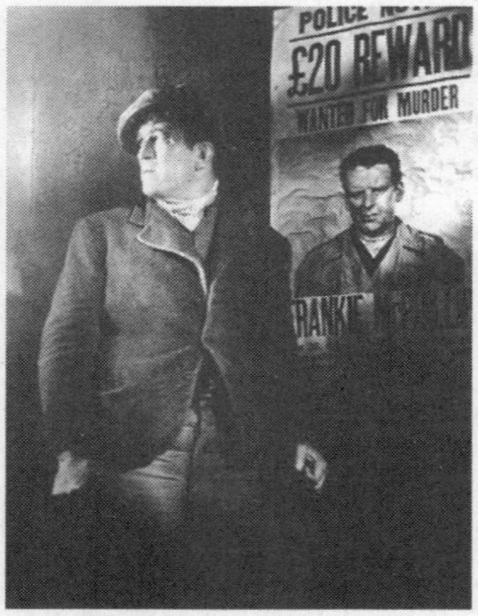

The Informer (1935)
John Ford's classic drama tells the tale of hard-drinking Gippo Nolan, who informs on a buddy to collect a reward during the Irish Rebellion. Victor McLaglen won an Oscar for his brilliant performance. 91 min.
05-1344 *$14.99*

Vanity Fair (1932)
The second Hollywood filming (and first sound version) of Thackeray's classic drama stars a young Myrna Loy as Becky Sharp, a society girl who uses those around her to get what she wants. 67 min.
08-5053 Was $19.99 *$14.99*

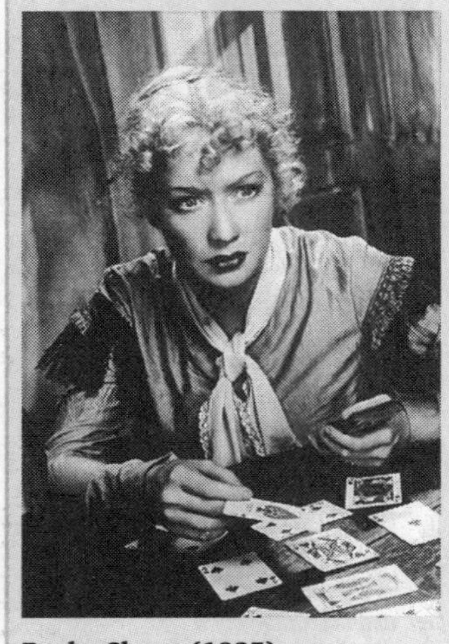

Becky Sharp (1935)
Delightful adaptation of Thackeray's "Vanity Fair" features Miriam Hopkins as the self-centered and manipulative anti-heroine Sharp. Frances Dee, Cedric Hardwicke, Billie Burke and Nigel Bruce also star in this, the first full-Technicolor film. 83 min.
10-3088 *$19.99*

Vanity Fair (1967)
Emmy Award-winning British production based on the William Thackeray "novel without a hero" stars Susan Hampshire as scheming Becky Sharp, who climbs the ladder of 19th-century English society and steps on more than one friend along the way. 250 min.
04-3463 *$39.99*

Vanity Fair (1998)
William Makepeace Thackeray's masterful novel is turned into a sumptuous saga focusing on Becky Sharp, a beautiful, smart but poor woman determined to make her mark in society. Along with her friend Amelia, who enjoys the privileges of a well-to-do life, the pair's fortunes are followed, from the mansions of early 19th-century London to the battlefields of Waterloo. Natasha Little, Frances Grey and Nathaniel Grey star. 300 min. on six tapes.
53-6613 *$79.99*

Dusty Ermine (1936)
The Austrian Alps provide the backdrop for this thrilling crime story about a woman involved with crooks like her forger uncle and counterfeiting brother. Will the woman's romance with a law officer help her family when they're threatened by rival criminals? June Baxter, Anthony Bushell and Margaret Rutherford star. AKA: "Hideout in the Alps." 74 min.
68-8963 *$19.99*

They Never Come Back (1932)
Having broken his arm in the ring, prizefighter Regis Toomey retires and becomes a nightclub bouncer. When he befriends a pretty exotic dancer, circumstances force his boxing comeback, bum left arm and all. 67 min.
68-8106 *$19.99*

After Midnight (1933)
It's fame and romance among the first-nighters when a brilliant playwright discovers just the girl to star in his new work, and the combo stands Broadway on its ear. Alan Dinehart and Anita Page do the Neil Simon/Marsha Mason bit in this glittering backstage drama. AKA: "I Have Lived." 69 min.
68-8108 *$19.99*

Motorcycle Squad (1937)
Exciting "B" film concerning a police officer who is dishonorably discharged so he can get inside info on a gang of crooks and bring them to justice. Kane Richmond, Wynne Gibson star. 63 min.
68-8112 *$19.99*

Shadows Of The Orient (1937)
Interesting Monogram crime drama about a young woman (Esther Ralston) and her involvement with an immigration official (Regis Toomey) whose dogged attempts to block a gang from smuggling Chinese illegal aliens in through Mexico even have him dropping them out of planes (and you thought Proposition 187 was tough!). With Sidney Blackmer. 72 min.
68-8114 Was $19.99 *$14.99*

Hong Kong Nights (1935)
Customs agents head to the mysterious East and press their case against gun smugglers to a fiery conclusion. A truly exciting film, the follow-up to "Our Daily Bread" for action star Tom Keene (alias George Duryea, Richard Powers). 59 min.
68-8412 Was $19.99 *$14.99*

Little Women (1970)
A lavish BBC production of Louisa May Alcott's tale of four sisters who share their lives, loves, sorrows and joys during the 1800s. Janina Faye, Angela Down and Patrick Troughton star. 205 min.
04-2714 Was $34.99 *$19.99*

Little Men (1935)
Strong-willed Jo Marsh (Erin O'Brien-Moore) from "Little Women" has grown up and taken on the responsibility of running a school for wayward boys in this delightful sequel to the beloved story. With Ralph Morgan, Frankie Darro, Dickie Moore. 90 min.
10-1358 Was $19.99 *$14.99*

Little Men (1940)
The sequel to Louisa May Alcott's "Little Women" finds Jo March (Kay Francis) married and headmistress at an unconventional school for boys. Jack Oakie, George Bancroft, Ann Gillis co-star. 84 min.
10-3033 *$19.99*

Little Men (1998)
Mariel Hemingway stars as the now-grown Jo March in this heartwarming family drama based on Louisa May Alcott's follow-up novel to "Little Women." Along with her husband, Hemingway opens a country school for troubled boys, but are they ready for the bundles of trouble that come their way? Chris Sarandon, Ben Cook, Michael Caloz also star. 98 min.
19-2703 Was $19.99 *$14.99*

Honky Tonk Girl (1937)
Dangerous curves...Wrong way...Soft shoulders! He read the warning signs, but he just couldn't stop himself. The startling tale of hitchhikers and prostitutes that every parent should see, starring Mary Chauning. AKA: "Highway Hell."
68-8418 *$19.99*

The Wrong Road (1937)
They're young, they're in love, and now Richard Cromwell and Helen Mack have gone to jail for stealing $100,000 from the bank where he worked. Upon their release, insurance company detective Lionel Atwill tries to help them turn their lives around...and recover the missing loot. Marjorie Main also stars. 53 min.
68-8424 *$19.99*

Passing Of The Third Floor Back (1935)
Conrad Veidt stars in this atmospheric allegory about a mysterious stranger who arrives at a boardinghouse and begins to help its pathetic denizens. An eerie, often surreal drama. 80 min.
68-8459 *$19.99*

When Thief Meets Thief (1937)
In a change-of-pace role, Douglas Fairbanks, Jr. plays a cat burglar who is smitten with one of his victims...who just happens to be engaged to his two-timing ex-partner! Lively drama with impressive stunts and trial scenes. With Valerie Hobson and Alan Hale; directed by Raoul Walsh. 85 min.
68-8536 *$19.99*

Thoroughbred (1935)
A down-on-his-luck reporter wins an unknown horse in a dice game and soon discovers that the animal is lightning on four hoofs. A young woman helps the reporter with the horse, but the two soon come in contact with a nefarious race-fixer. Toby Wing, Kenne Duncan and Wheeler Oakman star.
68-9123 *$19.99*

Behind The Green Lights (1935)
A ruthless gangster is brought down by a two-fisted policeman, but, much to his pursuer's dismay, the bad guy gets off with the aid of the cop's lawyer girlfriend. What's more, his next crime is a jewelry store heist that leads to the girl's father being shot! Norman Foster, Judith Allen star.
68-9237 *$19.99*

The Wages Of Sin (1938)
Seamy melodrama at its finest! Poor Marjorie supports her struggling family, but lands in trouble when she gets involved with hothead hood Tony. Soon, she's on the road to nowhere, working as a prostitute out of Tony's apartment and, later, Fat Pearl's brothel. Constance Worth, Willy Castello star. 76 min.
79-5493 Was $24.99 *$19.99*

Victims Of Passion (1938)
Groundbreaking abortion drama involving the arrest of a doctor accused of killing during an abortion. The doctor is acquitted and goes back to work, but a society woman's secretary and daughter soon are involved with the physician. Willy Castello and Lona Andre star. AKA: "Race Suicide."
79-5566 Was $24.99 *$19.99*

The Clairvoyant (1935)
Unusual British fantasy/drama stars Claude Rains as a phony mentalist who doesn't know what to do when he suddenly gains the ability to actually predict the future and is put on trial for causing a mine accident he foresaw. With Fay Wray, Jane Baxter. AKA: "Evil Mind."
88-1111 *$19.99*

Party Girl (1930)
Douglas Fairbanks, Jr. is a company president's son blackmailed into marrying one of the girls of a Times Square escort service that supplies bimbos for businessmen's parties. 61 min.
68-8137 Was $19.99 *$14.99*

Should A Girl Marry? (1939)
After being released from an 18-month jail term, a female thief must battle her greedy, amoral husband over a secret she's been entrusted with by a dying prison pal. Anne Nagel and Warren Hull star in this melodrama. 61 min.
09-2246 Was $24.99 *$14.99*

Secret Of Dr. Kildare (1939)
Years before TV, dedicated young medico James Kildare and his irascible mentor, Dr. Gillespie, were played by Lew Ayres and Lionel Barrymore in a popular film series. In this, the third installment, Kildare tries to cure an heiress' psychosomatic blindness while convincing Gillespie to take a much-needed vacation. Helen Gilbert, Laraine Day also star. 84 min.
08-1041 *$14.99*

Dr. Kildare's Strange Case (1940)
Accepting a position at a prestigious research hospital, Dr. Kildare (Lew Ayres) strives to save a mental patient suffering from a stranger disorder through experimental brain surgery. Compelling entry from the MGM drama series also stars Lionel Barrymore, Laraine Day. 76 min.
10-4009 *$19.99*

The Last Mile (1932)
A gut-wrenching, realistic look at life on death row, based on a play by John Wexley, stars Howard Phillips as a wrongly convicted prisoner awaiting execution, Preston Foster as a hardened criminal and Albert J. Smith as a cruel turnkey. 69 min.
09-1886 Was $19.99 *$14.99*

I Married A Spy (1938)
Mix of wartime drama, suspense and romance stars Brigitte Horney as a German-born French girl in World War I who escapes from a German concentration camp to becomes a spy for the Allies. Later, to avoid being deported, Horney weds French soldier Neil Hamilton. 59 min.
09-5332 *$19.99*

The Zero Hour (1939)
Three-hankie tearjerker about a young Broadway actress who becomes a success thanks to her producer. The two fall in love and set out to marry, but an auto accident leaves the producer paralyzed. Will their romance survive? Frieda Inescort, Otto Kruger and Jane Darwell star. 53 min.
09-5343 *$19.99*

His First Command (1929)
William Boyd, in a pre-Hopalong Cassidy role, is a pampered playboy who, in order to impress the daughter of a cavalry officer, enlists in the army. Dorothy Sebastian (later Mrs. Boyd). 60 min.
09-1983 Was $24.99 *$19.99*

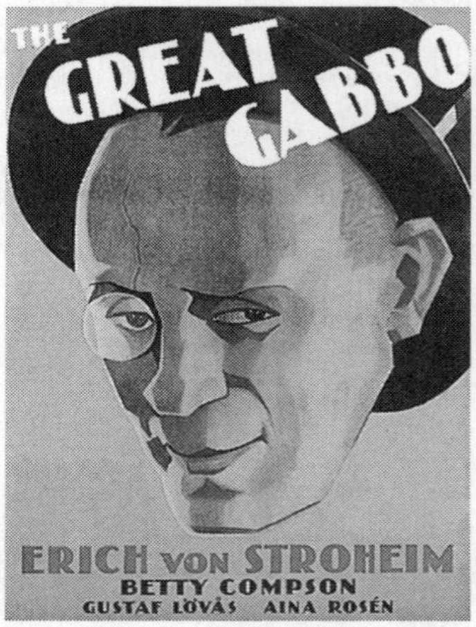

The Great Gabbo (1929)
Erich Von Stroheim gives a mesmerizing performance in this early talkie drama about an unbalanced ventriloquist whose dummy becomes an extension of his personality and begins to take over his life. With Betty Compson, Marjorie King. 96 min.
10-3036 *$19.99*

Barnum Was Right (1929)
In order to win over his sweetheart and her father, who wants his daughter to marry someone else, a poor young man tries to turn a dilapidated mansion into a profitable investment. Glenn Tryon, Merna Kennedy star.
10-9242 Was $19.99 *$14.99*

The Flying Scotsman (1929)
In one of Ray Milland's earliest roles, he plays the lover of a woman who stops a terrible plot carried out by a railroad engineer seeking vengeance on a coworker. Moore Marriott, Pauline Johnson and Alec Hurley star. 60 min.
17-9014 Was $19.99 *$14.99*

Alibi (1929)
Acclaimed for its stylized sets from art director William Cameron Menzies, this early crime drama stars Chester Morris as a gangster who reunites with his mob pals after being released from prison and gets involved in a deadly robbery. Harry Stubbs, Mae Busch, Regis Toomey also star. 84 min.
53-6320 *$24.99*

Painted Faces (1929)
Intriguing courtroom story starring Joe E. Brown as a circus clown serving on a jury during a murder trial who urges his fellow jurors to find the suspect innocent. It's eventually revealed that the clown is actually involved more closely to the case than originally believed. Helen Foster, Richard Tucker, William B. Davidson also star. 74 min.
68-8960 *$19.99*

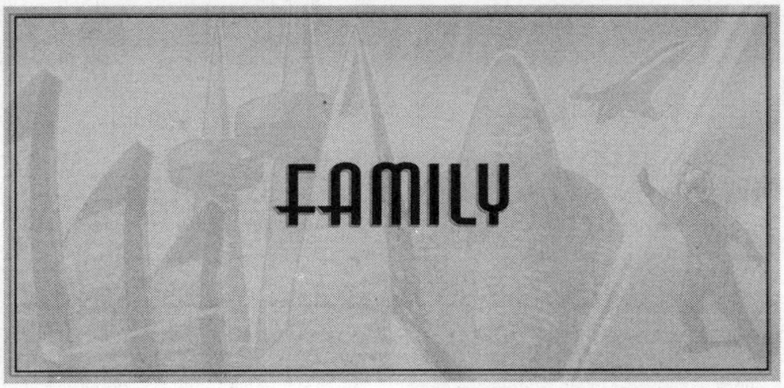

The Incredible Adventures Of Wallace & Gromit
A trio of ticklers from Nick Park's Oscar-winning clay animation couple, naive Wallace and his put-upon dog Gromit. Included on this video are "A Grand Day Out" (1992), about Wallace's desperate quest to obtain cheese for his crackers; "The Wrong Trousers" (1993), where the pair get mixed up with a scheming penguin, stolen diamonds and a pair of "automated techno trousers"; and "A Close Shave" (1995), with window cleaner Wallace falling for the owner of a local wool shop. 85 min.
19-5025 □*$19.99*

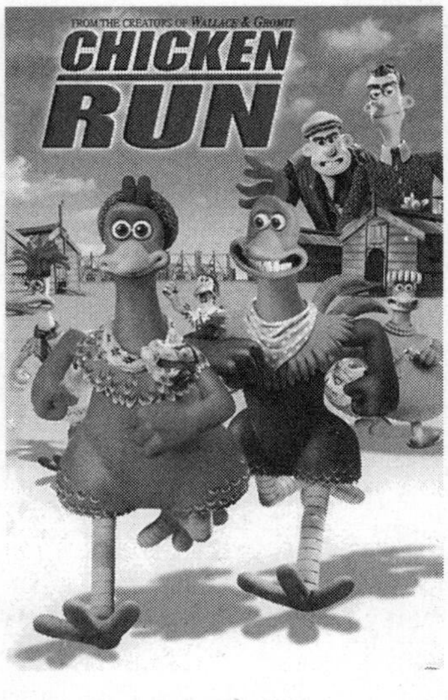

Chicken Run (2000)
From "Wallace & Gromit" creators Nick Park and Peter Lord comes this marvelous claymation feature set at Tweedy Chicken Farm in 1950s England. When Ginger, a mild-mannered hen, learns that the farm's owners plan to turn all of its inhabitants into chicken pies, she enlists the help of an American rooster named Rocky to plan a risky "great escape" to freedom. Mel Gibson, Miranda Richardson and Julia Sawalha provide the voices in this egg-citing family film. 84 min.
07-2953 □*$26.99*

Lapitch The Little Shoemaker (2000)
Setting out from his tiny village to see the world, a shoe-making mouse named Lapitch finds his trip filled with one wild adventure after another in this charming feature-length animated film. 75 min.
04-5709 □*$12.99*

The Scarecrow (2000)
A witch's magic spell turns a lonely man of straw into a being of flesh and blood, but it will take some help from a feisty field mouse for the scarecrow to save an orphan girl from a nasty count in this delightful animated feature. 90 min.
19-2979 □*$14.99*

The Road To El Dorado (2000)
Musical animated adventure set in Spain in 1519, where con artist pals Miguel and Tulio, who have acquired a map to the legendary golden city of El Dorado, become stowaways on Cortes' journey to America. After they are jailed on the explorer's ship, they escape to El Dorado, where they face off against an evil high priest and Tulio falls for Chel, a Mayan girl. Voices by Kevin Kline, Kenneth Branagh, Rosie Perez and Armand Assante; features songs by Elton John and Tim Rice.
07-2930 □*$24.99*

Little Bytes (2000)
From fun songs like "Hammer Time" and "Quazar Rap" to the rib-tickling adventures of the "Fat Cat on a Diet" and the lessons learned in "Bunkie and Booboo," parents and children alike will love this collection of short computer animated films which will provide plenty of entertainment and education for young children. 49 min.
50-8729 *$14.99*

Journey Home: The Animals Of Farthing Wood (1996)
Fox, Badger, Weasel and all the creatures who call Farthing Wood their home must leave it behind when humans start moving into the area and begin searching for a new place to live, in this British-made animated tale for the whole family. With the voice of Ralph Macchio.
04-3604 *$14.99*

The Legend Of The North Wind (1996)
Evil hunters plan to kill the creatures protected by a sacred Indian pact in the Great Bay of Whales. The only people who may be able to stop them are Elliott, his sister Anne, and their Native American friend Watuna. They embark on a dangerous journey against the hunters and the "Legend of the North Wind." John Ratzenberger narrates this animated tale. 74 min.
88-7002 *$14.99*

FernGully: The Last Rainforest (1992)
Wonderful, environmentally-conscious animated feature, about a human boy who is joined by a group of fairies on an adventure through the Amazon rain forest that is in danger of being destroyed by a greedy logging company. Robin Williams, Tim Curry, Christian Slater and Samantha Mathis provide the voices. 76 min.
04-2559 Was $24.99 □*$14.99*

FernGully 2: The Magical Rescue (1997)
Crysta, Pips, Batty Koda and all your favorite inhabitants of the enchanted rainforest are back in an all-new, song-filled feature that finds them on a quest into the outside world, where they must rescue a trio of baby animals taken from the forest. 75 min.
04-3603 Was $19.99 □*$14.99*

We're Back! A Dinosaur's Story (1993)
The Big Apple has had its share of strange visitors, but none compare to the friendly, talking dinosaurs who find themselves transported to modern-day New York in this animated family feature from Steven Spielberg's Amblin studios. John Goodman, Jay Leno, Walter Cronkite, Martin Short and Julia Child supply voices. 72 min.
07-2057 Was $24.99 □*$14.99*

Hercules & Xena: The Animated Movie: The Battle For Mount Olympus (1997)
Kevin Sorbo and Lucy Lawless bring their heroic alter egos into the cartoon arena in this exciting feature-length adventure that finds the Son of Zeus and the Warrior Princess in action against a horde of magical and monstrous menaces set upon them by scheming Hera, who teams with the Titans to take over Olympus. 90 min.
07-2562 Was $19.99 □*$14.99*

Donkey Kong Country: The Legend Of The Crystal Coconut (1999)
The barrel-throwing video game legend leaps into his own computer-animated, feature-length adventure, as Donkey Kong and his son Diddy set sail on a pirate ship voyage that's more fun than a barrel of...well, you know. 88 min.
06-2925 □*$19.99*

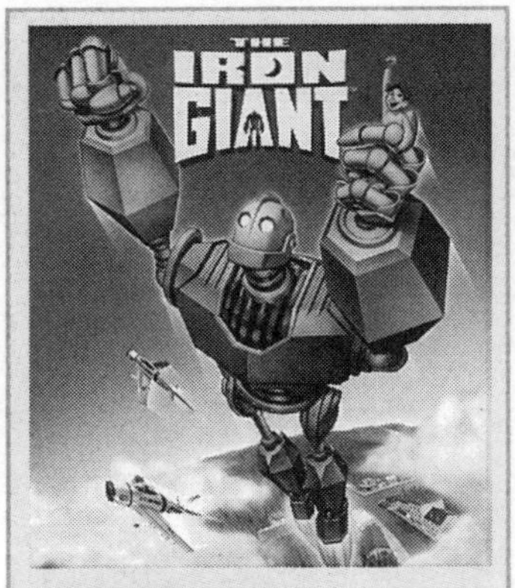

The Iron Giant (1999)
This wonderful animated fable is set in a New England town in 1957 and focuses on a young boy named Hogarth who desperately wants to find a pet his mother would approve of. Instead, he finds a 50-foot-tall robot from outer space that eats metal. While Hogarth and his metallic visitor become close pals, a nasty government agent tries to capture the alien. With voices by Jennifer Aniston, Harry Connick, Jr., Eli Marienthal. 87 min.
19-2911 □*$22.99*

The Iron Giant (Letterboxed Version)
Also available in a theatrical, widescreen format.
19-2925 □*$22.99*

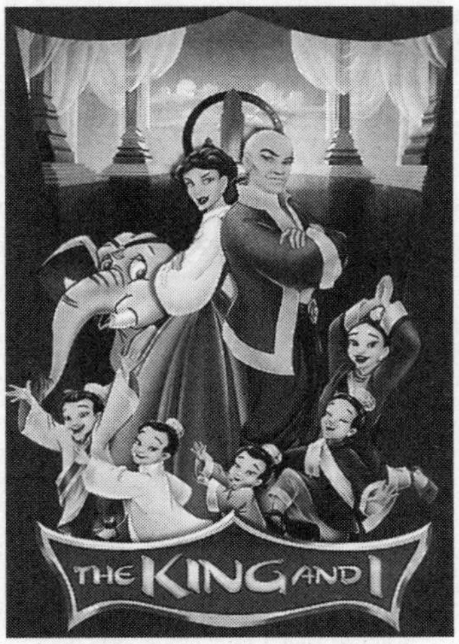

The King And I (1999)
The beloved Rodgers and Hammerstein musical becomes a charming animated tale for all ages, as British governess Anna Owen and her son arrive in Siam to teach the royal family's children. Along the way Anna befriends the headstrong king, while she and her charges must stop a scheming advisor from claiming the throne. "Getting to Know You" and "Shall We Dance" are among the classic songs featured; voices by Miranda Richardson, Martin Vidnovic, Ian Richardson. 90 min.
19-2871 Was $19.99 □*$14.99*

Anna And The King (1999)
The remarkable true story of the English schoolteacher who travelled with her young son to 1860s Siam to serve as instructor to the royal household is told in animated form. Watch as Anna's Western ways conflict with those of the obstinate monarch, and as Anna's son Louis and the crown prince learn to work together in order to save the kingdom. 50 min.
89-5224 *$14.99*

The Mighty Kong (1996)
The classic "giant ape meets girl" story becomes an exciting, song-filled animated adventure. Follow the Mighty Kong as he's taken from his jungle island home to New York, where he escapes and threatens to destroy the city unless the woman who's captured his heart can stop him. Jodi Benson and Dudley Moore supply voices; music by Richard and Robert Sherman ("Mary Poppins"). 78 min.
19-2695 □*$19.99*

Quest For Camelot (1998)
Lively animated saga with music details the adventures of Kayley, a knight's spunky daughter who teams with a two-headed dragon and a blind squire to retrieve the sword Excalibur from the evil Ruber in the England of King Arthur. Jessalyn Gilsig, Cary Elwes, Gary Oldman, Don Rickles, Pierce Brosnan and Eric Idle supply the voices; soundtrack by Celine Dion, LeAnn Rimes, Steve Perry. 86 min.
19-2748 Was $19.99 □*$14.99*

Jirimpimbira (1995)
A young African boy seeking food and water for his starving village receives a set of magical bones that can make his thoughts come true, but before using them to save his people he first learns a valuable lesson about greed and friendship. Diahann Carroll, James Avery and Meshach Taylor supply voices for this cartoon based on a folk story. 25 min.
19-9162 *$12.99*

The First Snow Of Winter (1999)
Fine family animated film about Sean, a little duck who misses his flight South when an airplane knocks him out of the sky. While preparing for the oncoming winter, Sean is befriended by a pal named Voley, who shows him how to gather food and get ready for the cold as well as watch out for the fox. Tim Curry and Carol Kane provide voices. 30 min.
02-3370 □*$14.99*

Bartok The Magnificent (1999)
You're sure to go "batty" for this feature-length animated tale featuring the hapless winged hero from "Anastasia," who must rescue his new friend Prince Ivan from the nasty witch Baba Yaga. Voices by Hank Azaria, Tim Curry, Kelsey Grammer and Jennifer Tilly. 80 min.
04-3857 Was $19.99 □*$14.99*

Balto (1995)
Thrilling animated adventure, based on the true story of a half-husky/half-wolf dog named Balto who overcame many dangers to deliver vital medicine to the snow-trapped town of Nome, Alaska, in 1925. Kevin Bacon, Bridget Fonda, Bob Hoskins and Phil Collins lend their voices to this inspiring family tale. 78 min.
07-2401 Was $19.99 □*$14.99*

Once Upon A Forest (1993)
A wonderfully animated environmental adventure in which a group of cute creatures, including a mole, a hedgehog and a wood mouse, attempt to save their friend and their forest from the destruction caused by a runaway chemical truck. Ben Vereen and Michael Crawford provide voices. 71 min.
04-2688 Was $24.99 □*$14.99*

Ninja Turtles: The Next Mutation
The shell-backed superheroes are back—and they're not alone! Raphael, Michaelangelo, Leonardo and Donatello get some timely help from their new female ally, a turtle named Venus De Milo, as they go up against the dangerous Dragon Lord in this feature-length adventure. 80 min.
04-3679 □*$14.99*

Night Of The Headless Horseman (1999)
William H. Macy, Tia Carrere, Mark Hamill and Luke Perry lend their voices to this well-made and atmospheric animated adaptation of the Washington Irving tale about the timid 18th-century schoolteacher of Sleepy Hollow and his encounter with the ghostly night rider. 63 min.
04-3979 *$12.99*

Faeries (1999)
Lively animation from England tells of two children who, while having a fun vacation on a farm, are transported to the magical Fairyland. But after one of them eats a special cake, they must complete three special tasks before they can return home. Jeremy Irons, Kate Winslet and Dougray Scott provide the voices. 75 min.
06-3012 □*$19.99*

The Pebble And The Penguin (1995)
Shy and chubby penguin Hubie may get his chance to win the lady bird of his dreams when he finds a brilliant emerald to use as a "betrothal pebble," but along the way he's got to deal with kidnappers, killer whales and a mean-hearted rival. This enchanting Don Bluth production features voices by Martin Short, James Belushi and Tim Curry and music by Barry Manilow. 74 min.
12-2981 Was $19.99 □*$14.99*

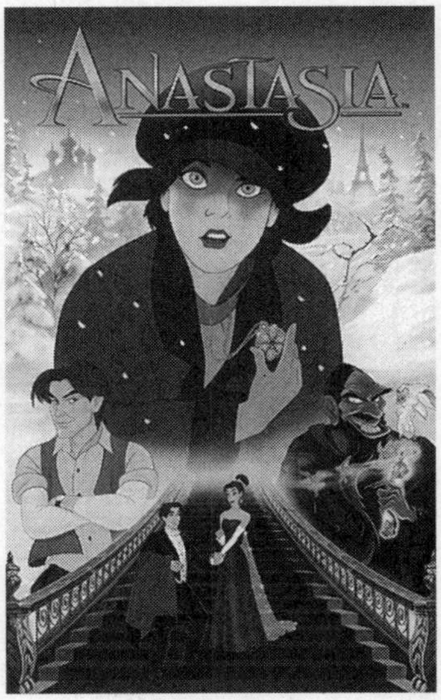

Anastasia (1997)
Dazzling, music-filled animated adaptation of the story of an amnesiac young woman in '20s Russia who is groomed by a pair of con artists to pose as the Princess Anastasia, sole survivor of the family of Czar Nicholas, in order to collect a reward. No one suspects that she is the real princess except the evil mage Rasputin, whose curse led to her family's downfall. Meg Ryan, John Cusack, Kelsey Grammer, Angela Lansbury and Christopher Lloyd supply voices. 94 min.
04-3606 Was $19.99 □*$14.99*

Anastasia (Letterboxed Version)
Also available in a theatrical, widescreen format. Includes behind-the-scenes footage on the making of the film.
04-3611 □*$26.99*

Babes In Toyland (1997)
Victor Herbert's classic operetta becomes a charming animated "toy story," as Jack and Jill and other favorite Mother Goose characters must save Christmas by stopping the nasty Barnaby from putting the Toyland Factory out of business. James Belushi, Lacey Chabert, Bronson Pinchot, Christopher Plummer and Charles Nelson Reilly supply voices. 74 min.
12-3196 Was $19.99 ❑*$14.99*

Cats Don't Dance (1997)
A small-town feline heads to California in the 1930s with dreams of becoming a movie star, only to find he and his fellow animal actors are doomed to bit player status, in this colorful and song-filled cartoon salute to the Golden Age of Hollywood. Scott Bakula, Jasmine Guy, Kathy Najimy and Natalie Cole are among the voice talents; songs by Randy Newman. 77 min.
18-7761 Was $19.99 ❑*$14.99*

Rover Dangerfield (1991)
In this funny animated story with music, Rodney Dangerfield provides the voice for the lead character, a streetwise, high-rolling canine from Las Vegas who finds love and wins respect at a nearby farm. Everybody will love this shaggy dog story, wonderfully animated by the creators of "The Brave Little Toaster." 78 min.
19-1914 Was $19.99 ❑*$14.99*

Pippi Longstocking (1997)
Astrid Lindgren's pig-tailed, mischievous 9-year-old heroine makes her animated debut in this song-filled feature, as Pippi and her pals set out on a wild series of adventures. 75 min.
19-2611 ❑*$19.99*

Pippi Longstocking: Pippi's Adventures On The South Seas (1999)
Get ready for an exciting voyage with the irrepressible Pippi, as she and her pals join set sail with Pippi's sea captain dad. Watch as they search for the fabled Cave of Pearls and fend off pirates in this animated feature. 70 min.
44-2216 ❑*$14.99*

A Troll In Central Park (1994)
A wondrous animated fantasy from animator Don Bluth about Stanley, a sweet-natured troll who is sent from his home in Troll Land to danger-filled New York City. After settling in Central Park, Stanley uses his magic to help a young girl and her brother in trouble. Dom DeLuise, Cloris Leachman and Hayley Mills provide the voices. 76 min.
19-2293 ❑*$19.99*

The Thief And The Cobbler (1996)
From Richard Williams, the animation genius behind "Who Framed Roger Rabbit," comes this beautiful, music-filled fantasy which took 30 years to complete. The story tells of an apprentice cobbler and a nameless thief who live in Baghdad and have to help a princess and her subjects from being invaded by an army of one-eyed men. With voices by Matthew Broderick, Vincent Price and Jennifer Beals. AKA: "Arabian Knight."
11-2091 ❑*$14.99*

Toonsylvania (1997)
Looking for some monstrously madcap adventures? Why not join demented medico Dr. Vic Frankenstein, his hapless hunchbacked aide Igor, and lunkheaded creature Phil for a frightfully funny feature-length tale culled from the hit Saturday morning TV series. 88 min.
07-2782 *$14.99*

The Pagemaster (1994)
A shy young boy learns valuable lessons about courage and the joy of reading, thanks to a mysterious librarian who sends him into an animated realm where three talking books guide him through such classic adventures as "Treasure Island," "Moby Dick" and "Jack and the Beanstalk." Macaulay Culkin and Christopher Lloyd star in this mix of live-action and cartoon excitement; Whoopi Goldberg, Leonard Nimoy and Patrick Stewart supply voices. 76 min.
04-2931 Was $19.99 ❑*$14.99*

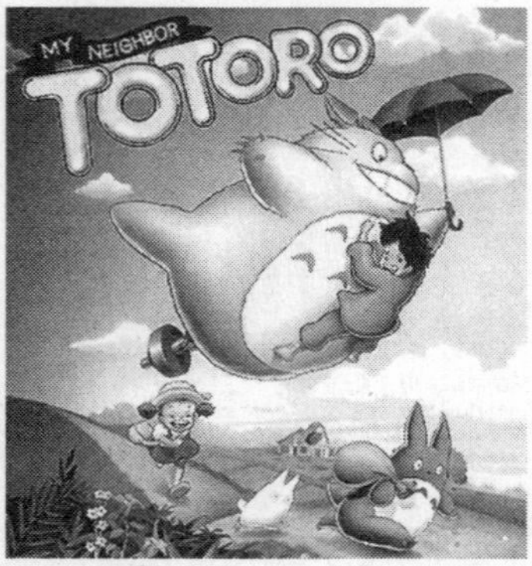

My Neighbor Totoro (1993)
Wonderful animated adventure about two young sisters in Japan who befriend the "Totoros," fuzzy forest creatures who are able to fly over mountains and make giant trees grow overnight...and who are invisible to adults. This delightful story features fantastic animation that will win over all ages. 87 min.
04-2837 Was $19.99 ❑*$14.99*

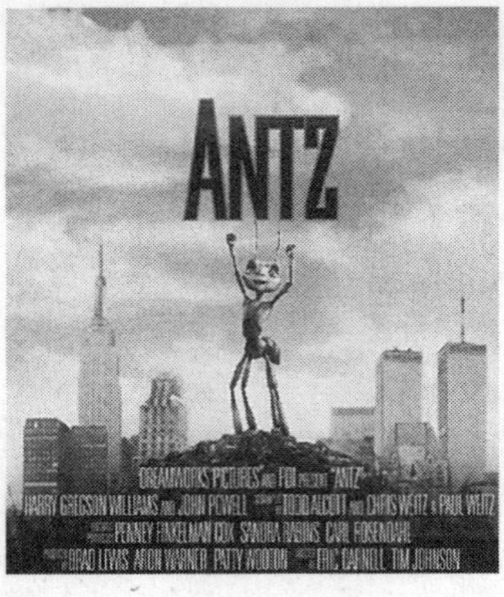

Antz (1998)
Take an up-close look at the everyday ant-ics of an ant colony where a neurotic worker named Z (voiced by Woody Allen) sets out to, with the help of his soldier buddy Weaver (Sylvester Stallone), prove his individuality and win the love of Princess Bala (Sharon Stone). Dazzling computer animation and a witty look at insect life make this a treat for all ages. Other voices include Dan Aykroyd, Anne Bancroft, Gene Hackman, Jennifer Lopez. 83 min.
07-2715 Was $19.99 ❑*$14.99*

Little Monsters: The Adventures Of Koby & The Oakie Dokeys (1998)
By day they're ordinary-looking household objects, but at night Koby and his pals come to life as miniature monsters. Their goal is to frighten everyone they meet, but when invading alien duckmen begin kidnapping children, it's up to the Little Monsters to save the day in this silly and scary animated feature. 88 min.
88-7021 *$14.99*

Aladdin And The Adventure Of All Time (1999)
In this fantastic animated adventure, Aladdin and his friend Paige have an incredible journey on a magic carpet that includes visits to English kings, Egyptian queens, a Tyrannosaurus Rex and Blackbeard the Pirate. With voices by E.G. Daily and Ed Gilbert. 81 min.
21-9208 *$29.99*

Puss In Boots: The Animated Storybook (1998)
A young man is trained to become a hero and win the hand of a beautiful princess by his ally—a wisecracking walking and talking cat—in this lively animated feature. Voices by Judge Reinhold, Vivian Schilling, Dan Haggerty and Michael York as Puss in Boots. 66 min.
88-7019 *$14.99*

Doug's 1st Movie (1999)
Jim Jenkins' pre-teen hero of his own cable and Saturday morning cartoon series now becomes a film star, as Doug Funnie and his pal Skeeter find a "monster" living in pollution-ravaged Lucky Duck Lake. Will Doug's discovery help him win Patti Mayonnaise's heart at last, or will he help save "Herman" the monster from a nasty industrialist? 77 min.
11-2344 Was $19.99 ❑*$14.99*

Rock-A-Doodle (1992)
Chanticleer's a rockin' rooster who leaves the barnyard behind him for a taste of life singing in the big city, but when the farm is threatened with no more sun, only his crowing can save the day. Song-filled cartoon tale from the Don Bluth studios features the voices of Glen Campbell, Sandy Duncan, Ellen Greene, Phil Harris, Christopher Plummer. 74 min.
44-1894 Was $19.99 ❑*$14.99*

The Swan Princess (1994)
Inspired by "Swan Lake," this animated, musical fairy tale tells of an evil wizard who kidnaps beautiful Princess Odette and turns her into a swan. She can't become human again until she agrees to marry the sorcerer, but coming to help her are a frog, a turtle, a bird and Prince Derek, her true love. Jack Palance, John Cleese and Steven Wright supply the voices. 90 min.
02-5050 Was $24.99 ❑*$14.99*

The Swan Princess II: Escape From Castle Mountain (1997)
The adventures of Princess Odette, Prince Derek, and their animal allies continue in this fanciful family feature filled with action and humor, as they must save their kingdom from the schemes of Clavius, an evil magician who wants to become ruler. 75 min.
18-7772 Was $19.99 *$14.99*

The Swan Princess III And The Mystery Of The Enchanted Treasure (1998)
In this all-new, song-filled cartoon feature, a nasty sorceress named Zelda kidnaps Princess Odette in order to force Prince Derek to turn over a magical treasure known as the Forbidden Arts. Can Derek, Jean-Bob the frog, Speed the turtle and Puffin the parrot rescue Odette in time? 75 min.
02-3195 Was $19.99 ❑*$14.99*

Babar: King Of The Elephants (1999)
See how an orphaned elephant named Babar is brought to the big city and cared for by a kindly old lady, and how he returns to his jungle home to meet his true love and become ruler of his fellow pachyderms, in this delightful animated feature based on the timeless children's books. 79 min.
44-2204 ❑*$19.99*

Snow White And The Seven Dwarfs (1992)
Colorful animation helps tell the story of the beautiful Snow White and her animal friends as they meet the Seven Dwarfs in the forest. 40 min.
45-5526 ❑*$12.99*

The Brave Little Toaster (1987)
Charming animated feature follows the adventures of five plucky household appliances (toaster, radio, lamp, electric blanket, vacuum cleaner) as they leave their summer cottage home behind and set out to find their "master" in the big city. A wonderful film for all ages; voices by Phil Hartman, Jon Lovitz, Deanna Oliver. 90 min.
11-1563 Was $22.99 ❑*$14.99*

The Brave Little Toaster Goes To Mars (1998)
All of your favorite animated appliance pals are back in an all-new feature-length saga that finds them blasting off into outer space on a quest to save their owner's new baby. Includes the voices of Carol Channing, Farrah Fawcett and Wayne Knight. 73 min.
11-2236 Was $19.99 ❑*$14.99*

The Brave Little Toaster To The Rescue (1999)
The cartoon adventures of the heroic bread-burner and his fellow appliances continue, as they put their voltages together to save a family of cats from being shipped off to a testing lab, in this song-filled feature. 74 min.
11-2314 Was $19.99 ❑*$14.99*

An American Tail (1986)
Engaging animated feature from Don Bluth that tells the story of Fievel Mouskewitz, a young mouse who flees Russia for America, where the streets are paved with cheese. He becomes separated from his family upon reaching New York, and his quest to find them makes for wonderful adventure. 80 min.
07-1520 ❑*$19.99*

An American Tail: Fievel Goes West (1991)
The adventures of plucky little Fievel Mouskewitz and his family continue in the Wild West in this charming animated sequel, as the mouse becomes "deputy" in a frontier town and helps bring some feline felons to justice. John Cleese, Dom DeLuise, Amy Irving and James Stewart provide voices. 75 min.
07-1795 ❑*$19.99*

An American Tail: The Treasure Of Manhattan Island (2000)
Everyone's favorite young rodent, Fievel the mouse, is back in an all-new cartoon feature. Join Fievel and his pals Tiger and Tony as the search for a fortune buried beneath the streets of New York takes them on a wild adventure. Voices by David Carradine, Lacey Chabert and Dom DeLuise. 80 min.
07-2823 ❑*$19.99*

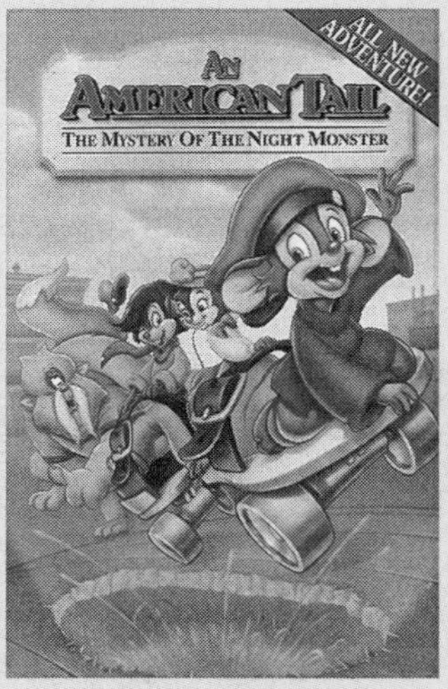

An American Tail: The Mystery Of The Night Monster (2000)
Who—or what—is responsible for the disappearance of mice off the streets of New York? The search for the rodent-grabbing culprit sends Fievel and his pals, along with intrepid mouse reporter Nellie Brie, on an exciting feature-length adventure. Dom DeLuise, Lacy Chabert and Robert Hays supply voices.
07-2885 ❑*$14.99*

Linnea In Monet's Garden (1993)
A charming animated adaptation of the best-selling children's book, following a little girl in 19th-century Europe who takes a trip to Paris and visits the garden of Claude Monet, where the artist's colorful paintings come to life. 30 min.
70-5069 Was $19.99 *$14.99*

The Pirates Of Dark Water (1990)
Dive into a world of animated fantasy and adventure in this feature-length tale from Hanna-Barbera and the co-creator of "An American Tail." On an ocean-covered world, young Prince Ren and his allies search for the treasures that will free his kingdom from pirate rule. 90 min.
72-1053 ❑*$29.99*

Treasure Island (1996)
Robert Louis Stevenson's classic adventure tale is wonderfully brought to life in this animated feature in which such legendary characters as Long John Silver and Jim Hawkins are portrayed as animals. 93 min.
88-7006 *$19.99*

All Dogs Go To Heaven (1989)
An amiable, streetwise mutt returns to Earth to get even with the gamblers who rubbed him out and winds up helping a poor orphan girl along the way in this charming animated fable from Don Bluth ("The Land Before Time"). Burt Reynolds, Loni Anderson and Dom DeLuise lend their voices to the canine caper. 85 min.
12-2051 Was $19.99 ❑*$14.99*

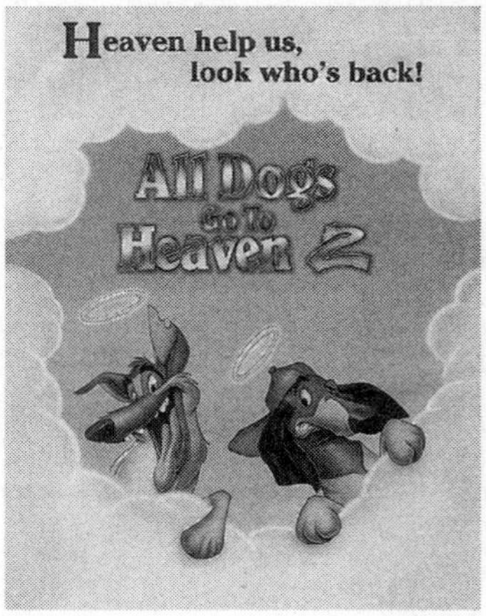

All Dogs Go To Heaven 2 (1996)
Angelic canines Charlie and Itchy are back on Earth, sent down to find Gabriel's stolen horn. They land in San Francisco, where they have to keep the powerful instrument out of the paws of the nasty Red, who will have all pooches exiled to Devil's Island if he has his way. Charlie Sheen, Sheena Easton and Dom DeLuise provide the voices to this tune-filled sequel. 83 min.
12-3100 Was $19.99 ❑*$14.99*

Twice Upon A Time (1983)
Inventive animated adventure produced by George Lucas about a gang of bad creatures who want to produce nightmares for the world's population. Only a dog and his master have a chance to save the day! Fast-paced tale has been praised by animation fans and is considered a little-seen classic. Voices by Lorenzo Music and Marshall Efron. 75 min.
19-1824 ❑*$14.99*

Cartoons For Big Kids (1989)
Animation maven Leonard Maltin salutes the all-ages humor of Bugs Bunny, Daffy Duck, Screwball Squirrel and crew in a cartoon collection featuring adult-oriented satire, celebrity caricatures and surprisingly sexy gags. Includes "Red Hot Riding Hood," "King-Size Canary," "The Big Snooze" and "The Great Piggy Bank Robbery." 44 min.
18-7134 *$19.99*

Heidi's Song (1983)
Delightful animated tale of Heidi and her grandfather. Lively musical numbers and great fun for the entire family. Voices of Lorne Greene, Sammy Davis, Jr. 94 min.
14-3028 *$19.99*

The Chipmunk Adventure (1987)
Follow Simon, Theodore and the irrepressible Alvin on a round-the-world hot air balloon race. Exciting locations, dangerous jewel thieves, laughs and great songs make this an animated treat for the whole family. 78 min.
40-1332 Was $19.99 ❑*$14.99*

Alvin And The Chipmunks Meet Frankenstein (1999)
Everyone's favorite famous singing rodents—Alvin, Simon and Theodore—have a Halloween encounter with a mad scientist and the legendary monster in this song-filled, feature-length chipmunk tale. 78 min.
07-2783 Was $19.99 ❑*$14.99*

Alvin And The Chipmunks Meet The Wolfman (2000)
Things get hairy for Alvin and his siblings when they get mixed up in some wacky werewolf hijinks in this howlarious Halloween cartoon feature. 78 min.
07-2889 ❑*$14.99*

The Flight Of Dragons (1986)
Dazzling feature-length animated fantasy from the producers of "The Hobbit." A young man from the present is brought back in time to help stop an evil wizard and his dragon allies from taking over the world. John Ritter, James Earl Jones, Harry Morgan and Larry Storch supply voices. 95 min.
19-2126 Was $59.99 ***$14.99***

Silas Marner (1982)
An award-winning animated adaptation of George Eliot's famous novel about a miserly recluse whose heart is thawed when an adorable baby girl enters his life. Animated by Alison de Vere. 28 min.
53-7706 ***$19.99***

Journey Through Fairyland (1988)
Magical cartoon feature follows a young boy into a land of flower sprites, where he learns a valuable lesson about life. Splendid animation is mixed with classical music by Debussy, Tchaikovsky, Rimsky-Korsakov and others in a film that's been called a Japanese "Fantasia." 90 min.
69-5078 ***$14.99***

The Brave Frog (1989)
Can a good-hearted treefrog named Jonathon find happiness when he moves to Rainbow Pond and must prove himself to King Leopold and the other animals that call the pond home? Find out in this colorful, exciting animated feature for the frog-lover in you. 91 min.
80-1080 ***$14.99***

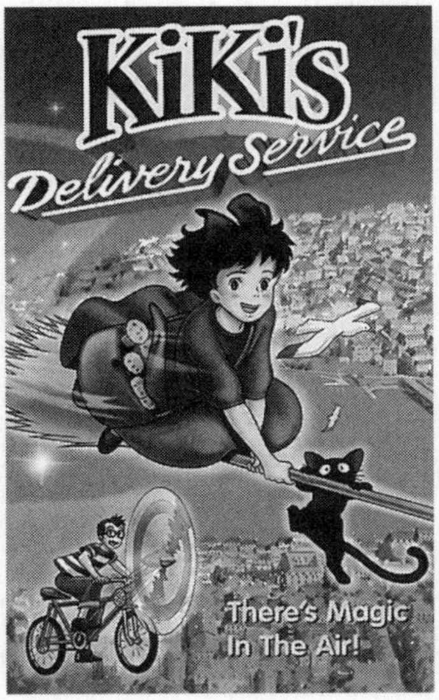

KiKi's Delivery Service (1989)
A box-office hit in its native Japan, this charming animated feature follows the whimsical adventures of a young witch named KiKi who, with her black cat Jiji, takes to the skies to help a bakery owner deliver his goods on time and winds up making new friends along the way. Kirsten Dunst, Janeane Garofalo, Phil Hartman, Matthew Lawrence and Debbie Reynolds supply the voices. AKA: "Majo No Takkyubin." 105 min. Dubbed in English.
11-2266 Was $19.99 □***$14.99***

Rainbow Brite And The Star Stealer (1985)
An exciting animated feature starring everyone's favorite colorful cutie, Rainbow Brite, and her friends in Rainbow Land. Together with the help of an outer space prince they must solve the mystery of the missing stars and save the galaxy from eternal darkness. 85 min.
19-1480 □***$14.99***

The Secret Of NIMH (1982)
An animated, fascinating family favorite about a widowed mouse who seeks the help of some mysterious, intelligent rats to save her family. Featuring the vocal talents of Peter Strauss, Dom DeLuise and Hermione Baddeley; listen for the voice of Shannen Doherty as Teresa. 83 min.
12-1252 □***$14.99***

The Secret Of Nimh 2: Timmy To The Rescue (1998)
The music and the magic is back in this new installment that continues the delightful tale of Timmy Brisby, the mouse with the heart of gold who grows up and learns that with the right amount of bravery, courage and trust, there isn't anything he can't do. Ralph Macchio, Eric Idle, Harvey Korman and Catherine O'Hara lend their voices to this feature-length cartoon. 70 min.
12-3261 ***$14.99***

The Care Bears Movie (1985)
From the toy shelf to the big screen to your home, those ubiquitous bringers of good cheer and happiness come from their home of Care-a-lot to help defeat an evil spirit. Animated fantasy narrated by Mickey Rooney; songs by Carole King and John Sebastian. 88 min.
47-1420 □***$14.99***

Care Bears Movie II: A New Generation (1986)
See how it all began! Meet the bears and their cuddling cousins when they were but wee cubs and find out how they became the custodians of caring. Will they fall victim to nasty Dark Heart's plan to eliminate all goodness? Featuring songs by Debbie Allen and Stephen Bishop. 77 min.
02-1626 Was $19.99 □***$14.99***

The Last Unicorn (1982)
Fanciful animated fable about a beautiful white unicorn who sets out on a quest to find others of her kind. Voices by Alan Arkin, Jeff Bridges, Mia Farrow, Angela Lansbury and Rene Auberjonois. 93 min.
27-5474 □***$14.99***

Cat City (1989)
Full-length animated fun filled with laughs and thrills, as a group of feline secret agents try to stop a mouse scientist from launching his latest invention: a weapon that will shrink the cats of Cat City down to rodent-sized proportions. 90 min.
50-2040 ***$59.99***

The Phantom Tollbooth (1970)
Live-action and animation blend in this musical fantasy tale of a young man who passes through a magic tollbooth into a world where bickering numbers and letters come alive. Butch Patrick stars, with the voices of Mel Blanc, June Foray and Hans Conried. Animation by Chuck Jones. 90 min.
12-1221 ***$19.99***

Puff The Magic Dragon (1979)
Magical animated retelling of the story of the fun-loving dragon from Honah Lee who teaches a lesson in self-esteem to little Jackie Draper. Songs by Peter, Paul and Mary; Burgess Meredith supplies Puff's voice. 30 min.
47-1315 Was $19.99 ***$12.99***

Robinson Crusoe (1970)
All-new animated rendition of the classic adventure story by Defoe, as shipwrecked Robinson Crusoe and faithful friend Friday must fend off enemies both natural and human on their island home. 55 min.
12-1539 ***$14.99***

The Water Babies (1978)
Live-action segments are mixed with animated sequences in this charming British fantasy about a London boy who enters a magical undersea kingdom where talking fish and aquatic creatures lead him on an exciting odyssey. James Mason, Billie Whitelaw, David Tomlinson and Tommy Pender star. 85 min.
53-1337 ***$14.99***

Winnie-The-Pooh (BBC) (1974)
With pictures based on the work of illustrator Ernest H. Shepard, A.A. Milne's classic stories of Winnie-the-Pooh, Piglet, Roo and Christopher Robin come vividly to life. A group of children visit Hundred Acre Wood, and Pooh and pals greet them in this BBC production. 57 min.
04-3215 ***$14.99***

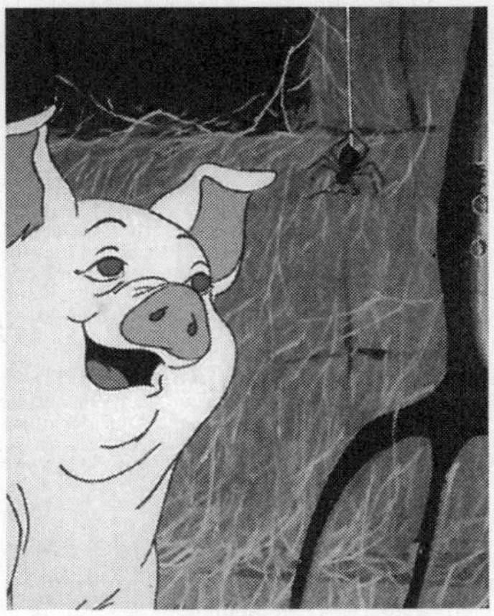

Charlotte's Web (1973)
Enjoyable and enchanting animated musical adaptation of E.B. White's classic barnyard tale about a shy piglet, slated for the breakfast table, who's befriended by a spider who saves his life with her "magic" web. Featuring the voice talents of Debbie Reynolds, Henry Gibson, Paul Lynde and Don Messick. 94 min.
06-1008 □***$14.99***

shinbone alley (1971)
Charming, song-filled animated feature based on Don Marquis' "archy and mehitabel" stories. Eddie Bracken and Carol Channing supply the voices of the cockroach and cat couple who share adventures amid the backways of New York. Songs include "I Am Only a Poor Humble Cockroach," "Ladybugs of the Evening," "Come to Meeoww." 83 min.
16-1121 ***$14.99***

Banjo The Woodpile Cat (1979)
Delightful animated story of a kitten who just can't stay out of trouble! It takes a trip to the big city to make him realize that "there's no place like home!" Seven years in the making, this wonderfully animated short was an early effort from director Don Bluth, produced in his garage independently from his Disney bosses. 49 min.
47-1583 □***$12.99***

The Cricket In Times Square (1973)
Charming animated story of a musically gifted cricket living in downtown New York who, with the help of a cat and mouse, brings joy into the hearts of the jaded citizens. 30 min.
27-5147 ***$12.99***

Gulliver's Travels Beyond The Moon (1966)
Japanese-made, "in name only" animated sequel to the Jonathan Swift story follows a young boy as he dreams of a journey he makes with the famed Gulliver, a dog, a crow and a toy soldier to a planet controlled by robots. 85 min.
09-5005 ***$19.99***

Alakazam The Great! (1961)
Animated fable from Japan about a young monkey prince who must face several trials on a quest to learn humility. Frankie Avalon, Jonathan Winters, Dodie Stevens and Arnold Stang provide the voices. 84 min.
44-1431 □***$14.99***

Panda And The Magic Serpent (1961)
Lovely animated fable from Japan focusing on the romance between a young man and a beautiful woman who is in reality an immortal mystical being. An evil wizard attempts to destroy them, and it's up to the man's animal friends (a panda, a raccoon, etc.) to save the day. Marvin Miller narrates. 74 min.
27-5052 Was $19.99 ***$14.99***

The Land Before Time (1988)
Antediluvian animated fable from animator Don Bluth ("An American Tail") follows five baby dinosaurs as they search for their missing families in the danger-filled world of 70 million years ago, learning to trust one another along the way. 69 min.
07-1622 □***$19.99***

The Land Before Time II: The Great Valley Adventure (1994)
Littlefoot the brontosaurus and his prehistoric buddies are back in this all-new, feature-length adventure, as a trip from peaceful Great Valley to the "Mysterious Beyond" has them dodging egg-stealing dinosaurs and tyrannosaurs, landslides, and other dangers. 74 min.
07-2207 □***$19.99***

The Land Before Time III: The Time Of The Great Giving (1995)
After a meteorite cuts off Great Valley's water supply, Littlefoot and his tiny dino comrades set out on a danger-filled quest to find a new source in this full-length animated dinosaur tale filled with action, comedy and song. 71 min.
07-2361 □***$19.99***

The Land Before Time IV: Journey Through The Mists (1996)
In their most exciting adventure yet, prehistoric pals Littlefoot, Ducky, Cera, Petrie and Spike travel through the unexplored "Land of the Mists" in order to find a special flower that can cure Littlefoot's ailing grandfather. It's an animated journey that blends laughs, danger and a lesson in friendship. 74 min.
07-2454 □***$19.99***

The Land Before Time V: The Mysterious Island (1997)
The search for a new food supply for their dinosaur families leads Littlefoot, Ducky, Spike and company to the title island and a reunion with their old pal Chomper the T-Rex in this exciting feature-length cartoon tale. 74 min.
07-2573 □***$19.99***

The Land Before Time VI: The Secret Of Saurus Rock (1998)
It's a secret that holds the key to the survival of the prehistoric denizens of the Great Valley, and it's up to Spike, Duckie, Petrie, Cera and Littlefoot to discover it in the dino-pals' sixth animated adventure. 77 min.
07-2699 □***$19.99***

The Land Before Time VII: The Stone Of Cold Fire (2000)
The appearance of a strange fireball in the sky sends Littlefoot, Ptery and the rest of the pint-size prehistoric critters on a trek to the Smoking Mountains to recover the mysterious object in this all-new, feature-length "Land Before Time" cartoon. 75 min.
07-2919 □***$19.99***

The Land Before Time Sing-Along Songs
Who says dinosaurs didn't sing? Join Littlefoot, Cera, Chomper and their friends in these wonderful collections of musical moments from the "Land Before Time" films, along with fun facts about the real world of prehistoric animals. Each tape runs about 30 min.

The Land Before Time: Sing-Along Songs
07-2519 □***$14.99***

The Land Before Time: More Sing-Along Songs
07-2807 □***$14.99***

The Adventures Of Sinbad (1960)
Marvelously animated adventure saga from Japan in which the young Sinbad and his companion, Ali, search for an island where priceless jewels are guarded by monstrous demons. With help from a magic carpet, Sinbad finds the island, meets a pretty princess and tackles various villains. 76 min.
09-2401 ***$19.99***

Alice Of Wonderland In Paris (1966)
"In-name-only" sequel to the Lewis Carroll favorite follows the animated adventures of a young girl named Alice as she travels to Paris and meets such memorable characters from children's literature as Anatole the bicycle-riding mouse, French schoolgirl Madeline, and others. Carl Reiner and Howard Morris are among the voice talents. AKA: "Alice in Paris." 52 min.
09-1124 ***$14.99***

The Hunting Of The Snark/Jabberwocky
Two timeless pieces of "Alice in Wonderland" author Lewis Carroll's "nonsense poetry" are brought to life in animated form in this wonderful program for all ages. Narrated by James Earl Jones. 27 min.
70-5174 ***$14.99***

Mad Monster Party? (1968)
Boris Karloff and Phyllis Diller lend their voices to this spooky shindig that mixes marionettes, comedy and shivers. Old Dr. Frankenstein is retiring and throws a monster mash to announce his replacement. Dracula, the Werewolf, the Mummy, Dr. Jekyll and many other ghouls show up for some scary fun. 94 min.
53-1422 ***$24.99***

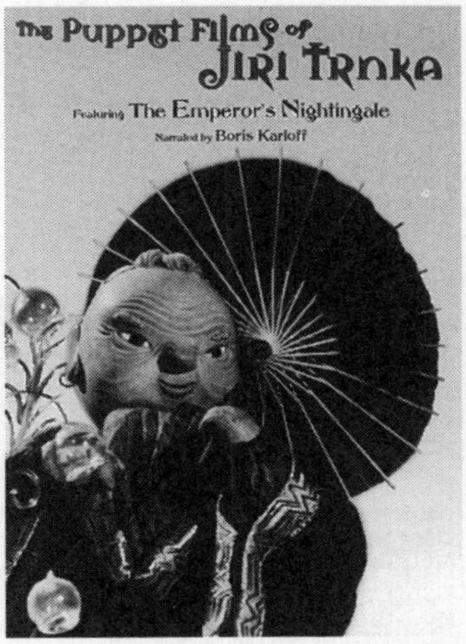

The Puppet Films Of Jiri Trnka
Remarkably lifelike stop-motion animation was the hallmark of Jiri Trnka, a Czech puppeteer and filmmaker whose works continue to delight young and old alike. This two-tape collection features Trnka's feature-length 1949 classic "The Emperor's Nightingale," with narration by Boris Karloff, along with the shorts "The Hand," "The Story of the Bass Cello," "A Merry Circus," "A Drop Too Much" and "The Song of the Prairie," and a documentary on his work. 156 min. total.
50-4918 ***$29.99***

Johnny The Giant Killer (1967)
This animated adventure from France tells the exciting tale of a boy named Johnny who teams with his friends to kill a giant. When the boy and his pals are captured, they are turned into miniature size and must battle all sorts of creatures. A Saturday matinee favorite. 74 min.
59-5044 Was $19.99 ***$14.99***

The Singing Princess (1967)
Julie Andrews supplies the magical voice for this musical animated feature that's an enchanting, fun journey to the days of the Arabian Nights. Genies, magical lamps and beautiful singing fill the screen. 66 min.
64-1028 ***$19.99***

Gay Purr-ee (1963)
Judy Garland, Robert Goulet and Red Buttons supply the voices to this animated musical delight about a country cat who journeys to turn-of-the-century Paris and finds love, danger and a possible marriage in Pittsburgh(!) during her adventures. "Wizard of Oz" songwriters "Yip" Harburg and Harold Arlen penned the music and Chuck Jones co-scripted this feature from the creators of "Mr. Magoo." 85 min.
19-1825 Was $59.99 □***$14.99***

Magic Horse (1959)
The first full-length animated film from the Soviet Union. Based on a popular children's book, the story involves a boy who befriends an enchanted horse that helps him learn who's been stealing his family's wheat. 54 min.
53-9319 Was $59.99 ***$14.99***

The Emperor's Nightingale (1949)
The Hans Christian Andersen fable comes to life through the wonderful stop-motion puppetry of Czech animator Jiri Trnka, framed by a live-action story of a lonely boy who dreams of a Chinese monarch and the bird whose song changes his life. Boris Karloff narrates. 57 min.
10-7235 Was $19.99 ***$14.99***

Thomas The Tank Engine & Friends

The lovable locomotive whose stop-motion animated adventures on "Shining Time Station" won him legions of fans now stars in his own video series. Join Thomas and his railroad comrades as they ride into a trackload of trouble, yet always learn a valuable lesson in the nick of time. Each tape runs about 40 min. There are eight volumes available, including:

Thomas The Tank Engine: Races, Rescues & Runaways
08-8774 ❑*$12.99*

10 Years Of Thomas The Tank Engine & Friends
08-8781 ❑*$12.99*

Thomas The Tank Engine: Spills, Chills & Other Thomas Thrills
08-8817 ❑*$12.99*

Thomas The Tank Engine: Make Someone Happy
08-8857 ❑*$12.99*

The Wind In The Willows

Climb aboard for a wild ride with that auto-loving amphibian, Toad of Toad Hall, as he tears along the English countryside—and drives his pals Mole, Ratty and Badger to distraction—in this lively animated feature based on the perennially popular children's book. 71 min.
02-3372 ❑*$12.99*

The Wind In The Willows (1987)

One of the most beloved characters in children's literature, the irascible and daredevil Mr. Toad of Toad Hall, drives his friends Ratty, Mole and Badger to distraction in this song-filled cartoon adaptation of Kenneth Grahame's book. Voices by Charles Nelson Reilly, Roddy McDowall, Jose Ferrer and Eddie Bracken. 96 min.
19-2128 Was $19.99 *$14.99*

The Wind In The Willows (1994)

From the people who brought you "The World of Peter Rabbit" and "The Snowman" comes this marvelous animated version of Kenneth Grahame's classic chronicling the adventures of Rat, Mole, Badger and Toad on the riverbank. Alan Bennett, Michael Palin, Rik Mayall and Michael Gambon provide the voices; Vanessa Redgrave narrates. 74 min.
10-2745 *$14.99*

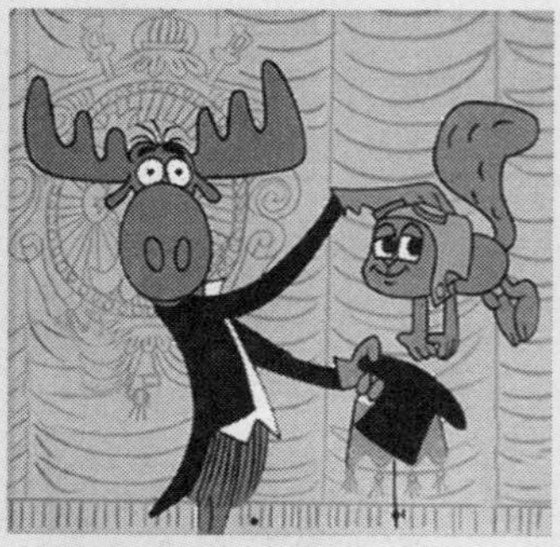

Rocky & Bullwinkle

"Hey, Rocky, watch me pull the funniest animated TV series of all time out of my hat!" Follow the classic capers of Rocky the Flying Squirrel and his antlered amigo, Bullwinkle J. Moose, as they foil the nasty plans of Boris Badenov and Natasha Fatale. These special video editions feature each show complete and uncut, along with "Bullwinkle's Corner," "Mr. Know-It-All," "Fractured Fairy Tales," "Peabody's Improbable History" and other surprises.

Rocky & Bullwinkle: Jet Fuel Formula
A simple cake recipe gets our heroes mixed up in a search for a "Jet Fuel Formula," as Rocky and Bullwinkle have to deal not only with Boris and Natasha, but also moonmen Gidney and Cloyd. Twenty shows; 440 min. on three tapes.
09-5436 *$59.99*

Rocky & Bullwinkle: Box Top Robbery
Boris launches a fiendish plot to seize control of the world's economy by printing up counterfeit cereal box tops! Can Bullwinkle's prized box top collection save the day? Six shows; 132 min.
09-5437 *$19.99*

Rocky & Bullwinkle: Metal-Munching Mice
Who—or what—is making off with the TV antennas of Frostbite Falls? Rocky and Bullwinkle set out to find the answer, but can they stop the outer space menace of "Metal-Munching Mice"? Eight shows; 176 min. on two tapes.
09-5438 *$29.99*

Rocky & Bullwinkle: Greenpert Oogle
When a remote island loses its legendary fortune-telling Oogle bird, they search for a substitute prognosticator and wind up kidnapping...Bullwinkle? Six shows; 132 min.
09-5439 *$19.99*

Rocky & Bullwinkle: Upsidaisium
When Bullwinkle inherits a mine filled with the priceless anti-gravity metal "Upsidaisium," he and Rocky become the targets of Boris and Natasha as well as their boss, the mysterious Mr. Big. Eighteen shows; 396 min. on three tapes.
09-5440 *$59.99*

Rocky & Bullwinkle: Rue Britannia
A birthmark on Bullwinkle's foot (hoof?) taps him as the heir to Abominable Manor in England, but will he and Rocky get there before some scheming relations bump them off for the inheritance? Four shows; 88 min.
09-5441 *$19.99*

Rocky & Bullwinkle: Wailing Whale
The search for missing ships lands the moose and squirrel deep in the belly of "Wailing Whale" Maybe Dick, and deep undersea in the aquatic city of Submerbia. Seven shows; 154 min.
09-5444 *$19.99*

Rocky & Bullwinkle: Buried Treasure
A newspaper contest hunt for "Buried Treasure" lands Bullwinkle in the not-so-tender clutches of mobster Baby Face Braunschweiger (better known as Boris You-Know-Who) and his gang. Seven shows; 154 min.
09-5442 *$19.99*

Rocky & Bullwinkle: The Last Angry Moose
Will Bullwinkle's "ultry sultry look" win him a shot at Hollywood stardom as matinee idol "Crag Antler," or will scheming Boris and Natasha seize the chance to empty the moose's money mattress? Two shows; 44 min.
09-5443 *$19.99*

Rocky & Bullwinkle: Bumbling Brothers Circus
When big top siblings Hugo and Igo Bumbling are faced with bankruptcy, Rocky uses his flying skills—and Bullwinkle puts tissue paper to comb to tame lions—in order to save their circus. Five shows; 110 min.
09-5445 *$19.99*

Rocky & Bullwinkle: Mucho Loma
The fellows are up to their necks (or, in Bullwinkle's case, his knees) in "Mucho Loma" when they have a south-of-the-border encounter with desperate desperado Zero. Three shows; 66 min.
09-5446 *$19.99*

Rocky & Bullwinkle: Pottsylvania Creeper
Bullwinkle's entry at the Frostbite Falls flower show could wind up overrunning the town thanks to Boris Badenov, who gave the moose a seed from a fast-growing "Pottsylvania Creeper." Three shows; 66 min.
09-5447 *$19.99*

Rocky & Bullwinkle: The Ruby Yacht
Could Bullwinkle's favorite bathtub toy boat actually be the priceless "Ruby Yacht" of Omar Khayyam, and what will happen to the hapless moose if it is? Three shows; 66 min.
09-5448 *$19.99*

Rocky & Bullwinkle: Bullwinkle's Testimonial Dinner
Bullwinkle's quest for a clean shirt to wear to a banquet being held in his honor takes him and Rocky all the way to China, where Boris and Natasha have some "laundering" plans of their own. Three shows; 66 min.
09-5449 *$19.99*

Rocky & Bullwinkle: The Weather Lady
Disaster strikes Frostbite Falls when the town's weather-predicting mechanical fortune teller is stolen. Rocky and Bullwinkle wind up posing as riverboat gamblers as they try to retrieve it. Three shows; 66 min.
09-5450 *$19.99*

Rocky & Bullwinkle: Louse On 92nd Street
A simple trip to the market for onions turns into a hostage drama for Bullwinkle, who mistakes some crooks' getaway car for a taxi. Three shows; 66 min.
09-5451 *$19.99*

Rocky & Bullwinkle: Wossamotta U.
Bullwinkle in college? It happens when he and Rocky become the star football players for the formerly winless "Wossamotta U." squad, but will Boris, Natasha and Fearless Leader fix the big game? Six shows; 132 min.
09-5452 *$19.99*

Rocky & Bullwinkle: Moosylvania Saved
It's up to Bullwinkle to rescue his sacred (and swampy) ancestral homeland from Boris and Natasha's latest villainy in "Moosylvania Saved." Four shows; 88 min.
09-5453 *$19.99*

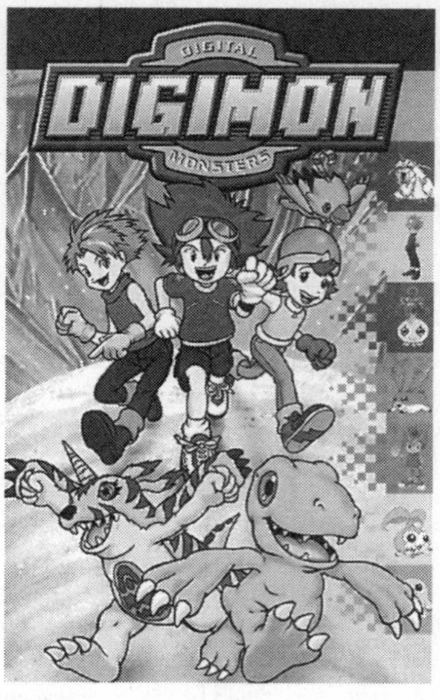

Digimon

Get ready for the animated ride of your life, as seven youngsters find themselves trapped in a strange world filled with "digital monsters" known as Digimons. Helping the good Digimons learn to "digevolve" into mighty fighters, the kids search for the way home in the hit Saturday morning TV series. Each tape features three episodes and runs about 75 min.

Digimon, Vol. 1
Includes "And So It Begins," "The Birth of Greymon" and "Garurumon."
04-3890 ❑*$14.99*

Digimon, Vol. 2
Includes "Biyomon Gets Firepower," "Kabuterimon Electro Shocker" and "Togemon in Toy Town."
04-3959 ❑*$14.99*

Digimon, Vol. 3
04-3972 ❑*$14.99*

Digimon 3-Pack
Volumes 1-3 of the "Digimon" saga are available in a boxed set.
04-3973 Save $5.00! *$39.99*

Calvin & The Colonel

"Amos 'n Andy's" Freeman Gosden and Charles Correll supplied the voices for this early '60s animated effort, which they also created. The series told of Southern animals Calvin, an amiable bear, and the Colonel, a sly fox, who attempt to adjust to a big city in the North. Each tape features two episodes and runs about 55 min.

Calvin & The Colonel, Vol. 1
Includes "The Thanksgiving Dinner" and "Sister Sue's Sweetheart."
09-5306 *$14.99*

Calvin & The Colonel, Vol. 2
Includes "Sycamore Lounge" and "Wheeling and Dealing."
09-5307 *$14.99*

Calvin & The Colonel, Vol. 3
Includes "The Costume Ball" and "Nephew Newton's Fortune."
09-5435 *$14.99*

The Last Polar Bears

An adventurous grandfather, accompanied by his trusty dog Roo, journeys to the North Pole in search of the fabled Great Bear Ridge, home of the last polar bears. Wonderful animated tale features narration by Nigel Hawthorne. 30 min.
04-5750 *$9.99*

Spot

The hero of the popular books by Eric Hill stars in this terrific video series, designed especially for toddlers. Using colorful, storybook animation, lovable pooch Spot and his friends come to life on tapes that include interactive, lift-the-flap booklets. Except where noted, each tape runs about 30 min. There are seven volumes available, including:

Where's Spot?
11-1723 ❑*$12.99*

Spot Goes To The Farm
11-1724 ❑*$12.99*

Spot Goes To A Party
11-1793 ❑*$12.99*

Spot And His Grandparents Go To The Carnival
11-2208 ❑*$12.99*

Discover Spot
Special double-length tape runs 65 min.
11-2420 ❑*$19.99*

Woody Woodpecker: 50th Anniversary Edition, Vol. 1

The wacky woodpecker created by Walter Lantz celebrates a half-century in this fast and furious collection. Includes Woody's first starring cartoon, 1941's "The Cracked Nut," along with "Banquet Busters," "The Redwood Sap" and "Born to Peck." 30 min.
07-1660 ❑*$14.99*

Woody Woodpecker: 50th Anniversary Edition, Vol. 2

Woody's greatest pecks, including "The Coo Coo Bird," "Ace in the Hole" "Well Oiled" and "Arts and Flowers." 30 min.
07-1661 ❑*$14.99*

Man's Best Friend

Some of the doggone funniest cartoons you ever saw, as Woody Woodpecker and his pals face canine calamities. "Helter Shelter," "Dig That Dog," "Private Eye Pooch," "Crazy Mixed Up Pup," "Man's Best Friend," "Dog Tax Dodgers," "Swiss Misfit" and "Get Lost! Little Doggy" are included. 51 min.
07-1336 *$14.99*

Wild And Woody

That wacky, wascally woodpecker wounds up laughs in the Wild West in these classic cartoon comedies. Includes "Puny Express," "Stage Hoax," "Short in the Saddle," "Hot Noon," "Pistol Packin' Woodpecker," "Panhandle Scandal," "Wild and Woody" and "Woodpecker Wanted." 51 min.
07-1337 *$14.99*

The World Of Andy Panda

What's black and white and funny all over? Andy Panda, of course, as you'll see in this Walter Lantz Cartoon collection. "Apple Andy," "Andy Panda's Pop," "Nutty Pine Cabin," "Meatless Tuesday," "Under the Spreading Blacksmith Shop," "Good-Bye, Mr. Moth," "Crow Crazy," "The Wacky Weed" and the Oscar-nominated "The Poet and the Peasant." 62 min.
07-1338 *$14.99*

Cartoonal Knowledge: Farmer Gray Goes To The Dogs (Cats, Monkeys & Lions)

More of the put-upon barnyard boss' silent cartoon antics, courtesy of the Paul Terry studios. "Small Town Sheriff," "The Medicine Man," "Monkey Shines," "Coast to Coast," "The Huntsman," "Cracked Ice" and "Mouse's Bride." 55 min. Silent with music score.
09-2176 Was $24.99 *$19.99*

Jack And The Beanstalk

Take some magic beans, add a young boy named Jack who's good at climbing, and toss in a hungry, treasure-hoarding giant, and you get this lively, song-filled animated retelling of the beloved fairy tale. Ben Savage, Sara Gilbert and Tone Loc supply voices. 75 min.
04-5721 ❑*$14.99*

Anastasia

Exciting, song-filled animated tale follows the struggle of the beautiful young Russian princess after her family is betrayed by the cruel Rasputin. Forced to flee for her life, Anastasia loses her memory and is aided by a handsome soldier named Alexander. 48 min.
04-5515 *$14.99*

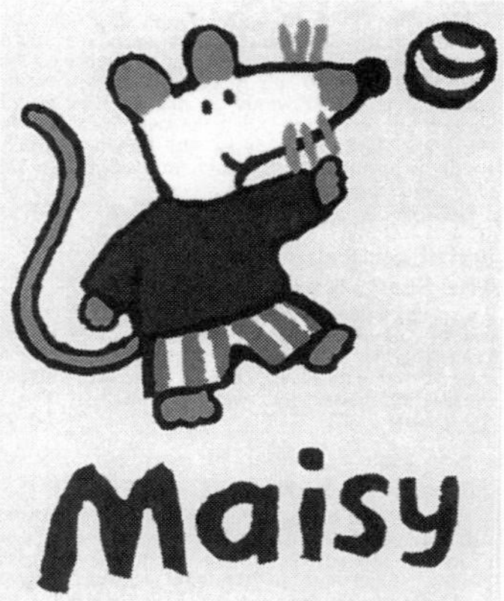

Maisy

Maisy is a mischievous little mouse who enjoys having fun with her friends and exploring the world around her. Now her popular cable TV exploits are on home video with these animated mouse tales designed to entertain and educate pre-schoolers. Each tape runs about 40 min. There are eight volumes available, including:

Count With Maisy
07-2870 ❑*$12.99*

Maisy's Colors And Shapes
07-2871 ❑*$12.99*

Maisy's Birthday
07-2872 ❑*$12.99*

Maisy's Winter Fun
07-2913 ❑*$12.99*

Warner Bros. Cartoons

Early Warner Brothers Cartoons
Eight nifty black and white Merrie Melodies before the Bugs and Daffy era with that toe-tappin' music of the '30s—"Lady, Play Your Mandolin!," "One More Time," "Freddy the Freshman," "You Don't Know What You're Doin'," "Red-Headed Baby," "I Love a Parade," "Smile, Darn Ya, Smile" and "The Shanty Where Santy Claus Lives." 55 min.
62-1016 *$19.99*

Bugs Bunny Superstar (1975)
Nine of the finest, funniest cartoons in Warner Bros. history (including "What's Cookin' Doc?," "Wild Hare," "My Favorite Duck" and "I Taw a Putty Tat") are assembled here, along with rare interviews with animation legends Tex Avery, Bob Clampett and Chuck Jones. Orson Welles narrates. 90 min.
12-1754 *$14.99*

The Bugs Bunny/ Road Runner Movie (1979)
The work of beloved Warner Bros. cartoon director Chuck Jones is featured in this feature-length compilation that mixes vintage shorts (including "Bully for Bugs," "Duck Amuck," "Rabbit Fire" and "What's Opera, Doc?") with all-new footage hosted by Bugs and a special look at the never-ending chase between the Road Runner and Wile E. Coyote. 98 min.
19-1021 *$14.99*

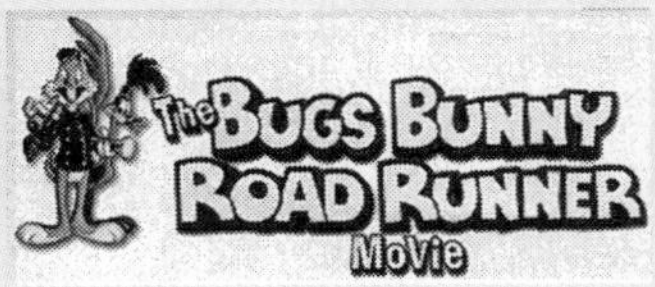

The Looney, Looney, Looney Bugs Bunny Movie (1981)
Eh, what's up, doc? How about a feature-length compilation of the greatest Warner Bros. cartoons from director Friz Freleng ever, plus all-new footage? Among the classic shorts spotlighted are "Knighty Knight Bugs," "Sahara Hare," "The Unmentionables," "Birds Anonymous" and many more, with Bugs, Yosemite Sam, Sylvester and Tweety and all your favorites. 79 min.
19-1193 *$14.99*

Happy Birthday, Bugs! (1990)
Here's a 50th birthday salute to the world's most "wascally wabbit," featuring clips of Bugs' greatest bits and guest appearances from a host of stars, including Milton Berle, Bill Cosby, John Goodman, Martin Mull, Fred Savage and William Shatner. Bugs is joined by pals Porky Pig, Daffy Duck and other classic Warner Bros. characters. 47 min.
19-1785 *$14.99*

Space Jam (1996)
It's a slammin' mix of live-action and animation, as basketball superstar Michael Jordan is "hijacked" into the cartoon world of Bugs Bunny, Daffy Duck and the rest of the Looney Tunes crew to help them when they're forced to play a game of hoops against a gang of alien behemoths who've stolen the talents of the NBA's top players. Wayne Knight, Bill Murray, and the voices of Danny DeVito and Billy West are also featured. 88 min.
19-2490 Was $19.99 *□$14.99*

Stars Of Space Jam: Bugs Bunny
The ever-resourceful rabbit needs all his wits when he plays lab "guinea pig" in "Hot Cross Bunny," squares off against outlaw Nasty Canasta in "Barbary Coast Bunny," keeps a construction worker from making him a "Homeless Hare," becomes a gorilla couple's "baby" in "Apes of Wrath," and more. 42 min.
19-2474 *□$12.99*

Stars Of Space Jam: Road Runner & Wile E. Coyote
The comic chase goes on and on in this compilation of Road Runner and Coyote cartoon capers. Along with the duo's first appearance in "Fast and Furry-ous," you'll see Wile E. run through the entire Acme catalog for help catching his prey in "Gee Whiz-z-z-z," "Zoom and Bored," "Hook, Line and Stinker" and others. 39 min.
19-2476 *□$12.99*

Stars Of Space Jam: Tazmanian Devil
The always-hungry devil from Down Under tries to get his teeth into Bugs Bunny and Daffy Duck in these classic Warner Bros. cartoons. Included are Taz's debut in "Devil May Hare," plus "Bedevilled Rabbit," "Ducking the Devil," "Bill of Hare" and more. 40 min.
19-2478 *□$12.99*

Stars Of Space Jam: Daffy Duck
The dizzy duck takes off to new heights of hilarity as "Stupor Duck," tries selling insurance to Porky Pig in "Fool Coverage," gets in the middle of a feud between Foghorn Leghorn and the hound dog in "The High and the Flighty," is threatened with becoming a hillbilly couple's Thanksgiving dinner in "Holiday for Drumsticks," and more. 41 min.
19-2475 *□$12.99*

Stars Of Space Jam: Sylvester & Tweety
That "tweet widdle birdie" has his wings full trying to avoid becoming dinner for the "bad old puddy tat" in such animated treats as "Canary Row," "Puddy Tat Twouble," "Sandy Claws," "Snow Business," "Tweet Zoo" and others. 43 min.
19-2477 *□$12.99*

Tweety: Tweet & Lovely
Here's a sweet "tweet" for fans of the lovable little canary and his always-hungry pursuer, Sylvester: 10 of their funniest Warner cartoons in one "tweemendous" compilation. Included are "Birds Anonymous," "Fowl Weather," "A Pizza Tweety Pie," "Tugboat Granny," "Rebel Without Claws" and more. 66 min.
19-2855 *$14.99*

Tweety: Home Tweet Home
How can one itty-bitty bird get into so many scrapes? Watch as Tweety tries to avoid becoming Sylvester's next meal in "Red Riding Hoodwinked," "Bad Ol' Putty Tat," "Snow Business," "Dog Pounded," "The Jet Cage" and five more classic cartoon chases. 70 min.
19-2856 *$14.99*

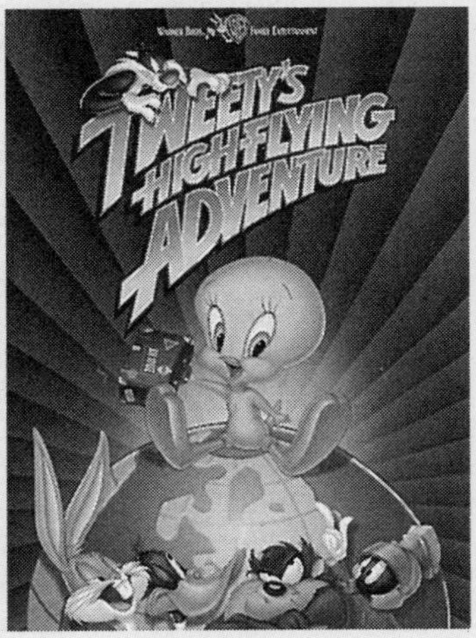

Tweety's High Flying Adventure (2000)
Everyone's favorite cartoon canary is now the star of his very own feature! Sent by Granny on a trip around the world to collect 80 cat paw prints in 80 days, Tweety has some exciting adventures with a variety of Looney Tunes characters—including a bird-hungry "bad ol' putty tat" named Sylvester. 70 min.
19-2991 *□$19.99*

Superior Duck
"Look, up in the sky. It's a bird...it's a plane..." Actually, it is a bird, as Daffy Duck puts on the tights and sets out to fight for justice—and fails hilariously—in this all-new cartoon from director Chuck Jones. Also includes "The Stupor Salesman," "Golden Yeggs," "Stork Naked," "Design for Leaving," "Show Biz Bugs." 40 min.
19-2613 *□$14.99*

Bugs Bunny's Easter Funnies
The Easter Bunny takes ill just before it's time for his annual egg delivery, and the call goes out for auditions for a "stand-in." Can a certain "Oscar-winning rabbit" win the job and make sure the Technicolor henfruit gets out in time?
19-1923 *$12.99*

Bugs Bunny's Creature Features
Have a spook-tacularly funny time with these Warner Bros. cartoons with a Halloween theme. See Bugs fall victim to the "Invasion of the Bunny Snatchers" and Daffy Duck star in "The Duxorcist" and "Night of the Living Duck." 25 min.
19-1993 *□$14.99*

Bugs Bunny's Halloween Hijinks
There's nothing but "treats" for viewers when Bugs Bunny and his Looney Tunes pals find themselves meeting all manner of ghosts, witches and monsters (who lead such innn-teresting lives!) in two Halloween adventures. 50 min.
19-2982 *□$14.99*

From Hare To Eternity
Set sail for laughs with an all-new animated Warner Bros. short from director Chuck Jones, as Bugs Bunny crosses swords once more with pint-sized pirate Yosemite Sam. Also includes "High Diving Hare," "Bully for Bugs," "Rabbit Fire," "My Bunny Lies Over the Sea" and "Ballot Box Bunny." 41 min.
19-2612 *□$14.99*

Carrotblanca
Your favorite Warner Bros. animated stars bite the hand that feeds them in this collection of movie-themed cartoons. Along with Bugs Bunny making like Bogey in "Carrotblanca," there's also "Box-Office Bunny," "Dripalong Daffy," "Hare Do," "The Scarlet Pumpernickel" and the newly-colorized "You Ought to Be in Pictures." 45 min.
19-2456 *$12.99*

Bugs Bunny: Big Top Bunny
It's three rings of rascally rabbit fun with this collection of classic Warner Bros. cartoons featuring the one and only Bugs Bunny. Included are "Big Top Bunny," "Water, Water Every Hare," "Rabbit Rampage," "Abominable Snow-Rabbit," "Hook, Line and Stinker," "Bugs Bunny Gets the Boid," "Rabbit's Kin," and more. 70 min.
19-2893 *□$14.99*

Chariots Of Fur: Road Runner And Wile E. Coyote
After more than 30 years, animation legend Chuck Jones returned to direct an all-new cartoon featuring his duelling desert-dwelling creations. Along with "Chariots," there are five other Road Runner/Coyote classics, including "Beep Beep," "Hook, Line and Stinker," "Operation: Rabbit" (guest-starring you-know-who) and others. 39 min.
19-2457 *$12.99*

Sing Along: Looney Tunes
Join that rockin' rabbit, Bugs Bunny, and his pals Daffy Duck, Tweetie, Elmer Fudd and others for a fun-filled collection of classic cartoon bits and "merry melodies" that viewers can sing along to. Songs include "Jeepers Creepers," "The Daring Young Hare on the Flying Trapeze," "The Three Little Bops," "Tea for Two" and more, plus Bugs' TV theme song, "This Is It." 30 min.
19-2702 *$12.99*

Marvin The Martian: Space Tunes
"Oh, it will make me *very* angry if you Earthlings miss this collection of my greatest attempts to blow up your planet!" See Marvin's debut opposite Bugs Bunny in "Haredevil Hare"; and watch him tangle with "space hero" Daffy Duck in "Duck Dodgers in the 24 1/2th Century"; also included on this tape are "Hare-Way to the Stars," "Mad as a Mars Hare," "Spaced Out Bunny" and more. 83 min.
19-2894 *□$14.99*

Taz's Jungle Jams
"BPPPHHHATTBLLLAAAHHHRRRAAAWWW!" That's Tasmanian Devil-speak for "don't miss this fun-filled video featuring all five of my classic Warner Bros. cartoon appearances, plus other jungle-themed gems." Included are "Devil May Hare," "Ducking the Devil," "Bill of Hare," "Dr. Devil and Mr. Hare," "Bushy Hare," "Nelly's Folly" and more. 67 min.
19-2968 *$14.99*

Pinky And The Brain
They went from "Animaniacs" to their own hit series, and now Acme Labs' duo of mischievous mice are ready to launch the Brain's latest schemes to take over the world (unless Pinky somehow manages to goof up his plans). Each tape runs about 45 min.

Pinky And The Brain: World Domination Tour
19-2452 *$12.99*

Pinky And The Brain: Mice Of The Jungle
19-2608 *$12.99*

Pinky And The Brain: Cosmic Attractions
19-2609 *$12.99*

Tiny Toon Adventures
They're the students of Acme Tooniversity and the next generation of Warner Bros. cartoon stars. Now Buster Bunny and Babs Bunny (no relation), Plucky Duck, Hamton Pig, Dizzy Devil and the rest of the Tiny Toon crew (plus Bugs, Elmer and the original gang) come to home video. Each tape features two episodes and runs about 45 min. There are seven volumes available, including:

Tiny Toon Adventures: The Best Of Buster And Babs
19-2055 *□$14.99*

Tiny Toon Adventures: Tiny Toons In Two-Tone Town
19-2057 *□$14.99*

Tiny Toons Night Ghoulery
19-2453 *□$12.99*

Animaniacs
After being locked away for over 50 years in the studio water tower, the zany trio of Yakko, Wakko and Dot have broken loose on TV and home video. Follow the Animaniacs and their pals, Mindy and Buttons, Slappy Squirrel, and Pinky and the Brain, in these wild cartoon capers. Each tape runs about 40 min. There are six volumes available, including:

Animaniacs: Animaniacs Stew
19-2258 *□$12.99*

Animaniacs Sing-Along: Yakko's World
19-2259 *□$12.99*

Animaniacs: You Will Buy This Video
19-2261 *□$12.99*

Animaniacs: Spooky Stuff
19-2449 *□$12.99*

Animaniacs: Wakko's Wish
The appearance of a magical "wishing star" sends screwball siblings Wakko, Yakko and Dot on a wild search to find where it landed and, by touching it, make their wish come true in this feature-length adventure. 70 min.
19-2917 Was $19.99 *$14.99*

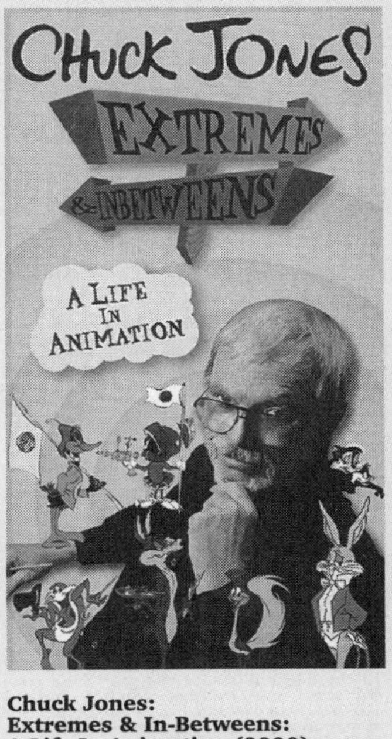

Chuck Jones: Extremes & In-Betweens: A Life In Animation (2000)
He brought road runners and coyotes, love-starved skunks and dancing frogs to animated life, and this wonderful program salutes the life and career of Warner Bros. cartoon director Chuck Jones. Along with clips from such Jones works as "Duck Dodgers in the 24 1/2th Century," "What's Opera, Doc?," "One Froggy Evening," "How the Grinch Stole Christmas" and others, there are comments from colleagues and guests Matt Groening, Leonard Maltin, Steven Spielberg and Robin Williams. 85 min.
19-5003 *$19.99*

The Ketchup Vampires
A teenager whose family of "vegetarian vampires" prefer drinking ketchup to that other red stuff has his hands full trying to keep a valuable vampirism manual away from some bloodsucking relatives in this spooky and silly animated tale narrated by horror hostess Elvira. 90 min.
69-5277 *$14.99*

The BFG (Big Friendly Giant)
The best-selling book by Roald Dahl ("Willy Wonka and the Chocolate Factory") has been turned into a first-rate animated feature that tells of the relationship between Sophie, a young orphan, and a 24-foot giant. The two team to tackle an army of bad giants who like to terrorize small children. 95 min.
69-5279 *$14.99*

This Land Is Your Land
The timeless music of Woody Guthrie serves as the basis for an animated odyssey that shows children the rich heritage of American folk music. Among the songs performed by Woody and Arlo Guthrie are "This Land Is Your Land," "Jig Along Home," "Howjido?," "All Work Together" and others. 28 min.
27-5567 *□$14.99*

Sonic The Hedgehog: The Movie
The super-speedy, little blue star of video games dashes into his very own full-length animated adventure, as Sonic and his pals must save the planet Robotropolis from Dr. Robotnik's most diabolical invention yet: a robotic duplicate of Sonic! Follow them in this fast and funny cartoon saga. 60 min.
20-8360 Was $19.99 *$14.99*

Blue's Clues

Designed with pre-schoolers in mind, this popular Nickelodeon show lets viewers follow the clues left by a fun-loving animated dog named Blue as she goes from one activity to another. Each tape features two episodes and runs about 50 min. There are 11 volumes available, including:

Blue's Clues: Blue's Birthday
06-2757 □$12.99

Blue's Clues: Blue's Big Treasure Hunt
06-2846 □$12.99

Blue's Clues: Blue's Big Pajama Party
06-2894 □$12.99

Blue's Clues: Magenta Comes Over
06-2957 □$12.99

Blue's Big Musical Movie (2000)

It's the ever-curious pooch Blue's first feature and she's in trouble! Seems that there's a big backyard show today and partner Tickety-Tock has lost her voice. Now, Blue, Steve and the rest of the gang have to play "Blue's Clues" to find a new singer. Features the new feline character Periwinkle and a special vocal appearance by Ray Charles. 78 min.
06-3031 □$19.99

Rocko's Modern Life

He's a put-upon wallaby who can't quite cope with the hassles of day-to-day existence, even with the "help" of his bovine pal, Heffer, and dog Spunky, and now Rocko's Emmy-winning misadventures are on home video. Each tape runs about 60 min. There are four volumes available, including:

Rocko's Modern Life: Machine Madness
04-5291 □$12.99

Rocko's Modern Life: With Friends Like These...
04-5292 □$12.99

Hey Arnold!

He's your typical 9-year-old who lives with his grandparents, is the unwilling boyfriend of a bossy girl named Helga, and has a head shaped like a football. Join Arnold, his best friend Gerald and the whole gang for some wild escapades in the popular Nickelodeon cartoon series. Each tape runs about 60 min. There are five volumes available, including:

Hey Arnold!: The Helga Stories
06-2590 □$12.99

Hey Arnold!: Partners
06-2731 □$12.99

Brothers Flub

They're the unlikeliest heroes who ever flew into outer space. Follow the out-of-this-world exploits of interplanetary delivery guys and squabbling siblings Fraz and Guapo in these animated video collections from the popular Nickelodeon series. Each tape runs about 45 min.

Brothers Flub, Vol. 1: Doom Wears Funny Tights
04-5732 □$12.99

Brothers Flub, Vol. 2: Plan C: Panic
04-5733 □$12.99

CatDog

They may not always get along, but Cat and Dog are stuck with each other...literally. Follow the conjoined critters' comical exploits as they try not to drive each other crazy in these episodes from the popular Nickelodeon cartoon series. Each tape runs about 60 min.

CatDog: Together Forever
06-2831 □$12.99

CatDog: CatDog vs. The Greasers
06-2832 □$12.99

Gullah Gullah Island

Songs, cute puppets and lessons highlight this fun-filled series from Nick, Jr., in which Binyah Binyah Polliwog finds himself in lively, heart-warming adventures with the Daise family and their friends. Each tape runs about 30 min. There are five volumes available, including:

Gullah Gullah Island: Sing Along With Binyah Binyah
04-5353 □$12.99

Gullah Gullah Island: Play Along With Binyah And Friends
04-5427 □$12.99

Gullah Gullah Island: Feelings
06-2680 □$12.99

Maurice Sendak's Little Bear

The popular series of Sendak-illustrated children's books are now a collection of acclaimed animated tales. Join Little Bear and his friends Cat, Duck, Hen and Owl for fun-filled adventures and lessons about the world around them. Each tape, which also includes an introduction by Sendak, runs about 35 min. There are eight volumes available, including:

Little Bear: Meet Little Bear
06-2575 □$12.99

Little Bear: A Kiss For Little Bear
06-2940 □$12.99

Little Bear: Little Bear's Band
06-2938 □$12.99

Aaahh!! Real Monsters

Some of the creepiest, crawliest critters can be found in these frightfully funny animated tales from the creators of "Rugrats." Meet Ickis, Oblina and Krumm, three mutant monsters-in-training out to make life difficult for humans. Each tape runs about 60 min.

Aaahh! Real Monsters: Meet The Monsters
04-5377 □$12.99

Aaahh! Real Monsters: Monsters' Night Out
04-5378 □$12.99

Rugrats

From the playpen to your TV, the funny and refreshing Nickelodeon animated series has earned Emmy Awards and the adoration of children and parents nationwide. Follow the adventures of one-year-old Tommy Pickles, his toddler pals Chuckie, Phil and Lil, and the "sweet " Angelica, who all prove to be much wiser than their parents think. Each tape runs about 45 min. There are 18 volumes available, including:

Rugrats: Phil And Lil: Double Trouble
06-2522 □$12.99

Rugrats: Runaway Reptar
06-2855 □$12.99

Rugrats: Make Room For Dil
06-2892 □$12.99

Rugrats: I Think I Like You
06-2938 □$12.99

Rugrats: Discover America
06-2971 □$14.99

The Rugrats Movie (1998)

The diaper-clad daredevils of cable TV's hit cartoon series crawled their way onto the big screen in this hit feature-length ride. With the Pickles household thrown into a tizzy over the arrival of new baby Dil, the toddlers decide to make things right by revving up the Reptar Wagon and taking Tommy's little brother back to the "hopsicle," only to wind up lost in the woods and forced to fend for themselves. 81 min.
06-2830 □$26.99

Adventures From The Book Of Virtues: Collector's Set

Based on William Bennett's best-seller, this six-part collection of animated tales follows two children and the group of talking animals who share with them fables, myths and historical stories from around the world to illustrate such important principles as "Courage," "Honesty," "Compassion," "Work," "Responsibility" and "Self-Discipline." 180 min. total. NOTE: Individual volumes available at $14.99 each.
18-7734   Save $30.00! $59.99

Classic Jonny Quest

In 1964, Hanna-Barbera broke new ground in TV animation with the thrilling screen adventures of young Jonny Quest, his scientist father, East Indian pal Hadji and bodyguard Race Bannon as they travelled the world, encountering strange menaces and mysteries. Each volume features two episodes and special bonus cartoons, and runs about 60 min.

Classic Jonny Quest: Bandit In Adventure's Best Friend
The danger-loving dog joins his master on a search for giant mutant creatures on "Danger Island," and helps Jonny and Hadji in a jungle odyssey in "Attack of the Tree People."
18-7601 $14.99

Classic Jonny Quest: Race Bannon In An Army Of One
Government agent-turned-tutor Race Bannon gives Jonny a crash course in escaping from laser-wielding saboteurs in the Sargasso Sea in "Mystery of the Lizard Men," then has doppelganger problems, courtesy of Dr. Zin, in "Double Danger."
18-7602 $14.99

Classic Jonny Quest: Hadji In Mysteries Of The East
Learn how the young Indian boy came to join the Quest team in "Calcutta Adventure," followed by Hadji and Jonny tackling modern-day buccaneers in "Pirates from Below."
18-7603 $14.99

Classic Jonny Quest: Dr. Zin In Master Of Evil
The sinister Asian scientist lives up to his billing when he dispatches "The Robot Spy" to steal Dr. Quest's latest invention, then pursues a fabulous treasure in "Riddle of the Gold."
18-7604 $14.99

Jonny Quest vs. The Cyber Insects (1995)
An attack on an experimental orbital space station by the fiendish Dr. Zin and his army of cybernetic alien organisms sends Jonny and his family and friends on their most breathtaking adventure yet in this feature-length cartoon thriller. 90 min.
18-7605 $14.99

Jonny Quest: The Real Adventures

The boy-hero of '60s cartoon fame gets a high-tech revamping in this all-new animated series. Join teenager Jonny, Hadji, Dr. Quest, Jessie and Race Bannon as they explore the frontiers of earth, space and virtual reality and face an array of bizarre dangers. Each tape features two episodes and runs about 50 min.

Jonny Quest: The Real Adventures, Vol. 1: Escape To Questworld
18-7667 $14.99

Jonny Quest: The Real Adventures, Vol. 2: The Alchemist
18-7668 $14.99

Jonny Quest: The Real Adventures, Vol. 3: Rage's Burning Wheel
18-7669 $14.99

Jonny Quest: The Real Adventures, Vol. 4: The Darkest Fathoms
18-7670 $14.99

The Neverending Story: The Animated Adventures Of Bastian Balthazar Bux

All your favorite characters from the popular live-action movies are back in this all-new cartoon saga, as young Bastian returns to the magical land of Fantasia to help the Empress save her realm from wicked Sorceress Xayide and her Black Giants. 90 min.
19-2463   □$14.99

Tex Avery's Screwball Classics, Vol. 1

He was the master of the animated sight gag and put the gold in the Golden Age of Cartoons. Now see some of Tex's wildest and funniest MGM classics: "Swing Shift Cinderella," "Bad Luck Blackie," "Lucky Ducky," "Magical Maestro" and more. 60 min.
12-1845 $14.99

Tex Avery's Screwball Classics, Vol. 2

Second screwy selection of cartoon cacophonies from ink-and-paint legend Avery includes the infamous "Red Hot Riding Hood" (the '40s inspiration for Jessica Rabbit), "Wild and Woolfy," "Northwest Hounded Police" and more. 60 min.
12-1905 $14.99

Tex Avery's Screwball Classics, Vol. 3

The sight gags come fast and furious in this latest collection of outlandish cartoons from Avery's MGM heyday. Included are Screwball Squirrel in "The Screwy Truant," "Hound Hunters" with George and Junior, "Batty Baseball" and more. 44 min.
12-2160 $14.99

Tex Avery's Screwball Classics, Vol. 4

More terrific and innovative animation entries from gagmeister Avery. Travel to Mars in "TV of Tomorrow," see a lonely flea find love in "What Price Fleadom," laugh at the Harpo-wigged inhabitant of "The Cuckoo Clock" and more. 46 min.
12-2405 $14.99

Droopy And Company

Droopy Dog, one of Tex Avery's greatest creations, is featured in this hilarious compilation of the laid-back canine's greatest adventures. Included here are "Officer Pooch," "One Droopy Knight," "Sheep Wrecked," "Mutts About Racing," "Grin and Share It" and "The Hungry Wolf." 44 min.
12-2404 $14.99

MGM Cartoon Magic

Seven classic cartoon treats from the Golden Age of Animation, including three from Tex Avery. Features "Screwball Squirrel," "King-Size Canary," "Little Rural Riding Hood," "Blue Danube," and more. 53 min.
12-1295 $14.99

Jules Verne Adventure Classics 3-Pack

Three of Verne's most incredible tales become memorable animated films with all-animal casts in this three-tape boxed set. Included are "20,000 Leagues Under the Sea," "Around the World in 80 Days" and "Journey to the Center of the Earth." 258 min. total. NOTE: Individual volumes available at $14. 99 each.
88-7013   Save $15.00! $29.99

Underdog

"There's no need to fear," because everyone's favorite super-powered canine is on home video! Watch as humble, lovable Shoeshine Boy becomes Underdog and protects the world as well as sweet Polly Purebred) against such foes as Simon Barsinister and Riff Raff. Each tape features three complete stories and runs about 40 min.

Underdog vs. Simon Barsinister
04-5739 $12.99

Underdog vs. Riff Raff
04-5740 $12.99

Underdog vs. Overcat
04-5741 $12.99

It's The Great Pumpkin, Charlie Brown (1966)
While the rest of the Peanuts kids go out for a night of trick-or-treating (and Snoopy sets out to find the Red Baron), Linus and Sally sit in the pumpkin patch to await the arrival of the Great Pumpkin. 25 min.
06-2220 ❑$12.99

You're Not Elected, Charlie Brown (1972)/It Was A Short Summer, Charlie Brown (1969)
Grade school politics have never been funnier, as Linus runs for class president and (in an attempt to corner the blockhead vote) picks Charlie Brown as his running mate. Next, summer camp with the gang is highlighted by a wrist-wrestling contest between Lucy and the Masked Marvel, a funny-looking kid with a big nose. 49 min.
06-2223 ❑$12.99

A Charlie Brown Thanksgiving (1973)
Charlie Brown feels like the biggest turkey of all time when Peppermint Patty invites herself—and the whole crew—over to his house for Thanksgiving dinner. Good thing master chefs Snoopy and Woodstock are there to save the day. 24 min.
06-2226 ❑$12.99

It's The Easter Beagle, Charlie Brown (1974)
Springtime means laughtime for the "Peanuts" gang in this animated tale. Frying Easter eggs, a "rigged" egg hunt, and an appearance by the Easter Beagle and his feathered assistant are just some of the treats in store. 25 min.
06-2185 ❑$12.99

It's A Mystery, Charlie Brown (1974)
When an unknown thief makes off with Woodstock's new nest, Snoopy turns from beagle to bloodhound to track down the culprit. Which of the Peanuts gang is guilty in this cartoon whodunit? 25 min.
10-3232 ❑$12.99

Be My Valentine, Charlie Brown (1975)
The course of true love runs anything but smooth for the "Peanuts" crew in this Valentine's treat, as Linus' candy for his teacher winds up in Sally's hands, Snoopy and Woodstock exchange gifts, and Charlie Brown faithfully waits for his first card. 25 min.
06-2229 ❑$12.99

You're A Good Sport, Charlie Brown (1975)
Good Grief! You'll have a ball when Woodstock hits the tennis courts, the gang takes up motocross, and Charlie Brown doesn't give up on placekicking with Lucy. 25 min.
10-3234 ❑$12.99

It's Arbor Day, Charlie Brown (1976)
The "Peanuts" gang is gripped by Arbor Day fever, showing off their green thumbs by turning the baseball field into a botanical garden. Will having a tree on his pitcher's mound turn Charlie Brown into a better ballplayer? 25 min.
10-3243 $12.99

You're In Love, Charlie Brown (1967)/It's Your First Kiss, Charlie Brown (1977)
Charlie Brown proves he's the master of unrequited love in this romance-filled double feature. First, the final week of school finds Charlie trying to get a note to the Little Red-Haired Girl of his dreams. Next, guess who gets to escort the Homecoming Queen to the big dance? 49 min.
06-2230 ❑$12.99

Play It Again, Charlie Brown (1971)/She's A Good Skate, Charlie Brown (1980)
In order to win his heart, Lucy lands Schroeder a musical gig at a PTA show...but the Beethoven-loving prodigy will have to play rock music! After that, see Peppermint Patty take to the ice, as Snoopy coaches her for a skating competition. 49 min.
06-2352 ❑$12.99

What A Nightmare, Charlie Brown (1978)/ It's Magic, Charlie Brown (1981)
A late-night pizza binge sends the sleeping Snoopy into a dream where he's an overworked sled dog in the frozen Yukon. Next, the beagle tries his hand at legerdemain and winds up levitating Lucy into the air and making Charlie Brown invisible. 49 min.
06-2351 ❑$12.99

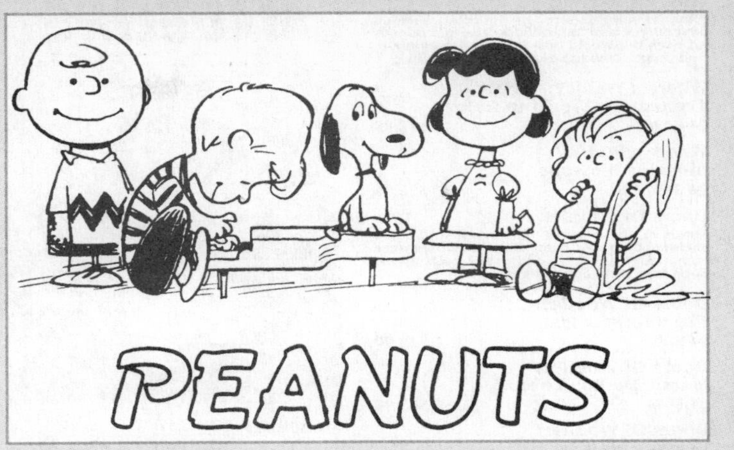

A Charlie Brown Celebration (1982)
Delight in the antics of the "Peanuts" crew as Peppermint Patty winds up in obedience school, Sally takes on the "other woman" in Linus' life, Lucy tries yet again to catch Schroeder's eye, and Charlie Brown tries yet again to kick a football. 48 min.
10-3240 ❑$12.99

What Have We Learned, Charlie Brown? (1983)
While on a student exchange program in France, Charlie Brown, Linus, Peppermint Patty and Marcie visit Normandy Beach and a WWII cemetery and learn how Americans fought and died to defend freedom. 23 min.
10-3242 ❑$12.99

It's An Adventure, Charlie Brown (1983)
Of course, comic strip fans know that every day's an adventure with the kids from "Peanuts," and you'll see why in this cartoon special that has Peppermint Patty and Marice serving as gold caddies, Lucy trying to break Linus of his blanket habit, and Charlie Brown becoming a hero to his fellow summer campers. 47 min.
71-7084 ❑$12.99

He's Your Dog, Charlie Brown (1968)/It's Flashbeagle, Charlie Brown (1984)
When Snoopy's antics begin upsetting the neighborhood, Charlie Brown decides that a term in (gasp!) obedience school is the only answer. Then, Snoopy takes his passion and makes it happen on the dance floor, but will his nightly escapades catch up with him? 50 min.
06-2192 $12.99

Life's A Circus, Charlie Brown (1980)/Snoopy's Getting Married, Charlie Brown (1985)
Smitten with a pretty circus poodle, Snoopy runs away from home for a new life under the big top. Next, is the fun-loving bachelor dog ready to walk down the aisle (with brother Spike serving as "best beagle")? 48 min.
06-2405 ❑$12.99

Happy New Year, Charlie Brown (1986)
The Peanuts kids decide to throw the biggest New Year's Eve bash ever, but while Peppermint Patty is looking for a midnight kiss from Charlie Brown, he's trying to finish a vacation homework assignment by reading "War and Peace" in one night! 24 min.
06-2227 ❑$12.99

You're The Greatest, Charlie Brown (1979)/ Snoopy's Reunion (1988)
Everyone's favorite loser tries out for the Junior Olympics, but he's got stiff competition in the decathlon from a masked rival with a big nose. Next, it's beagles galore when Snoopy hosts a gathering of his many brothers and sisters. 48 min.
06-2191 ❑$12.99

Snoopy The Musical (1988)
He's been a WWI fighter ace, an author, a lawyer and a top shortstop, and now Snoopy (along with faithful sidekick Woodstock) is a song-and-dance star! Join the beloved beagle and the whole Peanuts gang in a musical look at a dog's life. 50 min.
06-2329 ❑$12.99

Charlie Brown's All Stars (1966)/ It's Spring Training, Charlie Brown (1988)
Get a double dose of diamond doings with the world's losingest baseball team. First, Charlie Brown has to choose between getting his team into a real league or letting the girls and Snoopy play. Then, a businessman promises the team uniforms...if they can win a game! 48 min.
06-2408 ❑$12.99

It's The Girl In The Red Truck, Charlie Brown (1988)
The first "Peanuts" special to mix animation and live-action takes Snoopy's desert-dwelling brother, Spike, for the ride of his life when he hitches a ride with a pickup-driving girl named Jenny. 48 min.
06-2409 ❑$12.99

Why, Charlie Brown, Why? (1990)
When a classmate is hospitalized with a serious illness, the Peanuts kids learn some important lessons about caring and friendship in this very special animated adventure. 25 min.
06-2334 ❑$12.99

It Was My Best Birthday Ever, Charlie Brown! (1997)
A roller-skating trip home from a party turns into a romantic adventure for Linus when he meets the girl of his dreams. But will she be able to make it to Linus' birthday bash? Find out in this home video premiere "Peanuts" special. 25 min.
06-2610 ❑$12.99

It's The Pied Piper, Charlie Brown (2000)
When his town is overrun by soccer-playing, river-dancing mice, Charlie Brown recruits Snoopy to play Pied Piper Beagle and get rid of the rodents. This tape includes an 11-minute tribute to "Peanuts" creator Charles Schulz. 25 min.
06-3013 ❑$12.99

Race For Your Life, Charlie Brown (1977)
It's anything but a vacation for the Peanuts kids when they go to summer camp and are challenged by a gang of bullies to a danger-filled raft race in this full-length cartoon romp. 75 min.
06-1050 $14.99

Bon Voyage, Charlie Brown (1980)
The Peanuts crew travels to Europe (with Snoopy and Woodstock stowing away), and finds adventure, laughs and even romance while there in this feature-length animated film. 75 min.
06-1005 ❑$14.99

You're A Good Man, Charlie Brown (1985)
Songs from the hit Broadway musical are featured in this animated rendition, with the entire Peanuts gang trying to cope with losing ball games, endless lunch hours and the hunt for the Red Baron. 49 min.
10-3278 $12.99

You Don't Look 40, Charlie Brown! (1990)
Celebrate four decades of "Peanuts" with this special salute to Charlie Brown, Snoopy, Lucy, Linus and company. Charles Schulz discusses his comic-strip creations and looks back at favorite stories and characters, while you relive memorable moments from the "Peanuts" animated specials, and more. 47 min.
06-2524 ❑$12.99

The Charlie Brown & Snoopy Show
The gang from "Peanuts" made their Saturday morning TV debut in this series of animated stories taken from their funniest comic strip adventures. Each tape runs about 45 min. There are nine volumes available, including:

The Charlie Brown & Snoopy Show, Vol. 1
06-2189 ❑$12.99

The Charlie Brown & Snoopy Show, Vol. 2
06-2190 ❑$12.99

The Charlie Brown & Snoopy Show, Vol. 3
06-2221 ❑$12.99

The Charlie Brown & Snoopy Show, Vol. 4
06-2222 ❑$12.99

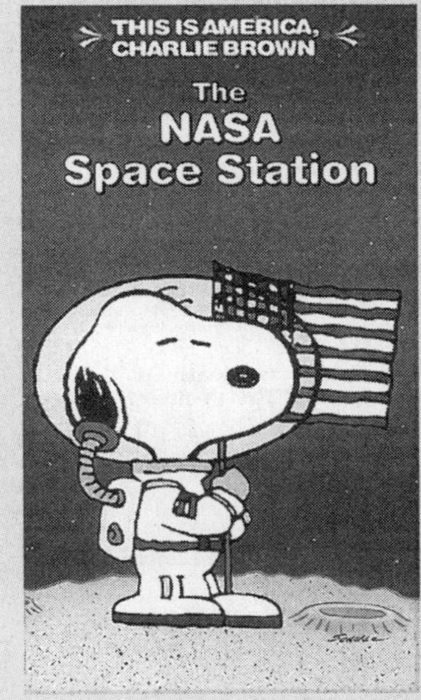

This Is America, Charlie Brown
Take a trip through the great moments of American history, and meet the men and women responsible for them, with the "Peanuts" crew in this acclaimed animated series. Each tape runs about 25 min.

This Is America, Charlie Brown, Vol. 1: The Great Inventors
06-2187 ❑$12.99

This Is America, Charlie Brown, Vol. 2: The Wright Brothers At Kitty Hawk
06-2188 ❑$12.99

This Is America, Charlie Brown, Vol. 3: The Building Of The Transcontinental Railroad
06-2224 ❑$12.99

This Is America, Charlie Brown, Vol. 4: The Mayflower Voyagers
06-2228 ❑$12.99

This Is America, Charlie Brown, Vol. 5: The NASA Space Station
06-2327 ❑$12.99

This Is America, Charlie Brown, Vol. 6: The Birth Of The Constitution
06-2328 ❑$12.99

This Is America, Charlie Brown, Vol. 7: The Smithsonian And The Presidency
06-2336 ❑$12.99

This Is America, Charlie Brown, Vol. 8: The Music And Heroes Of America
06-2337 ❑$12.99

Precious Moments: Simon The Lamb
An accident with "rainbow paint" from an angel leaves poor Simon the only blue lamb in his flock, but a snowstorm gives him a chance to prove his "true blue" worth to the other lambs in this animated tale narrated by Pat Boone. 25 min.
04-5615 $12.99

Archie's Weird Mysteries: Archie & The Riverdale Vampires
It's the scariest thing to happen in Riverdale since Pop raised prices of his soda shop, as the town is invaded by a horde of bloodsucking monsters. It's up to Archie, Betty, Veronica, Jughead and friends to save the day in this feature-length adventure.
07-2890 $14.99

Alexander And The Terrible, Horrible, No Good, Very Bad Day
For every kid who's ever gone through a "rotten day," this animated adaptation of the popular children's book, showing how Alexander puts up with problems ranging from scoldings and bullies to a cavity in one of his teeth, will let them see their problems aren't unique. 30 min.
04-5657 $12.99

Cartoon Festival: The Cat Came Back
It's a collection of award-winning animation that's sure to delight the entire family. Featured are "The Log Driver's Waltz," "The Dingles," "Summer Legend" and the Oscar-nominated "The Cat Came Back." 40 min.
19-3940 $14.99

Rotten Ralph
Ralph's not a bad cat...at least, he doesn't mean to be. The pesky pet who makes life a mess for Sarah and her family in the popular children's books now stars in his own home video series, featuring wonderful stop-motion animation. Each tape runs about 60 min.

Rotten Ralph, Vol. 1
Includes "Boogie Woogie Ralph," "Kung Fu Kitty," "The Whole Rotten Truth" and more.
04-3970 □*$12.99*

Rotten Ralph, Vol. 2
Includes "Ralph's Kitten," "Grandma's Visit," "World Cup Ralph" and more.
04-3971 □*$12.99*

Dragon Tales
Get ready to soar into fun-filled stories as 6-year-old Emmy and her little brother Max are joined by their magical dragon pals—big and not-so-brave Ord, shy little Cassie, and two-headed siblings Zak and Wheezie—in this charming and educational animated series. Each tape runs about 40 min. There are four volumes available, including:

Dragon Tales: Big Brave Adventures
02-3446 □*$12.99*

Dragon Tales: Let's All Share!
02-3447 □*$12.99*

Dragon Tales: You Can Do It!
02-3448 □*$12.99*

Where's Waldo?
Why, he's right here, in fun-filled cartoon adventures that take Waldo and his friends all over the world and let the viewer try to find them. Each tape runs about 25 min.

Where's Waldo?: Around The World In A Daze
04-3486 *$12.99*

Where's Waldo?: Birthday Blowout
04-3487 *$12.99*

Doors Of Wonder
Some of the world's best-loved and most acclaimed stories from children's literature come alive in these animated collections. Each tape runs about 30 min.

Doors Of Wonder: The Rainbow Fish
04-5503 □*$12.99*

Doors Of Wonder: Mama, Do You Love Me?
04-5644 □*$12.99*

Doors Of Wonder: Famous Fred
04-5671 □*$12.99*

Doors Of Wonder: George And Martha: Best Friends
04-5726 *$12.99*

Iron Man: The Origin Of Iron Man
Learn how millionaire industrialist Tony Stark became the armored avenger known as Iron Man in this exciting episode from the syndicated animated series. 25 min.
04-3484 *$12.99*

Iron Man: The Death Of Tony Stark/The Crimson Dynamo
The armor-plated avenger who "fights and fights with repulsor rays," in two episodes from the 1960s, must tackle the deadly dual menace of the Titanium Man and the Crimson Dynamo (sorry, Mr. McCartney, no Magneto). 44 min.
04-3784 □*$14.99*

Fantastic Four: The Origin Of The Fantastic Four
An experimental spaceflight runs afoul of cosmic rays, and four ordinary people are transformed into the Human Torch, the Invisible Woman, Mr. Fantastic and the ever-lovin', blue-eyed Thing, in the fantastic foursome's cartoon series' debut episode.
04-3482 *$12.99*

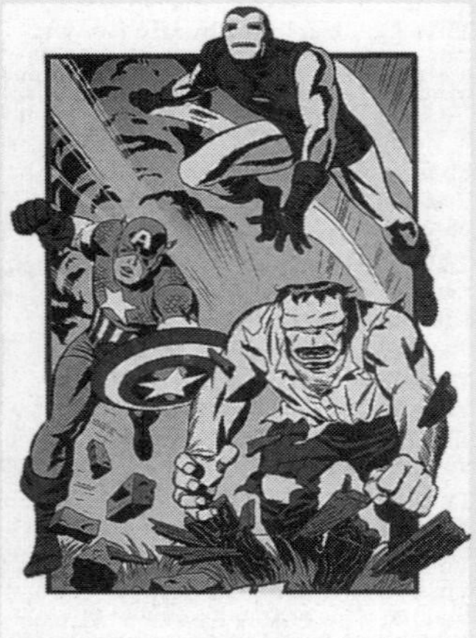

Captain America: The Origin Of Captain America/ The Fantastic Origin Of Red Skull
Learn how a 4-F weakling named Steve Rogers was turned into the shield-slinging superhero of World War II, and witness the creation of his greatest foe, in two thrilling tales from Cap's 1960s cartoon series. 44 min.
04-3782 *$14.99*

The Incredible Hulk: Return Of The Beast
"Is he man...or monster...or both?" Doc Bruce Banner and his emerald green alter ego are at odds once more in an episode from the hit syndicated cartoon series. 25 min.
04-3483 *$12.99*

The Incredible Hulk: Origin Of The Hulk/ The Power Of Bruce Banner
"Belted with gamma rays," scientist Bruce Banner is transformed into the green-skinned goliath known as the Incredible Hulk in two '60s animated adventures sure to thrill all "Hulkamaniacs." 44 min.
04-3783 *$14.99*

The Mighty Thor: Enter Hercules/ Battle Of The Gods
Verily, thou hast ne'er seen animated action such as is beheld in these two epics from the '60s, as the golden-haired thunder god pits his strength and his Uru hammer against the Olympian might of Hercules. Excelsior! 44 min.
04-3785 *$14.99*

Sub-Mariner: Atlantis Under Attack/To Conquer A Crown
The underwater super-hero who made pointed ears popular years before Mr. Spock needs all his sea-spawned strength in this '60s animated double bill, as Prince Namor defends his realm from the evil Attuma. Imperius Rex! 44 min.
04-3786 *$14.99*

Spider-Man: The Hobgoblin
Swinging in from his hit Fox animated series, the amazing Spider-Man squares off in battle against one of his strangest and deadliest foes, the horrifying, high-flying Hobgoblin. 25 min.
04-3485 *$12.99*

The Amazing Spider-Man: The Origin Of Spider-Man/ The Killowatt Kaper
Thanks to a radioactive spider bite, timid student Peter Parker can do "whatever a spider can," only to learn that "with great power comes great responsibility" in the original episode from his '60s animated series. Next, Spidey must ground the high-voltage villainy of Electro. 44 min.
04-3787 *$14.99*

Marvel's Greatest Avengers 3-Pack
It's an even better bargain than a Merry Marvel Marching Society membership kit: "Captain America," "The Incredible Hulk" and "Iron Man" in a boxed collector's set that also includes a vintage Marvel comic reproduction, a commemorative medallion, and a limited edition lithograph. Nuff said!
04-3788 *$24.99*

Marvel's Mightiest Super-Heroes 3-Pack
Face front, true believers, with this special boxed set featuring "The Amazing Spider-Man," "Mighty Thor" and "Sub-Mariner," plus a vintage Marvel comic reproduction, a commemorative medallion, and a limited edition lithograph.
04-3789 *$24.99*

X-Men
Marvel Comics' misunderstood mutant super-heroes are on home video! Cyclops, Jean Grey, Rogue, Storm and Wolverine, under the leadership of Professor X, fight all manner of menaces to make the world safe for humanity and mutantkind in the hit animated TV series. There are 13 volumes available, including:

X-Men: Beyond Good And Evil, Parts 1-4
Includes four episodes. 80 min.
07-2932 *$14.99*

X-Men: Night Of The Sentinels, Parts 1 & 2/ Days Of Future Past, Parts 1 & 2
Includes four episodes. 80 min.
07-2933 *$14.99*

X-Men: Savage Land Savage Heart, Parts 1 & 2/ Dark Phoenix Saga, Parts 1-4
Includes six episodes. 120 min.
07-2934 *$14.99*

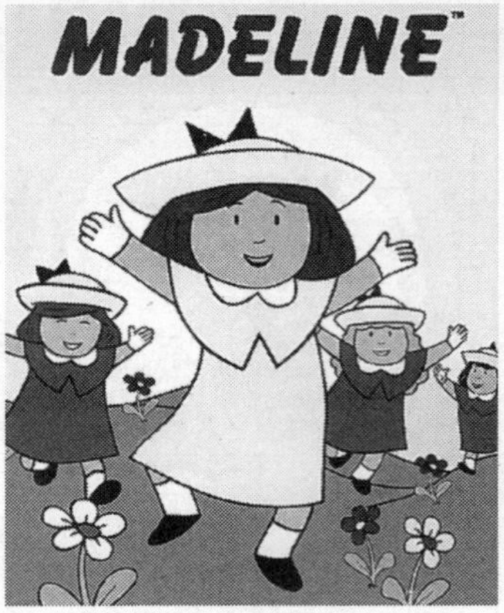

Madeline
She's the charming little girl whose adventures at her Parisian school have entertained readers for generations, and now Madeline and her friends star in a delightful animated series. Each tape runs about 25 min. There are 17 volumes available, including:

Madeline: Madeline At Cooking School
04-5587 □*$12.99*

Madeline: Madeline And The Gypsies
04-5591 □*$12.99*

Madeline: Madeline And The Soccer Star
04-5593 □*$12.99*

Madeline: Madeline's Rescue
04-5594 □*$12.99*

Madeline: Lost In Paris (1998)
Has little Madeline found a family at last? It looks that way as a long-lost uncle arrives at her vine-covered Paris school from Vienna, but Madeline, Miss Clavel and the girls soon find themselves involved in a dangerous hoax and an exciting adventure. Jason Alexander, Lauren Bacall and Christopher Plummer lend their voices to this song-filled, feature-length cartoon tale. 74 min.
11-2315 Was $19.99 □*$14.99*

Earthworm Jim
He was an ordinary, dirt-loving worm, until the day he crawled into a powerful cyber-suit and was transformed into a star-hopping hero. See Jim blast off into space to save beautiful Princess What's-Her-Name from such intergalactic menaces as Evil the Cat and Queen Slug-for-a-Butt in these wild animated adventures. Each tape features two episodes and runs about 40 min.

Earthworm Jim: Bring Me The Head Of Earthworm Jim/Sword Of Righteousness
07-2402 □*$12.99*

Earthworm Jim: Conquerer Worm/Day Of The Fish
07-2403 □*$12.99*

Earthworm Jim: Assault And Battery/Trout!
07-2404 □*$12.99*

The Adventures Of Corduroy
The fun-loving toy bear from Don Freeman's popular book series has all sorts of magical experiences in these animated stories. Each tape runs about 27 min. There are four volumes available, including:

The Adventures Of Corduroy: The Puppy
06-2514 □*$12.99*

The Adventures Of Corduroy: The Dinosaur Egg
06-2551 □*$12.99*

Poky And Friends
He's been one of the best-loved characters in children's books for years, and now the Poky Little Puppy and his pals Saggy Baggy Elephant, Scuffy the Tugboat and others come to home video. Each tape in this series features five animated tales and runs about 30 min.

Poky And Friends: Starring Poky Little Puppy
04-5672 □*$12.99*

Poky And Friends: Starring Saggy Baggy Elephant
04-5673 □*$12.99*

Poky And Friends: Starring Scuffy The Tugboat
04-5674 □*$12.99*

Asterix In Britain
Charming animated adventure saga, based on the popular French comic strip, as Asterix and his Gallic Warrior Band take on the legions of Caesar when they attempt an invasion. 85 min.
69-5131 *$14.99*

Asterix vs. Caesar
Asterix and pal Obelix battle Caesar and his Roman countrymen in this animated adventure. See the Gallic pair try to save a beautiful princess and her handsome prince from the dreaded lions. 85 min.
69-5157 *$14.99*

Champagne And The Talking Eggs
Danny Glover narrates this heartwarming animated children's tale, based on a Creole folk tale, about a young girl and her quest to overcome adversity and realize her dreams. 38 min.
70-5161 *$14.99*

Before Mickey: An Animated Anthology
This insightful documentary looks at the world of animation before Mickey Mouse appeared in the late 1920s. Different animation forms are showcased here, including line drawings, cut-outs and more, along with films of different lengths. Among the examples here are Winsor McCay's "Gertie the Dinosaur" and works by Otto Messmer and the Fleischer Brothers. 120 min.
76-7460 *$49.99*

Animation Legend Winsor McCay
A pioneer in the fields of comics and screen animation, all of McCay's surviving silent cartoons are featured on this collection. Included are his first work, an adaptation of his strip "Little Nemo" (1911), "How a Mosquito Operates" (1912), "Gertie the Dinosaur" (1914), "The Sinking of the Lusitania" (1918) and more, along with rare clips from later McCay projects. 100 min.
80-5022 *$39.99*

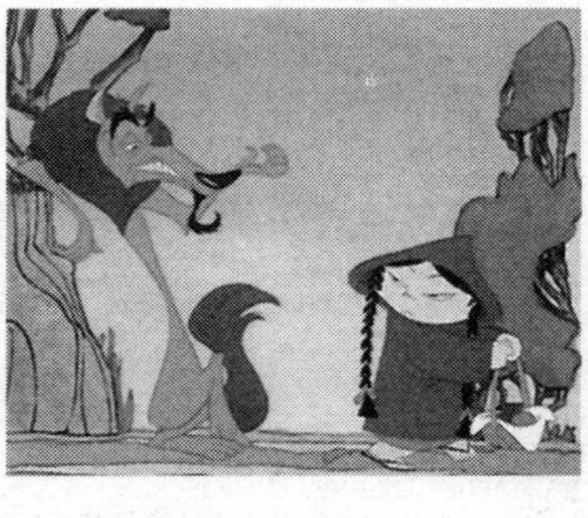

Happily Ever After: Fairy Tales For Every Child
The fairy tales of old get a face-lift with a new racially diverse presentation in these animated programs which feature exciting musical scores and celebrities supplying the voices. Narrated by Robert Guillaume; each episode runs about 30 min. There are 14 volumes available, including:

Happily Ever After: The Golden Goose
A simple-minded peasant's son must perform three seemingly impossible tasks to win the hand of a beautiful princess, and the title bird holds the key to his success. Voices by Sinbad, Loretta Devine and Richard Lewis.
44-2143 □*$12.99*

Happily Ever After: The Pied Piper
Samuel L. Jackson, Wesley Snipes and Grant Shaud lend their voices to a fresh look at the tale of the pipe-playing rat-catcher who saves the town of Hamlyn.
44-2144 □*$12.99*

Happily Ever After: Pinocchio
A bluesy African-American milieu adds to the enjoyment of the story of the puppet who longs to be a real boy. Will Smith, Chris Rock and Della Reese supply voices.
44-2145 □*$12.99*

Happily Ever After: Goldilocks
The yellow-tressed housebreaker and food thief runs into bear trouble in this cartoon adventure. Voices by David Alan Grier, Lou Rawls, Ben Vereen and Alfre Woodard.
44-2222 □*$12.99*

Happily Ever After: The Twelve Dancing Princesses
Hector Elizondo, Daisy Fuentes and Liz Torres are among the voices in this Latino-flavored telling of the fairy tale favorite.
44-2223 □*$12.99*

Happily Ever After: Thumbelina
The tiny girl with big wishes comes to animated life. Debbie Allen, Edward James Olmos, Rosie Perez and Antonio Sabato, Jr. supply voices.
44-2224 □*$12.99*

Happily Ever After: Puss 'N Boots
A South Pacific setting is given to this popular tale, voiced by Pat Morita and David Hyde Pierce.
44-2225 □*$12.99*

Scared Silly
Frightfully funny collection of creepy old cartoons including "The Cobweb Hotel," "The Screaming Bishop," "The Haunted House," "Hollywood Capers" and "The Friendly Ghost," featuring Casper's film debut. 60 min.
15-9032 Was $19.99 ***$14.99***

Jem
Beautiful record company executive Jerrica moonlights as Jem, glamorous lead singer for the hip band The Holograms, in this fun- and song-filled animated series that follows the all-girl combo around the globe. Each tape features two episodes and runs about 50 min.

Jem, Vol. 1: Passport To Rock
Includes "World Hunger Shindig" and "Adventure in China."
15-5512 ***$12.99***

Jem, Vol. 2: Fashion Fiasco
Includes "In Stitches" and "Culture Clash."
15-5557 ***$12.99***

Speed Racer:
The Original TV Classics
Rev up for animated action with the teen driver of the world's fastest, most gadget-laden car, the Mach 5, in the '60s Japanese cartoon series, featuring Speed, Trixie, Pops, Sparky and those pesky stowaways, Spridle and Chim Chim. Adventure's waiting just aheaaaaaad! Each tape runs about 50 min.

Speed Racer: Car With A Brain
15-1171 □***$14.99***

Speed Racer: The Great Plan
27-5454 □***$14.99***

Speed Racer:
The Fastest Car On Earth
27-5456 □***$14.99***

Speed Racer: The Movie
Two classic adventures with everyone's favorite daredevil driver are combined with other vintage TV cartoons and commercials in this feature-length package. Speed and the gang try to help a girl whose father wages war against autos as "The Car Hater," then face their ultimate challenge in "The Race Against the Mammoth Car." 80 min.
27-5453 Was $19.99 ***$14.99***

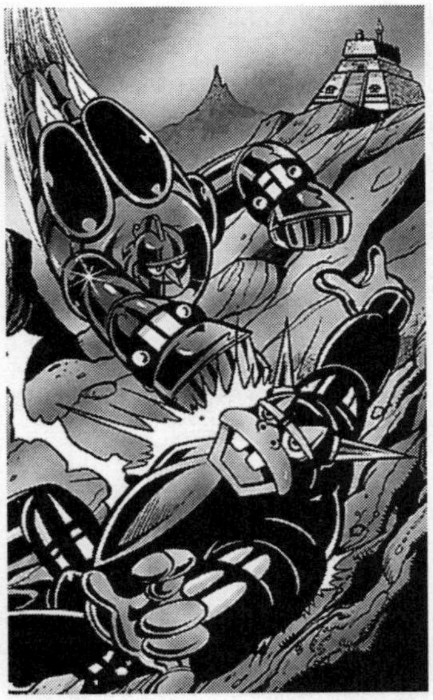

Gigantor
He's bigger than big, taller than tall, quicker than quick and stronger than strong. He's Gigantor, the space-age robot who teams with his teen controller Jimmy to battle high-tech villains in this animated Japanese series. Except where noted, each program runs about 75 min. There are eight volumes available, including:

Gigantor, Vol. 1
Features "Struggle at the South Pole," "Battle at the Bottom of the World" and "Sting of the Spider."
17-7006 ***$24.99***

Gigantor, Vol. 2
Features "Return of the Spider," "The Spider's Revenge" and "Secret Valley."
17-7007 ***$24.99***

Gigantor Retrospective 30, Vol. 1
Includes "World in Danger" and "The Smoke Robots." 50 min.
17-7028 ***$24.99***

Gigantor Retrospective 30, Vol. 2
Includes "Badge of Dager" and "The Freezer Ray." 50 min.
17-7029 ***$24.99***

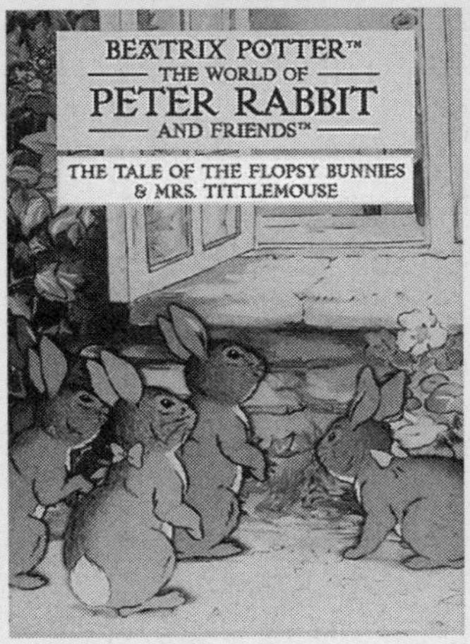

The World Of
Peter Rabbit And Friends
The authorized series based on Beatrix Potter's timeless children's stories is presented with animation that utilizes the original watercolors by the artist. Each program is introduced by Niahm Cusack as Potter, and voices are provided by some of England's top actors. Each tape runs 30 min.

The Tale Of The Flopsy Bunnies And Mrs. Tittlemouse
In this delightful animated adventure, Benjamin Bunny marries Flopsy Bunny and the two have six little Flopsy Bunnies who cause all sorts of mischief. When the youngsters get in trouble after falling asleep in Mr. McGregor's garden, Mrs. Tittlemouse tries to save the day.
10-2680 Was $19.99 ***$14.99***

The Tale Of Peter Rabbit And Benjamin Bunny
Little Peter learns he should listen to his mother's advice, and bold Benjamin has an adventure in the woods, in these two wonderful rabbit tales.
10-2399 Was $19.99 ***$14.99***

The Tale Of Samuel Whiskers
Mrs. Tabitha Twitchit has lost one of her kittens, and must find poor Tom before hungry old rat Samuel Whiskers turns him into "kitten dumpling roly-poly pudding."
10-2400 Was $19.99 ***$14.99***

The Tailor Of Gloucester
With the mayor's Christmas Day wedding getting closer, the Tailor of Gloucester must meet the deadline he's been given.
10-2428 Was $19.99 ***$14.99***

The Tale Of Pigling Bland
Country-dweller Pigling Bland sees his day at the marketplace become an unexpected adventure when he helps the lovely Pig-wig, who's been stolen by a wicked farmer.
10-2483 Was $19.99 ***$14.99***

The Tale Of Tom Kitten And Jemima Puddle-Duck
Tom Kitten and his sisters, Moppet and Mittens, learn that the garden of Farmer McGregor is not a good place to play, and would-be mother Jemima Puddle-Duck seeks a site to hatch her eggs that's better than the farmer's yard.
10-2427 Was $19.99 ***$14.99***

The Tale Of Mrs. Tiggy-Winkle And Mr. Jeremy Fisher
When Lucie loses her handkerchiefs she is helped by kindly Mrs. Tiggy-Winkle, a hedgehog washerwoman, and meets Mr. Jeremy Fisher, a frog who tells her of his incredible fishing trip.
10-2484 Was $19.99 ***$14.99***

Beatrix Potter Platinum Collection
This special three-tape collection of the beloved Beatrix Potter stories includes "The Tale of Peter Rabbit and Benjamin Bunny," "The Tailor of Gloucester" and "The Tale of the Flopsy Bunnies and Mrs. Tittlemouse."
10-2709 ***$44.99***

The Tale Of Mr. Tod
Benjamin and Flopsy Bunny's seven little offspring are swiped by a badger, and Benjamin and Peter Rabbit try to track down the culprit at the nasty fox Mr. Tod's hideout.
10-2710 Was $19.99 ***$14.99***

The Tale Of Two Bad Mice & Johnny Town-Mouse
This animated version of Beatrix Potter's tale tells of Poor Timmy Willie, a country mouse who is accidentally transported into the city, where he befriends suave Johnny Town-Mouse. The two set off on all sorts of adventures.
10-2711 Was $19.99 ***$14.99***

The Tale Of Peter Rabbit
Delightful animated adaptation of Beatrix Potter's "The Tale of Peter Rabbit" featuring Carol Burnett, who narrates, supplies the voices for two characters and sings. Follow Peter's escapades in Mr. McGregor's garden. 27 min.
27-5358 □***$14.99***

Show Me A Story Collection
The classic children's fables of Beatrix Potter come to life in this unique three-tape series that features narration by storyteller Sydney Walker accompanying Potter's original illustrations, plus a special "read-along" section for kids' participation. 135 min. total. NOTE: Individual volumes available at $12.99 each.
27-5583 Save $9.00! □***$29.99***

The Tailor Of Gloucester
A poor tailor, charged with making a formal outfit for the town's mayor, receives some unexpected help from the mice who live in his shop in this live-action musical based on the timeless Beatrix Potter tale. Ian Holm, Benjamin Luxon and Thora Hird star. 45 min.
44-2061 Was $19.99 ***$14.99***

Tales Of Beatrix Potter
Pirouettes meet Peter Rabbit in this family production by the Royal Ballet, in which dancers bring to life such beloved Potter characters as Jemima Puddle-Duck, Mr. Jeremy Fisher and others. 86 min.
63-1682 ***$12.99***

The Magic Flute
The Mozart operatic fantasy is turned into an exciting animated tale with music, as a young prince uses an enchanted flute to help save a beautiful princess. Voices by Mark Hamill, Samantha Eggar, Michael York, Joely Fisher. 44 min.
19-9098 □***$12.99***

The Transformers
They're more than meets the eye, these shape-shifting robots who protect Earth against the wrath of the evil Decepticons in these exciting animated tales of action and adventure. Each collector's set features three two-episode tapes and runs about 150 min. total. NOTE: Individual volumes available at $12.99 each.

Transformers 3-Pack #1: Vols. 1-3
Includes "Prime Threat," "Revenge of the Decepticons" and "Programmed for Evil."
15-5510 Save $9.00! ***$29.99***

Transformers 3-Pack #2: Vols. 4-6
Includes "The Key to Vector Sigma," "Return to Cybertron" and "Evolution Revolution."
15-5556 Save $9.00! ***$29.99***

Transformers 3-Pack #3: Vols. 7-9
Includes "The Return of Optimus Prime," "Evil Experiment" and "Grimlock the Hero."
15-5585 Save $9.00! ***$29.99***

Transformers: The Movie (1986)
Full-length animated action with the shape-shifting robots of toy store fame. In the near future the Autobots and Decepticons begin their final battle for power, but a sinister living planet could doom them all. Voices by Judd Nelson, Robert Stack, Orson Welles. NOTE: This is the uncut version that has not been seen in the U.S. since 1986. 90 min.
27-5202 Was $19.99 ***$14.99***

The Amazing Bunjee Venture
When a brother and sister take their inventor dad's time machine for a test spin back, they're rescued from becoming a dinosaur's lunch by Bunjee, a funny, furry critter with an inflatable trunk. Follow their adventure in this cartoon treat. 43 min.
70-3073 ***$12.99***

G.I. Joe
From the toy store to the TV screen, here are the exciting, animated adventures of the top secret defense force code-named "G.I. Joe." Watch as the members of the Joe team protect America from the evil cabal known as Cobra. Each collector's set features three two-episode tapes and runs about 150 min. total. NOTE: Individual volumes available at $12.99 each.

G.I. Joe 3-Pack #1: Vols. 1-3
Includes "Worlds Without End," "Revenge Is Not Always Sweet" and "Crime Doesn't Pay."
15-5511 Save $9.00! ***$29.99***

G.I. Joe 3-Pack #2: Vols. 4-6
Includes "Lady Luck," "Cosmetic Chaos" and "Money Is Everything."
15-5552 Save $9.00! ***$29.99***

G.I. Joe 3-Pack #3: Vols. 7-9
Includes "Captives of Cobra," "The Traitor" and "Nothing But Lies."
15-5581 Save $9.00! ***$29.99***

G.I. Joe: The Movie (1987)
Go, Joe! In this feature-length, battle-packed animated adventure, the Joes are our only hope against a threat from Cobra that could result in utter, total world destruction! With the voices of Don Johnson, Burgess Meredith, Sgt. Slaughter. 93 min.
69-5005 ***$14.99***

The Halloween Tree
While trying to save their friend Kip from the ghosts of Halloween, four youngsters join a mysterious figure named Moundshroud, who takes them on a globetrotting trip through the centuries where they learn about friendship and the meaning of Halloween. Leonard Nimoy and Lindsay Crouse supply the voices for this fine animated adaptation of Ray Bradbury's tale. 70 min.
18-7509 Was $19.99 □***$14.99***

Casper Saves Halloween
It's every ghost's favorite holiday, but this Halloween finds Casper trying to stop his buddy Hairy Scary from spooking humans, while he helps some orphans with their trick-or-treating. Other fun-filled Casper cartoons round out the show. 115 min.
19-2981 □***$14.99***

Mad Mad Mad Monsters (1972)
This hilarious animated spoof of the classic horror films has Dr. Frankenstein bringing together Dracula, Wolf Man, Mummy, and all of his scary pals for his creature's wedding to his new "monstress." Your kids will go crazy with laughter. 45 min.
04-5610 □***$12.99***

Witch's Night Out (1978)
Gilda Radner supplies the voice of an inept witch who has one night to prove her magical abilities in this animated Halloween treat with the funniest monsters you ever saw. 30 min.
27-5121 ***$14.99***

Monster Mash (2000)
It's an animated "graveyard smash," as the classic novelty song by Bobby "Boris" Pickett is brought to life (if that's the correct word) by Dracula, the Frankenstein Monster and a host of creepy, kooky creatures. 65 min.
07-2891 ***$14.99***

The Great Easter Egg Hunt
Join a rabbit named Whiskers as he and his Toyland friends set out on an exciting adventure, tracking down a magical, wish-granting egg, in this animated Easter treat. 44 min.
27-5584 ***$12.99***

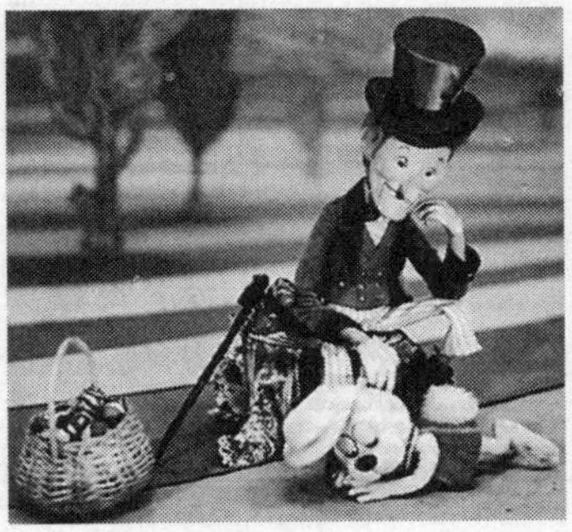

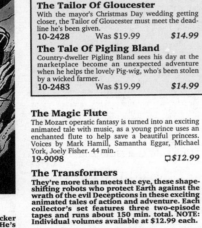

Here Comes Peter Cottontail (1971)
Hippity hoppity, a fun-filled Easter adventure's in store for any child who watches this animated rabbit tale (tail?), as that beloved bringer of eggs and candy comes hopping down the bunny trail. Told and sung by Danny Kaye; with the voice talents of Vincent Price and Casey Kasem. 53 min.
27-5314 ***$12.99***

The First Easter Rabbit (1976)
The animated, tuneful tale of Stuffy, the toy bunny who is brought to life by the good fairy and charged with delivering Easter eggs to the children of the world, is narrated by Burl Ives. Adapted from the beloved book "The Velveteen Rabbit," the story also features voices by Robert Morse and Stan Freberg. 25 min.
19-2048 ***$12.99***

The Easter Bunny Is Comin' To Town (1977)
Presented in "Animagic," a stop-motion animation process, this Rankin-Bass tale narrated by Fred Astaire tells of how a rabbit named Sunny came to the town of Kidville, a city populated by children, and helped create the traditions of Easter. 50 min.
19-2049 ***$14.99***

Yogi The Easter Bear (1993)
Yogi's appetite leads him to eat the candy for Jellystone Park's Easter Jamboree, and he and Boo-Boo have to find replacement sweets in a hurry. But when they learn the Easter Bunny has been kidnapped the pair launch a rescue mission—and learn the secrets of Easter from Mildred, the Magic Easter Chicken in the process. 55 min.
72-1093 □***$14.99***

The Mouse On The Mayflower (1968)
Delightful animated look at the first Thanksgiving, as seen through the eyes of a pilgrim mouse who helps the settlers find Plymouth and make friends with the Indians. Tennessee Ernie Ford and Eddie Albert supply voices. 48 min.
27-5409 ***$12.99***

The Berenstain Bears And Cupid's Surprise (1982)
Valentine's Day becomes un-bearable for Brother when a mysterious admirer has him trying to guess her identity in this animated special. 30 min.
53-1133 ***$12.99***

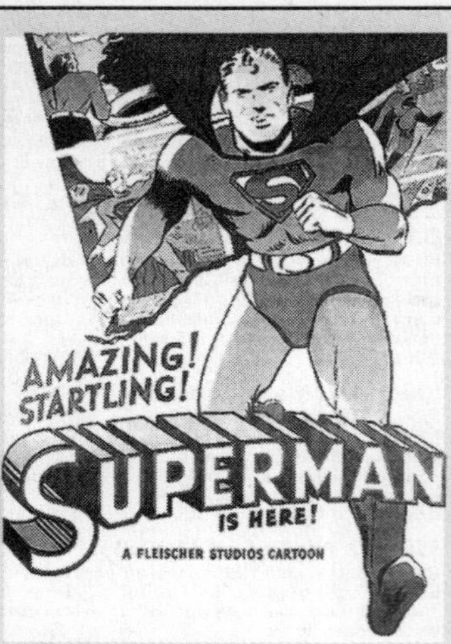

Superman: The Complete Collection
Great Krypton! Watch as Superman leaps into action in this collection that contains all 17 of the Fleischer Studios' timeless classics from the '40s in color. Includes "Japoteurs," "Secret Agent," "Electric Earthquake," "Volcano," "Showdown," "The Mechanical Monsters," and more. 142 min.
62-1264 — *$19.99*

Super Powers: Superman
It's "up, up and away" with eight animated adventures starring the Ace of Action. See Superman battle against arch-fiend Lex Luthor, human computer Brainiac, the power-sucking Parasite and other mighty menaces. 60 min.
19-1419 — *$14.99*

Super Powers: Batman
Holy home video! The Dynamic Duo are here, in five cartoon capers. Watch as Batman and Robin protect Gotham City from super-criminals like the Joker, Riddler, Catwoman and Penguin with their detective work. 60 min.
19-1420 — *$14.99*

Super Powers: Aquaman
Get wet and wild when you watch these eight animated undersea adventures. Aquaman, his young ally Aqualad and their pet walrus Tusky keep Atlantis safe from invaders like the fiendish Fisherman and Brain. 60 min.
19-1421 — *$14.99*

Super Powers: Superboy
Join the Boy of Steel and his super-dog Krypto in Smallville for eight fun-filled animated escapades, as they battle robot soldiers, interplanetary hijackers and other adversaries. 60 min.
19-1422 — *$14.99*

The Adventures Of Batman & Robin
The Caped Crusaders take on an array of their strangest, deadliest foes in these stylishly animated tales from the acclaimed Saturday morning TV series. Each tape features two episodes and runs about 45 min. There are eight volumes available, including:

The Adventures Of Batman & Robin: Two-Face
19-2347 — *$12.99*

The Adventures Of Batman & Robin: The Joker
19-2348 — *$12.99*

The Adventures Of Batman & Robin: The Penguin
19-2523 — *$12.99*

Batman: Mask Of The Phantasm (1993)
Derived from the hit animated TV series, this exciting, dark adventure features the deadliest case of Batman's career. A mysterious figure is killing Gotham City's crime bosses and everyone thinks the Caped Crusader is to blame, but the Phantasm's secret reaches deep into Bruce Wayne's past. Kevin Conroy, Dana Delany, Mark Hamill and the great Dick Miller supply the voices. 77 min.
19-2212 — Was $19.99 — □*$14.99*

Batman & Mr. Freeze: Subzero (1997)
The frigidly fiendish Mr. Freeze unleashes a chilling crimewave across Gotham City in order to restore his cryogenically preserved wife back to life, and the last element he needs for his plan could cost Batgirl her life. Batman and Robin must race against time to save her in this exciting feature-length animated saga that's too "cool" to miss. 67 min.
19-2548 — Was $19.99 — □*$14.99*

Batman Beyond
In the Gotham City of the 21st century, a new breed of super-criminals has risen to prey on the citizens, and a new Dark Knight, mentored by a retired Bruce Wayne, swoops in to keep the streets safe. Follow the rebirth of Batman in this hit animated series. Except where noted, each tape features three episodes and runs about 75 min. There are five volumes available, including:

Batman Beyond: Disappearing Inque
19-2912 — □*$12.99*

Batman Beyond: Spellbound
19-2949 — □*$12.99*

Batman Beyond: Crush
19-2950 — □*$12.99*

Batman Beyond: The Movie (1998)
See how young Terry McGinnis, seeking to avenge his father's murder, became the new Winged Crusader in this special two-part pilot episode. 45 min.
19-2831 — □*$14.99*

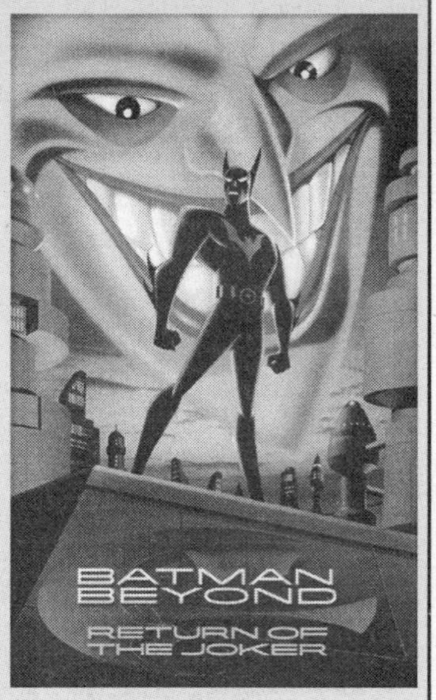

Batman Beyond: Return Of The Joker (2000)
Future masked manhunter Terry McGinnis faces his deadliest test ever when that maniacal Clown Prince of Crime, the Joker, reappears to stake his claim to Gotham City. And when his mayhem seriously injures Bruce Wayne, the new Batman must take on his most dangerous foe alone, in this feature-length animated saga. 70 min.
19-2994 — □*$19.99*

The Batman/Superman Movie (1997)
The world's finest heroes team up in this feature-length epic from their popular animated TV series, but will even the combined forces of the Dark Knight and the Man of Steel be enough to save Metropolis from the super-weaponry of Lex Luthor and the manic menace of the Joker, who's got a Kryptonite surprise for Superman? Voices by Kevin Conroy, Tim Daly, Dana Delany and Mark Hamill. 80 min.
19-2716 — *$14.99*

Superman: The Last Son Of Krypton (1996)
"It's a bird." "It's a plane." It's the Man of Steel in his first feature-length animated film, the debut adventure of the hit TV series. Follow Superman on his odyssey from his doomed home planet to the city of Metropolis, as he begins his never-ending battle for truth and justice. Tim Daly, Dana Delany, Clancy Brown supply voices. 75 min.
19-2462 — *$14.99*

Yogi Bear: Love Bugged Bear
When Cupid's arrows start flying in Jellystone Park, even Yogi isn't immune, and soon pursuing pretty she-bears is more important than pilfering picnic baskets. Also includes special "bonus toons." 60 min.
18-7724 — *$12.99*

Hulk Hogan's Rock 'N' Wrestling
There's animated grappling, giggles and good times ahead, as the one and only Hulkster teams up with pals Andre the Giant, Captain Lou and Hillbilly Jim to thwart the schemes of nasty Rowdy Roddy Piper, Mr. Fuji and their cohorts. Each tape runs about 45 min. There are six volumes available, including:

Hulk Hogan's Rock 'N' Wrestling, Vol. 1
Includes "Small But Mighty" and "Ten Little Wrestlers."
31-5216 — *$12.99*

Hulk Hogan's Rock 'N' Wrestling, Vol. 2
Includes "Amazons Just Wanna Have Fun" and "The Wrong Stuff."
31-5217 — *$12.99*

Hulk Hogan's Rock 'N' Wrestling, Vol. 3
Includes "Bucket" and "Four-Legged Pickpocket."
31-5218 — *$12.99*

Aesop's Fables
Bill Cosby stars as the legendary storyteller of ancient Greece whose fables always contained a message. Watch and learn as Aesop tells a group of children some of his famous tales. 30 min.
40-1129 — *$14.99*

Silverhawks: The Original Story
Exciting, feature-length animated thriller featuring the Silverhawks, men and women who soar through the stars on wings of silver and protect the planets from the evil MonStar. 101 min.
40-1217 — Was $19.99 — *$14.99*

Goodnight Moon And Other Sleepytime Tales
Having trouble putting your little ones to bed? This video features some of the best-loved children's bedtime stories of all time, with performances by Tony Bennett, Natalie Cole, Billy Crystal, Lauryn Hill, Susan Sarandon and others.
44-2219 — *$12.99*

Tubby The Tuba
The classic animated fantasy about a tuba's search for its own melody, featuring the voices of Dick Van Dyke, Pearl Bailey and Jack Gilford. 81 min.
47-1140 — Was $19.99 — *$12.99*

Santo Bugito
Get ready to get buggy with the six-legged inhabitants of Santo Bugito, Texas, a desert town filled with fun-loving Latino insects who know how to fiesta, in these animated tales from the creators of "Rugrats." There are three volumes available, including:

Santo Bugito, Vol. 1
Includes five episodes. 116 min.
50-8300 — *$14.99*

Santo Bugito, Vol. 2
Includes four episodes. 93 min.
50-8392 — *$14.99*

What-A-Mess
He's a fun-loving pooch who gets into one mess after another. He's What-A-Mess, the scruffy Afghan dog from Frank Muir's popular book series, and now he and all his friends can be found in these delightful animated videos.

What-A-Mess At The Seaside And Other Tales
50-8459 — *$12.99*

What-A-Mess And The Cat-Next-Door And Other Tales
50-8460 — *$12.99*

The Best Of George Pal
Creator of the award-winning "Puppetoon" series, this master animator is highlighted by his U.S. and European works. Films in black and white are "The Sleeping Beauty," "Cavalcade of Music," "Captain Kidding" and "Sky Pirates." Color films are "Tubby the Tuba," "Philips Broadcast 938," "Ship of the Ether," "Madcap Models," "John Henry and the Inky-Poo," "The Little Broadcast" and "Jasper in a Jam." 70 min.
62-1015 — *$19.99*

Little Lulu And Little Audrey
Two "little" ladies team for one big hour of cartoon fun featuring "Musicalulu," "The Dog Show Off," "Chick and Double Chick," "Loose in a Caboose," "A Bout with a Trout," "Tarts and Flowers" and "Bargain Counter Attack." 58 min.
62-1323 — *$19.99*

Cartoonies: Little Lulu
The star may be little, but the laughs are big in this fun-filled potpourri of Lulu's classic cartoon scrapes. See "Dog Show Off," "Lulu at the Zoo," "Big Drip," "I'm Just Curious" and others. 49 min.
63-1106 — *$14.99*

Bravestarr
The sharpest-shootin', hardest-ridin' tin star west of the Milky Way, Marshal Bravestarr, saddles up for outer space adventure while trying to keep the planet of New Texas free of intergalactic evildoers. Each tape runs about 60 min. There are five volumes available, including:

Bravestarr, Vol. 1: Taming The Western Galaxy
69-5052 — *$14.99*

Bravestarr, Vol. 2: High Noon In Texas
69-5077 — *$14.99*

Bravestarr, Vol. 3: Battling For Justice On The New Texas Frontier
69-5090 — *$14.99*

The Addams Family Cartoons
The drawings of Charles Addams and the hit TV show inspired these animated episodes which follow Gomez, Morticia and family a zany tour across America, with voices by Jackie Coogan, Ted Cassidy, Janet Waldo, Lennie Weinrib and Jodie Foster. Except where noted, each tape runs about 30 min. There are seven volumes available, including:

The Addams Family: The Circus Story
72-1069 — *$12.99*

The Addams Family: In New York
72-1070 — *$12.99*

The Addams Family: The Reluctant Astronauts
72-1076 — *$12.99*

The Powerpuff Girls
They're "sugar, spice and everything nice"—plus a dash of Chemical X—and now pint-sized superheroes Blossom, Bubbles and Buttercup are ready to defend the city of Townsville against the forces of evil. Join the kindergarten crusaders in these fun-filled animated adventures from their hit Cartoon Network series. Each tape runs about 70 min.

The Powerpuff Girls: Bubblevicious
72-1116 — □*$14.99*

The Powerpuff Girls: Monkey See, Doggie Do
72-1117 — □*$14.99*

The Powerpuff Girls: Birthday Bash
72-1119 — □*$14.99*

The Powerpuff Girls: Dream Scheme
72-1120 — □*$14.99*

The Tale Of Tillie's Dragon
Looking for someone to play with in her castle home, a lonely girl named Tillie makes friends with Herman, a fun-loving dragon. But how will Tillie's uncle, a descendant of St. George, react to her new pal? See what happens in this enchanting animated story. 50 min.
76-9114 — *$14.99*

The Jungle Book
Rudyard Kipling's classic tale of Mowgli's adventures in the jungle with a group of animal friends receives an exciting animated treatment.
45-5497 — *$12.99*

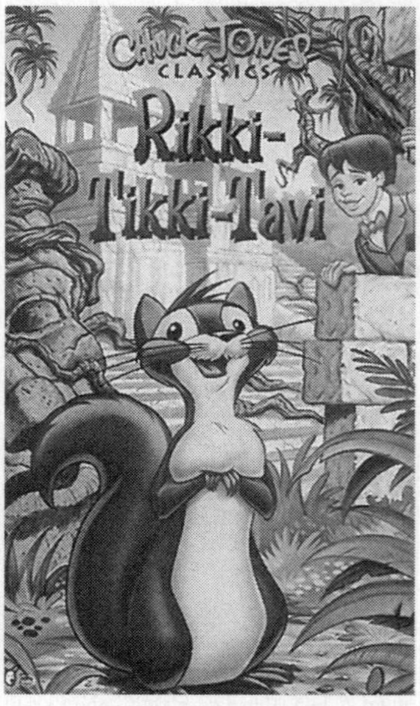

Rikki-Tikki-Tavi (1975)
Animated story based on Kipling's tale of a pet mongoose in British-ruled India who protects his young master from a vicious cobra. Superior animation from the Chuck Jones studio highlights this family adventure. Narrated by Orson Welles. 30 min.
27-5120 — □*$12.99*

The White Seal (1975)
Animated tale based on a Kipling story, as a young seal pup grows up from a mischievous infant to an adult who must save his herd from hunters. 30 min.
27-5149 — *$12.99*

The Adventures Of Mowgli (1996)
Lovingly animated adaptation of Rudyard Kipling's stories involving Mowgli and his experiences with Baloo the bear, Bagheera the panther and other creatures. Voices are supplied by Charlton Heston, Sam Elliott and Dana Delany. 92 min.
76-9095 — *$14.99*

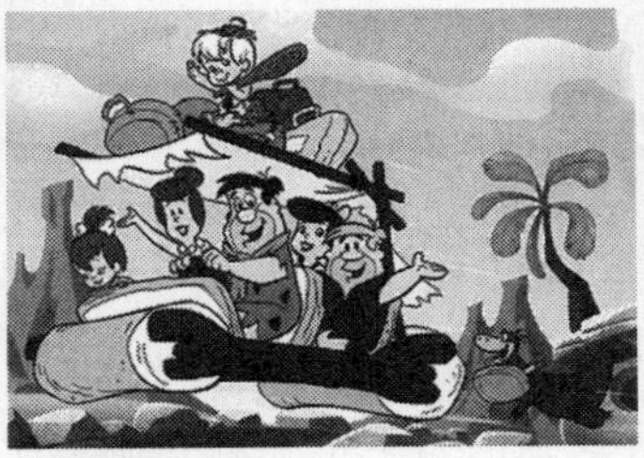

THE FLINTSTONES

The Flintstones: Stone-Age Adventures
Six of your favorite tales featuring "the modern Stone Age family" are gathered together in one video. Join Fred, Barney, Betty and Wilma for "Split Personality," "The Twitch" and more.
19-2935 🗨$14.99

The Flintstones: Fearless Fred Strikes Again
Wilma's birthday, a talking dodo named Doozy, and "The Buffalo Convention" in Frantic City all add up to trouble for Fred and Barney. Next, it's "Mother-in-Law's Visit," and Fred makes a valiant effort to get along with her. 50 min.
72-1079 $14.99

The Flintstones: Babe In Bedrock
The babe is none other than Pebbles, spotlighted in two great episodes. See the chaos that erupted on the day Pebbles was born in "Dress Rehearsal," followed by Fred's efforts to enter "Daddy's Little Beauty" in a contest for grown-ups. 50 min.
72-1080 $14.99

The Flintstones: Hooray For Hollyrock
For such a small town, Bedrock has had more than its share of celebrity visits. Watch what happens when the Flintstones and Rubbles play host to two of them in "Ann-Margrock Presents" and "The Return of Stoney Curtis" (both with the voices of their real-life counterparts). 50 min.
72-1081 $14.99

The Flintstones: I Yabba-Dabba Do! (1996)
It's the wedding of the year—somewhere around 70,000 to 60,000 B.C., we think—when Pebbles and Bamm-Bamm decide to tie the knot and throw their parents into one marital mishap after another in this feature-length "Flintstones" tale. 92 min.
18-7722 $14.99

Cartoons That Time Forgot, Vol. 1: All Singing! All Dancing!
Animator extraordinaire Ub Iwerks' early '30s works are presented in this fabulous cartoon collection, featuring music by Carl Stalling, later of "Looney Tunes" fame. Included here are "Fiddlesticks!," "The Soup Song," "Old Mother Hubbard," "Mary's Little Lamb," "Summertime," "The Brementown Musicians," and more. 75 min.
53-7766 $24.99

Cartoons That Time Forgot, Vol. 2: Down And Out With Flip The Frog
Ub Iwerks' Depression-era cartoon hero, Flip the Frog, is showcased in this innuendo-filled collection. Included here are "The Milkman," "The New Car," "The Office Boy" and "Movie Mad," all of which were produced between 1931 and 1933. 76 min.
53-7767 $24.99

Cartoons That Time Forgot, Vol. 3: Things That Go Bump In The Night
The dark and fantastic side of Ub Iwerks' animation can be seen in this spooky sampler that offers "Stratos-Fear," "Jack Frost," "A Chinaman's Chance," "Spooks," and many more, including a clip from the lost Willie Whopper cartoon, "Hell's Fire." 75 min.
53-7768 $24.99

Cartoons That Time Forgot, Vol. 4: Willie Whopper's Fantastic Adventures
The invention of Ub Iwerks, Willie Whopper was a "little boy with a big imagination" whose "tall tales" were flavored with wild sight gags and innovative background design. He's the star of nine shorts, including "Sinbad the Sailor," "Good Scout," "Insultin' the Sultan," "Tom Thumb" and the never-before-seen "The Air Race." 75 min.
53-7769 $24.99

Ub Iwerks' Famous Fairytales
Classic animation from the man who helped create Mickey Mouse. Includes "The Headless Horseman," "Aladdin and the Wonderful Lamp," "The King's Tailor," "Dick Whittington's Cat," "Mary's Little Lamb," "Jack and the Beanstalk" and "Puss in Boots." 56 min.
62-1290 $19.99

Monster Rancher
Eleven-year-old video game champion Genki is going to need his skills when he's magically transported to a strange land filled with a menagerie of creatures and in danger of being conquered by the wicked Master Moo. Follow Genki, his pal Holly, and their monster allies as they battle to save the world in these exciting animated stories. Each tape features three episodes and runs about 75 min.

Monster Rancher, Vol. 1: Let The Games Begin!
20-8523 $14.99

Monster Rancher, Vol. 2: Catch A Tiger By The Tail!
20-8524 $14.99

Monster Rancher, Vol. 3: Fast Friends And Fiendish Foes!
20-8590 $14.99

Nursery Rhymes
Mother Goose goes video in this animated collection of the classic children's fables. See Simple Simon, Little Bo Peep, Old King Cole and, of course, Mother Goose herself. 60 min.
27-5151 $12.99

The Velveteen Rabbit
All-new animated rendition of the classic children's story, as a little stuffed bunny must undergo many hardships in his quest to become "real." Narrated by Christopher Plummer. 30 min.
27-5167 🗨$14.99

Phantom 2040: The Ghost Who Walks
In the 21st-century city of Metropia, Kit Walker becomes the legendary Phantom and battles a deadly "virtual reality" game in order to stop a ruthless businesswoman from wreaking ecological havoc on Earth in this feature-length thriller. 97 min.
27-5549 $14.99

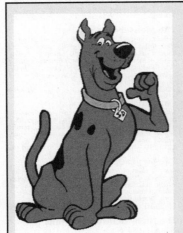

Theodore Tugboat
These uplifting animated stories will thrill and delight preschoolers as they follow the adventures of Theodore, a tiny tugboat with a heart of gold who spends his days in Big Harbor exploring with an array of boat buddies. Each volume contains three episodes and runs about 45 min.

Theodore Tugboat: Theodore's Friendly Adventures
Includes "Theodore and the Unsafe Ship," "A Joke Too Far" and "Hank and the Sunken Ship."
18-7818 🗨$12.99

Theodore Tugboat: Theodore Helps A Friend
Includes "Theodore and the Hunt for Northumberland," "Bedford's Big Move" and "Guysborough Makes a Friend."
18-7819 🗨$12.99

Theodore Tugboat: Big Harbor Bedtime
Includes "Emily and the Sleep Over," "Theodore's Bright Night" and "Foduck and the Shy Ship."
18-7820 🗨$12.99

Theodore Tugboat: Underwater Adventures
Includes "Night Shift," "Rebecca and the Big Snore" and "Hank Stays Up Late."
18-7900 🗨$12.99

Towser
Have a howling good time as you follow the misadventures of a trouble-prone dog named Towser with these delightful cartoon collections. Each tape runs about 65 min.

Towser, Vol. 1
22-1585 $14.99

Towser, Vol. 2
22-1586 $14.99

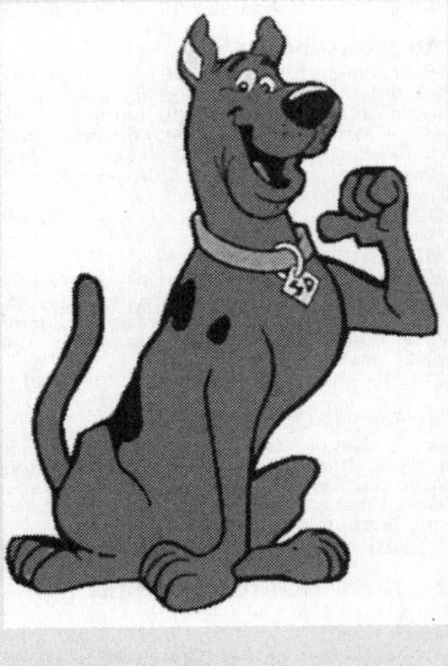

Classic Scooby-Doo
Goofy Great Dane Scooby-Doo and pals Shaggy, Freddy, Velma and Daphne try to solve their greatest mirthful mysteries in these classic programs. Each 60-minute tape includes two episodes of the ever-popular Hanna-Barbera series, plus special bonus cartoons.

Classic Scooby-Doo: Scooby-Doo And A Mummy, Too
18-7635 $12.99

Classic Scooby-Doo: Foul Play In Funland
18-7636 $12.99

Classic Scooby-Doo: Which Witch Is Which?
18-7637 $12.99

Classic Scooby-Doo: A Gaggle Of Galloping Ghosts
18-7638 $12.99

Classic Scooby-Doo: Mystery Mask Mix-Up
72-1112 $12.99

Classic Scooby-Doo: That's Snow Ghost
72-1113 $12.99

Classic Scooby-Doo: The Haunted House Hang-Up
72-1114 $12.99

Scooby-Doo Meets The Boo Brothers
To collect the fortune in jewels bequeathed to him by Uncle Beauregard, Shaggy and his pals Scooby-Doo and Scrappy-Doo must survive a night in a haunted Southern Mansion and deal with a trio of spectral siblings in this full-length adventure. 91 min.
14-3177 $14.99

Scooby-Doo: Arabian Nights
This feature-length Scooby-Doo adventure finds the daffy dog and Shaggy heading to Arabia, where they're going to be food tasters for the Caliph. Mistaken identities and silly situations soon ensue, and Yogi Bear as a genie and Magilla Gorilla as Sinbad are in on the fun. 80 min.
18-7639 $14.99

Scooby-Doo's Greatest Mysteries
He's been pulling the masks off of would-be ghosts, witches and other monsters for 30 years, and now the all-time favorite adventures of Scooby-Doo and "those meddling kids" have been gathered in one mystery-packed video. Included are "Jeepers, It's the Creeper," "Hassle in the Castle," "A Clue for Scooby-Doo" and "The Rage Backstage." 95 min.
72-1115 🗨$14.99

Scooby-Doo's Creepiest Capers
Grab a box of Scooby Snacks and get ready for a "spooktacular" collection of the monster-chasing mutt's eeriest episodes, as Scooby and the gang tussle with Count Dracula, the Frankenstein Monster and other classic creeps. 90 min.
72-1118 🗨$14.99

Scooby-Doo Goes Hollywood (1979)
Everyone's favorite mystery-solving mutt decides he's tired of the monster-chasing business and wants to branch out as an actor. Joined by his "agent" Shaggy, Scooby takes to the screen as a cowboy hero, disco star and more in this riotous Tinseltown spoof. 51 min.
14-3003 🗨$14.99

Scooby-Doo On Zombie Island (1998)
Hey Scooby, it's time to catch that villain! Scooby, Shaggy, and the rest of the gang get together to take on a bunch of scary zombies on an island in the bayou. A mysterious and hilarious feature-length adventure the whole family can enjoy, as long as somebody brings the Scooby Snacks. 70 min.
72-1111 🗨$19.99

Scooby-Doo And The Witch's Ghost (1999)
The ghost-hunting Great Dane and his pals have their work cut out for them when they meet up with a noted horror author and visit a New England town that appears to be haunted by the spirit of a vengeful witch in this feature-length mystery. 70 min.
19-2892 🗨$19.99

Scooby-Doo And The Alien Invaders (2000)
Sure, he's defeated ghosts, vampires, zombies, witches and other terrestrial terrors, but can Scooby-Doo handle a mystery from outer space? Watch as Scoob and the gang tackle a UFO menace in this out-of-this-world feature-length tale. 80 min.
72-1122 🗨$19.99

Dangermouse
He's the James Bond of the rodent world, and with loyal aide Penfold in tow, Dangermouse always gets his foe. Everyone will enjoy these exciting and witty animated adventures, as our heroes strive to keep the world safe for mousedom. Each tape runs about 60 min.

Dangermouse, Vol. 1
44-1210 $14.99

Dangermouse, Vol. 2
44-1232 $14.99

Dangermouse, Vol. 3
44-1262 $14.99

Dangermouse, Vol. 4
44-1291 $14.99

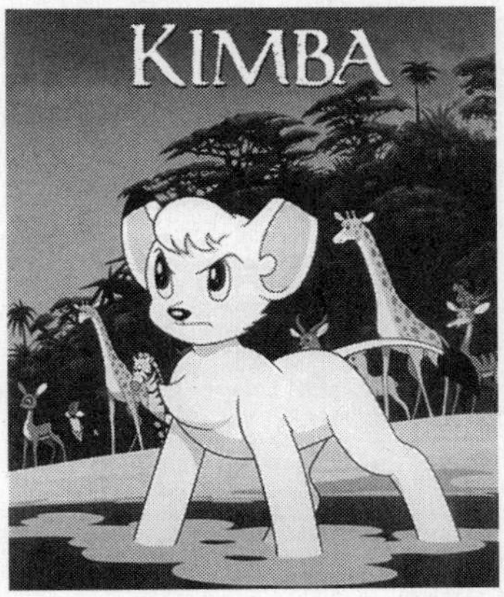

Kimba The White Lion
First airing on Japanese TV in 1965, this popular animated series from "Astro Boy" creator Osamu Tezuka followed the adventures of an orphaned lion cub named Kimba. Escaping from captivity and returning to his jungle home, Kimba assumes his role as king of the animals and works with his friends to keep their realm free and safe. Each tape features four episodes and runs about 100 min.

Kimba The White Lion, Vol. 1: The King Is Dead, All Hail The King
20-8525 $14.99

Kimba The White Lion, Vol. 2: Trials Of A Jungle King
20-8526 $14.99

Kimba The Lion Prince
The white lion known as Kimba is featured in these two-episode, 60-minute programs from the ever-popular animated series that captivated youngsters in the mid-1960s. Follow the adventures of Kimba, the young son of slain lion king Caesar, who tries to protect his African homeland from enemies.

Kimba The Lion Prince: Legend Of The Claw
58-8202 $12.99

Kimba The Lion Prince: River Battle
58-8203 $12.99

Kimba The Lion Prince: Jungle Thief
58-8204 $12.99

Kimba The Lion Prince: Insect Invasion
58-8205 $12.99

The New Adventures Of Kimba The White Lion
Two decades after he first debuted on TV in the 1960s, the lovable lion prince was revamped by his creator, famed Japanese cartoonist Osamu Tezuka, for this exciting, all-new animated series. Follow Kimba and his pals as they battle animal and human enemies to keep the jungle safe. Each tape runs about 65 min. There are six volumes available, including...

The New Adventures Of Kimba The White Lion, Vol. 1: The Successor Of Legend
85-1159 🗨$19.99

The New Adventures Of Kimba The White Lion, Vol. 2: The Vow Of Peace
85-1165 $14.99

The New Adventures Of Kimba The White Lion, Vol. 3: Poachers And Puzzles
85-1166 $14.99

Holiday Favorites

Christmas TV Classics
Timeless episodes from some of TV's best-loved vintage series, all with a holiday theme. Ozzie plays Scrooge in a PTA play on "Ozzie and Harriet," "Captain Gallant of the Foreign Legion" celebrates Christmas with his son, Danny Thomas helps "Make Room for Daddy" on Christmas, and Charles Boyer stars in the TV yule drama "The Gift." 120 min. total.
01-5137 Was $29.99 *$14.99*

Buster & Chauncey's Silent Night
Learn how the legendary Christmas song "Silent Night" was created in this animated fantasy about two musical mice who accidentally create a Christmas miracle after befriending a poor orphan girl. Features voices by Marie Osmond, Phil Hartman and Tom Arnold. 49 min.
02-3190 □*$12.99*

The Nuttiest Nutcracker
Computer animation, the voices of Jim Belushi, Cheech Marin and Phyllis Diller, and the music of Peabo Bryson help bring this unique version of "The Nutcracker" to you. In this story, a teenage girl dreams of the Nutcracker Prince, the Sugar Plum Fairy, the Mouse King and some talking foods while waiting for her parents to come home during a snowstorm. 48 min.
02-3358 □*$14.99*

The Nutcracker Prince (1990)
Lovely, lively animated version of the perennial holiday favorite about the romance between a princess and a brave nutcracker that comes to life to defend her against the evil Mouseking. Voices by Kiefer Sutherland, Megan Follows and Peter O'Toole; music by Tchaikovsky. 74 min.
19-1902 Was $19.99 □*$14.99*

Richard Scarry's The Best Christmas Surprise Ever
Have yourself a Scarry little Christmas with this fun-filled animated special that presents three stories with the author's popular characters. 25 min.
02-8761 *$12.99*

Scrooge (1935)
An early British rendition of Dickens' classic tale. Sir Seymour Hicks co-wrote the screenplay and stars in the title role, and the excellent supporting cast includes Maurice Evans, Robert Cochran and Mary Glynne. 61 min.
17-1079 *$19.99*

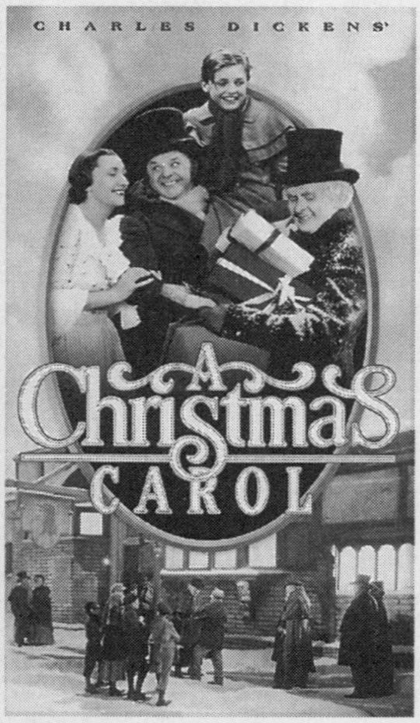

A Christmas Carol (1938)
Classic version of the holiday favorite. Reginald Owen stars as Ebeneezer Scrooge, the skinflint whose very soul is in danger unless he can learn the true spirit of Christmas. Gene Lockhart stars as Bob Cratchit and Leo G. Carroll plays Marley's ghost. Truly a fine holiday treat for all. 70 min.
12-1473 Was $19.99 *$14.99*

A Christmas Carol (Color Version) (1938)
"That wonderful holiday favorite with Reginald Owen as Scrooge is now available in vibrant color? The Dickens, you say!"
12-1004 Was $19.99 *$14.99*

A Christmas Carol (1951)
Superb treatment of Dickens' classic, too good to be shown only at Christmas. Alastair Sim is quintessential miser Scrooge. Also stars Patrick Macnee, Jack Warner, Kathleen Harrison. 86 min.
08-1045 Was $19.99 *$14.99*

A Christmas Carol (Color Version) (1951)
"That wonderful holiday favorite with Alastair Sim as Scrooge is now available in vibrant color? The Dickens, you say!"
08-1450 Was $19.99 *$14.99*

A Christmas Carol With Fredric March
An annual holiday treat on '50s television was this episode from the "Shower of Stars" variety series. Academy Award-winner March teams with Basil Rathbone for a lively musical rendition of the Dickens fable. 60 min.
10-1290 Was $19.99 *$14.99*

A Christmas Carol (1971)
Winner of the Academy Award for Best Animated Short Subject, director Richard Williams' faithful adaptation of the holiday perennial favorite features Alastair Sim reprising his most famous film role, as the voice of consummate miser Ebeneezer Scrooge. Sir Michael Redgrave narrates. 30 min.
19-9021 □*$14.99*

The Stingiest Man In Town (1978)
A new variation on the Charles Dickens classic "A Christmas Carol," featuring Walter Matthau doing the voice of Ebeneezer Scrooge, and Tom Bosley, Theodore Bikel, Robert Morse and Dennis Day in support. 50 min.
19-1804 *$12.99*

A Christmas Carol (1984)
A marvelous performance by George C. Scott as repentant pinchpenny Ebeneezer Scrooge fuels this acclaimed adaptation of Dickens' beloved holiday fable. The stellar cast also includes David Warner, Susannah York, Frank Finlay, Edward Woodward and Nigel Davenport. 100 min.
04-3258 □*$14.99*

Scrooged (1988)
That irrepressible little Dickens, Bill Murray, stars in this riotous reworking of "A Christmas Carol" as a commercial, callous TV exec who receives laugh-packed lessons in having holiday spirit from some antagonistic apparitions! Gonzo cast includes John Forsythe, Karen Allen, Carol Kane, Bobcat Goldthwait, David Johansen, many others. 111 min.
06-1682 □*$14.99*

Ms. Scrooge (1997)
Cicely Tyson plays the title role of the cold-hearted businesswoman who receives a spectral lesson in holiday spirit in this distaff version of Dickens' "A Christmas Carol." Katherine Helmond, Michael Beach also star. 87 min.
06-2930 □*$79.99*

Ebenezer (1997)
Oscar-winner Jack Palance has the title role in this Old West retelling of Dickens' "A Christmas Carol." Ebenezer is a mean-spirited old crook who goes through a holiday odyssey when he is visited by three ghosts who show him the error of his ways. Rick Schroder and Amy Locane co-star. 94 min.
88-7017 *$14.99*

An All Dogs Christmas Carol (1998)
Charlie, Itchy and their cartoon canine pals offer up a doggie spin on Charles Dickens' immortal story in this feature-length Yuletide tale, visiting a mean old bulldog who wants to ruin the holidays as the Ghosts of Christmas Past, Present and Future to show him the error of his ways. Voices by Ernest Borgnine, Dom DeLuise, Sheena Easton and Charles Nelson Reilly. 73 min.
12-3262 □*$14.99*

A Christmas Carol (1999)
Patrick Stewart takes on the role of Dickens' Yuletide tightwad Ebeneezer Scrooge, who receives a lesson in the Christmas spirit from some ghostly do-gooders, in this faithfully rendered film that's sure to become a holiday favorite. 93 min.
19-2986 □*$14.99*

A Christmas Carol
Miserly Ebeneezer Scrooge, put-upon Bob Cratchit and his family, the spectre of Jacob Marley and a trio of holiday spirits are all vividly portrayed in this wonderful animated rendition of the Charles Dickens story. Ed Asner, Tim Curry, Whoopi Goldberg and Michael York are among the voice talents. 72 min.
04-3519 Was $19.99 □*$14.99*

Madeline: Madeline's Christmas
In this special holiday-themed adventure with Ludwig Bemelman's good-hearted—but trouble-prone—French schoolgirl, a sudden blizzard could force Madeline to spend her Christmas taking care of a bunch of ailing friends. 25 min.
04-5573 □*$12.99*

A Very Merry Casper Christmas
This Harveytoon holiday treat features four animated tales with such characters as Casper the Friendly Ghost ("True Boo," "Ice Scream"), Baby Huey ("Jumping with Toy") and Herman and Katnip ("Mice Meeting You"). 22 min.
07-2809 *$12.99*

The Gingham Dog And The Calico Cat
Popular songstress Amy Grant and guitar great Chet Atkins tell the story of two cute Christmas gifts that fall off Santa's sleigh and into a great forest. After arguing, they learn to trust each other, and bring their love to their new family.
07-5008 *$14.99*

Bump In The Night: 'Twas The Night Before Bumpy
When Bumpy hatches a scheme to sneak up to the North Pole and steal Santa's bag of gifts for himself, he and pals Squishington and Molly learn a valuable holiday lesson in this clay animation Christmas fable. 63 min.
08-8768 *$14.99*

The Twelve Days Of Christmas
An outrageous animated Christmas fantasy in which Sir Carolboomer and his squire, Hollyberry, steal the Christmas list of the hard-to-please Princess Silverbelle. Accidentally, Carolboomer takes the answers to the king's crossword puzzle and Hollyberry tries to fill the list...all leading to the origin of the famous song. The voice of Phil Hartman is featured. 30 min.
10-2532 Was $19.99 *$12.99*

The Mousehole Cat
Based on an English legend and a famous children's book, this delightful animated holiday adventure tells about a cat named Mowzer who lives in the fishing village of Mousehole with an elderly fisherman named Tom. When the arrival of the Great Storm Cat in the harbor threatens the town's Christmas, Tom and Mowzer team to tame it. 25 min.
10-2689 *$14.99*

Christmas Homes
America's most incredibly decorated, most extravagantly lit homes are highlighted in all of their holiday splendor. Accompanied by favorite carols, this terrific tour of festive homes is sure to get you in a jolly holiday mood. 35 min.
10-2759 *$9.99*

The Magic Of Christmas
Enjoy an array of Yuletide scenes in this program that takes you all around the country. Witness a Rocky Mountain winterland, New York City's outdoor decorations, Vermont snowfalls, Colorado sleigh rides and more. 59 min.
10-2760 *$12.99*

The Night Before Christmas
This animated program looks at Clement Clark Moore's classic, "A Visit from St. Nicholas," which came to be known as "The Night Before Christmas." Learn how the Columbia University professor wrote the poem for his ailing daughter, who requested a special story which Moore couldn't find. 28 min.
10-2762 *$12.99*

The Nutcracker
Tchaikovsky's famed ballet is colorfully brought to life in this wonderful animated production involving a 7-year-old girl, a mysterious nutcracker gift and the malicious seven-headed Mouse King. 50 min.
10-2764 *$12.99*

Rudolph The Red-Nosed Reindeer (Merry Christmas Rudy)
Three classic holiday-themed cartoons are featured on this special collection: Max Fleischer's original animated short based on the classic song "Rudolph the Red-Nosed Reindeer"; Fleischer's beloved Grampy bringing cheer to some orphans in 1936's "Christmas Comes But Once a Year"; and a live-action telling two children the cartoon tale of "The Christmas Toyshop." 30 min.
10-2818 *$12.99*

The Christmas Toy
Kermit the Frog narrates this Christmas tale about a stuffed tiger named Rugby who thinks that he'll be under the tree again this year when his owner opens his presents. When he isn't wrapped up again, Rugby sets out to do it himself, but faces the danger of losing his power to come alive if he is caught. 50 min.
11-1753 *$12.99*

Muppet Family Christmas
Kermit, Fozzie, Miss Piggy and the rest of the gang head off to a fun-filled holiday at Fozzie's mom's farmhouse. Along with the snow, the Yuletide cheer and a few special visits from Sesame Street friends, they have a magical time never to be forgotten, and sing a few songs to boot. 42 min.
11-1947 *$12.99*

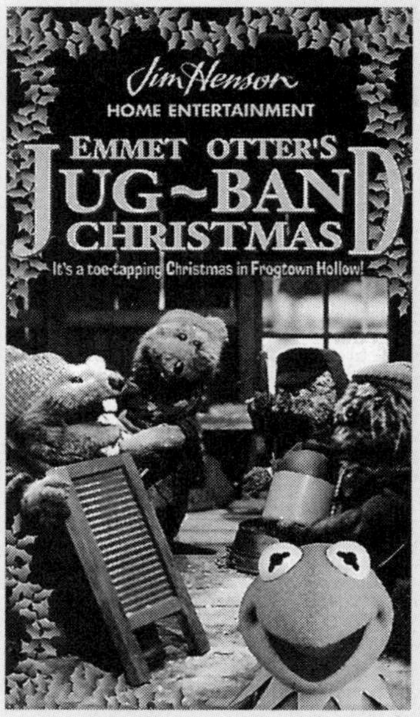

Emmet Otter's Jug-Band Christmas
Kermit the Frog takes you on a musical holiday journey with this children's book adaptation with a Muppet twist. In it, Emmet and his Ma put everything on the line to give each other a nice Christmas by entering a talent show contest. 48 min.
11-1073 *$12.99*

Christmas Eve On Sesame Street
As Sesame Street busily prepares for the holiday, Oscar the Grouch asks Big Bird how Santa Claus is able to squeeze his girth down all those chimneys. Hot on the trail of the answer, Big Bird learns the true meaning of Christmas. 60 min.
46-1041 □*$12.99*

Elmo Saves Christmas (1996)
Little Elmo doesn't want the holiday fun to end, but when his wish that every day would be Christmas is granted, he learns an important lesson in this "Sesame Street" special featuring guest stars Maya Angelou, Charles Durning and Harvey Fierstein. 55 min.
04-5468 □*$12.99*

MGM Cartoon Christmas
Yule certainly like this collection of four holiday animated treats, featuring "Alias St. Nick," the 1939 Oscar-nominated anti-war fable "Peace on Earth," "The Pups' Christmas" and "The Peachy Cobbler." 35 min.
12-1721 *$14.99*

Mary-Kate And Ashley Olsen: To Grandmother's House We Go
While on a Christmas trip to Grandma's house, Mary-Kate and Ashley get involved with Santa's elves, cops and a winning lottery ticket. Guests include Rhea Perlman and Jerry Van Dyke. 89 min.
19-2362 □*$14.99*

Will Vinton's Claymation Christmas Celebration
Have a happy holiday with the stop-motion creations of "California Raisins" inventor Will Vinton. Enjoy the merriment with a cast that includes singing camels, ice-skating penguins and the Paris Bellharmonic Orchestra. 24 min.
27-5497 *$12.99*

Arthur's Perfect Christmas
In this holiday special, Arthur and his friends celebrate Christmas, Chanukah and Kwanzaa, but he learns some lessons during the holiday season, too. 55 min.
02-5748 *$12.99*

Santa's Special Delivery
In this animated holiday tale, Santa's elves have updated his list of good and naughty children onto a computer disc, but an accidental deletion could spell the end of Christmas unless a young computer whiz can help Santa save the day. With the voice of Rik Mayall. 30 min.
02-5749 *$12.99*

Teletubbies: Christmas In The Snow
This two-tape holiday set features Tinky Winky, Dipsy, Laa-Laa and Po finding Teletubbyland covered in snow in "It's Snowing!" and building a snowy pal and learning how children from different countries celebrate Christmas in "The Snow Tubby." 90 min.
18-7919 *$29.99*

The Christmas Tradition
The joyous spirit of Christmas comes to life in a performance by the Stratford Chamber Choir from Stratford-Upon-Avon, England, of many classic holiday songs, along with charming images from 2,000 years worth of seasonal art. 60 min.
22-1834 *$19.99*

Miracle On 34th Street (1947)
The perennial holiday film classic about a Macy's department store Santa Claus who insists he's the real item. Edmund Gwenn stars in his Academy Award-winning role of "Kris Kringle," Maureen O'Hara plays a doubting store executive, Natalie Wood is her daughter, and John Payne is the lawyer who defends Gwenn in court. 96 min.
04-3060 ❑*$14.99*

20th Century Fox Hour: The Miracle On 34th Street (1955)
A long-lost TV version of the classic tale of Santa Claus and feuding department stores stars Thomas Mitchell as Kris Kringle, along with Macdonald Carey, Teresa Wright, Ray Collins and Hans Conried. 47 min.
09-2323 *$14.99*

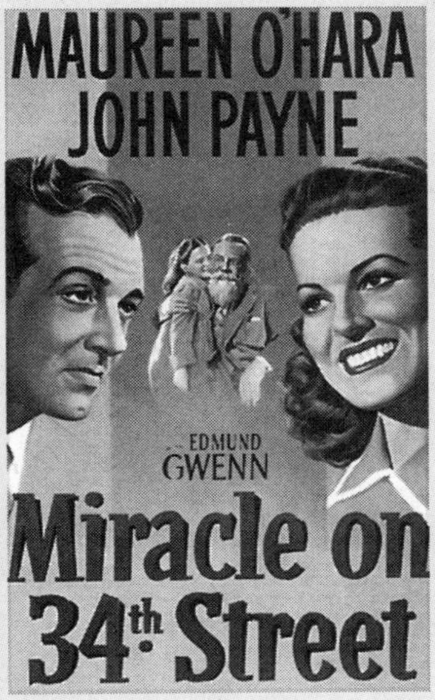
MAUREEN O'HARA
JOHN PAYNE
EDMUND GWENN
Miracle on 34th Street

Miracle On 34th Street (1994)
What happens when a department store Santa Claus claims to be the genuine article? Richard Attenborough is the jolly Kris Kringle who teaches those around him a lesson in Christmas spirit in this colorful updating of the beloved Yuletide story. With Elizabeth Perkins, Dylan McDermott, Mara Wilson. 113 min.
04-2993 ❑*$14.99*

The Flintstones: Christmas In Bedrock
In this double bill of holiday-themed "Flintstones" tales, Fred and Wilma help a mischievous boy learn about the Christmas spirit, followed by Fred's foray into department-store Santa duty. 60 min.
18-7693 ❑*$12.99*

A Flintstone Christmas (1977)
Fred and Barney become Stone Age Santas when a Yuletide visit to Bedrock leaves the real Kris Kringle with a sprained ankle in this animated holiday adventure. 49 min.
10-2217 *$12.99*

The Flintstones Christmas Carol (1993)
It's "Yabba-Dabba-Bah, Humbug!" when Fred is cast as Ebenezer Scrooge in Bedrock's stage production of "A Christmas Carol" and begins taking the role a little too much to heart. Can Wilma, Pebbles and the Rubbles restore his holiday spirit before it's too late? 90 min.
72-1102 *$14.99*

Scooby-Doo's A Nutcracker Scoob
Ghosts and mysteries don't take time off for the holidays, and neither do Scooby and the gang in these two wintry whodunits. See them put a spooky snow monster on ice in "Alaskan King Coward," followed by a haunted Christmas show at a children's home in "A Nutcracker Scoob." 60 min.
18-7694 ❑*$12.99*

A Jetson Christmas Carol
Flint-hearted space sprockets mogul Mr. Spacely plays Scrooge to George Jetson's Cratchit in a space-age updating of the Dickens tale that's sure to be a holiday hit in any galaxy. 30 min.
72-1012 *$12.99*

'Twas The Night Before Christmas
When a town is afraid that Santa will overlook it on Christmas Eve, it's up to a clockmaker—and the mice who live in his house—to save the day in this animated special. With the voices of Joel Grey, Tammy Grimes and "Lonesome" George Gobel. 24 min.
19-1802 *$12.99*

Bugs Bunny's Looney Christmas Tales
Eh, what's cooking in this holiday program, Doc? Why, it's Bugs Bunny and pals, enacting "A Christmas Carol" and "'Twas the Night Before Christmas" in their favorite fashion. 25 min.
19-1805 *$12.99*

Hello Kitty: Santa's Missing Hat
In this animated tale, feline friends Kitty and Mimi discover that their pals don't believe in Santa Claus and are soon hurled into a series of wild adventures when a hat from a Santa display blows into the forest. Also on this tape is "The Christmas Eve Gift," in which Keroppi and his pals help Twinkle the little star shine bright on Christmas night. 55 min.
27-5532 ❑*$12.99*

The Littlest Angel
A little boy-turned-neophyte angel learns that staying out of trouble in Heaven isn't as easy as one would think, until he sets out to find a present to give to the Christ child, in this animated rendition of Charles Tazewell's perennially popular holiday story. 24 min.
27-5570 ❑*$12.99*

Jingle Bells
A family learns a valuable lesson in togetherness and the Christmas spirit in this warm and funny animated holiday tale. Voices by Jason Alexander, Don Knotts and Shelley Long. 48 min.
27-5575 ❑*$14.99*

O' Christmas Tree
Ed Asner, Tim Conway and Marie Osmond lend their voices to this delightful holiday cartoon about a lonely little tree who discovers the holiday spirit. 48 min.
27-5576 ❑*$14.99*

We Wish You A Merry Christmas
Learn how a town's rediscovery of the holiday spirit leads to the invention of Christmas carols in this song-filled animated gem. Travis Tritt narrates and sings the title tune; voices by Nell Carter, Lacey Chabert. 48 min.
27-5577 ❑*$14.99*

The Tangerine Bear
Based on the popular children's book, this wondrous holiday story tells of the Tangerine Bear, a doll with its mouth sewn upside down. After months of being neglected in a toy store window, the bear is adopted by a loving family just in time for Christmas. Trisha Yearwood narrates and provides songs; voices by Jonathan Taylor-Thomas, Tom Bosley, Jenna Elfman and Howie Mandel. 61 min.
27-5589 ❑*$14.99*

Maxine's Christmas Carol
The wisecracking elderly woman of Hallmark card fame gets her own funny Christmas special, as the cranky characters learns a few lessons at Yuletide. 30 min.
27-5591 *$14.99*

Red Skelton's Christmas Dinner
Happy holidays are in store as the irrepressible Red recounts the story of Freddie the Freeloader's attempts to bring holiday cheer to fellow hoboes Vincent Price and Imogene Coca. "Merry Christmas to all...and may God bless!" 60 min.
27-6446 *$12.99*

Barney's Night Before Christmas
Maybe the mice weren't stirring, but the dinosaurs certainly were in this fun-filled holiday video, as Barney, B.J. and Baby Bop travel to the North Pole and get a guided tour of Santa's workshop from St. Nick himself! 60 min.
50-8322 *$14.99*

Wee Sing: The Best Christmas Ever!
Here is a merry, merry Yuletide program that's animated and offers non-stop fun. Kids will love singing the holiday's favorite songs! 56 min.
50-4162 ❑*$12.99*

Veggie Tales: The Toy That Saved Christmas
When the children of Dinkletown are brainwashed by a greedy toy manufacturer into thinking that Christmas is all about getting gifts, one brave little doll sets out to teach the kids about the first Christmas and the true meaning of the holiday in this animated Yuletide tale.
50-8058 *$14.99*

Christmas Yule Log Fireplace (3-Hour Version)
Have an old-fashioned holiday just like Grandma and Grandpa used to have (well, not *just* like them) with this video of a crackling Yule log in a fireplace. You'll almost feel the flames, as a selection of the best-loved Christmas carols and songs play on the soundtrack. Perfect for holiday parties! 180 min.
50-8604 *$19.99*

An Old-Fashioned Christmas
Reader's Digest presents this Yuletide delight which mixes scenes of holiday cheer and festiveness with 44 Christmas songs, including "Silver Bells," "The Little Drummer Boy," "Winter Wonderland," "I'll Be Home for Christmas" and more. 120 min.
50-8640 *$39.99*

Christmas Unwrapped: The History Of Christmas
Ever wonder how such holiday customs as gift giving, Santa Claus and Christmas trees got their start, or if Jesus was really born on December 25th? Join host Harry Smith for a fun-filled look at the origins of these and other Christmas traditions. 50 min.
53-6310 *$19.99*

In The Christmas Spirit
Get yourself in the Christmas mood with this selection of classic holiday songs set to scenes of winter wonderlands and holiday nights. Gospel great Mahalia Jackson is joined by Willie Nelson to provide the music for "The Twelve Days of Christmas," "Joy to the World," "Silent Night" and many other gems. 60 min.
53-6555 *$14.99*

Silent Mouse
Here's a family holiday story about the famous Christmas carol "Silent Night," set in an Austrian town on Christmas Eve in 1887, where an unusual tale of mice and men unfolds. Lynn Redgrave serves as storyteller; also includes accompanying book.
53-7446 Was $24.99 *$19.99*

Fenwick
Fun-filled mix of live-action and animation help bring to life this tale of Santa's most lovable elf, Fenwick. Journey to the North Pole and follow the elf who watches the reindeer and his adventures. With Walter Slezak, Johnnie Whitaker and a song by Anita Bryant. 30 min.
78-3026 *$14.99*

The History Of Santa Claus
Ho-ho-ho! The history of St. Nick is told in this entertaining program that takes you all over the world to explore one of the most adored figures in history. The spirited story looks at ancient shamanic cave paintings, pagan gods and Santa's reindeer-populated North Pole home. 50 min.
80-7052 *$19.99*

The Story Of The Carol
Tune-filled history of Christmas carols that traces their beginnings from the first printed carol in 1521 to their condemnation by Puritans to their revival during the Victorian era. 52 min.
80-7074 *$19.99*

The Spirit Of Christmas
Wonderful winter scenes of snowy mountains, festive light displays, family holiday gatherings and other Yuletide sights are set to a soundtrack of traditional carols and songs, making for a delightful Christmas experience. 51 min.
83-1360 *$14.99*

Christmas Greetings From The Alps
Yodel-ay-he-ho-ho-ho! Enjoy the holiday season in the Alps with traditional Christmas and Advent fairs in small Austrian villages, a sleigh ride through the snow-covered valleys, a traditional Alpine Christmas dinner, a Santa Claus festival and lots more. 59 min.
89-7006 *$14.99*

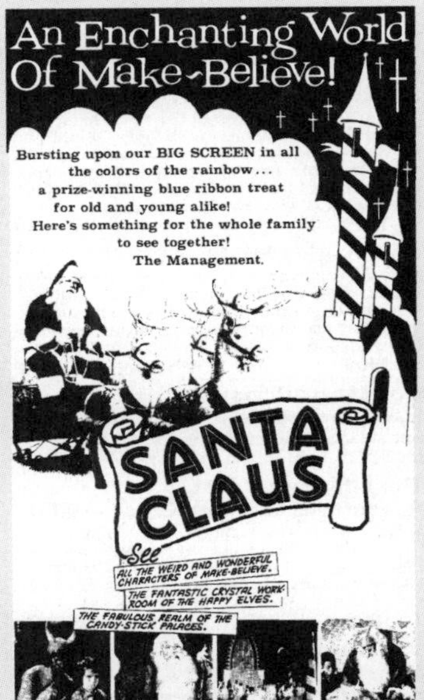
An Enchanting World Of Make-Believe!
Bursting upon our BIG SCREEN in all the colors of the rainbow . . . a prize-winning blue ribbon treat for old and young alike! Here's something for the whole family to see together! The Management.
SANTA CLAUS
See
ALL THE WEIRD AND WONDERFUL CHARACTERS OF MAKE-BELIEVE.
THE FANTASTIC CRYSTAL WORK-ROOM OF THE HAPPY ELVES.
THE FABULOUS REALM OF THE CANDY-STICK PALACES.

Santa Claus (1959)
Santa Claus teams up with Merlin the Magician to stop the Devil from spoiling the world's Christmas (or at least Mexico's) in this magical fantasy. St. Nick gets help from his kid pals, and even his mechanical reindeer(!) make an appearance. With Joseph Moreno as Santa; produced by K. Gordon Murray and directed by Rene Cardona ("Guyana: Cult of the Damned"). 94 min.
68-8460 *$19.99*

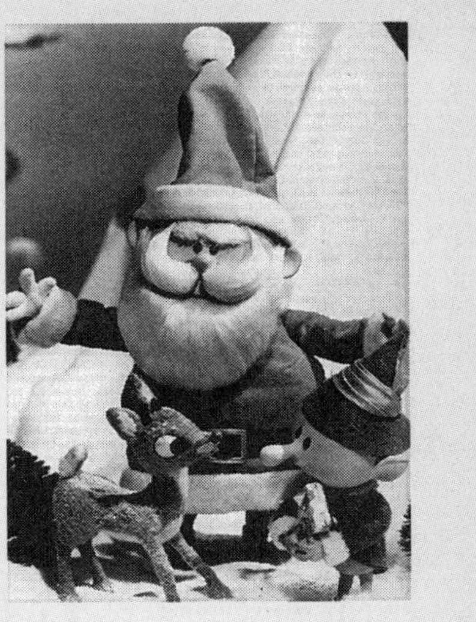

Rudolph The Red-Nosed Reindeer (1964)
It's sure to be a holly, jolly Christmas for fans of this animated classic, narrated by Burl Ives. The talented reindeer escapes the clutches of the Abominable Snowman ("Bumbles bounce!"), in time to lead Santa's team. With help from Herbie the dentist elf and Yukon Cornelius, a silver and gold treat! 55 min.
27-5306 ❑*$12.99*

Rudolph's Shiny New Year (1979)
When the coming of New Year's Day is threatened, who else can be called on to save the holiday but the intrepid red-nosed reindeer? With the voices of Red Skelton, Frank Gorshin, Morey Amsterdam. 51 min.
19-1997 *$12.99*

Rudolph And Frosty's Christmas In July (1979)
Now Christmas comes twice a year, as two of your favorite holiday characters team up to solve the mystery of Rudolph's unshiny nose in a delightful animated festival. Red Buttons, Mickey Rooney, Ethel Merman, Shelley Winters and Jackie Vernon supply the voices. 97 min.
19-1998 *$12.99*

Rudolph The Red-Nosed Reindeer: The Movie (1998)
The world's most beloved Christmas critter is back, crimson nose and all, in a brand-new, feature-length musical featuring eight holiday songs—including a performance by Paul and Linda McCartney—certain to entertain the entire family. Whoopi Goldberg, John Goodman, Eric Idle, Bob Newhart, Sarah Jessica Parker, Debbie Reynolds and Richard Simmons supply the voices. 90 min.
10-2801 *$22.99*

A Charlie Brown Christmas (1965)
Everybody's favorite loser gets chosen to direct the annual Christmas play, but can Charlie Brown help the gang (and Snoopy) learn the true meaning of the season? The first "Peanuts" animated TV special remains a beloved holiday favorite. 23 min.
06-2225 ❑*$12.99*

It's Christmastime Again, Charlie Brown (1992)
And the imminent arrival of the holiday means more crises for the "Peanuts" kids, from Snoopy's turn as a sidewalk Santa to the annual trial of another Christmas play to perform. 23 min.
06-2525 ❑*$12.99*

How The Grinch Stole Christmas (1966)
From high atop Mt. Crumpet, the nasty Grinch hatches a scheme to take away Christmas from the good folk in Whoville, but he soon gets a dose of the holiday spirit himself. Boris Karloff narrates and supplies the Grinch's voice in Chuck Jones' beloved animated adaptation of the Dr. Seuss tale. Also included is "Horton Hears a Who," the good Doctor's story of an elephant's devotion to his too-tiny-to-see friends. 53 min.
19-2881 ❑*$14.99*

Cricket On The Hearth (1967)
Roddy McDowall, Danny Thomas and Marlo Thomas lend their voices to this animated rendition of the charming Charles Dickens holiday tale about a courageous cricket who helps a poor toymaker and his daughter one Christmas morning. 50 min.
04-5572 *$12.99*

The Little Drummer Boy (1968)
A lonely orphan, shunned by all and filled with sorrow, finds the true secret of happiness when he serenades a Bethlehem newborn on his tin drum. Greer Garson narrates this stop-action animation classic. 30 min.
27-5303 ❑*$12.99*

The Little Drummer Boy II (1976)
A wonderful animated sequel to the classic family program about the young boy who played his drum for the Christ child. Voices by Greer Garson and Zero Mostel. 23 min.
19-1800 *$12.99*

Frosty The Snowman (1969)
"Happy Birthday!" A snowman is brought to life with a magic top hat, but has to outrun the third-rate magician who lost it, in this belly-womping animated delight featuring the voices of Jackie Vernon, Billy DeWolfe and Jimmy Durante. 30 min.
27-5304 □*$12.99*

Frosty's Winter Wonderland (1976)
The lovable snowman is back, but his plans to marry the (snow)woman of his dreams are threatened by wicked Jack Frost. With the voices of Jackie Vernon, Andy Griffith, Shelley Winters. 23 min.
19-1996 *$12.99*

Frosty Returns (1992)
Frosty the lovable Snowman returns, befriending a little girl named Holly for some snowy fun. But when evil tycoon Mr. Twitchell sprays the snow away with one of his inventions, winter may be lost, and Holly and Frosty must stop him before it's too late. John Goodman supplies the voice of Frosty; Jonathan Winters narrates. 25 min.
27-5436 □*$12.99*

Santa And The Three Bears (1969)
Because they're usually hibernating in December, bears always miss out on all the Christmas fun. This year, though, two mischievous cubs stay up and leave their cave, getting into several hilarious and exciting adventures before meeting Santa himself, in this cartoon treat for the whole family. 60 min.
46-5034 *$12.99*

Santa Claus Is Coming To Town (1970)
Fred Astaire narrates this stop-action animation version of the Kris Kringle legend which tells how the jolly fellow met his future bride, started a workshop managed by elves and came to be known as "Santa Claus" by the world's grateful children. 53 min.
27-5305 □*$12.99*

A House Without A Christmas Tree (1972)
Sensitive holiday drama about a family celebration of Christmas, featuring Jason Robards, Jr. as a widower father who doesn't understand his 10-year-old daughter's request for a special tree. Lisa Lucas, Mildred Natwick also star. Followed by "The Easter Promise" and "The Holiday Treasure." 90 min.
04-3224 *$14.99*

A Very Merry Cricket (1973)
Classic Christmas animation, featuring the voice of Mel Blanc. Tucker the Mouse, Harry the Cat and Chester the Cricket all join to give New York a special Christmas gift, as Chester plays "Silent Night" on his wings. Charming holiday fare. 30 min.
27-5133 *$12.99*

Yes, Virginia, There Is A Santa Claus (1974)
Emmy Award-winning animated show about the little girl who writes to the editor of the New York Sun after being teased by her friends because of her belief in Santa Claus. Classic, touching holiday tale. 30 min.
06-1306 *$12.99*

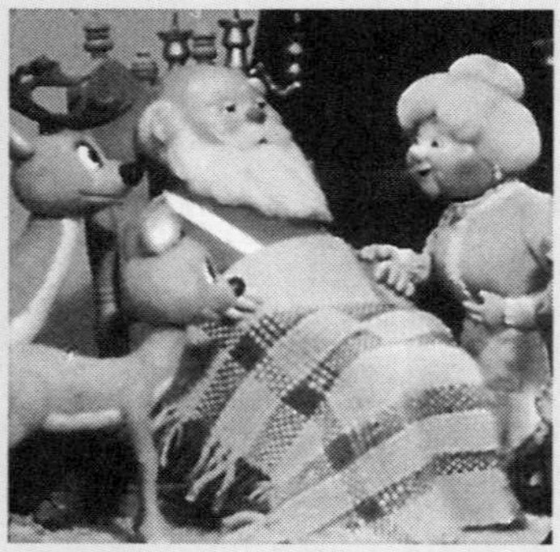

The Year Without A Santa Claus (1974)
When Kris Kringle feels unwanted and decides to sit the holidays out, it's up to Mrs. Claus and two elves to convince him that the world's children still care. Fun-filled special with the voices of Mickey Rooney, Shirley Booth and Dick Shawn includes the hit songs "Heatmiser" and "Snowmiser." 50 min.
19-2000 *$14.99*

The First Christmas: The Story Of The First Christmas Snow (1975)
Stop-motion animation helps tell the tale of a blind boy in 19th-century France who wishes to experience snow at Christmas and receives a Yuletide miracle. Voices by Angela Lansbury and Cyril Ritchard. 23 min.
19-1799 *$12.99*

Young Pioneers' Christmas (1976)
Moving family drama about a young pioneer couple in the Dakota Territory of the 1870s who overcome their own tragedy to offer a holiday gift of friendship. Linda Purl, Roger Kern, Robert Hays star. 94 min.
19-9074 □*$12.99*

The Christmas Coal Mine Miracle (1977)
In 1951, a small mining town is gripped by fear when several miners are trapped in an unsafe mine. When the townspeople work feverishly to free the trapped men, holiday spirit and comradeship abound. Kurt Russell, Melissa Gilbert star. 97 min.
04-3169 Was $59.99 □*$29.99*

Nestor The Long-Eared Christmas Donkey (1977)
Roger Miller, Brenda Vaccaro and Paul Frees supply the voices for this enchanting, stop-motion version of the favorite fable about the kind, little burro, ridiculed for his ears, who took a special ride to Bethlehem. 23 min.
19-1801 *$12.99*

The Gift Of Love (1978)
An orphaned heiress in 1900s New York falls in love with a poor but honest immigrant in this moving adaptation of O. Henry's Christmas story, "Gift of the Magi." Marie Osmond, Timothy Bottoms, David Wayne and June Lockhart star. 96 min.
27-9087 □*$24.99*

Jack Frost (1979)
Jack decides to spend a day on Earth as a human, and winds up falling in love with a mortal girl, in this wonderful, wintry animated tale. Buddy Hackett, Robert Morse and the inimitable Larry Storch supply voices. 50 min.
19-2002 *$12.99*

A Christmas Without Snow (1980)
A recently divorced woman, trying to make a new life for herself and her son in a small town, finds direction when she joins a church choir. Warm family holiday drama stars Michael Learned, John Houseman. 96 min.
04-3127 Was $59.99 □*$14.99*

The Snowman (1982)
An Oscar-nominated animated short that imaginatively combines music and mime to tell the tale of a young boy whose snowman comes to life during his Christmas Eve dream, a dream which sends the pair on a journey to each other's world. Based on the children's book by Raymond Briggs. 26 min.
45-5015 *$14.99*

Father Christmas (1991)
A charming and unusual animated tale of Father Christmas, who is a stuffy Englishman in real life. He decides to retire from his annual toy-delivering chores to do some travelling, but soon finds that he is much better suited to pleasing the world's children. Based on the books by Raymond Briggs, author of "The Snowman." 26 min.
27-5438 □*$14.99*

The Bear (1998)
A bear with a heart of gold finds a young girl's beloved teddy bear, accidentally dropped into his home at the zoo, and magically shows up in the girl's bedroom to return the toy in this animated adventure of the joys of friendship, trust and giving. Based on the holiday book by Raymond Briggs ("The Snowman"). 30 min.
11-2795 □*$12.99*

A Christmas Story (1983)
A hilarious and totally enjoyable yarn about a young boy's attempts at getting what he really wants for Christmas—a Red Ryder Air Rifle. His experiences with his parents, his trip to see Santa and the whimsical dialogue from Jean Shepherd make this gem ideal for any time of the year. Darren McGavin, Melinda Dillon, Peter Billingsley. 93 min.
12-1364 Was $19.99 *$14.99*

Santa Claus: The Movie (1985)
Ho, Ho, Ho, and away we go! Can Santa and his two young helpers rescue runaway elf Dudley Moore from the clutches of evil businessman John Lithgow and save Christmas? Dazzling family holiday extravaganza also stars David Huddleston as St. Nick. You'll believe eight reindeer can fly. 112 min.
03-1509 □*$12.99*

One Magic Christmas (1985)
Mary Steenburgen stars as a despondent young mother who gets a lesson in the Christmas spirit from "guardian angel" Harry Dean Stanton in this delightful holiday fantasy for all ages from the Disney studios. With Gary Basaraba, Elizabeth Harnois. 88 min.
11-1365 Was $19.99 *$14.99*

One Magic Christmas (Letterboxed Collector's Edition)
Also available in a theatrical, widescreen format.
08-8777 *$14.99*

The Life And Adventures Of Santa Claus (1985)
L. Frank Baum, the author of "The Wizard of Oz," wrote the story that this animated marvel is based on. Here's the tale of Santa Claus and how he became the man who delivered toys at Christmas. Superior family fun! 49 min.
19-1803 *$12.99*

The Best Christmas Pageant Ever (1986)
Warm and wonderful holiday special stars Loretta Swit as the "caretaker" for several delinquent youngsters. How she keeps them in line while staging the town's annual Christmas play makes for a heartfelt story of love and faith. 69 min.
55-1150 *$19.99*

A Hobo's Christmas (1987)
Holiday-themed holiday drama, guaranteed to tug on the heartstrings, stars Barnard Hughes ("da") as an elderly drifter returning to the family he left behind 20 years earlier. Gerald McRaney, Wendy Crewson, William Hickey also star. 94 min.
74-5038 *$12.99*

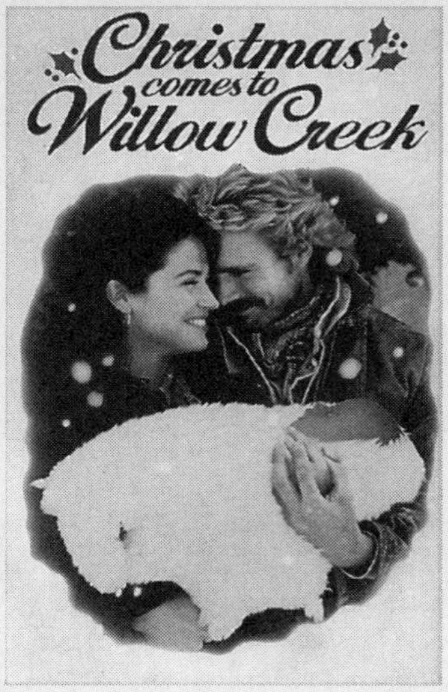

Christmas Comes To Willow Creek (1987)
Heartwarming holiday tale reunites "The Dukes of Hazzard" stars Tom Wopat and John Schneider as feuding brothers who come together to help deliver Christmas gifts to a remote village in Alaska. Hoyt Axton, Kim Delaney co-star. 93 min.
27-5443 □*$12.99*

The Night They Saved Christmas (1987)
A geologist is hired to work on a project near the North Pole and moves his family to the Arctic, only to learn the job is endangering the area's most famous resident—Santa Claus! Delightful family holiday drama stars Paul LeMat, Jaclyn Smith, Paul Williams, and Art Carney as Santa. 95 min.
58-5061 *$14.99*

A Very Brady Christmas (1988)
The ever-popular "Brady Bunch" attempts to get together for a family holiday celebration, but will their Christmas be marred by tragedy? Second TV "reunion" movie stars Robert Reed, Florence Henderson, Ann B. Davis, Barry Williams, Maureen McCormick. 94 min.
06-2050 Was $59.99 □*$14.99*

Pee-wee's Playhouse Christmas Special (1988)
"Ho ho ho" is today's secret word, and you're all invited to the playhouse for a holiday funfest with Pee-wee Herman, his regular cast of crazies from his hit TV show, and such special guest stars as Little Richard, Joan Rivers, Charo, Dinah Shore, Frankie and Annette, and Santa himself. 49 min.
71-7156 *$12.99*

The Simpsons Christmas Special (1989)
America's favorite cartoon family made their episode-length debut in this Yuletide adventure. A less-than-expected Christmas bonus, some last-minute shopping, and a Christmas Eve visit to the dog track for Homer and Bart all add up to a hectic, hilarious holiday, Simpson-style. 23 min.
04-2475 Was $24.99 □*$12.99*

Prancer (1989)
A young girl discovers a wounded reindeer that she recognizes as the fabled member of Santa's sleigh team and sneaks him home to her family's farm in order to nurse him back to health in this charming family holiday tale. Sam Elliott, Cloris Leachman, Abe Vigoda and Rebecca Harrell star. 103 min.
73-1088 Was $19.99 □*$14.99*

The Kid Who Loved Christmas (1990)
In this warm Christmas drama, a young orphan fights against the authorities to spend the holidays with his adoptive father, a travelling musician. The all-star cast includes Michael Warren, Della Reese, Cicely Tyson and Sammy Davis, Jr. in his final role. 118 min.
06-2049 Was $59.99 □*$14.99*

All I Want For Christmas (1991)
Engaging holiday family comedy about a young girl who uses all sorts of wacky methods to reunite her divorced parents in time for Christmas. Jamey Sheridan, Harley Jane Kozak, Ethan Randall, Thora Birch and Lauren Bacall star. 92 min.
06-2009 Was $19.99 □*$14.99*

A Wish For Wings That Work (1992)
"Bloom County" auteur Berke Breathed created this wacky animated holiday story about flight-fancying penguin Opus, who will do just about anything to take to the friendly skies. Joined by Bill, his flaky feline friend, Opus asks Father Christmas to make him aerodynamically unchallenged. 30 min.
07-2021 □*$12.99*

The Santa Clause (1994)
This smash holiday hit stars Tim Allen as a grumpy divorced dad looking after his Christmas-loving son at Yuletide. After the real Kris Kringle slips off his roof, Allen reluctantly steps into the red suit finding he has assumed the responsibility of delivering toys to kids around the world. Judge Reinhold, Wendy Crewson and Peter Boyle also star. 97 min.
11-1894 Was $19.99 □*$14.99*

The Thieves Christmas (1994)
Ernest Borgnine excels as a grandfather who takes out a storybook to read to his family at Yuletide and relates the tale of a group of thieves who like Christmas because it enables them an opportunity to steal things, but eventually learn a lesson about the holiday. 60 min.
78-3021 *$14.99*

The Forgotten Toys (1995)
A doll and a teddy bear, both abandoned by their owners in favor of new high-tech gifts they receive on Christmas, set out in search of new homes in this heartwarming animated story based on the popular children's book "The Night After Christmas." With the voice of Bob Hoskins. 30 min.
04-5467 *$12.99*

The Town That Santa Forgot (1995)
In this animated holiday tale, a selfish little boy's massive want list to Santa becomes the key to restoring the Christmas spirit to a neglected town. 45 min.
18-7692 □*$12.99*

A Pinky And The Brain Christmas (1995)
Narf! That fiendishly clever lab mouse, the Brain, and his addle-brained sidekick, Pinky, disguise themselves as reindeer as part of their plan to use Santa's global toy run to take over the world in this Yuletide adventure from the hit TV series. Also includes "That Smarts!" 30 min.
19-2451 □*$12.99*

The Christmas Box (1995)
Moving holiday drama, based on the best-selling book by Richard Paul Evans, stars Maureen O'Hara as a rich widow who hires a family as live-in help and Richard Thomas as the family's workaholic head, who learns a lesson on the true meaning of the season. Annette O'Toole also stars. 92 min.
58-5251 □*$14.99*

THE NIGHTMARE BEFORE CHRISTMAS

The Nightmare Before Christmas: Special Edition (1993)
A wonderfully bizarre and visually stunning Yuletide treat from Tim Burton, who uses stop-motion animation to tell the story of Jack Skellington, the bored Pumpkin King of Halloweenland. When he accidentally discovers Christmastown, Jack decides to kidnap Santa Claus and take charge of the holiday in his own spooky style. Catherine O'Hara, Chris Sarandon and Danny Elfman (who also composed the score) supply voices. Special video edition includes a "making of" featurette, Burton's early short films "Vincent" and "Frankenweenie," and more. 143 min. total.
11-2491 Letterboxed □*$22.99*

Jingle All The Way (1996)
When harried dad Arnold Schwarzenegger promises his son he'll get the season's most popular item, a Turbo-Man action figure, on December 25th and then forgets to buy it, his Christmas Eve becomes a comical store-to-store quest to find the sold-out toy that pits him against another Turbo-seeker, maniacal mailman Sinbad, in this wild holiday comedy for the whole family. Phil Hartman, Rita Wilson also star. 85 min.
04-3518 Was $19.99 □*$14.99*

A Different Kind Of Christmas (1996)
Warm holiday story involving a high-profile city attorney who has more than her share of problems after her good-hearted father dies. He used to play Santa year-round for the kids and never disappointed them with gifts. Even after his passing, kids keep coming to the house, causing problems for the lawyer with the zoning board. Shelley Long, Barry Bostwick and Nathan Lawrence stars.
10-2862 *$14.99*

Mrs. Santa Claus (1996)
Angela Lansbury is a delight in this music-filled Yuletide tale that follows Kris Kringle's wife on a magic sleigh ride that ends with an emergency landing in New York City. Mrs. Claus begins brightening up the Big Apple with her holiday cheer, but will Santa find her in time to save Christmas? Charles Durning, Michael Jeter also star; Jerry Herman supplies songs and lyrics. 91 min.
88-1141 □*$14.99*

Annabelle's Wish (1997)
One Christmas Eve, an adorable calf named Annabelle who would like to be one of Santa's reindeer meets up with Kris Kringle and helps him deliver a special holiday gift to a little boy. Charming animated tale features songs by Alison Krauss and Randy Travis and the voices of Cloris Leachman, Jerry Van Dyke and Jim Varney. 54 min.
88-1143 □*$14.99*

How The Toys Saved Christmas (1997)
In this magical holiday animated film, Granny Rose's illness prevents her from helping Santa deliver toys for Christmas. Mr. Grimm takes over the job, but he has devious plans to sell them to the highest bidder. When the toys hear of this scheme, they decide to deliver themselves. Mary Tyler Moore and Tony Randall provide the voices for this Yuletide adventure. 78 min.
11-2209 □$14.99

I'll Be Home For Christmas (1998)
California college student Jonathan Taylor Thomas' plans to spend Christmas vacation in Mexico with girlfriend Jessica Biel are changed when his father offers him a car if he'll spend the holiday with his family in New York. Problem is, Thomas' rival for Biel has left him stranded in the desert and glued into a Santa suit. His 3,000-mile trek makes for hilarious holiday fun. Gary Cole also stars. 86 min.
11-2356 Was $19.99 □$14.99

Richie Rich's Christmas Wish (1998)
Your favorite poor little rich boy is back in this hilarious sequel that stars David Gallagher in the title role. This time around, Richie finds out what it would be like if he was never born when he ruins a Christmas delivery to needy children by mistake. It's up to him to make things right and save the holidays for everyone. Also stars Martin Mull and Lesley Ann Warren. 85 min.
19-2739 Was $19.99 □$14.99

A Season For Miracles (1999)
This touching holiday tale tells of two small children who are taken in by their aunt after a well-meaning social worker tries to relocate them in foster homes, away from their mother. The aunt brings the kids to the magical town of Bethlehem, where they adopt false identities, but eventually their happy Christmas is jeopardized. Patty Duke, Kathy Baker, Carla Gugino and Laura Dern star in this "Hallmark Hall of Fame" presentation. 99 min.
27-5593 Was $19.99 $14.99

Must Be Santa (1999)
When it's time for Santa to become an angel, a down-on-his-luck loser named Floyd is recruited to fill his boots. But with only a few days left until Christmas, Floyd tries to use his new job to impress his estranged daughter, only to wind up threatening the holiday for all the world's children! Family comedy stars Arnold Pinnock, Deanna Milligan and Dabney Coleman. 92 min.
07-2924 □$14.99

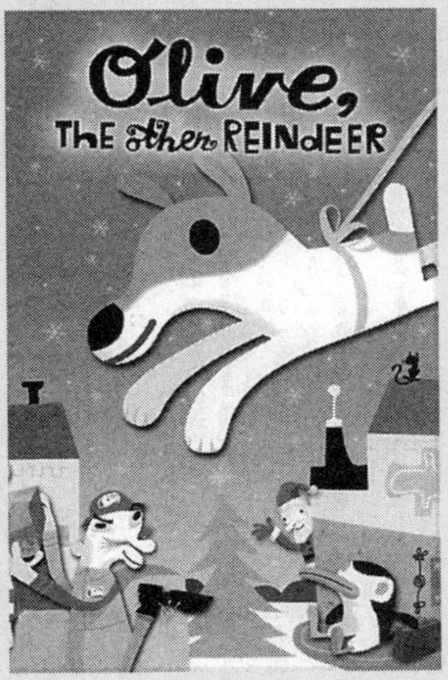

Olive, The Other Reindeer (1999)
In this unusual and delightful holiday tale animated by "Simpsons" creator Matt Groening, a spirited dog named Olive (voiced by Drew Barrymore) offers to stand in for an injured Blitzen and help Santa complete his Christmas Eve toy run. Other voice talents include Ed Asner, Dan Castellaneta, Tim Meadows and Michael Stipe. 69 min.
04-3964 □$14.99

The Life And Adventures Of Santa Claus (2000)
Ever wonder how Kris Kringle started giving out Christmas gifts to the world's children, and how he manages to do so in just one night? Find out Santa's life story in this animated tale based on the book by L. Frank Baum. Robby Benson, Dixie Carter and Hal Holbrook supply voices.
07-2931 $14.99

Grandma Got Run Over By A Reindeer (2000)
The demented Yuletide tune you thought they'd never turn into a cartoon is now a wild animated holiday treat. When an encounter with Santa's sleigh leaves Grandma Spankenheimer unhurt but with amnesia, she's taken to the North Pole to recuperate. Can her grandson find her and help Grandma regain her memory in time to save the family's Christmas? 50 min.
19-2990 $14.99

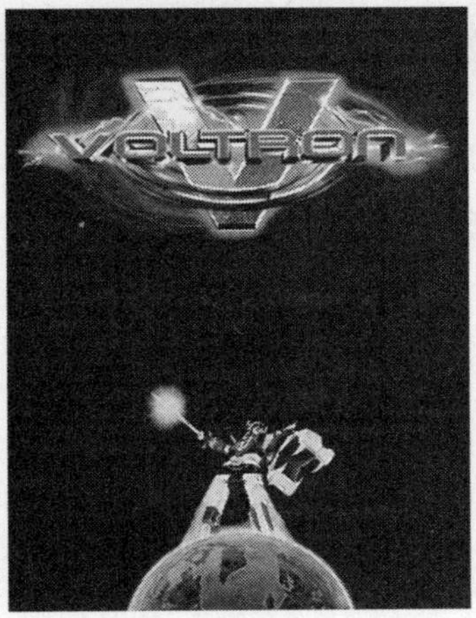

Voltron: The Third Dimension
The saga of the Voltron Force continues in this all-new, computer-animated series, as the team must battle space pirates and the vengeful Prince Lotor, who is fueled by greed and an obsession with Princess Allura. Each tape features two episodes and runs about 45 min.

Voltron: The Third Dimension, Vol. 1: Escape From Bastille 12
Includes "Escape From Bastille 12" and "Red Lions Break Loose."
68-2031 $14.99

Voltron: The Third Dimension, Vol. 2: Building The Forces Of Doom
Includes "Building the Forces of Doom" and "Lost Souls."
68-2032 $14.99

Voltron: Defenders Of The Universe
One of the most popular animated series to ever come from Japan, these are the original '80s adventures of the five-in-one hero. Watch as the Voltron Force merge their lion robots to create Voltron and lead the interplanetary Alliance against evil King Zarkon and other menaces. Each tape features two episodes and runs about 70 min.

Voltron: Defenders Of The Universe, Vol. 1: Fleet Of Doom
Includes "Fleet of Doom" and "The Alliance Strikes Back."
68-2033 $14.99

Jane Hissey's Old Bear Stories
Travel to an enchanted world where bears and their pals come to life, thanks to stop-motion animation. Based on Jane Hissey's popular stories, these 30-minute tapes will delight children of all ages. There are four volumes available, including:

Old Bear Stories: Friends, Friends, Friends
04-5435 $12.99

Old Bear Stories: Happy Birthday Old Bear
04-5436 $12.99

The Wizard's Tales
Some of the greatest kids' stories ever are presented in this series, produced with beautifully rendered, colorful animation. Each tape runs about 50 min. There are 13 volumes available, including:

The Wizard's Tales: The Emperor's New Clothes
50-8678 $14.99

The Wizard's Tales: The Pied Piper Of Hamlin
50-8679 $14.99

The Wizard's Tales: The New Adventures Of Robin Hood
50-8680 $14.99

The Wizard's Tales: The New Adventures Of William Tell
50-8681 $14.99

The Wizard's Tales: White Fang
50-8682 $14.99

The Wizard's Tales: The Count Of Monte Cristo
50-8683 $14.99

The Wizard's Tales: Frank Enstein
50-8684 $14.99

The Wizard's Tales: Hans And The Silver Skates
50-8685 $14.99

The Mr. Potato Head Show
He's entertained youngsters for decades, and now the superstar spud is featured in his own TV show that mixes puppetry, live-action and computer animation. Join Mr. Potato Head and his food friends as they deal with both the cancellation of his show and an alien invasion. 73 min.
85-1190 $14.99

C-Bear And Jamal
It's not always easy being a child, but 10-year-old Jamal gets some help from his best friend—a hip-talking teddy named C-Bear—and learns how to get along with the kids in his neighborhood, all the while chilling to some fun-filled music and having a great time, in these cartoons from the hit TV series. Featuring the voice talents of George Wallace, Kim Fields and Paul Rodriguez.
54-9173 $14.99

Rainbow Fish
The flashily-colored fish from Marcus Pfister's award-winning books swims into his very own fun-filled animated video series. Join Rainbow and his piscatorial pals as they explore their undersea home. Each tape features four stories and runs about 45 min.

Rainbow Fish: Fintastic Friends
04-5728 □$12.99

Rainbow Fish: High Tide Heroes
04-5729 □$12.99

Our Friend, Martin
Two youngsters assigned to do a school report on the life of Dr. Martin Luther King take a trip back in time and become pals with a boy who turns out to be the young King. Animation is mixed with live-action documentary footage in this moving family film that shows the importance of King's message. Voices by Ed Asner, Angela Bassett, Danny Glover, Whoopi Goldberg, Susan Sarandon, Oprah Winfrey and others. 60 min.
04-3762 □$14.99

Wondrous Myths & Legends
Follow Lisa and Nick, a pair of time-travelling teens, and their dog Zeus as they enter a magical cavern and are whisked away to a series of thrilling encounters with characters from world fable and mythology in this animated series. Each two-episode tape runs about 45 min.

Wondrous Myths & Legends: Discovery
Includes "The Magic of Pegasus, The Winged Horse" and "The Riddle of the Sphinx."
04-5730 □$12.99

Wondrous Myths & Legends: Enchantment
Includes "The Mystery of the Loch Ness Monster" and "The Valor of St. George, The Dragonslayer."
04-5731 □$12.99

The Wubbulous World Of Dr. Seuss
Two giants in the field of children's entertainment come together in this delightful live-action series, as the Jim Henson studio brings to life such beloved Dr. Seuss characters as the Cat in the Hat, Yertle the turtle, Horton the elephant and others for fun-filled stories loaded with imagination and song. Each tape features two episodes and runs about 50 min. There are six volumes available, including:

The Wubbulous World Of Dr. Seuss, Vol. 1
Includes "The Cat in the Hat Takes a Nap" and "Cat's Play."
02-3252 $14.99

The Wubbulous World Of Dr. Seuss, Vol. 2
Includes "The Cat in the Hat Cleans Up His Act" and "Make Yourself at Home."
02-3253 $14.99

The Wubbulous World Of Dr. Seuss, Vol. 3
Includes "The Cat in the Hat Builds a Door-a-Matic" and "The Cat in the Hat's Art House."
02-3297 $14.99

Dr. Seuss Beginner Book Videos
The fun-filled series of easy-to-read storybooks for youngsters, featuring favorite stories by Dr. Seuss and other authors, is now on home video. Children can follow along with the on-screen titles, colorful illustrations and accompanying narration (some by top Hollywood stars). Each tape runs about 30 min.

The Cat In The Hat
Dr. Seuss's troublemaking cat with the red and white hat makes quite a mess for a brother and sister one rainy day in this storybook double feature that also has the "what do you want to be?" tale "Maybe You Should Fly a Jet! Maybe You Should Be a Vet!"
04-5525 □$12.99

Green Eggs And Ham
Will a fox, a box, a goat or a boat help Sam I Am convince his fussy friend to try the title dish? "Ten Apples Up on Top" and "The Tooth Book," also by Dr. Seuss, round out this three-story treat.
04-5526 □$12.99

The Cat In The Hat Comes Back
It's the return of the cat whose manners aren't so hot. Should Sally and her brother let him in their home? We say they should not! Two other Dr. Seuss stories, "There's a Wocket in My Pocket!" and "Fox in Socks," are included.
46-1058 □$12.99

Dr. Seuss's ABC
The letters of the alphabet are imaginatively illustrated with animals from the good doctor's whimsical menagerie. Then, delight to "I Can Read with My Eyes Shut!" and "Mr. Brown Can Moo! Can You?"
46-1060 □$12.99

Hop On Pop
Hop! Hop! Poor Pop becomes a trampoline for his youngsters in Dr. Seuss's silly rhyming story. You'll also see "Marvin K. Mooney, Will You Please Go Home Now!" and "Oh Can You Say?"
46-1061 □$12.99

Are You My Mother?
From the pen of P.D. Eastman comes the harrowing tale of a just-hatched bird who sets off in search of his mother. Also featured on this video are "Go, Dog. Go!" and "The Best Nest."
46-1086 □$12.99

Horton Hatches The Egg
Narrator Billy Crystal proves "an elephant's faithful one hundred percent" in this beloved Dr. Seuss tale of friendship and loyalty, followed by "If I Ran the Circus."
46-1089 □$12.99

Yertle The Turtle
John Lithgow leads viewers on this excursion into Dr. Seuss-land about a cranky turtle king and his subjects. Other stories include "Gertrude McFuzz" and "The Big Brag."
46-1090 □$12.99

Horton Hears A Who!
"A person's a person, no matter how small" is the motto of Horton the elephant as he saves his tiny friends, the Whos, and their flower home in the Dr. Seuss story narrated by Dustin Hoffman. Also included is "Thidwick the Big-Hearted Moose."
46-1092 □$12.99

Dr. Seuss's Sleep Book
Madeline Kahn tells the story of how a tiny bug's yawn soon has everyone in the neighborhood getting ready for bedtime, followed by "Hunches in Bunches."
46-1112 □$12.99

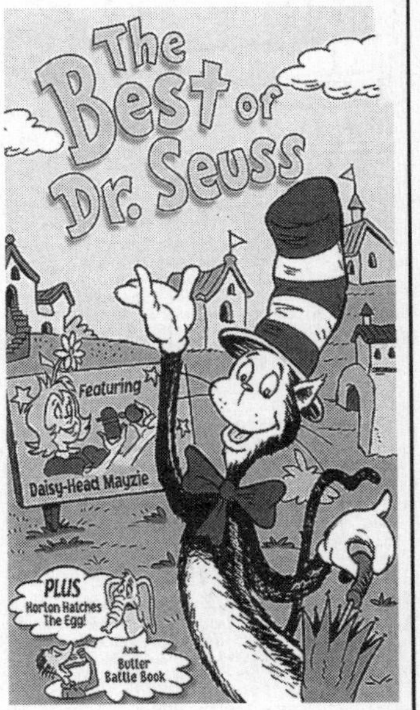

The Best Of Dr. Seuss
Three timeless tales from the perennially popular children's author have been gathered for this fun-filled animated video. Watch as "Daisy-Head Mayzie" becomes a celebrity, thanks to a flower growing out of her head; follow the elephant who meant what he said and said what he meant in "Horton Hatches the Egg"; and learn about the futility of conflict in the parable "The Butter Battle Book." 57 min.
19-5000 $14.99

In Search Of Dr. Seuss (1994)
A whimsical inquiry into the life and work of children's favorite Dr. Seuss that mixes music, live-action and animation to tell his story. Reporter Kathy Najimy joins Matt Frewer's Cat in the Hat to investigate the truth behind "Yertle the Turtle," "The Grinch Who Stole Christmas" and "The Lorax." Christopher Lloyd, Robin Williams and Eileen Brennan are also featured. 90 min.
18-7548 $12.99

Cartoon Madness: The Fantastic Max Fleischer Cartoons
Their studio gave Hollywood some of its first and finest animated cartoons and brought Koko the Clown, Betty Boop, Popeye and Superman to the screen. Now Leonard Maltin hosts this salute to the pioneering duo of Max and Dave Fleischer, with clips from their greatest cartoons. 94 min.
63-1603 □*$14.99*

Koko The Clown, Vol. 1
Koko, as created by Max Fleischer, was perhaps the most imaginative silent cartoon series, as evidenced here: "The Tantalizing Fly," "Perpetual Motion," "Bubbles," "The Clown's Little Brother," "The Ouija Board," "In the Good Old Summertime," "Koko the Kop," "Modeling." 55 min. Silent with music track.
62-1078 *$19.99*

Koko The Clown, Vol. 2
Another collection of innovative silent cartoons with the Fleischer Brothers' put-upon punchinello. Included are "Koko in Reverse," "Koko's Storm," "Koko's Barnyard" and many more. 50 min. Silent with music track.
62-1306 *$19.99*

Koko The Clown Cartoons (1927-1929)
From "Out of the Inkwell" comes Max and Dave Fleischer's silent cartoon clown, ready once more to blur the line between film and reality. Join Koko and his canine pal Bimbo for 10 of their funniest animated short subjects, including "Chemical Koko," "Koko the Kid," "Koko's Conquest," "Koko's Reward," more. 70 min.
63-1551 *$19.99*

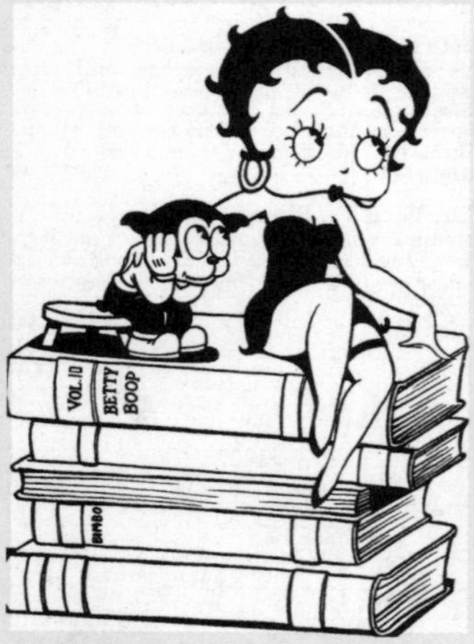

Betty Boop: The Definitive Collection
For over 60 years her saucy animated antics have entertained audiences, and now the Fleischer Studio's flirty flapper "Boop-oop-a-doops" her way through a fun-filled collection of her greatest cartoons.

Betty Boop: The Definitive Collection, Vol. 1: The Birth Of Betty
See Betty's screen debut (as a dog!) in 1930's "Dizzy Dishes," plus early appearances in "Barnacle Bill," "Silly Scandals," "Bimbo's Express," "Minding the Baby" and more. 62 min.
63-1843 □*$9.99*

Betty Boop: The Definitive Collection, Vol. 2: Pre-Code
Betty's at her jazziest (and raciest) in this collection of pre-1934 delights that includes "Boop-Oop-a-Doop," "A Hunting We Will Go," "Betty Boop for President," guest star Cab Calloway in "Minnie the Moocher" and "Snow White," "Kitty from Kansas City" with Rudy Vallee, and others. 108 min.
63-1844 □*$9.99*

Betty Boop: The Definitive Collection, Vol. 3: Surrealism
The wild sight gags and storylines that were a Fleischer trademark are well evidenced in this compilation. Included are "Bimbo's Initiation," "Crazy Town," "Betty Boop's May Party," "Just a Gigolo," "Is My Palm Read?," "Betty Boop's Ker-Choo" and more. 110 min.
63-1845 □*$9.99*

Betty Boop: The Definitive Collection, Vol. 4: Musical Madness
Betty's a singing, dancing bundle of cartoon energy in "Any Little Girl That's a Nice Little Girl," "Let Me Call You Sweetheart," "I Heard," "Sally Swing" and others, and "Mother Goose Land," "Poor Cinderella," "Dizzy Red Riding Hood," "Betty in Blunderland" and "Jack and the Beanstalk" are among her fairy-tale adventures seen here. 106 min.
63-1846 □*$9.99*

Betty Boop: The Definitive Collection, Vol. 5: Curtain Call
The cartoon cutie steals the show in "Betty Boop's Crazy Inventions," "Betty Boop Limited," "Keep in Style" and "The New Deal Show," among others. Then, Betty's joined by the ever-inventive Grampy for "Betty Boop and Grampy," "Grampy's Indoor Outing," "House Cleaning Blues," "Service with a Smile" and more. 110 min.
63-1847 □*$9.99*

Betty Boop: The Definitive Collection, Vol. 6: Betty's Boys
The men in her life range from lifeguards to monarchs, and you'll meet a few of them in "Betty Boop's Big Boss," "Betty Boop's Lifeguard," "Betty Boop and the Little King," "Betty Boop's Rise to Fame," "Betty Boop with Henry, the Funniest Living American" (who can argue with that?) and more. 108 min.
63-1848 □*$9.99*

Betty Boop: The Definitive Collection, Vol. 7: Betty's Travels
Join the on-the-go Betty for "When It's Sleepy Time Down South," "When My Ship Comes In," "So Does an Automobile," "Whoops! I'm a Cowboy," "The Scared Crows" and other animated gems, including the debut of that precocious pup, Pudgy, in "Betty Boop's Little Pal." 100 min.
63-1849 □*$9.99*

Betty Boop: The Definitive Collection, Vol. 8: Betty And Pudgy
The cartoon canine capers continue in this howlingly funny volume that includes "Happy Me and Merry You," "Pudgy Takes a Bow Wow," "Ding Dong Doggie," "Pudgy the Watchman," "Baby Be Good" and others. 94 min.
63-1850 □*$9.99*

Betty Boop: The Definitive Collection Complete Set
All eight volumes are also available in a "boop"iful boxed collector's set that includes a "Boopliography" booklet.
63-1851 *$79.99*

Betty Boop Confidential
Animation's "Boop-Oop-a-Doop Girl" is spotlighted in a song-filled special video program featuring the cartoon coquette's greatest screen appearances. "Betty Boop's Rise to Fame," "Dizzy Dishes," "Minnie the Moocher," "Mother Goose Land" and "Poor Cinderella" are among the classic adventures. 82 min.
63-1898 □*$9.99*

Betty Boop: Animated Sex Appeal
And that's just what Betty delivers in a cartoon compilation offering a fun-filled retrospective of the screen siren's career. "Barnacle Bill," "Is My Palm Read?," "Crazy Inventions," and "Betty Boop and Grampy" are among the eight classic shorts included. 56 min.
09-1117 *$14.99*

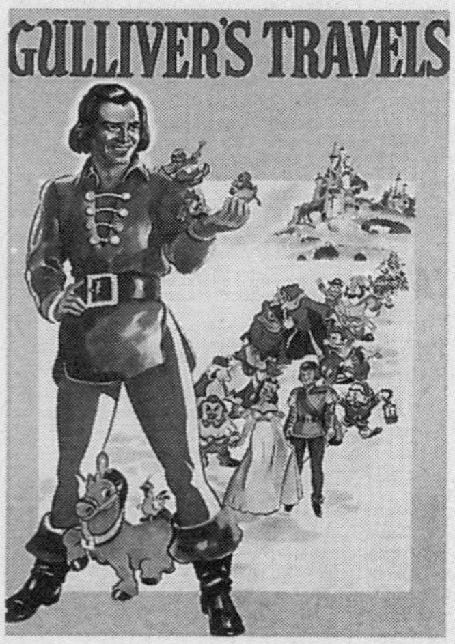

Gulliver's Travels: 60th Anniversary Collector's Edition (1939)
The Fleischer Studio's animated rendition of Jonathan Swift's novel follows the adventures of the traveller who washes up on the shore of the island of Lilliput, whose inhabitants are one inch tall. After a frightening first impression, Gulliver helps the tiny populace resolve a feud that has interrupted the wedding of Prince David and Princess Glory. This special video version with fully restored color and sound also includes a documentary on the Fleischer Studio, previews, and the Gabby shorts "King for a Day" and "Swing Cleaning." 110 min. total.
53-6577 *$14.99*

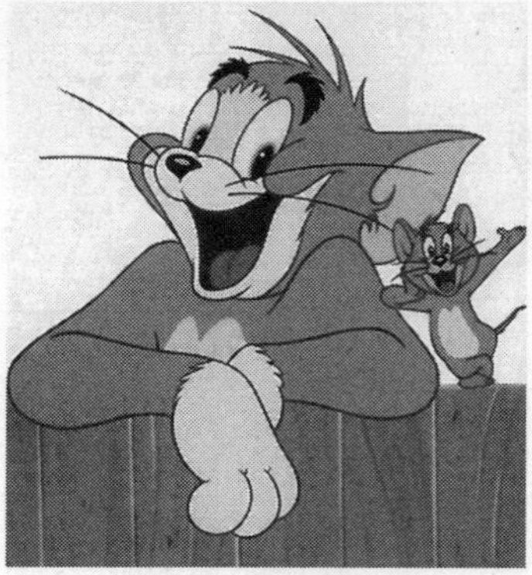

Tom & Jerry's Festival Of Fun
How much fun can a cat and mouse offer? You'll see cartoon zaniness reach its limits in this collection of classic T & J shorts, including "The Truce Hurts," "Sufferin' Cats," "Little Quacker," "Touché, Pussycat," and more. 43 min.
12-2400 □*$12.99*

Tom And Jerry's Greatest Chases
The Oscar-winning cat-and-mouse duo are spotlighted in this collection of 12 of their funniest cartoon romps. Included are "Yankee Doodle Mouse," "Salt Water Tabby," "Mouse in Manhattan," "The Cat Concerto," "Solid Serenade" (featuring Tom's rendition of "Is You Is or Is You Ain't My Baby?"), "Johann Mouse," "Dr. Jekyll and Mr. Mouse," "Jerry's Diary" and more. 89 min.
19-2933 □*$14.99*

Tom And Jerry: Wild & Wacky Adventures
There's six—count 'em—six crazy cartoon capers with those perennial animated antagonists, Tom and Jerry, in this wild and wacky collection. Shorts include "Downhearted Duckling," "Fit to Be Tied," "Hatch Up Your Troubles," "Puppy Tale," The Flying Sorceress" and "Polka Dot Puss." 42 min.
19-2934 □*$12.99*

Tom And Jerry: The Movie (1993)
After 50 years of catfights, that frisky feline and resourceful rodent appear in their first feature-length adventure—and talk, too! The former arch-enemies unite to save a young girl from her mean aunt and help her find her father. Features a number of new songs by Henry Mancini. 84 min.
27-6841 Was $19.99 □*$14.99*

Just Me And My Dad
A camping trip for Little Critter and his father provides important lessons in work, sharing, and the parent-child bond in this fun-filled animated tale based on Mercer Mayer's book. 25 min.
04-5656 *$12.99*

Tarzan Of The Apes
The orphaned child who was raised in the African jungle by apes and would grow up to become master of his domain becomes an animated hero in this song-filled, feature-length adventure based on Edgar Rice Burroughs' novels. Follow Tarzan as he meets Jane and is forced to choose between two worlds. 48 min.
04-5637 *$12.99*

Hercules
Thrill to the exploits of the strongest man in all of Greece as the mighty Hercules battles strange creatures, evil magicians and even the gods of Olympus to claim his rightful heritage in a cartoon saga. 48 min.
04-5500 □*$14.99*

Mu Lan
When her retired general father is unable to rejoin the army and help put down a rebellion, a fiery Chinese girl named Mu Lan disguises herself as a boy and joins the soldiers in order to maintain her family's honor. See how she becomes a hero to her people in this exciting animated adventure. 50 min.
08-8652 *$12.99*

The Pink Panther
Think pink with that sophisticated cat, the Pink Panther, in an animated potpourri of crazy capers in which the felicitous feline always gets the upper paw. Each tape runs about 40 min. There are seven volumes available, including:

The Pink Panther: Jet Pink
Includes "Jet Pink," "In the Pink of the Night," "Little Beaux Pink," "The Pink Blueprint," the Oscar-winning short "The Pink Phink," and three more.
12-3186 *$12.99*

The Pink Panther: Pink Bananas
Includes "Pink Bananas," "Pink Aye," "Pink Pranks," "Supermarket Pink" and four more.
12-3187 *$12.99*

The Pink Panther: Pink Elephant
Includes "Pink Elephant," "Pink Blue Plate," "Pinkfinger," "Yankee Doodle Pink" and four more.
12-3188 *$12.99*

The Pink Panther: Pink-A-Rella
Includes "Pink-A-Rella," "Tickled Pink," "Pinkadilly Circus," "Pink Arcade" and four more.
12-3189 *$12.99*

The Cats And Mice Of Paul Terry
Years before his crime-stopping Mighty Mouse burst onto the scene, animator Paul Terry released hundreds of shorts during the '20s, seven of which are featured here, including "The Wild West," "Short Vacation," "China Doll," "Sunny Italy" and "Ship Ahoy." 55 min.
09-1980 Was $24.99 *$19.99*

Kid Fun! Winky Dink And You/ Farmer Al Falfa
Jack Barry is the host for the early animated misadventures of Terrytoon's Farmer Al Falfa, plus the interactive exploits of boy-hero Winky Dink and his dog, Woofer. 30 min.
10-7309 Was $29.99 *$14.99*

Felix!
He was the screen's first animated series star, and Felix the Cat remains popular to this day. Among the amusing and innovative silent cartoons of animator Otto Messmer's mischievous hero featured are Felix's screen debut in "Feline Follies" (1919), an encounter with the New York Yankees in "Felix Saves the Day" (1922), an all-star assemblage in "Felix in Hollywood" (1923), the surrealistic "Comicalamities" (1928) and more. Silent with music score. 60 min.
80-5021 *$39.99*

Felix The Cat Cartoon Compilation
Featured in this kitty cartoon collection are 10 classic Felix tales from Otto Messmer: "April Maze" (1930), "Felix All Puzzled" (1936), "Felix Dines and Pines" (1926), "Felix Gets Broadcasted" (1923), "Felix Goes West" (1924), "Felix in Fairyland" (1924), "Felix Turns the Tide" (1924), "Futuritzy" (1928), "Non-Stop Fright" (1927) and "Polly-Tics" (1928).
10-6006 *$14.99*

Fun With Gumby
The green fellow and his equine pal Pokey star in this selection of mirth-filled animated episodes, including "The Kachinas," "Tree Trouble," "Lion Drive," "The Magic Show" and "Yard Work Made Easy." 30 min.
10-2578 *$12.99*

Gumby's Greatest Adventures
Ol' "Green Slab of Clay" and his pal Pokey have all sorts of exciting adventures in this collection that includes "Gumby Racer," "Gold Rush Gumby," "The Black Knight" and "The Blockheads," and six more. 50 min.
10-2702 *$12.99*

Gumby: The Movie (1994)
A feature-length Claymation spectacular with Gumby and his rock-band pals, The Clayheads, battling two Blockheads who want to kidnap them and create evil duplicates. Also featured are pony pal Pokey, Tara, the green slab's galfriend, and a dinosaur named Prickle. 90 min.
19-3851 *$19.99*

The Best Of Aesop's Fables
A giant-sized collection of the Van Beuren Studios animation series from the '30s, with animals in human clothing singing songs and giving humorous lessons. 120 min.
10-7431 Was $29.99 *$14.99*

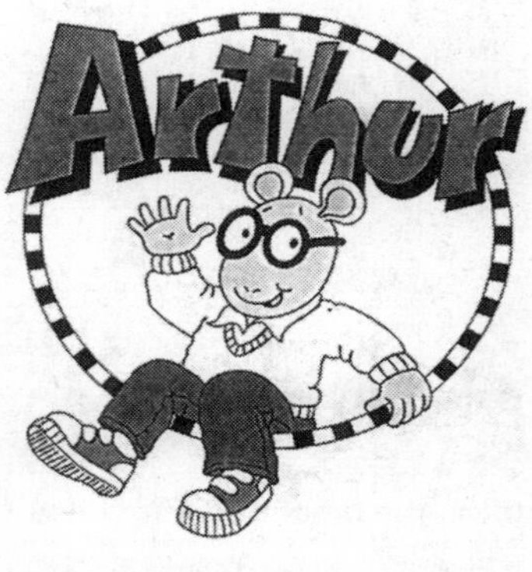

Arthur The Aardvark
He's the lovable, bespectacled critter whose books are popular with children around the world, and now Arthur, his sister D.W., and their friends are the stars of their own fun-filled animated series. Except where noted, each tape features two stories and runs about 30 min. There are 21 volumes available, including:

Arthur's Computer Adventure
Includes "Arthur's Computer Adventure" and "Arthur vs. the Piano."
04-5639 □*$12.99*

Arthur Gets Lost
Includes "Arthur Gets Lost" and "Arthur Cleans Up."
04-5665 □*$12.99*

Arthur's Scary Stories
This frightfully fun-filled collection features three Halloween-themed episodes. 40 min.
04-5735 □*$9.99*

Arthur: The Music Video
Special tape includes "Arthur's Almost-Live, Not-Real Music Festival," "The Ballad of Buster Baxter" and "D.W. and the Crazy Bus Song." 40 min.
04-5680 □*$12.99*

Pokémon

They're the lovable "pocket monsters" who jumped from video games to TV stardom in their native Japan, and now the animated adventures of the Pokémon—and the people out to catch them—can be yours on home video. Each tape features three episodes and runs about 75 min.

Pokémon, Vol. 1:
I Choose You! Pikachu!
85-1160   *$14.99*

Pokémon, Vol. 2:
Mystery Of Mount Moon
85-1162   *$14.99*

Pokémon, Vol. 3:
Sisters Of Cerulean City
85-1163   *$14.99*

Pokémon, Vol. 4: Poké-Friends
85-1175   *$14.99*

Pokémon, Vol. 5: Thunder Shock!
85-1176   *$14.99*

Pokémon, Vol. 6:
Seaside Pikachu
85-1317   *$14.99*

Pokémon, Vol. 7:
Psychic Surprise
85-1316   *$14.99*

Pokémon, Vol. 8:
Primeape Problems
85-1318   *$14.99*

Pokémon, Vol. 9: Fashion Victims
85-1319   *$14.99*

Pokémon, Vol. 10:
Fighting Tournament
85-1320   *$14.99*

Pokémon, Vol. 11:
Great Race
85-1324   *$14.99*

Pokémon, Vol. 12:
Pikachu Party
85-1325   *$14.99*

Pokémon, Vol. 13:
Wake Up Snorlax
85-1462   *$14.99*

Pokémon, Vol. 14: Jigglypuff Pop
85-1463   *$14.99*

Pokémon, Vol. 15: Charizard!
85-1488   *$14.99*

Pokémon, Vol. 16: Totally Togepi!
85-1489   *$14.99*

Pokémon, Vol. 17:
Picture Perfect!
85-1501   *$14.99*

Pokémon, Vol. 18: Water Blast!
85-1502   *$14.99*

Pokémon, Vol. 19:
Our Hero Meowth
85-1504   *$14.99*

Pokémon, Vol. 20:
The Final Badge
85-1505   *$14.99*

Pokémon, Vol. 21:
The Po-Ké Corral!
85-1507   *$14.99*

Pokémon, Vol. 22:
Hang Ten, Pikachu
85-1508   *$14.99*

Pokémon: The First Movie (1999)
With a title that's either promise or threat, the hard-to-catch critters star in their very own animated feature. On a remote island, scientists have created a clone Pokémon named Mewtwo who wants his fellow creatures to join him in rebelling against their human trainers. Can Pokémon catcher Ash and his allies, along with the lovable Pikachu, defeat Mewtwo in battle and stop him? Also included is the short "Pikachu's Vacation." 90 min.
19-2948   ☐*$19.99*

Pokémon The Movie 2000 (2000)
Ash, Misty and their Pokémon pals are back in their most exciting showdown yet in this exciting feature-length tale, as they must stop a fanatical collector from capturing four legendary Pokémon whose powers keep Earth's natural forces in balance. Also included is the short "Pikachu's Rescue Adventure." 102 min.
19-5015   ☐*$22.99*

Lucky Luke

The quick-on-the-draw frontier lawman whose comic book exploits have delighted European audiences for over 50 years comes to life in this fast-paced, funny animated series. Except for the double-length "Ma Dalton," each tape features one episode and runs about 26 min. There are 13 volumes available, including:

Lucky Luke: Ma Dalton/
The Daltons In The Blizzard
75-7203   *$12.99*

Lucky Luke: Billy The Kid
75-7205   *$12.99*

Lucky Luke: The Stagecoach
75-7206   *$12.99*

Crayola Presents:
The Ugly Duckling
It's one exciting adventure after another when Ugly, a misfit duckling, teams with an ambitious young mouse named Scruffy, seeking fame and fortune in the theater. This fun-filled family outing features eight original songs. 85 min.
88-1152   *$12.99*

Crayola Presents:
The 3 Little Pigs: The Movie
The fun never stops with the timeless tale of the porcine siblings who are taught a lesson in the value of sturdy home construction by a big, hungry wolf. 65 min.
88-1171   *$12.99*

Crayola Presents:
Percy The Park Keeper
Join the lovable park keeper and the animal friends he cares for in two stories based on Nick Butterworth's popular children's books: "The Rescue Party" and "One Snowy Night." 77 min.
88-1175   ☐*$12.99*

Sherlock Hound

He's a calculating canine with a snout for mystery, and along with comrade Dr. Watson, Sherlock Hound sets off in search of crimes to solve in these thrilling animated adventures. Each tape runs about 60 min.

Sherlock Hound:
The Dogs Of Bowserville
69-5112   *$14.99*

Sherlock Hound:
The White Cliffs Of Rover
69-5135   *$14.99*

Sherlock Hound In
Moriarty Unleashed
69-5150   *$14.99*

Dexter's Laboratory: Ego Trip
The pint-sized boy genius leaps from TV's Cartoon Network into his own feature-length animated adventure. Follow Dexter through time as he and his future selves must combine their brains and, yes, brawn to keep history on the right course. 60 min.
72-1121   *$14.99*

Dink The Little Dinosaur

Dink is a pint-sized brontosaurus and the star of these animated adventures in which he joins his dino pals for fun and thrills in a land before time known as Dinosaur Valley. Each tape features five episodes and runs 55 min. There are six volumes available, including:

Dink The Little Dinosaur:
Phantom Of The Cave
72-1087   ☐*$12.99*

Dink The Little Dinosaur:
Shyler's Island
72-1089   ☐*$12.99*

Dink The Little Dinosaur: Rivals
72-1090   ☐*$12.99*

Postman Pat
The lovable letter-carrier whose stop-motion animated antics made him a hit with kids in England comes to America with these delightful video collections. Join Postman Pat and his feline helper Jess as they deliver mail and good tidings to the village of Greendale. Each tape runs about 75 min.

Postman Pat, Vol. 1:
Postman Pat Takes The Bus
68-5295   *$19.99*

Postman Pat, Vol. 2:
Postman Pat And The Tuba
68-5296   *$19.99*

Dragon Ball
In this family series from Japan, an enchanted land of evil monsters and magic is the setting for adventure and laughs. Join karate-obsessed alien lad Goku and his allies Krillin and Bulma as they race a wicked king's minions to find the seven mystical Dragon Balls. Except where noted, each tape features two episodes and runs about 45 min. There are seven volumes available, including:

Dragon Ball:
Curse Of The Blood Rubies
See how Goku's quest began in this double-length tale. 48 min.
68-1812   *$12.99*

Dragon Ball, Vol. 1:
Secret Of The Dragon Ball
Includes "Secret of the Dragon Ball" and "The Emperor's Quest."
68-1813   *$12.99*

Dragon Ball, Vol. 2:
The Nimbus Cloud Of Roshi
Includes "The Nimbus Cloud of Roshi" and "Oolong the Terrible."
68-1814   *$12.99*

Dragon Ball:
The Saga Of Goku Boxed Set
All six "Dragon Ball" volumes, plus the "Curse of the Blood Rubies" adventure, are also available in a boxed collector's set.
68-1882   Save $18.00!   *$59.99*

Dragon Ball:
Sleeping Princess In Devil's Castle
Sent on a quest by a would-be martial arts mentor, Goku and Krillin must rescue a princess being held prisoner in Devil's Hand. They have their work cut out for them when her captor turns out to be a vampire named Lucifer who's planning to ravage the Earth with his ogre army in this double-length adventure. 38 min.
89-5202   *$14.99*

Dragon Ball Z
The saga of now-grown martial arts expert Goku continues, as his brother Raditz arrives on Earth. This is no happy family reunion, however, as Raditz tells Goku and his son Gohan they must take over the planet for their alien Saiyan masters in this action-packed animated series from Japan. There are 32 volumes available, including:

Dragon Ball Z, Vol. 1: Arrival
85-1100   ☐*$14.99*

Dragon Ball Z, Vol. 2: The Saiyans
85-1101   ☐*$14.99*

Dragon Ball Z, Vol. 3: Snake Way
85-1104   ☐*$14.99*

Mike Mulligan And
His Steam Shovel
The shovel's name is Mary Anne, and she and Mike set out to prove they can dig a cellar as fast as any new-fangled machine in this cartoon version of the popular children's book. 25 min.
79-3002   *$12.99*

Vera The Mouse:
Mr. Mole's Surprise
Marjolein Bastin's lovable characters come to life in this animated mouse tale that finds Vera coming to the rescue when everyone is too busy feuding to remember Mr. Mole's birthday. 30 min.
88-1203   *$12.99*

Dragon Ball Z, Vol. 4:
Pendulum Room
85-1120   *$14.99*

Dragon Ball Z:
The Saiyan Conflict Boxed Set
Volumes 1-8 are also available in a special collector's set.
85-1234   Save $20.00!   *$99.99*

Dragon Ball Z:
The Namek Saga Boxed Set
Volumes 9-17 are also available in a special collector's set.
85-1235   Save $20.00!   *$114.99*

Dragon Ball Z:
Captain Ginyu: Assault
Includes three episodes. 63 min.
89-5204   *$14.99*

Dragon Ball Z:
Captain Ginyu: Double Cross
Includes four episodes. 82 min.
89-5206   *$14.99*

Dragon Ball Z:
Frieza: The Summoning
Includes three episodes. 63 min.
89-5208   *$14.99*

Dragon Ball Z:
Frieza: Transformation
Includes four episodes. 82 min.
89-5210   *$14.99*

Dragon Ball Z: Frieza: Revealed
Includes three episodes. 60 min.
89-5212   *$14.99*

Dragon Ball Z:
Frieza: Death Of A Prince
Includes three episodes. 59 min.
89-5214   *$14.99*

Dragon Ball Z
The Movie: Dead Zone
In the first "Dragon Ball Z" full-length adventure, nasty would-be world conqueror Garlic Jr. raises a stink when he kidnaps Gohan as part of his plan to trap Goku and his allies in the oblivion of the "Dead Zone." Will the heroes be able to escape in time? 45 min. In Japanese with English subtitles.
85-1102   *$24.99*

Dragon Ball Z The Movie:
Dead Zone (Dubbed Version)
Also available in a dubbed-in-English edition.
85-1103   *$19.99*

Dragon Ball Z The Movie 2:
The World's Strongest
Goku's always prided himself on his strength, but that may not be such a good thing, as mad scientists Dr. Wheelo and Dr. Kochin kidnap Piccolo and Master Roshi as part of their scheme to put Wheelo's brain in Goku's super-strong body, in this feature-length saga. Uncut version; 60 min. In Japanese with English subtitles.
85-1147   *$24.99*

Dragon Ball Z The Movie 2:
The World's Strongest
(Dubbed Version)
Also available in a dubbed-in-English edition.
85-1148   *$19.99*

Dragon Ball Z The Movie 3:
The Tree Of Might
Evil takes root when a menacing alien plants a tree that begins absorbing all of Earth's life energy as it grows. It's up to Goku and the Special Forces fighters to stop the pernicious plant and its cultivator in this hard-hitting feature-length adventure. Uncut version; 60 min. In Japanese with English subtitles.
85-1130   *$24.99*

Dragon Ball Z The Movie 3: The
Tree Of Might (Dubbed Version)
Also available in a dubbed-in-English edition.
85-1131   *$19.99*

Dragon Ball Z Trilogy:
Uncut Movie Boxed Set
All three "Dragon Ball Z" features, in their uncut version, are also available in a special collector's set. Dubbed in English.
85-1415   *$59.99*

The Berenstain Bears
From the best-selling books by Stan and Jan Berenstain come the cartoon exploits of the lovable Bear family. Mama, Papa and the cubs show just how much trouble a woodland family can get into, even when strangers aren't sleeping in their beds. Each tape features three episodes and runs about 36 min. There are six volumes available, including:

The Berenstain Bears, Vol. 1
Includes "The Messy Room," "The Terrible Termites" and "Life With Papa."
02-3311 ❑*$12.99*

The Berenstain Bears, Vol. 2
Includes "The Truth," "Save the Bees" and "The Forbidden Cave."
02-3312 ❑*$12.99*

The Berenstain Bears, Vol. 3
Includes "Learn About Strangers," "The Disappearing Honey" and "The Substitute Teacher."
02-3313 ❑*$12.99*

Godzilla: The Series
Based on the monstrous 1998 hit film, this thrilling animated series finds scientist Dr. Nick Tatopoulos playing "mother" to a new Godzilla, hatched from an egg left behind by the original green behemoth. Watch as Godzilla defends the planet against an array of monsters, mutants and other menaces.

Godzilla: The Series, Vol. 1
Includes "Trouble Hatches." 45 min.
02-3345 ❑*$12.99*

Godzilla: The Series, Vol. 2
Includes "Monster War." 60 min.
02-3346 ❑*$12.99*

The Real Ghostbusters
Peter, Ray, Egon and Winston—and their ghostly pal Slimer—are up to their proton packs in hereafter heavies and phantasmagorical fun in these animated unearthly exploits. Each tape runs about 25 min. There are eight volumes available, including:

The Real Ghostbusters: Knock, Knock
02-1659 *$14.99*

The Real Ghostbusters: Play Them Ragtime Boos
02-1660 *$14.99*

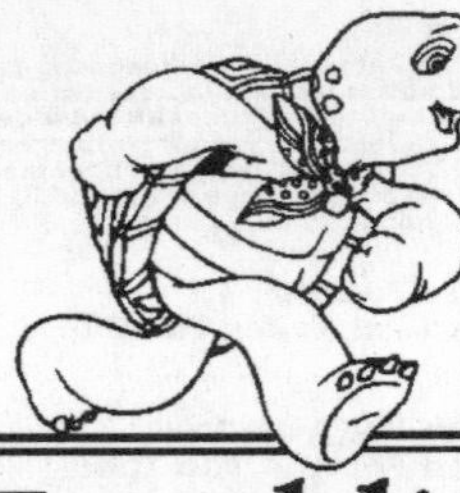

Franklin

Franklin
The fun-loving turtle who's the star of his own book series now comes to home video with these entertaining and educational animated tales. Except where noted, each tape features two stories and runs about 25 min. There are 13 volumes available, including:

Franklin's Valentines
Includes "Franklin's Valentines" and "Franklin's New Friend."
02-9024 *$12.99*

Franklin Plants A Tree
Includes "Franklin Plants a Tree" and "Franklin's Garden."
02-9193 ❑*$12.99*

Franklin's Blanket
Includes "Franklin's Blanket" and "Franklin Camps Out."
02-9215 *$12.99*

Franklin And The Green Knight
The arrival of Spring to Woodland will also mean that Franklin's new baby brother or sister will be born, so the intrepid little turtle sets out on a knightly quest to end Winter in this feature-length tale. 75 min.
02-9217 ❑*$19.99*

The Best Of Franklin
This best-of collection starring the popular turtle with a hat features "Franklin's New Friend," "Franklin and the Secret Club," "Franklin Is Messy," "Franklin Plays the Game," "Franklin and the Red Scooter" and "Franklin's Fort." 70 min.
02-9175 *$19.99*

Beauty And The Beast
A young girl teaches a bitter monster the meaning of love in this beautifully animated rendition of the classic children's fable. Mia Farrow narrates. 26 min.
02-7471 *$14.99*

Storytime!
Some of the all-time favorite children's tales, including "The Three Little Pigs," "Little Red Riding Hood" and "Henny Penny," are depicted in animated form and narrated by singer Arlo Guthrie. 25 min.
71-7151 *$12.99*

Aaron's Magic Village
After Aaron and his pet goat arrive in their aunt and uncle's hometown, they discover the place has come under attack by an evil sorcerer. Can he and his animal pal stop the sorcerer from casting a horrible spell? Isaac Bashevis Singer's stories have received a fine animated adaptation, featuring music and lyrics by Michel Legrand and Sheldon Harnick. 80 min.
02-3106 *$19.99*

Men In Black: The Series
Protecting the Earth from the cartoon scum of the universe, super-secret government agents "J" and "K" are on the lookout for alien invaders, strange creatures and other menaces in these animated tales based on the hit film. Each volume features two episodes and runs about 50 min.

Men In Black: The Series, Vol. 1
Includes "The Long So-Long Syndrome" and "The Irritable Bow-Wow Syndrome."
02-3284 *$12.99*

Men In Black: The Series, Vol. 2
Includes "The Neutralizer Syndrome" and "The Elle of My Dream Syndrome."
02-3285 *$12.99*

Noddy
He's the little wooden boy who took Europe by storm, and now his whimsical animated adventures in Toyland are on home video. Join Noddy and his pals Big Ears, Martha Monkey, Dinah Doll, Clockwork Mouse and the rest in these delightful tales. Each tape features two episodes, plus original music videos, and runs about 60 min.

Noddy: Noddy Gives A Birthday Party
02-9089 *$14.99*

Noddy: Noddy Makes A New Friend
02-9090 *$14.99*

Rupert
The delightful comic strip bear is the star of 12 fantastic tales. Rupert meets sea serpents and other fabulous creatures in these superb stories. 57 min.
04-3213 *$14.99*

Shelley Duvall's Bedtime Stories
From the creator of the popular "Faerie Tale Theatre" comes this animated series based on best-selling children's books. Shelley Duvall has enlisted some of the world's biggest stars to narrate these enchanting tales. Each program runs 25 min. There are 13 volumes available, including:

Elbert's Bad Word/Weird Parents
Two favorites by Audrey Wood are presented, featuring Ringo Starr narrating "Elbert" and Bette Midler relating "Weird Parents."
07-1844 ❑*$14.99*

There's A Nightmare In My Closet/There's Something In My Attic
Three tales of childhood fears of the dark by author Mercer Mayer are featured. Michael J. Fox reads "Nightmare," Christian Slater narrates "There's an Alligator Under My Bed" and "There's Something in My Attic" is read by Sissy Spacek.
07-1903 ❑*$14.99*

Patrick's Dinosaurs/What Happened To Patrick's Dinosaurs
Any kid who ever dreamed of owning a prehistoric menagerie will enjoy Martin Short narrating Carol and Donald Carrick's "Patrick's Dinosaurs" and "What Happened to Patrick's Dinosaurs."
07-1904 ❑*$14.99*

My New Neighbors/Rotten Island
Billy Crystal relates what happens when a boy moves to a strange neighborhood in "My New Neighbors," and Charles Grodin tells of the shocking day a flower bloomed on monster-laden "Rotten Island."
07-2167 *$14.99*

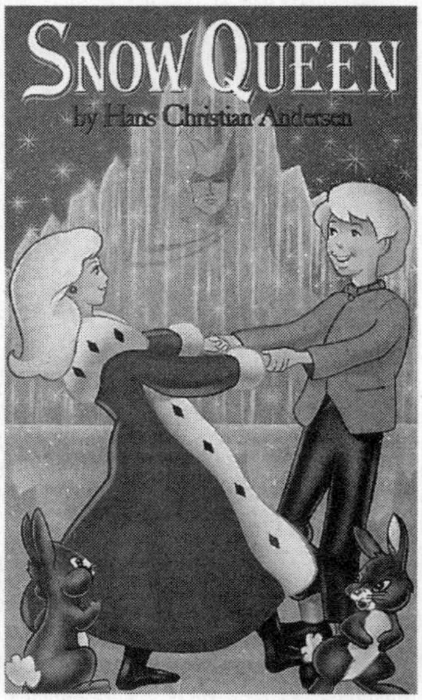

The Snow Queen
An enchanting animated version of Hans Christian Andersen's timeless tale of a young girl who journeys to a faraway land to find her friend, imprisoned by the heartless Snow Queen. 70 min.
69-5221 *$14.99*

The Snow Queen (1998)
When her brother Tom is abducted by the wicked Snow Queen, a young girl named Ellie sets out on a daring adventure to rescue him. Hans Christian Andersen's fable is turned into a fun- and song-filled animated feature. 79 min.
19-2787 ❑*$14.99*

The Snow Queen's Revenge (1999)
The cool, cruel Snow Queen is back with another invention to spread her wintry will across the world, and siblings Ellie and Tom are back with their animal friends to stop her, in this all-new cartoon adventure. 66 min.
19-2923 ❑*$14.99*

The World Of Hans Christian Andersen (1971)
Animated retelling of the life of the famed fantasy writer, with all the charm and loving characters of his fairy tales. 73 min.
02-1422 Was $19.99 *$14.99*

Thumbelina (1994)
From Don Bluth, the creator of "An American Tail," comes this wondrous musical story based on Hans Christian Andersen's beloved fairy tale. Thumbelina, the thumb-sized girl born to normal-sized parents, searches for the fairy prince of her dreams in the danger-filled forest. Voiced by Jodi Benson, Carol Channing, Charo and Gilbert Gottfried; music by Barry Manilow. 86 min.
19-2242 Was $24.99 ❑*$19.99*

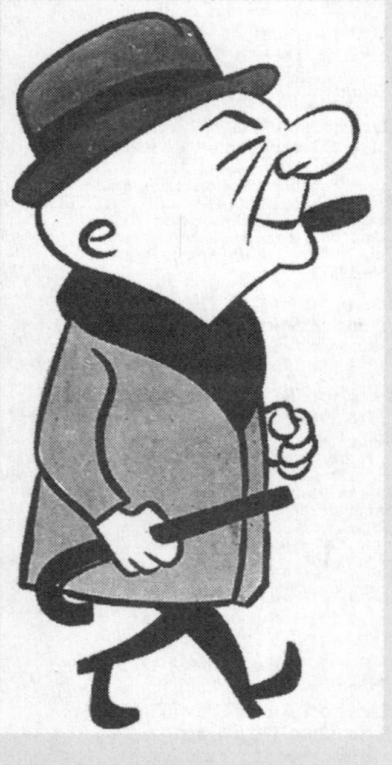

Columbia Pictures Cartoons, Vol. 1: Starring Mr. Magoo
The myopic misanthrope stars in four animated shorts, including "Barefaced Flatfoot" (1951), "Bungled Bungalow" (1950), "Bwana Magoo" (1959) and "Destination Magoo" (1954). 27 min.
02-1004 Was $19.99 *$14.99*

Columbia Pictures Cartoons, Vol. 2: Starring Mr. Magoo
That man of unique vision, Quincy Magoo, stars once more in four animated classics, including "Magoo Beats the Heat" (1956), "Magoo Breaks Par" (1957), "Magoo Goes West" (1956) and "Magoo Goes Overboard" (1957). 26 min.
02-1005 Was $19.99 *$14.99*

Columbia Pictures Cartoons, Vol. 3: Gerald McBoing Boing
The little boy who speaks only in sound effects stars in a quartet of delightful animated adventures, including the Oscar-winner "Gerald McBoing Boing" (1950), "Gerald McBoing Boing on the Planet Moo" (1956), "Gerald McBoing Boing's Symphony" (1953) and "How Now McBoing Boing" (1954). 29 min.
02-1003 Was $19.99 *$14.99*

Columbia Pictures Cartoons, Vol. 4: Cartoon Classics
Animated adventures include "The Emperor's New Clothes" (1953), "The Jay Walker" (1956), "The Man on the Flying Trapeze" (1954) and "Christopher Crumpet's Playmate" (1955). 27 min.
02-1006 Was $19.99 *$14.99*

Columbia Pictures Cartoon, Vol. 5: Starring Mr. Magoo
Those near-sighted bunglings continue, with "Stage Door Magoo" (1955), "Magoo's Glorious Fourth" (1957), "Sloppy Jalopy" (1952), "Magoo's Homecoming" (1959), "Trouble Indemnity" (1950), "Fuddy Duddy Buddy" (1951) and "Magoo's Masquerade" (1957). 45 min.
02-1149 Was $19.99 *$14.99*

Columbia Pictures Cartoons, Vol. 6: Cartoon Classics
UPA animated classics include "The Popcorn Story" (1950), "Pete Hothead" (1952), "Christopher Crumpet" (1953), "A Unicorn in the Garden" (1953), "Ballet-Oops" (1954), "Four Wheels and No Brake" (1955), "The Rise of Duton Lang" (1955) and "The Family Circus" (1951). 55 min.
02-1193 Was $19.99 *$14.99*

Columbia Pictures Cartoons, Vol. 7: Starring Mr. Magoo
UPA's clumsy curmudgeon stars in "Grizzly Golfer" (1951), "Pink and Blue Blues" (1952), "Magoo's Masterpiece" (1953), "Madcap Magoo" (1955), "Meet Mother Magoo" (1956), "Magoo's Canine Mutiny" (1956), "Magoo's Young Manhood" (1958) and "Terror Faces Magoo" (1959), the final theatrical release for UPA. 54 min.
02-1205 Was $19.99 *$14.99*

Columbia Pictures Cartoons, Vol. 8: Starring Mr. Magoo
"Oh, Magoo, you've done it again!" Quincy's further adventures include: "Gumshoe Magoo" (1958), "Safety Spin" (1953), "Dog Snatcher" (1952), "Captains Outrageous" (1952), "Magoo's Private War" (1957), "Rockhound Magoo" (1957), "When Magoo Flew" (1955) and "Scoutmaster Magoo" (1958). 52 min.
02-1619 Was $19.99 *$14.99*

Columbia Pictures Cartoons, Vol. 9: Cartoon Classics
Eight of UPA Studio's most-heralded animated shorts include: "The Tell-Tale Heart" (1953), "Gerald McBoing Boing" (1951), "A Unicorn in the Garden" (1953), "Ragtime Bear" (1949), "Rooty Toot Toot" (1952), "Madeline" (1952), "Magoo's Puddle Jumper" (1956) and "Robin Hoodlum" (1948), the studio's first release. 50 min.
02-1762 Was $19.99 *$14.99*

Columbia Pictures Cartoons, Vol. 10: Starring Mr. Magoo
Eight cartoon cavalcades starring Mr. Magoo, including "Love Comes to Magoo" (1958), "Calling Dr. Magoo" (1956), "The Explosive Mr. Magoo" (1958), "Hotsy Footsy" (1952), "Kangaroo Courting" (1954), "Magoo Goes Skiing" (1954), "Magoo's Check-Up" (1955) and "Magoo's Cruise" (1958). 55 min.
02-1799 Was $19.99 *$14.99*

Columbia Pictures Cartoons, Vol. 11: Starring Li'l Abner
Made by Columbia at the height of the comic strip's popularity, these five animated visits to beautiful downtown Dogpatch include "Amoozin' But Confoozin'" (1944), "Sadie Hawkins Day" (1944), "A Peekoolyar Sitcheeayshun" (1944), "Porkuliar Pig" (1944) and "Kickapoo Juice" (1944). 35 min.
02-1935 Was $19.99 *$14.99*

Columbia Pictures Cartoons, Vol. 12: Starring Mr. Magoo
You haven't seen anything yet! Eight more foggy mishaps with the goggle-eyed geezer, including "Magoo Makes News" (1955), "Magoo's Express" (1955), "Magoo Slept Here" (1953), "Magoo's Lodge Brother" (1959), "Matador Magoo" (1957), and more. 55 min.
02-1946 Was $19.99 *$14.99*

Columbia Pictures Cartoon Classics Collector's Edition: Mister Magoo
The cantankerous Quincy Magoo, voiced by the one and only Jim Backus, bumbles his way through one mess after another in this collection of his Oscar-winning antics. Included are Magoo's debut in "Ragtime Bear" (1949); the Academy Award-winners "Magoo's Puddle Jumper" (1956) and "When Magoo Flew" (1954) and nominees "Trouble Indemnity" (1950) and "Pink and Blue Blues" (1952); and the final Magoo short, "Terror Faces Mr. Magoo" (1959). 42 min.
02-3131 *$14.99*

Mr. Magoo: 1001 Arabian Nights (1959)
Animated look at Mr. Magoo's voyage to the magical world of Aladdin, genies, a beautiful princess and the Wicked Wazir. Feature-length adventure with Jim Backus as the voice of Mr. Magoo. 76 min.
02-1256 Was $19.99 *$14.99*

Hello Kitty And Friends
These cartoon programs from Japan offer the adorable Kitty and her fellow feline Mimi, fun-loving frog Keroppi, and other animal pals in exciting adventures and fairy tale take-offs. Kids everywhere are sure to fall in love with Kitty and her friends. Each tape runs about 45 min. There are 10 volumes available, including:

Hello Kitty: Wizard Of Paws
12-3227 □$14.99

Hello Kitty: Kitty And The Beast
12-3228 □$14.99

Keroppi: Let's Play Baseball
27-5503 □$14.99

Hello Kitty: The Dream Thief
27-5536 $14.99

The Very Hungry Caterpillar
Five fanciful stories by best-selling children's writer Eric Carle come to life in this animated collection designed for pre-schoolers. Along with the title story, there's also "Papa, Please Get the Moon for Me," "The Very Quiet Cricket," "The Mixed-Up Chameleon" and "I See a Song." 30 min.
11-1905 $12.99

Inspector Gadget: Gadget's Greatest Gadgets
The original cartoon sleuth whose body has a gadget for getting out of every scrape he falls into is back in this all-new feature-length caper. Join Inspector Gadget (voiced by Don Adams), his niece Penny and their dog Brian as they go up against the diabolical Dr. Claw's most evil plan to date. 65 min.
11-2386 □$14.99

The Little Engine That Could
A wonderful animated treatment of the classic children's book about the brave Little Engine that comes to the rescue of the stranded Birthday Train using its courage and repeating the words "I think I can, I think I can..." 30 min.
07-1916 □$12.99

William's Wish Wellingtons, Vol. 1
A young boy lets his imagination run wild—thanks to a pair of magical red Wellingtons (boots to you Yanks) that grant his wishes—in these episodes from the enchanting British animated series.
04-3908 □$14.99

To Boo Or Not To Boo
Watch as Casper the Friendly Ghost "doth make cowards of us all"—well, the grown-ups, anyway—in three laugh-raising, scare-raising cartoons: "To Boo or Not to Boo," "Frightday the 13th" and "Spooking of Ghosts," plus Herman and Katnip in "Frighty Cat." 22 min.
07-2786 □$12.99

Casper's Cartoon Classics
This spooky collection features five Casper shorts from Famous Studios and Paramount Pictures from the late 1940s and 1950s. Included is the first Casper cartoon, "Casper, The Friendly Ghost," plus "Spooky About Africa," "There's Good Boos Tonight," "A-Haunting We Will Go" and "Boo Moon." 45 min.
69-5275 $12.99

Casper's Haunted Christmas
Kibosh, the ruler of all ghosts, wants Casper to scare at least one person before Christmas day. But when kindly Casper ignores the request, the Ghostly Trio hires the friendly ghost's cousin Spooky to perform the deed. Features music by Randy Travis.
07-2910 $19.99

Rabbit Ears Video
Movies Unlimited is proud to present this award-winning series that features music and stories from around the world. Famous actors narrate each tale, presented in "dissolve animation" storybook form. Except where noted, each tape runs about 30 min. There are 25 volumes available, including:

Jack And The Beanstalk
Michael Palin of Monty Python fame narrates an enchanting version of the classic tale of a young man's adventures with a dim-witted giant. Eurythmics' Dave Stewart supplies the music.
07-5003 $14.99

Davy Crockett
A colorful look at legendary frontiersman Davy Crockett, known for his feistiness and his heroics at the Alamo. Nicolas Cage lends his voice to Davy, and string master David Bromberg performs the music.
07-5013 $14.99

John Henry
The American folk tale of John Henry, the "steel-drivin' man" who pits his strength against a steam drill, is told commandingly by Denzel Washington, with music by blues great B.B. King.
07-5020 $14.99

Follow The Drinking Gourd
This inspirational story, based on the famous folk song, tells of a family's escape from slavery via the Underground Railroad. Morgan Freeman tells the tale, set to Taj Mahal's score.
07-5021 $14.99

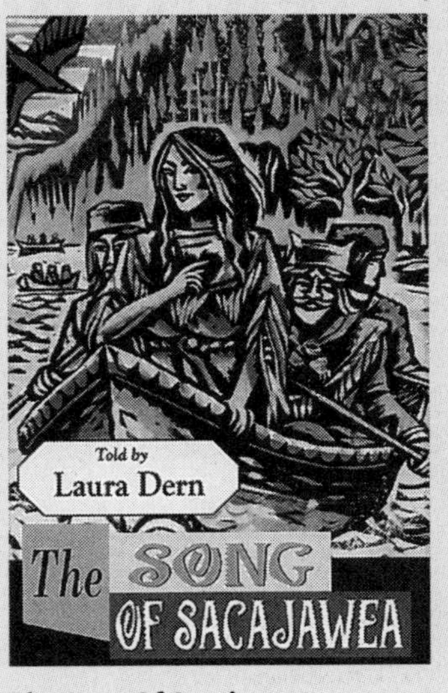

The Song Of Sacajawea
The true story of the teenage Native American woman who assisted explorers Lewis and Clark on their expedition is wonderfully recounted by actress Laura Dern and features music by instrumentalist David Lindley.
07-5027 $14.99

Squanto And The First Thanksgiving
The extraordinary and factual account of the Native American who was sold into slavery in Spain and who returned to North America to help the Pilgrims survive at Plymouth is given an exciting treatment by reader Graham Greene ("Dances With Wolves") and woodwind virtuoso Paul McCandless.
07-5029 $14.99

The Tale Of Jeremy Fisher/ The Tale Of Peter Rabbit
From the pen of Beatrix Potter comes these two animated classics of children's literature, as rascally Peter disturbs Farmer McGregor's carrots and bucolic bullfrog Jeremy tries his hand at fishing. Narrated by Meryl Streep.
45-5348 $14.99

How The Rhinoceros Got His Skin/ How The Camel Got Its Hump
What parent wouldn't want Jack Nicholson telling their child bedtime stories? Here he relates two of Kipling's "Just So" stories, as bad behavior earns each animal a distinctive physical trait. Bobby McFerrin provides the music. 30 min.
45-5349 $14.99

The Emperor And The Nightingale
Hans Christian Andersen's timeless tale of a Chinese ruler whose love of the nightingale's song leads him to obtain a mechanical bird is narrated by actress Glenn Close. 40 min.
45-5350 $14.99

The Legend Of Sleepy Hollow
A classic tale of Americana, Washington Irving's story of schoolmaster Ichabod Crane's nocturnal encounter with the fearsome Headless Horseman is read by Glenn Close.
45-5441 $14.99

The Three Billy Goats Gruff And The Three Little Pigs
Two of the best-loved tales for tikes are brought to life here, as it falls to the cleverest siblings in each family to outwit a greedy troll and a hungry wolf. Holly Hunter narrates.
45-5472 $14.99

Paul Bunyan
Comic master Jonathan Winters reads the enchanted animated myth about mighty lumberjack Paul Bunyan and his mighty feats. Leo Kottke composed the folksy music score and Rick Meyerowitz, of National Lampoon fame, handled the art.
45-5489 $14.99

The Elephant's Child
Animated version of Rudyard Kipling's "Just So" story, about how the elephant came by his distinctive sniffer is given a hearty narration by Jack Nicholson.
46-1007 $12.99

The Velveteen Rabbit
Animated version of beloved Margery Williams tale about a toy hare who is loved so long and so deeply by a child that it comes to life. Meryl Streep narrates.
46-1010 $12.99

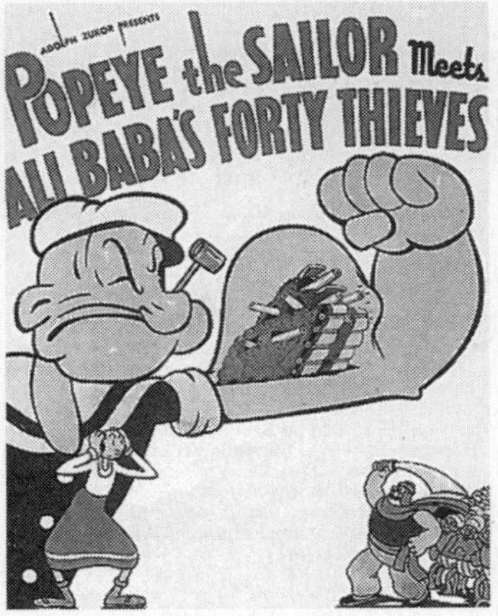

Popeye Festival
Three exciting and unique 20-minute cartoons by the Fleischer Studios in the late '30s, using early Technicolor and a three-dimensional process. Watch the spinach-chomping sailor, Olive Oyl and Wimpy in "Popeye the Sailor Meets Sinbad the Sailor," "Popeye the Sailor Meets Ali Baba's Forty Thieves" and "Popeye the Sailor in Aladdin and His Wonderful Lamp." 54 min. total.
10-1108 Was $19.99 $14.99

Popeye, Vol. 1
The "musckle"-bound mariner is "strong to the finish" in a collection of eight classic cartoons from the '30s and '40s. Included are "Little Swee' Pea," "I'm in the Army Now," "The Paneless Window Washer," "I Never Changes My Altitude," "A Date to Skate," "Customers Wanted," "With Poopdeck Pappy" and "Me Musical Nephews." There's even a vintage '60s TV spot for Popeye and Bluto "Soakies." 55 min.
10-9777 $14.99

70 Years Of Popeye
Celebrate seven decades of spinach-swallowing exploits with this deluxe collection of Popeye, Olive Oyl, Wimpy, Bluto and company's best animated adventures, all restored with enhanced soundtracks and effects. Shorts include "Popeye for President," "Assault and Flattery," "Gopher Spinach," "Fright to the Finish," "Customers Wanted," and more. 100 min.
53-6753 $14.99

The Best Of Popeye
Cast off for 15 color cartoon voyages with the squint-eyed sailor who makes spinach growers happy and grammarians wince. Includes "Taxi-Turvy," "Private Eye Popeye," "Floor Flusher," "Assault and Flattery," "Out to Punch," "Parlez Vous Woo," " Fright to the Finish," "Gopher Spinach" and seven more from Paramount Pictures. 100 min.
62-1344 $14.99

Astro Boy
Relive those childhood memories with these classic animated adventures featuring Osamu Tezuka's super-powered adolescent robot. Watch Astro Boy battle futuristic bad guys in these inventive, intelligent outings. Each tape contains two episodes and runs about 50 min. There are 17 volumes available, including:

Astro Boy, Vol. 1
Includes "The Birth of Astro Boy" and "The Monster Machine."
17-7001 Was $24.99 $19.99

Astro Boy, Vol. 2
Includes "The Terrible Time Gun" and "One Million Mammoth Snails."
17-7002 Was $24.99 $19.99

Astro Boy, Vol. 3
Includes "Super Brain" and "Mystery of the Amless Dam."
17-7003 Was $24.99 $19.99

Astro Boy 30th Anniversary Collector's Series, Vol. 1
Includes "Vampire Vale" and "Phoenix Bird."
17-7022 $14.99

Astro Boy 30th Anniversary Collector's Series, Vol. 2
Includes "Cleopatra's Heart" and "Funnel to the Future."
17-7023 $14.99

Astro Boy 30th Anniversary Collector's Series, Vol. 3
Includes "The Deadly Flies" and "Astro Boy Goes to School."
17-7024 $14.99

Astro Boy: The Lost Episode: The Beast From 20 Fathoms
Long unseen, this "Astro Boy" episode was produced in 1963 by several guest animators. In it, Astro Boy meets an evil creature at the bottom of a lake that hypnotizes nearby workers. Also includes "The Snow Lion," in which Astro discovers that a mysterious snow is actually the start of an alien invasion. 50 min.
17-7036 $14.99

Sunday Morning Funnies
There'll be plenty of brick-tossing, spinach-eating, rocket-blasting excitement when some of your favorite comic-strip characters come to life in these fun-filled animated adventures.

Sunday Morning Funnies: Barney Google And Snuffy Smith
15-5521 $12.99

Sunday Morning Funnies: Beetle Bailey
15-5522 $12.99

Sunday Morning Funnies: Betty Boop
15-5523 $12.99

Sunday Morning Funnies: Blondie & Dagwood, Vol. 1
15-5524 $12.99

Sunday Morning Funnies: Cool McCool
15-5526 $12.99

Sunday Morning Funnies: Flash Gordon
15-5527 $12.99

Sunday Morning Funnies: Hagar The Horrible
15-5528 $12.99

Sunday Morning Funnies: Krazy Kat
15-5529 $12.99

Sunday Morning Funnies: Popeye, Vol. 1
15-5530 $12.99

Sunday Morning Funnies: Popeye, Vol. 2
15-5531 $12.99

Pegasus
The winged horse of Greek myth fame takes flight once more, to battle the monstrous Chimaera and live among the stars, in this charming animated tale read by Mia Farrow. 25 min.
71-7166 □$14.99

The Magic Pearl
A brother and sister, with the help of an enchanted pearl that protects them, accompany their grandmother on a magical journey that brings them face to face with dragons, witches and other wonders in this animated adventure based on Chinese folk tales. 63 min.
08-8732 □$12.99

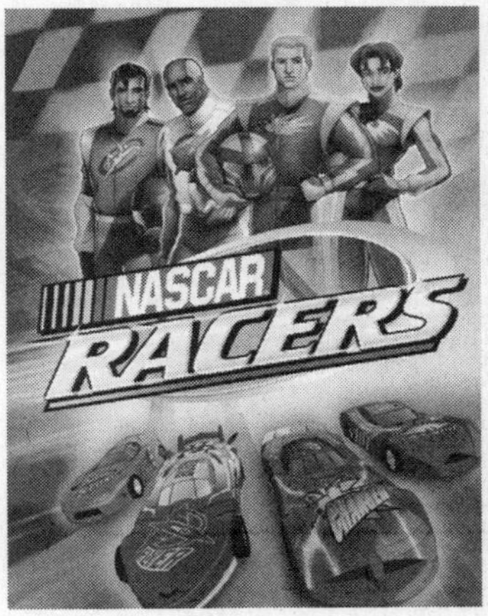

NASCAR Racers
The high-speed excitement of NASCAR racing zooms into animated form with these episodes from the hit Saturday morning TV series. Join Mark, Carlos, Steve and Megan—the hard-driving heroes of Team Fastex—as they take on devious Team Rexcor in thrilling competitions on the tracks of New Motor City. Except where noted, each tape runs about 60 min.

NASCAR Racers, Vol. 1: Start Your Engines
Special feature-length adventure runs 90 min.
04-3935 $14.99

NASCAR Racers, Vol. 2: Take It To The Limit!
04-3976 $14.99

NASCAR Racers, Vol. 3: Fastex vs. Rexcor/Get In The Driver's Seat!
04-3977 $14.99

NASCAR Racers 3-Pack
Rev up some savings with this special collection of Volumes 1-3 of "NASCAR Racers."
04-3978 Save $5.00! $39.99

Walt Disney

Disney's Beginnings
Eight early efforts by the pioneering American animator. Included are one of the "Newman Laugh-O-Grams" made for a Kansas City theatre in the early '20s; "The Four Musicians of Bremen" (1922); Oswald the Lucky Rabbit in 1927's "Great Guns" and "The Mechanical Cow"; and the 1925 live-action/animated shorts "Alice Rattled by Rats," "Alice's Egg Plant," "Alice's Orphan" and "Alice Solves the Puzzle." Silent with music score. 55 min.
62-1135 *$19.99*

Snow White And The Seven Dwarfs (1937)
The first feature-length cartoon from Walt Disney remains a masterpiece of animation to this day. Follow beautiful Snow White as she flees the clutches of her evil stepmother and finds refuge in the cottage of the Seven Dwarfs. (Remember them all? Bashful, Doc, Dopey, Grumpy, Happy, Sleepy and Sneezy.) Songs include "Heigh Ho," "Someday My Prince Will Come," "Whistle While You Work." 84 min.
11-1780 *$59.99*

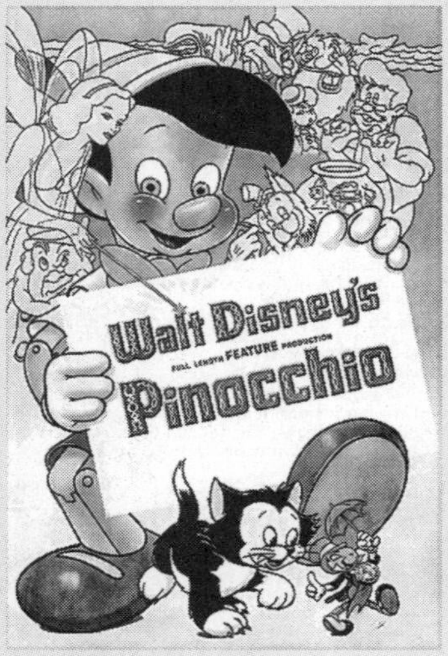

Pinocchio: 60th Anniversary Edition (1940)
Disney's second animated feature, the story of the mischievous puppet who longs to be a real boy, is back on video with a remastered print. Join Pinocchio and pal Jiminy Cricket as they journey from Gepetto's toy shop to mysterious Pleasure Island and an encounter with Monstro the whale. Songs include "When You Wish Upon a Star," "Hi-Diddle-De-De." Special edition includes the featurette "The Making of 'Pinocchio'," with rare behind-the-scenes footage. 88 min.
11-2358 *$22.99*

Dumbo (1941)
A magical Walt Disney tale about a shy, floppy-eared circus elephant who gets lessons in confidence from his rodent pal, Timothy the Mouse, and some tips in aerodynamics from four conniving crows. Songs include "Pink Elephants on Parade" and "Baby of Mine." 64 min.
11-1025 *$22.99*

Bambi (1942)
The Disney crew worked for four years to animate Felix Salten's woodland tale, resulting in some of the studio's most memorable characters (young fawn Bambi and pals Thumper and Flower) and unforgettable moments (the death of Bambi's mother and the forest fire). Bambi's rise to king of the forest makes for classic family fare. 69 min.
11-1477 *$39.99*

Saludos Amigos (1943)
Made to bolster wartime relations between the U.S. and South America, this unusual mix of travelogue and cartoons follows Walt Disney and his staff on a south-of-the-border tour. Animated sequences that complement their stops feature Goofy as an Argentinean gaucho, Donald Duck fishing at Bolivia's Lake Titicaca and meeting Brazilian parrot Joe Carioca, and a brave little mail plane named Pedro crossing the Andes. 75 min.
11-2418 *$19.99*

The Three Caballeros (1945)
Donald Duck joins his two South-of-the-Border friends, Jose Carioca and Panchito, in this classic mixture of live-action and animation. Highlight is the piñata sequence, in which Donald takes a magic serape ride through Mexico. Also includes the classic shorts "Don's Fountain of Youth" and "Pueblo Pluto." 71 min.
11-1045 Was $24.99 *$19.99*

Make Mine Music (1946)
Originally conceived as a contemporary counterpart to "Fantasia," the Disney animators covered an array of musical and artistic styles with this feature-length compilation. Among the highlights are "The Whale Who Wanted to Sing at the Met," with Nelson Eddy performing as Willie, the operatic whale; Jerry Colonna telling the story of "Casey at the Bat"; a surreal interpretation of Benny Goodman's "After You're Gone"; the Prokofiev classic "Peter and the Wolf"; the Andrews Sisters' "Johnny Fedora and Alice Blue Bonnet" and more; 67 min.
11-2419 *$19.99*

Fun And Fancy Free (1947)
Jiminy Cricket is your host for this Disney feature made up of two animated stories. "Bongo," narrated by Dinah Shore, follows a runaway circus bear who escapes into the forest and looks for acceptance from his ursine comrades. Next, some magic beans send Mickey Mouse, Donald Duck and Goofy up into the clouds for an encounter with a shape-changing giant named Willie in "Mickey and the Beanstalk," introduced by Edgar Bergen and Charlie McCarthy. 73 min.
11-2110 *$26.99*

Melody Time (1948)
The last of Walt Disney's '40s "musical vignette" features, this wonderful mix of animated and live-action sequences includes Roy Rogers and The Sons of The Pioneers relating the story of "Pecos Bill"; The Andrews Sisters singing about "Little Toot" the tugboat; Dennis Day as the voice of "Johnny Appleseed"; Donald Duck and his "Three Caballeros" compadres in "Blame It on the Samba," and much more. 75 min.
11-2235 *$19.99*

The Adventures Of Ichabod And Mr. Toad (1949)
Two of literature's unlikeliest heroes had their stories told in cartoon form in this Disney double bill. Bing Crosby narrates Washington Irving's "The Legend of Sleepy Hollow," as colonial schoolteacher Ichabod Crane has a nocturnal encounter with the Headless Horseman, while the car-loving Toad of Toad Hall makes life crazy for Ratty, Mole and Badger in an adaptation of Kenneth Grahame's "The Wind in the Willows," narrated by Basil Rathbone.
11-2313 *$22.99*

Alice In Wonderland (1951)
Walt Disney's fanciful adaptation of the Lewis Carroll classic. Follow young Alice down the rabbit role into Wonderland, where strange and funny characters like the Mad Hatter, Cheshire Cat and Tweedledum and Tweedledee dwell. 'Tis brillig! 75 min.
11-1026 *$22.99*

Peter Pan (Restored 45th Anniversary Edition) (1953)
J.M. Barrie's boy who wouldn't grow up takes to the skies in the beloved Disney cartoon feature. Join Peter, Tinker Bell and the Darling children on a fun-filled trip to Never-Never Land, where wicked Captain Hook and an always-hungry crocodile lie in wait. "Never Smile at a Crocodile" and "You Can Fly" are among the songs. This restored limited edition also includes a "making of" featurette. 76 min.
11-1501 *$26.99*

Lady And The Tramp (1955)
The doggone funniest love story you'll ever see, this charming Disney animated feature follows the rocky romance between a proper cocker spaniel and a streetwise mutt from opposite sides of the tracks. Features the voice talents of Peggy Lee, Barbara Luddy, Stan Freberg and Alan Reed. Songs include "Bella Notte," "He's a Tramp," "We Are Siamese." 75 min.
11-1428 Remastered *$29.99*

Lady And The Tramp (Letterboxed Version)
Also available in a theatrical, widescreen format.
11-2769 *$29.99*

Sleeping Beauty: Restored Collector's Edition (1959)
One of the Disney studio's most stunning animated features was this rendition of the fairy tale favorite. Can handsome Prince Phillip rescue Princess Aurora and awaken her from the curse placed on her by the evil sorceress Maleficent? Tchaikovsky's timeless music, along with such original songs as "Once Upon a Dream," adds to the enjoyment. Also included is a special featurette on the making of the film. 75 min.
11-1354 *$29.99*

101 Dalmatians (1961)
One of Disney's most popular animated films details the adventures of London-based canine couple Pongo and Perdita, who produce 15 cute puppies, only to have them snatched by the merciless Cruella De Vil. Pongo and Perdita set out from their masters' home and enlist the help of England's animals to track down their missing offspring. Songs include "Dalmatian Plantation" and "Cruella De Vil." 79 min.
11-1606 *$19.99*

The Sword In The Stone (1963)
Follow the adventures of young would-be knight Wart and his tutor, the slightly muddled mage Merlin, in this delightful Disney animated feature. See a wizard's feud between Merlin and the Mad Madam Mim, a thrilling jousting contest and the magical sword embedded in a stone. 79 min.
11-1278 *$22.99*

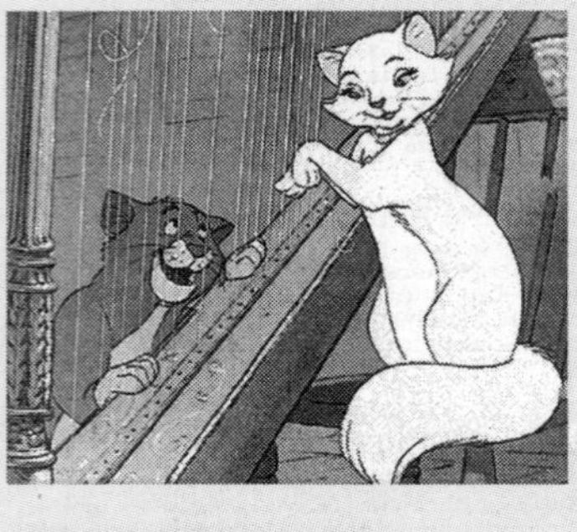

The Aristocats (1970)
A pampered Parisian cat named Duchess and her three children are in line to inherit a fortune from their owner, but a scheming butler has other plans. It takes some help from a pair of detective dogs and an alley cat named O'Malley to save Duchess and her brood in this tune-filled Disney cartoon outing. Eva Gabor, Phil Harris, Pat Buttram and Scatman Crothers are among the voice talents. 79 min.
11-1988 *$22.99*

Bedknobs And Broomsticks (1971)
Animation and live actors are blended in this dazzling Disney adventure about an amateur witch and a group of plucky orphans who team up to defend England from Nazi invaders. Angela Lansbury, David Tomlinson, Roddy McDowall star. 117 min.
11-1002 Was $24.99 *$19.99*

Robin Hood (1973)
He swings through the forest, robbing the rich to help the poor, but now he's a fox! What's more, Little John's a bear, Friar Tuck's a badger, and evil Prince John's a lion. Disney's thrilling animated version of the timeless legend features the voices of Roger Miller, Peter Ustinov, Terry-Thomas and Phil Harris. 83 min.
11-1135 *$22.99*

Pete's Dragon (1977)
An orphan boy befriends a comical, sometimes invisible dragon, but greedy villains want the beast for themselves. Wonderful musical fantasy from Disney blends live-action and animation. Mickey Rooney, Helen Reddy, Sean Marshall and Charlie Callas, as the dragon's voice, star. 128 min.
11-1011 *$22.99*

The Rescuers (1977)
A Disney animated favorite, this fun-filled adventure follows two mice and a seagull who set out to save a young girl being held captive in a swamp by the evil Madame Medusa. Songs include "Tomorrow Is Another Day" and "Someone's Waiting for You." Voices are supplied by Bob Newhart, Eva Gabor, Geraldine Page and Joe Flynn. 76 min.
11-1619 *$26.99*

The Rescuers Down Under (1990)
That intrepid pair of mouse adventurers, Bernard and Miss Bianca, journey via "albatross express" to Australia to help free a young boy and his eagle pal from the clutches of a villainous poacher. With the voices of Bob Newhart, Eva Gabor, John Candy and George C. Scott. 90 min.
11-1574 *$22.99*

The Fox And The Hound (1981)
Two childhood chums, a bloodhound pup and a fox cub, grow up to find themselves on opposite sides of a hunting party in this bittersweet Disney animated tale that that features the voices of Mickey Rooney, Kurt Russell, Pearl Bailey, Sandy Duncan and Pat Buttram. 83 min.
11-1739 *$22.99*

The Black Cauldron (1985)
A young would-be hero and a feisty princess team up to stop the wicked Horned King from obtaining a seemingly ordinary cauldron that is a source of unlimited magical power in this animated adventure from Disney. Lavishly drawn and filled with fantastic creatures, the film features the voices of John Hurt, Nigel Hawthorne, Susan Sheridan and Grant Bardsley. 80 min.
11-2251 *$22.99*

The Great Mouse Detective (1986)
Lively animated feature from Disney Studios about the adventures of Basil of Baker Street, the Sherlockian rodent out to crack a case involving England's royal family masterminded by the diabolical Professor Ratigan. Voices are supplied by Vincent Price, Barrie Ingham and Alan Young. 72 min.
11-1616 *$26.99*

Who Framed Roger Rabbit (1988)
The mind-blowing, Oscar-winning blend of Raymond Chandler and Tex Avery stars Bob Hoskins as a seedy private eye in a '40s Hollywood populated by humans and animated "toons" who must clear cartoon star Roger Rabbit of a murder charge. With Christopher Lloyd and the voices of Charles Fleischer and Kathleen Turner; cameos by Mickey Mouse, Bugs Bunny, Daffy and Donald Duck and others. 104 min.
11-1478 Was $19.99 *$14.99*

The Best Of Roger Rabbit
P-P-P-Paleeease don't miss this collection featuring the hapless hare, his gorgeous wife Jessica, and that mischievous Baby Herman in a trio of original "Maroon Cartoons" made by the Disney Studios. Included are "Tummy Trouble," "Roller Coaster Rabbit" and "Trail Mix-Up." 30 min.
11-1978 *$12.99*

Oliver & Company (1988)
Dickens' classic story "Oliver Twist" goes to the dogs—and cats—in this vibrant and fun-filled animated romp from Disney. An orphaned kitten named Oliver, left alone in the city, is taken in by a daring dog named Dodger and joins his pack of streetwise mutts. Joey Lawrence, Billy Joel, Bette Midler, Cheech Marin and Robert Loggia supply voices; songs by Joel, Midler and Huey Lewis. 73 min.
11-2021 *$29.99*

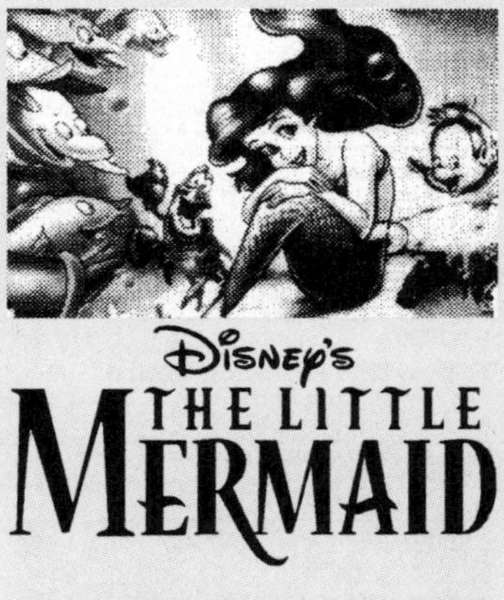

The Little Mermaid (1989)
One of the most delightful Disney animated films in years, this charming adaptation of the Hans Christian Andersen fable follows young Ariel on her quest for true love with a land-dwelling prince, much to the distress of her sea king father. Wonderful, Oscar-winning score (including "Under the Sea," "Part of Your World" and "Kiss the Girl") and an array of memorable aquatic characters fuel this all-ages treat. 83 min.
11-1500 *$26.99*

The Little Mermaid II: Return To The Sea (2000)
The aquatic adventures continue in this all-new animated feature. Young Princess Melody, daughter of Ariel and Eric, dreams of a life under the sea, but first she'll need the help of friends old (Sebastian and Scuttle) and new (Dash and Tip) to overcome the evil schemes of sea witch Ursula's sister, Morgana. 75 min.
11-2458 *$26.99*

The Little Mermaid: Ariel's Undersea Adventures
There's plenty of fun and excitement "under the sea" with Ariel and her pals Sebastian and Flounder in this animated series from Disney that takes place before the events in the hit movie. Each tape runs about 45 min. There are four volumes available, including:

The Little Mermaid: Double Bubble
11-1669 *$12.99*

The Little Mermaid: Ariel's Gift
11-1734 *$12.99*

The Little Mermaid: In Harmony
11-1735 *$12.99*

DuckTales The Movie: Treasure Of The Lost Lamp (1990)
The world's richest drake, Scrooge McDuck, and nephews Huey, Dewey and Louie are off to the desert in search of the fabled treasure of Collie Baba in this feature-length "DuckTales" saga loaded with daredevil escapes, evil magicians, and strange genies with the voice of Rip Taylor. 74 min.
11-1551 Was $22.99 ❑*$14.99*

Aladdin (1992)
Follow the heroic beggar boy who finds a magic lamp and calls on its wacky blue genie (voiced by Robin Williams) to help him win the hand of a princess about to be wed to an evil vizier. Disney's animated spin on the Arabian Nights fable mixes music, romance, laughs and adventure; the Academy Award-winning score includes "Friend Like Me" and "Whole New World." 87 min.
11-1691 ❑*$39.99*

The Return Of Jafar (1994)
The beloved characters from Disney's award-winning hit "Aladdin" are back for all-new adventures (and five new songs, to boot) in the studio's first animated feature made for home video. Wicked Jafar escapes from his imprisonment to create new troubles for Aladdin, Princess Jasmine, the genie (voiced by Dan Castellaneta) and the rest of the crew. 66 min.
11-1776 ❑*$19.99*

Aladdin And The King Of Thieves (1996)
All of Agrabah is preparing for the long-awaited marriage of Aladdin and Princess Jasmine, but a visit from the marauding Forty Thieves and a quest for Aladdin's long-lost father may postpone the wedding, in this thrill-packed all-new tale that features music, excitement, and the return of Robin Williams as the voice of the Genie. 80 min.
11-2004 ❑*$24.99*

A Goofy Movie (1995)
In his first big-screen animated feature, Goofy, the lovable Disney canine, causes trouble for his son Max's social life. It seems that Max is trying to impress pretty Roxanne at school, but Dad's, er, goofiness keeps getting in the way. In order to iron things out, Goofy takes Max on a fishing trip that he hopes will help strengthen their relationship. 78 min.
11-1893 ❑*$19.99*

An Extremely Goofy Movie (2000)
When son Max goes off to college, poor Goofy finds life in his empty home boring, so, much to Max's dismay, pop enrolls to finish his own college education. Now the pair have to learn to get along as classmates as well as father and son in this all-new feature-length laughfest. Voices by Pauly Shore, Bebe Neuwirth, Vicki Lewis. 79 min.
11-2384 ❑*$24.99*

Here's Goofy!
A-Hyuk! That garrulous, gangling, gregariously goony goof is at his bumbling best in this trio of ticklers from the Disney archives: "For Whom the Bull Tolls," "Lion Down," and "A Knight for a Day." 22 min.
11-1406 *$12.99*

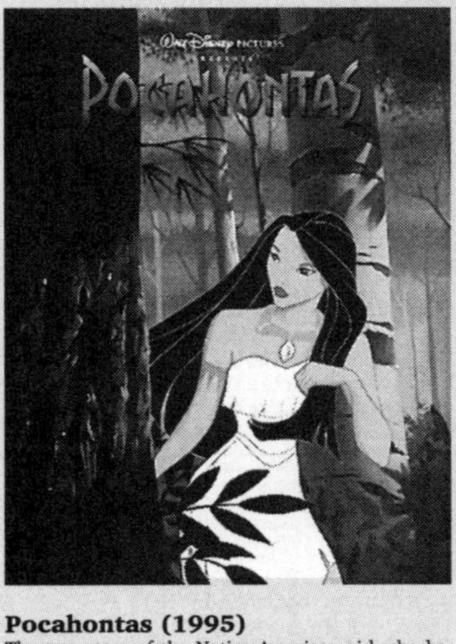

Pocahontas (1995)
The true story of the Native American girl who became a peacemaker between her people and English settlers in the early 1600s served as the basis for Disney's wonderful animated mix of drama, adventure and romance. With the voices of Mel Gibson as Captain John Smith and Irene Bedard as Pocahontas; songs include "Colors of the Wind." 81 min.
11-1956 ❑*$22.99*

Pocahontas II: Journey To A New World (1998)
Taking up where the Academy Award-winning 1995 film left off, this all-new animated feature follows Pocahontas on a voyage to London, where she hopes to win fair treatment of her people from the English king. Waiting for her across the ocean, however, are old friends and enemies and unexpected danger. Song-filled adventure features voices by Irene Bedard, Billy Zane, Donal Gibson, Jean Stapleton and David Ogden Stiers. 72 min.
11-2238 ❑*$22.99*

Toy Story (1995)
The first feature-length computer-animated film, this Oscar-winning treat for all ages takes place in a child's room where, when no one is around, the toys come to life, and where a pull-string cowboy named Woody (voiced by Tom Hanks) fears losing his "favorite plaything" status to new arrival Buzz Lightyear (Tim Allen), a high-tech spaceman figure who thinks he's real. Other voices include Jim Varney, Annie Potts and Don Rickles; songs by Randy Newman. Special edition includes a "making of" documentary, a music video, and the Oscar-winning short "Tin Toy." 81 min.
11-2005 ❑*$22.99*

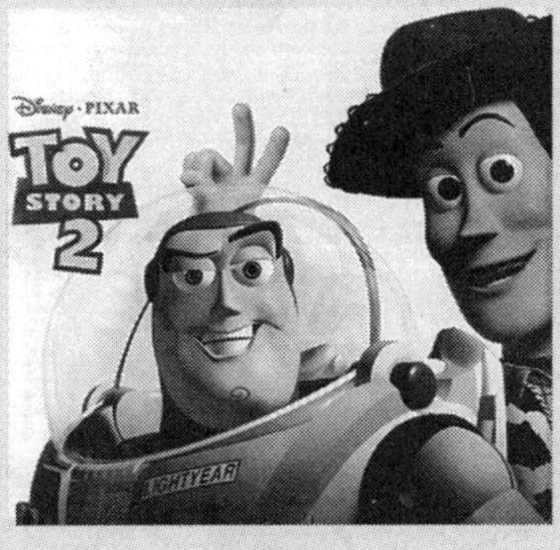

Toy Story 2 (1999)
When Woody is mistakenly left in a yard sale and taken by a fanatical toy collector, it's up to Buzz, Slinky Dog, Mr. Potato Head and the gang to stage a rescue. But once Woody is reunited with his long-forgotten pals from the '50s TV puppet show he starred in, will he *want* to be rescued? Funny, exciting and even touching, this wonderful sequel to the computer-animated hit features voices by Tim Allen, Tom Hanks, John Ratzenberger, Don Rickles, Jim Varney, Joan Cusack and Kelsey Grammer. 95 min.
11-2459 ❑*$26.99*

Buzz Lightyear Of Star Command: The Adventure Begins (2000)
Prepare yourself for a journey "to infinity...and beyond!," as the high-flying hero from the "Toy Story" films stars in his very own animated feature. Join Buzz (voiced by Tim Allen), his Star Command crew, and the Little Green Men as they do battle with the diabolical Emperor Zurg. With the voices of Linda Hamilton, Stephen Furst, Wayne Knight. 70 min.
11-2439 ❑*$24.99*

James And The Giant Peach: Special Edition (1996)
From the co-creators of "The Nightmare Before Christmas" comes this dazzling mix of live-action and stop-motion animation, based on Roald Dahl's book. A young English orphan mistreated by his aunts goes on a remarkable journey when he enters a huge, magical peach and befriends the wisecracking insects who want to ride the fruit across the ocean to New York. Paul Terry, Joanna Lumley star, with Richard Dreyfuss, Jane Leeves and Susan Sarandon supplying voices. Special video edition includes a "making of" featurette, the original theatrical trailer, Randy Newman's music video for "Good News" and more. 90 min. total.
11-2492 Letterboxed ❑*$22.99*

The Hunchback Of Notre Dame (1996)
The Disney Studio's magnificently animated version of Victor Hugo's classic adds lively music and an uplifting message to the story of Quasimodo, deformed bellringer of the Paris cathedral, who falls in love with Gypsy dancer Esmerelda. Voices are supplied by Tom Hulce, Demi Moore, Kevin Kline and Jason Alexander; score by Alan Menken and Stephen Schwartz. 91 min.
11-2084 ❑*$26.99*

Mulan (1998)
The timeless Chinese folk tale of a heroic young woman who takes drastic measures to save her family and country is given an exciting animated treatment by the Disney studio. After her father is unable to answer a call to arms to battle the invading Huns, Mulan disguises herself as a man and enlists in the army. Ming-Na Wen supplies the voice of Mulan, with Eddie Murphy as her companion, a wisecracking little dragon named Mushu; other voices include B.D. Wong, Lea Salonga and Donny Osmond. 88 min.
11-2269 ❑*$22.99*

Hercules (1997)
Turning their attention to the Greek myths, the Disney animators have dressed up the story of the legendary strongman into a lively and colorful cartoon saga. Will fan adulation and merchandise deals keep heroic Hercules from reclaiming his Olympian heritage and saving his father, Zeus, and the other gods from the sinister schemes of Hades, lord of the underworld? Tate Donovan, James Woods, Danny DeVito, Susan Egan, Rip Torn and Charlton Heston are among the voices. 93 min.
11-2191 ❑*$22.99*

Hercules: Zero To Hero (1999)
You've seen him as the fully-grown hero of ancient Greece, but what was Hercules like as a headstrong, super-strong teenager? Find out how Herc learned to use his powers for good in this all-new, feature-length follow-up to Disney's 1997 animated hit. Voices by Tate Donovan and James Woods. 70 min.
11-2347 ❑*$19.99*

Mighty Ducks: The Movie: The First Face-Off (1996)
From live-action films to real hockey team, the Mighty Ducks take the next logical step, becoming cartoon heroes in this feature-length adventure. These Ducks are interstellar, hockey-playing heroes who defend the Earth by taking on evil Dragaunus and his minions in a no-holds-barred ice match. Voices are supplied by Ian Ziering, Dennis Franz and Jim Belushi. 66 min.
11-2093 ❑*$14.99*

The Lion King II: Simba's Pride (1998)
The saga of jungle lord Simba and his family continues in this all-new, song-filled feature, as his headstrong and independent daughter, Kiara, sets out on a trek to the forbidden Outlands. There she meets Kovu, scion of the evil Scar, but the cubs' friendship will face a severe test. Voices by Matthew Broderick, Neve Campbell, Nathan Lane and Ernie Sabella. 75 min.
11-2267 ❑*$26.99*

Timon's & Pumbaa's Wild Adventures
The scene-stealing warthog and meerkat team from "The Lion King" are back and looking for fun (plus a few grubs and bugs to eat) in their own series of wacky animated exploits. Each video runs about 30 min. There are six volumes available, including:

Timon & Pumbaa's Wild Adventures: True Guts
11-1975 ❑*$12.99*

Timon & Pumbaa's Wild Adventures: Don't Get Mad, Get Happy!
11-1997 ❑*$12.99*

Timon & Pumbaa's Wild Adventures: Quit Buggin' Me!
11-1999 ❑*$12.99*

A Bug's Life (1998)
From the creators of "Toy Story" comes this fun-filled animated feature with an all-insect cast. When a trouble-prone ant named Flik's mishaps antagonize a group of grasshoppers threatening his colony, he locates a gang of misfit bugs and brings them back to help save the day. The invertebrate voices are supplied by Dave Foley, Denis Leary, Julia Louis-Dreyfus, Roddy McDowall, David Hyde Pierce and Kevin Spacey. 95 min.
11-2300 ❑*$22.99*

A Bug's Life (Letterboxed Version)
Also available in a theatrical, widescreen format.
11-2312 ❑*$26.99*

Tarzan (1999)
Disney's lovely and lively adaptation of Edgar Rice Burroughs' famed story tells how an orphaned child in 1900s Africa is rescued by a female gorilla and raised with apes, growing up to become the feral king of the jungle. When a scientific expedition arrives in the wilds, Tarzan befriends Jane, a professor's daughter, and battles nasty poachers. Voices supplied by Tony Goldwyn, Minnie Driver, Glenn Close and Rosie O'Donnell; music by Phil Collins. 88 min.
11-2810 ❑*$26.99*

Fantasia 2000 (1999)
Disney's updating of their 1940 mixture of classical music and spectacular animation features the original "The Sorcerer's Apprentice" along with seven new episodes. Among them: "The Steadfast Tin Soldier," featuring Shostakovich's Piano Concerto No. 2; Donald Duck in a Noah's Ark tale set to "Pomp and Circumstance"; a flying flamingo sequence for Saint-Saens' "Carnival of the Animals"; and Gershwin's "Rhapsody in Blue," represented by cartoons in the style of artist Al Hirschfeld. Hosts include James Earl Jones, Steve Martin, Bette Midler, and Penn & Teller.
11-2468 ❑*$26.99*

Winnie The Pooh And The Honey Tree (1965)
Pooh Bear, Christopher Robin, Rabbit, Eeyore, Piglet and the other delightful A.A. Milne characters make their Disney debut in this animated featurette. Poor Pooh's stomach wants "hunny," and he'll stop at nothing to get it! Includes the songs "Winnie the Pooh" and "Rumbly in My Tumbly." 25 min.
11-1325 ❑*$12.99*

Winnie The Pooh And The Blustery Day (1969)
A storm sweeps through the Hundred Acre Woods in this Oscar-winning Disney cartoon short, bringing with it floods, winds and the irrepressible Tigger, all of which adds up to problems for Pooh and his pals. Includes the song "The Wonderful Thing About Tiggers." 24 min.
11-1326 ❑*$12.99*

Winnie The Pooh And Tigger Too (1974)
Poor Tigger is driving Pooh and his friends crazy with his bouncing up and down, until one day he gets stuck in a tree and Rabbit helps him...on the condition that he never bounces again! 25 min.
11-1327 ❑*$12.99*

The Many Adventures Of Winnie The Pooh (1977)
Honey-loving Pooh Bear, Christopher Robin and the whole crew are here in this feature-length compilation of Disney's adaptations of the A.A. Milne stories. Along with "Winnie the Pooh and the Honey Tree," "Winnie the Pooh and the Blustery Day" and "Winnie the Pooh and Tigger Too," there's also a behind-the-scenes look at the making of the cartoons. 83 min.
11-1989 ❑*$29.99*

Winnie The Pooh And A Day For Eeyore (1981)
That perennially downcast donkey is in a bigger funk than ever when it seems that his friends have forgotten his birthday...but Pooh and his pals come through to make it the finest party ever! 25 min.
11-1403 ❑*$12.99*

Winnie The Pooh Storybook Classics: Gift Set
Save some money for your "hunny" with this four-tape collection featuring "Winnie the Pooh and the Honey Tree," "Winnie the Pooh and the Blustery Day," "Winnie the Pooh and Tigger Too" and "Winnie the Pooh and a Day for Eeyore."
11-1461 Save $8.00! *$44.99*

Pooh's Grand Adventure: The Search For Christopher Robin (1997)
Young Christopher Robin is off to school, but a misunderstanding sends Winnie the Pooh, Piglet, Tigger and the rest of the Hundred Acre Woods animals on a quest to find and "rescue" him in this charming, song-filled animated feature. 70 min.
11-2111 ❑*$24.99*

Winnie The Pooh: Sing A Song With Pooh Bear
Join Winnie the Pooh and all his Hundred Acre Wood friends—and sing along with them—as Pooh's search for a song to call his own leads the animals on a fun-filled adventure in music. 45 min.
11-2278 ❑*$14.99*

Winnie The Pooh: A Valentine For You
It's up to Pooh, Piglet and company to help cure Christopher Robin's lovesickness when he's smitten by a pretty classmate in this Valentine-themed adventure. 30 min.
11-2385 ❑*$14.99*

Winnie The Pooh: Sing A Song With Tigger
His top is made out of rubber, his bottom is made out of springs, and now you can sing along with Pooh Bear's boisterous striped pal that includes favorite songs from Disney's Winnie the Pooh films, including three tunes from "The Tigger Movie." 31 min.
11-2387 ❑*$14.99*

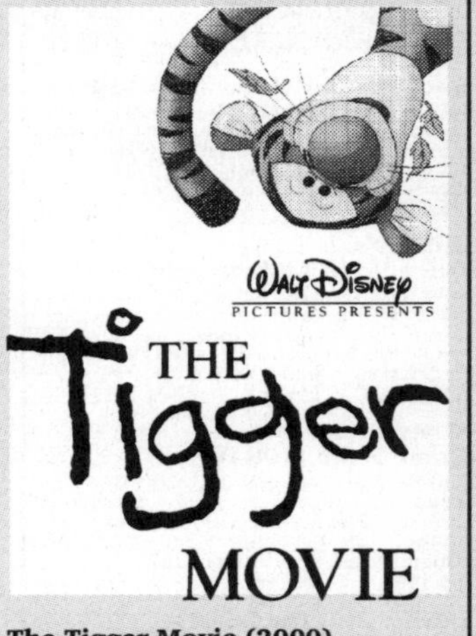

The Tigger Movie (2000)
The "bouncy, trouncy, flouncy, pouncy" stuffed cat from the Hundred Acre Woods hops his way into his very own, song-filled feature-length adventure. After years of assuming that he's "the only one," Tigger sets out on a quest to find others of his kind, with some help from Winnie the Pooh, Piglet, Roo and company. 70 min.
11-2457 ❑*$24.99*

Pooh Learning
That lovable bear Winnie the Pooh and such friends as Tigger and Christopher Robin help kids learn important lessons about manners, friendship and responsibility in this series. Each tape includes a set of flashcards designed to help kids learn while they laugh along with Pooh. Each tape runs about 45 min. There are six volumes available, including:

Pooh Learning: Making Friends
11-1766 ❑*$12.99*

Pooh Learning: Helping Others
11-1767 ❑*$12.99*

Pooh Learning: Working Together
11-2030 *$12.99*

Donald's Scary Tales
Donald Duck and his pals get into the Halloween spirit with three delightfully diabolical tales: "Donald Duck and the Gorilla" (1944), "Duck Pimples" (1945), and "Donald's Lucky Day" (1939). 22 min.
11-1590 ❑*$12.99*

A Walt Disney Christmas
An animated Christmas card from Walt Disney. Mickey, Donald and the gang celebrate the holidays in this Yuletide cartoon collage. 46 min.
11-1030 ❑*$12.99*

Jiminy Cricket's Christmas
Everybody's favorite "conscience" is your host for a Yuletide cartoon sampler, featuring holiday hilarity with Donald Duck, Chip and Dale, Goofy and much more. 45 min.
11-1360 ❑*$12.99*

Rolie Polie Olie: A Rolie Polie Christmas
Join the lovable robot Rolie and his dog spot in this holiday-themed episode of the Emmy-winning Disney Channel animated series. 22 min.
11-2472 *$12.99*

The Small One (1978)
A warm-hearted Disney cartoon featurette about a young boy who must part with his beloved pet donkey, only to find that they both will play an important role in the first Christmas. 25 min.
11-1236 ❑*$12.99*

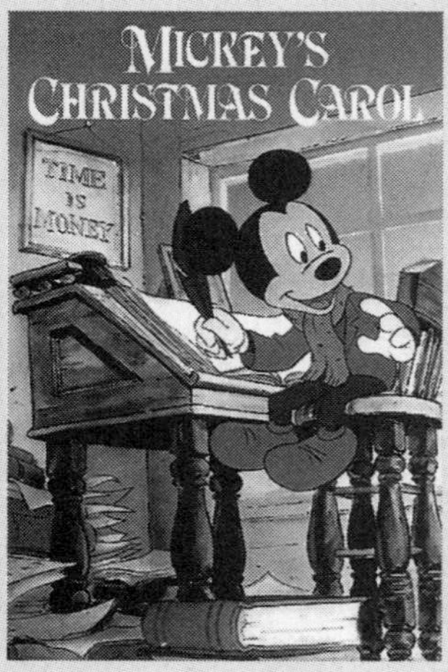

Mickey's Christmas Carol (1983)
All of Disney's beloved characters make a long-overdue return to the screen in this animated adaptation of the Dickens fable. Mickey is Bob Crachit, Uncle Scrooge plays (of course) Ebeneezer Scrooge, and so on. 25 min.
11-1131 ❑*$12.99*

Mickey's Once Upon A Christmas (1999)
Celebrate the holidays with Mickey, Minnie, Donald, Goofy, Pluto and other favorite Disney characters with this heartwarming feature-length cartoon that features the gang sharing their favorite Christmas memories. 70 min.
11-2355 ❑*$19.99*

Where The Toys Come From (1984)
Amazing stop-action animation highlights this charming tale of two Christmas toys, a camera named Zoom and a pair of binoculars named Peepers, who try to find their "roots." Follow their exciting and funny tour through a factory where toys come alive. 68 min.
11-1138 *$12.99*

Beauty And The Beast: The Enchanted Christmas (1997)
All the beloved characters from Disney's acclaimed 1991 animated film are back in this all-new, feature-length holiday tale that presents an untold chapter in the story of Belle, who wants to decorate the enchanted castle for Christmas, and her beastly suitor. Robby Benson, Tim Curry, Angela Lansbury and Paige O'Hara are among the voices. 80 min.
11-2176 ❑*$26.99*

101 Dalmatians Christmas (1998)
Will a Christmas Eve visit from a trio of spotted spectres help the wicked Cruella De Vil turn away from her puppy-napping ways and give her the holiday spirit? Find out in this fun-filled animated Yule special based on the popular Disney films and TV series. 44 min.
11-2779 ❑*$12.99*

Winnie The Pooh: Seasons Of Giving (1999)
Pooh Bear and his pals set out to find the perfect holiday gift, only to learn a valuable lesson in the Christmas spirit, in this feature-length animated tale. 70 min.
11-2357 ❑*$19.99*

Silly Symphonies: Animals Two By Two
Three ticklish teamings of funny fauna from Disney's "Silly Symphonies." "Father Noah's Ark" (1933) finds an arkful of animals setting sail in history's most famous voyage; "Peculiar Penguins" (1934) travels to the Arctic Circle to frolic with our "tuxedoed" friends; and the Academy Award-winning "The Tortoise and the Hare" (1935) follows the literary rivals' great race. 27 min.
11-1432 *$12.99*

Disney Favorite Stories
Now you can watch and read along to some of the best-loved animated adaptations of classic tales, all with the special Disney touch, in this delightful series of videos. Each tape features an illustrated storybook on the box.

Three Little Pigs (1933)
"Who's Afraid of the Big Bad Wolf?" Not the brave little porkers who confound him through their heavy-duty construction methods in this classic Disney cartoon that won a Best Animated Short Academy Award. Also included on this tape are "The Big Bad Wolf" (1934) and "Three Little Wolves (1936)."
11-2022 ❑*$12.99*

Mickey And The Beanstalk (1947)
Professor Ludwig Von Drake narrates this hilarious spin on the fairy tale favorite, as Mickey, Donald Duck and Goofy shimmy up the stalk to find fantastic treasure and a shape-shifting giant named Willie. 29 min.
11-1457 ❑*$12.99*

Paul Bunyan/ Little Hiawatha (1958)
Frontier heroes come in all sizes in this double bill of cartoon tales. Join tree-size lumberjack Paul Bunyan and his blue ox Babe as they clear a path from coast to coast, followed by the story of the young Indian who dreams of becoming a warrior brave.
11-1857 ❑*$12.99*

The Prince And The Pauper (1990)
In his first theatrical short in decades, Mickey Mouse takes on the title roles of the beggar boy and the crown prince who trade places. All your favorite Disney characters are here in this adaptation of the Mark Twain classic. 24 min.
11-1564 ❑*$12.99*

Sweetheart Stories
The course of true love runs hilariously in this trio of vintage Disney animated shorts starring Mickey, Minnie, Donald, Pluto and the gang. Included are "Mickey's Rival" (1936), "In Dutch" (1946) and "Nifty Nineties" (1941). 23 min.
11-1971 ❑*$12.99*

Gargoyles: The Series
By day they sit atop the skyscrapers of New York, but at night these ancient creatures come to life and take to the skies, using their awesome strength to battle evildoers in this animated adventure series. Each tape runs about 45 min.

Gargoyles: Deeds Of Deception
11-1986 ❑*$12.99*

Gargoyles: Brothers Betrayed
11-1987 ❑*$12.99*

Gargoyles: The Force Of Goliath
11-1995 ❑*$12.99*

Gargoyles: The Hunted
11-1996 ❑*$12.99*

Disney Sing-Along Songs
Now youngsters (and adults) can watch and join in on their favorite tunes from classic Disney features (just follow the bouncing mouse head and the onscreen lyrics) in this toe-tapping series. Each tape runs about 30 min. There are 22 volumes available, including:

Disney Sing-Along Songs: Zip-A-Dee-Do-Dah
11-1364 ❑*$12.99*

Disney Sing-Along Songs: Heigh-Ho
11-1404 ❑*$12.99*

Disney Sing-Along Songs: You Can Fly!
11-1453 ❑*$12.99*

Disney Sing-Along Songs: Very Merry Christmas Songs
11-1463 ❑*$12.99*

Disney Sing-Along Songs: The Twelve Days Of Christmas
11-1748 ❑*$12.99*

Disney Sing-Along Songs: Under The Sea
11-1505 ❑*$12.99*

Disney Sing-Along Songs: Disneyland Fun
11-1573 *$12.99*

Disney Sing-Along Songs: Happy Haunting—Party At Disneyland!
11-2768 ❑*$12.99*

Frank And Ollie (1995)
The lifelong friendship and creative collaboration of Hollywood animators Frank Thomas and Ollie Johnston, who began working together for Walt Disney in the mid-'30s and retired 40 years later as two of the studio's venerable "Nine Old Men," are the focus of this acclaimed documentary by Thomas' son, Theodore. The pair talk about their lives and their art, a history of animation that ranges from "Snow White and the Seven Dwarfs" and "Bambi" to "101 Dalmatians" and "The Jungle Book." 89 min.
11-2291 ❑*$19.99*

So Dear To My Heart (1949)
The whole family can enjoy this sensitive film from Disney Studios which mixes live-action with animated scenes. A young boy enters his misfit black sheep at the country fair to win the coveted first prize. Bobby Driscoll, Burl Ives, Beulah Bondi star. Songs include "Lavender Blue (Dilly Dilly)," "Stick-to-it-ivity." 82 min.
11-1331 Was $24.99 ❑*$19.99*

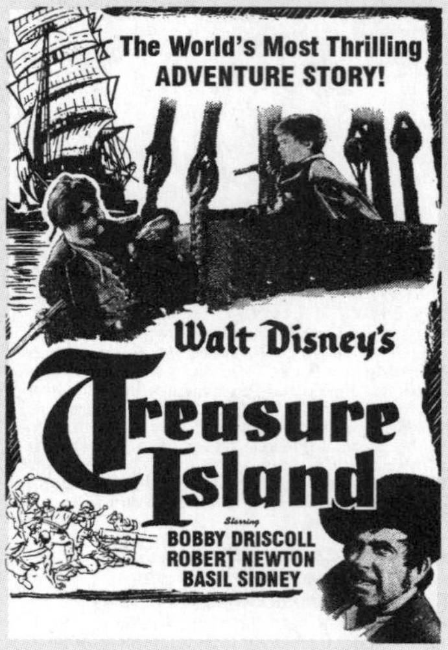

Treasure Island (1950)
Set sail on board the Hispaniola with young Jim Hawkins (Bobby Driscoll) and rapscallious Long John Silver (Robert Newton) in Disney's filming of the beloved pirate saga. With Finlay Currie, Basil Sydney. 96 min.
11-1031 Was $19.99 ❑*$14.99*

The Story Of Robin Hood And His Merrie Men (1952)
Richard Todd takes to the woods in this lavish Disney filming of the tale of literature's most beloved outlaw. Peter Finch co-stars as the evil Sheriff of Nottingham; with Joan Rice, James Robertson Justice. 84 min.
11-1424 *$14.99*

The Living Desert (1953)
Oscar-winning Disney nature documentary that looks at the American desert, a region that at first appears to be devoid of life, but has a surprising diversity of flora and fauna. See the amazing adaptations animals have developed to survive in this inhospitable climate. 69 min.
11-1282 *$14.99*

The Vanishing Prairie (1954)
Learn how snakes, owls, prairie dogs and other wildlife survive in a challenging world that's increasingly threatened by man's encroachment, the great American plains, in this entry from Disney's "True Life Adventure" series. 60 min.
11-1242 *$14.99*

Secrets Of Life (1956)
Take a remarkable look at rarely-seen worlds of nature, courtesy of Walt Disney. This "True Life Adventure" uses special cameras and time-lapse photography to let you watch plants grow; follow frogs, fish and other pond animals; and marvel at the life inside a drop of water. 69 min.
11-1243 *$14.99*

White Wilderness (1958)
Join the Disney camera team on an expedition to the top of the world in this Academy Award-winning live-action film. Polar bears, seals, walruses and other Arctic animals are seen in their natural environs. 72 min.
11-1241 *$14.99*

Jungle Cat (1960)
A day in the life of a South American jaguar is filled with all sorts of dangers. Watch hunter become hunted as the jungle cat faces wild pigs, alligators, boa constrictors and other menaces in this Disney "True Life Adventure." 69 min.
11-1283 *$14.99*

20,000 Leagues Under The Sea (1954)
Jules Verne's classic undersea drama is given the superlative Disney treatment. James Mason is Captain Nemo, builder of the fantastic submarine Nautilus, and Paul Lukas, Kirk Douglas and Peter Lorre are his less-than-willing guests. Oscar-winning special effects. 127 min.
11-1012 ❑*$19.99*

The Wonderful World Of Disney
From 1954 to 1990 and on all three major networks, the Disney studios treated audiences to original animated adventures, live-action comedies and dramas, wildlife documentaries and specials on their weekly TV series. Now some of the favorite episodes are available on video in these double features.

The Yellowstone Cubs (1963)/ Flash, The Teen-Age Otter (1961)
In this delightful double feature of live-action animal adventures, a pair of mischievous bear cubs create havoc in Yellowstone National Park, followed by a curious otter's overcoming of natural and man-made obstacles to return home. 96 min.
11-1301 *$12.99*

Dad, Can I Borrow The Car? (1972)/ The Hunter And The Rock Star (1980)
Kurt Russell narrates a light-hearted look at America's love affair with cars that uses live-action and animated vignettes. Next, Timothy Hutton plays a singer who tries to save a tiger from hunters. 103 min.
11-1303 *$12.99*

Fire On Kelly Mountain (1974)/ Adventure In Satan's Canyon (1974)
A young Forest Service lookout gets his first taste of danger when lightning sparks a raging forest fire in the first episode. Next, a river trek for an Olympic kayaking hopeful and his coach becomes a perilous race through rapids. 95 min.
11-1304 *$12.99*

Three On The Run (1978)/ Race For Survival (1978)
With the help of their grandfather and a rag-tag dog team, two brothers try to win a sledding race. Then, a greyhound must race against time for help when his master crashes their plane in the African veldt. 95 min.
11-1306 *$12.99*

Run, Appaloosa, Run (1966)/The 101 Problems Of Hercules (1966)
Enter the rough-and-tumble world of rodeo riding with a young Indian girl and her magnificent appaloosa horse, Sky Dancer. Then, if you think you have problems, check out the predicaments a pack of hard-working sheepdogs must face. 98 min.
11-1334 *$12.99*

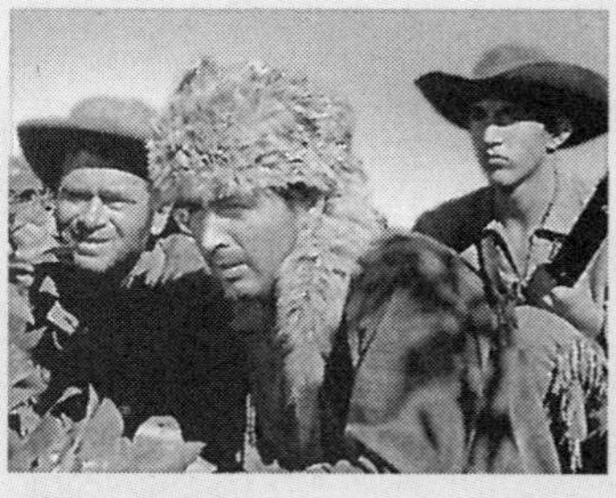

Davy Crockett, King Of The Wild Frontier (1955)
Compiled from three episodes of the hit TV series, this rousing Disney adventure stars Fess Parker as the man who was "born on a mountaintop in Tennessee." Follow Crockett from his days as an explorer and settler, to his Congressional career, and to the fateful last stand at the Alamo. Buddy Ebsen, Hans Conried, Kenneth Tobey also star. 90 min.
11-1004 Was $19.99 ❑*$14.99*

Davy Crockett And The River Pirates (1956)
Frontier hero Fess Parker is back (and looking none the worse for having died at the end of the first film) and ready to take on the mighty Mississippi in this feature-length adventure. Watch Davy and legendary keelboatman Mike Fink in a race to New Orleans, then see the duo team up to stop river bandits disguised as Indians. With Buddy Ebsen, Jeff York. 81 min.
11-1015 Was $19.99 ❑*$14.99*

The Great Locomotive Chase (1956)
Based on a true story (the same one that inspired Buster Keaton's "The General"), this rousing Disney Civil War drama stars Fess Parker as the leader of a band of Union soldiers known as Andrew's Raiders, who commandeer a Southern train and are pursued by Confederate forces. With Jeffrey Hunter, Jeff York. 85 min.
11-1068 *$14.99*

The Great Locomotive Chase (Letterboxed Version)
Also available in a theatrical, widescreen format.
08-8845 *$14.99*

Westward Ho, The Wagons! (1956)
Exciting western action is in store as a wagon train scout must get his charges safely through a hostile wilderness populated by horse rustlers and hostile Indians. Fess Parker, George Reeves, Kathleen Crowley star. 90 min.
11-1310 *$14.99*

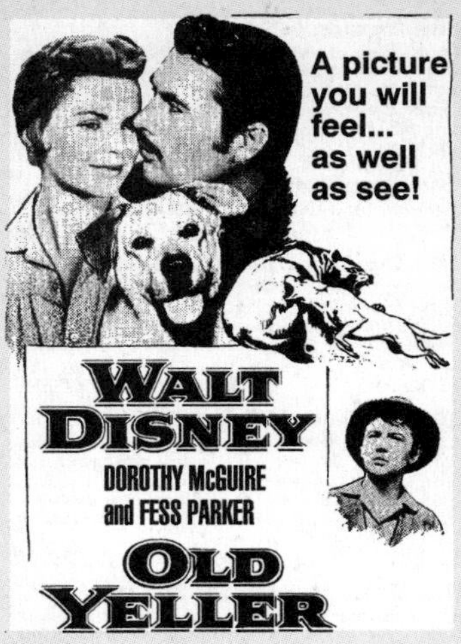

A picture you will feel... as well as see!
WALT DISNEY
DOROTHY McGUIRE and FESS PARKER
OLD YELLER

Old Yeller: Restored 40th Anniversary Edition (1957)
Disney's deeply moving family drama set in the Texas frontier of the 1860s, about a farm family who find their lives changed by the stray yellow dog they take in. Fess Parker, Dorothy McGuire, Tommy Kirk, Kevin Corcoran star. 89 min.
11-1029 ❑*$19.99*

Johnny Tremain And The Sons Of Liberty (1957)
Return to the days of the American Revolution, as young apprentice silversmith Johnny Tremain joins with Paul Revere, James Otis and other Boston area leaders in the fight for independence from England in this live-action Disney feature based on Esther Forbes' book. Hal Stalmaster, Jeff York, Luana Patten and Sebastian Cabot star.
11-1067 Was $19.99 *$14.99*

The Light In The Forest (1958)
Can a young white boy (James MacArthur), taken from his frontier family and raised by Indians, survive in the "civilized" world when he's returned to his relatives after a peace treaty signing? Sensitive live-action Disney adventure, based on the book by Conrad Richter, also stars Wendell Corey, Fess Parker and Carol Lynley (her film debut).
11-1346 Was $19.99 *$14.99*

The Shaggy Dog (1959)
Thanks to a magical ring, a teenager is transformed into a sheepdog and has to perform an act of bravery in order to change back in this doggone funny film, Disney's first live-action comedy. Fred MacMurray, Tommy Kirk, Annette Funicello, Jean Hagen star. 104 min.
11-1032 Was $19.99 ❑*$14.99*

The Shaggy D.A. (1976)
Dean Jones takes over the role of the now-grown Wilby Daniels, a lawyer whose campaign for district attorney could wind up in the doghouse—literally—when the magic ring turns him into a sheepdog again. Suzanne Pleshette, Keenan Wynn, Tim Conway co-star.
11-1209 Was $19.99 *$14.99*

Kidnapped (1960)
Robert Louis Stevenson's classic adventure about a young boy who is robbed of his inheritance and sold into servitude by his scheming uncle. Spirited action film stars James MacArthur, Peter Finch, Bernard Lee; look for Peter O'Toole in his film debut. 94 min.
11-2113 *$19.99*

Daniel Boone (1960)
Dewey Martin starred as the buckskin-clad trailblazer who tamed the wilderness of 18th-century America in this exciting Disney adventure series. With Kevin Corcoran, Diane Jergens, William Herrin. Each tape runs about 50 min.

Daniel Boone, Vol. 1: The Warrior's Path
11-2161 ❑*$9.99*

Daniel Boone, Vol. 2: And Chase The Buffalo
11-2162 ❑*$9.99*

Daniel Boone, Vol. 3: The Wilderness Road
11-2163 ❑*$9.99*

Daniel Boone, Vol. 4: The Promised Land
11-2164 ❑*$9.99*

Pollyanna (1960)
Beloved Disney family tale about a warm-hearted 12-year-old orphan who goes to live with her aunt in a small New England village at the turn of the century and manages to win over the townsfolk with her optimistic attitudes. Hayley Mills, Jane Wyman, Karl Malden, Agnes Moorehead star. 134 min.
11-1037 ❑*$19.99*

Swiss Family Robinson (1960)
Adventure classic from Walt Disney about a shipwrecked family who try to make a paradise out of the South Seas island on which they're stranded. They battle the elements, tame wild animals and square off against a nasty gang of pirates. John Mills, Dorothy McGuire, Sessue Hayakawa, Tommy Kirk and James MacArthur star. 126 min.
11-1040 ❑*$19.99*

The Absent-Minded Professor (Color Version) (1961)
One of the most popular of Disney's live-action films was this whimsical comedy. Fred MacMurray stars as the addled academian who invents a miraculous anti-gravity substance he calls "flubber" and uses it to propel his school's basketball team to victory and send his Model T on a flight around Washington. With Nancy Olson, Keenan Wynn, Tommy Kirk. 97 min.
11-2196 Was $19.99 *$14.99*

Son Of Flubber (1963)
The first sequel made by the Disney studio returns Fred MacMurray to the role of addled academician Ned Brainard. Among the crazy creations he comes up with to save his college are "flubbergas," a "dry rain" gun, and more. With Nancy Olson, Keenan Wynn, Tommy Kirk. 100 min.
11-1111 Was $19.99 *$14.99*

Flubber (1997)
Robin Williams bounces into the "Absent-Minded Professor" role first played by Fred MacMurray in an energetic and effects-filled remake of the Disney favorite. Williams' creation of a high-energy, gravity-defying goo with a mind of its own could save the college where he and long-suffering fiancée Marcia Gay Harden work, but a crooked businessman will stop at nothing to learn the secret of Flubber for himself. Christopher McDonald, Raymond Barry also star. 94 min.
11-2227 Was $19.99 ❑*$14.99*

Babes In Toyland (1961)
Grand Disney adaptation of the holiday musical favorite "March of the Wooden Soldiers" stars Tommy Sands and Annette Funicello as Mother Goose Land lovers Tom Piper and Mary Contrary, Ray Bolger as wicked Mr. Barnaby, and Ed Wynn as the addle-brained Toymaker. 105 min.
11-1053 *$14.99*

The Parent Trap (1961)
Hayley Mills plays a dual role in this classic Disney comedy of teenage twin sisters who meet for the first time at summer camp and concoct a scheme to reunite their divorced parents. Maureen O'Hara, Brian Keith, Charlie Ruggles co-star. 124 min.
11-1083 ❑*$19.99*

The Parent Trap (1998)
This remake of the 1961 Hayley Mills favorite features Lindsay Lohan as Hallie and Annie, twins separated at birth, who realize they're siblings while attending summer camp, and decide to swap identities in order to reunite parents Dennis Quaid and Natasha Richardson. With Simon Kunz and Lisa Ann Walter. 128 min.
11-2808 Was $19.99 ❑*$14.99*

Greyfriars Bobby (1961)
Touching family drama from Disney about a Scottish shepherd and his devoted terrier. After the old man's death, Bobby becomes a pet to the local village. Donald Crisp, Laurence Naismith star. 89 min.
11-1280 *$19.99*

Nikki, Wild Dog Of The North (1961)
A Malamute pup belonging to a trapper in the Canadian wilderness befriends an orphaned bear cub which the trapper takes with them in his canoe. When the boat overturns, the two animals, tied together, must cooperate as they learn to fend for themselves. Winning Disney adventure stars Jean Coutu. 73 min.
11-1373 *$14.99*

Big Red (1962)
Touching Disney drama in the "Old Yeller" mold, focusing on a beautiful Irish Setter and the boy who cares for it. Adventure and heartfulness abound in this classic, filmed in gorgeous Quebec, Canada. Walter Pidgeon, Gilles Payant star. 89 min.
11-1096 *$14.99*

Big Red (Letterboxed Version)
Also available in a theatrical, widescreen format.
08-8818 *$14.99*

The Legend Of Lobo (1962)
Live-action Disney adventure follows the life of a wolf named Lobo, from his first days in the holt as a cub through adulthood, as he learns to hunt for himself and avoid a two-legged enemy named Man. Rex Allen narrates, with music by The Sons of the Pioneers. 67 min.
11-1246 *$14.99*

Sammy, The Way-Out Seal (1962)
Fun-filled comedy about two young brothers who bring home a surprise stowaway from their seashore vacation: a mischief-making seal. The boys can't hide their pet for too long, though, sending their family and the whole town for a loop. With Jack Carson, Robert Culp, Michael McGreevey and Billy Mumy. 89 min.
11-1372 *$14.99*

The Incredible Journey (1963)
The original film version of Sheila Burnford's popular book, and one of Disney's best-loved live-action adventures. A cat and two dogs traverse over 200 miles of rugged Canadian wilderness and face many hardships and dangers in order to be reunited with the family that owned them. 80 min.
11-1123 Was $19.99 ❑*$14.99*

Homeward Bound: The Incredible Journey (1993)
A magical live-action adventure from the Disney studios about a golden retriever, a cat and a bulldog puppy who are separated from their human family and must travel across the Sierra Nevada Mountains to find them. Fun, excitement and stunning photography are in store, along with voices by Michael J. Fox, Sally Field and Don Ameche. 84 min.
11-1692 Was $19.99 ❑*$14.99*

Homeward Bound II: Lost In San Francisco (1996)
The three peripatetic pets are off on an odyssey through the urban wilderness when a mishap at the airport strands the trio in San Francisco and forces them to survive on the city streets while befriending local dogs and cats. Exciting and funny follow-up to the family hit features the voices of Sally Field, Michael J. Fox, Ralph Waite and Sinbad. 89 min.
11-2019 Was $19.99 ❑*$14.99*

Summer Magic (1963)
Delightful Disney family film, based on the book "Mother Carey's Chickens," about widow Dorothy McGuire and her children working to keep their family together in a small town in turn-of-the-century Maine. Hayley Mills, Eddie Hodges, Deborah Walley and Burl Ives also star. 100 min.
11-1154 Was $19.99 ❑*$14.99*

The Moon-Spinners (1964)
A teenager on vacation in Greece with her aunt becomes involved in a search for jewel thieves and finds adventure, danger and romance in this thrilling Disney drama. Hayley Mills, Peter McEnery, Eli Wallach, Joan Greenwood and Pola Negri star. 118 min.
11-1210 Was $19.99 ❑*$14.99*

The Misadventures Of Merlin Jones (1964)
Tommy Kirk and Annette Funicello star in this slapstick Disney comedy about a college "genius" whose latest invention, a mind-reading machine, backfires and lands him in hot water with a judge. With Leon Ames. 90 min.
11-1285 *$14.99*

The Monkey's Uncle (1965)
Wacky teen inventor Merlin Jones is up to his old tricks in this comedy for the whole family, trying out the "sleep-teaching" experiment he performed on his pet chimp on some schoolmates who need his help to pass a big test. Tommy Kirk, Annette Funicello, Leon Ames, Arthur O'Connell star. 90 min.
11-1286 *$14.99*

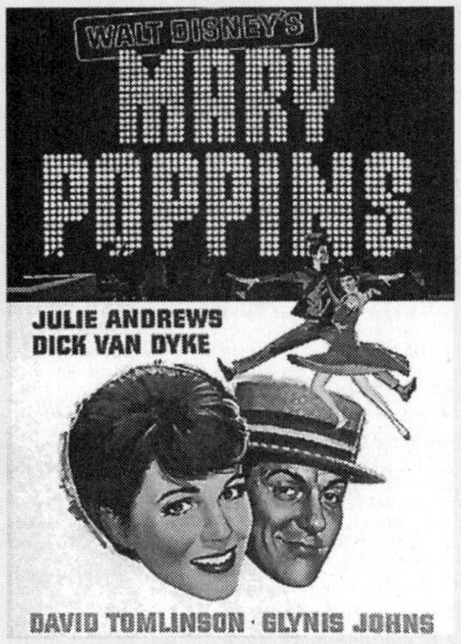

WALT DISNEY'S
MARY POPPINS
JULIE ANDREWS
DICK VAN DYKE
DAVID TOMLINSON · GLYNIS JOHNS

Mary Poppins (1964)
Julie Andrews won an Oscar in her film debut as the "supercalifragilisticexpialidocious" nanny who brings magic and joy to the Banks family in turn-of-the-century London. Fanciful adaptation of P.L. Travers' books co-stars Dick Van Dyke, David Tomlinson, Glynis Johns and Ed Wynn. The score by Richard and Robert Sherman includes "A Spoonful of Sugar," "Let's Go Fly a Kite," "Chim Chim Cheree." 139 min.
11-1013 ❑*$22.99*

That Darn Cat (1965)
A funny feline frolic about how a mischievous cat helps lead owner Hayley Mills and FBI agent Dean Jones to a hostage held by bank robbers Neville Brand and Frank Gorshin. Great support from Dorothy Provine, Elsa Lanchester and Ed Wynn. 116 min.
11-1153 Was $19.99 ❑*$14.99*

That Darn Cat (1997)
The '60s Disney favorite gets a lively updating in this frenetic family comedy, as bored teenage Christina Ricci stumbles onto a kidnapping plot with the help of her pet cat D.C. Only novice FBI agent Doug E. Doug will believe Ricci's story as they set out to crack the case. With Dyan Cannon, Peter Boyle and original "That Darn Cat" co-star Dean Jones. 89 min.
11-2154 Was $19.99 ❑*$14.99*

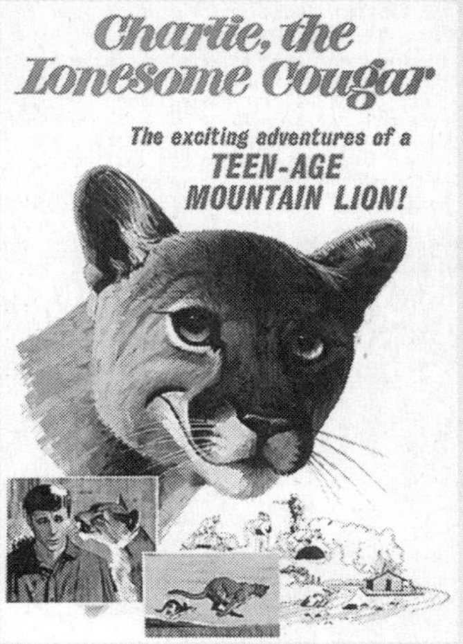

Charlie, the Lonesome Cougar
The exciting adventures of a TEEN-AGE MOUNTAIN LION!

Charlie, The Lonesome Cougar (1967)
Delightful comedy-adventure from Disney about an abandoned cougar kitten raised by loggers as their camp's "mascot," but forced to learn to fend for himself in the wilderness years later. Rex Allen narrates. 75 min.
11-1245 *$14.99*

The Happiest Millionaire (1967)
The last Disney film to be overseen by Walt himself, this lively musical follows the exploits of the rich, eccentric Biddle family, whose lavish home contains live alligators and a Bible-and-boxing school, in 1916 Philadelphia. Fred MacMurray, Greer Garson, Geraldine Page, Tommy Steele and, in their screen debuts, John Davidson and Lesley Ann Warren. The Sherman Brothers ("Mary Poppins") score includes "I'll Always Be Irish," "Let's Have a Drink on It" and "Fortuosity." 144 min.
11-1099 *$14.99*

The Happiest Millionaire (Letterboxed Collector's Edition)
Also available in a theatrical, widescreen format.
08-8761 *$14.99*

The Horse In The Gray Flannel Suit (1968)
A horse named Aspercel takes Madison Avenue by storm in this live-action Disney comedy starring Dean Jones as a harried ad executive who sees the steeplechase steed as the answer to getting closer to his daughter and saving his job. Diane Baker, Lloyd Bochner, Ellen Janov and Kurt Russell also star. 112 min.
11-1371 Was $19.99 ❑*$14.99*

The Love Bug (1969)
A Volkswagen named Herbie with a mind of his own helps new owner Dean Jones find success at the race-track and romance with pretty Michelle Lee in this Disney favorite that spawned three sequels. With Buddy Hackett, David Tomlinson. 108 min.
11-1008 ❑*$19.99*

Herbie Rides Again (1975)
It's high-octane fun when that feisty little automobile, Herbie the Love Bug, returns to help an old lady save her home from a building developer. Ken Berry, Stefanie Powers, Helen Hayes, Keenan Wynn star. 88 min.
11-1036 Was $19.99 ❑*$14.99*

Herbie Goes To Monte Carlo (1977)
The free-wheeling Volkswagen returns for all-new mischief in Monaco. While owner Dean Jones is racing in Europe, Herbie tries to keep him away from smugglers who have hidden jewels in the car. Julie Sommars and Don Knotts also star in this souped-up laughfest. 91 min.
11-1136 Was $19.99 *$14.99*

Herbie Goes Bananas (1980)
There's full-throttle Disney family fun South of the Border, as that lovable little car revs his engine to help his new owners win a race in Brazil. Harvey Korman, Cloris Leachman and Charles Martin Smith are Herbie's human co-stars. 91 min.
11-1137 Was $19.99 *$14.99*

The Love Bug (1997)
Everyone's favorite Volkswagen, Herbie, is back, playing matchmaker for Alexandra Wentworth and mechanic/racer Bruce Campbell and squaring off against his "evil twin," in this fun-filled updating of the Disney classic. With John Hannah, Kevin J. O'Connor, and a cameo by original "Love Bug" star Dean Jones. 88 min.
11-2407 ❑*$99.99*

The Boatniks (1970)
It's a shipful of laughs as a young Coast Guard officer in an ocean resort tangles with a gang of inept seafaring jewel thieves. All smiles on deck with Robert Morse, Phil Silvers, Stefanie Powers, Wally Cox and Norman Fell. 99 min.
11-1098 *$14.99*

The Computer Wore Tennis Shoes (1970)

A freak electrical accident turns an average college student named Dexter Riley (Kurt Russell) into a genius by filling his brain with the campus' new computer's memory banks. Can Russell use his new-found smarts to save the college by winning a quiz show? Fun-filled Disney comedy also stars Joe Flynn, Cesar Romero, William Schallert. 90 min.
11-1221   Was $19.99   ☐$14.99

Now You See Him, Now You Don't (1972)

Accident-prone collegian Dexter Riley (Kurt Russell) makes like Claude Rains after he invents an invisibility spray and uses it to halt the takeover of his financially-strapped school by gangster Cesar Romero, who has his own designs on the fantastic potion. Joe Flynn, Jim Backus, William Windom and Joyce Menges co-star in the second entry in the Disney series. 88 min.
11-1222   ☐$14.99

The Strongest Man In The World (1975)

Put-upon collegian Dexter Riley (Kurt Russell), who gained super-smarts in "The Computer Wore Tennis Shoes" and vanished in "Now You See Him, Now You Don't," becomes a campus Hercules when he eats a breakfast cereal that contains an experimental strength formula. Joe Flynn, Cesar Romero, Eve Arden and Phil Silvers co-star. 92 min.
11-1253   Was $19.99   ☐$14.99

The Barefoot Executive (1971)

Kurt Russell plays a TV network mailroom clerk whose girlfriend's pet chimp can select the top-rated show in any time slot. Russell uses the ape's ability to climb up the corporate ladder, but when the secret is exposed, everyone wants the program-picking primate for themselves. Slapstick satire also stars Joe Flynn, Wally Cox, Heather North. 95 min.
11-1224   Was $19.99   ☐$14.99

Napoleon And Samantha (1972)

Following his grandfather's death, an orphan boy (Johnny Whitaker) and his pet lion are joined by a fellow runaway (Jodie Foster, in her film debut) on an exciting odyssey across the American Northwest. Action-filled Disney feature also stars Michael Douglas as the mountain man who befriends the youngsters. 91 min.
11-1332 $14.99

Napoleon And Samantha (Letterboxed Version)

Also available in a theatrical, widescreen format.
08-8772 $14.99

One Little Indian (1973)

Offbeat Western comedy/drama from Disney stars James Garner as an AWOL Cavalry soldier who finds his escape complicated when he gets involved with an Indian boy and a camel. Co-stars Clay O'Brien, Vera Miles and Jodie Foster. 90 min.
11-1307 $14.99

One Little Indian (Letterboxed Version)

Also available in a theatrical, widescreen format.
08-8844 $14.99

The Castaway Cowboy (1974)

Exciting family film stars James Garner as a Texas cowpoke who is shipwrecked on the Hawaiian island of Kauai in the late 1800s. Rescued by a young boy, Garner comes to the aid of the lad's mother, widowed farmer Vera Miles, and helps her save her land from villain Robert Culp. 91 min.
11-1110 $14.99

Superdad (1974)

In this comedy from the Disney studios, Bob Crane is a father who begins immersing himself in the activities of his teenage daughter and her buddies, from water-skiing to surfing, in order to get closer to her. With Kurt Russell, Kathleen Cody, Barbara Rush, Joe Flynn, Dick Van Patten. 93 min.
11-1207 $12.99

The Island At The Top Of The World (1974)

A rescue expedition to a volcanic region of the Arctic finds a remote valley where a tribe of Viking warriors has lived unchanged for centuries. The explorers must fight natural and man-made menaces to escape in this exciting Disney adventure. David Hartman, Donald Sinden, Mako star. 95 min.
11-1057 $14.99

The Island At The Top Of The World (Letterboxed Version)

Also available in a theatrical, widescreen format.
08-8728 $14.99

The Bears And I (1974)

Vietnam vet Patrick Wayne, eager to start a new life in the Pacific Northwest wilderness, gets more than he bargained for when he becomes a "parent" to three bear cubs and gets involved in a dispute between townsfolk and Indians. With Chief Dan George, Andrew Duggan. 88 min.
11-1244 $14.99

The Bears And I (Letterboxed Version)

Also available in a theatrical, widescreen format.
08-8773 $14.99

Escape To Witch Mountain (1975)

Two young children with supernatural powers, while searching to learn their origin, are pursued by an evil business magnate who wants to control them in this exciting Disney thriller. Eddie Albert, Ray Milland, Kim Richards and Ike Eisenmann star. 94 min.
11-1005   ☐$19.99

One Of Our Dinosaurs Is Missing (1975)

Set in London, this thrilling Disney family adventure stars Helen Hayes and Joan Sims as nannies who must recover secret microfilm hidden in dinosaur fossils by a British lord. Also after the microfilm is a crafty Chinese intelligence agent, played by Peter Ustinov. Clive Revill and Derek Nimmo also star. 101 min.
11-1343 $14.99

Gus (1976)

Gus, a field goal-kicking mule from Yugoslavia, is enlisted by the owner of the hapless California Atoms to help his football team. Soon, the animal's efforts help the Atoms win games, despite the efforts of some crooks to cool Gus' hot streak. Ed Asner, Don Knotts, Tim Conway, Gary Grimes, Bob Crane, Dick Enberg and Stu Nahan of "Captain Philadelphia" fame star. 96 min.
11-1019   ☐$19.99

The Littlest Horse Thieves (1976)

In Yorkshire, England, in 1909, three children try to liberate a group of ponies that are being mistreated in the coal mines. The children's efforts ignite sympathy from the miners, who threaten to strike unless conditions are changed. Alastair Sim, Peter Barkworth and Maurice Colbourne star in this Disney live-action drama. 104 min.
11-1317 $14.99

The Littlest Horse Thieves (Letterboxed Version)

Also available in a theatrical, widescreen format.
08-8758 $14.99

The World's Greatest Athlete (1976)

Losing college coaches John Amos and Tim Conway find the answer to their prayers when, while on an African vacation, they discover super-athletic jungle boy Jan-Michael Vincent. Winning Disney comedy also stars Roscoe Lee Browne, Howard Cosell. 89 min.
11-1355 $14.99

No Deposit, No Return (1976)

Great family comedy about two kids who are left to stay with their grandfather while their mother vacations in Hong Kong. The siblings hire a pair of bumbling crooks to "kidnap" them so they can fly out to be with her. David Niven, Don Knotts, Darren McGavin, Kim Richards and Brad Savage star. 112 min.
11-1358 $19.99

Candleshoe (1977)

Orphan Jodie Foster is trained by a pair of con artists to pass herself off as wealthy widow Helen Hayes' long-lost granddaughter in this exciting family adventure. David Niven, Leo McKern, Vivian Pickles also star. 101 min.
11-1157 $14.99

Candleshoe (Letterboxed Version)

Also available in a theatrical, widescreen format.
08-8771 $14.99

The Cat From Outer Space (1978)

A U.F.O. crash lands on Earth and its occupant, a telepathic alien feline called Jake, turns to a local physicist for help in repairing his ship before Army scientists track him down. Fun-filled family fare from the Disney studios stars Ken Berry, Sandy Duncan, Harry Morgan, Roddy McDowall. 103 min.
11-1079 $14.99

The Cat From Outer Space (Letterboxed Version)

Also available in a theatrical, widescreen format.
08-8733 $14.99

Hot Lead And Cold Feet (1978)

Rip-roaring western comedy stars Jim Dale in a dual role as twin brothers (one a ruthless gunslinger, the other a meek missionary) who compete in a wild obstacle race to see who'll control the family fortune and a frontier town. With Don Knotts, Karen Valentine, Darren McGavin. 90 min.
11-1006 $14.99

A JOURNEY THAT BEGINS WHERE EVERYTHING ENDS

THE BLACK HOLE

The Black Hole (1979)

Dazzling special effects highlight this Disney sci-fi spectacle, as the crew of an exploratory spaceship becomes the prisoners of an obsessed scientist and his robot allies at the edge of a mysterious black hole. Maximilian Schell, Ernest Borgnine, Robert Forster, Yvette Mimieux, Anthony Perkins star. 105 min.
11-1003 $14.99

The Black Hole (Letterboxed Version)

Also available in a theatrical, widescreen format.
08-8724 $14.99

The North Avenue Irregulars (1979)

In this hit Disney comedy, Edward Herrmann is a newly appointed minister who causes controversy by delegating church responsibilities to a group of feisty neighborhood women, including Barbara Harris, Cloris Leachman and Karen Valentine. When Herrmann discovers that city officials are tied to a bookie ring, he and the women tackle local criminals. With Susan Clark, Patsy Kelly. 100 min.
11-1009 $14.99

The North Avenue Irregulars (Letterboxed Version)

Also available in a theatrical, widescreen format.
08-8757 $14.99

Unidentified Flying Oddball (1979)

When klutzy astronaut Dennis Dugan takes off on a routine space flight, he doesn't expect to be thrown back through time to the court of King Arthur, but that's what happens in this laugh-filled updating of "A Connecticut Yankee in King Arthur's Court." Ron Moody, Kenneth More co-star. 92 min.
11-1341 $14.99

Unidentified Flying Oddball (Letterboxed Version)

Also available in a theatrical, widescreen format.
08-8734 $14.99

The Watcher In The Woods (1980)

An American family rents an English manor house that is haunted by the spirit of a young girl, and only the family's two children and an elderly woman can solve the unearthly reason for her presence. Scares, Disney-style, with Bette Davis, Lynn-Holly Johnson, Carroll Baker, Kyle Richards. 83 min.
11-1049   Was $19.99 $14.99

The Watcher In The Woods (Letterboxed Collector's Edition)

Also available in a theatrical, widescreen format.
11-2273 $14.99

The Last Flight Of Noah's Ark (1980)

Down-and-out pilot Elliott Gould is hired to fly a planeload of animals to a Pacific island for missionary Genevieve Bujold, but runs into trouble when the plane is forced to land on a remote island and a pair of young stowaways is discovered. Comedy/adventure also stars Ricky Schroder, Tammy Lauren. 97 min.
11-2274 $14.99

The Last Flight Of Noah's Ark (Letterboxed Collector's Edition)

Also available in a theatrical, widescreen format.
11-1056 $14.99

Amy (1981)

A poignant and inspiring drama about a young woman who leaves her wealthy but domineering husband after their deaf son dies to take a job as a teacher in a backwoods school for the deaf. Jenny Agutter, Barry Newman star. 100 min.
11-1027 $14.99

The Devil And Max Devlin (1981)

Disney-produced comedy featuring Elliott Gould as a mean-spirited landlord who is sent "down under" after he's run over by a bus. The devil, played by Bill Cosby, makes an offer: find three untainted souls for Hell and Max is free. Susan Anspach, Adam Rich also star. 95 min.
11-1033 $14.99

Condorman (1981)

There's loads of high-flying comedy and thrills when a shy cartoonist gets mixed up with spies while visiting Europe and becomes his own comic-strip hero, the winged Condorman. Michael Crawford, Barbara Carrera, Oliver Reed star. 90 min.
11-1034 $14.99

Condorman (Letterboxed Version)

Also available in a theatrical, widescreen format.
08-8727 $14.99

The Journey Of Natty Gann (1985)

A young girl undertakes a danger-filled journey across 1930s America to join her father and is aided by a teenage hobo and a tame wolf in this exciting family drama. Meredith Salenger, John Cusack and Ray Wise star. 101 min.
11-1324 $19.99

Miracle Down Under (1987)

A group of settlers in the arid bush country of 19th-century Australia face one obstacle after another in their struggle to tame the frontier in this rousing family adventure. Stars Dee Wallace Stone, John Waters; directed by George Miller ("The Man from Snowy River"). 101 min.
11-1442   ☐$29.99

Not Quite Human (1987)

A scientist builds an artificial human and sends the android teen—whom he names Chip—to school with his human daughter to learn how to interact with real people. But the inventor's former employers, a ruthless toy company, try to steal the plans to his creation. Alan Thicke, Joseph Bologna, Jay Underwood and Robyn Lively star.
11-1709   ☐$19.99

Still Not Quite Human (1992)

The further adventures of Chip the teenage android find him going into battle against a nasty business tycoon who has abducted his inventor "dad." Chip creates his own creature, a Dad lookalike, and then faces dastardly robot Spartacus. Alan Thicke, Jay Underwood, Ken Pogue, Betsy Palmer star.
11-1711   ☐$39.99

WHITE FANG

White Fang (1991)

Sprawling, beautiful filmization of Jack London's classic tale. A boy discovers adventure and camaraderie with an orphaned Alaskan husky in the Klondike during the Alaskan Gold Rush. Klaus Maria Brandauer and Ethan Hawke star in this thrilling, family-oriented epic. 107 min.
11-1559   Was $19.99   ☐$14.99

White Fang 2: Myth Of The White Wolf (1994)

This sequel to Disney's hit treatment of the Jack London story finds White Fang's owner, Henry, being discovered by a Native American girl who brings him to her tribe. Along with White Fang, Henry is recruited to track down a missing caribou herd whose migration has been halted by a nasty miner. With Scott Bairstow, Charmaine Craig and Joss Ackland. 106 min.
11-1824   Was $19.99   ☐$14.99

Wild Hearts Can't Be Broken (1991)

Sensitive, true-life story of Sonora Webster, an orphan living in Depression-era Georgia who joins a travelling carnival as the rider in their "diving horse" attraction. A bad dive leaves her blind, but she overcomes her handicap to become a star rider at Atlantic City's famed Steel Pier. Gabrielle Anwar, Cliff Robertson, Michael Schoeffling star. 89 min.
11-1584   Was $19.99   ☐$14.99

The Mighty Ducks (1992)
"Slap Shot" meets "The Bad News Bears" in this surprise hit comedy with Emilio Estevez as a cynical lawyer who's given community service after a driving violation. His duty: coach an inept pee-wee ice hockey team. Along the way, players and coach learn some valuable lessons about winning. Lane Smith, Joss Ackland co-star. 104 min.
11-1675   Was $19.99   ☐$14.99

D2: The Mighty Ducks (1994)
The ragtag bunch of rink rejects who skated their way to a championship (no, not the '94 Rangers!) and coach Emilio Estevez are back for all-new ice-capades, as the Ducks represent the United States in the Junior Goodwill Games hockey event and take on a polished squad from Iceland. Michael Tucker, Kathryn Erbe co-star. 106 min.
11-1804   ☐$14.99

D3: The Mighty Ducks (1996)
After winning an important tournament, the Ducks travel to an exclusive academy for some further education and a chance to flex their hockey muscles. But they find lots of roadblocks in their way, from the strong-armed tactics of the varsity team to a replacement for coach Emilio Estevez. Jeffrey Nordling and David Selby also star. 104 min.
11-2098   ☐$14.99

A Far Off Place (1993)
Enthralling, gorgeously photographed African adventure about two teenagers who are left to fend for themselves in the Kalahari desert after their camp is attacked by poachers. They enlist the help of a great white hunter and a Bushman in order to survive in the jungle. Reese Witherspoon, Ethan Randall, Jack Thompson and Maximilian Schell star. 107 min.
11-1733   Was $19.99   ☐$14.99

Heidi (1993)
An orphaned girl is sent to live with her reclusive grandfather in the Swiss Alps and wins the bitter old man over with her bright spirit, but their happiness is threatened in this enchanting Disney Channel production. Jason Robards, Jane Seymour and Patricia Neal head the superb cast. 165 min.
11-1813   Was $19.99   ☐$14.99

The Jungle Book (1994)
The first live-action remake by the Disney studio of one of their animated films, this exciting adventure stars Jason Scott Lee as Kipling's wild child Mowgli, raised by wolves in the Indian jungle and thrust back into "civilization" 20 years later to find romance, a jealous rival, and a search for a lost treasure. With Lena Headey, Sam Neill, Cary Elwes, John Cleese. 111 min.
11-1877   Was $19.99   ☐$14.99

The Jungle Book (Letterboxed Version)
Also available in a theatrical, widescreen format.
11-1882   Was $22.99   ☐$14.99

The Jungle Book: Mowgli's Story (1998)
Follow the early days of the "man-cub" who could talk to the animals in this all-new, live-action Disney feature that serves as a "prequel" to the 1994 film, as Mowgli and his adopted wolf family face an array of friends and foes in the jungles of India. Brandon Baker stars as Mowgli; voices by Eartha Kitt, Brian Doyle Murray, Kathy Najimy. 77 min.
11-2778   Was $19.99   ☐$14.99

Iron Will (1994)
Enthralling, true-life family saga about the adventures of Will Stoneman, a teenager from a turn-of-the-century South Dakota farm who enters a grueling 500-mile dog sled race from Winnipeg, Canada, to Minneapolis in order to win the $10,000 prize to help his debt-ridden family. Mackenzie Astin, Kevin Spacey and David Ogden Stiers star. 109 min.
11-1792   Was $19.99   ☐$14.99

Blank Check (1994)
After his bike is run over by a notorious mobster, an 11-year-old boy is handed a blank check, which he promptly fills in for $1 million and begins having the time of his life, investing in go-carts, gadgets, a chauffeur and even a girlfriend. Then the gangster returns, wondering where his cash went. Brian Bonsall, Miguel Ferrer, Karen Duffy, Michael Lerner star. 93 min.
11-1796   Was $19.99   ☐$14.99

Squanto: A Warrior's Tale (1994)
This stirring true story centers on Squanto, the Native American brave abducted by English traders and taken to Great Britain, where he's put on display. After fleeing from his captors, Squanto befriends a clergyman who inspires him to return to America, where he seeks peace between the Indians and the Pilgrim settlers. Adam Beach, Mandy Patinkin and Michael Gambon star. 102 min.
11-1887   Was $89.99   ☐$14.99

Angels In The Outfield (1994)
Convinced that the key to reuniting with his estranged father is to pray for the hapless California Angels to win the pennant, a boy finds his request answered by some heavenly helpers only he can see. A charming and fun-filled updating of the '50s diamond comedy, co-starring Danny Glover as the brash California manager and Christopher Lloyd as his angelic counterpart; with Tony Danza, Brenda Fricker. 102 min.
11-1853   Was $19.99   ☐$14.99

Angels In The Endzone (1997)
Sports-loving angel Al (Christopher Lloyd), who turned a baseball team around in "Angels in the Outfield," is back to lend a little heavenly help to a hapless high-school football squad in this family fun-filled follow-up.
11-2246   Was $19.99   ☐$14.99

Tall Tale: The Unbelievable Adventure (1995)
Mythical folk heroes Pecos Bill, John Henry, and Paul Bunyan and Babe the Blue Ox come to life to help a young boy save his family's farm from a greedy industrialist after it in this exhilarating Disney adventure. Patrick Swayze, Oliver Platt, Scott Glenn, Roger Aaron Brown and Nick Stahl star.
11-1927   Was $89.99   ☐$14.99

Heavyweights (1995)
The less-than-athletic kids of Camp Hope—a camp for overweight children—put their pound problems aside and join forces to overthrow the camp's tyrannical new fitness instructor and challenge the rival youths across the lake in a hilarious sports competition. Rousing underdog comedy stars Aaron Schwartz, Tom McGowan and Ben Stiller. 97 min.
11-1928   Was $89.99   ☐$14.99

The Big Green (1995)
Trying to build self-confidence in her new students, British-born teacher Olivia D'Abo starts a youth soccer team in a small Texas town with help from deputy sheriff Steve Guttenberg, and quicker than you can say "goalgoalgoalgoal," the ragtag bunch is heading for the state championship in this high-kicking family comedy. 99 min.
11-1959   Was $19.99   ☐$14.99

A Kid In King Arthur's Court (1995)
Mark Twain's "A Connecticut Yankee" story gets a contemporary updating in this live-action Disney romp, as a California Little Leaguer falls through the Earth during an earthquake and finds himself in fabled Camelot, where he uses 20th-century technology to help Merlin save King Arthur's throne and woos a pretty princess. Thomas Ian Nicholas, Joss Ackland, Paloma Baeza star. 90 min.
11-1960   Was $19.99   ☐$14.99

Tom And Huck (1995)
Those immortal Mark Twain heroes, Tom Sawyer and Huck Finn, are given the Disney treatment in this colorful and exciting family film. Jonathan Taylor Thomas (TV's "Home Improvement") is Tom and Brad Renfro ("The Client") is Huck. Follow their adventures with Becky Thatcher, Injun Joe and other characters along the Mississippi. With Eric Schweig. 92 min.
11-2006   Was $19.99   ☐$14.99

Operation Dumbo Drop (1995)
Set in Vietnam in 1968, this raucous comedy with sensitive moments stars Ray Liotta and Danny Glover as Green Berets given the assignment of transporting a huge elephant to a friendly village whose people lost their previous pachyderm to the Viet Cong. Joining them on this impossible mission that takes them 200 miles through the jungle are Denis Leary, Doug E. Doug and Corin Nemec. 108 min.
11-1967   Was $89.99   ☐$14.99

First Kid (1996)
Secret Service agent Sinbad dreamed of working in the White House, but he didn't count on acting as an official babysitter for the president's bratty son. After helping the boy cope with his always-busy father and uptight mom, however, kid-watcher and "first kid" become close pals. Brock Pierce, Robert Guillaume also star in this sweet and silly family comedy. 103 min.
11-2078   Was $99.99   ☐$14.99

101 Dalmatians (1996)
The Disney animated classic gets a hit live-action reworking with Glenn Close as the flamboyant Cruella De Vil, an evil fashion mogul looking for the perfect fur coat and setting her sights on canine couple Pongo and Perdita's spotted litter. Jeff Daniels and Joely Richardson co-star as the dogs' human owners. 103 min.
11-2108   ☐$14.99

Oliver Twist (1997)
Charles Dickens' perennially popular orphan boy, who struggles to escape a life of hardship on the streets of Victorian London, comes to life in this feature-length drama from TV's "The Wonderful World of Disney." Alex Trench stars as Oliver, with Elijah Wood as the Artful Dodger and Richard Dreyfuss as Fagin.
11-2211   Was $19.99   ☐$14.99

Jungle 2 Jungle (1997)
Wall Street broker Tim Allen gets a big surprise when he travels to the wilds of Venezuela to get divorce papers signed by long-estranged wife JoBeth Williams, a doctor living with a remote native tribe: he's the father of a 13-year-old son! A comical "culture clash" erupts when Allen brings the jungle-raised boy back to New York with him for a visit in this frantic family outing. With Martin Short, Lolita Davidovitch and Sam Huntington. 105 min.
11-2137   Was $19.99   ☐$14.99

Air Bud (1997)
He's the strangest looking basketball player since Dennis Rodman—a golden retriever named Buddy who uses his snout to sink baskets and is ready to lead his new owner's school's team to victory—in this fun family tale. Kevin Zegers, Bill Cobbs, Wendy Makkena, Michael Jeter and Buddy, as himself, star. 98 min.
11-2193   Was $19.99   ☐$14.99

Air Bud: Golden Receiver (1998)
In this sequel to the hit canine comedy, Buddy the pooch lends his athletic prowess to his pal Josh's losing football team, serving as a star receiver. While Buddy and Josh help their once-hapless team, two mysterious Russians try to kidnap the dog for their travelling circus. With Kevin Zegers, Gregory Harrison, Cynthia Stevenson and Nora Dunn. 91 min.
11-2809   Was $19.99   ☐$14.99

Air Bud: World Pup (2000)
Move over, Pelé, because everyone's favorite golden retriever is back again, and this time soccer is the name of his game. Buddy gets to kick the ball around with U.S. women's champions Brandi Chastain, Brianna Scurry and Tisha Venturini. He also manages to become a father of several cute pups that he must eventually save from some clumsy kidnappers. 83 min.
11-2469   ☐$19.99

BRENDAN FRASER

George Of The Jungle (1997)
Brendan Fraser tries to "watch out for that tree" as the cartoon jungle hero with the rock-hard body—and the head to match—in this laugh-filled live-action adventure. See how young George is raised by the faithful Ape, watch his first meeting with the lovely Ursula, and witness George running amuck in the big city to save her from her rapscallious fiancé. With Leslie Mann, Thomas Hayden Church, and John Cleese as the voice of Ape. 92 min.
11-2192   Was $19.99   ☐$14.99

Mail To The Chief (1999)
Randy Quaid is U.S. President A. Thorton Osgood III, who, while in the middle of re-election plans, is persuaded by his Chief of Staff to correspond with ordinary citizens on the Internet. Using the name "Average Joe," Quaid begins exchanging messages with "Big Jack W"—in reality, a 13-year-old who offers sage political advice. With Holland Taylor, Bill Switzer. 90 min.
11-2484   ☐$99.99

Smart House (1999)
A widower and his young son and daughter win a "Smart House"—a fully computerized home—in a contest. Named PAT (Persona Applied Technology), the house can be programmed to do just about anything. When the boy realizes his father is getting close to the Smart House's annoying creator, he programs PAT to be like his mother, and eventually it comes to life. Kevin Kilner, Katey Jessica Steen and Ryan Merriman star. 90 min.
11-2486   ☐$99.99

Angels In The Infield (2000)
After he makes a disastrous mistake in a game that costs his team the pennant, pitcher Patrick Warburton has a tough time. But when his 13-year-old daughter wishes for some heavenly help, it comes in the form of David Alan Grier, a deceased ballplayer trying to earn his wings. Rebecca Jenkins, Kurt Fuller and Colin Fox also star.
11-2479   ☐$99.99

RocketMan (1997)
Hapless NASA computer expert Harland Williams is tapped to replace a grounded scientist on the first manned flight to Mars, and nearly wrecks the mission with his ineptitude, in this spaced-out slapstick comedy from the Disney studio. Jessica Lundy, William Sadler, Beau Bridges also star. 94 min.
11-2231   Was $19.99   ☐$14.99

Rodgers & Hammerstein's
Cinderella

Rodgers & Hammerstein's Cinderella (1997)
Teen pop star Brandy plays the title role, and Whitney Houston is the fairy godmother who makes her dreams come true, in this lavish rendition of Rodgers and Hammerstein's musical take on the timeless fairy tale. The wonderful supporting cast includes Jason Alexander, Whoopi Goldberg and Bernadette Peters. Songs include "In My Own Little Room," "Impossible," "Ten Minutes Ago." 88 min.
11-2210   Was $19.99   ☐$14.99

Beverly Hills Family Robinson (1997)
Marsha Robinson, the host of a TV cooking show, thinks she's going on a pleasant vacation with her family on a yacht, but a band of pirates and a dangerous storm help land the clan on a sparsely inhabited island. While trying to make the best of the situation, the Robinsons realize the importance of family. Dyan Cannon, Martin Mull and Sarah Michelle Gellar star. 91 min.
11-2446 $99.99

Toothless (1997)
After getting hit by a car and finding herself in Limbo, dentist Kirstie Alley is dismayed to learn that, before moving on in the afterlife, she must spend time as the Tooth Fairy! Alley's antics as she tries to master flying and the teeth-for-change racket makes for wild family fun. Lynn Redgrave, Dale Midkiff also star.
11-2247   Was $19.99   ☐$14.99

Mr. Magoo (1997)
Leslie Nielsen stumbles his way into one mishap after another as he brings the myopic misadventures of the cartoon codger to life. When a mix-up after a museum theft puts Magoo in possession of a priceless stolen gem, he becomes the target of both the jewel thieves and federal agents. Kelly Lynch, Ernie Hudson, Malcolm McDowell and Matt Keeslar as Magoo's nephew, Waldo, also star. 88 min.
11-2256   Was $19.99   ☐$14.99

The Garbage-Picking Field Goal-Kicking Philadelphia Phenomenon (1998)
Tony Danza is the sanitation engineer with the golden foot who puts his talent to use as the newest member of the Philadelphia Eagles, only to discover that success on the gridiron threatens his homelife, in this fast-paced family film.
11-2248   Was $19.99   ☐$14.99

Goldrush (1998)
A young woman (Alyssa Milano) leaves her upper-class home and joins a group of fortune-hunters seeking gold in 1890s Alaska in this exciting family adventure. Bruce Campbell, William Morgan Shepherd, Stan Cahill also star. 89 min.
11-2376   ☐$99.99

Safety Patrol (1998)
When a crime wave strikes a grade school, the best chances for catching the crooks lie with the school district's incompetent head of security (Leslie Nielsen) and an accident-prone new student (Bug Hall). Todd Hurst, Lainie Kazan and "Weird Al" Yankovic also star in this slapstick caper comedy. 92 min.
11-2277   ☐$99.99

Ruby Bridges (1998)
The moving true story of a 6-year-old New Orleans girl who caught the country's attention when she became her elementary school's first black student in 1960 is told in this "Wonderful World of Disney" production. Michael Beach, Penelope Ann Miller, Lela Rochon, and Chaz Monet as Ruby star. 88 min.
11-2395   ☐$99.99

Noah (1998)
In this modern retelling of the famous Biblical story, Tony Danza plays the man who has 40 days to build a floating zoo, collect the animals two by two and join his sons before it rains. Wallace Shawn, Lloyd Berry, Jane Sibbett co-star. 90 min.
11-2417   ☐$99.99

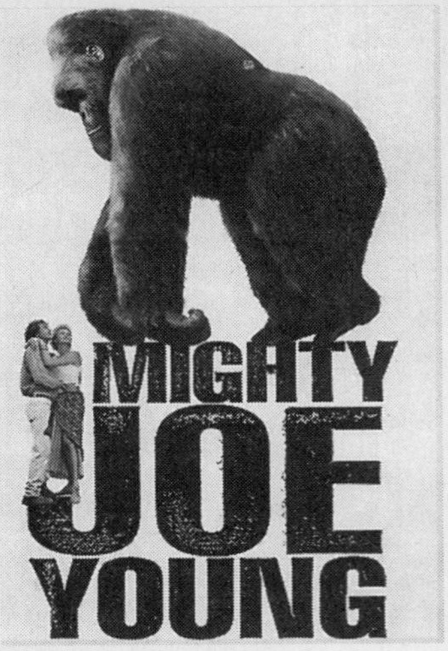

Mighty Joe Young (1998)
Disney's updating of the 1949 adventure classic stars Charlize Theron as a young woman whose best friend since both of them were orphaned is a 15-foot-tall gorilla named Joe. When poachers threaten the safety of their African jungle home, Theron agrees to a plan by scientist Bill Paxton to take Joe to a California nature preserve, but mishaps lead to the ape escaping onto the streets of L.A. David Paymer, Rade Sherbedgia also star. 114 min.
11-2309 Was $19.99 ❑*$14.99*

A Knight In Camelot (1998)
In this delightful variation on Mark Twain's "A Connecticut Yankee in King Arthur's Court," Whoopi Goldberg plays a computer expert whose malfunctioning PC sends her back in time to medieval England. Using her trusty laptop, she amazes the Camelot inhabitants, while trying to figure a way to get back to the present. With Michael York, Amanda Donohoe. 89 min.
11-2371 ❑*$99.99*

Murder She Purred: A Mrs. Murphy Mystery (1998)
Based on Rita Mae Brown's Mrs. Murphy novels, this entertaining family mystery stars Ricki Lake as a would-be crimesolver who is aided by a cat named Mrs. Murphy and a dog named Tucker, two sleuthing pets who can talk to each other. With Bruce McGill, Ed Begley, Jr. 88 min.
11-2408 ❑*$99.99*

My Date With The President's Daughter (1998)
Hallie, the teenage daughter of the President of the United States, desperately wants to go out on a date, but that's difficult because of security reasons. She finally gets her chance when she meets geeky Duncan, but their romantic night is packed with all sorts of obstacles and funny incidents. Dabney Coleman, Will Friedle and Elisabeth Harnois star. 90 min.
11-2416 ❑*$99.99*

Tourist Trap (1998)
What should have been a fun-filled—and trouble-free—RV vacation for Daniel Stern and Julie Hagerty and their kids turns into a series of comical catastrophes in this road trip romp for the whole family. David Rasche, Paul Giamatti also star. 89 min.
11-2428 ❑*$99.99*

Flash (1998)
Compelling family drama set in a small Georgia town where Connor, a teenage boy, is given a horse named Flash by his father. But Connor's family's financial status has forced Dad to join the Merchant Marines, leaving the boy with his elderly grandmother. Eventually, Connor learns a lesson about life by making important sacrifices. Lucas Black, Ellen Burstyn, Brian Kerwin star. 90 min.
11-2445 ❑*$99.99*

Principal Takes A Holiday (1998)
John, a prank-loving high school senior, will collect a $10,000 gift from his parents if he can graduate without pulling another trick. When his latest trick, however, leaves the school without a principal, John finds a drifter to take the man's place—and get his mischief-filled records erased in the process! Zachery Ty Bryan, Kevin Nealon and Jessica Steen star in this family comedy. 89 min.
11-2455 ❑*$99.99*

Mr. Headmistress (1998)
Con artist and former convict Harland Williams is on the run from the police, so he hides out at an all-girls' school where he poses as the headmistress. Can he fool everyone, including stodgy assistant headmistress Katey Sagal? With Shawna Waldron and Janet Wright. 89 min.
11-2456 ❑*$99.99*

Summer Of The Monkeys (1998)
A boy sees his opportunity to purchase a pony he adores when he captures four runaway circus chimps with reward money hanging over their heads. Of course, it isn't always so simple to let go of four friends who steal your heart. Wilford Brimley and Michael Ontkean star.
11-2780 Was $19.99 ❑*$14.99*

My Favorite Martian (1999)
Christopher Lloyd is the antennae-headed extraterrestrial stranded on Earth after his ship crashes, and Jeff Daniels is the TV reporter who agrees to disguise him as "Uncle Martin" in exchange for an exclusive story, in Disney's laugh- and effects-filled updating of the popular '60s sitcom. The supporting cast includes Daryl Hannah, Elizabeth Hurley, Wallace Shawn and original TV Martian Ray Walston. 94 min.
11-2334 Was $19.99 ❑*$14.99*

Annie (1999)
Everyone's favorite plucky Depression-era heroine returns to save the day in this all-new presentation of the beloved family musical. Alicia Morton stars in the title role, with Kathy Bates playing scheming orphanage owner Miss Hannigan and Victor Garber as Annie's plutocratic foster pop, Daddy Warbucks. Alan Cumming, Audra McDonald also star. 90 min.
11-2383 ❑*$19.99*

Selma, Lord, Selma (1999)
After hearing a speech by Martin Luther King, an 11-year-old African-American girl takes part in the landmark 1965 civil rights march that threatened to tear Alabama apart. Jurnee Smollett, MacKenzie Astin, Yolanda King and Clifton Powell star in this stirring "Wonderful World of Disney" production. 88 min.
11-2396 ❑*$99.99*

Perfect Game (1999)
Young Cameron Finley dreams of being a baseball star. But when he learns that coach Patrick Duffy picked him and eight other "talentless" kids to fill out his team as part of a bet, they turn to a new skipper, retired minor-leaguer and coach Ed Asner, for help in this fun-filled family diamond tale. Tracy Nelson co-stars. 99 min.
11-2421 Was $19.99 ❑*$14.99*

The Duke (1999)
British nobility goes to the dogs—literally—in this rollicking Disney comedy. An elderly duke wills his estate and title to his faithful canine companion Hubert, but can the new Duke of Dingwall and his human allies stop a scheming relative from taking it all away? James Doohan, Courtnee Draper, Jeremy Maxwell and John Neville star. 88 min.
11-2422 Was $19.99 ❑*$14.99*

A Saintly Switch (1999)
Veteran NFL quarterback David Alan Grier and pregnant wife Vivica A. Fox gain a new appreciation for each other and their family when their kids use a magic spell found in their new house to transfer each parent's spirit into the other's body. Fun-filled family comedy also stars Rue McClanahan, Al Waxman; directed by Peter Bogdanovich. 88 min.
11-2465 ❑*$99.99*

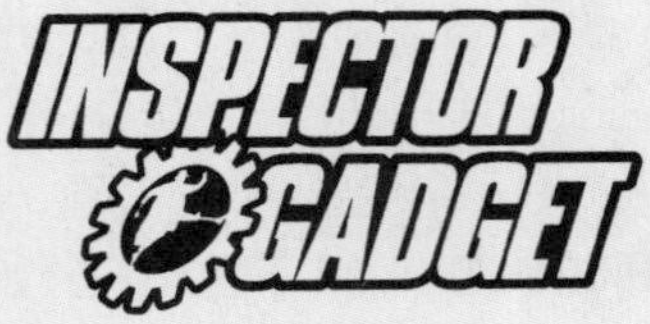

Inspector Gadget (1999)
The popular cartoon crimefighter springs into live-action in this fun-filled adventure starring Matthew Broderick as a hapless security guard who is transformed into a cybernetic super-cop by scientist Joely Fisher. With help from niece Michelle Trachtenberg, a talking car and a host of wacky accessories, Gadget "go goes" against Rupert Everett's evil Claw, who's out to destroy Riverton City. With Dabney Coleman, Andy Dick. 78 min.
11-2364 Was $19.99 ❑*$14.99*

Zenon: Girl Of The 21st Century (2000)
Based on the popular comic strip, this family sci-fi comedy tells of Zenon, a 13-year-old girl who has lived on a space station since she was five. As a punishment for misbehaving, her parents send Zenon to live with relatives on Earth, but can she adapt to "ground-level" culture and get along with other kids her age? Kirsten Storms, Raven-Symone and Stuart Pankin star. 97 min.
11-2480 ❑*$99.99*

Geppetto (2000)
Drew Carey stars in the title role of the lonely toymaker whose wish for a child is granted in the form of a puppet named Pinocchio, in this lively, song-filled rendition of the beloved children's story. With Julia Louis-Dreyfus, Brent Spiner, and Seth Adkins as Pinocchio. 89 min.
11-2437 Was $19.99 ❑*$14.99*

Life-Size (2000)
A girl tries to use magic to bring her late mother back to life, but the spell goes awry and changes her favorite fashion doll into a real woman. Supermodel Tyra Banks portrays the enchanted charmer in this fun-filled Disney fantasy that also stars Lindsay Lohan ("The Parent Trap") and Jere Burns. 89 min.
11-2438 Was $19.99 ❑*$14.99*

Model Behavior (2000)
A small-town high school girl (Maggie Lawson) longs to be more popular, while a New York teen supermodel (also Lawson) seeks a break from her tightly-controlled life, away from the glamour. The two switch places, and humor and romance follow in this Disney reworking of "The Prince and the Pauper." With Jason Timberlake of 'NSYNC, Kathie Lee Gifford and Cody Gifford. 90 min.
11-2464 ❑*$99.99*

Snow Day (2000)
When a record snowstorm shuts down the city of Syracuse, a teenager seizes the chance to win the girl of his dreams with the help of his female pal, who harbors secret feelings for him. Meanwhile, his little sister has her own "snow day" goal: to stop the hated Snowplow Man in his chain-tired tracks. Fun-filled family comedy stars Mark Weber, Zena Grey, Chevy Chase, Jean Smart and Chris Elliott. 89 min.
06-3030 Was $99.99 ❑*$14.99*

Family Tree (2000)
The residents of a small town learn an important lesson, thanks to a young boy's fight to save a very special tree, in this moving family drama. Robert Forster, Naomi Judd, Andy Lawrence, Matt Lawrence and Cliff Robertson star. 90 min.
19-2975 ❑*$19.99*

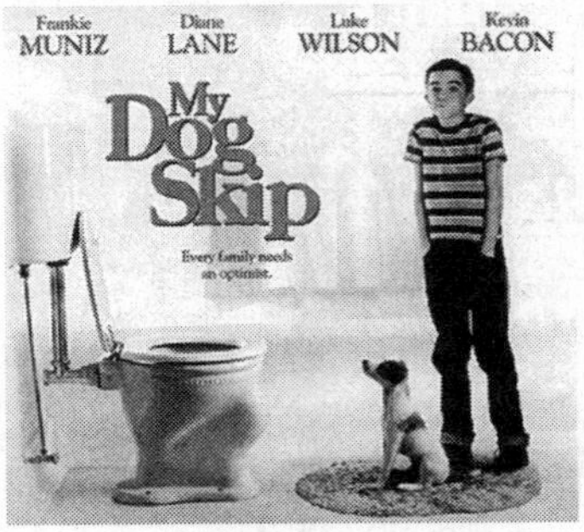

My Dog Skip (2000)
A life-changing friendship forms between a 9-year-old boy in a small town in '40s Mississippi and the precocious terrier he receives as a birthday present in this heartwarming family tale, based on the memoirs of writer Willie Morris. Frankie Muniz (TV's "Malcolm in the Middle"), Diane Lane, Kevin Bacon and Luke Wilson star. 93 min.
19-2983 ❑*$22.99*

Thomas And The Magic Railroad (2000)
From the popular TV program "Thomas the Tank Engine & Friends" comes the little engine's first movie. The Magic Railroad that connects the land of the talking trains to the human world is in danger of being shut down by evil diesel engines, and it's up to Thomas—along with some help from human pals Alec Baldwin, Peter Fonda and Mara Wilson—to foil the plans of Diesel 10 and his henchmen. 84 min.
02-3470 ❑*$22.99*

Mom, Can I Keep Her? (2000)
Timmy Blair, a 12-year-old boy with a busy father, a troublesome stepmother and difficulties at school, makes friends with a 500-pound gorilla who follows him home from school. Soon, Timmy and his new companion are causing all sorts of chaos. Gil Gerard, Kevin Dobson, Justin Berfield, Alana Stewart and Terry Funk star; Fred Olen Ray ("Hollywood Chainsaw Hookers") directs. 90 min
21-9202 *$29.99*

Tons Of Trouble (2000)
There's a trunkful of adventure and laughs in store when a group of kids try to save a friendly elephant from becoming a poacher's prey in this tale for the whole family. John Laughlin, R.D. Call, Lee Purcell and Karen Black star. 92 min.
86-1152 ❑*$99.99*

Snoopers (2000)
Four young treasure-hunters have the adventure of their lives when they try to track down a legendary lost jewel in this exciting family film. Rebecca Keeling, Aled Roberts, Christine Kaufmann star. 100 min.
86-1153 ❑*$99.99*

Ballet Shoes (1991)
The popular family story from Noel Streatfield focuses on three poor orphans who live a sheltered life with their guardian. They are accepted to ballet school, but can their desire help them overcome their dire financial situation? With Angela Thorne, Elizabeth Roman and Sarah Price. 120 min.
53-6817 *$19.99*

Jock Of The Bushveld (1992)
Fine family adventure saga set in turn-of-the-century Africa and focusing on a man who seeks to make a fortune prospecting for gold along with Jock, his trusted dog. When the man gets into all sorts of trouble, Jock helps him out. Gordon Mulholland, Wilson Dunster star. 92 min.
78-3032 *$14.99*

George's Island (1991)
High adventure greets a 10-year-old orphan when he escapes from his cruel foster parents and joins his salty old Grandpa on a trip to a mysterious island where Captain Kidd and ghostly pirates rule the roost. Ian Bannen, Sheila McCarthy and Maury Chaykin star. 89 min.
02-2194 Was $89.99 *$14.99*

Monkey Trouble (1994)
Lovingly rendered family film about a little girl named Eva who wants to have a pet, but is forbidden by her mother and stepfather. She befriends Dodger, a kleptomaniacal monkey who has escaped its mean organ grinder owner, and the two have a series of exciting and funny adventures. Harvey Keitel, Mimi Rogers, Thora Birch, and Finster as Dodger star. 93 min.
02-2654 Was $19.99 ❑*$14.99*

Born Wild (1995)
An inspiring and enchanting drama for the whole family, starring Brooke Shields as a documentary filmmaker in Africa who teams with a conservationist to rescue two orphaned leopard cubs from natural enemies, as well as man. With Martin Sheen, John Varty. 98 min.
02-2830 Was $89.99 ❑*$14.99*

Prince Brat And The Whipping Boy (1995)
In this family adventure, a young prince with a nasty attitude is kidnapped along with a poor orphan boy, and their identities are confused by the inept culprits. After a series of exciting events, the prince learns a lesson about royalty and friendship. Truan Munro, Nic Knight, Mathilda May, George C. Scott and Vincent Schiavelli star. 96 min.
02-2837 Was $89.99 ❑*$14.99*

Magic In The Water (1995)
A lonely young girl goes with her older brother and divorced dad for a summer vacation at a lakeside British Columbia town where reports of a "sea monster" have circulated for years. When the child sees and makes friends with the gigantic "Orky," the pair form a special bond that helps them both in this enchanting family film. Mark Harmon, Sarah Wayne, Harley Jane Kozak star. 101 min.
02-2868 Was $19.99 ❑*$14.99*

Buddy (1997)
Buddy is an adorable baby gorilla who becomes the newest member of eccentric socialite Rene Russo's animal-filled household, but can Russo resist the temptation to raise Buddy like a human child and "civilize" him? Based on a true story, this charming family film from Jim Henson Productions also stars Robbie Coltrane, Alan Cumming. 85 min.
02-3127 Was $19.99 ❑*$14.99*

Madeline (1998)
Based on the beloved series of children's books by Ludwig Bemelman, this endearing family film tells of Madeline, an orphan who lives at a charity-run boarding school in Paris and has a knack for continually getting into trouble, particularly with Miss Clavel, the school's supervisor. Frances McDormand, Nigel Hawthorne and Hatty Jones star. 89 min.
02-3217 Was $24.99 ❑*$14.99*

The Sand Fairy (1991)
A children's fantasy from England about a little, magical creature found by five children while vacationing at a manor home near the seashore who offers to make their wildest dreams come true. Based on the book "Five Children and It" by Edith Nesbit. 139 min.
04-2706 Was $29.99 *$14.99*

Captains Courageous (1995)
Lively adaptation of the Rudyard Kipling novel follows the adventures of a spoiled businessman's son who is picked up after being lost at sea by a fishing vessel and learns valuable lessons in maturity and courage from one of the ship's crew. Robert Urich, Kenny Vadas, Duncan Fraser star. 93 min.
58-5223 Was $79.99 ❑*$14.99*

Little Ninjas (1990)
There's plenty of high-kicking family fun in this tale of three mite-sized martial artists who get mixed up in a rebellion on a South Seas island and are given the map to a priceless treasure. The island's wicked prime minister chases the kids halfway around the world to regain the map. Douglas Ivan, Steven Nelson star. 85 min.
68-1257 Was $89.99 ❑*$14.99*

Frankenstein & Me (1995)
A young boy's obsession with monster movies leads him to recover a missing carnival sideshow exhibit—"the actual authentic Frankenstein" monster—and try to bring the body back to life. Offbeat live-action family adventure stars Jamieson Boulanger, Burt Reynolds, Louise Fletcher. 91 min.
68-1827 Was $99.99 ❑*$14.99*

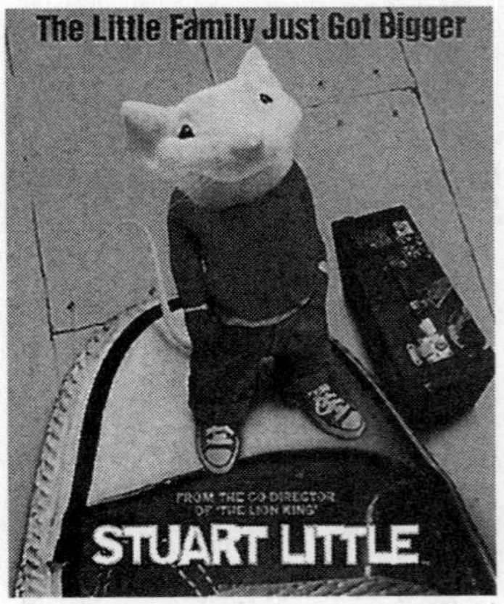

Stuart Little (1999)
Amazing computer animation and the voice of Michael J. Fox help bring to life E.B. White's tiny mouse hero in this delightful live-action family film. Adopted by Manhattanites Geena Davis and Hugh Laurie, young Stuart must win over new "brother" Jonathan Lipnicki while avoiding the clutches of the family cat, Snowbell (voiced by Nathan Lane). 85 min.
02-3418 ❑*$24.99*

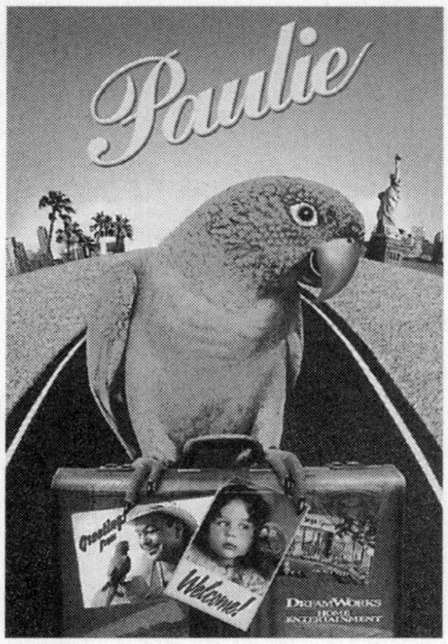

Paulie (1998)
The entire family will enjoy this warm and funny film about a wisecracking parrot that can say a whole lot more than "Paulie want a cracker" and goes on a cross-country adventure to be reunited with the little girl who raised him. Jay Mohr lends his voice to the lovable little bird (and also has a human role); with Hallie Kate Eisenberg, Cheech Marin, Bruce Davison. 91 min.
07-2661 Was $22.99 ❑*$14.99*

Pocahontas: The Legend (1995)
Lavishly filmed treatment of the Pocahontas legend with Sandrine Holt playing the Powhatan Indian princess who saves the life of British explorer Captain John Smith (Miles O'Keeffe) after he is captured by her tribe. Tony Goldwyn co-stars. 96 min.
10-2623 *$19.99*

The Amazing Panda Adventure (1995)
A young boy travels to China to see his father, who works at a preserve for the endangered panda population. When poachers capture a young cub, the boy and a female preserve worker try to rescue it. Lively family adventure with great scenery and cuddly animals stars Stephen Land, Ryan Slater and Yi Ding. 85 min.
19-2412 Was $19.99 ❑*$14.99*

Dad, The Angel & Me (1995)
Warm family story starring Judge Reinhold as a prize-winning self-help expert who learns how to practice what he preaches after his ex-wife dies and he has to care for his estranged 10-year-old daughter—with the help of guardian angel Carol Kane. Alan King, Stephi Lineburg co-star. 90 min.
10-3409 *$14.99*

Gold Diggers: The Secret Of Bear Mountain (1995)
Two teenage girls living in a coastal town in the Pacific Northwest share the adventure of a lifetime when they set out on a search for a fabled fortune in hidden gold. Thrilling family action film stars Anna Chlumsky and Christina Ricci; with Polly Draper, Diana Scarwid, David Keith. 94 min.
07-2412 Was $99.99 ❑*$14.99*

Ed (1996)
Hilarious family comedy featuring "Friends" star Matt LeBlanc as a minor-league pitcher who suffers from "stage fright" whenever he takes to the mound in a game and who overcomes his problem with the help of a most unusual teammate—a slick-fielding chimpanzee third baseman named Ed! Jayne Brook, Jack Warden co-star. 95 min.
07-2430 Was $99.99 ❑*$14.99*

No Worries (1998)
A brave and wise-beyond-her-years 11-year-old girl helps her parents run a sheep farm in the drought-plagued Outback of Australia. Together, they triumph over such adversities as recession, impending foreclosures, and a terrifying dust storm. Stars John Hargreaves and Geraldine James.
10-2798 *$14.99*

A Very Unlucky Leprechaun (1998)
After moving to Ireland, 9-year-old Molly and her father can't stay out of trouble when they inherit "Misfortune Mansion," an estate that promises bad luck to anyone who owns it. With large sums of tax money owed on the mansion, Molly calls on a leprechaun for help. Tim Matheson, Lisa Thornhill and Warwick Davis star. 92 min.
21-9164 *$24.99*

The Kid With The X-Ray Eyes (1998)
An imaginative 12-year-old boy named Bobby finds a mysterious pair of glasses that enable him to see through objects. After having some fun with his X-ray specs, Bobby finds himself calling on his uncle to get him out of trouble with cops, thieves and the CIA. Robert Carradine, Justin Berfield and Diane Salinger star. 84 min.
21-9188 Was $24.99 *$14.99*

Kid Cop (1996)
Eager to follow in the footsteps of his policeman father, an 11-year-old puts on the badge and joins with his dad's former partner to solve a series of local crimes in this pint-size police tale. Jeremy Lelliott, Edward Albert, Alexandra Paul star. 93 min.
06-2817 Was $29.99 ❑*$14.99*

Johnny Mysto: Boy Wizard (1997)
Aspiring magician Toran Caudell ("Hey Arnold!") tries his latest disappearing trick, using a magical ring given to him by the Great Blackmoor. When his sister is transported back to the days of Camelot, he joins Blackmoor on a wild journey filled with danger and fun. Ian Abercrombie and Russ Tamblyn co-star. 87 min.
06-2664 Was $29.99 ❑*$14.99*

Little Ghost (1997)
A lonely 12-year-old boy who is down in the dumps gets a new lease on life with help from a centuries-old ghost named Sophie who inhabits a castle his mother wants to turn into a health spa. When the boy finds out his mom's boyfriend wants to cheat her out of her money, he and Sophie team up to ruin the plan. With James Fitzpatrick, Sally Kirkland. 88 min.
06-2666 Was $29.99 ❑*$14.99*

Beanstalk (1994)
One of the world's favorite fairy tales gets a 1990s updating in this live-action family fantasy, as young Jack befriends a mad scientist whose experimental "seed pods" send the lad on a climb into the clouds and a meeting with a family of giants. J.D. Daniels, Amy Stock Poynton, Richard Moll and Margot Kidder star. 96 min.
06-2281 Was $89.99 ❑*$14.99*

Magic Island (1995)
Thirteen-year-old Jack is thrust into a magical world of pirates and adventure where he encounters the nasty Blackbeard himself. The salty seadog thinks the boy knows how to find some lost treasure, and Jack faces a mermaid and land sharks before he leads the pirate to the riches. Zachery Ty Bryan, Lee Armstrong and Edward Kerr star. 88 min.
06-2393 Was $89.99 ❑*$14.99*

Barney's Great Adventure: The Movie (1998)
The lovable, singing purple dinosaur's big-screen debut is here to charm your family on home video! A trip to the farm becomes a song- and fun-filled adventure for a group of kids when they join Barney on a hunt for a magical egg that contains... Trevor Morgan, Diana Rice and, yes, Baby Bop also star. 75 min.
02-8908 Was $22.99 ❑*$14.99*

The Return Of The Sand Fairy (1993)
A sequel to "The Sand Fairy" that finds four children sent to live in the country with their stern great-aunt who discover a fabulous troll-like creature in their travels. With help from the fairy, the kids visit the future, become invisible, try to win over their aunt and help a poor country girl and her father. 139 min.
04-2882 Was $29.99 *$14.99*

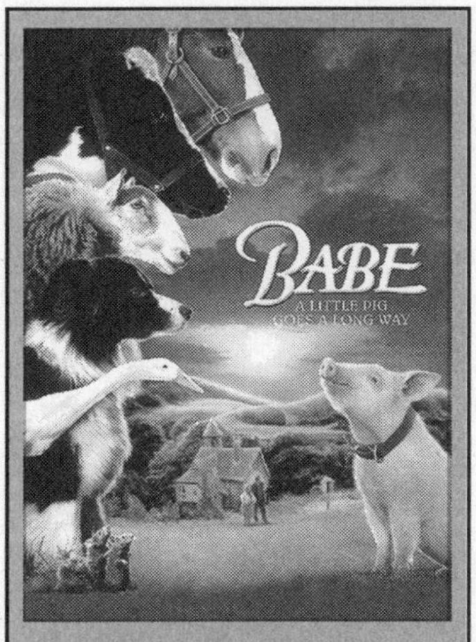

Babe (1995)
An orphaned piglet named Babe is won by a farmer at a fair and is taken home to a barnyard where the animals have the ability to talk to one another. There, a border collie becomes Babe's foster mother and helps him avoid becoming a ham dinner by teaching him the fine art of sheep-herding. Live-action and animatronic animals are seamlessly mixed in this fun-filled, heartwarming tale for the whole family. James Cromwell stars. 92 min.
07-2375 Was $19.99 ❑*$14.99*

Babe: Pig In The City (1998)
The little pig with a big heart is back in an all-new adventure. When Farmer Hoggett is injured, Babe and Mrs. Hoggett travel to a county fair to rescue the farm, but mishaps strand them in a strange and menacing city, where Babe befriends a hotel's menagerie of animal guests to save the day. James Cromwell, Magda Szubanski and Mickey Rooney star. 96 min.
07-2729 Was $19.99 ❑*$14.99*

The Right Connections (1997)
Heartwarming hip-hop comedy about a group of siblings who, with the help of retired rap star MC Hammer and cab driver Melissa Joan Hart, enter a music contest in order to help their out-of-work mom through financial difficulties. With Meshach Taylor, Elizabeth Hart, Brian Hart and Alexandra Hart-Gilliams. 97 min.
06-2736 ❑*$99.99*

Shadow Of The Knight (1998)
A young boy interested in knights and medieval lore is in for the adventure of his life when he meets a live dragon who helps him battle a nasty knight. Exciting family fantasy feature with a bright young cast. 91 min.
06-2816 Was $29.99 ❑*$14.99*

Dunston Checks In (1996)
A posh L.A. hotel is the setting for a mess of monkeyshines (okay, apeshines) when a thief's trained orangutan escapes and runs amok in the building, confounding the staff and making friends with the manager's young son. Energetic comedy for the whole family stars Jason Alexander, Faye Dunaway, Rupert Everett, Eric Lloyd and Sam the simian as Dunston. 88 min.
04-3313 Was $19.99 ❑*$14.99*

Rusty: The Great Rescue (1998)
He's Rusty, a feisty beagle whose orphaned young owners have moved to their grandparents' animal shelter. But when some scheming crooks set their sights on the kids' trust fund, Rusty rallies his animal pals to save the day in this fun-filled family feature. Hal Holbrook, Rue McClanahan, Laraine Newman star, with critter voices supplied by Suzanne Somers, Bobcat Goldthwait and Rodney Dangerfield. 90 min.
04-3744 ❑*$19.99*

Mystic Knights Of Tir Na Nog (1998)
This high-energy, action-packed feature, the pilot to the hit Fox Kids TV series, follows four young knights who join forces with the Little People and set out on a magical quest to locate the mystical warrior and fire dragon who will help them defeat wicked Queen Maeve. With Lochlainn O'Mearain and Lisa Dwan. 80 min.
04-3835 ❑*$14.99*

The Silver Stallion: King Of The Wild Brumbies (1994)
In the tradition of such classic stories as "The Black Stallion" and "National Velvet" comes this superb family adventure about a silver horse named Thowra who captivates the young daughter of a writer. Caroline Goodall, Ami Daemion and Russell Crowe star. 93 min.
06-2205 Was $89.99 ❑*$14.99*

Harriet The Spy (1996)
When precocious 11-year-old Harriet sets out to sharpen her espionage and writing skills by investigating her schoolmates' and neighbors' lives and keeping a detailed (and brutally honest) journal of her observations, she never imagines the trouble that ensues when her notebook falls into the hands of her "subjects." Lively family film, based on the popular Louise Fitzhugh book, stars Michelle Trachtenberg and Rosie O'Donnell. 102 min.
06-2538 Was $19.99 ❑*$14.99*

The Incredible Genie (1997)
Shy-but-smart Simon befriends a 4,000-year-old genie with questionable wish-granting skills. When the genie's magic goes awry, he attracts the attention of an evil government scientist. Now, Simon and his new, ages-old pal have to work together to stop the scientist. Matt Koruba, Stacie Randall and Tom Fahn star. 91 min.
06-2673 Was $29.99 ❑*$14.99*

The Education Of Little Tree (1997)
Wonderfully realized film version of Forrest Carter's acclaimed novel tells of the struggles faced by an 8-year-old part-Cherokee boy in the 1930s. Facing prejudice and the threat of being sent to an institution after his parents' deaths, the boy goes to live with his grandparents in the Smoky Mountains. With James Cromwell, Tantoo Cardinal and Joseph Ashton. 117 min.
06-2718 Was $99.99 ❑*$14.99*

In The Doghouse (1998)
Wacky family comedy starring Matt Frewer as a man who loses his job because Benny, his dog, ruins his relationship with an important client. But Frewer and family soon catch a break when Rhea Pearlman, an agent for animals, decides to make Benny a star. Then the pooch is dognapped! 90 min.
06-2861 ❑*$99.99*

The Real Macaw (1998)
Set in Australia, this thrilling and heartfelt family adventure stars Jason Robards as an elderly man whose ancient pet macaw offers the location of buried treasure. Robards grandson sets out to locate the booty, but when he discovers a resort has been built on its location he has to devise another plan. With Jamie Croft, Deborra-Lee Furness and the voice of John Goodman. 92 min.
06-3004 ❑*$19.99*

A Little Princess (1995)
A magical adaptation of the children's gem by Frances Hodgson Burnett detailing the adventures of the daughter of a British Army captain living in India in 1914. When her father is called to military service, the girl is sent to a New York girls' school, where she enchants her classmates and annoys the stern headmistress with her fantastic stories. Liesel Matthews, Eleanor Bron star. 97 min.
19-2384 Was $24.99 ❑*$19.99*

Baby Huey's Great Easter Adventure (1998)
The oversized duckling who doesn't know his own strength waddles from cartoons to his very own live-action feature. Join Baby Huey and his human pals as they save their town's Easter celebration and stop a nasty showman and a mad scientist who want to "ducknap" Huey. Joseph Bologna, Harvey Korman, David Leisure and Maureen McCormick star. 89 min.
02-3281 Was $19.99 ❑*$14.99*

Baby Geniuses (1999)
Deep in a top secret lab, nasty researchers Kathleen Turner and Christopher Lloyd try to crack the language barrier that will enable them to understand the "babble" of babies, who are born with the knowledge of the universe. One of the test subjects escapes and sets out with his pint-size pals to stop their scheme. Lively family comedy also stars Kim Cattrall, Peter MacNichol and Dom DeLuise. 95 min.
02-3348 Was $24.99 ❑*$14.99*

Father And Scout (1995)
Bob Saget plays a father who wants to show his son what kind of great dad he is during a camping trip. City slicker Saget is more at home making jokes than tying knots and pitching a tent, but when he's put on the spot in a tight situation, Dad comes through with shining colors. Stuart Pankin and Brian Bonsall co-star. 92 min.
02-5061 Was $89.99 ❑*$14.99*

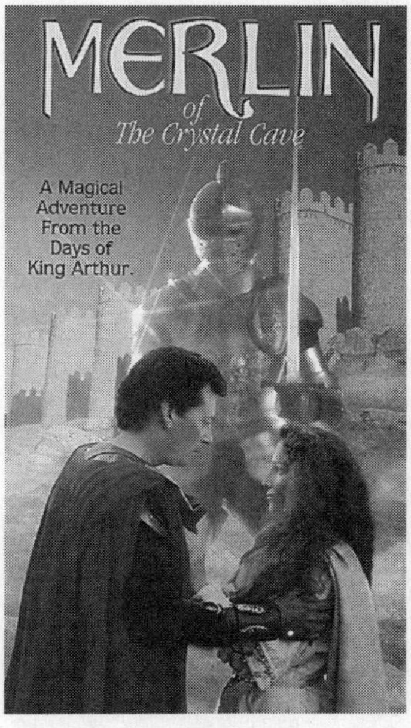

Merlin Of The Crystal Cave (1991)
Arthurian legend lovers of all ages will want to see this enchanting BBC production, based on the novel by Mary Stewart. Follow the adventures of the boy who would grow up to become Merlin, and see how he first discovered his magical heritage, in this live-action fantasy. 159 min.
04-2635 Was $19.99 *$14.99*

A Pig's Tale (1995)
This family comedy is set at Kamp Kipperman, where a group of loser campers known as "the Pigs" take on "the Wolves," a snobby group of kids who terrorize anyone who gets in their way. With help from a wacky counselor, however, the Pigs have a shot at beating their rivals at their own game—and getting the girl in the process. Joe Flaherty stars. 94 min.
02-8434 Was $89.99 *$14.99*

The Last Game (1995)
Heartfelt family drama features Shereen Neville as a hearing-impaired teenager who works to gain respect from her father and siblings by trying out for her high school basketball team. When a medical problem stands in the way of Neville's father coaching her on the court, her brother steps in to help. With Joey Travolta. 75 min.
64-3445 *$14.99*

Slappy And The Stinkers (1998)
A group of misfit kids spending the summer at a snooty private school gets into a variety of comical misadventures, from turning a leaf-blower into a flying machine to "rescuing" a seal lion named Slappy, in this exciting family feature. B.D. Wong, Bronson Pinchot, Jennifer Coolidge and Joseph Ashton star. AKA: "Stinkers." 79 min.
02-3142 Was $19.99 ❑*$14.99*

Far From Home: The Adventures Of Yellow Dog (1995)
Hair-raising family adventure in which a teenage boy and his faithful Labrador Retriever are swept into the ocean while on a boating trip with the boy's father. The pair are then thrust into a series of frightening situations in which they face a pack of bobcats, wolves and the forces of nature. Jesse Bradford, Mimi Rogers and Bruce Davison star. 81 min.
04-2950 Was $19.99 ❑*$14.99*

Rugged Gold (1994)
Compelling family drama in which Don and Martha Martin and their son move to the Alaskan wilderness in 1954. They face a series of dangerous adventures that test their courage and their strength as a family, including encounters with a grizzly bear, an earthquake and the disappearance of Don when Martha is pregnant. Jill Eikenberry, Art Hindle and Graham Greene star. 95 min.
10-2868 *$19.99*

The River Kings (1991)
Set in 1920s Australia, this family saga tells of a fatherless teenager who takes a job as a deckhand on the steamer Lazy Jane. The boy befriends the colorful crew and its captain, and also finds competition from the Lady Mabel, a boat competing for business along the Murray River. Bill Kerr, Edward Hepple and Willie Fennell star. 240 min.
10-2867 *$19.99*

Gordy (1995)
In this unique family adventure, a talking pig named Gordy loses his Dad to a sausage factory, then sets out to find his mother and siblings, who have been taken from their farm home. During his travels, Gordy meets a group of country singers, becomes a model and saves the grandson of a millionaire. Doug Stone, Kristy Young star. 89 min.
11-1942 □*$14.99*

Kazaam (1996)
NBA superstar Shaquille O'Neal slams home the fun in this magical family fantasy, playing a rapping, 3,000-year-old genie named Kazaam. Freed from his boombox captivity by a young boy, O'Neal uses his powers to help his new friend cope with school bullies and search for his estranged father. With Francis Capra, Ally Walker. 93 min.
11-2067 Was $99.99 □*$14.99*

Tower Of Terror (1997)
Steve Guttenberg, Kirsten Dunst and the "Tower of Terror" Disney World attraction are the stars of this family mystery yarn. Guttenberg, a '30s tabloid journalist, investigates the disappearance of five people, including a child movie star. With Nia Peeples and Melora Hardin. 89 min.
11-2372 □*$99.99*

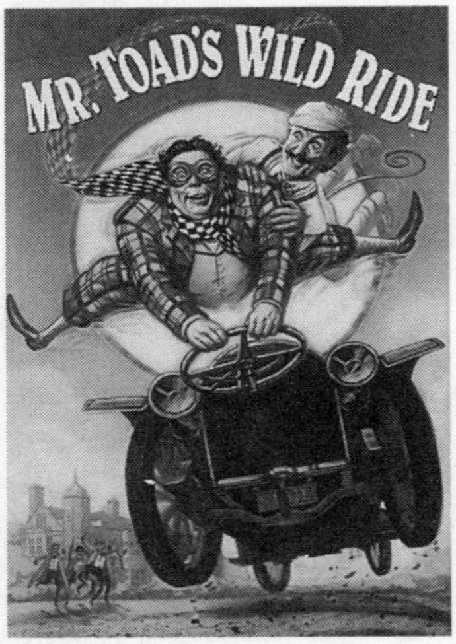

Mr. Toad's Wild Ride (The Wind In The Willows) (1996)
Writer/director Terry Jones plays the title role of the irresponsible, auto-loving lord of Toad Hall, who needs the help of loyal chums Mole, Ratty and Badger to keep his ancestral home from falling into the hands of the wily Weasels, in this lively rendition of the timeless children's tale. Steve Coogan, Nicol Williamson, and Jones' Monty Python pals Eric Idle, John Cleese and Michael Palin also star.
11-2151 Was $19.99 □*$14.99*

Casper (1995)
"The friendliest ghost you know" stars in his first live-action feature, befriending a teenage girl whose "spectre therapist" father is hired to clear out the mansion inhabited by Casper and his rude, crude companions, the Ghostly Trio. Humor, drama and tenderness all mix in this spirited family hit. Christina Ricci, Bill Pullman, Cathy Moriarty, Eric Idle star. 101 min.
07-2330 Was $19.99 □*$14.99*

Casper: A Spirited Beginning (1997)
Learn when and how Casper opted out of the scaring folks "afterlifestyle" and set out to be a friendly ghost in this spooky and silly follow-up to the hit live-action film. Steve Guttenberg, Lori Loughlin, Rodney Dangerfield and Brendon Ryan Barrett star. 90 min.
04-3499 Was $19.99 □*$14.99*

Casper Meets Wendy (1998)
Casper is back with a new friend, Wendy the Good Little Witch. Can they use their powers to combat a wicked warlock's devious plot? Second "spooktacular" sequel stars George Hamilton, Cathy Moriarty, Shelley Duvall, Teri Garr and Hilary Duff as Wendy. 88 min.
04-3709 Was $19.99 □*$14.99*

A Simple Wish (1997)
An 8-year-old girl wishes for a "fairy godmother" to come down and help her would-be singer dad land a role in a Broadway musical, but what she gets is a well-meaning bumbler named Murray whose broken magic wand causes one comic calamity after another. Martin Short, Mara Wilson, Kathleen Turner and Robert Pastorelli star in this funny family fantasy. 90 min.
07-2576 □*$14.99*

3 Ninjas (1992)
Take "The Karate Kid" and blend in a little "Home Alone," and you get this terrific family action film about three brothers who are trained in the martial arts by their grandfather and get to use their skills to fight a crooked arms dealer and his henchmen. Chad Power, Michael Treanor, Victor Wong star. 87 min.
11-1648 Was $19.99 □*$14.99*

3 Ninjas Kick Back (1994)
Those high-kicking ninja kids face danger, excitement and even romance when they head to Japan to help Grandpa award a priceless dagger to the winner of a martial arts tournament. While battling Grandpa's old enemy, they meet a pretty girl who teaches them some lessons about self-defense and life. Max Elliott Slade, Sean Fox and Victor Wong star. 93 min.
02-2647 Was $19.99 □*$14.99*

3 Ninjas Knuckle Up (1995)
While vacationing with their martial arts expert grandfather, the ninja brothers befriend a Native American girl and find themselves embroiled in a battle between the girl's people and weaselly businessmen. There's action, laughs and lessons learned in this third installment of the popular series, featuring Victor Wong, Charles Napier and Vincent Schiavelli. 93 min.
02-2778 Was $89.99 □*$14.99*

3 Ninjas: High Noon At Mega Mountain (1998)
The Three Ninjas—Colt, Rocky and Tum Tum—face their greatest foe yet when they go up against the evil Medusa (Loni Anderson), who has taken over their revered Mega Mountain Amusement Park. Using their martial arts mastery, the kids team up with TV action star Dave Dragon (Hulk Hogan) to save the day. Jim Varney, Victor Wong also star. 94 min.
02-3194 Was $19.99 □*$14.99*

Balloon Farm (1999)
The acclaimed children's story by Jerdine Nolen Herold has been turned into a whimsical movie starring Rip Torn as Harvey Potter, the owner of the only government-sanctioned balloon farm. Keeping tabs on the process of raising the floating "plants" is a young girl who must stay out late to figure out Torn's secret. With Mara Wilson and Laurie Metcalf. 92 min.
11-2435 □*$99.99*

Fluke (1995)
Touching, often funny family drama about a driven businessman who is killed in a car accident and reincarnated as a dog. As memories of his human life come back to him, Fluke tries to reunite with his wife and son and come to terms with his new existence. With Matthew Modine, Nancy Travis, Eric Stoltz, Max Pomeranc and the voice of Samuel L. Jackson. 95 min.
12-3014 Was $89.99 □*$14.99*

Warriors Of Virtue (1997)
A young boy is magically transported to a mystical land whose ruthless ruler is draining it of a precious element in order to gain immortality for himself. The boy teams up with the Warriors of Virtue—five kangaroo-like martial arts fighters—to save the world in this dazzling live-action family fantasy. Mario Yedidia, Angus MacFadyen star. 103 min.
12-3182 Was $19.99 □*$14.99*

Richie Rich (1994)
He's the boy with all the bucks, and who better to play him than Macaulay Culkin? Watch Culkin bring the comic-book favorite to life in this fun-filled family comedy, as Richie, his faithful butler Cadbury, and a gang of kids he befriends rescue his parents and the Rich family fortune from scheming Lawrence Van Dough. John Larroquette, Jonathan Hyde co-star. 95 min.
19-2330 Was $19.99 □*$14.99*

Free Willy (1993)
Moving family drama about a troubled 12-year-old boy who gets a job at an adventure park, where he befriends the star attraction, a 7,000-pound killer whale named Willy. When the boy realizes Willy is miserable in captivity, he plans a way to release him to the ocean. Jason James Richter, Michael Madsen and Lori Petty star. 111 min.
19-2148 Was $19.99 □*$14.99*

Free Willy 2: The Adventure Home (1995)
This whale-of-a-sequel to the popular film finds teenager Jason James Richter having a troubling and adventurous summer vacation when he tries to deal with his arrogant half-brother and save the now-freed Willy and his family from a disastrous oil spill fire. With Michael Madsen, Jayne Atkinson and August Schellenberg. 98 min.
19-2404 Was $19.99 □*$14.99*

Free Willy 3: The Rescue (1997)
When an illegal whale hunt in the Pacific Northwest threatens Willy and his family, his human pal Jessie (Jason James Richter), working as an assistant on a marine research boat, teams up with the young son of one of the poachers to stop the animals from being killed. Thrilling third entry in the series also stars Annie Corley, Patrick Kilpatrick. 86 min.
19-2614 Was $19.99 □*$14.99*

A Cry In The Wild (1991)
In the tradition of "The Black Stallion" and "White Fang" comes this thrilling, beautifully-filmed tale of a brave boy's experiences battling the elements and ferocious animals in the Canadian wilds after his plane crashes. Jared Rushton, Pamela Sue Martin and Ned Beatty star. 82 min.
12-2248 Was $79.99 □*$14.99*

White Wolves: A Cry In The Wild II (1993)
While on a two-week trip through the Cascade Mountains, a group of teens shoot the rapids, explore caves and go face-to-face with difficult terrain and dangerous weather in this sequel to the popular family adventure. Ami Dolenz, Matt McCoy and Mark Paul Gosselaar star. 74 min.
21-9035 Was $89.99 *$14.99*

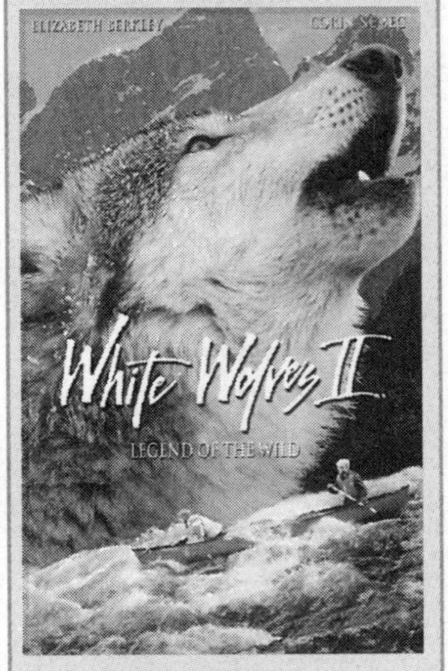

White Wolves II: Legend Of The Wild (1996)
A group of misfit teens take a wilderness expedition to help a naturalist save a nearly-extinct band of wolves. When their leader is injured, the young people battle whitewater rapids, deadly predators and tensions between themselves. Jeremy London, Corin Nemec, Ele Keats, Ernie Reyes, Jr. and Elizabeth Berkley star. 87 min.
21-9117 Was $99.99 *$14.99*

Cry Of The White Wolf: White Wolves III (1998)
After their plane crashes, two teenagers on their way to juvenile offenders camp depend on their injured Native American pilot to teach them how to survive in the Sierra wilderness with its treacherous canyons, ferocious grizzly bears and dangerous rapids. Rodney A. Grant, Mercedes McNab and Mick Cain star. 82 min.
21-9158 Was $24.99 *$14.99*

Joey (1997)
There's plenty of adventure and fun down under in this family film about an Australian boy who teams up with the daughter of the U.S. ambassador to rescue a baby kangaroo and return it to its home in the wild. Ed Begley, Jr., Jamie Croft, Alex McKenna star.
12-3234 □*$14.99*

True Heart (1997)
A boy and girl lost in the wilderness after a plane crash get help from an Indian and a fabled wild bear as they cope with surviving and battle a band of poachers. Kirsten Dunst, Zachery Ty Bryan, Dey Young and Michael Gross star in this thrilling family adventure saga. 92 min.
12-3275 Was $59.99 □*$14.99*

Born To Be Wild (1995)
Spirited family adventure-comedy about a troubled teenager who gets a new best friend: Katie, a 400-pound gorilla who communicates by sign language. After Katie's former owner kidnaps her and makes her an attraction at a flea market, the teen attempts a daring rescue. Wil Horneff, Helen Shaver and Peter Boyle star. 99 min.
19-2367 Was $19.99 □*$14.99*

War Of The Buttons (1995)
The feud between two rival groups of boys in a small Irish town "escalates" into a junior war game where the factions fight for the buttons off each other's clothes in this family film that mixes comedy and drama. Colm Meaney, Johnny Murphy star. 95 min.
19-2430 Was $89.99 *$19.99*

A Rat's Tale (1997)
Can a resourceful rodent from New York named Monty find true love with the "uptown" Isabella and at the same time keep humans from destroying their world? Traditional marionettes and live actors mix with modern special effects to create a charming children's fable. With Lauren Hutton, Jerry Stiller and Beverly D'Angelo. 90 min.
19-2676 Was $19.99 *$14.99*

A Tale Of Cinderella (1996)
The fairy tale favorite about true love, magic, and the importance of properly fitting footwear gets a lively retelling in this lavish live-action musical for the whole family. Christianne Tisdale, star of Broadway's "Beauty and the Beast," shines in the title role. 129 min.
19-2517 □*$19.99*

The Phoenix And The Magic Carpet (1994)
While staying in England with their mother, three American children discover a mysterious carpet and egg in a secluded cottage. From the egg hatches a magical phoenix who turns the rug into a flying carpet that takes the kids on an exciting journey to a tropical island. Fantastic family adventure stars Dee Wallace Stone and Peter Ustinov. 89 min.
19-9127 Was $89.99 *$14.99*

The Skateboard Kid (1993)
A boy who recently moved to town is troubled by the fact the neighborhood skateboard thrashers want nothing to do with him. Zack is looking for a change of luck—and he gets it, when he finds a magical talking skateboard! Timothy Busfield, Bess Armstrong and Dom DeLuise (as the voice of "Rip") star. 83 min.
21-9040 Was $89.99 *$14.99*

The Skateboard Kid 2 (1994)
Another teenager uses another magical board to become a champ on wheels, but a group of local thrashers try to destroy his chance of winning a local tournament. When the going gets tough, the skateboard goes wild. Dee Wallace Stone, Bruce Davison and Andrew Stevens star.
21-9081 *$14.99*

Revenge Of The Red Baron (1993)
Grandpa Spencer (Mickey Rooney) was a fighting ace in World War I, and now he has to go into battle again against Germany's infamous Red Baron, who has returned to gain revenge on his family. Meanwhile, Grandpa's family is having its share of problems, so he must regain his glory to save his family and stop his old nemesis. Laraine Newman and Ronnie Schell co-star. 81 min.
21-9050 Was $89.99 *$14.99*

Looking For Trouble (1996)
A tomboy named Jamie tries to rescue an elephant named Trouble from a cruel circus master. Jamie finds friendship and pachyderm-sized thrills in this family adventure starring Susan Gallagher and Holly Butler.
21-9128 *$24.99*

Invisible Mom (1997)
Ten-year-old Josh has problems at school because of his goofy inventor father. But when Dad concocts an invisibility potion, Josh wants to give it a try. Then Mom drinks it and wackiness ensues. Dee Wallace Stone, Barry Livingston and Russ Tamblyn star. 92 min.
21-9137 Was $24.99 *$14.99*

Invisible Mom 2 (1999)
Eddie, a 12-year-old orphan, is taken in by a wacky inventor and his sometimes unseen wife, but is surprised when two mysterious cousins appear to adopt him. When he learns he has inherited millions, Eddie also discovers that the cousins have a plan to do him in to the get the cash. That's when his new mother turns invisible to help him! Dee Wallace Stone, Mickey Dolenz, Mary Woronov star. 80 min.
21-9191 *$24.99*

Vulcan (1998)
A young boy finds an egg that became unearthed by a volcano. The egg soon hatches a gigantic pterodactyl with whom the boy has a series of wild adventures. Tom Taus, Vernon Wells, Diana Barton, Nick Nicholson and Robert Vaughn star in this family fantasy. 82 min.
21-9175 *$24.99*

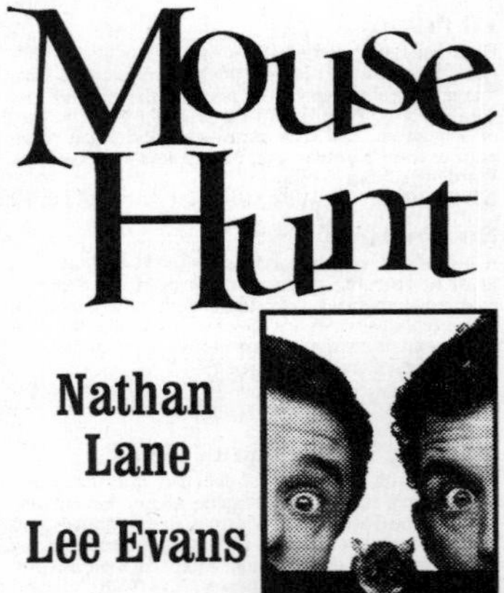

Mouse Hunt (1997)
Hilarity of the wackiest order is in store when the Smuntz Brothers (Nathan Lane and Lee Evans) inherit a dilapidated mansion from their string manufacturer father. Their renovation plans, after learning the house is really worth a fortune, hit a snag when they come across the lone occupant: a pesky rodent that continually eludes the brothers' frenzied extermination tactics. Christopher Walken co-stars. 97 min.
07-2615 Was $16.99 □*$14.99*

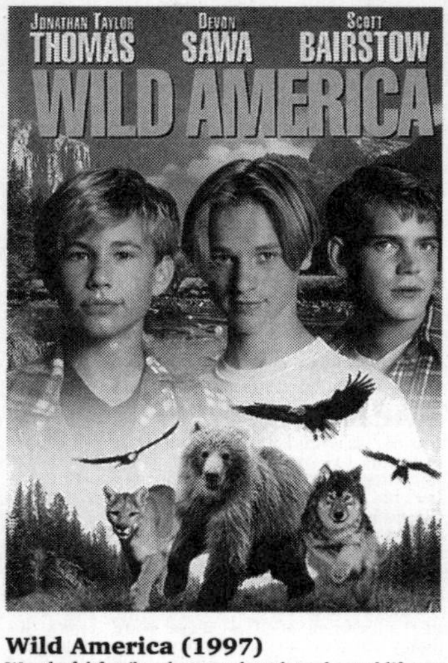

Wild America (1997)
Wonderful family adventure based on the real-life exploits of the teenage Stouffer brothers, who set out on their own in the summer of 1967 to film wild animals in their natural habitat, a cross-country odyssey filled with action, danger and fun. Jonathan Taylor Thomas, Devon Sawa, Scott Bairstow star. 102 min.
19-2597 Was $19.99 ❑$14.99

Fairytale: A True Story (1997)
In the English countryside of 1917, two schoolgirls' claim to have photographs of fairies that inhabit the woods near their home makes the youngsters instant celebrities and stirs an international debate with opponents as diverse as believer Sir Arthur Conan Doyle and skeptic Harry Houdini. This fanciful spin on a true incident stars Florence Hoath, Elizabeth Earl and Paul McGann, with Peter O'Toole as Doyle and Harvey Keitel as Houdini. 99 min.
06-2682 Was $99.99 ❑$14.99

Alone In The Woods (1997)
Ten-year-old Justin accidentally gets into the wrong van while his family is on their way to grandmother's cabin on Thanksgiving. He soon discovers that he's sharing the van with a billionaire toy magnate's daughter, who's been kidnapped by bumbling crooks. Can the two kids team to stop them? Laraine Newman, Chick Vennera star. 81 min.
21-9149 $24.99

The White Pony (1999)
In this children's adventure saga that mixes fantasy and wildlife elements, a 12-year-old girl with a dream of owning a pony encounters a magical leprechaun, her evil cousin and a fairy tale princess while seeking that special pony on her uncle's farm. Carly and Natalie Anderson, Olivier Gruner, Warwick Davis star. 86 min.
21-9194 $24.99

King Of The Wind (1993)
Exciting family adventure about a poor stable boy whose devotion to an Arabian horse leads him to a journey that stretches from the African desert to France and England. Richard Harris, Glenda Jackson, Nigel Hawthorne and Navin Chowdhry star. 101 min.
27-5452 Was $89.99 ❑$14.99

The Girl From Mars (1991)
A bright but eccentric teenager obsessed with space is convinced she's really an alien. When strange things begin happening around her, her schoolmates and teachers start believing her claims, but what is the truth behind the "Girl from Mars"? Magical live-action family film stars Sarah Sawatsky, Edward Albert, Christianne Hurt and Eddie Albert. 91 min.
27-5560 ❑$14.99

Teenage Mutant Ninja Turtles (1990)
Cowabunga! Those pizza-eating, hip-talking, reptilian ronin leap from comics and cartoons to the big screen in their live-action hit adventure. Can Michaelangelo, Raphael, Leonardo and Donatello rescue their teacher from the clutches of the evil Shredder? You'll believe a turtle can swing nunchukas after seeing this wild blend of action and comedy. 93 min.
27-6672 $14.99

Teenage Mutant Ninja Turtles II: The Secret Of The Ooze (1991)
The Fab Four of the reptile world are back and up to their shells in trouble, as the Shredder and a gang of martial arts mavens use the toxic waste that created the Turtles to produce their own monsters and threaten the world. Live-action Turtlemania continues; with Paige Turco, David Warner and special guest Vanilla Ice. 88 min.
02-5001 ❑$14.99

Teenage Mutant Ninja Turtles III: The Turtles Are Back...In Time (1993)
Leonardo, Raphael, Donatello and Michaelangelo join reporter pal April O'Neill in an adventure that sends them time-travelling back to feudal Japan, where they get caught in a battle between clans of rival samurais. Elias Koteas, Paige Turco and Stuart Wilson star in this "turtle-riffic" epic. 95 min.
02-2431 ❑$14.99

Stanley's Dragon (1994)
A teenage boy strikes up a most unusual friendship when he finds and makes a "pet" of a tame dragon in this whimsical live-action family fantasy with a bright young cast. 91 min.
27-5561 ❑$14.99

Zeus And Roxanne (1997)
The unlikely friendship that develops between a spunky little dog named Zeus and a mischievous dolphin known as Roxanne also inspires a relationship between Zeus's owner, songwriter and widower Steve Guttenberg, and single mom Kathleen Quinlan, a marine biologist studying Roxanne, in this delightful family film. 98 min.
44-2089 Was $19.99 ❑$14.99

Ava's Magical Adventure (1994)
You have to understand, Ava is a two-ton circus elephant who has one wild adventure after another when a 10-year-old helps her run away from the big top in this magical family feature. Timothy Bottoms, Georg Stanford Brown, Priscilla Barnes and Remy Ryan star. 97 min.
46-5597 $14.99

Keeping The Promise (The Sign Of The Beaver) (1997)
Follow the trials and tribulations of a pioneer family as they struggle to survive in the forests of Maine in the early 1700s. Keith Carradine and Annette O'Toole star in this exciting and moving family drama, based on Elizabeth George Speare's novel. 93 min.
50-3568 ❑$29.99

The Treasure Seekers (1998)
Five motherless children struggle to save their inventor father from financial ruin in this family classic from author Edith Nesbit. Together, they learn that love, togetherness, and never giving up can help them accomplish anything. Stars Nicholas Farrell, Camilla Power, Ben Simpson, James Wilby. 105 min.
50-5889 ❑$29.99

Kayla: A Cry In The Wilderness (1997)
Beautifully realized family drama about a young boy in despair over his polar explorer father's death who comes out of his shell when he encounters a wolf who resembles the dog who led his father's sled. Tod Fennell, Meredith Henderson and Henry Czerny star. 96 min.
50-8637 $19.99

Children Of The New Forest (1998)
Hair-raising adventure and powerful drama highlight this adaptation of Captain F. Marryat's acclaimed family tale set in 17th-century England. After his father dies, teenager Edward Beverley cares for his younger sisters and brother while trying to elude the evil Reverend Corbould and Oliver Cromwell's army. Malcolm Storry and Tom Wisdom star. 105 min.
53-6653 $19.99

Walking Thunder (1994)
A young man and his family are stranded in the Rocky Mountains in 1850, facing a bitter struggle for survival against Indians, outlaws and a giant bear the Sioux call Walking Thunder. The pioneers' encounter with the huge creature changes their lives forever in this family adventure epic starring John Denver and James Read and narrated by Brian Keith. 90 min.
58-2002 $89.99

Nacho Chihuahua: The Movie (1998)
He's a Nacho, Nacho Chihuahua, and when he and feisty gal pal El Nina leave their homeland to find Nacho's South of the Border homeland, they find danger when they're chased by a pack of wild canines. Will they find Nacho's doggy roots and be happy? John Hardison and Melanie Maxey star in this wacky family farce. 55 min.
58-8277 $14.99

Adventures In Dinosaur City (1992)
Three hip teens find themselves zapped into a prehistoric world inhabited by all sorts of outrageous dinosaurs, then team with a crime-fighting Tyrannosaurus and his pals to save Dinosaur City from melting down. Omri Katz and Shawn Hoffman star in this fascinating, special effects-filled fantasy. 88 min.
63-1560 Was $89.99 ❑$14.99

Bigfoot: The Unforgettable Encounter (1995)
When a young boy lost in the woods comes face to furry chest with the legendary man-beast, a friendship is born that will see the pair fend off bounty hunters and reporters in order to keep Bigfoot free. Exciting adventure tale for the whole family stars Matt McCoy, Zachery Ty Bryan, David Rasche. 86 min.
63-1753 Was $89.99 ❑$14.99

Dark Horse (1992)
A powerful family drama about a young woman who finds herself caring for a horse after she's sent to a farm for her troublemaking deeds. Soon, a whole new world opens for her, but an accident threatens to change her newfound happiness. Mimi Rogers, Ed Begley, Jr. and Ari Meyers star. 98 min.
27-6768 $14.99

Grizzly Falls (1999)
A journey to the Pacific Northwest to capture a live grizzly bear turns into a harrowing, thrilling adventure for an explorer and his son when the boy is captured by a bear and his father sets out to save him. Bryan Brown, Tom Jackson, Oliver Tobias and Richard Harris star. 94 min.
27-7204 Was $49.99 ❑$14.99

Storybook (1995)
In this family fantasy, 8-year-old Brandon and his dog Leo are thrust into a magical land called Storyland after finding an enchanted book. Soon, Brandon joins forces with Woody the Woodsman, Pouch the Boxing Kangaroo and Hoot the Wise Owl to bring happiness to the kingdom by defeating Queen Evilia. Swoosie Kurtz, William McNamara star. 88 min.
63-1770 Was $89.99 ❑$14.99

Two-Bits & Pepper (1995)
When two young girls are kidnapped by a pair of bumbling crooks (both played by Joe Piscopo), it's up to the girls' brave pet horses, Two-Bits and Pepper, to gallop to the rescue in this exciting and funny family film. With Lauren Eckstrom, Rachel Crane and Dennis Weaver. 90 min.
63-1827 Was $99.99 ❑$14.99

Behind The Waterfall (1995)
Tommy and his sister are sent to live with their aunt after their father dies. Along with his cousin, Alex, Tommy learns to believe in himself with help from Mr. Connors, a local storyteller. Gary Burghoff, Luke Baird and Alyssa Hansen star. 94 min.
66-6068 ❑$14.99

Second Chances (1998)
This moving true story tells of a little girl struggling to find normalcy in her life after a car crash injures her leg and kills her father. Damaged physically and emotionally by the experience, she withdraws from people around her until she shows interest in a crippled horse named Ginger. Kelsey Mulrooney, Stuart Whitman, Isabel Glasser and Tom Amandes star.
66-6078 $19.99

Doom Runners (1998)
This lively family adventure with sci-fi elements tells of a group of children who move from one world to another to escape the evil, mind-sucking Dr. Kao. Their destination is New Eden, but first they encounter all sort of danger. Tim Curry, Lea Moreno and Nathan Jones star. 87 min.
67-9004 ❑$14.99

The Sweetest Gift (1998)
Two Florida families—one black, the other white—struggle with a host of similar problems in this touching drama. Diahann Carroll and Helen Shaver are the mothers facing problems of race, poverty and absent fathers. With Tisha Campbell. 90 min.
67-9005 ❑$14.99

Time At The Top (1999)
A 14-year-old girl uses her building's elevator to transport her from contemporary Philadelphia to the City of Brotherly Love in 1881. There she meets another teenager her own age whose problems she tries to solve using her time machine. Timothy Busfield, Elisha Cuthert star. 96 min.
67-9006 ❑$14.99

Big And Hairy (1998)
A boy named Picasso moves with his folks to Chicago. Picasso is having trouble making friends and isn't very good at basketball, but things turn around when he befriends a teenage Sasquatch called "Ed" who turns out to be a pal and a great basketball player to boot. Richard Thomas and Chilton Crane star in this family comedy that's like "Air Bud"—with the Abominable Snowman! 94 min.
67-9007 ❑$14.99

Shiloh (1997)
Based on the award-winning children's novel, this moving family drama follows a boy who tries to rescue a beagle puppy from its abusive owner and learns a valuable lesson on growing up in the process. Michael Moriarty, Rod Steiger and Blake Heron star. 93 min.
19-2538 ❑$19.99

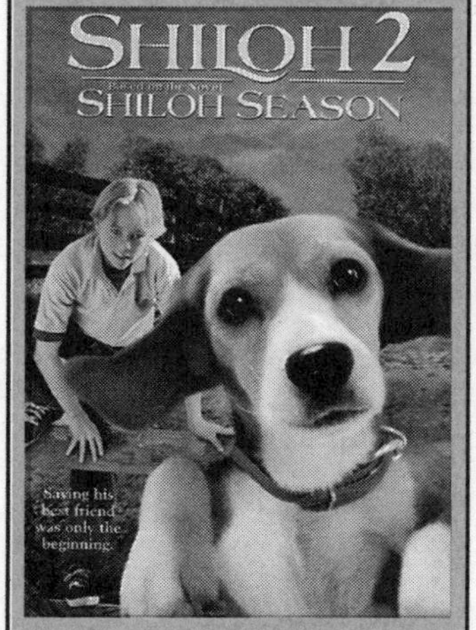

Shiloh 2: Shiloh Season (1999)
The adventures of young Marty and his canine best friend, Shiloh, continue in this all-new feature, as the pair learn an important lesson in the healing power of love. Zachary Browne, Michael Moriarty and Rod Steiger star. 96 min.
19-2866 ❑$19.99

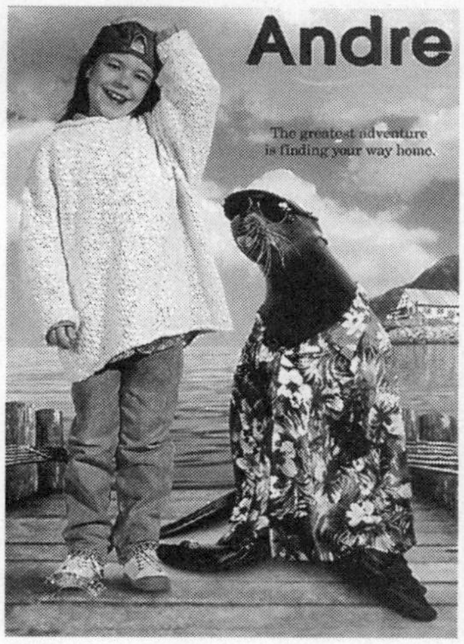

Andre (1994)
Based on a true story, this fun-filled family feature tells the tale of an orphaned seal pup who is taken in by a little girl in a New England coastal town and becomes a local celebrity and tourist attraction. Tina Majorino, Keith Carradine, Chelsea Field, and Tory the sea lion as Andre the seal star. 96 min.
06-2287 Was $19.99 ❑$14.99

Soccer Dog (1998)
A young boy faces trouble from the soccer teammates in his new town until he befriends Lincoln, a dog on the run from the local dogcatcher. When a player gets injured, Lincoln steps in and quickly becomes the "Pele of Poochdom," inspiring other families to test their pets' sports expertise. James Marshall, Olivia D'Abo and Jeremy Foley star. 98 min.
02-3276 Was $19.99 ❑$14.99

The Devil's Arithmetic (1998)
A gripping and intense filming of Jane Yolen's novel, this family drama stars Kirsten Dunst as a rebellious Jewish teen who learns a powerful lesson about her family's faith and the Holocaust when she's miraculously sent back in time to a Polish concentration camp in 1941. Paul Freeman, Brittany Murphy and Mimi Rogers also star; introduced by co-producer Dustin Hoffman. 101 min.
67-9016 ❑$14.99

Tin Soldier (1995)
Inspired by Hans Christian Andersen's "The Steadfast Tin Soldier," this fantasy tells of a 12-year-old boy who just can't seem to fit in at school. When he gets in trouble after befriending some of the school's bad kids, a tin soldier magically comes to life and helps the boy solve his problems. Jon Voight stars and directs; with Dom DeLuise, Ally Sheedy. 99 min.
63-1768 Was $89.99 ❑$14.99

Escape From Wildcat Canyon (1998)
A fishing trip for a boy and his grandfather turns into a battle for survival when their plane crashes in a remote mountainous area. Exciting family adventure saga stars Dennis Weaver, Michael Caloz, Peter Keleghan. 96 min.
67-9017 ❑$14.99

Sea People (1999)
In this whimsical story, a 14-year-old loner who lives in a small coastal town in Nova Scotia and dreams of swimming the English Channel one day saves an elderly man after he jumps off a bridge. After the rescue, she's taken to his home and meets his peculiar family, whom she comes to believe are related to mermaids. Hume Cronyn, Joan Gregson and Tegan Moss star. 92 min.
67-9028 ❑$14.99

The Adventures Of Galgameth (1996)
A young prince seeking to avenge his father's death at the hands of an evil knight who also seized control of the kingdom gets some help from a magical statue of a lizard-like creature that comes to life and can grow to gigantic size in this live-action fantasy for the whole family. Devin Oatway, Stephen Macht star. 100 min.
68-1840 Was $19.99 ❑$14.99

Star Kid (1998)
A shy, sci-fi-loving 12-year-old doesn't wish upon a star for help in dealing with a school bully and overcoming his fears, but aid arrives from outer space anyway when he climbs into a super-powered alien cybersuit nicknamed "Cy" that crash-lands near his home. Enjoyable family adventure stars Joseph Mazzello, Corinne Bohrer, Richard Gilliland. 110 min.
68-1874 Was $99.99 ❑$14.99

A Kid In Aladdin's Palace (1998)
In this fantastic follow-up to "A Kid in King Arthur's Court," young Thomas Ian Nicholas meets up with a genie who takes him back to the days of the Arabian Nights, where he must team up with a beautiful princess and save Aladdin from the schemes of his evil brother. With James Faulkner, Rhona Mitra and Taylor Negron. 89 min.
68-1884 ❑$14.99

Summer's End (1998)
The friendship between a retired black doctor and a young neighbor boy is tested by a racist incident in their town's past in this moving family drama. James Earl Jones, Brendan Fletcher and Wendy Crewson star. 101 min.
67-9015 ❏*$14.99*

Mr. Music (1998)
A teenage boy is picked as the new vice president of talent for a failing record company, but when he learns his selection was purely for publicity purposes, the teen sets out to save the firm and revive the career of its former rock star head. Jonathan Tucker and Mick Fleetwood star. 92 min.
67-9018 ❏*$14.99*

The Adventures Of A Two-Minute Werewolf (1991)
A 13-year-old horror film fan gets the shock of his life when, after seeing a particularly scary movie, he begins turning into a werewolf...but only for two minutes at a time! Howlingly funny family tale stars Lainie Kazan, Barrie Youngfellow. 46 min.
70-3138 *$12.99*

Journey To Spirit Island (1991)
It's the adventure of a lifetime when two city kids on vacation in the Pacific Northwest join a Native American brother and sister for a wilderness odyssey filled with danger and fun. Moving family-themed drama stars Brandon Douglas, Gabriel Damon, Bettina. 93 min.
71-5267 ❏*$12.99*

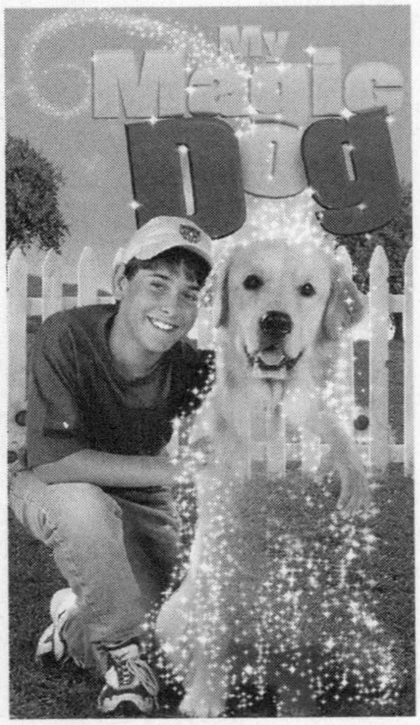

My Magic Dog (1997)
A boy's best friend is his dog...especially when that dog is Lucky, a magical mutt that is totally invisible to everyone except Toby, his 8-year-old master. Watch the fun as Lucky helps Toby save his inheritance from a nasty aunt in this live-action fantasy for the whole family. Leo Millbrook, Russ Tamblyn and John Philip Law star. 98 min.
83-1184 Was $39.99 *$14.99*

Me And The Kid (1993)
A would-be burglar turns kidnapper when he's interrupted by a young boy who feels neglected by his rich parents, but the unlikely pair wind up having so much fun on the run that the boy doesn't want to go home! Danny Aiello, Joe Pantoliano, Cathy Moriarty and Alex Zuckerman star in this family-themed road movie. 97 min.
73-1140 Was $89.99 ❏*$14.99*

Napoleon (1997)
Join an adventurous puppy named Napoleon as he sets out on an exciting and fun-filled odyssey across the wilds of Australia, and watch as he gains a menagerie of new friends, in this charming live-action family feature. Jamie Croft, Bronson Pinchot, Joan Rivers and Casey Siemaszko supply voices. 81 min.
73-1288 ❏*$14.99*

My Family Treasure (1993)
A young boy learns of his family history when his mother and eccentric grandfather tell him a story about a priceless Fabergé egg. Given to the grandfather by the Czar during the Russian Revolution, the boy's mother attempted, years later, to return to the Soviet Union to recover the treasure. Dee Wallace Stone and Theodore Bikel star in this family-oriented adventure. 95 min.
74-3001 *$79.99*

Treehouse Hostage (1998)
Infamous counterfeiter Jim Varney thinks he escaped scot free from prison, but a 10-year-old's backyard trap makes him the boy's unwilling treehouse "guest" and the focus of the his summer school project in this wild family comedy. Joey Zimmerman, Debby Boone also star. 90 min.
68-1920 ❏*$99.99*

Biokids (1991)
Five kids are given incredible powers by an elderly scientist and use their abilities to fight the evil force of Exxor which threatens world peace. Wild sci-fi yarn in the tradition of "Infra-Man." Sammy Lagmay, B. Roco star. 92 min.
68-3002 *$14.99*

Mystery Monsters (1997)
A trio of puppet creatures on a popular children's TV show are even more amazing than the audience imagines...because they're really beings from another dimension held prisoner by the show's host! It's up to a young boy and girl to rescue the Mystery Monsters in this thrilling fantasy adventure for the whole family. Ashley Cafagna, Tim Redwine star. 81 min.
75-5015 Was $89.99 *$14.99*

The Secret Kingdom (1997)
When some youngsters discover a miniature city and its inhabitants living underneath their family's kitchen sink, a magical adventure begins in which the kids must stop the tiny residents from waging war. Billy O., Jamieson K. Price, Tricia Dickson star. 85 min.
75-5020 Was $49.99 *$14.99*

Little Bigfoot (1996)
A brother and sister on vacation in the country make a unique friend when they find a young Bigfoot in the woods and set out to protect his forest home from loggers. Live-action family adventure stars Ross Malinger, Kelly Packard, P.J. Soles and Matt McCoy. 99 min.
63-1870 Was $49.99 ❏*$14.99*

Little Bigfoot 2: The Journey Home (1997)
The furry little creature is back for more family fun, as he meets three youngsters in the woods and turns their quiet camping vacation into a thrilling and hilarious adventure. Stephen Furst, Michael Fishman, Taran Nolan Smith and Tom Bosley star. 93 min.
86-1128 *$59.99*

The Werewolf Reborn! (1998)
What was supposed to be a pleasant vacation to visit her older cousin in his European homeland turns into a (literally) hair-raising adventure for a teenage girl when his village is attacked by what appears to be a werewolf. Spooky family film stars Ashley Cafagna, Len Lesser and Robin Downes. 70 min.
75-5031 Was $29.99 *$14.99*

Frankenstein Reborn! (1998)
Has the world's most famous monster come back to life? It sure looks like it when 13-year-old Anna Frankenstein's curiosity over her uncle's experiments leads her to his secret lab—and face to face with the creature he's assembled from dead bodies! Chills and thrills in the "Goosebumps" tradition; Jaason Simmons, Ben Gould star. 70 min.
75-5032 Was $29.99 *$14.99*

Teen Knight (1998)
Five kids win a stay at a high-tech medieval theme park located in an ancient castle. During an electrical storm, the castle is transported back in time and the kids have to fight knights, sorcerers and fire-breathing dragons. Kristopher Lemche, Caterina Scorsone and Paul Soles star. 90 min.
75-5035 Was $49.99 *$14.99*

Phantom Town (1998)
The search for their missing parents leads three siblings to a desert ghost town that is home to a mysterious, sinister presence. Can the youngsters defeat the evil force and save their parents? Spooky family adventure stars John Patrick White, Taylor Locke, Belinda Montgomery. 90 min.
75-5038 Was $49.99 *$14.99*

The Excalibur Kid (1998)
A young man is transported back in time to the days of Camelot, where he must help the young King Arthur reclaim the magic sword Excalibur and save Merlin the magician from an attack by an evil sorceress. Jason McSkimming, François Klanfer star. 90 min.
75-5040 Was $49.99 *$14.99*

Shapeshifter (1999)
With the help of a 360-year-old wizard, a teenage boy gains magical shape-changing powers and uses them to save his secret agent parents and defeat some plutonium thieves in this exciting live-action family fantasy. Paul Nolan, Catherine Blythe star. 90 min.
75-5047 *$49.99*

Teen Sorcery (1999)
Dawn, a new student at Pilgrimtown High School, teams with her friends to battle Mercedes, head cheerleader and evil spirit, for possession of the powerful Devilstone in this thrilling fantasy-adventure for the whole family. A.J. Cook, Nadia Litz and Lexa Doig star. 90 min.
75-5054 *$49.99*

Planet Patrol (1999)
Four teenagers known as "The Planet Patrol Team" battle Lord Doom, who has targeted the Earth as the home for his repulsive creatures, including a savage robot, a living dinosaur skeleton and a "killer monster." Michael David, Anthony Furlong and Robert Garcia star. 72 min.
75-5057 *$49.99*

Clockmaker (1998)
An eccentric old man controls time for the entire world with his eerie timepieces and weird gadgets. But when a young boy finds his way up into the clockmaker's apartment, he accidentally pushes a wrong button that sends him and his curious friends through a time-bending adventure in the past that could change everything in the present. With Anthony Medwetz and Katie Johnston. 90 min.
75-5028 Was $49.99 *$14.99*

The Flintstones (1994)
The "modern Stone-Age family" goes live-action in this Bronto-sized blockbuster produced by Steven Spielberg. John Goodman stars as Fred Flintstone, who doesn't realize that his promotion at the quarry is part of an embezzlement scheme by an unscrupulous executive. Elizabeth Perkins, Rick Moranis, Rosie O'Donnell, Elizabeth Taylor and Halle Berry also star. 91 min.
07-2196 Was $19.99 ❏*$14.99*

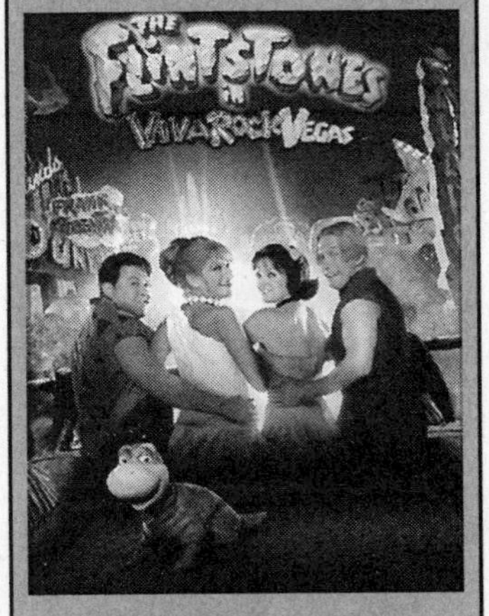

The Flintstones In Viva Rock Vegas (2000)
Take a look back at the early days of Bedrock's two favorite couples and see how they met and fell for one another in this second live-action feature. The gang is off to Rock Vegas for a good time, unaware that scheming casino owner Chip Rockefeller has designs on Wilma...and her family's fortune. Mark Addy, Stephen Baldwin, Kristen Johnston, Jane Krakowski and Thomas Gibson star. 91 min.
07-2926 ❏*$99.99*

Star Games (1997)
A family adventure saga set on a faraway planet where a 10-year-old prince escapes from an evil empire by piloting a spaceship to Earth. There he meets a young Earthling boy who helps him in his quest to destroy the intergalactic bad guys. Tony Curtis, Travis Clark and Trevor Clark star.
82-5062 *$29.99*

Billy Frankenstein (1999)
A young boy named Billy Frank gets the surprise of his life when he learns that he's a distant relative of Dr. Frankenstein. When his family inherits the infamous Frankenstein Castle, there are more surprises—and scares—in store, including some unexpected guests. Vernon Wells, Tommy Kirk and Darran Norris star in this family fright fest from the indefatigable Fred Olen Ray. 92 min.
82-5134 *$34.99*

The Shrunken City (1998)
In this exciting fantasy adventure for the whole family, two youngsters find the bottled city of Shandar, which was magically reduced in size centuries earlier. Can the kids help Shandar's revived inhabitants defend themselves from extra-dimensional attackers and return to normal? Michael Malota, Agnes Bruckner, Steve Valentine star. 90 min.
75-5025 Was $49.99 *$14.99*

Breakout (1998)
Wild and exciting family adventure in which the son of an inventor who has discovered a new, environmentally safe form of energy is kidnapped by dastardly oil tycoons out to blackmail his father. The son is a technical wizard who, along with a group of ninja pals, gives his captors more than they bargained for. With Robert Carradine, James Hong and J. Evan Bonifant. 86 min.
76-9108 Was $19.99 *$14.99*

Kid Witch (1997)
After being abandoned by her parents, Diedre, a young witch-in-training, is taken in by a new foster family who don't know of her powers. Diedre soon attempts to win over her foster mother by calling on her supernatural abilities. With Russ Tamblyn, Michael Bauer. 90 min.
82-5140 *$34.99*

Boys Will Be Boys (1997)
When their parents leave them home alone so they can attend a company barbecue, two young brothers trash their house, then have to get rid of their dad's scheming business rival and clean up before their folks get back home. Fun-filled family fare with Randy Travis, Julie Haggerty, Jon Voight, Michael DeLuise and Dom DeLuise, who also directed. 89 min.
83-1198 Was $29.99 ❏*$14.99*

Clubhouse Detectives (1996)
Fun-filled family adventure about a boy who can't convince any adult about a crime he witnesses occurring in a neighbor's house, and how he and his gang of school-age sleuths set out to solve the mystery themselves. With a bright young cast. 85 min.
83-1119 Was $39.99 *$14.99*

The Legend Of Wolf Mountain (1992)
Three children are abducted by escaped convicts and taken in the Utah wilderness in this thrilling family adventure. The youngsters get away from their captors, but it takes the aid of a mystic Indian "wolf spirit" to help them survive in the wild. Bo Hopkins, Robert Z'Dar, Vivian Schilling and Mickey Rooney star. 88 min.
80-1049 Was $89.99 ❏*$14.99*

Get A Clue (1998)
When "Turtle" Wexler moves into a new town with her family, their house turns out to be right next to the "haunted" Westing mansion! She sneaks into the house one night and begins to unravel a surprising mystery in this live-action adventure, based on the acclaimed children's book "The Westing Game." Ashley Peldon, Diane Ladd, Sally Kirkland and Ray Walston star. 95 min.
83-1253 Was $29.99 *$14.99*

Invisible Dad (1997)
Lots of kids wish their parents would disappear once in a while, but Doug Bailey's father really has, thanks to a mysterious machine in their garage. How the Invisible Dad causes a riot at home and work while Doug tries to figure out how to get him to reappear for good makes for wild family fun. With a bright young cast. 90 min.
83-1188 Was $29.99 *$14.99*

Jungle Boy (1998)
In the tradition of "The Jungle Book" comes this family adventure about a boy raised by a monkey and an elephant in the jungles of India. His life is changed with the arrival of a woman and an evil poacher in search of a sacred statue. Asif Mohammad Seth, Jeremy Roberts and Lea Moreno star. 92 min.
83-1247 Was $29.99 *$14.99*

Mysterious Museum (1999)
A visit to a museum turns into a time-travelling adventure for a brother and sister when a magical painting sends them back to the 17th century. Can they stop a nasty wizard from making off with the enchanted jewel they need to get back home? Andrew James Trauth, Brianna Brown star. 80 min.
75-5061 *$49.99*

Little Heroes (1991)
A terrific family-oriented drama about a poor girl and her loyal dog named Fuzz who must come to the rescue of their only friend, a gruff, old farmer. Raeanin Simpson, Katherine Willis and Keith Christensen star. 78 min.
80-1011 Was $79.99 *$14.99*

My Teacher Ate My Homework (1998)
J.R. Black's "Shadowzone" kid's book series comes to life with this fun family adventure about Jesse and Cody, two kids enjoying middle school until a mysterious doll comes to life and causes trouble for them and everyone around them. Shelley Duvall, Margot Kidder, Gregory Smith Star and John Neville star. 91 min.
83-1254 Was $29.99 *$14.99*

The Robin Hood Gang (1997)
Two youngsters come to the rescue of their neighbors when they find a suitcase filled with money in their apartment building. Trouble is, the loot belongs to a bank robber who'll stop at nothing to get it back in this fast-paced family comedy in the "Home Alone" tradition. With a bright young cast. 86 min.
83-1282 Was $29.99 *$14.99*

P.U.N.K.S. (1998)
A group of pre-teen misfits gets revenge on their school's troublemakers—and save the day for one boy's dad in the process—when they "borrow" a nasty businessman's invention that turns weaklings into hulks. Henry Winkler, Randy Quaid and Cathy Moriarty star. 93 min.
83-1285 Was $29.99 *$14.99*

The Indian In The Cupboard (1995)
Enchanting adaptation of the popular children's book centering on Omri, a young boy whose cupboard has the power to bring inanimate figures to life. Little Bear, a tiny Indian, comes alive, along with a Texas cowboy named Boone. When the two characters begin to fight, Omri learns some important lessons about life. Hal Scardino, Litefoot and David Keith star. 97 min.
02-2816 Was $19.99 ❏*$14.99*

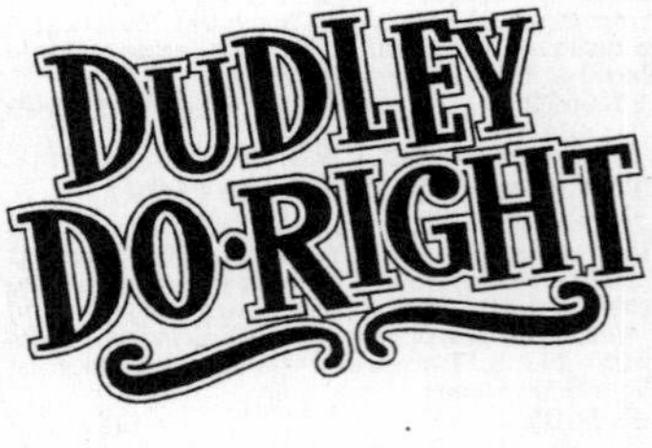

Dudley Do-Right (1999)
Jay Ward's much-loved cartoon hero is brought to life with Brendan Fraser as the fearless—and brainless—Mountie who must get his man, arch-fiend Snidely Whiplash (Alfred Molina). When Whiplash gains financial control of Semi-Happy Valley, as well as the hand of Dudley's gal, Nell (Sarah Jessica Parker), Dudley and his trusted Horse must come to the rescue. 83 min.
07-2802 Was $99.99 ❏*$14.99*

Treasure Of Pirate's Point (1998)
Ray and his friends befriend a reclusive descendant of legendary pirate Captain Vane who convinces them that treasure might be hidden nearby. While trying to recover the loot, the boys foil an evil plan to destroy their town and learn an important lesson about friendship. Asher Metchik and William Sheppard star in this exciting family adventure. 88 min.
83-1289 Was $29.99 *$14.99*

Angel In Training (1997)
A 12-year-old basketball whiz gets some divine help from a guardian angel in saving her father's business from a scheming rival. Wonderful family comedy features a bright young cast. 90 min.
83-1382 Was $29.99 *$14.99*

The Adventures Of Young Brave (1998)
Two children searching in the wilderness for a fortune in buried gold get some unexpected help from the mystical spirit of an Indian lad named Horton Laughing Feather in this exciting family adventure with a bright young cast. 92 min.
83-1393 Was $29.99 *$14.99*

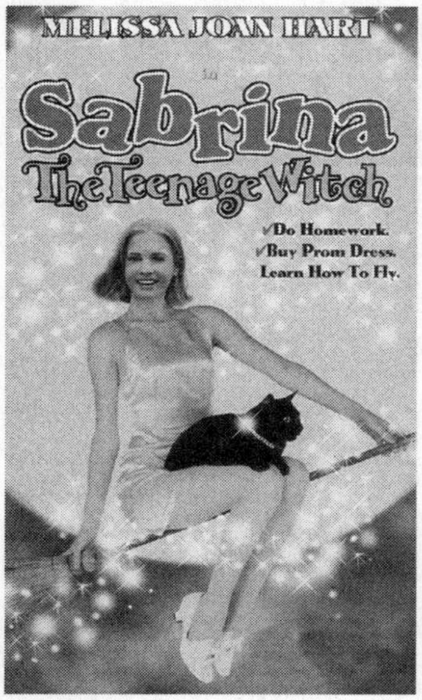

Sabrina The Teenage Witch (1996)
The high school enchantress who was featured in Archie comics and cartoons comes to life in the fun-filled pilot to the hit TV series. Sixteen-year-old Sabrina discovers her magical heritage after she moves in with her two otherworldly aunts, but will she use her powers to help her find true love? Melissa Joan Hart, Sherry Miller and Charlene Fernetz star. 91 min.
88-1095 Was $99.99 ❑*$14.99*

Fly Boy (1999)
Engaging family story in which a 10-year-old boy and his grandfather, a former World War II flying ace, decide to take a final flight in their favorite antique plane. Little do they know what adventures they'll get into. With a bright young cast. 86 min.
83-1396 Was $29.99 *$14.99*

A Kid Called Danger (1999)
Lively family adventure in which young Dane "Danger" McGuire tries to emulate his policeman father by getting involved in perilous situations. With help from a group of deputies, he uses all sorts of spying techniques to catch a jewel thief even the cops can't find. 90 min.
83-1411 Was $29.99 *$14.99*

Mystery Kids (1999)
Two youngsters investigate the mysterious disappearance of a high school girl in hopes of collecting a $5,000 reward. At first believing she's been murdered, the kids discover she's been working as a rock singer in a bar because of problems with her parents and try to help her out. Brighton Hertford, Christine Lakin star. 88 min.
83-1439 Was $29.99 *$14.99*

The Prince And The Surfer (1999)
This contemporary treatment of Mark Twain's "The Prince and the Pauper" tells about a prince who switches positions with a California skateboarder. Trouble starts when the prince takes a liking to the surfer's girlfriend and his look-alike gets entangled in royal matters. Robert Englund, Timothy Bottoms and Arye Gross star. 90 min.
83-1465 Was $29.99 *$14.99*

The Million Dollar Kid (1999)
Young Shane and his family are thrilled to learn they've just won a $50 million lottery, but the search for the winning ticket becomes a wild hunt that turns the neighborhood upside-down and pits Shane against some nasty crooks in this family comedy. Richard Thomas, Maureen McCormick, C. Thomas Howell, Cory Feldman star. 89 min.
83-1496 Was $29.99 *$14.99*

Arthur's Quest (1999)
A young man named Arthur gets a crash course in responsibility—and British history—when he frees the legendary sword Excalibur from its rocky resting place and is paid a visit by Merlin the magician in this family fantasy saga. Eric Christian Olsen, Brion James, Clint Howard and Catherine Oxenberg star. 92 min.
83-1529 Was $29.99 *$14.99*

The Modern Adventures Of Tom Sawyer (1998)
In this fun-filled updating of the Mark Twain story, Tom's traded in his river rafting for rollerblading, but he and his pals still manage to get into some wild exploits as he tries to catch young Becky's eye. Phillip Van Dyke, Bethany Richards star. 92 min.
83-1530 Was $29.99 *$14.99*

My Uncle: The Alien (1996)
The president's teenage daughter goes to Los Angeles to visit a children's shelter. When she discovers the shelter is in desperate need of money, she devises a plan to help, but she soon runs into trouble on the streets of L.A. Thankfully, a friendly alien creature tries to help her. Hailey Foster and Jay Richardson star. 90 min.
86-1107 Was $89.99 ❑*$14.99*

Hollywood Safari (1997)
Exciting family drama set in the Hollywood hills, where a family that trains animals for the movies must find their escaped tame mountain lion before it's shot by police who are pursuing another big cat—a vicious killer. David Leisure, Debby Boone, Ted Jan Roberts and John Savage star. 99 min.
86-1118 ❑*$59.99*

Buck And The Magic Bracelet (1997)
A teenager and his dog are the only survivors of a camp of prospectors in the Old West that is attacked by an outlaw gang. Setting out to bring the crooks to justice, but lost in the wilderness, the boy is aided by an Indian medicine man who gives him a mystical bracelet in this dramatic family adventure. Matt McCoy, Abby Dalton, Felton Perry star. 99 min.
86-1129 *$59.99*

From The Mixed-Up Files Of Mrs. Basil E. Frankweiler (1995)
Feeling unappreciated by their parents, two children run away from home and set up residence inside New York's Metropolitan Museum of Art, where they become involved in a mystery surrounding a statue and its eccentric former owner. Funny family adventure, based on the popular book, stars Lauren Bacall, Jesse Lee, Jean Marie Barnwell. 92 min.
88-1029 Was $79.99 ❑*$14.99*

Johnny & Clyde (1995)
Ten-year-old Johnny is forced to dog-sit Clyde, a "criminal canine" who needs to be led down the straight and narrow. The two reluctant partners become friends in a wild series of scrapes and adventures in this funny family film. John White, Michael Rooker star. 84 min.
88-1032 Was $89.99 ❑*$14.99*

Gulliver's Travels (1996)
The classic satire by Jonathan Swift is marvelously brought to life in this special effects-filled production that stars Ted Danson as Dr. Lemuel Gulliver, the 18th-century Englishman whose amazing odyssey takes him to the tiny nation of Lilliput; Brobdingnag, land of giants; the flying island of Laputa; and to the Houyhnhnms, intelligent horses. The all-star cast also includes Mary Steenburgen, James Fox, Peter O'Toole, Alfre Woodard. 179 min.
88-1086 Was $24.99 ❑*$14.99*

Saltwater Moose (1997)
A city boy spending the summer on his grandmother's farm in Nova Scotia joins a local girl on an exciting adventure when they befriend a bull moose stranded on an isolated island and set out to bring him a mate. Johnny Morina, Katharine Isobel, Timothy Dalton and Lolita Davidovich star. 90 min.
88-1164 ❑*$14.99*

The Legend Of Sleepy Hollow (1999)
Washington Irving's classic chiller about a quiet town in 18th-century New York state and its ghostly vistor receives an effective translation in this family treat. Brent Carver stars as Ichabod Crane, the skeptical schoolmaster who has a fateful encounter with the Headless Horseman. With Rachel Lefevre, Paul Lemelin. 91 min.
88-1213 ❑*$14.99*

The Giant Of Thunder Mountain (1997)
Exciting family adventure about a young girl named Amy who sets out with her two brothers to search for a giant who lives on top of Thunder Mountain and has been accused of provoking lots of mischief. When the giant becomes the target of the townspeople, Amy has to help him before they get to him. Richard Kiel, Noley Thornton star. 88 min.
88-7011 *$19.99*

Fly Away Home (1996)
Stirring, gorgeously filmed family adventure focusing on a young girl who goes to live in Canada with her estranged inventor father after her mother dies. The girl becomes "parent" to a flock of newly-hatched geese and, when they reach maturity, learns to fly an ultra-light plane so she can lead her charges to a winter home in the United States. Anna Paquin, Jeff Daniels, Dana Delany star; directed by Carroll Ballard ("The Black Stallion"). 107 min.
02-2995 Was $19.99 ❑*$14.99*

Kids Of The Round Table (1995)
For young Alex and his friends, knights and castles were things of make-believe. That is, until the legendary wizard Merlin arrives, with sword Excalibur in tow, to offer the kids a fantastic adventure and a lesson in good versus evil. Malcolm McDowell, Johnny Morina, Michael Ironside star. 89 min.
58-5220 Was $79.99 ❑*$14.99*

Magic Kid (1993)
A 13-year-old martial arts master finds his trip to California turns dangerous when his uncle, a third-rate talent agent, gets in trouble with a powerful mobster. With help from his idol, Don "The Dragon" Wilson, the youngster tackles the gangster and his henchmen. Stephen Furst, Shonda Whipple, Ted Jan Roberts co-star. 90 min.
86-1075 Was $19.99 ❑*$14.99*

Magic Kid 2 (1994)
Teen karate whiz Ted Jan Roberts has gone on since the first film to become star of the hit TV series "Ninja Boy," but when he gets tired of the Hollywood grind some weaselly studio execs hatch a plot to force him to stay! Exciting martial arts action and comedy for the whole family. With Stephen Furst, Dana Baron.
86-1082 Was $89.99 ❑*$14.99*

Annie (1982)
The hit Broadway musical about the feisty Depression-era comic-strip heroine becomes a fun-filled family treat. Follow Annie and her dog Sandy as they leave the orphanage for the opulent mansion of Daddy Warbucks. Carol Burnett, Albert Finney, Tim Curry, Bernadette Peters and Aileen Quinn, in the title role, star. 127 min.
02-1150 Was $19.99 ❑*$14.99*

Annie: A Royal Adventure! (1995)
Sequel to the ever-popular "Annie" follows the red-headed moppet, her dog Sandy, and Daddy Warbucks to England, where he is scheduled to be knighted. At the same time, evil Lady Hogbottom plots to blow up Buckingham Palace and become Queen of England. Can Annie and company stop them? Joan Collins, George Hearn, Ashley Johnson star. 92 min.
02-2828 *$14.99*

Cold River (1982)
A captivating family adventure about a family that finds danger and wild animals while on a trip through the Adirondack Mountains. Suzanne Weber, Pat Petersen star. 94 min.
04-1646 Was $59.99 *$14.99*

The Neverending Story (1984)
Enter a fantastic world where the strongest power is the power of the imagination. A young boy comes across a book that can project the reader into its story. You'll see a land of flying dragons, evil tigers, racing snails, and a warrior-child who must save it from destruction. 94 min.
19-1356 ❑*$14.99*

The Neverending Story II: The Next Chapter (1991)
Special effects-filled sequel to the hit family fantasy follows the young hero in a quest to save a beautiful princess. On his odyssey, he befriends some fabulous creatures while battling some horrible ones. With John Wesley Shipp and Jonathan Brandis. BONUS: Includes "Box-Office Bunny," the first Bugs Bunny theatrical cartoon in 26 years. 90 min.
19-1861 Was $19.99 ❑*$14.99*

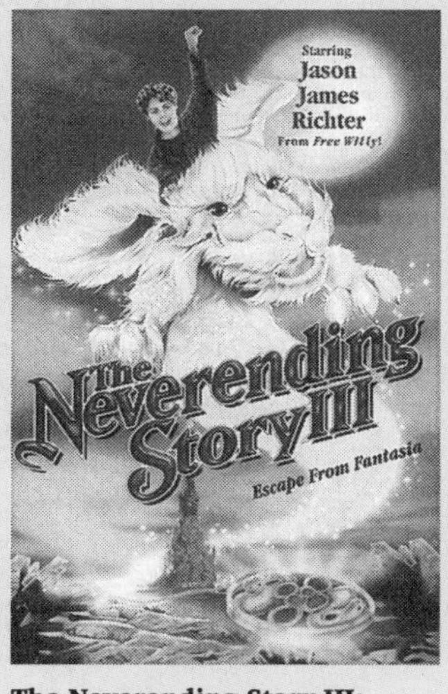

The Neverending Story III: Escape From Fantasia (1996)
Spectacular special effects and a true sense of wonder highlight the third installment in the popular fantasy series. In it, the young hero and his new step-sister find themselves facing danger and adventures in the magical land of Fantasia. Jason James Richter of "Free Willy" fame stars. 95 min.
11-2090 ❑*$14.99*

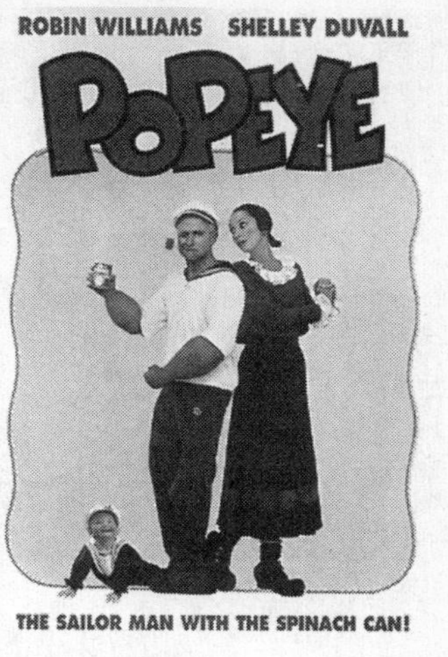

Popeye (1980)
Robin Williams as Popeye and Shelley Duvall as Olive Oyl bring the beloved cartoon characters to life in director Robert Altman's fun musical that's a delight for kids of all ages. With Paul Dooley, Ray Walston, Paul L. Smith. 114 min.
06-1080 *$14.99*

Dream Chasers (1984)
An 11-year-old boy dying of cancer befriends an elderly antique shop owner and retreats into a fantasy world of Western outlaws. The two become "bandits" in an attempt to escape from the problems life has handed them. Touching family drama stars Harold Gould and Justin Dana.
04-3070 *$14.99*

The New Adventures Of Pippi Longstocking (1988)
One of children's literature's most endearing heroines is back on the screen. Join pig-tailed scamp Pippi and her pals as they run away from home and get involved in a search for buried pirate treasure. Eileen Brennan, Dick Van Patten, Dennis Dugan and Tami Erin as Pippi star. 100 min.
02-1898 Was $19.99 ❑*$14.99*

Brenda Brave (1989)
When her grandmother slips and breaks her legs, young Brenda helps out by taking over her job of selling peppermint sticks in the town square. Brenda's loving and selfless ways bring her a wonderful and surprising reward at Christmastime in this charmer from Astrid Lindgren, author of "Pippi Longstocking." With Mathilda Lindgren, Majlis Granlund. 30 min.
70-5114 Was $19.99 *$14.99*

The Light Princess (1985)
Flavorful and fun adaptation of George MacDonald's fantasy concerning a princess who has been cursed with the inability to take things seriously. Wonderful animation mixes with live-action in this memorable BBC treat. Stacey Dorning, John Fortune star. 56 min.
04-3190 Was $19.99 *$14.99*

My Family And Other Animals (1987)
Wonderful adventure of a young boy whose family moves from England to a tropical paradise where he uncovers fantastic wildlife and unusual insects. A grand saga that's educational, funny and thrilling, this BBC production is based on the life of naturalist Gerald Durrell and his novelist brother, Lawrence. 230 min.
04-3216 *$24.99*

The Last Winter (1989)
This acclaimed story of innocence, hope and change chronicles a 10-year-old country boy who tries to adapt to his family's move to the city. Winner of many international awards, the film stars Gerard Parkes and David Ferry. 103 min.
04-3251 Was $59.99 ❑*$29.99*

The Night Train To Kathmandu (1988)
Milla Jovovich stars as a young girl who dreads accompanying her parents on a trip to remote Nepal...until she meets a handsome guide who takes her on an adventure-filled journey through the Himalayas. Exciting family drama also stars Pernell Roberts. 102 min.
06-1609 Was $19.99 ❑*$14.99*

The Worst Witch (1986)
Delightful live-action family fantasy about a young enchantress who seems unable to impress her witchy elders. Fairuza Balk, Diana Rigg, Tim Curry and Charlotte Rae star. 70 min.
46-5577 Was $79.99 *$14.99*

The Adventures Of Milo And Otis (1989)
Outstanding live-action charmer for the whole family focuses on the forays of a pair of farmyard friends, a kitten and puppy, as they are whisked from their home and embark on a series of adventures through the countryside. Dudley Moore narrates. 76 min.
02-1974 Was $19.99 ❑*$14.99*

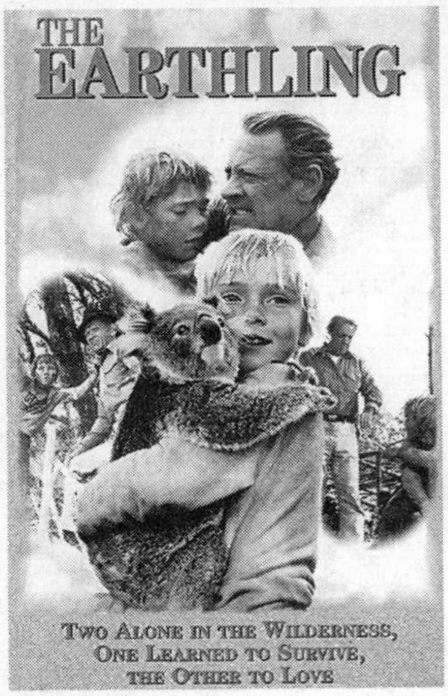
THE EARTHLING
TWO ALONE IN THE WILDERNESS, ONE LEARNED TO SURVIVE, THE OTHER TO LOVE

The Earthling (1980)
William Holden is a terminally ill survivalist in the Australian Outback who teaches a lonely orphan boy (Ricky Schroder) the necessary skills to survive in the wilderness. 96 min.
47-1072 Was $59.99 *$14.99*

The Secret Garden (1949)
Wonderful family melodrama stars Margaret O'Brien as an orphan who comes to live with her reclusive uncle and his handicapped son in their dilapidated mansion. The two children begin caring for the run-down garden on the grounds (with sequences filmed in color), and the resulting change affects all the residents. Herbert Marshall, Dean Stockwell, Elsa Lanchester co-star. 92 min.
12-2260 *$14.99*

The Secret Garden (1984)
The charming children's classic from the pen of Frances Hodgson Burnett comes to life, as a pensive orphan girl finds the courage to face the harsh world with the help of a hidden, magical hideaway. Splendid BBC production stars Sarah Hollis Andrews, David Patterson and John Woodnutt. 107 min.
04-3191 Was $19.99 □*$14.99*

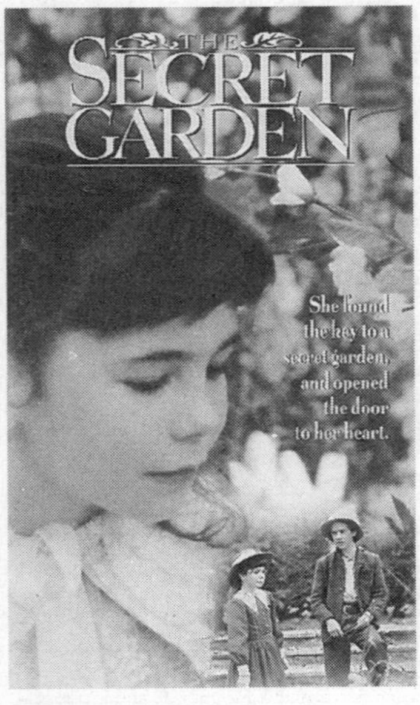
THE SECRET GARDEN
She found the key to a secret garden, and opened the door to her heart.

The Secret Garden (1987)
A gorgeous "Hallmark Hall of Fame" version of the story that inspired the hit Broadway musical. This fanciful family drama, set in Victorian England, tells the tale of a lonely orphan girl who finds a world of wonder in the garden of a large estate. Gennie James, Derek Jacobi, Barret Oliver, Jadrien Steele star. 100 min.
63-1576 □*$14.99*

The Secret Garden (1993)
A magical adaptation of Frances Hodgson Burnett's classic from director Agnieszka Holland ("Europa, Europa") focuses on an orphan girl who leaves India to live with her uncle in a dreary manor in England. There she befriends her invalid cousin and discovers a garden with fantastic healing powers. Kate Maberly, Heydon Prowse and Maggie Smith star. 102 min.
19-2164 Was $24.99 □*$19.99*

Sleeping Beauty (1989)
Tahnee Welch is the princess who causes time to freeze with a drop of blood in this magical musical version of the ageless story. Morgan Fairchild and Nicholas Clay are Beauty's royal parents, and Sylvia Miles is the shunned Red Fairy who curses their kingdom with sleep and thorns. 90 min.
12-2470 *$14.99*

The Capture Of Grizzly Adams (1982)
Dan Haggerty returns as the famed wilderness man in this feature-length drama based on the TV series. Framed for a murder he didn't commit, Adams must leave the safety of the forest in order to keep his niece from being sent to the orphanage, even if it means his capture. With Chuck Connors, Kim Darby, June Lockhart. 96 min.
14-3305 *$12.99*

The Legend Of Grizzly Adams (1990)
Mountain man Adams and his grizzly bear pal, Martha, embark on a trek to see old pals and wind up helping in the capture of a band of inept gold thieves, who learn a lesson from the rugged pair. Gene Edwards and Acquanetta star in this scenic family saga. AKA: "The All-New Adventures of Grizzly Adams: The Legend Continues." 75 min.
08-1559 *$19.99*

Grizzly Mountain (1994)
Two youngsters travel back in time to the Orgeon Territory of the 1870s to help a famed mountain man defend a sacred Native American mountain from greedy land swindlers in this exciting adventure for the whole family. TV's Grizzly Adams, Dan Haggerty, stars along with Kim Morgan Greene, Martin Kove, and Dylan and Megan Haggerty. 96 min.
80-1087 Was $19.99 □*$14.99*

Red Riding Hood (1989)
A maiden's visit to her grandmother is filled with danger when she encounters an evil king's henchman, a man who can become a hungry wolf at will. Song-filled version of the Brothers Grimm standard stars Craig T. Nelson, Isabella Rossellini and Amelia Sharkey ("Dreamchild"). 84 min.
12-2469 *$14.99*

The Magic Snowman (1988)
This charming story tells of a snowman that talks to the boy who built him and helps his family when a fishing drought threatens their livelihood, while later teaching the lad a valuable lesson when he tries to beat the local bully in a skating contest. Justin Fried stars, with Roger Moore as "The Voice." 85 min.
27-5450 Was $39.99 □*$12.99*

Big Shots (1987)
Two young boys, one white and one black, team up for a series of exciting adventures and daredevil escapes while driving from Chicago to Louisiana in a stolen car. Lots of laughs, scares and heart-warming drama. Ricky Busker, Darius McCrary. 91 min.
40-1363 Was $19.99 □*$14.99*

The Bear (1989)
A spectacular adventure story for all ages that has been hailed as one of the best nature films ever made. An orphaned cub must fend for itself before being befriended by an adult Kodiak bear in the beautiful, dangerous Canadian wilderness. Directed by Jean-Jacques Annaud ("Quest for Fire"). 93 min.
02-2011 Was $19.99 □*$14.99*

The Golden Seal (1983)
Wonderful family adventure set in the Aleutian Islands, where Steve Railsback awaits the return of a fabled golden seal who arrives at the islands every seven years. Railsback plans to capture the creature and collect a big reward, but his young son wants the seal saved. Penelope Milford, Michael Beck and Torquil Campbell also star. 94 min.
53-1144 Was $19.99 *$14.99*

Dennis The Menace: Dinosaur Hunter (1987)
Hank Ketcham's irascible 5-year-old finds a dinosaur bone in his backyard, and when Mr. Wilson learns that Dennis and his discovery are drawing the attention of reporters and scientists, he knows he's in for trouble. William Windom, Victor Dimattia and Jim Jansen star. 118 min.
68-1283 Was $89.99 □*$14.99*

Dennis The Menace (1993)
The irascible comic-strip tike who can't stop getting into everyone's hair makes it to the big screen in this slapstick-happy farce from producer John Hughes. While staying with Mr. Wilson (Walter Matthau), Dennis (Mason Gamble) is kidnapped by a sinister thief named Switchblade Sam (Christopher Lloyd). With Lea Thompson, Joan Plowright. 96 min.
19-2149 Was $19.99 □*$14.99*

Dennis The Menace Strikes Again (1998)
In this fun-filled follow-up to the 1993 family hit, trouble abounds when young Dennis (Justin Cooper) discovers that his neighbor Mr. Wilson (Don Rickles) has been targeted by two scheming con men. Dennis becomes determined to save his friend, and hilarious mischief and mayhem ensues. With George Kennedy, Carrot Top, and Betty White. 75 min.
19-2731 Was $19.99 □*$14.99*

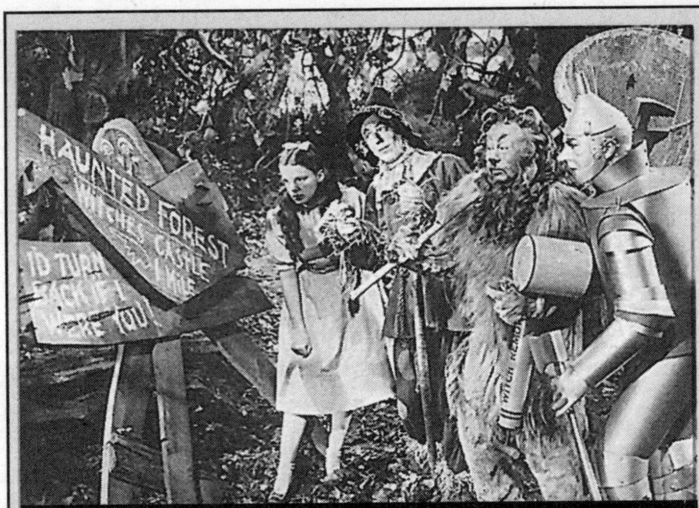
HAUNTED FOREST
WITCHES CASTLE

The Wizard Of Oz

The Patchwork Girl Of Oz (1914)
Produced by Oz scribe L. Frank Baum's own film company, this silent fantasy follows young Ojo (Violet MacMillan) and the "living doll" Scraps (Pierre Couderc) on their journey to the Emerald City, where familiar Oz characters abound. 80 min. Silent with music score and narration.
10-7075 *$19.99*

The Magic Cloak Of Oz (1914)
Fanciful silent adaptation of L. Frank Baum's story "Queen Zixi of Ix," about a magical cloak, woven by fairies, that offers its wearer one special wish. Violet MacMillan stars; directed by Baum. 45 min. Silent with music score and narration.
10-9088 *$19.99*

His Majesty, The Scarecrow Of Oz (1914)
For the final Oz film from his studio, L. Frank Baum wrote and directed this effects-filled tale that borrows from several of his books. The wicked witch Mombi freezes Princess Gloria's heart so she can take over Oz, and Dorothy, the Tin Woodman and the Scarecrow must save the day. Violet MacMillan, Frank Moore star. 65 min. Silent with music score and narration.
10-9089 *$19.99*

The Wizard Of Oz (1925)
Rarely-seen silent adaptation of Baum's classic, scripted and directed by '20s comic Larry Semon. A young woman named Dorothy (Semon's wife, Dorothy Dwan) finds herself in Oz, where she helps stop a royal feud and exposes the humbug Wizard. Semon co-stars as the Scarecrow, and Oliver Hardy plays the Tin Woodsman. 96 min. Silent with music score and narration.
09-1968 Was $29.99 *$24.99*

L. Frank Baum's Silent Film Collection Of Oz
This special boxed set includes Baum's own film company's productions of "The Patchwork Girl of Oz," "The Magic Cloak of Oz" and "His Majesty, The Scarecrow of Oz," plus the 1925 version of "The Wizard of Oz."
78-3037 Save $30.00! *$39.99*

The Wizard Of Oz: Special Edition (1939)
Follow Dorothy over the rainbow and down the Yellow Brick Road, along with the Scarecrow, Tin Woodsman, Cowardly Lion and Toto, too, for fun and adventure in the Emerald City. Judy Garland, Ray Bolger, Jack Haley, Bert Lahr, Margaret Hamilton and Frank Morgan star in one of the most beloved films of all time. The Harold Arlen-E.Y. "Yip" Harburg score includes "We're Off to See the Wizard," "Follow the Yellow Brick Road" and more. Special edition includes the documentary "The Wonderful Wizard of Oz: The Making of a Movie Classic," hosted by Angela Lansbury and featuring rare outtakes, and the original theatrical trailer. 101 min.
19-2891 □*$24.99*

The Wizard Of Oz: Deluxe Gift Set
The ultimate gift for Ozophiles, this beautiful boxed set includes a restored print of the 1939 MGM classic; a "making of" documentary hosted by Angela Lansbury and featuring rare outtakes and interviews; a reproduction of the original script; a set of black-and-white stills; and color theatrical poster reproductions.
12-2832 *$49.99*

The Marvelous Land Of Oz (1980)
An exciting stage version of L. Frank Baum's second Oz book features the further adventures of the Tin Woodsman and Scarecrow, plus new friends like Jack Pumpkinhead, young Tip, and the bombastic Wogglebug. Wonderful songs and life-like costumes make this play a special treat. 104 min.
07-1100 *$39.99*

Return To Oz (1985)
Disney's dazzling "sequel" to "The Wizard of Oz" has young Dorothy coming back to the Emerald City and finding its famed inhabitants under the spells of the evil Nome King and Princess Mombi. Helping Dorothy in her quest to free the city are new Ozian pals Jack Pumpkinhead, clockwork man Tik-Tok and Billina the talking hen. Fairuza Balk, Nicol Williamson, Jean Marsh star. Special video version includes a 1999 interview with Balk. 109 min.
11-1234 *$14.99*

Return To Oz (Letterboxed Version)
Also available in a theatrical, widescreen format.
08-8770 *$14.99*

The Wonderful Wizard Of Oz (1987)
Join Dorothy Gale and her friends as they travel to the Emerald City in this all-new animated rendition of the classic American fairy tale. Margot Kidder narrates. 93 min.
02-1831 *$12.99*

The Marvelous Land Of Oz (1987)
When General Jinjur and her all-girl army take over the Emerald City, a boy named Tip joins the Scarecrow, Tin Woodsman, and Dorothy to look for Oz's rightful ruler in this animated version of the second Baum tale. Margot Kidder narrates. 90 min.
02-1848 *$12.99*

Ozma Of Oz (1988)
Dorothy returns to Oz and teams up with a friendly clockwork man named Tik Tok, along with old pals like the Scarecrow and Tin Woodsman to save Princess Ozma in this animated feature. Margot Kidder narrates. 90 min.
02-1879 *$12.99*

The Emerald City Of Oz (1988)
The wicked Nome King has set his sights on becoming lord of Oz, and with an army of strange creatures he just may succeed unless Princess Ozma, Dorothy and the Emerald City residents can find a solution. Magical animated Oz fable, narrated by Margot Kidder. 90 min.
02-1902 *$12.99*

The Wizard Of Oz In Concert (1998)
An all-star cast that includes Jewel as Dorothy, Jackson Browne as the Scarecrow, Roger Daltrey as the Tin Woodsman, Nathan Lane as the Cowardly Lion and Debra Winger as the Wicked Witch of the West takes the stage at Lincoln Center for a wonderful live performance. All your favorite songs from the MGM musical are here, along with special appearances by Natalie Cole, Joel Grey, Dr. John, David Sanborn, Phoebe Snow, and The Boys Choir of Harlem. 95 min.
18-7839 *$14.99*

The Wizard Of Oz (Animated)
Follow the yellow brick road to fantastic adventure with Dorothy, Toto, Cowardly Lion, Scarecrow and Tin Woodsman as they search for the Wizard in this animated program based on the L. Frank Baum classic. 30 min.
45-5528 □*$14.99*

Lion Of Oz (2000)
A storm during a balloon ride separates a young lion from his circus pal Oscar and lands him in the magical land of Oz. There the Wicked Witch of the East sends him on a quest where he and his new friends will prove his courage in this animated rendition of the book by Roger S. Baum, great-grandson of Oz creator L. Frank Baum. Voices by Jason Priestly, Tim Curry, Dom DeLuise and Bobcat Goldthwait. 75 min.
04-5753 *$14.99*

Anne Of Green Gables (1934)
Homespun heart-tugger from L.M. Montgomery's novel stars Anne Shirley (formerly child star Dawn O'Day, who legally adopted the name of this film's character) as the pig-tailed orphan who captures the hearts of the family she goes to live with in the country. 79 min.
18-7058 *$19.99*

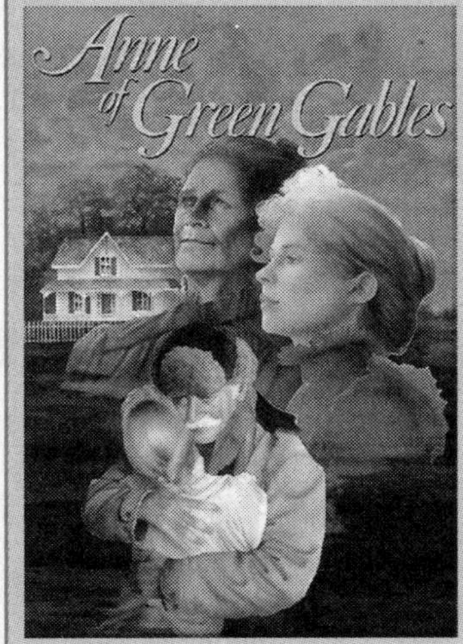

Anne Of Green Gables (1985)
L.M. Montgomery's charming orphan heroine comes to life in this award-winning adaptation filmed in the Canadian Maritimes. Young Anne's life is traced from her meeting with her adoptive family to her emergence as a young woman. Megan Follows, Colleen Dewhurst, Patricia Hamilton, Richard Farnsworth star. 202 min.
11-1441 *□$29.99*

Anne Of Avonlea (1987)
Megan Follows returns as the feisty, independent Anne, here beginning a new life as a teacher in the town of Avonlea, in this continuation of the classic family drama. With Colleen Dewhurst, Wendy Hiller. 224 min.
11-1492 *□$29.99*

Lantern Hill (1990)
A young girl must overcome many obstacles as she tries to reunite her parents in this heartfelt family drama from the creator of "Anne of Green Gables." Sam Waterston, Colleen Dewhurst, Marion Bennett star. 112 min.
11-1549 *□$29.99*

Tales From Avonlea
Produced by the Disney Channel, this acclaimed series (also known as "Road to Avonlea") brings to life the stories by "Anne of Green Gables" author L.M. Montgomery, as young Sara Stanley leaves her home in Montreal to begin a new life with relatives in the picturesque town of Avonlea, on Canada's Prince Edward Island, at the turn of the century. Each tape features two episodes.

Tales From Avonlea, Vol. 1: The Journey Begins
Sara's arrival at her Aunt Hetty's house is met by jealous pranks from her cousins and a decision to run away in "The Journey Begins," while Felicity and Sara spend a revealing weekend by themselves in "The Proof of the Pudding." 106 min.
11-1729 *□$14.99*

Tales From Avonlea, Vol. 2: The Gift Of Friendship
In "The Quarantine at Alexander Abraham's," a dare to sneak into the home of a notorious recluse puts Sara and Mrs. Lynde in the middle of a smallpox scare. Next, guest star Colleen Dewhurst plays a spinster who is shocked by a visit from a "lost love" in "The Materializing of Duncan." 93 min.
11-1730 *□$14.99*

Tales From Avonlea, Vol. 3: Magical Moments
In order to win the island's spelling bee, Felix gets a "magic crystal" from "The Witch of Avonlea." Next, Sara may have to return to Montreal when her father comes to take her home in "Nothing Endures But Change." 100 min.
11-1917 *□$14.99*

Tales From Avonlea, Vol. 4: Felicity's First Date
Can a steady diet of romance novels prepare Felicity for the real thing when she falls for a handsome cricket player in "How Kissing Was Discovered?" And when Aunt Hetty injures her back, she's not happy with the schoolteacher who fills in for her in "Aunt Hetty's Ordeal." 97 min.
11-1918 *□$14.99*

The Red Fury (1984)
A touching story about a 10-year-old Indian boy who battles prejudice and finally makes friends with a schoolmarm and a rancher. He also grows fond of a horse, and learns how to care for it. William Jordan, Katherine Cannon star. 105 min.
10-1378 Was $29.99 *$14.99*

The Quest (1986)
"E.T.'s" Henry Thomas is an inquisitive young boy in the Australian Outback, pursuing the secrets behind a legendary monster. Against the advice of an old medicine man, he allows his obsessive quest to put his life in danger. Tony Barry co-stars. 94 min.
53-3062 *$14.99*

Mac And Me (1988)
Enchanting family fantasy about an alien being from another planet who comes to Earth and befriends a crippled boy, teaching him lessons about love and independence. Jade Calegory, Jonathan Ward, Christine Ebersole star. 91 min.
73-1030 *$14.99*

Spy Trap (1988)
A quartet of junior high school kids concoct a way to raise money for a teacher's emergency surgery: develop "top-secret military plans" and sell them to the unsuspecting Russians! Soon, they're sought by the KGB and CIA. Danielle DuClos, Elya Baskin star. 96 min.
80-1046 Was $89.99 *$14.99*

The Littlest Viking (1989)
Everyone knows what fierce warriors the Vikings were, but for one 12-year-old prince, proving he's worthy of being a Viking means a series of harrowing, fantastic adventures. Exciting, fun-filled family drama, filmed in Scandinavia, stars Kristian Tonby, Per Jansen. 93 min.
80-1081 *$14.99*

Runaway Ralph (1988)
Funny, family-themed tale based on Beverly Cleary's motorcycle-riding mouse stories stars Fred Savage as the camper who calls on his talking rodent friend to help him after he's accused of stealing a watch. Sara Gilbert, Ray Walston co-star. 42 min.
70-3057 *$14.99*

The Mouse And The Motorcycle (1991)
Winning adaptation of the popular children's book about a young boy and his friend, a talkative mouse who takes to the boy's toy motorcycle. Features Ray Walston, John Byner, and the voice of Billy Barty. 41 min.
70-3058 *$12.99*

Toby McTeague (1986)
This fine family feature concerns a teenaged boy from the Canadian wilderness who assists his father in the breeding of championship sled huskies. When Dad is injured before the regional races, Toby begs for the chance to take his place—but he must learn that such responsibility is not earned lightly. Winston Rekert, Yannick Bisson. 94 min.
53-3117 *$14.99*

Seven Little Australians (1984)
Based on the popular children's book by Ethel M. Turner, this heartwarming drama follows the ups and downs of seven siblings in 1880s Australia, their stern but loving army officer father, and the trials they face together when the children's mother passes away. Stars Elizabeth Alexander, Barbara Llewellyn. 200 min. on two tapes.
50-8098 *$29.99*

The Princess Bride (1987)
Fun, fetching fantasy for the family from Rob Reiner, following the fairy tale quest of a young swashbuckler to rescue the title heroine from the evil machinations of her husband-to-be, a wily prince. Robin Wright and Cary Elwes are the young lovers; Billy Crystal, Mandy Patinkin, Wallace Shawn, Andre the Giant and Peter Falk. 98 min.
53-1726 Was $19.99 *□$14.99*

On Our Own (1988)
From the creators of "Where the Red Fern Grows" comes this touching tale of four children who are ordered into a foster home after their father leaves them and their mother dies. Escaping from welfare officials, the kids set out on their own and head out to find their estranged Uncle Jack. Sam Hennings and Scott Warner star. 84 min.
66-6066 *□$14.99*

The River Pirates (1989)
Take an unpredictable adventure with Willie and his friends as they go head-to-head against a group of hoods causing fear for an entire town. With help from his wise grandfather, Willie organizes his pals and goes after the pirates, deep in the swamps of the Mississippi. Richard Farnsworth, Maureen O'Sullivan and Ryan Francis star. AKA: "Good Old Boy." 108 min.
68-1314 Was $89.99 *$14.99*

The Haunted Mansion Mystery (1983)
The mansion belongs to a missing miserly old man who is said to have hidden a fortune in his house, but when two teenagers try to solve his disappearance they find an even bigger mystery. Family thriller stars Christian Slater, Tristine Skyler. 42 min.
70-3139 *$12.99*

White Fang: To The Rescue (1974)
White Fang, the gallant German Shepherd, proves his loyalty when he fends off wild bears and a gold thief to save the life of a boy in Canada's Northwest territories. With Henry Silva, Maurizio Merli. 100 min.
78-3028 *$14.99*

The Legend Of Cougar Canyon (1976)
Action and splendor mix in this live-action adventure set in the Navajo territory of the Southwest. When a goat leaves its herd and wanders into the infamous Cougar Canyon, two young boys set out to rescue it and must face a dangerous mountain lion. Holger Kasper, Johnny Guerro star. 74 min.
10-2696 *$12.99*

Across The Great Divide (1977)
Two orphans are stranded in the wilderness in 1876. In order to get to the land which is theirs in Oregon, they need the help of a rugged mountain man to cross the treacherous Rockies. Robert Logan, Heather Rattray, Mark Hall star.
03-1138 *$14.99*

Challenge To Be Free (1976)
A fur trapper is pursued by the law in the forbidding wilderness of the Arctic in this exciting family frontier adventure. Mike Mazurki, Vic Christy star. 90 min.
03-1173 *$14.99*

Pinocchio (1977)
This delightful, song-filled live-action adaptation of Carlo Collodi's classic children's story stars Sandy Duncan as the mischievous marionette and Danny Kaye as woodcarver Geppetto. With Flip Wilson, Liz Torres. 90 min.
08-1070 Was $19.99 *$14.99*

The Adventures Of Pinocchio (1996)
The beloved Carlo Collodi story receives an enchanting treatment that mixes live-action and fantastic animatronic effects. Martin Landau plays lonely puppetmaker Geppetto, who carves out a wooden son that springs to life and sets off on a series of adventures. Jonathan Taylor Thomas is Pinocchio; Genevieve Bujold, Bebe Neuwirth, Rob Schneider and Udo Kier also star. 94 min.
02-5109 Was $19.99 *□$14.99*

Starbird & Sweet William (1975)
An Indian youth survives a plane crashes in the remote Southwest. There, he finds himself at odds with the beautiful wilderness, but he gets help from a rascally bear cub. A. Martinez, Don Haggerty star in thisexciting family adventure in the "Wilderness Family" tradition. AKA: "The Adventures of Starbird." 95 min.
08-1445 *$14.99*

The Boy Who Talks To Whales (1975)
A teenage boy spends the summer in a California town with his uncle, a man who claims to have communicated with a whale named Gigi. When Gigi is missing, the boy and his uncle must track her down. The beautifully filmed story stars Victor Jory, Byrd Baker and Andy Gordon. AKA: "The Man Who Talks to Whales." 75 min.
10-2496 *$12.99*

International Velvet (1978)
Grand continuation of the "National Velvet" story stars Tatum O'Neal as Sarah, the niece of the now-grown Velvet Brown who seeks to become an Olympic rider and follow in her aunt's footsteps. Moving and inspiring family drama also stars Christopher Plummer, Anthony Hopkins, Nanette Newman. 127 min.
12-1299 *$19.99*

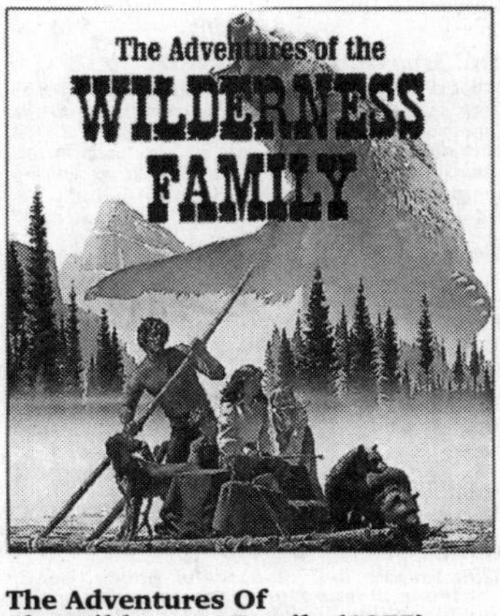

The Adventures Of The Wilderness Family (1975)
Beautiful shot-in-Utah adventure about a family who leaves the bustle of the city behind to try and live "the simple life" in a log cabin in the woods. Robert Logan, Susan Damante Shaw star.
03-1130 *□$14.99*

Mountain Family Robinson (1979)
The third entry in the exciting adventure series finds the Robinsons' pioneer existence in jeopardy when the government threatens to take over their land. Robert Logan, Heather Rattray, George "Buck" Flower star. AKA: "Wilderness Family Part III."
03-1151 *$14.99*

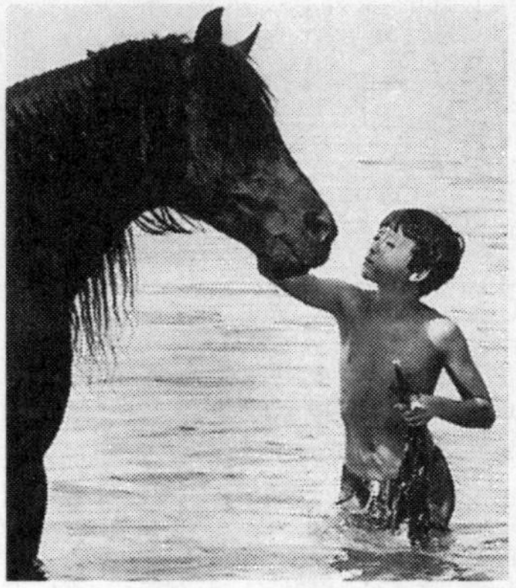

The Black Stallion (1979)
Beautiful adventure based on William Farley's best-selling series. A young boy is shipwrecked off the African coast with a magnificent horse and gains its trust. Later the pair become champion racers. Mickey Rooney, Teri Garr and Kelly Reno star. 117 min.
12-1910 Was $19.99 *□$14.99*

The Black Stallion Returns (1983)
Beautifully filmed sequel to "The Black Stallion" follows the further adventures of the prize steed and its owner, young Kelly Reno. The stallion's original owner, an Arab sheik, wants to run the horse in an up-coming race. Teri Garr, Vincent Spano co-star. 104 min.
12-2041 Was $19.99 *□$14.99*

The Adventures Of Black Stallion (1990)
Mickey Rooney returns to the role of trainer Henry Daly in this pilot film for the hit family TV series. In this thrilling story, Rooney and a determined young jockey take the Black Stallion to France to compete against international contestants in the Prix de Chantilly. With Richard Ian Cox, Marianne Filali. 90 min.
10-2866 *$14.99*

Pollyanna (1973)
A rigid New England town receives a healthy dose of sunshine from Eleanor Porter's energetic and enthusiastic "glad girl," a young orphan who comes to live with her Aunt Polly, even going so far as to play matchmaker for her dower caretaker. 155 min.
04-2715 Was $24.99 *$14.99*

The Little Prince (1974)
Antoine de St. Exupery's classic novel is transformed into a heartwarming musical-drama. Richard Kiley is a downed pilot in the desert who finds a young visitor from outer space. Gene Wilder and Bob Fosse also star. 88 min.
06-1034 *$14.99*

Grizzly And The Treasure (1974)
Ezra Lambert moves with his family to the Yukon Territory in 1898 in hopes of finding gold. Meanwhile, his wife and young son are more interested in the area's natural beauties. When Ezra finds his gold, he is attacked by a baby grizzly his son has adopted, and his injury puts them in peril through the savage winter. Andrew Gordon, Susan Backline star in this family saga. 88 min.
10-2690 *$12.99*

Peter Lundy And The Medicine Hat Stallion (1977)
In Nebraska Territory during the 1860s, teenager Peter Lundy (Leif Garrett), is upset when his father sells his prized horse, Domingo. Lundy joins the newly formed Pony Express and is eventually reunited with Domingo. Together, they become the swiftest team in the Pony Express. Mitchell Ryan, Bibi Besch and Milo O'Shea also star. 105 min.
10-2869 *$14.99*

Young And Free (1978)
Thrilling frontier adventure for the whole family, as a young boy is left to survive on his own when his parents die on a wagon train expedition. He grows to manhood, and must decide to rejoin civilization or return to the wilderness. Erik Larsen, Ivy Angustain star. 87 min.
27-6068 Was $39.99 *$29.99*

Danny (1979)
Danny is a racehorse abandoned by his spoiled rich girl owner after an accident. A new mistress, however, shows him the love and faith he needs to become a champion in this endearing family drama. Rebecca Page stars. 90 min.
27-6165 *$29.99*

The Little Dragons (1978)
If you thought "The Karate Kid" had moves, wait till you see these junior judo masters as they track down a band of kidnappers. Karate, comedy, action with Ann Sothern, Tony Bill, Charles Lane and the inimitable Joe Spinell. AKA: "Kung Fu Kids." 90 min.
44-7005 *$19.99*

Marco (1973)
A dazzling musical adventure based on the life of Marco Polo that is great family fare. Desi Arnaz, Jr. stars as the famed explorer who opened China for Europe, and Zero Mostel is the elderly emperor, Kublai Khan. Action, comedy and music combine for an exciting and delightful film. 109 min.
46-5015 *$19.99*

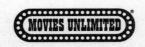

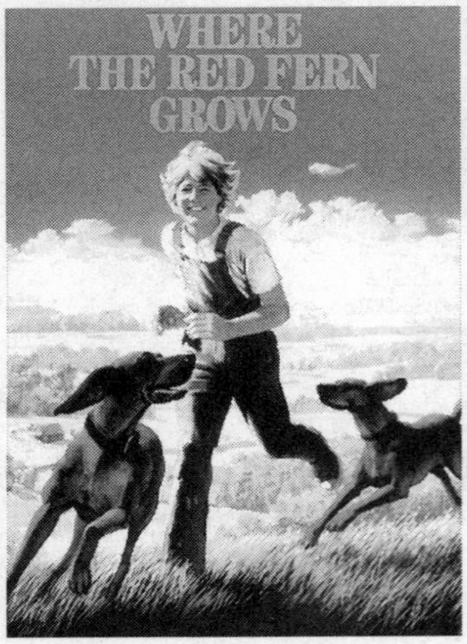

Where The Red Fern Grows (1974)
In the Oklahoma Dust Bowl of the '30s, a young boy and his grandfather purchase a pair of hunting dogs and train them for a state coonhunting competition. Wonderful family adventure, with songs performed by Andy Williams, stars James Whitmore, Beverly Garland, Stewart Peterson. 97 min.
27-5418 □$14.99

Where The Red Fern Grows, Part 2 (1992)
This poignant sequel to the family favorite is set in the Louisiana woods, where two children experience growing up with help from wise Grandpa, some hound dogs and a couple of raccoons. Doug McKeon, Lisa Whelchel, Chad McQueen and Wilford Brimley star. 92 min.
08-1507 Was $89.99 $14.99

Willy Wonka And The Chocolate Factory (1971)
Gene Wilder stars as Willy, maker of Oompa Loompas, Everlasting Gobstoppers and other sweet treats, as he leads a group of children on a tour of his magical candy factory. Based on a Roald Dahl book, this music-filled fantasy includes the song "The Candy Man." With Jack Albertson, Peter Ostrum. 100 min.
19-1358 □$24.99

The Witches (1990)
An enchanting, thrilling fantasy starring Anjelica Huston as the leader of a coven of evil witches who wants to turn all of England's children into mice. A young boy accidentally stumbles into their meeting and is transformed into a rodent, but he and his grandmother have a plan to turn the tides on the sorceress. Nicolas Roeg directs, with special effects by Jim Henson. Mai Zetterling co-stars. 92 min.
19-1826 □$14.99

Matilda (1996)
Director Danny DeVito turns Roald Dahl's story into a dark and whimsical fantasy about a smart, book-loving young girl whose parents send her to a boarding school run by mean-spirited Mrs. Trunchbill. After Matilda discovers she has telekinetic powers, she uses them to teach the cruel principal a lesson. With Mara Wilson, Embeth Davidtz, Rhea Perlman and DeVito. 98 min.
02-2941 Was $22.99 □$14.99

Where The Lilies Bloom (1973)
A compassionate story of four children in rural North Carolina who decide to band together and fend for themselves after their father dies in order to avoid being separated by the state. Julie Gholson, Jan Smithers and Harry Dean Stanton star; scripted by Earl Hamner, Jr. 97 min.
12-2461 $14.99

The Legend Of Black Thunder Mountain (1979)
After their dad is captured by some crooks and they're left on their own on a remote mountain, two children will need some help from the animals, an Indian boy, and the mysterious "Mad Mountain Man" to survive in this thrilling wilderness adventure. Holly Beemer, Steve Beemer, Keith Sexson star.
14-6053 $12.99

C.H.O.M.P.S. (1979)
A young inventor creates a mechanical pooch to act as a watchdog. Complications arise when an argument with his boss threatens his job and a corporate rival hires some crooks to steal the artificial bow-wow. Wesley Eure, Valerie Bertinelli, Chuck McCann and Red Buttons star in this family favorite based on a story by cartoon creator Joseph Barbera.
19-1522 $14.99

The Sea Gypsies (1978)
Fine family fare about an adventurous widower who sets out on an around-the-world sailing trip with his two daughters and a female journalist. When they're stranded on an isolated island near Alaska they decide to remain and start a new life. Robert Logan, Mikki Jamison-Olsen star. 101 min.
19-1551 Was $19.99 $14.99

Seven Alone (1975)
After their parents die, seven children trek 2,000 miles out West during the early 19th century. Dewey Martin, Aldo Ray. Marvelous family film! 100 min.
47-1192 Was $19.99 $14.99

Blue Fin (1978)
When a tuna boat is wrecked during a storm and the crew is left helpless, only the captain's young son can save them. Exciting family film stars Hardy Kruger, Greg Rowe. 93 min.
53-1347 $14.99

Robinson Crusoe And The Tiger (1973)
An unusual take on the "Robinson Crusoe" story looks at the legend from an animal's-eye viewpoint. Hugo Stiglitz and Ahui star. 109 min.
53-1384 $14.99

The Moon Stallion (1978)
A young blind woman named Diana has "visions" of a mysterious white moon stallion with ties to the legend of King Arthur. When an evil warlock learns of these visions, he kidnaps Diana, who must depend on her bravery to stop him. Stars John Abineri, Joy Harrington. 95 min.
53-8555 $19.99

Mr. Superinvisible (1972)
Disney perennial Dean Jones is a scientist working on a cure for the common cold, but the serum he develops turns him invisible! When foreign spies hear of his discovery, the result is hilarious, fast-paced family comedy fun. See it while you can! 90 min.
64-3018 $29.99

Salty (1971)
Clint Howard stars as the lovable tike who adopts a cute sea lion who gets into all sorts of trouble in this family adventure. With Mark Slade and Nina Foch. 90 min.
47-3093 $19.99

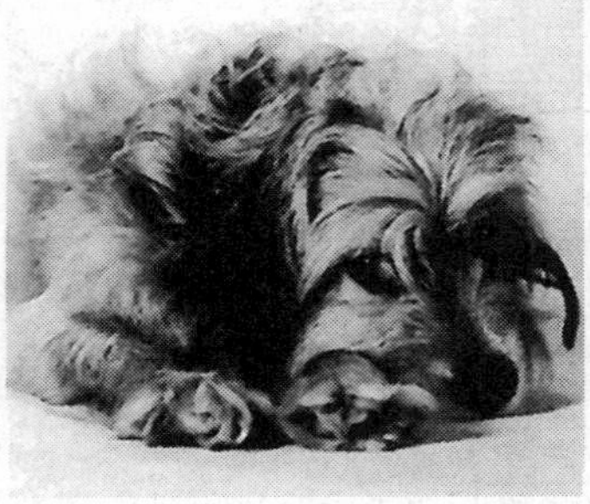

Benji (1974)
America's most huggable hero makes his screen debut, as marvelous mutt Benji finds a family to call his own, fights kidnappers, and even finds true love. Deborah Walley, Edgar Buchanan, and Higgins as Benji star; Charlie Rich sings the theme song. 87 min.
47-1049 Was $19.99 $14.99

For The Love Of Benji (1978)
Canine movie star Benji travels with his owners to Greece, but loses hem at the airport. From there, it's one harrowing adventure after another as he faces police and stray dog packs and gets involved with smugglers. 90 min.
47-1054 Was $19.99 $14.99

Oh! Heavenly Dog (1980)
What do you get when Chevy Chase meets Benji? Zany fun, that's what! Chevy's reincarnated as the precocious pup, and secret agents, the beautiful Jane Seymour and outrageous comedy play parts in this canine chase caper. Omar Sharif, Robert Morley and the great Alan Sues also star. 103 min.
04-1760 Was $19.99 □$14.99

Benji At Marineland (1981)
America's most huggable hero pays a visit to Marineland—and gets into all sorts of aquatic adventures—in this exciting video. You'll believe a dog can scuba dive! 60 min.
47-1230 $14.99

Benji The Hunted (1987)
After becoming lost at sea, Benji washes ashore in a hostile land...and becomes responsible for teaching an abandoned pack of baby cougars the art of survival. An engaging adventure for all ages. 88 min.
11-1454 □$14.99

Benji: The TV Series
That lovable and resourceful pooch, Benji, befriends a young prince from outer space and his robot ally, who have landed on Earth to escape from sinister Hunters who attacked their home planet, in these adventures from the hit kid's TV series "Benji, Zax & the Alien Prince." Each volume runs about 25 min. There are four volumes, including:

Benji In Benji Call Home
64-1303 $14.99

Benji In Double Trouble
64-1351 $14.99

Benji In Ghost Town
64-1352 $14.99

After School Specials
Designed for teenagers and their families, these award-winning, highly acclaimed dramas aired regularly on ABC and used top-notch casts and talent to handle important topics with sensitivity. Each tape runs about 45 min.

Beat The Turtle Drum (1977)
Melissa Sue Anderson plays a girl who is devastated when a freak accident involving a horse leads to her sister's death. In order to overcome her grief, Anderson tries to understand the tragedy by talking to people she believes can help her. Katy Kurtzman also stars in this touching and uplifting drama from Constance Greene's novel. AKA: "As Very Good Friends."
67-2013 $39.99

Trouble River (1977)
High adventure ensues when Dewey and his feisty grandmother travel by raft down an Oregon river to protect the young man's mother, who is about to give birth. Assisted by his trusty dog, Dewey faces dangerous rapids, Indians and raging fires. Michael LeClair, Nora Denney and Hal England star; based on Betsy Byars' story.
67-2014 Was $49.99 $39.99

Gaucho (1978)
Gaucho, a young man from Puerto Rico, believes his brother will help his mother realize her dreams of returning to their homeland, but his hopes dashed when the brother marries a white girl. When Gaucho drifts into a life of crime by becoming a runner for a a local hood, his uncle tries to set him straight. Panchito Gomez, Phillip R. Allen star; based on the Gloria Gozalez story.
67-2015 Was $49.99 $39.99

A Special Gift (1979)
In this "After School Special," a young boy who has been raised on a farm secretly desires to become a ballet dancer. But when he lands the lead in a production of "The Nutcracker," he has to deal with the reaction of his father and fellow students. Stephen Austin, Bill Sorell star; based on Marcia Simon's book.
67-2012 Was $49.99 $39.99

First Step (1981)
In this Emmy-winning story, a high school student trying for years to deal with her divorced mother's alcoholism is helped by a boy in a similar situation, but is it too late to keep her family from totally falling apart? Bonnie Bartlett, Amanda Wyss star. AKA: "She Drinks a Little."
67-2008 $39.99

Schoolboy Father (1981)
Rob Lowe drew lots of attention in this story that casts him as a teenager whose summer camp romance results in a child. When he learns that the girl wants to put the baby up for adoption, Lowe decides he wants to raise it himself, but a "trial adoption" shows him how difficult parenthood can really be. With Susan Spelman, Dana Plato and Nancy McKeon.
67-2009 $39.99

Ace Hits The Big Time (1981)
The popular book for young adults has been transformed into a top-notch "After School Special" focusing on Ace, a kid new to New York, who befriends a local gang called the Purple Falcons, then finds himself falling in love, cast in a low-budget movie and at odds with rival gang members. Rob Stone, James LeGros star.
67-2010 Was $49.99 $39.99

The Night Swimmers (1982)
A widowed country-western star ignores his teenage daughter and two young sons while he goes out on the road, leaving them to fend for themselves and have fun with such diversions as midnight visits to a neighbor's pool. When one swim lands the kids in trouble, the father's new girlfriend helps him see how much his family needs him. With Trey Wilson, Mallie Jackson, Jason Hervey.
67-2011 Was $49.99 $39.99

Did You Hear What Happened To Andrea? (1983)
Teenagers Andrea and David hitch a ride home and find their decision has tragic consequences when, after David is dropped off, Andrea is raped by the unknown driver. As Andrea's parents struggle to help her cope with what happened, David sets out to find the culprit—but can Andrea face him in court? Michele Greene, Moosie Drier star; from Gloria Miklowitz's story. AKA: "Andrea's Song."
67-2016 $39.99

The Borrowers (1973)
This TV version of the famed book by Mary Norton tells of a young boy who discovers his family's house is also inhabited by another brood: the mouse-sized Clocks. Featuring a lively score by Rod McKuen and delightful performances by Eddie Albert, Judith Anderson, Tammy Grimes, Barnard Hughes and Dennis Larson. 81 min.
10-9779 $14.99

The Borrowers (1993)
Superb family epic adapted from Mary Norton's books tells of a tiny family who live under the floorboards of an English house and "borrow" things from the "normal"-sized occupants. When the teenage daughter wants to see the big world, she encounters a human for the first time while on a "borrowing" spree. Ian Holm, Penelope Wilton, Sian Phillips star. 170 min.
18-7479 Was $59.99 □$14.99

The Return Of The Borrowers (1996)
This sequel to the popular children's story continues the adventures of the mouse-sized Clock family, as they are forced to venture out of their secretive, housebound existence and into the outside world, where many dangers—including gigantic "human beans"—await them. Ian Holm, Penelope Wilson and Sian Phillips star. 165 min.
18-7681 □$14.99

The Borrowers (1998)
If anything's ever gone missing in your house, chances are it's now in the tiny hands of the Borrowers, a race of four-inch-tall beings who live within the homes of humans. It's up to one brood of Borrowers to help their normal-sized "hosts" win back their home from greedy lawyer John Goodman, who plans to demolish it, in this enchanting live-action family tale, based on the books by Mary Norton. With Jim Broadbent, Celia Imrie, Bradley Pierce. 86 min.
02-8865 □$22.99

Mooch Goes To Hollywood (1971)
They say every dog has his day, and when this pooch gets his he wants to spend it in the town that made Rin Tin Tin a star. Mooch's visit to Tinseltown stars Vincent Price, Jill St. John, Jim Backus and James Darren with narration by Zsa Zsa Gabor. 55 min.
75-7008 Was $19.99 $14.99

The Bushbaby (1969)
A British girl living in Africa with her parents is accidentally left behind on the trip home. Joined by a servant and her pet, a tree-dwelling lemur or "bushbaby," she sets out on a cross-country journey to find her father's friends, but must dodge the authorities when it's mistakenly assumed the girl was abducted. Lou Gossett, Jr., Margaret Brooks, Donal Huston star. 100 min.
12-2746 $19.99

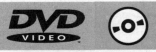

Hansel & Gretel (1965)
The Brothers Grimm story about a brother and sister's adventures in the forest with a witch and her building-code-violating gingerbread house is given a fun-filled translation in this German production narrated by Paul Tripp. 50 min.
15-5204 $14.99

Rumpelstilzchen (1965)
The famed fairy tale comes to life in this live-action film about a little man who can spin gold out of straw and makes a pact with a pretty girl to inherit her first born. The only way she can get out of the deal is to guess his name. Werner Kruger, Liane Croon star. 72 min.
15-5214 $14.99

Beauty And The Beast (1963)
A fanciful telling of the classic story that teaches how true beauty is more than "skin deep." Lovely Lady Althea of Sardi is betrothed to marry handsome Duke Eduardo, unaware that a curse turns him into a hideous monster at night. Joyce Taylor, Mark Damon and Eduard Franz star in this fairy tale favorite. 76 min.
12-2542 □$14.99

Little Red Riding Hood (1963)
Hey, there, Little Red Riding Hood fans, this movie's looking good. It's everything the Big Bad Wolf would want. Watch as the gal with the redhead meets the nasty wolf at Grandma's cottage. A K. Gordon Murray production with Maria Garcia. 72 min.
15-5215 $14.99

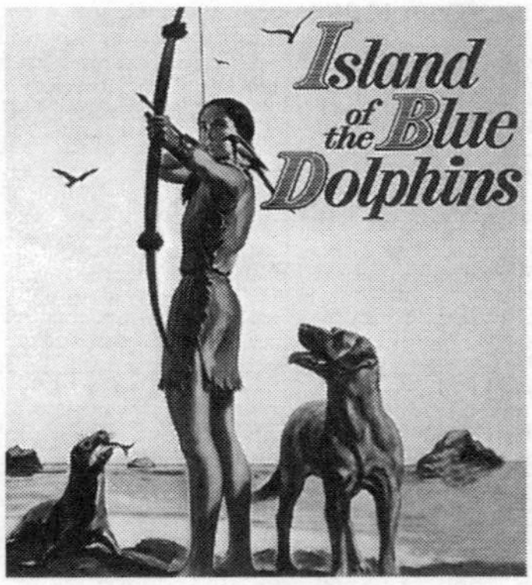

Island Of The Blue Dolphins (1964)
Uplifting family adventure tells the true story of Karana, a 19th-century Indian girl who becomes stranded on an island off the California coast. Based on the children's classic by Scott O'Dell. Celia Kaye, Larry Domasin and George Kennedy star. 99 min.
07-1311 Was $59.99 $14.99

Zebra In The Kitchen (1965)
Frantic family favorite stars Jay North (TV's "Dennis the Menace") as a boy who has a plan to help the inhabitants of the city zoo, including the puma he had to give up as a pet: unlock their cages and set them free. Soon, hippos, elephants and monkeys (and zebras) are taking over the town. Martin Milner and Andy Devine also star in this Ivan Tors ("Flipper") production. 92 min.
12-2456 Was $19.99 ❏*$14.99*

Namu, My Best Friend (1966)
First-rate live-action nature story starring Robert Lansing as a marine biologist studying a killer whale in the Pacific Northwest who comes under attack by the local fishermen, who believe the whale is a threat to their salmon harvests. The real Namu stars, along with Lee Meriwether and some spectacular photography. AKA: "Namu, The Killer Whale." 89 min.
12-2744 *$14.99*

The Adventures Of Tom Sawyer (1938)
David O. Selznick produced this lavish adaptation of Twain's book detailing the exploits of Tom and his pals in Hannibal, Mo. Tommy Kelly stars, with Jackie Moran as Huck Finn, Ann Gillis as Becky, and Victor Jory as Injun Joe; Walter Brennan, Margaret Hamilton co-star. 91 min.
04-1356 *$19.99*

Tom Sawyer (1973)
Musical adaptation of Mark Twain's tale stars Johnnie Whitaker and Jeff East as best friends Tom Sawyer and Huck Finn, getting in and out of trouble along the Mississippi. Jodie Foster, Celeste Holm and Warren Oates co-star; music by Richard and Robert Sherman ("Mary Poppins"). 80 min.
12-2045 Was $19.99 ❏*$14.99*

Tom Sawyer (2000)
Everyone's favorite raft-riding rascals, Tom Sawyer and Huck Finn, are a cat and a fox, respectively, in this colorful, tuneful animated adaptation of the beloved Mark Twain story. Rhett Akins, Lee Ann Womack, Don Knotts, Betty White and Hank Williams, Jr. are among the voices; songs by Womack, Williams, Charlie Daniels and others. 89 min.
12-3297 ❏*$14.99*

The Adventures Of Huckleberry Finn (1939)
Mickey Rooney stars as the barefoot troublemaker created by Mark Twain, finding fun and danger as he travels the Mississippi with his black friend Jim. Rex Ingram and William Frawley co-star. 89 min.
12-1048 *$24.99*

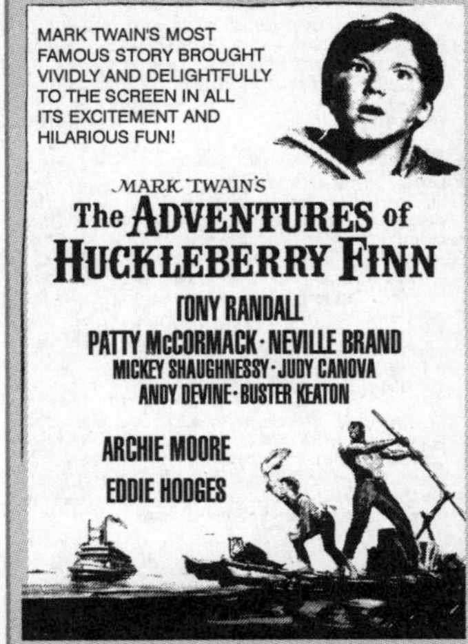
MARK TWAIN'S MOST FAMOUS STORY BROUGHT VIVIDLY AND DELIGHTFULLY TO THE SCREEN IN ALL ITS EXCITEMENT AND HILARIOUS FUN!
MARK TWAIN'S
The ADVENTURES of HUCKLEBERRY FINN
TONY RANDALL
PATTY McCORMACK · NEVILLE BRAND
MICKEY SHAUGHNESSY · JUDY CANOVA
ANDY DEVINE · BUSTER KEATON
ARCHIE MOORE
EDDIE HODGES

The Adventures Of Huckleberry Finn (1960)
Cast off for a raft ride down the Mississippi you'll never forget in this fine rendition of Mark Twain's timeless adventure. Eddie Hodges is Huck, former boxer Archie Moore his comrade, Jim, and Tony Randall, Neville Brand, Andy Devine, John Carradine and Buster Keaton are some of the folk they encounter on their perilous journey. 107 min.
12-2182 Was $19.99 *$14.99*

Huckleberry Finn (1974)
Jeff East and Paul Winfield star as rascally Huck and his pal Jim, off on an exciting, perilous trip down the Mississippi in this tune-filled version of the Mark Twain favorite. Songs by Richard and Robert Sherman ("Mary Poppins"); with Harvey Korman, David Wayne and Natalie Trundy. 114 min.
12-2743 *$14.99*

Huckleberry Finn (1975)
Ron Howard has the title role in this musical version of the Twain classic, which expands on the stories in the book. Also stars Jack Elam, Donny Most and a special appearance by Royal Dano as Mark Twain. 74 min.
04-1360 Was $19.99 ❏*$14.99*

The Adventures Of Huckleberry Finn (1985)
Lavishly filmed adaptation of Mark Twain's classic about the thrilling exploits of a young boy and his escaped slave pal on the Mississippi River. This "American Playhouse" production features Richard Kiley, Barnard Hughes, Lillian Gish, Frederic Forrest, Jim Dale and a fine turn by Patrick Day as Huck. 240 min.
27-6819 *$69.99*

The Adventures Of Huckleberry Finn (1985) (Feature Version)
The "American Playhouse" production of Mark Twain's classic is also available in a special, feature-length edition. 121 min.
07-1327 *$19.99*

Huck & The King Of Hearts (1993)
Modern-day updating of Mark Twain's "Hucklberry Finn," about a young boy named Huck and his adult friend, Jim, who leave their rural Missouri home on a cross-country search for the lad's long-lost grandfather. Chauncey Leopardi, Graham Greene, Joe Piscopo, Dee Wallace Stone and John Astin star. 103 min.
46-5583 *$14.99*

The Adventures Of The Prince And The Pauper (1969)
Mark Twain's popular story about a poor boy who trades places with the young Edward VI of England, then finds himself crowned king, comes to life in this fanciful production filmed in Ireland. Ken Shaffel and Gene Bua star. 68 min.
15-5242 *$14.99*

Mark Twain's A Connecticut Yankee
Fanciful live version of Mark Twain's classic about a New England resident who is thrust into the mythical city of Camelot. Stars Richard Basehart, Roscoe Lee Browne and Paul Rudd.
52-1055 Was $69.99 *$24.99*

A Young Connecticut Yankee In King Arthur's Court (1996)
A guitar-playing 20th-century teen gets zapped back through the centuries to medieval England in this hilarious updating of the Mark Twain fantasy. Michael York, Theresa Russell, Nick Mancuso and Philippe Ross star. 95 min.
58-5224 Was $79.99 ❏*$14.99*

The Notorious Jumping Frog Of Calaveras County
A grade-schooler who delights in hustling his classmates with rigged bets puts himself and his "victims" into the Mark Twain story about a frog-jumping contest and the rascal who thinks he has the race in the bag. Billy Jacoby, Steven Spencer star. 24 min.
70-3011 *$12.99*

The Private History Of A Campaign That Failed (1980)
Mark Twain's remembrances of his experiences in the Confederate Army paint a stirring anti-war message. Pat Hingle leads a pack of young soldiers into battle, but when faced with danger, they retreat. Plus: Edward Herrmann stars in the short, "War Prayer." 89 min.
07-1239 *$19.99*

Life On The Mississippi (1980)
The glorious days of riverboats in the 1850s come to life in this beautiful saga. Robert Lansing is the riverboat pilot whose ship sails for Americana excitement. Kurt Vonnegut introduces the tale. 115 min.
07-1241 *$19.99*

The Mysterious Stranger (1982)
An irreverent fantasy classic from Mark Twain about a young printer's apprentice who daydreams about a magical European castle where magic really exists. Chris Makepeace, Lance Kerwin and Fred Gwynne star. 89 min.
07-1238 *$19.99*

The Innocents Abroad (1983)
Mark Twain, a San Francisco reporter, journeys around the world to write a series of articles about the great cities. Italy, Greece, France and Egypt are visited by the great humorist in this exciting and witty adventure. Craig Wasson, Brooke Adams, David Ogden Stiers. 116 min.
07-1242 *$19.99*

Pudd'nhead Wilson (1984)
Mark Twain's satire on slavery, relationships and human foibles, focusing on lawyer Pudd'nhead Wilson and his experiences in West Virginia. Ken Howard. 87 min.
07-1240 *$19.99*

Charlie's Ghost: The Secret Of Coronado (1994)
A young boy without any friends finally finds one when he meets the ghost of legendary Spanish explorer Coronado in this enchanting comedy for the whole family. Based on a story by Mark Twain; Cheech Marin, Trenton Knight, Anthony Edwards and Linda Fiorentino star. 92 min.
46-5599 Was $89.99 *$14.99*

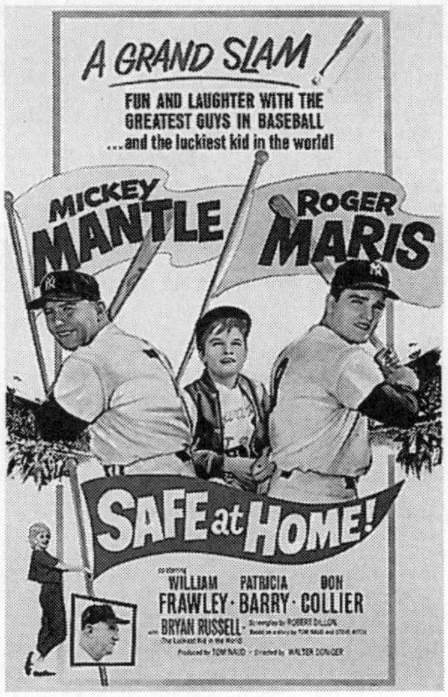
A GRAND SLAM!
FUN AND LAUGHTER WITH THE GREATEST GUYS IN BASEBALL ...and the luckiest kid in the world!
MICKEY MANTLE
ROGER MARIS
SAFE at HOME!
WILLIAM FRAWLEY · PATRICIA BARRY · DON COLLIER
BRYAN RUSSELL

Safe At Home! (1962)
The best family film to ever star Mickey Mantle and Roger Maris! A young boy brags to his friends that his father is best friends with the Yankees stars, then travels alone to Spring Training to persuade Mick and Rog to come to bat for him. Bryan Russell, Patricia Barry and William Frawley also star. 84 min.
02-2854 *$14.99*

Maya (1965)
Stunning nature photography highlights this tale of a boy who reunites with his hunter father in India and, after a disagreement, sets off on an adventure rife with danger. The boy befriends a young native on a mission to deliver two elephants to a sacred temple. Jay North, Clint Walker and Sajid Kahn star. 91 min.
12-2745 *$19.99*

Sleeping Beauty (1965)
Based on the beloved fairy tale, this story concerns a young girl who falls into a deep sleep thanks to a spell cast by a wicked witch. Picturesque kiddie matinee favorite was produced in Germany and narrated by Paul Tripp. With Karin Hardt, Fritz Genschow; music by Milton DeLugg ("The Gong Show").
15-5203 *$19.99*

Born Free (1966)
Classic family adventure film, based on Joy Adamson's book, tells the amazing true story of Elsa, an orphaned lion cub who is raised in an African game compound, and how her adoptive "parents" train her to be re-released into the wild. Virginia McKenna, Bill Travers star; features the Oscar-winning title song. 96 min.
02-1026 *$14.99*

Living Free (1972)
Sequel to "Born Free" follows the Adamsons (Susan Hampshire, Nigel Davenport) as they return to the veldt to seek out Elsa the lioness, now nearing the end of her life. Do they bring her cubs to shelter in captivity, or let them continue to live free...? 91 min.
02-1629 *$14.99*

Christian The Lion (1977)
Heartwarming, true story of a lion cub born in London who is brought to Kenya and must be trained to live in the wild. "Born Free" stars Bill Travers and Virginia McKenna appear along with Christian. A timeless story of emotional ties between man and animals that is perfect for family viewing. 87 min.
48-1087 Was $29.99 *$19.99*

Born Free/Living Free Boxed Set
The moving true saga of Elsa the lion and her offspring is also available in a special two-tape boxed collection.
02-2789 Save $10.00! *$19.99*

Ring Of Bright Water (1969)
"Born Free" stars Bill Travers and Virginia McKenna return in this moving family tale about a would-be writer who moves from London to the Scottish highlands with his pet, a mischievous otter named Mij. Based on a true story. 109 min.
04-1323 *$14.99*

Peter Pan With Mary Martin (1960)
One of the Golden Age of Television's most beloved memories is now on home video. Mary Martin shines as the mischievous Peter, taking to the sky to foil rapscallious Captain Hook, played by Cyril Ritchard. Favorite songs like "I'm Flying" and "Never-Never Land" make this color rendition of the popular play a treat for all ages. 104 min.
10-2278 Was $19.99 *$14.99*

Peter Pan (1999)
Olympic gymnast Cathy Rigby re-creates her Broadway role as James Barrie's "boy who wouldn't grow up" in this dazzling revival of the '50s musical treasure. Follow Peter, Wendy, John and Michael as they journey to Neverland and do battle with Captain Hook and his pirate crew. Songs include "I'm Flying," "I Gotta Crow" and others. 104 min.
50-8608 *$19.99*

My Side Of The Mountain (1969)
Beautiful natural scenery highlights this positive children's adventure about a 13-year-old Canadian boy who runs away from home to brave the harshness of the mountain wilderness. Stars Theodore Bikel and Ted Eccles. 100 min.
06-1280 Was $29.99 *$14.99*

Tomboy And The Champ (1961)
With the odds against her, a young farmgirl enters her beloved cow into a contest, determined to win the much-coveted blue ribbon, in this sentimental family favorite. Stars Candy Moore, Ben Johnson and Jesse White. 92 min.
08-1355 Was $59.99 *$19.99*

Indian Paint (1964)
Western drama for the whole family follows the adventures of a young Plains Indian boy and the wild colt he tames and grows to love. Johnny Crawford, Jay (Tonto) Silverheels star. 90 min.
08-1363 Was $19.99 *$14.99*

Thunderbirds Are Go! (1966)
When a manned Earth-to-Mars mission is destroyed shortly after take-off, it's up to the Tracy family and the Thunderbirds team to find the saboteurs and keep the next launch safe in this exciting feature-length adventure. 93 min.
12-1271 Was $19.99 *$14.99*

Thunderbird 6 (1968)
The maiden voyage of Skyship One turns into a deadly trap when Alan Tracy and Lady Penelope are taken hostage. Can the rest of the Thunderbirds and their amazing land, sea and air ships save the day? 89 min.
12-1297 Was $19.99 *$14.99*

Chitty Chitty Bang Bang (1968)
A magical car that can fly like a plane or float like a boat leads an eccentric inventor and his children into amazing adventures in this delightful song-filled fantasy. Dick Van Dyke, Sally Ann Howes, Lionel Jeffries and Benny Hill star; based on Ian Fleming's book. 145 min.
12-1909 Was $19.99 ❏*$14.99*

Clarence, The Cross-Eyed Lion (1965)
Wonderful family adventure, set in an African animal care compound, that led to the TV series "Daktari." Marshall Thompson and Cheryl Miller are a father/daughter team who must protect their charges from poachers, with some help from cross-eyed "kitty" Clarence and Doris the chimp. 92 min.
12-2181 *$19.99*

Snow White (1965)
Made-in-Germany version of the Brothers Grimm fairy tale in which Snow White, whose father has remarried a wicked woman, becomes the brunt of her stepmother's jealousy after a mirror pronounces her "the fairest in the land." Snow gets help from seven dwarves and a handsome Prince Charming to fend off stepmom's evil plans. Elke Arendt, Addi Adametz star; narrated by Paul Tripp. 77 min.
17-9027 Was $19.99 *$14.99*

Snow White & Rose Red (1966)
The famed fairy tale by the Brothers Grimm is brought to life in this German production. Sisters Snow White and Rose Red see a prince turned into a bear by an evil dwarf and set out to save him by stopping the spell. With Rosemarie Seehofer. 55 min.
15-5248 *$14.99*

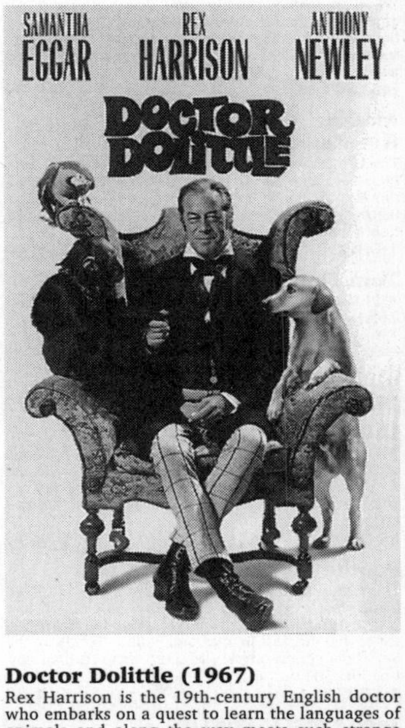
SAMANTHA EGGAR
REX HARRISON
ANTHONY NEWLEY
DOCTOR DOLITTLE

Doctor Dolittle (1967)
Rex Harrison is the 19th-century English doctor who embarks on a quest to learn the languages of animals and along the way meets such strange creatures as the two-headed Pushmi-Pullyu, the Great Pink Sea Snail, and Anthony Newley. Song-filled family gem also stars Samantha Eggar, Richard Attenborough. 145 min.
04-1048 Was $19.99 ❏*$14.99*

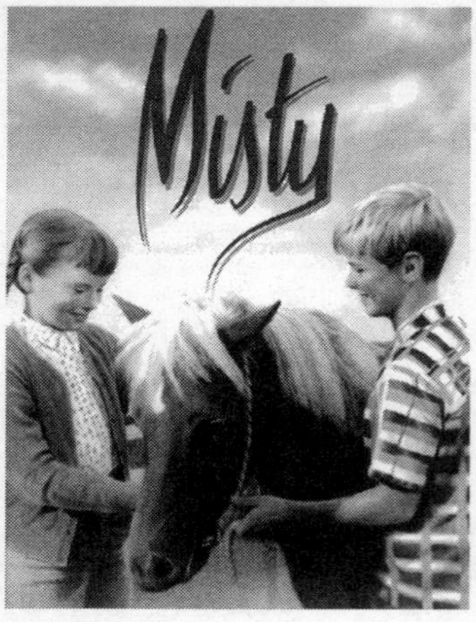

Misty (1961)
Touching story about brother and sister orphans who live with their grandparents on Chincoteague Island off the Virginia coast and take part in the annual wild pony round-up and auction. Based on Marguerite Henry's perennial best-seller, this family drama stars Arthur O'Connell, Pam Smith and future Hollywood executive David Ladd. 93 min.
06-1858 *$14.99*

Flipper (1963)
They call him Flipper, that daring, dynamic dolphin who's "faster than lightning," and when a shark attacks the boy who cared for him after a life-threatening spearing, Flipper swims to the rescue. Heartfelt family adventure stars Chuck Connors, Luke Halpin, and Mitzi as Flipper. 91 min.
12-2047 Was $19.99 □*$14.99*

Flipper's New Adventure (1964)
Filmdom's finny friend is back in his second feature-length tale, as Flipper and human chum Luke Halpin travel to the Bahamas and foil some modern-day buccaneers and their blackmail plot. With Pamela Franklin, Brian Kelly. 95 min.
12-2179 Was $19.99 *$14.99*

Flipper (1996)
Exciting and moving family drama, based on the popular '60s TV series and films, stars Elijah Wood as a troubled Chicago youth who goes to spend the summer in Florida with fisherman uncle Paul Hogan and finds a dolphin whom he names Flipper. The pair become friends as they cope with dangers both natural and man-made. 96 min.
07-2453 □*$14.99*

Puss 'N Boots (1967)
Live rendition of the Brothers Grimm fable about an ingenious feline who helps to win a miller a wife and a fortune by using trickery and neat planning. Margritta Sone and Christa Oenicke star. 63 min.
15-5205 *$14.99*

The Never Never Princess (1968)
When an envious chambermaid wants the hand of a dashing prince, she poses as his real wife-to-be to take her place at the altar. Fanciful songs and lively entanglements highlight this fairy tale production featuring narration by Paul Tripp. 79 min.
08-1807 *$14.99*

Aladdin And His Magic Lamp (1968)
Travel back to the time of the Arabian Nights, where men were men and Genies were Genies. Watch Aladdin and his magic lamp that produces a giant Genie who grants him three wishes in this Russian production. 68 min.
15-5216 *$14.99*

Tom Thumb (1967)
This Mexican import, based on the Brothers Grimm story, was filmed in 1958, but released in the U.S. in 1967. A tiny boy and his six brothers encounter a nasty ogre, a magic wand and seven dirty girls when they try to help their woodcutter father. With Cesareo Quesada. 76 min.
15-5241 *$14.99*

Lad: A Dog (1962)
Timeless live-action family drama, based on the book by Albert Payson Terhune, follows intrepid collie Lad as he befriends a young invalid girl and gives her courage. Peter Breck, Angela Cartwright, Carroll O'Connor and Lad star. 98 min.
19-2300 Was $19.99 *$14.99*

Paddle To The Sea (1967)
This Oscar-nominated story, inspired by the heralded picture book by Holling C. Holling, tells of a young Native American boy who carves a wooden figure in a canoe and places it in a stream. Follow "Paddle to the Sea's" dangerous odyssey as it travels to its final destination. 30 min.
19-3957 *$14.99*

Jack Frost (1966)
A charming live-action fantasy from Russia about a young girl left in the woods by her cruel stepmother, and how the magical inhabitants of the forest come to help. 82 min. Dubbed in English.
53-7283 Was $29.99 *$14.99*

Shipwreck Island (1961)
Exciting adventure yarn focusing on eight boys who find themselves battling the elements and wild animals on a deserted island. In the tradition of "Swiss Family Robinson," this film offers thrills, fine photography and a sense of imagination. With Paplio Calvo, Charlito Maldonando. 93 min.
53-6018 *$19.99*

Gentle Giant (1967)
Beloved family drama about a young boy who befriends a black bear in the Florida Everglades, much to the distress of his parents and the townsfolk. Family adventure that later became TV's "Gentle Ben" stars Dennis Weaver, Vera Miles, Clint Howard, and Ben the bear. 93 min.
63-1096 *$12.99*

The Man Who Wagged His Tail (1961)
Peter Ustinov stars in this delightful "shaggy dog" story about a cruel slumlord turned into a mutt by a tenant who writes fairy tales. AKA: "An Angel Passed Over Brooklyn." 91 min.
68-8237 *$19.99*

The Pied Piper Of Hamelin (1957)
Based on the fabulous Grimm fairy tale, this wonderful family favorite stars Van Johnson as the Pied Piper, who entices a village of children into a magical mountain after their townspeople fail to keep a promise. With Jim Backus, Claude Rains, and Kay Starr. 87 min.
03-1196 *$19.99*

The Brave One (1956)
This simple and charming drama about a Mexican boy's efforts to save his beloved pet bull from a certain death in the arena was marked by controversy (blacklisted scripter Dalton Trumbo, writing under a pseudonym, won an Academy Award), but remains a warm story for the entire family. Michel Ray, Rodolfo Hoyos star. Restored, remastered edition; 100 min.
08-1557 Letterboxed *$14.99*

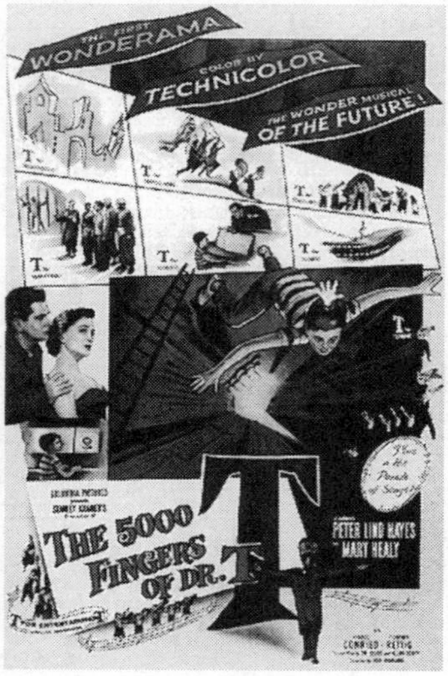

The 5,000 Fingers Of Dr. T (1953)
Unusual musical fantasy, co-scripted by Dr. Seuss, follows a young boy's nightmares about his tyrannical piano teacher. Hans Conried is the fiendish Dr. Terwilliker, who keeps 500 boys locked in his bizarre castle and makes them practice day and night. The often surreal cult favorite for all ages co-stars Tommy Rettig, Peter Lind Hayes, Mary Healy. 92 min.
02-2093 Was $19.99 □*$14.99*

A Dog Of Flanders (1959)
The world-renowned, heart-rending children's classic by Ouida is beautifully rendered in this shot-on-location film about a young Belgian boy (David Ladd), who longs to be a great painter, his grandfather (Donald Crisp), and the course their lives take after befriending a sickly stray dog. Co-stars Theodore Bikel. 96 min.
06-1281 Was $59.99 *$14.99*

A Dog Of Flanders (1999)
An orphan boy in 19th-century Belgium struggles to realize his late mother's dream and become a great artist, finding support from his kindly grandfather, a friend who serves as a model, and a shaggy dog he saves from a cruel master and who becomes his constant companion. Wonderful adaptation of the classic children's story stars Jeremy James Kissner, Cheryl Ladd, Madylin Sweeten, Jack Warden, Jon Voight. 101 min.
19-2947 Was $19.99 □*$14.99*

DVD VIDEO
ASK ABOUT OUR GIANT DVD CATALOG!

Heidi (1953)
Johanna Spyri's classic tale of the little girl from the mountains and her kindly grandfather is told in this Swiss production, featuring location scenes in the majestic Alps. Heinrich Gretler stars. 98 min.
08-8004 Was $19.99 *$14.99*

Heidi (1968)
The sweetheart of the Swiss Alps comes alive in this fine family film based on Johanna Spyri's classic tale. Jennifer Edwards is the adventurous Heidi, Walter Slezak her kindly grandfather. Maximilian Schell, Jean Simmons also star; script by Earl Hamner, Jr. 110 min.
47-1321 *$19.99*

The New Adventures Of Heidi (1978)
Can the sweetheart of the Swiss Alps find her way amid the man-made mountains of Manhattan when she and her grandfather come to America? Find out in this charming, song-filled updating of the perennially popular story. Katy Kurtzman, Burl Ives, John Gavin star.
75-7129 *$14.99*

Courage Mountain (1989)
A new, exciting adaptation of the classic "Heidi" story finds the Swiss girl now a teenager struggling to escape from a horrible Italian orphanage during World War I. Charlie Sheen plays the brave young man who attempts a daring rescue in this family-flavored adventure. With Leslie Caron, Jan Rubes and Juliette Caton. 92 min.
02-2029 Was $19.99 □*$14.99*

It's A Dog's Life (1955)
A delightfully frisky family fable about a bull terrier named Wildfire who rises from poverty in the "Bow-wow-ery" and life as a dogfight participant to the lap of luxury when a servant and his wealthy employer take him in. Jeff Richards, Edmund Gwenn and Dean Jagger star; the voice of Wildfire is supplied by Vic Morrow. AKA: "Bar Sinister." 87 min.
12-2457 *$19.99*

Gypsy Colt (1954)
Wonderful family outing about a young girl who is forced into selling her prize horse to a racing stable because of family financial problems. The horse breaks out of its new home and sets out on a 500-mile trek to find the beloved girl. Donna Corcoran, Ward Bond, Frances Dee, Lee Van Cleef star. 62 min.
12-2747 *$19.99*

Good-Bye, My Lady (1956)
Beloved family melodrama loaded with pathos and warmth stars Brandon de Wilde as a young orphan boy who adopts a stray dog that becomes his best friend. With Walter Brennan, Phil Harris, and an early appearance by Sidney Poitier. 95 min.
19-1745 *$14.99*

The Red Balloon (1956)
One of the most charming films ever made, this French short subject follows a young boy who makes friends with a bright red balloon and shows their travels one day through Paris. Using no dialogue, the story is told through music and everyday sounds. 34 min.
53-1797 *$14.99*

The Red Balloon (1956)/ White Mane (1952)
Two classic live-action family films are available on one tape. Along with the delightful French story of a boy and his "pet" balloon, there's the moving tale of a proud, fierce white horse and the small lad who eventually tames him. 72 min. total.
22-5680 *$24.99*

Stowaway In The Sky (1960)
"Red Balloon" director Albert Lamorisse looks at a different kind of aerial odyssey in this feature-length adventure. A young boy stows away on his grandfather's antique hot-air balloon for a breathtaking journey across the French countryside. Andre Gille, Pascal Lamorisse star; narrated by Jack Lemmon. 82 min.
22-5925 *$19.99*

John & Julie (1955)
Two English youngsters set out on their own to see the coronation of Queen Elizabeth II in London—150 miles away from their rural homes. John and Julie's journey via bike, bus, train and foot is filled with exciting adventures and colorful characters in this family feature. Colin Gibson, Lesley Dudley, Wilfred Hyde-White and Peter Sellers, as a police constable, star. 82 min.
70-5136 Was $24.99 *$14.99*

Hans Christian Andersen (1952)
Danny Kaye stars as the Danish cobbler-turned-storyteller extraordinaire in a fanciful family favorite, loosely based on Andersen's life. Lavish sets and ballet sequences and a Frank Loesser score that includes "Inchworm," "Thumbelina" and "The Ugly Duckling" add to this timeless fantasy. 112 min.
44-1830 Was $19.99 *$14.99*

The Red Shoes
Magnificently staged rendition of Hans Christian Andersen's timeless fairy tale from the Children's Theater Company of Minneapolis. Andersen himself tells a little girl the story of selfishness and its price. 79 min.
07-1334 *$39.99*

The Tin Soldier (1992)
The classic Hans Christian Andersen story concerning a toy soldier who would rather win over a beautiful paper ballerina than fight in a war is presented in a stunning stage version featuring the Ottawa Ballet and narrated by Sally Struthers. 63 min.
69-5274 *$19.99*

tom thumb (1958)
Wonderful Grimm fairy tale for all ages, filled with superb music, dazzling special effects and lots of hilarious situations. Tom, a 5 1/2-inch-tall fellow, is forced to help a few nasty robbers, played by Peter Sellers and Terry-Thomas. Russ Tamblyn is tom; George ("The Time Machine") Pal directs. 93 min.
12-1352 Was $19.99 □*$14.99*

The Wonderful World Of The Brothers Grimm (1962)
Spectacular star-laden George Pal production features three favorite fables framed by a story concerning the sibling tale-weavers. Lush and colorful effort stars Laurence Harvey and Karl Boehm as the Grimms, with Claire Bloom, Walter Slezak, Buddy Hackett, Yvette Mimieux, Jim Backus. 129 min.
12-1913 *$19.99*

Alice In Wonderland (1951)
Made at the same time as Disney's better-known cartoon feature, master puppeteer Leo Bunin's lively version of Lewis Carroll's madcap classic features unique stop-action puppets faithful to the original illustrations. Carol Marsh stars as Alice. 80 min.
27-6292 *$24.99*

Alice Through The Looking Glass (1966)
Step through the mirror in this song-filled adaptation of young Alice's return visit to the fantastic world of Wonderland. Judi Rolin stars as Alice, with Jimmy Durante, Ricardo Montalban, Agnes Moorehead, Jack Palance and the Smothers Brothers heading up the all-star cast.
53-1346 *$14.99*

Alice's Adventures In Wonderland (1972)
Journey through the looking-glass with Lewis Carroll's plucky heroine and encounter the White Rabbit, the Mad Hatter, and all of Wonderland's strange residents. All-star British cast includes Dudley Moore, Ralph Richardson, Michael Crawford and Peter Sellers. 96 min.
47-1272 Was $19.99 *$14.99*

Alice In Wonderland (1981)
Tuneful live stage version of Carroll's classic children's story follows Alice down the rabbit hole to the bizarre world of Wonderland. Performed by the Children's Theatre Company of Minneapolis. 81 min.
07-1301 *$39.99*

Alice In Wonderland (1985)
Lewis Carroll's classic fantasy receives a spectacular rendition from producer Irwin Allen, with songs by Steve Allen. Follow the young Alice (Natalie Gregory) as she meets the likes of the March Hare (Roddy McDowall), the Cheshire Cat (Telly Savalas), the Duchess (Martha Raye), a dancing Caterpillar (Sammy Davis, Jr.) and the White Rabbit (Red Buttons). 90 min.
19-2129 *$19.99*

Alice Through The Looking Glass (1985)
The further adventures of Alice are chronicled in this music-filled extravaganza in which Carroll's child heroine encounters the Mock Turtle (Ringo Starr), Tiger Lily (Sally Struthers), Tweedledum and Tweedledee (Steve Lawrence and Edie Gorme), the Walrus (Karl Malden) and others. 90 min.
19-2130 *$19.99*

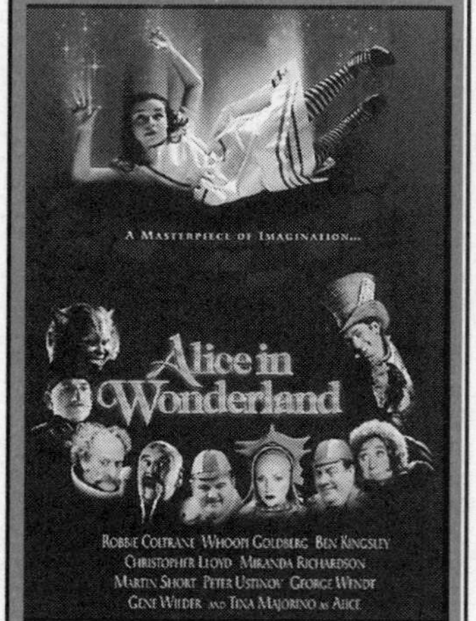

Alice In Wonderland (1999)
Lewis Carroll's timeless tale of a young girl's odyssey through an enchanted land filled with strange characters, where nothing is as it seems, becomes a dazzling, effects-filled adventure. The all-star cast includes Whoopi Goldberg as the Cheshire Cat, Miranda Richardson as the Queen of Hearts, Martin Short as the Mad Hatter, Gene Wilder as the Mock Turtle, and Tina Majorino as Alice. 129 min.
88-1195 Was $19.99 □*$14.99*

372 · FAMILY
MOVIES UNLIMITED
CALL · 1-800-4-MOVIES

Bush Christmas (1946)
No, it's not George, Barbara and the boys singing "Jingle Bells" by the fireplace. It's a superb family adventure about a group of Australian children heading home through the mountains of New South Wales for the holidays. After accidentally telling thieves about their father's horses, they must try to stop them, calling on their survival skills to save the family ranch. With Clyde Combo, Chips Rafferty.
12-3321 *$14.99*

Who Killed Doc Robbin? (1948)
Great fun and suspense by Hal Roach as a gang of youngsters investigate strange doings in an old house. Larry Olsen stars. AKA: "Curley and His Gang in the Haunted Mansion." 50 min.
01-1186 *$19.99*

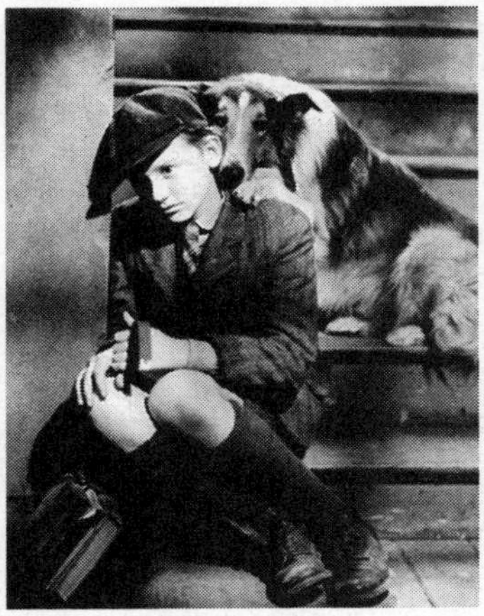

Lassie Come Home (1943)
The beloved collie made her (actually, his) screen debut in this touching family classic. A poor British family sells their dog in order to make ends meet, but Lassie escapes and makes a hazard-filled journey back home. Roddy McDowall, Donald Crisp, Nigel Bruce and Elizabeth Taylor co-star. 90 min.
12-2048 Was $19.99 *$14.99*

Son Of Lassie (1945)
Terrific sequel to "Lassie Come Home" finds Lassie's son, Laddie, helping master and RAF pilot Peter Lawford defeat the Nazis in Europe during World War II. Exciting and bittersweet canine drama with Donald Crisp, June Lockhart and Nigel Bruce. 100 min.
12-2462 Was $19.99 *$14.99*

Courage Of Lassie (1946)
Heartfelt Lassie saga, with the precocious collie nursed back to health by young Elizabeth Taylor following a hunting accident. A job working on a sheep ranch and a tour of duty in the Pacific in World War II(!) follow for Lassie. Frank Morgan, Tom Drake co-star. 93 min.
12-2458 Was $19.99 *$14.99*

Hills Of Home (1948)
A poignant "Lassie" adventure featuring Edmund Gwenn as a kindly Scottish doctor who tries to cure the famous collie of her fear of water. When the doctor gets in trouble, Lassie attempts a daring aquatic rescue. Donald Crisp, Tom Drake and Janet Leigh also star. 97 min.
12-2765 Was $19.99 *$14.99*

Challenge To Lassie (1949)
Heartfelt family drama with the ever-faithful canine keeping a daily vigil on her master's grave, until a hard-hearted policeman chases Lassie away. Will the townsfolk come to her aid? Edmund Gwenn, Donald Crisp, Geraldine Brooks star. 76 min.
12-2180 Was $19.99 *$14.99*

The Painted Hills (1951)
She's called Shep here, but it's the one and only Lassie who stars in this family drama and helps out her owner, a gold prospector whose crooked partner wants to dupe him out of his rightful share of the profits. Paul Kelly, Gary Gray, Bruce Cowling star. 70 min.
12-2766 Was $19.99 *$14.99*

Lassie (1994)
The most famous dog in movie history makes her return to the screen, as Lassie befriends a big city family adjusting to life on a Virginia farm. The clever collie helps a young boy cope with his mother's death and father's remarriage, while saving the family's sheep ranching business from a nefarious neighbor. Thomas Guiry, Helen Slater, Frederic Forrest, Richard Farnsworth star. 95 min.
06-2280 Was $89.99 *$14.99*

The Story Of Lassie
Who better than June Lockhart to host this look at the doggone amazing film and TV career of America's favorite collie? See how Lassie leapt from books to Hollywood stardom in the 1940s with "Lassie Come Home"; how she went to have one of the longest-running shows in TV history; and how the Weatherwax family has trained "Lassies" for decades. 63 min.
50-7604 *$14.99*

Curley (1947)
With his "Little Rascals" series winding down, producer Hal Roach used this film as the first in a planned line of kids gang comedies. When their teacher gets married, Curley and his pals plan a series of stunts to win her back. Larry Olsen, Frances Rafferty, Walter Abel star. AKA: "Adventures of Curley and His Gang." 53 min.
01-1156 Was $19.99 *$14.99*

The Adventures Of Rusty (1945)
The first in a series of films made by Columbia Pictures in the '40s, this family drama follows a young boy trying to adjust to his widowed father's remarriage. When he finds a neighbor's injured German shepherd and nurses it back to health, the pair form an inseparable friendship. With Ted Donaldson, Margaret Lindsay, Conrad Nagel and Ace the Wonder Dog as Rusty. 67 min.
02-2736 *$14.99*

Son Of Rusty (1947)
Danny (Ted Donaldson) and his canine pal, Rusty (Flame), befriend a new neighbor who happens to own a female dog, but when it's rumored that the man is an ex-convict, it's up to Danny to learn the truth. With Tom Powers, Ann Doran. 70 min.
02-2737 *$14.99*

Rusty's Birthday (1949)
It's anything but a celebration when the beloved German shepherd winds up missing and alone, until he's taken in by another family. Will Danny ever see Rusty again? Ted Donaldson, Jon Litel, Ann Doran and Flame the dog star. 61 min.
02-2738 *$14.99*

My Friend Flicka (1943)
Magnificent family adventure saga starring Roddy McDowall as a boy who adopts a beautiful but wild horse against the wishes of his father. Preston Foster, Rita Johnson and Jeff Corey co-star in this colorful favorite. 89 min.
04-2448 *$14.99*

Reg'lar Fellows (1941)
Alfalfa Switzer, of "Little Rascals" fame, stars in this wacky comedy about a gang of kids who foil a hold-up. Based on the cartoon strip popular at the time. 67 min.
09-2049 Was $29.99 *$14.99*

Danny Boy (1946)
Family-themed adventure about a heroic pooch who returns to America after serving as a Marine mascot in World War II but is dognapped by a group of crooks. After Danny escapes from his captors, he later attacks them on the street and is put in the pound. Will Danny's young owner save him in time? Robert "Buzz" Henry, Ralph Lewis and Ace, the Dog, star. 53 min.
09-5044 *$19.99*

The Return Of Rin Tin Tin (1947)
A young Robert Blake stars in this heartfelt family drama about a withdrawn war refugee child who finds a friend in a runaway German shepherd (Rin Tin Tin III). With Donald Woods, Claudia Drake. AKA: "The Adventures of Rin Tin Tin." 65 min.
10-8347 Was $19.99 *$14.99*

The Yearling (1946)
Marjorie Kinnan Rawlings' timeless story of a young boy in the Florida backwoods and his love for a fawn is a classic Oscar-winning drama for the entire family. Gregory Peck, Jane Wyman, Chill Wills and Claude Jarman, Jr. star. 129 min.
12-1456 *$19.99*

Swiss Family Robinson (1940)
Classic rendition of Johann Wyss' family adventure stars Thomas Mitchell as the father who must make the best for his brood after a shipwreck strands them on a tropical isle. Co-stars Freddie Bartholomew, Tim Holt, Edna Best. 92 min.
17-3002 *$19.99*

The New Swiss Family Robinson (1998)
In this family-oriented adventure saga, the Robinson family escapes from pirates and finds themselves on a tropical island where they must use their ingenuity to survive and figure out how to get back to civilization. Jane Seymour, David Carradine and James Keach star. 90 min.
50-8669 *$19.99*

A Boy, A Girl, And A Dog (1946)
Little Kippy and Button volunteer their beloved pooch for combat duty during World War II and he paws his way to topdog status in the Pacific Theater. Lovable mutt of a movie co-stars Harry Davenport and Lionel Stander. 86 min.
17-3070 *$19.99*

The Great Mike (1944)
Touching and thrilling tale of a young boy who wants to turn a milk-cart horse into a racing winner. A daring rescue from the kid's pooch saves the steed and helps to crack a gambling ring in this family-flavored outing. With Stuart Erwin and Carl "Alfalfa" Switzer. 72 min.
50-4147 *$14.99*

The Enchanted Forest (1945)
Fantasy-filled story about a young boy who is lost in the woods and rescued by an old hermit. The hermit raises the child and teaches him about the wonders of nature, but five years later the boy's mother returns to find him. Heartwarming tale stars Edmund Lowe, Brenda Joyce and Harry Davenport. 77 min.
70-1067 Was $19.99 *$14.99*

Mickey McGuire's Gang
Before he made a splash at MGM, Mickey Rooney was Mickey McGuire in a series of shorts from 1927 to 1933 based on the popular "Toonerville Trolley" comic strip. With black shoe polish darkening his hair, Mickey was ringleader of a group of adventurous youngsters that included Billy Barty. Each tape features two episodes and runs about 40 min.

Mickey McGuire's Gang: Mickey's Stampede/Mickey's Helping Hand
Mickey and pals are the underdogs in the big football game in "Stampede." And Mickey and his gang try to make Christmas fun in Toonerville in "Helping Hand."
66-6073 *$14.99*

Mickey McGuire's Gang: Mickey's Race/Mickey's Thrill Hunters
There's a surprise entry in Toonerville's Derby Day, thanks to the kids, in "Race." And Mickey and pals start a window-washing service in "Thrill Hunters."
66-6074 *$14.99*

Mickey McGuire's Gang: Mickey's Revolution/Mickey's Big Business
Mickey and his pals start a "Revolution" by adding holes to the Toonerville golf course. Next, an Olympics-style competition is turned into a wacky chariot race in "Big Business."
66-6075 *$14.99*

Mickey McGuire's Gang: Mickey's Mix-Up/Mickey's Wildcats
Mickey defends his pal in court when he's accused of dognapping in "Mix-Up." And in "Wildcats," Mickey and company discover a little baby in a cabinet.
66-6076 *$14.99*

Mickey McGuire's Gang: Mickey's Luck/Mickey's Ape Man
Mickey McGuire and crew try to help a volunteer fire department, but have no "Luck." Then, inspired by a Tarzan look-alike contest at a local theater, the kids head to the zoo in "Ape Man."
66-6077 *$14.99*

Mickey McGuire's Gang: Boxed Set
This deluxe five-tape collector's set includes "Mickey's Stampede/Mickey's Helping Hand," "Mickey's Race/Mickey's Thrill Hunters," "Mickey's Revolution/Mickey's Big Business," "Mickey's Mix-Up/Mickey's Wildcats" and "Mickey's Luck/Mickey's Ape Man."
66-6072 Save $15.00! *$59.99*

Mickey The Great
A rare chance to catch Mickey Rooney and Billy Barty before they got big: five "Our Gang"-like comedies from the '30s "Mickey McGuire" series. Young Joe Yule, Jr. was so popular in the title role he took the name "Mickey" as his permanent showbiz moniker. 51 min.
09-2050 Was $24.99 *$19.99*

Elephant Boy (1937)
Sabu made his film debut as a young Indian boy who dreams of reuniting with his family's beloved elephant after the animal is given away to a mean-spirited new owner. Exciting family adventure film, and a "boss' fave" at Movies Unlimited, co-stars W.E. Holloway, Allan Jeayes. Directed by Zoltan Korda; based on Rudyard Kipling's "Toomai of the Elephants." 81 min.
44-1835 *$14.99*

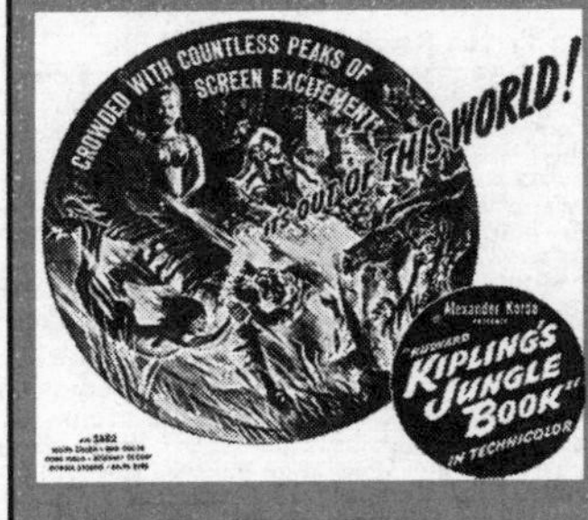

Jungle Book (1942)
The epic Kipling fantasy of a boy raised by wolves in the Indian jungle is beautifully brought to the screen by Alexander and Zoltan Korda. Sabu stars as Mowgli, who grows up to return to his village and save them from the menace of Shere Kahn, the tiger. With Joseph Calleia, Rosemary DeCamp. 105 min.
10-2054 *$14.99*

Rudyard Kipling's The Second Jungle Book: Mowgli And Baloo (1997)
Return to Kipling's magical, danger-filled jungle in this exciting prequel to the 1994 live-action adventure. Follow 10-year-old Mowgli and his animal allies Baloo the bear, Bagheera the panther and Grey Wolf as they face enemies from their kingdom, as well as those from the world of man. Jamie Williams, Bill Campbell, Roddy McDowall star. 88 min.
02-3077 Was $19.99 *$14.99*

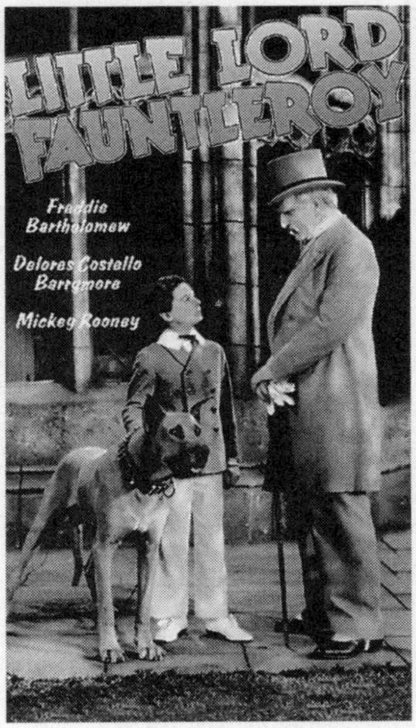

Little Lord Fauntleroy (1936)
Frances Hodgson Burnett's famous story of a New York street urchin who finds out he is the heir to a fortune and a British title, and must travel to Victorian England to claim them. Freddie Bartholomew, Mickey Rooney and Guy Kibbee star in this family favorite. 102 min.
04-1198 Was $19.99 *$14.99*

Little Lord Fauntleroy (1994)
The time-honored tale from Frances Hodgson Burnett relates the story of young Ceddie Errol, a well-mannered boy from New York who learns he is the sole heir to his titled grandfather's British estate. Travelling to England, his kindness softens his crusty grandfather's heart. Stars Michael Benz, George Baker and Betsy Brantley. 100 min.
04-3542 *$14.99*

Peck's Bad Boy (1934)
First talking version of the classic family heartbreaker stars Jackie Cooper as a mischievous lad who discovers he's adopted when a meddlesome aunt and her obnoxious brat come to stay and try to split up him and his pa. With Thomas Meighan, Jackie Searle. 70 min.
10-1371 *$19.99*

Peck's Bad Boy With The Circus (1938)
Young Peck wants to win the big race at camp and join the circus. He joins, but his misadventures with mom's sleeping pills have the lion act in big trouble. Tommy Kelly, Edgar Kennedy, Ann Gillis and Spanky McFarland. 66 min.
09-1413 Was $29.99 *$24.99*

Ferocious Pal (1934)
Move over, Rin Tin Tin! Here comes Kazan, the Wonder Dog. He ain't no Elia and he has nothing to do with Shaquille O'Neal. Set in Oregon, this adventure features the pooch as the animal locals think is killing all the area sheep, but Kazan's owner knows better. Harry Dickinson, Henry Roquemore star. 54 min.
10-9335 *$19.99*

The Best Of Shari Lewis' Lamb Chop & Friends
Culled from eight seasons of the Emmy-winning entertainer's "Lamb Chop's Play Along" and "Charlie Horse Music Pizza" series, this special video retrospective features Shari and her puppet pals in a song-filled, fun-filled salute. Tunes include "The Song That Doesn't End," "My Dog Has Fleas," "Do Re Mi," "I Love a Parade," "Uncle Lew's Stew" and many more. 50 min.
04-5635 *$12.99*

Kukla, Fran And Ollie, Vol. I
Puppeteer Burr Tillstrom was the man behind the Kuklapolitan Players, lending a hand to Kukla the clown, Oliver J. Dragon and the gracious Fran Allison. Two episodes of the entertainment and education series are included, announced by Hugh Downs. 60 min.
01-9039 *$19.99*

Kukla, Fran And Ollie: Premiere Collector's Edition
Created by Burr Tillstrom, this perennially popular kid's series featured the comical, song-filled exploits of hostess Fran Allison and her puppet pals: solemn, bulb-nosed Kukla; wisecracking Oliver J. Dragon; and the rest of the Kuklapolitan Players. This five-tape set includes "Tis the Season to Be Ollie," "Madame O's Merry Musicale," "Get on the Dragon Wagon," "Be a Clown, Be a Clown" and "Kukla Discovers America." 225 min. total. NOTE: Individual volumes available at $14.99.
67-2006 Was $89.99 *$69.99*

Our Gang Classics
Here's three silent "Our Gang" classics with early series stars Mary Kornman, Jackie Davis, Mickey Daniels, Joe Cobb and Jackie Condon. Includes "Champeen" (1922), involving a grudge match; the dreamlike fantasy "Mary, Queen of Tots" (1925); and "Uncle Tom's Uncle" (1926), a loose adaptation of the famous story. 75 min.
59-7005 Was $59.99 ***$24.99***

Our Gang's Greatest Hits
Best-loved comedies include the silents "Shivering Spooks," "Big Business," and the long-suppressed "Lodge Night" with Sunshine Sammy and Farina; also, the sound classics "Bear Shooters" and "School's Out." 113 min.
62-1321 ***$19.99***

Our Gang Festival
Spanky, Darla, Alfalfa and Buckwheat stir up trouble in this trio of comedy shorts. First up, Alfalfa is in the mood for opera in "Follies of 1938"; "School's Out" (1930) finds Jackie Cooper coming between his teacher and the altar; finally Jackie, Farina and the gang become great white hunters in "Bear Shooters" (1930).
10-1293 Was $19.99 ***$14.99***

Our Gang Comedy Festival, Vol. 1
Everyone's favorite movie kid gang is back in an all-new collection full of laughs. There's three classic shorts with all your favorites: Spanky, Alfalfa, Darla, Buckwheat, Chubby, Farina and Froggy, plus a rare '30s bicycle commercial with Spanky and a '50s TV reunion from "You Asked for It." 60 min. total.
10-2169 ***$12.99***

Our Gang Comedy Festival, Vol. 2
A wonderful collection of films highlighting the 20-year run of the "Our Gang" comedy short subjects. All of your favorite little rascals are here: Alfalfa, Spanky, Buckwheat, Darla, Farina, Jackie and others, plus scenes from an "Our Gang"-like series with Shirley Temple, a personal appearance by Pete the Pup, and more. 75 min.
10-2245 ***$19.99***

The Original Our Gang Comedies: "Don't Lie"
Five classic kid comedies starring Spanky, Alfalfa, Darla, Froggy, Buckwheat and company. The gang cause a movie mix-up in "The Big Premiere" (1940), put on a homemade circus in "Clown Princes" (1939), bromide problems in "Bubbling Troubles" (1940), spend a day as "Farm Hands" (1943), and learn a lesson in truth in "Don't Lie" (1942). 53 min.
12-1510 ***$14.99***

Our Gang Comedies: The Best Of Alfalfa
If you're "in the mood" for comedy shorts starring the cow-licked kid, here's: "Alfalfa's Double" (1940), in which he trades places with a look-a-like named Cornelius; "Alfalfa's Aunt" (1939), in which his aunt's stories inspire his imagination; "Clown Princes" (1939), about a Little Rascals benefit circus for Porky; and "Time Out for Lessons" (1939), where Alfalfa learns school is more important than football. 40 min.
12-2941 ***$12.99***

Our Gang Comedies: The Best Of Spanky
Oh, that Spanky! See the cherubic tike film a movie with his pals in "The Big Premiere" (1940); help a teacher get her job back in "Come Back, Miss Phipps" (1941); get suckered into doing the work for a wealthy kid in "Unexpected Riches" (1942); and join the gang in an overnight sleepout in order to get the early bites in "Goin' Fishin'" (1940). 40 min.
12-2942 ***$12.99***

Our Gang Comedies: The Best Of Buckwheat
You'll laugh with delight and yell "o-tay"! as Buckwheat and his pals use smelly cleaner after getting splashed with mud in "Mighty Lak a Goat" (1942); stop a gang with their reporting in "Going to Press" (1942); try to retrieve a lost baseball in "Kiddie Cure" (1940); and visit an ill Darla in the hospital with goodies they like in "Men in Fright" (1938). 40 min.
12-2943 ***$12.99***

The Little Rascals
Spanky, Alfalfa, Darla, Buckwheat and the rest of the troop are back—and better than ever!—in this collection from the cherished Hal Roach series. Hosted by Leonard Maltin, these programs offer pristine quality, uncut adventures, many of them unseen in this fashion for decades. Each tape features four episodes and runs about 70 min.

The Little Rascals, Vol. 1
Pete the Pup helps the Little Rascals stop Grandma from getting swindled in "Fly My Kite" (1931); rich kid Wally gets some kicks from a mule in "Honky-Donkey" (1934); Spanky gets pelted by pea-shooters while performing Shakespeare in "Beginner's Luck" (1935); and in "Reunion in Rhythm" (1937) some of the original "Our Gang" alumni return for a song-filled revue.
58-5134 ***$12.99***

The Little Rascals, Vol. 2
The fire's on and the Rascals come to the rescue in "Hook and Ladder" (1932); a camping trip gets scary for the crew in "The First Round-Up" (1934); in "Teacher's Beau" (1935), Spanky and Alfalfa plot to get their teacher "unhitched"; and the "He-Man Woman Haters' Club" is a big success—until Alfalfa falls for Darla—in "Hearts Are Thumps" (1937).
58-5135 ***$12.99***

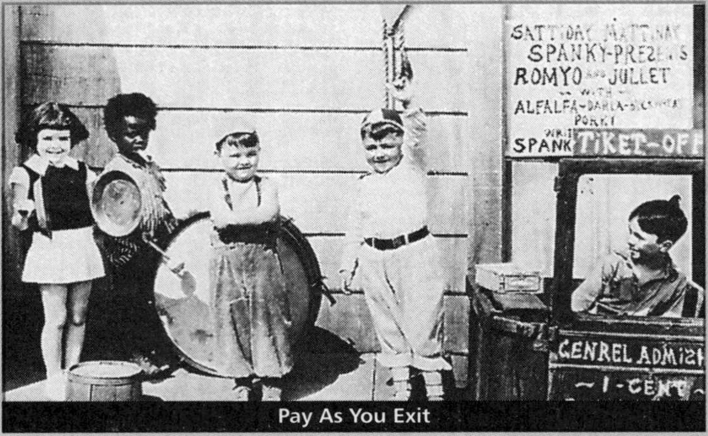

Pay As You Exit

The Little Rascals

The Little Rascals, Vol. 3
Jackie, Chubby and Farina have some unusual gifts for teacher Miss Crabtree in "Teacher's Pet" (1930); Jackie's feelings for Miss Crabtree in "School's Out" (1930) lead him to scare a "rival"; Chubby and Jackie battle for Miss Crabtree's affections in "Love Business" (1931); and Spanky and Alfalfa's elaborate hooky scheme could cost them a trip to the circus in "Spooky Hooky" (1936).
58-5136 ***$12.99***

The Little Rascals, Vol. 4
Brisbane attempts to memorize a poem about picking daffodils in "Readin' and Writin'" (1932); the gang discovers that "Uncle George" is really "Bumbo the Wild Man" in "The Kid from Borneo" (1933); the gang tries to gain the attention of a truant officer's daughter in "Sprucin' Up" (1935); and Buckwheat plays Juliet to Alfalfa's onion-breath "Romyo" in "Pay As You Exit" (1936).
58-5137 ***$12.99***

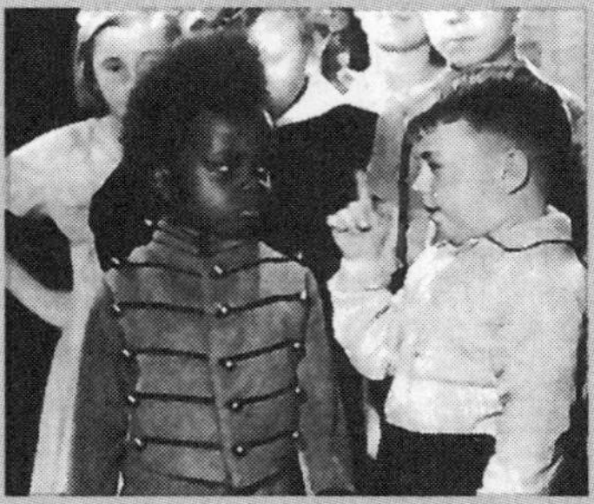

The Little Rascals, Vol. 5
Farina talks Wheezer into taking his baby brother back to the hospital in "Bouncing Babies" (1929); a pet show goes to the dogs when the gang gets in trouble in "Pups Is Pups" (1930); Stymie helps Wheezer save Petey from the pound in "Dogs Is Dogs" (1931); and Alfalfa boxes meanie Butch in the ring, with a little help from Buckwheat and Porky, in "Glove Taps" (1937).
58-5138 ***$12.99***

The Little Rascals, Vol. 6
Rich Dickie Moore has Dr. Stymie cure his stiff neck with a mule ride in "Free Wheeling" (1932); the gang plays "Man on the Flying Trapeze" to gain attention at a radio audition in "Mike Fright" (1934); Waldo plays football instead of violin at his mother's luncheon in "Washee Ironee" (1934); and Spanky has a plan to save Alfalfa's skin from the nasty Butch in "Fishy Tales" (1937).
58-5139 ***$12.99***

The Little Rascals, Vol. 7
The kids help save an old lady's general store from being bought out in "Helping Grandma" (1931); "Spanky" (1932) finds the tike taking the spotlight in a production of "Uncle Tom's Cabin"; Spanky has to get his baby sister to sleep before joining in a football game in "Little Papa" (1935); and Alfalfa and Spanky pose as G-men to get Buckwheat and Porky's firecrackers in "Two Too Young" (1936).
58-5140 ***$12.99***

The Little Rascals, Vol. 8
In "Shiver My Timbers" (1931), the Little Rascals find their high seas fantasies become a reality; the kids then trade places with orphans during a train ride in "Choo-Choo!" (1932); un-fore-gettable hijinks ensue when the Rascals play golf in "Divot Diggers" (1936); and in the Oscar-winning "Bored of Education" (1936),Miss Lawrence catches Spanky and Alfalfa with phony toothaches.
58-5141 ***$12.99***

The Little Rascals, Vol. 9
Jackie Cooper's attempts to get into his locked house prompt his neighbors to think he's a robber in "When the Wind Blows" (1930); Stymie has to save his dog Pete from the dogcatcher in "The Pooch" (1932); the gang is stuck at a strict boarding school where every meal seems to be "Mush and Milk" (1933); and Alfalfa and Butch are rivals in Spanky's talent contest in "Framing Youth" (1937).
58-5142 ***$12.99***

The Little Rascals, Vol. 10
Spanky and Stymie bake a birthday cake for Dickie's mom in "Birthday Blues (1932); Wally must sacrifice Pete the Pup after he's blamed for breaking his sister's doll in "For Pete's Sake!" (1934); the gang brews a plot to help Scotty and his Grandpa's lemonade stand in "The Lucky Corner" (1936); and Spanky, Buckwheat and Alfalfa join two vaudeville midgets in a wacky school play in "Arbor Day" (1936).
58-5143 ***$12.99***

The Little Rascals, Vol. 11
The hand of maid Mary Ann is decided in a swordfight between Jackie and Speck in "The First Seven Years" (1930); the gang constructs a fire engine to compete against rich Jerry in "Hi'-Neighbor!" (1934); Alfalfa warbles "I'm in the Mood for Love" while filling in for Darla on a radio show in "The Pinch Singer" (1936); and Spanky and Alfalfa dance at a ballet recital in "Rushin' Ballet" (1937).
58-5144 ***$12.99***

The Little Rascals, Vol. 12
Joe and Chubby square off in the ring in "Boxing Gloves" (1929); Spanky and pals are pirates in search of gold in "Mama's Little Pirate" (1934); Alfalfa prefers opera to crooning in "Our Gang Follies of 1938" (1937); and in "Hide and Shriek" (1938), detective Alfalfa searches for Darla's missing candy with help from deputies Porky and Buckwheat.
58-5145 ***$12.99***

The Little Rascals, Vol. 13
The Little Rascals are back to their old tricks, particularly door-to-door salesmen Wheezer and Stymie, who befriend a little rich girl in "Bargain Day" (1931); the crew helps capture crooks at a party in "Free Eats" (1932); "Night 'n' Gales" (1937) finds the Rascals annoying Darla's dad during a storm and at his birthday dinner in "Feed 'Em and Weep" (1938).
58-5174 ***$12.99***

The Little Rascals, Vol. 14
Spanky comes face-to-face with a burglar in "Bedtime Worries" (1933), and gets his own mug shot by a photographer in "Wild Poses" (1933), featuring Laurel and Hardy in cameos; in "Mail and Female" (1937), Alfalfa tries to retrieve a love letter he sent to Darla; and the Gang puts on their own horse race in "Derby Day" (1923)
58-5175 ***$12.99***

The Little Rascals, Vol. 15
"Railroadin'" (1929), the second sound "Our Gang" short, has the tykes encountering adventure in a railroad yard; Spanky and pals learn a lesson after they run away from home in "Roamin' Holiday" (1937); Alfalfa squares off in a boat race for Darla's affections against Waldo in "Three Men in a Tub" (1938); and the kids release all sorts of animals in "Cat, Dog & Co." (1929).
58-5176 ***$12.99***

The Little Rascals, Vol. 16
The Gang eludes a truant officer in an amusement park in "Fish Hooky" (1933); Spanky and Alfalfa's hooky scheme is ruined when they have to baby-sit in "Canned Fishing" (1938); the Rascals await the Tooth Fairy's riches in "The Awful Tooth" (1938); and in "Dogs of War" (1923), the Rascals wreak havoc at a movie studio and Harold Lloyd makes a cameo appearance.
58-5177 ***$12.99***

The Little Rascals, Vol. 17
The Little Rascals try to stop poachers during a camping trip in "Bear Shooters" (1930); Spanky, Darla and pals show an old woman how to have fun in "Second Childhood" (1936); in "Three Smart Boys" (1937), the Gang stages an "epidemic" to close school; and Alfalfa has to prove his football expertise when he comes home from military school in "The Pigskin Palooka" (1937).
58-5178 ***$12.99***

The Little Rascals, Vol. 18
The talkie debut of "Our Gang" takes place in "Small Talk" (1929), in which the orphaned crew are adopted by society folks; the group goes fishing while Spanky baby-sits in "Forgotten Babies" (1933); Alfalfa's aspirations of taming wild animals are put to the test when he encounters a bear in "Bear Facts" (1938); and Joe gets a new sibling from Farina in "Baby Brother" (1927).
58-5179 ***$12.99***

The Little Rascals, Vol. 19
The Rascals turn a school play into a pie-throwing fight in "Shivering Shakespeare" (1930); with help from a magic lamp, an elderly couple exposes the ills of an orphanage in "Shrimps for a Day" (1934); the Gang pools their talent for a big show in "Our Gang Follies of 1936" (1936); and Alfalfa battles the Masked Marvel in "Came the Brawn" (1938).
58-5180 ***$12.99***

The Little Rascals, Vol. 20
Farina enters his brother in a baby contest in "Lazy Days" (1929); the Gang ignores a policeman's warnings and stop by a haunted house in "Moan & Groan, Inc." (1929); Stepin Fetchit helps the gang after a taffy pull in "A Tough Winter" (1930); and in "Little Daddy" (1931), authorities try to separate Stymie from Farina, his guardian.
58-5181 ***$12.99***

The Little Rascals, Vol. 21
In order to get his parents closer, Wheezer fakes an illness in "Big Ears" (1931); the Gang believes they have found a magic lamp in "A Lad an' a Lamp" (1932); in "Anniversary Trouble" (1935), the kids confuse the treasury cash with Alfalfa's father's money; and Spanky skips church for a fishing trip that turns creepy in "Little Sinner" (1935).
58-5182 ***$12.99***

The Little Rascals Five-Pack
Join Spanky, Alfalfa and the crew in Volumes 1-5 of the "The Little Rascals" series.
27-7325 Save $15.00! ***$49.99***

The Little Rascals 10-Pack
Alfalfa, Buckwheat, Darla and Spanky will delight you for a long time when you purchase this collection of Volumes 1-10 of the "The Little Rascals."
27-7326 Save $30.00! ***$99.99***

General Spanky (1937)
"Our Gang" stars "Spanky" McFarland, "Alfalfa" Switzer and "Buckwheat" Thomas made their only feature film appearance together in this Civil War comedy, as the trio rescue a plantation owner-turned-Confederate soldier from a Yankee firing squad. With Phillips Holmes, Ralph Morgan. 71 min.
12-2258 ***$19.99***

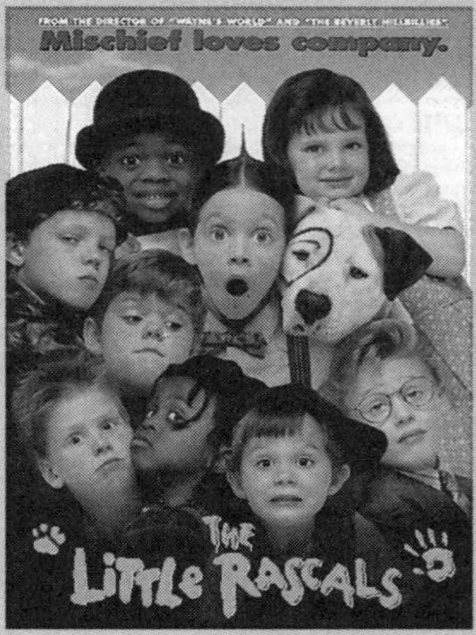

The Little Rascals (1994)
The mischievous spirit (and several stories from) Hal Roach's "The Little Rascals" have been resurrected in this splashy family farce in which Spanky tries to keep "The He-Man Woman Hater's Club" exclusively male, causing problems for Alfalfa, who has fallen in love with a—ugh!—girl named Darla. Bug Hall, Travis Tedford and Brittany Ashton Holmes star. 83 min.
07-2232 Was $24.99 ***$14.99***

The Our Gang Story: 20 Years & 200 Episodes
Rare footage takes you behind the scenes of the classic "Our Gang"/"Little Rascals" series, as the careers of "Rascals" Alfalfa, Buckwheat, Froggy and the rest are showcased in this program. Included is the 1952 reunion on "You Asked for It" and a madcap race with Jackie Cooper, the Marx Brothers and Carole Lombard. A collector's treat! 45 min.
10-2577 ***$19.99***

Black Beauty (1933)
An early version of Anna Sewell's classic tells of a beautiful horse whose steeplechase abilities are what the Cameron estate is banking upon. But when the horse is injured, its racing days are threatened and its original family comes to its aid. Esther Ralston, Alexander Kirkland star. 70 min.
10-1601 *$19.99*

Courage Of Black Beauty (1957)
Wholesome heartwarmer tells the tale of a young boy (Johnny Crawford) who raises a foal into a prized horse and the effect the animal has on the boy's strained relationship with his father. J. Pat O'Malley, John Bryant co-star. 77 min.
27-6466 Was $19.99 *$14.99*

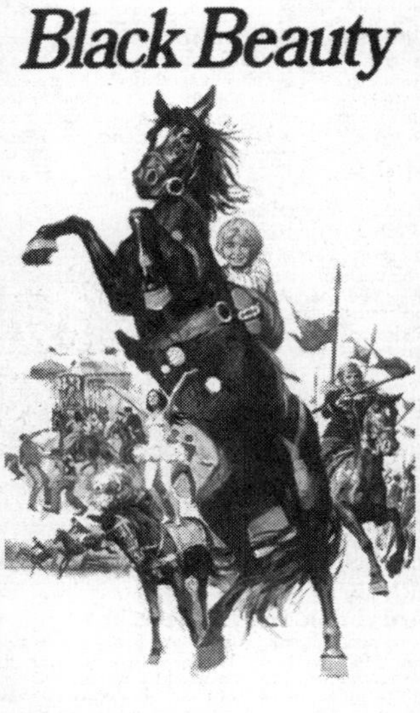

Black Beauty (1971)
Moving, classic family drama about the friendship and understanding between a boy and his horse. Mark Lester ("Oliver") stars as the boy who loses, but finally is reunited with, Black Beauty. Walter Slezak co-stars. 109 min.
06-1279 *$14.99*

Black Beauty (1994)
A gorgeously filmed adaptation of Anna Sewell's timeless book which faithfully follows the adventures of a beautiful ebony horse from her birth and upbringing to her experiences with various owners. Narrated by Black Beauty herself, this is an exciting and tender tale sure to delight the entire family. With Sean Bean, David Thewlis, Eleanor Bron and Peter Cook. 88 min.
19-2272 □*$19.99*

The New Adventures Of Black Beauty
The classic story of Anna Sewell's family favorite continues in this all-new live-action series. The tale centers on Vicky, a 12-year-old English girl who travels with her stepmother to New Zealand, where she befriends a magnificent black horse. Each two-episode tape runs about 120 min.

The New Adventures Of Black Beauty: Set 1
This two-tape boxed set includes "Vol. 1: The Old World/A Horse Like Beauty" and "Vol. 2: Breaking In/Ride a Black Horse." 120 min. total.
50-2835 *$29.99*

The New Adventures Of Black Beauty: Set 2
This three-tape boxed set includes "Vol. 3: Deceptive Appearances/Fear of Water," "Vol. 4: Treasure Hunt/The Birdman" and "Vol. 5: Different Races/A Question of Justice." 180 min. total.
50-2977 *$39.99*

Children Of The Wild (1937)
Police dog Silver Wolf is blamed for a child's death, but (wait a minute...he's trying to tell us something) the truth is she was stolen to an eyrie by a giant eagle. The animal actors are equal to the charming juveniles in this fangs and talons actioner. AKA: "Killers of the Wild." 58 min.
09-2055 Was $29.99 *$14.99*

Ultraman, Vol. 1
Hayata, the Beta Capsule! It's the original '60s "Ultraman" series, the UHF favorite in which ace pilot Hayata uses his Beta Capsule to become the giant alien superhero Ultraman, so he and the Science Patrol can battle huge monsters across the Japanese landscape. Includes the first episode "Ultra Operation #1," "Shoot the Invader," "Go Science Patrol" and "Five Seconds Until Apocalypse." 110 min.
20-7636 *$24.99*

Mighty Morphin Power Rangers: The Movie (1995)
The high-kicking sextet of TV action heroes "go, go" big-time in their first feature film, facing the messy menace of a sinister slimelord named Ivan Ooze. But when Ivan steals their "morphin" energy, the now-powerless Rangers must travel to a distant planet to gain new abilities that will help them save planet Earth. 96 min.
04-3249 Was $19.99 □*$14.99*

Turbo: A Power Rangers Movie (1997)
Fans of super-charged superhero excitement need look no further than this all-new Power Rangers feature. The Rangers need all their new Turbo powers—plus the help of some old and new allies—to stop an evil interstellar villainess from destroying the Earth. 85 min.
04-3470 Was $19.99 □*$14.99*

Power Rangers In Space (1998)
Get ready to "go, go" into the final frontier, as the karate-chopping quintet uses its new Astro Megaship to blast off into space and defend Earth from the sinister Dark Specter and his henchwoman Astronema in this feature-length adventure. 80 min.
04-3763 □*$14.99*

Power Rangers Lost Galaxy (1999)
The super-suited heroes "morph" into yet another incarnation in this full-length pilot for the hit TV series, as five teenagers from the Earth colony Terra Venture become Power Rangers and battle the intergalactic menace of Scorpius and his minions.
04-3855 *$14.99*

Power Rangers Lost Galaxy: The Return Of The Magna Defender (1999)
Have the Rangers met with a new ally or an enemy when Magna Defender, the rogue warrior whose son was killed by Scorpius years earlier, returns in this special feature-length adventure? 60 min.
04-3892 *$14.99*

Power Rangers Lightspeed Rescue (2000)
The power is passed on to a new breed of ranger. See how a quintet of teen heroes becomes the Lightspeed Power Rangers and use their Rescue Zords to battle the demented Diabolico and his monster minions in this feature-length thriller. 70 min.
04-3939 *$14.99*

Power Rangers Power Payback
It's "Morphing Time" once again with the original Power Rangers band. Thrill to the adventures of the teenage monster-fighting quintet in these classic compilations.

Power Rangers Power Playback: Red Ranger Adventure
Includes "Day of the Dumpster" and "Wanna Be a Ranger."
04-3913 *$12.99*

Power Rangers Power Playback: Pink Ranger Adventure
Includes "No Clowning Around" and "Bloom of Doom."
04-3914 *$12.99*

Power Rangers Power Playback: Black Ranger Adventure
Includes "Happy Birthday Zach" and "Putty on the Brain."
04-3915 *$12.99*

Power Rangers 3-Pack
Power up some savings with this three-tape collection that includes "Power Rangers Lost Galaxy," "Power Rangers Lost Galaxy: The Return of the Magna Defender" and "Power Rangers Lightspeed Rescue."
04-3975 Save $5.00! *$39.99*

Wishbone
Hot-diggity-dog! Direct from PBS comes this series featuring canines in the roles of literature's greatest characters. Boasting great production values, superb costumes and tour-de-force performances from the lead pooch, a wily white mutt, and his cohorts. Except where noted, each tape runs about 30 min. There are 11 volumes available, including:

Wishbone: The Slobbery Hound
02-8402 *$14.99*

Wishbone: The Prince And The Pooch
02-8405 *$14.99*

Wishbone: Mary Shelley's Frankenstein
02-8546 *$14.99*

Wishbone: Bone Of Arc
02-8547 *$14.99*

Wishbone: Dog Days Of The West
Everyone's favorite daredevil dog becomes a frontier hero—and the Wild West will never be the same—in this feature-length family adventure based on the acclaimed PBS series. 90 min.
50-4720 *$14.99*

Wishbone In The Legend Of Sleepy Hollow
A Halloween scavenger hunt sends Wishbone and Joe to the old Murphy home, where Joe once saw a ghost. Meanwhile, "Ichabod Crane" Wishbone has his own spirit problems with the infamous Headless Horseman of Sleepy Hollow. 60 min.
50-5974 *$14.99*

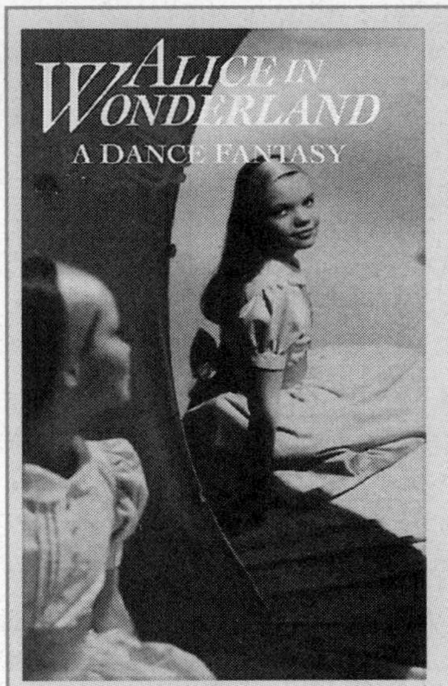

Alice In Wonderland: A Dance Fantasy
Lewis Carroll's classic children's tale becomes a wonderful ballet experience for the whole family, combining dancers, mimes and acrobatic artists, in this production featuring the Prague Chamber Ballet and Czech Philharmonic Orchestra. 27 min.
22-7123 *$19.99*

The Magic Flute Story: An Opera Fantasy
Mozart's classic story of young lovers and the magical flute that helps bring them together is told in a special condensed version, featuring a live cast singing in German with English-language narration and designed to introduce children to the world of opera. 42 min.
22-7148 *$19.99*

Hansel And Gretel: An Opera Fantasy
Two lost and hungry children, a house made of gingerbread, and a wicked witch add up to fun and excitement in this acclaimed 1954 production that mixed puppetry with stop-motion animation to bring Englebert Humperdinck's operetta to life. Singers include Anna Russell, Mildred Dunnock, Frank Rogier. 72 min.
22-7160 *$19.99*

Bizet's Dream
A young girl named Michelle living in 1875 Paris receives valuable lessons on playing the piano and bringing her estranged parents back together from her new music teacher, composer Georges Bizet, in this visually stunning family drama. Features music from "Carmen Suites," "L'Arlésienne" and "The Pearl Fishers." 53 min.
04-5357 *$19.99*

Bach's Fight For Freedom
After reluctantly becoming an aide to a struggling composer named Johann Sebastian Bach, a young boy learns a valuable lesson in self-reliance while helping Bach achieve his dreams in this music-filled drama. Includes selections from the Brandenberg Concertos, "Jesu, Joy of Man's Desiring" and more. 53 min.
04-5406 *$19.99*

Liszt's Rhapsody
This compelling, music-filled tale follows the life of a young Franz Liszt before he became a famous composer, when, acclaimed as a pianist, he lived a life similar to contemporary rock stars. What Liszt really wanted to do was write his own music, and this film shows how a young Gypsy violinist helped him realize his dream. 53 min.
04-5433 *$19.99*

Strauss: The King Of 3/4 Time
Living in the shadow of his famous father and driven to make a name for himself, Johann Strauss, Jr. comes to the aid of a put-upon stable boy and forms a friendship that transforms both their lives in this compelling entry in the "Composer's Specials" series. 50 min.
04-5454 *$19.99*

Rossini's Ghost
After the initial performance of his latest opera, "The Barber of Seville," is a disappointing failure, composer Gioacchino Rossini receives some otherworldly encouragement from an invisible little girl. 50 min.
04-5486 *$19.99*

Handel's Last Chance
In 18th-century Dublin, an impoverished young boy who dreams of being a singer befriends the composer George Frideric Handel, who fears his music is falling out of favor. Together they receive a chance to prove themselves, through the premiere of Handel's most beloved work, "The Messiah." 50 min.
04-5489 *$19.99*

Composer's Specials Boxed Set
This deluxe six-tape collector's set includes the live-action family dramas "Bach's Fight for Freedom," "Bizet's Dream," "Handel's Last Chance," "Liszt's Rhapsody," "Rossini's Ghost" and "Strauss: The King of 3/4 Time."
04-5490 Save $20.00! *$99.99*

Who's Afraid Of Opera?: Complete Set
Renowned soprano Joan Sutherland is joined by a group of puppet friends to enact famous scenes from the world's best-loved operas in this entertaining and educational four-tape series for the whole family. "Faust," "Rigoletto," "La Traviata," "Daughter of the Regiment," "The Barber of Seville," "Lucia di Lammermoor," "Mignon" and "La Perichole" are featured. 240 min. total. NOTE: Individual volumes available at $14.99 each.
22-1321 *$59.80*

The Adventures Of Peer Gynt
Award-winning puppeteer Jim Gamble helps Henrik Ibsen's classic story and Edward Grieg's music come to life with his fanciful and colorful creations of Peer Gynt, Green Hilda, Whirling Dervishes and the Mountain King. 30 min.
89-7001 *$14.99*

Carnival Of The Animals
Superior puppet production of Camille Saint-Saens' story of a young boy who writes a musical for an imaginary carnival in which household objects turn into clowns, elephants and other things. From master puppeteer Jim Gamble and featuring full orchestration. 30 min.
89-7005 *$14.99*

The Nutcracker
Jim Gamble's amazing puppets help bring Tchaikovsky's famed piece to life. Sugar Plum fairies, toy soldiers, Cossack acrobats, Chinese dragons and other puppets are used, along with the Berlin Symphony Orchestra, to make this a memorable production. 30 min.
89-7016 *$14.99*

Peter And The Wolf
This production showcases Jim Gamble's amazing puppets to enact Prokofiev's fabled story and teach children about music in the process. People, animals and animated instruments spring to life as puppets in this endearing tale. 30 min.
89-7020 *$14.99*

Cinderella...Frozen In Time
Olympic gold medalist Dorothy Hamill skates her way to the royal ball, taking the title role in this family spectacle that features the Ice Capades skaters in a lively musical telling of the fairy tale favorite. Narrated by Lloyd Bridges.
04-5405 *$14.99*

Sleeping Beauty On Ice
The timeless fairy tale of true love and long catnaps; the haunting music of Tchaikovsky; Olympic skaters Robin Cousins and Rosalynn Somners. Combine these elements and you have an enchanting ice spectacle for young and old alike. 62 min.
22-1078 Was $29.99 *$24.99*

The Nutcracker: A Fantasy On Ice (1983)
Tchaikovsky's beloved ballet is given a more wintry flavor than ever before in this adaptation performed on ice skates. Dorothy Hamill is Clara and Robin Cousins is the Nutcracker in this delightfully graceful holiday treat. 85 min.
68-1046 Was $24.99 *$12.99*

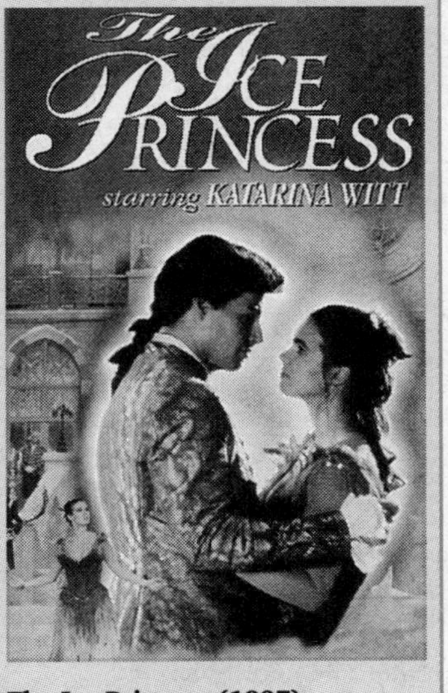

The Ice Princess (1997)
The timeless story of Cinderella forms the basis for this enchanting, song-filled ice-skating spectacle starring Olympic champion Katarina Witt as Ella, the simple maid who captures a handsome prince's heart. With Christopher Barker, Vernon Dobtcheff. 60 min.
53-9977 Was $19.99 *$14.99*

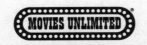

Shirley Temple

Shirley Temple: The Early Years: Dora's Dunkin' Donuts
Here are four short comedies made by the *very* young Temple shortly before she made a big splash in features. Temple stars with Andy Clyde in "Dora's Dunking Doughnuts" (1932), followed by "Managed Money" (1934), and "The Pie-Covered Wagon" (1932) and "War Babies" (1933) from the "Baby Burlesks" series. 58 min.
67-5031 $14.99

Shirley Temple: The Early Years: What's To Do
More rarely-seen shorts with everyone's favorite moppet are offered in this collection that features "What's to Do," "Kid in Africa," "Kid in Hollywood" and "Polly-Tix in Washington." 47 min.
67-5032 $14.99

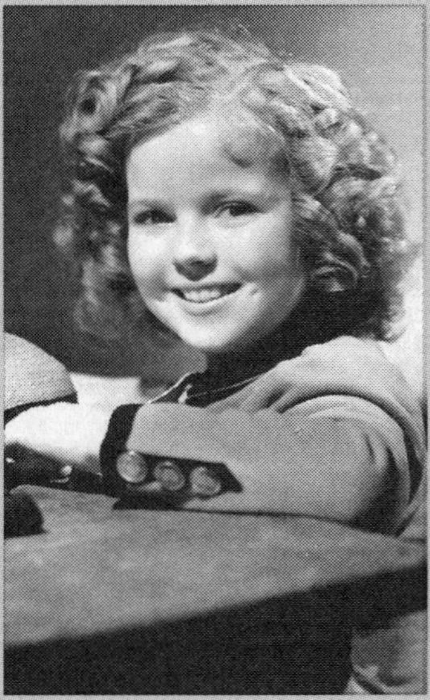

Shirley Temple: The Early Years: Merrily Yours
Shirley Temple shines in four short comedies, all filmed before she was five years old, that showcase her performing talents. Included on this program are "Merrily Yours," "Pardon My Pups" and "Glad Rags to Riches," plus the 1976 documentary "Shirley Temple: The Biggest Little Star of the Thirties." 58 min.
67-5033 $14.99

The Red-Haired Alibi (1932)
Before she became a big star and a household name, Shirley Temple played a small but crucial role in this crime drama. She's the daughter of a criminal who tries everything she can to keep him out of jail. But her attempts only go so far when Dad gets into more trouble. With Merna Kennedy, Theodore Von Eltz and Grant Withers. 70 min.
10-9985 $14.99

Stand Up And Cheer (1934)
Will Rogers had the idea for this Depression-beater about a big variety show staged by "Secretary of Entertainment" Warner Baxter to lift the nation's spirits. The host of talent includes six-year-old Shirley Temple, Stepin Fetchit, Theresa "Aunt Jemima" Gardenia, and John Boles, and songs include "Baby Take a Bow" and "We're Out of the Red." 69 min.
04-2199 □$19.99

Baby Take A Bow (1934)
The first starring vehicle for Shirley Temple was a musical drama about an ex-con struggling to stay straight and the adorable daughter who keeps him away from shady criminals and a persistent cop. James Dunn and Claire Trevor co-star. 76 min.
04-2203 □$19.99

Baby Take A Bow (Color Version)
04-2944 □$14.99

Bright Eyes (1934)
Irresistible orphan Shirley Temple charms a rich old coot, his lovely niece and an adventurous flyer who compete for adoption rights. This is the movie that features America's Sweetheart doing her classic rendition of "On the Good Ship Lollipop." With Jane Darwell, James Dunn. 90 min.
04-2200 □$19.99

Bright Eyes (Color Version)
04-2792 □$14.99

Little Miss Marker (Color Version) (1934)
The classic Damon Runyon tale received its first—and most-beloved—cinematic treatment with Shirley Temple as the cute youngster left to bookie Adolphe Menjou as a gambling marker. Her influence leads Menjou to try to mend his ways and marry his nightclub singer girlfriend. Dorothy Dell, Charles Bickford also star. 79 min.
07-2443 □$14.99

Now And Forever (Color Version) (1934)
Con man Gary Cooper is reunited with young daughter Shirley Temple, who lived with relatives after her mother's death, and takes the tike with him on his scams while trying to get to know her better. For the sake of the child, girlfriend Carole Lombard tries to talk Cooper into going straight, but can this crook say goodbye to crime for good? With Charlotte Granville. 82 min.
07-2444 □$14.99

Curly Top (1935)
How would America have ever gotten through the Depression without Shirley Temple tapping and charming her way into our hearts? Here she's a plucky orphan who plays matchmaker for her big sister with a handsome millionaire. With John Boles, Rochelle Hudson, Arthur Treacher; songs include "Animal Crackers in My Soup," "When I Grow Up." 75 min.
04-1232 □$19.99

Curly Top (Color Version)
04-2819 □$14.99

Our Little Girl (1935)
When her doctor dad ignores his family for his career and her mother receives amorous attention from a neighbor, poor Shirley Temple runs away from home in an attempt to bring her parents back together in this early soaper. 64 min.
04-2204 □$19.99

Our Little Girl (Color Version)
04-2949 □$14.99

The Littlest Rebel (1935)
When her father is arrested by Union soldiers and wrongly sentenced to death as a Confederate spy, singing Southern belle Shirley Temple goes all the way to President Lincoln to save his life. Features John Boles, Bill Robinson. 70 min.
04-1011 □$19.99

The Littlest Rebel (Color Version)
04-2820 □$14.99

The Little Colonel (1935)
One of Shirley Temple's best-loved films, with the million-dollar moppet playing peacemaker between her ex-Confederate officer grandfather and her mother, who married a Yankee. Features the classic "stair dance" between Temple and Bill "Bojangles" Robinson; with Lionel Barrymore. 80 min.
04-1013 □$19.99

The Little Colonel (Color Version)
04-2818 □$14.99

Poor Little Rich Girl (1936)
Sent off by her widowed father to attend a private school, chipper gamine Shirley Temple runs away and joins a song and dance duo in this spry musical treat for the whole family. Co-stars Jack Haley, Alice Faye, Gloria Stuart; songs include "Oh My Goodness," "Military Man." 72 min.
04-1007 □$19.99

Poor Little Rich Girl (Color Version)
04-2817 □$14.99

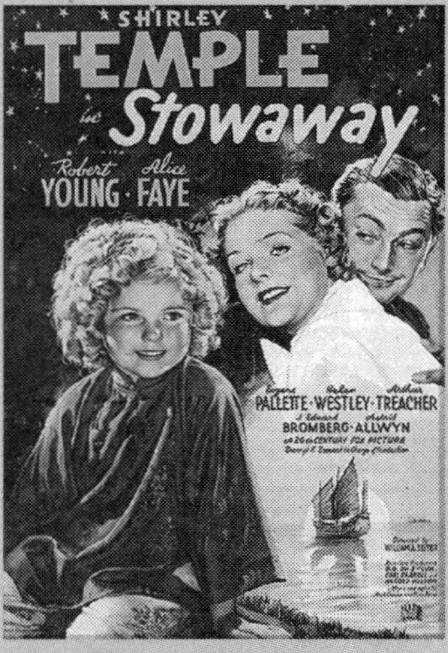

Stowaway (1936)
This is the film where Shirley Temple "speaks and sings Chinese," according to the ads. She's the ward of a group of murdered missionaries in China who hides in an ocean liner bound for America. Along the way she's adopted by Robert Young and Alice Faye, sings "I Wanna Go to the Zoo" and "That's What I Want for Christmas," and imitates Jolson and Cantor! 86 min.
04-1005 □$19.99

Stowaway (Color Version)
04-2901 □$14.99

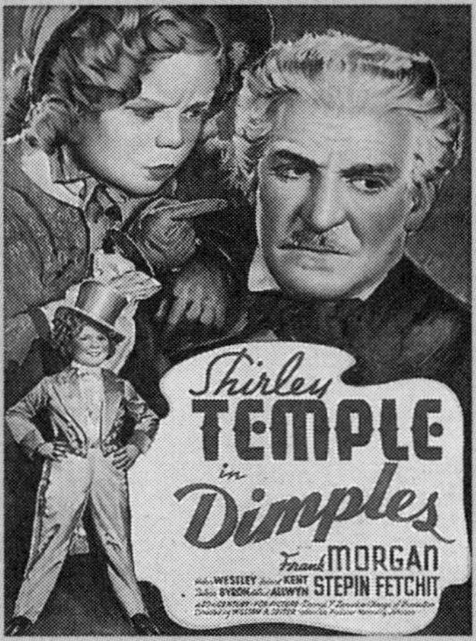

Dimples (1936)
Street performer Shirley Temple is cared for by rapscallious grandfather Frank Morgan in turn-of-the-century New York when a society matron offers to adopt her in this tuneful tearjerker. Songs include "Oh Mister Man Up in the Moon" and "Dixie-Anna"; Bill Robinson arranged the dancing. 78 min.
04-1025 □$19.99

Dimples (Color Version)
04-2793 □$14.99

Captain January (1936)
Lighthouse keeper Guy Kibbee saves Shirley Temple from the boating accident that drowns her folks and the two lead a happy life with their salty pals until a truant officer interferes. Sentimental favorite with great songs, including Shirley's delightful dance routine with Buddy Ebsen, "At the Codfish Ball." 78 min.
04-2201 □$19.99

Captain January (Color Version)
04-2883 □$14.99

Wee Willie Winkie (1937)
Orphan Shirley Temple lives in colonial India with Granddad and plays mascot to British troops in her own pint-sized uniform. A Kipling-based adventure well-suited to the talents of director John Ford, with plenty of teary sentiment for the dimpled darling. Co-stars Victor McLaglen. 100 min.
04-2198 □$19.99

Wee Willie Winkie (Color Version)
04-2821 □$14.99

Heidi (Color Version) (1937)
Shirley Temple is the little Swiss orphan girl who reaches the hearts of her gruff grandfather and teaches a crippled girlfriend to walk again in this classic version of Johanna Spyri's novel. With Jean Hersholt, Arthur Treacher, Helen Westley and Pauline Moore. 88 min.
04-2794 □$14.99

Little Miss Broadway (1938)
As the perky charge of a group of vaudevillians living in a boarding house, Shirley Temple helps them put on a variety show to pay the rent and even wins over landlady Edna May Oliver. With George Murphy, Jimmy Durante; songs include "Be Optimistic," "When You Were Sweet Sixteen." 70 min.
04-1009 □$19.99

Little Miss Broadway (Color Version)
04-2896 □$14.99

Just Around The Corner (1938)
When her architect father loses his job, it's up to little Shirley Temple to talk a miserly tycoon into creating new jobs to help out Depression-riddled America. Winning musical tale also stars Bill Robinson, Charles Farrell, Bert Lahr; songs include "I'll Be Lucky with You," "I'm Not Myself Today." 70 min.
04-1015 □$19.99

Just Around The Corner (Color Version)
04-2940 □$14.99

Rebecca Of Sunnybrook Farm (1938)
It's not really based on the classic story, but this tale of a child's becoming a radio star is a must-see for Shirley Temple fans. Little Shirley sings "Crackly Corn Flakes," "Old Straw Hat," and a medley that includes "Good Ship Lollipop." Randolph Scott, Jack Haley, Bill Robinson co-star. 80 min.
04-1234 □$19.99

Rebecca Of Sunnybrook Farm (Color Version)
04-2816 □$14.99

Susannah Of The Mounties (1939)
Next to that underage Brooklyn kid in the war picture, the surest kiss of death in movies is to play Shirley Temple's natural parents. This time an Indian attack does the deed, and the perennial orphan is adopted by rugged R.C.M.P. Randolph Scott. Great frontier action, plus Shirley teaching Scott to tap dance. 77 min.
04-2202 □$19.99

Susannah Of The Mounties (Color Version)
04-2822 □$14.99

The Little Princess (1939)
Warmly remembered tearjerker stars Shirley Temple as a Victorian waif searching for her father, a soldier who was reported killed in the Boer War. With Cesar Romero, Arthur Treacher, Ian Hunter; Shirley's first color film. 93 min.
04-2205 □$14.99

The Blue Bird (1940)
Second of three screen versions of the Maurice Maeterlinck fantasy about a brother and sister searching for a magic bird of happiness in a dream kingdom. Glorious color production stars Shirley Temple, favorite movie villainess Gale Sondergaard, Nigel Bruce and Spring Byington. 83 min.
04-2206 □$14.99

Young People (Color Version) (1940)
Filmdom's pluckiest orphan, Shirley Temple, finds herself parentless once again, until retiring vaudevillians Jack Oakie and Charlotte Greenwood adopt her. The family moves to a small town that doesn't take to "show folk," but Shirley sets out to change their feelings. Songs include "Tra-La-La," "Fifth Avenue" and the title tune. 78 min.
04-2959 □$14.99

The Story Of Seabiscuit (1949)
Fanciful fiction mixes with actual events in this lively biodrama of the famed racehorse. Shirley Temple stars as the niece of a charismatic horse trainer who falls in love with a young jockey. Against her wishes, the jockey is persuaded by her uncle to ride Seabiscuit and become a champion. Barry Fitzgerald, Lon McCallister also star. 93 min.
12-2463 $19.99

Shirley Temple's Storybook Theatre (1958)
Everyone's favorite little girl grew up to host this '50s television series, which adapted the best-loved fairy tales and kid's stories and featured top stars. Each tape runs about 50 min.

Mother Goose
Mother Goose (Elsa Lanchester) travels to Wayfair, and tries to save the town's annual fair, which has been cancelled by young Polly Baker's (Shirley Temple) father, the mayor (Billy Gilbert). With Rod McKuen, Lloyd "Crash" Corrigan.
55-1001 $14.99

Hiawatha
J. Carroll Naish and Pernell Roberts are among the guest stars in the Native American fable set "by the shores of Gitchy-Goomy."
55-1003 $14.99

Sleeping Beauty
The classic fairy tale of the young woman cast in a spell that sends her to sleep and the prince who revives her is beautifully translated. Nancy Marchand, Judith Evelyn and Alexander Scourby star.
73-5049 $14.99

The Emperor's New Clothes
Eli Wallach stars as the conniving tailor who convinces vain monarch Sebastian Cabot that his invisible rainment really exists.
73-5062 $14.99

Ali Baba And The Forty Thieves
"Open Sesame" is the password to adventure as poor Ali finds a bandits' cave loaded with treasure. Thomas Gomez and Nehemiah Persoff are the guest stars.
73-5063 $14.99

Shirley Temple Triple Pack
With the money you save on this boxed collector's set featuring Shirley in the colorized versions of "Baby Take a Bow," "Curly Top" and "Heidi," you'll be able to put a few extra animal crackers in your soup.
04-3956 Save $5.00! $39.99

Shirley Temple Tribute
A nostalgic medley of highlights from the tap-happy tot's illustrious career, as Shirley does what she does best in an assortment of song-and-dance numbers accompanied by vintage newsreel footage of Shirley at play on the lot and celebrating birthdays at home, film trailers, two comedies, "The Pie-Covered Wagon" and "Merrily Yours," and much more. 90 min.
10-7535 Was $19.99 $14.99

Shirley Temple Scrapbook
Highlights from the career of America's Little Sweetheart are featured with clips from Depression-era films, as well as at-home footage that provide rare glimpses into Shirley's private life. 60 min.
50-6299 $19.99

Shirley Temple: America's Little Darling
The legend of Hollywood's greatest childhood star is recounted in this marvelous documentary which looks at the reasons for her popularity, features clips from such favorites as "The Little Colonel," "Stowaway" and "The Little Princess," and offers anecdotes by Cesar Romero, Alice Faye and Jane Withers. Narrated by Tommy Tune. 60 min.
50-7173 Was $19.99 $14.99

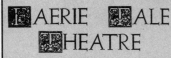

Faerie Tale Theatre

Faerie Tale Theatre

Movies Unlimited proudly presents this fabulous series, produced and hosted by actress Shelley Duvall, which features some of Hollywood's top performers in lively (and sometimes irreverent) spins on the world's best-loved fairy tales and fables. Each tape runs about 60 min.

The Tale Of The Frog Prince
When a frog is actually an enchanted prince, he's only a kiss away from true love. Robin Williams plays the amphibious beau, Teri Garr is a skeptical princess, and Rene Auberjonois is her father, the king. Monty Python's Eric Idle directed.
04-1632 □*$12.99*

Sleeping Beauty
The music of Tchaikovsky, Christopher Reeve as the dynamic prince, Beverly D'Angelo as the wicked fairy, and Bernadette Peters as the enchanting (and enchanted) princess add up to a memorable family viewing experience.
04-1633 □*$12.99*

Rapunzel
From high atop a tower, a beautiful woman lets down her hair so love can climb the golden stair. Shelley Duvall plays the maiden, Jeff Bridges the dashing prince, and Gena Rowlands the wicked witch. Live-action and animation mix with gorgeous sets and stunning costumes.
04-1634 □*$12.99*

Jack And The Beanstalk
Exciting rendition of the beloved tale about a young man's journey up the beanstalk to a giant's home. Dennis Christopher is Jack, while Elliott Gould and Jean Stapleton play Mr. and Mrs. Giant. Mark Blankfield and Katherine Helmond also star.
04-1636 □*$12.99*

Beauty And The Beast
The classic parable about how love can bring beauty to even the ugliest spirit. Klaus Kinski is the beastie; lovely Susan Sarandon his lady fair.
04-1668 □*$12.99*

Hansel And Gretel
A magical adaptation of the fantasy about a brother and sister's adventures at a gingerbread house and with the nasty witch who lived there. Ricky Schroder, Joan Collins, Paul Dooley star.
04-1710 □*$12.99*

The Emperor's New Clothes
The classic tale of vanity and its downfall stars Dick Shawn as a foppish ruler and Art Carney and Alan Arkin as the convincing tailors who sell him "invisible garments" which only "intelligent" people can see.
04-1812 □*$12.99*

Cinderella
Jennifer Beals is the good-hearted girl whose fairy godmother, played by Jean Stapleton, helps her become the belle of the ball. Matthew Broderick is the handsome prince in this lavish re-creation of the family favorite.
04-1813 □*$12.99*

Puss 'N Boots
That foxy cat with a trick up his sleeve is brought to life by Ben Vereen, and master Gregory Hines needs his help to defeat an ogre and win the hand of a beautiful princess. This fun fantasy was written by cartoonist Jules Feiffer.
04-1814 □*$12.99*

The Little Mermaid
Pam Dawber stars as Hans Christian Andersen's sea heroine, who must choose between living in the ocean with her family or on land with handsome sailor Treat Williams. Helen Mirren, Brian Dennehy also star.
04-1875 □*$12.99*

The Three Little Pigs
When Big Bad Wolf Jeff Goldblum gets his stomach set for a pork chop dinner, it's up to practical pig Billy Crystal to save foolish brothers Stephen Furst and Fred Willard in a hilarious retelling of the fairy tale favorite.
04-1876 □*$12.99*

Rip Van Winkle
The iconoclastic Harry Dean Stanton stars as Rip, who, after making merry with some little people nods off for awhile...only to wake up some 20 years later! Francis Coppola directs the Washington Irving favorite, which co-stars Talia Shire.
04-1895 □*$12.99*

Faerie Tale Theatre Gift Set
All 12 volumes are also available in a money-saving set.
58-5205 Save $36.00! *$119.99*

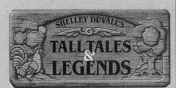

American Tall Tales & Legends

From "Faerie Tale Theatre" creator Shelley Duvall comes this delightful live-action series that focuses on some of the country's most famous heroes and heroines. Some of the characters were real, some were larger than life, but all are unforgettable. Each tape runs about 50 min. There are nine volumes available, including:

American Tall Tales & Legends: Annie Oakley
04-3099 *$12.99*

American Tall Tales & Legends: Casey At The Bat
04-3107 *$12.99*

American Tall Tales & Legends: Johnny Appleseed
04-3203 *$12.99*

American Tall Tales & Legends: Darlin' Clementine
04-3204 *$12.99*

American Tall Tales & Legends: The Legend Of Sleepy Hollow
04-3205 *$12.99*

Shelley Duvall's Mother Goose Rock 'N Rhyme
Shelley Duvall, creator of "Faerie Tale Theatre," produced and stars in this music-filled extravaganza of nursery rhymes and good ol' times. Mother Goose was never so hip or colorful, as Teri Garr, Howie Mandel, Bobby Brown, Paul Simon and others play various storybook characters. 90 min.
03-1740 *$12.99*

BeetleBorgs: Curse Of The Shadow Borg
They're big, they're bad, and now TV's BeetleBorgs are on home video in a feature-length action saga. Join the three youngsters who have the power to transform into armor-plated superheroes called "Borgs" and their ghostly pal Flabber as they try to solve the mystery of the menacing Shadow Borg before it's too late. 90 min.
04-3437 □*$14.99*

Animorphs
"Nothing is as it seems" in this exciting live-action TV series based on the popular kids' books. Alien invaders known as Yeerks are infiltrating the Earth, and the only people able to combat them are five young people given the ability to change their form into any animal they touch. Each tape features three episodes and runs about 75 min.

Animorphs, Part 1: The Invasion Begins
02-3268 □*$14.99*

Animorphs, Part 2: Nowhere To Run
02-3299 □*$14.99*

Animorphs, Part 3: The Enemy Among Us
02-3335 □*$14.99*

Animorphs, Part 4: The Legacy Survives
02-3336 □*$14.99*

The Baby-Sitters Club
Ann Martin's popular stories about seven junior high girls who form their own baby-sitting company now comes to home video with these live-action adventures. Each tape runs about 30 min. There are 11 volumes available, including:

The Baby-Sitters Club: Dawn And The Haunted House
10-2299 *$14.99*

The Baby-Sitters Club: The Baby-Sitters Remember
19-3456 *$14.99*

The Baby-Sitters Club: Jessi And The Mystery Of The Stolen Secrets
19-3457 *$14.99*

The Baby-Sitters Club: Dawn And The Dream Boy
19-3554 *$14.99*

The Baby-Sitters Club: The Movie (1995)
From the popular book series comes this sensitive, fun-filled adventure about the summer the seven members of "The Baby-Sitters Club" decide to start a day-care camp. Their plans are immediately challenged when the girls face all sorts of problems, including the return of estranged fathers, meddlesome neighbors and romantic predicaments. With Schuyler Fisk, Peter Horton, Brooke Adams. 92 min.
02-2858 Was $19.99 □*$14.99*

Mrs. Piggle-Wiggle
When kids or their parents get in tough situations, they call on Mrs. Piggle-Wiggle, a red-headed master of solving problems. Played by Jean Stapleton, she teaches kids how to deal with important and not-so important crises in a fun, whimsical way. Produced by Shelley Duvall and featuring such guest stars as Christopher Lloyd and Joan Cusack, each tape runs about 60 min.

Mrs. Piggle-Wiggle, Vol. 1
Includes "The Not-Truthful Cure" and "The Radish Cure."
07-2216 □*$14.99*

Mrs. Piggle-Wiggle, Vol. 2
Includes "The Pet Forgetters Cure" and "The Never-Want-to-Go-to-Bedders Cure."
07-2217 □*$14.99*

Mrs. Piggle-Wiggle, Vol. 3
Includes "The Answer-Backer Cure" and "The Chores Cure."
07-2218 □*$14.99*

The Adventures Of Timmy The Tooth
Using amazing electronic puppetry, this whimsical series is set in Flossmore Valley, where Timmy the Tooth, pal Brushbrush and a group of oddball friends have all sorts of song-filled and healthy adventures. Who needs the Tooth Fairy when Timmy's around? Each tape runs about 30 min. There are 10 volumes available, including:

The Adventures Of Timmy The Tooth: Molar Island
07-2233 □*$9.99*

The Adventures Of Timmy The Tooth: Timmy In Space
07-2235 □*$9.99*

The Adventures Of Timmy The Tooth: The Brush In The Stone
07-2367 □*$9.99*

Joanie Bartels: Simply Magic, Vol. 1
Leading children's entertainer Joanie Bartels takes you to the Caribbean where you'll do the Limbo Rock, enjoy a poolside splash party and experience some awesome magic and music. 45 min.
02-7833 *$14.99*

Pat The Bunny: Sing With Me
Generations of youngsters have grown up reading (and patting) the book. Now the beloved bunny plays cartoon host for a fun-filled video in which a group of youngsters hop, play and sing along to songs and activities based on the book. Among the 10 tunes are "The Things You Can Do," "That's Me in the Mirror" and, of course, "Pat the Bunny." 30 min.
04-5646 □*$12.99*

Wee Sing
An acclaimed sing-along series for children ages 2-8, these videos feature live-action and puppets in a variety of fun-filled settings where they perform favorite tunes. Except where noted, each tape runs about 55 min. There are 11 volumes available, including:

Wee Sing Favorites: Classic Songs For Kids
07-2420 *$12.99*

Wee Sing In The Marvelous Musical Mansion
50-2430 □*$12.99*

Wee Sing: Grandpa's Magical Toys
50-4123 *$12.99*

Wee Sing: Wee Sing In Sillyville
50-4124 *$12.99*

Baby Songs
It's MTV for the sandbox set with these programs filled with fun songs that will set baby's toes a-tappin' and have kids singing along. Each tape runs about 30 min. There are nine volumes available, including:

Baby Songs: Good Night
08-8706 □*$12.99*

Baby Songs: Animals
08-8834 *$12.99*

Baby Songs: Play-Along Songs
08-8881 *$12.99*

Baby Songs: Baby's Busy Day
71-7042 □*$12.99*

David Jack: Making Music, Making Friends
Popular kiddies entertainer David Jack will enchant youngsters with this live concert that features dancing dinosaurs, singing cavegirls and songs like "Dinosaur Dip," "Gotta Hop!" and "Miranda and the Panda."
10-2537 *$12.99*

Wheels On The Bus: Sing Along Down On The Farm
The magical "Wheels on the Bus" crew includes a talking steering wheel, a group of kids and Koko the Kangaroo. In this adventure, they explore a farm and invite kids to sing-along to "Old MacDonald," "Poison Ivy" and "Itsy Bitsy Spider." 30 min.
10-2706 *$14.99*

Pete Seeger's Family Concert
Folk singing maestro Pete Seeger presents some of his favorite sing-along songs in a concert from the banks of the Hudson River. Included are such favorites as "Skip to My Lou," "This Land Is Your Land," "Abi-Yo-Yo," "Guantanamera" and more. 45 min.
45-5525 *$14.99*

Peter, Paul And Mary: Peter, Paul And Mommy, Too
The award-winning folk trio turn their attentions to the younger set in this live concert filmed at the Brooklyn Academy of Music. Children's tunes like "Puff the Magic Dragon," "Home on the Range" and "I Know an Old Lady Who Swallowed a Fly" are featured, along with popular songs like "This Land Is Your Land" and "Blowin' in the Wind" (always a kiddie fave). 60 min.
19-3403 *$14.99*

Joe Scruggs: Live From Deep In The Jungle
It's a veritable menagerie of mirth and music from award-winning children's music star Joe Scruggs. Let Joe take you on a silly song-filled safari, as he encounters some outrageous animal characters. 51 min.
50-5386 *$14.99*

Joe Scruggs: Joe TV
Your youngsters will be saying "I want my Joe TV!" when they see this delightful family program featuring the jovial Joe Scruggs, who takes some of his favorite songs and turns them into outrageous music videos. 31 min.
50-5387 *$14.99*

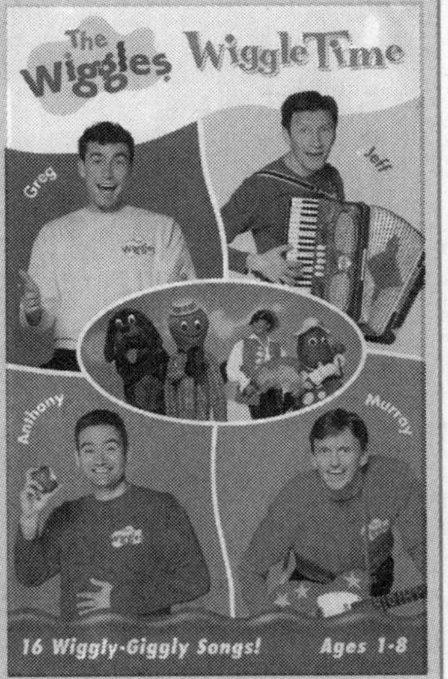

The Wiggles
This Australian quartet has wiggled their way to incredible success Down Under and in England, and now their upbeat, fun-filled brand of song and comedy is available in the States. Join Murray, Jeff, Anthony and Greg, along with Dorothy the Dinosaur, Henry the Octopus, Captain Feathersword and Wags the Dog, for bouncy pre-school fun. Each tape runs about 40 min.

The Wiggles: Wiggle Time
Includes the songs "Get Ready to Wiggle," "Here Comes a Bear," "Uncle Noah's Ark," "Ponies" and more.
50-7616 *$14.99*

The Wiggles: Yummy Yummy
Includes the songs "Hot Potato," "Numbers Rhumba," "Monkey Dance" and, for all you Barry Reisman fans out there, "Havenu Shalom Alachem."
50-7617 *$14.99*

Billy Jonas: Bangin' And Sangin'
This children's sing-along is perfect for audience participation as entertainer Billy Jonas delights kids in a live concert, perorming "Some Houses," "Bangin' and Sangin'" and "One," as well as favorites "Pharaoh, Pharaoh," "Lean on Me" and more. 41 min.
55-9043 *$19.99*

Storybook Adventures
Some of children's literature's most beloved works have been portrayed in these colorful live-action renditions that are certain to delight and tickle the imaginations of little ones the world over. Each tape runs about 30 min.

Storybook Adventures: A Pocket For Corduroy
A teddy bear left behind in a laundromat searches for its owner in "A Pocket for Corduroy"; next, follow the journey of "The Remarkable Riderless Runaway Tricycle" as it escapes from the trash heap.
10-2661 *$12.99*

Storybook Adventures: A Boy, A Dog And A Frog
Mercer Mayer's three famous "Frog" books are brought to life in this collection that includes "A Boy, a Dog and a Frog," "Frog Goes to Dinner" and "Frog on His Own."
10-2662 *$12.99*

Goosebumps
The frighteningly popular series of spooky kid's books by R.L. Stine makes its way to home video with these live-action tales guaranteed to give you the shivers. Each tape runs about 45 min.

Goosebumps Triple Pack 1
This three-tape set opens with a girl using "The Haunted Mask" to get back at her tormentors, but at a price. A brother and sister spend "A Night in Terror Tower" at a wax museum, and a girl doesn't heed her botanist father's warning to "Stay Out of the Basement." NOTE: Individual volumes available at $14.99 each.
04-3641 Save $20.00! *$24.99*

Goosebumps Triple Pack 2
Come face-to-"face" with terror again in "The Haunted Mask II," leading off this three-tape "Goosebumps" collection. Also included are a family who learn some shocking facts about their new neighbors in "Welcome to Dead House" and a boy's encounter with a bayou beast in "The Werewolf of Fever Swamp." NOTE: Individual volumes available at $14.99 each.
04-3642 Save $20.00! *$24.99*

Ultimate Goosebumps: One Day At Horrorland, Parts 1 & 2
The Morris family's visit to Zoo Gardens becomes a trip into terror when they find themselves in Horrorland, a monster-run theme park where patrons pay...with their lives.
04-3726 *□$12.99*

Ultimate Goosebumps: Werewolf Skin, Parts 1 & 2
A young camera buff isn't ready for what develops when he visits his aunt and uncle in remote Wolf Creek, where the woods are crawling with man-beasts!
04-3727 *□$12.99*

Ultimate Goosebumps: Bride Of The Living Dummy/An Old Story
Could wedding bells be in the air when Slappy, the sinister ventriliquist's dummy with a mind of his own, meets the "doll" of his dreams? Next, two young brothers are getting old before their time, thanks to their aunt's cooking.
04-3728 *□$12.99*

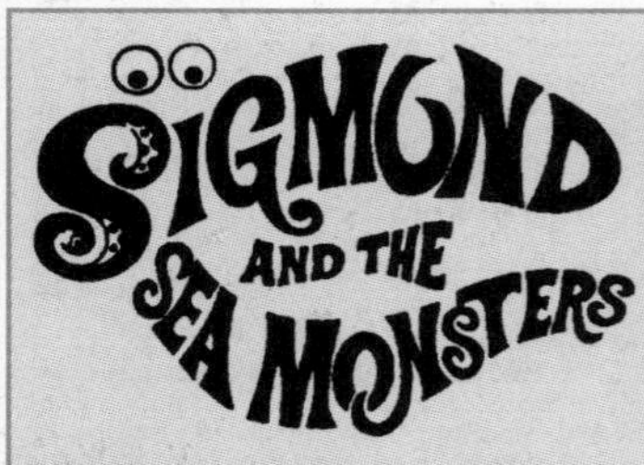

Sigmund And The Sea Monsters
Kicked out of his home for failing to scare humans, a cute little sea monster named Sigmund Ooze is taken in by brothers Johnny (Johnny Whitaker) and Scott (Scott Kolden), who have to hide their new friend from prying eyes and his monstrous family. Each tape features two episodes and runs about 50 min.

Sigmund And The Sea Monsters, Vol. 1
Includes "Happy Birthdaze" and "The Nasty Nephew."
15-5492 *$12.99*

Sigmund And The Sea Monsters, Vol. 2
Includes "Monster Rock Festival" and "Ghoul School Days."
15-5493 *$12.99*

Sigmund And The Sea Monsters, Vol. 3
Includes "The Curfew Shall Ring Tonight" and "Sweet Mama Redecorates" and comes with a limited edition Sigmund plush toy.
15-5542 *$14.99*

Sigmund And The Sea Monsters: The Complete Box Set
No need to "shell" out a lot of "clams" to own your very own six-tape boxed collection that features all 29 episodes from the Krofft Brothers favorite. 12 hrs. total.
15-5562 *$79.99*

The Bugaloos
Courage, Harmony, I.Q. and Joy are the fabulous flying quartet known as the Bugaloos. Join them as they soar over Tranquility Forest with their firefly pal Sparky, singing and foiling the nasty schemes of Benita Bizarre (Martha Raye), in this Saturday morning fantasy series from Sid and Marty Krofft. Each tape features two episodes and runs about 50 min.

The Bugaloos, Vol. 1
Includes "The Love Bugaloos" and "If I Had the Wings of a Bugaloo."
15-5496 *$12.99*

The Bugaloos, Vol. 2
Includes "Lady, You Don't Look Eighty" and "Benita the Beautiful" and comes with a limited edition Sparky plush toy.
15-5543 *$14.99*

Lidsville, Vol. 1
Falling into a mysterious magician's oversized hat draws young Mark (Butch Patrick) into Lidsville, a land of living headwear. Can the heroic hats and Weenie the Genie help Mark avoid the nasty Hoodoo the Magician (Charles Nelson Reilly) and get back home? Includes "Let's Hear It for Whizzo" and "Is There a Mayor in the House." 50 min.
15-5497 *$12.99*

Far Out Space Nuts, Vol. 1
After mistaking the "launch" button for "lunch," hapless NASA workers Barney (Chuck McCann) and Junior (Bob Denver) find themselves lost in outer space and having close encounters of the comedy kind in this Sid and Marty Krofft '70s Saturday morning fave. Includes "Tower of Taget" and "Secrets of Hexagon." 50 min.
15-5498 *$12.99*

H.R. Pufnstuf
A young boy named Jimmy ("Oliver!'s" Jack Wild) and Freddy, his talking flute, are abducted and taken to Living Island by the evil Witchiepoo (Billie Hayes), who wants Freddy for herself. It's up to the island's mayor, a lovable dragon named H.R. Pufnstuf, to rescue the pair and help them search for their way home, in the beloved Krofft brothers series. Each tape features two episodes and runs about 50 min.

H.R. Pufnstuf, Vol. 1
Includes "The Stand-In" and "The Golden Key."
15-5490 *$12.99*

H.R. Pufnstuf, Vol. 2
Includes "The Birthday Party" and "The Box Kite Kaper."
15-5491 *$12.99*

H.R. Pufnstuf, Vol. 3
Includes "You Can't Have Your Cake" and "Horse with the Golden Throat" and comes with a limited edition Pufnstuf plush toy.
15-5540 *$14.99*

H.R. Pufnstuf, Vol. 4
Includes "Dinner for Two" and "A Tooth for a Tooth" and comes with a limited edition Witchiepoo plush toy.
15-5541 *$14.99*

H.R. Pufnstuf: The Ultimate Box Set
All 17 episodes from the popular Saturday morning series are available in this "Puftastic" four-tape collector's set. 8 1/2 hrs. total.
15-5516 *$59.99*

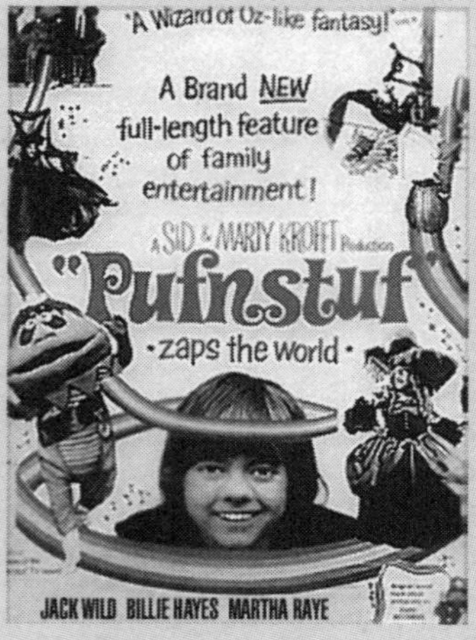

Pufnstuf (1970)
Sid and Marty Krofft's 1960s TV favorite gets the big screen treatment, as young Jimmy (Jack Wild), his pal Pufnstuf, and the creatures of Living Island try to save Freddie the Flute from wicked Witchiepoo (Billie Hayes), who swiped the instrument so she can win a "Witch of the Year" competition. "Mama" Cass Elliott, Martha Raye, Billy Barty also star; songs include "Pufnstuf," "Fire in the Castle" and "Happy Hour." 95 min.
07-2907 *□$14.99*

H.R. Pufnstuf Live At The Hollywood Bowl (1972)
The seven-foot-tall dragon "who's your friend when things get rough" is joined by his pal Jimmy (Jack Wild), the nasty Witchiepoo, and all the other characters from the popular Sid and Marty Krofft Saturday morning series in a laugh- and song-filled live show from the famed Hollywood Bowl. Adding to the groovy fun is a guest appearance by the Brady Bunch Kids. 50 min.
15-5374 *$14.99*

Land Of The Lost (1974)
While on a rafting trip, forest ranger Rick Marshall and his kids Will and Holly are sucked through a whirlpool and transported to a mysterious world where dinosaurs, ape-men and strange reptilian beings known as Sleestaks live. Live-action and stop-motion animation are mixed in this exciting sci-fi/adventure series from Sid and Marty Krofft. Each tape features two episodes and runs about 50 min.

Land Of The Lost, Vol. 1
Includes "The Stranger" and "Tag Team."
15-5494 *$12.99*

Land Of The Lost, Vol. 2
Includes "The Search" and "The Paku Who Came to Dinner."
15-5495 *$12.99*

Land Of The Lost, Vol. 3
Includes "Circle" and "Zarn."
15-5576 *$12.99*

Land Of The Lost, Vol. 4
Includes "Elsewhen" and "Split Personality."
15-5577 *$12.99*

Land Of The Lost (1991)
This new version of Sid and Marty Krofft's live-action family series follows the adventures of Tom Porter (Timothy Bottoms), his two children, a jungle girl and a monkey-boy in a hidden jungle land filled with dinosaurs, evil lizard-men and other creatures. Each tape features two episodes and runs 45 min. There are six volumes available, including:

Land Of The Lost: Tasha/Something's Watching
14-3338 *$14.99*

Land Of The Lost: Jungle Girl/Shung, The Terrible
14-3339 *$14.99*

Land Of The Lost: Kevin vs. The Volcano/Day For Knight
14-3341 *$14.99*

The Lost Saucer, Vol. 1
Bumbling aliens Jim Nabors and Ruth Buzzi land their ship on Earth and accidentally blast off with two kids they befriended on board. Watch as they explore strange new worlds in search of the way back in two installments from the mid-'70s kid TV fave. Included are "Where Did Everybody Go?" and "Get a Dorse." 50 min.
15-5571 *$12.99*

Electra Woman And Dyna Girl, Vol. 1
Before hitting it big as a daytime diva, soap star Deidre Hall joined Judy Strangis as a team of laser-powered superheroines who battle all sorts of wild villains in a segment of Saturday morning's "The Krofft Supershow." Two "electrafantastic" adventures are featured here: "The Sorcerer's Golden Trick" and "Glitter Rock." 50 min.
15-5572 *$12.99*

Wonderbug, Vol. 1
He's just a broken-down heap called Schlepcar, until, with a toot of his magic horn, he changes into the amazing super-vehicle known as Wonderbug! Join this crime-fighting car and his young pals as they battle crooks in episodes from their "Krofft Supershow" series: "The Wonderbug Express" and "Shlepfoot." 50 min.
15-5573 *$12.99*

The World Of Sid & Marty Krofft: Boxed Set
Go back to those psychedelic days of '70s Saturday morning TV with this "Pufariffic" three-tape set featuring episodes from the Brothers Krofft's beloved live-action series. You'll see one adventure each from "H.R. Pufnstuf," "The Bugaloos," "Lidsville," "Sigmund & the Sea Monsters," "Land of the Lost," "Far Out Space Nuts," "ElectraWoman & DynaGirl," "Bigfoot & Wildboy," "Pryor's Place" and others. 390 min. total.
15-5484 *$29.99*

Young Ivanhoe (1995)
A "prequel" of sorts to Sir Walter Scott's famed novel, this thrilling live-action family drama follows young Ivanhoe on his quest to become a knight, an odyssey that brought him into contact with such legendary figures as Robin Hood and the Black Knight. Stacy Keach, Margot Kidder, Nick Mancuso and Kris Holdenried star. 96 min.
58-5221 Was $79.99 *□$14.99*

Kidnapped (1996)
A young man seeking his family inheritance is betrayed by a cruel uncle and pressed into service at sea, where he joins with an older sailor in a quest for freedom and vengeance, in this exciting adaptation of the Robert Louis Stevenson classic. Armand Assante, Brian McCardie star. 142 min.
58-5225 Was $79.99 *□$14.99*

The Way Of The Wind
Thrilling true story of a 30,000-mile sailboat odyssey that takes you from the Pacific and Hawaii to the infamous Bermuda Triangle and mysterious Greek Isles. 125 min.
64-1021 Was $29.99 *$19.99*

The Ransom Of Red Chief
What happens when two dimwitted drifters kidnap a 10-year-old boy and hold him for ransom, only to find that he's trickier than they think? O. Henry's rambunctious short story stars Jack Elam, Strother Martin. 22 min.
70-3092 *$12.99*

The Revenge Of Red Chief
The lovable frontier con artists from the pen of O. Henry are back to their old tricks, pretending to be "rainmakers" in a drought-stricken town. When Red Chief discovers what they're doing, look out! Alan Hale, Noah Beery and Jack Elam star. 22 min.
70-3095 *$12.99*

The Ghost Of Thomas Kempe
A young boy learns that a little magic can be a dangerous thing when he accidentally releases the spirit of a 17th-century sorcerer. Can he get the ghost to return to his resting place before he's blamed for all the silly spectre's antics? 60 min.
70-3141 *$12.99*

Barnaby And Me
Delightful family film from Australia about a young girl who tries to "push" her mother into a relationship with a free-spirited man. Sid Caesar, Juliet Mills and Barnaby the talking koala star. 90 min.
71-5000 *$14.99*

Voyage Into Space (1970)
Culled from episodes of the Japanese "Johnny Sokko" TV series, this feature-length sci-fi tale finds young Sokko and his flying robot battling the dangerous Dracolon, a monster sent out to destroy Tokyo. With Mitsundbu Kaneko and Akyo Ito.
68-9244 *$19.99*

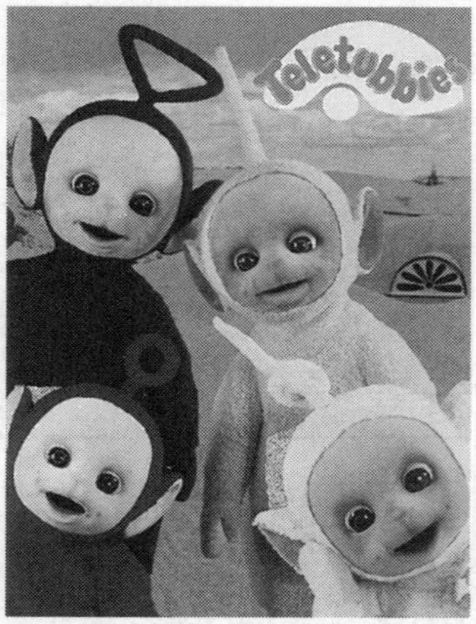

Teletubbies
"Over the hills and far away," the Teletubbies have come to home video! Your pre-school children will have their social, physical and cognitive needs reinforced while watching Tinky Winky, Dipsy, Laa-Laa and Po learn self-esteem, friendship, and other important values of growing up. Each tape runs 60 min. There are eight volumes available, including:

Teletubbies: Here Come The Teletubbies
18-7821 *□$14.99*

Teletubbies: Dance With The Teletubbies
18-7822 *□$14.99*

Teletubbies: Favorite Things
18-7861 *□$14.99*

Teletubbies: Big Hug!
18-7892 *$14.99*

Teletubbies: Bedtime Stories And Lullabies
18-7909 *□$14.99*

The Muppet Movie (1979)
Follow the fantastic, music-filled adventures of Kermit the Frog and Fozzie Bear as they travel across the country to seek fame and fortune in Hollywood. Miss Piggy, Scooter, Rowlf and all your Muppet favorites are on hand, as well as Steve Martin, Bob Hope, Richard Pryor, Charles Durning, Edgar Bergen, Mel Brooks and other human guests. 94 min.
11-1649 ❑*$14.99*

The Great Muppet Caper (1981)
The Muppets tackle a mystery when Kermit, Fozzie Bear and Gonzo investigate the robbery of the fabulous Baseball Diamond, owned by fashion queen Diana Rigg. Miss Piggy is the prime suspect in the case, but there's more to the crime, and the Muppets try to get to the bottom of it. Charles Grodin, John Cleese also star. 98 min.
11-1650 ❑*$14.99*

The Muppets Take Manhattan (1984)
Kermit, Miss Piggy, Fozzie and crew head for the "Big Apple" in this sparkling musical-comedy for young and old alike. Appearing with the Muppets are Joan Rivers, Art Carney, Brooke Shields and other stars. Will Kermie and Miss P. tie the knot? 94 min.
04-1791 ❑*$14.99*

Muppet Treasure Island (1996)
Set sail for a hilarious and exciting adventure for the whole family when the Muppets take on Robert Louis Stevenson's classic pirate tale. Join captain Kermit the Frog, Fozzie, Gonzo, Rizzo and company as they join with young Jim Hawkins and the rascally Long John Silver (Tim Curry) on a search for a fabled fortune in gold. 99 min.
11-2020 ❑*$19.99*

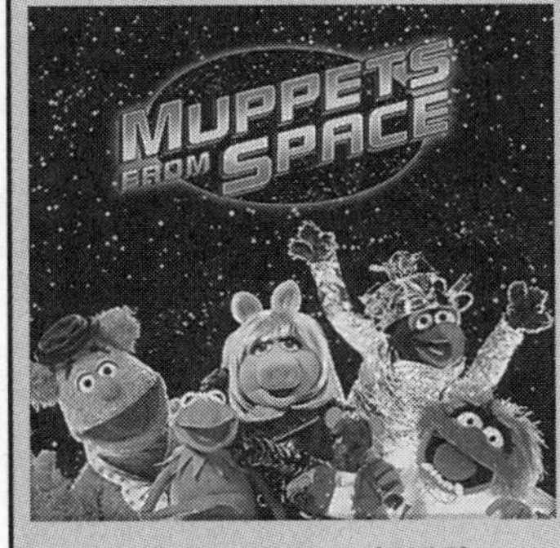

Muppets From Space (1999)
After receiving strange messages in his breakfast cereal, big-beaked Muppet Gonzo sets out on a quest to find his roots...but is even he ready for the news that he's not from Earth? Now Gonzo, his rat pal Rizzo, Kermit, Miss Piggy and the rest of the Muppet gang have to deal with alien-hunting government agents and Gonzo's wild family in this fun-filled adventure. Human guest stars include Jeffrey Tambor, Andie McDowell, Rob Schneider. 88 min.
02-3365 Was $19.99 ❑*$14.99*

Sesame Street Presents: Follow That Bird (1985)
Call the FBI! Big Bird has left Sesame Street to live with other birds, and the Muppet gang are out to bring him back. Delightful comedy for kids of all ages also stars Bert, Ernie, Oscar, Grover and The Count, with cameos by John Candy, Sandra Bernhard, Chevy Chase, Waylon Jennings and other humans. 88 min.
19-1479 ❑*$19.99*

The Tale Of The Bunny Picnic (1986)
From Jim Henson's Muppet crew comes this delightful bunny-tale with a cast of crazy rabbits whose plans for a peaceful picnic go comically awry. 51 min.
11-1654 ❑*$12.99*

Jim Henson's The StoryTeller

The Storyteller (1994)
This Emmy-winning family series from the Jim Henson Company stars John Hurt as the title talespinner, whose recountings of classic European fairytales and folk stories come to life through live actors and puppetry. Each tape features two episodes and runs about 45 min.

The Storyteller: Sapsorrow/The Luck Child
A beautiful princess leaves her home to avoid an arranged marriage and is magically disguised as the furred and feathered "Sapsorrow"; and when a newborn peasant turns out to be a "Luck Child" destined to rule, the nasty king tries to thwart the prophecy.
02-3373 ❑*$12.99*

The Storyteller: The Soldier & Death/A Story Short
A young soldier receives a magical sack that can catch and hold whatever he wants, but when he manages to snare Death, he learns the folly of his ways. Next, the Storyteller tells how he was once charged with telling a story a day for one year to a king...or else.
02-3374 ❑*$12.99*

The Storyteller: Greek Myths: Perseus And The Gorgon/Daedalus And Icarus
The tales of Ancient Greece come to life, as young hero Perseus must avoid the petrifying gaze of the Gorgon Medusa in order to slay her and fulfill a prophecy. Then, inventor Daedalus and his son create waxen wings that let them fly, until Icarus strays too near the sun.
02-3405 ❑*$12.99*

The Storyteller: Greek Myths: Theseus And The Minotaur/Orpheus And Eurydice
In a test of courage, young Prince Theseus of Athens must defeat a savage beast that's half-man and half-bull. Next, Orpheus takes his gift of song into the underworld on a quest to bring his true love Eurydice back to the land of the living.
02-3406 ❑*$12.99*

The Adventures Of Elmo In Grouchland (1999)
Lovable red Muppet Elmo loses his beloved blue blanket after a tug-of-war with Zoe. The blanket lands in Grouchland, a scary, faraway place populated by creepy creatures, smelly trash and an evil character named Huxley. Can Elmo use his wits and courage to get his prized blankie back and escape? Mandy Patinkin and Vanessa L. Williams star in this song-filled "Sesame Street" production that also features Oscar, Cookie Monster and Big Bird. 73 min.
02-3388 Was $19.99 ❑*$14.99*

Clarence And Angel
A 12-year-old boy, teased by his classmates because he can't read, is befriended by another boy who uses the sights and sounds of their inner city environment to teach him to read. Moving family drama in a modern urban setting stars Darren Brown, Mark Cardova. 75 min.
76-7005 *$59.99*

Barnaby And Me
Delightful family film from Australia about a young girl who tries to "push" her mother into a relationship with a free-spirited man. Sid Caesar, Juliet Mills and Barnaby the talking koala star. 90 min.
71-5000 *$14.99*

Pepito's Dream
The award-winning "Pepito" books served as the basis for this family film produced by the United Nations about a boy who wishes to end disturbances in his own neighborhood. He travels to the U.N. and urges people everywhere to stop fighting one another. 27 min.
20-7079 *$14.99*

Happy Birdy: Hey It's Your Birthday!
It's a musical birthday greeting for children of all ages, featuring sing-a-longs that are perfect for birthday parties, and a huge flying creature. 60 min.
22-7083 *$14.99*

Chuck E. Cheese In The Galaxy 5000
Everyone's favorite pizza-eating rodent stars in his very own live-action adventure, as Chuck E. and his pals travel to a distant world and take part in the most exciting rocket-car race this side of the Milky Way, the Galaxy 5000, in order to help young Charlie save his aunt and uncle's farm. There's action, slaughs and songs galore for the whole family. 62 min.
89-5192 *$12.99*

S-Club 7 In Miami (1999)
What's a British pop singing group to do when their "American debut" leaves them stranded and working in a run-down Florida hotel? Well, for Bradley, Hannah, Jo, Jon, Paul, Rachel and Tina—the seven fun-loving teens known as S-Club 7—it's a chance to take part in wild, fun- and song-filled adventures. Each tape features three episodes and runs about 105 min.

S-Club 7 In Miami, Vol. 1
04-3936 ❑*$14.99*

S-Club 7 In Miami, Vol. 2
04-3937 ❑*$14.99*

Mary-Kate & Ashley Olsen: Our First Video
The cute twin sisters from ABC-TV's hit sitcom "Full House" now star in their own home video, performing in seven music videos from their album, "Brother for Sale." "I Am the Cute One," "No One Tells the President What to Do," "Identical Twins" and "Mom's Song (We'll Think We'll Keep You)" are featured. 30 min.
02-7911 *$12.99*

The Adventures Of Mary-Kate And Ashley
The adorable Olsen twins make the jump from TV stars to detectives in these exciting whodunits, as the girls, along with Clue the basset hound, promise to "solve any crime by dinner time." Each tape runs about 25 min. There are 10 volumes available, including:

The Case Of The Logical i Ranch
02-8132 ❑*$12.99*

The Case Of The Shark Encounter
19-3894 ❑*$12.99*

Mary-Kate & Ashley Olsen: Double, Double, Toil And Trouble
It's twice the tricks and twice the treats in this Halloween-themed adventure, as the sisters try to help their aunt, who's been trapped by a witch's spell. Cloris Leachman, Meshach Taylor also star. 93 min.
19-2361 ❑*$14.99*

Mary-Kate & Ashley Olsen: Our Music Video
Eight of the girls' favorite songs, including "Too Much to Do," "Footprints on the Moon" and others, have been gathered for this special "best of" video that also features jokes and comic antics. 30 min.
19-3990 ❑*$12.99*

You're Invited To Mary-Kate & Ashley's Christmas Party
The Olsen girls have planned a holiday happening that no one will want to miss, from skiing and bobsledding fun and cookie baking to carolling and a surprise visit from that jolly man in the red suit (no, not Uncle Jesse!). 30 min.
19-3992 ❑*$12.99*

You're Invited To Mary-Kate & Ashley's Ballet Party
Looking for some party fun that will keep you on your toes? Then join the Olsen twins for a backstage visit at Lincoln Center with the world-famous New York City Ballet. 30 min.
19-4014 ❑*$12.99*

You're Invited To Mary-Kate & Ashley's Fashion Party
The always stylish Olsen Twins are your guides for a tour of the Fashion Institute of Design and Merchandising to learn how clothes are designed, made and sold, followed by the girls taking to the runway for their very own fashion show. 30 min.
19-4058 ❑*$12.99*

You're Invited To Mary-Kate & Ashley's Greatest Parties
It's three...three...three parties in one, courtesy of the lovable Olsen girls and this video that features the fun-loving twins in "Mary-Kate & Ashley's Birthday Party," "Mary-Kate & Ashley's Mall Party" and "Mary-Kate & Ashley's Sleepover Party." 90 min.
19-4080 ❑*$14.99*

You're Invited To Mary-Kate & Ashley's School Dance Party
It's the eve of the big school dance, and while Ashley's wondering about her run for Queen of the Dance, Mary-Kate is wondering if she'll have a date. This special video also includes highlights from "Mary-Kate & Ashley Olsen: Our Music Video." 60 min.
19-4081 ❑*$14.99*

The Amazing Adventures Of Mary-Kate & Ashley
They're the cutest sleuths who ever cracked a case, and on this program Mary-Kate and Ashley Olsen are up to their identical ears in fun and mystery. Included are "Case of the Hotel Who-Done-It," "Case of the Sea World Adventure" and "Case of the U.S. Space Camp Mission." 90 min.
19-4082 ❑*$14.99*

How The West Was Fun (1994)
When a greedy businessman plans to take over their great-grandmother's dude ranch and turn it into an environmentally unfit theme park, Mary-Kate and Ashley Olsen go to work, trying to fend off the culprit and save the ranch. Martin Mull, Michelle Greene and Patrick Cassidy also star. 93 min.
19-2458 ❑*$14.99*

It Takes Two (1995)
The lovable "Full House" twins, Mary-Kate and Ashley Olsen, make their big-screen debut with this delightful family comedy that mixes "The Prince and the Pauper" with "The Parent Trap" to tell the story of identical strangers, a feisty orphan and a motherless rich girl, who team up to bring together prospective parents Kirstie Alley and Steve Guttenberg. 101 min.
19-2436 Was $19.99 ❑*$14.99*

Billboard Dad (1998)
When sisters Mary-Kate and Ashley Olsen have a personal ad placed on a Hollywood billboard in order to find the perfect wife for their father, they never expect the flurry of responses that follow...or that the woman he falls for would be their worst enemy's mother! There's plenty of laughs in this feature-length family comedy. 90 min.
19-2761 ❑*$19.99*

Passport To Paris (1999)
Those irascible twins find adventure and a little romance when they travel to Paris to visit their grandfather. Even though they have a strict chaperone on their heels, Mary-Kate and Ashley encounter two French boys (and have dinner with them at the Eiffel Tower), shop at French boutiques and take in some sight-seeing. With Peter White, Ethan Peck.
19-2928 ❑*$19.99*

Switching Goals (1999)
Soccer-playing sibs Mary-Kate and Ashley Olsen turn their league upside-down when they switch identities and play on each other's team in this kickin' comedy for the whole family. 85 min.
19-4074 ❑*$19.99*

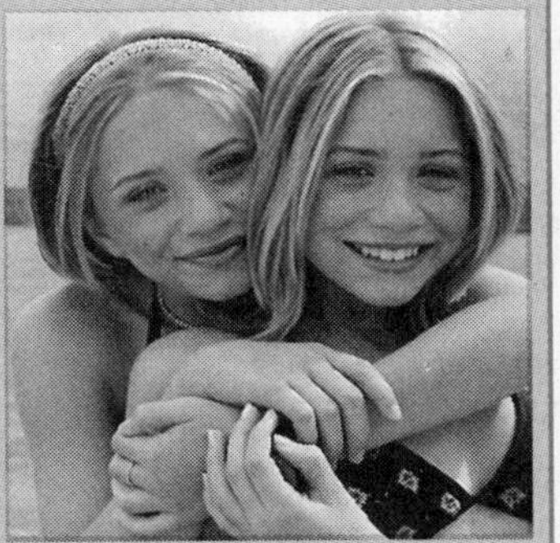

Our Lips Are Sealed (2000)
Mary-Kate and Ashley Olsen are in deep trouble when they get on the bad side of a nasty gangster, and the Witness Protection Program can't keep them safe because they keep blowing their cover. The girls finally wind up "down under" in Sydney, but can they stay cool with their Aussie pals while avoiding crooks looking for them in this fun-filled family feature. 95 min.
19-5004 *$19.99*

Pee-wee's Playhouse
The secret word is "video," as Pee-wee Herman's award-winning TV series is available once more. The gang's all here (Miss Yvonne, Chairy, Captain Carl, Jambi, and Conky) for fun and laughs in the playhouse, with the effervescent Pee-wee as your host. Each tape features two episodes and runs about 50 min. There are 16 volumes available, including:

Pee-wee's Playhouse, Vol. 1
Includes "Open House" and "Pee-wee Catches a Cold."
12-3109 ❑*$12.99*

Pee-wee's Playhouse, Vol. 2
Includes "I Remember Curtis" and "Conky's Breakdown."
12-3110 ❑*$12.99*

Pee-wee's Playhouse, Vol. 3
Includes "Store" and "Playhouse in Outer Space."
12-3111 ❑*$12.99*

Pee-wee's Playhouse: Vols. 1-8 Gift Set
The first eight volumes of Pee-wee's show are also available in this boxed collector's set.
12-3113 *$99.99*

Pee-wee's Playhouse: Vols. 9-16 Gift Set
Have plenty of Playhouse in your house with this boxed set that includes volumes 9 to 16.
12-3155 *$99.99*

Babies At Play
Designed for kids from ages 9 months to 4 years, this series features babies and toddlers playing, learning and experiencing family life with new and favorite songs. Each tape runs about 35 min.

Babies At Play: In Their Favorite Places
19-2358 ❑*$14.99*

Babies At Play: On A Fun, Rainy Day
19-2359 ❑*$14.99*

Baby Love: Babies Being Babies
And is there anything more entertaining than babies being babies? This delightful video features an array of adorable infants crawling, walking, playing, eating, crying and laughing, along with music and sound effects. It's all the fun, with no one to clean up after! 30 min.
22-1454 *$14.99*

Singing Babies
Kids love to see babies, and this video offers babies "singing" children's favorites, set to colorful backgrounds with fun-filled props like trains, stuffed animals and costumes. Using adult mouths with kid's faces, this delightful effort includes such tunes as "Mary Had a Little Lamb," "Ten Little Indians," "This Old Man" and more. 30 min.
76-7476 *$14.99*

Bear in the Big Blue House

Bear In The Big Blue House
Pre-school kids (and their parents) will love this hit series from the Jim Henson studio. Join lovable Bear and the animal pals who share his house as they learn the value of honesty, friendship and family through wonderful music and creative storytelling. Except where noted, each tape runs about 50 min. There are 12 volumes available, including:

**Bear In
The Big Blue House, Vol. 1**
Includes "Home Is Where the Bear Is" and "What's in the Mail Today?"
02-3206 $12.99

**Bear In
The Big Blue House, Vol. 2**
Includes "Friends for Life" and "The Big Little Visitor."
02-3207 $12.99

**Bear In
The Big Blue House, Vol. 3**
Includes "Dancing' the Day Away" and "Listen Up."
02-3244 $12.99

**Bear In The Big Blue House:
Visiting The Doctor With Bear**
02-3442 $12.99

**Bear In The Big Blue House:
Halloween & Thanksgiving**
02-3462 $12.99

How To Be A Ballerina
For every little girl who's ever wanted to be a dancer, this fun instructional video, hosted by Royal Academy of Dance instructor Debra Bradnum, features a primer on basic ballet positions and movements guaranteed to keep your youngsters on their toes. 45 min.
04-5502 $14.99

The Busy World Of Richard Scarry
His books have delighted young readers for decades, and now the beloved animal characters of author Richard Scarry have fun and offer gentle lessons about the world in this charming animated series. Each tape runs about 25 min. There are 15 volumes available, including:

The Best Birthday Present Ever
02-8256 $12.99

**Richard Scarry's
Now I Know My 1 2 3's**
02-8681 $12.99

**Richard Scarry's
Practice Makes Perfect**
02-8849 $12.99

**Richard Scarry's Best Sing-Along
Mother Goose Video Ever!**
04-5533 $12.99

**Richard Scarry's
Best ABC Video Ever!**
46-1068 $12.99

**Richard Scarry's
Best Counting Video Ever!**
46-1069 $12.99

**Richard Scarry's
Best Learning Songs Video Ever!**
46-1109 $12.99

Our Mr. Sun
Frank Capra produced, wrote and directed this classic from the Bell Telephone Science Program. Dr. Frank Baxter and Eddie Albert examine the power of the sun with help from Father Time (voiced by Lionel Barrymore). 60 min.
15-5173 $14.99

The Alphabet Conspiracy
Dr. Frank Baxter teams up with the Mad Hatter to show a young girl the wonders of language by illustrating its importance and how communication works. Hans Conried stars and Friz Freleng supplied the animation. 56 min.
15-5174 $14.99

Strange Case Of The Cosmic Rays
Animation, puppetry and fascinating facts combine to tell the story of the atom in an easy-to-understand style. Frank Capra directed and Shamus Culhane ("Betty Boop") animated this amazing journey from the Bell Science series. 55 min.
15-5176 $14.99

Hemo The Magnificent
Take a trip through the human body and learn about the wonders of that most important of muscles, the heart, and the circulatory system in this animated entry from the '50s Bell Science film series, written and directed by the legendary Frank Capra. 54 min.
15-5189 $14.99

About Time
A very "timely" film, this Bell Science documentary uses animated vignettes and live-action scenes starring Les Tremayne and Richard Deacon to explain how time is measured and used in science and our everyday lives. 53 min.
15-5190 $14.99

Unchained Goddess
What is weather? This question is explained with help from the Goddess of Weather and her pals, Wind, Clouds and Rain. Frank Capra produced, wrote and directed this look at climate that's filled with animation and incredible live footage of hurricanes and tornadoes. 54 min.
15-5196 $14.99

Learn to Read with Phonics

Learn To Read With Phonics
Children can now master the elements of reading in this program that features reading expert Barbara Phipps and her pal Snoothyguzzlesmort. Letter recognition, proper writing technique, special vowel sounding drills and putting sounds together to make words are among the subjects covered. 75 min.
10-2576 $12.99

Learning To Read
With Phonics: Set
This award-winning series will help youngsters learn to read at a quicker pace using special techniques designed by educators. Tapes in the five-part set include "Letters and Words," "Long and Short Vowels," "Reading and Counting," "Sight Words" and "Soundable Words." NOTE: Individual volumes available at $14.99 each.
10-2846 Save $5.00! $59.99

The Magic School Bus

The Magic School Bus
Based on the award-winning Scholastic books, this animated series, seen on PBS, star Lily Tomlin as the voice of Ms. Frizzle, a teacher who leads her class through a series of amazing adventures. Malcolm Jamal Warner, Carol Channing, Tyne Daly and Dom DeLuise also provide voices. Each tape runs about 30 min. There are 20 volumes available, including:

**The Magic School Bus
Inside Ralphie**
19-3739 $12.99

**The Magic School Bus
Goes To Seed**
19-3903 $12.99

**The Magic School Bus
Gets Ants In Its Pants**
19-3987 $12.99

**The Magic School Bus
In A Beehive**
19-4051 $12.99

**The Magic School Bus:
Greatest Adventures**
Three of the all-time favorite "Magic School Bus" episodes, as chosen by kids across America, are featured on one special video. Included are "Busasaurus," "In a Pickle" and "Lost in Space." 90 min.
19-4083 $14.99

**The Magic School Bus:
Creepy, Crawly Fun**
Think you're brave enough to watch three creepy, crawly tales of Ms. Frizzle and the kids, all on one tape? Featured here are "Going Batty," "Inside a Haunted House" and "Spins a Web." 90 min.
19-4084 $14.99

Table Manners For Kids:
Tots To Teens
Marjabelle Young Stewart, etiquette expert to the children of many First Families, shows young people ages 6-16 the proper way to dine. Set at a Victorian mansion, Ms. Stewart uses her expertise and demonstrates a variety of dining settings, from family meals and prom night to dinner at the White House. 30 min.
22-5718 $14.99

Baby Einstein
This popular series mixes music, fun and learning to help teach babies, toddlers and pre-schoolers about specific subjects in a unique way. Toys, familiar objects, words and poetry are all utilized to provide a special experience. Each tape runs about 30 min.

Baby Einstein
Colorful toys and real-world objects are used in tandem with vocabulary words from foreign language to help kids learn. For infants aged 1 month to 18 months.
27-7230 $14.99

Baby Mozart
Brightly colored toys, sound effects and Mozart's music meld to enlighten kids and introduce them to classical melodies. For infants and toddlers aged 1 month to 36 months.
27-7231 $14.99

Baby Bach
Child-friendly musical segments help expose your baby to the expressive music of Johann Sebastian Bach. For infants and toddlers from 1 to 36 months of age.
27-7232 $14.99

Baby Shakespeare
Kids can explore vocabulary through poetry and visuals as 12 common words are introduced by Bard, a word-loving dragon. For children aged 1 year to 4 years.
27-7233 $14.99

Baby Van Gogh
Charming puppetry, live-action sequences and classical music are used by "Vincent Van Goat" to introduce kids to the world of art. For children aged 1 year to 4 years.
27-7234 $14.99

Works
Curious kids eager to learn how everyday things are made and put together will enjoy this fun- and fact-filled video series that takes them to factories, workshops and other locales to learn the "how" and "why" of the world around them. Each tape runs about 30 min.

Works: Fun And Games
04-5706 $12.99

Works: How Do They Do That?
04-5707 $12.99

Works: In My House
04-5715 $12.99

Works: Fabulous Food
04-5716 $12.99

Miss Christy's Dancin'
Celebrity choreographer and children's dance specialist Christy Curtis is featured in this series of programs designed to help kids learn dance steps of all types. The steps are made simple and easy to follow, so get into the groove today. Each tape runs about 30 min. There are four volumes available, including:

Miss Christy's Dancin': Jazz
10-1533 $19.99

Miss Christy's Dancin': Ballet
10-1534 $19.99

Miss Christy's Dancin': Tap
10-1535 $19.99

Nighty Night
For every parent who ever had trouble getting their kids off to bed, this video mix of adorable baby animals getting ready for sleep and gentle, soothing music is just the answer. 20 min.
10-1752 $12.99

Kids For Character
A passel of favorite children's TV stars, including Barney, Babar, Shari Lewis and Lamb Chop, the Magic School Bus gang and others, offer entertaining and informative lessons on the "Six Pillars of Character": trustworthiness, respect, responsibility, fairness, caring and citizenship. 60 min.
50-5167 $14.99

Kids For Character:
Choices Count!
Youngsters will learn how their actions affect others and how to choose the right way to behave in this song- and fun-filled special featuring appearances by characters from such kidvid hits as "Bananas in Pajamas," "The Big Comfy Couch," "Wishbone" and others. Tom Selleck hosts. 60 min.
50-5562 $14.99

William Wegman's Mother Goose
Everyone's favorite costumed canines meet everyone's favorite bedtime stories in this colorful, comical take on the Mother Goose legend, as the Wegman dogs bring to life 24 nursery rhymes, including "Three Men in a Tub," "Patty Cake, Patty Cake" and many more. 30 min.
04-5527 $12.99

Alphabet Soup
World famous artist William Wegman has made a career photographing his photogenic dogs, and now he brings pooches Fay Ray, Chundo, Crooky and Batty to home video in a delightful program that helps kids learn the ABCs. See the Weimaraners in all sorts of domestic situations relating to the alphabet. 30 min.
19-3800 $12.99

How To Raise A Street Smart Child
When that nice-seeming stranger approaches your child, will they know how to react? Daniel J. Travanti hosts this acclaimed program that shows parents how to educate their children to recognize and avoid potential dangers. 43 min.
44-1481 Was $19.99 *$14.99*

All About Kids' Safety
Entertaining, informative primer on child safety, focusing on bike, street and fire care and what kids should do in emergency situations. Produced by the animators of "Sesame Street," this tape will help youngsters with important household and outdoor tips. 49 min.
50-2142 *$19.99*

Origami For Kids
The ancient Japanese art of paper folding is taught in easy-to-learn style by experts Katsuhiko Takeshige and Jill Meuninck, as kids learn how to create frogs, cicadas, cranes, swans, hats, paper boats, drinking cups and more. 60 min.
53-6909 *$14.99*

Introduction To Puppet Making
Puppeteer Jim Gamble shows how, using household items, kids can produce wonderful finger, book and rod puppets and make marionettes. Youngsters will be amazed and entertained at Jim's fun-filled creations, which they can now make themselves. 30 min.
89-7010 *$14.99*

Bonjour Les Amis: Complete Set
Language expert Marie-Pierre Moine, using songs and animated sequences featuring a lovable French feline named Moustache, teaches beginning French for children ages 4 to 9 in this three-tape series. 150 min. total. NOTE: Individual volumes available at $19.99 each.
27-6858 Save $5.00! *$54.99*

Hola Amigos: Complete Set
Say "hola" (hello) to Paco the Chihuahua, who lives with the Perez family in Veracruz, Mexico, and joins them in all sorts of fun-filled adventures that help teach basic Spanish words and phrases. Children ages 4 to 9 will enjoy learning a new language with this three-tape series. 165 min. total. NOTE: Individual volumes available at $19.99 each.
27-7028 Save $5.00! *$54.99*

Show & Tell: Bats & Balls
It's "Take Me Out to the Ball Factory," as Chicago White Sox star third baseman Robin Ventura leads youngsters on a cross-country video tour to see how baseballs, bats and gloves are made. 46 min.
50-7450 *$14.99*

Show & Tell: News & Comics
Get the scoop on how a daily newspaper is published in this four-star kids' video that takes you behind the scenes at the Chicago Tribune. Go from how newsprint is made and reporters covering stories to an up-close look at the massive printing presses in action, plus a visit with "Dick Tracy" artist Dick Locher as he draws and colors a Sunday comic strip. 30 min.
50-7539 *$14.99*

Marsalis On Music: Complete Set
Acclaimed jazz and classical music performer Wynton Marsalis brings hois terrific talents to video with this four-tape series in which he taches kids the finer points of music appreciation. Guest stars, classic orchestras and Marsalis' own jazz group help him trumpet the benefits of music education in "Wynton on Form," "Wynton on the Jazz Band," "Wynton on Practice" and "Wynton on Rhythm." 200 min. total. NOTE: Individual volumes available at $19.99 each.
04-5394 *$79.99*

Wimzie's House
Join 5-year-old bird/dragon monster Wimzie, her family and her friends as they explore everyday adventures and problems in this acclaimed PBS series that uses puppets to entertain and gently educate. Each tape features two episodes and runs about 45 min.

Wimzie's House: It's Magic Time
04-5681 *$12.99*

Wimzie's House: You're Special
04-5682 *$12.99*

Wimzie's House: Babies Have It Made
04-5719 *$12.99*

Wimzie's House: Pet Tales
04-5720 ❑*$12.99*

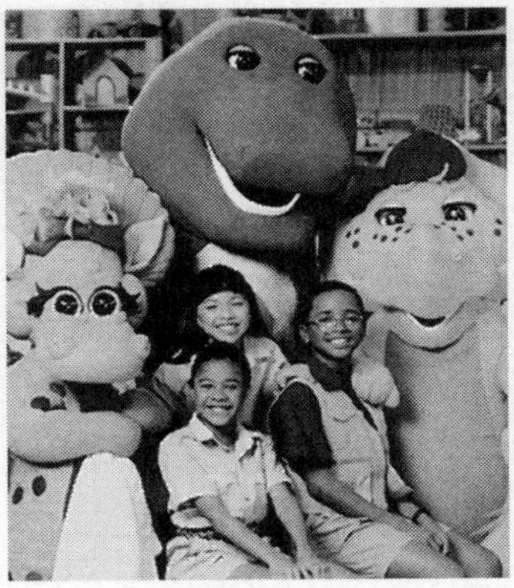

Barney And Friends
Everyone's favorite friendly purple dinosaur, his prehistoric pals Baby Bop and BJ, and all his human friends are here for some super-dee-duper sessions of games, songs and educational fun. Except where noted, each tape runs about 30 min. There are 23 volumes available, including:

Barney Goes To School
50-2052 *$14.99*

Barney Songs
50-2912 *$14.99*

Barney Live! In New York City
Live on the stage of the legendary Radio City Music Hall, the world's friendliest purple-and-green dinosaur is joined by Baby Bop, BJ and new pal the Winkster for a dazzling song-filled show that includes all your favorite Barney tunes. 80 min.
50-4915 Was $19.99 ❑*$14.99*

Sing & Dance With Barney
Celebrate 10 years of the beloved dinosaur's "purple reign" with this special program, as Barney is joined by friends old and new for a sing-along party. Among the favorite songs performed are "The More We Get Together," "Itsy Bitsy Spider," "Do Your Ears Hang Low," "Baby Bop Hop" and many more, including, of course, "I Love You." 56 min.
50-5431 *$14.99*

Barney's Adventure Bus
"His name is Barney, and he is the adventure bus driver!" Hop on board and let the prehistoric purple one take you on a fun-filled ride that includes a castle-building stop in the Land of Make Believe, a lesson in pizza-making at Barney's Purple Pepperoni Pizzeria, a musical jamboree with Baby Bop and more. 50 min.
50-5559 *$14.99*

Barney: More Barney Songs
50-8245 ❑*$14.99*

Barney's Rhyme Time Rhythm
Proving he's not a "Not Ready for Rhyme Time Player," Barney and special guest Mother Goose host a colorful tea party and help the kids act out some of their favorite nursery rhymes, including "Hickory Dickory Doc," "Simple Simon," "Old King Cole," "One, Two Buckle My Shoe" and others. 50 min.
50-8384 ❑*$14.99*

Michael Jordan's Playground
Your young hoop fans will enjoy this high-flying look at NBA superstar Michael Jordan in action. Exciting basketball footage, an up-front interview with Michael on working to achieve your goals and doing your best, and the music video "Anything's Possible" are featured. 40 min.
04-2413 Was $19.99 ❑*$14.99*

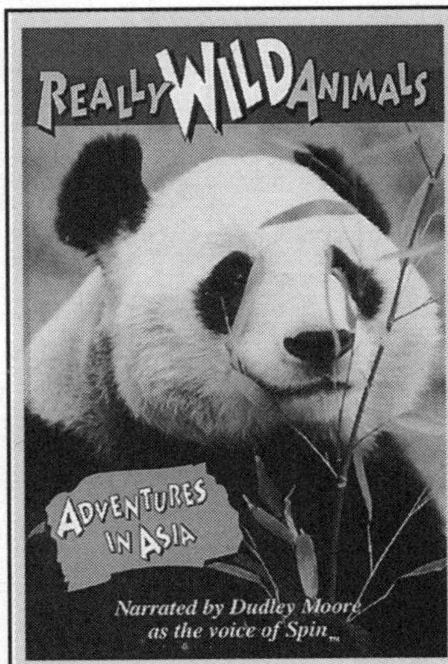

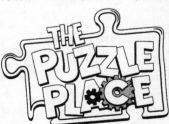

Really Wild Animals
Produced by National Geographic for kids of all ages, these videos entertain and inform children about the animal kingdom. With superb photography, original music and an animated host named Spin (voiced by Dudley Moore), the series travels around the world and under the sea in its quest for excitement. Each tape runs about 45 min. There are 13 volumes available, including:

Really Wild Animals: Adventures In Asia
02-2639 ❑*$14.99*

Really Wild Animals: Swinging Safari
02-2548 ❑*$14.99*

Really Wild Animals: Amazing North America
02-2638 ❑*$14.99*

Really Wild Animals: Dinosaurs And Other Creature Features
02-2886 ❑*$14.99*

Horses A To Z
Children who love horses will enjoy this terrific tape that's ideal for the novice rider. There's thoroughbreds, draft horses and cute and cuddly ponies. Whether you seek rodeo action or want to learn how to care for your horse, this one's for you. 30 min.
10-2697 *$12.99*

Zoboomafoo
From nature-loving sibs Martin and Chris Kratt comes this top-rated PBS program made especially for preschoolers. Zoboo is a lemur from Madagascar who leaps from place to place teaching children about the wonders of wildlife. Live-action, animation, guessing games and songs are among the highlights in each episode. Each tape runs about 45 min.

Zoboomafoo: Zoboo's Little Pals
18-7917 *$14.99*

Zoboomafoo: Play Day At Animal Junction
18-7918 *$14.99*

See How They Grow
Based on the best-selling children's books, this series follows different animals in their habitat from infancy through maturity, and offers an intimate glimpse of the creature's habits. They're fluffy, creepy, cuddly and furry! There are 10 volumes available, including:

See How They Grow: Farm Animals
04-5358 ❑*$12.99*

See How They Grow: Wild Animals
04-5359 ❑*$12.99*

See How They Grow: Jungle Animals
04-5443 *$12.99*

Audubon's Animal Adventures
From the National Audubon Society comes a wonderful documentary series that the whole family can enjoy, as you take an up-close look at some of the animal kingdom's most remarkable and resourceful members. Each tape runs about 30 min. There are 13 volumes available, including:

Audubon's Animal Adventures: Wolf Adventures
44-2094 ❑*$12.99*

Audubon's Animal Adventures: Dolphin Adventures
44-2095 ❑*$12.99*

Audubon's Animal Adventures: Bat Adventures
44-2128 ❑*$12.99*

I Love Dinosaurs!
That's what millions of kids (and quite a few adults) across America are saying, and in this video you'll join some young dino-fans on a fossil dig and come face to face with a Tyrannosaurus Rex named Sue!
19-2944 ❑*$12.99*

Dinosaurs Of The Jurassic And Other Periods
Through the magic of clay animation, the Triassic, Jurassic and Cretaceous Periods come to life as you visit the Earth 64 million year ago—when the central plains of North America were underwater; prehistoric life lived in subtropical swamps; and tyrannosaurs roamed the countryside. 45 min.
58-8174 *$14.99*

Animal Tales
It's a real-life Aesop's Fables with this charming family series that features films of critters from around the world in wildlife adventures that teach simple, gentle lessons to youngsters. Each two-tape gift set runs about 110 min. total. NOTE: Individual volumes available at $14.99 each.

Animal Tales: Series 1 Gift Set
Includes Vol. 1 ("The Lost Cubs"/"The Bully"/"Down Under in a Tree"/"Happy Birthday, Archie") and Vol. 2 ("The Lonely Tiger"/"The Bad Luck Donkey"/"The Gorilla Who Wouldn't Say Thank You"/"Smile"). NOTE: Individual volumes available separately at $14.99.
89-5028 *$19.99*

Animal Tales: Series 2 Gift Set
Includes Vol. 3 ("It All Began with a Blueberry Pie"/"You Can Be Anything"/"Learning to Fly"/"All A'Chore, Who's Going A'Chore") and Vol. 4 ("Take a Bath, Stinky"/"The Chocolate Rock"/"Octavious and the Sea Witch"/"How to Build Your Very First Dam!"). NOTE: Individual volumes available separately at $14.99.
89-5029 *$19.99*

The Baby Animals Collection
If you enjoy watching those cute little creatures romp, explore and have fun in the great outdoors—and who doesn't—then this three-video set is for you. Delightful wildlife footage will entertain young and old in "Baby Animal Fun," "Catch Me If You Can" and "The Wonder of Baby Animals." 140 min. total. NOTE: Individual volumes available at $19.99 each.
65-7003 Save $20.00! *$39.99*

The Magic Of Baby Animals
Magical indeed is this enthralling and entertaining program that lets viewers visit young Emperor penguins in the Antarctic, witness the birth of a baby sea otter, swing from tree to tree with orangutans in Southeast Asia, and marvel at the tender love between mothers and their babies of all species. 50 min.
65-7007 *$12.99*

Animal Antics: Boxed Set
Set in and around an old English schoolhouse, this delightful live-action series follows the adventures of a group of wild and domestic animals through the course of a year. Included in the four-tape set are "Spring," "Summer," "Autumn" and "Winter." 195 min. total. NOTE: Individual volumes available at $12.99 each.
69-5306 Save $12.00! *$39.99*

Baby Animals At Uncle Larry's Farm
It's time for family fun down on the farm, as Uncle Larry welcomes one and all to watch these delightful little critters frolic and play, each with their own sing-along song. You'll see calves, goats, ducklings, chicks, kittens, piglets, bunnies and more. 30 min.
76-7417 *$12.99*

All About Animals
Developed with pre-schoolers in mind, this National Geographic mixes games, songs and rhyming fun with amazing wildlife footage to teach 2- to 5-year-olds the wonders of the animal kingdom. Each tape runs about 30 min. There are six volumes available, including:

All About Animals: Bundles Of Babies
See how young bears, turtles, penguins and other critters are cared for and learn to fend for themselves.
19-2951 ❑*$12.99*

All About Animals: Special Animal Secrets
See what's unique about chameleons, kangaroos, zebras and other animals.
19-2952 ❑*$12.99*

All About Animals: Peekaboo Pals
How do animals avoid being seen by predators? Learn some of their hiding tricks here.
19-2953 ❑*$12.99*

Banana Zoo: Boxed Set
A lovable cartoon chimp named Banana serves as host for this exciting live-action wildlife series that offers youngsters a light-hearted look at the animal kingdom's diverse members. Included in the four-tape set are "Animal Songs," "Endangered Species," "Funny Fellows" and "Predators." 104 min. total. NOTE: Individual volumes available at $12.99 each.
83-1339 Save $17.00! *$34.99*

Jack Hanna's Animal Adventures: Complete Set
You've seen him on David Letterman and "Good Morning America," and now Columbus Zoo director Jack Hanna delights young and old alike with a three-tape boxed set of fun, fascinating looks at the animal kingdom. Included are "Baby Boomers," "Gorilla Quest" and "It's Elephant Time!" 125 min. total. NOTE: Individual volumes available at $14.99 each.
86-9008 *$34.99*

THE PUZZLE PLACE

The Puzzle Place
The creators of "Reading Rainbow" and "Storytime" bring you this terrific series in which kids journey to a magical realm where they'll discover what makes them different from and similar to other children through music, puppets and puzzles. Each tape runs about 55 min. There are six volumes available, including:

The Puzzle Place: Deck The Halls
04-5388 *$14.99*

The Puzzle Place: Accentuate The Positive
04-5449 *$14.99*

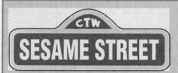

Sesame Street
Sunny day...Everything's A-OK when children's television favorites help youngsters learn any time of the day with the simple push of a button. Each tape features a specific educational goal or activity, from learning the ABC's to counting to discovering the importance of self-esteem. Except where noted, each volume runs about 30 min. There are 31 volumes available, including:

Do The Alphabet
Children and parents can sing their way through the ABCs with Big Bird, who joins special guest Billy Joel to teach Baby Bear the alphabet, in this special "Sesame Street" program that's never been seen on TV. 45 min.
04-5431 $12.99

Cookie Monster's Best Bites
There's nothing "crumby" about this delicious collection of music and skits featuring everyone's favorite big blue baked goods consumer. Actress Annette Bening pays Cookie a visit, there are silly songs, and more. 30 min.
04-5432 $12.99

Put Down The Duckie: An All-Star Musical Special
What will it take to get Ernie to leave his beloved rubber buddy, if only for a little while? An array of special musical guests try to convince him to "Put Down the Duckie" in this special "Sesame Street" tale. 45 min.
04-5441 $12.99

Sleepytime Songs & Stories
Seeing the "Sesame Street" gang get ready for sleep makes bedtime much easier for children (and especially for their parents).
04-5453 $12.99

Get Up And Dance
Big Bird shakes his tail feathers and teaches kids how to have fun while putting their best feet forward in this song-filled "Sesame Street" dance video.
04-5497 $12.99

Quiet Time
"Hush, little baby, don't say a word. Mommy's got a video with Big Bird." Spend "down time" with the feathered fellow and pals Telly Monster, Oscar, Rosita, and "Rent" star Daphne Rubin-Vega.
04-5504 $12.99

Kids' Favorite Songs
Who better than the "Sesame Street" gang to offer their spin on some of the all-time favorite children's tunes? Join Elmo for a "Top Ten Countdown" that includes "I've Been Working on the Railroad," "Row, Row, Row Your Boat," "Twinkle, Twinkle Little Star," "She'll Be Comin' 'Round the Mountain" and many more. 30 min.
04-5643 $12.99

Let's Make Music
Elmo, Oscar and company are joined by the cast of the hit stage show "Stomp" for a toe-tappin' look at rythymn and making music.
04-5736 $9.99

Learning About Letters
The alphabet from A to Z, as demonstrated by Big Bird and Cookie Monster.
46-1001 $12.99

Getting Ready To Read
Big Bird and Oscar use rhymes and stories to show how words sometimes look and sound alike.
46-1003 $12.99

Learning About Numbers
Who but The Count could teach youngsters about the numbers from 1 to 20?
46-1005 $12.99

Rock & Roll!
DJ Jackman Wolf answers the requests of Sesame Street pals who shake, rattle and roll to tunes like "The Word Is No" and "Count Up to Nine."
46-1071 $12.99

Sing Yourself Silly!
A manic musical masterpiece featuring a slew of Sesame Street friends. Among the highlights are Oscar the Grouch singing "Everything in the Wrong Place Ball," "Honker Duckie Dinger Jamboree" by Ernie, and guest James Earl Jones doing "Jellyman Kelly."
46-1076 $12.99

Sesame Street Visits The Firehouse
For your little firefighter, this video trip by Big Bird and his friends to the local firehouse is sure to delight. See how firefighting equipment works, take a ride in an engine, see a real conflagration and more. 30 min.
46-1077 $12.99

Elmocize
Everyone's favorite little red Muppet learns the importance of physical fitness, as well as how much fun getting in shape can be, with help from musical guest star Cyndi Lauper in this kid-style exercise video.
04-5451 $14.99

Elmopalooza!
It's an all-star music and laughfest with the jolly red fellow, his fellow Sesame Street Muppets, and such special guests as Celine Dion, Gloria Estefan, The Fugees, The Mighty Mighty Bosstones, Rosie O'Donnell, Chris Rock and others. 55 min.
04-5564 $12.99

The Adventures Of Elmo In Grouchland: Sing And Play
Join the lovable Elmo and his new best friend, Grizzy the Grouch, in this special song-filled adventure that features three tunes from the movie, "The Adventures of Elmo in Grouchland." 30 min.
04-5676 $12.99

Elmo's World
It's a big world for someone who's only three years old, and in this special video you can join the "Sesame Street" favorite, as Elmo, his pet goldfish Dorothy and his friend Mr. Noodle use their imagination to explore dancing, music and books. 50 min.
04-5727 $12.99

Elmo's Sing-Along Guessing Game
Children can guess (and sing) along with the "Sesame Street" crew in this video quiz show that features such tunes as Big Bird's "My Best Friend," and "I Love My Eyebrows" by Kermit the Frog.
46-1082 $12.99

The Best Of Elmo
Little red Elmo, one of "Sesame Street's" most popular residents, takes the spotlight in this program, singing his best-loved songs. It's wacky, funny and educational kid's entertainment in the finest "Sesame Street" mold.
46-1101 $12.99

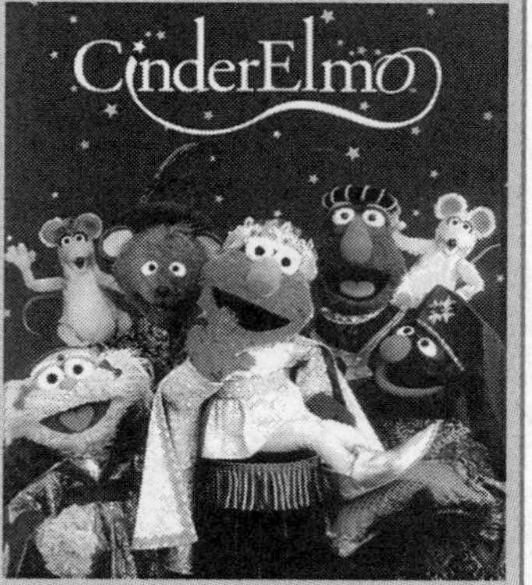

CinderElmo (1999)
One of the world's best-loved fairy tales is given a "Sesame Street" treatment in this delightful special. Watch as the one and only Elmo plays the put-upon title character and gets a chance, courtesy of his Fairy Godperson, to attend a fancy ball and win the hand of Princess Charming. With Keri Russell, Oliver Platt, Kathy Najimy and French Stewart. 50 min.
04-5708 $12.99

Sesame Street Kids' Guide To Life
This all-new series from the "Sesame Street" crew features entertaining stories with an educational message for children, plus special family activities and parenting tips for moms and dads. Each tape runs about 45 min.

Big Bird Gets Lost
Separated from Maria during a trip to a department store, Big Bird gets some help from guest star Frances McDormand in remembering what to do when you're lost.
04-5559 $12.99

Learning To Share
When Elmo's friend Zoe comes over to join him for playtime, it's up to guest star Katie Couric to help he learn that it's more fun to share his toys with Zoe than not.
04-5430 $12.99

Telling The Truth
It's no lie that guest star Dennis Quaid has to set Elmo and Telly Monster straight on the importance of being truthful to others.
04-5495 $12.99

Sesame Street: 25 Wonderful Years— A Musical Celebration! (1994)
Join in the song-filled merriment when Ernie, Bert, Grover, Cookie Monster and Big Bird celebrate 25 years of the most famous street on TV. Favorite tunes like "Rubber Ducky" and "It's Not Easy Being Green" are featured in a magical program. 60 min.
46-1100 $12.99

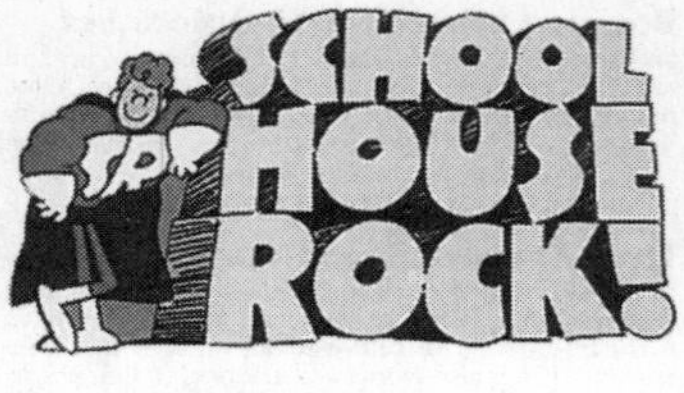

Schoolhouse Rock
Filled with hummable tunes and colorful animated segments, this Saturday Morning favorite has captivated "Generation X"-ers and contemporary children alike. These programs feature classic and new animated footage that help youngsters learn about math, science, English and history. Each tape runs 30 min.

Schoolhouse Rock: Money Rock
Includes "Dollars and Sense," "Where the Money Goes," "Tax Man Max," "Tyrannosaurus Debt" and more.
11-2239 $14.99

Schoolhouse Rock: Grammar Rock
Includes "Interjections!," "The Tale of Mr. Morton," "A Noun Is a Person, Place or Thing," "Lolly, Lolly, Lolly, Get Your Adverbs Here," the ever-popular "Conjunction Junction" and more.
19-9115 $14.99

Schoolhouse Rock: America Rock
Includes "Fireworks," "No More Kings," "The Great American Melting Pot," "I'm Just a Bill," "Three-Ring Government" and others.
19-9116 $14.99

Schoolhouse Rock: Multiplication Rock
Includes "My Hero, Zero," "Elementary, My Dear," "I Got Six," "Figure Eight," "Little Twelvetoes" and more.
19-9117 $14.99

Schoolhouse Rock: Science Rock
Includes "Do the Circulation," "Telegraph Line," "Electricity, Electricity," "Interplanet Janet" and others.
19-9118 $14.99

Schoolhouse Rock 4-Pack
Get a lesson in saving some dough with this special set that includes "America Rock," "Grammar Rock," "Multiplication Rock" and "Science Rock."
19-9119 Save $10.00! $49.99

Becoming A Master: The Ultimate Pokémon Experience
Forget Wacky Packages...forget pogs...the hot fad at the turn of the millennium is Pokémon cards. Learn about how the craze started in Japan, which cards to look for and how to trade for them, and how to play the game with this two-tape set. 80 min.
05-5116 $19.99

Good Housekeeping: Kids In Motion
Who said you can't learn math skills and physical fitness at the same time? Not America's funniest housekeeper, Scott Baio, who hosts this interactive learning tape for kids. Learn mind and body coordination and watch song and dance routines that help teach numbers and movement.
04-3134 $12.99

Ei Ei Yoga
Easy-to-follow yoga exercises for youngsters are mixed with a barnyard setting in this fun-filled fitness program hosted by farmer Yogi Oki Doki (in reality celebrated yoga teacher Max Thomas). Kids will enjoy improving strength, flexibility and stamina with the moves demonstrated here. 38 min.
70-7238 $14.99

Mini-Muscles: A Fitness Adventure
Tired of your kids sitting on the couch and watching videos without getting exercise? Why not sit them on the couch and let them watch this video? Join host Cindy Crawford and guests Kobe Bryant and Radu for a fun-filled animated adventure that shows how exercise can be fun and stress the importance of keeping fit. 30 min.
10-1750 $12.99

Dance! Workout With Barbie
Now kids of all ages can get a chance to exercise with America's favorite doll, the always-lovely Barbie! Live-action and animation mix to bring Barbie and her fitness-minded, fun-loving pals to you! Look for "Party of Five" star Jennifer Love Hewitt as a young workout partner. 30 min.
11-1612 Was $19.99 $14.99

Chicken Fat: The Youth Fitness Video
Inspired by the popular song written by Meredith Wilson ("The Music Man") for President Kennedy's Council on Physical Fitness, this exercise video links the past with the present, offering footage of JFK discussing youth fitness and a workout program for kids only. 30 min.
76-7333 $14.99

Tae-Bo Junior, Vol. 1
Tae-Bo master Billy Blanks brings his winning formula of exercise, strengthening and positive reinforcement to the youngsters in this awesome workout kids will love.
50-8471 $29.99

Nature Art For Kids
Kids can learn the wonders of nature and how to be creative with this video that offers many interesting arts-and-crafts projects for them. Olivia and Rebecca are the hosts for a primer that will teach children how to plant a wild flower and herb garden, create paper flowers, weave miniature rugs, create yard dolls, fashion jewelry and lots more. 60 min.
53-6908 $14.99

All About Hardworking Tugboats
Join Captain Evans and Captain Bob in the wheelhouse of a tugboat as they help ships from all over the world "park" in the harbor. Also, you'll witness the power of a little tug, check out its two engines and join longshoremen as they load and unload containers of freight. 30 min.
10-2549 $12.99

All About Fast-Moving Trains
Learn everything you wanted to about trains of all kinds as you join Engineer Gus and Engineer Sam on a fun-filled educational journey. You'll see coal engines, travel at 100 m.p.h. on the Super Train, meet model train collectors and more. 30 min.
10-2550 $12.99

All About Heavy Construction Equipment
Join "Hard Hat Harry," the construction genie, as he shows you some of the most astounding building equipment around. Check out a king-sized piledriver hammering away, a heavy off-road dump truck and a barrier mover that can make a two-lane highway in seconds. 60 min.
10-2551 $12.99

Big Machines: Road Construction
Look out! Here comes a brigade of awesome machines specializing in devouring old roads, clearing the way for new construction. Witness huge bulldozers thundering through the landscape and gigantic machines of all sorts. Kids will be enthralled by the activity captured on this video. 30 min.
58-8158 $12.99

Big Buildings: Demolition & Reconstruction
Things go boom big-time in this explosive production that shows huge buildings going down, explosions that'll amaze you, and construction equipment at work. Be a "Demolition Boy" or "Girl" after checking out this video. 30 min.
58-8159 $12.99

Big Trucks: Tractors & Trains
They haul cargo and freight. They chug along at great speeds, carrying goods and passengers coast to coast. See these impressive big machines at work, whether it be on the rails or on the road. 30 min.
58-8161 $12.99

Real Wheels
Get rollin' with this exciting live-action children's series that puts them up close and behind the wheel of all manner of things that move. Each tape runs about 30 min. There are 20 volumes available, including:

There Goes A Fire Truck!
19-3504 $12.99

There Goes A Bulldozer!
19-3505 $12.99

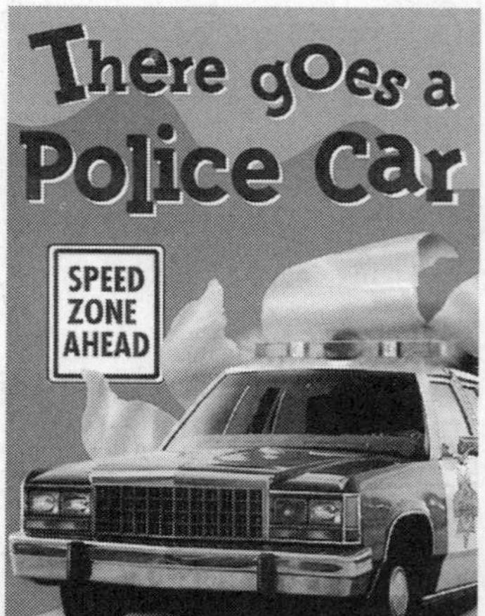

There Goes A Police Car!
19-3565 $12.99

There Goes A Train!
19-3566 $12.99

There Goes A Truck!
19-3567 $12.99

There Goes A Helicopter!
19-3700 $12.99

There Goes A Dump Truck
19-4048 $12.99

Mexico

Maria Candelaria (1946)
Mexican-made tragedy stars legendary beauty Dolores Del Rio as the daughter of a woman who was stoned to death because she posed nude for a rakish painter. Dolores tempts destiny when poverty forces her to sit for the artist herself. 96 min. In Spanish with English subtitles.
53-7271 *$39.99*

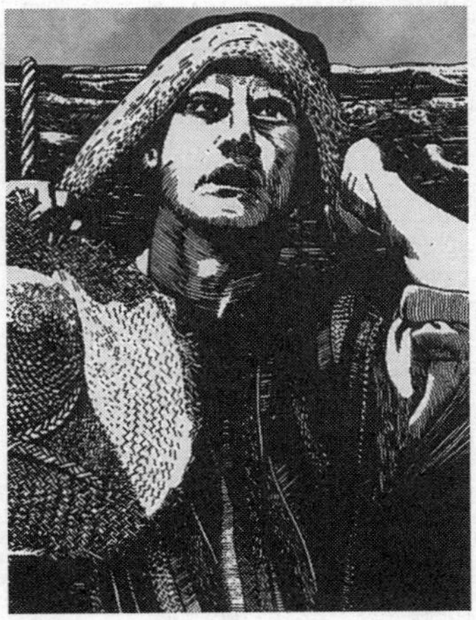

Macario (1961)
A haunting Mexican fantasy/drama, based on a story by the author of "The Treasure of the Sierra Madre." A peasant is visited by Death and given the power to heal the sick, but this gift soon proves to be a curse. Ignacio Lopez Torres stars; directed by Roberto Gavaldon. 91 min. In Spanish with English subtitles.
53-7347 Was $69.99 *$29.99*

Yanco (1964)
Magical Mexican fable of a young boy who learns to play a special violin called Yanco, believed by his fellow villagers to contain an evil spirit. A unique exercise in pure cinema, the story is told only through visuals, music and sound effects. 94 min.
53-7094 Was $39.99 *$29.99*

Reed: Insurgent Mexico (1971)
Dramatic filmization of the accounts of the Mexican Revolution by journalist John Reed (the subject of Warren Beatty's "Reds"), including his adventures with Pancho Villa's army from 1913 to 1914. Claudio Obregon stars. 104 min. In Spanish with English subtitles.
53-8226 Was $59.99 *$29.99*

Place Without Limits (El Lugar Sin Limites) (1977)
When the female owner of a run-down brothel in a Mexican village is threatened by a visiting truck driver, her father—a transvestite who wears glamorous dresses and does a steamy Flamenco dance—steps in to save the day. Based on a novel by Chilean author José Donoso, director Arturo Ripstein's outrageous tale stars Roberto Colo ("Los Olvidados"). 110 min. In Spanish with English subtitles.
70-3472 Letterboxed *$29.99*

Doña Herlinda And Her Son (1986)
What happens when a meddling mother tries to arrange a marriage for her son, while at the same time inviting his male lover to move in with them? Outrageous comedy of sexual mores and maternal possessiveness from Mexico stars Guadalupe Del Toro, Marco Antonio Trevino; written and directed by Jaime Humberto Hermosillo. 90 min. In Spanish with English subtitles.
53-7130 Was $79.99 *$39.99*

Esmeralda Comes By Night (1997)
This fanciful and sexy romantic fable from Mexican director Jaime Humberto Hermosillo ("Doña Herlinda and Her Son) tells of Esmeralda, a nurse with five husbands who is arrested for bigamy as she's about to wed spouse number six. Her allure proves so strong that she sparks the interests of a police inspector and other citizens of Mexico City. With Maria Rojo, Claudio Obregon. 103 min. In Spanish with English subtitles.
02-5198 *$99.99*

Cabeza De Vaca (1992)
A historical saga set in 1528, where a survivor of a Spanish expedition off the Florida coast searches for his countrymen in the American wilderness. He discovers an Indian tribe called the Iguase, learns their culture and becomes their leader, but must take a stand against invaders from his homeland. With Juan Diego. 108 min. In Spanish with English subtitles.
21-9041 Was $89.99 *$24.99*

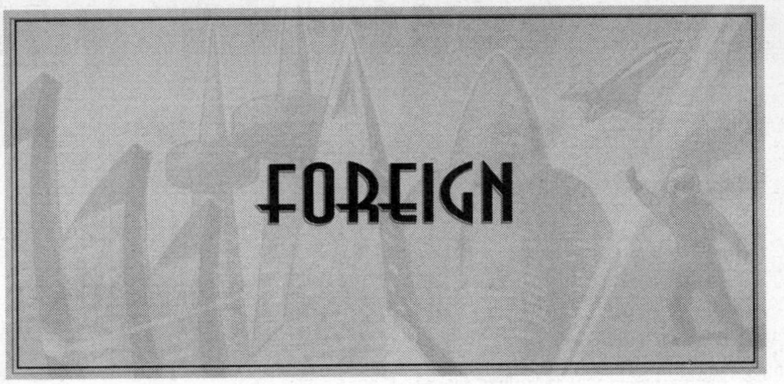

Cronos (1992)
A bizarre take on vampirism, this Mexican horror-fantasy tells of an alchemist who creates a scarab-like device that will give its user eternal youth and even restore life to the dead...but at a chilling price. Centuries later, an aging antique store owner finds the device and falls under its spell, but a dying millionaire wants it for himself. Federico Luppi, Claudio Brook, Ron Perlman star. 92 min. In English and Spanish with English subtitles.
68-1323 Was $89.99 *$14.99*

Cronos (Dubbed Version)
Also available in a dubbed-in-English edition.
68-1324 Was $89.99 *$14.99*

Forbidden Beach (La Playa Prohibida) (1984)
A powerful and brutal drama with Oedipal overtones from Mexico, Enrique Gomez Vadillo's tale follows a teenage boy whose overly protective attitude towards his widowed mother grows dangerous when she takes up with a handsome engineer while they're on vacation at the beach. Sasha Montenegro, Jose Alonzo star. 84 min. In Spanish with English subtitles.
78-5082 *$49.99*

Danzón (1993)
Stylishly sensual story set in Mexico City about a telephone operator whose tame life is made exciting whenever she partakes in ballroom dancing. When her partner of six years fails to attend the dance one night, she tries to track him down amongst the eccentric people of the city. Maria Rojo stars. 103 min. In Spanish with English subtitles.
02-2489 Was $89.99 *$19.99*

Salon Mexico (1994)
A remake of a popular 1948 Mexican film, director Jose Luis Garcia Agraz's stylish drama is set in a 1930s dance hall where a dancer and her lover have killed each other after a violent fight. As a police inspector looks into the crime, the woman's tragic story is revealed through flashbacks. Maria Rojo, Alberto Estrella, Manuel Ojeda star. 110 min. In Spanish with English subtitles.
53-6853 *$29.99*

Highway Patrolman (1992)
Director Alex Cox ("Repo Man," "Sid and Nancy") returns to form with a stylish story of a naive Mexican patrolman whose idealism is threatened when he realizes he can't escape from the corruption around him. Roberto Sosa and Vanessa Bauche star in this hybrid of road movie and western laced with humor. 104 min. In Spanish with English subtitles.
53-8922 *$89.99*

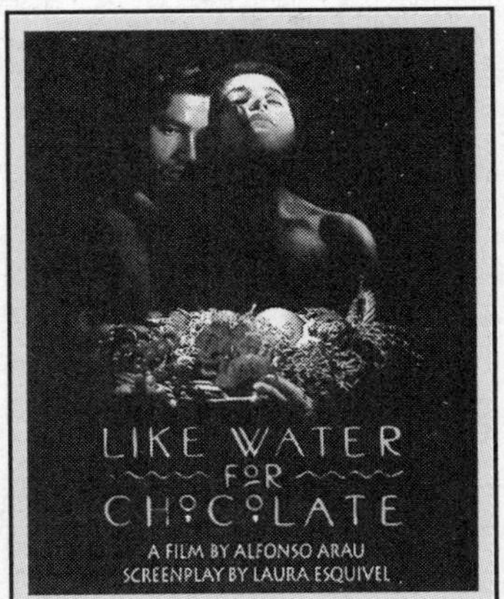

Like Water For Chocolate (1993)
The most popular Latin American film of all time is an enchanting story of romance and eroticism, set in early 20th-century Mexico and focusing on a family's youngest daughter. Put upon by her mother and siblings, she uses her magical abilities to control people's emotions through the food she cooks. Lumi Cavazos stars; directed by Alfonso Arau and based on a novel by his wife, Laura Esquivel. 105 min. Dubbed in English.
11-1803 Was $89.99 *$19.99*

Frida (1984)
The moving life story of controversial 20th-century painter Frida Kahlo is recounted in this engrossing drama that uses the Mexican artist's works as settings for surreal flashback sequences. Ofelia Medina, Max Kerlow star. 108 min. In Spanish with English subtitles.
53-7302 Was $79.99 *$29.99*

Midaq Alley (El Callejón De Los Milagros) (1995)
One of the most acclaimed Mexican films ever, director Jorge Fons' adaptation of Egyptian author Naguib Mahfouz's novel moves the story from Cairo to Mexico City. The lives and loves of the owner of a neighborhood cantina, his family and neighbors, and the bar's patrons are movingly interwoven, from the barman's infatuation with a male clerk to a barber's obsession with a beautiful prostitute. Ernesto Gómez Cruz, Bruno Bichir, Margarita Sanz and Salma Hayek star. 140 min. In Spanish with English subtitles.
53-6329 Was $89.99 *$19.99*

Return To Sender (1994)
When her neighbor complains to the police about her noisy parties, a young woman concocts an elaborate prank to play on the middle-aged bachelor, sending him anonymous love letters. The man's search for the "secret admirer" drives him to desperate actions that change both people's lives in this compelling Mexican drama. Fernando Torre Laphame, Thiare Scanda star. 97 min. In Spanish with English subtitles.
53-6855 *$29.99*

All Of Them Witches (Sobrenatural) (1995)
Haunted by a friend's murder in a neighboring apartment, a young woman searches for answers to what happened and is drawn into a dangerous world of black magic cults and sinister secrets. Mexican filmmaker Daniel Gruener's gripping chiller, filmed with haunting images, stars Susana Zabaleta, Alejandro Tomassi. 100 min. In Spanish with English subtitles.
53-6854 *$29.99*

Untamed Women (1995)
In this unusual, insightful look at changing gender roles in modern Mexican society, four unhappily married women from a small town leave their families behind and move to Guadalajara for a chance at a new life. Will what they find be worth what they gave up, or will it be worse? Patricia Reyes Spindola, Regina Orozco star. 116 min. In Spanish with English subtitles.
53-6856 *$29.99*

Between Pancho Villa And A Naked Woman (1995)
Tiring of her boyfriend's inability to commit, a woman dumps him in favor of a younger lover. Can a visit by the ghost of famed outlaw Pancho Villa help the spurned man regain his pride and win her back? Offbeat and thoughtful romantic fantasy from Mexico stars Diana Bracho, Arturo Rios, and Jesus Ochoa as Villa. 100 min. In Spanish with English subtitles.
53-6857 *$29.99*

The Last Call (1995)
The line between fiction and reality becomes blurred for an actor who lands a part in a play that changes his formerly close relationship with his son, with tragic consequences. Director Carlos Garcia Agraz's powerful drama stars Alberto Estrella, Arcelia Ramirez, Abraham Ramos. 94 min. In Spanish with English subtitles.
53-6858 *$29.99*

Deep Crimson (Profundo Carmesi) (1996)
Based on the real-life murders that inspired 1970's "The Honeymoon Killers," director Arturo Ripstein's compelling mix of suspense and perverse dark comedy stars Daniel Gimenez Cacho as a would-be ladies' man in '40s Mexico who robs the women who reply to his lonelyhearts ads. He meets his match in overweight nurse/embalmer Regina Orozco, who becomes Cacho's lover and takes his scheme to a deadly new level. 109 min. In Spanish with English subtitles.
53-6545 *$99.99*

Who The Hell Is Juliette? (1997)
A fascinating mix of fact and fiction, Mexican filmmaker Carlos Marcovich's low-key, non-linear debut feature juxtaposes the life stories of two young Latin American women—impoverished, streetwise Havana youth Yuliet Ortega and Mexican-born model and aspiring actress Fabiola Sanchez—and shows how a chance meeting changes their lives. Salma Hayek appears in a cameo as herself. 91 min. In Spanish with English subtitles.
53-6385 Was $79.99 *$24.99*

Latin America

Nueba Yol (A Funny Way To Say New York) (1996)
A charming, highly acclaimed effort from the Dominican Republic about Balbuena, a Dominican widower who receives a travel visa and heads for New York City in hopes of finding happiness and fortune. Instead, he faces labor, romantic and financial problems. Can he overcome them to make a happy life for himself? Luisito Marti stars. 105 min. In Spanish with English subtitles.
50-5360 *$19.99*

Nueba Yol 3 (1997)
Balbuena is back in this hilarious, observant follow-up to the hit "Nueba Yol" (the director thought sequels were usually lousy, so he went directly to #3). In this outing, Balbuena recovers from a gunshot wound and finds a way around a new government immigration law by trying to fake a marriage and remain in the U.S. Luisito Marti stars. 105 min. In Spanish with English subtitles.
50-8306 *$29.99*

Shoot To Kill (1990)
When her son is killed during a routine police round-up, a woman must battle corrupt officials in order to prove he was an innocent victim in this compelling drama from Venezuela. 90 min. In Spanish with English subtitles.
53-9593 *$59.99*

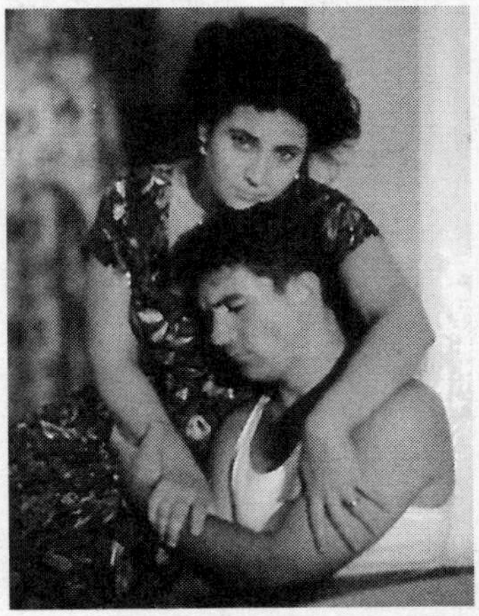

Terranova (1991)
Antonio Banderas is featured in this drama set in Venezuela in the 1950s and chronicling the relationship between the matriarch of a humble Italian immigrant family and Noemi, an aristocratic landowner. As the women discuss their frustrations, they form a strong bond. With Marisa Laurito, Mimi Lazo. 82 min. In Italian with English subtitles.
53-8985 Was $79.99 *$39.99*

Knocks At My Door (1992)
Gripping political drama set in a remote Latin American village preyed upon by armed government death squads. A rebel fugitive is hidden away by two nuns at the risk of their own lives. Director Alejandro Saderman's acclaimed adaptation of a Venezuelan stage-play stars Elba Escobar, Veronica Oddo, and playwright Juan Carlos Gene as the town's mayor. 105 min. In Spanish with English subtitles.
53-6365 Was $89.99 *$19.99*

The Marijuana Story (1951)
The title may lead you to believe this is an exploitation item, but it's not. In fact, this Latin American import tells of a man's struggle against drugs which claimed his wife's life. The further he gets involved with drugs, the more apparent it becomes that he will be a victim, too. Pedro Lopez Lagier stars. In Spanish with English subtitles.
79-5673 Was $24.99 *$19.99*

Sugar Cane Alley (1984)
Award-winning drama by Euzhan Palcy set on a sugar plantation in 1930s Martinique, where an old woman struggles to send her grandson to school and give him a better life. Garry Cadenat and Darling Legitimus star in this realistic look at Third World colonial life. AKA: "Rue Cases Negres." 107 min. In French with English subtitles.
03-1465 Was $89.99 *$29.99*

Third World Cop (1999)
Capone is a rebellious Jamaican cop who has just been transferred back to his hometown in order to clean up the streets. A run-in with his old friend Ratty, whom Capone learns is working for a local mob boss whose gun-running ring he is trying to shut down, forces the two men into a frenetic showdown in this reggae-flavored crime drama. Paul Campbell, Mark Danvers star. 98 min.
02-9270 *$19.99*

The Tigress (1990)
One of the most compelling images in Latin American literature's "Magic Realism" school, that of the strong-willed "Superwoman," is depicted in this drama from Ecuador. An independent and sexually aggressive woman known as "the Tigress" lives with her sisters in a remote jungle outpost and uses her sexuality to manipulate those around her, but what will happen when her youngest sibling plans to marry? 80 min. In Spanish with English subtitles.
87-7013 *$59.99*

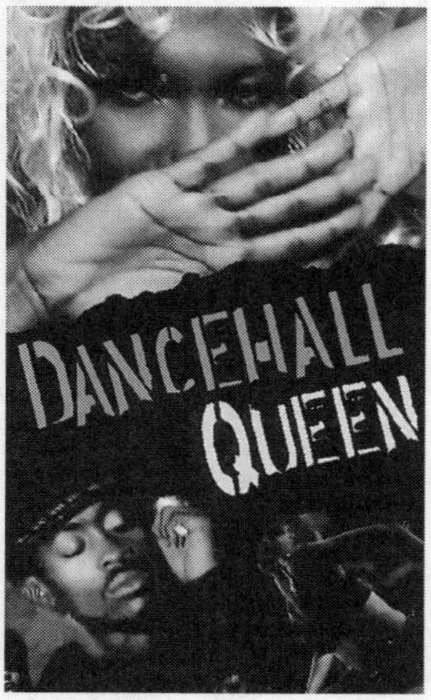

Dancehall Queen (1997)
Gritty, song-filled drama, set amid the ghettos and glittery dance clubs of Jamaica's capital city of Kingston. A single mother struggling to support her family as a street vendor spends her nights on the dance floor and sees an upcoming contest as her chance for a better life. Grace Jones, Beenie Man, The Marley Girls and others are featured on the reggae soundtrack. 95 min.
02-8776 *$19.99*

Johnny 100 Pesos (1995)
Based on a true story, this Chilean drama follows an attempted armed robbery at a video store that turns into a hostage situation. As the police try to end the standoff non-violently, the accompanying media frenzy starts to center on the youngest criminal, 17-year-old Johnny, who is made into a symbol of national turmoil. Armando Araiza, Patricia Rivera star. 95 min. In Spanish with English subtitles.
53-8630 Was $89.99 *$19.99*

Alias, La Gringa (1991)
An unusual prison drama with political overtones, this Peruvian film follows a criminal with a genius for breaking out of jail cells. After his latest escape, he returns to help the imprisoned intellectual who aided him, but a riot traps La Gringa inside. 100 min. In Spanish with English subtitles.
53-9594 *$59.99*

Rodrigo D: No Future (1990)
A raw and powerful look at youths struggling to survive in Medellin, Colombia, "the murder capital of the world." Called "a revolutionary piece of filmmaking," this unflinching story focuses on Rodrigo and his friends, trapped in a lifestyle filled with violence and drugs. 93 min. In Spanish with English subtitles.
53-7614 *$79.99*

Confessing To Laura (1990)
The 1948 assassination of Colombian political leader Jorge Elieser Gaitán and the nationwide turmoil that followed forms the basis for this compelling drama, as three people find themselves trapped in a house by the rioting and spending an emotional night together. 90 min. in Spanish with English subtitles.
53-9591 *$59.99*

The Green Wall (1970)
Poetic drama from Peru about a couple and their young son who abandon life in hectic Lima for a cabin in the jungle. When a government official contests their land claim, the father travels to the city to straighten out matters, which provokes him to reflect on his past. Armando Robles Godoy's autobiographical film stars Julio Aleman, Sandra Riva and Raul Martin. 110 min. In Spanish with English subtitles.
53-9273 Was $79.99 *$29.99*

La Boca Del Lobo (1988)
A young Peruvian soldier must decide whether to listen to his conscience or obey orders when his dictatorial commander tries an entire village for treason after siding with a revolutionary group. Francisco Lombardi's gripping drama was a hit at many film festivals. 111 min. In Spanish with English subtitles.
53-7401 *$79.99*

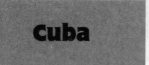

Cuba

Bitter Sugar (1996)
A caustic and unflinching look at the fervor—and failure—of Castro's Cuba, director/co-writer Leon Ichaso's drama follows the love affair between Gustavo, an idealistic young Communist, and Yolanda, a dancer who sells her body to foreign tourists and dreams of emigrating to America, in a turmoil-filled Havana. 102 min. In Spanish with English subtitles.
53-8147 Was $89.99 *$19.99*

Portrait Of Teresa (1979)
One of the masterworks of contemporary Cuban cinema, this documentary-like film focuses on a housewife's decision to get involved with politics and social change, much to the chagrin of her more traditional husband. This controversial, frank film stars Daisy Granados and Adolfo Llaurado. 115 min. In Spanish with English subtitles.
53-7385 *$79.99*

Death Of A Bureaucrat (1966)
A slapstick comedy from Cuba? Unreleased for 13 years, Tomás Gutiérrez Alea's satirical look at governmental red tape follows a young man's attempt to retrieve his late uncle's union card for his aunt. The problem is, the card was buried with uncle's body and an exhumation permit must be obtained! 87 min. In Spanish with English subtitles.
53-7549 *$69.99*

Memories Of Underdevelopment (1968)
The first film from Castro's Cuba to be released in America. An anti-revolutionary intellectual living in Havana expresses contempt for the new regime, until he is forced to confront his own past. Intriguing blend of drama and documentary footage from writer Edmundo Desnoes and director Tomás Gutiérrez Alea. 104 min. In Spanish with English subtitles.
53-7353 *$69.99*

The Last Supper (1976)
Cuban filmmaker Tomás Gutiérrez Alea ("Memories of Underdevelopment") directed this morality tale about a powerful slave owner who decides to change his ways and invites 12 of his slaves to a dinner where they are asked to re-enact the Last Supper. With Silvano Rey, Nelson Villagra. 110 min. In Spanish with English subtitles.
53-7423 *$79.99*

Up To A Certain Point (1985)
A sly and incisive mix of romantic comedy and social satire from Cuba's Tomás Gutiérrez Alea that follows a Havana writer whose research into his culture's sense of "machismo" leads him into an affair with an attractive female dockworker and a re-examination of his own views towards women. Oscar Alvarez, Mirta Ibarra star. 72 min. In Spanish with English subtitles.
53-8093 *$89.99*

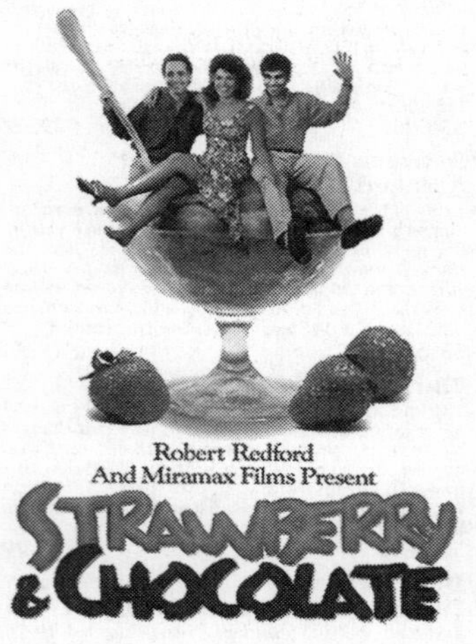

Strawberry And Chocolate (1994)
Nominated for an Academy Award for Best Foreign Film, this acclaimed effort from Cuba's Tomás Gutiérrez Alea ("Memories of Underdevelopment") studies the relationship between a straight political science student and a flamboyant, art-loving young man who happens to be gay. With Jorge Perrugorria, Vladimir Cruz. 104 min. In Spanish with English subtitles.
11-1954 Was $89.99 *$19.99*

Guantanamera! (1998)
From Cuba's Tomáas Gutiérrez Alea ("Strawberry and Chocolate") comes this effervescent social and romantic comedy in which a funeral procession for a renowned singer that includes the deceased's politically active niece and government worker son-in-law keeps crossing paths with a truck driver who used to be the niece's student. Mirta Ibarra, Carlos Cruz. 104 min. In Spanish with English subtitles.
53-6263 *$99.99*

8-A Ochoa (1992)
This stirring look at Cuba under Castro's rule details the trial and execution in 1989 of General Arnaldo Ochoa, a high-ranking officer and hero of the revolution. Ochoa is arrested with others following a party during which he advocated the resignation of Fidel Castro and his brother. After being accused of illegal drug trafficking, Ochoa faces a firing squad. Orlando Jiménez-Leal directs. 84 min. In Spanish with English subtitles.
53-8903 Was $89.99 *$29.99*

Argentina

Chronicle Of A Boy Alone (1964)
Banned by government censors for nearly 30 years, this harrowing and graphic Argentinian drama focuses on an 11-year-old boy who is abandoned by his family and taken into a brutal state-run orphanage, where physical and emotional abuse are a way of life. Diego Puente, Tino Pascali star. 86 min. In Spanish with English subtitles.
78-5080 *$59.99*

Don Segundo Sombra (1969)
The novel by Ricardo Guiraludes is the basis for this fine Argentinean drama about a young boy whose mentor, Don Segundo Sombra, is an old gaucho who teaches him moral lessons through stories and examples he sets. This unique production was filmed without a script, following the novel page by page in the sites where it took place. 110 min. In Spanish with English subtitles.
53-8227 Was $59.99 *$29.99*

Funny Dirty Little War (1983)
The return to power of dictator Juan Peron in the mid-'70s is savaged in this acclaimed Argentinean satire, as one tiny village tries to remain free despite interference from without and within. Co-scripted and directed by Hector Olivera. 80 min. In Spanish with English subtitles.
53-7158 Was $59.99 *$29.99*

A Shadow You Soon Will Be (1995)
A band of misfits travels about the Argentinean countryside on a meandering odyssey that serves as an allegory for the country's evolving society in this bittersweet adaptation of the popular Osvaldo Soriano novel. Miguel Angel Sola, Pepe Soriano star; directed by Hector Olivera ("Funny Dirty Little War"). 105 min. In Spanish with English subtitles.
53-8648 Was $89.99 *$29.99*

Camila (1984)
In 1840s Argentina, a young socialite falls in love with a Jesuit priest. The pair secretly marry and run away to start a new life together, but their identities are uncovered and they are eventually condemned to death for "sacrilege." Based on a true story, director Maria Luisa Bemberg's controversial, emotional tale of doomed love stars Susu Pecoraro, Imanol Arias. 105 min. In Spanish with English subtitles.
53-1411 Was $59.99 *$29.99*

I Don't Want To Talk About It (1993)
An offbeat love story in the style of Buñuel and Fellini, director Maria Luisa Bemberg's enchanting comedy/drama stars Marcello Mastroianni as a highly eligible bachelor who shocks an Argentinean town when he proposes to a local woman's teenage dwarf daughter. With Luisina Brando, Alejandra Podesta. 105 min. In Spanish with English subtitles.
02-2751 Was $89.99 *$19.99*

I, The Worst Of All (1995)
The final film by Argentinean director Maria Luisa Bemberg, this elegant and sensual costume drama chronicles the life of 17th-century Mexican writer and poet Sister Juana Ines de la Cruz, whose works won her the admiration of the peasantry, the ire of the Spanish Inquisition, and the patronage of an aristocrat, whose wife shared a passionate relationship with the writer. Assumpta Serna, Dominique Sanda star. 107 min. In Spanish with English subtitles.
70-5093 Was $59.99 *$29.99*

The Dark Side Of The Heart (1992)
A lyrical and erotic drama from the "magic realism" school, Argentinean director Eliseo Subiela ("Man Facing Southeast") follows an obsessed young poet's search for the perfect woman—one "who can fly." He finds his ideal in a prostitute, but she wants their relationship to remain on a "professional" level. Dario Grandinetti, Sandra Ballesteros star. 127 min. In Spanish with English subtitles.
53-8293 *$89.99*

Wild Horses (1996)
A satirical "road movie" from Argentina that blends in elements of "Dog Day Afternoon" and "Thelma and Louise." An elderly anarchist's attempt to recover money due him at a bank backfires into a robbery and lands him $500,000 and a young banker who becomes the older man's hostage, then his partner, in a cross-country run from the law that turns them into media heroes. Hector Alterio, Leonardo Sbaraglia star. 122 min. In Spanish with English subtitles.
53-9910 *$89.99*

Heat (1966)
The lusciously endowed Isabel Sarli stars for husband-director Armando Bo in this sultry, erotic drama that finds Sarli shipwrecked on a deserted island. She recalls her past experiences, which include serving as a sexual plaything for an evil man. She soon discovers that she's the prize desired by three of the island's sea lion hunters. Dubbed in English.
79-5606 Was $24.99 *$19.99*

Naked Temptation (1967)
"Fuego" star Isabel Sarli goes wild in this super-scorching sensual drama, playing a low-cut dress-wearing, bosom-swaying wayward woman who tries to tease and please a woman-hating hermit. Ms. Sarli ignites the screen in an unforgettable shower scene—and every other scene! Although this rare film ends in abrupt fashion, it's still a sultry sizzler. Dubbed in English.
79-5893 Was $24.99 *$19.99*

The Female: Seventy Times Seven (1968)
Acclaimed Argentinean director Leopoldo Torre Nilsson ("The House of the Angel") had his 1962 film starring sex bomb "Fuego" star Isabel Sarli re-edited with more erotic sequences when it arrived in America six years later. The result is a torrid, whacked-out tale with Sarli as a hooker who recalls her life and loves with two men. With Francisco Rabal. Dubbed in English.
79-6219 Was $24.99 *$19.99*

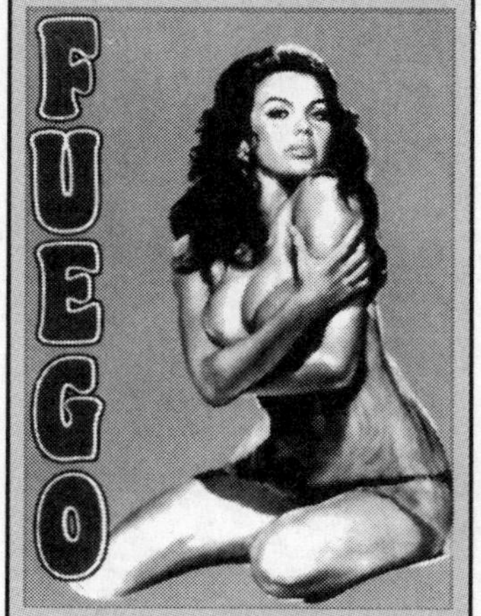

Fuego (1969)
An overheated drama from Argentina that was a drive-in fave in the '70s. Sultry Isabel Sarli stars as a village sexpot who plays with the town's men like they were toys, until one day when a love-starved man persuades her to marry him. Her games of passion, however, don't end. Dubbed in English.
79-5892 Was $24.99 *$19.99*

Extasis Tropical (1972)
Isabel Sarli, the Argentinean star of "Fuego," turns in another smoldering performance as a woman who comes to a small island and finds jealousy and lust rampant far away from society. Armando Bo also stars in this adult-flavored shocker. Spanish language version; no subtitles.
53-7432 *$39.99*

Times To Come (1988)
An Argentinean science-fiction thriller that's been favorably compared to "Blade Runner." In a futuristic city, the authoritarian government is shaken when an accidental shooting occurs at an anti-government demonstration. 98 min. In Spanish with English subtitles.
53-7399 Was $79.99 *$39.99*

Veronico Cruz (1988)
The winner of major awards at the Berlin Film Festival is a powerful study of a young Indian boy, born in a remote area of Argentina, whose life is threatened during the Falklands War. Directed by Miguel Pereira. 106 min. In Spanish with English subtitles.
53-7400 Was $79.99 *$39.99*

A Place In The World (1995)
A beautiful and evocative film from Argentina and Uruguay, Adolfo Aristarain's drama looks at a 12-year-old boy's coming of age in a small, impoverished village. Meanwhile, the boy's parents—a teacher who heads a collective of shepherds and a doctor—battle big business while trying to preserve their political beliefs. 120 min. In Spanish with English subtitles.
53-8936 *$89.99*

Autumn Sun (1996)
Set in Buenos Aires, this touching romantic drama centers on a middle-aged Jewish woman in need of a Jewish man in order to impress her old-fashioned brother. An ad in a local publication gets one response, but when the woman learns that "Saul Levin" is really "Raul Ferrero," she tutors him in the customs of her people. Norma Aleandro and Federico Luppi star. 103 min. In Spanish with English subtitles.
75-1012 *$79.99*

Life According To Muriel (1997)
After her husband abandons her and her young daughter, a woman leaves Buenos Aries and heads for Argentina's countryside. A freak accident leaves them without their possessions, but an inn-keeper offers her help and, along with the inn-keeper's own children, a makeshift family forms. Florencia Camiletti, Jorge Perugorria star. 97 min. In Spanish with English subtitles.
22-9048 *$79.99*

The Official Story (1985)
An Argentinean school teacher begins to question the "official" history of her nation that she tells her students, and in researching the bloody events of the late '70s discovers shocking facts that reach into her own family. 1986's Best Foreign Film Oscar winner, this gripping drama of human rights stars Norma Aleandro, who was an exile herself during Argentina's "dirty war." 110 min. In Spanish with English subtitles.
07-8065 *$19.99*

Brazil

Dona Flor And Her Two Husbands (1978)
Spicy and witty Brazilian sex comedy with the lovely Sonia Braga as a recent widow who remarries and finds her new husband to be kind, but unstimulating. One night the ghost of her ne'er-do-well first husband visits her, and she learns to enjoy the best of both worlds. 106 min. In Portuguese with English subtitles.
19-1094 Was $79.99 *$19.99*

Amor Bandido (1978)
Graphic sex scenes and a sordid look at life on the wild side in Rio de Janeiro highlight this controversial film from Bruno Baretto. Set in Rio's Copacabana Beach section, the film explores the tenuous relationship between a police chief investigating the murders of cab drivers and his prostitute daughter. Paulo Gracindo and Cristina star. 94 min. In Portuguese with English subtitles.
53-7442 Was $79.99 *$19.99*

The Story Of Fausta (1988)
A bawdy, sexy romp from Bruno Baretto about a feisty cleaning woman who attracts the attentions of an old widower, hoping their relationship will get her out of her marriage and the shanty town she lives in. Betty Faria stars. 90 min. In Portuguese with English subtitles.
53-9434 Was $79.99 *$19.99*

Four Days In September (1997)
The true story of the 1969 abduction of the American ambassador to Brazil by young people protesting their homeland's authoritarian regime is recounted in director Bruno Baretto's acclaimed drama. Alan Arkin stars as ambassador Charles Elbrick, who comes to form a bond of understanding with his idealistic captors. With Pedro Cardoso, Marco Ricca. 107 min. In Portuguese with English subtitles.
11-2258 Was $99.99 *$19.99*

Bossa Nova (2000)
Breezy romantic tale from Bruno Barreto ("Dona Flor and Her Two Husbands") stars real-life wife Amy Irving as a fortysomething widow who moves to Rio from the U.S. for a change of pace. While teaching English to the locals, she falls for Brazilian lawyer Antonio Fagundes, who is trying to get over his failed marriage. 95 min. In English and Portuguese with English subtitles.
02-3466 *$99.99*

Black Orpheus (1958)
The Greek myth of doomed lovers Orpheus and Eurydice is transferred to contemporary Rio de Janeiro's festive Carnival in Marcel Camus' Oscar-winning film, a lively blend of sight and sound. Breno Mello, Marpessa Dawn star. 103 min. In Portuguese with English subtitles.
22-5542 Restored *$29.99*

Black God And White Devil (1964)
This Brazilian masterwork, directed by Glauber Rocha, chronicles a peasant's change from preacher to bandit, battling the area's wealthy landowners. 102 min. In Portuguese with English subtitles.
53-9275 Was $59.99 *$39.99*

How Tasty Was My Little Frenchman (1973)
This perverse comedy featuring extensive nudity from Nelson Pereira do Santos, one of the leading filmmakers of Brazil's "Cinema Novo" of the 1960s and 1970s, focuses on a 16th-century French explorer who attempts to befriend a group of cannibalistic Indians in the Brazilian jungle who have captured him. 80 min. In French and Tupi with English subtitles.
53-8225 *$89.99*

Xica (1976)
Exotic, erotic tale from Carlos Diegues is set during Brazil's diamond boom of the 1700s, as a strong-willed slave uses her wits and her sensuality to capture the fortunes of her masters. Zeze Motta stars as the alluring, legendary "Empress of Brazil." 109 min. In Portuguese with English subtitles.
53-7824 *$89.99*

Bye, Bye Brazil (1980)
An exotic, erotic fantasy about a magician and his troupe as they travel through the country from village to village and examine the changing face of Brazil. Jose Wilker, Betty Farina star. 115 min. In Portuguese with English subtitles.
19-1095 Was $79.99 *$19.99*

Quilombo (1984)
Brazil's Carlos Diegues ("Bye Bye Brazil") directed this engaging film with fascinating music about a 17th-century jungle community founded by runaway slaves. 114 min. In Portuguese with English subtitles.
53-7597 Was $89.99 *$29.99*

Pixote (1981)
Director Hector Babenco's acclaimed look at the harrowing world of Brazil's street children as seen through the eyes of a 10-year-old Sao Paolo boy whose life is one of poverty, drugs and prostitution. Fernando Ramos da Silva, who was picked off the streets to star in the title role, was later killed by police in 1987. In Portuguese with English subtitles.
02-1110 Was $89.99 *$29.99*

Hour Of The Star (1985)
A remarkable directorial debut for Suzana Amaral, this Brazilian drama follows the bittersweet adventures of a young woman who moves from a large city to the more remote northeast country. Marcelia Cartaxo stars. 96 min. In Portuguese with English subtitles.
53-7132 *$79.99*

Happily Ever After (1986)
Sizzlingly sensual drama from Brazil concerning an ordinary housewife who is compelled to pursue a handsome lowlife through the decadent underworld he inhabits in order to possess him. 110 min. In Portuguese with English subtitles.
75-1005 *$69.99*

The Dolphin (1987)
Eroticism and mysticism are blended in this Brazilian fantasy-drama based on an Indian legend. A dolphin comes ashore on the night of the full moon, assumes human form, and seduces the women of a nearby village, but his continued presence leads to a dangerous resolution. Carlos Alberto Riccelli, Cássia Kiss star. 95 min. In Portuguese with English subtitles.
53-7652 Was $79.99 *$19.99*

Luzia (1988)
Provocative Brazilian drama about a beautiful rodeo rider (Claudia Ohana) who is caught in the middle of a dangerous conflict between ruthless ranch owners and squatters. Thales Pan Chacon, José De Abreu co-star. 112 min. In Portuguese with English subtitles.
53-7610 Was $79.99 *$19.99*

Savage Capitalism (1993)
An offbeat mix of soap-opera melodrama and political satire from Brazil, following the romance between a reporter and an influential mining executive and the nationwide turmoil that results when the business-man's wife, long thought dead, shows up alive. 86 min. In Portuguese with English subtitles.
53-9596 *$59.99*

The Man In The Box (1994)
Years before "EDtv" and "The Truman Show," Brazilian filmmaker Luiz Alberto Pereira directed and starred in this fanciful satire about a TV repairman who, after a bizarre lightning strike, finds his every movement broadcast across the country 24 hours a day. Pereira quickly becomes a national celebrity, but his family (and soccer fans eager to watch the World Cup) are less than thrilled. 100 min. In Portuguese with English subtitles.
70-3478 *$59.99*

Foreign Land (1995)
Lively noirish thriller co-directed by Walter Salles ("Central Station") is set in 1990 Brazil, when a new president tried to slow the country's economic crises by freezing personal bank accounts. A young man named Paco, leaving to visit his late mother's Spanish homeland, agrees to deliver a violin case to Portugal that, unknown him, is filled with stolen diamonds. Fernando Alves Pinto, Fernanda Torres and Tcheky Karyo star. 100 min. In Portuguese with English subtitles.
53-6968 *$89.99*

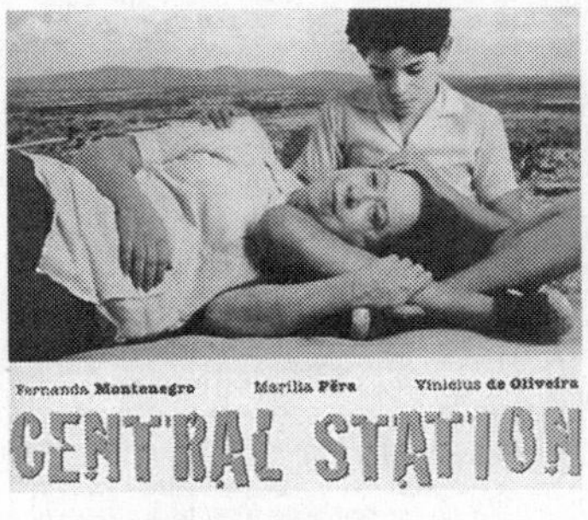

Central Station (1998)
Garnering Academy Award nominations for Best Foreign Film and Best Actress, this touching Brazilian drama follows a young boy whose mother is killed near Rio de Janeiro's Central Station. Befriended by an elderly newsstand owner, the pair set out on a difficult journey into the country's remote Northeast region to find the boy's father. Fernanda Montenegro, Vinicius de Oliveria star. 115 min. In Portuguese with English subtitles.
02-3322 Was $99.99 *$21.99*

Tieta Of Agreste (1997)
Sonia Braga ("Kiss of the Spider Woman") stars in this moving tale of honor and redemption as a country girl who returns to her native village after a 26-year absence to help defend them from a group of ruthless outsiders who are threatening to construct a highly toxic plant outside of town. From the novel by Jorge Amado. 115 min. In Portuguese with English subtitles.
53-6245 Was $89.99 *$19.99*

Portugal

The Jester (1987)
A pointed political allegory from Portugal, director Jose Alvaro Morais' drama is set shortly after the 1974 military junta that ended that country's war with rebellious colonies in Africa. A stage director resorts to selling guns to finance his staging of the popular historical play "The Jester," which tells of the formation of the Portuguese state in the 12th century. 127 min. In Portuguese with English subtitles.
87-7010 *$59.99*

The Convent (1995)
Mousy American professor John Malkovich, hoping to prove that Shakespeare was a Spanish Jew, brings wife Catherine Deneuve on a research trip to a Portuguese monastery. The monastery's sinister guardian wants Deneuve, and uses a voluminous library and a beautiful assistant to try to divert Malkovich's attention. Directed by Manoel de Oliveira. 90 min. In English, and French and Portuguese with English subtitles.
53-9728 Was $89.99 *$19.99*

Voyage To The Beginning Of The World (1997)
A French-born actor (Jean-Yves Gautier) seeking out his Portuguese roots while starring in a movie there sets out to find the aunt he's never met. Accompanied by the film's aged director (Marcello Mastroianni, in his final role), the pair set off on a wistful voyage of discovery in this heartfelt tale from writer/director Manoel de Oliveira. 95 min. In Portuguese with English subtitles.
78-9038 *$79.99*

The Jew (1996)
Set in 18th-century Portugal during the brutal reign of the Spanish Inquisition, director Jom Tob Azulay's compelling drama tells the story of popular playwright Antonio da Silva, who publicly converted to Christianity, but retained his Jewish faith and faced the wrath of the Church hierarchy. Felipe Pinheiro, Dina Sfat star. 85 min. In Portuguese with English subtitles.
70-5125 Was $79.99 *$29.99*

Spain

Belle Epoque (1994)
This Oscar-winner for Best Foreign Film is an amorous comedy set in Spain in 1931 and concerns an Army deserter who meets an eccentric old painter after fleeing his post. The soldier takes residence at the artist's house, and soon learns that he has four gorgeous single daughters, each with a hankering for their visitor. Jorge Sanz stars. 109 min. In Spanish with English subtitles.
02-2660 *$19.99*

Belle Epoque (Dubbed Version)
Also available in a dubbed-in-English edition.
02-2714 *$19.99*

Tierra (1995)
Set in the wine country of Spain, this unusual mix of romance and allegorical drama follows a mysterious insect exterminator named Angel (Carmelo Gomez). Called in to save the vineyards after a woodlice plague has altered the taste of the local wine, Angel falls in love with two disparate women. But is Angel what he appears to be, a divine messenger, or a madman? Emma Suarez, Silke co-star in Julio Medem's haunting tale. 125 min. In Spanish with English subtitles.
22-9038 Was $79.99 *$29.99*

The Red Squirrel (1995)
While wandering the beach contemplating suicide, a troubled former rock star witnesses a motorcycle crash and rescues a young woman. When it's learned she's suffering from amnesia, the musician claims they are lovers and invents an imaginary life for her. Julio Medem's quirky and compelling drama stars Emma Suarez, Nancho Novo. 104 min. In Spanish with English subtitles.
53-8647 Was $89.99 *$29.99*

Lovers Of The Arctic Circle (1998)
A brazenly romantic saga from Spain's Julio Medem looks at the relationship of Otto, a young man obsessed with aviation, and Ana, his stepsister and secret lover. The two meet in a forest and form a bond when they are young and, even after Otto's father marries Ana's mother, continue a passionate relationship over the years. Najwa Nimri, Fele Martínez star. 108 min. In Spanish with English subtitles.
02-5215 *$99.99*

Thesis (1996)
Edgy thriller from Spain's Alejandro Amenabar ("Open Your Eyes") stars Ana Torrent as a college student who, while researching her thesis on violence, discovers a "snuff movie" in which a student's murder is captured on film. Her investigation points to school officials' involvement in the film. 121 min. In Spanish with English subtitles.
22-9029 Was $79.99 *$29.99*

Open Your Eyes (Abre Los Ojos) (1997)
Spanish filmmaker Alejandro Amenábar's surreal psychological suspenser stars Eduardo Noriega as a handsome lothario who accepts a ride home from a jealous ex-flame. The trip ends in a crash that kills the woman and leaves Noriega's face hideously scarred, but his troubles are only beginning as the lines between illusion and reality, between life and death, are blurred. Penélope Cruz, Najwa Nimri also star. 117 min. In Spanish with English subtitles.
27-7127 Was $99.99 *$14.99*

Pedro Almodovar

Pepi, Luci, Bom (1980)
If you're looking for a film with lesbians, sado-masochism, drug use and a bearded lady, look no further than Pedro Almodovar's first feature. This wild affair shows the complications that occur after an heiress submits to a sexual roundelay with a seedy cop in order to have him overlook a drug charge. Carmen Maura and Eva Siva star. 80 min. In Spanish with English subtitles.
53-7711   Was $79.99   *$39.99*

Labyrinth Of Passion (1982)
Pedro Almodovar's outrageous screwball farce is set in Madrid, where all sorts of whacked-out characters partake in far-out feats. You'll meet nymphomaniac punk rockers, a laundress with healing powers, an incestuous gynecologist and a bizarre terrorist in this saucy, sexy movie. Cecilia Roth, Antonio Banderas, Imanol Arias star. 100 min. In Spanish with English subtitles.
53-7407   Was $79.99   *$39.99*

WHAT HAVE I DONE TO DESERVE THIS !

What Have I Done To Deserve This? (1984)
Poor Gloria feels trapped in her squalid existence as a housewife and cleaning woman in Madrid's slums...her husband is an insensitive boor, her children are seducing men and selling heroin, and her mother-in-law brings home a pet lizard! But must it all lead to murder by hambone? Wonderful dark comedy from director Pedro Almodovar stars Carmen Maura, Angel De Andres-Lopez. 100 min. In Spanish with English subtitles.
53-7192   Was $79.99   *$39.99*

Dark Habits (1984)
Spanish filmmaker Pedro Almodovar spins a blackly funny tale of a nightclub singer who flees when her lover dies of a drug overdose and takes refuge in a convent, only to find that the sisters' eccentricities outdo anything in the outside world. Christina Pascual, Carmen Maura, Julieta Serrano star. 116 min. In Spanish with English subtitles.
53-7214   Was $79.99   *$39.99*

Women On The Verge Of A Nervous Breakdown (1988)
The cliché about fury and women scorned is mild indeed compared to Pedro Almodovar's tale of an actress' search for the lover who dumped her via her answering machine. A variety of vengeful women, Muslim terrorists, mambo-playing taxis and spiked gazpacho all play a part in the darkly comic proceedings. Carmen Maura, Antonio Banderas star. 92 min. In Spanish with English subtitles.
73-1054   *$19.99*

Tie Me Up! Tie Me Down! (1990)
In perhaps his most outrageous and controversial film up to then, Pedro Almodovar follows the strange relationship that grows between obsessive ex-mental patient Antonio Banderas and porno actress Victoria Abril, whom he kidnaps so she can become his bride. Bizarre sexual scenes originally earned this offbeat comedy an "X" rating that the producers dismissed. 105 min. In Spanish with English subtitles.
02-2491   Letterboxed   *$14.99*

Against The Wind (1990)
Controversial drama stars Antonio Banderas as a man who decides to move to a remote area after being involved in an incestuous relationship with his sister. A year later, his sister decides to visit him, prompting emotional sparks to fly. Emma Suarez also stars in this unusual love story. 89 min. In Spanish with English subtitles.
53-8144   Was $79.99   *$19.99*

Loyola, The Soldier Saint (1952)
Moving biodrama about St. Ignatius of Loyola, 16th-century founder of the Jesuit order, and his heroic life, from his experiences as a young page in the Spanish court to his religious awakening after being wounded in battle, and subsequent studies. Rafael Duran and Maria Rosa Jiminez star. 93 min. Dubbed in English.
55-9006   Was $69.99   *$29.99*

High Heels (1991)
A sexy incestual farce from Pedro Almodovar about a young woman who finds her beautiful mother returning to her life after years of abandonment. Tensions soon flare, as the daughter's husband—a former lover of the mother—is found dead. But who killed him? Marisa Paredes, Victoria Abril and Miguel Bosé star. 113 min. In Spanish with English subtitles.
06-2001   *$89.99*

Kika (1994)
Kika is a gorgeous Madrid make-up artist who tries to live a quiet life with her photographer lover Ramon. Leave it to a maid and Ramon's stepfather (both of whom want to seduce Kika); the maid's brother, an escaped rapist; a tabloid TV hostess and other assorted oddballs to turn Kika's world upside-down in this kinky comedy from Pedro Almodovar. Verónica Forqué, Peter Coyote, Victoria Abril star. 109 min. In Spanish with English subtitles.
68-1342   Was $89.99   *$14.99*

The Flower Of My Secret (1996)
In this erotic farce by Pedro Almodovar, a successful author of steamy romances is having trouble writing, so her agent starts penning books under her name. At the same time, her son has been swiping her serious writings from the trash and selling them in order to finance his dream of becoming a flamenco dancer. Marisa Paredes and Juan Echanove star. 107 min. In Spanish with English subtitles.
02-2975   Was $99.99   *$24.99*

Live Flesh (1997)
A young man's quest to become the world's greatest lover takes an unforeseen twist when he's wrongly convicted of shooting a policeman during a fight with his girlfriend. Released from jail after six years, he's shocked to learn his old flame has married the now-paraplegic ex-cop, and sets out to avenge his imprisonment, in this sizzling and typically offbeat tale from Pedro Almodovar. Liberto Rabal, Francesca Neri star. 100 min. In Spanish with English subtitles.
73-1289   Was $99.99   *$19.99*

ALL ABOUT MY MOTHER

All About My Mother (1999)
When her teenage son is run over and killed, Madrid nurse Cecilia Roth sets out to fulfill the boy's wish to find the father he never knew. Roth's quest to locate the father—now living as a transvestite prostitute in Barcelona—brings her into the lives of a variety of fellow "lost souls" and a nun pregnant with the missing man's baby. Winner of the Best Foreign Film Academy Award, Pedro Almodovar's "screwball drama" paean to motherhood (in all forms) also stars Penélope Cruz, Antonia San Juan. 102 min. In Spanish with English subtitles.
02-3440   *$99.99*

Moonchild (1989)
A 12-year-old orphan living in Europe believes he's the chosen child god prophesied about since ancient times by a tribe in Africa. The boy sets out to find his destiny in this stunning erotic fantasy filled with intimate, magical images. With Maribel Martin; Agustin Villaronga directs. 120 min. In Spanish with English subtitles.
78-5079   *$69.99*

The Spirit Of The Beehive (1973)
Haunting drama, set in a small village shortly after the Spanish Civil War, centers around the dream world of a 10-year-old girl who sees the film "Frankenstein" and becomes obsessed with finding the monster's soul. Ana Torrent, Isabel Telleria, Juan Margallo star. 95 min. In Spanish with English subtitles.
22-5592   *$29.99*

Caresses (1997)
Unfolding like a pansexual "La Ronde," Spanish director Ventura Pons' interconnected series of 11 vignettes follows a variety of couples—gay and straight, married and unmarried—through the course of an evening in a Barcelona neighborhood. Based on a play by Sergi Belbel, the erotic, darkly funny tale stars Rosa Maria Sarda, Sergi Lopez, Laura Conejero. 96 min. In Spanish with English subtitles.
01-1572   Letterboxed   *$79.99*

The Fencing Master (1992)
The romance and intrigue are as sharp as the edge of a sword in this elegant drama set in pre-revolutionary Spain. A legendary fencing teacher is secretly hired to instruct a beautiful and mysterious noblewoman whom he begins falling in love with, but things turn deadly when another of his pupils is found dead, killed by the swordsman's signature thrust to the throat. Omero Antonutti and Assumpta Serna star. 88 min. In Spanish with English subtitles.
53-9911   *$89.99*

How To Be A Woman And Not Die In The Attempt (1997)
In this battle-of-the-sexes farce, Carmen Maura, Pedro Almodovar's favorite actress, plays a journalist attempting to juggle a chaotic life that includes marriage to her third husband, three children, her career and her love life. Antonio Resines also stars. 96 min. In Spanish with English subtitles.
83-5000   *$79.99*

Butterfly Wings (1991)
What is normally a joyous event, the birth of a child, brings long-suppressed feelings of jealousy and resentment to the surface for the members of a dysfunctional family in this emotional, award-winning drama from Spanish director Juanma Bajo Ulloa. 105 min. In Spanish with English subtitles.
53-9595   *$59.99*

Mouth To Mouth (1997)
An out-of-work Madrid actor, while waiting for a screen test that could land him a role in a Hollywood film, takes a job as an operator at a male phone-sex service. He becomes a hit thanks to his acting experience, but soon becomes ensnared in an offbeat love triangle with a plastic surgeon and his sexy wife. Funny and sexy comedy stars Javier Bardem, Aitana Sanchez-Gijon. 97 min. In Spanish with English subtitles.
11-2253   Was $99.99   *$19.99*

Mary My Dearest (Maria De Mi Corazon) (1983)
Scripted by acclaimed author Gabriel Garcia Marquez, this offbeat and darkly funny tale follows a woman who convinces an old flame, a small-time crook, to go straight and join her in a travelling magic show. While on the road, however, the woman is wrongly locked up in a sanitarium. Maria Rojo, Hector Bonilla star; Jaime Humberto Hermosillo directs. 100 min. In Spanish with English subtitles.
53-7661   Was $79.99   *$29.99*

Details Of A Duel: A Question Of Honor (1989)
Sergio Cabrera directed this absurdist farce about a teacher and butcher who battle themselves in a fight to the death in the Andes during the 1950s, cheered on by the town's clergy, militia and bureaucrats. 97 min. In Spanish with English subtitles.
70-5032   *$59.99*

Skyline (1984)
Bittersweet comedy dealing with a Spanish photographer who emigrates to New York in the hope of starting a career. Once there, he falls in love and must choose between his two worlds. 84 min. In English and Spanish with English subtitles.
53-7784   *$39.99*

Carlos Saura

Peppermint Frappe (1967)
Surrealistic tale of romance and obsession from director Carlos Saura about a respected and religious doctor whose infatuation with the wife of his best friend Pablo overwhelms him and leads him to attempt to fashion his into a double for his unattainable love. Geraldine Chaplin stars in a dual role as the wife and nurse. 92 min. In Spanish with English subtitles.
22-5993   Letterboxed   *$29.99*

CRIA!

Cria! (1976)
Director Carlos Saura's haunting drama of a woman (Geraldine Chaplin) looking back on how, as a child, she dealt with the deaths of her parents. In flashbacks, the young woman (Ana Torent) learns to cope through visions of her late mother (also played by Chaplin). AKA: "Cria Cuervos," "Raise Ravens," "The Secret of Anna." 107 min. In Spanish with English subtitles.
53-7090   Letterboxed   *$29.99*

Elisa, Vida Mia (Elisa, My Life) (1977)
Carlos Saura directed this penetrating study of an ailing man, writing his memoirs from the point of view of his estranged daughter, who is surprised when she returns home. When they share their recollections, they find a special bond. Fernando Rey and Geraldine Chaplin star. AKA: "Elisa, My Love." 125 min. In Spanish with English subtitles.
53-8018   Was $59.99   *$29.99*

Deprisa, Deprisa (1981)
Cautionary tale of crime and murder set in the slums of Madrid. Three young hoodlums team up with a spunky waitress, who is having an affair with one of them, to rob a bank. When the carefully planned crime turns deadly, they find their lives slowly falling apart. Directed by Carlos Saura; Jose Antonio Valdelomar, Jesus Arias Aranzeque star. 99 min. In Spanish with English subtitles.
22-5987   Letterboxed   *$29.99*

Ay, Carmela! (1991)
Marvelous mix of drama and satire from director Carlos Saura about a husband-and-wife entertainment team who are captured by Fascists during the Spanish Civil War and must fashion their show for a theatre-loving official in order to stay alive. Carmen Maura, Andres Pajares and Gabino Diego star. 105 min. In Spanish with English subtitles.
44-1850   Was $89.99   *$19.99*

Sevillanas (1992)
Using music and dance, director Carlos Saura captures the passion and spirit of the Spanish culture with this visual essay on the art of Flamenco. From the 17th century to modern dances and guitar interpretations of songs from Seville, the film is a joyous tribute to Flamenco, and features artists such as Lola Flores, Rocio Jurado, Manolo Sanlucar and Paco de Lucia. 55 min.
53-8504   *$39.99*

Outrage (1993)
Spanish reporter Antonio Banderas, sent to cover a travelling circus, falls in love with a beautiful trick-shooter. But a brutal assault on the woman leads to a violent revenge, and a doomed flight for freedom, in this compelling drama by Carlos Saura. With Francesca Neri, Lali Ramon. AKA: "Dispara." 108 min. In Spanish with English subtitles.
83-1075   Was $89.99   *$14.99*

Flamenco (1995)
Continuing his cinematic fascination with indigenous Spanish dance and music, director Carlos Saura brings nearly 300 performers before the camera in an abandoned, mirror-covered train station in Seville. The result is a dazzling, sensual display of sight and sound, featuring such flamenco notables as Pepe de Lucia, Merche Esmerelda and Joaquin Cortes. 100 min. In Spanish with English subtitles.
53-6337   Letterboxed   *$99.99*

TANGO

Tango (1998)
Sumptuously filmed tribute to tango dancing from Spain's Carlos Saura ("Flamenco") tells of a disabled dancer producing a film about tango who falls in love with his shady investor's gorgeous girlfriend. The premise allows Saura an opportunity to stage spectacular dance sequences. Miguel Angel Flores and Cecilia Narova star. 115 min. In Spanish with English subtitles.
02-3351   Was $99.99   *$21.99*

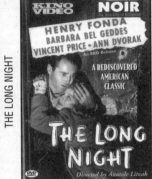
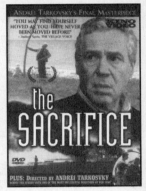

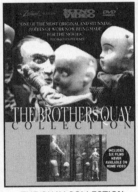

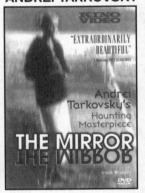
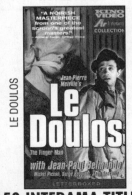

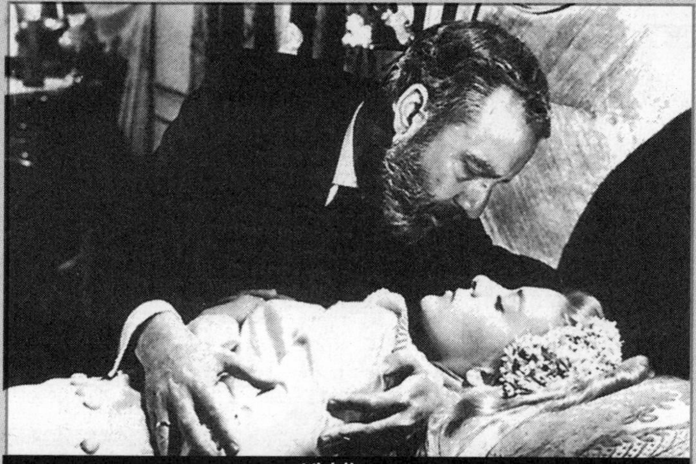

Viridiana

Luis Buñuel

Fall Of The House Of Usher (1928)
Luis Buñuel's stunning silent adaptation of Poe's tale of a dying, decadent family features a fantastic, surrealistic atmosphere through the pioneering camera work of Jean Epstein. 45 min. Title cards in French.
53-7028 *$29.99*

Un Chien Andalou (1928)/ Land Without Bread (1932)
A double feature of early Luis Buñuel films. First is the director's amazing silent collaboration with surrealist Salvador Dali that explores distortion as an artistic technique. Next, Buñuel's gripping documentary look at the harsh peasant life in Northern Spain. 51 min. Silent; and narrated in English.
53-7428 *$29.99*

L'Age D'Or (1930)
The cause of riots in the streets during its premiere in Paris, the second film collaboration of Luis Buñuel and Salvador Dali is a series of bizarre, bewildering images that mock religious hypocrisy while framing a surprisingly sentimental love story. One of the milestones in cinematic surrealism; Lya Lys, Gaston Modot, Max Ernst star. 60 min. In French with English subtitles.
53-7156 *$39.99*

Land Without Bread (1932)
Luis Buñuel's landmark documentary view of poverty and its toll on the human spirit focuses on the inhabitants of the poorest region of Northern Spain. 27 min. With English commentary.
53-7095 *$19.99*

Mexican Bus Ride (1946)
Class disparity and the endless cycle of life and death are the subjects of this rarely seen Buñuel film. A young boy travels by bus to settle his mother's will in the city, accompanied by a prostitute, a priest, a pregnant woman and some goats and chickens. 100 min. In Spanish with English subtitles.
53-7270 *$39.99*

The Great Madcap (El Gran Calavera) (1949)
A likable and sometimes slapstick satire of advertising, evangelicalism and class conflict, Luis Buñuel's comedy follows a wealthy man whose carefree spending attitudes alarm his greedy relatives. 90 min. In Spanish with English subtitles.
01-1473 Was $79.99 *$29.99*

Los Olvidados (1950)
Luis Buñuel's compelling and often surrealistic look at juvenile delinquency in the slums of Mexico, as a young boy falls in with a gang and its bullying leader. AKA: "The Young and the Damned." 81 min. In Spanish with English subtitles.
09-1751 Was $29.99 *$24.99*

El (This Strange Passion) (1952)
"Strange" indeed is the obsessive love that drives a newly married, middle-aged man to suspect his beautiful young wife of infidelity in Luis Buñuel's gripping psychological drama of jealousy and paranoia. Arturo de Cordova, Delia Graces star. 88 min. In Spanish with English subtitles.
53-6001 Was $59.99 *$24.99*

El Bruto (1952)
"The Brute" is a working-class tough hired by a Mexico City slumlord to keep the victimized tenants in line in this insightful drama by master filmmaker Luis Buñuel. Stars Pedro Armendariz, Andres Soler, Katy Jurado. 81 min. In Spanish with English subtitles.
53-7149 Was $59.99 *$29.99*

Illusion Travels By Streetcar (1953)
Lampoon of religion and government, courtesy of Luis Buñuel during his Mexican period. After restoring an antiquated streetcar, two men learn that the vehicle will be taken out of commission. They decide to take one last drive, in which they pick up an unusual array of passengers. With Lilia Prado and Carlos Navarro. 90 Min. In Spanish with English subtitles.
53-7529 *$59.99*

Diamond Hunters (1956)
Rarely seen Luis Buñuel effort mixes "Wages of Fear"-styled thrills with the director's darkly satiric outlook on religion and human nature. After fleeing a diamond field in the Amazon, a group of misfits comes to depend on each other for survival in the jungle. The discovery of a crashed airplane sends them back to their greedy, violent ways. Simone Signoret, Michel Piccoli star. AKA: "Death in the Garden." 97 min. Dubbed in English.
10-9304 *$19.99*

Nazarín (1958)
Attacking the hypocrisy in organized religion while celebrating the strength of personal faith, Luis Buñuel's allegorical drama details a rural Mexican priest's travails as he tries to follow Christ's precepts. Francisco Rabal, Marga Lopez star. 92 min. In Spanish with English subtitles.
53-7315 *$69.99*

Fever Mounts At El Pao (1959)
Luis Buñuel's political allegory follows the rise to leadership of a minor official in a Latin American republic and his corruption by the power he is given. Gerard Philipe, Jean Servais star. 97 min. Dubbed in English.
53-7531 *$39.99*

The Young One (1960)
A racist sheriff on a Carolina island rapes a 13-year-old girl and uses a black musician to take the blame in Luis Buñuel's intense, English-language drama about racial tensions. With Zachary Scott, Bernie Hamilton and Kay Meersman. 95 min.
53-7813 *$59.99*

Viridiana (1961)
Irony is written on every page of the script in Buñuel's sharply satiric drama. After would-be nun Sylvia Pinal is raped by uncle Fernando Rey, who then kills himself, she turns his estate over to a horde of derelicts, but in Buñuel's world no good deed goes unpunished. 90 min. In Spanish with English subtitles.
01-1249 Was $39.99 *$24.99*

The Exterminating Angel (1962)
One of director Luis Buñuel's greatest triumphs. A daring, surreal satire on the bourgeoisie, this film centers on a group of people at a sumptuous party who are forced to starve after they discover they can't leave. Enrique Rambla stars. 95 min. In Spanish with English subtitles.
01-1317 *$24.99*

The Criminal Life Of Archibald De La Cruz (1962)
Provocative psychological drama from Luis Buñuel concerning a boy who, witnessing the murder of his governess, is convinced he willed it...and grows up with an often perversely funny obsession with death. Ernesto Alonso stars. AKA: "Rehearsal for a Crime." 91 min. In Spanish with English subtitles.
17-3009 *$29.99*

Simon Of The Desert (1965)
Buñuel's acerbic featurette follows a devout Mexican who emulates St. Simon Stylites by standing atop a pillar in the desert for over six years in order to be closer to God. Satan arrives to tempt Simon, appearing as a nubile schoolgirl and Jesus and finally taking him dancing in a 1960s discotheque. Claudio Brook, Silvia Pinal star. 45 min. In Spanish with English subtitles.
01-1264 *$29.99*

Belle De Jour (1967)
This unseen-for-years masterwork from Luis Buñuel stars Catherine Deneuve as the bourgeois wife of a surgeon who seeks a way out of her dull life through kinky fantasies and by becoming a prostitute at a local brothel. Jean Sorel, Michel Piccoli and Genevieve Page co-star. 100 min. In French with English subtitles.
11-1955 Was $89.99 *$19.99*

Tristana (1970)
Set in 1920s Spain, Luis Buñuel's masterfully acerbic drama stars Catherine Deneuve as a beautiful young woman who rejects the smarmy romantic advances of her guardian, hypocritical nobleman Fernando Rey. After running away with artist Franco Nero, illness forces Deneuve to return to Rey's care, but she uses the situation to gain the upper hand in this tug-of-war between the sexes. 98 min. In Spanish with English subtitles.
22-5863 Letterboxed *$29.99*

"THE DISCREET CHARM OF THE BOURGEOISIE"

The Discreet Charm Of The Bourgeoisie (1972)
Luis Buñuel's classic satire is filled with savage wit and some of the director's most surrealistic images. Fernando Rey, Delphine Seyrig and Stephane Audran star in this incredibly bizarre look at an elegant dinner party with a mysteriously absent host. Academy Award-winner for Best Foreign Film. 101 min. In French with English subtitles.
03-1413 Letterboxed *$29.99*

Killing Grandpa (1991)
Charming dark comedy about an elderly engineer whose suicide attempt leaves him comatose and near death. While his children congregate at his estate awaiting their inheritance, the gorgeous young half-sister of the estate's handyman arrives and, thanks to her prowess in bed, rejuvenates the elderly man to good health. Federico Luppi stars. 114 min. In Spanish with English subtitles.
53-8924 *$89.99*

Intruso (1993)
After teaming for "Lovers," director Vincente Arande and star Victoria Abril reunite for this erotic, eerie effort. After being married for 10 years, a couple welcomes a childhood friend into their home as a guest. But rather than re-creating their happy friendship from years ago, the reunion becomes a strange and troubled experience. 90 min. In Spanish with English subtitles.
53-8937 *$89.99*

Baton Rouge (1988)
Sensual and stylish thriller from Spain stars Carmen Maura as a wealthy but troubled woman who is framed for her husband's murder by psychiatrist Victoria Abril and fortune-seeking gigolo Antonio Banderas. But the scheme begins to unravel into a series of deadly double-crosses. 90 min. In Spanish with English subtitles.
53-8616 Was $89.99 *$29.99*

In A Glass Cage (Tras El Cristal) (1986)
A former Nazi death camp doctor, living in hiding with his family in Spain, is injured and placed in an iron lung. Soon a young male nurse joins the household, seduces the doctor and his daughter, and confesses a shocking secret. Bizarre and darkly fascinating Spanish drama stars David Sust, Gunter Meisner; written and directed by Agustin Villaronga. 110 min. In Spanish with English subtitles.
53-7191 *$79.99*

Letters From Alou (1990)
A compassionate human drama focusing on the adventures of Alou, an African immigrant who faces prejudice and exploitation while working his way to Barcelona to meet a friend. Despite the hurdles he faces, Alou remains optimistic about life in the new land. Mulie Jarju stars; directed by Montxo Armendariz. 100 min. In Spanish, French and Senegalese with English subtitles.
53-7969 Was $79.99 *$29.99*

The Grandfather (1999)
This Oscar-nominated effort is set in turn-of-the-century Spain, where an elderly man named Rodrigo returns from America to his hometown in hopes of discovering which of his affectionate granddaughters is his true heir. At the same time, Rodrigo's widowed daughter-in-law goes to great lengths to stop his search. With Fernando Fernán-Goméz, Cristina Cruz. 146 min. In Spanish with English subtitles.
11-2453 ❑*$99.99*

The Miracle Of Marcelino (1955)
An orphaned boy in Spain is left in the care of a group of Franciscan monks, who all become his "father," and makes an imaginary friend out of a statue of Christ in this warm and winning drama for the whole family. Pablito Calvo, Fernando Rey star. 98 min. In Spanish with English subtitles.
53-8221 Was $59.99 *$29.99*

The Miracle Of Marcelino (Dubbed Version)
Also available in a dubbed-in-English edition. 90 min.
08-1444 Was $19.99 *$14.99*

Jamon Jamon (1993)
Hilarious, highly erotic sex farce set in a small Spanish town where the pregnant daughter of a local prostitute plans to wed her lover. Unhappy with her future daughter-in-law's pedigree, the groom's rich mother hires the town's hunkiest guy to seduce the would-be bride and halt the marriage plans. Anna Galiena, Penélope Cruz and Stefania Sandrelli star. 95 min. In Spanish with English subtitles.
71-5305 Was $19.99 *$14.99*

Italy

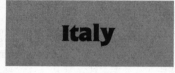

What A Woman! (1958)
Sophia Loren is a sultry sex kitten whose provocative photograph catches the interest of a wealthy entrepreneur who plans to turn her into a star. She becomes a sensation, but the poor photographer who snapped the attention-getting shot also has an interest in Sophia. Marcello Mastroianni and Charles Boyer also star. AKA: "Lucky to Be a Woman." 95 min. Dubbed in English.
53-6065 Was $29.99 *$19.99*

Death Of A Friend (1959)
Directed by Franco Rossi and co-scripted by Pier Paolo Pasolini, this subtle, compassionate film focuses on the seedy exploits of a young pimp who persuades his childhood friend to join him in his easy-going criminal lifestyle. Gianni Garko and Spiros Focas star. 87 min. In Italian with English subtitles.
53-6260 Letterboxed *$29.99*

The Great War (La Grande Guerra) (1959)
A pardoned criminal (Vittorio Gassman) becomes a reluctant inductee in the Italian army in World War I and joins another soldier in dodging the battlefront in this wry wartime comedy/drama. Co-stars Alberto Sordi, Silvana Mangano. 117 min. In Italian English subtitles.
53-7331 Was $59.99 *$39.99*

1860 (1933)
A forerunner to Italy's post-war neo-realist movement, director Alessandro Blasetti's sumptuously filmed epic depicts the events surrounding Garibaldi's defeat of the king of Naples by his troops, as witnessed by two peasants in 1860. Considered a masterpiece, the film excels at portraying its many characters with unusual depth. 72 min. In Italian with English subtitles.
01-1466 *$29.99*

The Iron Crown (1941)
A staggering epic by noted director Alessandro Blasetti that mixes history and fantasy in its ancient setting. A young hero, raised by lions, uses a magical crown to rescue an imprisoned princess. 100 min. In Italian with English subtitles.
53-7394 Was $59.99 *$39.99*

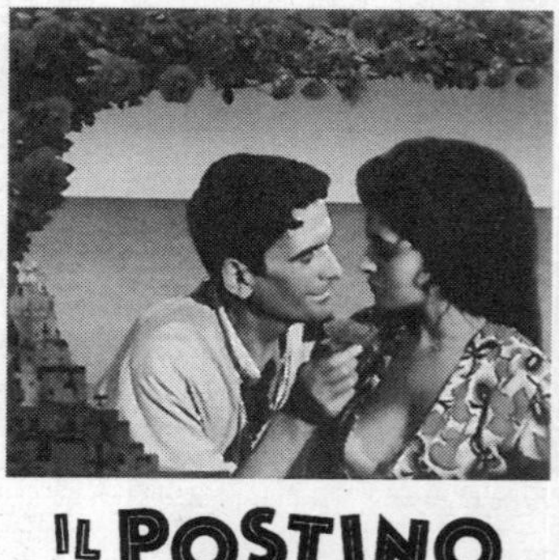

IL POSTINO THE POSTMAN

Il Postino (The Postman) (1995)
Lovely romance set in a small Italian town during the 1950s where exiled Chilean poet Pablo Nerudo has taken refuge. A shy mailman befriends the poet and uses his words—and, ultimately, the writer himself—to help him woo a woman with whom he has fallen in love. With Philippe Noiret and Massimo Troisi (who died a day after filming ended). 108 min. In Italian with English subtitles.
11-1946 Was $99.99 *$19.99*

The Station (1992)
A wistful romantic comedy from Sergio Rubini, set during one rainy night in a remote Italian train station, whose only occupants, a shy station master (Rubini) and a young woman who just left her heartless fiancé, begin to fall in love. Margherita Buy co-stars. 92 min. In Italian with English subtitles.
53-7741 Was $89.99 *$19.99*

Alberto Express (1992)
At the age of 40, Alberto has a big problem: his parents want their children to pay back the money spent on raising them before starting a family on their own, and now Alberto is about to have his first child and he's broke. This whimsical comedy stars Sergio Castellitto, Nino Manfredi and Jeanne Moreau. 90 min. In French and Italian with English subtitles.
53-7779 Was $89.99 *$19.99*

The Flavor Of Corn (1992)
A handsome professor falls under the spell of an adolescent boy after arriving on an isolated Italian island. They share a rare intimacy and friendship, much to the dismay of the professor's manipulative girlfriend. This sensitive handling of a controversial theme features nudity and sexual imagery. With Lorenzo Lena. 93 min. In Italian with English subtitles.
78-5059 *$69.99*

Acla (1992)
Acclaimed, controversial account of a 12-year-old boy who is sold to work in underground sulfur mines by his destitute parents. After encountering child abuse and beatings, the boy decides to escape, unaware of the horrifying repercussions he and his parents may face. Features nudity, strong language and mature sexual situations. Stars Luigi Maria Burruano. 86 min. In Italian with English subtitles.
78-5070 *$69.99*

Flight Of The Innocent (1993)
After witnessing his criminal family being slaughtered by merciless rival gangsters, a 10-year-old boy flees for his life, first to his cousin's home in Rome, then to the wealthy family of a boy kidnapped by his parents. Highly acclaimed directing debut of Carlo Carlei mixes raw violence and poignancy. With Manuel Colao. 105 min. In Italian with English subtitles.
12-2939 Was $89.99 *$19.99*

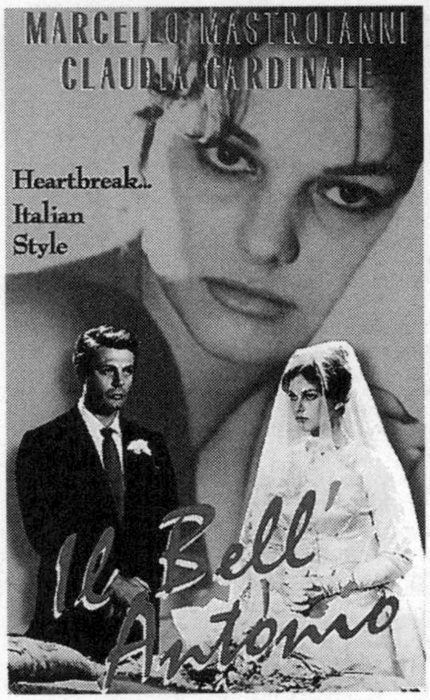

Il Bell'Antonio (1960)
A delightfully bawdy and droll Italian comedy starring Marcello Mastroianni as Antonio, a legendary local lothario who is persuaded by his family to return to his Sicilian hometown to wed village beauty Claudia Cardinale. A scandal erupts after the wedding night reveals Antonio to be impotent and the marriage is annulled! Mauro Bolognini; co-scripted by Pier Paolo Pasolini. 115 min. In Italian with English subtitles.
53-7939 Was $59.99 *$24.99*

Lina Wertmuller

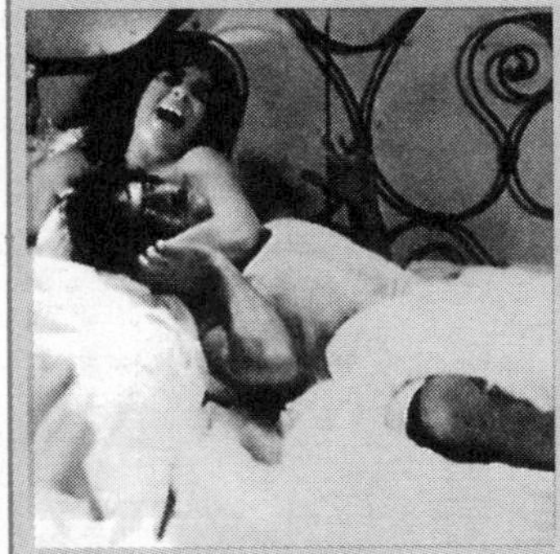

The Seduction Of Mimi

The Seduction Of Mimi (1972)
Sicilian laborer Giancarlo Giannini is the hapless man in the middle of struggles both political (between the Mafia and the Communists) and romantic (between his wife and a leftist mistress) in director Lina Wertmuller's acclaimed mix of social satire and bedroom farce. With Mariangela Melato, Turri Ferro. 89 min. In Italian with English subtitles.
53-8890 *$29.99*

Love And Anarchy (1973)
A simple farmer falls in with antifascist rebels in 1930s Italy and is sent to the city to assassinate Mussolini. Seeking refuge in a bordello whose madame lost her lover to the brown shirts, the would-be assassin begins to have doubts about his mission and falls in love with one of the prostitutes. Giancarlo Giannini, Mariangela Melato and Lina Polito star in director Lina Wertmuller's insightful political drama. 129 min. In Italian with English subtitles.
53-8887 *$29.99*

Swept Away (1975)
Directed by Lina Wertmuller, this farce on class struggle chronicles the tumultuous love affair between a communist and a capitalist marooned on an island. Giancarlo Giannini, Mariangela Melato star. 116 min. In Italian with English subtitles.
76-1033 Letterboxed *$29.99*

Seven Beauties (1976)
Giancarlo Giannini stars in Lina Wertmuller's dark seriocomedy as a small-time hood in WWII Italy trying to support his sisters. His desperate attempts to stay alive take him from jail to a mental hospital, and eventually put him in the hands of an obese concentration camp commandant (Shirley Stoler). 115 min. In Italian with English subtitles.
76-1037 *$29.99*

Seven Beauties (Dubbed Version)
Also available in a dubbed-in-English edition.
02-1016 *$29.99*

A Night Full Of Rain (1978)
Lina Wertmuller's first English-language production features Candice Bergen as a feminist photographer whose marriage to chauvinistic, Communist writer Giancarlo Giannini provokes an all-out battle of the sexes. With Jill Eikenberry, Anne Byrne and Michael Tucker. 104 min.
19-1846 Was $59.99 *$19.99*

Sotto...Sotto (1985)
Hearty laugh at both sex and sexism in Lina Wertmuller's inimitable manner. A blustering husband starts tailing suspects when he finds out his wife's attentions are straying...and blows his stack when he finds out the "other man" is a woman. Funny and farcical. 104 min. In Italian with English subtitles.
02-1628 Was $69.99 *$19.99*

Ciao, Professore! (1994)
A tender and often hilarious comedy from Lina Wertmuller centering on a teacher who is mistakenly assigned to a third-grade class in an impoverished town in Southern Italy. The teacher soon faces the Mafia, truancy and pupils with family problems while trying to steer his students in the right direction. Paolo Villaggio stars. 91 min. In Italian with English subtitles.
11-1849 Was $99.99 *$19.99*

The Worker And The Hairdresser (1996)
Politics makes strange—but happy—bedfellows in Lina Wertmuller's sexy political satire. With the 1994 Italian general elections drawing to a conclusion, labor organizer and die-hard Communist Tullio Solenghi tries to forget his party's losses by seducing pro-business right-winger Veronica Pivetti, but she manages to turn the tables on him. 104 min. In Italian with English subtitles.
53-6398 Letterboxed *$24.99*

The Lina Wertmuller Collection
Four of the acclaimed director's finest films—all in their subtitled versions—have been gathered in a money-saving collector's set: "Love and Anarchy," "The Seduction of Mimi," "Seven Beauties" and "Swept Away."
53-6366 Save $20.00! *$99.99*

Cinema Paradiso (1989)
A charming, bittersweet tribute to the power of movies which won 1989's Best Foreign Film Academy Award. A film director looks back on his childhood in Sicily, where he served as an apprentice to the projectionist at his small town's only movie theater. Giuseppe Tornatore directs; Philippe Noiret and Jacques Perrin star. 123 min. In Italian with English subtitles.
44-1731 Was $89.99 *$19.99*

Cinema Paradiso (Dubbed Version)
Also available in a dubbed-in-English edition.
44-1982 *$19.99*

Everybody's Fine (Stanno Tutti Bene) (1991)
From Giuseppe Tornatore, the director of "Cinema Paradiso," comes this poignant comedy-drama starring Marcello Mastroianni as an elderly man who travels across Italy to visit his five grown children. His bittersweet adventures include stops in Rome, Naples Florence and Milan. Michelle Morgan, Valeria Cavalli co-star. 120 min. In Italian with English subtitles.
02-2207 *$19.99*

Rorret (1987)
A creepy Italian homage to the suspense cinema, set in a movie house whose disturbed owner shows only horror films and likes to spy on the frightened female patrons from behind the screen. Eventually, he begins living out his stalking fantasies. Re-created scenes from thrillers like "Psycho" and "Peeping Tom" are a highlight. Lou Castel, Anna Galiena star. 105 min. In Italian with English subtitles.
53-7701 Was $79.99 *$29.99*

Le Bal (1983)
Delightful French-Italian drama by Ettore Scola that traces the history of a French dance hall and the people who go there. Using no dialogue, a rich evocative score and a recurring cast, we watch these people as they meet, fall in and out of love and learn about life. Music by Chopin, Irving Berlin and The Beatles. 112 min.
19-1320 *$79.99*

The Story Of Boys And Girls (1991)
A group of friends and family members congregate to celebrate an engagement and partake in a sumptuous feast of food and wine. Eventually, they begin revealing secrets about their lives, lusts and jealousies, and even the maid becomes involved in a romantic tryst. Directed by Pupi Avati. 92 min. In Italian with English subtitles.
53-7676 Was $89.99 *$19.99*

The Conviction (1994)
From controversial director Marco Bellocchio ("Devil in the Flesh") comes this study of a man and woman locked in a museum overnight who engage in a love-making session. When the man reveals that he had the museum keys all along, the woman charges him with rape, leading to an emotional trial. With Claire Nebout, Vittorio Mezzogiorno. 92 min. In Italian with English subtitles.
53-8104 Was $89.99 *$19.99*

Lamerica (1994)
Amid the poverty and turmoil of post-Communist Albania, two con artists from Italy arrive with a scheme to get government money by setting up a fraudulent manufacturing plant. But when the native figurehead of their "company" vanishes, one of the men sets off to find him and winds up losing his money, clothing and very identity. Gianni Amelio's acclaimed comedy/drama stars Enrico Lo Verso, Michele Placido. 116 min. In Italian with English subtitles.
53-9883 Was $89.99 *$29.99*

Forever Mary (1990)
Gritty, heartfelt drama set in an Italian reformatory where the teenage boys face brutal gang attacks and sexual assaults. In this tense atmosphere a 16-year-old transvestite prostitute falls for a mild-mannered teacher trying to improve the inmates' lives. Filled with physical and psycho-sexual violence, as well as unexpected tender moments. Micele Placido, Alessandro Di Sanzo star. 100 min. In Italian with English subtitles.
53-7654 *$79.99*

Iris Blond (1996)
Witty tale of a talented musician named Romeo who seeks help from a tarot card reader after his latest girlfriend dumps him. She sees a new love in his future, but that love does not come with the singer Romeo meets on a cruise ship, but rather with a waitress with whom he starts a musical lounge act. This quirky romantic comedy with an edge stars Carlo Verdone, Claudia Gerini. AKA: "I'm Crazy About Iris Blond." 113 min. In French and Italian with English subtitles.
11-2415 *$99.99*

Big Deal On Madonna Street (1957)
A band of inept burglars and ne'er-do-wells attempts to break into a pawnshop and loot its safe, only to see their elaborate plan disintegrate in front of them. Hilarious Italian comedy, remade as "Crackers," stars Vittorio Gassman, Marcello Mastroianni, Claudia Cardinale and Toto. 91 min. In Italian with English subtitles.
22-5831 *$29.99*

Le Soldatesse (1966)
Set during the occupation of Italy in World War II, this drama tells of a group of Athenian prostitutes brought to brothels in the Northern part of the country for the pleasure of Italian soldiers. The focus is on the women and three military escorts who help them get to their destination. Anna Karina stars. AKA: "The Camp Followers." 97 min. In Italian with English subtitles.
10-9449 *$19.99*

Taviani Brothers

Saint Michael Had A Rooster (1971)
Freed after spending 10 years in jail for political crimes, a dedicated revolutionary in 19th-century Italy is told by a younger group of anarchists that the ideals that kept him going through his imprisonment have no place in their movement. Based on a story by Leo Tolstoy, this allegorical early drama from Paolo and Vittorio Taviani stars Giulio Brogi. 87 min. In Italian with English subtitles.
53-9937 Was $79.99 *$19.99*

Allonsanfan (1974)
When the reign of Napoleon is over, Europe restores the old order. Few revolutionaries remain, and one just released from prison must choose between the privileges of his aristocratic background and the political ideas of his followers. Marcello Mastroianni and Laura Betti star in this historical drama from the Taviani Brothers. 115 min. In Italianwith English subtitles.
53-7114 *$29.99*

Padre Padrone (1977)
Powerful study of a poor Sardinian boy who grows to manhood while learning to confront his dictatorial father. Paolo and Vittorio Taviani's drama stars Omero Antonutti, Saverio Marconi. 117 min. In Italian with English subtitles.
76-1038 Was $29.99 *$19.99*

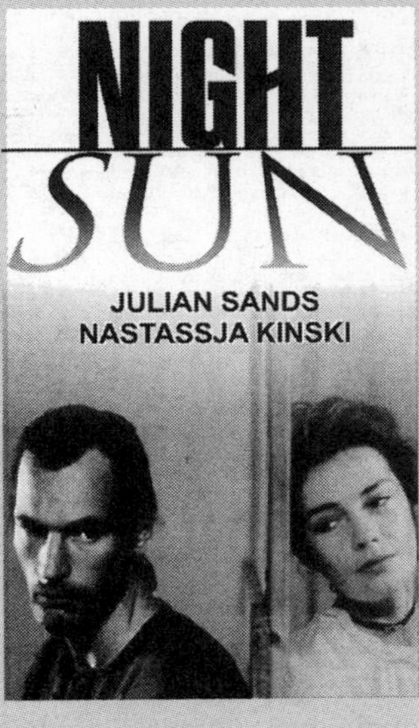

Night Sun (1990)
Based on Tolstoy's "Father Sergius," this lush drama by Paolo and Vittorio Taviani stars Julian Sands as an 18th-century Italian nobleman who, upon learning his fiancée was a courtesan to the king, leaves his aristocratic lifestyle behind and becomes a monk. Nastassja Kinski, Charlotte Gainsbourg also star; Sands' voice was dubbed by Giancarlo Giannini. AKA: "Il Sole Anche di Notte." 112 min. In Italian with English subtitles.
53-6591 *$19.99*

Wild Flower (Fiorile) (1994)
An epic story of intrigue and romance from the Taviani brothers ("Padre Padrone") focusing on the Benedettis, a family in Tuscany cursed when an ancestor stole coins which belonged to one of Napoleon's regiments. Against the backdrop of sweeping social and political changes, the effects this act has on the family is portrayed. 118 min. In Italian with English subtitles.
02-2629 Was $89.99 *$19.99*

Elective Affinities (La Affinita Elettive) (1996)
Based on a novel by Goethe, this pastoral drama from the Taviani Brothers examines stars Isabelle Huppert and Jean-Hughes Anglade as a married couple whose quiet life in a Tuscan villa is thrown into emotional disarray by the arrival of two guests: Anglade's handsome architect friend and Huppert's beautiful goddaughter. 98 min. In Italian with English subtitles.
53-6330 Was $89.99 *$19.99*

The Taviani Collection
The filmmaking siblings are saluted with a special set that includes "Elective Affinities," "Night Sun," "Padre Padrone" and "St. Michael Had a Rooster."
53-6605 *$69.99*

Roberto Rossellini

Return Of The Pilot (Una Pilota Ritorna) (1942)
Produced under the "guiding hand" of the Fascist government, the second feature directed by Roberto Rossellini follows a downed Italian pilot's imprisonment in an English POW camp. This rare find is presented here in an Italian-language version without subtitles. 87 min.
53-8605 *$59.99*

Man With A Cross (1943)
War-ravaged Italy during the summer of 1942 serves as the backdrop for this rare, neo-realistic drama from Roberto Rossellini which depicts the virtuous efforts of a chaplain providing aid to soldiers and peasants under bombardment from Russian artillery fire. AKA: "L'uomo Della Croce." 76 min. In Italian with English subtitles.
53-7335 Was $59.99 *$39.99*

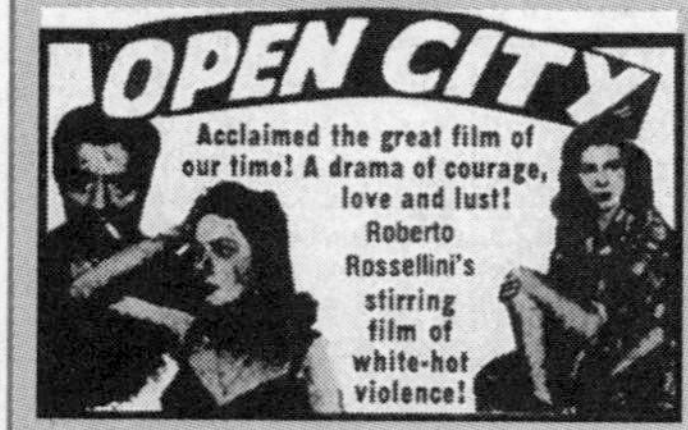

Open City (1945)
Director Roberto Rossellini's moving drama follows a leader of the WWII Italian underground and his fight against the Nazi occupation of Rome. Much of the film shows actual scenes of people and their struggles in war-torn Italy. A brave achievement! 105 min. In Italian with English subtitles.
09-1757 Was $29.99 *$24.99*

Germany In Year Zero (1947)
Roberto Rossellini's neo-realistic look at life amid the shambles that the once-proud city of Berlin had become. A stirring drama and a valuable document on the effects of war. With Franz Gruger and Edmund Meschke. 78 min. In German with English subtitles.
53-7124 *$29.99*

Paisan (1948)
Roberto Rossellini's film is composed of six stories following the Allied advance from Sicily to the Po Valley to liberate Italy during World War II. 115 min. In Italian with English subtitles.
09-1768 Was $29.99 *$24.99*

Machine To Kill Bad People (1948)
Rarely seen Robert Rossellini effort set in a small Italian village after World War II where a photographer is given a special camera that has the ability to petrify, then kill, those who are shot with it. The man plans to use the camera to rid the world of bad people, but eventually learns it's hard to distinguish between good and evil. With Gennaro Pisano. 80 min. In Italian with English subtitles.
10-9451 *$19.99*

The Miracle (1948)
Perhaps the most controversial film of its time, Roberto Rossellini's drama stars Anna Magnani as a pregnant peasant girl who is convinced her condition is the result of an immaculate conception and faces the scorn of her village for her claim. Denounced by the Catholic Church in America and the subject of court censorship battles. 40 min. In Italian with English subtitles.
53-7508 *$29.99*

Amore (1948)
An homage to the great Anna Magnani, Roberto Rossellini's two-part film features the Italian actress in Cocteau's one-act play "The Human Voice," in which she speaks to an unseen lover on the phone, and the controversial "The Miracle," which casts her as a peasant who believes she has given birth to the new Messiah. AKA: "Woman," "Ways of Love." 78 min. In Italian with English subtitles.
53-7623 Was $59.99 *$24.99*

Stromboli (1949)
The affair between director Roberto Rossellini and married star Ingrid Bergman became one of film-dom's biggest scandals, overshadowing this powerful drama. Bergman is a Czech war refugee trapped in a loveless marriage in a small Italian fishing village. This is the rare, filmed-in-English version of the film, restored to its original length. 107 min.
53-7378 *$59.99*

Stromboli (Subtitled Version)
Also available in an Italian-language edition with English subtitles.
53-7625 Was $29.99 *$19.99*

Europa '51 (1952)
American socialite Ingrid Bergman, looking for meaning in her life following her son's suicide, devotes herself to helping the poor and needy in Rome, but her husband has her judged insane and placed in an asylum. Compelling drama from Roberto Rossellini also stars Alexander Knox, Giulietta Masina. AKA: "The Greatest Love." 110 min. Filmed in English.
53-8338 *$39.99*

Voyage In Italy (1953)
Compelling Roberto Rossellini drama stars Ingrid Bergman and George Sanders as a married couple who travel to Italy to visit a house they've inherited. While there, their already strained relationship is put to the test. With Maria Mauban, Paul Muller. AKA: "Strangers." Filmed in English. 83 min.
53-7336 Was $29.99 *$19.99*

Fear (1954)
In their final film collaboration, director Roberto Rossellini and star Ingrid Bergman create a compelling drama of an unhappily married woman who enters into an affair, only to be blackmailed by her lover's ex-girlfriend. AKA: "Angst." 91 min. Original, English-language version.
08-5019 *$39.99*

General Della Rovere (1960)
A masterpiece from Roberto Rossellini, this is a prime example of the Italian neo-realist style of filmmaking. Vittorio DeSica plays a petty con who poses as a general. However, his masquerade backfires, as the plan goes to his head. 139 min. In Italian with English subtitles.
01-1340 *$29.99*

Vanina Vanini (1961)
Roberto Rossellini blends neo-realism with costume melodrama in this tale set in 19th-century Italy, as a revolutionary is sent to kill a traitor. AKA: "The Betrayer." 125 min. In Italian with English subtitles.
53-7359 *$39.99*

Era Notte A Roma (1961)
Roberto Rossellini returns to the stunning neo-realist form of his earlier classics with this powerful drama. Allied POWs attempt to hide in occupied Rome during WWII. With Giovanna Ralli and Leo Genn. 140 min. In Italian with English subtitles.
53-7368 *$59.99*

The Rise Of Louis XIV (1966)
Acclaimed as one of the most historically accurate films ever made, Roberto Rossellini's interpretation of the early years of the Sun King focuses on the young monarch's domination of fashion, which eventually led to his control of France's entire power structure. With Jean-Marie Patte and Raymond Jourdan. AKA: "The Taking of Power by Louis XIV." 102 min. In French with English subtitles.
53-7126 Was $59.99 *$24.99*

Socrates (1970)
Produced for Italian television, this biographical drama from Roberto Rossellini focuses on the struggles faced by the Greek philosopher after a former student-turned-tyrannical ruler is overthrown. Put on trial by the city-state of Athens, Socrates must defend himself against charges of subversion. Jean Sylvere, Anne Caprile star. 120 min. In Italian with English subtitles.
53-7393 *$29.99*

Blaise Pascal (1971)
Stunning cinematic portrait from director Roberto Rossellini of the 17th-century French theologian, with Pierre Arditi in the lead. 131 min. In Italian with English subtitles.
53-7168 *$59.99*

The Age Of The Medici (1972)
Roberto Rossellini directed this epic tribute to Florentine art, featuring a gallery of priceless masterpieces, that traces its history through the lives of the famed Renaissance merchant family. 255 min. Filmed in English.
53-7373 *$129.99*

The Messiah (1975)
Rarely-seen final effort from neo-realist great Roberto Rossellini begins with an overview of Old Testament Israeli history, then looks at the life of Jesus through such simple activities as work, travel and everyday conversation. An American investor threatened to re-edit the film, but a protracted legal battle allowed this uncut, original director's cut to be preserved. With Pier Maria Rossi, Mita Ungaro. 145 min. In Italian with English subtitles.
22-9030 *$59.99*

Rossellini On Rossellini
One of the leading lights of Italy's "neorealist" film movement of the '40s and '50s, director Roberto Rossellini talks openly about his films and his controversial personal life in this compelling documentary. 60 min. In Italian with English subtitles.
22-1630 *$19.99*

Please see our index for these other Roberto Rossellini titles: *RoGoPaG • Seven Deadly Sins*

Allegro Non Troppo (1977)
Director Bruno Bozzetto's pastiche of "Fantasia" is a witty, wonderful voyage for the imagination, as fabulous animated sequences set to classical works by Debussy, Ravel, Stravinsky and Vivaldi are mixed with comical live-action segments featuring Maurizio Nichetti ("The Icicle Thief"). 85 min. In Italian with English subtitles.
22-5809 *$29.99*

West & Soda (1990)
The "spaghetti" westerns of Sergio Leone meet Three Stooges-esque comedic anarchy in this madcap animated ride from Italy's Bruno Bozzetto ("Allegro Non Troppo"). A delightful, colorful spoof. 90 min.
76-7106 *$29.99*

The Best Of Bruno Bozzetto (1997)
The award-winning Italian master of animated film introduces each of the four segments that make up this collection of his witty and offbeat cartoon shorts. Included are "Self-Service," "Life in a Tin," "Sigmund," "Mr. Rossi Wins an Award," "Big Bang," "Man and His World," "Grasshoppers" and many more. 81 min. In Italian with English subtitles.
22-5970 Was $29.99 *$19.99*

Acqua E Sapone (1983)
Sparkling Italian comedy about a teenage fashion model on a three-day assignment in Rome. Unknown to her or her over-protective mother, the "priest" hired to chaperone her is an impostor! Ribald farce stars Natasha Hovey, Carlo Verdone. 100 min. In Italian with English subtitles.
02-1608 Was $59.99 *$19.99*

The Icicle Thief (1989)
Italy's answer to Woody Allen, actor-director Maurizio Nichetti, fashions a hilarious, inventive farce. After a power failure jolts the airwaves, reality and fantasy blur, and a model from a TV commercial finds herself in a '40s-style movie, forcing the film's director (Nichetti) to enter the film and set things right. Acclaimed mix of slapstick and satire co-stars Catterina Sylos Labini and Heidi Komarek. 84 min. In Italian with English subtitles.
53-7594 Was $89.99 *$19.99*

Volere Volare (1993)
A surreal and sexy mix of animation and live action from Maurizio Nichetti, the creator of "The Icicle Thief." A cartoon-obsessed technician whose specialty is dubbing sound effects into classic cartoons falls in love with a prostitute. But how can the lonely soundman find true love when he's turning into an animated character himself? 92 min. In Italian with English subtitles.
02-5032 Was $89.99 *$19.99*

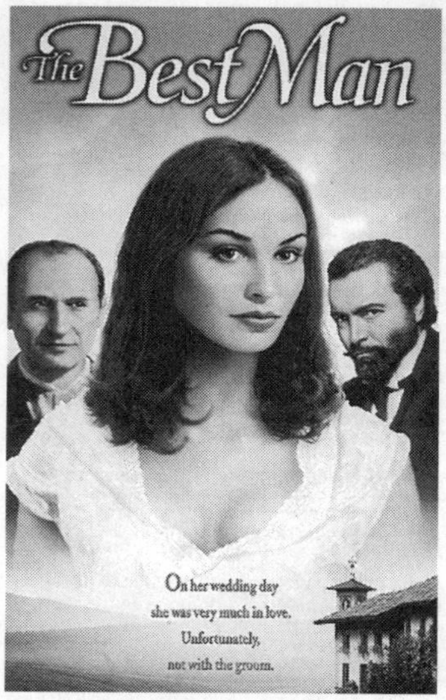

The Best Man (1997)
Set on the final day of the 19th century, this romantic work from Italy's Pupi Avati ("The Story of Boys and Girls") centers on the arranged marriage of beautiful, young Francesca to older, lecherous Edgardo. Complications ensue when Francesca falls for Angelo, Edgardo's best man. With Inès Sastre, Dario Cantarelli and Diego Abatantuono. 101 min. In Italian with English subtitles.
07-2728 Was $89.99 *$14.99*

Where Is Picone? (1984)
When a man disappears in an ambulance on the way to the hospital, his wife teams up with a small-time crook to unravel the mystery. What they discover is shocking, considering that the man was so upright and respectable...or was he? Colorful, humorous suspenser stars Giancarlo Giannini and Lina Sastri. 110 min. In Italian with English subtitles.
53-7117 *$29.99*

Michelangelo Antonioni

Il Grido (1957)
Michelangelo Antonioni's warm-up for his classic "L'Avventura" details the saga of an American working in a Po Valley sugar refinery who attempts to win the hand of a recent widow. Steve Cochran, Alida Valli and Betsy Blair star. AKA: "The Outcry." 115 min. In Italian with English subtitles.
53-7366 Was $59.99 *$24.99*

L'Avventura (1960)
A scathing examination of Italy's aristocratic classes set within the framework of a mystery story, director Michelangelo Antonioni's groundbreaking film chronicles the disappearance of a wealthy woman. While searching for her, the woman's lover and best friend become romantically involved. Monica Vitti, Gabrielle Ferzetti star. 145 min. In Italian with English subtitles.
22-5703 *$29.99*

La Notte (1961)
As dark and moody as its title, this Antonioni drama chronicles one evening in the life of a couple (Marcello Mastroianni, Jeanne Moreau) who have tired of life together. Moreau leaves her husband at a party and wanders the streets, while Mastroianni tries to woo Monica Vitti, until fate brings the pair back together. AKA: "The Night." 125 min. In Italian with English subtitles.
53-7473 *$39.99*

The Eclipse (1962)
Completing the trilogy that began with "L'Avventura" and "La Notte," Michelangelo Antonioni follows heroine Vittoria (Monica Vitti) as she trades her older lover for a brash Rome stockbroker. A drama of occluded values in modern society co-starring Alain Delon ("Swann in Love"). 123 min. In Italian with English subtitles.
53-7286 *$19.99*

Red Desert (1964)
Antonioni's landmark work on the isolating effects of modern culture focuses on a depressed housewife (Monica Vitti) and her desperate search for meaning in her life. In addition to stunning color cinematography, the film features a haunting electronic score. With Richard Harris and Carlo Chionetti. 116 min. In Italian with English subtitles.
53-7127 Letterboxed *$19.99*

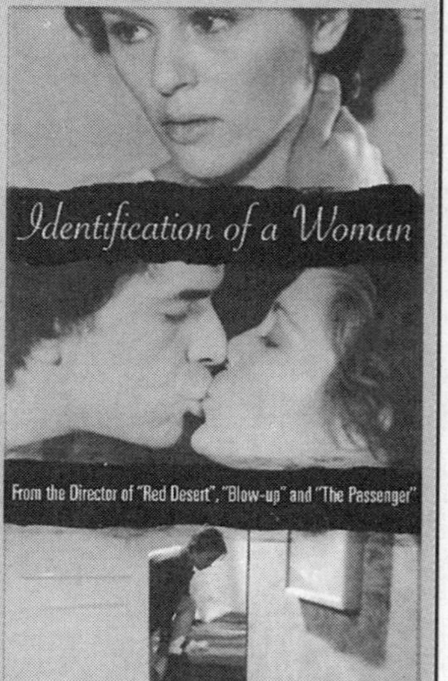

Identification Of A Woman (1982)
As he tries to cope with both a divorce and the search for a female lead for his latest work, filmmaker Tomas Milian has affairs with two very different women—socialite Daniela Silverio and actress Christine Boisson—in this sensual drama from director Michelangelo Antonioni. 131 min. In Italian with English subtitles.
53-6811 *$79.99*

Please see our index for these other Michelangelo Antonioni titles: *Blow Up • Love In The City • Zabriskie Point*

Women Without Names (1949)
Rarely-seen film set in post-World War II Italy, where women without passports were herded into detention centers. Simone Simon is a detainee who plans to seduce a camp worker, marry him and gain her freedom. Lesbianism, sexuality and abortion are among the subjects examined in this unflinching story. 94 min. In English and French and Italian with English subtitles.
53-8054 *$29.99*

The Forbidden Christ (1950)
The only film made by noted author Curzio Malaparte, this powerful Italian drama stars Raf Vallone as a soldier and ex-P.O.W. who returns to his Tuscany village and launches a bitter search for vengeance after learning that his Resistance fighter brother was betrayed to and killed by the Nazis. With Gino Cervi, Elena Varzi. 98 min. In Italian with English subtitles.
53-6110 *$24.99*

Anna (1951)
Hot off her sexy appearance in "Bitter Rice," Silvana Mangano turns in another much-talked-about performance as a nun working at a hospital who treats a former lover after he's shot by a rival. This meeting leads Mangano to recall her sordid experiences with both men, and how they led her to join the convent. With Raf Vallone, Vittorio Gassman. 97 min. In Italian with English subtitles.
10-9444 *$19.99*

Variety Lights (1951)
Federico Fellini's debut directorial effort (with Alberto Lattuada) has all the familiar emblems of his private mythology—a tawdry circus, provincial villages and an attraction for the grotesque. A talented dancer charms a rundown travelling show before moving on to classier arenas. Carla Del Poggio, Peppino De Filippo, Giulietta Masina star. 93 min. In Italian with English subtitles.
53-7285 *$29.99*

Love In The City (1953)
A unique series of five "hidden camera" vignettes, all supposedly based on true stories, that looks at romance, Roman style. The directors putting the mostly non-professional casts through their paces include Michaelangelo Antonioni, Federico Fellini, Dino Risi, Alberto Lattuda, Francesco Maselli and Cesare Zavattini. 90 min. In Italian with English subtitles.
01-1304 Was $29.99 *$19.99*

The Doll That Took The Town (1957)
Although only 20 years old when she made this film, Virna Lisi excels as an aspiring actress who is found lying unconscious on a road outside of Milan. She appears to be another victim of a wave of crime and rape that has troubled the countryside, but when police find the culprits, more questions arise over the incident. With Haya Harareet. 79 min. Dubbed in English.
09-2951 *$19.99*

Bread And Chocolate (1974)
A much-requested title at Movies Unlimited, director/co-scripter Franco Brusati's bittersweet comedy/drama stars Nino Manfredi as an Italian immigrant who moves to Switzerland in hopes of finding a job to support his family, but is caught in a clash of cultures and a series of misadventures. With Anna Karina, Johnny Dorelli. 109 min. In Italian with English subtitles.
53-6104 Was $59.99 *$24.99*

The Tree Of Wooden Clogs (1978)
Ermanno Olmi's heartfelt look at peasant life in Lombardy, Italy at the turn of the century won the Golden Palm Award at Cannes. The story involves the various generations of four families who work as sharecroppers on an estate. Filled with moving moments and fascinating acting from non-professionals; Luigi Ornaghi, Francesca Moroggi star. 185 min. In Italian with English subtitles.
53-7444 Was $79.99 *$19.99*

Palombella Rossa (1989)
The funniest movie to ever mix water polo, amnesia and Italian Communism, writer/director/star Nanni Moretti's surrealistic farce follows a high-ranking politician who loses his memory during a water polo game and attempts to regain it...without leaving the swimming pool. 87 min. In Italian with English subtitles.
53-7926 Was $89.99 *$19.99*

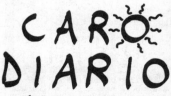

CARO DIARIO
(DEAR DIARY)

Caro Diario (Dear Diary) (1994)
A funny and whimsical comedy from acclaimed Italian filmmaker Nanni Moretti, who wrote, directed, and stars as himself. At odds with his art and his life, Moretti takes off on his motorbike on a personal odyssey across the countryside, and is seen in a trio of vignettes questioning his movies, meeting "Flashdance" star Jennifer Beals, and consulting doctors over a strange body itch. 100 min. In Italian with English subtitles.
18-7529 Was $89.99 *☐$19.99*

The White Sheik (1951)
The first solo turn as director for Federico Fellini is a wonderful romp that follows the misadventures of two mismatched newlyweds: the sensual wife who runs off to meet her favorite "photo strip" hero on a location shoot, and the stodgy husband who must cover for her indiscretions. Alberto Sordi, Brunella Bovo, Leopoldo Trieste star. 86 min. In Italian with English subtitles.
22-5828 *$29.99*

I Vitelloni (1953)
Almost the foreign predecessor of "Diner," this early Fellini triumph follows a group of teenage boys as they face, with dreaded anticipation, their future in the small Italian coastal town they call home. Franco Interlenghi, Alberto Sordi star. 104 min. In Italian with English subtitles.
53-7163 *$59.99*

La Strada (1954)
Federico Fellini's Oscar-winning study of members of a travelling circus troupe, as a brutal strongman uses a simple-minded woman who loves him, forcing her to find solace with a good-hearted clown. With Anthony Quinn, Giulietta Masina, Richard Basehart. 107 min. In Italian with English subtitles.
22-5702 *$29.99*

Il Bidone (The Swindle) (1955)
A trio of swindlers preying on the local peasantry is the focus of Federico Fellini's engrossing drama. Broderick Crawford plays the cold-hearted gangleader, with Richard Basehart, Franco Fabrizi and Giulietta Masina. 98 min. In Italian with English subtitles.
53-7346 Was $59.99 *$19.99*

The Swindle (Dubbed Version)
Also available in a dubbed-in-English edition. 85 min.
68-8829 *$19.99*

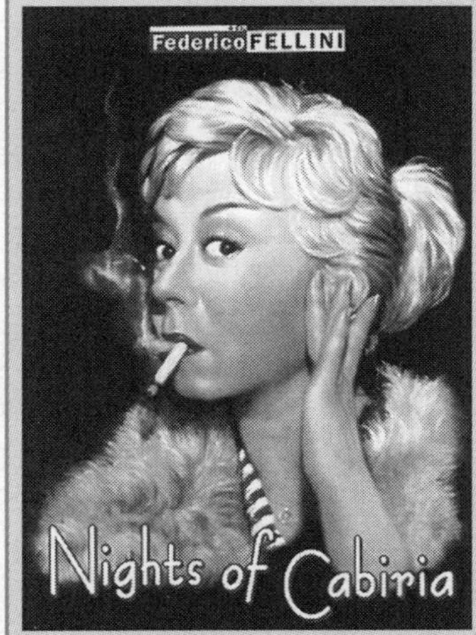

Nights Of Cabiria (1957)
The winner of 1957's Best Foreign Film Oscar, Fellini's moving drama stars Giulietta Masina as an impoverished prostitute who dreams of a better life. Full of poignancy and bittersweet revelations, the film inspired "Sweet Charity." Remastered director's cut includes a seven-minute sequence that was excised after pressure from the Catholic Church, a 40-minute interview with Fellini's assistant, and original and reissue theatrical trailers. 154 min. total.
53-7536 Remastered *$29.99*

Nights Of Cabiria (Dubbed Version)
Also available, in the unrestored version, in a dubbed-in-English edition. 111 min.
09-1929 *$29.99*

La Dolce Vita (1961)
Federico Fellini's masterpiece about the decadent life in Rome and how it affects a gossip columnist. Contains many classic scenes. Marcello Mastroianni, Anita Ekberg, Anouk Aimee. 175 min. In Italian with English subtitles.
63-1007 *$24.99*

8 1/2 (1963)
Federico Fellini's masterpiece about the confusing troubles of a filmmaker trying to get a project off the ground. A dazzling piece of personal cinema. Marcello Mastroianni, Claudia Cardinale. 135 min. In Italian with English subtitles.
50-6286 Was $59.99 *$19.99*

Juliet Of The Spirits (1965)
Director Federico Fellini's dazzling, surrealistic portrait of the sexual fantasies and neuroses of a young woman trying to break out of an unhappy marriage. Giulietta Masina, Mario Pisu, Sylva Koscina star. 142 min. In Italian with English subtitles.
54-9098 *$29.99*

Juliet Of The Spirits (Letterboxed Version)
Also available in a theatrical, widescreen format. 137 min.
50-8336 *$19.99*

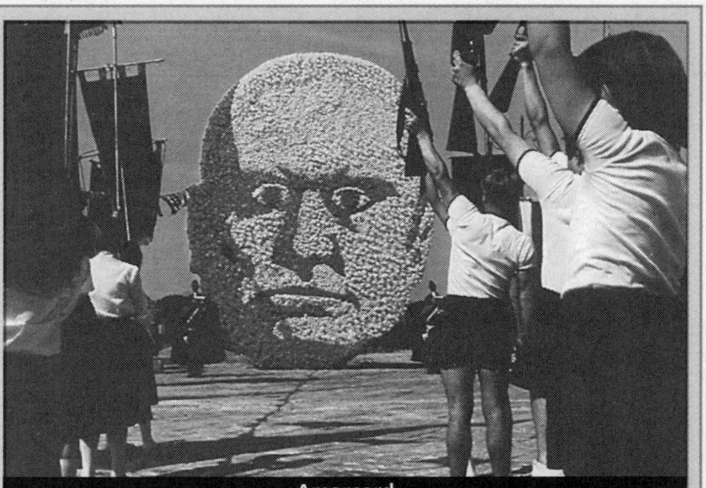
Amarcord

Federico Fellini

Fellini Satyricon (1969)
A decade before "Caligula," Federico Fellini crafted this visually stunning look at the decadence and debauchery of Ancient Rome. Based on contemporary accounts, the succession of bizarre beings, orgiastic lifestyles and amoral attitudes reflect Fellini's views of '60s youth. With Martin Potter, Capucine, Hiram Keller. 128 min. In Italian with English subtitles.
12-3277 *$19.99*

Fellini Satyricon (Letterboxed Version)
Also available in a theatrical, widescreen format.
12-1774 *$19.99*

Fellini: A Director's Notebook (1970)
A surreal documentary by the master himself, shot during the filming of his wildest creation, "Fellini Satyricon." This time capsule follows Fellini as he visits sets for an abandoned project, travels to ancient Rome, visits a slaughterhouse and tries to cast all sorts of eccentrics for his films. There's also Giuletta Masina offering scenes cut from "Nights of Cabiria" and more. 52 min.
53-8049 Was $29.99 *$19.99*

Ciao, Federico! (1970)
This privileged view of Federico Fellini filming "Satyricon" is a wild assemblage of encounters between a passionate creator who makes no distinction between work and existence, and the exotic cast hired to bring to life his vision of depraved Ancient Rome. Directed by Gideon Bachman. 60 min.
70-7013 Was $29.99 *$19.99*

The Clowns (1971)
An enchanting and nostalgic documentary about the life of circus clowns that manages to be a spoof of the genre itself. Fellini displays his mastery for comedy in this affectionate look at a small Italian circus, and even makes a gag appearance himself. 90 min. In Italian with English subtitles.
53-6011 Was $24.99 *$19.99*

Fellini's Roma (1972)
In this filmic salute to his beloved Eternal City, Fellini juxtaposes scenes of himself as an adult shooting a movie on the streets of Rome, with childhood memories of tenement life in WWII Italy, vaudeville performers, clerical fashion shows and his first visit to a bordello. Peter Gonzales and Stefano Majore co-star as the young Fellini. 119 min. In Italian with English subtitles.
12-2264 *$19.99*

Amarcord (1974)
The title is from the Italian for "I remember," and that's what director Federico Fellini does in this heartfelt autobiographical drama. The life and times of a coastal village at the dawn of the Fascists' regime are chronicled through the eyes of an adolescent boy. Winner of the Best Foreign Film Academy Award; with Puppela Maggio, Magali Noel. 127 min. In Italian with English subtitles.
22-5827 Letterboxed *$29.99*

Orchestra Rehearsal (1979)
Set in a decaying medieval chapel, this allegorical Federico Fellini drama chronicles the internal squabbles of the members of an orchestra as they prepare for an upcoming TV documentary, and how the musicians eventually unite to rebel against their German conductor's authoritarian manner. Balduin Bass, Clara Colosimo star; score by Nito Rota. 72 min. In Italian with English subtitles.
53-9815 Was $79.99 *$19.99*

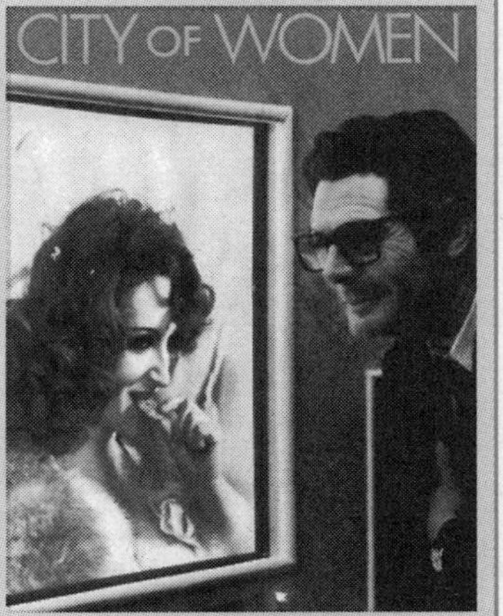

City Of Women (1980)
A dreamlike exploration by Fellini into the mysterious realm of the female psyche. Marcello Mastroianni stars as the hapless dream traveller who finds himself trapped in a feminist convention and then is placed on the frontline of the battle of the sexes in a series of surrealistic images. 104 min. In Italian with English subtitles.
53-7351 Was $89.99 *$19.99*

And The Ship Sails On (1984)
Federico Fellini's look at the loss of personal and global innocence, set on a luxury liner in mid-1914. An odd lot of passengers finds themselves at odds with one another, as the ship serves as a metaphor for Europe at the dawn of World War I. Freddie Jones, Victor Poletti, Janet Suzman star. 132 min. In Italian with English subtitles.
02-1366 Letterboxed *$29.99*

Ginger And Fred (1986)
Take a look at television through the eyes of Federico Fellini in this whimsical story of former dance partners (Marcello Mastroianni and Giulietta Masina) who are reunited after 30 years for a campy TV special and hesitantly restart their love affair. 128 min. In Italian with English subtitles.
12-1637 *$19.99*

Intervista (1987)
While making a film at Rome's famed Cinecitta Studios, Federico Fellini reminisces about his life and his work. His remembrances lead to sequences that mix reality and fantasy and appearances by the director's favorite performers, Marcello Mastroianni and Anita Ekberg. 108 min. In Italian with English subtitles.
72-9016 Was $19.99 *$14.99*

Masina Directed By Fellini 3-Pack
Celebrate one of Italian cinema's most famed collaborations (on and off the screen) with this collection that includes "La Strada," "Nights of Cabiria" and "Variety Nights."
22-6041 Save $10.00! *$79.99*

Please see our index for these other Federico Fellini titles: *Love In The City • Spirits Of The Dead*

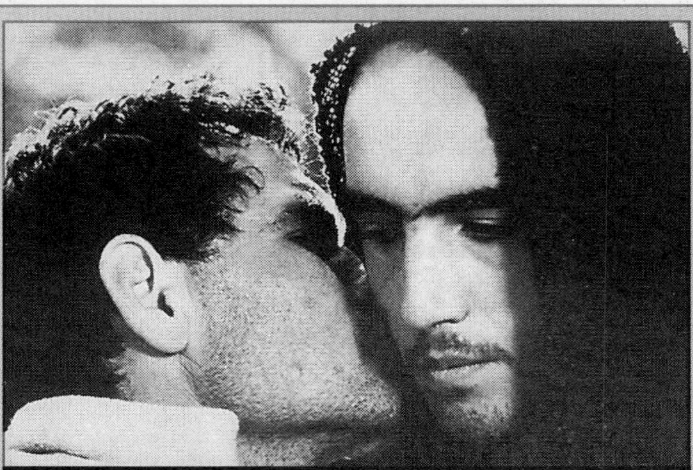

The Gospel According To St. Matthew

Pier Paolo Pasolini

Accattone! (1961)
A graphic slice of Italian street life, this documentary-styled drama by Pier Paolo Pasolini recounts a pimp's efforts to leave his past life behind him when he falls in love with a young woman. Fine crime film uses a non-professional cast. 120 min. In Italian with English subtitles.
01-1481 *$29.99*

Mamma Roma (1962)
Anna Magnani stars as an ex-prostitute trying to build a better life for herself and her teenage son, but the temptations of city life and a money-hungry former pimp may doom her efforts, in this emotional and often-censored drama from Pier Paolo Pasolini. 110 min. In Italian with English subtitles.
53-8345 Was $79.99 *$29.99*

Love Meetings (1964)
Pier Paolo Pasolini's humorous cinéma-vérité study of sexual habits in Italy, featuring appearances by author Alberto Moravia and psychologist Cesare Musatti. Experts and Everymen share their tales of love, homosexuality, prostitution, non-marital relationships and more. 90 min. In Italian with English subtitles.
01-1447 Was $79.99 *$29.99*

The Gospel According To St. Matthew (1964)
A totally original filmic version of the story of Jesus. Director Pier Paolo Pasolini combines non-professional actors, magnificent Italian locales, and a stirring classical score for a moving and surprisingly reverent biographical drama. Deluxe, letterboxed print from the Pasolini Foundation and the Museum of Modern Art. 135 min. In Italian with English subtitles.
01-1449 Was $79.99 *$29.99*

The Gospel According To St. Matthew (Dubbed Version)
Also available in a dubbed-in-English edition.
08-1498 *$19.99*

The Hawks And The Sparrows (1967)
Comic Pier Paolo Pasolini fable about a man and his son's journey through life, and the magical crow that offers them advice. The film traces the duo from the year 1200, where they are monks under the guidance of St. Francis of Assisi, through modern times, where they come face to face with Communism. With Toto and Ninetto Davoli. 88 min. In Italian with English subtitles.
01-1448 Was $79.99 *$29.99*

Oedipus Rex (1967)
The classic Greek tragedy of a young man's dark destiny is brought to the screen by Italian filmmaker Pier Paolo Pasolini, who sandwiches the tale within a modern-day prologue and epilogue. Silvana Mangano, Franco Citti, Alida Valli star. Deluxe, letterboxed print from the Pasolini Foundation and the Museum of Modern Art. 110 min. In Italian with English subtitles.
01-1450 Was $79.99 *$29.99*

Teorema (1969)
Is wanderer Terence Stamp, who moves into a middle-class Milan household, a messenger from Heaven or Hell? Director Pier Paolo Pasolini isn't saying, letting the audience decide in this offbeat drama about how the stranger's presence affects those he meets. With Massimo Girotti, Silvana Mangano, Laura Betti. 93 min. In Italian with English subtitles.
01-1425 *$24.99*

Porcile (Pigsty) (1969)
Director Pier Paolo Pasolini's darkly comic duet of stories starts with a tale of cannibalism set in war-torn medieval Italy, followed by the strange romance between a Nazi industrialist's son and the pigs on his family's estate that eventually eat him alive. Contains some gore and male nudity. Pierre Clementi, Ugo Tognazzi, Jean-Pierre Leaud star. 99 min. In Italian with English subtitles.
53-6043 Was $79.99 *$29.99*

The Decameron (1970)
Eight ribald tales from Boccaccio's medieval literary classic are brought to the screen by Italian filmmaker Pier Paolo Pasolini for the first entry in his "Trilogy of Life." The highlight: a man who poses as a deaf-mute in order to win the favors of a convent filled with sex-hungry nuns. 116 min. Deluxe letterboxed print; In Italian with English subtitles.
01-1458 *$29.99*

The Canterbury Tales (1971)
The bawdy humor your English Lit teacher played down is brought back in full force in Pier Paolo Pasolini's quartet of stories, centering around religious hypocrisy and sexual misadventures. Pasolini himself appears as author Geoffrey Chaucer; with Josephine Chaplin, Hugh Griffith. 109 min. Filmed in English.
01-1428 *$29.99*

Arabian Nights (1974)
The concluding chapter in director Pier Paolo Pasolini's earthy "Trilogy of Life," this erotic, exotic series of vignettes centers around an Arabian prince's search for his lost love, a slave girl, and the stories his party tells to pass the time. Sumptuous sets and Pasolini's trademark unbridled sensuality highlight this unique film. 130 min. In Italian with English subtitles.
01-1390 *$29.99*

Pasolini "Trilogy Of Life" Set
Cinema enthusiasts will want this special set featuring Pasolini's unique film adaptations of "The Decameron," "The Canterbury Tales" and "Arabian Nights."
01-1482 Save $10.00! *$79.99*

Medea (1970)
Maria Callas, in her only dramatic non-singing role, stars in this version of the Greek myth about the sorceress whose ambitions and sins drove her to murder her own children. Co-stars Giuseppe Gentile, Luarent Terzieff; Pier Paolo Pasolini directs. In Italian with English subtitles. 100 min.
22-3023 *$39.99*

Salo: The 120 Days Of Sodom (1977)
Pasolini's last film was also his most graphic and controversial. A group of Fascist leaders kidnaps local teenagers and subjects them to degradation, rape, mutilation and murder, with the youths' suffering symbolizing the horrors of Mussolini's Italy. A hellish tale of explicit sex and violence, available here in a new, uncut print from the Pasolini Foundation and the Museum of Modern Art. 115 min. In Italian with English subtitles.
50-8783 Letterboxed *$59.99*

Whoever Says The Truth Shall Die (1981)
Telling documentary examines the life and work of Italian filmmaker, poet and radical politico Pier Paolo Pasolini, whose murder in 1975 may have been, as purported here, the result of a right-wing conspiracy. 90 min. In English and Italian with English subtitles.
53-9023 *$59.99*

Nerolio (1996)
This intriguing film looks at the life of controversial filmmaker and poet Pier Paolo Pasolini before his death, focusing on his homosexual compulsions, his desire for young men and his need for unrestrained self-expression. Marco Cavicchioli and Vincenzo Crivello star. 82 min. In Italian with English subtitles.
53-8982 *$79.99*

Please see our index for the Pier Paolo Pasolini title: *RoGoPaG*

Malicious (1973)
The voluptuous Laura Antonelli shines as a woman who is hired to clean up after a widower and his three adolescent sons, but winds up being lusted after by the entire household, in this saucy Italian comedy. With Turi Ferro, Alessandro Momo. 97 min. Dubbed in English.
06-1038 Was $49.99 *$19.99*

And The Wild, Wild Women (1960)
Acclaimed actresses Anna Magnani and Giuletta Masina star in this rough-and-tough prison epic from Italy. The story centers on a young girl's experiences in a female hoosegow, where she witnesses the harsh cruelties of prison life. Cristina Gajoni also stars. AKA: "Hell in the City." 85 min. Dubbed in English.
68-9122 *$19.99*

We The Living (1942)
Italian-made version of Ayn Rand's novel, suppressed by Mussolini as "subversive" and unseen for many years, stars Alida Valli and Rossano Brazzi as idealistic young lovers opposing the Communist regime in post-revolutionary Russia. An epic drama of the struggle between individualism and totalitarianism, this is the re-edited version that was overseen by Rand herself. 174 min. In Italian with English subtitles.
50-1849 *$89.99*

Ape Woman (1964)
An outrageous satirical drama, based on a true story, from Italian master of the mirthful macabre Marco Ferreri ("La Grande Bouffe"). Con artist Ugo Tognazzi convinces Annie Girardot, a beautiful young woman covered from head to toe with fur, to join him as a popular sideshow attraction, and even marries her "for love" when she threatens to leave him. Dubbed in English.
79-6018 Was $24.99 *$19.99*

Bitter Rice (1948)
Silvana Mangano became an international sensation with her performance as a shapely city woman working in the rice fields of Italy's Po Valley after World War II. The sexy Mangano is caught in a love triangle with the respectable Raf Vallone and the unscrupulous Vittorio Gassman, in this Neo-Realist classic. 106 min. In Italian with English subtitles.
09-2392 *$19.99*

Seeking Asylum (1979)
In one of his first film roles, Roberto Benigni plays an unconventional preschool teacher whose comically eccentric ways endear him to his charges but put him at odds with the school's strict supervisors. Directed by Marco Ferreri. 112 min. In Italian with English subtitles.
50-5624 *$19.99*

Johnny Stecchino (1993)
Funny farce from Italy, directed by and starring comic Roberto Benigni ("Life Is Beautiful") as a shy bus driver whose life takes some hilarious turns when he's mistaken for a mob boss. Nicoletta Braschi also stars. 100 min. In Italian with English subtitles.
02-2488 Was $89.99 *$19.99*

The Monster (1996)
Roberto Benigni co-wrote, directed and stars in this wacky mistaken identity farce which became the most popular movie in Italy's history. Benigni plays a struggling con artist who finds his life gets more difficult when he's mistaken for a rapist and serial killer who has been terrorizing the area. With Michel Blanc and Nicoletta Braschi. 111 min. In Italian with English subtitles.
02-3071 Was $99.99 *$24.99*

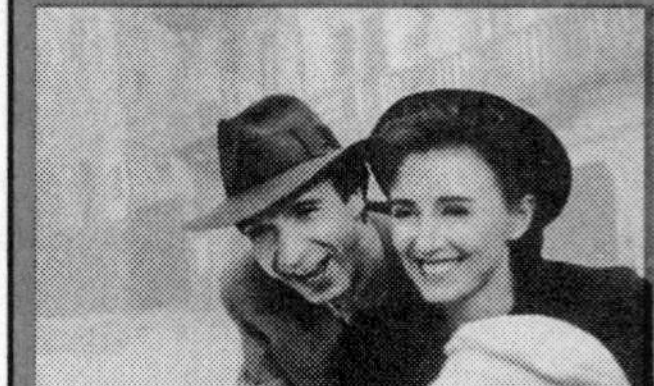

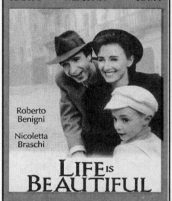

Life Is Beautiful (1998)
Alternately harrowing and funny, this Oscar-winning Holocaust story features writer/director/star Roberto Benigni as a Jewish innocent living in a small Italian village with his wife and son in 1939. When father and son are sent to a concentration camp, Benigni uses games and humor to shield the boy from the surrounding horrors. Nicoletta Braschi and Giorgio Cantarini also star. 116 min. In Italian with English subtitles.
11-2332 Was $99.99 *$19.99*

Life Is Beautiful (Dubbed Version)
Also available in a dubbed-in-English edition.
11-2333 Was $99.99 *$19.99*

Divorce—Italian Style (1962)
Marvelous, Oscar-winning farce starring Marcello Mastroianni as a man facing mid-life crisis who discovers it's easier to kill his annoying wife than divorce her. Eventually, he falls for a gorgeous younger woman, played by Stefania Sandrelli. With Daniela Rocca. 104 min. In Italian with English subtitles.
53-6039 Was $39.99 *$24.99*

Divorce—Italian Style (Dubbed Version)
Also available in a dubbed-in-English edition.
53-6810 *$24.99*

Seduced And Abandoned (1964)
A hilarious look at a Sicilian playboy's downfall, from the director of "Divorce, Italian Style," Pietro Germi. A family demands justice when a girl is used by her sister's fiancée in this witty, biting comedy. Saro Urzi, Stefania Sandrelli star. 118 min. In Italian with English subtitles.
01-1268 Letterboxed *$24.99*

The Unfaithfuls (1960)
Gina Lollobrigida, May Britt and Irene Papas star in this comedy with serious moments about a group of rich society members whose corrupt and adulterous ways are exposed by a blackmailer. Co-written by Franco Brusati ("Bread and Chocolate") and produced by Dino De Laurentis and Carlo Ponti, the film was released overseas in 1953. 91 min. Dubbed in English.
08-1737 *$14.99*

RoGoPaG (1962)
Four top European directors contributed episodes to this acclaimed anthology film (and their initials to the strange title). Roberto Rossellini chronicles an airline stewardess coping with an amorous passenger; a post-WWIII love story is supplied by Jean-Luc Godard; an actor in a religious drama being made by Orson Welles dies on the cross in Pier Paolo Pasolini's controversial segment; and Ugo Gregoretti follows a couple's battle against modern consumerism. 126 min. In French and Italian with English subtitles.
53-8128 Was $79.99 *$24.99*

Madame (1962)
Sophia Loren is at her lustiest in this bawdy romp set during Napoleonic times. She plays the ex-laundress of Napoleon who falls for a sergeant in his army. When he's declared missing in action, she attempts to find him by joining a group of prostitutes on their way to the battle zone. Robert Hossein also stars. AKA: "Madame Sans-Gene." 104 min. Dubbed in English.
59-7019 *$89.99*

The Organizer (1964)
Controversial and highly praised political drama stars Marcello Mastroianni as a professor who has fled Genoa and lands in Turin, where he witnesses the horrible conditions encountered by textile workers. While he dodges would-be assassins, Mastroianni organizes the laborers into forming a union. With Annie Girardot, Bernard Blier. 126 min. In Italian with English subtitles.
53-6114 Letterboxed *$24.99*

The Little Nuns (1965)
Two nuns from a remote Italian village travel to Rome, hoping to talk the owner of an airline into changing the flight paths of his planes which are destroying their convent's beloved fresco. Charming comedy with a fine cast that includes Catherine Spaak, Sylva Koscina. 100 min. Dubbed in English.
09-5023 *$19.99*

Peddlin' In Society (1947)
Four comedy stories in one film, highlighted by a tale starring Anna Magnani as a vegetable vendor who wins the lottery, begins living among high society types, then sees her fortune fall. Vittorio De Sica co-stars and co-scripted; Gennaro Righelli. 90 min. In Italian with English subtitles.
10-8213 *$29.99*

Sacco And Vanzetti (1971)
An Italian-made drama that follows the controversial real-life story of two anarchist Italian immigrants who were convicted and sentenced to death in America in the 1920s for murdering two people during a shoe store robbery. Was their execution due to their unpopular political beliefs? This film ponders the question with stirring results. With Gian Maria Volante, Riccardo Cucciolla. 120 min. Dubbed in English.
08-1131 *$14.99*

Sacco And Vanzetti (Letterboxed Version)
Also available in a theatrical, widescreen format.
08-1828 *$19.99*

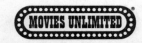

Where The Hot Wind Blows! (1958)
Set in a small town in Southern Italy, this steamy melodrama looks at the amorous adventures of the town's inhabitants, from peasants to bosses. Among those involved in the heated relationships are Gina Lollobrigida, Marcello Mastroianni, Yves Montand and Melina Mercouri, whose husband, Jules Dassin, directs. AKA: "The Law." 114 min. Dubbed in English.
09-2257 Was $29.99 ***$24.99***

Joyful Laughter (Risate Di Gioia) (1960)
Delightful, stylish Italian comedy of two inept pick-pockets planning a big score on New Year's Eve and the klutzy actress who keeps thwarting their efforts. Hilarious romp through Rome stars Anna Magnani, Ben Gazzara, Fred Clark and the legendary Toto. AKA: "The Passionate Thief." 106 min. In Italian with English subtitles.
53-7532 Was $59.99 ***$39.99***

Scent Of A Woman (Profumo Di Donna) (1975)
An entertaining Italian comedy, later remade by Hollywood with Al Pacino, with an award-winning performance by Vittorio Gassman as a blinded army captain who sets out to seduce beautiful women with his sharpened remaining senses. Alessandro Momo co-stars. 103 min. In Italian with English subtitles.
53-8975 ***$89.99***

In The Name Of The Pope King (In Nome del Papa Re) (1977)
Magnificent historical drama of the struggle to unify Italy, focusing on the magistrate of the beleaguered Papal State. When terrorists blow up the barracks of government troops, the official (a monsignor) discovers that his illegitimate son is among the suspects. With Nino Manfredi and Cesare Costa. 115 min. In Italian with English subtitles.
53-7116 ***$29.99***

Vittorio De Sica

The Children Are Watching Us (I Bambini Ci Guardano) (1942)
The break-up of a marriage as seen through the eyes of a couple's 4-year-old son is the focus of this powerful, early neo-realist film from director Vittorio De Sica that was his first dramatic directorial effort. Isa Pola, Luciano De Ambrosis star. 89 min. In Italian with English subtitles.
22-5884 ***$29.99***

Shoeshine (1946)
This neo-realist drama from Vittorio De Sica has been hailed as one of the greatest films of all time. Two streetwise boys use their experience shining Allied soldiers' boots to enter the black market, but eventually their activities lead them to a brutal reform school. Winner of a special Academy Award; with Franco Interlenghi and Rinaldo Smordoni. 93 min. In Italian with English subtitles.
53-8533 ***$59.99***

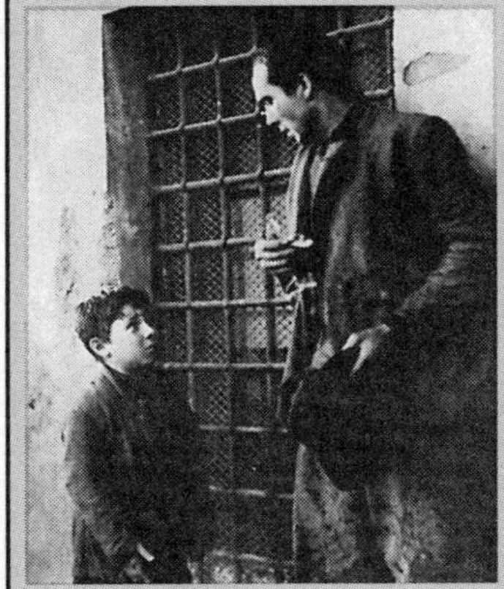

The Bicycle Thief (1949)
Many critics consider this Oscar-winning classic to be one of the greatest films ever made. Vittorio De Sica used non-professional actors to tell the simple, human tragedy of a working man whose bike, which he needs for his job, is stolen, sending him and his son on a harrowing search through the streets of Rome. 90 min. In Italian with English subtitles.
53-8155 ***$69.99***

Miracle In Milan (1951)
Compassionate, neo-realist masterwork from Vittorio De Sica is set in post WWII Italy, where beggars roam the streets. A young orphan is given a magic dove by the ghost of the woman who raised him, and he quickly tries to better the lives of the street people around him. With Francesco Golisano and Paolo Stoppa. 96 min. In Italian with English subtitles.
22-5398 Was $39.99 ***$29.99***

The Gold Of Naples (1954)
Director Vittorio De Sica's serio-comic collection of vignettes examining Neapolitan life and love includes a bullying crook who moves into the home of childhood chum Toto in "The Racketeer"; Sophia Loren as the love-starved wife of a pizza maker in "Pizza on Credit"; De Sica as "The Gambler," squandering his wife's family fortune; and "Theresa," with Silvana Mangano as a prostitute who agrees to a stranger's marriage proposal. 107 min. In Italian with English subtitles.
53-8337 ***$39.99***

The Gold Of Naples (Dubbed Version)
Also available in a dubbed-in-English edition. 87 min.
53-7330 ***$19.99***

Umberto D (1955)
Director Vittorio De Sica's touching drama follows a retired Italian civil servant determined to retain his independence and dignity while subsisting on a meager pension. Carlo Battisti, Maria Pia Casilio star. 88 min. In Italian with English subtitles.
22-5811 Was $29.99 ***$19.99***

The Roof (Il Tetto) (1956)
Vittorio De Sica directed this gently funny tale of a newlywed couple looking for a home of their own in crowded Rome after World II. Gabriella Pallotta, Giorgio Listuzzi star. 98 min. In Italian with English subtitles.
01-1305 ***$29.99***

Two Women (1961)
Sophia Loren deservedly won her Oscar for her moving portrayal as an Italian woman in WWII's waning days who is, along with her daughter, raped and left to die by Allied Moroccan soldiers. Raf Vallone, Jean-Paul Belmondo, Eleanora Brown co-star; Vittorio De Sica directs. 99 min. Dubbed in English.
53-1696 Was $19.99 ***$14.99***

Marriage Italian Style (1964)
Classic Italian comedy from Vittorio De Sica featuring Marcello Mastroianni as a man about to wed who recalls his wartime romance with lusty prostitute Sophia Loren upon learning she is about to die. After Mastroianni agrees to marry her instead, Loren miraculously recovers, giving her an opportunity to have the relationship on her own terms. Sophia is featured in some incredibly sexy outfits in this Oscar-nominated gem. 102 min. In Italian with English subtitles.
59-7042 ***$89.99***

Yesterday, Today And Tomorrow (1964)
Sophia Loren and Marcello Mastroianni shine in Vittorio De Sica's saucy, comedic trilogy about three women (all played by Loren) who use their sexuality to get what they want from the men in their lives. The final episode features a still-steamy striptease scene that is one of Loren's most famous ever. Winner of the Best Foreign Film Academy Award. 118 min. Dubbed in English.
77-7012 ***$19.99***

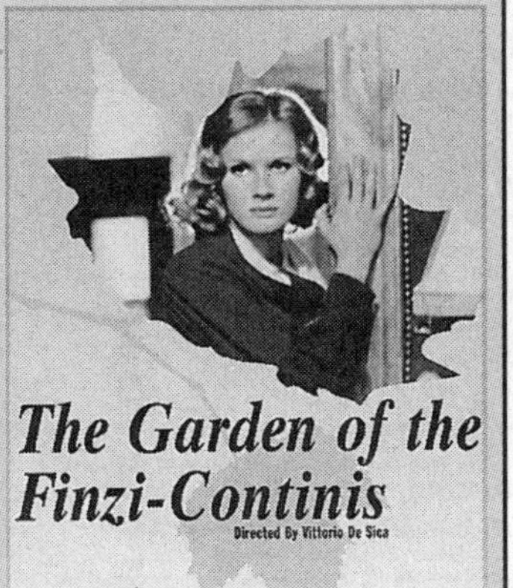

The Garden Of The Finzi-Continis (1971)
Director Vittorio De Sica's Oscar-winning drama centers around an upper-class Jewish family living in Fascist Italy, oblivious at first to the growing tide of anti-Semitism that soon threatens their existence. Dominique Sanda, Helmut Berger, Fabio Testi star. 94 min. In Italian with English subtitles.
40-1370 Restored ***$19.99***

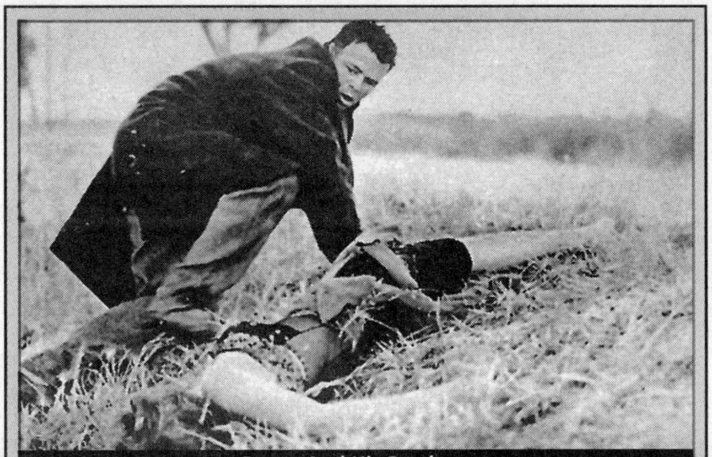

Rocco And His Brothers

Luchino Visconti

Ossessione (1942)
Not seen in America for over 30 years, Italian filmmaker Luchino Visconti's first film is an unauthorized rendition of "The Postman Always Rings Twice" that closely follows the plot of James Cain's classic novel, while adding Visconti's distinctive neo-realist touches. Clara Calamai, Massimo Girotti star. 140 min. In Italian with English subtitles.
53-7154 ***$29.99***

La Terra Trema (1947)
Although a financial misfire upon its initial Italian release, this Luchino Visconti drama has emerged as a classic of the neo-realistic movement. Non-professional actors tell the simple human tale of a small fishing village whose lifeblood is being drained by greedy northern entrepreneurs. 161 min. In Italian with English subtitles.
53-7334 Was $59.99 ***$29.99***

Senso (1953)
Luchino Visconti's classic story of love and war, set amidst the war between Austria and Venice in the 1860s. Farley Granger and Alida Valli star as a member of the bourgeoisie and an aristocrat in this study of emotional relationships. AKA: "The Wanton Countess." 117 min. In Italian with English subtitles.
53-7472 ***$29.99***

White Nights (1957)
A sentimental and uncharacteristically dreamlike Luchino Visconti drama, based on a story by Dostoyevsky. Shy clerk Marcello Mastroianni meets beautiful Maria Schell on a bridge where she waits for the return of her sailor lover. Smitten, Mastroianni tries to convince her that the sailor's never coming back and to go dancing with him. 94 min. In Italian with English subtitles.
53-7530 Was $59.99 ***$39.99***

Rocco And His Brothers (1960)
Heartfelt, controversial social drama by Luchino Visconti that follows a mother and her four sons as they move from rural Italy to the slums of Milan. Alain Delon and Renato Salvatori star as the two oldest sons, both in love with prostitute Annie Girardot. With Claudia Cardinale. 134 min. In Italian with English subtitles.
62-1311 ***$29.99***

Sandra Of A Thousand Delights (1963)
Luchino Visconti's powerful drama stars Claudia Cardinale as a woman who travels back to her home town in Italy in order to attend a memorial ceremony for her Jewish father, who was killed in a concentration camp. The woman discovers that her mother may have had something to do with her father's death. Jean Sorel, Michael Craig co-star. 100 min. In Italian with English subtitles.
53-7466 Was $39.99 ***$29.99***

The Damned (1969)
The decadence and perversion that accompanied the Nazis' rise to power in '30s Germany is graphically chronicled, via the slow degeneration of a wealthy weapons-building family, in Luchino Visconti's shocking drama. Dirk Bogarde, Ingrid Thulin, Helmut Berger and Charlotte Rampling star. 146 min. Dubbed in English.
19-1121 ***$59.99***

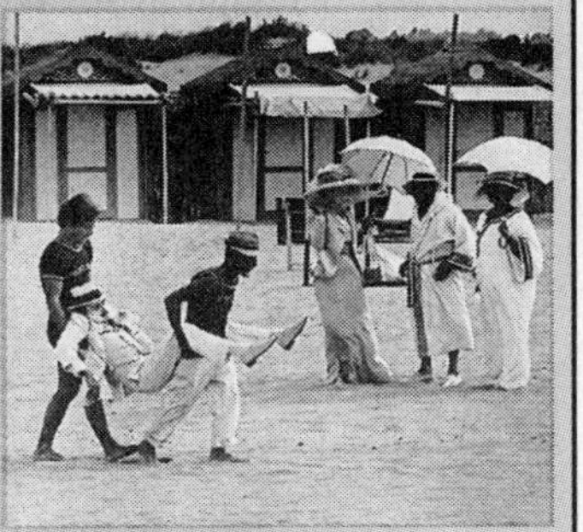

Death In Venice (1971)
Luchino Visconti's brilliant version of Thomas Mann's classic story. Dirk Bogarde stars as a jaded, middle-aged German composer on holiday on Venice who spots a handsome young boy on the beach. His doomed obsession with the youth renews his interest in living. With Silvana Mangano, Bjorn Andresen. 130 min. Filmed in English.
19-1123 ***$59.99***

Ludwig (1972)
Luchino Visconti's sumptuously decadent epic on the life of the 19th-century "Mad King of Bavaria" stars Helmut Berger in the title role. The film chronicles Ludwig's platonic affair with Austrian princess Elizabeth (Romy Schneider), his affection for young men, his patronage of struggling composer Richard Wagner (Trevor Howard) and his mysterious death. With Silvana Mangano, Gert Frobe. 231 min. In Italian with English subtitles.
53-8582 Letterboxed ***$24.99***

The Innocent (1976)
The final work by director Luchino Visconti is a lush, erotic drama set in late 19th-century Italy. Aristocrat Giancarlo Giannini has an affair with widow Jennifer O'Neill, ignoring long-suffering wife Laura Antonelli...until she begins seeing a young author. 125 min. In Italian with English subtitles.
53-7001 ***$29.99***

The Queen Of Sheba (1953)
Set in the year 1000 B.C., this Biblical epic tells the story of King Solomon, the ruler of Israel, who finds his son, Prince Rehoboam, involved with the beautiful queen of the rival city of Sheba. Gino Cervi and Leonora Ruffo star in this grand-scale epic. 103 min. Dubbed in English.
09-2211 ***$19.99***

Woman Of Rome (1956)
Latin lollapalooza Gina Lollobrigida is a cynical prostitute whose fall begins with nude modelling, and ends when she rejects the love of the only man who truly cares about her. Daniel Gelin co-stars. 93 min. In Italian with English subtitles.
10-7324 Was $29.99 ***$19.99***

Girl With A Suitcase (1961)
Claudia Cardinale exudes lust as a young woman from the wrong side of the tracks who finds romance with an ex-lover's teenage brother. The relationship brings trouble into both their lives, but will she leave him for a worldly musician? Jacques Perrin, Corrado Pani also star. 111 min. In Italian with English subtitles.
55-9023 ***$29.99***

The Long Night Of 1943 (1960)
Co-written by Pier Paolo Pasolini, this acclaimed story is set in Italy's Po Valley, where an attractive pharmacy worker who cares for her partially paralyzed husband begins a clandestine affair with her former fiancé. Belinda Lee, Gino Vervi star. 106 min. Dubbed in English.
09-2369 ***$19.99***

Bellissimo: Images Of The Italian Cinema (1987)
A panoramic view of Italian cinema, spanning over 40 years, with film clips and interviews with some of the most influential artists of the Italian film industry, including Marcello Mastroianni, Federico Fellini, Sophia Loren and many others. A must for any foreign film buff. 110 min. In Italian with English subtitles.
53-7115 *$29.99*

Marcello Mastroianni: I Remember (1997)
Completed shortly before his death in 1996, this marvelous, clip-filled film memoir from one of the world's best-loved actors features Mastroianni looking back on his four-decade career of more than 170 movies. With characteristic grace and humor he dismisses his "Latin Lover" sobriquet, talks about the American actors who influenced him, and shares anecdotes about Fellini, De Sica and other colleagues. 199 min.
53-6750 *$89.99*

The Battle Of Algiers (1965)
Acclaimed drama of the Algerian struggle for independence from France in the 1950s. While focusing on one small band of rebels making their last stand, the film adopts a semi-documentary look while detailing the bloody fighting. Directed by Gillo Pontecorvo. 123 min. In Italian with English subtitles.
76-1001 *$29.99*

La Scorta (1993)
Set in Mafia-influenced Trapani, Sicily, this tightly wound political suspenser focuses on four honest men who are assigned to protect an investigating magistrate from corrupt killers who assassinated his predecessor. Claudio Amendola and Carlo Cecchi star in Ricky Tognazzi's film, which features music by Ennio Morricone. 92 min. In Italian with English subtitles.
53-8926 *$89.99*

Mille Bolle Blu (1993)
Set on a single block in Rome on the night before a solar eclipse, this exuberant film focuses on the neighborhood kids as they spy on their elderly neighbors. They uncover secret loves, inept criminals and a trumpeter who awaits the most important day of his life. With Stefano Dionisi, Nicoletta Boris. 83 min. In Italian with English subtitles.
53-9732 *$89.99*

Bernardo Bertolucci

The Grim Reaper (1962)
Groundbreaking directorial debut by Bernardo Bertolucci (made at the age of 22) is a gripping, stark drama examining the brutal slaying of a prostitute in a Rome park. Scripted by Pier Paolo Pasolini; Francesco Rulu, Marisa Solinas star. 100 min. In Italian with English subtitles.
53-7476 *$29.99*

Partner (1968)
An early work by Bernardo Bertolucci, based on Dostoyevsky's "The Double." A young man's quiet and orderly life is suddenly thrown into chaos when he meets his doppelganger and loses his grip on his very sanity. Pierre Clementi, Tina Aumont star. 110 min. In Italian with English subtitles.
01-1437 *$19.99*

BERNARDO BERTOLUCCI'S
THE SPIDER'S STRATAGEM

The Spider's Stratagem (1970)
Atmospheric political mystery by Bernardo Bertolucci, set in a town in Italy's Po Valley. A young man whose anti-fascist father was killed by the village in the '30s visits 15 years later and is coldly received. Giulio Brogi, Alida Valli star; based on a Jose Luis Borges story. 90 min. In Italian with English subtitles.
53-7438 Was $59.99 *$29.99*

Tragedy Of A Ridiculous Man (1982)
Bernardo Bertolucci's seriocomic story, set in the Italian countryside, tells about a cheese manufacturer who faces an emotional struggle when he must decide whether to raise ransom money for his kidnapped son. Ugo Tognazzi, Anouk Aimee and Laura Morante star. 117 min. In Italian with English subtitles.
19-1845 *$59.99*

Please see our index for these other Bernardo Bertolucci titles: *1900 • Besieged • The Last Emperor • Last Tango In Paris • The Sheltering Sky • Stealing Beauty*

Switzerland

The Last Chance (1945)
German exile Leopold Lindtberg directed this powerful drama while living in Switzerland. Set in 1943 in Northern Italy, the story follows an escaped American and a British POW who encounter a resourceful farmer, a beautiful woman and a courageous priest while on their way to neutral Switzerland. With E.G. Morrison. 104 min. In English and other languages with English subtitles.
09-2952 *$19.99*

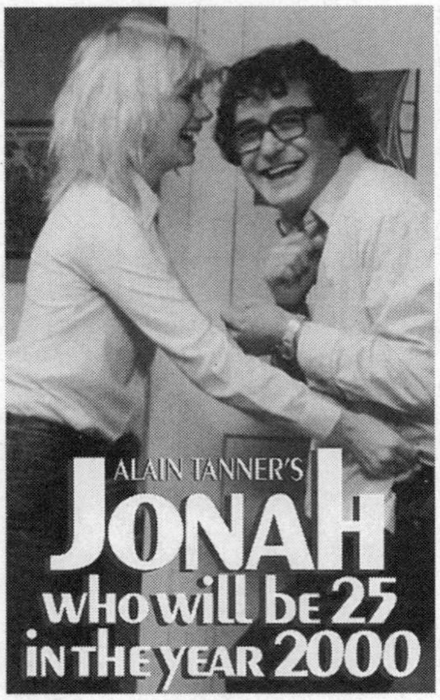
ALAIN TANNER'S
JONAH
who will be 25
IN THE YEAR 2000

Jonah Who Will Be 25 In The Year 2000 (1976)
Alain Tanner's spirited comedy looks at eight veterans of the political upheaval of the late 1960s who confront their hopes, dreams and disappointments as they attempt to face the future. Among the characters are an altruistic supermarket worker, a disillusioned journalist and a sexy, mystical secretary. Miou-Miou, and Myriam Meziere star. 110 min. In French with English subtitles.
53-7696 Was $89.99 *$29.99*

Charles: Dead Or Alive (1969)
The debut feature from Swiss filmmaker Alain Tanner ("Jonah Who Will Be 25 in the Year 2000") is a thought-provoking treatise on non-conformity and its cost. François Simon stars as a successful watchmaker who abruptly sheds his middle-class lifestyle and moves in with an artist and his mistress. With Marcel Robert, Maya Simon. 93 min. In French with English subtitles.
53-6350 *$89.99*

La Salamandre (1971)
From Alain Tanner directed a sensuous and incisive story of a woman who draws the obsessive interests of a journalist and a novelist after she's accused of shooting her guardian. Jacques Denis, Jean-Luc Bideau and Bulle Ogier star. 125 min. In French with English subtitles.
53-8007 *$89.99*

The Invitation (1973)
An afternoon garden party for a group of employees in a business office turns into a revealing series of encounters as the festivities wear on and social pretenses are dropped in this compelling character study from Swiss filmmaker Claude Goretta. Jean-Luc Bideau, Francois Simon star. 100 min. In French with English subtitles.
22-5885 *$29.99*

Messidor (1981)
Alain Tanner's controversial film follows a female college student and a salesgirl who meet while hitchhiking and launch a crime spree across Switzerland, which they discover has a seamy side kept hidden to tourists. Clémentine Amouroux and Catherine Rétoré star. 120 min. In French with English subtitles.
53-8331 Was $89.99 *$29.99*

In The White City (1983)
Haunting chronicle from director Alain Tanner of a sailor who goes AWOL in Lisbon and, with his Super 8mm camera, begins capturing the sights of the city and his life. Bruno Ganz stars in this memorable mood piece. 106 min. In English and Portuguese, German and French with English subtitles.
53-7679 *$89.99*

France

Award-Winning French Shorts
From France and Canada come three unique short films: "Le a la Menthe" (not subtitled), "La Fin de Ete" and "Le Poulet" (both subtitled in English). 59 min.
53-7026 *$29.99*

French Animation Festival
An engrossing gallery of Gallic animated short subjects, ranging from four pre-1923 works by pioneer filmmaker Emile Cohl to more recent cartoons from the '40s and '60s. Includes "Fantasmagorie" (1909), "Bonehead Is Shipwrecked" (1912) and "La Flute Magique" (1945). No dialogue.
53-7034 *$29.99*

Poison Ivy (1953)
Flavorful espionage effort with Eddie Constantine as a fed fighting sharks and gold smugglers in Casablanca. This European production is filled with action, nice locales and Eddie acting cool, a la "Alphaville."
68-9139 *$19.99*

Dishonorable Discharge (1958)
An unofficial reworking of "To Have and Have Not" with Eddie Constantine as a down-and-out American sailor hired to pilot a cruise ship for a group of tourists. Little does Constantine know that there's also dynamite, illegal drugs and treasure-seekers on the trip. With Lino Ventura, Lise Bourdin. Dubbed in English.
79-6511 *$19.99*

Women Are Like That (1960)
Eddie Constantine's ace spy Lemmy Caution is elected by the French secret service to stop a group of counterfeiting creeps operating out of Europe and Asia. Caution masquerades as a gangster while trying to top the thugs, but finds time to romance French babes Françoise Prévost and Françoise Brion. AKA: "Comment Qu'elle Est!"
79-6557 Was $24.99 *$19.99*

There's Going To Be A Party (1961)
Secret agent Eddie Constantine goes on a top secret mission to rescue a fellow operative being held behind bars. He soon learns that the captive is a double agent, and Constantine must stop him before more damage is done. With Barbara Laage, Claude Cerval. Dubbed in English.
68-8952 *$19.99*

Ladies' Man (1962)
Before and after he played the character in Jean-Luc Godard's "Alphaville," Eddie Constantine starred as hard-boiled spy Lemmy Caution in a series of light-hearted thrillers. Here he uncovers danger and romance among the rich and famous on the French Riviera.
68-8831 *$19.99*

Your Turn, Darling (1963)
Slick secret agent Lemmy Caution (Eddie Constantine) investigates the murder of a female American spy and the abduction of a scientist and uncovers a spy ring in the process in this tongue-in-chic French thriller. Christian Minazzoli also stars. 93 min. Dubbed in English.
68-8763 *$19.99*

It Means That To Me (1963)
A trench-coated, down-on-his-luck reporter (Eddie Constantine) is framed on espionage charges by the government, and then hired to transport secret microfilm. Jean-Louis Richard and Rosita also star in this spy thriller. Dubbed in English.
68-8765 *$19.99*

As If It Were Raining (1963)
Eddie Constantine stars in this espionage thriller that finds secret agent Lemmy Caution traveling to Spain to stop an embezzlement scheme. Elisa Montes also stars.
68-8832 *$19.99*

There Goes Barder (1964)
A shady ship-owner hires con artist Eddie Constantine to be a security agent in this noirish thriller co-starring May Britt. 92 min. Dubbed in English.
68-8766 *$19.99*

Make Your Bets, Ladies (1964)
Exciting Eddie Constantine outing with Eddie playing a special agent searching for missing NATO weapons and encountering a scientist who has invented a ring that emits a paralysis spray. With Nelly Benedetti and Danny Ceccaldi. Dubbed in English.
68-8953 *$19.99*

Hail Mafia (1965)
Two-fisted crime drama starring Eddie Constantine as an American hiding in France who is confronted by two thugs out to get him: Henry Silva, a hit man hired by a construction company, and Jack Klugman, who has a vendetta against him. Elsa Martinelli also stars.
68-8933 *$19.99*

Attack Of The Robots (1966)
Lemmy Caution (Eddie Constantine) is back in one of his most bizarre cases ever, as the super agent gets mixed up in a scientist's plot to turn ordinary citizens into mind-controlled political assassins. With Fernando Rey; Jess Franco directs. 88 min. Dubbed in English.
09-1506 Was $29.99 *$24.99*

Jean Cocteau

The Blood Of A Poet (1930)
Director Jean Cocteau's first film, an important entry in the French avant-garde cinema, tells the haunting story of a poet who "lives" what he writes. The four autobiographical vignettes explore Cocteau's dreams, fears, opium addiction, and obsession with death. Stars Pauline Carton, Lee Miller. 55 min. In French with English subtitles.
53-7381 *$29.99*

The Eternal Return (1943)
Jean Cocteau adapts the Tristan and Isolde legend in this poetic drama. A young man falls in love with his uncle's wife, yet his loyalty to his uncle prevents him from openly expressing his love, and his sense of honor leads to tragedy. Jean Marais stars. 100 min. In French with English subtitles.
22-5782 *$24.99*

Beauty And The Beast (1946)
Jean Cocteau's imaginative, surrealistic adaptation of the Marie de Beaumont fairy tale is cinematic poetry at its finest. Jean Marais and Josette Day star as the grotesque beast and the young beauty, whose love restores his soul. 93 min. In French with English subtitles.
22-5649 Remastered *$24.99*

The Eagle With Two Heads (L'Aigle A Deux Tetes) (1948)
Adapted from his own successful stageplay, this Jean Cocteau costume drama stars Jean Marais as a 19th-century anarchist and double for his tiny European country's late king. Sneaking into the palace to assassinate queen Edwige Feuillére, the would-be revolutionary winds up falling in love with his target. 93 min. In French with English subtitles.
01-1493 *$29.99*

Les Parents Terribles (1948)
A young man brings his new-found love home to meet his parents, but neither he nor his domineering mother realize that the woman of his dreams is also his father's mistress. Emotionally layered and daring comedy-drama from Jean Cocteau, based on his play, stars Jean Marais, Yvonne De Bray, Gabrielle Dorziat. AKA: "The Storm Within." 98 min. In French with English subtitles.
01-1494 *$29.99*

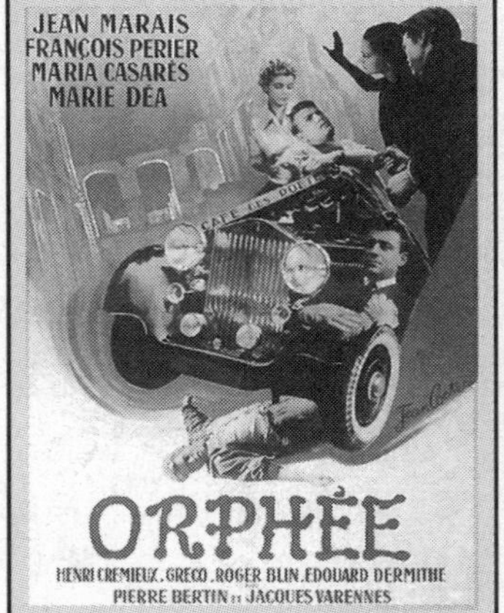
JEAN MARAIS
FRANÇOIS PERIER
MARIA CASARES
MARIE DEA
ORPHÉE
HENRI CREMIEUX . GRECO . ROGER BLIN . EDOUARD DERMITHE
PIERRE BERTIN ET JACQUES VARENNES

Orpheus (1949)
Jean Cocteau directed this unusual mixture of real and unreal, as the personification of Orpheus finds himself pursued by death in the form of a strange, beautiful woman driving a Rolls Royce. Jean Marais, Maria Casares star. 95 min. In French with English subtitles.
53-1607 *$19.99*

The Testament Of Orpheus (1960)
The final film by Jean Cocteau is a surreal tour de force that looks over his life, his art and his cinematic oeuvre. Laden with fanciful camerawork (including color sequences), characters from Cocteau's previous movies, and cameos by such luminaries as Pablo Picasso, Charles Aznavour, Yul Brynner, Roger Vadim and Brigitte Bardot, the drama serves as a fitting farewell. 79 min. In French with English subtitles.
22-5498 *$29.99*

Cocteau's Orphic Cycle
"Blood of a Poet," "Orpheus" and "The Testament of Orpheus" are also available in a collector's set.
22-5984 *$79.99*

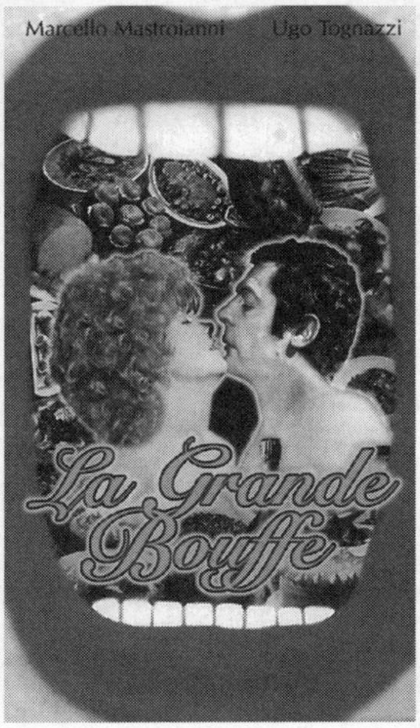

La Grande Bouffe (1973)
A judge, a chef, a pilot and a TV personality decide to end their lives of boredom by partaking in a session of total debauchery in a Paris villa. Their goal: to eat themselves to death. Along the disgusting road to ruin, they partake in wild sex with a teacher and some prostitutes. Marcello Mastroianni, Philippe Noiret and Ugo Tognazzi star in Marco Ferreri's notorious cult favorite. 130 min. In French with English subtitles.
01-1505 *$19.99*

Don't Touch The White Woman! (1974)
The battle of Little Big Horn becomes a battle over trinkets and souvenir stands in Marco Ferreri's anachronistic farce. Marcello Mastroianni stars as an egotistical General Custer who watches over a curio shop run by Indian scout Ugo Tognazzi that sells, among other items, stuffed and mounted Indians. Mastroianni's final battle with Sitting Bull (Alain Cuny) takes place in a desolate Paris marketplace. Catherine Deneuve, Michel Piccoli also star. 110 min. In French with English subtitles.
50-5625 *$19.99*

The Crucible (1957)
Jean-Paul Sartre wrote the screenplay for this French adaptation of the Arthur Miller play set amid the Salem Witch Trials of the 1690s. The hysteria that grips a New England town when several girls accuse a couple of consorting with the devil was Miller's response to "red scare" America of the '50s. Simone Signoret, Yves Montand, Mylene Demongeot star. 108 min. In French with English subtitles.
53-6095 *$39.99*

Mayerling (1937)
Exquisite French romance based on the tragic true story of 19th-century Austria's Crown Prince Rudolf, whose affair with an aristocratic woman in response to a loveless marriage forced on him by his father ended in tragedy. Charles Boyer and Danielle Darrieux star as the doomed lovers. 90 min. In French with English subtitles.
22-5888 Remastered *$29.99*

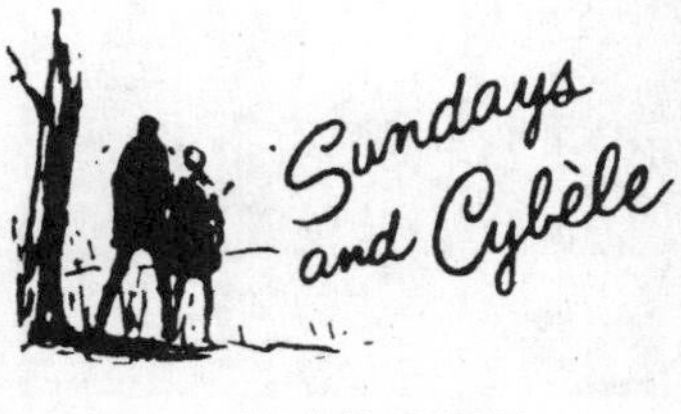

Sundays And Cybèle (1962)
The Best Foreign Film Oscar-winner of 1962 stars Hardy Kruger as a shell-shocked pilot who, after returning home from the Indochinese war, develops a sensitive and ultimately tragic friendship with a 12-year-old girl (Patricia Gozzi). 110 min. In French with English subtitles.
01-1241 *$24.99*

Sundays And Cybèle (Letterboxed Version)
The subtitled edition is also available in a theatrical, widescreen format.
53-7783 Was $59.99 *$29.99*

Sundays And Cybèle (Dubbed Version)
Also available in a dubbed-in-English edition.
09-2360 *$24.99*

Crime And Punishment (1935)
The first and still the best filmization of Dostoyevsky's classic novel benefits from taut direction by Pierre Chanal and masterful performances by Pierre Blancher as the compulsive student/murderer Raskolnikov and Harry Baur as his canny adversary, Inspector Porfiry. 110 min. In French with English subtitles.
53-9042 *$59.99*

Extenuating Circumstances (1936)
A judge and his wife are stranded in a seedy city on the outskirts of Paris and attempt to convert its denizens into law-abiding citizens in this delightful story starring Michel Simon and Arletty. 90 min. In French with English subtitles.
87-1007 *$39.99*

Poil De Carotte (1931)
The affecting story of a young boy and his relationship with his parents—a loving father and a cold, uncaring mother. With Robert Dunen and the celebrated Harry Baur. 90 min. In French with English subtitles.
53-7051 *$29.99*

The Sorceress (1956)
Haunting and sensual fantasy/drama about a French engineer sent to a remote Swedish town to oversee construction of a road. Once there, he becomes entranced by a beautiful young woman who lives in the woods and has been accused of being a witch by the villagers. Marina Vlady, Nicole Courcel star. 91 min. In French with English subtitles.
55-9015 *$29.99*

Double Verdict (1955)
Intriguing thriller in which a husband accused of killing his wife is acquitted by a hung jury. When the man is released from custody, he begins dating—and eventually marries—the daughter of an industrialist who served on the jury. And when he suspects that his new son-in-law is really a murderer, he must stop him. Serge Sauvion stars. Dubbed in English.
79-6552 *$29.99*

Ruy Blas (1948)
Jean Cocteau scripted this intriguing costume drama based on the Victor Hugo novel of political intrigue, mistaken identity and romance in 17th-century Spain. Jean Marais plays a dual role as a student and a nobleman-turned-bandit, with Danielle Darrieux as the queen; Pierre Billon directs. 90 min. In French with English subtitles.
87-1017 *$39.99*

Volpone (1939)
Ben Johnson's tale of the merchant who feigns mortal illness just to watch his would-be heirs scramble for their share in the will has seldom been better told than in this Maurice Tourneur effort. Harry Baur stars. 95 min. In French with English subtitles.
01-1373 *$29.99*

Lady Chatterley's Lover (1955)
Director Marc Allegret's French film version of D.H. Lawrence's controversial celebration of physical love was itself the subject of considerable controversy. 102 min. In French with English subtitles.
01-1120 Was $29.99 *$19.99*

Obsession (1954)
Trapeze artists Michele Morgan and Raf Vallone fall in love, but Morgan doesn't know of Vallone's past—he thinks he killed a man. An injury to Vallone's arm and a new partner with ties to his past add to the suspense in this French melodrama. With Jean Gaven; Jean Delloney directs. 105 min. Dubbed in English.
10-8147 *$29.99*

Nana (1955)
Emile Zola's classic about a courtesan who seduces the rich men of France is given a fine treatment, with Charles Boyer and Martine Carol. 118 min. In French with English subtitles.
08-5035 *$29.99*

The Heart Of A Nation (1943)
Smuggled out of wartime France one reel at a time, this absorbing drama chronicles three generations of a Montmarte family coping with the occupation of their country, from the Franco-Prussian war of 1871 to the arrival of the Nazis. Stars Louis Jouvet, Raimu; narrated by Charles Boyer. 111 min. Dubbed in English.
10-9172 *$19.99*

La Symphonie Pastoral (1946)
Based on a novel by Andre Gide, this moving drama stars Michele Morgan as a blind orphan who is taken in by the family of pastor Pierre Blanchar, who becomes consumed by guilt over his love for the girl. With Jean Desailly; directed by Jean Delannoy. 105 min. In French with English subtitles.
22-5883 *$29.99*

Renoir Shorts
Two rare short features, an adaptation of Hans Christian Andersen's "The Little Match Girl" (1927) and the risqué "The Charleston" (1928), provide insight into the development of expressionistic master filmmaker Jean Renoir. Silent with English titles.
10-7328 *$29.99*

La Chienne (1931)
Early triumph for Jean Renoir concerns a meek businessman and gifted amateur artist (Michel Simon) who becomes hopelessly infatuated with a gregarious hooker (Janie Mareze) and is oblivious to her exploitation of his talents. Well-crafted, blackly funny film was remade as "Scarlet Street." Georges Flament costars. 93 min. In French with English subtitles.
53-7311 *$59.99*

Boudu Saved From Drowning (1932)
Slapstick French satire that inspired "Down and Out in Beverly Hills." Michel Simon is the tramp fished out of the Seine by a Paris bookseller and taken to his home, only to bring chaos into the family. With Charles Granval, Marcelle Hania; Jean Renoir directs. 87 min. In French with English subtitles.
53-7002 Was $29.99 *$19.99*

Madame Bovary (1934)
Early film adaptation of the infamous Gustave Flaubert novel, scripted and directed by Jean Renoir, stars Valentine Tessier as the bored wife who embarks on a series of hedonistic affairs that lead to her downfall. 102 min. In French with English subtitles.
53-6002 *$39.99*

Underground (The Lower Depths) (1935)
Jean Renoir directs this acclaimed version of Maxim Gorky's famed play, changing the setting from Russia to Paris. Louis Jouvet plays a financially ruined nobleman who learns about life from a street thief in the slums. Jean Gabin, Jany Holt, Suzy Prim co-star. 91 min. In French with English subtitles.
10-8209 *$29.99*

The Crime Of Monsieur Lange (1935)
When the boss embezzles the company funds and is declared dead while fleeing the country, the workers at a publishing firm band together to produce a very successful series of "Arizona Jim" cowboy stories. All is well until the boss returns to cash in. Funny and allegorical tale from Jean Renoir stars Renee Lefevre, Jules Berry. 90 min. In French with English subtitles.
53-7246 *$59.99*

A Day In The Country (1936)
Jean Renoir's classic adaptation of the de Maupassant story of a Parisian merchant's Sunday outing with his family. While the men fish, the women go off in a boat with some handsome strangers...and the results are not so surprising! With Silvia Bataille, Georges Darnoux. 40 min. In French with English subtitles.
53-7860 *$39.99*

La Marseillaise (1937)
Incredible spectacle by Jean Renoir that lavishly documents the French Revolution from the summer of 1789 to the final collapse of Louis XVI's monarchy. A vivid re-creation of a turning point in world history from one of cinema's grand masters. 130 min. In French with English subtitles.
01-1374 *$29.99*

Grand Illusion (1937)
Director Jean Renoir's masterful study of wartime honor and courage stars Jean Gabin, Pierre Fresnay and Marcel Dalio as French officers in World War I who are captured and sent to a German prison camp run by aristocratic commandant Erich von Stroheim. The bonds between captor and inmate form the basis for this compelling drama. Restored edition includes an introduction by Renoir. 117 min. In French with English subtitles.
22-5503 Remastered *$29.99*

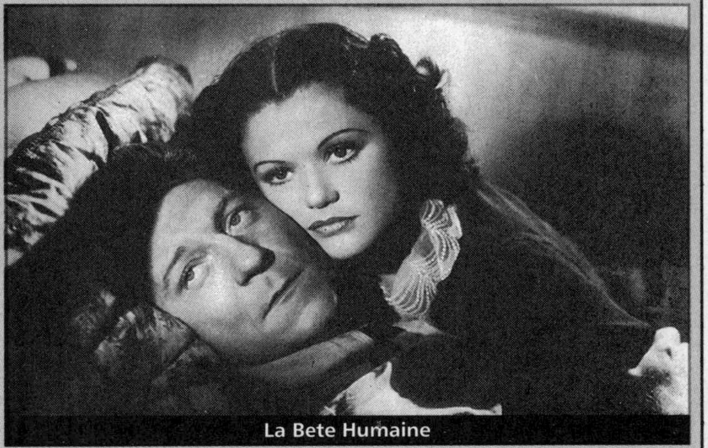
La Bete Humaine

Jean Renoir

La Bete Humaine (1938)
Director Jean Renoir's story of the son of a drunkard finding that his own abstinence from liquor is no escape from self-hatred and haunted memories. 101 min. In French with English subtitles.
09-1762 Was $29.99 *$19.99*

Rules Of The Game (1939)
A weekend shooting party at an upper-class French estate is the setting for director Jean Renoir's witty, acerbic look at the jaded and amoral lifestyles of the aristocracy in the days before World War II. Denounced at its premiere, the drama is now recognized as a masterpiece of world cinema. Roland Toutain, Nora Gregor, Marcel Dalio and Renoir star. 110 min. In French with English subtitles.
22-5502 Restored *$29.99*

The River (1951)
Made after his brief sojourn to Hollywood in the '40s, Jean Renoir's first color film is a lyric study of a British family living in postwar India, and the effect that a visiting relative, a wounded soldier, has on the household's three teenage girls. Nora Swinburne, Adrienne Corri, Radha, Thomas E. Breen star. 99 min. Filmed in English.
22-5578 Restored *$29.99*

The Golden Coach (1952)
Jean Renoir helmed this French-Italian co-production about a Commedia dell'Arte company touring 1800s South America, and how leading lady Anna Magnani ensnares three local men with her charms. With Duncan Lamont, Odoardo Spadaro; this is the original, English-dialogue version. 103 min.
53-7169 Remastered *$24.99*

Elena And Her Men (1956)
Director Jean Renoir elevates Ingrid Bergman to a modern Venus in this classic, about a Polish princess in 1880s Paris who grooms a series of talented lovers for success in the political world. An eloquent tale of affairs of the heart and affairs of state with Mel Ferrer and Jean Marais. AKA: "Paris Does Strange Things." 98 min. In French with English subtitles.
53-7196 *$59.99*

French Can-Can (1956)
Paris of the 1880s is visually re-created with brilliant strokes by Jean Renoir in this backstage musical. The early days of the Moulin Rouge and the entrepreneur who began it are backdrops for beautiful, high-kicking chorus girls and their swirling petticoats. Stars Jean Gabin and Maria Felix. 93 min. In French with English subtitles.
53-7197 *$59.99*

Picnic On The Grass (1959)
A whimsical romance full of nostalgic and fantastic plot elements, courtesy of director Jean Renoir. A candidate for the United States of Europe presidency runs on a platform of artificial insemination, but during one pastoral summer picnic his views on love and sex are changed, thanks to a country lass. Paul Meurisse, Catherine Rouvel star. 91 min. In French with English subtitles.
53-7152 *$59.99*

The Elusive Corporal (1962)
Jean Renoir directs this passionate account of a Frenchman, captured by the Nazis, who dreams of being back in Paris. A great film. Jean-Pierre Cassel, Claude Brasseur. 109 min. Dubbed in English.
09-1415 Was $29.99 *$24.99*

The Little Theatre Of Jean Renoir (1969)
Renoir wrote, directed and served as host for this delightful quartet of fables, ranging from a bittersweet look at a bum standing outside a fancy restaurant and an operatic salute to an electric floor waxer to a tender love ballad and a most unusual love triangle. The cast includes Jeanne Moreau, Nino Fornicola, Marguerite Cassan, Pierre Olaf, Fernand Sardou. 100 min. In French with English subtitles.
53-7250 *$59.99*

Please see our index for these other Jean Renoir titles: *Diary Of A Chambermaid • The Southerner*

Brigitte Bardot

Le Trou Normand (1952)
Sentimental Gallic farce about a village simpleton who inherits an inn, but must pass his grade school exam first. French comic Bourvil stars; look for Brigitte Bardot in her film debut. AKA: "Crazy for Love." 82 min. In French with English subtitles.
53-7016 *$29.99*

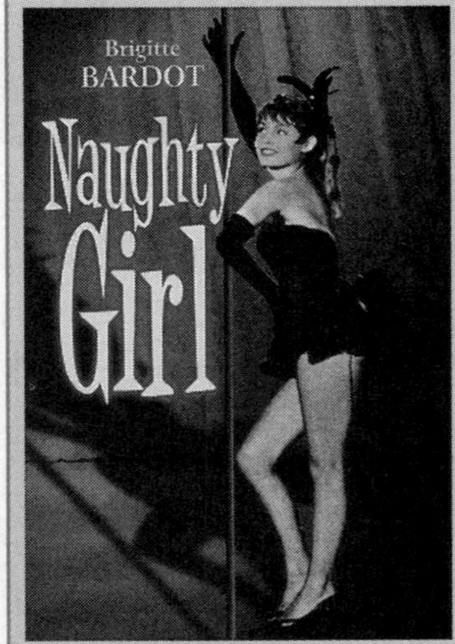

Naughty Girl (Cette Sacrée Gamine) (1956)
And when it came to racy French films in the '50s, that title could mean only one thing: the gorgeous Brigitte Bardot! Here she plays the bored daughter of a Parisian nightclub owner. Entrusted to the care of a lounge singer, Bardot winds up involved with counterfeiters and on stage in sizzling dance numbers. Jean Bretonniere, Bernard Lancret also star. AKA: "Mam'zelle Pigalle," "That Naughty Girl." 83 min. In French with English subtitles.
08-8849 Letterboxed *$14.99*

That Naughty Girl (Dubbed Version)
Also available in a dubbed-in-English edition.
77-7014 *$19.99*

Plucking The Daisy (1956)
Paris schoolgirl Brigitte Bardot anonymously pens a steamy best-seller, prompting her father to ship her to a convent. Not even her sheltered new home can keep Bardot out of trouble, as she teases men throughout Europe and eventually turns stripper. Includes the original theatrical trailer. AKA: "Mademoiselle Striptease," "Please, Mr. Balzac." 99 min. In French with English subtitles.
22-6047 Letterboxed *$19.99*

Her Bridal Night (1956)
In this sparkling romantic farce, a young Brigitte Bardot plays the beautiful girl chosen for a magazine layout by fashion entrepreneur Louis Jourdan. The layout's bridal theme prompts Bardot and Jourdan to get closer and romantic sparks fly. AKA: "The Bride Is Much Too Beautiful." 85 min. Dubbed In English.
53-6084 Was $19.99 *$14.99*

And God Created Woman (1957)
The original spicy French drama that brought gorgeous Brigitte Bardot to American audiences. Here the beautiful Bardot plays a bored young wife who cavorts with her brother-in-law and a handsome millionaire on the sunny shores of St. Tropez. With Jean-Louis Trintignant, Curt Jurgens; Roger Vadim directs. 91 min. In French with English subtitles.
67-5042 Letterboxed *$19.99*

And God Created Woman (Dubbed Version)
Also available in a dubbed-in-English edition.
47-1001 *$19.99*

Une Parisienne (1958)
Brigitte Bardot turns in a turned-on performance as the sexy daughter of the Premier of France newly married to her father's aide. When she thinks hubby is cheating on her, Bardot tries to do the same with elderly prince Charles Boyer at a posh Riviera resort, but the tryst falls apart when they both develop head colds. With Henri Vidal. 99 min. In French with English subtitles.
22-6048 Letterboxed *$19.99*

The Night Heaven Fell (1958)
Brigitte Bardot is a young woman living in a convent who helps con artist Stephen Boyd elude authorities while she is vacationing in Spain. The two start a steamy relationship, but if Bardot only knew Boyd killed her uncle and seduced her aunt, things would be different. Alida Valli and Cantinflas also star; Roger Vadim directs. 91 min. In French with English subtitles.
22-6049 Letterboxed *$19.99*

Come Dance With Me (Do You Want To Dance With Me?) (1959)
A thriller/sex comedy with Brigitte Bardot absolutely gorgeous as a woman involved in a murder plot with her feuding dentist husband, his shrewish new girlfriend and Bardot's suspicious father. When her hubby becomes a chief suspect in the case, Bardot goes undercover to help him. With Henri Vidal, Dawn Addams. AKA: "Sexy Girl." 91 min. In French with English subtitles.
08-8848 Letterboxed *$14.99*

Please Not Now! (1961)
Sexy hi-jinks meet screwball laughs in this romantic romp featuring Brigitte Bardot as a model whose boyfriend leaves her for an American heiress. Following the couple to a ski resort, Bardot gets her revenge with the help of a wild toboggan ride, a loony swami, and a good old-fashioned custard pie fight. Also included is a sizzling nude dance sequence. With Michel Subor, Claude Brasseur. AKA: "La Bride Sur le Cou," "Only for Love." 89 min. In French with English subtitles.
08-8850 Letterboxed *$14.99*

Le Repos Du Guerrier (1962)
Lovely Brigitte Bardot shines in this French drama by then-husband Roger Vadim, detailing the doomed love affair between a young woman and her suicidal lover. With Robert Hossein. AKA: "Warrior's Rest." 100 min. In French with English subtitles.
10-3172 *$19.99*

Viva Maria! (1965)
Spirited, rip-roaring comedy starring Brigitte Bardot as the daughter of an Irish anarchist who joins circus performer Jeanne Moreau in a song-and-dance act that takes them across South America. The pair are touched by the impoverished conditions they see there and become revolutionaries in order to help their cause. George Hamilton also stars; Louis Malle directs. 119 min. In French with English subtitles.
12-2862 *$19.99*

A Coeur Joie (1967)
Everyone's favorite French pastry, the lovely Brigitte Bardot, stars in this farcical tale of marital infidelity and its repercussions. 100 min. In French with English subtitles.
10-3169 *$19.99*

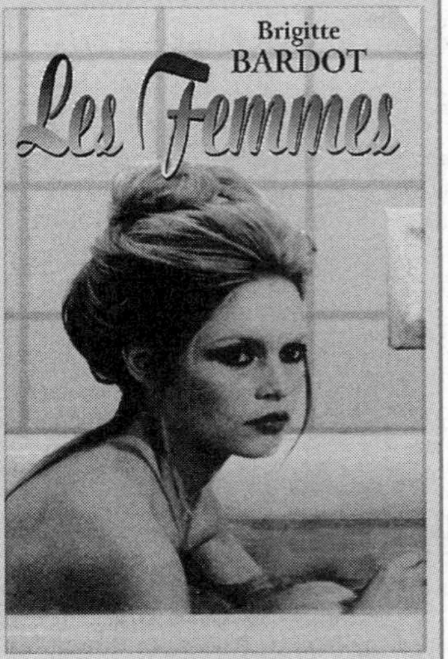

Les Femmes (The Women) (1969)
Brigitte Bardot stars in this Gallic romp as the new secretary for idea-starved author Maurice Ronet, who finds inspiration for both his writings and his romantic fantasies with his free-spirited employee. Annie Duprey, Christina Holm also star; directed by Jean Aurel. 86 min. In French with English subtitles.
08-8847 *$14.99*

The Women (Les Femmes) (Dubbed Version)
Also available in a dubbed-in-English edition.
48-1107 Was $59.99 *$14.99*

Don Juan (Or If Don Juan Were A Woman) (1973)
Brigitte Bardot and ex-husband Roger Vadim reteamed for this sexy, distaff spin on the Don Juan legend. While confessing to her cousin, a priest, Bardot recounts her life story and talks about the many men she seduced and led to their downfall. With Jane Birkin, Mathieu Carrière. AKA: "Ms. Don Juan." 94 min. In French with English subtitles.
20-1004 Letterboxed *$19.99*

Ms. Don Juan (Dubbed Version)
Also available in a dubbed-in-English edition. 90 min.
67-5043 *$19.99*

The Brigitte Bardot Collection
Along with "Come Dance with Me," "Les Femmes," "Naughty Girl" and "Please Not Now!," this boxed collector's set also includes the exclusive documentary "Brigitte Bardot...Take One," featuring Bardot's life story in her own words, rare newsreel footage and film clips, and narration by Julie Delpy.
08-8851 Save $10.00! *$49.99*

Please see our index for these other Brigitte Bardot titles: *Dear Brigitte • Doctor At Sea • Helen Of Troy • Rum Runners • Shalako • Spirits Of The Dead • A Very Private Affair*

Seven Deadly Sins (1952)
Top French and Italian filmmakers and performers collaborated on this anthology film about the seven deadly sins (plus one). Lust, greed, laziness and more are stylishly covered by such directors as Yves Allegret, Jean Dreville, Roberto Rossellini and others. Gerard Philipe, Michelle Morgan star. 113 min. In French and Italian with English subtitles.
55-9005 Was $69.99 *$19.99*

The Seven Deadly Sins (1961)
Following in their predecessors' footsteps, a second group of European filmmakers (Claude Chabrol, Philippe De Broca, Jacques Demy, Jean-Luc Godard, Eugene Ionesco, Edouard Molinaro, Roger Vadim and others) took on Man's fatal flaws with this seven-part collection of witty, satirical vignettes. Jean-Pierre Aumont, Claude Berri, Eddie Constantine, Micheline Presle star. 113 min. In French with English subtitles.
53-6490 Letterboxed *$29.99*

Liebelei (1932)
Max Ophuls' first big success is a gorgeously filmed tale of romance and codes of honor in late 19th-century Vienna. A handsome soldier finds love with the daughter of a violinist, but discovers his past affair with a baroness coming back to haunt him. With Magda Schneider (Romy's mother), Wolfgang Liebeneiner. 82 min. In German with English subtitles.
53-8610 Was $39.99 *$24.99*

La Signora Di Tutti (1934)
Early film from Max Ophuls benefits from Isa Miranda's star-making performance as young woman whose life is compromised by the attraction that she holds for men. 90 min. In Italian with English subtitles.
53-7309 Was $59.99 *$29.99*

De Mayerling A Sarajevo (Mayerling To Sarajevo) (1940)
Before he went to the U.S., Max Ophuls ("La Ronde") completed this account of the relationship between Archduke Franz-Ferdinand and his wife, Countess Sophie, and how their assassination led to World War I. The film focuses on their aristocratic lifestyle and the opposition they met from the Austro-Hungarian court. With John Lodge, Edwige Feuillére. 89 min. In French with English subtitles.
01-1521 *$29.99*

La Ronde (1950)
A film which started an often-imitated cinematic style, this elaborate, lively satire on sexual behavior follows lovers and the loveless in majestic Viennese manors. Max Ophuls directs; with Simone Simon, Simone Signoret and Danielle Darrieux. 97 min. In French with English subtitles.
22-5784 *$29.99*

Le Plaisir (House Of Pleasure) (1951)
The brilliant Max Ophuls directs three classic stories by Guy de Maupassant: "La Maison Tellier," "Le Masque" and "Le Modele." With Danielle Darrieux, Jean Gabin and Pierre Brasseur. 95 min. In French with English subtitles.
53-7050 Was $29.99 *$19.99*

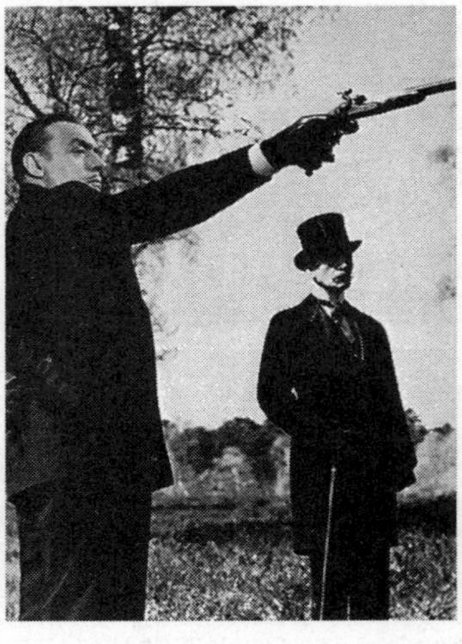

The Earrings Of Madame De... (1954)
Max Ophuls' lavish costume drama that traces a 18th-century French countess's doomed affair with a handsome diplomat, and how the titular baubles, sold by the countess, keep turning up at pivotal moments. Danielle Darrieux, Charles Boyer, Vittorio De Sica star. 105 min. In French with English subtitles.
10-7445 Was $39.99 *$19.99*

Lola Montes (1955)
Lush romantic drama that was filmmaker Max Ophuls' last work. Martine Carol is mesmerizing as the 19th-century courtesan whose lovers included composer Franz Liszt and King Ludwig I of Bavaria, living out her final years sharing her life story in a travelling circus. Co-stars Peter Ustinov, Will Quadflieg. 110 min. In French with English subtitles.
53-6332 *$29.99*

Liliom (1935)
Charming French fantasy, directed by Fritz Lang, that was the original inspiration for Rodgers and Hammerstein's beloved "Carousel." Charles Boyer is a man taken to Heaven after he dies and placed before a celestial trial in order to gain his wings. Original French-language version; no subtitles.
17-3077 *$29.99*

Carnival In Flanders (1936)
Lushly rendered and utterly charming satire from Jacques Feyder concerning the 17th-century conquest of a Flemish village by Spanish invaders. The seductive wiles of the female townsfolk save the day after the men turn tail and run! 90 min. In French with English subtitles.
01-1378 *$24.99*

Club Des Femmes (1936)
The lives and destinies of several women, all residents of a "women only" hotel, are examined in this masterpiece of storytelling. With Danielle Darrieux and Elsie Argel. 90 min. In French with English subtitles.
53-7029 Was $39.99 *$29.99*

The Man From Nowhere (1937)
Engaging comedy classic, adapted from Pirandello's "The Late Mathias Pascal," concerning a meek librarian who gets another shot at life when his domineering wife and mother-in-law believe he's been killed. Pierre Blanchar, Ginette LeClerc star; Pierre Chanal directs. 98 min. In French with English subtitles.
53-9043 *$59.99*

La Maternelle (1933)
A moving French drama, set in a day care nursery in Paris' Montmartre slum district, focuses on the growing relationship between a nurse and a young girl abandoned by her prostitute mother. Madeleine Renaud, Paulette Elambert star in Jean Benoit-Levy and Marie Epstein's emotionally gripping film. AKA: "Children of Montmartre." 83 min. In French with English subtitles.
01-1464 *$29.99*

Mauvaise Graine (1933)
The first film Billy Wilder directed (with Alexander Esway) outside of Germany concerns a young Parisian who has his car taken from him and sold by his tough physician father. Deciding to steal another auto, he's seen by a gang of car thieves and soon joins them, falling in love with a gang member's sister. With Danielle Darrieux, Pierre Mingand. 77 min. In French with English subtitles.
53-8611 Was $39.99 *$24.99*

Le Golem: The Legend Of Prague (1935)
Classic fantasy tale set in old Prague, where a vicious dictator rules his Jewish constituents with an oppressive hand. The Jews call on the Golem, a giant, destructive clay statue, to defend them and put an end to the dictator's ways. Harry Baur, Roger Carl and Charles Dorat star; directed by Julien Duvivier. 96 min. In French with English subtitles.
53-7499 *$59.99*

The Charterhouse Of Parma (1948)
Based on the acclaimed novel by Stendhal, this story concerns a young Archbishop whose love for a young woman makes him think of leaving the Church. But his aunt, who happens to be secretly in love with him, will stop at nothing to have him continue his life of celibacy. Gérard Philipe, René Faure star. In French with English subtitles.
87-1005 Was $69.99 *$49.99*

The Story Of A Cheat (1936)
One of the most acclaimed French films of all time, writer/director/star Sacha Guitry's witty dark comedy follows an elderly gentleman at a Parisian sidewalk cafe as he looks back (via dialogue-free flashbacks) on a life filled with schemes and cons from which he prospered. With Marguerite Moreno, Jacqueline Delubac. 83 min. In French with English subtitles.
53-8072 *$59.99*

Panique (Panic) (1946)
Moody crime drama from Julian Duvivier was the first filming of George Simenon's novel, remade as 1990's "Monsieur Hire." Michel Simon stars as a Parisian loner suspected of killing a young woman. He gets involved with a beautiful neighbor whose husband knows more about the crime than she leads on. With Viviane Romance and Paul Bernard. 96 min. In French with English subtitles.
01-1239 Was $29.99 *$19.99*

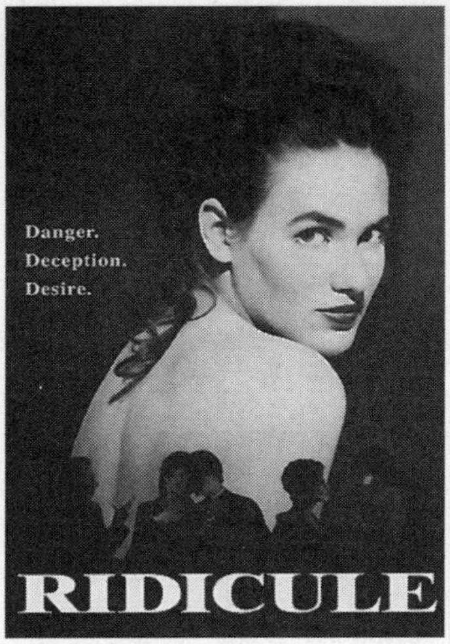
Danger.
Deception.
Desire.
RIDICULE

Ridicule (1996)
Beautifully produced satire of aristocratic society set in and around the court of Louis XVI shortly before the French Revolution and centering on a young engineer who uses his razor-sharp wit to mix with Versailles' movers and shakers in order to get help for his sick countrymen. Charles Berling, Fanny Ardant star; Patrice Leconte ("Monsieur Hire") directs. 103 min. In French with English subtitles.
11-2123 Was $94.99 *$19.99*

Beaumarchais The Scoundrel (1996)
Swashbuckling epic based on the true story of legendary French playwright Pierre-Augustin Caron de Beaumarchais. Among his numerous exploits were writing the story for "The Marriage of Figaro," spying on Great Britain for King Louis XV, and joining Benjamin Franklin in the American Revolution. Stars Fabrice Luchini, Michel Serrault and Manuel Blanc. 100 min. In French with English subtitles.
53-6205 *$94.99*

Overseas (1992)
Acclaimed drama which looks at the lives, loves and dreams of three sisters living in French-ruled Algeria in the mid-1950s. One sibling yearns for a man's company while her naval officer husband is away; another runs a vineyard while her husband reads; and the third sister is a nurse who ignores her boyfriend's wish to marry. Marianne Basler, Nicole Garcia star. 96 min. In French with English subtitles.
53-7685 Was $89.99 *$19.99*

Chasing Butterflies (La Chasse Aux Papillons) (1993)
Set in and around two chateaux in a French village, Otar Iosseliani's droll comedy tells of the chateaux' eccentric residents. In one lives an elderly woman and her energetic cousin; an obsessively clean realtor and his smarmy son occupy the other. A series of unusual occurrences play parts in the story. 115 min. In French with English subtitles.
53-8330 *$79.99*

Diary Of A Seducer (1995)
Romantic intrigue, suspense and dark humor all play a part in writer/director Daniele Dubroux's offbeat tale about a bored psychology student (Chiara Mastroianni, daughter of Marcello Mastroianni and Catherine Deneuve, in her film debut) whose life takes a strange turn when she reads a copy of Kierkegaard's "Diary of a Seducer" belonging to a fellow student. Melvil Poupaud, Jean-Pierre Leaud also star. 95 min. In French with English subtitles.
53-9885 Was $89.99 *$19.99*

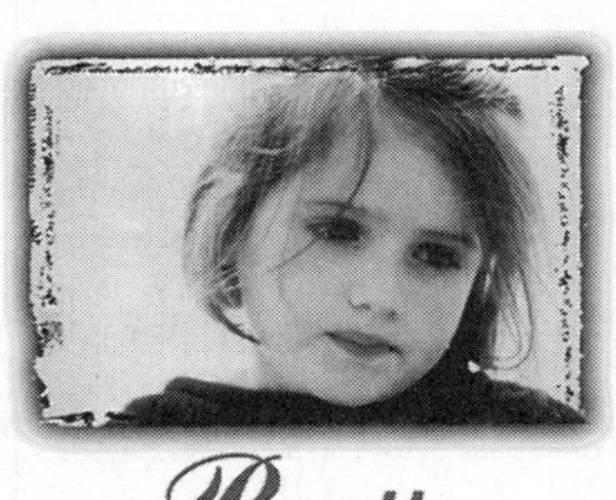
Ponette

Ponette (1996)
After her mother is killed in an auto accident, a 4-year-old girl struggles to come to terms with the reality of her death, a struggle that becomes harder when her father sends the child away to live with relatives. Writer/director Jacques Doillon's emotional drama features an outstanding performance by young Victorie Thivisol in the title role. 92 min. In French with English subtitles.
53-9989 Was $89.99 *$29.99*

Van Gogh (1993)
Daring portrait of the legendary Dutch painter from director Maurice Pialat ("A Nous Amour") concerning Van Gogh's inspirations for his work, as well as his turbulent personal life and emotional problems. Jacques Dutronc and Alexandra London star. 155 min. In French with English subtitles.
02-2490 Was $89.99 *$19.99*

La Petite Apocalypse (1993)
A Polish writer is little prepared for the culture clash that erupts when he leaves his homeland and moves to France, only to wind up living in his ex-wife's attic, in this satire from director Costa-Gavras. Pierre Aditti, Andre Dussollier and Czech filmmaker Jirí Menzel star. 110 min. In French with English subtitles.
53-6473 *$19.99*

La Vie De Bohéme (1993)
From Aki Kaurismäki, the acclaimed director of "Leningrad Cowboys Go America" and "The Match Factory Girl," comes this darkly humorous story of three struggling artists—an Albanian painter, a French poet and an Irish composer—who share their miseries, loves and dreams while sharing a cramped Paris apartment. Matti Pellonpää stars. 100 min. In French with English subtitles.
53-7993 Was $89.99 *$19.99*

Un Coeur En Hiver (1993)
A beautiful concert violinist involved in an affair with an instrument repairman finds herself attracted to her lover's mild-mannered friend. This intense, lyrical drama stars Daniel Auteuil and Emmanuelle Béart and was directed by Claude Sautet ("A Simple Story"). 100 min. In French with English subtitles.
63-1632 Was $89.99 *$14.99*

La Sentinelle (1992)
Unusual and provocative thriller from director Arnaud Desplechin tells of a student studying medicine who discovers a severed, mummified head in his luggage upon returning home from a trip. The student soon becomes obsessed with trying to determine the origin of his find. Emmanuel Salinger stars in this acclaimed suspenser. 139 min. In French with English subtitles.
53-6538 Was $89.99 *$19.99*

Barjo (1992)
Adapted from a novel by Philip K. Dick ("Blade Runner"), this off-kilter tale from director Jerome Boivin ("Baxter") focuses on a promiscuous wife and mother whose home life is disrupted when her weird, UFO-obsessed brother moves in. Anne Brochet, Hippolyte Girardot and Richard Bohringer star. 85 min. In French with English subtitles.
53-7929 Letterboxed *$19.99*

The Elegant Criminal (1992)
Based on a true story, this compelling French drama tells of a 19th-century French aristocrat whose murder trial held the nation's attention as much for the shocking nature of his crimes as for his debonair, charismatic attitude. Daniel Auteuil, Jean Poiret, Jacques Weber star. 120 min. In French with English subtitles.
53-7724 Was $89.99 *$19.99*

Cross My Heart (1992)
Compassionate coming-of-age tale focusing on a boy in the eighth grade who tries to keep his mother's death a secret in order to avoid being sent to a state orphanage. When his two friends learn of the boy's predicament, they help him by signing his report cards, learning to cook and shielding him from adults. Sylvain Copans stars. 105 min. In French with English subtitles.
53-7780 Was $89.99 *$19.99*

Tom And Lola (1992)
A one-of-a-kind fantasy about a pair of children who have been isolated since birth because of damaged immune systems. The nude, hairless children form a supernatural bond together in a quest to find a new world and also encounter a 12-year-old boy who thinks they are space aliens. Cecile Magnet and Marc Barman star. 98 min. In French with English subtitles.
78-5061 *$69.99*

Jean-Luc Godard

Godard/Truffaut Shorts (1957)
A double bill of early shorts from two giants of French cinema. Godard's "All the Boys Are Named Patrick" follows a young man's loves and infidelities, while "Les Mistons" by Truffaut looks at a group of teens who, mystified by romance, decide to follow a pair of lovers. 39 min. total. In French with English subtitles.
53-7035 *$29.99*

Breathless (1958)
Seminal early French New Wave film features Jean-Paul Belmondo as a small-time crook on the run after he kills a policeman, with Jean Seberg as his American girlfriend he calls on to hide him from authorities. Jean-Luc Godard directs; from a story idea by François Truffaut. 89 min. In French with English subtitles.
08-5061 Was $29.99 *$24.99*

A Woman Is A Woman (1961)
When her live-in lover refuses her request to marry and raise a family together, a stripper pretends to fall for another man in order to make him jealous. Lighthearted menage a trois tale from writer/director Jean-Luc Godard stars Anna Karina (then Mrs. Godard), Jean-Paul Belmondo, Jean-Claude Brialy. 80 min. In French with English subtitles.
53-7251 Was $59.99 *$29.99*

My Life To Live (1963)
One of Godard's cinematic breakthroughs stars Anna Karina as a woman whose separation from her husband prompts her hand as an artist, then as a prostitute. Divided into 12 various segments, the film showcases such Godardian touches as jump-cuts, long takes and allusions to other films and literary works. With Saddy Rebbot, Gerard Hoffman. AKA: "Vivre Sa Vie." 85 min. In French with English subtitles.
50-1133 Was $59.99 *$29.99*

Band Of Outsiders (1964)
Two bumbling burglars are coaxed by a female acquaintance into robbing her rich aunt, but problems mount almost immediately in this fast-paced thriller by Jean-Luc Godard that blends Hollywood crime drama clichés, slapstick comedy and romance. Anna Karina, Claude Brasseur, Sami Frey star. 97 min. In French with English subtitles.
53-7003 Was $29.99 *$24.99*

Le Gai Savoir (1965)
In one of his most experimental and controversial films, scripter/director Jean-Luc Godard adapts Jean Jacques Rousseau's "Emile" into a two-person drama that breaks the language of cinema down to its basic elements. Jean-Pierre Leaud, Juliet Berto star. 96 min. In French with English subtitles.
53-7641 *$39.99*

Pierrot Le Fou (1965)
Filmed without a script "improv"-style at each day's shooting, Jean-Luc Godard's acclaimed and introspective drama follows a bored family man (Jean-Paul Belmondo) who flees with his lover (Anna Karina) when a dead gangster turns up in her apartment. Haunting, poetic drama with an unforgettable ending also stars Dirk Sanders; look for director Sam Fuller playing himself. 110 min. In French with English subtitles.
53-9104 Letterboxed *$29.99*

Alphaville (1965)
Jean-Luc Godard's offbeat, stylish blend of American private eye thrillers and European science fiction stars Eddie Constantine as detective Lemmy Caution, whose latest case involves retrieving a scientist headquartered on a mysterious computer-ruled planet. With Akim Tamiroff, Anna Karina, Howard Vernon. 100 min. In French with English subtitles.
22-5857 Letterboxed *$29.99*

Alphaville (Dubbed Version)
Also available in a dubbed-in-English edition.
50-1203 *$19.99*

Two Or Three Things I Know About Her... (1966)
Jean-Luc Godard's fascinating study of 24 hours in the life of a woman and a city, focusing on bourgeois housewife Marina Vlady, who leads a double life. One day a week she leaves her husband and young child in the suburbs and works as a prostitute in downtown Paris. Anny Duperey, Roger Montsoret star. 84 min. In French with English subtitles.
53-8622 Letterboxed *$89.99*

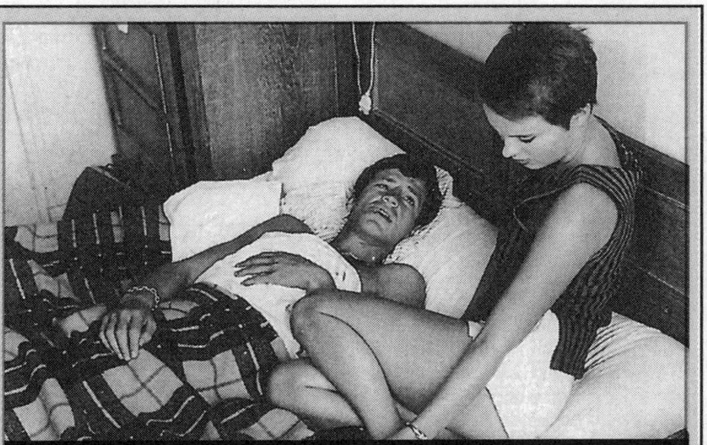
Breathless

Masculine-Feminine (1966)
In his film salute to the then-nascent '60s "youth culture," writer/director Jean-Luc Godard depicts the turbulent affair between writer Jean-Pierre Leaud (Truffaut's "Antoine Doinel" films) and would-be rock singer Chantal Goya in mod Paris. 103 min. In French with English subtitles.
62-1213 *$19.99*

Weekend (1967)
Jean-Luc Godard's celebrated attack on bourgeoisie values, the Vietnam War and boring filmmaking follows a couple's weekend journey which is interrupted by a massive traffic jam that leads the drivers to violence, rape, political diatribes and other surprises. With Mirielle Darc, Jean Yanne, Jean-Pierre Leaud. 105 min. In French with English subtitles. End of synopsis.
53-7596 Was $79.99 *$29.99*

Ici Et Ailleurs (Here And Elsewhere) (1970)
This collaboration between Ann-Marie Miville and Jean-Luc Godard began in 1970 as a documentary chronicling the Palestinian uprising through footage shot in Middle East camps. But following a massacre by Jordanian forces, the filmmakers decided to study how video captures history by focusing on a French family watching the events on TV. 55 min. In French with English subtitles.
53-9676 *$59.99*

Numero Deux (1975)
Jean-Luc Godard uses experimental techniques, mixing video with numbered film sequences, to examine three generations of a middle-class family in France and how their sexual drives and emotions relate to political and social factors. Pierre Oudry and Sandrine Battistella star. 88 min. In French with English subtitles.
53-9675 *$59.99*

Comment Ca Va? (How's It Going?) (1976)
Jean-Luc Godard looks at the inner workings of a Communist-leaning newspaper where the boss and staff decide to make a video called "How Communists Manufacture Information." The story leads Godard to comment on the media and technology by introducing layers of video imagery. With Ann-Marie Miéville. 78 min. In French with English subtitles.
53-9677 *$59.99*

Passion (1983)
This comedy on the nature of filmmaking stars Jerzy Radziwilowicz as a director determined to make the ultimate artistic film. Complications mount when he begins affairs with two different women and his movie begins to fall apart. Directed by Jean-Luc Godard. 88 min. In French with English subtitles.
53-6186 Was $49.99 *$19.99*

First Name: Carmen (1983)
A spontaneous mix of slapstick, eroticism and deep thoughts, Jean-Luc Godard's irreverent satire of "Carmen" stars Maruschka Detmers as a femme fatale who plans to rob a bank while pretending to film a movie. Godard himself appears in his first comedy as a once-great director now confined to a local madhouse. 85 min. In French with English subtitles.
53-7300 *$19.99*

Detective (1985)
Director Jean-Luc Godard intertwines two tales of money, murder, prizefighting and gangsters—all set in a French resort hotel—in this stylized salute to classic Hollywood crime dramas. Presented in a non-linear style of storytelling, the film also offers Godard's views on modern life in France. Nathalie Baye, Claude Brasseur, Johnny Hallyday and Jean-Pierre Leaud star. 95 min. In French with English subtitles.
53-6187 Was $49.99 *$19.99*

For Ever Mozart (1996)
Once again blurring the line between art and reality, director Jean-Luc Godard presents the absurdist travails of a veteran filmmaker who travels with his family and colleagues to the war-weary city of Sarajevo, Bosnia. Hoping to put on a production of a play by Alfred de Musset, the company meets with crises ranging from personal feuds to capture by armed forces. Madeleine Assas, Ghalia Lacroix, Vicky Messica star. 85 min. In French with English subtitles.
53-6353 *$89.99*

The Godard Collection
The innovative filmmaker is feted with a collector's set of six of his greatest works: "Detective," "First Name: Carmen," "My Life to Live," "Passion," "Pierrot Le Fou" and "A Woman Is a Woman."
53-6604 Save $30.00! *$119.99*

Please see our index for these other Jean-Luc Godard titles: *Aria • RoGoPaG • Six In Paris*

Head Against The Wall (1958)
The first non-documentary feature by Georges Franju ("Eyes Without a Face") concerns a psychiatrist whose new patient has been institutionalized in an asylum for defying his wealthy, manipulative father. The subject gave Franju an opportunity to delve into the harrowing state of mental health in France at the time. Pierre Brasseur, Anouk Aimee star. AKA: "The Keepers." 95 min. In French with English subtitles.
10-6018 **$19.99**

Be Beautiful, But Show Up! (1957)
Comic caper film about a blonde sweetie who takes the rap for a jewel robbery after the car used in the heist is found by police. An inspector attracted to the woman poses as a hood to win her over and learn the real story behind the robbery. Henri Vidal, Mylene Domeneot, Jean-Paul Belmondo, Alain Delon and Roger Hanin star. AKA: "Just Another Pretty Face." Dubbed in English.
79-6508 **$19.99**

Cafe Au Lait (1994)
One part François Truffaut and one part Spike Lee, this warm and funny French comedy follows a West Indian woman living in Paris who is pregnant, but doesn't know which of her two lovers (a black Muslim law student or a rapping Jewish bike messenger) is the father. Writer/director/co-star Mathieu Kassovitz's modern menage also stars Julie Mauduech, Hubert Kounde. 94 min. In French with English subtitles.
53-8615 **$89.99**

La Separation (1994)
Penetrating drama stars Daniel Auteuil as a children's book illustrator and dedicated father to his young son who gets a rude awakening when live-in companion Isabelle Huppert tells him that she is romantically involved with another man. Director Christian Vincent focuses on how Auteuil deals with this devastating confession. 85 min. In French with English subtitles.
53-6528 **$89.99**

Marcel Pagnol

Marius (1931)
Alexander Korda directs the first of Marcel Pagnol's "Marseilles Trilogy," which introduces the many delightful and fascinating characters of the city's waterfront and their tangled relationships. Stars Jules Raimu, Orane Demazis and Pierre Fresnay. 125 min. In French with English subtitles.
01-1123 **$39.99**

Fanny (1932)
In the second part of the "Marseilles Trilogy," Marius (Pierre Fresnay) answers the call of the sea, abandoning Fanny (Orane Demazis) with his child, while Cesar (Raimu) plays matchmaker; Marc Allegret directs Pagnol's charming screenplay. 126 min. In French with English subtitles.
01-1113 Was $39.99 **$19.99**

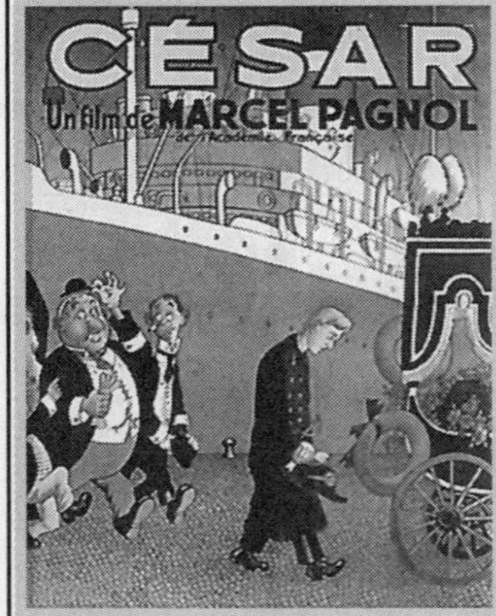

Cesar (1936)
Pagnol himself directed the final film in his trilogy, in which the characters come to grips with tragedy and separation. The entire series was later remade as the 1961 film "Fanny." 117 min. In French with English subtitles.
01-1111 **$39.99**

The Fanny Trilogy
Marcel Pagnol's lyric film series consisting of "Marius," "Fanny," and "Cesar" is available in a special collectors' set.
53-7579 **$99.99**

Angèle (1934)
Moving melodrama of country life about a simple girl who shames her family with a Marseilles pimp and is imprisoned by her father in the cellar. Notable for Marcel Pagnol's innovative location shooting; with Oriane Demazis, Fernandel and Jean Sevais. 150 min. In French with English subtitles.
53-7248 **$59.99**

Topaze (1935)
Pagnol's first self-produced rendering of his hit play (a result of his anger at Hollywood's script doctoring of the 1932 version) benefits from sterling performances by Louis Jouvet as the mousy professor-turned-cocky mountebank and Edwige Feuillère as his boss' intrigued mistress. 92 min. In French with English subtitles.
53-7310 **$59.99**

Topaze (1951)
A straight-arrow school teacher is fired from his job for being "too honest" and winds up finding satisfaction as an unscrupulous businessman. Marcel Pagnol directs from his own play, with Fernandel and Helene Perdriere. 90 min. In French with English subtitles.
53-7054 **$29.99**

Harvest (1937)
The sole inhabitant of a deserted French farming community falls in love with a young woman he rescues in the woods, and together they bring the village and its fields back to life, in this lyrical Marcel Pagnol drama, based on Jean Giono's novel. Gabriel Gabrio, Orane Demazis and Fernandel star. AKA: "Regain." 103 min. In French with English subtitles.
01-1314 **$59.99**

The Baker's Wife (1938)
A charming Pagnol fable about a simple country baker whose debut in a new town is spoiled when his younger wife runs away with a local shepherd. His steadfast (and unfounded) belief in his bride's fidelity becomes the marvel and blessing of the whole village. Raimu and Ginette Leclerc star. 130 min. In French with English subtitles.
53-7195 **$59.99**

Le Schpountz (1938)
A bumbling village grocer is the victim of a prank by a film crew shooting in his town and arrives at their Paris studio ready to become a movie star. Hilarious and endearing comedy from Marcel Pagnol stars Fernandel, Charpin, Odette Roger. AKA: "Heartbeat." 135 min. In French with English subtitles.
53-8179 **$59.99**

The Well-Digger's Daughter (1941)
Insightful and heart-rending French drama made under the steady hand of filmmaker Marcel Pagnol that revolves around a pregnant woman (Josette Day) abandoned by her aviator lover and rejected by her unsparing father. 142 min. In French with English subtitles.
01-1313 **$29.99**

Letters From My Windmill (1954)
A trilogy of humorous, touching tales from 19th-century writer Alphonse Daudet, adapted for the screen by Marcel Pagnol. A gourmand clergyman is tempted by the Devil on Christmas Eve, a group on monks save their order by making liqueur, and a miller tries to stave off a mechanized competitor. 134 min. In French with English subtitles.
01-1312 **$59.99**

Jean De Florette (1986)
The first of two epic dramas from Claude Berri based on Marcel Pagnol's novels. Moving with his family to a small provincial town to claim a family farm, the hunchbacked Jean (Gerard Depardieu) is tricked by a greedy landowner (Yves Montand) who blocks the spring that waters his land, yet Jean refuses to be driven away. With Daniel Auteuil, Elisabeth Depardieu. 122 min. In French with English subtitles.
73-1019 **$19.99**

Manon Of The Spring (1986)
Claude Berri's acclaimed companion piece to "Jean de Florette" stars Emmanuelle Béart as Jean's now-grown daughter and details how her discovery of the plot against her father leads to a fitting vengeance...and a startling revelation. Yves Montand, Daniel Auteuil, Hippolyte Girardot also star. 112 min. In French with English subtitles.
73-1020 **$19.99**

My Father's Glory (1991)
Author Marcel Pagnol's childhood reminiscences about life in the South of France at the turn of the century make up this bittersweet look at the joys and pains of growing up. Yves Robert's film focuses on a boy's relationship with his schoolteacher father and his adventures at the family's summer home in the mountains. Phillippe Caubere, Nathalie Roussel star. 110 min. In French with English subtitles.
73-1117 Was $79.99 **$19.99**

My Mother's Castle (1991)
The continuation of Marcel Pagnol's adventures begun in "My Father's Glory" follows the young protagonist's experiences in a prestigious school, his Christmas in the country, and how his family trespasses on a private road en route to their holiday home. Phillippe Caubere, Nathalie Roussel star. 98 min. In French with English subtitles.
73-1118 Was $79.99 **$19.99**

Le Bourgeois Gentilhomme (1958)
The timeless comedy of "nouveau riche" pretentiousness by Moliere is performed in this hilarious, music-filled show from the famed Comèdie Française troupe. 97 min. In French with English subtitles.
09-1276 Was $29.99 **$19.99**

Miracle Of Saint Therese (1959)
Inspirational French drama follows the brief but meaningful life of St. Theresa of Lisieux, a Carmelite nun who moved everyone around her with her faith and devotion until her death in 1897 at the age of 24. Frances Descaut, Jean Debucourt star. 90 min. Dubbed in English.
55-9018 **$29.99**

Maria Chapdelaine (1934)
This love triangle set against the harshness of the Canadian Yukon established Jean Gabin as a major star. Gabin is the trapper vying with Jean-Pierre Aumont for Madeleine Renaud's affections. PLEASE NOTE: Print quality varies, but this is the finest extant. 75 min. In French with English subtitles.
01-1376 **$29.99**

La Bandera (1935)
Fleeing from his native France, accused murderer Jean Gabin joins the Spanish Foreign Legion. In a strife-torn region of North Africa, he finds solace with Arab beauty Annabella, but a relentless police officer is soon on Gabin's trail, in this compelling and romantic adventure. AKA: "Escape from Yesterday." 98 min. In French with English subtitles.
87-1018 **$69.99**

Pepe Le Moko (1937)
The first film version of the story of famed Algerian criminal Le Moko, played by Jean Gabin. In his hideaway in the Casbah, he eludes police, but a beautiful woman proves to be his undoing. 90 min. In French with English subtitles.
09-1957 **$19.99**

Grisbi (1953)
The model for many French New Wave films that followed, this superb crime drama stars Jean Gabin as an aging gangster who agrees to one last robbery, but is undone by the jealousy and treachery of his colleagues and their women. Jeanne Moreau, Lino Ventura also star; directed by Jacques Becker. AKA: "Honour Among Thieves," "Touchez Pas Au Grisbi." 94 min. In French with English subtitles.
53-9820 **$19.99**

Four Bags Full (1956)
Jean Gabin stars as a rogue in WWII Germany transporting a slaughtered pig (in four suitcases!) from a butcher to the black market, trying to avoid watchful Nazis and other pitfalls along the way. Serio-comic gem questioning wartime morality also stars Bourvil. 82 min. In French with English subtitles.
62-1274 **$29.99**

Les Miserables (1957)
Inspiring and rarely seen rendition of Victor Hugo's classic novel, with Jean Gabin as Jean Valjean, a petty thief who tries desperately to put the past behind him while Police Inspector Javert relentlessly pursues him. Also stars Daniele Delorme and Bernard Blier. 240 min. Dubbed in English.
10-1190 Was $39.99 **$29.99**

Le Cas Du Dr. Laurent (1958)
Intriguing and effective film stars Jean Gabin as a country doctor who faces persecution for his advocacy of natural childbirth. The actual birth sequences which garnered this film so much notoriety are frankly and affectingly handled; Nicole Courcel, Sylvia Monfort co-star. 93 min. In French only.
10-7238 Was $29.99 **$24.99**

Le Gentleman D'Epsom (1962)
Sly French spoof of high society with Jean Gabin ("Grand Illusion") as the wily Duke who fleeces his wealthy friends at the racetrack. 83 min. In French with English subtitles.
10-3170 **$19.99**

La Horse (Erbarmungslos) (1970)
Based on a true story, this powerful French drama stars Jean Gabin as a strong-willed farm owner who must defend his land and his family from a gang of heroin traffickers. With Udo Kier, Dominique Zardi; directed by Pierre Granier Deferre. 100 min. In French with English subtitles.
87-1019 **$69.99**

A Jury Of One (1974)
This gripping drama stars Sophia Loren as the mother of a young man accused of murdering a young girl. In order to free her son, Loren kidnaps the sickly wife of an influential judge. A number of surprising complications lead to a stunning ending in this film from director Andre Cayette. With Jean Gabin, Michel Albertini. AKA: "The Verdict." 95 min. Dubbed in English.
59-7099 **$89.99**

Le Chat (1975)
Jean Gabin and Simone Signoret are an elderly married couple whose relationship has soured. Gabin's feelings for Signoret are transferred to his cat in this penetrating study which won several international awards. 90 min. In French with English subtitles.
10-9763 **$14.99**

L'Annee Sainte (1978)
The great French actor Jean Gabin's last film casts him as a gangster from the old school who escapes from jail with a friend and attempts to recover stolen cash in Rome. On the way there, however, the crooks discover that their plane is being hijacked by international terrorists. In French with English subtitles.
87-1004 Was $79.99 **$39.99**

Tati Double Feature
Two early short films starring French comic master Jacques Tati. Tati's attempt to start a tourist bus service goes awry in "Gai Dimanche" (1931), and he plays a farmhand-turned-boxer in "Swing to the Left" (1936). 54 min. total. French language; no subtitles.
53-7475 **$24.99**

Jour De Fete (1948)
Comic genius Jacques Tati is captured at his finest in his feature debut. Tati portrays a village postman who is determined to make his service state-of-the-art, but whose blundered attempts to do so drive the townsfolk crazy! 79 min. In French with English subtitles.
53-1686 **$29.99**

Sylvia And The Phantom (1950)
A young girl staying in a haunted family castle is wooed by the ghost of her grandmother's former lover in this whimsical French comedy. Jacques Tati and Odette Joyeux star. 93 min. In French with English subtitles.
22-5759 Was $29.99 **$24.99**

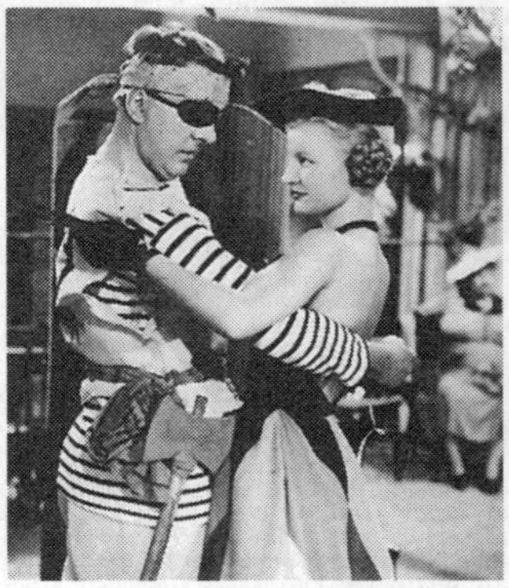

"Mr. Hulot's Holiday"

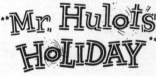

Mr. Hulot's Holiday (1954)
Writer/director Jacques Tati introduced his most famous character, the always bemused and odd-walking Mr. Hulot, in this hilarious, classic homage to silent screen comedy. A peaceful seaside resort turns into chaos when Hulot arrives, trying hard to relax. The sparse dialogue in the film is not central to the plot and is in French. 85 min.
22-5648 **$24.99**

Mon Oncle (1958)
French comic genius Jacques Tati harkens back to the days of silent farce in this delightful look at one man's struggles against modern society, as Mr. Hulot tries to cope with life in his brother-in-law's fully-mechanized house while teaching some valuable lessons to his young nephew. 110 min. In French with English subtitles.
22-5758 **$29.99**

My Uncle (Dubbed Version)
Also available in a dubbed-in-English edition.
53-1480 **$19.99**

Playtime (1967)
A financial failure upon its first release, but now recognized as a gem of film comedy, creator/star Jacques Tati's spoof of 20th-century city life follows Gallic Everyman Mr. Hulot on a dizzying trip through contemporary Paris, where he gets caught up with a group of American tourists and becomes the unwitting cause of a new "high-tech" nightclub's destruction. Some of the sparse dialogue was written by Art Buchwald. Restored, 120-minute version. In French with English subtitles.
22-5872 Letterboxed **$29.99**

Traffic (1971)
The driving of a new, gadget-laden camping vehicle from the Paris factory to an Amsterdam auto show should be an easy task, but when Mr. Hulot (director/co-writer/star Jacques Tati) gets behind the wheel, the result is one comic calamity after another. Maria Kimberly, Marcel Fraval co-star. 89 min. Dubbed in English.
22-5757 Letterboxed **$29.99**

Parade (1974)
Mostly silent comic gem, courtesy of France's legendary Jacques Tati, follows the misadventures of two children who go behind the scenes at a provincial circus. Director Tati also appears as a harried circus performer. 88 min. In French; no subtitles.
22-5440 Restored **$29.99**

The Hypothesis Of The Stolen Painting (1978)
Innovative Chilean-born filmmaker Raul Ruiz directed this black-and-white mystery about an art collector's attempt to find a missing work by 19th-century French artist Frederic Tommerre. Filled with unusual visuals and gorgeous cinematography; the tape includes "Dog's Dialogue," a short by Ruiz. 78 min. In French with English subtitles.
70-3156 *$59.99*

Life Is A Dream (1986)
Filmmaker Raul Ruiz takes the 17th-century play about a young prince, who discovers that all of existence is a dream that one only awakens from at death, and transplants the theme to a contemporary tale of a movie-obsessed Chilean revolutionary whose real memories and reel memories are becoming more inseparable. Sylvain Thirolle, Roch Leibovici star. AKA: "Mémoire des Apparences." 100 min. In French with English subtitles.
87-7009 *$59.99*

Three Lives And Only One Death (1996)
The legendary Marcello Mastroianni plays four different characters in a quartet of stories by writer/director Raul Ruiz. A salesman leaves his wife and has a surprising meeting with her new husband 20 years later; a professor-turned-beggar befriends an unusual hooker; a young couple inherit both a mansion and a mysterious butler; and a businessman is visited by an imaginary family. Anna Galiena, Melvil Poupaud, Chiara Mastroianni also star. 123 min. In French with English subtitles.
53-9912 *$89.99*

Genealogies Of A Crime (1998)
In this thriller from iconoclastic director Raul Ruiz, a dark and stormy night brings together a group of psychiatrists trying to solve the murder of an analyst. The evening eventually leads to an investigation into reincarnation and revenge beyond the grave. Catherine Deneuve plays both an inquisitive lawyer and the dead analyst. With Michel Piccoli. 113 min. In French with English subtitles.
78-9026 *$79.99*

The Crazy Stranger (Gadjo Dijo) (1998)
Eager to find the woman whose taped singing has captivated him, a young Frenchman ventures into the vibrant, insular Gypsy community of rural Romania and is taken under the wing of an elderly musician with his own plans for the stranger. A moving, song-filled salute to Gypsy culture from Algerian-born director Tony Gatlif, the film stars Romain Duris, Isidor Serban. 97 min. In French and Romany with English subtitles.
53-6548 *$89.99*

Un Aire De Famille (Family Resemblances) (1996)
Celebrating with acerbic and dark humor the universal nature of dysfunctional families, director Cedric Klapisch ("When the Cat's Away") follows a birthday gathering for the sister of a Paris cafe owner that quickly devolves into backbiting, dredging up old feuds, and alcohol-fueled revelations. Jean-Pierre Bacri and Agnes Jaoui (who wrote the play this film is based on) star; with Catherine Frot, Claire Maurier. 105 min. In French with English subtitles.
53-6420 Was $89.99 *$19.99*

Forbidden Games (1952)
A touching drama focusing on a girl who loses her parents in an air raid and is taken in by a poor family. Brigitte Fossey stars as the girl and George Poujouly is the family's son who befriends her. René Clément directed; winner of the 1952 Oscar for Best Foreign Film. 102 min. In French with English subtitles.
53-1694 *$29.99*

Gervaise (1956)
Set in 19th-century Paris, René Clément's powerful adaptation of Emile Zola's story centers on a young mother who struggles against poverty and her husband's alcoholism to raise her children in a noble fashion. Maria Schell and Francois Perier star. 121 min. In French with English subtitles.
22-5783 *$29.99*

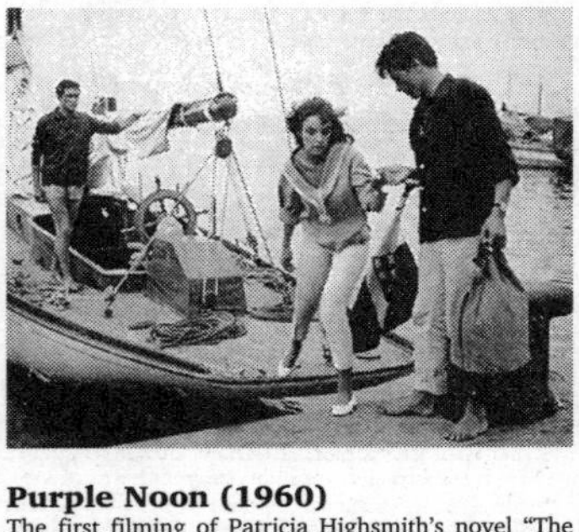

Purple Noon (1960)
The first filming of Patricia Highsmith's novel "The Talented Mr. Ripley" was this "sea noir" thriller by director Rene Clement. Alain Delon is the ne'er-do-well who befriends playboy Maurice Ronet and is hired by Ronet's father to shepherd him home from Italy. Delon hatches a scheme to claim Ronet's money and identity for himself. With Marie Laforet. AKA: "Blazing Sun," "Plien Soliel." 125 min. In French with English subtitles.
11-2086 Was $94.99 *$19.99*

François Truffaut

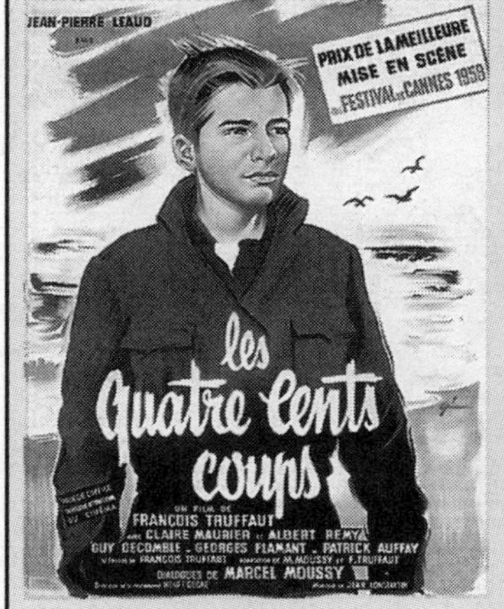

The 400 Blows (1959)
François Truffaut's debut feature directorial work, and the first of his "Antoine Doinel" series, stars Jean-Pierre Leaud as 12-year-old Doinel, who begins a life of petty crime in response to a troubled home life, until he uses his inner strength to overcome his situation. 98 min. In French with English subtitles.
22-5518 Was $39.99 *$29.99*

Les Mistons (1957)/ Antoine & Colette (1962)
Two François Truffaut rarities are offered on this tape. "Les Mistons" is a 17-minute short about a group of boys who follow an older woman with whom they are infatuated; Gerard Blain stars. And Jean-Pierre Leaud's Antoine Doinel is in love with music student Marie-France Pisier in "Antoine & Colette," a 30-minute segment from the anthology film "Love at 20." 47 min. In French with English subtitles.
53-6526 *$19.99*

Stolen Kisses (1968)
The cinematic life story of Antoine Doniel (Jean-Pierre Leaud) continues in Truffaut's third installment. Released from the army, Doniel takes jobs as a hotel clerk, detective, shoe salesman and a TV repairman and romances different women, including a boss's wife, before reuniting with his true love. With Delphine Seyrig and Claude Jade. 90 min. In French with English subtitles.
53-6524 *$19.99*

Bed And Board (1970)
Franccois Truffaut's fourth Antoine Doinel comedy finds Doinel getting married, becoming a father, having an affair with a Japanese woman and trying to patch up his troubled marriage with his childhood sweetheart. Claude Jade and Hiroko Berhauer also star. 100 min. In French with English subtitles.
53-6525 *$19.99*

Love On The Run (1979)
The final entry in Truffaut's semi-autobiographical Antoine Doinel film series finds Doinel (Jean-Pierre Leaud) in his 30s and a recent divorcé, but still a romantic and in search of "true love." Marie-France Pisier co-stars. 95 min. In French with English subtitles.
22-5520 Letterboxed *$29.99*

Shoot The Piano Player (1960)
An important early film from the French New Wave, François Truffaut's dark mystery stars Charles Aznavour as a concert pianist-turned-bar musician involved with the underworld. With Marie Dubois. 84 min. In French with English subtitles.
22-5540 Letterboxed *$29.99*

Jules And Jim (1961)
Truffaut's lushly moving look at three people in love...with each other. Their ups and downs over the years make for a memorable "menage a trois" that goes beyond most conventional relationships. Jeanne Moreau, Oskar Werner, Henri Serre star. 105 min. In French with English subtitles.
22-5524 Letterboxed *$29.99*

The Soft Skin (1964)
Jean Desaily and Françoise Dorleac star as illicit lovers in François Truffaut's tense, moody look at a businessman's extramarital affair. The relationship eventually ends, but Desaily's problems compound when his wife discovers his infidelity. 120 min. In French with English subtitles.
22-5525 Letterboxed *$29.99*

The Bride Wore Black (1968)
Paying homage to Alfred Hitchcock, François Truffaut spins a suspenseful story of a woman (Jeanne Moreau) tracking down and killing the five men who accidentally murdered her fiancé on their wedding day. Jean-Claude Brialy, Charles Denner co-star. 107 min. In French with English subtitles.
12-2261 *$19.99*

Mississippi Mermaid (1969)
Suspenseful Truffaut film about a wealthy tobacco planter (Jean-Paul Belmondo) whose mail-order bride (Catherine Deneuve) leaves him, taking with her his money. After hiring a detective to track her down, Belmondo finds her himself...or does he? 110 min. In French with English subtitles.
12-2266 *$19.99*

The Wild Child (1970)
Engrossing François Truffaut drama, based on a true story, follows an orphaned boy who is found living in the woods in 18th-century France. Unable to communicate, the child is to be sent to an asylum until a doctor takes him in and tries to educate him. Jean-Pierre Cargol plays the feral boy cut off from the world, and Truffaut appears as his mentor. 86 min. In French with English subtitles.
12-2271 *$19.99*

Two English Girls (1972)
Lyrical, beautifully photographed Truffaut study of a pair of English sisters (one artistic and liberated, the other a moody idealist) who both fall for a young Parisian recuperating at their seaside home. Jean-Pierre Leaud, Kika Markham, Stacey Tendeter star. 108 min. In French with English subtitles.
22-5519 Letterboxed *$29.99*

Day For Night (1973)
Winner of the Best Foreign Film Oscar, this engrossing character study details the lives of a cast and crew filming a love story. Truffaut is featured as, naturally, the film's director, obsessed with controlling the actors on- and off-camera. Jacqueline Bisset, Valentina Cortese and Jean-Pierre Leaud also star. 120 min. Dubbed in English.
19-1122 *$59.99*

The Story Of Adele H. (1975)
A haunting true story of romantic obsession, François Truffaut's elegant drama stars Isabelle Adjani as the daughter of author Victor Hugo, vainly pursuing the soldier who broke off their engagement while writing endlessly of love in her journals. Bruce Robinson, Sylvia Marriott co-star. 97 min. In French with English subtitles.
12-2269 *$19.99*

Small Change (1976)
François Truffaut's salute to the innocence and wisdom of children, this wistful comedy/drama looks at the lives, joys and problems of the youngest residents of a small French town. The non-professional cast of child actors adds to the film's charm. 104 min. In French with English subtitles.
12-2268 *$19.99*

The Green Room (1979)
Inspired by the writings of Henry James, François Truffaut directs and stars in this story of an obituary writer for a magazine in post-WWI Paris who continually worships the memory of his deceased wife. Eventually, he meets a woman who tries to show him what he's missing from life. With Nathalie Baye. 94 min. In French with English subtitles.
12-2561 *$19.99*

The Last Metro (1981)
François Truffaut's look at the lives and loves of the members of a Paris theatre troupe during World War II. Catherine Deneuve plays the group's boss and lead actress, who shelters her Jewish husband from the Nazis in the theatre basement, but finds herself falling for fellow actor Gerard Depardieu. Jean Poiret, Heinz Bennent co-star. 135 min. In French with English subtitles.
22-5521 Letterboxed *$29.99*

The Woman Next Door (1981)
Two former lovers, both now married to others, find they are new neighbors, and they cannot help renewing their passionate, painful affair. Gerard Depardieu and Fanny Ardant star in François Truffaut's masterful study of obsessive emotion. 106 min. In French with English subtitles.
22-5523 Letterboxed *$29.99*

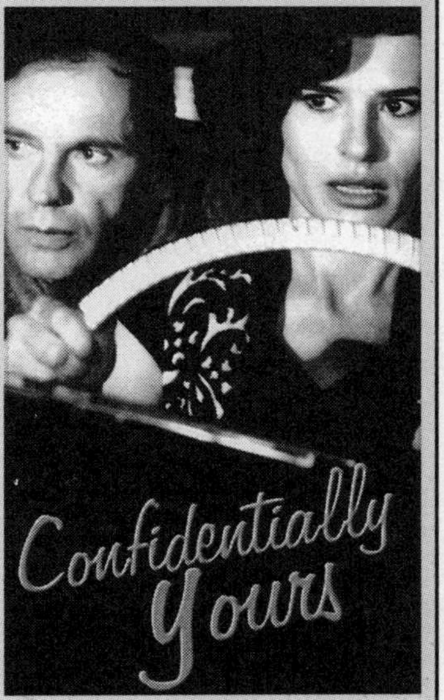

Confidentially Yours (1983)
When businessman Jean-Louis Trintignant is framed for the murder of his wife and her lover, secretary Fanny Ardant steps in, complete with trench coat, to clear her boss. François Truffaut's last film, a delightful paean to Hitchcock and '40s "film noir," is a stylized, witty romp. 110 min. In French with English subtitles.
22-5522 Was $29.99 *$19.99*

François Truffaut: Stolen Portraits (1993)
The director who helped create the French "New Wave" of the '50s and '60s and who went on to become one of the world's best-known filmmakers is the focus of this revealing documentary. Clips from such Truffaut classics as "The 400 Blows," "Stolen Kisses" and "The Woman Next Door," interviews with Gerard Depardieu, Eric Rohmer and other colleagues and friends, and archival footage of Truffaut help chronicle the man and his movies. 93 min.
53-8404 Was $89.99 *$19.99*

François Truffaut Collection I
The acclaimed French director is feted with a special collection of six of his best films: "Confidentially Yours," "The 400 Blows," "The Last Metro," "Love on the Run," "Shoot the Piano Player" and "Two English Girls."
53-6553 Save $20.00! *$119.99*

François Truffaut Collection II
This six-tape collection of works by François Truffaut includes "Bed and Board," "Jules and Jim," "Les Mistons/Antoine & Colette," "The Soft Skin," "Stolen Kisses" and "The Woman Next Door."
53-6527 Save $10.00! *$119.99*

Please see our index for the François Truffaut title: ***Fahrenheit 451***

Love Etc. (1996)
After meeting through a personals ad, pretty art restorer Charlotte Gainsbourg and shy bank clerk Yvan Attal fall in love and marry. Things become complicated when Attal's best friend, teacher and ladies' man Charles Berling, decides he's in love with Gainsbourg as well in Marion Vernoux's ménage a trois comedy/drama, based on Julian Barnes' "Talking It Over." 105 min. In French with English subtitles.
53-6758 *$89.99*

Nelly And Monsieur Arnaud (1996)
This tender, bittersweet romance from director Claude Sautet stars Michel Serrault as a middle-aged French businessman who hires beautiful young Emmanuelle Béart to type his memoirs. The gentle relationship that grows between the unlikely pair is threatened when Béart falls for Serrault's editor. 103 min. In French with English subtitles.
53-8815 Was $89.99 *$29.99*

My Sex Life (Or How I Got Into An Argument) (1996)
A Parisian assistant professor of philosophy who's been working for years to finish his dissertation finds that his personal life is becoming as complicated as his professional life. Acclaimed seriocomic look at the romantic foibles of French twentysomethings from director/co-scripter Arnaud Desplechin stars Mathieu Amalric, Emmanuelle Devo. 178 min. In French with English subtitles.
53-9985 Letterboxed *$19.99*

Salut Cousin! (1996)
A country bumpkin from Algeria arrives in Paris to grab a suitcase of dresses for the family business back home. He hooks up with his cousin, an urbanized immigrant with dreams of becoming a rap star. When the suitcase is lost, a series of comic misadventures in the City of Lights ensues. Gad Elmaleh and Mess Hattow star in this farce. 90 min. In Algerian and French with English subtitles.
82-5050 *$79.99*

French Twist (1996)
Funny French sex romp about a dancer-turned-housewife who decides to teach her philandering husband a lesson by inviting her new lover, a lesbian disc jockey, to live with them. Zesty and erotic situations abound in this farce. With Victoria Abril, Alain Chabat and Josiane Balasko, who also directed. 100 min. In French with English subtitles.
11-2043 *$94.99*

Late August, Early September (1998)
Called "a French 'Big Chill'" by critics, director Olivier Assayas' essay on friendship, love and mortality chronicles a year in the life of struggling writer Mathieu Amalric and his social circle. Among the group: ex-flame Jeanne Balibar, unstable new lover Virginie Ledoyen, and fellow author François Cluzet, who is faced with a serious illness. 112 min. In French with English subtitles.
53-6741 Letterboxed *$89.99*

The Holes (1973)
Gerard Depardieu, Philippe Noiret and Charles Denner star in this fun-filled farce about the day a group of tourists, some policemen, and a few buildings are suddenly swallowed up by the ground in Paris. 92 min. Dubbed in English.
79-1001 *$14.99*

Vincent, Francoise, Paul And The Others (1975)
Three men come to depend on their friendship and their sense of humor as they all try to cope with the onset of middle age in this charming Gallic serio-comedy by Claude Sazutet. Yves Montand, Michel Piccoli, Stephane Audran and Gerard Depardieu star. 118 min. In French with English subtitles.
53-7323 Was $29.99 *$19.99*

Barocco (1976)
A taut and twisting noir-flavored drama from France, starring Gerard Depardieu as a crook who kills his double and takes over all aspects of the man's life, including girlfriend Isabelle Adjani, with whom he launches a blackmail scheme against a local politician. With Marie-France Pisier, Jean-Claude Brialy. 102 min. In French with English subtitles.
53-8109 Was $79.99 *$29.99*

This Sweet Sickness (1977)
An obsessive man designs a house with hopes of persuading his now-married childhood girlfriend to live there. At the same time, another woman remains in love with the man while he ignores her. Gerard Depardieu and Miou-Miou star. 105 min. In French with English subtitles.
70-3278 Letterboxed *$24.99*

Bye Bye Monkey (1978)
The first English-language film from Italian director Marco Ferreri ("La Grande Bouffe") is a typically off-the-wall satire of capitalism, sexual politics and modern society, set in a grimy Manhattan neighborhood. James Coco plays a museum owner, with Gerard Depardieu as Coco's assistant, who becomes part of a feminist group's rape revenge scheme, and Marcello Mastroianni as a man who wills his pet chimpanzee a fortune. Geraldine Fitzgerald, Mimsy Farmer also star. 94 min.
50-5622 *$19.99*

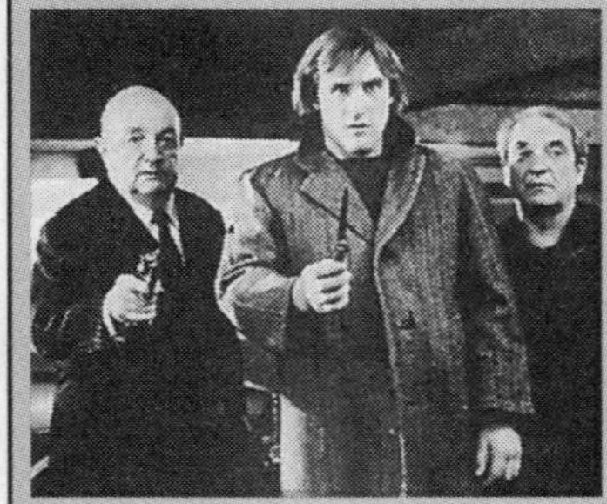

Buffet Froid (1980)
Anarchic and hilarious thriller stars Gerard Depardieu as a death-obsessed drifter drawn into an absurd murder plot featuring a bureaucrat who plans his own assassination, a missing knife that turns up in a subway rider's belly, and a killer who's afraid of the dark. Surreal direction from Bertrand Blier; Bernard Blier, Michel Serrault also star. 95 min. In French with English subtitles.
53-7247 Was $59.99 *$19.99*

Loulou (1980)
Isabelle Huppert and Gerard Depardieu star in Maurice Pialat's unusual romance about a woman who leaves her middle-class husband for a free-spirited jock she meets in a Paris disco. Rich in characterization and erotic content, the film also stars Guy Marchand. 110 min. In French with English subtitles.
53-7384 Was $89.99 *$29.99*

La Chevre (1981)
Before the hit "Les Comperes," Gerard Depardieu and Pierre Richard teamed up in this slapstick Gallic comedy as two bumblers assigned to bring home the missing daughter of a business mogul. 91 min. In French with English subtitles.
75-1001 *$69.99*

The Return Of Martin Guerre (1983)
A young man leaves his 16th-century French village and comes back years later, but is it really him? An unforgettable romantic mystery based on a true story, rich in period flavor and highlighted by magnetic performances from Gerard Depardieu and Nathalie Baye. Restored director's version; 123 min. In French with English subtitles.
53-1273 Letterboxed *$29.99*

Tartuffe (1984)
Moliere's masterpiece serves as an awesome directorial debut for Gerard Depardieu, who also stars as the charismatic charlatan who manipulates a merchant and his family, makes passes at the man's wife and disrupts the daughter's engagement. Francois Perier and Elizabeth Depardieu also star in the classic satire of religious and sexual hypocrisy. 140 min. In French with English subtitles.
53-7557 *$79.99*

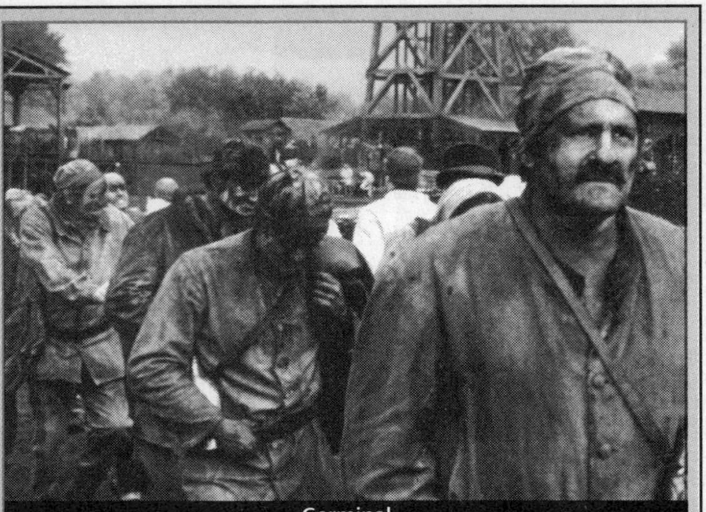

Germinal

Gerard Depardieu

Fort Saganne (1984)
An epic adventure saga starring Gerard Depardieu as a French peasant who joins the Foreign Legion and is assigned to a remote post in the Sahara Desert. Although he is denied a promotion to officer because of his background, Depardieu becomes a fearless leader. Catherine Deneuve, Philippe Noiret and Sophie Marceau co-star. 180 min. In French with English subtitles.
53-8021 Was $89.99 *$29.99*

Police (1985)
Gerard Depardieu is a tough but understanding cop who falls in love with the girlfriend of an Algerian drug dealer and finds the more involved he becomes with the woman, the closer his ties get to the underworld. Sophie Marceau and Sandrine Bonnaire also star; directed by Maurice Pialat ("A Nos Amour"). 113 min. In French with English subtitles.
53-7595 Was $79.99 *$29.99*

Under The Sun Of Satan (1987)
A film of conflict and contrast, Maurice Pialat's allegorical drama stars Gerard Depardieu as a 1920s village priest whose obsession with the power of evil leads him into a bizarre encounter with a mysterious stranger. Jean-Christophe Bouvet, Sandrine Bonnaire co-star. 98 min. In French with English subtitles.
53-7322 Was $79.99 *$29.99*

Camille Claudel (1989)
Isabelle Adjani earned an Academy Award nomination for her moving portrayal of the sculptress whose collaboration/love affair with Auguste Rodin ended in bitterness, paranoia and madness. Gerard Depardieu co-stars as Rodin in Bruno Nuytten's stirring biodrama. 149 min. In French with English subtitles.
73-1089 Was $79.99 *$19.99*

Cyrano De Bergerac (1990)
The hardest-working man in French show business, Gerard Depardieu, shines in his acclaimed portrayal of Rostand's large-nosed poet, swordsman, social gadfly and unlikely romantic hero. This lavish French production of the classic drama also stars Anne Brochet as Roxanne, Vincent Perez and Jacques Weber. 138 min. In French with English subtitles.
73-1108 Was $89.99 *$19.99*

Uranus (1991)
Director/co-scripter Claude Berri's compelling and thought-provoking drama is set in a small French town after World War II. A local businessman and a bar owner put their reputations, their careers and their lives on the line when they help a friend and ex-German collaborator hide from government officials. Jean-Pierre Marielle, Gerard Depardieu, Michel Blanc and Philippe Noiret star. 100 min. In French with English subtitles.
44-1908 Was $89.99 *$19.99*

All The Mornings Of The World (Tous Les Matins Du Monde) (1993)
Award-winning French drama, set in the 17th century, follows a reclusive composer who takes an outgoing student under his wing, only to find to his protégé disrupting his life...and the lives of his two daughters. Gerard Depardieu, Jean-Pierre Marielle, Anne Brochet star. 110 min. In French with English subtitles.
11-1779 Was $89.99 *$19.99*

Germinal (1994)
Claude Berri's epic, based on Emile Zola's novel, stars Gerard Depardieu as a rugged mine worker who faces strikes, mine cave-ins, political strife and low wages as he attempts to make a living for his wife and seven children. Miou-Miou, Renaud and Jean Carmet also star. 160 min. In French with English subtitles.
02-2657 Was $89.99 *$19.99*

Colonel Chabert (1994)
Ten years after being wounded in the devastating 1807 Battle of Eylau, army officer Gerard Depardieu returns to Paris in hopes of continuing his life. But when he discovers that his wife has claimed his fortune, has remarried, and fails to recognize him as her former husband, Depardieu hires a dynamic lawyer to seek justice. Fanny Ardant co-stars in this adaptation of Honoré de Balzac's novel. 111 min. In French with English subtitles.
63-1762 Was $89.99 *$14.99*

A Pure Formality (1995)
A wicked cat-and-mouse thriller from director Giuseppe Tornatore ("Cinema Paradiso") pits police inspector Roman Polanski against murder suspect Gerard Depardieu, who claims to be a noted author but cannot prove his identity. As Depardieu is interrogated by Polanski, lies, secrets and distortions are revealed. With Sergio Rubini. 107 min. In French with English subtitles.
02-2840 *$89.99*

The Machine (1996)
High-tech Gallic spin on the Jekyll/Hyde story, starring Gerard Depardieu as a psychiatrist/inventor whose latest device, a brain transfer machine, merges his mind with that of a patient of his—a homicidal psychopath—and puts everyone around him in deadly danger. With Nathalie Baye, Didier Bourdon. 96 min. In French with English subtitles.
02-8587 Was $94.99 *$14.99*

The Machine (Dubbed Version)
Also available in a dubbed-in-English edition.
02-8588 Was $94.99 *$14.99*

The Count Of Monte Cristo (1998)
One of the world's best-loved adventure classics is brought to life in this French mini-series. Gerard Depardieu stars as Edmund Dantes, betrayed and sent to jail for a crime he didn't commit. Escaping after many years, Depardieu uses a fabulous treasure he recovers to help him gain his revenge. Ornella Muti, Jean Rochefort also star. 480 min. on four tapes. In French with English subtitles.
53-6682 *$89.99*

Balzac: A Life Of Passion (1999)
The life and times of Honoré de Balzac come to life in this lavish French TV production featuring Gerard Depardieu as the 19th-century writer. Follow Balzac's struggles with his demanding mother (Jeanne Moreau), his romances with Madame de Berney (Virna Lisi) and the married Countess Eva Hanska (Fanny Ardant), and the creation of his epic "La Comédie Humaine." 210 min. In French with English subtitles.
53-6969 *$49.99*

Please see our index for these other Gerard Depardieu titles: *1492: Conquest Of Paradise • 1900 • Bogus • Danton • Dead Tired • Green Card • Hamlet • Jean De Florette • The Last Metro • The Man In The Iron Mask • My Father, The Hero • The Secret Agent • Unhook The Stars • The Woman Next Door*

Olivier Olivier (1993)
The disappearance of a 9-year-old French boy causes his family tremendous upheaval and leads to the father's abandonment. Six years later, a boy is found in Paris who is reported as the missing youth, but his family is suspicious of the child's identity. With François Cluzet; directed by Agnieszka Holland ("Europa Europa"). 110 min. In French with English subtitles.
02-2560 Was $89.99 *$19.99*

Between Heaven And Earth (1993)
Provocative drama focusing on a single career woman who becomes pregnant following a one-night stand. Her unborn baby tells her he doesn't want to be born, citing a world filled with turmoil, but she tries to persuade him otherwise. Carmen Maura ("Law of Desire") stars with Jean-Pierre Cassel. 80 min. In French with English subtitles.
74-3004 Letterboxed *$79.99*

The Accompanist (1994)
In France during World War II, a young pianist begins working for a glamorous opera singer with a husband adept at using people. The shy musician learns of the secrets in her mentor's life, idolizes her and begins living vicariously through her. Richard Bohringer, Elena Safonova and Romane Bohringer star; music by Schubert and Mozart. 111 min. In French with English subtitles.
02-2652 Was $89.99 *$19.99*

Pigalle (1995)
In Pigalle, the red-light district of Paris ruled by criminal gangs and populated by pimps, hookers and druggies, a love story unfolds involving a "private dancer" and her male hustler lover. This intoxicating film from writer-director Karim Dridi looks at society's castoffs and the world they call their own. Vera Briole and Francis Renaud star. 97 min. In French with English subtitles.
82-5051 *$79.99*

Thieves (Les Voleurs) (1996)
In this engrossing drama from André Téchiné, Catherine Deneuve is a philosophy professor whose involvement with a beautiful tomboy leads to danger when the tomboy seduces a cop whose family is comprised of professional car thieves. Daniel Auteuil and Laurence Cote also star. 116 min. In French with English subtitles.
02-3099 Was $94.99 *$19.99*

The Eighth Day (1996)
This sensitive drama from Belgian director Jaco Van Dormael ("Toto the Hero") focuses on Harry, a successful salesman who becomes unhinged when his wife leaves him and his children refuse to talk to him. Then he meets Georges, a young man with Down's Syndrome, and the two form a special bond that changes Harry's life forever. Daniel Auteuil, Pascal Duquenne star. 108 min. In French with English subtitles.
02-8669 Was $94.99 *$14.99*

Nais (1945)
French comic Fernandel stars in this bittersweet tale of a country hunchback in love with a beautiful country girl. Produced by Marcel Pagnol, the film mixes sentiment and comedy superbly. 105 min. In French with English subtitles.
09-2168 Was $29.99 *$24.99*

Forbidden Fruit (1952)
French comic great Fernandel tries a change-of-pace role, playing a country physician who rebels against his overbearing wife and mother by having an affair with an amoral young woman. Based on a novel by Georges Simenon, the film also stars Francoise Arnoul. AKA: "The French Touch." 94 min. Dubbed in English.
62-1365 *$19.99*

Ali Baba And The 40 Thieves (1954)
French comic Fernandel stars in this fun-filled adaptation of the Arabian Nights story. He's the thief who encounters all sorts of adventures when he discovers a cave full of treasures while trying to purchase a new wife for his mean master. Paul Misraki also stars. 92 min. In French with English subtitles.
87-1006 Was $69.99 *$29.99*

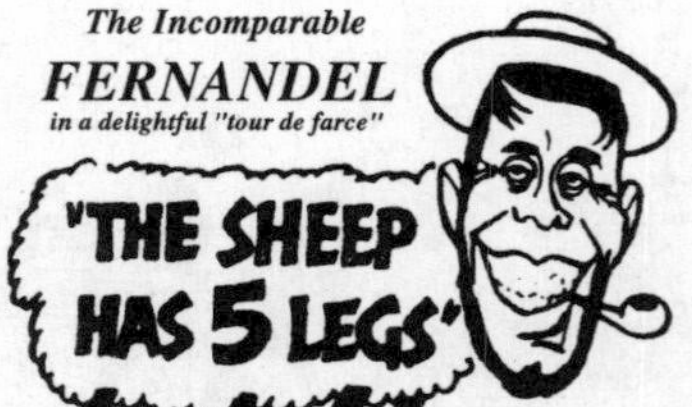

The Sheep Has Five Legs (1955)
It's "The Family Jewels," Fernandel style, as France's foremost funnyman executes a six-role tour de force. The plot concerns a plot to reunite an aged vintner with his five estranged sons: an arrogant hair dresser, a sourpussed sea dog, a mild romance columnist, a harried priest and a chronic hypochondriac. 95 min. In French with English subtitles.
01-1399 *$19.99*

The Dressmaker (1956)
Sparkling Gallic comedy of a women's couturier and his relationship with his jealous wife. With Fernandel and Suzy Delair. 92 min. In French with English subtitles.
53-7032 Was $39.99 *$24.99*

Les Anges Du Peche (1943)
The first film from cinema master Robert Bresson ("Au Hazard Balthazar") is an intense drama about a novice nun who wants to help a murderous woman find redemption. The two women are drawn to each other in different ways and for different reasons in this striking yet subtle tale. With Renee Foure, Jany Holt. AKA: "Angel of the Streets." 91 min. In French with English subtitles.
53-6264 *$29.99*

The Ladies Of The Bois De Bologne (1945)
For his second feature film, director Robert Bresson adapted (with co-scripter Jean Cocteau) a Diderot story about a woman who concocts an elaborate scheme of vengeance against her former lover, fixing him up with another woman with a dark secret in her past. Maria Casarès, Paul Bernard star. AKA: "Ladies of the Park." 83 min. In French with English subtitles.
53-6096 Was $59.99 *$24.99*

Diary Of A Country Priest (1950)
Moving French drama detailing the travails of a frail young priest as he is assigned to his first parish, a small provincial town where his devotion and fortitude are put to the test. Claude Laydu, Jean Riveyre star; directed by Robert Bresson. 120 min. In French with English subtitles.
53-7859 *$59.99*

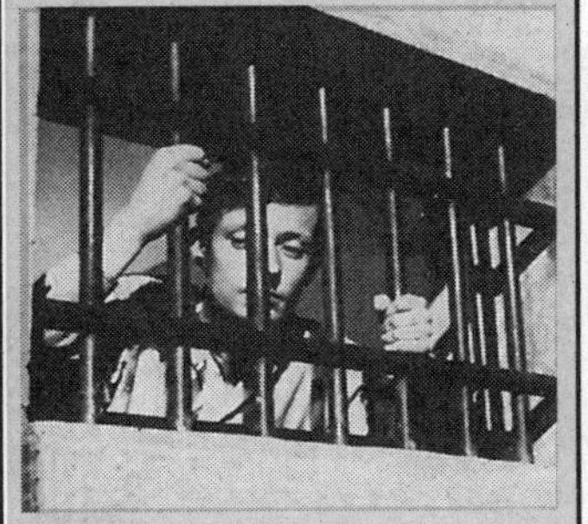

A Man Escaped (1956)
Starkly filmed true story about a French Resistance fighter imprisoned by the Nazis who plots a daring escape with a teenage cellmate. Robert Bresson directs this fascinating drama that uses shadowy atmospherics, realistic sets and non-professional actors for maximum impact. François Leterrier stars. 100 min. In French with English subtitles.
53-7967 Was $69.99 *$19.99*

Pickpocket (1959)
A young man finds himself drawn deeper and deeper into a criminal lifestyle, and neither his friends nor the woman who loves him can stop him, in Robert Bresson's powerful French New Wave crime drama. Martin Lassalle, Marika Green. 71 min. In French with English subtitles.
53-7256 Was $59.99 *$19.99*

Mouchette (1966)
The final 24 hours in the sad life of a young girl in rural France are vividly portrayed on the screen by writer/director Robert Bresson, from a brutal rape and the death of her mother to, ultimately, her suicide. Dark, emotionally gripping drama stars Nadine Nortier, Marie Cardinal. 90 min. In French with English subtitles.
53-6071 Was $59.99 *$24.99*

A Gentle Woman (Une Femme Douce) (1971)
Robert Bresson's stunning study of a young woman whose marriage to a pawnbroker leads her to contemplate his murder, then her suicide, stars Dominique Sanda (then a 20-year-old fashion model) in a striking debut as the despondent wife. With Guy Frangin. 87 min. In French with English subtitles.
53-8329 Was $79.99 *$29.99*

Lancelot Of The Lake (1975)
The final days of Camelot are given a dark depiction in this mystical costume drama from director Robert Bresson. Luc Simon plays Lancelot, who returns with the other Knights of the Round Table from the failed quest for the Holy Grail to renew his doomed affair with Guinevere. Laura Duke Condominas, Vladimir Antolek-Oresek also star. AKA: "The Grail." 80 min. In French with English subtitles.
53-8092 Was $79.99 *$29.99*

The Devil, Probably (1977)
Director Robert Bresson's compelling and controversial look at contemporary angst among France's twentysomething crowd follows the emotional, ideological and romantic travails of five young people who look for solace in activism, religion, love and drugs. Antoine Monnier, Tina Irissari star. 95 min. In French with English subtitles.
53-8813 Was $89.99 *$29.99*

L'Argent (1983)
Based on Leo Tolstoy's short story "The False Note," this harrowing drama from director Robert Bresson follows a counterfeit 500-franc bill as it passes from hand to hand, focusing on a hapless deliveryman whose life is ruined by the note. Christian Patey, Caroline Lang, Vincent Risterucci star. 82 min. In French with English subtitles.
53-7920 Was $79.99 *$29.99*

When The Cat's Away (1997)
Freewheeling Gallic comedy about a withdrawn young modeling agency assistant who returns from vacation and discovers that her cat has escaped from the eccentric neighbor who was caring for it. The woman's search through her Paris neighborhood for the missing feline turns into a wild and exciting adventure filled with colorful characters. Garance Clavel, Zinedine Soualem star. 90 min. In French with English subtitles.
02-3133 Was $99.99 *$19.99*

Will It Snow For Christmas? (1996)
The daily hardships of a French farm woman and her seven illegitimate children, who toil as virtual slaves for their domineering father and struggle to find any degree of happiness or warmth, are movingly detailed in this acclaimed debut feature from Sandrine Veysset. Dominique Reymond, Daniel Duval, Jessica Martinez star. 90 min. in French with English subtitles.
53-6351 *$89.99*

Mondo (1996)
Filled with wonder and pathos, this acclaimed film from writer/director Tony Gatlif ("Latcho Drom") follows the adventures of a 10-year-old orphaned Gypsy boy on the streets of Nice, France, and the eclectic characters he meets in his search for a family. Ovidiu Balan, Pierette Fesch star. 80 min. In French with English subtitles.
53-6348 *$89.99*

Life Of Jesus (1997)
Far from the religious drama its title implies, this powerful French drama follows the slacker-like existence of a 20-year-old epileptic man who spends his time riding around on his motorbike with his unemployed pals, and the violence that erupts when the son of an Arab family makes a play for the man's girlfriend. David Douche and Kader Chaatouf head the mostly non-professional cast. 96 min. In French with English subtitles.
53-6417 Was $89.99 *$19.99*

After Sex (Post Coitum) (1997)
A successful, married Parisian book editor (director/co-writer/star Brigitte Roüan) enters into a passionate affair with a client's roommate, a handsome engineer half her age, but her growing obsession with him threatens their relationship, her job and her family. Erotic and emotionally charged drama also stars Boris Terral, Patrick Chesnais. 97 min. In French with English subtitles.
53-6562 Letterboxed *$94.99*

Marius And Jeanette (1997)
Leftist politics and sentimental romance are blended in this disarmingly simple tale from director/co-scripter Robert Guediguian. Set in and around a shuttered factory in Marseilles, the film follows the relationship that develops between security guard Marius and Jeanette, a feisty former worker and single mother. Ariane Ascaride, Gerard Meylan star. 102 min. In French with English subtitles.
53-6637 Letterboxed *$94.99*

Western (1997)
Simple and engaging "road comedy" about a Spanish shoe salesman working in France's Brittany region who befriends a Russian immigrant...after he steals and wrecks the salesman's car. The odd couple set off on a quest to find the immigrant a woman to fall in love with and meet a variety of colorful characters along the way. Sergi Lopez, Sacha Bourdo star. 121 min. In French with English subtitles.
53-6711 Letterboxed *$89.99*

Women (Elles) (1997)
As befits its French/Portuguese co-production nature, this look at the family, job and health crises faced by a group of fortysomething friends—among them TV journalist Carmen Maura, bisexual beautician Marisa Berenson, divorced caterer Marthe Keller and widowed professor Miou-Miou (who's having an affair with Keller's son)—mixes Gallic romantic comedy and Latin drama for an emotionally compelling film. 97 min. In French with English subtitles.
53-6841 *$89.99*

A Self Made Hero (1997)
In director Jacques Audiard's audaciously dark comedy, a cowardly salesman in post-WWII France invents a past for himself as a heroic Resistance fighter and becomes an admired and successful figure. Filmmaker Mathieu Kassovitz ("Hate") stars as the chameleon-like milquetoast who gets caught up in his own false memories. 105 min. In French with English subtitles.
53-9997 Letterboxed *$89.99*

Dry Cleaning (Nettoyage A Sec) (1997)
The staid lives of a fortysomething couple who run a dry cleaning shop in a small French town are turned upside-down when they get involved with a pair of cross-dressing siblings performing at a local nightclub. And when the brother of the duo winds up taking a job at the shop and catches the eye of both the husband and wife, something's got to give. Anne Fontaine's tale of sexual tension stars Miou-Miou, Charles Berling, Stanislas Merhar. 98 min. In French with English subtitles.
78-9040 *$79.99*

The Dreamlife Of Angels (1998)
Highly praised debut effort from Eric Zonca focuses on the complex relationship between two young women in Northern France. Homeless Isa befriends Marie while at work in a garment factory. While Isa shares the apartment where Marie is housesitting, the two grow close, only to have differences drive them apart. Natacha Regnier, Elodie Bouchez star. 113 min. In French with English subtitles.
02-3360 Was $99.99 *$14.99*

Eric Rohmer

The Girl At The Monceau Bakery (1962)/Suzanne's Career (1963)
These two short films were the first chapters in French director Eric Rohmer's six-part "Moral Tales" series, which he described as "a cinema of thoughts rather than actions." A young man, mourning the absence of a woman he admired from afar, finds solace with "The Girl at the Monceau Bakery," while "Suzanne's Career" looks at two friends' rivalry over a beautiful girl. 78 min. total. In French with English subtitles.
53-8957 *$19.99*

La Collectionneuse (1966)
Set on the sunny shores of St. Tropez, Eric Rohmer's third "Moral Tales" film follows the sexual gamesmanship between a bikini-clad young beauty who enjoys adding men to her "collection" and the two older friends who struggle to overcome their baser instincts and become her latest conquests. Haydee Politoff, Patrick Bauchau star. 90 min. In French with English subtitles.
53-8528 *$19.99*

My Night At Maud's (1969)
The fourth of Eric Rohmer's "Moral Tales" stars Jean-Louis Trintignant as a devout Catholic man in love with a young woman he spies at church. Too shy to court her, Trintignant's fidelity is put to the test when he spends the night at the home of sexy, free-thinking Francoise Fabian. With Marie-Christine Barrault. 110 min. In French with English subtitles.
03-1577 Was $29.99 *$19.99*

Claire's Knee (1971)
Long before "Pauline at the Beach," Eric Rohmer explored the stormy division between love and lust with this "Moral Tales" comedy that follows the relationship between a diplomat and his fiancée while they're on vacation. Jean-Claude Brialy, Aurora Cornu star. 106 min. In French with English subtitles.
03-1562 *$19.99*

Chloe In The Afternoon (1972)
For his final "Moral Tales" installment, Eric Rohmer follows a happily married French executive through his inner struggles against the seductive charms of an old flame he meets by chance one day. Zouzou, Bernard Verley, Francoise Verley star in this whimsical story. 97 min. In French with English subtitles.
53-7148 *$19.99*

Moral Tales Boxed Set
All six of Rohmer's "Moral Tales" films are also available in a five-tape collector's set.
53-8958 Save $20.00! *$79.99*

The Marquise Of O (1976)
Based on the Heinrich von Kliest novella, this German-made drama from French filmmaker Eric Rohmer stars Edith Clever as the widowed German noblewoman who is raped in her sleep by an officer with the invading Russian army. When she learns she is pregnant, the Marquise weds the count who, unknown to her, was her assailant. Bruno Ganz, Volker Frachtel star. 102 min. In German with English subtitles.
53-6423 *$19.99*

Perceval (1978)
Fabrice Luchini essays the title role of the Arthurian knight on a quest for the Holy Grail in Eric Rohmer's lush and offbeat drama based on the medieval French poem. Shot on stylized painted sets, the film mixes theatre, mime and rhyming verse to tell its story of a young man's redemption. With Andre Dussollier, Arielle Dombsale. 140 min. In French with English subtitles.
53-6422 *$19.99*

The Aviator's Wife (1980)
Convinced that his girlfriend is cheating on him, a young man gets help from a younger girl in spying on a pilot he believes is "the other man" in this tale of romance gone awry, the first of director Eric Rohmer's "Comedies and Proverbs." Philippe Marlaud, Marie Riviére, Anne-Laure Meury star. 104 min. In French with English subtitles.
53-6421 *$19.99*

A Good Marriage (Le Beau Mariage) (1982)
Charming romantic comedy from French filmmaker Eric Rohmer about a young woman who one day decides she's bored with the single life and wants a husband...any husband. Her search for a prospective mate makes for whimsical fare. Stars Beatrice Romand, Andre Dussollier. 97 min. In French with English subtitles.
03-1499 *$19.99*

Full Moon In Paris (1984)
Lighthearted Eric Rohmer look at a young woman who feels her life is incomplete. She leaves her live-in lover to spend time by herself and "experience loneliness," only to find that things are just as bad, if not worse. Pascale Ogier, Tcheky Karyo star. 101 min. In French with English subtitles.
03-1498 Was $59.99 *$19.99*

Summer (1986)
Funny and touching comedy from director Eric Rohmer follows the travels and travails of a fiercely independent young woman in her frustrated attempts to have a pleasurable vacation...and a meaningful relationship. Marie Riviere, Vincent Gauthiere star. 98 min. In French with English subtitles.
07-8103 Was $29.99 *$19.99*

Boyfriends And Girlfriends (1988)
A witty roundelay of couplings and uncouplings between four young people in modern-day Paris provides a fitting capstone to writer/director Eric Rohmer's "Comedies and Proverbs" series. Emmanuelle Chaulet, Sophie Renoir, Eric Viellard star. 102 min. In French with English subtitles.
73-1044 *$19.99*

The Four Adventures Of Reinette And Mirabella (1989)
An episodic and at times deceptively simple comedy from Eric Rohmer, focusing on the relationship between two very different French girls (one from Paris, the other a farm lass) who become roommates. Joelle Miquel, Jessica Forde star. 95 min. In French with English subtitles.
53-7515 Was $69.99 *$29.99*

A Tale Of Winter (1994)
The second in Eric Rohmer's "Tales of the Four Seasons" (after "A Tale of Springtime") this sensual and witty film centers on Félicié, a beautiful young woman torn between two men whose life becomes even more complicated when a lover from years earlier reappears. Charlotte Véry and Hervé Furie star. 114 min. In French with English subtitles.
53-8228 *$89.99*

A Summer's Tale (1996)
A French student plans to spend the summer in a seaside town on the Brittany coast, all in hopes of running into a girl he thinks he may be in love with. Along the way, however, his friendships with a pretty waitress and another woman wind up complicating the already tenuous relationship, in director Eric Rohmer's third "Tales of the Four Seasons" film. Melvil Poupaud, Amanda Langlet, Aurelia Nolin star. 113 min. In French with English subtitles.
53-6894 *$89.99*

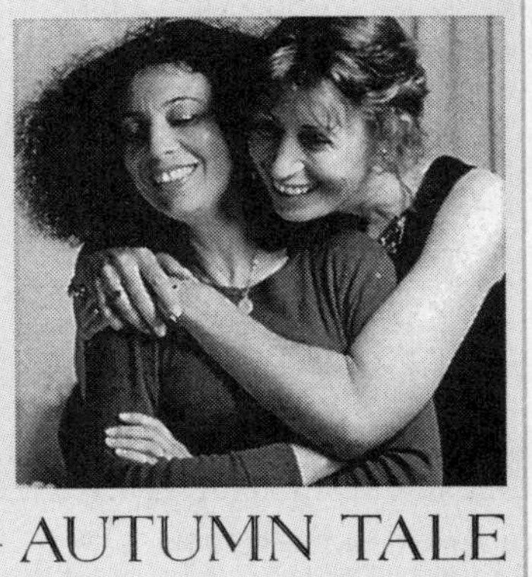

Autumn Tale (1999)
The final entry in Eric Rohmer's "Tales of the Four Seasons" series is set in Southern France, where Magali, a lonely woman who runs her family's winery, longs for male companionship. Trying to help her find a mate are friend Isabelle and Rosine, Magali's son's girlfriend, who tries to unite her with her ex-lover, a college philosophy professor. Beatrice Romand and Marie Riviere star in this sophisticated sparkler. 110 min. In French with English subtitles.
02-9168 Was $99.99 *$14.99*

Rendezvous In Paris (1996)
Eric Rohmer's anthology about romantic follies in the City of Lights tells three poignant stories: a college student arranges a date with a stranger in a cafe after learning her lover has been unfaithful; a woman has an illicit affair with a young man after she decides to leave her fiancé; and a painter on a date at the Picasso Museum falls for another woman. With Mathias Megard, Clara Bellar. 100 min. In French with English subtitles.
53-8900 Was $89.99 *$29.99*

The Eric Rohmer Collection
This special collector's set includes "The Aviator's Wife," "Boyfriends and Girlfriends," "Full Moon in Paris," "The Good Marriage," "The Marquise of O," "Perceval" and "Summer."
53-6424 Save $20.00! *$119.99*

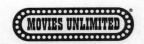

René Clair

Entr'acte (1924)/ The Crazy Ray (1924)
Two experimental silent fantasies from noted French filmmaker René Clair. In "Entr'acte," he enlisted such famed dadaists as Man Ray, Marcel Duchamp and Georges Auric to appear in a tale of inanimate objects coming to life. Next, a scientist's new invention stops all of Paris in its tracks. 62 min. total. Silent with organ score.
53-7455 Was $49.99 ***$39.99***

Phantom Of The Moulin Rouge (1924)
A young aristocrat, depressed when his fiancée breaks up with him, meets a doctor who performs an experiment on him that allows his spirit to leave his body. Can the "phantom" save his girl from marrying a blackmailing publisher and return to his body before the doctor is accused of murder? Albert Préjean, Sandra Milovanoff and Georges Vaultier star; René Clair directs. Silent with music score.
68-9264 ***$19.99***

The Italian Straw Hat (1927)
French silent farce about the hilarious altercation that erupts when the horse of a groom on his way to his wedding eats the hat of a married woman while she's trysting with her soldier boyfriend. Director René Clair's trademark irreverent visual style is evident. 108 min.
53-7862 ***$39.99***

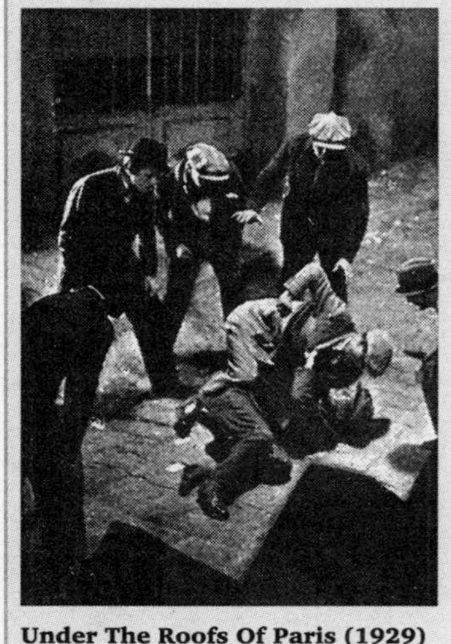

Under The Roofs Of Paris (1929)
One of the first French sound films, director René Clair's charming and romantic comedy/drama follows the ménage a trois that develops between a Parisian street singer and the beautiful Romanian girl he loses to his best friend when he's jailed for a crime he didn't commit. Lively songs are mixed with tender melodrama. Albert Prejean, Pola Illery star. 96 min. In French with English subtitles.
22-6076 Remastered ***$29.99***

Le Million (1931)
Lighthearted, fast-moving French musical comedy about two penniless artists who win a fortune in the lottery...if they can just reclaim the winning ticket from an opera singer's jacket. René Lefèvre, Annabella, Paul Olivier star; René Clair directs. 89 min. In French with English subtitles.
09-1496 Remastered ***$29.99***

A Nous La Liberte (1931)
René Clair wrote and directed this classic satire about an escaped convict who becomes a wealthy phonograph company owner, and the complications that follow when a prison friend is released and comes looking for a job. The film's dehumanizing portrayal of factory life was an inspiration for Chaplin's "Modern Times." Henri Marchand, Raymond Cordy star. 87 min. In French with English subtitles.
53-6068 Was $29.99 ***$24.99***

Quatorze Juillet (Bastille Day) (1932)
René Clair directed this tale of the romance between a Parisian taxi driver and a young flower girl who find themselves seeking refuge from a gang of mobsters. Anabella, Georges Rigaud, Paul Oliver star. 85 min. In French with English subtitles.
62-1342 ***$19.99***

Beauty And The Devil (La Beauté Du Diable) (1950)
A lavish reworking of the "Faust" legend from René Clair, starring Gérard Philipe as Dr. Faust, who agrees to sell his soul to Mephisto in exchange for eternal youth, the love of a gypsy woman and the power to make gold. The surprise comes when Mephisto attempts to collect his end of the bargain. With Michel Simon. 97 min. In French with English subtitles.
01-1502 ***$29.99***

Beauties Of The Night (Les Belles De Nuit) (1952)
René Clair directed this tale of a young music teacher who escapes from his drab life through fantastic dreams in which he meets beautiful women while he's a popular musician, a military officer and a celebrity. Gérard Philipe, Martine Carol and Gina Lollobrigida star. AKA: "Night Beauties." 89 min. In French with English subtitles.
01-1501 ***$29.99***

Les Grandes Manoeuvres (1955)
In a garrison town shortly before World War I, handsome soldier Gérard Philipe wagers with his comrades he can seduce and abandon a local woman chosen at random. Things change, however, when he falls for his intended target, beautiful divorcée Michéle Morgan. René Clair's first color film is a pastoral and charming romantic fable. With Yves Robert and a young Brigitte Bardot. 106 min. In French with English subtitles.
01-1541 ***$29.99***

Clair In The 30's 2-Pack
The savings are "Clair" when you purchase "Under the Roofs of Paris" and "Le Million" in a special two-pack.
22-6077 Save $10.00! ***$49.99***

Please see our index for these other René Clair titles: *And Then There Were None • The Flame Of New Orleans • I Married A Witch • It Happened Tomorrow*

La Jetee (The Pier) (1962)
Chris Marker's unique short film, the inspiration for Terry Gilliam's "12 Monkeys," uses still images to tell the story of a post-atomic world where survivors live in underground vaults, and where one man's memory of a woman's face provides the key to a time-travel experiment. 29 min. In French with English subtitles.
53-7017 Was $29.99 ***$19.99***

La Joli Mai (1962)
Acclaimed cinéma vérité look at Paris and its constituents at an important point in time, the summer of 1962. Parisians comment on the Algerian War, rioting, politics and living in the City of Lights. An invigorating documentary from filmmaker Chris Marker. 180 min. In French with English subtitles.
53-9303 ***$39.99***

Love And The Frenchwoman (1961)
Seven Gallic directors, including René Clair, Henri Decoin, Jean Delannoy and Jean-Paul Le Chanois, cast their cameras on life and romance as seen through the lives of various French women, from "Childhood," "Adolescence" and "Virginity" through to "Marriage," "Adultery," "Divorce" and "A Woman Alone." Humorous and touching anthology features Jean-Paul Belmondo, Martine Carol, Annie Girardot, Dany Robin. 135 min. In English and French with English subtitles.
55-9017 ***$29.99***

Love And The Frenchwoman (Dubbed Version)
Also available in a dubbed-in-English edition.
53-9315 ***$29.99***

The Devil In The Flesh (1949)
The first filmization of the Raymond Radiquet novel, controversial in its day and recognized as a classic of French cinema. Superlative story of the forbidden love between a teenage boy and a soldier's fiancée stars Micheline Presle, Gerard Philipe, Claude Autant-Lara directs. 110 min. Dubbed in English.
10-7218 ***$29.99***

Dedee D'Anvers (1949)
Seamy, sensational story of the tawdry triangle between a dockside bar floozy, her brutish bouncer boyfriend, and the seadog who wants to take her away from it all. Simone Signoret, Bernard Blier, Marcel Pagliero, Dalio star. AKA: "Dedee," "Woman of Antwerp." 95 min. In French with English subtitles.
10-7219 ***$29.99***

L'Ecole Buissonniere (1951)
An inspirational French drama that depicts the doogged attempts of a progressive teacher (Bernard Blier) to instill in his students the same enthusiasm for learning that he demonstrates, only to meet with interference from old-fashioned parents. AKA: "Passion for Life." 84 min. In French with English subtitles.
01-1465 ***$29.99***

Girl In His Pocket (1960)
A science-fiction comedy from France starring Jean Marais as a professor whose latest experiment has turned his beautiful lab assistant into a three-inch statue, thus giving him the perfect place to hide her from his fiancée. With Genevieve Page, Jean-Claude Brialy. AKA: "Nude in His Pocket." 73 min. Dubbed in English.
68-8804 ***$19.99***

Qui Etes-Vous Mr. Sorge (1961)
Gripping French drama based on the true story of Richard Sorge, a German reporter who was arrested and convicted of espionage in WWII Japan. Thomas Holtzman, Keiko Kishi star. 130 min. In French with English subtitles.
10-3175 ***$19.99***

Antoine Et Antoinette (1947)
The staid—and stale—marriage between a hot-headed Parisian print shop worker and his flirtatious store clerk wife gets a break when their lottery ticket turns out to be a winner. Problem is, they can't find it. Roger Pigaut and Clair Maffei are the title couple in this comedic slice of French "neo-realism" from Jacques Becker. 78 min. In French with English subtitles.
01-1551 ***$29.99***

Rendez-Vous De Julliet (1949)
Acclaimed drama from director Jacques Becker follows a group of free-spirited, jazz-loving young people in post-WWII Paris and the problems that arise when a would-be filmmaker wants his friends to join on a film shoot in Africa. Daniel Gélin, Brigitte Auber star. 110 min. In French with English subtitles.
01-1550 ***$29.99***

Modigliani (1957)
The life of troubled painter Amedeo Modigliani is chronicled in Jacques Becker's stirring biography. Modigliani's paintings and nude sketches are captured, as well as his entangled romances with his mistress, writer Beatrice Hastings, and a young art student. Gérard Philipe, Anouk Aimee, Lilli Palmer and Lino Ventura star. AKA: "Montparnasse 19." 120 min. In French with English subtitles.
53-7843 ***$59.99***

Le Trou (The Hole) (1959)
The final film from director Jacques Becker was a fact-based drama about five convicts who undertake an elaborate escape plot by tunneling through the prison vaults into the Paris sewers. Suspicions arise that one of the inmates may be a traitor, threatening their plans. A mostly non-professional cast and the lack of a musical score add to the realism of this suspenseful tale. AKA: "The Night Watch." 123 min. In French with English subtitles.
22-6031 ***$29.99***

Paris Belongs To Us (1959)
A young woman, curious about the death of a stranger, joins an acting troupe he was involved with and hears of a global conspiracy that has marked the other members for death. A bizarre blend of drama, suspense, and paranoid fantasy, this early New Wave feature stars Betty Schneider, Giani Esposito, Jean-Claude Brialy, with cameos by Claude Chabrol and Jean-Luc Godard. Jacques Rivette directs. 138 min. In French with English subtitles.
62-1310 ***$29.99***

The Nun (La Religieuse) (1966)
Banned for several years by the French government, this moving drama follows a teenage girl in 18th-century France who is forced by her impoverished family to enter a convent. The spartan life and abusive superiors drive her to try and leave. Anna Karina, Francisco Rabal, Liselotte Pulver star; directed by Jacques Rivette. 155 min. In French with English subtitles.
53-7512 Letterboxed ***$24.99***

Celine And Julie Go Boating (1974)
Director Jacques Rivette's hypnotic and surreal drama, based in part on the writings of Henry James, follows flamboyant nightclub magician Celine (Juliet Berto) and withdrawn librarian Julie (Dominique Labourier) on a strange visit to a country mansion where two women vie for the affections of a widower with an invalid daughter. With Marie-France Pisier, Barbet Schroeder. 193 min. In French with English subtitles.
53-8868 ***$89.99***

La Belle Noiseuse (1990)
A compelling examination of the artist's drive to create, director Jacques Rivette's acclaimed drama stars Michel Piccoli as a once-renowned painter worn down by years of inactivity and the beautiful Emmanuelle Beart as the young woman who becomes his model and muse, inspiring him to pick up the brushes again. 240 min. In French with English subtitles.
53-7922 ***$89.99***

Divertimento (1993)
Director Jacques Rivette "reconstructed" his 1990 film "La Belle Noiseuse" into this shorter version that also includes all-new scenes. A young woman comes into the life of a famous but burned-out artist and rekindles his creativity. Emmanuelle Beart, Michel Piccoli star. 126 min. In French with English subtitles.
53-8125 ***$89.99***

Joan The Maid: The Battles (1993)
Directed by Jacques Rivette ("La Belle Noiseuse"), this first installment in his look at the life of Joan of Arc focuses on Joan's attempts to convince the French people that she has been sent by God, and how she leads them against the English in the Battle of Orleans. Sandrine Bonnaire stars. 112 min. In French with English subtitles.
53-6630 ***$49.99***

Joan The Maid: The Prisons (1993)
The second entry in Jacques Rivette's saga tells of how Joan was left by her men in Compiegne and taken prisoner by the British. She is carried to Rouen, bound in chains and eventually charged with witchcraft, leading to her burning at the stake. Sandrine Bonnaire stars. 115 min. In French with English subtitles.
53-6631 ***$49.99***

Joan The Maid: Boxed Set
Both films are also available in a boxed collector's set.
53-6632 Save $10.00! ***$89.99***

A Bullet In the Gun Barrel (1958)
Gritty crime drama co-directed by Michel Deville ("La Lectrice") centers on three pals who fought together in Vietnam and use $75,000 from another friend to open a nightclub in France. When that friend resurfaces as a mob boss, he demands his money back, and now the trio have to pull of a heist to get it. With Roger Hanin, Pierre Vaneck and Mijanou Bardot (Brigitte's sister). AKA: "A Slug in the Heater," "Une Balle Dans Le Canon." Dubbed in English.
79-6550 ***$19.99***

Moderato Cantabile (1959)
Based on a Marguerite Duras story, Peter Brook's stark and moody drama stars Jeanne Moreau as a wealthy industrialist's bored wife. After witnessing the aftermath of a murder at a local cafe, Moreau becomes obsessed with the crime and takes up with blue-collar worker Jean-Paul Belmondo, who may or may not know about the killing. 90 min. In French with English subtitles.
87-1009 ***$69.99***

Monsieur Vincent (1947)
Inspiring biography of 16th-century French priest St. Vincent de Paul and his message of love, charity and faith. With Pierre Fresnay and Aime Clariond. 112 min. In French with English subtitles.
62-9018 ***$29.99***

Monsieur Vincent (Dubbed Version)
Also available in a dubbed-in-English edition.
10-1630 ***$29.99***

End Of The World (La Fin Du Monde) (1930)
Abel Gance's long-lost doomsday thriller is seen here in a truncated "roadshow" version that played American theatres in 1934. The story focuses on an astronomer who discovers that a comet heading towards Earth in 30 days may destroy the planet. The disbelieving population loses their cool when they discover the prediction is real. With Victor Francen and Gance. 54 min. In French with English subtitles.
79-5640 ***$19.99***

Lucrezia Borgia (1935)
Pioneering filmmaker Abel Gance ("Napoleon") examined another controversial chapter in European history with this lavish melodrama about the 15th-century Italian family whose lust for power reached even the Papal throne, and whose treachery made them infamous. Edwige Feulliere plays the title role; with Gabriel Gabrio, Roger Karl. Also included are two of Gance's silent short films, "Au Secours!" (1923) and "La Folie du Docteur Tube" (1916). 138 min. total. In French with English subtitles.
50-8597 ***$19.99***

Beethoven (1936)
Focusing on the famed composer's stormy romances and his growing deafness, this compelling biodrama from director Abel Gance offers an insightful study of genius and madness, magnificent visuals and dramatic use of sounds. Harry Baur, Jean-Louis Barrault, Jany Holt star. AKA: "Un Grand Amour de Beethoven." 116 min. In French with English subtitles.
53-7459 Was $29.99 ***$19.99***

J'Accuse (1939)
Anti-war sentiment meets horrific fantasy in Abel Gance's powerful, disturbing masterwork about an inventor, the sole survivor of a doomed WWI platoon. When he learns his discoveries are to be used by the military, the angry veteran calls on his dead comrades and other soldiers to rise from their graves in protest. Victor Francen, Jean Max star. 125 min. In French with English subtitles.
53-7591 ***$29.99***

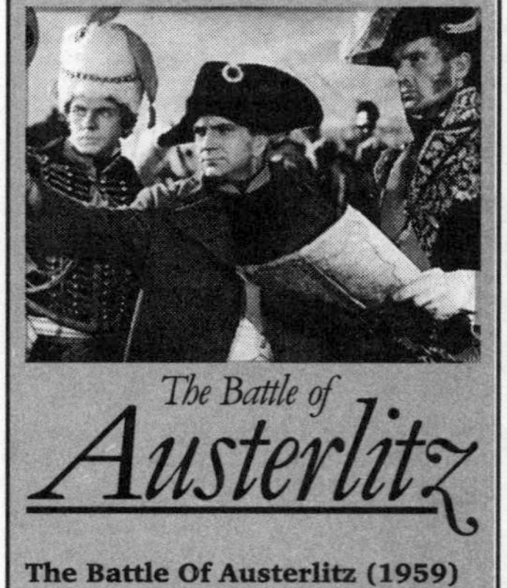

The Battle Of Austerlitz (1959)
Thirty years after his epic "Napoleon," director Abel Gance returned to the life of the Little Corporal with this look at the decisive 1805 conflict between French forces and the armies of Austria and Russia. The international cast includes Rossano Brazzi, Claudia Cardinale, Jack Palance, Vittorio De Sica, Orson Welles and Pierre Mondy as Napoleon. 118 min. Dubbed in English.
10-9321 ***$19.99***

Please see our index for the Abel Gance title: *Napoleon*

Devil Of Paris (1964)
After he accidentally kills a man, nobleman Jean Marais heads to Paris, where he poses as a commoner while trying to find the dead man's missing daughter who has been kidnapped into slavery. Marais saves her and decides to help other ordinary citizens, but an enemy discovers his true identity and tries to use it against him. Dany Robin also stars. Dubbed in English.
79-6161 Was $24.99 ***$19.99***

Le Gendarme De Saint-Tropez (1964)
The first entry in a successful series starring Louis De Funès as an ambitious police officer transferred to a laid-back station in the resort town of St. Tropez. Just as he adjusts to his new environment, his daughter begins having a bit too much fun. In French with English subtitles.
87-1002 Was $69.99 ***$39.99***

Le Gendarme À New York (1966)
Inspector Louis De Funès and his somewhat less-than-crack squad of St. Tropez police officers have their work cut out for them when a visit to America turns into a series of comical calamities in this satirical sequel. With Michel Galabru, Genevieve Grad. 100 min. In French with English subtitles.
87-1010 ***$69.99***

Les Grandes Gueules (1965)
An engrossing human drama from France about two ex-convicts whose sole motive in taking jobs as lumberjacks in a remote logging camp is revenge. Stars Lino Ventura and Bourvil. AKA: "Jailbird's Vacation." 125 min. In French with English subtitles.
10-3214 ***$19.99***

Six In Paris (1965)
Directors Claude Chabrol, Jean Douchet, Jean-Luc Godard, Jean-Daniel Pollet, Eric Rohmer and Jean Rouch contributed segments to this anthology film centering on amusing, romantic and dramatic incidents, each set in a different Parisian neighborhood. Stephane Audran and Barbet Schroeder star. 93 min. In French with English subtitles.
53-7841 ***$69.99***

Life Upside Down (La Vie A L'Envers) (1965)
Compelling, award-winning examination of a Paris real estate developer who deserts his friends, his job and his new wife to retreat into his own detached world. But is it a choice to be detested, pitied or admired? Charles Denner and Anna Gaylor star in this provocative film, directed by Alain Jessua. 115 min. In French with English subtitles.
53-7968 Was $79.99 ***$29.99***

How Not To Rob A Department Store (1965)
A small-time, down-on-his-luck criminal teams with an old friend who thinks he has become successful to pull off a payroll heist from a department store during the Christmas season. Complicating matters are a group of delinquents who rob a fake Santa of stolen cash. Jean-Claude Brially and Marie Laforet star in this comic caper. Dubbed in English.
79-6513 ***$19.99***

L'Odeur Des Fauves (1966)
A photojournalist with a reputation for uncovering scandal begins to feel remorse for the people whose lives he has hurt in this French drama with Maurice Ronet, Josephine Chaplin, Vittorio De Sica. 86 min. In French with English Subtitles.
10-3173 ***$19.99***

Mademoiselle (1966)
Jeanne Moreau turns in an unforgettable performance as a psychotic, sexually repressed young teacher in a small French town who commits arson, starts floods and kills livestock, then persuades the townspeople to believe that her lover, a woodcutter, is responsible. Ettore Manni co-stars; Tony Richardson directs. 99 min. In French with English subtitles.
12-2856 ***$19.99***

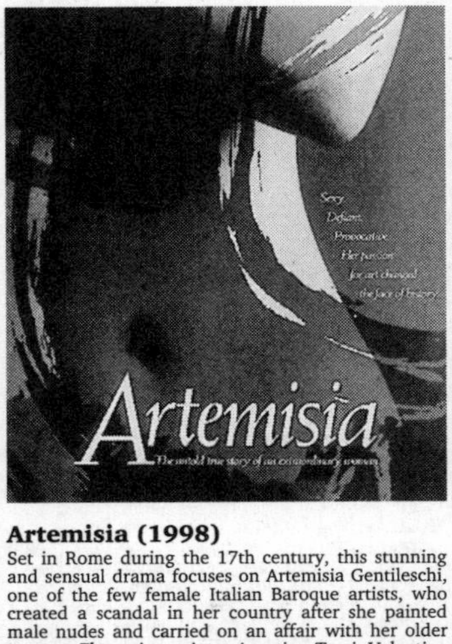

Artemisia (1998)
Set in Rome during the 17th century, this stunning and sensual drama focuses on Artemisia Gentileschi, one of the few female Italian Baroque artists, who created a scandal in her country after she painted male nudes and carried on an affair with her older mentor, Florentine painter Agostino Tassi. Valentina Cervi, Michel Serrault star. 95 min. In French with English subtitles.
11-2805 Was $99.99 ***□$19.99***

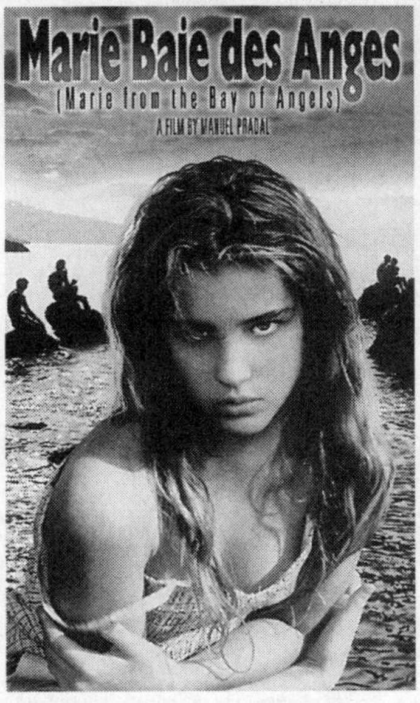

Marie Bai Des Anges (Marie From The Bay Of Angels) (1998)
Set on the French Riviera, this sumptuous, sensual and unsettling story tells of 15-year-old Marie, a beautiful, streetwise thief living off the U.S. sailors who frequent her town. She carries on a relationship with Orso, another teenage thief, but is their lifestyle too predatory to make the union work? Vahina Giocante and Frederic Malgras star. 90 min. In French with English subtitles.
02-3270 Was $99.99 ***$19.99***

The Chambermaid On The Titanic (1998)
From Spanish director Bigas Luna ("Jamon Jamon") comes a compelling and heartfelt drama about a French foundry worker who wins a trip to England to see the famed liner set off on its ill-fated maiden voyage. His chance (and unconsummated) encounter with a maid the night before the ship sails is turned by him into a passionate, romantic tale that makes him a celebrity. Olivier Martinez, Romance Bohringer and Aitana Sanchez Gijon, in the title role, star. 96 min. In French with English subtitles.
53-6561 ***$94.99***

Sitcom (1998)
A seemingly normal French family is turned into sex-crazed, murderously uninhibited maniacs, thanks to bites from a pet rat that the father brings home one day, in this outrageous, taboo-breaking dark comedy from François Ozon. Evelyne Dandry, Marina de Van star. 80 min. In French with English subtitles.
53-6710 Letterboxed ***$94.99***

See The Sea (1998)
Set on a French resort island in the Sea of Biscay, director François Ozon's quietly unsettling thriller follows an English woman on vacation with her infant daughter. The arrival of a mysterious backpacker who pitches her tent next to the woman's cottage and begins insinuating her way into her life leads to sinister consequences. Sasha Hails, Marina de Van star. Also included is Ozon's short film "The Summer Dress," about a gay man who has a fateful beachside encounter with a woman. 67 min. total. In French with English subtitles.
53-6740 Letterboxed ***$89.99***

Jeanne And The Perfect Guy (1998)
Directed by Mathieu Demy in the tradition of father Jacques' "Umbrellas of Cherbourg," this musical romance centers on Jeanne, an uninhibited woman who thinks she's found the perfect guy in Olivier, whom she meets on the public transit. But getting in the way of their relationship is the fact that Olivier is HIV-positive due to a past drug problem. Virginie Ledoyen ("The Beach") stars alongside Demy. 98 min. In French with English subtitles.
78-9042 ***$79.99***

East-West (1999)
In this Academy Award nominee for Best Foreign Film, Russian émigrés are invited to return home by Stalin following World War II. But when a doctor, his French-born wife and their young son arrive from Paris, they're shocked to find most of their fellow returnees arrested and killed. The family is given a small apartment in Kiev, but living in a world of fear and suspicion leads the wife to plan an escape. Sandrine Bonnaire, Oleg Menshikov and Catherine Deneuve star in this effort from Régis Wargnier ("Indochine"). 125 min. In French with English subtitles.
02-3467 ***$99.99***

School Of Flesh (1998)
Based on a story by Yukio Mishima, this sensual drama stars Isabelle Huppert as a fashion designer desperate for a relationship. She gets involved with young, bisexual hustler Vincent Martinez, who also works as a bartender at a gay club. The two carry on a wild affair in which the power between them continually shifts. In French with English subtitles. 102 min.
02-3380 Was $99.99 ***$21.99***

The 317th Platoon (1965)
An intense, intimate study of men at war, focusing on a French squad of auxiliary soldiers stationed in Laos shortly before the fall of Dien Bien Phu in 1954. The squad is comprised of 41 Laotians and four Frenchmen, and the film examines their relationships and anguish in the face of death. Pierre Shoendoerffer ("La Crabe Trambour") directs; Jacques Perin and Bruno Cremer star. 94 min. In French with English subtitles.
53-7460 ***$59.99***

Outpost Indochina (1965)
Near the end of the Vietnamese war for independence, a group of refugees is sent by French soldiers to "Madman's Fort," where the rigors of duty have driven men insane. When the enemy surrounds the fortress, broadcasting propaganda with loudspeakers, the soldiers and their charges try to keep their wits about them. With Jacques Harden, Jean Rochefort. Dubbed in English.
79-6453 Was $24.99 ***$19.99***

The Tall Blonde Man With One Black Shoe (1973)
A power struggle at the French Secret Service spills into the life of an innocent concert violinist who fiddles obliviously while rival spies and hit men try to set him up for a final bow. Director Yves Robert's daffy hit, remade in America as "The Man with One Red Shoe," stars Pierre Richard as the marked-for-mayhem musician. 90 min. Dubbed in English.
09-1749 ***$19.99***

The Mother And The Whore (1973)
One of only a handful of features made by filmmaker Jean Eustache, this sparse, intense meditation on emotional detachment among Paris' young intelligentsia in the early '70s is considered by many to be a defining entry in the French New Wave. Jean-Pierre Leaud, Bernadette Lafont and Françoise Leburn are the unequally happy sides in a romantic triangle that leads to a cathartic resolution. 215 min. In French with English subtitles.
53-6389 ***$94.99***

La Permission (The Story Of A Three Day Pass) (1967)
A black American soldier on a three-day pass has a whirlwind romance with a young French girl, but their fragile relationship is unable to stand against the forces that oppose it. Bittersweet drama directed by Melvin Van Peebles stars Harry Baird and Nicole Berger. 87 min. In French with English subtitles.
53-6012 Was $59.99 ***$19.99***

Train Of Life (1998)
In order to escape the approaching Nazis, the Jewish residents of a remote Eastern European village carry out a wild plan suggested by the "town fool": refurbish a train, pose as stormtroopers and prisoners, and "deport" themselves safely across the Russian border. Laughter and tears are mixed in this poignant tale from writer/director Radu Mihaileanu; Lionel Abelanski, Clément Harari, Rufus star. 103 min. In French with English subtitles.
06-2974 ***$89.99***

The Dinner Game (1998)
Laughter is the main course in this acclaimed Gallic farce. Snide publisher Thierry Lhermitte delights in attending dinner parties where he and his society friends must bring "idiots"—unsuspecting average people with quirky or obsessive interests—for everyone's amusement. Lhermitte thinks he's found a gem in taxman/matchstick sculptor Jacques Villeret, but a bad back leaves him trapped in his apartment and at the "idiot's" mercy. With Daniel Prévost, Alexandra Vandernoot. 81 min. In French with English subtitles.
07-2821 ***□$99.99***

The Killing Game (1967)
Wild satire involving a rich young man whose claim that he has lived the incredible adventures created by a comic artist inspires the artist to invent new situations with the young man as a hero. But life imitates art too closely when the fan takes things a little too seriously. Jean-Pierre Cassel and Claudine Auger star. 95 min. In French with English subtitles.
53-8020 Was $39.99 ***$29.99***

Bertrand Tavernier

The Clockmaker (1974)
Film critic Bertrand Tavernier made his feature directorial debut with this gripping study of a watchmaker in a small town who re-evaluates his life after his son is accused of murdering a local factory owner. Philippe Noiret, Jean Rochefort and Sylvain Rougerie star in this masterfully told tale. 105 min. In French with English subtitles.
50-1033 Letterboxed ***$24.99***

Spoiled Children (1977)
A filmmaker takes refuge away from home in a high-rise apartment to work on his new script. Instead of serenity, he finds romance with a beautiful young woman who recruits him to help the building's tenants in a fight against their landlord. Michel Piccoli and Christine Pascal star; Bertrand Tavernier directs. 113 min. In French with English subtitles.
53-7811 Was $59.99 ***$29.99***

The Judge And The Assassin (1979)
Bertrand ("Round Midnight") Tavernier's riveting intrigue about the intensified relationship between an unscrupulous judge and a suspected child killer. Philippe Noiret, Michel Galabru and Isabelle Huppert star. 130 min. In French with English subtitles.
53-7377 Was $79.99 ***$29.99***

Coup De Torchon (1981)
Dark, haunting seriocomedy from director Bertrand Tavernier transfers Jim Thompson's Southern potboiler "Pop. 1280" to 1930s French Africa. Phillipe Noiret stars as a put-upon colonial police chief who uses his official powers to get back at his enemies while cleaning up the region's criminal element. With Isabelle Huppert, Guy Marchand. 128 min. In French with English subtitles.
70-5039 Letterboxed ***$29.99***

A Sunday In The Country (1984)
An aging painter's regular weekly visit from his family becomes a day of discovery all around in this poignant, exquisitely photographed fin de siecle drama by Bertrand Tavernier. Acclaimed French stage actor Louis Ducreux makes his film debut as the elderly artist; with Sabine Azema, Michel Aumont. 94 min. In French with English subtitles.
12-1676 Letterboxed ***$24.99***

Life And Nothing But (1989)
Bertrand Tavernier's powerful, critically acclaimed drama stars Philippe Noiret as a WWI French soldier in charge of identifying and burying war dead who attempts to help two women seeking word on their missing men. Sabine Azema, Pascale Vignal also star. 135 min. In French with English subtitles.
73-1112 Was $79.99 ***$19.99***

L.627 (1992)
A gritty policier from Bertrand Tavernier detailing the life of Paris narcotics cop Lulu, who goes to great lengths to keep the streets safe from drug dealers. Immersed in a seedy world of junkies and prostitutes, Lulu frets about relations with both a loving wife and a drug-addicted hooker. Didier Bezace stars. 145 min. In French with English subtitles.
63-8147 Was $79.99 ***$24.99***

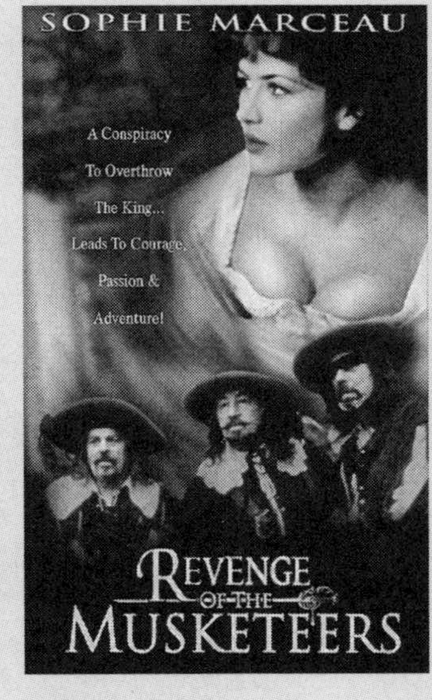

Revenge Of The Musketeers (1994)
The legendary swordsmen of 17th-century France are called back into action by D'Artagnan's daughter (Sophie Marceau) when her convent home offers sanctuary to a corrupt nobleman's escaped servant and a conspiracy that threatens the monarchy is exposed. Director Bertrand Tavernier's rousing drama also stars Sami Frey, Philippe Noiret, Claude Rich. AKA: "Daughter of D'Artagnan." 130 min. In French with English subtitles.
11-2340 Was $99.99 ***□$19.99***

Capitaine Conan (1996)
Epic war saga from Bertrand Tavernier is set in the Balkan hills of Romania near the end of World War I. The fearless leader of a troop of French guerrillas, who continued fighting in the region after the armistice was signed, must defend two of his men on murder charges in a court-martial trial. Philippe Torreton and Samuel Le Bihan star in this award-winning drama, based on the autobiographical novel by Roger Vercel. 130 min. In French with English subtitles.
53-6194 Letterboxed ***$24.99***

Please see our index for the Bertrand Tavernier title: *Round Midnight*

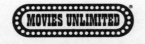

Claude Chabrol

Le Beau Serge (1958)
Recognized as one of the first films of the French New Wave, Claude Chabrol's directorial debut is a somber tale of two friends in a small town. Jean-Claude Brialy returns from Paris to his home village and finds Gerard Blain a drunkard with a troubled marriage. 97 min. In French with English subtitles.
53-7170 *$19.99*

Les Cousins (1958)
Two very different young men (one a cocky urbanite, the other a quiet farmboy) room together in Paris while studying law, but the pressures to succeed and the attentions of a beautiful girl soon shatter their friendship. Award-winning drama by Claude Chabrol stars Jean-Claude Brialy, Gerard Blain. 110 min. In French with English subtitles.
53-7171 Was $59.99 *$19.99*

Les Bonnes Femmes (1960)
Before he shifted to atmospheric mysteries, Claude Chabrol directed this compassionate and archly ironic look at four shopgirls whose dreams of a batter life lead them to try music hall singing, a pleasure-seeking binge, an unhappy marriage and a doomed search for "true love," respectively. Clothilde Joano, Stephane Audran star. 95 min. In French with English subtitles.
53-6911 Letterboxed *$24.99*

La Route De Corinthe (The Road To Corinth) (1968)
When a NATO security officer investigating the electronic jamming of U.S. missile sites in Greece is murdered, his widow and an intelligence agent search for the killers behind the deadly sabotage scheme. Claude Chabrol's sly espionage spoof stars Jean Seberg, Maurice Ronet, Michel Bouquet. AKA: "Who's Got the Black Box?" 97 min. In French with English subtitles.
53-6314 *$29.99*

Who's Got The Black Box? (Dubbed Version)
Also available in a dubbed-in-English edition.
68-9102 *$19.99*

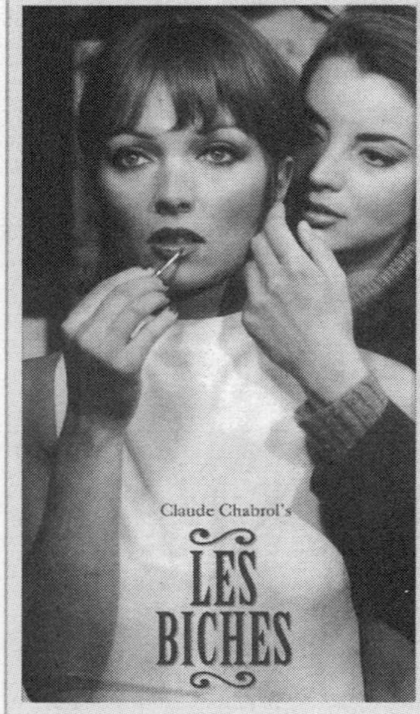

Les Biches (1968)
Claude Chabrol's homage to Hitchcock with a kinky spin is set in St. Tropez, where an affair unfolds between a bored society woman and a young girl. The affair is eventually threatened by the presence of a handsome architect. Stephane Audran, Jean-Louis Trintignant star. AKA: "Bad Girls." 95 min. In French with English subtitles.
53-7674 Was $79.99 *$24.99*

La Rupture (1970)
After a man attacks his son while under the influence of drugs, his parents hire an investigator to discredit their daughter-in-law, a former barmaid, in order to win custody of the child. Besides being a top-notch psychological suspenser, Claude Chabrol's film tellingly comments on class distinction. Stephane Audran and Michel Bouquet star. AKA: "The Breakup." 124 min. In French with English subtitles.
53-7812 Was $79.99 *$19.99*

Le Boucher (1971)
Claude Chabrol, "the French Alfred Hitchcock," directed this alternately pastoral and terrifying mystery set in a quiet village. A lonely schoolteacher begins an affair with the town butcher, but their romance is interrupted when an unknown killer begins preying on the local children. Stephane Audran, Jean Yanne star. 90 min. In French with English subtitles.
53-7695 Was $79.99 *$24.99*

Nada (1974)
A French terrorist group kidnaps an American ambassador and holds him hostage in a remote farmhouse, but as the situation drags on it becomes apparent that authorities are more concerned with eliminating the group than freeing the ambassador. Unusual and compelling drama from Claude Chabrol stars Fabio Testi, Mariangela Melato, Maurice Garrel. 107 min. In French with English subtitles.
53-6313 *$29.99*

Une Partie De Plaisir (A Piece Of Pleasure) (1974)
Claude Chabrol's dark depiction of modern marriage, the story of a couple whose love for one another is slowly disappearing, due mainly to the husband's tyranny and selfishness. Based upon actual experiences in the lives of Paul and Danielle Gegauff, who star in the film. 97 min. In French with English subtitles.
53-7046 *$79.99*

Les Innocent Aux Mains Sale (1975)
From acclaimed director Claude Chabrol comes this noir-ish plot twister about a woman who sets out with her young lover to murder her rich but impotent husband. However, things get fishy when her lover disappears, she finds herself accused of murder, and her husband shows up not quite dead. Romy Schneider, Paolo Giusti and Rod Steiger star. 121 min. Filmed in English.
20-1034 *$79.99*

The Horse Of Pride (1980)
Intriguing departure for Claude Chabrol takes a fond and telling look at the lives of the peasants of Breton in the early 1900s through their loves, tragedies and triumphs. Jacques Dufilho, Francois Cluzet star; strikingly lensed by Jean Rabier. 118 min. In French with English subtitles.
53-7312 Was $59.99 *$24.99*

Story Of Women (1988)
A dark and emotional fact-based drama by famed French director Claude Chabrol. Isabelle Huppert stars as a mother in Nazi-occupied France who makes a living by performing illegal abortions, until she is arrested and tried for her crime. With Francois Cluzet, Niels Tavernier. 108 min. In French with English subtitles.
53-7463 Was $79.99 *$29.99*

Betty (1993)
Claude Chabrol's audacious examination of the life of Betty, a mysterious woman who recounts her fall from Parisian bourgeois society into the world of alcoholism and depravity to a curious listener in a bar. Marie Trintignant, Stephane Audran and Jean-François Garreau star in this stirring film. 103 min. In French with English subtitles.
53-8009 *$89.99*

L'Enfer (1994)
French cinema's suspense master, Claude Chabrol, offers up a man's chilling descent into mistrust, paranoia and deadly rage. François Cluzet stars as a hotel owner who suddenly begins suspecting beautiful wife Emmanuelle Beart of being unfaithful and turns violently jealous. 100 min. In French with English subtitles.
53-8190 Was $89.99 *$19.99*

La Cérémonie (1996)
Claude Chabrol's taut thriller tells of a French bourgeois family who hire a prim young woman as their housekeeper. Trouble starts when the housekeeper befriends a local woman who has a hatred for the family and the two form an intimate bond that leads to the unravelling of dark secrets and sinister impulses. Sandrine Bonnaire, Isabelle Huppert, Jacqueline Bisset star. 110 min. In French with English subtitles.
53-8901 Was $89.99 *$29.99*

The Swindle (Rien Ne Va Plus) (1997)
A stylish tale of romantic deceptions and elaborate cons, director Claude Chabrol's 50th film stars Isabelle Huppert and Michel Serrault as a team of French scam artists. The pair's relationship—business and personal—may be threatened by their latest scheme, in which Huppert attaches herself to the money courier for a crime syndicate, but who is betraying whom? With Francois Cluzet, Jean-Francois Balmer. 105 min. In French with English subtitles.
53-6665 Letterboxed *$94.99*

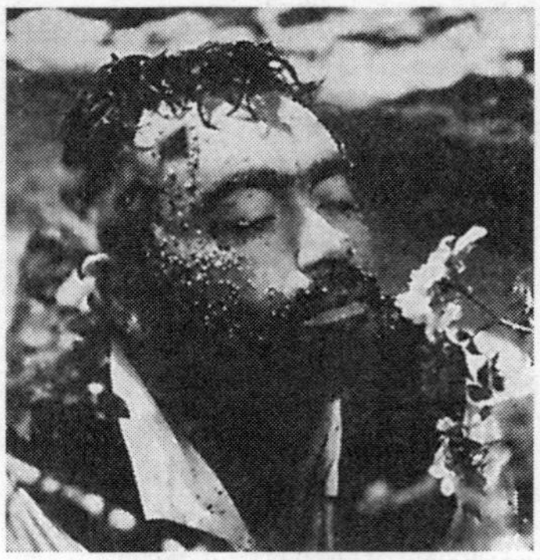

An Occurrence At Owl Creek Bridge (1962)
Based on the short story by Ambrose Bierce, this is the classic dialogue-free short film dealing with a man's final moments on the gallows before being hanged for Civil War sabotage. Academy Award and Cannes Grand Prix winner. 29 min.
09-1798 Was $19.99 *$14.99*

The First Time (1967)
Claude Berri's sequel to "The Two of Us" is set in 1952 and follows young artist Claude (Alain Cohen) and his friends as they try to meet girls and partake in sex for the first time. Charles Denner and Delphine Levy co-star in this charming tale. 83 min. In French with English subtitles.
53-6083 *$29.99*

Irma Vep (1997)
Writer/director Olivier Assayas' satirical look at the French movie industry stars Jean-Pierre Leaud as a once-hot filmmaker whose comeback attempt is a remake of the classic silent serial "Les Vampires," with Hong Kong action star Maggie Cheung (playing herself) in the lead. Language problems, an amorous costume lady and a nervous breakdown by the director are among the on- and off-the-set crises. 96 min. In English and French with English subtitles.
53-9958 Letterboxed *$19.99*

The Shameless Old Lady (1966)
Endearing adaptation of a Bertolt Brecht story about an old woman who, after spending her life caring for her husband and family, decides to cut loose and live life to its fullest. She buys a car, goes on a vacation and befriends a prostitute. Starring Sylvie, Malka Ribovska and Victor Lanoux. 95 min. In French with English subtitles.
53-9300 Was $29.99 *$19.99*

Salut L'Artiste (1973)
Marcello Mastroianni turns in a wonderful tour de force performance as a charming character actor who will tackle any role for his art, while juggling romantic liaisons with his wife and mistress. Jean Rochefort and Francoise Fabian also star in this spry farce directed by Yves Robert ("My Father's Glory"). 96 min. In French with English subtitles.
53-7621 Was $79.99 *$29.99*

We Are All Naked (1966)
Disturbing, acclaimed drama about a dysfunctional family living on the Normandy shore in Northern France whose members include an alcoholic father, his nymphomaniac wife, a retarded son, an innocent daughter and an indifferent niece. When the mother tries to stop her son's bizarre sex habits, tragedy ensues. Alain Saury stars; directed by Claude Pierson. Dubbed in English.
79-5854 Was $24.99 *$19.99*

The Sucker (Le Corniaud) (1965)
A French businessman on vacation in Italy becomes the unwitting dupe of smugglers when he's involved in an auto accident and is given a car stuffed with drugs and mob money to drive across the border in this slapstick comedy. Bourvil and Louis de Funes star; Gerard Oury directs. 90 min. In French with English subtitles.
87-1014 *$39.99*

La Grande Vadrouille (1966)
The team behind "The Mad Adventures of Rabbi Jacob"—actor Louis De Funes and director Gerard Oury—collaborated on this story about three Allied parachutists who are forced to land in German-occupied Paris in 1943 and stay in hiding with the conductor of the Paris Opera and a house painter. With Bourvil. 122 min. In French with English subtitles.
87-1008 Was $69.99 *$39.99*

Delusions Of Grandeur (1976)
Slapstick comedy, adventure and fine performances mix in this farce set in 17th-century Spain and based on a story by Victor Hugo. Louis De Funes is a nasty nobleman who sends servant Yves Montand to spy on the King and Queen. When Montand saves their lives, he's made tax collector and begins redistributing the wealth. Karin Schubert co-stars. 105 min. In French with English subtitles.
53-9311 *$69.99*

Murder At 45 R.P.M. (1961)
A famous singer carries on an affair with her accompanist which causes her husband to leave her. Soon, the husband is murdered, and the lovers suspect each other is the killer. Things get creepier when the dead hubby leaves a recorded message. With Danielle Darrieux, Michel Auclair. Dubbed in English.
68-8828 *$19.99*

Special Police (1985)
A police inspector involved in investigating a criminal organization known as the Movement, which is tied to several important politicians, is forced to protect the sister of an old friend who is killed by hit men seeking evidence gathered against the Movement. Richard Berry, Carole Bouquet star. 92 min. In French with English subtitles.
87-1003 Was $59.99 *$39.99*

Conseil De Family (Family Business) (1986)
A satiric and ironic comedy about deception, thievery and other familial duties from director Costa-Gavras. French pop star Johnny Hallyday plays the safe-cracking patriarch who reluctantly lets his son follow in his footsteps, but soon finds that, thanks to the boy's electronic genius, business is booming. Remi Martin, Fanny Ardant, Guy Marchand also star. 111 min. In French with English subtitles.
01-1542 *$29.99*

Max, Mon Amour (1986)
In the tradition of the films of Luis Buñuel comes Nagisa Oshima's romantic story about a man, a woman and a chimp. When a British diplomat discovers that his wife has been carrying on an affair with an ape, he invites "Max" to share their Paris apartment. With Anthony Higgins, Charlotte Rampling and Victoria Abril. 94 min. In English and French with English subtitles.
53-7940 Was $89.99 *$29.99*

Red Kiss (Rouge Baiser) (1986)
Set in Paris in the 1950s, this acclaimed film focuses on a 15-year-old, America-obsessed girl who falls for an American photographer she meets while attempting a pro-Stalinist demonstration. A sexy, heartfelt coming-of-age tale that mixes politics and romance. With Charlotte Valandrey, Lambert Wilson and Marthe Keller. 110 min. In French with English subtitles.
53-9301 Was $79.99 *$19.99*

Next Summer (1986)
Follow the loves, angers, jealousies and devotions that keep three generations of a family together in this warm French feminist drama by Nadine Trintignant. Acclaimed cast includes Claudia Cardinale, Philippe Noiret, Fanny Ardant, Jean-Louis Trintignant. 100 min. In French with English subtitles.
75-1006 *$69.99*

Life Is A Long Quiet River (1987)
Two families—one wealthy and polite, the other slovenly and unscrupulous—discover that their babies were switched at birth 12 years ago, setting into motion a series of wacky events. A screwball social satire from Etienne Chatiliez ("Tate Danielle") which was a huge hit in France; with Helene Vincent. 89 min. In French with English subtitles.
53-7795 *$79.99*

L'Année Des Meduses (1987)
Sizzlingly sensual drama that stars Valerie Kaprisky ("Breathless") as a nubile French Riviera Lolita whose boundless passions spell deadly trouble for all men who will not, or cannot, satiate them. Caroline Cellier, Bernard Giraudeau co-star. 110 min. In French with English subtitles.
75-1003 *$69.99*

36 Fillette (1988)
A sensual and poignant coming-of-age drama about a 14-year-old French girl who vows to "become a woman" during a family vacation, but finds the road to adulthood a slippery one. Catherine Breillat's sensitive tale stars Delphine Zentout, Jean-Pierre Leaud. 88 min. In French with English subtitles.
53-7491 Was $79.99 *$19.99*

A Propos De Nice (1929)
Jean Vigo's first film, and one of only three the innovative director ever made, is a droll and ironic contrast between the upper class beach visitors of the French resort town and the impoverished residents of Nice's slums. 25 min.
53-7478 Was $24.99 *$19.99*

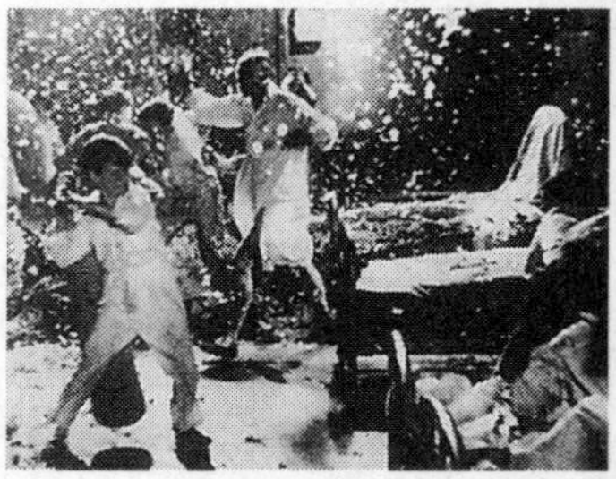

Zero De Conduite (1933)
Director Jean Vigo's celebrated tale of two boys returning to a French boarding school after the holidays and rebelling against petty dictatorship. 42 min. In French with English subtitles.
09-1759 Was $29.99 *$19.99*

L'Atalante (1934)
One of world cinema's most enduring classics, Jean Vigo's lyrical romance (his final film before his untimely death) relates the simple love story between a barge captain (Jean Dasté) and his young bride (Dita Parlo) who, after a troubled start, struggle through the loneliness of their separation. Co-stars Michel Simon, Gilles Margaritis. 87 min. In French with English subtitles.
01-1121 Was $39.99 *$19.99*

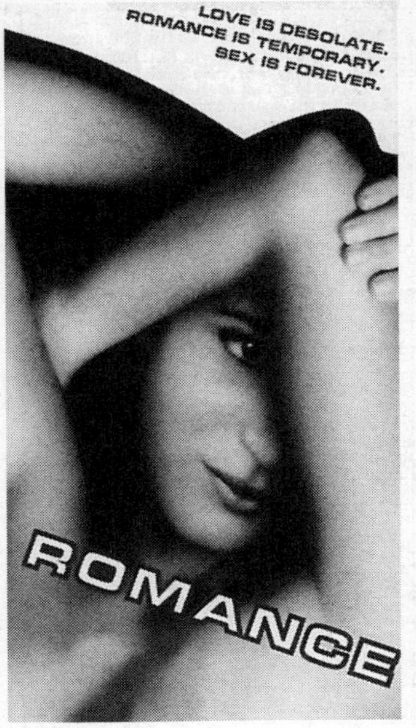

Romance (1999)
One of the most sexually graphic mainstream movies ever made, French filmmaker Catherine Breillat's erotic exploration of the connection—or the lack thereof—between love and sex stars Caroline Ducey as a teacher frustrated by her model boyfriend's lack of interest in lovemaking. Cruising the streets and bars of Paris, Ducey has a series of encounters ranging from a handsome stud (Euro porn star Rocco Siffredi) to a colleague (François Berleand) with a bondage fetish. Unrated director's cut. In French with English subtitles.
68-1969 *$69.99*

Sorceress (1988)
Set in a 13th-century French village, this historical drama details the rivalry between a Dominican monk and a woman who uses herbs to heal the sick. The monk deems the woman a "heretic" and plots to have her burned at the stake. Directed by Suzanne Schiffman, François Truffaut's longtime collaborator, and starring Tcheky Karyo and Christine Boisson. 96 min. In French with English subtitles.
70-7066 *$29.99*

Sorceress (Dubbed Version)
Also available in a dubbed-in-English edition.
70-7264 *$29.99*

Chocolat (1988)
Effective study of the waning days of French colonial Cameroon, as shown through the eyes of the young daughter of a harried bureaucrat. Impressive and personal directorial debut for scenarist Claire Denis stars Isaach du Bankole, Guila Bosche, Francois Cluzet. 105 min. In French with English subtitles.
73-1070 Was $79.99 *$19.99*

No Fear, No Die (1993)
From Claire Denis, the acclaimed director of "Chocolat," comes this exotic drama set in France, where an African immigrant teams with a West Indian man to supply fighting cocks to a sleazy bar. When the African falls for the saloonkeeper's mistress, emotions explode. Isaach de Bankole, Solveig Dommartin star. 97 min. In French with English subtitles.
70-5064 Was $29.99 *$19.99*

I Can't Sleep (1995)
As much a character study as it is a murder mystery, director/co-scripter Claire Denis' compelling look at urban alienation in contemporary Paris follows a variety of intersecting stories, from a killer of elderly women to a West Indian musician and carpenter trying to provide for his family. Richard Courcet, Beatrice Dalle star. 110 min. In French with English subtitles.
53-8649 Letterboxed *$89.99*

Nenette And Boni (1996)
The do-nothing existence of Boniface, a 19-year-old pizza chef who finds release through writing in his autobiographical journal and fantasizing about the local baker's wife, is shaken when his estranged younger sister, Nenette, shows up pregnant and looking for help. Director Claire Denis's funny and emotional tale stars Gregoire Colin, Alice Houri. 103 min. In French with English subtitles.
53-9996 Letterboxed *$89.99*

Marquis (1990)
A bizarre blend of anthropomorphic satire, puppetry and animation, and bawdy humor from French artists Henri Xhonneux and Roland Toper, based on writings by the Marquis de Sade. In 1789, a hedonistic canine aristocrat, held in the Bastille for blasphemy, carries on philosophical debates with his penis, which has a mind (and mouth) of its own. Roosters, rats, cows and horses also populate this "adults only" look at a decadent society on the verge of revolution. 88 min. In French with English subtitles.
70-5051 Was $59.99 *$29.99*

Eyes Without A Face (Les Yeux Sans Visage) (1959)
Released in its English-language run as " The Horror Chamber of Dr. Faustus," this is the original Gallic version of the chillingly poetic shocker about a surgeon's murderous attempts to restore the disfigured face of his daughter. Grand Guignol masterpiece by Georges Franju stars Pierre Brasseur, Edith Scob, Alida Valli. 88 min. In French with English subtitles.
53-7290 Remastered *$29.99*

Tales Of Paris (1962)
Four stories about romance in the City of Lights: "Tale of Ella," about a nightclub singer and a producer; "Tale of Antonia," focusing on a married woman's revenge on a former lover; a woman seduces her friend's husband to prove his unfaithfulness in "Tale of Francoise"; and "Tale of Fanny," about an innocent girl and a rock star. Catherine Deneuve, Dany Saval, Johnny Hallyday star. 85 min. In French with English subtitles.
10-8210 *$29.99*

Judex (1964)
A stylish revamping of the silent French serial of the same name, director Georges Franju's elaborate thriller follows masked vigilante Judex's campaign against a crooked banker and his own villainous female counterpart. Channing Pollock, Michel Vitold, Francine Bergé star. 103 min. In French with English subtitles.
01-1118 Was $29.99 *$19.99*

Bandits Of Orgosolo (1964)
Superlative work regarding a Sardinian shepherd who must take flight after being unjustly accused as a bandit...and who is ironically forced into notorious thievery by life on the run. Michele Cossu, Peppeddu Cuccu star. 98 min. Dubbed in English.
10-7240 Was $29.99 *$14.99*

Franz (1972)
A haunting and tragic love story directed by and starring Jacques Brel. The relationship between a former mercenary and an introverted woman (Barbara) is forever doomed through intervention from family and friends. 90 min. In French with English subtitles.
10-3213 *$19.99*

Cartouche (1963)
An exciting, lighthearted Gallic adventure starring Jean-Paul Belmondo as a Parisian thief-turned-highwayman who becomes the terror of 18th-century France and Claudia Cardinale as the beautiful Gypsy for whom he falls. With Jean Rochefort, Marcel Dalio; co-written and directed by Philippe de Broca ("King of Hearts"). 115 min. In French with English subtitles.
53-6072 *$29.99*

Cartouche (Dubbed Version)
Also available in a dubbed-in-English edition.
09-2406 *$24.99*

That Man From Rio (1964)
A spoof of spy movies from director Philippe de Broca ("King of Hearts") finds French pilot Jean-Paul Belmondo tracking his girlfriend (Françoise Dorleac) after she's kidnapped by South American Indians in search of priceless statues. 114 min. In French with English subtitles.
12-2859 *$19.99*

King Of Hearts (1967)
Beloved Philippe de Broca comedy stars Alan Bates as a Scots WWI soldier who must defuse a German bomb left in a French town. The town, however, has been taken over by a group of asylum inmates, and they want to make Bates their leader. Genevieve Bujold, Pierre Brasseur co-star. 101 min. In French with English subtitles.
12-2025 Letterboxed *$19.99*

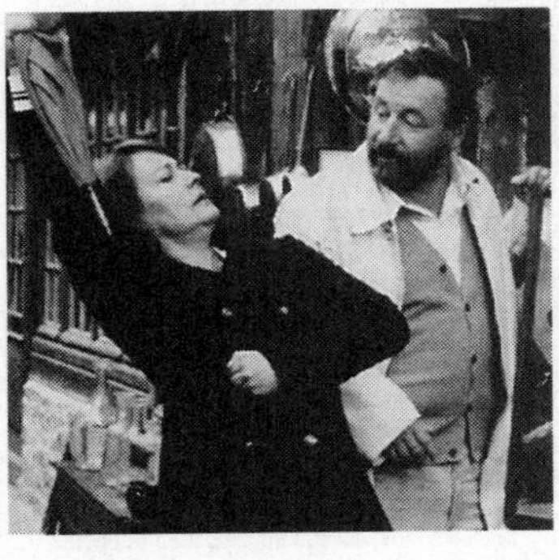

Dear Detective (1977)
Mystery, romance and comedy mix in this delightful tale from director Philippe De Broca ("King of Hearts"). Annie Girardot stars as a divorced police inspector whose latest case—the murders of three government officials—has her literally bumping into an old flame, professor Philippe Noiret, who may or may not be a suspect. AKA: "Dear Inspector," "Tendre Poulet." 90 min. In French with English subtitles.
87-1013 *$39.99*

The Green House (1996)
Set in the final days of World War II, this wonderfully touching drama from director Philippe De Broca ("King of Hearts") stars Claude Rich as an elderly Paris zookeeper who tries to shield his 8-year-old granddaughter from the brutal reality of her Resistance fighter father's death by telling her fanciful stories of his exploits. 93 min. In French with English subtitles.
70-5103 Was $59.99 *$29.99*

3 Men And A Cradle (1985)
The lives of three happy-go-lucky French bachelors are turned upside-down when a former lover of one leaves a baby on their doorstep, and they become (at first) reluctant fathers. The original French farce co-stars Roland Giraud, Michel Boujenah, Andre Dussolier. 106 min. In French with English subtitles.
47-1714 *$19.99*

Mama, There's A Man In Your Bed (1989)
Wonderful Gallic comedy about a self-absorbed businessman who's blind to his wife's affair and a plot to take over his company, and the no-nonsense black cleaning woman who helps him plot his revenge while he stays with her family. Daniel Auteuil and Firmine Richard are the odd couple in this tale from writer/director Coline Serreau ("Three Men and a Cradle"). 107 min. In French with English subtitles.
44-1794 Was $89.99 *$19.99*

La Cage Aux Folles (1980)
The original French comedy that became one of the most popular foreign films of all time. A pair of middle-aged homosexuals run a gay nightclub on the Riviera, and when the son of one plans to get married, they must make a valiant effort to appear "normal" for his future in-laws. Ugo Tognazzi and Michel Serrault star in this funny and touching love story. 106 min. In French with English subtitles.
12-2026 *$19.99*

La Cage Aux Folles II (1981)
The wild and crazy adventures of the "happiest" couple on the French Riviera continue. This time, a lovers' spat leads Ugo Tognazzi and Michel Serrault into a caper involving spies and government secrets. 102 min. In French with English subtitles.
12-3324 *$19.99*

La Cage Aux Folles 3: The Wedding (1985)
France's oddest couple are at it again in a wild farce in which drag queen Michel Serrault must marry and sire an heir in order to inherit a family fortune, a fortune that he and Ugo Tognazzi need to save their nightclub. Another comedy in the outrageous "La Cage" tradition. 88 min. Dubbed in English.
02-1605 *$19.99*

A Slightly Pregnant Man (1980)
Zany French bedroom farce with a twist, as Catherine Deneuve and Marcello Mastroianni find themselves proud parents-to-be, only he's carrying the baby. 100 min. Dubbed in English.
15-1062 *$12.99*

Voyage En Douce (1981)
The Gallic precursor of sorts to "Thelma and Louise," this heartfelt comedy-drama stars Geraldine Chaplin and Dominique Sanda as two women trapped in stale relationships who decide to set out on an odyssey of romantic fantasies and self-discovery. Directed by Michel Deville. 95 min. In French with English subtitles.
53-8058 *$79.99*

La Vie Continue (1982)
A tender film, directed by Moshe Mizrachi, about a woman played by Annie Girardot learning to cope with life's problems—including the death of her husband. Dubbed in English.
02-1174 *$59.99*

I Married A Dead Man (1982)
Compelling French mystery starring Nathalie Baye as a young woman fleeing her abusive lover who befriends a newlywed couple on a train. When the train crashes, killing the couple, Baye is mistaken by the dead man's parents as their daughter-in-law and moves in with them. Someone, though, knows Baye is living a lie...but who? With Francis Huster, Richard Bohringer. AKA: "J'ai Epousé une Ombre." 110 min. Dubbed in English.
41-5000 *$19.99*

Elle Voit Des Nanins Partout (1983)
Weird and wild take on fairy tales, based on the famed Cafe Theatre Show. Here Little Red Riding Hood's mission is to deliver wine for her father's liquor company, Tom Thumb is "raised" by the Nuns of Eternal Help and Snow White and Prince Charming don't exactly live happily ever after. 83 min. In French with English subtitles.
53-9309 *$69.99*

L'Ete Meurtrier (1984)
The ever-seductive Isabelle Adjani stars in this haunting French drama as a woman who plots an elaborate scheme of seduction and murder against three men who raped her mother years ago. 134 min. In French with English subtitles.
07-1503 *$59.99*

La Discrete (1990)
A compelling and wittily dark look at love, this French drama follows a writer who, after his girlfriend dumps him, swears to get even on all women. His plan is to woo (and abandon) a woman chosen at random and then publish an account of the affair, but his selected target has other plans. Fabrice Luchini, Judith Henry star. 96 min. In French with English subtitles.
53-7919 *$89.99*

Dr. Petiot (1990)
This macabre, true tale is set during the Nazi occupation of Paris and centers on an eccentric physician who lures Jews to his home with promises of helping them, only to rob, murder and incinerate them. An acclaimed, ominous film, featuring Michel Serrault in a chilling title performance; directed by Christian De Chalonge. 98 min. In French with English subtitles.
70-3296 Was $79.99 *$29.99*

Le Quai Des Brumes (Port Of Shadows) (1938)
Marcel Carné's classic tale of a dockworker who finds romance with a young woman he meets in a town he has fled to after committing a murder. Their relationship is eventually threatened by her ill-mannered guardian. This atmospheric story stars Jean Gabin and Michele Morgan. 89 min. In French with English subtitles.
53-8019 Was $59.99 *$39.99*

Bizarre, Bizarre (1939)
Riotous French comedy of errors from director Marcel Carné and scripter Jacques Prévert about a mystery writer whose household is thrown into turmoil by an unexpected weekend guest. Michel Simon, Louis Jouvet star. 90 min. In French with English subtitles.
01-1271 *$29.99*

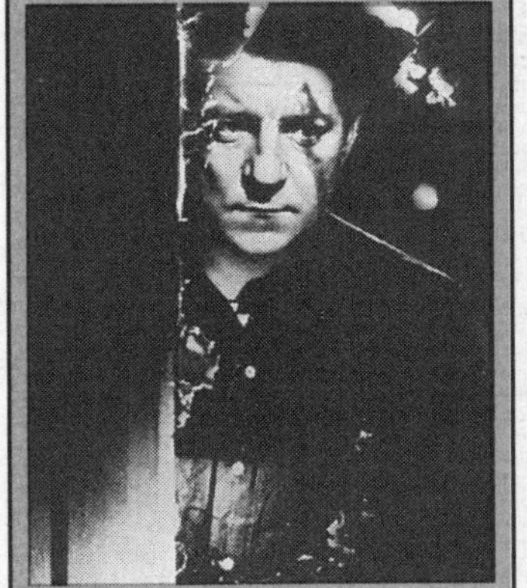

Le Jour Se Leve (Daybreak) (1939)
Jean Gabin is superb in Marcel Carné's classic example of French "poetic realism," about a lonesome romantic who locks himself in his apartment after killing a rival for his beloved's affection, then flashes back through the tragic events that led him to his current state of despair. Co-stars Jules Berry, Arletty and Jacqueline Laurent. Restored version; 88 min. In French with English subtitles.
22-5735 Was $39.99 *$29.99*

The Devil's Envoys (Les Visiteurs Du Soir) (1942)
The Devil sends two doomed souls to 15th-century Earth to seduce and lead a betrothed couple astray, but one of the diabolical minions falls in love with his charge. Haunting allegorical fable from Marcel Carné and Jacques Prévert, filmed during the Nazi occupation, stars Jules Berry, Alain Cuny, Arletty. 120 min. In French with English subtitles.
22-5455 Was $39.99 *$29.99*

The Cheaters (1958)
A change of pace from "Children of Paradise" director Marcel Carné, this Gallic JD drama stars Jacques Charrier as a Parisian college student who gets involved with a crowd of rowdy delinquents as they defy the rules of society, involving themselves in everything from blackmail to bizarre love triangles. With Andréa Parisy, Pascale Petit. AKA: "Les Tricheurs," "Youthful Sinners." 117 min. Dubbed in English.
68-9259 *$19.99*

La Merveilleuse Visite (1974)
Based on a story by H.G. Wells, writer/director Marcel Carné's final feature is a bittersweet comic fantasy about an injured angel who lands near a French village. He's nursed back to health by the local priest, but the heavenly visitor's behavior in town causes an uproar. Gilles Kohler, Jean-Pierre Castaldi star. 102 min. In French with English subtitles.
53-6070 Was $59.99 *$24.99*

Josepha (1982)
Two struggling actors who can't stop bickering realize that their relationship is not working out and that they may not be suited for marriage. Captivating dissection of companionship stars Miou-Miou, Claude Brasseur and Bruno Cremer. 114 min. In French with English subtitles.
53-7970 Was $59.99 *$29.99*

Grain Of Sand (1982)
Riveting psychological drama concerning a woman who finds herself isolated from her past and present benefits from an excellent performance by Delphine Seyrig and exceptional first-time direction from Pomme Meffre. 90 min. In French with English subtitles.
53-9017 *$59.99*

Act Of Aggression (1982)
Catherine Deneuve and Jean-Louis Trintignant shine in this riveting suspense drama about a man who goes to the edge in order to avenge the death of his murdered wife. 110 min. In French with English subtitles.
53-9313 *$69.99*

Notorious Nobodies (Illustres Inconnus) (1984)
Striking plea for human dignity tells eight separate, concurrent stories, from different corners of the globe, of individuals being stripped of their most fundamental rights by their governments. Stanislav Stanojevic directs. 102 min. In French with English subtitles.
53-9013 *$59.99*

Seventh Heaven (1999)
A repressed French wife suffering from kleptomaniacal impulses and a lack of sexual responsiveness has her homelife—and love life—changed after a visit to a hypnotherapist, but is her husband able to handle the changes? Director Benoit Jacquot's ("A Single Girl") compelling look at a marriage in metamorphosis stars Sandrine Kiberlain, Vincent Lindon. 91 min. In French with English subtitles.
53-6610 *$89.99*

The Double Life Of Veronique (1991)
Two women with identical looks, birthdates and names unknowingly have their lives interconnect in this mesmerizing, beautifully crafted thriller. When one of the women dies, a puppeteer familiar with both Veroniques tries to uncover the mystery behind her death. Irene Jacob plays the dual title role; directed by Krzysztof Kieslowski. 96 min. In French and Polish with English subtitles.
06-1999 *□$89.99*

Delicatessen (1991)
A kinetically comic blend of dark humor and satire from France, set in a post-apocalyptic world where food is so scarce that the residents of an apartment house have taken to hiring "handymen," killing them, and supplying the remains to the landlord, a butcher, for processing. Complications arise when the butcher's daughter falls for the hapless new arrival. Marie-Laure Dougnac, Dominic Pignon star. 95 min. In French with English subtitles.
06-2036 *$89.99*

The City Of Lost Children (1995)
Moody, striking fantasy from the creators of "Delicatessen" telling the grim fairy tale of a scientist living on a mysterious rig who has children kidnapped so he can tap into their dreams. Trouble occurs when a circus strongman joins forces with a child gang leader to save his kidnapped younger brother. Ron Perlman, Daniel Emilfork stars. 112 min. In French with English subtitles.
02-2912 Was $94.99 *$19.99*

The City Of Lost Children (Dubbed Version)
Also available in a dubbed-in-English edition.
02-2913 Was $94.99 *□$19.99*

Frantic (1958)
Louis Malle made his directorial debut with this early French New Wave thriller about two lovers who plan to murder the woman's husband, only to see their "perfect crime" come apart at the seams. Jeanne Moreau, Maurice Ronet star. AKA: "Elevator to the Gallows." 90 min. In French with English subtitles.
09-1778 Was $29.99 *$24.99*

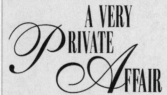

A VERY PRIVATE AFFAIR

A Very Private Affair (1962)
Louis Malle directed and co-wrote this sexy drama that examines how fame overwhelms and destroys the life of a gorgeous actress. Brigitte Bardot, Marcello Mastroianni star. 95 min. Dubbed in English.
12-1224 Was $59.99 *$19.99*

Au Revoir Les Enfants (1987)
Acclaimed French drama, based in part on events in the life of writer/director Louis Malle, that depicts life in a Nazi-occupied town in World War II. The focus is on an adolescent boy's friendship with a Jewish youth who must be hidden in their boarding school from German soldiers. Gaspard Manesse, Raphael Fejto, Peter Fitz star. 103 min. Dubbed in English.
73-1031 Was $99.99 *$19.99*

May Fools (1990)
Director Louis Malle continues the semi-autobiographical tone of "Au Revoir les Enfants" with this seriocomedy set in a French country manor in 1968. Relatives gathered for the clan's matriarch's funeral (and to squabble over her estate) find that their own bickering mirrors the turmoil sweeping France in the late '60s. Michel Piccoli, Miou-Miou star. 108 min. In French with English subtitles.
73-1095 Was $79.99 *$19.99*

Please see our index for these other Louis Malle titles: *Alamo Bay • Atlantic City • Crackers • Damage • Plucking The Daisy • Pretty Baby • Spirits Of The Dead • Vanya On 42nd Street • Viva Maria!*

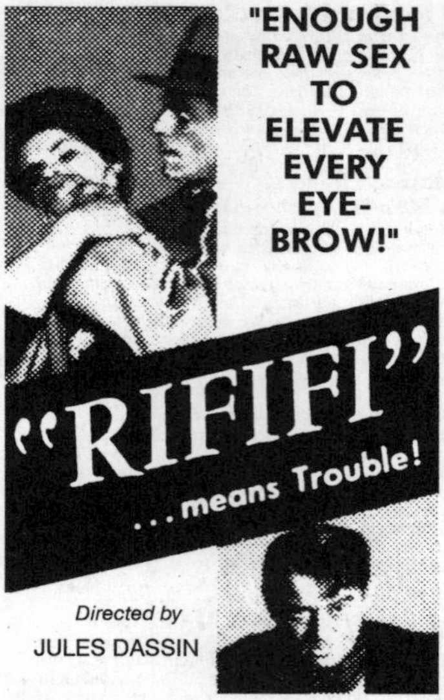

Rififi (1956)
Jules Dassin's groundbreaking French crime drama, with a memorable dialogue-free opening scene, follows four thieves who pull a jewel heist and watch their "perfect crime" fall apart before their eyes. Jean Sevais, Carl Mohner and Dassin, under the alias "Perlo Vita," star. 115 min. In French with English subtitles.
09-1710 Was $29.99 *$24.99*

Eyes Of The Bird (1984)
A Uruguayan prison is the setting for this powerful, true-to-life account of life behind bars in Latin America. Members of the International Committee of the Red Cross are granted access to interview prisoners and soon learn of torture and other injustices. Gabriel Auer directs. 80 min. In French with English subtitles.
53-9308 *$89.99*

The Lovers On The Bridge (Les Amants Du Pont-Neuf) (1991)
Ignored by audiences and critics until its 1999 American re-release, writer/director Leos Carax's lavishly downbeat romance stars Juliette Binoche as a would-be painter suffering from a disease slowly robbing her of her eyesight. Making her way to Paris' fabled Pont-Neuf Bridge, she falls in with alcoholic vagrant Denis Lavant, and the two begin a doomed love affair. 126 min. In French with English subtitles.
11-2393 Was $99.99 *□$19.99*

Le Chambon: Le Colline Aux Mille Enfants (1996)
During World War II, the village of Le Chambon-sur-Lignon, under the guidance of Christian pastors, risked reprisal from the Nazis to offer refuge to 5,000 people, many of them Jews and children. The townspeople's moving story is recounted in this historical drama. Patrick Raynal, Jip Wijngaarden, Dora Doll star. 118 min. In French with English subtitles.
50-8260 *$24.99*

La Femme Nikita (1991)
Exciting, sexy and violent thriller about a beautiful junkie, condemned to die for murdering a policeman, who is given a second chance by becoming a secret political assassin for the government. Nikita eventually falls in love with a grocery clerk who has no idea of her real identity. Anne Parillaud and Jeanne Moreau star; directed by Luc Besson ("Subway"). 117 min. In French with English subtitles.
68-1204 *$19.99*

A Paper Wedding (1991)
Intimate, powerfully acted tale of a 39-year-old college professor (Genevieve Bujold) who finds her Mr. Right in the person of her sister's boyfriend, a Chilean refugee who must marry in order to avoid deportation. The teacher agrees to marry the handsome refugee, but her feelings for him complicate matters. With Manuel Aranguiz, Dorothy Berryman. 90 min. In French with English subtitles.
75-1008 *$79.99*

Toto The Hero (1992)
Reality and fantasy blend in this acclaimed, darkly comedic study of an elderly man who believes that his life was radically altered when he was switched at birth. Seeking vengeance for the deed, the man recounts the events that led to his disappointing existence. Michel Bouquet and Mirelle Perrier star. AKA: "Toto le Heros." 94 min. In French with English subtitles.
06-2096 *□$89.99*

The Hairdresser's Husband (1992)
This whimsical look at sexual desire stars Jean Rochefort as a man who has been obsessed with hairdressers since he was a child. When he approaches middle age, he finally finds the perfect woman who can fulfill his dreams: a beautiful coiffeuse (Anna Galiena). Directed by Patrice Leconte ("Monsieur Hire"). 84 min. In French with English subtitles.
06-2107 Was $89.99 *□$19.99*

Baxter (1991)
A hilarious Gallic farce about a bull terrier with an attitude. The cantankerous canine has problems with pats on the head, babies, old ladies and owners...especially owners. Original, provocative and nasty satire told from the dog's eye view. 82 min. In French with English subtitles.
53-7684 Was $89.99 *$19.99*

Hate (1995)
Acclaimed, no-holds-barred drama follows four troubled youths in Paris through a 24-hour period. While one of the quartet of friends lies in a hospital after being beaten in a riot, his three cronies—one an Arab, one black and one Jewish—cruise their grimy neighborhood, try to score drugs, and get into trouble with police. AKA: "La Haine." 95 min. In French with English subtitles.
02-8617 Was $19.99 *$14.99*

Son Of The Shark (1995)
Powerful, mysterious French true-life drama about Martin and Simon, two homeless juvenile delinquent brothers who terrorize their small French town. After scaring adults with their crimes, the siblings are put into separate foster homes, only to escape to provoke more trouble. Ludovic Vandendaele, Erick Dasilva star. 85 min. In French with English subtitles.
53-8314 Was $89.99 *$19.99*

My Life And Times With Antonin Artaud (1995)
Paris, 1946: Antonin Artaud, poet, actor and founder of "The Theatre of Cruelty," is released from a mental hospital and befriended by a young poet, Jacques Prevel. Artaud soon depends on Prevel for the drugs he's addicted to, and an unusual relationship develops between the men. Sami Frey, Marc Barbé star. 93 min. In French with English subtitles.
53-8524 Letterboxed *$19.99*

The Disenchanted (1990)
An offhand remark by her boyfriend to prove her love for him by sleeping with the ugliest man she can find sends a 17-year-old Parisian girl on a strange and haunting series of encounters with family, friends, and a series of men. Compelling drama from director Benoit Jacquot stars Judith Godrèche, Therese Liotard. 78 min. In French with English subtitles.
70-5147 Was $79.99 *$24.99*

Mina Tannenbaum (1995)
Acclaimed drama traces four decades in the lives of two Jewish women living in Paris, from their birth in 1958 and their first meeting as children in ballet class, through the rigors of adolescence and up to the '90s, where business pressures and a rivalry over a man test their friendship. Romane Bohringer and Elsa Zylberstein star in director Martine Dugowson's film that mixes the real and surreal. 128 min. In French with English subtitles.
53-8621 *$89.99*

Ivan And Abraham (1995)
Set in 1930s Poland, this powerful French drama movingly depicts the friendship between two boys, Christian Ivan and Jewish Abraham. Fearful of political turmoil and growing anti-Semitism, the boys leave their homes and, accompanied by Abraham's teenage sister and a young Communist student who loves her, set out on their own in the countryside. Roma Alexandrovitch, Sacha Iakovlev star. 105 min. In Polish, Russian and Yiddish with English subtitles.
53-8869 Letterboxed *$89.99*

Bye-Bye (1995)
Intense story about Ismael and Mouloud, two teenage brothers from Paris who leave the city to live with their uncle and his family in Marseilles after a family tragedy. The siblings are soon travelling down different paths, as one gets involved with drugs and crime, while the other tries to save him. Sami Boyajila stars. 107 min. In French with English subtitles.
53-8895 Was $89.99 *$19.99*

Augustin (1995)
Augustin, an insurance salesman, desperately wants to be a great dramatic actor, but doesn't realize that his drolly charming personality and small roles in commercials have already marked him as a top comic performer. This quirky farce stars Jean-Chrétien Sibertin-Blanc and Thierry Lhermitte. Also includes the Oscar-winning short "Omnibus." 70 min. total. In French with English subtitles.
53-9730 *$59.99*

Candide (1962)
The 18th-century satire by Voltaire is modernized as a young man is taught by his professor to accept fate, then finds he has a rocky road until he reaches happiness. Along the way, he joins the Army, is taken prisoner and is tortured. Then, he arrives in America and things turn around. Jean-Pierre Cassel, Dahlia Lavi, Michel Simon star. 93 min. Dubbed in English.
10-8226 *$29.99*

The Rat Trap (1962)
French singer-turned-actor Charles Aznavour excels in a dramatic role in this tale that finds him searching for a new life in Paraguay. Down on his luck, Aznavour meets beautiful Marie Laforêt, but the two get involved in smuggling guns. Aznavour lands in prison, Laforêt becomes a prostitute, and both eventually try to leave the country in order to save their lives. Dubbed in French.
79-6559 Was $24.99 *$19.99*

Lafayette (1963)
An all-star, lushly filmed look at the life of Marquis de Lafayette, the French nobleman who helped the American Revolution and George Washington's raagged army. Michel Le Boyer, Pascale Audret, Orson Welles, Jack Hawkins, Edmund Purdom and Vittorio De Sica star. 60 min. Dubbed in English.
09-2217 Was $29.99 *$24.99*

Cleo From 5 To 7 (1961)
Ninety minutes in the life of Cleo (Corinne Marchand), a young woman who has been told by a palm-reader that she has cancer and must wait for test results. A unique and revealing drama directed by Agnes Varda ("Vagabond"); with Antoine Bourseiller. 90 min. In French with English subtitles.
53-7123 Remastered *$29.99*

Le Bonheur (Happiness) (1965)
Noted for its colorful, pastoral images and Mozart-filled score, both of which offset the harsh drama contained within, Agnes Varda's controversial early work follows a young carpenter who, though he loves his wife and children, decides to take a mistress. Jean-Claude Drouot, Marie-France Boyer star. 85 min. In French with English subtitles.
22-5923 Remastered *$29.99*

Lion's Love (1969)
A free-wheeling Sixties excursion featuring famed Warhol Factory actress Viva and the creators of "Hair," Gerome Ragni and James Rado. The three counterculture figures discuss such topics as metaphysics and the dangers of milk consumption, and casually drift into a menage a trois; Agnes Varda directs. Complete, unrated version; 115 min. Filmed in English.
53-8048 Letterboxed *$39.99*

Vagabond (1986)
Award-winning film from Agnes Varda that presents a "Rashomon"-like chronicle of a willful, beautiful young drifter through the reflections of those whose lives she touched. Sandrine Bonnaire is magnetic in the title role. 105 min. In French with English subtitles.
07-8099 *$29.99*

Jacquot (1993)
Director Agnes Varda fashions a sensitive look at the early years of her late husband, filmmaker Jacques Demy ("The Umbrellas of Cherbourg"). With narration and musical numbers, the film follows Demy's life as a youth obsessed with puppets, as a teen living through the Nazi occupation, and as a young artist. With Philippe Maron. 118 min. In French with English subtitles.
02-2579 Was $89.99 *$19.99*

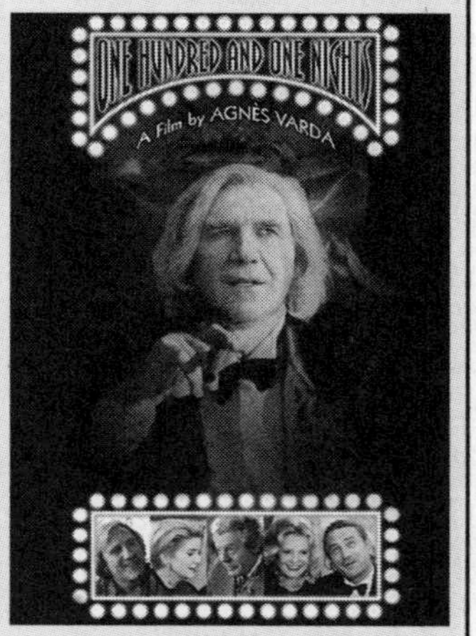

One Hundred And One Nights (1995)
Conceived as a celebration of the centennial of motion pictures, Agnes Varda's lush fantasy travels back and forth in time to track the career of 100-year-old filmmaker Simon Cinema (Michel Piccoli) and the many colleagues and students who come to his home to pay tribute to him. Julie Gayet, Mathieu Demy also star; special appearances by Anouk Aimee, Jean-Paul Belmondo, Robert De Niro, Catherine Deneuve, Gerard Depardieu, Harrison Ford, Gina Lollobrigida, Marcello Mastroianni, Jeanne Moreau and many others. 101 min.
53-6666 Letterboxed *$19.99*

The Agnes Varda Collection
This special collector's set includes the Varda films "Cleo from 5 to 7," "Le Bonheur" and "Vagabond."
22-5924 Save $10.00! *$79.99*

Passion Of Slow Fire (1963)
Superior crime drama about a French college professor accused of murdering an American student boarding at his house. When he becomes the prime suspect, his obsession with the murder leads him into an affair that turns deadly. Jean DeSailly, Alexandra Stewart and Yves Robert star. AKA: "The End of Belle," "La Morte De Belle." 91 min. Dubbed in English.
68-9132 *$19.99*

Symphony For A Massacre (1963)
From director Jacques Deray ("Borsalino") comes a complex "film noir" about a young member of a drug-smuggling ring who decides to swipe cash from his superiors. Making problems worse is an affair with his partner's wife and his counterfeiting partner. Michel Auclair, Daniella Rocca and Michele Mercier star in this atmospheric crime melodrama. Dubbed in English.
79-6430 Was $24.99 *$19.99*

La Silence De La Mer
(The Silence Of The Sea) (1947)
Written and directed by Jean-Pierre Melville ("Bob Le Flambeur"), this intense film is set in Nazi-occupied France, where a German officer is the unwelcome houseguest of a French farmer and his niece. The pair vow never to speak to their "visitor," and listen stoically as he expresses his opinions on a variety of different subjects. Howard Vernon stars. 86 min. In French with English subtitles.
01-1520 *$29.99*

Les Enfants Terribles (1950)
The unmistakable influence of scriptwriter Jean Cocteau is evident in Jean-Pierre Melville's atmospheric melodrama about a Parisian brother and sister and their friends, and how their forbidden relationships lead to tragic consequences. Nicole Stephane, Edouard Dermit star in this Quentin Tarantino favorite. 107 min. In French with English subtitles.
53-7325 *$29.99*

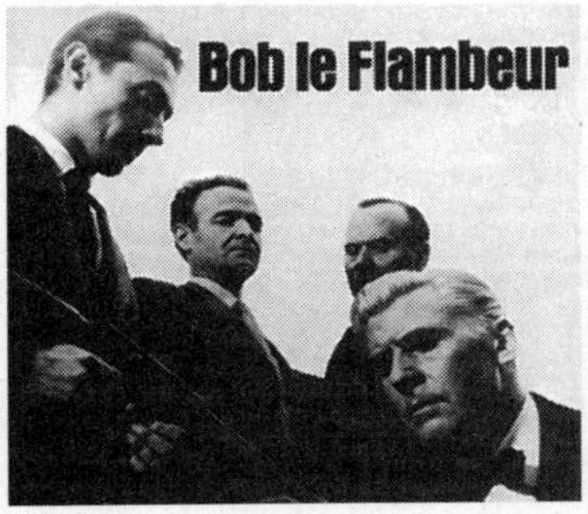

Bob Le Flambeur (1955)
Bob waits with his gang for one last score. It arrives when he decides to go after 800 million francs from the Deauville Casino. One of the greatest gangster films from "French New Wave" mentor Jean-Pierre Melville. 97 min. In French with English subtitles.
53-7941 *$59.99*

Léon Morin, Priest (1961)
In Jean-Pierre Melville's stirring drama set in occupied France during World War II, a leftist-leaning widow falls in love with a young priest. She attempts to seduce him, but he deflects her attempts, forcing the relationship to become more complex. Jean-Paul Belmondo, Emmanuelle Riva star. 118 min. In French with English subtitles.
53-7704 *$59.99*

Le Doulos (1962)
Jean-Paul Belmondo stars as a police informer playing both sides against the middle with a ruthless convict and the local gendarmes. Hit men, caper schemes, and fierce gun battles punctuate this absorbing thriller, directed by Jean-Pierre Melville. 108 min. In French with English subtitles.
53-7194 Letterboxed *$24.99*

Le Samouraï (1967)
The moody and atmospheric French thriller from director Jean-Pierre Melville that counts Quentin Tarantino and John Woo among its admirers stars Alain Delon as Jef, a cool and detached hit man who works by his own version of the samurai Bushido, or code of honor, and is pursued by both the police and his own mob employer. With François Périer, Nathalie Delon. In French with English subtitles.
53-8959 Letterboxed *$29.99*

L'Homme Blesse (1984)
Award-winning French drama that chronicles the awakening homosexual feelings in an 18-year-old boy when an encounter in a railway station with a brutish older man kindles urges he cannot understand. Audacious, moving tale stars Jean-Hughes Anglade, Vittorio Mezzogiorno; Patrice Chereau directs. 90 min. In French with English subtitles.
53-7161 Was $79.99 *$39.99*

Those Who Love Me
Can Take The Train (1998)
A Paris-to-Limoges train ride for the funeral of a brash, charismatic artist brings together a disparate group of people—the friends, family, and former lovers (both male and female) of the dead man—in director Patrice Chereau's complex character study. As the crowded journey progresses, new romances, old jealousies and time-tested friendships come to the surface. Jean-Louis Trintignant, Charles Berling, Pascal Greggory, Vincent Perez star. 122 min. In French with English subtitles.
53-6762 *$79.99*

The Little Thief (1989)
The last film co-scripted by François Truffaut is a charming and seductive work about the exploits of a precocious young girl who takes up a life of crime in her quest to grow up. Charlotte Gainsbourg stars; Claude Miller directs. 108 min. In French with English subtitles.
44-1730 Was $89.99 *$19.99*

Every Other Weekend (1989)
Compelling drama featuring Nathalie Baye as a television actress whose fame has faded. She decides she would like to revive her relationship with her two children, whom she has neglected for her career. Can she win over their love? Miki Manojlovc also stars. 100 min. In French with English subtitles.
53-9733 *$89.99*

Beau Père (1981)
Director Bertrand Blier ("Get Out Your Handkerchiefs") once again walks the fine line between controversy and exploitation with this touching seriocomedy. Burned-out pianist Patrick Dewaere takes in estranged 14-year-old stepdaughter Ariel Besse after her mother's death, only to be shocked by her request that he be her first lover. Maurice Ronet, Nathalie Baye also star. 120 min. In French with English subtitles.
03-1715 *$19.99*

My Man (Mon Homme) (1997)
French cinema's master of twisted romantic comedy, Bertrand Blier, once again mixes social satire and dark humor with pathos in this story of a prostitute who's more interested in the sexual pleasure she gives her clients and herself than the money, and whose search for the "perfect man" to fulfill her life reaches an unexpected end with a shabby bum who becomes her pimp. Anouk Grinberg, Gerard Lanvin star. 95 min. In French with English subtitles.
53-9963 Letterboxed *$29.99*

La Petite Sirene
(The Little Mermaid) (1985)
Unusual, charming romance about a 14-year-old French girl, obsessed with Hans Christian Andersen's "The Little Mermaid," who falls in love with a 40-year-old garage mechanic. Subtly erotic fable stars Laura Alexis and Philippe Leotard. 104 min. In French with English subtitles.
70-3044 Was $59.99 *$19.99*

A Single Girl (1996)
After confessing to her boyfriend that she is pregnant, a young woman sets off for her first day of work as a room service waitress in a posh Paris hotel. Her at times funny, at times antagonistic, interactions with co-workers and guests as she contemplates her future form the basis of Benoit Jacquot's drama. Virginie Ledoyen, Benoit Magimel star. 90 min. In French with English subtitles.
53-7065 Was $89.99 *$19.99*

Spirits Of The Dead (1968)
Three top European directors offer their interpretations of short stories by Edgar Allan Poe in this acclaimed anthology. Roger Vadim's "Metzengerstein" stars Jane Fonda and Peter Fonda as cousins involved in an unrequited romantic relationship; Alain Delon searches for his doppelganger in Louis Malle's "William Wilson," co-starring Brigitte Bardot; and a film shoot in Rome leads to a fatal wager for actor Terence Stamp in "Never Bet the Devil Your Head," directed by Federico Fellini. AKA: "Histories Extraordinaires." 117 min. In French with English subtitles.
01-1511 Letterboxed *$19.99*

Zou Zou (1934)
The star of several lavish French musical dramas in the '30s and '40s, the legendary Josephine Baker co-stars with Jean Gabin in this backstage tale of a laundress who fills in for the leading lady on opening night and becomes a sensation. 92 min. In French with English subtitles.
53-9106 *$24.99*

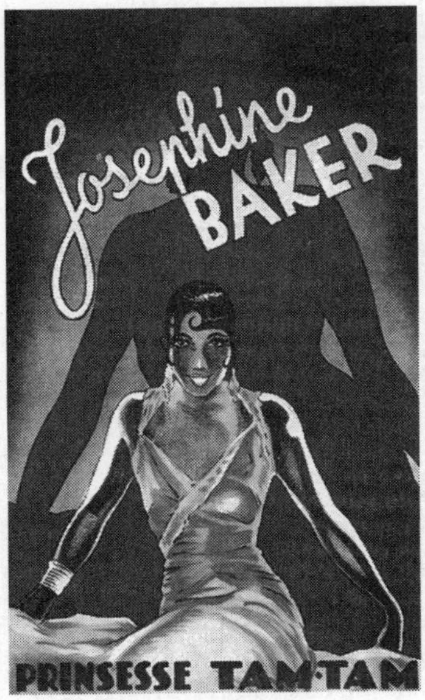

Princess Tam Tam (1935)
Josephine Baker plays an African native brought to France by a writer and coached so she can be passed off as an Indian princess in this "Pygmalion"-like comedy that also showcases Baker in stunning musical sequences. With Albert Prejean, Germaine Aussey. 77 min. In French with English subtitles.
53-9105 *$24.99*

The French Way (1940)
Josephine Baker stars in this delightful film as a night-club owner trying to open her club and act as matchmaker to two young lovers whose families are constantly feuding. Combines all the classic elements: a "Romeo and Juliet" love story, a happy ending, and the great chanteuse singing four songs! 72 min. In French with English subtitles.
62-1217 *$29.99*

Les Choses De La Vie
(Things Of Life) (1970)
An architect has an affair with a younger woman but still has feelings for his wife and son. The woman puts him on the spot, forcing him to make a decision about their future and, in fact, his whole life. Romy Schneider, Michel Piccoli and Lea Massari star. 90 min. In French with English subtitles.
53-7435 Was $79.99 *$29.99*

The Infernal Trio (1974)
A pair of sisters who marry men and then kill them for their estates and a conniving lawyer come together in a bizarre, albeit highly profitable, "love" triangle in this delicious Gallic black comedy. Romy Schneider, Michel Piccoli star. 100 min. In French with English subtitles.
53-7338 Was $59.99 *$29.99*

Les Violons Du Bal (1974)
Michel Drach's highly acclaimed drama begins with the director trying to raise funds to make the film that follows, a semi-autobiographical tale about a 9-year-old Jewish boy and his family's experiences in German-occupied France during World War II. Jean-Louis Trintignant stars. 108 min. In French with English subtitles.
53-7703 Was $79.99 *$29.99*

The Widow Couderc (1974)
A sly, witty thriller featuring Simone Signoret as a widow who has the affair of her life when she falls for escaped murderer Alain Delon. Lots of nail-biting tension and fine performances. 92 min. In French with English subtitles.
53-9297 *$69.99*

Immoral Tales (1974)
A quartet of racy tales await in this classic example of European erotica from director Walerian Borowczyk. Two teenage cousins spend an arousing day at the beach; a young woman, locked in a room by her mother, discovers the joys of self-love; Paloma Picasso portrays the bloodthirsty Countess Bathory; and the infamous Borgia family engages in a shocking, incestuous affair. With Lise Danvers, Florence Bellamy. 103 min. In French with English subtitles.
59-1025 Letterboxed *$19.99*

A Pain In The A— (1974)
The writer and director of "La Cage Aux Folles" come up with a zippy dark comedy about a Mafia hit man and a suicidal klutz who become involved in some shady dealings together. Later Americanized as "Buddy Buddy"; Jacques Brel, Lino Ventura star. 90 min. In French with English subtitles.
70-5037 Was $59.99 *$29.99*

Icy Breasts (1975)
This precursor to "Sea of Love" stars Alain Delon as a detective trying to protect his beautiful client from killing the men in her life. Mirelle Darc also stars in this intriguing thriller, directed by George Lautner. 105 min. In French with English subtitles.
53-9307 *$69.99*

Dracula, Father And Son (1976)
Christopher Lee dons the cape once more in this French spoof of the legendary bloodsucker. Forced from their Romanian castle home by Communist forces, Lee and his less-than-successful vampiric offspring, who has yet to bite a single neck, find themselves rivals for the attentions of a beautiful woman who looks like the "boy's" mother. Bernard Menez, Catherine Breillat also star; directed by Edouard Molinaro ("La Cage Aux Folles"). AKA: "Dracula and Son." 110 min. Dubbed in English.
02-1132 *$29.99*

La Marge (1976)
Controversial director Walerian Borowczyk ("Immoral Tales") delivers an erotically-charged drama starring "Emmanuelle's" Sylvia Kristel as a Parisian prostitute who partakes in a torrid affair with client Joe Dallesandro after his wife commits suicide. 90 min. In French with English subtitles.
59-7106 *$99.99*

The Lacemaker (1977)
Isabelle Huppert is unforgettable as a 19-year-old beauty salon worker who falls in love with a literature student, then falls apart when he leaves her. Claude Goretta's bittersweet romance takes an insightful look at relationships, class distinction and desire. 107 min. In French with English subtitles.
22-5401 Letterboxed *$29.99*

Madame Rosa (1977)
Winner of the Best Foreign Film Academy Award, this moving French drama stars Simone Signoret as an aging madame who cares for the children of prostitutes in Paris' Arab-Jewish ghetto. She and a young halfbreed boy develop a special friendship. With Samy Ben Youb, Claude Dauphin and filmmaker Costa-Gavras. 105 min. In French with English subtitles.
53-6048 Was $59.99 *$24.99*

Le Crabe Tambour (1977)
Offbeat French drama that garnered three of that country's Cesar Awards. Three ex-soldiers reminisce about a colorful officer with whom each served in various parts of the world, their exploits being shown in flashback. Jean Rochefort, Claude Rich, Jacques Dufilho and Jacques Perrin as "Le Crabe Tambour" star. 120 min. In French with English subtitles.
53-7249 *$59.99*

A Woman At Her Window (1977)
A superb performance from Romy Schneider highlights this romantic drama set in Greece in 1936. She plays an aristocrat who falls in love with a political activist after a series of shallow affairs with noblemen. Philippe Noiret, Victor Lanoux co-star. 110 min. In French with English subtitles.
53-8017 Was $79.99 *$29.99*

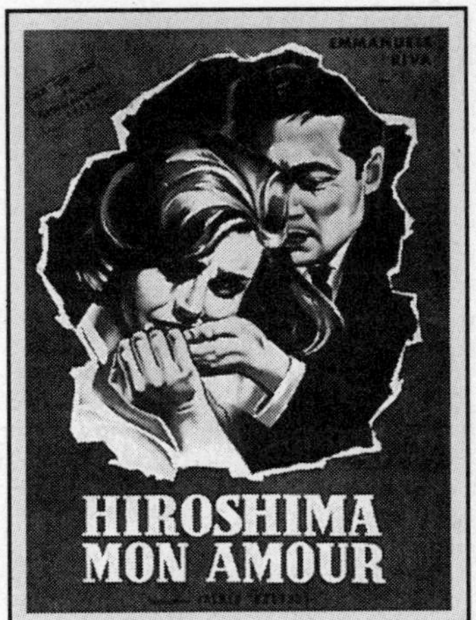

Hiroshima, Mon Amour (1959)
Director Alain Resnais' classic haunting story of two people, a beautiful French actress (Emmanuelle Riva) and a Japanese architect (Eiji Okada), who find escape from dark memories in a brief but meaningful love affair, weaves complex images and flashbacks in its depiction of the horrors of war. 91 min. In French with English subtitles.
22-5917 *$29.99*

Last Year At Marienbad (1962)
Bizarrely captivating and equally ambiguous drama juxtaposes time and memory, fantasy and reality, and the past and present, with Giorgio Albertazzi as a man who relentlessly tries to convince a woman (Delphine Seyrig), a guest at a posh chateau, that they met a year earlier and had planned to meet again. Alain Resnais and novelist Alain Robbe-Grillet's collaboration co-stars Sacha Pitoeff. 93 min. In French with English subtitles.
62-1138 Was $29.99 *$24.99*

Last Year At Marienbad
(Letterboxed Version)
Also available in a theatrical, widescreen format.
53-9939 *$19.99*

Muriel (1963)
Compelling French drama by director Alain Resnais about two people trapped in their past: a widow who has an affair with an old flame, and her stepson, obsessed with the death he witnessed of a young girl during the Algerian conflict. Delphine Seyrig, Jean-Baptiste Thierree star. 116 min. In French with English subtitles.
53-7151 Was $59.99 *$19.99*

La Guerre Est Finie (1966)
Alain Resnais' "New Wave" classic stars Yves Montand as a revolutionary opposing the Spanish government who returns to his Paris apartment, where he meets a young student, learns of his associates' troubles in Madrid, and visits his mistress. The events lead him to reconsider his life. Ingrid Thulin, Genevieve Bujold co-star. 120 min. In French with English subtitles.
53-6081 *$29.99*

Stavisky (1974)
Alain Resnais' elegant chronicle of Serge Stavisky, a charming Russian promoter whose financial thievery and bribery of government officials nearly brought down the French government in the 1930s. Jean-Paul Belmondo, Charles Boyer, Anny Duperey, Michel Lonsdale, Gerard Depardieu star; music by Stephen Sondheim. 117 min. In French with English subtitles.
53-7611 Letterboxed *$24.99*

Mon Oncle D'Amerique (1980)
Witty treatise on human behavior from Alain Resnais observes the interactions of three people: a manager at a textile plant (Gerard Depardieu), an actress (Nicole Garcia) and a media mogul (Roger Pierre). Interspersed with this trio's stories is commentary on how laboratory rats and humans relate to one another. 123 min. In French with English subtitles.
53-1616 Letterboxed *$29.99*

The Last Adventure (1977)
After trying a scam which involved flying his plane through Paris' Arc de Triomphe, pilot Alain Delon joins his racing mechanic pal and a sculptress on a dangerous trip down the Congo in search of a downed plane filled with riches. Lino Ventura, Joanna Shimkus co-star; Robert Enrico ("An Occurrence at Owl Creek Bridge") directs. In French with English subtitles.
87-1001 Was $69.99 *$39.99*

L'Etat Sauvage (1978)
Powerful political drama set in a newly independent African nation in the 1960s. When he discovers his estranged wife living with a black politician, a French U.N. official takes radical steps to ruin his career and life. Director Francis Girod examines prejudice from several viewpoints. Jacques Dutronic, Marie-Christine Barrault, Claude Brasseur star. 111 min. In French with English subtitles.
53-7426 *$59.99*

Fantastic Planet (Collector's Edition) (1973)
Director René Laloux's spellbinding animated marvel follows the travails of the Oms—tiny humans kept as pets by the giant, blue-skinned Traags on a distant world—and how one Om escapes from his captivity and begins a rebellion. Wonderful Czech/French feature was based on Stefan Wul's novel "Om En Série." This special video edition also includes three early cartoon shorts by Laloux: "Les Dents du Singe" (1960), "Les Temps Morts" (1964) and "Les Escargots" (1965). 74 min. In French with English subtitles.
08-8711 Letterboxed ***$14.99***

Rendez-Vous (1987)
Explosive, erotic French drama stars sultry Juliette Binoche ("The Unbearable Lightness of Being") as a would-be actress who falls into a violently passionate triangle with two roommates. Lambert Wilson, Wadceck Stanczak, Jean-Louis Trintignant co-star; André Techine directs. 82 min. In French with English subtitles.
53-7375 ***$29.99***

My Favorite Season (Ma Saison Preferee) (1993)
After suffering a stroke, an elderly woman moves into the home of daughter Catherine Deneuve's family. The stressful situation worsens when the woman's son, obsessive surgeon Daniel Auteuil, arrives for a Christmas dinner, as old wounds are reopened and dormant passions are reawakened. Director André Téchiné's emotional drama also stars Jean-Pierre Bouvier, Chaira Mastroianni (Denueve's real-life daughter). 122 min. In French with English subtitles.
53-9814 Letterboxed ***$19.99***

Wild Reeds (1995)
Set in 1962, André Techiné's acclaimed tale of politics and coming-of-age sexuality focuses on three teenagers attending a French boarding school. A boy discovers he has feelings towards a male friend who, in turn, has fallen for the daughter of one of his teachers. Further complicating matters is the arrival of a student with radical political views. Gael Morel, Stephane Rideau star. In French with English subtitles.
53-8578 Was $89.99 ***$29.99***

Le Corbeau (The Raven) (1943)
Early French drama by Henri-Georges Clouzot that focuses on the growing paranoia and suspicion in a small town when an anonymous person begins sending poison pen letters to the residents. 90 min. In French with English subtitles.
62-1204 ***$19.99***

Jenny Lamour (1948)
Riveting mystery from Henri-Georges Clouzot ("Diabolique") concerning a pair of forlorn lovers who become implicated in the slaying of a sleazy film producer. Gripping tale stars Suzy Delair, Bernard Blier, Simone Renant. AKA: "Quai Des Orfevres." 102 min. Dubbed in English.
10-7217 ***$29.99***

Manon (1949)
Acclaimed post-war drama from France which follows the sad and sordid descent of a teenage girl, who dared to love a resistance fighter, into prostitution. Henri-Georges Clouzot directs; Cecile Aubry, Michel Auclair star. 87 min. In French with English subtitles.
01-1394 Was $39.99 ***$19.99***

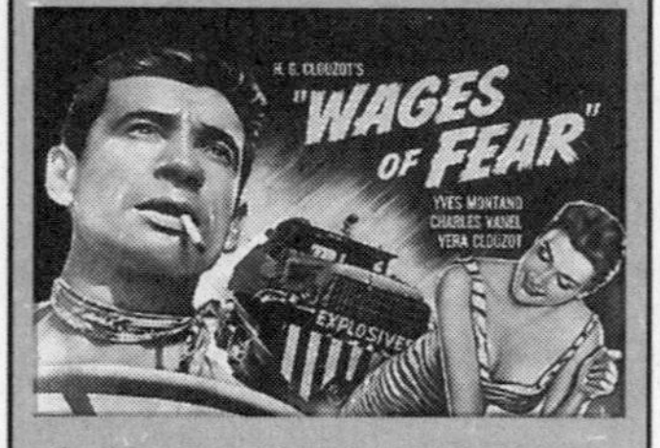

The Wages Of Fear (1953)
Henri-Georges Clouzot's spellbinding tale of a team of four men hired to drive two trucks loaded with nitroglycerine across 300 miles of mountainous South American terrain. Yves Montand, Charles Vanel star in a gem of cinematic suspense and adventure. Restored European version; 148 min. In French with English subtitles.
22-5499 Was $39.99 ***$29.99***

Diabolique (1955)
Taut thriller from Henri-Georges Clouzot that rivals Hitchcock's best. A cruel schoolmaster is murdered by his wife and his mistress...or is he? A frightening tale of suspense and desperation with Simone Signoret, Vera Clouzot and Paul Meurisse. 116 min. In French with English subtitles.
22-5541 Restored ***$29.99***

Diabolique (Dubbed Version)
Also available in a dubbed-in-English edition.
08-9009 Was $39.99 ***$29.99***

Clouzot Suspense 2-Pack
This money-saving package features two classics from the French master of cinematic suspense: "Diabolique" and "The Wages of Fear."
22-5985 Save $10.00! ***$49.99***

Indochine (1992)
A striking epic of romance and politics and winner of the Best Foreign Film Oscar, starring Catherine Deneuve as a privileged French plantation owner living in Indochina in the 1930s who finds herself in an embittered fight over her naval officer lover with her adopted, native teenage daughter. Vincent Perez and Linh Dan Pham also star. 156 min. In French with English subtitles.
02-2524 Was $89.99 ***$19.99***

The Umbrellas Of Cherbourg (1963)
Jacques Demy's haunting romantic drama, unique for having all of its dialogue sung, stars beautiful Catherine Deneuve as a widowed shopkeeper's daughter who discovers she is pregnant by her soldier boyfriend and, fearing for her family's security, agrees to marry another man. With Nino Castelnuovo, Ellen Farner; the Michel Legrand score includes "I Will Wait for You," "Watch What Happens." 91 min. In French with English subtitles.
27-6057 Letterboxed ***$29.99***

The Young Girls Of Rochefort (1967)
Gloriously filmed musical romance from Jacques Demy ("The Umbrellas of Cherbourg") tells of twin sisters (played by real-life sisters Catherine Deneuve and Françoise Dorléac) who long for love and a way out of the seaside town where their mother runs a small cafe. Gene Kelly, Michel Piccoli and Jacques Perrin are the men who enter their lives. With Danielle Darrieux and George Chakiris. This restored version was supervised by Demy's wife, Agnes Varda. 125 min. In French with English subtitles.
11-2463 ***□$99.99***

Roads To The South (1978)
Yves Montand stars as a writer who left his native Spain during the Franco takeover and returns decades later to confront the changes in his homeland and his life. Miou-Miou also stars in this emotional drama directed by Joseph Losey. 100 min. In French with English subtitles.
53-7488 Was $79.99 ***$29.99***

Lucie Aubrac (1997)
A remarkable true story of love and courage, director Claude Berri's WWII drama stars Carole Bouquet as Aubrac, a pregnant woman in occupied Lyon who risks her life to save husband Daniel Auteuil, a Resistance leader captured and sentenced to death by the Nazis. With Patrice Chéreau, Heino Ferch. 116 min. In French with English subtitles.
02-9186 Was $99.99 ***$14.99***

A Simple Story (1978)
Romy Schneider turns in a tour de force performance as a 39-year-old woman who faces a mid-life crisis and decides to change her life following an abortion. This sensuous and thought-provoking film from director Claude Sautet also stars Claude Brasseur and Bruno Cremer. 110 min. In French with English subtitles.
70-5040 Was $59.99 ***$29.99***

French Fried Vacation (1978)
A Club Med-like resort is the setting for wild and racy fun in the sun in this Gallic beachside bedroom romp. Josiane Balasko, Michel Blanc, Gerard Jugnot and Thierry Lhermitte star. AKA: "Les Bronzes." 98 min. In French with English subtitles.
87-1015 ***$39.99***

The Associate (1979)
Michel Serrault stars as a French businessman who can't get ahead until he invents a fictional English "partner," only to find that his creation gets all the credit. Lively Gallic spoof of high finance also stars Claudine Auger. 94 min. In French with English subtitles.
53-1663 ***$29.99***

War Of The Buttons (1963)
An acclaimed story of the war between two factions of young French boys, battling with slingshots and donkeys for the belts and buttons found on the opposing side's clothing. The war games become more elaborate, as one group decides to go into combat without clothing! A charming satire from Yves Robert ("My Father's Glory"). 88 min. In French with English subtitles.
78-5065 ***$39.99***

Subway (1985)
Luc Besson's surreal journey into the lives of those living in the catacombs of Paris' Metro. Christopher Lambert stars as a hood on the run, Isabelle Adjani is his would-be lover/victim, trying to choose between a life of leisure or Lambert. Colorful, mixture of humor, suspense and cynicism. 104 min. Dubbed in English.
04-1955 ***$19.99***

The Visitors (Les Visiteurs) (1992)
A record-breaking hit in its native France, Jean-Marie Poire's fantasy/comedy stars Jean Reno and Christian Clavier (who co-scripted with Poire) as a 12th-century knight and his squire who, thanks to a wizard, are transported to modern-day France and must battle autos, appliances and such strange notions as democracy and bathing. With Valerie Lemercier. 107 min. In French with English subtitles.
11-2107 Was $94.99 ***$19.99***

Little Indian, Big City (1994)
The original French comedy that was Americanized as 1997's "Jungle 2 Jungle," with Thierry Lhermitte as a Paris businessman who learns he has a 12-year-old son who's been raised with natives in the South American jungle and tries to "civilize" the boy by bringing him back to France with him. Ludwig Briand, Patrick Timsit, Miou Miou also star. 90 min. Dubbed in English.
11-2245 Was $99.99 ***□$19.99***

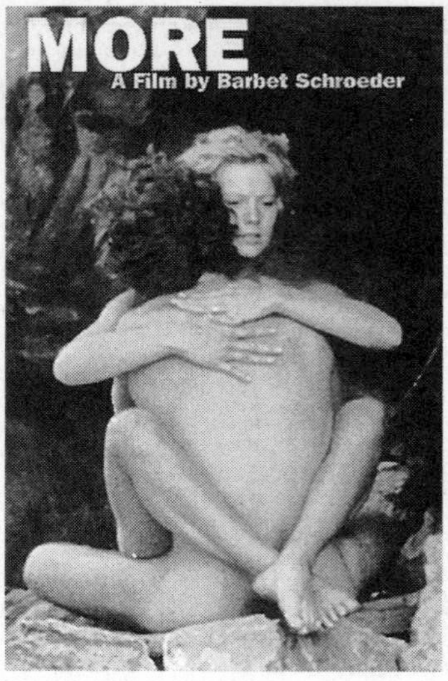

More (1969)
The first effort from Barbet Schroeder ("Reversal of Fortune") is an authentic '60s time capsule, detailing the adventures of a German student whose search for meaning in life takes him to Paris and the Mediterranean and involves him with wild sex, drug addiction, and more. With Mimsy Farmer, Klaus Grünberg; music by Pink Floyd. 110 min. In English and French, German and Spanish with English subtitles.
19-1854 Letterboxed ***$29.99***

Maitresse (1976)
In the kinky tradition of "The Night Porter" comes this look at sexual obsession. Burglar Gerard Depardieu becomes infatuated with beautiful dominatrix Bulle Ogier and is drawn into her life, a world where middle-class "normalcy" masks a reality of anonymous sex, bondage games and pain. Directed by Barbet Schroeder. 112 min. In French with English subtitles.
19-1858 Letterboxed ***$29.99***

Peppermint Soda (1977)
The young daughters of a divorced Jewish couple encounter tough teachers, first love and dreaded holidays with their father in Diane Kurys' bittersweet comedy about the joys and pain of adolescence, set in 1950s Paris. With Eléonore Klarwein and Odile Michel. 97 min. In French with English subtitles.
53-7827 Was $79.99 ***$29.99***

Cocktail Molotov (1980)
Diane Kurys ("Entre Nous") directed this story, set in 1968, which tells of a teenage girl who leaves home after a quarrel with her parents and heads to a kibbutz in Israel. A group of friends try to find her, but their trip is filled with unexpected problems, including the student riots they encounter. Elise Caron, Philippe Lebas star. 100 min. In French with English subtitles.
53-6493 Letterboxed ***$29.99***

Entre Nous (1983)
Two of France's leading actresses, Miou Miou and Isabelle Huppert, shine in this look at the 30-year friendship of two very different women. A funny and tender story from director Diane Kurys, based in part on her mother's life. 112 min. In French with English subtitles.
12-1387 ***$19.99***

Love After Love (1994)
Acclaimed romantic seriocomedy from director Diane Kurys follows a year in the life of authoress Isabelle Huppert, tracing her love affairs and how their outcomes affect those people around her and her lovers. With Hippolyte Girardot, Bernard Giraudeau. 104 min. In French with English subtitles.
53-8353 Letterboxed ***$19.99***

Diva (1982)
A wildly colorful and complex French thriller from director/co-scripter Jean-Jacques Beineix whose marvelously convoluted plot involves a young Paris mail carrier obsessed with an opera star who refuses to make records, a tape spelling out police corruption, Taiwanese mobsters, New Wave assassins, and a wild chase through the Paris Metro. Frederic Andrei, Richard Bohringer, Gerard Darmon and Wilhelmenia Wiggins Fernandez star. 123 min. In French with English subtitles.
12-1237 ***$29.99***

Cousin, Cousine (1975)
Delightful comedy that twists the old "kissing cousins" cliché. Victor Lanoux and Marie-Christine Barrault become cousins through their marriages, but soon after the weddings, they begin a passionate and funny love affair. Later Americanized as "Cousins." 95 min. In French with English subtitles.
76-1015 Letterboxed ***$29.99***

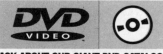

Mr. Klein (1975)
Alain Delon is Robert Klein, an art dealer in occupied France who purchases valuable works from Jews trying to flee the country for a song. But when Nazi officials mistake him for a second Mr. Klein—this one a Jewish resistance leader—Delon becomes obsessed with finding his "other self." Jeanne Moreau, Suzanne Flon also star in director Joseph Losey atmospheric thriller. 124 min. In French with English subtitles.
70-5126 ***$29.99***

A Man And A Woman (1966)
One of cinema's great romances, this lyrical Claude Lelouch love story between a script girl (Anouk Aimee) and an auto racer (Jean-Louis Trintignant) captured worldwide acclaim and the hearts of a generation. 102 min. Dubbed in English.
19-1553 ***$19.99***

A Man And A Woman: 20 Years Later (1986)
Director Claude Lelouch reteams with stars Anouk Aimee and Jean-Louis Trintignant for this romantic, nostalgic treat. Script girl Aimee is now a producer...and her attempts to make a film about her affair with Trintignant rekindles the old fire. 112 min. In French with English subtitles.
19-1554 Was $19.99 ***$14.99***

Les Misérables (1995)
Claude Lelouch's magnificent interpretation of Victor Hugo's classic novel moves the 19th-century story to World War II, where French furniture mover Jean-Paul Belmondo gets involved in a series of significant events, from helping a Jewish family escape the Nazis to participating in the French Resistance movement. With Michel Boujenah, Anne Girardot. 178 min. In French with English subtitles.
19-2440 Was $94.99 ***$29.99***

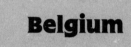

Belgium

The Red Dwarf (1998)
A twisted tale of loneliness and rejection, this surreal Belgian film follows a diminutive law office clerk (Jean-Yves Thual) who begins an unlikely affair with a client, an aging opera star (Anita Ekberg) looking to divorce her unfaithful husband. When Ekberg breaks off the affair, a jealous Thual strangles her and runs away with a travelling circus, where he is befriended by a teenage acrobat. Dyna Gauzy, Arno Chevrier also star. 101 min. In French with English subtitles.
02-3421 ***$99.99***

The Sexual Life Of The Belgians (1995)
Belgian director Jan Bucquoy's risqué comedy focuses on the adventures of Jan, a young man whose attempts to get intimate with members of the opposite sex are continually thwarted. During the sexual revolution of the 1960s, Jan finally fulfills his desires, but marriage eventually disrupts his life. 85 min. In French with English subtitles.
70-5096 Was $59.99 ***$29.99***

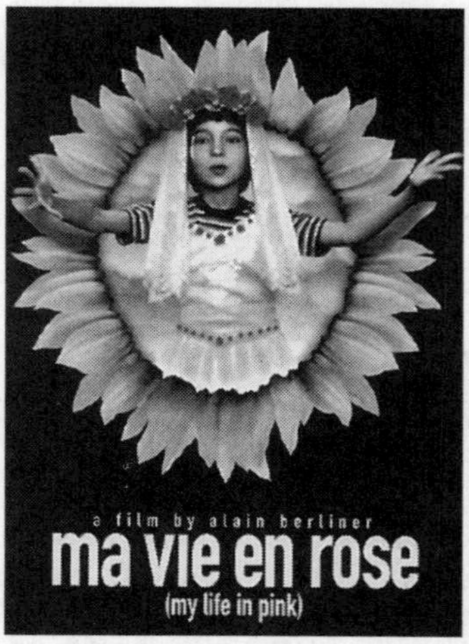

Ma Vie En Rose (My Life In Pink) (1997)
Seven-year-old Ludovic enjoys playing dress-up with lipstick and high heels and plans to marry a male classmate...which would be fine, except that Ludovic is a boy. His gender-bending play is met with bemusement at first by his parents, but the family soon faces scorn and ostracism by their suburban Belgian community . A lyrical, funny and touching look at sexual identity, director/co-writer Alain Berliner's acclaimed tale stars Michèle Laroque, Jean-Philippe Ecoffey and Georges du Fresne. 89 min. In French with English subtitles.
02-3179 Was $99.99 ***$24.99***

Chantal Akerman

Akermania, Vol. 1
Three Chantal Akerman short films are collected on this tape: "J'Ai Faim, J'Ai Froid (I'm Hungry, I'm Cold)" looks at the adventures of two runaway teens in Paris; "Saute Ma Ville" is the story of a lonely woman (Akerman) who literally seals herself in her apartment; and "Hotel Monterey" is a silent look at a New York pension hotel. 89 min. In French with English subtitles.
70-3183 Was $59.99 ***$19.99***

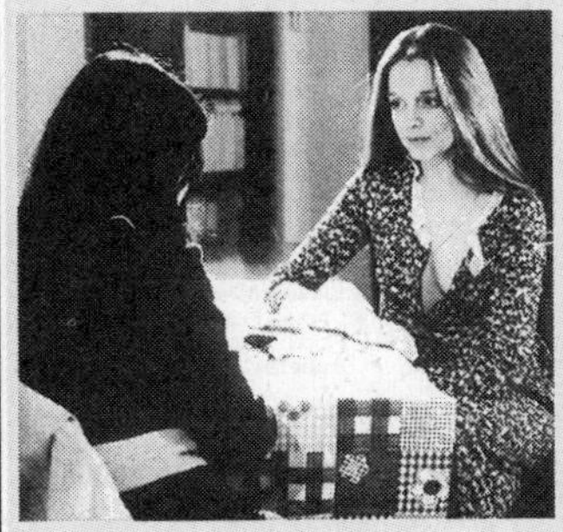

Je Tu Il Elle (1974)
The first feature by independent Belgian filmmaker Chantal Akerman is a stark, dramatic look at a woman's coming to terms with her life. Akerman stars as the isolated heroine who leaves her spartan apartment and embarks on a series of adventures on the way to the home of a former lesbian lover. 90 min. In French with English subtitles.
70-3028 ***$29.99***

News From Home (1976)
A "city symphony of New York," presented by Belgian filmmaker Chantal Akerman, capturing the Big Apple in all its glory and sordid splendor through looks at its residents and their daily routines. Strikingly photographed, the film includes letters from the director and her mother. 90 min. In English and French with English subtitles.
70-3046 Was $79.99 ***$24.99***

Les Rendezvous d'Anna (1978)
A woman filmmaker journeys across Europe, and along the way has affairs with a variety of men, in this Belgian drama by Chantal Akerman. Aurore Clement, Helmut Green star. 120 min. In French with English subtitles.
70-3029 ***$29.99***

Toute Une Nuit (1982)
An arresting nighttime walk down the streets of Brussels, courtesy of director Chantal Akerman, this film flows from door to door and story to story as it follows the many personal dramas that unfold. A child running away from home, a wife's meeting with her lover, a voyeuristic encounter and other vignettes are featured. 90 min. In French with English subtitles.
70-3030 ***$29.99***

The Eighties (Les Annees 80) (1983)
One of the most unique movie musicals ever made, Chantal Akerman's film-within-a-film first chronicles the auditions, rehearsals and preparations for her musical comedy set in a shopping mall, "Window Shopping," followed by the actual performance. 82 min. In French with English subtitles.
70-3031 ***$79.99***

Window Shopping (1986)
Chantal Akerman's salute to classic MGM musicals details the romantic involvements of a group of people based at a stylish Paris shopping mall. Entanglements occur between a young storekeeper, a hairdresser and others in this bouncy but cynical salute to l'amour. With Delphine Seyrig, Charles Denner, Lio and John Berry. In French with English subtitles.
70-3045 ***$29.99***

Night And Day (1991)
A wry and racy romantic comedy about a young woman in Paris who manages to have full-time relationships with two friends who work opposite shifts as taxi drivers. Director Chantal Akerman's menage a trois tale stars Guilane Londez, Thomas Langmann, Francois Negret. 90 min. In French with English subtitles.
53-7925 Was $89.99 ***$19.99***

Please see our index for the Chantal Akerman title: *A Couch In New York*

Rosetta (1999)
A young woman, living with her mother in a seedy trailer park, desperately yearns to escape her edge-of-poverty existence. Will she be forced to choose between a better life and her only friend? Émilie Dequenne and Fabrizio Rongione star in this acclaimed, understated drama from Belgian brothers Luc and Jean-Pierre Dardenne. 95 min. In French with English subtitles.
02-9219 ***$79.99***

Man Bites Dog (1992)
An extraordinary commentary on screen violence, chronicling the life of a ruthless, loquacious serial killer who murders people for the fun of it. A TV news crew filming a documentary on the psychopath is eventually lured into his maniacal path. Scathingly funny and horribly disturbing. Uncut, NC-17 director's version; 96 min. In French with English subtitles.
53-7804 Was $89.99 ***$19.99***

Daens (1992)
This compelling true story focuses on Father Pieter Daens, who spoke out against the miserable conditions in factories and drew the wrath of Church officials, businessmen and the monarchy. Eventually, Daens is elected to Parliament, where he continues his controversial campaign for the working class. Jan Decleir stars. 134 min. In Flemish and French with English subtitles.
53-8421 Was $89.99 ***$19.99***

Farinelli (1994)
Sumptuously filmed drama, based on a true story, focuses on the difficult relationship between a renowned castrato singer in 18th-century Europe and his older brother, a mediocre composer. Thanks to efforts by Frederic Handel, their love for the same woman and questions about the singer's past, a bitter rivalry ensues. With Stefano Dionisi, Enrico Lo Verso. 110 min. In French with English subtitles.
02-2801 Was $89.99 ***$19.99***

La Promesse (1996)
Unforgettable, lyrical drama tells of Igor, a teenage thief whose father is a master swindler specializing in sneaking illegal immigrant workers into his Belgian city. Much to the dismay of his father, Igor tries to change his sordid lifestyle by helping Assita, an African refugee whose husband they killed. Jérémie Renier, Olivier Gourmet star. 93 min. In French with English subtitles.
53-6280 Letterboxed ***$94.99***

Hombres Complicados (1997)
Petty thief Roger is in deep hock with hoods, so, in order to beat the heat, he convinces his estranged customs officer brother Bruno to join him and their wives on a road trip. Their journey turns out to be a wild one, filled with danger, sex and scary loan sharks. With Dirk Roofthoot, Josse de Pauw. 83 min. In Flemish and French with English subtitles.
01-1563 ***$29.99***

Netherlands

Keetje Tippel (Katie's Passion) (1975)
Haunting Dutch drama from Paul Verhoeven about a young girl (Monique van de Ven) forced by her impoverished mother to walk the streets. Rutger Hauer also stars as the handsome stranger who may be her salvation...or her destruction. 90 min. In Dutch with English subtitles.
53-7301 ***$29.99***

Rembrandt—1669 (1977)
Superlative Dutch biodrama recounts the final year in the life of the legendary painter, as the aging Rembrandt attempts to balance a tempestuous personal life with his still-vibrant creative drive. Authentic settings and costumes add to the charm of this stirring film. Frans Stelling, Tom de Koff star. 114 min. In Dutch with English subtitles.
53-7723 Was $79.99 ***$29.99***

A Flight Of Rainbirds (1981)
This serio-comic take on love and sex was one of the most popular Dutch films ever released. Jeroen Krabbe stars as both a repressed biologist, who dreams he must lose his virginity or die, and his slick alter ego, who tries to help him find an appropriate woman. 94 min. In Dutch with English subtitles.
70-3186 Was $79.99 ***$29.99***

On Top Of The Whale (1982)
This Dutch film, one of the most offbeat comedies ever made in any land, chronicles the attempts of a pair of anthropologists to study the last remaining members of a dying Indian tribe whose entire language consists of one word, spoken with different inflections. An eccentric millionaire's mansion is the setting for this satirical look at the scientific community. 93 min. In Dutch with English subtitles.
53-7519 ***$59.99***

A Question Of Silence (1984)
Controversial Dutch drama in which three women, strangers to one another, murder a man out of hatred for male-ruled society. At their trial, a female court psychiatrist appointed to examine them comes to sympathize with their views and questions her own beliefs. Cox Habbema, Edda Barends star in this film from Marleen Gorris. 92 min. In Dutch with English subtitles.
70-5036 Was $59.99 ***$29.99***

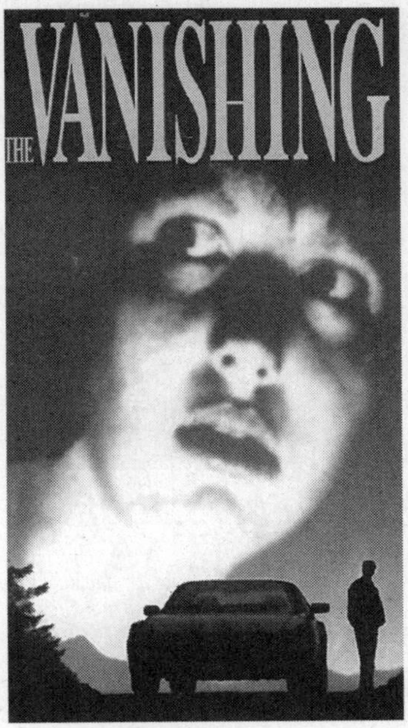

The Vanishing (1988)
In this haunting thriller, a young man stages an obsessive search for his girlfriend who mysteriously vanished during a car trip. After three agonizing years of looking for the woman, he gets an opportunity to meet the diabolical person who kidnapped her. Bernard-Pierre Donnadieu, Gene Bervoets and Johanna Ter Steege star. 107 min. In French and Dutch with English subtitles.
53-7644 Was $89.99 ***$19.99***

The Outsider (1983)
Rutger Hauer plays a Dutch detective who becomes romantically involved with the widow of a powerful drug dealer. But the woman has a sordid dark side, as Hauer soon discovers in this exotic actioner. With Rijk de Gooyer and Willeke Van Ammelroy. AKA: "Outsider in Amsterdam." 90 min. Dubbed in English.
64-3296 ***$14.99***

Ciske The Rat (1984)
Powerful and graphically brutal Dutch drama about a precocious 11-year-old boy who is caught in the middle of a feud between his separated parents. The turmoil leads him to commit a violent and shocking crime that lands him in prison. Danny De Munk, Willeke Van Amelrooy star. 107 min. In Dutch with English subtitles.
78-5084 ***$59.99***

Antonia's Line (1995)
Marleen Gorris' winner of the Academy Award for Best Foreign Film centers on an elderly woman who recalls her life in a small Dutch village on the day of her death. Her remembrances involve five generations of women and some of their men, including her artist daughter and her granddaughter, a musical prodigy. With Willeke Van Ammelrooy, Els Dottermans. 102 min. In Dutch with English subtitles.
02-8983 Letterboxed ***$19.99***

1-900 (1995)
A provocative, sexually charged film from Theo van Gogh (Vincent's great-nephew) looks at two lonely professionals who meet through a phone sex line. Their electronic relationship becomes increasingly personal, and each seeks more intimate contact, even though they've agreed never to meet or learn each other's names. Ariane Schluter, Ad van Kempen star. 90 min. In Dutch with English subtitles.
53-9729 Was $89.99 ***$19.99***

The Dress (1996)
The effect that a dress has on the women who own it—from a bored housewife to a lonely bag lady—and the men they encounter while wearing it is the focus of this unusual comedy/drama from Dutch filmmaker Alex van Warmerdam, who co-stars as a lecherous train conductor. With Henri Garcin, Ariane Schluter. 103 min. In Dutch with English subtitles.
53-6471 ***$19.99***

Character (1997)
This Academy Award-winner for Best Foreign Film is a stylish suspense film set in Rotterdam during the 1920s and details the events that occur after the brutal murder of the town's hated bailiff. Arrested for the crime is the bailiff's son, a lawyer, who tells his tragic life story to a detective. Mike Van Diem's effort stars Jan Decleir. 114 min. In Dutch with English subtitles.
02-3214 Was $99.99 ***$24.99***

The Delivery (1999)
In this stylish Dutch thriller, two men in desperate need of cash agree to help a drug kingpin by transporting $25 million worth of Ecstasy from Amsterdam to Barcelona. The trip should be a breeze, but things turn dangerous when they encounter terrorists and a mysterious woman named Loulou. With Freddy Douglas and Aurelie Meriel. 100 min. Dubbed in English.
68-2012 ***□$69.99***

Crocodiles In Amsterdam (1990)
Nina is a hot-headed rebel, while flighty Gino is content to drift through life. The friendship that develops between them forms the basis of this funny and touching female bonding film from director Annette Apon. 88 min. In Dutch with English subtitles.
01-1507 ***$39.99***

For A Lost Soldier (1993)
A nostalgic and poignant coming-of-age drama, starring Jeroen Krabbe as a choreographer suffering from creative block who reminisces about how, as a teenager after World War II, he was befriended by a Canadian soldier who became his first love. With Maarten Smit, Andrew Kelley. 92 min. In English and Dutch with English subtitles.
53-8064 Was $89.99 ***$19.99***

The Forbidden Quest (1993)
Using astonishing stock footage, this pseudo-documentary from Dutch director Peter Delpeut ("Lyrical Nitrate") chronicles an imaginary 1905 Norwegian expedition to the South Pole. The doomed voyage is recounted by the expedition's sole survivor, the ship's carpenter, in Ireland in 1941. 75 min. Filmed in English.
53-8450 ***$59.99***

Egg (1988)
A hit at the Cannes Film Festival, this is the engaging, often hilarious story of a banker who finds a lonely schoolteacher through a personal ad. Danniel Danniel directed this fresh romantic fable that's in the tradition of Jacques Tati and Buster Keaton. 58 min. In Dutch with English subtitles.
53-7386 ***$59.99***

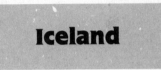

Iceland

Children Of Nature (1994)
Nominated for an Oscar for Best Foreign Film, this touching romance focuses on an elderly farmer who rekindles the love he shared with a childhood sweetheart when they both move to a Reykjavik old age home. Together, the couple take off in an incredible adventure that helps them rediscover their lives. With Gisli Halldorsson. 85 min. In Icelandic with English subtitles.
53-7943 Was $89.99 ***$19.99***

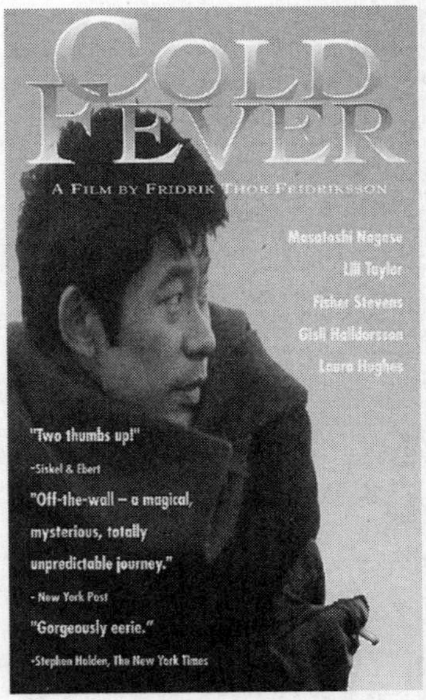

Cold Fever (1996)
From director Fridrik Thor Fridriksson ("Children of Nature") comes this offbeat tale about a hard-working Japanese executive whose family convinces him to forego a Hawaii golfing vacation to travel to Iceland, where his parents were killed in an accident, and perform a traditional ceremony in their memory. "Culture clash" drama stars Masatoshi Nagase, Lili Taylor and Fisher Stevens. 85 min. In English and Icelandic and Japanese with English subtitles.
53-8873 Was $94.99 ***$19.99***

Devil's Island (1996)
Set in a 1950s Reykjavik "neighborhood" comprised of leftover U.S. Army Quonset huts, director Fridrik Thor Fridriksson's culture clash comedy/drama focuses on the rivalry between siblings Danni, who tries to woo a neighbor girl, and Baddi, who returns from a stay in America with an Elvis haircut and a rebel attitude. Baltasar Kormákur, Sveinn Geirsson star. 103 min. In Icelandic with English subtitles.
53-6790 ***$89.99***

The Juniper Tree (1987)
Haunting fantasy drama from Iceland stars alternative rock singer Björk as a young woman who, after her mother is executed as a witch, flees with her older sister across the harsh Icelandic wilderness. At an isolated farm, the older sibling uses a spell to win the heart of a widowed farmer, and Björk and the farmer's son seek to end the romance. 78 min. Filmed in English.
15-5324 *$19.99*

Remote Control (1994)
A hilarious farce from Iceland (dare we say the funniest film to ever come from Iceland?) involving amateur mobsters, metalheads, a missing TV remote control and hostage goldfish. With Björn Jörundur Fridbjörnsson, Helgi Björnsson. 85 min. In Icelandic with English subtitles.
02-2721 *$89.99*

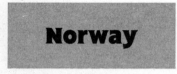

Norway

Edvard Munch (1976)
A monumental biography of Norwegian expressionist painter Edvard Munch (Geir Westby) and the effect his upbringing in Christiana (later Oslo), Norway, had on his work. Director Peter Watkins employs non-professional actors to play Munch and the troubled people in his life and takes an insightful look at the creative process. 167 min. In Norwegian and German with English subtitles.
53-7950 Was $79.99 *$29.99*

The Last Lieutenant (1994)
Ready for a well-earned retirement with his wife, an elderly Norwegian Merchant Marine officer volunteers for service when his country faces invasion by Germany in 1940. Confronted with the army's lack of readiness, the former lieutenant assembles his own band of volunteers for a resistance movement. Compelling and human war drama stars Espen Skjonberg, Rut Tellefsen. 102 min. In Norwegian with English subtitles.
22-9033 Was $79.99 *$29.99*

Cross My Heart And Hope To Die (1994)
A memorable tale of innocence lost, this film won international acclaim for its portrayal of a lonely schoolboy who falls under the influence of a charismatic older boy. What begins as a prank turns serious as the pair find themselves entangled in a dark secret that threatens to turn their world upside-down. Martin Dahl Garfalk, Jan Devo Kornstad star. 96 min. In Norwegian with English subtitles.
22-9039 *$79.99*

Kristin Lavransdatter (Director's Cut) (1995)
Liv Ullmann's second turn behind the camera is a rich, entrancing film set in Norway during the 14th century. A young woman is faced with a horrible dilemma: should she marry the man she truly loves or the man chosen for her by her family? Elisabeth Matheson, Erland Josephson star; cinematography by Sven Nykvist. 180 min. In Norwegian with English subtitles.
22-6050 *$39.99*

Zero Kelvin (1995)
Set in a isolated cabin in the frozen wilderness of Greenland in the 1920s, this acclaimed adventure film from Norwegian director Hans Petter Moland follows the desperate struggle for survival over the course of a bitter winter by three men: a thrill-seeking writer, a reclusive scientist, and a world-weary trapper. Gard B. Eidsvold, Stellan Skarsgård star. 113 min. In Norwegian with English subtitles.
53-7110 Letterboxed *$24.99*

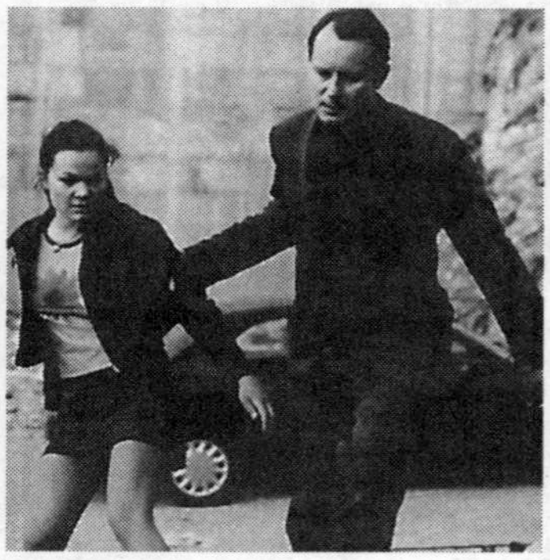

Insomnia (1997)
Sent to investigate a woman's brutal murder in a remote town in Northern Norway, a Swedish detective haunted by his past makes a mistake that leads to death and a desperate attempt to hide the truth. Director Erik Skjokdbjaerg's compelling thriller, set against the relentless light of the Arctic summer, stars Stellan Skarsgard, Sverre Anker Ousdal, Maria Bonnevie. 97 min. In Norwegian with English subtitles.
22-6032 Letterboxed *$29.99*

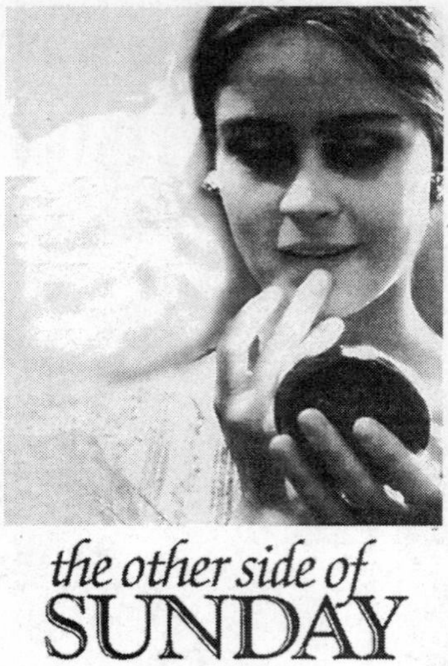

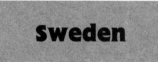

The Other Side Of Sunday (1996)
In 1950s Norway, teenager Maria is eager to wear earrings and date boys like her girlfriends, but must bow to the wishes of her strict clergyman father. A chance encounter with an older woman who attends her father's church leads to a surprising revelation and a lesson in growing up in this gently subversive comedy/drama. Marie Theisen, Bjørn Sundquist star. 103 min. In Norwegian with English subtitles.
53-6327 Was $89.99 *$19.99*

Mendel (1997)
A young Jewish boy must adjust to a new way of life when he and his family are relocated from post-WWII Germany to a tiny Norwegian village in writer/director Alexander Rosler's heartwarming and funny coming-of-age tale. Thomas Jungling Sorenson, Hans Kremer star. 85 min. In Norwegian with English subtitles.
70-5145 Was $79.99 *$29.99*

Junk Mail (1997)
Offbeat comedy from Norway involving a shabby Oslo mailman who turns voyeur when he begins secretly hanging out in the home of a hearing-impaired woman on his route. He eats her cereal, checks out her drawers and, after falling asleep under her bed, saves her from committing suicide. Robert Skjaerstad, Andrine Saether star. 83 min. In Norwegian with English subtitles.
82-5102 *$89.99*

Sweden

Private Confessions (Enskilda Samtal) (1997)
The cinematic reminiscences of scripter Ingmar Bergman continue under the direction of Liv Ullmann. Pernilla August and Samuel Fröler repeat their "Best Intentions" portrayals of Bergman's parents, as a series of dialogues are followed back and forth in time to depict August's crisis of faith and an affair she had with a younger man. Max von Sydow co-stars as August's uncle. 127 min. In Swedish with English subtitles.
22-6052 Letterboxed *$29.99*

The Last Dance (1993)
Colin Nutley ("House of Angels") directed this lively tale of two couples—Claus and Tove, and Lennart and Liselott—whose love for ballroom dancing keeps them friendly despite the jealousy shared amongst themselves. When Liselott is found murdered, the emotions that may have led to the deed are revealed. With Helena Bergstrom. 109 min. In Swedish with English subtitles.
53-6112 Was $59.99 *$24.99*

The Man On The Roof (1976)
Based on a novel by Maj Sjowall and Per Wahloo ("The Laughing Policeman"), Bo Widerberg's innovative and gripping thriller follows a madman's rooftop campaign of revenge against the police. Carl Gustav Lindstedt stars as homicide detective Martin Beck. 110 min. In Swedish with English subtitles.
53-8292 *$89.99*

The Man From Mallorca (1984)
What begins as a simple robbery at a Stockholm post office grows into a complex and deadly case, and two police officers charged with investigating the crime become caught up in a conspiracy with ties to their department and government officials. Compelling police thriller from writer/director Bo Widerberg stars Sven Wollter, Tomas von Brömssen. 106 min. In Swedish with English subtitles.
53-9995 *$89.99*

The Ox (1991)
Longtime Ingmar Bergman cinematographer Sven Nykvist made his directorial debut with this Oscar-nominated drama involving a man who returns from prison after serving time for killing his boss's ox for food and finds that his wife has committed unspeakable acts. Max Von Sydow, Liv Ullmann and Erland Josephson star. 93 min. In Swedish with English subtitles.
71-5289 *$19.99*

The Emigrants (1972)
Stirring, gorgeously photographed look at a group of Swedish peasants who leave their homeland in the mid-19th century and journey to America, where they settle in Minnesota in hopes of finding a better life for themselves. Liv Ullmann and Max Von Sydow star in Jan Troell's lyrical drama. 151 min. Dubbed in English.
19-2172 *$29.99*

The New Land (1972)
A sweeping sequel to "The Emigrants" finds the Swedish settlers searching for happiness in America while fighting such hardships as severe weather and a disastrous search for gold in the Southwest. Liv Ullmann and Max Von Sydow star under Jan Troell's sensitive direction. 159 min. Dubbed in English.
19-2173 *$29.99*

Freud Leaving Home (1991)
"Freud" is the nickname of a 25-year-old Jewish woman still living in her parents' home in Stockholm. When her disparate and combative relatives begin arriving for her mother's 60th birthday, Freud sees this as an opportunity to break away and start living her own life. Offbeat and touching seriocomedy stars Gunilla Roor, Ghita Norby. 100 min. In Swedish with English subtitles.
70-5106 *$59.99*

Elvira Madigan (1967)
One of the most beautifully photographed films ever made, this haunting romance from Sweden details the tragic affair between a 19th-century army officer and a free-spirited circus star. Pia Degermark, Thommy Berggren star; Bo Widerberg directs. 90 min. In Swedish with English subtitles.
54-7032 Was $24.99 *$19.99*

Like It Never Was Before (1995)
A staid and strait-laced man who takes his family on a seaside vacation has his life turned upside-down by an encounter with a handsome hotel handyman in this skewed black comedy from Sweden, scripted by popular gay writer and stand-up comic Jonas Gardell. Loa Falkman, Simon Norrthon star, 108 min. In Swedish with English subtitles.
53-8987 *$79.99*

The Slingshot (1994)
Wonderfully realized coming-of-age story set in Sweden during the 1920s and centering on Roland, the 10-year-old son of a Jewish mother and a handicapped Socialist father, who faces adversity from his conservative teacher, non-Jewish classmates and boxing brother while devising some clever uses for condoms. Jesper Salén stars. 102 min. In Swedish with English subtitles.
02-2724 Was $89.99 *$19.99*

The White Lioness (1996)
The discovery of a murdered girl in rural Sweden leads a small-town police inspector down a twisted path that culminates in South Africa and a plot to assassinate President Nelson Mandela in this gripping thriller based on Henning Mankell's novel. Rolf Lassgard, Jesper Christensen star. 104 min. In English and Swedish with English subtitles.
22-9044 *$79.99*

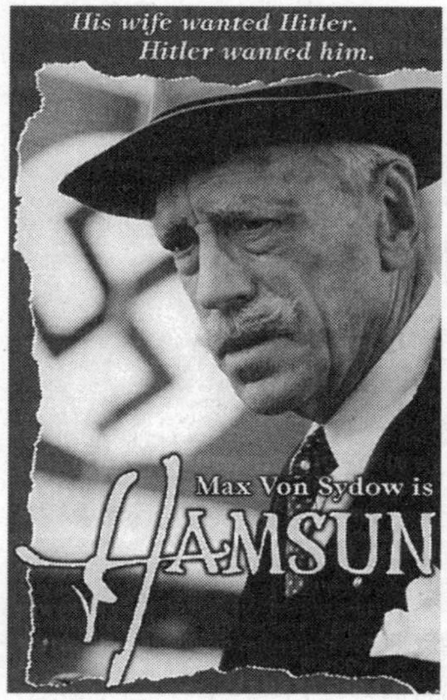

Hamsun (1997)
The gripping and compelling true story of Knut Hamsun, the Nobel Prize-winning Norwegian author who stunned his country when he sided with Hitler during World War II, not for Nazi ideals, but due to his deep hatred of Great Britain. With Max Von Sydow, Ghita Norby, Ernst Jacobi; directed by Jan Troell. 156 min. In Danish, German, Norwegian and Swedish with English subtitles.
70-5137 *$29.99*

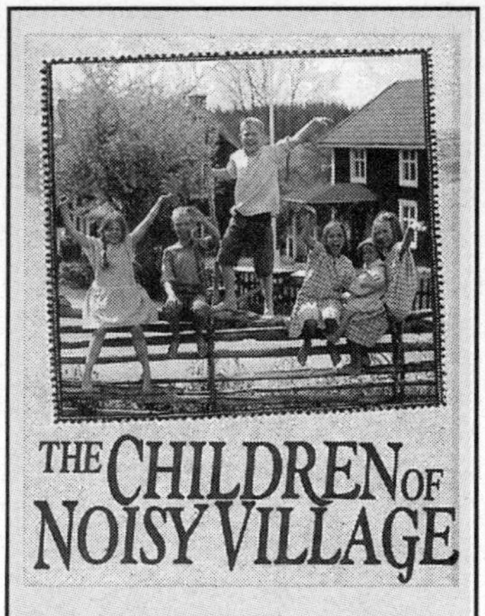

The Children Of Noisy Village (1986)
Enchanting family film from Lasse Hallstrom ("My Life as a Dog") detailing the adventures of six loquacious kids in their village, shortly before World War II. They explore the countryside, invent fun-filled games and enjoy themselves during a much simpler time. Based on a book by Astrid Lindgren ("Pippi Longstocking"). AKA: "The Children of Bullerby Village." 88 min. Dubbed in English.
70-5095 Was $24.99 *$19.99*

More About The Children Of Noisy Village (1987)
Take another trip back to the tiny village in the Swedish countryside where the children's imaginations lead them into a series of magical and exciting adventures, as Astrid Lindgren's wonderful characters return in this charming tale directed by Lasse Hallstrom. 85 min. Dubbed in English.
70-5140 Was $24.99 *$19.99*

Noisy Village 2-Pack
Both "Noisy Village" films are also available in a money-saving collection.
53-6792 Save $10.00! *$29.99*

My Life As A Dog (1987)
Charming Swedish look at the adult world through a child's eyes. An 11-year-old boy in the late '50s is sent to stay with relatives in the country when his mother becomes seriously ill, and learns valuable lessons about love, separation and growing up from the locals. Anton Glanzelius, Tomas von Bromssen star. 101 min. In Swedish with English subtitles.
06-1554 *$19.99*

My Life As A Dog (Dubbed Version)
Also available in a dubbed-in-English edition.
06-1528 *$19.99*

The Women On The Roof (1996)
Directed by Carl-Gustaf Nykvist (son of cinematographer Sven Nykvist), this provocative erotic drama is set in Stockholm before World War I and looks at the complex relationship that develops between two women—Linnea, new to an apartment building, and Anna, a photographer with a boyfriend. Helena Bergstrom stars. 86 min. In Swedish with English subtitles.
53-6115 Was $59.99 *$24.99*

Jerusalem (1996)
In the late 19th century, a small Swedish village is sharply divided by the arrival of a radical and charismatic preacher who seeks followers to join him on a pilgrimage to Jerusalem to await Christ's return. Based on a true story, director Bille August's ("Pelle the Conquerer") adaptation of Selma Lagerlöf's novel stars Maria Bonnevie, Olympia Dukakis, Ulf Friberg and Max von Sydow. 166 min. In English and Swedish with English subtitles.
53-9988 Was $89.99 *$29.99*

Expectations (Svenska Hjältar) (1997)
Adapted from author Reidar Jönsson's novel "Swedish Heroes," director Daniel Bergman's understated drama follows the daily lives of several seemingly unconnected individuals, from a newly separated ladies' magazine writer and a pair of young lovers to a prodigal son trying to reconcile with his fisherman father. With Lena Endre, Hans Klinga, Anki Lidèn. 95 min. In Swedish with English subtitles.
22-6051 Letterboxed *$29.99*

Dreaming Of Rita (1993)
An elderly cameraman, despondent over the death of his wife, tries to find a woman in Copenhagen he knew years earlier who resembled Rita Hayworth in the movie "Gilda." The man's beautiful daughter leaves her husband and baby to join her father on the trip, which turns out to be a whimsical journey filled with romance and surprises. Per Oscarsson stars. 108 min. In Swedish with English subtitles.
70-5086 Was $59.99 *$29.99*

Ingmar Bergman

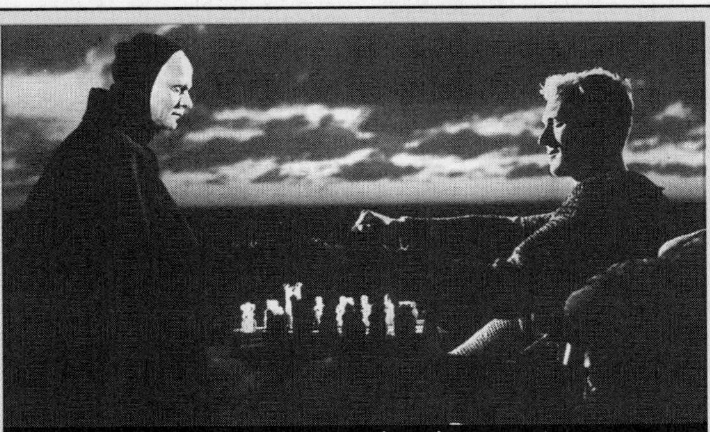
The Seventh Seal

Torment (1944)
Ingmar Bergman's first screenplay explores the tortured relationship between a young student, his sadistic teacher and the girl they're both involved with. When the teacher murders the girl in a fit of sexual rage, the youth turns him in, only to lead himself down a road of bitterness and hatred. Mai Zetterling, Gunnar Bjornstrand star; Alf Sjoberg directs. 90 min. In Swedish with English subtitles.
53-1719 *$29.99*

Night Is My Future (1947)
Emotional early effort from Ingmar Bergman follows a musician who is blinded in an accident. Driven to the depths of despair, he is saved by the love of a sympathetic woman. Birger Malmsten, Mai Zetterling star. 87 min. Dubbed in English.
09-1752 Was $29.99 *$24.99*

Port Of Call (1948)
Ingmar Bergman's moving study of a sailor and his love for a dance hall girl, haunted by her unhappy background. Bergman's respect for Italian neo-Realist film shows in this character study. 100 min. In Swedish with English subtitles.
53-1151 Was $29.99 *$19.99*

The Devil's Wanton (1949)
An early work from Ingmar Bergman, examining the lives and dreams of several very different people (filmmaker, poet, prostitute, and others). Lyrical and touching, the drama also asks stark questions about man's place in the world and the "silence" of God. 78 min. In Swedish with English subtitles.
09-1658 Was $29.99 *$24.99*

Three Strange Loves (Torst) (1949)
An early triumph from Ingmar Bergman, following a rail journey across the countryside of post-WWII Germany by a couple whose marriage has become a similarly barren wasteland. Eva Henning, Birger Malmsten star; look for Bergman in a cameo as a train passanger. AKA: "Thirst." 84 min. In Swedish with English subtitles.
53-1695 Was $29.99 *$19.99*

Summer Interlude (1950)
One of Ingmar Bergman's favorites among his own films, the story of a ballerina who discovers the diary of a now-deceased love and finds a catharsis for her life through reliving the joys and sorrows of their affair. Maj-Britt Nilsson, Alf Kjellin star. AKA: "Illicit Interlude." 95 min. In Swedish with English subtitles.
53-1720 *$29.99*

Monika (1952)
Typical of the films that marked his early "summer" period was this Ingmar Bergman drama of two young people whose brief love affair leads to pregnancy, marriage and turmoil. Harriet Andersson, Lars Ekborg star. AKA: "Summer with Monika." 96 min. In Swedish with English subtitles.
22-5600 *$29.99*

Secrets Of Women (1952)
A trio of women, connected by their marriage to three brothers, talk about their romantic experiences in this lighthearted episodic examination of fidelity and infidelity by Ingmar Bergman. Anita Bjork, Eva Dahlbeck star. 114 min. In Swedish with English subtitles.
22-5672 Was $39.99 *$29.99*

Sawdust And Tinsel (1953)
Ingmar Bergman's powerful look at life in a small circus in turn-of-the-century Sweden, filled with memorable characters, philosophical insights, and brilliant performances from Harriet Andersson and Ake Gronberg. 83 min. In Swedish with English subtitles.
22-5673 *$29.99*

A Lesson In Love (1954)
One of Bergman's rare but witty entries into comedy, this sex farce traces a gynecologist whose indiscretions have been discovered by his wife...and his connivances to win her back after she runs to the arms of his best friend. Gunnar Björnstrand, Eva Dahlbeck star. 95 min. In Swedish with English subtitles.
53-1685 *$29.99*

Smiles Of A Summer Night (1955)
Utterly charming Bergman comedy about the sexual liaisons and moral dilemmas encountered by eight weekend visitors to a lush country estate in the late 1800s. This classic romance inspired both Stephen Sondheim's "A Little Night Music" and Woody Allen's "A Midsummer Night's Sex Comedy." Harriet Andersson, Ulla Jacobsson star. 108 min. in Swedish with English subtitles.
22-5676 Remastered *$29.99*

Dreams (1955)
Insightful drama of desire and obsession from Ingmar Bergman follows a day in the lives of a modeling agency owner and her top model and each women's doomed love affair. Harriet Andersson, Eva Dahlbeck, Gunnar Bjornstrand star. AKA: "Journey Into Autumn." 86 min. In Swedish with English subtitles.
53-1439 *$29.99*

The Seventh Seal (1956)
Ingmar Bergman's most acclaimed film is a haunting allegory set in the Middle Ages, where a disillusioned knight (Max von Sydow) returning home from the Crusades is challenged by Death to a game of chess, with humans as pawns. Bibi Andersson, Gunnar Bjornstrand co-star in the bleak, stunning drama. 96 min. In Swedish with English subtitles.
22-5736 *$29.99*

Wild Strawberries (1957)
Ingmar Bergman's masterwork about an aging professor who, while on his way to receive an honorary degree, recalls the failures and selfishness of his life. Brilliant acting by Victor Sjostrom, Bibi Andersson, Ingrid Thulin. 90 min. In Swedish with English subtitles.
22-5598 *$29.99*

The Magician (1958)
A mesmerist who runs a travelling magic troupe in 19th-century Sweden meets opposition from local officials in Ingmar Bergman's eerie, penetrating drama. Max von Sydow, Erland Josephson and Ingrid Thulin star. AKA: "The Face." 98 min. In Swedish with English subtitles.
53-1539 Remastered *$29.99*

The Virgin Spring (1959)
A young peasant girl's defilement and murder, her father's oath of vengeance, and a spring that blossoms from the ground where the girl was killed...these are the elements in Ingmar Bergman's Oscar-winning drama of life and renewal, based on an ancient Scandinavian legend. Max Von Sydow, Brigitta Valberg star. 88 min. In Swedish with English subtitles.
53-1538 *$29.99*

The Devil's Eye (1960)
In hopes of curing an eye problem he blames on a parson's daughter's chastity, the Devil sends Don Juan back to Earth to seduce her. Jarl Kulle and Bibi Andersson star in this comedic allegory from Ingmar Bergman. 90 min. In Swedish with English subtitles.
22-5971 *$29.99*

Through A Glass Darkly (1961)
Evocative, Oscar-winning effort from Bergman concerning a woman's slow descent into insanity, as her husband and family take her to a secluded island following her release from a sanitarium. One of the director's best; stars Harriet Andersson, Gunnar Bjornstrand, Max von Sydow. 91 min. In Swedish with English subtitles.
22-5737 *$29.99*

Winter Light (1962)
Ingmar Bergman's penetrating examination of an aloof priest coming to terms with humanity's (and his own) lack of faith. Intense, stark and thought-provoking; with Gunnar Bjornstrand, Ingrid Thulin, Max von Sydow. 80 min. In Swedish with English subtitles.
22-5738 *$29.99*

The Silence (1963)
One of Ingmar Bergman's most acclaimed works follows two sisters (one lesbian, the other a free-spirited unwed mother) whose stay in an isolated village brings out repressed angers and desires. Moving allegorical drama stars Ingrid Thulin, Gunnel Lindblom. 95 min. In Swedish with English subtitles.
22-5639 *$24.99*

All These Women (1964)
Ingmar Bergman goes the satirical route with this story about a womanizing cellist who uses his music to attract women. A writer working on a biography of the musician is continually sidetracked by his conquests. Jarl Kulle, Georg Funkquist, Bibi Andersson star. AKA: "Now About All These Women." 80 min. In Swedish with English subtitles.
09-5264 *$19.99*

Persona (1966)
Ground-breaking meditation by Bergman on personality and metaphysics involves a mute actress who depends upon a surrogate nurse to speak and, ultimately, to feel for her. Bibi Andersson, Liv Ullmann star. 83 min. In Swedish with English subtitles.
12-2558 *$19.99*

The Shame (1968)
A masterpiece from Ingmar Bergman starring Liv Ullmann and Max von Sydow as married musicians who flee their war-torn country to find peace on an isolated island. But when the fighting spreads to the island, their relationship goes through some complex, dramatic changes and makes them question their involvement with each other and the outside world. 103 min. In Swedish with English subtitles.
12-2557 *$19.99*

Hour Of The Wolf (1968)
A haunting drama from Ingmar Bergman featuring Max von Sydow as a painter who lives with pregnant wife Liv Ullmann on a secluded island. The two begin receiving disturbing "visits" from what might be ghosts, and a secret from von Sydow's past is revealed. Erland Josephson, Ingrid Thulin also star. 88 min. In Swedish with English subtitles.
12-2559 *$19.99*

The Passion Of Anna (1970)
A stark, psychological drama from Ingmar Bergman starring Max von Sydow as a former convict living on an isolated island farmhouse who becomes involved with a handicapped woman (Liv Ullmann). Their relationship with each other—and another couple (Erland Josephson and Bibi Andersson)—forms the core of this compelling story. 100 min. In Swedish with English subtitles.
12-2555 *$19.99*

The Ritual (Riten) (1970)
Themes of love, art, censorship and hypocrisy are explored in writer/director Ingmar Bergman's drama, originally made for Swedish television. A three-person theatrical troupe's planned performance of a controversial work is held up by a close-minded judge who attempts to seduce the company's actress. Ingrid Thulin, Anders Ek, Erik Hell star. 75 min. In Swedish with English subtitles.
22-5814 Was $39.99 *$29.99*

Cries And Whispers (1972)
A terminally ill woman is looked after by her two sisters and the family maid, and each woman's view of mortality and life's meaning is eloquently depicted in Ingmar Bergman's acclaimed drama. Liv Ullmann, Ingrid Thulin and Kari Sylwan star; Oscar-winning cinematography by Sven Nykvist. 95 min. In Swedish with English subtitles.
22-5674 Remastered *$29.99*

The Magic Flute (1974)
Mozart's classic fantasy opera about a princess' abduction by an evil sorcerer is brought to the screen by master filmmaker Ingmar Bergman, and it's a heavenly match for opera and movie fans alike. Ulric Cold, Birgit Nordin, Erik Saeden, Irma Urrila star. 134 min. In Swedish with English subtitles.
06-1362 *$29.99*

Scenes From A Marriage (1974)
One of Ingmar Bergman's most intimate and acclaimed works, a harrowing and claustrophobic look at the 20-year history and disintegration of a marriage, was first made as a mini-series for Swedish television. Liv Ullmann stars as the distraught spouse struggling to cope after learning of husband Erland Josephson's infidelity. 170 min. In Swedish with English subtitles.
22-5813 Letterboxed *$29.99*

From The Life Of The Marionettes (1980)
Made during his brief "exile" in Germany, this brutal and provocative work from Ingmar Bergman looks at the troubled relationship between a businessman and his fashion designer wife, and how an encounter with a prostitute drives the man to a shocking crime. Robert Atzorn and Christine Buchegger, whose characters were first seen in "Scenes from a Marriage," star. 104 min. In German with English subtitles.
22-5900 *$29.99*

Autumn Sonata (1978)
Ingmar Bergman's electrifying drama stars Ingrid Bergman as a noted concert pianist whose reunion with estranged daughter Liv Ullmann leads her to face feelings of guilt concerning her career and their relationship. Erland Josephson also stars. 92 min. In Swedish with English subtitles.
22-5786 Was $39.99 *$29.99*

Fanny And Alexander (1983)
Eloquent Ingmar Bergman portrayal of two children in 1900s Sweden whose carefree lives are thrown into turmoil when their actor father suddenly dies and their mother remarries a stern minister. Ewa Froling, Erland Josephson, Pernilla Alwin and Bertil Guve star; cinematography by Sven Nykvist. 200 min. In Swedish with English subtitles.
53-1149 Was $39.99 *$19.99*

The Making Of Fanny And Alexander (1983)
A behind-the-scenes view of Ingmar Bergman's semi-autobiographical masterpiece, directed and edited by the filmmaker himself, with insights on the creative process of an acknowledged master creating a work he has called the summation of his illustrious career.
53-7304 *$29.99*

After The Rehearsal (1984)
A penetrating study by Ingmar Bergman into the questions of love, solitude, ambition and longing. On the eve of his latest production, a womanizing stage director (Erland Josephson) pursues a young actress (Lena Olin) and is visited by one of his old flames (Ingrid Thulin). 72 min. In Swedish with English subtitles.
02-1407 Was $59.99 *$19.99*

The Best Intentions (1992)
Ingmar Bergman wrote the script for Bille August's acclaimed drama based on the lives of his parents. Set in a small, frigid Swedish town, the film chronicles the often-difficult relationship between Bergman's father, a poor minister, and his mother, a strong-willed woman from a wealthy family. With Samuel Fröler, Pernilla August and Max Von Sydow. 182 min. In Swedish with English subtitles.
71-5282 Was $89.99 *$29.99*

Sunday's Children (1993)
The rift between a 10-year-old Swedish boy and his preacher father becomes worse as time passes and carries over into the son's adulthood in this compelling, emotional drama, written by Ingmar Bergman and directed by his son, Daniel. Thommy Berggren, Henrik Linnros star. 118 min. In Swedish with English subtitles.
70-5077 Was $59.99 *$29.99*

The Ingmar Bergman Collection
Three of the master director's finest are included in this money-saving collector's set: "The Seventh Seal," "Wild Strawberries" and "The Virgin Spring."
22-5856 Save $30.00! *$59.99*

Miss Julie (1950)
Dramatic adaptation of the Strindberg play of social and sexual domination. A noblewoman lets her servant seduce her when her engagement is broken, but this leads to her disgrace and eventual destruction. Anita Bjork and Ulf Palme star; directed by Alf Sjoberg. 90 min. In Swedish with English subtitles.
53-1431 *$29.99*

The Doll (1962)
Compelling tale of loneliness and delusion, with Per Oscarsson as a Stockholm department store guard who brings home a mannequin that he imagines comes to life and talks to him, encouraging him to steal expensive gifts for her. Gio Petre co-stars in the title role. 95 min. In Swedish with English subtitles.
10-9177 *$29.99*

The Mozart Brothers (1986)
"Amadeus" meets the Marx Brothers in this satiric libretto from Sweden, as an operatic company rebels against their new director's extremely avant-garde ideas for staging their production of "Don Giovanni." Susanne Oldstein directed and co-wrote with star Etienne Glaser. 111 min. In Swedish with English subtitles.
70-5017 *$24.99*

House Of Angels (1993)
Whimsical, seductive fable that shows how the arrival of a sensuous nightclub singer and her gay, cross-dressing traveling companion affects the residents of a Swedish town when the singer moves there after inheriting her grandfather's estate. Rikard Wolff and Helena Bergström star in Colin Nutley's acclaimed comedy. 119 min. In Swedish with English subtitles.
02-2580 Was $89.99 *$19.99*

Denmark

The Celebration (1998)
In this highly-acclaimed effort from Thomas Vinterberg and the guerrilla-like film collective Dogma 95, three grown children gather at an estate to honor their father on his 60th birthday. The happy occasion turns ugly when the partygoers get drunk and reveal some unsettling secrets about the past and the patriarch. With Henning Motizen, Ulrich Thomsen. 106 min. In German with English subtitles.
02-9109 Was $99.99 *$14.99*

Ladies On The Rocks (1983)
Move over, Thelma and Louise! Here are Micha and Laura, two disillusioned women who take to the road with their wacky cabaret act on a journey of self-discovery. Helle Ryslinge, Anne Marie Helger star. 100 min. In Danish with English subtitles.
53-7680 Was $79.99 *$29.99*

Babette's Feast (1987)
A special dinner prepared by their French maid proves to be a memorable evening for two sisters whose austere lives have kept them apart from the world in 1988's Oscar winner for Best Foreign Film. Moving Danish comedy/drama stars Stephane Audran, Bodil Kjer, Birgitte Federspiel. 102 min. In Danish with English subtitles.
73-1032 *$19.99*

The Hideaway (1991)
After a lonely 12-year-old boy shields a young punk from police, he finds his fantasies have turned darkly dangerous in this tender, tough drama from Denmark's Niels Grabol. Mixing gripping psychological insight with coming-of-age situations, the film tackles sensitive issues with depth and candor. 70 min. In Danish with English subtitles.
78-5064 *$59.99*

Sofie (1993)
The acclaimed directorial debut of actress Liv Ullmann tells a sensitive, powerful story. Set in 19th-century Copenhagen, the drama focuses on a 28-year-old Jewish woman whose devotion to her family persuades her to sacrifice her love for a Gentile man and marry within her religion. Erland Josephson, Karen Lise Mynster, Ghita Norby star. 145 min. In Danish with English subtitles.
74-3003 Letterboxed *$79.99*

Heart Of Light (1999)
This gorgeously filmed, intense drama tells of an Inuit family living in Greenland who is torn apart when their troubled teenage son goes on a killing rampage. Unable to deal with the tragedy, the father abandons the rest of the family and, after meeting a mystical hermit, reconsiders his past. Rasmus Lyberth stars. 92 min. In Inuit and Danish with English subtitles.
22-9047 *$79.99*

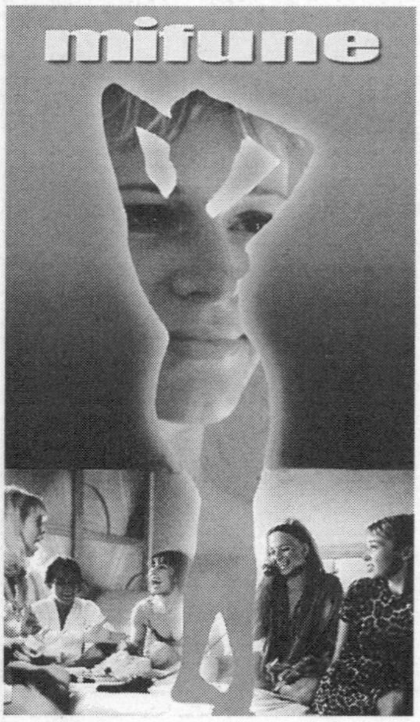

Mifune (1999)
This no-frills Dogma '95 production tells the darkly humorous tale of a newly married Copenhagen businessman who must return to his rural family's ramshackle farm and his retarded brother, neither of which he told his wife about, after his father dies. The situation gets even more complicated when he falls for the ex-hooker housekeeper he hires to live on the farm. With Anders W. Berthelsen, Jesper Asholt and Iben Hjejle ("High Fidelity"). 102 min. In Danish with English subtitles.
02-3452 *$99.99*

The Parson's Widow (1920)
A young parson, newly installed in a country village, is shocked to learn that, according to local custom, he must be wed to his predecessor's widow, an elderly harridan who has now driven three husbands to their graves. The parson joins forces with his fiancée to concoct a plan to do away with her. Carl Dreyer's humorous tale stars Hildur Calberg. 60 min. Silent with music score.
10-9423 *$14.99*

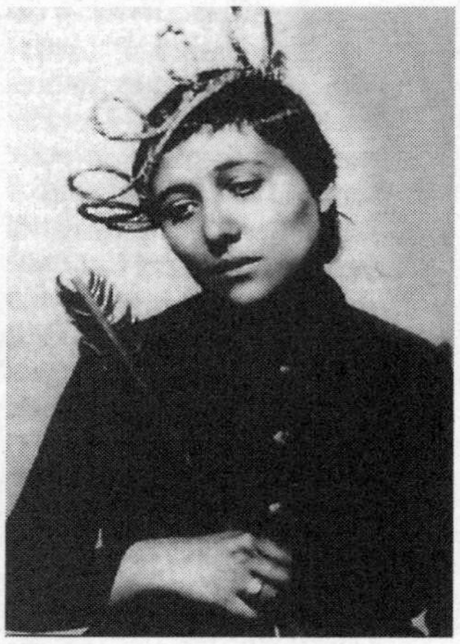

La Passion De Jeanne D'Arc (1928)
Danish director Carl Theodor Dreyer was commissioned by producers in France to create a film portrait of a French historical figure, and the result was this masterpiece of world cinema. Renée Falconetti, in her only film role, is impeccable as the 15th-century war heroine whose leadership of French forces against England ends in her capture and trial on charges of heresy and sorcery. 82 min. Silent with music score.
53-8617 Remastered *$29.99*

Vampyr (1932)
One of the earliest and best vampire-based horror films, Carl Theodor Dreyer's moody, dreamlike thriller of a man haunted by visions of being buried alive contains several hauntingly surreal scenes. 75 min. In German with English subtitles.
09-1779 *$24.99*

Day Of Wrath (1943)
A woman in 17th-century Denmark, recently married to an older pastor, falls in love with her stepson. When the husband dies after learning of their affair, she is accused of witchcraft. Intense and moving drama stars Thorkild Roose, Lisbeth Movin; Carl Dreyer directs. 93 min. In Danish with English subtitles.
22-6080 Remastered *$29.99*

Ordet (1955)
Carl Dreyer's touching and poetic examination of the life of a farming family in rural Denmark, and what happens when one of the three sons plans to wed the daughter of a neighbor with whom his stern father has religious differences. Henrik Malberg, Emil Hass Christensen star. 126 min. In Danish with English subtitles.
22-6081 Remastered *$29.99*

Gertrud (1964)
The final film by Danish director Carl Theodor Dreyer, this heartfelt drama follows a woman who leaves her loveless marriage and embarks on a series of doomed affairs. Nina Pens Rode, Axel Strobye star. 117 min. In Danish with English subtitles.
53-7104 Was $49.99 *$29.99*

Gertrud (Letterboxed Version)
Also available in a theatrical, widescreen format.
22-6082 Remastered *$29.99*

The Carl Dreyer Collection
The legendary Danish filmmaker is saluted with this special three-tape set that includes "The Passion of Joan of Arc," "Ordet" and the letterboxed version of "Gertrud."
22-6083 Save $15.00! *$74.99*

Hunger (1966)
A stunning performance by Per Oscarsson fuels this drama about a writer in 19th-century Norway who, unable to sell his work, lives in abject poverty and turns down charity out of pride, preferring to scrounge in garbage while retaining faith in his abilities. 100 min. In Danish with English subtitles.
53-7506 *$49.99*

Pusher (1996)
Called a Scandinavian "Trainspotting" by critics, this edgy Danish drama follows a small-time Copenhagen drug dealer who loses his stash during a police raid and only has two days to pay off a big debt to his boss, or face the consequences. Kim Bodnia, Zlatko Buric, Laura Drasbaek star. 105 min. In Danish with English subtitles.
70-5175 Was $79.99 *$24.99*

The Element Of Crime (1983)
A diabolical slaughterer of little girls becomes the quarry for an obsessed police detective in a drab, post-apocalyptic Europe. This Danish futuristic thriller was shot entirely in sepiatone and won acclaim at the Cannes Film Festival. Directed by Lars von Trier ("Zentropa"); Michael Elphick and Esmond Knight star. 104 min. Filmed in English.
48-1169 Letterboxed *$19.99*

The Kingdom (1995)
Originally produced for European television, this creepy, darkly humorous soap opera from Morten Arnfred and Lars von Trier follows the unusual people who populate a Copenhagen hospital. Among them are a Swedish surgeon who hates Danes, an official who hides when the facility is inspected and the ghost of a young girl who haunts the premises. With Ernst Hugo Haregard. 265 min. In Danish with English subtitles.
88-1055 Was $24.99 *$14.99*

The Idiots (1999)
This controversial, shot-on-video Dogma 95 production from Lars Von Trier focuses on a group of young people who partake in "spassing"—acting as mentally disturbed people in public places in order to shock the middle class and affirm the dignity of the disabled. Threatened with an NC-17 rating for sexual scenes, the producers decided to use strategically placed black bars. With Bodil Jorgensen, Jens Albinus. In Danish with English subtitles.
02-9274 *$99.99*

Finland

Ariel (1989)
An offbeat and satiric comedy from Finland, following a laid-off miner on a cross-country odyssey in his white Cadillac. Along the way he picks up a divorcee, and the two launch a crime spree. Turo Pajala, Susanna Haavisto star. 74 min. In Finnish with English subtitles.
53-7586 *$79.99*

Leningrad Cowboys Go America (1990)
Offbeat comedy, headed for cult status, detailing the misadventures of an awful rock band from Finland who head to America (with a dead member in tow) to seek fame and fortune. En route from New York to Mexico for a gig at a wedding, the group discovers the joys of the seamier side of the U.S.A. With Matti Pellonpää, Kari Vaananen. 80 min. In English and Finnish with English subtitles.
73-1110 Was $79.99 *$19.99*

The Match Factory Girl (1990)
Dark comedy from Finnish director Aki Kaurismäki ("Leningrad Cowboys Go America") involving a young factory worker whose oppressive life slides even further downward when the man she loves stops seeing her. This time, however, she plans to cope with her problem in a unique way. The tape includes the Leningrad Cowboys short "Those Were the Days." 75 min. In Finnish with English subtitles.
53-7832 *$79.99*

Zombie And The Ghost Train (1991)
Are there "slackers" in Scandinavia? Yes, says Finnish director Mika Kaurismäki in this nihilistic comedy about a young drifter who goes from job to job when he's not sponging off his girlfriend. His dream is to land a gig playing bass with the rock band Ghost Train, who are seen in the film but never heard. 88 min. In Finnish with English subtitles.
70-5076 Was $59.99 *$29.99*

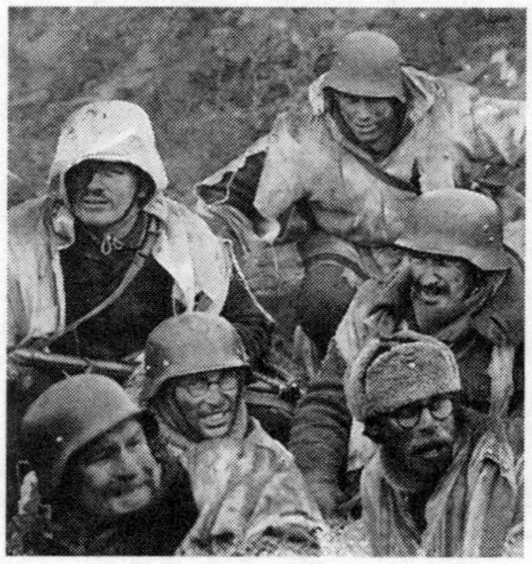

The Winter War (Talvisota) (1990)
The heroic struggle of the 1939-1940 Russo-Finnish War, in which Finland's tiny army defended its homeland against the Soviet Union's superior numbers and firepower for 105 days in bitter Arctic conditions, is recounted in a gripping drama that realistically depicts the lives of the soldiers. 125 min. In Finnish with English subtitles.
65-3001 *$29.99*

Pathfinder (1988)
Action-packed, Oscar-nominated epic based on an ages-old Lapland legend about a teenage boy who, while plotting revenge against the savage warriors who slaughtered his family, comes of age. Stunningly filmed in breathtaking Scandinavian locales by director Nils Gaup ("Shipwrecked"). With Mikkel Gaupa, Helgi Skulason. 88 min. In Lapp with English subtitles.
53-7542 Was $79.99 *$19.99*

Germany

Congress Dances (Der Kongress Tanzt) (1931)
Delightful costume comedy about the mishaps of a saleswoman seeking both financial and romantic gain at the 1815 Congress of Vienna. A long-buried classic with Lilian Harvey and Conrad Veidt. WARNING: Print quality varies, but this is the finest extant. 92 min. In German with English subtitles.
01-1375 *$29.99*

Maedchen In Uniform (1931)
Highly controversial when first released, this drama of a lonely student in a girls' boarding school and her infatuation with a female teacher is recognized as a classic of early German cinema. Hertha Thiele, Dorothea Wieck star; directed by Leontine Sagan. 90 min. In German with English subtitles.
22-5741 Was $29.99 *$24.99*

My Song Goes 'Round The World (1934)
Beautiful location footage of Venice and the magnificent voice of German tenor Josef Schmidt (whose rising career was cut short when the Nazis came to power and learned he was Jewish) highlight this atmospheric musical about a would-be opera singer's search for success and love. With John Loder, Charlotte Ander. 77 min. In German with English subtitles.
10-7221 *$29.99*

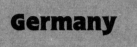

THE
THREEPENNY
OPERA

The Threepenny Opera (1930)
Well-made German version of the famed Brecht/Weill play about life in Victorian London's underworld. Lotte Lenya stars as Jenny, and Rudolf Forster is Mackie Messer; directed by G.W. Pabst. 113 min. In German with English subtitles.
22-5742 Was $39.99 *$29.99*

Kameradschaft (1931)
Gas explosions collapse a mine on the French/German border, trapping a group of French miners within. When rescue operations west of the border prove futile, a daring mission is mounted by a crew of German miners. Inspiring plea for unity by director G.W. Pabst. 78 min. In German with English subtitles.
53-1684 *$29.99*

Mistress Of Atlantis (1932)
The English-language version of G.W. Pabst's elegant fantasy-adventure (filmed simultaneously in French and German as "L'Atlantide"), this rare film features Brigitte Helm ("Metropolis") as Antinea, the seductive, evil ruler of the lost civilization whose palace is filled with the remains of those who died for her love. John Stuart, Gibb McLaughlin also star. 79 min.
01-1220 *$59.99*

The Broken Jug (1935)
Wonderful German "rural comedy" features Emil Jannings as the wise village judge who dispenses justice in a unique style. Angela Salloker, Paul Dahlke also star. 82 min. In German with English subtitles.
10-9266 *$29.99*

Black Roses (1936)
German-made tragedy stars Lilian Harvey ("Congress Dances") as a Russian ballerina in turn-of-the-century Finland who sacrifices herself to the Tsar's brutal provincial governor to save the life of her true love, a rebel Finnish sculptor. AKA: "Did I Betray?" 93 min. Dubbed in English.
17-3081 *$29.99*

The Blum Affair (1949)
A fascinating and frightening examination of German anti-Semitism between the wars, as a Jewish businessman wrongly accused of murder battles police indifference and the false witness of the real killer. Kurt Erhardt, Paul Bildt and Claus Becker star. 109 min. In German with English subtitles.
10-7323 Was $29.99 *$19.99*

The Last Bridge (1954)
Compelling, award-winning war drama featuring Maria Schell as a German physician captured by Yugoslavian Partisans during World War II. After refusing to help her wounded captors, she decides to offer medical assistance, realizing that all people are worthy of her expertise. With Bernhard Wicki, Carl Mohner. 90 min. In German with English subtitles.
53-6656 *$29.99*

MOVIES UNLIMITED

Young Toerless (1966)
The debut feature of director Volker Schlöndorff ("The Tin Drum") is a dramatic parable of Nazi German society set in a boys' school. A shy student wants to report a group of bullies who harass a classmate, but keeps silent under threats from the attackers. Matthieu Carriere, Marian Seidowsky and famed horror queen Barbara Steele star. 90 min.
22-6099 Letterboxed *$29.99*

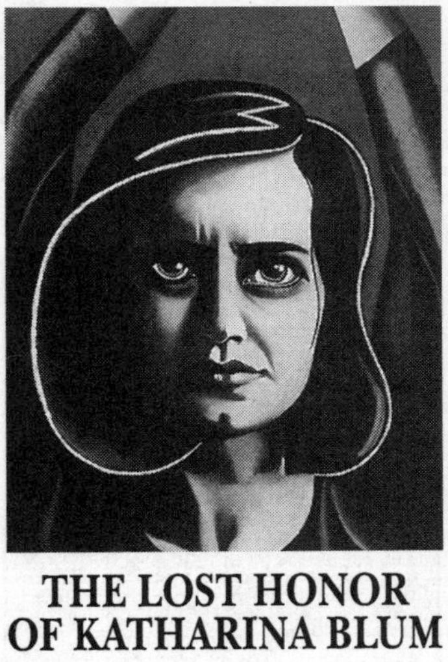

The Lost Honor Of Katharina Blum (1975)
Volker Schlöndorff and Margarethe von Trotta co-wrote and directed this highly praised (and highly politicized) adaptation of the Heinrich Böll novel. A young woman has a one-night stand with a man who turns out to be a suspected terrorist under government surveillance and becomes a target of media and police harassment. Angela Winkler, Mario Adorf, Jurgen Prochnow star. 109 min. In German with English subtitles.
22-6098 Letterboxed *$29.99*

Le Coup De Grace (1976)
Powerful drama set against the backdrop of the 1919 Latvian Communist revolt. A young woman falls in love with a German officer whose unit is stationed on her family's estate. Spurned by him, she takes up with the revolutionaries and their cause. Margarethe von Trotta, who co-scripted with director/husband Volker Schlöndorff, stars. 98 min. In French and German with English subtitles.
76-1045 Letterboxed *$29.99*

The Tin Drum (1979)
Fantastic and moving tale about the rise and fall of Nazi Germany as seen through the eyes of a "man-boy" (David Bennett) who "refuses to grow" in order to ignore the horrors around him, venting his anger through a toy drum. Director Volker Schlöndorff's adapatation of the Gunter Grass novel won the Best Foreign Film Academy Award. 142 min. In German with English subtitles.
19-1156 Letterboxed *$39.99*

The Ogre (Der Unhold) (1996)
German filmmaker Volker Schlöndorff ("The Tin Drum") continues his cinematic exploration of the banality of evil with this compelling drama. Simple-minded French mechanic John Malkovich, falsely accused of molesting children, avoids prison by joining the army at the start of World War II. Captured by the Germans, Malkovich is drawn into the Nazi cause and becomes a recruiter of boys for a Hitler Youth camp. Volker Spengler, Armin Mueller-Stahl, Marianne Sägebrecht also star. 117 min. Filmed in English.
53-6560 Letterboxed *$24.99*

Winter Sleepers (1997)
"Run Lola Run's" Tom Tykwer directed this eerie ensemble drama set in a snowbound German town where five characters' lives intersect. There's Laura, a nurse who aspires to be an actress; roommate Rebecca, a translator involved with ski instructor Marco; and René, a projectionist whose accident with farmer Theo while driving Marco's car sets into motion a series of unusual complications. With Marie-Lou Sellem, Floriane Daniel and Heino Ferch. 124 min. In German with English subtitles.
53-6967 *$89.99*

Run Lola Run (1999)
Knockout exercise in style and tension follows a flame-haired German punkette as she races to get 100,000 marks and deliver it to her petty crook boyfriend, who lost a bag of money he was taking to his violent boss, in 20 minutes. Lola's frantic trek through the streets of Berlin is followed through three different scenarios and three very different outcomes. Franka Potente, Moritz Bleibtreu star; directed by Tom Tykwer. 81 min. In German with English subtitles.
02-3381 Was $99.99 *$19.99*

Run Lola Run (Dubbed Version)
Also available in a dubbed-in-English edition.
02-3432 *$19.99*

Rebel Flight To Cuba (1959)
Thrilling, over-the-top airplane disaster effort from Germany in which a priest, a minister, a rabbi, an unhappy countess, a fugitive Nazi and a pregnant mother are among the passengers on a plane being hijacked to Cuba. Linda Christian and Peter Van Eyck star in what might have been the inspiration for all those "Airport" films. Dubbed in English.
53-8053 *$29.99*

Der Stern Von Afrika (1957)
Exciting aerial footage highlights this German war drama based on the real-life story of WWII Luftwaffe ace Hans-Joachim Marseille, whose unconventional attitude and daring exploits helped him down over 150 enemy planes and earned him the nicknames "the Star of Africa" and "the Eagle of the Desert." Joachim Hansen, Marianne Koch star. 105 min. In German with English subtitles.
65-3008 *$29.99*

Der Stern Von Afrika (Dubbed Version)
Also available in a dubbed-in-English edition.
65-3002 *$29.99*

Naked In The Night (1958)
Fifties sexploitation dramas weren't the exclusive property of American studios, as this German melodrama of loose women and the men to whom their wicked, wicked ways lead them amply demonstrates. Eva Bartok and Alexander Kerst star in the sordid tale of fallen frauleins. Dubbed in English.
68-8749 *$19.99*

The Testament Of Dr. Mabuse (1933)
Fritz Lang's second film featuring the criminal mastermind finds Mabuse a harmless asylum inmate, but a new crime wave has a police inspector looking for a connection. The thriller's not-always subtle parallels between Mabuse and Hitler led to a Nazi ban and forced the director to flee Germany. With Rudolph Klein-Rogge, Otto Wernicke. 120 min. In German with English subtitles.
22-5743 *$24.99*

The Crimes Of Dr. Mabuse (1933)
This dubbed-in-English version of Lang's "The Testament of Dr. Mabuse" features an opening sequence that depicts Germany in shambles after a Second World War (in 1939!). 76 min.
09-2385 *$19.99*

The Thousand Eyes Of Dr. Mabuse (1960)
For his final film, director Fritz Lang resurrected his legendary scientific super-criminal. Set in a luxury hotel in Berlin, the thriller follows a pair of detectives investigating a string of murders and learning that someone who thinks he is the infamous Mabuse is using an electronic spy center inside the hotel as his base of operations. Gert Frobe, Wolfgang Preiss, Dawn Addams, Peter Van Eyck star. 99 min. In German with English subtitles.
53-6851 Letterboxed *$24.99*

The Thousand Eyes Of Dr. Mabuse (Dubbed Version)
Also available in a dubbed-in-English edition.
17-3044 *$19.99*

Return Of Dr. Mabuse (1961)
Follow-up to Fritz Lang's classic films finds the diabolical doctor plotting to take over Munich with prison inmate zombies he helped to create. Gert Frobe, Lex Barker, Daliah Lavi and Wolfgang Preiss star in this shadowy thriller. 88 min.
68-8559 *$19.99*

The Invisible Dr. Mabuse (1962)
Wolfgang Preiss re-creates his role as the German evil genius, Dr. Mabuse, who stops at nothing to obtain an invisibility potion. Detective Lex Barker is the only one who can stop him, before his unseen legions take over the world. AKA: "The Invisible Horror." 89 min.
68-8140 *$19.99*

The Testament Of Dr. Mabuse (Terror Of The Mad Doctor) (1962)
A remake of Fritz Lang's 1933 film opens with the mad Mabuse (Wolfgang Preiss) imprisoned and hypnotizing a professor into carrying out his evil schemes. With Gert Frobe, Senta Berger, Walter Rilla. 88 min.
68-8787 *$19.99*

Dr. Mabuse vs. Scotland Yard (1963)
Germany's answer to Fu Manchu takes over the body of a professor and uses his "hypno-ray" gun and tries to take over England (whose royal family includes a "Princess Diana"). Wolfgang Preiss, Sabine Bettmann, Klaus Kinski, Peter Van Eyck star. 90 min. Dubbed in English.
09-1659 Was $29.99 *$14.99*

The Death Ray Of Dr. Mabuse (1964)
The final German-made Dr. Mabuse entry stars Wolfgang Preiss as the evil Mabuse, who plots to control the world by using a concave mirror that condenses energy into a death ray. Peter Van Eyck also stars. AKA: "The Secret of Dr. Mabuse."
68-8935 *$19.99*

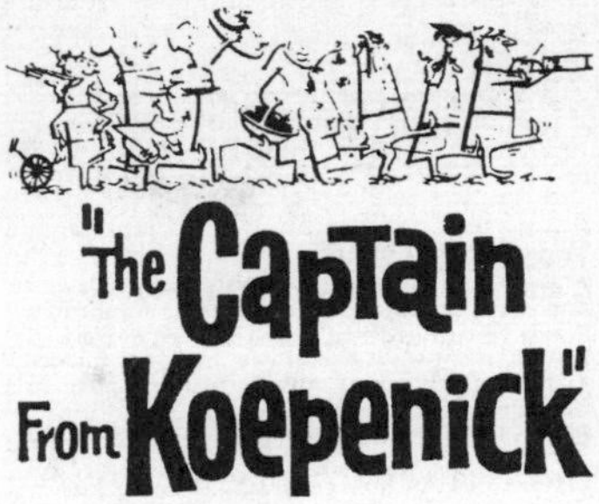

The Captain From Koepenick (1957)
Comic classic from Germany, based on a true incident, recounts the story of a mousy cobbler (Heinz Ruhmann) who gets back at the system by impersonating an Army officer and plunges the town into chaos! 93 min. In German with English subtitles.
01-1392 Was $24.99 *$19.99*

Punishment Battalion 999 (1959)
On the Eastern Front during World War II, a German battalion consisting of soldiers being punished for different crimes is sent on a suicide mission while under fire from Russian troops. This realistic, unusual war drama stars Werner Peters and George Thomas. AKA: "Penal Battalion 999." 103 min. In German with English subtitles.
65-1059 *$29.99*

Whisky And Sofa (1966)
Frothy romantic comedy starring Maria Schell as an architect who enters a design contest in Trieste. Pushy and calculating, Schell falls in love with the mannered son of the chief of a rival company, and romantic complications ensue. Carl Michaels, Nadia Gray also star. 85 min. Dubbed in English.
09-2325 *$19.99*

The All-Round Reduced Personality (1977)
Edda is a West Berlin photojournalist and single mother who joins up with a group of female photographers to create a series of photo essays on social issues. When their work is rejected by the sponsors, Edda places her pictures on billboards around the city in hopes of making a statement. Helke Sander wrote, directed and stars in this landmark effort. 98 min. In German with English subtitles.
53-6283 *$59.99*

Knife In The Head (1978)
In a riveting performance, Bruno Ganz plays a biogeneticist who is shot in the head during a police raid while visiting his estranged wife in a left-wing youth center. After losing his memory and physical coordination, Ganz finds himself in the middle of political intrigue. Angela Winkler also stars; directed by Reinhard Hauff. 108 min. In German with English subtitles.
53-7966 *$79.99*

Germany In Autumn (1978)
A number of Germany's major filmmakers, including Rainer Werner Fassbinder, Alexander Kluge and Volker Schlöndorff, contributed to this meditation on political terrorism in their country and the state of the people and politics after the kidnapping and murder of industrialist Hans Martin Schleyer. 124 min. In German with English subtitles.
70-3291 Was $79.99 *$29.99*

David (1979)
A young Jewish boy in Germany is separated from his family during the Holocaust, and is helped by friends as he tries to avoid capture. Moving drama directed by Peter Lilienthal, the film was the first made in Germany by a Jew to depict the horrifying acts of the Nazi regime. 106 min. In German with English subtitles.
53-7129 Was $79.99 *$29.99*

Germany, Pale Mother (1980)
Based on the life story of writer/director Helma Sanders-Brahms, this compelling drama stars Eva Mattes as a German newlywed whose husband joins the army at the start of World War II. After learning she is pregnant and giving birth, Mattes and her child wander the war-torn German countryside and endure a series of harrowing experiences, including Mattes' rape by American soldiers. With Ernst Jacobi, Angelika Thomas. 123 min. In German with English subtitles.
53-7545 *$89.99*

Céleste (1981)
The relationship between the dying author Marcel Proust and his housekeeper is depicted by filmmaker Percy Adlon ("Bagdad Cafe") in this moving, beautifully photographed drama, based on the real Céleste's memoirs. Eva Mattes, Jürgen Arndt star. 107 min. In German with English subtitles.
53-7548 Was $79.99 *$29.99*

The Boat Is Full (1981)
Exceptional drama about a group of people trying to escape Nazi Germany by seeking asylum in Switzerland. They pose as family, and are taken in by an innkeeper's wife. However, when Nazi authorities discover the group's true identities, the innkeeper's wife, her husband and the townspeople must make a difficult decision. Tina Engal, Curt Bois star. 104 min. In German with English subtitles.
70-5035 Was $59.99 *$29.99*

Das Boot: The Director's Cut (1982)
One of the most acclaimed German films of all time, director Wolfgang Petersen's harrowing drama looks at World War II through the eyes of a weary U-boat crew, with stunning photography that vividly depicts the cramped, claustrophobic feelings of life onboard a submarine. Jurgen Prochnow stars as the ship commander. This expanded, remastered edition also includes an introduction by Petersen. 209 min. In German with English subtitles.
02-3047 Letterboxed *$24.99*

Das Boot: The Director's Cut (Dubbed Version)
Also available in a dubbed-in-English edition.
02-3048 *$24.99*

The Second Awakening Of Christina Klages (1977)
For her first solo directorial effort, German filmmaker Margarethe von Trotta creates a compelling mix of action and social polemic. Tina Engel stars as Christa, a young woman forced into robbing a bank when the funding for the day care center she runs is cut and then flees to Portugal after her lover and accomplice is killed by police. Sylvia Reize, Marius Müller-Westernhagen co-star. 93 min. In German with English subtitles.
01-1534 *$39.99*

Sisters, Or The Balance Of Happiness (1979)
The emotional and psychological bonds that keep two women—a successful, controlling secretary and her insecure younger sister, a college student—tied to one another are explored in Margarethe von Trotta's compelling study. Jutta Lampe, Gudrun Gabriel, Jessica Früh star. 96 min. In German with English subtitles.
01-1533 *$39.99*

Sheer Madness (1982)
Two disparate German women, one a staid college professor (Hanna Shygulla), the other an eccentric artist (Angela Winkler), strike up a friendship that is tested by the world around them in this acclaimed drama from director Margarethe von Trotta ("Rosa Luxemburg"). AKA: "Friends and Husbands." 106 min. In German with English subtitles.
12-1423 *$39.99*

Marianne & Juliane (1982)
Set during the turbulent 1970s, Margarethe von Trotta's film studies the relationship between two sisters, a feminist editor and a radical involved with a political terrorist group. Barbara Sukowa, Jutta Lampe and Rudiger Volker star in this powerful drama. 106 min. In German with English subtitles.
53-8010 *$59.99*

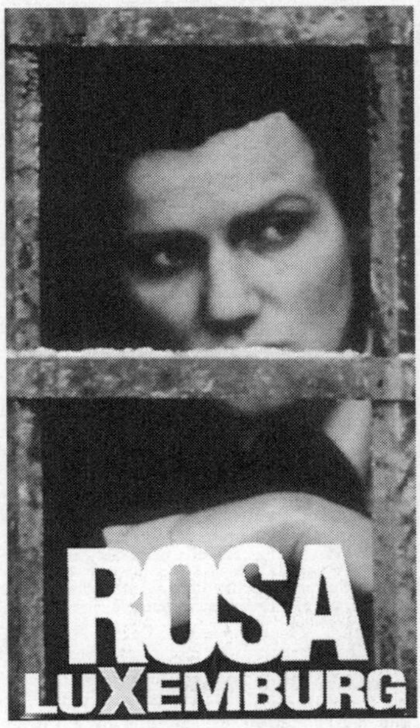

Rosa Luxemburg (1985)
Critically hailed biography that traces the life, works and death of the indefatigable woman who helped found the Socialist Democratic Party in early 20th-century Germany. Barbara Sukowa's award-winning title performance is a wonder to behold in Margarethe von Trotta's painstakingly crafted drama. 122 min. In German with English subtitles.
53-7951 Was $79.99 *$29.99*

The Promise (1995)
Two teenage lovers in 1961 East Germany plan an escape together to the West, but fate strands them on opposite sides of the Berlin Wall. The love between them burns on for decades, until the 1989 fall of Communism allows an emotional reunion, in this powerful drama by director Margarethe von Trotta ("Rosa Luxemburg"). Corinna Harfouch, Meret Becker star. 115 min. In German with English subtitles.
02-5083 Was $89.99 *$19.99*

Werner Herzog

Signs Of Life (1968)
Werner Herzog's first feature is a disturbing portrait of a German soldier wounded during World War II who is sent to a peaceful island with his wife and two other soldiers to recuperate. While there, the soldier guards a fortress and eventually questions his own sanity. Peter Brogle stars. 90 min. In German with English subtitles.
53-8230 *$79.99*

Even Dwarfs Started Small (1970)
"Lord of the Flies" meets "The Terror of Tiny Town" in Werner Herzog's bizarre parable about a group of dwarfs and midgets imprisoned on a remote island. During the island's governor's absence, the little people run amok in an orgy of rebellious and violent behavior. Helmut Döring, Gerd Gickel, Gisela Hertwig star. 96 min. In German with English subtitles.
08-8799 *$19.99*

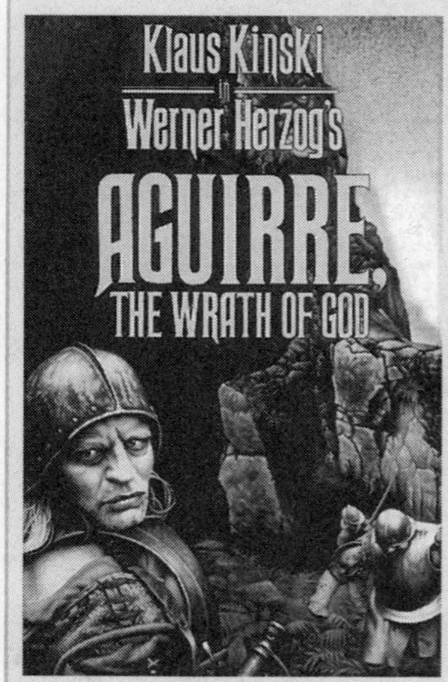

Aguirre: The Wrath Of God (1972)
A band of Spanish conquistadors travels into the Amazon jungle searching for the legendary city of El Dorado, but their leader's obsessions soon turn to madness in a compelling drama by Werner Herzog. Klaus Kinski stars as the driven Aguirre. 94 min. In German with English subtitles.
14-6064 Was $59.99 *$14.99*

Woyzeck (1978)
A quiet, repressed military orderly is driven to insanity and, ultimately, murder by those around him in this visually gripping drama by Werner Herzog. Klaus Kinski gives a typically fevered performance as the harried Woyzeck; with Eva Mattes. 82 min. In German with English subtitles.
53-7517 Letterboxed *$14.99*

Nosferatu The Vampyre (1979)
Werner Herzog's moody reworking of F.W. Murnau's 1922 horror classic features Klaus Kinski in an eerie performance as the titular character, a bald, bat-eared creature of the night. With Isabelle Adjani as the beautiful Lucy Harker and Bruno Ganz as Jonathan Harker. 107 min. In German with English subtitles.
59-7058 Letterboxed *$14.99*

Nosferatu The Vampyre (English-Language Version)
Also available in a filmed-in-English edition.
08-8694 Letterboxed *$14.99*

Fitzcarraldo (1982)
Herzog's monumental drama about human aspiration, filmed on location in the Amazon jungle, stars Klaus Kinski as a rubber plantation owner whose dream of an opera house in the wilderness drives him to move a boat across a mountain in order to claim the land he needs. With Claudia Cardinale. 157 min. Dubbed in English.
19-1258 Letterboxed *$19.99*

Cobra Verde (Slave Coast) (1988)
For what proved to be his last film with frequent star Klaus Kinski, writer/director Werner Herzog crafted this lush historical drama featuring Kinski as an 19th-century Brazilian peasant-turned-bandit who is hired to travel to West Africa to revive the slave trade. As the manic Kinski befriends the equally unstable king of Dahomey, he raises up an army of women warriors to try and topple the ruler. Includes the original theatrical trailer. 110 min. In German with English subtitles.
08-8888 Letterboxed *$14.99*

Herdsmen Of The Sun (1988)
Werner Herzog directed this incredible chronicle of the tribal rites of the Woodabe, nomads in the African Sahara who consider themselves the most beautiful people in the world. The film captures a festival in which the young men don make-up, beads and feathers in the hope of being selected by a woman as a mate. 52 min. Filmed in English.
53-7645 *$59.99*

My Best Fiend (1999)
The fruitful but often bizarre collaboration between actor Klaus Kinski and filmmaker Werner Herzog is chronicled in this incisive documentary directed by Herzog. The actor-director tandem led to such works as "Aguirre, The Wrath of God" and "Nosferatu the Vampyre," but, as revealed here, their intense natures often clashed in violent confrontations. 100 min. In German with English subtitles.
08-8880 Letterboxed *$14.99*

A Virus Knows No Morals (1986)
An unsettling comedy about AIDS from German underground filmmaker Rosa von Praunheim. Nurses roll dice to see which AIDS patient will die next, a gay bathhouse owner is confronted with the disease and gay terrorists kidnap the Minister of Health. Unusual, to say the least. 82 min. In German with English subtitles.
70-5003 *$39.99*

Anita: Dances Of Vice (1987)
Unflinching, innovative depiction of the wild life of Anita Barber, infamous nude dancer and cabaret star of post-WWI Berlin. Barber's bisexuality and drug abuse are candidly depicted in director Rosa von Praunheim's unusual biodrama, shot in the style of '20s German expressionism. 85 min. In German with English subtitles.
70-5016 *$39.99*

I Am My Own Woman (1993)
The stranger-than-fiction life story of Charlotte von Mahlsdorf, a 65-year-old transvestite and gay rights activist from Germany, is the focus of director Rosa von Praunheim's moving mix of documentary interviews and dramatic re-creations. Von Mahlsdorf recounts how his struggle to live his life pitted him against Nazi officials, East Germany's Communist rulers, and skinhead attacks. 91 min. In German with English subtitles.
53-8062 Was $79.99 *$19.99*

Neurosia (1995)
While hosting a salute to his work, gay German filmmaker Rosa von Praunheim is shot and killed by an unknown assailant. When murderer and victim both vanish, a beautiful tabloid reporter sets out to uncover the truth behind the crime on a bizarre odyssey that takes her from von Praunheim's family in Germany to the sex clubs of New York. Described as a gay "Citizen Kane," von Praunheim's off-the-wall satire also stars Desirée Nick. 87 min. In German with English subtitles.
70-5111 Was $59.99 *$29.99*

The White Spider (1963)
An enigmatic master detective with a hidden identity tries to stop a diabolical plot to control the world in this terrific German-made crime drama. With Karin Dor, Joachim Fuchsberger. 102 min. Dubbed in English.
68-8965 *$19.99*

Hypnosis (1966)
A ventriloquist's assistant goes on a killing spree to get control of the act but is tripped up by his obsessive fear of the talking dummy. Rare West German suspenser stars Eleanor Rossi-Drago. "It's me, Winchell, Knucklehead Smif, and I'm not gonna take it anymore!" AKA: "Dummy of Death." 86 min. Dubbed in English.
68-8330 *$19.99*

Devil In Silk (1968)
A wife's insane jealousy and a faked suicide attempt sends husband Curt Jurgens to the arms of his secretary. When she really does kill herself, the struggling composer is tried for her murder. Well-acted German courtroom drama co-stars Lilli Palmer. 105 min. Dubbed in English.
68-8363 *$19.99*

Heimat (1984)
A groundbreaking drama that captivated West German audiences on TV and in theatres, director Edgar Reitz's 16-hour epic chronicles German history from the end of World War I to the early '80s, as seen through the eyes of the members of a family of Rhineland farmers. 924 min. on nine tapes. In German with English subtitles.
53-9716 *$149.99*

The Wannsee Conference (1984)
Chilling docudrama re-creates the January, 1942 meeting of German officials in the Berlin suburb of Wannsee that led to the "Final Solution" and sentenced millions to death. Their casual discussion of death camps, gas chambers and body counts is a bitterly ironic look at one of humanity's darkest moments. 85 min. In German with English subtitles.
22-5675 *$19.99*

The Nasty Girl (1990)
A provocative drama from director Michael Verhoeven focusing on a German girl who attempts to uncover her hometown's past during World War II. Her quest turns out to be more difficult than she imagined when skeletons from the townspeople's closets resurface and death threats become frighteningly real. Lena Stolze, Hans-Reinhard Muller star. 94 min. In German with English subtitles.
44-1851 Was $89.99 *$19.99*

All Of Me (1990)
A witty and offbeat comedy about the unusual love triangle that develops between a German transvestite cabaret singer, his wife and a young Polish man while the singer is on tour in Warsaw. Georgette Dee stars in Bettina Wilhelm's gender-bending tale. 76 min. In German with English subtitles.
70-3466 *$39.99*

Flaming Ears (1991)
Described as a "futuristic sci-fi lesbian fantasy," this bizarre, violent German feature is set in a post-apocalyptic city in the 28th century, where the personal and romantic lives of three women (a comic book artist, a pyromaniacal performance artist and a reptile-loving alien) intertwine. 84 min. In German with English subtitles.
01-1506 *$39.99*

Europa Europa (1991)
Writer/director Agnieszka Holland's acclaimed, controversial film tells the amazing true story of a Jewish teen who escapes from the Polish ghetto and poses as a Nazi to escape the camps. Eventually, he joins a Hitler youth school and the German army, and must hide his true identity from a girl he cares for. Marco Hofschneider, Julie Delpy star. 115 min. In German and Russian with English subtitles.
73-1119 Was $89.99 *$19.99*

Terror 2000 (1992)
This politically-incorrect saga meshes sex, violence and humor in its tale of a husband-and-wife detective team sent to a German refugee camp to find a Polish family and a social worker. During the search, the sleuths are kidnapped by neo-Nazis, and it's soon learned that their interests are as strange as the people around them. With Udo Kier, Gary Indiana. 79 min. In German with English subtitles.
01-1559 *$29.99*

Maybe...Maybe Not (1994)
A frantic and funny gender-bending comedy...from Germany? Writer/director Sonkë Wortmann's romantic roundelay follows a handsome womanizer who moves in with a gay friend with an unrequited crush on him after his girlfriend kicks him out. When she learns she's pregnant, she goes to make up with him, and is shocked to find the two men in a "compromising position." Til Shweiger, Katja Riemann, Rufus Beck star. AKA: "Der Bewegte Mann." 93 min. In German with English subtitles.
27-7000 *$94.99*

Kaspar Hauser (1994)
The true story which was the basis for Werner Herzog's 1975 movie is re-examined in this effort which won several major German film awards. In the early 1800s, the heir to the throne of the Duchy of Baden is kidnapped and imprisoned for 12 years, eventually appearing on the streets of Nuremberg as a crippled "wild man." André Eisermann stars. 137 min. In German with English subtitles.
53-8865 *$79.99*

Jacob The Liar (1974)
The original film version of Jurek Becker's moving Holocaust novel, this acclaimed East German drama features Vlastimil Brodsky as a resident of a Jewish ghetto in Poland who overhears war news on a Gestapo radio. Pretending to own an illegal radio, he passes the news on to his fellow prisoners and quickly becomes a hero, making up stories of Allied victories to keep hope alive. Erwin Geschonneck, Henry Hubchen, Armin Mueller-Stahl also star. 96 min. In German with English subtitles.
53-6585 *$39.99*

The Inheritors (1984)
A chilling look at the neo-Nazi movement in modern Europe, this acclaimed drama focuses on a teenage German boy who becomes involved in a fascist organization that uses violence and terrorism. Written and directed by Walter Bannert. 90 min. Dubbed in English.
53-1805 *$19.99*

Men... (1985)
Engaging comedy of the sexes from Doris Dörrie centers on a happily married advertising executive who discovers his wife is having an affair with an iconoclastic artist. In order to get the goods on his wife, he rents a room next to her lover and eventually befriends him. With Heiner Lauterbach. 96 min. In German with English subtitles.
53-7946 Was $79.99 *$29.99*

Beyond Silence (1998)
Touching story of Lara, a young girl who serves as the interpreter for her hearing-impaired parents. After she is given a clarinet by her aunt, Lara's decision to pursue a career in music leads to a bitter division between herself and her mother and father. Sylvie Testud, Tatjana Trieb and Howie Seago star. 107 min. In German with English subtitles.
11-2299 Was $99.99 *$19.99*

A Man Like Eva (1983)
Loosely based on actual events in the life of German filmmaker Rainer Werner Fassbinder, this fascinating drama stars actress Eva Mattes as the director, seducing actors and actresses and browbeating the film crew while trying to complete his latest work. Co-written and directed by Radu Gabrea. 92 min. In German with English subtitles.
53-7162 *$79.99*

Brother Of Sleep (1996)
This acclaimed mystical drama from Joseph Vilsmaier ("Stalingrad") is set in a small 19th-century Alpine village where a young man's incredible musical talents both astonish and frighten the locals, and where his relationship with a young woman eventually leads to conflict and tragedy. André Eisermann, Ben Becker star. 133 min. In German with English subtitles.
02-3073 *$94.99*

Stalingrad (1995)
One of the most realistic depictions of war ever filmed, this stunning epic chronicles the six-month siege of the Russian city by German forces in World War II, a battle in which over 2,000,000 lives were lost. Told from the point of view of a German soldier, this powerful saga offers astonishing battle sequences. 150 min. In German with English subtitles.
53-8657 Letterboxed *$29.99*

Stalingrad (Dubbed Version)
Also available in a dubbed-in-English edition.
53-8658 Letterboxed *$29.99*

Beware Of A Holy Whore (1970)
Unflinchingly honest account of the world of filmmaking from Rainer Werner Fassbinder centered around the relationships of a German film crew staying at a Spanish seaside hotel, awaiting the arrival of the temperamental director. Lou Castel, Eddie Constantine, Hanna Schygulla star. Music by Leonard Cohen and Elvis Presley. 103 min. In German with English subtitles.
53-8164 Was $79.99 *$19.99*

I Only Want You To Love Me (1976)
R.W. Fassbinder's penetrating drama focuses on Peter, the put-upon son of innkeepers, who moves to the city with his wife in order to forget his tough upbringing and continuous criticism from his father. Eventually, the strains of work, marriage and money lead him to murder. Vitrus Zeplichal stars. 104 min. In German with English subtitles.
01-1513 Was $39.99 *$29.99*

Shadow Of Angels (1976)
A prostitute named Lily Brest is so beautiful, people can't believe she's really a hooker. A rich real estate investor helps her see that her real talent may be talking to her clients, but their secrets and disturbing confessions lead her into depression and contemplating taking her own life. With R.W. Fassbinder, who co-adapted his own play. 103 min. In German with English subtitles.
01-1514 *$39.99*

Satan's Brew (1976)
Called Fassbinder's most outrageous effort, this darkly humorous tale is about a has-been poet who kills his mistress, then assumes the identity of Stefan George, a 19th-century homosexual German romantic poet. A mix of slapstick, Theatre of the Absurd, and satire, the film stars Max Raab and Margit Cartensen. 112 min. In German with English subtitles.
53-8165 Was $79.99 *$19.99*

The Stationmaster's Wife (1977)
A weak stationmaster becomes the laughingstock of his village when his manipulative wife carries on a series of affairs with the townspeople, including a butcher and a hairdresser. Rainer Werner Fassbinder's erotic drama concerning the "destructiveness of love" stars Kurt Raab and Elisabeth Trissenaar. 111 min. In German with English subtitles.
53-7797 Was $29.99 *$19.99*

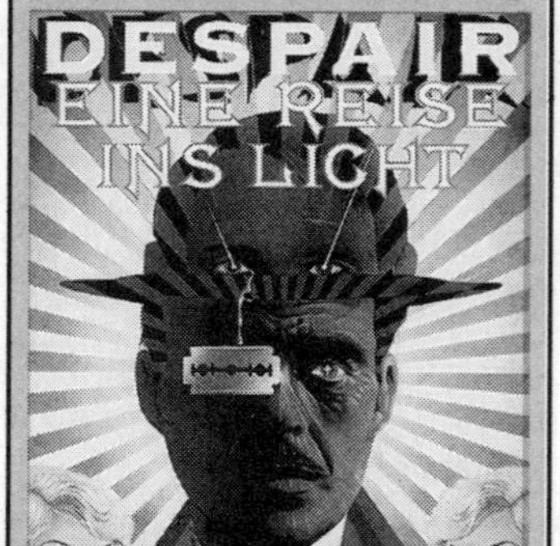

Despair (1978)
Filmed in English, Rainer Werner Fassbinder's translation of Nabokov's novel stars Dirk Bogarde as a Jewish-Russian chocolate manufacturer in pre-Nazi Berlin. Seeking refuge from his boring life, Bogarde takes the identity of a stranger with whom he has little resemblance. With Andrea Ferreol. 119 min.
19-1265 *$29.99*

Wings Of Desire (1988)
A hauntingly beautiful tale from German filmmaker Wim Wenders, depicting a black-and-white Berlin as seen through the eyes of angels who pass unnoticed to follow the people they're assigned to watch. Bruno Ganz stars as the seraph who yearns for a taste of humanity after falling for circus performer Solveig Dommartin; with a delightful cameo by Peter Falk. 130 min. In German with English subtitles.
73-1041 *$19.99*

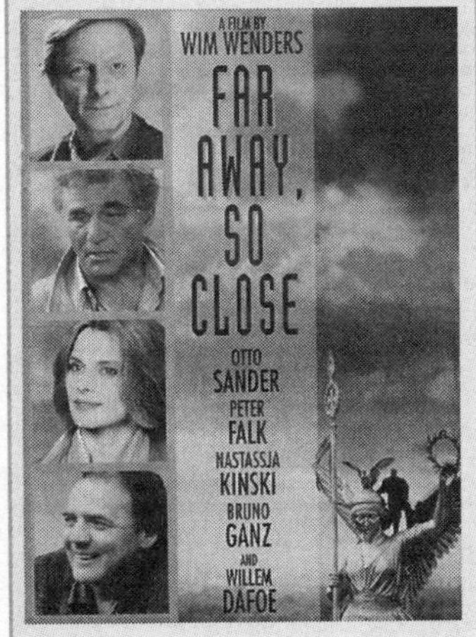

Faraway, So Close (1993)
Wim Wenders' lushly filmed sequel to "Wings of Desire" is set in post-Cold War Berlin and follows an angel who assimilates into the real world and is faced with danger when he becomes an aide to a dealer in arms and pornography. Otto Sander, Nastassja Kinski, Horst Buchholz star, with cameos by Peter Falk and Mikhail Gorbachev. 146 min. In English, French and German with English subtitles.
02-2634 Was $89.99 *$14.99*

Notebook On Cities And Clothes (1990)
A documentary as offbeat and thought-provoking as its subject, German filmmaker Wim Wenders' look at Japanese fashion designer Yohji Yamamoto slowly transforms from a straight biographical piece into an insightful examination of fashion, cinema and the nature of creativity. 80 min.
53-7753 Was $59.99 *$29.99*

Lisbon Story (1995)
A sound engineer travels to Portugal, where a film director friend is supposed to be working on a documentary, but upon his arrival discovers the director missing and a silent, unfinished film on the editing table. The engineer wanders the streets of Lisbon, recording the sounds of the city for the movie and searching for his friend, in this lyrical and allegorical drama from Wim Wenders. Rudiger Vogler, Patrick Bauchau star. 100 min. In English, and German and Portuguese with English subtitles.
53-9938 Letterboxed *$19.99*

Please see our index for these other Wim Wenders titles: *The End Of Violence • Until The End Of The World*

Bandits (1997)
One part "Thelma & Louise" and one part "The Harder They Come," director/co-scripter Katja von Garnier's vibrant drama follows a rock band made up of four female convicts. An unexpected chance for freedom comes when they overpower an abusive guard and escape in a police van, but while the girls elude authorities, their demo tape gets radio airplay, and soon The Bandits are the nation's hottest band. Jutta Hoffmann, Nicolette Krebitz, Katja Riemann, Jasmin Tabatabai star. 109 min. In German with English subtitles.
02-3415 Was $99.99 *$21.99*

The Charm Of La Boheme (1936)
A unique and heart-rending drama woven around the grand opera "La Boheme." With Jan Kiepura and Martha Eggerth. 93 min. In German with English subtitles.
53-7058 Was $39.99 *$19.99*

An Orphan Boy Of Vienna (1937)
Delightful family tale of a young foundling who is taken into a prestigious music school and looked after by a kindly nun. The Vienna Choir Boys star in this musical drama. 87 min. In German with English subtitles.
09-1683 Was $29.99 *$24.99*

Romance In A Minor Key (1943)
Marianne Hoppe and Paul Dahlke star in this story about a husband who discovers that his wife has acquired a valuable pearl necklace. Produced during World War II, this is a rare example of filmmaking under the Nazi regime. In German with English subtitles.
10-9268 *$29.99*

Angry Harvest (1986)
Remarkable German drama that chronicles the intense love-hate relationship between a Jewish woman fleeing the Nazis and the Polish landowner whose farm she hides on. Agnieszka Holland's compelling tale stars Elisabeth Trissenaar, Armand Mueller-Stahl. 102 min. In German with English subtitles.
75-1004 *$69.99*

The Invincibles (1994)
In this thriller, Simon, a leader of a special police unit, discovers that his former partner who supposedly committed suicide is the leader of a gang involved in counterfeiting. Simon gets tangled in a web of murder and double-crosses and is suspected to have taken part in kidnapping a government official. Herbert Knaup stars. 115 min. In German with English subtitles.
53-6451 *$39.99*

Under The Bridge (1945)
Two bargemen on the River Havel fall in love with the same woman in this drama featuring Carl Raddatz, Gustav Knuth and Hannelore Schrothe. Directed by Helmut Kutner. In German with English subtitles.
10-9267 *$29.99*

The Blue Light (1932)
The mystical fantasy of an ethereal mountain girl, a hidden treasure, and her rejection by the people of the village below was the first film directed by Leni Riefenstahl. An enthralling adaptation of the romantic German legend; with Riefenstahl and Bela Balazs. 70 min. In German with English subtitles.
53-7057 Was $29.99 *$19.99*

Tiefland (1954)
Twelve years in the making, Leni Riefenstahl's final finished film is the romantic story of a Gypsy dancer, set against lushly photographed pastoral settings. Although an extremely controversial film, attacked for alleged use of slave labor during production, this is a worthwhile last look at a unique and influential talent. Riefenstahl also stars. 98 min. In German with English subtitles.
53-7069 *$29.99*

The Life And Loves Of Mozart (1959)
Fascinating study of the musical genius' poverty-stricken later years, featuring Oscar Werner in a tour de force title performance. The film focuses on Mozart's extramarital involvement with a beautiful singer, political controversies caused by his librettist, and his magnificent music. With Johanna Matz. 87 min. Dubbed in English.
17-9039 *$19.99*

Mozart: A Childhood Chronicle (1976)
Before "Amadeus," German filmmaker Klaus Kirschner brought the great composer's early years to life in this sweeping epic. A child prodigy who was writing scores at the age of six, young Mozart's relationship to his family is depicted using actual letters from his parents and sister. 224 min. In German with English subtitles.
53-7135 Was $149.99 *$99.99*

Forget Mozart (1986)
Fascinating study of the life of Mozart, styled like a detective thriller. After the composer dies, the head of Prague's secret police investigates his life, questioning his wife, his lyricist and his nemesis, Salieri. Armin Mueller-Stahl, Tidof and Catarina Raacke star. 93 min. In German with English subtitles.
01-1468 Was $79.99 *$29.99*

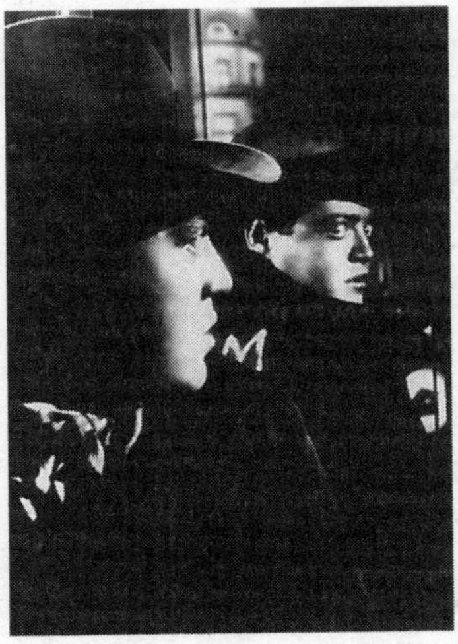

M (Restored Version) (1931)
Harrowing images, shadows and symbolism permeate Fritz Lang's first sound film, a classic of the German cinema. Peter Lorre is unforgettably chilling as a psychotic child killer stalking the streets of Berlin even as he is hunted by both the police and the city's underworld, intent on taking the heat off themselves. This remastered edition includes the often missing final scene and a restored soundtrack. 106 min. In German with English subtitles.
22-5918 *$19.99*

Dragon Chow (Drachenfutter) (1987)
A lively and imaginative look at friendship and business in the face of adversity. A Pakistani political refugee befriends an Oriental waiter and the two open a Chinese restaurant in West Germany. With Bhasker and Ric Young. 75 min. In German, Urdu and Mandarin with English subtitles.
53-7425 *$69.99*

The Harmonists (1999)
Compelling true story of the Comedian Harmonists, a popular comic singing group in Germany who were forced to disband in 1934 due to persecution directed at them because of their three Jewish members. With Ben Becker, Ulrich Noethen; directed by Joseph Vilsmaier ("Stalingrad"). 115 min. In German with English subtitles.
11-2374 Was $99.99 *$19.99*

Czechoslovakia

Cassandra Cat (1963)
Winner of the Cannes Special Jury Prize, this Czech fantasy tells of a magician who has a special pet: a cat with glasses that sees people in their true colors. Honest people are unchanged, while cheats are gray and adulterers appear yellow. Whimsy and social commentary meld in this unusual outing, starring Jan Werich. AKA: "The Cat." 87 min. Dubbed in English.
10-9448 *$19.99*

Intimate Lighting (1965)
The debut feature from Czech-born director Ivan Passer ("Cutter's Way"), this gentle seriocomic look at culture clash and dreams deferred follows a renowned cellist who leaves his big city home with his wife to visit a friend now working as an orchestra director in a small village. Zdenek Bezusek, Vera Kresadlova star. 73 min. In Czech with English subtitles.
22-6090 *$29.99*

Closely Watched Trains (1966)
A masterpiece from Czechoslovakia that won the Best Foreign Film Oscar, Jiri Menzel's touching seriocomedy chronicles the coming of age of a young railroad worker during the Nazi occupation. His experiences with the opposite sex are hilarious and winning. Vaclav Neckar stars. 93 min. In Czech with English subtitles.
02-1321 *$29.99*

My Sweet Little Village (1986)
Oscar-nominated and entirely charming Czech film concerning the various and sundry eccentrics who populate a tiny town, particularly a sweetly knuckleheaded young trucker who'd rather face the big city than the wrath of his pushed-to-the-brink partner. Good fun from Jiri Menzel, director of "Closely Watched Trains." 100 min. In Czech with English subtitles.
53-6101 Was $59.99 *$24.99*

All My Good Countrymen (1968)
Sharply funny Czech satire, banned upon its initial release, that chronicles the bemused reactions of a small village to encroaching socialism and bureaucracy. 115 min. In Czech with English subtitles.
53-9014 *$59.99*

Diamonds Of The Night (1968)
Harrowing, brilliantly told story of two Jewish youths who escape a concentration camp-bound train and flee for their survival marked Jan Nemec's feature directorial debut; Ladislav Jansky, Antonin Kumbera star. The short film "A Bite to Eat" is included. 80 min. In Czech with English subtitles.
53-9015 *$59.99*

A Report On The Party And The Guests (1968)
Jan Nemec's banned satire on conformity and persecution follows a group of picnickers who's set upon by a pack of bullies, only to be delivered to saviors that are even worse. Searing look at abusive authority stars Ivan Vyskocil, Jan Klusak. 70 min. In Czech with English subtitles.
53-9019 *$59.99*

Adrift (1971)
Jan Kadar received universal acclaim for this tale of a happily married, morally rigid fisherman who becomes obsessed with the naked woman he saves from drowning. Jealousy and guilt rage as she ignores him while he ignores his ill wife. Rade Markovic, Paula Pritchett star in this sensual drama. 103 min. In Czech with English subtitles.
53-6073 *$29.99*

The Elementary School (1991)
Sensitive story from "Kolya" director Jan Svêrák tells an autobiographical tale of a 10-year-old boy's coming-of-age experiences and his village's new schoolteacher. 100 min. In Czech with English subtitles.
53-8925 *$89.99*

Mandragora (1997)
A bored Czech teenager tries to escape his drab life by fleeing to Prague, only to fall into a seamy underworld of drugs and male prostitution, in this powerful drama by writer/director Wiktor Grodecki ("Not Angels But Angels"). Mirek Caslavka, Pavel Skripal star. 135 min. In Czech with English subtitles.
78-5088 Letterboxed *$39.99*

Wolf Trap (1957)
Considered a landmark in Czech cinema, Jiri Weiss' drama tells of a town veterinarian who falls in love with his own adopted daughter. The psychological ramifications of the affair are what drives this emotional tale. Jiri Sejbalova, Jana Brejchova star. 95 min. In Czech with English subtitles.
53-9679 *$29.99*

The Coward (1961)
Set in a Slovak village during the final days of World War II, this gripping thriller from director Jiri Weiss focuses on a cowardly schoolteacher who risks his life to save victims of the Nazis. Oleg Strizhenov, Dana Smutna star. 113 min. In Slovak with English subtitles.
53-9680 *$29.99*

Murder Czech Style (1967)
Superb black comedy about a portly office clerk who thinks he gets his first chance at true love—then discovers that his wife is having a heated affair. Directed by award-winning documentary filmmaker Jiri Weiss; Rudolf Hrusinsky, Kveta Fialova star. 90 min. In Czech with English subtitles.
53-9678 *$29.99*

Loves Of A Blonde (1965)
A heartfelt Czech comedy-drama from director Milos Forman about a young woman who works in a shoe factory and dreams of bettering her life with the right man. She falls for a pianist from Prague, but the relationship takes a sour turn when they travel to meet his parents. Hana Brejchova stars. 88 min. In Czech with English subtitles.
22-5548 Was $39.99 *$29.99*

The Firemen's Ball (1968)
Director Milos Forman's acclaimed satire follows the goings-on in a small Czech town whose fire brigade commander is about to step down. His retirement party turns into a slapstick disaster that also manages to poke fun at Marxist politics. Vaclav Stockel, Josef Kolb star. 73 min. In Czech with English subtitles.
22-5678 *$29.99*

The Shop On Main Street (1965)
A moving, memorable Czech drama that won the Best Foreign Film Academy Award. Ida Kaminska stars as an elderly Jewish shopkeeper in Nazi-occupied Slovakia who is befriended by a Slovak man assigned to watch over her. Co-directed by Ján Kadár and Elmar Klos. 128 min. In Czech with English subtitles.
22-5632 *$29.99*

Scenes From The Surreal
This program features three works by noted Czech animator Jan Svankmajer ("Alice"): "Darkness Light Darkness," "Manly Games" and "Death of Stalinism." Also included is "Jan Svankmajer: The Animator of Prague," a documentary on how the inventive artist blends clay animation, live-action, stop-motion techniques and magical surrealism for his dreamlike films. 58 min.
70-5050 Was $49.99 *$19.99*

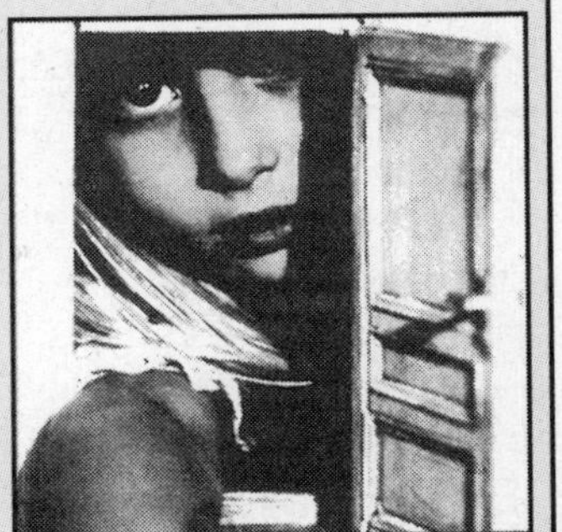

Alice (1988)
Fascinating version of Lewis Carroll's "Alice's Adventures in Wonderland," presented in both live action and animation by Czech master of the surreal, Jan Svankmajer. For adults and children, the film is provocative, eerie and wholly original. 84 min. Dubbed in English.
70-5000 Was $29.99 *$19.99*

Faust (1994)
Czech animator Jan Svankmajer's startling adaptation of the "Faust" legend is a mysterious mix of stop-motion animation, pixilation, puppetry and live action. The story concerns Faust's pact with Lucifer in which he swaps his soul for 24 hours of pleasure. But Faust is soon turned into an actor, then a puppet on a stage. With Petr Sepek. 97 min. Dubbed in English.
53-8607 Was $79.99 *$24.99*

Conspirators Of Pleasure (1996)
With a cast of humans that seem as odd and detached as any of his puppet stars of prior films, Czech director Jan Svankmajer examines the intricate sexual proclivities—from a man who abuses an effigy of his neighbor while wearing a chicken costume to a woman who enjoys having her toes sucked by fish—of a seemingly unconnected group of fetishists in this dialogue-free satire. 83 min.
53-6413 Was $79.99 *$24.99*

Romeo, Juliet And Darkness (1960)
Stirring Holocaust drama about a student who hides a Jewish girl from the Nazis in occupied Czechoslovakia and becomes her only link to the outside world. The two eventually fall in love, but their relationship leads to tragedy. Ivan Mistrik, Dana Smutna star; Jiri Weiss directs. AKA: "Sweet Light in a Dark Room." 96 min. In Czech with English subtitles.
53-9681 *$29.99*

Ecstasy (1933)
The landmark Czech drama that featured teenage Hedy Lamarr's notorious nude swim scene. Lamarr (billed as Hedwig Kiesler) plays a child bride who flees from a loveless marriage and has an affair with an engineer. Co-stars Zvonimir Rogoz, Leopold Kramer. 82 min. In Czech with English subtitles.
53-6013 *$19.99*

Ecstasy (Dubbed Version)
Also available in a dubbed-in-English edition. 67 min.
10-3026 *$19.99*

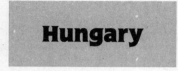

Hungary

The Little Valentino (1979)
Offbeat Hungarian seriocomedy, small in story but rich in detail, follows one day in the aimless life of the title character, a 20-year-old driver's assistant who gets by on his wits and some petty theft. 102 min. In Hungarian with English subtitles.
53-9280 *$59.99*

Sunday Daughters (1980)
A tough social drama studying a 16-year-old girl's journey from a brutal juvenile prison and daring escape to her love affair with the son of a woman who helps her. Directed by Janosz Rozsa. 100 min. In Hungarian with English subtitles.
53-9128 *$59.99*

Maria's Day (1985)
During the course of a birthday party, an aristocratic family reviews their lives and their politics, and takes an introspective look at their contemporary lives and how their relation to poet Sandor Ptofi has affected them. 113 min. In Hungarian with English subtitles.
53-9126 *$59.99*

The Round Up (1966)
Miklos Jancso's groundbreaking film created a stir when it was shown at Cannes. This controversial drama paints a cynical picture of the police state as it follows Hungarian outlaws, peasants and herdsmen who are placed in a prison stockade and asked to identify rebels. 90 min. In Hungarian with English subtitles.
53-6046 Letterboxed *$59.99*

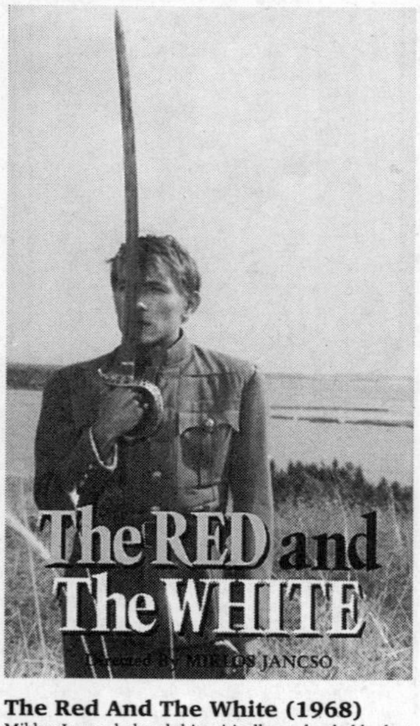

The Red And The White (1968)
Miklos Jancso helmed this critically applauded look at the 1918 Russian Revolution through Hungary's point of view. The Hungarian Army and the Red Army battle the counter-revolutionary Whites in this brilliantly photographed drama. 92 min. In Hungarian with English subtitles.
53-7389 Letterboxed *$24.99*

Hungarian Rhapsody (1983)
Hungary's great Miklos Jancso directs this political drama focusing on the struggles of a nobleman who leads peasants against his ruling class brother and his associates in Hungary in 1911. With Gyorgy Cserhalmi. 101 min. In Hungarian with English subtitles.
53-9285 *$69.99*

Father (Diary Of A Week) (1967)
Moving Hungarian film that studies a young man's search for the truth behind his father's death during World War II. Istvan Szabo directs. 89 min. In Hungarian with English subtitles.
09-1299 Was $29.99 *$24.99*

25 Fireman's Street (1973)
During their last night together before the building is demolished, the residents of a boarding house share their memories, hopes, and fears of an uncertain future in this moving Hungarian drama by director Istvan Szabo. 97 min. In Hungarian with English subtitles.
53-7140 *$69.99*

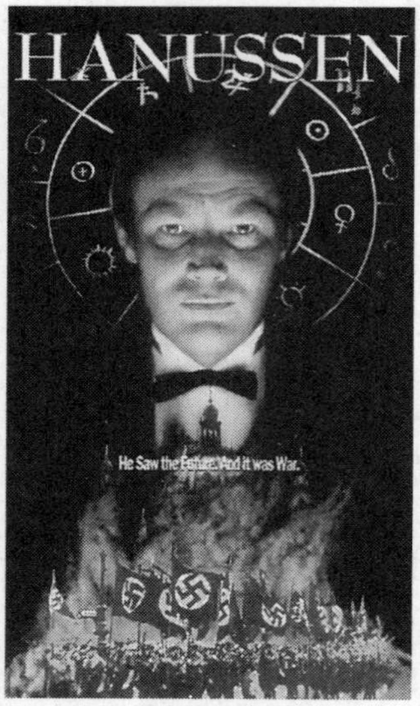

Hanussen (1988)
Klaus Maria Brandauer reteams with "Mephisto" director Istvan Szabo for a fascinating tale about an Austrian WWI soldier who gains power to see into the future after he's shot in the head. When the Nazis seize power, the psychic must decide whether to side with or battle against them. With Erland Josephson and Walter Schmidinger. 117 min. In German with English subtitles.
02-2031 Was $79.99 *$19.99*

Magic Hunter (1996)
When a Budapest policeman receives special bullets guaranteed to hit his targets from a sinister superior, he doesn't know the last bullet is sure to hit whom the superior—an incarnation of Satan—desires. Gary Kemp and Sadie Frost star in this mystical tale. 106 min. In Hungarian with English subtitles.
70-5115 Was $79.99 *$29.99*

Stand Off (1989)
Gripping, intense tale of two teenage brothers who hold 16 girls hostage in a dormitory for five days, demanding money and a flight out of Budapest. This thriller in the tradition of "The Desperate Hours" was directed by Gyula Gazdag ("A Hungarian Fairy Tale") and features director Istvan Szabo ("Mephisto") in a rare acting role. 97 min. In Hungarian with English subtitles.
53-7482 *$79.99*

A Hungarian Fairy Tale (1989)
Political satire meets heartfelt whimsy in this magical tale about a fatherless boy who is considered a nonentity in his Hungarian town until he can find an appropriate surrogate parent. David Vermes, Maria Varga star; co-written and directed by Gyula Gazdag. 97 min. In Hungarian with English subtitles.
53-8527 Was $89.99 *$19.99*

My Twentieth Century (1990)
Identical twin sisters who were separated at birth take very different life paths before they are re-united 20 years later while travelling on the Orient Express in this award-winning Hungarian seriocomedy set at the turn of the century. Dortha Segda stars as the two siblings; scripted and directed by Ildiko Enyedi. 104 min. In Hungarian with English subtitles.
53-7631 Was $89.99 *$19.99*

The Annunciation (1993)
A truly unique account of the dark history of humanity from the Garden of Eden to modern times as portrayed by children aged 8 to 14. Follow the plight of 14-year-old Adam as he encounters adventures in ancient Greece, the French Revolution, rapists, concubines and a deceptively sweet, blonde-haired Lucifer. 101 min. In Hungarian with English subtitles.
78-5056 *$69.99*

Woyzek (1994)
Compelling version of the classic George Büchner story involving a trainyard flagman whose emotional distress stems from his poverty, his horrible job, a strange medical experiment with which he's involved and the discovery of his wife's adulterous affair with a policeman. János Szász directs. 93 min. In Hungarian with English subtitles.
01-1562 *$29.99*

Cold Days (1966)
Based on true incidents, this gripping and disturbing Hungarian drama looks at the 1946 trial of four men charged with leading Nazi-ordered massacres of Jews and Serbians during World War II, drawing parallels between their actions and Communist crackdowns in the '60s. 102 min. In Hungarian with English subtitles.
53-9278 *$59.99*

The Girl (1968)
The first film by Hungarian director Marta Meszaros is a heartfelt drama about a young woman who leaves her orphanage home to be reunited with her mother, but finds that they live in two different worlds. 86 min. In Hungarian with English subtitles.
53-7146 *$69.99*

Riddance (1973)
A young woman who works in a factory falls in love with a university student, but his embarrassment at her station in life tests the strength of their relationship in this moving Hungarian movie by Marta Meszaros. 84 min. In Hungarian with English subtitles.
53-7145 *$69.99*

Adoption (1975)
Award-winning tale of two women from Hungary, centering around the unlikely friendship that develops between a middle-aged widow whose married lover won't give her the child she wants and a teenager eager to set out on her own. Directed by Marta Meszaros. 89 min. In Hungarian with English subtitles.
53-7144 *$69.99*

The Witness (1968)
Suppressed by the Hungarian government for 12 years, Peter Basco's savage political satire is set in Poland in 1949, where a loyal party member is groomed by a protective friend to serve as a witness against a government minister falsely accused of treason. With Ferenc Kállai. 108 min. In Hungarian with English subtitles.
53-7776 *$59.99*

Sinbad (1970)
The wistful, sensual memories of an aging Don Juan, as he thinks about the many women in his life, form a visually compelling drama by Hungarian painter-turned-filmmaker Zoltan Huszaruk. 98 min. In Hungarian with English subtitles.
53-7139 *$69.99*

Love (1971)
Touching drama by Hungarian filmmaker Károly Makk about a political reformer who is imprisoned. His wife must care for his aging mother while he's in jail, and they tell the mother that he's working in America in order to keep her spirits up. Lili Darvas, Ivan Darvas star. 92 min. In Hungarian with English subtitles.
53-7487 *$59.99*

Cat's Play (1973)
A widowed teacher living alone in Budapest finds her quiet life (and relationship with an old flame) upset by a chance meeting with a woman she knew during World War II in this insightful drama from Hungarian director Károly Makk. Margit Dayka, Elma Bulla star. 115 min. In Hungarian with English subtitles.
53-9473 Was $59.99 *$29.99*

A Very Moral Night (1977)
Set in a Hungarian bordello, this fanciful film tells the story of a naive student who catches the eye of the cynical madam and becomes the house's "mascot." With Iren Psota, Margit Makay; directed by Károly Makk. 96 min. In Hungarian with English subtitles.
53-7709 *$39.99*

Nobody's Daughter (1976)
This drama concerns an 8-year-old girl who is taken from her orphanage by a farmer who plans to make money on her. She escapes the abuse and cruelty of his home only to encounter more difficult times with a wealthy family. Czinkoczi Zsuzsi stars. 90 min. In Hungarian with English subtitles.
53-7725 *$59.99*

Bad Guys (1979)
A goulash western? This fascinating look at the end of the outlaw era in Hungary, set in the 1860s, follows a group of desperadoes who hold a town at bay and the authorities who wage a war against them. Janos Derzsi, Djoko Rosic star. 93 min. In Hungarian with English subtitles.
53-7483 *$69.99*

The Nice Neighbor (1979)
A sharp-witted but selfish tenant of an apartment complex uses his skills to deceive his neighbors and gets a bigger apartment when the complex is torn down. A masterful performance from star Laszlo Szabo and keen direction from Zsolt Kezdi-Kovacs highlight this look at manipulation. 90 min. In Hungarian with English subtitles.
53-9286 *$59.99*

The Memories Of A River (1989)
When a young girl is found drowned in the river Tisza, tensions mount as a group of Jewish raftsmen is accused of the crime. What makes matters worse is that the district attorney in charge of prosecuting the case decides to force the young son of one of the accused to testify against his own father. 131 min. In Hungarian with English subtitles.
53-6211 *$59.99*

The Midas Touch (1989)
In this much-acclaimed political allegory, a flea market merchant discovers he has the power to turn ordinary objects into gold, a talent that is put to the test during the bloody revolution of 1956. Karoly Eperjes, Judit Pogany star. 100 min. In Hungarian with English subtitles.
53-7546 *$79.99*

We Never Die (1994)
A lusty, carefree romp from director Róbert Koltai centering on a naive teenager who joins his uncle on an excursion to sell wooden hangers during the 1960s. The uncle promises his nephew that their trip will include "grub, booze and women," and the youth soon witnesses his uncle's promises come true. 90 min. In Hungarian with English subtitles.
53-8028 *$79.99*

Bolshe Vita (1996)
Tragic coming-of-age story set during the 1989 fall of Communism in Hungary. A disparate group of people—two girls from England and America, a pair of Russian musicians, and a Russian engineer-turned-knife salesman—meet and befriend each other in a Budapest nightclub. Their lives are forever changed by the turmoil surrounding them. With Alexei Serebryakov and Helen Baxendale. 90 min. In Russian with English subtitles.
53-6210 *$79.99*

Eastern Europe

A Friend Of The Deceased (1998)
Nominated for an Academy Award for Best Foreign Film, this absurdist comedy tells of a linguist scrambling for work as a translator in Kiev. Unable to find employment—and discovering that his wife is having an affair—he hires a hit man to kill him. Then he meets a prostitute, and their relationship changes his outlook on life. 100 min. In Ukrainian with English subtitles.
02-3232 *$99.99*

Cabaret Balkan (1999)
Serbian filmmaker Goran Paskaljevic ("Someone Else's America") offers an unforgettable look at a place where brutality and death are everyday parts of life. Set in 1995 Belgrade, the interlinking stories follow a series of events—from a fender-bender to a bus hijacking—that push the war-weary residents into violent confrontations. Nebojsa Glogovac, Lazar Ristovski, and Nikola Ristanovski as the "master of ceremonies" star. 102 min. In Serbo-Croatian with English subtitles.
06-2961 *$79.99*

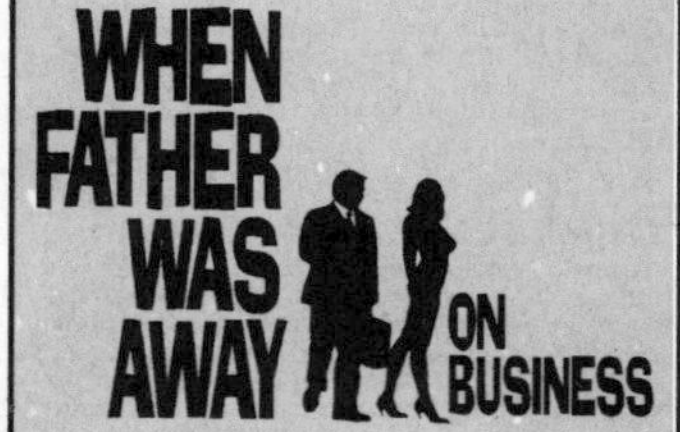

When Father Was Away On Business (1985)
Acclaimed political satire from director Emir Kusturica is set in Yugoslavia in the 1950s and follows the experiences of a 6-year-old boy whose father has, unknown to the youth, been sent to a labor camp after being found with a government official's mistress. 144 min. In Serbian with English subtitles.
53-9433 Was $89.99 *$19.99*

Time Of The Gypsies (1990)
An epic drama from Emir Kusturica, the director of "When Father Was Away on Business." An orphaned Gypsy boy leaves his small town and joins a strange caravan of misfits on a journey to Italy. The trek includes many magical stops and fascinating, surrealistic moments. With Davor Dujmovic and Ljubica Adzovic. 136 min. In Romany and Serbo-Croatian with English subtitles.
02-2041 Was $79.99 *$19.99*

Underground (1995)
A half-century of Yugoslavian history is traced through the stormy relationship of two opportunistic men in Emir Kusturica's award-winning drama. Blacky (Lazar Ristovski) and Marko (Miki Manojlovic) are black marketeers raiding German supply posts in WWII Belgrade. A rivalry for money and a woman leads Marko to keep Blacky and a group of refugees "protected" in a cellar for years after the war's end, producing arms for him to sell to both sides of the country's ongoing conflicts. 167 min. In Serbian with English subtitles.
53-6233 Was $94.99 *$29.99*

Black Cat, White Cat (1998)
Bosnian-born filmmaker Emir Kusturica's acclaimed comedy/drama follows the slapstick rivalry between criminal Gypsy families in a Slovenian town. When a botched caper and a sizeable debt lead to plans for an arranged marriage between the clans, nothing goes as planned as mishaps and misunderstandings escalate. Zabit Mehmedovski, Florijan Ajdini star. 129 min. In Romany and Serbo-Croatian with English subtitles.
02-9185 Was $99.99 *$14.99*

Man Is Not A Bird (1966)
Remarkable debut directorial effort from director Dusan Makavejev ("The Coca-Cola Kid") that follows the turbulent relationship between a factory engineer and a hairdresser in a small Yugoslavian mining town. 80 min. In Serbian with English subtitles.
53-9024 *$59.99*

Love Affair: Or, The Case Of The Missing Switchboard Operator (1967)
Blackly funny glimpse at sex and politics chronicles the tale of a young operator who falls for a garbageman...at least, until a more desirable man catches her eye. Early triumph for director Dusan Makavejev ("Montenegro"). 70 min. In Serbian with English subtitles.
53-9018 *$59.99*

Innocence Unprotected (1968)
A typically offbeat and fascinating movie from director Dusan Makavejev, this black comedy blends scenes from the first sound Serbian film, interviews 20 years later with the cast and crew, and WWII newsreels. The result is a funny and at times bitter collage of heroic strongmen, romantic melodramas, political repression and more. 78 min. In Serbian with English subtitles.
53-9462 *$59.99*

W.R.: Mysteries Of The Organism (1971)
Director Dusan Makavejev's multi-layered exploration of the connection between sexual and political liberty follows the romance between a Yugoslav woman and a Russian skater, and is framed by Stalinist propaganda films, scenes of '60s New York street life, and footage of psychologist Wilhelm Reich (the title's "W.R."). 84 min. In English and Serbian with English subtitles.
53-9107 *$79.99*

Sweet Movie (1975)
A shocking and provocative cult favorite, this blend of dark comedy and futurist satire from maverick Yugoslav filmmaker Dusan Makavejev follows the interwoven fates of a beauty pageant queen, a Texas oil millionaire, a rock star, a sailor from the Battleship Potemkin and other offbeat characters. Carol Laure, Pierre Clementi star. 97 min. In English and other languages with English subtitles.
53-9090 *$79.99*

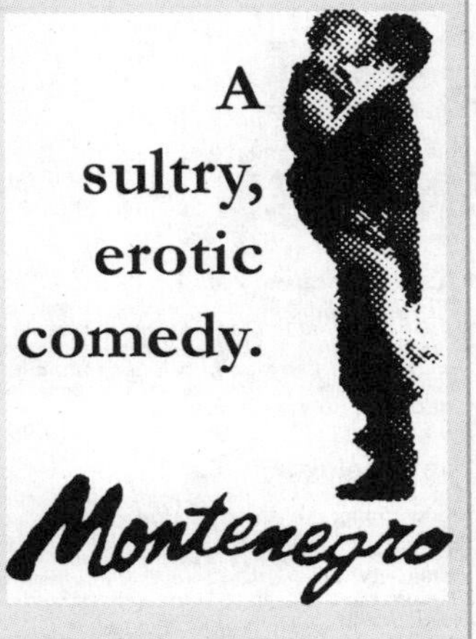

Montenegro (1981)
Dusan Makavejev's wild sex farce stars Susan Anspach as a repressed American housewife hoping to satisfy her erotic desires while living in Sweden with her family. She finds an outlet for her sexuality when she stops at a bizarre club, where she performs a kinky dance and has an illicit affair. With Erland Josephson. 97 min. In English, and Serbo-Croatian and Swedish with English subtitles.
44-1041 *$19.99*

Gorilla Bathes At Noon (1995)
Yugoslavia's Dusan Makavejev's whimsical political comedy concerns an expatriate Russian soldier (Svetozar Cvetkovic) who has decided to remain in Berlin after the fall of Communism. Riding around the city on his bike, Cvetkovic observes the changes made in the city while trying to meet girls, visiting the animals in the zoo, and proudly waving his Soviet flag. 83 min. In German and Russian with English subtitles.
53-6282 *$59.99*

Goodbye 20th Century (1999)
Wild tale from Macedonia comprised of three parts. It starts in a post-apocalyptic future where religious zealots try to kill a man "cursed" with immortality. Haunted by past events, the man goes back to 1900 for a bizarre wedding, then to New Year's Eve 1999, where a psychotic Santa Claus, living corpses and a barber-prophet are encountered. With Nikola Ristanovski, Lazar Ristovski. 83 min. In Macedonian with English subtitles.
73-9366 *$39.99*

Someone Else's America (1996)
Poignant comedy-drama depicting the friendship between a Spanish native operating a ramshackle bar in Brooklyn and an illegal Yugoslavian immigrant who works as a janitor. Both men strive to reach their vision of the American Dream. Tom Conti, Miki Manojlovic star. 116 min. In English and Serbo-Croatian with English subtitles.
53-8962 *$89.99*

Hey Babu Riba! (1987)
Four teenage pals on a rowing team and the pretty girl coxswain who paces them into manhood share an obsession with Marlboros, Glenn Miller, Esther Williams, and the hardships of life in '50s Yugoslavia. Jovan Acin's appealing coming-of-age drama stars Gila Videnovic, Relja Baisc. 112 min. In Serbo-Croatian with English subtitles.
73-1043 *$19.99*

The Harms Case (1988)
Acclaimed, highly stylized Yugoslavian biodrama chronicles the life story of Danil Harms, an early 20th-century Russian poet who was censored, persecuted and finally silenced by the Communist regime. 90 min. In Serbo-Croatian with English subtitles.
87-7006 *$59.99*

Tito And Me (1992)
Quirky comic fable set in Belgrade in 1954 and focusing on a pudgy 10-year-old boy who is enamored with Yugoslavia's reigning dictator, Marshall Tito. The boy gets an opportunity to visit Tito's homeland with an orphan girl he's in love with, but the trip turns out to be filled with all sorts of unexpected nuisances. 104 min. In Serbo-Croatian with English subtitles.
53-7928 Was $89.99 *$19.99*

When I Close My Eyes (1993)
The first independent film to come out of Slovenia, director Franci Slak's compelling thriller follows a young woman who uses a robbery at the rural post office where she works to steal some money for herself. Her fascination with the thief leads her on a search to track him down. Petra Govc, Mario Selih star. 94 min. In Slovenian with English subtitles.
53-8457 *$89.99*

Vukovar (1995)
Set against the turmoil of post-Cold War Yugoslavia, this gripping drama tells of two childhood friends—one Croat, the other Serb—who get married, only to have their relationship threatened by the war between their people. Director Boro Draskvoic's somber tale, winner of several international awards, was filmed in the bombed-out title city even as fighting continued. 94 min. In Serbo-Croatian with English subtitles.
53-8923 *$89.99*

Pretty Village Pretty Flame (1997)
As complex and compelling as its subject matter, director Srdjan Dragojevic's acclaimed look at the long-running Bosnian civil war travels back and forth from 1980 to 1992 as it follows the friendship between two boys—a Serb and a Muslim—that is later transformed into hatred and leaves them on opposite sides of the conflict. Dragan Bjelogric stars. 125 min. In Serbo-Croatian with English subtitles.
53-9582 Was $89.99 *$19.99*

The Wounds (Rane) (1998)
Set between 1991 to 1996, this knockout Bosnian crime drama traces how two young men named Pinki and Kraut become dangerously violent criminals under the tutelage of a master hood and smuggler who teaches them about prostitutes, drugs and gold chains. Dusan Pekic, Milan Maric star; directed by Srdjan Dragojevic ("Pretty Village Pretty Flame"). 103 min. In Serbo-Croatian with English subtitles.
70-5191 *$79.99*

The Countess (1989)
A teenage drug addict in Bulgaria in 1968 is sent to a treatment clinic/re-education camp, but upon her release continues in a pattern of self-destructive behavior that comes to represent the struggle for individuality in a repressive society, in director Peter Popzlatev's intense drama, based on a true story. 118 min. In Bulgarian with English subtitles.
87-7007 *$59.99*

Canary Season (1994)
Young Malin is released from prison and confronts his mother, who tells him of her background before and after the Communist takeover of Bulgaria. He learns of how she was raped and forced to marry her rapist, sent to a labor camp after being falsely accused of prostitution, and witnessed a political murder. Plamena Getova stars. 133 min. In Bulgarian with English subtitles.
73-9263 *$59.99*

The Oak (1991)
Stylish and edgy road movie set against the backdrop of Romania during the fall of Communism. A schoolteacher sets out on a free-wheeling journey after her father, a chief of the country's secret police, is murdered. Maia Morgenstern, Razvan Vasiliescu star; Lucian Pintilie directs. 105 min. In Romanian with English subtitles.
53-7965 *$89.99*

An Unforgettable Summer (1994)
Set in '20s Romania, this powerful drama from director Lucian Pintille ("The Oak") follows an army officer who is sent, along with his family, to a remote frontier outpost. While his wife befriends the area's residents, the officer is torn when, after border skirmishes with bandits, he's ordered to execute local farmers. Claudiu Bleont, Kristin Scott-Thomas star. 82 min. In Bulgarian, French and Romanian with English subtitles.
53-8417 *$89.99*

City Unplugged (1993)
This gritty crime story from the Baltic state of Estonia tells of a young engineer recruited by the Russian mob to cause a blackout to cover their $900 million robbery of the National Treasury. Because of his pregnant wife, the engineer must go along with the plan, but its results may alter him forever. Ivo Uukkivi, Milena Gulbe star. In Estonian with English subtitles.
82-5033 *$59.99*

Invisible Adversaries (1977)
Austrian filmmaker Valie Export's little-seen, quirky tales have earned her a cult following, as in this sci-fi drama of a photographer who uncovers an alien plan to take over the planet by increasing people's aggressive tendencies. Visually stunning and sexually frank film stars Susanne Widl, Peter Weibel. 112 min. In German with English subtitles.
53-9099 *$59.99*

Menschenfrauen (1980)
Described as "a human view of a woman's place in a man's world," Valie Export's drama focuses on a faithless family man's relationship with his wife and with the three other women in his life. 100 min. In German with English subtitles.
53-9100 *$59.99*

The Practice Of Love (1984)
While covering a murder investigation, a reporter uncovers leads that implicate her two lovers. Offbeat drama that combines "film noir" suspense with a pointed look at male-female relationships, courtesy of Austria's Valie Export. 90 min. In German with English subtitles.
53-9101 *$59.99*

THE INHERITORS

The Inheritors (1998)
This acclaimed film from Austria's Stefan Ruzowitzky tells of seven farmworkers who inherit their boss's farm after he is murdered. They soon encounter great opposition from local landowners and townspeople, who plot to take control of the property. Sophie Rois and Simon Schwarz star. 94 min. In German with English subtitles.
02-3376 Was $99.99 *$14.99*

Funny Games (1998)
An affluent family's vacation at their lakeside summer home is shattered by the arrival of two handsome and seemingly polite young men who intimidate the family with increasingly hostile and brutal actions, eventually taking them hostage. Disturbing and at times surreal look at the nature of violence from Austrian filmmaker Michael Haneke stars Frank Giering, Ulrich Mühe. 103 min. In German with English subtitles.
53-6338 Letterboxed *$19.99*

Greece

Stella (1955)
Rarely seen film features Melina Mercouri in her movie debut, as a young bouzouki player refuses to be bound by the constraints of conventional morality and subsequently pays the price. Compelling early work from Michael Cacoyannis ("Zorba the Greek"). 95 min. In Greek with English subtitles.
53-9079 Was $59.99 *$19.99*

A Girl In Black (To Koritsi Me Ta Mavra) (1956)
Effective early effort by director Michael Cacoyannis concerning a callow young author attracted to the daughter of the once-proud family he boards with...and the shocking tragedy that follows. Surprising look at provincial Greek life stars Ellie Lambeti, Dimitris Horn. 120 min. In Greek with English subtitles.
53-9080 Was $59.99 *$19.99*

A Matter Of Dignity (1957)
Michael Cacoyannis directs this compelling look at a Greek upper class family who try to jiggle relationships and a sense of security as they face bankruptcy. Ellie Lambeti and George Pappas star in this expert drama. 101 min. In Greek with English subtitles.
53-9287 Was $59.99 *$19.99*

The Cacoyannis Collection
"A Girl in Black," "A Matter of Dignity," "Stella" and the powerful documentary "Attila '74: The Rape of Cyprus" are also available in a boxed collector's set.
54-6792 Save $10.00! *$69.99*

Aunt From Chicago (1960)
Hilarity abounds in this Greek comedy about a retired general who sends for his Chicago-based sister in hopes she'll help him find husbands for his strictly-raised daughters. Instead, she introduces the gals to booze, rock music and men. Georgia Vassiliadou shines in the title role. 75 min. In Greek with English subtitles.
10-9450 *$19.99*

Lysistrata (1987)
The classic anti-war satire by Aristophenes is brought to the screen with all of its wit and earthy humor intact, as the women of ancient Athens refuse their husbands' sexual advances until they stop feuding with neighboring city-states. Jenny Karezi, Costas Kazakos star. 97 min. In Greek with English subtitles.
53-7380 *$39.99*

Red Lanterns (1963)
The lives, loves and desires of five prostitutes are spotlighted in this acclaimed effort that delves into the reasons they have chosen their sordid lifestyle and how the love for a sailor affects one of them. Set in the Greek port city of Piraeus, the film stars Jenny Karezi and George Foundas. 85 min. In Greek with English subtitles.
53-6091 *$29.99*

Man With The Red Carnation (1982)
Hard-hitting, true-life historical drama about Nikos Bellyogiannis, a leftist leader in post-Civil War Greece who is hunted down with other dissenters and tried as a spy. Mikis Theodorakis ("Zorba the Greek") composed the music. 110 min. In Greek with English subtitles.
53-7467 *$39.99*

The Cannon And The Nightingale (1966)
A trio of vignettes about the occupation of Greece by successive Italian, German and British troops, ranging in tone from a comic tale of a clock-obsessed fascist who is hoodwinked by villagers to a dark episode involving the torture of a Greek peasant by Nazi soldiers. 90 min. In Greek with English subtitles.
53-7279 *$39.99*

Z (1969)
Gripping political thriller, based on actual incidents in 1960s Greece, stars Yves Montand as a liberal opposition leader who is killed in a suspicious accident and Jean-Louis Trintignant as an official investigating the case. Winner of the Best Foreign Film Oscar; written and directed by Costa-Gavras. 127 min. In French with English subtitles.
76-1027 Letterboxed *$29.99*

Antigone (1962)
Irene Papas is impeccable as Sophocles' tragic heroine who defies the edict of the ruler of Thebes and bestows the rites of burial on her slain brother, thereby bringing about her own death. Co-stars Manos Katrakis. 88 min. In Greek with English subtitles.
53-6003 Was $59.99 *$29.99*

Special Request (1980)
At a nightclub in junta-ruled Greece in 1973, a pair of police officers are murdered for giving offense to a celebrated ex-con, a symbolic blow against absolute police authority that makes a hero out of the gunman. Katerina Gogou stars. 96 min. In Greek with English subtitles.
53-7281 *$39.99*

Path Of God (1984)
A young woman, seeking to escape her depressing existence, enters a convent, only to again fall victim to the exploitation she thought she left behind. 88 min. In Greek with English subtitles.
53-7109 *$39.99*

The Travelling Players (O Thiassos) (1975)
A landmark film in the Greek cinema, director Theo Angelopoulos' sweeping, allegorical drama follows a troupe of actors in the early 1950s. Their performances of a popular folk drama—as well as their private lives—serve as a metaphor for the political turmoil that rocked Greece throughout the 20th century (the film itself was made in secrecy during the end of military rule). Eva Kotamandiou, Petros Zarkadis star. 230 min. In Greek with English subtitles.
53-6352 *$89.99*

Landscape In The Mist (1988)
Highly acclaimed drama from filmmaker Theo Angelopoulos focusing on two Greek children whose search for their lost father in Germany is filled with meetings with unusual strangers, surreal sights and danger. A poignant, beautifully photographed film starring Michalis Zeke and Tania Palaiologou. 125 min. In Greek with English subtitles.
53-7840 *$79.99*

ULYSSES' GAZE

Ulysses' Gaze (1995)
In this stunning, award-winning epic from Greece's Theo Angelopoulos ("Landscape in the Mist"), Harvey Keitel plays a Greek filmmaker who travels across the Balkans to find lost film shot by cinematic pioneers from the region. During his journey, Keitel encounters different women and witnesses war's effect on the region. 173 min. In English and Greek with English subtitles.
53-8935 Was $89.99 *$29.99*

Rembetiko (1983)
It was the sad popular music of Greek cafes and hash joints in the '30s and '40s, and Rembetiko became a metaphor for the tragic life of songstress Marika Ninou. Moving depiction of the singer's sufferings for her art and due to Turkish persecution stars Sotiria Leonardou. 110 min. In Greek with English subtitles.
53-7278 Was $59.99 ***$39.99***

Heavy Melon (1983)
Charming comedy-drama of a young man's breakaway from his small Greek village and his search for fame and fortune. A delightful adaptation of a universal theme. Stars Katerina Gogou. 92 min. In Greek with English subtitles.
53-7107 ***$39.99***

The End Of The Game (1984)
A disturbing tale of obsession, rape and murder about six people on a weekend holiday who are provoked to the point of madness when a nude woman sunbather lights outside their retreat. Katerina Gogou stars. In Greek with English subtitles.
53-7280 ***$39.99***

Poland

Dr. Judym (1976)
Acclaimed tale of a young physician from a working-class family who helps the poor after making great sacrifices. Stars Jan Englert, Jerzy Kamas. 94 min. In Polish with English subtitles.
53-9178 ***$49.99***

Cupid's Bow (1978)
This movie attracted much controversy in Poland due to its erotic content. Set in Cracow after World War I, the film details a woman's struggle for independence. 119 min. In Polish with English subtitles.
53-9176 ***$49.99***

Roman Polanski

Two Men And A Wardrobe (1958)/ Fat And The Lean (1961)
Two award-winning silent shorts from a young Roman Polanski. "Two Men and a Wardrobe" (1958) uses slapstick humor in an allegory about freedom, as two men push a wardrobe out of the sea. Also, "Fat and the Lean" (1961) details a master-slave relationship that features Polanski as the slave. 35 min.
53-9331 Was $49.99 ***$29.99***

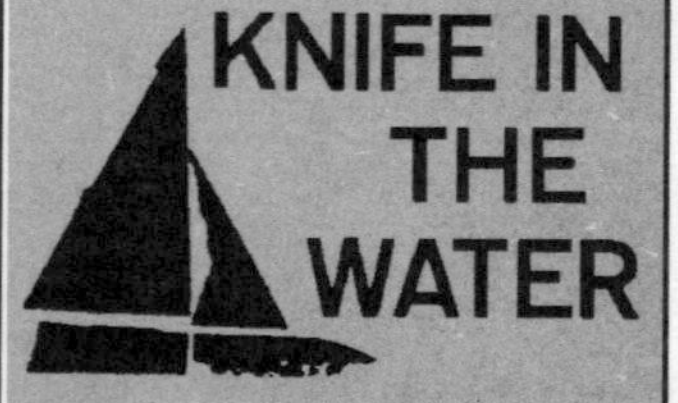

Knife In The Water (1962)
Director Roman Polanski's first feature is a subtly chilling tale about a married couple who pick up a young hitchhiker and invite him to join them on a boating trip. Once there, tempers flair during a storm and passions lead to violence. Leon Niemczyk, Jolanta Umecka star. 94 min. In Polish with English subtitles translated by Polanski.
22-5886 Remastered ***$29.99***

Mammals (1963)
Early silent film by Roman Polanski which garnered the young director acclaim. Two former friends encounter Death on an icy plain, where a sledge finally turns them into arch-rivals. 10 min.
53-9330 ***$29.99***

Diary Of Forbidden Dreams (1973)
Sydne Rome and Marcello Mastroianni star in director/co-scripter Roman Polanski's offbeat, erotic story of a beautiful hitchhiker in a remote area of the Italian Riviera who finds herself trapped in a strange mansion. AKA: "What?" 94 min. Dubbed in English.
20-5027 ***$19.99***

Please see our index for these other Roman Polanski titles: *Bitter Moon • Chinatown • Death And The Maiden • The Fearless Vampire Killers • Frantic • Macbeth • The Ninth Gate • Repulsion • Rosemary's Baby • The Tenant*

Knights Of The Teutonic Order (Krzyzacy) (1960)
An acclaimed, sprawling epic about Poland during medieval times, featuring a huge cast and based on the novel by Henryk Sienkiewicz. Directed by Aleksandar Ford, and starring Andrzej Szalawski and Grazyna Staniszewska. 142 min. In Polish with English subtitles.
53-9487 ***$59.99***

Knights Of The Teutonic Order (Dubbed Version)
Also available in a dubbed-in-English edition.
53-9271 ***$59.99***

Border Street (1948)
Set during the Warsaw uprising of 1943, this film chronicles the struggle of a tailor who attempts to save his daughters and others from the Nazis. A powerful, much-acclaimed drama. 101 min. In Polish with English subtitles.
53-9328 Was $89.99 ***$39.99***

Mother Joan Of The Angels (1960)
Based on the same true incident that inspired Ken Russell's "The Devils," this Polish drama is set in a 17th-century convent where a priest investigating claims of demonic possession becomes involved in a bizarre, forbidden love. Lucyna Winnicka, Mieczyslaw Voit star; Jerzy Kawalerowicz directs. AKA: "The Devil and the Nun." 108 min. In Polish with English subtitles.
53-8065 ***$59.99***

The Passenger (1963)
The chance meeting on a cruise ship between a woman who was a guard at Auschwitz and one of her former charges sets off a series of bitterly powerful memories of life in the prison camp. After director Andrzej Munk was killed in an auto accident during filming, the crew and Munk's colleagues worked to complete this moving drama. Aleksandra Slaska, Anna Ciepielewska star. 63 min. In English and Polish with English subtitles.
53-6113 Letterboxed ***$24.99***

Colonel Wolodyjowski (1969)
Set in the year 1668, this historical epic follows the military career of the famed colonel at the time of the Turkish invasion of Poland's Eastern frontier. 160 min. In Polish with English subtitles.
53-9173 ***$49.99***

The Doll (Lalka) (1969)
Set in 19th-century Poland, this is an exceptional tale of the romance between a social climbing man and a beautiful, cool aristocratic woman. Beata Tyszkiewicz, Mariausz Dmochowski star. 159 min. In Polish with English subtitles.
53-9177 ***$49.99***

Family Life (1971)
After living six years in Warsaw, a young engineer returns to his family's run-down country home to attempt to put things right with his alcoholic father and mentally ill sister in this moving drama by Krzysztof Zanussi. Daniel Olbrychski, Jan Kreczmar star. 93 min. In Polish with English subtitles.
53-8069 ***$69.99***

Hands Up (1971)
Groundbreaking drama from Jerzy Skolimowski ("Moonlighting"), banned for years in Poland due to its anti-Communist sentiments, traces the reunion of a group of Stalinist medical students, now complacent physicians. 78 min. In Polish with English subtitles.
53-9136 ***$49.99***

The Deluge (Potop) (1973)
Nominated for a Best Foreign Film Academy Award, this epic historical drama follows the love affair between a would-be soldier and a young gentlewoman, set against the Polish-Swedish War of the 17th century. Daniel Olbrychski, Matgorzata Braunek star. 180 min. In Polish with English subtitles.
53-8070 ***$69.99***

The Peasants (1973)
Based on a novel by Wladyslaw Reymont, this epic film looks at a father and son's love for the same woman. It's set in a small Polish village at the turn of the century, and features richly observed scenes of country traditions and folklore. 184 min. In Polish with English subtitles.
53-9207 ***$69.99***

Balance (1974)
Probing drama from master director Krzysztof Zanussi looks at a woman who must make a difficult decision in her life after she meets with an old acquaintance: should she leave her husband and child to be with him? With Marek Piwowski and Maja Komorowska. 99 min. In Polish with English subtitles.
53-9162 ***$49.99***

Casimir The Great (1975)
Historical study of Poland's most revered monarch traces the life of Casimir III, the last king of the Piast dynasty, from the death of his father to his decisive battle against the Knights of the Teutonic Order in the first half of the 14th century, which ended two centuries of disunity within his country. Stars Krzysztof Chamiec. 148 min. In Polish with English subtitles.
53-9169 Letterboxed ***$69.99***

Nights And Days (1976)
The loves and struggles of a Polish family are filtered through the historical events of the mid-to-late 1800s in this bravura mix of political and family drama. A unique look at oppression and exile, with the January, 1864 Uprising as a focal point. With Jadwiga Baranska. 255 min. In Polish with English subtitles.
53-9205 ***$69.99***

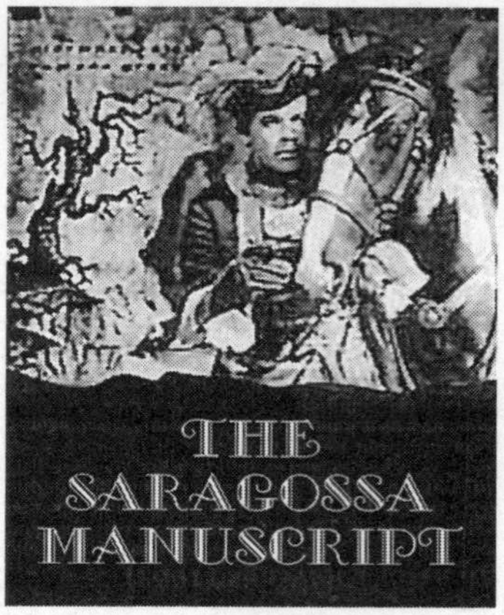

The Saragossa Manuscript (1965)
This hallucinatory epic follows the exploits of a Belgian officer in Spain during the Napoleonic Wars who encounters a series of bizarre adventures while perusing the illustrations of an old book and meeting such memorable characters as seductive sisters, a hermit, a Gypsy, and a Cabalist. This mind-bending film gained cult status after turning up on The Grateful Dead's Jerry Garcia's favorite films list. 174 min. In Polish with English subtitles.
53-6809 ***$59.99***

Kung-Fu (1979)
Banned for many years in Poland, this drama looks at the paths taken by three university friends who begin their careers at the same time. The country's ambiguous moral climate during the 1970s is perfectly captured by director Janusz Kijowski. 110 min. In Polish with English subtitles.
53-9132 ***$49.99***

Enigma Secret (1979)
Suspenseful thriller about how three Polish mathematicians decipher a Nazi secret coding machine. 158 min. In Polish with English subtitles.
53-9179 ***$39.99***

Housemaster (1979)
Poland after World War II serves as the backdrop for this intriguing tale of a deceptive game played by an ailing aristocrat and his servant. Wojciech Marczewski directs; Tadeusz Lomnicki stars. 85 min. In Polish with English subtitles.
53-9270 ***$39.99***

Fever (1981)
Agnieszka Holland ("Europa Europa") directed this ultra-realistic, expansive view of revolutionary fervor, struggles for independence and the birth of anarchism and political terrorism. 115 min. In Polish with English subtitles.
53-9135 ***$49.99***

Provinicial Actors (1983)
In this unique comedy from Agnieszka Holland, the leading actor in a rural theatrical troupe faces the end of his marriage when his loving but emotionally unstable wife begins to fret about his plans to become a big star. Tadeusz Huk, Halina Labonarska star. 104 min. In Polish with English subtitles.
53-8224 ***$79.99***

Interrogation (1982)
After a one-night stand with a military officer, a woman is detained and persecuted for five years by the secret police in this acclaimed Polish drama set in 1950s Warsaw. Stars Krystyna Janda (who won the Best Actress prize at Cannes in 1990, the film being banned in Poland for eight years), Adam Ferency; directed by Richard Bugajski. 118 min. In Polish with English subtitles.
53-7587 ***$79.99***

The Mother Of Kings (1982)
Acclaimed drama from director Janusz Zaorski focuses on the life of a poor widow throughout the worst moments in Poland's history, including World War II and the Stalinist regimes. This stark and powerful film incorporates stunning newsreel footage to tell its compelling story. With Teresa Wojcik. 126 min. In Polish with English subtitles.
53-7829 ***$49.99***

Austeria (The Inn) (1982)
Poignant drama set at the beginning of World War I, as a group of Orthodox Polish Jews flees from the invading Cossack army and takes refuge overnight in a remote country inn. There, new relationships are formed while others are severed, romances bloom, and faith is put to the test. Franciszek Pieczka stars. 110 min. In Polish with English subtitles.
53-7995 ***$69.99***

Krzysztof Kieslowski

Camera Buff (1979)
A Polish worker spends two-months salary on an 8mm camera to photograph his infant daughter and is soon enlisted by his employers to start a film club and shoot the everyday incidents that occur at work. Eventually, the film fan goes too far, catching his bosses in a less-than-desirable light. Krzysztof Kieslowski directs. 112 min. In Polish with English subtitles.
53-8008 ***$89.99***

Blind Chance (1982)
Filmmaker Krzysztof Kieslowski's fascinating "what if" study of a man's life choices examines three different career paths that were open to the protagonist: physician, political dissident, and party activist. Boguslaw Linda stars. 122 min. In Polish with English subtitles.
53-9137 ***$49.99***

No End (1984)
Poland under martial law in 1982 is the setting for this powerful drama from director Krzysztof Kieslowski ("The Double Life of Veronique"). After her husband's death, an attorney's widow attempts to help one of his clients, a worker accused of organizing anti-government strikes. Grazyna Szapolowska, Jerzy Radziwilowicz star. 108 min. In Polish with English subtitles.
53-7923 Was $79.99 ***$29.99***

The Decalogue (1988)
Originally made for Polish TV, director Krzysztof Kieslowski's acclaimed series of short films follows the residents of a Warsaw apartment complex through stories based on and illuminating—at times tangentially—each of the Ten Commandments, bringing the edicts to life and showing their relevancy to modern society. In Polish with English subtitles.

The Decalogue, Vol. 1
A college professor's unswerving faith in the accuracy of computers leads to tragedy when his son goes skating on a frozen lake calculated to be safe in "I Am the Lord Thy God; Thou Shalt Have No Other Gods Before Me." Next, a terminally ill man's wife, pregnant with a child that isn't his, asks a doctor a question that will determine if the child lives or dies in "Thou Shalt Not Take the Name of the Lord Thy God in Vain." 110 min.
53-6734 ***$19.99***

The Decalogue, Vol. 2
In "Remember the Sabbath Day, To Keep It Holy," a married cab driver receives a Christmas Eve message from his former lover. Then, a mysterious letter from her late mother could forever change the relationship between a young woman and her father in "Honor Thy Father and Mother." 112 min.
53-6735 ***$19.99***

The Decalogue, Vol. 3
A neophyte lawyer comes to question the death penalty during the trial of a young drifter who savagely murdered a taxi driver in the graphic "Thou Shalt Not Kill." Next, "Thou Shalt Not Commit Adultery," a postal worker's spying on a beautiful, promiscuous neighbor via telescope leads to a fateful meeting. 115 min.
53-6736 ***$19.99***

The Decalogue, Vol. 4
The theft in "Thou Shalt Not Steal" is of identity and affection, as a young woman runs away with the illegitimate child who was being raised as her sister by the woman's mother. Next, an ethics professor faces her past when a Holocaust survivor she had failed to help hide from the Nazis confronts her in "Thou Shalt Not Bear False Witness Against Thy Neighbor." 110 min.
53-6737 ***$19.99***

The Decalogue, Vol. 5
Unable to have sexual relations with his wife due to illness, a once-philandering doctor urges her to take a lover, only to be consumed with jealousy, in "Thou Shalt Not Covet Thy Neighbor's Wife." Then, a pair of feuding brothers find a stamp collection inherited from their father is more a curse than a blessing in "Thou Shalt Not Covet Thy Neighbor's Goods." 115 min.
53-6738 ***$19.99***

The Decalogue: Complete Set
All five volumes are also available in a boxed collector's set.
53-6739 ***$99.99***

Krzysztof Kieslowski: I'm So-So...
The Polish-born director, best known in America for his ten-film series "The Decalogue" and the French-made "Three Colors" trilogy, talks candidly about his life and art in this wonderful documentary, filled with clips from throughout his career, filmed shortly before his death in 1996. 56 min.
70-5149 Was $29.99 ***$19.99***

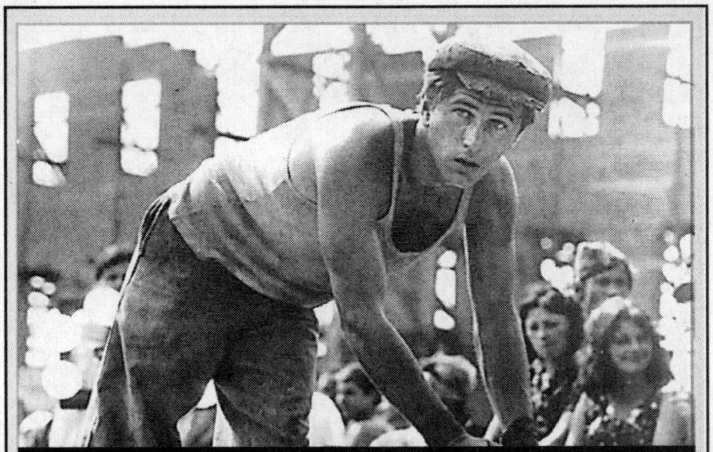

Man Of Marble

Andrzej Wajda

A Generation (1955)
The striking debut feature from director Andrzej Wajda (and the first film in his "war trilogy") follows a young Polish man who joins the anti-Nazi Resistance during the Warsaw uprising and risks his life to help escapees avoid capture. Tadeusz Lomnicki, Urzula Modrzynska, Roman Polanski star. 85 min. In Polish with English subtitles.
22-5704 *$24.99*

Kanal (1957)
After the German destruction of Warsaw that followed the 1944 ghetto uprising, a small band of Polish soldiers and partisans attempts to escape through the city's sewers. Tadeusz Janczar stars in Andrzej Wajda's gripping war drama. 96 min. In Polish with English subtitles.
22-5705 *$24.99*

Ashes And Diamonds (1958)
Andrzej Wajda's haunting look at Poland on the final day of World War II, as a young Resistance fighter shoots the wrong man and is captured by the newly appointed Communist authorities. Zibigniew Cybulski, Eva Krzyzeska star. 105 min. In Polish with English subtitles.
22-5706 Remastered *$24.99*

War Trilogy Complete Set
The complete Andrzej Wajda "war trilogy" ("A Generation," "Kanal," "Ashes and Diamonds") is also available in a money-saving set.
22-5707 Save $15.00! *$59.99*

Innocent Sorcerers (1960)
Life in contemporary Poland is the focus of this ironic seriocomedy by Andrzej Wajda which follows the stormy romantic life of a young doctor and part-time jazz player. Tadeusz Lomnicki, Krystyna Stypulkowska, Roman Polanski and Jerzy Skolimowski (who co-scripted) star. 86 min. In Polish with English subtitles.
53-8066 *$59.99*

Siberian Lady Macbeth (1962)
1800s Czarist Russia is the setting for Polish director Andrzej Wajda's masterful drama, filmed in Yugoslavia. A woman takes a young lover when her husband is away, then poisons her stepfather and plots to kill her spouse. Olivera Markovic, Ljuba Tadic star. AKA: "Fury Is a Woman." 93 min. In Serbo-Croatian with English subtitles.
53-6038 Was $59.99 *$24.99*

Birch Wood (1971)
The great Andrzej Wajda ("Danton") directed this powerful tale of two brothers, one of whom is near death but high in spirits, while the other is a grieving widower envious of his brother's hopeful attitude. 100 min. In Polish with English subtitles.
53-9138 *$49.99*

The Wedding (1973)
Andrzej Wajda's milestone film concerns a peasant's daughter whose marriage to a poet brings out a wedding party that includes intellectuals, a journalist, a priest and others. Rumors of war erupt during the gathering, guests arm themselves, and the lines between fantasy and reality begin to blur. With Ewa Zietek. 103 min. In Polish with English subtitles.
53-7962 *$49.99*

Land Of Promise (1974)
Around the turn of the century, three industrialists—a Pole, a German and a Jew—open a textile factory in Lodz, Poland, but soon encounter problems with their employers, who complain about the work and pay. Andrzej Wajda directed this Oscar nominee for Best Foreign Film. With Daniel Olbrychski. 161 min. In Polish with English subtitles.
53-7828 *$89.99*

Man Of Marble (1977)
Andrzej Wajda's masterpiece about Polish life after World War II follows a film student's efforts to make a documentary about a lauded bricklayer whose life was ruined when he interfered with political affairs. Stylistically similar to "Citizen Kane," the film remains quite controversial and was followed by "Man of Iron" in 1981. With Jerzy Radziwilowicz, Krystyna Janada. 160 min. In Polish with English subtitles.
53-7440 Was $89.99 *$29.99*

Man Of Iron (1980)
Andrzej Wajda's sequel to "Man of Marble" employs fictional characters against the backdrop of historical events that span from the Gdansk student reform movement of 1968 to the Solidarity strikes of 1980. The story concerns a journalist whose subjective reporting on the leader of a shipyard strike (and son of the worker hero of "Man of Marble") leads her to question her own political interests. Jerzy Radziwilowicz stars. In Polish with English subtitles. 140 min.
12-2857 *$19.99*

Without Anesthesia (1978)
A famed Polish TV news correspondent returns home from an assignment to find that his wife has been having an affair and is ready to leave him. Director Andrzej Wajda follows the newsman's personal and professional breakdown in achingly intimate fashion. Zbigniew Zapasiewicz stars. AKA: "Rough Treatment." 111 min. In Polish with English subtitles.
53-8060 Was $79.99 *$29.99*

The Maids Of Wilko (1979)
Following service in World War I, a bachelor on vacation returns to the place of his birth to try to rekindle relationships with the five sisters who live on a nearby estate, but soon realizes that they, like the times, have changed. Andrzej Wajda's engaging tale stars Daniel Olbrychski. AKA: "The Young Ladies of Wilko." 111 min. In Polish with English subtitles.
53-7961 *$59.99*

The Conductor (1980)
A Polish-born director (John Gielgud) returns to his birthplace following 50 years in the United States. The aging man impresses his native audience when he conducts the local orchestra, but wins few favors with the orchestra's younger leader. With Krystyna Janda; Andrzej Wajda directs. 101 min. In Polish with English subtitles.
53-7947 *$79.99*

Danton (1983)
Polish director Andrzej Wajda's brilliant historical drama detailing the battle of wills and ideas between the leaders of the French Revolution—a conflict that ended at the guillotine—stars Gerard Depardieu in the title role and Wojceich Pszoniak as the power-obsessed Robspierre. 138 min. In French with English subtitles.
02-1322 Letterboxed *$29.99*

Korczak (1990)
A powerful, true Holocaust drama from Andrzej Wajda, set in Poland after the Nazi invasion of 1939 and focusing on a Jewish doctor who refuses to leave his country and the Warsaw orphanage he oversees. Finally, in 1942, he is forced to join his daughter and the children on a journey to Treblinka. Written by Agnieszka Holland; Wojtek Pszoniak stars. 118 min. In Polish with English subtitles.
53-7796 *$79.99*

Sarah's House (1984)
A sexy, offbeat horror film about a beautiful woman who takes on lovers, then puts them under a spell, leading them to degradation and death. Then, one day, she meets her match. 70 min. In Polish with English subtitles.
53-9208 *$49.99*

I Like Bats (1985)
An Eastern European version of "Martin." A beautiful female vampire seeks help from a psychiatrist when she realizes she'd rather be human. 90 min. In Polish with English subtitles.
53-9189 *$49.99*

Train To Hollywood (1986)
Funny, near-surreal comedy about a beautiful girl, living in a small Polish town, who is obsessed with Marilyn Monroe. Will the dreams that she nurtures while working on a train dining car take her to Tinseltown? Directed by Radoslaw Piwowarski. 96 min. In Polish with English subtitles.
53-9129 *$49.99*

Greta (1986)
Intriguing drama about the adventures of a 10-year-old Polish boy who escapes from a labor camp and comes into contact with an SS officer, an Army deserter and an understanding girl his own age. Directed by Krzysztof Gruber. 60 min. In Polish with English subtitles.
53-9134 *$49.99*

Kingsize (1988)
Part modern-day fantasy and part satire of the then-ruling Communist regime, this offbeat Polish comedy is set in a world where two races dwell: the normal-sized residents of Kingsize and the toy-scale "brownies" of Drawerland. See what happens when the wee folk (who are all male) invent a serum that lets them grow and experience women for the first time! Jacek Chmielnik stars. 108 min. In Polish with English subtitles.
53-7996 *$69.99*

Crows (Wrony) (1994)
Scorned by her schoolmates and neglected by her work-driven single mother, a 9-year-old Polish girl decides to create her own family by running off with a younger friend who will be her "daughter." Wonderfully moving drama from writer/director Dorota Kedzierzawska stars Karolina Ostorozna and Kasia Szczepanik. 66 min. In Polish with English subtitles.
53-6349 *$89.99*

With Fire And Sword (1999)
Lavish Polish spectacle set in the mid-17th century when Cossacks plan on attacking Poland while the Polish ruling class battles among themselves. A beautiful princess is desired by a dashing soldier, but her evil fiancé tries to kidnap her in order to keep her away from him. Izabella Scorpupco, Michal Zebrowski star. 180 min. In Polish with English subtitles.
53-6804 *$49.99*

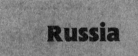

Russia

Enthusiasm (1931)
The legendary Dziga Vertov directed this look at the coal miners of the Don Basin and the effects of the Five-Year Plan on their lives and work. Notable for its unique use of natural sounds mixed with music, the film has no dialogue. 84 min.
53-7098 Was $39.99 *$29.99*

Road To Life (1931)
A pioneering film in Russia for its use of sound to further plot and characterization, this drama focuses on a group of ruthless orphan youths who roam the countryside begging and stealing following the Revolution. They are incarcerated by the Children's Commission, an organization that attempts to reform them. 100 min. In Russian with English subtitles.
53-8050 *$39.99*

Deserter (1933)
This major rediscovery from V.I. Pudovkin tells of a German shipyard worker who faces his company's harsh treatment when he defies his corrupt union and joins a workers' strike. Hoping to make a new life for himself, the worker is sent by an envoy to the USSR, where he is rejuvenated by the workers' spirit. Boris Livanov stars in the drama, known for its groundbreaking sound. 100 min. In Russian with English subtitles.
53-9787 *$29.99*

Peter The First, Part I (1937)
Vladimir Petrov's epic drama of the founder of the Russian Empire is matched in scope only by the work of his contemporary, Eisenstein. In the first of the two-film series Peter I (Nikolai Simonov) regroups his armies after a defeat by Sweden and founds as his "second headquarters" the city of St. Petersburg. 99 min. In Russian with English subtitles.
53-7182 *$39.99*

Peter The First, Part II (1938)
In the conclusion to Petrov's film biography, the legendary Tsar sweeps across Scandinavia in a stunning military victory, faces dissent from the nobility as he modernizes Russia, and must decide if his own son is guilty of treason. Nikolai Simonov, Alla Tarasova star. 121 min. In Russian with English subtitles.
53-7183 *$39.99*

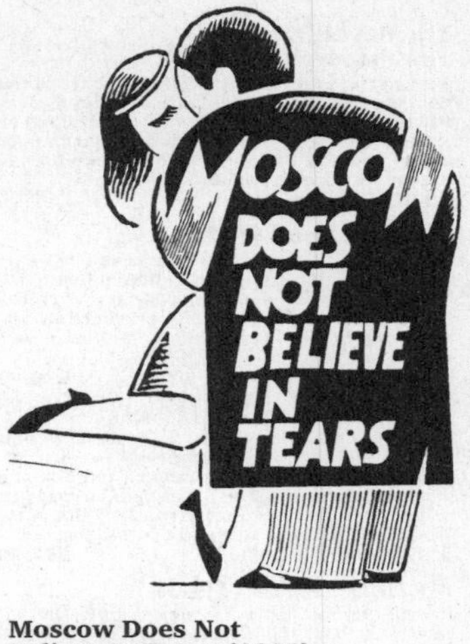

Moscow Does Not Believe In Tears (1981)
Russian drama that won the Academy Award for Best Foreign Film examines the trials and tribulations of three women from small towns who set out to make new lives for themselves in '50s Moscow. With Irina Muravyova and Vera Alentova. 150 min. In Russian with English subtitles.
53-7817 Was $59.99 *$29.99*

The Cranes Are Flying (1957)
Moving Russian drama that garnered several international film awards. Tatyana Samoilova stars as a young woman whose fiancé goes off to fight in World War II and is killed in battle. Alexi Batalov, Vasily Merkuryev co-star. 91 min. In Russian with English subtitles.
65-1017 Was $49.99 *$29.99*

The Seagull (1971)
A lavish Russian production of "favorite son" Anton Chekhov's timeless drama, set on a remote country estate and centering on the hopeless loves of the home's residents and visitors. Alla Demidova, Yuri Yakovlev star. 99 min. In Russian with English subtitles.
10-7446 *$29.99*

Oblomov (1980)
Adapted from Goncharov's 19th-century novel, the satiric tale of a Czarist Russian landowner literally cushioned from care when he retires permanently to bed stars Oleg Tabakov as the worthless Oblomov, for whom aristocratic indulgence becomes a kind of heroism. 142 min. In Russian with English subtitles.
53-7258 Was $59.99 *$29.99*

Kindergarten (1984)
A spacious and exuberant film-poem from director/writer Yevgeny Yevtushenko tells the semi-autobiographical tale of a young boy tramping across Russia during World War II with his trusty violin. Klaus Maria Brandauer and Sergej Gusak star. 143 min. In Russian with English subtitles.
53-7266 *$59.99*

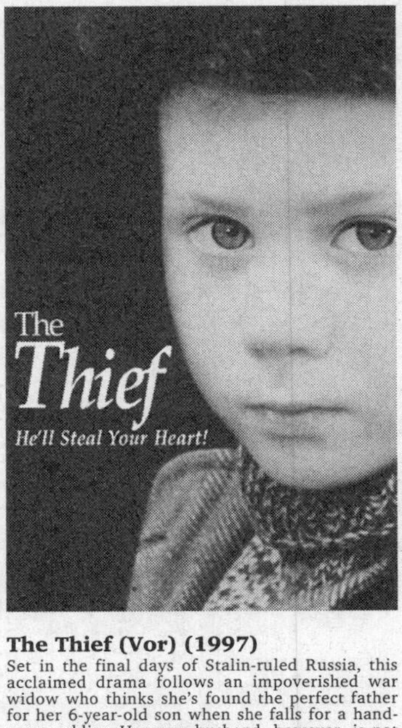

The Thief (Vor) (1997)
Set in the final days of Stalin-ruled Russia, this acclaimed drama follows an impoverished war widow who thinks she's found the perfect father for her 6-year-old son when she falls for a handsome soldier. Her new husband, however, is not what he appears, and his sly ways both fascinate and repel his stepson. Vladimir Mashkov, Ekaterina Rednikova, Misha Philipchuk star. 92 min. In Russian with English subtitles.
02-3302 Was $99.99 *$21.99*

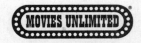

The Revolt Of The Fishermen (1935)
German theater director Erwin Piscator directed this expressionistic slice of Soviet cinema about a young sailor who joins scab workers when fishermen go on strike. When one of the strikers is killed, a graveside service leads to a bloody revolt. With Alexei Diky. In Russian with English subtitles.
10-9258 *$29.99*

My Childhood (1938)
The first part of director Mark Donskoi's film trilogy based on "The Autobiography of Maxim Gorky" follows the writer as a 4-year-old living in poverty with his stern grandfather and doting grandmother. Varvara Massilitinova stars. 100 min. In Russian with English subtitles.
53-7635 *$39.99*

My Apprenticeship (1939)
Young Maxim Gorky is taken in by a middle-class family who renege on their promise of an education. He later teaches himself to read and sets out on a journey of discovery across Russia in this second part of Donskoi's cinematic biography. AKA: "Out in the World." 100 min. In Russian with English subtitles.
53-7636 *$39.99*

My Universities (1940)
Reaching manhood and entering university, Gorky is introduced to the political arena and joins the radical factions that were to ignite the Bolshevik Revolution in Mark Donskoi's concluding chapter of the writer's life story. AKA: "University of Life." 100 min. In Russian with English subtitles.
53-7637 *$39.99*

Don Quixote (1957)
One of the last Russian films to play the U.S. before relations soured during the Cuban Revolution, this well-made adaptation of the Cervantes classic stars noted Soviet actor Nikolai Cherkassov as the would-be knight and Yuri Tolubeyev as Sancho Panza. Special English-dubbed version made in cooperation with British filmmakers. 110 min.
53-7186 *$59.99*

The Magic Weaver (1965)
In this Russian fable, a soldier making his way home from a long stint in the military attempts to rescue the kidnapped mother of a little boy. She's an expert weaver, abducted by the evil Czar of Water and held captive in his underwater kingdom. With Mikhail Kuznetsov. AKA: "Maria, the Wonderful Weaver." 87 min. Dubbed in English.
10-9412 *$14.99*

The Overcoat (1959)
Mastreful film adaptation, not released in America until 1965, of Nikolai Gogol's story of a poor, dispirited clerk and the effect that a brand new overcoat has on his life. Rolan Bykov and Yuri Tolubeyev star; directed by popular Russian actor Aleksei Batalov. 78 min. In Russian with English subtitles.
53-7100 *$29.99*

Guerrilla Brigade (1939)
Inspirational war drama by Ukrainian filmmaker Igor Savchenko, a colleague of Eisenstein. Set during the 1917 Revolution, this moving tale depicts Ukrainian and Russian workers and soldiers working together for the common good in a plea for Soviet unity. 90 min. In Russian with English subtitles.
53-7391 *$59.99*

No Greater Love (1943)
A gripping WWII drama starring Vera Maretskaya as a Russian woman who turns her villagers into partisans for revenge against the German troops, who have killed her infant son and husband. 74 min. Dubbed in English.
53-9320 *$59.99*

Inspector General (1954)
An illiterate worker is mistaken for the Czar's Inspector General in this version of Gogol's famous play which was also the basis for the 1949 Danny Kaye film. Performed by members of Moscow's Art Theater and directed by Vladimir Petrov. 128 min. In Russian with English subtitles.
53-9318 *$49.99*

Othello (1955)
This Russian translation of Shakespeare's tragedy of the jealous Moor driven to murder was heralded at the Cannes Film Festival upon its release. Sergei Bondarchuk, later one of the Soviet Union's top directors, excels in the title role. Directed by Sergei Yutkevich. 108 min. Dubbed in English.
53-6089 *$29.99*

The Twelfth Night (1956)
Shakespeare's charming comedy of would-be lovers and mistaken identity is given a lyrical, handsomely filmed treatment in this Russian production. Klara Luchko, Alla Larionova star. 88 min. Dubbed in English.
53-6093 *$29.99*

King Lear (1971)
Famed author Boris Pasternak ("Doctor Zhivago") wrote the screenplay for this Russian rendition of Shakespeare's classic play of love betrayal and redemption. Grigori Kozintsev directs. 140 min. In Russian with English subtitles.
53-7022 *$29.99*

Ballad Of A Soldier (1959)
The adventures of a young soldier on leave during WWII is the simple plot for one of the most moving films of the Russian cinema. Starring Vladimir Ivashov as the young soldier. Directed by Grigori Chukhrai. 88 min. In Russian with English subtitles.
62-1056 Was $29.99 *$24.99*

A Summer To Remember (1960)
A touching, realistic drama of family life, as seen through the eyes of a 6-year-old Russian boy. Stars Borya Barkhatov and noted actor/director Sergei Bondarchuk as the boy's stepfather. 81 min. In Russian with English subtitles.
53-7103 *$29.99*

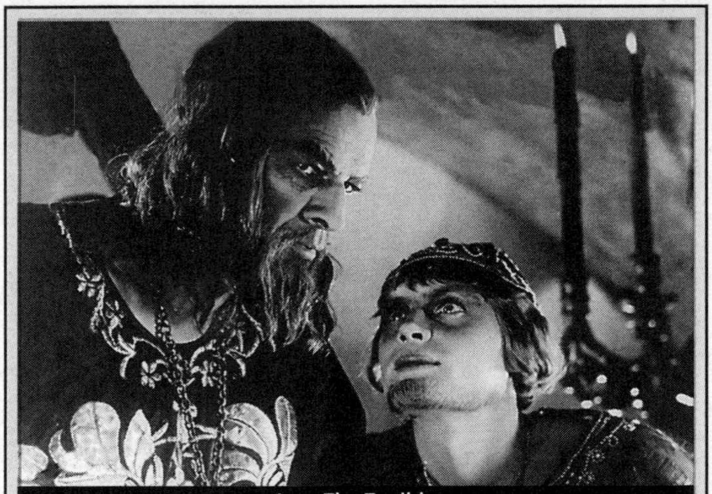

Ivan The Terrible

Sergei Eisenstein

Strike (1924)
Sergei Eisenstein's first directorial effort is an outstanding depiction of the plight of workers under the czarist regime, with an ill-fated strike at the heart of the drama. 94 min. Silent with music.
53-7102 Was $29.99 *$24.99*

Battleship Potemkin (1925)
Eisenstein's classic true-life silent drama, recognized as one of the greatest films of all time. The 1905 revolt of Russia's peasant class against the Czar's forces is shown in a gripping series of images and vignettes, including the groundbreaking "Odessa Steps" montage scene. 67 min. Silent with music score.
63-1449 *$19.99*

October (Ten Days That Shook The World) (1927)
Eisenstein blended characteristic montage sequences with sublime religious symbolism in his silent chronicle of the 1917 Bolshevik uprising, based in part on the book by John Reed. This newly remastered version includes a music score by Shostakovich. 104 min.
22-1220 Remastered *$29.99*

The General Line (1929)
A poor farm woman helps the people of her village combine their land and form a cooperative in this pro-Soviet drama that was seminal filmmaker Sergei Eisenstein's final silent movie. 70 min. Silent with music score.
53-7018 *$29.99*

Que Viva Mexico (1932)
She astonishing images of Sergei Eisenstein's long-lost history of Mexico, unfinished due to financial problems, are restored with the help of the film's original editor, Grigory Alexandrov. A quartet of stories captures the tranquillity of Mexico's jungles, the struggles of colonial peasant life, a romantic look at bullfighting, and the glory of the 1910 revolution. 84 min. Russian narration with English subtitles.
53-7265 Was $59.99 *$24.99*

Alexander Nevsky (1936)
One of the classics of Soviet cinema, Sergei Eisenstein's lavish spectacle recounts the invasion of Russia by the Teutonic Knights in the 13th century. Nikolai Cherkasov stars as the title hero, with music by Prokofiev. 108 min. In Russian with English subtitles.
22-1223 Remastered *$29.99*

Ivan The Terrible, Part 1 (1943)
Filmed during the early '40s and released in two parts in 1947 and 1959 (due in part to pressure from the Stalinist regime), Eisenstein's monumental historical epic brings to life the 16th-century Russian leader's struggle to unite his people. Nikolai Cherkasov stars as the young Ivan, fighting the Mongol invaders. Score by Sergei Prokofiev. 99 min. In Russian with English subtitles.
22-1221 Remastered *$29.99*

Ivan The Terrible, Part 2 (1946)
The concluding chapter in Eisenstein's film biography follows Ivan's battle against enemies inside the Russia he has tenuously brought together. Includes the lavish banquet sequence, filmed in color. 85 min. In Russian with English subtitles.
22-1222 Remastered *$29.99*

Eisenstein (1958)
Soviet-made documentary that looks at the career of the cinematic pioneer. Features many of his innovative and dramatic scenes from such films as "Battleship Potemkin," "October/Ten Days That Shook the World," and "Ivan the Terrible." 48 min.
09-1100 Was $24.99 *$19.99*

Sergei Eisenstein: Autobiography
Based on the groundbreaking Russian filmmaker's memoirs, this fascinating documentary mixes Eisenstein's own reminiscences with rare archival footage and clips from "Battleship Potemkin," "Alexander Nevsky" and other movies to examine how his career was affected by life under Lenin and Stalin. 86 min.
50-8337 *$19.99*

My Name Is Ivan (1962)
Andrei Tarkovsky directed this story of a young man who turns military spy as a means of avenging the slaughter of his family at the hands of the Nazis. Exciting and well-acted, a rare view of World War II through Soviet eyes. With Kolya Burlaiev, Valentin Zubkhov. 84 min. In Russian with English subtitles.
53-7125 Was $59.99 *$19.99*

Andrei Rublev (1966)
Landmark Russian historical drama by Andrei Tarkovsky recounts the tempestuous life of the 15th-century icon painter, a man torn between his devotion to his faith and his art and the struggles of local peasants against the nobility. Filmed in color and black-and-white and banned for many years; Anatoli Solonitsyn stars. 185 min. In Russian with English subtitles.
10-7548 Was $29.99 *$19.99*

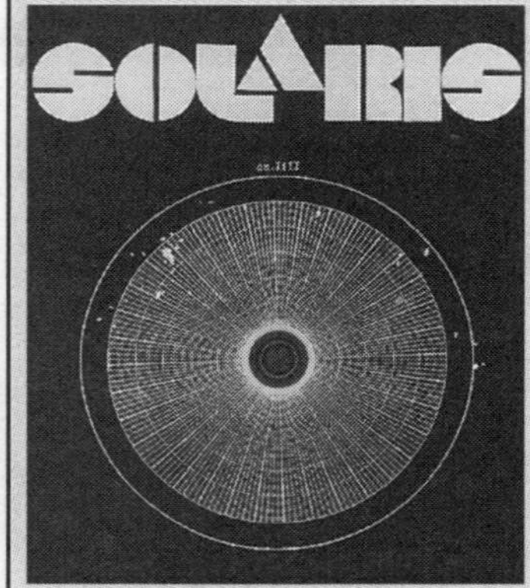

Solaris (1972)
A monumental science-fiction film from director Andrei Tarkovsky, based on a novel by Stanislas Lem. A psychologist leads an investigative team to the planet Solaris to investigate a strange, sentient force that covers its surface. Donatas Banionis and Natalya Bondarchuk star. Special letterboxed edition. 167 min. In Russian with English subtitles.
53-7583 Was $79.99 *$19.99*

The Mirror (1975)
Combining autobiographical accounts of life during World War II, political allegory, dream sequences and newsreel footage, maverick Russian director Andrei Tarkovsky creates a haunting cinematic vision in this internationally acclaimed drama. 90 min. In Russian with English subtitles.
53-7756 Was $59.99 *$29.99*

Stalker (1979)
Stunning, brilliant science fiction from director Andrei Tarkovsky ("Solaris") about a journey taken by a scientist and a writer to a dangerous forbidden zone where fantastic powers can fulfill man's greatest desires. Led by a bald guide known as the Stalker, the men encounter a series of difficult obstacles before they reach their destination. 160 min. In Russian with English subtitles.
53-7754 Was $89.99 *$19.99*

Nostalghia (1984)
The first film made outside his native Russia by director Andrei Tarkovsky is a hauntingly beautiful portrait of a Russian poet and musicologist who travels to a spa village in Italy's Tuscany region on a research project. Even as he longs to return to his homeland and his family, the poet is drawn to his lovely interpreter and fascinated with a local professor-turned-mystic. Oleg Jankovksy, Erland Josephson, Domiziana Giordano star. 120 min. In Italian with English subtitles.
53-8932 Letterboxed *$29.99*

The Sacrifice (1985)
Foreboding and unforgettable tale of life after nuclear disaster that was the final work of director Andrei Tarkovsky. This winner of the Special Jury Prize at Cannes stars Erland Josephson; cinematography by Sven Nykvist. 145 min. In Russian and Swedish with English subtitles.
07-8098 *$29.99*

Directed By Andrei Tarkovsky (1988)
The brilliant Russian director of thought-provoking films as "Solaris" and "The Mirror" is profiled by his friend and editor, Michal Leszczylowski, in this engrossing behind-the-scenes documentary made on the set of Tarkovsky's final work, "The Sacrifice." AKA: "The Genius, The Man, The Legend: Andrei Tarkovsky." 100 min. In Russian and Swedish with English subtitles.
53-9284 Was $59.99 *$29.99*

The Errors Of Youth (1989)
Russian filmmaker Boris Frumin's bleak look at Soviet life, shut down by the government in the middle of filming in 1979, was completed years later when the director was invited to return from America. A young man leaves army service unsure of his future and drifts through a series of jobs and relationships, eventually working in Leningrad's black market. AKA: "Wild Oats." 87 min. In Russian with English subtitles.
53-9646 *$59.99*

Viva Castro! (1993)
A small Russian town in 1965 is the setting for this funny and emotional coming-of-age tale about a young man whose father disappears after stealing coins from a local museum and whose mother is sent to a prison work farm for the crime. With Pavel Zharkov, Sergey Dontsov; directed by Boris Frumin. 82 min. In Russian with English subtitles.
53-9648 *$59.99*

Commissar (1965)
Banned in Russia for 20 years, this powerful drama tells the story of a Red Army Commander who is forced to stay with a Jewish family after realizing she is pregnant. During her stay, she assimilates into the family's world and eventually must decide whether to stay with her troops or with her child. Alexander Askoldov's film stars Nonna Mordukova and Rolan Bykov. 105 min. In Russian with English subtitles.
53-7405 *$59.99*

To See Paris And Die (1995)
This acclaimed effort from Alexander Proshkin centers on a gifted piano prodigy who has a chance to travel to Paris for a major competition. The young boy's opportunity is jeopardized because of his mother's past, and she must consider an important sacrifice for her son. With Tatyana Vasilyeva. 110 min. In Russian with English subtitles.
53-8938 *$89.99*

A Chef In Love (1996)
At once funny, tragic and romantically moving, this acclaimed drama from the Republic of Georgia stars Pierre Richard as a world-weary French chef whose visit to a Georgian town in the 1920s revives his interest in his craft—and whose affair with a younger local woman renews his zest for life. Micheline Presle, Jean-Yves Gautier also star. 95 min. In French, Georgian and Russian with English subtitles.
02-3125 Was $99.99 *$19.99*

Brother (1997)
Playing like a '30s Hollywood gangster flick transposed to post-Communist Russia, Alexei Balabanov's stark, moody drama follows a young man who returns home to St. Petersburg from military service. With job prospects and his future looking bleak, he reluctantly joins with his brother, a Russian Mafia hit man, to fulfill a contract on a rival mobster. Sergei Bodrov, Jr., Victor Suhorukov star. 96 min. In Russian with English subtitles.
53-6386 *$79.99*

Shadows Of Forgotten Ancestors (1964)
Lyric Russian fantasy set in a remote mountain village, where a young man tries to cope with the loss of his lover and his family, only to find himself lost in the past. Striking color sequences and bizarre occult scenes highlight Sergei Paradjanov's compelling tale. AKA: "Wild Horses of Fire." 99 min. In Ukrainian with English subtitles.
22-5579 Restored ***$29.99***

The Color Of Pomegranates (1969)
Censored by Soviet officials, Sergei Paradjanov's lavish film follows 18th-century Armenian poet Sayat Nova's incredible life, from carpet weaver's apprentice to archbishop to martyr. The lyrical, image-laden work led to the director's imprisonment in 1974. Also includes "Hagop Hovnatanian," Paradjanov's short on the artist. AKA: "Red Pomegranate," "Sayat Nova." 80 min. In Armenian with English subtitles.
53-7403 Was $59.99 ***$29.99***

The Legend Of Suram Fortress (1985)
Sergei Paradjanov's fantasy, based on an ancient legend, about a young man who agrees to be entombed in order to save his Georgian comrades in their fight against invaders. With Levan Outchanechvili. 89 min. In Georgian with English subtitles.
53-7406 Was $59.99 ***$29.99***

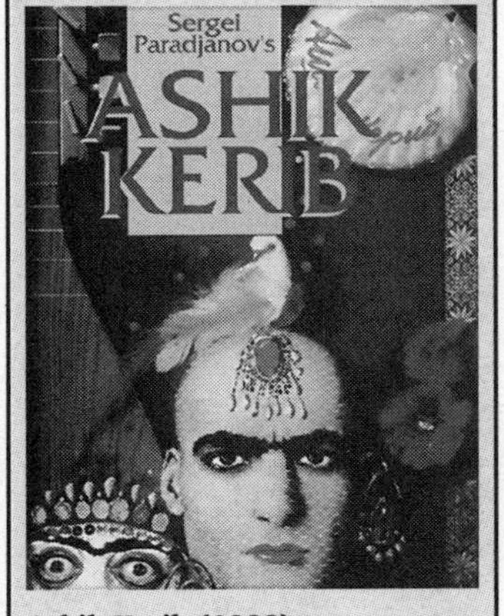

Ashik Kerib (1988)
Sergei Paradjanov's final film is a sumptuously realized saga about a wandering minstrel who goes on a wondrous journey filled with adventure and danger in order to marry the daughter of a wealthy merchant. 75 min. In Armenian with English subtitles.
53-7815 Was $59.99 ***$29.99***

Paradjanov: A Requiem (1994)
One of the most innovative directors of the post-WWII Russian cinema, Sergei Paradjanov was censored, persecuted and even imprisoned by Soviet authorities for his outspoken views and his homosexuality. Rare interviews and clips from some of Paradjanov's most memorable movies paint an unforgettable picture of the late filmmaker. 57 min. In English and Russian with English subtitles.
53-7047 ***$29.99***

A Small Favor (1984)
After agreeing to deliver a package given to him by a stranger on a train, a touring Russian pop singer finds that the mission, which takes him to a quiet village, will open up secrets in his past and change his life in ways he never imagined. Simple and heartfelt tale stars Nikolai Karachentsov, Liya Akhedzhakova. 80 min. In Russian with English subtitles.
22-9036 ***$79.99***

Window To Paris (1995)
Unusual fantasy from Russia about a group of St. Petersburg residents who find a strange "spatial ladder" in the closet of a deceased neighbor that instantly takes them from their frozen homeland to the sunny streets of Paris. Agnés Soral, Sergueï Dontsov, Victor Mikhailov star. 92 min. In Russian and French with English subtitles.
02-2810 ***$89.99***

The Lady With The Dog (1960)
Based on the wistful story by Chekhov, this Russian drama details the affair between a banker in turn-of-the-century Yalta and the beautiful woman he spies in the park walking her dog, and the choice the couple must make between togetherness or their unhappy marriages. 86 min. In Russian with English subtitles.
53-7180 ***$29.99***

Come And See (1986)
During the 1943 Nazi invasion, a Russian boy (Alexsei Kravchenko) joins freedom fighters and is transformed by endless horrors into a broken soul. A devastating work by Elim Klimov, testifying to hundreds of incidents of village genocide. 142 min. In Russian with English subtitles.
53-7261 ***$59.99***

Leo Tolstoy (1984)
The life and times of the author of "War and Peace" and "Anna Karenina" are given a fascinating account that shows new insight into his masterful work. 103 min. In Russian with English subtitles.
53-7404 ***$59.99***

Beshkempir (The Adopted Son) (1999)
From the former Soviet republic of Kyrgyzstan in Central Asia comes a simple and heartfelt look at a fun-loving adolescent boy's coming to terms with his place in his family and his village's society when he learns he was adopted. Director Aktan Abdykalykov's acclaimed drama stars Mirlan Abdykalykov, Adir Abilkassimov. 81 min. In Kyrgyzstani with English subtitles.
53-6667 Was $89.99 ***$19.99***

Scarecrow (1985)
Schoolchildren copy the attitudes of their parents without the pretense to civility in director Rolan Bykov's commentary on the sometimes cruel world of teenagers. Effective performances by Christina Orbakaita and Yury Nikulin are supplemented by a sixth-grader ensemble. 130 min. In Russian with English subtitles.
53-7262 ***$59.99***

Little Vera (1988)
"Glasnost" struck the Soviet cinema with this sexually frank seriocomedy about a young girl who dreams of romance and escaping her dingy industrial hometown. Sultry Natalya Negoda stars in Vasily Pichul's controversial look at modern Russian life. 110 min. In Russian with English subtitles.
01-1438 Was $89.99 ***$29.99***

War And Peace (1968)
Finally released in a Russian-language version, this epic adaptation of Tolstoy's Napoleonic novel took five years and $100,000,000 to make! Grand vignettes of human drama are framed with astounding battle scenes, including one that featured over 120,000 extras. Winner of the Best Foreign Film Oscar; Sergei Bondarchuk directs. 403 min. on three tapes. In Russian with English subtitles.
22-1274 Was $99.99 ***$59.99***

War And Peace (Dubbed Version)
Also available in the dubbed-in-English edition seen in American theatres. 360 min. on three tapes.
22-1011 Was $79.99 ***$49.99***

Crime And Punishment (1970)
Rigorously faithful rendition of Dostoyevsky's immortal novel as lensed by director Lev Kulijanov stars Georgi Taratorkin as Raskolnikov and Innokenti Smoktunovsky as Porfiroy; Victoria Fyodorova co-stars. 224 min. In Russian with English subtitles.
10-7579 Was $39.99 ***$29.99***

Tchaikovsky (1971)
The life, loves and work of brilliant composer Peter Ilich Tchaikovsky are the focus of this compelling biographical drama that features music conducted by noted Hollywood composer Dimitri Tiomkin and a stirring lead performance by Innokenti Smoktunovsky. 153 min. In Russian with English subtitles.
53-7816 ***$59.99***

Siberiade (1979)
From the reign of Nicholas II through to the Cold War and the '60s, the lives of two families (one wealthy and aristocratic, the other working-class) located in the remote frontier region of Siberia are traced in this award-winning saga from director Andrei Konchalovksy. Nikita Mikhalkov, Lyudmilla Gurchenko star. 206 min. In Russian with English subtitles.
53-8015 Was $79.99 ***$29.99***

Taxi Blues (1990)
A compelling drama that uses the growing conflict between two Muscovites, a loyal-to-the-state cab driver and a free-thinking jazz saxophonist, to symbolize the tumult in the Soviet Union during the final years of Gorbachev's rule. Piotr Zaitchenko and Russian rocker Piotr Mamonov star; written and directed by Pavel Lounguine. 110 min. In Russian with English subtitles.
53-7699 Was $89.99 ***$29.99***

Second Circle (1990)
When his father dies, a young man's struggles to deal with his passing—as well as the spiritual crisis the death stirs inside him—in this moving drama from Russian director Alexander Sokurov. 90 min. In Russian with English subtitles.
87-7005 ***$59.99***

Mother And Son (1997)
This visually and emotionally stunning Russian film from director Aleksandr Sokurov tracks the relationship between a dying woman and her adult son as they come to terms with their feelings and her imminent death. Gudrun Geyer, Aleksei Ananishnov star. 73 min. In Russian with English subtitles.
53-6941 ***$89.99***

Sideburns (1991)
Yurii Mamin uses humor to warn against fascism in Russia in this story about a group of reactionaries who wear 19th-century garb and want to eliminate all Western influences in their homeland. The local party enlists them as a "cleaning service" and they soon begin attacking innocent civilians. 110 min. In Russian with English subtitles.
53-9475 ***$59.99***

House Built On Sand (1991)
What starts out as a love letter prank between a group of friends in pre-WWII Russia leads to unforeseen and tragic political ramifications in director Niyole Adomenaite's compelling drama of life among the Soviet intelligentsia during the Stalin era. 75 min. In Russian with English subtitles.
87-7008 ***$59.99***

Close To Eden (1992)
An Oscar-nominated co-production of France and Russia, Nikita Mikhalkov's gorgeously photographed, cross-cultural fable focuses on the friendship between a simple Mongolian shepherd and a Russian road builder comforted by modern technology. With Vladimir Gostukhin and Badema. 109 min. In Russian with English subtitles.
06-2155 ***$89.99***

Luna Park (1992)
Set in Russia at the height of its recent political and social chaos, this gritty, acclaimed drama focuses on a group of anti-Jewish, fascist skinheads who hang out in a battered amusement park. Andrei, the thugs' leader, is in for some life-altering revelations when he searches for his long-missing father. 107 min. In Russian with English subtitles.
53-8006 Was $89.99 ***$29.99***

Moscow Parade (1993)
Set in Moscow in the summer of 1939, this acclaimed film focuses on a former aristocrat unhappily married to a chief in the secret police and the death of her family at the hands of the KGB. When she meets a mysterious man with a strange plan, her life heads off into a new direction. Singer Ute Lemper stars. 103 min. In Russian with English subtitles.
70-5066 Was $79.99 ***$29.99***

Burnt By The Sun (1995)
Winner of the 1994 Academy Award for Best Foreign film, Nikita Mikhalkov's sweet-natured drama unfolds during a summer day in 1936 when a retired soldier, his beautiful wife and their young daughter are visited by the wife's charismatic former lover. Oleg Menchikov stars along with Mikhalkov and his daughter, Nadia. In Russian with English subtitles. 134 min.
02-2808 Was $89.99 ***$19.99***

Africa

Quartier Mozart (1992)
Set in Cameroon's capital city of Yaounde, this enchanting mix of fantasy, feminist drama and social satire tells of a working-class schoolgirl who, with the help of a local sorceress, enters a male body for a new look at the sexual politics and games that make up her society. 80 min. In French with English subtitles.
53-8472 ***$59.99***

Jit (1993)
Punctuated by the beat of African jit-jive music, this exuberant romantic fantasy from Zimbabwe centers on a young man infatuated with a taller, older woman with a gangster boyfriend. With advice from an ancestral spirit, the young man tries to make the woman his bride. Michael Raeburn stars; features music by Oliver Mtukudzi and the Bhundu Boys. 98 min. Filmed in English.
22-5785 Was $79.99 ***$29.99***

Faces Of Women (1985)
The conflict between centuries of local African tradition and the increasing Westernization of modern life, and how two women learn to cope with it, is the focus of this funny, heartfelt tale from the Ivory Coast. Eugénie Cissé Roland, Sidiki Bakaba star; Désiré Ecaré directs. 103 min. In French with English subtitles.
53-8059 ***$89.99***

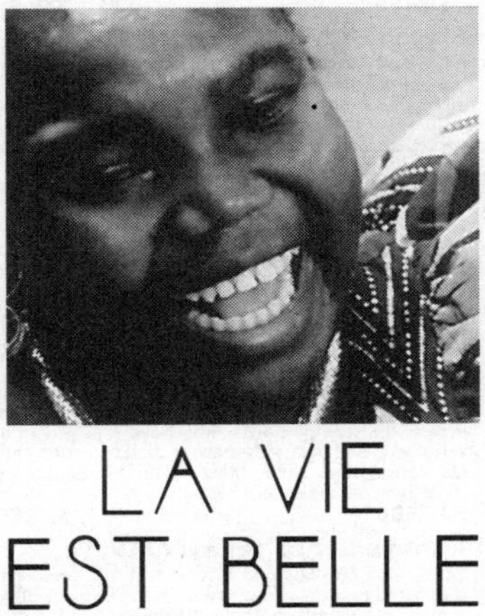

La Vie Est Belle (1987)
A lively and compelling film from Zaire that follows the travails of a village musician (played by international pop performer Papa Wemba) who moves to the capital city of Kinshasa in order to become a star. He's forced to take a job as a houseboy and falls for an upper-class girl, but it will take a witch doctor's aid for things to work out in this blend of comedy, romance and song. With Bibi Krubwa, Kanku Kasongo. 85 min. In French with English subtitles.
53-8471 ***$59.99***

The Magic Garden (1960)
An unusual musical drama from South Africa made with an all-black cast and set in a minority township where some stolen "magic money" has strange effects on the lives of those who come in contact with it. 63 min.
09-1323 Was $29.99 ***$24.99***

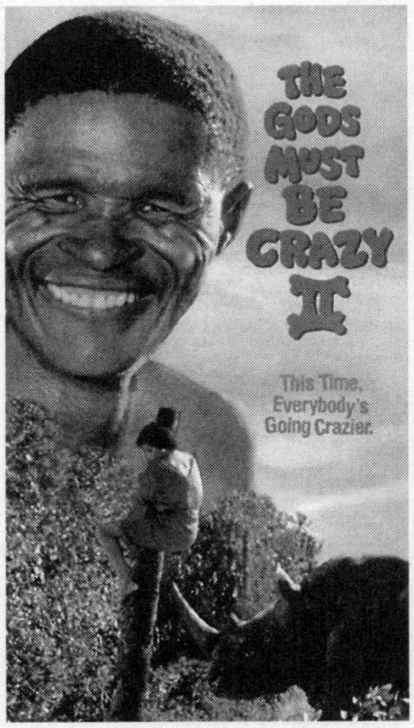

The Gods Must Be Crazy II (1990)
Bushman N!xau ventures forth once more from his feral homeland into the "civilized" world to recover his children, who stowed away in the truck of some ivory poachers, and once more must deal with the problems of modern society in the second slapstick feature from Jamie Uys. 97 min.
02-2046 Was $89.99 ***$19.99***

Soweto Green (1994)
A wickedly funny fable from South Africa focuses on two stories at the same time. First, a professor and his American bride move from Beverly Hills back to his home in Soweto's slums. Meanwhile, a liberal white Afrikaner returns to his rich family, only to find he must abandon his black fiancée and marry the woman they have chosen. John Kani, L. Scott Caldwell star.
54-9203 ***$59.99***

The Quarry (2000)
After killing a Baptist minister near a small South African coastal town, an unnamed man (John Lynch) takes his victim's identity and assumes his post at a nearby church. Soon, he's offering help to such parishioners as a racist cop and two brothers with criminal interests. Jonny Phillips also stars. 112 min. In English and Afrikaans with English subtitles.
70-5189 ***$79.99***

Man Of Ashes (Rih Essed) (1986)
On the eve of his wedding, a Tunisian woodcarver is overcome with anxiety due to a disturbing incident that happened to him and his best friend years earlier, an incident that sends them to a fateful encounter with a prostitute. Director Nouri Bouzid's compelling drama stars Imad Maalal, Khaled Ksouri. 109 min. In Arabic with English subtitles.
53-6888 ***$19.99***

Halfaouine: Boy Of The Terraces (1990)
This comic coming-of-age story set in exotic Tunisia focuses on a 13-year-old boy who becomes aware of his sexual desires after he sees nude women in a Turkish bathhouse which he has visited with his mother. The boy's awakenings lead him to explore an outlet for his sexuality, but he is continually frustrated by others' actions. 98 min. In Arabic with English subtitles.
53-8943 ***$79.99***

Honey & Ashes (1996)
Three women living in North Africa struggle to control their own lives and destinies in this potent drama. Young Laila carries on an affair against her father's wishes, while Naima, a successful doctor, is forced into pre-arranged marriage and Amina attempts to battle her abusive husband. A Tunisian "Thelma & Louise"! Nozha Khouadra, Amel Ledhili star. 80 min. In Arabic and French with English subtitles.
22-9026 ***$79.99***

The Silences Of The Palace (1996)
French-ruled Tunisia in the 1950s is the setting for a sumptuously filmed look at political and sexual power. Alia, a young native servant girl, attempts to overcome the harsh treatment by her French colonialist masters in this stunning coming-of-age story with a feminist twist. Amel Hedhili stars. 127 min. In Arabic and French with English subtitles.
75-1011 ***$79.99***

Touki Bouki (1973)
A landmark in the New African Cinema, Senegalese director Djibril Diop Mambety's drama depicts with laughter and tears the struggles of two young lovers from Dakar who dream of travelling to Paris and finding a better life. 85 min. In Wolof with English subtitles.
53-8474 *$59.99*

Hyenas (1992)
This masterful comedic parable about greed from Senegal's Djibril Diop Mambety ("Touki Bouki") tells of a kindly grocer living in an impoverished village whose life is disrupted when a wealthy woman returns to the village, claiming he seduced and abandoned her years earlier. In order to get revenge, the woman offers the villagers millions if they kill the shopkeeper. 113 min. In Wolof with English subtitles.
53-8942 *$79.99*

Alexandria...Why? (Iskindiria...Leh?) (1978)
The first film in noted Egyptian director Youssef Chahine's autobiographical "Alexandria Trilogy," this compelling tale of romantic and political awakening in WWII Egypt chronicles a movie-mad schoolboy's dreams of becoming a filmmaker, as well as a series of doomed love affairs that cross cultural barriers. Moshen Mohiedine, Nagla Fathi star. 133 min. In Arabic with English subtitles.
53-6889 *$19.99*

An Egyptian Story (Hadota Misreya) (1982)
While undergoing open-heart surgery, filmmaker Yeshia (Mohiel Dine) looks back on his past, and the at-times conflicted artistic, political and personal sides of his life that have led him to where he is. Director Youssef Chahine's mix of post-WWII Middle East history, his own experiences and "All That Jazz" also stars Nour El Cherif. 127 min. In Arabic with English subtitles.
53-6890 *$19.99*

Alexandria Again And Forever (Iskindiria Kamen Oue Kamen) (1990)
Taking over in the role of his on-screen alter ego Yehia, writer-director Youssef Chahine deals with success for his films and a growing obsession with the lead actor of his latest project. Clips from Chahine's previous works, as well as footage from the Berlin Film Festival, are deftly worked into the proceedings. 105 min. In Arabic with English subtitles.
53-6891 *$19.99*

The Alexandria Trilogy: Complete Set
All three entries in director Youssef Chahine's acclaimed film series—"Alexandria...Why?," "An Egyptian Story" and "Alexandria Again and Forever"—are available in a money-saving collection.
53-6892 Save $10.00! *$49.99*

Nasser 56 (1996)
Filmed like a 1950s newsreel, this inventive pseudo-documentary focuses on Egyptian president Gamal Abdel Nasser's efforts to nationalize the Suez Canal in 1956. The film shows how Egypt dared to defy world superpowers like the United States and its Western allies with its actions. With Ahmad Zaki as Nasser. 140 min. In Arabic with English subtitles.
22-9011 *$39.99*

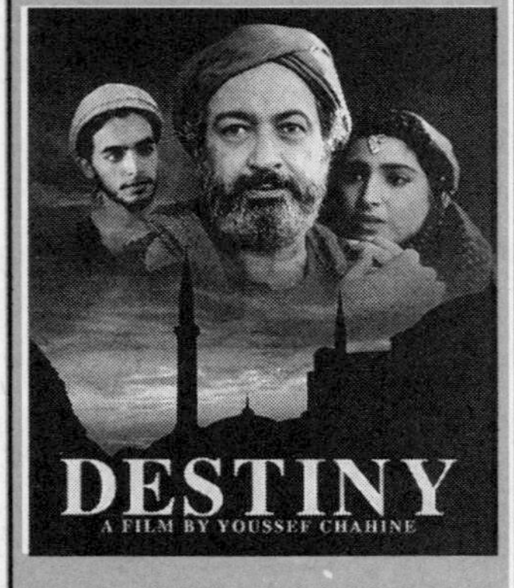
DESTINY
A FILM BY YOUSSEF CHAHINE

Destiny (al-Massir) (1997)
A vibrant, emotional look at a little-seen part of European history, director Youssef Chahine's colorful film is set in Muslim-ruled 12th-century Spain. The son of a French scholar burned at the stake for copying the writings of an Arab philosopher travels to Andalusia, where the ruling caliph faces pressure from religious fundamentalists to reject the philosopher's ideas and ban his works. Melodrama, comedy and lively musical numbers all play equal parts. Nour el-Cherif, Mahmoud Hemeida star. 135 min. In Arabic with English subtitles.
53-6638 Letterboxed *$89.99*

Wend Kuuni (God's Gift) (1982)
A mute homeless boy is found wandering in the African bush by a peddler and taken back to the man's village to live with his family in this gently moving tale from Burkina Faso. Serge Yanago, Joseph Nikiema star; directed by Gaston J.M. Kaboré. 70 min. In Moré with English subtitles.
53-8473 *$59.99*

Yaaba (1989)
A young boy tries to befriend an elderly woman who was cast out of his village over fears she was a witch. When his cousin is stricken with fever, he begs for the woman to help him find a shaman to cure her. Winner of the International Critics Prize at Cannes, this eloquently simple drama established Burkina Faso's Idrissa Ouedraogo as a leading force in new African cinema. Noufou Ouedraogo, Fatimata Sanga star. 90 min. In Mòoré with English subtitles.
53-6611 *$89.99*

Tilai (The Law) (1994)
Directed by acclaimed filmmaker Idissa Ouedraogo ("Yaaba"), this witty and tragic drama from Burkina Faso details a young man's secret affair with a former fiancée now married to his father. Rasmane Ouedraoio, Ina Cissé star. 81 min. In Moré with English subtitles.
53-8229 *$79.99*

Guimba The Tyrant (1995)
Set in a fictitious kingdom in pre-colonial Africa, this cautionary and satirical fable from Malian filmmaker Cheick Oumar Sissoko follows the efforts of the power-mad ruler to marry his dwarf son off to the land's most beautiful woman. The spoiled son, however, demands to wed the woman's stout mother instead, forcing Guimba to send her husband into exile. Issa Traore, Lamie Diallo star. 93 min. In Bambara and Peul with English subtitles.
53-6489 Letterboxed *$79.99*

Israel

Echoes Of Conflict (1986-1989)
The new wave of Israeli filmmakers is represented by three powerful efforts: "Night Movie" follows an Israeli soldier and an Arab youth thrown together by circumstances in Tel Aviv; "Don't Get Involved," in which a tortured Argentinean relives horrific memories in Israel; and "The Cage," focusing on an Israeli bartender's discovery of a former co-worker's past. 91 min. In Hebrew with English subtitles.
53-7615 Was $79.99 *$29.99*

Hill 24 Doesn't Answer (1955)
Intriguing drama, the first film made entirely in Israel, that depicts the nation's 1948 struggle for independence. By depicting the lives of four members of Israel's army (an American, a native-born Jew, an ex-member of the British protectorate and a Yemenite woman) as they fight to hold Hill 24, the war is put into a human perspective. Edward Mulhare, Arich Lavi, Michael Wager star. Filmed in English. 101 min.
53-7236 *$79.99*

They Were Ten (1961)
Against overwhelming odds and prejudice, a group of Russian Jews in the late 1800s immigrate to Palestine to organize a settlement there. Moving Israeli-made drama depicts their lifelong struggle for a homeland; co-written and directed by Baruch Dienar. 105 min. In Hebrew with English subtitles.
53-7240 *$79.99*

Siege (1970)
An Israeli woman widowed in the Six Day War is pressured by her husband's friends to remain perpetually mournful and isolated in his memory. A moving drama about a common circumstance of life in Israel, with Gila Almagor and Dahn Ben Amotz. 95 min. In Hebrew with English subtitles.
48-5022 *$79.99*

But Where Is Daniel Wax? (1974)
Israel's answer to "The Big Chill" looks at a high school reunion where a pop singer and a doctor reminisce about their youth and wonder whatever happened to their class's most popular student. Lior Yaeni, Michael Lipkin star. 95 min. In Hebrew with English subtitles.
53-7503 *$89.99*

My Michael (1975)
Based on a novel by Amos Oz, this drama from Israel depicts the stormy marriage between two people in Jerusalem, and the wife's growing dissatisfaction with her station. Efrat Lavie, Oded Kotler star. 95 min. In Hebrew with English subtitles.
53-7238 *$79.99*

Kuni Lemel In Tel Aviv (1977)
The Jewish farmboy and folk hero of 100 years ago is updated to present-day Brooklyn in this song-filled comedy. An elderly man offers $5 million to the first of his two grandsons who marries a nice Jewish woman and settles in Israel. Mike Burstyn and Mandy Rice-Davies star. 90 min. In Hebrew with English subtitles.
48-5115 *$79.99*

An Intimate Story (1980)
Shattering drama from Israel about the floundering marriage of a couple living in a kibbutz. Hava Alberstein, Alex Peleg star. In Hebrew with English and French subtitles.
48-5006 *$79.99*

Yiddish Films

His Wife's Lover (1931)
Famed Yiddish comedy starring Ludwig Satz as an actor who dons the disguise of an elderly man in order to charm a younger woman. When he reveals his real identity the relationship is put to the test. With Michael Rosenberg. 77 min. In Yiddish with English subtitles.
53-7500 *$59.99*

Uncle Moses (1932)
Classic Yiddish adaptation of the Sholom Asch story about a Lower East Side sweatshop owner who treats his laborers badly but eventually falls in love with daughter of one of his discontented workers. Maurice Schwartz, Judith Abarbanel star. 87 min. In Yiddish with English subtitles.
48-5112 *$59.99*

Yidl Mitn Fidl (Yiddle With A Fiddle) (1937)
Molly Picon stars as a violin player who disguises herself as a boy to travel with a musical show. An engaging portrait of Eastern European Jewish life filmed in Poland before the war, with classic vaudeville routines and songs. 92 min. In Yiddish with English subtitles.
48-5052 *$89.99*

Mamele (1938)
The warmhearted story of a widower's youngest daughter charged with keeping house for her helpless family features several exuberant songs by Molly Picon, queen of Yiddish musical-comedy. 95 min. In Yiddish with English subtitles.
48-5051 *$89.99*

The Cantor's Son (1937)
A Yiddish counterpart to "The Jazz Singer," about a talented émigré who, after living in poverty, becomes a singing sensation in New York City. Based on the life of star Moishe Oysher; with Florence Weiss. 90 min. In Yiddish with English subtitles.
48-5084 *$79.99*

The Dybbuk (Der Dibuk) (1937)
Noted as one of the greatest Yiddish films ever made, this story of unfulfilled love and broken promises tells of how the spirit of a young man enters the body of his beloved after the couple are kept apart by her father. Avrom Marevsky and Lili Liliana star in this spellbinding Polish effort. 120 min. In Yiddish with English subtitles.
48-5091 *$49.99*

A Brivele Der Mamen (1938)
One of the last Yiddish movies filmed in Warsaw is the sentimental story of a Jewish mother holding her family together in New York following their emigration from the Polish Ukraine. Stars Lucy Gehrman, Misha Gehrman and Edmund Zayenda. 100 min. In Yiddish with English subtitles.
48-5050 *$89.99*

Mirele Efros (1938)
A classic study in the relations between mothers and daughters-in-law, focusing on a dignified widow's conflict with her son's new wife. With Berta Gersten and based on Jacob Gordin's play. 80 min. In Yiddish with English subtitles.
48-5072 *$79.99*

The Singing Blacksmith (1938)
Classic Yiddish charmer set in Eastern Europe (but filmed in New Jersey!), about an alcoholic, womanizing blacksmith who meets the woman of his dreams, then attempts to change his life. Directed by Edgar G. Ulmer, the film features some fine musical moments. With Florence Weiss, Michael Rosenberg. AKA: "Yankl Der Shmid." 90 min. In Yiddish with English subtitles.
48-5092 *$89.99*

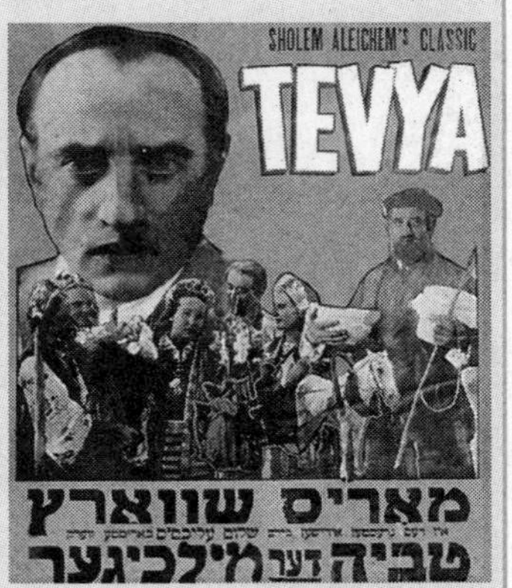
SHOLEM ALEICHEM'S CLASSIC
TEVYA
מאריס שווארץ
טביה דער מילכיגער

Tevye (1939)
Sholom Alechem's story served as the basis for "Fiddler on the Roof." In this powerful production, Maurice Schwartz plays Tevye the Milkman, whose daughter falls in love with a Gentile. With Miriam Riselle and Leon Liebgold. 96 min. In Yiddish with English subtitles.
48-5086 *$89.99*

Overture To Glory (1940)
An inspirational classic of the Yiddish cinema and splendid showcase for the talents of star Moishe Oysher. A cantor abandons his wife and child for a career in opera, but is uncomfortable with city life and returns to his village on Yom Kippur. 85 min. In Yiddish with English subtitles.
48-5049 *$89.99*

Beyond The Walls (1984)
Gripping drama of humanity and prejudice from Israel was nominated for Best Foreign Film. Arabs and Israelis confined in prison together and kept at each other's throats must overcome their mutual hatred in order to survive. 104 min. In Hebrew with English subtitles.
19-1471 *$79.99*

Beyond The Walls (Dubbed Version)
Also available in a dubbed-in-English edition.
19-1472 *$79.99*

The Wooden Gun (1979)
Set in the strife-torn town of Tel Aviv in the mid-'50s this incisive Israeli drama depicts the gap that separates two groups of young people living there: the native-born Israelis, or "Sabras," and the European immigrants who sought refuge from the Holocaust. 91 min. In Hebrew with English subtitles.
53-7241 *$79.99*

Hide And Seek (1980)
Set in pre-1948 Palestine, this Israeli film movingly depicts the tribulations of growing up as faced by a group of Jewish adolescents. Gila Almagor, Chaim Hadaya, Efrat Lavie star. 90 min. In Hebrew with English subtitles.
53-7235 *$79.99*

Noa At Seventeen (1982)
A young Israeli girl is torn between finishing high school and joining her friends on a youth movement kibbutz, a personal dilemma which reflects the ideological struggle going on in the early days of the Israeli nation. Compelling Israeli drama stars Dalia Shimko, Idit Zur. 86 min. In Hebrew with English subtitles.
53-7239 *$79.99*

Hamsin (1983)
The relationship between a Jewish landowner and an Arab laborer in Galilee is threatened when the government announces a plan to confiscate Arab lands in the area. A powerful dramatization of Israel's bitter social divisions, starring Shlomo Tarshish and Yasin Shawap. 90 min. In Hebrew with English subtitles.
48-5024 *$79.99*

The House On Chelouche Street (1973)
Moving parable about a teenage boy who's moved from Europe with his widowed mother to British-occupied Tel Aviv in 1946 and how his involvements with a labor dispute and an older woman push him into adulthood. Directed by Moshe Mizrahi ("Madame Rosa"). 111 min. In Hebrew with English subtitles.
09-1502 Was $29.99 *$19.99*

Women (Nashim) (1997)
Set in late 19th-century Jerusalem, director Moshe Mizrahi's unusual romantic drama stars Michal Bat-Adam as a woman who, after 15 years in a childless marriage, convinces her husband to take a younger woman as his second wife so that his family line might continue. Amos Lavi also stars. 90 min. In Hebrew with English subtitles.
70-3477 *$79.99*

Wedding In Galilee (1987)
In first-time director Michel Khleifi's Cannes Festival winner, the head of a Palestinian village gets a one-day curfew suspension from the Israeli mayor so his son's wedding can be celebrated in traditional Arab fashion. Ali El Akili, Bushra Karaman star. 113 min. In Arabic and Hebrew with English subtitles.
53-7306 Was $79.99 *$24.99*

Fictitious Marriage (1988)
A high school teacher living in Jerusalem leaves his family for a trip to New York, but instead travels to Tel Aviv. There he's mistaken as an Arab laborer and discovers what modern Israel is really like when he joins an Arab work force on a construction job. Shlomo Bar-Aba, Irit Sheleg star. 90 min. In Hebrew with English subtitles.
48-5094 *$89.99*

Cup Final (1992)
Set in the Middle East during the 1982 Israeli invasion of Lebanon, this compelling film tells the story of an Israeli soldier who is captured by PLO fighters while en route to Beirut. He seems to be in lots of trouble until he discovers that the PLO leader shares his love for soccer. 107 min. In Hebrew with English subtitles.
70-5057 *$59.99*

Atalia (1985)
Penetrating drama set on a kibbutz about the romance between an alienated war widow, considered an outsider by the people around her, and a younger man. Michal Bat-Adam and Yiftach Katzur star in this acclaimed story. 90 min. In Hebrew with English subtitles.
48-5093 *$89.99*

Take Two (1985)
A fresh, sexy romantic farce from Israel about a playboy cinematographer who gets more than he bargained for when a new American assistant moves in. She proves critical of his work and his lifestyle in this comedy set in Tel Aviv. 100 min. Filmed in English.
53-9288 *$89.99*

Late Summer Blues (1987)
An acclaimed film from Israel detailing the experiences shared by a group of teens shortly before their induction into the armed forces during the 1970 Suez War, as each young man and woman questions their future and the end of their innocence. 101 min. In Hebrew with English subtitles.
22-5397 Restored *$29.99*

Pick A Card (Afula Express) (1996)
Winner of several Israeli Academy Awards, this enchanting fable tells of David and Batya, a married couple who move from their small town to Tel Aviv so David can pursue his dream career as a magician. While Batya works as a grocery clerk to make ends meet, David befriends a master magician and attempts to hone his limited skills. Zvika Hadar, Esti Zackheim star. 94 min. In Hebrew with English subtitles.
22-9027 *$79.99*

Saint Clara (1996)
Science fiction and teenage angst are blended in this unusual film from Israel about a young girl who uses her clairvoyant abilities to help her classmates and throw her school into chaos. Along with co-director Ari Fulman and Ori Sivan's futuristic drama, this video also includes the short "Personal Goals," about a son trying to live up to his father's dreams of him becoming a soccer star. 101 min. total. In Hebrew with English subtitles.
53-6131 *$79.99*

Under The Domim Tree (1996)
In this acclaimed coming-of-age tale from Israel's Eli Cohen ("The Quarrel"), a teenage girl who survived the Nazi concentration camps takes refuge in a kibbutz with other holocaust survivors in the 1950s. Struggling with her haunted memories, the girl finds solace with her friends under the peaceful Domim tree. With Kaipo Cohen. 102 min. In Hebrew with English subtitles.
53-8660 Was $89.99 *$19.99*

Sallah (1965)
Topol stars in this Oscar-nominated look at the adventures of a family of Oriental Jews who have immigrated to the newly formed state of Israel in 1949. Comedy and drama mix as a father searches for suitable housing while attempting to marry off his daughter (Geula Noni). 105 min. In Hebrew with English subtitles.
48-5070 *$79.99*

Chronicle Of A Disappearance (1996)
The "disappearance" of the title refers to the loss of Palestinian identity under Israeli rule, and through a series of documentary-like glimpses of everyday Palestinian life, filmmaker Elia Suleiman offers funny, pointed and emotional looks at the clashing and blending of the two cultures. 88 min. In Arabic with English subtitles.
53-6472 Was $89.99 *$19.99*

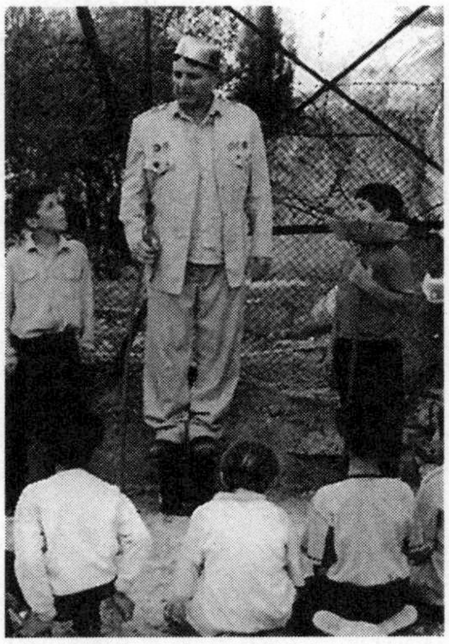

The Milky Way (1997)
Set in an Israeli-occupied Palestinian village in 1964, director Ali Nassar's poignant drama examines the tense relationship between the displaced residents and the region's government-backed ruler, the Mukhtar. The situation becomes even more strained when the Mukhtar's son is killed and an outspoken young metalkworker is suspected. Sufiel Haddad, Mohammad Bakri star. 104 min. In Arabic and Hebrew with English subtitles.
53-6612 *$79.99*

Turkey

The Horse (1982)
Simple but universal drama from Turkey about a working-class father's attempts to earn enough money to send his son to school. Director Ali Ozgenturk's story was viewed by some (including the Turkish government, who arrested him) as an indictment of the country's rulers. 116 min. In Turkish with English subtitles.
53-7138 *$69.99*

The Wall (1983)
The last film by Turkish director Yilmaz Guney ("Yol"), made while he lived in exile in France, depicts the harrowing lives of young boys in an Ankara prison dorm, and their attempts to revolt in order to be transferred to another jail. 117 min. In Turkish with English subtitles.
53-7142 *$69.99*

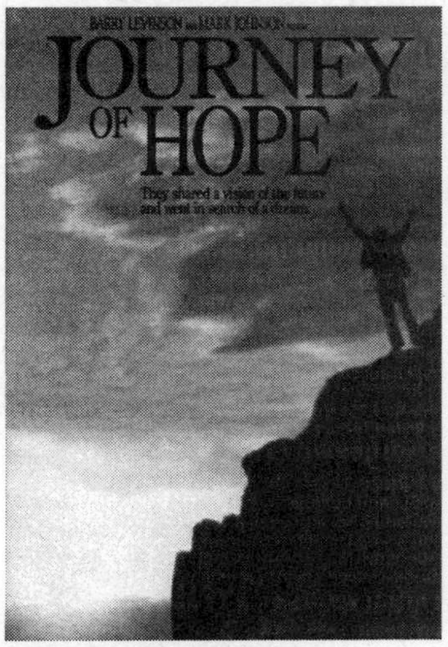

Journey Of Hope (1991)
The winner of the 1991 Academy Award for Best Foreign Film is a passionate drama about a poor Kurdish couple who decide to make a better life for themselves and their seven children by moving to Switzerland from their native Turkey. Their dangerous journey is chronicled in this stirring film, directed by Xavier Koller. 111 min. In Turkish and German with English subtitles.
44-1853 Was $89.99 *$19.99*

Iran

The Suitors (1989)
An off-kilter comedy from Iranian-born Ghasem Ebrahimian, set in Manhattan, about an Iranian couple whose sacrificial slaughter of a lamb prompts their apartment building's super to call in the police. The situation goes from bad to absurd when the police are joined by the SWAT team, who think they have terrorists on their hands. 106 min. In Farsi with English subtitles.
70-5019 Was $59.99 *$29.99*

The Last Act (1991)
In order to gain their inheritance, a brother and sister in 1930s Tehran plot to drive their late brother's wife insane by hiring actors to pose as servants and stage increasingly terrifying occurrences in her home. Offbeat and atmospheric mystery stars Farimah Farjami, Niku Kheradmand. 110 min. In Farsi with English subtitles.
53-6359 *$29.99*

The Legend Of A Sigh (1991)
A female writer in the Azerbaijani region of Northern Iran gets help in overcoming her creative block from a handsome spirit who helps her experience the lives of four women from different segments of society. Writer/director Tahmineh Milani's feminist-flavored fantasy/drama stars Mahshid Afsharzadeh, Yarta Yaran. 105 min. In Farsi with English subtitles.
53-6360 *$29.99*

The Need (1991)
Once rivals, two adolescent boys overcome the animosities between them to become friends in this moving drama from Iranian director Alireza Davudneshad. 81 min. In Farsi with English subtitles.
53-9743 *$39.99*

The Peddler (1987)
A compelling and brutally honest look at life for the poorest residents of contemporary Tehran, this drama from Iranian director Mohsen Makhmalbaf is comprised of three separate stories: an impoverished couple try to find someone to adopt their newborn daughter; a mentally troubled man turns to his elderly mother for company; and a young street peddler arouses the anger of his competitors. In Farsi with English subtitles.
53-9741 *$39.99*

The Cyclist (1989)
The divisions between rich and poor in contemporary Iranian society are the focus of this powerful and visually striking social drama from director Mohsen Makhmalbaf. 75 min. In Farsi with English subtitles.
53-9742 *$39.99*

Once Upon A Time, Cinema (1992)
Acclaimed Iranian director Mohsen Makhmalbaf salutes his homeland's first filmmakers with this haunting drama set in the last days of the Qajar dynasty. A Chaplin-like travelling movie showman arrives at the Persian court and attempts to win the Shah over to the new medium. Included are clips from such early Iranian films as "A Banquet in Hell," "The Cow," "Downpour" and more. Ezzatollah Entezami, Mehdi Hashemi star. 100 min. In Farsi with English subtitles.
53-6357 *$29.99*

Gabbeh (1997)
A radiant and romantic fable set among a nomadic tribe in Iran. Gabbeh, a young woman named after the traditional hand-woven carpet, weaves a tale as colorful and intricate as her namesake, recounting the story of a man who loves her, but is forbidden by Gabbeh's father to marry her. Mohsen Moharami's mystical drama stars Shaghayegh Djodat. 75 min. In Farsi with English subtitles.
53-6415 Letterboxed *$94.99*

The Sealed Soil (1977)
Directed by Iran's first female director, Marva Nabili, this drama tells of a woman in pre-revolution Iran who decides to rebel against traditional ways and turns down a string of marriage proposals. Her decisions pit her against her family and lead to a nervous breakdown. 90 min. In Farsi with English subtitles.
70-3464 Was $79.99 *$29.99*

The Key (1986)
A 4-year-old Iranian boy is left home to mind his infant brother and tend to food cooking in the oven while his mother goes out shopping in director Ebrahim Forouzesh's intimate tale that mixes laughter and pathos. 76 min. In Farsi with English subtitles.
53-9745 *$39.99*

Nargess (1992)
A handsome young thief, trained by his older lover, is tempted to mend his ways when he falls for the daughter of a poor but honest family. He has trouble sticking to the straight and narrow, however, in Iranian filmmaker Rakhshan Bani-etemad's controversial drama that looks at life outside of her homeland's strict Islamic code of conduct. Farimah Farjami, Atefeh Razavi star. 100 min. In Farsi with English subtitles.
53-6355 *$29.99*

Travellers (Mosaferan) (1992)
A time of celebration and joy turns into an event of mourning, when the family of a woman is killed in a traffic accident on her wedding day, in this powerful and richly-drawn Iranian drama. Mozhdeh Shamsai, Jamileh Sheikhi star. 90 min. In Farsi with English subtitles.
53-6358 *$29.99*

Zinat (1994)
A compelling look at the changing role of women in contemporary Iran, this acclaimed drama follows a woman who runs a health clinic in a remote region of Southern Iran and must choose between her work and her heart when her fiancé's mother demands she quit her job. Atefeh Razavi, Hassan Joharchi star. 88 min. In Farsi with English subtitles.
53-6356 *$29.99*

Leila (1996)
A powerful look at the clash between modernity and tradition in contemporary Iran, director Dariush Mehrjui's drama follows a recently married middle-class couple who discover that the wife cannot have children. The husband's family, particularly his mother, pressures him to take a second spouse so that the line can continue. Leila Hatami, Ali Mossaffa star. 129 min. In Farsi with English subtitles.
70-5180 *$79.99*

Children Of Heaven (1997)
A simple and heartwarming tale for all ages, this acclaimed drama from writer/director Majid Majidi follows two young siblings in an Iranian city as they try to keep the loss of the sister's only shoes from their parents. Sharing the brother's sneakers, they search for a way to get another pair without straining their family's limited finances. Mir Farrokh Hashemian, Bahare Seddiqi star. 83 min. In Farsi with English subtitles.
11-2343 Was $99.99 *$19.99*

The Color Of Paradise (1999)
Beautifully rendered effort from Iran's Majid Majidi centers on an 8-year-old blind boy named Mohammad whose poor, widowed father has no interest in raising him. After he's taken in along with his two sisters by his grandmother, Mohammad is cared for by a blind carpenter who hopes to train the boy as his apprentice. Mohsen Ramezani stars. 90 min. In Farsi with English subtitles.
02-3459 *$99.99*

Where Is The Friend's Home? (1989)
An offbeat and lyrical "road movie" from Iranian director Abbas Kiarostami that follows a traveller as he sets out to visit a friend, a trip that becomes an odyssey through hauntingly beautiful locales. 90 min. In Farsi with English subtitles.
53-9744 *$39.99*

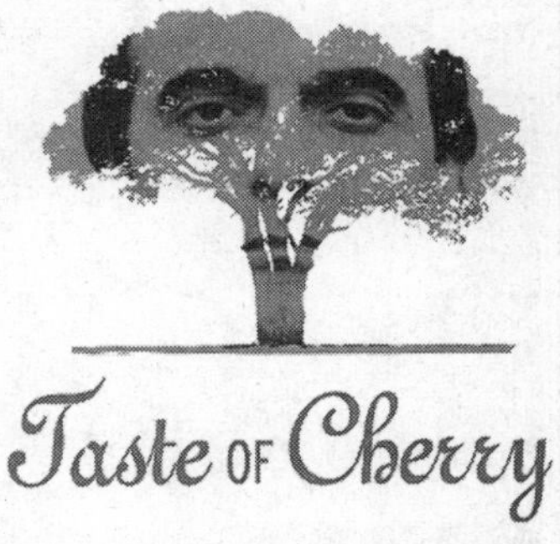

Taste Of Cherry (1997)
A simple and thoughtful study on life and death that aroused controversy in its native Iran, director Abbas Kiarostami's acclaimed drama follows a Tehran man who drives around the city picking up people in his truck and seeking someone willing to help him end his life. Each passenger offers reasons why the man should go on living. Homayon Ershadi stars. 95 min. In Farsi with English subtitles.
22-6019 Letterboxed *$29.99*

India

Spices (1986)
Searing story set in 1940s India directed by Ketan Mehta, one of India's premier filmmakers. A woman eludes tax collectors and takes a job at a pepper factory in this acclaimed feminist tale. 98 min. In Hindi with English subtitles.
70-7078 *$29.99*

Genesis (1986)
In this lyrical and allegorical drama from noted Indian director Mrinal Sen, the quiet existence of a weaver and a farmer, sole residents of a ruined village, is shattered by the arrival of a mysterious woman with whom both men fall in love. Shabana Azmi, Om Puri, Naseeruddin Shah star. 105 min. In Hindi with English subtitles.
87-7011 *$59.99*

The Mahabharata (1988)
India's epic Hindu poem of feuding royal clans and divine intervention is turned into a majestic three-part drama with a multinational cast by maverick British director Peter Brook. The struggle for power between two dynasties, the righteous Pandavas and the evil Kauravas, is the backdrop for a story of devotion, courage and dharma (duty). Full-length version; 318 min. on three tapes. Filmed in English.
70-3018 *$99.99*

The Mahabharata (Theatrical Version)
Peter Brook's sweeping drama is also available in its feature-length version. 180 min. on two tapes.
70-3295 *$49.99*

The Eye Above The Well (1988)
Everyday life in a village in the Kerala state of Southwestern India, and how the customs and culture of the region's people are passed from generation to generation, are the focus of this lush and lyric drama from Dutch-born director Johan van der Keuken. 94 min. In Malayalam with English subtitles.
87-7012 *$59.99*

In Custody (1994)
Producer Ismail Merchant's directorial debut is a compelling drama about a college professor in India whose interview with a once-famous poet takes him into a whirlwind of unexpected problems involving his subject and his feuding wives, the university and the professor's own family. Shasi Kapoor and Om Puri star. 123 min. In Urdu and Hindi with English subtitles.
02-2722 *$29.99*

DVD VIDEO
ASK ABOUT OUR GIANT DVD CATALOG!

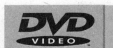

Pather Panchali

Satyajit Ray

Pather Panchali (1955)
The hardships of daily life for an Indian family are seen through the eyes of a young boy named Apu, who dreams with his sister of leaving their remote Bengal village to visit the big city, in this lyrical drama, the groundbreaking first film in director Satyajit Ray's "Apu Trilogy." Subir Bannerjee, Karuna Bannerjee star; music by Ravi Shankar. 113 min. In Bengali with English subtitles.
02-2923   Was $29.99 $19.99

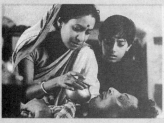

Aparajito (1958)
The second installment of Ray's acclaimed series follows Apu from childhood to adolescence, as tragedy tests his family and he wins the chance to go to college in Calcutta. Pinaki Sen Gupta, Smaran Ghosai and Karuna Bannerjee star. 113 min. In Bengali with English subtitles.
02-2924   Was $29.99 $19.99

The World Of Apu (1959)
Forced to curtail his studies due to a lack of funds, Apu's dreams of becoming a writer are challenged when he enters into an arranged marriage and brings his new wife to Calcutta in the moving finale to Satyajit Ray's story of Indian life. Soumitra Chatterjee, Sharmila Tagore star. 106 min. In Bengali with English subtitles.
02-2925   Was $24.99 $19.99

Apu Trilogy: Complete Set
The complete trilogy is also available in a collector's set.
02-2926 $59.99

Jalsaghar (The Music Room) (1958)
Forced to sell his decaying family mansion to pay his bills, an Indian aristocrat decides to use his remaining money to mount an extravagant concert of classical indigenous music in this emotional tale from Satyajit Ray. Chabi Biswas, Padma Devi star. 100 min. In Bengali with English subtitles.
02-3095 $19.99

Two Daughters (1961)
A matched set of insightful tales from director Satyajit Ray regarding love as seen through a young woman's eyes. The first story deals with a girl's devotion to her employer, "The Postmaster." In "The Conclusion," a bride's flight from forced marriage leads to charming consequences. 112 min. In Bengali with English subtitles.
53-1698 $19.99

Devi (1962)
Absorbing tale from director Satyajit Ray regarding a young girl who is treated as a reincarnated deity after her father-in-law has a vision...and soon can't help but wonder if it is true. Sharmila Tagore, Chhabi Biswas star. AKA: "The Goddess." 95 min. In Bengali with English subtitles.
10-7227   Was $29.99 $19.99

The Big City (Mahanagar) (1963)
Satyajit Ray chronicled the changing role of women in an increasingly Westernized Indian society in this blend of comedy and drama. In order to keep her impoverished family going, a timid housewife takes a job selling knitting machines door to door, and soon gains a newfound self-confidence. Anil Chaterjee, Madhabi Mukherjee star. 131 min. In Bengali with English subtitles.
02-3097 $19.99

Charulata (The Lonely Wife) (1964)
Feeling neglected by her political writer husband, a woman becomes attracted to his cousin, a poet, who comes to live with them. Based on a story by noted Indian writer Rabindranath Tagore and set in 19th-century Calcutta, Satyajit Ray's lush tale of the disintegration of a marriage stars Madhabi Mukherjee in the title role. 117 min. In Bengali with English subtitles.
02-3094 $19.99

Days And Nights In The Forest (1970)
Insightful drama by Satyajit Ray follows four Calcutta men on their respective vacations. While each man is on holiday, he has a romantic encounter of varying degrees of seriousness and intensity that affects his life. 120 min. With English subtitles.
53-7642 $39.99

The Adversary (1971)
After graduating from college, a young Indian man finds life in Calcutta much tougher than he ever imagined as he copes with unemployment and mounting personal hardships. Satyajit Ray directed this compelling, neo-realist drama. 110 min. With English subtitles.
53-7643 $19.99

Distant Thunder (1974)
Famine strikes Bengal in 1942 when the army seizes available food supplies for soldiers and leaves the civilian populace to scramble for survival. Satyajit Ray's vivid drama was the top prize winner at the Berlin International Film Festival. 95 min. In Hindi with English subtitles.
53-7269 $49.99

The Middleman (Jana Aranya) (1975)
After unsuccessfully hunting for a job in his chosen field, a Calcutta university graduate becomes a "middleman" for a shady business operation and must make difficult choices between ethics and survival. Satyajit Ray's powerful look at contemporary Indian society stars Pradip Mukherjee, Satya Banerjee. 131 min. In Bengali with English subtitles.
02-3096 $19.99

The Stranger (Agantuk) (1991)
The final film from acclaimed director Satyajit Ray, this warm comedy of manners tells the story of a man who returns to his native Calcutta after 35 years of travelling the world to visit his niece and her family. But is this man really the long-lost uncle, or an impostor looking to make off with an inheritance? 120 min. In Bengali with English subtitles.
70-5101   Was $59.99 $29.99

Satyajit Ray: Introspections
The famed Indian filmmaker talks candidly about his years behind the camera, the philosophy behind his art, and his personal life in this fascinating Museum of Modern Art documentary. 55 min.
22-1631 $19.99

Fire (1997)
The subject of bans and protests throughout India, this taboo-breaking erotic tale focuses on the relationship of Sita, the wife of a grocery store owner in New Delhi, and Radha, her sister-in-law and wife of a celibate swami. The two women break out of the doldrums of their marriages when they discover their attraction to one another, and a forbidden lesbian tryst ensues. Shabana Azmi and Nandita Das star. 104 min. Filmed in English.
53-6281   Letterboxed $29.99

Earth (1998)
The religious bloodshed evolving from the 1947 partition of India and Pakistan is seen through the eyes of an 8-year-old Parsee girl in this powerful drama from director Deepa Mehta ("Fire"). As young Lenny watches with her Hindu nanny, the forced migration of Hindus from Pakistan to India, with Muslim refugees making the reverse trip, leads to intolerance and violence. Maaia Sethna, Nandita Das star. 104 min. In Hindi, Parsee, Punjabi and Urdu with English subtitles.
53-6929   Letterboxed $94.99

Southeast Asia

My Village At Sunset (1992)
One of the leading figures in modern Cambodian cinema is no less than the country's ruler, King Norodom Sihanouk. Here he serves as writer/director to bring to the screen a moving tale of a dedicated young doctor who moves to a rural province to aid land mine victims, only to become involved in a love affair that leads to jealousy and death. Prince Norodom Sihamoni, San Chariya and Mam Kanika star. 63 min. In Cambodian with English subtitles.
53-6295 $29.99

See Angkor And Die

See Angkor And Die (1993)
After he's diagnosed with a terminal illness, a man travels to the ruined city of Angkor to spend his last days in contemplation, leaving his wife behind in Phnom Penh to think about remarrying. How each person looks to the future is interwoven with the history and music of ancient Cambodia in this lyrical drama written and directed by King Sihanouk. Roland Eng, Mam Kakina star. 81 min. In Cambodian with English subtitles.
53-6294 $29.99

Peasants In Distress (1994)
Set against the 1993 Cambodian Civil War, this haunting drama follows a rebel army commander who falls in love with a local peasant woman. When the officer's jealous deputy kills a U.N. soldier, the rebels are forced to take the peasants hostage and take them into the jungle. Written and directed by King Sihanouk. 75 min. In Cambodian with English subtitles.
53-6297 $29.99

An Ambition Reduced To Ashes (1995)
In this unusual, allegorical tale directed by King Sihanouk, a seemingly young prince in modern-day Cambodia falls in love with a beautiful girl, but is warned by his Merlin-like mentor to wed her and consummate the marriage would lead to his death and prevent him from fulfilling his destiny as his country's savior. 44 min. In Cambodian with English subtitles.
53-6296 $29.99

The Last Days Of Colonel Savath (1995)
Filmmaking monarch King Sihanouk of Cambodia continues to chronicle his country's tumultuous recent past with a powerful tale set during the 1975 fall of Phnom Penh to the Khmer Rouge. An army colonel loyal to the monarchy cannot stop his superior from giving support to Pol Pot's forces; meanwhile, the colonel's doctor father tries to treat the victims of the Communists' bloody attacks. 34 min. In Cambodian with English subtitles.
53-6298 $29.99

The Dumb Die Fast, The Smart Die Slow (1991)
A noir-flavored thriller from Thailand, this compelling film follows an escaped prisoner who finds refuge in a remote village and gains employment with the town's richest man. Things go smoothly until his boss' scheming wife learns his secret and forces the fugitive to help her steal her husband's money. Surasak Wongthai, Ungkana Timdee star. 110 min. In Thai with English subtitles.
53-6292   Was $39.99 $29.99

Sunset At Chaopraya (1996)
Set in Japanese-occupied Thailand during World War II, director Euthana Mukdasanit's moving drama follows the doomed romance that grows between a Thai woman and a Japanese man whose love draws them together, but who are pulled apart by their devotion to their homelands. Thongchai McIntyre, Appasiri Nitiphon star. 134 min. In Thai and Japanese with English subtitles.
53-6293 $39.99

The Scent Of Green Papaya (1994)
The first effort from Vietnam nominated for a Best Foreign Film Oscar is director Tran Anh Hung's lyrical story of Miu, who becomes a servant for a family in 1950s Saigon at the age of 10 and later continues her service as a domestic for a wealthy young composer. The film focuses on Miu's joy in preparing and cooking food and finding solace in nature's beauty. 104 min. In Vietnamese with English subtitles.
02-2744   Was $89.99 $19.99

Cyclo (1996)
A powerful tale set in the underworld of post-war Vietnam, this gripping drama from director Tran Anh Hung ("The Scent of Green Papaya") follows a Ho Chi Minh City pedicab driver struggling to support his sisters and grandfather and who is forced to deal with a charismatic crime ring boss when his bicycle is stolen. Le Van Loc, Tony Leung ("A Bullet in the Head") stars. 123 min. In Vietnamese with English subtitles.
53-8940 $89.99

A Smart Lady (1994)
In this tale from Burma, a beautiful, young orphaned woman who works for her aunt, selling fish in a small village, attracts the eye of such men as a college student, a musician and a former monk. Her expertise in business brings great financial success—and her own private bodyguard, who becomes jealous of the attention she gets. With Mi Thien Kywe. 114 min. In Burmese with English subtitles.
53-6453 $29.99

That's The Way I Like It (1998)
In Singapore in 1977, teenage supermarket worker Adrian Pang's obsession with "Saturday Night Fever" leads him to take dance lessons in order to enter a disco contest in which he hopes to make enough money to buy a prized Triumph motorcycle. Filled with good humor, nostalgia and neat dance numbers, this winner also stars Madeline Tan, Anna Belle Francis. 92 min. Dubbed in English.
11-2414   Was $99.99 $14.99

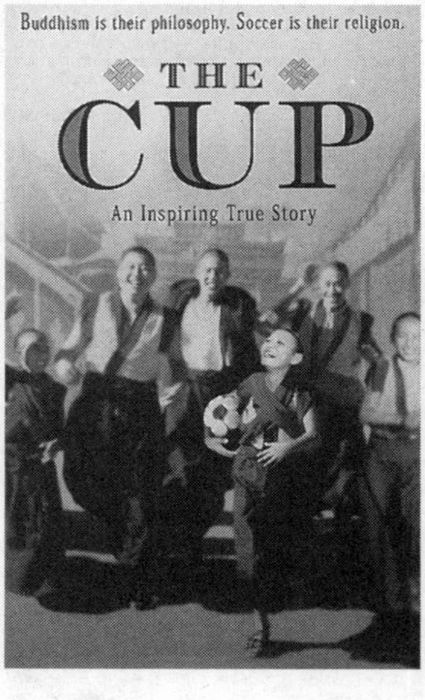

Buddhism is their philosophy. Soccer is their religion.

THE CUP
An Inspiring True Story

The Cup (1999)
Filmed in the central Asian country of Bhutan and written and directed by Khyentse Norbu (recognized by Buddhists as an incarnation of a 19th-century Tibetan saint) this warm and winning story tells of a teenage monk-in-training in India who is obsessed with soccer. After getting in trouble for watching the World Cup games on TV, the young man and his fellow students concoct a scheme to bring the games inside the monastery walls. Jamang Lodro and Neten Chokling lead the incredible cast of non-professionals. 94 min. In Hindi and Tibetan with English subtitles.
02-5239 $99.99

China/ Hong Kong

The Reincarnation Of Golden Lotus (1989)
Exotic, sexually charged tale of a woman who escapes Mao's repressive regime by marrying a wealthy Hong Kong man. She indulges in several sadomasochistic affairs, and, through flashbacks, realizes she may be the reincarnation of an Imperial courtesan. Joi Wong, Eric Tsang star in Clara Law's acclaimed, kinky drama. 99 min. In Chinese with English subtitles.
53-7673 *$89.99*

Autumn Moon (1992)
An offbeat and warm seriocomedy from acclaimed director Clara Law, set in present-day Hong Kong. A food- and sex-craving Japanese tourist strikes up a friendship with a teenage Chinese girl whose parents are preparing to move the family to Canada. Masatoshi Nagase, Li Pui Wai star. 108 min. Filmed in English and in Cantonese with English subtitles.
70-5085 Was $59.99 *$29.99*

Temptation Of A Monk (1993)
A compelling blend of human drama and costume adventure, director Clara Law's tale of honor and betrayal in 7th-century China follows a disgraced general who takes refuge in a Buddhist temple while plotting revenge against the rival general who led to his downfall. Wu Hsin-Kuo, Zhang Fengyi, Lisa Lu and Joan Chen, in a dual role, star. 118 min. In Mandarin with English subtitles.
53-8222 Was $89.99 *$19.99*

Yellow Earth (1984)
Set in Northern China in 1939, this compelling drama centers on a 14-year-old peasant girl whose life is changed forever when a Communist Army soldier arrives in her remote village to collect folk songs for his superiors. Photographed by Zhang Yimou ("The Story of Qiu Ju") and directed by Chen Kaige ("Farewell My Concubine"). 89 min. In Mandarin with English subtitles.
53-7831 *$19.99*

Life On A String (1991)
From director Chen Kaige comes this lyrical, haunting drama about an elderly blind man who, along with a sightless student, travels from village to village singing folk songs on a pilgrimage of enlightenment. Liu Zhong Yuan, Huang Lei star. 107 min. In Mandarin with English subtitles.
53-7987 Letterboxed *$24.99*

Temptress Moon (1997)
Set amid the decadent elegance of 1920s Shanghai, director Chen Kaige's moving drama stars Leslie Cheung as a hustler who works for a powerful crime ring and is sent to seduce beautiful heiress Gong Li, whose family mistreated Cheung as a boy. 115 min. In Mandarin with English subtitles.
11-2203 Was $99.99 ▢*$19.99*

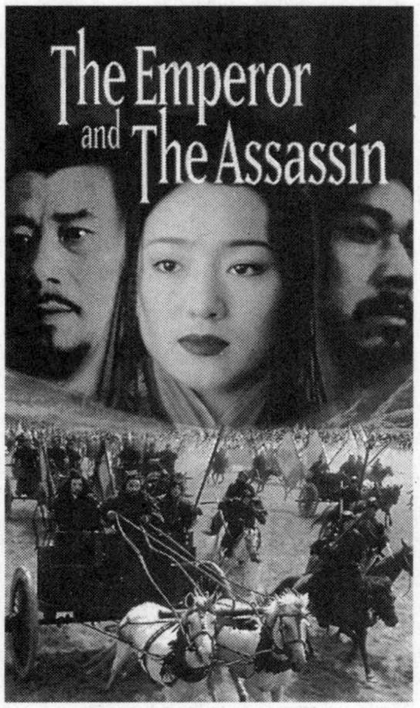

The Emperor And The Assassin (1999)
Epic historical saga from Chen Kaige ("Farewell My Concubine") is set in the 3rd century B.C., when Ying Zheng of the Qin state invades the rival Han state with 250,000 troops and a plot to control China's territories. The plan involves his concubine, a childhood friend and an unstable assassin. Gong Li, Li Xeujian, Zhang Fenghi star. 161 min. In Mandarin with English subtitles.
02-3434 ▢*$99.99*

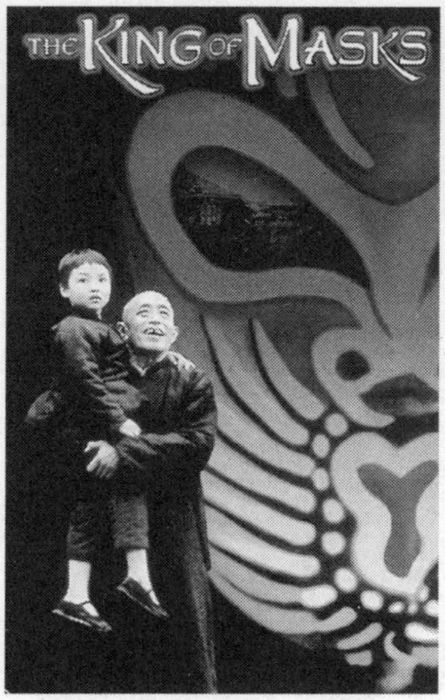

The King Of Masks (Bian Lian) (1996)
An elderly street performer in 1930s China, eager for a male heir to whom he can pass on the tricks of his trade, purchases an 8-year-old from a "baby market," only to discover that his new "grandson" is actually a girl. Forbidden by tradition from teaching her his craft, a bond nevertheless grows between the two that is tested in this moving drama from director Wu Tianming. Zhu Xu, Zhou Ren-ying star. 101 min. In Mandarin with English subtitles.
02-3407 Was $99.99 *$21.99*

Girl From Hunan (1986)
The first film from the People's Republic of China to receive worldwide release in nearly 40 years was this surprisingly frank study of sexuality in feudal China. The haunting drama relates the strife-filled life of a woman promised in marriage to a young boy and her illicit affair with a farmhand. 99 min. In Mandarin with English subtitles.
53-7662 Was $79.99 *$29.99*

Horse Thief (1987)
A compelling and beautifully photographed film from the People's Republic of China, telling the story of a villager who is expelled, along with his family, for stealing a horse and forced to live in the harsh wilderness. 88 min. In Mandarin with English subtitles.
53-7518 Letterboxed *$59.99*

Crows & Sparrows (1949)
Considered a milestone in Chinese cinema, this Neo-Realist drama, filmed just before the Communist takeover, centers on a greedy landlord hoping to sell his boarding house and flee to Taiwan, leaving his tenants to fend for themselves. The diverse group struggles for survival as the Red Army approaches their residence. With Zhao Dan; directed by Zheng Junli. 108 min. In Mandarin with English subtitles.
53-6109 Was $59.99 *$24.99*

Stage Sisters (1965)
Acclaimed filmmaker Xie Jin's mixture of human melodrama and government "message film" follows the ups and downs of two actresses through the turmoil of World War II and the Communist revolution. 112 min. In Mandarin with English subtitles.
87-7004 *$59.99*

China, My Sorrow (1989)
An inspiring tale about a young boy whose love song for a girl leads him to arrest by Mao's police for obscenity and lands him in a remote re-education center. He befriends a wise monk and a teenage rebel, while rediscovering his own sense of freedom. Directed by Dai Sijie. 86 min. In Mandarin and Cantonese with English subtitles.
53-7787 Was $79.99 *$29.99*

Women's Story (1989)
Unusual social drama from China follows three peasant women who, in order to get away from their rural village's rigid, gender-assigned roles, go to the big city to sell their wool. 96 min. In Mandarin with English subtitles.
87-7003 *$59.99*

The Blue Kite (1993)
Much-applauded, beautifully photographed drama focusing on a boy's experiences growing up in China in the 1950s and 1960s during the rise of Chairman Mao, and facing continuous political, social and familial turmoil. Banned in the People's Republic of China, Tian Zhuanghuang's film was hailed as one of the best of 1994 by several film critics. 138 min. In Mandarin with English subtitles.
53-8146 Letterboxed *$29.99*

A Virtuous Widow (1997)
A young woman in a Northwest Chinese village is forced to choose between her undying love for an unconventional peddler and her loyalty to her father when he betroths her to a kind and gentle doctor. With Zhang Lu, Chang Rong, Li Wei. 96 min. In Mandarin with English subtitles.
53-6224 Letterboxed *$49.99*

Red Firecracker, Green Firecracker (1994)
A stunning and sensual drama, set in turn-of-the-century China, about a young woman who becomes the head of her family's fireworks factory because there is no male heir. Treated like a man and forbidden to marry, she is caught between her duty and her heart when she falls in love with a handsome artist. Ning Jing, Wu Gang star. 117 min. In Mandarin with English subtitles.
88-1028 Was $89.99 ▢*$19.99*

The Story Of Xinghua (1994)
Compelling drama about a crooked grocer and his put-upon wife, whom he beats, abuses and cheats on. When she falls in love with a sensitive, educated plantation worker and eventually becomes pregnant by him, her husband goes to great lengths to ruin both of their lives. Jiang Wenli stars. 89 min. In Mandarin with English subtitles.
88-1085 Was $94.99 *$19.99*

Red Cherry (1995)
This harrowing tale of survival tells the story of two Chinese orphans who struggle to live through the turmoil of the German invasion of Russia during World War II. Based upon true events, the film was China's highest-grossing film of 1996 and nominated for a Best Foreign Film Academy Award. Guo Ke-Yu, Xu Xiaoli star. 120 min. In Mandarin with English subtitles.
53-6183 Was $89.99 *$19.99*

Blush (1995)
In the aftermath of the Communist takeover of China in 1949, two Shanghai prostitutes who were co-workers and close friends find their lives taking very different, yet later intertwining, turns—turns centered around a wealthy young man attracted to both of them—in this lyrical drama based on a novel by Su Tong ("Raise the Red Lantern"). Wang Ji, He Saifei star. 119 min. In Cantonese with English subtitles.
70-5122 Was $79.99 *$29.99*

Women From The Lake Of Scented Souls (1995)
When her mentally ill son asks for a wife, a wealthy woman trapped in an unhappy marriage purchases a young peasant girl for him, just as she herself was sold away years earlier. Will she recognize the sad similarities between her life and her new daughter-in-law's in time to prevent history from repeating itself? Siqin Gaowa stars. 106 min. In Mandarin with English subtitles.
74-3017 *$89.99*

The Emperor's Shadow (Qin Song) (1996)
Set in feudal China's Qin dynasty, director Zhou Xiaowen's compelling drama focuses on two step-brothers who grow up to assume very different destinies: one as a brutal warlord attempting to unite the country, the other a musician who has an affair with the emperor's daughter. Ge You, Jiang Wen star. 123 min. In Mandarin with English subtitles.
53-6597 Was $89.99 *$19.99*

A Mongolian Tale (1996)
Set amid the vast wilderness of the Inner Mongolian steppes, this compelling Chinese drama follows an elderly woman who serves as surrogate mother to two orphaned children. When the youngsters mature, the woman hopes to have them marry, but the boy leaves to go to school and returns three years later to a very changed situation. Dalarsurong, Tengger star. 100 min. In Mongolian with English subtitles.
53-9913 *$89.99*

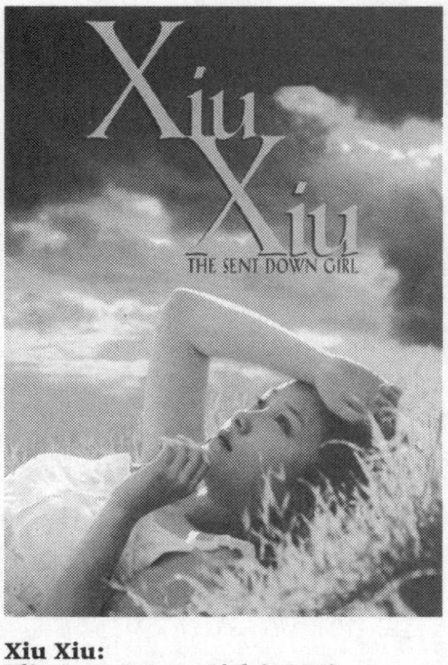

Xiu Xiu: The Sent Down Girl (1998)
The directorial debut of actress Joan Chen is a moving drama that was banned in China for its sexual and political content. The film is set in the early 1970s during the Chinese "Cultural Revolution," where a teenage girl is sent from her city home to isolated Tibet, where she falls in love with a horse trainer. After he leaves her, she attempts to get back home, but first must service a series of men that can help her. Lu Lu and Lopsang star. 100 min. In Mandarin with English subtitles.
83-1401 Was $99.99 *$14.99*

Red Sorghum (1988)
Exotically rendered epic from China, set during the 1930s invasion by Japan. A young woman arrives at a remote winery to marry the elderly vintner to whom she is betrothed, but enters into an affair with a servant and must suffer the consequences of her actions. Gong Li, Jiang Wen star in Zhang Yimou's fascinating, award-winning drama. 91 min. In Mandarin with English subtitles.
53-7628 *$89.99*

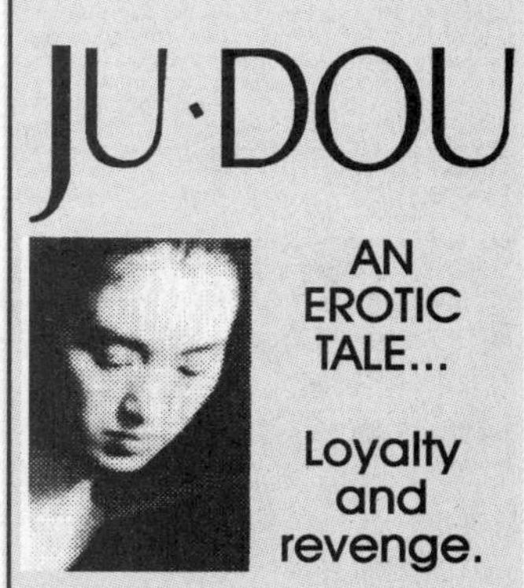

Ju Dou (1990)
A controversial 1990 Best Foreign Film Oscar nominee, this beautiful, politically charged drama, set in northern China in the '20s, tells the story of a young woman who is sold into marriage to an elderly tycoon. Eventually, she is secretly impregnated by his cowardly nephew, and, years later, her son uncovers the mystery of his birth. Directed by Zhang Yimou. 98 min. In Mandarin with English subtitles.
27-6725 Was $79.99 *$19.99*

Raise The Red Lantern (1991)
Set in Northern China in the 1920s, this drama from Zhang Yimou tells the story of a young woman (Gong Li) who leaves her hostile stepmother following her father's death and becomes the fourth wife of a wealthy patriarch. She soon realizes that rivalries exist between the other wives, one of whom is plotting to destroy her. 125 min. In Mandarin with English subtitles.
73-1124 Was $79.99 *$19.99*

The Story Of Qiu Ju (1992)
Highly acclaimed, ironic tale from director Zhang Yimou ("Raise the Red Lantern") concerning a Chinese woman's dogged quest for justice when her husband is beaten by the village elder. Gong Li and Lei Lao Sheng star in this powerful and darkly comic story of political hypocrisy. 100 min. In Mandarin with English subtitles.
02-2559 Was $89.99 *$19.99*

To Live (1994)
Acclaimed director Zhang Yimou chronicles the stormy, war-torn history of 20th-century China, as seen through the personal turmoils of one family through four generations, in this compelling and moving drama. Ge You, Gong Li star. 132 min. In Mandarin with English subtitles.
88-1011 Was $89.99 *$19.99*

Shanghai Triad (1995)
This exotic gangster epic from Zhang Yimou ("To Live") traces the inner workings of Shanghai's most prominent crime syndicate in the 1930s, as witnessed by a 14-year-old boy. When the boy becomes the servant for a promiscuous singer (and the crime boss's mistress), he learns of the cruelty and dealings of the Triad gangs. Gong Li stars. 109 min. In Mandarin with English subtitles.
02-2910 Was $94.99 *$24.99*

Not One Less (1999)
This change-of-pace effort from epic stylist Zhang Yimou ("Raise the Red Lantern") focuses on a 13-year-old girl who gets to serve as a substitute teacher in a village school when the schoolmaster is called to his mother's deathbed. A series of funny and moving episodes occur as the young instructor begins to excel at the job. With Wei Minzhi. 106 min. In Mandarin with English subtitles.
02-3451 *$99.99*

Frozen (1997)
Shot without government approval in 1994 and smuggled piecemeal out of the country, this unusual Chinese drama follows a performance artist's plans to make his death a work of art. Embedded in a block of ice, he'll melt it with his body heat until he dies from hypothermia. Based on a true story, filmmaker Wu Ming's (a pseudonym that translates to "no name") look at the repressed Chinese counterculture stars Jia Hongshen, Ma Xiaoqing. 95 min. In Mandarin with English subtitles.
53-6686 Was $89.99 *$19.99*

Begging Swordsman (1984)
A young apprentice swordsman is charged by his master to combat an evil criminal and his gang of henchmen. Unbeknownst to their master, however, the swordsman's classmate tags along under the guise of a beggar. Features Wong Ling and Yeung Ming. 123 min. In Cantonese with English subtitles.
53-9854 Letterboxed *$49.99*

Chow Yun Fat

The Postman Strikes Back (1981)
After four mercenaries discover that the cargo they've been hired to escort is actually stolen weapons on their way to an enemy trying to overthrow the government, they turn patriots to stop them. Action-packed thriller set in turn-of-the-century China (but filmed in Korea) stars Leung Kar Yan, Chow Yun Fat, Cherrie Cheung. In Cantonese with English subtitles.
53-9762 *$49.99*

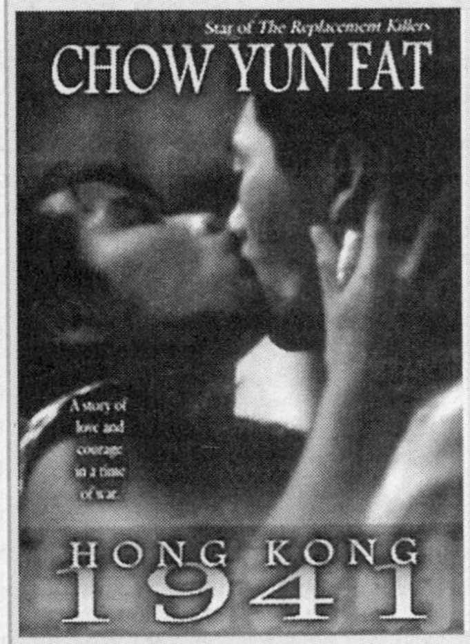

Hong Kong 1941 (1984)
International sensation Chow Yun Fat stars in this tragic love story set in war-torn Hong Kong on the eve of the Japanese invasion in 1941. Chow and Alex Man both fall in love with terminally ill Cecilia Yip, who was saved from the streets by Chow. 118 min. In Cantonese with English subtitles.
53-5035 Letterboxed *$59.99*

Hong Kong 1941 (Dubbed Version)
Also available in a dubbed-in-English edition.
53-5034 Letterboxed *$59.99*

Tragic Hero (1987)
Chow Yun Fat excels as Chi, a Hong Kong gangster who faces brutal retaliation from Yung (Alex Man), the brother he overlooked when he chose his other sibling as head of his operations years earlier. Chi's plans to retire are threatened when Yung follows him to his retreat. With Danny Lee, Andy Lau. 96 min. In Cantonese with English subtitles.
53-6916 Letterboxed *$19.99*

An Autumn's Tale (1987)
This change of pace for action hero Chow Yun Fat finds him as a streetwise New York cab driver helping out his pretty young cousin, who has come to the city to study acting. Cherie Chung and Danny Chan also star. 98 min. In Cantonese with English subtitles.
53-8477 *$49.99*

City On Fire (1987)
An explosive action excursion from Hong Kong starring Chow Yun Fat as an undercover cop set on stopping a motley band of jewel thieves. Ringo Lam called the shots to this riveting story that's been called the inspiration for Quentin Tarantino's "Reservoir Dogs." 100 min. In Cantonese with English subtitles.
53-9388 Was $69.99 *$49.99*

Code Of Honor (1987)
Hong Kong underworld saga featuring Chow Yun Fat as the son of a gang leader who is mysteriously assassinated after one of his underlings squeals on him. Chow returns to the city from Australia to unite with his brother and keep the Japanese mob from moving in. With Mei Fei-Lung, Danny Lee. AKA: "The Brotherhood." 90 min. In Cantonese with English subtitles.
53-9755 *$49.99*

Rich And Famous (1987)
The prequel to "Tragic Hero" features Chow Yun Fat as a gang chief out to avenge those responsible for the death of his brother. At the same time, Chow falls for a pretty woman whom he wishes to marry, but will his rivals disrupt his wedding plans? With Andy Lau, Danny Lee. 104 min. In Cantonese with English subtitles.
53-9765 Was $49.99 *$19.99*

City War (1988)
Hong Kong action hero Chow Yun Fat is a policeman who teams with Ti Lung to try to stop a maniacal drug dealer recently freed from prison. Spectacular action and Chow at his coolest are the highlights of this Far Eastern thriller. 96 min. In Cantonese with English subtitles.
53-8499 *$49.99*

Wild Search (1989)
Loner cop Chow Yun Fat's investigation into gun-running in rural Hong Kong leads him to a crime victim's 4-year-old daughter, a witness in her mother's death. While Chow falls for the girl's aunt and tries to bond with her craggy grandpa, he faces the evil criminals and their hit man. Directed by Ringo Lam ("Full Contact"). 98 min. In Cantonese with English subtitles.
53-9807 *$49.99*

Inside Story (1990)
A young man tries to escape his past with the underworld, but finds himself drawn back into the world of the Triads when his father is killed in a brutal power struggle. Chow Yun Fat stars in a story of power, loyalty and betrayal. 94 min. In Cantonese with English subtitles.
53-9789 *$49.99*

Prison On Fire II (1991)
This sequel to the action hit finds hardened prisoner Chow Yun Fat trying to keep an uneasy peace between Mainland Chinese and Hong Kong inmate factions. But when a sadistic guard murders a Hong Kong prisoner and frames another inmate for the crime, Chow is branded as an informer and must fight to survive. Chen Sung Yung also stars in this Ringo Lam film. In Cantonese with English subtitles.
53-8428 Letterboxed *$49.99*

Full Contact (1993)
In this rousing action yarn from director Ringo Lam ("City on Fire"), Chow Yun Fat plays a bouncer and sometime thief working out of a Bangkok nightclub who joins a pal in a hijacking scheme involving a ruthless, flamboyant crook named Judge. But Chow and his friend are duped by Judge and his gang, and soon find themselves in a blazing battle of wills. 96 min. In Cantonese with English subtitles.
53-8429 *$49.99*

Treasure Hunt (1994)
Lively comic thriller with Chow Yun Fat as a CIA agent in China who infiltrates a Shaolin temple in order to stop a smuggling ring. During his assignment, Chow falls in love with a holy woman who has supernatural powers. Wu Chien Lien and Roy Chiao star. 105 min. In Cantonese with English subtitles.
53-6860 *$19.99*

God Of Gamblers 2 (1994)
Rousing sequel to the popular Hong Kong hit finds ace gambler Chow Yun Fat enjoying a peaceful retirement in France until his pregnant wife is murdered by a jealous rival. Chow's road to revenge leads from Mainland China to Taiwan, as he looks after an orphan boy, befriends a band of petty thieves, and meets his nemesis head-on at cards. 124 min. In Cantonese with English subtitles.
53-8464 Letterboxed *$49.99*

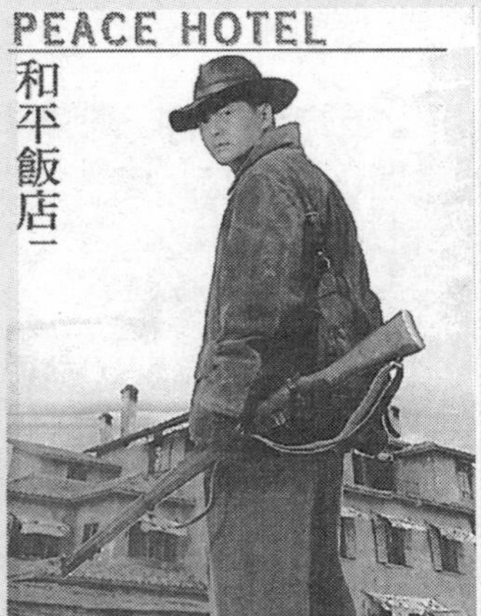

Peace Hotel (1995)
Inspired by American westerns, this stunning John Woo production (his last Hong Kong effort) stars Chow Yun Fat as a former killer in the 1920s who opens a remote desert hotel for fugitives seeking protection. When a female swindler wanted for murdering her boss connives her way in, Chow finds himself facing a gang looking for his new guest. With Cecilia Yip. In Cantonese with English subtitles.
53-8465 Letterboxed *$49.99*

Please see our index for these other Chow Yun Fat titles: *A Better Tomorrow I-III • Anna And The King • The Corrupter • Hard Boiled • The Killer • Once A Thief • The Replacement Killers*

Aces Go Places II (1983)
Freewheeling jewel thief Sam Hui and policeman partner Karl Maka reunite in a thriller filled with death-defying stunts, Keystone Kops-style shenanigans and hip spy humor. The plot? King Kong and Baldy go against Clint Eastwood lookalike "Filthy Harry" and a Henry Kissinger clone. AKA: "Mad Mission 2." 100 min. In Cantonese with English subtitles.
53-9380 *$49.99*

Aces Go Places III: Our Man From Bond Street (1984)
A James Bond look-alike and Peter Graves are featured in director Tsui Hark's entry in the popular action-comedy series. Heroes King Kong (Sam Hui) and Baldy (Karl Maka) battle international spies and villains intent on stealing England's Crown Jewels. With Richard Kiel ("Jaws" from the 007 series) and an "Oddjob"-type character. AKA: "Mad Mission 3." 96 min. In Cantonese with English subtitles.
53-9810 *$49.99*

Aces Go Places 4 (1986)
The fourth entry in this popular series finds King Kong and Baldy trying to thwart international spies in New Zealand and Hong Kong who are trying to recover a "brain prism" that can impart super-intelligence and psychic powers to the user. Sam Hui, Karl Maka and Sally Yeh star; directed by Ringo Lam. In Cantonese with English subtitles.
53-9780 *$49.99*

Aces Go Places V: The Teracotta Hit (1990)
It looks like the end of Sam Hui and Karl Maka's partnership—that is, until they're framed for the theft of priceless antique treasures and must work together to deal with Hong Kong and Mainland Chinese authorities, mobsters and the real crooks. Conan Lee, Leslie Cheung and Nina Li Chi also star. 103 min. In Cantonese with English subtitles.
53-6229 *$49.99*

Lethal Panther (1990)
Sibelle Hu is beautiful agent Betty Lee in this sexy, hair-raising actioner in which she attempts to stop the nasty Chinese leader of the toughest Filipino gang in the world while battling a Japanese hit woman. With Yoko Miyamato. 90 min. Dubbed in English.
53-8884 *$14.99*

Lethal Panther 2 (1992)
In this sequel, Yukari Oshima plays an Interpol agent who joins forces with a Hong Kong police inspector and a bitter Filipino cop to halt a Yakuza crime boss operating out of Manila. With Carina Lau. 88 min. Dubbed in English.
53-8885 *$14.99*

Swordsman (1990)
Rousing period adventure from producer Tsui Hark and director King Hu (among others) details the exploits of Fox, a Ming Dynasty sword expert, who gets help from an older warrior in finding a priceless scroll. While on his quest, Fox comes into contact with strange musical instruments and lethal swordswomen. With Sam Hui, Cecilia Yip, Jacky Cheung. In Cantonese with English subtitles.
53-9770 Letterboxed *$49.99*

Swordsman II (1991)
Jet Li takes over the role of the young blademaster in this furious, stunt-filled sequel. Li and his fellow students are out to recover the magical Sacred Scroll, stolen by an evil sorcerer who castrates himself to use their power and is slowly changing into a woman! With Rosamund Kwan, Lau Shin, and Brigitte Lin as the transgendered Asia the Invincible. In Cantonese with English subtitles.
53-8455 *$49.99*

The East Is Red (1993)
Sex-changed sorceress Brigitte Lin turns on her feminine charms and macho heroism in the third "Swordsman" saga, fighting off Japanese and Spanish invaders while searching for her true identity. The film is highlighted by incredible martial arts sequences and a bizarre relationship between Lin and former female lover Joey Wong, who has adopted Lin's old masculine persona. In Cantonese with English subtitles.
53-9771 Letterboxed *$49.99*

The Swordsman Saga Collection
All three films in Tsui Hark's action-packed "Swordsman" trilogy, "Swordsman," "Swordsman II" and "The East Is Red," are also available in a collector's set.
53-9772 Save $70.00! *$79.99*

18 Shaolin Golden Boys (1996)
Treasure hunters seeking Chinese national artifacts discover a stash hidden in the old Shaolin Temple. To find it, the hunters must recover a map that has been separated into three pieces, but that job is easier said than done. Yu Rong Guang stars. 90 min. In Cantonese with English subtitles.
53-9799 *$49.99*

Bloody Friday (1996)
As his name implies, the "Friday Killer" strikes only on the sixth day of the week and all of his victims are call girls. Can Inspector Hung stop the killing spree—even at the cost of losing his family? Simon Yam stars. 94 min. In Cantonese with English subtitles.
53-9794 Letterboxed *$49.99*

Killer Has No Return (1996)
A professional killer attends a wedding to rub out the unsuspecting groom, but before he can do his job, another wedding guest is murdered. In the ensuing chaos, the "innocent" assassin is framed for the murder, and soon finds himself the target of a police and gangland manhunt. Wang Xi stars in this Hong Kong actioner. 90 min. In Cantonese with English subtitles.
53-8991 *$49.99*

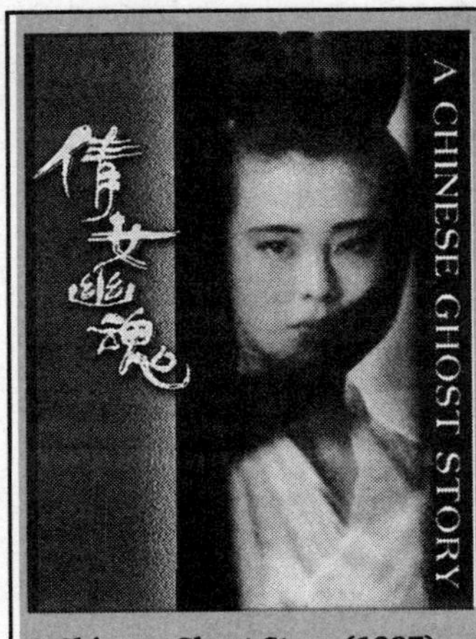

A Chinese Ghost Story (1987)
Fascinating supernatural story focusing on the relationship between a young tax collector and a seductive female ghost he meets in a haunted temple. The young man joins a Taoist hermit to storm the gates of Hell in order to bring the girl to human form. Horror, farce and special effects mix; Leslie Cheung, Wong Tse Hsien star. 93 min. In Cantonese with English subtitles.
53-9387 *$49.99*

Chinese Ghost Story, Part II (1990)
The fantastic series continues, as four teenagers, led by Leslie Cheung's Ning, find themselves in the middle of a nasty, supernatural war between an evil wizard and a corrupt general. The teens encounter decomposing corpses, a demon posing as a Buddha, a Taoist swordsman and a ferocious monster. In Cantonese with English subtitles.
53-8498 *$49.99*

A Chinese Ghost Story 3 (1990)
Tsui Hark's third entry in the popular series takes place 100 years after the Tree Devil has been defeated by ghost killers in China. An elderly priest and his young protégé's journey through the countryside to recover a golden Buddha is disrupted by the return of the Tree Devil and a series of ghostly happenings. Tony Leung stars. 109 min. In Cantonese with English subtitles.
53-6896 *$49.99*

A Chinese Ghost Story: The Tsui Hark Animation (1997)
A dazzling blend of anime-style characters and computer-generated animation, turning the popular 1987 Hong Kong film into a feature-length cartoon adventure. A young man's debt-collecting trip takes a detour into a town of ghosts, where he meets a beautiful spirit. Will their otherworldly romance survive the ghost's soul-sucking mistress and a pair of feuding exorcists? 83 min.
85-1327 *$19.99*

Dangerous Duty (1996)
A police crackdown on an illegal cigarette smuggling ring goes sour when the only witness becomes the target of a professional killer. It's up to Hong Kong's finest to track the cold-blooded assassin while they try to protect the witness from any harm. Max Mok stars. 90 min. In Cantonese with English subtitles.
53-8994 *$49.99*

The Wild Couple (1996)
A Triad leader is stripped of $6,000,000 by a pair of inept cons and left for dead. They escape before the cops arrive, kidnapping the daughter of a rich couple in the process, then go on the lam with gangsters and the police on their trail. Roy Cheung stars. 97 min. In Cantonese with English subtitles.
53-9844 *$49.99*

The Great Jetfoil Robbery (1996)
A shipment of $10 million in transit by jetfoil to Hong Kong is seized by armed thieves who redirect the boat to a secret island hideout and vanish without a trace, leaving the Hong Kong and Macau police scrambling to solve the case. Tony Chun Chung stars. 82 min. In Cantonese with English subtitles.
53-9845 *$49.99*

Banana Club (1996)
No, it's not a club that loves Hanna-Barbera TV characters. It's the name of a group of disc jockeys on a popular radio show who dispense logic on love and other matters over the airwaves. Michael Chow and Tam Siu Wan star in this comedy that's fun-fe-fun-fun. 96 min. In Cantonese with English subtitles.
53-9846 Letterboxed *$49.99*

Robotrix (1991)
In this wild sex-and-sci-fi actioner, a deranged scientist transfers his mind into an android body and goes on a brutal rampage of rape and murder. A policewoman who is killed trying to stop the rampaging robot is brought back to life as a rather voluptuous android in order to help corral the high-tech criminal. Amy Yip, Chikako Aoyama star. 99 min. Dubbed in English.
20-8621 Letterboxed *$24.99*

Mission To Kill (1984)
The amazing Simon Yam stars in this fast and furious actioner detailing a jewelry robbery carried out by a group of highly skilled smugglers. When one of the crooks has the gems stolen from his associates, the others use force to get him. The problem worsens when the police get involved in the proceedings. Norman Tsui also stars. 92 min. Dubbed in English.
53-9967 *$14.99*

Tiger Cage (1988)
This Hong Kong policier was directed by Yuen Wo Ping, stunt coordinator for "The Matrix." There's mucho macho action as two cops battling the drug trade discover some of their associates on the force are involved in cocaine-smuggling proceedings. Jacky Cheung, Donnie Yern and Simon Yam star. In Cantonese with English subtitles.
53-6506 *$49.99*

Killer's Romance (1989)
Simon Yam is the son of a Japanese Triad boss who is assassinated by a rival Chinese mobster. Yam takes personal vengeance against the killers, but his involvement with a beautiful artist he must eliminate could jeopardize his mission—and his life—in this bullet-riddled thriller, loosely based on the Japanese comic book "Crying Freeman." With Joey Wang. 91 min. Dubbed in English.
53-9841 *$14.99*

Mission Kill (1991)
Double- and triple-crosses are the norm in this wild actioner in which private detective Moon Lee becomes a target of Colombian drug lords after she helps Interpol break a cocaine operation in Southeast Asia. Simon Yam is an FBI agent assigned to guard her, but his true mission could cost Lee her life. Dubbed in English.
53-9842 *$14.99*

Man Wanted (1995)
Explosive Hong Kong police saga featuring "Full Contact's" Simon Yam as an undercover cop on the trail of a notorious drug smuggler. Yam believes the crime kingpin was killed in a sting operation, but gets a big surprise when he reappears, setting the stage for a showdown in Hong Kong's seedy Mongkok district. With Yu Rong Guang. 92 min. In Cantonese with English subtitles.
53-8600 Letterboxed *$19.99*

Man Wanted (Dubbed Version)
Also available in a dubbed-in-English edition.
53-8905 Letterboxed *$19.99*

Scarred Memory (1996)
Vicious criminal Simon Yam is injured in a skirmish and finds himself in the hospital with amnesia. To complicate matters, the physician assigned to care for Yam is a rape victim that the criminal assaulted in the past. 90 min. In Cantonese with English subtitles.
53-9843 *$49.99*

Yes Madam 5 (1996)
Hong Kong police inspector Cynthia Khan finds her on-again, off-again relationship with her gangster boyfriend tested when they're on the trail of a missing computer disc containing incriminating Triad evidence. With Chin Siu-Hour. 90 min. In Cantonese with English subtitles.
53-9798 Letterboxed *$49.99*

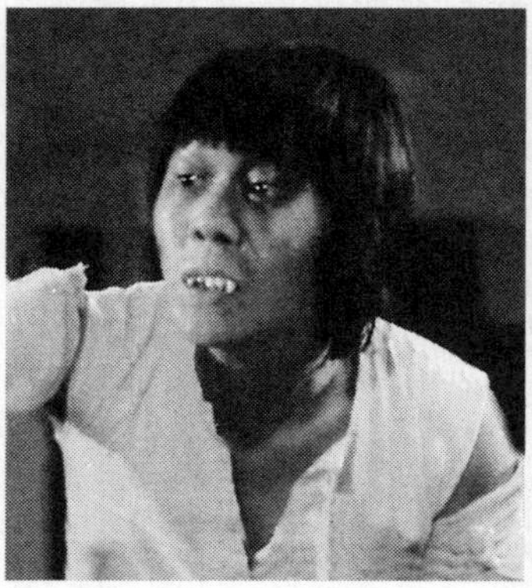

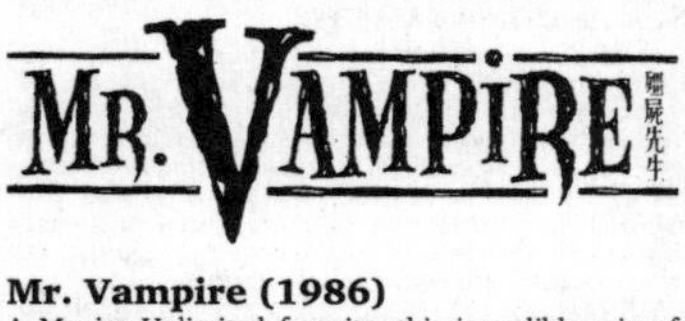

Mr. Vampire (1986)
A Movies Unlimited favorite, this incredible mix of horror, martial arts and slapstick comedy from Hong Kong spawned several sequels. A greedy businessman's father dies and comes back as a yellow-fanged ghoul, and a vampire-hunter and his two bumbling aides must stop him. And we haven't even mentioned the hopping zombies! Lam Ching Ying stars; (Ricky) Lau Chang Wei directs. 94 min. In Cantonese with English subtitles.
53-9407 Letterboxed *$19.99*

Mr. Vampire (Dubbed Version)
Also available in a dubbed-in-English edition.
53-6564 Letterboxed *$19.99*

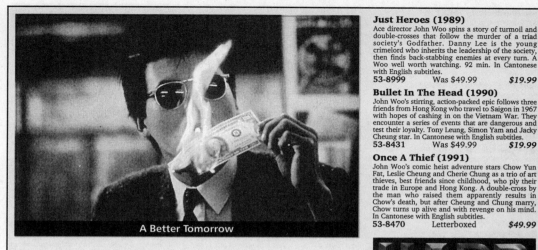

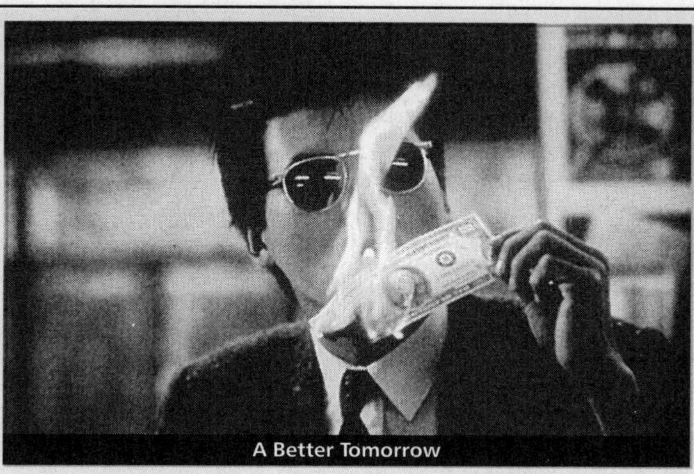
A Better Tomorrow

John Woo

Last Hurrah For Chivalry (1978)
This early John Woo effort is a period actioner about Kao, a man who seeks assistance from two swordsmen in an effort to defend his family from a ruthless enemy. But the swordsmen soon discover that Kao has another plan, and their friendship with him is tested. With Wei Pei and Damian Lau. 108 min. In Cantonese with English subtitles.
53-8876 Letterboxed *$19.99*

Last Hurrah For Chivalry (Dubbed Version)
Also available in a dubbed-in-English edition.
53-8877 Letterboxed *$19.99*

Heroes Shed No Tears (1985)
John Woo's first modern action outing is a slam-bang saga set in "the Golden Triangle," where the Thailand government hires a group of mercenaries to capture a drug-smuggling Army general. The action really starts after the capture occurs, and the soldiers-of-fortune have to make it through the perilous jungle. Eddy Ko, Lam Ching-Ying star. 93 min. In Cantonese with English subtitles.
53-9940 Letterboxed *$19.99*

Heroes Shed No Tears (Dubbed Version)
Also available in a dubbed-in-English edition.
53-9941 Letterboxed *$19.99*

A Better Tomorrow (1986)
Masterful thriller from leading Hong Kong filmmaker John Woo ("The Killer") tells the saga of three friends who run a successful counterfeiting ring. When one is sent to prison, his partner becomes more ruthless when he takes over the operation. Highlighted by stunning action sequences; with Chow Yun Fat, Ti Lung and Leslie Cheung. 95 min. In Cantonese with English subtitles.
53-9392 *$49.99*

A Better Tomorrow III (1988)
The third installment in the action series follows Chow Yun Fat to Saigon, where he hopes to use a cache of cash to rescue his captive uncle and cousin. While in Vietnam, Chow meets a gunslinging, gang-leading beauty whom he recruits to help him. Anita Mui, Tony Leung also star; directed by Tsui Hark and produced by John Woo. 114 min. In Cantonese with English subtitles.
53-8430 *$49.99*

A Better Tomorrow, Part II (1988)
Dynamite sequel to the hit actioner focuses on the twin brother of the original's leading character as he teams with a female cop and a reformed crook to battle a group of tough criminals. Featuring an audacious shoot-out finale, John Woo's film pays homage to Sergio Leone and American gangsters in an intoxicating style. With Chow Yun Fat and Leslie Cheung. 100 min. In Cantonese with English subtitles.
53-9393 *$49.99*

The Killer (1989)
One of the most astounding action movies ever produced, John Woo's electrifying crime drama focuses on an assassin-for-hire who agrees to do one more job in order to pay for the operation of a beautiful singer he accidentally blinded. Filled with wild shoot-outs, surprising humor and schmaltzy melodrama, the film stars Chow Yun Fat, Danny Lee and Sally Yeh. 111 min. In Cantonese with English subtitles.
53-7693 Was $19.99 *$14.99*

The Killer (Letterboxed Version)
The subtitled version is also available in a theatrical, widescreen format.
53-8908 Was $19.99 *$14.99*

The Killer (Dubbed Version)
Also available in a dubbed-in-English edition.
53-7694 Was $19.99 *$14.99*

Just Heroes (1989)
Ace director John Woo spins a story of turmoil and double-crosses that follow the murder of a triad society's Godfather. Danny Lee is the young crimelord who inherits the leadership of the society, then finds back-stabbing enemies at every turn. A Woo well worth watching. 92 min. In Cantonese with English subtitles.
53-8999 Was $49.99 *$19.99*

Bullet In The Head (1990)
John Woo's stirring, action-packed epic follows three friends from Hong Kong who travel to Saigon in 1967 with hopes of cashing in on the Vietnam War. They encounter a series of events that are dangerous and test their loyalty. Tony Leung, Simon Yam and Jacky Cheung star. In Cantonese with English subtitles.
53-8431 Was $49.99 *$19.99*

Once A Thief (1991)
John Woo's comic heist adventure stars Chow Yun Fat, Leslie Cheung and Cherie Chung as a trio of art thieves, best friends since childhood, who ply their trade in Europe and Hong Kong. A double-cross by the man who raised them apparently results in Chow's death, but after Cheung and Chung marry, Chow turns up alive and with revenge on his mind. In Cantonese with English subtitles.
53-8470 Letterboxed *$49.99*

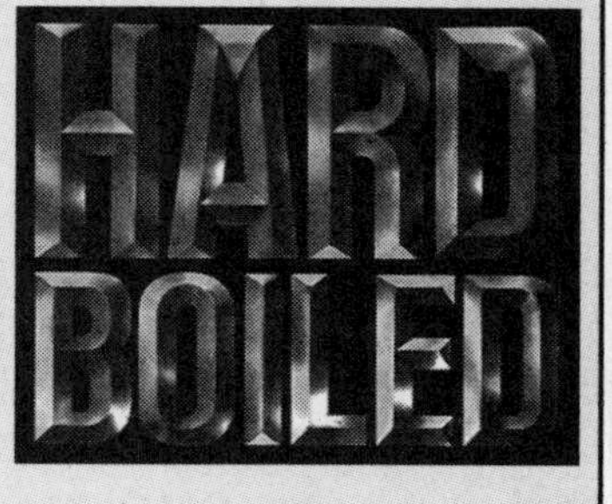

Hard Boiled (1992)
After his partner is killed in a shoot-out with a gun-smuggling ring, a veteran police inspector (Chow Yun Fat) reluctantly teams up with a maverick undercover cop (Tony Leung) to bring the mobsters down. Director John Woo takes the action genre to new heights in this bullet-riddled thriller that climaxes with an unbelievable showdown in a hospital. 127 min. In Cantonese with English subtitles.
53-8154 Letterboxed *$14.99*

Hard Boiled (Dubbed Version)
Also available in a dubbed-in-English edition.
53-8011 Was $19.99 *$14.99*

The John Woo Collection
A double-shot of Hong Kong action auteur John Woo is available in this boxed set that includes "The Killer" and "Hard Boiled." In Cantonese with English subtitles.
53-8525 Save $10.00! *$29.99*

The John Woo Collection (Dubbed Version)
Also available in a dubbed-in-English edition.
53-8526 Save $10.00! *$29.99*

Please see our index for these other John Woo titles: *Blackjack* • *Broken Arrow* • *Face/Off* • *Hard Target* • *Mission: Impossible 2* • *Once A Thief*

The Intruder (1981)
After he discovers that his mother has been killed, a young man goes berserk and takes the law into his own hands to seek revenge. Liu Yen Fang and Chou Tui Fang star. In Cantonese with English subtitles.
53-6697 *$49.99*

The Thundering Sword (1967)
This Shaw Brothers production spotlights astonishing swordplay as it tells the story of the quest for an invincible blade used to slaughter the members of a righteous clan. The search also leads to a swordsman with incredible skills who may hold the secret to the weapon. With Cheng Pei Pei, Sui Pui Pui. In Cantonese with English subtitles.
53-6308 *$49.99*

Snake Deadly Act (1979)
Classic martial arts thriller about the trouble-addicted son of a tycoon who gets in all sorts of hot water with a local casino boss. The young man is trained by a mysterious fighter in the art of snake first fighting, but is soon shocked to discover that his father is involved in sleazy dealings. Wilson Tong (who also directed), Ng Kun Lung star. 90 min. In Cantonese with English subtitles.
54-9153 Letterboxed *$19.99*

The Miracle Fighters (1982)
Offbeat martial arts comedy/fantasy from Yuen Wo Ping, fight choreographer for "The Matrix." The evil Sorcerer Bat has a scheme to sieze power by passing off a young man as the prince who was kidnapped years earlier. When his guardian is killed, the pseudo-prince looks to two aged masters to teach him super-natural fighting skills. Yuen Yat, Yuen Shun star. 92 min. In Cantonese with English subtitles.
53-6507 *$49.99*

Date In Portland Street (1996)
A struggling art student decides to leave Hong Kong and study overseas, even though he will have to leave his devoted wife behind. Two years later, they reunite in a cheap motel room in Hong Kong's Mongkok district. It's there they realize that love doesn't conquer all. 119 min. In Cantonese with English subtitles.
53-9851 Letterboxed *$49.99*

Young And Dangerous 2 (1996)
A group of reckless hoods from Hong Kong's mean streets who have risen in the Triad underworld find themselves battling Taiwanese gangsters and crooked politicians in this fast and furious actioner from Hong Kong. Jordan Chan, Anthony Wang star. 100 min. In Cantonese with English subtitles.
53-9959 Letterboxed *$49.99*

Beyond Hypothermia (1996)
Unusual action thriller from Patrick Leung, former assistant to John Woo. Wu Chien Lien is a beautiful assassin who is literally an ice-cold killer since her body temperature never rises above 32° Celsius. She begins a relationship with a chef, but her dangerous line of work keeps getting in the way of leading a normal life. 95 min. In Cantonese with English subtitles.
76-2092 Letterboxed *$24.99*

Intruder (1997)
And they say a good woman is hard to find these days... A drop-dead beautiful woman (no pun intended) begins a road trip of cold-blooded murder throughout China to Hong Kong, all in the name of love for her criminal husband. With Wu Chien Lien, Lai Yiu Cheung and Moses Chan. 87 min. In Cantonese with English subtitles.
53-6222 Letterboxed *$79.99*

Best Of The Best (1996)
A rookie cop fresh out of the police academy encounters a Vietnamese assassin on his first day of work. Determined to take the hit man down, he joins the Special Duties Unit, where he must prove his mettle to himself, his superiors and his stepbrother, a fellow cop and SDU trainee. With Jackie Cheung. 97 min. In Cantonese with English subtitles.
53-8992 Letterboxed *$49.99*

Tai Chi II (1996)
An astonishing amalgamation of adventure, martial arts sequences and romance, this saga tells of a young Tai Chi master who goes against evil British merchants involved in China's opium trade and also must face jealous suitors in order to win the hand of a pretty revolutionary. With Jacky Wu and Christy Chung. 95 min. In Cantonese with English subtitles.
53-8651 Letterboxed *$19.99*

Tai Chi II (Dubbed Version)
Also available in a dubbed-in-English edition.
53-6910 Letterboxed *$19.99*

Duel To The Death (1982)
Set during the Ming Dynasty, this swordplay spectacle tells of a duel that's fought in China every 10 years, pitting a Japanese ninja against a Shaolin warrior. When a scroll containing martial arts secrets is swiped, the contest takes on new meaning to the participants. Damian Lau, Flora Cheung star. 90 min. In Cantonese with English subtitles.
53-8842 Letterboxed *$19.99*

Duel To The Death (Dubbed Version)
Also available in a dubbed-in-English edition.
53-8843 Letterboxed *$19.99*

Angel's Mission (1988)
Interpol agent Yukari Oshima is called on to investigate a Hong Kong prostitution ring, cutting her vacation short. While trying to gather clues for the case, she discovers that her own mother is the main madam of the ring. Shoot-outs, martial arts battles and lively action sequences ensue in this "Angel" outing. With Ron Van Lee. 95 min. Dubbed in English.
53-9775 *$14.99*

Angel Of Kickboxer (1989)
A social worker teams with a no-nonsense Hong Kong police detective to try to thwart a nasty loan shark's plan to rob a local goldsmith. The action comes fast and furious with Yukari Oshima as the martial arts expert heroine; John Lam and David Koh also star. 100 min. Dubbed in English.
53-9773 *$14.99*

Angel The Kick Boxer (1993)
A ruthless band of international criminals serves as a punching bag for heroic supercop Yukari Oshima in this Hong Kong martial arts action flick. Along for the ride are Pauline Chan, Wong Chi Yeung and Cynthia Rothrock (in scenes from her film "Honor and Glory"). 91 min. In Cantonese with English subtitles.
53-6235 *$49.99*

Angel On Fire (1995)
Guns, kicks and gorgeous Cynthia Khan showcase this Hong Kong action confection in which an unscrupulous supermodel double-crosses a group of hoods and steals a priceless relic. Hot on her trail are an Interpol agent, who's helped by a comical cabby. Waise Lee and Yeung Pan Pan also star. 87 min. Dubbed in English.
53-9774 *$14.99*

The Assassin (1993)
Stunning martial arts epic is set in the 18th century, as a farmer, accused of kidnapping his girlfriend, is sent to prison and has his eyes sewn shut! In order to be released, he must fight seven prisoners, then serve a band of killers as their master swordsman. With Zhang Feng Yi, Rosamund Kwan. 95 min. In Cantonese with English subtitles.
76-2091 Letterboxed *$24.99*

Taxi Hunter (1993)
Anthony Wong is an insurance salesman who goes on a one-man revenge spree when his pregnant wife dies after a cab driver refuses to take her to the hospital. Wong decides to act as judge, jury and executioner, targeting Hong Kong's taxi drivers. With Yu Rong Guang. 95 min. In Cantonese with English subtitles.
76-7475 Letterboxed *$24.99*

Ashes Of Time (1994)
This effort from "Chungking Express" director Wong Kar-Wai is a complex period story set on Mainland China and starring Leslie Cheung as a middleman who hires swordsman Tony Leung for killings. Trouble brews when Cheung is hired to kill Leung by the brother of a woman he jilted. And that's just a portion of the proceedings! 95 min. In Cantonese with English subtitles.
76-2090 Letterboxed *$29.99*

Burning Paradise (1994)
Fong Sai Yuk and Hong Kei Koon, two fabled Chinese heroes, team in this exhilarating historical actioner that finds them trying to help a group of monks escape a forbidden, booby trap-filled fortress overseen by a religious zealot and his fighting followers. Lee Tian San and Willie Kwai star; Ringo Lam ("City on Fire") directs. In Cantonese with English subtitles.
53-5885 Letterboxed *$19.99*

Michelle Yeoh

Royal Warriors (1986)
Michelle Khan (Yeoh) turns in a dynamic performance in this awesome actioner, playing an undercover Hong Kong cop whose Japanese partner's wife and child are killed by crooks in retaliation for the deaths of their colleagues. Together the cops set out on their own campaign of revenge. With Hiroyuki Sanada. AKA: "In The Line of Duty." 85 min. In Cantonese with English subtitles.
53-9768 Letterboxed *$59.99*

Royal Warriors (Dubbed Version)
Also available in a dubbed-in-English edition.
53-9890 Letterboxed *$59.99*

Magnificent Warriors (1987)
Action star Michelle Yeoh brings her deadly charms and daredevil stunts to this action-packed thriller, portraying a pilot and spy for China fighting against the Japanese during World War II. Her mission: rescue a heroic Chinese leader from the hands of a ruthless Japanese general and his advancing army. Don't get in Yeoh's way. 92 min. In Chinese with English subtitles.
53-5032 Letterboxed *$19.99*

Magnificent Warriors (Dubbed Version)
Also available in a dubbed-in-English edition.
53-5033 Letterboxed *$19.99*

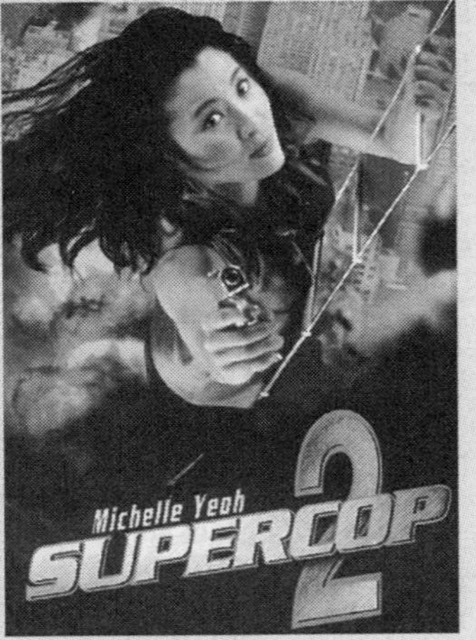

Supercop 2 (1992)
Reprising her role in "Police Story 3," Michelle Yeoh plays a tough Mainland Chinese police officer who heads to Hong Kong to stop a group of jewel thieves from her native land. Complications arise when Yeoh finds out her ex-boyfriend is among the crooks. Features tremendous stunts and a cameo appearance (in drag!) by Jackie Chan. AKA: "Once a Cop," "Project S." 94 min. Dubbed in English.
11-2369 Was $99.99 *$14.99*

The Heroic Trio (1992)
Furious action and fantasy mix as three rival Hong Kong superbabes unite to combat a powerful wizard who's kidnapping newborn babies. There's Wonder Woman, a martial arts expert who runs across telephone wires; Chat, the leather-clad, cycle-riding "Thief Catcher"; and the mysterious Invisible Girl. Maggie Cheung, Anita Mui and Michelle Yeoh star. 112 min. In Cantonese with English subtitles.
53-8463 Letterboxed *$19.99*

The Heroic Trio (Dubbed Version)
Also available in a dubbed-in-English edition.
53-6452 Letterboxed *$19.99*

Executioners (1995)
The rip-roaring sequel to "The Heroic Trio" finds Wonder Woman, Thief Catcher and Invisible Girl facing off against the evil, masked Black Knight, who is controlling the sparse supply of uncontaminated water after a nuclear explosion. Maggie Cheung, Michelle Yeoh and Anita Mui star. 100 min. In Cantonese with English subtitles.
53-9727 Letterboxed *$19.99*

Butterfly Sword (1993)
Set in feudal China, this unpredictable tale of court intrigue and martial arts madness follows two rival eunuch "uncles," a powerful lady and her two helpers, and a letter that will reveal a traitor out to overthrow the Ming Dynasty. Featuring spectacular aerial fight sequences, the film stars Michelle Khan and was helmed by Ching Siu-Tung of "Swordsman" fame. AKA: "Comet, Butterfly and Sword." 86 min. In Cantonese with English subtitles.
53-9804 *$49.99*

Comet, Butterfly And Sword (Dubbed Version)
"Butterfly Sword" is also available in a dubbed-in-English edition.
82-7007 *$39.99*

Wonder Seven (1994)
Director Ching Siu-Tung ("A Chinese Ghost Story") transposes the fantasy martial arts of the "Swordsman" series into the urban sprawl of a John Woo epic in this story of a group of secret agents assigned to keep the peace in pre-Communist Hong Kong. Stars Michelle Yeoh and Hung Yan-Yan ("Double Team"). 90 min. In Cantonese with English subtitles.
53-8998 *$79.99*

Wing Chun (1995)
Michelle Yeoh stars as Wing Chun, a woman who invents her own special brand of kung fu to defeat bandits and scare men away in this period action-comedy. Filled with stunning and often hilarious fight sequences, this fast-paced film showcases one of China's top female stars as one of Asia's earliest independent women. 93 min. In Cantonese with English subtitles.
53-8462 Letterboxed *$19.99*

Please see our index for these other Michelle Yeoh titles: *Supercop • Tomorrow Never Dies • Twin Warriors*

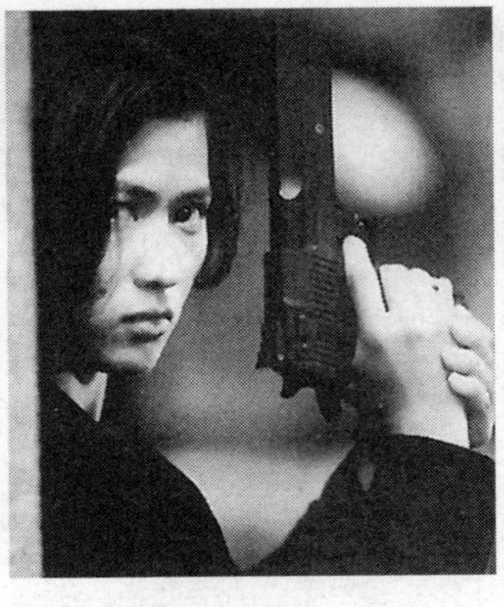

Black Cat (1991)
In this reworking of "La Femme Nikita," Jade Leung plays the reckless young woman turned into an emotionless, mini-skirt-wearing assassin through a microchip implanted in her skull and training by a secret government operative. Simon Yam also stars. In Cantonese with English subtitles.
53-8496 *$19.99*

Black Cat 2 (1992)
Exciting sequel to the hit Hong Kong confection features Jade Leung as a sexy government hit woman who has her memory erased in order to serve as bodyguard for Russian Prime Minister Boris Yeltsin, who's targeted by assassins. Robin Shou Wan-Bo also stars in this action-packed film. In Cantonese with English subtitles.
53-8502 *$49.99*

Iron Monkey (1993)
Amazing flying stunts highlight an enthralling historical actioner in which a doctor disguises himself as the Robin Hood-like bandit "Iron Monkey" at night to help his townspeople. A well-meaning monk who has become friendly with the doctor is blackmailed into finding the mysterious Monkey. Yo Rong-Guang stars in this action classic. 86 min. In Cantonese with English subtitles.
53-9719 Letterboxed *$19.99*

The Iron Monkey (Dubbed Version)
Also available in a dubbed-in-English edition.
53-6504 Letterboxed *$19.99*

Iron Monkey 2 (1996)
Donnie Yen adapts the Iron Monkey persona and fights evil warlords throughout China. During a battle against arms smugglers, Yen faces an infamous assassin known as the Snow Fox, whose martial arts prowess may just cage this Monkey. With Billy Chow and a searing amalgamation of foot kicks. 90 min. Dubbed in English.
53-6825 *$19.99*

A Chinese Odyssey, Part 1: Pandora's Box (1994)
This unique take on the legend of the Monkey King stars comic Stephen Chiau as a bandit chieftain who is a modern incarnation of the fabled trickster. When he finds himself in the middle of a feud between two immortal sisters, Chiau uses a time-travel device—and lands 500 years in the past, where he faces his original persona. 86 min. In Cantonese with English subtitles.
53-8587 Letterboxed *$49.99*

A Chinese Odyssey, Part 2: Cinderella (1994)
As the "Monkey King" saga reworking continues, Stephen Chiau's bandit must deal with romantic entanglements, the ferocious King Bull, grotesque animal-headed fighters, gigantic spiders and zombies 500 years in the past. Terrific slapstick, fantastic creatures, lots of action, a marvelous entry in Hong Kong cinema. 98 min. In Cantonese with English subtitles.
53-8588 Letterboxed *$49.99*

The Untold Story (1993)
This hideous true-life story tells of a demented restaurant chef who uses human parts in his special dumplings and the inept police who tried to catch him. The Hong Kong shocker spawned a cycle of popular "true crime" films and features lots of grisly sequences. With Anthony Wong, Danny Lee. 95 min. In Cantonese with English subtitles.
53-8601 Was $89.99 *$19.99*

A Moment Of Romance 2 (1993)
A girl from Mainland China smuggles herself into Hong Kong, hoping to make a better tomorrow for herself. After falling into a life of prostitution, she witnesses a Triad gang hit, and soon finds herself on a gangster's assassination list. Wu Chien Lien, Aaron Kwok star. In Cantonese with English subtitles.
53-8969 Letterboxed *$49.99*

Twist (1994)
When a Federal Reserve armored car is robbed and $170 million is reported missing, policeman Danny Lee ("The Killer") is put on the spot, given only 48 hours to interrogate suspected mob members. Lee also directed this crackerjack crime drama co-starring Simon Yam. In Cantonese with English subtitles.
53-8974 *$49.99*

Fallen Angels (1995)
Considered by many to be director Wong Kar-Wai's masterpiece, this unconventional film intertwines two tragic tales of love and redemption: a woman in love with a contract killer, and a mute ex-convict who finds himself involved in an awkward romance with a girl named Cherry. Stars Leon Lai Ming, Takeshi Kaneshiro and Michele Reis. 97 min. In Cantonese with English subtitles.
53-6255 Letterboxed *$79.99*

Happy Together (1997)
This Cannes favorite centers around a gay Chinese couple, living as expatriates in Buenos Aires, who are always on the verge of going their separate ways. However, they find out things about themselves they never could have imagined when they meet a mysterious man from Taiwan. Tony Leung, Leslie Cheung and Chang Chen star; directed by Wong Kar-Wai. 97 min. In Cantonese with English subtitles.
53-6254 Letterboxed *$79.99*

Fire Dragon (1994)
Adrenaline-spiked amalgam of martial arts, romance, fantasy, comedy and costume drama in which Brigitte Lin plays the title role, a flame-inducing masked assassin who teams with an evil prince in a plot to kill the prime minister. When she learns of her partner's true nature, Lin shifts her allegiance and joins with a fortune teller to stop him. 90 min. In Cantonese with English subtitles.
53-6508 *$49.99*

The Three Swordsmen (1994)
High-powered Hong Kong swordplay highlights this period adventure based on a popular comic strip. Set in Imperial China, the story centers on three sword experts sent by the emperor to transport two prisoners to a deserted area. Wild, flying blade battles ensue as the swordsmen have to get the criminals to their destination before the ice they're packed in (!) melts. With Brigitte Lin, Andy Lau. In Cantonese with English subtitles.
53-8584 Letterboxed *$49.99*

Angel Of The Road (1993)
A struggling entrepreneur in the seedy trucking business finds himself getting into trouble. This Hong Kong actioner features Max Mok and Loletta Lee. 90 min. In Cantonese with English subtitles.
53-9754 *$49.99*

Armageddon (1989)
Hong Kong action flick about two hardened cops who are forced to confront their troubled past when they take a violent stand against a ruthless Triad kingpin who is recruiting mercenaries from Mainland China to do his dirty work. Directed by Wong Siu Chun. In Cantonese with English subtitles.
53-6237 *$49.99*

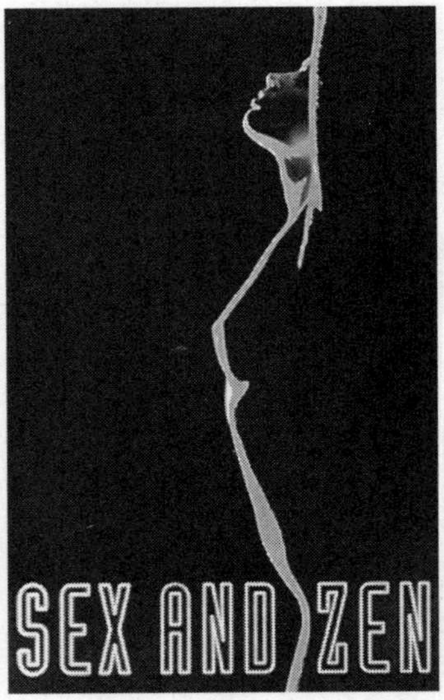

Sex And Zen (1993)
One of the most outrageous films ever made, this Hong Kong fable tells the story of an oversexed scholar who isn't happy with his love life with his huge-breasted wife. After he sleeps with different women, he decides to get a penis transplant—from a horse! His life then becomes a series of wild and raucous encounters that take eroticism—and comedy—to new levels. Lawrence Ng and Amy Yip star. 99 min. In Cantonese with English subtitles.
53-8340 *$94.99*

Sex And Zen (Dubbed Version)
Also available in a dubbed-in-English edition.
53-8904 *$94.99*

Sex And Zen II (1996)
A criminal known as the "Mirage Woman" is on the lam, thanks to her unique ability to steal the life forces out of her sexual partners. She hooks up with the dim-bulb son of a lothario, then sleeps with his father, while she finds time to play games with a court officer. This carnal martial arts sequel stars Hsu Chi. 88 min. In Cantonese with English subtitles.
53-9791 Letterboxed *$49.99*

Lethal Girls 2 (1995)
Action-crammed Asian exciter in which a Hong Kong cop is accidentally thrust into the world of drug smugglers and the dark side of Chinese security forces when he's on assignment on Mainland China. With Yukari Oshima ("Lethal Panther 2"), Mark Chang. 85 min. Dubbed in English.
53-8886 *$14.99*

01:00 (1995)
Spooky stuff from Hong Kong, this anthology of ghost stories based on "urban legends" all set at or around 1 o'clock in the morning includes tales about a nurse working the night shift in a haunted hospital; a psychology student challenged to interview a ghost for a project; and a pair of cops who discover a camera that can take spirits' pictures. In Cantonese with English subtitles.
53-8970 Letterboxed *$49.99*

03:00 A.M. (1998)
Spirits abound in this three-chiller follow-up to "01:00 A.M." A young girl's mysterious suicide, a legendary "ghost villa" on the banks of a river and a haunted construction site all add up to horror, Chinese-style. With Jordan Chan and Cheung Tat Ming. 95 min. In Cantonese with English subtitles.
53-6223 *$79.99*

The Girls In The Hood (1995)
So sordid you have to take a shower after watching it, this drama tells of four young women who live on Hong Kong's mean streets, selling themselves as "no-bath girls" to strangers in exchange for a place to sleep. They also have to face dangerous customers, crooked cops and a bisexual stalker. 90 min. In Cantonese with English subtitles.
53-8972 Letterboxed *$49.99*

The Adventurers (1995)
Superlative actioner focusing on a young fighter pilot who joins a CIA operative to find the arms-smuggling billionaire responsible for his parents' deaths. The search leads him to Thailand and San Francisco, where he marries the villain's daughter in hopes of finishing off her father. Andy Lau stars; directed by Ringo Lam ("City on Fire"). In Cantonese with English subtitles.
53-9734 Letterboxed *$19.99*

Full Throttle (1995)
Andy Lau plays a champion racing driver who pursues his dreams of glory at any cost. After he is almost killed in a devastating accident, he attempts to regain his courage with help from his devoted girlfriend. Highlighted by exciting racing footage. 108 min. In Cantonese with English subtitles.
53-9796 Letterboxed *$49.99*

Private Eye Blues (1994)
Entertaining Hong Kong actioner featuring Jacky Cheung as a down-and-out private detective who takes the assignment of tracking down a teenage girl in Hong Kong and returning her to the mainland. When law agencies and gangs join in the search, Cheung finds himself in trouble as well. With Kathy Chow Hoi Mei. In Cantonese with English subtitles.
53-9763 *$49.99*

The Phantom Lover (1995)
This beautifully filmed take on the "Phantom of the Opera" story is set in 1930s China, where a once-glorious opera house is the setting for romance and intrigue. The lead singer of a theatrical troupe is recruited by the theater's disfigured architect to rekindle his love for a merchant's daughter, whose hand has been promised to a corrupt politician's son. Leslie Cheung, Wu Chien-lien star in this film from Ronny Yu ("The Bride with White Hair"). 102 min. In Cantonese with English subtitles.
53-6932 Letterboxed *$59.99*

The Phantom Lover (Dubbed Version)
Also available in a dubbed-in-English edition.
53-6933 *$59.99*

Organized Crime And Triad Bureau (1995)
Explosive Hong Kong actioner starring Danny Lee ("The Killer") as an unconventional police officer who teams with a group of renegade enforcers to track down a notorious jewel thief and his mistress who are hiding out on a small island near Hong Kong. Cecilia Yip and Anthony Wong also star in this thriller. 91 min. In Cantonese with English subtitles.
53-8427 Letterboxed *$19.99*

Organized Crime And Triad Bureau (Dubbed Version)
Also available in a dubbed-in-English edition.
53-8902 Letterboxed *$19.99*

Dragon From Shaolin (1996)
During his search for Buddha, Little Dragon, a kung fu master from the Shaolin Temple, joins forces with a street orphan and soon becomes entangled in a series of wild adventures. This martial arts-filled family adventure stars Sik Siu Loong, Fok Siu Man and Yuen Biao. 89 min. In Cantonese with English subtitles.
53-6431 Letterboxed *$19.99*

Dragon From Shaolin (Dubbed Version)
Also available in a dubbed-in-English edition.
53-6432 Letterboxed *$19.99*

Tsui Hark

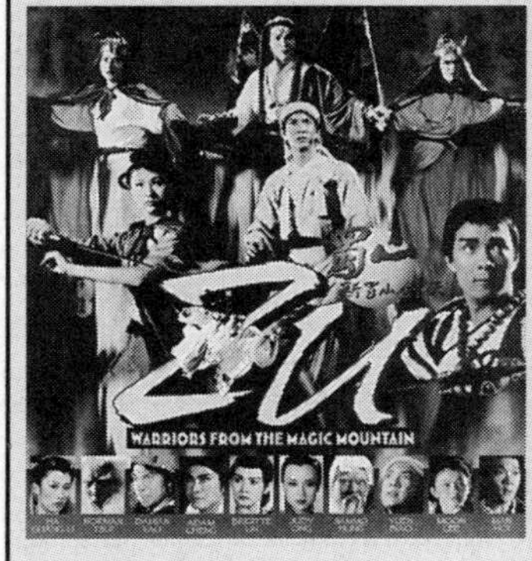

Zu: Warriors From The Magic Mountain (1983)
John Carpenter's "Big Trouble in Little China" was influenced by this fantastic Hong Kong epic of magic, action and ghosts from Tsui Hark ("A Chinese Ghost Story"). Set in ancient China, the story tells of a young warrior who must travel through the enchanted Zu Mountains in order to retrieve twin swords that can defeat dangerous demons. With Yuen Biao, Adam Cheng, Sammo Hung, Brigitte Lin. 98 min. In Cantonese with English subtitles.
53-8976 Letterboxed *$19.99*

Zu: Warriors From The Magic Mountain (Dubbed Version)
Also available in a dubbed-in-English edition.
53-8977 Letterboxed *$19.99*

Peking Opera Blues (1986)
One of the finest films to emerge from Hong Kong's New Wave, director Tsui Hark's story juggles incredible acrobatics, humor, stunning art direction, and political and feminist themes in a story set in 1910s China. The focus is on the experiences of three women, one of whom is a general's daughter involved with revolutionary guerrillas. Ling Ching-Hsai, Sally Yeh and Cherie Cheung star. 104 min. In Cantonese with English subtitles.
53-9414 Was $49.99 *$19.99*

Once Upon A Time In China, Part 3 (1993)
The third chapter of Tsui Hark's saga on the life of Wong Fei-Hong stars Jet Li as the famed martial artist in a wild action tale set in early 20th-century China. In Beijing to visit his father, Li finds himself taking part in a Lion Dance contest, stopping a Russian assassin from killing the president, and trying to patch thing up with girlfriend Rosamund Kwan. In Mandarin with English
53-8523 Was $49.99 *$19.99*

Once Upon A Time In China, Part V (1994)
The continuing adventures of folk hero Wong Fei-Hong (Chiu Man-Chuk) find the kung fu master and his band of loyal students clashing with pirates who have taken control of the South China Sea, terrorizing locals and magistrates in their wake. Director Tsui Hark's mix of gunplay and martial arts also features Rosamund Kwan. 101 min. In Cantonese with English subtitles.
53-9808 Letterboxed *$19.99*

Green Snake (1993)
Based on a Chinese folktale, Tsui Hark's lush fantasy epic features Maggie Cheung and Joey Wong as snake spirit siblings who can assume human form. After Wong falls in love with and marries a nerdy scholar, the sisters meet their match from a strident monk who is immune to their flirtatious ways. 98 min. In Cantonese with English subtitles.
53-9809 Was $49.99 *$19.99*

The Blade (1996)
Master filmmaker Tsui Hark ("A Chinese Ghost Story") adapts the classic "One-Armed Boxer" premise for the 1990s, focusing on the adopted son of a swordmaker who loses his arm to bandits. The young man uses his father's broken sword to seek revenge in this tale of love, honor, good, evil and vengeance. With Chiu Man Chuk. In Cantonese with English subtitles.
53-8968 Letterboxed *$19.99*

Shanghai Grand (1996)
This stylish offering from producer Tsui Hark tells the tale of a Taiwanese soldier/spy (Leslie Cheung) who arrives in Shanghai and allies himself with an up-and-coming Triad member (Andy Lau). Complications arise for the two when they find themselves competing for the love of the same woman. 107 min. In Cantonese with English subtitles.
53-9839 *$79.99*

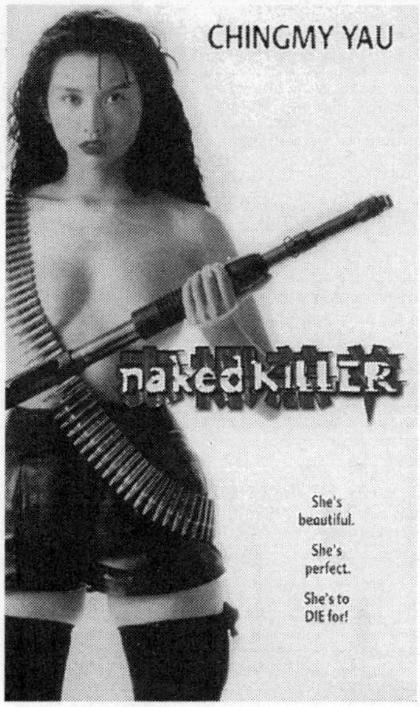

Naked Killer (1992)
This outrageous sex-and-violence hoedown from Hong Kong stars Chingmy Yau as a gorgeous leather-clad sweetie who enjoys offing rapists. After Yau murders a mobster, his gang goes after her, and she seeks tips from a lethal female killer. Both women meet their match when the killer's former protégé, lesbian Carrie Ng, comes looking for them. 88 min. In Cantonese with English subtitles.
53-6785 Letterboxed *$19.99*

Naked Killer (Dubbed Version)
Also available in a dubbed-in-English edition.
53-6786 Letterboxed *$24.99*

Raped By An Angel (1993)
He looks like a nice guy, but on the inside Mark Cheng is an evil rapist who also enjoys killing the women after he violates them. After a woman is murdered, her friend lures the culprit into a nasty trap. Also known as "Naked Killer II," this film has nothing to do with the original except for cast members Chingmy Yau, Simon Yam and Carrie Ng. In Cantonese with English subtitles.
53-9764 Letterboxed *$49.99*

Legendary Couple (1995)
A Hong Kong take on "Natural Born Killers" featuring Simon Yam and Chingmy Yau as a notorious pair of contemporary Robin Hoods who go to violent extremes in their robbery efforts. Mixing shoot-outs, humor and sex, this film delivers the goods with kinetic style. 95 min. In Cantonese with English subtitles.
53-6286 Letterboxed *$49.99*

Lover Of The Last Empress (1995)
Historical spectacle gets a sensual treatment in this "Category III" ("Adults Only") saga set during the last Chinese dynasty and starring Chingmy Yau as the Imperial concubine who uses sex, murder and help from the Emperor's brother to become the most powerful woman in China. Tony Leung also stars. 97 min. In Cantonese with English subtitles.
53-6287 Letterboxed *$49.99*

Chingmy Yau Series: Boxed Set
The luscious Chingmy Yau stars in three sexy and adventurous films available in one boxed set: "Legendary Couple," "Lover of the Last Empress" and "Raped by an Angel."
53-6285 Save $70.00! *$79.99*

Satin Steel (1994)
Pesky detective Jade Leung joins by-the-book investigator Anita Lee to track down nasty arms dealers in Singapore in this slam-bang actioner that puts a Hong Kong spin on the "Lethal Weapon" buddy movies. The dynamic duo are forced into using their kickboxing and shooting abilities to stop the top criminal and his sidekick with a bionic arm. 84 min. In Cantonese with English subtitles.
53-9737 Letterboxed *$49.99*

The Spike Drink Gang (1995)
Nasty effort from Hong Kong based on the true exploits of a gang that spikes convenience store drinks with drugs, then robs, kidnaps or rapes their victims for a profit. The gang is led by a former prison guard who was fired because of his unruly conduct. Yvonne Yung Hung and Tsui Kam-Kong star. 92 min. In Cantonese with English subtitles.
59-7108 Letterboxed *$24.99*

The Red Headkerchief (1996)
Dramatic tale set in Japanese-occupied China during World War II. A landlord, in spite of the turmoil around him, is driven by love for his country and his family to hold a lavish wedding for his adopted son, only to have the day slowly turn to chaos and confusion. Zhao Yansong, Li Fazeng star. 95 min. In Cantonese with English subtitles.
53-6221 *$49.99*

Beast Cops (1998)
Gritty Hong Kong actioner stars Anthony Wong as a crooked cop with a gambling addiction who finds himself under fire when by-the-book police official Michael Wong invades his turf. You're never quite sure who is the crook and who's on the up and up in this super-stylish tale from Gordon Chan ("Fist of Legend"). 110 min. In Cantonese with English subtitles.
53-6429 Letterboxed *$19.99*

Beast Cops (Dubbed Version)
Also available in a dubbed-in-English edition.
53-6430 Letterboxed *$19.99*

Her Name Is Cat (1998)
Stylish actioner stars Almen Wong as a lovely, lethal Mainland China assassin tracked to Hong Kong by cop Michael Wong after she kills local triad bosses. After a hit on a politician goes wrong and Cat's thuggish ex searches for her, she teams with the cop to elude him and others after her. 95 min. In Cantonese with English subtitles.
53-6661 *$24.99*

Her Name Is Cat (Dubbed Version)
Also available in a dubbed-in-English edition. 89 min.
82-5141 *$89.99*

The Suspect (1998)
Riveting political thriller from Ringo Lam ("Full Contact") centering on a former convict asked by two friends to kill a presidential candidate. When he refuses and the politician is murdered, he becomes a prime suspect in the crime. Louis Koo, Julian Chang star. 108 min. In Cantonese with English subtitles.
53-6713 Letterboxed *$19.99*

The Suspect (Dubbed Version)
Also available in a dubbed-in-English edition.
53-6714 Letterboxed *$19.99*

The Day The Sun Turned Cold (1994)
Inspired by a true story, this fascinating thriller from China tells of a welder who enters a police station to report the poisoning death of his father by his mother 10 years before. The local police chief opens the case and uncovers the unsettling truth behind the man's accusation. Siqin Gowa stars. 99 min. In Mandarin with English subtitles.
53-8590 Letterboxed *$79.99*

Return To A Better Tomorrow (1994)
In-name-only installment in the John Woo-Tsui Hark franchise that centers on an up-and-coming Triad boss who is betrayed by his closest lieutenant, then embarks on a road to retribution, aided by his best friend and an undercover cop. Directed by Wong Jing ("High Risk"). In Cantonese with English subtitles.
53-8973 *$49.99*

Kick Boxer (1992)
In this enthralling historical adventure, Yuen Biao plays a kung fu expert and pupil of Wong Fei-Hong (the character featured in "Once Upon a Time in China") who joins forces with a no-nonsense police chief to try to stop the opium trade. Lu Sho Ling also stars. 85 min. Dubbed in English.
82-7031 *$39.99*

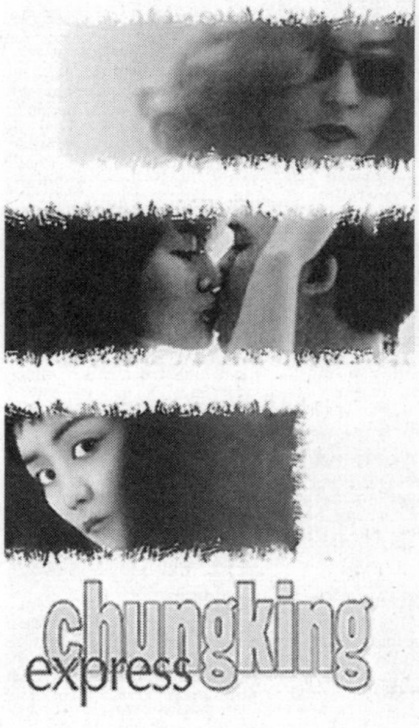

Chungking Express (1994)
At once funny and touching, this comedy/drama of life, love and take-out food in contemporary Hong Kong follows the barely-connected romances of two city policemen. One man pines for his long-gone girlfriend while meeting a mysterious woman in a bar; the other becomes the object of obsession for a gaminish sandwich shop worker. Brigitte Lin, Tony Leung, Faye Wang star; written and directed by Wong Kar-Wai. 102 min. In Cantonese with English subtitles.
11-2076 Was $94.99 *$19.99*

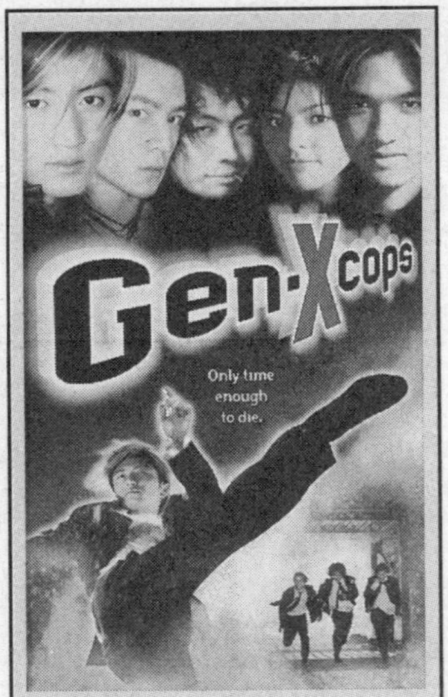
Gen-X cops
Only time enough to die.

Gen-X Cops (1999)
"The Mod Squad" gets an Asian twist with this Hong Kong drama. A trio of volatile twentysomething police recruits are the city's last chance to stop a Japanese crime ring from wreaking havoc with a stolen shipment of weapons. Intense action and daredevil stunts will blow you away. Nicholas Tse, Stephen Fung, Sam Lee and Toru Nakamura star; look for a cameo by co-producer Jackie Chan. 113 min. Dubbed in English.
02-3420 *$99.99*

Laboratory Of The Devil (1991)
Allegedly based on declassified WWII documents, this gruesome shocker from China is set in 1945 and tells of Japan's horrific experiments on Chinese, Korean and Mongolian prisoners in Camp 731. A doctor and his wife try to stop the hideous experiments. This gory, uncut tale is the second part in the "Man Behind the Sun" trilogy. With Wang Gang. 95 min. In Cantonese with English subtitles.
82-5026 *$49.99*

Saviour Of The Soul (1992)
Spiked with wild aerial fights, this stunning live-action salute to Japanese anime tells of master criminal Silver Fox (Aaron Kwok), out for revenge against soldiers-of-fortune Andy Lau and Anita Mui, who killed one of Silver Fox's friends. Silver Fox poisons Mui, and the only antidote can be supplied by the mysterious Pet Lady. 94 min. In Cantonese with English subtitles.
53-6180 Letterboxed *$49.99*

Saviour Of The Soul II (1992)
Comic book-styled sequel-of-sorts relates the legend of the Ice Woman in Snowy Mountain, a legendary beauty who has attracted many fans, none of whom have returned to civilization after meeting her. A martial artist obsessed with the Ice Woman meets her and finds himself battling the evil Devil King. Rosamund Kwan, Andy Lau star. In Cantonese with English subtitles.
53-6181 Letterboxed *$49.99*

Dragon Inn (1992)
In this remake of the seminal 1966 martial arts film "Dragon Gate Inn," a deadly storm strands sword-wielding lovers Tony Leung and Brigitte Lin in a remote desert inn along with the vicious government eunuch and his minions that are pursuing them. What's more, the inn's owner, Maggie Cheung, earns extra money by luring men to their deaths and selling the remains for "spicy meat buns"! 93 min. In Cantonese with English subtitles.
53-6411 Letterboxed *$19.99*

Weekend Lover (1993)
A compelling drama about disillusioned Chinese youth centers on three young people, including a teenage boy imprisoned for killing another boy for a girl he loves. 96 min. In Cantonese with English subtitles.
53-9848 *$49.99*

School On Fire (1988)
Ringo Lam turns his eye for gritty action on a high school in Hong Kong's seedy Kowloon district. In this world of teeny-bopper gang violence and drugs, an innocent girl tries to report a gang-related murder and finds her world turned upside-down by vengeful criminals and manipulative police. Fanny Yuen stars. 114 min. In Cantonese with English subtitles.
53-9781 *$49.99*

Snake Fist (1994)
A slick and violent melodrama set in Mainland China tells the tale of a wealthy businessman whose life is threatened by the Chinese Triads. It's up to a team of Interpol agents to protect the man and track down the killers. Bridgette Lin ("Swordsman II") plays the gender-bender game once again as a female assassin disguised as a man. 90 min. In Cantonese with English subtitles.
53-8996 *$49.99*

An Erotic Ghost Story (1990)
The breastacular Amy Yip is one of three fox-fairies in human form who entice and bewitch all they meet. However, they could be in trouble when they run into a scholar who arouses their desires. Based on a Chinese literary classic, this film offers lots of heated encounters. Yip-eee! 84 min. In Cantonese with English subtitles.
53-9793 Was $49.99 *$19.99*

An Erotic Ghost Story (Dubbed Version)
Also available in a dubbed-in-English edition.
53-6514 Was $49.99 *$19.99*

Legacy Of Rage (1987)
In his only film made in Hong Kong, Brandon Lee plays an auto junkyard worker and martial arts expert who is framed for killing a cop by a close friend and sent to prison. When Lee learns of the set-up, he teams with a fellow inmate to stop his friend, who has become a mobster since Lee's imprisonment. With Bolo Yeung. 82 min. In Cantonese with English subtitles.
53-9758 Was $49.99 *$19.99*

Legacy Of Rage (Dubbed Version)
Also available in a dubbed-in-English edition.
59-7014 Was $89.99 *$19.99*

Wicked City (1992)
Combine "The Killer," "Alien Nation" and "Scanners" and you might get this wild Hong Kong actioner based on a popular Japanese comic series. Human society is infiltrated by the Reptoids, shape-shifting beings with fantastic psychic powers who want to take over the world. Two anti-Reptoid task force agents must stop the creatures' latest scheme, but one of them falls for a beautiful Reptoid. Jacky Cheung, Leon Lai, Michelle Li star. 88 min. In Cantonese with English subtitles.
53-8354 Letterboxed *$14.99*

Wicked City (Dubbed Version)
Also available in a dubbed-in-English edition.
53-8357 Was $19.99 *$14.99*

Zen Of Sword (1992)
Wild sword-and-magic mayhem from Hong Kong focuses on a prince and princess who find themselves on opposite sides of the battlefield when their families go to war against each other. Egged on by his aunt, the prince uses his amazing swordfighting prowess to defeat his clan's arch rival—and his lover's family. With Michelle Lee. In Cantonese with English subtitles.
53-8497 *$49.99*

Dr. Lamb (1992)
Inspired by the true story of the "Hong Kong Cab Murderer," this ultra-gory Hong Kong production is a no-nonsense shocker about a deranged taxi driver out to rid the world of prostitutes. After killing the women, the cabby dismembers, photographs and (often) has sex with them. With Danny Lee, Simon Yan. In Cantonese and Mandarin with English subtitles.
53-8506 *$49.99*

Rebekah (1997)
Heavy on nudity and sex, this "Category III" sizzler from Hong Kong tells of a failed singer who goes into another line of "entertainment," recruiting gorgeous beauty queens for her highly profitable escort service. When a scandal threatens to halt her enterprise, Rebekah steps forward to save herself. Mei-Lan Choi stars. 90 min. In Cantonese with English subtitles.
59-7109 Letterboxed *$29.99*

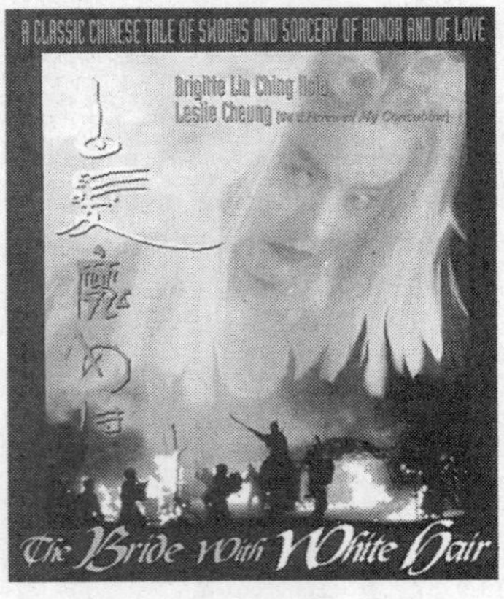
A CLASSIC CHINESE TALE OF SWORDS AND SORCERY OF HONOR AND OF LOVE
Brigitte Lin Ching Hsia
Leslie Cheung
The Bride With White Hair

The Bride With White Hair (1993)
Hong Kong fantasy at its most amazing is on display in this tale of a woman raised in the mountains by wolves and in the service of an evil cult led by a twisted pair of siblings. Her romance with a martial arts master from a rival school leads to a battle of magic and astonishing swordplay. Brigette Lin, Leslie Cheung star in this surprise-filled thriller. 92 min. In Cantonese with English subtitles.
53-8598 Letterboxed *$19.99*

The Bride With White Hair II (1993)
A continuation of the popular sword-and-sorcery saga finds enchantress Brigitte Lin leading a group of female warriors to defeat the evil clan she resigned from in the first film. Here she uses kung-fu hair that shoots out and stabs people to seek revenge. With Leslie Cheung. 80 min. In Cantonese with English subtitles.
53-8599 Letterboxed *$19.99*

From Beijing With Love (1994)
Hilarious James Bond spoof, Hong Kong style, with Stephen Chow as an incompetent, knife expert secret agent in search of a priceless dinosaur skull that's been stolen. Chow joins forces with pretty agent Anita Yuen and the two fall for each other—even though Yuen has plans to kill him. The laughs and stunts come fast and furious. In Cantonese with English subtitles.
53-9717 Letterboxed *$49.99*

Rikki Oh (Story Of Ricky) (1991)
One of the most outrageously violent action films ever made, this Hong Kong adaptation of a popular Japanese comic book is set in a high-security prison of the near future. When kung fu master Rikki (Fan Siu Wang) is sent there for massacring the drug dealers who killed his girlfriend, he uses his deadly skills to battle the sadistic warden's henchmen, becoming a hero in the process. Witness a man being strangled by another man's intestines, eyeballs popping out, and the infamous "head-smashing" shot seen on TV's "The Daily Show"! With Frankie Chin, Yukari Oshima. 90 min. Dubbed in English.
20-8291 *$19.99*

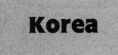

Taiwan

A Time To Live And A Time To Die (1985)
Set in late 1950s Taiwan, director Hou Hsiao-Hsien's semiautobiographical drama poignantly depicts the growing gap between generations of a family that left mainland China during the Communist takeover and whose older members still long to return home. Yu An-Shun, Tian Feng star. 137 min. In Taiwanese with English subtitles.
87-7002 *$59.99*

Dust In The Wind (1987)
A teenage boy and girl move from their rural Taiwanese village with dreams of finding success in the capital city of Taipei, but find that urban life is filled with its own hardships, in this moving drama from Hou Hsiao-Hsien. Wang Ching-Wen, Hsing Shu-Fen star. 109 min. In Mandarin and Taiwanese with English subtitles.
87-7001 *$59.99*

Eat Drink Man Woman (1994)
Acclaimed comedy-drama from Ang Lee ("The Wedding Banquet") about Chu, a widowed master chef facing such problems as losing his sense of taste, his three daughters' strong desire for leaving home and a marriage-minded widow next door. In order to solve some of his predicaments, Chu calls on his cooking expertise. Sihung Lung, Kuei-Mei Yang, Chien-Lien Wu star. 124 min. In Mandarin with English subtitles.
88-1002 Was $89.99 *$19.99*

Vive L'Amour (1996)
This beautifully filmed, erotic epic is set in Taipei, Taiwan, where a seductive real estate agent and a street merchant carry on a heated affair in a vacant apartment. A young gay man who has taken refuge in the same apartment gets involved with the couple, and a bizarre love triangle ensues. Yang Kuei-Mei stars in Tsai Ming-Liang's effort. 118 min. In Taiwanese with English subtitles.
53-8832 Letterboxed *$19.99*

Korea

Peach Blossoms (1987)
A forbidden night of passion between a woman and an escaped convict leads to the birth of Peach, a beautiful girl who is told that the curse accompanying her birth will bring tragedy to her family. Lee Dae Keun and Mam King Won star in this Korean-made drama. 117 min. In Cantonese with English subtitles.
53-6218 *$49.99*

Why Has Bodhi-Dharma Left For The East? (1989)
The first major Korean film to be released theatrically in the United States, writer/director Bae Yong-kyun's 10-years-in-the-making Zen saga traces a few days in the lives of an elderly Buddhist monk, his young disciple, and an orphan boy in a hermitage in the mountains. As the monk prepares for his imminent death, he shares his teachings with his two charges and helps them find the paths they are to follow in life. Visually stunning and as enigmatic as its title, the film stars Yi Pan-yong, Sin Won-sop. 135 min. In Korean with English subtitles.
80-5026 Letterboxed *$29.99*

Jungle Story (1996)
A dedicated soldier is discharged from the army and forced to take part in civilian life. However, when he takes a job in a record store, he discovers his true talent as a singer, which leads him to musical stardom. Offbeat, song-filled Korean drama stars Yoo Dao Hye, Jae Wan Won. 91 min. In Cantonese with English subtitles.
53-6217 Letterboxed *$49.99*

The Gingko Bed (1996)
Epic tale of tragic love and redemption that revolves around a college art lecturer who is reunited with a love from a former life when he comes across an antique gingko bed. However, their reignited passions also bring about the evil spirit of the military general that kept them apart before. Stars Suk-Kyu Han and Hee-Kyung Jin. 88 min. In Korean with English subtitles.
76-7411 *$69.99*

Japan

Anathan (1953)
Josef von Sternberg's final film, considered a forgotten masterpiece by critics, details the adventures of a young woman marooned on a Pacific island inhabited by Japanese marines who don't know World War II ended. Japanese dialogue, with English narration by the director. Also included is a 1944 von Sternberg documentary, "The Town."
53-7370 *$59.99*

The Funeral (1985)
Darkly funny tale of a contemporary Japanese family's skewed attempts to conduct a traditional Buddhist service for their late patriarch. Controversial, compelling comic effort from Juzo Itami stars Tsutomu Yamazaki, Nobuko Miyamoto. 114 min. In Japanese with English subtitles.
63-1284 *$19.99*

Tampopo (1986)
Off-the-wall entry from Japan concerns the put-upon owner of a noodle restaurant and the bizarre drifters who try to aid her in making her place a success. Tremendous, tangential comedy that may be the first cinematic celebration of the joy of eating. Nobuko Miyamoto, Tsutomu Yamazaki star under Juzo Itami's direction. 114 min. In Japanese with English subtitles.
63-1283 *$19.99*

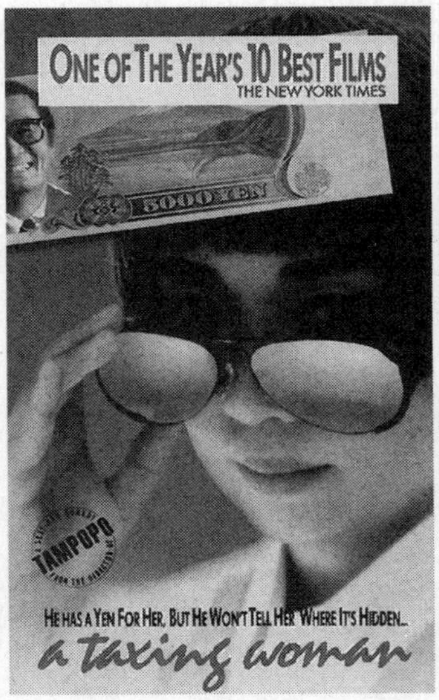
ONE OF THE YEAR'S 10 BEST FILMS
THE NEW YORK TIMES
HE HAS A YEN FOR HER, BUT HE WON'T TELL HER WHERE IT'S HIDDEN...
a taxing woman

A Taxing Woman (1987)
Writer/director Juzo Itami ("Tampopo") takes comedic aim once again at Japanese life with this winning look at a job-obsessed tax collector (Nobuko Miyamoto) who sets her sights on bringing a wealthy "love hotel" owner (Tsutomu Yamazaki) to justice. Before long, the pair of enemies are brought together, in a sly satire with universal appeal. 127 min. In Japanese with English subtitles.
53-7268 Was $79.99 *$19.99*

A Taxing Woman's Return (1989)
Relentless Japanese tax inspector Nobuko Miyamoto is back to take on felonious businessmen, corrupt politicians, and a priestly con artist in the satiric sequel from writer/director Juzo Itami. 127 min. In Japanese with English subtitles.
53-7382 Was $79.99 *$29.99*

Minbo (Or The Gentle Art Of Japanese Extortion) (1994)
A controversial satire from Juzo Itami ("Tampopo") about a female attorney hired to clear out a hotel overrun by mobsters who specialize in blackmail and intimidation. Nobuko Miyamoto stars in this darkly humorous film that enraged Japan's Yakuza to the point that they attacked director Itami. 123 min. In Japanese with English subtitles.
22-5836 Was $79.99 *$29.99*

The Juzo Itami Collection
Three of the iconoclastic Japanese filmmakers best works are featured in a special collector's set: "The Funeral," "Tampopo" and "A Taxing Woman."
53-6668 Save $10.00! *$49.99*

Snow Country (1957)
Sensitive romantic drama explores the torment of a Tokyo artist torn between his family and their sophisticated lifestyle and a woman at an idyllic mountain retreat with whom he has fallen in love. Ryo Ikebe stars; directed by Shiro Toyoda. 133 min. In Japanese with English subtitles.
45-5452 Was $29.99 ***$19.99***

Traitors Of The Blue Castle (1958)
Intrigue and drama play a role in this Japanese samurai thriller, as a Shogun's right-hand man plots the eventual overthrow of his lord. Kanjuro Arashi, Ryuzaburo Nakamura star; Tatsuo Yamada directs. 100 min. In Japanese with English subtitles.
01-1433 ***$69.99***

I Was Born, But... (1932)
An early example of the "shomin-geki" domestic drama that was to mark director Yasujiro Ozu's career. After seeing their father demean himself to gain favor with his boss, two young boys launch a hunger strike in order to win an explanation. Tatsuo Saito, Hideo Sugahara star. 89 min. In Japanese with English subtitles.
53-6547 ***$89.99***

Record Of A Tenement Gentleman (1947)
Yasujiro Ozu's bittersweet tale concerns an abandoned child who decides to make a grumpy, independent woman his surrogate mother. After a period of uncertainty, the woman realizes how the child has enhanced her life. With Choko Lida and Hohi Aoki. 72 min. In Japanese with English subtitles.
53-8223 ***$79.99***

Late Spring (1949)
Contemporary look at everyday life in postwar Japan, centering on an elderly man's attempts to find a suitable husband for his reluctant daughter before it's "too late." Director Yasujiro Ozu's penchant for richly drawn character studies is well-evidenced; Chishu Ryu stars. 107 min. In Japanese with English subtitles.
53-7292 ***$49.99***

Early Summer (1951)
Groundbreaking Japanese drama by director Yasujiro Ozu ("Floating Weeds") about a young woman who rebels against an arranged marriage presents a fascinating look at postwar Japanese society. Setsuko Hara, Chishu Ryu star. 135 min. In Japanese with English subtitles.
45-5417 Was $59.99 ***$29.99***

Tokyo Story (1953)
An elderly couple leave their small town to visit their grown children in Tokyo, but receive a chilly reception and are welcomed only by a son's widow, in this moving drama by Yasujiro Ozu. Chishu Ryu, Chiyeko Higashiyama and Setsuko Hara star. 139 min. In Japanese with English subtitles.
53-7320 ***$79.99***

Equinox Flower (1958)
Yasujiro Ozu continues his fascination with Japan's middle class in his first color film, a beautifully designed domestic comedy-drama about the problems faced by a Tokyo businessman's daughter who decides to marry without her father's consent. Shin Saburi stars. 118 min. In Japanese with English subtitles.
53-7668 ***$79.99***

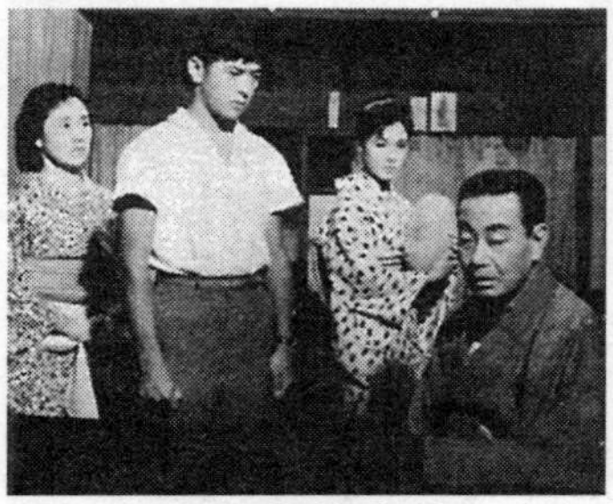

OZU'S FLOATING WEEDS

Floating Weeds (1959)
Yasujiro Ozu directed this beautiful look at a theatrical troupe's visit to a remote island town, where the group's leading actor has an emotional reunion with an old flame and the son he never knew. 128 min. In Japanese with English subtitles.
22-5637 ***$29.99***

Good Morning (Ohayo) (1959)
Told by their father to shut up after he refuses to buy a TV for their home, two Japanese boys take him at his word and begin a vow of silence that soon has the whole family at odds with their friends and neighbors in this satirical comedy from director Yasujiro Ozu. Chishu Ryu, Kuniko Miyake star. 93 min. In Japanese with English subtitles.
22-5891 ***$29.99***

An Autumn Afternoon (1963)
The final film by director Yasujiro Ozu follows in his tradition of heartfelt dramas examining the changing roles in Japanese family life. Postwar Tokyo is the setting for this intimate look at a father preparing for his only daughter's wedding. Chishu Ryu, Shima Iwashita, Mariko Okada star. 112 min. In Japanese with English subtitles.
53-7630 ***$79.99***

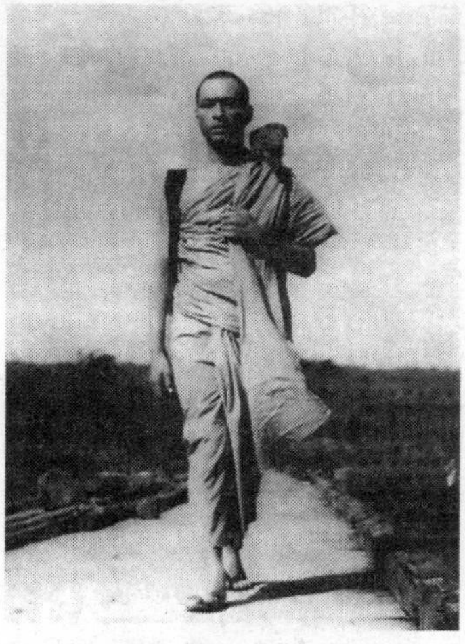

The Burmese Harp (1956)
Moving anti-war drama from Japan about a wounded soldier in the Burmese jungles during the last days of World War II. Sent out to the mountains to persuade renegade fighters to surrender, the harp-playing soldier undergoes a spiritual change and becomes obsessed with burying war dead. Shoji Yasui stars; directed by Kon Ichikawa. 116 min. In Japanese with English subtitles.
22-5733 ***$29.99***

Enjo (1958)
Based on a novel by Yukio Mishima, this stunning drama from director Kon Ichikawa follows a young man who enters Kyoto's fabled Golden Pavillion to become a monk. As he becomes more and more despaired by what he sees as the temple's corruption by the outside world, the man commits a shocking act to "save" it. Raizo Ichikawa, Toshiro Mayazumi star. AKA: "Conflagration." 98 min. In Japanese with English subtitles.
53-8111 ***$79.99***

Fires On The Plain (1959)
Gritty, powerful anti-war drama from Japan focuses on a doomed unit of soldiers in the closing days of the Philippine campaign and their degeneration into barbarism as their situation becomes hopeless. Dark humor and an unflinching sense of realism drive director Kon Ichikawa's sentiments home. Eiji Funakoshi stars. 105 min. In Japanese with English subtitles.
53-1612 Letterboxed ***$29.99***

Odd Obsession (1959)
Effective, highly stylized drama from Japan concerning an elderly man who, despairing of his waning potency, goads his beautiful young bride into having an affair with his doctor. Remarkable effort stars Machiko Kyo, Ganjiro Nakamura; Kon Ichikawa directs. 96 min. In Japanese with English subtitles.
53-1699 ***$29.99***

Being Two Isn't Easy (1962)
The lighter side of director Kon Ichikawa ("Fires on the Plain") is shown in this touching comedy about a toddler's fascination with the world around him. The 2-year-old hero is seen pondering the moon, learning to climb stairs, and watching his feisty grandmother's conflicts with his mother. With Fujiko Yamamoto. 88 min. In Japanese with English subtitles.
22-5720 Was $29.99 ***$19.99***

An Actor's Revenge (1963)
Kon Ichikawa's powerful story focuses on a female impersonator in a 19th-century Kabuki troupe who takes the matter of revenge in his own hands when he attempts to murder three men responsible for the death of his parents. The film features a superb performance from Kazuo Hasegawa in the lead. AKA: "Revenge of a Kabuki Actor." 114 min. In Japanese with English subtitles.
53-7948 Was $79.99 ***$29.99***

Zero Woman (Director's Cut) (1995)
She's gorgeous, sexy and deadly: she's Rei, a special agent for Japan's covert police department, Section Zero. When the Yazuka abducts the witness to a brutal crime, Rei goes on a rampage of sex, violence and death to get her back. Natsuki Ozawa, Ken Kosugi (Sho's son) star. AKA: "Zero Woman 2." Unrated version; 90 min. In Japanese with English subtitles.
20-8091 Letterboxed ***$29.99***

Zero Woman (Director's Cut)(Dubbed Version)
Also available in a dubbed-in-English edition.
20-8146 ***$29.99***

Zero Woman: The Accused (1996)
The lovely and lethal lawman known as Rei is back, but this time she may have met her match when she's assigned to track down an assassin as skillful as she is. And if that's not bad enough, Rei's fellow Section Zero agents are after her, as well. Mai Taichira stars in this explosive, erotic actioner; with Yujin Kitagawa. 77 min. In Japanese with English subtitles.
20-8605 Letterboxed ***$29.99***

Remembering The Cosmos Flower (1998)
Moving drama about a teenage girl who moves back to Japan with her mother after spending several years abroad. When it's learned that the girl contacted AIDS from a blood transfusion in South America, she is shunned by the community, until a childhood friend helps her cope and confront the neighbors' prejudice. Akane Oda, Megumi Matsushita star. 103 min. In Japanese with English subtitles.
22-9042 ***$79.99***

The Samurai Trilogy (1955)
This acclaimed action series brought the story of legendary Japanese warrior Musashi Miyamoto to life, with the inestimable aid of director Hiroshi Inagaki and star Toshiro Mifune. All three are in Japanese with English subtitles.

Samurai I: Musashi Miyamoto
The then-callow warrior falls in with the wrong side in a civil war and tastes defeat instead of glory. Only the love of a village girl and the ministrations of a priest stand between Miyamoto and deterioration. Academy Award winner for Best Foreign Film. 92 min.
22-5642 ***$29.99***

Samurai II: Duel At Ichijoji Temple
Bolstered by renewed self-worth, Miyamoto turns to rigorous discipline to hone his fighting skills. He is put to the test by his own deadly training, as well as eager swordsmen looking to build their reputations, and must forsake his love to follow a warrior's path. 102 min.
22-5643 ***$29.99***

Samurai III: Duel At Ganryu Island
Miyamoto squares off against his lifelong nemesis, Kojiro Sasaki, in a battle that will prove to be their final confrontation. Incredible swordplay marks this conclusion to the Miyamoto saga. 102 min.
22-5644 ***$29.99***

The Samurai Trilogy: Complete Set
Inagaki's groundbreaking action trilogy is also available in a money-saving collector's set.
22-5645 Save $20.00! ***$69.99***

After Life (Wandafuru Raifu) (1998)
What one memory of your life would you want to live over and over? In this compelling and heartfelt fantasy from Japanese filmmaker Hirokazu Kore-eda ("Maborosi"), the newly dead are met in a "way station" by a celestial staff who help them in choosing and then re-creating the memory—be it good or bad—that will be all they take with them into eternity. Arata, Erika Oda, Taketoshi Naito star. 118 min. In Japanese with English subtitles.
53-6895 Letterboxed ***$94.99***

The Razor: Sword Of Justice (1972)
Samurai action meets kinky sexual antics in this outrageous initial entry in a series about "Razor" Hanzo Itami, an honest cop with an extreme style, working in Japan in the late 1800s. "Razor" investigates a woman who happens to be serving as mistress to both his corrupt boss and a well-connected political prisoner. With "Zatoichi" star Shintaro Katsu; features graphic sex and violence. 90 min. In Japanese with English subtitles.
20-7625 Letterboxed ***$29.99***

The Razor: The Snare (1973)
"Razor" Itami (Shintaro Katsu) takes no prisoners as his investigation into the death of a girl from an illegal abortion leads him to a convent where young women are forced into bizarre orgies with corrupt officials. His "interrogation" of the high priestess puts Itami at odds with a crooked treasurer who is above the law...but not "The Razor's" brand of justice. 89 min. In Japanese with English subtitles.
20-7708 Letterboxed ***$29.99***

The Razor: Who's Got The Gold? (1973)
A beautiful ghost near an imperial castle, a missing shipment of gold, some counterfeit money and an orgy involving government officials' wives all add up to trouble for indefatigable 19th-century Japanese cop Hanzo Itami in this third entry in the sex- and violence-filled series. Shintaro Katsu stars. 84 min. In Japanese with English subtitles.
20-7797 Letterboxed ***$29.99***

Osaka Elegy (1936)
Kenji Mizoguchi paints a compelling look at a woman's place in Japanese society by centering on a telephone operator in a pharmaceutical company who serves as mistress to her boss until he fires her. In order to help her debt-ridden father and student brother, she turns to a life of prostitution. Isuzu Yamada stars. 71 min. In Japanese with English subtitles.
22-5787 Was $59.99 ***$29.99***

Sisters Of The Gion (1936)
A moving depiction of the condition of women in Japan, as seen through the eyes of two geisha sisters. Considered one of the finest efforts of director Kenji Mizoguchi and the best pre-WWII Japanese film; with Yoko Umemura and Isuzu Yamada. 66 min. In Japanese with English subtitles.
53-7128 Was $59.99 ***$29.99***

The Story Of The Last Chrysanthemum (1939)
Kenji Mizoguchi's chronicle of a young man unwilling to follow in the family tradition of Kabuki acting features the director's trademark empathetic depiction of women and a stylized, painterly quality. 142 min. In Japanese with English subtitles.
53-7356 Was $59.99 ***$29.99***

The 47 Ronin, Part I (1941)
The fact-based story of honor and devotion in 18th-century Japan was filmed several times, but never as stunningly as in director Kenji Mizoguchi's thrilling two-film epic. This first chapter shows how feudal lord Asano was tricked by Lord Kira, a jealous rival, and forced to commit harakiri, and how his loyal samurai warriors vow to avenge his death. Chojuro Kawarazaki, Yoshizaburo Arashi star. 111 min. In Japanese with English subtitles.
45-5446 ***$29.99***

The 47 Ronin, Part II (1942)
In the dramatic conclusion to Mizoguchi's samurai saga, Lord Kira gathers all available forces to suppress an impending attack by Lord Asano's men. However, the samurai feign disloyalty to their late master as part of their plan of vengeance. 113 min. In Japanese with English subtitles.
45-5447 ***$29.99***

The 47 Ronin, Parts I & II
Both films are also available in a special collector's set.
22-5893 Save $10.00! ***$49.99***

Utamaro And His Five Women (1946)
Gorgeously stylized look at the life of a painter in 18th-century Tokyo who finds inspiration from the prostitution, drunken parties and underworld figures that surround him. Directed by Kenji Mizoguchi. 89 min. In Japanese with English subtitles.
53-7825 ***$69.99***

Life Of Oharu (1952)
Dramatic look at one woman's harsh life in Japan's feudal society by director Kenji Mizoguchi. After shaming her family by loving a peasant and forced to become a concubine, she sinks deeper and deeper, until she ends up an aging prostitute. Kinuyo Tanaka, Toshiro Mifune star. 136 min. In Japanese with English subtitles.
09-1546 Remastered ***$29.99***

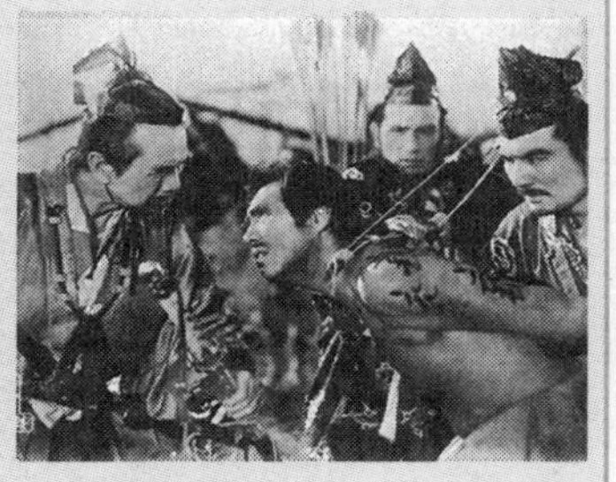

Ugetsu (1953)
Haunting Japanese drama of two peasants who leave their families to find success and wealth in the war-torn Japan of the 16th century. Directed by Kenji Mizoguchi. 96 min. In Japanese with English subtitles.
22-5634 Remastered ***$24.99***

A Geisha (1953)
Kenji Mizoguchi's much-acclaimed but rarely seen masterpiece dissects Japanese social changes after World War II by studying the relationship between a novice Geisha and her passive, elderly mentor. Michiyo Kogure stars. 86 min. In Japanese with English subtitles.
53-7842 ***$79.99***

Sansho The Bailiff (1954)
In Mizoguchi's poetic masterpiece, a young man in feudal Japan—a slave since childhood—prepares for his escape to search for his exiled father and mother, who was sold into prostitution. Stars Yoshiaki Hanayagi. 125 min. In Japanese with English subtitles.
22-5779 Was $39.99 ***$29.99***

The Taira Clan Saga (1955)
Director Kenji Mizoguchi brings to the screen a powerful drama set in medieval Japan, as the struggle for power of a samurai family faces tests from without and within. AKA: "Shin Heike Monogatari." 108 min. In Japanese with English subtitles.
53-7153 ***$39.99***

Princess Yang Kwei Fei (1955)
Gorgeously filmed drama from Kenji Mizoguchi about a maid who marries the emperor of China, then finds her life destroyed by the petty jealousies and intrigue that surround her in her new royal position. This "Cinderella" story is part fairy tale and part ghost story, and stars Masayuki Mori and Machiko Kyo. 91 min. In Japanese with English subtitles.
53-7773 Was $79.99 ***$29.99***

Street Of Shame (1956)
Kenji Mizoguchi's last work casts an unflinching eye at the lives of various occupants of a Tokyo brothel. This moving, powerful film engendered a wave of sentiment that culminated in Japan's 1957 outlawing of prostitution. Machiko Kyo, Ayako Wakao star. 88 min. In Japanese with English subtitles.
53-1586 Was $79.99 ***$29.99***

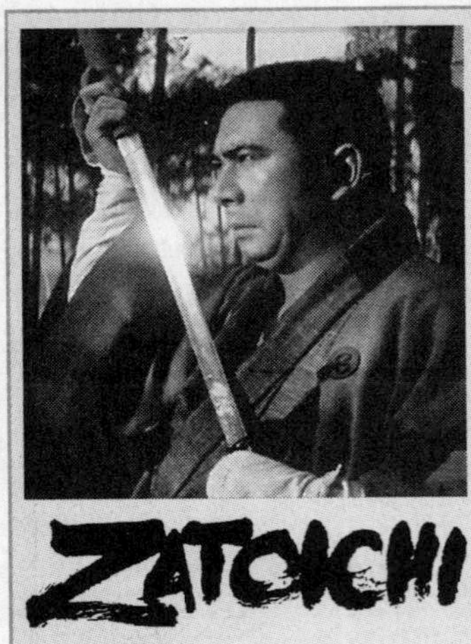

The Return Of Masseur Ichi (1962)
The second "Zatoichi" film finds the sightless samurai involved in two adventures. First, he uses his cane sword to fight gangsters hired by a warlord after he discovers that Zatoichi knows about his lawlessness. Then Zatoichi encounters a one-armed samurai who once competed with him for the same woman. With Shintaro Katsu. 73 min. In Japanese with English subtitles.
53-8045 Letterboxed *$19.99*

Masseur Ichi, The Fugitive (1963)
Zatoichi, the blind swordsman, learns there's a bounty on his head after he defends himself against an assailant. When Zatoichi investigates the bounty, he finds a gang war involving notorious swordsmen and killers, as well as a samurai married to one of his former loves. With Shintaro Katsu. 86 min. In Japanese with English subtitles.
53-8326 Letterboxed *$19.99*

Masseur Ichi Enters Again (1963)
Zatoichi returns to the village of his youth and soon reacquaints himself with his former teacher, Yajuro Banno. Banno's younger sister falls in love with the blind swordsman, but the marriage plans are disrupted when he learns of Banno's involvement in a kidnapping plot. With Shintaro Katsu. 91 min. In Japanese with English subtitles.
53-8663 Letterboxed *$19.99*

Masseur Ichi And A Chest Of Gold (1964)
While paying his respects to a former foe in a small town, masseur-swordsman Zatoichi and a criminal friend are accused of stealing a chest of gold. A cat-and-mouse game ensues as Zatoichi attempts to find the missing loot and prove their innocence. Shintaro Katsu, Mikiko Tsubouchi star; directed by Kazuo Ikehiro. 83 min. In Japanese with English subtitles.
53-7765 Letterboxed *$19.99*

Masseur Ichi On The Road (1964)
After rival Yakuza gangs try to enlist the services of Zatoichi, the blind gambler/masseur is sidetracked and decides to help the chambermaid daughter of a rich merchant to safety after a powerful lord attempts to rape her. Zatoichi battles reward-seeking opportunists and thugs while trying to get the girl home. Shintaro Katsu stars. 85 min. In Japanese with English subtitles.
53-8047 Letterboxed *$19.99*

Zatoichi's Flashing Sword (1964)
After fleeing from revenge-seeking gangsters, Zatoichi (Shintaro Katsu) finds himself caught in the middle of a feud between Yakuza heads who are battling over control of a ferry service. Zatoichi sides with a benevolent crime boss, whom he surprises with his sword expertise. Naoko Kubo also stars. In Japanese with English subtitles.
53-8512 Letterboxed *$19.99*

The Blind Swordsman And The Chess Expert (1965)
Sightless swordsman Zatoichi befriends an expert chess player named Jumonji, and the two encounter danger, tragedy and a group of unsuspecting hoods while on a journey by ship. Shintaro Katsu and Mikio Narita star; directed by Kenji Misumi. 87 min. In Japanese with English subtitles.
53-7763 Letterboxed *$19.99*

The Adventures Of A Blind Man (1965)
Thrill-filled, swords-a-flying adventure erupts when Zatoichi helps a woman track down the killers of her father, a town leader. He discovers that gangsters trying to shield their sleazy activities are the culprits and, using his cane swords, goes to work to stop their murderous ways. Shintaro Katsu stars. 86 min. In Japanese with English subtitles.
53-8327 Letterboxed *$19.99*

The Blind Swordsman's Revenge (1965)
Swordsman and masseur Zatoichi visits the man who taught him massage, but finds that he has mysteriously died and his daughter has been forced into prostitution by a local Yakuza boss. Zatoichi attempts to rescue the young woman through his incredible prowess with a sword. Shintary Katsu stars. 84 min. In Japanese with English subtitles.
53-8664 Letterboxed *$19.99*

The Blind Swordsman's Vengeance (1966)
Thrilling entry in the "Zatoichi" series finds him trying to grant a dying man's last wish: to deliver a bag of money to a person he knows nothing about. Zatoichi is led to a peaceful town overrun by gangsters whom he must battle in order to fulfill his promise. With Shintaro Katsu, Shigeru Amachi; directed by Tokuzo Tanaka. 83 min. In Japanese with English subtitles.
53-7764 Letterboxed *$19.99*

The Blind Swordsman's Cane Sword (1967)
The swordsman-gambler's winnings at a dice game with Yakuza members lead to a deadly cane fight. His weapon is recognized by a master swordsmith who claims it was created by his teacher and will break during its next battle. Zatoichi swears off fighting forever—or does he? With Shintaro Katsu. 93 min. In Japanese with English subtitles.
53-8328 Letterboxed *$19.99*

Zatoichi Challenged! (1967)
Zatoichi helps a dying woman by taking her young son to see his father in a small town. But when Zatoichi and the boy arrive and discover that the man is forced into working for a gangster in illegal activities, Zatoichi steps in to battle the crime boss. Shintaru Katsu stars in this outing, which inspired the Rutger Hauer film "Blind Fury." 87 min. In Japanese with English subtitles.
53-8662 Letterboxed *$19.99*

The Blind Swordsman Samaritan (1968)
Zatoichi (Shintaro Katsu) is hired by a Yakuza boss to kill a young man with a large debt, but discovers after finishing his assignment the gangster wanted the man killed in order to get to his beautiful sister. Zatoichi steps in to help the girl fight off her unwanted admirer. 84 min. In Japanese with English subtitles.
53-8046 Letterboxed *$19.99*

The Blind Swordsman And The Fugitives (1968)
A group of criminals enlists the massage services of Zatoichi, but flees when their leader recognizes him as a master swordsman. The thieves soon join forces with another gang of ruffians and proceed to terrorize the countryside, prompting Zatoichi to take action against swords, daggers and even gunfire. Shintaro Katsu stars. In Japanese with English subtitles.
53-8513 Letterboxed *$19.99*

Zatoichi Meets Yojimbo (1970)
It's the samurai showdown action fans have dreamed about, as blind swordsman Zatoichi (Shintaro Katsu), tired of his violent life, returns to his native village. In his absence, however, a corrupt warlord has taken over, and itinerant bodyguard Toshiro Mifune is charged with taking out Zatoichi. 116 min. In Japanese with English subtitles.
53-7118 Letterboxed *$29.99*

Blind Woman's Curse (1970)
Set in turn-of-the-century Japan, this atmospheric mix of crime drama, samurai action and supernatural suspense details the battle between warring Yakuza factions, and what happens when a female gang boss accidentally blinds another woman from a rival clan during a fight. Teruo Ishii directed this final entry in the "Rising Dragon" trilogy. AKA: "Kaidan Nobori Ryu," "The Tattooed Swordswoman." 83 min. In Japanese with English subtitles.
53-8362 Letterboxed *$39.99*

Violated Paradise (1963)
A strange mix of softcore drama and "mondo"-themed documentary, this Japanese film follows an innocent young woman who leaves her rural home to start a new life in cosmopolitan Tokyo, but finds big-city life too decadent for her tastes. Along the way, viewers are treated to topless abalone fisherwomen, geisha ceremonies, Ginza nightclub shows and unusual religious ceremonies. Kazuko Mine stars. Narrated in English.
79-5441 Was $24.99 *$19.99*

Misa The Dark Angel (1997)
Misa Kuroi is a good witch, but wherever she goes, evil follows. When a young girl is burned to death, Misa investigates the incident by enrolling at the Saint Salem School for Girls and joining the Drama Club, whose members are spending the summer at a haunted house where bizarre horrors await. Based on a popular Japanese comic book series; With Hinako Saeki, Ayaka Nanami. 90 min. In Japanese with English subtitles.
20-8112 Letterboxed *$29.99*

Village Of Dreams (1998)
From director Yoichi Higashi comes this film about twin brothers who recall their childhood in a rural fishing village. Whether it be fishing for eels, causing mischief at school, or getting visits from the spirits of the dead, they discover the joys and mysteries of their past in ways that they never could have imagined. With Miekó Harada, Keigo Matsuyama and Shogo Matsuyama. 112 min. In Japanese with English subtitles.
53-6204 Letterboxed *$89.99*

Grave Of The Fireflies (1988)
Based on an award-winning story, this beautifully animated story tells of an orphaned teenager and her young sister who try to survive the effects of American bombing in a Japanese city after World War II. 88 min. In Japanese with English subtitles.
20-7132 Letterboxed *$19.99*

Grave Of The Fireflies (Dubbed Version)
Also available in a dubbed-in-English edition.
20-8137 Letterboxed *$29.99*

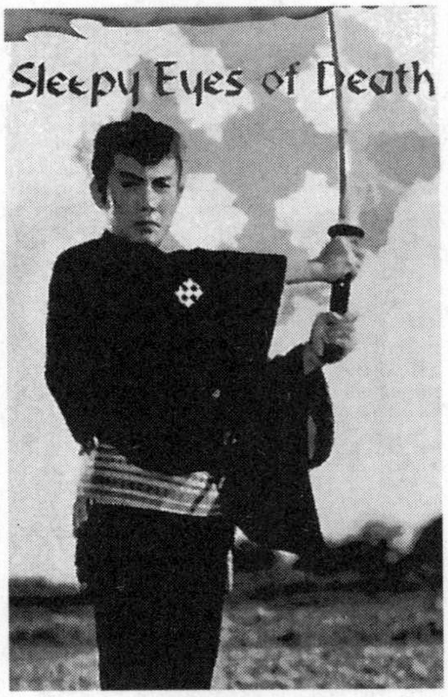

Sleepy Eyes Of Death: The Chinese Jade (1963)
Meet "Son of the Black Mass" Kyoshiro Nemuri (Raizo Ichikawa), a half-breed, red-haired samurai who slices down anyone that stands in his way with his incredible "Full Moon Cut" style. In this first film in the popular action series, a seductress attempts to set Nemuri against her master's enemy, the protector of an invaluable document. AKA: "Kyoshiro Nemuri: Book of Killing." 82 min. In Japanese with English subtitles.
20-7627 Letterboxed *$29.99*

Sleepy Eyes Of Death: Sword Of Adventure (1963)
Kyoshrio Nemuri, the half-breed samurai with the lethal swordfighting technique, is drugged, captured and prepared to be made a sexual slave to the Shogun's depraved daughter. He escapes her clutches, but soon finds himself fending off assassins out to kill the woman's elderly guardian. Wild samurai epic stars Raizo Ichikawa. AKA: "Kyoshiro Nemuri: Showdown." 83 min. In Japanese with English subtitles.
20-7754 Letterboxed *$29.99*

Sleepy Eyes Of Death: Full Circle Killing (1964)
The blood-filled saga of the "Full Moon Killer" continues, as a violent beheading on a shadowy street corner leads master swordsman Raizo Ichikawa into an encounter with a sadistic young nobleman and his domineering mother. Yuko Hamada also stars. In Japanese with English subtitles.
20-7841 Letterboxed *$29.99*

Sleepy Eyes Of Death: Sword Of Seduction (1965)
The murder of her handmaidens by another deviant daughter of the Shogun (this one a bloodthirsty opium addict) leads masterless samurai Kyoshiro Nemuri, "Son of the Black Mass," into a deadly series of confrontations—including a meeting with his Portuguese missionary father!—in this exciting entry in the violent "chambara" series. Raizo Ichikawa stars. AKA: "Kyoshuro Nemuri: Seductive Sword." 87 min. In Japanese with English subtitles.
20-7974 Letterboxed *$29.99*

Sleepy Eyes Of Death: Sword Of Fire (1965)
When a ruthless mob of fanatics targets an innocent girl who is posing as a washerwoman for death, it's up to Kyoshiro Nemuri (Raizo Ichikawa) to use his deadly samurai skills and blazing blade to deal out his brutal brand of justice to those who would bring her harm. AKA: "Kyoshiro Nemuri: Flaming Sword." 83 min. In Japanese with English subtitles.
20-8102 Letterboxed *$29.99*

Sleepy Eyes Of Death: Sword Of Satan (1965)
Feeling responsible for the death of a woman who tried to sell her body to him, wandering swordsman Kyoshiro (Raizo Ichikawa) vows to look after her young son, who is the sole heir to a recently deceased feudal lord. Pursued by foes who want him dead, the lad's only hope rests with the "Fool Moon Killer" in this explosive actioner. AKA: "Kyoshiro Nemuri: Devilish Sword." 75 min. In Japanese with English subtitles.
20-8414 Letterboxed *$29.99*

Weird Love Makers (1960)
A Tokyo pickpocket whose best friend is a prostitute tries to rip off the wrong person and finds himself in prison, where he makes friends with another convict. When they are released, the two men move in with the prostitute, but they're soon in the middle of all sorts of sordid situations. Directed by Koreyoshi Kurahara. In Japanese with English subtitles.
79-5557 Was $24.99 *$19.99*

Late Chrysanthemums (1954)
The best-known work by Japanese filmmaker Mikio Naruse, noted for his strong female characters and downbeat dramatic style, chronicles the lives of four middle-aged geishas who react in different ways to the changes that lie before them. Haruko Sugimura, Yuko Mochizuki star. 101 min. In Japanese with English subtitles.
70-3237 Was $79.99 *$19.99*

When A Woman Ascends The Stairs (1960)
A harsh and unflinching look at one woman's life, a Ginza barmaid who fears that, as she faces her 30th birthday and the loss of her job, she will have to turn to prostitution to support herself. Compelling drama from Mikio Naruse stars Hideko Takamine, Masayuki Mori. 110 min. In Japanese with English subtitles.
70-3236 Letterboxed *$19.99*

Cruel Story Of Youth (1960)
Director Nagisa Oshima ("In the Realm of the Senses") looks at restless youth in this electrifying drama about a teenage street tough and his girlfriend who form a sexual extortion racket preying on middle-aged men. With Yusuke Kawazu and Miyuki Kuwano. 96 min. In Japanese with English subtitles.
53-7698 Was $79.99 *$29.99*

The Sun's Burial (1960)
An electrifying New Wave juvenile delinquent drama from Nagisa Oshima in the same style of his earlier "Cruel Story of Youth." The film focuses on rival teenage gangs in Japan and is set in crime-ridden slums populated with pimps and prostitutes. With Kayoko Honoo. 87 min. In Japanese with English subtitles.
53-7952 Was $79.99 *$29.99*

Violence At Noon (1966)
From Nagisa Oshima comes this fascinating study of a sex murderer, his protective wife, and the first woman he raped, all of whom live on a commune in Tokyo. The women remain strangely protective of the man for different reasons, but eventually their views shift. 99 min. In Japanese with English subtitles.
53-7669 Was $79.99 *$24.99*

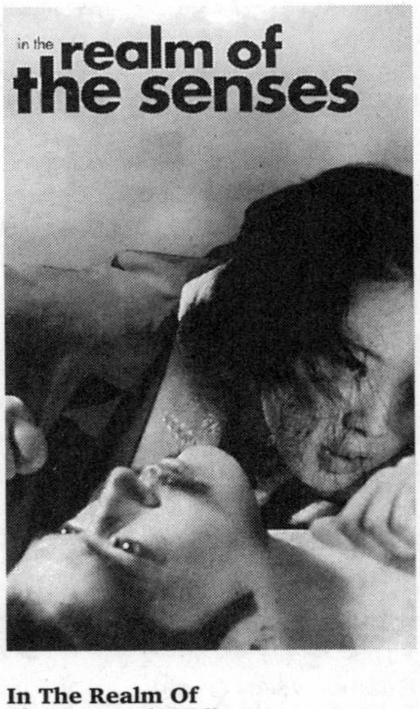

In The Realm Of The Senses (1976)
Banned by U.S. customs upon its arrival, Nagisa Oshima's sexual shocker tells about the bizarre, true-to-life love affair between a gangster and a prostitute in '30s Japan. Highlighted by lush visuals and graphic sex, as well as a violent, disturbing finale. With Tatsuya Fuji and Eiko Matsudo. 100 min. In Japanese with English subtitles.
53-9146 Was $89.99 *$19.99*

In The Realm Of The Senses (Dubbed Version)
Also available in a dubbed-in-English edition.
53-8142 Was $89.99 *$19.99*

In The Realm Of Passion (1978)
Set in Japan in 1895, this beautifully filmed story focuses on the all-consuming romance between a young soldier and an older woman, the wife of a rickshaw operator. The lovers kill the woman's husband, but his ghost appears to haunt them and his former village. From Nagisa Oshima, director of "In the Realm of the Senses." AKA: "Empire of Passion." 108 min. In Japanese with English subtitles.
53-7602 Was $89.99 *$19.99*

432 · FOREIGN
MOVIES UNLIMITED
CALL · 1-800-4-MOVIES

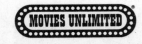

The Island (1961)
A fine example of pure cinema from Japan's Kaneto Shindo, telling the story of a peasant family living on a small island. Unique and touching film relies only on visuals, sound and music; no dialogue is used. 96 min.
09-1758 Was $29.99 ***$24.99***

Onibaba (1964)
Genuinely scary fantasy set in feudal Japan, where a widowed peasant woman and her mother-in-law survive by luring soldiers away from their comrades and slaying them for their armour, until a man comes between them. Kaneto Shindo's violent and eerie film caused a sensation in its first stateside release. Nobuko Otawa, Jitsuko Yoshimura star. 104 min. In Japanese with English subtitles.
53-7287 Letterboxed ***$29.99***

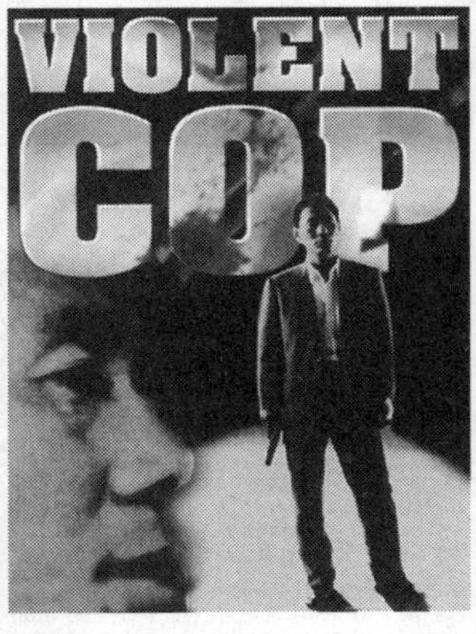

Violent Cop (1989)
After gaining popularity as a stand-up comic and TV actor, Takeshi "Beat" Kitano shocked audiences and critics by making his directorial debut with this brutal crime drama. Kitano plays a lone wolf policeman who puts his badge on the line to exact a savage vengeance on the drug gang that raped his sister and left his partner hospitalized. Maiko Kawakami also stars. 103 min. In Japanese with English subtitles.
53-6598 Letterboxed ***$19.99***

Boiling Point (3-4x Jugatsu) (1990)
After an angry encounter with local Yakuza members leads to their coach being savagely beaten by the hoods, two members of a junior baseball team seek revenge, but their trip to Okinawa to buy a gun lands them in the company of a psychotic Yakuza outcast. Takeshi "Beat" Kitano's violent and darkly comic tale stars Masahiko Ono and Kitano as the amoral gangster Uehara. 98 min. In Japanese with English subtitles.
53-6599 Letterboxed ***$19.99***

Violent Cop/ Boiling Point Combo
Both slam-bang Takeshi Kitano thrillers are available in a money-saving collection that can't be "Beat."
53-6602 Save $30.00! ***$89.99***

A Scene At The Sea (1992)
In a change of pace from his violent gangster films, writer/director Takeshi Kitano follows a deaf-mute garbage collector who finds a discarded surfboard on his work route and sets out, accompanied by his deaf girlfriend, to become a surfer. Kurodo Maki, Hiroko Oshima star. 101 min. In Japanese with English subtitles.
01-1580 ***$59.99***

Sonatine (1993)
"New Wave" Japanese Yakuza tale from Takeshi "Beat" Kitano mixes intense action and light humor, offering Kitano as a weary gangster called on by his boss to take his men to Okinawa, where they're slated to straighten out a turf war with rival hoods. When things turn bloody, Kitano and company seek some temporary relaxation at a beach house. 94 min. In Japanese with English subtitles.
11-2796 Was $99.99 ***□$19.99***

Kids Return (1996)
A pair of trouble-making high school bullies go on to take different career paths—one as a boxer, the other as a Yakuza hood—and a reunion at their old stomping grounds years later leads to unexpected consequences. Sentiment mixes with violence in Takeshi "Beat" Kitano's moody drama. Ken Kaneko, Masanobu Ando, Leo Morimoto star. 107 min. In Japanese with English subtitles.
01-1579 ***$59.99***

Fireworks (Hana-Bi) (1998)
Triple-threat Takeshi Kitano's poetic, explosive police saga showcases Kitano as Nishi, a detective distraught by a number of troubles in his life, including his wife's illness, his partner's handicapped status after an ambush and a debt he owes to a loan shark. Pushed to the edge, Nishi decides to pull off a bank robbery. 103 min. In Japanese with English subtitles.
53-6279 Was $94.99 ***$29.99***

Prisoner Maria: The Movie (1995)
Wrongly sent to prison for killing the drug dealer responsible for her husband's death, Maria's only chance to win release and be reunited with her son is to enter a top-secret training program and become a covert government assassin. In this intense actioner, a high-ranking politician's son who's behind a series of savage murders must be taken out before the police catch him. Noriko Aota, Tetsuo Kurata star. 75 min. In Japanese with English subtitles.
20-8400 Letterboxed ***$29.99***

Prisoner Maria: The Movie (Dubbed Version)
Also available in a dubbed-in-English edition.
20-8401 Letterboxed ***$29.99***

Score (1995)
Explosive Japanese crime drama about a bank robber known as Chance. Bailed out of prison by a mobster who uses his expertise to pull off a series of heists, Chance's final job for his "savior" is a jewelry store robbery that erupts into a violent string of double-crosses and mayhem. Hitoshi Ozawa, Osamu Ebara star. 87 min. In Japanese with English subtitles.
20-8537 Letterboxed ***$29.99***

Lady Ninja: Reflections Of Darkness (1996)
It's girl-on-girl martial arts action, with a good deal of risqué eroticism, in this offbeat actioner set in medieval Japan. When a sexual scandal threatens to topple a powerful shogun, his advisor hires a band of female ninjas to locate the ruler's many mistresses before his enemies do...and eliminate them! 90 min. Dubbed in English.
02-9212 Letterboxed ***$19.99***

Reborn From Hell: Samurai Armageddon (1996)
Explosive action and occult fantasy mix in this tale of seven legendary fighters who are reincarnated by an evil sorcerer out to take over the world, and the one-eyed swordsman who stands in their way. Yuko Moriyama, Tomoroh Taguchi star. Uncut, unrated version; 83 min. In Japanese with English subtitles.
20-8161 Letterboxed ***$29.99***

Reborn From Hell: Samurai Armageddon (Dubbed Version)
Also available in a dubbed-in-English edition.
20-8162 Letterboxed ***$29.99***

Day-Dream (1964)
What a day for a daydream, particularly if you're in the mood for a deranged tale of a beautiful nightclub singer and an art student who are drugged by their dentist and begin to have bizarre dreams, strange sexual interludes and masochistic encounters. Is it safe? Not for the squeamish! Directed by Tetsuji Takechi. In Japanese with English subtitles.
79-5931 Was $24.99 ***$19.99***

King Of The Mongols (1964)
Exciting historical action yarn from Japan in which a young samurai attempts to save a city under attack by the vicious Mongol, Kubla Khan. The samurai is blinded and his mother is killed by Khan's men, but he battles on. Hashizo Okawa and Jun Tazaki star. Dubbed in English.
79-6164 Was $24.99 ***$19.99***

Velvet Hustler (1967)
In this exciting Japanese Yakuza yarn, a gangster goes on the lam after killing the leader of his own crime family. But when he's closely followed by fellow crooks and the cops, he decides to hide in plain sight as an enforcer for a group of prostitutes. Tetsuya Watari stars in Toshio Masuda's effort. AKA: "Crimson Comet." 97 min. In Japanese with English subtitles.
53-6494 Letterboxed ***$29.99***

Boneless (1968)
An interesting examination of Japanese culture, released in theaters as an exploitation item, which delves into the world of obsession, adultery, blackmail and complex schemes. Directed by Seichi Fukuda. 76 min. In Japanese with English subtitles.
79-5531 Was $24.99 ***$19.99***

Double Suicide (1969)
Compelling Japanese drama, based on a traditional Bunraku puppet play (which is performed within the film itself) about a unhappily married shopkeeper who enters into a suicide pact with his mistress. Kichiemon Nakamura and Shima Iwashita (who plays both Nakamura's wife and his lover) star. 104 min. In Japanese with English subtitles.
45-5431 Was $59.99 ***$29.99***

Lady Snowblood (1973)
One of the first female stars of Japanese swordplay cinema, Meiko Kaji, is the title anti-heroine, wandering the countryside of turn-of-the-century Japan seeking revenge on the thieves who murdered her father and raped her mother. Based on a popular comic book series, this violent action tale also stars Shin Kishida and future director Juzo Itami ("Tampopo"). 97 min. In Japanese with English subtitles.
20-7973 Letterboxed ***$29.99***

Lady Snowblood: Love Song Of Vengeance (1974)
Captured and condemned to death for her deadly rampage in the first film, Meiko Kaji, the swordswoman known as Lady Snowblood, is given a chance to escape the hangman by going undercover and recover incriminating documents from a political subversive. Things get complicated when Kaji falls for the radicals' leader (Juzo Itami), but romance doesn't get in the way of the action. 89 min. In Japanese with English subtitles.
20-8003 Letterboxed ***$29.99***

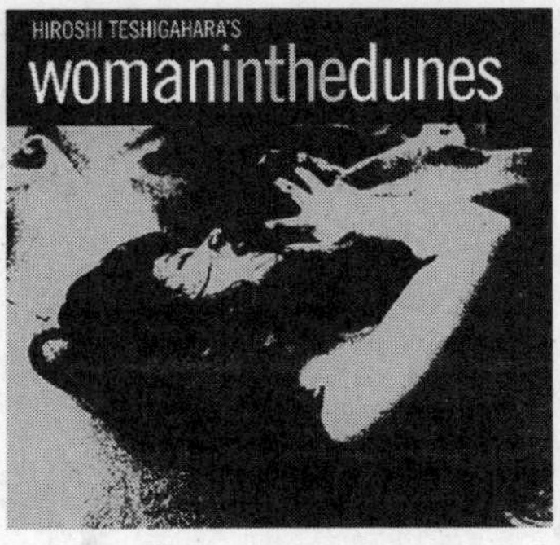

Woman In The Dunes (1964)
A haunting, allegorical Japanese film. A naturalist visiting a remote desert town is left by the villagers in an inescapable pit with a woman, but for what purpose? Hypnotic, passionate and suspenseful; directed by Hiroshi Teshigahara. 123 min. In Japanese with English subtitles.
80-5029 Was $89.99 ***$29.99***

Slave Widow (1969)
Striking sexual drama from Japan's Mamoru Watanabe in which a widow left with a huge debt consents to a sexual slave relationship with the man to whom her husband owed money. She soon experiences sexual satisfaction...then the man's son falls in love with her. 79 min. In Japanese with English subtitles.
79-5530 Was $24.99 ***$19.99***

Hunter In The Dark (1980)
An action-packed and erotic "yakuza" gangster film set in the 18th century and centering on a once-powerful clan whose members, among them a tough mobster and an amnesiac killer, wish to resurrect the gang and return to their glory days. Filled with magnificent camerawork and expertly staged action scenes, Hideo Gosha's film plays like Sergio Leone by way of "The Godfather." Tatsuya Nakadai, Sonny Chiba star. 138 min. In Japanese with English subtitles.
70-3187 Was $79.99 ***$29.99***

Swords Of Death (1971)
Suspenseful tale of a swordsman drawn into a web of deceit and vengeance when he kills a man in a fight. Superior action scenes and surprising swordplay, starring Kinnosuke Nakamura and Rentaro Mikuni. 76 min. In Japanese with English subtitles.
53-7086 ***$69.99***

Wife To Be Sacrificed (1974)
Noted for his compelling, erotic dramas of kinky sexuality, Japanese filmmaker Masaru Konuma spins a twisted tale of a woman who charges her husband with battery and divorces him when he flees. Three years later, he returns to abduct his ex-wife and draw her into a bizarre world of bondage and domination. Naomi Tani stars. 80 min. In Japanese with English subtitles.
01-1575 ***$39.99***

Sandakan No. 8 (1974)
Nominated for a Best Foreign Film Oscar, this drama tells the true story of Japanese women who were sold as prostitutes in Borneo during the "rubber plantation" years of the early 1900s, and who returned home to face scorn from those around them; directed by Kei Kumai. 121 min. In Japanese with English subtitles.
53-7011 ***$69.99***

A Woman Called Sada Abe: Beyond The Realm Of The Senses (1975)
Made shortly before Nagisa Oshima's more famous "In the Realm of the Senses," this erotic drama sticks closer to actual events to tell the story of a merchant's daughter in 1930s Japan who is cast out by her family after she is raped. Eventually moving to Tokyo, she becomes a Geisha and begins a passionate, violent affair with a married businessman that ends in a shocking act. Junko Miyashita, Hideaki Ezumi star. 80 min. In Japanese with English subtitles.
01-1576 ***$39.99***

Sure Death! (1984)
The first in a series of films based on the popular Japanese martial arts TV series "Hissatsu," this tongue-in-cheek historical actioner stars Makoto Fujita as Mondo, a henpecked and put-upon constable in 19th-century Tokyo who is secretly the head of a group of master assassins. When a rival clan of killers sets out to eliminate their competition, Mondo and his allies prepare for a final battle to the death. 123 min. In Japanese with English subtitles.
20-8004 Letterboxed ***$14.99***

Rikisha-Man (1958)
A masterful drama of unrequited love starring Toshiro Mifune as a plucky rickshaw driver who befriends a fatherless boy and becomes enamored of his wealthy mother, despite the gulf between their social stations. Directed by Hiroshi Inagaki ("Samurai"). 105 min. In Japanese with English subtitles.
53-7010 ***$69.99***

The Saga Of The Vagabonds (1959)
In feudal Japan, warlords levy crushing taxes on farmers in order to finance their own violent activities. When one province's warfund is stolen during delivery, the local noble joins up with the bandits in an attempt to redistribute the money in this lively adaptation of the Robin Hood legend. Stars Toshiro Mifune. 115 min. In Japanese with English subtitles.
53-7082 ***$69.99***

Samurai Saga (1959)
Delightful adaptation of "Cyrano de Bergerac," with the action switched to Japan of 1599, where a gallant samurai, cursed with a monstrous nose, falls in love with a ravishing princess who has fallen in love with his handsome comrade. With Toshiro Mifune and Yoko Tsukasa. 112 min. In Japanese with English subtitles.
53-7083 ***$49.99***

The Gambling Samurai (1960)
Returning to his birthplace after a long absence, samurai Toshiro Mifune exacts patient but deadly retribution against the petty officials who oppress the townspeople and caused the suicide of his sister. 93 min. In Japanese with English subtitles.
53-7008 ***$59.99***

I Bombed Pearl Harbor (1960)
Compelling look at the Pacific campaign of World War II through Japanese eyes stars Toshiro Mifune as Admiral Isoroku Yamaguchi, commander of the Japanese task force that attacked the Hawaiian naval base on December 7, 1941, and Yosuke Natsuki as a young officer who takes part in some of the war's most decisive battles. AKA: "Storm Over the Pacific." 98 min. Dubbed in English.
55-9024 Was $29.99 ***$19.99***

Samurai Assassin (1965)
In what is considered by many to be the greatest samurai film of all time, the legendary Toshiro Mifune stars as a masterless swordsman who joins a plot to assassinate an advisor of the emperor in order to gain favor and become a samurai. Based on an actual event during the Edo period of the mid-19th century. Directed by Kihachi Okamoto . AKA: "Samurai." 122 min. In Japanese with English subtitles.
20-8103 Letterboxed ***$29.99***

Sword Of Doom (1967)
Powerful and violent story of a young man (Tatsuya Nakadai) who adopts the way of the samurai as a means to gain vengeance. Toshiro Mifune is magnificent as the teacher who readies the youngster for his ultimate battle. Kihachi Okamoto directs. 120 min. In Japanese with English subtitles.
53-1683 Letterboxed ***$29.99***

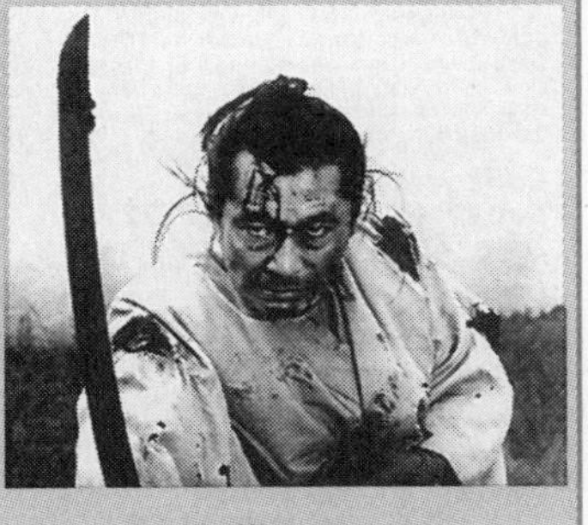

Samurai Rebellion (1967)
Set in 18th-century Japan, this compelling mix of action and drama from director Masaki Kobayashi ("Harikiri") stars Toshiro Mifune as a warrior torn between duty and family when the local ruler demands that Mifune's daughter-in-law, a former mistress to the overlord, be returned to him. With Takeshi Kata, Yoko Tsukasa. AKA: "Rebellion." 121 min. In Japanese with English subtitles.
22-5919 Letterboxed ***$29.99***

Red Lion (1969)
Stablehand Toshiro Mifune is asked by crooked government officials to impersonate a powerful military officer. Indending to return to his home village in glory, where Mifune realizes he had become a pawn of an evil magistrate bleeding the villagers dry for tax money he sets out to put things right. Shima Iwashita, Nobuko Otowa also star. 115 min. In Japanese with English subtitles.
20-7972 Letterboxed ***$29.99***

Samurai Banners (1969)
In 16th-century Japan, scheming warrior Toshiro Mifune rises to a position of influence in the house of a powerful warlord, but finds his loyalty tested when he and his lord fall for the same woman and a renegade priest raises an army and launches an attack. Yoshiko Samuka, Kinnosuke Nakamura also star. AKA: "Under the Banner of the Samurai." 166 min. In Japanese with English subtitles.
20-7975 Letterboxed ***$34.99***

Incident At Blood Pass (1970)
Toshiro Mifune reprises his role as the antihero samurai Yojimbo for the final time in this action-packed Japanese epic that has him teaming with doctor Shintaro Katsu (of "Zatoichi" fame) to hijack a Shogunate gold convoy. Of course, it doesn't go as planned. Directed by Inagaki Hiroshi. AKA: "Ambush." 118 min. In Japanese with English subtitles.
20-8101 Letterboxed ***$29.99***

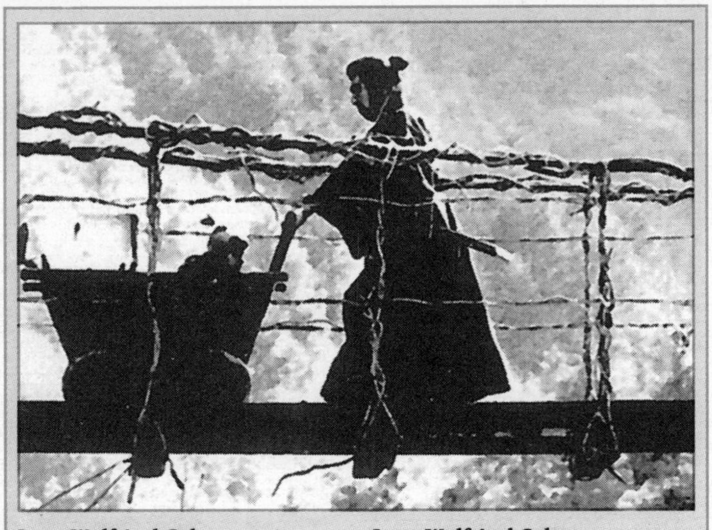

Lone Wolf And Cub: Sword Of Vengeance (1972)
Wildly violent first entry in the infamous "Baby Cart" samurai series that led to the Americanized "Shogun Assassin" feature. The story focuses on Itto Ogami, lethal court executioner for the Yagyu clan. Falsely accused of treason, Itto's wife is killed and he is forced to roam the countryside with his infant son. Tomisaburo Wakayama, Fumio Watanabe star. AKA: "Lone Wolf with Child: Lend a Child...Lend an Arm." 83 min. In Japanese with English subtitles.
20-7624 Letterboxed *$29.99*

Lone Wolf And Cub: Baby Cart At The River Styx (1972)
Swordsman-for-hire Itto Ogami is hired to kill a defector out to sell his clan's valuable dye-making process. To reach his target, Ogami must battle not only three bodyguards known as "The Gods of Death," but also a female ninja sent by the Yagyu clan to eliminate him and his son. 81 min. Japanese with English subtitles.
20-7626 Letterboxed *$29.99*

Lone Wolf And Cub: Baby Cart To Hades (1972)
The third "Baby Cart" film finds wandering assassin Tomisaburo Wakayama aiding a prostitute who killed her pimp, only to be captured and nearly beaten to death by the Yakuza. A local family's official then hires the "Lone Wolf" to kill a corrupt governor who killed the clan's leader and stole their estate. This violent actioner was retitled "Lightning Swords of Death" for a brief American release. 89 min. In Japanese with English subtitles.
20-7707 Letterboxed *$29.99*

Lone Wolf And Cub: Baby Cart In Peril (1973)
The father of a martial arts student who was raped by her teacher and is now endangering their clan with her quest for revenge reluctantly hires Itto Ogami to engage her in a duel to the death. Now wearing a grotesque tattoo across her chest as a reminder of the assault, the woman opens her shirt in the heat of battle to distract her opponents. AKA: "Lone Wolf with Child: Heart of a Parent, Heart of a Child." 81 min. In Japanese with English subtitles.
20-7753 Letterboxed *$29.99*

Lone Wolf And Cub: Baby Cart In The Land Of Demons (1973)
After being tested by them in violent battle, itinerant swordsman Itto Ogami is hired by retainers of a powerful but insane warlord to stop their master's plan to install his mistress's daughter, disguised as a boy, as his heir, a move which will spell the clan's downfall. This fifth "Lone Wolf" actioner is considered by many to be the best film in the series. AKA: "Lone Wolf with Child: Tread Lightly on the Path to Hell." 89 min. In Japanese with English subtitles.
20-7796 Letterboxed *$29.99*

Lone Wolf And Cub: White Heaven In Hell (1974)
In the concluding chapter to the original "Lone Wolf" film series, Itto Ogami and son Daigoro face the ultimate challenge from corrupt clan ruler Retsudo Yagyu, who dispatches his knife-wielding daughter, his illegitimate son from a rival clan, and a trio of tunnel-burrowing warriors to kill them, leading to a final battle in a frozen wilderness. Tomisaburo Wakayama, Akihiro Tomikawa star. AKA: "Lone Wolf with Child: Daigoro! We're Going to Hell!" 84 min. In Japanese with English subtitles.
20-7840 Letterboxed *$29.99*

Harakiri (1962)
Compelling Japanese costume drama from director Masaki Kobayashi ("Kwaidan"), about a 17th-century samurai in search of a lord to serve. When one ruler turns him down, he is compelled by the society's rigid code of honor to commit ritualistic suicide. Tatsuya Nakadai, Shima Iwashita star. 135 min. In Japanese with English subtitles.
22-5789 Letterboxed *$29.99*

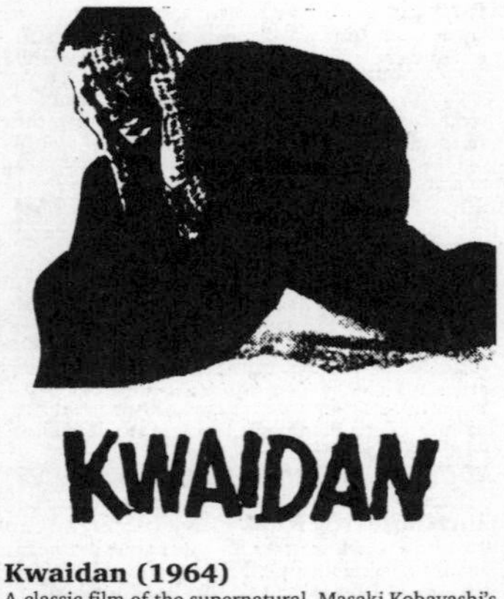

Kwaidan (1964)
A classic film of the supernatural, Masaki Kobayashi's tetralogy of ghost tales depicts a woman whose love for her samurai husband lasts beyond death, a love-starved snow spirit, a demon-fighting priest and a haunted cup of tea. 164 min. In Japanese with English subtitles.
22-5543 Letterboxed *$29.99*

Blowback: Love And Death (1990)
Left for dead by the crooks who double-crossed him and killed his partner, a Japanese hood named Joe turns the Philippines upside-down in his campaign of vengeance, but will the help of a beautiful bar owner be enough when he goes up against a ruthless crime boss named Wildcat? High-octane action tale stars Riki Takeushi, Mie Yoshida, Mike Monty. AKA: "Blowback 2." 90 min. In Japanese with English subtitles.
20-8597 *$29.99*

Traffic Jam (Jutai) (1991)
Contemporary Japanese culture is satirized in this darkly humorous account of a young Tokyo couple and their two kids who take a long car trip to see the husband's parents. What starts as a pleasurable trip, however, becomes a disaster as strange incidents make the long journey seem interminable. Music is performed by Kenny G. 108 min. In Japanese with English subtitles.
01-1498 Was $79.99 *$29.99*

Tetsuo II: Body Hammer (1991)
Writer/director Shinya Tsukamoto continues his cinematic exploration of the merging of human and machine, as a job-obsessed Japanese "salaryman" finds himself turning into the latest cybernetic mutant. At the same time, he pursues the mysterious skinheads who kidnapped his son through the glass-and-steel canyons of modern Tokyo. Tomoroh Taguchi, Nobu Nakaoka star. Uncut, NC-17 version; 83 min. In Japanese with English subtitles.
02-8995 *$19.99*

Tokyo Fist (1995)
From mondo filmmaker Shinya Tsukamoto ("Tetsuo: The Iron Man") comes this offbeat drama about an insurance salesman (played by the director) who takes to the gym to train when an old high school classmate, now a troubled pro boxer, comes for a visit and tries to move in on the salesman's fiancée. Dark comedy and violent action mix in Tsukamoto's unique style. Unrated version; 85 min. In Japanese with English subtitles.
02-8866 *$19.99*

Himatsuri (Fire Festival) (1985)
An epic drama of eternal conflict from Japan, centering on the life of a self-centered woodsman whose lack of caring for those around him seals his ultimate fate. Visually poetic drama laced with mythic elements, directed by Mitsuo Kanagimachi. 120 min. In Japanese with English subtitles.
40-1220 *$59.99*

Gonza The Spearman (1986)
A compelling tale of a Japanese lord whose tradition of leaving his wife and family in alternating years leads to tragic results. A stunning film starring Hiromi Go and Shima Iwashita and directed by Masahiro Shinoda ("Double Suicide"), one of Japan's top "New Wave" directors . 126 min. In Japanese with English subtitles.
53-7388 Was $79.99 *$24.99*

Summer Vacation: 1999 (1989)
At a rural boarding school, four male students (played by teenage girls) who remained behind for summer vacation find themselves caught up in a strange game of sexual tension, jealousy and reincarnation. Unusual and bittersweet tale from director Shusuke Kaneko, based on a popular comic strip, stars Eri Miyajima, Miyuki Nakano. 90 min. In Japanese with English subtitles.
53-7550 *$69.99*

The Ninja Dragon (1990)
Mobsters meet martial arts in this explosive Japanese actioner from anime master Go Nagai, as Yakuza leaders are killed by mysterious, unstoppable foes, and the daughter of one gang boss is protected by three mystical ninja fighters. Kenji Otsuki, Rikiya Yasuoka and pro wrestler Cutie Suzuki star. 70 min. In Japanese with English subtitles.
20-5136 *$29.99*

Rikyu (1991)
Magnificent historical epic from Hiroshi Tesgigahara ("Woman in the Dunes"), focusing on the tumultuous events surrounding the life of Sen-No Rikyu, the revered advisor and tea master to the powerful Lord Toyotimi in 16th-century Japan. Filled with sweeping battle scenes and moral complexity, this is a film not to be missed. With Rentaro Mikuni and Tsutomu Yamazaki. 116 min. In Japanese with English subtitles.
75-1009 *$79.99*

The Silk Road (1992)
A spectacular adventure film focusing on the fight between merchants and rebel armies for possession of the Silk Road, an important roadway for transporting goods to Chinese cities. A young man is forced into becoming a warrior when he braves a rebel attack, and sets out to rescue a princess held captive. Toshiyuki Nishida stars. 99 min. In Japanese with English subtitles.
68-1233 Was $89.99 *$12.99*

Spanking Love (1994)
After his top actress walks out on him, an adult filmmaker begins scouring the streets of Tokyo looking for a replacement. He finds a mysterious woman named Yukie and follows her to the S&M club where she works, but is he ready to enter her world of pain and pleasure? Find out in this erotically charged drama. 100 min. In Japanese with English subtitles.
20-8546 Was $79.99 *$24.99*

Sanctuary: The Movie (1995)
Based on the popular Japanese comic strip and animated series, this gritty live-action drama chronicles the journey of two young men from the genocide of Cambodia to the vice-riddled streets of Tokyo, as one man tries to make his way in politics while the other becomes part of the Japanese mob. Hiroshi Abe, Masanori Sera star. 103 min. In Japanese with English subtitles.
20-7641 *$34.99*

Weather Woman (1995)
The forecast is for outrageous, racy fun in this Japanese comedy based on a comic-book and cartoon series. A determined TV weather girl sends her station's ratings into the stratosphere when she flashes her underwear to the viewing audience, but will her newfound fame be sidetracked by a scheming rival? Kei Mizutani, Yasuyo Shirashima star. 84 min. In Japanese with English subtitles.
20-8362 *$29.99*

Tokyo: The Last Megalopolis (1997)
In the early 20th century, a renegade psychic kidnaps a young woman whose powers will help him revive a malevolent spirit that was trapped beneath Tokyo a thousand years earlier. Only a mystical priest and his allies stand between the city and its destruction in this tale of supernatural horror and action. Shintaro Katsu, Kyusaku Shimada star. 135 min. In Japanese with English subtitles.
20-8076 *$19.99*

Baptism Of Blood (1996)
Twisted Japanese shocker about a beautiful film star afflicted with a disfiguring disease. A sinister scientist offers the actress her only chance: transplanting her brain into her teenage daughter's body! The operation works...or does it? Rie Imamura, Risa Akikawa star. 93 min. In Japanese with English subtitles.
20-8385 *$29.99*

Fudoh: The New Generation (1996)
As emotional as it is violent, this powerful Japanese drama follows a young man eager for revenge against his Yakuza boss father for his brother's brutal murder. Gathering up his own crime empire, the vengeful son launches an all-out war for control of the streets. Takeshi Caesar, Mickey Curtis, Tamaki Kenmochi star. 100 min. In Japanese with English subtitles.
20-8452 Letterboxed *$29.99*

Tokyo Blue: Case 1 (1998)
Girls and guns are both in ample supply in this steamy Japanese crime drama. Beautiful police detectives Mika and Rin have their hands full when the government asks them to track down an ex-con who has the means for making perfect counterfeit cash. 100 min. Dubbed in English.
20-8389 *$19.99*

PB82: Police Branch 82 (1998)
Law enforcement was never so lovely—or so lethal—as in this explosive Japanese action tale about two gorgeous, gun-toting female detectives who are assigned to recover a stolen religious statue and wind up in some sexy, violent confrontations. Haruni Inoue, Mamiko Tayama, Liliko star. 90 min. Dubbed in English.
20-8596 *$19.99*

Gate Of Hell (1954)
Winner of the Academy Award for Best Foreign Film, this exciting, colorful epic from Teinosuke Kinugasa details the doomed love between a soldier and a married noblewoman in 12th-century Japan. Machiko Kyo, Kazuo Hasegawa star. 86 min. In Japanese with English subtitles.
22-5732 *$29.99*

The Pornographers (1966)
Director Shohei Imamura attacked Japan's anti-pornography codes with this scathing satire of three men who make their living through the shooting of 8mm blue movies. Outrageous black comedy stars Shoichi Ozawa, Sumiko Sakamoto. 128 min. In Japanese with English subtitles.
53-7316 Letterboxed *$29.99*

Vengeance Is Mine (1979)
A harrowing look at the darker side of life in modern Japan, Shohei Imamura's filming of a novel based on true events tells in flashback the life of a habitual criminal (Ken Ogata), a life of deprivation and anger that culminates in murder. 143 min. In Japanese with English subtitles.
45-5458 Letterboxed *$29.99*

Eijanaika (1981)
Shohei Imamura directed this epic that mixes elements of corruption, drama and eroticism in telling the story of Japan's Samurai class losing power and prestige to the Imperial government and American businessmen in 19th-century Tokyo. 151 min. In Japanese with English subtitles.
53-7390 Was $79.99 *$24.99*

Black Rain (1989)
The first Japanese film to look at the death and devastation caused by the atomic bombing of Hiroshima, this graphic and powerful drama follows the lives of various survivors who attempt to continue with their lives while the ever-present danger of radiation sickness looms over them. Directed and co-written by Shohei Imamura. 123 min. In Japanese with English subtitles.
53-7581 Was $79.99 *$19.99*

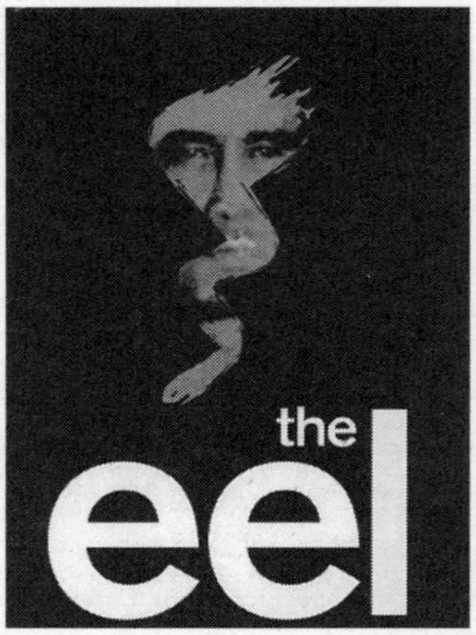

The Eel (Unagi) (1997)
Released from prison eight years after killing his unfaithful wife, Japanese "salaryman" Koji Yakusho, accompanied by the pet eel ("He listens to what I say") he kept behind bars, tries to start a new life as a barber in a small town. Misa Shimizu is the woman who becomes Yakusho's assistant and is attracted to him, but has a tragedy in her own past, in this unusual character study from Shohei Imamura. 117 min. In Japanese with English subtitles.
53-6805 Letterboxed *$94.99*

Dr. Akagi (1998)
Set on a remote Japanese island near the end of World War II, director Shohei Imamura's moving drama stars Akira Emoto as the island community's only doctor. Struggling to cope with a mounting hepatitis epidemic (an obsession that earns him the nickname "Dr. Liver"), Emoto gets help from an odd array of assistants, among them a teenage prostitute, a drug-addicted surgeon, and an escaped Dutch POW. Kumiko Aso, Jyuro Kara also star. AKA: "Kanzo Sensei." 128 min. In Japanese with English subtitles.
53-6586 *$79.99*

Akira Kurosawa

Sanshiro Sugata (The Judo Saga) (1943)
The nascent cinematic style of Akira Kurosawa is evident in this, his first outing as director. A 19th-century jujitsu student is engrossed by the disciplines of judo, culminating in a heated engagement with his beloved's father. Susumu Fujita, Denjiro Okochi star. 82 min. In Japanese with English subtitles.
45-5445 Was $29.99 *$19.99*

The Men Who Tread On The Tiger's Tail (1945)
Based on a popular Kabuki play, this early film from director Akira Kurosawa follows a fugitive clan lord and his six loyal aides as they flee through medieval Japan to escape the wrath of the lord's brother, a vengeful shogun. Hanshiro Iwai, Denjiro Okochi, Susumu Fujita star. 60 min. In Japanese with English subtitles.
22-5830 *$39.99*

No Regrets For Our Youth (1946)
Stirring drama of a frivolous, self-centered girl who grows in body and spirit amid the ruin and tumult of post-war Japan. Her changes reflect the hope for a new national rebirth in this, the first major work by Akira Kurosawa. Denjiro Okochi, Eiko Miyoshi star. 110 min. In Japanese with English subtitles.
53-7339 Was $29.99 *$19.99*

One Wonderful Sunday (1947)
A sentimental slice of postwar Japanese life, this early Akira Kurosawa work follows a disillusioned veteran and his fiancée through what they hope will be a romantic weekend afternoon in downtown Tokyo. The most famous scene has the girl asking the audience for applause to build up her boyfriend's spirits. Chieko Nakakita, Isao Numasaki star. AKA: "Wonderful Sunday." 108 min. In Japanese with English subtitles.
22-6011 *$19.99*

The Drunken Angel (1948)
Moving Akira Kurosawa drama, set in the lower-class section of a Japanese city, stars Toshiro Mifune as a dedicated doctor who tries to improve the lives of those around him. 102 min. In Japanese with English subtitles.
53-7007 Remastered *$19.99*

Quiet Duel (1949)
In Akira Kurosawa's stark drama, Toshiro Mifune is a young, virgin doctor working in a small hospital who contracts syphilis from a patient. Troubled by his conscience, Mifune decides to secretly treat himself and not marry the woman he had planned to. With Takashi Shimura. 95 min. In Japanese with English subtitles.
10-9445 *$19.99*

Stray Dog (1949)
On the streets of postwar Tokyo, a rookie police detective searches for his missing gun. Gritty Akira Kurosawa drama blends American "film noir" stylings with a look at the moral vacuum that formed in Japan following World War II. Toshiro Mifune, Takashi Shimura, Ko Kimura star. 122 min. In Japanese with English subtitles.
45-5420 *$29.99*

Scandal (1950)
Painter Toshiro Mifune sues a magazine for printing a scandalous story that links him to a popular singer, then hires a lawyer of questionable motives to represent him. Akira Kurosawa's drama is filled with irony and wry commentary on Japan's acceptance of American culture. With Yoshiko Yamaguchi. 104 min. In Japanese with English subtitles.
10-9446 Remastered *$19.99*

Rashomon (1950)
A rape and murder in medieval Japan are recounted in four flashback sequences, as seen through the eyes of the three people involved and a witness to the incident. Each version differs from the others, leaving viewers to draw their own conclusions on what actually transpired. Akira Kurosawa's breakthrough drama stars Toshiro Mifune, Machiko Kyo. 83 min. In Japanese with English subtitles.
22-5734 Remastered *$29.99*

The Idiot (1951)
Akira Kurosawa transposes Dostoyevsky's classic from Russia to Japan as he tells the story of an epileptic soldier and a wealthy businessman who vie for the love of a beautiful woman. Their obsessions lead to murder in this stark, brilliantly acted film featuring Toshiro Mifune and Masayuki Mori. 166 min. In Japanese with English subtitles.
53-7663 *$89.99*

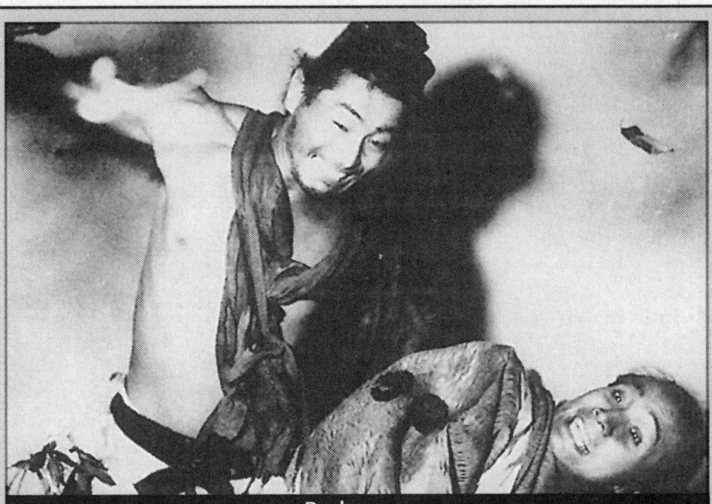
Rashomon

Ikiru (1952)
Thoughtful tale from Akira Kurosawa about a petty bureaucrat who, after he learns he has terminal cancer, tries to set his life in order and searches for the meaning of his existence. Takashi Shimura stars in this haunting, inspiring drama. 140 min. In Japanese with English subtitles.
22-5633 *$39.99*

The Seven Samurai (1954)
One of the greatest action epics ever, Akira Kurosawa's masterwork is set in 16th-century Japan, where a small village hires a group of professional warriors to protect itself from roving bandits. Fabulous battle scenes are mixed with characters filled with emotion and humanity. Toshiro Mifune, Takashi Shimura star. 208 min. In Japanese with English subtitles.
22-5638 Remastered *$34.99*

I Live In Fear (1955)
Compelling Akira Kurosawa drama, and one of the first Japanese efforts to deal with the atomic bomb, stars Toshiro Mifune as an industrialist whose fear of a nuclear war and attempts to move his family to a "safe" country drive him to madness and financial ruin. With Eiko Miyoshi. AKA: "The Record of a Living Being." 105 min. In Japanese with English subtitles.
10-9447 Remastered *$19.99*

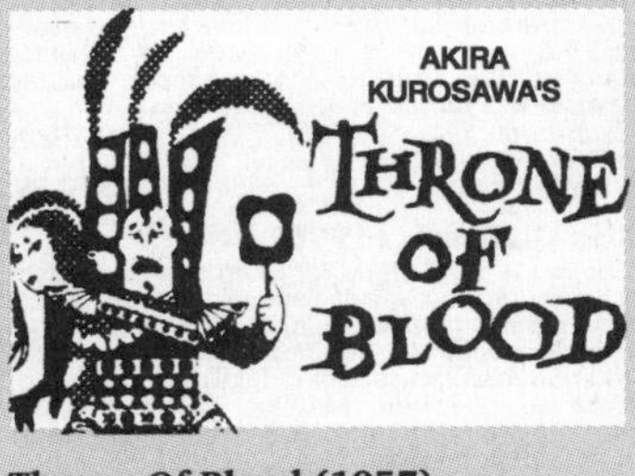

Throne Of Blood (1957)
Akira Kurosawa transforms "Macbeth" into an outstanding samurai saga starring Toshiro Mifune as the tragic ruler fated by the forewarnings of three witches. Also stars Isuzu Yamada, Takashi Shimura. 105 min. In Japanese with English subtitles.
22-5636 *$39.99*

The Lower Depths (1957)
Adapted from a play by Maxim Gorky, Akira Kurosawa's dark seriocomedy follows the adventures of a boarding home's odd residents, especially the love triangle that develops between the landlady, her sister, and a thieving boarder. Toshiro Mifune, Isuzu Yamada star. 125 min. In Japanese with English subtitles.
45-5456 *$29.99*

The Hidden Fortress (1958)
One of the main inspirations for "Star Wars," this Kurosawa epic is set in feudal Japan, where wily general Toshiro Mifune must escort a deposed princess and her clan's fortune through enemy territory, with some unwilling help from two bungling thieves. 139 min. In Japanese with English subtitles.
22-5635 Letterboxed *$29.99*

The Bad Sleep Well (1960)
Reflecting his fondness for American crime films and motifs, this Akira Kurosawa drama stars Toshiro Mifune as a young construction company executive who blames the company for his father's death and marries his boss's lame daughter in order to insinuate himself and expose their corrupt business practices. Based on a story by Ed McBain; with Masayuki Mori, Takashi Shimura. 151 min. In Japanese with English subtitles.
45-5430 Letterboxed *$29.99*

Yojimbo (1961)
Toshiro Mifune stars as the war-weary samurai who is caught in the middle of a feud between rival factions in a village. One of Kurosawa's greatest films is also a sly commentary on action movies in general and helped inspire "A Fistful of Dollars." 110 min. In Japanese with English subtitles.
22-5778 Letterboxed *$29.99*

Sanjuro (1962)
Akira Kurosawa's sequel to "Yojimbo" features Toshiro Mifune as a lonely samurai warrior who joins forces with some young fighters to stop corruption and end the reign of terror of a wicked warlord. Humor, incredible swordplay and Mifune's mighty performance are among the highlights of this epic. 96 min. In Japanese with English subtitles.
22-5788 Letterboxed *$29.99*

Samurai-For-Hire 2-Pack
Two of Akira Kurosawa's samurai classics, "Yojimbo" and "Sanjuro," are available in this money-saving collection.
22-5982 Save $10.00! *$49.99*

High And Low (1963)
Industrialist Toshiro Mifune hunts the kidnapper of his chauffeur's son in this drama from Akira Kurosawa. At once a fine detective story and brilliant allegory on the nature of class differences, as represented by the businessman, his servant and the kidnappers. Based on a story by Ed McBain. 142 min. In Japanese with English subtitles.
07-8122 Letterboxed *$29.99*

Red Beard (1965)
In early 19th-century Japan, Red Beard (Toshiro Mifune) is the head of a shoestring public health clinic who tries to turn his new assistant, a greedy and unrealistic young intern, into a real doctor. This striking film from Akira Kurosawa also stars Yuzo Kayama. 185 min. In Japanese with English subtitles.
22-5780 Letterboxed *$39.99*

Dodes'ka-Den (1970)
Telling drama by Akira Kurosawa about a group of people living in a Tokyo slum. Life's complexities and uncertainties have overtaken them, yet they get by on illusion and imagination. 140 min. In Japanese with English subtitles.
53-1504 *$29.99*

Dersu Uzala (1975)
A Russian expedition in 19th-century Siberia is saved from death by a Mongolian native guide, and a friendship develops between the group's leader and the simple, resourceful hunter. Epic drama by Akira Kurosawa, based on a true story and filmed on location in the Soviet Union, won the Best Foreign Film Academy Award. Maxim Munzuk, Yuri Solomon star. 137 min. In Russian with English subtitles.
53-8016 Letterboxed *$39.99*

Kagemusha (1980)
Sprawling Akira Kurosawa epic of a petty thief in feudal Japan who is spared from death in order to impersonate a recently killed warlord, and who begins to take on the fiery drive of his predecessor. Tatsuya Nakadai stars. 160 min. In Japanese with English subtitles.
04-1309 Was $29.99 *$19.99*

Ran (1985)
Akira Kurosawa's spellbinding transposition of "King Lear" to feudal Japan chronicles Lord Hideatora's attempt to pass down his kingdom to his sons, which results in its violent and chaotic downfall. Tatsuya Nakadai stars, with Akira Terao, Jinpachi Nezu and Daisuke Ryu as his sons, and Mieko Harada as ruthless Lady Kaede. 160 min. In Japanese with English subtitles.
04-1978 Letterboxed *$29.99*

Akira Kurosawa's Dreams (1990)
Eight mesmerizing tableaus explore the subconscious at various stages of an elderly man's life in this visually stunning work from the master Japanese filmmaker. A boy's meeting with the spirits of a forest, a snowbound encounter with an "angel of death," and a novice painter's search for Van Gogh are some of the fascinating episodes Kurosawa brings to the screen. 120 min. In Japanese with English subtitles.
19-1830 *$89.99*

Rhapsody In August (1991)
Akira Kurosawa's sensitive drama tells of four children whose visit to their grandmother rekindles her frightening memories of August 9th, 1945, when an atomic bomb was dropped on Nagasaki. The children learn about the horrors of war, and when an American cousin arrives, more dark secrets of the past are revealed. Sachiko Murase and Richard Gere star. 98 min. In Japanese with English subtitles.
73-1153 Was $79.99 *$19.99*

Kurosawa Noir 3-Pack
Three film noir classics by Akira Kurosawa are offered in this three-tape set that includes "The Bad Sleep Well," "High and Low" and "Stray Dog."
22-5986 Save $10.00! *$79.99*

Early Kurosawa 3-Pack
A trio of the internationally acclaimed filmmaker's early works have been gathered in this three-tape collection: "No Regrets for Our Youth," "One Wonderful Sunday" and "Sanshiro Sugata."
22-6010 Save $10.00! *$49.99*

Rare Kurosawa 3-Pack
This special collector's set features three of the filmmaker's seminal and more obscure works: "Drunken Angel," "I Live in Fear" and "Scandal."
22-6088 Save $10.00! *$49.99*

The Bondage Master (1996)
An illegal doctor and expert in the erotic art of bondage and domination becomes the prime suspect when a model, bound in his unique style, is found strangled. Can he track down the real killer before the police or the dead woman's lover, head of a ruthless crime gang, find him in this sensual thriller? Yukijiro Hotaru, Yoriko Ikuta star. 83 min. In Japanese with English subtitles.
20-8623 *$29.99*

Angel Dust (1996)
An intense and stylish thriller from Japan, following a female police psychologist who uses her ability to merge minds with those of the killers she seeks to investigate a series of bizarre murders of women on the Tokyo subway. A chance meeting with a former lover, now working to deprogram cult members, leads to a terrifying and deadly conclusion. Kaho Minami stars; directed by Sogo Ishii. 116 min. In Japanese with English subtitles.
53-8870 Letterboxed *$29.99*

Youth Of The Beast (1963)
Fresh from his success with the cops-and-gangsters drama "Detective Bureau 23: Damn the Villains!," maverick filmmaker Seijun Suzuki helmed this audacious sequel. Police detective Jo Shishido winds up on the outs with his superiors as he takes on rival Yakuza gangs in order to avenge a friend's murder. Suzuki's surreal filmic style came into its own with this acclaimed thriller. AKA: "Wild Beast of Youth." 91 min. In Japanese with English subtitles.
22-6020 Letterboxed *$29.99*

Gate Of Flesh (1964)
Controversial for its explicit nudity (a rarity in Japanese films at the time), Seijun Suzuki's erotic drama follows four prostitutes banding together for survival in American-occupied post-WWII Japan. Their solidarity is tested when they take in a wounded black marketeer that each woman is attracted to. Yumiko Nogawa, Satoko Kasai, Jo Shishido star. 90 min. In Japanese with English subtitles.
22-6021 Letterboxed *$29.99*

Story Of A Prostitute (1965)
In the second of her "Flesh Trilogy" movies made with director Seijun Suzuki, Yumiko Nogawa ("Gate of Flesh") plays a Chinese prostitute who agrees to service a garrison of 1,000 Japanese soldiers in Manchuria during World War II. The savage commander wants Nogawa all to himself, but she risks his wrath by falling for one of his officers. Tamio Kawachi, Isao Tamagawa co-star. AKA: "Joy Girls." 86 min. In Japanese with English subtitles.
22-6022 Letterboxed *$29.99*

Tokyo Drifter (1966)
From iconoclastic filmmaker Seijun Suzuki, whose stylized crime films put him at odds with critics and his studio, comes a lightning-fast gangster drama that blends elements of American film noir and Italian spaghetti westerns. Tetsuya Watari is Tetsu, a top Yakuza member who's double-crossed by his Tokyo boss and who wanders Japan, always watching his back (and always ready to break into song!), until the inevitable showdown. 83 min. In Japanese with English subtitles.
22-5951 Letterboxed *$29.99*

Fighting Elegy (1966)
A teenager in '30s Japan, obsessed with fighting and the martial arts, is driven to join with militaristic right-wingers when he cannot be with the young woman he loves from afar. Seijun Suzuki's compelling drama, a pointed look at the nationalism that led Japan into World War II, stars Hideki Takahashi, Junko Asano. AKA: "Born Fighter," "Elegy to Violence." 86 min. In Japanese with English subtitles.
22-6023 Letterboxed *$29.99*

Branded To Kill (1967)
At once a brutal action film and a parody of the genre and its critics, this bullet-riddled saga of the Japanese mob's "No. 3 Killer"—and how a mishap on a job turns him into the target of the "No. 1 Killer"—led to director Seijun Suzuki's being dropped by his studio, but is now recognized as a surrealistic classic. Jo Shishido, Mariko Ogawa star. 91 min. In Japanese with English subtitles.
22-5952 Letterboxed *$29.99*

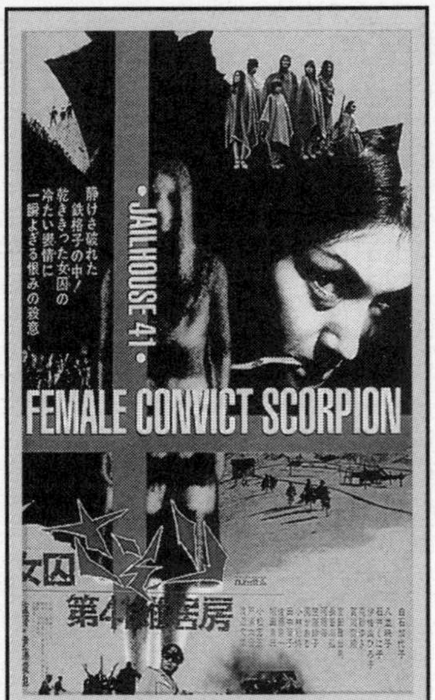

Female Convict Scorpion: Jailhouse 41 (1972)
The second in a series of popular Japanese "women-in-prison" films made in the '70s, this wild actioner stars Meiko Kaji as Matsu, a woman convicted of trying to kill her crooked cop boyfriend. Nicknamed "Scorpion" and vowing revenge, Matsu faces torture by the warden and fights for survival as she plots to escape by hijacking a visitors bus. 89 min. In Japanese with English subtitles.
50-8614 Letterboxed *$19.99*

Scorpion's Revenge (1998)
"Zero Woman" producers Hideo Sugimoto and Shinsuke Yamazaki revived the '70s "Scorpion" films with this thriller. A young woman who is wrongly convicted of killing her boyfriend in an explosion winds up in an L.A. women's prison. Surrounded by brutal torture and forbidden lust, she joins with a fellow inmate to attempt an escape. Yohko Saitoh, Kristin Norton star. 86 min. In Japanese with English subtitles.
20-8383 *$29.99*

Maborosi (1995)
A lyrical and thoughtful drama from Japan about a young mother who is haunted by the sudden death of her husband. Five years later, she agrees to an arranged marriage with a widowed fisherman who lives with his son in a remote seaside village, but will this new life fill the void in her heart? Makiko Esumi, Takashi Naitoh, Tadanobu Asano star; directed by Hirokazu Kore-eda. 110 min. In Japanese with English subtitles.
53-6130 Was $89.99 *$29.99*

Shall We Dance? (1997)
A married Tokyo businessman, smitten with a beautiful woman he spies in the window of a dance school, impulsively signs up for lessons and a chance to be near her. What he gains instead is a newfound sense of freedom on the dance floor and a renewed relationship with his wife. Writer/director Masayuki Suo's charming comedy stars Koji Yasuyo, Tamiyo Kusakari. 119 min. In Japanese with English subtitles.
11-2222 Was $99.99 *$19.99*

Black Tight Killers (1966)
In director Yasuharu Hasebe's outrageous, '60s-flavored crime thriller, a combat photographer must save his stewardess girlfriend from American gangsters and Japanese Yakuza after a cache of WWII gold hidden by her father. Complicating the hero's mission is a group of go-go girl assassins who toss records to dispatch their targets. Pop singer Akira Kobayashi, Chieko Matsubara star. 87 min. AKA: "Don't Touch Me, I'm Dangerous." 87 min. In Japanese with English subtitles.
50-8613 Letterboxed *$19.99*

Narayama Bushi-Ko (1958)
The original cinematic version of "The Ballad of Narayama" centers on an impoverished village where, upon reaching 70, inhabitants must go to a remote mountaintop and prepare to "meet the gods." This compelling effort fuses elements from Kabuki theater and modern film techniques. With Kinuyo Tanaka; directed by Keisuke Kinoshita. 97 min. In Japanese with English subtitles.
53-8589 Letterboxed *$79.99*

The Ballad Of Narayama (1983)
Shohei Imamura's passionate, graphic depiction of life in a 19th-century Japanese village beset by years of lean harvests where the old are taken to the mountains to die. An elderly woman, resigned to her fate, tries to solve her family's problems before her final trip. Sumiko Sakamoto, Ken Ogata star. 130 min. In Japanese with English subtitles.
22-5451 Letterboxed *$29.99*

The Dog Of Flanders (1998)
One of the most beloved children's stories of all time takes on new dimensions with this wonderful animated rendition. Set in 19th-century Belgium, the story follows a young orphan boy who finds the strength to live his life and realize his dream of becoming artist, with some help from his loyal dog. 108 min. In Japanese with English subtitles.
85-1335 *$24.99*

The Ladies' Phone Sex Club (1996)
Your dream girl is just a call away in this steamy, silly Japanese comedy, as top phone sex worker Lulu's quest to reach 1,000 clients is complicated by a mysterious female caller who winds up taking Lulu to new heights of ecstasy. Who is she, and what's her connection to Lulu's pantyhose-obsessed boss? Sho Kawaide, Shoichiro Akaboshi star. 88 min. In Japanese with English subtitles.
20-8622 *$29.99*

Moon Over Tao—Makaraga (1997)
A dazzling sci-fi fantasy, set in feudal Japan, from director Keita Anemiya ("Zeiram"). Three warriors join forces to recover a fabled mystical sword, but standing in their way are an evil sorcerer, the alien beings who left the sword on Earth, and their lethal monster, Makaraga. Yuko Moriyama stars. 96 min. In Japanese with English subtitles.
20-8238 Letterboxed *$29.99*

Nobody (1999)
A quiet evening in a bar for three Japanese "salarymen" turns into a twisted fight for survival in this compelling suspense tale. A chance remark about the trio sitting at the next table leads to one of the men being severely beaten. When they meet one of the assailants by chance and attack him, leaving him for dead, the businessmen begin receiving threatening calls from their mysterious, unknown enemies. Masaya Kato, Riki Rakeuchi, Hideo Nakano star. 100 min. In Japanese with English subtitles.
22-9043 *$79.99*

Bad Boys (1960)
The first feature film by noted Japanese documentary filmmaker Susumu Hani is a compelling look at life in a boy's reform school. Shot on location and starring real-life inmates, the gritty drama won worldwide acclaim. 90 min. In Japanese with English subtitles.
53-7639 *$39.99*

She And He (1963)
A housewife becomes bored with her lonely existence in a high-rise building and befriends an impoverished ragpicker, a move that meets with angry disapproval from her husband, in this moving and emotional drama by Susumu Hani. Sachiko Hidari, Kikuji Yamashita star. 110 min. In Japanese with English subtitles.
53-7640 *$39.99*

Nanami: First Love (1968)
Engrossing, erotic Japanese drama concerning a young man whose life has been a history of sexual trauma, and his obsession with a sensuous prostitute. Controversial and captivating work from Susumu Hani. 104 min. In Japanese with English subtitles.
09-1900 Was $29.99 *$24.99*

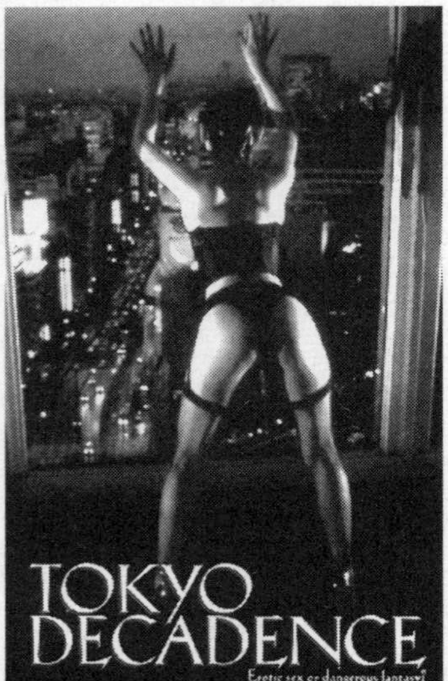

Tokyo Decadence (1993)
Explicit, ultra-kinky story exploring the life of a beautiful 22-year-old prostitute named Ai who takes the submissive role in sado-masochistic relations with Japanese businessmen. As the woman engages in acts of extreme depravity, she dreams of being rescued by one of her clients. Miho Nikaido stars. AKA: "Topazu." 112 min. In Japanese with English subtitles.
72-9021 Was $89.99 *$29.99*

Tokyo Decadence (Dubbed Version)
Also available in a dubbed-in-English edition.
72-9022 Was $89.99 *$29.99*

Miscellaneous

2000 SEEN BY...

2000 Seen By...
A group of international filmmakers were commissioned by French television companies to create their cinematic views on the new millennium. The results are an idiosyncratic batch of movies that range in style, tone and subject from director to director.

The Sanguinaires (1997)
A travel agent tired of all the new millennium hype arranges to join friends and family on a remote island near Corsica for a vacation from Christmas to New Year's Day. The plan is to rough it, without technology, but some of the guests protest his enforcement of the rules and a power struggle takes place between the agent and a friendly young tour guide. Frédéric Pierrot, Catherine Baugué star; directed by Laurent Cantet. 68 min. In French with English subtitles.
53-6975 *$19.99*

Tamas & Juli (1997)
Directed by Ildiko Enyedi ("My Twentieth Century"), this magical film tells of a miner who receives an invitation to meet a woman in a bar in a small Hungarian town on New Year's Eve, 1999. But the man can't meet her because of his work schedule, and soon a host of other hurdles comes between them. With Márta Angyal, Dávid Jánosi. 60 min. In Hungarian with English subtitles.
53-6976 *$19.99*

The Book Of Life (1998)
American indy Hal Hartley ("Flirt") helemed this quirky tale in which Jesus and sexy assistant Magdalena are sent by God to break the seven seals on the Book of Life—now on a computer disc—and bring about the end of the world. At the same time, the Devil, disguised as a drunk, chats with a gambler and waitress at a hotel bar. Martin Donovan, PJ Harvey and Thomas Jay Ryan star. 63 min.
53-6970 *$19.99*

The First Night Of My Life (1998)
As 1999 winds down, raucous parties take place throughout Madrid. At the same time, the pregnant Paloma and husband Miguel prepare to go to her parents' house for a celebration. But signals get crossed and Paloma's father sets out to pick them up. When his car breaks down, a series of other bizarre "millennial" events occur. With Leonor Watling, Juanjo Martinez; Miguel Albaladejo directs. 84 min. In Spanish with English subtitles.
53-6971 *$19.99*

The Hole (1998)
As the year 2000 approaches, rain permeates the city of Taipei, whose residents are afflicted with an epidemic that makes people fear light and crawl like cockroaches. A plumber trying to fix a leak in an apartment building leaves a hole between apartments that has a profound effect on two of the building's residents. Tsai Ming-Liang's eerie allegory features unusual lip-synched musical sequences. With Lee Kang-Sheng, Yang Kuei-Mei. 95 min. In Mandarin with English subtitles.
53-6972 *$19.99*

Life On Earth (1998)
This poetic film follows African filmmaker Abderrahmane Sissako's half-fictional, half-documentary return to his home village of Sokolo in Mali to visit his father as the new millennium approaches. What he finds is a society virtually unchanged by technology, free from the frenzy that has captured the "first world." 61 min. In Bambara and French with English subtitles.
53-6973 *$19.99*

Midnight (1998)
As fireworks fall over Rio de Janeiro's Copacabana beach with the dawn of a new millennium, destiny brings together an escaped prisoner and depressed middle class teacher who was recently deserted by the man she loved. With Fernanda Torres, Luis Carlos Vasconcelos; co-directed by Walter Salles ("Central Station"). 72 min. In Portuguese with English subtitles.
53-6974 *$19.99*

The Wall (1998)
From Alain Berliner ("Ma Vie en Rose") comes a millennial parable involving Albert, the owner of a frite (French fry) stand based at the border betweem Belgium's French and Flemish-speaking regions. When the government erects a barrier that bisects the stand and places French-speaking Albert on the Flemish side, he becomes a stranger in his own country. Daniel Hanssens, Pascale Bal star. 67 min. In Flemish and French with English subtitles.
53-6977 *$19.99*

2000 Seen By...: Collection
All eight films in the "2000 Seen By..." series are also available in a money-saving set including "The Book of Life," "The First Night of My Life," "The Hole," "Midnight" and others.
53-6978 Save $40.00! *$119.99*

This Special Friendship (1964)
A landmark in the depiction of gay relationships in world cinema, this moving French drama, set in a Jesuit boarding school, shows how a student turns in one of his peers for writing another student a love letter, then finds himself attracted to a younger classmate. Francis Lascombrade stars. 99 min. In French with English subtitles.
78-5012 *$59.99*

The Best Way (1978)
A boy's camp's macho sports instructor, confused by his sexual attraction to the camp's effeminate drama teacher, begins a campaign of intimidation and harassment against the man in this intense French film. Patrick Dewaere, Patrick Bouchitey star. 95 min. In French with English subtitles.
78-5005 *$59.99*

We Were One Man (1980)
Acclaimed French drama, set at the end of World War II, details the relationship that grows into love between a French peasant and the wounded German soldier he nurses back to health. Serge Avedikian, Piotr Stanisias star. 90 min. In French with English subtitles.
78-5013 *$59.99*

Noir Et Blanc (1986)
Inspired by a Tennessee Williams story, this kinky drama of obsession tells of a sado-masochistic relationship that develops between a shy accountant and a black masseuse. As their interest in each other gets greater, so does their attraction to pain. Francis Frappat and Jacques Martial star in this Cannes prize winner. 82 min. In French with English subtitles.
53-8157 *$79.99*

Le Jupon Rouge (1987)
The romantic relationship between human rights activist and concentration camp survivor Alida Valli and her younger lover, fashion designer Marie Christine Barrault, is strained when Barrault finds herself attracted to another woman in this unusual and provocative French drama from director Genevieve Lefebvre. 90 min. In French with English subtitles.
78-9017 *$39.99*

Sand And Blood (1989)
Searing sexual drama about the bizarre relationship between a wealthy doctor and a celebrated young matador. Directed by newcomer Jeanne Labrune, the film contrasts the brutality of bullfighting with the intimacy of their homosexual liaison. Sami Frey, Patrick Catalifo star. 101 min. In French with English subtitles.
53-7424 *$89.99*

Full Speed (1998)
This intelligent, highly-charged coming-of-age tale concerns the relationships of four young people in the South of France. Novelist Quentin is involved with free-spirited student Julie, who is smitten with Quentin's sexy rap singer friend Jimmy. Meanwhile, Quentin falls for Samir, a gay Algerian. Pascal Cervo, Stephane Rideau star. 86 min. In French with English subtitles.
78-9025 Was $39.99 *$19.99*

You Are Not Alone (1980)
This controversial Danish drama sensitively depicts the friendship between two boys in a boarding school, a relationship that grows into an attraction that neither fully understands. 90 min. In Danish with English subtitles.
78-5014 *$79.99*

Friends Forever (1986)
Acclaimed, erotically-charged look at a 16-year-old teen's experiences at a new school that was a hit at several international gay film festivals. The young man finds himself drawn to two other students: an androgynous, independent young man and a moody, blonde leader of a group of troublemakers, who eventually admits his homosexuality. 95 min. In Danish with English subtitles.
78-5031 *$79.99*

Pretty Boy (1993)
This powerful portrait of a taboo subject details the adventures of a 13-year-old runaway boy who turns hustler in order to survive on Copenhagen's streets. After leaving his mother, the boy experiences gang violence, sadomasochism, friendship with an androgynous girl and first love with Denmark's downtrodden. 86 min. In Danish with English subtitles.
78-5066 *$39.99*

Dear Boys (1980)
A humorous and telling story of an aging gay writer who tries to rejuvenate his sex life when he becomes obsessed with a young man who ignores his advances, but the writer devises other methods of seduction to get the man interested in him. Features extensive nudity and mature sexual situations. 90 min. In Dutch with English subtitles.
78-5075 *$69.99*

To Play Or To Die (1991)
Powerful drama about a shy boy who is continually made the target of a group of sadomasochistic bullies at an all-boys' school. Despite the terror inflicted upon him, the boy is attracted to the gang's handsome leader and plots to get even during a weekend alone together. Geert Hunaerts stars in this provocative story that features nudity. 50 min. In Dutch with English subtitles.
01-1476 Was $39.99 *$29.99*

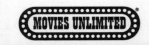

Ernesto (1979)
Sensitive Italian coming-of-age drama, set in a 1910s seaside town, chronicles an affair between an office boy and an older dockworker, and the effect the relationship has on his life. Martin Halm, Virna Lisi star. 98 min. In Italian with English subtitles.
78-5008 *$59.99*

Vito And The Others (1992)
A haunting, hypnotic, no-holds-barred look at the life of a 12-year-old boy from Naples whose journey through puberty includes experiences with abusive relatives, imprisonment, rape, male prostitution and drug abuse before he fights to regain his innocence. Savage, disturbing and powerful, this film deals with mature sexual themes. With Nando Triola. 90 min. In Italian with English subtitles.
78-5042 *$79.99*

Men Men Men (1996)
This raucous comedy from Christian De Sica (son of Vittorio) looks at the lives of four gay friends in Italy. Film producer Sandro has just come out of the closet; Vittorio deals with his lover leaving him—for a woman!; Dado, an orthopedic doctor, loves looking at hunks in an examining room; and Tony, a tailor, can't break from his mother's shadow. 84 min. In Italian with English subtitles.
53-6708 *$79.99*

Lola & Billy The Kid (1999)
Compelling drama focusing on teenager Murat, a Turk living in Berlin, who hides his homosexuality from his cab-driving brother Osman, still traumatized by another brother's decision to live as a transvestite named Lola. But when Lola and male hustler boyfriend Billy the Kid enter Murat's life, an edgy situation gets even more complicated. Baki Davrak stars. 90 min. In German and Turkish with English subtitles.
76-2107 *$79.99*

Steam: The Turkish Bath (1999)
Francesco, an unhappily married Italian architect, inherits a steam bath in Istanbul from his recently deceased aunt and decides to leave his wife in Rome while he goes to prepare the property for sale. When Francesco arrives in Turkey, he realizes how important the bath is to the community and questions his sexuality when he falls for the caretaker's handsome son. With Alessandro Gassman. 96 min. In Italian with English subtitles.
78-9043 *$79.99*

Angel (Angelos) (1982)
The first gay-themed film to receive wide distribution in its native Greece, director George Katakouzinos' acclaimed drama follows a young Athens man who falls for a handsome sailor. Leaving his impoverished home and abusive father to be with his lover, Angel is soon reduced to working the city's streets as a transvestite prostitute. Michael Maniatis, Dionyssis Xanthos star. 120 min. In Greek with English subtitles.
01-1577 *$39.99*

Meteor And Shadow (1985)
His writings made him a national hero, but his controversial politics and openly gay lifestyle led to his downfall. The life of early-20th century Greek poet Napoleon Lapathiotis is compellingly portrayed in this poignant drama from director Takis Spetsiotis. Takis Mschos, George Kentros star. 101 min. In Greek with English subtitles.
01-1578 *$39.99*

Another Way (1982)
Groundbreaking lesbian drama from Hungary follows the relationship between the beautiful journalist wife of an army officer and an outspoken reporter with whom she shares an office. At first frightened, their romance blossoms as they are swept away by their own flirtations. 100 min. In Hungarian with English subtitles.
53-7600 Was $89.99 *$29.99*

El Sacerdote (The Priest) (1970)
From the director of "El Diputado" comes this controversial account of a priest experiencing mid-life depression whose obsession with sexual fantasies leads him to make a tough decision: should he renounce his calling or stay and battle the demons of the flesh that may destroy him? With Simon Andreau; features nudity. 72 min. In Spanish with English subtitles.
78-5072 *$79.99*

El Diputado (1978)
An intriguing political thriller laced with homoerotic themes, this explicit Spanish drama depicts a street hustler who is forced by the secret police to help entrap a politician in a blackmail scheme, only to fall for his target. Jose Sacristan, Jose Alonso star. 111 min. In Spanish with English subtitles.
78-5007 *$69.99*

Colegas (1982)
When a young man gets his friend's sister pregnant, the two men are forced by circumstances into a life of crime and hustling on the street in this raw and powerful Spanish drama that features explicit nudity. Jose Luis Manzano, Antonio Gonzalez star. 117 min. In Spanish with English subtitles.
78-5006 *$69.99*

Los Placeres Ocultos (1977)
The first openly gay film to be released in post-Franco Spain, this compelling drama follows the doomed relationship between a middle-aged banker and a young student. Simon Andreu, Tony Fuentes star. 97 min. In Spanish with English subtitles.
78-5009 *$69.99*

Tú Solo (1984)
Despite opposition from his father, 16-year-old Miguel pursues a career in bullfighting when he studies at a famed school for matadors in Madrid. There, he gets a coming-of-age lesson in brutality and Spanish machismo. This unique drama features nudity and bullfighting sequences not for the squeamish. 96 min. In Spanish with English subtitles.
78-5073 *$59.99*

Extramuros (Beyond The Walls) (1985)
Set in Spain during the Inquisition, this strange tale of lesbian love in a convent tells of Sister Angela, who injures her hands and fakes the miracle of stigmata. With help from her lover, Sister Ana, Sister Angela usurps the Mother Superior, but soon has to answer to those who question her "miracle." Carmen Maura stars. 120 min. In Spanish with English subtitles.
78-9004 Was $29.99 *$19.99*

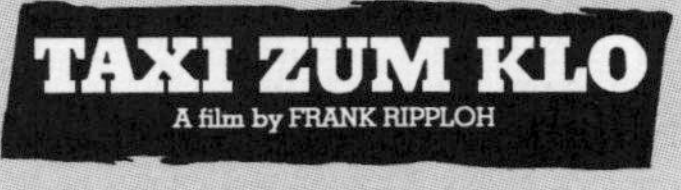

Taxi Zum Klo (1981)
Groundbreaking autobiographical film from director Frank Ripploh about homosexual life in West Germany, focusing on the adventures of a schoolteacher. Although sexually explicit, the film is also funny, fascinating and charming in a unique way. 92 min. In German with English subtitles.
50-1189 Was $79.99 *$39.99*

Seduction: The Cruel Woman (1985)
A masterpiece of kinkiness from Germany about a hot-blooded dominatrix who decides to take on a female lover in order to fulfill her sexual fantasies. A stylish, erotic glimpse into the world of bondage, set in Hamburg, from "Virgin Machine" creator Monika Truett. Stars Mechtild Grossman, Udo Kier and Sheila McLaughlin. 84 min. In German with English subtitles.
70-5018 Was $59.99 *$29.99*

Virgin Machine (1988)
A haunting and erotic lesbian love story about a female reporter who travels to San Francisco for a story about romance, and falls for a streetwise stripper who works at an all-woman club. 84 min. In English and German with English subtitles.
70-5001 Was $59.99 *$29.99*

Westler: East Of The Wall (1986)
In this poignant gay love story, a romance blossoms between a West Berlin resident and an East Berlin waiter, but they soon discover their love is not meant to be when political forces disrupt their relationship. A favorite at festivals, this gritty film was directed by Wieland Speck. 94 min. In German with English subtitles.
78-9008 *$39.99*

Coming Out (1989)
Philipp has known that he's been gay since he was very young but has struggled to ignore his feelings and live a "normal" life, even dating and moving in with a woman. But when a chance meeting with a young man turns into a loving relationship, Philipp must finally come to terms with who he is. The first gay-themed film to come from East Germany, this acclaimed drama stars Matthias Freihof, Dirk Kummer. 108 min. In German with English subtitles.
53-6928 *$79.99*

The Blue Hour (1991)
A popular male prostitute living in a Berlin apartment building tries to help his next door neighbor when her writer boyfriend leaves her. The unconventional couple soon become romantically involved, but will their relationship end when her boyfriend returns? A provocative, sexy film festival favorite. 87 min. In German with English subtitles.
01-1484 Was $39.99 *$29.99*

Street Kid (Gossenkind) (1991)
Unflinching account of a tough, 14-year-old male hustler on Dusseldorf's mean streets whose sexual relationship with a family man leads to unleashed passions and uncompromising pursuits. This controversial film looks at teenage prostitutes and other urban denizens in a realistic yet sympathetic manner. With Winfried Glatzeder. 89 min. In German with English subtitles.
78-5045 *$69.99*

Via Appia (1993)
A German airline steward brings a film crew with him to Rio de Janeiro's gay underground in search of the man with whom he had a brief romantic liaison and left the message "welcome to the AIDS club." Featuring graphic sexual content, violence and one explicit scene, this film looks at the seedy "Via Appia" section of Rio. 90 min. In German and Spanish with English subtitles.
53-9476 *$49.99*

Siegfried (1986)
Set in 1934, this controversial, sensitive film chronicles the relationship between an art entrepreneur and a young circus acrobat. There are homosexual undertones in their relationship, which stunned filmgoers. 91 min. In Polish with English subtitles.
53-9220 *$49.99*

Outcasts (1986)
After being cast out of his home by his abusive father, a teenager is taken in by an aging photographer in this sensual, moving film, the first gay-themed movie released by Taiwan. 102 min. In Mandarin with English subtitles.
78-5011 Was $69.99 *$49.99*

Pink Ulysses (1989)
A unique take on the "Ulysses" tale is presented in this homoerotic epic that focuses on the hero's return to Troy after a 20-year exile. Iron-muscled men in loincloths, steamy sexual encounters and a Penelope who has incestuous feelings towards her handsome son are among the hallmarks of this mostly silent effort from Norway. 98 min.
53-9643 *$39.99*

Lakki—The Boy Who Grew Wings (1993)
Sensitive tale of a young teen ignored by his desperate mother and his obnoxious father who flees to the streets, where he befriends an older punk rocker. Seeking refuge, the teen instead faces abuse and soon grows strange wings on his back. Features nudity and adult themes. 104 min. In Norwegian with English subtitles.
78-5076 *$69.99*

Sebastian (1995)
The relationship between two teenage best friends takes on an uncertain new dimension when one boy decides he's romantically attracted to the other in this compelling Norwegian drama from the creators of "Lakki—The Boy Who Grew Wings." Hampas Bjorek, Nocolai Broch star. 88 min. In Norwegian with English subtitles.
78-5083 *$59.99*

Amazing Grace (1992)
Writer/director Amos Gutman ("Drifting") looks at the friendship and romantic relationship that develops between an 18-year-old gay Israeli and his upstairs neighbor, an older man who has returned from living in New York and fears he may be HIV-positive, in this complex and compelling drama. Rivka Michaely, Sharon Alexander star. 95 min. In Hebrew with English subtitles.
53-8063 *$79.99*

Okoge (1993)
A young woman discovers that she prefers the company of gay men and becomes involved in a relationship with homosexual lovers she meets on a beach. As the relationship continues, the woman recounts the events that led to her attraction. This powerful, sensitive and satiric film stars Misa Shimizu and was directed by Takehiro Nakajima. 120 min. In Japanese with English subtitles.
53-7964 Was $79.99 *$39.99*

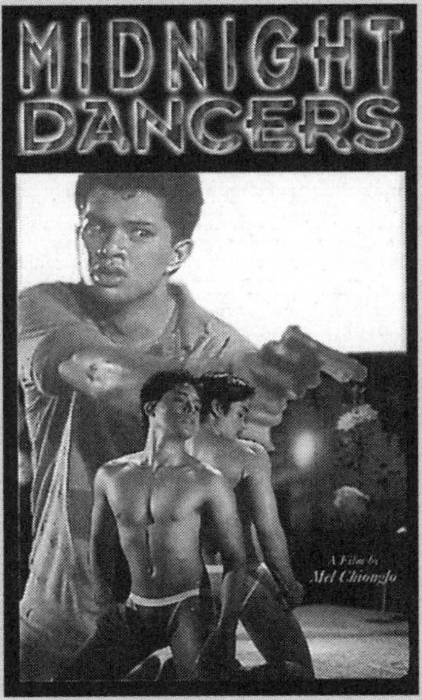

Midnight Dancers (1994)
Banned in the Philippines, this powerful drama salutes "Macho Dancer" as it tells the story of three native Filipino brothers who work as prostitutes and exotic dancers in a gay Manila nightclub. A series of dangerous situations make them reconsider their lifestyles and try to make a change. Unrated version; 118 min. In Filipino with English subtitles.
70-5094 Was $59.99 *$29.99*

Miguel/Michelle (1998)
A Filipino lad named Miguel leaves his family and boards a plane for America to make something of himself. No one is prepared, however, when the return trip reveals what he's made of himself is a beautiful woman now known as Michelle, in this wild, touching transgender farce from director Gil M. Portes. 106 min. In Tagalog with English subtitles
70-3479 *$39.99*

Freedom Is Paradise (1989)
The first Russian film shot in actual Soviet prisons and reformatories, this unflinching film centers on a teenage boy who attempts to escape the confines of a barbaric prison. When he learns that his father is still alive, he must undertake a grueling trip to find him. Not for the squeamish, this film contains nudity and sexual themes. 75 min. In Russia with English subtitles.
78-5219 *$69.99*

Lessons At The End Of Spring (1989)
A teenage boy's trip to the movies turns into a nightmare when a terrifying confrontation with police leads to imprisonment and sadistic shower room encounters, decrepit detention facilities and tomb-like prison cells. Set in the last months of the Kruschchev regime, this film features extensive male nudity and brutality of all sorts. 75 min. In Russian with English subtitles.
78-5220 *$69.99*

100 Days Before The Command (1990)
Banned after its release by Soviet censors, this compelling look at a group of young Red Army recruits banding together to overcome the constant brutality and violence that surrounds them features a surprising homoerotic undercurrent and an emsemble cast made up mostly of actual soldiers. Vladmir Zamansky, Armen Dzhigarkhanyan star. 71 min. In Russian with English subtitles.
01-1581 *$39.99*

Almost Privates (1999)
In celebration of their pal's 18th birthday, three of his friends join him for a raucous romp through an Eastern European city that ends with the quartet of hunky fellows deciding to enlist in the army. After medical inspections, showers and more, they soon discover that military life may not be for them after all. Features frontal nudity. 81 min. In English and Russian; no subtitles.
78-5089 *$49.99*

Bugis Street (1995)
The first film released in America from Singapore has been called "Snow White and the Seven Drag Queens." Hiep Thi Le ("Heaven and Earth") is a young woman who becomes a maid at a hotel in the red light district of Singapore in the 1960s. Little does she know that the residents are all transvestites and transsexuals who service young men and eventually teach the young woman about life. 100 min. In English and Cantonese with English subtitles.
76-7399 Was $79.99 *$39.99*

I Like You... I Like You Very Much (1994)
In this revolutionary gay film from Japan, a young man lives a seemingly happy life with his college student boyfriend—until he sees a hunky young man at a train stop. The attraction leads to complications as all of the characters question their sexuality in this no-holds-barred look at homosexual relations in the Land of the Rising Sun. 58 min. In Japanese with English subtitles.
01-1515 *$39.99*

Muscle (1994)
Disquieting and explicit, director Hisyasu Sato's homoerotic drama follows an editor at a muscle magazine whose obsession with bodybuilding and physical perfection draws him into a sadomasochistic world of pleasure and pain. Graphic scenes of violence and sexual situations mark this "adults only" tale. Takeshi Ito, Simonn Kumai star. 60 min. In Japanese with English subtitles.
78-9014 *$39.99*

Kizuna
This groundbreaking adult animated series from Japan centers on a gay romance between a fencing expert and the son of an Osaka mobster. Based on a popular Japanese comic book by Kazuma Kodaka, the two-part series features inventive animation and an erotic storyline. Each volume runs about 30 min. In Japanese with English subtitles.

Kizuna, Vol. 1 (1998)
Fencing champion Ranmaru Samejima is paralyzed in a hit-and-run incident whose intended target was Enjoji, his lover and the son of a powerful mob boss from Osaka. The two young men get closer during Sam's rehabilitation and move in together. But Sagano, Enjoji's half-brother, enrolls at their Tokyo college and soon realizes he's also attracted to Sam.
73-9141 *$29.99*

Kizuna, Vol. 2 (1998)
Sagano begins to interfere with the relationship between Enjoji and Sam, and things become more complicated when Masanori Araki, the junior boss of Enjoji and Sagano's father's mob family, arrives in Tokyo for a "visit."
73-9142 *$29.99*

East Palace, West Palace (1998)
Acclaimed and controversial effort from China centers on a gay writer arrested in a Beijing park for cruising. After surprising the policeman questioning him with a kiss, the lawman becomes interested in the writer romantically, leading to a one-night exploration of secret lives, sado-masochistic desires and other topics. With Si Han, Hu Jun. 90 min. In Mandarin with English subtitles.
78-9036 *$59.99*

Show Me Love (2000)
Elin and Agnes are two teenage girls growing up in a small Swedish town. Elin is bored with her life in a community where things are deemed outdated before they ever reach her, while Agnes is a shy, lonely lesbian who has a crush on Elin. The two form a relationship that explores their emotions and helps them come to terms with life. Alexandra Dahlström and Rebecca Liljeberg star. AKA: "F***ing Amal." 89 min. In Swedish with English subtitles.
78-9045 Letterboxed *$79.99*

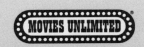

HISTORICAL & WAR

Sally Hemings: An American Scandal (2000)
Fascinating historical drama chronicles the controversial relationship between founding father and third president Thomas Jefferson and his mulatto slave Sally Hemings, who came to Monticello at the age of 14 and was involved with Jefferson for 38 years. Sam Neill, Carmen Ejogo, Mare Winningham and Diahann Carroll star. 173 min.
27-7338 *$49.99*

The Crossing (2000)
With his ragtag army on the verge of surrender, the last chance for him and his young nation lay with a desperate Christmas night attack. The true story behind George Washington's 1776 crossing of the ice-covered Delaware River to surprise British forces in Trenton, New Jersey, is told in this grand historical drama. Jeff Daniels stars as Washington; with Roger Rees, Nigel Bennett. 100 min.
53-6729 *$19.99*

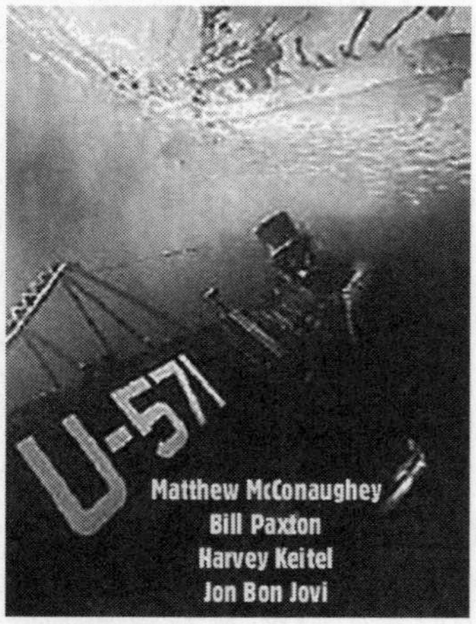

U-571 (2000)
During World War II, neophyte officer Matthew McConaughey heads up a secret U.S. Navy mission to retrieve a German encoding device from a disabled U-boat in the Atlantic. The operation succeeds, but the American sub is destroyed. Can the crew fix the damaged U-boat and make it home while staving off the enemy? Based on a true (albeit British) story, this gripping war drama also stars Bill Paxton, Harvey Keitel, Jon Bon Jovi. 117 min.
07-2929 *❑$99.99*

The Inner Circle (1991)
An epic historical film focuses on the experiences of the man who was the personal projectionist for Josef Stalin, and how his domestic life was sacrificed for his devotion to the State. Tom Hulce, Lolita Davidovich and Bob Hoskins star in this lavishly produced drama. 122 min.
02-2222 *❑$19.99*

A Midnight Clear (1992)
Set in Europe during the final months of World War II, this powerful drama tells the story of six American G.I.s who encounter a company of non-combative German soldiers. The two groups attempt to initiate a Yuletide peace between them, but the gestures ultimately lead to a tragic misunderstanding. Ethan Hawke, Frank Whaley, Kevin Dillon and Gary Sinise star. 107 min.
02-2312 Was $19.99 *❑$14.99*

The Last Butterfly (1993)
This poignant Holocaust story stars Tom Courtenay as a French actor imprisoned by the Germans and forced to perform in Terezin, a model city created by the Nazis to show the world how "well" they're treating the Jews. Brigitte Fossey, Freddie Jones, Ingrid Held also star. 106 min.
02-2718 Was $89.99 *❑$19.99*

The Brylcreem Boys (1997)
In the neutral Ireland of 1941, Allied and German prisoners of war are kept in an unusual POW camp that allows inmates to visit the neighboring village. In this offbeat setting, a downed Canadian pilot and his German counterpart engage in a rivalry for the love of a local woman. Unusual wartime drama stars Bill Campbell, Angus MacFadyen, Gabriel Byrne and Riverdance dancer Jean Butler in her film debut. 106 min.
02-8808 *❑$14.99*

A Royal Scandal (1996)
1820s England was shocked when King George IV attempted to divorce his wife, Queen Caroline, by charging her with adultery. Their trouble-plagued and controversial marriage is chronicled in this lavish and wickedly witty BBC production. Richard Grant, Susan Lynch star; Ian Richardson narrates. 110 min.
04-3425 *$24.99*

Flight Of The Intruder (1991)
1972. A maverick U.S. pilot, frustrated with his meaningless flying missions over Vietnam, teams with a rowdy pal for a rogue attack on an enemy air base in Hanoi. Willem Dafoe, Danny Glover, Brad Johnson and Rosanna Arquette star in John Milius' military thriller. 115 min.
06-1851 *❑$14.99*

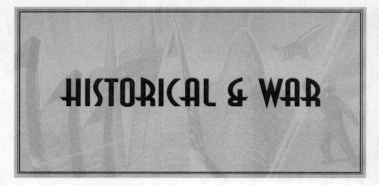

Mosley (1998)
He was a charismatic speaker and political showman who brought England to the brink of dictatorship. Jonathan Cake stars as '30s Fascist leader Oswald Mosley in this compelling biodrama that chronicles his rise and fall from power. Eric Allan, Windsor Davies also star. 240 min. on two tapes.
44-2235 *❑$29.99*

Dr. Bethune (1990)
Donald Sutherland turns in a towering performance as Dr. Norman Bethune, the Canadian expatriate who worked with the Loyalists during the Spanish Civil War and served under Chairman Mao during China's fight against Fascism. Helen Mirren and Helen Shaver also star in this stirring true story. 115 min.
53-7942 Was $89.99 *$19.99*

Ill-Gotten Gains (1997)
Filmed before "Amistad," this mesmerizing drama is set in 1869 and depicts the uprising of 24 slaves being held captive on the ship the Argon Miss off the coast of Guinea in West Africa. "Amistad" star Djimon Hounsou, Akosua Busia and the voice of Eartha Kitt are featured in this striking historical drama in which modern-day vernacular is used.
54-9191 *❑$24.99*

Hostile Waters (1997)
In 1986, an accidental collision between U.S. and Soviet submarines off the American coast crippled the Russian craft and led to a tense stand-off that could have instigated a nuclear conflict. Rutger Hauer, Martin Sheen and Max von Sydow star in a gripping real-life thriller. 92 min.
44-2138 Was $89.99 *❑$14.99*

My Little Assassin (1999)
As a teenager, she was seduced by one of the world's most notorious rulers; as an adult, the government sent her back to kill him. Gabrielle Anwar stars as Marita Lorenz, who had an affair with Fidel Castro and, after she was exiled to America, was talked by her CIA operative mother into returning to Cuba to take part in an assassination plot. Joe Mantegna co-stars as Castro; with Jill Clayburgh, Robert Davi. 90 min.
54-9195 *$59.99*

Class Of '61 (1992)
Set against the backdrop of the Civl War, this sweeping story tells of three West Point cadets whose loyalties are developed by the hardships of war. Confederate lieutenant Shelby Peyton courts fellow cadet Devin O'Neill's sister, while O'Neill and another classmate, George Armstrong Custer, pursue Washington socialites. Christien Anholt, Andre Braugher star. 95 min.
07-2317 *❑$89.99*

Texas (1994)
James E. Michener's sprawling epic traces the Lone Star State's struggle for independence against Mexico and details the efforts of settlers Sam Houston and Stephen Austin battling Mexican general Santa Ana, and Davy Crockett, Col. William Travis and Jim Bowie facing scores of enemy troops at the siege of the Alamo. David Keith, Stacy Keach, John Schneider star. 180 min.
63-1736 Was $49.99 *❑$19.99*

A Woman At War (1994)
A compelling and inspiring real-life WWII drama in the tradition of "Schindler's List." Martha Plimpton plays a young Jewish woman in occupied Belgium who, with the help of businessman/lover Eric Stoltz, infiltrates the headquarters of the Gestapo in order to save people from the Nazi death camps. 115 min.
63-1750 *❑$89.99*

A Dangerous Man: Lawrence After Arabia (1994)
Ralph Fiennes stars as famed British officer-turned-Arab rebel leader T.E. Lawrence in this compelling drama that follows his struggle to gain Arab independence in the wake of World War I. At the 1919 Paris Peace Conference, however, Lawrence finds himself in a different kind of battle. Denis Quilley, Paul Freeman, Siddig El Fadil also star. 104 min.
08-8636 *$19.99*

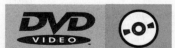

DVD VIDEO
ASK ABOUT OUR GIANT DVD CATALOG!

Fall From Grace (1995)
At the height of World War II, a team of American and British intelligence agents execute an elaborate scheme to deceive Hitler and pave the way for D-Day—but how many of them will survive? Compelling espionage thriller stars James Fox, Michael York, Gary Cole, Patsy Kensit and Tara Fitzgerald. 180 min.
19-3839 *$69.99*

Eye Of The Eagle III (1991)
The third installment in this gung-ho series stars Steve Kanaly as the brave leader of a group of grunts behind enemy lines on a dangerous mission in the swamps of Vietnam. Intense action-packed war story also stars Ken Wright and Carl Franklin. 90 min.
21-9007 *$14.99*

Beyond The Call Of Duty (1992)
Explosive Vietnam War saga stars Jan-Michael Vincent as an American commander who leads a band of renegades on a dangerous mission up the Vietcong-controlled Mekong River. With Eb Lottimer, Jillian McWhirter. 92 min.
21-9020 *$14.99*

Kill Zone (1993)
David Carradine is a renegade colonel who leads his men on a dangerous mission, raiding a jungle outpost in Cambodia during the Vietnam War. Football great Tony Dorsett also stars in this gung-ho actioner.
21-9034 *$14.99*

Saint Joan (1957)
Otto Preminger's film, based on George Bernard Shaw's play, catapulted Iowa's Jean Seberg to stardom, as she portrayed the famed teenager in 15th-century France whose claim of hearing angels leads to her commanding an army against English invaders and, later, being tried for heresy and sent to the stake. Richard Widmark, Richard Todd and John Gielgud also star. Special video edition includes a short feature on the making of the movie. 131 min. total.
19-2218 Was $19.99 *$14.99*

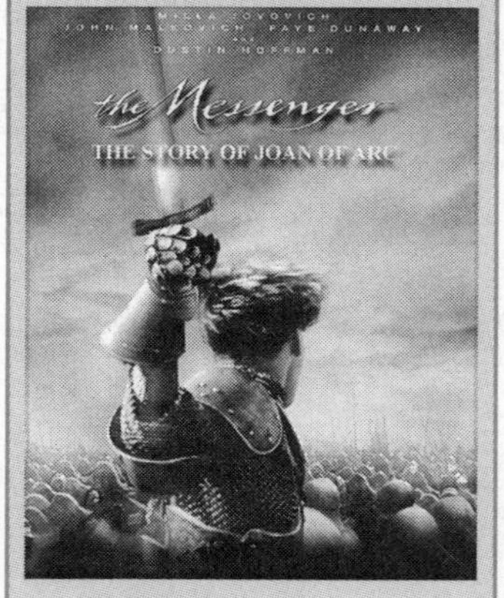

The Messenger: The Story Of Joan Of Arc (1999)
French filmmaker Luc Besson's ("The Fifth Element") lavish historical biodrama about the visionary peasant girl who inspired a nation stars Milla Jovovich as Joan. Driven by faith to lead her people against England, her battle against political enemies led to her capture, trial and execution. John Malkovich, Faye Dunaway, and Dustin Hoffman as "the Conscience" also star. 148 min.
02-3419 Was $99.99 *❑$14.99*

Joan Of Arc (1999)
She was a visionary, a warrior, a heroine and a martyr, all before the age of 20. Leelee Sobieski stars as the French peasant girl whose divine visions led her to become a military leader in the Hundred Years' War against England—and also led to her downfall—in this compelling historical drama. The supporting cast includes Jacqueline Bisset, Powers Boothe, Neil Patrick Harris, Shirley MacLaine, Peter O'Toole and Peter Strauss. 140 min.
27-7123 Was $19.99 *❑$14.99*

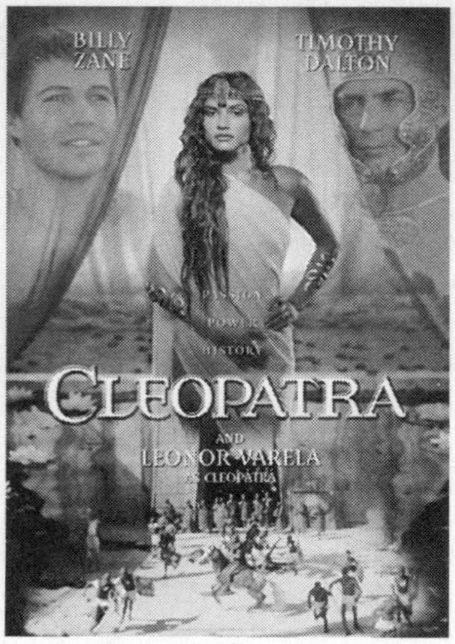

Cleopatra (1999)
By the time she was 20 she was ruler of Egypt, and she used her beauty and cunning to win the hearts of two of Rome's mightiest rulers. Leonor Varela stars as the seductive Queen of the Nile, with Timothy Dalton as Julius Caesar and Billy Zane as Marc Antony, in this sweeping historical drama. 139 min.
88-1197 Was $19.99 *❑$14.99*

All The King's Men (1999)
Comprised of servants and staff from King George V's Norfolk estate, Britain's Sandringham Company left England in 1915 and took part in the battle of Gallipoli, where they vanished to a man without a trace. One of World War I's most remarkable mysteries is explored in this drama that follows the men before the conflict and the search for their whereabouts after. David Jason, David Troughton, Stuart Bunce and Maggie Smith star. 120 min.
08-8843 *❑$19.99*

Horatio Hornblower: Boxed Set (1998)
C.S. Forester's 19th-century seafaring hero comes to life in this set of four feature-length adventures starring Ioan Gruffudd in the title role. Follow the ambitious young Hornblower on board the HMS Indefatigable as he rises through the ranks of the British Navy during the turmoil of the Napoleonic Wars. Included in the series are "The Duel," "The Fire Ships," "The Duchess and the Devil" and "The Wrong War." 400 min. on four tapes.
53-6460 *$59.99*

A Bright Shining Lie (1998)
This stirring adaptation of Neal Travis' award-winning book stars Bill Paxton as Lt. Col. John Paul Vann, a military advisor sent to Saigon in 1962 to help South Vietnam's battle against the Communist North. After revealing his critical findings to a reporter, Vann is dismissed from his job, but returns years later as a civilian advisor during the Johnson administration. With Vivian Wu, Donal Logue and Amy Madigan. 118 min.
44-2173 Was $99.99 *❑$14.99*

Vendetta (1999)
In the late 19th century, thousands of Italian immigrants settled in New Orleans and established themselves in the local shipping industry. The rivalry between the newcomers and wealthy businessmen boils over into a trumped-up murder trial for 19 Italian men and a bitter chapter in American history. Christopher Walken, Bruce Davison, Clancy Brown and Joaquim de Almeida star. 117 min.
44-2214 *❑$99.99*

Heroes & Villains: Boxed Set (1995)
Featured in this three-tape collection of British biodramas are "Full Throttle," with Rowan Atkinson as determined 1920s race car driver Sir Henry Birkin; "Queen of the East," featuring Jennifer Saunders as Lady Hester Stanhope, a 19th-century socialite-turned-adventurer; and "The Last Englishman," focusing on the life of British war hero Col. Alfred Wintle, played by Jim Broadbent. 150 min. total. NOTE: Individual volumes available at $19.99 each.
53-6650 Save $20.00! *$39.99*

Malcolm X: Death Of A Prophet (1991)
Morgan Freeman plays the late activist and Black Muslim leader in this look at Malcolm X's final days before his assassination. Newsreel footage and interviews are mixed with dramatic re-creations to bring history to life. Yolanda King, the daughter of Martin Luther King, Jr., plays Malcolm's wife, Betty Shabbaz. Ossie Davis narrates. 60 min.
53-7589 *$19.99*

Amelia Earhart: The Final Flight (1994)
Diane Keaton plays the 1930s aviatrix whose incredible accomplishments and mysterious disappearance while en route on an around-the-world flight made her a legend. Rutger Hauer co-stars as Earhart's navigator, Fred Noonan, and Bruce Dern is her husband, publisher G.P. Putnam. 95 min.
18-7508 *❑$89.99*

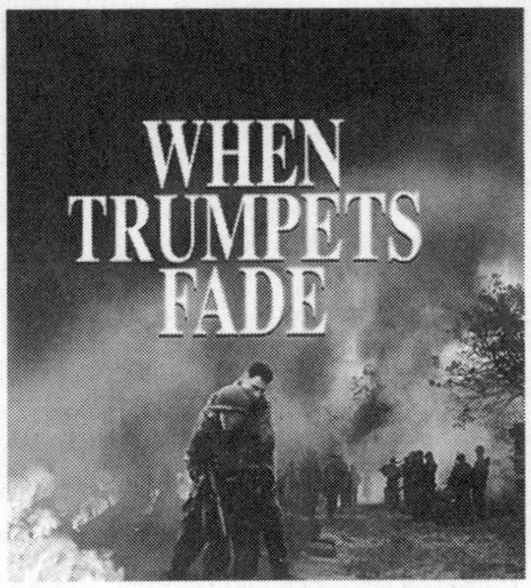

When Trumpets Fade (1998)
Shattering WWII drama depicting the 1944 Battle of Hurtgen Forest, when shell-shocked Allied forces must secure a bridge flanked by enemy tanks. With the troops in bad shape, four renegade soldiers, including a medic, an angry sergeant, a new recruit and a recently promoted private, must complete the assignment. Ron Eldard, Frank Whaley, Martin Donovan and Dwight Yoakam star. 92 min.
44-2171 Was $99.99 ❑*$14.99*

Doomsday Gun (1994)
What if the world's most powerful weapons fell into the hands of one of the world's most ruthless dictators? It nearly happened, as shown in this real-life thriller with Frank Langella as a scientist/arms designer who, with American, British and Israeli spies watching, agreed to build his experimental "supergun" for Iraqui ruler Saddam Hussein. Alan Arkin, Kevin Spacey co-star. 106 min.
44-1973 Was $89.99 ❑*$19.99*

The Walking Dead (1995)
Gritty war drama set in Vietnam in 1972, where a no-nonsense black Marine sergeant leads his men—four African-Americans and one white soldier—through the jungle to find any survivors of a POW camp left by the Viet Cong. As the platoon faces imminent danger, they reveal the reasons they've become Marines. Joe Morton, Allen Payne and Eddie Griffin star. 90 min.
44-1995 Was $19.99 *$14.99*

The Tuskegee Airmen (1995)
The inspiring real-life story of the "Fighting 99th," the black pilots who overcame prejudice to fight for America in the Second World War, is told in this exciting drama that features thrilling aerial sequences and a stellar cast that includes Laurence Fishburne, Andre Braugher, Cuba Gooding, Jr. and John Lithgow. 106 min.
44-2044 Was $19.99 ❑*$14.99*

Path To Paradise (1997)
International terrorism on America's shores became a bloody reality with the February, 1993 bombing of New York's World Trade Center. Learn the amazing true story of the Muslim extremists who planned a citywide bombing attack and the government agents who brought them to justice in this real-life thriller. Peter Gallagher, Marcia Gay Harden, Art Malik star. 94 min.
44-2120 ❑*$99.99*

Mission Of The Shark (1991)
A riveting true story concerning the tragic sinking of the Navy cruiser USS Indianapolis towards the end of World War II and the subsequent court-martial of its skipper, highly-decorated Captain Charles McVay. Stacy Keach, Richard Thomas and Carrie Snodgress star. 92 min.
72-9011 Was $89.99 *$14.99*

The Last Wargame (1993)
A group of campers out in the woods playing war games with paint pellets have to suddenly put their survival techniques to use when a renegade neo-Nazi and his heavily armed trainees assault them. Mark Coyan, Kelly Flynn star. 75 min.
73-9122 *$29.99*

Tides Of War (1994)
In a last-ditch effort by the Nazis to win World War II, they plan to use a British isle outpost to launch a missile on Washington, D.C. A German naval officer in charge of clearing the island has lost his loyalty for Hitler and plans to sabotage the effort. David Soul, Ernest Borgnine and Yvette Heyden star. 91 min.
74-3005 *$89.99*

The Bruce (1996)
Set in the late 13th century, this historical drama tells of Robert the Bruce, the Scottish patriot who leads his people's quest for independence against England's Edward I and is crowned King of the Scots. Oliver Reed, Brian Blessed, Sandy Welch and Michael Van Wijk star in this saga. 92 min.
80-7269 *$24.99*

Britannic (1999)
Stirring historical drama dealing with the English luxury liner, sister ship to the Titanic, that served as a hospital ship in World War I. Posing as a governess so she can search for a rumored German spy on board, British undercover agent Amanda Ryan falls for chaplain Edward Atterton, but an explosion puts theirs—and everyone else's—lives in danger. Jacqueline Bisset, John Rhys-Davies, Bruce Payne also star. 96 min.
85-1503 *$19.99*

Rob Roy (1995)
Stirring historical adventure set in the Scottish highlands during the early 1700s and starring Liam Neeson as Robert Roy MacGregor, a cattle drover forced to become an outlaw and fight for his freedom and honor when a scheming British nobleman steals money due MacGregor. Jessica Lange, Tim Roth and John Hurt also star in this epic, featuring compelling performances and expert battle scenes. 139 min.
12-2986 Was $19.99 ❑*$14.99*

One Man's Hero (1999)
Set during the U.S.-Mexican War of the 1840s, this exciting historical drama chronicles the story of the Saint Patrick Battalion. Irish immigrants who joined the U.S. Army after being promised citizenship, but instead met with prejudice and opted to settle in Mexican-owned land, the men known as the "San Patricios" fought for their adopted home against overwhelming odds. Tom Berenger, Patrick Bergin, Daniela Romo star. 122 min.
12-3299 ❑*$99.99*

Ironclads (1990)
Historical epic about the Civil War's most famous sea battle: the clash between mighty Ironclad ships, the Monitor and the Merrimack. A Union officer goes undercover with help from a beautiful Southern belle to try to uncover the South's secret ship-design information. Leslie Harmon, Alex Hyde-White and Virginia Madsen star. 94 min.
18-7299 Was $79.99 ❑*$14.99*

Iran: Days Of Crisis (1991)
This explosive drama looks at the taking of 60 Americans by militants in Iran in November, 1979, and how the nation, the captors and the hostages' families react to the situation. The personal side of the story focuses on hostage John Limbert and his Iranian-born wife. Arliss Howard, Alice Krige, Jeff Fahey, George Grizzard and Valerie Kaprisky star. 185 min.
18-7363 ❑*$89.99*

The Sound And The Silence (1993)
A superb biodrama that looks at the life of 19th-century inventor Alexander Graham Bell. John Bach stars as the Scottish-born Bell, whose experiences with his deaf mother and teaching the hearing-impaired led to his experiments with sound and the development of the telephone. With Ian Bannen, Elizabeth Quinn and Brenda Fricker. 93 min.
18-7462 ❑*$89.99*

George Wallace (1997)
Gary Sinise gives a spellbinding performance as the Alabama governor who came to symbolize the segregated South in director John Frankenheimer's acclaimed biodrama. Wallace's rise to power and bitter campaign against school integration and civil rights, his two presidential campaigns, the 1972 assassination attempt that left him paralyzed, and his apologies for his racist past are all depicted. Joe Don Baker, Angelina Jolie, Clarence Williams III and Mare Winningham also star. 180 min.
18-7784 Was $99.99 ❑*$19.99*

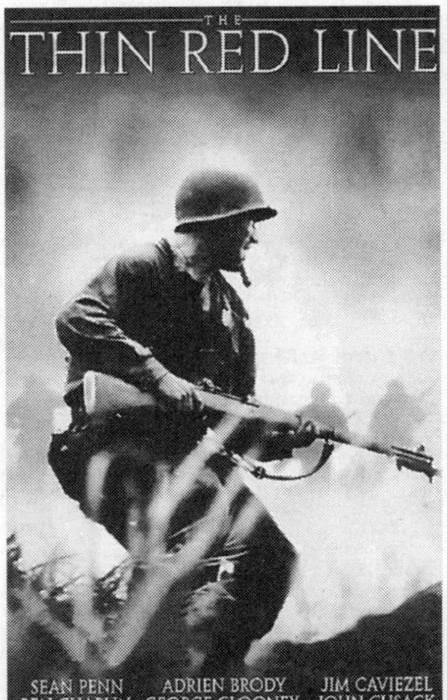

The Thin Red Line (1998)
Returning to the screen after a 20-year absence, writer/director Terence Malick adapts James Jones' semi-autobiographical novel set during the pivotal WWII battle of Guadalcanal in the South Pacific. The brutal realities of combat are seen primarily through the eyes of a U.S. army company headed by officers Elias Koteas and Sean Penn. Also in the ensemble cast are Jim Caviezel, Ben Chaplin, George Clooney, Woody Harrelson, Nick Nolte and John Travolta.
04-3845 Was $99.99 ❑*$14.99*

The Thin Red Line (Letterboxed Version)
Also available in a theatrical, widescreen format.
04-3876 ❑*$19.99*

Kingfish: A Story Of Huey P. Long (1995)
John Goodman turns in a tour-de-force performance as Huey P. Long, the controversial governor of '30s Louisiana known as much for his corruption and sparring with politicians and the wealthy as for his social reforms and helping the poor. Matt Craven, Anne Heche also star. 96 min.
18-7553 Was $89.99 ❑*$14.99*

Andersonville (1996)
Powerhouse historical drama from director John Frankenheimer focusing on the infamous Confederate prison camp where the deplorable conditions led to a bloody altercations between warring factions of prisoners in 1864. The principals involved are a young Union corporal (Jarrod Emick), a veteran sergeant (Frederic Forrest) and the camp's creepy commander (Jan Triska). 168 min.
18-7643 Was $49.99 ❑*$19.99*

Glory And Honor (1998)
They endured the worst elements of nature that man could experience to reach the top of the world, but while one returned home to a hero's welcome, the other faded into obscurity. Now the incredible true story of Commander Robert Peary, his African-American aide Matthew Henson, and their pioneering trek to the North Pole is retold in this acclaimed drama starring Henry Czerny as Peary and Delroy Lindo as Henson. 94 min.
18-7812 Was $79.99 ❑*$14.99*

The Hunley (1999)
Set in the South in 1864, this historical drama stars Armand Assante as Lt. George Dixon, a Confederate officer determined to use a hand-powered, submersible vessel and save war-torn Charleston, S.C. Donald Sutherland is General Beauregard, Assante's superior, who is wary of the ship's abilities because of past disasters. Alex Jennings, Christopher Bauer co-star. 94 min.
18-7879 Was $99.99 ❑*$14.99*

Memphis Belle (1990)
Thrilling World War II adventure centering on the final flight of the legendary Memphis Belle, a B-17 bomber with Dresden as its target. Meet the gung-ho members of its young crew (played by Eric Stoltz, Matthew Modine, Billy Zane and Harry Connick, Jr., among others) and be mesmerized by amazing flight sequences. With John Lithgow, David Strathairn. 106 min.
19-1838 Was $19.99 ❑*$14.99*

Born To Ride (1991)
Macho man John Stamos stars as a motorcycle-riding rebel who leads a group of young cyclists in a daring raid on the Nazis during World War II. John Stockwell, Teri Polo also star in this rousing, revving action film. 88 min.
19-1907 Was $19.99 ❑*$14.99*

The Man Who Captured Eichmann (1997)
Riveting true story about Peter Malkin, the Israeli secret agent who played a large part in finding and capturing notorious Nazi Adolf Eichmann in Argentina, 15 years after World War II. Robert Duvall, Arliss Howard, Jeffrey Tambor and Joel Brooks star. 96 min.
19-2529 Was $99.99 ❑*$19.99*

Rough Riders (1997)
They came from all walks of life, and, under the command of a brash young colonel named Theodore Roosevelt, their charge up Cuba's San Juan Hill during the Spanish-American War made history. Learn the true story behind the men of the 1st U.S. Volunteer Cavalry Regiment, the "Rough Riders," in this rousing historical drama. Sam Elliott, Gary Busey and, as Roosevelt, Tom Berenger star. 187 min.
19-2615 Was $99.99 ❑*$19.99*

Mountains Of The Moon (1990)
An epic, true-life saga detailing the adventures of British explorers Richard Burton and Lt. John Speke, whose perilous journey took them to the source of the Nile River in 1854. A mesmerizing tale, featuring beautiful photography, powerful performances and superb direction by Bob Rafelson ("Five Easy Pieces"). With Patrick Bergin and Ian Glen. 140 min.
27-6678 Was $89.99 ❑*$14.99*

Behind The Lines (Regeneration) (1997)
A Scottish military hospital in World War I is the setting for this unusual and gripping drama based on Pat Barker's novel "Regeneration." Psychiatrist Jonathan Pryce, charged with helping patients recover and sending them back to the front, begins to question his work during sessions with three men: hero-turned-anti-war author James Wilby, budding poet Stuart Bunce, and shell-shocked soldier Jonny Lee Miller. 105 min.
27-7182 ❑*$99.99*

Field Of Fire (1991)
When an American military expert is shot down behind enemy lines during the Vietnam war, General Corman (David Carradine) enlists a squadron of soldiers to stage a daring rescue. Intense jungle war drama also stars David Anthony Smith, Scott Utley. 96 min.
44-1867 Was $19.99 *$14.99*

Citizen Cohn (1992)
James Woods turns in a riveting performance as attorney Roy Cohn, Senator Joseph McCarthy's right-hand man during the Communist witch hunts of the 1950s, an arch-opponent of the Kennedys, and a friend of FBI leader J. Edgar Hoover. This dynamic film pulls no punches in its depiction of the ruthless, power-hungry Cohn. With Pat Hingle, Joe Don Baker and Frederic Forrest. 112 min.
44-1929 Was $19.99 ❑*$14.99*

Victoria The Great (1937)
First-rate biography of England's Queen Victoria, featuring Anna Neagle in a tour-de-force performance in the lead. The film traces her early days, her courtship and marriage to Prince Albert, her dealings with Disraeli, Wellington and Abraham Lincoln, and the Diamond Jubilee celebration of her rule. The film is notable for its use of Technicolor during the "Empress of India" scene. With Anton Walbrook, Walter Rilla. 110 min.
09-5085 Was $19.99 *$14.99*

Queen Victoria: Evening At Osborne (1991)
She ruled England for over 60 years, and her name has come to define the era of the British Empire's zenith. Prunella Scales ("Fawlty Towers") stars in an acclaimed performance as the aged Queen Victoria, looking back over her reign and recalling, in the monarch's own words, matters ranging from global politics to her family and private life. 51 min.
44-2215 *$24.99*

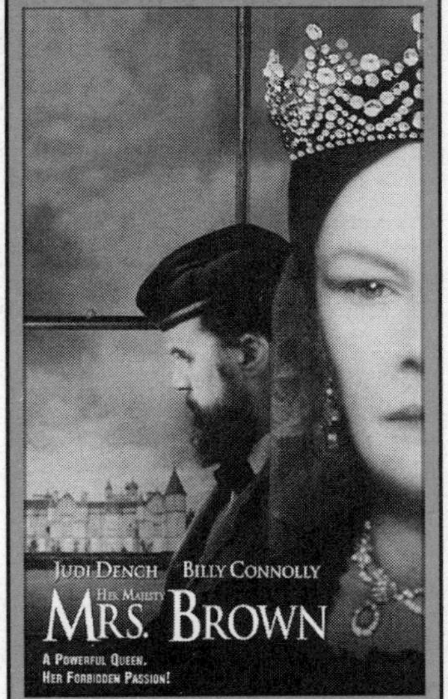

Mrs. Brown (1997)
The unique and controversial relationship that developed between Britain's Queen Victoria, who sequestered herself away in Windsor Castle following the death of her husband Albert, and Scottish stableman John Brown, who became the queen's confidant and pushed her to get on with her life and duties, is explored in this sensitive drama featuring standout performances from Judi Dench as Victoria and Billy Connolly as Brown. With Antony Sher, David Westhead. 105 min.
11-2232 Was $99.99 ❑*$19.99*

Michael Collins (1996)
Liam Neeson stars as the charismatic fighter for Irish independence in the early 20th century in writer/director Neil Jordan's striking historical biodrama that traces Collins' role in the 1916 Easter Uprising, his use of guerrilla warfare tactics against the British, and the signing of the 1921 peace treaty that divided Ireland, precipitated decades of civil war, and led to Collins' assassination a year later. Aidan Quinn, Stephen Rea, Alan Rickman and Julia Roberts also star. 133 min.
19-2498 Was $19.99 ❑*$14.99*

Michael Collins (Letterboxed Version)
Also available in a theatrical, widescreen format.
19-2590 ❑*$19.99*

Young Bess (1953)
Lavish historical drama about the incredible early life of Queen Elizabeth I (Jean Simmons), chronicling her relationship with her father, Henry VIII (Charles Laughton); her half-brother Edward VI's rise to power; and her romance with a married naval officer (Stewart Granger). With Deborah Kerr, Guy Rolfe. 112 min.
12-2936 *$19.99*

Elizabeth R (1972)
Glenda Jackson earned two Emmy Awards for her portrayal of England's strong-willed "Virgin Queen" in this acclaimed six-part "Masterpiece Theatre" presentation that traces Elizabeth I's 45-year reign, an era marked by religious strife, court intrigue and military triumphs. The cast includes Ronald Hines, Vivian Pickles, Nicholas Selby, Robin Ellis. 540 min.
04-2978 Was $149.99 ❑*$99.99*

Elizabeth (1998)
She overcame the intrigues of her half-sister to escape the executioner and ascend to the throne of England, and was forced to ignore the dictates of her heart to keep her crown. Cate Blanchett is superb in the title role in this lush biodrama that looks at the early years of Elizabeth I's reign. Geoffrey Rush, Joseph Fiennes and Kathy Burke also star. 124 min.
02-9073 Was $99.99 ❑*$14.99*

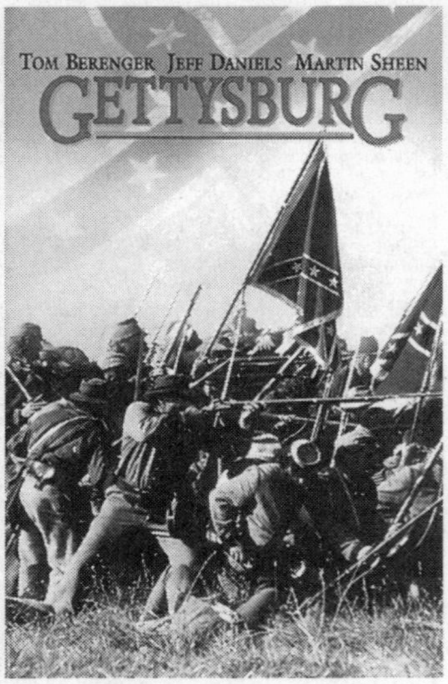

Gettysburg (1993)
The bloody, three-day Civil War battle that took place in July of 1863 and saw 53,000 lives lost is depicted in spectacular style in this epic film marked by incredible fighting sequences and a memorable cast that includes Tom Berenger, Martin Sheen, Stephen Lang, Jeff Daniels and Richard Jordan. Based on the acclaimed book "The Killer Angels." 254 min.
18-7466 Letterboxed ❑$24.99

Black Robe (1991)
Gorgeously photographed, true-life story details the efforts of a Jesuit priest who takes a danger-filled journey to the Canadian wilderness during the winter of 1634 to convert a group of Indians. Lothaire Bluteau, Aden Young and Sandrine Holt star; directed by Bruce Beresford ("Driving Miss Daisy"). 101 min.
68-1226 ❑$14.99

Black Robe (Letterboxed Version)
Also available in a theatrical, widescreen format.
68-1846 *$14.99*

The Madness Of King George (1994)
Marvelously acted, meticulously crafted story about King George III, the British monarch deemed "mad" by his subjects and court officials as a mysterious illness causes his behavior to grow increasingly erratic. While loyal aides seek to cure him, the king's scheming son and his followers try to gain the throne. Nigel Hawthorne, Helen Mirren and Rupert Everett star. 110 min.
88-1015 Was $19.99 ❑$14.99

The Truce (1998)
Based on Italian author Primo Levi's autobiographical book "The Reawakening," this moving drama stars John Turturro as an Auschwitz survivor struggling to reclaim his humanity as he tries to reach his homeland in the turmoil of post-WWII Europe. With Rade Serbedzija, Teco Celio; directed by Francesco Rosi ("Three Brothers"). 117 min.
11-2275 Was $99.99 ❑$19.99

Sharpe's (1993-97)
Set in Spain during the Napoleonic Wars, this action-packed mini-series stars Sean Bean ("Patriot Games") as Richard Sharpe, a dashing British officer who operates behind French lines, risking his life to defeat Napoleon's forces. Assumpta Serna and Elizabeth Hurley also star. Each installment runs about 100 min.

Sharpe's: Collection Set 1
"Sharpe's Rifles," "Sharpe's Eagle," "Sharpe's Company" and "Sharpe's Enemy" are offered in a deluxe set.
53-9608 *$69.99*

Sharpe's: Collection Set 2
The episodes "Sharpe's Honour," "Sharpe's Gold," "Sharpe's Battle" and "Sharpe's Sword" are available in this collector's set.
53-9657 *$89.99*

Sharpe's: Collection Set 3
The episodes "Sharpe's Regiment," "Sharpe's Siege" and "Sharpe's Mission" are available in this collector's set.
53-9888 *$69.99*

Sharpe's: Collection Set 4
This special collector's set includes "Sharpe's Revenge," "Sharpe's Justice" and "Sharpe's Waterloo."
53-9889 *$69.99*

Sharpe The Legend
In this salute to Richard Sharpe, a British soldier recounts the legendary leader's heroic deeds on the battlefield and romantic entanglements off of it. Sean Bean, Michael Mears and Elizabeth Hurley star in this program that includes many of "Sharpe's" finest moments. 90 min.
53-9983 *$19.99*

The Final Days (1989)
Intense historical drama, based on the best-selling book by "All the President's Men" reporters Bob Woodward and Carl Bernstein, follows the Watergate crisis and the downfall of President Nixon, powerfully played by Lane Smith. The fine cast includes Richard Kiley, Ed Flanders, Gary Sinise, Theodore Bikel. 150 min.
63-1811 Was $89.99 ❑$14.99

Hiroshima (1995)
An audacious, hypnotic look at the finals days of World War II and the events that led to the August, 1945 atomic bombing of Japan, which follows the actions of Allied and Japanese leaders through dramatic re-creations, eyewitness accounts and captivating newsreel footage. Filmed in black-and-white, this engrossing film stars Wesley Addy, Kohji Takahashi, Richard Masur, and Kenneth Welsh as President Truman. 165 min.
88-1026 Was $19.99 ❑$14.99

Nostradamus (1994)
The 16th-century mystic and seer whose prophecies are said to have predicted the rise of Hitler, the JFK assassination and other events is the subject of this moody, compelling biographical drama. Tcheky Karyo stars as Nostradamus, with support from F. Murray Abraham, Rutger Hauer, Julia Ormond and Amanda Plummer. 118 min.
73-1190 Was $89.99 ❑$14.99

Stalin (1992)
The public and private life of Russian dictator Joseph Stalin is chronicled in an impressive biodrama that features a towering title performance by Robert Duvall. With amazing authenticity Stalin's treacherous rise to power, his purges against real and imagined enemies, his alliance with Hitler and his troubled personal life are traced. Maximilian Schell, Julia Ormond and Jeroen Krabbe co-star. 173 min.
12-2641 Was $89.99 ❑$19.99

Dieppe (1993)
This epic study of one of the most tragic battles of World War II looks at the 1942 conflict that took place on the beaches of France through the real-life military and political leaders and a fictional group of Canadian soldiers who are ordered into a disastrous attack on the German-held town. Victor Garber, Gary Reineke and Robert Joy star; directed by John N. Smith ("The Boys of St. Vincent"). 208 min. on three tapes.
53-6955 *$39.99*

Ride With The Devil (1999)
Fascinating Civil War epic from director Ang Lee ("The Ice Storm") centers on four members of the "Missouri Irregulars," pro-Southern bushwhackers who attacked Union loyalists throughout the volatile border state. After staying at a homestead of Confederate sympathizers during the winter, the group stages a daring raid on nearby Lawrence, Kansas, with tragic results. Tobey Maguire, Skeet Ulrich, Jeffrey Wright, James Caviezel and pop singer Jewel star. 139 min.
07-2886 ❑$99.99

Grey Owl (1999)
Audiences in North America and Europe in the 1930s filled halls to hear Archie Grey Owl, a Canadian Ojibway Indian, speak on conservation. What the listeners never knew until years later, however, was that "noble savage" Grey Owl was really an English trapper who came to Canada decades earlier. Pierce Brosnan and Annie Galipeau star in director Richard Attenborough's ("Gandhi") compelling, breathtaking biodrama. 118 min.
02-3408 Was $99.99 ❑$14.99

Christopher Columbus (1949)
Sumptuously mounted look at the sailor and explorer, his voyage to the Americas, and his impact on the world. Fredric March stars as Columbus, with wife Florence Eldridge cast as Spain's Queen Isabella. Francis L. Sullivan, Kathleen Ryan, Derek Bond also star. 104 min.
88-1128 *$19.99*

Christopher Columbus (1985)
A lavish, historically detailed account of the adventures of the man whose exploits changed the course of world history. This epic film follows Columbus' relationship with Queen Isabella, his earlier journeys and his courageous explorations. Starring Gabriel Byrne, Eli Wallach, Oliver Reed, Nicol Williamson, Faye Dunaway. 128 min.
19-1956 Was $89.99 *$14.99*

1492: Conquest Of Paradise (1992)
Ridley Scott's version of the story of Christopher Columbus stars Gerard Depardieu as the explorer whose fearless pursuit of a new trading route to the East led to treachery and carnage when he attempted to "civilize" the natives of the "New World." Sigourney Weaver and Armand Assante also star in this gorgeously filmed epic. 142 min.
06-2115 Was $29.99 ❑$24.99

1492: Conquest Of Paradise (Letterboxed Version)
Also available in a theatrical, widescreen format.
06-2116 Was $29.99 ❑$24.99

Christopher Columbus: The Discovery (1992)
Thrilling biopic chronicles adventurer Christopher Columbus' attempts to lead an expedition across the Atlantic and his subsequent arrival in the "New Land." The all-star cast includes Marlon Brando as the inquisitor Torquemada, Tom Selleck as King Ferdinand, Rachel Ward as Queen Isabella and George Corraface as Columbus. 121 min.
19-2015 Was $19.99 ❑$14.99

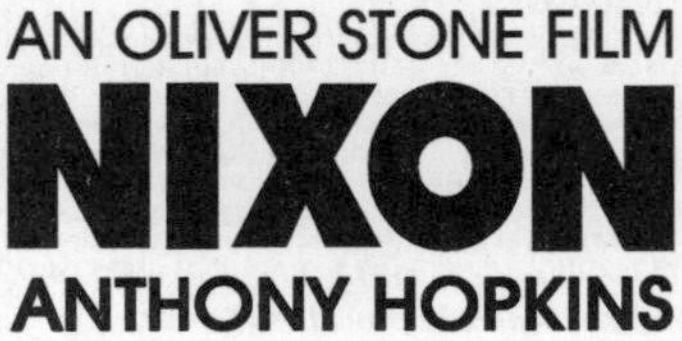

Nixon (1995)
Oliver Stone's epic look at the life of Richard M. Nixon showcases Anthony Hopkins in a tour-de-force performance as the embattled 37th president. Following Nixon from his troubled Quaker upbringing through his checkered political career and the scandal of Watergate, the film offers insight into the man behind the public image. With Joan Allen, Ed Harris, David Hyde Pierce, Paul Sorvino and Bob Hoskins. Special video version includes footage not shown in theatres. 191 min.
11-2024 Was $19.99 ❑$14.99

Kissinger And Nixon (1995)
Ron Silver and Beau Bridges play the respective title roles in this compelling historical drama that juxtaposes Kissinger's efforts to negotiate a peace treaty between North and South Vietnam in 1972 with the bitter political rivalries inside the Nixon White House that often put advisor and president on opposite sides. Matt Frewer, George Takei also star.
18-7616 Was $79.99 ❑$14.99

The Siege Of Firebase Gloria (1988)
As Tet Offensive troops swarm American footholds all over Vietnam, a Marine company and their hidebound sergeant dig in against an entire Viet Cong regiment. Heroic jungle combat featuring R. Lee Ermey and Wings Hauser. 95 min.
27-9035 *$24.99*

Hope And Glory (1987)
Director John Boorman takes a look back at the London Blitz of World War II, as seen through the eyes of a child, in this haunting, semi-autobiographical seriocomedy. Sebastian Rice-Edwards is the boy who sees the war as a grand adventure; with Sarah Miles, Sammi Davis, Ian Bannen and Charley Boorman. 113 min.
53-1727 Was $19.99 ❑$14.99

Jenny's War (1985)
In this powerful true story, Dyan Cannon plays an American schoolteacher who seeks her son, held captive in a Nazi POW camp in mid-1941. Going against all the odds, she eludes Hitler's army and enters the camp with a rescue plan. With Elke Sommer and Robert Hardy. 192 min.
02-2316 *$59.99*

Sadat (1983)
The life and times of Egyptian President Anwar El Sadat is chronicled in this exciting film that stars Louis Gossett, Jr. in an acclaimed title role performance. The film covers Sadat's achievements in Mideast politics, his Nobel Peace Prize and his tragic assassination. With Madolyn Smith and John-Rhys Davies. 191 min.
02-2333 Was $59.99 *$24.99*

The Beast (1988)
A Russian tank crew in Afghanistan, cut off from their main force, is besieged by native rebels in this engrossing and allegorical war drama. Steven Bauer, George Dzundza, Jason Patric star. 109 min.
02-1909 Was $89.99 *$14.99*

84 Charlie Mopic (1989)
An Army filmmaking crew in Vietnam is assigned to follow a reconnaissance unit on a jungle patrol and compile documentary footage. The result is an unusual and engrossing war drama that combines the narrative storyline with the "film-within-a-film" scenes of soldiers' everyday life. Acclaimed film stars Jonathan Emerson, Richard Brooks; Patrick Duncan directs. 95 min.
02-1967 Was $89.99 *$19.99*

Shogun (1980)
Suspense, romance, politics and intrigue mix in this breathtaking, feature-length version of the popular mini-series about the battle for power in 17th-century Japan. Richard Chamberlain, Toshiro Mifune and Yoko Shimada star. 124 min.
06-1074 Was $29.99 *$14.99*

Shogun: The Complete Mini-Series (1980)
James Clavell's epic tale of discovery, love and the conflict of two worlds in 17th-century Japan is now available in a special four-cassette set, containing the complete landmark TV mini-series. Richard Chamberlain, Toshiro Mifune, Yoko Shimada star. 545 min. on four tapes.
06-1275 *$249.99*

Walker (1987)
The bloody two-year rule of 1850s Nicaragua by lunatic American man-at-arms William Walker, after an invasion sponsored by U.S. business interests, is the basis for this blackly funny Alex Cox ("Sid & Nancy") film that parallels 19th-century history, sometimes anachronistically, with current events. Ed Harris, Peter Boyle and Marlee Matlin head the eccentric cast. 95 min.
07-1577 *$79.99*

Hitler's SS: Portrait In Evil (1985)
Penetrating war drama focusing on two brothers from Berlin who take opposite sides during World War II. Helmut, a student and opportunist, joins the SS, while Karl becomes a chauffeur for the stormtroopers. The siblings find themselves struggling against each other throughout the war. John Shea, Bill Nighy, Lucy Gutteridge, Tony Randall and José Ferrer star.
10-9517 *$14.99*

War And Love (1984)
Tender drama about two Jewish teenagers in war-torn Warsaw who fight against the Nazi invaders in the Ghetto Uprising but are captured and must search for each other after the war ends. Written by Abby Mann. 112 min.
12-1533 *$79.99*

Hell On The Battleground (1988)
Cut off from the rest of their platoon and trapped behind enemy lines, two veteran soldiers find that war is indeed hell in a blazing combat thriller. William Smith, Ted Prior, Fritz Matthews star. 91 min.
14-3382 *$12.99*

Salvador (1986)
"Platoon" creator Oliver Stone draws a disturbing parallel between America's involvements in Vietnam and Central America in this acclaimed drama. James Woods stars as an American journalist caught in the turmoil of the 1980 El Salvador revolution; with Jim Belushi, John Savage, Michael Murphy. 123 min.
47-1638 ❑$14.99

The Eagle And The Turtle (1988)
This compelling historical docudrama tells the story of Colonial American inventor David Bushnell, who developed a one-man submarine and attempted to get the American Army to use his craft against the British fleet during the Revolutionary War. An exciting look at a little-known part of the country's past. 37 min.
50-2476 *$19.99*

King (1982)
During one of the most turbulent times in American history, one man stood out as a leader for brotherhood and non-violence. Paul Winfield stars in this biographical drama of the life of Dr. Martin Luther King, Jr.: preacher, fighter for civil rights and humanitarian. With Cicely Tyson, Ossie Davis, Howard Rollins. 254 min. on three tapes.
73-1138 ❑$29.99

Gandhi (1982)
An epic masterpiece that won nine Academy Awards, including Best Picture, Actor and Director. Ben Kingsley turns in a commanding performance as Mahatma Gandhi, spiritual leader of the people of India, a peaceful man who taught tolerance and non-violence in frenzied times. Richard Attenborough directs. Candice Bergen, Edward Fox, John Gielgud and Martin Sheen. 188 min.
02-1233 *$29.99*

Utu: The Director's Cut (1983)
Action-filled drama set in British-ruled New Zealand in the 1870s, where a Maori native serving as a scout for the British army rebels when his family and village are massacred by colonial soldiers. Anzac Wallace, Bruno Lawrence, Kelly Johnston star. Special video version includes brutal scenes of warfare restored by director Geoff Murphy. 124 min.
04-2021 Letterboxed *$24.99*

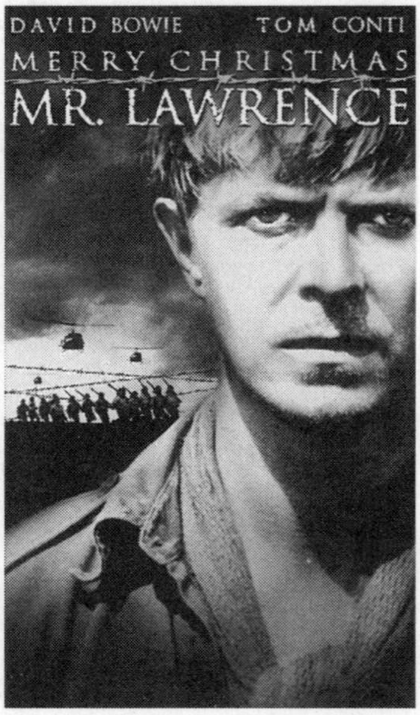

Merry Christmas, Mr. Lawrence (1983)
Powerful examination of the clash between European inmates and their Japanese captors in a WWII prisoner of war camp. David Bowie turns in a fascinating portrayal as a man going head to head against the camp's commanding officer. With Tom Conti, "Beat" Takeshi Kitano and Ryuichi Sakamoto (who also composed the film's score). 124 min.
07-1201 *$14.99*

Day One (1989)
Acclaimed look at the top-secret Manhattan Project, America's atomic bomb program, focusing on the stormy collaboration between Army colonel Leslie R. Groves and controversial scientist J. Robert Oppenheimer. Fine performances from Brian Dennehy, David Strathairn, Richard Dysart and Michael Tucker highlight this riveting true-life tale. 141 min.
14-3412 ❑$89.99

The Killing Fields (1984)
Engrossing true drama of courage and friendship between a journalist and his translator during the fall of Cambodia at the end of the Vietnam War. Sam Waterston is American reporter Sydney Schanberg; Oscar-winner Haing S. Ngor is captured Cambodian native Dith Pran. Roland Joffe directs. 142 min.
19-1430 ❑$14.99

The Hanoi Hilton (1987)
Harrowing drama that chronicles the 11-year captivity of a diverse group of American soldiers in a North Vietnamese POW camp. Devastating blend of "Stalag 17" and "Platoon" benefits from fine ensemble performances by Michael Moriarty, Jeffrey Jones, Paul LeMat, Lawrence Pressman, David Soul, Aki Aleong. 123 min.
19-1597 ❑$14.99

Lionheart (1987)
An enchanting adventure about a group of children in search of King Richard I during the Children's Crusade of the 13th century. Eric Stoltz and Gabriel Byrne star; directed by Franklin J. Schaffner ("Patton"). 104 min.
19-1755 Was $19.99 ❑$14.99

Bridge To Hell (1989)
Deadly firefights and explosive WWII action with a small band of escaped Allied POWs trapped behind enemy lines. Their suicide mission: to cross a heavily fortified bridge to freedom and demolish it behind them. Andy Forest and Jeff Connors star. 94 min.
19-7036 $59.99

The Walking Major (1988)
The inspirational story of Major Charles Allen, whose heroic exploits spanned three U.S. wars. A courageous battle commander, he became a legend for his annual 826-mile march to raise money for a Japanese orphanage. Dale Robertson, Frank Sinatra, Jr. and Toshiro Mifune star. 90 min.
23-5039 $29.99

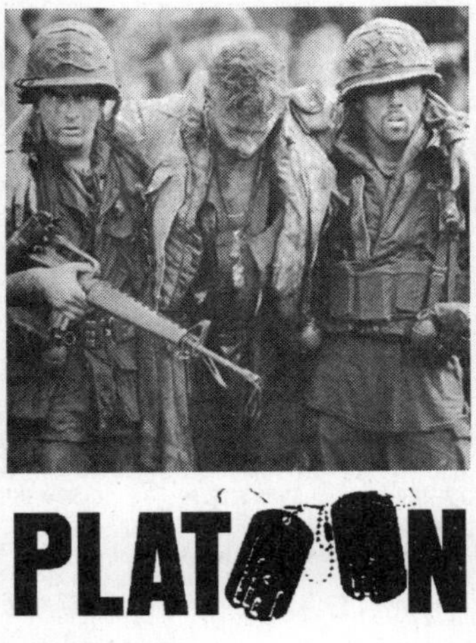

Platoon (1986)
Winner of Academy Awards for Best Picture and Best Director, this harrowing drama chronicles Vietnam frontline combat as seen through the eyes of young grunt Charlie Sheen (and drawn from the real-life experiences of creator Oliver Stone). Fine support from Tom Berenger and Willem Dafoe as the unit's bitterly competitive topkicks; with Johnny Depp, Forest Whitaker. 120 min.
47-1834 Was $19.99 ❑$14.99

Escape From Sobibor (1987)
This powerful, true-life saga details the efforts of a Russian Army officer leading a group of prisoners in a daring escape from a Nazi extermination camp during World War II. Rutger Hauer, Alan Arkin and Joanna Pacula star in this tale of courage against insurmountable odds. 120 min.
27-6757 Was $89.99 $14.99

Edward And Mrs. Simpson (1980)
Edward Fox and Cynthia Harris star in this award-winning biographical drama of the romance between King Edward VIII and the woman for whom he gave up his throne. Spectacular scenery and a superb cast highlight the story. 270 min. total.
44-1305 $29.99

Lion Of The Desert (1981)
Perhaps the finest historical battle film to be funded by a dictator (Libya's Col. Muammar Qaddafi), this sweeping war story stars Anthony Quinn as Omar Mukhtar, a Bedouin teacher-turned-guerrilla leader who headed the Libyan rebellion against the invading forces of Fascist Italy in the 1920s. With Oliver Reed, John Gielgud and Rod Steiger as Mussolini. This remastered video edition also includes a documentary on the making of the film and the original theatrical trailers. 206 min. total.
27-6063 Letterboxed $29.99

The Bunker (1981)
Anthony Hopkins received an Emmy Award for his tour-de-force portrayal of Adolf Hitler in this forceful look at the dictator's final days in his underground fortress in Berlin. With Richard Jordan as Albert Speer, Cliff Gorman as Joseph Goebbels, and Susan Blakely as Eva Braun. 150 min.
44-1961 Was $19.99 $14.99

The Plot To Kill Hitler (1990)
Forceful, true look at a group of German officers who, in 1944, plan to stop Hitler by assassinating him. Brad Davis, Madolyn Smith, Ian Richardson and Rupert Graves star. 93 min.
19-2237 Was $19.99 ❑$14.99

The Empty Mirror (1997)
Had he survived past the end of World War II, what would Adolf Hitler have thought about his reign of terror and his twisted legacy to the world? In this surreal psychodrama, a defeated Hitler (Norman Rodway) reflects from an underground bunker on his life, as visions of Goebbels (Joel Grey), Eva Braun (Camilla Soeberg) and Sigmund Freud (Peter Michael Goetz) visit him and WWII newsreel footage plays around him.
07-2857 Was $99.99 $19.99

Max And Helen (1989)
Powerful, true story about the Holocaust, focusing on the plight of an engaged couple from Poland who battle incredible odds to survive after the Nazis send them to a work camp. Treat Williams and Alice Krige star, and Martin Landau appears as Nazi hunter Simon Wiesenthal, who uncovers shocking secrets about their experiences years later. 94 min.
18-7215 ❑$14.99

Private War (1989)
A corporal training for a spot on a special forces unit discovers that the squadron's leader may be the killer behind a recent series of deadly "accidents." Martin Hewitt and Joe Dallesandro star in this powerful war drama. 95 min.
63-1374 $89.99

Shaka Zulu (1986)
An epic mini-series that traces the turbulent life of Shaka, the 19th-century Zulu tribal leader who united his people into one great nation that reached across Southern Africa until his downfall and murder. Henry Cele, Edward Fox, Trevor Howard and Christopher Lee head the cast in this remarkable, controversial production. 300 min.
68-1325 $14.99

Anzacs: The War Down Under (1985)
Everybody's favorite Aussie, Paul Hogan, stars in the story of the Australian and New Zealand Army Corps and their contributions in World War I, from the carnage of Gallipoli to the foxholes of France. With Andrew Clarke and Jon Blake. 165 min.
69-5026 Was $79.99 $19.99

Blunt: The Fourth Man (1984)
In 1951 the defection of three top British officials to the Soviet Union made headlines around the world, but until now the whole story couldn't be told. Anthony Hopkins stars as Anthony Blunt, the "fourth man" in the Philby/Burgess/MacLean spy scandal, in this compelling real-life espionage thriller. With Ian Richardson, Michael Williams. 86 min.
75-7091 Was $19.99 $14.99

Prisoners Of War (1988)
A woman is held captive in a Japanese prison camp during World War II. She must call on her wits and courage to escape from her sadistic captors. Jack Headley and Barbara Shelly star in this top-notch WWII adventure. 79 min.
78-1059 $19.99

The Wall (1982)
This dramatic and emotional historical drama recounts the Warsaw Ghetto uprising of 1943, when Jewish detainees fought valiantly against overwhelming numbers of German soldiers in an attempt to stave off extermination. Filmed on location in Poland, the film stars Tom Conti, Lisa Eichhorn, Rachel Roberts, Eli Wallach, Rosanna Arquette and Dianne Wiest. 150 min.
44-2043 Was $19.99 $14.99

The Right Stuff (1983)
Spectacular adventure of the birth of the Space Age and America's Mercury astronauts combines sweeping action, humor and human drama. Sam Shepard, Scott Glenn, Ed Harris, Barbara Hershey and Dennis Quaid star; written and directed by Phil Kaufman from Tom Wolfe's novel. 192 min.
19-1322 ❑$29.99

The Right Stuff (Letterboxed Version)
Also available in a theatrical, widescreen format.
19-2822 ❑$24.99

Hamburger Hill (1987)
It was one of the most brutal campaigns of the Vietnam War, and for one group of 14 American soldiers it was the closest they'd come to Hell on Earth. Brutal, factual war drama stars Michael Dolan, Steven Weber, Don Cheadle and Tom Quill. 104 min.
47-1831 $14.99

Hamburger Hill (Letterboxed Version)
Also available in a theatrical, widescreen format.
27-7057 $14.99

The Bastard (1978)
Epic presentation of John Jakes' American Bicentennial saga stars Andrew Stevens as the illegitimate son of an English nobleman who journeys through England, France and Revolutionary America to gain his rightful inheritance. Kim Cattrall, Buddy Ebsen, Lorne Greene, William Shatner and Tom Bosley also star. 189 min.
07-1723 Was $79.99 $29.99

The Rebels (1979)
The Kent Family Chronicles of John Jakes continue in this sequel to "The Bastard," as Philip Kent (Andrew Stevens) fights for American independence while at last confronting his father, the Duke of Kentland, face-to-face. Don Johnson, Doug McClure, Richard Basehart, Kim Cattrall and Tanya Tucker star. 180 min.
07-1735 Was $79.99 ❑$29.99

The Seekers (1979)
The third installment in John Jakes' historical trilogy focuses on Jarod Kent, who leaves the abusive household of his guardian brother to explore the Northwest Territory. Randolph Mantooth, Timothy Murphy, Ross Martin, George Hamilton and Delta Burke star. 200 min.
07-1737 Was $79.99 ❑$29.99

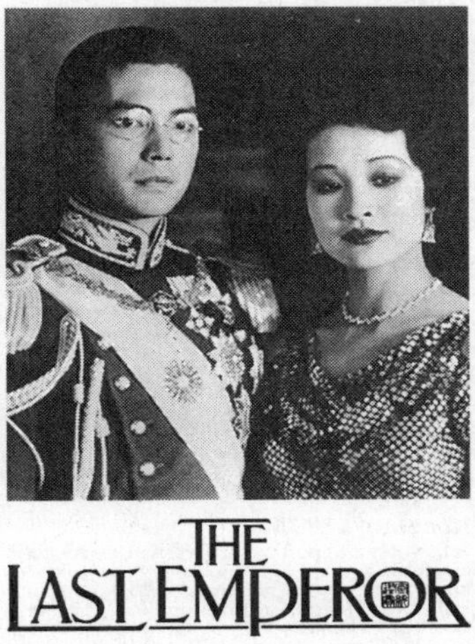

The Last Emperor (1987)
Bernardo Bertolucci's stunning historical drama, winner of nine Oscars including Best Picture and Director, follows the tragic life of Pu Yi: child ruler of Imperial China, dissolute playboy in exile, Japanese puppet leader, prisoner of the Communists. Filmed throughout China and in Peking's Forbidden City, this exquisite film stars John Lone as the adult monarch, Joan Chen, Lisa Lu and Peter O'Toole. 162 min.
53-1731 Was $29.99 ❑$14.99

The Last Emperor (Letterboxed Director's Cut)
Also available in the original director's cut in a theatrical, widescreen format. 218 min.
27-7100 ❑$24.99

The Key To Rebecca (1985)
Based on Ken Follett's novel, this WWII thriller stars Cliff Robertson as a British Army officer who battles a half-German, half-Arab spy (David Soul) in a dangerous cat-and-mouse game in North Africa. Season Hubley, Anthony Quayle, Robert Culp also star. 190 min.
14-3393 Was $24.99 $14.99

Edward The King (1975)
He was seen as a pampered playboy by many and spent 60 years waiting to ascend to the throne of England, only to rule for less than a decade. Timothy West stars as Edward VII, the eldest son of Queen Victoria who overcame his wild youth to earn the title Edward the Peacemaker, in this lavish mini-series. With Annette Crosbie, Francesca Annis, and Sir John Gielgud as Disraeli. 780 min. on six tapes.
82-9054 $129.99

Pacific Inferno (1985)
An intense WWII thriller based on a true incident. Japanese use American POWs to recover a cache of silver General MacArthur abandoned. Jim Brown, Richard Jaeckel. 90 min.
74-1006 $12.99

From Hell To Victory (1979)
A group of friends from different countries meet at a Paris cafe in 1939 and vow to return every year, a promise that will be difficult to keep when World War II puts them on opposite sides. Heartfelt war drama stars George Peppard, George Hamilton, Capucine, Horst Buchholz, Sam Wanamaker. 98 min.
03-1316 Was $19.99 $14.99

A Woman Called Moses (1978)
Cicely Tyson stars as Harriet Tubman, the escaped slave who risked her life to guide hundreds of fellow slaves to freedom via the Underground Railroad, in this moving biodrama. Will Geer, Robert Hooks, John Getz star; narrated by Orson Welles. 200 min.
54-9077 $89.99

The Jewel In The Crown (1984)
The visually stunning, emotionally stirring drama of love, betrayal, honor and deception, set against the final decades of British rule in India, is available in a deluxe eight-tape collector's edition. Dame Peggy Ashcroft, Tim Pigott-Smith, Geraldine James and Charles Dance star; adapted from Paul Scott's "Raj Quartet." 750 min.
06-5000 Was $149.99 $99.99

Attack At Dawn (1986)
Two Japanese brothers serving as soldiers in the 1937 invasion of Northern China's Manchuria region are beaten by their commanding officers and reduced to unquestioning "killing machines" whose own lives are to be willingly sacrificed in this gripping look at the dehumanizing brutality of war. Neil Fontane stars. 85 min. Dubbed in English.
73-9368 $19.99

Casablanca Express (1989)
Nazi commandos hijack the train carrying British Prime Minister Winston Churchill, and only one man can save him, in this fast-paced WWII thriller. Jason Connery, Glenn Ford, Donald Pleasence star. 90 min.
40-5013 Was $19.99 $14.99

Young Winston (1972)
Richard Attenborough's stirring epic of Winston Churchill's early years, from his days as a war correspondent in India and heroics in the Boer War to his failures and ultimate triumphs in the political arena and the halls of Parliament. Simon Ward, Robert Shaw, Anne Bancroft, John Mills and Edward Woodward star. 124 min.
02-1582 Was $59.99 $19.99

The Liberators (1977)
Klaus Kinski stars as a U.S. soldier sentenced to death in World War II for attempted rape and murder. He escapes behind enemy lines, only to find he must fight for his life against Nazi and Allied forces. 91 min.
48-1101 $59.99

The Magnificent Adventurer (1976)
Brett Halsey stars in this action-filled biodrama as Benvenuto Cellini, 16th-century Italian artist, goldsmith and ladies' man. 94 min.
48-1102 $59.99

The Lindbergh Kidnapping Case (1976)
The real-life trial has remained a center of controversy to this day. Did the uneducated Bruno Hauptmann kidnap and murder Charles Lindbergh's infant son, or was he set up by the law? Compelling "docudrama" stars Cliff DeYoung, Anthony Hopkins, Joseph Cotten, Martin Balsam and Denise Alexander. 150 min.
02-1743 $69.99

The Hiding Place (1975)
The award-winning wartime drama, based on the real-life exploits of Corrie tenBoom, a Dutch woman who was sent to a Nazi concentration camp with her sister for aiding Jewish refugees. Inspiring, life-affirming story stars Julie Harris, Eileen Heckart, Arthur O'Connell and Jeanette Clift. 145 min.
63-1173 $19.99

No Drums, No Bugles (1973)
Martin Sheen stars in this based-on-legend Civil War story of a conscientious objector on the run from the authorities, hiding in the wilderness and surviving alone for three years. 90 min.
71-1003 Was $19.99 $14.99

Winstanley (1975)
In the mid-1600s an obscure religious sect known as the Diggers, under the lead of reformer Gerard Winstanley, founded a short-lived agrarian commune in Surrey, England. Film scholar Kevin Brownlow's meticulously accurate drama recounts the group's efforts to start what some have called "the world's first communist movement," and the violent reaction they faced with local villagers and clergy. Miles Halliwell, David Bramley star. 96 min.
80-5039 $29.99

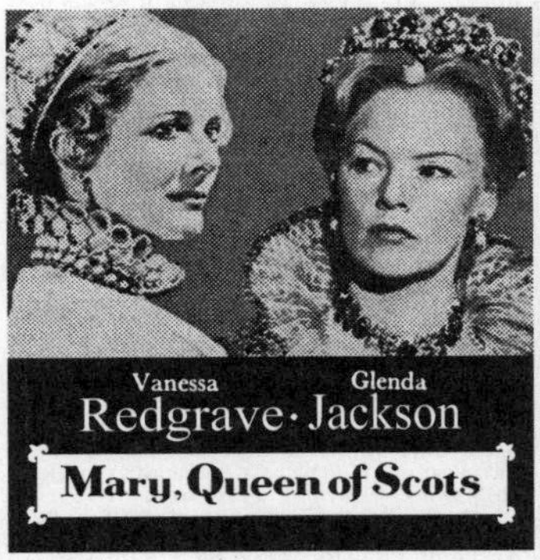

Mary, Queen Of Scots (1971)
Vanessa Redgrave stars as the strong-willed Mary Stuart, whose Catholic faith put her at odds with Glenda Jackson's Queen Elizabeth I of England, as well as scheming half-brother Patrick McGoohan, for control of the Scottish throne, in this lavish historical drama. Timothy Dalton, Trevor Howard also star. 129 min.
07-2839 ❑$14.99

The Fifth Day Of Peace (1972)
In the aftermath of World War I, two German soldiers are tried and executed for desertion by their commander, even though the Allies forbade German military trials. Riveting drama, based on a true story. Franco Nero, Helmut Schneider star. 103 min.
16-1098 *$14.99*

Operation Daybreak (1976)
Gripping, true-life World War II tale centering on a group of Czech soldiers who leave their British training ground and return to their homeland in hopes of assassinating Nazi leader Reinhard Heydrich. Timothy Bottoms, Anthony Andrews and Joss Ackland star. 102 min.
19-2221 Was $19.99 *$14.99*

Breaker Morant (1979)
Bruce Beresford's stirring war drama follows the true story of three Australian soldiers in the Boer War put on trial for the killing of civilians. Were they guilty, or were they merely scapegoats for the actions of their superiors? Edward Woodward, Bryan Brown, Jack Thompson star. 107 min.
27-6596 *$19.99*

The Day That Shook The World (1977)
Powerful historical drama examining the events that led to the assassination of Archduke Ferdinand and his wife, which led to WWI. An epic production highlighted by a fine cast which includes Christopher Plummer, Florinda Bolkan and Maximilian Schell. 111 min.
15-1176 Was $29.99 *$19.99*

Mayflower: The Pilgrims' Adventure (1979)
Fleeing persecution in their homeland, they undertook a perilous journey to seek freedom in an unknown land. The true story of the Pilgrims' 1620 voyage to America is compellingly recounted in this historical drama. Richard Crenna, Anthony Hopkins, Michael Beck, Jenny Agutter star. 96 min.
44-2205 *$14.99*

Riel (1979)
Louis David Riel was a 19th-century freedom fighter who battled for the independence of his people, a sect of half-Indian, half-French natives, in the Western Canadian frontier. Raymond Cloutier, Robert Blay, William Shatner and Christopher Plummer star in this true epic.
46-5005 *$14.99*

Pancho Villa (1972)
Telly Savalas plays the legendary outlaw-turned-revolutionary leader of turn-of-the-century Mexico. Action-filled historical drama also stars Anne Francis, Clint Walker, Chuck Connors. 90 min.
46-5240 *$14.99*

The Hindenburg (1975)
What really happened on that fatal day in 1937 when the great German dirigible exploded just before landing? Was it an accident or sabotage? Suspenseful, special effects-filled thriller that speculates on the airship's final flights stars George C. Scott, Anne Bancroft, Charles Durning, Gig Young, Burgess Meredith. 125 min.
07-1119 Was $19.99 *$12.99*

Give 'Em Hell, Harry (1975)
James Whitmore earned an Academy Award nomination for this filming of his acclaimed one-man stage show in which he portrays Harry S Truman, the man from Missouri who took over the presidency at one of the country's most difficult times and made many friends (and enemies) with his plain speaking ways. 103 min.
14-3007 *$19.99*

Truman (1995)
The remarkable true story of "The Man from Independence," Harry Truman, is brought to life in this memorable drama featuring a tour-de-force performance by Gary Sinise. Follow Truman's remarkable life—from his beginnings as a failed farmer to the presidency—and his achievements in the White House. With Diana Scarwid, Tony Goldwyn and Lois Smith. 130 min.
44-2026 Was $19.99 ❏*$14.99*

Suicide Patrol (1976)
In World War II Italy, Allied forces must abandon a strategic island to Nazi forces, but a small squad of commandoes remains to sabotage the island. Wartime thriller stars Pierre Richard, Gordon Mitchell. 90 min.
48-1069 *$49.99*

The Gypsy Warriors (1978)
Two high-spirited Army captains (Tom Selleck and James Whitmore, Jr.) receive help from a family of Gypsies while on a mission in Nazi-occupied France to retrieve a deadly toxin. 77 min.
07-1509 Was $39.99 *$14.99*

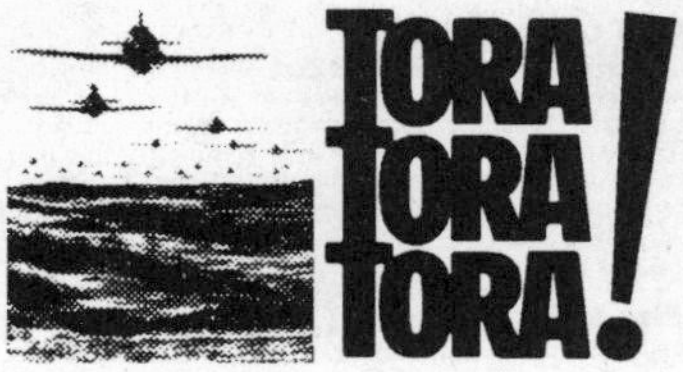

Tora! Tora! Tora! (1970)
Epic U.S.-Japanese co-production details the events surrounding the bombing of Pearl Harbor from both sides, leading to the beginning of World War II. Martin Balsam, Jason Robards, Jr., Soh Yamamura, E.G. Marshall and James Whitmore lead the cast. Featuring impressive battle sequences, the film was once to be co-directed by Akira Kurosawa. 144 min.
04-1163 *$14.99*

Tora! Tora! Tora! (Letterboxed Version)
Also available in a theatrical, widescreen format.
04-3657 *$19.99*

Man Of Legend (1971)
Falsely accused of espionage during World War I, a German soldier escapes and flees to Africa, where he joins the French Foreign Legion and becomes romantically involved with a rebel Moroccan chieftain's daughter. Peter Strauss, Tina Aumont, Luciana Paluzzi star. 95 min.
08-1292 *$14.99*

Lady Hamilton (1970)
The real-life love affair between English country lass-turned-married noblewoman Lady Emma Hamilton and naval hero Lord Horatio Nelson inspired this lush costume drama, based on the historical novel by Alexandre Dumas. Michele Mercier, Richard Johnson, John Mills star. AKA: "The Making of a Lady." 87 min.
08-1682 *$14.99*

Holocaust (1978)
A landmark television event and winner of eight Emmy Awards, this powerful drama tells the story of two men, a Jewish physicist and a lawyer-turned-SS officer, and their families in Nazi Germany during the period of 1935-1946. Michael Moriarty, Meryl Streep, Fritz Weaver, Blanche Baker, Tovah Feldshuh, James Woods and Joseph Bottoms head an exceptional cast. 450 min.
14-3025 Was $99.99 *$39.99*

The McKenzie Break (1970)
Top-notch war drama set in a POW camp in Scotland during World War II. After hearing of a planned prison break, Irish intelligence officer Brian Keith clashes with the sly U-Boat captain (Helmet Griem) behind the plot and allows the escape to occur, betting that the prisoners will lead the Allies to more German forces. With Ian Hendry. 106 min.
12-2831 Was $79.99 *$14.99*

A Bridge Too Far (1977)
Spectacular World War II saga about a 1944 Allied mission behind enemy lines in Holland that ends in disaster. The electrifying all-star cast includes Michael Caine, Sean Connery, Gene Hackman, Anthony Hopkins, Laurence Olivier, Ryan O'Neal, Robert Redford and Liv Ullmann; Richard Attenborough directs. 175 min.
12-2046 Was $29.99 ❏*$24.99*

A Bridge Too Far (Letterboxed Version)
Also available in a theatrical, widescreen format.
12-3078 ❏*$24.99*

Peter O'Toole

Lawrence Of Arabia (1962)
David Lean's epic biography of the British army officer who became a leader to Arab rebels won seven Academy Awards, including Best Picture, and features Peter O'Toole in his starring debut. With Alec Guinness, Omar Sharif, Anthony Quinn and Jack Hawkins. Also includes a documentary on the making of the film and the original theatrical trailer. 225 min.
02-2345 Letterboxed ❏*$24.99*

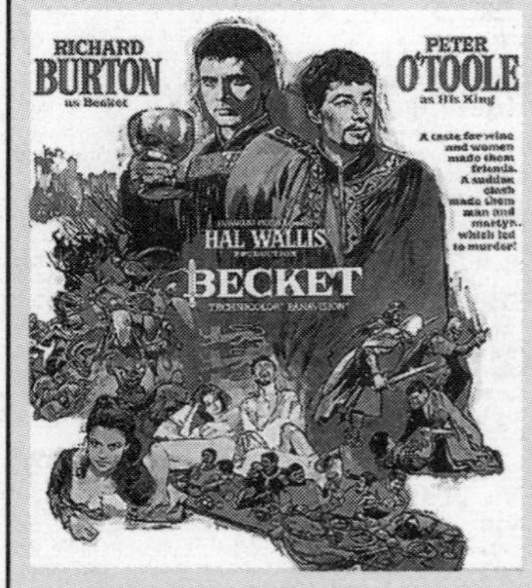

Becket (1964)
The volatile relationship between King Henry II and Thomas à Becket, ranging from the King's consecration of Becket to the position of Archbishop of Canterbury to the two devoted friends' ultimate schism over the role of the realm in ecclesiastical policy, is accurately rendered in this historical drama starring Peter O'Toole, Richard Burton and Sir John Gielgud. 148 min.
50-6017 Letterboxed *$19.99*

Lord Jim (1965)
Majestic adaptation of Joseph Conrad's classic tale about the fabulous adventures of a seaman in the Orient. Peter O'Toole is super in the title role. James Mason, Curt Jurgens, Daliah Lavi. Richard Brooks directs. 154 min.
02-1212 *$19.99*

The Night Of The Generals (1967)
Top-notch suspense thriller with a wartime background. A Nazi general kills prostitutes, and a Nazi agent must investigate the case. Peter O'Toole, Omar Sharif, Tom Courtenay. 148 min.
02-1405 *$19.99*

Goodbye, Mr. Chips (1969)
Lovely musical adaptation of the popular story stars Peter O'Toole as the mild-mannered English school teacher who falls in love with vivacious dancehall girl Petula Clark. Michael Redgrave, George Baker co-star; Herbert Ross directs. 151 min.
12-2116 *$19.99*

Murphy's War (1971)
A powerhouse performance by Peter O'Toole propels this tale of a WWII seaman determined to wreak his revenge on the German U-boat whose treacherous attack left him the sole survivor. Directed by Peter Yates. 108 min.
06-1375 Was $19.99 *$14.99*

Man Of La Mancha (1972)
Lush filming of the hit Broadway musical follows Cervante's errant knight, Don Quixote, and his quest for "The Impossible Dream." Peter O'Toole stars as Quixote and his creator, along with James Coco, Sophia Loren, Harry Andrews. Songs include "Dulcinea," "It's All the Same." 130 min.
12-2207 Was $19.99 *$14.99*

The Ruling Class (1972)
Outrageously funny satire features an Oscar-nominated performance by Peter O'Toole as a British earl who thinks he's Jesus Christ. Wicked barbs are thrown along the way at the Church and the aristocracy, and there's supporting turns by Alastair Sim, Harry Andrews and other top British actors. 142 min.
53-1092 *$39.99*

Rosebud (1975)
Action-crammed political thriller from Otto Preminger about a group of international beauties on a luxury yacht who are kidnapped by PLO terrorists, and a secret agent and an Israeli operative who team to rescue them. Peter O'Toole, Cliff Gorman, Peter Lawford, Richard Attenborough, Isabelle Huppert, Kim Cattrall and former New York City mayor John Lindsay star. 126 min.
12-2919 *$19.99*

Rogue Male (1976)
Peter O'Toole plays a man who finds himself dodging Nazis in 1939 Germany after he escapes his captors following a thwarted attempt at killing Adolph Hitler. Alastair Sim, John Standing also star. 100 min.
73-9092 *$19.99*

The Stunt Man (1980)
A complex and entertaining blend of suspense, action and comedy, as an escaped fugitive (Steve Railsback) finds "safety" working as a stunt man on a film set run by a crazed director (Peter O'Toole), whose calls for "realism" could cost him his life. Also stars Barbara Hershey, Alex Rocco. 129 min.
04-1195 Was $29.99 *$19.99*

MASADA

Masada (1981)
Feature-length version of the award-winning mini-series. Peter O'Toole is the Roman general ordered to crush the Jewish uprising in Israel; Peter Strauss the rebel leader fighting for freedom. Their last stand: the "city in the mountain" called Masada. A dramatic true story of courage and faith. 131 min.
07-1053 Was $59.99 *$19.99*

Masada (Mini-Series)
The complete mini-series is also available in a four-tape collector's set. 394 min.
07-2787 *$29.99*

My Favorite Year (1982)
Peter O'Toole turns in a devilishly funny performance as a boozing '30s matinee idol hired to appear on a '50s TV variety show, and Mark Linn-Baker as the young writer charged with keeping him sober. Wonderful comedy co-stars Joseph Bologna, Jessica Harper, Lainie Kazan. 92 min.
12-1256 Was $19.99 ❏*$14.99*

My Favorite Year (Letterboxed Version)
Also available in a theatrical, widescreen format.
12-3225 ❏*$14.99*

Kim (1984)
Rudyard Kipling's classic adventure tells the story of a teenage orphan boy out to find his true identity in India in the 1890s. He befriends two men on his quest—a Buddhist, who sees the boy as a perfect disciple, and a British spy, who recruits him for a dangerous mission. Peter O'Toole, Bryan Brown and Ravi Sheth star. 135 min.
22-5959 *$19.99*

Creator (1985)
Science fiction, romance and comedy blend in an offbeat tale of a college biology professor trying to "re-create" his deceased wife, but falling for a beautiful assistant. Peter O'Toole, Mariel Hemingway, Virginia Madsen and Vincent Spano star. 108 min.
44-1333 Was $69.99 *$14.99*

Wings Of Fame (1990)
An offbeat and satiric look at the nature of fame and notoriety. Peter O'Toole plays a renowned film star who is gunned down and finds himself wandering through a celebrity- and pseudo-celebrity-filled afterlife with the man who killed him, obsessed writer Colin Firth. 109 min.
06-2169 ❏*$89.99*

The Dark Angel (1991)
Suspenseful tale set in Victorian England stars Peter O'Toole as a treacherous uncle who dreams of gaining the family inheritance. The only thing standing in his way is the young niece coming to live with him—but will she survive the stay? With Beatie Edney, Jane Lapotaire, Guy Rolfe. 148 min.
04-2583 Was $89.99 *$19.99*

The Rainbow Thief (1995)
Peter O'Toole and Omar Sharif shine in this wonderful seriocomedy about a small-time con man who, in the hopes of making off with a fortune, befriends the black sheep heir of a wealthy family. Christopher Lee co-stars. 87 min.
19-2410 Was $89.99 ❏*$19.99*

Phantoms (1998)
Who—or what—is responsible for the deaths of hundreds of people in a Colorado ski town? Two sisters and the local sheriff and his deputies are the sole survivors, but their search for the truth leads them to a eccentric professor and an ancient menace striking from deep within the earth. Gripping horror tale, based on Dean Koontz's novel, stars Peter O'Toole, Rose McGowan, Ben Affleck, Joanna Going and Liev Schreiber. 91 min.
11-2257 Was $19.99 ❏*$14.99*

Coming Home (1998)
A boarding school student in '30s England is taken in by a friend's well-to-do family at their lush Cornish estate while her own parents are overseas, and in the ensuing years learns lessons in friendship, love and courage, in this moving adaptation of Rosamunde Pilcher's novel. Emily Mortimer, Penelope Keith, Joanna Lumley, David McCallum and Peter O'Toole star. 205 min. on four tapes.
50-8151 Was $59.99 *$39.99*

Please see our index for these other Peter O'Toole titles: *The Bible • Caligula • Club Paradise • Fairytale: A True Story • Gulliver's Travels • How To Steal A Million • Joan Of Arc • Kidnapped • The Last Emperor • The Lion In Winter • Molokai: The Story Of Father Damien • The Nutcracker Prince • What's New, Pussycat?*

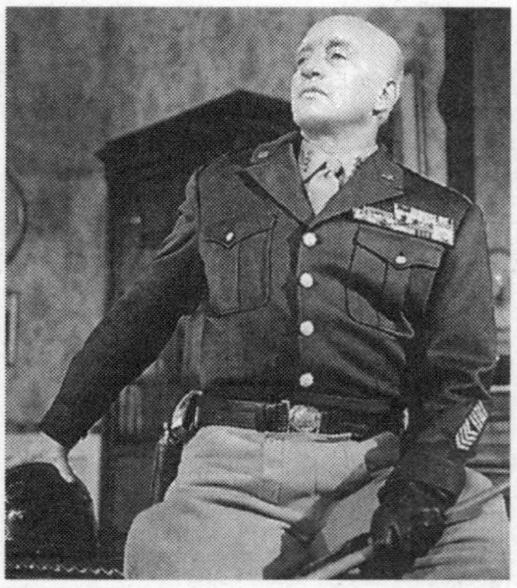

Patton (1970)
George C. Scott won (and turned down) a Best Actor Academy Award for his portrayal of the brilliant, no-nonsense WWII general in director Franklin Schaffner's epic screen biodrama. Winner of six other Oscars, including Best Picture, the film also stars Karl Malden, Stephen Young, Tim Considine; scripted by Francis Ford Coppola. 171 min.
04-1110 Was $19.99 *$14.99*

Patton (Letterboxed Version)
Also available in a theatrical, widescreen format.
04-3656 *$19.99*

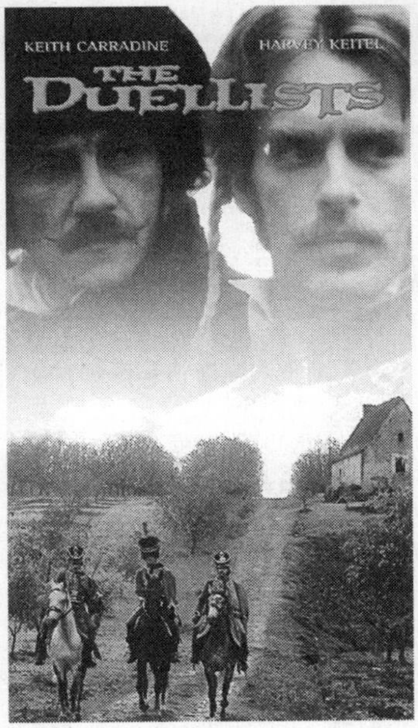

The Duellists (1978)
Ridley Scott's gorgeously lensed directorial debut adapts Joseph Conrad's story of two offciers in Napoleon's army who carry on a fierce and increasingly brutal series of duels that spans two decades. Harvey Keitel and Keith Carradine are the bound-by-honor rivals; Christina Raines, Edward Fox, Albert Finney also star. 101 min.
06-1014 Was $49.99 **$14.99**

The Eagle Has Landed (1977)
A superior WWII thriller about a Nazi plot to sneak paratroopers into England and kidnap Churchill. The top-notch cast includes Michael Caine, Donald Sutherland, Robert Duvall, Donald Pleasence. 134 min.
04-1055 **$12.99**

The Only Way (1971)
Harrowing true drama of the struggles of Danish Jews to escape Nazi persecution following their country's invasion during World War II. Jane Seymour, Martin Potter star. 86 min.
08-1173 Was $29.99 **$19.99**

Fireball Forward (1972)
During World War II, American soldier Ben Gazzara is given a group of hard-luck GIs and tries to turn them into a troop of tough fighting men. Eddie Albert, Dana Elcar and Ricardo Montalban also star. 100 min.
81-1097 **$14.99**

The Last Valley (1970)
Famed author James Clavell scripted and directed this historical adventure set in 17th-century central Europe, when the continent was embroiled in the Thirty Years' War. Wanderer Omar Sharif, a former teacher who lost his family in the conflict, seeks refuge in a village hidden in a remote valley. The peace is soon shattered, though, by the arrival of army captain Michael Caine and his men. With Nigel Davenport, Per Oscarsson. 125 min.
04-1346 **$14.99**

The Last Valley (Letterboxed Collector's Edition)
Also available in a theatrical, widescreen format.
08-8709 **$14.99**

Zeppelin (1971)
Action-packed World War I thriller starring Michael York as a young man who is contracted by Britain to uncover confidential German plans involving a new zeppelin. He gets more than he bargains for when he goes on a test flight aboard the ship and discovers that the Germans plan to steal the Magna Carta. Elke Sommer and Anton Diffring also star. 101 min.
19-1841 Was $19.99 **□$14.99**

Hell In The Pacific (1968)
Gripping WWII drama stars Lee Marvin and Toshiro Mifune as American and Japanese soldiers who find themselves stranded on a small Pacific island. Their hatred turns to a grudging respect, but the reality of war brings them back to conflict. John Boorman directs. 103 min.
04-1385 **$14.99**

Hell In The Pacific (Letterboxed Collector's Edition)
Also available in a theatrical, widescreen format.
08-8707 **$14.99**

Constantine And The Cross (1962)
Lavish historical saga stars Cornel Wilde as Constantine, who uses his military expertise to eventually become Emperor of Rome, and who was led by a vision to convert to Christianity and end the Roman persecution of the Church. With Christine Kaufmann, Belinda Lee. 120 min.
08-1561 Letterboxed **$14.99**

The Blue Max (1966)
George Peppard, Ursula Andress, James Mason star in the story of a German combat pilot in World War I and his quest for that most-coveted medal. With spectacular aerial combat sequences. 155 min.
04-1014 **$19.99**

Sinai Commandos (1968)
Set in the Sinai desert during the Six-Day War, this action-packed thriller deals with a suicide squad whose mission is vital to the survival of Israel. 99 min.
10-1025 Was $19.99 **$14.99**

The Private Life Of Henry VIII (1933)
Charles Laughton won an Oscar for his flamboyant portrayal of England's most-married monarch. Laughton's real-life spouse, Elsa Lanchester, is royal wife Anne of Cleves, and the supporting cast includes Merle Oberon, Robert Donat and Binnie Barnes. Classic costume drama directed by Alexander Korda. 98 min.
10-4027 Was $19.99 **$14.99**

A Man For All Seasons (1966)
Splendid film account of the conflict between England's King Henry VIII and Sir Thomas More over the monarch's divorcing of his first wife and break with the Catholic Church. Paul Scofield, Robert Shaw, Wendy Hiller and Orson Welles head an impressive cast; Fred Zinnemann directs. Winner of six Oscars, including Best Picture. 134 min.
02-1046 **$19.99**

Anne Of The Thousand Days (1969)
The ill-fated romance of King Henry VIII of England and his second wife, Anne Boleyn, is recounted in this lavish drama. Richard Burton, Genevieve Bujold, Irene Papas and Anthony Quayle star. 145 min.
07-1280 Was $19.99 **$14.99**

Thirty-Six Hours Of Hell (1977)
Blazing jungle warfare action set in the South Pacific, as American and Japanese forces vow to fight to the last man in a savage, bloody campaign. Thrill-packed drama stars Richard Harrison, Pamela Tudor. 95 min.
48-1109 **$19.99**

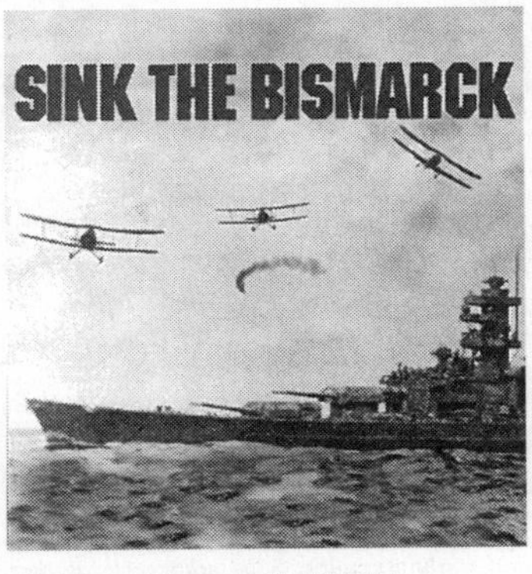

Sink The Bismarck! (1960)
One of the finest war dramas ever made, showing the true story of how the British Navy planned and executed the destruction of the mighty German WWII battleship. Superb cast includes Kenneth More, Carl Mohner, Dana Wynter, Michael Hordern. 97 min.
04-2334 **$19.99**

Ski Troop Attack (1960)
Produced and directed by Roger Corman, this effective wartime thriller makes good use of amazing action sequences depicting a ragtag band of soldiers who are assigned the impossible task of infiltrating Nazi territory to destroy a vital railway bridge. Stars Michael Forest and Richard Sinatra. 63 min.
10-7054 Was $19.99 **$14.99**

Desert Commando (1967)
Roosevelt, Churchill and Stalin are the targets of an assassination commando unit, and the only one who knows of the mission is Capt. Fritz Shuller, a Nazi officer. But will his conflicting morality get in the way of the mission? Ken Clark, Horst Frank and Gianni Rizzo star. 101 min.
10-9168 **$19.99**

Battle Of Blood Island (1960)
Two American soldiers, a Christian and a Jew trapped on a Pacific isle, must make peace between themselves before they can meet the challenge of the Japanese, who plan to bomb their outpost. With Richard Devon and Ron Kennedy. 64 min.
10-7562 Was $19.99 **$14.99**

Attack And Retreat (1965)
World War II saga with an international cast about a squadron of Italian soldiers who band together with Russian prisoners once treated harshly by the Nazis to defeat their German enemies. Arthur Kennedy and Peter Falk are featured. AKA: "Italiano Brava Gente." 140 min.
10-9122 **$19.99**

The Ravagers (1965)
John Saxon stars in this tough war saga set in the Philippines during World War II. When the Japanese come to an island to retrieve a shipment of gold, they are met by Filipino rebels. A Filipino leader breaks into a convent the Japanese have taken and falls for a beautiful American woman protected by nuns. Bronwyn Fitzsimmons also stars. 88 min.
10-9721 **$19.99**

The Nun And The Sergeant (1962)
In the tradition of "The Dirty Dozen" comes this war adventure in which Robert Webber (a "Dozen" co-star) leads a group of criminal soldiers behind enemy lines during the Korean War for an important mission. When Webber and company reach their targeted area, they encounter an American nun with an injured leg and a group of schoolgirls. Anna Sten, Hari Rhodes also star. 73 min.
09-5079 **$19.99**

Hawaii (1966)
Lush and atmospheric epic based on the James A. Michener novel chronicling the efforts of missionaries to bring "civilization" to the islanders in the 1820s. Stellar cast includes Julie Andrews, Max Von Sydow, Richard Harris, Gene Hackman, Jocelyn Lagarde, Carroll O'Connor. Newly restored version; 188 min.
12-2049 Was $29.99 **□$24.99**

Hawaii (Letterboxed Version)
Also available in a theatrical, widescreen format.
12-3079 **□$24.99**

633 Squadron (1964)
Cliff Robertson is a World War II air ace leading a group of British flyers into Norway to bomb a Nazi munitions factory. He's helped by a Norwegian resistance fighter whose sister he eventually falls in love with. George Chakiris, Maria Perschy and Harry Andrews co-star; filled with spectacular aerial footage. 94 min.
12-2313 **$19.99**

The Charge Of The Light Brigade (1968)
Large-scale battle sequences, a great cast and a surprisingly satirical script highlight Tony Richardson's epic chronicle of the events leading to the fateful battle between English and Russian forces in the Crimean War. Trevor Howard, John Gielgud, Harry Andrews, David Hemmings and Vanessa Redgrave star in this saga inspired by Tennyson's poem. 130 min.
12-2853 **$19.99**

Imperial Venus (1962)
Lush (and racy) French-Italian historical drama stars Gina Lollobrigida as Paolina Bonaparte, sister of Napoleon and a rebellious noblewoman known as "The Princess of Sin." With Stephen Boyd, Raymond Pellegrin. 120 min.
08-1290 **$14.99**

Operation Crossbow (1965)
Lavish World War II epic concerning a British mission to stop Nazis from firing deadly rockets targeted at England. Richard Johnson, George Peppard, Trevor Howard, Sophia Loren, Tom Courtenay and Jeremy Kemp lead the impressive cast in this action-packed effort. 116 min.
12-2507 **$19.99**

Caesar The Conquerer (1961)
Italian spectacle starring American Cameron Mitchell as the great Roman emperor and conquerer who finds opposition from his senate when he seeks more forces for his Gallic campaign. When his ward and her lover are captured by the Gauls, Caesar springs into action in a battle against Vercingetorix, their leader. 103 min.
68-8942 **$19.99**

Then There Were Three (1961)
Six GIs in Europe loose track of fellow members of their troop and allow a stranger to join them as they search for the lost soldiers. Little do they realize that the stranger is actually a Nazi spy with orders to kill an underground leader. Frank Latimore, Alex Nichol and Sidney Clute star. 74 min.
09-5081 **$19.99**

Is Paris Burning? (1966)
The Allied landing at Normandy, and the desperate battle to reach Paris before it can be destroyed by the Germans, is vividly depicted in this all-star WWII drama. The international cast includes Jean-Paul Belmondo, Charles Boyer, Leslie Caron, Kirk Douglas, Gert Frobe, Yves Montand, Anthony Perkins and Orson Welles; written by Gore Vidal and Francis Ford Coppola. 173 min.
06-1834 Was $29.99 **□$24.99**

Guerrillas In Pink Lace (1964)
George Montgomery's unique war drama focuses on a group of showgirls stranded in the Philippines in 1941 at the height of the Japanese invasion. The women show off their military prowess after Montgomery helps train them to become top-notch fighters. With Joan Shawlee, Valerie Varda. 96 min.
08-1695 **$14.99**

The White Warrior (1961)
Unusual casting finds strongman Steve Reeves in a story by Leo Tolstoy as Hadji Murad, who leads his mountain warriors against the army of Russian ruler Nicholas I while battling a rival for his girlfriend's hand. Georgia Moll, Renato Baldini also star; photography by Mario Bava. 86 min.
09-5043 Was $19.99 **$14.99**

King Rat (1965)
George Segal plays a POW in a Japanese camp who uses his wits to outsmart the enemy—and fellow prisoners. Tom Courtenay, James Fox. 133 min.
02-1172 **$19.99**

Lost Command (1966)
Anthony Quinn is a glory-seeking soldier, fighting France's doomed cause in colonial Indochina and Algeria, whose climb through the ranks is stalled when an Arab terrorist infiltrates his command. Fine international cast features George Segal, Alain Delon and Claudia Cardinale. 129 min.
02-1882 **$69.99**

PT 109 (1964)
The inspiring story of World War II Navy Lieutenant John F. Kennedy and his fight to keep his crew alive when their boat is sunk in the South Pacific stars Cliff Robertson as the young Kennedy. With Ty Hardin, Robert Culp, Robert Blake. 140 min.
19-1247 **□$19.99**

PT 109 (Letterboxed Version)
Also available in a theatrical, widescreen format.
19-2540 **□$19.99**

The Missiles Of October (1974)
Compelling dramatization of the 1962 Cuban Missile Crisis that had the United States and Russia on the brink of World War III. William stars as President John F. Kennedy, Martin Sheen is Bobby Kennedy, and Howard DaSilva is Soviet leader Nikita Khrushchev. 150 min.
50-6171 Was $39.99 **$19.99**

Robert Kennedy And His Times (1985)
Acclaimed biodrama of Senator Robert F. Kennedy traces his political career and private life from 1946, when he campaigned for older brother John's congessional race, to his run for the presidency and assassination in a Los Angeles hotel in 1968. Brad Davis, Veronica Cartwright, Cliff De Young, Ned Beatty, Beatrice Straight and Jack Warden star. 309 min.
02-2137 Was $59.99 **$24.99**

Ruby (1992)
"The man who shot the man who shot JFK" is superbly portrayed by Danny Aiello in this compelling speculative drama, as Dallas nightclub owner Jack Ruby's Mafia connections draw him deeper and deeper into a Mob-sponsored plot to assassinate the President. Sherilyn Fenn, Arliss Howard co-star. 110 min.
02-2232 Was $19.99 **$14.99**

Marilyn & Bobby: Her Final Affair (1995)
The long-rumored affair between Marilyn Monroe and Robert F. Kennedy is the basis for this powerful speculative drama that addresses the possible ties between the romance and Monroe's death in 1962. Melody Anderson, James Kelly and Jonathan Banks star. 95 min.
19-3829 **$89.99**

The Kennedys Of Massachusetts (1995)
A compelling examination of the stormy life of "America's Royal Family," from Joseph Kennedy's marriage to Rose Fitzgerald to JFK's election as President of the United States. William Petersen, Annette O'Toole, Charles Durning, Steven Weber, Tracy Pollan and Campbell Scott head the cast of this acclaimed three-part saga. 278 min.
73-1230 **$29.99**

A Place In Hell (1965)
An isolated island in the Philippines becomes a battleground for Marines and Japanese soldiers in this tense WWII drama. Guy Madison, Monty Greenwood, Helen Chanel star. 106 min.
48-1078 **$49.99**

Attack! (1956)
Compelling WWII drama from director Robert Aldrich ("The Dirty Dozen") set in Belgium in 1944, where cowardly American captain Eddie Albert has placed one of his small platoons in danger, sending them into a combat zone without protection. Led by lieutenant Jack Palance, the soldiers must fight their way back from the front. Lee Marvin, Richard Jaeckel and Buddy Ebsen also star.
12-3084 **$19.99**

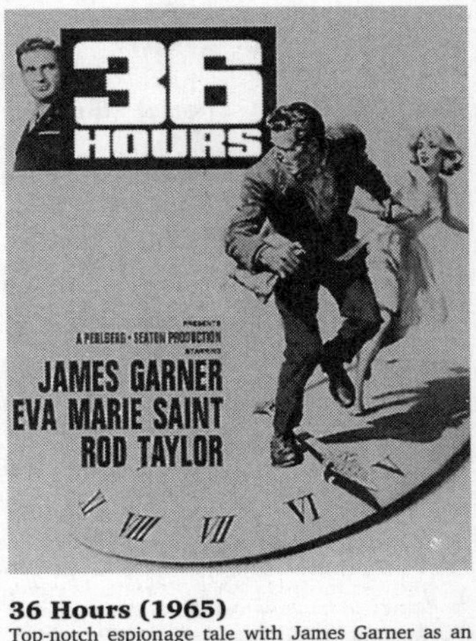

36 Hours (1965)
Top-notch espionage tale with James Garner as an American agent carrying confidential war plans who is abducted by Nazis shortly before the D-Day invasion. After being drugged, Garner is convinced the war has ended and urged to reveal secrets of the Allied invasion by psychiatrist Rod Taylor. With Eva Marie Saint and Alan Napier. 115 min.
12-2805 **□$19.99**

Triple Cross (1967)
A British safecracker doing time in the Channel Islands at the outbreak of World War II offers to spy for the Germans in exchange for cash, then cuts the same deal with British Intelligence during his first mission back home. Christopher Plummer, Yul Brynner and Romy Schneider star in this thriller. 126 min.
19-2222 Was $29.99 ***$19.99***

Once Before I Die (1964)
Exciting WWII action, as a band of American soldiers and one woman trapped behind enemy lines in the Philippines must fight to stay alive. Directed by John Derek, who also stars with then-wife Ursula Andress; with Ron Ely, Richard Jaeckel. 97 min.
19-2446 ***$19.99***

Five For Hell (1967)
Summer, 1944: five misfit soldiers of fortune are sent on a suicide mission into Nazi-held Europe. No one expected them to come out alive, but then no one asked them. Exciting WWII thriller stars Klaus Kinski. 88 min.
20-5086 ***$19.99***

The Steel Claw (1961)
George Montgomery wrote, directed and stars in this WWII story of a one-handed officer who, while waiting for his retirement from the military, stages one last strike, leading Filipino forces against Japanese troops. With Charita Luna. 96 min.
27-6410 ***$14.99***

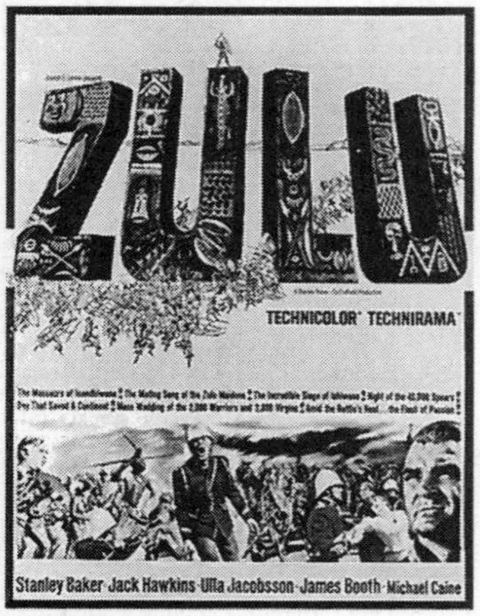

Zulu (1964)
A British outpost in 1879 Colonial Africa becomes the last stand for an Army unit in this classic adventure epic. Stories of the people involved are contrasted against breathtaking battle scenes. Stars Michael Caine, Stanley Baker, James Booth. 138 min.
53-3002 Was $19.99 ***$14.99***

Zulu (Letterboxed Version)
Also available in a theatrical, widescreen format.
65-3006 ***$19.99***

The Dirty Dozen: Special Edition (1967)
Lee Marvin, Ernest Borgnine, Charles Bronson, Jim Brown, John Cassavetes, Telly Savalas and Donald Sutherland head the cast of this highly entertaining WWII saga about 12 convict GIs who receive a chance to redeem themselves by taking on a dangerous mission deep inside German lines. Robert Aldrich directs. Special video version includes an introduction by Borgnine, the "making of" documentary "Operation Dirty Dozen" and the original theatrical trailer. 166 min. total.
19-2957 □***$19.99***

The Dirty Dozen: Special Edition (Letterboxed Version)
Also available in a theatrical, widescreen format.
19-2958 □***$19.99***

The Dirty Dozen: The Next Mission (1985)
Lee Marvin and Ernest Borgnine reprise their roles from the original film, as a new dozen is recruited from Army prisons for a suicide mission behind enemy lines. Ken Wahl, Richard Jaeckel, Larry Wilcox co-star. 97 min.
12-1860 ***$19.99***

Cavalry Command (1965)
Exciting war story set in the Philippine jungle. The U.S. Army sends a Cavalry unit to fight rebels, but the soldiers must also fight for the respect of the local villagers. John Agar, Richard Arlen star. 82 min.
15-5167 ***$59.99***

The Battle Of El Alamein (1968)
The world's mightiest tank armadas are hot on each other's tracks. It's the U.S. Army vs. Rommel in a battle for desert supremacy. George Hilton, Michael Rennie. 92 min.
16-1057 ***$14.99***

The Commandos (1968)
The Italian commandos, led by some stalwart Americans, must secure an important North African oasis before the Allies land. Lee Van Cleef, Jack Kelly. 100 min.
16-1062 ***$14.99***

From Hell To Borneo (1964)
George Montgomery stars as a hard-bitten soldier of fortune ready to defend his private island with hard fists and hot lead against gangsters and plunderers. 90 min.
27-6474 Was $19.99 ***$14.99***

Simon Bolivar (1969)
Historical action drama stars Maximilian Schell and Rosanna Schiaffino in the story of the 19th-century South American military leader who gained independence for five countries and is recognized as the "George Washington of Latin America." 120 min.
48-1067 ***$49.99***

Royal Hunt Of The Sun (1969)
Historical epic featuring Robert Shaw as Spanish explorer Francisco Pizarro, who befriends Incan leader Atahullpa (Christopher Plummer) in order to gain control of the natives' fabled treasure. Nigel Davenport, Michael Craig and James Donald also star in this stirring adaptation of Peter Shaffer's play. 88 min.
50-5978 ***$12.99***

Culloden (1964)
Originally produced for British TV, director Peter Watkins' "You Are There"-style docudrama chronicles the 1746 battle between the English army and the Highland Jacobite forces of Scotland's Charles Edward Stuart that ended "Bonnie Prince Charlie's" attempt to take the throne of England. 60 min.
53-7362 ***$29.99***

Chasing The Deer (1994)
Stirring epic set in Scotland during the 1700s and detailing events that led to the Battle of Culloden. After hearing that Euan, his son, has been taken prisoner by the Jacobites, father Cameron joins their ranks in hopes of ensuring his son's safety. But when Euan is taken in by opposing Hanoverian troops, father and son eventually square off in battle. Brian Blessed, Iain Cuthbertson star. 92 min.
80-7268 ***$29.99***

The Battle Of The Last Panzer (1968)
Rugged battle sequences highlight this WWII adventure, as an Allied tank crew finds itself cut off behind enemy lines and bracing for final combat. Guy Madison, Stan Cooper star. AKA: "Comando al Infierno," "Hell Commandos." 90 min.
20-1051 Was $59.99 ***$14.99***

Commando Attack (1967)
Wartime thriller about a band of misfits sent behind enemy lines to destroy a secret German transmitter and pave the way for the Allied invasion. Michael Rennie stars. 90 min.
48-1096 ***$19.99***

Dirty Heroes (1969)
Thrilling wartime story set in 1945 Holland, where a hidden fortune is the prize fought over by Nazi forces and escaped Allied prisoners. John Ireland, Adolfo Celi, Curt Jurgens star. 117 min.
55-1029 ***$19.99***

The Fall Of The Roman Empire (1964)
Epic drama set against the grandeur and decadence of ancient Rome. Stephen Boyd is the rightful heir to the imperial throne who must battle demented usurper Christopher Plummer in order to save Sophia Loren from death. The stellar cast also features James Mason, Omar Sharif, Alec Guinness. 153 min.
64-1189 ***$29.99***

Sunrise At Campobello (1960)
Ralph Bellamy and Greer Garson are Franklin and Eleanor Roosevelt in this acclaimed drama of the famed leader's lifelong struggle with polio and his attempts to re-enter politics in the '20s after a crippling attack. Hume Cronyn and Jean Hagen also star. 143 min.
19-1404 ***$19.99***

Eleanor And Franklin (1976)
The lives of Franklin D. Roosevelt and wife Eleanor, from FDR's boyhood and their courtship to his struggle with polio and election to the Presidency in 1932, were traced in this Emmy Award-winning two-part biodrama. Jane Alexander and Edward Herrmann star in the title roles, with support from Rosemary Murphy, David Huffman, Ed Flanders and Pamela Franklin. 205 min.
44-1924 Was $24.99 □***$19.99***

Eleanor: First Lady Of The World (1982)
Jean Stapleton plays the incredible Eleanor Roosevelt in this fascinating biodrama that chronicles her life after FDR's death and her work as U.S. delegate to the new United Nations. Joyce Van Patten, E.G. Marshall and Joyce Van Patten co-star. 96 min.
02-2298 Was $59.99 ***$19.99***

World War II: When Lions Roared (1994)
They were three world leaders united against a common enemy, but their own differences and forceful personalities threatened their fragile alliance. John Lithgow stars as Franklin D. Roosevelt, Bob Hoskins is Winston Churchill, and Michael Caine is Joseph Stalin in this compelling biodrama about a trio of men whose decisions still affect the course of world events. With Ed Begley, Jr., Jan Triska. 186 min.
50-7175 ***$39.99***

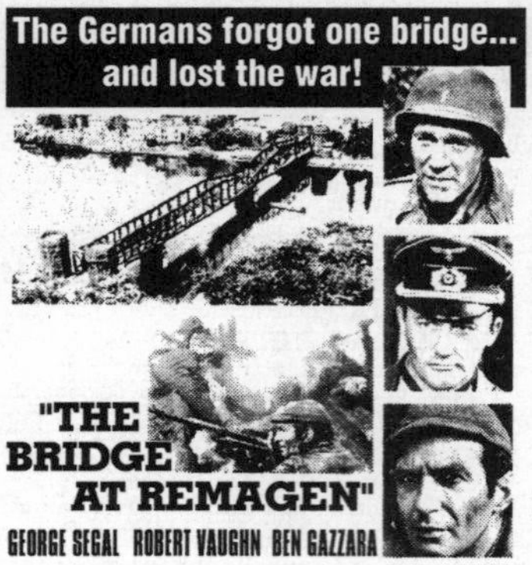

The Bridge At Remagen (1969)
Highly-charged WWII picture about the last bridge standing over the Rhine and the efforts of American and German troops to control it. George Segal, E.G. Marshall, Bradford Dillman and Ben Gazzara are the Americans; Robert Vaughn leads the Nazis. 116 min.
12-2315 ***$19.99***

The Man Who Never Was (1956)
Amazing true-life WWII thriller stars Clifton Webb as a British intelligence officer who conceives an elaborate hoax to dupe the Nazis, planting plans for a false Allied invasion of Greece on a British corpse recovered by the enemy. Stephen Boyd is the German spy trying to verify the dead man's fabricated identity. With Robert Flemyng, Gloria Grahame. 103 min.
04-2436 ***$19.99***

Drums In The Deep South (1951)
The Civil War is the battleground for emotions and loyalties when a group of West Point comrades find themselves fighting on opposite sides. Guy Madison, Barbara Payton, Craig Stevens star; directed by William Cameron Menzies. 87 min.
08-8030 Was $19.99 ***$14.99***

The Silent Enemy (1959)
Rousing true-life actioner recalls the exploits of a decorated British frogman who slipped away from his outfit and almost single-handedly destroyed an Italian base. Laurence Harvey and Michael Craig star. 92 min.
08-8112 ***$19.99***

Appointment In London (1953)
One mission away from completing his goal of 90 bombing runs, WWII British pilot Dirk Bogarde is grounded and assigned to desk duty, but plots to get back in the air one last time. Compelling war drama also stars Ian Hunter, Bryan Forbes, Dinah Sheridan. 96 min.
09-5327 ***$19.99***

A Hill In Korea (1956)
Atmospheric war story about a British Army patrol sent to a Korean village populated by enemy soldiers. Making their way to the town at night, the patrol encounters danger as they attempt to carry out their mission. With George Baker, Stephen Boyd, Harry Andrews, Robert Shaw and Michael Caine (in his film debut).
10-9257 ***$14.99***

Halls Of Montezuma (1951)
Top-notch Marine Corps WWII drama, centering on a squadron's dangerous mission to capture a Japanese-held post and learn the location of an enemy rocket site. Richard Widmark, Jack Palance, Robert Wagner, Richard Boone, Jack Webb and Karl Malden star, under the direction of Lewis Milestone. 113 min.
04-1291 ***$14.99***

D-Day, The Sixth Of June (1956)
The mammoth campaign of the Allied invasion is contrasted with the fears and desires of the men involved in this sprawling war saga. Robert Taylor, Richard Todd, Edmond O'Brien star. 106 min.
04-1847 Was $19.99 ***$14.99***

Omar Khayyam (1957)
An impressive production on the life of the medieval Persian poet with Cornel Wilde in the title role, fighting to save the Shah from court treachery while falling for a royal fiancée. Debra Paget, Raymond Massey and Michael Rennie co-star in this thrilling biopic by director William Dieterle. 100 min.
06-1978 □***$12.99***

Angels One Five (1954)
The inner workings of British air power during World War II are the focus of this effort starring Jack Hawkins, Michael Denison and Dulce Grey. Witness the courage of the fliers and the ingenuity of the people of the control room as they battle Axis forces in the air. 97 min.
10-9474 ***$19.99***

Quo Vadis (1951)
Ancient Rome is the setting for this grand spectacle, centering on an Imperial soldier's love for a Christian woman and his struggle to save her from the wrath of Nero. Robert Taylor, Deborah Kerr and Peter Ustinov star in a dramatic epic of faith and courage, and the birth of the Christian Church. 171 min.
12-1561 Was $29.99 □***$19.99***

Up Periscope (1959)
Edmond O'Brien plays the tough, by-the-book captain of a submarine whose problems with a young demolitions expert (James Garner) may get in the way of a dangerous mission involving the recovery of a secret Japanese code. Thrilling, intelligent WWII story co-stars Andra Martin, Alan Hale, Jr. and Warren Oates. 111 min.
19-1955 ***$14.99***

Land Of The Pharaohs (1955)
Spectacular Egyptian epic by director Howard Hawks and co-author William Faulkner about an aging king who must deal with palace intrigue, multiple wives and rebellious slaves while overseeing the construction of his final resting place—the Great Pyramid. Jack Hawkins is the Pharaoh, and Joan Collins is a scheming princess. With Alexis Minotis, James Robertson Justice. 103 min.
19-1950 Was $29.99 ***$19.99***

Lafayette Escadrille (1958)
Spectacular aerial sequences highlight this high-flying epic involving the young American volunteers of the famous French air group during World War I. Tab Hunter, Etichika Choureau, Jody McCrea star, with early appearances by Clint Eastwood and David Janssen. Director William Wellman's story was based in part on his own WWI exploits. 93 min.
19-2076 Was $19.99 ***$14.99***

John Paul Jones (1959)
Robert Stack plays the famous American naval hero in this exciting historical epic which follows Jones' struggles commanding a small fleet of ships during the Revolutionary War, his adventures helping Russia after the war, and his final years living in France. Marisa Pavan, Charles Coburn and Macdonald Carey also star; Bette Davis has a cameo appearance as Catherine the Great; look for a young Mia Farrow as an extra. 126 min.
19-2174 Was $29.99 ***$19.99***

Breakthrough (1950)
This ultra-realistic World War II saga examines the effects of war on a diverse group of infantrymen marching through Normandy, among them a rugged captain, a naive lieutenant and a soldier with political ambitions. John Agar, David Brian, Bill Campbell and Frank Lovejoy star. 91 min.
19-2223 Was $19.99 ***$14.99***

Darby's Rangers (1959)
This thrilling war saga traces the efforts of Major William Darby (James Garner), who organized American troops during World War II and led them in campaigns against the Nazis in Europe and Africa. Jack Warden, Edward Byrnes and Etchika Choureau also star. 121 min.
19-2075 Was $19.99 ***$14.99***

The Tanks Are Coming (1951)
Exciting World War II story centering on the Third Armored Division's efforts against the Germans in 1944. After the master sergeant of the batallion is killed, a no-nonsense soldier takes command, leading the troops into combat. Steve Cochran, Philip Carey and Mari Aldon star; based on a story by Samuel Fuller. 90 min.
19-2344 Was $19.99 ***$14.99***

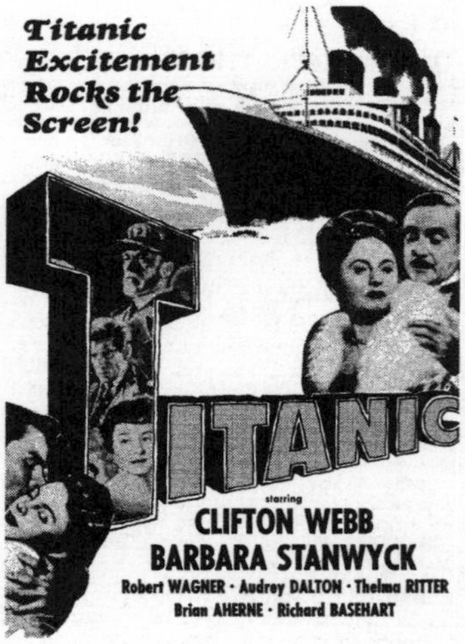

Titanic (1953)
The fateful maiden voyage of the luxury liner Titanic is stirringly re-created in this Oscar-winning saga that follows the personal dramas of several passengers and the ship's deadly encounter with an iceberg in the North Atlantic. Clifton Webb, Barbara Stanwyck, Robert Wagner, Audrey Dalton, Thelma Ritter and Richard Basehart star. 98 min.
04-2286 Was $19.99 □***$14.99***

Titanic (1996)
Its 2,000 passengers came from all walks of society, from millionaires to petty thieves, and this lavish depicting of the luxury liner's ill-fated voyage recounts the personal dramas as well as the horrific collision with an iceberg that sank her. George C. Scott, Peter Gallagher, Eva Marie Saint, Marilu Henner and Tim Curry star. 165 min.
88-1136 Was $99.99 □***$14.99***

Of Human Bondage (1949)
A young Charlton Heston makes an early appearance as a crippled medical student hopelessly infatuated with a cruel Cockney waitress in this retelling of the Somerset Maugham classic. Felicia Montealegre, Guy Sorel co-star in this "Westinghouse Studio One" presentation. 60 min.
09-1943 Was $24.99 *$14.99*

Wuthering Heights (1950)
"Westinghouse Studeo One" production of Emily Bronte's immortal love story stars a pre-Hollywood Charlton Heston as the ever-moody Heathcliff and Mary Sinclair as Catherine. 51 min.
09-1880 Was $24.99 *$14.99*

The Willow Cabin (1950)
Terrific romantic tale, from "Westinghouse Studio One," starring Charlton Heston as a talented surgeon whose involvement with an unpredictable British actress is harmed by war and memories of his former wife. 59 min.
09-2304 *$14.99*

A Bolt Of Lightning (1951)
Exciting Revolutionary War story featuring Charlton Heston as Boston attorney and patriot James Otis, who battled the British troops' right to search colonists' homes. Romney Brent and Anne Seymour co-star in this "Westinghouse Studio One" production. 60 min.
09-2225 Was $24.99 *$14.99*

The Greatest Show On Earth (1952)
Ladies and gentlemen...Welcome to Cecil B. DeMille's Oscar-winning look at life under the big top. See lion-tamers and acrobats! Be amazed at death-defying stunts and incredible train wrecks! Witness superb acting by Charlton Heston, James Stewart, Cornel Wilde, Betty Hutton and Dorothy Lamour! 149 min.
06-1109 Was $29.99 *$24.99*

Ruby Gentry (1952)
Steamy Southern melodrama with Jennifer Jones as a woman from the wrong side of the tracks who weds a wealthy landowner for spite when lover Charlton Heston takes another as his wife. With Karl Malden; King Vidor directs. 82 min.
04-1625 Was $59.99 *$14.99*

The Naked Jungle (1953)
Classic adventure drama stars Charlton Heston as a Brazilian plantation owner whose domain is under siege by a 20-mile-long army of killer ants, an unstoppable swarm that devastates anything in its path. Awesome special effects supervised by producer George Pal; with Eleanor Parker, Abraham Sofaer. 95 min.
06-1519 *$19.99*

Arrowhead (1953)
Militant cavalry scout Charlton Heston and renegade Apache Jack Palance are deadly enemies locked on a fatal collision course when tribal warfare threatens settlers in an exciting Western drama. With Brian Keith, Milburn Stone and Katy Jurado. 105 min.
06-1671 *$14.99*

The Private War Of Major Benson (1955)
Hard-nosed Army officer Charlton Heston, after rousing the ire of his superiors, is placed in charge of an ROTC unit of schoolboys at a military academy run by nuns and winning comedy. With Julie Adams as the school nurse, and Tim Considine, Steve Hovey and Sal Mineo as some of Heston's "men." 104 min.
07-2511 *$14.99*

Three Violent People (1956)
Powerful mix of frontier action and character study with Charlton Heston as an ex-Confederate officer who returns to the family ranch with new bride Anne Baxter and faces problems from carpetbaggers and his jealous brother, and a secret from Baxter's past. With Tom Tryon, Gilbert Roland, Forrest Tucker. 100 min.
06-2077 *$14.99*

The Buccaneer (1958)
Swashbuckling action galore set during the War of 1812, as General Andrew Jackson (Charlton Heston) enlists the aid of pirate Jean Lafitte (Yul Brynner) in stopping the British navy. With Claire Bloom, Charles Boyer, Inger Stevens. Anthony Quinn directed this remake of the C.B. DeMille (who served as producer) classic. 121 min.
06-1844 *$14.99*

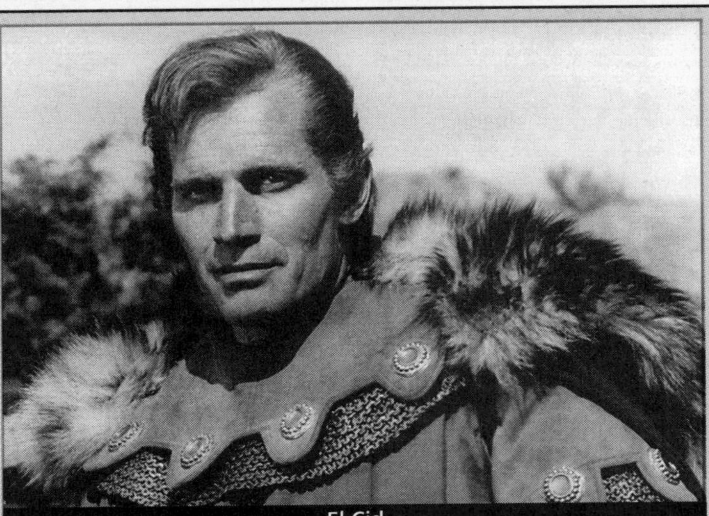
El Cid

Charlton Heston

Ben-Hur (1959)
Eleven Oscars, including Best Picture, went to this classic version of the Lew Wallace story of Palestine at the time of Christ. Charlton Heston and Stephen Boyd are friends torn asunder by their beliefs and driven by vengeance that culminates in the breathtaking chariot race scene. With Hugh Griffith, Martha Scott; William Wyler directs. 211 min.
12-1002 Was $29.99 *$24.99*

Ben-Hur (Letterboxed Version)
Also available in a theatrical, widescreen format.
12-3037 Was $29.99 *$24.99*

El Cid (1961)
Charlton Heston essays the title role as the famed warrior who led his men in driving the Moors out of medieval Spain. Lavish in detail and mammoth in scope, director Anthony Mann's epic tale also stars Sophia Loren, Herbert Lom, Raf Vallone. Restored version includes extra footage not previously available; 182 min.
64-1188 Restored *$29.99*

Diamond Head (1962)
Lush drama about the personal crises of a plantation family in Hawaii stars Charlton Heston as the dictatorial head and Yvette Mimieux as his strong-willed sister. With George Chakiris, James Darren. 107 min.
02-1740 Was $69.99 *$19.99*

55 Days At Peking (1963)
Charlton Heston, Ava Gardner and David Niven are American and British citizens caught between forces in the bloody Boxer Rebellion of 1900 China. Suspense and action on an epic scale. Nicholas Ray directs. 154 min.
64-1190 *$29.99*

Major Dundee (1965)
Sprawling Western epic from director Sam Peckinpah featuring Charlton Heston as a rough-hewn Union officer heading across the Mexican border with a troop of outcasts in search of a tribe of Apache Indians responsible for raiding an Army outpost. Richard Harris, Jim Hutton, James Coburn, Senta Berger and Warren Oates co-star. 124 min.
02-2700 *$14.99*

The Agony And The Ecstacy (1965)
The battle of wills between Michelangelo and Pope Julius II over the artist's painting of the Sistine Chapel ceiling is a sumptuous historical drama with great performances from stars Charlton Heston and Rex Harrison and spectacular re-creations of the chapel. Carol Reed directs. 138 min.
04-1001 Was $19.99 *$14.99*

Will Penny (1968)
Fine latter-day Western drama stars Charlton Heston as an itinerant ranch hand who works for farm wife Joan Hackett while fighting deranged preacher Donald Pleasence and his murderous offspring. Lee Majors, Anthony Zerbe, Bruce Dern, Ben Johnson also star. 109 min.
06-1668 *$14.99*

The Omega Man (1971)
Charlton Heston stars in this adaptation of Richard Matheson's "I Am Legend" as the only human survivor of the Last War. By day, he's alone, but at night, he must contend with a crazed army of vampire-like mutants, out to destroy any hints of civilization...including Heston! Fast-paced futuristic thriller co-stars Rosalind Cash and Anthony Zerbe. 98 min.
19-1494 *$14.99*

Skyjacked (1972)
Intense, high-flying drama with Charlton Heston as a pilot on a commercial flight hijacked to Moscow by mysterious passenger James Brolin. At the same time, the plane's crew must take care of a pregnant woman who goes into labor while Heston deals with his relationship with ex-girlfriend and stewardess Yvette Mimieux. With Claude Akins, Jeanne Crain and Susan Dey.
12-3086 *$19.99*

Call Of The Wild (1972)
Jack London's immortal classic about survival in the frozen North and the loyalty of a great dog comes to life in this excellent family film. Charlton Heston stars. 105 min.
50-6285 Was $19.99 *$14.99*

Soylent Green (1973)
In the year 2022, New York—and the world—is a mess, thanks to overpopulation, pollution and modern-day savagery. The government has a secret that will cure all of society's ills, and Charlton Heston is out to get it! Chuck Connors, Leigh Taylor-Young, Edward G. Robinson. 100 min.
12-1069 Was $19.99 *$14.99*

Midway (1976)
Spectacular World War II drama of the events leading to the courageous battle of the Pacific. Breathtaking war footage and superb special effects, with a stellar cast, including Charlton Heston, Henry Fonda, Glenn Ford and Robert Mitchum. 132 min.
07-1061 Was $19.99 *$14.99*

The Prince And The Pauper (1978)
Star-studded version of Mark Twain's classic details the adventures of identical youths who change places—from royalty to peasantry and vice versa—in Tudor England. Mark Lester, Raquel Welch, Oliver Reed, George C. Scott and Charlton Heston star. AKA: "Crossed Swords." 113 min.
03-1338 *$14.99*

The Prince And The Pauper (Letterboxed Version)
Also available in a theatrical, widescreen format.
08-8884 *$14.99*

The Mountain Men (1980)
A sweeping, funny, violent adventure dedicated to the first heroes of the American West—the trappers who braved the Rocky Mountains in the 1830s. Charlton Heston, Brian Keith, Victory Jory star. 102 min.
10-2612 *$14.99*

The Awakening (1980)
Charlton Heston stars as an archeologist who breaks into an Egyptian tomb and unleashes a vengeful spirit that takes over his daughter's body and demands his death. With Stephanie Zimbalist, Susannah York. 101 min.
19-1067 *$14.99*

A Man For All Seasons (1988)
For the sake of his faith and his duty, he defied his king and risked his life. The award-winning play by Robert Bolt about Sir Thomas More and his stand against the actions of England's King Henry VIII is brought to life with a cast that includes Sir John Gielgud, Vanessa Redgrave, and Charlton Heston as More. 168 min.
18-7108 *$79.99*

Treasure Island (1989)
A lavish, marvelously acted version of Robert Louis Stevenson's classic about buried treasure and pirates. Charlton Heston is wonderful as scheming scalawag Long John Silver; Oliver Reed, Christopher Lee and Christian Bale co-star. 131 min.
18-7216 Was $79.99 *$14.99*

A Thousand Heroes (1994)
The incredible real-life drama of United Airlines Flight 232, a jumbo jet that left Denver for Chicago on July 19, 1989. Somewhere over the skies of Iowa, the plane's engines exploded, and miraculously, 200 passengers escaped the ensuing crash. Charlton Heston, Richard Thomas and James Coburn star. 95 min.
21-9059 Was $89.99 *$14.99*

The Avenging Angel (1995)
In this exciting historical adventure, Tom Berenger plays Miles Utley, a Mormon called on in childhood to protect religious leader Brigham Young. When he gets older, Utley finds his allegiance to Young questioned after he becomes the focus of a conspiracy plot. Charlton Heston co-stars as Young; with James Coburn. 99 min.
18-7551 Was $89.99 *$14.99*

Alaska (1996)
When their pilot father's plane vanishes on a supply run in the rugged Alaskan wilderness and officials call off the search, two plucky teens and a polar bear cub they save from a villainous poacher brave the elements on their own perilous rescue mission. Thrilling family adventure stars Thora Birch, Vincent Kartheiser, Dirk Benedict and Charlton Heston; directed by Heston's son, Fraser. 109 min.
02-2989 Was $19.99 *$14.99*

Charlton Heston: For All Seasons
Examine the epic career of one of Hollywood's most beloved actors, whose films span half a century. Whether he is parting the Red Sea in "The Ten Commandments," winning a chariot race as "Ben-Hur," or speaking out on political issues, Charlton Heston is a talent and a force to be reckoned with. 50 min.
81-3004 Was $19.99 *$14.99*

Please see our index for these other Charlton Heston titles: *Almost An Angel • Any Given Sunday • Beneath The Planet Of The Apes • The Big Country • The Dark Mist • The Four Musketeers • The Greatest Story Ever Told • Hamlet • Hercules • In The Mouth Of Madness • Julius Caesar • Khartoum • Major Dundee • Planet Of The Apes • Solar Crisis • The Ten Commandments • The Three Musketeers • Tombstone • Touch Of Evil • True Lies • The Wreck Of The Mary Deare*

Men Of The Fighting Lady (1954)
Based on a series of articles written by James Michener, this exciting and powerful war film chronicles the heroics of a group of aircraft carrier pilots during the Korean War. Walter Pidgeon, Van Johnson, Louis Calhern and Keenan Wynn star, along with some impressive action sequences. 79 min.
12-2312 *$19.99*

Above And Beyond (1953)
Stirring account of the atomic boming of Hiroshima, focusing on Col. Paul Tibbets, the tough Air Force pilot who commanded the Enola Gay. Realistic aerial footage, a detailed depiction of the mission's preparation and a powerful take on the human side of the story propel the film. Robert Taylor, Eleanor Parker and James Whitmore star. 122 min.
12-2920 *$19.99*

The Moonraker (1957)
Colorful historical saga set in 1651 during the latter part of the English Civil War and detailing the efforts of Earl Anthony of Dawlish, a Royalist fighting Oliver Cromwell's Roundheads, who attempts to smuggle Prince Charles Stuart from England to France. George Baker, Sylvia Syms, Peter Arne star. 82 min.
53-6088 Was $29.99 *$19.99*

Flat Top (1952)
Set in 1944, this expert war saga stars Sterling Hayden as the tough commanding officer of the aircraft carrier, the USS Prnceton. His no-nonsense style comes into conflict with new air group commander Richard Carlson. Featuring actual combat footage, the film also features John Bromfield and William Phipps. 83 min.
63-1084 *$12.99*

The Egyptian (1954)
Hollywood's '50s penchant for Bible-based "sword and sandal" epics sometimes sent viewers further back in time, as in this tale of romance, intrigue and murder amidst the pyramids. Edmund Purdom, Jean Simmons, Peter Ustinov, Michael Wilding, Gene Tierney and Victor Mature star. 140 min.
04-2247 *$19.99*

5 Fingers (1952)
True-life, first-rate espionage account of L.C. Moyzisch, the spy known as "Cicero," a valet at the British Embassy in Turkey who sells secret files to Germany during World War II, only to discover that they may have double-crossed him for his efforts. James Mason, Danielle Darrieux and Michael Rennie star; Joseph L. Mankiewicz directs. 108 min.
04-2781 *$19.99*

Between Heaven And Hell (1956)
Expert war drama stars Robert Wagner as a prejudiced Southern landowner who learns the error of his ways while fighting in the Pacific during World War II. Supporting cast includes Terry Moore, Broderick Crawford, Buddy Ebsen, Harvey Lembeck, Frank Gorshin and Carl "Alfalfa" Switzer. 94 min.
04-2455 *$14.99*

Atrocities Of The Orient (1959)
Bizarre propagandistic entry concerning the Japanese over-running of the Philippines. Two Filipino soldiers wage a private rebellion against the Nipponese, here portrayed in the most mindlessly sadistic light imaginable. The film was cobbled together with parts of other films, including "Beast of the East," "Outrages of the Orient" and "Nightmare in Red China."
62-1259 *$19.99*

Go For Broke! (1951)
They were the 442nd Regiment...a squad of loyal Japanese-Americans who had to battle prejudice as well as the Axis enemy. Van Johnson stars as their contemptuous topkick, whose bigotry gives way to respect in the crucible of war. 90 min.
12-2311 $19.99

Torpedo Run (1958)
Powerful World War II drama studies submarine commander Glenn Ford's obsession with destroying a Japanese aircraft carrier, an obsession stemming from a tragedy that befell his wife and daughter years before. Ernest Borgnine and Diane Brewster co-star. 69 min.
12-2066 $19.99

Napoleon (1955)
Was he a national hero or a tyrant and madman? Orson Welles, Maria Schell, Yves Montand and Erich Von Stroheim star in this action-packed biographical drama that follows Napoleon from his early rise to power in revolutionary France to his last days at Elba. Daniel Gelin and Raymond Pellegrin portray the young and mature Napoleon; written and directed by Sacha Guitry. 121 min.
50-1266 $19.99

Eagle In A Cage (1971)
An inventive historical drama focusing on Napoleon's early days in exile on St. Helena. British envoy Lord Sissal approaches "the Little Corporal," offering to help him escape from prison if he agrees to help organize an attack on Prussia. John Gielgud, Ralph Richardson, Billie Whitelaw and Kenneth Haigh star. 97 min.
10-9511 $14.99

The Diary Of Anne Frank (1959)
The awesome inhumanity of the Holocaust is brought into agonizingly personal perspective in George Stevens' adaptation of young Frank's memoirs. Millie Perkins is the Jewish girl who, with her parents and another family, hides in the attic of an Amsterdam building to escape the Nazis. Joseph Schildkraut, Diane Baker, Lou Jacobi and Oscar-winner Shelley Winters also star. Original theatrical version; 171 min.
04-1044   Was $24.99   ❑$14.99

The Sea Shall Not Have Them (1954)
The superbly performed British drama takes place during WWII and focuses on a crew of seamen fighting for life on a raft while adrift at sea. Michael Redgrave, Dirk Bogarde. 91 min.
63-1087   Was $39.99 $14.99

The Dam Busters (1954)
Thrilling British WWII drama, based on a true story, follows a scientist who comes up with a way to destroy a series of German dams vital to the Nazi war effort and the RAF crew charged with carrying out the dangerous mission. Richard Todd, Michael Redgrave, Basil Sydney star; look quickly for Robert Shaw and Patrick McGoohan. 102 min.
44-1089 $14.99

Fighter Attack (1954)
A bombing raid over Italy in 1944 turns disastrous for Allied flyer Sterling Hayden when his plane is shot down and he must, with the help of a beautiful resistance fighter, reach safety. Thrilling WWII actioner also stars Joy Page, J. Carrol Naish. 80 min.
63-1326   Was $19.99 $14.99

Samuel Fuller

I Shot Jesse James (1949)
Maverick filmmaker Sam Fuller's directorial debut uses slam-bang stylistic touches and lots of close-ups in a unique approach to the Jesse James legend. The focus is on Bob Ford (John Ireland), who guns down the notorious outlaw for the reward money that will help him marry his childhood sweetheart. Barbara Britton, Reed Hadley also star. 81 min.
10-9851 $14.99

The Baron Of Arizona (1950)
A little-known piece of American history becomes a fascinating historical drama by Samuel Fuller. Vincent Price stars as James A. Reavis, who in the mid-1800s forged documents that turned the Arizona Territory over to a woman whom he later married, setting himself up as owner of the state. Ellen Drew, Reed Hadley. 97 min.
10-1363 $14.99

The Steel Helmet (1951)
Scripted and shot in just three weeks, Samuel Fuller's gritty Korean War drama is one of the finest genre entries ever made. Gene Evans is the wounded army sergeant who joins a beleaguered platoon holed up in a Buddhist temple. An unglamourized look at the realities of warfare, the film also stars James Edwards as a black medic and Harold Fong as a captured North Korean officer. 84 min.
10-1367 $14.99

Pickup On South Street (1953)
Sam Fuller's classic crime thriller stars Richard Widmark as a New York pickpocket whose latest heist carried an unexpected bonus—microfilm stolen by Communist spies—that puts him on the run from government agents as well as the spy ring. Gritty melodrama also stars Richard Kiley, Jean Peters, Thelma Ritter. 80 min.
04-2408 $19.99

China Gate (1957)
One of the first war films to be set in Vietnam (Indochina back then), Samuel Fuller's tale of a French-led guerrilla mission against a Communist ammo dump stars Gene Barry, Lee Van Cleef, Angie Dickinson as an Asian woman and a rare dramatic turn by Nat King Cole. 95 min.
63-1325 $19.99

Underworld U.S.A. (1961)
Seeking revenge on the gangsters who murdered his father years earlier, Cliff Robertson infiltrates the mob and attacks it from within in this gritty crime drama from writer/director Samuel Fuller. Co-stars Richard Rust, Dolores Dorn. 99 min.
02-1837   Was $69.99 $19.99

Merrill's Marauders (1962)
Director Samuel Fuller's two-fisted war story is set in 1942 and focuses on a troop of brave American volunteer soldiers who help the British prevent an invasion of India by the Japanese. Jeff Chandler stars as the infantry's leader; Ty Hardin, Peter Brown and Claude Akins also star. 98 min.
19-2077   Was $19.99 $14.99

Shock Corridor (1963)
Maverick filmmaker Samuel Fuller wrote and directed this unflinching drama that follows reporter Peter Breck into an asylum. Feigning insanity in order to learn the truth about an inmate's death, he soon falls into his own madness. Violent, emotional thriller also stars James Best, Hari Rhodes, Constance Towers. Restored version features special color scenes. 101 min.
22-5775   Letterboxed $19.99

The Naked Kiss (1964)
A taut melodrama on human depravity and redemption that has garnered a cult audience. Prostitute Constance Towers tries to leave the city streets behind her and start again in a quiet small town, but once there she uncovers a dark secret that threatens her new life. Writer/director Sam Fuller's lurid tale, with an unforgettable opening, also stars Michael Dante, Anthony Eisley. 90 min.
22-5776   Letterboxed $19.99

Dead Pigeon On Beethoven Street (1972)
Samuel Fuller's little-seen thriller involves a detective who goes undercover to stop the group of seedy, drug-dealing blackmailers responsible for his partner's murder. Glenn Corbett, Christa Lang and Anton Diffring star in this mystery showcasing Fuller's trademark tough-as-nails style. 92 min.
62-1394 $19.99

The Big Red One (1980)
Lee Marvin is a grizzled army sergeant leading the soldiers of the First Infantry Division (aka The Big Red One) from one battlefield to the next across Africa and Europe. Robert Carradine, Mark Hamill, Kelly Ward and Bobby DiCicco are among the young recruits in his charge. Samuel Fuller's autobiographical flag-waver was reportedly slated to be filmed in the '50s with John Wayne. 113 min.
19-1753   Was $19.99 $14.99

Tigrero: A Film That Was Never Made (1995)
This acclaimed documentary chronicles the aborted efforts of director Sam Fuller to make an action film in the Brazilian rain forest in 1954. Forty years after he explored the region for the movie, Fuller's incredible footage is revealed, and he and filmmaker Jim Jarmusch return to the Amazon and its inhabitants, the Karajá Indians; directed by Mika Kaurismäki. 75 min.
74-3029 $89.99

Please see our index for the Samuel Fuller title: *Shark! (Maneater)*

Audie Murphy

The Red Badge Of Courage (1951)
Based on Stephen Crane's classic novel of a young boy's coming of age as a Union Army recruit during the Civil War. Audie Murphy is excellent as Henry Fleming, who matures from a timid youth into a self-assured man and, finally, a hero. Also stars Bill Mauldin and Arthur Hunnicutt. 70 min.
12-1454 $24.99

The Duel At Silver Creek (1952)
A murderous gang of claim-jumpers have marshal Stephen McNally in their pocket, thanks to beautiful leader Faith Domergue, so it falls on deputy Audie Murphy, whose family was killed by the outlaws, to bring them to justice in this frontier drama directed by Don Siegel. 77 min.
07-2518   ❑$14.99

HIRED GUNSLINGER IN A LAWLESS LAND!

GUNSMOKE

Starring AUDIE MURPHY color by TECHNICOLOR

SUSAN CABOT · PAUL KELLY

with CHARLES DRAKE · MARY CASTLE

Gunsmoke (1953)
Hired by scheming frontier land baron Donald Randolph to run rancher Paul Kelly off his property, itinerant gun-for-hire Audie Murphy winds up switching sides and must battle Randolph's henchmen. Taut western drama also stars Susan Cabot, Mary Castle. 79 min.
07-2841   ❑$14.99

Ride Clear Of Diablo (1954)
With the help of veteran gunslinger Dan Duryea, Audie Murphy straps on the irons and sets out to avenge his father's and brother's murders at the hands of corrupt sheriff Paul Birch and his henchmen in this frontier thriller. With Susan Cabot, Abbe Lane, Russell Johnson. 81 min.
07-2842   ❑$14.99

To Hell And Back (1955)
The most decorated soldier of World War II, Audie Murphy, plays himself in this film biography of his exploits. A gritty, unflinching look at a reluctant hero, the war classic also stars Charles Drake, Marshall Thompson and David Janssen. 106 min.
07-1410 $14.99

Walk The Proud Land (1956)
True-to-life (for its time) frontier drama stars Audie Murphy as Indian agent John Philip Clum, who strove to guarantee self-government for the Apaches while convincing Geronimo to surrender to the authorities. Jay Silverheels also stars as Geronimo, with Pat Crowley and Anne Bancroft as an Apache woman. 89 min.
07-2516   ❑$14.99

Suspicion: "The Flight" (1957)
In a rare TV appearance, Audie Murphy stars as an ex-Navy flyer hired to transport a mysterious passenger. Thrills and surprises abound in this TV suspenser that also features Jack Warden, Susan Kohner and Everett Sloane. 60 min.
10-9853 $14.99

No Name On The Bullet (1959)
When notorious gunman-for-hire Audie Murphy arrives in a small frontier town, the locals know he's not there for a vacation. Who Murphy's target is, and the reason behind his mission of death, makes for a compelling western drama. With Joan Evans, Charles Drake, Edgar Stehli. 77 min.
07-2517   ❑$14.99

The Texican (1966)
Action-packed sagebrusher starring Audie Murphy as a former lawman, on the run after being framed, who returns from Mexico to search for the person responsible for the death of his newspaperman brother. Before long, Murphy discovers that a crooked saloon keeper is behind both deeds. With Broderick Crawford, Diana Lorys. 86 min.
02-2908 $14.99

A Time For Dying (1970)
A young man is eager to make a name for himself in the Old West as a bounty hunter, and along the way he has some eye-opening encounters for the heroes and outlaws of the time. Dramatic look at western heroes stars Richard Lapp, Victor Jory as Judge Roy Bean, and, in his last role, Audie Murphy as Jesse James. 87 min.
53-7284 $39.99

Lady Godiva (1955)
Maureen O'Hara plays history's original "streaker" in this costume (or, in the title heroine's case, uncostumed) drama set in medieval England. As the Normans and Saxons vie for power, nobleman's wife O'Hara makes her famous ride through the Canterbury streets to prove Saxon loyalty (except for a tailor named Peeping Tom). With George Nader, Eduard Franz, Victor McLaglen; look quickly for Clint Eastwood as "1st Saxon." 89 min.
07-2491 $14.99

Retreat, Hell! (1952)
A massive offensive by Chinese forces at the Changjin Reservoir forced U.S. Marines to make a withdrawal that one leatherneck summed up as "advancing in the opposite direction." Gritty combat tale of courage against overwhelming odds stars Frank Lovejoy, Richard Carlson, Russ Tamblyn. 95 min.
63-1327   Was $19.99 $14.99

Torpedo Alley (1953)
Fellow submarine officers must share a hazardous espionage mission in the Korean War, as well as their love for a gorgeous Navy nurse, in a taut combat drama. Mark Stevens, Douglas Kennedy, Dorothy Malone star. 84 min.
63-1328   Was $19.99 $14.99

SS: Strike At Dawn (1959)
Gripping war film set in 1943, when 20,000 beleaguered Yugoslav partisans fought 120,000 SS troops along the Sutjeska River. The wounded partisans are separated from the rest of their army and must fight against insurmountable odds for their lives. Branko Plesa, Nikola Popovic and Nada Skrinjar star.
79-6542   Was $24.99 $19.99

Guerrilla Girl (1953)
Furious action abounds in this tale of an iron-willed Gypsy woman (Marianna) who isn't afraid of meeting the Nazi invaders with flying lead. Helmut Dantine also stars.
68-8911 $19.99

Scott Of The Antarctic (1948)
Dramatic true-life adventure of the British explorer who led his country's Antarctic expeditions and strove to be the first to reach the South Pole. John Mills, Kenneth More, Derek Bond star. 105 min.
59-5045   Was $19.99 $14.99

The Desert Fox (1951)
James Mason shines in his portrayal of General Erwin Rommel, head of Nazi Germany's famed Afrika tank corps. Film follows his career from his victories and ultimate defeat in WWII to his downfall as a conspirator in a plot to assassinate Hitler. Jessica Tandy, Cedric Hardwicke co-star. 88 min.
04-1041 $19.99

The Desert Rats (1953)
This follow-up to "The Desert Fox" focuses on English Captain MacRoberts (Richard Burton), who bravely commands an Australian battalion defending Tobruk against Rommel and his Afrika Korps. Robert Newton, Torin Thatcher and James Mason (in a cameo as Rommel) are also featured; Robert Wise directs. 88 min.
04-2439   ❑$19.99

Battle Cry (1955)
Follow the brutal training and trial by combat of a squad of Marines bound for the Pacific Theatre in WWII in this hard-hitting Raoul Walsh classic. Van Heflin, James Whitmore, Aldo Ray, Tab Hunter star. 149 min.
19-1205 $19.99

The Gift Horse (1952)
Fine British military drama featuring Trevor Howard as a demanding, no-nonsense commander of a battleship who wins the respect of his men after he guides them out of a conflict with the Germans. Richard Attenborough, Sonny Tufts and James Donald co-star. AKA: "Glory At Sea." 100 min.
27-6383 $19.99

Adventures Of Tartu (1943)
Robert Donat, Valerie Hobson. A beautiful girl! A dangerous mission! Exciting drama set in WWII. British spy works with Czechs in effort to destroy Nazi factory. 103 min.
01-1187 $19.99

To The Shores Of Tripoli (1942)
Spoiled rich youth John Payne finds out a hitch in the Marine Corps isn't the same as a vacation in the Hamptons, but under the eye of D.I. Randolph Scott he becomes a full-fledged leatherneck. Rousing WWII flag-waver also stars Maureen O'Hara, Henry (Harry) Morgan, Maxie Rosenbloom. 86 min.
04-1293 $14.99

Wilson (1944)
Exceptional biography of Woodrow Wilson, chronicling his rise from college administrator and political theorist to governor of New York and President of the United States during World War I, which led to his fight for a League of Nations. Alexander Knox excels in the title role; Charles Coburn, Geraldine Fitzgerald, Thomas Mitchell and Vincent Price co-star. 154 min.
04-2285 *$19.99*

Wake Island (1942)
One of the first Hollywood films to honestly deal with American front line forces in WWII, this blistering saga recounts the true story of a handful of Marines who fought off an overwhelming Japanese land, air and sea attack for 16 days. Brian Donlevy, Robert Preston, William Bendix star. 88 min.
07-1409 *$14.99*

A Yank In Libya (1942)
He was about 30 years too early to take care of Qaddafi, but American news correspondent Walter Woolf King makes short work of a Nazi plot to arm Arab tribesmen in this wartime espionage thriller. With Joan Woodbury, H.B. Warner, Parkyakarkus. 65 min.
08-1460 Was $19.99 *$14.99*

Submarine Base (1943)
A former gangster who has taken refuge on a small island helps stop a group of Nazis who have landed nearby come looking for fuel for their U-boats. More problems arise when a merchant marine who was once a cop recognizes the ex-con. John Litel, Fifi D'Orsay and Alan Baxter star in this WWII adventure. 65 min.
08-1736 *$14.99*

Flying Blind (1941)
Thrilling, you-are-there aerial battle scenes highlight this actioner about spies stealing important dynamo from army bomber. Richard Arlen, Jean Parker. 69 min.
08-5020 Was $19.99 *$14.99*

The North Star (1943)
Hollywood's answer to President Roosevelt's call to arms to support our Russian allies was this war drama depicting one Ukrainian village's efforts to survive the atrocities imposed upon them by Nazi invaders. Stars Anne Baxter, Farley Granger, Dana Andrews, Walter Brennan, Walter Huston; Lewis Milestone directs from Lillian Hellman's script. AKA: "Armored Attack!" 102 min.
08-8068 Was $19.99 *$14.99*

Pimpernel Smith (1941)
A simply superb story about a daring, mysterious stranger who rescues artists and intellectuals from the Nazis during WWII. Thrills, suspense and some witty observations on Nazi customs. Leslie Howard directed and produced. 120 min.
09-1573 Was $29.99 *$19.99*

Salute John Citizen (1942)
Similar to "Mrs. Miniver," this inspiring essay focuses on an ordinary English family faced with the Nazi blitzkrieg of London. Two sons go off to war, mom and dad fight daily troubles like rationing, bombs and sacrifice, while the daughter goes to work in a bomb factory. Peggy Cummins, Stanley Holloway. 74 min.
09-1582 Was $29.99 *$24.99*

Battle For Music (1943)
Unusual, semi-documentary film centering on the London Philharmonic Orchestra during World War II. As German bombings destroy the Orchestra's hall and instruments, a benefit concert provides much-needed funds. Hay Petrie, Mavis Clarke and J.B. Priestly, playing himself, star. 75 min.
10-1606 *$19.99*

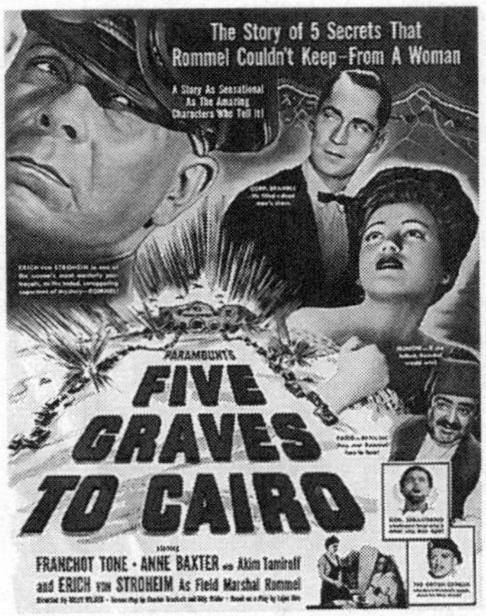

The Story of 5 Secrets That Rommel Couldn't Keep–From A Woman
PARAMOUNT'S
FIVE GRAVES TO CAIRO
FRANCHOT TONE · ANNE BAXTER with Akim Tamiroff and ERICH von STROHEIM As Field Marshal Rommel

Five Graves To Cairo (1943)
In a remote oasis hotel in the Sahara Desert, British soldier Franchot Tone impersonates a servant in order to get information from the inn's newest "guests": invading Afrika Korps tank troops and their commander, Gen. Irwin Rommel (Erich von Stroheim). Things get tricky when Tone learns the servant was really a German spy in this WWII espionage tale from director/co-writer Billy Wilder. With Anne Baxter, Akim Tamiroff. Includes original theatrical trailer. 97 min.
07-2514 ❑*$14.99*

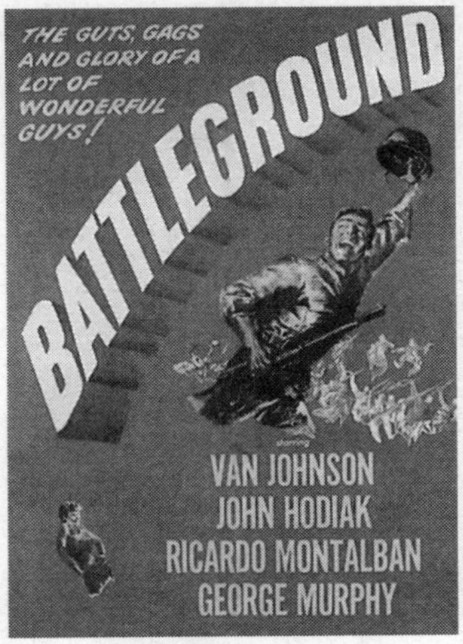

THE GUTS, GAGS AND GLORY OF A LOT OF WONDERFUL GUYS!
BATTLEGROUND
VAN JOHNSON
JOHN HODIAK
RICARDO MONTALBAN
GEORGE MURPHY

Battleground (1949)
An Oscar-winning account of the Battle of the Bulge, and the American foot soldiers who were trapped by the Germans in Bastogne during the fighting. Van Johnson, John Hodiak, Ricardo Montalban and George Murphy star in this stirring wartime drama, directed by William Wellman. 118 min.
12-2073 *$19.99*

Air Force (1943)
Rousing war classic from director Howard Hawks detailing the plight and flight of a B-17 Flying Fortress bomber as it travels from San Francisco to Pearl Harbor to important battles in the Pacific Theatre. The cast is led by John Garfield, John Ridgely, Gig Young and Arthur Kennedy; stunning newsreel and aerial fighting footage are featured. 124 min.
12-2310 *$19.99*

Black Dragons (1942)
Bela Lugosi and Clayton ("The Lone Ranger") Moore star in this exciting war-time tale about Japanese espionage in America and the ringleader, a Nazi doctor. 60 min.
09-1544 Was $19.99 *$14.99*

Black Dragons (Color Version)
Thanks to computerized color, the only thing black about Bela and his spy ring now are their deeds!
63-1520 Was $19.99 *$14.99*

The Day Will Dawn (1942)
Top-notch British WWII thriller set during the Nazi occupation of Norway. A foreign correspondent, an old salt and his beautiful daughter unite to sabotage a secret U-boat base being built in their home town. Stars Deborah Kerr, Hugh Williams and Ralph Richardson. 100 min.
09-1985 Was $29.99 *$24.99*

Submarine Alert (1943)
Tankers transporting oil to Allied bases are being torpedoed, and a German-born radio operator goes undercover and joins the Nazis in order to spy on their operation. Richard Arlen and Wendy Barrie star in this exciting WWII suspenser. 68 min.
09-2254 Was $29.99 *$24.99*

Unsung Heroes (1942)
A motherless teenager volunteers his beloved dog for Army service. Before the dog is sent on its assignment to stand alongside sentries at outposts, the pooch and its owner tangle with a band of German saboteurs. Heartfelt, exciting WWII story with Billy Lee and Addison Richards. AKA: "War Dogs." 64 min.
09-2349 Was $29.99 *$14.99*

Pastor Hall (1940)
Compassionate war drama about a German pastor whose anti-Nazi stance lands him in a concentration camp. Facing death, he manages to escape and tries to return to his parish before his captors catch up to him. Inspired by a true story, this Boulting Brothers production stars Nova Pilbeam, Wilfred Lawson. 97 min.
09-5080 *$19.99*

2000 Women (1944)
During the German occupation of France in World War II, women detainees at a converted spa help to conceal three downed British airmen from their Nazi captors. P.O.W. actioner stars Phyllis Calvert, Flora Robson. AKA: "House of 1000 Women." 97 min.
09-5281 *$14.99*

The Immortal Battalion (1944)
Sir Carol Reed directed this absorbing WWII drama about an army officer (David Niven) who whips a unit of British conscripts into a crack squad to face Rommel's North Africa Korps. Co-stars Stanley Holloway, Stanley Hartnell. AKA: "The Way Ahead." 91 min.
10-1065 *$19.99*

The Captive Heart (1948)
A Czech officer in a German prison camp poses as a dead British officer, going so far as to write to the dead soldier's wife and falling in love with her! Fine look at British POWs and their captors features excellent performances from Michael Redgrave, Basil Radford, Rachel Kempson. 96 min.
10-1144 Was $19.99 *$14.99*

Hangmen Also Die (1943)
The 1942 assassination of Nazi collaborator Reinhard Heydrich in Prague inspired director/co-writer Fritz Lang to create this fictional account of the incident. Brian Donlevy plays the killer, a Czech freedom fighter who is hidden by professor Walter Brennan, then must decide whether to give himself up when the Gestapo begins rounding up civilians. With Anna Lee, Gene Lockhart; Bertolt Brecht worked with Lang on the story. 134 min.
10-1387 *$24.99*

40,000 Horsemen (1941)
Action-packed historical adventure focusing on the brave men of the Australian Light Horse Regiment, which fought in Palestine in World War I. While the exciting efforts of the regiment are at the center of the film, there's also a romantic subplot about the relationship between a soldier and a beautiful French girl. With Grant Taylor, Chips Rafferty and Betty Bryant. 100 min.
10-9309 *$19.99*

Lady From Chungking (1943)
No, this isn't a movie about that woman on the chow mein commercials. Anna May Wong stars as the brave leader of Chinese guerrillas who organizes a group of farmers to battle the invading Japanese in pre-Pearl Harbor World War II. With Harold Huber, Mae Clarke. 71 min.
10-9340 Was $19.99 *$14.99*

Madame Curie (1943)
Greer Garson reteams with her "Mrs. Miniver" co-star, Walter Pidgeon, for this compelling biodrama of the 19th-century husband-wife scientists who struggled for years to prove their discovery of radium. Co-stars Robert Walker, Henry Travers, Dame May Whitty. 113 min.
12-2372 *$19.99*

Background To Danger (1943)
A rousing World War II thriller set in Turkey and starring George Raft as an American agent posing as a machinery salesman who finds himself caught between Nazi and Russian spies while trying to retrieve a secret map. Brenda Marshall, Sydney Greenstreet, Peter Lorre and Turhan Bey also star in this first-class suspense yarn that features a slam-bang car chase. 80 min.
12-2628 *$19.99*

The White Cliffs Of Dover (1944)
A sensitive look at war and its effect on soldiers' loved ones. Irene Dunne is an American woman who moves to England, where she faces tragedies in two world wars as her husband, then her son, die while defending their country. Inspired by Alice Duer Miller's epic poem, the film also stars Alan Marshall, Frank Morgan, Peter Lawford and Roddy McDowall; look for a young Elizabeth Taylor. 126 min.
12-2638 *$19.99*

Journey Together (1946)
Top-notch British WWII drama stars Richard Attenborough and Jack Watling as two Englishmen from divergent backgrounds who train and fight together as R.A.F. fliers. Edward G. Robinson has a memorable cameo as the duo's American instructor; look quickly for Rex Harrison. 95 min.
10-7564 *$19.99*

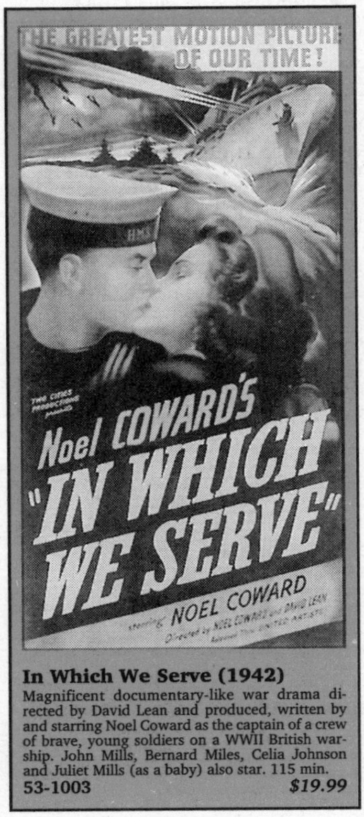

THE GREATEST MOTION PICTURE OF OUR TIME!
Noel COWARD'S
"IN WHICH WE SERVE"
NOEL COWARD

In Which We Serve (1942)
Magnificent documentary-like war drama directed by David Lean and produced, written by and starring Noel Coward as the captain of a crew of brave, young soldiers on a WWII British warship. John Mills, Bernard Miles, Celia Johnson and Juliet Mills (as a baby) also star. 115 min.
53-1003 *$19.99*

A Walk In The Sun (1945)
Terrific WWII drama from director Lewis Milestone follows one infantry platoon in battle from the time they land on an Italian beach to their bloody drive to claim an enemy-held farmhouse six miles inland. Top-notch cast includes Dana Andrews, Richard Conte, John Ireland, Lloyd Bridges, Norman Lloyd and Huntz Hall. 112 min.
67-5026 *$14.99*

Guilty Of Treason (1949)
Charles Bickford gives a compelling performance in this effective account of the outspoken Cardinal Mindszenty, whose anti-Communist stand caused a major stir in the 1940s. Also stars Paul Kelly. 86 min.
10-1199 Was $19.99 *$14.99*

The Black Book (1949)
Lavish and exciting historical epic about the quest for a book containing important information sought by both peasants and aristocrats during the French Revolution. Robert Cummings, Arlene Dahl and Richard Hart star; directed by Anthony Mann ("Winchester '73"). AKA: "Reign of Terror." 84 min.
10-1392 *$19.99*

We Dive At Dawn (1943)
Before "Das Boot" and "The Hunt for Red October" came this intense submarine thriller that follows the crew of a British sub scoping out a German battleship during World War II. John Mills and Eric Portman head the top-notch cast. 98 min.
10-1393 *$19.99*

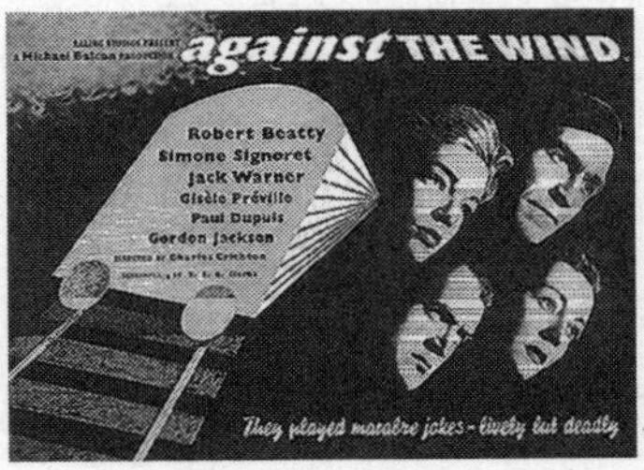

against THE WIND
Robert Beatty
Simone Signoret
Jack Warner
Gisèle Préville
Paul Dupuis
Gordon Jackson
They played macabre jokes–lively but deadly

Against The Wind (1949)
Thrilling, realistic war adventure from Ealing Studios concerning a group of gallant British volunteer spies who parachute into Nazi-occupied territory to destroy an office containing important documents. Documentary-like training and fighting scenes are supplemented by a cast that includes Robert Beatty, Jack Warner and Simone Signoret. 95 min.
17-9001 *$19.99*

Spitfire (1943)
Exciting, true-life tale of Reginald Mitchell, the man who designed the Spitfire, the plane that enabled the RAF to turn the tide against the German Luftwaffe in the Battle for Britain. Stars Leslie Howard (his final film), David Niven; directed by Howard. AKA: "The First of the Few." 117 min.
10-2012 Restored *$19.99*

Gung Ho! (1943)
Randolph Scott, Rod Cameron, J. Carroll Naish and Robert Mitchum star in this blood-and-guts Marine saga which heralds the true story of Carlson's Raiders in the Pacific during World War II. 88 min.
10-2049 Was $19.99 *$14.99*

Hitler—Dead Or Alive (1942)
Based on fact, this riveting and well-crafted spy thriller explores the events surrounding an offer of $1 million by an American businessman for the capture of Adolf Hitler and three ex-cons who embark on the hazardous mission. Stars Ward Bond and Russell Hicks. 72 min.
10-7055 *$19.99*

Eureka Stockade (1949)
During the early 1850s, the Australian government, fearing that gold-seeking miners have neglected the land in favor of immediate wealth, harasses the men, who are then forced to build a stockade for defense. Chips Rafferty, Peter Finch. 103 min.
10-7058 *$19.99*

The Foreman Went To France (1943)
An effective and often lighthearted WWII thriller about a factory foreman tagged by British military leaders to enter newly occupied France to retrieve machine parts that are vital to the war effort. Stars Clifford Evans, Constance Cummings and Tommy Trinder. AKA: "Somewhere in France." 89 min.
10-7065 Was $19.99 *$14.99*

Aerial Gunner (1943)
While recuperating in an Army hospital, pilot Richard Arlen recounts his aerial training and wartime experiences: the rigorous flight instruction, a rivalry with his sergeant for the hand of a girl, and a fight against the Japanese on a South Pacific island. Chester Morris, Lita Ward and Jimmy Lydon also star. 100 min.
53-6075 *$19.99*

The Purple Heart (1944)
Following their capture by the Japanese after being shot down on a bombing run, eight American fliers are placed on trial as war criminals and tortured for information. Harrowing tale of courage, based on true incidents, stars Dana Andrews, Richard Conte, Farley Granger, Sam Levene, Richard Loo; producer Darryl F. Zanuck co-scripted. 99 min.
04-1292 *$14.99*

Nine Men (1943)
Superb war drama focusing on a group of British soldiers fighting against Axis troops in North Africa who must fend for themselves when their commander is killed. Produced by Ealing Studios, the film stars Jack Lambert and Gordon Jackson. 65 min.
10-8451 Was $19.99 *$14.99*

U-Boat Prisoner (1944)
Exciting, true-life tale of an American swabbie who poses as a Nazi to stop a German submarine. After infiltrating the ship, he relays its whereabouts to a U.S. destroyer. With Bruce Bennett, Erik Rolf and John Abbott. 65 min.
10-9065 *$19.99*

Minesweeper (1943)
Story of a Navy deserter who re-enlists in the military with an alias when World War II breaks out and is given a chance to help his country by dismantling an enemy mine. Richard Arlen, Jean Parker, Russell Hayden and a young Robert Mitchum star. 67 min.
17-9063 *$19.99*

Ships With Wings (1942)
Superior aerial battle footage propels this war drama about a pilot (John Clements) who, after being court-martialled from the R.A.F., takes his shot at redemption by sacrificing himself by nosediving into a dam and flooding a German post. Co-stars Leslie Banks, Jane Baxter. 89 min.
17-9073 *$19.99*

They Raid By Night (1942)
A group of commandos flies into Norway to rescue a Norwegian general captured by the Nazis, then one of the commandos realizes his former girlfriend is working on the other side. Lyle Talbot, June Duprez, Charles Rogers star. 80 min.
17-9079 *$19.99*

Bombardier (Color Version) (1943)
Bomber pilot trainees Pat O'Brien and Randolph Scott lock horns over their philosophies of carrying out a bombing mission and over the love of Anne Shirley in this effective wartime drama. Co-stars Eddie Albert, Barton MacLane, and Robert Ryan in his film debut. 99 min.
18-7433 *$29.99*

Corregidor (1943)
Moving drama that focuses upon a hopeless love triangle between a trio of army surgeons during the blazing height of combat in the Philippines of World War II. Telling period romance stars Otto Kruger, Elissa Landi, Donald Woods, Frank Jenks. 69 min.
39-1954 *$19.99*

Home Of The Brave (1949)
A knock-out drama about a black soldier's problems on a Pacific island during WWII—mostly from comrades in his own platoon! Lloyd Bridges, Frank Lovejoy, James Edwards star. 85 min.
63-1085 *$19.99*

The Navy Way (1944)
Well-rendered rouser from the height of WWII that centers on a group of seadogs-to-be, including a pug who isn't happy about being shipped out before his title shot. Keep 'em flying with Robert Lowery, Jean Parker, Bill Henry, Roscoe Karns. 74 min.
10-7190 *$19.99*

The Dawn Express (1942)
Wartime intriguer about Nazi spies pursuing a formula that doubles the potency of gasoline and the noble American scientists who oppose them. Michael Whalen stars. AKA: "Nazi Spy Ring." 63 min.
68-8278 *$19.99*

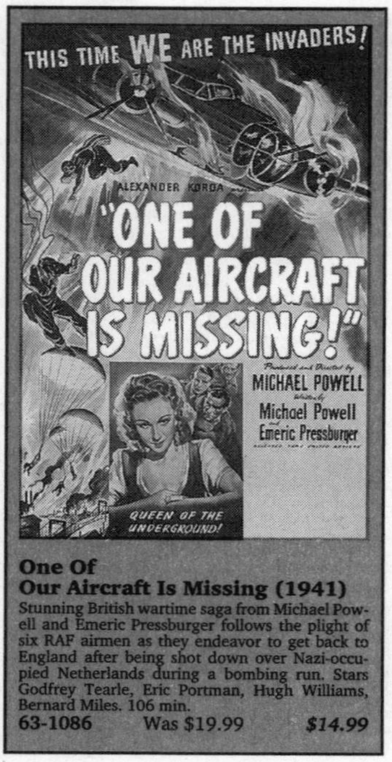

One Of Our Aircraft Is Missing (1941)
Stunning British wartime saga from Michael Powell and Emeric Pressburger follows the plight of six RAF airmen as they endeavor to get back to England after being shot down over Nazi-occupied Netherlands during a bombing run. Stars Godfrey Tearle, Eric Portman, Hugh Williams, Bernard Miles. 106 min.
63-1086 Was $19.99 *$14.99*

Wings Over The Pacific (1945)
The peaceful existence of an American World War I veteran and his daughter on a remote Pacific island is shattered when two pilots, an American and a Nazi working for the Japanese, crash their planes there. When the Axis scout learns of the island's oil reserves, the American flyer must try to stop him. Inez Cooper, Edward Norris, Montagu Love also star. 60 min.
10-9064 Was $19.99 *$14.99*

The Exile (1947)
Max Ophuls directed and Douglas Fairbanks, Jr. produced, wrote and starred in this stirring dramatization of the restoration of Charles II to England's throne after the defeat of Cromwell. With Nigel Bruce, Maria Montez and Paula Corset (later Corday). 94 min.
53-7360 *$39.99*

Bonnie Prince Charlie (1948)
Lavish historical adventure starring David Niven as the title character, a dashing young prince who returns to Scotland from France in 1745 and leads his fellow Scots against British monarch George II. Margaret Leighton, Judy Campbell, Jack Hawkins and Finlay Currie also star in this Alexander Korda presentation. 115 min.
10-9238 Was $19.99 *$14.99*

The Young Mr. Pitt (1942)
Epic historical drama starring Robert Donat as William Pitt the Younger, the English statesman and prime minister who revived his failing career by leading Britain against Napoleon and his forces. Robert Morley plays Charles James Fox, Pitt's former political foe, who comes to respect him. With Phyllis Calvert; directed by Carol Reed. 115 min.
10-9306 *$19.99*

San Demetrio, London (1947)
True-to-life Ealing Studio World War II drama about a merchant marine tanker that is stranded at sea, and the courageous crew who helps bring it back to shore. Walter Fitzgerald, Robert Beatty and Mervyn Johns star. 93 min.
17-9023 *$19.99*

Convoy (1940)
Noted for its depiction of World War II in a realistic manner, this story is set on a small English cruiser patrolling the North Sea that is attacked by a German battleship. Clive Brook, John Clements, Edward Chapman star. 95 min.
17-9047 Was $19.99 *$14.99*

Cottage To Let (1948)
Rarely seen British thriller set in Scotland during World War II. A man excavating a bombsight discovers a spy, and sets out to stop his diabolical efforts. Leslie Banks, Alastair Sim and John Mills star. Directed by Anthony Asquith ("The Winslow Boy"). AKA: "Bombsight Stolen."
68-8474 *$19.99*

Samurai (1945)
Outrageous, low-budget propaganda yarn about an American-raised Japanese orphan who decides to turn against his adopted country and help plot the Japanese invasion of California. Paul Fung and Luke Chan also star. 75 min.
68-8736 *$19.99*

The Fighting Sullivans (1944)
Patriotic, emotional WWII melodrama recounts the true story of five closeknit brothers who served and died together at Guadalcanal, from their small town boyhood to their final battle. Thomas Mitchell, Selena Royle, John Alvin, John Campbell, James Cardwell, George Offerman, Jr. and Edward Ryan co-star in this sentimental favorite. AKA: "The Sullivans." 111 min.
55-9000 *$29.99*

Guadalcanal Diary (1943)
Made almost simultaneously with the American assaults on Japanese-held islands in the Pacific, this gritty look at the day-by-day struggles of a "melting pot" Marine squadron stars Anthony Quinn, Lloyd Nolan, William Bendix, Richard Jaeckel, Lionel Stander, Preston Foster and Richard Conte. 93 min.
04-1290 *$14.99*

A Wing And A Prayer (1944)
A precursor to "Top Gun," this stirring war story focuses on a group of new Naval recruits on an aircraft carrier, battling the Japanese in the Pacific. Don Ameche, Dana Andrews, Richard Jaeckel and William Eythe star; remarkable combat footage. 97 min.
04-2459 *$14.99*

The Lion Has Wings (1939)
Exciting documentary footage is featured in this propaganda effort tailored for British audiences during World War II. Michael Powell was one of the directors of this flag-waving study of the brave people who endure the tumultuous effects of the war. Merle Oberon, Ralph Richardson, Flora Robson star. 76 min.
53-6056 Was $29.99 *$14.99*

The Spy In Black (U-Boat 29) (1939)
Exciting WWI spy melodrama about a German submarine officer who smuggles himself into England to learn the sailing date of the British fleet. The first collaboration of Michael Powell and Emeric Pressburger co-stars Conrad Veidt, Valerie Hobson and Marius Goring. 77 min.
53-1785 Was $19.99 *$14.99*

Bataan (1943)
Classic WWII thriller set in the Philippines, where American and Filipino forces fight time and the Japanese army to complete a vital bridge. Robert Taylor, Thomas Mitchell and George Murphy head the cast; great combat scenes. 114 min.
12-1577 *$19.99*

Paul Muni

Scarface (1932)
One of the earliest and most powerful gangster films ever made, courtesy of producer Howard Hughes, director Howard Hawks and co-writer Ben Hecht. Paul Muni became a star with his portrayal of blood-thirsty mobster Tony Carmonte (modelled after "Scarface" Al Capone). With Ann Dvorak, Boris Karloff, Osgood Perkins (father of Anthony) and coin-flipper George Raft. 90 min.
07-1027 *$14.99*

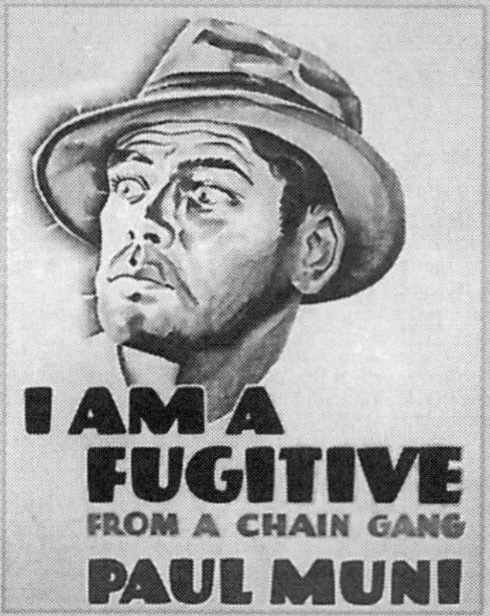

I Am A Fugitive From A Chain Gang (1932)
A powerful social drama that still packs a punch today. Mervyn LeRoy's searing look at the prison system stars Paul Muni as a drifter sentenced to 10 years' hard labor who escapes and builds a new life in Chicago, but is later recaptured. With Helen Vinson, Preston Foster. 93 min.
12-2374 *$19.99*

The Story Of Louis Pasteur (1936)
One of the finest Warner Bros. biodramas of the '30s, nearly all of which seemed to star Paul Muni. Here Muni, in his Oscar-winning turn, plays the famed 19th-century French scientist who fought to promote his vaccines for anthrax and hydrophobia. Josephine Hutchinson, Fritz Leiber co-star. 85 min.
12-1976 *$19.99*

The Good Earth (1937)
Paul Muni and the Oscar-winning Luise Rainer star in this sprawling epic of the troubles faced by Chinese peasants in pre-communist China. Fabulous sets, unforgettable special effects—including the famed locust attack sequence—and exceptional acting make this adaptation of Pearl Buck's novel a treasure not to be missed. 138 min.
12-1115 *$19.99*

The Life Of Emile Zola (1937)
Winner of three Oscars, including Best Picture, this moving biographical drama stars Paul Muni as the famed 19th-century French author. Joseph Schildkraut co-stars as Captain Louis Dreyfus, whose sensational trial brought Zola to prominence and served as a stirring tribute to the fight for justice. 116 min.
12-1839 *$19.99*

Juarez (1939)
Another magnificent portrayal by Paul Muni, this time as Mexican leader Benito Juarez, who valiantly fought for his country's freedom from Spain during the 1860s. Bette Davis, Brian Aherne, John Garfield and Claude Rains add stellar supporting turns; William Dieterle directs. 132 min.
12-2140 *$19.99*

Commandos Strike At Dawn (1942)
Gripping, human war drama stars Paul Muni as a Norwegian fisherman who escapes to England when the Nazis invade his village and returns to lead a commando raid on a German airstrip and rescue his daughter. With Anna Lee, Sir Cedric Hardwicke, Ray Collins, Lillian Gish; look for Lloyd Bridges as a soldier. 100 min.
02-1855 *$19.99*

Angel On My Shoulder (1946)
Witty fantasy comedy that plays like the flip side of "Here Comes Mr. Jordan" (and scripted by that film's writer). Gangster Paul Muni, killed by his double-crossing partner, comes back to Earth for revenge after making a deal with the Devil, delightfully played by "Mr. Jordan's" Claude Rains. Anne Baxter co-stars. 101 min.
08-8072 Was $19.99 *$14.99*

The Last Angry Man (1959)
Paul Muni received a fifth Academy Award nomination for his role as an idealistic physician working 45 years in a Brooklyn tenement. The saintly doctor's principles are threatened when TV producer David Wayne coerces his participation in a network profile. 100 min.
02-1917 Was $69.99 *$19.99*

Please see our index for the Paul Muni title: *A Song To Remember*

Under The Red Robe (1936)
High drama concerning Cardinal Richelieu's oppression of the Huguenots in 17th-century France. With Conrad Veidt, Raymond Massey. 82 min.
01-1080 Was $19.99 *$14.99*

Tudor Rose (1936)
Intrigue-filled historical drama set in England during the days following the death of flamboyant monarch Henry VIII, concentrating on the ascension of young Lady Jane Grey to the throne. Cedric Hardwicke, John Mills and Nova Pilbeam star. AKA: "Lady Jane Grey," "Nine Days a Queen." 80 min.
01-1221 *$19.99*

Lady Jane (1986)
Historical tale of passion and political intrigue that recounts the story of Lady Jane Grey, a teenager installed by conspirators as the Queen of England in the 16th century. Helena Bonham Carter, Cary Elwes, John Wood, Patrick Stewart co-star. 140 min.
06-1379 Was $79.99 *$14.99*

The Crusades (1935)
The master of cinematic historical spectacle, Cecil B. DeMille, turned his attention to medieval times with this sweeping drama of England's King Richard the Lion-Hearted leading his armies into battle in the Holy Land against the Muslim forces of Saladin. Henry Wilcoxon, Loretta Young, Ian Keith, Joseph Schildkraut and Catherine DeMille star. 126 min.
07-2245 *$14.99*

William Tell (1934)
In the 14th century, the Swiss people find themselves in danger of losing their land and liberty to the evil emperor. One man, the archer William Tell, becomes a patriot, leading his countrymen against the emperor's tyrannical rule in this thrilling historical epic that has many parallels to the the rise of Nazism at the time. Hans Marr, Conrad Veidt star.
09-2356 *$19.99*

Torpedoed! (1937)
Lively war-related drama in which England faces the threat of war with once-friendly Bianco, a south-of-the-border country experiencing revolt. When the British consul's daughter is kidnapped by revolutionaries, the British Admiralty dispatches a Navy cruiser to restore order. H.B. Warner, Richard Cromwell star. 67 min.
09-2378 *$19.99*

Abraham Lincoln (1930)
D.W. Griffith's first talkie is a moving, down-to-earth look at the life of America's 16th preisdent, from Lincoln's boyhood and his days as an Illinois lawyer to Wahington and the turmoil of the Civil War. Walter Huston stars in the title role; with Una Merkel, Kay Hammond. 90 min.
10-1119 *$19.99*

Abe Lincoln In Illinois (1940)
Moving and dignified film version of Robert Sherwood's Pulitzer Prize-winning play stars Raymond Massey as the rail-splitting country lawyer-turned-politician, following Lincoln's life from his early days through the debates with Stephen A. Douglas and his 1860 election to the presidency. With Ruth Gordon, Gene Lockhart. 110 min.
05-1086 *$19.99*

The Day Lincoln Was Shot (1998)
Rob Morrow stars in this gripping true-life drama as John Wilkes Booth, the renowned actor and Confederate sympathizer who assassinated President Lincoln in 1865. The film follows the days leading up to the fateful night at Ford's Theater, and continuing to Booth's escape and the showdown that resulted in his death. Lance Henriksen co-stars as Lincoln; with Donna Murphy, Jean Louisa Kelly. 95 min.
18-7813 Was $79.99 *$14.99*

The Iron Duke (1935)
George Arliss stars as the Duke of Wellington, who crushed Napoleon and rescued Louis XVIII from his enemies. Exciting drama co-stars Gladys Cooper and A.E. Matthews. 88 min.
10-3079 Was $19.99 *$14.99*

The Marines Are Coming (1934)
Action and romance spark this tale set in the Central American jungles, where a pair of Marines fight enemies and compete for the same woman. When the woman's Mexican boyfriend interrupts the American soldiers' intentions, trouble ensues. William Haines, Esther Ralston and Conrad Nagel star. 71 min.
10-3381 *$19.99*

Inside The Lines (1930)
World War I is the setting for espionage in this tale of the Germans' using a female agent to infiltrate an important British officer's house. Betty Compson, Montagu Love. 73 min.
09-1505 Was $29.99 *$14.99*

Viva Villa (1934)
Thrilling biography starring Wallace Beery as Mexican bandit and revolutionary Pancho Villa. The film follows Villa's life, from his revenge against the soldier who killed his father to his Robin Hood-like actions, robbing the rich landowners to help the poor, to his triumphs and misfires as a revolutionary leader and politician. Fay Wray, Stuart Erwin and Joseph Schildkraut also star. 115 min.
12-2637 **$19.99**

Crimson Romance (1934)
Two Yankee friends mad for dogfighting and adventure join the German Luftwaffe at the outbreak of WWI, but their loyalty and romantic view of combat are tested when America belatedly enters the fight. Ben Lyon, Jason Robards, Sr. and Erich von Stroheim star. 70 min.
09-2053 Was $29.99 **$19.99**

DuBarry, Woman Of Passion (1930)
Norma Talmadge is the headstrong, 18th-century French courtesan who became mistress to the king. William Cameron Menzies served as art director in this handsomely produced period piece. Co-stars Conrad Nagel and William Farnum. 88 min.
10-7074 Was $19.99 **$14.99**

Forgotten Women (1931)
Unusual for its time, this WWI drama follows the exploits of a group of women serving at an ambulance patrol station near the front and shows how they cope with everything from romantic triangles to the harsh realities of combat. Evelyn Brent, Marceline Day, Louise Fazenda, Irene Rich star; directed by William "One Shot" Beaudine. AKA: "The Mad Parade." 58 min.
10-9976 **$19.99**

Spy Of Napoleon (1936)
First-rate historical saga about a girl who is sent to spy on traitors during dispute the between Napoleon and the Bismark of Prussia. Richard Barthelmess, Dolly Haas. 77 min.
09-1605 Was $29.99 **$24.99**

Drums Of Destiny (1937)
Thrilling costume drama set in Spanish-ruled Florida in 1817, where an American army officer tries to save his brother, condemned to death by a cruel local official. Tom Keene, Edna Lawrence, Budd Buster star. 60 min.
09-5002 **$19.99**

Rasputin And The Empress (1932)
Large-scale historical epic teams the Barrymores—John, Ethel and Lionel—for the only time on screen. John plays the dashing Royal Prince Paul Chegodieff, who battles with evil monk Rasputin (Lionel) over Russia's throne and for the confidence of Empress Alexandra (Ethel). Ralph Morgan also stars. 123 min.
12-2634 **$19.99**

The Night They Killed Rasputin (1962)
Unusual telling of the Rasputin story centering on the efforts of Prince Yousoupoff to assassinate "The Mad Monk," who used his hypnotic powers to entrance Russia's royal family. John Drew Barrymore stars as Rasputin; Edmund Purdom, Gianna Maria Canale co-star. 87 min.
68-8734 **$19.99**

Nicholas And Alexandra (1971)
Epic historical account of Czar Nicholas and his wife, and the revolution they faced. The screen glitters with magnificent sets, lavish locations and fine acting by Michael Jayston, Janet Suzman, Jack Hawkins and Laurence Olivier. 180 min.
02-1252 Was $69.99 **$29.99**

Anastasia: The Mystery Of Anna (1986)
Lavish, romantic version of the mysterious story of Anna Anderson, the woman who claimed to be the surviving daughter of Russia's Czar Nicholas II, and the international scrutiny that followed her claim. Amy Irving, Olivia de Havilland, Omar Sharif, Rex Harrison and Susan Lucci star. 190 min.
58-5045 Was $29.99 □**$14.99**

Rasputin: Dark Servant Of Destiny (1996)
An electrifying chronicle of the life of the infamous "holy man" who won favor with Russian ruler Nicholas II and Empress Alexandra after mysteriously helping their hemophiliac son. Alan Rickman is masterful as Rasputin, whose thirst for decadence and disdain for authority led to his downfall in 1916. With Ian McKellen, Greta Scacchi and David Warner. 104 min.
44-2059 Was $99.99 **$19.99**

Rhodes Of Africa (1936)
Walter Huston stars as South African empire builder Cecil Rhodes, discoverer of the world's richest diamond mine, colonial prime minister and christener of scholarships and countries. Great location shooting enriches this fine biography co-starring Oscar Homolka and Peggy Ashcroft. 94 min.
68-8343 Was $19.99 **$14.99**

Rhodes: The Life & Legend Of Cecil Rhodes (1997)
He made his fortune in the diamond fields of South Africa, and his quest to bring the continent under British rule made him both a hero and villain whose legacy lives on to this day. Martin Shaw stars as 19th-century businessman and statesman Cecil Rhodes in this sweeping British mini-series. Frances Barber, Neil Pearson also star. 336 min. on three tapes.
04-3577 □**$59.99**

All Quiet On The Western Front (1930)
One of the first and most powerful war films ever made, director Louis Milestone's adaptation of the Erich Maria Remarque novel follows a group of idealistic young German soldiers in the final days of the Great War. Winner of Best Picture and Director Academy Awards. Lew Ayres, Louis Wolheim, John Wray star. Restored version; 131 min.
07-1034 Was $19.99 **$14.99**

All Quiet On The Western Front (1979)
Richard Thomas is a naive WWI German recruit and Ernest Borgnine the grizzled sergeant who shows him the brutal realities of war in this compelling new version of the classic novel. Co-stars Patricia Neal, Donald Pleasence; Delbert Mann directs. 131 min.
04-1273 Was $59.99 **$12.99**

Catherine The Great (1934)
Alexander Korda production with Douglas Fairbanks, Jr. and Elisabeth Bergner is dramatic story of Catherine's many loves and her rise to power. AKA: "The Rise of Catherine the Great." 92 min.
10-4007 **$19.99**

Young Catherine (1990)
An all-star cast is featured in this lavish historical drama of romance and royalty, focusing on the 18th-century Russian empress's rise to power. Married at 16 to the heir to the Imperial throne, Catherine must deal with court intrigue, her husband's misrule, and a secret lover. With Vanessa Redgrave, Christopher Plummer, Franco Nero, Marthe Keller and Julia Ormond in the title role. 180 min.
18-7292 □**$89.99**

She Goes To War (1929)
Top-notch drama directed by Henry King ("Twelve O'Clock High") about a spoiled rich girl's experiences in the trenches during World War I. Eleanor Boardman stars as the woman who joins her cowardly fiancée on the front lines of France, then gets into the heat of battle. An early talkie with musical score and some dialogue. 50 min.
09-2137 Was $24.99 **$19.99**

Disraeli (1929)
George Arliss won the Academy Award for his tour-de-force performance as the 19th-century Prime Minister of England whose leadership and wits helped his country win control of the Suez Canal over Russia. Florence Arliss, Joan Bennett and David Torrence also star. 90 min.
12-2583 **$19.99**

The Prime Minister (1941)
Stirring biodrama of the life of British leader Benjamin Disraeli stars John Gielgud in the title role and follows Disraeli from his early days as a writer through his stormy Parliament career and Downing Street tenures during the Victorian Era. With Diana Wynyard, Fay Compton. 94 min.
10-9338 Was $19.99 **$14.99**

Disraeli (1979)
The life of the Jewish law student and novelist who turned to politics and became one of England's most revered and influential statesmen is traced in this compelling British mini-series. Ian McShane stars as Benjamin Disraeli, whose seven years as prime minister helped to shape the Victorian world. 220 min. on four tapes.
50-8164 Was $79.99 **$49.99**

Flying Fool (1929)
Starring William Boyd and Marie Prevost, this is the story of two brothers, one of whom is now a World War I flying ace. Problems erupt when they both fall in love with the same woman. Directed by Tay Garnett ("Postman Always Rings Twice").
62-1212 **$19.99**

New From First Look Pictures

FIRST LOOK PICTURES

© 2000 Artwork and Design First Look Pictures

Mesmer
(1994)
This intriguing film looks at Dr. Franz Anton Mesmer, the 18th-century Austrian physician who drew controversy and an incredible following with his use of hypnotism and magnetism for healing. Alan Rickman turns in a tour-de-force performance as Mesmer; Amanda Ooms and Jan Rubes co-star. Scripted by Dennis Potter ("The Singing Detective"). Director's cut: 107 min.
83-5011 $24.99

Also available on DVD
Standard; Soundtrack: English Dolby Surround; theatrical trailer.
D1-7053 DVD $24.99

Alegria
(1994)
This lovely romantic fantasy from "Cirque de Soleil" artistic director Franco Dragone is about a disgruntled street mime who saves the life of an 11-year-old boy, when he's almost run over by a train carrying travelling circus performers. Frac meets and falls for Giuletta, a circus singer, but must first deal with her disapproving father. Ren Bazinet, Julie Cox and Frank Langella star. 93 min.
83-5007 Was $79.99 $14.99

Also available on DVD
Widescreen; Soundtracks: English 5.1 and Dolby; audio commentary by Dragone; "making of" featurette; music video; music performance; theatrical trailer.
D1-6860 DVD $24.99

A Soldier's Tale
(1988)
Penetrating and romantic WWII drama stars Gabriel Byrne as a British soldier stationed in France who falls for a beautiful woman (Marianne Basler) accused of being a collaborator. When an American G.I. (Judge Reinhold) with his own plans for the woman appears, Byrne is forced to make some difficult decisions. 96 min.
63-1509 $14.99

Also available on DVD
Standard; Soundtrack: English mono; theatrical trailer; scene access.
D1-7054 DVD $24.99

Necromaniac (2000)
Harry Russo is a monster of a man, given to episodes of inhuman brutality. Witness his unbelievable wrath as he takes to the streets of Las Vegas with bloodlust, searching for anyone who will satisfy his desires. With help from the homicidal Rubberneck, Harry proves to his mutilated victims that he is truly evil! Joe Giancaspro stars. WARNING: Not for the squeamish! 80 min.
73-9336 *$29.99*

Serial Killer Massacre (2000)
Serial killer Ted teams with mass-murdering Leah for a violent rampage that leads to love between two psychotic animals. A disagreement between the perverse pair leads them to battle each other. May the sickest murderer win! Stephanie Beaton and Jeff Murphy star. 85 min.
73-9361 *$29.99*

Tales From The Cannibal Side (2000)
This diabolical trilogy is definitely not for the squeamish: "Weekend in the City" involves a woman who has a strange desire to be eaten alive; in "Trick or Treat," Stacy's Halloween fun turns to terror when she becomes a holiday treat; and "Meat's Meat" concerns a family that enjoys butchering their own "vittles." With Stephanie Beaton, Trish Mayer. 85 min.
73-9362 *$29.99*

AMERICAN PSYCHO

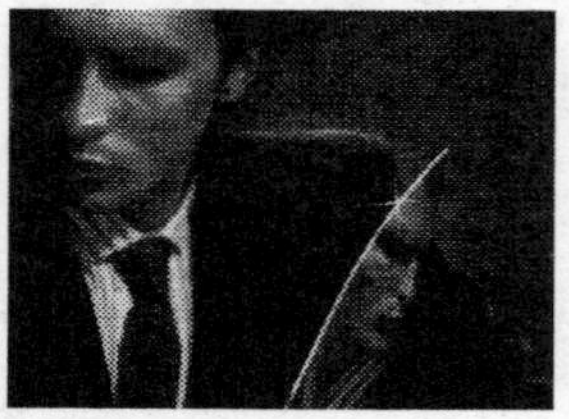

Killer Looks.

American Psycho (Unrated Version) (2000)
Brett Easton Ellis' infamous 1991 novel is turned into a darkly humorous horror show that slyly skewers 1980s values. Director Mary Harron ("I Shot Andy Warhol") casts Christian Bale as the slick, sick Wall Street player who doubles as serial killer, putting away people who annoy him and the women with whom he has loveless sexual encounters. Chloe Sevigny, Willem Dafoe and Reese Witherspoon also star. Unrated edition includes the controversial menage-a-trois sequence. 103 min.
07-2902 □*$99.99*

SideShow (2000)
Get ready to "freak out," as a sinister sideshow boss hatches a scheme to beef up his talent roster by transforming a pair of female runaways into hideous attractions, in this bizarre shocker from director Fred Olen Ray. Jamie Martz, Jessica Keenan, Phil Fondacaro, Brinke Stevens and Ross Hagen star. 90 min.
75-5078 *$99.99*

Believe (2000)
Ben Stiles, a man who loves to scare people, gets a dose of his own medicine when the ghost of Wickwire House beckons him and a friend into a supernatural world. As Ben tries to uncover the truth behind this haunting, he realizes that he'll need more than a sixth sense to stir the echoes in this house on haunted hill. With Ben Gazzara, Jan Rubes, Andrea Martin. 97 min.
82-5176 *$89.99*

Da Hip Hop Witch (2000)
What happens when five young, white suburbanites get lost in the tough-as-nails projects while on a search for the "hip hop witch"? The question is answered in disturbing found footage presented in this urban-flavored shocker. With appearances and music by Mobb Deep, Rah Digga, Eminem, Vanilla Ice and Stacii Jae Johnson. 94 min.
83-1558 *$99.99*

Final Destination (2000)
A high school student has a terrifying vision of a plane crashing right before he and his classmates are to head to Paris on a senior trip. Seven people leave the plane and watch in horror as the premonition comes true. Have the survivors truly cheated death, or, as they begin dying in mysterious ways, are they merely living on borrowed time? Devon Sawa, Ali Larter, Kerr Smith star in this unusual chiller from "X-Files" veterans Glen Morgan and James Wong. 98 min.
02-5237 □*$99.99*

Octopus (2000)
The daring crew of a nuclear submarine must brave a tumultuous stretch of ocean in order to transport a terrorist to America to be prosecuted. When he manages to escape to another ship, they must battle a gigantic octopus terrorizing the vessel as they try to recapture their prisoner. Jay Harrington, David Beecroft and Carolyn Lowery star. AKA: "Dead Eye Six." 99 min.
68-2029 *$69.99*

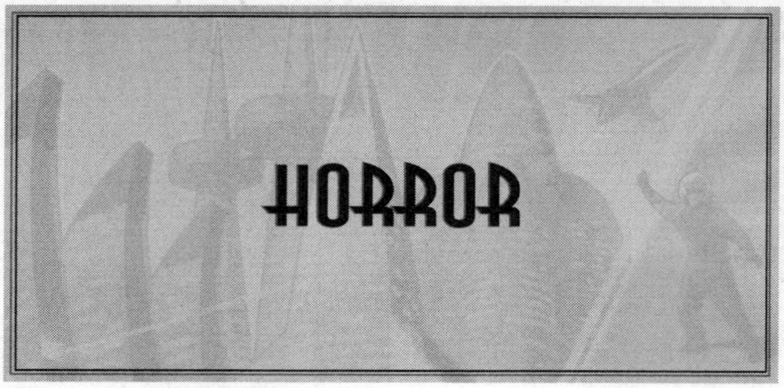

The Doorway (2000)
Four college students taking refuge in an old Georgian mansion uncover a doorway to demonic spirits and depraved passions. Who are they gonna call? How about paranormal expert and ghostbuster Roy Scheider, who must close the doors to Hell. Lauren Woodland and Suzanne Bridgman also star. 91 min.
20-9217 *$99.99*

Bloody Murder (2000)
The summer camp legend of chainsaw killer Trevor Moorehouse becomes a terrifying reality when a group of campers playing a game of Hide and Seek discover that their counselors are disappearing one after another. If the maniac is really alive, how can he be stopped? Jessica Morris, Peter Guillemette star. 90 min.
27-7337 □*$99.99*

Prison Of The Dead (2000)
An eccentric rich kid plans a high school reunion in the form of a funeral that's set to take place in an abandoned witches' prison. While holding a seance using a Ouija board, the former classmates unleash three executioners from their graves. Now they have to figure out how to stop the undead ghouls! Patrick Flood and Debra Mayer star. 90 min.
75-5079 *$89.99*

Voodoo Academy (2000)
A young college student named Christopher studies religion at a university. Little does he know that the school's chief financier has a plan to raise an ancient voodoo army of the undead. Christopher must stop the creep before he does the voodoo that he does so welllllll! Riley Smith, Rhett Jordan and Debra Mayer star. 85 min.
75-5080 *$89.99*

The Dummy (2000)
Paul is an aspiring ventriloquist who, along with his dummy sidekick Tommy, is a hit with the ladies. But when Paul's friend Donna discovers the sinister truth behind the duo's off-stage relationship, Tommy may just take matters into his wooden hands in this terror tale in the tradition of "Dead of Night" and "Magic." Writer/director Keith Singleton and Jocelyn Dondeville star. 90 min.
82-5230 *$59.99*

Night Life (1990)
A freak electrical accident in a mortuary revives four dead teenagers, and the quartet of adolescent zombies sets out in search of "food," sex and general horror (just like normal teens). Shocks and graveyard humor abound. Scott Grimes, Cheryl Pollack, John Astin star. 92 min.
02-2062 *$79.99*

Severed Ties (1992)
A scientist experimenting with human limb regeneration becomes the horrified host to a reptilian arm that has its own violent, murderous instincts. "Body Parts" meets "The Alligator People" in this frightening tale starring Oliver Reed, Elke Sommer, Garrett Morris and Johnny Legend. 95 min.
02-2258 Was $19.99 *$14.99*

The Harvest (1994)
Intense thriller focusing on a screenwriter living in Central America who investigates a gruesome black market in human organ trade after he discovers one of his body parts is missing. Miguel Ferrer, Leilani Sarelle, Harvey Fierstein and Henry Silva star. 97 min.
02-2600 Was $89.99 □*$14.99*

The Unborn (1991)
A diabolical horror outing about a mother-to-be who discovers that what she's carrying is something other than human! Brooke Adams, James Karen, Jane Cameron star in this frightening shocker offering state-of-the-art special effects. 85 min.
02-2123 *$89.99*

The Unborn II (1993)
Sequel to the hit shocker tells of a secret fertility experiment that has created a batch of monster children. A mother with one child joins her friend in protecting the little creeps before a relentless woman tries to destroy all of them. Michelle Greene and Scott Valentine star.
21-9055 Was $89.99 *$14.99*

Ghost In The Machine (1994)
A suspense-packed high-tech shocker about a serial killer whose soul infiltrates electrical systems after he is executed. A woman, her teenage son and a brilliant computer hacker join forces to try to stop this diabolical, unpredictable murderer. Karen Allen, Chris Mulkey and Wil Hornief star. 93 min.
04-2799 Was $89.99 □*$29.99*

School's Out (1999)
On the eve of a graduation night party, a college coed is brutally murdered on campus. Now the students are on edge, as a stalker haunts their corridors and classrooms. Is school out for them...forever? Katharina Wackernagel stars in this Euro-shocker. 90 min.
82-9062 *$89.99*

Brain Dead (1990)
Take a terrifying trip inside the human mind, as a doctor's experiments in erasing bad memories through "surgical resculpturing" of the brain backfires, with shocking results. Suspenseful tale written by "Twilight Zone" scripter Charles Beaumont stars George Kennedy, Bud Cort, Bill Pullman and Bill Paxton. 85 min.
12-2088 *$14.99*

Lucinda's Spell (1998)
The last descendant of Merlin must father a child on the eve of a Celtic holiday in order to preserve his family's mystical bloodline. In New Orleans, a magical prostitute must win this honor for personal reasons by waging a war against evil witches who want to bear the child for their own wicked purposes. Christina Fulton, Shana Betz and Leon Herbert also star. 105 min.
20-8624 *$69.99*

Wax Mask (1997)
Two women are thrown into a world of terror when they discover that a string of mysterious deaths in the city of Rome is connected to a macabre wax museum, and that the artist/owner of the museum is himself linked to the murder of one girl's parents years earlier, in this chilling remake of "House of Wax." Daniele Auber, Umberto Balli and Gianni Franco star. AKA: "Gaston Leroux's the Wax Mask." 98 min.
50-8730 *$29.99*

That Little Monster (1994)
A rare find, this edgy fright film tells of a strange couple who hire a young babysitter to watch their child. Little does the hired hand know that the little kid is actually a little terror! "Phantasm's" Reggie Bannister, Melissa Baum and the great Forrest J. Ackerman star in this effective terror tale.
68-9277 *$19.99*

Children Of The Night (1992)
A vampire and his children use a small town as their feeding ground, and only three strangers who serve as vampire hunters can stop them. This shocking, blood-drenched thriller stars Ami Dolenz, Karen Black, Garrett Morris and Peter DeLuise. 92 min.
02-2287 Was $19.99 *$14.99*

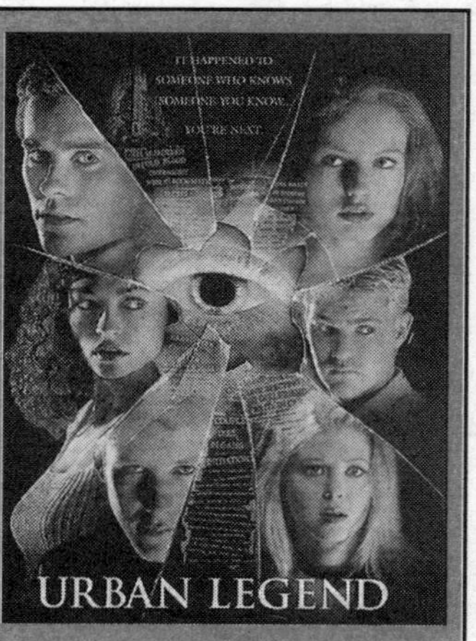

Urban Legend (1998)
It doesn't have to be Halloween for disturbing behavior to run rampant at Pendleton College. The place turns into Splatter University, after the student bodies taking a course on famous yarns sure to make them scream start turning up dead. Who has time to write an essay on what they did last summer when faced with this frightmare? Alicia Witt, Jared Leto, Rebecca Gayheart and Robert Englund star. 101 min.
02-3278 Was $99.99 □*$14.99*

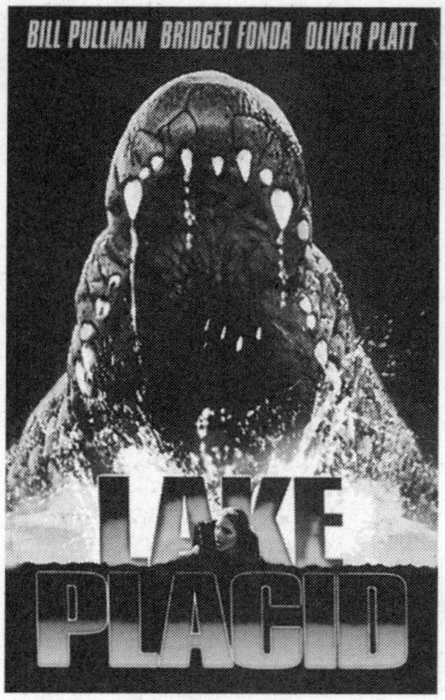

Lake Placid (1999)
The arrival of a gigantic, man- (and cow-) eating crocodile turns a peaceful New England lakeside region into a killing field in this bone-chilling horror thriller with a biting script courtesy of "Ally McBeal" creator David E. Kelly. Bill Pullman, Bridget Fonda, Oliver Platt, Betty White star. 82 min.
04-3916 Was $99.99 □*$14.99*

Popcorn (1991)
Fright and fun mix as a diabolical phantom haunts an all-night terror film festival. The audience doesn't realize this dastardly fiend is really killing people, so they cheer him on as "vintage" flicks like "Attack of the Amazing Electrified Man" and "Mosquito" unspool on the big screen. Dee Wallace Stone, Ray Walston, Jill Schoelen, Tony Roberts and Tom Villard star. 93 min.
02-2086 *$89.99*

Alligator II: The Mutation (1991)
This sequel to the cult shocker shows what happens when a sewer-dwelling alligator feasts on dead experimental animals and grows to monstrous proportions. The creature terrorizes the city and must feast on flesh to survive. Steve Railsback, Dee Wallace Stone, Joseph Bologna and Brock Peters star. 92 min.
02-2147 Was $19.99 *$14.99*

Guilty As Charged (1992)
In this darkly comic, over-the-top shocker, Rod Steiger plays a demented fellow who plays judge and jury to murderers by tracking them down, then killing them in his electric chair. The executioner runs into trouble when he tries to help a corrupt politician. Lauren Hutton and Isaac Hayes co-star. 95 min.
02-2206 Was $89.99 *$19.99*

Man's Best Friend (1993)
Scary shocker starring Ally Sheedy as a TV reporter whose investigation of a research facility leads her into discovering Max, a ferocious, genetically enhanced canine. With heightened senses and incredible strength, the dog is the most powerful—and dangerous—creature alive. Can it be stopped? Lance Henriksen, Fredric Lehne co-star. 87 min.
02-2612 Was $19.99 □*$14.99*

Ghoulies 4 (1994)
Those little terrifying critters (oops, sorry—wrong movie) are summoned from the Netherworld during a black magic ritual. Now, all they have to do is get home, but when they meet a dominatrix who happens to be a serial killer, trouble abounds. Peter Liapis, Stacie Randall and Barbara Alyn Woods ("Eden") star. 84 min.
02-2636 *$89.99*

Brainscan (1994)
A teenage computer wizard is thrown into a world of horror when he plays an interactive video game in which he commits all sorts of murderous deeds. He's soon visited by the Trickster, a terrifying, computer-generated killer who forces him to partake in a series of even more frightening games. Edward Furlong, Frank Langella and T. Ryder Smith star. 96 min.
02-2656 Was $19.99 □*$14.99*

The Girl With The Hungry Eyes (1994)
Horror and hot sexual interludes highlight this steamy shocker about a gorgeous model who kills herself in a Miami hotel room in the 1930s, but returns to life 60 years later as a vampire when the hotel is about to be demolished. Using her amazing body and stunning looks, she searches Miami for new victims and fresh blood. Christina Fulton, Isaac Turner star. 85 min.
02-2761 □*$89.99*

Bats (1999)
Fans of "nature run amok" chillers will find this one right up their belfry, as the residents of a small West Texas town find themselves under attack by hordes of flying predators. It's up to sheriff Lou Diamond Phillips and researchers Dina Meyer and Leon to find out what (or who) is turning the animals "batty" and how to stop them. 91 min.
02-3409 Was $99.99 □*$14.99*

The Vampire Conspiracy (1997)
A group of college sorority sisters are in big trouble during "Hell Week": they've been picked to become baby-breeding sex slaves for a group of cyber-vampires looking to rule the world. And you thought panty raids were trouble! Shocks and sexy naked ladies such as Heather Lemire and Jasmine Jean are showcased in this erotic odyssey. 90 min.
73-9180 *$29.99*

Hideaway (1995)
Jeff Goldblum is an antiques dealer who is brought back from the brink of death after a car accident. After experiencing harrowing hallucinations, Goldblum discovers he's psychically linked to another near-death returnee, a satanic serial killer who seeks his teenage daughter as his next victim. Based on a Dean Koontz novel, this shocker also stars Christine Lahti and Alicia Silverstone. 103 min.
02-2783 Was $19.99 □*$14.99*

In The Mouth Of Madness (1995)
John Carpenter's eerie excursion features Sam Neill as an insurance investigator hired by a Manhattan publisher to locate a popular horror writer who has disappeared. Joining forces with a pretty editor, the investigator finds the small-town setting of the author's novels and encounters fictional terrors that have come to life. Jurgen Prochnow, Julie Carmen, Charlton Heston co-star. 95 min.
02-5055 Was $19.99 □*$14.99*

The Good Son (1993)
Superior shocker starring Macaulay Culkin as the diabolical child with dark secrets and a frightening sadistic streak who terrifies his cousin (Elijah Wood) when he comes to live with him and his unknowing parents. Wendy Crewson, David Morse and Daniel Hugh Kelly co-star. 88 min.
04-2764 Was $89.99 □*$14.99*

Cemetery Man (1993)
Wildly inventive and erotic horror-comedy from Italy's Michele Soavi ("The Church") detailing the unsettling adventures of bored cemetery supervisor Rupert Everett, the simple-minded gravedigger he befriends, and the "customers" who start coming back to life. Everett's morbid world view changes when he falls for a beautiful—and deceased—woman. Francois Hadji-Lazaro, Anna Falchi co-star. AKA: "Dellamorte, Dellamore." 100 min.
04-3390 Was $99.99 □*$29.99*

Campfire Tales (1998)
Four teenagers get into a car wreck on a deserted road and, while they wait for help to arrive, build a fire to stay warm and pass the time by swapping scary stories. But what they don't realize is that the biggest horror of all is yet to come: a killer with a hook is stalking them! Jacinda Barrett (MTV's "The Real World"), Christine Taylor and Ron Livingston star. 103 min.
02-5190 Was $99.99 □*$19.99*

The Vampyr (1992)
Eroticism, fright and song blend in this unusual horror tale from the BBC. Ripley, a bloodsucker trapped in his tomb since 1793, is set free on a London construction site and begins a sinister mission to claim the lives of three girls in three days. Based on composer Heinrich Marschner's 19th-century work, the operatic shocker stars Omar Ebrahim. 115 min.
04-2766 Was $89.99 *$29.99*

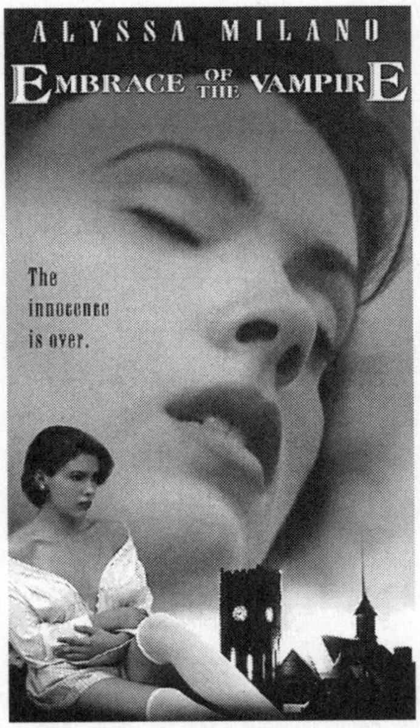
ALYSSA MILANO
EMBRACE OF THE VAMPIRE
The innocence is over.

Embrace Of The Vampire (1995)
Seductive bloodsucker saga with Alyssa Milano as a sexy college student drawn into the erotic world of a handsome vampire who appears in her torrid dreams of forbidden lust. Will she choose her caring, collegiate boyfriend or the kinky demon of the dark? Charlotte Lewis, Martin Kemp and Jennifer Tilly also star. Unrated version; 93 min.
02-5051 Was $19.99 □*$14.99*

I Know What You Did Last Summer (1997)
"Scream" scripter Kevin Williamson turns in another hip horror outing with this spine-tingling suspenser in which four teens involved in a fatal accident toss their victim's body into the sea and agree to keep the events a secret. One year later, though, a mysterious hook-wielding figure has come looking for revenge. Sarah Michelle Gellar, Jennifer Love Hewitt, Ryan Phillippe and Freddie Prinze, Jr. star. 101 min.
02-3155 Was $19.99 □*$14.99*

I Know What You Did Last Summer (Letterboxed Version)
Also available in a theatrical, widescreen format.
02-3210 □*$19.99*

I Still Know What You Did Last Summer (1998)
Just when you thought it was safe to eat Gorton's fish sticks again, the murderous, slicker-sporting hookman is back for revenge, terrorizing college chums Jennifer Love Hewitt and Brandy and their boyfriends in a Caribbean resort during a raging storm. Freddie Prinze, Jr. and Mekhi Phifer co-star in this still-scary shocker that we *know* you'll love. And remember, the capital of Brazil is Brasilia. 100 min.
02-3300 Was $19.99 □*$14.99*

The Addiction (1995)
This eerie, intellectual bloodsucking odyssey from Abel Ferrera ("Bad Lieutenant") tells of a New York philosophy student who is bitten by a female vampire and soon begins preying on the derelicts of Greenwich Village. When her bloodlust grows too great, she seeks help from a fellow vampire. Lili Taylor, Christopher Walken, Annabella Sciorra star. 82 min.
02-8451 Letterboxed *$14.99*

Tales From The Darkside: The Movie (1990)
Creepy horror and laughs anthology-style, written by Stephen King, George Romero and Michael McDowell ("Beetlejuice") and based on the hit TV show. A hit man is hired to kill a murderous cat, an artist marries "the perfect woman," and a college student tries to stop a mummy on the prowl. Christian Slater, David Johansen, Rae Dawn Chong, William Hickey, Julianne Moore and Deborah Harry star. 90 min.
06-1769 *$14.99*

The Craft (1996)
A misfit girl newly enrolled in a Los Angeles high school befriends three other troubled teens and, after showing them she has a knack for casting spells, is welcomed into their secret club dedicated to witchcraft. Soon, the girls are using their powers on a cocky jock, a racist student and others. Robin Tunney, Fairuza Balk, Neve Campbell, Rachel True star. 101 min.
02-2939 Was $19.99 □*$14.99*

The Craft (Letterboxed Version)
Also available in a theatrical, widescreen format.
02-3150 □*$19.99*

Wheels Of Terror (1990)
High-octane horror, as a small town's residents become the moving targets for a murderous, mysterious black sedan. Who, or what, is behind the wheel, and can it be stopped? Joanna Cassidy, Arlen Dean Snyder star. 86 min.
06-1798 □*$79.99*

Nightmare On The 13th Floor (1991)
Strange things are happening at a Victorian hotel. The sealed-off 13th floor holds deadly secrets and may be the key to the horrific events that have frightened resident Michele Greene. With Louise Fletcher and James Brolin. 85 min.
06-1896 *$89.99*

Body Parts (1991)
A frightening horror excursion about a criminal psychologist who loses his arm in a car accident, then receives a new one from a deceased criminal. Soon, the transplanted limb controls the world of the psychologist, leading him into the realm of terror. Jeff Fahey, Brad Dourif and Lindsay Duncan star; written and directed by Eric Red ("The Hitcher"). 88 min.
06-1914 Was $19.99 □*$14.99*

Child Of Darkness, Child Of Light (1991)
A young priest investigating two alleged virgin pregnancies learns the unborn children are the key to an ancient prophecy of the Antichrist and the end of the world. Anthony John Denison, Sela Ward, Brad Davis star. 85 min.
06-1956 *$89.99*

Dust Devil (1993)
A ritualistic, mythical serial killer comes to life and seeks souls in order to become more powerful. While the gruesome murderer is on a rampage, three people's lives intersect. Can they escape the "Dust Devil"? Robert Burke, Chelsea Field and Zakes Mokae star; directed by Richard Stanley ("Hardware"). 87 min.
06-2156 □*$89.99*

The Fury Within (1998)
When the seemingly perfect world of wife and mother Ally Sheedy is threatened by her husband's request for a divorce, a deadly supernatural force overwhelms the family. Chilling tale of suspense co-stars Costas Mandylor, Steve Bastoni. 91 min.
06-2835 □*$69.99*

Temptress (1995)
Photographer Kim Delaney returns from a trip to India with overwhelming sexual energy and strange pictures of the ancient goddess of death, Kali. Is she possessed by Kali's spirit? After a mysterious murder, her boyfriend thinks so, but can he rid her of the spirit without killing her? Chris Sarandon, Corbin Bernsen and Ben Cross co-star. 93 min.
06-2392 Was $89.99 □*$19.99*

The Relic (1997)
First-rate shocker stars Penelope Ann Miller as a feisty biologist working at a Chicago museum that's been the site of a gruesome murder. Sharp detective Tom Sizemore is on the case and, along with Miller, he uncovers Brazilian artifacts which have something to do with the flesh-eating mythical monster wreaking all the havoc. Linda Hunt and James Whitmore also star. 110 min.
06-2605 Was $99.99 □*$14.99*

Twists Of Terror (1998)
A couple in the remote countryside are terrorized by a mysterious pursuer; the victim of a dog attack finds himself in a bizarre hospital; and a love triangle between two playboys and a beautiful woman takes a deadly twist. Jennifer Rubin, Françoise Robertson and Nick Mancuso star in three twisted tales of suspense. 90 min.
06-2836 Was $69.99 □*$14.99*

The Apartment Complex (1999)
Destitute grad student Chad Lowe takes a job as a manager of a creepy Hollywood apartment complex populated by bizarre tenants. Among them are an oversexed psychic, two beautiful stunt actresses who enjoy wrestling with each other, and assorted weirdoes. Lowe is eventually accused of killing the former manager, who is found in the swimming pool. Tobe Hooper directs. 99 min.
06-3002 □*$69.99*

Castle Freak (1995)
The always-outrageous Stuart Gordon ("Re-Animator") turns in a pulse-pounding shocker about a castle in Italy that houses unspeakable horrors—and a frightening monster! A married couple and their young daughter inherit the place and move in, unaware of the terrors they face. Jeffrey Combs, Barbara Crampton and Jonathan Fuller star. Unrated director's cut; 95 min.
06-9000 Was $89.99 *$14.99*

The Vampire Journals (1996)
A contemporary bloodsucking saga that follows the quest of a vampire to destroy the bloodline of the monster who turned him into one of the undead. His ultimate target: the vicious vampire master Ash, who lives in a luxurious sanctuary deep in Eastern Europe. 90 min.
06-9002 Was $89.99 *$14.99*

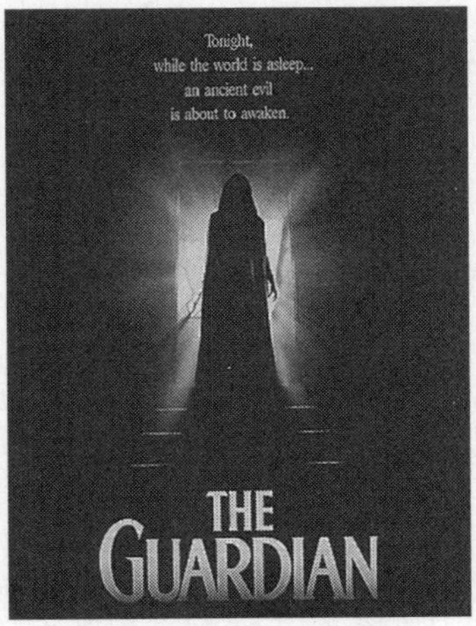
Tonight,
while the world is asleep...
an ancient evil
is about to awaken.
THE GUARDIAN

The Guardian (1990)
"Exorcist" director William Friedkin helmed this terror tale about a young couple who hire a nanny to care for their newborn, unaware that she's part of a nature-worshipping druid cult with a penchant for human sacrifice! Jenny Seagrove, Dwier Brown, Carey Lowell star. 92 min.
07-1652 Letterboxed *$14.99*

The Eighteenth Angel (1998)
From David Seltzer, the author of "The Omen," comes this shocker about a teenage girl who, after her mother's death, is joined by her father when she pursues a modeling career in Italy. Unsettling events soon occur, and eventually the girl learns that a bizarre priest holds the secret to her mother's death. Christopher McDonald, Stanley Tucci, Maximilian Schell and Rachel Leigh Cook star. 90 min.
02-3215 Was $99.99 □*$14.99*

Bleeders (1998)
Centuries of inbreeding have turned a branch of a once-noble French family into a grotesque clan of tunnel-dwelling, blood-drinking mutants. Now their remote island home is being visited by a distant relative and his wife as he searches for his "roots." The bad news is, he's found them; worse news is, *they've* found him! Rutger Hauer, Roy Dupuis star. AKA: "Hemoglobin." 89 min.
83-1260 Was $99.99 *$14.99*

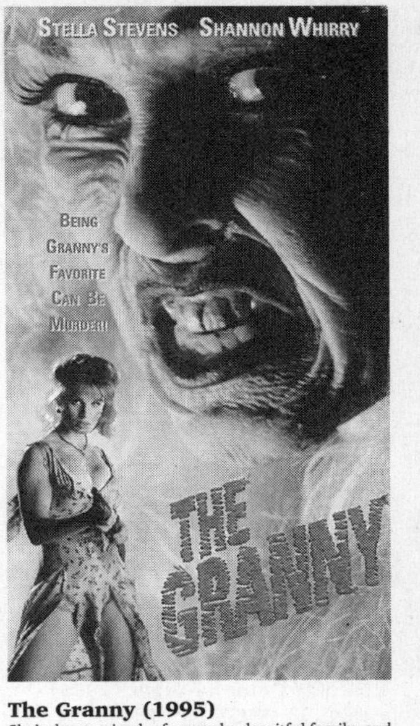
STELLA STEVENS SHANNON WHIRRY
BEING GRANNY'S FAVORITE CAN BE MURDER!
THE GRANNY

The Granny (1995)
She's the matriarch of a greedy, deceitful family, and only her granddaughter truly cares for her. When Granny dies, her clan cheats the granddaughter out of her rightful inheritance, but an ancient potion revives the craggy old lady, who has plans for murderous revenge. Stella Stevens and Shannon Whirry star. 85 min.
19-3712 Was $89.99 *$14.99*

High Desert Kill (1990)
The badlands of New Mexico are the setting for this story about three pals on a hunting expedition who find themselves manipulated in bizarre ways by an alien force. Anthony Geary, Marc Singer and Chuck Connors star. 93 min.
07-1666 *$79.99*

I'm Dangerous Tonight (1990)
A creepy shocker about a college student who turns an ancient Aztec cloak into a dress, then finds that she has unleashed a supernatural power. Mädchen Amick ("Twin Peaks"), Dee Wallace Stone and Anthony Perkins star; Tobe Hooper ("Poltergeist") directs. 92 min.
07-1691 *$79.99*

Strays (1992)
A family moves into a remote country house only to find that the woods around it are filled with untamed cats. Soon, swarms of feral felines begin to threaten their home and their lives in this horrifying thriller with Kathleen Quinlan and Timothy Busfield. 83 min.
07-1885 *$89.99*

Black Magic (1991)
A horrific, black (magic) comedy about a man haunted by his dead cousin. Travelling to South Carolina to conquer his fears, he meets his cousin'g beautiful ex-girlfriend, but gets a warning from the persistent ghost that she may be a witch. Judge Reinhold, Rachel Ward, Anthony LaPaglia star. 94 min.
07-1892 □*$89.99*

Vampire's Embrace (1998)
Creepy shocker in which two beautiful vampire twins, who have been dormant since the 1700s, rise from the dead and attempt to survive in modern-day New York. One of the sisters finds love with a human, but her sibling attempts to stop the relationship. 85 min.
73-9223 *$19.99*

The Haunting Of Seacliff Inn (1995)
A young couple having marital problems purchase a Victorian house and open a bed-and-breakfast in hopes of helping their troubled marriage. Soon, they are haunted by an evil ghost and discover a hidden room with clues to the house's secret history. Ally Sheedy and William R. Moses star. 94 min.
07-2346 □*$89.99*

Killer Tongue (1995)
Outrageous horror yarn tells of Johnny and Candy, a bank-robbing couple with their share of problems: Johnny faces creepy guards while in prison and Candy, well, she has grown a huge, evil tongue after unknowingly eating a piece of comet in her cornflakes. Melinda Clarke, Jason Durr, Robert Englund and Doug Bradley star in this over-the-top terror treat destined for cult status. 97 min.
83-1399 Was $99.99 *$14.99*

The Crying Child (1996)
What starts out as a peaceful vacation at an island cottage turns into a bizarre and otherworldly mystery for a young couple when they hear the sobbing sounds of an unseen child. Chilling suspenser stars Mariel Hemingway, Finola Hughes, Kin Shriner. 93 min.
07-2470 □*$89.99*

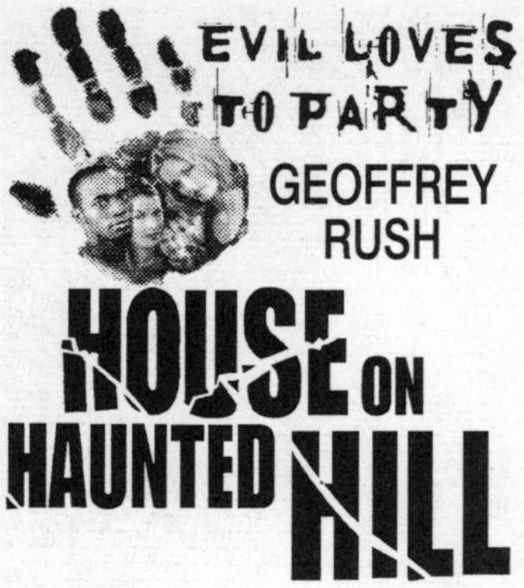

House On Haunted Hill (1999)
In this effects-filled remake of the '50s William Castle thriller, eccentric amusement park owner Geoffrey Rush holds a bizarre birthday party for his wife in an abandoned mental asylum. Five guests are offered $1 million each if they survive a night in the supposedly haunted building, but some sinister forces are out to make sure no one collects. Taye Diggs, Peter Gallagher, Famke Janssen and Chris Kattan also star. 93 min.
19-2962 Was $99.99 □$14.99

Tales From The Crypt Presents Demon Knight (1995)
Join the Crypt Keeper as he hosts the first big-screen installment of the TV fight fave, a tale of the battle between good and evil that is simply "gore-geous." A fiendish fellow called "The Collector" calls up a legion of the living dead to retrieve a mystic key from one of the residents of a run-down New Orleans hotel. Billy Zane, William Sadler, Jada Pinkett star. 92 min.
07-2320 Was $19.99 □$14.99

Tales From The Crypt Presents Bordello Of Blood (1996)
The bloodsucking beauties who ply their trade in this "gorehouse" offer their clients the night of their lives...and then take their lives as payment! It's up to a sarcastic ex-cop to lead the assault against these voluptuous vampires in the second fright feature from the Cryptkeeper. Dennis Miller, Angie Everhart, Erika Eleniak and Corey Feldman star. 87 min.
07-2478 Was $99.99 □$14.99

An American Werewolf In Paris (1997)
In the long-awaited follow-up to "An American Werewolf in London" (were the creatures waiting for the Chunnel to open?), a young man on a European trek with his buddies falls for a beautiful French woman who, unknown to him, carries the curse of the beast. Chills, laughs and amazing transformation effects galore; Tom Everett Scott, Julie Delpy, Vince Vieluf star. 98 min.
11-2244 Was $19.99 □$14.99

Tale Of The Mummy (1998)
A series of grisly murders and a robbery in a London museum lead police detectives to the granddaughter of an archeologist who may know who's behind the incidents. It turns out that the wrapped corpse of an evil, ancient Egyptian priest has been revived, and is now stalking in search of human blood. Jason Scott Lee and Christopher Lee star in Russell Mulcahy's salute to the classic Hammer films. AKA: "Talos the Mummy." 100 min.
11-2345 Was $99.99 □$14.99

The Minion (1998)
Dolph Lundgren plays a medieval Knight Templar sent to modern times to retrieve a key recovered during an archeological dig in New York City. The key, which opens the door to the Antichrist, is also sought by the Antichrist's servant, a ghost known as the Minion. With Françoise Robertson. AKA: "Fallen Knight," "Knight of the Apocalypse." 96 min.
11-2444 □$99.99

Vampire's Seduction (1998)
Ultra-kinky approach to the classic bloodsucking story in which Dracula's lesbian daughter puts Wally Van Helsing into a trance, forcing him to find gorgeous women to replenish the vampire race. Tina Krause, John Fedele and "Scream Queen" Debbie Rochon star. 75 min.
73-9221 $19.99

The Vagrant (1992)
A horror movie tinged with dark humor, this film chronicles the plight of a young executive who discovers that his snazzy new house is also the living quarters for a demented derelict. Soon, the demonic loafer begins playing sick games with his "landlord," and mysterious murders occur. Bill Paxton, Michael Ironside and Marshall Bell star. 91 min.
12-2543 Was $89.99 □$14.99

Haunting Fear (1991)
A woman fears that something spooky is going on...and she's right! Her unfaithful husband conspires with his murderous mistress to make her mad. Fred Olen Ray's erotic horrorthon is based on Edgar Allan Poe's "The Premature Burial" and stars Jan-Michael Vincent, Brinke Stevens and Karen Black (surprise!). 88 min.
15-5200 Was $79.99 $19.99

Fertilize The Blaspheming Bombshell (1991)
In a desolate desert, a group of Satanists search for a bride to bear their leader's child. When a beautiful young woman arrives on the scene, they think they've found the right person, little suspecting she's out to avenge the murder of her sister. Bo Hopkins, Sheila Cann and Robert Tessier star. AKA: "Mark of the Beast," "Triangle of Death."
15-5209 $14.99

Frankenstein (1993)
A superb version of Mary Shelley's horror classic that's quite faithful to the original. Patrick Bergin is Dr. Frankenstein, a demented scientist who artificially gives life to a hideous creature (Randy Quaid). The monster eventually revolts against its creator, attempting to bring to him the same tragedies he experiences. John Mills, Lambert Wilson co-star. 117 min.
18-7454 Was $89.99 □$14.99

Sleepstalker: The Sandman's Last Rites (1995)
A young boy witnesses his parents' murders at the hands of a demented killer known as the Sandman, who is caught and sent to Death Row. Before he is executed, the Sandman makes a pact with a mysterious stranger and is given occult powers to continue his bloody reign. His first target: the now-grown boy. Sinister suspenser stars Michael Harris, Jay Underwood. 102 min.
18-7535 $99.99

From Dusk Till Dawn (1996)
Outrageous horror-action outing, courtesy of director Robert Rodriguez ("Desperado") and screenwriter Quentin Tarantino, stars George Clooney and Tarantino as unbalanced siblings on a Southwest crime spree who take preacher Harvey Keitel and his children hostage. Their odyssey becomes a fight for survival when the sleazy Mexican roadside bar they stop in turns out to be a hangout for vampires. With Salma Hayek, Juliette Lewis, Cheech Marin and Fred Williamson. 108 min.
11-2023 Was $19.99 □$14.99

From Dusk Till Dawn (Letterboxed Version)
Also available in a theatrical, widescreen format.
11-2157 □$19.99

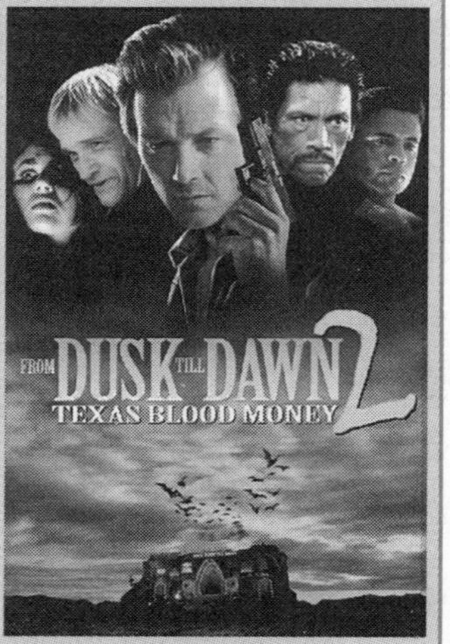

From Dusk Till Dawn 2: Texas Blood Money (1999)
It's more gunplay and bloodsucking in this action-packed sequel to the cult hit thriller, as the partners of the bankrobbing Gecko brothers come looking for them south of the border and get mixed up with a brood of bloodthirsty vampires. Robert Patrick, Bruce Campbell, Bo Hopkins and Tiffani-Amber Thiessen star. 88 min.
11-2305 Was $19.99 □$14.99

From Dusk Till Dawn 3: The Hangman's Daughter (1999)
The third entry in the popular horror series is a prequel set in the war-torn Mexican frontier of the early 1900s. American writer Ambrose Bierce and a group of stagecoach passengers get mixed up with bandits, a sadistic hangman and his rebellious child, and a tavern with an unusual night-time clientele. Sonia Braga, Michael Parks, Tamuera Morrison, Rebecca Gayheart and Danny Trejo star. 94 min.
11-2375 Was $99.99 □$14.99

Full Tilt Boogie (1997)
This revealing, behind-the-scenes look at the production of the 1996 cult horror-thriller "From Dusk Till Dawn" follows the film's 10-week shoot in the middle of the California desert. Director Robert Rodriguez, writer/co-star Quentin Tarantino, and actors George Clooney, Harvey Keitel and Juliette Lewis are featured joking around and talking candidly about their careers and the movie. 100 min.
11-2477 □$99.99

Psycho: Special Edition (1998)
Director Gus Van Sant's audacious, near shot-for-shot remake of the classic Hitchcock shocker stars Anne Heche as Marion Crane, a woman who embezzles $400,000 from her employer, but finds terror in the shower of her room at the Bates Motel, run by the eccentric Norman Bates (Vince Vaughn). William H. Macy, Viggo Mortensen and Julianne Moore also star. Special edition includes a "making of" documentary. 104 min.
07-2753 Was $99.99 □$14.99

Trapped Alive (1993)
Spine-tingling shocker about two young women whose trip to a Christmas party is interrupted by three escaped convicts who abduct them in their car. The quintet crashes down a deserted mine, where an unknown, unseen horror pursues them as they attempt to escape. Alex Kubik, Elizabeth Kent and Cameron Mitchell star. 92 min.
16-9145 $14.99

Quest For The Lost City (1990)
Horror and adventure are mixed in this north-of-the-border thriller, as a young boy uses a map left to him by his late archeologist father to locate an underground lost city. On the lad's trail are some murderous cultists and the mysterious "Zap Rowsdower." With Christian Malcom, Bruce Mitchell, Shane Marceau. AKA: "The Final Sacrifice." 90 min.
16-9154 $14.99

The Ghost Brigade (1994)
During the Civil War, a Confederate colonel and a Union captain join forces with a beautiful runaway slave to combat a brigade of ghostly soldiers wreaking havoc. Action, thrills and horror mix in this unusual thriller starring Corbin Bernsen, Adrian Pasdar, Martin Sheen and Cynda Williams. 80 min.
18-7542 Was $89.99 □$14.99

Ripper Man (1996)
A former cop and amateur hypnotist is suspected of being a serial killer known as "Ripper Man," whose murders are similar to those of Jack the Ripper. Since no one will believe the ex-policeman, he must find the killer and stop his reign of terror to clear his name. Mike Norris, Timothy Bottoms and Charles Napier star. 93 min.
18-7727 Was $99.99 $14.99

Primal Rage (1990)
Bo Svenson and Patrick Lowe star in this terrifying thriller about a horrifying experiment gone awry. It seems that some of the students on the college campus have been transformed into ruthless killers. This frat pack is out for blood! 91 min.
19-1815 Was $19.99 $14.99

Midnight Cabaret (1990)
What use is dying alone in your room? Come to the Cabaret, ol' chum, where a beautiful nightclub dancer encounters a real demon and brutal murders after she partakes in a satanic stage performance. Laura Harrington, Michael Des Barres, Thom Matthews and Lisa Hart Carroll star. 94 min.
19-1817 $19.99

Innocent Blood (1992)
This erotic horror-comedy from John Landis could be called "A European Bloodsucker in Pittsburgh." Anne Parillaud ("La Femme Nikita") plays a sexy vampire who drains the blood of mob boss Robert Loggia, who in turn returns from the dead to indoctrinate his fellow hoods into the vampiric underworld. Anthony LaPaglia, Don Rickles co-star. 113 min.
19-2034 Was $19.99 □$14.99

Mr. Stitch (1995)
A modern-day "Frankenstein" story starring Rutger Hauer as a diabolical doctor who creates a creature from different corpses' body parts. Possessed of incredible intelligence and superior strength, the creature is haunted by the disturbing memories of its different donors. Wil Wheaton, Nia Peebles co-star; directed by "Pulp Fiction" co-scripter Roger Avary. 98 min.
19-3918 $89.99

Immortal Sins (1991)
A couple inherits a Spanish castle but are unaware of the horrors that await them there. The husband is soon seduced by a woman insisting she's his distant cousin. Little does he know that the woman is really a demon fulfilling a centuries-old curse. Cliff De Young, Maryam D'Abo and Shari Shattuck star. 90 min.
21-9006 Was $89.99 $14.99

Confessions Of A Serial Killer (1992)
Gruesome thriller based on the confessions of Henry Lee Lucas that delves into the world of one of the most notorious mass murderers in history. The killer, here named Daniel Ray Hawkins, recounts his horrifying deeds up to his capture by the Texas Rangers. Dennis Hill and Robert A. Burns star. 80 min.
21-9015 $89.99

To Sleep With A Vampire (1992)
A nightstalking bloodsucker eager to learn about daytime life in the mortal world teams with a gorgeous stripper seeking her son, who lives with her estranged husband. Their shared misery creates an erotic bond that can turn deadly at any time. With Scott Valentine and the lovely Charlie Spradling ("Meridian"), who has some revealing nude scenes. 81 min.
21-9025 Was $89.99 $14.99

Evil Clutch (1991)
This horror-comedy offers campy thrills and gore galore as it tells the story of a sadistic demon living within a seductive young woman. When the demon needs blood, look out! A diabolical descent into the world of horror, not for the squeamish! 88 min.
15-5223 Was $79.99 $14.99

The Prophecy (1995)
An unusual shocker starring Christopher Walken as an evil angel Gabriel, whose jealousy over God's interest in humans leads him to instigate a war on Earth. Trying to stop him are good angels, led by Simon (Eric Stoltz), a detective who once studied for the priesthood, and a schoolteacher. With Elias Koteas, Virginia Madsen and Amanda Plummer. AKA: "God's Army." 97 min.
11-1966 Was $19.99 □$14.99

The Prophecy II (1997)
Christopher Walken returns as Gabriel, the diabolical angel out to kill nurse Jennifer Beals, whose unborn child, fathered by a rival angel, is destined to save Earth from a coming "holy war." Russell Wong, Eric Roberts and Glenn Danzig also star in this theological terror tale. 83 min.
11-2204 Was $19.99 □$14.99

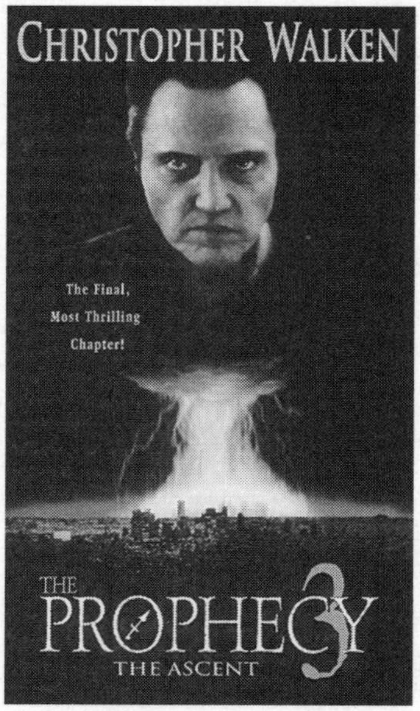

The Prophecy 3: The Ascent (1999)
The third seraphic shocker finds Gabriel (Christopher Walken) once again fighting "on the side of the angels," as he tries to defend the half-human Danyael from angel of genocide Pyriel, who is out to destroy the world. Kayren Butler, Vincent Spano, Scott Cleverdon also star. 84 min.
11-2402 Was $99.99 □$14.99

Last Gasp (1995)
When a man inherits the spirit of an Indian chieftain, he soon is transformed into a killer seeking human flesh. This terror tale stars Robert Patrick and Joanna Pacula. 90 min.
19-3759 $89.99

Demon Possessed (1993)
After a college student is injured in a snowmobile accident, he and his cronies take refuge in a deserted children's camp once run by a mysterious cult. A session with a Ouija board unleashes a demonic spirit who takes over the injured youth's body for its own sinister purposes. With Dawn Laurrie and Eve Montgomery. 97 min.
16-9126 $14.99

Savage Lust (1992)
It's a bloodlust that lures three couples into a rundown mansion one dark, stormy night, and that savage lust, born from a violent crime years earlier, will reach out from beyond the grave to claim this new collection of victims. Brutal and graphic shocker stars Jennifer Delora, William Russell. 90 min.
16-9129 $14.99

Project Vampire (1993)
A vengeance-seeking vampire plans to dominate the world through a diabolical scheme in which no mortals will be spared. Can anyone stop this bloodsucker with an attitude? Brian Knudson, Mary-Louise Gemmill, Christopher Cho star. 92 min.
16-9140 Was $19.99 $14.99

Dracula Rising (1993)
A woman who is haunted by visions from an ancient past travels to Europe and discovers the source of her fears: 500 years ago, she was burned at the stake. She then encounters Vlad Dracula, who recognizes her as the reincarnation of his long-lost love. Christopher Atkins and Stacey Travis star in this Roger Corman production. 85 min.
21-9028 Was $89.99 $14.99

Vampire Centerfolds (1997)
A young college cheerleader journeys to Hollywood, where she lands a part in a vampire film featuring a group of gorgeous actresses whom she eventually discovers are being transformed into sex-obsessed bloodsuckers. Elaine Juliette Williamson and Liddy Roley star in this kinky, nudity-filled shocker. Unrated director's cut edition; 135 min.
73-9178 $39.99

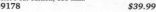

Carrie (1976)
The classic horror film from director Brian DePalma and writer Stephen King stars Sissy Spacek as a tormented high school student who learns she has psychic powers, and uses them in a bloody campaign of vengeance. Also stars Nancy Allen, John Travolta, P.J. Soles and Piper Laurie. 97 min.
12-1820　　Was $19.99　　☐*$14.99*

Carrie (Letterboxed Version)
Also available in a theatrical, widescreen format.
12-3175　　　　　　　　　　☐*$14.99*

Salem's Lot: The Miniseries (1979)
A writer returns to the small New England town where he grew up and soon finds the people there are threatened by a sinister undead presence that has claimed the town as its own. Stephen King's chilling novel is effectively brought to life by director Tobe Hooper. David Soul, Bonnie Bedelia, Lance Kerwin, Ed Flanders and James Mason star. 185 min.
19-2041　　Was $29.99　　　　*$24.99*

Salem's Lot: The Movie
The Stephen King shocker is also available in its European theatrical version, featuring scenes too violent for American TV. 111 min.
19-1307　　　　　　　　　　*$14.99*

Creepshow (1982)
George A. Romero and Stephen King team up for this series of frightening tales told in the style of the old E.C. comics. You'll see terrifying monsters, icky bugs, sadistic revenge, outer space goo. Hal Holbrook, Leslie Nielsen, E.G. Marshall, Ted Danson star. 120 min.
19-1241　　Was $19.99　　　　*$14.99*

Creepshow 2 (1987)
George Romero and Stephen King team once more for a new terrifying trilogy of tales! A wooden Indian out for vengeance, a man-eating slime rising from a lake, a hit-and-run victim that won't stay dead...they're waiting for you! George Kennedy, Dorothy Lamour, Lois Chiles star. 87 min.
70-1172　　　　　　　　　　☐*$14.99*

Christine (1983)
She's a 1958 Plymouth with jealousy and evil under her hood, and when Christine becomes a nerdish teen's driving obsession, she helps him get back at his tormentors. Keith Gordon, Alexandra Paul, Harry Dean Stanton star in this John Carpenter shocker, based on Stephen King's best-seller. 116 min.
02-1307　　　　　　　　　　☐*$14.99*

The Dead Zone (1983)
Suspense thriller by Stephen King and David Cronenberg about a man who awakens from a coma to discover he has the ability to see into the future. Christopher Walken stars as the troubled, gifted man. Brooke Adams, Martin Sheen, Tom Skerritt. 103 min.
06-1206　　　　　　　　　　*$14.99*

Cujo (1983)
Another dog-gone terrifying film from Stephen King, as a rabid St. Bernard traps a woman and her young son in their damaged car, refusing to let them escape and forcing them to fight to stay alive. Dee Wallace, Danny Pintauro, Ed Lauter star. 95 min.
14-3386　　　　　　　　　　*$14.99*

Children Of The Corn (1983)
A creepy adaptation of Stephen King's short story stars Linda Hamilton and Peter Horton as two travellers who land in a small Nebraska town inhabited by kids who sacrifice adults to "he who walks behind the rows." 93 min.
53-1185　　　　　　　　　　*$14.99*

Firestarter (1984)
From the pen of Stephen King comes this journey into supernatural terror. Drew Barrymore is a cute, young girl with a special gift—the ability to set things on fire, thanks to a haywire scientific experiment. Martin Sheen, George C. Scott, Louise Fletcher also star. 115 min.
07-1226　　Was $19.99　　☐*$14.99*

Cat's Eye

Stephen King

Stephen King's Nightshift Collection: The Woman In The Room/The Boogeyman (1984)
An attorney, tired of caring for his terminally ill mother, is convinced by a death row client to "help" her along to death; while a father's demand that his children overcome their fear of a "boogeyman" in the closet leads to terror, in two short tales based on stories by King. 58 min.
14-3420　　　　　　　　　　*$14.99*

Stephen King's Silver Bullet (1985)
A small town is terrorized by a series of grisly murders, and two young people are convinced that the killer is a werewolf. Chilling tale from fright fave King stars Gary Busey, Cory Haim, Megan Follows. 95 min.
06-1327　　　　　　　　　　☐*$14.99*

Cat's Eye (1985)
A trio of horror tales laced with laughs from monster maven Stephen King. An unusual "aversion therapy" for smokers, a nighttime stroll atop a 30-story building and a child's toy troll that becomes real are the ingredients for scares. James Woods, Alan King, Robert Hays and Drew Barrymore star. 93 min.
12-1996　　　　　　　　　　☐*$14.99*

Stephen King's Silver Bullet (1985)
A small town is terrorized by a series of grisly murders, and two young people are convinced that the killer is a werewolf. Chilling tale from fright fave King stars Gary Busey, Cory Haim, Megan Follows. 95 min.
06-1327　　　　　　　　　　☐*$14.99*

Maximum Overdrive (1986)
A highway truck stop learns the true meaning of "heavy metal" when mysterious forces bring all the vehicles and machinery in the area to life and fill them with a lust for blood. Written and directed by Stephen King, the fast-paced thriller stars Emilio Estevez, Pat Hingle and Yeardly Smith; look quickly for Marla Maples. 97 min.
40-1234　　Was $19.99　　☐*$12.99*

Trucks (1997)
Based on the same Stephen King short story that inspired 1986's "Maximum Overdrive," this high-octane thriller is set in a small town located near the infamous "Area 51." The residents are suddenly cut off from civilization when a convoy of mysterious, driverless trucks take over the roads. With Timothy Busfield and Brenda Bakke. 99 min.
68-1893　　Was $99.99　　☐*$14.99*

Pet Sematary (1989)
The man who's put more scares into people than the I.R.S., Stephen King, adapted his own best-seller about a mysterious Indian burial ground with resurrective powers, and how one family's desperate decision leads to a terrifying return. Dale Midkiff, Fred Gwynne, Denise Crosby star. 102 min.
06-1680　　　　　　　　　　☐*$14.99*

Pet Sematary (1989)
The man who's put more scares into people than the I.R.S., Stephen King, adapted his own best-seller about a mysterious Indian burial ground with resurrective powers, and how one family's desperate decision leads to a terrifying return. Dale Midkiff, Fred Gwynne, Denise Crosby star. 102 min.
06-1680　　　　　　　　　　☐*$14.99*

Misery (1990)
Nail-biting thriller from Stephen King's best-selling novel, as a successful author (James Caan) is rescued from a car crash in the woods by his number-one fan, a whacked-out nurse (Oscar-winner Kathy Bates) with a strange take on hero worship. Richard Farnsworth, Lauren Bacall also star; directed by Rob Reiner and scripted by William Goldman. 104 min.
02-5002　　Was $89.99　　☐*$14.99*

Graveyard Shift (1990)
From the chillingly prolific pen of Stephen King comes this terrifying tale about a small town where the biggest employer is a mill that keeps hiring workers...and losing them to whatever inhabits the basement level. Stephen Macht, David Andrews, Brad Dourif star. 87 min.
06-1828　　　　　　　　　　☐*$14.99*

Stephen King's It (1990)
Seven childhood friends return to the New England town where they grew up in order to stop an evil force that threatened them years earlier and has returned to renew its murderous ways. Terrifying adaptation of King's best-selling shocker stars Harry Anderson, John Ritter, Richard Thomas, Annette O'Toole and Tim Curry as Pennywise the clown. 193 min.
19-2032　　Was $29.99　　☐*$24.99*

Stephen King's Golden Years (1991)
A lab experiment backfires, and an elderly janitor caught in the explosion receives the "gift" of slowly growing younger. Now he must run for his newly-extended life from the government and corporation officials who want to learn his secret...at any cost! This special edition of Stephen King's suspenseful TV series includes the never-broadcast ending. Keith Szarabajka, Frances Sternhagen, Ed Lauter star. 232 min.
14-3295　　Was $24.99　　　　*$14.99*

Sometimes They Come Back (1991)
In this Stephen King terror tale, Tim Matheson returns to teach in his hometown after a 20-year absence. But the horrifying memories of the past begin haunting him, and he comes face-to-face with a gang of hoods who were killed in a car crash with his brother. Robert Rusler, Brooke Adams and William Sanderson co-star. 97 min.
68-1243　　　　　　　　　　☐*$14.99*

Stephen King's Sleepwalkers (1992)
In his first film written directly for the screen, King tells the story of a teenage boy and his beautiful mother who appear perfectly normal, but turn into catlike demons called "sleepwalkers" at night. State-of-the-art shock effects highlight this diabolical and erotic thriller starring Alice Krige, Brian Krause and Mädchen Amick. 89 min.
02-2281　　Was $19.99　　☐*$14.99*

The Tommyknockers (1993)
Stephen King's hit book is the basis for this fright film starring Jimmy Smits and Marg Helgenberger as residents of the New England town of Haven who discover a strange object in the nearby woods. The object's unearthly powers soon threaten the town's residents. John Ashton, Joanna Cassidy and Traci Lords also star. Theatrical version; 120 min.
68-1277　　Was $89.99　　☐*$12.99*

The Tommyknockers (Full-Length Version)
Also available in its original four-part version, as seen on TV. 168 min.
68-1355　　Was $89.99　　☐*$14.99*

The Dark Half (1993)
In George A. Romero's terrifying adaptation of Stephen King's shocker, Timothy Hutton plays a college professor who also writes pulp chillers under a nom de plume in his spare time. When Hutton retires his alter ego after penning a serious novel, the sinister pseudonym begins taking over his body. Amy Madigan, Julie Harris and Michael Rooker also star. 121 min.
73-1135　　Was $19.99　　☐*$14.99*

The Stand (1994)
"The end of the world is just the beginning" in the stunning TV mini-series based on Stephen King's apocalyptic best-seller. A biological warfare experiment goes awry, wiping out nearly all of the world's population, and the remaining survivors are drawn by unknown forces towards the ultimate showdown between the powers of good and evil. Gary Sinise, Molly Ringwald, Jamey Sheridan, Ruby Dee, Miguel Ferrer, Laura San Giacomo and Rob Lowe head the cast in this epic fantasy, available here in a deluxe six-hour, four-tape set.
14-3427　　Was $99.99　　　　*$39.99*

Dolores Claiborne (1995)
Creepy adaptation of Stephen King's novel starring Kathy Bates as the title character, a Maine woman suspected of killing her employer. When estranged daughter Jennifer Jason Leigh returns to Bates' home, she begins questioning the events that led to the death of the father she adored 15 years earlier. Christopher Plummer, Judy Parfitt also star. 131 min.
02-2804　　Was $19.99　　☐*$14.99*

Dolores Claiborne (Letterboxed Version)
Also available in a theatrical, widescreen format.
02-2822　　　　　　　　　　☐*$19.99*

The Mangler (1995)
Director/co-scripter Tobe Hooper ("Poltergeist") adapts Stephen King's short story about a small town's industrial laundry and the lethal machine inside it that seems to have a thirst for human blood. Robert Englund is the sinister businessman who knows "The Mangler's" dark secret; with Ted Levine. Unrated director's cut; 106 min.
02-5057　　Was $19.99　　☐*$14.99*

Stephen King's The Langoliers (1995)
In this eerie adaptation of Stephen King's novella, 10 passengers on a nighttime transcontinental flight awaken to discover that the rest of the plane's passengers and crew have disappeared and no one on the ground answers their distress calls. Dean Stockwell, David Morse, Patricia Wettig and Bronson Pinchot star. 180 min.
63-1772　　　　　　　　　　☐*$14.99*

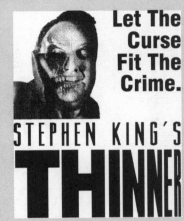
Let The Curse Fit The Crime.
STEPHEN KING'S THINNER

Stephen King's Thinner (1996)
Setting his sights on weight-obsessed America, the ever-prolific King penned this chiller about an obese attorney who hits and kills a Gypsy woman with his car. Cleared of any wrongdoing, he is cursed by the woman's father and begins dropping pounds...and dropping...and dropping, until he must gorge himself to stay alive. Robert John Burke, Michael Constantine, Joe Mantegna, Kari Wuhrer and Joie Lenz star. 92 min.
63-1869　　Was $99.99　　☐*$14.99*

Stephen King's Thinner (Letterboxed Version)
Also available in a theatrical, widescreen format.
63-1881　　　　　　　　　　*$14.99*

The Night Flier (1997)
Terror takes to the skies in this chilling rendition of the short story by Stephen King. Rival tabloid reporters Miguel Ferrer and Julie Entwisle investigate reports of a string of gruesome murders at remote airfields—murders that seem to be the work of a vampire who uses a plane to travel to each "refueling stop." With Dan Monahan, Merton H. Moss. 97 min.
44-2163　　Was $99.99　　☐*$14.99*

Storm Of The Century (1999)
Stephen King's bloody blizzard epic is set on an island off the coast of Maine where the residents must face twin evils: a devastating snowstorm and the arrival of a murderous stranger with psychic powers and a deadly agenda. Trying to stop the killer is Timothy Daly as a butcher who doubles as the town's lawman. With Colm Feore, Debrah Farentino. 248 min.
68-1921　　Was $79.99　　　　*$24.99*

Please see our index for these other Stephen King titles: *Apt Pupil • The Green Mile • The Running Man • The Shawshank Redemption • The Shining • Stand By Me • Tales From The Darkside: The Movie*

Tobe Hooper's Night Terrors (1993)
The director of "Poltergeist" and "The Texas Chainsaw Massacre" unleashes his most diabolical horror entry yet, as Robert Englund stars as the Marquis De Sade, evil practitioner of depravity. The Marquis returns from the past to terrorize a woman forced into a creepy cult devoted to him. With Zoe Trilling, William Finley. 98 min.
19-7100 Was $89.99 ❏*$19.99*

Arachnophobia (1990)
Who said spiders have to be the size of tractor-trailers to be scary? When a small California town is overrun by the lethal offspring of a South American spider, only the new local doctor (Jeff Daniels) and a Rambo-esque exterminator (John Goodman) can save the day in this hit "thrill-omedy." With Harley Jane Kozak, Julian Sands. 109 min.
11-1543 ❏*$19.99*

Demon Keeper (1994)
A con artist who uses the occult for swindling people is caught by a supernatural investigator and put on the spot during a seance. Forced to conjure a real spirit, he accidentally brings forth an evil demon with destructive powers. Edward Albert, Dirk Benedict star. 90 min.
21-9057 Was $89.99 *$14.99*

Watchers II (1990)
This sequel to the hit scare-a-thon features Marc Singer as an AWOL Marine who is befriended by a super-intelligent golden retriever that can communicate with him. The canine leads him to an animal psychologist, then attempts to warn both of them of a monstrous genetic mutation on the rampage. Tracy Scoggins and Jonathan Farwell also star. 101 min.
27-6681 Was $19.99 *$14.99*

Watchers 3 (1994)
The jungles of South America provide the backdrop for this second sequel to Dean Koontz's best-seller. A scientific experiment produces a golden retriever named Einstein with a 175 IQ and a monstrous creature known as "The Outsider." When the ferocious monster gets loose in the jungle, the government enlists a group of former military convicts to join Einstein to try to capture it. Wings Hauser stars.
21-9075 Was $89.99 *$14.99*

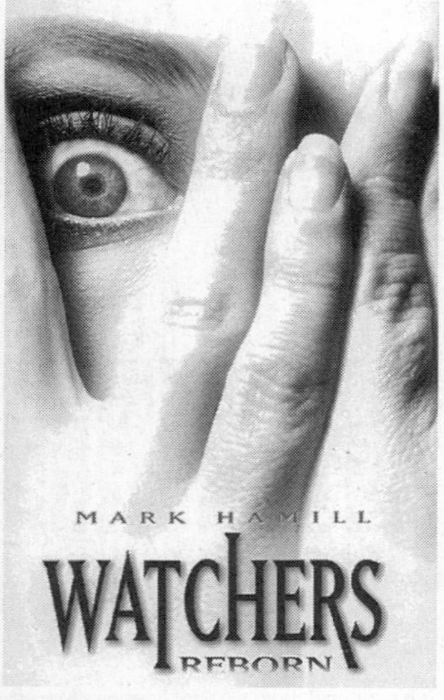

Watchers Reborn (1998)
When his partner is gruesomely murdered, Detective Jack Murphy discovers that the only clue is a golden retriever. Joining forces with a female doctor, Murphy discovers that the pooch is a super-intelligent dog has been programmed to track down a killing machine known as the Outsider. Now, dog and humans must stop him. Mark Hamill, Lisa Wilcox and Lou Rawls star. 83 min.
21-9160 Was $59.99 *$14.99*

Rattled (1996)
A huge den of rattlesnakes attack a peaceful community and a family finds their lives threatened. This is one thriller that's sure to rattle you! With William Katt, Shanna Reed, Ed Lauter and Bibi Besch. 90 min.
07-2423 ❏*$99.99*

Blood Song (1994)
A beautiful woman discovers an unfinished symphony in an antique piano and hires a dashing composer to complete it. As the composer attempts to finish the work, murder, ghostly appearances and other strange goings-on occur. Ben Cross, Jennifer Burns and Beverly Garland star in this Gothic shocker. AKA: "Haunted Symphony." 100 min.
21-9071 Was $99.99 *$14.99*

Club Vampire (1998)
From Andy Ruben of "Stripped to Kill" fame comes this sensual bloodsucking story set at Club Vampire, a not-so gracious oasis where vampires draw unsuspecting prey into the purgatory of the undead. John Savage, Starr Andreeff and Ross Malinger star. 90 min.
21-9171 *$59.99*

Night Hunter (1996)
Kickboxing sensation Don "The Dragon" Wilson is the son of vampire hunters who fell victim to the ageless bloodsuckers. Armed with an Uzi and helped by a tabloid reporter, Wilson seeks revenge on the fanged creeps, who have taken such human jobs as investment bankers to disguise their nefarious ways. With Maria Ford, Melanie Smith. 86 min.
21-9112 Was $99.99 *$14.99*

The Death Artist (1996)
Busboy and would-be sculptor Walter Paisley accidentally kills someone, then hides the body by sculpting over it. Soon, he's the talk of the art world, but the only way to find new subjects is to murder more people. This remake of the Roger Corman cult fave "A Bucket of Blood" stars Anthony Michael Hall, Justine Bateman and Shadoe Stevens. 80 min.
21-9127 Was $99.99 *$14.99*

Spectre (1997)
Haunting horror yarn in which a family moves to an old mansion in Ireland only to discover the place is inhabited by the ghost of a young girl. After a priest and clairvoyant die mysteriously, the family finds the girl's body and attempts to give her a proper burial. Then the terror really begins. Greg Evigan and Alexandra Paul star. 83 min.
21-9135 *$99.99*

The Haunted Sea (1997)
The captain of a steamer, his crew and a young scholar board an abandoned ship where they discover ancient Aztec figurines once stolen by Spanish conquistadors. After discovering that the ship's captain has died, the group must fend off spirits who have inhabited the treasure. James Brolin, Joanna Pacula and Krista Allen star. 74 min.
21-9145 *$59.99*

Knocking On Death's Door (1999)
Creepy haunted house shocker about two paranormal scientists who attempt to document the existence of ghosts in Hillside House in New England. Among the spirits they encounter is one of a murdered young boy, and they set out to uncover the facts behind his death. David Carradine, Brian Bloom and Kimberly Rowe star. 92 min.
21-9185 *$59.99*

The Haunting Of Hell House (1999)
A Henry James story is the basis for this horror yarn starring Michael York as a professor haunted by the ghost of his late daughter in a spooky, haunted house. Andrew Bowen and Claudia Christian, Aideen O'Donnell also star. AKA: "Henry James' The Haunted Rental." 88 min.
21-9195 *$59.99*

Blood & Donuts (1996)
Horror and black comedy mix in this tale of a vampire who awakens from a 25-year sleep and heads to a local donut shop in search of a late-night "snack," only to wind up getting involved in the personal lives of a waitress and a cab driver. Gordon Currie, Justin Louis, Helene Clarkson star, with a special appearance by David Cronenberg. 89 min.
27-6994 Was $99.99 ❏*$14.99*

Cupid (1996)
"Cupid...draw back your bow...and kill whomever stands in your way!" That's what happens when a handsome man's obsession over a beautiful woman—his perfect woman—gets the best of him. While she is smitten with him, too, some people stand in their way, including the woman's wild sister, her ex-boyfriend and his unpredictable sister. Zack Galligan, Ashley Laurence. 94 min.
27-7006 Was $99.99 ❏*$14.99*

Spirit Lost (1996)
After moving into a 200-year-old seaside house, a would-be painter and his beautiful wife are lured into a bizarre tale of obsessive love from beyond the grave, thanks to the ghost of an ex-lover of the home's builder, in this sinister suspenser. Leon, Regina Taylor, Cynda Williams. 90 min.
27-7007 Was $99.99 ❏*$14.99*

Bram Stoker's Burial Of The Rats (1996)
The author of "Dracula" takes center stage in this Roger Corman-produced thriller in which Stoker is kidnapped by two kinky female outlaws and taken to a bizarre, woman-run society where inhabitants worship rats, hate men and display dazzling swordsmanship. Stoker eventually risks his life by falling in love with one of his captors. With Adrienne Barbeau, Maria Ford. 85 min.
21-9114 Was $99.99 *$14.99*

The Clown At Midnight (1998)
Midnight....and the kiddies are screaming! The college kiddies, that is! A group of students get together to restore a crumbling opera house, and soon they start turning up dead. Who is behind the killings? Do they have a link to a past murder at the theater? Scream, sing, do whatever you can to get out of the opera, Doc! With Christopher Plummer, Margot Kidder, James Duval. 91 min.
27-7103 Was $89.99 ❏*$14.99*

DVD VIDEO
ASK ABOUT OUR GIANT DVD CATALOG!

The Curse Of The Blair Witch (1999)
What really happened in Maryland's Black Forest Hills in 1994? This cable TV documentary that kick-started the "Blair Witch" phenomenon offers insight into the mystery—and the terrifying legend behind it—through interviews with a historical expert, townspeople, and friends and family of the missing film students. 44 min.
27-7136 *$14.99*

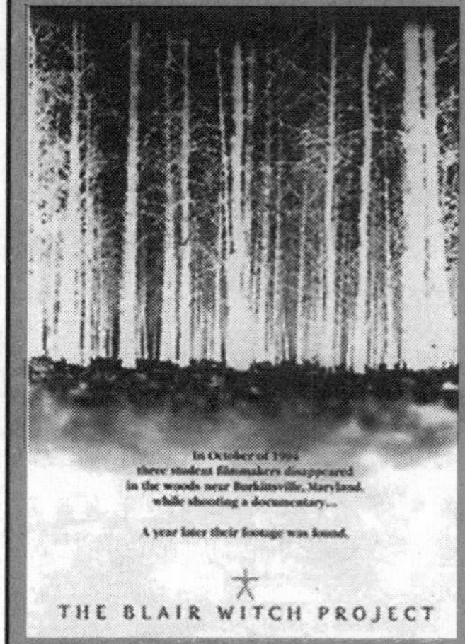

The Blair Witch Project (1999)
The ultra-scary, low-budget horror hit that traces the disappearance of three college students in rural Maryland in 1994 while filming a documentary about the region's fabled Blair Witch. What unfolds, through the surviving footage found of their expedition, is a series of unsettling experiences that become more frightening the more the trio learn and the further they go. With Heather Donohue, Michael Williams and Joshua Leonard. Video version includes footage not shown in theaters. 87 min.
27-7138 Was $19.99 ❏*$14.99*

The Blair Witch Two-Pack
This set includes the feature "The Blair Witch Project" and the documentary "The Curse of the Blair Witch."
27-7142 Save $10.00! *$19.99*

Head Of The Family (1996)
Demented shocker about the Stackpools, a reclusive family of mutants ruled by their telepathic brother, a huge, disembodied head, who like to kidnap and torture unwary victims. A man and his girlfriend decide to off her annoying hubby by sending him to the Stackpool house. Weird stuff from the Charles Band factory of fun. With J.W. Perra, Blake Bailey and Jacqueline Lovell. 82 min.
75-5010 Was $89.99 *$14.99*

Full Eclipse (1993)
With crime running rampant in Los Angeles of the near future, an elite squad of cops receives a secret serum, giving them enhanced speed and strength, and is charged with cleaning up the streets by any means necessary. Now one officer learns the bizarre secret behind the squad's powers and must choose to stand with them or against them. Action-filled chiller stars Mario Van Peebles, Patsy Kensit, Bruce Payne. Unrated version; 97 min.
44-1958 Was $19.99 *$14.99*

The Coroner (1999)
A mad coroner who doesn't care if his subjects are dead or not before he performs autopsies gets to ply—and enjoy—his diabolical trade. A potential victim is terrorized by the scalpel-slinging, not-so-good doctor, but she'll stop at nothing to stop him from slicing and dicing again! Jane Longenecker and Dean St. Louis star. 79 min.
21-9203 *$49.99*

Disturbed (1990)
Malcolm McDowell plays the sex-obsessed head psychiatrist at a mental hospital. When a beautiful but depressed ex-model is admitted, the not-so-good doctor tries a therapeutic approach that borders on horror. Priscilla Pointer, Geoffrey Lewis and Pamela Gidley co-star. 96 min.
27-6703 *$12.99*

Tales From The Hood (1995)
Creepiness and comedy abound as three black youths are greeted by Mr. Simms, a mortician, when they arrive at his funeral parlor trying to find some lost drugs. Mr. Simms tells them terrifying tales of his clients involving the supernatural and racism, child abuse, gang violence and police brutality. Clarence Williams III, Wings Hauser, David Alan Grier star. 98 min.
44-2001 Was $19.99 ❏*$14.99*

Tales From The Hood (Letterboxed Version)
Also available in a theatrical, widescreen format.
44-2156 Was $19.99 *$14.99*

Strangeland (1998)
From the "twisted" mind of rocker Dee Snider comes a horrific tale of suspense. Snider, who also scripted, stars as a demented hacker named Captain Howdy who lures teens into his basement torture chamber through the Internet. When a policeman's daughter becomes his latest victim, a desperate hunt begins. Kevin Gage, Elizabeth Peña and Robert Englund co-star. 91 min.
27-7106 Was $99.99 ❏*$14.99*

Blood Moon (1991)
The daughter of a Hollywood star and her boyfriend are next on the death list of a murderer whose targets have all been sexually promiscuous college students. Will they find the killer before he finds them, and what role does their biology teacher play in this mystery? Leon Lissek, Christine Amor star. 104 min.
27-6718 *$14.99*

Nightscare (1993)
British actress and model Elizabeth Hurley stars in this shocker in which a renowned neurologist and a top homicide detective try to track down a deranged psycho who's gained bizarre psychic powers by a series of behavior modification experiments. Craig Fairbrass, Keith Allen co-star. AKA: "Bedlam." 89 min.
27-6948 ❏*$12.99*

Ancient Evil: Scream Of The Mummy (1999)
Six young anthropology students discover the remains of an ancient mummy and accidentally unleash his plan to kill all mankind. Russell Richardson, Brenda Blondell and Ariauna Albright star in this shocker. 86 min.
82-5232 *$89.99*

The Willies (1990)
A group of campers gets the heck scared out of them when strange incidents occur at their tent site. Can the hatchet murderer be close? Who puts the millions of bugs in the chubby camper's bed? The answers to these and other questions awaits... With Sean Astin, James Karen, and an appearance by Kirk Cameron. 92 min.
46-5499 Was $89.99 *$12.99*

Beware! Children At Play! (1995)
Grisly shocker about a group of kids living in backwoods country who are mysteriously lured into a cannibalistic cult. Before you can say "Hatfield" or "McCoy," the tikes are carrying out a furious feud with their elders which leads to all sorts of incredibly violent altercations. Unrated version; 90 min.
46-8008 Was $69.99 *$14.99*

Frostbiter (1995)
This chilling shocker tells of a group of hunters on a remote island who mistakenly unleash the wrath of a demonic monster known as the Frostbiter, who has the ability to freeze everything in sight. A Troma release, so you know what you're getting! Ron Asheton, Lori Baker star. AKA: "Wrath of the Wendigo." Unrated, extra-gory version; 93 min.
46-8014 Was $69.99 *$14.99*

Mardi Gras For The Devil (1993)
A satanic serial killer is stalking the streets of New Orleans during the annual festival and a police detective becomes obsessed with stopping the murders. But this killer is possessed by supernatural powers and looking for new souls to sacrifice. Horrific thriller stars Michael Ironside, Robert Davi, Lesley-Anne Down and Margaret Avery. AKA: "Night Trap." 95 min.
46-5564 *$89.99*

Demon Wind (1990)
In the tradition of "Evil Dead" comes this ghoulish terror tale. A teenager and his friends confront a supernatural power that exists in a deserted farmhouse. Eric Larson and Francine Lapenee star. 97 min.
46-5491 Was $89.99 *$12.99*

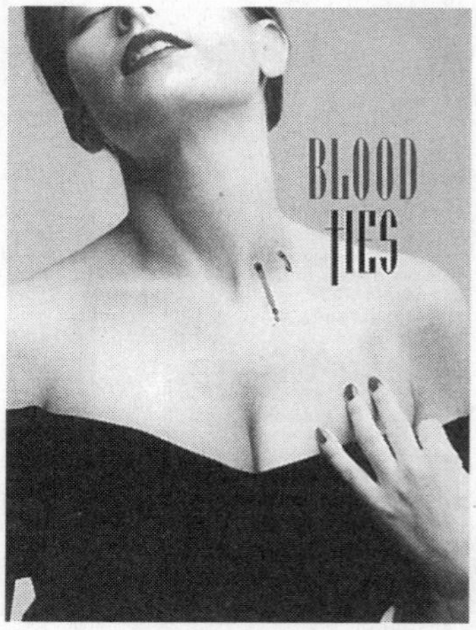

Blood Ties (1993)
The Carpathian family are vampires who have assimilated into society and have controlled their bloodlust. But now they are the ones being hunted and killed, and must fight back to preserve their undead legacy. A stylishly erotic fright film starring Michelle Johnson, Bo Hopkins and Patrick Bauchau; directed by Jim McBride ("The Big Easy"). 84 min.
21-9047 Was $89.99 *$14.99*

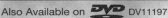
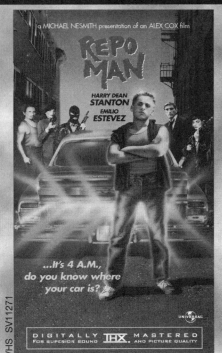

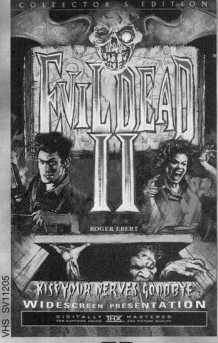

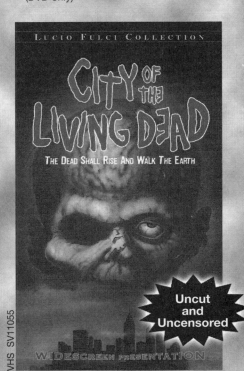

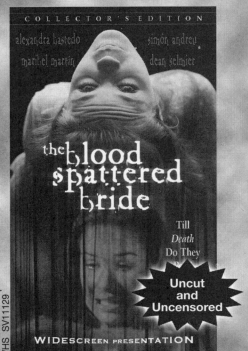

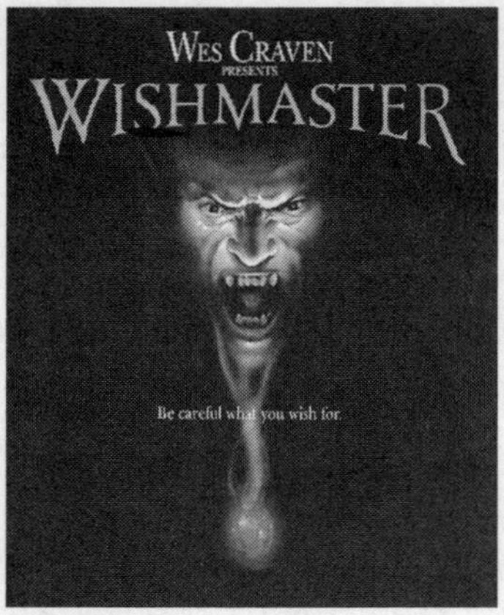
WES CRAVEN
PRESENTS
WISHMASTER
Be careful what you wish for.

Wishmaster (1997)
Your fondest wishes will come true—with a terrifying catch attached—when a not-so-gentle genie is set free from 700 years of captivity and uses his sinister powers on modern-day Los Angeles. Terrifying tale of supernatural horror stars Tammy Lauren, Andrew Divoff, Robert Englund, Tony Todd, Kane Hodder. 90 min.
27-7043 Was $99.99 ❑*$14.99*

Wishmaster 2: Evil Never Dies (1999)
"The Not-So Gentle Genie That Terrorized Los Angeles" is back, this time awakened by a female thief during a robbery and in search of 1001 souls so he can start the apocalypse now and unleash other evil genies on Earth. The quest takes the evil one to Las Vegas, along with the thief and a priest, and "Glitter Gulch" is turned into "Gore Gulch." Andrew Divoff, Holly Fields star. 96 min.
27-7124 Was $99.99 ❑*$14.99*

Paranoia (1998)
Twenty years after her family was brutally murdered by a serial killer, Jana Mercer has isolated herself in a New York City apartment. But her security-tight home may not be enough, because the killer is back—and stalking Jana on the Internet! And you thought dealing with America Online's billing department was scary! Larry Drake, Brigitte Bako and Sally Kirkland star. 87 min.
64-9034 *$99.99*

Modern Vampires (1999)
In this hip horror saga, a community of bloodsuckers living in L.A. finds their existence threatened when one of them, vampire seductress Natasha Gregson Wagner, gains notoriety as the "Hollywood Slasher." Leading ghoul Casper Van Dien tries to help her, while vampire hunter Rod Steiger and his gang-banging crew attempt to destroy the creatures. With Natasha Lyonne. 95 min.
64-9049 *$99.99*

The Ugly (1998)
This stylishly disturbing horror tale from New Zealand tells of a deranged serial killer who agrees to be interviewed in jail by a noted psychiatrist. As he recounts his story, from a tortured childhood to the events that led to his rampage, the doctor is slowly drawn into his psychotic world. Rebecca Hobbs and Paolo Rotondo star in a surprise-filled shocker. Unrated version; 94 min.
68-1897 Was $99.99 ❑*$14.99*

The Eternal (1998)
An American couple whose marriage has degenerated into drinking and arguments tries to set things right with a trip to the wife's family home in Ireland. Once there, however, she is haunted by a sinister family secret and a 2,000-year-old terror. Offbeat chiller stars Alison Elliott, Jared Harris, Christopher Walken. AKA: "Trance." 95 min.
68-1926 ❑*$99.99*

King Cobra (1999)
An experiment by a team of scientists goes haywire and a mutant snake—a mix of African King Cobra and Diamondback Rattler—escapes. Thirty feet long with a desire for human prey, the serpent is heading for a nearby town's annual beerfest. Everyone's in trouble now—even those Budweiser frogs! Pat Morita, Scott Brandon and Hoyt Axton star. 93 min.
68-1931 Was $99.99 ❑*$14.99*

Dean Koontz's Mr. Murder (1999)
Dean Koontz's diabolical thriller is brought to life, as Stephen Baldwin plays a novelist who unknowingly becomes part of an experiment after a genetically manufactured clone is produced from his blood. Seven years after the experiment, the writer learns of the clone—and that it's trained to destroy his family. With Thomas Haden Church, Julie Warner, James Coburn. 132 min.
68-1934 ❑*$99.99*

The Day Of The Beast (1995)
Father Angel, a priest and theological professor, travels to Madrid to fight the devil, whose Christmas Eve arrival he believes will herald the Apocalypse. In need of help for his mission, the kindly holy man recruits a heavy metal slacker and a popular TV psychic to meet evil head-on in this tenacious, darkly humorous terror tale from Spain. 99 min. Dubbed in English.
68-1951 ❑*$69.99*

Kill Me Tomorrow (1999)
The lives of several young people in a small town are disrupted by the appearance of a mysterious new girl who lures away the local hot-shot from his girlfriend. But no one suspects that she's a witch whose sinister thirst for souls leads to seduction, possession and murder. Suspenseful shocker from indie filmmaker Patrick McGuinn features a bright young cast. 80 min.
70-5179 Was $69.99 *$39.99*

Thriller Zone (1995)
Three tales of terror are offered in this anthology: "The Last Hand," in which a group of card players are visited by a devilish new player; "The Final Hour," with William Forsythe as a futuristic prisoner waiting for an appeal; and "Fanatical Extremes," a "digest version" of 1982's "The Last Horror Film," with cabby Joe Spinell stalking actress Caroline Munro in Cannes. 60 min.
72-4023 *$29.99*

Ticks (1994)
This is not a movie about killer clocks. Rather, it's about prehistoric wood ticks, mutated to monstrous size by steroids dumped into the water by marijuana growers. The disgusting critters wreak havoc on a group of teens on a wilderness weekend. Ami Dolenz, Rosalind Allen, Peter Scolari and Clint Howard star. 85 min.
63-1674 Was $89.99 ❑*$12.99*

The Paperboy (1994)
A woman returning to her hometown to settle her late mother's estate befriends a lonely 12-year-old paperboy. When the woman becomes intimate with an old high school flame, she is stalked by a deranged murderer. Can it be the paperboy, who's looking for more than a tip? Alexandra Paul, William Katt, Marc Marut star. 93 min.
63-1732 Was $89.99 ❑*$14.99*

Deranged: The Chronicles (1993)
Everything you wanted to know about the 1974 horror classic "Deranged" is offered on this program. First, take a trip to killer Ed Gein's house with producer Tom Karr in "The Ed Gein Story," which also features make-up man Tom Savini showing how he achieved the film's gruesome effects. Next, "Behind the Scenes," has stills, radio commercials and more. 90 min.
59-8008 *$29.99*

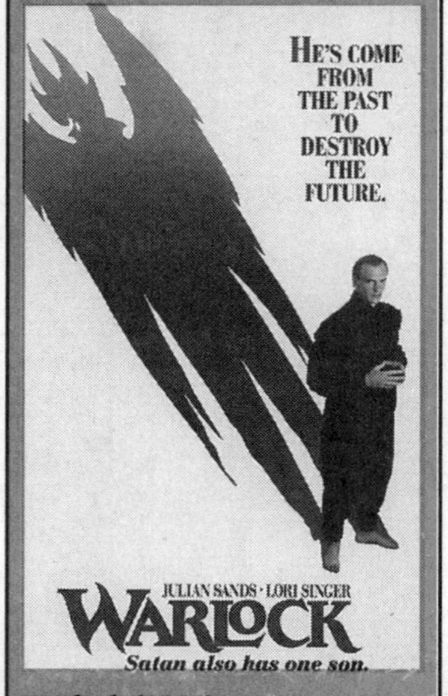
HE'S COME FROM THE PAST TO DESTROY THE FUTURE.
JULIAN SANDS · LORI SINGER
WARLOCK
Satan also has one son.

Warlock (1991)
Spared from a hot date with the stake in 1690s Salem, a male witch is transported to 1990s L.A., where he continues his search for a satanic tome that will grant him all the powers of Hell. Can a 17th-century witchfinder follow him through time? Sinister shocker stars Julian Sands, Richard E. Grant, Lori Singer, Mary Woronov. 103 min.
68-1192 ❑*$14.99*

Warlock: The Armageddon (1993)
Sequel to the hit horror flick involves the return of the Warlock (Julian Sands) to contemporary California to battle two young people who don't realize they are defending 17th-century runestones which contain evil power. Chris Young, Paula Marshall and Joanna Pacula also star in this special effects-filled shocker. 98 min.
68-1285 Was $89.99 ❑*$14.99*

Warlock III: The End Of The Innocence (1999)
The third outing in this popular scare series stars Ashley Laurence as a woman haunted by mysterious dreams after inheriting a 16th-century mansion. When some college friends arrive at the premises, Laurence stays, but she and her pals are soon visited by a stranger with a secret satanic agenda for all of them. Bruce Payne and Angel Boris also star. 94 min.
68-1944 Was $79.99 ❑*$14.99*

Witchboard 2: The Devil's Doorway (1993)
This sequel to the supernatural smash focuses on an artist (Ami Dolenz) who finds a Ouija board in her new loft that leads her face-to-face with a murderer who was once a tenant in the apartment. Larraine Newman, Timothy Gibbs also star. 98 min.
63-1653 Was $89.99 *$14.99*

Witchboard: The Possession (1995)
Two teenagers inherit an old ouija board that has the power to lead them into a terrifying netherworld, but after trying it, one of them becomes possessed by the board's unholy spirit in this third "Witchboard" shocker. David Nerman, Locky Lambert star. 93 min.
63-1796 Was $89.99 ❑*$14.99*

Rumpelstiltskin (1996)
Forget that lovable gnome from the children's story. This Rumpelstiltskin is a diabolical demon brought into 20th-century Los Angeles by an antique "wishing stone," and the young mother responsible for his release must stop his terrifying rampage. Kim Johnston Ulrich, Tommy Blaze and Max Grodenchik star. 91 min.
63-1842 Was $99.99 ❑*$14.99*

Serpent's Lair (1996)
Diabolical and erotic terror yarn in which a couple encounter a gorgeous sorceress after moving into their dream house. After the husband has a steamy liaison with the bewitching beauty, a terrifying odyssey begins that leads to a confrontation with the ultimate evil. Jeff Fahey, Lisa B., Patrick Bauchau star. 90 min.
63-1852 Was $99.99 ❑*$14.99*

Mad At the Moon (1992)
After her marriage, a young frontier bride discovers that her husband is the victim of a horrific curse. She seeks help from his brother, a handsome gambler, and soon learns that this monstrous mystery plagues the entire family. Mary Stuart Masterson, Hart Bochner and Fionnula Flanagan star in this Western-flavored chiller. 98 min.
63-1856 ❑*$89.99*

Voodoo Soup (1995)
A truly bizarre, darkly comic horror story about a voodoo queen and king who pool their talents and find happiness, cannibalism and lots of pretty women in Southern California. Penthouse Pets Taylor Wayne and Heidi Lynn are featured in this piece of weirdo mystical mayhem.
72-4024 *$29.99*

Creep (1995)
Kathy Willets, "America's Favorite Nymphomaniac," shows off her greatest assets when she stars in this shocker, playing a deranged woman who joins her deranged brother in committing bloody murders. Can a female detective stop their reign of terror? This sleazo shocker also stars Joel D. Wynkoop. Uncut, unrated version; 90 min.
59-8011 Was $29.99 *$19.99*

Trail Of Blood (1995)
The true story of the "Green River Killer," who was responsible for a series of murders in Washington state in the 1980s, is brought to frightening life in this shocker directed by noted artist Ari Roussimoff. David Huberman, Madonna Chavez, Joe Coleman and William Kotzwinkle star in this terror tale in the tradition of "Henry: Portrait of a Serial Killer."
50-5308 *$49.99*

Desecration (1999)
A 16-year-old boy, haunted by the death of his mother years earlier, accidentally kills a nun at his school. Soon after the nun's spirit begins haunting the teen, part of a series of bizarre and deadly incidents that culminates in a final showdown in Hell. Dante Tomaselli's surreal, symbol-laced horror outing stars Danny Lopes, Irma St. Paule. 88 min.
50-8394 *$19.99*

Dream Stalker (1991)
Eerieness and eroticism mix in this creepy horrorthon about a young fashion model who faces tragedy when her fiancé is killed in a motorcycle accident. But Brittany is soon haunted by Ricky, who goes on a murderous rampage in order to have his former lover all to himself. Mark Dias and Valerie Williams star. 85 min.
53-5171 Was $19.99 *$14.99*

Habit (1997)
Intriguing modern-day vampire saga about Sam, a Greenwich Village alcoholic, whose new girlfriend is great at sex, but keeps leaving him with strange little cuts around his body. He begins to have his suspicions: Is she a real-life bloodsucker? With Larry Fessenden (who also directed), Meredith Snaider. 112 min.
53-6303 Was $89.99 *$14.99*

5 Dark Souls (1997)
Ultra-gory horror offering in which a group of teens take their less popular classmates to the Wisconsin woods in order to make a real snuff movie, "just to see what it's like to kill someone." After one of the teens is sacrificed in a strange ritual, the two survivors must flee in order to save their lives. Matthew Winkler and Karen Dilloo star. 94 min.
59-8016 *$24.99*

5 Dark Souls 2 (1998)
Four years after a group of teens murdered their classmates, Professor Olivia Clark is writing a dissertation on the killings. Unfortunately, everyone she contacts about the crimes is eventually discovered dead. Will she be next? This shocking sequel stars Tina Ona Paukstelis and Karen Dilloo.
59-8018 *$29.99*

All You Can Eat (1996)
Unsettling pseudo-documentary focusing on LuAnn Lester, "the fattest woman in the world." Ms. Lester agrees to talk to a tabloid reporter and soon her bizarre life unfolds, from her breakthrough birth to tales of cannibalism and stories of incredible humiliation. Kathryn Szumibi and Don Schuchart star. 90 min.
59-8015 *$29.99*

Eyes Are Upon You (1997)
Two men in deep debt to mobsters try to score some quick cash by robbing a house. Little do they know that the woman who resides in the house is a demon with seductive and destructive powers. Brinke Stevens, Tom Savini and Sam Nicotero star in this shocker with gore and nudity.
59-8017 *$29.99*

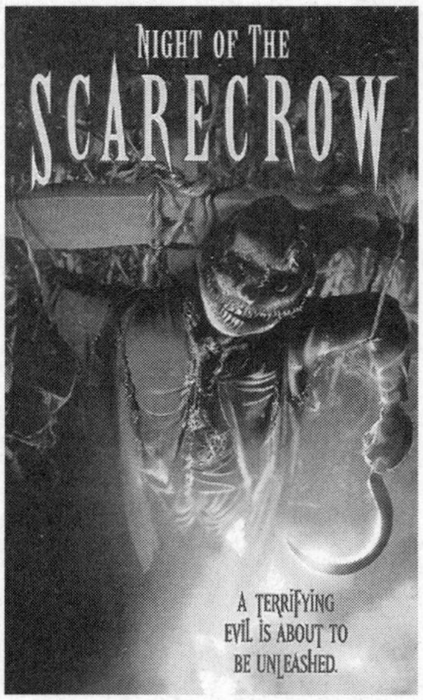
NIGHT OF THE
SCARECROW
A TERRIFYING EVIL IS ABOUT TO BE UNLEASHED.

Night Of The Scarecrow (1995)
That's "scarecrow" with a capital "SCARE," as the residents of a small farm town with a dark secret reap a harvest of terror when the Scarecrow comes out of the fields looking for a few good souls to claim. Spellbinding shocker stars Elizabeth Barondes, Bruce Glover, Howard Swain and Gary Lockwood. 90 min.
63-1801 Was $89.99 ❑*$14.99*

Body Bags (1993)
John Carpenter presents this trio of terror-ific tales that are guaranteed to give you a jolt. There's evil serial killers ("The Gas Station"), hair-raising horror ("Hair") and supernatural shocks ("Eye," directed by Tobe Hooper). Stars include Robert Carradine, Deborah Harry, Mark Hamill, Sheena Easton and David Warner. 95 min.
63-1665 Was $89.99 ❑*$14.99*

The Woman In Black (1993)
A creepy Victorian ghost story about a solicitor who journeys to a small town to settle the debt of a deceased woman. After facing the superstitious ways of the townspeople, he helps save a young Gypsy girl and then witnesses a sinister woman cloaked in black who has put a curse on the village. Adrian Rawlins and Clare Holman star. 100 min.
53-9544 Was $39.99 *$19.99*

Psychic (1991)
In this chilling shocker, a college student has a horrifying dream involving the woman he loves. Is she the next victim of a serial killer? If so, how can he stop the culprit from killing her, and who will believe him? Michael Nouri, Catherine Mary Stewart and Zach Galligan star. 92 min.
68-1219 ❑*$89.99*

Mirror Mirror (1990)
A young girl is drawn into the world of black magic and becomes involved in a deadly supernatural game. This tale of unrelenting horror stars Karen Black, William Sanderson, Yvonne DeCarlo, Rainbow Harvest. 105 min.
71-5215 Was $19.99 *$14.99*

Mirror Mirror 2: Raven Dance (1994)
The horror is back in the form of an antique mirror that's possessed and brings terror to a young girl stalked by her evil stepsister. Spooky special effects and creepy atmosphere highlight this shocking sequel starring Roddy McDowall, Sally Kellerman and Tracy Wells. 91 min.
55-1418 Was $89.99 *$14.99*

Mirror Mirror III (1996)
Mirror, mirror on the wall...what's the creepiest and sexiest movie of them all? The answer could be this installment in the popular series, in which a brooding artist discovers the magical looking glass in an abandoned mansion and soon becomes obsessed with a beautiful woman who haunts his dreams. Billy Drago, David Naughton and Monique Parent star. 100 min.
82-5024 Was $19.99 *$14.99*

Stigmata (1999)
When a mysterious religious relic given to Pittsburgh hairdresser Patricia Arquette leads to her manifesting the wounds of the crucified Jesus on her body, "de-bunker" priest Gabriel Byrne is sent by the Vatican to investigate. As Arquette's "possession" escalates and threatens her life, Byrne uncovers a secret that could rock the foundation of Christianity. Unusual supernatural thriller also stars Jonathan Pryce, Nia Long. 102 min.
12-3294   Was $99.99   ☐$14.99

Hellblock 13 (1999)
As she's led by executioner Gunnar Hansen down the "final mile," demented serial killer Debbie Rochon tries to ply him with a terrifying trilogy of tales regarding some of the prison's late occupants. A mother suspected of drowning her children, a woman who uses the occult to get rid of her white trash hubby, and a dead biker chick's "return" to her gang make for a spellbinding series of sinister stories. With Amy R. Swain, J.J. North.
46-8055 $59.99

The Unearthing (1994)
A woman who learns she is pregnant thinks she has the perfect plan for her unwanted unborn child: marry the heir to a wealthy estate and then present his dying mother with her "grandchild." Her perverse plot, however, leads to horrific consequences in this frightening film that mixes elements of "The Evil Dead" and "The Shining." Tina Ona Paukstelis, Norman Moses star. 83 min.
46-5593 $79.99

Beyond Sanity (1997)
From direct-to-video helmers Kevin Lindenmuth ("Addicted to Murder") and Mick McCleery comes these four early shockers. A man kills a woman at her request; a mysterious drug is used by two losers; a seemingly sane man uses his car to kill people; and some robbers go against a tough security man with surprising results. Brett Heniss, Diane Phillips star. 56 min.
73-9227 $24.99

Bugged! (1996)
A homemaker with pest problems calls on exterminators to tackle the creepy crawlers, but soon her house is a battleground for the bug-killers and their monstrously mutated foes. Raid the video store now for this wild, off-the-wall horror-comedy from the good people at Troma. With Priscilla Basque. 90 min.
46-8015   Was $69.99 $14.99

Sucker The Vampire (1998)
A bloodsucking vampire uses his popular rock band to lure young female groupies to dine on. However, as a result of his many escapades, he contracts a deadly virus, and it's up to his loyal sidekick to save his master from a fate worse than undeath. Yan Birch, Alex Erkiletian and Monica Barber star. 91 min.
46-8030   Was $59.99 $14.99

Mr. Frost (1990)
A chilling tale of psychological horror, starring Jeff Goldblum as an enigmatic asylum inmate whose quiet facade belies the shocking murders he committed. As one doctor tries to learn his true identity, people around him find their inner passions released in violent action. Is he a master manipulator, or the Devil incarnate? Kathy Baker, Alan Bates co-star in this shocker. 92 min.
45-5494   ☐$89.99

Decampitated (1998)
Sleeping bags are transformed into body bags when seven campers on vacation wander into haunted Decamp Acres and are decapitated one by one in the most gruesome ways imaginable. Mike Hart and Jonathan Scott star in this pulse-pounding horror camp-out! 103 min.
46-8034   Was $59.99 $14.99

THE LAST BROADCAST
A FILM BY STEFAN AVALOS AND LANCE WEILER

The Last Broadcast (1998)
Eerily similar to "The Blair Witch Project" (and filmed at least a year before that film), this shot-for-$900 thriller unfolds like a documentary, focusing on two hosts of a cable access TV show who join two strange fans to hunt down the legendary Jersey Devil in the New Jersey Pine Barrens. When only one fan returns from the trip alive, he remains the prime suspect in the disappearances. With David Beard and Jim Seward.
50-8307   Letterboxed $19.99

The Horror Of The Hungry Humongous Hungan (1996)
A voodoo priestess calls on the mystical Hungan to curse a doctor's Frankenstein-styled experiments. But things go awry and the diabolical doc's creature goes haywire, heading for the nearby town to terrorize the locals. B.J. Moyer, David A. Yoakam star; Jack Palance narrates. 100 min.
46-8050 $14.99

Legend Of The Chupacabra (1997)
A group of college students goes to Texas to make a documentary on a legendary Latin-American creature known as the Chupacabra or "Goat Sucker." No one knows if it's mere folklore, a man in a costume, or something more sinister, but when the Chupacabra's mutilation of sheep is captured on tape, the students' investigation turns shocking. Katsy Joiner stars.
46-8052 $24.99

The Arrival (1990)
A 73-year-old man on the brink of death makes a miraculous recovery and even begins growing younger, thanks to an alien force that enters his body. But the gift comes with a terrifying price in human life! Shocker stars John Saxon, Michael J. Pollard, Joseph Culp. 107 min.
46-5515 $19.99

Drawing Blood (1999)
A struggling artist enters into a twisted relationship with a beautiful fellow painter—who just happens to be a vampire who drains her models of their blood after drawing them—in this offbeat horror tale filled with scares and dark humor. Kirk Wilson, Dawn Spinella, Leo Otero star. 90 min.
46-8063 $49.99

Dead Meat (1993)
In the tradition of Herschell Gordon Lewis comes this deranged shocker about a serial killer named the "Senses Taker," who leaves a trail of victims missing their ears, eyes, nose, mouth and hands. Can the police stop the culprit? And what part does a quiet gardener have in the case? Nick Kostopolous stars in this grisly independent production. 107 min.
50-2711 $29.99

Dimension In Fear (1999)
Filmed in and around Las Vegas, this psycho killer thriller from cult fave Ted V. Mikels ("10 Violent Women") tells of a female TV weather reporter who encounters a serial murderer while on her way to an assignment in the mountains. Taken captive, a local detective must find her before it's too late. The forecast: bloody! Nicole West, Liz Renay and Dolores Fuller star. 109 min.
50-5011 $24.99

Jugular Wine (1995)
Atmospheric and erotic bloodsucking epic about an anthropologist who encounters a group of vampires who attempt to initiate him into their dark world. Their scheme, however, is interrupted before he's transformed into a full-blown vampire, and he must find a way to stop his deteriorating physical condition. Shaun Iron stars, with cameos by Henry Rollins, Stan Lee and Frank Miller. 95 min.
50-5145 $39.99

The 13th Floor (1990)
A young woman comes face to face with terror as she encounters the spirit of a boy her father had electrocuted in the office that served as the murder site. Lisa Hensley and Tim McKenzie star. 86 min.
46-5485 $89.99 $12.99

Ice Cream Man (1995)
"I scream, you scream, we all scream for the Ice Cream Man!" This diabolical shocker tells of a demented frozen goodies vendor who terrorizes a suburban neighborhood. With a recent stint in a mental hospital and the memories of his ice cream man pal's murder years earlier, there's no telling what this popsicle pusher will do next. Clint Howard, Sandahl Bergman, David Naughton star. 85 min.
83-1030   Was $89.99 $14.99

Hush Little Baby (1997)
After being united with her biological mother, a woman thinks she has found all the missing pieces to the puzzle that has been her life. As the woman and her husband discover that close friends and family are missing, they realize that Mom has a dark and murderous side. Diane Ladd and Geraint Wyn Davies star. 91 min.
64-3425 $14.99

Mark Of The Devil 666 (1994)
Creepy, blood-stained thriller about a killer who selects victims for strange reasons, kills them, then leaves them to be discovered. A detective and reporter try to stop the killer before he strikes again. Mike Wynoff, Karen Dilloo star. WARNING: Contains gory, gruesome scenes. 99 min.
59-8014 $29.99

Nightfall (1998)
A FBI agent looking into a series of grisly murders in Seattle faces a foe unlike any he's ever pursued before: a bloodthirsty vampire who's creating his own legion of undead followers...among them the agent's late partner. Gripping and chilling suspenser stars Jeff Rector, Adam Smoot.
46-8039   Was $59.99 $14.99

Dead Dudes In The House (1992)
While restoring a crumbling, old house, eight friends come across the gravestone of former owner Annabelle, who killed her husband. When one of the pals smashes her headstone, Annabelle arises from her grave, wreaking frightening havoc to the group working in the house. James Griffith and John Dayton Cerna star.
46-8042 $14.99

Spirits (1990)
The demon hordes of the Netherworld terrorize two families living in a haunted house, and only one priest with a dark secret of his own can stop them in this chilling tale of possession and suspense. Erik Estrada, Carol Lynley. 88 min.
68-1222   ☐$89.99

Shadow Tracker: Vampire Hunter (1999)
He got his start in the jungles of Vietnam 30 years ago, and now he's called on to use his incredible talents to save a small town. He's Shadow Tracker, a man on a mission to hunt, then kill, the undead. While the police think a serial killer is responsible for a series of grisly murders, Shadow Tracker knows better. Bruce G. Hallenback and Amy Naple star. 120 min.
73-9280 $19.99

Tainted (1998)
Hip and sardonically funny chiller about a trio of "Gen-X" film buffs whose midnight movie trip is interrupted by a vampire's plan to infect a local hospital's blood supply with vampire hemoglobin. Sean Farley, Greg James star. 106 min.
46-8043   Was $59.99 $14.99

Wes Craven

Last House On The Left (1972)
Writer/director Wes Craven and producer Sean Cunningham's chilling take on, of all things, Bergman's "The Virgin Spring" still packs more shocks than most of its successors. After a gang of drug-dealing sadists murders two teenage girls, they take refuge in a suburban family's home, unaware it's the home of one of their victims. When the parents discover the truth, they exact a gruesome revenge. "To avoid fainting, keep repeating: It's only a movie...It's only a movie." David Hess, Fred Lincoln, Sandra Cassel star. 82 min.
47-1392   Was $59.99 $14.99

Chiller (1985)
Frozen at the brink of death for 10 years in a cryogenic experiment, a young man is revived and returns to his life. But something is different, and soon the most chilling horror imaginable begins. Spellbinding shocker from Wes Craven stars Michael Beck, Beatrice Straight and Laura Johnson. 104 min.
75-7092 $14.99

Deadly Friend (1986)
Chilling blend of horror and science fiction from Wes Craven, as a teenage whiz (Matthew Laborteaux) implants a robot brain into his girlfriend's body, creating a murderous, albeit attractive, monster. With Kristy Swanson, Anne Ramsey. 91 min.
19-1558   ☐$14.99

The Serpent And The Rainbow (1988)
Horror master Wes Craven pulls out all the stops in this chilling tale of voodoo and zombies in modern-day Haiti. A scientist sent to investigate claims of "walking dead" falls under the spells of the local houngans, and the terror begins. Bill Pullman, Cathy Tyson, Paul Winfield star. 92 min.
07-1587   Was $19.99 $14.99

Shocker (1989)
"Nightmare on Elm Street" creator Wes Craven brings a new unstoppable killer to the screen in this supercharged chiller. Mass murderer Horace Pinker survives the chair by becoming an electrical force that zips along power lines and possesses people's bodies. Jolting horror tale also includes some neat swipes at TV; Mitch Pileggi, Michael Murphy, Peter Berg star. 111 min.
07-1637   Was $19.99 $14.99

The People Under The Stairs (1991)
Wes Craven's horrific and satiric tale concerns the efforts of a young boy and two hoods who attempt to ransack a mysterious house, but soon discover it's inhabited by a psychopathic (and slightly Reaganesque) couple and the "guests" they keep locked up. Everett McGill, Wendy Robie and Brandon Adams star. 102 min.
07-1801   Was $19.99   ☐$14.99

Scream (1996)
Director Wes Craven's slyly self-referential shocker follows a group of teenage horror film fans in a small California town who are systematically slaughtered by a mysterious murderer. Newscaster Courteney Cox thinks this killer also did in Neve Campbell's mother the year before, even though the supposed murderer is behind bars. Skeet Ulrich, David Arquette and Drew Barrymore co-star. Also included is a special "making of" featurette. 126 min.
11-2122   Was $19.99   ☐$14.99

Scream (Letterboxed Version)
Also available in a theatrical, widescreen format.
11-2194   ☐$19.99

Scream Deluxe Kit
Horror buffs will "scream" indeed for this boxed collector's set that includes the letterboxed version of the film, a second edition with audio commentary by Craven and screenwriter Kevin Williamson, a commemorative phone card and exclusive art cards of the stars.
11-2195 $34.99

Scream 2 (1997)
The ghost-faced killer from the first film is gone, and the survivors are trying to get on with their lives. But when the debut of a horror movie based on the murders called "Stab" is marred by copycat killings, it becomes clear to everyone that a new round of terror is about to begin. Neve Campbell, Courteney Cox, David Arquette, Jerry O'Connell, Sarah Michelle Gellar and Jada Pinkett star in this spooky, witty sequel. 120 min.
11-2249   Was $19.99   ☐$14.99

Scream 2 (Letterboxed Version)
Also available in a theatrical, widescreen format.
11-2794   ☐$19.99

SCREAM 3

Scream 3 (1999)
The third time is a bloody charm in Wes Craven's cut-and-cut-up series. Neve Campbell's Syndey, now a recluse working for a women's crisis hot-line, travels to Hollywood, where cast members of film-within-a film "Stab 3" are being slaughtered and pictures of Campbell's mother are being left at the crime scene. Courteney Cox Arquette, David Arquette, Patrick Dempsey and Parker Posey co-star, with several surprising cameos. 117 min.
11-2440   Was $99.99   ☐$22.99

Please see our index for these other Wes Craven titles: *Music Of The Heart • A Nightmare On Elm Street • Swamp Thing • Vampire In Brooklyn • Wes Craven's New Nightmare*

The Dentist (1996)
From the folks who gave you "Re-Animator" comes this disturbing tale of a Beverly Hills dentist who goes over the deep end when he discovers his wife is having an affair. Soon, he's taking his rage out on his patients, making his own bloody cavities when there aren't any, and becoming a driller killer. Is he safe? No way! Corbin Bernsen and Linda Hoffman star. 93 min.
68-1821 Was $99.99 □**$14.99**

The Dentist 2 (1998)
Just when you thought it was safe to stop flossing, demented dental doc Corbin Bernsen escapes from the mental hospital and makes his way to a small town that looks like a perfect place to restart his practice...once he eliminates the current dentist, that is! Take a bite of terror, but don't forget to rinse and spit. With Clint Howard, Jillian McWhirter. 98 min.
68-1911 Was $99.99 □**$14.99**

To Die For 2: Son Of Darkness (1991)
Wild sequel to the "fang-tastic" chiller finds bloodsucker Vlad Tepish back, disguised as Dr. Max Schreck, and in search of a beautiful woman who will play mother to his new son. But Vlad's brother is jealous and will go to horrific lengths to stop him. Michael Praed, Steve Bond and Amanda Wyss star. 95 min.
68-1213 □**$89.99**

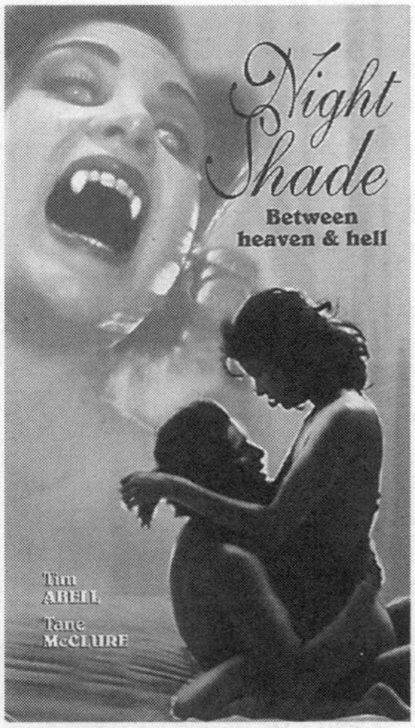
Night Shade
Between heaven & hell
Tim ABELL
Tane McCLURE

Night Shade (1996)
A man still haunted by his beautiful, young wife's death is shocked when he sees a woman who looks just like her in a club. His shock turns to terror when he discovers that this *is* his wife, come back from the grave as a seductive vampire, and that he can't resist her desire to be with him...forever. Erotic chiller stars Tane McClure, Tim Abell. 90 min.
70-5108 Was $29.99 **$19.99**

Psycho Sisters (1996)
After witnessing the rape and murder of their sister at the hands of out-of-control college students, siblings Jane and Jackie are sent to a mental hospital. Following their release, they embark on a deadly quest for revenge, looking to kill all men in their path and taking a "souvenir" of their work. Christine Taylor and Tina Krause star in this not-for-the-squeamish saga. 90 min.
73-8151 **$29.99**

Psycho Sisters (1998)
This remake of the 1996 "Psycho Sisters" tells of two institutionalized sisters who become serial killers in order to seek revenge against their younger sister's death. J.J. North, Theresa Lynn and Nancy Sirianni star in this wild, sexy and dangerous excursion into depravity. 95 min.
73-9216 Was $59.99 **$19.99**

Sorceress (1994)
A rising young lawyer's scheming wife tries to help him win a partnership by killing his competitor, but her victim's spouse is a witch who uses her black magic powers to exact a hellish revenge. Larry Poindexter, Linda Blair, Edward Albert and Julie Strain star in this mix of horror and sexy suspense. Uncut, unrated version; 93 min.
72-9044 Was $89.99 **$14.99**

Sorceress II: The Temptress (1999)
Each night, Greg Wrangler inexplicably encounters a strange world filled with beautiful women, sexual rituals and S&M practices. Led by Julie Strain, the women capture Wrangler's libido in order to steal his soul. Can he overcome his desires to save himself? Sandahl Bergman also stars in this sultry sequel. Uncut, unrated version; 82 min.
21-9187 **$59.99**

Color Me Blood Red Again (1995)
After two serial killers hide out in an art gallery, they discover that their grisly, dismembered victims are being hailed as real works of art. But from fame comes problems as their popularity eventually draws attention from the cops. Creepy sort-of-sequel to Herschell Gordon Lewis' "Color Me Blood Red." 90 min.
73-9152 **$19.99**

A Demon In My View (1992)
Hollywood's favorite "psycho," Anthony Perkins, gives a chilling performance in this tale about a serial killer who lives a seemingly normal life in an apartment house. His dark secrets are threatened when he's mistaken for another tenant by a jealous husband. With Sophie Ward, Stratford Johns. 98 min.
68-1242 □**$89.99**

Zombie Rampage (1992)
A young man gets into all sorts of trouble while waiting to meet his friends at a train station, finding himself trapped in a terrifying world whose inhabitants include zombies, serial killers and gangs. Hmmm...must've been the York-Dauphin El stop. Ed Dill and Erin Kehr star. 85 min.
73-9037 Was $19.99 **$14.99**

Dead Is Dead (1992)
A man seeking his brother's killers is dismembered by a mutant creature and left for dead. A woman revives him with an experimental drug, but a bad batch of the substance falls into the hands of drug pushers. Can they be stopped before the drug turns its users into walking dead? Mike Stanley, Connie Cocquyt star. 80 min.
73-9050 Was $79.99 **$19.99**

Goblin (1992)
In this frightening horror outing, a newlywed couple discovers that their new house was previously inhabited by a witchcraft-practicing farmer who raised a monstrous creature. Now, the monstrosity has escaped from a dark prison within the earth to terrorize the family. Jenny Admire, Tonia Monahan star. 75 min.
73-9057 Was $59.99 **$19.99**

Misbegotten (1997)
A couple trying to have a baby think their prayers have been answered when the wife becomes pregnant via an anonymous sperm donor. Little do they suspect that the donor is a homicidal sociopath who'll eliminate anyone that gets in the way of him and "his" child in this creepy chiller from director Mark L. Lester and scripter Larry Cohen. Kevin Dillon, Nick Mancuso and Lysette Anthony star. 96 min.
68-1878 □**$99.99**

The Landlady (1998)
"Yo, Adrian" becomes "Yaaaahhh, Adrian!" as Talia Shire plays a woman who kills her cheating husband, then takes a job as landlady of an apartment house. Shire goes to murderous lengths to make sure nobody interferes with her efforts to snag another spouse. Jack Coleman, Susie Singer and Bruce Weitz also star. 98 min.
68-1895 □**$99.99**

Pinocchio's Revenge (1996)
A man convicted of killing his young son is executed, but his public defender believes her client innocent. A mysterious Pinocchio puppet once buried with the dead boy falls into the hands of the lawyer's young daughter, and when the demonic wooden toy comes alive, there are no strings that can keep it from causing terror. Rosalind Allen stars. 96 min.
68-1816 Was $99.99 □**$14.99**

Dolly Dearest (1992)
A beautiful doll turns "doll-ibolical" when it attempts to possess a young girl, leaving a crew of corpses in its path. Who can stop the terrifying toy from taking over the tike? Only Daddy, who enters a nightmarish world to save his daughter. Denise Crosby, Sam Bottoms and Rip Torn star. 94 min.
68-1230 □**$12.99**

Milo (1998)
Sixteen years have passed since the mysterious murder of a classmate of four young girls. Now, all grown up, one of them is getting married, but what was supposed to be a happy day for the bride turns into a nightmare when the demonic young boy responsible for their friend's murder returns to wreak havoc upon them. Jennifer Jostyn, Antonio Fargas and Asher Metchik star.
64-9019 **$99.99**

Komodo (1998)
A young man is brought back by his pscyhologist to the remote island where his parents were killed years earlier. Unfortunately for them, and the biologist they meet there, the giant komodo dragons who killed the lad's folks are still around, and an oil company's evil actions are making the huge lizards angry...and hungry! With Kevin Zegers, Jill Hennessy. 90 min.
64-9064 **$99.99**

Hellgate (1990)
Three college students discover that the ghost stories they heard around the campfire about the Hellgate Hitcher are all too true. In fact, one of them is confronted by the ghostly spectre while driving down a road one night. The Hitcher happens to be a beautiful woman who lures travellers to death! With Ron Pallilo and Abigail Wolcott. 96 min.
68-1163 Was $89.99 **$12.99**

Tale Of A Vampire (1993)
After her lover tragically dies, a young woman is befriended by a mysterious scholar when she takes a job at a London library. She soon discovers that the scholar is, in fact, a vampire who is searching for his long-lost love. Julian Sands, Suzanna Hamilton star. 93 min.
68-1269 Was $89.99 □**$12.99**

Jack-O (1995)
A trio of graverobbers unknowingly stumbles upon the grave of Jack-O, a demon creature summoned by a warlock who was killed years earlier. Now, the people of Oakmoor Crossing face a frightening monster out for revenge. With "Scream Queens" Brinke Stevens and Linnea Quigley. 90 min.
72-9057 Was $89.99 **$14.99**

Laughing Dead (1998)
A post-apocalyptic Los Angeles filled with mutant cannibals, armed gangs and vampire legions that prey on helpless survivors is the setting for this low-budget but stylish sci-fi shocker, as a junkie haunted by a sinister secret takes on the ages-old vampire who's turning L.A. into his private "restaurant." Patrick Gleason, Nancy Rhee, John Hammond star. 88 min.
72-9281 **$59.99**

Feeding Billy (1997)
A lakeside weekend holds the promise of partying and wild fun for a group of friends. But, unknown to them, something is waiting for them at the lake...something that was hidden away years earlier and has come out looking for blood! Gruesome shocker stars Jennifer Maranzino, Jason Patzner and Ted Davis as "Billy." 63 min.
73-3007 **$14.99**

Leprechaun (1993)
Forget those breakfast cereal commercials on TV! This little fella is more murderous than mischievous, and when some young people make off with his gold, they'll need more than the "luck of the Irish" to escape the Leprechaun's wrath. Warwick Davis, Jennifer Aniston and Mark Holton star in a "magically delicious" horror frightfest. 92 min.
68-1258 Was $89.99 **$14.99**

Leprechaun 2 (1994)
That pint-sized purveyor of evil is back in this creepy sequel. The Leprechaun appears in the big city, searching for his pot of gold—and a gorgeous gal he wants to call his own. When the girl's boyfriend lifts one of the Leprechaun's gold coins, the tiny terror goes on a rampage. Warwick Davis stars. 85 min.
68-1315 □**$14.99**

Leprechaun 3 (1995)
The nasty little critter with the green hat goes wild in Las Vegas after discovering his magical gold shilling is missing. It seems that a down-on-his-luck college student has found it in a pawn shop and the Irish monstrosity is willing to kill to get the coin back. "Glitter City" becomes the "Emerald Isle of Death" in this outing. Warwick Davis stars. 93 min.
68-1362 Was $89.99 □**$14.99**

Leprechaun Boxed Set
It's "Faith and Be-gore-ahhh!" with this collector's set featuring the first three films starring the tiny terror.
68-1793 Save $5.00! **$39.99**

Leprechaun 4 In Space (1996)
The fourth appearance of the malicious Leprechaun is no lucky charm for the terrorized parties involved in his sinister shenanigans. The terrible troll holds a beautiful alien princess hostage on a distant planet, prompting Earth marines to stage a rescue mission. When the Celtic creep commandeers a spaceship, look out! With Warwick Davis, Debbe Dunning. 98 min.
68-1824 Was $99.99 □**$14.99**

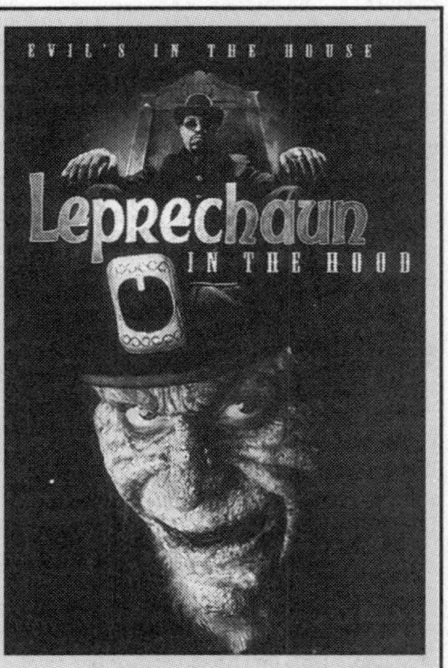
EVIL'S IN THE HOUSE
Leprechaun
IN THE HOOD

Leprechaun In The Hood (2000)
What, you've never heard of "black Irish"? The diminutive demon is brought back into the world by a trio of would-be rap stars who are raiding a music mogul's studio, and now the homeboys are faced with a horror they never imagined in this fifth entry in the shock series. Warwick Davis and Ice-T star. 91 min.
68-1979 □**$79.99**

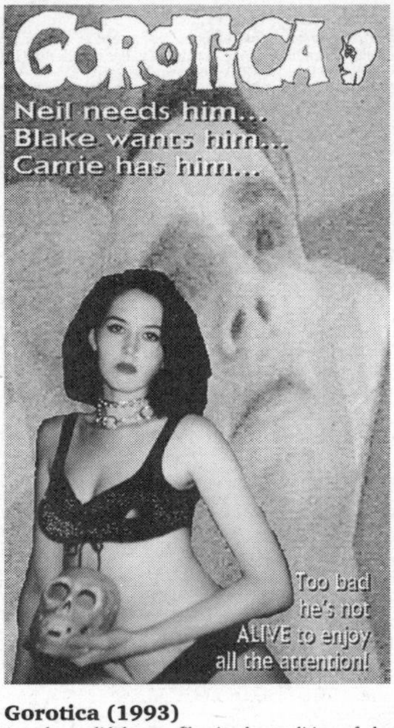
GOROTICA
Neil needs him...
Blake wants him...
Carrie has him...
Too bad he's not ALIVE to enjoy all the attention!

Gorotica (1993)
A truly sordid horror film in the tradition of the "Nekromantik" movies, this thriller tells of a bungled jewelry heist that leaves one of the two robbers dead. The dead man's friend goes on the run from the cops and picks up a strange woman who turns out to have an affection for kinkiness and corpses. Ghetty Chasun stars. WARNING: This film contains graphic violence and nudity. 60 min.
73-9058 Was $59.99 **$19.99**

Gorgasm (1993)
A detective investigating a murder discovers that the victim had a strange sexual fetish which involved pain, death and the search for "the ultimate climax." In learning more about this pursuit, the investigator delves into a world filled with sadism and torture. Gabriela and Rik Billock star in this terrifying tale filled with nudity and graphic violence. 85 min.
73-9068 **$49.99**

Gore Whore (1994)
From the fine folk who gave you "Gorgasm" and "Gorotica" comes this erotic, gruesome epic about a private eye searching for a missing lab assistant and a secret formula. He learns that the "assistant" is actually a dead hooker and the "formula," when mixed with human blood, keeps her alive. Audrey Street and D'Lana Tunnell star. WARNING: suggested for adults only. 70 min.
73-9075 **$19.99**

The Witching (1993)
A teenage boy gets more than he bargained for when he babysits for his grandmother and discovers he's the descendant of a 17th-century witch hunter. When Morgana, Queen of the Witches, begins to spin her devious spell to rule the world, the teenager must stop her. With Auggie Alvarez, Veronica Orr. 70 min.
73-9061 Was $19.99 **$14.99**

The Scare Game Double Feature (1993)
Get the goosebumps from two horror stories: "The Fine Art" involves a young couple whose residence is awfully close to the Cedar Hill Slayer's murderous route; and an evil wizard's apprentice collects souls in the frightening pastime called "The Scare Game." Lisa Morrison stars. 120 min.
73-9062 Was $29.99 **$19.99**

Dominion (1993)
A group of pre-pubescent vampires attempting to rule the world stage a rock concert that will help resurrect their leader, while two detectives and the gang leader's aged sister try to stop the baby-faced bloodsuckers' plan. 70 min.
73-9064 **$19.99**

Ozone (1993)
A cop is accidentally injected with a strange drug with mutative powers during a drug raid. When his partner mysteriously disappears, the cop finds himself searching for a monstrous crime kingpin while fighting bizarre changes in his own body. Tom Hoover and James L. Edwards star in this unusual mix of film noir and horror.
73-9065 Was $29.99 **$14.99**

Sinistre (1993)
A gore-iffic horror tale in which a group of crooks fleeing a bank robbery land in a deserted farmhouse inhabited by demons and a nasty axe murderer. "Green Acres" it ain't.
73-9095 **$14.99**

Shreck (1993)
Three fans living in the former house of a psychotic Nazi resurrect him during a seance and find themselves the targets of this bloodthirsty butcher. William Lantry and T.K. Malone star in this terror tale. 75 min.
73-9060 **$19.99**

Night Owl (1993)
Bloodsucking gets hip in this erotic, atmospheric shocker set in 1984. A young man searches for his sister, who has become the victim of a ruthless vampire preying on the hipsters and performance artists who frequent the downtown Manhattan club scene. John Leguizamo, Caroline Munro and Holly Woodlawn star. 77 min.
73-9102 Was $29.99 ***$19.99***

Savage Harvest (1995)
A demonic power that once attacked the Cherokee Indians on their "Trail of Tears" march is preparing to resurface in the modern day, as a group of people must battle monsters intent on possessing them. A gory shocker with Lisa Morrison and Ramona Midgett. 75 min.
73-9108 Was $29.99 ***$19.99***

Generation X-Tinct (1997)
Bobby and his "Generation X" pals are out for revenge after one of their chums is killed. They believe the culprit is a yuppie who drives a Mercedes. While the group of disaffected youth looks for the suspected killer, Bobby goes on a personal rampage. Move over, Mickey and Mallory—here comes Bobby! Mike Passion and Lonnie Jackson star. 86 min.
73-9212 ***$59.99***

Killing Spree (1990)
An unsettling shocker about a newlywed couple whose marriage is in danger because the husband thinks his wife is having affairs behind his back. Hubby uses ceiling fans, screwdrivers and a lawn mower to murder the culprits, but his victims have a habit of not staying dead too long. Gory, unrated creeper stars Tom Russo, Courtney Lercara. 88 min.
73-9138 Was $29.99 ***$19.99***

The Sandman (1995)
In this shocker from indy horrormeister J.R. Bookwalter, the denizens of the Yokum Trailer Park are being killed in their sleep by a mysterious entity with glowing red eyes. An insomniac writer begins investigating the strange deaths and soon finds himself face to face with a monstrous force that comes to people in their dreams. A.J. Richards stars. 90 min.
73-9140 Was $29.99 ***$14.99***

Potential Sins (1997)
A surprise party turns into a real surprise when the guest of honor decides to kill himself. Things get even darker as back-stabbing, adultery and murder come to the forefront when an unknown person begins killing the other party guests. Maybe it would have been better if they had held the party at Chuck E Cheese. 75 min.
73-9172 ***$19.99***

Ashes And Flames (1997)
Brooding psychological horror in the David Lynch tradition about two sisters abused by their father who seek redemption in a strange, surreal world, accompanied by a bizarre man who works at a mortuary. Sasha DeMarino stars. 91 min.
73-9215 Letterboxed ***$59.99***

Shatter Dead (1994)
Bloody and erotic horror film about a tough, gun-toting gal, who must battle gruesome (but articulate) zombies while on her way to her boyfriend's house, and another woman, who has a lesbian encounter with the Angel of Death. Disturbing and filled with offbeat humor, this independent shocker stars Stark Raven, Flora Fauna. 84 min.
73-9076 ***$24.99***

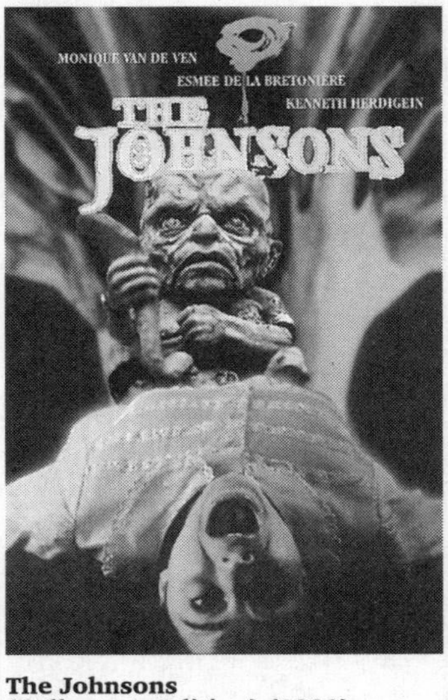

The Johnsons (Collector's Edition) (1992)
Offbeat, mystical Dutch horror film about a nature photographer who takes her teenage daughter on assignment with her to get the girl's mind off of troubling dreams of seven boys living in a blood-smeared house. A professor's discovery of a link between the dreams and a bizarre Indian ritual drives him to try to save the girl—and all of mankind—from an evil prophecy. Monique Van De Ven, Kenneth Herdigein star. AKA: "Xangadix." 98 min.
08-8730 Letterboxed ***$14.99***

Caress Of The Vampire (1995)
A beautiful female vampire reincarnated from the ancient Egyptian god of evil gets an erotic welcome to the modern world when she seduces a recently divorced woman. Nudity, lesbian liaisons and horror are the elements of this terror tale. With Paulina Monet. Unrated version; 75 min.
73-9150 ***$19.99***

Caress Of The Vampire, Vol. 2: Teenage Foot Ghoul-A-Go Go (1996)
An outrageous and satiric sequel to the horror hit that mixes gore, sex and ineptitude with equal relish. It involves a podiatrist with a foot fetish, a vampire who turns girls into bloodsuckers through blood enemas, and a zombie rock band. Unrated version; 75 min.
73-9157 ***$29.99***

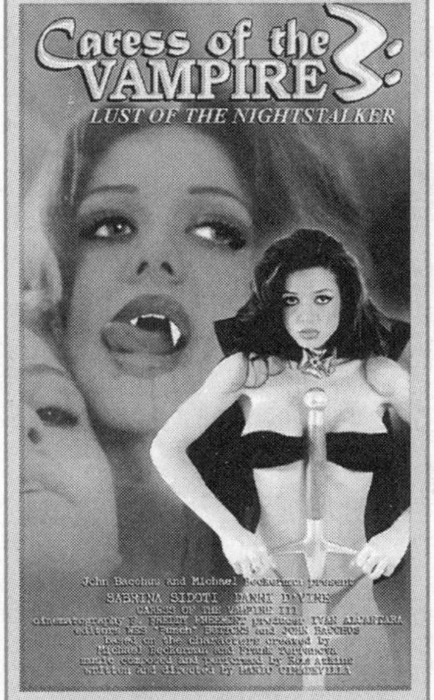

Caress Of The Vampire 3: Lust Of The Nightstalker (1999)
Lesbian desires meet bloodsucking creatures in the third entry in the erotically-charged series. Lette, a gorgeous vampire with a lust for beautiful hookers, is tracked by Kathy, a hot undercover detective. But when Lette seduces Kathy, the curvaceous cop realizes her life is at stake! Sabrina Sidoti and Danni D'Vine star in this nudity and violence-filled opus. 70 min.
73-9285 ***$19.99***

Outlaw Drive-In, Vol. 1: Horror-Comedy Double Feature
A double dip of frights and laughs: "Humanoids from Atlantis" (1992), in which a young documentary filmmaker and his girlfriend are confronted by an ancient creature near a lake; and "Reanimator Academy" (1992), about a college student obsessed with death who discovers he can restore life with a special serum. Gals, gore and more!
73-9105 ***$19.99***

The Ironbound Vampire (1998)
Ed Wood stock company members Conrad Brooks and Delores Fuller return to the screen together for the first time since "Glen or Glenda" in this tale of a former cop-turned-writer seeking a vampire in a strange sub-city of Newark. 75 min.
73-9224 ***$19.99***

Loons (1991)
This fright film with laughs tells of a family curse put upon the Loon family during the New England witch trials. Judge Loon condemns a real witch to death and all of his male descendants are cursed with lunacy. When a contemporary relative learns of this, he can't handle the consequences. 80 min.
73-9175 ***$19.99***

Twisted Tales (1996)
Three demented tales are presented in this eerie anthology, including "Nothing But the Truth," about a man whose exaggerations finally get the better of him; "The Shooting," in which a man in big trouble after a shooting is watched by his psychic girlfriend; and "Hungry Like a Bat," about a man obsessed with killing his pretty new neighbor. John Collins, Freddie Gano star. 90 min.
73-9145 ***$29.99***

Vamps: Deadly Dreamgirls (1996)
Welcome to "Vamps," a dance club that's different because it's owned by a gorgeous vampire and two eerie accomplices. When a pretty, down-on-her-luck woman gets a job at the club, she attracts the attention of Tasha, the lead bloodsucker. A battle ensues for the woman's soul between Tasha and a young priest. Jennifer Huss and Jenny Wallace star.
73-9146 Was $29.99 ***$19.99***

Ravage (1997)
Fiercely intense shocker about a criminal psychologist who witnesses the brutal slaying of his family by a serial killer. The psychologist attempts to track down the murderer and finds himself in a strange, violent underworld populated by brutal assassins. Mark Brazeale stars. 85 min.
73-9171 ***$29.99***

Hell's Belles (1996)
Two detectives investigating a rash of killings that may have been caused by vampires discover that their job has just gotten more dangerous when a group of party girls unwittingly opens a gateway to Hell. Rick Poll, Wendy Bednarz and Mick McCleary star in this special effects-filled shocker. AKA "Vampires and Other Stereotypes." 86 min.
73-9187 ***$29.99***

Death Magic (1997)
After five magicians get together to raise up the dead, Major Aaron Parker appears and proceeds to slay the descendants of the men who convicted him of mass murder in 1875. A night of terror and death takes place as the Major seeks revenge. Anne Caffrey and Keith DeGreen star. 93 min.
73-9213 ***$29.99***

Fatal Exam (1997)
A group of college kids participate in an experiment that turns deadly and find themselves racing against the clock to save themselves in this frightening direct-to-video terror tale. Mike Coleman and Carol Fitzgerald star. 112 min.
73-9226 ***$29.99***

Moonchild (1993)
"Mad Max" meets "The Howling" in this story of a man in search of his son after breaking out of prison in a futuristic America controlled by evil forces. The two happen to have been used in gene-splicing experiments that turned them into high-tech werewolves. Auggi Alvarez, Kathleen McSweeney star.
73-9094 ***$14.99***

The Paranormal (1998)
A movie theater becomes a gateway to another dimension, and the ravenous zombies that were flickering on the screen are leaping off it and looking for food. Can a parapsycholgist, his colleague, and two theater employees trapped inside the building resist this supernatural assault? Todd Norris, Audrey Crabtree star. 70 min.
73-3014 ***$14.99***

Bloodthirsty Cannibal Demons (1995)
A group of troublesome teens kill the owners of an abandoned theater, but get more than they bargain for when cannibal demons in the basement reawaken and go on a murderous rampage. Auggi Alvarez and Cheryl Metz star.
73-3018 ***$14.99***

Dead Things (1997)
If you cross "The Texas Chainsaw Massacre" with "Pulp Fiction" you'd get something like this gore-drenched crime thriller about two partners in drug dealing who join two other crooks in a daring prison break with the sheriff in hot pursuit. While stopping to deal with an injury, they run into the most sinister force the world has ever seen. Rico Love, Pat Stodden star.
73-3019 ***$14.99***

Vampire Holocaust (1997)
An ordinary evening turns into a trip to hell when a group of pals befriend a gang who have just used an old occult book to raise the dead from their graves. Hordes of zombies give the two factions trouble, but they believe they can meet the undead enemy head-on and defeat them in this outrageous gore bonanza. Nick Stodden and Coelle Peck star.
73-3020 ***$14.99***

Violent New Breed (1995)
Half-human, half-demon creatures spawned from Hell are populating the world with plans of enslaving the human race. The government launches a campaign to destroy these "Breeders," and when the leader of a special military unit discovers that his daughter has been kidnapped by the creatures, he sets out to stop them at any cost. Mark Glover, Nick Stodden, Rebecca Rose star, with a special appearance by Rudy Ray Moore.
73-9099 ***$19.99***

Zombie Bloodbath (1993)
When a nuclear power station in Kansas melts down, killing all area residents, the government responds with a cover-up by building new housing over the old reactor. But the new residents soon realize that the dead aren't really dead when they begin to rise, kill and eat human flesh. Auggi Alvarez, Frank Dunlay star.
73-3017 ***$14.99***

Zombie Bloodbath 2: Rage Of The Undead (1994)
A sequel to the gore hit details the eerie adventures of a group of college kids who go to a farmhouse for refuge, unaware that it's the past home of Satanic cult members and is currently occupied by three escaped convicts. Soon, the kids are fleeing for their lives from the cons, serial killers, zombies and a living scarecrow! Kathleen McSweeney, Dave Miller star.
73-9098 ***$14.99***

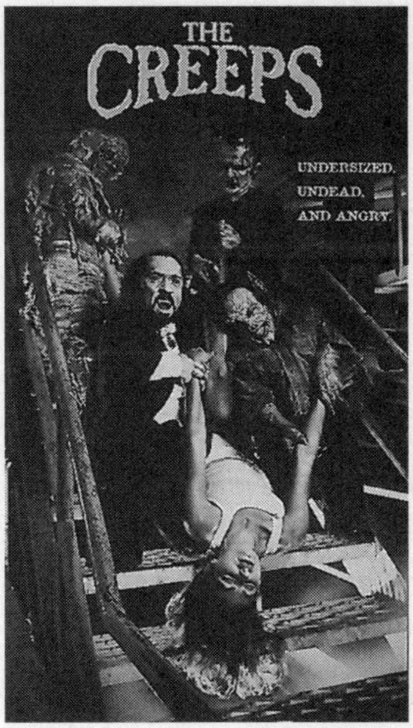

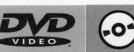

The Creeps (1997)
Mix "House of Frankenstein" with "The Terror of Tiny Town" and you just might get this terror tale of some three-foot-tall monsters—sawed-off simulacra of Dracula, the Frankenstein monster, the Mummy and the Werewolf—who are just as nasty and bloodthirsty as any full-sized fiends. Phil Fondacaro, Rhonda Griffin, Justin Lauer star. 80 min.
75-5017 Was $89.99 ***$14.99***

Addicted To Murder (1995)
A serial killer named Joel preys on women, slaughtering them in horrific fashion. Weary of his diabolical lifestyle, he decides to settle down with a childhood friend named Rachel—who happens to be a vampire! Mick McCleery and Laura McLauchlin star in this blood-drenched shocker from director Kevin Lindenmuth ("Vampires and Other Stereotypes"). 90 min.
73-9101 ***$29.99***

Addicted To Murder 2: Tainted Blood (1998)
New York City turns into a prime breeding ground for bloodsuckers in this sequel to the popular vampire epic. Who will become the next person to carry on the blood legacy? Will it be Tricia, who desires another life; Jonathan, a young vampire with an attitude problem; or Joel Winter, a serial killer? Sasha Graham, Mick McCleery and Ted V. Mikels star. 80 min.
73-9253 ***$29.99***

Evil Ambitions (1996)
An intrepid reporter working on a story uncovers a group of young women who are being sacrificed to a group of Satanists and their leaders. The reporter is close to getting the scoop, but first must face off against a sexy priestess, a corrupt politician and the Devil himself! With Debbie Rochon, Amber Newman and Bill Hinzman. Unrated version.
73-9301 ***$19.99***

Sacrifice Of The White Goddess (1998)
Savage horror and dangerous adventure mix in this tale of an archaeology student who joins forces with a female ne'er-do-well and a roguish trader and follows an ancient Mayan treasure map in search of gold. What they find during their journey is an eerie jungle where unknown horrors await. With a bright young cast. 106 min.
73-9257 ***$19.99***

Terror House (1998)
Three unsuspecting college students are lured into a house that is much more than haunted...it contains a half-human creature with a thirst for blood. Visited by a ghostly figure of a beautiful woman who may be trying to help them, one by one, they are stalked by the creature of death. Jon McBride, Bob Dennis, Mark Polonia star. 80 min.
73-9250 ***$29.99***

Carmilla (1998)
A vampire in Long Island? Look out, Ziggy Palffy! A beautiful bloodsucker preys on teenagers who live in a high rent district on the isle. How can she be stopped from feasting on them? And can her lesbian tendencies be curtailed? Maria Pechukas stars in this shocker packed with gore and sexy sequences.
73-9274 ***$39.99***

Retro Puppet Master (1999)
Travel back in time to the early days of "Puppet Master" Andre Toulon, who ran an avant-garde puppet theatre in pre-World War I Paris. When his love, Ilsa, is kidnapped by the servants of the ancient god Sutekh, Toulon activates his puppet creations to save her. Guy Rolfe, Greg Sestero and Brigitta Dau star. 90 min.
75-5056 ***$89.99***

Talisman (1998)
The end of the world is dawning! Theriel, the Black Angel, has been summoned from his resting place to bring about Armageddon. The only hope for humanity's salvation rests on the shoulders of a teenage boy and girl, but there is one problem: they have been choosing to assist the angel in its mission of evil. With Walter Jones, Ilinca Goia, Jason Adelman and Billy Parish. 90 min.
75-5030 Was $89.99 *$14.99*

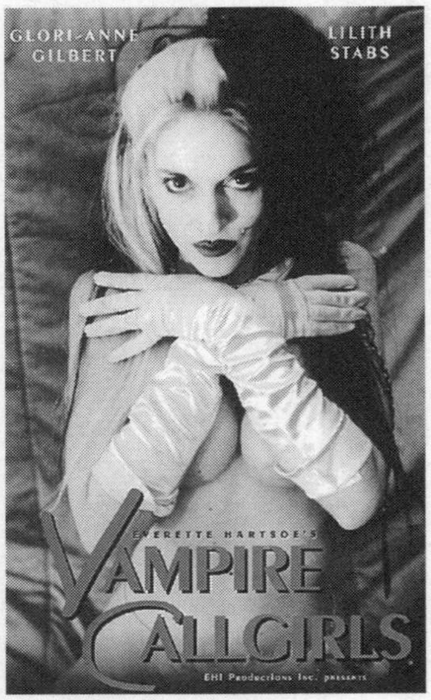

Vampire Callgirls (1998)
Sometimes, men just want to have fun. But when fun turns to kinky sex, then terror—look out! An escort service sends their best women to a fellow seeking a hot time in the old town. Little does he know that these gals come with extras: fangs and a desire for bloodsucking. Glori-Ann Gilbert stars in this sex and spewing hemoglobin bonanza.
73-9277 *$19.99*

Devil Souls (1997)
An archeologist uncovers a mysterious "wishing stone" alongside the remains of a 3,000-year-old mummy. As it passes from owner to owner the mystical stone grants people their darkest desires, but at the cost of their soul, culminating in hellish horror. This shocker features a vampire, a werewolf, a demon and a devil. 75 min.
73-9166 *$19.99*

Shrieker (1997)
Its cry is the sound of terror, and when the bloodthirsty creature known as the Shrieker is summoned, six people in a house become trapped, the targets in a deadly game of horror and suspense. Tanya Dempsey, Jamie Gannon, Parry Allen star. 80 min.
75-5021 Was $89.99 *$14.99*

Curse Of The Puppet Master (1998)
Andre Toulon's puppets rebel against their new master, Dr. Magrew, who has been experimenting with human assistants. After sitting around idly as the not-so good doctor has destroyed lives, they decide to put a stop to his murderous ways. George Peck, Emily Harrison and Josh Green star. 90 min.
75-5023 Was $89.99 *$14.99*

Foreverglades (1997)
Someone is taking out the top dogs at a prestigious enterprise, one by one. Who is it? Is it someone trying to stop their development in the Everglades? A reporter teams up with a psychic teenage with nightmarish visions to stop the killer before he, or she, kills them. 75 min.
73-9241 *$19.99*

Tale Of The Urban Werewolf (1997)
Horrific tale, "from the files of the Lawrence Psychiatric Institute," of a disturbed heroin addict who falls under an ancient curse and becomes a bloodthirsty cross between man and beast. Werewolves? Here wolves! John LaFleche, Nancy Ann Michaud star. 75 min.
73-9167 *$19.99*

V Is For Vampire (1997)
Laura Manning is a best-selling author and the world's top authority on vampires. There is a very good reason for her expertise, however: one mainly to do with her nocturnal "activities." If you value your life, don't go anywhere near her. 70 min.
73-9239 *$24.99*

Curvaceous Corpses (1998)
Poor Brace and Kelly; they're so desperate to have the most "realistic" murder scenes ever filmed, they'll do anything, like hire an actual killer to kill people. Do you think they'll be at the Independent Spirit Awards? Never know.
73-9240 *$24.99*

Living A Zombie Dream (1996)
Scream a little dream with this ultra-gory enterprise about a guy who lets his brother get sliced by a psycho killer after discovering his sibling was having an affair with his girlfriend. A guilt- and grief-stricken brother sets out to make amends by shooting the killer, but can the madman come back from the dead for a bloody zombie vengeance? 90 min.
73-9168 *$29.99*

Dark Descent (1997)
Horror video filmmaker Ron Bonk presents two early works: "I've Killed Before" is about a woman searching for a serial killer who murdered her best friend; and in "Permanent Waves," a woman believes she sees images of her dead, abusive husband from beyond the grave. Also includes behind-the-scenes footage from other works. 100 min.
73-9228 *$24.99*

The Dead Matter (1997)
Vampires, magical rings, and the living dead abound in this horror flick that will send you scurrying back under your bed. When a small group of close friends accidentally unearths a mysterious relic, they unleash a powerful force of evil beyond their worst nightmares.
73-9236 *$19.99*

Unnaturally Born Killer (1997)
Walter makes movies. Walter has a mean producer who wants all the blood, guts and sex that can possibly be put on screen. Walter decides the only thing to do is get the real thing, corpses and all. Have these guys ever heard of special effects? Ross Marshall stars. 90 min.
73-9237 *$24.99*

Ice Scream (1997)
Outrageous dark comedy in which an ice cream store owner, in order to increase declining sales, hires five beautiful women to scoop the treats. However, someone is a little too envious of his success, and once one of the girls is found murdered, the customers start to find a little more than cherries in their sherbet. Ed Wood regular Conrad Brooks and Tara Good star. 85 min.
73-9244 *$14.99*

Road Killer (1999)
A cold-blooded, maniacal killer carjacks four people and takes them on a shocking death ride to an unknown destination. How far will he take them on this long, strange trip? Kathleen L. Warner, Robert Margolis star. 90 min.
73-9284 *$59.99*

Zombie! vs. Mardi Gras (1999)
After being crippled by drunken Mardi Gras revelers, a young man seeks help from the dark world of the occult for revenge. During a Sumerian ritual, he unleashes a zombie from its sleep, and the creature soon turns Mardi Gras into the "Bloody Gras"!
73-9295 *$39.99*

Zombie Toxin (1998)
Gory effects and Monty Python-like humor highlight this British chiller about some devil worshippers who accidentally unleash a substance that turns residents of the English countryside into flesh-hungry zombies! At the same time, a Hitler look-alike and his henchman try to bottle the toxin in their "home brew" and create a zombie army to help them take over the world. 75 min.
73-9256 Letterboxed *$19.99*

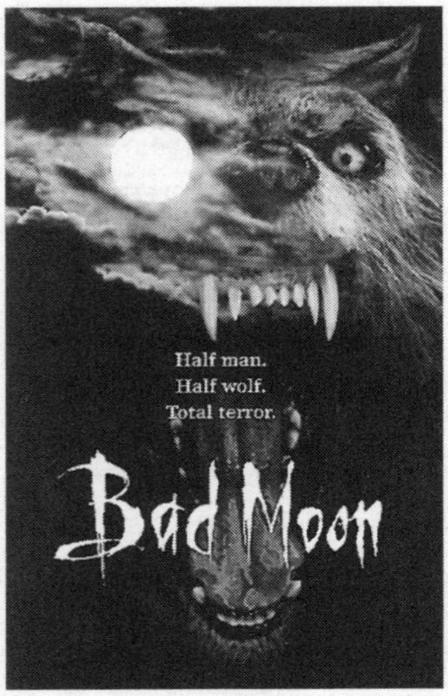

Bad Moon (1996)
A photojournalist returns home to the Pacific Northwest and moves in next door to his sister, her young son and their German Shepherd. A series of gruesome murders has police suspecting the dog, but the boy becomes convinced that his uncle is hiding a dark secret...one that the next full moon will reveal. Sinister shocker stars Michael Paré, Mariel Hemingway, Mason Gamble. 80 min.
19-2503 Was $99.99 *□$14.99*

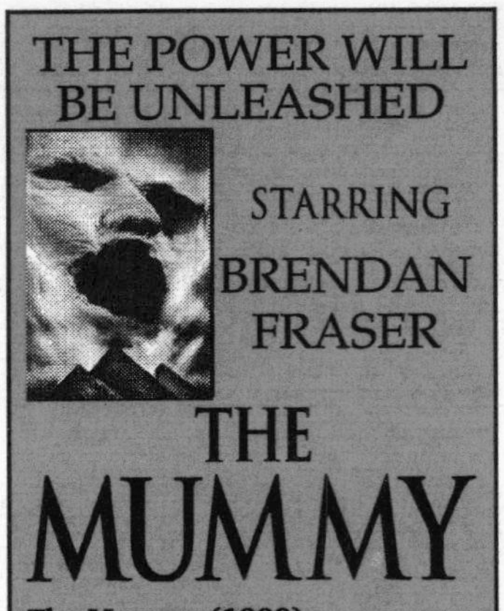

The Mummy (1999)
Buried alive more than 3,000 years ago, an ancient Egyptian priest is brought back to life by an archeological expedition in the 1920s and uses his arcane magic to call down a host of plagues upon the tomb raiders and reunite with his reincarnated love. Brendan Fraser, Rachel Weisz, John Hannah and Arnold Vosloo star in this effects-filled tale of timeless terror. 125 min.
07-2769 Was $19.99 *□$14.99*

The Mummy (Letterboxed Version)
Also available in a theatrical, widescreen format.
07-2770 Was $19.99 *□$14.99*

Only Darkness (1998)
A frustrated horror movie writer finds real life more frightening than reel life when he and a speechless young woman are terrorized by a mysterious cloaked killer. What is the killer's identity and motives? The answers couldn't be found in the writer's wildest works of fiction. Crispin Manson and Nicole Streak star in this unsettling shocker. 96 min.
73-9283 *$59.99*

Slaughter Day (1999)
Two construction workers find themselves in a precarious position when they face off against a crew of possessed hardhats and the Necronomicon Book of the Dead. Nothing less than the fate of the world is in the hands of the guys who usually hold hammers and saws! Blake Cousins and Joseph Ross star.
73-9292 *$24.99*

1-900 (1998)
A woman addicted to pleasuring others uses the information superhighway to meet her latest love interest. Little does she know that he might be a serial killer. Two detectives with different slants on life team to find the murderer, who uses adult chatlines and other high-tech outlets to meet his prey. Danielle Thys, Lance Gray star.
73-9293 *$29.99*

Snuff Kill (1997)
Gory shockathon in which a horror film buff and a rock singer team to make a bloody, torture-filled video. The horror movie fan is amazed at the realism of the effects, then discovers that the carnage is not so phony after all. The rocker is killing the actors for his own psychotic reasons! Al Darago and Mark Williams star in this disturbing terror filck. 90 min.
73-9302 *$19.99*

Savage Vows (1996)
The blood flows freely in this shocker from Wilkes-Barre, Pa., in which a man who recently lost his wife in an auto accident is joined at his home by six friends trying to console him. Their weekend turns into a time of terror as they're killed one by one by a mysterious foe seeking revenge. Armond Sposto, Mark Polonia star. 80 min.
73-9161 *$24.99*

The Shivers (1999)
Ultra-gory shocker about the Dread Mansion, an estate with a bloody past that's purchased by Rudy, who wants to turn it into a dance club. During a party, revelers are slaughtered and some of the attendees must travel between dimensions to stop the onslaught of ghouls and demons. This Todd Sheets production stars Rico Love and Nick Stodden. 95 min.
73-9286 *$19.99*

The Crier (1998)
Wicked, straight-to-video salute to the Mexican "Crying Woman" movies tells of a man who calls for the help of an old witch to bring his true love back to him. Little does he know that the witch will also unleash the incarnation of a sobbing woman who was killed 200 years earlier. Corey Elias and Lorena Gutierez star. 82 min.
73-9258 *$59.99*

Eternal Desires (1998)
After a bad date, Allison storms off to a deserted cemetery and is accidentally impaled on spikes sticking out of a broken tombstone. Allison dies, but is brought back to life by Lord Christopher, a mysterious vampire. Allison introduces her friend, Kristin, into her bloodsucking realm, where both women serve Lord Christopher. Rachel Moriello stars in this kinky scare story. 79 min.
73-9260 *$19.99*

Bad Magic (1998)
After his gangbanger brother is killed in a bank robbery, Renny goes to a West Indies witch doctor to seek help in finding revenge against the vicious gang responsible for his brother's death. Using the arts of voodoo he's taught, Renny gets all medieval on the killers as that ol' "Bad Magic" really has him in its spell. With Vince Simmons and Bruce Hardy as "Tobanga." 85 min.
73-9275 *$39.99*

Plenilunio (1998)
"Plenilunio" means "full moon" in Portuguese, and in this Brazilian shocker a monster takes residence in the woods near a small South American town and, during full moons, terrorizes a group of people who are on the staff of a cable TV show. And you thought "Daily News Live" with Bill Conlin was scary! Ricardo Islas and Martin Cabrera star. In Portuguese with English subtitles.
73-9276 *$24.99*

Rot (1999)
A woman contacts a deadly disease called "rot" from a corpse she with whom she was sexually involved, then passes the disease on to her close friend. Soon, the killer couple threaten friends and foes and encounter the Feds, along with the creepy scientist responsible for the "rot." Billy Scam, Tiffany Stinky and Joel D. Wynkoop star in this shocker. 90 min.
73-9304 *$19.99*

Lunatic! (1991)
At one time, this film was deemed too violent for video stores. After witnessing the proceedings, you'll believe it, as a depraved serial killer meets his female match while on his blood-strewn path of murder. The deadly pair go on a hideous rampage that's not for the squeamish. Michael Boland and Helena Richards star. 90 min.
73-9303 *$19.99*

I Strangle The Body Electric (1999)
When some of his "go-girls" die mysteriously, drug kingpin Joey Smack decides to go after some new talent. Little does he know that the Electric Cord Strangler may be behind the grisly killings. Sex, sadism and nudity abound in this deranged debacle starring Marie Mazur and Misty Mundae. 70 min.
73-9337 *$29.99*

Dark Romances, Vol. 1: Born Evil (1998)
The first entry in a creepy series in the creepiest "Grand Guignol" tradition tells of a creature of pure evil named Diana who dedicates her life to ruining others. See her strike in "The Black Veil" and "Listen to Midnight," a mix of erotica and horror. With Brinke Stevens, Elizabeth Moorehead and Dawn Wildsmith. 140 min.
73-9273 *$39.99*

The Vicious Sweet (1997)
A popular "Scream Queen" is about to hit the big time, but to everyone's surprise, she turns down a marriage proposal and a chance to work with a major director in a new film. It seems that the zombies and monsters from her past films have come alive, causing her much distress. Sasha Graham and Robert Licata star in this disturbing direct-to-video shocker. 90 min.
73-9229 *$29.99*

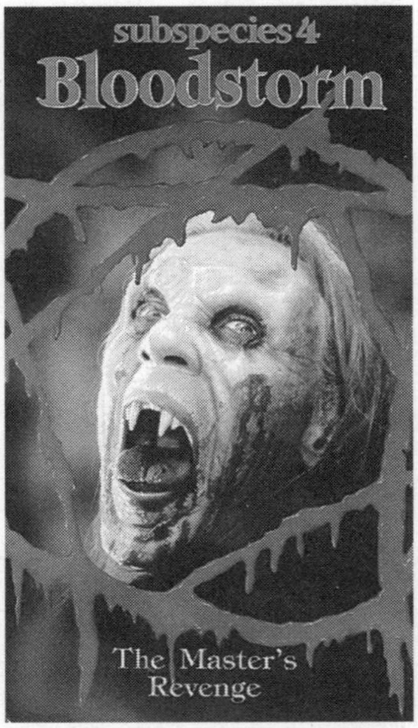

Subspecies 4: Bloodstorm (1998)
It's a battle for the world of the undead as vampire master Radu seeks to wrest control from a treacherous former disciple, and a young woman hovering between human and vampire seeks help to control her bloodlust, in this fourth entry in the chilling series. Anders Hove, Jonathon Morris, Denice Duff star. 90 min.
75-5033 Was $89.99 *$14.99*

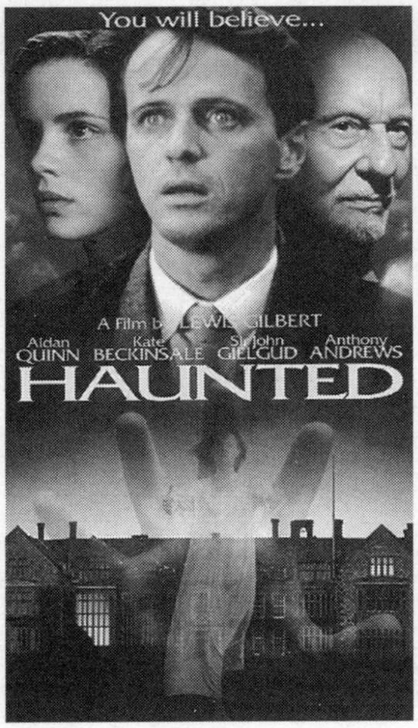
You will believe...
A Film by LEWIS GILBERT
Aidan QUINN
Kate BECKINSALE
Sir John GIELGUD
Anthony ANDREWS
HAUNTED

Haunted (1996)
Creepy thriller starring Aidan Quinn as an investigator looking into a haunting in the isolated British countryside. A series of eerie occurrences leads him to study the estate's family history, and soon he begins seeing the ghostly image of a young girl calling out to him. Kate Beckinsale and John Gielgud co-star. 108 min.
88-1074 Was $99.99 ***$14.99***

Creaturealm: From The Dead (1998)
Unusual direct-to-video terror outing about a make-up artist who decides to resurrect two horror stars after he finds out Hollywood has stopped making scary movies. Unfortunately, the two thespians turn out to be real ghouls who soon go on a monstrous rampage. Randal Malone and Sasha Graham star; featuring appearances by Conrad Brooks and Margaret O'Brien. 82 min.
73-9234 ***$39.99***

Canvas Of Blood (1999)
A college art teacher whose hand was disfigured in Vietnam goes off the deep end when his violinist daughter's hand is also crippled in a botched operation. When a crooked judge and lawyer leave him with no legal recourse, he uses his combat expertise to create a killer mechanical hand and seek revenge. With Jack McClernan, Marian Koubek. 80 min.
73-9307 ***$19.99***

Through Dead Eyes (1996)
A serial killer has puzzled a police detective, so he seeks help from a psychic for help. But when she proves baffled from the killings, the investigator goes to a retired cop who has handled a similar case for help. Is this a copycat case or is there some link between the murders? Find out in this pulse-pounding suspenser starring James Doohan and Kent Rulon. 90 min.
73-9309 ***$19.99***

Freak (1999)
A deformed and homicidal psychopath breaks out of a mental hospital and unleashes a nasty brand of terror on two sisters passing through the area and a van driver that accidentally unleashed him. As the killer's savage spree grows, the sisters and driver face off against him in the "freak's" childhood home. Amy Paliganoff, Travis Patton star. 85 min.
73-9312 ***$59.99***

Realm Of The Bizarre (1999)
These three tales of terror involve creepy characters, shocks and kinky sexual encounters. Included are "The Strange Case of Ezra Bumble," involving a murdering necrophiliac; "Bothered," about a divorced man's obsession with an adult cable TV actress; and "Homecoming," centered on a man's ghostly encounters in a house he inherited. 80 min.
73-9331 ***$19.99***

Poetic Seduction: The Dead Students Society (1999)
In this kinky chiller, Nora is a calculating serial killer who poses as a professor of literature in order to flirt, seduce, recite poetry to, and torture and murder students. Joining her in this devious game is her slow-witted brother Nikko. "Carpe Dead-'Em! Seize the Dead!" Roxanne Michaels, Joseph Anthony, Tina Krause and Conrad Brooks star. 85 min.
73-9287 ***$19.99***

Cutting Moments (1998)
A pizza delivery man's pooch becomes lethal thanks to strong drugs, in "Crack Dog"; a war vet has a unique way of telling his wife "Don't Nag Me"; an old man gets advice from an unlikely source—a "Bowl of Oatmeal"; a bored slacker joins some anarchists in "Principles of Karma"; and a faltering marriage leads to self-mutilation in "Cutting Moments," in this horror anthology. 80 min.
73-9232 ***$59.99***

Huntress: Spirit Of The Night (1996)
Red-haired beauty Tara returns to her ancestral home in North Wales for her father's funeral, but soon uncovers a dark family secret. As a sexual awakening stirs inside her, she falls victim to a centuries-old curse and becomes a feral she-beast with animal strength and instincts. Jenna Bodner stars; written by former Movies Unlimited employee James Sealskin. 86 min.
75-5012 Was $89.99 ***$14.99***

Fatally Yours (1995)
A gangland reincarnation thriller filled with sexy sequences, this unique thriller tells of a real estate agent who is mysteriously drawn to a dilapidated building. He purchases the property and soon resumes writing a crime novel he once started. Soon, the agent is visited by ghosts of 1920s gangsters. Rick Rossovich, Annie Fitzgerald, George Lazenby and Roddy McDowall star. 90 min.
76-9082 Was $19.99 ***$14.99***

Def By Temptation (1990)
A black college student travels to New York to visit a childhood friend and is introduced to a beautiful, sexy seductress who lures men to their death. Rousing blend of horror, eroticism and laughs from writer/director/co-star James Bond III also features Kadeem Hardison, Cynthia Bond, Bill Nunn and Samuel L. Jackson. 95 min.
77-5012 Was $19.99 ***$14.99***

Dahmer: The Secret Life Of Jeffrey Dahmer (1993)
The sensational, unsettling account of Jeffrey Dahmer, the demented Milwaukee serial killer whose ghastly murders and cannibalistic acts rocked the nation. This fictionalized chronicle of Dahmer's awful reign of terror is not for the squeamish! 100 min.
78-1191 ***$49.99***

Red Spirit Lake (1992)
Straight-to-video shocker tells of Marilyn, a descendent of witches, who arrives in snowy Angel Falls after her aunt is tortured and murdered. Then, the whole place goes berserk, as she meets two cretinous brothers, who have been operated on by aliens; a rich businessman who wants the estate for himself; hired killers; and other depraved people. Amanda Collins, R. Kern star.
79-6216 Was $24.99 ***$19.99***

Hideous! (1997)
Looking for disgusting, pickled freaks? Well, you've come to the right title, as an eccentric collector of human oddities thinks he's acquired his greatest specimen yet when he snags a mutant born of toxic sewage. The rightful owner of the critter decides to claim it for himself, prompting a war to erupt and many freaks to come to life. Michael Citriniti, Rhonda Griffin star. 82 min.
75-5014 Was $99.99 ***$14.99***

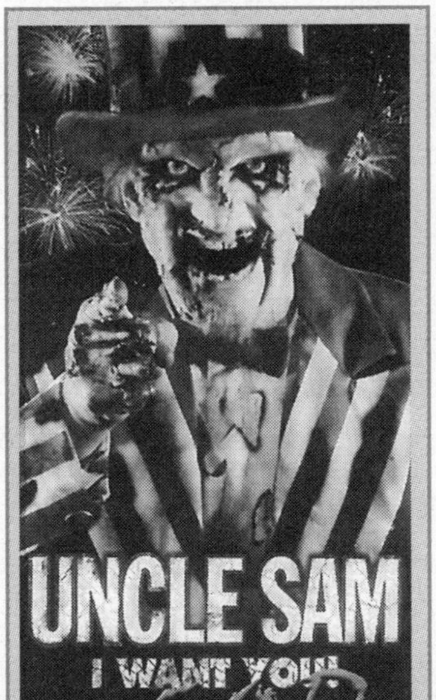
UNCLE SAM
I WANT YOU DEAD

Uncle Sam (1998)
The Fourth of July becomes the "Gore-th" of Ghoul-Eye when a Desert Storm chopper pilot, shot down by friendly fire and returned to his hometown, comes back to life as a patriotically-clad killer who vents his murderous wrath on flag burners, tax cheats and other "un-American" types. Offbeat horror tale from writer Larry Cohen and director William Lustig stars Timothy Bottoms, Robert Forster, Isaac Hayes and David Fralick. 91 min.
83-1235 Was $99.99 ***$14.99***

Uncle Sam (Letterboxed Version)
Also available in a theatrical, widescreen format.
83-1237 Was $99.99 ***$14.99***

We Await (1996)
In this wild and often shocking straight-to-video thriller, a con artist gets his just desserts when he finds a Christian couple he was trying to dupe are viciously murdered. Soon, the con man is held captive by the culprit—a lunatic—and his demented family. Among the clan members are a human dog and a woman about to give birth to a half-human, half-plant creation. With Thomas Angel. This tape also includes the short "Madball."
79-6476 Was $24.99 ***$19.99***

The Killer Eye (1998)
A brilliant ophthalmologist performs a groundbreaking experiment on a homeless subject which results in the man's death. But the man's eye soon comes to life, expands to gigantic size and seeks knowledge and hot babes. Jaqueline Lovell, Jonathan Norman and Nanette Bianchi star. Unrated director's cut; 80 min.
75-5036 Was $89.99 ***$14.99***

BRAM STOKER'S
The Mummy

Bram Stoker's The Mummy (1997)
A curse reaches out across the centuries, and an undead being from ancient Egypt seeks vengeance in modern-day San Francisco, in this chiller based on a story by the author of "Dracula." Louis Gossett, Jr., Amy Locane, Eric Lutes star. 99 min.
83-1180 Was $99.99 ***$14.99***

Ice From The Sun (1999)
The Presence, a being that terrorizes both the angels in Heaven and the demons in Hell, meets its match in Alison, a mortal, who faces unspeakable terror in order to destroy it. Alison—let's hope her aim is true. Ramona Midgett and Todd Tevlin star in this gore-drenched shocker.
73-9341 ***$39.99***

Dracula In Vegas (1999)
Bloodsuckers are common in Glitter Gulch, but Max is the real deal, a German vampire on the prowl for hookers and showgirls. Max may find true ghoulish love when he falls for a gorgeous coed named Christine. But will her presence weaken the blood-seeking ghoul? Maximillian Grabinger and April Leigh star.
73-9358 ***$24.99***

Freakshow (1995)
Two teens are treated to a quintet of terrifying tales, presented by a sinister barker known as the Freakmaster, when they visit a carnival sideshow. In this anthology-style shocker, the bizarre relics (a baby in a jar, a mummy, and more) all have a story behind them. With Gunnar Hansen and Veronica Carlson. 102 min.
74-3022 ***$89.99***

Funnyman (1996)
No, it's not a documentary about Bob Saget. It's a creepy horror yarn about a young man who wins the ancestral home of a mysterious figure in a game of poker and finds that the house comes with a resident demon—the comically creepy Funnyman. Tim James, Benny Young and Christopher Lee star. 90 min.
74-3033 ***$89.99***

Blood Dolls (1999)
Move over, Chucky! Step aside, Fats! Get lost, Gabbo! Here come the Blood Dolls, and they're looking for trouble. These deadly little critters are the creations of Virgil, a freaky billionaire who keeps go-go girls in a cage in his creepy home. And he's going to use the Blood Dolls for revenge, freaky style! Jack Maturin, Nicholas Worth star. 90 min.
75-5049 ***$89.99***

Totem (1999)
Six teenagers are drawn to a mysterious cemetery watched over by a mysterious Totem, which features the figures of the Three Masters of Death. The teens are soon made part of a ritual in which three of them will be killers and three will be victims. Jason Faunt, Marissa Tait and Eric W. Edwards star. 90 min.
75-5052 ***$89.99***

Ragdoll (1999)
Eager to get back at the thugs who beat him up, an African-American teenager uses his grandmother's magic to help him gain revenge, but what he summons is a tiny terror that cannot be stopped. Russell Richardson, Jennia Watson and Freda Payne star. 90 min.
75-5060 ***$89.99***

The Dead Hate The Living (1999)
A group of would-be filmmakers trying to make a low-budget horror movie find their work is turning into a documentary when they unwittingly revive an army of flesh-eating zombies. Trapped in an abandoned hospital, will this be their last film? Eric Clawson, Jamie Donahue, Matt Stephens star. 90 min.
75-5064 ***$89.99***

Star Time (1993)
A deranged TV fan is driven to the brink of suicide when his favorite show is cancelled, but is saved by an imaginary "agent" who makes him an offer: kill people and he'll gain small-screen stardom! Bizarre psycho-thriller stars Michael St. Gerard, John P. Ryan and Maureen Teefy. 85 min.
76-9044 ***$14.99***

The Horrible Dr. Bones (1999)
It's hip-hop horror like you've never seen, as an up-and-coming rap group gets a chance for the big time from legendary record mogul Dr. Bones. Trouble is, the not-so-good doctor plans to use their music as part of his plot to build a zombie army to take over the world! Darrow Igus, Sarah Scott, Larry Bates star. 90 min.
75-5073 ***$89.99***

Witchouse (1999)
Seven young people are invited by an odd classmate to a party in her family's New England mansion. Little do they suspect that someone else will be attending: the girl's resurrected ancestor, a witch out for revenge on the descendants of those who killed her 300 years earlier. Matt Raftery, Brooke Meuller, Ariauna Albright star. 90 min.
75-5046 ***$89.99***

Witchouse II: Blood Coven (2000)
After a haunted house is plowed over to make room for a shopping mall, four unmarked graves are unearthed. A professor and her students investigate the site, but an ancient witch and her coven appear to have returned to cause destruction and terror. Ariauna Albright, Elizabeth Hobgood and Andrew Prine star. 82 min.
75-5089 ***$99.99***

New York Vampire (1990)
After he fails to kill himself, a young man is seduced by a beautiful member of a vampire cult. Now forced to seek blood in order to survive, he and his lethal ladyfriend must dodge a detective determined to stop the cult's reign of terror. Tommy Sweeney, Julie Lynch star. 80 min.
73-9231 ***$59.99***

Screen Kill (1998)
Way-out direct-to-tape terror show about a horror movie fan and a theatrical rocker who team to make a fright film, only to have something go frighteningly awry while shooting a murder scene. The cinephile soon discovers that he and the rocker have real sinister sides. Al Darago, Ann Jagerman star. 80 min.
73-9233 ***$29.99***

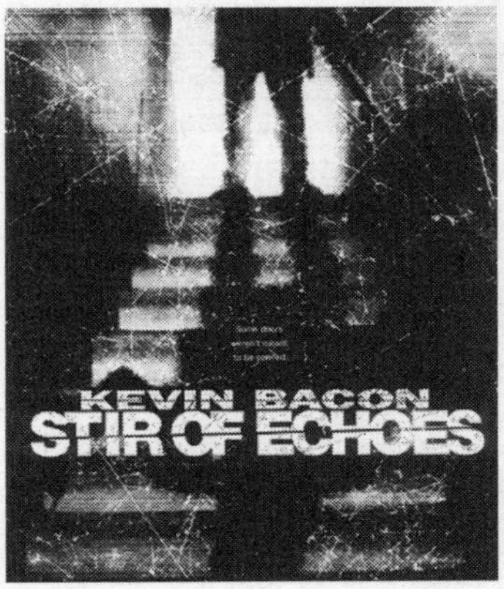
KEVIN BACON
STIR OF ECHOES

Stir Of Echoes (1999)
What begins as a hypnotism stunt at a party turns into a terrifying journey into the world beyond the grave, as Chicago telephone lineman Kevin Bacon begins receiving ghostly visions and must help the spirits rest in peace before they overwhelm his sanity and endanger his family. Kathryn Erbe, Illeana Douglas and Conor O'Farrell co-star in this eerie suspense thriller. 94 min.
27-7175 Was $99.99 ***$14.99***

Soultaker (1990)
A young couple injured in a car crash find their souls trapped in a netherworld between life and death, and are pursued by the evil Soultaker, who wants to possess their spirits for all eternity. Supernatural suspenser stars Joe Estevez, Vivian Schilling, Robert Z'Dar. 94 min.
80-1028 Was $19.99 ***$14.99***

Blood Thirsty (1998)
If you're into erotically-charged, bloodsucking sagas, you've gotta sink your teeth into this one, a story of a vampire gal named Whitney who finds passion and plasma with new roommate Celia. Monique Parent stars.
81-9068 ***$99.99***

Asylum Of Terror (1998)
A manor that used to house the criminally insane is turned into a haunted house for visitors who want spooky thrills. But these scare-seekers get more than they bargained for when one of the asylum's serial killing patients is on the loose—and starts killing patrons of his old, dark house!
81-9069 ***$99.99***

Kolobos (1999)
An aspiring artist has a frightening experience while making an experimental film. She and other members of the crew are trapped in a lodge where they are stalked by a stranger with a mutilated face. As they are picked off one by one, the survivors begin to turn against each other. Amy Weber, Linnea Quigley and Donny Ternnova star. 87 min.
81-9085 ***$69.99***

Twisted (1996)
Bryan Brown hosts this collection of macabre supernatural stories taken from the Australian TV series "Twisted Tales." They involve an airline passenger, a bored housewife, a con artist and a retiring killer, all of whom encounter bizarre experiences. Geoffrey Rush and Rachel Ward also star. 86 min.
88-7010 *$89.99*

Still Twisted (1996)
Are you ready for another quartet of creepy stories that are just a little bit...twisted? Join host Bryan Brown as you witness a woman trying to flee a hit-and-run accident, a ballroom dancer whose home hides a deadly secret, a killer-for-hire whose latest job has unforeseen consequences, and a woman trapped in a mysterious train station. 86 min.
88-7018 *$59.99*

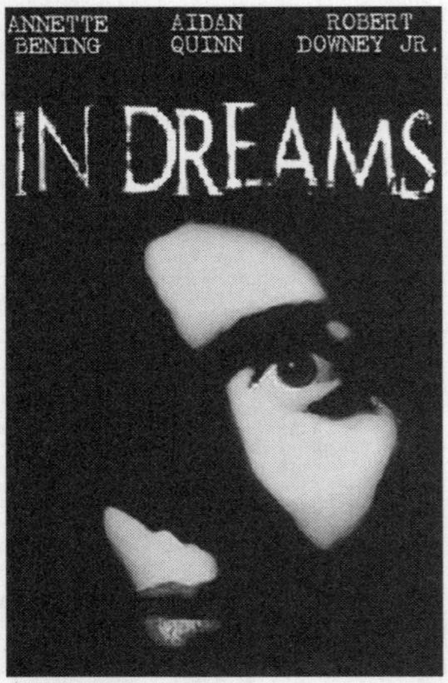

In Dreams (1999)
Eerie and suspenseful thriller from director Neil Jordan ("Interview with the Vampire") stars Annette Bening as a wife and mother haunted by disturbing visions of children being abducted and killed by psychopath Robert Downey, Jr. When her own daughter becomes Downey's latest victim, Bening must use her link to the madman's mind to find him and stop his rampage. Aidan Quinn, Stephen Rea also star. 100 min.
07-2752 Was $99.99 *$14.99*

Deadly Lessons (1996)
Ann could never fit in in high school, and she's not doing much better in college. In fact, things get pretty bad when her jock boyfriend is seduced away from her by a hip group of students. On the warpath, Ann looks for help from a mysterious childhood friend who teaches her lessons in mayhem, murder and revenge. Andrea Gall, Dana Wise star. 97 min.
82-5028 Was $89.99 *$19.99*

Shadow Creature (1996)
A 1950s horror feel with all the 1990s gore trimmings is one way to describe this scary outing in which a scientist investigating a series of grisly murders uncovers a formula which can lead to immortality and cause horrific mutations. "Mr. U.S.A" Shane Minor stars with Tracy Godard. 104 min.
82-5036 *$69.99*

Bloodletting (1997)
Blood-drenched shocker about a female serial killer fan whose obsessions lead her to America's most notorious murderer. She blackmails him into showing her how to kill people, and the two embark on a killing spree. Ariauna Albright, James L. Edwards star. 89 min.
82-5042 Was $89.99 *$19.99*

Annie's Garden (1996)
A beautiful young writer staying in a small town begins to suspect its good-looking, mysterious inhabitants are keepers of a hidden secret. When the woman falls in love with one of the townspeople and befriends his sister, she gets closer to the frightening truth. Yancy Butler, Grace Zabriskie and Charlotte Chatton star.
82-5045 *$99.99*

Immortal (1998)
A guitarist in a hot college rock band struggles with his deadly addiction to blood. This string-strumming ghoul finds that his bloodsucking tendencies get in the way of his relationship with his club manager girlfriend and his bandmates. Andrew Taylor, Meredith Leigh Sause and Mike Shaw star. 106 min.
82-5070 *$99.99*

Angel Of The Night (1998)
In this Danish production from director Shaky Gonzales, a young woman named Rebecca brings her best friend and boyfriend to a Gothic mansion she inherited from her grandmother. An old book reveals that Rebecca's great-grandfather was a vampire, leading her to try to resurrect the old bloodsucker. With Ulrich Thomsen. AKA: "Nattens Engel."
82-5166 *$89.99*

The Catcher (1997)
This catcher isn't into rye—he's into blood! After years in a mental hospital, Johnny MacIntosh returns to the same ball field where he bludgeoned his father to death. Soon, he's killing his new teammates with help from his dear, old, dead dad. And you thought Lance Parrish on the Phillies was brutal! David Heavener, Monique Parent and Joe Estevez star. 90 min.
82-5105 *$89.99*

I, Zombie (1998)
A young British man working on his PHD is attacked by a mysterious, seemingly dead woman while walking through a deserted ruin. Soon, the writer's mind and body begins to decay and he has a strong desire for human blood—and he'll stop at nothing to get it! Gile Aspen, Dean Sipling star in this gory shocker. 85 min.
82-5115 *$89.99*

Lycanthrope (1998)
A commando mission to rescue a missing team of scientists deep in the Amazon rain forest turns into a terrifying ordeal when the soldiers are attacked by a bloodthirsty man-beast. Robert Carradine, Michael Winslow star. 95 min.
82-5118 *$99.99*

Animals (1999)
It was supposed to be a peaceful family camping trip, but a fateful encounter with an escaped convict and his "animals" turns it into a spine-tingling fight for survival that has the family saying, "we gotta get out of this place." Scream queen Linnea Quigley stars. 90 min.
82-5119 *$69.99*

Lady Of The Lake (1998)
David inherits a family house near a lake after his uncle drowns and later encounters the beautiful Gypsy witch who haunts the lake, seducing and killing men to avenge her own brutal death. When the town librarian, an expert on the witch, is found dead, David discovers more about the deadly seductress of the lake. Erik Rutherford and Emidio Michetti star.
82-5127 *$99.99*

Granny (1999)
Wild horror opus in which a group of college pals' overnight reunion is disrupted by a psycho killer who appears to be an old woman. The friends are killed in horrifying ways by the gruesome granny and her axe. Who will survive her wrath? Katie Dugan and David Coleman star. 85 min.
82-5137 *$99.99*

In The Woods (1999)
There's horror in the woods, as two men on a hunting trip find the skull of a mysterious horned animal in a remote burial site. Bringing the relic home with them, they are unprepared for the supernatural menace their actions unleash. D.J. Perry, Aimee Tenaglia star. 90 min.
82-5151 *$99.99*

The Portrait (1999)
In this sexy, spooky take on "The Picture of Dorian Gray," Gabriella Hall ("Lolida 2000") poses for a photographer whose horrific but erotic works she has seen in an art gallery. When Hall tells him that she'd sell her soul to remain as young as she is in the photo, she doesn't realize what sort of devilish pact she made. Jenna Bodnar also stars. AKA: "Portrait of the Soul." 85 min.
82-5155 *$89.99*

Beyond Redemption (1999)
This suspense effort packed with supernatural thrills stars Andrew McCarthy as an atheist detective trying to track down a serial killer sacrificing respected people for some bizarre religious reason. Andrew McCarthy, Michael Ironside and Jayne Heitmeyer star. AKA: "Crack in the Mirror," "Twist of Faith." 97 min.
82-5177 *$89.99*

Disembodied (1998)
A deranged woman uses her power to dissolve and devour human flesh to keep herself—and her newly born mutant offspring—alive in this gruesome ode to "mother love." George Randolph stars. 90 min.
82-5092 *$99.99*

Mommy (1995)
Patty McCormack, the young title star of "The Bad Seed," has grown into a diabolical adult in this shocker. She's the mother of a young girl who murders her teacher after the child is passed over for a scholarship. Detective Jason Miller discovers that McCormack may also be responsible for the deaths of her two husbands. Majel Barrett, Brinke Stevens and Mickey Spillane also star.
88-5010 *$14.99*

Mommy (Letterboxed Version)
Also available in a theatrical, widescreen format.
08-1772 *$19.99*

Mommy's Day: Mommy 2 (1996)
Patty McCormack, the mother of all mothers, returns to wreak terror on all who stand in her way when she attempts to regain the love of her precious daughter. See Mommy smile. See Mommy kill! With Paul Peterson, Gary Sandy, Mickey Spillane. 88 min.
88-5011 Was $89.99 *$14.99*

Mommy's Day: Mommy 2 (Letterboxed Version)
Also available in a theatrical, widescreen format.
08-1773 *$19.99*

Evil Sister (1998)
After her sister is let out of a mental institution following a 15-year stay, Merrit isn't sure whether she's been cured of her problems or if she's been too much for the doctors to handle. Soon, Merrit's question is answered when she discovers her sister's satanic sensuality. Kim Farina, Joanne Lee Rubino star. 88 min.
82-5071 *$69.99*

Feast (1998)
Gory horror offering about a couple of serial-killing cannibals who get more than they bargained for when they confront a psychiatrist who has a few bizarre ideas of her own. Chuck Gavoian, Al Troupe, Sharon Mitchell and Ron Jeremy star in this unsettling tale. 88 min.
82-5073 *$69.99*

Trail Of A Serial Killer (1998)
In this tale of terror, a relentless serial killer draws the attention of FBI agent Christopher Penn and the obsessed Michael Madsen. The two follow clues emanating from notes left at the ghastly crime scenes to trace the murderer's trail. 95 min.
82-5085 *$89.99*

Voodoo Dawn (1998)
Released from a Louisiana prison, bank robber Michael Madsen steals a fortune from a powerful voodoo priestess as part of his plan to use black magic for revenge on the cop who killed his brother. Trouble is, the cash came with a curse, and soon everyone's life is in danger in this occult-flavored thriller. Rosanna Arquette, Balthazar Getty also star. 90 min.
82-5178 *$99.99*

Evil's Edge (1999)
It's lurking in the shadows, waiting for another body to claim: a Satanic force worshipped by a bizarre "family" of evildoers. When you're confronted by "Evil's Edge," you have two choices: join them or be destroyed! Be scared, be very scared, with this chiller starring Darlene Pergola, Al Lopez and Countess Vladermira. 90 min.
82-5184 *$99.99*

The Screaming (1999)
Desperate for a story, young Bob Martin finally gets his chance! He comes upon the Crystalnetics, an ancient cult that has roamed the Earth for centuries looking for a safe haven. But is the story of a lifetime worth the group's unending appetite for blood? Intense shocker stars Vincent Bilancio, Elizabeth Barris. 90 min.
82-5185 *$99.99*

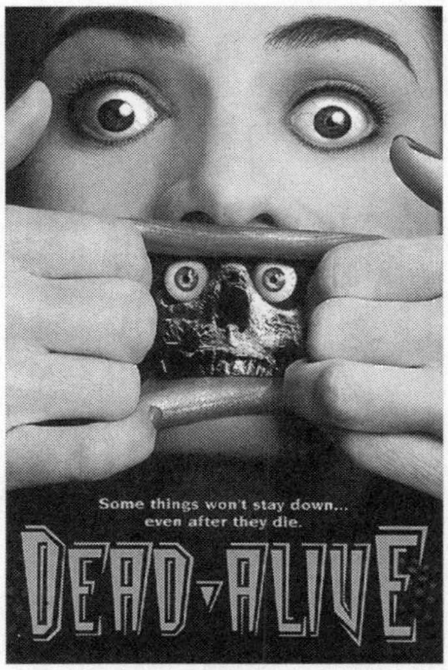

Dead Alive (1993)
Considered one of the most outrageous movies ever made, this gore-iffic horror-comedy from New Zealand's Peter Jackson ("Bad Taste") tells of a woman who has been turned into a zombie thanks to a bite from a cursed Sumatran rat-monkey. Soon, her friends and family are infected by the disease and turn into gruesome ghouls. Timothy Balme stars. Unrated version; 97 min.
68-1274 Was $89.99 *$14.99*

The Fear (1994)
A weekend retreat in the woods for a group of psychology students turns into a lethal lesson in the meaning of "fear," as each is subjected to demonic visions of their innermost phobias, thanks to a sinister spirit lurking in the woodwork named Morty. Terror tale stars Eddie Bowz, Ann Turkel, Erick Weiss, with appearances by Vince Edwards and horrormeister Wes Craven. 98 min.
83-1029 Was $89.99 *$14.99*

Skinner (1994)
Diabolical shocker stars Traci Lords as a woman troubled by horrific nightmares who learns that a blade-wielding psychopath is stalking and killing hookers in the city. As the murderous spree continues, Lords attempts to find the person behind the deaths. Ted Raimi and Ricki Lake also star. Uncut, unrated version. 90 min.
83-1033 Was $89.99 *$14.99*

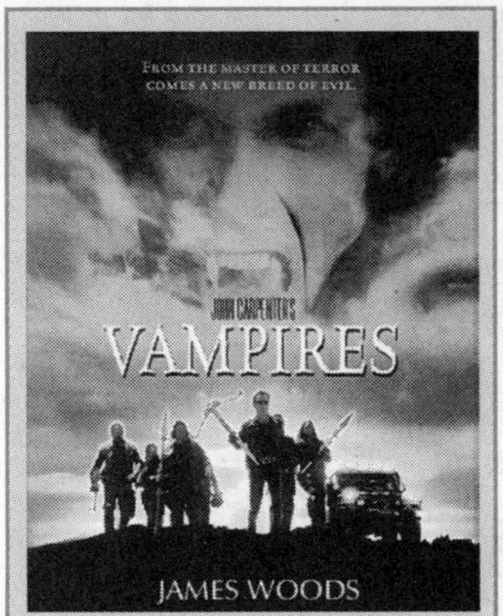

John Carpenter's Vampires (1998)
The director of "Halloween" sinks his teeth into the bloodsucker genre with this horrific gem. James Woods stars as the leader of a Vatican-backed band of vampire hunters battling the minions of a six-centuries-old nosferatu, who's seeking an ancient artifact that will allow them to stalk in the daytime. Daniel Baldwin, Thomas Ian Griffith, Cheryl Lee and Maximilian Schell also star. 108 min.
02-3274 Was $99.99 *$14.99*

The House That Screamed (1999)
Horror novelist Marty Beck rents a creepy house that he hopes will help inspire him for completing his latest terror tale. Little does he know that the place is inhabited by its dead past residents, as well as assorted monsters and ghouls. Bob Dennis, Robert Thomas star. 90 min.
82-5188 *$99.99*

Camp Blood (1999)
Two couples take a trip to Camp Blackwood, which, because of a bloodcurdling incident, came to be known as "Camp Blood" 10 years earlier. Soon, the killer responsible for murders a decade before is back—and ready to hack! Jennifer Ritchkoff and Michael Taylor star. 90 min.
82-5189 *$99.99*

The Reaper (1997)
In this shocker, Chris Sarandon is a writer whose best-selling book seems to have inspired a rash of brutal serial killings with pages of his book left with each victim. Sarandon retreats to a Maine hotel to finish his latest novel, but is recruited by a female detective to help in finding the murderer. Catherine Mary Stewart also stars. 97 min.
82-5190 *$99.99*

Shark (1996)
A ferocious, man-eating Great White Shark leaves its ocean home to terrorize a small upriver town in this horrifying thriller that stars Damian Brown and Monte Wheeler. 90 min.
82-5202 *$59.99*

The Evil Within (1994)
A grotesque life force from the center of the Earth enters the womb of a woman, turning her into a seductive murderess. Eventuallly, the woman gives birth to a hideous creature seeking blood and causing death and destruction. Emmanuelle Escourrou, Jean-François Gallotte star. 88 min.
83-1016 Was $89.99 *$14.99*

Vampyre (1991)
An evil vampire inhabits a ancient village, living off the blood of the townspeople and visitors. Only a mysterious stranger who arrives in town can stop the bloodsucker and his horrifying deeds. Modernized version of the Carl Dreyer silent classic stars Randy Scott Rozler and Cathy Seyler. 90 min.
86-1044 *$19.99*

I've Been Waiting For You (1999)
A series of deadly accidents plague a small-town high school. Could a new student be the reincarnation of a witch killed there 300 years earlier and returned from the grave for revenge? Sinister shocker, based on Lois Duncan's novel "Gallows Hill," stars Sarah Chalke, Soleil Moon Frye, Ben Foster and Markie Post. 90 min.
86-1143 Was $99.99 *$19.99*

Nadja (1995)
What better place for a hungry brother-sister pair of modern-day vampires to hang out than among the nocturnal denizens of New York's club scene? Stylish and offbeat, this bloodsucker shocker stars Elina Lowensohn, Suzy Amis, Martin Donovan and Peter Fonda as vampire-hunter Van Helsing. 92 min.
88-1040 Was $89.99 *$14.99*

Shadow Zone: The Undead Express (1996)
A young horror movie buff takes a non-stop ride into terror when a wrong turn in a subway tunnel leads him to a strange train whose undead occupant is looking for a way to return to the world of the living. Ron Silver, Chauncey Leopardi, Natanya Ross star, with a cameo by filmmaker Wes Craven. 98 min.
88-1123 Was $99.99 *$14.99*

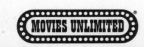

Prom Night (Collector's Edition)
The biggest night of any high school senior's year turns into a nightmare of terror, thanks to a mysterious killer who's gruesomely killing off disco-dancing teens (okay, so maybe he's doing the world a service!). Jamie Lee Curtis, Leslie Nielsen, Casey Stevens star. 91 min.
08-8576 Letterboxed *$14.99*

Prom Night III: The Last Kiss (1989)
And you thought the second trip to the prom was frightening! Thirty years after she dies in a fire at her high school, Mary Lou is back, haunting the hallways and having fun with classmates and the school's top jock. Casper was a friendly ghost; Mary Lou's not! Tim Conlon, Cyndy Preston and Courtney Taylor star. 97 min.
27-6671 Was $89.99 *$14.99*

Prom Night IV: Deliver Us From Evil (1991)
Take out the tuxes and the gowns, and look out! A monk who has something against sex escapes from a monastery and focuses his hate against four teenagers who are staying at their parents' summer house. Alden Kane, James Carver and Nikki DeBoer star. 95 min.
27-6760 Was $89.99 *$14.99*

The Doctor And The Devils (1985)
The crimes of notorious Victorian graverobbers Burke and Hare are re-created in this moody, chilling thriller, based on a story by Dylan Thomas. Timothy Dalton stars as a doctor whose quest for knowledge becomes an excuse for horror; co-stars Jonathan Pryce and Twiggy. 93 min.
04-1945 Was $79.99 ▢*$29.99*

Anguish: Collector's Edition (1987)
An unusual thriller with a twist: two girls in a dark theater are stalked by a creepy slasher, as they watch a movie about two girls in a dark theater who are stalked by a creepy slasher. Zelda Rubinstein ("Poltergeist"), Talia Paul, Michael Lerner star. 85 min.
04-2165 Letterboxed ▢*$14.99*

Q (Collector's Edition) (1982)
A gigantic winged reptile is loose in the skies over New York City, a bizarre Aztec cult is skinning its victims alive, and only a two-bit crook can help the police solve these seemingly unconnected crimes. Offbeat chiller from Larry Cohen stars Michael Moriarty, David Carradine, Richard Roundtree and Candy Clark. 92 min.
07-1164 Letterboxed *$14.99*

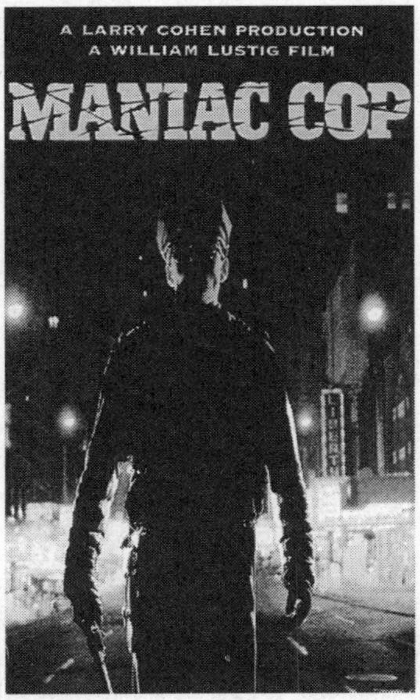

Maniac Cop (Collector's Edition) (1988)
Someone dressed as a police officer is cleaning up the mean streets of New York in the most brutal ways imaginable. A cop suspected in the killings must clear his name by finding the real murderer—an ex-officer who was sent to prison and killed by the inmates! Suspenseful shocker from the director of "Maniac" stars Tom Atkins, Bruce Campbell, Laurene Landon, Robert Zdar; written by Larry Cohen. Remastered version also includes theatrical and TV trailers and scenes not shown in American theaters. 85 min.
08-8554 Letterboxed *$14.99*

Maniac Cop 3 (1993)
You can't keep an undead cop down, as he's resurrected by an occult master and sent out after a group of corrupt officials and doctors who are responsible for framing a female officer for murder and leaving her hospitalized in a coma. Robert Z'Dar, Robert Davi, Gretchen Becker star. 85 min.
71-5273 ▢*$12.99*

Vampire At Midnight (1988)
It seems beyond belief, but a modern-day bloodsucker is stalking the streets of L.A.! Can a tough-as-nails cop bring down his undead quarry before the vampire attacks his own family? Intense shocker stars Jason Williams, Gustav Vintas. 93 min.
04-2175 Was $79.99 ▢*$29.99*

My Bloody Valentine (1980)
The sole survivor of a Valentine's Day mining disaster comes back to haunt the town of Valentine Bluffs when the younger residents ignore the warnings and hold a Valentine's party deep within the cavernous mine. 91 min.
06-1088 *$19.99*

The Sender (1982)
A suicidal patient is placed in a mental institution where an understanding psychiatrist discovers he has the ability to telepathically communicate his feelings and horrific nightmares to others. When the patient's mother appears at the hospital, their secret past is revealed. Kathryn Harrold, Zeljko Ivanek and Shirley Knight star in this intelligent shocker. 92 min.
06-1168 ▢*$19.99*

April Fool's Day (1986)
This comedy/chiller follows a gang of teens at a remote mansion where a maniac with no sense of humor is killing them one by one. Hey, put that axe down! Can't you take a joke? AAHHH! Deborah Foreman, Griffin O'Neal star. 88 min.
06-1380 Was $19.99 ▢*$14.99*

The Funhouse (1981)
The setting: an eerie, run-down carnival. The trapped: a group of teenagers. The horror: never-ending. A nonstop ride of scares and chills, directed by Tobe Hooper. With Elizabeth Berridge, Miles Chapin. 96 min.
07-1087 Was $19.99 *$14.99*

Ghost Story (1981)
A gloomy New England house, a dark, mysterious night and four old friends. These elements add up to a spell-binding, haunting tale filled with terror. Fred Astaire, Melvyn Douglas, Douglas Fairbanks, Jr., John Houseman. 110 min.
07-1097 Was $19.99 *$14.99*

Death Valley (1982)
A young boy, travelling to Arizona to visit his mother, finds an RV filled with the grisly handiwork of a deranged killer. The bad news is, no one believes him...except the slayer. Catherine Hicks, Paul LeMat, Peter Billingsley, Wilford Brimley star. 90 min.
07-1105 *$69.99*

Nightmares (1983)
We'll let you sleep on this one...if you can! A fearsome foursome of chilling vignettes about lurking psychos, rabid rats, demonic trucks and...killer video games? Emilio Estevez, Lance Henriksen, Christina Raines, Veronica Cartwright, Richard Masur and Moon Zappa star. 99 min.
07-1195 Was $59.99 *$14.99*

Revenge (1986)
A young man returns to his hometown because of his brother's death and uncovers a scarlet trail of murder and deception leading to an obscene cult of blood. Gore by the bucketful with Patrick Wayne, John Carradine. 98 min.
08-1327 *$19.99*

Terror At Tenkiller (1986)
Two girls spend a weekend at a lakeside resort to escape the urban jungle, but someone is following them...and killing anyone in the way. Is it the unbalanced boyfriend of one of the girls, or...someone even deadlier? Mike Wiles, Stacey Logan. 87 min.
08-1361 *$19.99*

The Last Slumber Party (1987)
Three carefree coeds decide to celebrate the end of school with a wild "pajama party," and when three guys show up there's even more fun...until the teens start dying one by one, that is. Shocker stars Jan Jensen, Nancy Meyer. 80 min.
08-1416 Was $19.99 *$14.99*

Terror (1984)
A family suddenly finds itself under attack from beyond in this pulse-pounding shocker. What is the terrifying secret behind their unearthly attacker? John Nolan stars. 86 min.
08-1422 *$14.99*

Blood Lake (1987)
"Come 'n' listen to a story 'bout a man named Jed, psychotic killer likes to see teenagers dead. Then one day he was stalking through the grove, and up from a teen come a-bubblin' Type O. Blood, that is. Red gold. Transylvania tea." 90 min.
08-1430 *$19.99*

My Brother Has Bad Dreams (1988)
Not even warm milk will cure the murderous nightmares of this troubled sibling, and when his dreams take on a deadly reality, there's no telling who'll die in his sleep. Bizarre chiller stars Nick Kleinholz, Marlena Lustic. 97 min.
08-1431 Was $29.99 *$19.99*

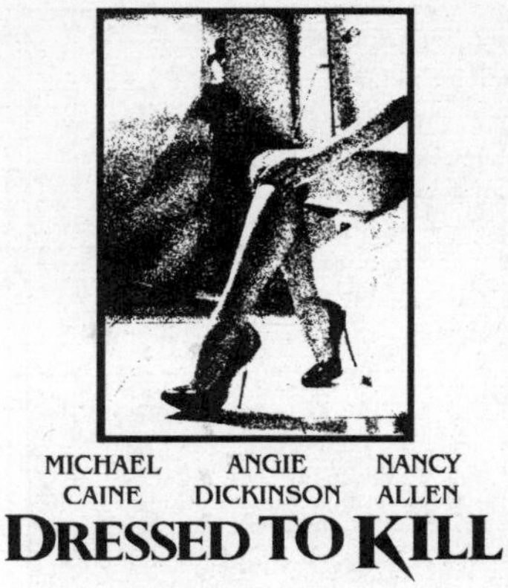

Dressed To Kill (1980)
A visit to the art museum leads to a fateful and fatal sexual encounter for bored housewife Angie Dickinson in this stylish, erotic suspenser from Brian De-Palma. Michael Caine is Dickinson's psychiatrist, who may hold the key to her murder; with Keith Gordon, Nancy Allen. 105 min.
19-1083 *$14.99*

Blood Cult (1985)
A quiet college campus is caught in a web of terror when a sinister blood coven begins killing students for an unholy ceremony in this horror film, the first made especially for video. Julie Andelman, Charles Ellis star. 89 min.
08-1275 *$19.99*

The Boogey Man (Collector's Edition) (1980)
Creepy shocker starts with a young boy stabbing his mother's lover to death as his sister watches in horror. The boy grows up to become mute while his sister mistakenly unleashes the dead lover's soul from a mirror. Fassbinder and Warhol cohort Ulli Lommel directs Suzanna Love and John Carradine. Includes original trailers. 83 min.
08-8700 Letterboxed *$14.99*

Boogeyman II (1983)
A little girl is haunted by a mirror. She tries to escape the clutches of a man possessed by the Boogeyman. Suzanna Love, Shannah Hall. 97 min.
23-5026 *$29.99*

Straight Jacket (1980)
A recovering alcoholic returns home after a series of psychic impressions and emotional disturbances, but soon finds things are equally unsettling in her house. Things get even creepier when she meets a former detective who once investigated a gruesome murder in the house. Aldo Ray, Kory Clark and Chuck Jamison star. 89 min.
10-9170 *$19.99*

Motel Hell (1980)
Just what could be the secret ingredient that makes Farmer Vincent's sausages so tasty? Guests of his motel know the answer. Or should we say *are* the answer? A zesty mix of humor, suspense and gore makes this cult hit an enjoyable treat. Rory Calhoun, Nancy Parsons, Wolfman Jack star. 106 min.
12-1587 Was $19.99 *$14.99*

The House Where Evil Dwells (1984)
When an American family moves to Japan, the spirits of three long-dead lovers possess their modern-day counterparts in order to re-enact the deadly triangle. Edward Albert, Susan George and Doug McClure star in a shocker of sinister terror. 88 min.
12-1410 Was $59.99 *$14.99*

A Stranger Is Watching (1981)
A TV newsreporter and her young daughter are kidnapped by a madman and held prisoner in the catacombs beneath New York's Grand Central Station. Shocking thriller stars Kate Mulgrew, Rip Torn and James Naughton. 98 min.
12-1213 *$19.99*

Pumpkinhead (1988)
A vengeful father calls upon the demon world to attack the men responsible for his son's death, and unleashes a grotesque creature who'll heed his summons for a price...in blood! Chilling tale of heartland horror stars Lance Henriksen, John DiAquino. 86 min.
12-1893 Was $19.99 *$14.99*

Pumpkinhead II: Blood Wings (1994)
Creepy Pumpkinhead is resurrected by a group of teenagers and the terror soon begins again. But this time, the creature carries the soul of a young boy who was brutally killed years earlier. Can the monster be destroyed and the child saved? Ami Dolenz, Linnea Quigley and "First Brother" Roger Clinton star. 88 min.
27-6887 Was $89.99 ▢*$14.99*

The Beast Within (1982)
A horrifying special-effects extravaganza about a boy who turns into a hideous werewolf and kills a slew of victims. Amazing transformation sequences highlight this terrifying film. Ronny Cox, Paul Clemens. 90 min.
12-1254 *$14.99*

House (1986)
A writer moves his family into an old mansion for "atmosphere" for his work, but gets a lot more than he bargained for...like ghosts, zombie soldiers, and gateways to other dimensions. Creepy thriller stars William Katt, Kay Lenz, Richard Moll, George Wendt. 97 min.
08-8447 *$14.99*

House II: The Second Story (1987)
Ascend another flight into terror as a man returns to his ancestral home in search of the hidden treasure buried with his great-grandfather, but finds that Grandpa's ghost isn't letting go! Dimension-spanning shocker stars Arye Gross, Jonathan Stark, Royal Dano and John Ratzenberger. 85 min.
08-8448 *$14.99*

House IV: Home Deadly Home (1991)
After her husband dies in a car crash, a woman and her daughter move into the family's decrepit summer home, only to discover an ancient force that unleashes supernatural terror. Filled with macabre humor and outrageous special effects, this outing stars Terri Treas, Scott Burkholder and William Katt. 89 min.
02-2154 Was $89.99 ▢*$14.99*

The Horror Show (1989)
Meat cleaver-wielding serial killer Max Jenke was supposed to have paid the ultimate price in the electric chair...trouble is, he just laughed it off! Now he's after the cop who brought him in! Lance Henriksen, Brion James, Rita Taggart star. 95 min.
12-1907 Was $19.99 *$14.99*

The Demon (1981)
The Demon...bloodthirsty, craving human flesh. The Demon...with an unstoppable killing urge. The Demon...holding a town terrified in its claws. The Demon...its next victim could be...YOU!!! Stars Cameron Mitchell, Jennifer Holmes. 94 min.
15-1096 *$19.99*

Child's Play (1988)
Gunned down in a toy shop, a homicidal psychotic casts his soul into a pudgy doll named Chucky, becoming a toy for a 6-year-old and a terror to the rest of Chicago. Mom Catherine Hicks and detective Chris Sarandon are two of Chucky's targets in this doll-icious horror hit. 87 min.
12-1139 Was $19.99 ▢*$14.99*

Child's Play 2 (1990)
Diabolical doll Chucky is back...and ready to hack! Mom's in a mental institution following the harrowing ordeal of going head-to-head with the killer children's toy. Her son is taken in by foster parents, but nothing can keep Chucky from terrorizing him again. With Alex Vincent, Jenny Agutter and the voice of Brad Dourif. 94 min.
07-1677 Was $19.99 ▢*$14.99*

Child's Play 3 (1991)
It's been eight years since Chucky was destroyed, but when toy manufacturers try to restart production of "Good Guy" dolls, the psychotic spirit enters a brand-new plastic shell and sets out to find a human body to possess. Chucky's scarifying antics at a military school are worth a 21-AAAHHH! salute. Justin Whalin, Perrey Reeves and Brad Dourif as Chucky's voice star. 89 min.
07-1730 Was $19.99 ▢*$14.99*

CHUCKY GETS LUCKY!

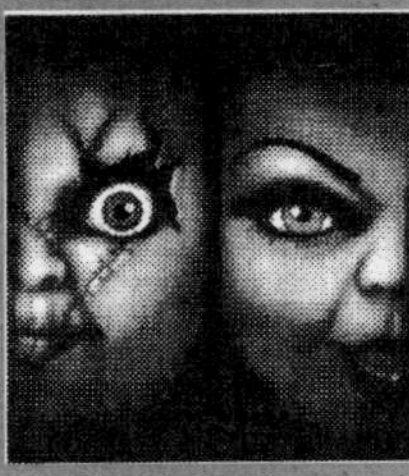

BRIDE OF CHUCKY

Bride Of Chucky (1998)
Thanks to some makeshift stitching and a voodoo spell from girlfriend Jennifer Tilly, demented doll Chucky is brought back to "life" in the fearsome fourth entry in the "Child's Play" series. But when Chucky's psychotic side emerges and Tilly is killed, there'll be two terrifying playthings looking for new human bodies to inhabit. With Katherine Heigl, Nick Stabile, John Ritter and Brad Dourif as the voice of Chucky. Special version includes 10 minutes of extra footage. 99 min.
07-2723 Was $99.99 ▢*$14.99*

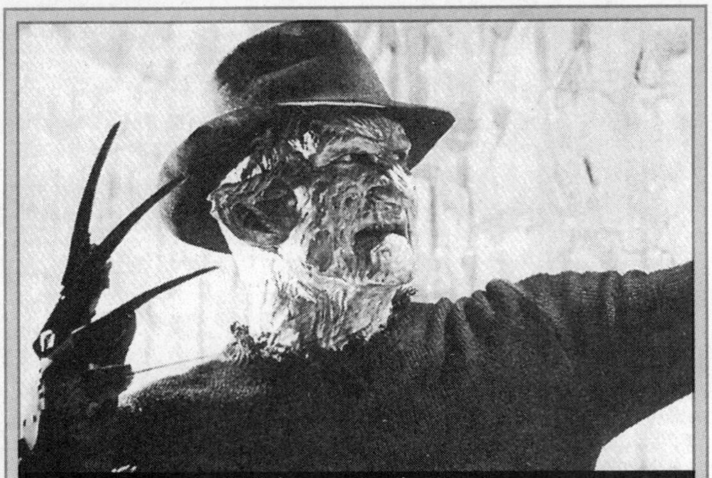

A Nightmare On Elm Street

A Nightmare On Elm Street (1984)
The debut of Ginsu-gloved dream demon Freddy Krueger, Wes Craven's chilling depiction of how Freddy terrorizes the sleeping teens of Springfield is a non-stop shocker that's a "cut" above the rest. With Heather Langenkamp, John Saxon, Johnny Depp and Robert Englund as Krueger. 92 min.
08-8404 ❏*$14.99*

A Nightmare On Elm Street (Letterboxed Version)
Also available in a theatrical, widescreen format.
03-1381 *$14.99*

A Nightmare On Elm Street, Part 2: Freddy's Revenge (1986)
A teenage boy moves to Elm Street and soon becomes a pawn in the supernatural schemes of frightful Freddie Krueger. Ripping good horror yarn stars Mark Patton, Kim Myers, Hope Lange and Robert Englund. 84 min.
08-8405 *$14.99*

A Nightmare On Elm Street, Part 3: Dream Warriors (1987)
Just when you thought it was safe to go back to bed...fearsome Freddy's back, and he's tormenting the dreams of some troubled teens under the care of the girl who survived his first rampage! Robert Englund, Heather Langenkamp, Craig Wasson, John Saxon and Patricia Arquette star. 96 min.
08-8406 *$14.99*

A Nightmare On Elm Street, Part 4: The Dream Master (1988)
The biggest cut-up in horror films returns! Fiendish Freddy Krueger (Robert Englund) has come back for revenge on the kids who "killed" him one film earlier, turning their dreams into deadly nightmares. Lisa Wilcox, Rodney Eastman star; directed by Renny Harlin ("Cliffhanger"). 93 min.
08-8411 *$14.99*

A Nightmare On Elm Street, Part 5: The Dream Child (1989)
For the young people of Elm Street, the nightmare never ends! Once more Freddy returns from the grave for revenge, focusing on the dreams of the unborn child of the one girl who can stop him (that's right, a pro-life horror film). Robert Englund, Lisa Wilcox and Kelly Jo Minter star. 90 min.
08-8416 *$14.99*

Freddy's Dead: The Final Nightmare (1991)
Yes, horror fans, the unthinkable has finally happened. Razor-gloved ghoul Freddy Krueger finally goes to his grave for good in this fright-fest, but before he does he's going to take the town of Springfield and his own daughter with him! Robert Englund as Freddy, Lisa Zane, Yaphet Kotto star, with cameos by Tom and Roseanne Arnold, Alice Cooper and Johnny Depp. Not in 3-D. 96 min.
02-5006 Was $19.99 ❏*$14.99*

Wes Craven's New Nightmare (1994)
Freddy may be dead in reel life, but not in real life, according to director Craven's diabolical return to the "Nightmare on Elm Street" series. A series of terrifying dreams leads to horror for actress Heather Langenkamp and her family, and talks with fellow "Nightmare" alumni Robert Englund, John Saxon and Craven (all playing themselves) convince her that Freddy Krueger is preparing to make the leap from fiction to reality. 111 min.
18-7534 Was $19.99 ❏*$14.99*

The Nightmare Collection Boxed Set
It's the collection that "Elm Street" fans have been dreaming about: all seven "Nightmare" films in a money-saving boxed set.
02-5214 Save $45.00! *$59.99*

Humanoids From The Deep (1980)
Preservation of the species and good old-fashioned loneliness get the best of some half-man, half-fish monsters as they leave their undersea home and attack a seaside town, abducting young women to bear their mutant offspring. Cult chiller that picks up where "The Creature from the Black Lagoon" left off stars Doug McClure, Vic Morrow, Ann Turkel. 82 min.
19-1009 Was $19.99 *$14.99*

Humanoids From The Deep (1997)
Just when you thought it was safe to go back you-know-where, along comes this reworking of the 1980 horror fave. Scientists experiment on serial killers by altering their genes with fish DNA, but instead of getting angry fish sticks, they create savage, amphibious monsters with a taste for human blood and a hunger for human women! Emma Samms, Robert Carradine, Justin Walker star. 85 min.
21-9142 *$59.99*

Eyes Of A Stranger (1981)
TV reporter Lauren Tewes is used to being watched, but when a psychotic neighbor begins following her and her deaf-mute sister, the attention turns dangerous. Spellbinding suspenser also stars Jennifer Jason Leigh, John DiSanti. 85 min.
19-1125 *$14.99*

Wolfen (1981)
A hypnotic, violent tale about a super breed of wolves that haunts the cities, preying on the weak and the sick. Albert Finney is the detective called on to unravel the bizarre mystery; with Gregory Hines, Edward James Olmos. 115 min.
19-1179 ❏*$14.99*

The Hand (1981)
It lives, it crawls, and suddenly, it kills. Michael Caine plays a cartoonist who loses his hand in an accident and later is haunted by it! Written and directed by Oliver Stone (who also appears as a bum). 105 min.
19-1188 *$14.99*

Sorority House Massacre (1986)
Forget panty raids; this campus is being ravaged by a "slice 'n' dice" killer who's after blood! You can lose a lot of good pledges that way! Horror film with a degree in gore stars Angela O'Neill, Wendy Martel, Pamela Ross. 74 min.
19-1563 Was $39.99 *$14.99*

Sorority House Massacre 2: Nighty Nightmare (1992)
A group of gorgeous gals—including Melissa Moore, Robyn Harris and Stacia Zhivago—know how to party, but when they spend their first night in a new sorority house they encounter a killer. The hook is that the killer has a hook...and knives...and other weapons. 80 min.
21-9017 Was $89.99 *$14.99*

Night Visitor (1989)
A young man turns peeping tom and spies on his gorgeous new neighbor, but the eyeful he gets includes a demonic cult murder! Can he convince the police of his bloodthirsty neighbors' activities before they get him? Horrifying thriller stars Derek Rydall, Elliott Gould, Shannon Tweed. 94 min.
12-1985 Was $79.99 *$14.99*

Dracula's Last Rites (1980)
If you're a vampire who doesn't feel like flapping his wings every night to search out victims, what would be the perfect job to have? Town mortician, of course! And Mr. Lucard uses his monstrous talents to keep business booming in this bloodsucking delight. Gerald Fielding, Victor Jorge star. 86 min.
12-2758 *$14.99*

Shock! Shock! Shock! (1987)
Described by its distributors as "a new low in slasher films," this frightfully funny spoof "cuts up" horror movie clichés old and new as its psycho killer star cuts up the cast one by one. Brad Isaac, Cyndy McCrossen star. 60 min.
15-5062 *$19.99*

City Of The Walking Dead (1983)
If you're a fan of "Dawn of the Dead," "Zombie" or "Gates of Hell," you'll want this gore-8 horror flick. Zombies everywhere. They're into blood and flesh and other things, the result of atomic radiation. With Mel Ferrer and Francesco Rabal. Umberto Lenzi directs. 92 min.
14-6006 *$14.99*

New Year's Evil (1980)
A nationally televised New Year's Eve punk rock party, being celebrated in all four time zones, sets an eerie stage for "Murders at Midnight" in this thriller with a twist ending. Roz Kelly, Kip Niven, Jed Mills star. 85 min.
19-7012 *$14.99*

Night School (1980)
Gruesome horror effort involving a series of ghastly knife killings at a Boston college and their connection to bizarre headhunter rituals of New Guinea. Rachel Ward, Leonard Mann star. 89 min.
19-2111 Was $19.99 ❏*$14.99*

Schizoid (1980)
Klaus Kinski plays a crazed psychologist determined to find the scissors-wielding murderer of his patients, one of whom, gossip columnist Mariana Hill, is receiving letters that may be from the killer. With Craig Wasson, Donna Wilkes, Christopher Lloyd. 89 min.
19-7011 *$19.99*

The Eyes Of The Panther (1989)
Ambrose Bierce wrote the story on which this horror tale is based. A mysterious panther brings a curse upon a pioneer family which makes the family's daughter answer the call of the wild. C. Thomas Howell and Daphne Zuniga star. 60 min.
19-7073 *$59.99*

Oasis Of The Zombies (1981)
German teens find themselves face-to-face with Nazi zombies when they try to undercover the hidden gold of Field Marshal Rommel in North Africa. Manuel Gellin, Frances Jordon also star in this Euro-shocker. AKA: "Bloodsucking Nazi Zombies." 80 min.
20-1069 *$14.99*

The Keeper (1982)
Stylish and disturbing Canadian shocker starring Christopher Lee as the chief of a mental hospital with a nefarious plan to insure his patients, then kill them to get their money and conquer the world. Tell Schreiber, Sally Gray also star.
20-5001 *$49.99*

Redneck Zombies (1988)
Revenooers, beware! A mess of mountain "home brew" is tainted with toxic waste, and before you can say "weeell, dogies!," a hillbilly clan is turned into radioactive cannibals ready to feast on some nearby campers. Shocks and laughs mix in this Troma Films concoction. Lisa D. Haven, William W. Decker star. 83 min.
20-5238 Was $69.95 *$19.99*

Blade Of The Ripper (1980)
This erotic Euro-shocker tells of the wife of an American diplomat stationed in Germany who begins to suspect that the man with whom she recently had a kinky, blood fetishistic affair may be the "Razor Killer" who's been terrorizing the city—and who may add her name to his list of murders. With Edwige Fenech, George Hilton. AKA: "The Next Victim."
21-5007 *$19.99*

The Prowler (1981)
A girl's school is terrorized by a bizarre bayonet killer. Hideous murders supplied by make-up artist Tom Savini ("Dawn of the Dead"). Cindy Weintraub, Christopher Goutman, Farley Granger star. 105 min.
23-5000 *$29.99*

Frankenstein Island (1982)
Wild Jerry Warren ("The Wild World of Batwoman") production in which a scientist-balloonist lands on an island where he encounters pirates, bikini-clad alien women, the floating head of John Carradine as Dr. Frankenstein and the monster itself. Robert Clarke, Steve Brodie, Cameron Mitchell and Andrew Duggan head the sublime "B" movie cast.
27-6105 *$19.99*

The Grim Reaper (1981)
This disturbing shocker from Italy's Joe D'Amato ("Trap Them and Kill Them") is set in the Greek islands where, an American student and her friends encounter a disfigured man who practices cannibalism. The psycho has a reason for eating people, though: to be forgiven for eating his own family after he was shipwrecked! With Tisa Farrow, George Eastman. AKA: "Antropophagus." 82 min.
27-6132 *$39.99*

The Ripper (1985)
A college criminology professor studying Jack the Ripper finds a ring that may have belonged to the infamous killer, but soon a new series of gruesome murders begins. Does the Ripper live again? Gory horrorfest stars make-up wizard Tom Savini. 104 min.
08-1293 *$19.99*

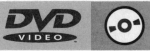

PRINCE OF DARKNESS

Prince Of Darkness (1987)
From John Carpenter comes this chilling tale of a primordial essence unleashed from its prison of seven million years by scientists. We don't know what the evil-looking liquid is in that ancient container, but with hordes of creepy crawlies around it, and a glow that turns folks into zombies, we bet it isn't Moxie. Donald Pleasence, Jameson Parker star. 102 min.
07-1576 Was $19.99 *$14.99*

Murder By Phone (1983)
Reach out and kill someone! A high-tech horror film about a deranged repairman who's learned how to make telephones deadly weapons. Richard Chamberlain and John Houseman star. AKA: "Bells." 80 min.
19-1314 Was $39.99 *$19.99*

Razorback (1984)
It's "Hooves"—a wild, giant, menacing boar loose in Australia's Outback! Gregory Harrison is out to stop him in this thrilling tale of nature gone awry. 95 min.
19-1401 Was $19.99 *$14.99*

Revenge Of The Zombie (1981)
Supernatural tale of violence and vengeance, when a biker gang breaks into a house and kills the father of two children with bizarre powers. Marilyn Burns, Jon Cedar and Fabian Forte star. AKA: "Kiss Daddy Goodbye." 92 min.
10-1404 *$19.99*

Blood Tide (1981)
A primitive Greek island becomes the center of a series of bloody murders caused by a horrifying monster. With James Earl Jones, Jose Ferrer, Lila Kedrova. 82 min.
14-6059 *$14.99*

The Wolfman (1982)
A creepy mansion in turn-of-the-century Georgia is the setting for this mesmerizing man-into-beast thriller from Southern shockmeister Earl Owensby (who also plays the title role). 91 min.
44-1093 *$14.99*

Prettykill (1987)
A high-class madam (Season Hubley) takes an innocent young thing (Suzanne Snyder) under her wing to teach her the tricks of the trade. Unfortunately the rookie is plagued by multiple personalities...some of which are very, very deadly. Susannah York, David Birney co-star. 95 min.
40-1336 Was $79.99 ❏*$19.99*

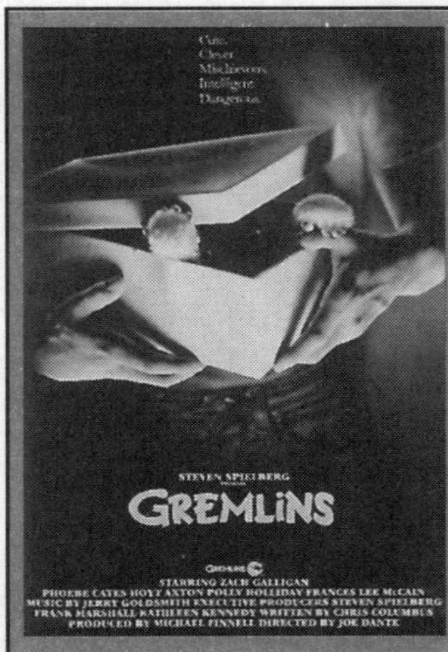

Gremlins (1984)
Gremlins may be cute and cuddly, but don't get them wet or feed them after midnight, or else you'll have more monsters than anyone can handle. "E.T." meets "The Thing" by way of "It's a Wonderful Life" in this horror gem from Joe Dante and Steven Spielberg; with Zach Galligan, Phoebe Cates, Hoyt Axton and the great Dick Miller. 111 min.
19-1461 ❏*$14.99*

Gremlins 2: The New Batch (1990)
Here they grow again! Those hellraising hobgoblins are back and running amuck in a TV mogul's high-tech New York skyscraper in Joe Dante's hit sequel that combines scares and laughs. Zach Galligan, Phoebe Cates, Dick Miller and John Glover star, with cameos by everyone from Christopher Lee and Leonard Maltin to John Wayne and Daffy Duck. 106 min.
19-1807 Letterboxed ❏*$14.99*

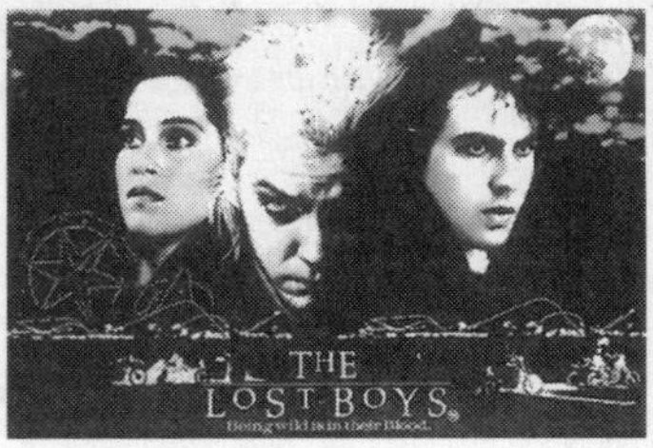
THE LOST BOYS

The Lost Boys (1987)
A new family moves into a small California town, and the teenage son is immediately taken with a local girl, only to discover that she (and most of the town youth) are vampires! It's up to his younger brother to save the day in this stylish and offbeat horror film. Jason Patric, Corey Haim, Jami Gertz, Kiefer Sutherland and Dianne Wiest star. 97 min.
19-1615 □*$14.99*

Necropolis (1987)
Shattering story of horror as a sensuous, centuries-old succubus stalks the streets of New York, stealing men's souls in her bid to complete an unholy pact for life eternal. Demon-filled descent into terror stars Lee Ann Baker, Jacquie Fitz. 76 min.
47-3221 *$12.99*

Cemetery High (1988)
It's a killer campus where S.A.T. stands for "Scream Aptitude Test," and where abused and terrorized coeds are getting bloody revenge on their male tormentors. Magna cum terror exercise stars Debbie Thibeault, Karen Nielsen. 80 min.
48-1164 *$19.99*

Don't Go To Sleep (1982)
Suspenseful supernatural shocker about the young daughter of a family who returns from the grave to join her living sister in a plot to kill other members of their family. Dennis Weaver, Valerie Harper and Ruth Gordon star. 93 min.
48-1180 *$29.99*

The Sinful Nuns Of St. Valentine (1980)
And they say nuns don't know how to have fun... Here, an insane Mother Superior and her convent of crazed, sex-starved sisters let loose their inhibitions and prey upon the nearby town's virgin girls. Based on the same story that inspired Ken Russell's "The Devils," Bruno Mattei's lurid "giallo" entry stars Franco Garofalo, Franca Stoppi. AKA: "The Other Hell." 93 min. In Italian with English subtitles.
50-5945 Letterboxed *$19.99*

The Dunwich Horror (1970)
From the pen of H.P. Lovecraft comes this classic tale of suspense and terror. A young girl becomes a pawn in a deadly game of sorcery and a heritage of blood is unleashed. Sandra Dee, Dean Stockwell and, in his last film, Ed Begley, Sr. star. 87 min.
53-1226 *$14.99*

From Beyond (1986)
The creators of "Re-Animator" have once again injected a sense of satire into another of H.P. Lovecraft's ghastly horror tales. A young scientist and a female psychiatrist discover a new dimension, where the ultimate pleasure is derived from "eating" another human's mind. Stars Jeffrey Combs and Barbara Crampton. 85 min.
47-1754 Was $19.99 □*$12.99*

The Unnamable (1988)
A house haunted by a centuries-old curse and a group of young people eager to dispel the myth are the elements in this other-worldly chiller based on a story by horror master H.P. Lovecraft. Charles King, Mark Kinsey Stevenson star. 87 min.
68-1090 *$12.99*

The Unnamable II (1992)
Shocking sequel returns to Miskatonic University, where a series of brutal murders is somehow connected to the spells of a 17th-century warlock and threatens to release a beautiful, demonic creature. Mark Kinsey Stephenson, John Rhys-Davies, David Warner, Julie Strain star. 104 min.
46-5554 □*$89.99*

Cthulhu Mansion (1991)
From the writings of horror master H.P. Lovecraft comes a tale of ancient terror and supernatural suspense, as a group of teens hiding out in the mansion of a carnival magician accidentally unleash a demonic force, and then must fight to stay alive. Frank Finlay, Brad Fisher, Melanie Shatner star. 92 min.
63-1490 Was $89.99 □*$12.99*

Necronomicon: Book Of The Dead (1996)
In this horrific anthology, H.P. Lovecraft (Jeffrey Combs) uncovers stories from the forbidden "Book of the Dead." Included are "The Drowned," about a man's drowned lover returning from the dead; "The Cold," in which a woman reveals her secret for cheating death to a reporter; and "Whispers," focusing on a pregnant policewoman's nightmarish near-death experiences. Bruce Payne, Maria Ford and David Warner also star. 96 min.
02-5110 Was $19.99 □*$14.99*

Wicked Games (1994)
The games are both wicked and bloody in this sinister slasher saga in which a mysterious, malevolent masked madman slaughters promiscuous people and other "deviants" in a small Southern town. Joel G. Wynkoop stars in this gory sequel to "Truth or Dare: A Critical Madness." 80 min.
73-9169 *$19.99*

Screaming For Sanity: Truth Or Dare 3 (1998)
Get ready for a disturbing tale of revenge, murder, and ultimate sin, as a copper-masked maniac kills those he believes to be profiting off the fame of serial killer Mike Stauber. Joel D. Wynkoop, Franklin E. Wales and Ken Blanck star. 101 min.
73-9245 *$29.99*

Necromancer (1988)
After she is savagely raped, a beautiful co-ed prays to Satan for power to gain her unholy vengeance. The bloody price, however, becomes too high when her own family is threatened! Sizzling shocker stars Elizabeth Cayton, Russ Tamblyn. AKA: "Necromancer: Satan's Servant." 88 min.
50-1685 Was $79.99 *$14.99*

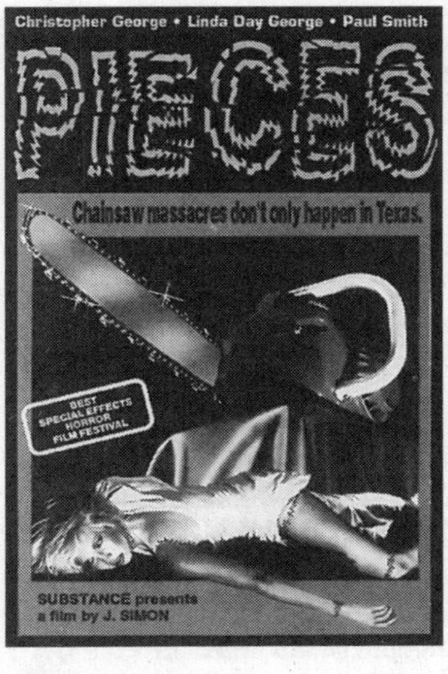
Christopher George • Linda Day George • Paul Smith
PIECES
Chainsaw massacres don't only happen in Texas.
BEST SPECIAL EFFECTS HORROR FILM FESTIVAL
SUBSTANCE presents
a film by J. SIMON

Pieces (1983)
What a chunk of terror! Remember "Texas Chainsaw Massacre"? The vroooooming of the chainsaw—the horror, the horror? Well, this one goes one step farther, into the realm of...of...AAHHH!! Gore city as a killer is on the loose, terrorizing a school with a chainsaw. Christopher George stars. 80 min.
47-1211 Was $19.99 *$14.99*

Pieces (Unrated Version)
Also available in an uncut, unrated version that's definitely not for the squeamish. 89 min.
59-7068 *$29.99*

The Great Alligator (1980)
Mel Ferrer owns an isolated resort in the African wilderness complete with hot and cold running alligators. Will Barbara Bach and Richard Johnson stop this menacing monster before more guests are devoured? 80 min.
50-6082 Was $19.99 *$14.99*

Death Spa (1989)
The demonic spirit of a gorgeous dead woman returns to the living to haunt the members of her husband's health spa. Each beautiful female member becomes possessed by evil and meets a grisly death. Lots of bloodbaths and nude baths in this wicked workout. With William Bumiller, Brenda Bakke and Merritt Butrick. Uncut, unrated version; 89 min.
50-6625 Was $79.99 *$19.99*

Zeder (1983)
A novelist's wife surprises him with a typewriter for an anniversary gift. But when he reads the typed ribbon imprint of the previous owner, a scientist attempting to prove the existence of "K-zones" where the dead can come back to life, the writer is propelled into a bizarre quest filled with occult groups and—just maybe—the undead. Unusual "zombieless zombie film" from "giallo" auteur Pupi Avati. Gabriele Lavia, Anne Canovas star. AKA: "Revenge of the Dead," "Zeder: Voices from Beyond." 98 min. Dubbed in English.
50-8335 *$19.99*

Revenge Of The Dead (Zeder) (Dubbed Version)
The retitled and dubbed-in-English edition of "Zeder" is also available. 90 min.
47-3004 *$19.99*

Dr. Bloodbath (1989)
This ultra-grisly shocker involves an abortion doctor who takes his job a little too far when he decides to murder his patients in the most diabolical ways possible. When his wife becomes pregnant, the not-so-good doctor has to perform the deed on his missus. Albert Ebkinazi and Irmigard Millard star. 60 min.
50-8401 *$19.99*

Swamp Thing (1982)
From the fog-shrouded Louisiana bayou, by way of comic books, comes SWAMP THING (Wow!), a scientist transformed into a green, muck-encrusted hulk of a monster with a heart. He has eyes for lovely government agent Adrienne Barbeau and battles villainous Louis Jourdan. Ray Wise, Dick Durock also star. 91 min.
53-1031 *$14.99*

The Return Of Swamp Thing (1989)
Comics' moss-covered man-brute is back, once more fighting undying archfoe Arcane (Louis Jourdan)! Can a seven-foot anthropomorphic plant find true happiness with his enemy's lovely niece (Heather Locklear)? Action and laughs abound; with Sarah Douglas and Dick Durock as Swampy. 88 min.
02-1957 *$14.99*

The Howling (1981)
Amazing special effects and a furry sense of humor highlight this Joe Dante scare-show about a TV anchorwoman on vacation at a remote California rest resort who finds it's home to a colony of werewolves. Co-written by John Sayles; Dee Wallace, Christopher Stone, Patrick Macnee, Slim Pickens, John Carradine and the great Dick Miller star. 91 min.
53-1076 *$14.99*

Howling II: Your Sister's A Werewolf (1985)
A young man, convinced his sister was murdered by a cult of werewolves, joins a lycanthropy expert on a mission to Transylvania to stop the terror at its source. Christopher Lee, Reb Brown, Annie McEnroe and Sybil Danning star in this horrific howler. 91 min.
63-1617 *$14.99*

Howling IV: The Original Nightmare (1988)
The successful erotic horror series continues, as a beautiful novelist seeking quiet at a country retreat is tormented by inhuman howls, terrible visions and hideous man-wolves. Heartpounder stars Romy Windsor. 94 min.
27-6603 *$14.99*

Howling V: The Rebirth (1989)
A group of people, stranded in an isolated castle, are marked for death when they witness an unholy secret, and the terror of "the Howling" rises once more. Latest entry in the beastly horror film series stars Philip Davis, Victoria Catlin. 99 min.
27-6660 Was $89.99 *$14.99*

The Howling VI: The Freaks (1990)
Ahh-ewww! Werewolves of the carnival! A midway sideshow is the backdrop for this excursion into evil, as a tortured man who lives in a cage awaits a visit from a vampire with the power to transform him into a werewolf. Outrageous special effects abound. With Carol Lynley, Antonio Fargas and Brendan Hughes. 102 min.
27-6709 *$14.99*

The Howling: New Moon Rising (1995)
A number of murders occur in a small California town after a motorcycle-riding stranger arrives. Meanwhile, in another nearby town, police are hot on the trail of a killer they believe is a werewolf. What connection does the stranger have to the gruesome killings? This "Howling" with a country-western angle stars Jim Lonzano. 90 min.
02-5066 Was $89.99 □*$19.99*

Fatal Pulse (1988)
A sorority house suffers a serious decline in membership when a sadistic killer brutally slays one sister after another, and soon only one coed is left...but not for long! Grisly shocker stars Michelle McCormick, Ken Roberts. 90 min.
69-5032 Was $79.99 *$19.99*

Evil Laugh (1988)
There's nothing funny about it to the teenagers who rented out an abandoned orphanage for their big party, only to find that the laugh belongs to a psycho killer who's staked the building out as his domain. Steven Baio, Tony Griffin, Kim McKamy. 90 min.
69-5070 *$79.99*

Violent Sh-t (1989)
Called "the goriest film ever made," this gross-out splatterthon is not for the squeamish—and maybe too strong for gorehounds, too! The film centers on the psychotic Karl the Butcher, a mass murderer who enjoys slaughtering everything in sight. Directed by Andreas Schnaas. 75 min. In German with English subtitles.
73-9066 *$49.99*

Violent Sh-t II: Mother Hold My Hand (1992)
Karl the Butcher, Jr. is doing disgusting stuff that would make his father proud, like avenging Dad's death in the most reprehensible ways imaginable: cutting, slashing and chopping. And Mama is giving Junior the orders! Andreas Diehn stars. 80 min. In German with English subtitles.
73-9067 Letterboxed *$49.99*

Zombie Doom!: Violent Sh-t III (1999)
An extreme gore fan's dream, this third excursion into zombiedom from German director Andreas Schnaas is the feverish flesh-ripping tale of Karl the Butcher, leader of a band of deranged walking dead looking to take a bite out of a group of shipwreck survivors. With Joe Neuman and Schnaas. WARNING: Contains graphic violence. 80 min. In German with English subtitles.
73-9335 *$29.99*

Christmas Evil (1983)
Hear those "slay" bells ring! Jolly old St. Nick is decking the halls red with blood and no one's safe from the maniac in the red and white suit in this holiday horror fest. Oh, he sees you when you're sleeping... AKA: "Terror in Toyland." 92 min.
67-1002 *$19.99*

Silent Night, Deadly Night 4: The Initiation (1990)
Just when you thought it was safe to trim the Christmas tree, more terror interrupts the holiday spirits. A blood-thirsty cult needs to initiate a new member. Their target: an inquisitive reporter with street smarts and beauty. Will she be able to stop them before she gets the membership card? Maud Adams, Clint Howard, Allyce Beasley and Tommy Hinkley star. 90 min.
27-6690 Was $89.99 *$14.99*

Silent Night, Deadly Night 5 (1991)
A young mute boy must learn who is responsible for the murderous playthings that have already tried to kill him once before. But someone's out to make sure that the child's next Christmas will be his last. Surely it can't be jolly toymaker Mickey Rooney, can it? With Tracy Fraim, Jane Higginson. 90 min.
27-6742 *$14.99*

Santa Claws (1996)
It's holiday-flavored horror laced with eroticism and dark comedy, as a cinema "scream queen" spends her Christmas battling a deranged neighbor who dresses in a Santa suit and begins killing the actress's friends and co-workers in order to have her all to himself. Debbie Rochon, Grant Kramer, John Mowod star; written and directed by John Russo ("Night of the Living Dead"). Uncut, unrated version; 85 min.
78-3036 Was $79.99 *$19.99*

Prime Evil (1988)
Beneath the streets of New York, a presence more sinister than any mere crook is growing. One young nun risks her life to infiltrate the ranks of a devil-worshipping cult, but her sacrifice may place her on the Satanists' altar. Supernatural thriller stars Christine Moore, William Beckwith. 87 min.
70-1243 Was $79.99 *$14.99*

Truth Or Dare... A Critical Madness (1986)
You used to play this all the time when you were little, right? But never in the manner that would disintegrate into a bizarre bloodbath that will numb you in its brutality as in this relentlessly grim thriller. Missed me, missed me...now you're going to kill me? 90 min.
50-1427 *$19.99*

The Devonsville Terror (1983)
A story of suspense and supernatural rites that is sure to frighten you, as a witch seeks vengeance on the descendants of the townsfolk who executed her 300 years earlier. Donald Pleasence, Robert Walker, Jr., Suzanna Love star. 82 min.
53-1088 Letterboxed *$14.99*

Slime City (1988)
An addictive homemade yogurt that changes health food nuts into crazy slime creatures piles up dozens of host bodies for the souls of a long-dead alchemist and his followers. A gooey cup of gore with lots of fright on the bottom starring Mary Huner and Robert Sabin. Features a "making of" documentary. 90 min.
72-5016 Was $79.99 *$19.99*

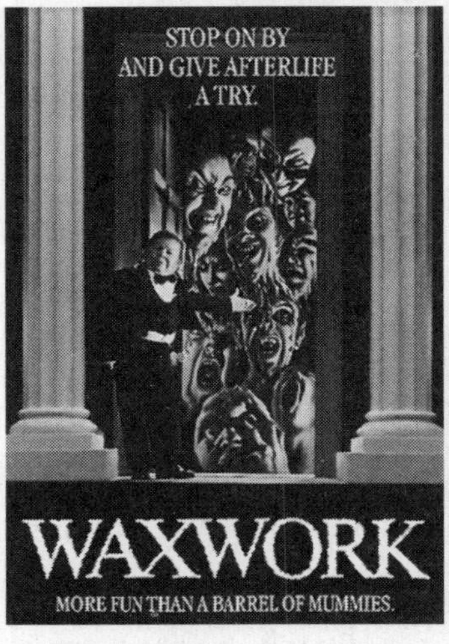
STOP ON BY
AND GIVE AFTERLIFE
A TRY.
WAXWORK
MORE FUN THAN A BARREL OF MUMMIES.

Waxwork (1988)
What is it about wax museums that makes them ripe subjects for horror films? Here a group of touring teens finds out the fiendish proprietor wants them to join his monstrous tableaux...permanently! Wax horrific with Zach Galligan, Miles O'Keeffe, Deborah Foreman and Patrick Macnee. Uncut version; 100 min.
47-1918 *$14.99*

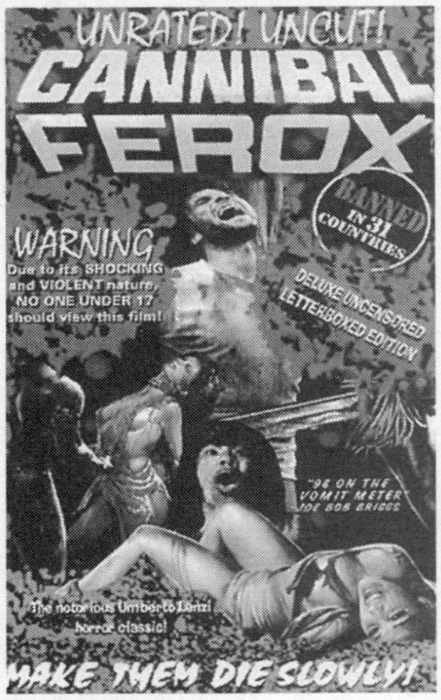
UNRATED! UNCUT!
CANNIBAL FEROX
BANNED IN 31 COUNTRIES
WARNING
Due to its SHOCKING and VIOLENT nature, NO ONE UNDER 17 should view this film!
DELUXE UNCENSORED LETTERBOXED EDITION
"96 ON THE VOMIT METER" JOE BOB BRIGGS
The notorious Umberto Lenzi horror classic!
MAKE THEM DIE SLOWLY!

Cannibal Ferox (Unrated Version) (1980)
Umberto Lenzi's notorious jungle cannibal adventure is considered one of the most disturbing films of all time, filled with unsettling, gory images. A college student and two friends travel to the Amazon, where they encounter drug dealers, nasty natives and some of the wickedest deaths ever captured on celluloid. Lorraine De Selle stars; this special edition features interviews and trailers. AKA: "Make Them Die Slowly," "The Woman from Deep River." 93 min.
20-8361 Letterboxed *$29.99*

Monster In The Closet (1987)
"Just when you thought it was safe to hang up your clothes"...a city is panicked when a mysterious creature begins coming out of people's closets and slaughtering them, and only a reporter and a beautiful scientist can stop it. Offbeat chiller stars Donald Grant, Denise DuBarry, Claude Akins, John Carradine. 90 min.
40-1334 *$14.99*

The Believers (1987)
A New York police psychiatrist uncovers links between a series of human sacrifices and the hovering presence of a mysterious voodoo cult. Graphic, unsettling descent into paranoia from director John Schlesinger stars Martin Sheen, Helen Shaver, Robert Loggia, Jimmy Smits. 114 min.
44-1507 Was $19.99 ❑*$14.99*

Dracula's Widow (1988)
When he started a tribute to a famous vampire in his waxworks, Raymond never dreamed he'd be welcoming the Countess Dracula herself, or that she'd turn the town into her own Chamber of Horrors! Sultry Sylvia Kristel ("Emmanuelle") stars. 85 min.
44-1560 Was $19.99 *$14.99*

Poltergeist (1982)
"They're here." Steven Spielberg and Tobe Hooper take you on a terrifying journey with a suburban family whose home is the focal point for an invasion from beyond the grave. Craig T. Nelson, JoBeth Williams, Zelda Rubinstein, Heather O'Rourke co-star. 114 min.
12-1228 Was $19.99 ❑*$14.99*

Poltergeist (Letterboxed Version)
Also available in a theatrical, widescreen format.
12-3178 ❑*$14.99*

Poltergeist II (1986)
"They're back!" The Freeling family finds itself under attack by vengeful spirits in the spooky sequel, and must enter a mystic realm to save their daughter. Frights and monsters galore; Craig T. Nelson, JoBeth Williams, Zelda Rubinstein, Julian Beck. 90 min.
12-1588 Was $19.99 ❑*$14.99*

Poltergeist III (1988)
Third entry in the spooktacular series has little Heather O'Rourke going to visit relatives in Chicago, unaware that the ghosts that have plagued her family are going with her, and soon a skyscraper becomes a battleground against the spirits. Tom Skerritt, Nancy Allen, Zelda Rubinstein co-star. 97 min.
12-1871 Was $19.99 ❑*$14.99*

Poltergeist: The Legacy (1996)
The feature-length pilot to the hit cable TV series based on the popular horror films stars Helen Shaver as a woman who unwittingly frees a bloodthirsty demon to prey upon mankind. Now a secret society known as "the Legacy" must return the monster to his world...or suffer a fate truly worse than death. With Derek de Lint, Martin Cummins. 85 min.
12-3181 ❑*$59.99*

Return Of The Living Dead, Part II (1987)
Just when you thought it was safe to bury Grandma...some foolhardy teens open barrels of "reanimation" vapor near a cemetery, and soon the dead and buried aren't staying that way, and are ready for some midnight snacking! Dana Ashbrook, Thom Mathews and James Karen star. 92 min.
40-1383 ❑*$14.99*

Return Of The Living Dead 3 (1993)
You can't keep a good flesh-easting zombie down, as a teenager learns to his horror when he sneaks into his father's Army research lab and uses an experimental gas on his deceased girlfriend. The results are less than romantic; in fact, they're downright terrifying! J. Trevor Edmond, Mindy Clarke, Kent McCord star. Uncut, unrated version; 97 min.
68-1300 ❑*$14.99*

Stepfather 2: Make Room For Daddy (1989)
Papa's got a brand new brood! Terry O'Quinn returns as Mr. Not-So-Nice Guy, escaping from a psychiatric hospital and posing as a therapist while continuing his demented search for the perfect fatherless family to claim...and murder! Meg Foster, Caroline Williams co-star. 93 min.
44-1717 Was $89.99 ❑*$14.99*

Stepfather 3 (1992)
And you thought he was finished! Well, now the mild-mannered murderer returns with a new face and a new fatherless family to terrorize. What's more, he gets a job at a garden nursery—a perfect place to bury things. Robert Wightman, Priscilla Barnes and Season Hubley star. 110 min.
68-1239 ❑*$89.99*

Dead And Buried (1981)
Lovecraftian horror excursion set in a small New England town where the local coroner has found a way to revive dead bodies...while listening to Big Band music! Sheriff James Farentino has to figure out why tourists are disappearing. Melody Anderson, Jack Albertson and Robert Englund co-star in this shocker scripted by "Alien" writers Ron Shussett and Dan O'Bannon. Unrated; 95 min.
47-1126 Was $79.99 *$29.99*

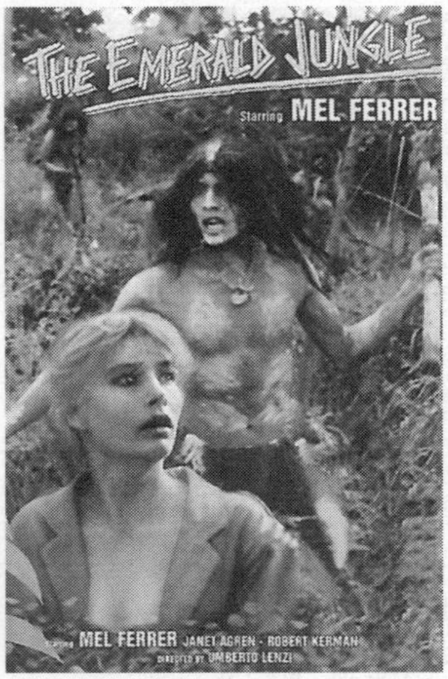
THE EMERALD JUNGLE
Starring MEL FERRER
MEL FERRER JANET AGREN · ROBERT KERMAN
DIRECTED BY UMBERTO LENZI

The Emerald Jungle (1985)
Frightening and gore-filled account of a woman who joins forces with an adventurer to search for her missing sister in the jungles of New Guinea. Their journey leads to a tribe of cannibals led by a deranged cult leader who uses sex and drugs to get his way. Not for the squeamish, this Umberto Lenzi outing stars Ivan Rassimov and Mel Ferrer. AKA: "Eaten Alive." 92 min.
14-6079 *$29.99*

Cameron's Closet (1989)
A lonely boy's closet seems to materialize his deepest fears and violent impulses, starting with the decapitation of his father. A well-written foray into psychic terror starring Mel Harris ("thirtysomething") and Tab Hunter. 87 min.
45-5462 *$14.99*

Out Of The Body (1988)
A primal force from another dimension takes over David Gaze's astral form and unleashes its savagery on beautiful, helpless women. Can he pull himself together in time to save them? Chilling experience stars Mark Hembrow. 89 min.
45-5463 *$79.99*

Underground Terror (1988)
Beneath the streets of New York City a mental patient named Boris heads a pack of misfits, freaks and murderers who stalk the weak and helpless in the subway's tiled horror chambers. Don't miss that train! Doc Dougherty stars. 92 min.
45-5464 *$79.99*

Stones Of Death (1988)
From their cave burial place, the remains of a serial killer and some cursed Indian artifacts launch an evil spirit to the dreams of nearby teenagers. Tom Jennings stars. 90 min.
45-5439 *$79.99*

Vicious (1988)
A very rich, very bored teenager falls in with a lawless band of thrill-seekers on a bloody spree. Graphic suspenser stars Tamblyn Lord and Craig Pierce. 90 min.
45-5453 *$79.99*

Blood Rage (1987)
A teenage couple are brutally murdered at a drive-in, and a disturbed child, one of a pair of twins, is arrested and institutionalized. Now, 10 years later he breaks out and plans a deadly family reunion. Shocker stars Louise Lasser. 87 min.
46-5352 *$79.99*

Bloody Wednesday (1985)
A seemingly normal day in a suburban restaurant turns into a day of terror when a disturbed gunman enters and opens fire on everyone inside. Shocking tale rent from today's headlines stars Raymond Elmendorf, Pamela Baker star. 89 min.
46-5353 *$19.99*

Thou Shalt Not Kill...Except (1987)
Marine sergeant Jack Stryker returns home from Vietnam to finds his girlfriend has been kidnapped and her grandfather murdered by a crazed, Manson-like cult. Along with some of his old war buddies, Stryker sets out to rescue her and exact their own brutal revenge. Intense low-budget thriller from writer/director Josh Becker stars Brian Schulz, Cheryl Hanson and filmmaker Sam Raimi ("The Evil Dead") as the cult leader. Special video version includes the original theatrical trailer and a deleted scene. 84 min.
46-5372 Letterboxed *$14.99*

Blood Hook (1986)
A group of college students travel to a Wisconsin fishing resort for a vacation, but some abominable angler is casting his line for humans! There's no exaggerating the full catch of terror in this una-bait-ed shocker directed by Jim Mallon ("MST3K's" own Gypsy). Mark Jacobs, Lisa Todd star. 87 min.
46-8002 *$14.99*

Girls School Screamers (1985)
Terror lurks in a Philadelphia-area mansion where a group of young female students and a nun uncover antiquated treasures...as well as scary spirits. Mollie O'Mara, Sharon Christopher star in this Troma release directed by John Finegan. 82 min.
46-8003 *$14.99*

Zombie Island Massacre (1984)
Former congressional wife and Playboy model Rita Jenrette has some revealing nude scenes in this horror outing about a group of tourists who have their Caribbean vacation disrupted by a group of voodoo-worshipping dancing girls and mysterious murderers. Rita also sings a song; with Tom Cantrell, David Broadnax.
46-8004 *$14.99*

Demented Death Farm Massacre...The Movie (1986)
John Carradine stars in this shocker about a group of jewel thieves on the run from the law who take refuge in a farm owned by hillbillies. They have a decision to make: surrender to the authorities or face all sorts of horrors. Ashley Brookes, Trudy Moore and George Ellis also star. AKA: "Death Farm."
46-8044 *$14.99*

Curse Of The Cannibal Confederates (1982)
A group of hunters and their girlfriends uncover a diary that helps revive a platoon of Confederate zombie soldiers seeking revenge against the Yankees who tortured them to death during the Civil War. The South does indeed rise—from its grave—in this gory shocker. Steve Sandkuhler, Judy Dixon star. AKA: "Curse of the Screaming Dead." 91 min.
46-8049 *$14.99*

Screamplay (1983)
A would-be screenwriter arrives in Hollywood and is given a chance to write a horror script. The quirky caretaker of an apartment building offers him a place to stay, but when he begins to use the building's residents in his story, several of them turn up dead. Offbeat mix of noir parody and slasher shocks stars director/co-scripter Rufus Butler Seder, Katy Bolger, George Kuchar.
46-8060 *$14.99*

House On The Edge Of The Park (1982)
Shockingly gory thriller from Ruggero Deodato ("Cut and Run") starring "Last House on the Left's" David Hess as a psychotic murderer into torturing his victims in the most despicable ways. Annie Belle also stars in this infamous fright fest. 91 min.
47-1508 *$29.99*

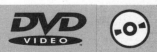

DVD VIDEO
ASK ABOUT OUR GIANT DVD CATALOG!

The Evil Dead: Collector's Edition (1983)
You axed for it—Movies Unlimited has it! It's Sam Raimi's original shocker about five college students who travel to a remote Tennessee cabin where they find an ancient book of magic. Inadvertently, they use the tome to summon a demonic force from another dimension that begins to possess them one by one. Bruce Campbell, Betsy Baker, Ellen Sandweiss star. Includes the original theatrical trailer. 85 min.
44-1152 *$14.99*

Evil Dead 2: Dead By Dawn (1987)
One part revamping of and one part extension to its predecessor, this audacious horror-comedy finds Ash (Bruce Campbell) forced to battle evil spirits that take over the woods, his girlfriend, and his own hand when he unwittingly plays recorded spells from the mysterious Book of the Dead while staying at a secluded cabin. With Sarah Berry, Denise Bixler. 85 min.
47-1776 *$14.99*

Evil Dead 2: Dead By Dawn: Collector's Edition
Also available in a theatrical, widescreen edition, which features a special digital transfer.
08-8637 Letterboxed *$14.99*

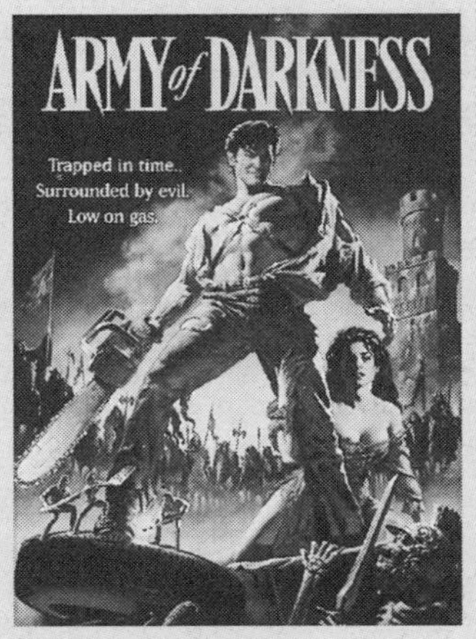
ARMY of DARKNESS
Trapped in time..
Surrounded by evil.
Low on gas.

Army Of Darkness (1993)
The outrageous "Evil Dead" series continues as cynical, chainsaw-wielding department store clerk Ash (Bruce Campbell) and his '73 Oldsmobile land in medieval England, where he battles pit-dwelling creatures, his villainous twin, and a battalion of the living dead. Hip humor and great special effects highlight Sam Raimi's action-horror yarn. Embeth Davidtz co-stars. Special video edition features the original "Rip Van Winkle" ending not shown in American theatres. 81 min.
08-8797 *$14.99*

Army Of Darkness (Letterboxed Collector's Edition)
Also available in a theatrical, widescreen format. Includes the theatrical trailer and the behind-the-scenes featurette "The Men Behind the Army," narrated by Campbell.
08-8798 *$14.99*

Death Warmed Up (1984)
Campy horror tale about a mad scientist on a deserted island who turns human beings into disgusting mutant killing machines. A gore-a-thon from New Zealand with Gary Day and Michael Hurst. 83 min.
47-1497 Was $69.99 *$29.99*

Igor And The Lunatics (1985)
A blood-spilling guru of gore and his team of brainwashed killer slaves take part in small-town community bloodbath. Not for the sheepish. Joseph Eero, Joe Niola star. 79 min.
47-1633 *$14.99*

C.H.U.D. II (1989)
Just when you thought it was safe to go back to the sewers...those dehumanized cellar-dwellers have returned...and no one is safe. Gerrit Graham, Robert Vaughn and Brian Robbins star in this icky outing. 84 min.
47-1986 *$12.99*

Hider In The House (1989)
Terrifying thriller stars Gary Busey as a psychopath who's released from an institution and finds a new place to live: the secret attic of a suburban family's home. Mimi Rogers, Michael McKean also star. 109 min.
47-2040 Was $89.99 *$14.99*

The Unholy (1988)
A young priest is sent to New Orleans to reopen a church, but finds that a demonic force has taken up residence there and was responsible for the death of his predecessors. Chilling horror tale stars Ben Cross, Hal Holbrook, Ned Beatty, Trevor Howard. 100 min.
47-1883 Was $19.99 *$14.99*

Voodoo (1995)
A college student learns to do background checks before pledging when he's drawn into a fearsome fraternity overseen by a voodoo priest who wants the initiate's girlfriend as a ritual sacrifice. Spellbinding shocker stars Corey Feldman, Sarah Douglas, Jack Nance. 91 min.
83-1056 Was $89.99 ***$14.99***

The Whispering (1996)
A sinister, seductive spirit lurking at the boundary between life and death softly and sensually lures unwary men into her clutches, and into the "great beyond," in this erotic chiller. Leif Garrett, Leslie Danon, Tom Patton star. 86 min.
83-1074 Was $89.99 ***$14.99***

The Surgeon (1996)
A hospital turns into a house of horror when a demented doctor begins practicing his own bizarre brand of medicine in this shocker that cuts like a scalpel. Isabel Glasser, James Remar, Peter Boyle and Malcolm McDowell star. 100 min.
83-1085 Was $99.99 ***$14.99***

Evil Ed (1996)
Filmed in Sweden, this demented horror film with moments of dark humor tells of Ed, a film editor specializing in art films who is reassigned to working on bloody horror opuses. Ed's new assignment eventually gets to him, turning him into a maniac killer not unlike the one featured in "Loose Limbs I-VII," a film he recently cut. Johan Rudeback stars. Extra gory, unrated version; 90 min.
83-1100 Was $99.99 ***$14.99***

Little Witches (1996)
There'll be the Devil to pay—literally—when an ancient occult tome transforms six curious Catholic schoolgirls into sexy witches with a passion for black magic. Terrifying tale features Jennifer Rubin, Zelda Rubinstein, Jack Nance. 91 min.
83-1118 Was $99.99 ***$14.99***

Werewolf (1995)
An archeological dig uncovers a skeleton that is half-man and half-beast, and soon an ancient curse is unleashed on the residents of a nearby town with the rising of the full moon. Howling good horror flick stars George Rivero, Adrianna Miles, Richard Lynch. 99 min.
83-1124 Was $99.99 ***$14.99***

Judge & Jury (1996)
A psychotic murderer is convicted and electrocuted, but comes back from the grave for revenge on the person who killed his wife during their last crime spree in this intense mix of action, suspense and otherworldly terror. David Keith, Martin Kove, Laura Johnson star. 98 min.
83-1126 Was $99.99 ***$14.99***

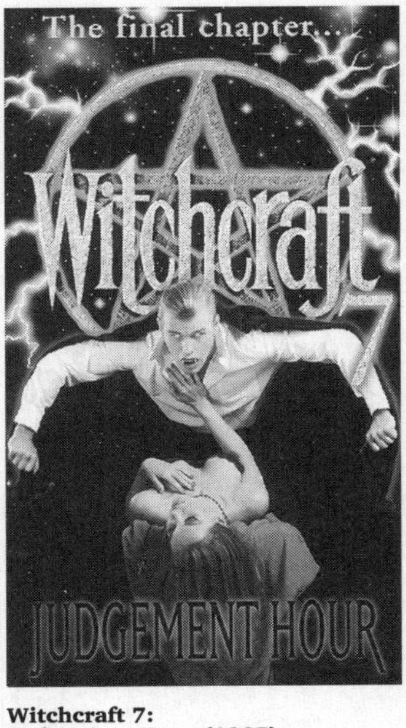

Witchcraft 7: Judgement Hour (1995)
An attorney caught between Heaven and Hell calls on his magical powers as he battles a group of nasty vampires. As he attempts to stop the fiendish bloodsuckers, he finds himself caught in a whirlwind of bloodlust, bizarre sexual rituals and supernatural forces. With David Byrnes, April Breneman and Playboy Playmate Alisa Christenson. Uncut, unrated version; 91 min.
83-1035 Was $89.99 ***$14.99***

Witchcraft: Salem's Ghost (1996)
Burned alive 300 years earlier in Salem for consorting with the Devil, a wicked warlock comes back from the grave, and soon an unwary couple are drawn into his sinister scheme of evil, debauchery and occult vengeance. Sensual shocker stars Lee Grober, Kim Kopf, David Weills. AKA: "Witchcraft VIII." Uncut, unrated version; 91 min.
83-1076 Was $99.99 ***$14.99***

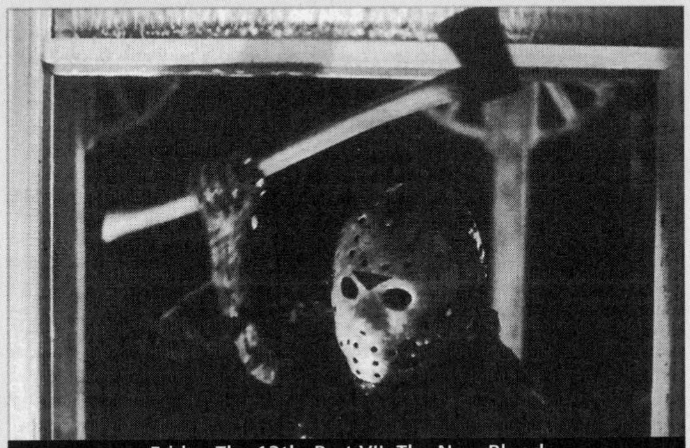
Friday The 13th, Part VII: The New Blood

Friday The 13th (1980)
The one, the only, the original! Many years after a rash of deaths, scenic Camp Crystal Lake reopens, complete with young, naive, sex-hungry counselors...and a maniacal killer. And who's this Jason they keep talking about? Adrienne King, Betsy Palmer, Kevin Bacon, Ari Lehman star. 95 min.
06-1079 ***$14.99***

Friday The 13th, Part 2 (1981)
Demented, deformed Jason Voorhees is back, and so are the gory camp killings. Blood, guts, knives, machetes, spears, icepicks, hammers in the head...the works! Amy Steel, John Furey, Warrington Gillette star. 89 min.
06-1099 ***$14.99***

Friday The 13th, Part 3 (1982)
Donning his trademark hockey mask for the first time, Jason takes terror to a new dimension in this third entry in the shock series. Look out, campers! Dana Kimmell, Paul Kratka, Richard Brooker star. Not in 3-D. 96 min.
06-1162 ***$14.99***

Friday The 13th: The Final Chapter (1984)
More carnage at Camp Crystal Lake, as hacksaw-swinging, spear-throwing, head-crushing Jason returns, and the only person able to stop him is a young boy. Kimberly Beck, Corey Feldman, Peter Barton, Crispin Glover, Ted White star. 91 min.
06-1227 □***$14.99***

Friday The 13th, Part V: A New Beginning (1985)
This time the horror isn't confined to camp, as a home for troubled teenagers is subjected to one shocking murder after another. Has hockey-masked hacker Jason returned from the grave, or is a new killer following in his bloody footsteps? John Shepard, Melanie Kinnaman, Corey Parker, Dick Wieand star. 92 min.
06-1285 □***$14.99***

Friday The 13th, Part VI: Jason Lives (1986)
And they said it couldn't be done! A lightning bolt brings everyone's favorite masked murderer back from the grave, and he's ready to pick (and axe) up where he left off, unless the youth who "killed" him the first time and the sheriff's daughter can stop him. Thom Mathews, Jennifer Cooke, Ron Palillo, C.J. Graham star. 87 min.
06-1414 □***$14.99***

Friday The 13th, Part VII: The New Blood (1988)
That's right, Jason's back and ready to rend, but this time his victims include a spunky teenage girl with deadly telekinetic powers. Has everybody's favorite ghoulish goalie finally met his match? Lar Park Lincoln, Terry Kiser, Heidi Kozak, Kane Hodder star. 90 min.
06-1587 □***$14.99***

Friday The 13th, Part VIII: Jason Takes Manhattan (1989)
It's the scariest thing to hit the Big Apple since Steinbrenner bought the Yankees! What will happen to the streets of New York when the unstoppable killer lands in search of fresh victims? Find out in the eighth installment in the interminable horror series. Jensen Daggett, Scott Reeves, Peter Mark Richman, Kane Hodder star. 96 min.
06-1703 □***$14.99***

Jason Goes To Hell: The Final Friday (1993)
This ninth (and, once again, final) entry in the series finds the immortal Jason both predator and prey, as he takes over different bodies while avoiding the police and a bounty hunter out to finish him for good. John D. LeMay, Kari Keegan and Kane Hodder star in this (literally) hellblazing shocker, presented in an uncut, unrated director's cut. 91 min.
02-2522 Was $19.99 □***$14.99***

Grim (1995)
A quiet suburb is turned into a bloody battlefield when a monstrous creature rises up from its underground lair in this chilling shocker with a bright young cast. 86 min.
83-1073 Was $89.99 ***$14.99***

The Fear: Halloween Night (1999)
"Fear" strikes back when Mike Hawthorne tries to cleanse his soul of his psychopathic father's spirit by inviting friends to congregate on Halloween Night and partake in an ancient ritual in which they face their most terrifying fears. Gordon Currie, Betsy Palmer and Stacy Grant star. 87 min.
83-1412 Was $99.99 ***$14.99***

Dead Of Night (1999)
On a remote, fog-shrouded island, a terrifying killer named Leo is waiting. As the dead of night spreads, Leo sets out to add some new victims to his list, in this sinister shocker. James Purefoy, Rachell Shelley, Chris Adamson star. 95 min.
83-1523 ***$79.99***

Evil Lives (1999)
In this twisted tale of a love that reaches from beyond the grave, an immortal being preys on college coeds, killing them in order to briefly bring back the spirit of his true love. Can his murderous obsession be stopped? Tristan Rogers, Tyrone Power, Jr., Arabella Holzbog star, with special appearances by Paul Bartel and Dawn Wells. 90 min.
83-1528 ***$99.99***

Small Kill (1993)
A deranged man tired of being ridiculed disguises himself as a female fortune-teller and bilks clients of their life savings while murdering all who get in his way. Two cops set out to stop the psycho, with help from a down-and-out alcoholic. Jason Miller, Gary Burghoff and Rebecca Ferratti star.
08-1515 Was $59.99 ***$19.99***

Jack Frost (1997)
Forget nipping at your nose; this Jack will be hacking at your limbs! A cold-blooded serial killer is caught in an accident with a truck carrying experimental genetic material during a snowstorm, turning him into a sinister snowman with icicle fangs. You'll never look at Frosty the same way again! Chris Allport, Eileen Seeley and Scott MacDonald star. 89 min.
83-1167 Was $99.99 ***$14.99***

Black Circle Boys (1998)
A high school student is drawn into a seductive world of drugs and Goth rock by the members of a secret occult society, and soon is threatened with the loss of more than just his life, in this chiller that puts a macho spin on "The Craft." Scott Bairstow, Donnie Wahlberg, Eric Mabius star, with appearances by John Doe, Lisa Loeb and Tara Subkoff.
83-1361 Was $99.99 ***$14.99***

Razor Blade Smile (1998)
Bullets and bloodsuckers mix in this horror/thriller about a lovely and lethal vampire named Lilith who "daylights" as a hit woman-for-hire. Lilith uses her guns and supernatural powers to bring down a crime cartel. Eileen Daly, Christopher Adamson, David Warbeck star. Unrated version; 101 min.
83-1400 Was $99.99 ***$14.99***

Happy Birthday To Me (1981)
This birthday is anything but a party, as a group of students are killed in a variety of gruesome ways, from suffocation to shish-kabobing. Melissa Sue Anderson, Sharon Acker, Glenn Ford star. 101 min.
02-1083 ***$69.99***

Alone In The Dark (1982)
A new doctor at an asylum sets out to befriend three of the more difficult cases, but during a power failure, the trio escapes and sets out to "repay" him in their own special way. Jack Palance, Martin Landau, Donald Pleasence and Erland Van Lidth star. 92 min.
02-1207 Was $19.99 ***$14.99***

Fright Night (1985)
What would you do if you thought your new neighbor was a vampire, and he had his eyes on your girl? Find out in this stylish blend of chilling horror and sly satire that stars Chris Sarandon as the suave bloodsucker and Roddy McDowall as a hammy horror film star hired to help stop him; with William Ragsdale, Amanda Bearse. 106 min.
02-1536 Was $19.99 □***$14.99***

Fright Night, Part II (1989)
Fearfully funny follow-up has the sister of the first film's vampire coming to town to lure William Ragsdale into her clutches and exact a bloodsucking vengeance. Can vampire killer Roddy McDowall stop her in time? Horrific chiller also stars Traci Lin, Julie Carmen. 108 min.
27-6647 ***$14.99***

The Bride (1985)
In the sexiest, most visually stunning rendition of the horror classic yet, Sting is mad genius Baron Frankenstein and Jennifer Beals the perfect woman he creates and tries to control. Co-stars Clancy Brown, Geraldine Page, David Rappaport and Quentin Crisp. 118 min.
02-1537 ***$14.99***

Rabid Grannies (1988)
These little old ladies aren't baking toll house cookies anymore! Not since a mysterious parcel from Hell turned them into bloodthirsty monsters in support hose! Outrageous combination of terror and laughs from the makers of "Surf Nazis Must Die" stars Danielle Daven, Jack Mayar. 89 min.
03-1724 ***$14.99***

Stuff Stephanie In The Incinerator (1989)
Get "Troma"-tized with this outrageous bad taste epic from the producers of "The Toxic Avenger." The elite meet to lie, kill, cheat and gross you out when they decide to rid the world of a sexy, snobby gal named Stephanie. M.R. Murphy, William Dame, and Catherine Dee, as Stephanie, star. 97 min.
03-1733 ***$14.99***

Blades (1988)
This is a movie that doesn't putt around! A possessed power lawn mower rips apart the members of a posh Wildwood, N.J., golf club. How can they stop the menacing, grass-guzzling machine? A Troma production, directed by Philadelphian John P. Finegan. 101 min.
03-1738 ***$14.99***

Bad Dreams (1988)
A young woman, the sole survivor of a Jonestown-like cult's mass suicide, awakes from a 14-year coma, but is stalked by the spectre of the cult's leader, in this chiller that's good for a week's worth of nightmares. Jennifer Rubin, Richard Lynch, Susan Ruttan star. 84 min.
04-1104 Was $89.99 □***$29.99***

Visiting Hours (1982)
In this hospital, your next visit may be your last. A female news commentator is stalked by a psychotic killer. When she goes into the hospital—look out! Lee Grant, William Shatner. 105 min.
04-1488 Was $59.99 ***$29.99***

The Entity (1983)
Based on a true story, this terrifying tale of demonic possession stars Barbara Hershey as a young woman who finds her body and soul assaulted by a demon from the realms of the subconscious. Ron Silver also stars. 125 min.
04-1621 Was $19.99 ***$14.99***

The Vindicator (1986)
A scientist is killed in a lab accident, but an unscrupulous colleague brings him back to life, a gruesome computerized creature on a mission of vengeance. High-tech horror with David McIlwraith, Pam Grier, Richard Cox. 92 min.
04-2000 Was $79.99 □***$29.99***

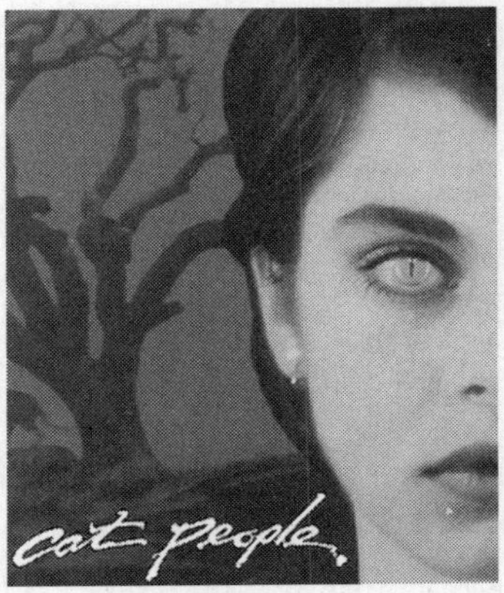

Cat People (1982)
Paul Schrader's moody, erotic remake of the 1942 classic. Nastassja Kinski is a virginal woman who learns from brother Malcolm McDowell that sex transforms members of their family into vicious black panthers, and only murder can return them to human form. Co-stars John Heard, Annette O'Toole, Ed Begley, Jr. 118 min.
07-1113 Was $19.99 ***$14.99***

Murder Weapon (1989)
A little sex, a little gore, a party for two beautiful young women and their closest male friends, and a mystery killer somewhere on the guest list. These are the elements for a chilling, suspenseful horror odyssey that stars Linnea Quigley, Karen Russell, and Lyle ("Let's Talk") Waggoner. 90 min.
73-9001 Was $79.99 *$19.99*

Skinned Alive (1989)
A mother and her young'uns travel the countryside, selling fine leather clothing out of their van. Thing is, they get their hides from the bodies of people they pick up on the road! Mary Jackson and Scott Spiegel star in a gory feast that promises you "a man turned inside out!!!" 90 min.
73-9003 Was $79.99 *$19.99*

Zombie '90: Extreme Pestilence (1993)
All-out gorefest concerning lethal chemicals that turn the people who live near a forest into zombies and the two doctors who try to stop the growing epidemic of the living dead. Matthias Kerl and Ralf Hess star in this unsettling shocker from the director of "Violent Sh-t." 80 min. Dubbed in English.
73-9059 *$29.99*

The Dead Next Door: Collector's Edition (1989)
Writer/director J.R. Bookwalter's shot-on-super 8 zombie opus follows an army of the living dead marching across America (and up to the White House!). An elite commando squad is sent to dispatch them, but runs into trouble when they find a religious cult that worships the zombies. This restored edition includes a behind-the-scenes look at the making of the movie. Pete Ferry, Scott Spiegel; listen for voicework by Bruce Campbell. 85 min.
73-9104 Was $39.99 *$29.99*

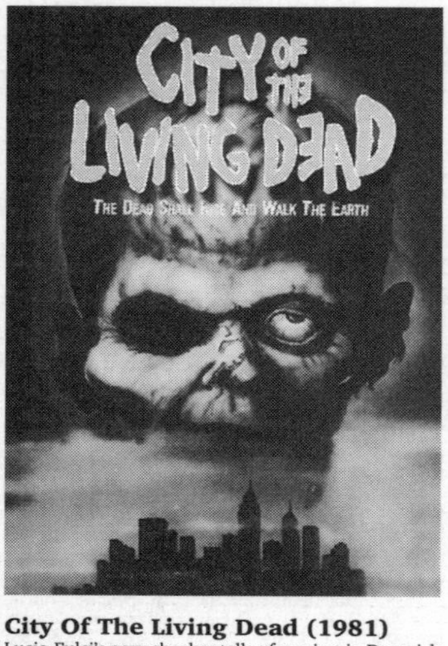

City Of The Living Dead (1981)
Lucio Fulci's gory shocker tells of a priest in Dunwich whose suicide opens the doors of Hell, unleashing unspeakable terror with corpses taking over the world. Reporter Christopher George tries to stop the onslaught of horror. With Janet Agren, Katherine MacColl. AKA: "The Fear," "The Gates of Hell," "Twilight of the Dead." 93 min.
58-1053 Letterboxed *$14.99*

The Gates Of Hell II: Dead Awakening (1997)
Dedicated to "Gates of Hell" director Lucio Fulci, this creepy frightfest tells of an occult group out to initiate members into its Darkness of Death sect. The group reawakens an ancient monster that soon wreaks terror. Tamara Hext and Tom Campitelli star in the in-name-only sequel. 87 min.
76-7332 *$19.99*

The Boogens (1981)
A long-abandoned silver mine is reopened 70 years after a deadly and mysterious cave-in, but the excavation unleashes the bloodthirsty tentacled creatures who were responsible for the first disaster and are eager for some fresh victims. Chilling horror tale from Sunn Classics ("In Search of Noah's Ark") stars Rebecca Balding, Fred McCarren. 95 min.
63-1880 ❑*$14.99*

Shiver (1980)
Creepy mix of satanic horror and Holocaust horrors, as a Nazi-hunter searching for the S.S. officer who killed his family tries to convince a cop and an author that a seemingly ageless musician is not only the same man, but is actually Satan. Marc Lawrence, Cameron Mitchell, Faith Cliff star. AKA: "Cataclysm," "The Nightmare Never Ends," "Satan's Supper." 87 min.
64-2417 *$14.99*

Scream Your Head Off (1982)
A man mouring his wife's death in a car accident seeks help in an unusual sanitarium, but after being subjected to shock therapy and drugs by a sexy psychiatrist, he begins kidnapping women and taking them to the clinic, where they are given similar treatment and sold into slavery. Bizzare chiller, footage of which was used in 1985's "Night Train to Terror," stars John Phillip Law, Richard Moll. 76 min.
64-3420 *$12.99*

Boarding House (1982)
Eerie shocker about a haunted house that plays host to a group of pretty young women. Soon, they are pretty terrified women, as the house's horrors run amuck. Alexandra Day stars.
58-1067 Was $19.99 *$14.99*

Torture Train (1986)
While riding home for Christmas vacation, two women wind up sharing a compartment with a pair of drugged-out punks and a mysterious woman who enjoys voyeurism. Soon, the girls are forced into disturbing torture and acts of brutality in this sordid shocker. With Patty Edwards and Kay Beal. 78 min.
59-7003 *$89.99*

A Return To Salem's Lot (1987)
All-new shocker from Larry Cohen ("It's Alive") follows a father and son who move into the sleepy New England town for a rest, only to learn that the residents sleep during the day. Bloodsucking scares galore with Michael Moriarty, Andrew Duggan, Ronee Blakley and Samuel Fuller. 101 min.
19-1639 ❑*$14.99*

Pet Sematary Two (1992)
Return to Ludlow, Maine, the site of the original "Pet Sematary," where a widower and his teenage son learn that what gets buried at the nearby Indian graveyard doesn't stay buried for long. Edward Furlong, Anthony Edwards and Clancy Brown star in this sequel to Stephen King's hit movie. 102 min.
06-2079 Was $89.99 ❑*$14.99*

Children Of The Corn II: The Final Sacrifice (1993)
After he discovers a cellar filled with dead bodies while on assignment in Nebraska, a tabloid reporter and his young son investigate the frightening finding. Soon more corpses are found, and the two learn that local children under the influence of a demonic spirit may be responsible for the murders. This sequel to Stephen King's story stars Terence Knox, Paul Scherrer. 93 min.
06-2142 Was $89.99 ❑*$14.99*

Children Of The Corn IV: The Gathering (1996)
The third sequel to Stephen King's story details what happens when a pretty medical student returns to her hometown and finds an evil spirit spreading terror throughout the area. Naomi Watts, William Windom and Karen Black star. 85 min.
11-2056 Was $19.99 ❑*$14.99*

Children Of The Corn V: Fields Of Terror (1998)
The corn—and the terror—is as high as an elephant's eye, as six college students' road trip takes a deadly detour and strands them in a remote rural town where the children are under the influence of a mysterious, malevolent force. Alexis Arquette, David Carradine, Stacy Galina, Fred Williamson and Ahmet Zappa star. 84 min.
11-2259 Was $19.99 ❑*$14.99*

Children Of The Corn 666: Isaac's Return (1999)
Just when you thought it was safe to stroll through the cornfield, horror returns. A woman en route to Nebraska to find her birth mother has an encounter with a strange man, and frightening events soon follow. Little does she know that he's the top husk of the evil children of the corn! John Franklin and Stacy Keach star in this continuation of Stephen King's story. 81 min.
11-2353 Was $99.99 ❑*$14.99*

Sometimes They Come Back...Again (1996)
In this horrifying sequel to the Stephen King thriller, a man's return to his hometown after the bizarre death of his mother brings him face-to-face with the evil forces that led to his sister's murder 30 years earlier. And now they have taken over his teenage daughter! Alexis Arquette, Hilary Swank, Michael Gross and Jennifer Aspen star. 98 min.
68-1808 Was $99.99 ❑*$14.99*

Sometimes They Come Back...For More (1999)
The third entry in the Stephen King-inspired series tells of two military officials who investigate the mysterious death of members of a remote government outpost in Antarctica. Upon arriving at the site, the officials meet the surviving members of the outpost and face a powerful, evil force. Clayton Rohner, Faith Ford, Damian Chapa and Max Perlich star. 89 min.
68-1937 Was $79.99 ❑*$14.99*

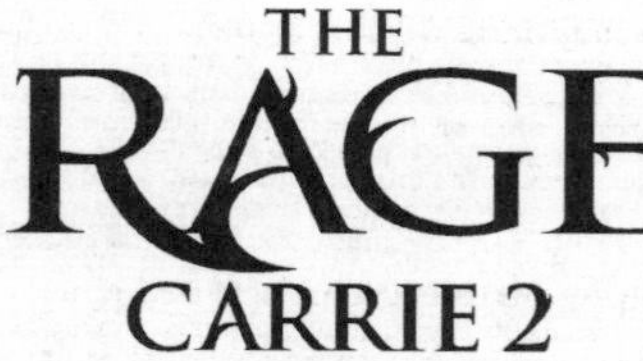

The Rage: Carrie 2 (1999)
Twenty-three years after Carrie White wreaked havoc at Bates High School, lonely teenager Emily Bergl's destructive telekinesis is triggered after her best friend is driven to commit suicide. As she lashes out against her nasty classmates and mean-spirited jocks, school counselor Amy Irving, sole survivor of Carrie's prom night pyrotechnics, tries to halt Bergl's rage. With Rachel Lang, Jeremy London, Mena Suvari. 105 min.
12-3283 Was $99.99 ❑*$14.99*

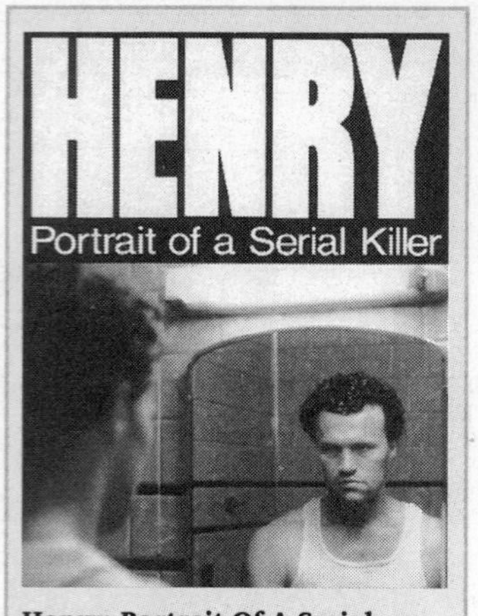

Henry: Portrait Of A Serial Killer: Director's Edition (1986)
A deeply disturbing, ultra-realistic account of the life of a cold-blooded serial killer. Based on the true story of Texan Henry Lee Lucas and presented in documentary-like fashion, the film paints a chilling picture of a murderer as it follows Henry's home life and his killing excursions. Not for the squeamish! Michael Rooker, Tom Towles and Tracy Arnold star. Uncut director's edition include interviews with John MacNaughton. 105 min.
50-6575 Was $29.99 *$19.99*

Henry: Portrait Of A Serial Killer 2 (1998)
A white-trash family has no idea of the horror that's in store for them when the father, a budding arsonist, opens their home to demented killer Henry (Neal Guintoli), who draws them into his violent lifestyle. Chilling follow-up to the 1986 cult favorite also stars Rich Komenich, Kate Walsh. 85 min.
50-7504 Was $29.99 *$19.99*

Death Nurse 2 (1987)
The "Death Nurse" is back—and ready to hack!—in this diabolical sequel that finds the carve-happy caregiver and her brother admitting street people to their clinic, then doing away with them in the most dastardly ways. Call the police! Call the army! Call your health insurance company! Priscilla Alden and Albert Eskinazi star. 92 min.
73-9324 *$19.99*

Cemetery Sisters (1987)
Two sisters who plan to own their own funeral home and cemetery team up to marry, then murder old men with moolah and collect the insurance money to start their business. The bodies start to pile up as the siblings' strange scheme gets bloodier and bloodier. Joan Simon and Leslie Simon star. 61 min.
73-9325 *$19.99*

Hide And Go Shriek (1987)
What begins as a fun-filled graduation party in a furniture store (hey, plenty of chairs!) for eight teenagers becomes a night of terror as they're slain, one by one, by a sinister stranger whose games turn deadly. Donna Baltron, Brittain Frye star. 90 min.
74-5002 *$29.99*

Lunch Meat (1987)
A group of teens plans a trip to the woods, unaware that a demented family of cannibalistic killers has claimed the territory. The box says, "WARNING: If decapitations, cannibalism, and brutal, savage acts of suspense and gore turn your stomach this film is not for you!!!" We say, "Nuff said!" 88 min.
76-7002 *$39.99*

Necromancer (1988)
After she is savagely raped, a beautiful co-ed prays to Satan for power to gain her unholy vengeance. The bloody price, however, becomes too high when her own family is threatened! Sizzling shocker stars Elizabeth Cayton, Russ Tamblyn. AKA: "Necromancer: Satan's Servant." 88 min.
50-1685 Was $79.99 *$14.99*

The Majorettes (1988)
OK, girls! Give me three black shrouds and a sis, boom, AAAAAHHHH! The school pep squad is sure losing a lot of pep, as a psychotic killer is leaving a trail of perky corpses in his wake. Kevin Kinklin and Terrie Godfrey star in this thriller from John Russo, co-creator of "Night of the Living Dead." 93 min.
47-1872 Was $59.99 *$19.99*

Rocktober Blood (1984)
Billy Eye Harper was one of the greatest rock legends to ever hit the stage...and not even death could halt his comeback! An onslaught of gore ensues, laden with heavy metal horror. Tray Loren, Donna Scoggins star; from Beverly and Ferd Sebastian ("Gator Bait"). 88 min.
47-1655 *$24.99*

Lone Wolf (1988)
A lethal lycanthrope is stalking the halls of the local high school, and two teenage computer buffs think they've found the monster...or has he found them? Grisly suspenser stars Dyan Brown, Kevin Hart. 97 min.
46-5406 *$79.99*

Horror Planet (1981)
An extraterrestrial monster assaults a young woman, who soon gives birth to a carnivorous killer baby. Will "mother love" prevail? "Alien" meets "Rosemary's Baby" in this shocker, which stars Judy Geeson and Jennifer Ashley. AKA: "Inseminoid." 93 min.
53-1164 *$14.99*

Raiders Of The Living Dead (1985)
Zombies go for the gusto—and lots and lots of human flesh—in this horrific horror outing in which a wacky doctor at an asylum turns criminals into the walking dead. Scott Schwartz ("The Toy" star-turned-porn performer) plays the kid who invents a laser gun to kill the creatures. With Donna Assali, and Zita Johann of "The Mummy" fame.
71-1048 *$14.99*

Grim Prairie Tales (1989)
Gather 'round the campfire, kids, and listen to a quartet of bizarre tales from the ol' West that'll leave your cowboy hat standing on end. James Earl Jones plays the storyteller who introduces you to a man who encounters terror on an ancient Indian burial ground, a young girl discovering a disturbing secret about her father, and more. Brad Dourif, William Atherton and Lisa Eichhorn co-star. 87 min.
71-5201 Was $19.99 *$14.99*

Midnight (1981)
Gore galore's in store for a frightened young fugitive who hops a ride with two seemingly nice boys...who deliver her to a baleful backwoods blood cult! Melonie Verlin, John Amplas and Lawrence Tierney star in this chiller from "Night of the Living Dead" co-writer John A. Russo; make-up and effects by Tom Savini. 88 min.
68-1050 *$79.99*

Midnight 2: Sex, Death & Videotape (1993)
Sequel to John Russo's popular horror film centers on the last surviving member of a crazed Pittsburgh family who stalks the streets with a camcorder in search of gorgeous women. He closely follows a beautiful bank teller who, unbeknownst to the stalker, has teamed with a detective to find her friend's killer. With Matthew Jason Walsh, Jo Norcia. 72 min.
73-9054 *$59.99*

The Slumber Party Massacre (1982)
Here's something different: a "mad slasher" movie created by women. When some co-eds have a pajama party, they don't count on a drill-wielding maniac turning up also. Michele Michaels, Robin Stille and Michael Villela star; written by Rita Mae Brown and directed by Amy Jones. 77 min.
53-1342 Was $39.99 *$14.99*

Slumber Party Massacre II (1987)
"Last night I dreamed I was drilled to death in my Maidenform bra..." Lissome lingeried lovelies come up against the Driller Killer in this horrifying, terrifying, scary shocker. With Crystal Bernard and Atanas Ilitch. 90 min.
53-1705 *$14.99*

Slumber Party Massacre 3 (1990)
Three high school gals have a bikini sleep-over, but little do they know that a psycho killer is stalking them. He's dressed to drill, and they're hardly dressed at all. Grrr-aw, Grrr-aw: this is a guaranteed big horror bit. With Hope Marie Carlton, Keely Christian, Maria Ford. 80 min.
21-9000 Was $89.99 *$14.99*

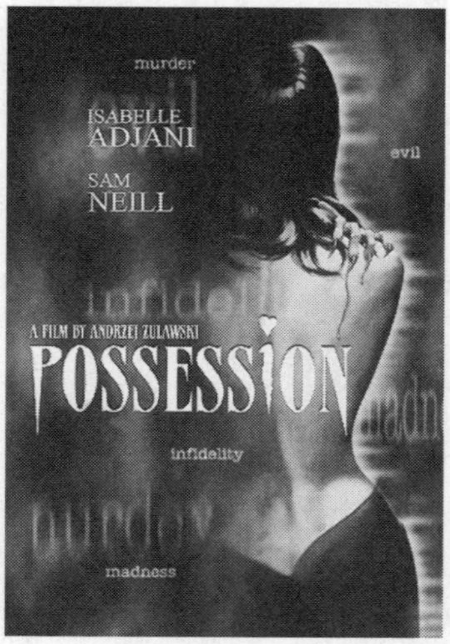

Possession: Collector's Edition (1983)
Disturbing Euro chiller stars Isabelle Adjani as a woman who begins to act strangely after husband Sam Neill returns home from an extended trip. As their relationship falls apart, Adjani's insecurities and desires manifest themselves in a bloodthirsty, tentacled creature that she gives "birth" to...and that becomes her lover. Restored director's cut features 40 minutes of footage not seen in America and the original theatrical trailers. 123 min.
47-1298 Letterboxed *$14.99*

Clive Barker

Clive Barker's Salome & The Forbidden
Featured on this collection are two early efforts from Clive Barker (both are silent with musical scores): "Salome" (1973) is a dark reworking of the legendary story; and "The Forbidden" (1975-1978) depicts the skinning of a man. Fans will note the appearance of Doug "Pinhead" Bradley and the lament configuration. An interview with Barker is also included. 70 min.
50-2924 *$19.99*

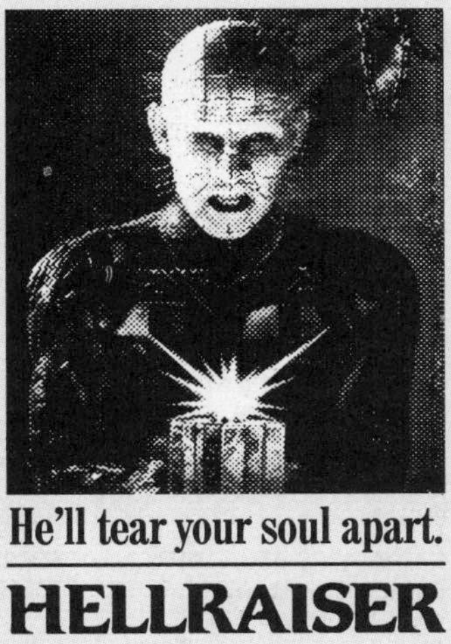

He'll tear your soul apart.
HELLRAISER

Hellraiser (1987)
British horror master Clive Barker penned and directed this chilling tale of a man who unwittingly opens a box that contains a doorway to a hellish netherworld. Trapped between life and death, he schemes with his sister-in-law to sacrifice his brother and restore his physical body. Andrew Robinson, Clare Higgins, Ashley Laurence and Doug Bradley as "Pinhead" star. 94 min.
70-1190 ❑*$14.99*

Hellraiser: Collector's Edition
This remastered special edition also includes interviews with Barker and the cast, plus original theatrical trailers. 118 min.
08-8502 Letterboxed *$14.99*

Hellbound: Hellraiser II (1988)
Sinister sequel continues the bizarre saga of the undead Cenobites, their deadly little puzzle boxes, and a disturbed young woman whose mind holds the link between this world and theirs. Horrific spine-tingler from Clive Barker will have you saying, "I don't wanna be a pin-head no more"; Claire Higgins, Ashley Laurence and Doug Bradley star. Uncut, unrated version; 98 min.
70-1251 *$14.99*

Hellbound: Hellraiser II: Collector's Edition (1989)
Special collector's edition includes interviews with producer Clive Barker, director Tony Randel and the cast, plus trailers. 108 min. total.
08-8561 Letterboxed *$14.99*

Hellraiser III: Hell On Earth (1992)
There's more terror and gore in store as the third outing of Clive Barker's horrific series involves a TV newswoman who must find a Cenobite box that has the power to send the evil, earthbound Pinhead back to Hell. Terry Farrell, Doug Bradley and Paula Marshall star. Unrated version features scenes not shown in theatres; 97 min.
06-2092 Was $89.99 ❑*$14.99*

Hellraiser: Bloodline (1996)
The unholy horror of Pinhead, his fellow Cenobites, and their bizarre little boxes reaches from 18th-century Europe to present-day New York to a space station in the distant future in the fright-filled fourth entry in the series. Doug Bradley, Bruce Ramsay and Valentina Vargas star in this shocker from noted director Alan Smithee. 81 min.
11-2066 Was $19.99 ❑*$14.99*

Hellraiser: Inferno (2000)
The fifth entry in the Clive Barker-created series stars Craig Sheffer as a Los Angeles detective who wakes up one morning to discover he's living in Hell. While some argue there's little difference between L.A. and Hell, the alarmed Sheffer realizes he must retrieve a puzzle box from the demonic Pinhead in order to return home. With Nicholas Turturro, Doug Bradley. 99 min.
11-2475 ❑*$99.99*

Candyman (1992)
Clive Barker's terrifying story "The Forbidden" is turned into an equally frightening film featuring Virginia Madsen as a modern folklore researcher whose investigation of a Chicago legend summons the spirit of a vengeance-seeking killer with a hook in place of one hand. Tony Todd and Vanessa Williams also star. 98 min.
02-2353 Was $19.99 ❑*$14.99*

Candyman: Farewell To The Flesh (1995)
The otherworldly, hook-wielding killer is beckoned back into this world, and now the Candyman is after the descendants of the family responsible for his damnation, in this spellbinding sequel that proves revenge can be sweet, indeed. Tony Todd, Kelly Rowan, Veronica Cartwright star. 99 min.
02-8269 Was $19.99 ❑*$14.99*

Candyman 3: Day Of The Dead (1999)
Summoned back from the land beyond the grave, the horrifying, hook-handed Candyman sets out to claim his last surviving descendant—sculptor Donna D'Errico—in this scarifying third entry in the sinister series. With Nick Corri, Alexia Robinson, and Tony Todd as Candyman. 93 min.
27-7145 Was $99.99 ❑*$14.99*

Lord Of Illusions (1995)
A private eye hired by a successful stage magician's wife to protect him can't stop a fatal stage "accident" caused by a demonic cult who want to revive their leader, dispatched by the magician to another dimension years earlier. Writer/director Clive Barker's spellbinding mix of Dashiell Hammett and H.P. Lovecraft stars Scott Bakula, Famke Janssen, Kevin J. O'Connor; special unrated director's cut includes scenes too intense for theatres. 120 min.
12-3019 Was $19.99 ❑*$14.99*

Quicksilver Highway (1998)
From the twisted imaginations of horror masters Stephen King and Clive Barker comes a terrifying tale of a storyteller whose listeners end up becoming the subjects of his stories. Christopher Lloyd, Matt Frewer and Veronica Cartwright star in this chiller that includes man-eating toy teeth and murderous dismembered hands; directed by Mick Garris ("The Stand"). 87 min.
04-3715 *$99.99*

Night Train To Terror (1985)
This is one train ride you won't want to miss! As a rock band breakdances its way through the titular train, God and Satan debate mankind's capacity for good or evil (which is depicted through segments from such other Philip Yordan-scripted films as "Death Wish Club," "Shiver" and more). John Phillip Law, Cameron Mitchell, Marc Lawrence, Ferdy Mayne star. 94 min.
10-1417 *$14.99*

Family Reunion (1989)
This shocker spans four decades and concerns a family vacation in which a youngster named Tom and his grandfather encounter a satanic cult headed by Tom's real father, who has plans to sacrifice his son. The grandfather saves Tom, but 40 years later a strange force draws them back to the site of the incident—now a ghost town! Pam Phillips and Mel Novak star. 90 min.
83-5002 Was $29.99 *$14.99*

Eye Of The Demon (1987)
Pamela Sue Martin and Tim Matheson are a young couple who purchase an old New England house only to discover that their neighbors are 250-year-old devil worshippers. With Woody Harrelson, Susan Ruttan, Barbara Billingsley. AKA: "Bay Coven," "Strangers in Town." 92 min.
68-1197 *$89.99*

Daughter Of Darkness (1989)
A beautiful American woman haunted by morbid dreams travels to Romania in search of her father. She discovers that Dad was a bloodsucking prince and is soon preyed upon by a sensuous vampire who hopes to turn the gal into a ghoul. Mia Sara, Anthony Perkins and Robert Reynolds star in this Stuart Gordon ("Re-Animator") film. 93 min.
68-1332 *$89.99*

Night Of The Zombies (1981)
Clouds of toxic gas from a top-secret military experiment kill the inhabitants of a city, but the true terror begins when the bodies come back to life as mindless ghouls with a taste for human flesh. A squads of trained soldiers is sent in to stop the zombie onslaught in this grisly shocker. Frank Garfield, Selan Karay star. AKA: "Cannibal Virus," "Zombie Creeping Flesh."
47-1254 *$19.99*

Cathy's Curse (1981)
Creepy horror from the good folks in Canada in which a family moves into a new house, only to find that their little girl has become possessed by the spirit of a dead relative. Can that dusty doll she found have anything to do with the "curse"? With Alan Scarfe, Beverly Murray.
14-6045 *$19.99*

The Midnight Hour: Collector's Edition (1988)
What starts out as an innocent Halloween party for the teens in a small New England town turns into a true horrorfest when some uninvited guests from beyond the grave crash the bash. With Shari Belafonte-Harper, Kevin McCarthy, LeVar Burton and Lee Montgomery. 97 min.
68-1120 Was $89.99 *$14.99*

The Sleeping Car (1989)
Forget Jason! Forget Chucky! Forget Freddy! Now it's The Mister, a horrifying ghost who frightens the frenzied young man living in his humble abode, an old railroad sleeping car. Mister, mister....argh! David Naughton and Kevin McCarthy star. 90 min.
68-1153 Was $89.99 *$12.99*

Demonwarp (1988)
Deep in the forest, a group of hunters searches. One man is looking for the monster that kidnapped his daughter, the others for a creature from the stars. Shocking story stars George Kennedy, Pamela Gilbert, Billy Jacoby. 91 min.
68-1085 *$79.99*

The Kiss (1988)
A young girl is less than thrilled by a visit from her mysterious aunt, but when bizarre things begin happening around them she realizes that her aunt has come to present her with a most sinister and deadly "gift." Chilling tale stars Joanna Pacula, Meredith Salenger, Mimi Kuzyk. 98 min.
02-1910 *$19.99*

976-Evil (1989)
A high school nerd, calling one of those phone lines, taps into an evil force from the pits of Hell...and now not having his parents' permission before dialing is the least of his problems! Terror calls collect in this chiller directed by Freddy Krueger himself, Robert Englund; Stephen Geoffreys, Sandy Dennis star. 105 min.
02-1958 *$14.99*

976-Evil 2: The Astral Factor (1991)
The diabolical 976 number is back, this time sending the spirit of a caller on murdering sprees while he sleeps. A young biker interested in the killings may be the only one to stop the terrifying toll service. Patrick O'Bryan, René Assa star. 93 min.
47-2067 *$14.99*

The Cursed Mountain Mystery (1989)
Two petty thieves steal a gemstone that bears a deadly curse and soon find that they unleashed an ancient warrior who carries the power of the curse. With Phil Avalon, boxer Joe Bugner and Tom Richards. 87 min.
02-2446 *$89.99*

Maniac (1980)
One of the most horrifying films ever made, this graphic shocker stars Joe Spinell as a crazed killer stalking the New York streets in search of female victims to become new additions to his scalp collection. With Caroline Munro, Gail Lawrence; special effects by Tom Savini. This remastered collector's edition includes previously unseen footage and original theatrical and TV trailers. 95 min.
03-1097 Letterboxed *$14.99*

The Wraith (1986)
A heartless pack of car-thieving punks had a good old time terrorizing the neighborhood...until a mysterious driver in an unworldly car started giving them a taste of their own medicine. Charlie Sheen, Nick Cassavetes, Sherilyn Fenn, Randy Quaid star. 92 min.
47-3215 *$12.99*

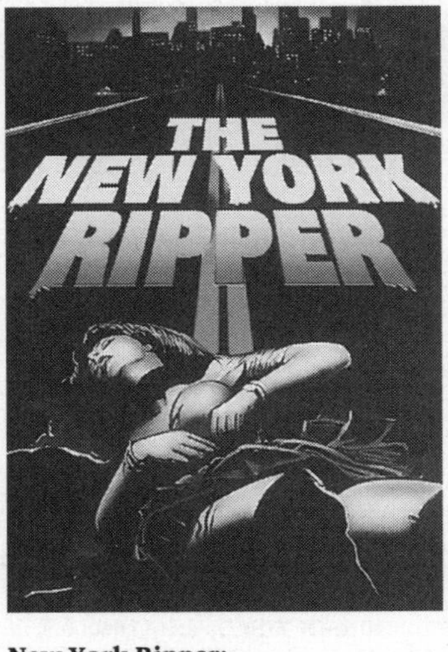

THE NEW YORK RIPPER

New York Ripper: Collector's Edition (1982)
Start spreading the blood...he's slashing today. if you want to wake up to the sound of a city that never stops screaming, then see Italian horror master Lucio Fulci's terrific tale of a psycho killer striking at the Big Apple's core. Jack Hedley, Almanta Keller, Howard Ross star. Includes the original theatrical trailer. 93 min.
68-1053 Letterboxed *$14.99*

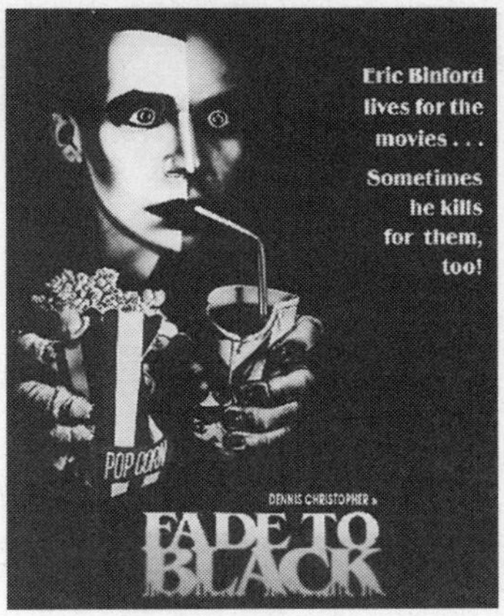

Eric Binford lives for the movies . . .
Sometimes he kills for them, too!
POP CORN
DENNIS CHRISTOPHER
FADE TO BLACK

Fade To Black (1980)
Dennis Chistopher stars as a deranged movie buff (we like him already!) whose obsession with Hollywood villains leads him to start bumping off his enemies while dressed as some of his favorite celluloid killers. With Linda Kerridge, Tim Thomerson. 102 min.
03-1157 *$14.99*

Fade To Black (Letterboxed Version)
Also available in a theatrical, widescreen format.
08-8785 *$14.99*

Night Of The Demons (1989)
Party Tips for Teens #23: When you look for a place to hold the gang's Halloween bash, don't choose abandoned funeral parlors. And if you do, for goodness' sake, don't summon bloodthirsty demons as a prank! William Gallo, Mimi Kinkade. 90 min.
63-1348 *$14.99*

Night Of The Demons 2 (1994)
In this diabolical sequel to the popular shocker, the students from St. Rita's Academy throw a party at a haunted house, only to have it disrupted by Angela, the hostess from Hell, and her ghoulish pals. The kids try to find refuge at a teen dance, but things get even scarier there! Bobby Jacoby and Amelia Kinkaide star in this special effects-filled terrorthon. 96 min.
63-1702 Was $89.99 ❑*$14.99*

Night Of The Demons 3 (1997)
Hull House reopens again with Angel as the horrific hostess welcoming a group of teens whose attempts to escape the law land them in deep trouble and a frightening situation they can't get out of. Amelia Kinkade, Vlasta Vrana and Larry Day star. 85 min.
63-1889 ❑*$99.99*

Chillers (1989)
Stranded together in an isolated bus stop, five travelers pass the time by sharing the nightmares that have been troubling them. A haunted swimming pool, an Aztec demon and some love-starved vampires are just some of the "chillers" in this spooky anthology. Jesse Emery, Laurie Pennington star.
86-1008 *$14.99*

Hell Night (1981)
As a college initiation prank, four freshmen must spend the night in a mansion where a family was brutally murdered years earlier, but neither they nor the seniors tormenting them know that the killer is back and looking for fresh blood. Grisly goodie stars Linda Blair, Vincent Van Patten, Peter Barton. 102 min.
03-1102 Was $19.99 *$14.99*

Hell Night (Letterboxed Collector's Edition)
Also available in a theatrical, widescreen format. Includes the original theatrical trailer and television ads.
08-8775 *$14.99*

Don't Answer The Phone (1980)
A psychotic Vietnam vet finds the female patients of a Los Angeles psychologist easy prey, following them from his office and strangling them with a stocking, in this disturbing chiller. Nicholas Worth, James Westmoreland star. AKA: "The Hollywood Strangler." 86 min.
03-1136 *$14.99*

Mother's Day (1980)
This mother turns out to be a bizarre old lady who sends her two demented sons out on an errand of terror. They kidnap some female campers and bring them home to "meet mom." Horrific thriller laced with sick satire stars Rose Ross, Billy Ray McQuade, Nancy Hendrickson. 91 min.
03-1177 Was $19.99 *$14.99*

Sleepaway Camp (1983)
If you thought the mosquitoes were bloodthirsty, you haven't met the camp cut-up. With ax, or knife, or chainsaw in hand, those frisky teen campers had better look out, or they'll be beside themselves...literally. With Mike Kerlin, Felissa Rose, Jonathan Tierston. 85 min.
03-1353 *$14.99*

Sleepaway Camp (Letterboxed Version)
Also available in a theatrical, widescreen format.
08-8858 *$14.99*

Dario Argento

The Bird With The Crystal Plumage (1970)
A modern-day Jack-the-Ripper stalks Rome, carving up pretty girls, and when an American tourist witnesses the latest killing he puts himself and his girlfriend in deadly danger. Suspenseful Dario Argento thriller stars Tony Musante, Suzy Kendall; music by Ennio Morricone. 98 min.
08-1136 Was $19.99 *$14.99*

The Bird With The Crystal Plumage (Letterboxed Version)
Also available in a theatrical, widescreen format.
08-1727 *$19.99*

Cat O' Nine Tails (1971)
Dario Argento directed this bloody thriller in the Hitchcock tradition about an investigative reporter who teams with a blind former newspaperman to find out who is killing all the people associated with a genetic laboratory. Karl Malden, James Franciscus and Catherine Spaak star. 112 min.
73-9044 *$19.99*

Deep Red (1975)
Dario Argento's striking terror tale involves a series of bizarre murders predicted by a dead psychic and probed by English jazz musician David Hemmings and reporter Daria Nicolodi. Delving into the case, the pair encounter a haunted house, a little girl who likes to impale lizards, and other creepy goings-on. Full-length director's cut features some scenes in Italian with English subtitles and also includes original theatrical trailers. AKA: "Deep Red Hatchet Murders," "Dripping Deep Red." 126 min.
81-1094 Letterboxed *$14.99*

Suspiria (1977)
A dancing school in a small German town is the setting for unholy terror, as modern-day witches seek to resurrect their coven's long-dead founder, in this fright fave from Italian scaremaster Dario Argento. Jessica Harper, Alida Valli, Joan Bennett and Udo Kier star; music by Argento and his band, Goblin. 95 min.
69-1146 Letterboxed *$19.99*

Inferno (1980)
An American music student in Rome returns home at the request of his sister, who is worried about strange occurrences in her New York apartment building. Upon arriving, the man discovers his sister has vanished and a sinister cult is using the building as their base of operations. Dario Argento's follow-up to "Suspiria" (and the second film in his unfinished "Three Mothers" trilogy) stars Leigh McCloskey, Daria Nicolodi, Irene Miracle. 107 min.
04-1899 ❑*$29.99*

Inferno (Letterboxed Version)
Also available in a theatrical, widescreen format. Includes an interview with Argento and the original theatrical trailer.
08-8846 *$14.99*

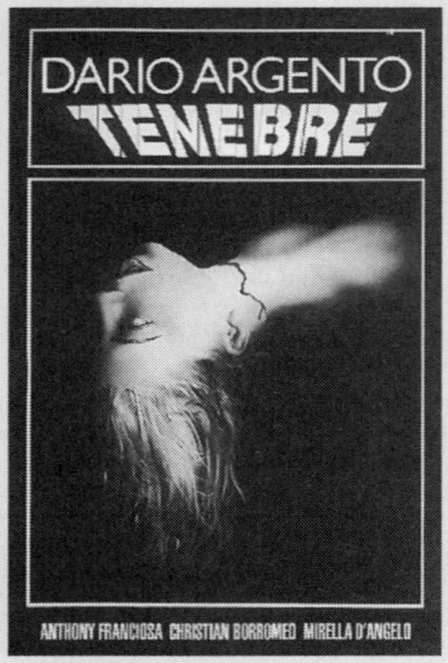

Unsane (Tenebre) (1982)
Little-seen great from suspense master Dario Argento. An American mystery novelist (Anthony Franciosa) visiting Rome becomes a prime suspect when a series of murders occurs that parallels his latest book. With John Saxon, Daria Nicolodi. 91 min.
05-1358 Was $19.99 *$14.99*

Tenebre (Letterboxed Version)
Also available in its uncut version, in a theatrical, widescreen format. Includes the original theatrical trailer and behind-the-scenes segments. 101 min.
08-8713 *$14.99*

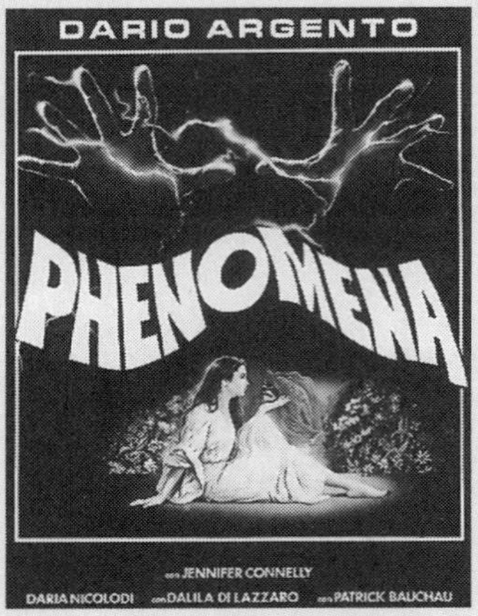

Creepers (Phenomena) (1984)
A deformed maniac is preying on the students of an isolated school. But he's met his match in one girl who can control insects with her, mind, and soon he's the prey in a bizarre, bloody bug battle. Jennifer Connelly, Donald Pleasence star; Dario Argento directs. 84 min.
03-1474 *$14.99*

Phenomena (Letterboxed Version)
Also available in its uncut version in a theatrical, widescreen format. Included are the original theatrical trailer, behind-the-scenes segments, music videos and an interview with Argento by Joe Franklin. 110 min.
08-8712 *$14.99*

Demons (1985)
Horror erupts in a movie theatre as the patrons of a film about Nostradamus begin to transform into slavering, bloodthirsty things from the depths of hell. Aren't you glad you're watching this at home? Gore-drenched effects and a great heavy metal score mark this Dario Argento production, directed by Lamberto Bava. Urbano Barberini, Natasha Hovey star. 88 min.
70-1096 Letterboxed *$14.99*

Demons II (1986)
What begins as an ordinary birthday party in a typical urban apartment building soon becomes a nightmare when hellish creatures appear from a TV set showing a horror film. Tenants are attacked, a dog turns into a zombie canine, and director Lamberto Bava shocks and impresses with his stunning technique. Dario Argento production stars Bobby Rhodes, Asia Argento. 91 min.
69-7015 Letterboxed *$14.99*

The Devil's Daughter (1990)
Dario Argento, Italy's master of the macabre, produced this frightening story about a legion of horrific creatures who use a beautiful school teacher to help them turn their evil on the human race. Kelly Curtis and Herbert Lom star in this stylish terror-fest. AKA: "The Sect." 112 min.
63-1479 ❑*$89.99*

Trauma (1993)
Dario Argento's diabolical shocker tells of a TV employee who teams with a beautiful runaway to track down a depraved cord saw killer known as "the Headhunter" who slaughtered the girl's parents. Piper Laurie, Asia Argento, Christopher Rydell, James Russo, Frederic Forrest and Brad Dourif star.
14-3429 *$12.99*

The Stendhal Syndrome (1996)
In Dario Argento's disturbing shocker, daughter Asia Argento is a sex crimes unit policewoman trying to track down a serial rapist in Italy. While at Florence's famed Uffizi museum, she falls victim to an illness that causes severe hallucinations. Upon recovery, she realizes that she has been raped by the man she is pursuing. With Thomas Kretschmann; music by Ennio Morricone. 101 min.
46-8062 Was $59.99 *$14.99*

Phantom Of The Opera (1998)
One of the all-time classic suspense stories is given a lavish rendition by Eurohorror auteur Dario Argento. Julian Sands stars as the twisted-in-body-and-soul denizen of the catacombs beneath the Paris Opera House, and Asia Argento is the beautiful singer who becomes his overwhelming obsession. With Andrea Di Stefano, Zoltan Barabas. 100 min.
83-1432 Was $99.99 *$14.99*

The Amityville Horror (1979)
Hit shocker, based on a true story and the best-selling book, stars James Brolin and Margot Kidder as a couple who come to believe their new Long Island home is haunted. With Rod Steiger. 117 min.
19-1087 *$14.99*

Amityville II: The Possession (1982)
How did the haunting of the Lutz family begin? Find out in this supernatural tale that awakens your worst fears. Follow a family's battle against terrifying demons. Burt Young, James Olson co-star. 104 min.
53-1043 Was $19.99 *$14.99*

Amityville 1992: It's About Time (1992)
The terror begins again as a businessman returns from New York with an antique clock. Little does he know of the timepiece's mystical powers. Soon, animals and objects take on minds of their own, friends and family turn on each other and horrifying incidents begin to occur. Stephen Macht, Shawn Weatherly, Megan Ward star. 95 min.
63-1540 Was $89.99 ❑*$14.99*

Amityville: A New Generation (1993)
A young artist picks up an antique mirror from a homeless man and soon learns of its dark secrets, as it brings terror to his family and allows him to experience a disturbing past he never knew existed. Co-stars David Naughton, Julia Nickson-Soul, Richard Roundtree, Ross Partridge and Terry O'Quinn. 92 min.
63-1623 Was $14.99 ❑*$12.99*

Amityville Dollhouse (1996)
If Barbie can have her own home, so can the demons of Amityville. Those creepy spirits inhabit a child's dollhouse and soon scare the heck out of all the family members. The place is so scary, even Ken and Skipper would avoid it. With Robin Thomas and Starr Andreef. 97 min.
63-1863 Was $99.99 ❑*$14.99*

House Of The Living Dead (1978)
What evils inhabit the attic of the Brattling manor? It's murderous and flesh-devouring, and it's not Grandma's portrait. Will lovely lady Marianne escape the horror that awaits her? Mark Burns, Shirley Anne Field star. 85 min.
08-1061 Was $29.99 *$19.99*

The Night Visitor (1970)
A man is put into an asylum. Once he's released, he's out to get his revenge on those who sent him there. Liv Ullmann and Max Von Sydow head the exceptional cast. 106 min.
08-1130 WasS $19.99 *$14.99*

What The Peeper Saw (1972)
Suspenseful chiller starring Britt Ekland as a newly married woman who has trouble getting stepson Mark Lester to like her. Ekland begins to suspect Lester was responsible for his mother's mysterious death, but is it merely her imagaination...or something more sinister? Hardy Kruger, Lili Palmer also star. AKA: "Night Child," "Night Hair Child." 97 min.
08-1154 Was $29.99 *$19.99*

Ghosts That Still Walk (1977)
A young boy becomes the receptacle for an evil otherworldly power, but when his worried grandparents take him to a psychic expert the true terror begins. Sinister shocker stars Matt Boston, Ann Nelson. 92 min.
08-1236 *$29.99*

Point Of Terror (1971)
A handsome young singer and the bored wife of an invalid music producer plan a perfect crime, only to unleash a vengeance from beyond the grave. Nerve-numbing terror. 88 min.
08-1257 Was $19.99 *$14.99*

Beast Of The Yellow Night (1971)
A man makes a deal with the Devil for power and wealth, only to learn the terrible price: he is turned into a loathsome rampaging monster. John Ashley stars. 87 min.
08-1269 Was $19.99 *$14.99*

Crypt Of The Living Dead (1973)
An isolated island is the setting for ageless terror when a female vampire is resurrected and starts prowling for victims. Andrew Prine, Mark Damon, Teresa Gimpera star. AKA: "Young Hannah: Queen of the Vampires." 81 min.
08-1276 Was $49.99 *$19.99*

Schizo (1979)
Somewhere, out there...the schizo is waiting for his next victim. He's got a sharp ax and a sharp wit, and no woman is safe. Lynn Frederick and Stephanie Beachum star in this shocker. AKA: "Amok," "Blood of the Undead." 109 min.
08-1314 *$14.99*

The Vampire Happening (1971)
Sensationally sexy, spooky spoof about a beautiful actress who returns to her ancestral home in Transylvania...and finds the skeletons in the family closet are still kicking! The vampire orgy sequence is a million yuks! Pia Degermark, Thomas Hunter. 101 min.
08-1331 Was $19.99 *$14.99*

The Vampire Happening (Letterboxed Version) (1971)
Also available in a theatrical widescreen format, which includes the original theatrical trailer.
08-8852 *$14.99*

Scream Bloody Murder (1978)
Matthew's mangled hand is replaced by a hook which he uses to kill his memories of his mother and her lover. Paul Ecenta, Suzette Hamilton star. 90 min.
08-1075 Was $19.99 *$14.99*

God Told Me To (1976)
Writer/director Larry Cohen delivers a controversial, way-out thriller starring Tony LoBianco as a New York cop trying to stop a series of bizarre sniper killings in which the shooters all say "God told me to." The man behind the bloodshed is a pale-skinned cultist who claims to be the product of a human-alien breeding. Sandy Dennis, Deborah Raffin and Andy Kaufman co-star. Special remastered edition. AKA: "Demon." 89 min.
08-8570 Letterboxed *$14.99*

The Curse Of Bigfoot (1972)
An elderly teacher tells his class about how, as a youngster, he was walking through an ancient Indian burial ground when he encountered Bigfoot, the legendary man-monster. William Simonsen and Robert Clymire star. 87 min.
10-9723 *$19.99*

Audrey Rose (1977)
A young girl is believed to be the reincarnation of another child killed in a crash in this spooky thriller. Robert Wise directs; Marsha Mason, John Beck, Anthony Hopkins star. 113 min.
12-1335 Was $19.99 *$14.99*

House Of Dark Shadows (1970)
The first of two movies based on the popular '60s gothic soap opera. Jonathan Frid stars as vampire Barnabas Collins, released from his 170-year nap to wreak havoc on the residents of Collinwood and search for the reincarnation of his true love. Joan Bennett, Kathryn Leigh Scott, Grayson Hall co-star. 98 min.
12-2084 Was $19.99 *$14.99*

Night Of Dark Shadows (1971)
David Selby and Kate Jackson are the newlyweds who soon learn that Selby's family estate is haunted by the cursed spirits of his ancestors in the spooky second entry in the "Dark Shadows" film series. With Grayson Hall, John Karlen, and Lara Parker as the bewitching Angelique. 95 min.
12-2085 Was $19.99 *$14.99*

What's The Matter With Helen? (1971)
Bizarre psychological shocker about two '30s Midwest mothers whose sons were convicted in a series of bloody murders. To escape the past, the women move to Hollywood and set up a school for would-be child actors, but a mysterious stranger won't let them forget. Shelley Winters, Debbie Reynolds, Dennis Weaver and Agnes Moorehead star. 101 min.
12-2475 Was $19.99 *$14.99*

Moon Of The Wolf (1972)
Ahh-ewww, werewolves are... are... are... everywhere! A small-town sheriff investigating a series of strange murders. What's going on? He thinks it could be a werewolf. David Janssen, Barbara Rush, Bradford Dillman. 74 min.
14-3026 Was $49.99 *$14.99*

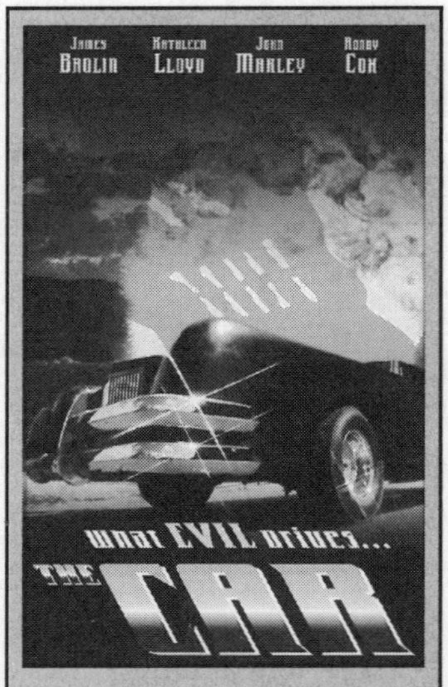

The Car (1977)
Much requested at Movies Unlimited, this terror tale stars James Brolin as a deputy sheriff in a Southwestern town who must try to stop a driverless black sedan that has taken a number of lives, including his superior's. John Marley, Kathleen Lloyd and R.G. Armstrong also star in this motorized monstrosity classic. 96 min.
08-8759 *$14.99*

The Car (Letterboxed Collector's Edition)
Also available in a theatrical, widescreen format; includes the original theatrical trailer.
08-8760 *$14.99*

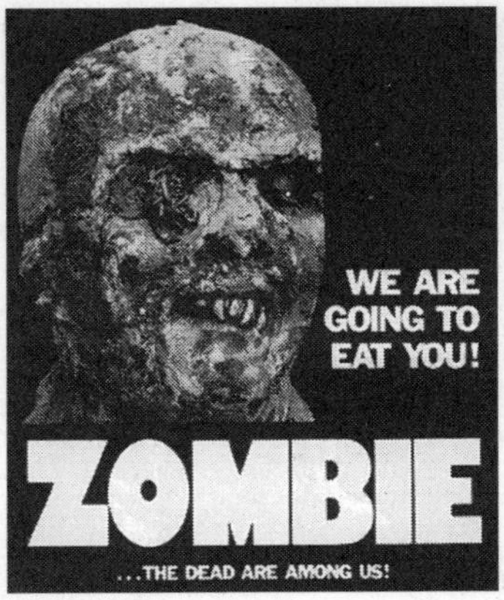
WE ARE
GOING TO
EAT YOU!
ZOMBIE
...THE DEAD ARE AMONG US!

Zombie (1980)
A gore-filled zombiethon from Italy's Lucio Fulci. Reporter Ian McCullough travels to a Caribbean island to investigate a series of murders and finds a diabolical doctor and hordes of flesh-eating ghouls. So shocking the film was given a self-imposed "X." Tisa Farrow and Richard Johnson also star. AKA: "Zombie 2: The Dead Are Among Us." 91 min.
69-1143 *$19.99*

Zombie (Letterboxed Collector's Edition)
Also available in a theatrical, widescreen format. This special edition includes liner notes and a new digital transfer.
08-8638 *$14.99*

American Gothic (1988)
So, that's why that guy had a pitchfork! A group of stranded campers are the "guests" of a demented family who desperately want them for dinner...and leftovers the next day. Rod Steiger, Yvonne DeCarlo, Michael J. Pollard star. 90 min.
68-1101 *$89.99*

Witchery (1988)
A mysterious hotel on a remote New England island is the setting for this terrifying tale of supernatural possession and demonic forces. Linda Blair, David Hasselhoff star. 96 min.
68-1121 *$79.99*

The Visitors (1989)
"A rustle in the walls...wet footprints in the attic...shadows creeping in the dark." An otherworldly force moves into a home and makes the family who already lives there very uncomfortable. Occult chiller stars Lena Endre, Keith Berkeley. 102 min.
68-1133 *$79.99*

The Beyond (1981)
An unrelenting nightmare begins when a young woman inherits a run-down New Orleans hotel and begins renovating it. The hotel was built over one of the gates of Hell which keep the undead out; now they're free to roam and kill! Katherine McColl, David Warbeck star; Lucio Fulci directs. AKA: "And You'll Live in Terror!," "Seven Doors of Death." Uncut version; 89 min.
27-6406 Letterboxed *$14.99*

Miss Morison's Ghosts (1981)
Inspired by true events, this haunting tale stars Wendy Hiller and Hannah Gordon as the principal and vice-principal of an Oxford college who supposedly encountered the ghosts of Marie Antoinette and her court at the Palace of Versailles. The women then caused great controversy among the academic community as they fought to be believed. 103 min.
53-6944 *$29.99*

The Creeping Flesh (1973)
Peter Cushing and Christopher Lee star in this unusual gothic chiller, as a scientist searching for the "ultimate evil" finds it locked within a prehistoric monster's skeleton, a skeleton that still lives. 89 min.
02-1133 *$49.99*

Nightwing (1979)
You'll go "bats" for this tale of Nature's revenge on Man. David Warner is an industrialist dynamiting sacred Indian caves, which unleashes a flood of angry vampire bats. Nick Mancuso is the naturalist who must find a way to eliminate the deadly swarms. 103 min.
02-1202 Was $19.99 *$14.99*

Jaws 2 (1978)
Just when you thought it was safe to turn on your VCR... there's another shark off the shores of Amity Beach, and it's up to police chief Roy Scheider to stop it. Heart-stopping suspense and terror on a par with the original. 117 min.
07-1020 Was $19.99 *□$14.99*

Jaws 3 (1983)
Like many travellers, man-eating sharks occasionally vacation in Florida, and the result is terror at an aquatic theme park when a mother great white comes looking for its offspring. Lou Gossett, Simon MacCorkindale, Bess Armstrong, Dennis Quaid star. Not in 3-D. 97 min.
07-1191 Was $19.99 *$14.99*

Please see our index for: *Jaws*

The Omen (1976)
Chilling horror classic stars Gregory Peck and Lee Remick as an ambassador and his wife, whose child may well be the prophesied Antichrist, Satan's ruler on Earth. Graphic gore effects and an Oscar-winning score by Jerry Goldsmith highlight this shocker. Co-stars David Warner, Billie Whitelaw, Leo McKern. 111 min.
04-3880 *$14.99*

Damien: Omen II (1978)
Damien, that little boy who's "cute as the Devil" in every sense of the phrase, is growing up and preparing to take on the world in this continuation of the horrifying series. William Holden and Lee Grant star as the adoptive parents who realize the truth...but is it too late? 107 min.
04-1034 Was $59.99 *$14.99*

The Final Conflict (1981)
The final chapter of the terrifying "Omen" trilogy. The satanic Damien Thorne becomes a presidential advisor—and control of the world is within his reach. Stars Sam Neill and Rossano Brazzi. 108 min.
04-1437 Was $59.99 *$14.99*

Omen IV: The Awakening (1992)
That ol' black magic is back, this time in the guise of a cute little girl. So sweet and innocent and...devilish! What's wrong? Could she have inherited the evil power of Damien Thorne? Faye Grant, Michael Lerner, Michael Woods star. 97 min.
04-2565 Was $29.99 *□$14.99*

The Omen Collection
"All four chilling 'Omen' films are also available in a money-saving boxed set? The devil, you say!"
04-3967 Save $10.00! *$29.99*

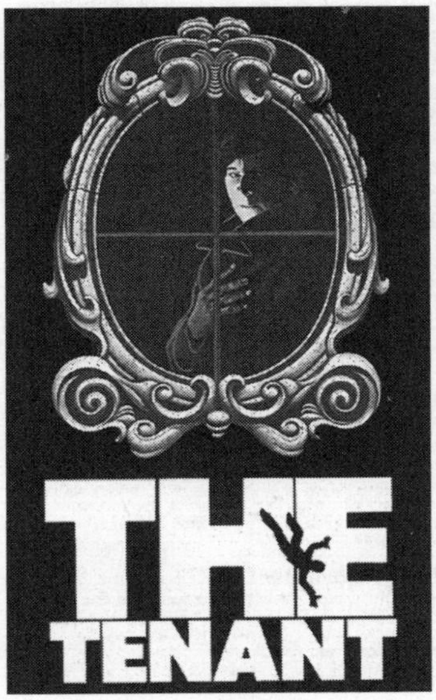
THE
TENANT

The Tenant (1976)
Roman Polanski directed and stars in this bizarre psycho-chiller about a man who moves into an apartment whose previous occupant killed herself, and soon becomes convinced her life is consuming his. With Isabelle Adjani, Melvyn Douglas, Shelley Winters. 125 min.
06-1183 Was $49.99 *$19.99*

Tintorera...Tiger Shark (1978)
Horror spectacular about a killer shark off the shores of Mexico, and the two men who vow to kill it...or be killed. Susan George, Andres Garcia star; from the director of "Survive." 85 min.
03-1183 Was $54.99 *$19.99*

Thirst (1979)
A secret vampirical society that "milks" and stockpiles its victims' blood kidnaps a beautiful businesswoman (Chantal Contouri) they believe to be descended from their founder, Countess Bathory. Stylish effects propel this spine-chilling horror parable that also stars David Hemmings and Henry Silva. 96 min.
03-1646 Was $19.99 *□$14.99*

When A Stranger Calls (1979)
Seven years ago, she was terrorized by a maniacal killer. Now he's escaped, and wants to pick up where he left off. Terrifying suspense story stars Carol Kane, Charles Durning, Colleen Dewhurst, and the classic line, "He's in the house!" 99 min.
02-1074 Was $19.99 *$14.99*

When A Stranger Calls Back (1993)
This frightening sequel to "When a Stranger Calls" finds original babysitter Carol Kane playing a student advisor to coed Jill Schoelen, who is being terrorized by a demented stalker. Both women must confront terrors from their past if they're to stop the maniac and stay alive. With Charles Durning. 94 min.
07-2053 *□$12.99*

Tombs Of The Blind Dead (Collector's Edition) (1971)
Seminal Spanish horror film about a group of travellers at a remote monastery whose graveyard contains the bodies of the Templars, 13th-century cultists who tortured and killed women and were put to death for their crimes, their eyes plucked out by crows. Now these unseeing zombies are out of their graves and, guided by sound, hunting for fresh victims. Oscar Burner, Lone Fleming star. Remastered, uncut version; 102 min. In Spanish with English subtitles.
08-8555 Letterboxed *$14.99*

The Return Of The Blind Dead (Collector's Edition) (1973)
Scary sequel to "Tombs of the Blind Dead" finds the village where the bloodthirsty Templars were killed centuries earlier under attack by the sightless living corpses. A group of survivors takes refuge in a church, but can they withstand the zombie onslaught? Tony Kendall stars in Amando de Ossario's gory saga. Remastered special edition includes the original theatrical trailer. AKA: "Return of the Evil Dead." 90 min. Dubbed in English.
08-8569 Letterboxed *$14.99*

The House On Skull Mountain (1974)
A voodoo master unleashes an army of zombies in this frightful flick, which stars Victor French, Mike Evans, Janee Michelle and Jean Durand. 85 min.
04-1882 Was $59.99 *□$29.99*

Race With The Devil (1975)
When two couples on vacation in the woods witness a witch cult's human sacrifice, they must run and then fight for their lives. Non-stop, brutal action thriller stars Peter Fonda, Warren Oates, Loretta Swit and Lara Parker. 90 min.
04-1897 *$14.99*

The Other (1972)
A chilling screen version of Thomas Tryon's classic suspense novel about a pair of twin boys, one good and the other evil, and a series of grotesque killings in a Connecticut farm community. Uta Hagen and Diana Muldaur star, with a hair-raising score by Jerry Goldsmith. 100 min.
04-2230 Was $59.99 *□$29.99*

The Mephisto Waltz (1971)
A journalist and his wife (Alan Alda, Jacqueline Bisset) are let in for some soul-swapping of the occult variety when he gets an interview with a reclusive pianist. Curt Jurgens and Barbara Parkins are incestuous Satanists in this three-scares-per-measure possession thriller. 108 min.
04-2234 Was $59.99 *$29.99*

Prophecy (1979)
A scary shocker about Nature run rampant. Talia Shire and Robert Foxworth are vacationing in Maine when bizarre creatures, the product of man's pollution, attack them. 102 min.
06-1040 *$19.99*

Bug (1975)
Huge cockroaches with the ability to set objects on fire terrorize a peaceful California community in this shocking William Castle production. Bradford Dillman, Joanna Miles. 100 min.
06-1135 *$19.99*

Let's Scare Jessica To Death (1971)
After being released from an institution, a young woman encounters all sorts of frightening happenings in a Connecticut farmhouse. But are the incidents real? Or are they part of a plot to scare Jessica to death? Zohra Lampert. 89 min.
06-1224 Was $49.99 *$19.99*

Tales That Witness Madness (1973)
Horror anthology from Amicus Films features Donald Pleasence and Jack Hawkins as psychiatrists analyzing the phobias of the patients at their clinic. There's ferocious, not-so imaginary tigers, a time-travelling bicycle, a human tree and a human sacrifice. With Joan Collins, Kim Novak, Suzy Kendall and Georgia Brown; Freddie Francis directs. 90 min.
06-1860 *$14.99*

Dracula (1979)
Broadway vamp Frank Langella brings an eerie sexuality to his version of the Count in this adaptation of the smash stage play. Laurence Olivier co-stars as Drac's nemesis, Van Helsing. With Donald Pleasence, Kate Nelligan. 109 min.
07-1016 Was $19.99 *$14.99*

The Devil's Wedding Night (1973)
In this erotically-charged Italian horror opus, Mark Damon plays twin archaeologists in search of the legendary ring of the Nibelungen in Transylvania. One of the siblings becomes a bloodsucker after coming under the spell of a beautiful female vampire, and the secrets to her bloody rituals are soon revealed. Sara Bey (Rosalba Neri) also stars.
08-1006 *$14.99*

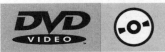

Shivers (1975)
The first feature from shockmaster David Cronenberg, a perverse chiller about parasitic bugs that inhabit the residents of a Canadian apartment complex and infect them with an insatiable sex drive, is presented in a special remastered edition that includes an exclusive interview with the filmmaker. Paul Hampton, Joe Silver and Barbara Steele star. AKA: "The Parasite Murders," "They Came from Within." 110 min. total.
08-8677 *$14.99*

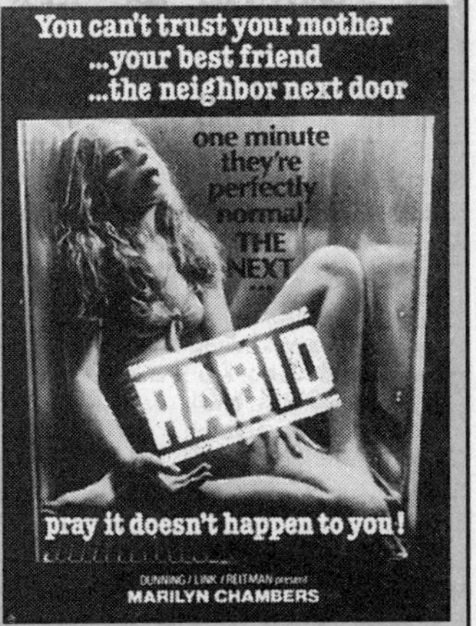
You can't trust your mother
...your best friend
...the neighbor next door
one minute
they're
perfectly
normal,
THE
NEXT
...
RABID
pray it doesn't happen to you!
MARILYN CHAMBERS

Rabid (1977)
Marilyn Chambers stars as an accident victim who undergoes experimental surgery, becoming a modern-day "vampire" (with a blood-sucking organ under her arm) and infecting Montreal with a madness plague. David Cronenberg's psycho-sexual chiller also stars Joe Silver, Frank Moore. 90 min.
19-1085 *$14.99*

Videodrome (1983)
A TV executive discovers an underground show where people are killed on camera, and is slowly drawn into a hallucinogenic world of living TV sets and programmable people. Dazzling blend of sci-fi suspense and erotic terror from David Cronenberg stars James Woods, Deborah Harry. 87 min.
07-1146 Was $19.99 *$14.99*

eXistenZ (1999)
In David Cronenberg's visionary thriller, Jennifer Jason Leigh is a game designer who has conceived a virtual reality game that hooks into peoples' bodies. When she is pursued by a radical anti-game group, Leigh joins forces with marketing trainee Jude Law on the lam in the dangerous, alternative world she has created. With Ian Holm, Willem Dafoe. 97 min.
11-2352 Was $99.99 *□$14.99*

Please see our index for these other David Cronenberg titles: *The Dead Zone • The Fly • M. Butterfly • Naked Lunch • Scanners*

Dr. Black, Mr. Hyde (1976)
There's a new twist on the classic shock story. As the kindly Dr. Pride's skin gets lighter, his soul gets darker, and soon an albino fiend is stalking the ghetto streets. Bernie Casey, Rosalind Cash and the inimitable Stu Gilliam star. 88 min.
08-1008 *$19.99*

Night Creature (1979)
Donald Pleasence stars as a millionaire big-game hunter whose private preserve is stalked by a deadly panther. Nancy Kwan and Ross Hagen co-star in this tense thriller. You'll never look at Kitty the same way again. 83 min.
08-1011 *$19.99*

The Resurrection Of Zachary Wheeler (1971)
Investigating the narrow escape from death of a presidential candidate, an inquisitive reporter sneaks into a compound and quickly encounters the sinister truth. Angie Dickinson, Bradford Dillman star. 100 min.
08-1032 *$14.99*

Ruby (1977)
The spirit of a dead gangster takes over the body of his deaf-mute daughter and seeks revenge on the girl's mother, a drive-in theatre owner, in this spellbinding shocker. Piper Laurie, Janit Baldwin, Stuart Whitman and Roger Davis star. 85 min.
08-1033 *$19.99*

Sisters Of Death (1978)
A young Claudia Jennings stars in this bizarre horror outing, playing a member of a secret all-girl cult called the Sisters. Jennings and her pals go to a compound run by the father of one of the girls, who died years earlier. What's more, Dad has a Gatling gun and a desire for revenge. Arthur Franz co-stars. AKA: "Death Trap."
08-1151 *$19.99*

The Beast In The Cellar (1971)
Two spinster sisters, a series of horrible murders and one monstrous half-human animal converge on a quiet and peaceful English hamlet. Beryl Reid, Flora Robson. 88 min.
19-7045 Was $59.99 *$19.99*

Vampires' Night Orgy (1973)
Thrillseekers visiting a European resort are unaware that the place is a sort of Club Med for swinging vampires. Talk about your bloodsucking tourist traps! White-knuckled horror from Spain stars Jack Taylor. AKA: "Orgy of the Vampires." 86 min.
68-8339 *$19.99*

It's Alive (1974)
Look out! A fanged mutant baby is on the loose! He's killed all the doctors in the delivery room! He got to the milkman too (but first raided his truck!). A first-class shocker that'll rattle you! John Ryan, Sharon Farrell star; Larry Cohen directs. 91 min.
19-1338 *$14.99*

It Lives Again (1978)
More killer babies on the loose—a whole playpen full of them! The father from "It's Alive" tries to stop this new breed of irksome infants. Frederic Forrest and Kathleen Lloyd are some new, not-so-proud parents. 91 min.
19-1339 *$14.99*

It's Alive III: Island Of The Alive (1987)
Five years earlier the fanged, cannibalistic children were taken to a deserted island. Now they're hungry...and homesick! Third entry in the horrifying series stars Michael Moriarty, Karen Black; written and directed by Larry Cohen. 94 min.
19-1617 Was $19.99 *$14.99*

Microwave Massacre (1979)
Deadpan comedian Jackie Vernon stars in this creepy comedy as a henpecked hard-hat who kills his nagging wife, then cooks up the remains in order to get rid of the evidence. He develops a taste for human flesh, and soon all types of women begin showing up on his dinner table. 80 min.
36-2007 *$59.99*

Count Yorga, Vampire (1970)
The bloodthirsty Count Yorga (Robert Quarry) comes to modern-day Los Angeles to satiate his lusts in this cult horror classic. Michael Murphy, Donna Anders, Roger Perry co-star. 90 min.
44-1281 Was $19.99 *$14.99*

The Return Of Count Yorga (1971)
Stylish bloodsucking saga finds the diabolical Count Yorga back for more blood and the neck of a gorgeous woman he meets at a benefit costume party. The vampire puts a spell on her, much to the horror of her fiancé. Robert Quarry, Mariette Hartley, Roger Perry star. 97 min.
73-1129 *$14.99*

Shriek Of The Mutilated (1974)
Early "splatter" treat features a group of college students who search on a desolate island for Bigfoot, only to find a greater, more human terror awaits. Jennifer Stock, Tawn Ellis star. 85 min.
47-3050 *$19.99*

Seeds Of Evil (1974)
Horrifying horticultural horror flick with Joe Dallesandro as a gruesome gardener who can transform into a tree and possesses evil powers over plants, who carry out his nefarious deeds. With Katharine Houghton. AKA: "The Gardener." 82 min.
48-1010 Was $29.99 *$19.99*

Edgar Allan Poe

The Fall Of The House Of Usher (1949)
A British film version of the classic Poe story about decadence and guilt, as brooding Lord Roderick Usher is frightened to the point of madness by the shrouded form of his sister, returned from the grave. Kay Tendeter, Irving Steen star. 70 min.
68-8029 *$19.99*

The Blancheville Monster (1963)
Alberto DeMartino ("The Tempter") directed this shocker, loosely based on Edgar Allan Poe's "The Fall of the House of Usher." It details the creepy goings-on at a house where an elderly, disfigured Englishman has buried his daughter...alive! Gerard Tichy and Joan Mills star. AKA: "Horror."
10-8097 Was $19.99 *$14.99*

Phantom Of The Rue Morgue (1954)
Originally made in 3-D for theatre showings, this horrific retelling of the Edgar Allan Poe story stars Karl Malden as Dr. Marais, who hypnotizes an ape and sends him out to kill all the women of Paris who have spurned his romantic advances (the doctor's, not the ape's). With Steve Forrest, Patricia Medina; look for a young Merv Griffin as a student. 84 min.
19-2249 Was $19.99 *$14.99*

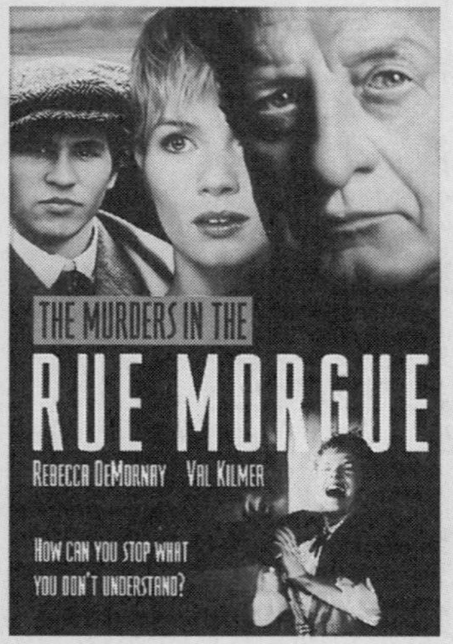
THE MURDERS IN THE
RUE MORGUE
REBECCA DEMORNAY VAL KILMER
HOW CAN YOU STOP WHAT
YOU DON'T UNDERSTAND?

The Murders In The Rue Morgue (1990)
The classic tale of murder and mystery by Poe is given a chilling adaptation in this stylish thriller. George C. Scott stars as detective Auguste Dupin, who must track down the killer terrorizing the citizens of Paris. Rebecca DeMornay, Val Kilmer co-star. 92 min.
68-1173 Was $89.99 *$14.99*

The Tell-Tale Heart (1960)
British version of the classic Poe chiller about a deformed loner who murders a romantic rival and hides the body beneath the floorboards of his house. Stars Lawrence Payne and Dermot Walsh. 78 min.
68-8402 *$19.99*

Dr. Tarr's Torture Dungeon (1972)
Loosely based on Edgar Allan Poe's "The System of Dr. Tarr and Professor Fether," this surreal Mexican shocker tells of a reporter who discovers that the asylum he's investigating for a story is actually being run by two of its inmates. Arthur Hansel and Claudio Brook also star; from the producers of "El Topo." 93 min. AKA: "House of Madness," "The Mansion of Madness."
69-1049 *$19.99*

The Black Cat (1980)
Italian horror maestro Lucio Fulci directs this creepy adaptation of Edgar Allan Poe's tale. A clairvoyant sends spirits from beyond the grave into a cat which then goes on a murderous spree. Patrick Magee and Mimsy Farmer star. 93 min.
15-5211 Was $19.99 *$14.99*

Web Of The Spider (1970)
Klaus Kinski plays Edgar Allan Poe in Antonio Margheriti's remake of his own "Castle of Blood." A skeptical journalist stays over in a haunted mansion on a dare and is subjected to a full-scale horror revue by the ghostly inhabitants. Anthony Franciosa stars. 93 min.
68-8316 Was $19.99 *$14.99*

The Spectre Of Edgar Allan Poe (1974)
Loose interpretation of the life of the enigmatic author depicts the horrors and degradation Poe's true love, Lenore, was subjected to within the walls of a mental institution headed by sadistic overseer Dr. Grimaldi (Cesar Romero). Co-stars Robert Walker, Jr. as Poe, Tom Drake and Mary Grover. 87 min.
48-1017 *$29.99*

The Oval Portrait (1988)
Eerie rendition of Edgar Allan Poe's tale of the doomed love between the daughter of a Union officer and the wounded Confederate soldier who came into her care...a love that death itself could not lay asunder. Gisele MacKenzie, Wanda Hendrix star. 89 min.
78-1003 *$19.99*

The Haunting Of Morella (1991)
A woman is convicted of witchcraft and executed as her husband and infant daughter watch. Eighteen years later, her soul returns to take over the body of her daughter and wreak horrific havoc. Shocker based on an Edgar Allan Poe tale stars David McCallum, Nicole Eggert and Maria Ford. 82 min.
21-9005 Was $89.99 *$14.99*

Edgar Allan Poe's Madhouse (1992)
Featured here are three creepy tales inspired by Poe's writings: a man thinks he's found the girl of his dreams, while she sees him as someone to sink her teeth into; winos discover some magic booze; and a stripper "reveals all" to a fan during the full moon. Tonia Monahan, Jenny Admire star. 85 min.
73-9038 *$19.99*

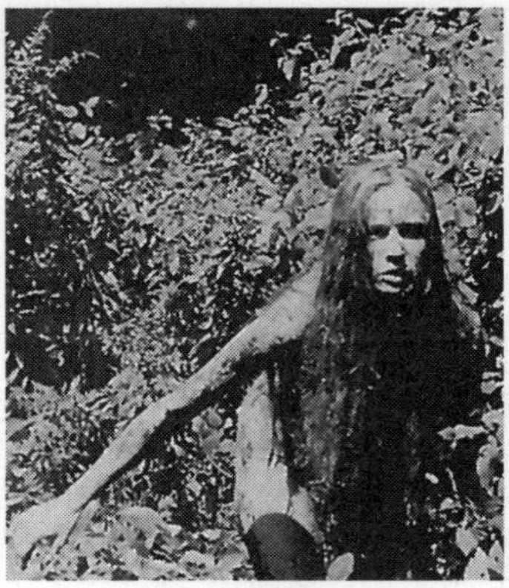

I Spit On Your Grave (1978)
One of the sickest, most disturbing movies ever made! After being savagely gang-raped and left for dead, a woman returns to plot her revenge. She chops, burns and mutilates her assailants. Not for the squeamish! Camille Keaton star. AKA: "Day of the Woman." Uncut version; 98 min.
20-1009 *$24.99*

I Spit On Your Grave (Letterboxed Collector's Edition)
Also available in a theatrical, widescreen format, which also includes the original theatrical trailer. 100 min.
08-8753 *$19.99*

The Changeling (1979)
Spine-tingling chiller with George C. Scott as a music teacher who moves into a house haunted by the spirit of a child killed there decades earlier. With Melvyn Douglas, Trish Van Devere, Barry Morse. 115 min.
44-1824 Was $19.99 *$14.99*

Tales From The Crypt (1971)
Five travellers are trapped in a tomb with the sinister Crypt Keeper (Sir Ralph Richardson), who tells them each a shocking story of their future—or is it their past?—in this chilling Amicus anthology based on the infamous E.C. horror comics of the '50s. Joan Collins, Peter Cushing, Richard Greene, Patrick Magee and Nigel Patrick star. 92 min.
46-5076 *$14.99*

Seven Deaths In The Cat's Eye (1972)
Gory murders galore when a cat-like creature appears to be preying on a small Scottish village. When the inhabitants of an isolated castle start emerging belly-up, the killer can only be one of the survivors...but which? Stars Anton Diffring, Jane Birkin. 90 min.
46-5280 *$19.99*

Night Screams (1977)
When his parents leave for a weekend trip, a high school football star invites his friends over for a wild party. Two escaped convicts who are definitely uninvited, however, show up, turning the bash into a bloodbath. Scares and shocks galore! Joe Manno, Megan Wyss star. 90 min.
46-5357 Was $29.99 *$14.99*

Squirm (1976)
This horror classic will make your skin crawl! A power line accidentally sets thousands of icky worms loose on the countryside. Soon, they're covering the place—they're in the shower, in the food, even in the egg cream. Don Scardino, Patricia Pearcy, Jean Sullivan star. 92 min.
47-1056 *$14.99*

The Love-Thrill Murders (1971)
Troy Donahue stars as Moon, the crazed leader of a cult of wild, spaced-out followers hell-bent on destroying the world of the privileged beautiful people. Moon kills all who do not obey! Chilling shocker more murderous than Manson! AKA: "Sweet Savior." 89 min.
47-1586 *$14.99*

The Black Panther (1977)
A harrowing look at Donald Neilson, the mass murderer known as the British Charles Manson, who committed some of England's most frightful murders. Stars Donald Sumpter, Debbie Farrington. 90 min.
47-1596 *$69.99*

The Legend Of Boggy Creek (1972)
Just what could be that hairy creature terrorizing the small Arkansas community? Legend has it that it's a seven-foot, 250-pound creature known for eluding its trackers. This docudrama was a huge box office success and spawned numerous imitators. 87 min.
47-1637 *$19.99*

When The Screaming Stops (1973)
Unusual horror film set in Europe's Rhine Valley, where a bewitching seductress lures the unsuspecting into her clutches, then turns into a reptilian monster and devours them. There's nudity, gore and even Teutonic myth in this frightfest from "Blind Dead" director Armado De Ossorio; the film includes red "fear flashes" as a warning. AKA: "Grasp of the Lorelei." 86 min.
47-3049 *$29.99*

Keep My Grave Open! (1974)
Gore-drenched story of a young lady who lives in a spooky old house with her mysterious husband. Anybody foolish enough to cross this threshhold meets with a gruesome demise! Filmed in Texas; Camilla Carr, Stephen Tobolowsky, Sharon Bunn star. 80 min.
48-1011 *$14.99*

The Witch Who Came From The Sea (1976)
There's little in the way of witchcraft, but plenty of seaside shivers, in this eerie shocker starring Millie Perkins as a Venice Beach barmaid who lures athletes and muscleman to her home, then castrates and kills them. With Rick Jason, Vanessa Brown. 84 min.
48-1047 *$49.99*

Garden Of The Dead (1972)
An isolated prison labor camp is the scene for horror and vengeance from beyond the grave when inmates doused with formaldehyde come back as bloodthirsty, unstoppable monsters. Duncan McLeod, Lee Frost star. AKA: "Tomb of the Undead." 60 min.
50-1307 Was $29.99 *$19.99*

The Bloodsucker Leads The Dance (1975)
What is the sinister, erotic secret that lures a group of beautiful young women to the remote island home of a monstrous Italian nobleman? Find out in this sensual "giallo" chiller. Femi Benussi, Giacomo Rossi Stuart and Krista Nell star. AKA: "The Passion of Evelyn." 89 min. Dubbed in English.
50-5765 Letterboxed *$19.99*

The Devil's Nightmare (1971)
Slick Belgian/Italian shocker about seven strangers who find their way to the house of a family cursed to have the firstborn daughter of each generation become an agent of the devil. One by one, the strangers are murdered by a horrifying woman in the manner of the deadly sin each represents. Erika Blanc, Jean Servais star. AKA: "The Devil Walks at Midnight," "Succubus." 93 min. Dubbed in English.
50-5942 Letterboxed *$19.99*

The Reincarnation Of Isabel (1973)
A Satanic cult, as part of an ancient rite to revive a witch who died 400 years earlier, must sacrifice a group of seven virgins. Trouble erupts when one of the prospective victim's lovers interrupts the rituals, and the witches turn into vampires and wreak havoc on the town. Rita Calderon and Mickey Hargitay star. 100 min. In Italian with English subtitles.
50-5943 Letterboxed *$19.99*

Don't Look In The Basement (1973)
Classic low-budget shocker set in an asylum where patients rebel against the new, sadistic female director after the former chief has been axed—literally! Will they stop her before she kills them all? With Ann McAdams, Rosie Holotik and William McGee as Sam, the lollipop-sucking inmate.
50-6002 Was $19.99 *$14.99*

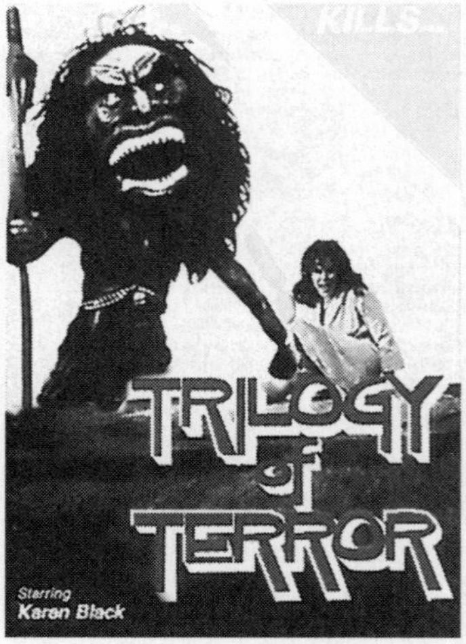
TRILOGY
of
TERROR
Starring
Karen Black

Trilogy Of Terror: Collector's Edition (1975)
Director Dan Curtis ("Dark Shadows") and fantasy writers Richard Matheson and William F. Nolan pooled their talents for this trio of scary stories. Karen Black stars in all three segments, playing feuding twin sisters, a blackmailed teacher, and a woman stalked by a living African fetish doll. With Robert Burton, Gregory Harrison, John Karlen. 72 min.
50-6185 *$14.99*

Trilogy Of Terror II (1996)
Brace yourself for another spine-tingling triple feature, courtesy of horror master Dan Curtis ("Dark Shadows"). A woman's "perfect" plan for killing her rich husband leaves her in a cemetery full of rats; an occult ritual brings a mother's drowned young son back to life, with horrifying consequences; and that nasty African doll from the first film is back for new victims. Lysette Anthony stars in all three vignettes; with Geoffrey Lewis, Matt Clark. 90 min.
06-2562 Was $79.99 *$14.99*

Werewolves On Wheels (1971)
You say you like growling, snarling man-beasts? You say you like red-hot biker action? Well, then, you can't miss with this horrifying tale of a motorcycle gang who take on a cult of Satanists. Billy Gray ("Father Knows Best"), Barry McGuire ("Eve of Destruction") star. 85 min.
48-1167 Was $19.99 ***$14.99***

Slave Of The Cannibal God (1979)
Searching in the jungles of New Guinea along with scientist Stacy Keach for her missing husband, lovely Ursula Andress is taken prisoner by a savage, man-eating tribe of natives who strip her, paint her body and prepare her for a bizarre and deadly ceremony. Brutal shocker from director Sergio Martino also stars Helmut Berger. 86 min.
20-1028 Was $49.99 ***$29.99***

Dr. Orloff's Invisible Horror (1970)
Howard Vernon returns as the demented Dr. Orloff, who, in this chiller, creates an invisible human in order to kidnap his partner's daughter, with whom he's obsessed. Britt Carva also stars. AKA: "The Invisible Dead." 80 min.
20-1058 ***$14.99***

Cold Eyes Of Fear (1971)
In this Italian-Spanish "giallo" film, a pair of crooks take a young lawyer and his girlfriend hostage in order to get back at the lawyer's father, who happens to be a judge. Giovanna Ralli, Leon Leonoir and Fernando Rey star in director Enzo Castellari's thriller set in the "Swinging London" of the '70s; music by Ennio Morricone. 91 min. Dubbed in English.
20-5157 Letterboxed ***$19.99***

Mardi Gras Massacre (1978)
Way down yonder in New Orleans...horror and human sacrifices are the name of the game, as a deranged Aztec priest starts carving up partygoers to offer to the god Quetzacoatl. Playboy Playmate Laura Misch, Curt Dawson star. 90 min.
23-5019 ***$29.99***

The Fiend (1971)
A withdrawn young man is taken into a bizarre religious cult, and soon his repressed passions are released in a violent orgy of sex and blood! Gory psycho-thriller stars Patrick Magee, Tony Beckley, Ann Todd. AKA: "Beware My Brethren." 87 min.
27-6385 ***$39.99***

Invasion Of The Blood Farmers (1972)
Nothing can stop a demonic tribe of druids in a remote New York valley as they kidnap young women for their blood, needed to ressurect the cult's queen from her glass coffin. From the director of "Shriek of the Mutilated"; Norman Kelly, Tanna Hunter star. 80 min.
21-5000 ***$19.99***

Trap Them And Kill Them (1977)
Italian shocker in which "Emannuelle's" Laura Gemser plays a newspaper reporter who tries to convince a group of flesh-eating Amazon natives that she's a goddess in order to save a fellow explorer, anthropologist Gabrielle Tinti. Wild exploitation mix of sex, nudity, unsettling gore and more from no-holds-barred helmer Joe D'Amato. Unrated version; 93 min.
20-5046 ***$29.99***

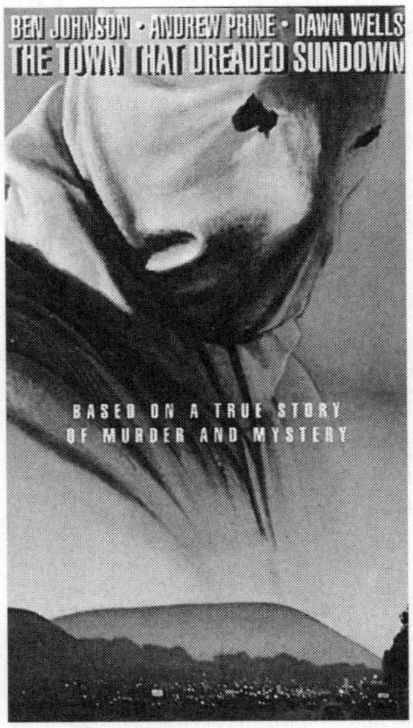

The Town That Dreaded Sundown (1977)
This true thriller focuses on a creepy, mysterious hooded killer who terrorized Texarkana in 1946. The beating and torture of two young lovers elicits the interest of a Deputy Sheriff and a tough Texas Ranger. Andrew Prine, Ben Johnson and Dawn Wells star. 90 min.
19-1282 ***$14.99***

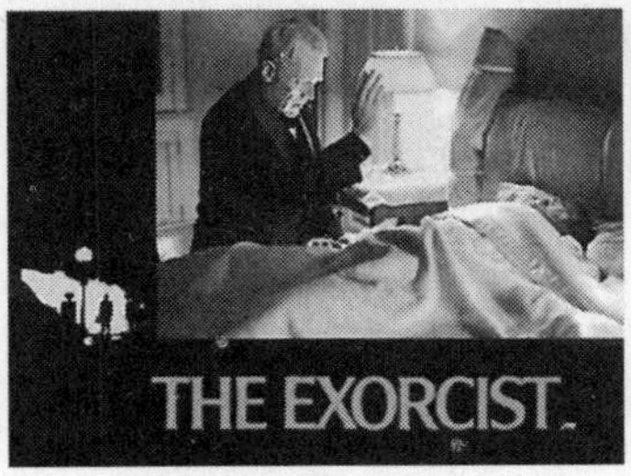

The Exorcist: 25th Anniversary Edition (1973)
Director William Friedkin's modern horror classic stars Linda Blair as the young girl possessed by the Devil, Ellen Burstyn as her terrified mother, and Max Von Sydow and Jason Miller as the priests who must confront the powers of Hell—and their own inner demons—to save Blair. Based on the best-selling William Peter Blatty novel. This special edition also includes the 30-minute documentary "The Fear of God: 25 Years of the Exorcist" and interviews with the cast and crew. 120 min.
19-2709 ***$19.99***

The Exorcist: 25th Anniversary Edition (Letterboxed Version)
Also available in a theatrical, widescreen format.
19-2715 ***$19.99***

The Exorcist: 25th Anniversary Edition Boxed Set
Also available in a boxed collector's set that features the letterboxed version of the movie, the "making of" documentary, a set of eight lobby card reprints, a commemorative book and a soundtrack CD.
19-2710 Letterboxed ***$49.99***

Exorcist II: The Heretic (1977)
John Boorman directed this underrated, terror-filled sequel that follows an 18-year-old Regan (Linda Blair), who once again is beset by an evil spirit. Louise Fletcher and Richard Burton co-star as a child psychologist and a heretical priest who explore new methods to treat the possessed teenager. With Max von Sydow, James Earl Jones and Ned Beatty. 118 min.
19-1033 ***$14.99***

The Exorcist III (1990)
William Peter Blatty, creator of the original "Exorcist," scripted and directed this all-new shocker of demonic possession. An executed serial killer has come back to resume his reign of terror (thanks to the powers of Hell), and the detective who caught him years earlier must stop him again. George C. Scott, Brad Dourif, Ed Flanders star. 105 min.
04-2416 ***$14.99***

House Of Whipcord (1975)
A beautiful model is taken prisoner and held in a bizarre private prison where women are subjected to brutality and degradation. Graphic British-made shocker stars Barbara Markham, Patrick Barr. 102 min.
27-6363 Was $39.99 ***$19.99***

Demon Lover (1976)
A group of teens accidentally unearth the secrets of the Devil, and unspeakable terror and horror are unleashed. A screamer with Gunnar Hansen ("Texas Chainsaw Massacre"), Val Mayerick. 87 min.
48-1012 ***$14.99***

Warlock Moon (1973)
Spine-tingling tale of a beautiful coed who becomes involved with a coven of witches. Stars Laurie Walters, Joe Spano. 89 min.
48-1016 ***$29.99***

Frogs (1972)
In this "rib-it-ing" nature-runs-amok affair, Ray Milland is a Everglades-based, wheelchair-bound chemical tycoon whose birthday party is interrupted by the arrival of scores of snakes, insects, snapping turtles and bullfrogs. Joan Van Ark, Sam Elliott, Adam Roarke and Judy Pace also star in one toad-infested terrorthon. 92 min.
19-1257 Was $59.99 ***$14.99***

The Pack (1977)
Gene and Roger would give this tale of wild dogs attacking villagers "two paws up." It's a terrifying tale of canines crunching—humans!! Joe Don Baker stars. 99 min.
19-1402 Was $19.99 ***$14.99***

The House Of Seven Corpses (1973)
In this creepy terror tale, a movie crew arrives at a supposedly haunted mansion to shoot a horror film, and the reading of passages from the Tibetan Book of the Dead unleashes vengeance-seeking spirits. John Carradine, John Ireland and Faith Domergue star. 84 min.
16-1037 ***$19.99***

Blood Couple (1973)
Creepy, atmospheric horror tale that has gained a wide cult following over the years details the terror faced by two archeologists who journey to Africa to study a lost Nigerian tribe. When one is stabbed by an ancient sacrificial knife, he is transformed into a vampire. Duane Jones, Marlene Clark star. AKA: "Blackout," "Double Possession," "Ganja and Hess." 83 min.
16-1111 ***$14.99***

Night Of The Sorcerers (1974)
Deep in the jungles of the Congo is a sacrificial altar to which beautiful young women, naked in their glory, are lured. Once there, vampire leopard women subject their flesh to depravities of all kinds. Simon Andreu and Kali Hansa star. 76 min.
48-1085 ***$49.99***

A Bell From Hell (1970)
A young man is trapped in a web of insanity and seduction when he's released from an asylum into the "care" of his demented aunt and her three daughters. Bizarre shocker stars Viveca Lindfors. 93 min.
48-1094 ***$49.99***

The Witches' Mountain (1971)
A coven of witches plans a bloody vengeance for the man who convinced his ex-lover, one of their number, to murder her daughter. Patty Shepard, John Caffari star. 83 min.
48-1105 Was $19.99 ***$14.99***

The Pyx (1973)
Creepy thriller starring Christopher Plummer as a detective investigating the death of drug-addicted hooker Karen Black and uncovering a Satanic cult. Donald Pilon, Terry Haig also star. AKA: "The Hooker Cult Murders." 101 min.
46-5279 Was $39.99 ***$19.99***

Disciple Of Death (1972)
Young maidens, beware! The Stranger, a being from beyond the grave, wants to sacrifice you to the Devil. Can the local deputy and minister stop the sinister ritual in time? Spell-binding suspense and horror; Mike Raven, Steve Bradley star. 82 min.
48-1043 ***$49.99***

Die Screaming, Marianne (1972)
A nightclub singer (Susan George) flees from a pack of killers who want to see that she doesn't make it to her 21st birthday, and in turn get their hands on her father's money. 81 min.
48-1045 ***$49.99***

Satan's School For Girls (1973)
What is behind the rash of suicides at the fashionable Salem Academy for Girls? Pamela Franklin tries to find out what demonic horror reigns there. With Kate Jackson, Cheryl Ladd. 74 min.
46-5110 ***$19.99***

The Haunted (1976)
What fury Ma Bell unleashed when a telephone booth was installed in a cemetery harboring the spirit of a vengeful Indian woman. The ancient curse is reawakened and a young girl becomes a victim to its evil cause. Aldo Ray, Virginia Mayo star. 93 min.
23-5006 ***$29.99***

Jess Franco

The Awful Dr. Orloff (1962)
Notorious Jess Franco shocker centering on a surgeon obsessed with repairing his scarred daughter by grafting parts of beautiful young women he has abducted. Aided by his blind, hunchbacked aide, Dr. Orloff proves how awful he really is in this diabolical, S&M-tinged story that spawned several sequels. With Howard Vernon, Perla Cristal. Complete, uncut version; 86 min.
79-5295 ***$24.99***

The Awful Dr. Orloff (Letterboxed Version)
Also available in a theatrical, widescreen format.
50-8595 ***$19.99***

Dr. Orloff's Monster (1964)
Sequel to "The Awful Dr. Orloff" about the disciple of a dead mad scientist who learns how to control corpses by radio, creating a zombie to do his murderous bidding. Gothic horror with Jose Rubio and Agnes Spaak. 88 min.
68-8164 Was $19.99 ***$14.99***

The Diabolical Dr. Z (1965)
Jess Franco's follow-up to "The Awful Dr. Orloff" finds the doc's daughter using her father's mind-control device to gain the will of a seductive cabaret singer whose extraordinarily long fingernails feature in her pseudo-sexual fantasies as piercing murder weapons. Mabel Karr, Howard Vernon star. AKA: "Miss Muerte." 85 min.
68-8060 ***$19.99***

Kiss Me Monster: Collector's Edition (1968)
Two beautiful spies posing as nightclub performers set out to learn the truth behind a demented professor's experiments on his remote Caribbean island. They encounter sexy lesbian killers and sweaty mutant bodybuilders who want to have their way with them. Janine Reynaud and Rossana Yanni star in this sordid Jesus Franco shocker. AKA: "Castle of the Doomed." 78 min.
08-8671 Letterboxed ***$14.99***

Two Undercover Angels: Collector's Edition (1969)
Shot back-to-back with "Kiss Me Monster," this Jesus Franco shocker reteams that film's sexy sleuths, Janine Reynaud and Rossana Yanni, in a bizarre mystery involving the disappearance of several women, a demented artist whose gruesome works resemble the missing girls, and his brutish sidekick. Adrian Hoven also stars. AKA: "Red Lips," "Sadisterotica." 80 min.
08-8755 ***$14.99***

Succubus: Collector's Edition (1969)
This Jesus Franco cult horror flick concerns Lorna, a beautiful and seductive dancer in an S&M club who may be possessed by a demon. This could be the reason behind Lorna's brutal killing of the club's patrons, her visions of seaside castles, the mannequins that magically come to life, and the women that can't keep their hands off each other. Or is it the drugs...or Lorna's collection of Aurora monster models? Janine Reynaud, Howard Vernon star. AKA: "Necromonicon." Includes the theatrical trailer. 76 min.
08-8670 ***$14.99***

Deadly Sanctuary (1970)
Shocking and perverse chiller, loosely based on the works of the Marquis DeSade, follows two sisters on a harrowing series of encounters in 17th-century France. Jack Palance and Klaus Kinski star in director Jess Franco's blend of horror and eroticism. 93 min.
27-6350 ***$39.99***

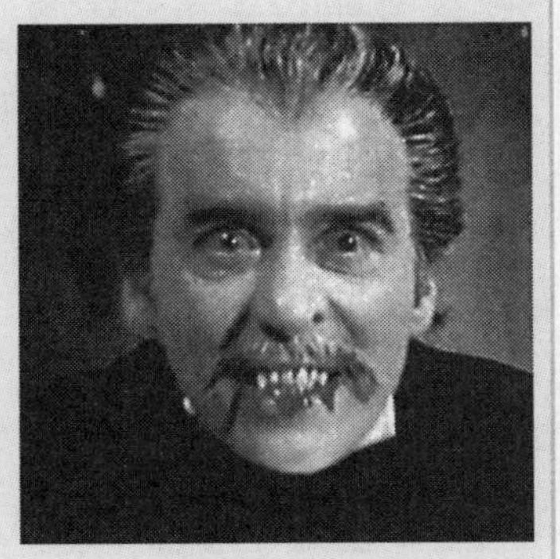

Count Dracula (1971)
Christopher Lee plays the Prince of Vampires in this frightening—and very faithful—adaptation of Bram Stoker's classic. Klaus Kinski plays the demented Renfield; Jess ("Jack the Ripper") Franco directs. 90 min.
63-1092 ***$14.99***

The Demons (1972)
Before a woman dies from a "witch test" in medieval England, she leaves a curse on the nobleman who sentenced her to death. Years later, her daughters become lesbian nuns whose kiss turns men into skeletons(!). Gruesome and erotic Jess Franco chiller stars Howard Vernon, Anne Lipert, Britt Nichols. 90 min.
48-1065 ***$49.99***

Female Vampire (1973)
In director Jess Franco's sexy spin on the classic vampire legends, an island resort learns too late the gruesome connection between a mysterious countess and the growing number of bloodless bodies they're finding. Lina Romay, Jack Taylor, Alice Arno and Franco star. AKA: "The Black Countess," "Erotikill," "Jacula," "The Last Thrill," "The Loves of Irina." 110 min.
50-8616 Letterboxed ***$19.99***

Jack The Ripper (1976)
Jess Franco does his take on the Jack the Ripper legend, as Klaus Kinski plays the doctor whose obsession with his mother's work as a prostitute sends him over the deep end, abducting, torturing and killing streetwalkers on London's foggy streets. Lina Romay, Josephine Chaplin also star.
47-1187 Was $19.99 ***$14.99***

A Virgin Among The Living Dead (1980)
An innocent young girl, returning to her family's remote ancestral home, is confronted with a chilling heritage of horror and death in this Jess Franco shocker. With Christina Von Blanc, Britt Nichols. AKA: "Zombie 4: Virgin Among the Living Dead." 90 min.
20-1061 ***$19.99***

Tender Flesh (1996)
Jess Franco's ultra-lurid excursion in shocks and S&M tells of a stripper hired by a wealthy couple to perform privately at a remote island. After being turned into a sex slave, she is then made the prey in a diabolical game where she is hunted down by the couple and her strip club boss. Monique Parent, Amber Newman and Lina Romay star. Uncut, 93-minute version.
73-9238 ***$49.99***

Blood Sabbath (1972)
Before he set daytime TV fans' hearts aflutter, Tony Geary played a guitarist who falls in love with a beautiful sea nymph but, in order to be with her, must let a witch queen have his soul. Unusual horror outing with erotic moments also stars Susan Damante and Dyanne Thorne of "Ilsa" fame.
50-1223 *$19.99*

Black Voodoo (1978)
A black nurse is possessed by the spirit of a religious fanatic who died on the operating table and is out for bloody revenge on everyone responsible in this sinister shocker from "B"-horrormeister Al Adamson. Jill Jacobson, Geoffrey Land, Marilyn Joi star. AKA: "Nurse Sherri." 90 min.
54-9133 *$19.99*

"Coffin Joe"

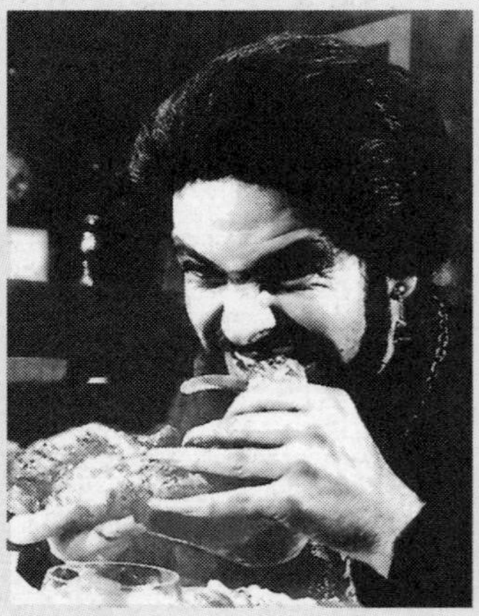

At Midnight I'll Take Your Soul (1963)
This gruesome masterpiece finds diabolical Coffin Joe (Jose Mojica Marins) in a small South American city in search of a woman who will bear him a son to continue his horrific legacy. A haunting excursion into the world of horror that mixes gore, blood, eroticism and moody atmospherics. In Portuguese with English subtitles.
79-5341 Was $24.99 *$19.99*

This Night I Will Possess Your Corpse (1968)
The sequel to "At Midnight I Will Take Your Soul" finds Coffin Joe in search of the perfect woman to bear him a perfect child. During his travels he takes some time and crushes people's heads, puts 50 tarantulas on innocent women and, in an extended color sequence, heads to Hell to witness all sorts of atrocities. In Portuguese with English subtitles.
79-5506 Was $24.99 *$19.99*

The Strange World Of Coffin Joe (1968)
A trio of terrifying tales from the demonic Coffin Joe about a strange dollmaker whose creations look "almost" real, the world of necrophilia, and a doctor ("Coffin Joe" himself) out to prove his theory that love is dead. Cruel and creepy! In Portuguese with English subtitles.
79-5342 Was $24.99 *$19.99*

The Awakening Of The Beast (1968)
Banned for 18 years by Brazilian authorities, this Coffin Joe outing goes way, way out in depicting the suffering of a drug-user whose LSD trips take him to the edge of torment. Ultra-violence, hallucinogenic imagery and out-and-out ghastliness are the "highlights." In Portuguese with English subtitles.
79-5343 Was $24.99 *$19.99*

Hallucinations Of A Deranged Mind (1970)
Shudder-expert Coffin Joe haunts the dreams of a young man (which gives the producer an opportunity to inject scenes from this sicko series that were banned by Brazilian authorities). From sexy to all-out gross-out, this film is not a hallucination. Just keep repeating: "It's only a 'Coffin Joe' movie, it's only a 'Coffin Joe' movie!" In Portuguese with English subtitles.
79-5394 Was $24.99 *$19.99*

Hellish Flesh (1970)
José Mojica Marins is a scientist trying to create an acid formula that can dissolve a human body. When his wife's boyfriend splashes the formula on his face and destroys his lab, a plot for revenge is set in motion. In this deranged outing, Marins adds scenes of eye surgery he underwent. In Portuguese with English subtitles.
79-5540 Was $24.99 *$19.99*

The End Of Man (1971)
José Mojica Marins gets serious as he explores faith and mysticism, playing a preacher with supposed supernatural powers. He has the ability to wake the dead and cure handicapped people, and is seen joining in the world of hippie psychedelia. Weird, weird stuff from the creator of "Coffin Joe." In Portuguese with English subtitles.
79-5507 Was $24.99 *$19.99*

When The Gods Fall Asleep (1972)
José Mojica Marins' sequel to "The End of Man" finds a preacher on another mission to save mankind when the gods fall asleep and evil takes over the world. After his release from an asylum, the preacher tries to save society by chastising manipulative women, interrupting Macuba rituals and virgin sacrifices and stopping duels. In Portuguese with English subtitles.
79-5658 Was $24.99 *$19.99*

The Bloody Exorcism Of Coffin Joe (1972)
Wait 'til you see what happens when Coffin Joe (José Mojica Marins) gets a hold of Christmas and waxes philosophic at the same time! Marins' visit to friends during the holidays prompts strange supernatural occurrences and the discovery of the friends' daughter's engagement to the son of Satan, leading to S&M rituals and a showdown between Marins and Coffin Joe! In Portuguese with English subtitles.
79-5539 Was $24.99 *$19.99*

The Strange Hostel Of Naked Pleasures (1975)
José Mojica Marins produced and stars in this eerie epic in which he plays the owner of a haunted hostel where guests make their wildest and most terrifying dreams come true. Not for the squeamish, this surrealist shocker was directed by "Coffin Joe" disciple Marcelo Motta. In Portuguese with English subtitles.
79-5508 Was $24.99 *$19.99*

Demons And Wonders (1976)
In a self-reflective mood, Coffin Joe chronicles his own amazing life in this autobiographical film that illustrates his live spook shows, his financial woes, his prison experiences, his hallucinations, his struggle to complete a film and more. Also featured is another documentary, "Fogo Fatuo," and his first effort. In Portuguese with English subtitles.
79-5827 Was $24.99 *$19.99*

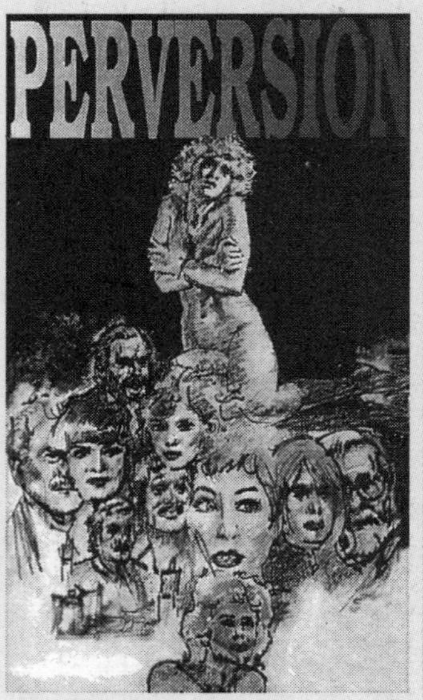

Perversion (1978)
Ultra-kinky, disturbing and savage film starring José Mojica Marins of "Coffin Joe" fame as a deranged millionaire with a penchant for bizarre and sadistic sexual encounters. Originally called "Rape," the film features such acts as Marins biting a young woman's nipple off. Not for the squeamish. In Portuguese with English subtitles.
79-5509 Was $24.99 *$19.99*

Coffin Joe's Visions Of Terror
A collection of trailers from the works of Brazil's maestro of macabre splatter, Coffin Joe. Included are previews for "At Midnight I Will Take Your Soul," "The Strange World of Coffin Joe," "Awakenings of the Beast," "Hallucinations of a Dangerous Mind" and a 20-minute color installment from "Trilogy of Terror." In Portuguese with English subtitles.
79-5505 Was $24.99 *$19.99*

Phantasm (1979)
Bizarre shocker about a cemetery that contains a gateway into another dimension and its sinister caretaker. Bill Thornbury, Michael Baldwin and Angus Scrimm as the Tall Man, and a flying "killer ball" star. 87 min.
53-1268 *$14.99*

Phantasm II (1988)
Get ready, horror fans, because "the ball is back!" The sinister cemetery keeper and his flying spheres are looking to recruit a few good souls in the hit sequel to the scarifying shocker. James Le Gros, Reggie Bannister, Paula Irvine and Angus Scrimm star. 97 min.
07-1595 *$14.99*

Phantasm III: Lord Of The Dead (1994)
Just when you thought the horror was over, the Tall Man and the killer ball are back in this thriller. The secret of the sphere is revealed as two young men return to the cemetery for a deadly encounter with the creepy caretaker. Reggie Bannister, A. Michael Baldwin, Angus Scrimm star. 91 min.
07-2203 *$89.99*

Phantasm: Oblivion (1998)
Are you prepared to revisit the cemetery where the customers don't stay buried? The fourth sinister entry in the shock series features never-before-seen footage from the original "Phantasm" and stars A. Michael Baldwin, Reggie Bannister, Bill Thornbury, Heidi Marnhout, and Angus Scrimm as the Tall Man. 90 min.
73-1293 Was $59.99 *$14.99*

Torso (1973)
With a hooded maniac savagely assaulting and dismembering their fellow coeds at a college campus, four friends decide a vacation at a country villa is a safe getaway. Big mistake, girls, because the killer is heading there after you! Suzy Kendall, Tina Aumont, John Richardson star in Sergio Martino's erotic chiller. Includes the American and European theatrical trailers. AKA: "The Bodies Bear Traces of Carnal Violence." 92 min.
46-5237 Letterboxed *$14.99*

Creature From Black Lake (1977)
Out in the mysterious swamps of Louisiana, a fearsome bayou beast lies waiting for its next victim. Could it be...you? Jack Elam, Dub Taylor, Dennis Fimple star in this horror treat. 95 min.
47-3013 Was $59.99 *$19.99*

Kiss Of The Tarantula (1977)
Willard had his rats and Timmy had Lassie, but this young girl has some eight-legged friends. When she can take no more of her classmates' teasing, she lets her little pets out for some exercise. Eric Price stars. 85 min.
50-6084 *$14.99*

The Blood-Spattered Bride (1972)
Classic mix of erotic thrills and atmospheric horror from Spain's Vicente Aranda is based on the bloodsucker classic "Carmila" and tells of a newlywed seduced by a lesbian vampire on her honeymoon. The new bride is soon involved in eerie happenings, bloody altercations and strange sexual situations. With Alexandra Bastedo, Simon Andreu. Includes the original theatrical trailer. AKA: "'Til Death Us Do Part." Uncut version; 101 min.
50-6085 Letterboxed *$14.99*

Tentacles (1977)
Forget sharks and piranha; there's eight times the horror in this tale of a giant octopus that reaches out and terrorizes a seaside community. Bo Hopkins, Henry Fonda, John Huston and Shelley Winters star; from the producers of "Beyond the Door." 90 min.
47-1105 Was $59.99 *$14.99*

Demon Witch Child (1974)
Atmospheric supernatural production from Spain's Armando De Ossorio ("Horror of the Zombies") in which an evil spirit takes over the body of a policeman's young daughter, turning her into a miniature witch whose demonic ways seem unstoppable. Maria Kosti, Dan Martin star. AKA: "The Possessed."
64-3007 *$19.99*

Pigs (1971)
You'll go hog wild over this demented little horror movie about a woman who kills her father before he rapes her, then seeks solace with a deranged pig farmer who uses the remains of his murder victims as food for his porkers. Marc Lawrence and Katharine Ross (not the one you think) star. AKA: "Daddy's Deadly Darling," "Horror Farm."
64-3121 *$19.99*

Saga Of The Draculas (1972)
Aging Count Dracula hopes to insure a suitably vigorous heir to his ghoulish dynasty, so he invites his pregnant niece to the castle and exchanges her evening wine with fresh blood, to give the unborn a taste of life among the undead. Tina Sainz stars. AKA: "Dracula: The Bloodline Continues." 90 min.
68-8050 *$19.99*

Frankenstein (1973)
Robert Foxworth is the scientist seeking to bring the dead to life, and Bo Svenson plays his unfortunate creation, in this retelling of Mary Shelley's classic chiller. With Susan Strasberg, John Karlen; produced by Dan Curtis ("Dark Shadows"). 126 min.
50-7044 Was $19.99 *$14.99*

Dead Of Night (1977)
High-chill trilogy of shockers, courtesy of producer Dan Curtis ("Dark Shadows"). From a "repossessed" car to a visit to a vampire's lair and a haunted beach house, you'll be on the edge of your seat. Patrick Macnee, Ed Begley, Jr., Joan Hackett star. 75 min.
50-7048 Was $29.99 *$19.99*

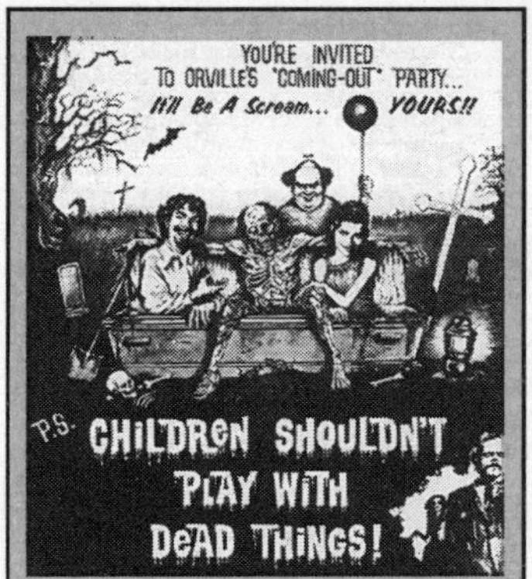

Children Shouldn't Play With Dead Things (1972)
Hippies and horror mix in this comedy-shocker from director Bob Clark ("Porky's"), who co-scripted with filmmaker Alan Ormsby. A group of actors and their director (Ormsby) go to a remote island to stage an occult ritual with the help of a freshly-dug up corpse named Orville, but they unwittingly launch an assault by the living dead. Jeffrey Gillen, Anya Ormsby also star. 91 min.
50-6087 Was $19.99 *$14.99*

Children Shouldn't Play With Dead Things (Letterboxed Collector's Edition)
Also available in a theatrical, widescreen format. Includes the original theatrical trailer.
08-8678 *$14.99*

The Invasion Of Carol Enders (1974)
A murdered woman gets an unholy chance at dealing retribution to her killer when her spirit takes over the innocent Carol Enders. Can she avenge herself before she becomes a victim for the second time? Bizarre shocker stars Meredith Baxter Birney, Christopher Connelly. 67 min.
50-7049 Was $19.99 *$14.99*

Nude For Satan (1974)
An Italian gothic thriller with many kinks, concerning a man whose efforts to help an injured woman take him to a strange castle inhabited by his and her "darker" halves. Lesbianism, whippings, black magic and more are in store with this shocker from director Luigi Batzella. With Rita Calderoni, James Harris, Renato Lupi. 95 min. In Italian with English subtitles.
50-8169 Letterboxed *$19.99*

Lady Frankenstein (1971)
If you thought Dr. Frankenstein was a madman, wait 'til you see the distaff side of the family! She's a real operator who's building a man to satisfy her cravings. Joseph Cotten, Sarah Bay and Mickey Hargitay star. 84 min.
53-1228 Was $19.99 *$14.99*

The Fog (1979)
An ancient curse on a sleepy coastal town brings back the vengeful spirits of shipwrecked sailors, who attack the town's inhabitants in the guise of a thick and murky fog. John Carpenter directs this gruesome shocker; Adrienne Barbeau, Jamie Lee Curtis, Hal Holbrook and Janet Leigh star. 91 min.
53-1402 *$14.99*

Doomwatch (1972)
Ecology mixes with horror in this sci-fi shocker, as a scientist finds himself trapped on a remote island where pollution and nuclear waste have turned the inhabitants into bizarre monsters. Ian Bannen, Judy Geeson and George Sanders star. 92 min.
53-1512 *$29.99*

Innocents From Hell (1975)
Two sisters are bound by a blood legacy of horror when they give themselves over to demonic possession in this chilling horror flick filled with sordid scenes of gore, plus lesbianism and more! With Tina Romero, Claudio Brook and Susana Kamini. AKA: "Sisters of Satan." 94 min.
55-1299 Was $24.99 *$19.99*

Good Against Evil (1977)
Supernatural shocker finds a priest racing to prevent a couple's marriage when he discovers that the bride-to-be has been possessed by an unknown evil. With Dan O'Herlihy, Dack Rambo and Elyssa Davalos. 78 min.
55-3016 *$19.99*

She Waits (1971)
A young woman, preparing to marry a handsome widower, becomes possessed by the spirit of the man's first wife, who returns from the grave to avenge her murder, in this sinister suspense tale. Patty Duke, David McCallum, Dorothy McGuire and Lew Ayres star. 74 min.
55-3035 *$19.99*

Craze (1973)
Sinister British thriller stars Jack Palance as an antiques dealer who is really the leader of a Satanic coven and practices blood sacrifices to an unholy idol. With Trevor Howard, Diana Dors, Julie Ege. AKA: "Demon Master," "Infernal Idol." 90 min.
58-1117 Was $19.99 *$14.99*

Nosferato In Brazil (1971)
An early effort from "Coffin Joe" sidekick Ivan Cardoso, shot in Super 8mm. It's a parody of the classic "Nosferatu" story in which the bloodsucker sets the bikini-clad beauties of Rio de Janeiro as his targets. Laughs, lewdness and blood are abundant in this outrageous outing. With Torquato Neto. In Portuguese with English subtitles.
79-5656 Was $24.99 ***$19.99***

The Secret Of The Mummy (1982)
Unsettling mix of scares, sex and satire from "Coffin Joe" pal Ivan Cardoso about a professor who revives the mummy of a 3,000-year-old psychopathic murderer. The mummy believes a radio station reporter is actually a woman who shunned his advances years earlier and tries to get her interested now. Anselmo Vasconcelos stars; Jose Mojica Marins guests. In Portuguese with English subtitles.
79-5653 Was $24.99 ***$19.99***

The Seven Vampires (1985)
A bored botanist's experiments with a carnivorous plant from Africa leads to terror when it kills him and leaves his wife suffering from a disease that rapidly ages her. That doesn't stop the gal from getting a job dancing at a nightclub where all who get close to her die. Warped and weird shocker from Ivan "The Terror" Cardoso. In Portuguese with English subtitles.
79-5654 Was $24.99 ***$19.99***

The Scarlet Scorpion (1986)
The writer of the radio serial "The Adventures of the Angel" becomes obsessed with his characters to the point he believes they have come to life. So, sadistic villains, superheroes and pretty heroines encounter thrills, chills and sexual kinkiness in a world of fiction. Or is it real? A wild and sexy satire on serials from Ivan "The Terror" Cardoso. In Portuguese with English subtitles.
79-5655 Was $24.99 ***$19.99***

Ivan Cardoso's Shocking Shorts
A terrifying compilation tape featuring Ivan Cardoso's "The Universe of Coffin Joe," a spellbinding documentary on his mentor that features interviews, film clips and footage of the horror auteur at work and play; trailers and outtakes from "The Secrets of the Mummy" and "The Seven Vampires"; and more. In Portuguese with English subtitles.
79-5657 Was $24.99 ***$19.99***

I Drink Your Blood (1971)
As gruesome as its title suggests, this gore classic is about a young man who gets even with a group of hippies by injecting rabid dog blood into their meat pies. Soon, the rabid rebels turn on a group of construction workers...and then themselves. Ronda Fultz, Lynn Lowrey star. 69 min.
79-5181 Was $24.99 ***$19.99***

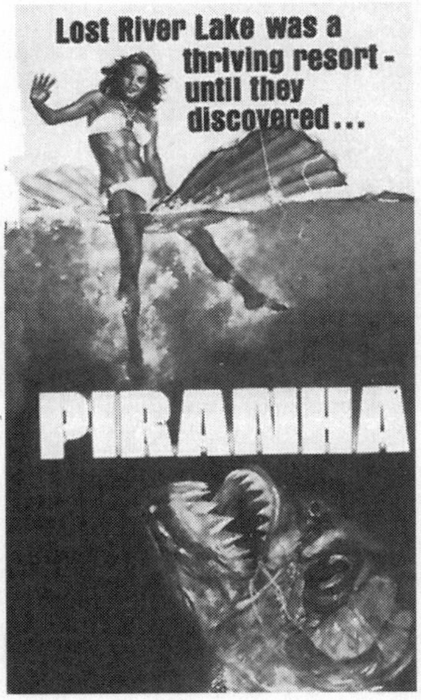

Piranha (1978)
A toothy little fright gem from director Joe Dante and scripter John Sayles that features bites at other genre films. A horde of man-eating fish, subjects of a military experiment, is accidentally released into a river and makes its way towards a family beach resort. Bradford Dillman, Heather Menzies, Kevin McCarthy, Paul Bartel and the great Dick Miller star. 90 min.
19-1252 ***$14.99***

Piranha (1995)
In producer Roger Corman's remake of his 1978 cult favorite, scientists William Katt and Alexandra Paul accidentally release killer piranhas into a river. The deadly creatures threaten everything that stands—and swims—in their wake, but can they be stopped before they reach the ocean and spawn? With Soleil Moon Frye and James Karen ("the Pathmark guy"). 84 min.
21-9124 Was $99.99 ***$14.99***

Halloween (1978)
John Carpenter's groundbreaking shocker that opened the floodgates for hundreds of (mostly inferior) imitators stills packs a scare-raising punch. Fifteen years after being placed in an asylum for killing his sister on Halloween, maniacal Michael Myers escapes and returns to his hometown in search of new victims. Jamie Lee Curtis (her film debut), Donald Pleasence, Nancy Loomis and P.J. Soles star. 93 min.
03-1014 ***$14.99***

Halloween (Letterboxed Version)
Also available in a theatrical, widescreen format.
08-8584 ***$14.99***

Halloween: Collector's Edition
Also available in a restored full-frame edition that includes original theatrical and TV trailers and the "making of" documentary "Halloween Unmasked 2000," featuring interviews with cast and crew.
08-8778 ***$14.99***

Halloween: Collector's Edition (Letterboxed Version)
The collector's edition is also available in a theatrical, widescreen format.
08-8779 ***$14.99***

Halloween II (1981)
The most terrifying night of the year continues, as unstoppable killer Michael Myers follows Jamie Lee Curtis and Donald Pleasence to the hospital for some "exploratory surgery" of his own. Guaranteed goosebumps! 92 min.
07-1091 Was $19.99 ***$14.99***

Halloween III: Season Of The Witch (1982)
A diabolical plot that will give 50 million children their most terrifying Halloween ever...a mad warlock out for blood...an army of robot assassins. All play elements in "the night nobody comes home!" Tom Atkins, Dan O'Herlihy. 98 min.
07-1139 Was $19.99 ***$12.99***

Halloween 4: The Return Of Michael Myers (1988)
Move over, Freddy and Jason, because Michael Myers is coming back! After spending 10 years in a prison asylum, Michael escapes and heads for the town where his bloody killing spree took place in order to find his niece. Donald Pleasence, Danielle Harris, Michael Pataki star. 88 min.
04-2227 ❑***$14.99***

Halloween 4: The Return Of Michael Meyers (Collector's Edition)
Also available in a theatrical, widescreen format that includes theatrical trailers for this film and the original "Halloween." 92 min.
08-8664 Letterboxed ***$14.99***

Halloween 5: The Revenge Of Michael Myers (1989)
Latest and scariest entry in the infamous horror film series follows unkillable killer Michael on his bloody rampage. But can the psychic link he shares with his young niece provide the key to ending his scourge? Donald Pleasence, Danielle Harris and Donald L. Shanks star. 96 min.
04-2296 Was $89.99 ❑***$14.99***

Halloween 5: The Revenge Of Michael Myers (Letterboxed Collector's Edition)
Also available in a theatrical, widescreen format. Includes the original theatrical trailer and an introduction by Harris and Cornell.
08-8885 ***$14.99***

Halloween: The Curse Of Michael Myers (1995)
The sixth installment in the ever-popular series finds masked monster Michael Myers returning to his Haddonfield hometown, where he's out to terrorize a young woman and her newborn baby. Donald Pleasence and Paul Rudd star in this shocker, reportedly the last in the series. 88 min.
11-2041 Was $19.99 ❑***$14.99***

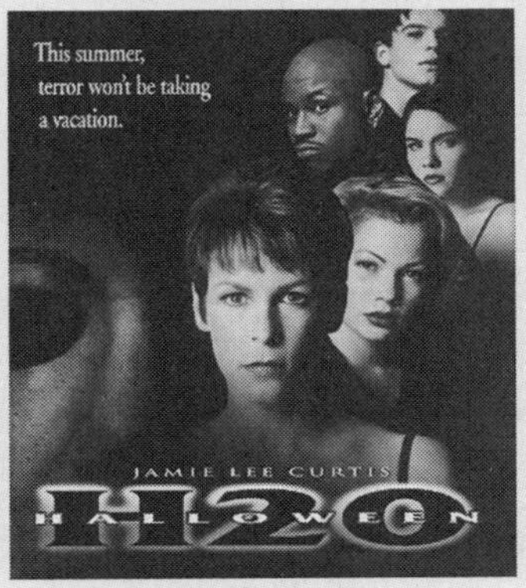

Halloween: H20 (1998)
Twenty years after Michael Myers terrorized the screen for the first time, the mysterious "Shape" is back, wreaking havoc once again for sister Jamie Lee Curtis, now a boarding school headmistress and single mother, as well as her teenage son and his pals. With Josh Hartnett, Michelle Williams, Adam Hann-Byrd, LL Cool J and, in a cameo, Janet Leigh. 86 min.
11-2271 Was $19.99 ❑***$14.99***

The Child (1973)
In the 1930s, a woman travels to a remote area where she plans to live with a widower and his 11-year-old daughter, who has supernatural powers. The young girl visits her mother's grave regularly and uses her powers to summon ghouls from beyond to help avenge her death. Rosalie Cole, Frank Janson and Laurel Barnet star. AKA: "Kill and Go Hide."
79-5646 Was $24.99 ***$19.99***

Meat Is Meat (1972)
A diabolical shocker with some macabre laughs about a deranged sausage maker from Vienna who adds his wife as an ingredient in his product. He uses more deceased females for his sausages, but his devious plan is halted when a police inspector finds other things in police canteen lunches. Victor Buono and Karin Field star. AKA: "The Mad Butcher." 90 min.
79-5647 Was $24.99 ***$19.99***

The Asphyx (1972)
The Asphyx is the essence of death living in all of us, but when it leaves, we die! A 19th-century scientist tries to isolate the Asphyx in order to gain immortality, but his experiments lead to frightening results. Robert Stephens, Robert Powell and Jane Lapotaire star in this shocker. AKA: "Spirits of the Dead."
79-5651 Was $24.99 ***$19.99***

Leather And Whips (1972)
Perverse Italian shocker stars Farley Granger as a wealthy author who hires gorgeous amateur sleuth Barbara Bouchet as his secretary, then engages the beauty in kinky sex games with his wife and starts writing a murder mystery that mirrors Bouchet's life. With Rosabla Neri. AKA: "Amuck."
79-5874 Was $24.99 ***$19.99***

Enter The Devil (1972)
A Texas satanic cult called "The Disciples of Death" wreak havoc with some disturbing human sacrifices. A deputy sheriff and anthropologist investigate and uncover some real surprises that eventually endanger their lives. Josh Bryant, Irene Kelly star.
79-5960 Was $24.99 ***$19.99***

School Of Fear (1971)
The arrogant gang leader of a group of boarding school teens gets into trouble for torturing a dog, prompting a visit from his father. Both mysteriously disappear for a while, then Dad resurfaces with a bullet in his head, a teacher commits suicide and someone is found gassed in a shower. Who is responsible? German-made shocker stars Joachim Fuchsberger, Conrad George.
79-5964 Was $24.99 ***$19.99***

The Legend Of Hell House (1973)
Superior haunted house story by Richard Matheson about a team of spirit hunters who search for the truth behind a mysterious mansion. Clive Revill, Gayle Hunnicutt, Roddy McDowall and Pamela Franklin star. 94 min.
04-1881 ❑***$19.99***

The Beast In The Cellar (1971)
Two spinster sisters, a series of horrible murders and one monstrous half-human animal converge on a quiet and peaceful English hamlet. Beryl Reid, Flora Robson co-star. 88 min.
19-7045 ***$19.99***

Guess What Happened To Count Dracula (1970)
Good question. We think he's turned into Count Adrian, the lead character of this fright film who sports a Van Dyke and a bad Hungarian accent. He also runs a weird nightclub where a young woman catches his attention. He has to draw blood from her neck, but her actor boyfriend tries to stop him. Des Roberts and Claudia Barron star.
79-5973 Was $24.99 ***$19.99***

Godmonster Of Indian Flats (1973)
Extremely obscure, hard-to-believe horror fest in which gas from an ancient mine causes a sheep to give birth to a huge, misshapen embryo that grows into an 8-foot mutant sheep. Soon, a corrupt mayor puts the monstrosity on display, much to the chagrin of the terrified townspeople. With Russ Meyer regular Stuart Lancaster, Christopher Brooks.
79-6015 Was $24.99 ***$19.99***

Teenage Passion Killer (1970)
A disturbing Canadian-made thriller about a group of troubled teens whose obsession with such practices as masturbation and petting leads to rape, murder and an explosive trial. Andrew Skidd, Robb Judd and Karen Martin star. AKA: "Teenage Psycho Killer."
79-6024 Was $24.99 ***$19.99***

Crypt Of Dark Secrets (1976)
A swamp shocker from New Orleans about Ted, a troubled Vietnam vet who returns from the dead after being robbed and killed by a trio of thieves. Ted wants revenge and gets help from Dambella, a naked witch with white eyeballs. A sheriff investigating the proceedings says "a lotta things in these swamps are unbelievable." After catching this one, who could argue with him? Ronald Tanet stars.
79-6417 Was $24.99 ***$19.99***

Axe (1973)
Super-shocking horror exploiter about three killers on the lam from the law who hide out in a desolate farm after terrorizing a helpless salesgirl. It turns out that the farm is actually inhabited by a little girl and her paralyzed grandfather. When the girl finds killers in her midst, she tries to stop them with her axe. Leslie Lee, Jack Canon star. AKA: "California Axe Massacre."
79-5645 Was $24.99 ***$19.99***

Exorcism's Daughter (1974)
This engrossing shocker set in a Spanish mental asylum focuses on a psychiatrist who discovers that his patient's mental problem stems from witnessing his mother being exorcised when he was younger. Francisco Rabal, Amilia Gade star. AKA: "House of Insane Women."
79-6117 ***$19.99***

The Exquisite Cadaver (1973)
Euro-shocker from Spain's Vicente Aranda ("Lovers") stars Carlos Estrada as a publisher who receives a package containing a severed hand. A telegram from the mysterious Capucine promises to explain the gruesome parcel, but when Estrada goes to meet her, he's drugged and taken to an estate where Capucine introduces him to the frozen, naked corpse of his ex-lover—who was her former lover as well!
79-6418 Was $24.99 ***$19.99***

The Dracula Saga (1972)
Sensuous vampire epic from Spain in which a young pregnant woman and her husband are invited to the Transylvanian castle of her grandfather, Count Dracula. While the hubby is enticed by some beautiful female bloodsuckers, the granddaughter soon learns that her unborn child is expected to carry on the family's heritage of horror. With Narcisco Ibanez Menta and Helga Line.
79-6420 Was $24.99 ***$19.99***

Vampire (1979)
Terrific contemporary bloodsucking story about a handsome millionaire in San Francisco who preys on gorgeous women for blood and the architect and ex-cop who try to stop him. Jason Miller, E.G. Marshall, Jessica Walter and Richard Lynch star; co-written and produced by Steve Bochco.
58-8134 ***$12.99***

It Happened At Nightmare Inn (1973)
Truly deranged, Italian-made shocker about two sisters, one dominant, the other meek, who run a small inn, and the murderous mania that develops when the dominant sibling begins slaying female guests. Judy Geeson stars. AKA: "A Candle for the Devil." 75 min.
68-8444 ***$19.99***

The Devil Times Five (1974)
Set in a Lake Arrowhead mountain lodge, this creepy thriller follows five young people, escapees from a hospital for the criminally insane, who terrorize the resort and its wealthy patrons. Gene Evans is the lodge's owner who tries to put a halt to the frightening proceedings; with Sorrell Booke, Leif Garrett. AKA: "People Toys."
03-1131 ***$19.99***

Beyond The Door (1974)
Post-"Exorcist" possession shocker starring Juliet Mills as the wife of a San Francisco record producer whose illicit affair with a Satanist leads to her pregnancy. Soon, she discovers she may be bearing a demon...and undergoes some horrific changes. Richard Johnson and Gabriele Lavia also star in this Italian-made fright fave. 97 min.
03-1155 ***$19.99***

Let Sleeping Corpses Lie (Collector's Edition) (1974)
An English experiment in controlling insects through ultrasonic waves has an unfortunate side effect: it brings the recently dead back to life! Now an army of zombies, who replenish their number by rubbing blood on corpses' eyelids, are marching across the countryside in Spanish director Jorge Grau's compelling slice of '70s Euro-horror. Ray Lovelock, Arthur Kennedy, Christina Galbo star. Also includes an interview with Grau and original trailers. AKA: "Don't Open the Window," "The Living Dead at the Manchester Morgue." 93 min.
08-8886 Letterboxed ***$14.99***

Crucible Of Terror (1971)
An occult-obsessed sculptor crafts a work of horror as he creates bronze statues of beautiful young women. That is, he doesn't use the girls as models...he pours hot wax and molten metal over his helpless victims! Mike Raven and Ronald Lacey star; directed by Ted Hooker (Philip Yordan). 90 min.
20-1036 ***$19.99***

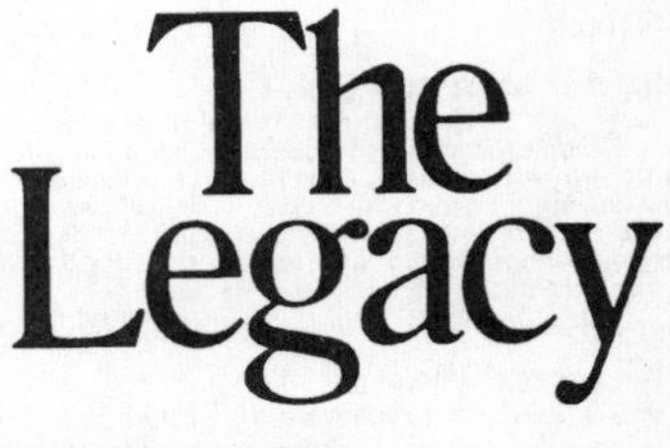

The Legacy (1979)
Katharine Ross and Sam Elliott are a young couple who travel to England for an inheritance, but learn to their horror that the legacy is one of evil and death. Chilling shocker of occult vengeance also stars Roger Daltrey and Charles Gray. 100 min.
07-1443 Was $19.99 ***$14.99***

Silent Night, Bloody Night (1973)
Flashback-filled fright fest starring Patrick O'Neal as a lawyer whose night at a former mental hospital is haunted by the building's past, when patients took over the place. Directed by Theodore Gershuny ("Sugar Cookies"), this curio features John Carradine and Warhol scene regulars Ondine, Jack Smith, Candy Darling and Mary Woronov. AKA: "Night of the Dark Full Moon." 90 min.
58-1036 *$19.99*

The Killing Kind (1973)
A young man, sent to prison for a gang rape he didn't take part in, comes out a vengeful lunatic, ready to kill the women he holds responsible for his conviction. Psycho shocker stars John Savage, Cindy Williams, Ann Sothern. 95 min.
58-1119 *$14.99*

The Corpse Grinders (1971)
A cat food company on the verge of bankruptcy hits upon a new recipe that sends their sales zooming, but the "secret ingredient" (check out the title!) begins turning ordinary household pets into man-eating killers. "Morris! Dinner ti...AAAHHH!" Sean Kenney, Monika Kelly star. 75 min.
59-5007 *$19.99*

Satan's Black Wedding (1976)
Here comes the bride, all drenched in blood! A small town is the center of occult activities and an unholy ritual will take place, unless the menace can be stopped. Ghoulish goodie stars Ray Miles, Lisa Milano.100 min.
59-5064 *$19.99*

The Wicker Man (1973)
Sophisticated and erotic thriller penned by Anthony Shaffer ("Sleuth") focuses on a police official who encounters a sinister pagan cult while attempting to find a missing girl on an island off the coast of Scotland. Edward Woodward, Christopher Lee, Ingrid Pitt, Britt Ekland and Diane Cilento star. 84 min.
63-1712 Was $79.99 *$14.99*

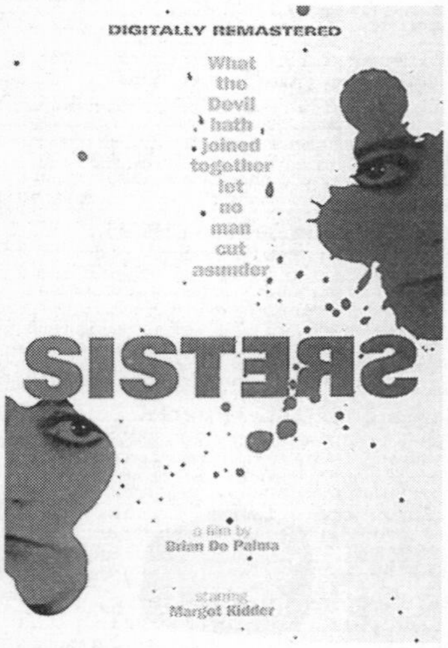

Sisters (1973)
Director/co-writer Brian De Palma's first foray into Hitchcockian screen suspense in a bloody thriller. Reporter Jennifer Salt witnesses Margot Kidder commit a murder, but cannot prove it to the authorities. As Salt digs into Kidder's past, she uncovers a twisted tale of dementia, homicide and the ultimate in "sibling rivalry." William Finley, Charles Durning also star; music by Bernard Herrmann. 93 min.
19-1084 Letterboxed *$19.99*

Snuff (1974)
"Filmed in South America...where life is cheap," the ads proclaimed. Now, you can see this notorious exploitation film for yourself. A Manson-like cult terrorizes the countryside, while an actress hired to star in a movie is actually killed on-camera. What is real? What is fiction? Find out in this gruesome tale from softcore auteurs Michael and Roberta Findlay. AKA: "The Slaughter." 80 min.
59-1003 *$29.99*

Murder Mansion (1970)
Murder and mayhem abound in this chiller, as a young couple joins other travellers spending the night in a creepy mansion in an otherwise deserted village. The building's mysterious occupant tells her "guests" the story of the undead horror that attacked the villagers...a horror that may have picked that night to return! Analia Gade, Ida Galli star. 85 min.
53-1800 *$14.99*

The Incredible Two-Headed Transplant (1971)
"Double your pleasure, double your horror" as mad scientist Bruce Dern grafts the head of a homicidal maniac onto the body of a simple-minded handyman. The result: a two-headed homicidal maniac! Leave it to hero Casey Kasem to save the day! With Pat Priest ("The Munsters"), John Bloom, and the theme song "It's Incredible." 88 min.
55-1130 *$19.99*

Caged Virgins (1970)
Shocking and sexy bloodsucking saga from France's Jean Rollin in which two cute teenage gals in mini-skirts discover that the mysterious chateau they have discovered is inhabited with vampires who enlist them as slaves. Marie Castel and Mirielle D'Argent star in this mix of erotica and ghoulishness. AKA: "Virgins and Vampires." 72 min.
79-5409 Was $24.99 *$19.99*

Les Raisins De La Mort (The Raisins Of Death) (1978)
A woman travelling in Southern France is assaulted by a corpse and escapes to the countryside, where she soon encounters legions of zombies. With help from two men, she learns that the vines in the area are infected by a pesticide responsible for the area's frightening inhabitants. Jean Rollin's gory shocker stars Marie-Georges Pascal. 83 min. In French with English subtitles.
50-2841 Letterboxed *$39.99*

Fascination (1979)
Erotically charged terror tale from Jean Rollin set at the turn of the century and focusing on a group of upper-middle class women addicted to drinking blood. Two of the bloodsuckers seek the body of a young hood, but when one of them falls in love with him, a shocking struggle ensues. Franca Mai stars. 87 min. In French with English subtitles.
50-2842 Letterboxed *$39.99*

The Night Of The Hunted (1980)
Jean Rollin's stylishly depraved horror opus features former porn star Brigitte Lahaie as an amnesiac woman who goes to Paris to get treatment but finds herself captive in a black tower. Held there with another woman, she's forced to comply to her captor's sadistic desires. Vincent Gardnere co-stars. Special video edition includes the original theatrical trailer and two erotic deleted scenes. AKA: "Night of the Cruel Sacrifice." 95 min. Dubbed in English.
50-8170 Letterboxed *$19.99*

Dracula (1973)
The celebrated vampire tale is given a scary, atmospheric treatment with Jack Palance playing a sympathetic Count. Nigel Davenport, Fiona Lewis and Sarah Douglas also star. Dan Curtis directs the script by Richard Matheson. 100 min.
50-7041 Was $29.99 *$19.99*

Criminally Insane (1973)
Ethel's mad...Ethel's bad...Ethel's 250 pounds of murderous mania, and when she's released from the asylum the streets (and screen) run red with blood. Shocker will make you believe a fat woman can swing a cleaver. Priscilla Alden, Michael Flood star. 61 min.
59-5065 Was $59.99 *$24.99*

Crazy Fat Ethel II (1987)
The asylum wasn't big enough to hold her...literally! Now, the two-ton terror is loose again, armed with a meat cleaver and a bad case of the munchies. Fearsome and fleshy follow-up to "Criminally Insane" stars Priscilla Alden and Michael Flood. 63 min.
50-1523 *$19.99*

Death Nurse (1987)
"Angel of mercy" Edith Mortly (Priscilla Alden) offers her charity charges plenty of Terrifying Lethal Care, feeding them rats and finding novel ways to dispose of those who pass on, in this chiller from the creators of "Criminally Insane" and "Crazy Fat Ethel II"—and featuring footage from those films. 80 min.
50-1541 *$19.99*

Crucible Of Terror (1971)
An occult-obsessed sculptor starts a trail of horror as he makes bronze statues from live, young beautiful women. He doesn't just use them as models...he pours bronze over them! Mike Raven, Ronald Lacey star; directed by Philip Yordan. 85 min.
59-5083 *$19.99*

The Hanging Woman (1972)
A young man arrives in a remote 19th-century village to claim his inheritance from his late uncle. What he finds is a widow into black magic, a scientist trying to revive the dead, an army of zombies, and, yes, a hanged woman. Creepy, erotic and darkly funny Euro-chiller stars Stelvio Rosi, Dyanik Zurakowska and Paul Naschy. AKA: "Beyond the Living Dead," "The Return of the Zombies," "Zombie 3: Return of the Living Dead." 90 min.
59-5086 *$14.99*

Werewolf Woman (1977)
A beautiful young woman is stricken with an ancestor's curse and assumes the form of a savage, bloodthirsty creature in director Rino di Silvestro's chiller. Ann Borel stars as the lovely lycanthrope; with Frederick Stafford, Dagmar Lassander. AKA: "Legend of the Wolfwoman," "She-Wolf." 90 min.
59-7043 *$79.99*

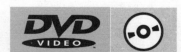

DVD VIDEO
ASK ABOUT OUR GIANT DVD CATALOG!

Vampyres: Collector's Edition (1975)
A man driving along a deserted country road stops to pick up two beautiful female hitchhikers, little suspecting that their version of "necking" is more intense than what he's used to. Sensual shocker of undead lusts stars Marianne Morris, Anulka Dziubinska. Includes the original theatrical trailers. AKA: "Blood Hunger," "Daughters of Dracula," "Satan's Daughters." 87 min.
69-1121 Letterboxed *$14.99*

Lemora: A Vampire's Tale (1973)
Surreal and sensual horror tale involving a teenage girl living in the 1930s who is summoned by a mysterious woman to see her gangster father, who had disappeared. During her journey, she encounters a group of undead creatures who want to turn her into a vampire. Cheryl Smith, Lesley Gilb star; includes a documentary on the film's making. 115 min. total.
59-8009 *$39.99*

Tam Lin (1972)
Ava Gardner plays a supernatural seductress who uses witchcraft to ensnare her younger lovers and keep herself eternally young in this offbeat chiller directed by Roddy MacDowall. Ian McShane, Stephanie Beacham, Cyril Cusack and Joanna Lumley also star. AKA: "The Devil's Widow." 106 min.
63-1915 *$14.99*

The School That Couldn't Scream (1973)
Italian horror thriller about a teacher at a girls' school who witnesses a murder while involved with one of the school's students. Fabio Testi stars in this eerie story.
68-8883 *$19.99*

Blood Mania (1971)
A doctor's sleazy abortion racket, a greedy daughter, her psychotic boyfriend, a blackmail scheme and murder are the elements that add up to terror in this "deadly nightmare" whose climax will, according to the film's makers, "jolt you out of your seat." Peter Carpenter, Maria De Aragon star.
71-5108 *$19.99*

Blacula (1972)
The "Dracula" plot is given a new treatment when William Marshall stars as an African prince cursed by Drac himself centuries ago to be one of the undead. He starts a reign of terror in modern-day L.A., while falling in love with a woman who may be the reincarnation of his dead wife. Denise Nicholas and Vonetta McGee co-star. 92 min.
73-1132 *$14.99*

Scream, Blacula, Scream (1973)
An occult ritual summons vampire William Marshall from spirit exile, and only the occult skills of voodoo priestess Pam Grier can send him back, ending the bloody clash of ghoulish hordes, bewildered police, and black magic. 96 min.
73-1014 Was $59.99 *$14.99*

J.D.'s Revenge (1976)
Suspenseful black-themed horror film that's a notch above the usual drive-in fare. A young law student becomes possessed by the spirit of a murdered '40s gangster out for revenge. Great New Orleans settings; Glynn Turman, Lou Gossett, Jr., Joan Pringle star. 96 min.
73-1099 Was $59.99 *$14.99*

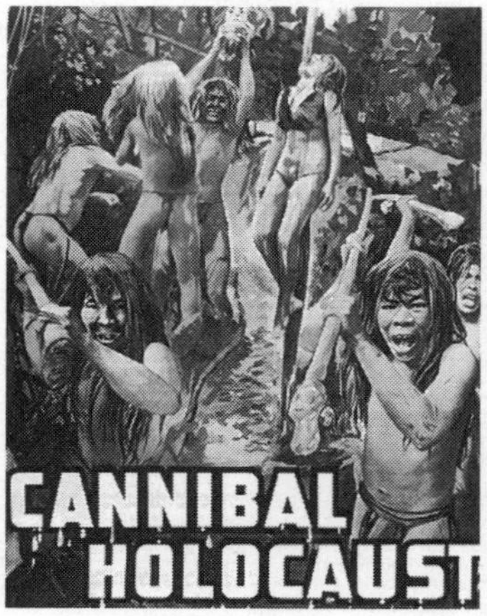

Cannibal Holocaust (1979)
This is one of the most notorious gore films ever and said to be the inspiration for "The Blair Witch Project." Four people on a documentary film crew searching for cannibals in the Amazon meet a tribe called the "Tree People" who give them shocking newsreel footage of another film team's horrific experiences. Disturbing sex sequences and violence abound. Includes a theatrical trailer and an interview with director Ruggero Deodato. Unrated version; 98 min.
59-7113 Letterboxed *$29.99*

The Bloodsuckers (1971)
A young man on vacation in Greece falls under the spell of a devil-worshipping cult that practices vampirism and sexual abandon. Can his fiancée and a retired major save him? Will he want to be saved? Patrick Macnee, Peter Cushing star. AKA: "Doctors Wear Scarlet," "Incense for the Damned." 80 min.
68-8744 *$19.99*

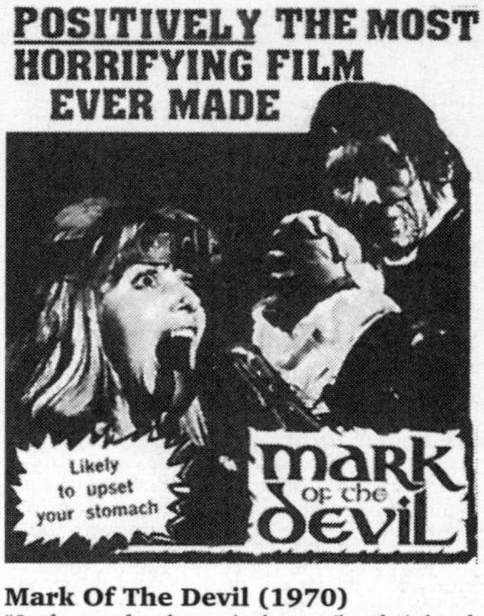

Mark Of The Devil (1970)
"Confess, confess that you've been guilty of witchcraft and illicit intercourse with the Devil in human form!" An unending nightmare of horror and violence, as an 18th-century European village is held under a spell of witchcraft and occult forces. Herbert Lom, Udo Kier star. 93 min.
62-1186 *$19.99*

Mark Of The Devil: Collector's Edition
Also available in a newly remastered version in a theatrical, widescreen format.
08-8562 Letterboxed *$19.99*

Mark Of The Devil, Part II (1972)
Those wacky, zany witch-hunters are at it again, torturing innocent maidens, burning nuns, and doing all sorts of nasty stuff! "At least 10 scenes you will positively not be able to stomach!" Reggie Nalder and Anton Diffring star. 88 min.
62-1218 *$19.99*

Frankenstein's Castle Of Freaks (1973)
It's a long way from the South Pacific to Castle Frankenstein for mad scientist Rosanno Brazzi, whose brain-transplant experiments result in terror unparalleled. With Michael Dunn, Edmund Purdom, and "Boris Lugosi" as Ook the Neanderthal Man. AKA: "House of Freaks." 88 min.
64-1017 *$19.99*

The Night Evelyn Came Out Of The Grave (1971)
Creepy, kinky Italian terror tale involving a sadistic English nobleman whose perverse ways with women initiate the appearance of his dead wife. Or so he thinks! It's actually his second wife plotting to get his inheritance. Anthony Steffen and gorgeous Erika Blank star. Uncut version; 99 min.
68-8870 *$19.99*

The Scream Of The Demon Lover (1971)
European Gothic shocker set in a mysterious castle and focusing on a biochemist who marries a mad doctor experimenting with rejuvenating flesh. The biochemist knows nothing of her new hubby's assistant, Igor, his supposed crimes against women, or the other horrors that await her. With Jennifer Hartley and Jeffrey Chase.
68-8927 *$19.99*

Bloodlust: The Vampire Of Nuremberg (1976)
Grisly shocker, based on a true story, about a disturbed, outcast young man who becomes a contemporary vampire, breaking into funeral homes and draining blood from corpses in a constant quest to quench his bloodlust. This disturbing German spectacle in the mold of the later "Nekromantik" films stars Fred Berhuff, Peter Ham. AKA: "Mosquito der Schander." 91 min. Dubbed in English.
73-9281 *$19.99*

Hitch Hike To Hell (1974)
Sordid tale of a disturbed young man who kills hitchhiking young women because they remind him of his sister, who ran away from home. The killings get sicker as the cops try to find this deranged Momma's boy. With Robert Gribbin, Kippi Bell and Russell Johnson ("The Professor" on "Gilligan's Island") as a cop on the case. 90 min.
79-5412 Was $24.99 *$19.99*

Death By Invitation (1971)
A woman who is the descendant of witches decides to wreak vengeance on the family that destroyed her clan 300 years earlier. Using her seductive charms to get revenge, she claws to death one fellow, cuts off a teenage girl's head, and more! Norman Paige, Shelby Leverington and Aaron Phillips star in this shocker. 81 min.
79-5482 Was $24.99 *$19.99*

The Wicked Caresses Of Satan (1973)
The medium known as Countess Claire plans to avenge her husband's mysterious death by teaming with a telepathic professor, a mindless zombie, a troll-like nerd and Satan himself. Claire and the prof infiltrate their way into a duke's chateau and plot the demise of their host and his friends. Sylvia Solar, Oliver Matthau star.
79-5644 Was $24.99 *$19.99*

The Dead Don't Die (1975)
An offbeat horror thriller written by Robert Bloch ("Psycho") that combines '30s private eyes, serial-type deathtraps and escapes, and an army of the living dead. George Hamilton, Ray Milland, Joan Blondell star. 78 min.
14-3050 *$12.99*

Snowbeast (1977)
It's mean and it snarls and it's attacking the people attending a winter carnival at a ski resort. How can you stop the monstrous Snowbeast? Bo Svenson, Yvette Mimieux, Robert Logan and Clint Walker star.
14-3076 *$14.99*

Psychomania (1974)
Filmed in 1971, this offbeat English chiller features George Sanders and Beryl Reid as parents who make a pact with a mysterious frog-worshipping cult to resurrect their dead biker son. Once the leather-clad zombie rides his bike out of his grave, he urges his old gang to kill themselves so they can join him in "immortality." Nicky Henson, Patrick Holt also star. AKA: "The Death Wheelers." 88 min.
10-1105 *$14.99*

Psychomania (Letterboxed Version)
Also available in a theatrical, widescreen format.
50-8577 *$19.99*

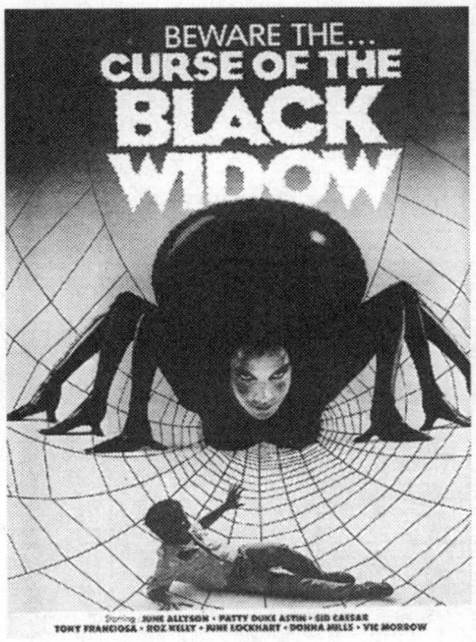

Curse Of The Black Widow: Collector's Edition (1977)
A series of bizarre murders in Los Angeles draws a private eye into a web of horror that leads him to a beautiful, wealthy woman haunted by a sinister curse. Tony Franciosa, Donna Mills, Patty Duke Astin, June Allyson and Vic Morrow star; directed by Dan Curtis. 97 min.
14-6042 Was $39.99 *$14.99*

Horror Express (1973)
Christopher Lee, Peter Cushing, Telly Savalas on a non-stop ride to Hell as one by one train passengers mysteriously disappear. AKA: "Panic on the Trans-Siberian Train." 90 min.
10-1125 Was $19.99 *$14.99*

Horror Express (Letterboxed Version)
Also available in a theatrical, widescreen format.
50-8390 *$19.99*

Barn Of The Naked Dead (1972)
The Nevada desert may seem an odd place to find a barn. But not when you're an ax-wielding homicidal maniac who, along with his radioactive mutant father, harvests a horrifying crop of human victims. Andrew Prine, Jennifer Ashley, Sherry Alberoni star; Alan Rudolph's directorial debut. 86 min.
10-1418 *$19.99*

Scream Of The Wolf (1974)
Dan Curtis of "Dark Shadows" fame directed this creeper about a legendary hunter who comes out of retirement to find a wolf that may also be turning into human form. Clint Walker, Peter Graves and Jo Ann Pflug star; Richard Matheson scripted. 78 min.
10-1597 *$19.99*

Frankenstein: The True Story (1973)
This eerie, much-requested adaptation of Mary Shelley's novel stars Michael Sarrazin as the creature given life by Victor Frankenstein (Leonard Whiting), who witnesses his creation turn uncontrollable after he's duped by his associate, Dr. Polidari (James Mason). David McCallum and Jane Seymour also star. 122 min.
10-2573 *$14.99*

The Eerie Midnight Horror Show (1977)
Sexual desires and horror mix as a pretty art student in Italy swipes a life-size religious statue and soon finds herself embroiled in terror, eroticism and possession. Stella Carnacina and Chris Auram star. AKA: "The Tormented," "The Sexorcists." 92 min.
14-6058 Was $79.99 *$29.99*

The Initiation Of Sarah (1978)
Sarah's a shy co-ed entering a bizarre sorority with a shocking secret. When the facts are revealed, Sarah must use her own dark powers to save herself. Kay Lenz, Morgan Fairchild and Shelley Winters star.
14-3045 *$12.99*

Autopsy (1974)
Trying to uncover the reason behind a series of violent apparent suicides that is paralyzing the city of Rome, pathologist Mimsy Farmer and priest Barry Primus discover a horrifying secret in this grisly slice of Italian horror, seen here in its uncut form. Includes the original American and European theatrical trailers. AKA: "Macchie Solari." 100 min.
08-8838 Letterboxed *$14.99*

Cannibal Man (1971)
This notorious Spanish production details the horrific life of Marcos, a slaughterhouse worker whose accidental murder of a man during a fight triggers his psychotic urges. He's soon killing others, then disposing of their remains in a most unusual—and disturbing—way. Vicente Parra and Emma Cohen star. Includes the original theatrical trailer. AKA: "Apartment on the 13th Floor," "Week of the Killer." 98 min.
08-8853 Letterboxed *$14.99*

Don't Torture A Duckling (1972)
This unsettling thriller from "giallo" maestro Lucio Fulci tells of a small town where several young boys have been found murdered. The chief suspect in the killings is a newly-arrived woman in town, who is working with a reporter to try to uncover the real culprit. Florinda Bolkan, Barbara Bouchet and Irene Papas star. Uncut version; 102 min.
08-8855 Letterboxed *$14.99*

Curse Of The Vampires (1970)
It's a family affair, bloodsucking-style, as a man returns to his old haunts to find that Mom's being held prisoner in the basement because Dad thinks she's a vampire. His worst fears are realized when she bites him, turning him into a creature of the night who seeks his fiancée for blood. Eddie Garcia and Amalia Fuentes star. 90 min.
09-5047 *$19.99*

Alice, Sweet Alice (1977)
Brooke Shields' first film role was in this moody thriller, shot on a miniscule budget in New Jersey and drenched in religious symbolism, featuring Shields as the younger sister of 12-year-old Alice, who dons a mask to scare those around her. But is Alice responsible for the gruesome killings that occur near a local church? With Paula Sheppard, Lillian Roth and wrestler Antonino Rocco. AKA: "Communion," "Holy Terror." 108 min.
10-1072 *$19.99*

Alice, Sweet Alice (Letterboxed Version)
Also available in a theatrical widescreen format; includes the original theatrical trailer.
08-8571 Remastered *$14.99*

Tenderness Of The Wolves: Collector's Edition (1973)
A powerful and haunting shocker from German filmmaker Ulli Lommel, loosely based on the same real-life case that inspired Fritz Lang's "M." Kurt Raab plays the bald-pated pedophile in post-WWII Germany who lures boys to his home and kills them. Jeff Roden, Margit Carstensen and famed director R.W. Fassbinder (who served as producer) co-star. 86 min. In German with English subtitles.
08-8784 Letterboxed *$14.99*

Asylum (1972)
Brace yourself for a crazed quartet of sinister stories, courtesy of Amicus Films and "Psycho" author Robert Bloch. See killer robot dolls, a dismembered murder victim's vengeance, a suit that brings its dead wearer back to life, and a tale of "schizo-murder," as told by the residents of an asylum. Peter Cushing, Britt Ekland, Herbert Lom, Robert Powell, Charlotte Rampling star. AKA: "House of Crazies." 88 min.
05-1132 *$19.99*

A Reflection Of Fear (1973)
Being stuck in the house with your estranged parents and dad's new lover would be hard on any young girl. Most kids, however, don't develop a split personality and go on a gore-filled rampage! Slashing, shocking suspenser stars Robert Shaw, Sally Kellerman, Sondra Locke, Mary Ure. 90 min.
02-1780 *$69.99*

The Brotherhood Of Satan (1971)
An underrated horror gem about a coven of witches responsible for the deaths of dozens of people in a small town and their search for a new member. Stars Strother Martin, L. Q. Jones and Alvy Moore. 92 min.
02-2688 *$14.99*

Blackenstein (1973)
Mary Shelley's tale of horror gets a new twist in this blend of horror and comedy. A ghetto surgeon is experimenting on organ and limb transplants, and succeeds in turning a wounded Vietnam into a super-strong monster (complete with '70s afro). John Hart, Ivory Stone and Liz Renay star. 85 min.
03-1078 Was $29.99 *$19.99*

Daughters Of Darkness (Collector's Edition) (1971)
Terrifying and erotic, Harry Kümel's surreal slice of Euro-horror stars Delphine Seyrig as bloodthirsty medieval noblewoman Elizabeth Bathory, who is revived into modern times along with her lesbian lover and becomes involved with a young couple staying at a seaside resort. With Andrea Rau, John Karlen. This restored director's cut includes 12 minutes of footage not shown in the U.S. 100 min.
08-8603 Letterboxed *$14.99*

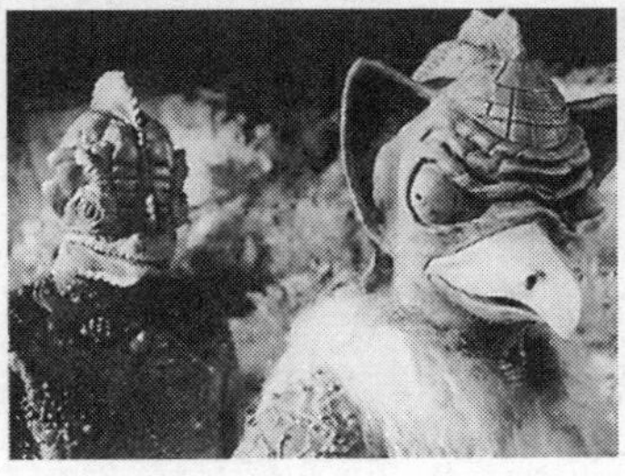

Gargoyles (1972)
While on an expedition in a mountainous region of Mexico, an anthropologist and his daughter stumble across a bizarre human-like skeleton that leads them into a terrifying encounter with a race of demonic-looking beings. Well-made chiller stars Cornel Wilde, Jennifer Salt, Scott Glenn, Grayson Hall and Bernie Casey as the chief gargoyle. 74 min.
08-1684 *$14.99*

The Flesh And Blood Show (1973)
Performers auditioning for a British "Grand Guignol" show are murdered in mysterious ways in this deranged thriller from director Pete Walker ("House of Whipcord"). Decapitations, drownings, psychotic elderly tramps, naked women...who could ask for anything more? With Jenny Hanley, Ray Brooks.
27-6281 Was $24.99 *$19.99*

I Dismember Mama (1972)
After he escapes from a mental hospital, deranged Zooey Hall sets out to kill his mother (who sent him there), but along the way attacks any "loose women" that cross his path. Eventually, he falls for a young girl, the daughter of his mother's housekeeper. Way-out shocker also features Greg Mullavey, Geri Reishl. AKA: "Poor Albert and Little Annie."
16-1091 *$29.99*

Legacy Of Blood (1971)
The children of a deceased millionaire are summoned to his estate, where they must stay the night in order in gain their inheritance. It soon becomes obvious that someone wants more than their fair share, as the heirs are murdered one by one. John Carradine, Faith Domergue, John Russell star. AKA: "Blood Legacy." 90 min.
16-1046 *$19.99*

Octaman (1971)
This revamping of "The Creature from the Black Lagoon," directed by that film's writer, tells of an eight-limbed, aquatic man-beast terrorizing explorers Kerwin Matthews and Pier Angeli in Mexico. With Jeff Morrow; features early makeup work by Rick Baker.
16-1106 *$14.99*

Whiskey Mountain (1977)
Two young couples are looking for treasure and find more than they bargained for in the haunted hills of Whiskey Mountain. Christopher George, Roberta Collins, Preston Pierce star. 95 min.
10-1305 *$19.99*

Suicide Cult (1977)
Horror, suspense, and occult terror await in this tale of a deadly struggle between the forces of Good and Evil for possession of a child whose coming has been foretold for centuries. 82 min.
14-6070 *$39.99*

Stanley (1972)
Slither on over and watch this chiller about a deranged Vietnam vet (Chris Robinson) who uses his pet rattlesnakes for revenge on those he thinks "wronged" him. With Alex Rocco, Susan Carroll. 96 min.
15-1119 *$19.99*

Hollywood Horror House (1975)
A lonely, faded movie queen is joined in her reclusive Hollywood mansion by a handsome young drifter. But this is no "Sunset Boulevard"; he's a psychotic killer into slashing women. John David Garfield (John Garfield's son), Miriam Hopkins, Gale Sondergaard, Joe Besser. AKA: "Savage Intruder." 80 min.
15-9031 Was $19.99 *$14.99*

Paul Naschy

Dracula vs. Frankenstein (1970)
No more peace-making missions for alien Michael Rennie, who stars in this sci-fi chiller as a visitor from the planet Ummo who settles in Transylvania and sends out a "fearsome foursome" of terror (Dracula, Frankenstein's monster, a mummy and a werewolf) to conquer the world. With Karin Dor, Paul Naschy. AKA: "Assignment Terror." 86 min.
10-9167 Was $19.99 *$14.99*

Fury Of The Wolfman (1970)
Sink your fangs into this furious (and furry-ous) frightmare about a scientist-turned-werewolf who becomes the "volunteer" for a female psychiatrist's bizarre mind-control experiments. Paul Naschy stars. 85 min.
53-1799 Was $29.99 *$19.99*

Dr. Jekyll vs. The Werewolf (1971)
A man marked with the sign of the beast seeks a cure from a descendant of the original Dr. Jekyll, only to swap his hairy, wolfish alter ego for a slightly less hirsute, slightly more human one—the cruel Mr. Hyde. With Paul Naschy. 85 min.
68-8057 Was $19.99 *$14.99*

Horror Rises From The Tomb (1972)
The flood of blood rises and rises as each modern-day victim falls to the monstrous incarnation of a French knight wrongfully beheaded in the 15th century. Paul Naschy stars. 89 min.
53-3124 *$14.99*

Count Dracula's Great Love (1972)
The Vampire Lord returns, using the blood of virgins to bring his daughter back to life until he falls for one of his potential victims. Paul Naschy stars as Dracula. 96 min.
68-8051 *$19.99*

The Werewolf vs. The Vampire Woman (1972)
When two co-eds are abducted by a vampire countess, a melancholy werewolf fated to die for love becomes their champion. Catchy European horror/eroticism stars Paty Shepard, Paul Naschy. AKA: "Shadow of the Werewolf." 86 min.
68-8165 *$19.99*

Vengeance Of The Zombies (1972)
The dead and decaying stalk the streets of London and set Scotland Yard on a chase, as a madman, bent on revenge, empties the graves and fills the streets with zombies. Paul Naschy stars. 90 min.
71-1032 *$19.99*

The Mummy's Revenge (1973)
Some people get all wrapped up in living; this fellow got all wrapped up in death! Now he's back, and he needs the blood of virgin females to stay "alive." Paul Naschy stars. 91 min.
48-1110 *$19.99*

Curse Of The Devil (1973)
A Mexican horror favorite with Paul Naschy as the descendant of a witch-hunter who gets a taste of his family's own medicine by being turned into a werewolf by a vengeful Gypsy. 73 min.
68-8443 *$19.99*

Devil's Possessed (1974)
Eerie horror outing set in France in the Middle Ages, where demented tyrant Field Marshal de Lancre (Paul Naschy) seeks a magical "philosopher's stone" while torturing the denizens of a small village. Shocks, savagery and atmosphere run wild in this production that's definitely not for the meek.
71-1025 *$19.99*

Exorcism (1974)
Paul Naschy goes "The Exorcist" route in this tale of a woman's unknowing involvement in a Satanic ceremony that leads her to be possessed by the spirit of her late father. After displaying all sorts of disturbing behavior, she turns to priest Naschy to exorcise the evil spirits. With Grace Mills, Maria Perschy.
71-1026 *$19.99*

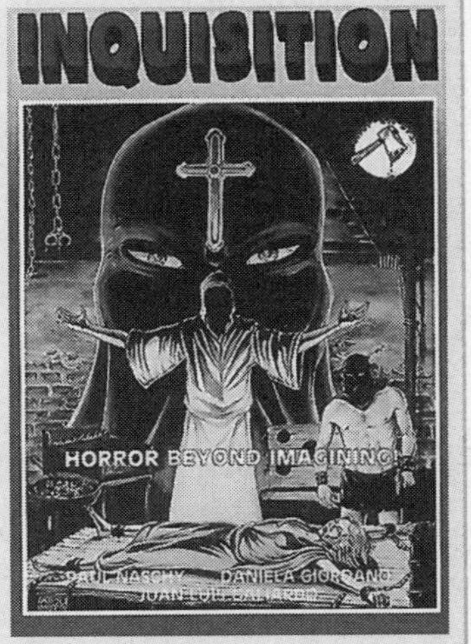

Inquisition (1976)
Superstition and religious fanaticism of the 16th century is brought to shocking life as you witness every gruesome detail of unspeakable horror. Paul Naschy is a witch-hunting judge who falls in love with the daughter of a warlock he's sentenced to die. Banned more than it was shown in theaters, this is not for the squeamish. 85 min.
50-1287 *$19.99*

Monsters Crash The Pajama Party (1965)
A bunch of partying teenagers have a haunted house encounter with a diabolical scientist in this obscure horror/beach-flick blend that was shown in theatres with a live act (when the mad doc orders his monstrous henchmen to find new victims, ushers in masks roamed the aisles for female patrons!). Wow! Peter James Noto stars.
68-8812 *$19.99*

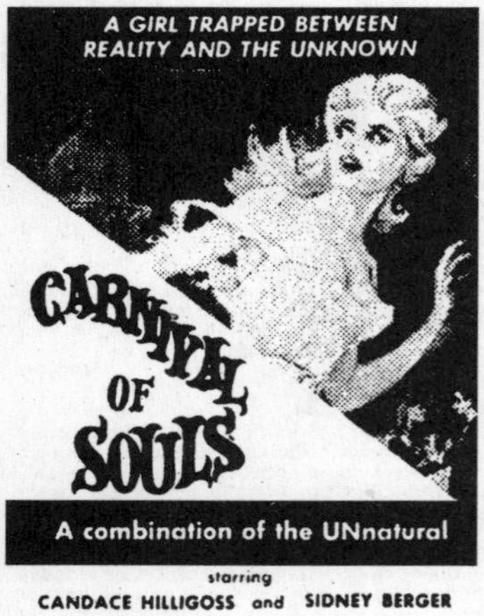
A GIRL TRAPPED BETWEEN REALITY AND THE UNKNOWN
CARNIVAL OF SOULS
A combination of the UNnatural
starring
CANDACE HILLIGOSS and SIDNEY BERGER

Carnival Of Souls (1962)
A car plunges off a bridge, and a young woman emerges, apparently unscathed. Wandering off, her odyssey takes her to a strange small town and a carnival pavilion whose patrons walk the line between the living and the dead. Director Herk Harvey's atmospheric low-budget chiller has achieved a cult following; Candace Hilligoss, Sidney Berger star. 87 min.
56-3000 *$19.99*

Carnival Of Souls: European Version (1962)
The horror cult fave is also available in a restored print, made for European release, that features scenes shot in the tinted "Super-Psychorama" process.
73-3005 *$19.99*

Carnival Of Souls (1998)
Produced by Wes Craven, this loose remake of the 1962 creeper focuses on Alex Grant, a young woman unable to shake witnessing her mother's horrible murder when she was a child. Visions of the killer dressed as a carnival clown keep haunting Alex. Is he still alive and stalking her? Bobbie Phillips, Larry Miller, Cleavant Derricks and Shawnee Smith star. 86 min.
68-1907 *□$99.99*

Face Of Terror (1962)
Years before "Death Becomes Her" came this nifty Mexican shocker with Fernando Rey as a scientist who invents a scar-removing serum which he uses on a disfigured woman. After she is transformed into a beauty, her true nature—that of a psychotic killer—is revealed. Lisa Gaye also stars.
68-8929 Was $19.99 *$14.99*

The Anatomist (1961)
Atmospheric rendering of the story of "Burke and Hare," involving graverobbers procuring cadavers for medical experiments. Alastair Sim, George Cole and Michael Ripper star in this creepy effort.
68-8938 *$19.99*

Crypt Of Horror (1963)
Christopher Lee, a nobleman concerned that a witch will possess his daughter, asks occult experts to observe her at home in hopes of detecting her descent into a world of evil. Jose Campos and Vera Valmont also star in this shocker based on "Carmilla." AKA: "Terror in the Crypt."
68-8939 *$19.99*

The Terrible People (1960)
A crackerjack Edgar Wallace story involving the ghost of a man hanged by mistake who returns to gain his sinister vengeance. Karin Dor and Joachim Fuchsberger star. 90 min.
68-8954 *$19.99*

Fortress Of The Dead (1965)
Rarely seen, atmospheric ghost story about the lone survivor of a decimated bunker at Corregidor who returns to the Philippines two decades later to encounter the spirits of his deceased comrades. John Hackett and Conrad Parkham star.
68-9062 *$19.99*

Hyena Of London (1964)
Inspired by an Edgar Wallace story, this thriller tells of a mad professor whose study of the "symptoms of evil" takes a new twist when he's turned into a maniac after injecting liquid from a killer's brain into his own noggin. Bernard Price, Tony Kendell star.
68-9063 *$19.99*

The Horrors Of Spider Island (1960)
A classic mix of horror, bad special effects and sexy beauties, this West German import tells of a talent scout and six gorgeous gals whose plane crashes on a deserted island inhabited by a giant spider whose bite turns the agent into a monster. This version of the film features a "skinny-dipping" sequence cut from most others. With Alex D'Arcy and Barbara Valentin. AKA: "It's Hot in Paradise." 86 min.
79-5299 Was $24.99 *$19.99*

Honeymoon Of Terror (1961)
After they get married in Las Vegas, newlyweds Frank and Marion head to Thunder Island for a great honeymoon. When they arrive at this cozy spot, they hear stories about a logger who went on a rampage of rape and murder. Now, the Bermuda Triangle's sounding like a better honeymoon love nest. Dwan Marlow and Doug Leith star. 57 min.
79-5483 Was $24.99 *$19.99*

The Blood Beast Terror (1968)
What is the sinister connection between a scientist's bizarre experiments on his daughter and the gruesome murders of young men in the village? Horror shocker stars Peter Cushing, Robert Flemyng. 91 min.
27-6342 Was $39.99 *$19.99*

The Bloody Dead (1967)
Klaus Kinski is at his demonic best in dual roles as twin brothers who return to their hometown to wreak havoc with the locals through a series of savage scientific experiments and torture, using a blue clawed hand. Based on an Edgar Wallace story, this shocker also stars Harald Leipnitz. AKA: "Creature with the Blue Hand." 80 min.
71-1049 *$14.99*

Black Mamba (1965)
Creepy shot-in-the Philippines effort from the John Ashley-Eddie Garcia Team ("The Beast with the Yellow Hand") tells of a voodoo witch who uses dolls and snakes to steal a child from a widowed woman. Ashley is a doctor who becomes a believer in black magic after he encounters the sorceress face to face. This rarity features extremely gory sequences. With Marlene Clarke. 92 min.
73-9316 *$19.99*

Track Of The Vampire (1966)
Notorious Roger Corman production tells the terror-filled tale of a Venice, Ca., artist (William Campbell) who believes he's the reincarnation of a 15th-century vampire and begins killing women by dipping them into molten wax and painting their bodies. Moody amalgamation of director Jack Hill's "Blood Bath," a Yugoslavian vampire film and new footage shot by Stephanie Rothman co-stars Marissa Mathes, Sandra Knight and Jonathan Haze.
68-8743 *$19.99*

Portrait Of Terror (1965)
Bizarre thriller features Patrick Magee as a deranged killer hiding out in a seedy Venice, California, hotel and William Campbell as an unbalanced artist looking to steal a valuable painting. Their seemingly unconnected tales come together in a story of desire, madness and murder. The footage of Magee covered in wax later turned up in the film "Track of the Vampire."
68-9087 *$19.99*

The Brainiac (1961)
A diabolical baron, burned at the stake 300 years earlier, returns to Earth as a super-tongued monster ready to suck out the brains of those who condemned him. Classic Mexican chiller stars Abel Salazar (who also produced), German Robles. 77 min.
68-8216 *$19.99*

Torture Chamber Of Dr. Sadism (1967)
Christopher Lee stars as the murderous Count Regula, who returns to the town that executed him to seek his bloody revenge. Chiller also stars Karin Dor and ex-Tarzan Lex Barker. AKA: "Blood Demon," "Castle of the Walking Dead." 81 min.
69-1075 *$19.99*

Mad Doctor Of Blood Island (1969)
John Ashley is the crazed Dr. Larca, conducting plant experiments on a desolate island. He accidentally turns his lab assistant into a blood-drinking monster with Chlorophyll. Oops! AKA: "Tomb of Living Dead."
69-1077 *$24.99*

Beast Of The Dead (1970)
Scary sequel to "The Mad Doctor of Blood Island" in which the evil Dr. Lorca unleashes a headless, green-blooded monster on a female newspaper reporter. John Ashley, Celeste Yarnall and Eddie Gomez star in this Filipino fright festival. AKA: "Beast of Blood." 78 min.
79-6167 *$14.99*

She-Freak (1967)
A conniving small-town waitress marries the wealthy owner of a travelling carnival that features a freak show. When hubby is murdered by her Ferris wheel operator boyfriend, she inherits the carnival and has new plans for the sideshow...but the freaks have a plan for her. A liberal reworking of "Freaks," this David F. Friedman production stars Claire Brennan. 87 min.
79-5543 Was $24.99 *$19.99*

Legend Of Horror (1966)
This horror yarn that's part-American and part-Argentinean is truly wild! Stanley, a psycho in prison for killing his uncle due to his "imperfect" eye, escapes from prison and goes on a murderous rampage. There's flashbacks, bizarre animation, stock footage from Roger Corman's Poe movies, Fawn Silver ("Orgy of the Dead") and a color ending (in a black-and-white movie). With Ben Daniels.
79-6016 Was $24.99 *$19.99*

It's Alive (1968)
From the always incredible schlockmeister Larry Buchanan ("Zontar, The Thing From Venus," "Beyond the Doors") comes this tale of a rancher who discovers a monstrous lizard-like creature in a cave and proceeds to find it unsuspecting travellers for meals. Tommy Kirk, Shirley Bond and Billy Thurman star.
79-6168 Was $24.99 *$19.99*

The Undertaker And His Pals (1967)
Sicko horror film about a mortician who hires motorcyclists to collect dead bodies so he can sell them to a diner which uses the cadavers as ingredients in their special dishes. Ray Dannis and Robert Lowery (star of the "Batman" serial) are featured in this ghastly terror-farce. 70 min.
82-5004 Was $24.99 *$19.99*

Burn, Witch, Burn! (1962)
Peter Wyngarde is living a charmed life, with a caring wife and a promising career as a college professor. Things take a bizarre turn when he finds out that spouse Janet Blair is a witch whose voodoo practices are responsible for his success. When he forbids her from using any more witchcraft, his job—and their lives—become jeopardized in this chiller based on Fritz Leiber's "Conjure Wife." AKA: "Night of the Eagle." 87 min.
12-3329 *$14.99*

Curse Of Nostradamus (1960)
This was the first in a series of four feature films culled from the 12-episode 1957 Mexican horror serial "Curse of Nostradamus." German Robles plays the 16th-century sage's vampiric son, who rises from the grave to challenge disbelieving foe Domingo Soler with a demonic crime wave and the abduction of Soler's daughter.
68-8403 *$19.99*

The Monster's Demolisher (1960)
Undead villain Nostradamus, Jr. is back with more monstrous menace in this second film in the south-of-the-border shock series, but can arch-enemy Duran stop him with an electronic device that emits signals harmful to bats? German Robles, Domingo Soler star.
68-8040 *$19.99*

Blood Of Nostradamus (1960)
You saw it on midnight and Saturday afternoon horror shows in your formative years, so why not check out this final entry in the German Robles "Nostradamus, Jr." series taken from a Mexican serial? Here, the vampire threatens the local police inspector, leading to a final showdown and a date with a stake. With Julio Aleman.
68-9246 *$19.99*

Castle Of The Creeping Flesh (1968)
A group of young aristocrats attends a hunting party at the isolated retreat of a demented count, only to learn that the invite said "B.Y.O.O."...Bring Your Own Organs for the host's bizarre experiments! Guess who won't be invited to any more parties! With Howard Vernon, Adrian Hoven. AKA: "Castle of Bloody Lust."
69-1103 *$19.99*

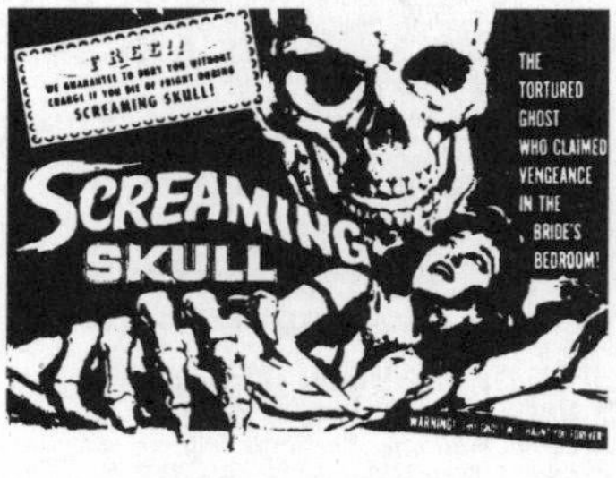
FREE!!
SCREAMING SKULL
THE TORTURED GHOST WHO CLAIMED VENGEANCE IN THE BRIDE'S BEDROOM!

The Screaming Skull (1958)
Macabre shocker about a young newlywed and former asylum patient who moves into the mansion her husband shared with his dead first wife. She soon begins seeing a skull wherever she goes. Is she still insane, or is there a more sinister answer? John Hudson, Peggy Webber star. 68 min.
68-8027 *$19.99*

Dementia (1955)
Highly stylized, dialogue-free "B" shocker, banned by New York censors, follows a young woman's descent into madness. Wandering through hellish city streets, she is accosted by a man in his apartment and pushes him out a window to his death. After cutting off his hand to retrieve her necklace, the woman winds up in a jazz nightclub (the horror!). Adrienne Barrett, Bruno Ve Sota star; songs sung by Marni Nixon. AKA: "Daughter of Horror." 60 min.
53-7569 *$24.99*

Daughter Of Horror (1957)
This is the revamped, retitled edition of the 1955 chiller "Dementia," featuring narration by none other than future "Tonight Show" sidekick Ed McMahon! 60 min.
56-3001 Was $19.99 *$14.99*

Curse Of The Undead (1959)
Bloodsuckers meet gunslingers in this offbeat shocker about a frontier preacher who uses bullets with crosses carved on them to battle a vampire who's bleeding the cattle ranchers dry—in every sense of the word. Eric Fleming ("Rawhide"), Michael Pate and Kathleen Crowley star. AKA: "Mark of the West." 79 min.
07-2427 *$14.99*

Horrors Of The Black Museum (1959)
Shocks are in store when a demented mystery writer enlists his hypnotized assistant to stage a number of gruesome murders, which he then uses in his books. Among the killing devices are a guillotine, ice tongs and, in a memorable opening scene, spiked binoculars. Michael Gough, June Cunningham and Graham Curnow star. Includes the rarely-seen opening sequence filmed in "Hypnovista." 94 min.
08-1621 *$14.99*

Horrors Of The Black Museum (Letterboxed Version)
Also available in a theatrical, widescreen format.
08-1721 *$19.99*

Barbara Steele

The Horrible Dr. Hichcock (1962)
Bizarre Gothic horror about a necrophiliac doctor who accidentally kills his wife during a "funeral game," then remarries to bring her back from the grave with his new wife's blood. Robert Flemyng, Barbara Steele star. 76 min.
63-1240 *$19.99*

Castle Of Blood (1964)
A poet is challenged by Edgar Allan Poe and Lord Blackwood to spend a night in an eerie castle, where phantoms involve him in re-enactments of their horrible deaths. Horror queen Barbara Steele stars. AKA: "La Danza Macabra." 85 min.
68-8326 *$19.99*

The Long Hair Of Death (1964)
Atmospheric shocker from director Anthony M. Dawson stars Barbara Steele as the daughter of a woman burned at the stake for witchcraft during the 16th century who returns from the dead seeking revenge. Moody scares and eroticism are featured; with Giorgio Ardisson, Halina Zalewska. 90 min.
79-5061 Was $24.99 *$19.99*

The Ghost (1965)
A woman murders her husband with dreams of owning his fortune in jewels, but when his spectre returns from the grave it's clear he's out for revenge...or is he? Bizarre chiller with British scream queen Barbara Steele, Peter Baldwin. 96 min.
50-1636 Was $29.99 *$19.99*

Nightmare Castle (1966)
Atmospheric European horror film about a doctor experimenting with the regeneration of human blood through electrical impulses. Barbara Steele stars in a dual role. 90 min.
01-1219 *$19.99*

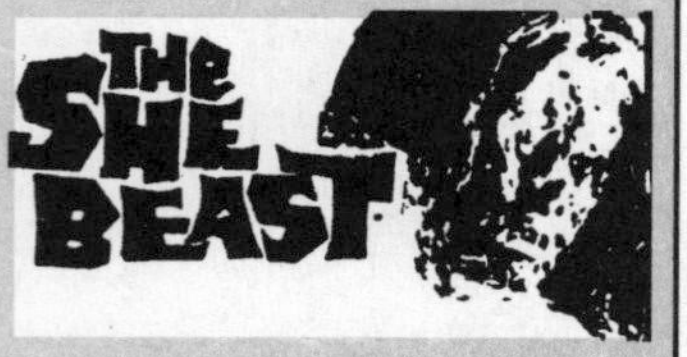
THE SHE BEAST

The She-Beast (1966)
The gorgeous Barbara Steele is the beast, a British tourist in Transylvania possessed by a witch. Ian Ogilvy and Mel Welles co-star in this spookfest, which also contains a bizarre anti-Communist subplot. 88 min.
50-1212 *$19.99*

Terror Creatures From The Grave (1966)
Dying by his wife's hand, a master occultist summons up forces of revenge from beyond eternity. Victims of the Black Death leave their ages-old resting place to stalk murdering widow Barbara Steele and inflict her with bubonic plague. 85 min.
68-8022 *$19.99*

An Angel For Satan (1966)
Scream queen Barbara Steele stars in this moody Italian shocker in which she plays a woman possessed by the spirit of a 200-year-old statue found on the bottom of the lake. Anthony Steffen, Claudio Gora co-star. In Italian; no subtitles.
68-8726 *$19.99*

Please see our index for these other Barbara Steele titles: *Black Sunday • The Capitol Conspiracy • The Monocle • Shivers • Young Toerless*

The House Of The Seven Gables (1940)
A mysterious New England house, a family fortune that drives brother against brother, and an ancient curse are the elements in this Gothic drama, based on Nathaniel Hawthorne's classic novel. Vincent Price, George Sanders, Margaret Lindsay and Nan Grey star. 89 min.
07-2624 □$14.99

Shock (1946)
Sinister psychiatrist Vincent Price murders his wife, only to find that a neighbor witnessed the crime. He then tries to convince the neighbor's husband that she's insane and puts her away. With Lyn Bari, Anabel Shaw. 66 min.
10-3040 Was $19.99 *$14.99*

House Of Wax (1953)
Horror classic, originally shown in 3-D, stars Vincent Price as the disfigured sculptor whose waxwork exhibits look a little too lifelike. With Phyllis Kirk, Carolyn Jones, and a young Charles Bronson. 88 min.
19-1341 Was $19.99 *$14.99*

The Bat (1959)
A jugular-ripping fiend called "The Bat" stalks his victims and a million dollars in securities hidden in a foreboding mansion. A leering Vincent Price co-stars with Agnes Moorehead in this chiller. 80 min.
62-1314 Was $19.99 *$14.99*

Tower Of London (1962)
Vincent Price, who was drowned in a wine vat in the 1939 version of the historical chiller, this time essays the role of the power-hungry King Richard III, who let nothing, not even murder, stand between him and the throne of England. With Michael Pate, Joan Freeman. 76 min.
12-2762 *$14.99*

Twice-Told Tales (1963)
A chilling trio of the best stories by Nathaniel Hawthorne are adapted in this awesome anthology. "Dr. Heidigger's Experiment," "Rappaccini's Daughter" and "The House of the Seven Gables" are brought to full, frightening life by Vincent Price, Sebastian Cabot, Mari Blanchard, Brett Halsey. 119 min.
12-1731 Was $19.99 *$14.99*

Diary Of A Madman (1963)
A magistrate in 19th-century Paris kills a prisoner in self-defense, but becomes the new unwilling host to a murderous demon that inhabited the dead man and compelled him to kill. Vincent Price, Nancy Kovack and Chris Warfield star in a chilling tale based on a Guy de Maupassant story. 96 min.
12-2755 *$14.99*

The Comedy Of Terrors (1963)
Delightfully macabre tale with Vincent Price and Peter Lorre as unsuccessful morticians (they've reused the same coffin for years) who must drum up business by resorting to murder, but find latest victim Basil Rathbone won't stay dead. Boris Karloff, Joyce Jameson, Joe E. Brown also star. 83 min.
44-1514 Was $79.99 *$14.99*

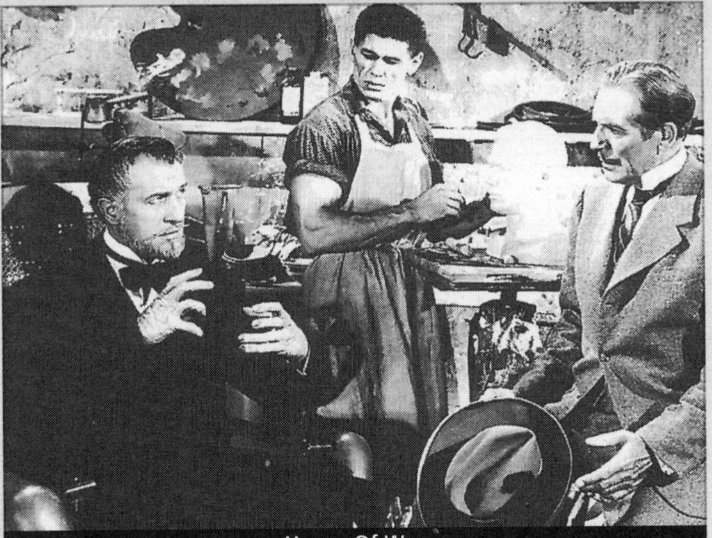

House Of Wax

Vincent Price

The Haunted Palace (1963)
Vincent Price turns in a classic creepy performance as the heir to a New England mansion who begins carrying out his evil ancestor's plans of practicing human sacrifices and creating a race of horrifying mutants. Debra Paget and Lon Chaney, Jr. also star in this Roger Corman production based on an Edgar Allan Poe poem and an H.P. Lovecraft story. 87 min.
44-1804 Was $59.99 *$14.99*

The Last Man On Earth (1964)
Vincent Price stars as the title character, the one human unaffected by a mysterious plague that has turned the world's population into diseased vampires. A frightening horror epic, based on Richard Matheson's "I Am Legend" and remade as "The Omega Man." With Franca Bettoia and Emma Danieli. 86 min.
68-8555 Was $19.99 *$14.99*

The Jackals (1967)
The South African plains are the setting for this adventure in which miner Vincent Price gets help from his no-nonsense, pistol-packing granddaughter when crooks try to steal his gold. Diana Iverson also stars. 105 min.
78-3025 *$14.99*

The Conqueror Worm (1968)
Lurid chiller stars Vincent Price as a corrupt "witch finder" in 17th-century England who uses his power to blackmail innocent women, until the fiancé of a murdered victim tracks him down for revenge. Moody tale of depravity and terror also stars Ian Ogilvy, Hillary Dwyer; Michael Reeves directs. AKA: "The Witchfinder General." 87 min.
44-1493 Was $59.99 *$14.99*

Cry Of The Banshee (1970)
The leader of a witches' coven swears vengeance against the magistrate who persecuted them, and calls forth a demon in human form to kill his family in this chilling costume thriller. Vincent Price, Sally Geeson star. 92 min.
44-1466 Was $59.99 *$14.99*

Scream And Scream Again (1970)
Vincent Price, Christopher Lee and Peter Cushing combine their frightful talents for this bizarre shocker about a doctor who's out to build his own race of super-beings...with the unwilling help of some organ transplant "donors." Don't watch this one alone...you won't be able to stop screaming! 94 min.
73-1147 *$14.99*

The Abominable Dr. Phibes (1971)
Vincent Price stars in his most sinister role, as a mad doctor who seeks revenge on the fellow physicians who failed to save his wife on the operating table. His method of killing each victim, based on the Old Testament plagues of Egypt (bees, locusts, hail, bats, etc.), makes for gruesomely witty fun. With Joseph Cotten, Terry-Thomas, and Virginia North as Vulnavia. 95 min.
73-1143 *$14.99*

Dr. Phibes Rises Again (1972)
Deranged scientist Anton Phibes (Vincent Price) returns, searching for an ancient Egyptian "elixir of life" to revive his late wife and ready to murder anyone in his way. Vivid, sly horror treat also stars Robert Quarry, Peter Cushing. 89 min.
73-1144 *$14.99*

Theater Of Blood (1973)
Vincent Price camps it up in the role of his career, as a supposedly dead ham actor who avenges himself on theatre critics, killing them in gory murders based on Shakespeare's plays! A rousing blend of horror and satire, co-starring Diana Rigg, Robert Morley, Ian Hendry and Milo O'Shea. 102 min.
12-1607 Was $59.99 *$14.99*

Escapes (1986)
Escape with host Vincent Price to the supernatural world of the eerie and uncanny. These five tales ("Something's Fishy," "Coffee Break," "Who's There," "Jonah's Dream" and "Think Twice") will keep you on the edge of your seat all night! 87 min.
46-5204 *$14.99*

Please see our index for these other Vincent Price titles: *Bagdad • Brigham Young—Frontiersman • Casanova's Big Night • Edward Scissorhands • The Fly • House On Haunted Hill • The Keys Of The Kingdom • Laura • Leave Her To Heaven • The Long Night • Master Of The World • The Raven • Return Of The Fly • Scavenger Hunt • Serenade • The Song Of Bernadette • Tales Of Terror • The Ten Commandments • The Thief And The Cobbler • The Three Musketeers • The Tingler • The Trouble With Girls • Up In Central Park*

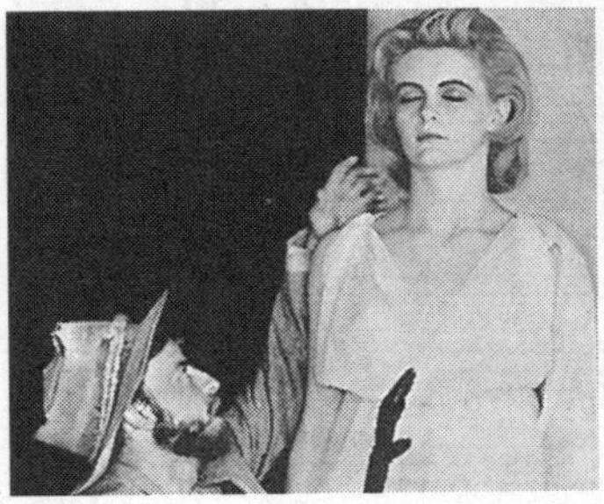

Manos, The Hands Of Fate (1966)
A vacationing family becomes the unwilling guests of a strange cult consisting of the caftaned "Master," his bevy of jealous wives, and a quirky handyman named Torgo in this bizarre low-budget chiller shot in El Paso, Texas. Writer/director Hal Warren stars, along with Tom Neyman, Diane Mahree, and John Reynolds as Torgo. 74 min.
68-8058 *$19.99*

Torture Garden (1967)
Hammer filmmaker Freddie Francis and "Psycho" author Robert Bloch team up for four sinister tales of terror and suspense. A demon cat, the ghost of Poe, a haunted piano and the curse of immortality are highlighted; Burgess Meredith, Jack Palance, Peter Cushing star. 93 min.
02-1471 *$59.99*

World Of The Vampires (1960)
A bloodsucking Count controls a coven of vampires by playing his bizarre pipe-organ made with human bones. Campiness and chills mix. Mauricio Garces. 83 min.
01-1333 Was $19.99 *$14.99*

Curse Of Nostradamus (1960)
In the first chapter of the Mexican-made Nostradamus, Jr. series, a second-generation vampire taunts an occult-debunking scientist with various supernatural crimes. Nobody likes a know-it-all, Doc. AKA: "The Blood of Nostradamus."
68-8403 *$19.99*

What Ever Happened To Aunt Alice? (1969)
This perversely refreshing horror tale in the Grand Guignol tradition stars Geraldine Page as a demented elderly woman whose method of digging herself out of debt includes murdering her housekeepers one by one and stealing their savings. Ruth Gordon co-stars as the friend of one of Page's victims who poses as a new employee to investigate her friend's disappearance. With Rosemary Forsyth, Mildred Dunnock. 101 min.
04-1353 Letterboxed *$14.99*

Daimajin (Majin: Monster Of Terror) (1966)
Well-done Japanese costume fantasy in which Majin, a giant stone warrior, rises from his mountain home to aid the children of a feudal lord murdered by an evil nobleman. When the nobleman murders a priestess and sends his warriors to stop Majin, the Asian Golem gets medieval on them. Miwa Takada, Jun Fujimaki star. 90 min. In Japanese with English subtitles.
20-8194 Letterboxed *$14.99*

Majin: Monster Of Terror (Dubbed Version)
Also available in a dubbed-in-English edition.
79-5813 *$19.99*

Return Of Daimajin (Return Of The Giant Majin) (1966)
The second of the "Daimajin" films finds the colossal warrior leaving its resting place in the middle of a lake to seek revenge against the villains who have destroyed a mystical statue. With Kojiro Horgo, Shiho Fujimura. 90 min. In Japanese with English subtitles.
20-8195 Letterboxed *$14.99*

Wrath Of Daimajin (Majin Strikes Again) (1966)
The residents of an impoverished village, suffering under the tyranny of a cruel warlord, cry out to the heavens for vengeance. Their prayers are answered in the immense form of the living stone samurai, Majin, in this final entry in Japan's "Daimajin" horror-fantasy series. Hideki Ninomiya, Shinji Hori star. 90 min. In Japanese with English subtitles.
20-8196 Letterboxed *$14.99*

Return Of Giant Majin (Wrath Of Daimajin) (Dubbed Version)
Also available in a dubbed-in-English edition.
79-5814 *$14.99*

The Invasion Of The Vampires (1961)
This spicy Mexican horror recipe makes a nice Terror Taco Grande using ingredients from lots of genre favorites. Want a vampire count named Frankenhausen? He's in there. The fiend's victims rising out of graves? It's in there. Hey Doc, is that real black garlic in that anti-vampire potion? Relax, it's in there! 78 min.
68-8042 *$19.99*

Blood And Roses (1961)
An erotic take on the horror tale "Carmilla" from Roger Vadim. A young woman obsessed with a vampire-like ancestor seeks to duplicate her relative's penchant for blood by attacking people at a masked ball. Annette Vadim, Mel Ferrer and Elsa Martinelli star. AKA: "Et Mourir de Plaisir." 74 min.
06-1967 □*$12.99*

The Skull (1965)
Peter Cushing is an occult collector who purchases the skull of the Marquis De Sade from a dealer in bizarre items. Soon, the skull haunts him, controls him and forces him to murder. Christopher Lee, Patrick Wymark and Jill Bennett also star in this shocker directed by Freddie Francis. 83 min.
06-1979 □*$12.99*

Horror Hotel (1960)
A curious co-ed in pursuit of her history studies visits a ramshackle Massachusetts town that had been the site of witch burnings...and lands in the clutches of a coven that has risen from the ashes! Foray into fiendish fight features Christopher Lee, Bella St. John. AKA: "The City of the Dead." 76 min.
10-1723 *$14.99*

Horror Hotel: Letterboxed Collector's Edition
Also available in a theatrical, widescreen format.
10-7245 *$14.99*

The Curse Of The Crying Woman (1961)
A favorite on "Chiller Theatre," "Dr. Shock" and other horror shows, this Mexican terror tale tells of a man and woman who become the victims of an ancient vampiric woman out to revive an anguished mummified corpse stricken with the curse of perpetual wailing. Abel Salazar, Rosita Ardenas and Rita Macedo star.
01-1287 *$19.99*

Doctor Of Doom (1962)
The classic thriller that launched Mexico's lucrative "female wrestler-monster-mad scientist" genre. Here the manic medico transplants a woman's brain into the body of a gorilla, while the victim's sister leads a group of her gal grappler allies for revenge. Lorena Velazquez, Roberto Cadeno star. 75 min.
10-8073 Was $19.99 *$14.99*

The Monster's Demolisher (1960)
This is a rare featurization of the classic Mexican vampire serial "Curse of Nostradamus." In these episodes, the kindly professor protects himself from the vampire Nostradamus, Jr. with an electronic device that emits signals harmful to bats.
68-8040 *$19.99*

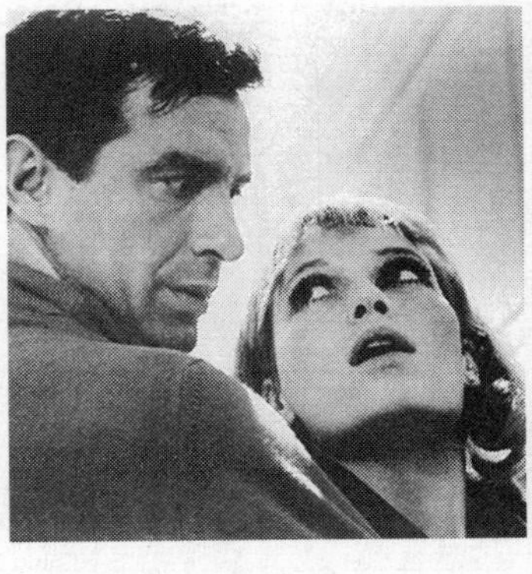

Rosemary's Baby (1968)
A masterpiece of movie terror, directed and scripted by Roman Polanski from Ira Levin's novel. A pregnant woman in a New York apartment building becomes increasingly suspicious of her husband's and neighbors' behavior, but cannot imagine the sinister forces behind it. Mia Farrow, John Cassavetes, Ralph Bellamy and Best Supporting Actress Oscar-winner Ruth Gordon star. 134 min.
06-1091 Was $19.99 *$14.99*

Night Of Bloody Horror (1968)
Years before "Simon and Simon" and "Major Dad," Gerald McRaney starred in this horror opus, playing a guy trying to get over the death of his girlfriend and the terror of his mother. He can't, and so he goes on an axe-wielding murder spree. Creepy, psychedelic stuff from the producers of "The Brain from Planet Arous." With Gayle Yellen.
58-1048 *$19.99*

Tomb Of Torture (1964)
A young woman is haunted by dreams of her past life as a bloodthirsty countess. Travelling to the countess's old castle with her father, she meets a reporter investigating the deaths of two local girls and soon discovers a monstrous secret alive within the building. Annie Alberti, Billy Gray, Adriano Micantoni star. AKA: "Metempsycho." 87 min.
62-7002 Letterboxed *$19.99*

Cave Of The Living Dead (1963)
From deep within a mysterious cavern comes terror, as women in a small village are found murdered. Can an Interpol agent find the horrifying link between the dead girls and a scientist working in a nearby castle? Thrilling German chiller stars Carl Mohner, Adrian Hoven, Wolfgang Preiss. 86 min.
62-7003 Letterboxed *$19.99*

Dr. Terror's House Of Horrors (1965)
From Britain's Amicus Studios comes the first in their anthology-styled horror films. Christopher Lee, Donald Sutherland, Peter Cushing and Michael Gough star in five creepy tales about female werewolves, Haitan Voodoo gods, vampires, crawling hands and vengeful creeping vines. 98 min.
63-1091 *$14.99*

Castle Of Evil (1966)
A small group of people travel to a Caribbean island for the reading of a mad scientist's will and face unspeakable horror in the form of a grisly robot created in his master's image. Frightful fun from a film that promised a free funeral "if you D.D. (Drop Dead) while watching." Stars Scott Brady, Hugh Marlowe and Virginia Mayo. 81 min.
63-1093 *$14.99*

The Devil's Mistress (1968)
Vicious rustlers terrorize an Indian settlement, unleashing supernatural forces when they murder an otherworldly brave and rape his vampiric squaw. Horror/western stars Joan Stapleton. 66 min.
68-8245 *$19.99*

Satanik (1968)
Italian horror yarn about an ugly lab technician who kills her boss and drinks his youth and beauty potion, embarking on a cruel spree of seduction, murder, and nightclub torch-singing. Based on a popular fantasy comic. 80 min.
68-8249 *$19.99*

Castle Of The Living Dead (1964)
Credited with Donald Sutherland's first film roles (he has two, one a grotesque hag in a dress), this is the story of Count Drago and his experiments with the mummification of living persons. Christopher Lee is the evil mastermind. 90 min.
68-8023 *$19.99*

The House In Marsh Road (1960)
A genial poltergeist in an old house protects the woman who has inherited it from a murder plot undertaken by her husband and his mistress. Patricia Danton stars. AKA: "Invisible Creature." 70 min.
68-8038 *$19.99*

The Devil's Hand (1961)
Robert Alda is a man who falls in love with a voodoo doll, the image of his ideal woman, and through it becomes an initiate in the Gamba, a cult with a hankering for human sacrifices. AKA: "The Naked Goddess." 71 min.
68-8043 Was $19.99 *$14.99*

Tormented (1960)
Sometimes chintzy, sometimes genuinely creepy, this chiller from Bert I. Gordon ("The Amazing Colossal Man") stars Richard Carlson as a pianist haunted by the spirit of his mistress, who fell to her death from a lighthouse. Hands crawl, heads appear, a seaweed-covered body surfaces...and you'll be tormented! With Juli Reding, Susan Gordon. 75 min.
68-8549 *$19.99*

Dead Eyes Of London (1961)
Klaus Kinski is just one of the villains in this sensational Edgar Wallace story, filmed previously as "The Human Monster." An evil reverend uses blind inmates at an institution to commit a series of profitable murders. AKA: "Dark Eyes of London." 95 min. Dubbed in English.
68-8056 *$19.99*

Bring Me The Vampire (1961)
Unusual Mexican horror/comedy about a group of artists who must spend the night in a deceased millionaire's mansion in order to inherit a share of his fortune. Also in attendance is the dead man's scheming brother, who sometimes become a vampire! With Joaquin Vargas. 80 min.
68-8247 *$19.99*

Creature Of Destruction (1967)
An unacknowledged remake of "The She Creature," about a cheap hypnotist who seizes the will of a young girl and forces her to commit murders in the style of a sea hag. Les Tremayne ("War of the Worlds") does the Kreskin bit.
68-8327 *$19.99*

Fangs Of The Living Dead (1968)
A vampire pesters his niece to join the undead and relinquish her castle inheritance. Late film by favorite Bob Hope co-star Anita Ekberg. Fangs for the memories, Anita. AKA: "Malenka, the Vampire." 94 min.
68-8250 *$19.99*

Scream Of Fear (1961)
Spine-tingling tale of suspense and murder, starring Susan Strasberg as a wheelchair-bound young woman who travels to her father's Riviera estate only to be told he's away on business. That night, she sees his dead body, and fears she may be next! With Ronald Lewis, Ann Todd, Christopher Lee. 81 min.
02-1930 *$69.99*

Creature Of The Walking Dead (1965)
A scientist moves into his grandfather's spooky castle. Discovering his musty lab and working notes, he retraces his experiments for reviving the dead...and up pops grampa with a need for blood! Rock Madsion, Ann Wells star in this Mexican-made shocker. 74 min.
68-8059 Was $19.99 *$14.99*

Dungeons Of Harrow (1962)
A shipwrecked couple fall prey to the suspect hospitality of a deranged count and become prisoners in his leprosy-infected dungeon. Altogether ooky horror sleaze starring Bill McNulty and Helen Hogan. AKA: "Dungeons of Horror." 74 min.
68-8163 *$19.99*

Bloody Pit Of Horror (1965)
Mickey Hargitay made this gruesome delight during a layover in Italy, where wife Jayne Mansfield was filming. The owner of a creepy castle is possessed by the spirit of a crimson-tighted ancestor and terrorizes a photographer and his models in the dungeon. Contains nine minutes of added footage; 83 min.
68-8198 Letterboxed *$19.99*

The Witch (1966)
A decrepit widow has the ability to transform herself into a beautiful young woman and works her magic to force a historian in a cursed mansion to murder his predecessor. Italian horror fantasy stars Rosanna Schiaffino. 109 min.
68-8317 *$19.99*

Swamp Of The Lost Monsters (1965)
Unusual mix of horror, Western and melodrama from Mexico about a deceased ranhcer's missing body, the family and friends who may have stolen it, a haunted swamp and the scaly monster who lives there. With a bright young Mexican cast. 76 min.
68-8329 *$19.99*

The Curse Of The Doll People (1960)
Four tourists interrupt a Haitian voodoo ceremony and are cursed by the witch doctor, who sends the titular knife-wielding midgets after them. A Mexican horror film that contains some genuinely creepy moments, this "Scream-In" favorite stars Ramon Gay, Elvira Quintana. 83 min.
68-8367 *$19.99*

Hands Of A Stranger (1962)
Atmospheric fright flick about an accident victim who has a murder victim's hands grafted onto his body and begins seeking vengeance on behalf of the hands' former owner. Paul Lukather, Joan Harvey star; look for a young Sally Kellerman. 95 min.
68-8432 *$19.99*

The Hands Of Orlac (1961)
Classic horror tale about a pianist who loses his hands in an accident and is given new ones in an experimental operation. Problem is, the hands came from a murderer, and soon seem to have a life of their own. Mel Ferrer, Christopher Lee, Donald Wolfit star. 87 min.
68-8441 *$19.99*

Anatomy Of A Psycho (1961)
A blast of wild '60s angst, with a creep and his gal wreaking revenge against the people who put his brother in the gas chamber. Ronnie Burns (where did George and Gracie go wrong?), Darrel Howe and Judy Howard star. 72 min.
68-8525 *$19.99*

Teenage Strangler (1964)
Leather jackets! Teenage dances! "Chickie" races! A high-school maniac with a penchant for murder! This made-in-West Virginia shocker is a drive-in schlock classic. Bill Bloom, Stacy Smith and Rick Harris are the teens who really scream. 65 min.
68-8548 *$19.99*

The Burning Court (1962)
Occult thriller about a family that is cursed by a witch whose prophecies become horrifically true. Bizarre excursion into the supernatural stars Charles Spaak, Jean-Claude Brialy and Nadja Tiller; directed by Julien Duvivier ("Pepe Le Moko").
68-8727 *$19.99*

Blood Thirst (1965)
Mystifying fright fest from the Philippines about a woman who becomes involved with sun cultists and seeks to retain her youth through ritual killings and bizarre experiments. With Robert Winston and Yvonne Nielson.
68-8741 *$19.99*

Seeds Of Sin (1968)
Ultra-rare—and ultra-bizarre—Andy Milligan effort about Carol, an oversexed woman, whose family reunion goes haywire when her demented relatives decide to scream and have sex with each other. And matters are made even worse when they are periodically killed. This unknown milestone in the cinema of strangeness stars Maggie Rogers and Candy Hammond. AKA: "Seeds."
79-6215 Was $24.99 *$19.99*

The Ghastly Ones (1969)
From the Shock King of Staten Island, Andy Milligan, comes this gruesome tale of revenge and bloodshed set in an eerie mansion. Three couples must spend the night to inherit a fortune, but they're dying one by one! Don Williams, Veronica Radburn star. 81 min.
56-3002 *$19.99*

Bloodthirsty Butchers (1970)
Inspired by the old "Demon Barber of Fleet Street" story that beget "Sweeney Todd," this shoestring-budget shocker from Andy Milligan details the demented exploits of a psychotic barber and his pastry chef compadre who turn butchered people parts into pies. With John Borske, John Miranda. 80 min.
36-2009 Was $24.99 *$19.99*

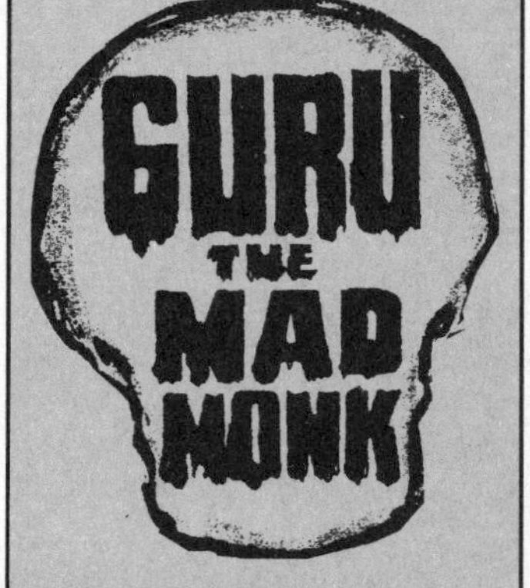

Guru The Mad Monk (1970)
Andy Milligan tops himself with this outré shocker about torture-loving Father Guru, who wields incredible power over his strange church of lost souls and is helped by a vampiress named Olga and a trusted hunchback sidekick. Set in "Mortavia" (but filmed at St. Peter's Church in Manhattan), the film stars Neil Flanagan and Jacqueline Webb.
51-1017 *$19.99*

The Man With Two Heads (1972)
Shocking variation of the "Dr. Jekyll and Mr. Hyde" story from Long Island auteur Andy Milligan. In 1830s England, a scientist uses a potion to transform himself into the hideous Mr. Blood. Denis De Marne, Julia Stratton star.
36-2010 Was $24.99 *$19.99*

The Body Beneath (1983)
"Filmed in the graveyards of England," this Andy Milligan tale of undead depravity follows a reverend who is the patriarch of a family of vampires looking for some "new blood" for his brood. Gavin Reed, Jackie Skarvellis, Susan Heard star. 85 min.
59-5076 Was $24.99 *$19.99*

Werewolf In A Girls' Dormitory (1961)
Those all-night pajama parties will never be the same again! A girls' school is the killing ground for a growling, snarling creature of the night in this "straight A" shocker. Curt Lowens, Barbara Lass, Carl Schell (Max's brother) star. AKA: "Lycanthropus." 80 min.
68-8515 Was $19.99 *$14.99*

The Vampire People (1966)
Filipino fright film with fangs tells the story of a bald-headed vampire whose lover is dying and arrives in town to (literally) steal the heart of her twin sister. The ghoul has a hunchback and a sexy gal as sidekicks and the power to turn invisible. Amalia Fuentes and Ronald Remy star. AKA: "The Blood Drinkers."
68-8742 *$19.99*

The Naked Witch (1963)
A college student researching the occult in Texas resurrects a woman who was falsely accused of practicing witchcraft in the 19th century. The woman then seeks vengeance against the descendants of the man who prosecuted her. Creepy horror thriller from noted schlockmeister Larry Buchanan. With Robert Short. 55 min.
68-8854 *$19.99*

The Embalmer (1966)
Extremely creepy horror yarn from Italy about a psychotic killer who terrorizes Venice by donning a nun's habit and a skull mask and stalking beautiful women, whom he then kills, stuffs and adds to his underground lair's statue collection. Gin Mart and Maureen Lidgard Brown star.
68-8918 *$19.99*

William Castle

House On Haunted Hill (1959)
A sinister host offers a group of people $10,000 each if they'll spend the night in his macabre mansion, then does his best (or worst) to see that no one collects! Spook-filled shocker from the legendary William Castle stars Vincent Price, Richard Long, Carol Ohmart and Elisha Cook, Jr.; not in "Emergo." 75 min.
04-1898 *$14.99*

The House On Haunted Hill (Letterboxed Version) (1959)
Also available in a theatrical, widescreen format.
46-8064 *$14.99*

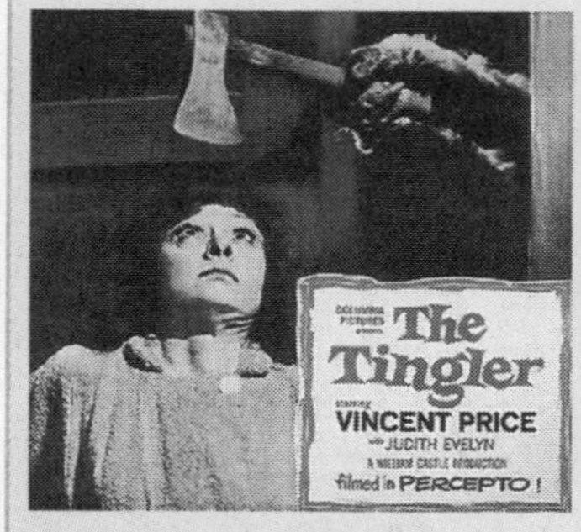

The Tingler (1959)
Famous as the film in which producer/director William Castle wired theatre seats to give customers mild electric jolts at key points, this offbeat chiller stars Vincent Price as a doctor who discovers that intense fear causes an insect-like creature to grow inside a person's spine, and only screaming can kill it. His theory, however, really gets put to the test when a "tingler" runs amok in a movie theatre! This version includes the color-tinted "bloody bathtub" sequence; with Darryl Hickman, Philip Coolidge, Judith Evelyn. 81 min.
02-2869 *$14.99*

13 Ghosts (1960)
Campy horror gem from William Castle about a family that inherits a mansion complete with hot and cold running poltergeists, a spooky housekeeper and a missing treasure. Martin Milner, Rosemary DeCamp and Margaret Hamilton star. 105 min.
02-2680 *$14.99*

Strait-Jacket (1964)
After 20 years in the booby hatch, Joan Crawford, convicted for the axe murders of her husband and his lover, finds peace at her daughter's home. But once dead bodies start popping up, she's convinced she's given decapitation another crack. Classic William Castle shocker, written by Robert Bloch ("Psycho"), reassures "It's only a movie...It's only a movie." 89 min.
02-1210 Was $59.99 *$19.99*

The Night Walker (1964)
A haunting suspense thriller from B-auteur William Castle, with Barbara Stanwyck as a wife whose blind husband dies in a mysterious accident. Soon after she has bizarre dreams, and several people claim to have seen her husband alive. Someone is trying to drive Stanwyck insane, but who? With Robert Taylor, Hayden Rorke; script by Robert Bloch ("Psycho"). 86 min.
07-1944 *$14.99*

I Saw What You Did: Collector's Edition (1965)
To liven up a night of baby-sitting, teens Sarah Lane and Andi Garrett make prank phone calls, dialing up strangers and saying "I saw what you did and I know who you are!" Unluckily for them, one of their victims is John Ireland, who just finished killing his wife and is coming after them! Joan Crawford co-stars as Ireland's love-starved neighbor in this nail-biter from director William Castle. Includes the original theatrical trailer. 82 min.
08-8783 Letterboxed *$14.99*

Please see our index for these other William Castle titles: *The Americano • Texas, Brooklyn And Heaven • Zotz!*

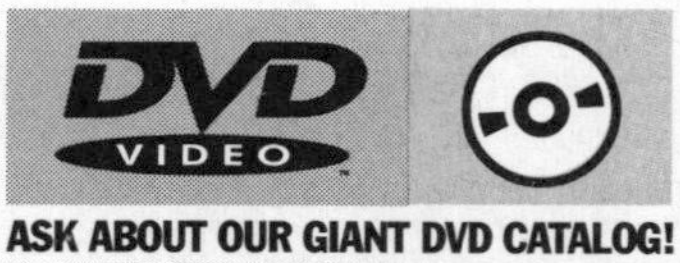

Nightmare In Wax (1969)
Heart-thumping terror abounds in a wax exhibit whose creator, embittered ex-film studio worker Cameron Mitchell, is killing actors and turning them into statues. Filmed on location in Hollywood's famed Movieland Wax Museum, this shocker also stars Berry Kroeger, Anne Helm. 95 min.
08-1158 Was $29.99 *$19.99*

Atom-Age Vampire (1961)
Italian-made shocker about a scientist who turns into a murdering beast in order to supply donors for his experiments to restore the scarred face of the woman he loves. Produced by Mario Bava. 71 min.
09-1554 Was $29.99 *$14.99*

Night Of The Bloody Apes (1968)
Mexican mayhem and madness, as a scientist trying to revive his dead son transplants a gorilla's heart in him, creating a bestial monster that attacks young women. Features bloody scenes of open heart surgery, semi-nudity, female wrestlers and rubber knives. With Carlos Lopez Moctezuma, Norma Lazareno. AKA: "Gomar The Human Gorilla."
10-1303 Was $24.99 *$19.99*

The Strangler (1964)
Leo's a good boy to his doting, wheelchair-bound mother. Little does she know that her son's fixation with her has turned him into a psychotic killer. Victor Buono, David McLean and Ellen Corby star. 89 min.
04-2001 *$14.99*

Crucible Of Horror (1969)
Forget "Mommie Dearest"! This British-made shocker is about a father who's so bad he drives his daughter and wife to kill him. Trouble is, he doesn't stay dead and returns to wreak vengeance. Michael Gough, Yvonne Mitchell, Sharon Gurney star. AKA: "The Corpse." 91 min.
12-2757 *$14.99*

Blood Of Dracula's Castle (1967)
Dracula and his undead wife go by the aliases of Count and Countess Townsend and keep their castle well-stocked with young women in the dungeon (for blood cocktails), a hunchbacked assistant, and butler John Carradine in this Al Adamson shocker. Alex D'Arcy, Paula Raymond also star. 84 min.
08-1141 Was $29.99 *$19.99*

Genii Of Darkness (1960)
In this third compilation of episodes from the little-seen "Curse of Nostradamus" vampire serial, the scholarly arch-rival of a modern vampire retrieves the ashes of the fiend's chief ancestor, a famous 16th-century occultist, from an ancient crypt.
68-8041 *$19.99*

The Mask (1961)
A psychiatrist is given custody of an ancient Aztec mask that gives whoever dons it weird (and three-dimensional!) visions and drives them to kill. Gimmicky matinee staple stars Paul Stevens, Claudette Nevins. Comes with two pairs of 3-D glasses. AKA: "Eyes of Hell," "The Spooky Movie Show." 85 min.
15-5106 *$14.99*

Ring Of Terror (1962)
A group of medical students launch an elaborate prank involving a cemetery, a school cadaver, and (gasp!) a ring on a classmate who claims to know no fear. With George Mather, Esther Furst, Austin Green, a cat named Puma, and some of the world's oldest collegians.
68-1014 Was $24.99 *$14.99*

The Haunting (1963)
A truly frightening film from director Robert Wise that will give your goosebumps goosebumps. A selected group of the curious gather in a supposedly haunted New England mansion and encounter the supernatural. Julie Harris, Richard Johnson, Russ Tamblyn and Claire Bloom star. 112 min.
12-1602 *$19.99*

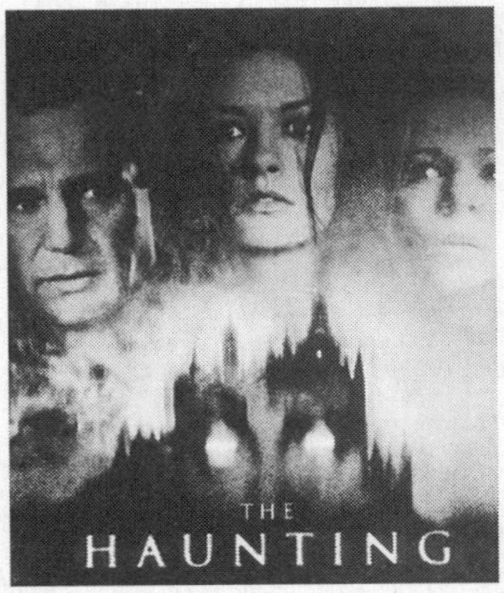

The Haunting (1999)
In this special effects-filled version of Shirley Jackson's "The Haunting of Hill House," Liam Neeson is a professor who recruits three people for experiments which he claims will help cure their insomnia. Little do they know that the house is haunted and they're in for the scariest evening of their lives! With Lili Taylor, Catherine Zeta-Jones, Owen Wilson and Bruce Dern; directed by Jan De Bont ("Speed"). 113 min.
07-2806 Was $19.99 ❑*$14.99*

Mario Bava

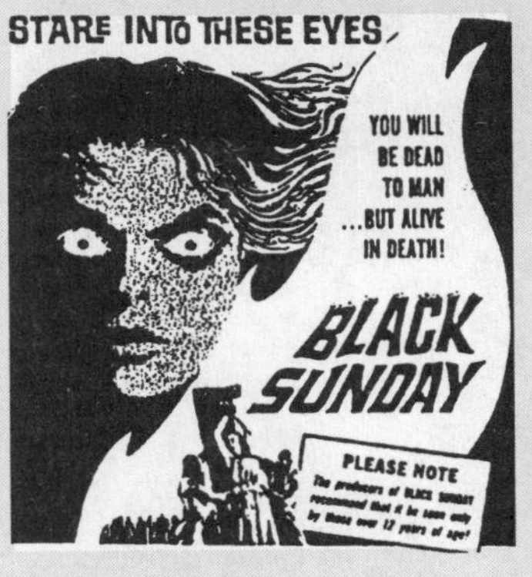

Black Sunday (1960)
The vampire fantasy from Mario Bava (his solo directorial debut) that made a horror goddess out of Barbara Steele. Condemned in the 1600s as a witch and gruesomely executed, Steele returns from the grave to massacre her family's survivors, including her look-alike descendant. With John Richardson, Ivo Garrani. AKA: "The Demon's Mask." 84 min.
68-8300 *$19.99*

Black Sunday (Uncut Letterboxed Version)
Also available in the uncut, European edition, in a theatrical, widescreen format. Includes the theatrical trailer. 87 min.
50-8342 *$19.99*

The Girl Who Knew Too Much (1963)
A vacation in Rome becomes a trip into terror for American tourist Leticia Román when she witnesses a murder. No one will believe Roman's story except doctor John Saxon, who thinks she saw the latest victim of the Alphabet Killer and may become his next target, in this compelling suspenser from Mario Bava. AKA: "Evil Eye," "La Ragazza Che Sapeva Troppo." 86 min. In Italian with English subtitles.
50-8596 Letterboxed *$19.99*

What! (1963)
Creepy Gothic shocker from Mario Bava in which sadistic Christopher Lee, the son of a wealthy count, tortures Daliah Lavi, his brother's wife and father's mistress. After Lavi kills Lee, his ghostly presence returns to haunt her and administer whippings on a nightly basis. AKA: "The Whip and the Body."
68-8922 *$19.99*

Blood And Black Lace (1964)
Disturbing thriller from Italian horror maestro Mario Bava set in a fashion house where gorgeous models are being killed by a masked murderer with metallic claws. Stylish shocker stars Cameron Mitchell, Eva Bartok and Thomas Reiner. 88 min.
68-8869 *$14.99*

Kill, Baby, Kill (1966)
A doctor investigating a young woman's apparent suicide in a Balkan village discovers the locals believe the ghost of a baron's daughter is responsible. Director Mario Bava's chiller stars G. Rossi Stuart, Erika Blanc. AKA: "Curse of the Living Dead," "Operation Fear." 83 min.
68-8246 *$19.99*

Danger: Diabolik (1968)
Colorful adaptation of a French comic strip stars John Phillip Law as a master criminal who enjoys pulling off such crimes as detonating tax offices and stealing priceless gold ingots. Marisa Mell, Michel Piccoli and Terry-Thomas also star; Mario Bava directs. 99 min.
06-1971 ❑*$12.99*

Bay Of Blood (1971)
This shocker from Italian maestro Mario Bava was a major inspiration for "Friday the 13th" and other gore films. It traces the events following the supposed suicide of Countess Federica, the owner of a bayside estate. A group of people vie for the property as a series of ghastly murders occur. Claudine Auger ("Thunderball") stars. AKA: "Twitch of the Death Nerve." 80 min.
50-6013 *$14.99*

Hatchet For A Honeymoon (1971)
They say wedding nights are tough, but it becomes downright deadly when a deranged dress designer begins hacking up young women in wedding gowns. Here comes the bride, all drenched in blood, in this matrimonial mayhem from director Mario Bava. Stephen Forsythe, Dagmar Lassander star. 93 min.
53-1801 Was $24.99 *$19.99*

Hatchet For A Honeymoon (Letterboxed Version)
Also available in a theatrical, widescreen format. 88 min.
79-6419 *$19.99*

Baron Blood (Collector's Edition) (1972)
Plans to renovate a 16th-century European castle as a tourist resort hit a horrifying snag when two college students accidentally revive the castle's former owner, a depraved nobleman who uses restored torture instruments for his sadistic pleasures. Joseph Cotten, Elke Sommer and Massimo Girotti star in Mario Bava's gory frightfest. Restored version features the original music score and scenes not shown in U.S. theaters. AKA: "Torture Chamber of Baron Blood." 90 min.
08-8527 Letterboxed *$14.99*

Lisa And The Devil (Collector's Edition) (1972)
Released in a re-shot, edited form in American theaters as 1975's "The House of Exorcism," this is the rarely-seen, uncut version of Mario Bava's chilling masterpiece of lust, murder and Satanic possession. Elke Sommer plays a woman driven by strange visions to a mansion inhabited by sadists, devil-worshippers, necrophiliacs...and lollipop-sucking butler Telly Savalas! With Alida Valli, Sylva Koscina. 116 min.
08-8528 Letterboxed *$14.99*

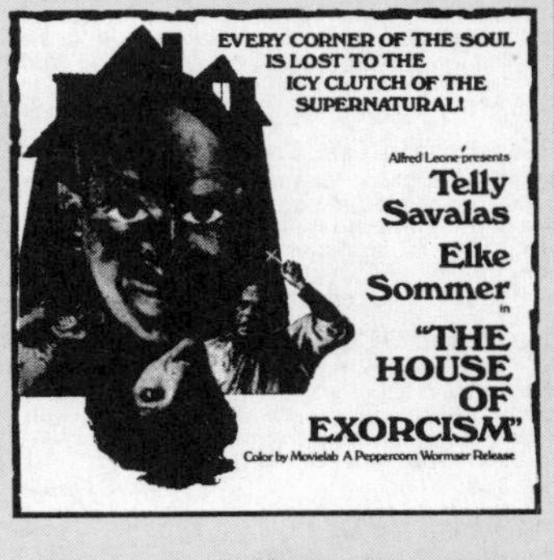

The House Of Exorcism (1975)
Mario Bava's shocker is also available in its stateside edition. 93 min.
50-6269 *$19.99*

The House Of Exorcism (Letterboxed Version)
Also available in a theatrical, widescreen format.
50-8540 *$19.99*

Shock (1977)
Released in America as "Beyond the Door II," Italian frightmaster Mario Bava's final feature follows a family whose young son seems to be able to talk to the dead. What will his "gift" reveal about the sinister truth behind his father's death, and what price will the boy's mother and her new husband pay? Daria Nicolodi, John Steiner star. Includes an interview with assistant director Lamberto Bava and the subtitled Italian theatrical trailer. 92 min.
08-8837 Letterboxed *$14.99*

Please see our index for the other Mario Bava title: *Erik The Conqueror*

Slaughter Of The Vampires (1962)
The terror mounts when a newlywed couple decides to honeymoon in an eerie old chateau...and the undead master of the house graciously offers them a bite! With Walter Brandi, Dieter Eppler. AKA: "Curse of the Blood Ghouls." 71 min.
27-6481 Was $24.99 *$19.99*

Mill Of The Stone Women (1962)
A mad doctor drains young women of their blood in an attempt to restore his daughter to life, leaving the bodies in a windmill turned into a wax museum. Bizarre horror tale from Europe. Wolfgang Preiss, Pierre Brice. AKA: "Icon." 94 min.
30-1041 *$14.99*

Death Curse Of Tartu (1967)
An archeological expedition deep in the Everglades uncovers a sacred Seminole burial mound and also finds a centuries-old curse that comes true, as a witch doctor named Tartu returns for a bloody vengeance. Can they kill Tartu a second time...before he kills them? 88 min.
44-7047 *$19.99*

Circus Of Fear (1967)
There's murder under the big top, and the police have no lack of suspects in this grisly shocker. Christopher Lee, Klaus Kinski, Leo Genn and Suzy Kendall star. AKA: "Psycho-Circus." 90 min.
50-3226 *$19.99*

The Fiendish Ghouls (1961)
Hammer-style gothic chiller set in 19th-century Edinburgh stars Peter Cushing as a doctor studying dead bodies supplied by a pair of thieves. The community becomes aware of the dastardly crimes after the duo kill the doctor's girlfriend, a pupil and an important official. With Donald Pleasence, George Rose. AKA: "Flesh and the Fiends," "Mania." 91 min.
17-9020 Was $19.99 *$14.99*

Scream Baby Scream (1969)
A demented beatnik artist kidnaps people and horribly disfigures them. Then he paints them, and his creations become the new craze in town, á la Corman's "Bucket of Blood." Ross Harris, Chris Martell star in this flashback-filled freak-out! AKA: "Nightmare House." 95 min.
21-5001 *$14.99*

Horror Castle (1963)
A newlywed couple moves into the husband's familial Rhineland castle expecting to start a new life, but a series of gruesome murders threatens their happiness...if not their lives. Christopher Lee stars as the scarred family retainer; with George Riviere, Rossana Podesta. AKA: "The Virgin of Nuremberg."
16-9006 *$19.99*

Night Tide (1963)
Unique suspenser stars Dennis Hopper as a sailor who falls for a sideshow mermaid...and discovers, to his danger, that her unearthliness may be more than just a mere carnival scam. Taut chiller co-stars Linda Lawson, Gavin Muir. 84 min.
17-3008 *$19.99*

Night Tide (Letterboxed Version)
Also available in a theatrical, widescreen format.
80-5031 *$29.99*

The Innocents (1961)
A masterpiece of cinematic suspense, director Jack Clayton's adaptation of Henry James' "The Turn of the Screw" stars Deborah Kerr as the new governess of a brother and sister in Victorian England. Strange occurrences and visions convince Kerr that the children are possessed by the spirits of two former employees of the house, but are the incidents real or in her mind? Michael Redgrave, Pamela Franklin, Martin Stephens also star. 100 min.
04-3278 ❑*$19.99*

The Turn Of The Screw (1974)
Lynn Redgrave stars in the chilling Henry James story as a Victorian governess who believes her young charges are possessed by long-dead spirits, setting her off on a fight to save their souls. With Jasper Jacob, Eva Griffith; directed by Dan Curtis. 118 min.
50-7046 Was $19.99 *$14.99*

The Turn Of The Screw (1999)
The classic ghost story by Henry James receives a fine treatment in this haunting film. Jodhi May stars as the repressed governess hired by a mysterious country squire to look after his children, and who begins seeing apparitions of two former estate workers. With Colin Firth, Pam Ferris. 120 min.
08-8842 Was $19.99 ❑*$14.99*

The Brain (1965)
A doctor becomes the victim of his own diabolical experiments when the disembodied brain of a sadistic millionaire takes over the scientist's body and begins a ghastly reign of terror. Peter Van Eyck, Anne Heywood star. 83 min.
27-6235 *$19.99*

Blood Beast Terror (1968)
What is the sinister connection between a scientist's bizarre experiments on his daughter and the gruesome murders of young men in the village? Horror shocker stars Peter Cushing, Robert Flemyng. 81 min.
27-6342 Was $39.99 *$19.99*

Psychomania (1963)
From the people who gave you "The Horror of Party Beach" comes this shocker filmed in Stamford, Connecticut, about an artist who likes to work with nude models who becomes a suspect in murders that occur at a girls' college. Lee Phillips and Jean Hale star. 90 min.
50-5717 *$14.99*

Brides Of The Beast (1968)
When a scientist and his wife land on a remote Pacific island, they discover the natives are more than restless; they're the slaves of a radiation-spawned monster that craves human women. Stars John Ashley, Beverly Hills, Kent Taylor. AKA: "Brides of Blood," "Grave Desires," "Island of Living Horror." 95 min.
21-5025 *$19.99*

I Eat Your Skin (1964)
Originally paired with "I Drink Your Blood," this gory goodie about a mad doctor who uses radioactive snake venom to help manufacture disgusting zombies stars William Joyce and Heather Hewitt; directed by Del Tenney ("Horror of Party Beach"). AKA: "Voodoo Blood Bath." 82 min.
59-1019 *$14.99*

Curse Of The Swamp Creature (1966)
A mad scientist is creating half-human, half-reptile monsters in his Everglades laboratory in this late night favorite from Larry ("Zontar") Buchanan. With John Agar, Francine York. 80 min.
62-1330 *$19.99*

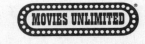

Four Sided Triangle (1953)
Two scientists settle a romantic rivalry over their blonde assistant by producing a clone of the woman with their new invention. Unfortunately, both the duplicate and the original both eyes for the same guy. No wonder these scientists go mad. Offbeat sci-fi tale from Hammer Studios stars Stephen Murray, Barbara Payton. 74 min.
68-8122 *$14.99*

Spaceways (1953)
Hammer Studios produced this mix of sci-fi and domestic drama starring Howard Duff as an American scientist suspected of killing his British wife and her lover and dumping their bodies in a space-bound satellite. In order to prove his innocence, Duff and fellow scientist Eva Bartok must go into space to recover the satellite. With Alan Wheatley. 78 min.
73-3022 *$19.99*

X The Unknown (1956)
Creepy sci-fi chiller from Hammer in which a “mud monster” revived by atomic experiments terrorizes Scotland while seeking new forms of radioactive material to stay alive. Dean Jagger is the scientist on the case, and Leo McKern, Anthony Newley, Edward Judd also star. 78 min.
08-8716 *$14.99*

The Abominable Snowman (1957)
Creepy, atmospheric Hammer production featuring Forrest Tucker as an adventurer and Peter Cushing as a botanist who team to search for the legendary man-beast known as the Yeti in the Himalayan region of Tibet. 91 min.
08-8718 Letterboxed *$14.99*

The Curse Of Frankenstein (1957)
The first fright flick from England’s Hammer Films started a new, more graphic trend in horror. Peter Cushing stars as the scientist whose obsession with creating life culminates with grotesque monster Christopher Lee. With Hazel Court. 83 min.
19-1455 *$14.99*

The Revenge Of Frankenstein (1958)
Hammer’s sequel to “Curse of Frankenstein” stars Peter Cushing as the Baron, who creates a new body from the limbs of cadavers for his handicapped assistant. Unfortunately, the new synthetic creation reverts back to its original form when beaten by a janitor and hospital patients. This creepy, surprisingly compassionate film features Michael Gwynne as the creature. 89 min.
02-2794 *$19.99*

Tales Of Frankenstein (1958)/ The Professor (1958)
Universal Pictures and England’s Hammer Films teamed to make a half-hour TV pilot based on Mary Shelley’s shocker; Anton Deffring and Don Megowan star. And in “The Professor,” Doug Hobart plays a laboratory-created lycanthrope who goes on a rampage. This terrifying double bill also features a 10-minute intermission of classic drive-in ads.
68-8912 Double Feature *$19.99*

The Evil Of Frankenstein (1964)
Peter Cushing makes his third appearance as the quintessential mad doctor. Here he and his assistant rescue the monster (Kiwi Kingston) from a glacier and attempt to revive him with help from a hypnotist. 84 min.
07-1476 Was $19.99 *$14.99*

Frankenstein Created Woman (1967)
Lively Hammer Films horror opus pulls a switcheroo on the monster legend, as Peter Cushing’s Baron Frankenstein implants a troubled male’s soul into a handicapped woman’s body and, with some plastic surgery, produces a beautiful creature (Playboy model Susan Denberg) with lots of issues and a menacing hatchet to help solve them. Includes TV and theatrical trailers. 92 min.
08-8656 Letterboxed *$14.99*

Frankenstein Must Be Destroyed (1969)
The brain’s the game for Baron Frankenstein (Peter Cushing), as he transplants the mind of a medical colleague into the body of an asylum worker, and neither patient is happy with the result. Spellbinding suspense and terror in the Hammer tradition; with Veronica Carlson, Simon Ward, Freddie Jones. 101 min.
19-2248 Was $19.99 *$14.99*

Frankenstein And The Monster From Hell (1974)
The final installment in Hammer’s Frankenstein series finds Peter Cushing as the not-so-good doctor, joining with a young disciple at a mental hospital where they perform some frightening experiments with the patients. Soon, they realize that they’ve created a monster! With Madeline Smith, David Prowse. 89 min.
06-1974 ❑*$12.99*

Horror Of Dracula (1958)
Christopher Lee adds a snaring animal presence to the bloodthirsty Count in this chilling Hammer classic, based on Stoker’s novel. Peter Cushing co-stars as intrepid vampire hunter Van Helsing. 82 min.
19-1456 *$14.99*

The Brides Of Dracula (1960)
Hammer’s sequel to “Horror of Dracula” stars David Peel as a young man who inherits the mantle and appetites (if not the name) of the bloodsucking count and sets out to make a teacher his latest victim. Peter Cushing returns as vampire hunter Dr. Van Helsing; with Yvonne Monlaur, Martita Hunt. 85 min.
07-1819 ❑*$14.99*

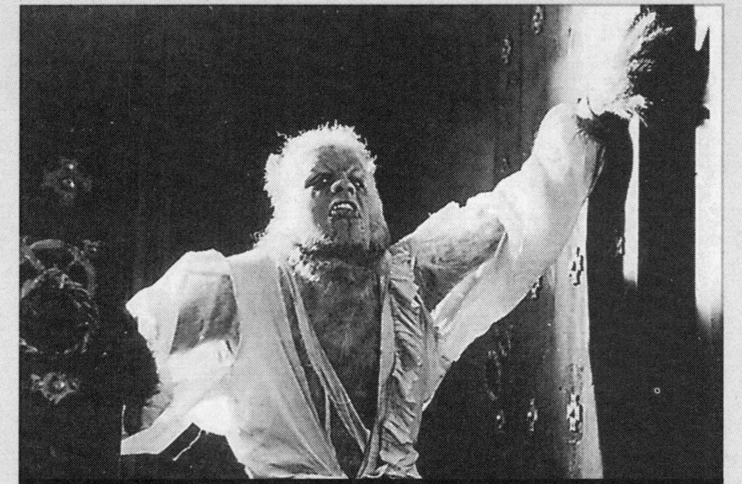
The Curse Of The Werewolf

Hammer Horror Classics

Dracula— Prince Of Darkness (1965)
Poetic, sensual entry in Hammer’s vampire series follows a group of travellers who get an unsettling welcome to Castle Dracula when Christopher Lee’s undead count is revived and goes right for the jugular with female visitors Suzan Farmer and Barbara Shelley. Special video release includes a behind-the-scenes “home movie” with commentary by Lee and his co-stars, plus original theatrical and TV trailers. 90 min.
08-8564 Letterboxed *$14.99*

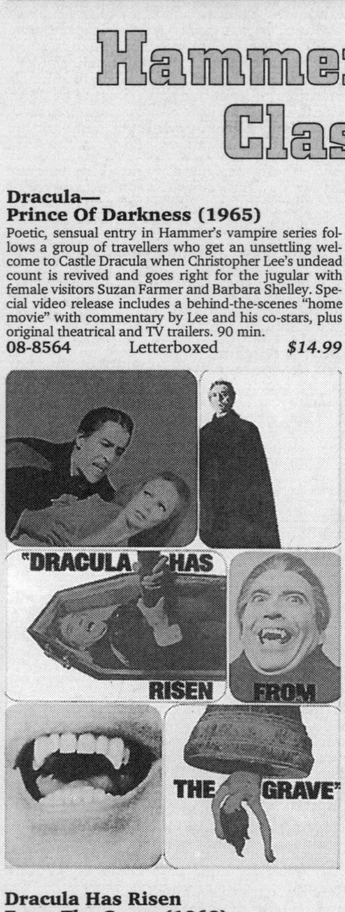

Dracula Has Risen From The Grave (1968)
The fourth film in Hammer’s “Dracula” series (and the third to star Christopher Lee in the title role) has the not-so-good Count returning from his watery resting place to terrorize the residents of an abbey. With Rupert Davies, Barbara Ewing, Barry Andrews. 92 min.
19-2038 Was $19.99 *$14.99*

Taste The Blood Of Dracula (1969)
You just can’t keep a good vampire down, as an English nobleman learns to his eternal regret when he resurrects Lord of Darkness Christopher Lee in this sanguine shocker from the Hammer studio. Ralph Bates, Linda Hayden, Isla Blair also star. 91 min.
19-2039 Was $19.99 *$14.99*

Dracula A.D. 1972 (1972)
Hippies and horror are mixed in this Hammer production in which a group of young people stage a black magic ritual and wind up resurrecting the undying Count Dracula (Christopher Lee) in the heart of psychedelic London. With Stephanie Beacham, Christopher Neame, and Peter Cushing as a descendant of Van Helsing. AKA: “Dracula Today.” 100 min.
19-2247 Was $19.99 *$14.99*

The Rites Of Dracula (The Satanic Rites Of Dracula) (1973)
This time it’s not just London, but the entire world that must beware the infamous bloodsucker (Christopher Lee), who masquerades as a reclusive billionaire as he launches a plan to use a deadly virus to destroy all life on Earth. Hammer chiller also stars Peter Cushing as Van Helsing, Michael Coles and Joanna Lumley. AKA: “Count Dracula and His Vampire Bride.” 88 min.
50-1652 *$19.99*

The Satanic Rites Of Dracula (Letterboxed Version)
Also available in a theatrical, widescreen format. Includes the British and American theatrical trailers.
08-8647 Was $19.99 *$14.99*

The Mummy (1959)
Hammer horror greats Christopher Lee and Peter Cushing return in this tale of supernatural vengeance. A 3,000-year-old mummy removed from his crypt and shipped to England is returned to life to murder the “defilers.” 88 min.
19-1457 *$14.99*

The Two Faces Of Dr. Jekyll (1960)
Atmospheric switcheroo on the Robert Louis Stevenson story, courtesy of Hammer Films, features Dr. Jekyll as a bearded, not-too handsome fellow and Mr. Hyde as a slick, good-looking charmer with a murderous way with the ladies. There’s eerie interludes and eroticism aplenty with Paul Massie, Dawn Addams and Christopher Lee. 87 min.
02-2795 *$19.99*

The Curse Of The Werewolf (1961)
An illegitimate child born on Christmas Day in 18th-century Spain is marked with the sign of the beast in this lurid lycanthrope tale from Hammer Films. Oliver Reed stars as the wolfman; with Yvonne Romain, Clifford Evans. 91 min.
07-1475 Was $39.99 ❑*$14.99*

The Maniac (1962)
Eerie British thriller in the “Psycho” mold. An artist visiting France is seduced by a beautiful girl and her stepmother, who wants him to help free her husband from an asylum. Murder, madness and plot twists abound in this Hammer shocker. Kerwin Matthews, Nadia Gray star. 86 min.
02-1131 *$49.99*

The Phantom Of The Opera (1962)
Herbert Lom tackles the role made famous by Lon Chaney and Claude Rains in this impressive production from Hammer Films. Lom plays the mysterious, deformed figure, obsessed with a beautiful singer, who haunts a London opera house. Michael Gough and Heather Sears also star. 85 min.
07-2287 ❑*$14.99*

Kiss Of The Vampire (1962)
Creepy bloodsucking epic from Hammer Films in which a young married couple arrive at a Bavarian mansion where their host turns out to be a vampire who practices black magic. A professor attempts to save the couple before they can be converted into creatures of the night? Clifford Evans, Noel Willman star. AKA: “Kiss of Evil.” 88 min.
07-2283 ❑*$14.99*

Paranoiac (1963)
Eerie effort from Hammer Studios in which a young woman believes she sees images of her brother, who committed suicide years earlier at a memorial service for her parents. This gives her other brother an opportunity to prove that she’s mentally unstable and attempt to collect the family inheritance. But who—or what—was that bizarre spectre? Janette Scott and Oliver Reed star. 80 min.
07-2288 ❑*$14.99*

Nightmare (1963)
Atmospheric Hammer shocker in which a teenager begins having horrific visions of her long-deceased mother, who killed the girl’s father years earlier. Who is behind the sinister plot to drive the young woman insane, and what will happen to her? David Knight, Moira Richmond and Jennie Linden star. 93 min.
07-2289 ❑*$14.99*

The Gorgon (1964)
Chilling Hammer production in which Megara, one of the mythological Gorgons with snakes in their hair and the ability to turn people into stone, haunts a German village. Peter Cushing, Christopher Lee and Barbara Shelley star in this atmospheric thriller. 83 min.
02-2695 *$14.99*

Rasputin—The Mad Monk (1966)
Christopher Lee’s most monstrous film portrayal may have been of a real person in this Hammer Films look at the charismatically menacing Russian holy man who used hypnosis to gain power in the court of Czar Nicholas II, where he seduced women and mercilessly crushed any potential rivals. Barbara Shelley co-stars. Special edition includes the original theatrical trailer. 92 min.
08-8565 Letterboxed *$14.99*

Plague Of The Zombies (1966)
Atmospheric, expertly realized Hammer horror set in a Cornish town where a local physician becomes suspicious of a rash of mysterious deaths. He soon finds out that a squire is using voodoo to resurrect the dead in order to have them work in his tin mine. John Carson, Brook Williams star in this shocker. Special edition includes original theatrical trailers. 90 min.
08-8566 Letterboxed *$14.99*

Prehistoric Women (1966)
Hoochy-koochy adventure from Hammer Studios starring the ravishing Martine Beswick as the mean leader of a tribe of sultry, rhino-worshipping females. A big-game hunter is transported back in time and becomes Beswick’s prisoner. When he escapes, he heads a rebellion against Beswick and her beauties. With Michael Latimer, Edina Romay, Carol White and Stephanie Randal. AKA: “Slave Girls.” 90 min.
08-8722 Letterboxed *$14.99*

The Witches (1966)
After a horrifying experience with voodoo in Africa, Joan Fontaine returns to England and takes a position as headmistress at a private school. She’s soon made aware of a coven of witches, led by a local journalist who plans to sacrifice a student. This Hammer production also features Kay Walsh, Alec McCowen. Includes theatrical and TV trailers. AKA: “The Devil’s Own.” 91 min.
08-8659 Letterboxed *$14.99*

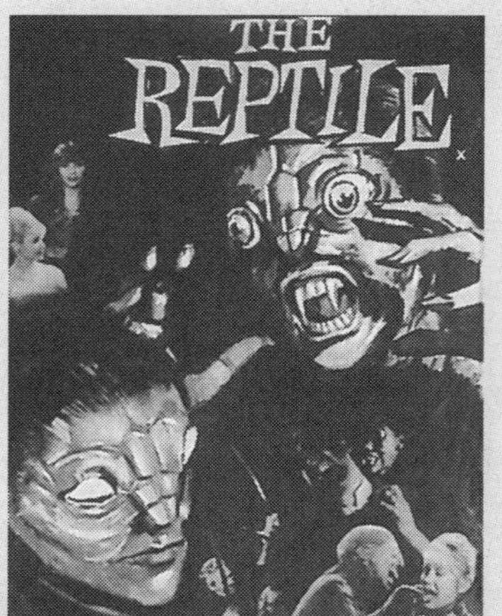

The Reptile (1966)
Classic Hammer shocker, set in a 19th-century Cornish village where a couple arrives to investigate the strange death of the husband’s brother. What they find is a series of killings whose victims appear to have been bitten by a snake and a chilling curse from the Asian jungle that turns one young woman into a savage, scaly horror. Jacqueline Pearce, Noel Willman star. Special edition includes the original theatrical trailer. 90 min.
08-8567 Letterboxed *$14.99*

The Mummy’s Shroud (1967)
“Beware the beat of the cloth-wrapped feet” in this Hammer chiller set in 1920s Egypt. An archeological team retrieves the remains of a young pharaoh, only to be confronted by the mummy of the ruler’s bodyguard. Andre Morell, Catherine Lacey, Eddie Powell star. Includes theatrical and TV trailers. 90 min.
08-8657 Letterboxed *$14.99*

The Devil Rides Out (1968)
Spooky Hammer Films outing showcases Christopher Lee as a British nobleman trying help his close friend, who has become involved with a Satan-worshipping cult. Lee's daughter is abducted by the sect, forcing him to perform a deadly ritual that draws him into conflict with the Devil himself. Charles Gray, Nike Arrighi also star. Includes original theatrical trailers. AKA: "The Devil's Bride." 95 min.
08-8658 Letterboxed **$14.99**

The Vampire Lovers (1970)
Erotic vampire thriller from Hammer Studios starring Ingrid Pitt as a beautiful woman with blood-sucking and lesbian tendencies who vampirizes the daughter and acquaintances of an exorcist. Peter Cushing, Dawn Addams and Pippa Steele co-star in this stylish shocker. 89 min.
73-1131 **$14.99**

Captain Kronos: Vampire Hunter (1972)
Sword and sorcery meets bloodsucking as a swashbuckling vampire hunter attempts to rid the countryside of fanged ghouls. Caroline Munro, Horst Janson star. 91 min.
06-1134 Was $49.99 **$19.99**

Honeymoon Of Fear (1972)
It's anything but a holiday for a young bride who is slowly being driven insane by her new husband to the brink of homicidal madness. Joan Collins, Peter Cushing, Judy Geeson and Ralph Bates star. AKA: "Fear in the Night." 85 min.
44-1055 **$19.99**

Demons Of The Mind (1972)
Every family has "roots," but the crazed Zorn clan's are dipped in blood! Madness, incest, paranoia, psychoses, bad attitudes...it's all here in this grisly Hammer shocker. Patrick Magee, Paul Jones star. AKA: "Blood Evil." 85 min.
63-1707 **$12.99**

The World Of Hammer: Complete Set
For over 30 years, England's Hammer Films was one of the world's leading producers of horror, science fiction and fantasy movies. In this 10-volume documentary series, you'll hear from the stars, see scenes from classic Hammer titles, and follow how the studio's style evolved. Included are "Christopher Lee," "Dracula and the Undead," "Frankenstein," "Lands Before Time," "Mummies, Werewolves and the Living Dead," "Peter Cushing," "Sci-Fi," "Thriller," "Vamp" and "Wicked Women." Hammer veteran Oliver Reed narrates. 250 min. total. NOTE: Individual volumes available at $12.99 each.
08-8869 Save $50.00! **$79.99**

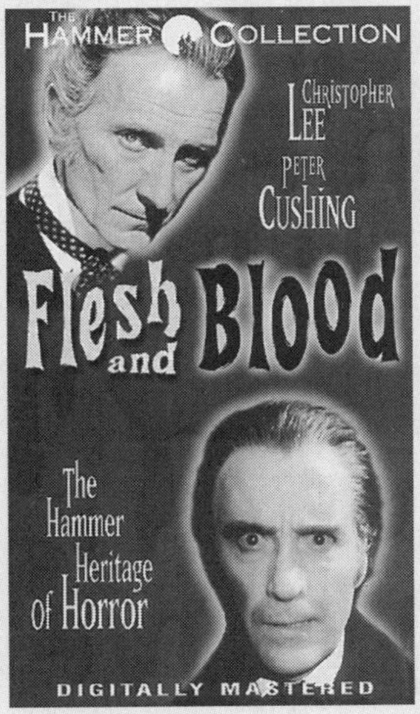

Flesh And Blood: The Hammer Heritage Of Horror (1997)
The British film studio that brought blood to the big screen and revolutionized the horror genre is saluted in a spine-chilling chronicle. Hosts Peter Cushing and Christopher Lee take you through the history of Hammer Films, from backstage battles to censorship problems. Clips from such Hammer classics as "Horror of Dracula," "Curse of Frankenstein," "The Devil Rides Out," "Quatermass and the Pit" and more are featured, along with interviews with Cushing, Lee, Raquel Welch and others. 100 min.
08-8731 **$14.99**

The Hammer Collection
Hammer home some chills with this boxed set that includes "Dracula—Prince of Darkness," "Plague of the Zombies," "Rasputin—The Mad Monk" and "The Reptile."
08-8609 Letterboxed **$59.99**

Voodoo Woman (1957)
Science meets sorcery in this A.I.P. shocker that features Tom Conway as a mad doctor who uses a voodoo spell to transform beautiful Maria English into a hideous beast ready to do his murderous bidding. With Lance Fuller, Mike "Touch" Connors, and the costume from the previous year's "The She Creature." 77 min.
02-2235 **$14.99**

Curse Of The Demon (1956)
A psychologist and occult "debunker" finds himself up against a centuries-old blood cult attempting to bring a demon to Earth, and must use lots of skills to pass the runes. Dana Andrews, Peggy Cummins and Niall MacGinnis star in a moody masterpiece of suspense and terror from Jacques Tourneur ("Cat People"). 81 min.
02-2691 **$14.99**

Serpent Island (1954)
An odyssey into the dark backwaters of the Caribbean turns into a deadly encounter with a giant jungle snake in this voodoo-flavored chiller from renowned B-auteur Bert I. Gordon. Sonny Tufts, Mary Munday star. 68 min.
05-1382 **$14.99**

Frankenstein's Daughter (1958)
Oliver Frankenstein carries on the family tradition by creating a monster with half a face (the other half is melting away) and by experimenting with drugs on a young girl who transforms into a grotesque creature. John Ashley, Sally Todd, Harold Lloyd, Jr. star. 85 min.
05-9011 **$14.99**

The Devil's Partner (1958)
Satanic possession is the theme of this desert-set tale about an old man who invites his own death in order to come back to life, phoenix-like, in a younger body. Ed Nelson and Edgar Buchanan star. 75 min.
68-8028 **$19.99**

The Horror Chamber Of Dr. Faustus (1959)
Having caused the disfigurement of his daughter in an auto accident, an obsessed plastic surgeon kidnaps Paris co-eds for a series of doomed attempts to graft their faces onto hers. Georges Franju's surrealist slasher film enjoys cult status. Pierre Brasseur, Edith Scob star. AKA: "Eyes Without a Face." 86 min. Dubbed in English.
68-8039 **$19.99**

Terror Is A Man (1959)
A crazed vivisectionist on a Philippine island operates on a wild panther, transforming it into a man-like beast, with killer instincts intact. Jungle horror filmed on location stars Francis Lederer. AKA: "Blood Creature." 89 min.
68-8120 **$19.99**

The Woman Eater (1959)
Searching for the key to immortality, British scientist George Coulouris steals a man-eating (or, in this case, woman-eating) tree from a tribe in the Amazon jungle. Back in his lab, Coulouris begins feeding the plant a steady diet of nubile victims, hoping to extract a life-prolonging serum from its sap. Unusual chiller also stars Vera Day, Joyce Gregg. 71 min.
68-8072 **$19.99**

Beast From Haunted Cave (1959)
A gang of gold thieves think they're safe once they reached their mountain hideout, unaware that the nearby cave is inhabited by a cobweb-covered "snow beast." Roger Corman's brother, Gene, served as producer for this beastly frightfest; Michael Forest, Frank Wolff, Sheila Carol star. 65 min.
68-8144 **$19.99**

The Phantom Of The Red House (1954)
An old, dark house...a group of inheritance seekers...a mysterious butler...a thunderstorm...a heroine named Mercedes Benz and a detective named Diogenes Holmes...musical numbers and comedy relief. It can only be a haunted house chiller from Mexico, courtesy of K. Gordon Murray! 90 min.
68-8436 **$19.99**

The Lonely Sex (1959)
A psycho killer kidnaps the daughter of a psychiatrist and keeps her locked in a secluded shack. The killer decides to confess to the crime, but is met by the girl's even more whacked-out roommate. A strong, creepy thriller, not for the squeamish. With Jean Evans, Karl Light.
68-8517 **$19.99**

The Head (1959)
The inventors of a serum that enlivens severed body parts settle their dispute over control of the business in a grisly fashion: the evil scientist makes himself the boss of the laboratory and his kindly partner the head. Stars Michael Simon and Horst Frank. AKA: "A Head for the Devil." 92 min.
68-8153 **$19.99**

I Bury The Living (1958)
New cemetery caretaker Richard Boone discovers that, by putting black pins on unoccupied lots shown on a map of the graveyard, he can kill the site's owner. Stylish low-budget creeper also stars Theodore Bikel, Peggy Maurer. 76 min.
68-8437 Was $19.99 **$14.99**

The New Invisible Man (1957)
A prison inmate receives an invisibility potion from his brainy brother and escapes, but delusional side effects ruin his ability to evade the police. A Mexican-made version of the classic H.G. Wells tale, starring Arturo De Cordova. 86 min.
68-8159 Was $19.99 **$14.99**

Creature From The Black Lagoon (1954)
A team of scientists on an expedition down the Amazon find more than they bargained for in the form of a water-breathing, half-human gillman, and soon the hunters become the hunted! Richard Carlson, Julia Adams, Richard Denning star in this classic sci-fi chiller. Not in 3-D. 79 min.
07-1693 **$14.99**

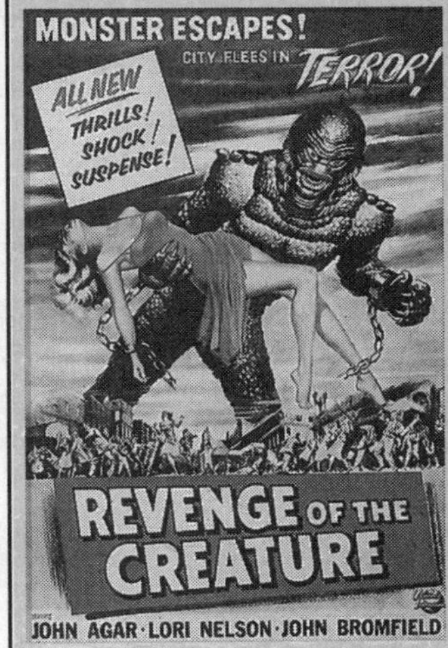

Revenge Of The Creature (1955)
The gargantuan gillman is taken from his Amazon abode to Florida's Marineland Aquarium by a group of scientists, but the change of locale doesn't suit the Creature well. He soon breaks out of his tank, frightening the tourists while clawing away at a pretty icthyologist. John Agar, Lori Nelson, John Bromfield star; look for Clint Eastwood, in his first film, as a lab assistant. 82 min.
07-1980 **$14.99**

The Creature Walks Among Us (1956)
In this third outing of the popular Universal horror series, scientists resuscitate the amphibious monster by mutating its lungs so it can live exclusively on land. But the petty jealousies of the humans throw the Creature into a tizzy, and it runs amok in San Francisco. Jeff Morrow, Rex Reason and Leigh Snowden star. 78 min.
07-1981 **$14.99**

The Creature Collectors' Set
They came from the Black Lagoon—and into your home! The original "Creature from the Black Lagoon," "Revenge of the Creature" and "The Creature Walks Among Us" are available in one great package.
07-2145 Save $5.00! **$39.99**

Ghost Ship (1952)
When a young couple purchase a yacht they are troubled by strange noises and haunting visions. A medium helps them learn of the "ghost ship's" spooky past, and what the strange visitors want. Dermot Walsh, Hazel Court star. 69 min.
08-1251 Was $19.99 **$14.99**

The Headless Ghost (1959)
Humor and horror mix as a group of American students staying at an English castle encounter a friendly ghost who asks for their help. They join him in a search for his spectral pal's lost head, but soon find trouble when a nasty third spirit gets involved. Richard Lyon, Clive Revill and Liliane Sottane star. 70 min.
08-1622 **$14.99**

The Headless Ghost (Letterboxed Version)
Also available in a theatrical, widescreen format.
08-1722 **$19.99**

Bride Of The Gorilla (1951)
Jungle action and voodoo terror in the African tropics, as doctor Raymond Burr marries beautiful Barbara Payton, only to find himself the victim of a man-beast's curse. Co-stars Lon Chaney, Jr. 65 min.
08-8022 Was $19.99 **$14.99**

Donovan's Brain (1953)
Great adaptation of the Curt Siodmak classic that stars Lew Ayres as the scientist who has preserved the living brain of a corrupt businessman...and who slowly succumbs to mental domination by it. With Nancy Davis (Reagan), Gene Evans. 83 min.
12-1730 Was $19.99 **$14.99**

The Return Of Dracula (1958)
An effective low-budget horror film that follows the infamous vampire from Transylvania to contemporary Southern California, where he impersonates a visiting artist and moves in with a small-town family. Francis Lederer, Norma Eberhardt star. AKA: "The Curse of Dracula." 77 min.
12-2761 **$14.99**

Teenage Zombies (1958)
"Teenage Zombies...it's only teenage zombies...they're all wasted," and a fiendish woman scientist wants to use them to take over the world in this campy shocker. Don Sullivan, Katherine Victor star. 71 min.
09-1555 **$14.99**

The Unearthly (1957)
Mad scientist John Carradine's experiments on human transplants have left him with two problems: a pesky undercover police officer and a cellar full of grotesque mutants! Campy horror film also stars Allison Hayes ("Attack of the 50-Foot Woman") and the inimitable Tor Johnson. 76 min.
15-5018 **$14.99**

The Bad Seed (1956)
Classic chiller about the terrorized mother of a seemingly sweet little girl with a perverse propensity for luring people to their deaths. All-time great shocker, based on a hit play, stars Nancy Kelly, Patty McCormack, Eileen Heckart. 129 min.
19-1527 Was $19.99 **$14.99**

Cult Of The Cobra (1955)
A group of American G.I.s in the Far East stumble upon the secret rituals of a snake-worshipping native cult. The head priestess follows the men back to the States and, using her power to transform herself into a cobra, begins killing them one by one. Slithery shocker stars Faith Domergue, Richard Long, David Janssen, Marshall Thompson. 80 min.
07-2077 **$14.99**

She Demons (1958)
Campy thriller about four people stranded on a Pacific isle fighting a Nazi doctor who turns native women into hideous beasts. Irish McCalla ("Sheena, Queen of the Jungle") stars. 80 min.
62-1191 Was $19.99 **$14.99**

The Monster Of Piedras Blancas (1958)
Cult horror classic about a crustacean monster on a rampage for blood along a deserted seacoast. Les Tremayne and Forrest Lewis star in this camp thriller. 72 min.
63-1385 **$14.99**

The Vampire's Coffin (1958)
In a sequel to "The Vampire," a fearless doctor who has dispatched a fiend with a stake through the heart retrieves the body to his laboratory. When a flunky loyal to the evil count removes the blessed charm, the vampire jolts back to life, and the reign of terror begins again. 86 min.
68-8020 **$19.99**

Zombies Of Mora Tau (1957)
Eager treasure-hunters have their work cut out for them when a sunken ship off the African coast is found be loaded with a fortune in diamonds...as well as an underwater army of the walking dead. Gregg Palmer, Allison Hayes, Morris Ankrum and Joel Ashley star. AKA: "The Dead That Walk." 70 min.
02-1470 **$59.99**

The Gamma People (1956)
When a pair of reporters travel to an isolated Balkan nation, they discover its demonic despot is subjecting the country's children to radiation treatments that either transforms them into mental prodigies...or blithering morons. Chiller stars Paul Douglas, Leslie Phillips. 79 min.
02-1639 **$14.99**

Giant From The Unknown (1958)
The giant spirit who's been rampaging through a superstitious California town turns out to be a really big Spanish conquistador revived by lightning. See, there had to be a logical explanation. Edward Kemmer and Sonny Baer star. 77 min.
68-8160 **$19.99**

The Electronic Monster (1957)
At a clinic where patients are hypnotized and filed away in morgue-style drawers as therapy, insurance investigator Rod Cameron finds an evil doctor who is programming them with an electronic device. AKA: "Escapement." 80 min.
68-8197 Was $19.99 **$14.99**

Man Beast (1956)
Journeying in the Himalayan wasteland to locate her missing brother, Virginia Maynor and her mountain guides come face to face with the dreaded Abominable Snowman and his deadly rampages. Lloyd Nelson co-stars. 67 min.
68-8211 Was $19.99 **$14.99**

The Professor (1958)
The insidious connection between communist expansion and the rise of domestic werewolves is revealed for the first time, in the Cold War horror tract "They" didn't want you to see! Extremely rare find starring John Copeland includes a selection of "wolfman" movie trailers.
68-8306 **$19.99**

Alias John Preston (1956)
A psychological "Jekyll and Hyde" thriller starring Christopher Lee as a well-to-do man plagued by horrible, bloody nightmares. Visiting his small town doctor for a sleeping potion, he receives a chilling explanation instead. 66 min.
68-8323 **$19.99**

The Devil's Commandment (1956)
An early Italian experiment in sensual terror from Riccardo Freda and cinematographer Mario Bava, detailing a doctor's attempts to keep the countess he loves eternally young, thanks to the blood of the local virgins. AKA: "I Vampiri." 90 min.
68-8368 **$19.99**

Fright (1956)
A woman believes she is the mistress of a 19th-century Austrian prince who died with him in a suicide pact. Eric Fleming plays the psychiatrist who tries to shock her out of her delusion. AKA: "Spell of the Hypnotist."
68-8235 *$19.99*

The Dead Talk Back (1957)
Obscure horror item in the tradition of Ed Wood concerning a scientist who develops a machine that can communicate with the dead and uses it to help the police solve a model's murder. Aldo Farmese, Scott Douglas star. 65 min.
68-8668 *$19.99*

Phantom Of The Opera (1943)
Winner of two Academy Awards, this lavish Technicolor retelling of the horror classic stars Claude Rains as the acid-scarred composer who seeks vengeance from beneath the Paris Opera House. Co-stars Nelson Eddy, Hume Cronyn, Leo Carillo, and Susanna Foster as the Phantom's love interest. 92 min.
07-1478 *$14.99*

Chamber Of Horrors (1940)
Superior suspense yarn based on Edgar Wallace's novel, "The Door with Seven Locks." Leslie Banks is a doctor out to eliminate a group of heirs with his underground lab/torture chamber. Lilli Palmer co-stars. 85 min.
08-1231 Was $19.99 *$14.99*

The Uninvited (1944)
An eerie ghost story with several memorable scares. Ray Milland and Ruth Hussey star as siblings who buy a house on England's Cornish coast, only to find signs that the house is haunted. A local girl with psychic abilities holds the key to the ghost's identity. With Gail Russell, Donald Crisp. 98 min.
07-1820 *$14.99*

The Mummy's Hand (1940)
The first entry in Universal's revived (no pun intended) "Mummy" series features Western star Tom Tyler as the bandaged Kharis, who sips a little tanaleaf tea and is sent to kill the defilers of an Egyptian tomb. George Zucco co-stars as the priest who brings Kharis to life, and Peggy Moran is the reincarnation of his long-lost love. 67 min.
07-1880 *$14.99*

The Mummy's Tomb (1942)
Lon Chaney, Jr. gets all wrapped up in the role of Kharis, the ancient mummy taken to America by an Egyptian high priest to wreak vengeance on the archeologists who disturbed his 4,000-year sleep. While in the States, Chaney finds himself attracted to the archeologist's pretty girlfriend. Dick Foran, Turhan Bey, Elyse Knox also star. 61 min.
07-1975 *$14.99*

The Mummy's Ghost (1944)
Finding the reincarnation of his ancient priestess in the form of a college student in New England, Lon Chaney, Jr.'s mummy goes on a rampage, trying to return her to her final resting place. John Carradine, George Zucco and Ramsay Ames also star in this terror favorite from Universal. 60 min.
07-1976 *$14.99*

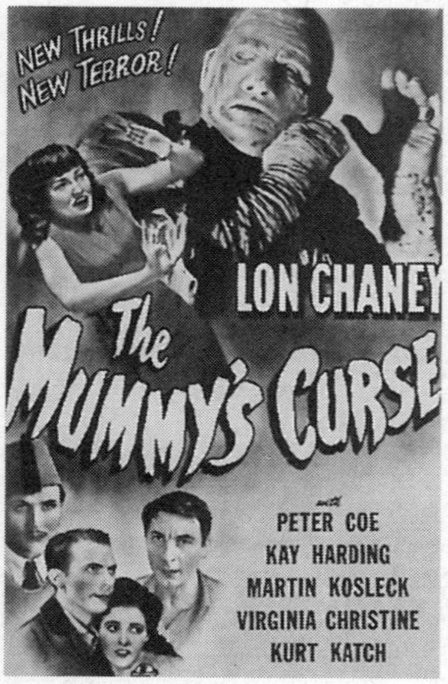

The Mummy's Curse (1944)
After being retrieved from their quicksand tomb from the third movie, Kharis the Mummy (Lon Chaney, Jr.) and his princess (Virginia Christine) are taken to Louisiana in order to be studied by scientists. Soon after their arrival, the creepy couple break out, causing horror in the bayou. Peter Coe and Dennis Moore co-star. 62 min.
07-1977 *$14.99*

The Mummy Collectors Set
Horror fans will get all wrapped up with this terrifying trio of Mummy movies from Universal Studios. The crypt includes "The Mummy," "The Mummy's Curse" and "The Mummy's Ghost." (Sorry, no "Mummy Dearest.")
07-2144 *$44.99*

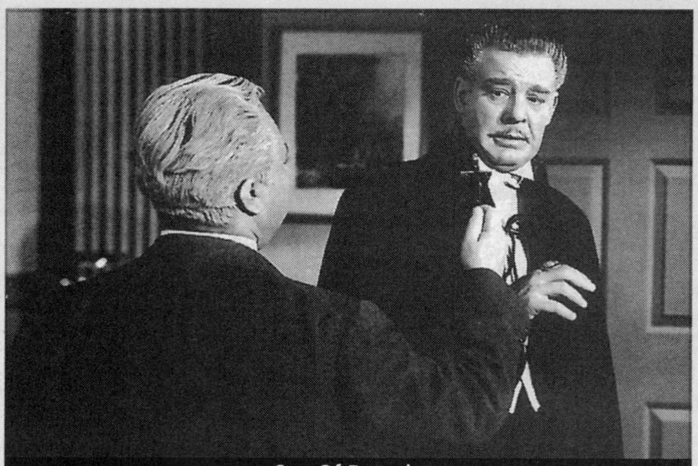

Son Of Dracula

Lon Chaney, Jr.

The Shadow Of Silk Lennox (1935)
An underground nightclub owner is called on the carpet for his dirty dealings by a G-man who has gone undercover. Lon Chaney, Jr., Dean Benton and Jack Mulhall star in this shadowy thriller. 60 min.
09-5107 *$19.99*

The Wolf Man (1941)
"Even a man who is pure in heart and says his prayers by night, may become a wolf when the wolf bane blooms and the autumn moon is bright." Lon Chaney, Jr. is marked with the sign of the beast in the classic chiller. With Claude Rains, Evelyn Ankers, Bela Lugosi and the ever-wizened Maria Ouspenskaya. 70 min.
07-1528 *$14.99*

The Ghost Of Frankenstein (1942)
Lon Chaney, Jr. replaces Boris Karloff as the legendary monster in the eerie fourth entry in Universal's series. Ygor (Bela Lugosi) saves the monster from a sulphur pit and takes him to Baron Frankenstein (Cedric Hardwicke), who plans on giving the creature a "normal" brain. Ralph Bellamy, Lionel Atwill, Evelyn Ankers also star. 68 min.
07-1974 *$14.99*

Frankenstein Meets The Wolf Man (1943)
Cursed lycanthrope Lon Chaney, Jr.'s search for a cure leads him to Castle Frankenstein and a fateful encounter with monster Bela Lugosi. Terrifying team-up also stars Ilona Massey, Maria Ouspenskaya. 72 min.
07-1439 *$14.99*

House Of Frankenstein (1945)
Universal pulled out all the stops for this monster medley that features Boris Karloff as a mad doctor who takes over a travelling sideshow whose main exhibits are the bodies of Dracula (John Carradine) and the Frankenstein Monster (Glenn Strange). Along the way, who should they pick up but the Wolf Man (Lon Chaney, Jr.)! With J. Carrol Naish, Elena Verdugo, Lionel Atwill. 71 min.
07-1824 *$14.99*

House Of Dracula (1945)
A monster-studded effort from Universal Studios in which an understanding doctor tries to cure the Wolf Man (Lon Chaney, Jr.) of his lycanthropy and Dracula (John Carradine) of his vampirism. Madness, and Drac-tainted blood, soon get the best of the good doc, leading him to search for and revive Frankenstein's Monster (Glenn Strange). With Onslow Stevens. 67 min.
07-1982 *$14.99*

Man Made Monster (1941)
Lon Chaney, Jr. makes his horror film debut, playing a carnival sideshow "electric man" who becomes a guinea pig for mad scientist Lionel Atwill's scheme to develop a race of supermen. Atwill adds more juice to Chaney, transforming him into a glowing, indestructible creature. Anne Nagel, Frank Albertson co-star. AKA: "The Electric Man," "The Atomic Monster."
07-2134 *$14.99*

Son Of Dracula (1943)
Lon Chaney, Jr. plays the infamous bloodsucker, travelling through Louisiana as Count Alucard (spell it backwards) and searching for a bride. Atmospheric and often overlooked, this Universal chiller co-stars Louise Allbritton, Evelyn Ankers. 78 min.
07-1574 *$14.99*

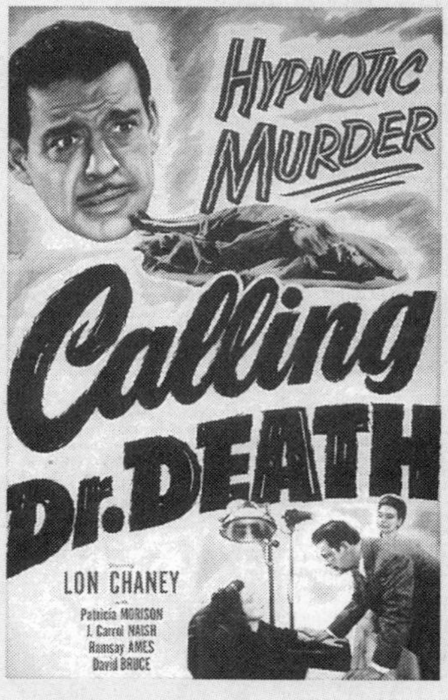

Calling Dr. Death (1943)/ Strange Confession (1945)
In "Calling Dr. Death," the first of six films he made for Universal based on the popular "Inner Sanctum" suspense radio program, Lon Chaney, Jr. plays a respected neurologist who can't remember if he's responsible for his unfaithful wife's murder. J. Carrol Naish, Patricia Morrison co-star. Next, chemist Chaney returns from South America looking for revenge on boss Naish in "Strange Confession," with Brenda Joyce. 125 min. total.
07-2548 Double Feature □*$14.99*

Dead Man's Eyes (1944)/ Pillow Of Death (1945)
After being blinded by acid thrown by jealous model Acquanetta, artist Lon Chaney, Jr.'s only chance at seeing again is a transplant...but does Chaney resort to murder to gain "Dead Man's Eyes?" With Jean Parker, Paul Kelly. Then, Chaney is a murder suspect again, accused of smothering his victims with the "Pillow of Death." Brenda Joyce co-stars. 131 min. total.
07-2549 Double Feature □*$14.99*

Weird Woman (1944)/ The Frozen Ghost (1945)
Based on Fritz Leiber's "Conjure Wife," "Weird Woman" stars Anne Gwynne as the island-raised new wife of professor Lon Chaney, Jr., who comes to believe his bride is using voodoo to get rid of his enemies. Ralph Morgan, Evelyn Ankers also star. The "Inner Sanctum" double bill continues with "The Frozen Ghost," as stage hypnotist Chaney is accused of killing an audience member and takes a job in a wax museum. With Evelyn Ankers, Milburn Stone. 126 min. total.
07-2550 Double Feature □*$14.99*

The Indestructible Man (1956)
Silent but deadly Lon Chaney, Jr. is an electrocuted criminal who, after being restored to life, seeks out the fellow bank robbers who sent him to the chair. Chilling screamer that promises "300,000 volts of horror." 70 min.
08-8076 *$19.99*

Manfish (1956)
A greedy treasure hunter kills and submerges his partner after they find pirate loot in the Caribbean. Picturesque suspenser, based on Poe's "Gold Bug" and "Tell-Tale Heart," stars Victor Jory, Lon Chaney, Jr. 78 min.
68-8219 *$19.99*

The Alligator People (1959)
When Beverly Garland's search for her missing husband in the Louisiana bayou ends with the discovery that he's the victim of a scientist whose limb-regeneration serum turns people into reptilian monsters, will she say "see ya later, alligator" to her scaly spouse? Classic low-budget chiller also stars Richard Crane, George Macready, and Lon Chaney, Jr. as a hook-handed Cajun. 74 min.
04-3670 *$14.99*

Face Of The Screaming Werewolf (1959)
Made as a Mexican horror comedy and re-edited into a straight American chiller for a 1965 re-release, this rare item features Lon Chaney, Jr. as a Mayan mummy who is revived by a thunderstorm and turns out to be a man-wolf beneath his bandages! With Ramon Guy, Rosita Arenas. AKA: "La Casa Del Terror." 60 min.
68-8370 *$14.99*

The Devil's Messenger (1961)
Compiled from three episodes of a Swedish TV show, this film stars Lon Chaney, Jr. as the Devil, who, along with a new female partner, recruits three people to join him in the underworld. Bizarre stuff, co-starring Karen Kadler, Michael Hinn and Gunnel Brostrom. 72 min.
68-8556 *$19.99*

Spider Baby (1964)
AKA "Cannibal Orgy," "The Liver Eaters" and even "The Maddest Story Ever Told," this gory goodie stars Lon Chaney Jr. as the manservant to a family of cannibals who helps out at mealtimes. Wonderful low-budget horror-comedy from director Jack Hill ("Switchblade Sisters") features a title song sung by Chaney himself! With Sid Haig, Carol Ohmart and Mantan Moreland. 80 min.
05-9024 Was $19.99 *$14.99*

Spider Baby: Special Collector's Edition
This remastered edition also includes footage from a 1994 "Spider Baby" reunion with stars Sid Haig and Mary Mitchell, director Jack Hill and host Johnny Legend.
73-9164 *$14.99*

House Of Black Death (1965)
Lon Chaney, Jr. and John Carradine play a pair of warlock brothers (although they never appear on-screen together!) who use their occult powers in a battle of good versus evil in this obscure shocker that also features witch, werewolves and belly dancers. With Tom Drake, Andrea King. AKA: "Blood of the Man Devil," "Night of the Beast." 80 min.
15-5503 *$14.99*

Gallery Of Horror (1967)
It's one portrait of terror and suspense after another when screen scream greats John Carradine and Lon Chaney, Jr. team up to take you on a guided tour of shocks. Among the creepy stories covered are "Spark of Life," "Monster Raid," "King Vampire," "The Witch's Clock" and "Count Alucard." With Rochelle Hudson, Ron Doyle. AKA: "Dr. Terror's Gallery of Horror." 83 min.
71-5001 Letterboxed *$19.99*

DRACULA VS. FRANKENSTEIN

Dracula vs. Frankenstein (1971)
A schlock classic from Al Adamson, highlighted by the battle between a curly-haired, goateed Dracula and a waxy-looking Frankenstein Monster. Horror, suspense, Lon Chaney, Jr., Angelo Rossitto, J. Carrol Naish, Regina Carrol, Russ Tamblyn, Forry Ackerman...what more could bad film fans ask for?
53-5010 *$14.99*

Please see our index for these other Lon Chaney, Jr. titles: *Abbott & Costello Meet Frankenstein • Battles Of Chief Pontiac • Behave Yourself • The Big Chase • Billy The Kid • Bird Of Paradise • The Black Castle • • The Black Pirates • The Black Sleep • Buckskin • The Bushwackers • Casanova's Big Night • Daniel Boone: Trail Blazer • The Defiant Ones • Flame Of Araby • Follow The Boys • Here Come The Co-Eds • The Haunted Palace • High Noon • Hillbillys In A Haunted House • I Died A Thousand Times • Jesse James • A Lion Is In The Streets • The Mummy's Curse • The Mummy's Ghost • The Mummy's Tomb • Overland Mail • Springfield Rifle*

The Beast With Five Fingers (1946)
Classic psychological chiller that relies more on mood than horror. The inhabitants of an isolated Italian villa, gathered for the will reading of a deceased pianist, are haunted by a mysterious entity. Has the dead man's hand come back for revenge? Peter Lorre, Robert Alda, Andrea King, J. Carrol Naish star. 88 min.
12-2471 *$19.99*

The Creeper (1948)
What begins as a medical experiment to aid doctors ends, as such trespassing-into-God's-domain-style projects often do, in terror when a scientist is transformed into a cat-like killer. Onslow Stevens, Ralph Morgan, June Vincent star. 64 min.
27-6632 *$19.99*

Strangler Of The Swamp (1946)
When the citizens of a small town lynch a man for a murder he did not commit, he vows revenge, and the curse of the Strangler begins striking down the guilty. One by one they are dragged down into the swamp to die. Rosemary La Planche, Charles Middleton and future filmmaker Blake Edwards star. 60 min.
45-5117 *$14.99*

The Woman Who Came Back (1945)
A woman believes she has been haunted for centuries by the spirit of a witch. Now, she finally has a chance to break the spell...but will anyone believe her enough to help? Nancy Kelly, Otto Kruger and John Loder star. 69 min.
45-5118 *$14.99*

Devil Bat's Daughter (1946)
Rosemary La Planche is suffering from nightmares in which her father visits her as a vampire thirsting for blood! She consults a psychiatrist, but the dreams grow more and more violent under his care. Could it be true? John James, Michael Hale also star. 66 min.
45-5119 *$14.99*

The Flying Serpent (1946)
Long before "Q," George Zucco played a deranged archeologist who tries to protect his Aztec treasure by summoning Quetzlcoatl, the ancient serpent-bird, to kill all those he believes are after the booty. Zucco places one of the creature's feathers over his intended victims, but he soon gets carried away with the bird bloodbath. With Ralph Lewis. 58 min.
50-8241 *$14.99*

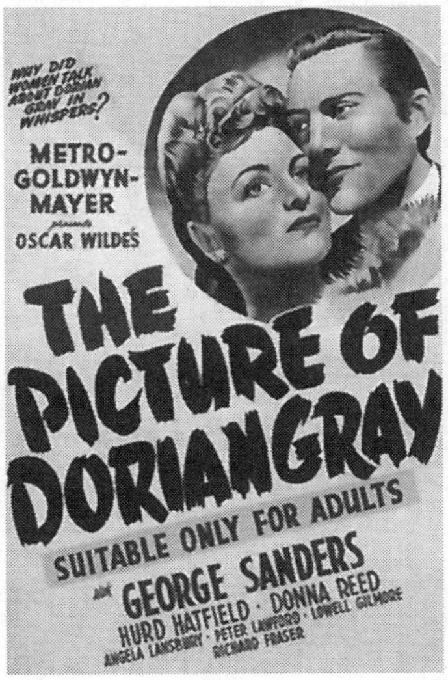

The Picture Of Dorian Gray (1945)
The sensational adaptation of Oscar Wilde's brilliant tale about a man who has an unholy fountain of youth—but his portrait reveals his true nature. George Sanders, Hurd Hatfield, Angela Lansbury; includes Technicolor sequences. 110 min.
12-1413 *$19.99*

Dorian Gray (1970)
Helmut Berger stars in this version of Oscar Wilde's classic "Picture of Dorian Gray," centering on a man who stays young while his portrait grows old. Richard Todd, Herbert Lom. AKA: "The Secret of Dorian Gray." 86 min.
63-1038 *$14.99*

The Picture Of Dorian Gray (1975)
Can the gift of eternal youth and beauty be a curse? It is in this gripping rendition of the Oscar Wilde shocker, produced by "Dark Shadows" creator Dan Curtis. Shane Briant, Nigel Davenport, Linda Kelsey and Charles Aidman star. 111 min.
50-7047 Was $19.99 *$14.99*

The Sins Of Dorian Gray (1983)
The timeless shocker gets a couple of new twists. The time is the 1980s...the attractive young Dorian is a woman (Belinda Bauer)...and it's her screen test that reflects the wear of time and sin while she remains eternally youthful! Anthony Perkins, Joseph Bottoms co-star. 95 min.
04-3149 *□$14.99*

The Monster And The Girl (1941)
When a man framed for murder by gangsters faces execution, a devious doctor persuades him to have his brain put into the body of a gorilla. After the operation, the man-creature goes ape, getting revenge on the hoods responsible for his death and his sister's involvement with prostitution. Paul Lukas, Ellen Drew and George Zucco star in this atmospheric creeper.
07-2139 *$14.99*

The Vampire's Ghost (1945)
Doomed by an ancient curse to roam the Earth throughout eternity, a centuries-old vampire menaces the west coast of Africa by night (and by day with the use of sunglasses) in this chiller. John Abbott, Grant Withers, Charles Gordon. 59 min.
10-7165 *$19.99*

Latin Quarter (1946)
In a Paris artist's community, a sculptor goes berserk over his wife's infidelity and kills her, plastering the body into his newest statue. Creepy suspense tale stars Derrick de Marney and Joan Greenwood. AKA: "Frenzy." 85 min.
68-8161 *$19.99*

House Of Darkness (1948)
A shocker from Britain starring Laurence Harvey as a man so obsessed with acquiring his stepbrother's mansion that he kills him, but then descends into madness prompted by disturbing visions of his victim's ghost. Leslie Brooks, John Stuart also star.
68-8928 *$19.99*

The Black Raven (1943)
A lonely roadside inn welcomes Death as a guest in this chilling story of maniacal murders among some stranded travellers. George Zucco, Charles Middleton, Noel Madison, Wanda McKay and Glenn Strange star. 65 min.
10-1139 Was $19.99 *$14.99*

Bluebeard (1944)
John Carradine stars in this harrowing tale about a 19th-century artist in Paris who cannot control his urge to kill his models once he has painted their portraits. Co-stars Jean Parker, Nils Asther; directed by Edgar G. Ulmer. 71 min.
10-3034 Was $19.99 *$14.99*

The Mad Monster (1942)
Demented scientist George Zucco's experiment goes haywire when an injection of wolf's blood transforms a big, slow-witted farmboy into a bloodthirsty monster in overalls. Shot-on-a-shoestring horror was filmed in five days to capitalize on Universal's success with "The Wolf Man." Co-stars Glenn Strange in his horror debut. 77 min.
10-7156 Was $19.99 *$14.99*

The Mad Ghoul (1943)
Diabolical but distinguished professor George Zucco discovers a life-preserving gas used by the ancient Egyptians and administers it on his young assistant when he discovers they're in love with the same woman. The stuff turns the assistant into a mummifying zombie, easily open to suggestions that he kill people or drop his engagement plans. Evelyn Ankers, David Bruce also star.
07-2135 *$14.99*

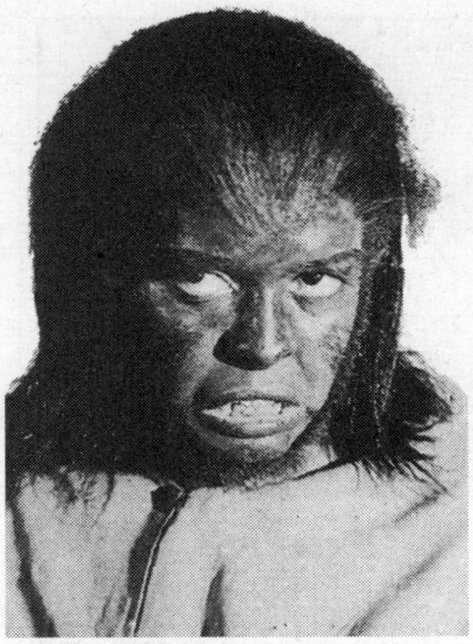

Captive Wild Woman (1943)
The first of three Universal "ape woman" chillers finds mad scientist John Carradine injecting an orangutan with a dying woman's blood, turning it into a beautiful she-creature that turns back into her murderous anthropoid state when her jealous streak is aroused. Evelyn Ankers, Milburn Stone, and Acquanetta as "Paula" co-star. 61 min.
07-2138 *□$14.99*

Jungle Woman (1944)
The alluring Aquanetta returns as half-woman, half-ape Paula, revived from death by doctor J. Carrol Naish to continue her deadly rampage that starts when jealousy turns her into a bloodthirsty jungle beast. With Evelyn Ankers, Milburn Stone and Douglas Dumbrille. 61 min.
07-2657 *$14.99*

Jungle Captive (1945)
This second sequel to "Captive Wild Woman" finds a new scientist (Otto Kruger) bringing Paula the Ape Woman (Vicky Lane) back to life, with plans to transplant his secretary's brain into the pulchritudinous primate's body. With Amelita Ward, Phil Brown, and Rondo Hatton as Kruger's assistant, Moloch. 64 min.
07-2656 *$14.99*

The Monster Maker (1944)
A deranged doctor infects a concert pianist with acromegaly germs, turning him into a deformed monster, and promises to cure him if he is given the victim's daughter's hand in marriage. J. Carrol Naish, Ralph Morgan, Wanda McKay star; from the director of "Terror of Tiny Town." 62 min.
09-1890 Was $19.99 *$14.99*

The Ghost Of Rashmon Hall (1947)
Eerie British ghost epic about a doctor who tries to rid his house of the spirits of a sailor, his wife and her lover. With Valentine Dyall and Ann Howard. AKA: "Night Comes Too Soon." 52 min.
68-8435 Was $19.99 *$14.99*

The Undying Monster (1942)
The heir to a British estate is afflicted with the curse of the werewolf and begins stalking the moors in search of prey. Atmospheric chiller, made to cash in on "The Wolf Man's" success, stars John Howard, Heather Angel, Bramwell Fletcher. 63 min.
10-7404 *$19.99*

Man With Two Lives (1942)
After a wealthy young man is killed in a car accident, he is restored to life at the same moment a gangster is executed. Their souls are switched and the young man is turned into a killer. Edward Norris, Marloi Dwyer star. 65 min.
10-8336 Was $19.99 *$14.99*

Dead Men Walk (1943)
Can you imagine dead men coming back from their graves to haunt their murderers? Well, they did a lot of that back in the '40s. George Zucco (in a dual role), Mary Carlisle and Dwight Frye star in this creepy, atmospheric, horror gem. 72 min.
08-1242 *$14.99*

King Of The Zombies (1941)
Campy fun by the ton as veteran mad doc George Zucco turns black men into automatons that follow the evil whims of Nazi subversives. With Dick Purcell, Henry Victor, Joan Woodbury, and, yes, Mantan Moreland. 67 min.
09-1344 *$19.99*

She-Wolf Of London (1946)
The foggy streets of London; watched over by constables, fussed over by tourists...and ravaged by a werewolf. A young woman rumored to have inherited her family's curse of lycanthropy believes she's responsible for the killings...but is she? June Lockhart, Don Porter and Sara Haden star. 62 min.
07-2659 *$14.99*

Werewolf Of London (1935)
The first attempt by Universal to add a lycanthrope to its stable of screen monsters, this chiller stars Henry Hull as a botanist who is attacked in Tibet by a wolfman and returns to his native England to find he has inherited the mark of the beast. Warner Oland, Valerie Hobson co-star. 75 min.
07-1829 *$14.99*

Dracula (Spanish-Language Version) (1931)
Filmed at night (how appropriate!) on the same Universal lots as the Bela Lugosi film being made simultaneously, this all-Spanish version of the horror classic was thought lost for decades. Lupita Tovar, Carmen Guerrero, and Carlos Villarias in the title role star in this chiller, hailed for its daringly erotic style and moody atmosphere. 104 min. Subtitled in English.
07-1830 *$14.99*

King Kong (1933)
Beauty meets beast atop the Empire State Building in one of fantasy cinema's finest moments, as the giant ape runs amok in New York. Fay Wray, Bruce Cabot, Robert Armstrong and "Kong, The Eighth Wonder of the World," star; special effects by Willis O'Brien. Restored version; 100 min.
05-1319 *$19.99*

The Son Of Kong (1933)
The adventure was still there, but the tone was much lighter in this sequel. Showman Carl Denham (Robert Armstrong) returns to Skull Island in search of a hidden treasure, but along the way he also finds Kong's friendlier offspring, a 25-foot albino ape. With Helen Mack, Frank Reicher. 70 min.
05-1123 *$19.99*

Mighty Joe Young (1949)
The producers of "King Kong" re-teamed with effects wizard Willis O'Brien for this classic tale of a showman who discovers a 10-foot-tall ape and the young woman who raised him in Africa and brings them back to America. Robert Armstrong, Terry Moore, Ben Johnson star. This special video edition includes the color-tinted orphanage fire scene, not seen since the film's first release. 94 min.
18-7135 Restored *$19.99*

Konga (1961)
You'll go ape over this Saturday matinee favorite from the 1960s featuring Michael Gough as a British scientist who discovers a serum that transforms a lab chimp into a gorilla. By hypnotizing the creature, Gough gets it to kill his enemies, and then it terrorizes London when it grows to king-size (or is that "Kong-size"?) proportions. With Margo Johns, Jess Conrad.
12-3320 *$14.99*

King Of Kong Island (1968)
Remote-control devices help turn monstrous gorillas into robots, but this practice is threatened when one of the descendants of King Kong tries to put a stop to the nefarious experiments. A Spanish-made shocker with Brad Harris, Marc Lawrence. AKA: "Eve the Savage Venus," "Eve the Wild Woman," "Kong Island."
08-1064 *$19.99*

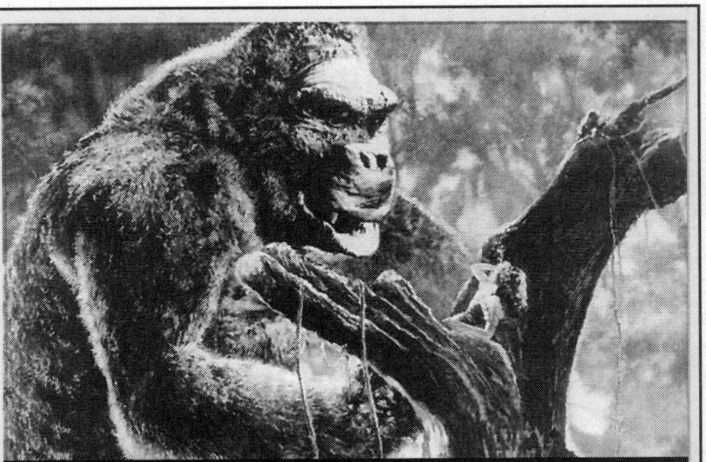
King Kong

The Mighty Gorga (1970)
At last...the world's wackiest monstrous monkey movie is on video! Desperate circus owner Anthony Eisley and great white huntress Megan Timothy head to the Congo in search of "a rare species of giant ape." Before they find Gorga,though, they must contend with a lost white tribe wearing Indian costumes who worship the hairy critter. With Scott Brady, Kent Taylor and Megan Timothy.
79-6416 Was $24.99 *$19.99*

King Kong (1976)
The Academy Award-winning remake of the timeless adventure. Jessica Lange, in her film debut, stars as the beauty who ensnares the 50-foot beast. Features a fight to the death atop the World Trade Towers as Kong battles Army helicopters. 134 min.
06-1029 *□$14.99*

King Kong Lives (1986)
Everybody's gonna cry "Watch out," because the mightiest monster of them all survived his 1976 plunge off the World Trade Center! The comatose Kong needs an artificial heart to survive—and a compatible blood donor is found when a giant female ape is discovered! Brian Kerwin, Linda Hamilton, John Ashton star. 105 min.
40-1305 *$12.99*

Mighty Peking Man (1977)
What happens when Hong Kong's film industry tries to rip off "King Kong"? You get this wild, off-the-wall thriller about an expedition into the Himalayan wilderness that finds not only a giant "missing link" to bring back, but a blonde, scantily-clad jungle woman who is the ape-like creature's only friend! Danny Lee, Evelyne Kraft star. AKA: "Goliathon." 90 min.
11-2426 Was $99.99 *□$19.99*

Crimes At The Dark House

Tod Slaughter

Murder In The Old Red Barn (1935)
English film actor Tod Slaughter appears in this adaptation of a popular stage melodrama, based on true events. A virtuous housemaid must defend herself from the lecherous advances of her evil employer, the local squire, until events lead to murder. AKA: "Maria Marten." 67 min.
68-8017 *$19.99*

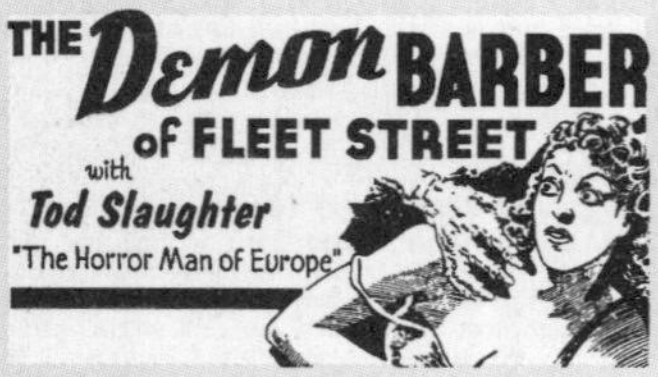
THE Demon BARBER
of FLEET STREET
with
Tod Slaughter
"The Horror Man of Europe"

The Demon Barber Of Fleet Street (1936)
Decades before the Broadway musical, British horror king Tod Slaughter starred as the razor-wielding Sweeney Todd. This dramatic rendition of the British folk tale may not have songs, but there are plenty of chills as Tod(d) knocks off client after client! 82 min.
15-5014 *$14.99*

The Ticket Of Leave Man (1937)
British crime thriller stars Tod Slaughter as "The Tiger," a ruthless criminal mastermind who baffles the police at every turn, only to be undone by a beautiful woman. 71 min.
09-1714 Was $29.99 *$24.99*

Crimes Of Stephen Hawke (1937)
Horror master Tod Slaughter is the king's money-lender, a fiend known as "The Spinebreaker" for the occasional rack of delinquent customer he serves up in his dungeon. And, they have to give back the toaster. Dusty, lurid camp thrills!
68-8026 *$19.99*

Never Too Late To Mend (1937)
A big, showy melodrama from "The Horror Man of Europe," Tod Slaughter. A rebuffed older suitor for a pretty maiden dispatches his rival by sending him to the prison he administers and delegates a brutal routine of torture. AKA: "It's Never Too Late to Mend." 67 min.
09-2311 Was $19.99 *$14.99*

The Face At The Window (1939)
In another gorged melodrama from the early English master of the form, Tod Slaughter and his deformed brother terrorize Paris, to draw police attention away from their real purpose—a daring bank robbery. 65 min.
68-8036 *$19.99*

Crimes At The Dark House (1940)
Wilkie Collins' "The Woman in White" served as the basis for this atmospheric mood piece about an insidious count (Tod Slaughter) who enlists the aid of a mental asylum escapee to double as the wife he murdered. Co-stars Hilary Eaves. 69 min.
10-7169 *$19.99*

The Curse Of The Wraydons (1946)
Tod Slaughter is the filmmaker behind this creepy tale of a former spy once defeated by Napoleon who has become a crazed inventor. Adopting the name "Springheeled Jack," he seeks revenge on the family of his brother. With Slaughter, Bruce Seton and Gabriel Toyne. 94 min.
09-5048 *$19.99*

The Greed Of William Hart (1948)
In this shocker, based on the infamous Burke and Hare, Tod Slaughter is a graverobber supplying cadavers to Edinburgh's medical students. When the fresh graves are empty, he helps death along a bit by murdering some of the local lowlife. 78 min.
68-8021 *$19.99*

Get That Girl (1932)
An action-packed thriller in which Richard Talmadge plays a guy who tries to save young heiress Shirley Grey from a mad doctor looking to perfect a process that turns people into mannequins. AKA: "Fear Mansion."
10-9091 Was $19.99 *$14.99*

Condemned To Live (1935)
A very unusual "B-Horror" film, produced by an independent film company but filmed on Universal's set. Ralph Morgan stars as the kindly village doctor who fears he may be the vampire killer who's been stalking the town. Mischa Auer, Maxine Doyle. 68 min.
01-1367 *$19.99*

After Dark (1932)
British-made "old dark house" thriller about some crooks who come to a creepy country estate in search of the stolen jewels they hid in an antique clock. Hugh Williams, Gretha Hansen, Ian Fleming star.
68-9225 *$19.99*

Secret Of The Loch (1934)
The first "talkie" about the Loch Ness monster stars Seymour Hicks as a loopy Scottish scientist who spots the famous serpent and Frederick Peisley as the reporter he convinces to go diving after it. 80 min.
68-8162 *$19.99*

The Monster Walks (1932)
A tour de force of chilling clichés, including suspicious cripples, weird servants, house guests, and a screaming gorilla hidden in the basement. Rex Lease, Vera Reynolds, Mischa Auer and Willie Best star in this campy old-house thriller. 63 min.
17-1070 Was $19.99 *$14.99*

Revolt Of The Zombies (1936)
Shuddersome horror, courtesy of the makers of "White Zombie." During World War I, an explorer (Dean Jagger) discovers the key to churning out zombie soldiers for the French army. 62 min.
18-3036 Was $19.99 *$14.99*

The Living Dead (1938)
Awe-inspiring and unusual shocker from Britain has a mad doctor methodically killing off people, amassing a fortune in insurance money and then rejuvenating his victims. Stars Gerald du Maurier and George Curzon. 63 min.
10-7059 Was $19.99 *$14.99*

The Ghost Walks (1934)
An ambitious playwright concocts an extravagant scheme to have his latest work produced...a scheme that backfires when the make-believe terrors he had planned become all too real. Stars John Miljan and June Collyer. 69 min.
10-7155 *$19.99*

The Love Wanga (1935)
A light-skinned voodoo priestess in Haiti falls for a white plantation owner, but when he spurns her affections for a beautiful socialite she uses the magicks at her command to put her rival in a coma and send zombies to kidnap her. A rarely seen "walking dead" shocker, starring Fredi Washington and Sheldon Leonard (as a black Haitian!). 56 min.
79-5517 *$19.99*

Midnight At Madame Tussaud's (1936)
A wealthy financier makes a wager that he can spend the night in the Chamber of Horrors at Madame Tussaud's Wax Museum, but the bet turns to something far more sinister when he finds himself the object of a murder scheme. Filmed at the actual London landmark. AKA: "Midnight at the Wax Museum." 66 min.
68-8033 *$19.99*

Mad Love (1935)
A classic of Hollywood horror, director Karl Freund's remake of "The Hands of Orlac" stars Peter Lorre (in his first American film) as a deranged doctor obsessed with an actress in Paris' gory Grand Guignol theatre. When her pianist husband loses his hands in an accident, Lorre transplants the limbs of an executed killer and attempts to make the couple think that the hands have a will of their own. Colin Clive, Frances Drake co-star. 68 min.
12-2473 *$19.99*

Dracula's Daughter (1936)
The moody and rarely-seen sequel to the 1931 Bela Lugosi classic (it starts out right where that film left off) stars Gloria Holden in the title role. Desiring to be cured of her vampirism, she goes to a doctor for help but winds up wanting him to become her undead consort. With Otto Kruger, Marguerite Churchill, and Edward Van Sloan as Dr. Van Helsing. 70 min.
07-1823 *$14.99*

Dr. Jekyll And Mr. Hyde (1932)
Fredric March earned an Academy Award for his work as the unfortunate physician and his brutish alter ego. Rouben Mamoulian's famed shocker also stars Miriam Hopkins, Rose Hobart. Original release print runs 97 min.
12-1922 *$19.99*

The Strange Case Of Dr. Jekyll & Mr. Hyde (1968)
Jack Palance stars as the mild-mannered scientist whose experiments in the nature of human evil unleash his brutish dark side and soon begin to control his life. With Oscar Homolka, Billie Whitelaw, Denholm Elliott. 120 min.
50-7045 Was $19.99 *$14.99*

The Strange Case Of Dr. Jekyll And Mr. Hyde (1989)
Chilling production of Stevenson's timeless terror tale stars Anthony Andrews as the good doctor who learns to unleash his bestial side and Laura Dern as the woman whose love for him may doom her. 60 min.
19-7067 Was $59.99 *$14.99*

Jekyll & Hyde (1990)
The time-honored tale of man's struggle between good and evil is vividly portrayed in this spine-tingling production featuring Michael Caine in the title roles of Dr. Henry Jekyll and his amoral counterpart. With Cheryl Ladd, Joss Ackland. 95 min.
68-1346 Was $89.99 *$14.99*

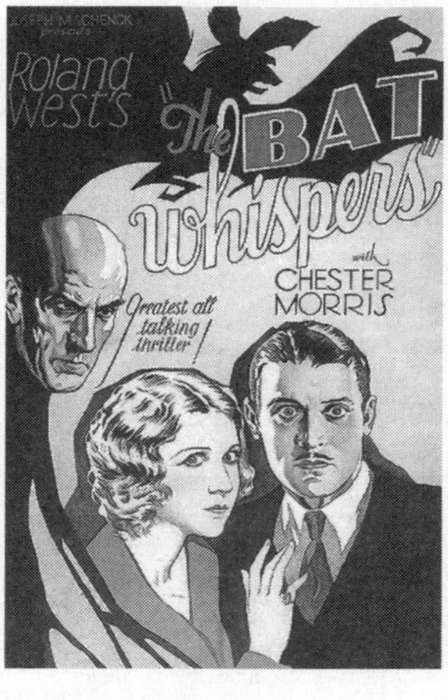
Roland West's
The BAT Whispers
with
CHESTER MORRIS
Greatest all talking thriller!

The Bat Whispers (1930)
The bat-masked baddie in this thriller, the first sound filming of Mary Roberts Rinehart's horror play, helped to inspire Batman's creation. A gothic mansion is the setting for mystery and terror as a wealthy spinster tries to learn a mysterious thief's identity. Chester Morris and Una Merkel star; directed by Roland West. This restored edition is presented in the original letterboxed edition, an example of an early photographic experiment. 88 min.
80-5030 Letterboxed *$29.99*

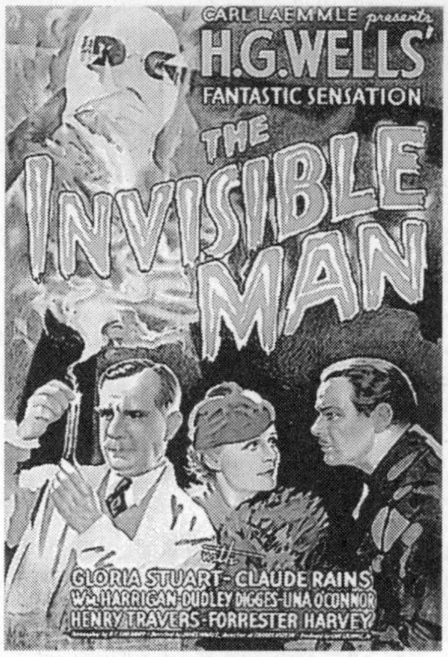
CARL LAEMMLE presents
H.G. WELLS'
FANTASTIC SENSATION
THE INVISIBLE MAN
GLORIA STUART - CLAUDE RAINS
WM. HARRIGAN - DUDLEY DIGGES - UNA O'CONNOR
HENRY TRAVERS - FORRESTER HARVEY

The Invisible Man (1933)
He's rarely seen in this, his film debut, but Claude Rains lends a sinister presence as H.G. Wells' "out of sight" scientist. Horror/fantasy classic also stars Gloria Stuart, William Harrigan, and quintessential town biddy Una O'Connor; James Whale ("Frankenstein") directs. 71 min.
07-1495 *$14.99*

The Invisible Man Returns (1940)
Actually, Vincent Price plays the brother of the original Unseen One. When he's framed for murder, Price has a scientist friend inject him with an invisibility serum so he can search undetected for the real killer. Great effects highlight this sequel; with Nan Grey, Cedric Hardwicke, John Dutton. 81 min.
07-1825 *$14.99*

Invisible Agent (1942)
The "Invisible Man" in this outing is a scientist's son who takes a special formula and travels to Europe to stop the Nazis' nefarious plan to attack America. See cigarettes floating in mid-air! Watch as Nazi soldiers get kicked in the rear by an unseen presence! Witness Peter Lorre as an evil Japanese officer! With Jon Hall, Ilona Massey, Sir Cedric Hardwicke. 82 min.
07-1978 *$14.99*

The Invisible Man's Revenge (1944)
A criminal enlists the aid of a scientist to turn him invisible so he can terrorize a wealthy couple in the hopes of gaining their fortune and their daughter. Jon Hall, Evelyn Ankers, Alan Curtis and John Carradine star in this creepy Universal production.
07-2136 *$14.99*

The Devil Doll (1936)
Horror classic from Tod Browning ("Dracula") stars Lionel Barrymore as a prison escapee who sends unique assassins after the men who wronged him...human beings shrunken to 12 inches high! Splendid special effects in this shocker, co-starring Maureen O'Sullivan, Henry B. Walthall. 79 min.
12-1729 *$19.99*

The Sphinx (1933)
Lionel Atwill ("Doctor X") deftly performs the dual role of a society-wheeling philanthropist and the deaf-mute brother he uses as an alibi for his secret murder spree. Sheila Terry, Theodore Newton also star. 63 min.
68-8009 *$19.99*

Murders In The Zoo (1933)
A demented zoologist dispenses of his amorous wife's lovers in a number of unsettling ways, including sewing their lips and leaving them in the desert for snakes to attack, while plotting to dump his spouse into a pool of crocodiles. Lionel Atwill, Charlie Ruggles, Randolph Scott and Gail Patrick star. 62 min.
07-2292 *$14.99*

A Woman Condemned (1934)
A famous singer suddenly disappears, only to be found murdered. A mysterious blonde is under suspicion for the killing, but when a reporter sets out to clear her name the trail leads to a sanitarium run by a mad scientist. Richard Hemingway, Lola Lane, Claudia Dell, Jason Robards and Mischa Auer star.
68-9261 *$19.99*

Mystery Of The Wax Museum (1933)
Lionel Atwill stars as the demented, crippled wax sculptor who discovers a gruesome shortcut to making his mannequins in this, the original "House of Wax." Terrific sets and two-color Technicolor are standouts. Fay Wray, Glenda Farrell, Frank McHugh star. 77 min.
12-1727 *$19.99*

Universal Studios Classic Monster Collection
How many scares, screams and shudders can you pack into one boxed set? Try this creepy eight-tape collection that includes "Bride of Frankenstein," "Creature from the Black Lagoon," "Dracula," "Frankenstein," "The Invisible Man," "The Mummy," "Phantom of the Opera" and "The Wolf Man."
07-2788 Save $20.00! *$99.99*

Bela Lugosi

The Deerslayer (1920)
In this silent version of James Fenimore Cooper's classic story, Bela Lugosi plays the courageous Indian warrior Chingachgook. The film details the adventures of a young boy raised by the Mohicans who helps a group of settlers against attacking Indians. Emile Mamelock also stars.
68-9137 *$19.99*

Daughter Of The Night (1921)
Long thought lost, this early Bela Lugosi thriller casts Bela as a French aristocrat who falls for a Soviet singer. Little does he know that she's actually the Russian underground's top spy. With Lee Parry, Violette Napierska. Silent with musical score.
68-9138 *$19.99*

Dracula (1931)
After starring in the title role on Broadway, Bela Lugosi became forever identified with the blood-sucking count in director Tod Browning's Gothic film adaptation. Follow Dracula from his Transylvanian castle to England as he ensnares the unwary in his diabolical schemes. With Dwight Frye, Helen Chandler, Edward Van Sloan. 75 min.
07-1007 *$14.99*

Dracula (New Musical Score)
The classic chiller is also available with an original musical score composed by Philip Glass and performed by the Kronos Quartet.
07-2773 *$14.99*

Murders In The Rue Morgue (1932)
Loosely based on the Poe story, this eerie and expressionistic horror piece stars Bela Lugosi as the mad Dr. Mirakle, whose Paris sideshow is a front for his bizarre experiments that involve kidnapping beautiful young women and injecting them with blood from his pet gorilla. Sidney Fox, Bert Roach co-star. 61 min.
07-1827 *$14.99*

Island Of Lost Souls (1932)
Inspired by an H.G. Wells story, this frightening horror classic stars Charles Laughton as the demented Dr. Moreau, who attempts to evolve animals into hideous human-like mutants in his "House of Pain." With Bela Lugosi, Richard Arlen, Kathleen Burke; sharp-eyed viewers can look for Buster Crabbe, Alan Ladd and Randolph Scott among the "ani-men." 71 min.
07-1983 *$14.99*

White Zombie (1932)
An overlooked but impressively moody early horror film set on a Haitian plantation whose workers are members of that most elite of clubs, the "living dead." Bela Lugosi stars as the leader of the zombies; with Madge Bellamy, Robert Frazer. 73 min.
68-8383 Was $19.99 *$14.99*

White Zombie (Color Version)
Forget the "white" part. Bela and his army of undead followers are a colorful crew, indeed, in this techno-tinted edition.
63-1521 *$19.99*

The Death Kiss (1933)
A movie studio is shrouded in mystery when its top star is murdered on the set, and everyone is a suspect. Bela Lugosi plays a temperamental actor who's the most likely suspect, alongside "Dracula" co-stars Edward Van Sloan, David Manners. This restored print features hand-tinted color sequences. 75 min.
08-5011 Was $19.99 *$14.99*

Chandu On The Magic Island (1934)
Condensed feature taken from the classic "Return of Chandu" serial starring Bela Lugosi at his best, saving the leading lady and using his mystical powers to become invisible. Do those sets look familiar? They did to King Kong. 67 min.
09-1350 Was $29.99 *$19.99*

The Raven (1935)
Grand exercise in terror and suspense stars Bela Lugosi as a plastic surgeon obsessed with the works of Poe and a beautiful patient who spurns his advances. Lugosi invites the woman, her fiancé and her father to his retreat and, with the aid of a criminal (Boris Karloff) he disfigured, imprisons and tortures them. With Irene Ware, Samuel Hinds. 62 min.
07-1837 *$14.99*

Murder By Television (1935)
A master electronics wizard and television inventor is murdered during a demonstration of T.V. Bela Lugosi is sinister in this campy whodunit. 55 min.
10-4021 Was $19.99 *$14.99*

The Mysterious Mr. Wong (1935)
Great mystery-adventure stars Bela Lugosi as a malevolent mandarin with an arcane scheme for conquest and Wallace Ford as the hard-nosed reporter who's out to stop him. 62 min.
62-1269 *$19.99*

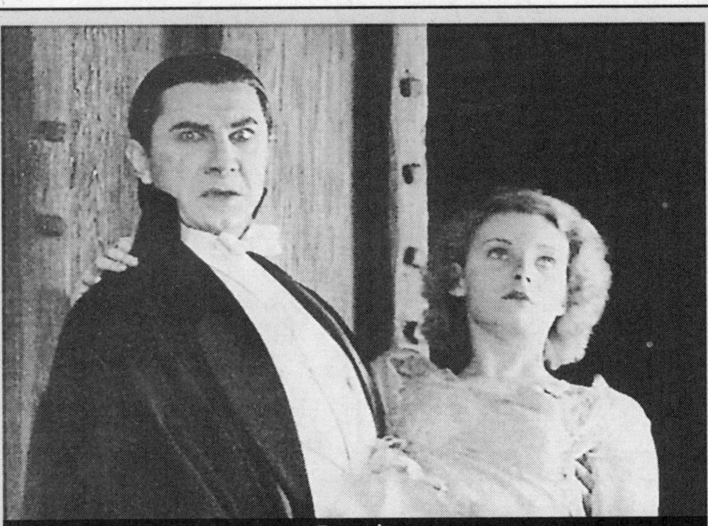
Dracula

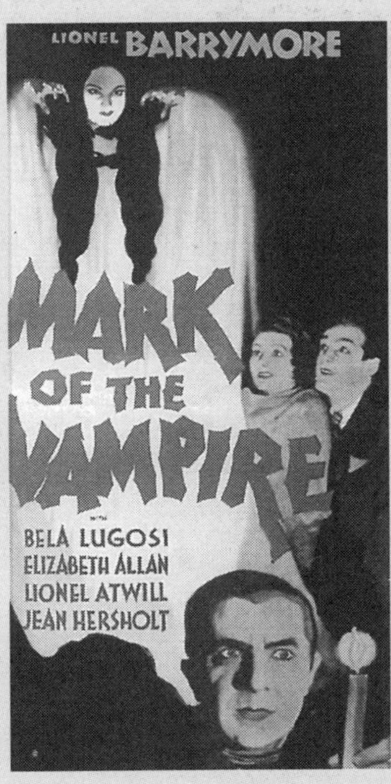

Mark Of The Vampire (1935)
Director Tod Browning helmed this chilling remake of his silent film "London After Midnight." Vampire hunter Lionel Barrymore arrives in a village terrified by a supposedly undead family (led by Bela Lugosi) living in a spooky castle where a murder victim was drained of blood. Atmospheric horror gem also stars Lionel Atwill, Elizabeth Allan, Carol Borland. 61 min.
12-1728 *$19.99*

Phantom Ship (1936)
Real-life maritime mystery of a 19th-century British freighter whose crew vanished in mid-ocean. Bela Lugosi stars. AKA: "The Mystery of the Mary Celeste." 64 min.
10-4025 *$19.99*

Postal Inspector (1936)
Ricardo Cortez stars as the hero of one of the government's unsung branches, hot on the trail of mail thief Bela Lugosi. Unusual crime thriller features a look at quack medical projects actually sold through the mail and newsreel footage of '30s floods in the eastern U.S. With Patricia Ellis, Hattie McDaniel. 60 min.
68-8005 Was $19.99 *$14.99*

The Human Monster (1939)
Moody thriller, based on an Edgar Wallace story, stars Bela Lugosi as the diabolical Dr. Orloff, who takes in blind vagrants and then tortures and kills them for the insurance money. With Greta Gynt, Hugh Williams. AKA: "Dead Eyes of London." 73 min.
08-1233 Was $19.99 *$14.99*

The Phantom Creeps (1939)
Bela Lugosi stars as the fiendish scientist Dr. Zorka, whose discovery of a mysterious substance from a fallen meteorite could spell doom for the free world. Action and danger with Robert Kent, Regis Toomey. 75 min.
10-3038 *$19.99*

The Gorilla (1939)
Haunted house hi-jinx with the Ritz Brothers as bumbling private eyes investigating a series of murders. Their main suspect...a gorilla? Patsy Kelly helps with the laughs; Lionel Atwill and Bela Lugosi supply the chills. 63 min.
62-1211 *$19.99*

The Black Cat (1941)
A group of conniving relatives gathers to wait for their wealthy aunt to die so they can collect the inheritance. One of them isn't that patient and murders her, but this is only the start of the killing of both heirs and the old woman's dozens of cats—who must die before the money is released—in this horror/comedy. Basil Rathbone, Hugh Herbert, Gladys Cooper, Alan Ladd, and Bela Lugosi as the estate's caretaker star. 71 min.
07-2658 *$14.99*

The Invisible Ghost (1941)
Bela Lugosi stars as a doctor unnerved by the apparent reappearance of his late wife. What follows is a web of deception, murder and terror. Betty Compson, Peggy Ann Young and Clarence Muse co-star. 64 min.
09-1782 Was $19.99 *$14.99*

Devil Bat (1941)
Kindly country doctor Bela Lugosi is not suspected to be the crazy fiend who trains his bats to attack anyone wearing a certain perfume. Also starring Dave O'Brien, of "Reefer Madness" fame. AKA: "Killer Bat." 69 min.
18-3024 Was $19.99 *$14.99*

Night Monster (1942)
In this thriller set in a spooky manor, a man whose legs have been amputated and who now wears fake limbs stalks the doctors responsible for his handicap. Ralph Morgan, Bela Lugosi and Lionel Atwill star. 73 min.
07-2293 *$14.99*

The Corpse Vanishes (1942)
Bela Lugosi is great in this horror tale of a sinister mad scientist who kidnaps and murders brides in order to rejuvenate his aging wife. Luana Walters, Minerva Urecal and Angelo Rossitto also star. 64 min.
10-3035 Was $19.99 *$14.99*

Bowery At Midnight (1942)
Creepy mystery starring Bela Lugosi as a psychology professor who uses a mission as a front for his criminal deeds. When people become aware of his activities, Lugosi has them killed and buried in a basement, then revives them with a special drug. John Archer and Wanda McKay co-star. 60 min.
17-9005 Was $19.99 *$14.99*

The Return Of The Vampire (1943)
Bloodsucker Bela Lugosi is on the prowl in war-torn London, starting his own bloody blitzkrieg in this effective low-budget chiller that also stars Nina Foch and Matt Willis as Lugosi's werewolf henchman. 69 min.
02-2705 *$14.99*

The Ape Man (1943)
Bela Lugosi is the doctor monkeying around with the forces of Nature, only to turn into a rampaging man-beast in this low-budget shocker from William "One Shot" Beaudine ("Billy the Kid vs. Dracula"). 64 min.
10-4001 Was $19.99 *$14.99*

One Body Too Many (1944)
Jack Haley, Jean Parker, Bela Lugosi. Mystery spoof in an eerie old house where an unknown murderer and a corpse keep popping up. 75 min.
18-3012 Was $19.99 *$14.99*

Scared To Death (1947)
A mad hypnotist, his dwarf sidekick, and a dead woman who relates the eerie circumstances that led to her demise all make for an eerie tale of horror. Bela Lugosi, George Zucco, Joyce Compton, Angelo Rossitto star; Lugosi's only color film. 67 min.
63-1518 Was $19.99 *$14.99*

Vampire Over London (1951)
The last entry in Britain's "Old Mother Riley" comedy series features Bela Lugosi as a coffin-sleeping scientist who just needs fuel for his robot, then look out, London! Arthur Lucan reprises his role as boisterous Irish charwoman Riley. AKA: "Mother Riley Meets the Vampire," "My Son, the Vampire." 74 min.
68-8001 Was $19.99 *$14.99*

Bela Lugosi Meets A Brooklyn Gorilla (1952)
What could possibly top a title like that? Mad scientist Bela needs human subjects he can turn into apes, when who should turn up at his jungle lab but Duke Mitchell and Sammy Petrillo, two Martin and Lewis clones whose act was the subject of several lawsuits. Reportedly filmed in two weeks for $20,000...and it shows! AKA: "The Boys from Brooklyn." 72 min.
09-1238 Was $19.99 *$14.99*

The Black Sleep (1956)
An all-star horror cast (Basil Rathbone, Bela Lugosi, Lon Chaney, Jr., John Carradine, Akim Tamiroff, Tor Johnson) is featured in this spooky tale of a 19th-century doctor who specializes in bizarre experiments and his castle full of mutants, madmen and other "victims." AKA: "Dr. Cadman's Secret." 80 min.
17-3017 *$19.99*

Mondo Lugosi
Acquaint yourself with the man behind the cape with this inquiring look at the famed Hungarian bloodsucker who chilled millions with his portrayal of Dracula. Contains rarely seen interviews, film clips and a sketch from "You Asked for It!" 60 min.
15-5040 *$19.99*

Bela Lugosi: Then And Now!
The man who played Dracula led an incredible, and often sad, life, and this program offers insight into his world with visits to his Hollywood homes and the studios where he did his work. Conrad Brooks, one of Bela's co-stars in "Plan 9 from Outer Space," adds insightful anecdotes about Lugosi the man and the legend. 50 min.
50-2239 *$19.99*

Please see our index for these other Bela Lugosi titles: *Black Dragons • Black Friday • Bride Of The Monster • Glen Or Glenda (I Changed My Sex) • Frankenstein Meets The Wolf Man • The Ghost Of Frankenstein • Ghosts On The Loose • International House • The Invisible Ray • Ninotchka • Plan 9 From Outer Space • The Return Of Chandu • The Saint's Double Trouble • Shadow Of Chinatown • Son Of Frankenstein • Spooks Run Wild • The Whispering Shadow • The Wolf Man • You'll Find Out*

Doctor X (1932)
Early horror classic stars Lionel Atwill as a Long Island researcher suspected to be responsible for a series of gory slayings. Remarkable sets, makeup, early Technicolor, and Fay Wray hollering away in this Grand Guignol great, co-starring Preston Foster, Lee Tracy, Mae Busch. 80 min.
12-1726 *$19.99*

The Vampire Bat (1933)
Top-notch cast, featuring Lionel Atwill, Dwight Frye, Melvyn Douglas and Fay Wray, in a spooky tale of a mad doctor murdering townspeople to find a substitute for blood. If you like "Famous Monsters of Filmland," you'll cherish this horror classic. 60 min.
17-1089 *$19.99*

The Crime Of Dr. Crespi (1936)
A loose treatment of Edgar Allan Poe's "The Premature Burial" with Erich von Stroheim as a mad scientist who finds a unique way to stop his romantic rival: inject him with a serum, leaving him in suspended animation, then bury him alive. Dwight Frye and Paul Guilfoyle also star. 61 min.
53-6051 *$29.99*

Ouanga (1935)
In this rarely seen, all-black fright film, a voodoo princess conjures a death spell for the fiancée of the man she loves. When that fails, she calls on two zombies to rise from their graves and kill the girl. Fredi Washington, Marie Paxton and Philip Brandon star.
68-8959 *$19.99*

The Bells (1926)
Silent melodrama of murder and guilt in a small European village stars Lionel Barrymore as the town's burgomeister, who harbors a murderous secret, and Boris Karloff as the sinister-looking mesmerist who may uncover Barrymore's crime. Along with the restored and tinted print, this video also includes René Clair's 1923 experiment in cinematic surrealism, "The Crazy Ray." 88 min.
53-6267 *$24.99*

Frankenstein (1931)
One of the all-time chillers. Boris Karloff became a screen legend for his portrayal of the monster brought to life by mad scientist Colin Clive. With Mae Clarke, Dwight Frye, Edward Van Sloan; restored version contains scenes not shown since the film's original release (how did that girl get in the lake?). 71 min.
07-1526 *$14.99*

Bride Of Frankenstein (1935)
Boris Karloff's back as the monster and Elsa Lanchester's got him! This teaming results in one of the greatest horror films ever, filled with terror, suspense, miniature people, mad doctors and wit. Colin Clive is the creator; Ernest Thesiger is Dr. Pretorious; James Whale directs. 75 min.
07-1227 *$14.99*

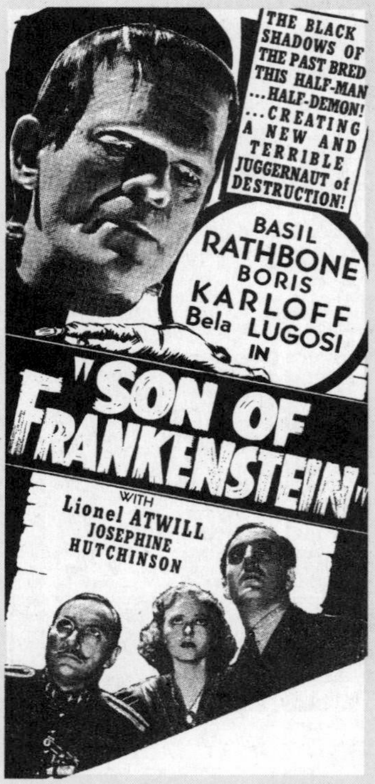

Son Of Frankenstein (1939)
Third entry in the series stars Basil Rathbone as Wolf von Frankenstein, returning to the ancestral estate with his family to atone for his father's mistakes. With the aid of crippled shepherd Ygor (Bela Lugosi), he brings the monster (Boris Karloff) back to murderous life. Lionel Atwill co-stars as the one-armed police inspector; wonderfully stylized sets add to the eeriness. 95 min.
07-1607 *$14.99*

The Mummy (1932)
Karloff is mesmerizing as the 3,700-year-old mummy brought to life when his tomb is uncovered by archeologists. He then sets out in a bloody path of vengeance while searching for his reincarnated lover. Edward Van Sloan, David Manners and Zita Johann co-star; Karl Freund directs. 72 min.
07-1319 *$14.99*

The Mask Of Fu Manchu (1932)
The infamous Oriental mastermind is expertly portrayed by Boris Karloff in this classic thriller. Fu and his equally evil daughter (Myrna Loy) raid the tomb of Genghis Khan for the ancient warlord's sword and mask, which are part of their plan for world domination. Lewis Stone, Karen Morely and Charles Starrett co-star. 67 min.
12-2474 *$19.99*

The Old Dark House (1932)
A classic mix of thrills, scares and laughs from "Frankenstein" director James Whale in which six travelers seek refuge from a storm in a decrepit mansion in Wales, only to be frightened by the creepy, eccentric family living there (especially hideously scarred butler Boris Karloff). With Charles Laughton, Melvyn Douglas, Ernest Thesiger, Gloria Stuart. 71 min.
53-8317 *$24.99*

The Ghoul (1933)
The first film starred in by Karloff in his native England, and Britain's first true horror feature, is the tale of a famed Egyptologist who returns from the dead to wreak vengeance on thieves of a sacred jewel. With Cedric Hardwicke, Ernest Thesiger, and the film debut of Ralph Richardson. 73 min.
68-8000 Was $19.99 *$14.99*

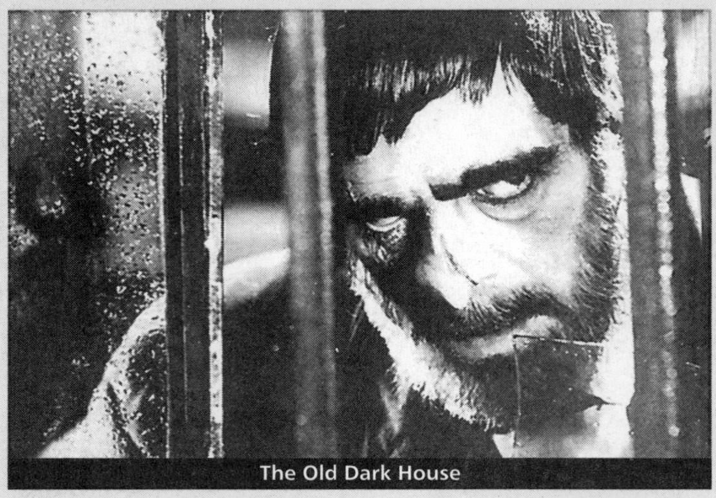
The Old Dark House

Boris Karloff

The Black Cat (1934)
Boris Karloff and Bela Lugosi teamed up for the first time in director Edgar G. Ulmer's macabre chiller that borrows the title (and little else) from Poe. A Balkan castle, built over a WWI graveyard, is the site for a bizarre battle of wills between psychiatrist Lugosi and devil-worshipper Karloff. With David Manners, Jacqueline Wells. 65 min.
07-1838 *$14.99*

The Black Room (1935)
Twice the horror from Karloff in this shocker. Boris stars as twin brothers, one good and one evil, under the influence of an ancient curse. The wicked one follows a path of depravity and evil that leads to the secret of the "black room." With Marian Marsh, Robert Allen. 67 min.
02-2686 *$14.99*

The Invisible Ray (1936)
A radioactive meteorite infects a scientist with a touch of death in this shocker that teams screen scream kings Boris Karloff and Bela Lugosi as rival researchers. With Frances Drake, Frank Laughton, Beulah Bondi. 81 min.
07-1477 Was $39.99 *$14.99*

The Man Who Lived Again (1936)
One of Karloff's best mad scientist roles was in this British melodrama, about a deranged inventor with a matter transfer machine he uses to switch men's brains from one body to another. AKA: "The Man Who Changed His Mind." 61 min.
68-8007 *$19.99*

Juggernaut (1937)
Unusual crime drama stars Boris Karloff as a doctor, forced to give up his research for lack of funds, who gets an offer of money from a millionaire's wife...if he'll help her murder her husband. 64 min.
09-1303 *$19.99*

The Man They Could Not Hang (1939)
A scientist is executed for his illegal work in organ transplants and suspended animation, but is revived by his assistant. Together the two plot a campaign of revenge. Boris Karloff, Byron Foulger, Lorna Gray star. 72 min.
02-2701 *$14.99*

Tower Of London (1939)
The bloody reign of King Richard III was the basis for this atmospheric Universal thriller. Basil Rathbone stars as the crippled monarch who eliminates all rivals to his throne with the help of bald, clubfooted executioner Boris Karloff. A young Vincent Price appears as a prince drowned in a wine vat; with Nan Grey, Barbara O'Neill. 92 min.
07-1828 *$14.99*

Before I Hang (1940)
A doctor (Boris Karloff) experimenting with ways of arresting the aging process becomes younger thanks to a blood transfusion, but the blood came from a condemned murderer! Edward Van Sloan and Evelyn Keyes co-star in this chiller. 71 min.
02-1352 Was $59.99 *$19.99*

Black Friday (1940)
Scientist Boris Karloff transfers the brain of a gangster into the body of an English professor injured in a car accident. When the academician takes on the characteristics of the hood and seeks revenge against a rival mobster (Bela Lugosi), Karloff faces the consequences of his well-intended but diabolical experiment. Stanley Ridges, Anne Nagel also star. 70 min.
07-2291 ☐*$14.99*

The Ape (1940)
Boris Karloff is a scientist experimenting with a cure for spinal disease: the transfusion of an ape's spinal fluid into humans. The result: monsters, shocks and screams. 62 min.
10-3004 *$19.99*

British Intelligence (1940)
Taut suspense and a sinister performance by Boris Karloff, as a German spy posing as a butler in the British War Office, highlight this film about a plot to bomb the English cabinet. A remake of "Three Faces East," with Margaret Lindsay. 62 min.
68-8003 *$19.99*

The Climax (1944)
After the success of their "Phantom of the Opera" remake, Universal re-used some of the same sets (and plot) for this thriller starring Boris Karloff as the Paris Opera House physician obsessed with a beautiful singer he believes to be the reincarnation of the star he murdered in a jealous rage years earlier. With "Phantom" star Susanna Foster, Gale Sondergaard, Turhan Bey. 86 min.
07-2426 *$14.99*

Lured (1947)
After her friend falls victim to a serial killer prowling the streets of London, American showgirl Lucille Ball agrees to work with Scotland Yard inspector Charles Coburn and serve as a decoy to trap the murderer. Glossy thriller from director Douglas Sirk also stars Boris Karloff and George Sanders as a dress designer and nightclub owner, respectively, who are among the prime suspects. 103 min.
53-6321 *$19.99*

The Strange Door (1951)
Based on a Robert Louis Stevenson story, this atmospheric Gothic chiller stars Charles Laughton as a 17th-century nobleman who seeks revenge on his brother, who married Laughton's true love, by imprisoning him in the dungeon of the family castle and marrying off his grown niece to a drunken scoundrel. Boris Karloff co-stars as Laughton's reluctant henchman; with Sally Forrest, Paul Cavanaugh. 81 min.
07-2429 *$14.99*

The Black Castle (1952)
A creepy gothic tale set in the 18th century and involving an Austrian count who kills humans for his own pleasure. An English aristocrat learns that two of his friends died at the hands of the count and now seeks revenge. Boris Karloff, Stephan McNally, Richard Greene and Lon Chaney, Jr. star. 82 min.
07-2290 ☐*$14.99*

Island Monster (1953)
Posing as a philanthropist, smuggler Boris Karloff must flee for his life from the police, taking a little girl hostage, in this Italian-made suspenser. AKA: "Monster of the Island." 87 min.
01-1371 Was $19.99 *$14.99*

Sabaka (1955)
Exciting adventure film in the style of "Jungle Book" about an Indian elephant boy who searches for the human sacrificial cult that killed his parents. Nino Marcel, Boris Karloff, Victor Jory and June Foray star. AKA: "The Hindu." 89 min.
68-8002 *$19.99*

Frankenstein 1970 (1958)
After three outings as the creature, Boris Karloff finally got to play the creator in this unusual horror outing set in the future year of 1970. Following in his infamous grandfather's footsteps, the scarred Baron Frankenstein allows an American TV crew to film in his familial castle so he can obtain money (and spare parts) to bring the Monster back to "life." With Tom Duggan, Jana Lund and former B-cowboy Donald "Red" Barry. 83 min.
19-2566 ☐*$14.99*

Corridors Of Blood (1958)
A 19th-century British doctor (Boris Karloff) experimenting with anesthetics becomes addicted to his new drug and is later blackmailed by two Burke & Hare types to assist in their graverobbing. Co-stars Christopher Lee. 86 min.
50-6224 *$14.99*

The Haunted Strangler (1958)
Set against the backdrop of Victorian society in London, this atmospheric thriller features Boris Karloff as a novelist investigating the case of the notorious "Haymarket Strangler," a man responsible for a series of gruesome murders. Eventually, Karloff realizes that he is the real culprit. With Jean Kent, Elizabeth Allan. AKA: "Grip of the Strangler." 78 min.
50-6220 *$14.99*

Black Sabbath (1964)
A terrifying trilogy of shockers from beyond the grave, hosted by Boris Karloff. A nurse steals a diamond ring from a corpse that doesn't take kindly to theft, a phone becomes a link between the living and the dead, and Karloff appears as a vampire who must prey on his loved ones. Directed by Mario Bava. AKA: "The Three Faces of Fear." 96 min.
44-1349 *$19.99*

Black Sabbath (Letterboxed European Version)
Also available in a theatrical, widescreen format. Includes footage not shown in the U.S. release and the Italian theatrical trailer. 92 min. In Italian with English subtitles.
50-2319 *$19.99*

Die, Monster, Die! (1965)
A recluse (Boris Karloff) given strange abilities from an unearthly meteor...a bloodthirsty cult worshipping obscene deities...and more chills per minute than the system can stand. Nick Adams, Suzan Farmer and Patrick Magee co-star in this shocker based on a short story by H.P. Lovecraft. 80 min.
44-1435 Was $19.99 *$14.99*

Cult Of The Dead (1968)
Zombies, an evil dwarf, a reptile woman, and scientist-turned-voodoo priest Boris Karloff turn up the terror on a South Pacific island. With Carlos East, Julissa. AKA: "The Snake People." 72 min.
48-1032 Was $19.99 *$14.99*

Alien Terror (1968)
Boris Karloff stars as a scientist who unearths an alien-designed "radioactive death ray" that can destroy anything in its path. Mexican-made sci-fi suspenser also stars Christa Linder, Yerye Beirute. AKA: "The Sinister Invasion," "Incredible Invasion." 90 min.
48-1066 *$14.99*

Dance Of Death (1968)
A group of greedy relatives gathered to claim their inheritance, harmless musical toys that become mechanical monsters, and the legendary Boris Karloff are the elements of this Mexican-made shocker. With Andres Garcia, Julissa. AKA: "House of Evil," "Macabre Serenade." 90 min.
68-8229 *$14.99*

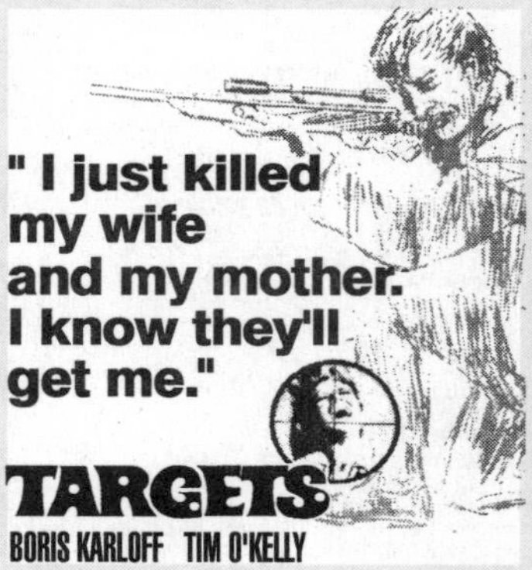

Targets (1968)
Mysterious sniper killings and a promotional appearance by an aging horror movie king. Two separate incidents. How do they relate to each other? Peter Bogdanovich's first film is both a harrowing account of a madman gone berserk and an affectionate tribute to star Boris Karloff. 90 min.
06-1137 Was $49.99 *$14.99*

The Torture Zone (1969)
The King of Horror, Boris Karloff, stars in this terror tale of a mad scientist who needs the blood of frightened women to feed to his creature. With Carlos East, Julissa. AKA: "Fear Chamber." 88 min.
68-8233 *$14.99*

Cauldron Of Blood (1970)
Boris Karloff and Viveca Lindfors star in this bloody tale of grisly murders and a blind artist who uses human skeletons for his sculptures. Karloff's last film. AKA: "Blind Man's Bluff." 95 min.
63-1095 *$14.99*

Please see our index for these other Boris Karloff titles: *Abbott & Costello Meet Dr. Jekyll & Mr. Hyde • Abbott & Costello Meet The Killer, Boris Karloff • Charlie Chan At The Opera • The Criminal Code • Dick Tracy Meets Gruesome • His Majesty, The American • House Of Frankenstein • The King Of The Kongo • King Of The Wild • Mad Monster Party? • Mr. Wong series • Old Ironsides • The Raven • Scarface • The Secret Life Of Walter Mitty • The Terror • Tonight or Never • Unconquered • You'll Find Out*

Exercise

10 Years Younger in 10 Hours
The Astonishing Deep-Muscle Exercise That Gives You A Perfect Figure
Callan Pinckney

Callanetics

Callanetics
Flatten your tummy, lift your bust and tone your entire body with Callan Pinckney. Callan illustrates her exercise techniques using precise motions that activate the body's more powerful muscles to tighten hips, buttocks and more. 60 min.
07-1451   Was $19.99   **$14.99**

Super Callanetics
Callan Pinckney, who transformed hundreds of thousands of bodies and lives with her original stress-free, deep-muscle workout, presents an advanced program of improved exercises for even faster age-reversing results. 90 min.
07-1592   Was $19.99   **$14.99**

Beginning Callanetics
Callan Pinckney returns with an all-new version of her celebrated deep-muscle, stress-free workout, specially designed for the novice exerciser or those whose fitness regimens have lapsed (shame!). 60 min.
07-1632   Was $19.99   **$14.99**

Quick Callanetics
There's no short cut to a great-looking body, but here's the next best thing. Join host Callan Pinckney for a quick and easy-to-follow series that focuses on specific "problem areas." Each tape runs about 25 min.

Quick Callanetics: Legs
07-1704   **$14.99**

Quick Callanetics: Stomach
07-1705   **$14.99**

Quick Callanetics: Hips And Behind
07-1706   **$14.99**

AM/PM Callanetics
Callan Pinckney presents a workout program designed for everyone's lifestyle needs. These two 20-minute workouts supplement each other: in the morning, energize and strengthen the body; in the evening, relax and rejuvenate. 40 min.
07-1874   Was $19.99   **$14.99**

The Kathy Kaehler Fitness System
The "fitness trainer to the stars" presents a complete exercise program featuring some of today's hottest starlets. See Kathy present "Step" training, fat burning, shaping and toning, and body sculpting with Penelope Ann Miller, Julianne Phillips, Jami Gertz, Tawny Kitaen and Beverly D'Angelo. 100 min.
02-2342   **$14.99**

The Grind Workouts
Eric Nies, hunky star of MTV's "The Real World" and "The Grind," leads the hip-hop troops in this workout series that mixes light-impact aerobic dance steps and a funky soundtrack. Each tape runs about 50 min. There are five volumes available, including:

The Grind Workout: Hip-Hop Aerobics
04-5341   **$14.99**

The Grind Workout: Strength & Fitness
04-5485   **$14.99**

LESSONS

Weight Watchers Workout Series
Aerobic champion Aileen Sheron is your guide to getting in shape the Weight Watchers way with this three-tape series. Whether you want to strengthen your cardiovascular system, increase your muscular power, relieve tension or help other areas of fitness, this series is for you. Each tape runs between 34-43 min.

Weight Watchers Workout Series: Low-Impact Aerobics
06-2402   ☐ **$12.99**

Weight Watchers Workout Series: Step And Sculpt
06-2403   ☐ **$12.99**

Body By Jake: Energize Yourself
The second workout by "body builder to the stars" Jake Steinfeld is a specially-conceived, grueling program that will keep you on your feet and keep the "spare tire" from around the tummy. 60 min.
07-1442   **$14.99**

Kari Anderson: Fitness Formula
This special three-part exercise program features one of the country's most popular fitness experts, the personable and well-informed Kari Anderson. Includes dynamic step choreography designed for all fitness levels; a complete abdominal program; and a special section on motivation. 60 min.
19-3480   **$14.99**

CLAUDIA SCHIFFER
PERFECTLY FIT BUNS

DESIGNED BY AND FEATURING CELEBRITY FITNESS TRAINER KATHY KAEHLER

Claudia Schiffer: Perfectly Fit
"Perfectly fit" is certainly how many people would describe top supermodel Schiffer, and in this series of target-trimming aerobic exercise videos Claudia is joined by fitness expert Kathy Kaehler as they demonstrate how you tighten and tone specific "trouble areas." Each tape runs about 40 min.

Claudia Schiffer: Perfectly Fit Abs
04-3266   ☐ **$14.99**

Claudia Schiffer: Perfectly Fit Legs
04-3267   ☐ **$14.99**

Claudia Schiffer: Perfectly Fit Buns
04-3268   ☐ **$14.99**

Claudia Schiffer: Perfectly Fit Arms
04-3269   ☐ **$14.99**

Jane Fonda's Complete Workout
For the aerobic completist, jumpin' Jane has produced an exercise program that's right for all fitness levels, combining aerobic moves, interval training, and low- and high-impact sessions. You can even follow specific sections for specific body "problem areas." 70 min.
19-1762   **$19.99**

Jane Fonda's Lean Routine Workout
A perfect low-impact/high-energy aerobics program from the Queen of Fitness. There's 20-, 40- and 60-minute segments for every fitness level, a section on interval aerobic training, and a special segment with tips on fat-burning, nutrition and weight control. 75 min.
19-1806   ☐ **$19.99**

Jane Fonda's Lower Body Solution
It's two...two...two workouts in one in this aerobic program with surefire tips on toning abdomens, buns and thighs. First, Jane leads a special shaping and tightening series of exercises, followed by a fat-burning regimen demonstrated by top Fonda fitness instructors. 60 min.
19-1903   ☐ **$19.99**

Jane Fonda's Step Aerobic And Abdominal Workout
The queen of aerobics presents a comprehensive workout that burns off fat and helps sculpt the lower body. With hot new music and a 10-minute abdominal workout, this program offers high-energy, low-impact conditioning. 60 min.
19-2003   **$19.99**

Jane Fonda's Favorite Fat Burners
No, it's not nine innings of "tomahawk chops." Jane has taken four of her best fat-burning workout routines and put them on this special low-impact aerobic program that's perfect for beginners and intermediate exercisers. There's also a segment on diet and nutrition. 70 min.
19-3449   **$19.99**

Jane Fonda's Yoga Exercise Workout
Ms. Fonda enters an exciting new exercise phase with this program that features a 20-minute stretch-and-tone routine, a 15-minute Yoga Sun Salutation progression and a 15-minute relaxation section. This "New Age" video is designed for all fitness levels. 65 min.
19-3498   **$19.99**

Jane Fonda's Personal Trainer Series
What would it be like to have video exercise pioneer Jane Fonda as your personal trainer? These programs, featuring a simple and effective workout regimen for all fitness levels, presented in two unique 20-25 minute programs, will provide you the answer. Each tape runs about 55 min.

Jane Fonda's Personal Trainer: Abs, Buns & Thighs
19-3835   **$19.99**

Jane Fonda's Personal Trainer: Total Body Sculpting
19-3836   **$19.99**

Jane Fonda's Personal Trainer: Low Impact Aerobics & Stretch
19-3837   **$19.99**

Jane Fonda's Easy Going Workout
The exercise tape for people in the "prime time" of their lives, this workout was designed by Jane for people who might have trouble with other programs. Now everyone can feel and look better with these workouts. 50 min.
40-1306   **$14.99**

Jane Fonda's Toning And Shaping
Jane returns with an all-new program for toning muscles. She teams with weight trainer Dan Isaacson for two 45-minute sessions in progressive weight training. Can be used with hand-held weights, ankle weights and free bench. Start the presses! 90 min.
40-1323   **$19.99**

Jane Fonda's Start Up
"More than just a warm-up," this special mini-workout from Jane will improve your muscle flexibility and tone, and it's just the ticket for a "quick start" to your workday or full-length exercise regimen. 25 min.
40-1365   **$14.99**

Heather Locklear Presents Your Personal Workout
The sexy star of "Melrose Place" has designed a workout program just for you! There are four different parts (kickstart, energy, power and grace) that can be mixed and matched to your advantage. Designed for women from 18 to 30, Heather's workout offers a winning way to keep fit. 60 min.
07-1662   Was $19.99   **$14.99**

Fabio Fitness Video
The world's most popular hunk shows you how to get into the sort of tip-top shape that he's in this thrilling exercise program. Joined by aerobics champ Brenda Dykgraaf, the fantastic Fabio shows people how to reduce body fat, boost energy, flatten tummies, and shape glutes and legs through exercises and weights. Be a Fabio—not a "Flabbio"! 60 min.
10-2432   **$19.99**

Tough Bodies
Exercise expert DePrise Brescia offers these top programs that help you increase strength, improve flexibility and endurance, and burn fat. Each program targets a specific area of the body with specific exercises. Each tape runs 45 min.

Tough Bodies: Cardiovascular Workout
10-2603   **$14.99**

Tough Bodies: Abs
10-2604   **$14.99**

Tough Bodies: Legs And Buns
10-2605   **$14.99**

Nude Personal Training
If you like to watch and do aerobics, this video's for you. This erotic delight features three hot-to-trot instructors showing you all the moves—in the nude! 35 min.
10-1683   **$14.99**

Nude Yoga

A Fully Instructional Yoga Tape, In The Nude!

Nude Yoga
Classic yoga postures performed by naked women? That's right! Now you can witness such yoga moves as "sun salutation" and "half spinal twist" with four beautiful, naked women offering a sexy and practical exercise demonstration. 45 min.
10-1616   **$19.99**

The New York Dancers Group Nude Exercise Program
This tape will not only keep you in shape, but will be a pleasurable experience over and over again. The first segment includes stretch and warm-up exercises. The other five (15 minutes each) exercises, performed by four beautiful nude female dancers. It will wow your eyes and tone your tummy. 60 min.
50-1135   **$59.99**

Nude Aerobics 2
What a workout you'll get as these gorgeous models strip down and exercise to some hot dance routines. And even if you don't lose a pound, it won't matter after watching Jasae, Tina, Sara, Amber and Lail sweat and stretch! WARNING: contains full frontal nudity. 60 min.
75-7088   **$19.99**

Nude Aerobics 3
Aerobics heads into a new dimension with this provocative workout program in which some of the world's wildest women go hog wild, getting in shape sans clothing. See Jasae (star of "Penthouse Forum Letters"), Tina, Sara and Amber in an outrageous exercise program. WARNING: contains full frontal nudity. 89 min.
75-7114   **$19.99**

Original 29 Minute Workout
Reduce and strengthen your upper body and arms, and trim your waistline and thighs, while improving overall circulation with this four-stage conditioning program.
10-2196 *$12.99*

Kathy Smith's Instant Workout
Three 20-minute mini-workouts help busy men and women keep themselves in top shape in a short amount of time. Each can be done alone or with fellow exercisers to get in shape the Kathy Smith way. 72 min.
03-1791 Was $19.99 *$14.99*

Kathy Smith: Kickboxing Workout
You're sure to get a "kick" out of this fitness video. Smith is joined by martial arts champ Keith Cooke for a hard-hitting workout that uses kickboxing moves for total body conditioning. 45 min.
04-5647 *$14.99*

Kathy Smith: Latin Rhythm Workout
Looking for a way to get "muy apto" that's "muy facil"? Then join Kathy for some lively dance workouts that combine Cha-Cha, Merengue and Salsa moves for a calorie-burning and body-toning exercise regimen. 45 min.
04-5697 *$14.99*

Kathy Smith: Ultimate Stomach And Thigh Workout
For anyone familiar with keeping those notorious troublespots tight and trim, Kathy has constructed this fat-burning and effective 4-phase program to strengthen and shape abdominals, thighs and buttocks for fantastic results. 85 min.
05-1442 Was $19.99 *$14.99*

Kathy Smith: Aerobox Workout
Exercise expert Kathy Smith teams with boxer Michael Olajide, Jr. for a superior workout that incorporates cardiovascular and toning routines with exercises to develop legs, abdomens and upper bodies. 62 min.
19-3507 Was $19.99 *$14.99*

Stretch To Win
Not just another exercise tape, this program shows you stretching regimens and special workouts designed to tone muscles and increase flexibility while burning off calories. Warm-up and relaxation exercises included. 30 min .
10-2154 *$12.99*

Stretching: The Video
Stretching is an essential part of any regular exercise program. But you'd be surprised how many people don't know how to do it correctly. Stretches for the neck, back, legs, hips, arms and shoulders are offered by experts Bob and Jean Anderson. 60 min.
50-4276 Was $29.99 *$19.99*

Jaclyn Smith: Workout For Beauty & Balance
All of you who were waiting for an exercise video from a former "Charlie's Angel" can now get pumping! The ever-gorgeous Jaclyn Smith leads you on her own personal fitness program, with a 25-minute calorie-burning dance routine, a 20-minute body-toning workout, and special beauty tips. 55 min.
04-2614 Was $19.99 ❑*$14.99*

Kathy Smith's Pregnancy Workout
Workout whiz Kathy Smith is joined by her daughter-to-be in a special fitness tape designed for use during and after pregnancy to keep all parties involved in the best of shape. 90 min.
05-1437 *$29.99*

Jane Fonda's Pregnancy, Birth And Recovery Workout
Jane shows you special exercises and fitness programs designed for pre-natal, birth and recovery periods, along with a special section on baby massage and infant care. 90 min.
40-1031 *$14.99*

Denise Austin's Pregnancy Plus Workout
Learn the best ways to stay in top physical shape for yourself and the "little one" with ESPN exercise guru Austin. Plus, a special 20-minute "shape-up" program for after delivery.
50-4543 Was $19.99 *$14.99*

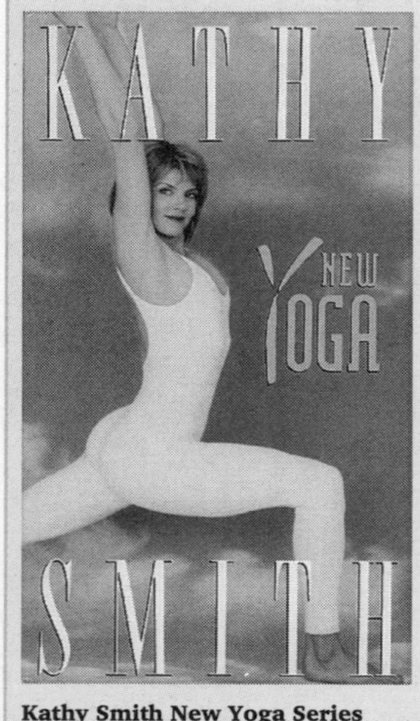

Kathy Smith New Yoga Series
Exercise queen Kathy Smith takes the mystery out of yoga to develop a fitness series that is accessible to all levels of expertise. Smith is joined by top yoga instructor Rod Stryker to demonstrate the easy-to-follow workouts. Each tape runs about 50 min.

Kathy Smith: New Yoga—Intermediate
19-3578 Was $19.99 *$14.99*

Kathy Smith: New Yoga—Basics
19-3744 Was $19.99 *$14.99*

Kathy Smith: New Yoga—Challenge
19-3745 Was $19.99 *$14.99*

Yoga With Linda Arkin 4-Pack
She was co-host of the "Alive and Well" fitness show, and in this four-part video series instructor Linda Arkin demonstrates Hatha Yoga techniques designed to strengthen and condition without excessive stress. Included are "Yoga for Flexibility," "Yoga for Relaxation and Rejuvenation," "Yoga for Strength" and "Yoga: Natural Body Tune-Up." 200 min. total. NOTE: Individual volumes available at $14.99 each.
19-3749 Save $20.00! *$39.99*

Basic Yoga
Members of the American Yoga Association led by Alice Christensen offer instruction for 21 different yoga exercises, as well as special breathing exercises, relaxation and meditation techniques, a limbering routine, and more. 65 min.
10-1505 *$19.99*

Ali MacGraw: Yoga Mind & Body
Model/actress Ali MacGraw demonstrates the yoga techniques that she has practiced for good health. With help from instructor Erich Schiffman, Ali incorporates breathing exercises and 13 Hatha-style Yoga stretches in this low-impact, stress-reducing workout. 55 min.
19-2271 ❑*$14.99*

Bryan Kest's Power Yoga: Complete Set
Noted yoga expert and "trainer to the stars" Bryan Kest hosts these easy-to-learn exercises that use yoga moves and disciplines to help build endurance, strength, flexibility and, focus while reducing stress. Volumes include "Energize," "Tone" and "Sweat." 165 min. total. NOTE: Individual volumes available at $14.99 each.
19-2527 *$44.99*

Lilias! Yoga Workout Series: Beginners
A comprehensive two-tape package will introduce you to the basics of a yoga fitness regimen. Segments look at "What Is Yoga?" with basic stretching and breathing exercises; how to maximize your moves through "Mindfulness"; the healing technique known as "The Inner Smile"; and "Meditation" techniques to aid mind and body. 120 min. total.
89-5064 *$19.99*

Lilias! Yoga Workout Series: Daily Routines For Beginners
Four episodes from Lilias' PBS show are combined in a special two-tape set to help you establish a daily Yoga workout schedule. There are special looks at easy ways to begin Yoga; using props to enhance workouts; moves to balance strength and flexibility; and using Yoga techniques to generate inner happiness. 120 min. total.
89-5067 *$19.99*

Lilias! Silver Yoga Series: Boxed Set
Designed by Lilias with the mature person in mind, this special two-tape series offers a relaxing beginning yoga routine that can improve flexibility, muscle tone and vitality while reducing stress. Included are "Morning Workout" and "Evening Workout." 120 min. total. NOTE: Individual volumes available at $19.99 each.
89-5135 *$29.99*

Lilias! Flowing Postures—Yoga For Beginners: Complete Set
Perfect for beginners and advanced users alike, this four-tape boxed set lets you join Lilias in easy-to-follow yoga workout programs designed for specific target areas. Included are "Arms & Abs," "Cardio Challenge," "Legs & Buns" and "Serenity Now." 140 min. total. NOTE: Individual volumes available at $14.99 each.
89-5155 Save $20.00! *$39.99*

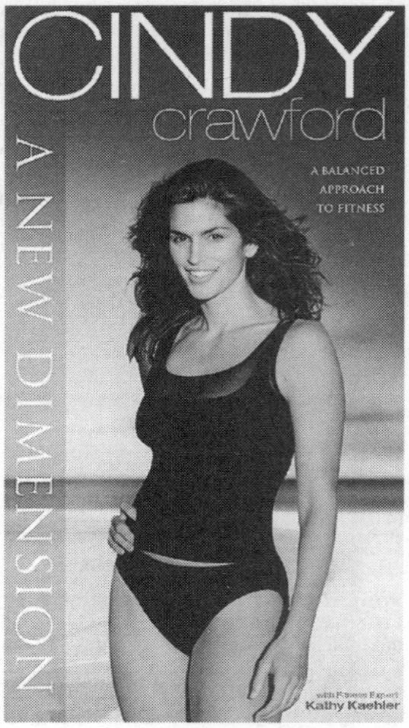

Cindy Crawford: A New Dimension
Designed with new moms (like Cindy) in mind but great for all sorts of exercisers, this program features Crawford and trainer Kathy Kaehler in two short workouts that ease you back into the routine and build energy and endurance, followed by a 40-minute regimen with cardio and strength-training intervals for the upper and lower body. 70 min.
10-1749 *$14.99*

Cindy Crawford: Shape Your Body Workout
You've seen her in commercials, on magazine covers, on MTV's "House of Style" and on Richard Gere's arm. Now the leggy supermodel takes video by storm starring in this music video-styled, non-aerobics fitness program with her trainer, Radu. 100 min.
10-2394 Was $19.99 *$14.99*

Cindy Crawford: The Next Challenge
For those of you who have already gone through a workout with Cindy (you lucky dogs!), here she is again with an even more intense exercise video. Natural body movements are combined into a cross-training-styled total body workout designed to tighten and tone muscles. 70 min.
10-2422 *$19.99*

T'ai Chi For Health
Tai Chi is a centuries-old Oriental discipline that strengthens mind and body while reducing stress and its effects. Get your muscles toned, your endurance stretched and your mind set in this unique fitness tape. 60 min.
08-8449 *$14.99*

Tai Chi For Young People
You're never too young to benefit from Tai Chi, says expert instructor Dr. Paul Lam. Based on the 42 Step International Competition Forms, the faster-paced exercises shown on this video were designed to improve fitness and concentration and work in conjunction with other sports. 70 min.
53-6845 *$24.99*

Tai Chi: 6 Forms/6 Easy Lessons
Aside from being the most widely practiced of the martial arts styles, Tai Chi has down-to-earth uses as effective exercise and meditative techniques. M.D. and Tai Chi expert Paul Lam presents a special fitness program that uses six basic "forms" and is suitable for beginning and advanced audiences. Includes an instructional booklet. 100 min.
53-9345 *$24.99*

Tai Chi For Arthritis
Can the ancient practice of Tai Chi forms and movements be an effective aid in reducing pain and increasing flexibility in arthritis patients? Yes, says renowned instructor Dr. Paul Lam, who demonstrates a series of easy-to-follow exercises. 80 min.
70-9080 *$24.99*

Tai Chi: The 24 Forms
Award-winning instructor Dr. Paul Lam is your guide through this easy-to-follow guide to basic Tai Chi movements and exercises. Precise step-by-step instructions and special breathing techniques are included. 120 min.
70-9089 *$29.99*

Tai Chi For Health
Raised in Hong Kong, martial arts instructor and healer Jason Chan has blended the teachings of East and West to develop the Infinite Tai Chi form of exercise movement. Following these easy-to-learn moves will help viewers restore vitality, inner strength and natural health. 42 min.
83-1312 *$14.99*

David Carradine's Tai Chi Workout
The star of TV's "Kung Fu" brings you "the fitness program that began 2,500 years ago." Ancient Oriental mental and physical disciplines are developed into a low-impact exercise and workout regimen designed to develop balance and coordination and reduce stress. 58 min.
50-3793 Was $29.99 *$19.99*

David Carradine's Chi Kung Beginners Workout
Learn the stress-relieving and healing potential of the Chi Kung ("energy skill") disciplines in this series of meditations, stretching and movement exercises, and self-massage techniques, as demonstrated by Carradine. 60 min.
89-5022 *$19.99*

David Carradine's Tai Chi Workout For Beginners
Perfect for all fitness levels and anyone looking for an easy-to-follow workout regimen, this program lets you join host Carradine in an opening stretching segment, a series of nine Chen Tai Chi moves, and other exercises designed to relax and improve mind and body. 60 min.
89-5023 *$19.99*

David Carradine's Tai Chi For Mind & Body: Boxed Set
Get a complete inner and outer workout, courtesy of host David Carradine and this two-tape set. "Mind" features relaxation exercises to relieve tension and stress and "recharge" your natural energy sources, while stretching moves, breathing techniques and muscle-toning exercises are demonstrated in "Body." 60 min. total. NOTE: Individual volumes available at $14.99 each.
89-5178 *$29.99*

David Carradine's Shaolin Cardio Kick Box For Beginners
Can the five animal movement forms of China's legendary Shaolin Boxers help 21st-century exercisers get in shape? Yes, says host David Carradine, who shows you a complete fitness program, from warm-up to cool-down, based on the moves of the Snake, Crane, Leopard, Tiger and Dragon. 40 min.
89-5179 *$19.99*

The Firm
One of the most popular exercise series ever is now available at Movies Unlimited. Now all of the body's major parts can be strengthened, stretched and toned by using these 45-to 60-minute programs. There are 19 volumes available, including:

The Firm: Body Sculpting Basics—Total Body Workout
02-8309 *$19.99*

The Firm: Low Impact Aerobics—Total Body Workout
02-8310 *$19.99*

The Firm: Total Body: Better Body And Buns
02-8987 *$19.99*

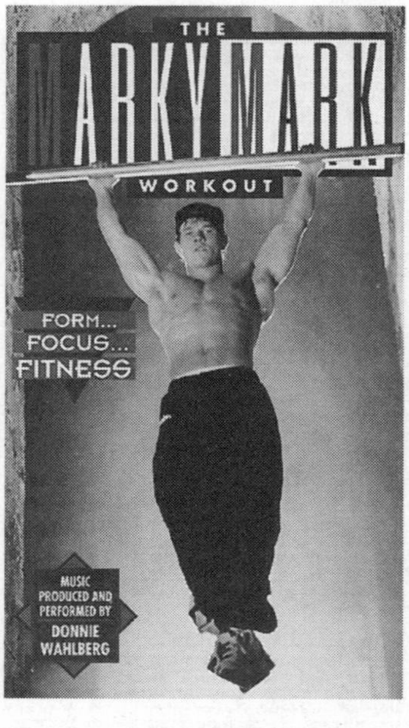

The Marky Mark Workout: Form, Focus, Fitness
He's a rap music sensation, a Calvin Klein model and a film star. Now, Marky Mark tells you his secrets for staying in shape and creating a great physique in a three-part workout designed for use at home and at the gym. "You Gotta Believe" you can get in shape with the Mark-man. 70 min.
10-2426 Was $19.99 *$14.99*

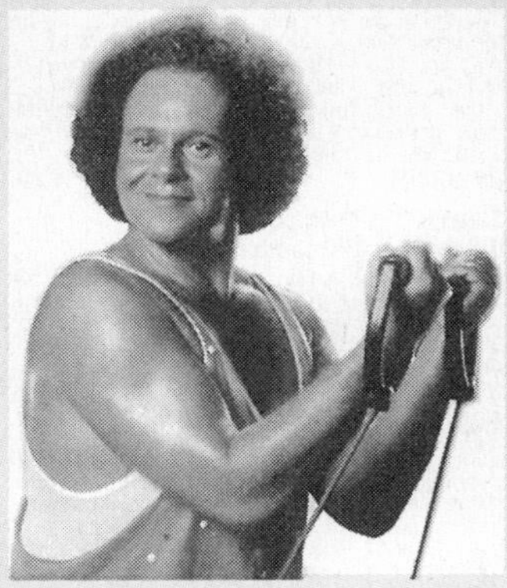

Richard Simmons: Sweatin' To The Oldies
Fitness guru Richard Simmons helps you get rid of excess poundage by rockin', rollin' and aerobicisin' to golden oldie tunes. Exercise is a pleasure as Richard leads you in a bump and grind session to such songs as "Dancing in the Streets," "Personality" and "It's My Party." 45 min.
19-1784 *$19.99*

Richard Simmons: Sweatin' To The Oldies, Vol. 2
Richard Simmons, the Svengali of the sweat set, shows you how to lose those extra inches in this music-filled exercise program. This incredibly popular workout tape features such songs as "Rescue Me," "Respect," "Oh, Pretty Woman," "Locomotion" and more.
10-2398 Was $19.99 *$14.99*

Richard Simmons: Sweatin' To The Oldies, Vol. 3
If you wanna dance, wanna sweat, wanna get in shape and wanna lose weight, let Richard Simmons help you out. This low-impact program is set to such tunes as "Do You Wanna Dance?," "Gimme Some Lovin'," "California Dreaming," "The Name Game" and others. Get into a healthy groove today! 60 min.
10-2425 Was $19.99 *$14.99*

Richard Simmons: Lose Weight And Celebrate
It's a complete weight-loss package with a Broadway beat as only Richard can put together! Get a Great White Way workout to such songs as "Hello, Dolly!," "Cabaret," "Don't Cry for Me, Argentina" and "Oklahoma!" with the one-hour "Broadway Sweat" and half-hour "Tone Up on Broadway" and "Broadway Blast Off" video programs; work your muscles with the Toning Cord system; and plan out your day's meals with the FoodMover brochures and Broadway Cookbook.
10-2884 *$49.99*

Richard Simmons: Sweat & Shout
Get sweaty at the sock hop when Richard sets his low-impact aerobics workout to such tunes as "Shout," "Mony Mony," "Someday We'll Be Together," "Dance to the Music" and others. Put on your dancing athletic shoes and get in shape! 60 min.
10-2530 *$19.99*

Richard Simmons: Stretchin' To The Classics
Let Richard Simmons say it: "Roses are red, violets are blue. Here is a stretch tape I made just for you. There's classical music you have loved and heard. And to your surprise, I don't utter a word. From the tips of your fingers to those 10 little toes, I'll get rid of your aches, your pain, and your woes." Featuring works by Grieg, Brahms, Pachelbel and others.
10-2546 *$19.99*

Richard Simmons: Get Down The Pounds U.S.A.!
It's the fitness program-in-a-box that the country's been waiting for! This special package from the one and only Richard includes three videotapes ("Dance Your Pants Off!," "Tonin' Downtown" and "Tonin' Uptown") loaded with fun- and music-filled exercise routines; the inspirational "Excuse Busters" booklet; a set of six special recipe cards; a pair of Tonin' resistance rings; the new and improved Pure to Go Plus water filter bottle; and more.
10-2789 *$39.99*

Richard Simmons: Move, Groove And Lose 2000
This package features Richard Simmons in the quick, 20-minute "Blast Off" video and the 60-minute "Groovin 'n the House," designed to help you sweat pounds away. Also included are the Food Mover, a pocket-sized food portion counter, the Food Mover Cookbook, the "Colors of Your Life" audiocassette and more.
10-2870 *$39.99*

Richard Simmons: Get Started
TV's exercise expert is back with a special program for the overweight and those who have never worked out before. This tape will launch you on the right fitness regimen for you, with tips on motivation, diet and nutrition. 60 min.
40-1065 *$19.99*

Richard Simmons: Reach For Fitness
A very special series of exercise programs, designed for people who are physically challenged, is featured along with diet and general health recommendations. Produced by Simmons in cooperation with leading physical therapists for a variety of conditions. 45 min.
40-1161 *$14.99*

Richard Simmons And The Silver Foxes
Everyone's favorite "chubby-challenger" is back in an all-new exercise program designed for older people, and he's brought along some top stars' parents: work out with Harry Hoffman, Sal Pacino, Jackie Stallone, Pauline Fawcett and Shirley Simmons. 45 min.
40-1224 *$19.99*

Donna Richardson: Step And Awesome Abs
You know her as one of ESPN's "Fitness Pros" and from Nike's "Body Conditioning" series. Now, Ms. Richardson stars in her own exercise program, demonstrating a fat-burning workout followed by great ab exercises. 60 min.
08-8287 Was $19.99 *$14.99*

CherFitness: A New Attitude
Snap out of it! Get in shape with the one and only Cher in a fabulous exercise tape that'll make you feel all sunny inside. A unique modular system lets you concentrate on specific problem body areas, while Cher offers the tips that have made her the top fitness proponent in show business. Includes music from Cher's "Love Hurts" album. 90 min.
04-2474 Was $19.99 *$14.99*

Knockout Workout 2-Pack: Kickboxing & Aerobic Boxing
This two-tape set features Stephanie Steele, famous kickboxing trainer and fitness expert, showing you the finer points of kickboxing and aerobic boxing. in "Kickboxing Workout," a high-energy, total body workout is offered for shaping and trimming. And "Aerobic Boxing Workout" can be applied to arms, backs, buttocks, thighs and abdominals. 95 min. total.
08-8873 *$14.99*

Regis Philbin: My Personal Workout
Who wants to feel like a million dollars? It's the one and only Reg in a dynamic exercise program that proves you don't have to be a youngster to keep fit. Philbin uses weights, special routines and aerobics for fitness purposes and is joined by wife Joy and TV co-host Kathie Lee Gifford. 50 min.
10-1471 Was $19.99 *$14.99*

Your Personal Best Workout With Elle MacPherson
The stunning supermodel/actress is joined by fitness training expert Karen Voight for a video to get you working toward your personal best in a unique exercise program that blends low-impact aerobics with target training. 45 min.
11-1851 Was $19.99 *$14.99*

Marilu Henner's Dancerobics
Looking for a fun fitness program, one that combines progressive dance steps with fat-burning aerobic exercises? Look no further than this tape with the star of "Taxi" and "Evening Shade" demonstrating her own daily workout regimen, a special "mini-workout" for those busy days, plus Henner's health and diet advice. 60 min.
10-3374 *$19.99*

Dixie Carter's Unworkout
The star of "Designing Women" shows you how to stay in shape with an invigorating, tension-reducing, non-aerobic workout. Dixie's Southern style will charm you in this program designed for women of all ages. 70 min.
07-1894 Was $19.99 *$14.99*

Dixie Carter's Yoga For You Unworkout
Dixie helps you "design" the perfect body-sculpting and stress-relieving techniques with this workout program that features two 20-minute no-impact routines for morning and evening, plus a 10-minute relaxation stop. 62 min.
07-2206 Was $19.99 *$14.99*

Joyce Vedral: The Bottoms Up Workout
Joyce Vedral, the 50sh exercise expert, leads you in a series of exercise programs that will help get rid of cellulite, shapelessness and fat. In each program, she offers terrific workout sets, tips on keeping fit and important health info. Each tape runs 45 min.

Joyce Vedral: The Bottoms Up Workout: Lower Body
10-2639 *$14.99*

Joyce Vedral: The Bottoms Up Workout: Upper Body
10-2640 *$14.99*

Joyce Vedral: The Bottoms Up Workout: Middle Body
10-2641 *$14.99*

Buns Of Steel: The New Generation
It's not just for buns anymore, as renowned exercise instructor Tamilee Webb leads you in these fat-burning, muscle-toning workouts designed for specific fitness levels and targeted body areas. Except where noted, each tape runs about 40 min.

Classic Arms & Abs Of Steel: Intermediate/Advanced
19-3628 *$12.99*

Classic Abs Of Steel: Beginner/Intermediate
19-3892 *$12.99*

Classic Abs Of Steel: Intermediate/Advanced
50-4438 *$12.99*

The Ballet Workout
If you've dreamed of being a dancer (or at least looking like one), this two-part exercise program will show you how to tighten and tone your body while improving one's carriage and posture. Renowned ballet star Melissa Lowe stars. 83 min.
22-1137 *$19.99*

The Ballet Workout II
Instructor Melissa Lowe shows dancers how to turn into graceful professionals with an improved carriage and a lithe, supple body. 70 min.
22-1293 *$19.99*

Exercise Can Beat Arthritis
If you have problems with arthritis, this is the workout for you. Let Valerie Sayce, noted physiotherapist, help alleviate arthritis pain, increase range of movement and strengthen muscles and joints. 40 min.
22-7074 Was $24.99 *$19.99*

Exercise Can Beat Arthritis: Getting Stronger
This companion to "Exercise Can Beat Arthritis" will show you fun and healthy workout programs meant to get rid of the pain in your bones and make the simple things in life normal again. 49 min.
22-7179 *$19.99*

Women At Large: Breakout
Being "big" and being "fit" aren't necessarily contradictory ideas. And this tape, hosted by the two women who founded Women at Large, will prove it to you, as a sensible, easy-to-follow exercise program is demonstrated. Feel better and be healthier! 60 min.
27-6567 *$12.99*

Paula Abdul's Get Up And Dance!
Now the chart-topping singer can be "Forever Your Exercise Girl," as you join Paula for an aerobic dance fitness program that uses low- and high-impact moves for a fat-burning workout that'll leave you "Spellbound." 54 min.
27-6932 *$14.99*

Denise Austin Series
Looking for a good way to get trim? Join up with "The Today Show's" exercise expert for these quick, tuneful low-impact regimens that'll improve cardiovascular strength and endurance while bringing you the taut and terrific shape you desire. There are 12 volumes available, including:

Denise Austin: Power Kickboxing
27-7345 *$14.99*

Denise Austin: Anti-Aging Cardio Dance Workout
27-7346 *$14.99*

Denise Austin: Totally Firm
27-7347 *$14.99*

Denise Austin: Hips, Thighs And Buttocks
27-7350 *$14.99*

Denise Austin: Rock Hard Abs
27-7351 *$14.99*

Denise Austin: Best Of Hit The Spot
27-7352 *$14.99*

Bodybuilding Encyclopedia
No, it's not working out with a set of Brittanicas. It's two-time Mr. Universe Manu Pluton demonstrating a comprehensive program of weight exercises, each targeting a specific set of muscles. Tone up and define legs, abdomen, back, chest, shoulders and arm muscles; designed for both men and women. 41 min.
50-3837 *$14.99*

Generation Xercise!
This series of workout videos featuring Debra Minghi, a renowned dancer, choreographer and fitness trainer, provides simple, low-impact exercises set to live music which are easy enough for beginners yet still challenging for higher-level fitness enthusiasts. Each tape showcases a different musical guest or style and runs about 60 min.

Generation Xercise!: Debra Minghi's Gospel Moves Workout
50-7623 *$14.99*

Generation Xercise!: Debra Minghi's Cardio Club DJ Workout
50-7624 *$14.99*

Body Control/ Weekly Workout 2-Pack
Based on the exercise techniques of Joseph Pilates, this two-tape set hosted by Lynne Robinson offers toning and conditioning workouts using slow, controlled muscle movements that also improve flexibility and posture. Included in the set are "Body Control" and "Weekly Workout." 180 min. total. NOTE: Individual volumes available at $19.99 each.
53-6696 Save $10.00! *$29.99*

Sexercise
"Scream Queen" fave Jewel Shepard stars in this enticingly erotic guide to staying in sexy shape. It's designed for partners who want to put some sexiness into their workout routine and features attractive, scantily-clad exercisers. Also on hand is the Naughty Nurse to dispense words of wowsome wisdom. 30 min.
55-9012 *$19.99*

Joan Lunden: Workout America
You've seen her as the perky co-host of "Good Morning America," and now Joan demonstrates the exercises that help make her so perky. With help from fitness expert Barbara Brant, Joan shows you how to stay in shape with dance aerobics and a toning routine. 60 min.
63-1739 *$14.99*

Oscar De La Hoya's Championship Boxing Workout
Pro and Olympic boxing champ Oscar De La Hoya is joined by Shawnae Jebbia, Miss USA 1998, in this invigorating workout video that combines boxing and skip aerobics to assist in burning calories and strengthening and toning muscle groups. 60 min.
73-9320 *$19.99*

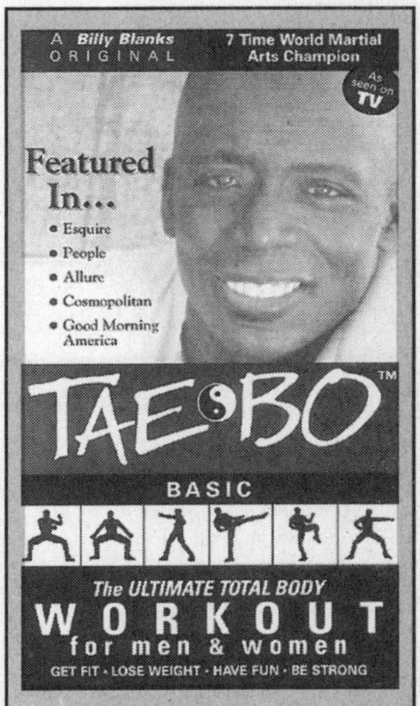

Tae-Bo (Two-Tape Set)
This smashing exercise program, developed by martial arts expert, top trainer and action film star Billy Blanks, combines Tae Kwon Do, boxing, dance and music for a spectacular workout that will keep you in physical and emotional shape. This two-tape package features both the basic and instructional workouts. 67 min. total.
50-8065 *$39.99*

Tae-Bo Workout: Advanced And Tae-Bo Live!
Billy Blanks is back in this pulse-pounding sequel to his original "Tae-Bo" videos. If you've completed the exercises in the first two tapes, graduate to this extreme workout featuring more complicated combinations guaranteed to make you sweat! 57 min.
50-8295 *$29.99*

Tae-Bo Four-Pack
Now you can own both of Billy Blanks' popular two-tape workout productions in one complete package. Both "Tae-Bo" and "Tae-Bo: Advanced and Tae-Bo Live" are available in this deluxe set. 180 min. total.
50-7583 Save $20.00! *$49.99*

Tae-Bo Gold
Billy Blanks of "Tae-Bo" fame offers an exercise program for older people who may have felt left out from the previous "Tae-Bo" outings. Based on the fundamental techniques of the original videos, this workout offers lots of important tips and techniques for seniors to stay in shape.
50-8472 *$29.99*

Tae-Bo Live
This four-tape set includes new moves, new music and new workouts featuring Tae-Bo creator Billy Blanks. Featured in the package are "Basic Workout," "Advanced Workout," "Instructional Workout" and "8-Minute Workout."
50-8659 *$59.99*

Aaron Lankford's Power Kicks
Kickboxing champ Aaron Lankford is featured in this power-packed workout that offers power-kicking, hand-foot combinations, kicking drills and a hand workout for upper body strength. 60 min.
73-9321 *$19.99*

The Cindy Margolis Total Body Fat Burn
She's America's most popular swimsuit model, the most downloaded woman on the Internet. Now, Cindy shows how she stays in shape with her personal workout that offers exercises to flatten stomachs, biceps, triceps, abs and more. Margolis is joined by Amy Fadhli and Sherry Goggin-Giardina, no slouches in the fitness department either. 33 min.
82-5063 *$14.99*

Targeted Sports Training Series
Get yourself in shape for your favorite outdoor activities with this unique series of fitness videos. Instructors Carey Bond and Blair French lead viewers through cardio- and body-conditioning exercises, an in-gym workout program, and performance enhancement tips for your sport. Each tape runs about 95 min.

Targeted Sports Training: Cycling
89-5168 *$19.99*

Targeted Sports Training: Running
89-5169 *$19.99*

Targeted Sports Training: Skiing
89-5170 *$19.99*

Bellydance: Fitness For Beginners: Boxed Set
It's been practiced throughout the world for centuries, and now it can be a popular and effective way to sculpt, tone and firm your body. Let instructors Veena and Neena Bidasha get your belly moving in a four-tape set of rhythmic workouts. Included are "Arms & Abs," "Basic Moves," "Fat Burning" and "Hips, Buns & Thighs." 120 min. total. NOTE: Individual volumes available at $14.99 each.
89-5230 Save $20.00! *$39.99*

Dance

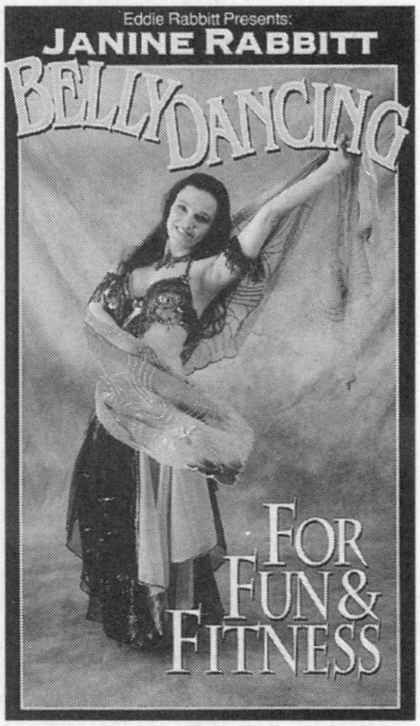

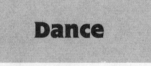

Belly Dancing For Fun And Fitness
Janine Rabbitt, wife of country star Eddie Rabbitt, shows you how to perfect your hoochy-coochy moves in this program that also offers tips on keeping in shape. Learn muscle control and dance methods, while improving posture, flexibility and grace. 55 min.
10-1469 Was $19.99 *$14.99*

Irish Dancing Made Easy
If you're itching to do a "funky ceili" but don't know how, this instructional video will teach you the basic steps for such Irish dances as the Reel, Irish Jig, Treble Jig and more.
50-2478 Was $29.99 *$19.99*

Swing Is King
Get into the swing groove with this instructional video from Hollywood dance instructor Nick Felix. Felix is the cat who taught some of the movie world's stars how to dance, and now he shows you the secrets to jumpin' and jivin' with the hottest swing moves. 60 min.
53-6341 *$14.99*

Learn To Dance In Minutes
Why be a wallflower any longer? Let Broadway dancer and instructor Cal Del Pozo take you out on the dance floor in a matter of (that's right!) minutes, with this series of instructional tapes. Each volume runs about 50 min.

Learn To Dance In Minutes: Salsa Merengue
10-1644 Was $19.99 *$14.99*

Learn To Dance In Minutes: The Basic Lessons
50-3827 Was $19.99 *$14.99*

Learn To Dance In Minutes: Swing & Slow Dances
50-3828 Was $19.99 *$14.99*

Learn To Dance In Minutes: The Latin Dances
50-3829 Was $19.99 *$14.99*

How To Lambada
It's dirty dancing meets spicy Brazilian salsa. Discover how to do the dance the whole world loves in this scintillating program. Hosted by Miranda Garrison, the choreographer of the film "The Forbidden Dance," and featuring stars of the movie, this is one tape you can cut the carpet to. 30 min.
02-2010 *$14.99*

Dance Moves: Kickin' It At The Clubs
Did your last date leave you on the nightclub floor when you started to do the Funky Chicken? Let MTV dancers and "Grind Workout" stars Kristen Denehy and Anthony Wiggins show you the hottest moves, as you visit a Greenwich Village dance studio, see steps demonstrated by acclaimed choreographer Jamie King, learn about Reggae and Latin dances, and more. 45 min.
04-5511 *$14.99*

How To Square Dance
This great introduction to the all-American pastime of square dancing features simple-to-learn methods to such steps as "The Promenade," "The Ladies Chain," "The Do-Si-Do," "The Allamande Left and Right" and more. 30 min.
10-1438 *$14.99*

Tap Dancing For Beginners
Learn how to tap step-by-step from Henry Le Tang, choreographer of "Sophisticated Ladies." The legendary Honi Coles makes an appearance. 31 min.
22-1046 Was $39.99 *$19.99*

Tap Dancing: Intermediate
Keep on tapping with this progressive, sound-by-sound method to tap dancing. You can be the next Gregory Hines if you follow these pointers designed for intermediate dancers. 40 min.
22-1232 Was $39.99 *$19.99*

Tap Dancing: Advanced
For those who are already tap-happy, try to perfect your steps with this program which includes close-ups of footwork, a focus on combination and routine, and original choreography. 40 min.
22-1233 Was $39.99 *$19.99*

I Hate To Exercise, I Love To Tap
Now you can have fun while tapping your way to fitness with that perky little red-headed bundle of energy, Bonnie Franklin, on this video. Franklin demonstrates basic tap dance steps and how to combine them to do popular routines like the Waltz Clog, the Time Step and more. 86 min.
22-1310 *$19.99*

The Land Of Sweet Taps
Now kids can learn how to tap dance the easy way, as basic sounds, rhythms and steps, including shuffles and digs, are taught by Rosemary Boross. Children can learn how to dance to such tunes as "The Peppermint Stick Strut" and "The Bubble Gum Bounce." 57 min.
22-1340 *$19.99*

Ballet Class For Beginners
World renowned ballet coach and teacher David Howard hosts an introduction for the novice dance student, emphasizing posture, placement and movement potential. 40 min.
22-1048 Was $39.99 *$19.99*

Ballet Class For Intermediate-Advanced
For the more experienced ballet students, famed instructor David Howard has produced a second series of lessons that expands on the techniques and classical vocabulary, stressing kinetic awareness and movement potential. 56 min.
22-1049 Was $39.99 *$19.99*

Bujones In Class
If you're interested in studying ballet, why not learn from the best: Fernando Bujones? Bujones demonstrates techniques for classical ballet, posture improvement and some of the steps which have made him a master in the art of dance. 60 min.
22-1054 Was $39.99 *$19.99*

I Can Dance!: Introduction To Ballet For Children
Professional dancer Debra Maxwell offers ballet lessons for boys and girls ages seven and up. This program encompasses a beginner's lesson: Pliés, Center Work and the five basic positions. 30 min.
22-1261 *$19.99*

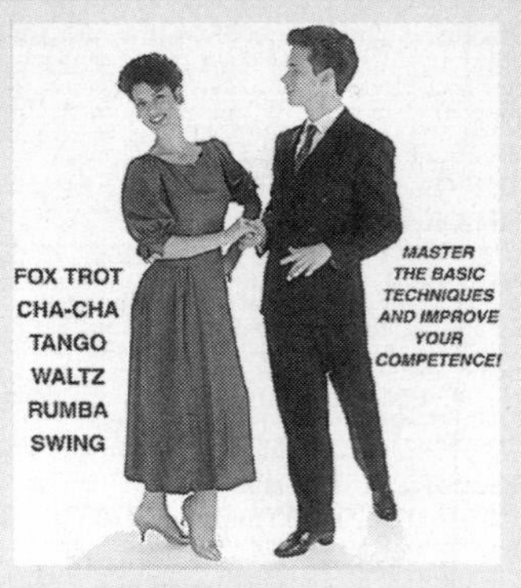

Ballroom Dancing For Beginners
Dazzle them at Roseland with this complete course in ballroom dancing from professional instructor and international competitor Teresa Mason. Lessons include elements of dance, dance positions, understanding music, and step patterns for the Fox Trot, Tango, Waltz, Rumba, Cha Cha and Swing. 57 min.
22-1104 Was $29.99 *$19.99*

Ballroom Dancing: Intermediate
Put those dancin' shoes back on for this superb sequel that will have you doing more complicated steps for the Fox Trot, Tango, Waltz, Rhumba, Swing and Cha-Cha. Let instructor Teresa Mason teach you how to cut the carpet. 48 min.
22-1227 Was $29.99 *$19.99*

Ballroom Dancing: Advanced
Popular social dances like the Fox Trot, Waltz, Tango, Rumba, Cha-Cha and Swing are featured in this advanced-level instructional program with dance wizard Teresa Mason. 60 min.
22-1290 Was $29.99 *$19.99*

Introduction To Ballroom Dancing
If you've dreamed of being queen (or king) of the Stardust Ballroom, here's your chance, as instructor Margot Scholz will have you gliding across the floor. Waltz, Cha Cha, Fox Trot, Swing and Rumba are all demonstrated. 68 min.
22-1131 *$19.99*

Swing Dancing With Teresa Mason
Get those zoot suits and bobby sox out of the attic, because the swingin' dances of the '30s and '40s are being discovered by a new generation. Let dance instructor Teresa Mason get you in the groove as she demonstrates East Coast Swing and West Coast Swing, Lindy, Jitterbug and Jive. 45 min.
22-1611 *$19.99*

Jazz Dance Class With Gus Giordano
The art of jazz dance is interpreted by internationally famous choreographer and innovator Gus Giordano. Classes include the Warm-Up, Basic Technique, Jazz Walks, Centre Barre, and the Professional Dancer, and include interviews and performance footage of the master. 63 min.
22-1105 Was $39.99 *$19.99*

Wedding Day Dancing
Looking to cut the carpet on your wedding day...or any day? This is the perfect video to teach you the steps for the waltz, the fox trot, the jitterbug and the "triple swing." The dances are carefully explained, the footwork clearly diagrammed and the instructors are experts Christopher Reilly and Elaine Bayless. Impress everyone (including yourself) on the big day. 90 min.
50-4450 *$19.99*

Polka 101: Basic Step And Level 1 Variations
You don't need the Schmenges to polka, as proven in this video featuring dance doyenne Mary Lou Kay and Eddie Blazonczyk of the Grammy-winning Versatones. All of the basic steps and their variations are featured. 60 min.
50-5262 *$29.99*

Fred Astaire Dance Series
About as light on your feet as a cross-eyed hippo? With the estimable aid of these instructional tapes from the first name in American dance, you'll be stepping in time with the best of them. Each program runs 40 min.

Fred Astaire Dance: Ballroom
Includes tips on how to Fox-Trot and Waltz.
64-1134 *$19.99*

Fred Astaire Dance: Top 40
Learn how to "dance dirty" and get down to Top 40 Rock.
64-1157 *$19.99*

Fred Astaire Dance: Swing
Do the Lindy and the Jitterbug in no time flat.
64-1158 *$19.99*

Dance Freestyle: Set
You know the Box Step, but does fast dance music leave you looking like Elaine from "Seinfeld"? This two-tape instructional program, hosted by top dance teacher Larry Gould, shows you how to combine basic moves and techniques to form your own "freestyle" dancing to Rock, Latin, Jazz, Swing and other types of music. 85 min. total.
89-5200 *$29.99*

Learn To Dance: 10 Steps For The Beginner
Tired of being a wallflower? This video lets you follow along at home to simple dance steps with live instructors and on-screen diagrams. Learn how to do the Basic Step, Key Step, Two-Step, Stroll, Box Step and others. 80 min.
89-5201 *$19.99*

Swing Craze
This instructional two-tape set will teach you to swing the night away as you first learn about the history of swing dancing, and where to find the coolest clothes and the hottest clubs. Then, several experts will show you the basic steps and progress to more advanced moves for your eventual night out on the town. 95 min.
64-3444 *$14.99*

Self-Defense

The World Of Martial Arts
You're being chased by a gang of muggers. What to do? Well, if you watched this important program detailing the fundamentals of self defense you wouldn't worry. No sweat—when you're a master.
07-1111 Was $29.99 *$19.99*

Women's Self-Defense & Fitness Program
Olympic champion Bruce Jenner and wife Kris are the hosts for this instructional video, as fifth-degree black belt and professional trainer Ken Herrera demonstrates exercises and training methods that promote fitness, along with self-defense tactics and tips. 60 min.
22-1370 *$19.99*

Karate And Self-Defense
Learn from karate master Ivan Rogers the basic stances and moves, special training exercises to keep the body limber, and 10 ways to protect yourself in specific situations. 88 min.
64-1025 Was $29.99 *$19.99*

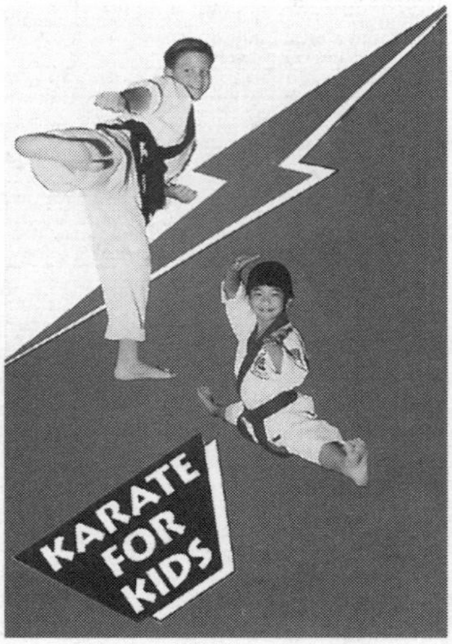

Karate For Kids
This three-part series is designed to help children find good health, fitness and positive values through karate. Great music and expert teachers help kids reach for the stars while kicking their feet. Each tape runs about 30 min.

Karate For Kids, Vol. 1: Easy Instruction And Exercise
22-1363 *$14.99*

Karate For Kids, Vol. 2: Intermediate Instruction And Exercise
22-1364 *$14.99*

Karate For Kids, Vol. 3: Advanced Instruction And Exercise
22-1365 *$14.99*

Sports

Magic Johnson: Put Magic In Your Game
The Lakers hoops wizard proves you can't take the playground out of the pro with a lesson in winning basketball fundamentals especially for children, illustrated with Magic's fabulous NBA highlights. 50 min.
04-2254 Was $19.99 ***$14.99***

Swoopes On Hoops: Basketball Basics
WNBA star Sheryl Swoopes shows you the finer points of basketball in this entertaining and informative video. The Houston Comets star offers exciting tips and important demonstrations on improving women's hoops games. 55 min.
22-1571 ***$14.99***

Gymnastic Excellence: Complete Set
Kids can learn the essentials of gymnastics with this four-tape series that covers all aspects of tumbling. Included in the set are "Pad Drills," "Beginning Tumbling," "Intermediate Tumbling" and "Advanced Tumbling." 166 min. total. NOTE: Individual volumes available at $39.99 each.
50-2966 Save $10.00! ***$149.99***

The Nature Of Hunting
A unique video that gives you a chance to see through a hunter's eyes and see what it's like stalking a wild mulie, trying to outsmart a big whitetail and calling in a turkey. Experience an intimacy with nature unlike any other. 60 min.
50-5160 ***$19.99***

Tony Gwynn's The Five Keys To Hitting
San Diego Padres hitting master Tony Gwynn offers the finer points to his success in this program that includes appearances from Joe Carter, Dwight Gooden, Tim Raines and Tommy Lasorda. Among the subjects covered are Hitting vs. Contact Hitting and the Stance. 30 min.
10-1524 Was $19.99 ***$14.99***

Play Ball The Major League Way: Complete Set
Get advice on playing the diamond from top major league coaches and instructors with this three-tape set that covers all the bases. Includes "Fielding," "Hitting and Baserunning" and "Pitching and Catching." 185 min. total. NOTE: Individual volumes available at $14.99 each.
13-5105 Save $5.00! ***$39.99***

Sports Clinic: Baseball
Play like an All-Star once you check into this diamond "clinic," hosted by World Series-winning manager Dick Williams. Learn about pitching, batting, running and defense from star players like Jerry Reuss, Gary Templeton, Terry Kennedy and Kurt Bevacqua. 80 min.
50-3189 ***$19.99***

LITTLE LEAGUE'S OFFICIAL HOW-TO-PLAY BASEBALL BY VIDEO

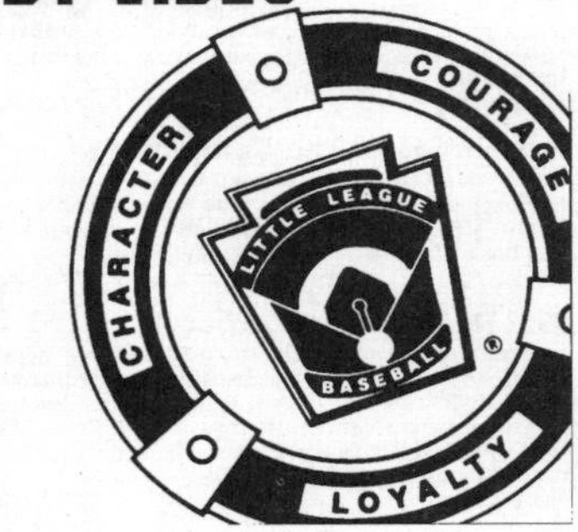

Little League's Official How-To-Play Baseball By Video
Now your junior Johnstones and young Yastrzemskis can learn the diamond basics in a tape designed for kids ages 7 to 13. Basics such as batting stance, base running, pitching and playing defense are covered. 90 min.
52-1078 ***$19.99***

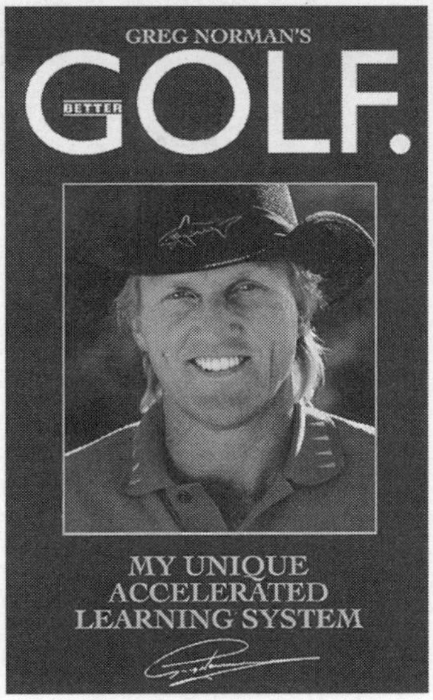

Greg Norman's Better Golf
Join golf champ Greg Norman and teaching wizard Butch Harmon for this instructional series designed for players at all skill levels. Featured are three 40-minute videos: "The Fundamentals," "Playing the Game" and "Tips and Drills."
04-3333 Was $79.99 ***$39.99***

Greg Norman: The Complete Golfer: Collector's Set
Golf's legendary "White Shark" demonstrates how to take a bite out of your score with this two-tape set. Includes "The Long Game" and "The Short Game." 110 min. total. NOTE: Individual volumes available at $19.99 each.
06-1855 ***$39.99***

Bad Golf Made Easier
There are many golf videos on the market, but only this one promises to "allow you to remain a bad golfer and still shave strokes off your game!" Join devious duffer Leslie Nielsen as he hilariously shows how to bend the rules to your benefit. Archie Hahn and Robert Donner also star. 53 min.
19-9018 Was $19.99 ***$14.99***

The 8-Step Swing
Expert Jim McLean's analysis on the golf swing has been broken down into eight different steps, and here he offers strategies on improving each of these areas. 106 min.
22-6074 ***$19.99***

Ben Crenshaw: The Art Of Putting
Come fill the cup, once you've mastered these putting pointers from PGA Champion Crenshaw. Grip, stance, stroke, reading greens, long putts, short putts, practice drills, so much more. 40 min.
50-3675 ***$14.99***

Sam Snead: The Complete Golf Lesson
The one and only "Slammin' Sam" is your tutor in an instructional video that covers all aspects of the game, from choosing equipment and the different types of grips and swings to working on specific problems for the tee, fairway and green. 60 min.
64-1315 ***$19.99***

Bobby Jones: How I Play Golf: Deluxe Gift Set
Legendary golfer Bobby Jones made a series of instructional films in the 1930s that captured his unique playing form. Now you can learn from one of the all-time greats with this four-tape boxed set that features "The Short Game," "The Long Game," "How to Break 90" and "A Round of Golf and Specialty Shots." 140 min. total. NOTE: Individual volumes available at $19.99 each.
64-1347 Save $10.00! ***$69.99***

Sports Clinic: Soccer
Hubert Vogelsinger, a top soccer coach, demonstrates the steps needed to make you a regular Pele. The most popular sport in the world can now be yours to master by using this tape. 75 min.
50-3215 ***$19.99***

Boxerobics
It's a "how-to" for fans of the "sweet science," as a quartet of boxing instructors lead you on an intense workout that includes work on the speed bag, heavy bag, skip rope and more to get you in fighting trim. 60 min.
78-3045 ***$14.99***

Chris Evert: How I Play Tennis Boxed Set
Her unique style and skill led her to three Wimbledon and seven French Open titles, and now tennis great Chris Evert shows you how to play the game on this invaluable three-tape series that lets you follow along with Chris as she demonstrates her winning moves. Included are lessons on "Groundstrokes," "The Serve & the Return" and "Specialty Shots." 126 min. total.
64-1373 ***$49.99***

Ice & Asphalt: The World Of Hockey
A fun and educational overview of the thrilling world of hockey, from the ice to the street and from the schoolyard to the rink. Luc Robataille hosts this show that includes tips from stars Chris Chelios, Pavel Bure, Mario Lemieux and Wayne Gretzky, as well as celebrity guests Scott Bakula, Alan Thicke and Richard Dean Anderson. There's also a trip to the NHL Hall of Fame. 59 min.
06-2436 ***$14.99***

Wayne Gretzky's Train To Win
Join "the Great One" in this video that offers excellent tips on training and hockey techniques. Gretzky is joined by Dr. Howie Wenger for a clinic on weight training, foot speed, acceleration, aerobic condition and nutrition. Endorsed by the NHL, this program is geared to your game to the high performance level. 75 min.
72-3023 ***$19.99***

Swim Lessons For Kids
Let your youngsters take the plunge, as this instructional video shows parents how to teach their children ages 3-12 how to swim. Swimming instructor Sue Royston covers floating, the crawl stroke and backstroke, breathing while swimming, and important safety tips for emergency situations. 40 min.
50-2448 ***$29.99***

Water Safety For Kids
A special video for youngsters that instructs them in important rules of swimming and water safety and shows them how to recognize and avoid dangerous situations. 15 min.
50-2624 ***$14.99***

Great American Trout Streams: Boxed Set
Get ready to "cast off" on a coast-to-coast tour of the country's top trout fishing locations. Host Tim Linehan also introduces you to fishin' magicians at each spot who share their tips for landing the big ones. Included in the three-tape set are "Eastern Rivers," "Rocky Mountain Rivers" and "Western Rivers." 285 min. total. NOTE: Individual volumes available at $19.99 each.
89-5174 Save $20.00! ***$39.99***

Bird Watching

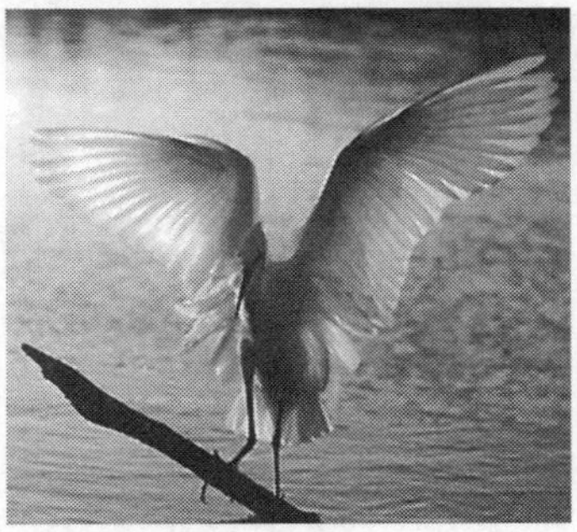

Audubon Society Videoguide To Birds Of North America
Renowned ornithologist Roger Tory Peterson is your host for this special program on American birds. Still and film footage, special animation techniques and graphics show each bird's natural habitat, feeding and nesting habits, bird calls and range.

Audubon Society Videoguide, Vol. 1
Includes loons, pelicans, ducks, geese and small waterfowl, hawks, vultures and falcons, and chicken-like birds. 94 min.
52-1076 ***$29.99***

Audubon Society Videoguide, Vol. 2
Includes herons, egrets, cranes, shore birds, gulls and terns. 60 min.
52-1086 ***$29.99***

Audubon Society Videoguide, Vol. 3
Includes pigeons and doves, cuckoos, owls, woodpeckers, kingfishers, hummingbirds and swifts. 60 min.
52-1087 ***$29.99***

Audubon Society Videoguide, Vol. 4
Includes swallows, crows, chickadees and nuthatches, wrens and thrushes. 60 min.
52-1088 ***$29.99***

Audubon Society Videoguide, Vol. 5
Includes vireos and warblers, finches, grosbeaks, buntings and sparrows. 60 min.
52-1089 ***$29.99***

Adventures In Birdwatching
Fans of our fine feathered friends will flock to this three-tape collection, culled from the popular "All-Bird TV" series, of up-close looks at some of the world's most interesting and beautiful birds. See New England songbirds and shorebirds along the Florida coast; avian predators from the Pacific Northwest and Southwest hummingbirds; and toucans and other exotic Central American species. 180 min. total.
81-3009 ***$49.99***

Pet Care

Just Call Me Kitty
"Miiidnight...and the kitties are sleeping!" Take a loving look at America's favorite felines with this purrrfectly wonderful video. See Persians, Maine Coons, Abyssinians and more, plus diet and grooming tips and other cat info. 60 min.
48-1138 ***$14.99***

Hamsters And Rabbits
These pets may be small in size, but they're big in fun and affection. Learn the "how-to's" of hamsters, from feeding and living quarters to the care of a "surprise" brood, followed by bunny basics on nutrition, health care and litter training (it can be done!). 45 min.
50-3949 ***$14.99***

Woof! Woof!! Uncle Matty's Guide To Dog Training
Dog expert to the stars Matthew Margolis offers a humane and innovative approach to canine training that covers all bases, from picking the proper puppy to making your new pet feel at home, from basic obedient commands to stopping problematical behavior problems. See how "Uncle Matty's" methods have worked for performers David Carradine, Louise Sorel and others. 70 min.
50-5412 ***$19.99***

Training The Family Dog
If Fido's a little too frisky, or Rover a bit rebellious, why not check out this video guide to basic discipline and easy ways to keep Trey in tow? 60 min.
68-1074 ***$19.99***

Arts & Crafts

Chinese Brush Painting
Traditional techniques of Chinese brush painting are shown by instructor Jane Evans, who goes over necessary materials and demonstrates how to create basic flower designs, plus more complicated subjects like birds, fish and landscapes. 90 min.
22-1383 ***$19.99***

Making Christmas Special
Make the Yuletide experience even more fun with tips on decorating your home, using fabric gift wrap and unusual alternatives to ribbons and bows, holiday craft projects for kids, do-it-yourself ornaments and garlands, and even how to prepare chocolate spoons and lace baskets. 50 min.
89-5052 ***$14.99***

Making Halloween Special
It's no trick to making original Halloween costumes (including robot, bee, fairy princess and French fries), creating spooky decorations, or whipping up party treats such as "spider soup" and "rotten apples" yourself. 50 min.
89-5053 ***$14.99***

Photography

How To Shoot Home Video: The Basics
The perfect introduction to home video, this tape covers Basic Camera Theory (F-stops, the iris, fade ins and outs), Sound, Lighting, Composition (framing, balance) and Directing/Continuity (establishing shots, camera angles, cut-aways). 30 min.
10-3116 ***$14.99***

The Art Of Erotic Photography
Learn how to take sexy shots while enjoying breathtaking scenery and beautiful women. Photographer John Kelly and four gorgeous models travel to a tropic isle where he demonstrates the art of centerfold photography. Contains nudity. 50 min.
50-1997 ***$24.99***

Food & Wine

Floyd Uncorked: Boxed Set
British TV gourmet Keith Floyd is joined by wine expert Jonathan Pedley for a robust and bubbly tour of the wine country of France in this four-volume series. Learn about the culture, history and distinctive product of each region in "The Alsace Region & Provence," "Burgundy & The Loire Valley," "The Languedoc-Roussillon Region & Champagne" and "The Rhone Region & The Bordeaux Region." 230 min. total.
80-7299 *$49.99*

California Wines: The White Varietals
For connoisseurs or those who can just about read a wine list, this instructional tape opens up a cellarful of marvelous white wines. You'll become acquainted with Chardonnay, Sauvignon Blanc, Johannesburg Riesling and more. 60 min.
10-3211 *$14.99*

California Wines: The Red Varietals
Your knowledge of California red wines will ripen with the viewing of this comprehensive guide. It'll show you how to "read" the color, how to chill, how to serve and how to select for any occasion. Wines covered are Cabernet Sauvignon, Merlot, Pinot Noir, Zinfandel and more. 60 min.
10-3212 *$14.99*

The Celebrity Guide To Entertaining
Looking to have a "Hollywood party, going a mile a minute?" Then let such stars as Tony Curtis, Whoopi Goldberg, Dudley Moore, Kelly LeBrock and Steven Seagal show you how to put together holiday and evening parties for two to 20 guests on a "plain folks" budget with this tape, hosted by Paula McClure and Spago maitre d' Bernard Erpicum. 62 min.
02-2466 *$14.99*

How To Enjoy Wine
Join oenophile Hugh Johnson for an encyclopedic look at the world of wine. From selecting, storing and decanting to tasting, reading a wine list and even how to open that stubborn cork, you'll learn all you need to know to be the smash of the cellar. 53 min.
22-5509 *$14.99*

Olympic Bartending
"Spin the Bottle" takes on a whole new meaning with this step-by-step guide to bartending flash from John "BD" Bundy, the champion mixologist who taught the hippy, hippy shake and other moves to Tom Cruise for the movie "Cocktail." 50 min.
76-7017 *$29.99*

The Art Of Dining: The Formal Dinner
Etiquette specialist Marjabelle Young Stewart offers tips on minding one's manners at a formal dinner. From invitations to seating and info on toasting, utensils and leaving the table, this program will make you say "Bon Appetit!" 36 min.
22-5483 *$14.99*

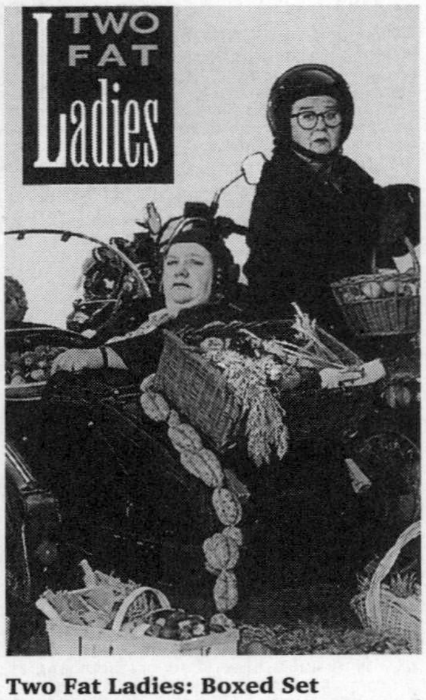

Two Fat Ladies: Boxed Set
This five-tape boxed set features the best recipes and antics of motorcycle-riding Brits Jennifer Paterson and Clarissa Dickson Wright. The feisty, fubsy TV Food Network faves show you how to prepare "Fish & Shellfish/Meat/Fruit & Vegetables," "Cakes & Baking/Game/Food in the Wild," "Lunch/Cocktail Party/Afternoon Tea," "Picnic/Breakfast/Dinner" and "A Christmas Feast." 377 min. total.
80-7236 *$79.99*

Quick And Easy Chinese Cooking
It's as simple as a "wok" down the block. So says Rocky Aoki, founder of Benihana, and on this tape he'll demonstrate some basic Chinese dishes that you'll learn to prepare at home in a snap. 30 min.
64-1090 *$14.99*

Chocolate, Chocolate, Chocolate
Chocoholics of the world will love this scrumptious salute to the joys of chocolate. See how the delicious delight is produced, poured, eaten, decorated and revered. You'll get a sweet tooth just by watching! 30 min.
64-1159 *$12.99*

Music Lessons

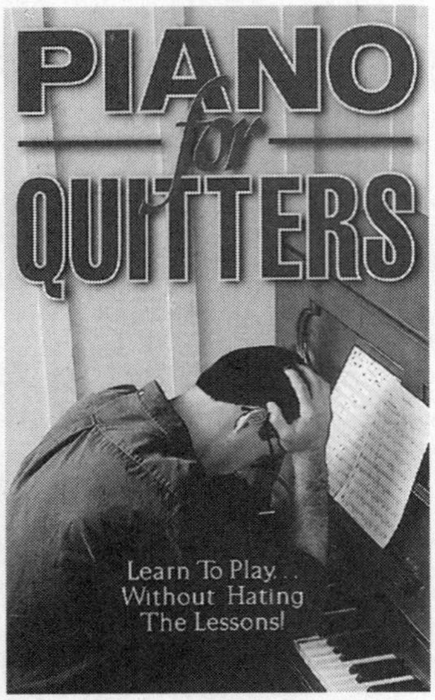

Piano For Quitters
Ever regret dropping out of those piano lessons you started taking as a child? Get ready to pound the ivories again, as instructor Marc Almond shares with you his proven method for playing the piano, a holistic approach based on those used by composers and musicians in the 1700s and 1800s. Perfect for returning students and new ones alike! 80 min.
50-3159 *$29.99*

Elementary Guitar With Barney Kessel
Renowned jazz musician Kessel guides the beginning strummer through the theory and practice of basic guitar. Tuning, tone production, music theory, chords and more explained. 77 min.
50-1147 Was $29.99 *$19.99*

Rock Guitar: A Guide From The Greats
Three of the top players of pop and rock—Richard Thompson, Michael Schenker and Ron Wood—offer advice of selecting your first guitar, chord positions and hand techniques, playing solos and more. There's also performance excerpts from guitar heroes Les Paul, B.B. King, Chuck Berry and Jimi Hendrix. 60 min.
63-7016 *$24.99*

Keyboards Today!
All-encompassing video series teaches novices the basic and finer points of keyboard playing. Each tape includes a workbook and flash cards that enable the would-be musician to review the important points demonstrated. Forget hours of tedious lessons, and pick up on this information-filled four-part series.

Keyboards Today!, Vol. 1
Learn the fundamentals of note reading, basic playing technique, accompaniment, and using the automatic chorder and manual chording.
50-4704 *$29.99*

Keyboards Today!, Vol. 2
After you finish watching this tape, most of the fundamentals featured here allow you to get going on almost any song.
50-4705 *$29.99*

Learn To Sing And Entertain
Joe Terry of Danny and The Juniors offers advice to would-be vocalists in this video how-to. He'll point out important techniques, show you how to gain confidence, how to use the microphone and body language, and how relaxation techniques can help your singing. There's even a segment on using a karaoke machine. 67 min.
50-4824 *$24.99*

Hobbies & Games

America's Best Model Trains
Classic and antique Lionel and American Flyer trains are presented in all their chugga-chugga glory in this program that offers the most incredible model train layouts in the country. It's all aboard trains that travel from level to level and room to room, through operating roundhouses and more. 45 min.
10-2582 *$12.99*

Play Chess, Vol. 1
It's been the world's favorite board game for centuries. Now beginners and novice players can learn about the rules of chess, basic moves and strategies, and more, courtesy of U.S. Chess Federation official Vince McCambridge. 50 min.
64-1101 *$19.99*

Play Chess, Vol. 2
Make your move beyond the basic game in this instructional video. Topics covered by chess masters Vince McCambridge and Bruce Pandolfini include making an aggressive opening, keeping control in the middlegame, common checkmate patterns, practicing with a chess computer and more. 65 min.
64-1213 *$19.99*

Max Maven's Mindgames
Look into my eyes...deeper...deeper...you will go to the counter, and you will get this tape starring master magician and psychic Max Maven. You will be amazed at his feats of mind reading, crazy card tricks, and magic with money, and you will see why he has astounded audiences on stage, television and film. 56 min.
07-1229 *$29.99*

Quick Tricks: Fun 'N Easy Magic
If you think that "legerdemain" is something that accountants do, maybe you should watch as mage Peter London demonstrates several easy "quick tricks" you can perform at home. 40 min.
64-1053 *$19.99*

The World Of Beanie Babies: The Unauthorized Collector's Video Guide
If you don't know "beans" about these adorable stuffed critters that kids love to collect and adults buy and sell for hundreds of dollars, this video guide to the Beanie Babies craze is for you. Learn about the history of Beanies, what makes some retired animals worth more than others, and other fascinating facts as you hear from collectors and visit Beanie shows. 50 min.
10-2808 *$14.99*

Minnesota Fats: How To Play Pool
Don't get caught behind the eight ball when someone challenges you to a game of pool. Minnesota Fats demonstrates the basics (stance, grip, line up, bridge and stroke), goes over the rules of the game, and even demonstrates some of his famous trick shots to guest Waylon Jennings. 60 min.
40-1171 *$14.99*

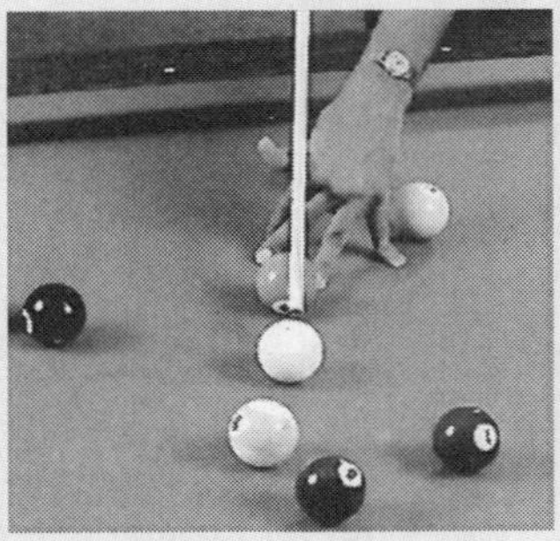

Byrne's Standard Video Of Pool & Billiards
If those tricky shots have left you behind the eight ball, get ready to rack up some fun by watching renowned pool teacher Robert Byrne on this video lesson series, as he demonstrates table top plays and strategies that'll have you sinking them faster than "Fast Eddie" Felson. There are four volumes available, including:

Byrne's Standard Video, Vol. 1: Basic To Advanced Techniques
Covers game basics such as grip, stance, using rakes and bridges, and stop, follow and bank shots.
50-3961 *$29.99*

Byrne's Standard Video, Vol. 2: Expert Techniques
Learn about such advanced techniques as jump and curve shots, sidespins, caroms and more.
50-3962 *$29.99*

Health & Personal Improvement

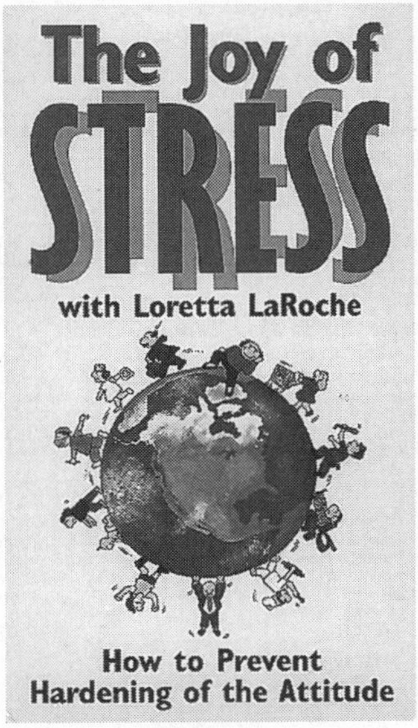

The Joy Of Stress
Humor is proven to be an indispensable tool in alleviating stress, and this program explores the concept of stress, its effect on mind, body and spirit and how humor aids in dealing with it. Hosted by Loretta LaRoche, stress management expert. 60 min.
50-5239 *$19.99*

Humor Your Stress
Using her light-hearted style and background in cognitive therapy, self-help speaker Loretta LaRoche helps you get a handle on stress and shows how humor can help people relax in a hectic world of over-achievers. Loretta also details the "eight steps to re-enlightenment" and the joys of rediscovering family and friends. 60 min.
50-5400 *$19.99*

Shirley MacLaine's Inner Workout
Sure, you've gotten your body in shape, but what about that all important "inner self"? Learning to relax and overcome stress can help you stay healthy, and transcendental screen star Shirley MacLaine goes out on a limb to share with you her own easy-to-follow relaxation and meditation exercises. 70 min.
47-1931 Was $29.99 *$14.99*

The Alexander Technique 2-Pack
For more than 100 years practitioners have used the Alexander Technique to ease back pain, relieve stress and improve well-being. Included in this two-tape set are "Alexander Technique: First Lesson," in which instructor Jane Kosminky demonstrates the basics with her guest, actor William Hurt; and "Alexander Technique: Solutions for Back Trouble," offering tips on overcoming and preventing back pain. 150 min. total. NOTE: Individual volumes available at $24.99 each.
53-6756 Save $10.00! *$39.99*

Letting Go Of Stress
Learn how to control stress in your daily life with the help of stress management instructor Frederick R. Honig. He teaches you how to implement the "wellness wheel," which enhances mental clarity, goal realization, health, vitality, relaxation, well-being and inner peace.
76-7281 *$19.99*

Oprah: Make The Connection
In this video companion to her best-selling self-help book, top talk show hostess Oprah Winfrey shares her step-by-step program for taking charge of your life and tips for healthier, happier living. 55 min.
11-2172 Was $24.99 *$14.99*

The Healthy Vegetarian
With this video, you'll learn about the healthy, vegetarian way of life. Tips on choosing the alternative eating style and how to get children interested in fruits and vegetables are offered, along with insight on shopping and cooking. Witness the impressive variety of foods available for vegans, too! 70 min.
50-5337 *$39.99*

How Can I Tell If I'm Really In Love?
Is "puppy love" real love? Should teenagers have sex? Does being in love really feel like "being on the Planet Z of Funness?" Young people can learn the answers to these and other questions about family life, dating and romance in this fun, informative tape that features advice from doctors and educators; Ted Danson and Justine and Jason Bateman host. 51 min.
06-1417 Was $24.99 *$14.99*

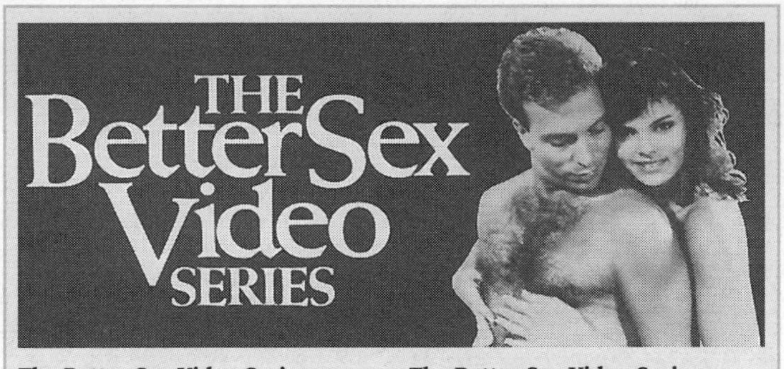

The Better Sex Video Series

This acclaimed series looks at different aspects of the sexual experience and how it can be improved between couples. Professional experts lend advice, and partners enact various sexual situations and fantasies in explicit segments. Informative, provocative, and artistically produced, these videos have been featured on many major TV talk shows.

The Better Sex Video Series, Vol. 1: Better Sexual Techniques

Five couples talk about and illustrate how improved communication skills enhanced their sexual relationships. 90 min.
50-4792 Was $29.99 *$19.99*

The Better Sex Video Series, Vol. 2: Advanced Sexual Techniques

A continuation of the first volume of the series, this program concerns techniques of good intercourse, oral sex, anal stimulation and more. 90 min.
50-4793 Was $29.99 *$19.99*

The Better Sex Video Series, Vol. 3: Making Sex Fun

Making loving fun is an essential element in relationships, and this program offers couples tips on playing role games, wearing different costumes and having sex in different rooms. 90 min.
50-4794 Was $29.99 *$19.99*

The Better Sex Video Series, Vol. 4: Exploring Sexual Fantasies

This tape will enable you to let your sexual fantasies become reality, as group sex, domination, sex with a stranger and other situations are explored. 85 min.
50-4795 Was $29.99 *$19.99*

The Better Sex Video Series, Vol. 5: Sharing Sexual Fantasies

Romantic sex, group sex, same-gender sex and other fantasies are explored in this guide to enhancing eroticism in your life. 75 min.
50-4796 Was $29.99 *$19.99*

The Better Sex Video Series, Vol. 6: Acting Out Your Sexual Fantasies

The reasons why people don't discuss their innermost desires are explained, and the benefits of partaking in fantasies are shown. Fantasies covered here involve romantic sex, sex in unusual places and sex with more than one partner. 76 min.
50-4797 Was $29.99 *$19.99*

The Better Sex Video Series, Vol. 7: Advanced Sexual Fantasies

Presented here is the latest data on sexual fantasies as well as segments from popular adult films. You'll learn about fantasies and guilt and get the answer to the question: Is it wrong to fantasize about someone else while making love to your partner? 55 min.
50-4798 Was $29.99 *$19.99*

The Better Sex Video Series, Vol. 8: You Can Last Longer

Now you can learn how to achieve better ejaculatory control by watching couples demonstrate intimate behavior, then discovering self-help techniques from noted therapists. Among the methods covered are the "Stop-Start" and the "Squeeze." 38 min.
50-4799 Was $29.99 *$19.99*

The Better Sex Video Series: Complete Set

All eight volumes in the "Better Sex Video Series" is available in this money-saving set.
50-4802 Save $20.00! *$139.99*

Alternative Medicine: Natural Medicine Chest And Home Remedies

Learn how to treat 50 common health conditions the natural way with this first-rate guide to alternative medicine. In expert, easy-to-understand fashion, you'll discover natural remedies for acne, allergies, backaches and lots more. Includes a 72-page reference book. 60 min.
50-5577 *$24.99*

Improving Your Intuition

"I wish I hadn't done that." "I should have bought that house." "I should have pursued that relationship." Does this sound familiar? If so, then this comprehensive new video is for you. Featuring some of the world's most renowned intuition experts, the program offers practical advice on listening to your "inner voice" and using your judgment to lessen life's laments and regrets. Also includes the six-page companion book "Intuition Exercise Guide." 45 min.
50-5872 *$29.99*

Dr. Wayne Dyer 2-Pack

Take charge of your life with this two-tape series of programs featuring the best-selling author of "Your Erroneous Zones" and "Everyday Wisdom." In "How to Get What You Really, Really, Really, Really Want," Dyer offers life-affirming techniques to build up one's self-image and drive at work and at home, while "Improve Your Life Using the Wisdom of the Ages" focuses on timeless, universal precepts and applies them to modern society. 160 min. total. NOTE: Individual volumes available at $19.99 each.
53-6847 Save $5.00! *$34.99*

Ancient Secrets Of Healing

Some of the most recent discoveries in health care are actually centuries old. Olympia Dukakis narrates this fascinating look at such long-practiced alternative medicine techniques as acupuncture, herbal medicine, homeopathy and guided imagery, as you explore the truth behind the claims and hear case stories from actual patients. 94 min.
50-8316 *$19.99*

Atkins' Answer: Dr. Atkins' New, Personalized "Weight Loss For Life" System

Dr. Atkins said "Let 'em eat steak." And steak and bacon and hamburgers they ate—and watched as the diet reduced their weight! This two-tape guide to the diet rage of the world features "Why It Works," an intro to rapid and permanent loss and "How It Works," a look at the simple keys for switching body metabolism to burn fat now! 60 min. total.
50-8375 *$39.99*

Healing Sexual Abuse: The Recovery Process

No matter how horrible it seems when sexual abuse occurs, a healthy and full recovery is possible. Hosted by therapist and author Dr. Eliana Gil, this video deals with such issues as incestual abuse, depression, suicidal feelings, and successful confrontations of the offenders. Includes a 32-page resource guidebook. 60 min.
50-5887 *□$19.99*

Alan Watts: The Art Of Meditation

Alan Watts, the late expert of Eastern thought, offers a step-by-step instructional video on the meditative disciplines of body posture, breath control and concentration. Also featured is Watts' colleague Elda Hartley's film, "Meditation: The Inward Journey," a look at how meditation is practiced in Muslim, Buddhist, Sufi, Christian and other cultures. 50 min.
70-9004 *$19.99*

Gay Youth

This important video helps "break the silence" regarding adolescent homosexuality and some of the disturbing statistics involving gay and lesbian teens. The program contrasts the tragic tale of 20-year-old suicide victim Bobby Griffith and the remarkable life of 17-year-old Gina Guiterrez. Learn how acceptance, support and information can make a difference. 40 min.
76-2082 *$39.99*

Trouble In Mind: Complete Set

Gain a better understanding of mental health topics and concerns with this 13-tape series that offers clear, concise explanations and practical advice from top medical professionals. Included are "Antisocial Personality Disorder," "ADD: Attention Deficit Disorder," "Borderline Personality Disorder," "Delirium," "Dementia," "Eating Disorder," "Mania," "Obsessive Compulsive Disorder," "Panic Disorder," "Paranoia," "Postpartum Depression," "Psychosomatic Illness" and "Schizophrenia." Jaclyn Smith hosts. NOTE: Individual volumes available at $29.99 each.
83-1492 Save $10.00! *$379.99*

Reflexology: The Timeless Art Of Self Healing

Does the key to better health lie at the bottom of your feet? Noted reflexology teacher and author Ann Gillanders demonstrates how nerve points in the foot correspond to every organ and system inside your body, and how simple pressure and massage moves can balance energies, reduce stress and alleviate health problems as diverse as PMS, headaches, backaches and insomnia. 75 min.
89-5099 *$24.99*

Larry Hagman's "Stop Smoking"

Do yourself a favor and quit that filthy habit once and for all with help from someone who's been there himself, Larry Hagman. Hagman shares all of his simple techniques that have made him a non-smoker. If J.R. can do it, so can you. 60 min.
40-1282 *$14.99*

Men Are From Mars, Women Are From Venus

His best-selling book on the behavioral and emotional differences between the sexes has changed thousands of lives. Now, in this ABC News program, Dr. John Gray presents his insights into building and strengthening relationships to six couples, in the hopes of mending their marital problems. 90 min.
50-7461 *$19.99*

Emotional Intelligence With Daniel Goleman

Most people are familiar with "IQ" (intelligence quotient), but psychologist/author Dr. Daniel Goleman says a better gauge of one's health and personal and professional prospects may come from measuring their "EQ" (emotional quotient) in five areas: empathy, managing emotions, motivation, self-awareness and social skills. Hear him discuss what your EQ says about you in this eye-opening program. 70 min.
90-1025 Was $19.99 *□$14.99*

Sexual Positions For Lovers

Four attractive couples demonstrate numerous lovemaking positions that are sure to enhance sexual pleasure. Covered in this informative tape are deeper penetration, G-Spot stimulation, prolonged intercourse and recommended positions for lovers with physical problems. Explicit sexuality is featured.
50-4800 Was $29.99 *$19.99*

Becoming Orgasmic

Women will learn methods to overcome the problems that prevent orgasm after watching this therapist-developed program. The tape offers masturbation techniques, ways to increase sexual desire, pointers on relaxation and recommendations on exploring bodies. WARNING: contains nudity and explicit material. 83 min.
50-4801 Was $29.99 *$19.99*

Power Of Seduction: How To Attract And Become The Perfect Lover

Leading sexologist Ava Cadell shows you the secrets to enhance your romantic and sexual relationship. Learn how to evaluate yourself, flirting techniques, undressing your lover, the G-Spot mystery, the art of erotic talk, discovering erogenous zones and more. 60 min.
50-5556 *$24.99*

Love Skills: A Guide To The Pleasures Of Sex

Specially made with couples in mind, this sensitively made yet visually explicit tape shows how to heighten your erotic awareness and enhance sexual experience. 56 min.
07-1251 *$29.99*

Warning: Food May Be Hazardous!

The hidden dangers in what you eat are explored in this important program that looks at foods and oils that can raise or lower cholesterol levels, how to read food labels, the truth behind coffee and sweets, and what foods to avoid at restaurants. 30 min.
58-8115 *$12.99*

Dr. Andrew Weil 3-Pack

He's a physician, a best-selling author, and one of the country's top health experts, and in this special three-tape set you'll see and hear Dr. Andrew Weil's practical advice on the topics of "8 Weeks to Optimum Health," "Eating Well for Optimum Health" and "Spontaneous Healing." 213 min. total. NOTE: "8 Weeks" and "Spontaneous Healing" are available separately at $14.99 each; "Eating Well" is available at $19.99.
53-6844 Save $10.00! *$39.99*

Massage: The Touch Of Love

Couples looking to learn how to rub each other the right way for a change can check out this beautifully photographed video guide to the sensual art of full body massage. 28 min.
07-1069 *$29.99*

Massage Your Mate

Rub your better half the right way for a change, after you master these Swedish and Shiatsu Acupressure techniques demonstrated by noted therapist Rebecca Klinger. Definitively explained in five chapters, this video will place you on the path to relaxation. 92 min.
22-7004 *$29.99*

The Healthy Massage Series

Stimulate muscles and promote relaxation with these healthful and sensuous Swedish and Shiatsu techniques. This easy-to-learn, three-part program has been acclaimed as the best available by professional therapists. Each tape runs about 30 min.

Healthy Massage, Vol. 1: The Scalp, Face, Neck And Chest

22-7046 Was $19.99 *$14.99*

Healthy Massage, Vol. 2: The Back

22-7047 Was $19.99 *$14.99*

Healthy Massage, Vol. 3: The Legs And Feet

22-7048 Was $19.99 *$14.99*

Deepak Chopra: Body, Mind & Soul: Complete Set

This two-tape set showcases Dr. Deepak Chopra and his beliefs and teachings. What is the body? What is the mind? Does the soul really exist? Dr. Chopra delves into these questions and also ponders the mechanics of perception, the seduction of the spirit and the keys to the active mastery of life. 120 min. total.
18-7632 *□$39.99*

Suzanne Somers: Somersize

TV/film star and pin-up fave Suzanne Somers shares her tips on starting and maintaining a healthy diet and lifestyle with this special two-tape program. "Eat Great, Lose Weight" features advice on proper eating and nutrition, while in "Think Great, Look Great" Somers presents stress-reduction and positive thinking exercises to inspire and motivate. Also includes companion audiocassettes, reference guide and recipe cards.
04-3424 *$29.99*

Child Care

Take Charge Of Your Pregnancy

Pregnancy needn't mean "confinement," especially with this liberating and authoritative guide to maternity management hosted by Candice Bergen. See how those baby boomers old enough to have their own babies are staying more active and healthier than ever before. 95 min.
04-2217 *□$29.99*

Strong Kids, Safe Kids

A timely and informative tape, produced by and starring Henry Winkler, that teaches kids to be wary of strangers and how to protect themselves. Designed for family viewing, the tape also features John Ritter, Mariette Hartley, and cartoon guests like the Flintstones and Scooby-Doo. 42 min.
06-1221 *$14.99*

The Joy Of Natural Childbirth

An exciting, informative hour on natural childbirth, with discussions, a look at the Lamaze Method and an actual birth sequence. Lorenzo Lamas, Jane Seymour, Kenny Rogers and Cindy Williams are featured. 60 min.
07-1257 *$29.99*

I Am Your Child (1997)

Tom Hanks hosts this program that examines Hampton Healthy Start, the innovative family development program used by the community of Hampton, Virginia, to help parents care for and teach their children during the first three years of life. Advice on child care is offered in segments with such guest stars as Michael J. Fox, Charlton Heston, Rosie O'Donnell, Colin Powell, Roseanne, Oprah Winfrey and President and Mrs. Clinton. Co-written and directed by Rob Reiner; theme by Barry Manilow. 45 min.
50-7451 *$19.99*

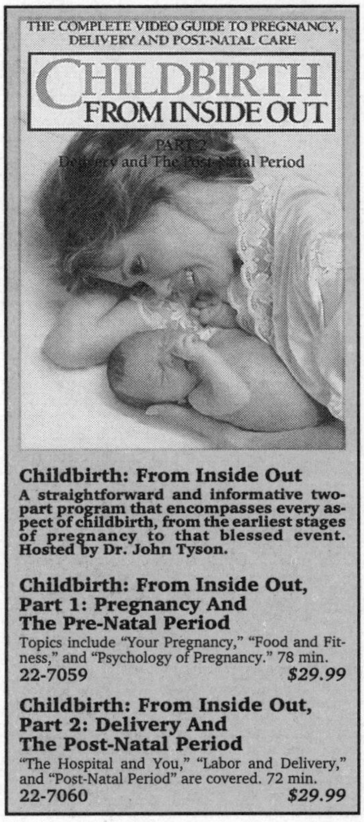

Childbirth: From Inside Out

A straightforward and informative two-part program that encompasses every aspect of childbirth, from the earliest stages of pregnancy to that blessed event. Hosted by Dr. John Tyson.

Childbirth: From Inside Out, Part 1: Pregnancy And The Pre-Natal Period

Topics include "Your Pregnancy," "Food and Fitness," and "Psychology of Pregnancy." 78 min.
22-7059 *$29.99*

Childbirth: From Inside Out, Part 2: Delivery And The Post-Natal Period

"The Hospital and You," "Labor and Delivery," and "Post-Natal Period" are covered. 72 min.
22-7060 *$29.99*

Child Development: The First Two Years
A comprehensive video guide to caring for your baby and encouraging physical and mental growth. Learn about nutrition, enhancing motor skills, language development and other topics in four age ranges: newborn to three months, three to six months, six to 12 months, and 12 to 24 months. 47 min.
22-7093 *$19.99*

Infant Massage: The Power Of Touch
Get your baby off to a healthy start with this video featuring easy to follow, step-by-step lessons in infant massage, demonstrated by a licensed neuromuscular therapist. A special "question-and-answer" session with health care professionals is included. 48 min.
22-7166 *$19.99*

When Baby Comes Home
Special made-for-video program will inform new parents on caring for the new arrival, answering questions on every subject from feeding and bathing to common ailments. 55 min.
50-6060 *$29.99*

Is Your Child Gifted?
Think your kid is smarter than most? This video offers tips on recognizing the signs of gifted children and help for nurturing your little genius. Learn how to develop you child's potential emotionally, intellectually, artistically and socially with this important guide. 60 min.
53-6907 *$14.99*

Brighter Baby
This video offers groundbreaking research on baby care and how different activities and behavior can affect your youngster. Hosted by medical expert Brenda Adderly, the program shows demonstrations of what works regarding a baby's development, from playing Mozart to baby massage to tips on how touch, sound and nutrition can enhance intelligence and well-being. 45 min.
53-6625 Was $19.99 *$14.99*

The Children Are Watching
Jane Seymour hosts this eye-opening look at how the actions of parents can, consciously or unconsciously, influence their teenage children. Four families are followed on camera, as anger, violence and other cyclical patterns of self-destructive behavior are revealed, and recommendations for counseling and support groups are offered. 58 min.
90-1043 *$19.99*

Jobs & Careers

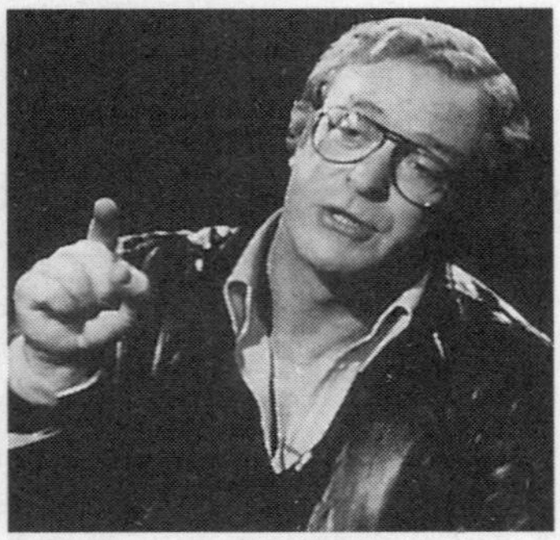

Michael Caine: Acting In Film
Academy Award-winning actor Michael Caine reveals some of the most precious secrets about his craft in this acclaimed video. Caine talks about using the cameras, using your face to get the most out of a reading and the importance of preparation. A fascinating and informative program from one of the world's best and busiest actors. 60 min.
50-1979 *$49.99*

How To Start A Career In Television, Movies And Commercials
Everything you wanted to know about getting in front of the show biz camera is on this program produced by people already in the industry. Covered are such points as how to get an agent; how to prepare your pictures and resumé; auditioning tips; and more. 55 min.
50-4813 *$24.99*

Syd Field's Screenwriting Workshop
Master screenwriting teacher Syd Field brings his highly successful seminar on writing scripts to video in this special two-tape set. The Hollywood guru guides you through "Getting Started," "Creating Character," "Writing the Screenplay" and "Rewriting the Screenplay." Learn the finer points of writing dialogue, structure, plot points and more. 124 min.
50-8239 *$79.99*

So You Want To Be An Actor?
For everyone who's dreamed of a Broadway career, this program offers practical advice on everything from casting calls and getting an agent to financial survival in New York. Hosts Jerry Stiller and Anne Meara add their insight into the how-tos of the acting game, along with tips from Roscoe Lee Browne, Uta Hagen, Christopher Walken and others. 75 min.
22-1699 *$19.99*

Computers

Bits & Bytes: Complete Set
Using animation and step-by-step instruction, this six-tape series on the personal computer world of the '90s explains "Basics," "Words," "Numbers," "Files," "Messages" and "Pictures" in a way that's both easy to understand and entertaining. 180 min. total. NOTE: Individual volumes available at $19.99 each.
14-9099 Save $20.00! *$99.99*

The Internet Show
Merge onto the information superhighway with this video that looks at the lighter side of the Internet, as well as its serious applications. Writers John Levine and Gina Smith show how cyberspace can change the world...and your life! 66 min.
18-7546 *$14.99*

Secrets Of The Internet
You've got a green light on the Information Superhighway with this three-part series that explores the wonders of the World Wide Web. Host Richard Karn ("Home Improvement") guides you through a universe of informative, entertaining Internet sites and shows how computer technology is revolutionizing the way we work, learn and play. Segments include "Caught in the Web," "Surfin' Safari" and "Hot Links." 145 min.
50-7524 *$19.99*

The Internet Video...Doing Donuts On The Information Superhighway
Along with a history of the Internet, this program offers such tips on finding an Internet provider and logging on; creating, sending and receiving e-mail; searching for databases around the world; logging into World Wide Web pages; and joining a Newsgroup. 60 min.
76-7157 *$19.99*

Video Guide For Understanding And Buying A Personal Computer
Considering purchasing a computer? Here's a must-have guide to the process, with tips on hardware and software, an overview of operating systems and insight on understanding the components. For IBM and IBM compatible PCs. 60 min.
76-7243 *$19.99*

Language

Signing Made Easy!
Learn how to communicate with a hearing-impaired person with this easy-to-follow instructional video. Actor Anthony Natale ("Mr. Holland's Opus") is your host for a primer on the sign language alphabet and over 300 words that will let your fingers do the talking. 55 min.
53-6859 *$19.99*

Basic English Grammar By Video
The basics of English grammar are taught in this program ideal for those wanting to brush up on our language as well as newcomers to the language.
52-1067 Was $79.99 *$24.99*

Say It With Sign
Considered the most comprehensive video series on sign language for the deaf and hearing-impaired, "Say It With Sign" includes lessons on cultural differences, family relationships and communication between the deaf and hearing worlds. Hosted by Lawrence and Nancy Solow, this Emmy-nominated series is a unique, inventive instructional series. There are 10 volumes available, including:

Say It With Sign, Vol. 1
Includes "Introduction to Sign Language," with commonly used signs as "Stop," "come here," "yes" and "no"; and "Signs You Already Know," which features signs for "thank you," "sick," "tired," "please" and the letters "O" and "K." 60 min.
50-4710 *$29.99*

Say It With Sign, Vol. 2
Includes "More Signs You Already Know" (focusing on words about parenthood and the alphabet from "A" to "D"); "Basic Conversation" (with the sing-song "Follow Me," the signs for "yesterday," "morning" and "wonderful"); "Special Signs You Need" and "Weather Signs I," with the sing-song "Oh, What a Beautiful Mornin'" and words about the weather. 120 min.
50-4711 *$29.99*

Joy of talking

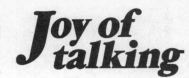

Joy Of Talking
Can't afford the inconvenience of language courses? Not interested in learning from a stuffy textbook? Everybody's talking about the Joy of Talking series, designed to teach a foreign language through mouth formations, facial expressions and body gestures. Each tape comes with an audiocassette and a pocket-sized phrase book, and runs about 65 min.

Joy Of Talking Spanish
68-1054 *$39.99*

Joy Of Talking French
68-1055 *$39.99*

Joy Of Talking German
68-1056 *$39.99*

Joy Of Talking Italian
68-1057 *$39.99*

Basic English For Hispanics By Video
Learn to read, write and speak a basic 1,000-word vocabulary in this tape, which reviews basic grammar and phrases using everyday situations. Contrasts English with Spanish. 90 min.
52-1071 Was $79.99 *$24.99*

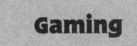

Gaming

Learn How To Win At Craps
Don't be intimidated when you step up to the table. Noted gaming authority John Patrick shows you betting strategies and play theories to lower the edge and let you leave the table with heavy pockets.

Beginner's Course
55-1040 *$39.99*

Advanced Craps
55-1125 *$39.99*

Intermediate Course
55-1225 *$39.99*

Learn How To Win At Roulette
Round and round the silver ball goes. Where she stops...you'll have a better idea if you let expert gambler John Patrick show you his systems to winning on the "wheel of fortune."

Basic Course
55-1041 *$39.99*

Advanced Roulette
55-1126 *$39.99*

Learn How To Win At Blackjack
Professional gamesman John Patrick says 21 is "one game you shouldn't play unless you're perfect." Watch as he demonstrates techniques for discipline and card-counting secrets.

Basic Course
55-1042 *$39.99*

Card Counting Course
55-1124 *$39.99*

Slots
You'll be the one holding up the one-armed bandit, once you view this potpourri of pointers from professional gambler John Patrick. Explore the differences between Progressive, Multi-line, Poker and Keno, dollar vs. quarter machines, how many coins to play at once, more. 50 min.
55-1123 *$39.99*

Horse Racing I: How To Interpret The Daily Racing Form Charts
"Here they come!" Noted gambling experts John Patrick and Rick Lang tell the would-be tout what information to look for in racing sheets and forms and, with the help of actual turf footage, show how to analyze race results. Make your trip to the track a more profitable experience. 112 min.
55-1234 *$39.99*

The Winning Strategies Series: Complete Set
You'll be "In Like Flint" at the casinos when host James Coburn and top gaming experts share their methods for improving the odds of the most popular games in your favor. This three-tape collection lets you in on the basic rules and successful strategies for "Blackjack," "Craps" and "Slots/Video Poker." 180 min. total. NOTE: Individual volumes available at $19.99 each.
89-5033 Save $10.00! *$49.99*

Play To Win: An Insider's Guide To Casino Gambling
Name your game and you'll find it here, along with important tips on how to beat the casinos at their own game. The instructor at the Las Vegas Hilton gives you the inside info on winning at blackjack, craps, roulette, slot machines and more. 74 min.
02-2305 Was $19.99 *$12.99*

Play To Win: Set
This three-tape set offers a primer on how to win at the casinos. Beat the odds, learn key strategies and approach the games with a surefire winning attitude after watching "Slots," "Blackjack" and "Craps." 120 min. total. NOTE: Individual volumes available at $14.99 each.
53-6818 Save $15.00! *$29.99*

The Lottery Video
Gamesman John Patrick reveals secrets of winning the popular Pick 6 Lotto with number selection methods based on the Unpopular Number Index, the Bell Curve Theorem and other major wheeling systems in use today. 45 min.
55-1242 *$24.99*

Miscellaneous

Help Save Planet Earth
Information and entertainment mix on this important and timely tape, as top stars talk about global environmental concerns and simple things we all can do to conserve. Ted Danson, Whoopi Goldberg, Jamie Lee Curtis, Beau and Lloyd Bridges and others are featured. 71 min.
07-1659 *$14.99*

8-Minute Makeovers
Make-up artist Claire Miller demonstrates the makeup techniques needed to complete the four basic looks: Classic, Romantic, Earthy, and Glamorous. Beauty tips, hairstyling advice, and makeup hints are combined to give you the most beautiful face possible. 60 min.
10-3112 *$14.99*

Why Do I Call You Sexy?
What do Farrah Fawcett, Victoria Principal, Ali MacGraw and Linda Gray have in common? Jose Eber! He's the famous hair styling expert who will show you celebrity hair care and fashion tips to help you look and feel sexy. 90 min.
40-1030 *$39.99*

The 9 Steps To Financial Freedom
Certified financial planner Suze Orman brings her ideas from her best-selling book to this video about how to overcome one's personal and psychological obstacles in the pursuit of wealth. Presented in a seminar format. 87 min.
90-1002 Was $19.99 *$14.99*

The Princeton Review
The world's leading test preparation course is now on tape, filled with important information for students taking the SAT. Included here are interviews with college admissions officers, an explanation of the SAT and test-taking techniques that are sure to help. 90 min.
19-3518 *$19.99*

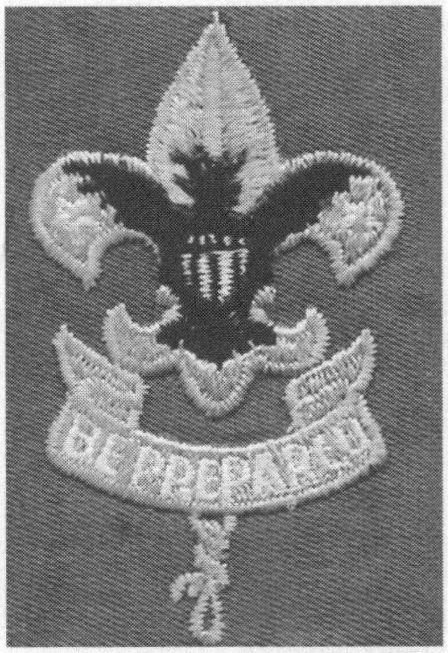

The Boy Scout Advancement Program: Complete Set
Now video can help youngsters "be prepared" as they climb the ladder up to Eagle Scout, courtesy of this official three-tape training series. The basics of scout lore, camping and hiking skills, first aid and physical fitness are demonstrated. Volumes include "Tenderfoot," "Second Class" and "First Class." 156 min. total. NOTE: Individual volumes available at $14.99.
06-3035 Save $15.00! *$29.99*

Journey Of Honor (1992)
Set in 1602, this action-packed adventure stars Sho Kosugi as a brave Samurai warrior who commands a ship sent from Japan to buy guns from the king of Spain. Battling shipboard spies, an evil duke and a nefarious sultan, the warrior attempts to complete his mission and claim the hand of the duke's fiancée. With Toshiro Mifune, Christopher Lee, David Essex. AKA: "Shogun Mayeda." 107 min.
07-1850 ❑$19.99

Billy Blanks Signature Series:
The King Of The Kickboxers (1991)/
Showdown(1994)
Before he was the king of "Tae-Bo Workout," Billy Blanks excelled in kung fu films, and here are two of his best. In "King of the Kickboxers," young martial artist Loren Avedon squares off against the evil Khan (Blanks) in order to avenge his brother's death. And in "Showdown," Blanks is an ex-cop-turned-sensei for a student involved in underground kickboxing. 194 min. on two tapes.
50-8308 $19.99

Full Contact (1993)
The action never stops in this martial arts-filled saga about a Fresno farmboy who hopes to avenge the death of his brother by seeking the murderer in the underground kickboxing circuit of Los Angeles. Kickboxing champs Jerry Trimble, Howard Jackson, Alvin Pounder and Gerry Blanck star. 96 min.
02-2473 Was $89.99 $14.99

Fatal Combat (1996)
The icy Arctic is the setting for this martial arts epic in which a wealthy broadcaster pits fighter against fighter in deadly martial arts bouts. When one bloodsport specialist is kidnapped and forced to fight, he breaks all the rules. Jeff Wincott and Phillip Jarrett star. 93 min.
02-2993 ❑$99.99

BRANDON LEE • POWERS BOOTHE
RAPID FIRE
UNARMED AND EXTREMELY DANGEROUS

Rapid Fire (1992)
Student Brandon Lee gets caught in the middle of a lethal drug war involving Chicago and Indo-Chinese mobsters, the FBI and a tough Chi-town detective. The fight sequences, which Lee helped stage, are among the most thrilling ever put on film. Nick Mancuso, Powers Boothe and Kate Hodge also star. 96 min.
04-2597 Was $19.99 ❑$14.99

The Perfect Weapon (1991)
Martial arts maven Jeff Speakman is a police detective who goes above the law when he sets out for justice by labeling a gang of Korean thugs "marked for death" in this bloodsport epic. Jeff's hard to kill, especially when his lionheart roars with vengeance. Wham! Bam! Speak-Man! John Dye and Mako co-star. 85 min.
06-1884 Was $89.99 ❑$14.99

Ring Of Steel (1994)
A former fencing champion becomes an outcast after accidentally killing an opponent in the ring, but is given a chance for a comeback when he battles bad guys in a decadent nightclub run by the mysterious "Man in Black." Eventually, the champion must face off against a psychotic fencer at the club. Robert Chapin, Carol Alt and Joe Don Baker star. 94 min.
07-2064 Was $89.99 ❑$14.99

Back In Action (1994)
A two-fisted cop teams with a martial arts expert and former Special Forces soldier to catch a ruthless drug ring who have taken the cop's girlfriend and the karate master's sister hostage. Roddy Piper, Billy Blanks and Bobbie Phillips star in this arresting actioner. 93 min.
07-2133 ❑$89.99

Triple Impact (1993)
Three martial arts champs join forces to defeat a global crime syndicate in a battle that ranges from backstreet fights in America to the jungles of Asia. Ron Hall, Dale "Apollo" Cook and Bridgett "Baby Doll" Riley are the stars of this smashing martial arts-filled saga. 97 min.
16-9134 $14.99

MARTIAL ARTS

Operation Golden Phoenix (1994)
In this rousing martial arts thriller, Jalal Merhi is a former CIA operative framed for stealing a priceless ancient pendant who busts out of prison and finds his way to Beirut. There, he uncovers the pendant's connection to an ancient treasure and must fight his former partner and an evil gangster to get to the goods. Loren Avedon, James Hong and Karen Sheperd co-star. 95 min.
07-2215 ❑$89.99

Night Of The Kickfighters (1991)
The kicks come fast and furious in this adrenaline-laden action flick, as a team of intelligence agents are charged with stopping terrorists armed with a top-secret weapon capable of destroying the world. Thrilling martial arts displays with world kickboxing champion Andy Bauman and Adam West. AKA: "Night Raiders." 87 min.
14-3405 $14.99

Blood Ring (1993)
A woman hires an old friend, a kickboxing champ, to help find her husband, who's been missing for months. The kickboxer soon discovers that the man is involved with an underground syndicate of fighters overseen by mobsters and is forced into action when he's captured. Dale "Apollo" Cook and Andrea Lamatsch star. 90 min.
16-9135 $14.99

Fist Of Steel (1991)
Kickfighting master Dale "Apollo" Cook is a futuristic warrior going up against an evil fighter named "Mainframe," who has been hired by "the syndicate" to destroy Cook in a fixed martial arts tournament. Gregg Douglass and Cynthia Khan also star in this foot-in-your-face epic. 97 min.
16-9138 $14.99

Gang Justice (1994)
Explosive thriller about a young Asian man named Paul whose family moves to America. After his father is crippled in a shootout and his mother remarries an American, Paul is forced to use his martial arts skills in a battle with a local gangleader...his new stepbrother! Jonathan Gorman, Nicole Rio and Erik Estrada star. 92 min.
16-9156 $14.99

Laser Mission (1990)
Brandon Lee, the son of martial arts master Bruce Lee, stars in this enthralling thriller filled with action and incredible fight sequences. He plays a renegade secret agent who must find the scientist responsible for a Soviet laser weapons formula. Ernest Borgnine and Debi Monahan also star. 83 min.
18-7230 ❑$14.99

Showdown In Little Tokyo (1991)
In this all-out action assault, Dolph Lundgren plays a tough cop who seeks vengeance for the death of his parents, murdered by a mobster when he was a youngster in Japan. With help from his wisecracking Asian partner (Brandon Lee), Lundgren takes to the dangerous streets of L.A.'s Little Tokyo in search of the killer. Tia Carrere co-stars. 76 min.
19-1909 Was $19.99 ❑$14.99

American Kickboxer 1 (1991)
Wave the flags and tighten the boots: Here come the American Kickboxers! Two expert footfighters tackle a rival kickboxer in a test of wills, strength and power that features the ultimate Yattle. John Barrett, Keith Vitali and Brad Morris star in this fight-filled actionfest. Stay tuned for the sequel. 93 min.
19-7081 Was $19.99 $14.99

American Kickboxer 2 (1993)
After her daughter is kidnapped and held for a $2 million ransom, a woman calls on both her L.A. cop ex-husband and a kickboxing champ and former lover to find the girl. These two dangerous men unite and enter a world where the only rule is that there are no rules. Dale "Apollo" Cook, Evan Lurie and Kathy Shower star. 91 min.
68-1266 Was $89.99 ❑$14.99

American Samurai (1992)
Two stepbrothers are trained from childhood by a master samurai in the deadly art of swordplay. But when one chooses to become a Yakuza gangster and the other a crusading journalist, the lines are drawn for a fight only one will survive in this exciting actioner. David Bradley, Mark Dacascos, Valarie Trapp star. 89 min.
19-7091 Was $19.99 ❑$14.99

Angel Fist (1993)
After her sister is savagely murdered, a beautiful martial arts maven goes to work, using her incredible skills for revenge. World Karate Association champ Cat Sassoon (that's right, Vidal's daughter) splits more than hairs in this thriller loaded with high-impact kicks, wild "Cat"-fighting sequences, and sexy co-stars Melissa Moore and Denise Buick. 80 min.
21-9032 Was $89.99 $14.99

Blood For Blood (1995)
A quiet policeman who has become a lethal human weapon draws upon his power to battle a Yakuza warlord when his family is put in danger. Lorenzo Lamas, James Lew and Mako star in this wild, kickboxing-filled thriller. 93 min.
27-6949 Was $89.99 ❑$12.99

Balance Of Power (1996)
Martial arts master Billy Blanks needs all of his power if he's going to take down a merciless Asian crime boss in this explosive action tale. With Mako, James Lew. 92 min.
27-7008 Was $99.99 ❑$14.99

The Dragon From Shaolin (1992)
He's one dragon who's never reluctant to unleash the full range of his swift and savage martial arts prowess. He's the one and only Brute Lee, and his vengeance on the soldiers who destroyed his order's temple is Brutal, indeed. 90 min.
41-7000 Was $29.99 $19.99

Bloodmatch (1991)
Martial arts champ Brick Bardo is put to the test when his brother is killed and he battles the world's greatest kickboxers in order to find the real murderer. Benny "The Jet" Urquidez, Thom Mathews and Hope Marie Carlton star. 85 min.
44-1820 Was $19.99 ❑$14.99

Street Knight (1993)
Kenpo karate expert Jeff Speakman plays an ex-L.A. cop whose search for a missing teenage gang member involves him with some renegade gang members planning a jewel heist. Christopher Neame also stars. 93 min.
19-7093 Was $19.99 ❑$14.99

To The Death (1993)
A champion kickboxer is lured out of retirement by a crooked fight promoter and soon discovers that the promoter's private kickboxing exhibitions end with the loser's death. Can the fighter team with an ex-opponent and escape with his life? John Barrett and Michel Qissi star. 90 min.
19-7096 Was $19.99 ❑$14.99

THE MYSTERY. THE LIFE. THE LOVE. THE LEGEND.
DRAGON
THE BRUCE LEE STORY

Dragon:
The Bruce Lee Story (1993)
Enthralling biography of late martial arts master Bruce Lee, covering his courtship and marriage to his American wife; his rise to karate prominence, competing in tournaments and teaching; and his meteoric but short-lived film career. Jason Scott Lee is dynamic in the title role; Lauren Holly and Robert Wagner also star. 120 min.
07-2024 Was $19.99 ❑$14.99

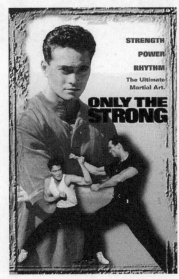
BlackBelt (1992)
A beautiful singer is the target for a deranged Vietnam veteran and must call on karate master Don "The Dragon" Wilson to help her fend off his deadly advances. This all-out martial-arts assault also features champions "Bad" Brad Hefton, Ernest Simmons, Mitch Borrow, Jim Graden, and others. 80 min.
21-9010 Was $89.99 $14.99

BlackBelt II: Fatal Force (1992)
A smashing martial arts spectacular starring world kickboxing champ Blake Bahner as a renegade L.A. detective who tackles a ring of drug dealers with his tough fists and swift kicks. With Roxanne Baird and Michael Vlastas. 83 min.
21-9027 Was $89.99 $14.99

Only The Strong (1993)
The 16th-century Brazilian mix of martial arts and dance known as "capoeira" is featured in this high-kicking, inspirational actioner. After fighting druglords in South America for the U.S. Army, a karate champ returns to his drug-infested former high school to teach the ancient art and stop the area's criminal activity. Mark Dacascos, Stacey Travis star. 96 min.
04-2751 Was $29.99 ❑$14.99

Kickboxer 2:
The Road Back (1991)
When his brother is murdered by an evil kickboxer angered after losing their match, a young fighter (Sasha Mitchell) is goaded by the killer's crooked manager to fight his man for his late brother's title. Slam-bang sequel to the martial arts actioner also stars Peter Boyle, Dennis Chan. 90 min.
44-1826 Was $19.99 ❑$14.99

Kickboxer 3:
The Art Of War (1992)
Sasha Mitchell is back, tackling all kickboxing culprits in this rip-snorting martial arts marathon. Mitchell lands in Rio, and soon finds himself in a murderous showdown against a drug-dealing mobster who has kidnapped a young girl. Dennis Chan co-stars. 92 min.
27-6789 Was $19.99 $12.99

Kickboxer 4:
The Aggressor (1993)
Could this be the final battle for kickboxer Sasha Mitchell? His arch-enemy, Tong Po, is determined to get rid of him once and for all, in the most exciting entry in the action-filled martial arts series yet. 90 min.
27-6865 $14.99

Redemption: Kickboxer 5 (1996)
Savage martial arts marathon involving a retired kickboxing champ out to avenge the death of a student who was murdered after he refused to join a renegade kickboxing federation. The search for vengeance takes him to South America, where he must fight to expose the group's leader's ruthless ways. Mark Dacascos, James Ryan star. 87 min.
68-1798 ❑$89.99

Dragon Fire (1993)
Futuristic kickboxing saga set in Los Angeles in the year 2050, where a rugged streetfighter seeks to avenge his brother's death by uncovering a killer in the dangerous world of kickbox matches of the future called "alley matches." Martial arts champs Dennis Kiefer, Rod Kei and Hyong Lee star; with Dominic La Banca. 93 min.
21-9043 Was $89.99 $14.99

China Heat (1990)
Enthralling stunts and non-stop action sequences are featured in this energized story about a group of female agents from China's elite task force who team with two New York City cops and their captain to get an international drug lord who has kidnapped two members of the force. Sibelle Hu and Sophia Crawford star. 90 min. Dubbed in English.
53-6165 $14.99

Jet Li

Shaolin Temple (1982)
In his first major film, an 18-year-old Jet Li brings his incredible Wu Shu skills to this period saga in which he seeks revenge for his father's death. After honing his martial arts abilities in the Shaolin Temple, Li is joined by a group of monks in his quest. With Yue Chen Wei, Yue Hai. 90 min. In Cantonese with English subtitles.
76-2104   Letterboxed   **$14.99**

Shaolin Temple (Dubbed Version)
Also available in a dubbed-in-English edition.
50-5060   **$39.99**

Kids From Shaolin (1983)
Jet Li's second effort is a sequel to "Shaolin Temple" and features the young martial arts master as the son of a Shaolin monk who's involved in a rivalry with a Wu Tang-following family on the other side of the river. Complications and extraordinary aerial fighting ensue when a star-crossed romance occurs. AKA: "Shaolin Temple II." 90 min. In Cantonese with English subtitles.
76-2102   Letterboxed   **$14.99**

Kids From Shaolin (Dubbed Version)
Also available in a dubbed-in-English edition.
82-7037   **$49.99**

Born To Defence (1986)
Jet Li directed and stars in this slam-banger, playing a young war veteran who, along with his former lieutenant, seeks a peaceful civilian life. But when his daughter and friend are mysteriously killed, Jet must find the killers and seek vengeance using his incredible Wu Shu fighting skills. 90 min. In Cantonese with English subtitles.
76-2103   Letterboxed   **$14.99**

Born To Defense (Dubbed Version)
Also available in a dubbed-in-English edition.
82-7039   **$39.99**

The Master (1989)
Jet Li's astonishing fighting abilities are showcased in this story directed by Tsui Hark. A martial arts expert who is also a specialist in herbal medicine is kidnapped by a ruthless student who sets his sights set on monopolizing the teachings of kung fu in America. Fellow student Li comes to the rescue. With Jerry Trimble, Billy Blanks. In Cantonese with English subtitles.
53-6505   **$49.99**

Dragon Fight (1989)
Martial arts master Jet Li teams with funnyman Stephen Chiao for this contemporary actioner that features lots of Wu Shu fighting. Li is a member of an acrobatics-martial arts team who finds himself in trouble when his troupe visits San Francisco. 96 min. In Cantonese with English subtitles.
53-9756   **$49.99**

Twin Warriors (The Tai Chi Master) (1993)
Ingenious fight sequences highlight this Jet Li actioner about two Shaolin Temple students who go their separate ways when Li decides to battle the government, while former best friend Chin Siu Ho fights for it—and its tyrannical eunuch leader. After a battle with Ho leaves Li without his memory, he goes on to develop the Tai Chi fighting style. Michelle Yeoh also stars. 93 min. Dubbed in English.
11-2430   Was $99.99   ☐**$14.99**

Lord Of The Wu Tang (1993)
Jet Li plays a sickly kid who overcomes his disabilities when he learns the Great Solar Stance and becomes a Shaolin martial arts expert. He then seeks vengeance for his parents' death at the hands of a clan leader. Spectacular fighting sequences highlight this film, which also stars Samo Hung. AKA: "Kung Fu Cult Hero." 105 min. In Cantonese with English subtitles.
54-9163   Letterboxed   **$19.99**

Kung Fu Master (1993)
Jet Li and Sammo Hung are kung-fu fighting to the max in amazing martial arts fantasy set in the Yuen Dynasty and pitting different sects against each other for two powerful golden swords. See Shaolin warriors battle the Ming faction, while Jet learns secrets from Sammo and uses the mysterious "solar" stance in battle. With Chingmy Yau. In Cantonese with English subtitles.
76-2100   Letterboxed   **$14.99**

The Legend (1993)
The amazing Jet Li stars in this explosive "Hong Kong-coction" of action, historical drama, romance and comedy. As young martial arts expert Fong Sai Yuk, Li takes part in a competition to win the hand of a reformed bandit's beautiful daughter and then must defend his father, a member of a secret society out to topple the corrupt Manchu governor. Michelle Reis, Sibelle Hu, Zhao Wen Zhou also star. AKA: "Fong Sai Yuk." 95 min. Dubbed in English.
11-2490   ☐**$99.99**

Last Hero In China (1993)
Jet Li is Chinese folk hero Wong Fei Hong, who relocates his martial arts school next to a brothel after experiencing financial problems. When he learns that several of the prostitutes are being kidnapped by nefarious members of the Boxer Society, Wong calls on his incredible fighting skills to stop the culprits. In Cantonese with English subtitles. AKA: "Deadly China Hero."
76-2101   Letterboxed   **$14.99**

Fist Of Legend (1994)
A high-flying salute to Bruce Lee's "The Chinese Connection" with Jet Li playing Lee's character Chen Zhen, a 1920s martial arts student out to avenge the death of his master, killed on the orders of an evil Japanese general. Rousing action and Li's charismatic performance will keep you riveted to this superb spectacle. With Chin Siu-Ho. 100 min. In Cantonese with English subtitles.
53-9718   Was $39.99   **$19.99**

Fist Of Legend (Dubbed Version)
Also available in a dubbed-in-English edition.
11-2390   Was $99.99   ☐**$14.99**

Bodyguard From Beijing (1994)
Mainland Chinese bodyguard Jet Li assigned to protect Christy Chung, a prosecution witness who is targeted by a host of assassins. Li's own future is threatened as well after the crimelord brother of an assassin he murdered comes after him. 95 min. In Cantonese with English subtitles.
76-2093   Letterboxed   **$29.99**

The Defender (Dubbed Version)
The Jet Li film "Bodyguard from Beijing," retitled for its 1999 American release, is also available in a dubbed-in-English edition. 93 min.
11-2451   ☐**$99.99**

New Legend Of Shaolin (1994)
It's stupendous action, Hong Kong-style, as Jet Li plays a martial arts master who has to find five kids with maps tattooed to their backs in order to get to a treasure hidden by rebel forces. In order to complete the mission, Li faces Imperial guardsmen, Tibetan monks and all sorts of dangerous weapons. In Cantonese with English subtitles.
53-8454   Was $49.99   **$19.99**

New Legend Of Shaolin (Dubbed Version)
Also available in a dubbed-in-English edition.
82-7035   **$39.99**

Shaolin Kung Fu (1994)
This engrossing documentary tells of the dedicated and painful training regimen of the legendary Shaolin monks and is hosted by martial arts film star Jet Li. Li recounts his training at the temple as a youth, with accompanying archival footage, and focuses on the still active monks and their superhuman feats. 90 min. In Cantonese with English subtitles.
53-8988   **$49.99**

My Father Is A Hero (1995)
Rousing and tender Jet Li actioner finds him playing a dedicated mainland Chinese cop who, unbeknown to his ailing wife and Kung Fu student son, is arrested as part of a plan to infiltrate a Hong Kong crime ring. When Li's wife dies, Hong Kong policewoman Anita Mui brings his son to the city, and the trio takes on the bad guys. With Tze Miu, Yo Rong Guang. 98 min. In Cantonese with English subtitles.
53-9761   Letterboxed   **$19.99**

Jet Li's The Enforcer (Dubbed Version)
Li's film "My Father Is a Hero," retitled for its 1999 American theatrical release, is also available in a dubbed-in-English edition. 100 min.
11-2413   Was $99.99   ☐**$14.99**

High Risk (1995)
Marvelous action spoof of Bruce Lee, Jackie Chan and "Die Hard" movies, with Jet Li as the stunt double of has-been action star Jacky Cheung who attempts to save a group of party-goers—including Cheung—being held hostage in a hotel by a deranged criminal out to steal the Russian crown jewels. Wild stunts, martial arts mayhem and sly humor abound. 100 min. In Cantonese with English subtitles.
53-8500   Letterboxed   **$19.99**

Once Upon A Time In China & America (1996)
Martial arts goes the western route in this action-filled saga starring Jet Li as Master Wong, who journeys with his aunt to the American West, where they encounter Indians, gunslingers and more! Kung-Fu master Sammo Hung directs this sixth entry in the series; with Rosamund Kwan, Hung Yan Yan ("Double Team"). 90 min. In English, and Cantonese with English subtitles.
53-9953   Letterboxed   **$19.99**

Dr. Wai In The Scripture With No Words (1996)
Jet Li is a timid writer who can't seem to complete his latest adventure saga. To make matters worse, he and wife Rosmund Kwan are having their share of problems. Jet fantasizes himself as the hero of his book, a dashing adventurer battling the Japanese for a fortune-telling box, while his wife is cast as the villainess. In Cantonese with English subtitles.
76-2096   Letterboxed   **$14.99**

Black Mask (1996)
High-energy action saga stars Jet Li as an artificially-enhanced super-soldier who escapes from the military and tries to live a peaceful life as a librarian. When he discovers that some of his former comrades are killing Hong Kong's top druglords and attempting to take over their business, Li becomes a masked vigilante, teaming with his police detective pal to beat the unstoppable killing machines. With Lau Ching Wan, Francoise Yip. 102 min.
27-7141   Was $99.99   ☐**$14.99**

Hitman (1998)
Jet Li's final Hong Kong film is an awesome mix of action and laughs, spotlighting the martial arts star as an impoverished soldier-turned-hit man out to join a $1 billion contest to take down the world's top assassin, "The King of Killers." Eric Tsang plays Crocodile Man, Li's "agent" and confidante; Simon Yam, Gigi Leung also stars. 109 min. In Cantonese with English subtitles.
53-6284   Letterboxed   **$24.99**

Romeo Must Die (2000)
In his first American film lead, Hong Kong sensation Jet Li plays an ex-cop who breaks out of the Chinese prison where he's been unjustly jailed and travels to Oakland, looking to avenge his brother's death. Li becomes romantically involved with Aaliyah, but the would-be lovers are caught on opposite sides of a deadly mob war waged by their fathers. Delroy Lindo, Isaiah Washington and Russell Wong also star in this action-packed, urban-flavored "Romeo and Juliet" revamping. 110 min.
19-2992   Was $99.99   ☐**$14.99**

Please see our index for these other Jet Li titles: *Lethal Weapon 4 • Once Upon A Time In China, Part 3 • Swordsman II*

Lethal Extortion (1993)
A group of ruthless international assassins abducts Russian models who are visiting Taiwan. Local police are overwhelmed, so a group of war veterans bands together to get the culprits. An explosive thriller that takes no prisoners. 99 min. Dubbed in English.
53-6133 *$14.99*

Cheetah On Fire (1993)
Thrill-a-second martial arts mayhem ensues when two Hong Kong inspectors enlisted to help the CIA extradite a criminal back to America find their crook kidnapped by a drug kingpin searching for a computer chip. Now, the CIA and the police join forces with the local army to get the criminal and halt the kingpin. Donnie Yen and Carrie Ng star. 87 min. Dubbed in English.
53-9993 *$14.99*

Thunder Run (1991)
Ho and Cheung, partners on the Hong Kong police force, see their Southeast Asia vacation take a turn for the worse when Ho is mistaken as a drug smuggler in Laos and Cheung has to pull off a risky prison escape to free his friend. Philip Lui and Alex Fong star. 91 min. Dubbed in English.
53-9994 *$14.99*

Mission Of Justice (1992)
A disillusioned cop goes underground when some of his friends die, and he discovers that a ruthless mayoral candidate has hired a group of savage ninja assassins to ignite violence and blackmail. Jeff Wincott, Brigitte Nielsen and Cyndi Pass star. 95 min.
63-1583 Was $89.99 □*$12.99*

Martial Outlaw (1993)
A Drug Enforcement Agency operative tracks a drug-dealing former KGB agent from Moscow to Los Angeles and soon discovers his brother, a hot-shot cop involved in the case, may be playing both sides of the fence. The two must combat a group of Soviet martial arts experts to finish the case. Jeff Wincott and Gary Hudson star. 89 min.
63-1657 □*$89.99*

Overkill (1995)
Martial arts skills must run in the Norris family, because Aaron Norris sure gets medieval in this actioner in which he plays a Los Angeles cop whose vacation in the South American jungles turns deadly when he faces an exploitative businessman. Michael Nouri, Pamela Dickerson also star. 92 min.
68-1823 □*$99.99*

Karate Cops (1991)
After his closest pal is killed, tough cop Alexander "Hawkeye" Hawkamoto seeks vengeance, going after the mobsters responsible for the deed. Soon, he and his partner are caught between the mob and the Yakuza. George Chung, Richard Norton and Chuck Jeffreys star.
72-4007 *$19.99*

Heroes Among Heroes (1993)
Donnie Yen shows off his spectacular martial arts skills in this period actioner set during the Ching Dynasty. He plays a beggar who gets addicted to opium and is manipulated by a prince to assassinate a nefarious general. Boasting incredible fight scenes, this film was directed by Yuen Woo-Ping, fight coordinator for "The Matrix." 91 min. In Cantonese with English subtitles.
76-2097 Letterboxed *$29.99*

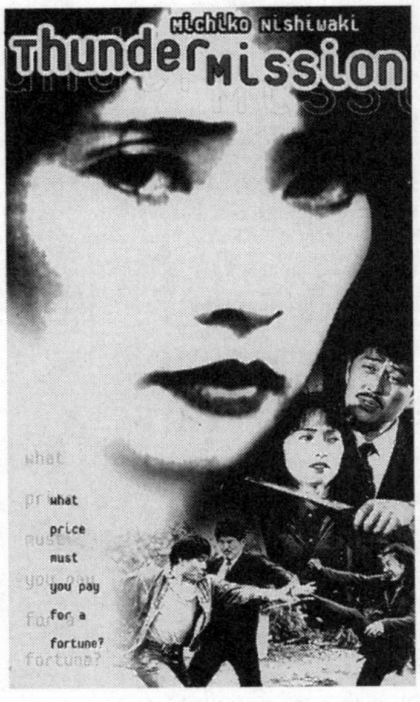
Michiko Nishiwaki
thunder mission
what
price
must
you pay
for a
fortune?

Thunder Mission (1992)
Japanese female kickboxing sensation Michiko Nishiwaki stars in a tale of half-sisters who find themselves targets of an assassin for no apparent reason. One sibling hires her boyfriend to help; the other her husband. But the secret behind the assassin soon unravels! 90 min. Dubbed in English.
53-6274 *$14.99*

Jean-Claude Van Damme

Monaco Forever (1983)
This sensual odyssey, set in the Riviera resort in 1956, tells the story of a young lady who takes off on a trip across Europe with an attractive stranger. During the journey, the pair have a fateful encounter with a handsome gay gentleman driving a Jaguar, played by Jean-Claude Van Damme in one of his earliest roles. Charles Pitt, Martha Ferris also star. 43 min.
23-5053 *$19.99*

Bloodsport (1988)
Every five years a clandestine martial arts competition is held where the victor is the last man alive. Into this secret society comes an outsider who must use all of his ninjitsu skills if he hopes to survive. Non-stop cinematic action; Jean-Claude Van Damme, Bolo Yeung, Forest Whitaker star. 92 min.
19-1663 Was $19.99 □*$14.99*

JEAN-CLAUDE VAN DAMME
KICKBOXER

Kickboxer (1989)
Martial arts sensation Jean-Claude Van Damme stars as an American who must learn the ancient and lethal art of kickboxing to avenge his brother's injury at the hands of a ruthless Thai fighter. Brutal action and a fight to the death make this a "must-see"! 97 min.
44-1711 Was $19.99 □*$14.99*

Death Warrant (1990)
High-kicking action star Jean-Claude Van Damme is a cop who goes undercover in the big house to solve a series of violent prison murders. When his cover's blown, he needs all of his fighting skills to get out alive. Thrilling tale laced with the martial arts prowess of "the muscles from Brussels" also stars Robert Guillaume, Cynthia Gibb. 90 min.
12-2164 Was $89.99 □*$14.99*

Double Impact (1991)
Are you ready for two Van Dammes? Here the action superstar plays a dual role, as twin brothers with very different methods of finishing a fight who unite on a mission of vengeance. Twice the thrills and twice the biceps in this slam-bang hit. With Geoffrey Lewis, Alan Scarfe, Bolo Yeung. 107 min.
02-2157 Was $19.99 □*$14.99*

Lionheart (1991)
Jean-Claude Van Damme stars as a tough member of the French Foreign Legion who deserts and heads to Los Angeles after he receives word that his brother is ill. Soon, he's partaking in underground bare-knuckle brawling to get cash to help his sibling. With Harrison Page and some astonishing action scenes. 105 min.
07-1692 Was $19.99 □*$14.99*

Universal Soldier (1992)
Two titans of movie muscledom, Jean-Claude Van Damme and Dolph Lundgren, team up in this sci-fi actioner. Killed while serving in Vietnam, they're brought back to life as bionic super-soldiers in a secret government program. But when Van Damme begins remembering his human past and escapes, Lundgren is sent to "terminate" his former comrade. With Ally Walker, Ed O'Ross. 102 min.
27-6786 Was $89.99 □*$12.99*

Universal Soldier (Letterboxed Version)
Also available in a theatrical, widescreen format.
27-7020 □*$14.99*

Universal Soldier: The Return (1999)
This theatrical sequel to the 1992 actioner features Jean-Claude Van Damme as the former "unisol" who must take on a rogue government supercomputer named S.E.T.H. that is leading the cybernetically-enhanced killing machines on a path of destruction. Michael Jai White, Heidi Schanz and pro wrestling star Bill Goldberg also star. 89 min.
02-3387 Was $99.99 □*$14.99*

Nowhere To Run (1993)
Jean-Claude Van Damme, in a change-of-pace role, plays an escaped convict who comes to the rescue of widow Rosanna Arquette and her two children when a ruthless contractor attempts to take over their land. There's action scenes aplenty, along with a surprising romantic angle. Kieran Culkin, Ted Levine and Joss Ackland co-star. 95 min.
02-2432 Was $19.99 □*$14.99*

Hard Target (1993)
Action-crammed reworking of "The Most Dangerous Game" stars Jean-Claude Van Damme as a merchant sailor living in New Orleans who uncovers a diabolical "contest" in which homeless Vietnam vets are hunted down and murdered by wealthy businessmen. Lance Henriksen and Yancy Butler co-star in Hong Kong director John Woo's smashing American debut. 97 min.
07-2046 Was $19.99 □*$14.99*

Timecop (1994)
At the dawn of the 21st century, time travel is a reality, and the technology is guarded by lawmen like Jean-Claude Van Damme. But when he must go back to stop his ex-partner from altering the past for personal gain, Van Damme is caught in a dangerous, time-hopping conspiracy involving a corrupt senator. Intriguing sci-fi actioner also stars Ron Silver, Mia Sara, Bruce McGill. 99 min.
07-2236 Was $19.99 □*$14.99*

Street Fighter (1994)
Video game fans, get ready for the biggest explosion of live-action excitement to ever hit the screen, as Colonel Guile (Jean-Claude Van Damme) leads his Allied Nation band of warriors in an assault on the forces of dictatorial General M. Bison (Raul Julia, in his final film role) to free kidnapped relief workers. Great fight scenes and special effects make this a winner. 102 min.
07-2274 Was $19.99 □*$14.99*

Sudden Death (1995)
When a group of terrorists led by a renegade special agent takes the vice president of the U.S. hostage during the final game of the Stanley Cup playoffs, fire marshal Jean-Claude Van Damme springs into action, trying to dismantle bombs planted throughout the Pittsburgh Civic Arena. High-energy "Die Hard on Ice" thriller also stars Powers Boothe, Dorian Harewood. 111 min.
07-2414 Was $99.99 □*$14.99*

Maximum Risk (1996)
Jean-Claude Van Damme is a French cop investigating the mysterious death of his long-lost brother in New York City's Russian enclave of Little Odessa. After discovering his sibling had worked for the Russian mob and had a secret file on illegal activities, Van Damme becomes a target of the FBI and mobsters. Natasha Henstridge co-stars; directed by Ringo Lam ("City on Fire"). 101 min.
02-3018 Was $99.99 □*$14.99*

The Quest (1996)
Making his directorial debut with this period actioner, Jean-Claude Van Damme plays a small-time thief in '20s New York who is shanghaied by gunrunners, sold into slavery, and forced to take part in a brutal martial arts competition with the world's toughest fighters. Roger Moore, James Remar, Janet Gunn also star. 95 min.
07-2433 Was $99.99 □*$14.99*

Double Team (1997)
And what a team it is when hard-kicking Jean-Claude Van Damme join forces with NBA bad boy Dennis Rodman in this stunt-filled tale. When government anti-terrorist agent Van Damme's family is targeted by mercenary leader Mickey Rourke, he turns to off-the-wall weapons master Rodman for help in bringing down the bad guys. Directed by Hong Kong action master Tsui Hark. 93 min.
02-3109 Was $99.99 □*$14.99*

Knock Off (1998)
High kicks meet high fashion in this explosive thriller starring Jean-Claude Van Damme as a jeans manufacturer in Hong Kong shortly before the 1997 Chinese takeover. When it's learned that the pants contain parts for an international weapons-smuggling scheme, Van Damme teams with wisecracking partner Rob Schneider to shut down the operation. Lela Rochon, Paul Sorvino also star. 91 min.
02-3254 Was $99.99 □*$14.99*

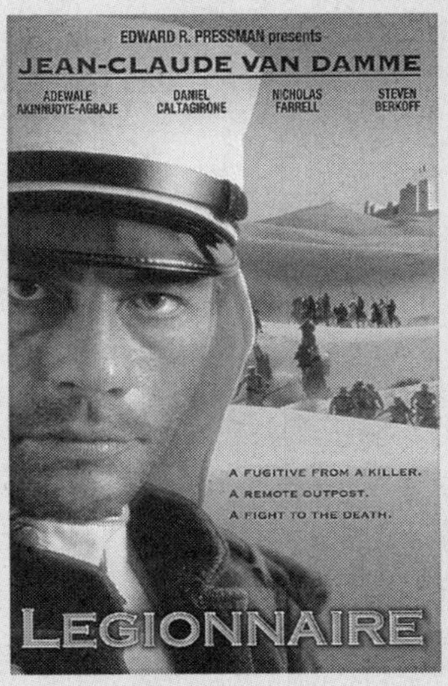
EDWARD R. PRESSMAN presents
JEAN-CLAUDE VAN DAMME
ADEWALE AKINNUOYE-AGBAJE
DANIEL CALTAGIRONE
NICHOLAS FARRELL
STEVEN BERKOFF
A FUGITIVE FROM A KILLER.
A REMOTE OUTPOST.
A FIGHT TO THE DEATH.
LEGIONNAIRE

Legionnaire (1998)
In 1920s France, boxer Jean-Claude Van Damme skips out on gangsters after he decides not to take a dive as promised and lands in the French Foreign Legion. Along with a group of new recruits, Van Damme faces the Legion's enemies in a remote Moroccan outpost. Steven Berkoff, Jim Carter also star in this lavish adventure saga. 120 min.
64-9031 Was $99.99 *$14.99*

Desert Heat (1999)
When a small desert town filled with eccentric citizens is terrorized by a group of thugs, drifter Jean-Claude Van Damme steps in to beat the creeps. An old-fashioned western premise gets "Van Dammed" in this exciting actioner with Pat Morita, Jaime Pressly, Larry Drake and Vincent Schiavelli, directed by John Avildsen ("Rocky"). AKA: "Inferno." 95 min.
02-3369 Was $99.99 □*$14.99*

The Van Damme Collection
If it's a "Damme" fine action film you're looking for, look no further than this special boxed set that includes "Double Team," "Knock Off" and "Maximum Risk."
02-3324 Save $20.00! *$24.99*

The Jean-Claude Van Damme Collection
Belgium's best import since waffles is saluted with this boxed set of three of Jean-Claude's action hits: "Cyborg," "Death Warrant" and "Double Impact."
12-3193 *$24.99*

Please see our index for the Jean-Claude Van Damme title: *Cyborg*

High Voltage (1994)
Donnie Yen excels in this high-octane thriller, playing a cop sent to the Philippines to escort an extradited crime witness. Yen eventually runs into the man responsible for killing his wife, and must walk the fine line between responsibility and revenge. Roy Cheung also stars. AKA: "Asia Cops: High Voltage." 95 min. In Cantonese with English subtitles.
76-2098 Letterboxed *$24.99*

Capital Punishment (1995)
Martial arts maestro Gary Daniels is recruited by the DEA to stop a new narcotic that is becoming a sensation on the streets. While trying to find the source of the drug, Daniels discovers a link between an evil drug kingpin and the police chief. David Carradine, Tadashi Yamashita also star. 90 min.
76-7338 *$59.99*

Expert Weapon (1993)
From Movies Unlimited alumnus Steven Austin ("American Streetfighter") comes this explosive martial arts opus, a kickboxing salute to "La Femme Nikita." After killing a cop, criminal Ian Jacklin is transformed into a killing machine by a secret government organization. Sam Jones, Judy Landers, Joe Estevez also star in this super-fine actioner. 90 min.
76-7353 *$59.99*

Black Belt Angels (1995)
When the Master Martial Arts School is about to shut down, Tae Kwon Do expert Matt Robbins and his teenage daughters decide to tackle a greedy mobster who holds the key to the school's future. The problem is that the mobster has his own band of ninjas and a showdown is on the horizon. Shawna Larson, Regekah Bertlett star. 82 min.
76-9079 *$14.99*

Shadow Dreams (1995)
A martial arts master whose family was killed by mobsters teams up with a heavyweight boxer whose career was ruined by the same crew. Using their incredible fighting skills, the two try to tackle some of the sleaziest crooks you've ever encountered. Jeong Sook Lee and Albert Myles star. 94 min.
78-3030 *$14.99*

Superfights: The Movie (1996)
A young man eager to enter the world of "Superfight" martial arts competitions is shocked to learn the organization's weaselly promoter is using the fighters as his own personal "crime army." Now the rookie must battle an armada of deadly opponents if he's to come out alive in this action-filled tale. Brandon Gaines, Keith Vitali, Kelly Gallant, Chuck Jeffreys star. 95 min.
78-3038 *$89.99*

Karate Wars (1992)
When a martial arts tournament with a million-dollar prize is cancelled, the would-be participants take their battle into the streets, where the only prize for winning is staying alive! Explosive karate action as you like it. 90 min.
81-9009 *$89.99*

Moving Target (1998)
Mark Kobain thinks he's being trained by martial arts masters when he takes an intense course at a remote cabin, but soon discovers that they're actually hunters, and he's about to become their human prey. A most dangerous game of death begins, but with Mark's skills and streetwise savvy, he's going to be a hard target with hopes of surviving the game. Greg Maye, Eugene Floyd star. 90 min.
81-9076 *$89.99*

Beyond Fear (1993)
A wilderness guide with an expertise in martial arts finds herself stalked by two desperate men seeking a videotape that features them involved in a vicious murder. Using her karate and survivalist skills, the guide attempts to protect the tape while being pursued through the forest. Mimi Lesseos stars. 84 min.
76-9050 Was $89.99 *$14.99*

Don Wilson

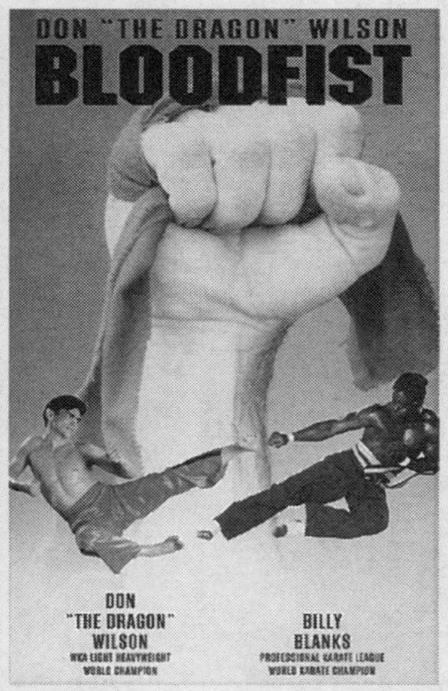
DON "THE DRAGON" WILSON
BLOODFIST
DON
"THE DRAGON"
WILSON
WKA LIGHT HEAVYWEIGHT
WORLD CHAMPION
BILLY
BLANKS
PROFESSIONAL KARATE LEAGUE
WORLD KARATE CHAMPION

Bloodfist (1989)
Kickboxing superstar Don "The Dragon" Wilson smashes his way into film fame with this martial arts thriller about a young man out to avenge his brother's murder. Stunning fight scenes; Billy Blanks, Rob Kaman co-star. 86 min.
12-2010 *$14.99*

Bloodfist II (1990)
The kickboxing world's biggest stars, including Don "The Dragon" Wilson, Maurice Smith, James Warring and Timothy Baker, are kidnapped to compete in savage death matches against chemically-induced killers on an island fortress, in this explosive film from producer Roger Corman. With Rina Reyes. 85 min.
12-2166 Was $89.99 *$14.99*

Bloodfist III: Forced To Fight (1991)
Don "The Dragon" Wilson returns in the third installment of this high-kicking martial arts series. He's in prison and accused of killing a black inmate. But even the prisoners at the new penitentiary he's been transferred to want him dead. Time to get a lesson in survival from fellow prisoner Richard Roundtree. 92 min.
31-9004 Was $89.99 *$14.99*

Bloodfist IV: Die Trying (1992)
Don "The Dragon" Wilson finds himself caught in a morass of CIA operatives, FBI agents and members of an arms cartel as he seeks to avenge the murder of his friend and the kidnapping of his daughter. Cat Sassoon, Amanda Wyss and James Tolkan co-star.
21-9022 Was $89.99 *$14.99*

Bloodfist V: Human Target (1993)
Don "The Dragon" Wilson plays an FBI operative who becomes amnesiac after trying to stop an international arms deal. Now he's caught between the FBI and the arms dealers, and must use his martial arts skills to hold them off until he learns his true identity. Denice Duff, Steve James also star.
21-9049 Was $89.99 *$14.99*

Bloodfist VI: Ground Zero (1994)
Don "The Dragon" Wilson goes head-to-head against terrorists with plans to detonate a nuclear warhead targeted for New York in this chop socky spectacular. Sexy Playboy model and kickboxing champ Cat Sassoon, Robin Curtis and former baseball great Steve Garvey also star. 86 min.
21-9072 *$14.99*

Futurekick (1991)
Kickboxing sensation Don "The Dragon" Wilson stars in this futuristic actioner as a cyborg bounty hunter tracking down a killer and breaking up a crime ring dealing in stolen body parts. Mesmerizing martial arts and sci-fi shocks; co-stars Meg Foster, Christopher Penn and Eb Lottimer. 80 min.
21-9001 Was $89.99 *$14.99*

Ring Of Fire II: Blood And Steel (1992)
Kickboxer extraordinaire Don Wilson is back in this action-loaded sequel, as a young doctor's fiancée is kidnapped by gang members whom he witnessed robbing a bank. Unable to get help from the police, the doctor calls on his martial arts skills and his old gang allies for help. With Maria Ford, Sy Richardson. 94 min.
86-1066 Was $89.99 *$14.99*

Ring Of Fire III: Lion Strike (1994)
It's anything but a peaceful vacation for martial arts master Dr. Johnny Wu (Don "The Dragon" Wilson) when he, his son Bobby and a beautiful forest ranger are caught in a deadly fight against the Global Mafia. High-kicking action tale also stars Bobbie Phillips, Robert Costanzo, Jonathan Wilson (Don's real-life son).
86-1085 Was $89.99 *$14.99*

Out For Blood (1993)
After his family is savagely murdered by drug dealers, a successful lawyer sets out to avenge their senseless deaths by turning into a vigilante the media dubs "Karateman." Caught between the mob and the law, he uses his amazing martial arts abilities to catch the killers. Don "The Dragon" Wilson stars. 90 min.
86-1071 Was $89.99 *$14.99*

Manhunt (1994)
Don "The Dragon" Wilson rescues a woman in trouble with some seedy criminals and finds himself framed for a murder. He's forced to go on the run, a fugitive from the authorities. Can he find the real culprit before the law throws him in jail? With Jillian McWhirter, Stephen Davies. AKA: "Bloodfist VII: Manhunt." 95 min.
21-9093 Was $89.99 *$14.99*

Virtual Combat (1995)
Kickboxing in cyberspace? You bet! Martial arts megastar Don "The Dragon" Wilson is the guard between the virtual and real worlds who must battle computer-generated adversaries and video game menaces in this dazzling mix of action and special effects. With Athena Massey, Loren Avedon. 93 min.
83-1058 Was $89.99 *$14.99*

Cyber Tracker 2 (1995)
Futuristic robot fighter Don "The Dragon" Wilson returns, karate moves intact, in this sequel to the popular sci-fi adventure. Here Wilson and his newscaster wife are framed for murder on live TV by cyborg duplicates. Stacie Foster, Stephen Rowe also star. 97 min.
86-1096 Was $89.99 *$14.99*

Hard Way Out (1996)
Former CIA operative Don "The Dragon" Wilson tries to put his past behind him and becomes a quiet math teacher and family man, but when a team of assassins attacks him and his son, Wilson must call on his old training to protect his loved ones. With Jillian McWhirter and John Patrick White. 84 min.
21-9123 Was $99.99 *$14.99*

Operation Cobra (1997)
When his partner is killed by an international crime ring in an explosion, Interpol agent Don "the Dragon" Wilson bucks his superiors and tracks the killers to India. In a land of exotic beauty and danger, Wilson sets out to deliver his own hard-kicking brand of justice. Tane McClure, Rick Hill co-star in director Fred Olen Ray's martial arts actioner. 82 min.
21-9154 Was $59.99 *$14.99*

Whatever It Takes (1997)
A pair of law enforcement agents goes undercover to break up an illegal steroid distribution ring working in the bulked-up world of pro wrestling and bodybuilding. Don "The Dragon" Wilson, Andrew "Dice" Clay and Fred "The Hammer" Williamson star in this ultra-intense actioner. 75 min.
85-1172 *$59.99*

Terminal Rush (1998)
Highly decorated ex-Army Ranger Don "The Dragon" Wilson has been having a tough time since he was thrown out of the corps for a crime he didn't commit. When a group of terrorists led by Roddy Piper takes over Hoover Dam, Wilson is the only one who can save the day. 94 min.
82-5090 *$89.99*

The Capitol Conspiracy (1999)
CIA agent Don "The Dragon" Wilson, tracking a radical anti-government group, uncovers a link between the people he's pursuing and his own mystery-shrouded past. His discovery makes Wilson a target for both sides of a bizarre conspiracy in this exciting thriller. With Alexander Keith, Barbara Steele; Fred Olen Ray directs. Aka: "The Prophet." 83 min.
21-9189 *$59.99*

Moving Target (2000)
Don "The Dragon" Wilson is a tourist in Ireland who finds himself battling terrorists after his girlfriend is kidnapped and he becomes a "moving target." To make matters worse, the bad guys put nuclear detonators in a case of beer. Watch out for the Guinness Stout! With Bill Murphy, Hilary Kavanagh. 86 min.
21-9207 *$59.99*

Spider Force (1992)
Stuart and Sharon are two of Hong Kong's finest, on assignment to stop drug smugglers from China. Sharon discovers that her uncle is the leader of the smugglers, and she and her partner track him to his remote island headquarters. But will they survive the Hong Kong police force's land, air and sea attack on the island? Carter Wong, Pauline Chan star. 90 min. Dubbed in English.
53-6166 *$14.99*

Lady Hunter (1992)
Offbeat comedy and wild martial arts action abound in this tale of a detective investigating threats made against a millionaire who falls for the man's beautiful but tough policewoman daughter. The sleuth and the cop team to get to the bottom of the trouble. Cynthia Khan and Anthony Wong star. 90 min. Dubbed in English.
53-6275 *$14.99*

Dragonball: The Magic Begins (1999)
In this live-action version of the popular animated series, evil King Horn attempts to retrieve the five Dragon Pearls he does not possess (he already has two of them) and conquer the universe. But can the owners of the pearls—Sparkle, Monkey Boy, Westwood, Turtle Man and Seetoe—stop him? C.K. Chan and T. Kim star in this high-octane family actioner. 95 min. Dubbed in English.
53-6824 *$19.99*

Legend Of The Drunken Tiger (1992)
The erratic style of martial arts popularized by Jackie Chan in the "Drunken Master" movies is the highlight of this costume karate opus in which a group of skilled fighters go against the evil Lord Wing of the 19th-century Ching Dynasty. Leading the fight is Cheong San, who's unstoppable when intoxicated. 98 min.
53-9778 *$14.99*

Crystal Hunt (1992)
Stunning martial arts fights highlight this rip-roarer in which a woman hires a noted professor to help find a crystal which can heal her ailing gangster father. When the professor is kidnapped, she joins forces with a policewoman and her associate to find him. Carrie Ng, Sibelle Hu and Donnie Yen star. 90 min. Dubbed in English.
53-9965 *$14.99*

Eat My Dust (1993)
Smashing suspense and high-powered action are showcased in this tale of a former gangster and the son of a murdered partner who leave South America for their Hong Kong homeland on a mission of revenge. Joined by a policewoman, they track down the killer, now the head of a powerful Triad. Michael Tsang, Mark Ng and Cynthia Lam star. 90 min. Dubbed in English.
53-9966 *$14.99*

Death Cage (1988)
American martial arts expert Joe Lewis and Hong Kong's Robin Shou star in this blast of kung fu action in which a group of fighters compete in fierce combat in the Death Cage. See such contestants as "Lady Lethal," "Bangkok Baz," "Monkey King," "Joe Cool," "Black Widows," "Crippled Master" and "Yellow Jacket." Wow! Dubbed in English.
54-9126 *$19.99*

Eastern Heroes (1991)
Robin Shou of "Mortal Kombat" fame stars in this actioner, playing a tough Hong Kong investigator taking on a gang of Vietnamese thugs who kidnapped the head of a big corporation. Shou learns that the tycoon actually hired the crooks to kill rival businessmen, and when he takes out the gang's leader, he finds his family in the U.S. in trouble. With Conan Lee. 91 min. Dubbed in English.
53-8632 *$14.99*

Fatal Chase (1992)
A senior detective, an unorthodox undercover cop and a female investigator snag a criminal named Dion in Hong Kong and take him back to the Philippines for prosecution. This Dion proves to be a wanderer, as he escapes the cops, forcing the trio to deal with a corrupt Manila police chief in order to catch the crook. Robin Shou stars. 96 min. Dubbed in English.
53-8633 *$14.99*

Interpol Connection (1992)
"Mortal Kombat" tough guy Robin Shou excels in this high-flying action yarn involving an evil heroin dealer who eludes a trio of police, then goes on a murderous rampage. The team, which includes a Hong Kong narc, a clumsy Manila cop and a female agent, find themselves in dangerous and funny situations. With Yukari Oshima. 91 min. Dubbed in English.
53-8634 *$14.99*

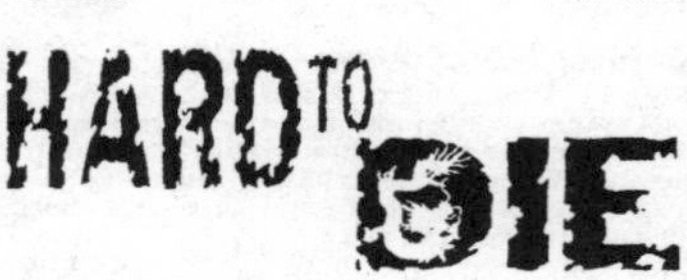
HARD TO DIE

Hard To Die (1990)
Wild action sequences highlight this high-energy story of a Hong Kong gangster pursued by a female police inspector, a dim-witted undercover agent and a female Japanese samurai out for revenge for her father's death. Sibelle Hu, Carrie Ng and Michiko Nishikawa star. 90 min. Dubbed in English.
53-6164 *$14.99*

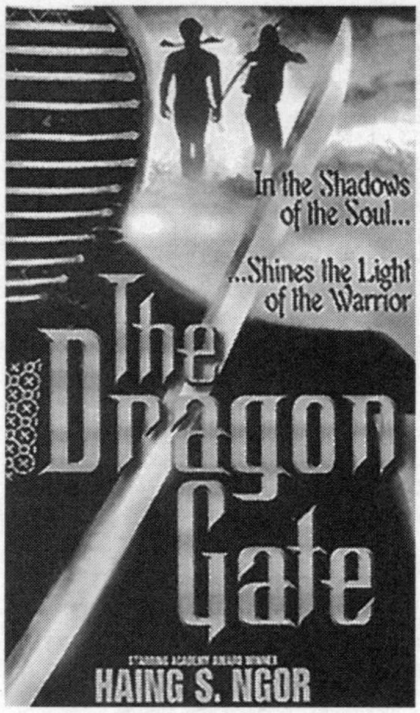
In the Shadows of the Soul...
...Shines the Light of the Warrior
The Dragon Gate
HAING S. NGOR

The Dragon Gate (1996)
After his girlfriend is kidnapped, a sword-wielding warrior must travel into another dimension to rescue her. Using his prowess in swordplay and martial arts, the man battles bloodthirsty assassins and an evil temptress. Dan Coplan, Dr. Haing S. Ngor, Geoffrey Lewis and Delia Sheppard star.
46-8036 Was $59.99 *$14.99*

Live By The Fist (1993)
A former Navy SEAL is framed for murder and put into a prison where men are judged by their fighting abilities. Sworn to a Zen code of nonviolence and tormented by penitentiary leader Khan, he must put aside his philosophy to whip his enemies and stay alive. Kickboxing champ Jerry Trimble, George Takei and Laura Albert star.
21-9037 Was $89.99 *$14.99*

One Man Army (1994)
Jerry Trimble, one of the world's leading kickboxing champs, investigates the death of his grandfather in a small town and finds corruption running rampant. It filters down from the top, as Trimble combats the sheriff and his cronies in this kick-'em-in-your-face outing. With Playboy Playmate Melissa Anne Moore.
21-9053 *$14.99*

Stranglehold (1994)
When a psychotic terrorist steals a deadly toxin from a chemical weapons facility and takes a congresswoman as hostage, stopping him falls on the shoulders of a former Secret Service agent (kickboxing champ Jerry Trimble), who uses his martial arts skills and espionage experience to stop his foe. Jillian McWhirter, Vernon Wells also star.
21-9074 *$14.99*

Desert Kickboxer (1992)
A Native-American border deputy uses his kickboxing skills to catch an international coke dealer and his posse of killers when they flee across the Mexican border. John Haymes Newton ("Superboy"), Judie Aronson and Paul L. Smith star in this action-laden story. 86 min.
44-1906 Was $19.99 *$14.99*

Blind Vengeance (1994)
Kickboxing champ Rod Kei plays Ricky Dirks, a world-famous fighter who discovers that his pretty new student not only brings romance with her, but a deadly martial artist from his past, as well. Cheryl Kalanoc, Carl Vanmeter co-star. 85 min.
48-1188 *$89.99*

Mission: Killfast (1999)
After an international arms dealer sells nuclear weapons to terrorists with the notion of blackmailing the rest of the world, America enlists karate expert Tiger Yang and his team to stop them. Featuring footage shot in 1984 as "Operation: Overkill," this Ted V. Mikels ("Astro-Zombies") production also stars Jewel Shepard. 97 min.
50-8281 *$24.99*

Tiger Street (1999)
A Tae Kwon Do master escapes from a Korea prison and heads for Denver, where he's recruited by an old friend to teach martial arts at the high school where he's employed. The master's success with a former drug dealer upsets the dealer's partner, and all-out war rages between teacher and thug. Julian Lee and Gary Sirchia star.
50-8602 *$39.99*

Phantom War (1990)
Smashing action yarn about a couple who survived Vietcong prison camps who decide to settle in London's Chinatown. Soon, they're facing another set of problems, from the man's flashbacks to Mafia druglords to old wartime nemeses. Highlighted by knockout displays of martial arts, this film stars Alex Man and Philip Ko. 80 min. Dubbed in English.
53-6134 *$14.99*

Cynthia Rothrock

Righting Wrongs (1986)
Knockout martial arts saga starring Yuen Biao as a lawyer who takes the law into his own hands when a key witness in his first major case is murdered. Cynthia Rothrock is the detective assigned to find the attorney, but eventually teams with him after another murder occurs. With Corey-Yuen-Kwai and Karen Shepherd. AKA: "Above the Law." 100 min. In Cantonese with English subtitles.
53-9990 Letterboxed *$19.99*

Righting Wrongs (Dubbed Version)
Also available in a dubbed-in-English edition.
53-9991 Letterboxed *$19.99*

Fight To Win (1990)
Inspired by a true story, this martial arts adventure tells of an explosive war over a coveted statue between a young self-defense expert and ruthless karate master. The young man calls on his elderly teacher for help and he recommends a new instructor: a woman. With Richard Norton, George Chung and, in an early role, Cynthia Rothrock. 88 min.
72-4002 *$19.99*

Martial Law 2: Undercover (1992)
Martial arts maestros Cynthia Rothrock and Jeff Wincott play members of an elite police squad investigating a colleague's death. They uncover a high-level call-girl ring and a crime kingpin protected by fighting experts, and Rothrock goes undercover to discover their connection to the killing. With Billy Drago. 92 min.
07-1843 ❑*$19.99*

Lady Dragon (1992)
Cynthia Rothrock stars in this action-packed saga about a woman out for revenge on the punks who killed her husband and left her to die. A martial arts teacher rescues her and trains her in the deadliest of fighting styles. With Richard Norton, Robert Ginty.
69-7082 *$19.99*

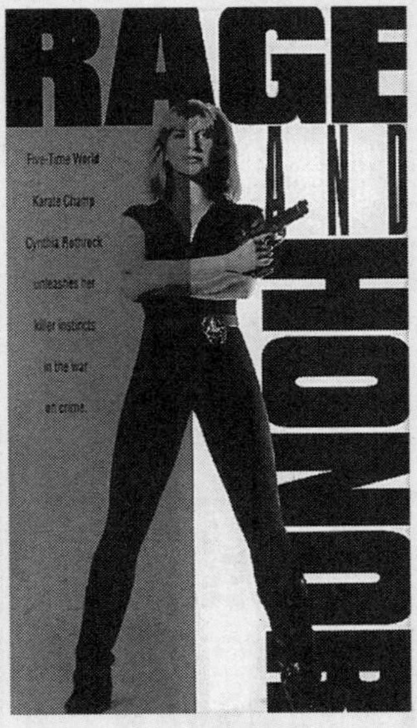

Rage And Honor (1992)
Inner-city high school teacher and martial arts expert Cynthia Rothrock discovers that evil cops are selling crack to her students. This calls for a stronger punishment than detention, so she decides to take on the criminal constables using her karate skills. Richard Norton and Catherine Bach also star. 93 min.
02-2341 Was $89.99 *$14.99*

Rage And Honor II: Hostile Takeover (1993)
Cynthia Rothrock returns in this high-kicking sequel that finds her travelling to Jakarta in order to stop a powerful banker from laundering huge amounts of drug money. While there, Rothrock teams with a fugitive police officer to uncover a web of deceit. Richard Norton co-stars. 98 min.
02-2518 Was $89.99 *$14.99*

Please see our index for these other Cynthia Rothrock titles: *Millionaires' Express • Night Vision*

The Tigers From Canton (1995)
Set during the Ching Dynasty, this action-packed kung fu saga follows a pair of martial artists from Northern and Southern China. Southern master Wong, dedicated to freeing his people from the opium trade, teams with his Northern counterpart, secret agent Timothy. Kidnapping, corruption and incredible fights play a part in this epic, based on the true exploits of Wong Fai Hong. 80 min.
82-7020 *$39.99*

A Kid From Tibet (1994)
A valuable golden urn is sought by Hong Kong lawyer E.G. Robinson, who learns that the item has been returned to where it belongs, in Potala Palace in Tibet. Robinson soon becomes embroiled in intrigue and political espionage as different parties attempt to retrieve the urn. Yuen Biao (who also directed), Yuen Wah, Nina Li Chi star. 82 min.
82-7025 *$39.99*

Revenge Of The Tiger (1994)
An all-out action assault involving the adopted martial arts expert son of a eunuch who, after finding his real father, becomes embroiled in a battle with the Emperor and his forces over the opium trade. Moral lessons and fierce fighting highlight this furious martial arts adventure starring Ma Jing Tao and Cheung Shen Kuang. 80 min.
82-7029 *$39.99*

Sword Of The Serpent (1993)
Astonishing sword-fighting sequences highlight this chop-sockey epic set in the final years of the Ming Dynasty, as a mysterious swordsman uses the special Gold Snake Sword to kill all evil rivals. While staying at a castle inhabited by his former lover, he faces her husband, a kung-fu master out to claim the sword for himself. Yuen Biao, Chang Min star. AKA: "The Sword Stained with Royal Blood." 87 min.
82-7030 *$39.99*

The Unconquered (1996)
Outstanding martial arts action highlights this tale about Manchurian emperor Chen Loong, who attempts to eradicate the Muslim inhabitants of China's Southwest regions, and a fiery rebel named Jackie, who uses his kung fu skills to fight to overthrow the Imperial forces. Ho Ha King stars. 87 min.
82-7034 *$39.99*

Deadend Of Besiegers (1992)
Furious, action-packed saga tells of a Japanese warrior who travels to China in order to learn more about the disciplines of the martial arts. During his excursion, he foils a coup and uses his expertise to get out of danger and save lives. Cynthia Khan stars with Yu Rong-Guang. 90 min. Dubbed in English.
82-7036 *$39.99*

To Be The Best (1993)
The girlfriend of a young member of the U.S. kickboxing team is kidnapped by a ruthless gambler out to fix an upcoming tournament. The kickboxer enlists the help of his father, his teammates and members of the opposing Chinese team to stop the threatening gambler. Mike Worth, Martin Kove, Alex Cord and Brittney Powell star in this high-energy kickathon.
86-1069 Was $89.99 ❑*$14.99*

Sword Of Honor (1994)
In order to avenge the murder of his partner, an undercover cop and martial arts expert embarks on a deadly one-man crusade. Action-laden thriller stars Steven Vincent Leigh, Sophia Crawford. 91 min.
86-1083 Was $89.99 ❑*$14.99*

The Power Within (1995)
A magical ring is placed on the finger of a young martial arts expert, and soon he's part of a fierce battle against an evil man who has possession of a similar ring that gives him unimaginable strength. With Ted Jan Roberts, Jacob Parker and Karen Valentine. 97 min.
86-1094 Was $89.99 ❑*$14.99*

Tiger Heart (1995)
A young man preparing for his freshman year of college gets a very different sort of education when he uses his martial arts skills to tackle the henchmen of a weaselly developer who wants to destroy his neighborhood. Fight-filled action tale stars T.J. Roberts, Robert LaSardo, Jennifer Lyons. 90 min.
86-1102 Was $89.99 ❑*$14.99*

Bloodsport III (1997)
In this all-out action assault, martial arts expert Daniel Bernhardt is out to avenge the death of his mentor by tackling a vicious warrior, the Beast, in a brutal fight known as the Kumite. In order to prepare for the match, Bernhardt turns to a great shaman for help. James Hong, John Rhys-Davis and Pat Morita also star. 92 min.
86-5002 *$99.99*

Bloodsport 4 (1999)
It's a battle to the death between fighters with nothing to live for, as karate-kicking cop Daniel Bernhardt goes undercover in a prison's death row and uncovers the Dark Kumite, the ultimate martial arts competition, being staged by a corrupt, sadistic warden. Stefanos Miltsakakis, Lisa Stothard also star. 100 min.
82-5110 *$89.99*

Kick Of Death (1997)
A star in Hong Kong's underground kickboxing battles named Shane dodges Triad mobsters and heads to America. After an altercation with a hit man, Shane takes the killer's identity, but runs into trouble when he meets a stripper and a fight promoter in Las Vegas. Vernon Wells, Michael Guerin and Brenda Maly star in this martial arts-filled film. 97 min.
88-5017 Was $89.99 *$14.99*

Enter The Ninja (1982)
The secret fighting rituals of the Ninja are featured in this two-fisted saga. A Westerner learns the rituals of the Ninja warriors, and uses them to take on the opposition. Franco Nero, Susan George, Sho Kosugi. 101 min.
12-1234 *$14.99*

Revenge Of The Ninja (1983)
Stand back for the action flick of the year. A brave Ninja, hoping to get away from his bloody past, goes to Los Angeles. But there he faces a drug-trafficker who may be his relative. Swift Ninja fighting that is truly unforgettable! Sho Kosugi and Arthur Roberts star. 88 min.
12-1321 *$14.99*

Ninja III: The Domination (1984)
Martial art and the supernatural mix as lovely telephone lineman Lucinda Dickey ("Breakin'") is given a mysterious sword and becomes possessed by the soul of a legendary Ninja master. With Sho Kosugi. 95 min.
12-1400 *$14.99*

Ninja Mission (1984)
When a top scientist and his lovely daughter are imprisoned in a maximum-security Soviet fortress, a CIA agent teams with a band of ninja warriors to rescue them...or die trying. Exciting blend of spy action and martial arts thrills stars Christopher Kohlberg, Hanna Pola. 96 min.
03-1438 *$14.99*

Ninja Champion (1980)
What is the secret this white-clad champion of the lethal martial arts hides behind a mask, and what is the real reason they come to the aid of Interpol agents tracking down a violent jewel smuggling ring? Watch this action-filled flick and find out! Philip Ching, Nancy Chan, Richard Harrison star. 90 min.
20-5155 *$19.99*

True Game Of Death (1980)
Was Bruce Lee murdered by a jealous movie mogul trying to put his independent film company out of business? That's what this martial arts drama proposes, and when stand-in Bruce Le takes the late star's place he is taken over by Lee's spirit to carry out a mission of vengeance. Action galore! 90 min.
21-1006 Was $29.99 *$19.99*

Duel Of The Masters (1988)
There'll be high-kicking, hard-fisted hell to pay when the most feared hit man in all the Orient squares off against his most feared rival...and only one will walk away! Chuck Taine, Llornu Durgo.
39-1956 *$19.99*

Dreadnaught (1981)
After his wife is killed by bounty hunters, a deadly kung fu criminal known as "White Tiger" goes off the deep end, killing all in his path. Can a timid laundry boy known as Mousey stop his murderous rampage when the police and even the famed Wong Fei Hung have failed? Yuen Biao and Kwan Tak Hing, star of 99 Wong Fei Hung films, star in this martial arts classic. 90 min. In Cantonese with English subtitles.
14-6161 Letterboxed *$19.99*

Dreadnaught (Dubbed Version)
Also available in a dubbed-in-English edition.
53-6339 Letterboxed *$19.99*

Bruce Li In New Guinea (1980)
Romance and adventure fill this slam-bang tale, as anthropologist Bruce Li uncovers an ancient serpent-worshiping cult on a remote island as he searches for the legendary Snake Pearl. Bolo Yeung also stars. 98 min.
16-1013 *$12.99*

Fists Of Fury II (1980)
Bruce Li returns in a mad rage of martial arts power to avenge the death of his brother and mother. 90 min.
16-1001 *$12.99*

Gymkata (1985)
Olympic gymnast and medal-winner Kurt Thomas follows in Bruce Jenner's footsteps in this action-packed tale of intrigue, espionage and Gymkata, an exciting blend of karate and gymnastics. Leaps, kicks, flips galore!
12-1471 *$79.99*

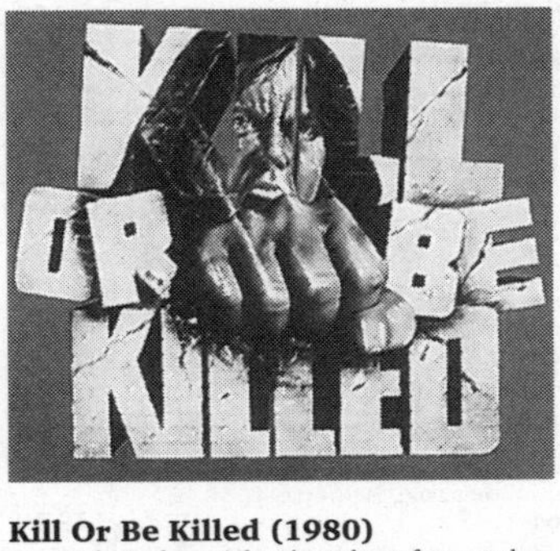

Kill Or Be Killed (1980)
A martial arts champ is lured to a desert fortress where he's to partake in an Olympic-like contest. When he finds out the contest is headed by a criminal mastermind—look out! He's quicker than a bullwhip, faster than a dart, stronger than a raging bull. James Ryan stars. 90 min.
03-1135 *$14.99*

Kickfighter (1989)
When an inspector on the Hong Kong anti-drug squad discovers his family has been murdered, he flees to Thailand. But soon he's in more trouble as he faces military drug cartels and tries to stop them and other drug dealers with help from a champion kickboxer. Yukari Oshima and Simon Yam star. 88 min. Dubbed in English.
53-6132 *$14.99*

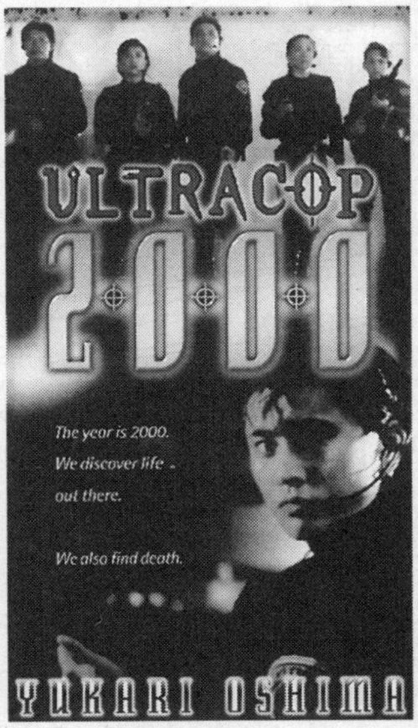

Ultracop 2000 (1993)
Move over, RoboCop! Here comes kickboxing babe Yukari Oshima as Ultracop, a futuristic freedom fighter, out to stop a Martian outlaw in the year 2000. There's all sorts of wild action sequences in this wild sci-fi actioner. Dubbed in English.
53-9956 *$14.99*

Tiger Angels (1993)
Yukari Oshima is hired by Cynthia Khan to act as a bodyguard for Khan's father, a businessman Khan fears will be kidnapped. When the deed occurs, both women must infiltrate the gangsters responsible for the job. Wild action, nifty stunts and gorgeous Oshima and Khan are sure to wow you! 90 min. Dubbed in English.
53-6862 *$14.99*

Angel Of Vengeance (1993)
Furious martial arts action ensues when Japanese kickboxing babe Yukari Oshima seeks revenge. She's the daughter of a mobster who has been killed in a gangster turf war, and Yukari is not gonna take it! 90 min. Dubbed in English.
53-6863 *$14.99*

Fatal Target (1994)
While vacationing in Manila, Japanese kickboxing dynamo Yukari Oshima and her policewoman friend are called into action to help authorities corral a group of smugglers. Complexity kicks in when it's learned that Yukari's cousin leads the smugglers. With Sharon Yeung Pan-pan. Dubbed in English.
53-9955 *$14.99*

Power Connection (1995)
Action? You better believe it! Two undercover cops assigned to halt drug-smuggling, counterfeiting and weapon-selling mobsters go head-to-head with members of a powerful Triad when they're true identities are revealed. Yukari Oshima and Philip Ko star. 88 min. Dubbed in English.
53-9992 *$14.99*

Guardian Angel (1996)
Yukari Oshima brings her martial arts prowess to this action spectacle in which she's an Interpol agent joined by two associates to battle international drug smugglers. When one of the agents is forced into fighting, a conflict occurs. Can it be resolved before things get out of control? 86 min. Dubbed in English.
53-9957 *$14.99*

The Shaolin Incredible Ten (1982)
Take a murdered Shaolin abbot, a missing Buddhist scripture, an army of kung fu soldiers led by a villain named Eagle Han, and some female ninjas. Stir all these ingredients into a tale of rebellion, murder and intrigue. The result...INCREDIBLE! Sue Lee, Elton Chong star. 87 min.
41-7004 Was $29.99 *$19.99*

Death Mask Of The Ninja (1987)
Two feudal princes, separated at birth, reunite and use their divergent martial arts styles in a fight to regain their kingdom. Joey Lee, Ton Chen, and Tiger Tung (not to be confused with the deli special of the same name) star. 95 min.
41-7005 Was $29.99 *$19.99*

Chuck Norris

Breaker! Breaker! (1977)
Pedal-to-the-floor action all the way as karate champion Chuck Norris leads a convoy of angry truckers in an action-packed assault on a Texas town. Co-stars George Murdock, Terry O'Connor, Don Gentry and Jack Nance. 86 min.
53-1041 *$14.99*

Good Guys Wear Black (1978)
The film that made Chuck Norris a star features the martial arts expert as a Vietnam veteran who discovers that his battalion's final, "suicide" mission may have been a CIA set-up and that a crooked politician is after him. See Chuck go feet-first through a speeding car's windshield! With Anne Archer, James Franciscus, Dana Andrews. 96 min.
44-1870 Was $19.99 *$14.99*

An Eye For An Eye (1981)
Chuck Norris stars as a San Francisco cop who quits the force after he's wounded and his partner killed by drug smugglers. Chuck doesn't need no stinking badge to deal a little vengeance to the crooks, just his fists and feet! With Christopher Lee, Richard Roundtree, Toru Tanaka. 103 min.
02-5058 *$14.99*

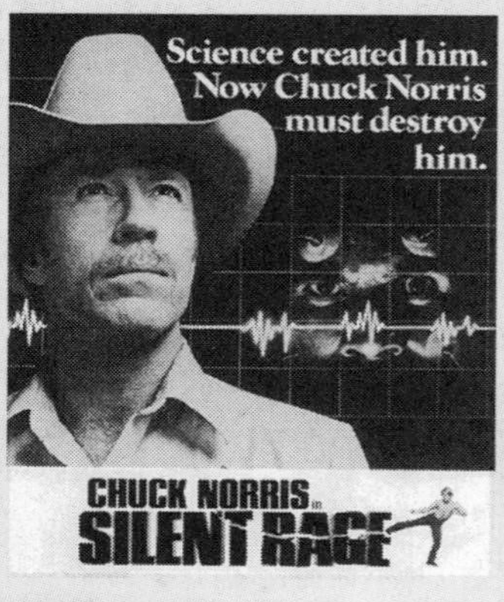

Silent Rage (1982)
Chuck Norris is a tough sheriff who faces a supernatural horror that is terrifying the town. Norris must call on his astonishing martial arts skills to battle the culprit!
02-1137 *$14.99*

Lone Wolf McQuade (1983)
Meet Chuck Norris. He's the meanest man in the world. Now he meets the toughest opponent ever—"Kung Fu's" David Carradine. The two battle it out in a way you've never seen before! Barbara Carrera. 107 min.
47-1147 *$14.99*

Missing In Action (1984)
Action ace Chuck Norris stars as a former Vietnam War P.O.W. who returns to Southeast Asia to rescue his comrades still being held in captivity. M. Emmet Walsh, James Hong also star. 101 min.
12-1405 *$14.99*

Missing In Action 2: The Beginning (1985)
Chuck Norris returns in an action-packed "prequel" that follows Norris and his crew's captivity in a Viet Cong P.O.W. camp. A daring escape through the jungle is their only chance for freedom, but who will survive? 96 min.
12-1449 *$14.99*

Invasion U.S.A. (1985)
When a Soviet-backed terrorist army attacks the Southeast U.S., only one man stands between them and victory: ex-CIA agent Chuck Norris. All-out action hit that pits Chuck against overwhelming odds. With Richard Lynch, Melissa Prophet. 108 min.
12-1541 *$14.99*

Code Of Silence (1985)
Chuck Norris scores big in this urban action thriller, playing a tough Chicago detective who must stop an underworld war by rescuing a gang boss' daughter. Exciting stunt work by Norris in this blockbuster hit.With Henry Silva, Dennis Farina. 100 min.
44-1313 *$14.99*

The Delta Force (1986)
Intense action-thriller from the pages of today's headlines, as Chuck Norris and Lee Marvin head up an elite anti-terrorist squad. When Arab guerrillas hijack a jetliner in the Middle East and hold the passengers hostage, only the Delta Force can save the day. With George Kennedy, Hanna Schygulla, Shelley Winters and Joey Bishop. 125 min.
08-8428 *$14.99*

The Hitman (1991)
Chuck Norris plays a cop left to die by his crooked partner in a gun battle who is rescued, then resurfaces with a new identity, working undercover for the Drug Enforcement Agency as a hit man. Soon, he finds himself in the middle of a war between the Mob, the Agency and Iranian drug dealers. Michael Parks, Alberta Watson co-star in this thrilling actioner. 94 min.
19-7086 Was $19.99 □*$14.99*

Hellbound (1993)
He's kicked the stuffing out of all sorts of screen villains, but Chuck Norris is up against his deadliest and most inhuman foe ever in this thriller, as Chicago cop Norris' probe of a murder leads him into a confrontation with a centuries-old Satanic disciple. With Sheree J. Wilson, Calvin Levels. 95 min.
19-2326 Was $89.99 □*$19.99*

Walker, Texas Ranger: One Riot, One Ranger (1993)
This pilot to the hit TV series features Chuck Norris as Cordell Walker, a tough Texas Ranger who teams with his slick, ex-gridiron star sidekick and a beautiful district attorney to smash a gang of bank robbers and three hoods who have victimized a teenage girl. Sheree J. Wilson, Clarence Gilyard co-star. 96 min.
19-7095 Was $19.99 □*$14.99*

Walker, Texas Ranger: Deadly Reunion (1994)
Chuck Norris kicks ass in this feature-length installment of his hit TV series. Texas Ranger Walker tracks down a deadly assassin who targets a presidential candidate. Sheree J. Wilson, Clarence Gilyard and Jonathan Banks also star. 92 min.
19-2342 Was $89.99 □*$19.99*

Top Dog (1995)
Chuck Norris has handled lots of screen challenges over the years, but this time he's up against his toughest one yet, as Norris plays a tough San Diego cop whose new partner is a clever canine named Reno! Watch Chuck break bones and Reno bury them in this fast-paced action/comedy. 93 min.
27-6930 Was $89.99 □*$14.99*

Forest Warrior (1996)
Chuck Norris is the titular character, a mythical frontiersman named John McKenna who helps a group of kids trying to stop unscrupulous businessmen from destroying a mountain and a beautiful forest. Action and environmental themes mix in this wilderness adventure. 98 min.
18-7716 Was $99.99 □*$14.99*

Please see our index for these other Chuck Norris titles: *Game Of Death • Return Of The Dragon • The Wrecking Crew*

Drunken Wu Tang (1983)
The Yuen Brothers are the stars of this outrageous chop-sockey enterprise that showcases dynamic martial arts brawls, aerial battles, some sex and bizarre creatures. The Brothers tackle a banana monster, robots, cluster bombs and Porcupine Back when they try to stop nasty Old Devil, a bad guy with supernatural powers. AKA: "Taoism Drunkard." 90 min.
54-9162 *$19.99*

Wu Tang Master (1986)
Extraordinary fighting tops this spectacular martial arts epic, the second sequel to "Miracle Fighters." The astounding Yuen Brothers attempt to jump, punch and kick their way out of a series of surreal hurdles in order to remain the world's top fighters. See them grapple with frogs, twins, the Ring Master and more! AKA: "Shaolin Drunkard." 90 min.
54-9166 *$19.99*

Rage Of The Master (1987)
X = The Commissioner; Y = The Ruthless Bandit; Z = The Kung Fu Fighter. X tries to capture Y. Instead, Y captures X. Z unintentionally rescues X, trying to steal X's horse. X and Z are recaught by Y, who poses as X until the real X reappears to save the day. Ng Ming Tsai, Tiger Yang star. 100 min.
55-1059 Was $59.99 *$19.99*

Bruce vs. Bill (1981)
Two Kung Fu masters (named, perhaps, Bruce and Bill?) go at it when they find out some buried treasure is missing. Bruce Le, Ma Cheung, Angela Yu Ching, Fung Ruen Chuen star. 87 min.
64-1001 *$19.99*

Bruce Is Loose (1981)
And he's strong as a moose. When he catches up with the killers who murdered his family, he'll fix their caboose, without accepting a truce. This one's a winner; how can you lose? Bruce Le stars. 76 min.
64-1023 *$19.99*

The Deadly Strike (1980)
A lone hero, appointed lawman in a terrorized town, selects seven desperate prisoners and whips them into a bone-crushing martial arts juggernaut willing to die at his command. Stars Bruce Li. 92 min.
64-1042 *$19.99*

The Big Rascal (1980)
"Fightin'...on a Sunday afternoon." You can be sure this is the Kung Fu movie for you, as two brothers grow up to become the martial arts protectors of their village, defending it against the "Evil Master." Ling Hu, Hing Lu star.
64-1063 *$19.99*

Treasure Of Bruce Le (1980)
When a remorseless Samurai steals precious secrets from a Buddhist monastery, it's up to Bruce and his crack squad of Kung Fu commandoes to retrieve them. Mayhem and mauling abound. 86 min.
64-1044 *$19.99*

The Magnificent Kick (1980)
Ever wonder what long-ago martial artist invented the "Kick Without Shadow," a lightning-fast move that leaves nothing standing? Well, his name was Wong-Fai-Hung, and his story is told in this exciting drama dripping with action scenes. With "an all-star kung fu cast." AKA: "Kick Without a Shadow." 90 min.
55-1112 Was $29.99 *$19.99*

Shaolin vs. Lama (1983)
The two-"L" llama, he's a beast; the one-"L" lama, he's an unstoppable martial arts killing machine. And when a group of them infiltrate a Shaolin temple, it's a battle to the death to prove whose is the superior fighting style. Pang Kam Man, Lo Yui star. 93 min. In Cantonese with English subtitles.
59-5034 *$19.99*

The Bone Crushing Kid (1981)
Sung, a young member of a theatrical troupe, learns martial arts and tries to use them against all who cause him trouble. Kam Lung stars in this ferocious fight-a-thon. 89 min. Dubbed in English.
53-6883 *$14.99*

Secret Of The Chinese Kung Fu (1980)
After being rescued from drowning by two sisters, Chang tries to repay them by battling a menacing thug named Kang who leads one of the area's top gangs. Lo Lieh, of "Five Fingers of Death" fame stars. 90 min. Dubbed in English.
53-6935 *$14.99*

Iron Thunder (1989)
Iron "Amp" Elmore, the world's heavyweight kickboxing champ, stars in this bone-crunching action opus in the tradition of "Enter the Dragon." The "Amp-Man" shows us his kicking prowess in and out of the ring. Bruce Lee would've been proud. With George M. Young and Julius Dorsey. 85 min.
54-9007 *$19.99*

The Fierce Boxer And Bruce (1981)
"Just how fierce is he," you ask? Well, fierce enough to challenge Kung Fu master Bruce Li to a deadly martial arts competition, where one wrong move could be your last! AKA: "The Fierce Boxer." 91 min.
64-1065 *$19.99*

Ghost Of The Ninja (1980)
When you're throwing stars, but not leaving scars, who're ya fighting? Ghost Ninja! When you draw your blade, and he starts to fade, who're ya fighting? Ghost Ninja! The bad guys don't have a ghost of a chance in this martial arts mishegas. Stars Jen Shih Kuan, Chen I Hsing. AKA: "Killer Wears White," "Killer in White." 114 min.
64-1067 *$19.99*

White Phantom (1987)
Magnificent martial arts melees are in store when a young American trained in the deadly art of the ninja must disable a ruthless crew of terrorists that is bargaining to acquire weapons-grade plutonium. Hard-fisted, blade-wielding high adventure with Bo Svenson, Jay Roberts, Jr. 90 min.
68-1071 Was $29.99 *$14.99*

Day Of The Panther (1987)
When one of their number is murdered by the martial arts-trained minions of an Australian drug lord, the frenetic fighting force known as the Panthers leaps into vengeance, guaranteeing a furious free-for-all. Eddie Stazak, John Stanton star. 86 min.
69-5046 *$79.99*

Fists Of Blood (1988)
"They killed his friend and kidnapped his lover." What to do? Well, when you're Jason Blade, you use your martial arts skills to see that no one, not even the ruthless drug lord behind these savage crimes, escapes justice. Stars Edward John Stazak, Zale Daniel, Paris Jefferson. AKA: "Strike of the Panther." 90 min.
69-5073 *$79.99*

Ninja Strike Force (1988)
No, Tito Santana and Rick Martel don't appear, but a cabal of nine deadly ninja warriors do, fighting to retrieve a mystic artifact that was stolen from them. Martial arts action as you like it. With Richard Harrison, Geoffrey Ziebart. AKA: "Ninja Operation 2: Way of Challenge." 89 min.
69-7012 *$19.99*

Ninja Masters Of Death (1985)
When the sinister cabal known as the Black Ninjas develops a secret plan to overthrow the government (sorry, we don't know which government), undercover martial arts agents challenge them in an amazing battle where your first mistake is your last. Daniel Wells, Chris Peterson, Karen McManus star. 90 min.
69-7019 *$19.99*

Ninja Commandments (1987)
The code of the Ninja demands harsh penalties for any couple who violate the marriage rules, but when an evil warrior tries to put Ninja Law above the Ten Commandments of Love, he soon meets his match. 90 min.
69-7021 *$19.99*

Zombie vs. Ninja (1987)
Sure, this black-clad assassin can defeat any foe alive, but will even his martial arts skills be enough to overcome the challenge of the undead! Horrific actioner stars Wang Li, Keth Uh Land.
69-7049 *$19.99*

Hands Of Death (1987)
The titular extremities belong to feuding bands of modern-day pirates who battle to the death over a fabulous treasure. Intense martial arts action with Richard Harrison, Mike Abbott. AKA: "Ninja Operation 7: Royal Warriors."
69-7031 Was $59.99 *$19.99*

Ninja Avengers (1987)
No, it's not Patrick Macnee in black pajamas and bowler. It's "good against evil in the ultimate clash of Ninja forces," and anyone who follows martial arts films knows what to expect: action, action, and more action! With Richard Harrison, Stuart Smith. AKA: "Ninja Operation 8: Champion on Fire."
69-7023 *$19.99*

Full Metal Ninja (1988)
"Killer ninja Eagle, you've got a peace symbol on your headband, and a pair of swords in your hands! What are you trying to prove?" "Sir, I think it's something about the duality of man, Sir!" Stars Pierre Kirby, Jean Paul and Renato Sala.
69-7044 *$19.99*

Ninja: The Final Duel (1986)
The head abbott of a famous Shaolin monastery is torn between accepting official recognition of his order's fighting ability or maintaining their pacifist reputation. When Japanese ninjas attack the monastery, the Shaolin masters are ordered not to fight, but the killing of a visiting Western monk forces them into action! Features incredible fight sequences. 88 min.
82-7009 *$39.99*

A Blood Stained Sword (1989)
An Imperial guard in Qing Dynasty China is ordered to kill a highly-valued concubine, but is banished when the emperor has second thoughts after the execution. During his exile, the guard is sought by a young martial arts students who needs his "magic" sword to avenge his teacher's murder, but the young man soon learns skill is more important than the sword when it comes to fighting. 90 min.
82-7022 *$39.99*

7 Lucky Ninja Kids (1989)
Magnificent Seven? You bet! Here are seven youngsters who happen to be martial arts experts, and when a top mafia type causes trouble, look for our gang to go, go, go. Chopsocky children in action. AKA: "7 Ninja Kids." 87 min.
78-1018 Was $19.99 *$14.99*

American Ninja (1985)
A young American man trained in the deadliest of the martial arts must use his skills to stop the ninja army of an international smuggler in this non-stop action film. Michael Dudikoff, Judie Aronson star. 90 min.
12-1489 *$14.99*

American Ninja 3: Blood Hunt (1989)
The black pajamas are passed on in this latest entry in the martial arts series, starring David Bradley as the homegrown ninja hero who faces his ultimate challenge when he fights a sinister cabal of assassins. Steve James, Marjoe Gortner co-star. 90 min.
19-7050 *$14.99*

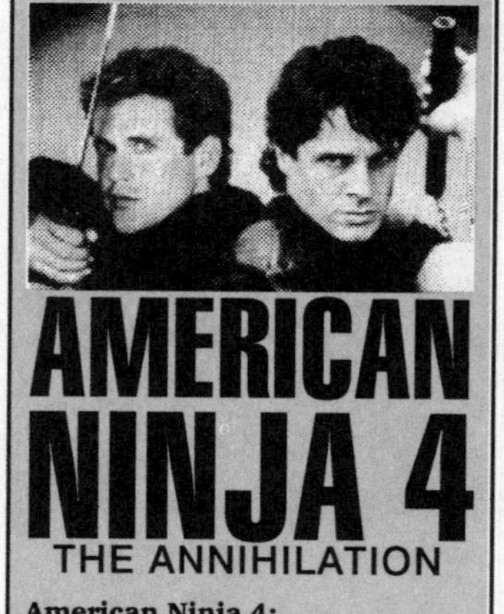

American Ninja 4: The Annihilation (1991)
Four Delta Force Commandos and a rescue team are captured by a clandestine ninja force and held captive in an African forest. It's up to Joe Armstrong, martial arts expert extraordinaire, to come out of retirement and tackle the dangerous escape mission. Michael Dudikoff and David Bradley star in this rip-roaring adventure. 99 min.
19-7082 Was $19.99 □*$14.99*

American Ninja 5 (1995)
When a scientist's beautiful daughter is kidnapped, American ninja David Bradley attempts to find her, but for this assignment he'll need the help of a youngster he has trained in the ways of the ninja. Pat Morita and Lee Reyes also star in this family-oriented entry in the popular series. 102 min.
19-7102 Was $89.99 □*$19.99*

Sammo Hung

Sting Of The Dragon Masters (1973)
If you build a fortress around your heart, these Kung Fu killers will kick it down! Angela Mao and Jhoon Rhee team up for twice the thrills and twice the excitement in a martial arts thriller that features an early supporting turn by Sammo Hung, who did the fight choreography. AKA: "When Taekwondo Strikes."
08-1291 *$19.99*

Enter The Fat Dragon (1978)
The Bruce Lee classic "Enter the Dragon" gets spoofed in this winning mix of laughs and martial arts action from director/star Sammo Hung. Hung plays a Lee-worshipping farmboy who arrives in Hong Kong to work for his uncle and winds up involved with crooks. Roy Chiao, Kin-Ming Lim and Yuen Biao also star. 91 min. In Cantonese with English subtitles.
20-8246 Letterboxed *$19.99*

Magnificent Butcher (1979)
Hyperkinetic martial arts epic that spoofs the popular Shaw Brothers efforts and features Yuen Biao, Sammo Hung and Wei Pei as students of famed teacher Wong Fei Hung. When Wong goes away on a business trip, pork vendor Hung is accused of rape and murder, prompting him and his pals to find the real culprits before their teacher returns. Kwan Tak Hing also stars as Wong. 107 min. In Cantonese with English subtitles.
53-6315 Letterboxed *$19.99*

The Magnificent Butcher (Dubbed Version)
Available in a dubbed-in-English edition.
53-6324 Letterboxed *$19.99*

The Odd Couple (1979)
Marvelous martial arts scenes highlight this film depicting an ongoing feud between sword master Sammo Hung and spear expert Lau Kar Wing. The two meet over a 10-year span to see who's weaponry is better, but after many draws, the aging warriors enlist students (Sammo plays Lau's student and vice versa) to carry on the rivalry. 90 min. In Cantonese with English subtitles.
54-9200 *$14.99*

Lightning Kung Fu (1980)
The three mighty masters of this electrifying art strike more than once in the same place, and if you try to spark with them, you're going to wind up bolting! Kung Fu clashes with John Li, Ayla Ranzz, Sammo Hung Kam-Bo, Condo Arlik. 94 min. AKA: "The Victim."
41-7006 Was $29.99 *$19.99*

The Filthy Guy (1980)
Sammo Hung shines in this kung fu fave that finds him as a poor orphan who works for a local village landlord named Chan. When Chan is threatened by some ruthless rivals, he and his son get a quick lesson in martial arts artistry from Hung, preparing them for the ultimate showdown. Carter Wong also stars. AKA: "Return of the Secret Rivals." 88 min. Dubbed in English.
50-5059 *$14.99*

The Prodigal Son (1981)
Masterful adventure featuring astonishing Wing Chun battles guaranteed to blow you away. Martial arts student Yuen Biao, upon discovering his father has been paying opponents to lose to him, goes to study under a real master. When the teacher is killed, Yuen must face off against the killer. Sammo Hung directed and co-stars. AKA: "Pull No Punches." 100 min. In Cantonese with English subtitles.
53-6137 Letterboxed *$19.99*

The Prodigal Son (Dubbed Version)
Also available in a dubbed-in-English edition.
53-6138 Letterboxed *$19.99*

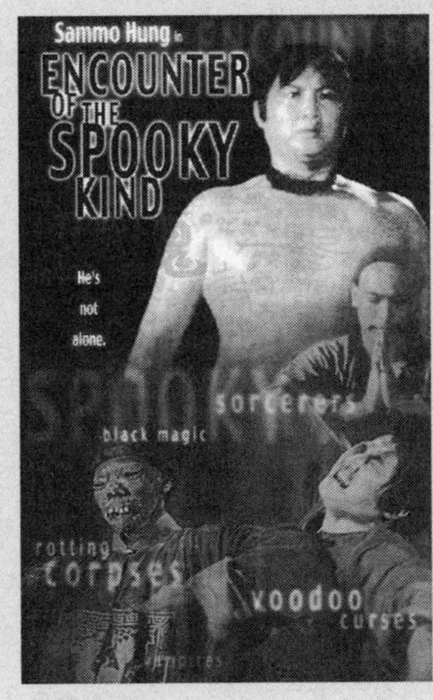

Encounter Of The Spooky Kind (1981)
An over-the-top "Hong Kong-coction" of horror, comedy and martial arts, this outrageous epic has director-star Sammo Hung fighting hopping vampires, ghosts and other menaces when his unfaithful wife's lover hires a Taoist priest to kill him. Hung is looked after by the priest's brother and becomes a pawn when the rival mages engage in a duel of spells. 90 min. In Cantonese with English subtitles.
53-6271 Letterboxed *$19.99*

Encounter Of The Spooky Kind (Dubbed Version)
Also available in a dubbed-in-English edition.
53-6272 Letterboxed *$19.99*

Millionaires' Express (1986)
Sammo Hung directed and stars in this all-star action spectacle as a petty crook in '30s China who returns to his impoverished hometown with a plan to save it by forcing a cross-country train packed with wealthy travellers to stop there. When a band of outlaws also after the train take over the town, Hung and his cohorts confront them in a wild and comical showdown. With Yuen Biao, Rosamund Kwan, Richard Norton and Cynthia Rothrock. AKA: "Shanghai Express." 107 min. In Cantonese with English subtitles.
53-9837 Letterboxed *$19.99*

Millionaires' Express (Dubbed Version)
Also available in a dubbed-in-English edition.
53-9838 Letterboxed *$19.99*

Eastern Condors (1987)
Hong Kong cinema's "round mound of martial arts rebound," Sammo Hung, directed and stars in this action-filled take on "The Dirty Dozen." A group of Chinese convicts are recruited by the U.S. military for a suicide mission deep in the jungles of Vietnam: destroy an abandoned American weapons depot before the Vietnamese find it. With Yuen Biao, Joyce Godenzi, Yuen Wah and Haing S. Ngor
53-8928 Letterboxed *$19.99*

Eastern Condors (Dubbed Version)
Also available in a dubbed-in-English edition.
53-8929 Letterboxed *$19.99*

Painted Faces (1988)
Set in the famed Peking Opera school in the 1950s, this acclaimed drama traces, with laughs and poignancy, the arduous training of the young students known as the "Seven Little Fortunes," whose alumni includes Hong Kong cinema legends Yeun Biao, Jackie Chan and Sammo Hung (who stars as his own teacher). In Cantonese and Mandarin with English subtitles.
53-9410 *$49.99*

Pedicab Driver (1989)
Lively romantic fable about a pedicab driver's love for a woman in Macao in the early 20th century. There's lightweight comedy and action in this change-of-pace effort from Sammo Hung, known for his fierce kung fu films. 98 min. In Cantonese with English subtitles.
53-9413 *$19.99*

Touch And Go (1991)
Hong Kong star Sammo Hung excels in this hair-raising thriller from Ringo Lam ("Full Contact") about a policeman obsessed in avenging the death of his close friend and partner. In fact, the cop's desire to even the score eventually threatens those around him. With Mo Shen Kwen. In Cantonese with English subtitles.
53-9806 *$49.99*

Don't Give A Damn (1994)
Sammo Hung is a gruff veteran cop who manages to antagonize his young boss, a customs agent he works with, and his girl. But Sammo's going to have to start getting along with his fellow cops if he wants to snag the crooks behind a botched drug deal before an all-out gang war breaks out. Takeshi Kaneshiro, Yuen Biao, Cathy Chow also star. 95 min. In Cantonese with English subtitles.
76-2095 Letterboxed *$24.99*

Please see our index for these other Sammo Hung titles: *Dragons Forever • Dreadnaught • The Heart Of The Dragon • Island Of Fire • Kung Fu Master • My Lucky Stars • Project A I & II • Twinkle, Twinkle Lucky Stars • Wheels On Meals • Winners And Sinners • Zu: Warriors From The Magic Mountain*

The Buddhist Fist (1980)
Boasting amazing stunts from director Yuen Wo Ping, this ferocious actioner concerns two orphaned brothers who are raised separately by Shaolin monks who train them in the lethal art of Buddhist Fist. A series of attacks on the monastery and a stunning revelation leads to the siblings squaring off against each other. Yurn Shun Yi stars. 90 min. Dubbed in English.
53-6764 Letterboxed *$19.99*

The Revengeful Swordsman (1980)
Wccchht! Wccchht! Wccchht! That sound you hear is the lightening swords of female martial arts maestro Chia Ling (Ga Ling) in this tale of revenge that finds Ling using her incredible dexterity with the blade to avenge the brutal death of her father. The action's so fierce, it'll leave you singing her praises: "Ch-ch-ch-Chia!" 88 min. Dubbed in English.
53-6830 *$14.99*

Shaolin Disciple (1980)
After his policeman father is killed by a notorious bandit named Tiger, a young man calls on a group of Shaolin monks for help in getting revenge. After learning the finer points of martial arts, the man goes up against the Tiger and his mysterious masked partner. Liu Gia-Yung and Kwok Fung star. 87 min. Dubbed in English.
53-6831 *$14.99*

Hit Man In The Hand Of Buddha (1981)
Korean martial arts champ Hwang Jang Lee is Wang Cheng, a man who calls on his incredible fighting prowess to deal with the creeps who stole his money. Filled with amazing stick-fighting sequences, this tale of robbery and deception is sure to wow martial arts mavens. 92 min. Dubbed in English.
53-6833 *$14.99*

The Young Avenger (1984)
Shaw Brothers star Wong Yue is the young funeral parlor worker who also practices incredible kung fu when not dressing corpses. It's wall-to-wall martial arts action, from beginning to end! 92 min. Dubbed in English.
53-6884 *$14.99*

Avenging Trio (1989)
Gordon Liu stars in this ferocious, fight-filled story about a no-nonsense police inspector who is targeted by a group of women seeking revenge for their criminal husbands, who were killed by the inspector. 90 min. Dubbed in English.
53-6918 *$14.99*

Secret Of The Chinese Kung Fu (1980)
"Five Fingers of Death" star Lo Lieh is featured in a high-kicking story about a man whose life is saved by two sisters who then recruit him to battle a group of thugs terrorizing the area. 90 min. Dubbed in English.
53-6920 *$14.99*

Emperor Of Shaolin Kung Fu (1980)
Enthralling swordplay, wild kung fu action and lavish settings and costumes highlight this epic set during the Ming Dynasty that finds a group of rebels going up against Emperor Lee Chi Shing in his palace. Their goal is to murder him, but they first face a brutal martial arts battle. Carter Wong, Yen Nan-Hsi and Lo Lieh star. 92 min.
53-6921 *$14.99*

The Secret Executioners (1983)
There's nothing secret about the explosive violence that erupts from the screen when a ruthless gangleader and a renegade cop square off in what's been called "one of the most dazzling displays of the martial arts ever filmed." Stars Wong Chen Li, Jim Norris. 90 min.
41-7008 Was $29.99 *$19.99*

Kung Fu For Sale (1985)
"KUNG-FU, BONE-CRUNCHING AND DEADLY: Good condition, forced to sell at 50% off retail. Call Shanghai 2-2222 after 6." The young warrior in this film doesn't actually take out such an ad, but he does wander the country pitting his skills in dangerous matches. Chong Hua, Dirk Morgna star. 95 min.
41-7009 Was $29.99 *$19.99*

Vengeance Of Snow-Maid (1982)
She's a flurry of ferocious female fighting fury, this young girl who lets nothing stand in her way as she battles to avenge her mother's rape at the hands of the infamous Golden Hair Mouse. Martial arts excitement and swordplay as you like it. Stars Mo Ka Kei-Chen Chen, Gim Allon. AKA: "Vengeance of Snow Maiden." 82 min.
41-7019 Was $29.99 *$19.99*

Hurricane Sword (1985)
A storm of martial arts mayhem is unleashed in this tale that has been called both "quick and bloody" and "a classic in the Far East." With Chen Sau Kei, Li Tai Shing. 86 min.
41-7022 Was $29.99 *$19.99*

Struggle Through Death (1981)
Held prisoner in the fortress of a cruel warlord and forced to work in his gold mines, two young friends use their martial arts skills to escape to freedom in this exciting saga. Jung Yiu, Jennifer Yang star. 93 min.
41-7023 Was $29.99 *$19.99*

Rivals Of The Dragon (1983)
The deadliest father-son fighting duo since Bruno and David Sammartino, Master Chan and Almond, are a joy to watch in this martial arts masterwork, as they put away mobsters and a karate gang boss called Wolf. Jeffrey Chan, Yuen Tak star. 86 min.
10-1297 *$19.99*

Bruce Lee: The Man/The Myth (1980)
He's a sixth-degree black belt who studied with the greatest martial arts hero the world has ever known. His name is Bruce Li, and this tribute to master Bruce Lee will astonish you. 90 min.
47-3003 Was $19.99 *$14.99*

Golden Sun (1984)
A young Kung Fu student decides to investigate the death of his hero, Bruce Lee, only to uncover a sinister conspiracy out to make him the next victim. Good thing Bruce's spirit is there to guide him! With Keung How.
48-1150 *$29.99*

Revenge Of Ninja (1988)
Martial arts meets mysticism in this tale of a ninja master whose powers stem from a medallion that he gives to a young woman. Soon the woman's boyfriend and the ninja must save her from an evil wizard and his gang, who are out to steal the medallion. Barry Prima, Dana Christina star. 90 min.
50-5110 Was $59.99 *$19.99*

Young Dragons: The Kung Fu Kids II (1989)
Three youths become the toast of the town with their thrilling stunts and the prize in a whirling hand-to-hand battle between the grandfather who trained them and their grandmother, a magical martial master. Chen Shun Yun and Yen Chin Kwok star. 100 min.
19-7055 *$59.99*

The Blind Fist Of Bruce (1981)
Village against village. Man against man. Arm against arm. Hand against hand. Kam Bo directed this dazzling display of damn good defense featuring the one and only Bruce Li.
50-5040 *$19.99*

Moonlight Sword And Jade Lion (1981)
No, we're not quite sure what the title means, either, but we do know this is a dramatic epic set in ancient China, where sects of martial arts masters fought to the death against the warriors of the ruling dynasties. Authentic battle scenes add to the action. With Mao Yin, Wong Do. 94 min.
41-7024 Was $29.99 *$19.99*

Raiders Of Buddhist Kung Fu (1982)
Exciting martial arts mayhem set in fin de siecle China, where a plan to overthrow the government leads to a "duel to the death" between two human killing machines (is one of them Dan Dierdorf?). Stars Liu Chia Hui, Mike Wong, T. Mark Reilly. 85 min.
10-1296 *$14.99*

Shaolin And Wu Tang (1983)
Two martial arts students who were once friends but joined rival schools become the pawns of a Manchu prince who uses magical powers to pit them and their fellow fighters against one another. Gordon Liu stars in and directs this wild, action-filled entry that also stars Adam Cheng. 90 min. In Cantonese with English subtitles.
53-6609 *$19.99*

Shaolin And Wu Tang (Dubbed Version)
Also available in a dubbed-in-English edition.
54-9165 *$19.99*

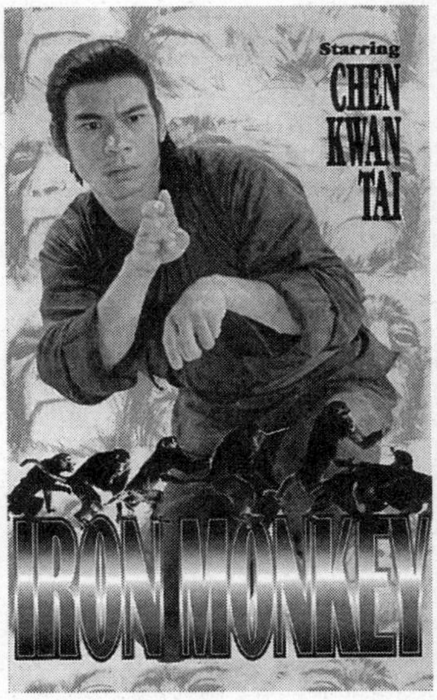

Iron Monkey (1984)
A young gambler, seeking revenge after his family is massacred by Manchu warriors, travels to a Shaolin temple, where he endures hardships and humiliation while training under the famous Bitter Monk. But his difficult times prepare him for a dangerous confrontation with the nasty chief of the Manchus. Chen Kwan Tai stars. 90 min. Dubbed in English.
54-9135 *$19.99*

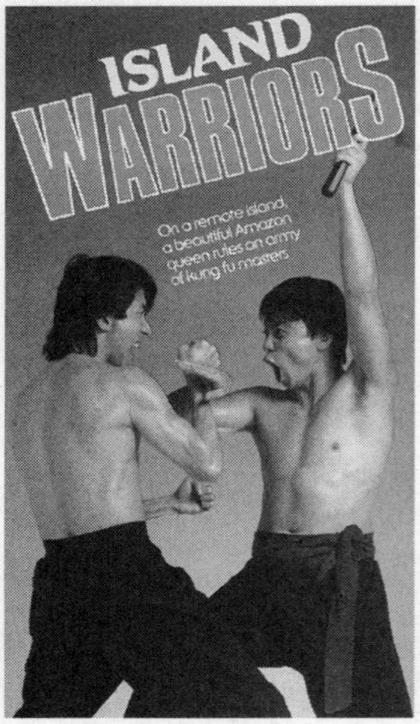

Island Warriors (1984)
A beautiful but lethal Amazon queen is the ruler of this uncharted desert isle where soldiers are trained in the deadliest of martial arts. Join Lee Shan, Wang Choi for thrilling karate action. 85 min.
64-1118 *$19.99*

A Bullet To Survive (1988)
A police inspector is ordered by his superiors to track down a fomer leader of a Vietnamese gang who recently escaped prison. The detective gets in the middle of a nasty underworld battle that pits rival gangs against each other. Fierce gunplay and martial arts action mesh in this look at the Hong Kong mafia, starring Man Su and Wai Ying Hung. 90 min.
82-7023 *$39.99*

In Sword We Trust (1985)
The commander of the Chinese Army is slaughter by the British and his head is hung for victory on a conquered fortress. The commander's daughter enlists the help of a group of rebels to retrieve the head and beat the British at their own game in this electrifying martial arts saga featuring swordfights and powerful hand-to-hand combat. Chu Shao, Jin Lee star. 82 min.
82-7028 *$39.99*

The Warriors Of Kung Fu (1982)
Yu-Ying, a kung-fu hero, teams with a woman seeking revenge for her father's murder to combat an evil gangster with ruthless ways. The finale features one of the greatest martial arts brawls of all time! Casanova Wong and Billy Yuen star. 86 min.
84-1012 Was $24.99 *$19.99*

Cage (1989)
It's the most brutal form of hand-to-hand combat imaginable: a steel cage, two men, no rules...and one survivor! Spectacular martial arts actioner stars Lou Ferrigno, Reb Brown, James Shigeta. 101 min.
73-1074 *$12.99*

Eagle vs. Silver Fox (1983)
When the Silver Fox, an evil martial arts maven, plans to restore the fallen Manchu Dynasty, the gallant Mighty Eagle tries to stop him. And you thought this one was about a fight between Don Henley and Charlie Rich. Wang Cheng Li and Mario Chan star. 86 min.
84-1014 Was $24.99 *$19.99*

Mystery Of Chess Boxing (1987)
In hopes of getting revenge for his father's murder at the hands of the destructive Ghost-Faced Killer, a young martial arts student teams with a master Chess Boxer, who happens to be the killer's arch-enemy. Spectacular Chess Boxing and Five Element fistfights highlight this effort starring Lee Yi Min and Jack Long. AKA: "Ninja Checkmate." 88 min.
54-9161 *$19.99*

Tattooed Hit Man (1976)
It you look at the pictures on his body, maybe you'll see the faces of his many victims. He's the Japanese Mafia's deadliest killer-for-hire, and his actions ignite the fuse of a bloody in this non-stop martial arts actioner. Bud Sugawara stars. 81 min.
03-1652 *$14.99*

Eagle's Claw (1978)
The martial arts schools of the Eagle's Claw and Praying Mantis have been locked in a rivalry for years, but when the Eagle's Claw leader dies, his head pupil defects to the Praying Mantis camp. This act prompts his former cohorts to stop him in an amazing battle. 86 min. Dubbed in English.
50-5014 *$14.99*

The New Game Of Death (1975)
After Bruce Lee's untimely death, Bruce Li must fulfill his legacy by getting to the Seven Star Tower and defeating seven of the world's top martial artists. Wild kung fu action highlights this salute to the master. 82 min. Dubbed in English.
53-6923 *$14.99*

The Hot, The Cool And The Vicious (1976)
High-flying leg-fighting is the highlight of this kick classic in which three martial artists set out to prove if the feet are mightier than the sword in daring competitions. Wong Too and Tommy Lee star. 93 min. Dubbed in English.
50-5020 *$14.99*

Spirits Of Bruce Li (1979)
This homage to the late, legendary Bruce Lee features Michael Chan Wai-Meng as a devoted fan of the martial arts hero who gets involved in a gang war and calls on his own skills to defeat them. 90 min. Dubbed in English.
50-5030 *$14.99*

72 Desperate Rebels (1972)
Kung fu action on a grand scale is presented in this epic set during the Ming Dynasty and detailing the adventures of pirate Pu Ho-Nien, who gathers 72 specialized fighters from various regions across China to battle the imperial government. With Pai Ying and Lung Ti. 93 min. Dubbed in English.
50-5032 *$14.99*

Amsterdam Connection (1979)
There's no people kicking off wooden shoes and leaping from windmills here, but you will find action that spans two continents, as detectives try to bust a film company that's a front for a drug and white slavery ring. With Chen Shing, Jason Pai Piu, Yeung Sze and Kid Sheriff (that's right, operator, "Kid Sheriff"). 90 min.
50-5035 Was $29.99 *$19.99*

Crack Shadow Boxer (1979)
A pair of offbeat adventurers join forces to save a village from invading bandits in this kung fu action saga that mixes drama with humor. Feng Ku, Chou Li Lung star. 91 min.
50-5036 Was $29.99 *$19.99*

The Bloody Fist (1972)
In other parts of the country, fighting takes over as daily activity. How do you get to see the finest Kung Fu action ever offered in just 90 minutes? Watch this one and you'll find out. With Chan Sing, Chan Kuan Tai, Liu Ta Chuan. AKA: "The Bloody Fists," "Death Beach." 90 min.
50-5038 *$19.99*

Militant Eagle (1974)
Nobles, villains and warriors fill the screen in authentically re-created battle sequences, going at it with incredible verve, seamless skill and downright nastiness. Choi Yue, Lu Ping, Pai Ying star. 90 min.
50-5041 Was $29.99 *$19.99*

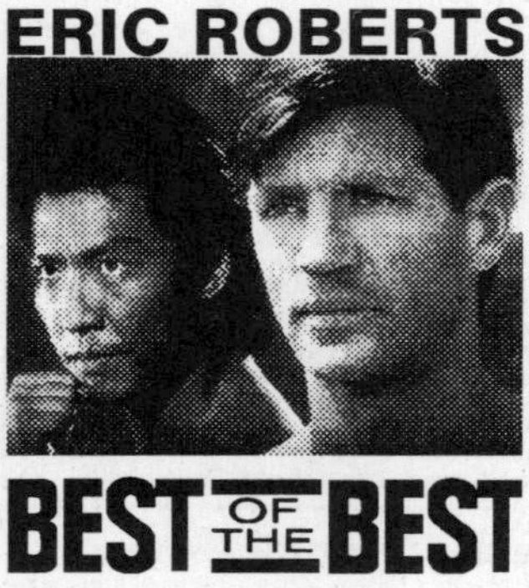

Best Of The Best (1989)
Rousing "Rocky"-styled drama of a martial arts tournament and the competitors who join forces to overcome their foes. Eric Roberts, James Earl Jones and Sally Kirkland head the impressive cast in this action-filled drama. 95 min.
45-5483 *$14.99*

Best Of The Best II (1993)
After their partner in a Las Vegas karate school is murdered in an underground match at a nightclub, a martial arts master, his young son and his other partner join together to seek vengeance against the culprit, a seedy nightclub owner. Eric Roberts, Phillip Rhee, Christopher Penn and Wayne Newton star in this smashing sequel. 100 min.
04-2673 Was $19.99 ❑*$14.99*

Best Of The Best 3: No Turning Back (1995)
Phillip Rhee returns as the martial arts champ, this time fighting racists terrorizing a small Southern town. When a Baptist minister disappears and his friend's Asian wife is terrorized, Rhee goes into action. With Gina Gershon, Christopher McDonald and Dee Wallace Stone. 90 min.
11-1958 Was $89.99 ❑*$19.99*

Best Of The Best: Without Warning (1998)
Phillip Rhee is back—and at his high-kicking best of the best—in this action-heavy outing. The martial arts expert finds himself taking on the Russian Mafia, who are out to nab high-tech software used to counterfeit money. With Ernie Hudson, Tobin Bell and Christopher Lemmon. 90 min.
11-2797 Was $99.99 ❑*$14.99*

The Bloody Fight (1972)
Bloody? You bet, especially when two young people attempt to avenge a murder and learn that justice may well be measured by the pint. Alan Tang, Yu In Yin, Tan Chin lead the hit (and kick) parade in this all-out actionfest. 89 min.
50-5042 Was $29.99 *$19.99*

Deadly Snail vs. Kung Fu Killer (1979)
Outrageous mix of fantasy and martial arts action tells of a daring duel between fairies in which Cheung saves the Sky Mussel Fairy, but soon finds himself in dire straits when his uncle drives him from his house. Cheung is forced to use his kung fu powers to battle gods, demons and bizarre creatures. 88 min. Dubbed in English.
50-5050 *$14.99*

Tough Guy (1970)
A pair of cops go undercover to break up a local crime ring, but if the going was tough before, it's downright deadly now in this explosive martial arts flick. Chen Xing, Charlie Chiang, Henry Yue Young star. AKA: "Kung Fu: The Head Crusher." 88 min.
50-5085 Was $29.99 *$19.99*

Shaolin Brothers (1979)
The livelihood of the Shaolin Temple is threatened by a drought, prompting two brothers from the monastery to travel from town to town in search of donations. When one of the siblings is killed by a rebel, the other goes ballistic seeking revenge. Features real abbots from the Shaolin Temple. 83 min. Dubbed in English.
50-5094 *$14.99*

Story In Temple Red Lily (1979)
At the end of the Sung Dynasty, the aging Emperor and his two children are under siege by rebel forces, and one imperial officer must battle to the death to defend them in this exciting karatefest. They could have fought anywhere—they chose Temple Red Lily! Stars Chia Lin, Tan Tao-liang. 88 min.
50-5108 Was $29.99 *$19.99*

The Invincible Killer (1979)
Triad member Michael Chan Wai-man decides to leave his gang and go straight. But this decision doesn't sit well with his gang leader, who sees Chan's actions as a betrayal and decides to frame him for a series of violent murders. Now the ex-gangster must clear his name and stop the violence. Chen Hui Min also stars. 91 min. Dubbed in English.
53-6829 *$14.99*

Six Directions Of Boxing (1977)
They're not east, west, north or south, but biff!, bam!, sock! and ker-pow! David Chiang ("Seven Blows of the Dragon") and Yuen Hsiao-Tien ("Drunken Master") star in this tale that's set during feudal times and tells the story of revolutionaries against secret police. 91 min. Dubbed in English.
53-6924 *$14.99*

The Invincible Kung Fu Trio (1974)
Everybody's kung fu fighting here, especially when a trio of tough grads from the Shaolin Temple named Hung Hey-Kwoon, Luk Ah-Choi and Fong Sai Yuk are put to the task, defending their honor and abilities. Chen Kwun-tai, star of "Crippled Avengers," is featured. 84 min. Dubbed in English.
53-6934 *$14.99*

99 Cycling Swords (1976)
"Five Fingers of Death" great Lo Lieh stars in this awesome actioner, playing the magistrate of a small town who is forced to hunt down rebels against the Manchu Dynasty. He hires four martial arts mavens to put the kibosh on the rebellion, but what will the ultimate result be? With Yueh Hua. 93 min. Dubbed in English.
53-6983 *$14.99*

Magnificent Fist (1978)
Carter Wong proves that one wong makes it right in this all-out action assault in which he leads a group of martial artist specialists against Japanese hoodlums who have taken over a small town in Northeastern China. A fistfighters delight! 87 min. Dubbed in English.
53-6984 *$14.99*

The Deadly Sword (1978)
The hand is not mightier than the sword in this kung fu thriller in which a police inspector uncovers the mysterious Green Dragon Society, a conspiracy and the secret behind the legendary Deadly Sword while looking into a burglary case. Based on a story by martial artist Ku Lung. 92 min. Dubbed in English.
53-6985 *$14.99*

The Last Duel (1977)
After being defeated by arch-rival Sze Mun in a duel, martial arts wizard Luk Siu-Feng tries to recuperate at a mysterious resort where he hears of a devious plan to slaughter all kung fu masters. This forces Luk to enlist Sze Mun to help stop the plan. 91 min. Dubbed in English.
53-6986 *$14.99*

Descendant Of Wing Chun (1978)
When an evil bandit escapes prison and gets revenge on his retired teacher's students, look out. The teacher, a scholar of the Wing Chun style of kung fu, goes head to head against the criminal in an awesome display of power and discipline. 92 min.
53-9779 *$14.99*

The Blazing Ninja (1973)
Martial arts masters set the scene aflame in this white-hot tale of deadly duels, spellbinding suspense and all-out action, set against the mysterious world of the ninja. Teng Hui Lee. 86 min.
08-8114 *$19.99*

Midnight Angels (1987)
The first film in a series of furious female Hong Kong actioners finds two sexy hit women being recruited by police to stop the Golden Dragon drug syndicate, run by the notorious Madame Sue. Moon Lee, Elaine Lui, Hideki Saijo and Yukari Oshima star. AKA: "Angel," "Iron Angels." Dubbed in English.
54-9125 *$59.99*

Midnight Angels II (1988)
Policewomen Moon Lee and Elaine Lui return in this slam-bang sequel that finds the Angels and their male partner on vacation in Malaysia. A holiday romance for Lui turns sour, however, when her boyfriend turns out to be part of a jungle militia plotting a revolution. With Alex Fong. AKA: "Angel 2," "Iron Angels II." Dubbed in English.
54-9170 *$59.99*

Devil Hunters (1989)
A huge drug deal goes awry when mysterious fighters interrupt the proceedings. The parties involved suspect each other, but the culprits are actually an elite martial arts brigade out to stop crime using their incredible fighting skills. Moon Lee and Sibelle Hu star. 90 min. Dubbed in English.
53-6140 *$14.99*

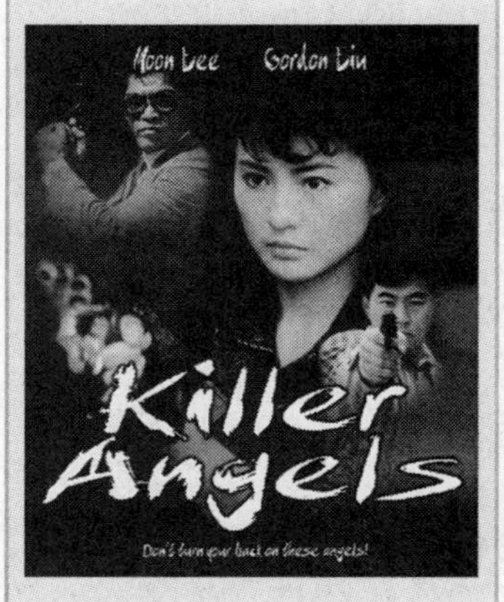

Killer Angels (1989)
Doll-faced and lethal Moon Lee kicks major league rears in this rousing Hong Kong actioner. See her and her sexy, kickfighting cohorts go up against the Ghost Shadow Gang, whose leader has revealed the identities of the secret "Angels." Features an astonishing final battle. With Gordon Liu. 92 min. Dubbed in English.
53-6141 *$14.99*

Beauty Investigator (1992)
Martial arts mistress Moon Lee teams with Yukari Oshima in this scorching actioner in which two policewomen go undercover as nightclub hostesses in order to find a serial rapist. They're soon investigating the club owner, a creep involved in arms smuggling who has hired a Japanese assassin to take them out. 90 min. Dubbed in English.
53-6139 *$14.99*

Kickboxer's Tears (1992)
If you're looking for high-kicking action with frisky femmes, look no further than this teaming of martial arts mistresses Yukari Oshima and Moon Lee. Here, Lee seeks revenge for her brother's death in a kickboxing match, killing his opponent and then taking on the dead man's boss, who sends his Japanese mistress, played by Oshima, after her. 90 min. Dubbed in English.
53-6273 *$14.99*

Angel Terminators II (1993)
When two rebellious teens insult the younger brother of a powerful Triad boss, they find that their lives are in serious trouble. Sibelle Hu and Moon Lee star in this tale of girls, guns and Hong Kong action. 93 min. In Cantonese with English subtitles.
53-6234 *$49.99*

Death Triangle (1993)
Moon Lee, Yukari Oshima and Cynthia Khan team for this energized actioner in which Lee and Khan vie for the attention of their superior officer. But Lee kills the officer him in a jealous rage, then frames Khan for the murder. In order to clear her name, Khan teams with tough gang leader Oshima. 90 min. Dubbed in English.
53-6861 *$14.99*

Little Heroes: Lost In China (1997)
Lovely action star Moon Lee is featured in this family-oriented actioner in which jewel thieves swipe rare gems that belong to a religious shrine in China. A detective and six kids who know their kung fu investigate the theft. 87 min. Dubbed in English.
53-6917 *$14.99*

A Gathering Of Heroes (1973)
"I, I wish I could fight...like the ninjas can fight. And nothing can stand in our way. We can be Kung Fu heroes, just for one day." Titanic teaming of martial arts masters features Lady Shang Fung, Alad N. Sain, Chan Xing, Thynwyt Duke. 92 min.
55-1076   *$19.99*

Ninja Blacklist (1972)
No, it's not Dalton Trumbo and the Tokyo Ten; it's chop sockey action the way America likes it, as renegade heroes team up to defeat karate killers. Are you now, or have you ever been a Kung Fu fan? Jo Micar Thee stars. AKA: "Kung Fu Blacklist," "Ninja Exterminator."
55-1079   *$19.99*

Single Fighter (1978)
A lone martial arts student searches for a list that names Chinese traitors during the Japanese invasion of 1931, but his fight for justice becomes a fight for life in this high-kicking thriller. Hing Lu, Ling Hu, Hling Luh star. 79 min.
58-1111   *$19.99*

Shaolin Kung Fu Mystagogue (1976)
In ancient China, two fighting factions of martial arts practitioners face off for the ultimate battle in a bone-splintering, brick-smashing, record-breaking explosion of hand-to-hand combat. With Hsu Feng, Carter Wong, Chang Yi.
64-1007   *$19.99*

Bruce The Superhero (1979)
It's a bird! It's a plane! It's Bruce Le dealing out iron fisted death against a blood-stained crime syndicate as they vie for possession of a fortune in gold. The hits just keep coming. 90 min.
64-1041   *$19.99*

Enter The Game Of Death (1978)
You'll never forget this classic with Bruce Le, as his search for stolen documents leads into a death duel with Kung Fu killers. Co-stars Cheung Lak, Lam Kum Fun, Yang See and Le Hai San. 88 min.
64-1069   *$19.99*

Return Of Bruce (1977)
The one and only Bruce Le, scion to the title of Martial Arts Movie Master, is back, taking on and defeating a gang of white slavers one by one (he wanted to fight them all at once, but that just isn't done). With Fei Meng. 90 min.
64-1084   *$19.99*

Bruce And Shao Lin Kung Fu (1977)
After humiliating the son of a feared warlord in pitched combat, Bruce Le finds himself marked for death by the vengeful father. See Bruce cut a bloody swath through an army of martial arts assassins. With Chang Lee, James Nam. AKA: "Bruce vs. Black Dragon." 85 min.
64-1087   *$19.99*

Fury Of King Boxer (1978)
When the tyrannical Manchus cast their evil shadow across the land, can one lone martial artist assemble a people's army and train them for battle? Exciting Kung Fu action epic stars Hu Yu Kidn, Masanori Murakami, Yu Wang. 85 min.
64-1119   *$19.99*

The Godfather Squad (1974)
Thrilling martial arts epic involving a group of drug smugglers who hire a high-kicking family of thugs to protect them. A kung fu star uses his abilities to try to stop the devious clan. Bruce Liang and Shirley Corrigan star.
68-8877   *$19.99*

Ninja, Grand Masters Of Death (1975)
After a prostitute is murdered, an Asian businessman is the prime suspect, but it's soon discovered that a renegade Ninja sect is actually responsible for the deed, poisoning the girl with a special solution. Can the sect be found before they strike again? Bruce Leih stars. 87 min.
68-8904   Letterboxed   *$19.99*

Supermanchu (1977)
Thugs wreak havoc at a small inn, killing the owners and raping their daughter. They don't count on the owners' martial arts expert son to seek revenge. This all-out action assault stars Chang Yi and Tien Mi.
68-8905   *$19.99*

Tiger Force (1975)
Chen Xing, Lotus Key and Chang Lee star in this action-packed, Japanese kung fu thriller. An undercover agent, who is also expertly trained in the martial arts, is called upon to help foil a kidnapping and put an end to an illegal drug ring.
68-9271   *$19.99*

Death Duel Of Mantis (1978)
Everyone knows that the "mantis stance" is one of the most subtle and deadly of the martial arts disciplines, and...what's that? You didn't know? Well, then, go no further until you see this thriller. With Fei Lung.
48-1151   *$29.99*

Ninja Destroyer (1970)
Death is his bread and mayhem his butter, and full, unfettered martial arts destruction is his all-natural strawberry jam. The Ninja Destroyer takes on all comers in this violent tale. Quing Lao, Bernard N. Michael, Reep Daggle.
50-1843   *$12.99*

ENTER JIM "DRAGON" KELLY

HE CLOBBERS THE MOB AS

BLACK BELT JONES

Black Belt Jones (1974)
Jim Kelly, the first black karate champ featured in "Enter the Dragon," is called on to defend his martial arts school against some violent thugs. Rousing, hands-a-flying action ensues with foot firmly planted in cheek. AAH-CHAA! Gloria Hendry co-stars. 85 min.
19-1343   Was $19.99   *$14.99*

Hot Potato (1976)
When a U.S. senator's daughter is kidnapped by an Oriental crime baron, only a crack squad of kung fu commandos led by Jim Kelly can rescue her...or they can die trying! Exciting actioner filled with martial arts mayhem co-stars George Memmoli, Irene Tsu. 87 min.
19-1599   Was $19.99   *$14.99*

The Tattoo Connection (1978)
The big, bad, bone-breaking Jim Kelly is back! He's on the trail of sinister smugglers who have made off with one of the largest diamonds in the world, and you can be sure he'll use all the power in his diamond-tough hands and feet to get it back! Pulverizing martial-arts action! With Chen Sin, Bolo Yung. 95 min.
53-1545   *$19.99*

Bruce Lee's Deadly Kung Fu (1976)
Bruce Li and his friend must learn to deal with discrimination against the Chinese in America, as a fight with some local martial arts students in San Francisco's Chinatown forces them to go on the run. Wang Chiata, Change Kuei and Ching Chi Min also star. AKA: "Bruce Lee's Secret," "Bruce Li's Jeet Kune Do," "A Dragon Story." 91 min.
68-9272   *$19.99*

The Runaway (1978)
A nasty battle ensues between loyalists of the Qing Dynasty in China and the empire's new ruler and his kung fu fighters. The brawl's over a treasure, and, after many loyalists are killed, the son of a murdered architect joins forces with an old monk to grapple against his foes for his people. With Mei Fong. 90 min. Dubbed in English.
82-7033   *$39.99*

The Five Deadly Venoms (1978)
Smashing Shaw Brothers epic in which an aging martial arts master dispatches one of his pupils to find out which former students have turned to a life of crime. All are masked and all are experts in different disciplines. Could the weasel be the Centipede, the Snake, the Scorpion, the Toad or the Lizard? Lo Meng, Philip Kwok star. "AKA: "Five Venoms." 96 min. Dubbed in English.
41-7025   Letterboxed   *$19.99*

The Return Of The 5 Deadly Venoms (1978)
Those poisonous practitioners of martial arts mayhem, the Venom Mob, strike out from the screen once more. Watch them launch a lethal campaign of vengeance in this smashing follow-up to "The Five Deadly Venoms." Kuo Chui, Lu Feng star. AKA: "Crippled Avengers," "Mortal Combat." Dubbed in English.
20-8244   Letterboxed   *$19.99*

Strike Of Thunderkick Tiger (1978)
The old adage "there is no honor among thieves" is proven in this kung fu thriller, as two gang members kill their leader for the map showing where their loot has been hidden. But when the map becomes missing, the pair's mutual mistrust turns into a violent showdown. With Casanova Wong, Charles Han. 84 min.
41-7007   Was $29.99   *$19.99*

Five Fingers Of Death (1973)
Legendary for launching the kung-fu mania of the 1970s, this Shaw Brothers production focuses on a martial arts student who learns the secret of the "Iron Fist" in order to defeat the criminal gang that has taken over a karate school. Filled with spectacular (and often outrageously gory) martial arts mayhem, the film stars Lo Lieh and Wang Ping. AKA: "King Boxer." 106 min.
77-1030   *$19.99*

Enter The Dragon

Bruce Lee

Fists Of Fury (1973)
In his first martial arts epic, Bruce Lee plays a naive country boy who chops and kicks his way through corruption and drug smuggling at an ice factory. With Maria Yi, James Tren. AKA: "The Big Boss." 105 min.
04-1115   *$14.99*

The Chinese Connection (1973)
Set in Japanese-occupied Shanghai in 1908, this Bruce Lee actioner follows him on a violent path of revenge against the foreign villains who killed his martial arts instructor. With Nora Miao, Bob Baker. 107 min.
04-1114   *$14.99*

Enter The Dragon: 25th Anniversary Edition (1973)
One of the biggest martial arts epics ever filmed finds karate master Bruce Lee hired by British agents to infiltrate the island fortress of a criminal mastermind during a deadly combat tournament. Lee's final completed film (although released before "Return of the Dragon") also stars John Saxon, Jim Kelly, Shih Kien and Bolo Yeung; look quickly for a young Jackie Chan. This restored anniversary version includes three minutes of footage not shown in America, an introduction by Lee's wife Linda, the original theatrical trailer and a 7 1/2-minute behind-the-scenes documentary. 103 min.
19-2679   ◻*$19.99*

Enter The Dragon (Letterboxed Version)
Also available in a theatrical, widescreen format.
19-2678   ◻*$19.99*

Enter The Dragon: Limited Edition Collector's Boxed Set
This special-edition collector's set features the letterboxed version of the movie, the CD soundtrack, a commemorative book, an eight-card set of lobby card reprints and a unique Senitype 8 1/2" x 10" blowup of a film frame.
19-2677   Letterboxed   *$49.99*

Return Of The Dragon (1974)
Bruce Lee travels to Rome to help a friend whose restaurant is being terrorized by gangsters. Top-notch fights, climaxed by a battle in the ruins of the Colosseum with future good-guy Chuck Norris; directed by Lee. AKA: "Way of the Dragon." 91 min.
04-1521   *$14.99*

The Green Hornet (1974)
Three episodes from the classic 1966 TV series that co-starred Bruce Lee as Kato, aide to mysterious masked crimefighter Van Williams, were combined to make this feature-length adventure. Watch Lee in all his fighting fury as he and the Hornet battle gangsters, karate killers, and even an "alien invasion." Remastered edition; 90 min.
08-8300   *$12.99*

Game Of Death (1979)
Completed and released six years after the death of Bruce Lee, this martial arts classic casts Lee as a Kung Fu star up against an evil syndicate. Bone-crunching battles, including the classic confrontation with Kareem Abdul-Jabbar. Chuck Norris, Gig Young. 100 min.
04-1460   *$14.99*

Fist Of Fear, Touch Of Death (1980)
Madison Square Garden is the setting for an international martial arts competition whose winner will be "the successor to Bruce Lee's title." Along with exciting contest footage featuring Bill Louie, Richard Barathy and others, this mix of documentary and action footage also features footage with Fred Williamson and Ron Van Clief and rare film clips of Lee himself. Adolph Caesar hosts. 90 min.
27-6515   Was $19.99   *$14.99*

Bruce Lee: The Curse Of The Dragon (1993)
The true story of legendary martial arts star Bruce Lee, told with interviews from people who knew him, rare footage and exciting film clips. James Coburn, Kareem Abdul-Jabbar and Chuck Norris are among Lee's pupils and friends featured on this program that also delves into "The Dragon's" mysterious death and the fatal accident that killed his son, Brandon. 90 min.
19-2114   Was $19.99   *$14.99*

Bruce Lee: The Legend
In a few short years, Bruce Lee became a worldwide film star and the most famous Kung Fu master of all time. This special documentary traces his life from his birth in Hong Kong to his tragic death, with clips from his screen action classics. 88 min.
04-1921   ◻*$14.99*

The Real Bruce Lee (1973)
A rare find sure to delight fans of the legendary martial arts star, this program features clips from four films the young Lee made in China ("The Little Dragon," "The Bad Guy," "Carnival," "Orphan Sam"), along with footage from his 1973 funeral and the full-length film "The Ultimate Lee," started by Lee but finished with a replacement. 120 min.
08-8454   *$14.99*

Bruce Lee And Kung-Fu Mania
The mastery of late martial arts expert Bruce Lee is chronicled in this look at his and others' Kung Fu classics. Witness the making of "Fists of Fury," learn of his tragic death, and see him battle Chuck Norris; also includes segments from "The Three Avengers," "Kung Fu Master" and more. 85 min.
10-2414   *$12.99*

Bruce Lee: The Immortal Dragon
Before his death in 1973 at the age of 32, Bruce Lee revolutionized the world of martial arts and overcame Hollywood prejudice to become an action film star around the globe. Learn about his life, from his boyhood in Hong Kong to his greatest screen successes, and hear about the man behind the myth from friends and family, including son Brandon, in this special episode from A&E's "Biography" series. 50 min.
53-9819   *$14.99*

Bruce Lee: The Lost Interview
A rare interview with Bruce Lee conducted in 1971, shortly after the release of "The Big Boss" ("Fists of Fury"). Lee discusses many subjects, including his philosophy of life, his personal approach to the martial arts, playing Kato on "The Green Hornet," his future plans, his celebrity students and more. 30 min.
76-7138   *$19.99*

Bruce Lee: The Master Collection Gift Set
Celebrate the life of the martial arts cinema's greatest star with this action-packed boxed set that includes "Fists of Fury," "The Chinese Connection," "Return of the Dragon" and "Game of Death," plus the exclusive documentary "Bruce Lee: The Legend."
04-3851   *$39.99*

Please see our index for the Bruce Lee title: *Marlowe*

Jackie Chan

Master With Cracked Fingers (1971)
A teenage Jackie Chan, in his first starring role, plays a young man who witnesses the murder of his father and, after honing his martial arts abilities with help from a hermit, tries to hunt down the killer. The film was unreleased for several years, until extra scenes with a double were added, and this special edition includes two alternate endings to the "Chan-tastic" saga. AKA: "Cub Fighter from Canton," "Little Tiger of Canton," "Snake Fist Fighter." 90 min. Dubbed in English.
54-9149 *$19.99*

Rumble In Hong Kong (1972)
Before "The Bronx," there was "Hong Kong," with Jackie Chan displaying his prowess in a (villainous!) supporting role. He's the bodyguard of a Hong Kong gangster who goes against a tough female cop in order to protect his boss. John Chang, Phoenix Chen also star. AKA: "Police Woman." 90 min. Dubbed in English.
54-9155 *$19.99*

Fist Of Anger (1973)
An early supporting turn by Jackie Chan highlights this action-packed martial arts thriller about members of a Chinese theater troupe during the Japanese occupation who use their skills to fight against their oppressors. AKA: "Eagle Shadow Fist," "Not Scared to Die." 80 min. Dubbed in English.
54-9154 *$19.99*

Hand Of Death (1975)
The only time Jackie Chan worked with legendary Hong Kong director John Woo was this actioner about a young Shaolin fighter (Dorian "Flash Legs" Tan) sent to bring down a turncoat student (James Tien) who is now a corrupt warrior. Tan and Chan join forces to battle Tien's minions, among them Sammo Hung as a crooked sheriff. Look for Woo's cameo as a scholar. AKA: "Strike of Death." 95 min.
53-9782 *$49.99*

New Fist Of Fury (1976)
In reality a sequel to Bruce Lee's "The Chinese Connection," this was the first film released to star Jackie Chan. As a pickpocket in occupied China during World War II, Chan seeks revenge when his girlfriend's martial arts school is destroyed by the Japanese. With "Chinese Connection" co-stars Nora Miao, Lo Wei. 119 min. Dubbed in English.
71-1024 *$19.99*

The Killer Meteors (1977)
In a rare bad guy role, Jackie Chan plays a mystical warlord known as "Immortal Meteor" who meets his match in martial arts warrior "Killer Weapon," played by Jimmy Wang Yu. 100 min. Dubbed in English.
64-3384 *$12.99*

To Kill With Intrigue (1977)
After his family is slaughtered, Jackie Chan seeks revenge and gets it from an unlikely source—a warrior queen who was responsible for the deaths, but falls in love with Chan and helps him train to become an unstoppable martial artist. With Chu Feng. AKA: "Jackie Chan Connection." 107 min.
71-1021 *$19.99*

Snake In The Eagle's Shadow (1978)
The film that revolutionized martial arts cinema was also Jackie Chan's first effort to mix comedy with a serious plotline and Chinese Opera-style fight sequences. Chan plays a rebellious young student who learns the snake style of kung fu in order to stop the Eagle Claw Gang. With Yuen Siu Tien. 94 min. Dubbed in English.
54-9141 Letterboxed *$19.99*

Spiritual Kung Fu (1978)
Jackie Chan is taught long-forgotten martial arts techniques by five ghostly guardians released from a crashed meteorite (!), and when he cuts loose against his foes, it's clear they don't have a "ghost" of a chance. With James Tien. AKA: "Karate Bomber." Dubbed in English.
71-1016 *$19.99*

Dragon Fist (1978)
No one's ever accused Jackie Chan of having "draggin' fists," and he proves why in this tale of a fighter out to avenge his master's murder. When Chan finds the repentant killer—who cut off a leg out of remorse—the two team up to defeat an evil warlord. James Tien, Nora Miao also star. 94 min. Dubbed in English.
71-1017 *$19.99*

In Eagle Shadow Fist (1978)
A trio of heroes-for-hire (Jackie Chan, Bruce Leung, James Tien) agrees to escort a young woman and her seriously ill brother through a countryside filled with such dangers as malevolent monks and an evil king in this kung-fu costume actioner. AKA: "Eye of the Dragon," "Magnificent Bodyguards." 90 min.
71-1020 *$19.99*

Half A Loaf Of Kung Fu (1978)
The humor that is a hallmark of Jackie Chan's cinematic work first appeared in this light-hearted costume actioner, in which Chan is a member of an elite bodyguard corps charged with safely delivering priceless jade. After they are waylaid by a group of ruthless robbers, Chan springs into action to battle the thieves. 96 min.
71-1022 *$19.99*

Jackie Chan's 36 Crazy Fists (1979)
Chan served as stunt coordinator—and also appears in special behind-the-scenes footage—in this incredible martial arts drama about a young orphan who is taught the ways of Kung Fu by an ancient monk and uses them against his father's killer. Liu Cha Yung, Ku Feng star. AKA: "Bloodpact," "The Master and the Boxer." 90 min. Dubbed in English.
14-1018 *$14.99*

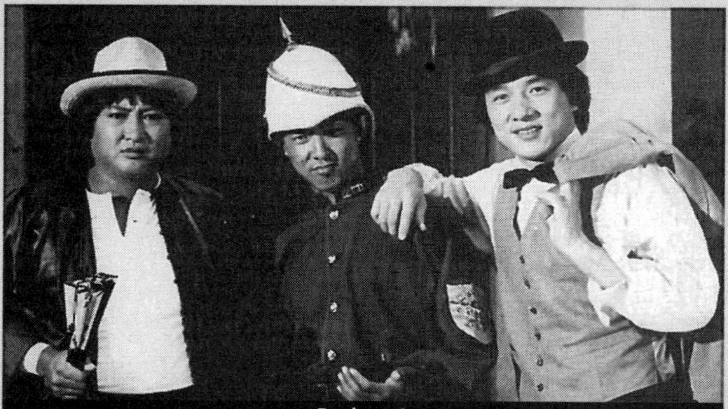

Project A

The Fearless Hyena (1979)
When young Jackie Chan sees his grandfather murdered by karate criminals, he vows vengeance. Years later, Chan uses a unique martial arts style called "Emotional Kung Fu," where he uses his body movements for laughing and crying to defeat his adversary. This explosive costume actioner marked Chan's debut as director/star. 97 min. Dubbed in English.
71-1015 *$19.99*

The Fearless Hyena, Part II (1980)
Jackie Chan returns—sort of—in this sequel that features Chan in unseen footage and outtakes from the first "Fearless Hyena," along with new scenes with a disguised double, to tell the story of Jackie and his brother battling to find their father's killer. 96 min. Dubbed in English.
71-1023 *$19.99*

The Young Master (1980)
When his foster brother gets mixed up with a shady martial arts school's activities and becomes wanted by the law, Jackie Chan tries to help him out and winds up having to clear his own name as well. With Wei Pei, Yuen Biao. 102 min. In Cantonese with English subtitles.
53-9430 Letterboxed *$19.99*

The Young Master (Dubbed Version)
Also available in a dubbed-in-English edition. 90 min.
53-8889 Letterboxed *$19.99*

Dragon Lord (1981)
Jackie Chan mixes comedy with remarkable martial arts expertise in this actioner that finds him an unwitting participant in a scheme to smuggle priceless treasures out of the Forbidden City. Directed by Chan; with Chan Wai-San, Mars. AKA: "Young Master in Love." 93 min. In Cantonese with English subtitles.
14-6147 *$49.99*

Project A (1983)
Amazing amalgamation of action, stunts and comedy, with Jackie Chan (who also directed) as a naval officer in early 1900s Hong Kong who teams with cop Yuen Biao and shady sailor Sammo Hung to tackle ruthless pirates on the South China Sea. Highlights include a wild bicycle chase and Jackie hanging from a clock à la Harold Lloyd. 105 min. Dubbed in English.
11-2429 Was $99.99 *❑$14.99*

Project A, Part II (1987)
Jackie Chan returns as the honest cop battling ornery crooks in turn-of-the-century Hong Kong in this incredible actioner filled with wild stunts and slapstick humor. Look for Chan's tribute to Buster Keaton and an incredible cat-and-mouse chase in an apartment. With Maggie Cheung. 101 min. In Cantonese with English subtitles.
53-9419 Letterboxed *$19.99*

Project A, Part II (Dubbed Version)
Also available in a dubbed-in-English edition.
53-6492 Letterboxed *$19.99*

Winners And Sinners (1983)
Knockout crime story with Jackie Chan as an ex-con who forms a cleaning business with four other former crooks looking to go straight. While working in a building, they run into a group of counterfeiters, and when fake printing plates are discovered in their van, the authorities and gangsters begin their chase. With Sammo Hung, Yuen Biao. AKA: "Five Lucky Stars." 102 min. In Cantonese with English subtitles.
53-8461 *$19.99*

Winners And Sinners (Dubbed Version)
Also available in a dubbed-in-English edition.
53-6163 Letterboxed *$19.99*

Wheels On Meals (1983)
A Jackie Chan spectacular with Jackie and Yuen Biao as fast-food cooks working out of a van in Barcelona, Spain. Their involvement with a pickpocketing prostitute who turns out to be a missing heiress sends them and private eye Sammo Hung (who also directed) into some truly outrageous martial arts brawls. With Lola Forner, Benny "The Jet" Urquidez, Herb Edelman. 107 min. In Cantonese with English subtitles.
53-9428 Letterboxed *$19.99*

Wheels On Meals (Dubbed Version)
Also available in a dubbed-in-English edition.
53-9964 Letterboxed *$19.99*

Fantasy Mission Force (1984)
A truly off-the-wall WWII actioner (with an abundance of loopy anachronisms), with Jackie Chan as part of an elite commando team sent to rescue a group of Allied generals kidnapped by the Japanese. Along the way the force must battle leopard-skinned Amazons, a haunted house full of ghosts, and other bizarre foes. With Brigitte Lin, Jimmy Wang Yu. 90 min. Dubbed in English.
71-1019 *$19.99*

Police Story (1985)
First installment in the hit thriller series starring Jackie Chan as a dedicated Hong Kong cop finds him trying to convince crime kingpin's secretary Brigitte Lin to testify against her boss. Chan is framed for murder and sought by his fellow officers as the action escalates, climaxing with an unbelievable shopping mall showdown. With Maggie Cheung, Bill Tung; directed by Chan. AKA: "Jackie Chan's Police Force." Dubbed in English.
02-5178 Was $29.99 *❑$14.99*

Police Story 2 (1988)
Demoted to patrolman status after his antics in the first film, police officer Jackie Chan finds himself and long-suffering girlfriend Maggie Cheung the targets of crime boss Bill Tung's revenge. Meanwhile, Chan must also defuse a gang of bomb-happy extortionists' plans to blow up downtown Hong Kong in this (literally) explosive sequel. 99 min. Dubbed in English.
02-5208 *$19.99*

Supercop (1996)
Incorruptible (and apparently indestructible) Hong Kong detective Jackie Chan is back in this stateside release of his 1992 film "Police Story 3: Supercop," joining forces with no-nonsense Mainland Chinese Michelle Khan to infiltrate and shut down an international drug ring. Along with Khan's chasing a train on a motorcycle, the highlight is Chan hanging from a helicopter ladder over the streets of Kuala Lumpur. 91 min. Dubbed in English.
11-2082 Was $19.99 *❑$14.99*

Jackie Chan's First Strike (1997)
Jackie does James Bond in this globehopping action tale, first released as "Police Story IV: First Strike." The search for a stolen Russian nuclear warhead sends top Hong Kong cop Chan from a snowy hideout in the Ukraine to an Australian aquarium, and gives Jackie the chance for breathtaking stunts, fighting on skis, inside a ladder, and underwater. With Jackson Lou, Chen Chen Wu. 85 min. Dubbed in English.
02-5129 Was $19.99 *❑$14.99*

Jackie Chan's First Strike (Letterboxed Version)
Also available in a theatrical, widescreen format.
02-5156 Was $19.99 *$14.99*

Operation Condor 2: The Armour Of The Gods (1985)
Retitled as a "prequel" for American release, this is the original "Raiders"-style action saga starring Jackie Chan as an adventurer who battles a mystic cult looking to swap his kidnapped ex-girlfriend for a priceless artifact he possesses. Among the film's amazing stunt scenes are Jackie's battle with a squad of stiletto-heeled Amazon warriors and a leap from a tree that nearly cost Chan his life! With Alan Tam, Rosamund Kwan. 86 min. Dubbed in English.
11-2802 Was $99.99 *❑$14.99*

Operation Condor (1997)
First released in 1991 as "Armour of God II: Operation Condor," this stunt-laden thriller finds Jackie Chan's globe-hopping treasure-hunter called on to locate a fortune in stolen Nazi gold hidden somewhere in the Sahara. Joined by three feisty female accomplices, Chan mixes it up with Arab assassins and a mercenary army and has a mind-blowing fight in a gigantic wind tunnel. Carol Cheng, Eva Cobo Garcia, Shoko Ikeda also star. 90 min. Dubbed in English.
11-2201 Was $19.99 *❑$14.99*

My Lucky Stars (1985)
Comic cops-and-robbers hijinks with lots of action, as Hong Kong cops Jackie Chan and Yuen Biao travel to Japan to track down a crooked ex-colleague who fled there with a fortune in stolen diamonds. When Biao is captured, Chan turns to an old orphanage pal (Sammo Hung, who also directed) and his "Lucky Stars," a band of hapless petty crooks, for help. 96 min. In Cantonese with English subtitles.
53-6603 Letterboxed *$19.99*

My Lucky Stars (Dubbed Version)
Also available in a dubbed-in-English edition.
53-9408 Letterboxed *$19.99*

Twinkle, Twinkle Lucky Stars (1985)
In this sequel to "My Lucky Stars," Hong Kong cops Jackie Chan and Yuen Biao, along with Chan's childhood pal Sammo Hung and his gang of thieves, "the Lucky Stars," have their vacation in Thailand interrupted when they must return home to protect a local drug lord from Thai assassins. With Rosamund Kwan, Richard Norton. AKA: "The Target." In Cantonese with English subtitles.
53-9769 *$49.99*

The Heart Of The Dragon (1985)
In this mix of astonishing martial arts action, drama and comedy, Jackie Chan plays a cop who wishes to leave his home in Hong Kong, but decides to stay to care for mentally disabled brother Sammo Hung. When Hung gets involved with crooks, Chan goes to work to save him. Emily Chu co-stars. AKA: "First Mission." 89 min. In Cantonese with English subtitles.
53-9435 Letterboxed *$19.99*

Dragons Forever (1988)
Shady lawyer Jackie Chan is hired by a crooked businessman whose chemical factory is accused of polluting a neighboring fish hatchery. When Chan falls for the hatchery owner's cousin and discovers the factory is a front for drug smuggling, he teams with pals Yuen Biao and Sammo Hung (who also directed) to shut the operation down. With Dick Wei, Benny "The Jet" Urquidez. 88 min. In Cantonese with English subtitles.
53-9394 Letterboxed *$19.99*

Dragons Forever (Dubbed Version)
Also available in a dubbed-in-English edition.
53-9397 Letterboxed *$19.99*

Miracles (1989)
Jackie Chan in a martial arts remake of Frank Capra's "Pocketful of Miracles"? That's what you get in this wild action/comedy, with Chan as a country bumpkin in 1930s Hong Kong who rescues a dying crime boss and becomes head of his gang. While Chan tries to deal with a rival mob, he must also help a peddler, whose roses he thinks bring him luck, pass herself off to her daughter's fiancé's family as a society woman. With Anita Mui, Richard Ng, Wu Ma. AKA: "Mr. Canton and Lady Rose." 106 min. Dubbed in English.
53-9406 *❑$99.99*

Island Of Fire (1990)
Jackie Chan joins fellow Hong Kong stars Sammo Hung, Tony Leung and Andy Lau in a fierce actioner about a cop (Leung) who goes undercover in prison to investigate a murder. Inside, he's forced to kill a corrupt official and is sent to death row, but a secret offer arrives for Leung and fellow inmates Chan, Hung and Lau. Jimmy Wang Yu also stars. In Cantonese with English subtitles.
53-8459 *$49.99*

Twin Dragons (1992)
There's twice the action, twice the laughs, and twice the Jackie Chans in this comedy-thriller that has Chan playing identical twins separated at birth. The grown-up Jackies, a streetwise Hong Kong mechanic and martial arts whiz and a refined symphony conductor from New York, meet and wind up switching identities to outwit Asian gangsters. With Maggie Cheung, Nina Li; directed by Tsui Hark and Ringo Lam. 90 min. Dubbed in English.
11-2341 Was $99.99 *❑$14.99*

City Hunter (1992)
Hired by a newspaper publisher to find his missing daughter, private eye Jackie Chan locates her on board a cruise ship that's about to be seized by a group of crooks planning to hold the wealthy passengers for ransom. Based on a popular Japanese comic book, this light-hearted action tale features a wild video game sequence with Chan playing the characters from "Streetfighter II." With Joey Wong, Richard Norton, Gary Daniels, Chingmy Yau. 98 min. In Japanese with English subtitles.
53-6454 *$19.99*

City Hunter (Dubbed Version)
Also available in a dubbed-in-English edition.
53-6455 *$19.99*

Crime Story (1993)
There's less emphasis on slapstick stunts and more on drama in this Jackie Chan thriller, based in part on a true story. Assigned to guard a wealthy Hong Kong builder from kidnapping threats, police inspector Chan must rescue the man from a mysterious group of abductors who may have connections within the police. With Kent Cheng. 104 min. Dubbed in English.
11-2125 Was $19.99 *❑$14.99*

Drunken Master II (1994)
Reprising one of his greatest roles, Jackie Chan plays the put-upon young master of a punch-drunk martial arts style who takes on crooked businessmen illegally selling Imperial Chinese treasures. The film's knockout fights take place under a train, in a busy marketplace, and in an iron foundry (where Chan lands on a bed of hot coals!). With Ti Lung, Johnny Lo, and Anita Mui as Jackie's mah-jongg crazy stepmother. 102 min. In Cantonese with English subtitles.
53-8458 Was $49.99 ***$19.99***

Rumble In The Bronx (1996)
From its bustling harbor to its scenic mountains, the Bronx has never been as action-packed as when Jackie Chan arrives from Hong Kong to work in his uncle's grocery and winds up battling marauding street gangs, motorcycle-riding babes, ruthless gem thieves and even a menacing hovercraft! The hits, kicks and death-defying stunts (all done by Chan) come fast and furious in this thrill-a-minute hit. With Anita Mui, Bill Tung, Francoise Yip. 91 min. Dubbed in English.
02-5097 Was $19.99 □***$14.99***

Rumble In The Bronx (Letterboxed Version)
Also available in a theatrical, widescreen format.
02-5112 Was $19.99 ***$14.99***

Jackie Chan's Who Am I? (1997)
All-out action assault with Jackie Chan as a CIA commando duped by his leader and left for dead while on a dangerous mission in Africa. After he's nursed back to health by a native tribe, an amnesiac Chan searches for clues to his true identity, but soon the bad guys are searching for Jackie as well. Stunt-filled adventure co-stars Michelle Ferre and Mirai Yamamoto. 108 min.
02-3271 Was $99.99 □***$14.99***

Mr. Nice Guy (1997)
TV chef/martial arts expert Jackie Chan whips up a mess of trouble when he comes to the aid of a plucky TV reporter carrying a videotape that links an untouchable crime kingpin with a gang of street hoods. It's up to Jackie to save the newsgal, his show's producer and his girlfriend from the bad guys in this stunt-filled soufflé directed by Sammo Hung. 87 min.
02-5183 Was $99.99 □***$14.99***

Rush Hour (1998)
Jackie Chan is a maverick Hong Kong cop who teams with fast-talking L.A. detective Chris Tucker to track down the kidnapped 11-year-old daughter of a Chinese consul. This high-energy buddy comedy is filled with Chan's wild stunts, Tucker's motor-mouthed antics and all sorts of outrageous action. With Elizabeth Peña, Tom Wilkinson and Philip Baker Hall. 97 min.
02-5194 Was $99.99 □***$14.99***

Rush Hour (Letterboxed Version)
Also available in a theatrical, widescreen format.
02-5206 □***$14.99***

Gorgeous (1999)
Taken with the writer of a mysterious love note she finds in a bottle, Qi Shi travels from Taiwan to Hong Kong to find him, only to discover the sender is gay photographer Tony Leung. While staying with him, Qi meets and falls for businessman Jackie Chan, who already has his hands (and feet) full dealing with an unscrupulous rival's attacks. Chan's action scenes are balanced with breezy romantic comedy in this change-of-pace outing. 99 min. Dubbed in English.
02-3441 □***$99.99***

Shanghai Noon (2000)
Jackie Chan makes the Wild West even wilder in this rambunctious ride, playing an Imperial Guard in China's Forbidden City in the 1880s who comes to America with three other guards in search of kidnapped princess Lucy Liu. After being separated from his compadres, Jackie teams with smooth-talking outlaw Owen Wilson to fight the princess's captors. With Xander Berkeley, Roger Yuan. 110 min.
11-2473 □***$99.99***

Jackie Chan: My Story
For the first time, the man who was crazy enough to hang off of a helicopter without a harness in "Supercop" talks about his career, his ambitions as an entertainer, and what makes him tick. Includes clips from some of Jackie's best death-dodging stunts from such films as "Crime Story," "Police Story," "Operation Condor" and more. 75 min.
53-6249 Was $24.99 ***$14.99***

Invincible Fighter: The Jackie Chan Story
Discover the real story of martial arts sensation Jackie Chan in this factual look at his life and career. Find out about Jackie's early days at Chinese opera school, his work as a film stuntman and his efforts to become Hong Kong's greatest star. Highlighted by rare footage and samples of Chan's amazing stuntwork.
54-9148 ***$19.99***

Please see our index for these other Jackie Chan titles: *An Alan Smithee Film: Burn Hollywood Burn • The Cannonball Run • Enter The Dragon*

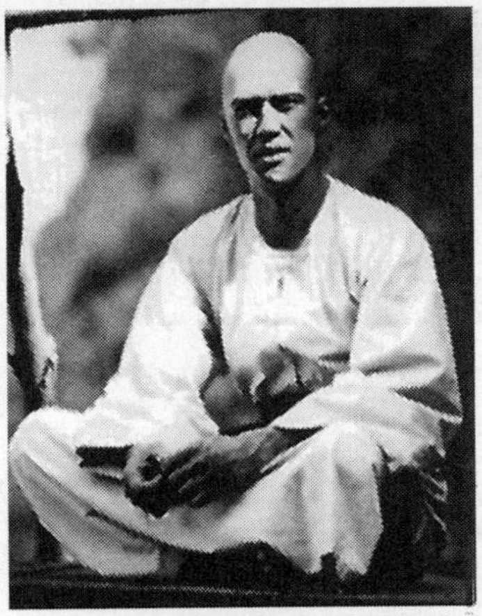

KUNG FU

Kung Fu (1971)
The movie that was the pilot for the "Kung Fu" TV series features David Carradine as a young Chinese-American priest who fights villains while working on the railroads out West. A tale of determination, skill and karate mastery. Barry Sullivan and Keye Luke also star. 75 min.
19-1347 ***$14.99***

Kung Fu: The Movie (1986)
David Carradine reprises his role as Kawi Chang Caine, caught up in a battle with a Chinese warlord who's shipping opium to America and a search for the son he never knew, in the action-filled sequel to the cult TV series. Brandon Lee co-stars as Caine's high-kicking son; with Mako, Martin Landau, Keye Luke. 93 min.
19-2035 Was $59.99 ***$14.99***

Chinese Hercules (1973)
After nearly killing his fiancée's brother, Chan Wai Man vows to never fight in anger again. But after he gets a job as a dockworker, his promise is shattered when he witnesses the abuses suffered by his fellow workers. Now he has to meet a martial arts powerhouse, Chinese Hercules (Bolo Yeung), enlisted by the crooked company bosses. Dubbed in English.
54-9146 ***$19.99***

Chinese Samson (1974)
Martial arts expert Bolo Yeung directed and stars in this opus in which he plays a Vietnamese killer whose arrival in a small town leads to an altercation with an abused, impoverished teacher, who has been developing a special "writing kung fu" style to use. AKA: "Writing Kung Fu." Dubbed in English.
54-9145 ***$19.99***

Chinese Goliath (1975)
Hong Kong bad boy Bolo Yeung is a Chinese warlord who hires a team of Japanese assassins to stop the activities of a group of revolutionaries. When the leader of the assassins saves a revolutionary's life, they team together to battle Yeung and his nefarious ways. Dragon Lee also stars. Dubbed in English.
54-9144 ***$19.99***

Bolo (1977)
Exciting martial arts thriller set in feudal China, as two prisoners are pardoned and sent to a remote village to protect it from marauding criminal cabals. They'll defend it...or die trying! Bolo Yeung, Mi Hsuen, Yang Sze star. AKA: "Bolo the Brute." 91 min.
50-5033 Was $29.99 ***$19.99***

Bloodfight (1990)
Bolo Yeung, who took on Bruce Lee in "Enter the Dragon" and Jean Claude Van Damme in "Bloodsport," now takes center stage in a martial arts drama unparalleled. Enter the "arena of death," where your first mistake is your last, with him...if you dare.
69-7054 Was $89.99 ***$19.99***

Shootfighter 2: Kill Or Be Killed (1996)
Hong Kong action master Bolo Yeung returns in this sequel to the martial arts hit, playing a kickboxing cop who joins an elite squad of policemen to stop a criminal mastermind supervising an illegal shootfighting ring in Miami. William Zabka, Michael Bernardo and Jorge Gil. 104 min.
02-2922 Was $99.99 □***$19.99***

Bolo Yeung Collection
You'll be "forever Yeung" with this three-tape set featuring the Bolo Yeung action hits "Chinese Goliath," "Chinese Hercules" and "Chinese Samson."
54-9137 ***$59.99***

Shatter (1976)
Stuart Whitman stars as Shatter, a top international assassin-for-hire who travels to Hong Kong for a hit that he thinks was arranged by the U.S. government, only to become ensnared in a deadly double cross. Shatter teams with a martial arts instructor to bring down a global drug cartel in this hard-hitting actioner from Hammer Films. Peter Cushing, Ti Lung co-star. AKA: "Call Him Mr. Shatter." 90 min.
08-8649 Letterboxed ***$14.99***

Death Machines (1976)
Just wind 'em up and watch them chop, kick, maim and murder. They're the human death machines, masters of deadly martial arts, and they must be stopped...at all costs! Kung fu cacophony stars Michael Chong, Ron Marchini. 93 min.
15-1099 ***$14.99***

The Dynamite Brothers (1974)
Explosive actioner set on the streets of Los Angeles, where a Chinese crimelord's efforts to take over the city's gambling and drug operations pit him against two "blood brothers." A Hong Kong-born martial arts master and a streetfighter from Watts, they've teamed up to clean up the town. Alan Tang, James Hong, Timothy Brown and Aldo Ray star. 90 min.
15-5277 ***$19.99***

Bruce Li: The Invincible (1977)
When it comes to Kung Fu action Bruce is the one, no Li. Watch as he leads students of a martial arts academy into a duel with bandits where the failing grade is death! With Wai Man Chen, Chen Sing. 93 min.
16-1002 ***$12.99***

Fighting Ace (1979)
It's "aces high" for a young man who undertakes a brutal regimen of martial arts training in order to avenge his parents' murder in one of the most violent explosions of action ever put to film. With Chung-Liang Liu, Juen-er Lung, Lung Chun Erl. 86 min.
41-7016 Was $29.99 ***$19.99***

Ten Tigers Of Shaolin (1979)
Action-filled Kung Fu spectacular about truth, justice and the Chinese way of life. Faster than a speeding train during rush hour in Manchuria; more powerful than a Great Wall; able to leap tall pagodas in a single bound...look...up on the rickshaw...it's the Ten Tigers of Shaolin. With Liang Hsiao, Li Jin Kun.
48-1036 ***$29.99***

Assassin (1978)
Thrill-packed martial arts melee set in the time of Feudal China. Cruel landlords and fearless fighters duel on foot and horseback with swords, fists, feet and more. Stars Hsu Feng, Roc Tien, Pai Ying. 90 min.
48-1041 ***$29.99***

Against The Drunken Cat Paws (1975)
Comedy, pathos, action and skill combine in this epic of a female martial arts student who is blinded by bandits and sets out for revenge. The catch... she's especially lethal when drunk, so she gets that way fairly often. Stars Chia Ling, Ou-Yang Ksiek. 94 min.
48-1084 ***$39.99***

Monkey In The Master's Eye (1972)
A lowly servant, taunted by those around him, goes away to study the martial arts. His former masters sure won't taunt him any longer, or it's "Hiiiyaaaa!" So Lo Go, Kai Bee Toi.
48-1093 ***$39.99***

Four Infernos To Cross (1975)
Martial arts excitement is mixed with history in a look at the Japanese occupation of Korea before and during World War II. Kyhee Kim, Musung Kwak. 90 min.
48-1074 ***$39.99***

Swordsman With An Umbrella (1970)
Forget Patrick Macnee on "The Avengers" or Burgess Meredith on "Batman." You haven't seen bumbershoot battles like the exciting (and historically accurate) fighting scenes in this tale of swordplay in old China. With Jiang Ming-Yu Er. 85 min.
41-7017 Was $29.99 ***$19.99***

The Fearless Young Boxer (1979)
I am just a fighter, tho my story's seldom told. I have squandered my existence while I use my karate skills to look for my father's killer.Casanova Wong stars.
48-1098 ***$39.99***

Death Challenge (1970)
Rival gangland factions war within the narcotics trade. This high adventure film uses gun fights, fist fights and karate to re-create the violent world of today's Hong Kong. Edwin Aro Cho, Susan Wong star.
48-1103 ***$39.99***

The Two Great Cavaliers (1973)
A fearsome young martial arts warrior, aided by his mysterious compatriot, must revenge the death of his fiancée by marauding Manchurians. Chen Shing, Shama Lhama Dhing Dhong. 95 min.
48-1116 ***$39.99***

The Furious Avenger (1976)
An ex-con, bent on avenging his family's murder, leaves a trail of blood and death along the way to a final battle with crazed samurai swordsmen. Hsiung Fei stars.
48-1119 ***$39.99***

Dance Of Death (1976)
Bone-crunching action with martial arts star Angelo Mao Ying as a woman seeking to learn kung fu from a pair of rival masters so she can avenge her family's murder. With Shek Tien, Chin Pei; fight choreography by Jackie Chan. AKA: "The Eternal Conflict."
48-1123 ***$39.99***

Dance Of Death (Letterboxed Subtitled Version)
Also available in a theatrical, widescreen format. In Chinese with English subtitles.
20-8245 ***$19.99***

The Eighteen Jade Arhats (1979)
What are arhats, you ask? Well, to be perfectly honest, we're not sure, but they give legendary power to martial artists and some people will kill to possess them. That's just what some villains do in this high-kicking thriller. Polly Shang, Lo Lieh star. AKA: "The Eighteen Claws of Shaolin," "The Eighteen Jade Pearls."
48-1183 ***$39.99***

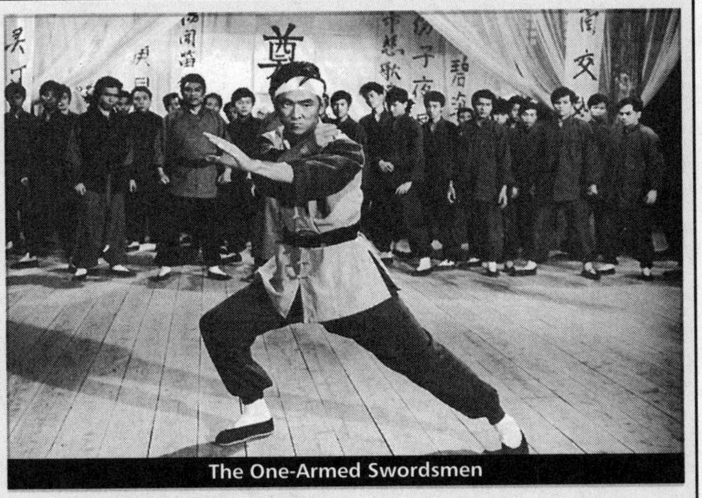
The One-Armed Swordsmen

The One-Armed Swordsmen (1968)
Maybe it takes two hands to handle a Whopper, but one is all a pair ofmartial arts masters needs to handle a similarly handicapped foe who killed their friends and besmirched their reputations. Jimmy Wang Yu, Lo Lieh and David Chiang star.
48-1099 ***$39.99***

Return Of The Chinese Boxer (1975)
And just in time, too, because Japanese spies are entering China to prepare for an invasion, and only his Kung Fu boxing skills can save his homeland. Jimmy Wang Yu reprises one of his greatest roles. 93 min. Dubbed in English.
48-1111 ***$39.99***

Return Of The Chinese Boxer (Letterboxed Version)
Also available in a theatrical, widescreen format.
20-8268 ***$19.99***

Master Of The Flying Guillotine (1975)
This second feature in the infamous "One-Armed Boxer" series is an over-the-top martial-arts marathon set in the 18th century, where a sightless martial arts master sets out for revenge against a one-armed rebel who killed his two disciples. The master uses an incredible flying device to do his dirty work. Jimmy Wang Yu stars in this outrageous actioner.
68-8903 ***$19.99***

Sonny Chiba

Soul Of Chiba (1973)
To avenge the murder of his beloved martial arts teacher by a fellow student who becomes part of an international drug cartel, fighting mad Sonny Chiba teams up with an undercover cop in Bangkok to attack the crooks' island fortress. Bronson Lee, Sue Shiomi and Bolo Yeung also star. 90 min. Dubbed in English.
54-9778 $19.99

IF YOU'VE GOT TO FIGHT—FIGHT DIRTY!

INTRODUCING THE INCREDIBLE SONNY CHIBA AS
THE STREET FIGHTER

The Street Fighter (1975)
The original, unrated, uncensored martial arts classic that thrilled and shocked audiences with its ultra-violent fight scenes stars Sonny Chiba as Terry Sugury, a mercenary karate master who runs afoul of Yakuza and Mafia villains when he agrees to protect an oil magnate's daughter from a kidnapping plot. Along the way eyes are gouged, body parts ripped off, and a head is smashed open—in slow-motion and X-ray footage! With Gerald Yamada, Doris Nakajima. 91 min.
04-1570 $12.99

The Street Fighter: Letterboxed Collector's Edition
Also available in a theatrical, widescreen format.
02-5077 $19.99

Return Of The Street Fighter (1976)
"The incredible Sonny Chiba" returns as killer-for-hire Terry Sugury, here hired to eliminate a stool pigeon behind bars. Chiba completes the assignment but earns the enmity of his employers, who send an army of assassins after him. Among the foes is Jungo, his arch-enemy from the first film. Yoko Ichji, Masafumi Suzuki co-star. 88 min.
04-1603 $12.99

Return Of The Street Fighter (Unrated Letterboxed Version)
The uncut, unrated edition is available in a theatrical, widescreen format.
02-5111   Was $19.99 $14.99

The Street Fighter's Last Revenge (1977)
A ruthless mob boss, striking factory workers, synthetic heroin manufacturers, a passel of machine gun-toting attackers and romance(!) all await unstoppable fighting machine Sonny Chiba in the third entry in the explosive "Street Fighter" series. With Gerald Yamada. 80 min.
20-1038 $12.99

Sister Street Fighter (1978)
After her narcotics agent brother is murdered by a merciless drug ring who then beats her and leaves her for dead, karate student Etsuko Shiomi enlists the aid of modern-day ninja Sonny Chiba to exact her vicious vengeance. Amazing martial arts action in the "Street Fighter" tradition. 91 min.
02-5078   Was $19.99 $12.99

Killing Machine (1975)
Following the end of World War II, former Japanese soldier and Shaolin martial arts master Sonny Chiba returns to Osaka to find black marketeers controlling the town. His campaign against them lands him in trouble with crooked lawmen and sends him to a remote village, where he establishes a Shaolin school. When the crooks show up there, all heck breaks loose. AKA: "Shaolin Fist." 85 min. Dubbed in English.
54-9139 $19.99

Golgo 13: Assignment: Kowloon (1977)
Sonny Chiba is perfectly cast as Golgo 13, the lethal killer-for-hire with his own code of honor and the star of a long-running Japanese comic book series. In this action-packed thriller, Golgo is hired to eliminate a drug-dealing Hong Kong businessman, only to find himself challenged by another hit man. AKA: "Kowloon Assignment." 93 min. In Japanese with English subtitles.
20-8380   Letterboxed $19.99

Golgo 13: Assignment: Kowloon (Dubbed Version)
Also available in a dubbed-in-English edition.
53-1598   Letterboxed $24.99

Assassin (1977)
Mean undercover cop Sonny Chiba masquerades as a killer-for-hire to get between rival Yakuza members out to control the Tokyo drug and gambling rackets. Pulling a "Yojimbo" (or "Fistful of Dollars" or "Last Man Standing"), Chiba plays one faction against the other, leading to dangerous consequences. With Fumio Watanabe. AKA: "Marijuana Trafficking Syndicate." Dubbed in English.
54-9142 $19.99

G.I. Samurai (1981)
A Japanese army unit out on maneuvers gets caught in a force-field which thrusts them back 400 years to feudal Japan. The soldiers are forced to face off against Samurai warriors who, despite primitive weaponry, prove to be incredibly skilled fighters. Sonny Chiba, Isao Natsuki star. AKA: "Time Slip." Dubbed in English.
54-9140 $19.99

Samurai Reincarnation (Dubbed Version) (1981)
Also available in a dubbed-in-English edition.
54-9143 $19.99

Immortal Combat (1994)
Explosive thrills meets martial arts mayhem meets sci-fi shocks, as action superstars Roddy Piper and Sonny Chiba team up to battle an army of unkillable ninja-trained warriors. Also with Meg Foster, Tiny Lister. 109 min.
83-1008   Was $89.99 $14.99

Sonny Chiba Collection
Japanese streetfighter Sonny Chiba slugs it out in this collection of five dubbed hits, including "Assassin," "G.I. Samurai," "Killing Machine," "Samurai Reincarnation" and "Soul of Chiba."
54-9136 $99.99

Hard As A Dragon (1978)
A vagabond skilled in the martial arts defends a weak, helpless man from a ruthless gang of criminals who are after him. The gang then frames the hero for murder, which leads to an explosive conclusion. Raymond Lui, Szu Chi Ying star.
68-9274 $19.99

Fists Like Lee (1976)
Lao Chen and Ling Kee Xing star in this obscure kung fu film about two feuding fighters who are unaware that they are actually brothers. But who is the real bad guy in this tale featuring plenty of martial arts action? AKA: "The Chinese Mack."
68-9273 $19.99

Shaolin Master Killer (1978)
A true milestone in martial arts movie history, this action-filled drama from director Lau Kar Leung ("Drunken Master II") stars Gordon Liu (Lau Ka Fai) as a shallow young man out to avenge his family's murder by Manchu assassins. Entering the Shaolin temple, Liu undergoes a grueling series of training exercises to master the fighting skills he'll need to gain his revenge. Lo Lieh, Wilson Tong also star. AKA: "Master Killer," "36th Chamber of Shaolin." 115 min. Dubbed in English.
20-8267   Letterboxed $19.99

Murder In The Orient (1973)
Martial arts expert Ron Marchini plays an American secret agent who is joined by a karate master to find two samurai swords that will lead him to millions in gold. Leo Fong also stars. 92 min.
78-3019 $14.99

Invincible Kung Fu (1978)
Two rival self-defense school owners combine their talents to fight an evil martial artist, but wind up banned from the area. Before they return to tackle the villain and his allies, the pair learn the lessons of kung fu art from a learned drunkard. Liang Hsiao Lung, Han Kuo Tsai star. 87 min.
82-7011 $39.99

The Legend Of The 7 Golden Vampires: Collector's Edition (1974)
Kung Fu goes batty in this energetic Hammer Films/Shaw Brothers production, as Professor Van Helsing (Peter Cushing) finds a clan of bloodsuckers in China under the command of Count Dracula and enlists the aid of a group of martial arts experts. With Julie Ege. Includes a theatrical trailer and is followed by "The Seven Brothers Meet Dracula," its American version. 164 min. total.
08-8648   Letterboxed $14.99

Shaolin vs. Ninja (1978)
Everybody's kung fu fighting in this martial arts marathon set in feudal China in which a Shaolin temple is the focus of a battle between the temple's fighting monks and black-clad Japanese ninjas. Chang Kwan Loong stars. 85 min.
82-7032 $39.99

Secret Of The Snake And Crane (1976)
Rich with historical flavor and martial arts action, this film follows the exploits of a group of warriors rebelling against the cruel lords of the Ching Dynasty. Their secret weapons: the fighting styles of the Snake and Crane. With "an all-star kung fu cast." 93 min.
55-1113   Was $29.99 $19.99

Return Of The Fist Of Fury (1971)
The fist is attached to the jackhammer arm of Bruce Le, and there's one on either side on his lean, mean bod. Watch him in action against the kung fu killers who murdered his brother! With Pei Chiu Tend, Janice Wong. 88 min.
64-1108 $19.99

Kung Fu Genius (1969)
Cliff Lok is a real kung fu genius who excels in a number of martial arts styles, but runs into conflict with the members of a local gym when he opens a competing school. When one of their fights leads to a young man's wounding, his brothel owner father enlists his deadly fan-wielding brother to lance Lok. With Wilson Tong, Hsiao Hou. 90 min. Dubbed in English.
20-5098   Letterboxed $19.99

The Little Big Master (1969)
He may be small, but his martial arts skills are big, and with his band of fighting beggars there's sure to be high times for action fans. Huang a Rait, Man Li Peng. 90 min.
48-1076 $39.99

Karate: The Hand Of Death (1964)
This action-packed precursor to the kung fu films of the 1970s features director Joel Holt as a tough American who gets in trouble and travels to Japan, where he uses his martial arts skills to stop a group of Asian thugs. Filmed in English in cooperation with the Japan Karate Association.
79-5474   Letterboxed $19.99

Bionic Ninja
High-tech meets "Hiii-yaaa!" in this thrilling martial arts tale, as a CIA agent trained in the arts of the ninja must get back a valuable scientific discovery from the KGB-backed Ninja Organization and its head, Number Zero. Kelly Steve, Alan Hammings, Rick Wilson star. 85 min.
10-1300 $19.99

Silver Dragon Ninja
Good ninjas who wear white and work for Interpol square off against black-clad evil ninjas in this action-packed martial arts story. Can the ninjas in black rule the world? Not if the ninjas in white, who get help from Hong Kong police, have any say in the matter. Harry Caine, Sam Yosida and Jim Gross star. 87 min.
10-1301 $19.99

Duel Of The Dragon
This film really cooks with martial arts action detailing the efforts of the grandson of the King of Chefs—a man who once cooked for the King—to find the mysterious stranger who killed his grandfather. Jackie Chen stars.
10-1692 $19.99

Challenge Of The Lady Ninja
Women's liberation comes to the martial arts, as a young Chinese woman learns the arts of the ninja in order to avenge her father's death at the hands of her traitorous uncle. See female ninja mud wrestling, razor-edged boomerangs, and much more!
10-2144 $12.99

Deadly Life Of A Ninja
Well, it ain't all sushi and sake, that's for sure! After receiving a ninja death threat, a man turns for help to an ex-ninjitsu student. More martial arts action and bizarre weaponry than one film can handle! Stars Ysing Le, K.T. Mullin.
10-2145 $12.99

Super Dragon's Dynamo
An expert criminal is named an official of a tycoon's company, and soon plots to murder his boss. The crook is hired over the tycoon's lazy son, who has been mistakenly charged with a crime and sent to prison. Once the son is released from jail, he plots revenge for his father's death. Champ Wang, Sherman Chow star in this guns-a-blazing Hong Kong actioner.
10-1691 $19.99

The Chinese Tiger: Master Of Kung-Fu
The Organization is a company of criminal experts specializing in drug peddling. They also have their hands in murder and smuggling and are considered unstoppable. Only "The Chinese Tiger," a master of kung fu, has a chance to stop them. See him pounce into action! 89 min.
10-1693 $19.99

Shaolin vs. Manchu
In this corner: Rock, a Shaolin disciple who is banished when a prostitute is found in his room. And in this corner: Jouan, the Manchu spy who framed Rock and has taken over the Shaolin temple for his own nefarious schemes. All right boys, shake hands and come out chopping, kicking and maiming! Romy Tso stars. 91 min.
41-7003   Was $29.99 $19.99

Fists And Guts
A rowdy, free-for-all compilation of some of the greatest kung-fu action ever, featuring chopsocky champs from China engaged in wild combat. It's a cavalcade of bone-crunching bodies you'll not soon forget. 94 min.
10-2514 $19.99

Ninja Mania
They wear hoods, carry swords and generally have mean dispositions. They are Ninjas, the dealiest in exotic killers, featured in movies, on TV, in comics and in cartoons. Now you can see the nastiest Ninjas in history in this action-packed compilation of film clips, including "A Life of Ninja," "Ninja in the Dragon's Den" and more. 86 min.
10-2516 $12.99

Cinema Of Vengeance
Marvelous look at the world of martial arts action movies, chronicling its beginnings in 1940s China to the ultra-violent efforts of John Woo and Jackie Chan today. Included are segments on Jimmy Wang, Bruce Lee, Bruce Li, Cynthia Rothrock, Samo Hung and producer George Tan. Rare interviews and film clips tell Nhe story of kung fu's greatest heroes and villains. 90 min.
53-8319 $19.99

Top Fighter
Marvelous look at the cinema's top martial arts fighters, focusing on such tough guys as Jackie Chan, Bruce Lee, Bolo Yeung, Jet Li, Jean-Claude Van Damme and many others. Interviews and film clips reveal Lee's "Jeet Kune Do" techniques; Chan's training regimen; and Van Damme's early years. 100 min.
54-9124   Was $59.99 $19.99

Top Fighter 2: Deadly China Dolls
Who are the deadliest female stars of the martial arts world? This video presents the wildest women in the movies, including Michelle Yeoh, Moon Lee, Cynthia Rothrock, Angela Mao, Amy Yip and Yukari Oshima.
54-9169 $14.99

The Deadliest Art (1990)
A "Who's Who" of the greatest martial arts film stars (Bruce Lee, Jackie Chan, Jean-Claude Van Damme, Sho Kosugi, Lee Van Cleef and others) are showcased in their roughest, toughest action scenes in this high-kicking collection. There's also behind-the-scenes looks at the weapons and fighting styles used in movies, appearances by Chuck Norris and Kareem Abdul-Jabbar, and more. 90 min. AKA: "The Best of the Martial Arts Films."
04-2558   Was $29.99 $14.99

東方巨龍
DRAGONS OF THE ORIENT
A documentary on the history of martial arts.

Dragons Of The Orient (1997)
A high-flying chronicle of the Shaolin martial arts, from their development over 1,500 years ago to their use by such modern film stars as Bruce Lee, Jackie Chan and Jet Li. Follow a female reporter and Li sparring partner Wang Chun on a tour of China that features expert demonstration of several martial arts disciplines, from footage of a young Li training at the Great Wall to a 100-year-old sword master. 88 min. In Cantonese with English subtitles.
53-6387 $19.99

Dragons Of The Orient (Dubbed Version)
Also available in a dubbed-in-English edition.
53-6388 $19.99

The Forbidden Dance (1990)
A beautiful Brazilian princess arrives in America in hopes of stopping a U.S. corporation from ruining Amazon rain forests. She falls for a handsome American and teaches him how to Lambada, the saucy dance of her country. Laura Herring and Jeff James star; music by Jose Feliciano and Kaoma. 97 min.
02-2016 *$19.99*

Lambada (1990)
A Beverly Hills teacher does the sexy Lambada dance at night at an East L.A. warehouse. His enthusiasm for cutting the carpet influences his pupils to do their schoolwork...until a jealous student threatens his lifestyle. J. Eddie Peck, Melora Hardin and Shabba-Doo star. 104 min.
19-7077 Was $19.99 *$14.99*

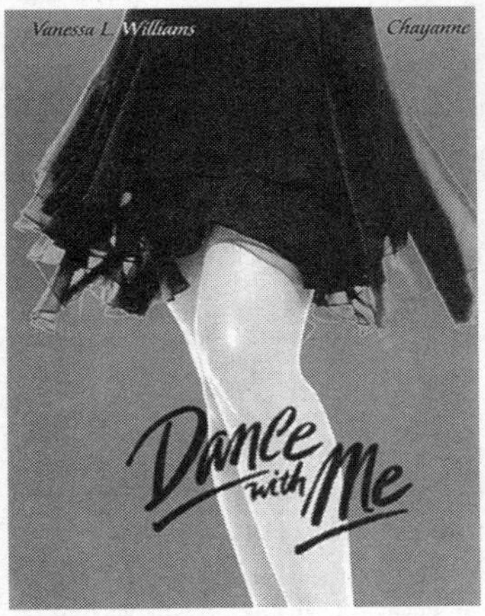

Dance With Me (1998)
Dance is the thing in this intoxicating story about a young Cuban who takes a handyman job at his estranged father's Houston dance studio. Everyone at the studio is getting ready for the World Open Dance contest in Las Vegas, and the young man reveals his own incredible talents when he teams with the studio's top dancer. Chayanne, Vanessa L. Williams and Kris Kristofferson star. 126 min.
02-3234 Was $94.99 ❑*$14.99*

Spice World (1997)
Britain's chart-topping all-girl quintet, The Spice Girls, makes the jump to screen stardom with a glitzy musical that could have been called "A Hard Day's Spice." Follow Sporty, Scary, Posh, Ginger and Baby Spice through a "typical" series of adventures—from an alien encounter and a best friend's going into labor to a media mogul out to squash "Girl Power"—as they prepare for a concert at London's Royal Albert Hall. With Richard E. Grant, and cameos by Roger Moore, Elton John, Elvis Costello. 93 min.
02-3165 Was $19.99 ❑*$14.99*

Double Platinum (1999)
In this musical drama, Diana Ross plays a singer who sacrificed her family life and relationship with daughter Brandy for a career in show business. After years apart, mother and daughter reunite, and now, with Brandy seeking her own music career, the two struggle to re-establish their bond. With Harvey Fierstein; features a hit soundtrack. 91 min.
02-3347 Was $19.99 *$14.99*

The Five Heartbeats (1991)
Lively look at a fictitious 1960s black vocal group, focusing on their beginnings, their ascension to the top of the charts and the ups and downs of each member. Robert Townsend co-wrote, directed and stars as the Heartbeats' talented songwriter; Michael Wright, Tico Wells, Diahann Carroll also star. 122 min.
04-2462 Was $89.99 ❑*$19.99*

Stepping Out (1991)
High-stepping musical-drama starring Liza Minnelli as a failed Broadway dancer who gives tap-dance (and life) lessons to a group of people in an old church. They're put on the spot when asked to dance in a benefit, but the difficult practice sessions bring the troupe together. Shelley Winters, Ellen Greene, Julie Walters co-star. 112 min.
06-1919 Was $89.99 ❑*$14.99*

Swing Kids (1993)
A musical-drama about the real-life German students who rebelled against the Hitler Youth movement by embracing the popular English and American cultures and dance styles of the day. The focus is on two close friends, one of whom is forced to join the youth group. Robert Sean Leonard, Christian Bale, Frank Whaley, Barbara Hershey and Kenneth Branagh star. 114 min.
11-1713 ❑*$19.99*

What's Love Got To Do With It? (1993)
The amazing life of singer Tina Turner has been translated into an exciting, compelling tale of survival in the entertainment industry. Witness Turner's early, troubled childhood, her stormy, abusive relationship with husband Ike, and her triumphant solo career and comeback. Angela Bassett and Laurence Fishburne turn in tour-de-force performances; the film features such songs as "Proud Mary" and the title tune. 118 min.
11-1771 Was $19.99 ❑*$14.99*

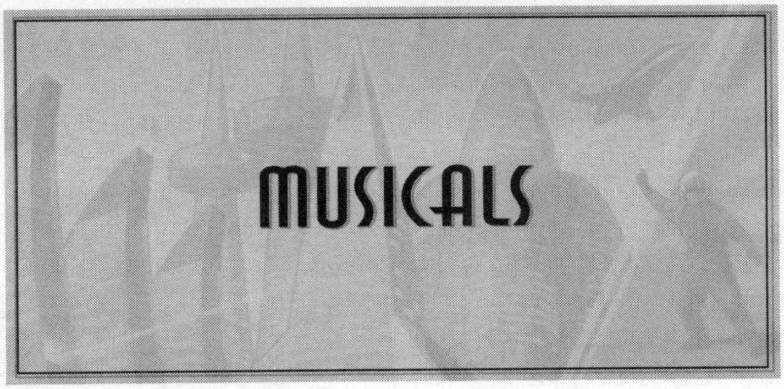

Monster Mash: The Movie (1995)
Car trouble forces a teenage couple to spend the night in an eerie castle inhabited by Dr. Frankenstein and his monster, Count and Countess Dracula, the Wolfman and his mother, and a mummy named Elvis in this song-filled horror spoof that features "Monster Mash" creator Bobby "Boris" Pickett as the mad doctor. With Candace Cameron, John Kassir, Mink Stole and Jimmie Walker. AKA: "Frankenstein Sings...The Movie." 82 min.
18-7574 Was $94.99 *$14.99*

Selena (1997)
Jennifer Lopez is magnetic in the title role of the Mexican-American singer who rose from the barrio of Corpus Christi, Texas, to become a Grammy-winning Tejano pop star and was on the brink of mainstream success before her tragic murder at the age of 23 in 1995. Edward James Olmos, Jon Seda co-star in this song-filled biopic. 128 min.
19-2579 Was $94.99 ❑*$19.99*

Selena (Letterboxed Version)
Also available in a theatrical, widescreen format.
19-2626 ❑*$19.99*

The Doors (1991)
A powerful depiction of the rise and fall of the seminal '60s band, highlighted by an uncanny performance by Val Kilmer as hard-living lead singer Jim Morrison. Oliver Stone's hypnotic film captures the intensity and spirit of the 1960s, features Doors classics like "Light My Fire" and "Love Her Madly" and boasts a supporting cast that includes Meg Ryan, Kyle MacLachlan, Billy Idol, Kevin Dillon, and Crispin Glover as Andy Warhol. 138 min.
27-6717 Was $89.99 ❑*$14.99*

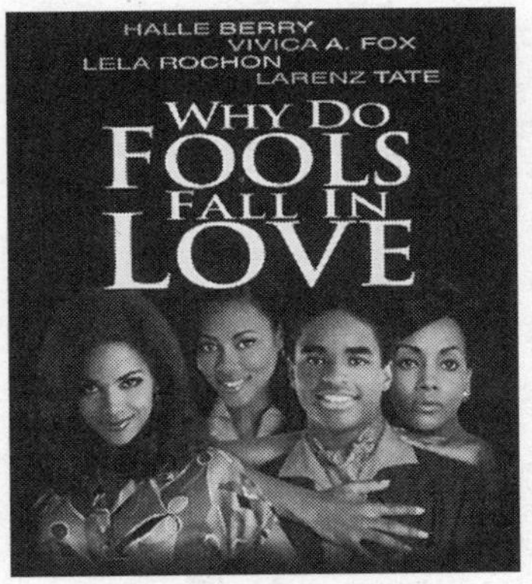

Why Do Fools Fall In Love (1998)
Decades after the drug overdose death of 1950s singing sensation Frankie Lymon, three ex-wives appeared in court to claim his estate. Lymon's meteoric success as a teen idol and tragic downfall are then traced in this darkly farcical look at show business and the role the women, all married to Lymon at the same time, played in the singer's life. Laurenz Tate, Halle Berry, Vivica A. Fox, Lela Rochon and Little Richard star. 116 min.
19-2783 Was $94.99 ❑*$14.99*

Mr. Rock 'N' Roll: The Alan Freed Story (1999)
Judd Nelson stars in this song-filled biodrama as the '50s Cleveland disc jockey who introduced America to a musical revolution and ushered in a new era in cultural integration, until scandal and a stormy personal life ended his career. A great '50s soundtrack and appearances by Fabian, Bobby Rydell, Paula Abdul, and Leon as Jackie Wilson add to the excitement. 91 min.
27-7178 Was $19.99 ❑*$14.99*

Alice (1981)
She remembers seeing the handsome young man jogging through the park. She remembers the sudden attempt on his life...and then blackness. She awakens into a world that appears normal...but the subtle differences grow increasingly nightmarish. Bizarre reworking of Lewis Carroll's classic tale blends music and intrigue; Sophie Barjac, Susannah York star. 80 min.
40-1199 Was $59.99 *$19.99*

Purple Rain (1984)
Risque rocker Prince stars as talented, withdrawn singer "The Kid" in this sizzling musical/drama that combines romance, comedy and dazzling on-stage performances by Prince and the Revolution, The Time and Apollonia 6. Songs include "When Doves Cry," "Let's Go Crazy," "Jungle Love." With Apollonia, Morris Day, Clarence Williams III. 111 min.
19-1349 Was $19.99 ❑*$14.99*

Under The Cherry Moon (1986)
The one and only Prince directs himself in this stylish black-and-white romantic drama laced with song, as a gigolo living on the French Riviera develops a fatal attraction to a gangster's daughter. Co-stars Kristin Scott Thomas, Jerome Benton. 98 min.
19-1543 Was $19.99 ❑*$14.99*

Graffiti Bridge (1990)
"Music is the power. Love is the message. Truth is the answer." That's the motto of Prince in this sequel to the smash hit "Purple Rain." His Royal Purpleness is a Minneapolis nightclub owner who squares off against business partner/rival Morris Day for the hand of beautiful Ingrid Chavez. Mavis Staples, George Clinton and Tevin Campbell join Prince on the soundtrack. 90 min.
19-1842 Was $89.99 *$14.99*

Bert Rigby, You're A Fool (1989)
A day-dreamy English coal miner with a habit of breaking into Fred Astaire numbers becomes a shaft-to-showbiz success in writer/director Carl Reiner's carefree tribute to the spirit of those grand old musicals. Robert Lindsay stars with Anne Bancroft, Jackie Gayle, Bruno Kirby and Corbin Bernsen. 94 min.
19-1709 Was $19.99 ❑*$14.99*

Salsa (1988)
A hot-blooded Hispanic dancer in L.A. changes partners as frequently as he changes steps on the way to a big Salsa dance contest. "Dirty Dancing" choreographer Kenny Ortega puts ex-Menudo Robby Rosas and Miranda Garrison through the sizzling Latin paces in this song-filled drama. 97 min.
19-7000 Was $19.99 *$14.99*

Absolute Beginners (1986)
Music mixes with drama in this slice of London teenage life, circa 1958, complete with early American rock, warring gangs of Mods Teddy Boys, and the start of the British sound. Director Julien Temple's stylish production stars Eddie O'Connell, Patsy Kensit and James Fox, with special appearances by David Bowie, Sade and Ray Davies. 107 min.
44-1434 ❑*$14.99*

A Chorus Line: The Movie (1985)
All the vibrant, colorful, song-filled, kinetic excitement of the Tony-winning Broadway musical comes to the screen, as the lives, hopes and struggles of a group of would-be dancers come to light during an audition. Richard Attenborough ("Gandhi") directs a talented cast, including Audrey Landers, Vicki Frederick, Terrence Mann and Michael Douglas as the play director. 118 min.
53-1491 ❑*$14.99*

Body Beat (1988)
In the style of "Flashdance" and "Dirty Dancing" comes this musical drama laced with sizzling dance numbers, as a tough young man from the city streets is hired to help save a financially strapped dance academy. Plenty of drama, romance and songs, plus a bright young cast. 90 min.
68-1106 *$29.99*

Sing (1989)
Entrancing musical set against the real-life Brooklyn high school competition that has served as the springboard to fame and fortune. A troubled young lass and an arrogant street punk learn lessons in fair play and love to the beat of an energetic pop score. Lorraine Bracco, Louise Lasser, Patti LaBelle star. 97 min.
02-1956 Was $89.99 *$19.99*

Beat Street (1984)
The Bronx is the hippest place in America, as breakdancers, graffiti artists, DJs and rap musicians converge for an exciting street scene. Grandmaster Melle Malle and Afrika Bhambatta are featured with Rae Dawn Chong in this Harry Belafonte production. 106 min.
47-1281 Was $59.99 *$14.99*

Krush Groove (1985)
An all-star, all-rap cast, including Sheila E., Run-DMC, Kurtis Blow, and the Fat Boys, brings the sound of the streets into the clubs and onto the screen in this smash hit musical, full of hit songs, romance and comedy. Blair Underwood co-stars. 97 min.
19-1484 Was $19.99 ❑*$14.99*

Cool As Ice (1991)
Rap master Vanilla Ice plays a motorcycling musician who rides into a small town with his band, then falls for a high school honor student. There's action, romance and rap songs galore in this flick that's cooler than ice. With Kristin Minter, Michael Gross and Candy Clark. 92 min.
07-1731 ❑*$89.99*

Fast Forward (1985)
The streets of New York come alive with dancing and music in a vibrant, song-filled tale of eight kids out to win a national dance competition. From jazz and ballet to soul and hip-hop, this movie has it all! Sidney Poitier directs a talented young cast. 110 min.
02-1460 Was $79.99 ❑*$14.99*

Tap (1989)
Gregory Hines, Sammy Davis, Jr. and some legendary hoofers star in a rousing dance showcase about a second-generation tapper and parolled jewel thief who's torn between the stage and returning to his lavish life of crime. A throwback to those classic MGM musicals, co-starring Suzzanne Douglas. 115 min.
02-1951 Was $19.99 ❑*$14.99*

The Pirate Movie (1982)
High-flying, fun-loving musical swashbuckler based on Gilbert & Sullivan's "Pirates of Penzance," with Kristy McNichol as a modern-day girl who daydreams about high sea adventures while on vacation in Australia. Co-stars Christopher Atkins, Ted Hamilton, Bill Kerr. 98 min.
04-1503 Was $59.99 *$29.99*

Flashdance (1983)
What a feeling! Jennifer Beals plays a beautiful young girl who works as a welder by day, but sexily dances at a smokey bar at night. Her dream: to become a ballet performer. Top-notch, hit-filled score; eye-opening dance numbers. Michael Nouri, Marine Jahan. 96 min.
06-1190 ❑*$14.99*

Footloose (1984)
Smash hit, filled with great pop music score, stars Kevin Bacon as a high-stepping city kid who goes against a music-hating preacher in a small town while falling for the clergyman's pretty daughter. Lori Singer, Dianne Wiest, John Lithgow. Music by Kenny Loggins, Deniece Williams and others. 107 min.
06-1218 *$14.99*

Fame (1980)
The Oscar-winning musical-drama based on New York's famed High School for the Performing Arts. The terms of several aspiring actors, singers, and dancers are followed in a moving style that blends gritty urban reality with vibrant song and dance numbers. Irene Cara, Gene Anthony Ray and Anne Meara star. 133 min.
12-1027 Was $19.99 *$14.99*

One-Trick Pony (1980)
Paul Simon scripted, scored and starred in this drama of a rock singer approaching middle age and faced with declining popularity and family tensions. Also stars Blair Brown, Rip Torn, Mare Winningham; appearances by Lou Reed, The B-52's, The Lovin' Spoonful and Tiny Tim. 98 min.
19-1012 Was $19.99 *$14.99*

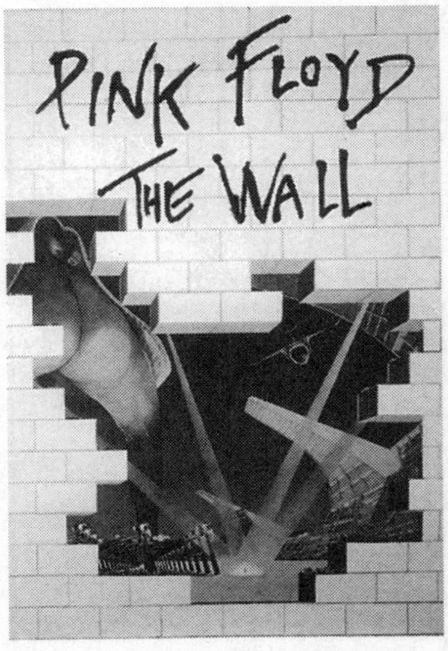

Pink Floyd: The Wall (1982)
Based on Pink Floyd's hit album, this dazzling rock musical stars Bob Geldof as Pink, a rock star tortured by his past and descending into madness. His breakdown is represented by striking live-action and animated sequences and such Floyd songs as "Another Brick in the Wall," "Comfortably Numb," "Goodbye Blue Sky," "The Trial" and others. With Bob Hoskins, Christine Hargreaves; Alan Parker directs. 95 min.
12-1289 *$19.99*

Little Shop Of Horrors (1986)
The film of the off-Broadway musical of the horror movie spoof...hilarious, tuneful story of a nerd and his man-eating plant stars Rick Moranis, Ellen Greene, Steve Martin and Levi Stubbs (of Four Tops fame) as the voice of Audrey II. Songs include "Suddenly Seymour," "Mean Green Mother from Outer Space." 94 min.
19-1567   Was $19.99   □$14.99

Hard To Hold (1984)
Teen idol Rick Springfield makes his film debut as a rock-and-roller who falls for a laid-back woman. Dynamic concert sequences and a non-stop rock score, including the hit, "Love Somebody," make this one to grab. Janet Eilber, Patti Hansen. 93 min.
07-1217   Was $69.99   □$14.99

1776 (1972)
A rousing musical celebration of our Founding Fathers and the birth of America. Meet Benjamin Franklin, Caesar Rodney, Tom Jefferson, Thomas McKean, John Adams, George Read, John Hancock—all singin', all dancin'. William Daniels, Blythe Danner, Howard DaSilva star. 141 min.
02-1170 $19.99

The Buddy Holly Story (1978)
The Oscar-winning biodrama of one of rock's first and most influential stars. Gary Busey stars as the horn-rimmed hero from Lubbock, Texas, who blended country and blues in hits like "That'll Be the Day," "Peggy Sue," and "Maybe, Baby"; he also performs the soundtrack. With Charles Martin Smith, Don Stroud. 113 min.
02-1811 $14.99

La Bamba (1987)
At the age of 17 he had three hit records and a brilliant future...until fate made him a legend. Hit biodrama of '50s rock and roller Ritchie Valens stars Lou Diamond Phillips as Valens, with music by Los Lobos, Brian Setzer and Marshall Crenshaw. Co-starring Esai Morales, Elizabeth Peña. 103 min.
02-1810   □$14.99

Jesus Christ Superstar (1973)
Innovative musical based on Andrew Lloyd Webber and Tim Rice's popular concept album features imaginative settings, marvelous dance numbers and fine performances to depict the events leading up to Christ's crucifixion. Stars Ted Neely, Carl Anderson, Joshua Mostel and Yvonne Elliman; Norman Jewison directs. 103 min.
07-1022   Remastered $14.99

Jesus Christ Superstar (Letterboxed Version)
Also available in a theatrical, widescreen format.
07-2597 $19.99

Sgt. Pepper's Lonely Hearts Club Band (1978)
Linking of Beatles' classic songs with an amusing story line. Bee Gees, Peter Frampton, Steve Martin, George Burns. 111 min.
07-1044   Was $19.99 $14.99

Grease: 20th Anniversary Edition (1978)
Get out your poodle skirts and penny loafers and get ready to rock-and-roll with John Travolta and Olivia Newton-John in the hit screen rendition of the Broadway musical look at '50s high school life. Songs include "Greased Lightning," "Summer Nights," "You're the One That I Want" and the title track. With Stockard Channing, Jeff Conaway, Didi Conn, Eve Arden. This remastered anniversary edition also includes new interview footage with the cast and director Randal Kleiser.
06-1023   Restored   □$14.99

Grease (Letterboxed Version)
Also available in a theatrical, widescreen format.
06-2734   □$14.99

Grease Gift Set
This special collector's set includes the movie, a copy of the original shooting script, and a soundtrack sampler CD.
06-2732 $19.99

Grease Gift Set (Letterboxed Version)
Also available in a theatrical, widescreen format.
06-2733 $19.99

Grease 2 (1982)
More marvelous musical fun! Rydell High is up in the air over a new Australian student. Is he the mysterious motorcycle master who's charming the Pink Ladies? Bouncy, bobby-sox up frivolity: songs, dancing, satire. Maxwell Caulfield, Michelle Pfeiffer, Lorna Luft, Tab Hunter. 115 min.
06-1149 $14.99

Grease 2-Pack
Both nostalgia-filled musicals, "Grease" and "Grease 2," are also available in a special boxed set.
06-2465 $29.99

Thank God It's Friday (1978)
Remember Disco? This movie shows the ups and downs of one wild dance hall on a Friday night. Terri Nunn and Jeff Goldblum star, and musical guests are The Commodores and Donna Summer. Includes Oscar-winning song "Last Dance." 89 min.
02-1167   Remastered $19.99

Don't Play Us Cheap (1973)
Melvin Van Peebles' film adaptation of his acclaimed Broadway musical, set in a boisterous Harlem party that's crashed by a pair of most unwelcome guests—two devilish minions sent up from the underworld to spoil everyone's fun. This funny, song-filled look at contemporary black life stars Esther Rolle, Avon Long, Rhetta Hughes, Mabel King. 95 min.
54-9129 $79.99

Song Of Norway (1970)
The life story of 19th-century Norwegian composer Edvard Grieg, who was forced more than once to choose between his music and love, is lavishly brought to the screen in this musical biodrama. Toralv Maurstad, Florence Henderson, Frank Porretta, Christina Schollin and Edward G. Robinson star. 142 min. on two tapes.
04-3080 $19.99

Lady Sings The Blues (1972)
Diana Ross is stunning in her portrayal of jazz and blues singer Billie Holiday, whose brilliant career was ruined by prejudice and drug addiction. Moving musical score and supporting roles by Billy Dee Williams and Richard Pryor. 144 min.
06-1031   Was $69.99 $24.99

Fiddler On The Roof (1971)
One of Broadway's greatest musicals comes to the screen with rousing dance numbers, emotionally charged performances, and such beloved tunes as "Sunrise, Sunset," "If I Were a Rich Man," "Do You Love Me?" and others. Topol stars as Tevye the Milkman, struggling to keep his family together and Jewish traditions alive in their turn-of-the-century Russian village. With Norma Crane, Molly Picon. 178 min.
12-1824   Was $29.99 $24.99

Fiddler On The Roof (Letterboxed Version)
Also available in a theatrical, widescreen format.
12-2907   Was $29.99   □$24.99

All That Jazz (1979)
A glittery, surrealistic musical by Bob Fosse. Roy Scheider is a demanding musical director trying to find meaning in his work and his life. Dazzling dance numbers include appearances by Ben Vereen, Jessica Lange and Ann Reinking. 123 min.
04-1006   □$14.99

That's Entertainment! (1974)
Unforgettable collection of sequences from MGM's greatest musicals. "Anchors Aweigh," "Babes in Arms," "Singin' in the Rain," "The Wizard of Oz," and more. Astaire, Crosby, Kelly, Minnelli, Sinatra and Rooney host. That's extravaganza, that's dance, that's song, that's entertainment. 122 min.
12-1020   Was $19.99 $14.99

That's Entertainment, Part 2 (1976)
Let your video recorder be the stage for this musical-comedy treat. More magical MGM moments with scads of stars, including Sinatra, Kelly, Astaire, Tracy and Hepburn, the Marx Brothers and more. 126 min.
12-1082   Was $19.99 $14.99

That's Dancing! (1985)
Gene Kelly, Liza Minnelli, Sammy Davis Jr., Mikhail Baryshnikov and Ray Bolger take you on a tour of Hollywood musicals. Famous dance scenes from "Oklahoma!," "The Wizard of Oz," "42nd Street," "Flashdance" and other films are seen, with stars from Fred Astaire and Ginger Rogers to Shirley Temple and John Travolta. 104 min.
12-1425 $19.99

That's Entertainment! III (1994)
Among the many musical highlights featured in this return trip to the MGM Studios library are unused numbers by Debbie Reynolds from "Singin' in the Rain" and Lena Horne from "Cabin in the Sky," Judy Garland's test footage for the lead role in "Annie Get Your Gun," Eleanor Powell dancing to "Fascinating Rhythm," and others. Hosts include Gene Kelly, Ann Miller, Mickey Rooney. 113 min.
12-2949   Was $19.99   □$14.99

The Slipper and the Rose
The Story of Cinderella

Richard Chamberlain   Gemma Craven

Annette Crosbie   Edith Evans

Christopher Gable   Michael Hordern

The Slipper And The Rose (1976)
The legend of Cinderella comes magically to life in this epic filmization of the classic fairy tale, featuring lavish settings and memorable music by the Sherman Brothers ("Mary Poppins"). Gemma Craven is Cinderella, Richard Chamberlain the handsome prince, and the supporting cast includes such British greats as Edith Evans, Margaret Lockwood and Kenneth More. 143 min.
50-8388   Letterboxed $19.99

Evita (1996)
Madonna is charismatically radiant in the title role of the hit musical, playing the born-to-poverty actress who seduced her way into power as the wife of Argentinean President Juan Peron and was both revered and hated by her countrymen until her death at the age of 33 in 1952. Director Alan Parker's adaptation of the Andrew Lloyd Webber/Tim Rice Broadway smash also stars Antonio Banderas and Jonathan Pryce; songs include "Don't Cry for Me, Argentina" and the Oscar-winning "You Must Love Me," written especially for the film. 135 min.
11-2152   Was $19.99   □$14.99

Evita (Letterboxed Version)
Also available in a theatrical, widescreen format.
11-2153   □$19.99

Hair (1979)
Let the sun shine in, in Milos Forman's adaptation of the super '60s play. Everything's a winner here—choreography, costumes, acting and the wonderful score that includes "Good Morning, Starshine," "Age of Aquarius" and others. Treat Williams, John Savage, Beverly D'Angelo. 121 min.
12-1776   Was $19.99 $14.99

The Wiz (1978)
The fabulous land of Oz rocks and dazzles in this glittering film version of the Broadway hit, a modernized, urban rendition of the Hollywood classic, with Diana Ross as a Manhattan schoolteacher easin' on down the road with the Scarecrow (Michael Jackson), the Tinman (Nipsey Russell) and the Lion (Ted Ross). With Mabel King, Lena Horne and Richard Pryor as the Wiz. 133 min.
07-1073   Was $19.99   □$14.99

Mame (1974)
Lucille Ball coaxes the blues right out of the horn in this brassy, big-screen musical extravaganza. She's the eccentric woman who teaches her young nephew how to make life fun. Beatrice Arthur, Robert Preston also star, with songs like "Mame" and "The Man in the Moon Is a Lady." 132 min.
19-1317   Was $19.99   □$14.99

Sparkle (1976)
Before "Dreamgirls," there was this musical drama, recalling the rise of a Supremes-like girl group from the ghetto to superstardom. Lonette McKee, Irene Cara, Dwan Smith and Philip Michael Thomas star. Features a score by Curtis Mayfield. 100 min.
19-1351   Was $19.99 $14.99

Cabaret: 25th Anniversary Edition (1972)
Bob Fosse's stylish musical, set amid the decadence of '30s Berlin, garnered eight Academy Awards. The plot revolves around singer Liza Minnelli's affair with writer Michael York and the exotic clientele that frequent the Kit-Kat Club. Joel Grey and Marisa Berenson co-star. This remastered anniversary edition includes original theatrical trailers and a behind-the-scenes featurette on the making of the film. 124 min.
19-1904   Remastered   □$19.99

That'll Be The Day (1974)
Acclaimed blend of "angry young man" and rock-and-roll drama stars David Essex as a British lad in the late '50s who must choose between a working-class existence with his wife and child or pursuing his dreams of musical stardom. Great oldies soundtrack; Ringo Starr, Billy Fury, Keith Moon co-star. 87 min.
63-1638 $14.99

ASK ABOUT OUR GIANT DVD CATALOG!

Godspell (1973)
One of the most requested titles at Movies Unlimited, this musical, based on the hit play, presents the Gospel According to St. Matthew as played out in modern Manhattan. Colorful costumes and exciting choreography highlight this favorite that features the songs "Day by Day," "Prepare Ye the Way of the Lord," "Light of the World" and others. With Victor Garber, David Haskell. 105 min.
66-6053 $19.99

Bye Bye Birdie (1963)
Some of Broadway's most memorable songs come from this satire of Elvis Presley's army induction. Conrad Birdie, the teenage idol, is drafted and agrees to sing a farewell song to a devoted fan on TV. Songs include "Kids," "Put on a Happy Face," "We Love You, Conrad," Stars Janet Leigh, Dick Van Dyke, Ann-Margret, Bobby Rydell and Paul Lynde. 112 min.
02-1030   Was $19.99 $14.99

Bye Bye Birdie (1995)
The Broadway favorite about a small town thrown into chaos when it's chosen for the final public appearance by a rock-and-roll idol about to enter the army, and the local girl picked to get Conrad Birdie's farewell kiss, gets a colorful rendition and three new songs in this Emmy-winning production. The cast includes Jason Alexander, Vanessa Williams, Chynna Phillips, George Wendt and Tyne Daly. 131 min.
88-1200 $14.99

Star! (1968)
Lavish musical biography of Gertrude Lawrence starring Julie Andrews as the legendary British stage performer whose life was devoted to entertaining people. Robert Wise's sumptuous production looks at Lawrence's early days, her friendship with Noel Coward and her romances. Songs include "Piccadilly" and "Someday I'll Find You." With Richard Crenna, Daniel Massey. AKA: "Those Were the Happy Times." Restored 172-min. version.
04-2710   Was $89.99   □$29.99

Sweet Charity (1969)
Shirley MacLaine stars as a lovelorn New York City prostitute who finds romance with a naive man who knows nothing about her line of work. Songs include "Big Spender" and "If My Friends Could See Me Now"; co-stars Chita Rivera and Sammy Davis, Jr.; Bob Fosse's directorial debut. 148 min.
07-1506   Was $19.99 $14.99

Half A Sixpence (1968)
Tommy Steele excels in this tune-filled adaptation of H.G. Wells' novel "Kipps." He plays a poor British draper who inherits a fortune and becomes part of England's wealthy aristocracy. Lavish production co-stars Julia Foster, Cyril Ritchard and Penelope Horner. 148 min.
06-1067 $19.99

Oliver! (1968)
Consider yourself right in when you watch this lively musical adaptation of the Dickens classic that garnered six Oscars, including Best Picture. Mark Lester stars as the plucky orphan lad, Jack Wild is his pal, the Artful Dodger, and Ron Moody is the rapscallious Fagin. Delightful score from composer Lionel Bart includes "Food, Glorious Food," "Where Is Love?" and more. With Oliver Reed, Hugh Griffith and Shani Wallis. 145 min.
02-3181   Remastered   □$19.99

The Ghost Goes Gear (1966)
Unseen in its complete form for decades, this "swingin' '60s" musical features British Invasion faves The Spencer Davis Group in a tale about a music festival to save a mansion that may or may not be haunted. Along with "Gimme Some Lovin'," "I'm a Man" and four more Spencer Davis hits, there are songs by Acker Bilk, The M6, Dave Berry and other English bands. With Jack Haig, Sheila White. 79 min.
08-8840   Letterboxed $14.99

The Unsinkable Molly Brown (1964)
Debbie Reynolds is the irrepressible backwoods gal who becomes a society leader in gold rush Denver in this vibrant musical by Meredith Willson. Ed Begley, Hermione Baddeley and Harve Presnell co-star; songs include "I Ain't Down Yet" and "Belly Up to the Bar, Boys." 128 min.
12-1418   Was $19.99 $14.99

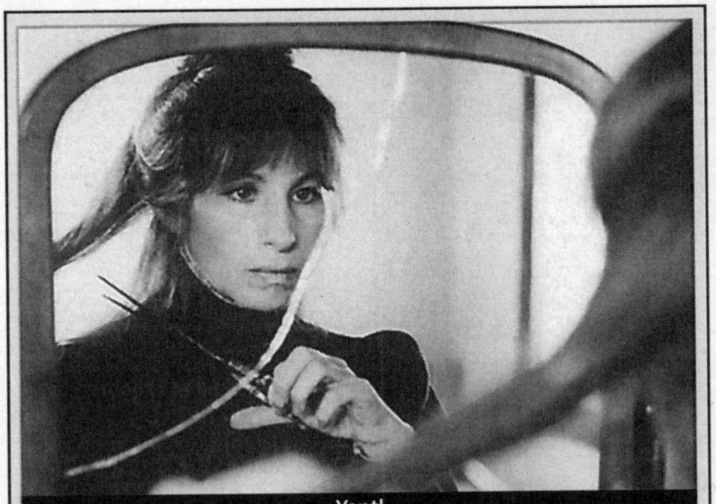
Yentl

Barbra Streisand

Funny Girl (1968)
Classic musical comedy based on the life of singer-actress Fanny Brice (Barbra Streisand) and her love affair with and marriage to gambler Nicky Arnstein (Omar Sharif). Songs include "People" and "Don't Rain on My Parade." 155 min.
02-1175 *$19.99*

Funny Lady (1975)
Streisand returns to the role that put her on the map, Ziegfeld superstar Fanny Brice. James Caan is sly and sexy as Fanny's second husband, composer/entrepreneur Billy Rose. Fine musical score belted out in the inimitable Streisand manner; Omar Sharif, Roddy McDowall, Ben Vereen also star. 137 min.
02-1617 Was $19.99 *$14.99*

Funny Girl/Funny Lady Gift Pack
People...people who get this deluxe boxed set featuring Streisand's Fanny Brice biodramas...are the luckiest people in the world!
02-2180 Save $5.00! *$29.99*

Hello, Dolly! (1969)
Lavish screen adaptation of the beloved Broadway musical stars Barbra Streisand as the turn-of-the-century New York matchmaker who falls for client Walter Matthau. Supporting turns by Michael Crawford and Louis Armstrong, and a score that includes "Before the Parade Passes By," "Just Leave Everything to Me" and the title song, add to the fun. 148 min.
04-1069 ❑*$19.99*

The Owl And The Pussycat (1970)
Boisterous call girl Barbra Streisand moves into the apartment of her neighbor, shy bookstore clerk George Segal, after his complaints about her "practice" get her evicted. Fast-paced romantic comedy, scripted by Buck Henry from the hit Broadway play, also stars Robert Klein, Alan Garfield; look for porn star Marilyn Chambers (aka Evelyn Lang) as Klein's girlfriend. 95 min.
02-2624 *$14.99*

On A Clear Day You Can See Forever (1970)
Delightfully romantic musical stars Barbra Streisand as a woman who believes she is reincarnated, and finds help and romance with sexy psychiatrist Yves Montand. Songs include "He Wasn't You" and "Come Back to Me"; also stars Jack Nicholson, Bob Newhart, Larry Blyden. 129 min.
06-1208 ❑*$14.99*

What's Up, Doc? (1972)
Writer-director Peter Bogdanovich's salute to the screwball comedies of the '30s and '40s stars Barbra Streisand and Ryan O'Neal in a wild chase through San Francisco over stolen jewels and prehistoric musical instruments. Madeline Kahn and Kenneth Mars co-star. 94 min.
19-1061 ❑*$14.99*

Up The Sandbox (1972)
Barbra Streisand stars in this offbeat look at a pregnant New York housewife who finds herself fantasizing about safaris in Africa and revolutions with Fidel Castro. David Selby, Jane Hoffman also star. 97 min.
19-1303 *$19.99*

For Pete's Sake (1974)
Devoted wife Barbra Streisand winds up involved with loan sharks, madames and mobsters as she tries to pay off cab-driver husband Michael Sarrazin's debts in this frenetic comedy. Estelle Parsons, Molly Picon also star. 90 min.
02-1038 *$14.99*

A Star Is Born (1976)
The third version of the story of a doomed show biz romance takes its focus to the world of rock music. Barbra Streisand and Kris Kristofferson make a magnetic couple, faced with choices about love and career. Oscar-winning song "Evergreen" is featured. 140 min.
19-1046 *$19.99*

The Main Event (1979)
Barbra Streisand and Ryan O'Neal re-team in this screwball comedy about a bankrupt businesswoman whose sole remaining asset is the contract of a has-been boxer. Patti D'Arbanville co-stars. 109 min.
19-1042 ❑*$14.99*

Yentl (1983)
Barbra Streisand wrote, directed, and stars in this funny, bittersweet tale of a young woman who, in early 1900s Europe, dresses as a man in order to study the Hebrew scriptures. Amy Irving, Mandy Patinkin. 134 min.
12-1938 ❑*$19.99*

Barbra: The Concert (1994)
People who love Barbra will not want to miss this special concert, captured during the final performances of her triumphant 1994 tour from Anaheim, California. Along with a 47-piece orchestra, Streisand performs an array of selections from her career, including "Guilty," "People," "Evergreen," a "Yentl" medley and "Somewhere." 103 min.
04-5241 *$29.99*

Nuts (1987)
Unforgettable drama stars Barbra Streisand as the daughter of wealthy socialites who want her declared insane so she won't have to stand trial for murder, and Richard Dreyfuss is the court-appointed attorney whom Streisand wants to prove her sane. With Karl Malden, Maureen Stapleton, Eli Wallach; Martin Ritt directs. 116 min.
19-1635 Was $19.99 ❑*$14.99*

The Prince Of Tides (1991)
Powerful drama stars Nick Nolte as a South Carolina football coach with a failing marriage who goes to New York City to help psychiatrist Barbra Streisand (who also directed) unravel his sister's emotional problems. Eventually, Nolte confronts his own dark secrets while falling in love with Streisand. Blythe Danner, Kate Nelligan and Jeroen Krabbe co-star. 132 min.
02-2229 Was $19.99 ❑*$14.99*

THE MIRROR HAS TWO FACES

The Mirror Has Two Faces (1996)
Based on a 1958 French film, director/star Barbra Streisand's warm and revealing romantic comedy follows Babs' frumpy Columbia professor on an odyssey from ugly duckling to glamorous sophisticate, all to kindle passion in her "platonic marriage" to fellow academician Jeff Bridges. With Pierce Brosnan, Mimi Rogers and Lauren Bacall. 127 min.
02-3021 Was $19.99 ❑*$14.99*

Please see our index for the Barbra Streisand title: *The Way We Were*

Stop The World— I Want To Get Off (1966)
The popular Anthony Newley-Leslie Briscusse musical is transformed into a lively film set in a circus ring and follows the travails of aggressive Mr. Littlechap, who will stop at nothing to find fame and success, even if it means stepping on the people around him. Tony Tanner and Millicent Martin star; songs include "What Kind of Fool Am I?," "Someone Nice Like You." 100 min.
19-2170 Was $29.99 *$19.99*

Camelot: 30th Anniversary Edition (1967)
Richard Harris stars as King Arthur in this lavish, Academy Award-winning film adaptation of Lerner and Loewe's musical take on the legend of the Knights of the Round Table, with Vanessa Redgrave and Franco Nero as doomed lovers Guenevere and Lancelot. Among the memorable tunes are "Camelot," "If Ever I Would Leave You," "What Do the Simple Folk Do?" Special remastered edition also includes original theatrical trailers. 180 min.
19-2488 Was $24.99 ❑*$19.99*

Camelot (Letterboxed Version)
Also available in a theatrical, widescreen format.
19-2487 Was $24.99 ❑*$19.99*

Having A Wild Weekend (1965)
In the wake of The Beatles' "A Hard Day's Night," fellow Britpop combo The Dave Clark Five hit the big screen with this bouncy musical in which pop singer/film stuntman Clark and his bandmates leave Swinging London behind for a remote island getaway, with a beautiful actress tagging along. Directed by John Boorman ("Deliverance"). Songs include "Catch Us If You Can," "Sweet Memories" and the title tune. AKA: "Catch Us If You Can." 91 min.
19-2515 ❑*$14.99*

Gypsy (1962)
Smash musical about the life of stripper Gypsy Rose Lee. Natalie Wood plays the vaudeville singer-turned-burlesque star, with Rosalind Russell as her abrasive stage mother. The Stephen Sondheim-Jule Styne score includes such gems as "Everything's Coming Up Roses," "Small World" and "You Gotta Have a Gimmick." With Karl Malden, Ann Jillian. Special video version includes two outtake musical numbers, screen tests of original Broadway cast, and the theatrical trailer. 153 min.
19-1316 Was $59.99 ❑*$19.99*

Gypsy (Letterboxed Version)
Also available in a theatrical, widescreen format.
19-2764 *$19.99*

Disk-O-Tek Holiday (1966)
A real find, this American re-edit of Britain's "Just for You" is a rock-'n'-roll knockout featuring Freddie Cannon, A Band of Angels, Peter and Gordon, The Rockin' Ramrods, Freddie and The Dreamers and many other groups. The slight story follows an aspiring teen idol and his girlfriend who harass disc jockeys Bob Foster, Arnie Ginsburg and Philly's own Hy Lit as they roam the country. Great stuff!
79-6224 Was $24.99 *$19.99*

The Fastest Guitar Alive (1967)
Mercy! The legendary Roy Orbison made his screen debut as a Confederate soldier who takes part in robbing a Union gold shipment, then is branded a criminal when the war ends. Roy sings eight songs and makes use of a shotgun guitar(!); with Sammy Jackson, Maggie Pierce, Iron Eyes Cody. 87 min.
12-1967 Was $19.99 *$14.99*

Crazy Baby (1968)
The mods and the rockers go head-to-head in a musical battle that drives the establishment wacky in this Italian opus that stars Ricky Shayne singing "Crazy Baby, I Got You" and "No No No No No." With Joachim Fuchsberger. AKA: "Battle of the Mods."
68-8946 *$19.99*

Good Times (1967)
Sonny and Cher's first and only starring film together was this breezy musical romp that features the pop duo as themselves. Ready to break into Hollywood but unhappy with the scripts studio head George Sanders offers them, Sonny imagines he and Cher in western, gangster and jungle movies in a series of comedic fantasy sketches. Songs include "I Got You Babe," "Just a Name," "Trust Me"; William Friedkin's ("The French Connection") directorial debut. 91 min.
08-8639 *$14.99*

Thoroughly Modern Millie (1967)
The "Roaring Twenties" live on in this Oscar-winning musical comedy of innocent girls, wild flappers, romance and crime. Julie Andrews and Mary Tyler Moore are the heroines, John Gavin the good guy, Carol Channing a dizzy heiress and Beatrice Lillie the head of a white slavery ring. 138 min.
07-1379 Was $19.99 *$14.99*

How To Succeed In Business Without Really Trying (1967)
Window washer Robert Morse takes a quick trip up the corporate ladder, thanks to a unique handbook, in the film version of the hit Broadway musical comedy. Frank Loesser score includes "I Believe in You," "Coffee Break"; with Rudy Vallee, Michele Lee. 119 min.
12-1687 Was $19.99 *$14.99*

How To Succeed In Business Without Really Trying (Letterboxed Version)
Also available in a theatrical, widescreen format.
12-3208 *$14.99*

West Side Story (1961)
Leonard Bernstein's classic street-wise musical, a modern-day "Romeo and Juliet," stars Richard Beymer and Natalie Wood as doomed lovers caught up in the violence of rival street gangs. Co-stars Rita Moreno. Winner of 10 Academy Awards, including Best Picture; co-directed by Robert Wise and Jerome Robbins. 155 min.
12-1771 Remastered ❑*$14.99*

A Funny Thing Happened On The Way To The Forum (1966)
There's "Comedy Tonight" and every night in Richard Lester's slapstick adaptation of the hit Broadway musical set in ancient Rome. Zero Mostel is the scheming slave who dreams of freedom, and Michael Crawford ("Phantom of the Opera") is his lovestruck master. With Phil Silvers, Jack Gilford, Annette Andre, Buster Keaton. 99 min.
12-2206 Was $19.99 *$14.99*

A Funny Thing Happened On The Way To The Forum (Letterboxed Version)
Also available in a theatrical, widescreen format.
12-3209 *$14.99*

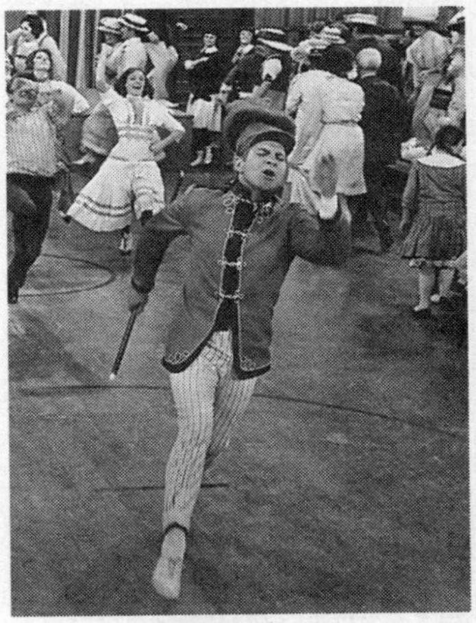

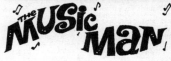

THE MUSIC MAN

The Music Man: Special Edition (1962)
Robert Preston is Professor Harold Hill, sly salesman who cons the good folk of 1910s River City, Iowa, into forming a youth band so he can sell them instruments and then skip town...until he falls for lovely librarian Shirley Jones. The hit Meredith Wilson musical includes "76 Trombones," "Trouble," "Till There Was You" and "Shipoopi"; with Hermione Gingold, Paul Ford, Ronny Howard and Buddy Hackett. This restored collector's edition includes a special introduction by Jones, the documentary "Right Here in River City: The Making of The Music Man," and the original theatrical trailer. 177 min. total.
19-1521 ❑*$19.99*

The Music Man: Special Edition (Letterboxed Version)
Also available in a theatrical, widescreen format.
19-2736 *$19.99*

Rock Baby, Rock It! (1957)
One of the rarer of the '50s rock musicals has kids fighting mobsters who want to use their dance club for a bookie parlor. Rockabilly pioneer Johnny Carroll and Kay Wheeler (founder of the Elvis Fan Club) star. 77 min.
15-5003 *$12.99*

Li'l Abner (1959)
The downhome denizens of Dogpatch, U.S.A. are a-singin' and a-dancin' in this film rendition of the Broadway musical. It's up to Abner and Mammy Yokum to save the day when their town is deemed "most useless in America" and marked for an A-bomb test! Al Capp's colorful characters are all here; with Peter Palmer, Leslie Parrish, Billie Hayes, Stubby Kaye, Julie Newmar. 113 min.
06-1835 ❑*$14.99*

Stars And Stripes Forever (1952)
Lively, tuneful biography of march master John Philip Sousa, starring Clifton Webb as the former Marine Corps band leader who started his own concert band and wrote some of America's most beloved patriotic songs. Robert Wagner, Debra Paget, Ruth Hussey co-star. 89 min.
04-2454 ❑*$19.99*

Red Garters (1954)
Rosemary Clooney, Jack Carson, Guy Mitchell, Pat Crowley and Gene Barry star in this high-spirited musical/comedy that pokes gentle fun at Western movies. A cowboy rides into a frontier town to catch his brother's killer, but also finds romance along the way. Songs include "A Dime and a Dollar," "Good Intentions," "Man and Woman." 91 min.
06-2074 ❑*$14.99*

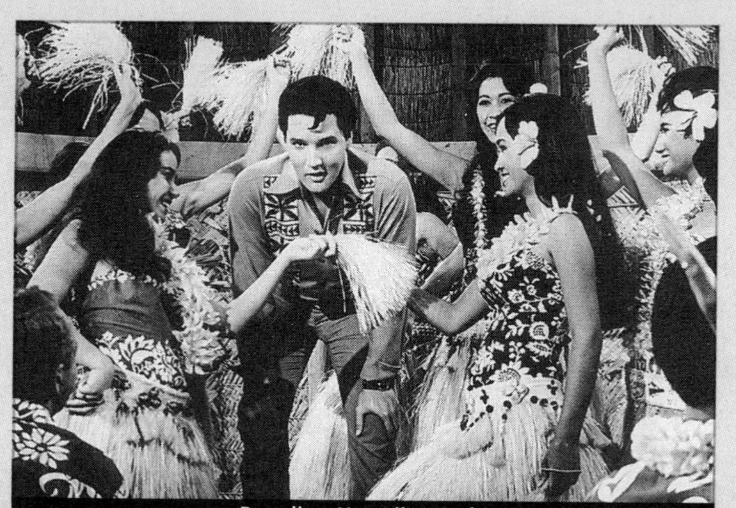

Paradise, Hawaiian Style

Elvis Presley

Love Me Tender (1956)
Elvis Presley's first movie finds him as a farm boy romancing his presumed-dead brother's fiancée during the Civil War. Songs include "Poor Boy," "We're Gonna Move" and the title tune. With Debra Paget, Richard Egan. 89 min.
04-1796 *$14.99*

Jailhouse Rock (1957)
"Warden threw a party in the county jail..." Perhaps the quintessential Elvis film has him as a young man in jail for killing a woman's attacker. Learning to play the guitar from a fellow inmate, Presley becomes a recording star after he's released. Along with the title song, Elvis performs "Treat Me Nice," "I Wanna Be Free" and more. With Mickey Shaughnessy, Judy Tyler, Dean Jones. Includes original theatrical trailer. 96 min.
12-1010 Was $19.99 ❏*$14.99*

Loving You (1957)
Small-town gas station attendant Elvis Presley is pushed into stardom by promoter Lizabeth Scott as part of her ex-husband's country band. With Wendell Corey, Delores Hart and a cameo by Presley's mother, Gladys. Songs include "Teddy Bear," "Got a Lot of Living to Do" and the title tune. 102 min.
19-1143 Remastered ❏*$14.99*

King Creole (1958)
One of Elvis Presley's finer acting roles came in this drama based on a novel by Harold Robbins. Elvis plays a singing busboy in New Orleans who gets a job from gangster Walter Matthau as a singer in a mob-owned nightclub. With Carolyn Jones, Dolores Hart, Vic Morrow; songs include "Hard-Headed Woman," "Crawfish" and the title tune. 115 min.
04-1215 ❏*$14.99*

G.I. Blues (1960)
For his first movie after serving in the Army, Elvis found himself back in uniform, playing a singing soldier stationed in Germany who makes a bet with his buddies that he can woo a nightclub singer (leggy Juliet Prowse), and winds up falling for her. Songs include "It's Not Good Enough for You," "Frankfurt Special" and the title tune. 104 min.
04-1213 ❏*$14.99*

Flaming Star (1960)
This unusual (for star Elvis Presley) frontier drama gave the singer a rare chance to flex his dramatic muscles, playing a half-breed forced to choose when tensions mount between white settlers and his mother's Kiowa people. With Barbard Eden, Steve Forrest, Delores Del Rio; directed by Don Siegel ("Dirty Harry"). 87 min.
04-1795 *$14.99*

Blue Hawaii (1961)
Tour guide Elvis sings 14 songs and still manages to drive sightseers around the islands in golf carts in this lush musical that features great locales and such tunes as "Blue Hawaii," "Can't Help Falling in Love with You" and "Rock-a-Hula Baby." With Angela Lansbury, Joan Blackman, Roland Winters. 103 min.
04-1211 ❏*$14.99*

Wild In The Country (1961)
Clifford Odets wrote the screenplay to this Elvis Presley drama about a backwoods youth whose desire to write is encouraged by a social worker. With Hope Lange, Tuesday Weld, John Ireland. 114 min.
04-1564 *$14.99*

Kid Galahad (1962)
Fine remake of the boxing classic stars Elvis Presley as a garage mechanic-turned-prize fighter who runs afoul of gangster Charles Bronson. Between bouts, Elvis manages to sing a song or two, including "King of the Whole Wide World" and "I Got Lucky." With Lola Albright, Gig Young. Includes original theatrical trailer. 95 min.
12-1636 Was $19.99 *$14.99*

Follow That Dream (1962)
And that's just what backwoods crooner Elvis Presley and pa Arthur O'Connell do, taking care of three plucky orphan kids as they set up housekeeping on unclaimed government land in Florida, in this fun-filled Presley vehicle that features such songs as "What a Wonderful Life" and "I'm Not the Marrying Kind." Joanna Moore, Simon Oakland co-star. Includes original theatrical trailer. 110 min.
12-1710 Was $19.99 ❏*$14.99*

Fun In Acapulco (1963)
After a big top accident leaves him with a fear of heights, trapeze performer Elvis Presley heads South of the Border and gets a job as a lifeguard/singer at an Acapulco resort. But will a rivalry with a cliff diver for the attentions of Ursula Andress force Elvis to confront his fears? "Viva el Amor," "Bossanova" and "No Room to Rhumba in a Sports Car" are among Presley's songs. 97 min.
04-1212 ❏*$14.99*

Roustabout (1964)
After he's run off the road and his motorcycle is smashed, Elvis Presley signs on as a worker with a travelling carnival run by Barbara Stanwyck and eventually becomes the show's singing star (performing "Poison Ivy League," "Carnival Time," "One-Track Heart" and more) in this song-filled drama that also stars Joan Freeman, Sue Ann Langdon. Look for Raquel Welch in her film debut. 101 min.
04-1217 ❏*$14.99*

Viva Las Vegas (1964)
In one of his biggest and best films, Elvis Presley is "just a devil with love to spare" as a race car driver looking to enter the Las Vegas Grand Prix and romancing sexy Ann-Margret. With Cesare Danova, William Demarest and the great Jack Carter as himself. Songs include "The Lady Loves Me," "What'd I Say" and the title tune. Includes original theatrical trailer. 86 min.
12-1110 Was $19.99 ❏*$14.99*

Kissin' Cousins (1964)
It's two...two...two Elvises in one movie! The King stars as both an Air Force officer and his cousin, a hillbilly whose family owns land that the government wants to use for a missile base. Wanna bet each Elvis gets a girl? Arthur O'Connell, Yvonne Craig also star. Songs include "Smokey Mountain Boy," "Tender Feeling." Includes original theatrical trailer. 95 min.
12-1848 ❏*$14.99*

Tickle Me (1965)
A light-hearted Elvis romp, with the handsome crooner playing a former rodeo star who sings on to work at a health ranch whose clientele includes bevies of beautiful girls. With Julie Adams, Jocelyn Lane. Songs include "If It Feels So Right" and "I'm Yours." 90 min.
04-1797 ❏*$14.99*

Harum Scarum (1965)
Elvis Presley stuff at its zaniest as pop idol Elvis finds himself kidnapped in a strange Middle East country with sheiks, sexy gals and songs. Fran Jeffries co-stars. "Golden Coins" and "Kismet" are among the tunes Presley croons. Includes original theatrical trailer. 95 min.
12-1377 Was $19.99 ❏*$14.99*

Girl Happy (1965)
It's musical fun under the sun at Spring Break in Ft. Lauderdale, as Elvis Presley lands his rock combo a gig in Florida...as long as he agrees to chaperone a mobster's coed daughter (Shelley Fabares). And when Fabares falls for Elvis, the fun really starts. This one features Presley performing "Spring Fever," "Startin' Tonight" and the classic "Do the Clam." With Harold J. Stone. Gary Crosby. 95 min.
12-1847 ❏*$14.99*

Paradise, Hawaiian Style (1966)
Back in the Aloha State once more, Elvis this time is an ex-airline pilot who starts a charter helicopter sightseeing service and finds himself coping with pretty tourists, FAA officals, and a chopper full of dogs! And remember, "Last one out of the water is a papaya picker!" Suzanna Leigh, James Shigeta co-star. Songs include "A Dog's Life," " "Sand Castles" and "Bill Bailey, Won't You Please Come Home?" 91 min.
04-1216 ❏*$14.99*

Frankie And Johnny (1966)
Elvis was her man, but he did her wrong, in this rollicking musical based on the timeless song and set on a 19th-century riverboat on the Mississippi. Donna Douglas co-stars as Presley's spurned lover, Frankie; with Harry Morgan, Nancy Kovack. Songs include "Everybody Come Aboard," "When the Saints Go Marching In" and the title tune. Includes original theatrical trailer. 87 min.
12-1709 Was $19.99 ❏*$14.99*

Spinout (1966)
With three women (a spoiled rich girl, a man-hungry author, and his band's drummer) out to snare him, racecar driver/singer Elvis Presley sure has his hands full in this one! With Shelley Fabares, Diane McBain, Carl Betz. Includes original theatrical trailer. 90 min.
12-1850 Was $19.99 ❏*$14.99*

Easy Come, Easy Go (1967)
When Navy underwater demolitions expert Elvis Presley finds gold in a sunken wreck during his final service dive, he comes back with an oddball crew to recover the treasure. Along with the high seas action, Elvis stops by a beatnik discotheque "at a freak-out that's out of sight!" and sings "Love Machine," "I'll Take Love" and the title tune. With Dodie Marshall, Pat Harrington. 95 min.
06-1015 *$14.99*

Double Trouble (1967)
The titular troubles that follow singer Elvis Presley around Europe in this breezy musical are a beautiful young heiress and some jewel thieves after both of them, but there's still plenty of time for him to do such songs as "Long-Legged Girl," "Could I Fall in Love?" and even "Old MacDonald"! With Annette Day, John Williams. Includes original theatrical trailer. 92 min.
12-1376 Was $19.99 *$14.99*

Clambake (1967)
Hey, Elvis, toss another clam in the pot! Here the King plays a bored Texas oil heir who switches places with a water-skiing instructor for some tuneful surfside action. With Shelley Fabares, Bill Bixby, Gary Merrill. Presley performs "The Girl I Never Loved," "Who Needs Money" and others. Includes original theatrical trailer. 97 min.
12-1635 Was $19.99 ❏*$14.99*

Speedway (1968)
Elvis Presley is fast in a car, with his lips, with his hips and on the guitar in this swingin' race car saga. He's romancing lovely I.R.S. agent Nancy Sinatra with "There Ain't No Nothin' Like a Song," "Let Yourself Go," "Your Time Hasn't Come" and others along the way. With Bill Bixby, Gale Gordon. Includes original theatrical trailer. 94 min.
12-1379 Was $19.99 ❏*$14.99*

Live A Little, Love A Little (1968)
Magazine photographer Elvis has to juggle two jobs (one for a stuffy, conservative publisher, the other with a "girlie" mag) but still finds time to belt out "Almost in Love," "Wonderful World" and more in this wild romp. Co-stars Michele Carey, Don Porter, Rudy Vallee. Includes original theatrical trailer. 89 min.
12-1849 Was $19.99 ❏*$14.99*

Stay Away, Joe (1968)
In a change-of-pace role, Elvis Presley plays a half-breed Indian trying to get government aid for his tribe's reservation. And he's a singing Indian, too (with such tunes as "Stay Away," "Lovely Mamie" and "All I Needed Was the Rain")! Burgess Meredith, Joan Blondell, Katy Jurado co-star. Includes original theatrical trailer. 101 min.
12-1851 Was $19.99 ❏*$14.99*

The Trouble With Girls (And How To Get Into It) (1969)
Offbeat Elvis Presley drama, with the King playing the manager of a touring Chautauqua company in the '20s, and the trouble that erupts when it arrives in a small town. With Marlyn Mason, Vincent Price, Dabney Coleman, Sheree North. Songs include "Clean Up Your Own Backyard" and "Swing Low Sweet Chariot." Includes original theatrical trailer. 97 min.
12-1852 Was $19.99 ❏*$14.99*

Charro! (1969)
Showing more smolder than hoochy-coochy, a brooding Elvis Presley stars as an ex-outlaw framed by his old gang for the theft of an antique cannon. Western drama, directed by "Gunsmoke" creator Charles Marquis Warren, also features Victor French and Lynn Kellogg. 98 min.
19-1661 *$14.99*

Elvis Meets Nixon (1997)
Ever wonder what events led to the famous picture of Elvis Presley shaking hands with President Nixon? This mock docudrama chronicles the wild 1970 weekend that culminated with a drugged-out Presley going to the White House, seeking to become a special federal drug agent, and Nixon seizing the photo op. Rick Peters and Bob Gunton play the respective title roles. 103 min.
82-5076 *$89.99*

Elvis: The Complete Story
Almost everything you ever wanted to know about Elvis is presented in this briskly paced documentary that covers his life, music career and movies though film clips, TV footage and interviews with some of his most prominent co-stars. Find out what made him tick, his devotion to his mother and the inspiration for his greatest hits. 120 min.
05-5086 *$19.99*

Elvis: All The King's Men: The King Collection
"The Memphis Mafia" were Elvis Presley's five closest friends and confidantes, and in this incredible five-part series they talk about the Elvis few knew with stunning revelations and amazing anecdotes. Volumes include "The Secret Life of Elvis," "Rocket Ride to Stardom," "Wild in Hollywood," "The King's Comes Back" and "Collapse of the Kingdom." This special set includes the bonus program "The Legend Lives On" and an audio-cassette of a secret phone conversation with Elvis. NOTE: Individual volumes available at $19.99 each.
50-5585 Save $20.00! *$79.99*

Elvis In Hollywood: The 50's
The early film career of Elvis Presley is covered in this fascinating program filled with film clips, home movies, interviews and documents made available through the Presley estate. See Elvis in such classics as "Love Me Tender," "Loving You," "Jailhouse Rock" and "King Creole." 65 min.
02-7917 *$19.99*

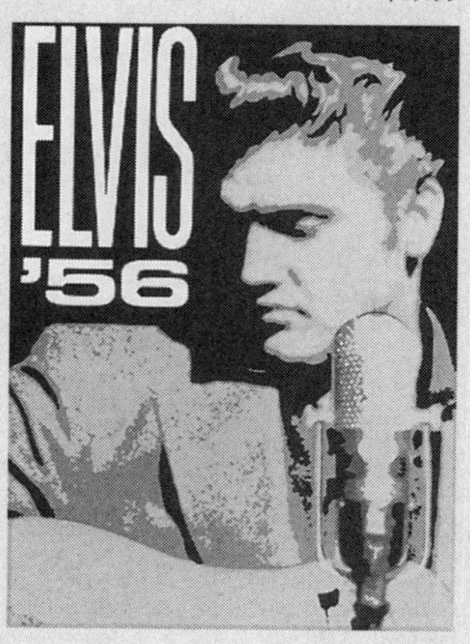

Elvis '56
In 1956, a 21-year-old singer named Elvis Presley was about to make the jump from local singer to a national celebrity. Levon Helm narrates this look at early Elvis, including rare concert footage, some of his first TV appearances, and never before shown backstage scenes. 61 min.
03-1582 *$19.99*

Rare Moments With The King
He's gone, but he's not forgotten, and this sampling of buried treasures featuring Elvis Presley will help keep the memory alive. Little-seen news footage, TV clips, comedy bits and more make this a must-have item. 60 min.
10-2122 *$12.99*

Elvis: Dead Or Alive?
The mysteries surrounding Elvis and his death are explored in this TV special hosted by Bill Bixby. A number of questions are probed, including: Why did Elvis cash in all his "paid-up" insurance policies before his death? Did organized crime set up Elvis in a $1 scam? And why were photos of the "death" scene and medical examiner's notes missing from files? 54 min.
10-2620 *$14.99*

Elvis In The Movies
This salute to the movies of Elvis Presley features trailers from all 33 films, including "Jailhouse Rock," "Love Me Tender," "Flaming Star," "Kid Galahad," "Kissin' Cousins," "Frankie and Johnny" and many more. 80 min.
10-2786 *$19.99*

Mondo Elvis
To these people, The King never died. Meet twin sisters who believe Elvis was their father, a woman whose husband divorced her because of her fanatical devotion to Elvis, and more Presley impersonators than should be gathered on one tape. A hilarious, fascinating look at the "outer fringes" of the Elvis cult. 30 min.
15-5024 *$14.99*

Why Elvis?
This documentary probes into the Elvis mythology, as nearly 100 people are interviewed, revealing stories about "The King" that have never left Memphis. Elvis' fame, influence and success are among the topics touched upon in this insightful program. 76 min.
22-1374 *$19.99*

Elvis: The Echo Will Never Die
For millions of his fans, Elvis Presley lives on, and this special look at his life and music was made for them. Join guests B.B. King, Tom Jones, Sammy Davis, Jr. and deejay Casey Kasem for interviews, rare home footage, concert clips and more. 50 min.
50-6192 *$19.99*

Elvis: King Of Entertainment
Some of the greatest moments of Elvis Presley's career have been preserved in this program. Follow the rise of Elvis from Tupelo to stardom with stops in between to perform "Heartbreak Hotel" on the Dorsey Brothers "Stage Show"; watch him joke around with Milton Berle and Steve Allen and make his historic appearances on "The Ed Sullivan Show"; and more. 93 min.
10-2785 *$19.99*

This Is Elvis
Documentary on "The King of Rock and Roll" featuring home movies, rare concert footage and newsreels. Told in a unique fashion by Elvis himself (through use of an impressionist), the film traces his life from boyhood to his sad, untimely death. Uncut, 144-minute version.
19-1212 Was $19.99 *$14.99*

Elvis: The Great Performances
Who better than Priscilla Presley to host this music-filled salute to the man who put rock and roll on the map? Loaded with rare concert clips, private home movies and family album photos, the program offers a glimpse at the public and personal sides of Elvis. "My Happiness," "Heartbreak Hotel," "Hound Dog," "Jailhouse Rock," "All Shook Up," "If I Can Dream" and "Always on My Mind" are among the songs featured. 90 min.
50-2016 *$19.99*

Elvis: 1st Filmed Performance
Lost for nearly 40 years, this historic film features the future king, Elvis Presley, in what is believed to be his first recorded performance. This collector's must-have offers the young Elvis performing in the small town of Sheldon, Texas, on August 7, 1955 and was filmed by Lois and Jim Robertson. The color footage runs 1:40 and is soundless. 30 min.
76-7432 *$24.99*

Elvis: The Lost Performances
An amazing find, these never-before-seen outtakes from the early '70s concert films "Elvis: That's The Way It Is" and "Elvis on Tour" feature the King singing "Hound Dog," "Heartbreak Hotel," "Teddy Bear," "All Shook Up," and more. A superb program, ideal for Presley collectors! 60 min.
12-2446 *$14.99*

Elvis '68 Comeback Special
Big classy TV extravaganza with lots of Elvis, taped with a live audience. His famous tunes and gospel numbers include "Heartbreak Hotel," "Hound Dog," "All Shook Up," "Jailhouse Rock," "Love Me Tender," "Guitar Man," "Falling in Love" and many more. 76 min.
03-1333 *$19.99*

Elvis: One Night With You (1968)
Never-before-seen footage of the King in an intimate concert setting highlights this collection of scenes that were deleted from his 1968 "Comeback" TV special. Elvis sings, reminisces and jokes with his audience in a style uniquely his. 53 min.
03-1453 *$19.99*

Elvis: Aloha From Hawaii (1972)
The classic TV special with Elvis in concert live in Honolulu. In his white sequined suit, festooned with leis from the audience, Elvis shows his stuff with 25 tunes, including "Hound Dog," "Burning Love," "Can't Help Falling in Love," "Suspicious Minds" and, of course, "Blue Hawaii." Special video edition includes the never-before-available song "No More." 72 min.
03-1349 *$19.99*

Elvis On Tour (1972)
Whether or not you ever had the chance to see "The King" live, this film chronicle of Elvis's 1971 North American tour gets you so close you'll reach out for one of his scarves. Along with rare backstage footage, witness Presley perform 29 tunes, including "Suspicious Minds," "Burning Love," "C.C. Rider," "That's All Right Mama" and more. Includes original theatrical trailer. 92 min.
12-1222 Was $19.99 ❑*$14.99*

Elvis: The Concert Collection
Catch "The King" in three classic concert performances—"68 Comeback Special," "Aloha from Hawaii" and "One Night with You"—in one lip-twitchin' boxed set.
02-8051 Save $10.00! *$49.99*

He Touched Me: The Gospel Music Of Elvis Presley, Vol. 1
Did you know the three Grammys Elvis won in his lifetime were all for "sacred/inspirational music"? Some of the King's greatest gospel songs, including "How Great Thou Art," "Peace in the Valley," "I Believe in the Man in the Sky," "His Hand in Mine," "Amazing Grace" and many more, are featured in this special program that also includes vintage performance footage and interviews with some of Elvis' friends. Sander Vanocur narrates.
44-4179 *$19.99*

He Touched Me: The Gospel Music Of Elvis Presley, Vol. 2
Get a further look at the King's spiritual side with this second program spotlighting Elvis' gospel recordings. Following Presley from his Vegas days to his death in 1977, the video features long-unseen film footage, reminiscences by colleagues and friends, and such songs as "I'm Saved," "Bosom of Abraham," "Put Your Hand in the Hand," "In the Ghetto" and many more. 90 min.
44-4182 *$19.99*

Elvis Gift Set
"Elvis is everywhere," especially in this limited-edition collection that includes "Blue Hawaii," "Fun in Acapulco," "G.I. Blues," "King Creole" and "Paradise, Hawaiian Style."
06-2646 Save $15.00! *$59.99*

The Golden Disc (1958)
Early British rock-and-roll musical centers on two youngsters who open a coffee bar and recording company. Their search for a singing star becomes unnecessary when they realize that their janitor has talent, but after the company begins cranking out the hits, another enterprise attempts a takeover. Lee Patterson, Mary Steele star with appearances from Sonny Stewart's Skittle Kings, the Teddy Kennedy Group and Don Rendell's Six. AKA: "The In-Between Age."
09-5086 *$19.99*

Top Banana (1954)
The cameras rolled in New York's famed Winter Garden Theatre for this film version of the hit Broadway musical comedy. Phil Silvers shines as a TV comic forced to add a "love interest" couple to his variety show who falls for his new female co-star. Along with classic vaudeville skits and jokes, there's such songs as "My Home Is in My Shoes," "A Word a Day" and "If You Want to Be a Top Banana." Rose Marie, Jack Albertson, Judy Lynn co-star. 84 min.
12-3026 ❑*$19.99*

Rock You Sinners (1957)
Early British rock 'n' roll musical about a hip disc jockey who gets his own TV show and is catapulted to stardom. Philip Gilbert stars; music by Tony Crombie and His Rockets, Rory Blackwell and The Blackjacks, others. 59 min.
09-1196 Was $24.99 *$19.99*

Expresso Bongo (1959)
Fast-talking promoter Laurence Harvey thinks he's found the next teen singing sensation when he spies bongo-playing troubadour Cliff Richard in a Soho coffeehouse. Join them on the rocky road to stardom in this classic British rock-and-roll musical that also stars Sylvia Sims, Yolonde Dolan. Songs include "Bongo Blues," "Love," "A Voice in the Wilderness." 111 min.
53-9188 Letterboxed *$24.99*

Gigi (1958)
Winner of nine Oscars, including Best Picture, this is the delightful story of an aspiring chanteuse in 1900s Paris. Leslie Caron, Maurice Chevalier star. "Thank Heaven for Little Girls" and "I Remember It Well" are featured on the Lerner/Loewe score. 116 min.
12-1045 Was $19.99 *$14.99*

Gigi (Letterboxed Version)
Also available in a theatrical, widescreen format.
12-2851 Was $19.99 *$14.99*

Seven Brides For Seven Brothers (1954)
One of MGM's most exciting musical-comedies is a tale of seven backwoods brothers and their quest of seven homespun beauties. Many classic songs, dance sequences, sets, color...it's wonderful! Howard Keel, Jane Powell star. Songs include "When You're in Love," "Sobbin' Women" and "Spring, Spring, Spring." 103 min.
12-1090 Was $19.99 *$14.99*

Seven Brides For Seven Brothers (Letterboxed Version)
Also available in a theatrical, widescreen format.
12-3207 *$14.99*

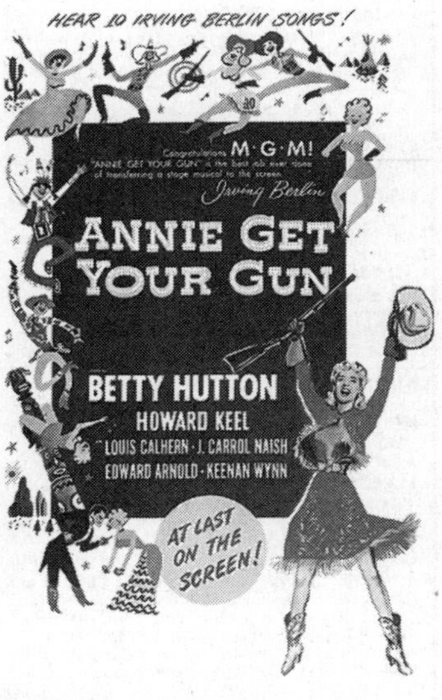

HEAR 10 IRVING BERLIN SONGS!
M·G·M!
ANNIE GET YOUR GUN
BETTY HUTTON
HOWARD KEEL
LOUIS CALHERN · J. CARROL NAISH
EDWARD ARNOLD · KEENAN WYNN
AT LAST ON THE SCREEN!

Annie Get Your Gun (1950)
One of the most-requested titles in Movies Unlimited history, this fun-filled film version of the Irving Berlin musical stars Betty Hutton (who replaced Judy Garland shortly after shooting began) as legendary Wild West sharpshooter Annie Oakley, who falls for fellow marksman Howard Keel. With Louis Calhern as Buffalo Bill Cody, and J. Carrol Naish as Sitting Bull; songs include "Anything You Can Do," "Doin' What Comes Natur'lly" and "There's No Business Like Show Business." Special 50th Anniversary Edition includes the theatrical trailer, an introduction by Keel, and rare musical outtakes with Garland. 107 min.
19-2993 ❑*$19.99*

Esther Williams

Bathing Beauty (1944)
In her first leading role for MGM, Esther Williams swims her way to stardom as an aquatic instructor at a girls' school who is wooed by songwriter Red Skelton. Breezy musical comedy also stars Basil Rathbone, Harry James and Xavier Cugat and their orchestras. Songs include "Tico-Tico," "I Cried for You," "Bim, Bam, Boom." 101 min.
12-2196 *$19.99*

The Thrill Of A Romance (1945)
Feisty and (for its time) spicy musical farce stars Esther Williams as an ever-swimming newlywed who does a backstroke over Army Air Corps hero Van Johnson, whom she meets at a mountain lodge while her hubby is summoned to Washington on business. With Henry Travers, Lauritz Melchior, and Xavier Cugat and Tommy Dorsey and their orchestras; songs include "Lonely Night," "I Should Care." 105 min.
12-2433 *$19.99*

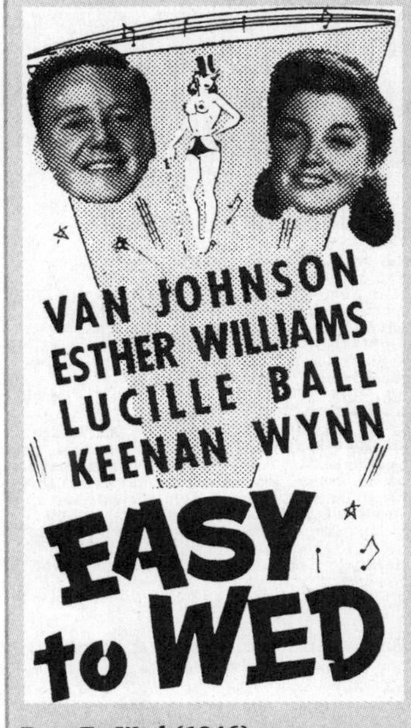

VAN JOHNSON
ESTHER WILLIAMS
LUCILLE BALL
KEENAN WYNN
EASY to WED

Easy To Wed (1946)
The screwball favorite "Libeled Lady" received a musical revamping from MGM, with Esther Williams playing the socialite who sues newspaperman Van Johnson after a less-than-flattering article is run about her. Lucille Ball and Keenan Wynn also star; songs include "Come Closer to Me," "Continental Polka" and (no kidding!) "It Shouldn't Happen to a Duck." 111 min.
12-3044 ❑*$19.99*

This Time For Keeps (1947)
Splashy Esther Williams tuner with the gal in the bathing suit as the star of Mackinac Island's "Aquacaper" show and longed for by the singing son of an opera star. Jimmy Durante does "Inky Dinka Do" and Lauritz Melchior performs "You Are So Easy to Love" and "La Donna E Mobile." Xavier Cugat and Dame May Whitty also appear. 105 min.
12-2791 *$19.99*

On An Island With You (1948)
Top-notch MGM musical fantasia with Esther Williams as a Hollywood star on location in Hawaii who is desired by swabby Peter Lawford. Ricardo Montalban, Jimmy Durante, Cyd Charisse and Xavier Cugat and his Orchestra also star; songs include "If I Were You," "Dog Song" and "Wedding Samba." 76 min.
12-2429 *$19.99*

Neptune's Daughter (1949)
Esther Williams supplies the aquatic splendor, Ricardo Montalban the Latin charm, and Red Skelton and Betty Garrett the laughs in this breezy MGM songfest about bathing suit designer Williams fending off the advances of playboy Montalban. Tunes include "My Heart Beats Faster," "Baby, It's Cold Outside"; with Keenan Wynn, Mel Blanc, and Xavier Cugat. 92 min.
12-1875 *$19.99*

Pagan Love Song (1950)
Lively musical romance with Howard Keel as a teacher in Tahiti who falls for American Esther Williams, whom he believes to be an island native. Rita Moreno co-stars in this MGM production showcasing dazzling swimming choreography and songs like "Singing in the Sun," "Tahiti" and "The House of the Singing Bamboo." 76 min.
12-2430 *$19.99*

Texas Carnival (1951)
Carnival dunk tank performers Esther Williams and Red Skelton get into trouble at a Texas resort when Red poses as a millionaire oil tycoon. Howard Keel, Ann Miller, Keenan Wynn and Glenn Strange co-star; songs include "It's Dynamite," "Young Folks Should Get Married" and "Deep in the Heart of Texas." 105 min.
12-2432 *$19.99*

Million Dollar Mermaid (1952)
Esther Williams splashes and shines in this highly Hollywoodized but wholly enjoyable biography of 1890s swimming sensation Annette Kellerman. Fine support from Victor Mature, Walter Pidgeon, Jesse White, plus Busby Berkeley's eye-popping, show-stopping water carnival. 115 min.
12-1921 Was $29.99 *$19.99*

Dangerous When Wet (1953)
Small-town girl Esther Williams tries to become famous by swimming the English Channel. Real-life husband Fernando Lamas is her love interest, and the supporting cast (Jack Carson, Charlotte Greenwood, Tom and Jerry) is top-notch in this song-filled, splashy gem. 95 min.
12-1527 Was $19.99 *$14.99*

Easy To Love (1953)
Spectacular choreography from Busby Berkeley highlights this breezy musical with Esther Williams as a secretary who romances other guys to get the attention of boss Van Johnson. See Esther swim with a chimp and water-ski with a group of pals in incredibly staged sequences; with Tony Martin, John Bromfield; songs include "Easy to Love," "Coquette," "Didja Ever." 96 min.
12-2427 *$19.99*

Jupiter's Darling (1955)
History is set to music, MGM-style, with Esther Williams in a waterproof toga as Amytis, who tries to stop Hannibal (Howard Keel) before he makes the trek through the Alps to take Rome. Marge and Gower Champion, George Sanders, William Demarest co-star; songs include "I Have a Dream" and "If This Be Slav'ry." 96 min.
12-2428 *$19.99*

Please see our index for these other Esther Williams titles: *Andy Hardy's Double Life • A Guy Named Joe • Take Me Out To The Ball Game • Ziegfeld Follies*

It's A Wonderful World (1956)
Two struggling British songwriters concoct an idea to reverse a popular song: claim it was written by an unknown foreign composer and cash in on its success. The plan works until... Terence Morgan, George Cole, Kathleen Harrison and Ted Heath and His Music are featured. Songs include "When You Came Along," "A Few Kisses Ago" and "The Hawaiian War Chant." 89 min.
08-1758 *$14.99*

Jamboree (1957)
"Boy pop singer meets girl pop singer" is the basic plot for this early rock 'n' roll musical, but the main reasons to watch are vintage performances by Fats Domino ("Wait and See"), Jerry Lee Lewis ("Great Balls of Fire"), Carl Perkins ("Glad All Over"), Philly's own Charlie Gracie and even Count Basie and Slim Whitman! Bob Pastine and Kay Medford (whose singing voice was dubbed by Connie Francis) star. AKA: "Disc Jockey Jamboree." 86 min.
19-2516 ❑*$14.99*

Happy Go Lovely (1951)
A brisk and breezy musical comedy about an American theater producer in Edinburgh who hires a young chorus girl in hope that her millionaire boyfriend may lay out the bucks. Stars David Niven, Cesar Romero and Vera-Ellen. Restored, uncut version; 98 min.
10-1201 *$19.99*

New Faces (1954)
Film version of the lively Broadway musical comedy revue features dazzling performances by Eartha Kitt (whose songs include "C'est Si Bon") and slapstick with Paul Lynde, Ronny Graham and Alice Ghostley (comedy routines written by Mel Brooks). 98 min.
10-1024 *$19.99*

New Faces (Letterboxed Version)
Also available in a theatrical, widescreen format.
10-1722 *$14.99*

Varieties On Parade (1952)
The spirit of vaudeville is captured in this film version of a vaudeville show featuring a wide range of performers including Jackie Coogan, Tom Neal, Eddie Dean, Eddie Garr and Ed Wood regular Lyle Talbot. 60 min.
10-9125 Was $19.99 *$14.99*

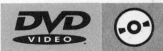

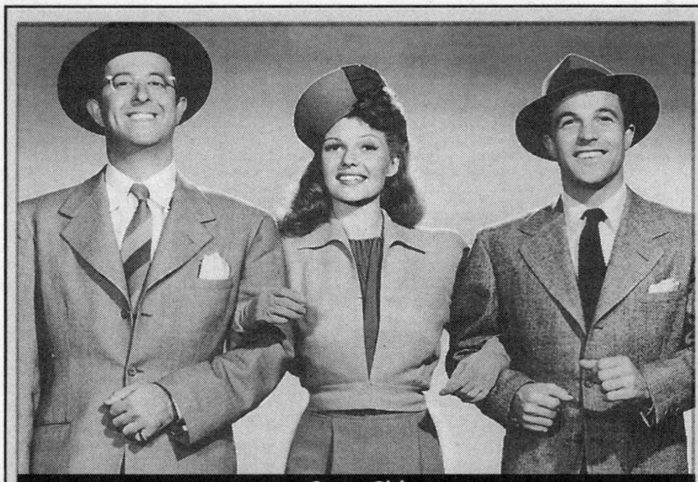

Cover Girl

Gene Kelly

Thousands Cheer (1943)
An Army base variety show is the setting for this high-energy musical, with Gene Kelly as a former trapeze artist who's trying to get out of the army and Kathryn Grayson the colonel's daughter he's fallen head over heels for. MGM's star-filled contribution to the war effort co-stars Mary Astor, John Boles, Lionel Barrymore, Mickey Rooney, Judy Garland, Red Skelton, Eleanor Powell, Lucille Ball, many more. Songs include "Honeysuckle Rose," "In a Little Spanish Town," "Yankee Doodle" and "Let Me Call You Sweetheart." 126 min.
12-1586 Was $29.99 ***$19.99***

DuBarry Was A Lady (1943)
There's fun and frolicking in 17th-century France when Red Skelton finds himself sent back in time to the regal court of Madame DuBarry. Lavish musical comedy also stars Gene Kelly, Lucille Ball, Zero Mostel and Virginia O'Brien; score includes Cole Porter's "Friendship." 101 min.
12-1598 Was $29.99 ***$19.99***

Anchors Aweigh (1945)
In their first film together, Gene Kelly and Frank Sinatra are two sailors who use their leave time to pursue Kathryn Grayson, entertain a young boy, and dance, dance, dance... Highlights include Sinatra singing "I Fall in Love Too Easily" and Kelly's Mexican hat dance and duet with Jerry the mouse. 140 min.
12-1686 Was $19.99 ***$14.99***

Living In A Big Way (1947)
Army lieutenant Gene Kelly returns from overseas to find that disheartened, spoiled wife Marie MacDonald wants a divorce. The two try to work things out with help from her parents, who realize Gene is the right fellow for their daughter. This MGM production boasts dazzling choreography and such songs as "It Had to Be You" and "Fido and Me." With Charles Winninger, Phyllis Thaxter. 104 min.
12-2787 ***$19.99***

On The Town (1949)
The wacky musical-comedy exploits of a trio of sailors on 24-hour leave in New York City, as they search for fun and romance. Gene Kelly, Frank Sinatra, Jules Munshin, Ann Miller, Vera-Ellen and Betty Garrett paint the Big Apple even redder while singing "New York, New York," "Come Up to My Place," "You're Awful" and more. 98 min.
12-1057 Was $19.99 ***$14.99***

Take Me Out To The Ball Game (1949)
Fast and fun turn-of-the-century musical teams Frank Sinatra and Gene Kelly as baseball players trying to deal with their team's new female owner (Esther Williams). The score incudes "O'Brien to Ryan to Goldberg"; Betty Garrett, Edward Arnold, Jules Munshin co-star under Busby Berkeley's direction. 93 min.
12-1715 Was $19.99 ***$14.99***

An American In Paris (1951)
The dancing of Gene Kelly and Leslie Caron, a classic score by George Gershwin and the romantic settings of the City of Lights make for a timeless musical delight. Winner of six Academy Awards, including Best Picture. Songs include "Embraceable You," "Nice Work If You Can Get It" and "Our Love Is Here to Stay." 113 min.
12-1001 Was $19.99 ❑***$14.99***

Singin' In The Rain (1952)
Gene Kelly, Debbie Reynolds and Donald O'Connor star in what is probably the most famous and best-loved of all screen musicals. Set in Hollywood at the end of the silent era, the film features such classic numbers as "Make 'Em Laugh," "Broadway Ballet," "You Were Meant for Me," and the title tune. Co-directed by Kelly and Stanley Donen. Also includes the original theatrical trailer. 103 min.
12-2388 Was $19.99 ***$14.99***

Brigadoon (1954)
New Yorkers Gene Kelly and Van Johnson stumble upon a magical Scottish village which comes alive every 100 years, where Kelly falls in love with enchantress Cyd Charisse and must decide to stay or return to his humdrum life. The classic Lerner and Loewe score includes "From This Day On," "I'll Go Home with Bonnie Jean," "The Heather on the Hill." 108 min.
12-1052 Was $19.99 ***$14.99***

Brigadoon (Letterboxed Version)
Also available in a theatrical, widescreen format.
12-3206 ***$14.99***

It's Always Fair Weather (1955)
Co-directors Gene Kelly and Stanley Donen ("Singin' in the Rain," "On the Town") reteam for this exuberant, top-notch musical. Three GI buddies (Kelly, Dan Dailey and Michael Kidd) meet 10 years after the war's end and discover they no longer have anything in common. 102 min.
12-1665 Was $29.99 ***$19.99***

Invitation To The Dance (1956)
A trio of stories told entirely in music and dance, directed and choreographed by star Gene Kelly. Includes "Circus," the story of a mime clown; "Ring Around the Rosey," about a ubiquitous bracelet; and "Sinbad, the Sailor," a masterful blend of live-action and animation. Co-stars Claire Sombert, Carol Haney and Igor Youskevitch. 95 min.
12-1245 Was $59.99 ***$19.99***

Les Girls (1957)
Lively Cole Porter songs highlight this musical comedy. Gene Kelly's a dancer touring Europe who romances each of the beautiful members of his troupe (Taina Elg, Mitzi Gaynor, Kay Kendall), which leads to funny complications and a hilarious courtroom climax. Songs include "Les Girls," "Flower Song," "Ladies in Waiting," and more. 114 min.
12-1531 Was $29.99 ***$19.99***

Xanadu (1980)
Space age look at music of today with Olivia Newton-John and Gene Kelly. Music by Electric Light Orchestra. Roller skating, dancing and fun for the whole family in this updating of 1947's "Down to Earth." 96 min.
07-1047 Was $79.99 ***$14.99***

Please see our index for these other Gene Kelly titles: *Cover Girl • For Me And My Gal • 40 Carats • Inherit The Wind • Let's Make Love • Love Is Better Than Ever • Marjorie Morningstar • North And South • Summer Stock • The Three Musketeers • Viva Knievel • Words And Music • Xanadu The Young Girls Of Rochefort • Ziegfeld Follies*

I Love Melvin (1953)
Light and funny MGM musical stars Donald O'Connor as a photographer's assistant who, in order to impress chorine Debbie Reynolds, tells her he can get her on the cover of Look magazine, then must make good on his promise. With Una Merkel, Jim Backus, Les Tremayne; songs include "A Lady Loves," "We Have Never Met as of Yet," "And There You Are." 76 min.
12-2198 ***$19.99***

Kismet (1955)
A glorious tune-filled story of a vagabond poet, his daughter and the colorful city of ancient Baghdad, starring Howard Keel, Ann Blyth and Sebastian Cabot. Score includes "Stranger In Paradise." 113 min.
12-1205 ***$19.99***

Show Boat (1951)
Spectacular MGM rendition of the beloved Hammerstein-Kern tale of show folk, gamblers and steamboats along the old Mississippi. The cast includes Howard Keel, Ava Gardner, Kathryn Grayson and Joe E. Brown as Captain Andy, with songs like "Where's the Mate for Me?," "Can't Help Lovin' that Man" and "Ol' Man River." 107 min.
12-1223 Was $19.99 ***$14.99***

Lili (1953)
Leslie Caron is a 16-year-old French waif who joins a travelling carnival and falls for callous magician Jean-Pierre Aumont. Her only friends are puppeteer Mel Ferrer's figures, who come to life to sing to her. Charming fantasy/musical features an Oscar-winning score that includes "Hi-Lili-Hi-Lo"; with Zsa Zsa Gabor, Kurt Kasznar. 81 min.
12-1298 Was $59.99 ❑***$19.99***

Lovely To Look At (1952)
The 1935 Kern-Harbach musical "Roberta" gets a splashy updating in this tale of three would-be Broadway producers (Red Skelton, Howard Keel, Gower Champion) who travel to Paris to run a dress salon. Ann Miller, Kathryn Grayson, Marge Champion and Zsa Zsa Gabor supply the feminine charms, and the songs include "Smoke Gets in Your Eyes," "I Won't Dance" and the title tune. 105 min.
12-2200 ***$19.99***

Two Weeks With Love (1950)
A bubbly musical-comedy starring Jane Powell and Debbie Reynolds as sisters who head to the Catskills with their family on vacation and find romance while singing and dancing to Busby Berkeley's elaborate choreography. Ricardo Montalban, Louis Calhern and Ann Harding co-star; songs include "Aba Daba Honeymoon." 92 min.
12-2118 ***$19.99***

The Glass Slipper (1955)
Dazzling ballet sequences and a haunting song score highlight this musical retelling of the "Cinderella" fable. Leslie Caron stars as poor Cinderella and Michael Wilding is her handsome prince. With Estelle Winwood, Keenan Wynn, Elsa Lanchester. 94 min.
12-2177 ***$19.99***

Kiss Me Kate (1953)
Cole Porter's musical delight stars Howard Keel and Kathryn Grayson as a husband-wife acting team whose latest play, "Taming of the Shrew," is interfering with their off-stage lives. The supporting cast includes Ann Miller, Keenan Wynn, Bobby Van and James Whitmore, and songs include "So In Love," "Brush Up Your Shakespeare" and "Wunderbar." 109 min.
12-1530 Was $19.99 ***$14.99***

Hit The Deck (1955)
Sailors Tony Martin, Vic Damone and Russ Tamblyn use their leave in San Francisco for sightseeing, family visits, romance and music, music, music. Splashy MGM musical co-stars Debbie Reynolds, Jane Powell, Ann Miller, Walter Pidgeon. Vincent Youmans score includes "More Than You Know," "A Kiss or Two," "Sometimes I'm Happy," "Ciribiribee." 112 min.
12-1874 ***$19.99***

Small Town Girl (1953)
Big city playboy Farley Granger runs afoul of the law after speeding through a sleepy hamlet, and is released into the custody of judge's daughter Jane Powell. Frothy MGM musical comedy also stars Ann Miller, Bobby Van, Nat King Cole; songs include "Take Me to Broadway," "I've Gotta Hear That Beat" (with Miller dancing around a disembodied orchestra). 93 min.
12-2017 ***$19.99***

Rodgers & Hammerstein

State Fair (1945)
The only original film score by Rodgers and Hammerstein sparks this lavish musical adaptation of the beloved tale of a family's adventures during their annual trip to the fair. Stars Jeanne Crain, Dana Andrews, Vivian Blaine, Dick Haimes and Charles Winninger. Songs include "Isn't It Kinda Fun!," "All I Owe Iowa," and the Oscar-winning "It Might as Well Be Spring." 100 min.
04-2352 Was $19.99 ***$14.99***

Oklahoma! (1955)
Rodgers and Hammerstein's fanciful Broadway ground-breaker stars Gordon MacRae and a debuting Shirley Jones as the cowhand and the country girl discovering love together. The memorable score includes "Oh What a Beautiful Morning" and "People Will Say We're in Love"; with Rod Steiger, Gloria Grahame and Eddie Albert. 143 min.
04-1571 Was $19.99 ❑***$14.99***

Oklahoma! (Letterboxed Version)
Also available in a theatrical, widescreen format.
04-3793 ***$19.99***

The King And I (1956)
East meets West with delightful results in this famed Rodgers and Hammerstein musical. Yul Brynner is the 19th-century Siamese monarch who hires English governess Deborah Kerr to teach his wives and children and winds up getting an education of his own. Features such classic songs as "Getting to Know You," "Hello Young Lovers" and "Shall We Dance." 133 min.
04-1083 Was $19.99 ❑***$14.99***

The King And I (Letterboxed Version)
Also available in a theatrical, widescreen format.
04-3791 ***$19.99***

Carousel (1956)
A haunting musical classic boasting a Rodgers and Hammerstein score that includes "If I Loved You," "What's the Use of Wonderin'" and "You'll Never Walk Alone." Gordon MacRae plays the carnival barker who returns from the dead to help his teenage daughter. Shirley Jones and Cameron Mitchell also star. 128 min.
04-2341 Was $19.99 ❑***$14.99***

Carousel (Letterboxed Version)
Also available in a theatrical, widescreen format.
04-3792 ***$19.99***

South Pacific (1958)
Popular Rodgers and Hammerstein musical about life on a lonely Pacific island post in World War II. Rossano Brazzi, Mitzi Gaynor and Ray Walston star. Great soundtrack includes "There's Nothing Like a Dame," "Some Enchanted Evening," "Happy Talk" and more; based on James Michener's "Tales of the South Pacific." 150 min.
04-1586 Was $19.99 ***$14.99***

South Pacific (Letterboxed Version)
Also available in a theatrical, widescreen format.
04-3794 ***$19.99***

Flower Drum Song (1961)
Rodgers and Hammerstein provide an unforgettable, dance-filled musical comedy set in San Francisco's Chinatown. A nightclub owner (Jack Soo) tries to cancel his arranged marriage to a girl from Hong Kong (Miyoshi Umeki) so he can woo a sexy saloon singer (Nancy Kwan). Songs include "I Enjoy Being a Girl," "Chop Suey" and "Don't Marry Me." 133 min.
07-1422 ***$19.99***

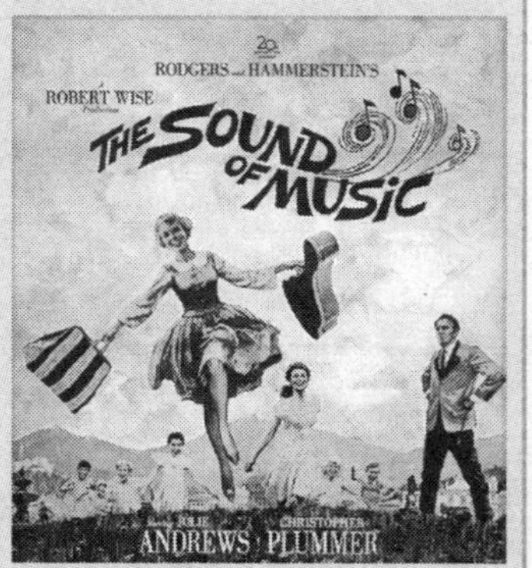

The Sound Of Music (1965)
One of the most popular film musicals of all time, the Rodgers and Hammerstein classic stars Julie Andrews as a novitiate who becomes governess to a large family in 1930s Austria and charms both her charges and their father (Christopher Plummer). Winner of five Oscars, including Best Picture; with Eleanor Parker, Richard Hadyn. Songs include "Do Re Mi," "My Favorite Things" and the title tune. 173 min.
04-1149 Was $24.99 ***$14.99***

The Rodgers & Hammerstein Collection
Oh, what a beautiful gift set...six Rodgers and Hammerstein film classics—"Carousel," "The King and I," "Oklahoma!," "The Sound of Music," "South Pacific" and "State Fair"—in one boxed collection.
04-3968 Save $25.00! ***$64.99***

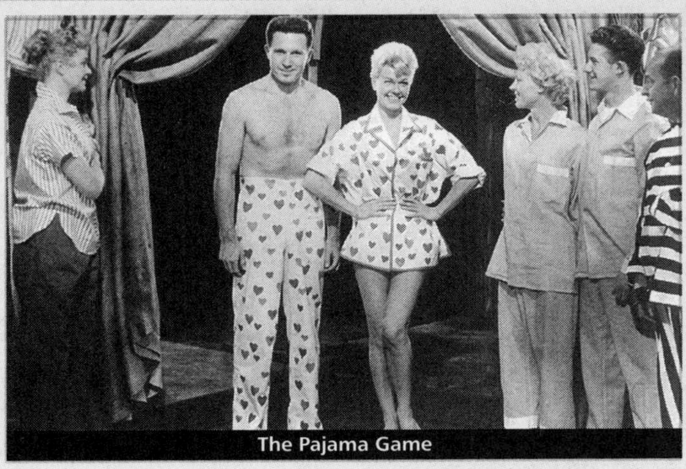

The Pajama Game

Doris Day

Romance On The High Seas (1948)
Lively romance and music can be found in this farce about adultery that marked Doris Day's screen debut. Wife Janis Paige suspects husband Don DeFore is cheating on her, and together they wind up on a Caribbean cruise where Day and Jack Carson get in the middle of the jealous couple's spying. Oscar Levant co-stars; songs include "Put 'em in a Box," "It's Magic"; choreography by Busby Berkeley. 99 min.
12-2246 *$29.99*

It's A Great Feeling (1949)
The stars are out in this musical comedy set on the Warner Bros. lot in Hollywood. Dennis Morgan and Jack Carson (as "themselves") play actors whose clashing egos result in funny feuding and hilarious double-crossing, and Doris Day is the waitress whom each man promises to make a star. Cameos include Gary Cooper, Joan Crawford, Edward G. Robinson. Score by Jules Styne and Sammy Cahn includes "Give Me a Song With a Beautiful Melody," "At the Cafe Rendezvous," and the title tune. 85 min.
12-2243 *$29.99*

My Dream Is Yours (1949)
Breezy musical comedy starring Doris Day as a young singer who wants to be a radio star and Jack Carson as a talent scout who wants to hel her make it in the business. There's supporting turns by Adolphe Menjou, Eve Arden and Franklin Pangborn; a dream sequence boasting Bugs Bunny and Tweety Pie; and songs like "My Dream Is Yours" and "Some Like You." 101 min.
12-2244 *$29.99*

Tea For Two (1950)
Musical comedy based on "No, No, Nanette" stars Doris Day as a would-be stage singer who, in order to win money for a Broadway play, must say "no" to every question asked her for 24 hours. Gordon MacRae, Gene Nelson, Eve Arden and Billy De Wolfe also star; features songs like "I Know That You Know," "I Want to Be Happy," "I Only Have Eyes for You" and "Oh Me, Oh My." 98 min.
19-1920 Was $29.99 *$19.99*

Lullaby Of Broadway (1951)
Stage singer Doris Day arrives in New York from London to visit her one-time star mother (Gladys George), unaware that her career has hit the skids thanks to alcoholism. A wealthy man and his valet attempt to keep the truth from her in this charming musical laced with comedy and pathos. Gene Nelson, S.Z. Sakall, Billy De Wolfe also star; songs include "Just One of Those Things," "Zing! Went the Strings of My Heart" and the title tune. 92 min.
19-1919 Was $29.99 *$19.99*

I'll See You In My Dreams (1951)
A music-filled biography of songwriter Gus Kahn (Danny Thomas), chronicling his early career in Chicago, his success with Ziegfeld in New York, his problems during the Depression era and his relationship with wife Grace LeBoy (Doris Day). Songs include "It Had to Be You," "Love Me or Leave Me," "Ain't We Got Fun," "I Never Knew" and more. With Frank Lovejoy. 110 min.
19-2060 Was $59.99 *$19.99*

On Moonlight Bay (1951)
Lively musical-comedy starring Doris Day as a tomboy in a small Indiana town before World War I who falls for college student Gordon MacRae, much to the dismay of her banker father. Partially based on Boothe Tarkington's "Penrod" stories, the film also stars Leon Ames, Rosemary DeCamp and Billy Gray; songs include the title tune, "Til We Meet Again," "Pack Up Your Troubles in Your Old Kit Bag." 95 min.
19-2061 Was $59.99 *$19.99*

By The Light Of The Silvery Moon (1953)
A spirited sequel to "On Moonlight Bay" starring Doris Day as a woman who meets all sorts of funny obstacles while awaiting her wedding day with World War I veteran Gordon MacRae. Songs include the title tune, "I'll Forget You" and "Ain't We Got Fun." With Leon Ames, Rosemary DeCamp, Mary Wickes and Merv Griffin. 101 min.
19-2059 Was $59.99 *$19.99*

Calamity Jane (1953)
Doris Day shines as the Old West's sassy female sharpshooter in a rip-roarin' musical comedy about her travels to Chicago to bring back a famed opera singer to save her town's dance hall, but winds up returning with her maid. Also stars Howard Keel, Allyn Ann McLerie, Philip Carey and Dick Wesson. Songs include the Oscar-winning "Secret Love," and more. 101 min.
19-1560 Was $19.99 *$14.99*

April In Paris (1953)
Doris Day is the perky chorus girl mistakenly sent to a Paris arts festival who finds love on an ocean liner with milquetoast diplomat Ray Bolger. Dancing, singing and sparkling romance ensue, with songs like "It Must Be Good," "That's What Makes Paree" and "The Place You Hold in My Heart." With Eve Miller, Claude Dauphin. 101 min.
19-1917 Was $19.99 *$14.99*

Lucky Me (1954)
A group of out-of-work entertainers find themselves relegated to kitchen work at a Miami hotel, but spunky Doris Day teams up with songwriter Robert Cummings to convince an oil tycoon to sponsor Cummings' new show. There's just one obstacle: the oilman's spoiled daughter keeps getting in the way. Breezy musical also stars Phil Silvers, Eddie Foy, Jr., Nancy Walker. 99 min.
19-1918 Was $29.99 *$19.99*

Young At Heart: 40th Anniversary Edition (1954)
Great musical/drama, based on the 1938 film "Four Daughters," with Frank Sinatra as a musician who comes to a small town to work with composer Gig Young and winds up stealing fiancée Doris Day from him. Top-notch score includes "Someone to Watch Over Me" and the title tune. With Dorothy Malone, Ethel Barrymore. This anniversary edition includes the film's original trailer and a reproduction of the theatrical poster. 117 min.
63-1730 *$14.99*

The Pajama Game (1957)
Labor relations take on a whole new meaning in George Abbott's filming of the hit Broadway musical, with garment worker activist Doris Day and factory foreman John Raitt playing the enemies-turned-lovers. "Steam Heat," "Hernando's Hideaway" and "I'm Not at All in Love" are among the memorable Adler/Ross tunes enhanced by Bob Fosse's choreography. Special video edition includes outtakes of the unused "The Man Who Invented Love" number and original theatrical trailers for Day's "Romance on the High Seas" and "Calamity Jane," and Adler and Ross' "Damn Yankees." 101 min.
19-1714 ❑*$19.99*

Please see our index for these other Doris Day titles: *Billy Rose's Jumbo • The Glass Bottom Boat • Love Me Or Leave Me • The Man Who Knew Too Much • Midnight Lace • Pillow Talk • Please Don't Eat The Daisies • Send Me No Flowers • The Thrill Of It All • That Touch Of Mink • The Tunnel Of Love • Where Were You When The Lights Went Out? • The Winning Team • Young Man With A Horn*

Give A Girl A Break (1953)
When his leading lady walks out, Broadway director Gower Champion must choose between rival starlets Marge Champion, Debbie Reynolds and Helen Wood to replace her. Glossy MGM musical, helmed by Stanley Donen, also stars Bob Fosse, Kurt Kasznar. Score includes "It Happens Every Time," "Applause, Applause," "In Our United State." 81 min.
12-2197 *$19.99*

Meet Me In Las Vegas (1956)
Rancher Dan Dailey is unsuccessful at the casinos until he finds a good luck charm, ballerina Cyd Charisse, in this star-studded musical salute to the City of Neon. With Agnes Moorehead, Paul Henreid, and cameos ranging from Frank Sinatra to Peter Lorre. Songs include "If You Can Dream," "The Girl with the Yaller Shoes," and "Frankie and Johnny" (sung by Sammy Davis, Jr.). 112 min.
12-2201 *$19.99*

Nancy Goes To Rio (1950)
Lively remake of the Deanna Durbin musical "It's a Date" stars Ann Sothern and Jane Powell as a mother/daughter acting duo vying for the same role in a new play...as well as the attentions of Barry Sullivan. "Time and Time Again," "Love Is Like This" and "Cha Bomm Pa Pa" are among the featured numbers; with Carmen Miranda, Louis Calhern. 99 min.
12-2351 *$19.99*

Athena (1954)
Unusual MGM musical extravaganza follows the romantic adventures of seven daughters of a health-conscious family who are named for heroines of Greek myth. Jane Powell, Debbie Reynolds, Virginia Gibson, Edmund Purdom, Vic Damone and Louis Calhern star; songs include "Love Can Change the Stars," "I Never Felt Better" and "The Girl Next Door." 95 min.
12-2682 *$19.99*

Rich, Young And Pretty (1951)
A young Texas girl (Jane Powell) joins her rancher father (Wendell Corey) on a trip to Paris that leads to romance with the Frenchman of her dreams (Vic Damone) and the discovery of her real mother, now living in Europe. Danielle Darrieux and Fernando Lamas also star; songs include "Dark Is the Night," "We Never Talk Much" and "Wonder Why." 95 min.
12-2687 ❑*$19.99*

The Merry Widow (1952)
Sumptuous treatment of Franz Lehar's opera, starring Lana Turner as a wealthy widow who is wooed by dashing Fernando Lamas in order to get her fortune and save his country. When Lamas really falls in love with her, he risks being court-martialed. Una Merkel also stars; songs include "Girls, Girls, Girls," "I'm Going to Maxim's" and "The Merry Widow Waltz." 105 min.
12-2689 ❑*$19.99*

Bundle Of Joy (1956)
Music-filled remake of the '30s comedy "Bachelor Mother" stars Debbie Reynolds as a department store clerk who finds an abandoned baby and can't convince people the child isn't hers. Reynolds' real-life hubby, Eddie Fisher, plays the store owner's son who falls for her. With Adolphe Menjou, Nita Talbot. Songs include "Lullaby in Blue," "All About Love."
08-1043 *$19.99*

Damn Yankees (1958)
A lifelong Washington Senators fan makes a deal with the devilish Ray Walston and is transformed into slugger Tab Hunter, ready to lead his club to the pennant, in the hit baseball-based musical comedy. Gwen Verdon is Walston's sultry sidekick, and the score includes "Heart" and "Whatever Lola Wants." 110 min.
19-1319 Was $19.99 ❑*$14.99*

The Desert Song (1953)
Lavish filming of the classic Sigmund Romberg operetta stars Gordon MacRae as a mild-mannered student in the Middle East who disguises himself as the dashing, mysterious El Khobar, leader of a native tribe known as the Riffs. He battles a group of nasty Arabs and romances Kathryn Grayson, the daughter of a general. With Raymond Massey. Songs include "One Alone," "Long Live the Night." 110 min.
19-2167 Was $29.99 *$19.99*

The Jazz Singer (1953)
Danny Thomas tackles the role played previously by Al Jolson and later by Neil Diamond. He's the son of a cantor who returns home following a stint in the military during the Korean War and decides he wants to pursue a career in the theater. His decision puts him at odds with his father, who wants Thomas to replace him at the synagogue. Peggy Lee and Eduard Franz co-star; songs include "Just One of Those Things" and "Living the Life I Love." 107 min.
19-2168 Was $29.99 *$19.99*

So This Is Love (1953)
Kathryn Grayson stars as famed Metropolitan Opera House soprano Grace Moore in this tune-filled biography that traces Moore's life from her Tennessee childhood to her struggle to achieve fame in New York. With Merv Griffin (his film debut), Walter Abel, Rosemary De Camp; songs include "The Kiss Waltz," "Ciribiribin," and selections from "The Marriage of Figaro," "Faust" and "La Boheme." 101 min.
19-2421 *$19.99*

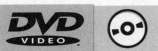

ASK ABOUT OUR GIANT DVD CATALOG!

Mario Lanza

That Midnight Kiss (1949)
Lush, semi-biographical account of the discovery of Mario Lanza, with the singer making his feature debut as a Philadelphia truck driver who gets a chance to show off his marvelous voice when a tempermental tenor walks out on an opera during rehearsal. Kathryn Grayson, Jose Iturbi and Ethel Barrymore also star; songs include "They Don't Believe Me," "Santa Lucia," "Celeste Aida." 98 min.
12-2501 *$19.99*

The Toast Of New Orleans (1950)
Mario Lanza shines in his second film as a Louisiana fisherman who is taken from the docks to center stage at the opera house. Great score includes the renowned "Be My Love." Kathryn Grayson, David Niven, Rita Moreno and J. Carrol Naish co-star. 97 min.
12-1716 Was $29.99 *$19.99*

The Great Caruso (1951)
Philadelphia's own Mario Lanza, in his best-remembered role, portrays the turn-of-the-century opera star who many say was the world's finest voice. Selections from famous operas highlight this beautiful screen biography. 109 min.
12-1062 Was $59.99 *$19.99*

Because You're Mine (1952)
The great Mario Lanza sings and marches in this MGM production about an opera singer's experiences in army training camp. Lots of music, laughs and a spectacular scene of Lanza singing while the world's flags wave. With soprano Doretta Morrow, James Whitmore and Paula Corday. 101 min.
12-2495 *$19.99*

The Student Prince (1954)
Edmund Purdom, with his voice dubbed by Mario Lanza, plays a handsome prince who, at his father's request, seeks to learn about life outside the castle in Heidelberg. He meets and falls in love with an innkeeper's beautiful daughter (Ann Blyth), but the difference in the lovers' status eventually threatens the romance. Songs include "Serenade," "Deep in My Heart" and "Golden Days." 107 min.
12-2499 *$19.99*

Serenade (1956)
Mario Lanza's superb voice highlights this classy soap opera in which he plays an aspiring opera singer who falls for Joan Fontaine, a socialite who intends to promote his career. When she dumps him, he lands in Mexico, falls in love with a matador's daughter (Sarita Montiel) and tries to resurrect his dreams of stardom. With Vincent Price; Lanza sings a wide range of opera favorites. 121 min.
19-2169 Was $29.99 *$19.99*

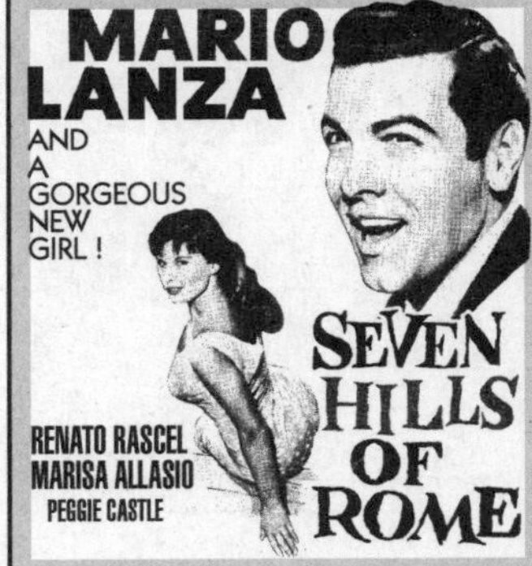

Seven Hills Of Rome (1958)
Following an absence from the screen, Mario Lanza made his return in this music-filled romance in which he plays a TV star who travels to Rome to rekindle his relationship with his girlfriend following an argument. But while overseas, Lanza finds true love with a pretty Italian girl. Renato Rascel and Marisa Allasio also star; songs include "Arrivederci Roma," "Italian Calypso." 104 min.
12-2881 *$19.99*

For The First Time (1959)
Mario Lanza's final movie casts him as an opera singer who attempts to raise money to help his deaf girlfriend by performing concerts throughout Europe. Although Lanza's health was faltering during the film's production, his voice is still magnificent. Among the numbers featured: "La Donna e Mobile," "Oh Mon Amour" and "Ave Maria." Zsa Zsa Gabor, Johanna von Koszian co-star. 97 min.
12-2879 *$19.99*

Frank Sinatra

Higher And Higher (1943)
Frank Sinatra made his film acting debut in this spry musical comedy about a broke aristocrat who tries to marry off his daughter into money. Leon Errol, Jack Haley, Victor Borge and Michele Morgan co-star. Songs include "You Belong in a Love Song," "A Lovely Way to Spend an Evening," "The Music Stopped," and more. 90 min.
62-5038 *$19.99*

Step Lively (1944)
A lively musical remake of "Room Service" has young playwright Frank Sinatra trying to get back money he loaned to a hot-shot producer. Gloria DeHaven, Anne Jeffreys, Walter Slezak, George Murphy. Songs include "Some Other Time," "As Long as There's Music," "Where Does Love Begin?," and more. 88 min.
18-7047 *$19.99*

It Happened In Brooklyn (1947)
Delightful musical charmer stars Frank Sinatra as a GI returning to his Brooklyn stamping grounds with dreams of making it in show-biz, Kathryn Grayson as the neighborhood teacher he falls for, and Peter Lawford as the snobby songwriter out to help Frank. With Jimmy Durante and Gloria Grahame; songs include "Time After Time," "Brooklyn Bridge." 104 min.
12-2120 *$19.99*

The Kissing Bandit (1948)
Musical adventure with Frank Sinatra as the son of a notorious California outlaw who follows in his father's bootsteps, becoming an hombre with a thing for smooching and tending to his inn. Kathryn Grayson also stars; Ricardo Montalban, Ann Miller and Cyd Charisse make special appearances. Songs include "Love Is Where You Find It" and "Señorita." 102 min.
12-2786 *$19.99*

Meet Danny Wilson (1952)
In one of his best performances, Frank Sinatra plays a talented but luckless singer who gets into trouble with a shady nightclub owner (Raymond Burr) and a sexy singer (Shelley Winters) he and his piano-playing partner (Alex Nicol) have fallen for. Tommy Farrell co-stars; Tony Curtis appears in an early role. Songs include "When You're Smiling" and "I've Got a Crush on You." 88 min.
07-2164 ❏*$14.99*

Guys And Dolls (1955)
Damon Runyon's colorful gangsters come to life in this lavish film adaptation of Frank Loesser's beloved Broadway musical. Frank Sinatra is Nathan Detroit, proprietor of "the oldest established permanent floating crap game in New York," and Marlon Brando is high-rolling gambler Sky Masterson; with Jean Simmons, Vivian Blaine, Stubby Kaye. The score includes "Luck Be a Lady," "Adelaide's Lament," "Sit Down, You're Rockin' the Boat." 149 min.
04-1583 Was $19.99 *$14.99*

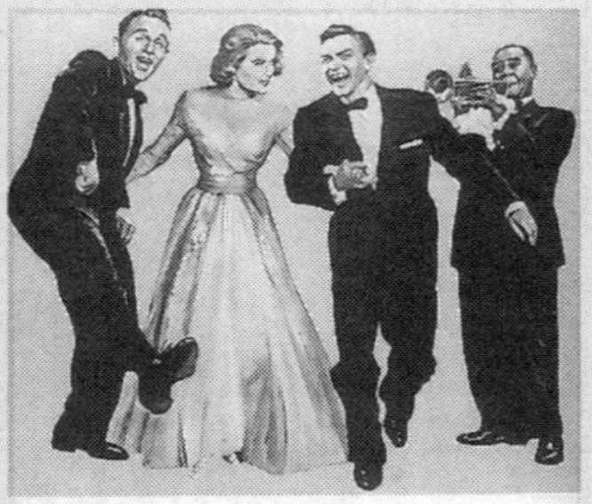
BING CROSBY
GRACE KELLY
FRANK SINATRA
High Society
CELESTE HOLM · JOHN LUND
LOUIS CALHERN · SIDNEY BLACKMER
LOUIS ARMSTRONG

High Society (1956)
Grace Kelly's last film was this lively musical remake of "The Philadelphia Story," with Grace (appropriately) as the Main Line gal who must choose between Bing Crosby and John Lund. Frank Sinatra, Celeste Holm and Louis Armstrong co-star; Cole Porter score includes "True Love," "Did You Evah?" and "You're Sensational." 107 min.
12-1417 Was $19.99 *$14.99*

Pal Joey (1957)
Frank Sinatra is the womanizing nightclub singer caught between his attraction to chorus girl Kim Novak and rich socialite Rita Hayworth in Rodgers and Hart's classic musical. Score includes "Bewitched, Bothered and Bewildered," "The Lady Is a Tramp," "My Funny Valentine." 111 min.
02-1787 *$19.99*

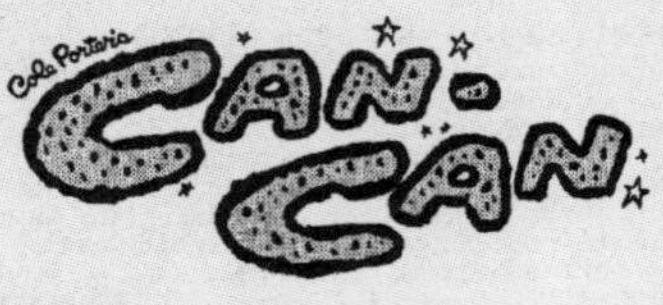
Cole Porter's
CAN-CAN

Can-Can (1960)
Any musical denounced during filming by Khrushchev as being "immoral" can't be all bad! Shirley MacLaine is the Gay Paree nightclub owner charged with indecency, and Frank Sinatra is the lawyer who defends, and falls in love with, her. Maurice Chevalier, Louis Jourdan co-star. Lively Cole Porter score includes "I Love Paris," "Let's Do It," "C'est Magnifique." 131 min.
04-1023 ❏*$14.99*

Robin And The Seven Hoods (1964)
The last of the "Rat Pack" films is set in Roaring Twenties Chicago, and Sinatra and crew play garrulous gangsters who rob from the rich and give to the poor...and themselves. Dean Martin, Sammy Davis, Jr., Bing Crosby, Peter Falk co-star; great score includes "My Kind of Town." 103 min.
19-1595 Was $19.99 *$14.99*

The Frank Sinatra Collection
The best shows from Frankie's '50s TV career have been assembled in this 10-tape boxed set. Along with eight episodes from Sinatra's half-hour variety show, with such special guest stars as Dagmar, Ella Fitzgerald, Sammy Davis, Jr., Elvis Presley, Lena Horne, Jack Benny, Jackie Gleason, Dean Martin and Bing Crosby, you'll also get a 1954 "Colgate Comedy Hour" rendition of "Anything Goes," with Sinatra, Ethel Merman and Bert Lahr, and the documentary "Hollywood Remembers Frank Sinatra." 8 hrs. total.
05-5042 *$69.99*

The Frank Sinatra Show, Vol. 1
Frankie sings, dances and laughs it up with '50s blonde bombshell Dagmar in this entertaining episode from his live musical variety show, telecast from New York. 60 min.
10-7003 *$19.99*

The Frank Sinatra Show, Vol. 3
It's "music, music, music" when Dean Martin and Bing Crosby visit with Frank in an early "Rat Pack" gathering, with distaff charm provided by special guest Mitzi Gaynor.
10-7961 *$19.99*

The Frank Sinatra Show, Vol. 4
Serviceman Elvis Presley is welcomed back to America in this special tribute. Along with a duet from Elvis and Frank, there's music by Sammy Davis, Jr. and Nancy Sinatra, comedy with Joey Bishop, and more.
10-7962 *$19.99*

The Frank Sinatra Show, Vol. 5
The theme for this episode is "A Toast to the Ladies," and among the women sharing the stage with Frank here are Lena Horne, Juliet Prowse, Barbara Heller and special guest star Eleanor Roosevelt.
10-7963 *$19.99*

The Frank Sinatra Show, Vol. 6
There's plenty of music and comedy in store when Sinatra welcomes the one and only Jack Benny to his show (although not, we hope, to play the violin). 60 min.
10-8330 *$19.99*

The Frank Sinatra Show, Vol. 7
Taking a break from his own hit variety series, Jackie Gleason makes a special guest appearance on Frank's show. 60 min.
10-8331 *$19.99*

Starring Frank Sinatra: The TV Years (1951/1959)
A double dose of the Chairman's early tube efforts. The "Bulova Watch Time" Christmas show features Frank making merry with comedian Ben Blue and Hollywood veteran Walter Slezak, and singing holiday favorites. Next, a "Timex Watch Hour" broadcast has Ella Fitzgerald, Juliet Prowse and Peter Lawford joining Sinatra for such songs as "Our Love Is Here to Stay," "I've Got the World on a String," "It's All Right with Me" and more. 112 min. total.
62-1363 *$19.99*

Please see our index for these other Frank Sinatra titles: *Anchors Aweigh • Assault On A Queen • Cast A Giant Shadow • Come Blow Your Horn • The Devil At 4 O'Clock • Dirty Dingus Magee • The First Deadly Sin • 4 For Texas • From Here To Eternity • Kings Go Forth • Lady In Cement • The Man With The Golden Arm • The Manchurian Candidate • Meet Danny Wilson • The Miracle Of The Bells • None But The Brave • Ocean's 11 • On The Town • Some Came Running • Suddenly • Take Me Out To The Ball Game • The Tender Trap • Tony Rome • Von Ryan's Express • Young At Heart*

The Eddie Cantor Story (1953)
Music-filled biodrama of the famed stage and screen star known as "Ol' Banjo Eyes" stars Keefe Brasselle as Cantor, whose comic mannerisms and singing made him a hit in the Ziegfeld Follies. With Marilyn Erskine, William Forest as Flo Ziegfeld, and Will Rogers, Jr. as Rogers, Sr. Songs include "Ma (He's Making Eyes at Me)," "Making Whoopie," "If You Knew Susie" and many more. 117 min.
19-2420 *$19.99*

You'll Find Out (1940)
Haunted house hodge podge of music, mystery and mirth, with Kay Kyser and his entourage getting in the way of three co-conspirators (Boris Karloff, Peter Lorre and Bela Lugosi), who don't intend to let a young debutante collect an inheritance. Co-stars Dennis O'Keefe, Helen Parrish and Ish Kabibble. 97 min.
01-1297 Was $49.99 *$19.99*

No No Nanette (1940)
Second screen version of the 1925 Broadway farce about a doting niece and her financially troubled uncle. Anna Neagle, Roland Young, Victor Mature and ZaSu Pitts lead the cast through such standards as "Tea for Two" and "I Want to Be Happy." 96 min.
17-3072 *$19.99*

Calendar Girl (1947)
Lively musical set in a turn-of-the-century boarding house where a painter and a composer become romantic rivals for a girl. Songs include "Have I Told You Lately?," "Calendar Girl," "New York's a Nice Place to Visit." Stars Jane Frazee, William Marshall and Victor McLaglen. 88 min.
17-9045 *$19.99*

London Town (1946)
An aging music hall performer returns to London believing he's the star of a new show. When he discovers that he's only slated to be the understudy, his daughter sabotages the revue's star in order to get him back into the spotlight. Lively comedy with music stars Sid Field, Kay Kendall and Petula Clark; music by Jimmy Van Heusen and Johnny Burke. AKA: "My Heart Goes Crazy." 93 min.
10-9305 *$19.99*

Doll Face (1945)
Stripper Vivian Blaine tries to make the jump to Broadway stardom, but her manager gets jealous when she falls for a writer hired to create her "biography," in this lively musical based on a play by Gypsy Rose Lee. With Dennis O'Keefe, Perry Como, Carmen Miranda; songs include "Chico-Chico," "Dig You Later," "Red Hot and Beautiful." 80 min.
01-1251 *$19.99*

We'll Meet Again (1942)
Inspired by the life of British "Forces' Sweetheart" Vera Lynn, who later became a star on BBC radio, this musical features Lynn as a woman who falls for a Scottish soldier, but soon finds herself jilted when he leaves her for her best friend. She leaves London and becomes a success entertaining the troops during World War II. Geraldo, Patricia Roc also star. 84 min.
10-9729 *$19.99*

Till The Clouds Roll By (1946)
Tune-filled look at the life of composer Jerome Kern stars Van Heflin, Robert Walker and a galaxy of guest stars, including Judy Garland, Frank Sinatra, Lena Horne, Tony Martin and Cyd Charisse. We are proud to offer the complete, uncut 137-minute version, as seen in theatres.
12-1094 *$19.99*

Best Foot Forward (1943)
A high-spirited musical romp with Lucille Ball as a movie star who decides on a whim to accept a young man's invitation to his military academy's prom. The tunes include "Buckle Down Winsockie," "Wish I May," and Harry James performing "Two O' Clock Jump." June Allyson, Nancy Walker, Tommy Dix. 95 min.
12-1579 Was $29.99 *$19.99*

Let's Go Collegiate (1941)
Spirited musical-comedy about a college crew team that enlists the help of a truck driver when their best oarsman is drafted. Songs include "Look What You've Done to Me," "Sweet 16" and "Let's Do a Little Dreaming." Stars Frankie Darro, Marcia Mae Jones and Jackie Moran. 62 min.
17-9060 *$19.99*

Betty Grable

Down Argentine Way (1940)
Betty Grable and Don Ameche are members of two feuding upper class families who meet while vacationing on the pampas and fall in love in this frothy musical fiesta that features Carmen Miranda in her film debut and a dazzling dance number by the Nicholas Brothers. 92 min.
04-2219 ❏*$19.99*

Moon Over Miami (1941)
Betty Grable, Carole Landis and Charlotte Greenwood leave the Texas prairie behind for Miami's palm trees and single millionaires in this breezy musical salute to the Sunshine State. With Don Ameche, Robert Cummings. 91 min.
04-2223 ❏*$19.99*

Footlight Serenade (1942)
Backstage Broadway musical features Betty Grable and John Payne as secretly married actors in the same show and Victor Mature as boxer-turned-thespian who sets his sights on Grable. Able support from Jane Wyman, Phil Silvers, Mantan Moreland; songs include "Are You Kidding?," "Living High." 81 min.
04-2221 ❏*$19.99*

Song Of The Islands (1942)
Lush Hawaiian scenery and a sarong-clad Betty Grable are just two of the treats on hand in this musical tale of two lovers whose fathers fight over a strip of land both men want. Victor Mature is Betty's burly love interest; Thomas Mitchell, Jack Oakie, Billy Gilbert co-star. 73 min.
04-2225 ❏*$19.99*

Springtime In The Rockies (1942)
Bickering Broadway performers Betty Grable and John Payne decide their relationship is at an end, so Betty joins up with Cesar Romero while Payne woos Carmen Miranda. Fun-filled musical romp features Harry James and His Orchestra, a supporting turn by a young Jackie Gleason, and Miranda's offbeat rendition of "Chattanooga Choo Choo." 91 min.
04-2226 ❏*$19.99*

Pin-Up Girl (1944)
Who else but Betty Grable, WWII's most famous pair of legs, could play the title role? In this musical comedy she's a secretary who masquerades as a singer and finds herself on the stage of a USO canteen performing for the troops. John Harvey, Joe E. Brown, Martha Raye co-star. 83 min.
04-2224 ❏*$19.99*

The Dolly Sisters (1945)
Betty Grable and June Haver sing and dance their way through the title roles in this breezy musical biodrama about the vaudeville duo who charmed America at the turn of the century. With John Payne, Frank Latimore, S.Z. Sakall. Songs include "I Can't Begin to Tell You," "I'm Always Chasing Rainbows," "Give Me the Moonlight." 114 min.
04-3264 ❏*$19.99*

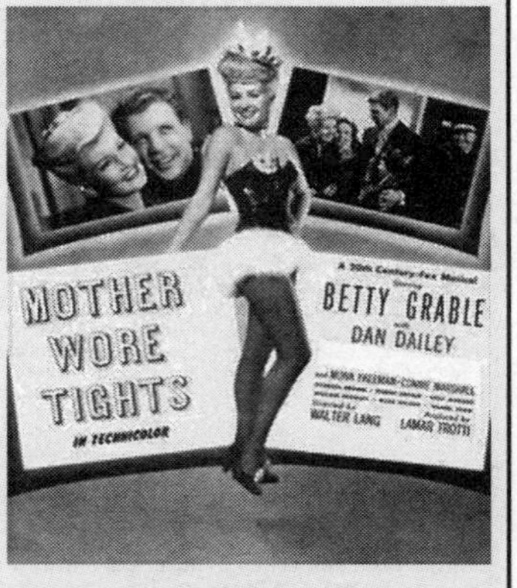
MOTHER WORE TIGHTS
BETTY GRABLE
DAN DAILEY
IN TECHNICOLOR
WALTER LANG
LAMAR TROTTI

Mother Wore Tights (1947)
In what she considered to be her favorite of her movies, Betty Grable plays a vaudevillian who retires to raise a family and, years later, plans a return to the stage, much to the dismay of her grown daughters. Along with an Oscar-winning Alfred Newman score and such tunes as "M-O-T-H-E-R," "Lily of the Valley" and "Put Your Arms Around Me Honey," the film features Dan Dailey, Connie Marshall, Mona Freeman and Señor Wences; Anne Baxter narrates.
04-3807 *$14.99*

The Farmer Takes A Wife (1953)
Lively musical set along the 1850s Erie Canal, with Betty Grable as a flatboat cook who is wooed by struggling farmer Dale Robertson. With Thelma Ritter, Eddie Foy, Jr.; songs include "On the Erie Canal," "Somethin' Real Special." 80 min.
04-2220 *$19.99*

Three For The Show (1955)
The Somerset Maugham play "Too Many Husbands" gets a musical revamping, with Betty Grable starring as a performer and war widow who marries Gower Champion, the songwriting partner of late spouse Jack Lemmon—then is shocked when Lemmon shows up alive and well. Marge Champion co-stars; songs include "I've Got a Crush on You," "Someone to Watch Over Me" and the title tune.
02-3166 *$19.99*

Please see our index for these other Betty Grable titles: *The Beautiful Blonde From Bashful Bend • College Swing • Follow The Fleet • Four Jills In A Jeep • The Gay Divorcee • Give Me A Sailor • How To Marry A Millionaire • I Wake Up Screaming • Pigskin Parade • A Yank In The RAF*

Pigskin Parade (1936)
A 15-year-old Judy Garland made her feature film debut in this spirited musical comedy that also starred Jack Haley as a Texas college football coach who takes his team, led by hard-throwing hillbilly Stuart Erwin, to Connecticut for a show-down with the Yale squad. Look for early appearances by Betty Grable, Tony Martin and Alan Ladd; songs include "It's Love I'm After," "You're Simply Terrific." 93 min.
04-3432 ❑*$19.99*

Thoroughbreds Don't Cry (1937)
Mickey Rooney and Judy Garland teamed up for the first time in this racetrack drama, with Rooney playing a young jockey pressured by his father into throwing a race. Garland works in a boarding house for aunt Sophie Tucker and sings "Got a New Pair of Shoes" and "Sun Showers." With C. Aubrey Smith, Ronald Sinclair. 80 min.
12-2387 *$19.99*

Everybody Sing (1938)
When her show biz family is faced with financial ruin, plucky Judy Garland teams up with servants Fanny Brice and Allan Jones to "put on a show" and save the day in this fun-filled MGM musical. The songs include "Swing, Mr. Mendelssohn," "I Wanna Swing"; with Billie Burke, Reginald Owen, Monty Woolley. 91 min.
12-2384 *$19.99*

Listen, Darling (1938)
In an early film role, Judy Garland is a spunky teenager who teams up with friend Freddie Bartholomew to find the right husband for her widowed mother. Mary Astor, Walter Pidgeon, Gene Lockhart also star in this spry musical-comedy that features such songs as "Zing! Went the Strings of My Heart" and "Ten Pins in the Sky." 75 min.
12-2386 *$19.99*

Babes In Arms (1939)
Busby Berkeley directs Mickey Rooney and Judy Garland in a rousing rendition of Rodgers and Hart's famed Broadway hit. They're children of vaudevillians who go on tour with their parents and their stage veteran friends and, after not being allowed to join them in performance, start their own show. With Charles Winninger, Grace Hayes. Songs include "Where or When," "Good Morning" and "I Cried for You." 96 min.
12-1414 Was $19.99 *$14.99*

Strike Up The Band (1940)
Judy Garland! Mickey Rooney! Busby Berkeley! Hey, let's put on a show! Mick's high school band's out to nab an award in Paul Whiteman's national radio contest. Songs include "Our Love Affair," "Nell of New Rochelle," "Do the Conga," "Sing, Sing, Sing" and "The Sidewalks of New York." 120 min.
12-1412 *$19.99*

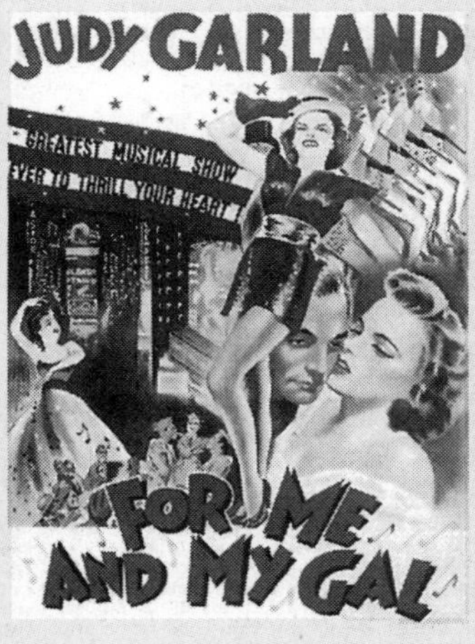

For Me And My Gal (1942)
Delightful romp set in pre-WWI vaudeville, with naive young singer Judy Garland being wooed away from her partners by sly-talking hoofer Gene Kelly (his film debut). George Murphy, Ben Blue and Keenan Wynn co-star in Busby Berkeley's blend of show tunes, drama, and wartime patriotism. 104 min.
12-1015 *$19.99*

Presenting Lily Mars (1943)
Charming and refreshing little tale with Judy Garland as a persistent actress who sets her heart on making it big on Broadway. Van Heflin is the producer whom she consistently nags. Songs include "Every Little Movement Has a Meaning of Its Own"; also stars Spring Byington and Marilyn Maxwell. 104 min.
12-1667 Was $24.99 *$19.99*

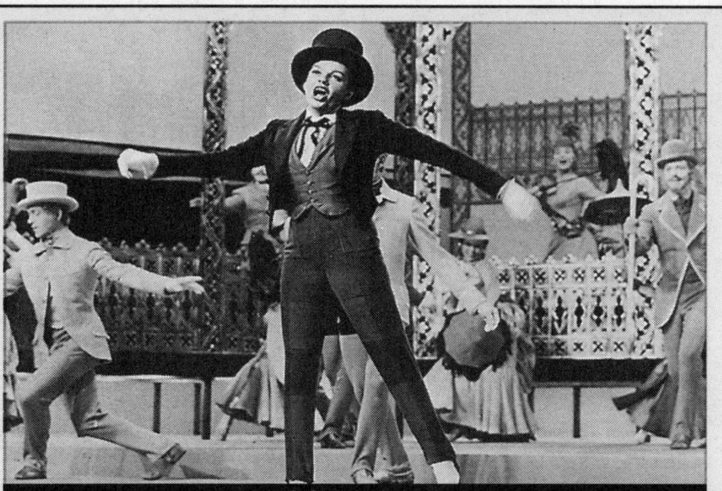

A Star Is Born

Judy Garland

Girl Crazy (1943)
Girl-chaser Mickey Rooney is sent to a small private school to mend his ways, but once he sees Judy Garland it's love at first sight, in this musical-comedy based on a Wheeler and Woolsey vehicle made a decade earlier. One of Mickey and Judy's best co-stars June Allyson, Nancy Walker and Tommy Dorsey and His Orchestra and features a classic Gershwin score, including "Embraceable You," "But Not for Me," "Fascinating Rhythm," "I Got Rhythm" and many more. 99 min.
12-1438 Was $19.99 *$14.99*

Meet Me In St. Louis (1944)
Charming Judy Garland stars in this captivating musical set in turn-of-the-century St. Louis and its World's Fair. Tom Drake is the boy of her dreams, Margaret O'Brien her precocious little sister. Songs include "Trolley Song," "Have Yourself a Merry Little Christmas" and the title song. 113 min.
12-1012 Was $19.99 *$14.99*

The Clock (1945)
Frothy romance stars Judy Garland as a New York secretary who meets and falls in love with soldier Robert Walker in Pennsylvania Station while he is on leave. During their courtship, they encounter all sorts of colorful characters in the Big Apple. Noted for its fabulous studio-bound sets, the film was directed by Vincente Minnelli and co-stars James and Lucille Gleason, Keenan Wynn and Marshall Thompson. 90 min.
12-2113 *$19.99*

The Harvey Girls (1946)
When America headed west, so did Fred Harvey's restaurant chain...and so did a lot of demure young waitresses who didn't know how wild the frontier was! Judy Garland and Ray Bolger star in this delightful musical that features "On the Atchison, Topeka and the Santa Fe." John Hodiak, Angela Lansbury co-star. 101 min.
12-1718 Was $19.99 *$14.99*

In The Good Old Summertime (1949)
Judy Garland and Van Johnson are music shop clerks who have secret "pen pal" lovers, not knowing that it's each other, in this charming musical version of "Shop Around the Corner." Sentimental Movies Unlimited favorite co-stars S.Z. Sakall, Spring Byington and Buster Keaton; look for a young Liza Minnelli with her mother in the finale. 102 min.
12-1529 *$19.99*

Summer Stock (1950)
Forget your troubles by watching Judy Garland and Gene Kelly in this favorite MGM musical about a farm overrun by a summer theater troupe. Features "Get Happy" and Kelly's "newspaper dance"; with Eddie Bracken, Marjorie Main, Phil Silvers. BONUS!: The 1936 musical short "Every Sunday," Garland's and Deanna Durbin's screen debut, is included. 110 min. total.
12-1689 *$19.99*

A Star Is Born (1954)
George Cukor directed this classic musical drama about the doomed marriage of an entertainer whose career is on the rise (Judy Garland) and her husband whose career is in decline (James Mason). Songs include "Born in a Trunk," "The Man That Got Away," "Lose That Long Face"; with Jack Carson, Charles Bickford. This is the re-released, 175-minute version.
19-1299 Was $29.99 *$19.99*

A Star Is Born (Letterboxed Version)
Also available in a theatrical, widescreen format.
19-2929 Was $24.99 *$19.99*

A Child Is Waiting (1963)
John Cassavetes directs Judy Garland in this touching tale about an overly involved teacher in a school for the mentally retarded and her wisely objective supervisor. The fine cast includes Burt Lancaster, Gena Rowlands and real-life handicapped children. 104 min.
12-2003 *$19.99*

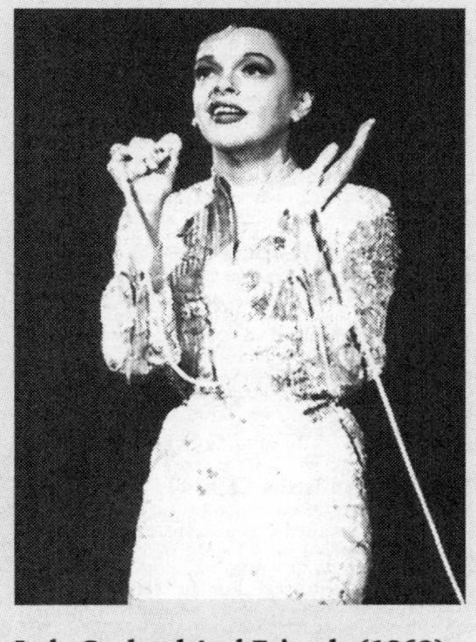

Judy Garland And Friends (1963)
A gem of a compilation from Judy's 1963 TV show, featuring her performing with guests Barbra Streisand, Ethel Merman and Liza Minnelli. Selections include "Happy Days Are Here Again/Get Happy" with Streisand; "The Best Is Yet to Come" with Liza; "There's No Business Like Show Business" with Garland, Merman and Streisand, and much more. A collector's delight! 54 min.
19-3301 *$14.99*

The Judy Garland Christmas Show (1963)
Judy is joined by her children, Liza Minnelli, and Lorna and Joey Luft, and guest stars Jack Jones and Mel Tormé in this charming live TV special. The songs include holiday favorites like "Have Yourself a Merry Little Christmas" and "Santa Claus Is Coming to Town," as well as "Wouldn't It Be Loverly," "Where Is Love?" and "Over the Rainbow." 59 min.
19-3238 *$14.99*

The Judy Garland Special (Judy And Her Guests) (1963)
Judy Garland sings "Get Happy" and guests Robert Goulet and Phil Silvers go drag to impersonate Judy in skits in this entertaining CBS special. 52 min.
09-1233 *$14.99*

Judy Garland: Live At The London Palladium (1964)
Garland's last appearance at the famed London venue was marked by moving renditions of classic songs and the first public appearance of Liza Minnelli, who performs with her mother. Included in this sensational program are "The Man That Got Away," "Once in a Lifetime," "Hello, Dolly!," "It's Just a Matter of Time," "San Francisco," "Chicago," "Over the Rainbow" and more. 55 min.
89-7012 *$14.99*

That's Entertainment: Judy Garland In Concert (1964)
Judy is featured in this program taken from two episodes of her 1963-64 CBS series. Songs include "Liza," "Lorna," "Rock-a-Bye Your Baby," "That's Entertainment!" and "America the Beautiful," plus a spiritual medley of "Swing Low, Sweet Chariot" and "He's Got the Whole World in His Hands" and a war medley (including "When Johnny Comes Marching Home" and "Give My Regards to Broadway"). 51 min.
89-7027 *$14.99*

The Best Of Judy Garland
Rare TV performances from the early '60s showcase Judy and show why she was one of the most dynamic live performers of all time. Songs featured include "Swanee," "The Man That Got Away," "Stormy Weather," "That's Entertainment!" and "Over the Rainbow." 52 min.
02-1485 *$14.99*

A Judy Garland Tribute
A stunning collection of movie memories, some never before available on video, saluting the one and only Judy. Trailers from over 20 of Garland's greatest films, outtakes and test footage (including her screen tests for "Annie Get Your Gun" and "The Valley of the Dolls"), film interview segments and scenes from Judy's stage appearances make for unforgettable entertainment. 150 min.
10-7560 *$19.99*

Judy Garland Scrapbook
Relive the glamour of the golden age of Hollywood musicals with a review of the career of its greatest singing star: out-takes, scenes from newsreels and clips from Judy's movies. 55 min.
50-6302 *$19.99*

Judy Garland: The Concert Years
Lorna Luft hosts this special look at mother Judy's incredible career, which includes comments from such acquaintances as Edward Albee, Tony Bennett, Alan King, Mort Lindsey, Rex Reed and Nelson Riddle. Songs include "Liza," "Lorna," "Get Happy," "Ol' Man River," "Swanee," "Consider Yourself," "Chicago" and "Over the Rainbow." 59 min.
89-7013 *$14.99*

Judy, Frank & Dean: The Legendary Concert (1962)
This milestone concert featuring Judy Garland, Frank Sinatra and Dean Martin was long believed to be lost, but Movies Unlimited has found it, and what a joy it is for music lovers. Directed by Norman Jewison, the program features "Just in Time," "When You're Smiling," "You Do Something to Me," "The Man That Got Away" and a finale in which Judy belts out "Swanee," "Rock-A-Bye Your Baby" and "San Francisco." 51 min.
89-7014 *$14.99*

Judy Garland's Hollywood
This two-part tape features the gala 1954 Hollywood premiere of "A Star Is Born," featuring Judy with then-husband Sid Luft and a passel of stage and screen luminaries on display. Also included is "Hollywood Home Movies," taken by ace Tinseltown cameraman Ken Murray and spotlighting Garland, Joan Crawford, Gary Cooper, Charlie Chaplin, Louis B. Mayer and Frank Sinatra. 58 min.
89-7036 *$14.99*

Please see our index for these other Judy Garland titles: *Andy Hardy Meets Debutante • Broadway Melody Of 1938 • Easter Parade • Gay Purr-ee • Judgment At Nuremberg • Life Begins For Andy Hardy • Love Finds Andy Hardy • Till The Clouds Roll By • The Wizard Of Oz • Words And Music • Ziegfeld Follies*

Good News (1947)
Raccoon coats, "Oh, you kid," ukuleles, "Varsity Drag"...it's college life in the '20s as seen by Betty Comden and Adolph Green ("Singin' in the Rain"). June Allyson and Joan McCracken are the campus coeds after grid star Peter Lawford. Songs include "French Lesson," "Best Things in Life Are Free" and "Pass the Peace Pipe." 93 min.
12-1591 Was $19.99 *$14.99*

Spotlight Scandals (1943)
An energetic musical farce about a small-town barber who finds show business success when he joins forces with a vaudeville comic. But when the comedian has an opportunity to fly high with a solo act, the barber drops out of the picture...until a successful reunion at a later date. Frank Fay, Billy Gilbert, Harry Langdon star. Songs include "The Restless Age." 69 min.
50-1300 *$19.99*

Look For The Silver Lining (1949)
This musical biography of actress Marilyn Miller chronicles the life of the star who started in vaudeville and became a Broadway sensation with help from her mentor, Jack Donahue, before she died at the age of 37. June Haver, Ray Bolger and Charlie Ruggles star. Songs include "Who," "Sunny," "A Kiss in the Dark," "Just a Memory" and "Time on My Hands." 100 min.
12-2769 *$19.99*

Summer Holiday (1948)
Eugene O'Neill's "Ah, Wilderness!" served as the basis for this Rouben Mamoulian musical starring Mickey Rooney as the eldest son in a New England family at the turn of the century. Gloria DeHaven, Walter Huston, Frank Morgan co-star. "It's Our Home Town," "Afraid to Fall in Love" and "The Stanley Steamer" highlight the score. 92 min.
12-2202 *$19.99*

Panama Hattie (1942)
Ann Sothern is the sassy saloon keeper whose Central American bar is a haven for fighting sailors, romancing couples, and sinister spies in this filming of the Cole Porter Broadway musical. Dan Dailey, Red Skelton, Virginia O'Brien, Lena Horne also star; songs include "It Was Just One of Those Things," "I've Still Got My Health," "The Son of a Gun Who Picks on Uncle Sam." 79 min.
12-2349 *$19.99*

Broadway Rhythm (1944)
There's a score of musical gems to be found in this lavish MGM production about a stubborn ex-vaudeville star tangling with his son, who happens to be the producer of his new show. George Murphy, Charles Winninger, Gloria DeHaven, Lena Horne and Tommy Dorsey and His Orchestra star; songs include "Milkman, Keep Those Bottles Quiet," "Pretty Baby" and "All the Things You Are." 112 min.
12-2683 □*$19.99*

Holiday In Mexico (1946)
Colorful MGM tuner starring Jane Powell as the daughter of the U.S. ambassador to Mexico (Walter Pidgeon) who, against her father's wishes, falls in love with an older man. With Jose Iturbi, Roddy McDowall, Ilona Massey, Jane Powell, Xavier Cugat (and, in a crowd scene, a teenage Fidel Castro!). Songs include "You, So It's You," "The Music Goes 'Round and 'Round" and "Walter Winchell Rhumba." 127 min.
12-2685 *$19.99*

Song Of Scheherazade (1947)
Lush Technicolor sets and lavish song sequences fuel this musical/drama starring Jean-Pierre Aumont as Russian composer Rimsky-Korsakov and Yvonne De Carlo as the sultry dancing girl he meets in Morocco and inspires to write his masterpiece, "Scheherazade." Brian Donlevy, Eve Arden also star; score includes "Flight of the Bumblebee," "Gypsy Song," "Navy March." 106 min.
07-2862 *$14.99*

Rhythm Hits The Ice (1942)
Musical-comedy about a country girl who inherits an ice show on a New England farm, then must battle an unscrupulous promoter to keep the skate spectacle going. Ellen Drew, Jerry Colonna, Richard Denning star. Songs include "Tequila," "The Guy with the Polka-Dotted Tie" and "After All." 79 min.
08-8016 Was $19.99 *$14.99*

Sensations Of 1945 (1945)
Campy musical stars Eleanor Powell, Dennis O'Keefe, C. Aubrey Smith, W.C. Fields, Cab Calloway, Sophie Tucker and Eugene Pallette. Loaded with specialty numbers; contains the now-famous number where Eleanor tap-dances her way inside a giant pinball machine. 86 min.
62-1018 *$19.99*

Luxury Liner (1948)
Spirited seafaring musical-comedy from MGM starring Jane Powell as a young woman who wants to play matchmaker for her father, luxury liner captain George Brent. The lucky woman for Dad is a widowed passenger, played by Frances Gifford. With Lauritz Melchior and Xavier Cugat; tunes include "I've Got You Under My Skin" and "Yes We Have No Bananas." 98 min.
12-2788 *$19.99*

Two Sisters From Boston (1946)
Two sisters from New England find romance and adventure at a New York nitery populated by all sorts of colorful characters. One sibling (June Allyson) gets entangled with an opera producer (Peter Lawford), while the other (Kathryn Grayson) becomes acquainted with the club's piano-playing owner (Jimmy Durante). With Lauritz Melchior; songs include "After the Show," "Nellie Martin." 112 min.
12-2793 □*$19.99*

Belle Of The Yukon (1944)
Set in the days of the great Canadian Gold Rush, this rousing musical stars Randolph Scott as a "reformed" con artist-turned-dance hall owner whose girlfriend, singer Gypsy Rose Lee, tries to keep him on the straight and narrow. Dinah Shore, William Marshall, Bob Burns co-star; songs include "Like Someone in Love," "Sleigh Ride in July," "Ev'ry Girl Is Different." 84 min.
12-3031 □*$19.99*

Ship Ahoy (1942)
What do you get when you mix music, dancing, comedy and spies? This entertaining concoction for one, starring Eleanor Powell as a tap dancer working on an ocean liner heading for Puerto Rico who is unknowingly recruited by spies to smuggle secret plans. Bert Lahr, Red Skelton, (an uncredited) Frank Sinatra, and Tommy Dorsey and His Orchestra (with Buddy Rich) also star. Songs include "Poor You" and "On Moonlight Bay." 96 min.
12-2688 □*$19.99*

Sonja Henie

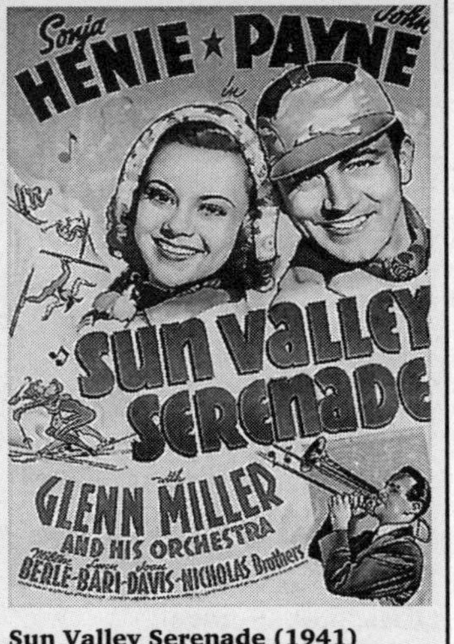

One In A Million (1936)
Olympic gold medalist Sonja Henie made her Hollywood debut in this musical-comedy boasting dazzling icebound sequences. She's a skater training for the Olympics (surprise!) who is discovered in Switzerland by talent agent Adolphe Menjou and brought to America to star in ice shows. The Ritz Brothers, Don Ameche co-star; songs include "We're Back in Circulation Again." 94 min.
04-2733 □*$19.99*

Thin Ice (1937)
A Swiss hotel's ski instructor shares her time on the slopes with a handsome ski enthusiast reporter whom she later discovers is a prince. Romance blossoms, much to the chagrin of diplomats who don't want the prince to wed a commoner. Sonja Henie excels in the film's several skating scenes; Tyrone Power, Arthur Treacher and Joan Davis co-star. 78 min.
04-2735 □*$19.99*

Happy Landing (1938)
Sonja Henie's fantastic skating abilities highlight this comedy with musical numbers in which playboy bandleader Cesar Romero and manager Don Ameche face off for her affections while on tour in Norway. Songs include "Hot and Happy" and "Yonny and His Oomphah." With Ethel Merman, Jean Hersholt. 75 min.
04-2731 □*$19.99*

My Lucky Star (1938)
After the son of a sporting goods store owner falls for a spunky sales clerk, he sends her to college to promote the shop's fashion wardrobe. Although her clothes cause jealousy among schoolmates and she gets involved with a teacher, she manages to skate in an ice show sponsored by the store. Sonja Henie, Richard Greene and Cesar Romero star; songs include "I've Got a Date With a Dream." 84 min.
04-2734 □*$19.99*

Second Fiddle (1939)
Minnesota schoolteacher Sonja Henie is tapped for Hollywood stardom by studio press agent Tyrone Power. Power creates a staged romance between Henie and co-star Rudy Vallee, but when she learns the love letters she's been receiving were fake, she heads back home, with true admirer Power following her. The Irving Berlin score includes "Back to Back," "I Poured My Heart Into Song." 86 min.
04-2729 □*$19.99*

Everything Happens At Night (1939)
In a rare serious role (but one that still leaves room for skating), Sonja Henie is the daughter of a political commentator hiding out in Switzerland, where rival newspapermen Ray Milland and Robert Cummings are fighting for the story on her father and wind up falling for her. Who will win Henie, and who'll settle for the scoop? 77 min.
04-2730 □*$19.99*

Sun Valley Serenade (1941)
Sonja Henie skates and Glenn Miller and his Orchestra blast out super tunes in this snow-capped musical-comedy. The Miller band arrives in an Idaho ski resort where pianist John Payne meets the Norwegian refugee (Henie) he has sponsored, and romance follows. Milton Berle, Lynn Bari, Dorothy Dandridge and the Nicholas Brothers co-star; songs include "Chattanooga Choo-Choo," "In the Mood," "I Know Why and So Do You." 86 min.
04-2453 □*$19.99*

Iceland (1942)
When the Marines land in Iceland during World War II, Reykjavik beauty Sonja Henie receives a whimsical offer of marriage from smart-alecky soldier John Payne, who doesn't know such actions are taken seriously in her country. Jack Oakie and Sammy Kaye and his Orchestra also star. Henie's incredible skatework and the song "There Will Never Be Another You" are highlights. 79 min.
04-2732 □*$19.99*

Wintertime (1943)
Large-scale skating musical with Sonja Henie as a Norwegian champion who lands in Canada with her wealthy uncle, who has purchased a dilapidated hotel. While being wooed by two men (Cesar Romero and Cornel Wilde), Henie organizes a dazzling ice show to raise cash to revive the resort. Carole Landis and Woody Herman and his Band also star; songs include "Later Tonight." 82 min.
04-2736 □*$19.99*

It's A Pleasure (1944)
Ice skating star Sonja Henie is the wife of a rough hockey player whose fighting ways get him suspended from the sport. While her popularity soars on the ice show circuit, his drinking hurts his chances at making it as a figure skater, which causes friction within the marriage. Michael O'Shea and Bill Johnson co-star in this drama. 90 min.
12-3002 □*$19.99*

Strictly G.I. (1942)
A quartet of special musical-comedy shorts made during WWII for the boys overseas. The all-star lineup includes Bob Hope, Judy Garland, Bing Crosby, Lana Turner, Frank Sinatra, Harpo Marx, Dorothy Lamour and more. All-singing, all-dancing, all-joking, all-flag-wavin' fun. 75 min.
01-5052 *$19.99*

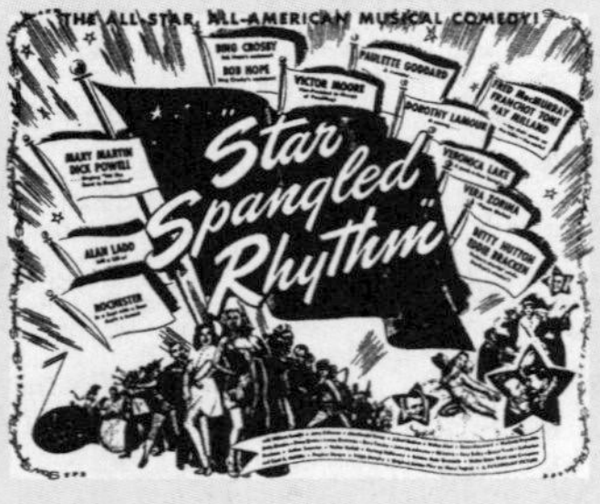

Star Spangled Rhythm (1942)
A parade of Hollywood's biggest stars were enlisted for this tuneful comedy starring Eddie Bracken as a sailor who brings his pals to Paramount Studios to meet his father, a guard and one-time cowboy star now posing as a movie honcho. Bing Crosby, Betty Hutton, Bob Hope, Alan Ladd, Mary Martin, Dick Powell and Victor Moore lead the cast; songs include "Hit the Road to Dreamland." 100 min.
07-2129 □*$14.99*

The Yanks Are Coming (1942)
Rah-rah tuner in which bandleader Henry King talks his musicians into enlisting in the armed forces during WWII in order to entertain the troops, but wind up serving as soldiers. Mary Healy, Maxie Rosenbloom and Parkyakarkus co-star. Songs include "Zip Your Lip," "There Will Be No Blackout of Democracy" and the title tune. 65 min.
09-5094 *$19.99*

Private Buckaroo (1942)
Vintage WWII musical with The Andrews Sisters and Harry James and his Orchestra jumpin' and jivin' through basic training. With Joe E. Lewis. 65 min.
10-4023 *$19.99*

Thank Your Lucky Stars (1943)
Warner Bros.' contribution to the war effort was this songfest featuring their star players performing numerous hits. The plot revolves around the mishaps of Eddie Cantor and a look-alike cab driver. Stars include Humphrey Bogart, Joan Leslie, Olivia de Havilland, John Garfield, Bette Davis singing "They're Either Too Young or Too Old" and Errol Flynn singing "That's What You Jolly Well Get." 127 min.
12-1633 *$29.99*

Jive Junction (1943)
Lively musical-comedy about a band of patriotic teens who turn a barn into a canteen for servicemen during WWII. Edgar G. Ulmer directs Dickie Moore, Tina Thayer. 62 min.
09-1583 Was $24.99 *$19.99*

This Is The Army (1943)
Ronald Reagan and Joan Leslie, and a cast of thousands. Irving Berlin's morale-booster tribute to the Armed Forces during WWII, and a memorable entertainment of song and dance. Kate Smith sings her heart out with "God Bless America." Colossal, rousing musical bit of nostalgia. 105 min.
10-1069 Was $19.99 *$14.99*

Stagedoor Canteen (1943)
The greatest collection of stars in an "All Out for Victory" musical blockbuster. The story is a simple soldier-meets-USO-girl love story, but what a supporting cast! Katharine Hepburn, Helen Hayes, George Raft, Paul Muni, Harpo Marx, Ed Wynn, Edgar Bergen and Charlie McCarthy, and more, with music by Benny Goodman, Count Basie, Guy Lombardo, and their orchestras. 132 min.
10-2002 *$19.99*

Four Jills In A Jeep (1944)
The "Jills" are Kay Francis, Carole Landis, Mitzi Mayfair and Martha Raye, four members of a USO show unit touring Europe and North Africa. Rousing musical comedy, based on the girls' real wartime exploits, also features Phil Silvers, Dick Haymes, and guest appearances by Alice Faye, Betty Grable, Carmen Miranda and Jimmy Dorsey and His Band. Songs include "Crazy Me," "How Blue the Night," "Over There." 89 min.
04-2929 *$14.99*

Follow The Boys (1944)
In this patriotic all-star show biz musical, former vaudeville star-turned-movie actor George Raft organizes a travelling show for the troops. The performers include W.C. Fields, who does his famous pool routine; Dinah Shore, Jeanette MacDonald and The Andrews Sisters, who turn in memorable musical moments; plus, Orson Welles, Marlene Dietrich, Donald O'Connor and Sophie Tucker. 111 min.
07-2176 □*$14.99*

Hollywood Canteen (1944)
Star-studded follow-up to "Stage Door Canteen," filled with Hollywood favorites, patriotic spirit and classic songs. The plot involves soldiers Dane Clark and Robert Hutton catching entertainment at the famed Canteen before being shipped to New Guinea, and Hutton meeting dream girl Joan Leslie. With the Andrews Sisters, Jack Benny, Bette Davis, Joan Crawford, Eddie Cantor and many more. 124 min.
12-2241 *$29.99*

Meet The Navy (1946)
A post-war musical treat, this British-made film follows the Royal Canadian Navy revue performing for Allied troops and the Royal Family. John Pratt, Margaret Hurst star. 81 min.
09-1503 Was $29.99 *$14.99*

New Orleans (1947)
The only feature film appearance of the legendary Billie Holiday, who performs "Farewell to Storyville," is just one of the highlights of this song-filled look at the (fictionalized) birth of jazz. When bandleader Louis Armstrong's sizzling new sound draws crowds to his gambling hall, New Orleans saloonkeeper Arturo de Córdova sets out to spread the music to the public. Kid Ory and Woody Herman are among the other jazz greats appearing; with Irene Rich, Shelley Winters. 90 min.
53-6784 *$24.99*

Carnegie Hall (1947)
Set in the legendary New York concert hall, this song-filled melodrama follows an Irish immigrant (Marsha Hunt) who gets a job at the newly-opened building. Among the artists appearing on stage are Ezio Pinza (performing from "Simon Di Boccanegra" and "Don Giovanni"), Artur Rubinstein ("Ritual Fire Dance") and Lily Pons ("Bell Song"), plus Jascha Heifetz, Risë Stevens, Vaughn Monroe and his Orchestra, Leopold Stokowski and more; Edgar G. Ulmer directs. 136 min.
53-6783 *$24.99*

Breakfast In Hollywood (1946)
Romantic comedy and Big Band music combine in this adaptation of a popular radio series. Features Bonita Granville, Billie Burke, Beulah Bondi, Spike Jones and His City Slickers, the Nat King Cole Trio and other top stars. 91 min.
09-1008 Was $29.99 *$24.99*

Delightfully Dangerous (1947)
Delightful musical comedy stars Jane Powell and Constance Moore as two sisters, one sedate and shy, the other a breezy stripper, competing for Ralph Bellamy. 80 min.
08-8020 *$19.99*

Frolics On Ice (1940)
Irene Dare, Edgar Kennedy in fine musical comedy/romance with several spectacular ice-skating production numbers. 65 min.
09-1018 Was $29.99 *$24.99*

Gaiety (1941)/ La Cucaracha (1934)
A South-of-the-Border musical mix is offered in this feature-length double bill. First is producer Hal Roach's romantic comedy, also known as "Fiesta," that features The Guadalajara Trio and lively folk dancers. Next up, is a lavish, Oscar-winning Latin American festival that was the first three-color Technicolor short subject. 65 min. total.
10-7575 Double Feature *$14.99*

Variety Girl (1947)
Practically the entire talent roster of Paramount Pictures lent their services to this all-star musical, made to benefit the Variety Club children's charity. Two young women with dreams of stardom come to Hollywood and work their way onto the studio's lot, running into such stars as Bob Hope and Bing Crosby, Ray Milland, Alan Ladd, Barbara Stanwyck, Paulette Goddard, Dorothy Lamour, Burt Lancaster, William Holden, Pearl Bailey, Sunny Tufts (Sonny Tufts?) and even Cecil B. DeMille. 93 min.
07-2712 □*$14.99*

Swing Hostess (1944)
Entertaining rags-to-riches-to-rags story features Benny Goodman vocalist Martha Tilton as an unemployed big band singer who takes a job as an operator at a jukebox company. After falling in love with a bandleader, she gets a chance to get back in the limelight by singing for his group. With Charles Collins. Songs include "Let's Capture This Moment." 76 min.
09-5093 *$19.99*

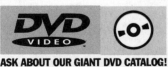

Words And Music (1948)
The renowned songwriting team of Richard Rodgers and Lorenz Hart are spotlighted in this musical biography that features an all-star cast performing their greatest works. Judy Garland, Gene Kelly, Cyd Charisse, Lena Horne and Mel Tormé star, with Tom Drake and Mickey Rooney as Rodgers and Hart. Songs include "I Wish I Were in Love Again," "Johnny One Note," "The Lady Is a Tramp," "Slaughter on Tenth Avenue," "Where or When" and more. 119 min.
12-1532 Was $29.99 ***$19.99***

Dance Hall (1941)
Dance hall singer Carole Landis is smitten with club manager Cesar Romero until she learns he's something of a Casanova. When he realizes Landis is no longer under his spell, Romero coaches his pal, composer William Henry, on winning her over. Enjoyable comic tuner features the songs "There's a Lull in My Life" and "There's Something in the Air." 70 min.
10-3160 ***$19.99***

Two Girls And A Sailor (1944)
Breezy musical with a wartime setting, as millionaire/sailor Van Johnson buys a building for showgirls June Allyson and Gloria DeHaven to use as a soldier's canteen. A dazzling array of guest performers, including Lena Horne, Jimmy Durante, Xavier Cugat and His Orchestra, Buster Keaton, Gracie Allen and the Harry James Orchestra, highlight the festivities. 124 min.
12-2018 ***$19.99***

Orchestra Wives (1942)
Vibrant tale of a newly-married Big Band trumpeteer whose marriage is considered a bad bet by the other band members and wives because of the schemes of a sultry lead singer. Glenn Miller and his Band, George Montgomery, Ann Rutherford, Cesar Romero, Lynn Bari and Jackie Gleason star. Songs include "I've Got a Gal in Kalamazoo," "At Last" and "Serenade in Blue." 98 min.
04-2452 ***▭$19.99***

The Fabulous Dorseys (1947)
Biography of the great bandleader brothers shows how they fought with each other, even from childhood. Tommy and Jimmy play themselves. Also starring Janet Blair, William Lundigan, Paul Whiteman and other musical greats; songs include "Marie," "Green Eyes," more. 88 min.
08-8066 ***$19.99***

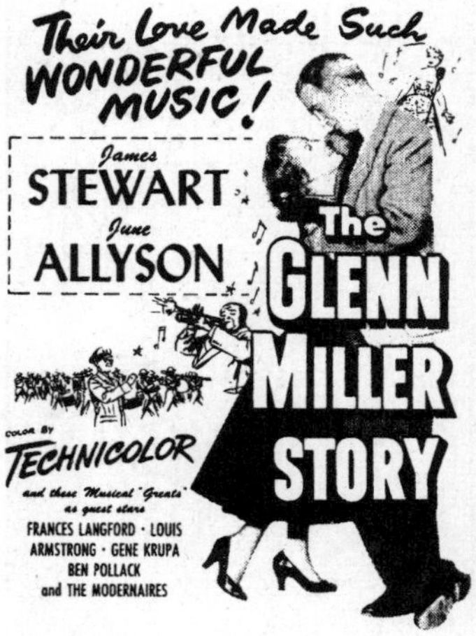

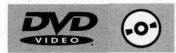

The Glenn Miller Story (1954)
The music of the Big Band era lives again in this famed biography of the musician and band leader. James Stewart shines in the title role, with June Allyson as his wife. Special musical guests include Louis Armstrong, Gene Krupa, Frances Langford and the Glenn Miller Orchestra, performing such classics as "Pennsylvania 6-5000," "Moonlight Serenade" and "Chattanooga Choo-Choo." 113 min.
07-1385 ***$19.99***

The Benny Goodman Story (1955)
The life story of the King of Swing is told in memorable fashion with a standout performance by Steve Allen in the title role. Donna Reed co-stars, and Sammy Davis Jr., Gene Krupa, Harry James, Lionel Hampton and many more make musical appearances. Goodman himself dubbed the clarinet playing. 116 min.
07-1516 ***$19.99***

The Gene Krupa Story (1959)
Sal Mineo shines in this much-loved film bio as the premier jazz drummer of his day. His rise to fame, his descent into drug addiction and struggle back are strikingly recounted. Krupa supplies the soundtrack; James Darren, Susan Kohner, Yvonne Craig co-star. 101 min.
02-1770 ***$19.99***

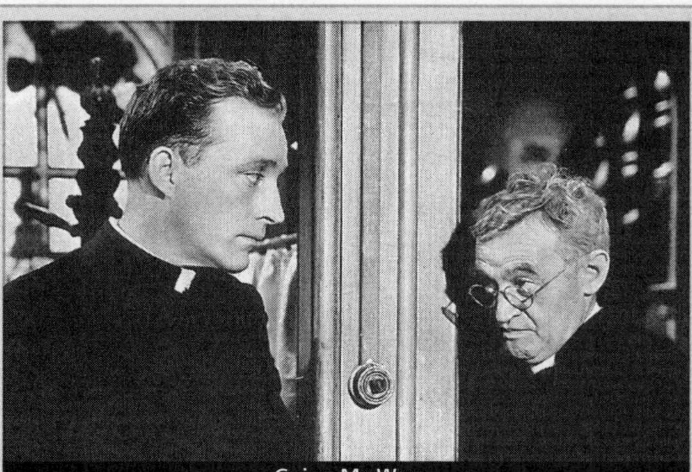
Going My Way

Bing Crosby

King Of Jazz (1929)
This spectacular jazz revue marked the birth of the Technicolor musical. Great bits include bandleader Paul Whiteman visiting a jungle inhabited by Oswald the Rabbit, Bing Crosby singing "Happy Feet," 500 cowboys singing "Song of Dawn," and George Gershwin's "Rhapsody in Blue." 93 min.
07-1163 Was $19.99 ***$14.99***

I Surrender, Dear: Bing Crosby And Ruth Etting (1932)
Two of the decade's most popular singers are featured in this musical trio of two-reelers from the '30s. Bing Crosby portrays himself in "I Surrender, Dear" (1931), as the radio star gets tangled up with a woman betrothed to a jealous Latin lover; Bing falls for the "Billboard Girl" (1932), whose brother is the one answering the singer's love letters; then, Ruth Etting crosses her stern physician husband in her pursuit of a singing career, in "Artistic Temper" (1932). 60 min.
09-2280 ***$19.99***

Going Hollywood (1933)
Delightful early MGM musical-comedy with Bing Crosby as a singer with aspirations of making it big in Hollywood who finds himself caught between a seductive actress (Fifi D'Orsay) and a pretty French teacher (Marion Davies). Songs include "After Sundown," "We'll Make Hay While the Sun Shines" and the title tune. With Patsy Kelly and Ned Sparks. 78 min.
12-2684 ***$19.99***

We're Not Dressing (1934)
Musical precursor to "Gilligan's Island" stars Bing Crosby as a deckhand on a ship populated by high-society types who gets to give the orders when the vessel shipwrecks on a South Seas island. Carole Lombard, George Burns and Gracie Allen, Ethel Merman, Leon Errol and Ray Milland co-star; songs include "It's a Lie," "May I?" and "She Reminds Me of You." 74 min.
07-2126 ***▭$14.99***

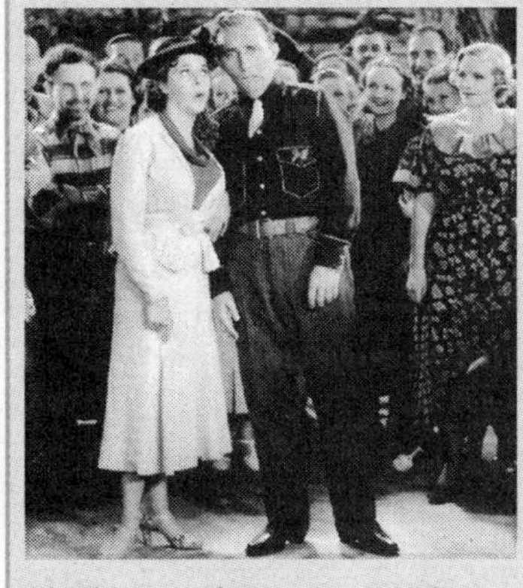

Rhythm On The Range (1936)
Singing rodeo cowboy Bing Crosby(!) is shepherding a prize bull from New York to a California dude ranch by freight train when he comes across a stowaway, runaway heiress Frances Farmer, in this lively musical comedy. The supporting cast includes Martha Raye (in her film debut), Bob Burns, and The Sons of the Pioneers (with a young Roy Rogers). 88 min.
07-2280 ***▭$14.99***

Waikiki Wedding (1937)
The Oscar-winning song "Sweet Leilani" is just one of the tunes in this breezy romance starring Bing Crosby as a pineapple company executive who accompanies a reluctant "Pineapple Princess" on a PR tour of the islands. With Shirley Ross, Martha Raye, Bob Burns, and Anthony Quinn as a native leader. 89 min.
07-2282 ***▭$14.99***

Rhythm On The River (1940)
After his wife leaves him, songwriter Basil Rathbone suffers from a creative block, so he enlists young tunesmiths Bing Crosby and Mary Martin to secretly write new numbers for him. The two meet and decide to take credit for their work, meeting Rathbone's wrath in the process. Oscar Levant and William Frawley co-star. Songs include "That's for Me" and "When the Moon Comes Over Madison Square." 94 min.
07-2125 ***▭$14.99***

Birth Of The Blues (1941)
New Orleans clarinetist Bing Crosby teams up with trumpet player Brian Donlevy and singer Mary Martin to form a band to play his new brand of Dixieland music and this tuneful (if not historically accurate) account of the beginnings of jazz. With Eddie "Rochester" Anderson, Jack Teagarden; songs include "St. Louis Blues," "Memphis Blues," "Melancholy Baby." 76 min.
07-2279 ***▭$14.99***

Holiday Inn (1942)
Irving Berlin's musical trip through the calendar featuring the film debut of "White Christmas." Bing Crosby is an entertainer who tires of the stage life and buys a country inn to relax, only to find he can't escape show biz, especially when hoofer Fred Astaire tries to woo Bing's girl. 101 min.
07-1075 Was $19.99 ***▭$14.99***

Going My Way (1944)
The timeless heartwarming tale about a priest whose unconventional methods annoy and delight his gruff superior. Bing Crosby and Barry Fitzgerald won Oscars for their roles, as did director Leo McCarey and the film itself. 126 min.
07-1074 Was $19.99 ***▭$14.99***

The Bells Of St. Mary's (1945)
Bing Crosby reprises his "Going My Way" role of dedicated priest Father O'Malley, who faces a challenge when he's sent to shore up a financially troubled parish and enters a battle of wits with strong-willed nun Ingrid Bergman. With Henry Travers. 126 min.
63-1001 ***$14.99***

The Bells Of St. Mary's (Color Version)
Father Crosby and Sister Ingrid Bergman never looked better than in this new-fangled, computer-tinted edition.
63-1265 Was $19.99 ***$14.99***

Here Come The Waves (1944)
Terrific tuner with Bing Crosby as a singing idol who joins pal Sonny Tufts in the Navy during World War II. Although he's seeking combat action, Bing becomes the director of benefit shows and soon falls in love with a woman who has an identical twin (both played by Betty Hutton). Songs include "Accentuate the Positive," "That Old Black Magic" and "I Promise You." 99 min.
07-2128 ***▭$14.99***

Welcome Stranger (1947)
"Going My Way" stars Bing Crosby and Barry Fitzgerald reunited, albeit with a different calling, in this tune-filled tale of a small town whose veteran doctor is at first put off by the arrival of his new colleague, who has a habit of breaking into song. Joan Caufield co-stars. 107 min.
07-2281 ***▭$14.99***

The Emperor Waltz (1948)
Uncharacteristically fluffy entertainment from writer-director Billy Wilder features Bing Crosby as a phonograph salesman in Austria who tries to pitch his product to the country's ruler while attempting to woo the emperor's niece (Joan Fontaine). Richard Haydn and Sig Rumann co-star; tunes include "I Kiss Your Hand, Madame," "Friendly Mountains" and the title song. 106 min.
07-2127 ***▭$14.99***

A Connecticut Yankee In King Arthur's Court (1949)
Bing Crosby stars in this fanciful musical version of Mark Twain's immortal classic, as a blacksmith is thrown back in time to 6th-century Camelot. He's immediately pegged a wizard by Merlin and forced to joust Sir Lancelot for the hand of King Arthur's niece (Rhonda Fleming). Co-stars Sir Cedric Hardwicke and William Bendix. 108 min.
07-1510 Was $29.99 ***$14.99***

Mr. Music (1950)
Frothy musical comedy fun with Bing Crosby as a semi-retired songwriter who is lured back to help an on-the-skids Broadway producer stage a comeback show. Nancy Olson, Charles Coburn and Tom Ewell co-star, with special appearances by Groucho Marx, Peggy Lee, and Marge and Gower Champion. Songs include "Life Is So Peculiar," "High on the List." 113 min.
06-2060 ***$14.99***

Just For You (1952)
Widower Bing Crosby has his hands full trying to juggle his Broadway producer job, his engagement to Jane Wyman, and the demands of raising two teenagers in this spry musical comedy. Songs include "Zing a Little Zong," "I'll Si-Si Ya in Bahia" and the title tune. With Natalie Wood, Robert Arthur, Ethel Barrymore. 95 min.
06-2122 ***$14.99***

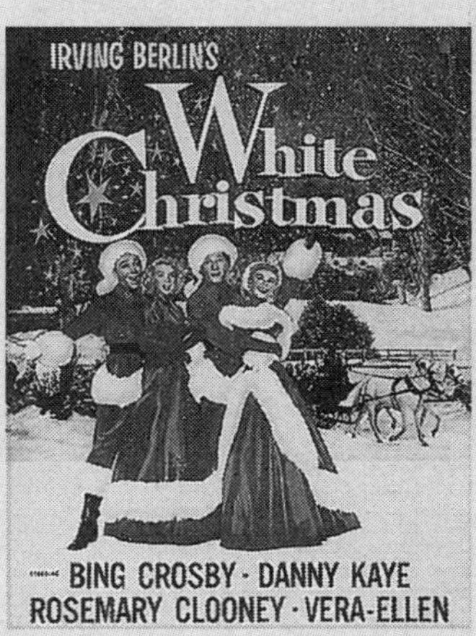

White Christmas (1954)
Movies Unlimited is proud to present the all-time holiday favorite complete with Irving Berlin score, Bing Crosby and Danny Kaye, Rosemary Clooney, Vera-Ellen, frolicking laughs and good times for all! A treat for the entire family. 120 min.
06-1305 ***▭$14.99***

White Christmas: Collector's Edition
Film buffs will be dreaming of this deluxe collector's edition of the Bing Crosby/Danny Kaye musical. Along with a letterboxed print of the movie, there is an 8x10 photo, a colorful brochure, a CD of the beloved Irving Berlin soundtrack, and many other bonuses.
06-2274 ***▭$59.99***

Bing Crosby Collector's Set
Catch some of B-B-Bing's finest musical moments in this set that includes the films "Here Come the Waves," "We're Not Dressing," "The Emperor Waltz" and "Rhythm on the River."
07-2130 Save $30.00! ***$29.99***

Bing Crosby Surprise Package
This triple treat of vintage TV features Bing joining host Perry Como for a song-filled "Kraft Music Hall" episode from 1960, followed by a 1954 interview at the Crosby home with Edward R. Murrow. Rounding out the package is a Wayne and Shuster special that looks at the careers of Crosby and Bob Hope. 110 min.
53-6306 ***$29.99***

Holiday Inn/ Going My Way Gift Set
You'll be "swingin' on a star" with the addition of this money-saving Bing Crosby two-pack to your video collection.
07-2449 Save $15.00! ***$14.99***

Please see our index for these other Bing Crosby titles: *Blue Skies • The Country Girl • Here Comes The Groom • High Society • Let's Make Love • Riding High • Road To Bali • The Road To Hong Kong • Road To Morocco • Road To Rio • Road To Singapore • Road To Utopia • Road To Zanzibar • Robin And The Seven Hoods • Star Spangled Rhythm*

The Stork Club (1945)
Betty Hutton plays a hat-check girl who pals up with hobo Barry Fitzgerald, who is actually a millionaire, in this frothy comedy with some memorable musical bits. Hutton belts out her famous "Doctor, Lawyer, Indian Chief." Co-stars Robert Benchley. 98 min.
10-4040 *$19.99*

Band Wagon (1940)
Inspired by a British radio series, this comedy with music focuses on some amateur comics who convert a haunted castle into a TV station, until some Nazi spies cause problems. Arthur Askey, Jack Hylton star. 85 min.
09-5250 *$19.99*

Zis Boom Bah (1941)
"Hey, kids, let's get together and put on a show!" That's the idea behind this raucous spoof about a vaudeville performer who's sent to college to spy on his bratty son. Music and comedy in equal doses, with Peter Lind Hayes, Mary Healy, Huntz Hall, Benny Rubin. 61 min.
09-1500 Was $19.99 *$14.99*

All-Black Musicals

Music And Comedy Masters, Vol. 1
A collection of nifty shorts featuring black performers is on tap here: "Ain't Misbehavin'" with Fats Waller and Louis Armstrong, "Blues and Boogie" with Maxine Sullivan and Nat King Cole, and "Murder in Swingtime" with Les Hite & Orchestra. 80 min.
10-8421 Was $19.99 *$14.99*

Music And Comedy Masters, Vol. 2
Terrific compendium of African-American greats performing from the golden age of jazz and be-bop. There's Cab Calloway ("Minnie the Moocher"), Mantan Moreland ("Showtime at the Apollo"), Hamtree Harrington ("Jittering Jitterbugs") and Bessie Smith ("St. Louis Blues"). 75 min.
10-8422 Was $19.99 *$14.99*

Music And Comedy Masters, Vol. 3
Marian Anderson, Sarah Vaughn, Duke Ellington, Lionel Hampton, Dinah Washington, Nipsey Russell and Nat King Cole are among the artists performing "Basin Street Review," "Symphony in Black" and other choice numbers. 80 min.
10-8423 Was $19.99 *$14.99*

Music And Comedy Masters, Vol. 4
A wonderful selection of classic musical shorts showcasing great black performers. Featured are Cab Calloway's "Jitterbug Party," the Nat King Cole Trio, Count Basie & Orchestra, Louis Armstrong and Duke Ellington, among others. 75 min.
10-8424 Was $19.99 *$14.99*

Music And Comedy Masters, Vol. 5
The talented African-American entertainers of yesteryear appear in this classic collection of musical shorts. Included here are "Sepian Swing" with Cab Calloway, "Stars on Parade" with Herb Jeffries, plus Dorothy Dandridge, Louis Armstrong, Bill "Bojangles" Robinson and others. 60 min.
10-8425 Was $19.99 *$14.99*

Music And Comedy Masters, Vol. 6
Superb compilation of classic shorts starring black music and comedy greats. Included are "Open the Door, Richard" with Dusty Fletcher, "Slow Poke" with Stepin Fetchit and "Spying the Spy," a rare all-black 1915 short on private detectives. 50 min.
10-8426 Was $19.99 *$14.99*

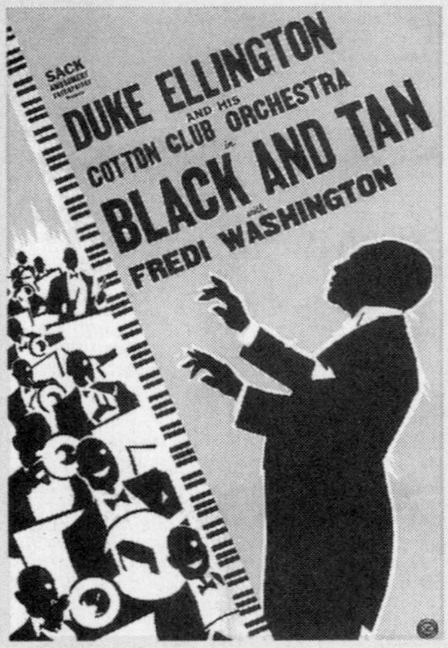

The Duke Is Tops (1938)/ Black And Tan (1929)
Vintage all-black musical about a woman who gets her big break and has to bid adieu to her boyfriend/producer. Big, sassy production numbers highlight this rare find, which was the film debut of the great Lena Horne. AKA: "The Bronze Venus." Next up, see the legendary Duke Ellington and his Cotton Club Orchestra performing "The Duke Steps Out," "Black Beauty," "Hot Feet" and "The Black and Tan Fantasy"
08-5014 *$19.99*

Sepia Cinderella (1936)
A songwriter's sudden success and fame leads him to abandon his girlfriend and start a fast slide down the "fast lane" in this all-black musical/drama. Billy Daniels, Sheila Guyse, Tondeleyo star. 70 min.
08-5072 *$19.99*

Burlesque In Harlem (1936)
Dewey "Pigmeat" Markham ("Here Comes the Judge") stars in this rousing, all-singin', all-dancin' spectacular set in a Harlem theater.The songs are lively, the dancing fleet of foot and the spirit contagious. 60 min.
15-9015 *$19.99*

Swing (1938)
Rousing all-black musical love story that follows the sometimes sad, sometimes rapturous relationship of an easy lover and a naive cook from the fields of Birmingham to the nightlife of Harlem. Cora Green, Hazel Diaz, Carmen Newsome, Alex Lovejoy star. 70 min.
01-1417 *$19.99*

Broken Strings (1940)
Clarence Muse co-scripted and starred in this all-black musical drama loosely based on "The Jazz Singer." Classical violinist and music teacher Muse is upset when his swing-loving son decides not to follow in his father's footsteps. 60 min.
09-1321 *$19.99*

Mystery In Swing (1940)
Unique all-black musical murder mystery! Someone killed suave trumpeter Prince Ellis by putting snake venom on his trumpet's mouthpiece. Was it Prince's wife, tired of his two-timing? Or any of the other women he was involved with? Or their men? Monte Hawley, Marguerite Whitten star. 66 min.
09-1843 Was $29.99 *$19.99*

Paradise In Harlem (1940)
All-black musical has fascinating glimpses into the life of black entertainers before WWII. Starring Mamie Smith. 83 min.
17-1105 *$19.99*

Stormy Weather (1943)
One of mainstream Hollywood's rare all-black musicals, showcasing Bill "Bojangles" Robinson's dancing and Lena Horne's singing and a romantic subplot. Also features Fats Waller, Cab Calloway and his orchestra, the Nicholas Brothers and Dooley Wilson ("Casablanca"). 77 min.
04-2039 □*$19.99*

Cabin In The Sky (1943)
Glossy all-black MGM musical with Eddie "Rochester" Anderson as a gambler whose soul becomes the prize in a contest between God and the Devil. Lena Horne, Ethel Waters, Rex Ingram, Louis Armstrong and Duke Ellington are featured; Vincente Minnelli's first directing assignment. 100 min.
12-1435 Was $24.99 *$19.99*

Big Timers (1945)
Rare and rip-roaring all-black musical concerning a poor young miss who catches the eye of an Army officer. Francine Everett, Duke Williams star; performances by Stepin Fetchit, Rocky Brown, Gertrude Saunders, many others. 36 min.
01-1401 *$19.99*

Beware (1946)
Louis Jordan and his Tympani Five swing out in this tremendous all-black musical. Their gig at Jordan's old college turns into a musical mission of mercy to save the alma mater from financial ruin. Valerie Black, Frank Wilson. 60 min.
01-1400 *$19.99*

Tall, Tan And Terrific (1946)
The owner of a Harlem nightclub is accused of shooting a gambler, and it's up to slapstick sleuth Mantan Moreland to catch the real killer in this all-black musical featurette. With Monte Hawley, Francine Everett. 40 min.
10-1311 *$19.99*

Boy, What A Girl! (1946)
A delightful musical-comedy featuring Tim Moore ("Kingfish" on TV's "Amos-N-Andy"). He plays a producer who dons women's clothing in order to make the show go on. Outstanding musical numbers and a cameo by Gene Krupa add to the fun.
17-1108 *$19.99*

Dirty Gertie From Harlem U.S.A. (1946)
All-black version of Somerset Maugham's "Rain." Gertie goes to Trinidad to hide from her boyfriend and finds fun and songs at a Harlem-style variety show. Francine Everett. 60 min.
62-1190 *$19.99*

Murder With Music (1946)
A reporter tries to get the "big story" on a notorious gangster in this all-black crime drama, laced with musical numbers. Nellie Hill, Noble Sissle. 57 min.
62-1189 *$19.99*

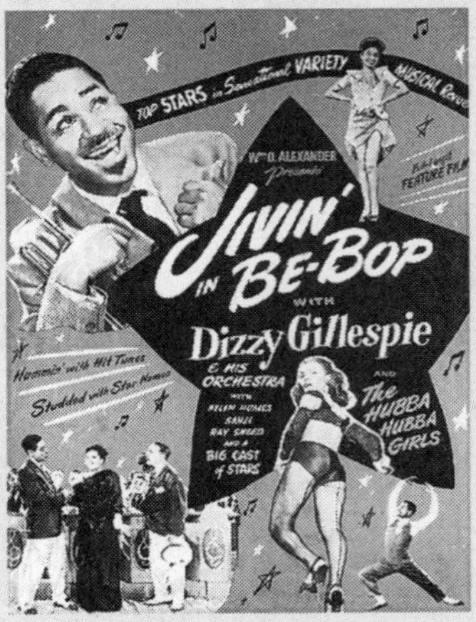

Jivin' In Bebop (1946)
Dizzy Gillespie and band are featured in this full-length musical that includes hits songs of the 1940s. 60 min.
01-1253 *$19.99*

Juke Joint (1947)
Fast and funny all-black musical comedy concerning a pair of vagabonds who try to repay their landlady's kindness by "rescuing" her daughters from some loose-living lads. Spencer Williams, July Jones, Inez Newman star. 70 min.
01-1408 *$19.99*

Junction 88 (1947)
All aboard for the express train to music, fun, laughs, and all points west! Rollicking all-black revue that keeps the entertainment running on time. "Pigmeat" Markham, Bob Howard, Wyatt Clark, Noble Sissie and his Orchestra star. 70 min.
01-1409 *$19.99*

Reet, Petite And Gone (1947)
Louis Jordan, the top saxophone player, stars in this all-black story of a swindled inheritance. Jazzy score includes "Let the Good Times Roll" and "That Chick's Too Young to Fry." 67 min.
09-1416 *$19.99*

Boardinghouse Blues (1948)
A troubled theatrical boardinghouse serves as the backdrop for this terrific all-black musical revue. Moms Mabley, Dusty Fletcher star; amongst the acts caught in performance are Lucky Millinder's band, Bull Moose Jackson, Una Mae Carlisle, Stump & Stumpy, and many more. 90 min.
01-1404 *$19.99*

Look Out Sister (1948)
Louis Jordan and the Tympani Five get in their licks on a dude ranch, of all places. Thrill as "Two-Gun" Jordan tears up the mortgage on the place and wins the fair lady's hand! Fine all-black musical fun with Suzette Harbin, Monte Hawley. 67 min.
01-1410 *$19.99*

Hi-De-Ho (1948)
Cab Calloway stars in this musical-drama as a bandleader caught between rival gangs. Jeni Le Gon, the Miller Brothers and Peter Sisters co-star. 64 min.
08-5068 *$19.99*

Miracle In Harlem (1948)
One of the best all-black films ever made: a superior blend of music, comedy, romance and drama. A Harlem "tycoon" plays possum when he discovers business would be better if he was dead. Stepin Fetchit, Sheila Guyse, Lynn Proctor Trio. 70 min.
17-1111 *$19.99*

Killer Diller (1948)
A superior cast of top black performers in a top-notch vaudeville show reminiscent of the old Apollo Theatre extravaganzas; Moms Mabley, Nat "King" Cole, Butterfly McQueen and a host of others are on view. 70 min.
17-1112 *$19.99*

Carmen Jones (1954)
Oscar Hammerstein II's all-black revision of Bizet's "Carmen," brought to the screen by Otto Preminger, showcases Harry Belafonte as a handsome soldier whose love for sexy, conniving Dorothy Dandridge leads him to murder. Pearl Bailey, Olga James and Diahann Carroll also star in this classic, a much-requested film at Movies Unlimited. 105 min.
04-2282 □*$19.99*

Alice Faye

365 Nights In Hollywood (1934)
Starstruck Illinois gal Alice Faye arrives in Hollywood dreaming of a movie career, but instead enrolls in a fly-by-night acting school run by two con men. When a wealthy man agrees to finance a film, the scheming school owners hatch a plot to sabotage it in this song-filled comedy, long thought to be a "lost film." With James Dunn, Frank Mitchell. 77 min.
73-3006 *$19.99*

On The Avenue (1937)
Frolicsome musical-comedy with Dick Powell as a Broadway impresario who produces a satirical musical starring Alice Faye as "The Richest Girl in the World." When the woman Faye plays appears at the theater outraged, Powell falls for her, setting in motion all sorts of wacky events. Madeleine Carroll and The Ritz Brothers co-star; among the Irving Berlin tunes is "I've Got Love to Keep Me Warm." 88 min.
04-2832 □*$19.99*

Alexander's Ragtime Band (1938)
Terrific tuner follows society boy Tyrone Power, who decides to play ragtime instead of classical music and forms his own group. While he struggles, singer/girlfriend Alice Faye opts for a Broadway stint and marriage to pianist Don Ameche. Years later, after World War I, Power and Faye tearfully reunite. Ethel Merman co-stars; "Now It Can Be Told" and "My Walking Stick" are among the more than two dozen Irving Berlin songs featured. 106 min.
04-2728 □*$19.99*

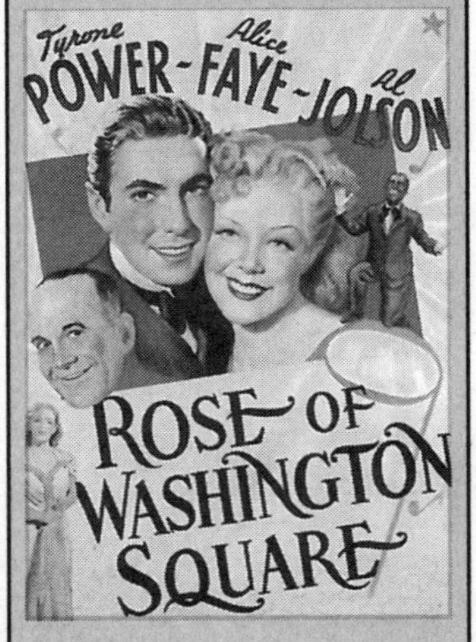

Rose Of Washington Square (1939)
Set in 1920s New York, this bouncy musical loosely based on the life of Fanny Brice, stars Alice Faye as the songstress who continually tries to keep con artist boyfriend Tyrone Power out of prison while her career as a Ziegfeld Girl takes off. Al Jolson, who plays the couple's friend, sings such songs as "My Mammy" and "California, Here I Come." Other tunes include "I Never Knew Heaven Could Speak." 86 min.
04-2833 □*$19.99*

Weekend In Havana (1941)
Macy's showgirl Alice Faye heads off on a Caribbean vacation, but after her ship encounters problems, the cruise company sends her to Havana with official chaperone John Payne. In the Cuban resort city, Faye meets a married gambler who takes a liking to her, while Payne realizes she's the gal for him. Cesar Romero and Carmen Miranda co-star. Songs include "Romance and Rhumba" and "Tropical Song." 81 min.
04-2835 □*$19.99*

Hello, Frisco, Hello (1943)
Lively and colorful musical set on the sprawling Barbary Coast, where entrepreneur John Payne opens a saloon and becomes romantically involved with socialite Lynn Bari, pushing main singing attraction Alice Faye out of his life. Misfortune and marital problems soon follow Payne around, while Faye finds fame in Europe. Can they reunite? Songs include Oscar-winner "You'll Never Know." 99 min.
04-2831 □*$19.99*

Please see our index for these other Alice Faye titles: *Four Jills In A Jeep • In Old Chicago • Poor Little Rich Girl • Stowaway*

Youth On Parade (1942)
First-rate musical-comedy about a group of college students who create an imaginary "perfect collegian," only to have a psychology teacher demand to meet her. Facing expulsion, the students hire a New York actress to portray her. With John Hubbard, Martha O'Driscoll, Ruth Terry and, in a small role, Yvonne DeCarlo; songs are by Sammy Cahn and Jule Styne. 72 min.
09-5252 *$19.99*

Perils Of Pauline (1947)
Betty Hutton, John Lund, Billy DeWolfe. Hutton explodes on the screen in this fine musical semi-biographical account of Pearl White's life as silent serial queen. 96 min.
10-2000 *$14.99*

The Three Musketeers (1939)
A rousing, musical take on Alexandre Dumas' classic starring Don Ameche as D'Artagnan, the brave young adventurer who joins forces with the swashbuckling Musketeers (played by the Ritz Brothers) to protect King Louis XIII from scheming Cardinal Richelieu. Lionel Atwill, Binnie Barnes, John Carradine also star. Songs include "My Lady" and "Song of the Musketeers." 73 min.
04-2727 *$19.99*

Mimi (1935)
Wonderful musical based on the novel that inspired "La Boheme." Douglas Fairbanks, Jr. and Gertrude Lawrence are magnificent as the struggling playwright in 1850s Paris and the waif whose love furnishes him with the inspiration he has long sought. Puccini's music is featured throughout. 92 min.
09-2042 Was $19.99 *$14.99*

Hats Off (1936)
Song-filled fluff with John Payne and Mae Clarke as press agents for two rival Texas towns, each of whom tries to one-up the other in the promotion of their town's impending exposition, while mixing in a little romance for good measure. This was future director Sam Fuller's first screen credit, as co-writer. Songs include "Let's Have Another," "Hats Off." 66 min.
09-3098 *$19.99*

Rainbow Over Broadway (1933)
A brother-sister songwriting team have to overcome the ambitions of their stepmother, a faded Broadway star looking to make a comeback, in order to realize their own dreams of success in this early musical-comedy. Joan Marsh, Lucien Littlefield, Frank Albertson star. 51 min.
09-3122 *$14.99*

Manhattan Merry-Go-Round (1937)
An oddball array of guest stars that includes Cab Calloway, Louis Prima, Gene Autry and Joe DiMaggio propels this musical comedy about a gangster who takes control of a recording studio. Phil Regan, Ann Dvorak, Leo Carillo star. 75 min.
01-1259 *$19.99*

Over She Goes (1937)
Lively musical-comedy about an elderly vaudevillian who inherits the title of "lord" and proceeds to invite some old pals to share in the fun. A woman he once promised marriage to appears on the scene and soon tries to sue the entertainer for breach of contract. John Wood, Claire Luce, Laddie Cliff star. 74 min.
09-5089 *$19.99*

Follow Your Heart (1936)
In her only film appearance, opera star Marion Talley plays a young singer who must decide on which career path to take. Should she follow her mother's footsteps into the world of opera? Michael Bartlett co-stars with Nigel Bruce. Features selections from "Lucia Di Lammermoor" and other operas; co-written by Nathaniel West and Lester Cole.
09-5251 *$19.99*

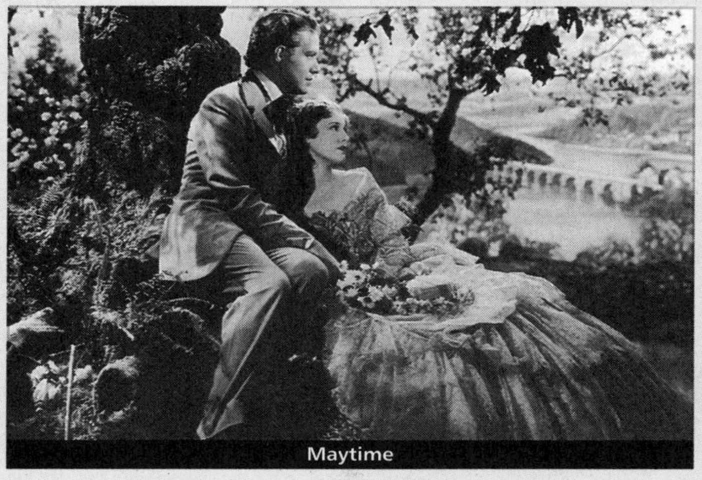

Maytime

Nelson Eddy & Jeanette MacDonald

The Merry Widow (1934)
Lavish early MGM musical, based on Franz Lehar's operetta, stars Jeanette MacDonald as the wealthy patron of a postage stamp European country whose sudden move to Paris throws the nation into a tizzy. Can playboy prince Maurice Chevalier woo her back? Delightful romantic comedy also stars Edward Everett Horton, Una Merkel; songs include "Girls, Girls, Girls," "Vilia" and "Merry Widow Waltz." 99 min.
12-1124 *$19.99*

The Cat And The Fiddle (1934)
Down-on-his-luck composer Ramon Novarro hopes his new operetta will save him, but a bounced check, an exiting orchestra and cast, and a drunken lead actress could lead to disaster. Enter would-be singer Jeanette MacDonald, who agrees to help Novarro avoid jail. Early MGM musical with Technicolor sequences also stars Frank Morgan; songs include Kern and Harbach's "The Night Was Made for Love." 88 min.
12-2497 *$19.99*

Naughty Marietta (1935)
Nelson Eddy and Jeanette MacDonald first teamed in this lively Victor Herbert operetta about the romance between a French princess and a swaggering soldier. Songs like "Ah, Sweet Mystery of Life" and "Tramp, Tramp, Tramp" highlight this delight. Frank Morgan, Elsa Lanchester co-star. 106 min.
12-1323 *$19.99*

Rose Marie (1936)
Nelson Eddy and Jeanette MacDonald are calling you, in this classic operetta. He's a mountie assigned to bring in her brother (James Stewart), but before long they fall in love. Great sets and songs, including "Indian Love Call." 110 min.
12-1443 *$19.99*

Rosalie (1937)
The music of Cole Porter, including "In the Still of the Night," highlights this romantic musical about a West Point cadet who falls for a European princess. Nelson Eddy, Eleanor Powell, Edna May Oliver, Frank Morgan and Ray Bolger star. 122 min.
12-1442 Was $24.99 *$19.99*

Maytime (1937)
One of the best films from Jeanette MacDonald and Nelson Eddy was this story of an opera star and a penniless singer who fall in love, but face problems and complications from her husband/manager. Songs include "Sweetheart." Co-stars John Barrymore, Herman Bing. 132 min.
12-1469 *$19.99*

The Firefly (1937)
Glowing musical set during the Napoleonic War stars Jeanette MacDonald as a spy who poses as a singer in a Madrid cafe in order to learn Napoleon's military secrets. She attempts to enlist wealthy Spaniard Allan Jones to her cause, and romantic and political intrigues ensue. With Warren William, Douglass Dumbrille; songs include "The Donkey Serenade," "A Woman's Kiss." 130 min.
12-2498 *$19.99*

The Girl Of The Golden West (1938)
Saloon keeper Jeanette MacDonald falls for dashing bandit Nelson Eddy in this musical romantic drama set in the Old West. With Walter Pidgeon, Buddy Ebsen, Monty Woolley; songs include "Señorita" "Who Are We to Say," "Ave Maria." 120 min.
12-1122 *$19.99*

Sweethearts (1938)
The time-worn stage chestnut is a "play-within-a-film" for this frothy Jeanette MacDonald/Nelson Eddy musical comedy, written by Dorothy Parker and Alan Campbell. MacDonald and Eddy play a married acting couple who plan to leave Broadway for Hollywood, but impresario Frank Morgan plots to stop them. With Ray Bolger, Florence Rice, Mischa Auer. 120 min.
12-1125 *$19.99*

Balalaika (1939)
Nelson Eddy is a Russian prince who falls in love with cafe singer Ilona Massey and arranges for her to perform at the Royal Opera, but her debut is rudely interrupted when the Russian Revolution erupts. Years later, the two reunite in Paris, where Eddy has gained fame as a crooner. Features a classic rendition of "Stille Nacht (Silent Night)." 91 min.
12-2878 *$19.99*

Let Freedom Ring (1939)
Politics and music mix when Harvard lawyer Nelson Eddy returns to his small Western hometown to find a railroad company muscling in on the townspeople. Eddy disguises himself as "The Hornet" and launches a battle against the evil company and its thugs. Edward Arnold, Virginia Bruce and Victor McLaglen co-star; tunes include "Dusty Road," "Love Serenade," "Home Sweet Home" and more. 100 min.
12-2880 *$19.99*

New Moon (1940)
Colorful 1700s New Orleans is the setting for adventure, romance and song in this Jeanette MacDonald-Nelson Eddy musical, the duo's sixth pairing. The score includes "Lover Come Back," "One Kiss," "Marianne," and "Wanting You"; with Mary Boland, George Zucco. 105 min.
12-1018 *$19.99*

BITTER SWEET

Bitter Sweet (1940)
The music of Noel Coward and the seventh screen pairing of Nelson Eddy and Jeanette MacDonald are the ingredients for movie magic. The duo are struggling to make ends meet in 1880s Vienna, but singer MacDonald's patron (George Sanders) has amorous intentions that lead composer Eddy to challenge him to a duel. 92 min.
12-1120 *$19.99*

The Chocolate Soldier (1941)
In order to test his wife's fidelity, opera singer Nelson Eddy disguises himself as a Russian suitor and tries to woo her. Much to his surprise, he succeeds! Lavish musical romance, based on the Oscar Straus operetta, co-stars Risë Stevens, Nigel Bruce; songs include "While My Lady Sleeps," "Sympathy." 102 min.
12-1121 *$19.99*

Cairo (1942)
Top-flight intrigue ensues when a war correspondent is recruited by a purported British spy to pass on top-secret information to a woman in Cairo. While in the city, the journalist falls for an American movie star, learns that his Cairo contact is actually a Nazi spy and finds himself in a frantic desert chase. Jeanette MacDonald, Robert Young, Reginald Owen and Ethel Waters star. 101 min.
12-2784 *$19.99*

Northwest Outpost (1947)
In this grand frontier musical/drama that was his last film, Nelson Eddy plays an ex-soldier who comes to the aid of Russian settlers in 19th-century California and falls in love with the wife of a jailed aristocrat. Ilona Massey, Joseph Schildkraut co-star. 91 min.
63-1387 *$19.99*

Three Daring Daughters (1948)
Jane Powell, Elinor Donahue and Ann B. Todd are the feisty siblings of divorced magazine editor Jeanette MacDonald who go to great lengths to reunite their parents. But the girls carry out their scheme while Mom's on an ocean cruise...meeting and marrying concert pianist Jose Iturbi! Songs include "Route 66," "Alma Mater" and many classical works. 115 min.
12-2792 *$19.99*

Jeanette MacDonald Scrapbook
The beloved screen operetta star as she appeared in the TV shows "Person to Person" with Edward Murrow and "This Is Your Life," as well as in original movie previews from many of her hits with Nelson Eddy. 90 min.
10-7430 *$19.99*

Please see our index for these other Nelson Eddy/Jeanette MacDonald titles: *Dancing Lady • Follow The Boys • Phantom Of The Opera • San Francisco*

Bobby Breen

Let's Sing Again (1936)
Eight-year-old boy soprano Bobby Breen, who earned a following on Eddie Cantor's radio show, made his screen debut as an orphan who gets a chance to sing opera in New York. Songs include "The Farmer in the Dell," "La Donna e Mobile" from "Rigoletto" and the title tune. 70 min.
17-3085 *$19.99*

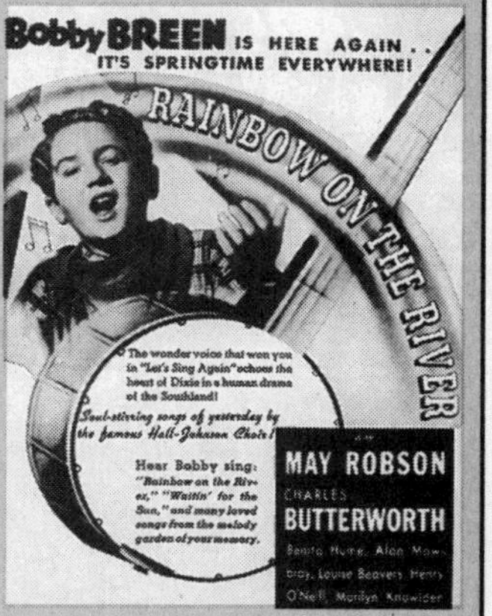

Rainbow On The River (1936)
Bobby Breen and May Robson star in a song-filled tale of a young orphan boy and the ex-slave caring for him in the post-Civil War South, until the child goes to live with a wealthy grandmother in New York. With Louise Beavers, Eddie "Rochester" Anderson. AKA: "It Happened in New Orleans." 83 min.
09-1279 *$19.99*

Make A Wish (1937)
While at summer camp in the Maine woods, little Bobby Breen befriends composer Basil Rathbone, who left the city to try and break his creative block, and is soon playing matchmaker for his widowed singer mother and Rathbone. Lively family musical also stars Marion Claire, Leon Errol; songs include "Music in My Heart," "Old Man Rip." 75 min.
09-1280 Was $29.99 *$19.99*

Breaking The Ice (1938)
When his widowed mother is forced to move in with her domineering brother and his family, Bobby Breen runs away from home and joins a travelling ice revue to earn money for her. Song-filled tale stars Charles Ruggles, Dolores Costello. 79 min.
09-1273 *$19.99*

Hawaii Calls (1938)
After being nabbed while trying to stow away on board an ocean liner en route to Hawaii, young Bobby Breen sings for his travel fare and, along with sidekick Pua, turns detective to recover stolen naval documents from crooks. Co-stars Ned Sparks, Pua Lani and Irvin S. Cobb. Songs include "That's the Hawaiian in Me," "Down Where the Trade Winds Blow" and "Aloha Oe." 65 min.
10-8143 *$14.99*

Way Down South (1939)
A young orphan (Bobby Breen) in antebellum Louisiana tries to regain his family's plantation from treacherous trustees in this song-laced drama that was scripted by co-star Clarence Muse, who played a loyal slave, and poet Langston Hughes. With Charles Middleton, Ralph Morgan.62 min.
10-7234 Was $29.99 *$19.99*

Escape To Paradise (1939)
Adorable little Bobby Breen plays a South American tourist guide who steers traveller Kent Taylor into a romance with native gal Maria Shelton in this spry musical-comedy. Songs include "Rhythm of the Rio," "Ay, Ay, Ay." 60 min.
10-8237 Was $19.99 *$14.99*

Fisherman's Wharf (1939)
A boy (Bobby Breen) adopted by a San Francisco fisherman decides to leave his home when the fisherman's sister-in-law moves in with her annoying son. Efforts are on to find Breen...but first, some musical numbers, including "Blue Italian Waters" and "Sell Your Cares for a Song." Leo Carillo, Lee Patrick and Slicker the Seal also star. 72 min.
10-8243 *$19.99*

Say It With Flowers (1934)
A number of cockney variety acts are featured in this musical about two poor flower sellers who are helped when a group of entertainers stage a benefit for them. Mary Clare, Ben Field and George Carney star. 71 min.
10-9726 *$14.99*

King Kelly Of The U.S.A. (1934)
Half-musical, half-comic, all-romantic misadventures of a young man who falls for a princess while on a transatlantic cruise. Guy Robertson, Irene Ware and Edgar Kennedy star. 64 min.
50-1907 *$12.99*

Reckless (1935)
In this snappy romantic drama spiced with musical numbers, Jean Harlow performs a change-of-pace role as a Broadway actress whose effect on men leads to jealousy, scandal and even murder. William Powell, Franchot Tone, May Robson, Ted Healy and Rosalind Russell star. Songs include "Reckless," "Ev'rything's Been Done Before" and the title tune. 96 min.
12-2300 *$19.99*

Sweet Adeline (1935)
A top-notch score by Kern and Hammerstein highlights this lively musical romance starring Irene Dunne as the sweetheart of a Hoboken beer garden in the Gay Nineties who falls for a dapper songwriter (Donald Woods). Songs include "Here Am I," "'Twas Not Long Ago," "Don't Ever Leave Me," and more. 87 min.
12-2500 *$19.99*

Lassie From Lancashire (1938)
English music hall comedy, as two aspiring young singers start out on the "rocky road to stardom" and soon fall in love. Marjorie Brown, Hal Thompson star. 67 min.
09-1657 Was $29.99 *$24.99*

One Night Of Love (1934)
Wonderful early film musical stars Grace Moore as an aspiring opera singer who falls in love with teacher Tullio Carminati. Selections from "Madame Butterfly," "Carmen" and other works highlight the Oscar-winning score; with Jane Darwell, Lyle Talbot. 80 min.
02-1987 *$19.99*

Sing While You're Able (1937)
A toy company owner and his daughter find a singing hillbilly in the Arkansas backwoods and take him back to the big city in hopes of helping their radio show ratings. Pinky Tomlin, Monte Collins and Toby Wing star in this musical farce. 65 min.
10-1353 *$19.99*

Dance Band (1935)
Rival bandleaders Charles "Buddy" Rogers and June Clyde enter their combos in a big contest, but before the finals the feuding pair fall in love in this spry musical comedy. With Steven Geray, Magda Kun. 60 min.
10-7029 Was $19.99 *$14.99*

Swing It, Professor (1937)
Fun and frothy musical comedy that stars Pinky Tomlin as a hardline musicologist who can't stand jazz...and after his obstinance costs him his job, he soon discovers that crazy rhythm ain't all that bad! With Milburn Stone, Mary Kornman. 62 min.
10-7187 Was $19.99 *$14.99*

Bittersweet (1933)
Splendid rendition of the Noel Coward classic about the woman wooed by an accomplished violinist, and who only after marriage discovers his tragic addiction to gambling. Masterful movie operetta stars Anna Neagle, Fernand Graavey. 76 min.
10-7241 *$19.99*

Love On Wheels (1932)
Spiffy British musical in which a worker at a shop tells a woman he's the manager in hopes of impressing her. When he's fired, she loses interest, but wins her back after catching a crook and being named the store manager. Jack Hulbert, Edmund Gwenn and Gordon Harker star. 80 min.
10-9725 *$19.99*

Madam Satan (1930)
For his only musical, Cecil B. DeMille chose this glossy tale about a neglected wife who adopts a mysterious alter ego in order to win back her husband. A spectacular dance party sequence set in a dirigible floating over New York City climaxes with the airship catching fire (this was seven years before the Hindenburg!). Kay Johnson, Reginald Denny, Lillian Roth, Roland Young star. 115 min.
12-2622 *$19.99*

Flirtation Walk (1934)
Musical-romance with Dick Powell as an army officer stationed in Hawaii who gets involved with Ruby Keeler, the general's engaged daughter. In order to avoid a scandal, the pair break up, but meet again years later when Powell's a West Point officer producing the annual play that turns out to star Keeler. With Pat O'Brien; songs include "I See Two Lovers" and the title tune. 98 min.
12-2728 ❑*$19.99*

The Goldwyn Follies (1938)
All singing, all dancing, all laughs and all in Technicolor...this lavish "film within a film" about a Hollywood mogul out to make the biggest movie of all time features Andrea Leeds, Kenny Baker, Edgar Bergen and Charlie McCarthy, Adolphe Menjou, the Ritz Brothers, and a score by George and Ira Gershwin. 115 min.
44-1859 Was $19.99 *$14.99*

Deanna Durbin

Three Smart Girls (1936)
The feature film debut of 14-year-old soon-to-be-star Deanna Durbin casts her as one of three sisters who go to great lengths to stop their father's marriage to a golddigger and reunite him with their mother. Nan Grey and Barbara Read play the other siblings, while Ray Milland, Alice Brady and Binnie Barnes also star. Songs include "Someone to Care for Me" and "My Heart Is Singing." 84 min.
07-2186 ❑*$19.99*

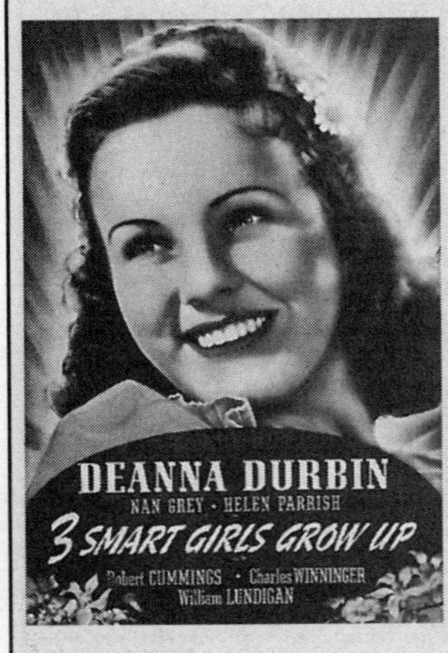

Three Smart Girls Grow Up (1939)
A delightful sequel to "Three Smart Girls" offers Deanna Durbin as a young woman getting involved with her sisters' love affairs and getting herself in a fix when one sister falls for the other's boyfriend. Nan Grey, Helen Parrish, Robert Cummings and Charles Winninger star. Songs include "Because" and "The Last Rose of Summer." 88 min.
07-2187 ❑*$19.99*

One Hundred Men And A Girl (1937)
Lively, music-filled fable starring Deanna Durbin as the feisty teen who talks famed conductor Leopold Stokowski into starting an orchestra consisting of unemployed musicians, including her trombonist father. Adolphe Menjou, Alice Brady and Billy Gilbert also star. The score includes a mix of popular tunes and classical works by Tchaikovsky and others. 84 min.
07-2185 ❑*$19.99*

Mad About Music (1938)
Worried about her age, vain Hollywood actress Gail Patrick decides she wants to forget about daughter Deanna Durbin, so she sends her to a Swiss boarding school. Durbin invents an explorer father to impress her mates, but when asked to prove he's real, she tries to find a suitable parent to play the role. With Herbert Marshall, Arthur Treacher. Songs include "I Love to Whistle." 96 min.
07-2374 ❑*$19.99*

That Certain Age (1938)
Smitten with her family's houseguest, visiting journalist Melvyn Douglas, teenager Deanna Durbin ignores former steady beau Jackie Cooper until Douglas sets things right in this song-filled romantic comedy that was co-scripted by Billy Wilder and Charles Brackett. Soundtrack includes "Be a Good Scout," "You're as Pretty as a Picture" and the title tune. 101 min.
07-2476 ❑*$19.99*

First Love (1939)
Modern "Cinderella" story starring Deanna Durbin as an orphan adopted by a wealthy but nasty family. When her relatives try to stop her from going to the ball, Deanna gets help from a family servant and meets her true love at the gala affair (as well as receiving her first screen kiss). Robert Stack co-stars. Songs include "Symphony," "Deserted," "Home Sweet Home." 85 min.
07-2371 ❑*$19.99*

It's A Date (1940)
Deanna Durbin stars in this frothy musical-comedy, playing the daughter of a popular actress (Kay Francis) who wishes to make it as a big-time star. She goes to Hawaii with mom, where she falls for a suave millionaire (Walter Pidgeon), but learns some lessons about life in the process. Songs include "Love Is All" and "Ave Maria." 103 min.
12-2242 *$19.99*

It Started With Eve (1941)
Ailing Charles Laughton wants to meet son Robert Cummings' future wife before he dies, but since she isn't immediately available, Cummings chooses a stand-in: spunky hat-check girl Deanna Durbin. Things get romantically complicated when Dad takes a liking to Deanna and Cummings' real fiancée arrives for a visit. Margaret Tallichet co-stars. 92 min.
07-2188 ❑*$19.99*

Nice Girl? (1941)
In one of her first "mature" screen roles, Deanna Durbin plays a lovestruck small-town girl who finagles a chance to drive visiting family friend Franchot Tone back to New York City. After her amorous overtures are rebuffed by Tone, Durbin returns home to find she's now the object of local gossip. With Robert Stack, Walter Brennan, Robert Benchley. Songs include "Love at Last," "Thank You America." Special video edition also includes an unused alternate ending. 96 min.
07-2475 ❑*$19.99*

His Butler's Sister (1943)
Small-town girl Deanna Durbin heads for New York to start her singing career and takes a job as a maid with half-brother Pat O'Brien, a butler working for a popular composer. O'Brien fires Durbin, hoping to shield her from the composer's romantic advances, but true love prevails. With Franchot Tone. Songs includes "In the Spirit of the Moment." 84 min.
07-2372 Was $19.99 ❑*$14.99*

The Amazing Mrs. Holliday (1943)
In a change-of-pace role, Deanna Durbin plays an American schoolteacher working in China who pretends to be a shipping magnate's widow so she can get a group of war orphans into the United States. Durbin still manages to sing some songs (including two in Chinese). With Edmond O'Brien, Barry Fitzgerald, Arthur Treacher. 98 min.
07-2707 ❑*$19.99*

Can't Help Singing (1944)
Beautiful Technicolor scenery and such Jerome Kern/E.Y. Harburg songs as "More and More," "Cal-i-for-ni-ay" and "Swing Your Sweetheart" highlight this lush costume musical starring Deanna Durbin as an 1840s senator's daughter who, against her father's wishes, heads west across the frontier to be with her cavalry officer beau. With Robert Paige, Ray Collins, Akim Tamiroff. 90 min.
07-2477 ❑*$19.99*

Lady On A Train (1945)
Funny and thrilling comedy-mystery showcasing Deanna Durbin as a woman who sees a murder from a train while en route to New York City. When the police ignore her story, she teams with a mystery writer to find the culprit. Durbin discovers the victim was a shipping tycoon, and begins investigating his wacky family. Ralph Bellamy, Edward Everett Horton, David Bruce co-star. 95 min.
07-2373 Was $19.99 ❑*$14.99*

Because Of Him (1946)
Eager for a shot at Broadway stardom, would-be actress Deanna Durbin works to become the protégé of veteran stage star Charles Laughton, over the objections of playwright Franchot Tone, in this breezy, song-filled romantic comedy. With Helen Broderick, Donald Meek. 98 min.
07-2708 ❑*$19.99*

Something In The Wind (1947)
Mistaken identity's the order of the day in a song-filled romantic comedy that finds singing disc jockey Deanna Durbin kidnapped by John Dall, who thinks she was involved with his tycoon grandfather. Can would-be singing star Donald O'Connor save her? With Charles Winninger, Jan Peerce; songs include "It's Only Love," "Turntable Song." 89 min.
07-2580 ❑*$19.99*

I'll Be Yours (1947)
Scripter Preston Sturges adapted the Ferenc Molnar play "The Good Fairy" to suit the talents of star Deanna Durbin. The result was this delightful musical comedy in which New York theater usherette Durbin tries to help handsome attorney Tom Drake land a job with meat-packing tycoon Adolphe Menjou. With William Bendix, Franklin Pangborn, Dudley Dickerson. 94 min.
07-2706 ❑*$19.99*

Up In Central Park (1948)
In turn-of-the-century New York, feisty Irish immigrant Deanna Durbin teams up with handsome young reporter Dick Haymes to help him bring down infamous politico "Boss" Tweed (Vincent Price). Lively adaptation of Sigmund Romberg's Broadway musical features such tunes as "Carousel in the Park," "Oh Say Do You See What I See?" and "When She Walks in the Room." 88 min.
07-2579 ❑*$19.99*

For The Love Of Mary (1948)
In her final film before retiring at the age of 27, Deanna Durbin plays a White House telephone operator who gets help from her unseen chief executive boss in straightening out her romantic problems. Edmond O'Brien, Jeffrey Lynn and Don Taylor co-star as Durbin's suitors in this breezy musical-comedy. Special video version includes an unused ending and song. 91 min.
07-2581 ❑*$19.99*

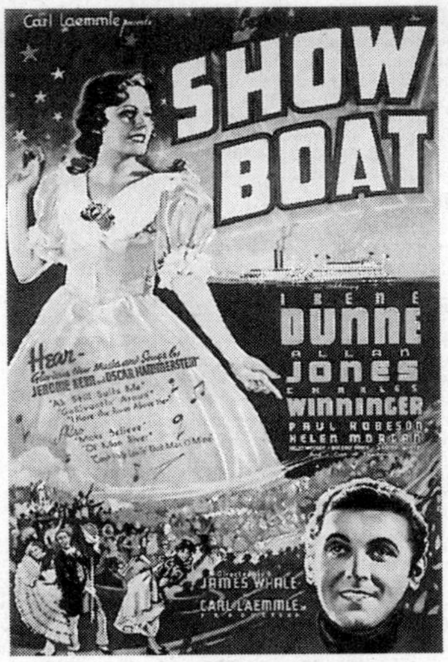

Show Boat (1936)
The second film version of the classic Hammerstein-Kern musical stars Irene Dunne, Allan Jones and Charles Winninger and features Helen Morgan torching off the songs "Bill" and "Can't Help Lovin' Dat Man" and the legendary Paul Robeson singing "Ol' Man River" and "Ah Still Suits Me." Directed by James Whale. 110 min.
12-2007 *$19.99*

The Voice Of Hollywood
A collection of six musical comedy shorts from the popular Tiffany Pictures series of the late '20s and early '30s. Performing in the studios of "radio station STAR" are such screen greats as Buster Keaton, Bert Wheeler and Robert Woolsey in solo turns, Lupe Velez, Ken Maynard, Marjorie Kane, Weber and Fields and many more. Songs, dancing, gags and even Laurel and Hardy look-alike waiters! 48 min.
62-1146 *$19.99*

42nd Street (1933)
Sensational Busby Berkeley musical that launched a thousand clichés; ailing Broadway director Warner Baxter puts his all into his last show, but when the leading lady breaks her ankle, plucky chorine Ruby Keeler must take her place. With Dick Powell, Bebe Daniels, Ginger Rogers. 89 min.
12-1914 Was $19.99 *$14.99*

Footlight Parade (1933)
One of Busby Berkeley's best, featuring out-of-this-world musical numbers and songs like "Honeymoon Hotel," "By a Waterfall," and "Shanghai Lil." James Cagney is a down-and-out stage producer who tries his hand at stupendous dance numbers. Joan Blondell, Ruby Keeler and Dick Powell co-star; directed by Lloyd Bacon. 105 min.
12-1916 Was $19.99 *$14.99*

Dames (1934)
Grand Busby Berkeley musical with dazzling production numbers, multitudes of chorus girls, and the beloved "let's put on a show" plot. Dick Powell, Ruby Keeler, Joan Blondell, ZaSu Pitts and Hugh Herbert star. Songs include "I Only Have Eyes for You," "Dames," "Girl at the Ironing Board." 90 min.
12-1915 Was $29.99 *$19.99*

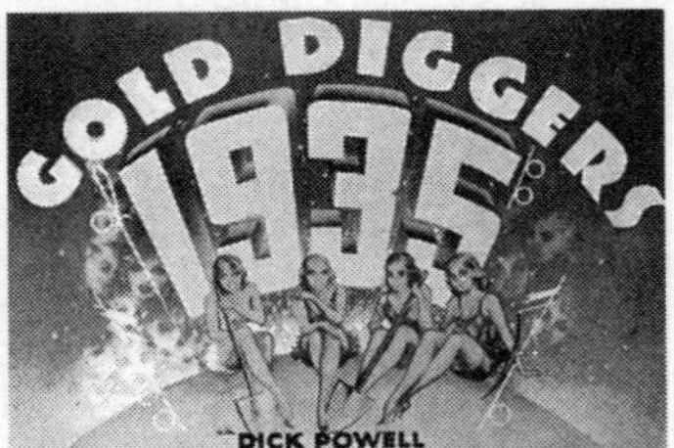

Gold Diggers Of 1935 (1935)
Pass on the plot concerning the types who populate a resort hotel and marvel at Busby Berkeley at the pinnacle of his form, including the Oscar-winning "Lullaby of Broadway" and the "baby grand ballet"; Dick Powell, Gloria Stuart, Adolphe Menjou, Glenda Farrell star. 95 min.
12-1918 *$29.99*

Billy Rose's Jumbo (1962)
Splashy and sensational filmed version of Rose's 1930s circus extravaganza benefits from a great Rodgers and Hart score, Busby Berkeley's magnificent musical sequences (his final filmwork), and spirited performances from Doris Day, Stephen Boyd, Jimmy Durante, and Martha Raye. 125 min.
12-1717 Was $29.99 *$19.99*

Flying Down To Rio (1933)
The credits in this breezy musical may list Dolores Del Rio first, but Fred Astaire and Ginger Rogers steal the show in their first film together. The story involves the romance between bandleader-pilot Gene Raymond and singer Del Rio, with the standout sequences including Fred and Ginger doing the "Carioca" together and dozens of chorus girls dancing on the wings of airplanes "in midair." 89 min.
05-1002 Was $19.99 ***$14.99***

Dancing Lady (1933)
Fast-paced, frothy musical comedy that set the tone for many of MGM's later works. Would-be Broadway star Joan Crawford is romanced by stage manager Clark Gable and playboy Franchot Tone, dances with Fred Astaire (his film debut), and even rehearses with Ted Healy and The Three Stooges. With Nelson Eddy, Robert Benchley. Truly something for everyone! 94 min.
12-1659 ***$19.99***

The Gay Divorcee (1934)
Cole Porter's Broadway hit became a perfect debut starring vehicle for dance legends-to-be Fred Astaire and Ginger Rogers, whose inevitable romance is sidetracked by a case of mistaken identity in an English seaside resort. With Betty Grable, Alice Brady. The score includes "Night and Day" and "The Continental," the first recipient of the Best Song Academy Award. 104 min.
18-7673 Was $19.99 ***$14.99***

Roberta (1935)
The lively dancing of Fred Astaire and Ginger Rogers highlights this Jerome Kern-Otto Harbach musical, set in Paris and featuring Irene Dunne and Randolph Scott. Look for an unknown Lucille Ball in the fashion show sequence! Score includes "Smoke Gets in Your Eyes" and "Lovely to Look At." 105 min.
12-1589 Was $29.99 ***$14.99***

Swing Time (1935)
Delightful musical stars Fred Astaire as a roguish gambler/dancer who is challenged by fiancé Betty Furness' father to come up with $25,000 to prove he's worthy of her hand. But after he falls in love with dance instructor Ginger Rogers, Fred'll do anything to keep from coming up with the bucks. The Jerome Kern-Dorothy Fields score includes "The Way You Look Tonight," "A Fine Romance." Also includes the original theatrical trailer. 103 min.
18-7657 Was $19.99 ***$14.99***

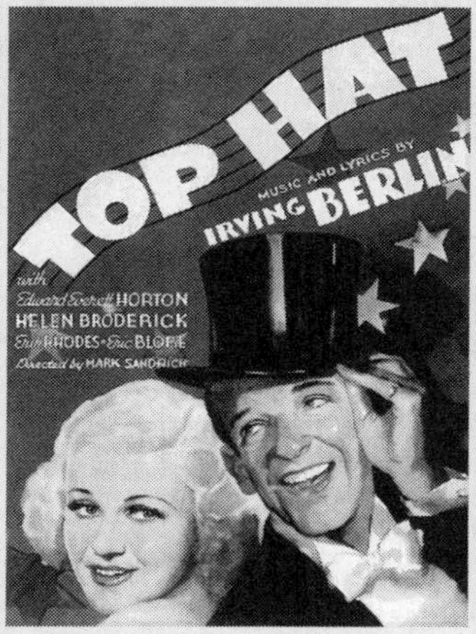

Top Hat (1935)
What is arguably the best of the Astaire-Rogers musicals features a classic Irving Berlin score, including "Cheek to Cheek" and "Isn't This a Lovely Day (To Be Caught in the Rain)?" Fred is an American dancer uprooted to London who falls for Ginger, an occupant at the same hotel. With Edward Everett Horton, Helen Broderick and Lucille Ball as a flower girl. 97 min.
05-1326 Was $19.99 ***❑$14.99***

Follow The Fleet (1936)
Fred Astaire's a gum-chewing sailor, Ginger Rogers' a dance hall hostess, and they dance together to some of Irving Berlin's best-loved songs, including "Let Yourself Go" and "We Saw the Sea." Co-stars Betty Grable, Randolph Scott; look quickly for Lucille Ball. 110 min.
05-1003 Was $19.99 ***$14.99***

A Damsel In Distress (1937)
The dancing talents of Fred Astaire (with new partner Joan Fontaine alongside), a marvelous musical score by the Gershwins, and comic relief from Burns and Allen combine in this enchanting romantic treat about an American dancer finding a place in his heart for a sheltered British aristocrat while in London. Co-written by P.G. Wodehouse and directed by George Stevens; songs include "Sing of Spring." 101 min.
18-7672 Was $19.99 ***$14.99***

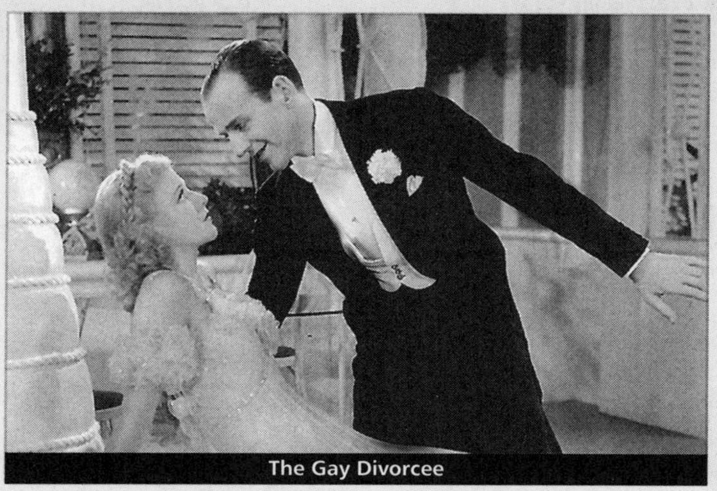
The Gay Divorcee

Fred Astaire

Shall We Dance (1937)
Russian ballet dancer Fred Astaire and musical-comedy star Ginger Rogers, both in need of a boost in their sagging careers, step into a headline-grabbing romance cooked up by her manager...and it's anyone's guess what romantic twists will follow. The classic Gershwin score includes "Let's Call the Whole Thing Off," "They All Laughed" and "They Can't Take That Away from Me." 108 min.
18-7674 Was $19.99 ***$14.99***

Carefree (1938)
Ginger Rogers walks into psychiatrist Fred Astaire's office to ask if she should marry her boyfriend, but before long the two are dancing out the door together. Fine Irving Berlin score includes "Change Partners" and "I Used to Be Color Blind." With Ralph Bellamy, Jack Carson. 83 min.
05-1001 ***$14.99***

The Story Of Vernon And Irene Castle (1939)
Fred and Ginger's last film together for RKO is a tuneful biography of the famous turn-of-the-century dance team. Wonderful dance numbers and a fine supporting cast, including Edna May Oliver and Walter Brennan, make this a fond farewell. Numbers include "Only When You're in My Arms," "Oh, You Beautiful Doll," "By the Beautiful Sea" and "Glow, Little Glow Worm." 93 min.
05-1005 Was $19.99 ***$14.99***

Second Chorus (1940)
Trumpet-playing college students Fred Astaire and Burgess Meredith vie for a place in Artie Shaw's band and the attentions of Paulette Goddard in this breezy musical that features such tunes as "Would You Like to Be the Love of My Life?," "Poor Mr. Chisholm" and "I'm Yours." 84 min.
10-2050 ***$14.99***

You'll Never Get Rich (1941)
A wonderful musical romp starring Fred Astaire as a choreographer who finds chorine Rita Hayworth has what it takes to be his dancing partner. Hoofing takes a back seat to Uncle Sam, though, when Astaire is drafted. "Since I Kissed My Baby Goodbye," "Dream Dancing" and "The A-stairable Rag" are among the Cole Porter songs; with Robert Benchley, Ona Massen. 88 min.
02-1184 ***$19.99***

You Were Never Lovelier (1942)
Fred Astaire reteams with Rita Hayworth for this top-notch musical comedy. He falls for the ravishing Rita after her father (Adolphe Menjou) fixes them up. Score includes "Dearly Beloved" and "I'm Old-Fashioned." 98 min.
02-1382 ***$19.99***

The Sky's The Limit (1943)
WWII pilot Fred Astaire falls for reporter Joan Leslie while he's on leave in this spry musical that features comedy relief from Robert Benchley, great dancing, and a score that includes "My Shining Hour" and "One for My Baby." 89 min.
18-7063 Was $19.99 ***$14.99***

Yolanda And The Thief (1945)
Fred Astaire is an amiable wanderer and con artist who takes a naive young girl (Lucille Bremer) "under his wing" in this charming MGM musical by Vincente Minnelli. With Frank Morgan, Mildred Natwick; songs include "Coffee Time." 108 min.
12-1596 Was $29.99 ***$19.99***

Blue Skies (1946)
A musical extravaganza filled with classic Irving Berlin tunes and detailing a love triangle involving nightclub owner Bing Crosby, chorus girl Joan Caulfield and hoofer Fred Astaire. Follow their relationships over a quarter-century, and enjoy dandy dancing, glorious color and songs like "Puttin' on the Ritz," "You Keep Coming Back Like a Song" and "White Christmas." 104 min.
07-2124 Was $19.99 ***❑$14.99***

Easter Parade (1948)
Fred Astaire and Judy Garland starring in their only movie together! After losing original partner Ann Miller, Astaire trains Garland and together they rise to stardom. The wonderful Irving Berlin score includes "Easter Parade," "A Couple of Swells," with Jules Munshin, Peter Lawford. 103 min.
12-1312 Was $19.99 ***$14.99***

The Barkleys Of Broadway (1949)
Fred Astaire and Ginger Rogers' final screen pairing is also a deft spoof of their public image, as they portray a popular but endlessly bickering husband and wife dance team. Includes the reprise of "They Can't Take That Away from Me" and the "Shoes with Wings On" number. Oscar Levant co-stars. 109 min.
12-1732 Was $19.99 ***$14.99***

Let's Dance (1950)
A Frank Loesser score and Fred Astaire's famed "Piano Dance" highlight this musical that teams Fred with Betty Hutton, an ex-showgirl who returns to the boards against the wishes of her society in-laws. With Lucille Watson, Roland Young. 112 min.
06-1672 ***$14.99***

Three Little Words (1950)
Another fine musical bio from MGM stars Fred Astaire and Red Skelton as songwriters Bert Kalmar and Harry Ruby. Numbers include "Who's Sorry Now?," "I Wanna Be Loved by You," "Thinking of You" and the title tune. Vera-Ellen, Keenan Wynn, Debbie Reynolds co-star. 102 min.
12-1733 ***$19.99***

Royal Wedding (1951)
Fred Astaire and Jane Powell are a brother/sister dance team performing in England during Queen Elizabeth II's coronation and finding romance along the way. Includes the amazing sequence of Fred dancing on the walls and ceiling of his hotel room. This is the complete 93-minute MGM print.
12-1089 ***$19.99***

The Belle Of New York (1952)
Fun flight of fancy that features Fred Astaire as a turn-of-the-century playboy set on romancing mission girl Vera-Ellen. Delightful duets through the clouds above remain a highlight. Marjorie Main, Keenan Wynn, Alice Pearce co-star. Songs include "Oops," "I Wanna Be a Dancin' Man" and "Bachelor's Dinner Song." 82 min.
12-1734 Was $29.99 ***$19.99***

The Band Wagon (1953)
A super MGM musical! It's a tune-filled tale about a has-been movie star who takes to Broadway to find a new career. Songs include "Dancing in the Dark," "Shine on Your Shoes," and "That's Entertainment." Stars Fred Astaire, Cyd Charisse, Jack Buchanan. 112 min.
12-1112 Was $19.99 ***$14.99***

Daddy Long Legs (1955)
Lavish, dance-filled extravaganza starring Leslie Caron as a French orphan whose schooling is sponsored by an anonymous American millionaire, played by Fred Astaire. The millionaire's secretary persuades her boss to visit the girl, and romance soon blooms. Terry Moore, Thelma Ritter co-star; songs include "Something's Got to Give." 126 min.
04-2451 ***❑$19.99***

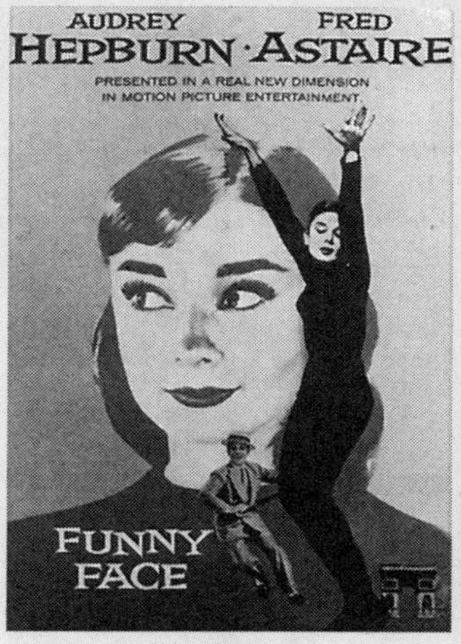

Funny Face (1957)
Fred Astaire is a fashion photographer, Audrey Hepburn the shy young girl he makes over into a top model in this lavish musical with a winning Gershwin score, including "He Loves and She Loves," "How Long Has This Been Going On?" and more. Co-stars Kay Thompson, Ruta Lee. 103 min.
06-1255 ***$14.99***

Silk Stockings (1957)
Cole Porter's stylish score, the dancing of Fred Astaire and Cyd Charisse and a hilarious supporting role for Peter Lorre highlight this musical remake of the classic comedy, "Ninotchka." 117 min.
12-1046 ***$19.99***

Finian's Rainbow (1968)
Fred Astaire plays codger Finian McLonergan, who thinks his magical pot-of-gold will grow and make him a millionaire until a real leprechaun, played by Tommy Steele, appears. Beautiful musical includes "How Are Things in Glocca Morra?" "Look to the Rainbow." Petula Clark, Keenan Wynn, Al Freeman, Jr. co-star. 141 min.
19-1318 ***$19.99***

A Family Upside Down (1978)
Show business legends Fred Astaire and Helen Hayes team up for the first time in this sensitive drama about an elderly couple who find they are becoming too dependent on their grown children after family patriarch Astaire suffers a heart attack. Co-stars Efrem Zimbalist, Jr., Patty Duke Astin. 100 min.
02-1375 ***$59.99***

The Fabulous Fred Astaire (1958)
Classic TV variety special with the one and only Astaire and co-star Barrie Chase in a song-filled "dance bash." Add to this a "Person to Person" interview by Edward R. Murrow at Fred's home and you have a magical salute to a timeless star. NOTE: The print quality of this rare find is sometimes below our usual standards. 71 min.
09-1116 Was $29.99 ***$19.99***

Another Evening With Fred Astaire (1959)
This sequel to the 1958 TV special "An Evening with Fred Astaire" features the legendary entertainer dancing to "Night Train," performing a medley that includes "Puttin' on the Ritz," and more. Among Fred's guests are Barrie Chase, Ken Nordine, and The Jonah Jones Quartet, with choreography by Hermes Pan. 52 min.
53-6076 ***$29.99***

Please see our index for these other Fred Astaire titles: *Broadway Melody Of 1940 • Ghost Story • Holiday Inn • On The Beach • The Over-The-Hill Gang Rides Again • The Towering Inferno • Ziegfeld Follies*

Heart's Desire (1937)
Accomplished Austrian tenor Richard Tauber stars in this British musical romance as a simple Viennese beer hall singer who is discovered by a famed impresario and offered a chance at fame on the London stage, but must surrender his love for a beauty back home. 79 min.
09-1288 Was $29.99 ***$24.99***

Happy (1934)
British musical-comedy involving a down-on-his-luck musician who invents an anti-theft device for cars, then hits the big time when he sells it to an insurance firm. The good luck continues when he marries the daughter of the insurance company boss. With Stanley Lupino, Laddie Cliff. 80 min.
09-5087 ***$19.99***

Mad About Money (1938)
Madcap musical mayhem unfolds when starving showgirl Lupe Velez poses as a cattle heiress to land a part in a movie. Lucky for her, singing silent star Harry Langdon is on hand to salvage her waning career. Songs include "Oh So Beautiful" and "Dustin' the Stars." 69 min.
10-7043 Was $19.99 ***$14.99***

Dancing Pirate (1936)
Early Technicolor treat tells the story of a Boston dance teacher who gets shanghaied by buccaneers who might make his next steps be off the plank! Frank Morgan, Charles Collins star; songs by Rodgers and Hart. Look for Rita Hayworth (Cansino) as a member of the Royal Cansinos. 83 min.
10-7243 ***$19.99***

Al Jolson

The Jazz Singer (1927)
The groundbreaking film that brought sound to the movies stars Al Jolson as the cantor's son who would rather sing on stage than in temple. Songs include "My Mammy," "Toot Toot Tootsie" and "Blue Skies"; with Warner Oland, May McAvoy and William Demarest. 90 min.
12-2238 Was $29.99 ***$19.99***

The Singing Fool (1928)
Warner Bros. and Al Jolson followed up their "Jazz Singer" success with this part-talkie, part-silent tearjerker. Songwriting waiter Jolie weds a singer and finds success on Broadway, but falls on hard times after his wife flees to France with their young son. With Betty Bronson, David Lee; songs include "Golden Gate," "I'm Sittin' on Top of The World," "Sonny Boy." 102 min.
12-2983 ***$19.99***

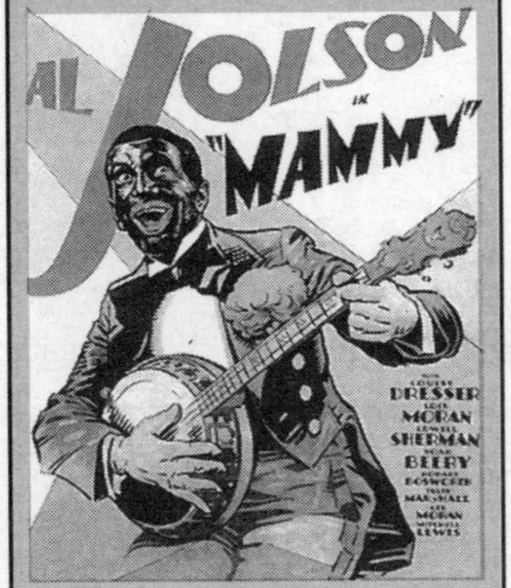

Mammy (1930)
Terrific Irving Berlin tunes and the ever-charismatic Al Jolson are the highlights of this intriguing film that finds Jolson, the star of a minstrel show, seeking help from his mother after accidentally shooting the show's emcee. Lois Moran, Louise Dresser and Mitchell Lewis co-star. Songs include "To My Mammy" and "Yes, We Have No Bananas." 84 min.
12-2967 ***$19.99***

Hallelujah, I'm A Bum (1933)
Classic early musical boasting tunes by Rodgers and Hart, rhyming dialogue and Al Jolson as a New York tramp who falls in love with the mayor's amnesiac girlfriend after rescuing her from a suicide attempt. With Madge Evans, Frank Morgan, Harry Langdon; songs include "I'll Do It Again," "You Are Too Beautiful." 82 min.
12-3077 Was $19.99 ***□$14.99***

Wonder Bar (1934)
An all-star Warner Bros. extravaganza set in a Paris nightclub where club owner Al Jolson and bandleader Dick Powell fall for dancer Delores Del Rio, who is fond of stage partner Ricardo Cortez, who in turn is pursued by rich Kay Francis. Among the lavish musical numbers, with choreography by Busby Berkeley, are "Don't Say Goodnight," "Why Do I Dream Those Dreams" and the outrageously tasteless (even for back then) "Goin' to Heaven on a Mule," with Jolson in blackface. 84 min.
12-2968 ***$19.99***

The Jolson Story (1946)
Larry Parks supplies the body, Al Jolson the voice, in one of Hollywood's best-loved musicals. Follow brash young Asa on his climb up the show biz ladder and into film history as the Jazz Singer. Songs include "Swanee," "April Showers," "Mammy"; with Evelyn Keyes, William Demarest. 128 min.
02-1632 ***$19.99***

Jolson Sings Again (1949)
The saga of legendary entertainer Al Jolson continues, from his entry into sound films and decline in the '30s to his comeback and rediscovery by a new generation of fans. Larry Parks returns as Jolie, who supplied his own singing voice. Barbara Hale, William Demarest co-star. 96 min.
02-1725 ***$19.99***

Please see our index for the Al Jolson title: *Rose Of Washington Square*

Broken Melody (1934)
British musical-drama stars John Garrick as a classical composer who escapes from Devil's Island, where he's being held on a murder charge, and finds inspiration for his art in the arms of his girlfriend. Merle Oberon, Margot Grahame also star. 84 min.
53-6020 ***$29.99***

Born To Dance (1936)
Hoofer Eleanor Powell has the title condition, and proves it to boyfriend James Stewart (who tries a few steps himself), in this MGM musical enhanced by a Cole Porter score that includes "Easy to Love" and "I've Got You Under My Skin." Buddy Ebsen, Virginia Bruce co-star. 105 min.
12-2016 ***$19.99***

Sunny Skies (1930)
Musical gridiron romp about football players giving the old college try (or a pint of blood if it'll help) to win the big game. Benny Rubin and Rex Lease are the singin' and slingin' jocks with a glee club between their goal lines. 70 min.
17-3083 Was $29.99 ***$19.99***

Marie Galante (1934)
After being shanghaied and taken to Panama, dance hall worker Ketti Gallian teams up with espionage agent Spencer Tracy to stop a sabotage plot against the Panama Canal. Intriguing adventure also stars Ned Sparks, Sig Rumann, and the great Helen Morgan, who sings two songs. 88 min.
10-7367 Was $19.99 ***$14.99***

Sitting On The Moon (1936)
A pair of songwriters fall for a former film star and her friend, but when a professional blackmailer claims he married the actress at a drunken wedding ceremony, the songwriter must prove otherwise. Roger Pryor, Grace Bradley, William Newell and Pert Kelton star; songs include "Lost in My Dreams," "How Am I Doin' with You?" and more. 60 min.
10-9109 Was $19.99 ***$14.99***

Millionaire Merry-Go-Round (1938)
Notable for featuring the screen debut of Maureen O'Hara (playing a secretary as "Maureen Fitzsimmons"), this lively British musical comedy follows a young cabaret singer who tries to hit the big time, with help from a friendly millionaire. Evelyn Dall, Harry Richmond, Florence Desmond star. AKA: "Kicking the Moon Around," "The Playboy."
10-9453 ***$19.99***

The Gay Desperado (1936)
Leo Carrillo, Pancho from "The Cisco Kid," is a music-obsessed Mexican bandit who apes the gangsters from American movies. In order to learn more about the Tinseltown thugs, he kidnaps singing cowboy Nino Martini and heiress Ida Lupino. This funny, tune-filled treat from Mary Pickford and Jesse Lasky features the songs "Cielito Lindo" and "The World Is Mine Tonight"; directed by Rouben Mamoulian ("The Mark of Zorro"). 85 min.
80-5045 ***$29.99***

Frankie And Johnny (1936)
Musical drama based on the famous barroom standard. Helen Morgan stars as cathouse singer Frankie, and Chester Morris is Johnny, the bounder who does her wrong (and pays for it). Music score by Victor Young. 68 min.
62-5002 ***$19.99***

The Great Ziegfeld (1936)
William Powell stars as Broadway's Glorifier of the American Girl in this lavish, song-filled biodrama that won three Academy Awards, including Best Picture. Stars like Fannie Brice and Ray Bolger play themselves, Luise Rainer and Myrna Loy are the impresario's lady loves, and the score includes "Rhapsody in Blue," "A Pretty Girl Is Like a Melody," "Makin' Whoopee" and "If You Knew Susie." Look quickly for Pat Nixon as an extra. 176 min.
12-1838 Was $29.99 ***$24.99***

Ziegfeld Follies (1946)
An MGM musical treat, with William Powell introducing the proceedings from Heaven as the great Ziegfeld. The all-star cast includes Judy Garland, Lucille Ball, Red Skelton, Fred Astaire, Gene Kelly. Vincente Minnelli directs. 110 min.
12-1258 ***$19.99***

Ziegfeld Follies: Collector's Edition
A deluxe edition fit for the master showman himself, featuring a restored version of the all-star musical with new stereophonic sound, the original theatrical trailer, and overture and exit music, and a CD of the film soundtrack.
12-2962 ***$29.99***

Glorifying The American Girl (1929)
This Flo Ziegfeld production is a classic example of the "backstage musical," featuring 75 glorified beauties, vintage music (composed by Irving Berlin), wonderful costumes and choreography and a rather thin plot. But who cares about the plot? Stars Rudy Vallee, Eddie Cantor and Helen Morgan. 95 min.
09-1793 ***$19.99***

Applause (1929)
Roaring '20s torch singer Helen Morgan is a fading burlesque star trying to shield her daughter from the seamy side of show business. In her first film role, the tragic Morgan mirrors her real-life association with ne'er-do-well men and does some cabaret tunes in her plaintive style. 80 min.
53-7276 ***$19.99***

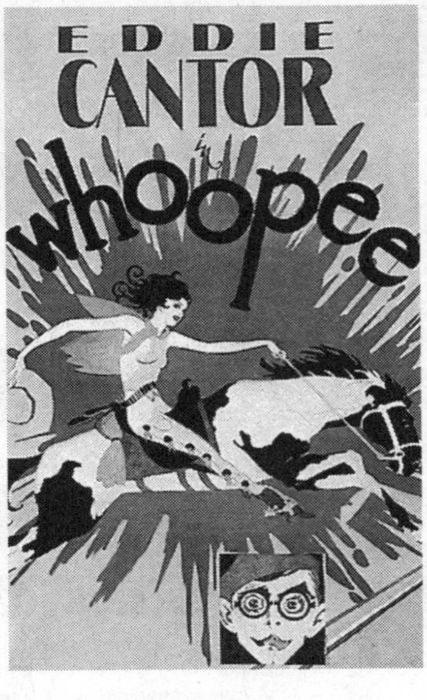

Whoopee! (1930)
Super-splashy early Technicolor musical stars Eddie Cantor as a hypochondriac whose move out West for his health results in crazy calamities. Choreography courtesy of Busby Berkeley; co-produced by Samuel Goldwyn and Flo Ziegfeld. 93 min.
44-1861 Was $19.99 ***$14.99***

Roman Scandals (1933)
Picturesque production numbers and zany comedy highlight this Eddie Cantor vehicle in which Ol' Banjo Eyes is transported back in time to Ancient Rome (that's probably why the empire fell!). With Ruth Etting, Edward Arnold and the choreography of Busby Berkeley. 92 min.
44-1862 Was $19.99 ***$14.99***

Kid Millions (1934)
Eddie Cantor's definitely one in a million in this riotous musical comedy about a Brooklyn boy who inherits a fortune from his archeologist father, but has to go to Egypt to claim it. Don't miss the ice cream factory scene, done in early Technicolor. With Ethel Merman, George Murphy, Ann Sothern; look for Lucille Ball as a "Goldwyn Girl" and Tor Johnson as a torturer. 90 min.
44-1981 Was $19.99 ***$14.99***

The Eddie Cantor Collection
Six of Eddie's musicals are available in a money-saving set: "The Kid from Spain," "Kid Millions," "Palmy Days," "Roman Scandals," "Strike Me Pink" and "Whoopee!"
44-2112 Save 10.00! ***$79.99***

The Broadway Melody (1929)
A seminal entry in the movie musical genre, this backstage drama of two sisters whose dreams of stage stardom are threatened when they both fall for the same man stars Anita Page, Bessie Love, Charles King. Winner of the second Best Picture Oscar; songs include "You Were Meant For Me," "Love Boat," "Give My Regards to Broadway." 102 min.
12-1836 Was $19.99 ***$14.99***

Broadway Melody Of 1938 (1937)
One of MGM's first, biggest and brightest all-star musicals, featuring the dazzling production numbers and memorable solos that became a trademark. Stars include Eleanor Powell, Robert Taylor, George Murphy, Sophie Tucker, Buddy Ebsen and Billy Gilbert; the highlight is Judy Garland's "Dear Mr. Gable." 110 min.
12-1597 Was $29.99 ***□$19.99***

Broadway Melody Of 1940 (1940)
Top-flight entertainment highlighted by a marvelous Cole Porter score ("Begin the Beguine"), exciting Fred Astaire-Eleanor Powell dance numbers, and some hilarious skits. Also stars George Murphy, Frank Morgan and Ian Hunter. Other songs include "I've Got My Eyes on You," "Between You and Me" and "I Concentrate on You." 102 min.
12-1666 ***$19.99***

Harmony Lane (1935)
A poignant biopic of 19th-century songwriter Stephen Foster woven together by his classic folk ballads. Douglas Montgomery stars as Foster, who leaves the ministry, becomes trapped in a loveless marriage, and in later years, is reduced to poverty and alcoholism. Songs include "Oh Susanna," "My Old Kentucky Home," and "Swanee River." With William Frawley. 85 min.
10-7051 ***$19.99***

I Dream Of Jeanie (1952)
Musical biography of composer Stephen Foster, tracing his life from his days as a bookkeeper to the successful writer of "My Old Kentucky Home," "The Old Folks at Home," "Oh Susanna," "Camptown Races" and others. Ray Middleton, Bill Shirley and Muriel Lawrence star. 90 min.
17-9058 ***$19.99***

The Vagabond Lover (1929)
Rudy Vallee croons his way through a zany musical about an amateur musician in search of work who impersonates a big band leader. With Sally Blaine, Marie Dressler. 66 min.
09-1272 ***$19.99***

Dance Of Life (1929)
A burlesque comic, inspired by the love of a good woman, becomes a success on Broadway, only to let it go to his head, in this early musical look at life behind the greasepaint, later remade as "Swing High, Swing Low." With Nancy Carroll, Hal Skelly, and the first credited screen appearance by pianist Oscar Levant. 115 min.
10-7345 ***$19.99***

Tanned Legs (1929)
Set at a seaside resort, this musical comedy-drama tells of a family comprised of a husband and wife seeking younger partners, a daughter who gets involved with a con man and another daughter who wants to straighten them all out. June Clyde, Arthur Lake, Nella Walker and Sally Blane star; songs include "With You, With Me" and "You're Responsible."
10-8381 Was $19.99 ***$14.99***

Evergreen (1934)
British musical starring Jessie Matthews is a comedy of mistaken identity. Among the classic Rodgers and Hart songs is "Dancing on the Ceiling." This was the first film from England to play Radio City Music Hall. 91 min.
62-1065 Was $19.99 ***$14.99***

First A Girl (1935)
This version of the story that inspired "Victor/Victoria" stars British singer Jessie Matthews as a seamstress's delivery girl. After she's recruited by a female impersonator stricken with laryngitis to pose as a man posing as a woman, Matthews becomes a sensation, but a mysterious woman and her friend try to find out what's really going on under the costume. Sonnie Hale, Anna Lee also star. 93 min.
73-3033 ***$14.99***

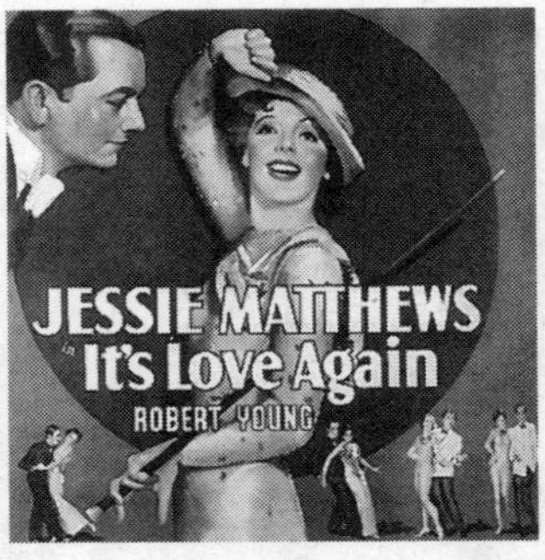

It's Love Again (1936)
A sparkling and vivacious musical/comedy about an ambitious newsman (Robert Young) who fabricates stories in order to compete with a female rival reporter (Jessie Matthews). Songs include "Heaven in Your Arms" and the title tune; look quickly for Terry-Thomas. 83 min.
10-7041 Was $19.99 ***$14.99***

Gangway (1937)
A musical-mystery starring Jessie Matthews as a British reporter on a ship headed for New York who is attempting to interview a jewel thief posing as a Hollywood actress. Soon, Matthews is suspected as the culprit by a detective and a gangster. With Liane Ordeyne, Barry Mackay. 90 min.
10-8242 ***$19.99***

Head Over Heels (1937)
A musical-comedy set in Paris, where two gangsters fall in love with the same girl, an American actress. Jessie Matthews, Robert Flemyng, Louis Borell star. Songs include "May I Have the Next Romance with You?," "Through the Courtesy of Love," "Don't Give a Good Gosh Darn" and more.
10-8370 ***$19.99***

Sailing Along (1938)
A lively British musical that stars Jessie Matthews as a woman who gives up her life on the stage for the love of a man (Barry Mackay). Jack Whiting, Roland Young also star in this tune-filled treat. 80 min.
10-8241 ***$19.99***

Candles At Nine (1944)
Popular British musical star Jessie Matthews stars as a young girl who must stay the night in a "haunted house" in order to inherit a fortune. Will the other greedy relatives do her in? Chills and laughs. 84 min.
09-1664 ***$19.99***

She Shall Have Music (1936)
Producer Julius Hagen gathered an array of top musical talents for this lively British showcase about a wealthy businessman's plans to broadcast a live show from on board his yacht. Jazzy treat stars Jack Hylton and his band, June Clyde, Gwen Farrar and Claude Dampier; music composed by Maurice Sigler. 81 min.
73-3009 ***$19.99***

Eye Of The Beholder (2000)

Electrifying erotic thriller starring Ewan McGregor as a high-tech British operative grappling with personal problems while trailing gorgeous serial killer Ashley Judd across the United States. Using his surveillance equipment to spy on Judd, McGregor eventually becomes smitten with the disguise-changing murderess. With Patrick Bergin, k.d. lang and Genevieve Bujold. 101 min.

02-3424   Was $99.99   ☐$14.99

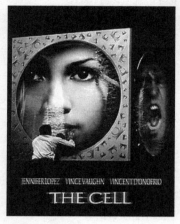

The Cell (2000)

Psychotherapist Jennifer Lopez, who uses experimental virtual reality technology to enter the minds of her patients, is recruited by the FBI to delve into the twisted subconscious of comatose serial killer Vincent D'Onofrio, whose latest abduction victim will die unless she can be found within 24 hours. Creepy, visually bold blend of suspense and high-tech horror also stars Vince Vaughn, Marianne Jean-Baptiste.

02-5242   ☐$99.99

The Golden Spiders (2000)

Rex Stout's portly super-sleuth Nero Wolfe comes to life in this thriller. Maury Chaykin stars as Wolfe, who, with aide de camp Archie Goodwin (Timothy Hutton), tries to help a boy who witnessed a woman in danger in a car. But when the boy is hit by the same car the next day, a deadly tale of blackmail, deception and high society suspects is revealed. With Saul Rubinek, Bill Smitrovich. 100 min.

53-6822 $19.99

Mercy (2000)

Ellen Barkin is a homicide detective investigating a bizarre series of killings in which the victims have been tortured in S&M style and had their eyelids cut off. Barkin's search leads her to prime suspect Peta Wilson, who guides her through the underground world of kinky, lesbian sex clubs that the victims had frequented. With Julian Sands, Wendy Crewson. 94 min.

02-3436   ☐$99.99

Jill The Ripper (2000)

Ex-San Francisco cop-turned-debt collector Dolph Lundgren returns to his detective roots when his younger brother is murdered. As other men are found killed in a similar fashion, Lundgren's search leads him into a clandestine world of power, intrigue and kinky sexual games...and closer to a seductive—and deadly—suspect. Erotic thriller also stars Danielle Brett. AKA: "Jill Rips," "The Leatherwoman." 93 min.

02-3439 $99.99

Deterrence (2000)

Intense doomsday thriller in the "Fail-Safe" mold. In the year 2008, Iraqi forces kill American soldiers and invade Kuwait. President Emerson (Kevin Pollak) is on the campaign trail, stuck in a snowbound diner in Colorado, when he hears the news. After a stand-off with Iraqi officials, he must decide whether to drop a nuclear bomb on Baghdad. Timothy Hutton, Sheryl Lee Ralph co-star. 104 min.

06-3009   ☐$99.99

Partners In Crime (2000)

Rutger Hauer is a small-town cop, investigating the disappearance of a wealthy businessman, who discovers that the FBI agent involved in the case is ex-wife Paulina Porizkova. When the missing man's body is found in a car on Hauer's property, he becomes the prime suspect in the case, and must team with Porizkova to find the real killer. 90 min.

27-7193   ☐$99.99

Premonition (2000)

Young journalist Ally Preston teams with old pro Christopher Lloyd to get the scoop on a series of eerie murders and encounters a man who can predict other people's deaths in the process. After getting involved with death-obsessed Adrian Paul, Preston reconnects to feelings she's lost after a near-fatal plane accident. AKA: "Convergence." 93 min.

27-7229   ☐$99.99

The Last Stop (2000)

Trapped inside an isolated mountain lodge by a raging blizzard, a group of strangers is targeted for murder when one of their number turns out to be a killer after a bag of stolen money, but which of them is the murderer? Gripping suspense tale stars Adam Beach, Rose McGowan, Jurgen Prochnow. 94 min.

64-9060 $99.99

MYSTERY & SUSPENSE

Hide And Seek (2000)

Daryl Hannah and Bruce Greenwood are a successful couple whose lives are turned into a nightmare when deranged duo Jennifer Tilly and Vincent Gallo kidnap the pregnant Hannah as part of their bizarre plan to raise the child as their own. With time running out, Greenwood devises a depserate plan to save her. AKA: "Cord." 100 min.

68-1996   ☐$79.99

Flypaper (2000)

The lives of three back-stabbing, double-dealing low-lifes collide on a sunny afternoon in California as they maim, fondle and rob each other in order to retrieve $1 million. Lucy Liu, Sadie Frost, Robert Loggia, Craig Sheffer and John C. McGinley star in this thriller in the tradition of "Pulp Fiction" and "2 Days in the Valley." 111 min.

68-1998   ☐$69.99

Goodbye Charlie (2000)

A defense attorney specializing getting violent criminals off the hook finds himself in hot water when he murders a woman he picked up in a bar. After confessing the crime to his friends, a plan is conceived in which one of the lawyer's client—a hit man—is selected to take the fall. Jeremy Klavens, Christian Desmond star in this intriguing thriller. 85 min.

73-9339 $59.99

The Stray (2000)

After striking a homeless man with her car, a beautiful restauranteur takes him back to her ranch to recuperate. As a friendship develops between the two grows into a romantic attraction, the stranger's sinister side begins to overwhelm and threaten his rescuer. Angie Everhart, Michael Madsen and Frank Zagarino star in this compelling thriller. 98 min.

86-1151   ☐$99.99

First Daughter (2000)

Mariel Hemingway is a Secret Service agent who, after guarding the president, is reassigned to keep tabs on the chief executive's teenage daughter. Hemingway finds herself in a race against time when the young woman is kidnapped by a militia group while on a hiking trip. Doug Savant, Gregory Harrison, Monica Keena and pro wrestler Diamond Dallas Page also star. 94 min.

02-3473   ☐$99.99

The Skulls (2000)

Working-class Yale student Joshua Jackson is recruited to join the university's most elite and secretive society, the Skulls. The group offers money, status and opportunity to its members, but when Jackson's journalism student friend is found dead in an apparent suicide, he discovers how far—and dangerous—its reach can be. Gripping suspenser also stars Paul Walker, Leslie Bibb, Craig T. Nelson. 107 min.

07-2928   ☐$99.99

Slow Burn (2000)

In this edgy thriller, Minnie Driver plays a woman who has spent most of her life in the Mexican desert in search of treasure her mother and grandmother sacrificed their lives for. But her quest comes to a halt when she's confronted by escaped cons James Spader and Josh Brolin, also looking for the loot, who take her hostage. 97 min.

27-7336 $99.99

Lady Audley's Secret (2000)

Steven Mackintosh's friend has disappeared and it seems that his aristocratic uncle's young wife, whom Mackintosh loves, may be involved. He must manage to resist the adulterous woman's advances until he can figure out the truth in this deceptive Victorian mystery. Neve McIntosh, Kenneth Cranham and Jamie Bamber also star 106 min.

53-6945 $29.99

Cut Up (2000)

A police photographer who left his position as investigator after an accidental killing of a young girl is enlisted by his former partner to look into a series of murders in New Orleans. The assignment brings back haunting memories from the past, leading him to face his worst nightmare.

73-9365 $29.99

Cold Blooded (2000)

Already paralyzed by bitter winter weather, a city is also in the icy grip of a serial killer who has claimed 12 victims. When police call a body they find a suicide, suspicious reporter Michael Moriarty digs into the case and, with help from a source inside the police force, must discover the chilling secret behind the murders. Gloria Reuben, Patti LuPone co-star. AKA: "Bad Faith." 97 min.

82-5228 $89.99

Red Ink (2000)

Based on the Atlanta child killings of the late '70s, this compelling thriller follows a reporter investigating the murders of several black teenage boys, as his search for a connection between the victims draws him deeper into danger. A bright young cast stars in this urban mystery. 100 min.

81-9119 $59.99

Code Of Ethics (1997)

After indulging in an on-line game, government computer whiz Melissa Leo finds the consequences of her recreation to be dire, as she is unexpectedly thrown into an extremely dangerous predicament in this high-tech thriller. 90 min.

82-5225 $59.99

Obsession Kills (1995)

Three people become involved with each other in this tense tale of lustful desire and avarice. Will a betrayal lead one of them to pay the ultimate price? Lisa Comshaw, Carrie Genzel and Sam Jones star. 90 min.

82-5226 $59.99

Newsbreak (1999)

Gripping thriller starring Michael Rooker as a tough investigative reporter who discovers a pattern of city-wide corruption involving construction company head Judge Reinhold and judge Robert Culp, who happens to also be Rooker's father. 95 min.

82-9064 $89.99

Delivered (1998)

In this shocker with humorous moments, a college dropout working as a pizza delivery boy arrives at a customer's house and finds the man murdered and himself a target of the killer. David Strickland, Ron Eldard, Leslie Stefanson and Nicky Katt star. AKA: "Death by Pizza." 90 min.

53-6982 $14.99

No Alibi (1999)

Businessman Dean Cain would never suspect that the gorgeous stranger drawing him into a steamy affair was sent by her lover, lowlife crook Eric Roberts, to track down a missing stash of drug money. But who betrays whom in this gripping suspense tale? Lexa Doig co-stars. 90 min.

64-9065 $99.99

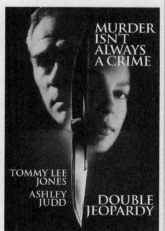

Double Jeopardy: Special Edition (1999)

Hit suspense thriller stars Ashley Judd as a Seattle wife and mother who is caught in a nightmare when she's convicted of killing husband Bruce Greenwood. Her dilemma worsens in prison when she learns her husband is not only alive, but had framed her for his "murder." Upon her release she devises a plan to gain a deadly revenge for which the law cannot punish her. Tommy Lee Jones co-stars as Judd's parole officer; with Annabeth Gish, Roma Maffia. Special edition includes a "making of" featurette. 105 min.

06-2947   Was $99.99   ☐$19.99

Relentless (1989)

The suspense, tension and action are just what the title says in this thriller. Judd Nelson is the psycho who mounts a campaign of murder in L.A. for revenge against the police force that turned him down, and Robert Loggia and Leo Rossi are the detective duo out to catch him. 92 min.

02-1983   ☐$19.99

Relentless 2: Dead On (1991)

Detective Leo Rossi is back to put his badge, his family and his life on the line in order to track down a serial killer before he strikes again. Suspenseful follow-up to the hit thriller also stars Ray Sharkey, Meg Foster, Miles O'Keeffe. 93 min.

02-2163   Was $89.99 $19.99

Relentless 3 (1993)

A savage and fiendishly clever killer is terrorizing the streets of L.A., but when he threatens the girlfriend of hard-edged detective Leo Rossi, what started out as a murder case becomes a bitter and personal fight to the finish. William Forsythe and Signy Coleman co-star. 84 min.

02-5030   Was $19.99   ☐$14.99

Relentless 4 (1994)

Sam Dietz returns, and this time he's on the trail of a serial killer with a passion for ritualistic executions. His search leads him to a beautiful psychiatrist with whom he has a torrid affair, risking his career and home life. Will this relationship bring him closer to the murderer? Leo Rossi, Famke Janssen and Colleen Coffy star. 91 min.

02-2713   Was $19.99   ☐$14.99

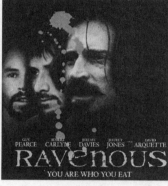

Ravenous (1999)

In this offbeat historical thriller laced with dark humor, Army captain Guy Pearce thinks he's being promoted for his "heroism" during the Mexican War. Instead, he's sent to a remote fort in the Sierra Nevadas inhabited by a group of outcasts. The arrival of a Scottish stranger, who tells them of a group of pioneers who had to resort to cannibalism to survive, leads to an ominous search and some "tasty" plot twists. Robert Carlyle, David Arquette, Jeffrey Jones also star. 101 min.

04-3859   Was $99.99   ☐$14.99

The Rain Killer (1990)

A vicious killer terrorizes Los Angeles, claiming his victims only when it rains. Two cops track the murderer throughout the city, from the seedy red light district to the top of society, but he always remains one step ahead of his pursuers. Ray Sharkey, Michael Chiklis and Tania Coleridge star. 94 min.

02-2079 $89.99

Genuine Risk (1990)

An erotic, modern-day film noir about a parolee who takes a job as a money collector for his criminal pal, and soon finds himself in love with the girlfriend of a dangerous mobster. Terence Stamp, Peter Berg, Michelle Johnson star. 89 min.

02-2082 $89.99

The Man Inside (1990)

A nail-biting, true-life thriller starring Peter Coyote as a journalist who risks his life when he goes undercover at his German newspaper to expose a government plot against new liberal factions in Europe. Jurgen Prochnow, Nathalie Baye also star. 93 min.

02-2095   Was $89.99 $19.99

No Secrets (1991)

Seductive thriller about three beautiful high school girls who travel to a secluded ranch for a vacation, and the handsome stranger who joins them. What does he want, and to what lengths will he go to get it? Amy Locane, Heather Fairchild, Traci Lind, Adam Coleman Howard star. 92 min.

02-2105 $89.99

Eye Of The Storm (1991)

An isolated motel in the Southwest desert is the setting for a dangerous romantic triangle, when an abandoned wife comes between two brothers who share a dark secret. Sexy, compelling thriller stars Dennis Hopper, Craig Sheffer, Lara Flynn Boyle. 98 min.

02-2242   Was $19.99 $14.99

Kiss Me A Killer (1991)

Two adulterous lovers find that the edges of their romantic triangle are sharp enough to kill in this steamy suspense story about a planned "perfect murder" that backfires. Julie Carmen, Robert Beltran, Guy Boyd star. 91 min.

02-2150 $89.99

Love Walked In (1998)
In a Florida resort town, a piano player and his lover, a beautiful singer, concoct a scheme to seduce and then blackmail a wealthy patron of the club where they perform in this steamy, modern-day noir thriller. Denis Leary, Aitana Sánchez-Gójon and Terence Stamp star. 91 min.
02-3169 Was $99.99 ❑$24.99

The Disappearance Of Kevin Johnson (1995)
When a wealthy British wannabe producer disappears after coming to Hollywood, a TV film crew from England attempts to investigate the mystery, interviewing the agents, actors and executives who came in contact with him. They soon uncover a number of bizarre secrets, but can they solve the puzzle? Pierce Brosnan, James Coburn and Dudley Moore appear as themselves. 106 min.
02-3176 Was $99.99 ❑$24.99

Johnny Skidmarks (1998)
Eerie, unsettling and darkly humorous crime melodrama starring Peter Gallagher as a police crime photographer who moonlights as a camera-clicker for a group of blackmailers targeting politicians and city officials. When Gallagher's seedy cronies turn up murdered, Gallagher wonders if Frances McDormand, his unstable new girlfriend, has anything to do with the killings. With John Lithgow and Charlie Spradling. 97 min.
02-3246 Was $99.99 ❑$24.99

The Assignment (1997)
The amazing real-life global manhunt for the international terrorist known as Carlos the Jackal forms the basis for this compelling espionage thriller. Aidan Quinn is an American naval officer whose amazing physical resemblance to Carlos leads CIA operative Donald Sutherland and Israeli agent Ben Kingsley to recruit him for a dangerous impersonation scheme to trap the murderous Jackal. 115 min.
02-3147 Was $99.99 ❑$14.99

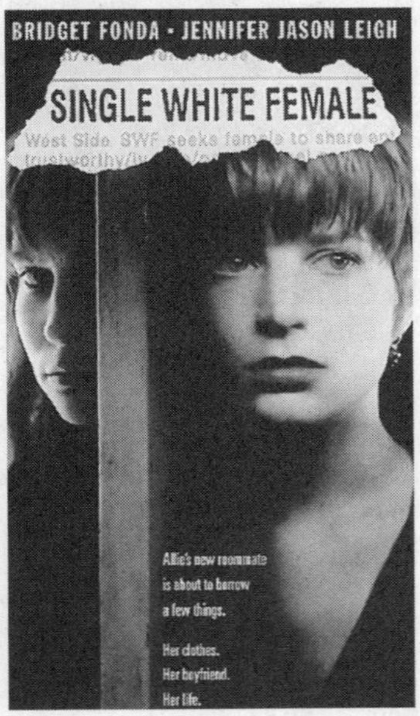

Single White Female (1992)
The hit erotic thriller stars Bridget Fonda as a young woman living in a New York apartment building who takes on a roommate when she learns her boyfriend is cheating on her. New roomie Jennifer Jason Leigh, a shy woman with self-image problems and a mysterious past, turns out to be a violent psychotic ready to take over Fonda's life. Barbet Schroeder ("Reversal of Fortune") directs. 107 min.
02-2334 Was $19.99 ❑$14.99

Indiscreet (1998)
When a private investigator is hired by a suspicious millionaire to follow the man's wife, the detective never expected to fall in love with the woman...and he certainly didn't plan to become a suspect when the client turns up murdered! Compelling and erotic suspense tale stars Luke Perry, Gloria Reuben, Peter Coyote and Adam Baldwin. 101 min.
02-3249 Was $99.99 $24.99

Implicated (1998)
A young woman thinks she's found the perfect lover, but a babysitting job for her boyfriend's boss turns into a kidnapping scheme and leaves her betrayed and fighting for her life. Exciting suspense thriller stars Amy Locane, William McNamara, Frederic Forrest, Priscilla Barnes and Richard Tyson. 95 min.
02-3303 ❑$99.99

Mute Witness (1995)
A mute American woman working as a special-effects artist on a film shooting in Russia accidentally stumbles onto a snuff movie being made on the set late one night. Unable to convince anyone of what she saw, the woman is pursued by the killers in this unusual thriller. Marina Sudina, Fay Ripley, Oleg Jankowskij star. 98 min.
02-2844 Was $19.99 ❑$14.99

Sunset Heat (1992)
A sexy suspenser about a photojournalist who returns to Los Angeles and encounters a drug scam, a murder and his girlfriend in danger. Michael Paré, Dennis Hopper, Adam Ant, Daphne Ashbrook and Tracy Tweed star in this atmospheric thriller. Uncut, unrated version; 94 min.
02-2293 Was $19.99 $14.99

Deadbolt (1992)
A young woman takes in a male roommate and thinks she's solved her security problems, but the terror is just beginning when he begins controlling her life and eventually makes her a prisoner in their apartment. Gripping suspense tale stars Justine Bateman, Adam Baldwin, Chris Mulkey and Michele Scarabelli. 95 min.
02-2310 Was $19.99 $14.99

Under Suspicion (1992)
A suspenseful, sexy thriller set in the 1950s in which a sleazy divorce attorney makes his living by setting up phony adultery cases with his wife. When one of their scams goes awry and the wife and a wealthy client die, the attorney and his mistress become prime suspects. Liam Neeson and Laura San Giacomo star. 100 min.
02-2247 Was $89.99 ❑$14.99

Fatal Instinct (1992)
A cop with a habit of breaking the rules investigates a savage killing, but is drawn into a steamy erotic obsession that could cost him his own life. This sexually charged thriller in the style of "Fatal Attraction" and "Basic Instinct" stars Michael Madsen, Laura Johnson. Uncut, unrated version; 95 min.
02-2260 Was $19.99 $14.99

Deep Cover (1992)
An unrelenting cop thriller starring Larry Fishburne as a cop who poses as a drug dealer in Los Angeles' seedy underworld. He partners with sleazy lawyer Jeff Goldblum and is quickly seduced by the criminal lifestyle. Eventually, he must decide which side of the law he's really on. Victoria Dillard and Charles Martin Smith co-star. 107 min.
02-2267 Was $19.99 ❑$14.99

One False Move (1992)
Terrific suspense-filled thriller about two ruthless drug dealers and a young woman who head from Los Angeles to a small Arkansas town after committing a series of brutal murders. Waiting for them are two L.A. cops and the local sheriff, who's hiding a secret from his past. Cynda Williams, Bill Paxton and Billy Bob Thornton star in director Carl Franklin's electrifying crime story. 106 min.
02-2276 Was $19.99 ❑$14.99

The Finishing Touch (1992)
The deaths of some of L.A.'s most gorgeous women are appearing on snuff films throughout the city. A detective suspects an avant-garde artist, but his hunches are halted when red tape interferes with the investigation. Soon, he finds his former wife involved in the case...and she has fallen for the suspect. Michael Nader and Shelley Hack star. 82 min.
02-2320 $89.99

Death Dreams (1992)
Christopher Reeve and Marg Helgenberger seem to have a perfect life together, enjoying wealth, social rank and beauty. Then their world unravels when their daughter tragically drowns, and things get quite eerie when the little girl contacts them from beyond with startling evidence about how she really died. 94 min.
02-2325 Was $19.99 $14.99

Sins Of Desire (1992)
Searching for the truth behind the death of her sister, who passed away after being treated at a mysterious sex therapy clinic, a woman goes undercover as a nurse. She soon becomes ensnared in the erotic games of the husband-and-wife team running the clinic and looks for help from a handsome private eye conducting his own investigation. Sexually charged thriller stars Tanya Roberts, Nick Cassavetes, Jan-Michael Vincent. 90 min.
02-2351 Was $89.99 $14.99

The Paint Job (1993)
Obsession and infidelity play equal parts in this thriller about a house painter whose love for his married neighbor opens the door to deceit and, possibly, murder. Will Patton, Bebe Neuwirth and Robert Pastorelli star. 90 min.
02-2511 $89.99

Past Midnight (1992)
In this steamy and exciting suspenser, Rutger Hauer plays a man who is recently released from prison after serving 15 years for murdering his pregnant wife. Sparks soon fly between Hauer and his parole officer (Natasha Richardson), who stakes her life on his innocence. Clancy Brown also stars. 100 min.
02-2399 Was $19.99 $14.99

Desperate Motive (1993)
A demented man and woman who have escaped from a mental hospital are determined to have a "normal" life, and, in order to do so, they visit the man's happily married cousin and set out to take over their hosts' identities. David Keith, Marg Helgenberger, William Katt and Mel Harris star in this intense shocker. 92 min.
02-2414 Was $19.99 $14.99

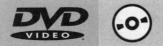

Poison Ivy (1992)
In this erotically-charged thriller, Drew Barrymore turns in a heated performance as a sly teenage seductress who befriends fellow troubled student Sara Gilbert, then seeks to insinuate her way into her family through devious methods. Tom Skerritt and Cheryl Ladd play Gilbert's troubled parents; with Leonardo DiCaprio. Unrated video version features extra footage not shown in theatres. 95 min.
02-2318 Was $19.99 ❑$14.99

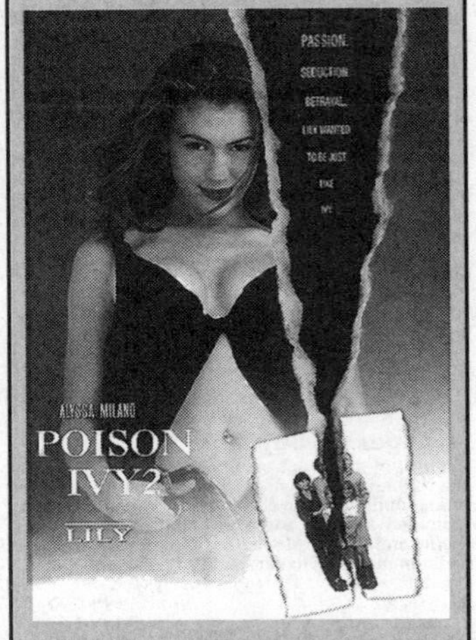

Poison Ivy 2: Lily (1995)
Ivy herself may be gone, but the erotic diaries she left behind are found by naive art student Alyssa Milano, who is inspired by them to pursue her sexual interests. A flirtation with an older, married professor, however, draws her into a dangerous affair with potentially fatal consequences. Scorching sequel, marked by Milano's revealing nude scenes, also stars Johnathon Schaech, Xander Berkeley. Uncut, unrated version; 112 min.
02-5075 Was $19.99 ❑$14.99

Poison Ivy: The New Seduction (1997)
She comes on like a rose, especially when she takes off her clothes. And Violet, Ivy's evil sister, does it with regularity, seducing fathers, boyfriends and anyone else in order to get her manipulative way. Scorching third entry in this hit series stars Jaime Pressly, Megan Edwards, Greg Vaughan and Michael Des Barres. Uncut, unrated version; 93 min.
02-5127 Was $19.99 ❑$14.99

Storyville (1992)
Atmospheric thriller stars James Spader as a New Orleans attorney running for political office who falls into a web of blackmail after a liaison with a prostitute in the seedy Storyville section of town. While fighting for his life and career, the young lawyer uncovers some unsettling skeletons from his own family closet. Joanne Whalley-Kilmer and Jason Robards, Jr. co-star. 112 min.
02-2332 Was $89.99 $19.99

Quake (1993)
A San Francisco surveillance expert (Steve Railsback) uses the tools of his trade to spy on a beautiful lawyer he works for. When an earthquake hits, the woman is left trapped, which offers the stalker an opportunity to kidnap her and fulfill his twisted desires. Erika Anderson ("Zandalee") and the great Dick Miller also star. 84 min.
02-2419 $89.99

Fatal Bond (1993)
Linda Blair is a young woman who becomes convinced that her lover is in fact a madman who has raped and murdered a number of women. Should she turn him in or protect him? Seductive thriller also stars Jerome Elhers, Stephen Leeder. 89 min.
02-2429 $89.99

Final Judgement (1993)
After being framed for murder, a priest known for his humanitarian work must infiltrate the sexual underworld of Los Angeles to find the real killer. Brad Dourif, Karen Black, Maria Ford and Isaac Hayes star in this intriguing mystery. 90 min.
02-2504 $89.99

Love, Cheat & Steal (1994)
After he learns that his gorgeous ex-wife has remarried, a convicted murderer breaks out of prison and returns to her home with deadly plans for the newlyweds. Eric Roberts, John Lithgow and Madchen Amick star. 95 min.
02-2614 Was $89.99 ❑$14.99

Under Investigation (1993)
The beautiful wife of an artist is a suspect in the murder of her husband's girlfriend. A cynical detective investigating the case falls for the wife, who stands to cash in on a $10 million insurance policy when hubby also turns up dead. Steamy suspenser stars Harry Hamlin, Joanna Pacula and Ed Lauter. 94 min.
02-2506 Was $19.99 ❑$14.99

Afraid Of The Dark (1992)
An acclaimed psychological terror tale involving a small boy with disintegrating eyesight who begins his own secret investigations into the brutal assaults against blind people in the area. When the boy finally faces the slasher, he must also confront his fear of the unknown. James Fox, Fanny Ardant, Ben Keyworth and Paul McGann star. 91 min.
02-2331 Was $19.99 $14.99

Red Rock West (1993)
Director John Dahl's smart, surprise-filled thriller stars Nicolas Cage as a down-and-out Texan who winds up in a Wyoming bar where he's mistaken for a hit man and accepts an offer from the bar owner's sexy wife (Lara Flynn Boyle) to bump off her husband. But when the real killer (Dennis Hopper) arrives, things can only get more complicated. J.T. Walsh co-stars. 98 min.
02-2529 Was $19.99 ❑$14.99

Double Obsession (1993)
Heather (Margaux Hemingway) has held a burning jealousy towards Claire (Maryam d'Abo) since they were college roommates and Claire fell in love with another student. Years pass and anger grows, and now Heather's out to get even. Inspired by a true story, this erotic suspenser also stars Frederick Forrest and Scott Valentine. 88 min.
02-2532 Was $89.99 $19.99

Deadly Currents (1994)
Intense thriller involving a former CIA agent who is exiled to the island of Curacao after being accused of killing a fellow agent. After making friends with a mysterious man living on the island, the ex-agent is confronted by South African secret police, his old partner and Chinese gangsters. William Petersen, George C. Scott and Julie Carmen star. 93 min.
02-2582 Was $89.99 ❑$14.99

They Watch (1994)
A supernatural thriller about a prominent Southern architect who re-evaluates his life when his 11-year-old daughter is killed. He travels to the Carolina backwoods, where he is drawn to a blind psychic who attempts to reunite him with his child. Patrick Bergin, Vanessa Redgrave and Valerie Mahaffey star. 100 min.
02-2604 $89.99

Blink (1994)
Intense thriller sparked with eroticism starring Madeleine Stowe as a blind woman who undergoes a cornea transplant and partially regains her eyesight, only to become the witness to a murder committed by a serial killer. Helping protect her and investigating the case is a tough Chicago detective, played by Aidan Quinn. With Laurie Metcalf, Peter Friedman. 106 min.
02-2623 Was $19.99 ❑$14.99

Never Talk To Strangers (1995)
Gripping sensual suspenser starring Rebecca De Mornay as a criminal psychologist whose meeting with mysterious, handsome stranger Antonio Banderas in a supermarket leads to kinky sexual liaisons. After an argument between the two, unsettling incidents occur, leading De Mornay to attempt to find out more about her new lover. With Dennis Miller, Len Cariou. 86 min.
02-2856 Was $19.99 ❑$14.99

Sensation (1994)
A beautiful co-ed becomes part of her handsome college professor's experiments in harnessing psychic abilities, but when her new powers tell her that the teacher was involved in the brutal sex slaying of a former student, it's easy to predict her life is in danger. Sexy thriller stars Eric Roberts, Kari Wuhrer, Ron Perlman, Ed Begley, Jr. 102 min.
02-2720 $89.99

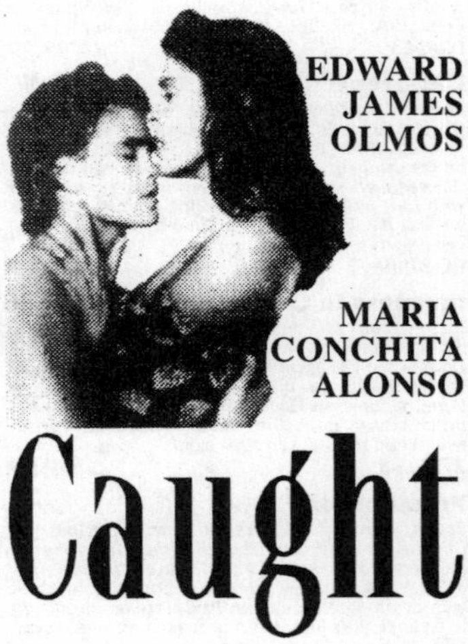

Caught (1996)
Heated contemporary film noir starring Edward James Olmos as the owner of a fish store who, along with wife Maria Conchita Alonso, provides a job and a room for a well-meaning homeless young man. While befriending Olmos, the young man carries on a torrid affair with Alonso, which eventually leads to danger. With Arie Verveen and Steven Schub. 109 min.
02-3059 Was $99.99 ❑$14.99

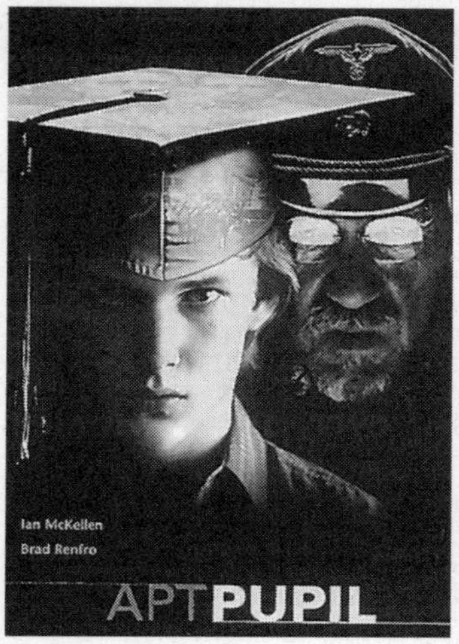

Apt Pupil (1998)
After he discovers that an elderly neighbor was a notorious Nazi death camp officer, a teenager obsessed with the Holocaust blackmails the man into graphically recounting the horrors of his past crimes. The cat-and-mouse game between the two reaches a murderous intensity in this suspenseful adaptation of Stephen King's story from director Bryan Singer ("The Usual Suspects"). Ian McKellen, Brad Renfro, Bruce Davison and David Schwimmer star. 112 min.
02-3304 Was $99.99 □*$19.99*

The Reunion (1999)
Louis, a salesman in his 30s obsessed with an embarassing incident that occured in high school, arranges an 18-year reunion to show that he's successful. At the gathering, a gun-waving Louis loses his cool at some of his former tormentors, prompting a high-tension hostage situation. Timothy Devlin, Mimi Langeland star. 90 min.
76-7481 *$79.99*

Heartless (1997)
After Mädchen Amick receives a heart transplant, she begins to have dreams about a lover she has never met. Learning where her donor's husband lives, Amick discovers that the woman was murdered and sets out to find the killer, even though suspicion leads to the man she now loves. Louise Fletcher also stars. 90 min.
82-5222 *$59.99*

Chapter Perfect (1996)
Lucky Vanous and Capricie Benedetti are writers of crime fiction who are about to begin the perfect novel. But when murders in their small community mirror the deaths of characters in the book, police chief Wilford Brimley wants some answers. Now Vanous must somehow prove his innocence in this deadly thriller. 90 min.
82-5223 *$59.99*

Under Pressure (1999)
Charles Sheen is a fireman known for his heroics in a time of danger. When his wife leaves him, Sheen goes off the deep end and soon terrorizes his next-door neighbor and her two children. Mare Winningham and John Ratzenberger also star in this thriller. AKA: "Bad Day on the Block." 88 min.
02-3342 Was $99.99 □*$19.99*

Judas Kiss (1999)
Steamy thriller set in New Orleans and focusing on the kidnapping of a computer company owner by a pair of crooks who run sex scams out of sleazy hotels. When the wife of a senator is accidentally killed during the kidnapping, a group of detectives is called into the investigation. Carla Gugino, Emma Thompson, Alan Rickman and Gil Bellows star in this sexy suspenser. 108 min.
02-3367 Was $99.99 □*$19.99*

Black & White (1999)
Rookie cop Rory Cochrane gets paired with tough and sexy veteran officer Gina Gershon, and the two soon have a torrid romance. But when a serial killer murdering some of the criminals Gershon has encountered continues his campaign of terror, Cochrane and investigator Ron Silver begin to wonder if the policewoman is responsible. Alison Eastwood also stars. 97 min.
02-3390 Was $99.99 □*$19.99*

Resurrection (1999)
Christopher Lambert is a rugged Chicago cop trying to hunt down a serial killer who has been killing people named after the 12 Apostles and piecing together various body parts to make a complete figure of Jesus. His diabolical plan has the city terrorized, and when he targets Lambert's wife and partner, the cop turns up the heat to catch him. With Leland Orser. 108 min.
02-3391 Was $99.99 □*$14.99*

Malice (1993)
Riveting, surprise-filled suspenser set at a New England woman's college where a series of rape-murders troubles the school's dean (Bill Pullman). A brash surgeon (Alec Baldwin), who has rented a room in the house being restored by the dean and his wife (Nicole Kidman), becomes a suspect in the crimes. Bebe Neuwirth, George C. Scott, Gwyneth Paltrow co-star. 106 min.
02-2566 Was $89.99 □*$14.99*

Bad Influence (1990)
Moody and erotic modern "film noir" starring Rob Lowe as a creepy drifter who befriends repressed Los Angeles yuppie James Spader, then leads him into a lifestyle of robbery, murder and sex in front of a video camera. Lisa Zane and Christian Clemenson also star in this solid thriller. 99 min.
02-2035 Was $19.99 *$14.99*

Jezebel's Kiss (1990)
A mysterious, beautiful young woman arrives in a small town, ready to use her sensuality to get what she wants: revenge for the death of a loved one. Sinister, erotic thriller stars Malcolm McDowell, Meredith Baxter Birney, Katherine Barrese. 95 min.
02-2057 *$79.99*

In The Heat Of Passion (1992)
A scorching thriller starring Sally Kirkland as a sensuous older woman involved with a young, down-on-his-luck actor. Their obsessive relationship reaches new sexual heights...and then her jealous husband discovers the steamy affair. With Nick Corri, Jack Carter. Uncut, unrated version features nudity and controversial sexual sequences not shown in theaters. 86 min.
02-2187 Was $89.99 *$19.99*

In The Heat Of Passion II: Unfaithful (1994)
Sizzling, erotic, in-name-only sequel involving a man having an affair with his stepdaughter who believes he's being followed after his wife is killed in a horrible accident. Suspense and sensuous encounters mount as the man finds himself caught in a web of danger. Barry Bostwick, Lesley-Anne Down and Teresa Hill star. Uncut, unrated version.
21-9073 Was $89.99 *$14.99*

Body Chemistry (1990)
Erotic thriller about a lab director working on human sexuality who gets more than he bargained for when he begins a torrid affair with a sexy government researcher. As their romance gets more serious, the woman's obsessive streak grows, and the liaison turns deadly. Marc Singer, Mary Crosby, Lisa Pescia star. 84 min.
02-2028 Was $79.99 *$19.99*

Body Chemistry 2: Voice Of A Stranger (1992)
A cop whose abuse-riddled childhood left him with a compulsive need for violent sex tries to get help from a female call-in radio therapist, but the professional relationship heats up and threatens both of them in this super-steamy sequel. Lisa Pescia returns as the sexy shrink; with Gregory Harrison, Robin Riker, Morton Downey, Jr. 84 min.
02-2240 Was $89.99 *$19.99*

Body Chemistry 3: Point Of Seduction (1993)
An aspiring writer attempts to sell the story of his friend's death to a slick producer, but first they must get the approval of a gorgeous TV newscaster, who may have killed him. When the producer falls in love with the suspected murderess, eroticism and danger meet. Steamy suspenser stars Andrew Stevens, Morgan Fairchild and Shari Shattuck.
21-9051 Was $89.99 *$14.99*

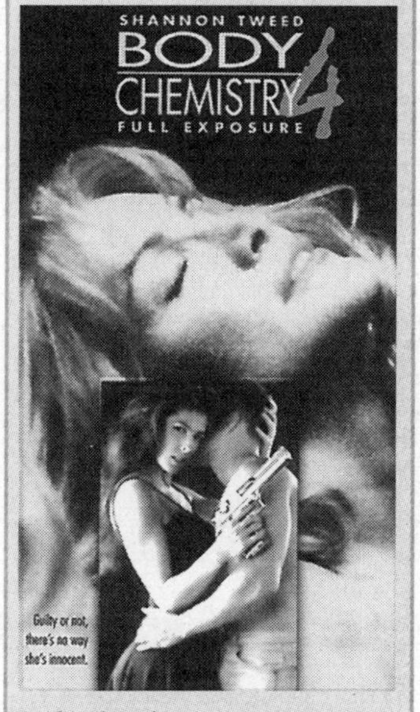

Body Chemistry 4: Full Exposure (1995)
A top-notch criminal attorney faces career and marital problems when he falls in love with a sex psychologist accused of murder. Their relationship turns into a wild series of sexual adventures that become dangerous. Shannon Tweed, Larry Poindexter, Larry Menetti star. Uncut, unrated version; 95 min.
21-9092 Was $89.99 *$14.99*

Every Breath (1993)
An ambitious but broke young actor is welcomed into a game of wild sex and elaborate game-playing when he gets involved with a wealthy European man and his gorgeous wife. Betrayal and murder ensue in this kinky thriller starring Judd Nelson, Patrick Bauchau and Joanna Pacula star. 88 min.
02-2558 □*$89.99*

Till The End Of The Night (1995)
A successful young architect learns that his beautiful wife has a hidden past—and a previous husband, too. As he begins to probe his wife's secrets, he learns that her ex-hubby is psychotic and still takes their nuptials seriously. With Scott Valentine, David Keith and Katherine Kelly Lang. 89 min.
02-2759 *$89.99*

Murdered Innocence (1996)
There's surprises aplenty in this dark thriller about a young mother who is brutally stabbed. Her husband is accused of the murder, but is killed by an overzealous cop. Or is he? Twenty years later, the cop's past comes back to haunt him. Jason Miller, Fred Carpenter and Ellen Greene star. 88 min.
02-2876 Was $99.99 □*$19.99*

Circumstances Unknown (1995)
Judd Nelson turns in a creepy performance as a jealous killer who plots to kill his happily married pals. What dark, hidden secret triggers Nelson's homicidal ways? Isabel Glaser and William Moses co-star. 91 min.
06-2345 □*$89.99*

Dangerous Pursuit (1990)
A visit by a top politico also brings to town a deadly professional assassin. A former lover who recognizes the hit man knows what he's there for, and must stop him...but he's recognized her, too! Gregory Harrison, Alexandra Powers and Scott Valentine star in this taut suspenser. 95 min.
06-1739 *$89.99*

The Kissing Place (1990)
He was abducted from his true family as an infant. Now he's 10, and desperately searching the streets of New York for them...unless the unbalanced woman he's called "Mom" finds him first! Meredith Baxter Birney, David Ogden Stiers and Nathaniel Moreau star in this mesmerizing mystery. 88 min.
06-1764 *$79.99*

Snow Kill (1990)
It's high action in the high mountains when a group of business pals on a survival weekend find themselves stranded in a horrible snowstorm. Things get worse when a gang of drug smugglers move in for an attack. Terence Knox, Patti D'Arbanville and Clayton Rohner star. 94 min.
06-1781 □*$89.99*

In Too Deep (1990)
A beautiful torch singer falls for a rock star, but their steamy affair takes a dangerous turn when he tries to draw her into a life of crime. Erotic thriller in the style of "Body Heat" stars Santha Press, Hugo Race, Dominic Sweeney. 106 min.
06-1849 □*$89.99*

Hitler's Daughter (1990)
A White House press aide discovers that one of three prominent Washington women is actually the child of the infamous dictator and will rise to even greater power in the next presidential election. Kay Lenz, Patrick Cassidy, Veronica Cartwright and Melody Anderson star in this tale of espionage and hidden identity. 88 min.
06-1880 □*$89.99*

The Secret Agent (1996)
Gripping thriller, based on Joseph Conrad's novel, stars Bob Hoskins as a meek shopkeeper in 1890s London who heads a clandestine anarchist group. Unknown to anyone around him, however, including wife Patricia Arquette, Hoskins is really in the employ of the Russian government, which sends him on a bombing mission that ends in chaos and tragedy. With Christian Bale, Gerard Depardieu, and an unbilled Robin Williams as "The Professor." 95 min.
04-3405 Was $99.99 □*$29.99*

Web Of Deceit (1991)
Linda Purl, James Read and Paul deSouza star in this gripping mystery about a female defense attorney on the trail of a horrible killer who may be closing in on her. 93 min.
06-1891 □*$89.99*

Nature Of The Beast (1995)
Intense suspenser about two men with deadly secrets who face each other while in the desert. One of them is a disturbed killer in the midst of a murder spree, the other ripped of a Las Vegas casino for a million dollars...but which one is which? Eric Roberts, Lance Henriksen and Brion James star. 91 min.
02-5067 □*$19.99*

Scissors (1991)
In this sinister thriller, Sharon Stone plays an emotionally frail woman who is given a rude awakening when she moves to the big city. Attacked by a man in her apartment building, she fights back with a pair of scissors, and soon the real and the imagined blend as she encounters her worst fears. Steve Railsback, Ronny Cox and Michelle Phillips also star. 105 min.
06-1895 □*$14.99*

Mortal Sins (1992)
After he hears the confession of a serial murderer, a priest, who is compelled to keep the admission confidential, must stage a race against time to stop the killer on his own. Christopher Reeve, Roxanne Biggs and Francis Guinan star in this top-notch thriller. 93 min.
04-2657 Was $19.99 □*$14.99*

When The Dark Man Calls (1995)
Twenty years after her parents are slain, a talk-radio psychologist is pursued by the same psychotic killer in this riveting suspenser. Joan Van Ark, Chris Sarandon star. 89 min.
06-2398 □*$89.99*

Deadly Desire (1990)
Jack Scalia stars in this erotic thriller as a former cop now doing security work who is hired by the seductive wife of a wealthy businessman, and soon finds himself in a dangerous web of intrigue involving double deals and, possibly, murder. Kathryn Harrold, Will Patton and Joe Santos co-star. 93 min.
06-1904 □*$89.99*

Outside The Law (1995)
While investigating a murder, a police detective is seduced by a gorgeous woman who turns out to be a prime suspect in the case. He soon carries on a torrid affair with the woman which leads him into a world of danger and desire. David Bradley, Anna Thomson and Ashley Laurence star. Unrated version; 95 min.
02-5054 Was $89.99 □*$19.99*

Fatal Exposure (1991)
In this electrifying thriller, a single mother picks up the wrong photos from a lab and soon finds herself and her children endangered by a maniacal killer. Hmmm...should have used Fotomat. Mare Winningham, Nick Mancuso and Christopher McDonald star. 89 min.
06-1913 □*$89.99*

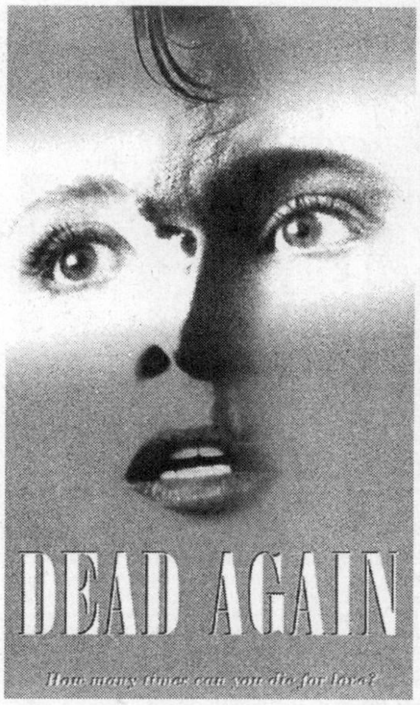

Dead Again (1991)
Stylish, witty psychological thriller starring Kenneth Branagh (who also directed) as an L.A. private detective who tries to help a beautiful amnesia victim (Emma Thompson), but discovers that they both may be reincarnations of the principals involved in a lurid murder case 40 years earlier. Andy Garcia, Derek Jacobi, Hanna Schygulla and Robin Williams co-star. 107 min.
06-1918 Was $89.99 □*$14.99*

One Good Turn (1996)
A man and his wife find their marriage threatened when one of the husband's old friends gets back into his life...and proceeds to terrorize both of them. Intense thriller in the "Unlawful Entry" mold stars James Remar, Lenny von Dohlen, Suzy Amis and John Savage. 90 min.
02-8483 Was $99.99 *$14.99*

Living In Peril (1997)
Ambitious young architect Rob Lowe happily moves to Los Angeles for what looks like a dream job, but soon is caught up in a terrifying game where death is the ultimate penalty. Gripping suspense story also stars James Belushi, Dean Stockwell, Dana Wheeler-Nicholson. 95 min.
02-5169 Was $99.99 □*$19.99*

Dead Connection (1994)
Intense thriller focusing on a tough Los Angeles cop trying to capture a murderer who lures women to hotel rooms, then kills them after listening to a phone sex line. When the cop discovers a reporter has some inside information on the killer, he teams with her to stop the crimes. Michael Madsen, Lisa Bonet star. 92 min.
02-8037 □*$14.99*

Clay Pigeons (1998)
Offbeat dark comedy/thriller stars Joaquin Phoenix as a Montana gas station attendant whose affair with his best friend's manipulative wife leads to a suicide, a murder, and Phoenix forced to hide two bodies. Just when he's sure things can't get worse, Phoenix is befriended by slick cowboy Vince Vaughn, and bodies start turning up all over the place. With Scott Wilson and Janeane Garofalo. 104 min.
02-9050 Was $99.99 *$14.99*

Where Sleeping Dogs Lie (1991)
A struggling novelist moves into a house where a family was brutally murdered five years earlier. The crime gives him the inspiration for a new work, but his research into what happened draws the unwanted attention from the killer. Suspenseful tale stars Dylan McDermott, Tom Sizemore and Sharon Stone. 92 min.
02-2349 Was $19.99 □$14.99

The Cold Light Of Day (1996)
Atmospheric suspenser with Richard E. Grant as a detective investigating a serial killer. When the prime suspect is found dead, Grant believes the culprit is still loose and, in order to find him, quits the force and tries to use one of the killer's young near-victims and her mother as "bait" for a trap. With Lynsey Baxter, Simon Cadell. 101 min.
02-8486 Was $19.99 $14.99

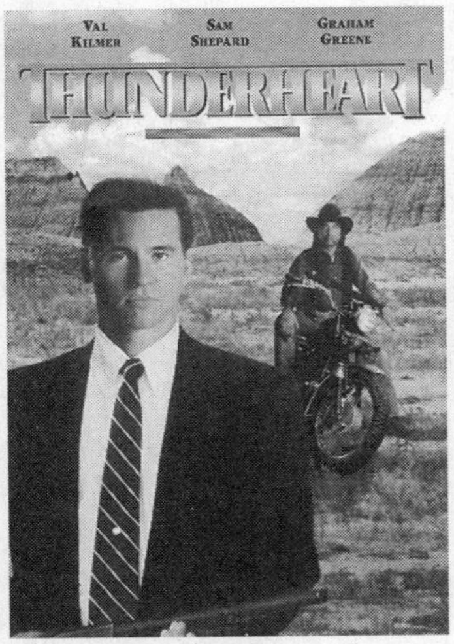

Thunderheart (1992)
A slick FBI agent of Native-American descent investigates a murder that occurred on a Sioux reservation in South Dakota. Joined by a tribal policeman and a veteran FBI operative, the agent gets closer to the killer, as well as his own heritage. Val Kilmer, Sam Shepard and Graham Greene star in this thriller inspired by the events depicted in the documentary "Incident at Oglala." 119 min.
02-2282 Was $19.99 □$14.99

Smilla's Sense Of Snow (1997)
Based on Danish author Peter Hoeg's best-selling novel, this unusual and compelling film stars Julia Ormond as Smilla, a young Inuit/American woman living in Copenhagen who, using her instinctive powers of perception and affinity for snow and ice, sets out to learn the true circumstances surrounding a neighbor boy's fatal fall. With Gabriel Byrne, Richard Harris and Vanessa Redgrave; Bille August ("Pelle the Conqueror") directs. 121 min.
04-3469 □$99.99

Murderous Vision (1991)
A killer is stalking the city, and when police fail to find him, a detective specializing in missing persons teams with a beautiful psychic to track down the murderer. Robert Culp, Bruce Boxleitner and Laura Johnson star in this supernatural-tinged mystery. 93 min.
06-1934 □$89.99

The Ten Million Dollar Giveaway (1991)
Riveting true story about the 1978 Lufthansa robbery at New York's Kennedy Airport, the largest cash heist in American history, masterminded by Jimmy "The Gent" Burke and his gang of motley mobsters. John Mahoney, Karen Young and Tony LoBianco star. 93 min.
06-1935 □$89.99

Intimate Stranger (1991)
An erotic thriller starring Deborah Harry as a struggling rock singer who takes a job as a phone-sex operator and comes into contact with a psychopathic killer during one of her calls. Soon, he's out to get her. James Russo, Tim Thomerson, Grace Zabriskie co-star. 96 min.
06-1940 Was $89.99 □$14.99

Born Killers (1992)
In this gripping thriller, an aspiring artist falls into a life of crime when he gets involved with a friend's get-rich-quick scheme. When he finds himself up to his ears in crime and the target of a hit man, only then does he see that he must become a "born killer" to survive. Thomas Edwards, John M. Craig, Emily Newman star. AKA: "Double Cross." 90 min.
76-7478 $79.99

Kafka (1991)
The life and writings of Franz Kafka inspired this fascinating film featuring Jeremy Irons as the title character, an aspiring author who pays his bills as an insurance clerk. When a friend disappears, Kafka attempts to find him, with the search leading him to an ominous castle. Theresa Russell, Armin Mueller-Stahl, Alec Guinness co-star; directed by Steven Soderbergh ("sex, lies and videotape"). 98 min.
06-2010 $89.99

Blind Man's Bluff (1992)
A top-notch cast stars in this intense suspenser about a blind professor who is unknowingly involved in a deadly frame job. Robert Urich, Lisa Eilbacher and Ron Perlman star. 86 min.
06-1953 $89.99

Killer Image (1992)
A man discovers that his brother's death may have something to do with the photos he took of a powerful senator and a prostitute. He attempts to find the killers, but gets caught in a deadly cat-and-mouse game with a cruel assassin. Michael Ironside, M. Emmet Walsh and Krista Errickson star. 97 min.
06-1954 □$89.99

Deadly Game (1992)
Roddy McDowall, Jenny Seagrove and Marc Singer lead the cast of this action-packed suspenser about a deranged millionaire who invites seven people to the desert for a most dangerous manhunt. 93 min.
06-1958 □$89.99

Blackmail (1992)
A highly-charged erotic suspenser about two grifters out to blackmail a wealthy gangster's wife. Soon, they are caught at their own game as a seedy detective wants to get in on the con. Susan Blakely, Dale Midkiff, John Saxon and Mac Davis star. 87 min.
06-1992 □$89.99

Love Kills (1992)
Steamy thriller about a beautiful heiress who falls in love with a man who may be an assassin hired by her duplicitous husband. Virginia Madsen, Jim Metzler and Lenny Von Dohlen star in this erotic mystery. 92 min.
06-1994 □$89.99

The Lightning Incident (1992)
A young, pregnant Santa Fe sculptor with psychic abilities becomes convinced that the bizarre nightmares troubling her are signs of a dark force after her child. When the baby is born, a devil-worshipping cult abducts it, and the woman must use her powers to find them. Nancy McKeon, Elpidia Carrillo and Polly Bergen star. 90 min.
06-2061 □$89.99

Treacherous Crossing (1992)
What starts out as a luxurious, peaceful honeymoon cruise on an ocean liner becomes a journey into suspense and terror, and the new bride may never get the chance to show off that Victoria's Secret peignoir if a mysterious killer gets to her first. Lindsay Wagner, Grant Show, Angie Dickinson, Joseph Bottoms and Charles Napier star. 88 min.
06-2064 □$89.99

Whispers In The Dark (1992)
A Manhattan psychiatrist (Annabella Sciorra) becomes enthralled by the sexual fantasies of a female patient, but when her own erotic dreams lead her to seek therapy, someone begins blurring fantasy and reality, and turning the dreams into deadly nightmares. Sizzling suspenser stars Deborah Unger, Jamey Sheridan, Anthony LaPaglia and Alan Alda. 103 min.
06-2068 Was $89.99 □$19.99

Body Language (1993)
Steamy thriller about a successful businesswoman with man trouble who hires a secretary to solve her problems. Little does she suspect that the "gal Friday" has some rather drastic solutions in store. Heather Locklear, Linda Purl and Edward Albert star. 93 min.
06-2084 □$79.99

Dirty Work (1992)
A tense thriller involving a drug-dealing bailbondsman who gets in trouble with the mob by taking their counterfeit money, then sets his partner up to take the fall. Kevin Dobson, John Ashton and Mitchell Ryan star. 88 min.
06-2094 □$89.99

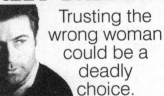

ALEC BALDWIN

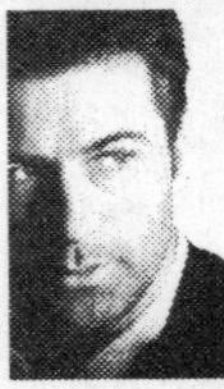

Trusting the wrong woman could be a deadly choice.

HEAVEN'S PRISONERS

Heaven's Prisoners (1996)
Alcoholic ex-cop Alec Baldwin rescues a young Salvadoran girl from a plane crash and, along with wife Kelly Lynch, adopts her. But he suspects the crash wasn't an accident, and his investigation leads to a number of dangerous characters tied to the New Orleans underworld. Mary Stuart Masterson, Teri Hatcher and Eric Roberts also star in this erotic, atmospheric suspenser. 135 min.
02-5108 Was $99.99 □$14.99

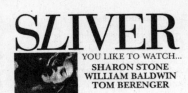

SLIVER

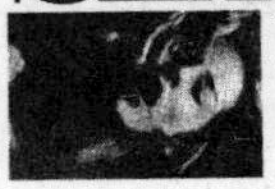

YOU LIKE TO WATCH...
SHARON STONE
WILLIAM BALDWIN
TOM BERENGER

Sliver (1993)
Sharon Stone scorches the screen with her supercharged erotic performance in this thriller, playing a New York book editor who finds herself caught up in a world of kinky thrills orchestrated by the voyeuristic owner (William Baldwin) of her apartment building. When a stalker terrorizes the building, Stone has Baldwin pegged as a prime suspect. Tom Berenger also stars. 106 min.
06-2146 Was $19.99 □$14.99

Sliver (Unrated Version)
Also available in an unrated edition, featuring scenes too hot for theatres. 108 min.
06-2241 Was $19.99 □$14.99

Rampage (1992)
A seemingly normal teenage boy goes on a horrifying killing spree and a liberal district attorney is assigned to prosecute him. Complicating matters is the fact the D.A. believes that the death penalty is appropriate, a punishment that goes against his usual beliefs. Michael Biehn, Alex McArthur and Nicholas Campbell star in William Friedkin's thriller (actually filmed in 1987). 92 min.
06-2108 Was $89.99 □$14.99

Jennifer 8 (1992)
Moody suspenser about a former L.A. cop who leaves the rigors of the city for a police beat in the country. He's soon involved with catching a serial killer whose targets are blind women, and holding the secret to the case may be a beautiful sightless woman. Andy Garcia, Uma Thurman, John Malkovich and Lance Henriksen star. 127 min.
06-2109 Was $19.99 □$14.99

Sunstroke (1992)
Diabolical thriller with Jane Seymour as a seductive woman who meets a handsome drifter with a secret while searching for her kidnapped child. Steve Railsback and Don Ameche also star. 91 min.
06-2113 □$89.99

Perfect Family (1992)
A single mother hires a handyman and his sister to care for her two young girls. At first, her new babysitters appear perfect, but soon strange things occur, and the family's future is soon threatened. Bruce Boxleitner, Jennifer O'Neill and Joanna Cassidy star. 92 min.
06-2121 □$89.99

The Temp (1993)
A young cookie executive (Timothy Hutton) on the fast track hires a beautiful, ultra-efficient temporary secretary (Lara Flynn Boyle) with aspirations higher than taking dictation—and she will wile, seduce and murder to reach them! Creepy corporate shocker also stars Faye Dunaway, Dwight Schultz. 99 min.
06-2123 Was $19.99 □$14.99

Writer's Block (1991)
A best-selling author is told by her publishers that it's time to retire her popular serial killer character. But a series of bizarre, copy-cat killings have begun to occur...and her stories seem to be coming to life. What can she do to stop the murders? Morgan Fairchild, Michael Praed and Joe Regalbuto star. 90 min.
06-2124 □$89.99

Are You Lonesome Tonight (1991)
Sultry thriller about a rich, gorgeous woman who discovers that her husband is carrying on a steamy affair with a phone-sex girl. She wants to investigate the romance further and is soon drawn into a web of suspense. With Jane Seymour and Parker Stevenson. 91 min.
06-1949 □$89.99

Fade To Black (1993)
After he captures a murder on his video camcorder, a voyeuristic professor finds himself in the middle of a plot involving deceit, murder and blackmail. Heather Locklear, Timothy Busfield and Cloris Leachman star. 84 min.
06-2158 □$89.99

Linda (1993)
A taut thriller in which a duplicitous woman carrying on a steamy affair with her neighbor plots to have her loving, mild-mannered husband framed for the murder of the neighbor's wife. Richard Thomas, Virginia Madsen and Ted McGinley star. AKA: "Lust for Murder." 88 min.
06-2195 □$89.99

The Cover Girl Murders (1993)
In this sizzling thriller, a group of gorgeous cover girl models are brought to a remote island for a shoot for a magazine's special swimsuit edition. Soon, competition gets so fierce that women are being found dead. Lee Majors, Jennifer O'Neill, Adrian Paul and supermodel Beverly Johnson star. 87 min.
06-2198 □$89.99

Dying To Remember (1993)
A fashion designer undergoes hypnotherapy and discovers that she was murdered in her past life. Hoping to find out more about the incident, she travels to San Francisco, where she learns the culprits are plotting another murder. Melissa Gilbert and Ted Shackleford star. 87 min.
06-2201 □$89.99

Tainted Blood (1993)
Raquel Welch stars in this intriguing suspenser, playing an investigative reporter tracking down a teenage twin of a serial killer. Alley Mills, Joan Van Ark and Kerri Green co-star. 86 min.
06-2168 □$89.99

Praying Mantis (1993)
A woman with a lengthy matrimonial record also has a history of husbands turning up dead. Her latest spouse discovers this and sets out to stop her before deadly divorce proceedings start again. Jane Seymour, Frances Fisher and Barry Bostwick star. 90 min.
06-2170 □$89.99

Rubdown (1993)
A baseball player-turned-Beverly Hills masseur discovers that he's the chief suspect in the murders of his clients. Jack Coleman, Catherine Oxenberg, Michelle Phillips, Alan Thicke and William Devane star. 88 min.
06-2173 □$89.99

Dancing With Danger (1994)
In this mix of romance and mystery, a private detective's steamy relationship with a taxi dancer leads him into a dark world where he's targeted for danger. Cheryl Ladd and Ed Marinaro star. 90 min.
06-2263 □$89.99

The Spider And The Fly (1994)
Involving thriller about two mystery writers who plot the perfect crime, then become chief suspects when a real murder occurs. Can they prove their innocence? Ted Shackelford and Mel Harris star. 87 min.
06-2269 □$79.99

Seduced By Evil (1994)
A journalist doing a story on a "New Age" shaman finds herself falling under the healer's seductive, deadly magic in this occult-flavored thriller starring Suzanne Somers, James B. Sikking, John Vargas. 88 min.
06-2282 □$79.99

Bitter Vengeance (1994)
An unfaithful husband thinks he's found the perfect "no-fault divorce" when he frames his wife for robbery and murder, but she launches her own plans for revenge in this taut suspenser. Virginia Madsen, Bruce Greenwood, Kristen Hocking star. 90 min.
06-2283 □$79.99

Jericho Fever (1993)
Intense suspenser in which disease specialists Stephanie Zimbalist and Perry King try to stop a group of terrorists from unleashing a lethal virus. 88 min.
06-2206 □$89.99

Dark Side Of Genius (1994)
The glamorous and trendy world of L.A.'s art gallery scene is the background for this seductive thriller, as a reporter's investigation of a parolled murderer whose lurid nude paintings have made him a celebrity lures her deeper and deeper into danger. Brent Fraser, Finola Hughes, Seymour Cassel, Moon Zappa star. 86 min.
06-2284 Was $89.99 □$19.99

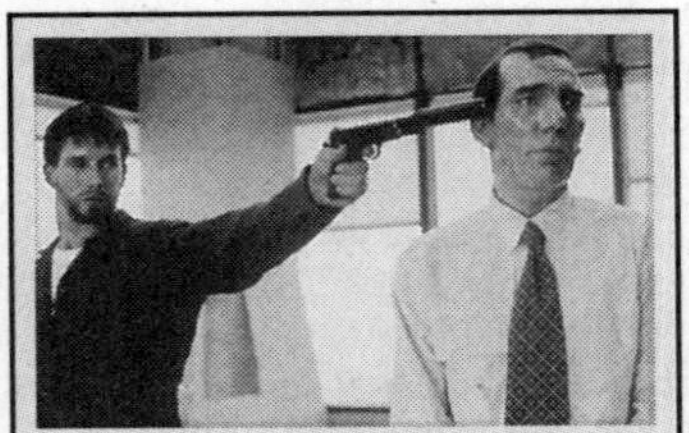

The Usual Suspects

The Usual Suspects (1995)
Four small-time criminals and a crooked former New York cop, brought together in a police lineup, pool their expertise for a multi-million-dollar heist. The caper lands them in California and in the grip of a feared and enigmatic crime boss named Keyser Soze, who blackmails the quintet into pulling a job that turns into a bloodbath. Wonderfully witty and complex thriller with more than one surprise twist stars Stephen Baldwin, Gabriel Byrne, Benicio Del Toro, Chazz Palminteri, Kevin Pollak and, in an Academy Award-winning turn, Kevin Spacey. 106 min.
02-8367 Was $19.99 □$14.99

The Usual Suspects: Limited Edition Collector's Set
This two-tape, numbered limited edition boxed collector's set features the letterboxed version of the Oscar-winning mystery; a second edition featuring running commentary from screenwriter Christopher McQuarrie and director Bryan Singer ("X-Men"). Plus, there's some real cool collectibles, including a copy of the final shooting script; a "Who is Keyser Soze?" lapel pin; a cast line-up pin; and a Zippo-type cigarette lighter imprinted with the movie's logo, all beautifully packaged in a large gift box.
02-8537 $39.99

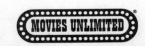

Fatal Past (1994)
A bodyguard hired to watch the mistress of a shady entrepreneur falls in love with the woman and is viciously punished by his employer. Soon, the bodyguard realizes that he and his lover share a fate that is connected to their past lives in 17th-century feudal Japan. Costas Mandylor and Kasia Figura star. 85 min.
06-2245 Was $89.99 ❑*$14.99*

Parallel Lives (1994)
An all-star cast is featured in this witty and intriguing tale of deception, murder, seduction and jealousy at a college reunion. Treat Williams, JoBeth Williams, Dudley Moore, Lindsay Crouse, Jill Eikenberry, Robert Wagner, Liza Minnelli and Gena Rowlands star; directed by Linda Yellen ("Chantilly Lace"). 105 min.
06-2292 Was $89.99 ❑*$14.99*

A Vow To Kill (1994)
After her husband dies in a car accident, beautiful Julianne Phillips gets over her grief when she falls in love with handsome Richard Grieco. After the two marry, Phillips learns a startling secret: her new husband is a devious kidnapper and she is his ticket to ransom money. Gordon Pinsent also stars. 91 min.
06-2315 ❑*$89.99*

As Good As Dead (1995)
Riveting thriller from cult favorite Larry Cohen ("Q") about a well-meaning woman who offers her identity to a sickly friend checking into the hospital. When her friend is murdered, the woman discovers that she was the intended victim. Judge Reinhold, Crystal Bernard and Traci Lords star. 88 min.
06-2344 ❑*$89.99*

Benefit Of The Doubt (1993)
Twenty-two years after he was sentenced to prison for killing his wife, ex-con Donald Sutherland returns to the home of daughter Amy Irving, who testified against him. He claims he wants to renew family relations, but she's certain his intentions are more sinister. Graham Greene and Christopher McDonald co-star. 92 min.
06-2179 ❑*$89.99*

The Substitute (1993)
An alluring substitute teacher with a disturbing secret in her past gives her high school students lessons in sexuality and horror when she seduces and terrorizes the teens in her class. Amanda Donohoe, Dalton James and Marky Mark star. 86 min.
06-2181 ❑*$89.99*

Accidental Meeting (1993)
After their involvement in an auto accident, two women with man trouble decide that swapping murder plans might solve their problems. After making their pact, however, both find themselves in a dangerous cat-and-mouse game. Linda Purl, Linda Gray, Leigh J. McCloskey and Kent McCord star. 91 min.
06-2234 ❑*$89.99*

Cover Me (1995)
Scorching erotic thriller about a cop (Courtney Taylor) who goes undercover as a nude model in order to find the killer of a group of fashion models. She becomes involved in the Los Angeles underground world of strip clubs, shower dancing and escorts. With Rick Rossovich and Paul Sorvino; features lots of kinky encounters. 94 min.
06-2389 Was $89.99 ❑*$19.99*

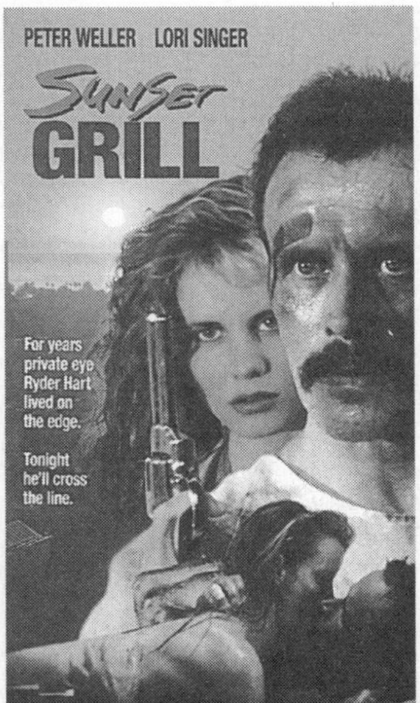

PETER WELLER LORI SINGER
SUNSET GRILL
For years private eye Ryder Hart lived on the edge.
Tonight he'll cross the line.

Sunset Grill (1992)
A private investigator's search for his wife's killers teams him up with a beautiful and enigmatic girl whose employer is involved with an international money racket. Will the pair learn how their problems are connected before it's too late? Action-filled and erotic thriller stars Peter Weller, Lori Singer, Stacy Keach. Uncut, unrated version; 104 min.
02-2350 Was $19.99 *$14.99*

On Dangerous Ground (1995)
Based on a story by best-selling author Jack Higgins, this compelling suspenser stars Rob Lowe as Sean Dillon, a former IRA operative recruited by British intelligence to recover a long-lost document that could jeopardize the transfer of Hong Kong to China. Kenneth Cranham, Deborah Moore, Jurgen Prochnow co-star. 105 min.
06-2670 Was $79.99 ❑*$14.99*

Midnight Man (1995)
Jack Higgins' Sean Dillon thinks he has settled down after getting married and retiring, but news of an assassination plot targeting members of the British Royal Family—a plan whose trigger man is an old enemy of Dillon's—forces him back into action. Rob Lowe, Deborah Moore, Kenneth Cranham star. 104 min.
06-2788 Was $79.99 ❑*$14.99*

Thunder Point (1996)
Kyle MacLachlan stars as ex-terrorist-turned-mercenary Sean Dillon, who is assigned by the British government to protect a woman in possession of a WWII document that could destroy the free world. Political extremists want her dead, and it's up to Dillon to keep the woman and the document safe, in this thriller based on Jack Higgins' novel. With Pascale Bussières, John Colicos. 95 min.
06-2749 ❑*$89.99*

The Windsor Protocol (1996)
British secret agent Sean Dillon (Kyle MacLachlan) is back in this riveting thriller that finds him trying to stop a group of Nazi sympathizers who hold a dangerous connection to a powerful senator. Macha Grenon, Alan Thicke and Shannon Whirry also star. 96 min.
06-2789 ❑*$79.99*

Tall, Dark And Deadly (1995)
Naive Kim Delaney is wooed by charming stranger Jack Scalia, but becomes frightened by his strange behavior and ends the relationship. She has no idea that he's responsible for the death of two people, and when he kills her rival at work, she's framed for murder. Todd Allen, Ely Puget co-star. 88 min.
06-2399 ❑*$89.99*

Playback (1995)
A red-hot sensual thriller about a fast-tracking business executive who has the biggest deal of his life sidetracked after he becomes involved with a sexy fellow employee looking to set him up and his boss tries to seduce his wife. Charles Grant, Tawny Kitaen, Shannon Whirry, George Hamilton and Harry Dean Stanton star. 91 min.
06-2401 Was $89.99 ❑*$19.99*

The Sister-In-Law (1995)
Twenty years after her parents were accidentally killed, a deranged woman seeks revenge on the family responsible by assuming a new identity. Her plan? Marry into the clan and destroy it from within by deception, adultery and murder! Stylishly seductive suspenser stars Kate Vernon, Craig Wasson, Shanna Reed. 95 min.
06-2407 ❑*$79.99*

The Crude Oasis (1995)
Eerie noirish thriller centering on a distraught housewife, involved in a bad marriage, who meets a man she keeps seeing in recurring nightmares at a local gas station. She follows him to the river one night and into a bar where mystery and danger await. Jennifer Taylor and Aaron Shields star in Alex Graves' film, shot for a mere $25,000. 82 min.
06-2471 ❑*$89.99*

Down, Out And Dangerous (1996)
A charming homeless man is taken in by a professional couple about to have a baby, but his well-meaning persona eventually disappears, as he transforms into a dangerous killer. Richard Thomas and Bruce Davison star in this gripping thriller. 90 min.
06-2473 ❑*$89.99*

Tails You Live, Heads You're Dead (1996)
What at first seems like a friendly encounter at a bar between two strangers eventually turns dangerous when one of the men reveals he's a serial killer and his new acquaintance is to be his next victim. With Corbin Bernsen, Ted McGinley and Tim Matheson. 91 min.
06-2474 ❑*$89.99*

Maternal Instincts (1996)
Delta Burke is a woman who desperately wants a baby. After she gets pregnant, complications force her to undergo an emergency hysterectomy. But Burke believes her gynecologist could have saved the child, and soon a deranged Delta begins terrorizing the doctor. With Beth Broderick, Garvin Sanford. 92 min.
06-2500 ❑*$99.99*

Where Truth Lies (1996)
Harrowing psychological suspenser stars John Savage as a renowned psychiatrist who goes from doctor to patient when, against his will, he's sent to a strange institute where the line between reality and fantasy is blurred, and where someone wants him insane...or dead. With Kim Cattrall, Sam Jones, Malcolm McDowell. 92 min.
06-2541 ❑*$99.99*

Contagious (1997)
Respected physician Lindsay Wagner is in a ferocious race against time in order to stop a deadly outbreak of cholera. The nightmare becomes personal when she learns her husband has been exposed to the disease. Elizabeth Peña and Tom Wopat co-star. 90 min.
06-2622 ❑*$99.99*

Through The Eyes Of A Killer (1992)
After a New York publishing executive breaks off her romance with the contractor who designed her home in a renovated loft building, he moves into secret compartments built into her apartment to spy on her and begin a campaign of terror. Spellbinding suspense tale stars Richard Dean Anderson, Marg Helgenberger, Tippi Hedren. 94 min.
06-2410 ❑*$79.99*

Scorpion Spring (1996)
A desperate drug runner on the lam takes a beautiful hostage with him through the desert and dupes two travellers into giving them aid. But all four people's lives are placed in jeopardy when they find themselves in a region controlled by a merciless narcotics kingpin. Intense thriller boasts a fine cast that includes Esai Morales, Matthew McConaughey and Ruben Blades. 89 min.
02-5122 Was $99.99 ❑*$19.99*

Mirage (1995)
Down-and-out ex-cop Edward James Olmos takes a job guarding Sean Young, the beautiful wife of a wealthy environmentalist, and is romantically drawn to her. Young, however, has multiple personality disorder (including an alter ego who's a stripper), and her affliction pulls her and Olmos into a bizarre game of deceit, treachery and murder. 92 min.
07-2357 ❑*$99.99*

Jade (1995)
From the typewriter of Joe Eszterhas ("Showgirls") comes this sensuous suspenser in which San Francisco Assistant D.A. David Caruso looks into the death of an art dealer who blackmailed public officials by photographing them in bed with hookers. Caruso's search leads to ex-lover Linda Fiorentino, a psychologist and call girl by night, now married to powerful lawyer Chazz Palminteri. This special, unrated edition, supervised by director William Friedkin, contains 12 minutes of footage too hot for theatres. 107 min.
06-2841 Was $89.99 ❑*$19.99*

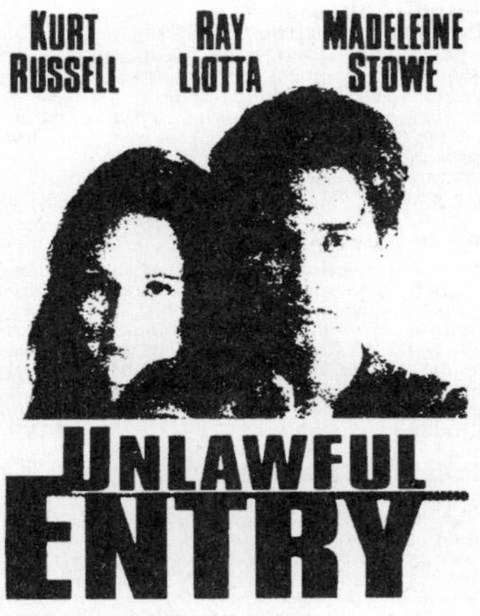

KURT RUSSELL
RAY LIOTTA
MADELEINE STOWE
UNLAWFUL ENTRY

Unlawful Entry (1992)
Intense suspenser about an upwardly mobile couple (Kurt Russell and Madeleine Stowe) who are confronted by a burglar and soon take measures to make their home safer. Offering assistance is "friendly" policeman Ray Liotta, who immediately becomes romantically obsessed with Stowe and will do anything to have her—including commit murder. Roger E. Moseley, Ken Lerner also star. 107 min.
04-2596 Was $19.99 ❑*$14.99*

Human Bomb (1996)
After moving to Germany to begin a new teaching position, Patsy Kensit and her class of third-graders are taken hostage by a masked gunman who demands 50 million marks to set them free. Jurgen Prochnow is the police official who matches wits with the diabolical criminal. 93 min.
06-2722 ❑*$99.99*

Gold Coast (1997)
Elmore Leonard's book is the basis for a first-rate thriller starring David Caruso as an ex-con who attempts to collect money owed to him by a powerful mobster. But when Caruso discovers that the mobster is dead, he must contend with his beautiful widow (Marg Helgenberger) and her no-nonsense enforcer. Barry Primus and Jeff Kober also star in this sensual suspenser. 109 min.
06-2723 ❑*$99.99*

Face Down (1997)
For New York private eye Joe Mantegna, a one-night stand with a beautiful client leads him into a deadly maze of deception and death. Can he clear his name of a false murder charge before becoming the killer's next victim? Steamy noir thriller also stars Kelli Maroney, Peter Riegert. 107 min.
06-2712 ❑*$69.99*

Innocent Lies (1995)
Seductive suspenser set in 1938 about a British detective investigating the alleged suicide of his friend who delves into the private lives of an English family living in France. Among the family members are a snooty, Nazi-connected widow, her sexy daughter and her guilt-ridden son. Gabrielle Anwar, Stephen Dorff, Adrian Dunbar and Joanna Lumley star. 88 min.
02-8329 ❑*$14.99*

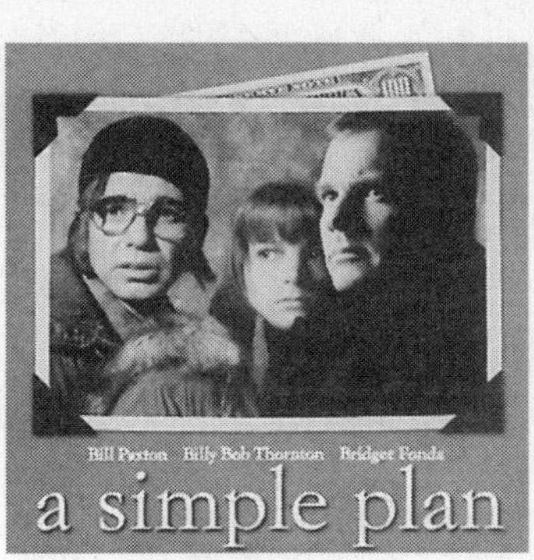

Bill Paxton Billy Bob Thornton Bridget Fonda
a simple plan

A Simple Plan (1998)
This intense tale tells of brothers Hank (Bill Paxton) and Jacob Mitchell (Billy Bob Thornton) who, along with friend Lou (Brent Briscoe), find a gym bag stuffed with $4.4 million in a crashed plane. What should be done with the money is the focus of Sam Raimi's atmospheric, tragic thriller of greed, American style. With Bridget Fonda. 121 min.
06-2852 Was $99.99 ❑*$14.99*

Aldrich Ames: Traitor Within (1998)
This riveting true story tells of the exploits of Aldrich Ames, the high level CIA director of Soviet counter-intelligence, who was convicted in 1994 of selling information on spies he, the CIA and the FBI recruited to the Soviets. Timothy Hutton, Joan Plowright and Elizabeth Peña star in this look at America's greatest traitor since Benedict Arnold. 97 min.
06-2858 ❑*$99.99*

Where's Marlowe? (1999)
Two down-on-their-luck film students tackle a documentary on L.A.-based detective Miguel Ferrer, but the further they get into production on the film, the more they're enmeshed in his latest case, involving cheating wives, crooked partners and dead bodies. Mos Def, John Livingston and Allison Dean star in this intriguing mix of thriller and mockumentary. 99 min.
06-3000 ❑*$99.99*

Happy Face Murders (1999)
In this true story, Ann-Margret plays an Oregon grandmother obsessed with TV detective shows whose attempts to pin a series of murders on her younger, abusive lover leads to her own implication in the crimes. When the real killer begins to take credit for the killings, detectives Marg Helgenberger and Henry Thomas start to investigate. 99 min.
06-3001 ❑*$69.99*

The Hunted (1998)
An ambitious insurance investigator heads into the mountains of the Pacific Northwest in search of a plane that crashed with $12 million on board. Once there, she encounters a mysterious recluse who, instead of taking her to the wreckage site, decides to go hunting...with her as his prey. Harry Hamlin and Mädchen Amick star in this suspenseful cat-and-mouse thriller. 96 min.
06-2754 Was $69.99 ❑*$14.99*

Wounded (1997)
Mädchen Amick plays a game warden trying to track down a grizzly bear poacher who has killed her fellow wildlife officer fiancé. When the FBI refuses to help her, Amick turns to a recovering alcoholic cop for aid in finding the murderer. Graham Greene and Adrian Pasdar also star in this rugged thriller. 91 min.
06-2790 ❑*$69.99*

Dirty Little Secret (1998)
Desperate for money, a young woman abducts the son of a wealthy sheriff, but captor and captive learn disturbing secrets about their pasts in this compelling thriller. Tracy Gold, Jack Wagner star. 92 min.
06-2839 ❑*$69.99*

A Prayer In The Dark (1997)
Nerve-numbing suspense story starring Lynda Carter as a religious woman whose faith and pacifism are put to the test when a brutal killer on the run from the law takes her family hostage. Colin Ferguson, Teri Polo also star. 91 min.
06-2649 ❑*$79.99*

Perfect Crime (1997)
When a female Marine Corps officer vanishes, her husband, also a soldier, becomes a suspect in her murder. Mitzi Kapture and Jasmine Guy star in this suspenser, based on a true story. 92 min.
06-2650 ❑*$79.99*

The Stepsister (1997)
When her wealthy father dies shortly after remarrying, a young woman begins to suspect her new stepsister of killing him. Can she prove her sibling's sinister plot, however, before becoming her next victim? Gripping thriller stars Bridgette Wilson, Rena Sofer, Alan Rachins and Linda Evans. 91 min.
06-2652 ❑*$99.99*

The Ticket (1997)
A winning lottery ticket looks to be the answer to the dreams of a pilot and his estranged family, but when their plane crashes in the wilderness while they're on the way to claim their money, it becomes clear that someone is after them and wants the ticket...at any price. Action-packed thriller stars Shannen Doherty, James Marshall. 88 min.
06-2653 ❑*$99.99*

Quicksand: No Escape (1992)
This thriller in the best "noir" tradition stars Donald Sutherland as an unscrupulous detective hired by the wife of an architect to uncover her husband's extra-marital affairs. But the detective's sleuthing links the husband to the killing of a vice cop and leads to blackmail. Tim Matheson and Felicity Huffman also star. 93 min.
07-1898 ❑*$89.99*

The Public Eye (1992)
Joe Pesci plays "Bernzy" Bernstein, a gutsy tabloid photographer whose striking photographs capture the seedy streets of '40s New York. When he's hired by a sharp femme fatale (Barbara Hershey) to snoop on a group of troublesome thugs, Bernstein plunges into a world of nasty scams and a dangerous gang war. 98 min.
07-1919 Was $89.99 ❑*$19.99*

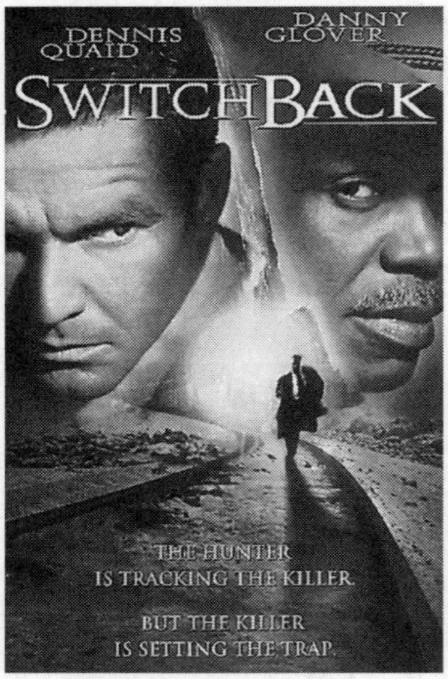

Switchback (1997)
Intense thriller concerns a serial killer wreaking havoc in and around the Rocky Mountains and the federal agent out to capture the murderer whom he believes is responsible for his son's kidnapping. Danny Glover, Dennis Quaid, Jared Leto and R. Lee Ermey star. 120 min.
06-2702 Was $99.99 ❑*$14.99*

Deadly Rivals (1993)
A bookish physicist falls for a mysterious woman while at a Miami convention. But when she's accused of being an enemy spy and a mob courier the pair get caught in a war between a crime boss, an undercover operative and an FBI agent. Andrew Stevens, Margot Hemingway, Cela Wise and Richard Roundtree star. 93 min.
07-1946 ❑*$89.99*

A Case For Murder (1993)
When a hot-shot lawyer's competitive colleague is found dead and his wife is the prime suspect, he hires a beautiful female attorney to help defend his spouse. The two counselors carry on a passionate affair, but the woman soon begins having her suspicions about her partner's involvement in the killing. Jennifer Grey, Peter Berg and Belinda Bauer star. 94 min.
07-2034 ❑*$89.99*

Caught In The Act (1993)
A struggling actor in deep financial trouble discovers that his bank account has thousands of dollars added to it. Soon, a beautiful woman enters his life and he's framed for murder. What do these things have in common, and will this real-life thriller be his last performance? Gregory Harrison, Leslie Hope star. 93 min.
07-2043 ❑*$89.99*

The Waiting Time (1999)
Zara Turner is a British Intelligence officer who attacks a former East German politician she believes was involved in her German lover's murder years earlier. Law clerk John Thaw agrees to travel to Berlin with Turner to investigate the matter, and soon the unlikely pair are thrown into a dangerous search for the truth in this post-Cold War thriller. With Hartmut Becker, Colin Baker. 149 min.
53-6946 *$29.99*

The Disappearance Of Christina (1993)
After his beautiful wife vanishes on a pleasure cruise, a high-powered entrepreneur becomes the prime suspect in her disappearance when the police discover that the woman was about to file for divorce. But her husband thinks she's still alive—and trying to frame him. John Stamos, Claire Yarlett, Robert Carradine and Kim Delaney star. 93 min.
07-2074 ❑*$89.99*

Malevolence (1998)
A young man, newly released from jail, is framed by a far-reaching conspiracy for the assassination of a renowned black politician in this gripping tale of Washington intrigue. Joe Cortese, Michael McGrady, Tom Bower star. 95 min.
06-2838 ❑*$69.99*

Breakdown (1997)
When married couple Kurt Russell and Kathleen Quinlan's car stalls on a remote Southwest highway, passing trucker J.T. Walsh offers to drive Quinlan to a cafe down the road while Russell stays behind. But when Russell reaches the diner and both Walsh and the people claim to have never seen him or his wife, a desperate and deadly search for the truth begins, in this hit suspense thriller. 95 min.
06-2637 Was $99.99 ❑*$14.99*

Breakdown (Letterboxed Version)
Also available in a theatrical, widescreen format.
06-2704 ❑*$14.99*

Last Rites (1998)
Awakening from a coma after a freak lightning strike saves him from the electric chair, serial killer Randy Quaid loses his memory but discovers he's gained psychic powers that enable him to save lives. A psychiatrist convinced he's changed works to have Quaid freed, but have his killing urges disappeared for good? Embeth Davidtz, A Martinez co-star. 88 min.
07-2754 ❑*$99.99*

Kidnapped In Paradise (1998)
Set in the Caribbean, this exotic thriller tells of a woman taken captive by an obsessive stalker during her tropical wedding celebration. The bride-to-be is taken to the creep's secret hideaway, and only sister Joely Fisher can rescue her. 91 min.
07-2756 ❑*$99.99*

Shattered Image (1998)
In this Hitchcockian thriller from director Raul Ruiz, Anne Parillaud and William Baldwin play two different characters in parallel stories. One tale concerns an heiress threatened by her husband on a Jamaican honeymoon; the other tells of a Seattle hit woman and the lover she's been contracted to kill. Graham Greene, Lisanne Falk also star. 103 min.
07-2757 Was $99.99 ❑*$19.99*

Blood, Guts, Bullets & Octane (1999)
No-budget thriller involves two used car dealers in serious financial trouble who agree to allow a vintage Pontiac convertible on their lot for a large sum of money. Little do they know that the FBI is looking for the car, which has its trunk wired to a bomb and has been associated with a score of dead bodies. Joe Carnahan, Dan Leis and Dan Harlan star. 87 min.
07-2775 Was $99.99 ❑*$19.99*

Rebecca (1996)
The suspenseful Gothic classic by Daphne du Maurier is given a lavish and atmospheric rendition in this adaptation that features Emilia Fox as the young woman who weds widower Charles Dance and moves into his remote Cornwall estate. There she is haunted by the memory of Dance's first wife, the beautiful Rebecca, and by sinister housekeeper Diana Rigg. 176 min. on two tapes.
08-8563 ❑*$29.99*

Into The Blue (1997)
A bankrupt English businessman gets a job as caretaker of a millionaire friend's estate on the Greek island of Rhodes. His upturn of fortune continues when he falls for a beautiful woman he meets in a local bar, but when she disappears and he's suspected of killing her, he begins to realize he's part of a deadly plot. Gripping British thriller stars John Thaw, Matthew Marsh, Abigail Cruttenden. 120 min.
08-8622 ❑*$19.99*

The Killing Device (1993)
Two scientists lose their government funding on a political assassination project. In retaliation, the scientists use their deadly device to kill the officials responsible for stopping their project. With Anthony Alda, Gig Rauch and Clu Gulager as the mysterious "Mr. Smitty." Uncut, unrated version; 93 min.
08-1523 Was $59.99 *$19.99*

The Sculptress (1996)
Compelling British suspenser, seen on PBS's "Mystery," follows a writer researching a book on Olive "The Sculptress" Martin, who was sentenced to life for killing and dismembering her mother and sister. As the author delves into Martin's story, she becomes convinced that she is hiding the truth behind the murders...but if Olive didn't kill her family, who did? Caroline Goodall, Pauline Quirke star. 180 min.
08-8627 ❑*$29.99*

The Ice House (1997)
The discovery of a body on an English estate leads local police to believe it's the long-missing husband of the estate's mistress, but the investigation to discover the dead person's identity creates more questions than it solves. Gripping mystery stars Penny Downie, Kitty Aldridge, Daniel Craig. 180 min.
08-8654 ❑*$29.99*

Painted Lady (1998)
When a wealthy and powerful art dealer is brutally murdered, a reclusive singer who's lived on his estate for over a decade becomes determined to bring his killers to justice and uncover the connection between his death and a painting that was stolen during the crime. Helen Mirren, Iain Glen, Franco Nero star. 204 min.
08-8661 ❑*$29.99*

Running Time (1997)
Like Hitchcock's "Rope," this thriller takes place in real time and in one seemingly continuous shot. Bruce Campbell plays an ex-con with a plan to rob the prison from which he has just been released after 10 years. With help from a high school pal, a safecracker and a driver, Campbell goes into action, but things soon go dangerously awry. Jeremy Roberts co-stars. 70 min.
08-8809 *$19.99*

Every Mother's Worst Fear (1998)
When her daughter is lured away from home after talking to a stranger on the Internet, desperate mother Cheryl Ladd works with the FBI to search the world of cyberspace and find the girl before it's too late in this compelling thriller. With Jordan Ladd, Ted McGinley. 92 min.
07-2705 ❑*$99.99*

Midnight Edition (1994)
An ambitious reporter is unknowingly lured into danger and has his family and career threatened when he begins writing a series of sympathetic interviews with a man convicted of the cold-blooded slaying of his family. Will Patton, Michael DeLuise and Nancy Moore Atchison star in this intense suspenser. 98 min.
07-2221 ❑*$89.99*

Indecency (1993)
A beautiful but unstable woman finds terror when she goes to work for a chic ad agency whose owner mysteriously commits suicide. She becomes romantically involved with her late boss's former husband, but begins to suspect that what looked like suicide could have been murder. Jennifer Beals, James Remar and Sammi Davis-Voss star. 88 min.
07-1947 ❑*$89.99*

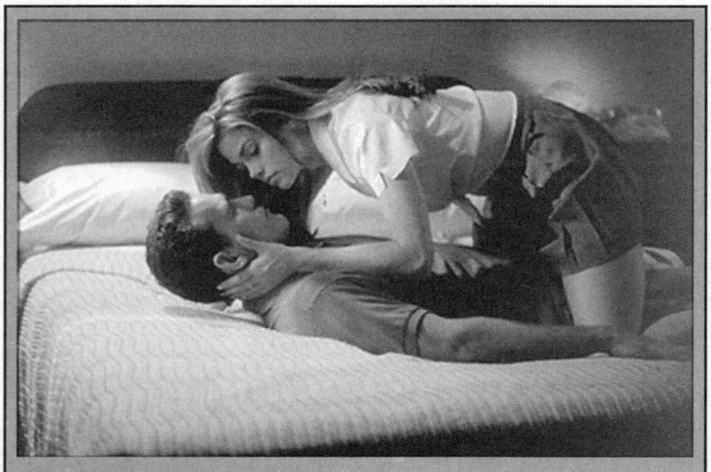

Wild Things (1998)
Swamp princess Neve Campbell and vixen Denise Richards are high school students who shock their posh South Florida town by accusing counselor Matt Dillon of rape, but that's only the beginning of the twisted, erotic goings-on in this steamy tale of deception, seduction and a multi-million-dollar scam. Kevin Bacon, Theresa Russell and Bill Murray also star; from director John McNaughton ("Henry: Portrait of a Serial Killer"). 108 min.
02-3208 Was $19.99 ❑*$14.99*

Wild Things (Letterboxed Version)
Also available in a theatrical, widescreen format.
02-3296 ❑*$19.99*

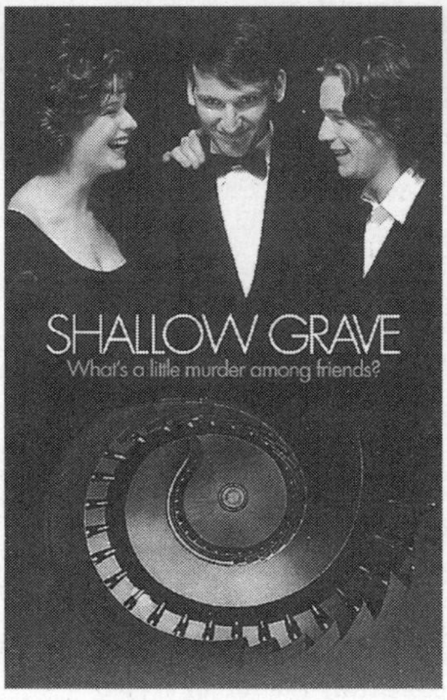

Shallow Grave (1994)
Darkly humorous thriller about three roommates—an accountant, a reporter and a doctor—who can't decide what to do when the newest resident in their home is found dead in his room with a suitcase filled with cash. A battle over the booty and the body rapidly escalates between the trio of "friends." Christopher Eccleston, Kerry Fox and Ewan McGregor star in this suspense gem from "Trainspotting" director Danny Boyle and scripter John Hodge. 92 min.
02-8244 Was $19.99 ❑*$14.99*

Deconstructing Sarah (1994)
A beautiful L.A. ad executive appears to be leading a normal, successful existence, but when her secret life of nocturnal trips into the city's sordid sexual underground catches up with her, the results could be deadly. Compelling, erotic suspenser stars Sheila Kelley, A Martinez, Rachel Ticotin. 92 min.
07-2239 ❑*$89.99*

Blindsided (1992)
An ex-cop acts as a middleman in a robbery scheme that goes wrong and is temporarily blinded. While on the beaches of Mexico he plots his revenge and becomes infatuated with a beautiful young woman who leads him further into a web of deceit. Jeff Fahey, Mia Sara and Ben Gazarra star in this thriller. 93 min.
07-1970 ❑*$89.99*

Dead Air (1994)
Nighttime radio disc jockey Gregory Hines receives a terrifying call on the air from a killer dispatching his victim. As the calls continue, he joins forces with a beautiful psychology student to uncover the mystery and find the culprit before he strikes again. Debrah Farentino co-stars. 91 min.
07-2278 ❑*$89.99*

Breach Of Conduct (1994)
The wife of a military officer living in a remote base in Utah falls for a mysterious stranger she later learns is the base's commander. After refusing his sexual overtures, the woman faces danger when she discovers the base's unspeakable secret. Peter Coyote and Courtney Thorne-Smith star. 93 min.
07-2321 ❑*$89.99*

Legacy Of Lies (1992)
A Chicago cop's investigation of a mistaken gangland shooting leads him to his father, a member of the Mob, and a grandfather he never knew. Soon, a ruthless struggle between three generations erupts in dishonor and violence. Michael Ontkean, Martin Landau and Eli Wallach star. 94 min.
07-1907 Was $89.99 *$14.99*

Hidden Obsession (1993)
A beautiful TV news reporter finds her vacation plans go awry when a killer who escaped from a nearby prison terrorizes her. A local police officer protects her and the two carry on a torrid affair, but things get scary again when the horror continues—after the murderer is captured! Jan-Michael Vincent and Heather Thomas star. 92 min.
07-1962 *$89.99*

Kill Cruise (1990)
The skipper of a yacht, feeling guilty over a friend's death, is hired by two beautiful British women to take them to Barbados. But what starts out as a pleasure cruise takes a dangerous turn thanks to stormy weather and the explosive jealousy of the women. Jurgen Prochnow, Patsy Kensit, Elizabeth Hurley star. AKA: "Der Skipper." 99 min.
07-1891 Was $89.99 ❑*$14.99*

DVD VIDEO
ASK ABOUT OUR GIANT DVD CATALOG!

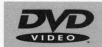

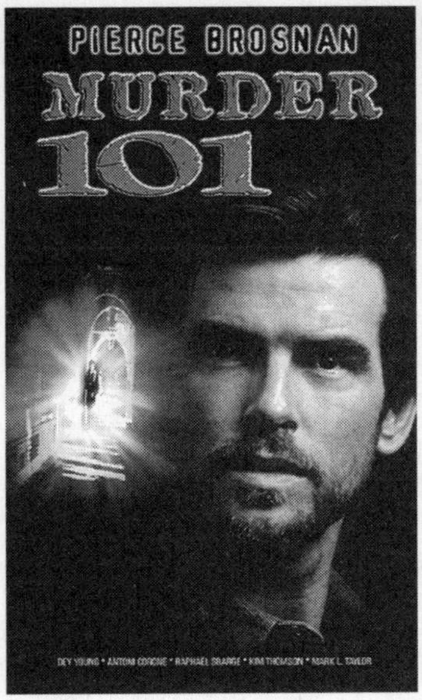
PIERCE BROSNAN
MURDER
101

Murder 101 (1991)
Pierce Brosnan plays a professor and mystery writer who gives his students a disturbing assignment: plan an unsolvable murder. Soon, he's put on the spot when a student he meets for a romantic liaison is found dead. Dey Young, Raphael Sbarge and Kim Thomson also star. 93 min.
07-1818 ❑$12.99

Slaughter Of The Innocents (1993)
An FBI Special Agent teams with his computer wizard son in an investigation to find a psychotic religious fanatic who has been preying on children for 15 years in Utah's Badlands. Scott Glenn, Jesse Cameron-Glickenhaus and Sheila Tousey star in this riveting psychological thriller. 104 min.
07-2083 Was $89.99 ❑$14.99

Dangerous Heart (1993)
The wife of a deceased undercover cop finds herself seduced by a sensitive businessman shortly after her husband's death. What she doesn't realize is that her new lover is the drug dealer responsible for her husband's demise. Tim Daly and Lauren Holly star in this suspenser. 94 min.
07-2123 ❑$89.99

The Hand That Rocks The Cradle (1992)
A woman accuses her gynecologist of molesting her, and the publicity drives him to suicide. The doctor's unstable young wife, in search of revenge, takes a job as a nanny with the woman's family and begins turning the kids against Mommy while trying to seduce Daddy. Hit thriller stars Rebecca De Mornay, Annabella Sciorra, Matt McCoy and Ernie Hudson. 110 min.
11-1620 Was $19.99 ❑$14.99

Curiosity Kills (1991)
After a young actress dies of mysterious causes, an aspiring actor moves into her apartment the next day. Suspecting foul play, the apartment building's handyman teams with a beautiful artist to uncover the true reason behind the death. C. Thomas Howell, Rae Dawn Chong and Courtney Cox star in this exciting puzzler. 86 min.
07-1687 $79.99

Red Wind (1991)
Lisa Hartman plays a psychiatrist specializing in abusive relationships who finds herself involved in a web of suspense when one of her patients claims to have murdered her husband. Philip Casnoff, Christopher McDonald co-star in this sexy suspenser. 93 min.
07-1862 ❑$79.99

Silhouette (1990)
Faye Dunaway stars as a successful architect who, while returning home through Texas, witnesses the vicious murder of a cocktail waitress and is forced to stay in town by the authorities. Can the police protect her from threats of death and locate her abducted daughter? David Rasche and Talisa Soto star in this suspense yarn. 89 min.
07-1719 $79.99

The Lookalike (1991)
A year after her daughter's tragic death, a woman sees the child's double and enlists a friend's help in proving what she saw wasn't her imagination. Melissa Gilbert-Brinkman, Diane Ladd and Frances Lee McCain star in this creepy thriller. 88 min.
07-1726 ❑$79.99

This Gun For Hire (1990)
Robert Wagner reprises the role made famous by Alan Ladd in this reworking of the classic Graham Greene thriller. Here Wagner is a hit man who discovers that his latest victim—a powerful politician—was a set-up. On the run from the law, he kidnaps a dancer while trying to find the people who conspired against him. Nancy Everhard co-stars. 89 min.
07-1729 $79.99

Death Benefit (1996)
When a young woman's mysterious death is ruled an accident, top attorney Peter Horton puts his career—and his life—on the line to prove she was actually the latest victim of demented serial killer Carrie Snodgress. Riveting suspenser also stars Wendy Makkena, Penny Johnson. 89 min.
07-2460 ❑$89.99

Tagget (1990)
An intense story of a Vietnam vet-turned-successful businessman (Daniel J. Travanti) who suffered horrible atrocities in Southeast Asia and realizes that something unsettling occurred on his last mission overseas. When he digs deeper for the facts, though, a conspiracy unravels. Roxanne Hart, William Sadler co-star. 89 min.
07-1734 ❑$79.99

Lies Of The Twins (1991)
Scorching thriller stars Isabella Rossellini as a fashion model involved with her handsome psychotherapist who becomes furious when she spies him with another woman. It turns out to be the doctor's twisted twin brother, and she is drawn into a deadly love triangle. Aidan Quinn plays the dual paramours; with Iman and Claudia Christian. 93 min.
07-1805 ❑$79.99

Dead In The Water (1991)
A riveting thriller starring Bryan Brown as a high-powered lawyer who will stop at nothing to achieve his dream....the killing of his rich wife. When he attempts to carry out his plans, however, he finds himself enmeshed in danger. With Teri Hatcher and Veronica Cartwright. 90 min.
07-1808 ❑$79.99

The Underneath (1995)
Steven Soderbergh reworks the 1949 thriller "Criss Cross" into an intense modern film noir featuring Peter Gallagher as a gambler who returns to his Austin, Texas, home to attend his mother's wedding and drop in on an ex-girlfriend. After he gets a job as an armored car driver, he plots a heist with his ex's dangerous new lover. With Alison Elliott, William Fichtner, Joe Don Baker. 100 min.
07-2341 Was $89.99 ❑$19.99

Out Of Annie's Past (1995)
A diabolical thriller starring Catherine Mary Stewart as a successful career woman with a loving family and a dark secret. When a bounty hunter threatens to expose her mysterious past, she finds herself caught in a web of deceit. Dennis Farina and Scott Valentine also star. 91 min.
07-2331 ❑$89.99

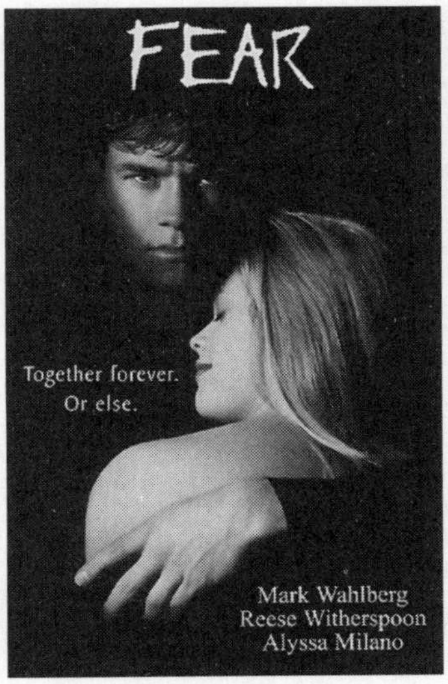
FEAR
Together forever.
Or else.
Mark Wahlberg
Reese Witherspoon
Alyssa Milano

Fear (1996)
In this creepy thriller, a pretty teenage girl thinks the handsome charmer she meets at a party is the man of her dreams, despite her stepfather's misgivings. But as their relationship sizzles, the new boyfriend turns more dangerously possessive, and soon the girl and her family fear for their lives. With Reese Witherspoon, Mark Wahlberg, William Petersen, Alyssa Milano. 96 min.
07-2437 Was $99.99 ❑$14.99

The Colony (1995)
When a family moves into a new neighborhood, they assume it's just what it appears to be: a safe, secure place to raise a family. But they soon find out that their privacy is an illusion and they are at the mercy of the development's powerful head, who will go as far as murder to protect his "dream environment." John Ritter, Hal Linden, Mary Page Keller star. 93 min.
07-2385 ❑$89.99

Night Owl (1993)
Her seductive voice fills the late-night airwaves and seduces men into obsession, madness and death. She's the "Night Owl," and a young speech therapist tries to track her down after she witnesses her friends succumb to the mysterious unseen voice. Jennifer Beals, James Wilder and Jackie Burroughs star. 91 min.
10-2589 $12.99

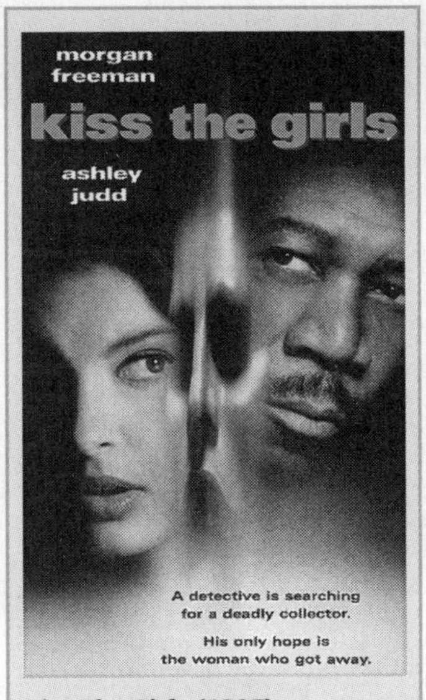
morgan
freeman
kiss the girls
ashley
judd
A detective is searching
for a deadly collector.
His only hope is
the woman who got away.

Kiss The Girls (1997)
When his North Carolina college student niece disappears and is thought to be the latest target of a psychopathic kidnapper calling himself "Casanova," Washington, D.C., police psychologist Morgan Freeman begins his own investigation. Together with doctor Ashley Judd, the only victim to escape captivity, they begin a desperate search for the maniac in this gripping hit suspense tale. Carey Elwes, Tony Goldwyn also star in this adaptation of James Patterson's thriller. 107 min.
06-2701 Was $99.99 ❑$14.99

Buried Alive II (1997)
In this suspenseful sequel to the claustrophobic thriller, Ally Sheedy plays a woman whose husband is preparing to leave with her inheritance and his mistress...after he puts her out of the way for good. Stephen Caffrey, Tim Matheson also star. 92 min.
07-2600 ❑$99.99

Evil Has A Face (1996)
Police sketch artist Sean Young attempts to help solve a kidnapping case, but soon finds herself in a mysterious situation that relates to her own childhood. She joins forces with a local sheriff to try to expose the killer and is soon thrust into a struggle for survival. William R. Moses, Chelcie Ross also star. 92 min.
07-2468 ❑$99.99

Trial & Error (1992)
A district attorney (Tim Matheson) campaigning for lieutenant governor has a potential lethal skeleton in his closet: five years ago, he may have sent the wrong man to Death Row, and now not only is an innocent man about to be executed, but the real killer is stalking Matheson's wife (Helen Shaver). 91 min.
07-1973 ❑$89.99

Sharon's Secret (1995)
After a 16-year-old girl becomes a chief suspect in her parents' brutal murders, her psychiatrist begins uncovering some disturbing secrets that eventually remind the doctor of a tragic event in her own past. Mel Harris, Candace Cameron and Alex McArthur star. 91 min.
07-2410 ❑$89.99

The Three Lives Of Karen (1997)
A woman about to be married meets a stranger who says he's her husband, leading her to explore her mystery-shrouded past and uncover a string of deadly secrets. Suspenseful thriller stars Gail O'Grady, Dennis Boutsikaris, Tim Guinee. 90 min.
07-2577 ❑$99.99

The Assassination File (1997)
Sherilyn Fenn is an FBI agent held responsible for the death of America's first black president. After two years of forced retirement, her partner calls her back into action when he finds evidence of a government conspiracy. In order to save her life and career, she must make the assassins known. Paul Winfield co-stars. 106 min.
07-2558 Was $99.99 ❑$14.99

Jane Street (1996)
Explosive and steamy thriller in which a woman named Kim is having one erotic nightmare after another that seem to point to the culprit in a series of grisly murders. As her deepest fantasies turn into frightening reality, Kim realizes that she could be his next victim. Linda Hoffman, D.K. Kelly, Carrie Stevens star. 87 min.
07-2677 $39.99

Striking Resemblance (1998)
Ultra-hot sensual suspenser in which a beautiful detective working on a series of killings gets romantically involved with the brother of one of the murder victims. Nicole Gian ("Intimate Obsessions"), Kevin Spirtas and Ash Adams star. 92 min.
07-2688 $39.99

Baby Monitor: Sound Of Fear (1997)
When a beautiful young nanny's affair with her infant charge's father becomes known to the man's wife, the unstable mother's plan for revenge threatens everyone's life, and the nanny must try to save the child, in this passionate, compelling suspenser. Josie Bissett, Jason Beghe star. 90 min.
07-2640 ❑$99.99

When Danger Follows You Home (1997)
After a troubled young patient left in the care of psychiatrist JoBeth Williams dies under mysterious circumstances, she is charged with manslaughter. The nightmare is just beginning, though, when Williams' own son is abducted, and the clues point to the dead youth's family, in this gripping suspense story. William Russ, Michael Manasseri also star. 92 min.
07-2641 ❑$99.99

Second Sight (1999)
This intense psychological suspenser tells of a police detective whose deteriorating eyesight forces him to enlist the help of a rival investigator to solve a case involving the murder of a college student. Clive Owen, Claire Skinner and Stuart Wilson star. 180 min.
08-8811 ❑$29.99

Letter To My Killer (1995)
When a couple comes across a letter written by a woman whose murder 30 years earlier was never solved, they are thrust into a conspiracy that is still around...and still deadly. Suspenseful tale stars Mare Winningham, Nick Chinlund and Rip Torn. 92 min.
07-2377 ❑$89.99

Twilight Man (1996)
Thrilling suspenser about a popular college professor who finds himself in constant danger when he becomes the target of a computer hacker's bizarre obsession. Tim Matheson and Dean Stockwell star. 99 min.
07-2504 Was $99.99 ❑$14.99

Donor Unknown (1995)
Suspenseful story of a hard-working insurance fraud investigator who collapses and is in dire need of a heart transplant. His wife arranges for a new heart to be supplied by a brilliant surgeon, but when the man starts delving into the doctor's methods, he uncovers a creepy conspiracy. Peter Onorati, Alice Krige and Sam Robards star. 93 min.
07-2415 ❑$99.99

Mrs. Bradley Mysteries: Speedy Death (1998)
Diana Rigg stars as Gladys Mitchell's unconventionally outspoken 1920s sleuth in this top-notch thriller. Here, with help from her trusted chauffeur George, Mrs. Bradley investigates the suspicious death of her goddaughter's boyfriend just before a party announcing their engagement. Neil Dudgeon, John Alderton also star. 90 min.
08-8830 ❑$19.99

Sex, Love & Cold Hard Cash (1993)
A high-priced hooker hires a tough-talking detective to find her manager, who has skipped town with her cash—and $20 million in mob money. Their search leads to a luxury cruise liner, where they come face-to-face with a Mafia hit squad. JoBeth Williams, Anthony John Denison and Robert Forster star. 86 min.
07-2026 ❑$89.99

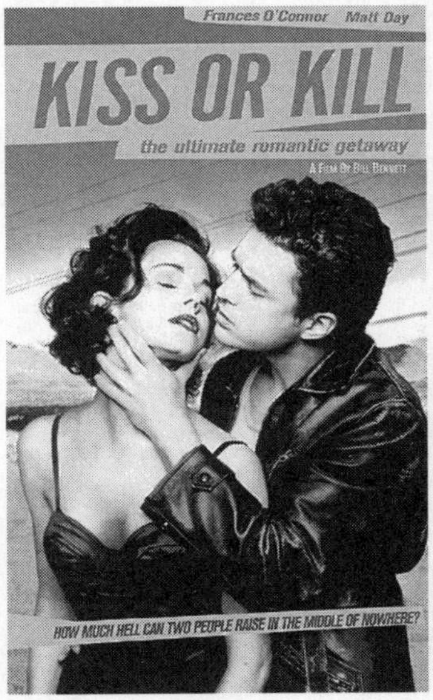
Frances O'Connor Matt Day
KISS OR KILL
the ultimate romantic getaway
HOW MUCH HELL CAN TWO PEOPLE RAISE IN THE MIDDLE OF NOWHERE?

Kiss Or Kill (1997)
A woman makes a living by luring men to hotels and then, with her lover's help, drugging and robbing them. The con artists find themselves in over their heads—and on the run from the law across the Australian Outback—when their latest victim accidentally dies and they find on him a video that incriminates a popular athlete in a sex scandal. Compelling thriller stars Frances O'Connor, Matt Day, Chris Haywood. 97 min.
07-2618 Was $99.99 ❑$19.99

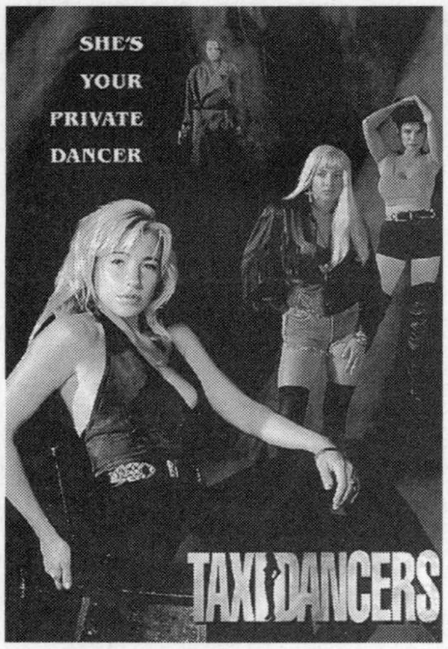

Taxi Dancers (1993)
A young woman seeking a career in show business arrives in Hollywood, only to find herself living in poverty on the streets. In order to make a living, she becomes an erotic dancer at a local club and gets involved with a mysterious gambler in trouble with gangsters. Brittany McCrena and Sonny Landham star in this exposé of the world of "taxi dancers." 97 min.
16-9147 *$14.99*

Consenting Adults (1992)
Kevin Kline is a suburban businessman whose life is turned upside down when new neighbor Kevin Spacey invites him to swap wives one night. The neighbor's wife soon turns up dead, Kline is accused of the murder and his wife (Mary Elizabeth Mastrantonio) takes up with Spacey. Rebecca Miller and Forest Whitaker also star in this erotic thriller from Alan J. Pakula ("Presumed Innocent"). 99 min.
11-1679 Was $19.99 ❑*$14.99*

Guilty As Sin (1993)
Gorgeous lawyer Rebecca De Mornay is hired by slick playboy Don Johnson when he's accused of murdering his wealthy wife. A love affair between the two ensues, but as Johnson begins taking over De Mornay's personal life and she begins doubting his innocence, she wonders if theirs is a "fatal attraction." Stephen Lang and Jack Warden co-star; Sidney Lumet directs. 107 min.
11-1736 Was $19.99 ❑*$14.99*

Eye Of The Killer (1999)
Kiefer Sutherland is an alcoholic detective who is haunted by the psychic powers he developed after an accident. Whenever he touches the belongings of a murder victim he is bombarded with horrific visions. But now a ruthless serial killer is back after a 10-year absence, and Sutherland must use his gift to finally capture a madman. Henry Czerny, Polly Walker also star. AKA: "After Alice." 100 min.
68-2025 ❑*$69.99*

The Tie That Binds (1995)
After her criminal parents botch a robbery and flee, a young girl is taken in by a young professional couple who plan to adopt her. Their happy family life doesn't last, though, when the child's real mother and father return to take back their daughter...no matter what the cost. Keith Carradine, Daryl Hannah, Moira Kelly, Vincent Spano and Julia Devin star. 99 min.
11-1968 Was $19.99 ❑*$14.99*

Escape Clause (1997)
A hot-shot ad executive may wind up just being shot when a stranger calls him, claiming to be a paid killer hired by the man's wife. Is he telling the truth, or is the mystery just beginning? Offbeat suspenser stars Andrew McCarthy, Paul Sorvino, Connie Britton. 99 min.
12-3179 ❑*$59.99*

The Innocent (1995)
In John Schlesinger's espionage thriller, Campbell Scott plays a telephone engineer hired by American intelligence officer Anthony Hopkins to infiltrate Russian communications for the CIA and British spies. Against the wishes of Hopkins, Scott becomes involved with Isabella Rossellini, a mysterious German seductress, which can only lead to danger. 99 min.
11-1991 ❑*$19.99*

Loaded (1996)
The first film from Anna Campion, sister of director Jane Campion ("The Piano"), is a haunting thriller about a group of friends who gather together in upstate New York to make a low-budget horror movie. After a day of shooting, they decide to have dinner, take drugs and reveal secrets to each other, which leads to a bizarre series of eerie incidents. Thandie Newton stars. 96 min.
11-2071 Was $99.99 ❑*$19.99*

Midnight Fear (1992)
Spine-tingling suspense in the manner of "The Silence of the Lambs," with David Carradine as a sheriff tracking down the maniac responsible for a brutal assault and murder. The trail leads to two brothers, one of whom is an escapee from a mental hospital. Craig Wasson, August West co-star. 90 min.
15-5257 *$79.99*

The Satan Killer (1993)
A brutal murderer stalking the area is nicknamed "the Satan Killer" by the media, but the detective on his trail has real incentive to stop him: his beautiful fiancée has just become the latest victim. Now the investigator must go undercover and act as judge, jury and executioner to put an end to the killer's reign of terror. Steve Sayre, Billy Franklin star. 90 min.
16-9137 *$14.99*

Ex-Cop (1993)
Although a heavy-drinking cop is kicked off the force when the police department decides to create a new image, he vows not to stop his pursuit of a deadly killer named the "Las Vegas Slasher." But after the murderer is tried and released from prison, he kidnaps the cop's daughter for revenge. Ric Savage and Sandy Hackett star in this terror-filled suspenser. 97 min.
16-9144 *$14.99*

Deadly Daphne's Revenge (1993)
A beautiful hitchhiker is abducted and assaulted by a group of men. When she attempts to bring them to justice, the men get in touch with a mob boss in order to silence her, unaware that one of their previous victims has escaped from an asylum and is looking for revenge! Brutal suspenser from Troma Films stars Anthony Holt, Laurie Tait Partridge. 98 min.
16-9152 *$14.99*

The Rich Man's Wife (1996)
Well-crafted suspenser stars Halle Berry as a woman who attempts to salvage her marriage to her wealthy, alcoholic husband. But when he's found brutally murdered, Berry must prove her innocence while fighting for her life against the real killer. Christopher McDonald, Peter Greene, Clive Owen also star. 95 min.
11-2105 Was $19.99 ❑*$14.99*

Albino Alligator (1997)
Kevin Spacey's directorial debut is a tightly-wound thriller in which three fugitive crooks land in a sleazy bar at 4 a.m., only to find themselves trapped when police sharpshooters surround the place. The criminals discover that the police are after somebody else in the tavern, but whom? Is it a worker, a customer or the owner? Matt Dillon, Faye Dunaway, Gary Sinise star. 94 min.
11-2129 ❑*$14.99*

Adrift (1993)
In hopes of helping their marriage, a couple takes a vacation, sailing their yacht through the South Pacific. After 10 days at sea, they rescue two people from a stranded boat, only to find themselves victims of their new shipmates, who terrify them with their deadly desires. Kate Jackson, Kenneth Welsh and Kelly Rowan star. 92 min.
14-3413 ❑*$89.99*

Stonebrook (1999)
A pair of college students think they've found a way to pay off those pesky tuition loans when they hatch a scheme to double-cross some local mobsters, but they quickly find themselves in over their head—and in deadly danger—in this suspenseful thriller. Seth Green, Brad Rowe, Zoe McLellan star. 90 min.
12-3317 ❑*$99.99*

In The Eyes Of A Stranger (1992)
In this thriller, Justin Bateman plays a woman targeted by mobsters after their stolen money is missing. They think she took the loot. Did she? With Richard Dean Anderson and Cynthia Dale.
10-3415 *$14.99*

Blind Witness (1991)
A pulse-pounding suspenser about a blind woman whose husband is killed by intruders in their home. When the culprits return to eliminate her, she uses her specially-equipped apartment to turn the tables on them. Victoria Principal, Paul LeMat, Stephen Macht star. 92 min.
14-3411 ❑*$89.99*

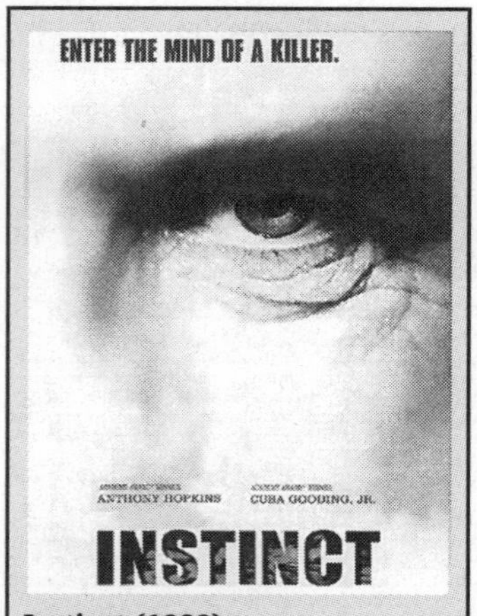

Instinct (1999)
Famous primatologist and animal activist Anthony Hopkins goes berserk in Rwanda and kills two park rangers. Refusing to talk, Hopkins is taken to a Florida mental institute where young psychiatrist Cuba Gooding, Jr. tries to delve into Hopkins' mind and find out what provoked his violent outburst. Donald Sutherland, Maura Tierney, John Ashton also star.
11-2359 Was $22.99 ❑*$14.99*

Heaven (1999)
Creepy psycho-sexual thriller featuring Martin Donovan as an embittered architect, going through a nasty divorce with wife Joanna Going, who takes a job working at his friend's exotic nightclub. There he meets a clairvoyant transvestite whose premonitions help, then haunt, Donovan. Danny Edwards and Richard Schiff also star. 103 min.
11-2362 Was $99.99 ❑*$19.99*

Shattered (1991)
Suffering from amnesia following a car accident with his wife, architect Tom Berenger begins finding clues that lead him to believe the crash wasn't an accident after all. Greta Scacchi, Corbin Bernsen, Joanne Whalley-Kilmer and Bob Hoskins also star in this gripping, erotic tale of straying spouses where what you don't remember can definitely hurt you. Wolfgang Petersen directs. 98 min.
12-2398 Was $89.99 ❑*$14.99*

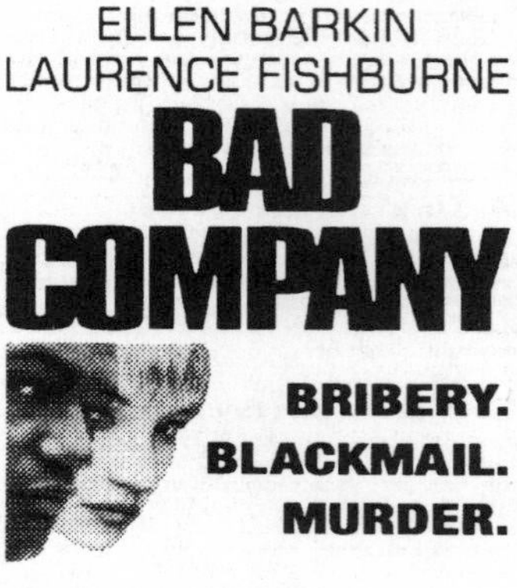

Bad Company (1995)
Former CIA agent Laurence Fishburne goes to work for a mysterious agency run by Ellen Barkin and Frank Langella that specializes in corporate espionage. After completing his first assignment, Fishburne receives an even more dangerous one from Barkin: help her "take out" Langella and join her in running the firm. Michael Beach, David Ogden Stiers co-star. 108 min.
11-1889 ❑*$14.99*

Liebestraum (1991)
Smoldering tale about a sexually explosive triangle formed by an architect, his college friend and his sensuous wife. Their attraction reflects a similar situation which occurred years earlier...and ended in a double murder. Haunting thriller stars Kevin Anderson, Bill Pullman, Pamela Gidley and Kim Novak. Uncut, unrated version; 109 min.
12-2406 ❑*$14.99*

Body Of Evidence (1993)
Scorching erotic thriller boasting a super-steamy performance by Madonna as a seductress accused of killing her rich, older lover during a kinky lovemaking session. While on trial for murder, her defense attorney (Willem Dafoe) is drawn into her wild style of sexual games. Joe Mantegna and Anne Archer also star. Uncut, unrated version contains scenes too hot for theatres; 101 min.
12-2725 Was $19.99 ❑*$14.99*

The Sketch Artist II: Hands That See (1994)
Jeff Fahey returns as police sketch artist Jack Whitfield, this time involved with a beautiful blind woman who is the only witness in the case involving a sexual psycho on a murderous spree. As Fahey gets drawn to the witness romantically, his life becomes more dangerous. Courteney Cox, Brion James and Jonathan Silverman co-star. 95 min.
12-2978 Was $19.99 ❑*$14.99*

The Set Up (1995)
Recently paroled security ace Billy Zane takes a job with a slick millionaire and constructs an impenetrable security system for a bank. But after getting involved with sultry Mia Sara and finding himself a prime suspect in a murder, his skills are put to the test when he's forced to rob the bank he just helped to secure. James Coburn and James Russo co-star. 95 min.
12-3013 Was $89.99 ❑*$19.99*

Hackers (1995)
Enthralling techno-thriller about a group of young cyberpunks who make a game of breaking into corporate computer systems, until they inadvertently tap into the files of a high-tech embezzler who frames the hackers in order to recover incriminating information from them. Jonny Lee Miller, Angelina Jolie and Fisher Stevens star. 104 min.
12-3021 Was $89.99 ❑*$14.99*

Unforgettable (1996)
From thriller specialist John Dahl ("The Last Seduction") comes this gripping suspenser starring Ray Liotta as a medical examiner haunted by the mysterious murder of his wife—a death for which he was once considered the prime suspect. With help from scientist Linda Fiorentino, Liotta injects himself with a memory-transfer chemical that allows him to see his wife's final moments. 114 min.
12-3097 Was $99.99 ❑*$14.99*

Secret Weapon (1990)
A thrilling, true-to-life story about an Israeli scientist who exposes his government's plans of building nuclear bombs, then faces a beautiful spy assigned to stop him. Griffin Dunne and Karen Allen star in this fascinating tale. 95 min.
18-7229 *$14.99*

Deceiver (1998)
As disturbing as it is darkly funny, this thriller from filmmaking brothers Josh and Jonas Pate takes viewers deep into the mind of a brilliant and wealthy man (Tim Roth) suspected in the murder of a Charleston, South Carolina, prostitute. As he is questioned by police, Roth uses his intellect to manipulate his interrogators and draw them into his twisted "games." Chris Penn, Michael Rooker and Renee Zellweger also star. AKA: "Liar." 102 min.
12-3254 Was $99.99 ❑*$14.99*

The Limbic Region (1997)
After a suspect in a rash of brutal murders in a small town is released for lack of evidence, a detective becomes obsessed with linking the man to the crimes. What follows is a decade-long battle of wills that ends in a shocking confrontation in this gripping thriller that stars Edward James Olmos, George Dzundza, Gwynyth Walsh. 96 min.
12-3180 ❑*$59.99*

The Lesser Evil (1998)
Told in flashback fashion, this gripping suspenser tells of four childhood friends who find themselves in trouble with authorities for what they did to some bullies years earlier. Now, the pals—a lumber company owner, a priest, a cop and a lawyer—must decide how to handle their dire situation. David Paymer, Arliss Howard, Tony Goldwyn and Colm Feore star. 97 min.
12-3284 Was $49.99 ❑*$14.99*

Break Up (1998)
Intriguing thriller stars Bridget Fonda as an abused wife who awakens in a hospital to discover hubby Hart Bochner was killed in a car crash and she is suspected of being responsible for his death. As detective Kiefer Sutherland gets closer to arresting Fonda, she goes on the run to find the real killer. Penelope Ann Miller, Steven Weber, Tippi Hedren also star. 101 min.
11-2361 Was $99.99 ❑*$14.99*

The Thomas Crown Affair (1999)
In this stylish reworking of the 1968 favorite, Pierce Brosnan is Thomas Crown, a playboy art thief whose recent purloining of a $100 million Monet draws the attention of insurance investigator Rene Russo and detective Denis Leary. Once Russo figures Brosnan is the culprit, the two play a wicked cat-and-mouse game that leads to a heated romance. With Faye Dunaway, Ben Gazzara. 113 min.
12-3290 Was $99.99 ❑*$14.99*

The Deadly Secret (1992)
Real estate mogul Joe Estevez seems to have it all: wealth, women and success. But when he is blackmailed over an incident from college in which he and a few friends killed a girl, Estevez has to stop the story and the blackmailer immediately. Tracy Spaulding, Reggie Cale and Douglas Stalgren co-star. 90 min.
16-9157 *$14.99*

Codename: Kyril (1990)
In this intense espionage yarn, a KGB agent is given a dangerous assignment: to find and exterminate an agent giving valuable secrets to British Secret Service. Little does he know that both sides are after him, and a British operative is out to stop him. Ian Charleson and Edward Woodward star. 90 min.
18-7278 *$79.99*

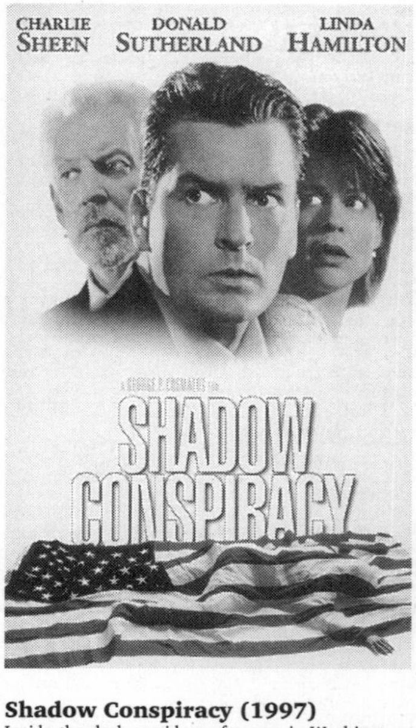

Shadow Conspiracy (1997)
Inside the dark corridors of power in Washington, a secret that could rock the foundations of the government falls into the hands of presidential aide Charlie Sheen. Now, with only reporter girlfriend Linda Hamilton and chief of staff Donald Sutherland to help him, Sheen must avoid a deadly killer-for-hire while trying to solve the mystery of the conspiracy. Gripping thriller also stars Sam Waterston, Stephen Lang. 103 min.
11-2156 Was $19.99 ❑*$14.99*

Dead On The Money (1991)
Stylish thriller in the "Double Indemnity" mold stars Amanda Pays as a woman who chooses a wealthy man (John Glover) over his cousin (Corbin Bernsen), a good-looking but poor man. Soon, she has a large insurance policy attached to her, and bizarre things begin to occur. Eleanor Parker also stars. 92 min.
18-7337 ❑*$89.99*

Incognito (1997)
Harry Donovan is the world's top art forger, but the murder charge that someone has framed him with is all too real. Now Harry's in a race across Europe to prove his innocence in this gripping tale of action and suspense. Jason Patric, Irene Jacob, Ian Richardson and Rod Steiger star; directed by John Badham. 108 min.
19-2741 Was $99.99 ❑*$14.99*

Goodbye Lover (1998)
Smart and stylish comic film noir from Roland Joffe ("The Killing Fields") starring Patricia Arquette as a conniving real estate salesperson having a torrid affair with brother-in-law Don Johnson. Arquette's plans to kill alcoholic hubby Dermot Mulroney hit several snags, and more than one murder is commited for detective Ellen DeGeneres to investigate. With Mary-Louise Parker, Ray McKinnon. 101 min.
19-2904 Was $99.99 ❑*$14.99*

Perfect Alibi (1995)
An heiress' sister's suspicions about her brother-in-law's affair with his new babysitter lead to deceit, blackmail and murder in this complex thriller spiked with surprises and sexiness. Teri Garr, Kathleen Quinlan, Lydie Denier and Hector Elizondo star. 100 min.
19-3713 *$89.99*

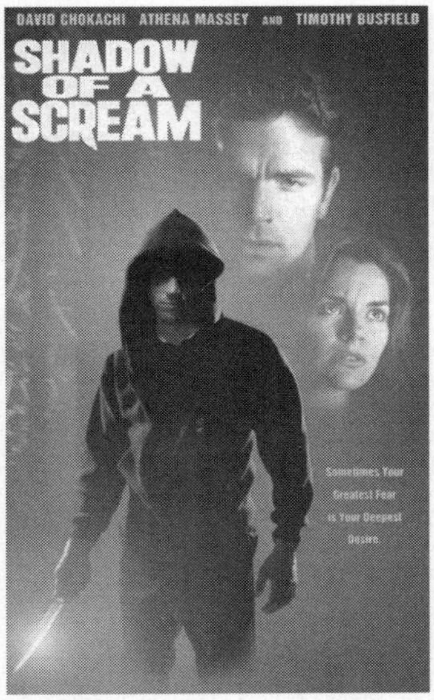

Shadow Of A Scream (1997)
Beautiful cop Athena Massey ("Undercover") goes back under the covers to investigate a murder suspect who has a penchant for rough sex with women he meets through personal ads. While posing as an interested party to the suspect's desires, she discovers her own kinky agenda as well. David Chokachi ("Baywatch") and Timothy Busfield also star. 84 min.
21-9139 Was $59.99 *$14.99*

Judicial Consent (1995)
Intense thriller starring Bonnie Bedelia as a judge whose love interest, a handsome law clerk, may be linked to the death of an attorney. Is the killer one of the attorney's girlfriends, Bedelia's jealous husband or an ambitious district attorney who happens to be the law clerk's former flame? Will Patton, Billy Wirth, Lisa Blount and Dabney Coleman co-star. 100 min.
19-3721 *$89.99*

Midnight Heat (1995)
Football player Tim Matheson finds himself in trouble after his team's owner, whose wife the jock was romantically involved with, is found murdered. Will he be able to scramble around the incriminating evidence and, ultimately, tackle the real killer? Mimi Craven, Stephen Mendel also star. 97 min.
19-3838 *$89.99*

Bodily Harm (1995)
Linda Fiorentino is a homicide detective who discovers that ex-lover Daniel Baldwin is the main suspect in the murder of a stripper. Torn between her feelings for Baldwin and her dedication to her job, Fiorentino must risk her life to discover the truth. With Gregg Henry, Joe Regalbuto. 90 min.
19-3850 *$89.99*

Hard Evidence (1994)
A successful businessman is seduced by his mistress into joining her on a "business trip," but when the trip turns out to be a drug-smuggling run and he's forced to shoot a federal agent, the man and his wife are caught up in a deadly trap. Suspenseful and steamy tale stars Gregory Harrison, Joan Severance, Cali Timmins. 100 min.
19-3870 *$69.99*

Power 98 (1995)
An L.A. radio "shock jock" and his new protégé have the hottest show on the airwaves, and ratings go even higher when a listener calls in and confesses to a murder. Is it a prank, or the beginning of a sinister and shocking series of killings? Compelling thriller stars Eric Roberts, Jason Gedrick, Jennie Garth. 90 min.
19-3974 Was $99.99 *$19.99*

The Arrogant (1991)
In this scorching sensual thriller, Sylvia Kristel shows that she's as wild as she was in her "Emmanuelle" films, playing a sexually charged woman whose desert encounter with a motorcycle-riding stranger leads her into a dangerous game of deceit. With Gary Graham. 86 min.
19-7084 Was $89.99 ❑*$19.99*

Roots Of Evil (1992)
A sexy, ultra-kinky thriller about a detective and his beautiful partner who attempt to track down a serial killer terrorizing the streets of Los Angeles. Soon, the trail leads to gangsters, prostitutes and sleazy characters. Alex Cord, Delia Shepard, Jillian Kesner, Brinke Stevens star. Unrated version; 95 min.
19-7090 Was $89.99 *$19.99*

Over The Line (1993)
Erotically-charged thriller starring Leslie-Anne Down as a college professor who's romantic fling with a student leads to danger. With John Enos and Michael Parks. 108 min.
19-7101 Was $89.99 *$19.99*

Play Murder For Me (1991)
Heated, erotic thriller stars Jack Wagner as a down-and-out saxophone player who meets his former lover (sexy Tracy Scoggins) while in Buenos Aires. He begins rekindling their romance, but the fire between them ignites her mobster husband's suspicions and sucks the saxman into a dangerous underworld scheme. 80 min.
21-9002 Was $89.99 *$14.99*

Ultraviolet (1992)
A female doctor living in Los Angeles and her forest ranger husband try to reconcile their marriage by meeting for a weekend in Death Valley. A few days of love and happiness become a nightmare when they investigate smoke in the distance and find a mysterious stranger. Esai Morales, Patricia Healy and Stephen Meadows star. 80 min.
21-9008 *$89.99*

Final Embrace (1992)
Enter the steamy, sex-soaked world of music videos in this suspenseful tale about a young woman trying to learn the truth behind her rock star sister's death. Will she be the next victim? Nancy Valen, Robert Rushler, Dick Van Patten star. 85 min.
21-9019 *$89.99*

Terror In Paradise (1992)
While on vacation on a tropical island, a couple seeks love but discovers they may have looked in all the wrong places. A group of ruthless terrorists are also on the island, and the couple are their new target. Joanna Pettet and Gary Lockwood star. 90 min.
21-9024 *$89.99*

Eyewitness To Murder (1993)
A young artist witnesses a murder, but is blinded when she is bludgeoned with a blow to the head. Two overworked detectives are put on the case, and must heep her safe as she finds her way through a dangerous world filled with stalking killers. Andrew Stevens, Adrian Zmed and Sherilyn Wolter star. 90 min.
21-9033 Was $89.99 *$14.99*

Caroline At Midnight (1993)
A gorgeous femme fatale devises a complex plan to get ahead which involves her crooked cop husband and his partner. After finding herself the target of a lethal female drug dealer, the woman carries on a torrid affair with a reporter whose knowledge of her past may be fatal. Mia Sara, Timothy Daly, Judd Nelson, Clayton Rohner and Virginia Madsen star. Ms. Sara is featured in several scorching nude scenes.
21-9048 Was $89.99 *$14.99*

Angel Of Destruction (1994)
An undercover cop investigating threats made against a controversial rock star is killed, and her kid sister wants to get to the bottom of it. She goes undercover, searching for the killer in a world filled with sex, drugs and rock-and-roll. Maria Ford and Charlie Spradling star in this steamy thriller. 80 min.
21-9058 Was $89.99 *$14.99*

Concealed Weapon (1994)
A struggling actor lands a role in a movie produced by a famous foreign filmmaker, but soon finds himself entangled with murder, the filmmaker's former mistress and the black market when he arrives on location in Yugoslavia. Daryl Haney, Karen Stone and Cassandra Leigh star.
21-9076 Was $89.99 *$14.99*

Serial Killer (1995)
A gorgeous female cop on the trail of a demented murderer becomes the hunted, as the maniac begins preying on her friends in order to lure her into a trap, in this gripping psychological thriller. Kim Delaney, Gary Hudson, Tobin Bell star. 94 min.
63-1808 Was $89.99 ❑*$14.99*

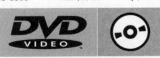

DVD VIDEO
ASK ABOUT OUR GIANT DVD CATALOG!

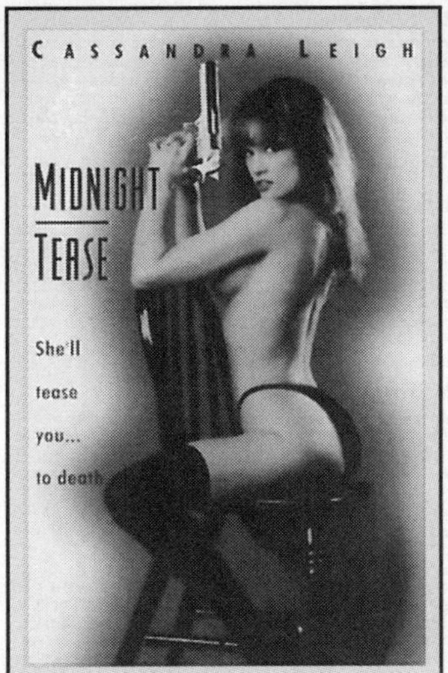

Midnight Tease (1994)
At a wild nightclub called Club Fugazi, beautiful strippers are being horrifically murdered. The lead dancer has been dreaming of these deaths and thinks she may have something to do with them...only her psychiatrist can persuade the cops that she's innocent. Cassandra Leigh and Rachel Dyer star in this heated thriller. Unrated version.
21-9069 Was $89.99 *$14.99*

Midnight Tease 2 (1995)
A beautiful young woman whose dancer sister was murdered goes undercover as a stripper to find the assailant. While performing her exotic dances, the killings continue, forcing her to play an erotic and dangerous game to catch the murderer. Kimberly Kelly, Tane McClure and Penthouse Pet Julie Smith star. Unrated version; 94 min.
21-9099 Was $89.99 *$14.99*

Lola's Game (1998)
A cop searching for his former girlfriend's killer is thrust into the underground of sex, drugs and rock and roll when his investigation leads to a game of deadly seduction involving a seductive singer. Doug Jeffrey, Joe Estevez and Elise Muller star. 82 min.
21-9167 *$59.99*

The Fiancé (1997)
A woman seeks sympathy from a stranger after suspecting her husband of cheating on her, but "the kindness of strangers" turns into a deadly romantic obsession. Hair-raising suspense story stars William R. Moses, Lysette Anthony, Patrick Cassidy. 94 min.
27-7041 Was $99.99 ❑*$14.99*

Stranger In The House (1997)
Mayhem, murder and mystery await in this gripping tale, as a jewelry heist that goes wrong and a publishing house executive's death lead to dangerous and potentially fatal happenings. Michelle Greene, Steve Railsback, Kathleen Kinmont star. 94 min.
27-7042 ❑*$59.99*

Murder In Mind (1997)
Stricken with amnesia after her husband is brutally murdered, Mary-Louise Parker attempts to find out what happened with help from a noted hypnotherapist. Will her restored memories make her a suspect? Nigel Hawthorne and Jimmy Smits co-star in this intriguing thriller. 89 min.
27-7065 ❑*$99.99*

Night Caller (1998)
A disturbed woman becomes obsessed with a radio psychologist she frequently calls for advice, and when she looks to a way to enter the doctor's life, no one will stand in her way. Shanna Reed, Mary Crosby and Tracy Nelson star. 94 min.
27-7071 ❑*$89.99*

Nightmare (1994)
After the maniac who kidnapped her daughter is captured and the child returned safely, Victoria Principal thinks her nightmare is over. But when the suspect is freed on a technicality and begins stalking her, the true terror begins. With Paul Sorvino, Jonathan Banks, Danielle Harris. 95 min.
21-9078 Was $89.99 *$14.99*

The Spy Within (1994)
A beautiful spy who uses sex to uncover secrets and a reclusive explosives expert learn that they are the targets of a covert assassination team. The two decide to team together to outsmart their pursuers in this steamy suspenser starring Theresa Russell, Scott Glenn, Katherine Helmond and Joe Pantoliano.
21-9084 Was $89.99 *$14.99*

Reflections In The Dark (1995)
With the clock ticking off the final seconds of her life, a woman set to be executed for her husband's murder reveals the truth behind the deed to a prison guard. The disclosure brings the two of them together in a last-minute quest for redemption. Mimi Rogers, Billy Zane and John Terry star. 95 min.
21-9087 Was $89.99 *$14.99*

Double Take (1997)
After identifying in a police line-up the man he saw kill a jewelry store clerk during a robbery, a writer is shocked to see the accused's double walking down the street and becomes convinced he put the wrong man behind bars. Can he and the suspect's girlfriend uncover the truth? Multi-layered mystery stars Craig Sheffer, Brigitte Bako, Costas Mandylor. 86 min.
27-7056 Was $99.99 ❑*$14.99*

Twisted Love (1995)
After being shunned by the hip crowd at her college, Janna kidnaps a handsome, star football player hurt in a motorcycle accident and begins planning their future together—without his consent! Soleil Moon Frye, Mark Paul Gosselaar and Lisa Dean Ryan star in this thriller.
21-9090 *$89.99*

Provocateur (1996)
The enticing Jane March plays a North Korean operative who goes undercover as a nanny in order to get important confidential documents from a U.S. colonel. Getting in the way of her assignment is the colonel's young daughter, whom she begins to care for, and his son, with whom she falls in love. Lillo Brancato, Nick Mancuso also star. 104 min.
27-7067 ❑*$99.99*

Showgirl Murders (1996)
Gorgeous Maria Ford is on the run from some ornery drug dealers, so she ducks into a sleazy bar—and soon turns it into the hottest strip spot in town. While enticing the clientele, she seduces the bar's owner and plots to bring about his wife's demise. Kevin Alper, Samantha Carter co-star.
21-9115 Was $89.99 *$14.99*

Sawbones (1996)
A demented surgeon who plays God with his patients is terrorizing a busy hospital, But who is he? Only one woman knows his identity. Can she stop him before she goes under the knife? Diabolical thriller stars Adam Baldwin, Don Harvey, Nina Siemaszko and Barbara Carrera. 85 min.
21-9116 Was $99.99 *$14.99*

Exposé (1997)
A congressman's seductive young daughter starts an extortion scheme with a few of her girlfriends and is soon seducing some of the country's most powerful leaders, until a lobbyist learns of their "game" and draws them into a deadly plan. Racy and suspenseful thriller stars Tracy Tutor, Kevin E. West, Daneen Boone. 83 min.
21-9143 *$59.99*

The Corporation (1997)
A mysterious computer company sends subliminal directives in its software to all who play their games, forcing users to buy more of their products and get involved in other, more sinister activities. A young executive is lured into the corporation and, after discovering their agenda, joins his wife in trying to stop them. Ian Ziering, Katherine Kelly Long, Dee Wallace Stone star. 81 min.
21-9132 *$99.99*

Don't Sleep Alone (1997)
A beautiful young woman takes the title advice to heart, but when she claims to have been assaulted by several attackers and her former lovers begin turning up dead, a pair of detectives must discover if this seductress is victim or killer. Compelling and erotic thriller stars Lisa Welti, Doug Jeffrey. 81 min.
21-9151 *$59.99*

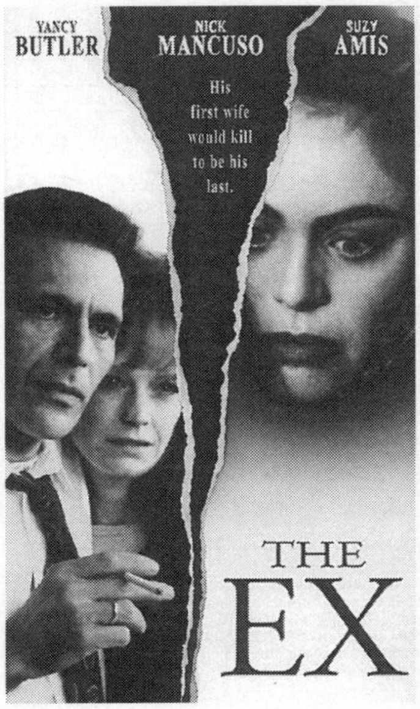

The Ex (1996)
"Fatal Attraction" meets "The First Wives Club" in this nerve-numbing suspenser about a divorced architect who finds his career, his new girlfriend, and his very life threatened by his insanely jealous ex-wife. Yancy Butler, Nick Mancuso and Suzy Amis star. 87 min.
27-7011 Was $99.99 *$14.99*

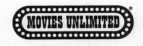

Dangerous Curves (1999)
Tantalizing and terrifying erotic thriller involving a handsome attorney whose search for his former lover finds him involved in a dangerous web of deceit and murder. Robert Carradine, Maxine Bahns and David Carradine star. 85 min.
21-9201 *$49.99*

Cost Of Living (1998)
In this contemporary film noir, rugged individualist Edie Falco finds herself asking for help from menacing people in her past when she's in trouble. One of the people she encounters is James Villermaire, a blue-collar worker who turns out to be both her antagonist and object of desire. With Caitlin Clarke. 101 min.
22-9019 *$89.99*

Blown Away (1993)
Erotic thriller about an activities director at a resort whose relationship with the manipulative teenage daughter of the owner has deadly consequences. Corey Haim, Corey Feldman and Nicole Eggert (TV's "Baywatch") star in this sizzling suspenser. Unrated version; 93 min.
27-6849 Was $89.99 ❑*$14.99*

Deception (1993)
Globe-trotting romantic thriller with Andie MacDowell as a woman determined to uncover the cause of her husband's mysterious death. But her investigation turns dangerous when she realizes he had been leading a double life. Liam Neeson and Viggo Mortensen also star. AKA: "Ruby Cairo." 90 min.
27-6863 Was $19.99 ❑*$14.99*

The Road Killers (1993)
In this thriller, four psychotic joyriders terrorize a family on vacation and eventually kidnap their teenage daughter. Forced into action, mild-mannered father Christopher Lambert takes matters into his own hands and goes after the punks. Craig Sheffer, Adrienne Shelly co-star. 89 min.
27-6920 Was $89.99 ❑*$14.99*

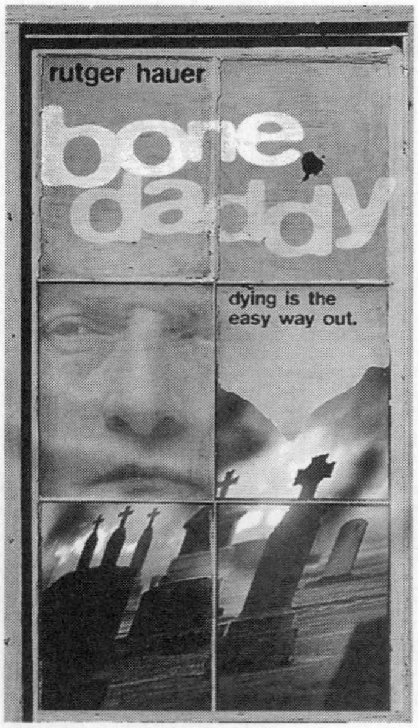

Bone Daddy (1998)
When former Chicago medical examiner Rutger Hauer writes a best-selling novel based on the exploits of a notorious serial killer known as Bone Daddy, he never expects the real murderer to come out of hiding. Now Hauer must race against time to track down Bone Daddy before his friends and family become the next victims. Chills and thrills in the tradition of "Silence of the Lambs"; with Barbara Williams, R.H. Thomson. 90 min.
27-7094 Was $89.99 ❑*$14.99*

Night Train To Venice (1993)
Creepy thriller with Hugh Grant as a passenger on a transcontinental train who encounters evil incarnate in the form of mysterious stranger Malcolm McDowell. Tahnee Welch also stars in this spellbinding suspenser. 98 min.
27-6921 ❑*$12.99*

Probable Cause (1995)
A veteran detective trying to track down a serial cop killer is assigned a beautiful new partner with whom he becomes romantically involved, but when the investigation points to her as a suspect, will he put his heart—and his life—on the line? Action-filled thriller stars Michael Ironside, Kate Vernon, Craig T. Nelson. 90 min.
27-6956 Was $89.99 *$19.99*

The Fixer (1997)
Jon Voight plays a legendary "fixer," a man who takes care of business behind the scenes, for everyone from mobsters to politicos. When he is almost killed, Voight questions his unsavory life and contemplates changing his ways. Brenda Bakke, J.J. Johnston and Miguel Sandoval also star. 105 min.
27-7088 ❑*$89.99*

Defenseless (1991)
Riveting psychological stunner stars Barbara Hershey as a successful lawyer who becomes romantically involved with one of her clients, a married man with ties to the adult film industry. When he is found murdered, she must defend the man's wife, an old school friend of hers, in court. Sam Shepard, J.T. Walsh and Mary Beth Hurt also star. 106 min.
27-6751 ❑*$14.99*

Lady Killer (1997)
Ben Gazzara is a cop on the edge when a serial killer strikes in the area where his daughter is attending college. To make matters worse, her boyfriend keeps turning up at the scene of the crime. The boyfriend claims he's been studying the killings for his acting career, but Gazzara think differently. With Alex McArthur, Reneé Altman. 74 min.
21-9146 *$59.99*

Shadow Dancer (1998)
When the lights go out at an L.A. strip club, one of the dancers on stage is savagely stabbed to death. All the evidence leads to a fellow stripper who hides a deadly secret in her past, but is she a killer...or the next victim? Erotically charged suspenser stars Gabriella Hall, Robert Donovan, Kate McNeil. 85 min.
21-9156 *$59.99*

Criminal Affairs (1998)
High intensity abounds in this suspenser set in the Maine woods where Mark and Robin are taken hostage in a remote cabin by Clint, an escaped convict. After Clint rapes Robin, it's revealed that they, in fact, were once lovers and her marriage to Mark was part of a scheme to extort money. Louis Mandylor, James Marshall and Renee Allmann star. 94 min.
21-9162 *$59.99*

The White Raven (1998)
Ace reporter Ron Silver latches onto the biggest—and deadliest—story of his career when a dying Nazi war criminal tells him about a priceless diamond missing since World War II. Now Silver is on the run from two governments and a global terrorist group in this riveting thriller. Joanna Pacula, Roy Scheider also star. 92 min.
27-7095 ❑*$49.99*

After Dark, My Sweet (1990)
Riveting tale of suspense and double-crosses, as an ex-boxer and asylum inmate joins up with a couple planning the kidnapping of a politician's child, unaware that he's to be used as their fall guy. Bruce Dern, Rachel Ward and Jason Patric star in the sexy thriller, based on a novel by Jim Thompson ("The Grifters"). 114 min.
27-6697 Was $89.99 ❑*$14.99*

Strip For Action (1999)
In this thriller, stripper Maria Ford and her dancer pal and boyfriend are taken hostage by a group of ruthless robbers who stole cash from her club. The three are taken on a plane by the thugs, and when the vehicle crashes on the way to Las Vegas, the women are forced to perform their erotic routines to please their captors. Nikki Fritz also stars. Unrated version; 77 min.
21-9190 *$59.99*

Homicidal Impulse (1992)
A young assistant D.A. finds his career has stalled...until he has a torrid affair with a sexy office intern who happens to be his boss's niece. Their passion soon ignites a scheme for advancement, and murder is part of the plan. Charles Napier, Scott Valentine and Vanessa Angel star in this scorching suspenser. Uncut, unrated version; 86 min.
27-6792 *$14.99*

The Minus Man (1999)
In this eerie suspenser directed by "Blade Runner" scripter Hampton Fancher, Owen Wilson is a serial killer who settles in a small Pacific Northwest town where he rents a room from troubled couple Mercedes Ruehl and Brian Cox, who helps him get a job at the post office. But even while holding a job and dating workmate Janeane Garofalo, Wilson can't stop killing people. With Sheryl Crow. 114 min.
27-7191 Was $99.99 ❑*$14.99*

The Reflecting Skin (1991)
Set in a Midwest town during World War II, this haunting thriller focuses on a young boy who witnesses the deaths of two friends and his father's suicide and is convinced that the widow living next door is responsible...and is a vampire! When his brother becomes romantically involved with the woman, the boy plots a way to stop her. With Viggo Motenson, Lindsay Duncan. 98 min.
27-6753 Was $89.99 *$19.99*

Cast A Deadly Spell (1991)
Set in a '40s Los Angeles where magic and monsters are commonplace, this fascinating film mixes the best of film noir with horror. Private eye Phillip Lovecraft (Fred Ward) battles a gangster, his zombie assistant and other creatures while on the trail of a book with mystical powers. David Warner, Julianne Moore, Clancy Brown co-star. 93 min.
44-1846 ❑*$89.99*

Witch Hunt (1994)
Hollywood detective Phillip Lovecraft returns (played now by Dennis Hopper) to investigate when a gorgeous actress's rich husband is found murdered by magic. Is the lovely thespian responsible or are there darker forces at work? Penelope Ann Miller and Julian Sands co-star in this diabolically funny suspense sequel to "Cast a Deadly Spell" from director Paul Schrader. 100 min.
44-1992 Was $19.99 ❑*$14.99*

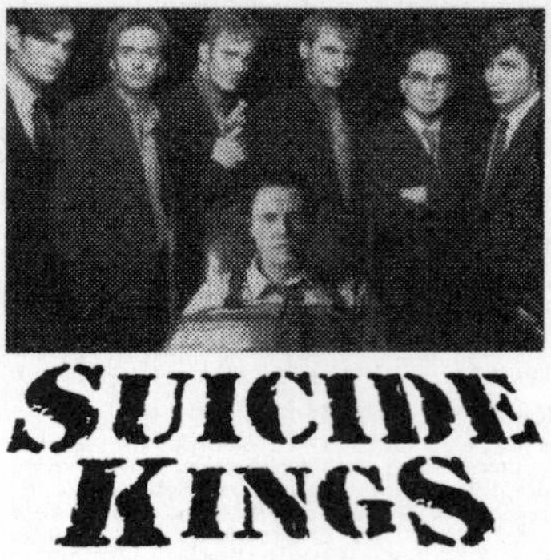

Suicide Kings (1997)
Slick, darkly funny thriller concerns five college preppies who get more than they bargained for when they abduct and hold for ransom retired wiseguy Christopher Walken in order to save the sister of one of them from the hands of a group of sadistic kidnappers. Henry Thomas, Sean Patrick Flanery, Jay Mohr, Denis Leary, Laura San Giacomo co-star. 103 min.
27-7077 Was $99.99 ❑*$14.99*

Executive Power (1997)
In a suspense thriller ripped from the headlines, a sexual scandal threatens to rock the White House, and the president's loyal staffers may have to put their lives on the line—literally—to protect the chief executive. Craig Sheffer, Joanna Cassidy, John Heard star. 115 min.
27-7098 ❑*$89.99*

Persons Unknown (1996)
An ex-cop working as a security expert is the victim in a game of seduction and deceit when a beautiful junkie and her sister use him to gain access to a drug ring's headquarters in this gripping thriller. Joe Mantegna, Kelly Lynch, J.T. Walsh, Jon Favreau and Naomi Watts star. 99 min.
27-7110 ❑*$89.99*

Memorial Day (1998)
After a stay in a mental hospital, former high-ranking Marine and government operative Jeff Speakman is called on to stop a group of terrorists piloting a Russian satellite with powers of great destruction. Teamed with a newscaster, Speakman uncovers a conspiracy that leads to U.S. officials. With Bruce Weitz, Stephanie Niznik and Paul Mantee. 95 min.
27-7113 ❑*$99.99*

Running Woman (1998)
In this thriller, Theresa Russell is a woman wrongly accused of killing her young son. After escaping police custody, she ventures into the seedy underworld of Los Angeles to find the real killer and prove her innocence. Andrew J. Robinson, Eddie Velez co-star. 84 min.
21-9168 *$59.99*

Never 2 Big (1998)
The seedy side of the music industry is revealed in this thriller in which a record company executive attempts to uncover the truth behind the murder of his sister, a rising R&B singer. He discovers that his own label may have been behind the killing in a deadly plan to boost sales. Ernie Hudson, Donnie Wahlberg, Nia Long and Shemar Moore star. 100 min.
27-7089 Was $89.99 *$14.99*

Exception To The Rule (1997)
A married gem dealer thinks his affair with a beautiful stranger was just a one-night stand, but the "other woman" has more on her mind than mere revenge, blackmailing the man into giving her a valuable shipment of diamonds and threatening his family and his life. Seductive thriller stars Kim Cattrall, Eric McCormack, Sean Young and William Devane. 98 min.
27-7116 ❑*$99.99*

Lured Innocence (1999)
A beautiful young woman thinks she's found a way out of her small-town home when she begins an affair with an older married man, but when the man's wife learns of their relationship things turn deadly. Intricate and erotic suspense tale stars Dennis Hopper, Marley Shelton, Talia Shire. 97 min.
27-7176 ❑*$99.99*

By Dawn's Early Light (1990)
A terrorist group explodes a nuclear missile over a Russian city, sending American and Soviet powers into a frenzy and forcing the U.S. to send out a B-52 bomber with the bunkers of Russian leaders as its target. Powers Boothe, Rebecca De Mornay, James Earl Jones and Martin Landau star. 100 min.
44-1737 Was $89.99 ❑*$14.99*

The Enemy Within (1994)
An intense reworking of the classic suspense film "Seven Days in May," starring Forest Whitaker as an officer with the Joint Chiefs of Staffs who suspects that his boss, high-ranking general Jason Robards, is plotting a military coup to topple weak U.S. president Sam Waterston. With Dana Delany. 86 min.
44-1978 Was $19.99 *$14.99*

Body Language (1995)
A successful defense attorney has the hots for a beautiful stripper and decides he will do anything to please her, even if it means killing her abusive boyfriend. Smoldering erotic suspenser stars Tom Berenger, Heidi Schanz and Nancy Travis. 95 min.
44-2016 Was $89.99 ❑*$19.99*

Widow's Kiss (1996)
After marrying seductive Beverly D'Angelo, widower Bruce Davison mysteriously dies, leaving son Mackenzie Astin his estate. But Astin is suspicious of his stepmother and a new stepbrother, so he hires a private investigator to look into her shadowy past. Dennis Haysbert also stars in this sexy suspenser. 103 min.
44-2047 Was $99.99 ❑*$14.99*

Deadly Voyage (1996)
A group of stowaways on a freighter bound for America are discovered by the crew and sadistically murdered one by one, but one man escapes and fights to stay alive long enough to reach port. Harrowing suspense film stars Omar Epps, Joss Ackland and David Suchet. 92 min.
44-2063 Was $19.99 ❑*$14.99*

Always Outnumbered, Always Outgunned (1998)
From "Devil in a Blue Dress" author Walter Mosley comes this atmospheric thriller starring Laurence Fishburne as Socrates Fortlow, a former convict who, following his release from prison, tries to help a murder witness, falls in love with his friend's wife and tries to run a murderer out of town. Cicely Tyson, Natalie Cole, Bill Nunn and Laurie Metcalf co-star. 110 min.
44-2172 Was $99.99 ❑*$14.99*

Dance With Death (1991)
A rash of murders of L.A.'s top strippers provokes the curiosity of a beautiful female reporter. In order to uncover the killer, she poses as an exotic dancer and investigates the sordid world of strip joints. Maxwell Caufield, Barbara Alyn Jones and Martin Mull star. 90 min.
44-1868 *$89.99*

Traces Of Red (1992)
Contemporary film noir starring James Belushi as a Palm Beach police detective who discovers that someone has been killing all of the women he has been involved with. Who is responsible for the killings, which have been marked by clues written in lipstick? Is it his partner (Tony Goldwyn) or a wealthy socialite (Lorraine Bracco) he's had a torrid affair with? 105 min.
44-1927 Was $89.99 ❑*$14.99*

Blind Side (1993)
A married couple accidentally kill a cop on a deserted backroad and become the target of a ruthless killer who witnessed the incident when he shows up at their door. To keep him quiet, will they have to pay the ultimate price? Steamy, suspenseful thriller stars Rebecca DeMornay, Ron Silver and Rutger Hauer. Uncut, unrated version; 89 min.
44-1938 Was $19.99 *$14.99*

Blue Ice (1993)
Michael Caine is a spy-turned-jazz club owner whose old skills are needed when he falls in love with an ambassador's seductive wife (Sean Young). Young is looking for Caine's help to track down her former lover, but along the way several of his friends turn up dead. Exciting suspenser also stars Bob Hoskins. 96 min.
44-1951 Was $89.99 ❑*$19.99*

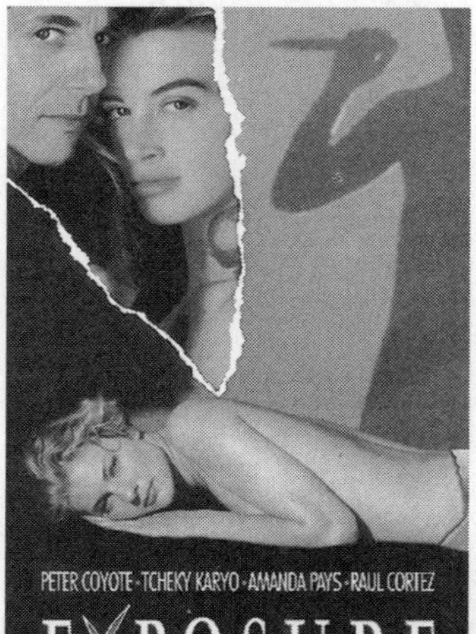

Exposure (1991)
In this intense thriller, Peter Coyote plays an American photographer working in Brazil who discovers that a young prostitute's murder may be the work of a company trafficking in drugs and arms dealing. Soon, his girlfriend is raped and he decides to tackle the assailants head-on. With Amanda Pays, Tcheky Karyo. 105 min.
44-1872 Was $19.99 ❑*$14.99*

Above Suspicion (1995)
After a drug bust shooting leaves him paralyzed, cop Christopher Reeve begins to suspect his wife and fellow officer brother of having an affair in this riveting suspenser that mixes adultery, deception, and a million-dollar murder scheme. With Kim Cattrall, Joe Mantegna, Edward Kerr. 95 min.
44-2018 Was $19.99 ❑*$14.99*

534 · MYSTERY & SUSPENSE
MOVIES UNLIMITED
CALL · 1-800-4-MOVIES

Caracara (1999)
Ornithological researcher Natasha Henstridge finds her isolated life interrupted when an FBI team uses her New York apartment for a stakeout and she's attracted to team leader Johnathon Schaech. But when she learns the truth about the "agent" and his deadly mission, Henstridge's life will be in danger. Compelling suspenser also stars Lauren Hutton. AKA: "The Last Witness." 93 min.
44-2228 ❑*$99.99*

Ultimate Desires (1991)
When one of her clients, a high-priced call girl, is found brutally murdered, a lawyer enters into a world of "sex for sale" in an attempt to find the killer, and soon finds repressed aspects of her own sexuality coming out. Erotic thriller stars Tracy Scoggins, Marc Singer, Brion James. 93 min.
46-5524 ❑*$12.99*

All-American Murder (1991)
Intriguing thriller about a rebellious college student who lands in his new school only to be made the suspect in the killing of a gorgeous coed. Soon, he finds everyone after him, but a local cop gives him 24 hours to find the real culprit. Christopher Walken, Joanna Cassidy and Charlie Schlatter star; directed by Anson Williams. 94 min.
46-5528 Was $89.99 *$14.99*

Double Exposure (1994)
A thrilling tale of lust, seduction and adultery about a possessive husband's discovery that his wife is unfaithful drives him to seek vengeance in dangerous ways. Ron Perlman, Jennifer Gatti and Dedee Pfeiffer star. 91 min.
46-5586 *$89.99*

Prey Of The Chameleon (1992)
A mysterious serial killer stalks female victims and, after murdering them, assumes their appearance and identities. A policewoman must stop the Chameleon from striking again in this offbeat and seductive thriller. Daphne Zuniga, Alexandra Paul, James Wilder star. 91 min.
46-5529 ❑*$89.99*

Blood & Concrete: A Love Story (1991)
Inventively quirky thriller about a small-time car thief who falls for a neurotic nightclub singer and soon finds himself caught in an underworld mess involving Hollywood mobsters, a wacky detective and a powerful aphrodisiac which everyone wants. Billy Zane, Jennifer Beals, Darren McGavin and Nicholas Worth star in this cutting-edge mystery. 97 min.
45-5521 Was $89.99 *$19.99*

The Grifters (1990)
In this seedy, emotionally-charged film noir set in contemporary Los Angeles, Anjelica Huston is the horse-playing mother of con artist John Cusack who doesn't like her son's romantic interest with sexual swindler Annette Bening. You never know who's duping whom in Martin Scorsese's acclaimed production, directed by Stephen Frears ("Dangerous Liaisons") and based on Jim Thompson's novel. 114 min.
44-1798 Was $19.99 ❑*$14.99*

Touch And Die (1991)
Martin Sheen plays a hard-drinking American journalist based in Rome whose investigation of a series of murders leads him to an intriguing underworld plot involving nuclear arms and dangerous arms dealers. Renee Estevez, David Birney and Franco Nero co-star in this suspenseful globe-trotting thriller. 108 min.
47-2063 ❑*$89.99*

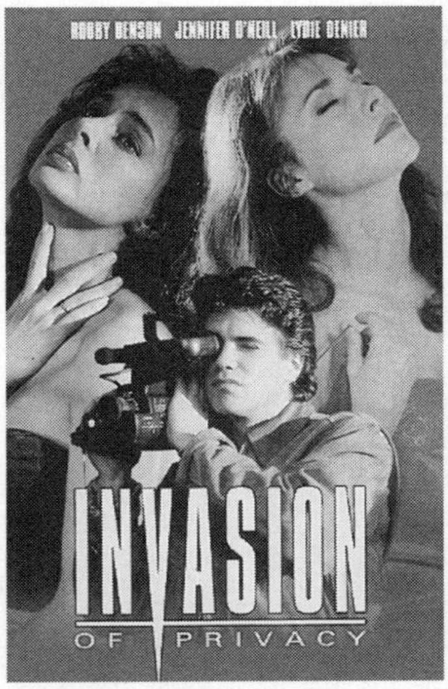

Invasion Of Privacy (1992)
Who said Robby Benson would never be in an erotic thriller? Benson plays a deranged prison inmate obsessed with glamorous reporter Jennifer O'Neill. After his parole he becomes her assistant, but when O'Neill rejects his advances, Benson turns his attentions to her beautiful, naive daughter (Lydie Denier). Steamy, unrated version; 97 min.
46-5551 Was $89.99 ❑*$14.99*

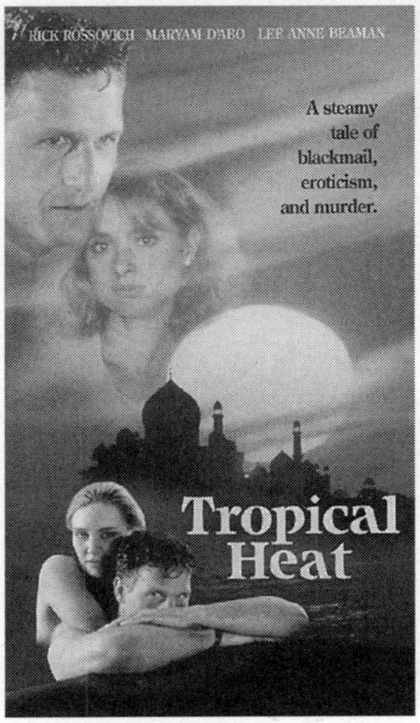

Tropical Heat (1993)
A whirlpool of eroticism and deception ensues when a Maharajah is killed on a safari and his widow seeks to collect a $5 million insurance claim. Along with her beautiful servant, the woman is followed in her mysterious travels by a Los Angeles detective investigating—and infatuated with—her. Rick Rossovich, Maryam D'Abo star. 88 min.
46-5569 Was $89.99 *$14.99*

Fatal Pursuit (1997)
The investigation into an $8 million diamond heist leads investigator Shannon Whirry to a criminal mastermind and his gorgeous assistant, both of whom will stop at nothing to keep the diamond for themselves. Malcolm McDowell, L.P. Brown and Charles Napier also star in this stylish and sexy caper offering. 105 min.
50-5655 Was $79.99 *$14.99*

A Gun, A Car And A Blonde (1997)
A wheelchair-bound recluse takes some tips from a friend involved in New Age beliefs and hypnotizes himself so he can enter his own world—the world of an old-fashioned gumshoe in Los Angeles. In his fantasy, he tries to find who is out to get a beautiful blonde who bears a resemblance to his real-life neighbor. With Jim Metzler, Billy Bob Thornton, Kay Lenz and Andrea Thompson. 110 min.
50-5746 Was $99.99 *$14.99*

Hindsight (1997)
The old saying goes: "Hindsight is 20/20," but this film proves "Hindsight" is also a steamy erotic tale about Hollywood at its most seductive. An aspiring actor's involvement with a studio executive's wife leads to a series of steamy and ultimately dangerous encounters with her and another gorgeous woman. Cyndi Pass, Kathy Shower and Robert Forster star. Unrated version; 97 min.
50-5777 *$39.99*

Night Eyes (1989)
A security expert gets more than he bargained for when he begins to videotape a sexy woman's every move. He soon becomes obsessed with his subject and doesn't see a plot of murder and blackmail unfolding around him. Andrew Stevens, Tanya Roberts star. Uncut, unrated version; 95 min.
46-5481 *$14.99*

Night Eyes...Fatal Passion (1995)
When a disturbed former patient begins following her, sexy psychiatrist Paula Barbieri goes to a handsome security whiz to help her set a seductive trap for the stalker. Passion-filled entry in the hit thriller series also stars Jeff Trachta, Andrew Stevens. Uncut, unrated version; 101 min.
46-5602 *$89.99*

Fever (1991)
An ex-con finds an unexpected ally in a successful lawyer as they attempt to save the woman they both love, who has been kidnapped by a seedy thug. In order to stop the creep from killing her, the two must commit three parole-breaking crimes, ranging from arson to murder. Armand Assante, Sam Neill and Marcia Gay Harden star in this feverish thriller. 99 min.
44-1829 Was $89.99 *$19.99*

The November Men (1997)
During the 1992 presidential campaign, a filmmaker begins shooting a suspense movie set in the election and starring an unbalanced ex-Marine as a would-be assassin. Is this just a work of fiction, or is someone planning the use the filming to mask a real-life assassination? Unusual and compelling thriller from director/co-star Paul Williams also features James Andronica (who wrote the script), Leslie Bevis and Robert Davi. 98 min.
46-8027 Was $59.99 *$14.99*

Fleshtone (1994)
A lonely artist who depicts murders in his paintings carries on a highly-charged affair with a gorgeous woman he meets through a phone-sex ad. After she becomes the subject for one of his paintings, she is killed, and the artist turns out to be the top suspect in her death. Martin Kemp and Lise Cutter ("Dangerous Curves") star. Uncut, unrated version; 89 min.
46-5590 Was $89.99 *$14.99*

A Brilliant Disguise (1994)
A beautiful, distraught artist seduces a handsome sportswriter she meets at a trendy restaurant. Their heated passion leads to a dangerous obsession, putting the writer's life in danger. Does the woman's psychiatrist hold the key to her secret desires? Lysette Anthony, Anthony John Denison and Corbin Bernsen star. 97 min.
46-5595 *$89.99*

Black Ice (1992)
A woman carrying on a secret affair with a married politician finds her life in danger after their relationship ends in violence. She offers a cab driver lots of cash to get her out of the country, but her government employers are right behind them. Taut, steamy thriller stars Joanna Pacula, Michael Ironside, Michael Nouri. Uncut, unrated version; 92 min.
46-5547 Was $89.99 *$14.99*

Betrayal Of The Dove (1993)
A sensual, surprising thriller about a divorced mother whose best friend arranges a blind date with a handsome doctor which leads to danger and a series of mysterious circumstances. Helen Slater, Billy Zane, Kelly LeBrock, Alan Thicke and Harvey Korman star. 93 min.
46-5560 Was $89.99 *$14.99*

A Murder Of Quality (1991)
Denholm Elliott stars as master British spy George Smiley in a compelling mystery based on a story by John le Carré. A letter from a former intelligence colleague who fears for her life brings Smiley to an exclusive boys' school, where murder is on the curriculum and societal privilege hides dark secrets. Glenda Jackson, Joss Ackland, Christian Bale also star. 103 min.
44-2233 *$19.99*

Year Of The Gun (1991)
Set during the tumultuous atmosphere in late '70s Italy when terrorists kidnapped prime minister Aldo Moro, this edgy thriller from John Frankenheimer stars Andrew McCarthy as an American journalist whose novel mirrors the real-life political events. Soon, he finds himself falling into a dangerous web of intrigue. Sharon Stone, Valeria Golino and John Pankow co-star. 111 min.
45-5516 Was $19.99 *$14.99*

Cat Chaser (1990)
Elmore Leonard's best-seller becomes a smoldering thriller starring Peter Weller as a Miami hotel owner (and ex-soldier) who involves himself in a dangerous relationship with the seductive wife of a ruthless millionaire. Kelly McGillis (in revealing nude scenes), Charles Durning and Frederic Forrest also star; Abel Ferrara ("Ms. 45") directs. Uncut, unrated version; 97 min.
47-2041 *$19.99*

Lethal Seduction (1996)
A crime boss discovers that his associates are being lured into sexual situations, then assaulted and murdered. The mobster wants to put a stop to the killings, but complicating matters is a cop trying to solve the case whose only suspect is a beautiful dark-haired woman seen at the scene of one of the crimes. Julie Strain, Joe Estevez and Chris Mitchum star. 90 min.
50-5465 Was $29.99 *$19.99*

Illusions (1992)
Following a stint in a mental hospital, a woman attempts to revive her strained marriage with her husband. But the arrival of her spouse's seductive sister—and their unusually close relationship—makes her more suspicious than ever before of hubby's motives. Robert Carradine, Heather Locklear, Ned Beatty and Emma Samms star. 95 min.
46-5544 Was $89.99 ❑*$14.99*

The Donor (1995)
A film stuntman wakes up after meeting a mysterious stranger to find out he was drugged, operated on, and is missing an organ. Attempting to track down the people responsible puts him in a deadly fight against the illegal trade in human body parts. Jeff Wincott, Michelle Johnson star. 94 min.
19-3779 *$89.99*

Trouble On The Corner (1999)
Unusual, sensual suspenser about a psychotherapist with a host of patients with sexual frustrations who comes to realize that his own marriage is unhappy. He becomes involved with an attractive model, which leads him into a mysterious and dangerous situation. Tony Goldwyn, Debi Mazar, Giancarlo Esposito, Edie Falco, Joe Morton and Tammy Grimes star. 104 min.
50-7540 *$74.99*

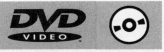

DVD VIDEO
ASK ABOUT OUR GIANT DVD CATALOG!

The Method (1998)
What happens when four actors take their "method" too far and start taking on the personae of real killers? Find out in this disturbing thriller that features Sean Patrick Flanery, Tyrin Turner, Nicholas Sadler, Natasha Gregson Wagner and Robert Forster. 97 min.
50-5976 *$89.99*

Real Killers (1998)
Disturbing thriller in the "Natural Born Killers" mold centering on Odessa and Kyle James, two brothers whose slaughter of their parents has landed them in prison, where they face the electric chair. The siblings become media sensations, and when they escape prison, they take a family as hostage. Dave Larsen, David Gunn and C.T. Miller star.
50-8238 Was $39.99 *$14.99*

Dead Heart (1998)
Bryan Brown stars in a taut, provocative thriller as a lawman who discovers a conspiracy of racism and corruption in rural Australia. Tensions begin to mount when an aboriginal prisoner is found dead in his cell and a native bootlegger having an affair with a white woman is murdered. With Ernie Dingo, Angie Milliken. 106 min.
53-6182 Was $89.99 *$19.99*

Element Of Doubt (1996)
Beth, an attractive, devoted schoolteacher, becomes suspicious of her new husband, an ambitious businessman. Is he trying to kill her or is she losing her grip on reality? This psychological thriller stars Nigel Havers and Gina McKee. 100 min.
53-6374 *$24.99*

The Life & Crimes Of William Palmer: Prince Of Poisoners (1998)
On the surface, Dr. William Palmer seems like a respectable, genteel physician to the residents of a small town in Victorian England. Eventually, it's revealed that Palmer is a swindler, womanizer and dastardly serial killer. This strange but true story stars Keith Allen, Jayne Ashbourne and Chloe Newsome. AKA: "Prince of Poisoners." 180 min.
53-6470 *$59.99*

Small Vices (1999)
Joe Mantegna plays Robert B. Parker's Spenser in this first-rate mystery that finds the Boston detective hired by lawyers to investigate the case of their client, a teenager with a rap sheet they believe is innocent of murdering a college student. The closer Spenser gets to the truth, the more danger he finds himself in. With Marcia Gay Harden. 100 min.
53-6614 ❑*$19.99*

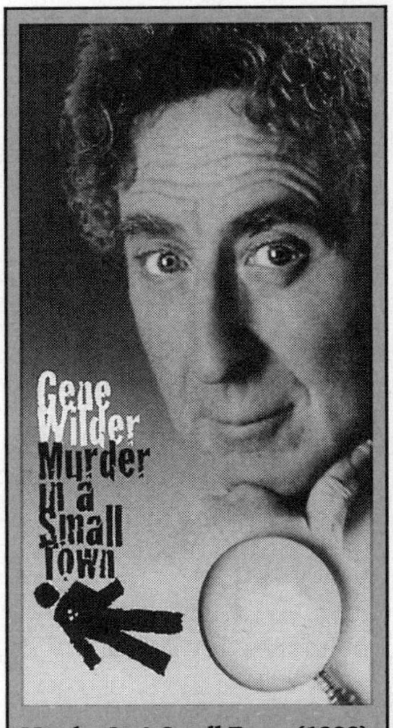

Murder In A Small Town (1998)
Gene Wilder co-scripted and stars in this compelling mystery, playing a successful Broadway director in the late '30s who retreats to a quiet Connecticut town after his wife is killed. When a local businessman is murdered, Wilder is drawn into investigating the crime, which proves to be linked to his own tragic past. Mike Starr, Terry O'Quinn also star. 100 min.
50-5630 *$19.99*

The Lady In Question (1999)
The murder of a well-known local philanthropist brings theater director-turned-amateur sleuth Larry "Cash" Carter (Gene Wilder) onto the case, but the string of suspects reaches across the Atlantic to Nazi Germany in this suspenseful whodunit. Claire Bloom, Mike Starr, Cherry Jones also star. 100 min.
53-6680 *$19.99*

Hidden Fears (1993)
Years after witnessing her husband's brutal murder, a young woman finds herself the next target in a series of killings by the people who made her a widow. Taut suspenser stars Meg Foster, Frederic Forrest, Wally Taylor. 90 min.
46-5581 *$89.99*

Framed (1993)
Based on a true story, this slam-bang thriller stars Timothy Dalton as Eddie Myers, a British criminal who absconded with millions in mob money and was thought to be dead when he was spotted while living the good life in Spain. After his arrest and return to England, Dalton agrees to cooperate with authorities...but has some plans of his own. With David Morrisey, Timothy West, Penélope Cruz. 115 min.
53-6814 *$29.99*

Georgia (1993)
Psychological suspenser starring Judy Davis as a lawyer who discovers that her real mother was a photographer who died under mysterious circumstances. As Davis begins to uncover the secrets of her past, she encounters deceit, danger and murder. With Julia Blake. 90 min.
53-7945 Was $19.99 *$14.99*

P.D. James: Devices And Desires (1995)
Classic P.D. James thriller set on the lonely East coast of England, where Commander Adam Dalgliesh of Scotland Yard investigates a number of vicious murders which may be the work of a serial killer, and a host of conflicting clues perplex the expert investigator. Roy Marsden, Susannah York star. 300 min. on six tapes.
53-8564 *$79.99*

P.D. James: A Mind To Murder (1996)
Roy Marsden returns as P.D. James' ace Scotland Yard investigator Adam Dalgliesh, this time trying to uncover the truth behind the mysterious death of a female colleague. Dalgliesh's investigation leads him to a high-society psychiatric clinic where the director has been murdered and nobody can be trusted. With Frank Finlay, David Hemmings. 100 min.
53-8812 *$19.99*

A Certain Justice (1998)
When a prominent British attorney is found stabbed to death in her office, Scotland Yard commander Adam Dalgliesh (Roy Marsden) and detective inspector Kate Miskin (Sarah Winman) quickly discover that the legal world guards its secrets as zealously as its criminal counterpart. Penny Downie co-stars; based on the P.D. James novel. 180 min. on three tapes.
08-8765 *□$29.99*

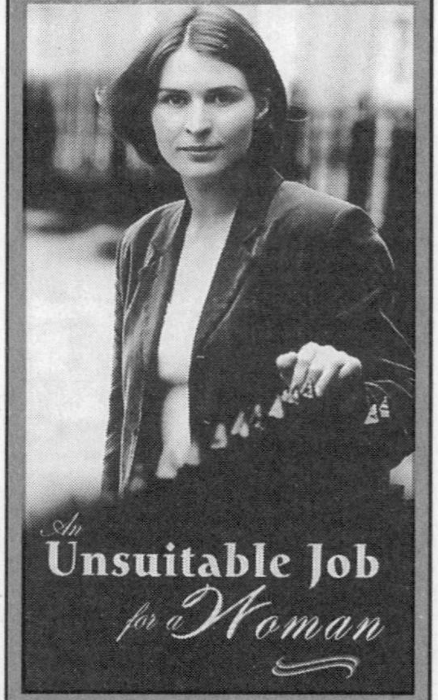

An Unsuitable Job For A Woman (1998)
From the best-selling crime novel by P.D. James comes a pair of intriguing mysteries. Cordelia Gray (Helen Baxendale) is plunged headfirst into the dangerous and exciting world of the private detective when she inherits a detective agency from her ex-policeman boss. Included are "Sacrifice" and "A Last Embrace." 330 min. on three tapes.
08-8662 *□$39.99*

An Unsuitable Job For A Woman, Series 2 (1998)
The further adventures of P.D. James' ace detective Cordelia Gray (played by Helen Baxendale) find her pregnant and trying to stop crooks and a killer with a surprising connection to Scotland Yard. Included are "Playing God" and "Living on Risk." 240 min. on two tapes.
08-8832 *□$29.99*

The Contract (1996)
British authorities are ecstatic when they think an East German designer of anti-tank missiles has defected. When they discover the defector is, in fact, the inventor's son, the government plans to use him to reel in the real thing. Kevin McNally, Stephan Meyer Kohloff star in this espionage thriller. 106 min.
53-8559 *$19.99*

Circle Of Deceit (1994)
Two years after terrorists killed his wife and young son, SAS officer Dennis Waterman is called back into action, assuming the identity of an IRA soldier recently killed. As Waterman infiltrates the organization, he tries to convince the dead man's family of his identity and soon falls in love with an IRA leader's daughter. Derek Jacobi, Peter Vaughan also star. 103 min.
53-9601 *$19.99*

The Kill-Off (1990)
Based on a story by Jim Thompson ("The Grifters"), this gritty film noir is set in a decrepit New Jersey seaside town where a bedridden woman controls the people around her by gossiping about their private lives. Soon, her chit-chat leads her adulterous husband, a stripper, a bar owner, herself and others into danger. Loretta Gross, Steve Monroe, Cathy Haase star. 100 min.
54-9123 *$69.99*

Masquerade (1992)
Adult sensation Teri Weigel stars in this ultra-erotic thriller as a female LAPD investigator sent to Italy to find out who is killing that country's top art dealers. Weigel teams with a Florence police captain to go undercover and infiltrate the high-stakes world of international art collectors. Nellie Marie Vickers also stars. Unrated version; 93 min.
59-7016 *$99.99*

Night Of The Cyclone (1990)
Kris Kristofferson plays a police lieutenant on a beautiful tropic island who persuades his model daughter to live with him, then uncovers some seedy goings-on which may involve her artist boyfriend. Marisa Berenson and Jeff Meek also star in this thriller brimming with lush locales and suspense. 90 min.
63-1403 *$14.99*

Femme Fatale (1991)
When a man's new wife vanishes, he teams with his artist pal to uncover the mystery. Soon they infiltrate L.A.'s avant garde art scene and get drawn into a world of double-crosses and conspiracies. Colin Firth, Lisa Zane, Billy Zane and Lisa Blount star in this steamy, noirish thriller. 96 min.
63-1417 Was $89.99 *□$12.99*

Total Exposure (1991)
Sizzling modern film noir about a private eye hired by a fashion photographer accused of killing a beautiful model. The clues lead the sleuth to a district attorney who may know more about the murder than he's letting on. Michael Nouri, Season Hubley, Jeff Conaway and Playboy centerfold Deborah Driggs star. 90 min.
63-1441 *□$89.99*

Lower Level (1991)
Erotic thriller about a beautiful architect who becomes the obsession of a deranged security guard. When the guard discovers she has a boyfriend, he stalks both of them in an empty high rise, following their every move, controlling every exit in the building. Elizabeth Gracen, Jeff Yagher and David Bradley star. 88 min.
63-1478 *$14.99*

Horseplayer (1991)
Intriguing, erotic suspenser about a lonely racing addict who is pulled into a dangerous sexual adventure involving a creepy artist and his beautiful girlfriend, who poses as his sister. Sammi Davis, Brad Dourif, M.K. Harris and Vic Tayback star in this haunting modern film noir. 89 min.
63-1510 *□$89.99*

Landslide (1992)
Greed, ambition, seduction and murder play important parts in this suspense-filled thriller involving an amnesiac geologist who begins learning about his life when he returns to the site of the accident that took his memory away. Anthony Edwards, Joanna Cassidy, Melody Anderson and Tom Burlinson star. 95 min.
63-1581 *□$89.99*

Double Vision (1992)
Kim Cattrall plays a medical student investigating the disappearance of her identical twin in London. To discover what happened to her sister, she assumes her identity and is quickly drawn into the kinky lifestyle she lived. Based on a story by Mary Higgins Clark; with Christopher Lee, Gale Hansen. 92 min.
63-1584 *□$89.99*

The Baby Doll Murders (1992)
A series of murders of beautiful young women, with the only clue a broken doll left at each crime scene, has police baffled. But when a pair of detectives uncover a common link to the murders, the discovery puts one of the men's wives in deadly jeopardy. Nerve-numbing suspenser stars Jeff Kober, Bobby DiCicco, Melanie Smith, John Saxon. 90 min.
63-1592 *□$89.99*

A Cry In The Night (1992)
A recently remarried woman has her dream life turned upside-down when, following the mysterious deaths of her newborn baby and her ex-husband, she learns that the police and even her new spouse suspect her of being responsible. Is she killer or victim? Carol Higgins Clark and Perry King star in this gripping psychological thriller based on Mary Higgins Clark's novel. 99 min.
63-1593 *□$89.99*

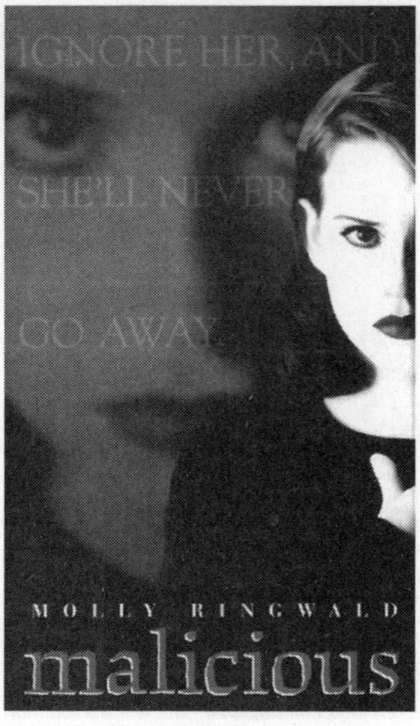

Malicious (1995)
Molly Ringwald has some scorching, revealing scenes in this thriller about a mysterious woman who seduces a handsome college athlete. When the athlete goes back to his girlfriend, the jealous Ringwald tries to win him back in devious and deadly ways. With Patrick McGaw, Mimi Kuzyk and Sarah Lassez. 92 min.
63-1792 Was $89.99 *□$14.99*

The Franchise Affair (1991)
Set in the sleepy village of Millford in 1947, this thriller concerns a scandal in which an elderly lady, her daughter and the residents of a country home known as "The Franchise" are accused of abducting, beating and starving a schoolgirl they wanted to be their servant. Patrick Malahide and Joanna McCallum star. 155 min.
53-9509 *$29.99*

Knight Moves (1992)
A chilling psychological thriller involving an arrogant chess master (Christopher Lambert) who is accused of murder. The police call in a psychologist (Diane Lane) to probe the mind of the suspect, but her inquiry leads to a steamy romance and danger. Tom Skerritt and Daniel Baldwin co-star. 105 min.
63-1604 Was $89.99 *□$12.99*

Terror Stalks The Class Reunion (1992)
After a music teacher is abducted by one of her former students, a young police detective races against the clock to find her. Kate Nelligan, Jennifer Beals and Geraint Wyn Davies star in this frightening tale from Mary Higgins Clark. 95 min.
63-1609 *□$89.99*

Weep No More My Lady (1993)
The best-selling thriller from Mary Higgins Clark is the basis for this tale of a hot-tempered actress who is found dead after she discovers that her sister is having an affair with her fiancé. Following the murder, a chateau becomes the center of deceit and intrigue. Daniel J. Travanti, Shelley Winters star. 92 min.
63-1624 *□$89.99*

The Wrong Man (1993)
Stylish, sensual noir thriller about an American sailor, accused of killing a smuggler in Mexico, who attempts to elude the authorities by hitching a ride with an expatriate and his sexy wife. Soon, the sailor finds himself involved with deception, danger and double-crosses. Rosanna Arquette, John Lithgow and Kevin Anderson star in this surprise-filled suspenser. 98 min.
63-1631 Was $89.99 *□$14.99*

Past Tense (1994)
A police detective and aspiring mystery writer has a romantic fling with his beautiful neighbor before she's found murdered. But after he receives phone calls from the dead woman and meets a new neighbor living in the house, the detective is drawn into a bizarre and deadly puzzle. Scott Glenn, Lara Flynn Boyle and Anthony LaPaglia star. 91 min.
63-1724 Was $89.99 *□$14.99*

Breaking Point (1994)
Retired Seattle cop Gary Busey finds himself fighting for more than just his life when a demented killer whom he tried to catch before at the cost of his sanity and marriage resurfaces in this ultra-intense psychological thriller. Kim Cattrall, Darlanne Fluegel also star. 95 min.
63-1733 Was $89.99 *□$12.99*

Illicit Dreams (1993)
A sex-starved housewife's erotic fantasies become real when she meets her dream lover, but the reality becomes fatal when her jealous husband finds out and decides he'd rather have her dead than let her go. Super-steamy suspenser stars Shannon Tweed, Andrew Stevens, Joe Cortese. Unrated version; 93 min.
63-1752 Was $89.99 *□$14.99*

Thicker Than Water (1993)
After his wife is killed in an auto accident, a man tries to rebuild his life and finds a new love, but the late wife's twin sister becomes obsessed with him and refuses to go away. Jonathan Pryce and Theresa Russell star in this sinister psychological suspenser. 150 min.
53-8074 Was $39.99 *$19.99*

The Secretary (1994)
Office politics takes a sinister turn in this suspenseful story about a female executive whose new secretary turns out to be a scheming psychopath who uses underhanded tricks and sexual manipulation to climb up the company ladder. Sheila Kelley, Mel Harris, Barry Bostwick star. 94 min.
63-1754 *□$89.99*

Stalked (1994)
A mysterious man who saves a woman's son from a tragic accident begins assimilating himself into her life. Their warm friendship soon turns frightening when he begins following her, monitoring her phone calls and planning their future together. What fuels his obsession and how far will it go? Marym D'Abo, Jay Underwood and Lisa Blount star. 95 min.
63-1761 *$69.99*

Dream Man (1995)
A female Seattle cop with the psychic ability to witness crimes as they are being committed carries on a dangerous affair with a dashing murder suspect. Has the slick playboy clouded her extra-sensory perceptions? Patsy Kensit, Bruce Greenwood and Andrew McCarthy star. 94 min.
63-1763 *□$89.99*

Bulletproof Heart (1995)
Tired hit man Anthony LaPaglia wants to retire from the business, but when an old mobster friend contracts him to kill beautiful Mimi Rogers, the only thing he can say is "yes." LaPaglia discovers that the seductive Rogers is not afraid of being whacked and begins to fall in love with her. With Matt Craven, Peter Boyle. 96 min.
63-1790 Was $89.99 *□$14.99*

The Wrong Woman (1995)
A woman (Nancy McKeon) framed for murder finds herself caught between the police and the real killer while trying to prove her innocence. Can she elude both of them in order to show the authorities she didn't commit the crime? With Chelsea Field, Stephen Shellen, Gary Hudson and Lyman Ward. 90 min.
63-1793 *□$89.99*

The Courtyard (1995)
After moving to California from New York, architect Andrew McCarthy has found the perfect job, girl and place to live. When a series of murders occurs in his apartment complex, McCarthy's dream life becomes a nightmare filled with creepy neighbors, strange noises, and a detective who thinks he's a prime suspect. With Mädchen Amick, Cheech Marin. 103 min.
63-1800 Was $89.99 *□$14.99*

The Grave (1996)
Haunting thriller in which North Carolina prison farm inmates Craig Sheffer and Josh Charles bribe a guard so they can escape and search for a treasure buried with its owner, a tight-fisted businessman in a decrepit mortuary. The danger gets greater when Sheffer's former girlfriend joins the pursuit. Gabrielle Anwar, Anthony Michael Hall, Eric Roberts also star. 90 min.
63-1833 Was $99.99 *□$14.99*

Closer And Closer (1995)
An altercation with a serial killer has left mystery writer Kaitlin Sanders partially paralyzed and living in seclusion in the Pacific Northwest. She finds herself in danger again when a killer begins imitating a character in her new book. Along with the FBI and local authorities, she tries to stop the culprit. Kim Delaney and Scott Craft star. 93 min.
64-3418 *$14.99*

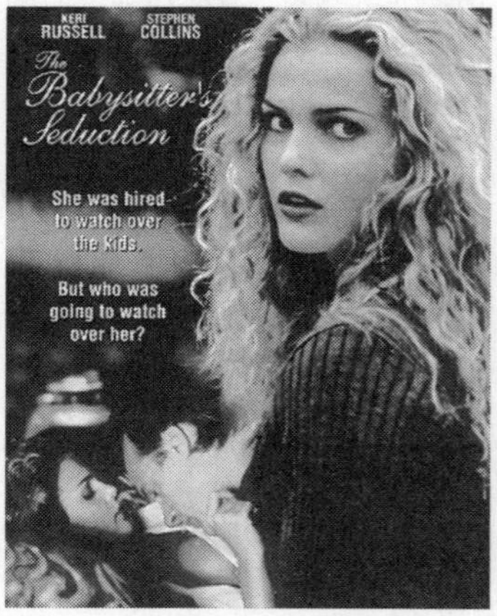

The Babysitter's Seduction (1995)
"Felicity" star Keri Russell is a young woman obsessed with married Stephen Collins and his family. When the wife suddenly dies, Russell becomes the family's full-time babysitter. Soon, however, her dream life becomes a nightmare filled with greed and deadly danger. 91 min.
64-3429 *$14.99*

Trade Off (1995)
Scorching erotic thriller starring Theresa Russell in the femme fatale role of a woman who seduces a distressed businessman, then tries to talk him into killing her abusive husband and his wife. Adam Baldwin, Megan Gallagher and Barry Primus also star in this steamy, noirish suspenser. 92 min.
63-1781   Was $89.99   ☐$14.99

Twin Sisters (1991)
Riveting, sexually-propelled thriller about a young woman who is recruited by a detective to impersonate her missing sister, a high-priced call girl. Stefanie Kramer, Susan Almgren, Frederic Forrest and James Brolin star. 92 min.
68-1228 $89.99

Play Nice (1992)
A tough-talking homicide detective enlists the help of a beautiful records office worker to track down a female serial killer who has been murdering her lovers "in the act." Steamy, sex-soaked suspenser stars Ed O'Ross, Robey and Michael Zand. Uncut, unrated version. 90 min.
68-1245 $89.99

Woman Undone (1995)
In this gripping thriller, Mary McDonnell plays a woman found near her burned-out car with her dead husband. When an autopsy reveals her husband has a bullet in his head, the secrets of McDonnell's marriage unravel. Randy Quaid and Sam Elliott also star. 91 min.
63-1819   Was $99.99   ☐$14.99

Exit (1996)
"Animal Instincts" star Shannon Whirry is seductive and stunning in this far-fetched story about an exotic dancer who uses her body and brains when the nightclub she works at is taken hostage by two thugs. There's lots of wild bumping and grinding in this thriller co-starring David Bradley. 90 min.
63-1828   ☐$99.99

Frame By Frame (1996)
Michael Biehn and Marg Helgenberger are two cops whose working relationship leads romance, but when Biehn's wife is killed by an Asian drug dealer, he suspects Helgenberger may have some ties to the murder. 97 min.
63-1829   ☐$99.99

Undertow (1996)
In this gripping suspenser, Lou Diamond Phillips and Mia Sara are a young couple who have to battle rugged mountain man Charles Dance in an intense fight for their lives. Co-written by Kathryn Bigelow ("Strange Days"). 90 min.
63-1830   ☐$99.99

Black Day, Blue Night (1996)
In this "Southwestern noir," two young women encounter a handsome drifter who leads them into danger when they get involved with $1 million in stolen cash and a vengeful police detective. With Gil Bellows, Michelle Forbes, J.T. Walsh and Mia Sara, who has revealing nude scenes. 99 min.
63-1832   ☐$99.99

Miami Hustle (1996)
Gorgeous con artist Kathy Ireland is drawn into a scam orchestrated by a gangster and involving millions of dollars. She soon finds her life in danger when the scam takes an unexpected turn. John Enos and Richard Sarafian also star. 80 min.
63-1867   ☐$99.99

Payback (1994)
After 13 years in prison, a man sets out to fulfill a deal he made with a deceased cellmate—kill the guard responsible for his buddy's death and he'll get a fortune in hidden loot. But once he meets the now-retired guard's sexy wife, a fatal love triangle develops. Steamy tale of double-crosses stars C. Thomas Howell, Joan Severance, Marshall Bell. Unrated director's cut; 93 min.
68-1336   Was $89.99   ☐$14.99

JENNIFER TILLY   GINA GERSHON
BOUND

Bound (1996)
Intense, erotic crime thriller with Gina Gershon as an ex-con who, after having a sexual liaison with neighbor Jennifer Tilly, joins forces with her to dupe gangster boyfriend Joe Pantoliano out of $2 million of laundered loot. This stylish, sizzling suspenser from the Wachowski Brothers ("The Matrix") features titillating sex scenes and lots of plot surprises. 105 min.
63-1864   Was $99.99   ☐$14.99

Bound (Letterboxed Version)
Also available in a theatrical, widescreen format.
63-1891   ☐$14.99

Servants Of Twilight (1991)
Based on the best-selling book by Dean R. Koontz, this thriller tells the eerie tale about a 6-year-old boy believed to be the Antichrist by a group of religious fanatics called "Servants of Twilight." The boy's mother enlists the help of a private detective to protect her and her son from the group's murderous threats. Bruce Greenwood, Belinda Bauer, Grace Zabriskie star. 96 min.
68-1216   ☐$12.99

Criminal Passion (1994)
A gorgeous female detective investigating the brutal murder of a young woman is drawn into an erotic affair with the victim's boyfriend, after he's cleared of the crime. But when the detective's partner and ex-lover discovers new evidence implicating the boyfriend, it becomes a deadly game to find the guilty party. Joan Severance and Anthony John Denison star in this scorcher. Unrated version; 96 min.
68-1312 $89.99

Final Mission (1994)
A special Air Force project installs virtual reality simulators into F-16 jet fighters, enabling the pilots to see further, fly faster and shoot more accurately. When flyers begin dying mysteriously, a project pilot investigates the problem. Billy Wirth, Steve Railsback and Corbin Bernsen star. 91 min.
68-1318 $89.99

Dangerous Touch (1994)
Dashing hustler Lou Diamond Phillips leads sexy talk show host Kate Vernon into a world filled with danger at every turn, but doesn't realize her desire for lust is greater than anticipated. After their relationship reaches a fever pitch, the two face each other in a game of blackmail and deceit. Unated version; 103 min.
68-1320   Was $89.99   ☐$14.99

Love Is A Gun (1994)
A police forensic photographer gets caught in a dangerous love triangle when he falls for a beautiful model who convinces him they were lovers once before. Soon past and present blur, and his dream affair turns into a deadly nightmare. Eric Roberts, Kelly Preston and Eliza Roberts star in this sexy suspenser. 92 min.
68-1330 $89.99

The Babysitter (1995)
Alicia Silverstone ("Clueless") plays the teenager an entire small town is obsessed with in this suspenser. What is the reason a married man lusts after her and another woman uses her to fantasize about an affair with a neighbor? When Silverstone's boyfriend gets involved in a malicious prank, tragic events occur, leading to...Silverstone again! With J.T. Walsh. 90 min.
63-1789   Was $89.99   ☐$14.99

Shattered Image (1994)
Former supermodel Bo Derek agrees to a quick-money kidnapping scam, but when the "crime" backfires and her husband is murdered, she turns to undercover FBI agent Jack Scalia to save her from the killers in this elaborate, sexy thriller. With John Savage, Dorian Harewood, David McCallum. 98 min.
68-1349 $89.99

Blood Of The Hunter (1995)
Set in Canada's Great White North, this suspenser stars Michael Biehn as a mysterious stranger who terrorizes the wife of a fur trader he has framed for murdering a postman. Who is this killer and why is he out to destroy the trader and his family? Gabriel Arcand also stars. 92 min.
68-1364   ☐$89.99

Exclusive (1992)
Suzanne Somers is a TV anchorwoman who exploits a mass homicide in order to boost her ratings. But soon after the ratings soar, her life goes into turmoil as she is viciously attacked and her college professor husband is accused of killing a student. Is there a connection—and what can she do to stop the dangerous situation? With Michael Nouri. 93 min.
64-3424 $14.99

Those Bedroom Eyes (1993)
After his wife is murdered, Harvard professor Tim Matheson thinks he has found the perfect replacement in Mimi Rogers. But soon fear sets in, and Matheson believes Rogers might be killed as well, so he sets out on a dangerous search for the killer. AKA: "A Kiss to Die For. 93 min.
64-3430 $14.99

Route 9 (1998)
Rural deputies Kyle MacLachlan and Wade Andrew Williams stumble upon a van with several dead occupants, a stash of drugs, and over a million dollars in cash along remote Route 9. Keeping the loot for themselves, the lawmen get caught up in an increasingly complex cover-up as they must elude their boss and federal agents. Gripping thriller also stars Peter Coyote, Amy Locane. 111 min.
64-9037 $99.99

A Murder Of Crows (1998)
Compelling suspense tale in which New Orleans lawyer Cuba Gooding, Jr. submits, under his own name, a mystery novel manuscript written by a man he thinks is dead. When it's learned that the book's killings are real unsolved cases, Gooding becomes the prime suspect and must uncover the truth behind the murders. Tom Berenger, Marianne Jean-Baptiste and Eric Stoltz co-star. 102 min.
64-9042 $99.99

Brown's Requiem (1998)
Based on "L.A. Confidential" author James Ellroy's novel, this thriller stars Michael Rooker as a former L.A. cop who makes ends meet as a repo man and private detective. Rooker is hired to follow a golf caddie's young sister, and soon finds a connection between her and her elderly sugar daddy, mobsters and the LAPD. With Selma Blair, Brion James and Harold Gould. 97 min.
64-9058 $99.99

Two Shades Of Blue (1998)
When best-selling author Rachel Hunter is accused of murder, she assumes the identity of her heroine and goes undercover to find the real killer. Her new life as a phone relay operator for the deaf involves her in a steamy and deadly conspiracy linked to her own trouble. Gary Busey, Marlee Matlin and Eric Roberts also star in this compelling and erotic thriller. 103 min.
64-9061 $99.99

Blowback (1999)
Police detective Mario Van Peebles thinks the nightmare is over when the Bible-quoting serial murderer he brought to justice is executed. But when the jurors from the killer's trial begin turning up dead, Van Peebles becomes convinced that it's not just a copycat...and that the madman is back for revenge. Pulse-pounding suspenser also stars James Remar, Stephen Caffrey. 95 min.
64-9062 $69.99

The Inspectors (1998)
Inspired by case files from the U.S. Postal Service, this gripping suspenser stars Lou Gossett, Jr. and Jonathan Silverman as postal inspectors trying to track down a mail-bomber terrorizing a Baltimore suburb. Evidence points to a Navy munitions expert, but where is he? With Tobias Mehler. 91 min.
67-9001   ☐$14.99

Safe House (1999)
Patrick Stewart is a one-time government agent suffering from Alzheimer's disease who believes a presidential candidate he was involved with in covert operations is out to kill him. To protect himself, Stewart stages complex drills in his surveillance-protected home with his caregiver. Hector Elizondo and Kimberly Williams also star in this unique thriller. 112 min.
67-9022   ☐$14.99

Fair Game (1991)
If you thought the battles in "War of the Roses" were tough, watch what happens when a vengeful husband puts his estranged wife in danger for her life, with some help from a lethal mamba snake. Suspenseful thriller stars Gregg Henry, Trudie Styler. 81 min.
68-1186 $89.99

Black Magic Woman (1990)
A love triangle charged with erotic passion turns into a deadly obsession in this sexy thriller of lust, revenge and murder. Mark Hamill, Amanda Wyss and Apollonia star. 91 min.
68-1187 $89.99

Highway Hitcher (1999)
A road trip for a man trying to forget his dead-end job and his wife's leaving him takes a deadly detour when the hitchhiker he picks up reveals he killed a woman. Gripping suspense tale stars William Forsythe, James LeGros, Elizabeth Peña. 89 min.
81-9092 $49.99

Suspicious Minds (1999)
Provocative sexpenser starring Patrick Bergin as a private detective hired to spy on the unfaithful wife of a wealthy businessman. When her lover is discovered murdered, the husband becomes the prime suspect, but further investigation leads Bergin to another suspect—and into the arms of the woman. With Jayne Heitmeyer, Gary Busey and Daniel Pilon. 93 min.
68-1930   ☐$99.99

Lulu On The Bridge (1998)
Novelist Paul Auster ("Smoke") wrote and directed this offbeat mystery starring Harvey Keitel as a jazz musician who has problems playing the saxophone after he's injured during a shooting. While recovering, Keitel finds a stone that is being sought by anthropologist Willem Dafoe and leads him to aspiring actress Mira Sorvino, with whom he has an affair. With Gina Gershon. 103 min.
68-1941   ☐$69.99

Agent Of Death (1999)
Facing a possible re-election loss, the President of the United States agrees to a fake kidnapping publicity stunt, but the hoax becomes real when a Secret Service operative turns double agent. Now the only person who can save the day is embittered CIA agent Eric Roberts, whose wife and daughter were killed during an assassination attempt on the President. Gripping thriller also stars Michael Madsen, Ice-T. 105 min.
68-1995   ☐$69.99

An Occasional Hell (1996)
An ex-cop and writer in a Southern town is asked by a beautiful woman to help her prove her innocence in the shooting death of her husband, a professor who was having an affair with a waitress, but as they're drawn to one another romantically, the truth behind the crime could prove deadly. Steamy suspenser stars Tom Berenger, Valeria Golino, Robert Davi, Kari Wuhrer. 93 min.
68-1828   Was $99.99   ☐$14.99

Martin Kemp   Kerry Hodge   Deborah Shelton
DESIRE
Power, Passion and Murder.

Desire (1995)
A killer is terrorizing Los Angeles, leaving his or her victims doused with Desire perfume. In order to find the culprit, the perfume company's sexy security chief goes undercover as a cop and soon finds herself encountering all sorts of suspects in this lurid thriller filled with strong sensuality. Kate Hodge, Deborah Shelton and Robert Miranda star. 90 min.
76-9083   Was $19.99 $14.99

Crimetime (1997)
From George Sluizer, the director of "The Vanishing," comes this intense thriller starring Stephen Baldwin as an actor playing a serial killer on a true crime TV show. Each new victim brings Baldwin and the program more attention, but the real culprit soon begins murdering just to see himself on TV. Pete Postlethwaite, Geraldine Chaplin, Sadie Frost and Karen Black also star. 95 min.
68-1832   ☐$99.99

Invasion Of Privacy (1997)
Josh and Theresa seemed like the perfect couple, but after he moves in with her, he begins to go into frightening rages. When Theresa discovers she's pregnant, she tries to hide out in a remote cottage, but Josh finds her and launches a terrifying reign of control that threatens her life. Johnathon Schaech, Mili Avital, David Keith and Naomi Campbell star. 95 min.
68-1833   Was $99.99   ☐$14.99

Sweet Murder (1993)
A beautiful young woman discovers that her shy and drab roommate is hiding a dark secret in her past. The roommate's desires to take on the persona of her new "friend" leads to murder. Helene Udy, Russell Todd and Embeth Davidtz star. 101 min.
68-1270 $89.99

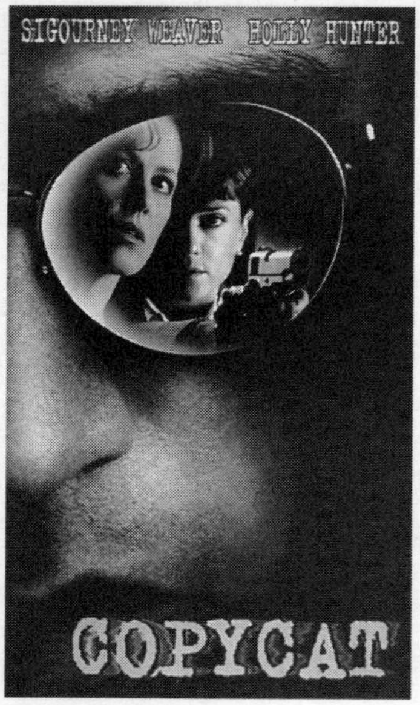
SIGOURNEY WEAVER HOLLY HUNTER
COPYCAT

Copycat (1995)
Gripping hit suspenser stars Holly Hunter as a San Francisco detective who seeks criminal psychologist Sigourney Weaver's help in solving a string of murders. They discover the culprit is basing his crimes on noted serial killers of the past, and Weaver could be his ultimate target. With Dermot Mulroney, William McNamara and Harry Connick, Jr. 123 min.
19-2427 Was $19.99 □$14.99

Iron Maze (1991)
Intense thriller set in a Pennsylvania mill town where an arrogant Japanese factory owner is found brutally beaten. A detective investigating the crime must discern the truth from the stories of two people: the victim's beautiful American wife and a former mill worker charged with the assault. Jeff Fahey, Bridget Fonda and J.T. Walsh star. 102 min.
71-5234 $19.99

Sex Crimes (1993)
A prominent political figure discovers that he's featured on a kinky porno tape. In order to save his career and personal life, he must infiltrate a web of blackmail and deceit in this high-energy erotic thriller. With Jack Klanz, Dave Schlesser and Margot Hope.
72-4006 Was $89.99 $19.99

Click:
The Calendar Girl Killings (1991)
Creepy thriller filled with eroticism and set in the world of high fashion photography, where a string of beautiful models are found dead. Ross Hagen, Gregory Scott Cummins, Troy Donahue, Keely Simms star.
72-4012 $19.99

Secret Sins (1994)
A wild, erotic thriller in which a beautiful woman working at a stock footage company discovers a TV star in a porno film clip. When the footage is found missing, the woman is falsely accused of stealing it. She enlists the help of a neighbor to help find the real culprits, but events take a sexy...and deadly...turn. Michelle McIntosh stars. 90 min.
72-4016 Was $59.99 $19.99

Child In The Night (1990)
A Seattle police detective teams with a child psychologist when the only witness to a murder is the victim's 8-year-old son. Shocked by the incident, the boy becomes unreachable, and it's up to the detective and psychologist to unravel his frightening story. Tom Skerritt, JoBeth Williams and Elijah Wood star. 93 min.
72-9000 Was $79.99 $14.99

Trade Secrets (1992)
A detective investigating the death of the heiress to a wine family's fortune is drawn to a beautiful family member who holds the key to the clan's darkest secrets. Erotic suspenser stars Sam Waterston, Lauren Hutton and Marisa Berenson. 91 min.
72-9010 Was $89.99 $14.99

Body Puzzle (1994)
A serial killer collecting body parts doesn't plan to stop the bloodshed until he gets them all. Strange clues left at each murder all seem to point to a beautiful woman, but is she the next victim or the maniac responsible for the killings? Chilling suspenser stars Joanna Pacula and was directed by Lamberto Bava (credited to "Larry Louis"). 98 min.
72-9033 Was $89.99 $14.99

Die Watching (1993)
A young video director records a number of Hollywood's hottest young starlets in kinky situations that satisfy his deranged fantasies. When he finds himself caught between a beautiful new discovery and her sexy friend, his murderous tendencies take over. Christopher Atkins, Tim Thomerson and Vali Ashton star. 92 min.
72-9019 Was $89.99 $14.99

True Crime (1995)
Crime-obsessed teenager Alicia Silverstone decides to launch her own investigation into the mutilation murder of a classmate. She finds a link between the killing and a travelling carnival, and teams with a handsome police cadet to uncover the culprit. But does her new ally know more than he's letting on? Kevin Dillon, Bill Nunn co-star. 94 min.
68-1368 Was $89.99 □$14.99

Danger Of Love (1995)
An unhappily married teacher has a passion-filled affair with a beautiful colleague, but on the very night he plans to call off the relationship, his wife is found brutally murdered. Is the killer the husband or the mistress...and who'll be the next victim? Seductive suspenser stars Joe Penny, Jenny Robertson, Richard Lewis, Fairuza Balk and Joseph Bologna. 95 min.
68-1783 $89.99

Separate Lives (1995)
Respected psychology professor Linda Hamilton, troubled by strange memories and dreams, hires ex-cop Jim Belushi to follow her day and night. What Belushi finds is that Hamilton is leading a subconscious second life in the city's erotic underworld. Suspenseful and sensual thriller also stars Vera Miles. 102 min.
68-1787 Was $89.99 □$14.99

In Dark Places (1997)
Following her father's death, Chapelle reunites with Chazz, her estranged half-brother, whom she decides must be killed in order to gain her father's fortune. Her plan involves luring Chazz and his friend Karl in a torrid love triangle. Joan Severance, Bryan Kestner and John Vargas star. 96 min.
68-1851 □$99.99

Top Of The World (1998)
A recently parolled convict rolls into Las Vegas with the intention of winning back his ex-wife. However, the stakes are raised when he is falsely accused of being a thief and finds himself the most hunted man in Nevada. Peter Weller, Tia Carrere, Dennis Hopper, Joe Pantoliano and David Alan Grier star. 98 min.
68-1890 □$99.99

Inferno (1998)
Ray Liotta awakens in the middle of the desert with amnesia. After befriending reclusive artist Gloria Reuben, Liotta tries to piece his life together and realizes he once had a huge batch of cash. Soon, his life is endangered when others looking for the loot try to find him. Armin Mueller-Stahl also stars. AKA: "Pilgrim." 94 min.
68-1997 □$79.99

The Perfect Tenant (1999)
In the tradition of "The Hand That Rocks the Cradle" comes this creepy thriller about a woman who rents out her guesthouse, over her daughter's objections, to a handsome, well-mannered young man. Little does she suspect that the tenant blames her for his father's suicide years earlier, and has planned out a deadly vengeance. Maxwell Caufield, Linda Purl, Tracy Nelson and Earl Holliman star. 93 min.
68-2004 □$69.99

Blue Desert (1991)
In this intense thriller, Courteney Cox plays a beautiful artist who heads to the desert for a vacation and soon finds herself befriended by a motorcycle-riding drifter. But the drifter is the quarry of the local lawman, and Cox must decide which man is really dangerous. Craig Sheffer and D.B. Sweeney also star. 98 min.
71-5217 $12.99

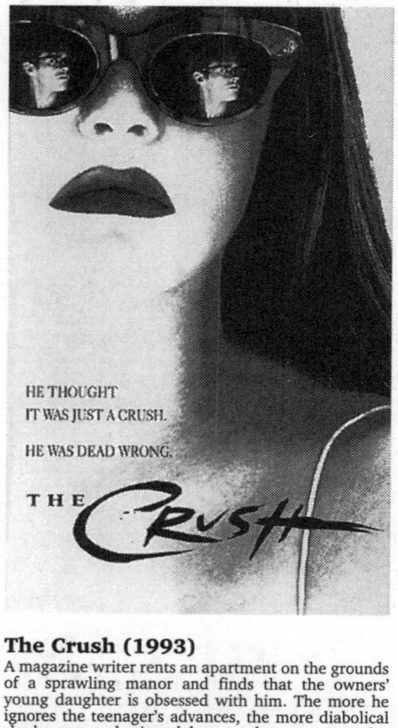
HE THOUGHT
IT WAS JUST A CRUSH.
HE WAS DEAD WRONG.
THE CRUSH

The Crush (1993)
A magazine writer rents an apartment on the grounds of a sprawling manor and finds that the owners' young daughter is obsessed with him. The more he ignores the teenager's advances, the more diabolical she becomes, plotting elaborate schemes to terrorize his new girlfriend and ruin his job and life. Cary Elwes, Jennifer Rubin, Alicia Silverstone star. 89 min.
19-2121 Was $19.99 □$14.99

Bodily Harm (1990)
A wealthy physician finds his life and practice threatened by a seductive patient who files a multi-million dollar malpractice suit against him. Who is the victim and who has murder in their heart forms the basis of this steamy mystery. Joe Penny, Lisa Hartman and Kathleen Quinlan star. 100 min.
72-9002 Was $79.99 $14.99

Body Shot (1993)
An L.A. photographer obsessed with shooting a gorgeous rock star for a tabloid newspaper discovers that she's been murdered and he's the prime suspect. Tantalizing, erotic thriller stars Robert Patrick and Michelle Johnson. 98 min.
72-9029 Was $89.99 $14.99

Casualties (1997)
Desperate to escape her brutal marriage to a violent cop, a woman turns for help to a handsome stranger who offers her a way out...but at what cost? Shocking suspense tale stars Caroline Goodall, Mark Harmon, Jon Gries. 85 min.
68-1857 Was $99.99 □$14.99

Lipstick Camera (1994)
A woman seeking a career in television news attempts to get her role model, a handsome newsman, to help her. When he refuses, she uses a friend's miniature camera to capture the newsman while he's on a mysterious assignment. What the camera reveals could give her the scoop of a lifetime...if she lives that long! Sizzling thriller stars Ele Keats, Terry O'Quinn, Charlotte Lewis. Unrated version; 93 min.
72-9031 Was $89.99 $14.99

Killing Obsession (1994)
After 20 years in prison, a psychotic killer is released and begins a search for Annie, the daughter of the woman he murdered. Although the murder occurred two decades earlier, he still thinks the woman—now 32—is 11 years old...and he plans to search through every "Annie" in the phone book until he finds the right one. John Saxon, John Savage and Kimberly Chase star. 95 min.
72-9036 Was $89.99 $14.99

Hard Drive (1994)
A man and woman share their secret desires through an interactive computer network. But when they want to make these fantasies a reality, they discover someone else is intercepting their communications and is steering them into new, dangerous areas. Steamy and erotic suspenser stars Matt McCoy, Edward Albert, Jr., Christina Fulton and Stella Stevens. Unrated version; 92 min.
72-9038 Was $89.99 $14.99

The Soft Kill (1994)
A no-nonsense private eye in Los Angeles is the main suspect when his girlfriend becomes a strangling victim, and with the police hot on his tail and more bodies being discovered, he must find out who's trying to frame him. Exciting thriller stars Michael Harris, Brion James, Corbin Bernsen and Carrie-Ann Moss. 95 min.
72-9040 Was $89.99 $14.99

Private Obsession (1994)
A beautiful fashion model is abducted and held prisoner by a demented fan who's determined to possess her all to himself. The woman must use her body and brains to turn the tables on her captor and attempt an escape in this scorching suspenser. Shannon Whirry, Michael Christian, Bo Svenson star. Ultra-steamy uncut version; 93 min.
72-9047 Was $89.99 $14.99

Virtual Desire (1995)
Stuck in a boring marriage, a man begins having a series of steamy affairs initiated by cruising the Internet. But there's a killer who's also on-line, and when the man's wife is found murdered, he becomes the prime suspect. Gail Harris, Julie Strain, Mike Meyer star. Uncut version; 92 min.
72-9058 Was $19.99 $14.99

Mother (1995)
M is for the manic way that mother Diane Ladd clings to her grown son, who wants to leave home. Mom, however, will stop at nothing to keep her baby boy with her, even...murder? Bizarre psychological shocker of obsessive love also stars Olympia Dukakis, Morgan Weisser, Ele Keats. 90 min.
72-9061 Was $79.99 $14.99

Public Access (1993)
The first feature from director Bryan Singer ("The Usual Suspects") is a creepy, award-winning account of life in small-town America. A public access TV show hosted by a mysterious stranger draws the attention of the people of Brewster, who are fascinated by the host's magnetic personality. Soon, many of the townspeople's disturbing lives are revealed. Ron Marquette stars. 90 min.
72-9065 Was $89.99 $14.99

Over The Wire (1996)
A telephone lineman overhears a conversation in which a woman makes arrangements for a hit man to murder her sister. The lineman sets out to prevent the killing, but soon discovers that getting involved with rival siblings leads to seduction—and danger. Shauna O'Brien, Griffin Drew star in this scorching thriller. Uncut, unrated version; 90 min.
72-9070 Was $99.99 $14.99

Dead On (1993)
Two married lovers think they've hit upon the perfect crime: murder each other's spouse and there'll be no motive to trace. But their scheme takes some unexpected turns in this ultra-steamy suspenser that mixes "Strangers on a Train" and "Fatal Attraction." Tracy Scoggins, Matt McCoy, Shari Shattuck and David Ackroyd star.
73-1139 □$14.99

Freeway (1996)
An edgy, erotic thriller in sheep's clothing, this creepy reworking of the "Red Riding Hood" story stars Reese Witherspoon as a teenager, sexually abused by her crack-smoking stepfather, who hitches a ride with a serial killer and faces a prison stint while trying to escape her home. Kiefer Sutherland, Brooke Shields, Dan Hedaya, Amanda Plummer also star. 102 min.
63-1862 Was $99.99 □$14.99

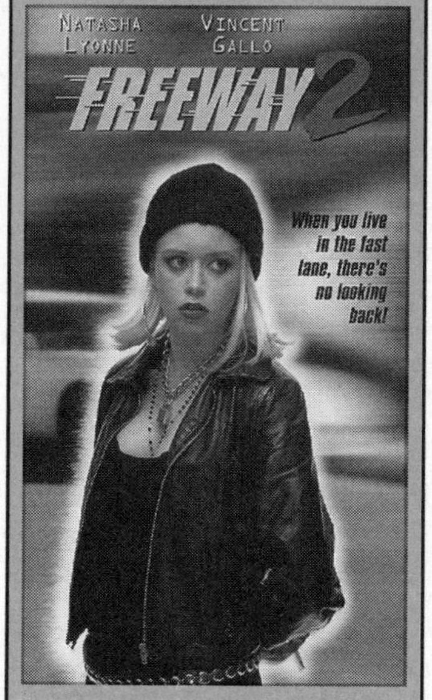
NATASHA LYONNE
VINCENT GALLO
FREEWAY 2
When you live in the fast lane, there's no looking back!

Freeway 2: Confessions Of A Trickbaby (1999)
Natasha Lyonne and Maria Celedonio are two teenage bad girls who escape from a juvenile prison and face violent altercations with several people they meet while on the lam. Their destination is Tijuana, where they hope to meet psychic Vincent Gallo, whose visions have had a powerful effect on them. But first they must elude a killer on their trail in this pseudo-sequel to "Freeway" from writer-director Matthew Bright. 90 min.
75-5055 $89.99

Silhouette (1998)
A group of people gather at the mansion of late millionaire Walter Huntington in hopes of learning of their inheritance from his will. Soon, the guests begin to die one at a time. Who is responsible for the murders? Taunya Dee, Clifford Dalton and Joe Wandell star. 90 min.
76-7398 $59.99

Whodunit? (1998)
This hip murder-mystery featuring an African-American cast tells of five friends who get together for a party and discover that an unexpected guest has been murdered. Soon, other guests are found dead and Solomon, one of the party-goers, attempts to uncover the killer. Chantal LaShon and Rockmond Dunbar star. 80 min.
76-7457 $19.99

China Moon (1994)
An atmospheric, surprise-filled film noir starring Ed Harris as a smalltown homicide detective involved with Madeleine Stowe, a gorgeous, mysterious woman. When Stowe's abusive husband dies, Harris and his partner are called in to conduct the investigation, and the detective soon becomes the prime suspect in the murder. Charles Dance and Benicio Del Toro co-star. 99 min.
73-1158 Was $89.99 □$14.99

Jigsaw (1999)
Talked into taking part in a drug deal that goes bad, a down-and-out prizefighter finds himself on the run from both sides of the law as he tries to figure out who killed his ex-girlfriend and left him to take the blame. Explosive suspense tale stars William Corino, Erica Ehm.
81-9097 $69.99

Killing For Love (1996)
In this sensual whodunit, a screenwriter upset at a producer for adding sex and violence to his scripts gets an invitation to spend a weekend at the producer's mountain cabin with his girlfriend and other couples. But soon fact and fiction mix as the guests are murdered one by one while in the throes of passion Lisa Haslehurst, Jay Richardson star. Uncut, unrated version; 90 min.
73-1256 $19.99

DVD VIDEO
ASK ABOUT OUR GIANT DVD CATALOG!

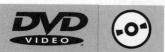

The Glass Cage (1996)
A scorching thriller set in New Orleans and featuring Charlotte Lewis as an exotic dancer involved with the mobster who owns the club where she performs. When her former flame takes a bartending job there, old passions re-ignite, but diamond smuggling, danger and that mobster get in the way of the ex-lovers' happiness. Richard Tyson, Eric Roberts also star. 96 min.
73-1257 *$19.99*

Final Justice (1994)
Three couples looking to spend a quiet weekend getaway at a remote lakeside cabin are instead caught in a deadly hostage situation in this taut thriller. James Brolin, Shawn Huff, Brent Huff star. AKA: "We the People." 90 min.
74-3035 *$89.99*

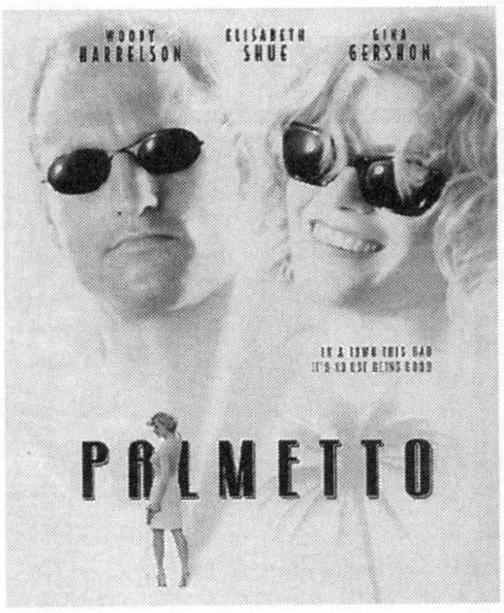

Palmetto (1998)
Atmospheric contemporary film noir showcasing Woody Harrelson as a former reporter and ex-con enlisted by Elisabeth Shue to take part in a kidnapping scheme involving her teenage stepdaughter in order to bilk her wealthy husband. Gina Gershon, Michael Rapaport and Chloe Sevigny also star in this steamy, set-in-Florida suspenser. 113 min.
19-2727 Was $99.99 *$14.99*

Midnight Blue (1996)
Martin, a lonely banker, has a heated sexual liaison with Martine, a beautiful woman, while on a trip to Atlanta. When Martin relocates to Los Angeles, he realizes that Georgine, his new boss's wife, looks exactly like Martine. After they have a seductive rendezvous, Martin finds himself drawn into a world of erotic deception. Damian Chapa, Annabel Schofield, Steve Kanaly and Dean Stockwell star. 95 min.
73-1262 *$19.99*

Russian Roulette (1993)
The Cold War is over, but for one American the danger has never been greater, as a teacher on vacation in Russia becomes involved in a deadly plot to smuggle Czarist treasures out of the country. Suspenser stars Barry Bostwick, Susan Blakely, E.G. Marshall. AKA: "Russian Holiday." 89 min.
76-9056 Was $19.99 *$14.99*

Improper Conduct (1994)
Erotically-charged thriller from the creator of "Night Eyes" about a woman who dies mysteriously after accusing her boss of sexual harassment. The woman's sister decides to use her own sensuality to get revenge. Steven Bauer, Tahnee Welch, Lee Anne Beaman, John Laughlin, Kathy Shower and Nia Peeples star. Unrated version; 97 min.
76-9063 Was $89.99 *$14.99*

The Mosaic Project (1993)
In this espionage adventure, two slackers from Fresno, California, accidentally discover computer chips that, when implanted in a brain, can transform a spy into a multi-lingual martial arts expert. When the government finds out of their discovery, it enlists them in a series of dangerous undercover assignments. Jon Tabler, Ben Marley, Julie Strain and Joe Estevez star. 89 min.
76-9075 Was $89.99 *$14.99*

Soft Deceit (1995)
A beautiful special police agent goes undercover to trap a clever criminal who's made off with a multi-million-dollar heist, but finds herself falling for her target, in this steamy thriller of deception and danger. Patrick Bergin, Kate Vernon, John Wesley Shipp star. 95 min.
18-7564 *$89.99*

The Beneficiary (1998)
In this sensual thriller, a woman doesn't know what's in store when she murders her wealthy, philandering husband and blames the murder on a fictional character she claims raped her. While waiting to collect on the insurance policy, she meets another man who learns of her scheme and wants in. Stacy Haiduk, Linden Ashby, Suzy Amis and Ron Silver star. 97 min.
73-1301 Was $59.99 *$14.99*

Almost Dead (1994)
When psychiatrist Shannon Doherty believes she's encountered the spirit of her late mother, who killed herself four years earlier, she returns to her hometown and learns that the search for the truth can be deadly. Spellbinding suspenser also stars Costas Mandylor.
76-9070 Was $89.99 *$14.99*

Crime Noir (1999)
Reminiscent of the classic crime dramas of the '30s and '40s, this stylish thriller follows a hard-up ex-policeman who is hired by a shady art collector to "recover" a valuable painting, but soon finds himself embroiled in a deadly case of deception, seduction and murder. With a bright young cast.
73-9340 *$39.99*

Cover Story (1994)
A man obsessed with a dead stripper attempts to piece together her past and soon finds himself exploring a world of ruthless street gangs, kinky underground cultures and sex nightclubs. William Wallace, Christopher McDonald, Robert Forster and Tuesday Knight star in this sensual suspenser. 93 min.
74-3008 *$49.99*

Condition Red (1995)
A male guard at a woman's maximum security prison falls in love with a seductive inmate and, when she tells him she's pregnant, helps arrange her escape. Now on the run from the law, the two are caught in a deadly and deceptive love triangle in this tense suspense tale shot in Philadelphia's Eastern State Prison. James Russo, Cynda Williams and Paul Calderon star. 85 min.
74-3027 *$89.99*

Broken Trust (1993)
After inheriting a large estate, a beautiful woman finds herself the target of her greedy relatives, who will stop at nothing to get a piece of the action. Intriguing, sensual thriller stars Nick Cassavetes, Kimberly Foster and Don Swayze. 85 min.
76-9048 Was $19.99 *$14.99*

The Ice Runner (1993)
A U.S. spy stationed in the Soviet Union is betrayed by the CIA and sent to a prison camp. After assuming the identity of a dead thief, he's transferred to a minimum security camp, but when the cruel camp commander suspects something isn't right, the dead man's wife is called in to expose him. Edward Albert, Victor Wong, Olga Kabo and Basil Hoffman star.
76-9052 Was $89.99 *$14.99*

Trial By Jury (1994)
Suspenseful courtroom thriller starring Joanne Whalley-Kilmer as a single mother on the jury for the trial of mobster Armand Assante. D.A. Gabriel Byrne thinks he's about to convict the hood, but when Whalley-Kilmer receives threats on her son's life if she votes "guilty," the fate of the trial is threatened. William Hurt also stars. 107 min.
19-2291 Was $19.99 *$14.99*

Diabolique (1996)
Suspenseful reworking of the classic 1955 French thriller features Sharon Stone as the mistress of boys' school headmaster Chazz Palminteri who plots with Isabelle Adjani, the man's wife, to murder him. After poisoning, then drowning Palminteri, the women think the deed is done...until his corpse disappears. Kathy Bates, Spalding Gray also star. 107 min.
19-2460 Was $99.99 *$19.99*

Blackwater Trail (1997)
Judd Nelson is a reporter who returns to his hometown to attend the funeral of a friend who killed himself. But Nelson suspects the death was actually a murder, and soon finds himself tracking down a serial killer who leaves passages from the Bible as clues. Dee Smart and Rowena Wallace also star. 100 min.
19-2530 Was $99.99 *$19.99*

Random Encounter (1998)
Elizabeth Berkley is a beautiful and talented executive whose sensual encounter with a mysterious stranger leads to a series of horrific events and terror. Can that stranger, who appeared handsome and charming, be responsible?
81-9058 *$99.99*

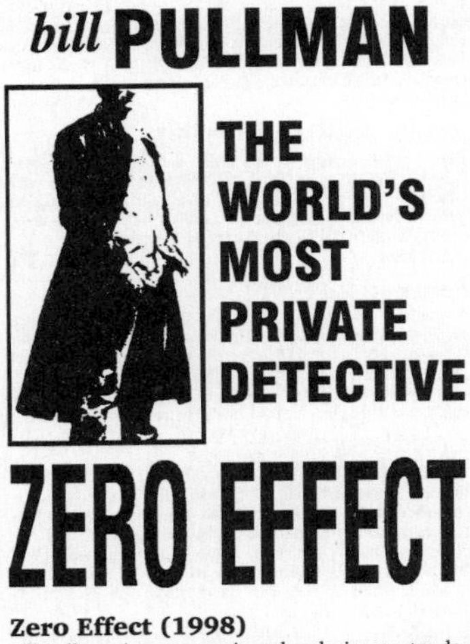

Zero Effect (1998)
Bill Pullman is an eccentric and reclusive master detective hired by wealthy Ryan O'Neal to find a lost key to a safety deposit box that holds evidence linking him to a crime. With help from hip attorney partner Ben Stiller, Pullman uses his unorthodox methods to find the key and sort out all of the surprises tied to the case. Written and directed by Jake Kasdan (Lawrence's son). 116 min.
19-2729 Was $99.99 *$14.99*

When The Bough Breaks (1994)
A female homicide investigator for the Texas Rangers draws a close bond with a mentally disturbed boy who appears to have a psychic connection to a serial killer stalking the Houston area. What does the child know, and will the investigator survive a series of harrowing events to uncover his secret? Ally Walker, Martin Sheen and Ron Perlman star. 103 min.
18-7526 *$89.99*

When The Bough Breaks II: Perfect Prey (1998)
A serial killer is preying on young women in the Lone Star State. Texas Ranger special investigator Audrey Macleah (Kelly McGillis) is determined to track down the murderer, but when the crimes prove to have a connection to Macleah's past, she realizes that she may be the killer's next prey. Spine-tingling suspenser also stars Bruce Dern, David Keith, D.W. Moffett. 99 min.
19-2790 *$99.99*

The November Conspiracy (1996)
A gorgeous reporter assigned to cover a senator's presidential campaign must fight for her life when, after a series of assassination attempts, she receives information that will expose a high-level Washington conspiracy. Gripping political thriller stars Paige Turco, Dirk Benedict, George Segal, Elliott Gould and Conrad Janis, who also directed. 103 min.
73-1265 *$14.99*

Night Of The Archer (1998)
Erotic suspenser in which Travis, a Las Vegas gambler on the run from mob hit men, lands at a mysterious chateau where Reggie, a hot-shot gambler and art dealer, is holding an archery competition for his bow-and-arrow expert daughter. When Reggie is found murdered, Travis is singled out as a suspect. Barbara Carrera, Joseph Bologna and Jeff Griggs stars. 100 min.
73-9294 *$59.99*

Asylum (1996)
An investigator experiencing emotional problems discovers that the only person who can help him—his psychiatrist—has committed suicide. Teamed with a mental patient, the investigator searches for answers to his doctor's death and eventually comes face to face with a deadly serial killer. Robert Patrick, Malcolm McDowell and Sarah Douglas star.
76-9096 Was $19.99 *$14.99*

Seeds Of Doubt (1998)
A beautiful reporter is convinced that an artist has been wrongfully imprisoned for murdering a model. After receiving no help from her police detective ex-lover, the reporter writes a series of articles that helps get the artist out of jail. But when strange things soon happen and a murder occurs, she begins to worry. Alberta Watson, Joe Lando and Peter Coyote star. 94 min.
76-9097 Was $19.99 *$14.99*

Teach Me Tonight (1998)
After her drug-dealing boyfriend is viciously murdered, Janey seeks help from her ex-lover's professor boss and his wife. Soon, Janey's enticed into kinky sexual interludes with the couple and learns of shocking evidence in her lover's death. Judy Thompson, Kim Yates and Jack Becker star. Unrated version features 19 minutes of scorching extra footage. 93 min.
76-9109 Was $39.99 *$14.99*

In A Moment Of Passion (1993)
An American actress carries on a scorching affair with the star of a movie she's making in Germany. But the series of horrifying murders occuring at an estate where the film's cast is staying makes the actress question her lover's true intentions. Maxwell Caulfield, Vivian Schilling and Jeff Conaway star. 100 min.
80-1058 Was $89.99 *$14.99*

Trapped (1994)
In this tale of seduction and lust, a wealthy lawyer plots to have his ex-centerfold wife murdered after he has a heated affair with her best friend. The attorney springs his wife's former lover from prison to commit the act, but an obsessed fan's plans disrupt the scheme. Paul Winfield, Pamela Bryant, James Van Patten star. Unrated version; 90 min.
81-9011 *$89.99*

The Best Revenge (1998)
After his wife is horribly tortured and murdered in El Salvador, a man heads to Los Angeles in search of the culprit. He believes he has found him in an American CIA advisor, but when he begins to carry out his plot of revenge, he realizes he may have the wrong person. Carlos Riccelli and Robert Pine star.
81-9062 *$99.99*

Cold Heaven (1992)
Theresa Russell and Mark Harmon heat up the screen in director Nicolas Roeg's mystifying thriller involving seduction, deception and death...and what lies beyond. James Russo, Will Patton, Talia Shire also star. 78 min.
80-1041 Was $89.99 *$14.99*

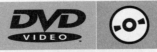

Rear Window (1998)
Christopher Reeve returns to acting in this gripping remake of the 1954 Alfred Hitchcock thriller, playing an architect confined to a wheelchair after a car accident. Unable to leave his apartment, Reeve begins spying on his neighbors and becomes convinced that one of them is a murderer. Daryl Hannah, Robert Forster and Richie Coster also star. 89 min.
88-1183 Was $19.99 *$14.99*

Friction (1997)
Struggling college student Natalie takes a job as an exotic dancer after she gets into financial trouble. Her gorgeous body and bold dance moves intoxicate the patrons of a men's club and she becomes a top draw. But Denise, another performer, becomes jealous, and plots a way to stop Natalie's success. Elizabeth Wagner, Jennifer Wolf star. Unrated version.
81-9030 *$14.99*

Stir (1998)
Following her husband's mysterious death in a hotel room, Kelly Bekins and her son return to the crime scene to try to bring closure to their pain. Instead, they begin to uncover a conspiracy of deceit after the boy realizes he witnessed his father's murder...and the killer comes after him. Traci Lords and Tony Todd star.
81-9055 *$89.99*

The List (1999)
High-class call girl Mädchen Amick orchestrates her own arrest so she can blackmail her clients. On her list are the names of some powerful figures, including judges, lawyers and even the governor of the state. Judge Ryan O'Neal faces a dilemma because many of his friends are on the list, and threats, an attack on Amick and a murder heighten the danger. With Ben Gazzara. 93 min.
81-9114 *$99.99*

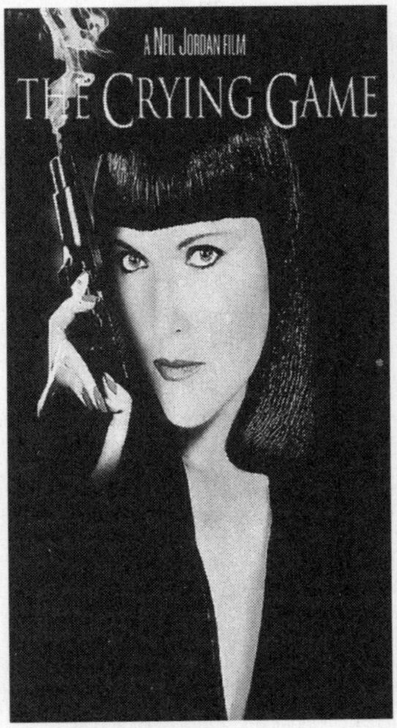

The Crying Game (1992)
Writer/director Neil Jordan's acclaimed, surprise-filled thriller about an I.R.A. fighter who leaves Ireland for England and begins an affair with a former prisoner's "girlfriend," a hairdresser working in London's seamy East End. But his old allies won't let the past stay buried, and an already volatile situation becomes deadly. Stephen Rea, Miranda Richardson, Forest Whitaker and Jaye Davidson star. 112 min.
27-6807 Was $19.99 *$14.99*

Perfect Assassins (1998)
Dr. Ben Carroway, an FBI profiler, must use a series of clues to track down a killer who has been terrorizing people on the streets. The clues lead Carroway to a compound in Mexico where killers are trained for murder without remorse or conscience. Andrew McCarthy, Robert Patrick, Nick Mancuso and Portia De Rossi star.
81-9064 *$99.99*

Captive (1998)
Intense thriller about an advertising exec who conspires with his female work partner to kidnap the son of their wealthy boss and cash in on a big ransom. After a series of dangerous misguided events occur, the man realizes that he may be a pawn in a more complicated plot concocted by his co-worker. Richard Grieco, Paul Hopkins and Marie-Josee Croze.
81-9065 *$99.99*

Trust Me (1995)
After she sees a video that features her senator boyfriend cheating on her, a young woman takes to the road with the tape and a charming young hit man. Soon, she's pursued by the senator's henchmen in this wild, unpredictable thriller. Theresa Tinling, Bob Morrisey and Adrian LaTourelle star.
82-5014 *$69.99*

Powder Burn (1996)
In this erotic suspense opus, a world-weary Beverly Hills private detective who once worked for the LAPD finds a simple case involving a cheating wife may involve murder, with him being set up to take the fall. Jay Irwin and Elizabeth Barry star.
82-5029 *$79.99*

Rift (1994)
Guilt and romantic longing play important parts in this New York independent film about a man who finally gets his chance with a woman he has obsessed over after her marriage dissolves. When he begins to have nightmares involving murder, he seeks help from a psychiatrist, but do the dreams have ties to reality? William Sage, Jennifer Bransford star. 85 min.
82-5034 *$59.99*

Starstruck (1996)
A sleazy Hollywood agent lands his clients "killer" jobs—acting in films in which they are really tortured and murdered. But the 10-percenter gets more than he bargained for when his niece appears for a casting call and he has to figure out a way to save her. Karen Black, Lawrence Tierney, Julie Strain and Joe Estevez star. 90 min.
82-5041 *$89.99*

Death And Desire (1997)
After his wife dies in a tragic accident, a fashion photographer throws himself into his work, oblivious to the beautiful models he works with. Eventually, he gets involved with the gorgeous editor of a fashion magazine, but when she becomes obsessed with him, he finds himself part of a deadly relationship. Tane McClure, Tim Abell star. Unrated version; 84 min.
82-5052 *$59.99*

Suicide Ride (1997)
A man desperate to end his own life makes an arrangement with a killer-for-hire, only to find himself trapped on the wrong side of the gun. Tim Quill, Matthias Hues and Frank Adonis star in this hard-hitting thriller. 86 min.
82-5056 *$89.99*

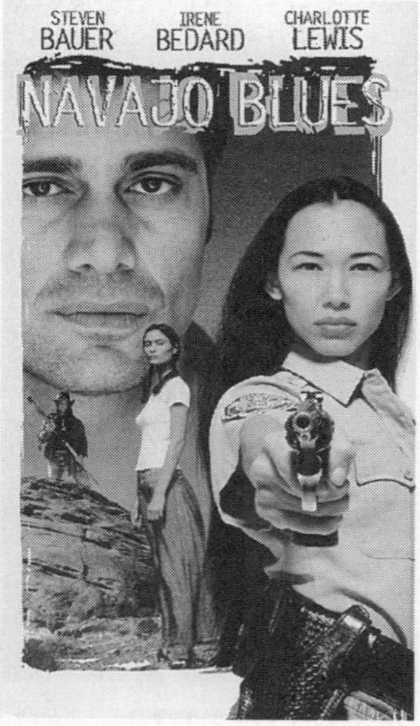

Navajo Blues (1997)
After his partner is murdered, police detective Nicholas Epps joins the witness protection program in order to dodge mob assassins. He becomes an Indian Affairs Liaison on the Navajo Indian reservation, but soon a series of murders and thefts put him on the defensive again. And the mobsters are hot on his trail, too. Steven Bauer, Irene Bedard and Charlotte Lewis star. 99 min.
83-1164 Was $99.99 *$14.99*

Seduction Of Innocence (1998)
Inspired by real events, this thriller stars Playboy Playmates T.J. Myers and Erica Palmer as two small-town girls who travel to Dallas to stay with Myers' older sister, a stripper working in a club run by the Mob. Only an undercover cop trying to stop the mobsters can stop them going down the same dangerous path. Unrated version; 103 min.
82-5057 *$59.99*

Blood Money (1999)
Lori Petty is an exotic dancer who finds her life threatened when she witnesses the murder of two Mafia assassins. Two police detectives try to protect Petty, but the hit squad will stop at nothing to find her. Michael Ironside, Currie Graham also star. 95 min.
82-5156 *$89.99*

Jaded (1999)
Ultra-sexy, somewhat disturbing thriller in which an innocent young woman is befriended by two hot women at a small-town bar, then discovers they have more in store for her than she originally thought. Carla Gugino, Rya Kihlstedt, Christopher McDonald and Anna Thomson star. 95 min.
82-5157 *$89.99*

Mischievous (1998)
At a 10-year high school reunion, a man reacquaints himself with an old flame he remembers as being emotionally unstable. He learns that she gets excited from a series of sexual dares, and he's soon part of her games. But things get dangerous as the dares turn into highly erotic cat-and-mouse games. Doug Jeffrey, Jennifer Burton ("Playtime") star. Unrated version; 95 min.
82-5059 *$79.99*

Starved (1998)
He uses flowers, candles and erotic notes to win over women he wants to meet. But it's not until it's too late that his latest target realizes her date is a psychotic who will abduct her and keep her captive as he tries to break her will. Lee Anne Beaman and Hal Adams star in this creepy suspenser based on a true story. 86 min.
82-5072 *$99.99*

Pressure Point (1998)
A CIA operative who has been falsely imprisoned has one chance for freedom. He must stop a radical militia targeting Washington, D.C., in this political thriller starring Steve Railsback, Larry Linville and Don Mogavero. 102 min.
82-5089 *$89.99*

Mind Lies (1998)
When his investigation into a series of fatal stabbings leads to his own brother becoming a suspect, a veteran detective teams with his estranged sibling to uncover the truth behind the murders. Gripping suspenser stars Dennis Christopher, Charles Hallahan, Tippi Hedren and Max Gail. 95 min.
82-5094 *$89.99*

Captured (1999)
A car thief picks the wrong target when he tries to swipe a high-tech Porsche but is trapped inside by its demented, power-infatuated owner. The owner puts the thief through hell by subjecting him to torture by remote control in a battle of wills that spirals out of control. Andrew Divoff and Nick Mancuso star in this wild thriller. 95 min.
82-5116 *$99.99*

Motel Blue (1998)
Intense thriller stars Soleil Moon Frye as a Department of Defense agent assigned to look into scientist Sean Young's life for security reasons. Frye discovers that Young's lavish lifestyle doesn't gel with her earnings and that she may be involved in selling secrets. With Seymour Cassel, Robert Vaughn. 96 min.
82-5131 *$89.99*

Nowhere Land (1998)
High-octane thriller starring "Starship Troopers" femme fighter Dina Meyer as a gutsy gal enlisted by the FBI to keep a key witness alive and away from mobsters. Peter Dobson, Jon Polito and Francesco Quinn also star. 88 min.
82-5182 *$59.99*

Tripfall (1999)
Corporate exec John Ritter, wife Rachel Hunter and their children take a much-needed vacation in California, where they draw the attention of crook Eric Roberts and his motley crew. Roberts and company kidnap Hunter and the kids, then ask Ritter for $1.2 million in ransom money. Can Ritter save them? 95 min.
82-5193 *$89.99*

The Witness Files (1999)
Special effects artist Yancy Butler must use her expertise to stay alive after she witnesses a brutal mob slaying. Posing as different characters in a variety of disguises, Butler finds that she can no longer tell who to trust and who is out to silence her for good in this gripping suspenser. David Nerman also stars. 97 min.
82-5196 *$99.99*

Psychopath (1997)
Mädchen Amick is a gorgeous D.A. who teams with a crafty police detective to track down a killer targeting female law students. With Bruce Dinsmore and Chris Mulkey. AKA: "Twist of Fate." 95 min.
82-5197 *$99.99*

Cappuccino (1997)
A '90s film noir with slick visuals and frightening twists. Nothing is what it seems when Victor, a successful young writer frustrated in his boring marriage, starts a passionate affair with a mysterious woman whom he only knows by what she drinks. His wife, trying to keep their marriage together, discovers the truth about her but realizes it may be too late. James Black, Angelle Brooks and Jennifer Lee star. 96 min.
73-9247 Was $59.99 *$19.99*

Deceptions (1990)
Harry Hamlin and Nicollette Sheridan sizzle in this thrilling contemporary film noir. He's the detective investigating the mysterious circumstances surrounding the death of her husband. His passion for her leads him into a web of intrigue and, possibly, murder. Robert Davi also stars. 105 min.
63-1397 *$14.99*

Deceptions II: Edge Of Deception (1995)
Scorching thriller focuses on a voyeuristic detective whose obsesssion with a gorgeous neighbor takes an unusual turn when, at the same time, he's pulled into a web of passion and betrayal by an attractive reporter. Soon, both romances intersect, leading the detective into danger. Mariel Hemingway, Stephen Shellen and Jennifer Rubin star. 100 min.
19-3778 *$89.99*

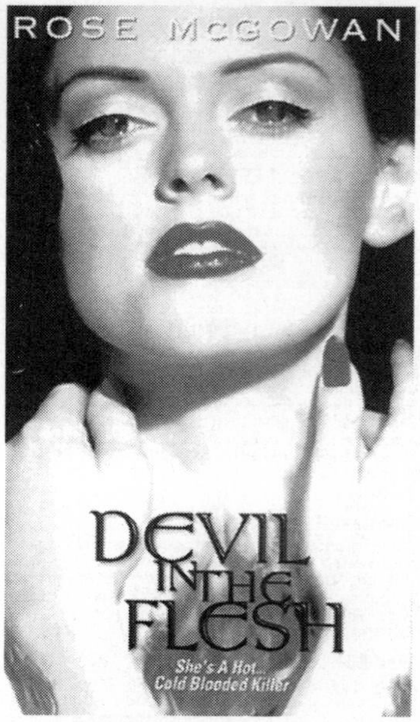

Devil In The Flesh (1998)
"Scream's" Rose McGowan is Debbie Strand, the new girl in school with some unusual things on her agenda. She tries to seduce her teacher and enjoys murdering fellow students using a variety of unusual objects. This nasty and kinky thriller also stars Alex McArthur and Sheri Rose. 92 min.
83-1287 Was $89.99 *$14.99*

Y2K: Year To Kill (1999)
On January 1, 2000, the Y2K bug has turned all of technology into a shambles. Looters and killers run rampant in the streets. Amidst this frightening turmoil, a reluctant young gang member discovers love with a woman, but can they avoid the danger that awaits them? Alex Anagnostou and Melody Moore star. 98 min.
82-5135 *$99.99*

Hidden Agenda (1999)
Kevin Dillon arrives in Berlin in hopes of seeing his brother, only to learn he's been killed in an accident. When he's offered a computer disc that belonged to his brother, Dillon suspects foul play and is soon enmeshed in espionage involving the CIA and the STASI, the former East German secret police. Christopher Plummer, J.T. Walsh and Michael Wincott also star. 97 min.
82-5147 *$89.99*

The Fall (1998)
This suspenser tells of Adam, a former prosecutor working on a novel, and Lisa, a financier, two Americans living in Paris who find themselves caught in a web of deception and danger. When Marta, a Budapest native, gets involved with the duo, a seductive game of cat-and-mouse ensues. Craig Sheffer, Jurgen Prochnow and Hélène de Fougerolles star. 90 min.
82-5159 *$89.99*

The Witness (1999)
A youngster accidentally overhears a devious developer's plans to burn a museum down in order to obtain the land, and now he and his friend must run for their lives as he tries to convince the authorities he's telling the truth. Nail-biting suspenser stars John Heard, Patrick Thomas, Chris Heyerdahl. 95 min.
82-5164 *$89.99*

Kate's Addiction (1999)
Desire turns deadly in this twisted suspense tale starring Kari Wuhrer as Kate, who goes off the deep end when she learns that friend Farrah Forke is going to get married and stops at nothing to halt the planned nuptials. With Matthew Porretta. 97 min.
82-5165 *$89.99*

Scorned 2 (1996)
A teacher having marital problems falls for a gorgeous student. When his wife discovers the illicit affair, she turns on her own seductive charms. But this sensual love triangle eventually leads to danger and, possibly, murder. Tane McClure and Wendy Schumacher star in this heated thriller. Uncut, unrated version; 102 min.
83-1121 Was $99.99 *$14.99*

The Killing Jar (1997)
In a picturesque town, Michael Sanford tries to piece together parts of his shattered memory in order to prove himself innocent of a brutal murder he's accused of. More murders occur, and Sanford finds himself in a race against time to stop them and save himself. Brett Cullen, Tamlyn Tomita and Wes Studi star. 101 min.
83-1131 Was $99.99 *$14.99*

The Boys Club (1997)
A remote clubhouse is a refuge from family and school pressures for a trio of adolescent boys, but it becomes a place of danger when they find a mysterious, wounded stranger hiding out there. Unusual and gripping suspense drama stars Chris Penn, Devon Sawa, Stuart Stone. 92 min.
83-1139 Was $99.99 *$14.99*

Stranger By Night (1994)
A serial killer is stalking the streets of the city, and two detectives investigating the bloody trail of bodies soon learn that the murderer may be one of their own. Intense suspenser stars Steven Bauer, William Katt, Jennifer Rubin. 96 min.
83-1021 Was $89.99 *$14.99*

Undercover (1994)
A beautiful detective trying to track down a murderer gets a job at a high-priced bordello catering to the city's rich and elite, but as she gets closer to solving the case she's drawn into a seductive world of sexual fantasy. Steamy and exciting thriller stars Athena Massey, Tom Tayback, Meg Foster. Unrated version; 93 min.
83-1028 Was $89.99 *$14.99*

Object Of Obsession (1994)
What began as a wrong number and grew into a passionate affair for a young woman and a handsome stranger turns into a twisted, dangerous showdown in this tale of sexual desire and fatal revenge. Erika Anderson, Scott Valentine, Liza Whitcraft star. 91 min.
83-1037 Was $89.99 *$14.99*

Dead Funny (1995)
Suspenseful mystery/comedy about a woman and her eccentric painter boyfriend who carry on a wild romance filled with passion and bizarre practical jokes. When the painter is found murdered on the kitchen table, his lover and a friend trace the relationship to try to figure out who the killer is. Elizabeth Peña, Andrew McCarthy and Paige Turco star. 81 min.
83-1039 *$89.99*

Terrified (1995)
A beautiful young woman whose husband killed her lover and then himself becomes the object of desire for a mysterious stalker who follows and assaults her. Is the nightmare over, or will the predator strike again? Spine-tingling suspenser stars Heather Graham, Lisa Zane. 95 min.
83-1077 Was $99.99 *$14.99*

Body Of Influence 2 (1996)
A sexy new patient spells temptation for a psychiatrist who falls under her seductive spell—and trouble when her jealous husband enters the picture—in this intense and erotic tale of fatal passions. Daniel Anderson, Jodie Fisher star. Uncut, unrated version; 90 min.
83-1084 Was $99.99 *$14.99*

Suite 16 (1996)
A seafront hotel on the French Riviera is the site of this kink-o-rama about a young Dutch man who blackmails older women for sexual favors. When he thinks he has killed one of the women, he takes refuge in the suite of a wealthy, wheelchair-bound Englishman, who spies on his new partner's erotic encounters. Pete Postlethwaite, Antonie Kamerling star. Uncut, unrated version; 93 min.
83-1114 Was $99.99 *$14.99*

Diary Of A Serial Killer (1997)
A writer accidentally stumbles onto a brutal murder and becomes the reluctant interviewer of the vicious killer, launching him down a terrifying trail of bodies that could end with his own death. Chilling suspense story stars Gary Busey, Michael Madsen, Arnold Vosloo, Julia Campbell. 92 min.
83-1183 Was $99.99 *$14.99*

Sweet Evil (1995)
A childless couple thinks their prayers have been answered when a young woman agrees to be a surrogate mother and moves in with them. Little do they suspect that the woman is the most "psycho" mother since Mrs. Bates, and she's got her own plans for "family togetherness." Bridgette Wilson, Scott Cohen and Peter Boyle star in this spine-chilling suspenser. 95 min.
83-1187 *$14.99*

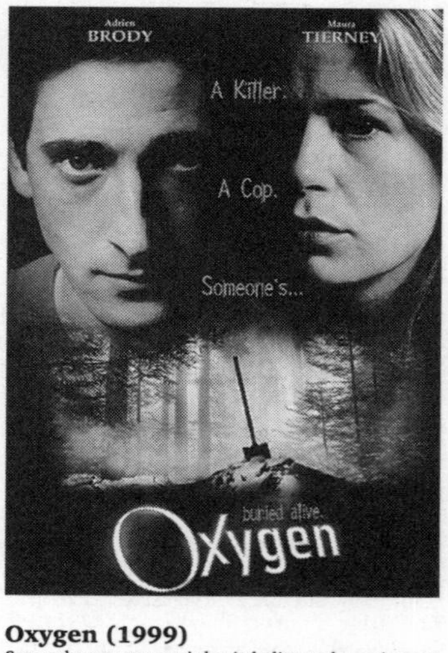

Oxygen (1999)
Somewhere a woman is buried alive and running out of air. Her only chance for survival lies with a troubled female cop who must confront her own demons if she is to win the battle of wits with the victim's abductor. Compelling suspense tale stars Maura Tierney, Adrien Brody, Dylan Baker. 92 min.
83-1494 Was $79.99 *$14.99*

The Settlement (1999)
Darkly comic thriller about two creeps who buy life insurance policies from the terminally ill, then bet on them to die on schedule. With their fortunes failing after some bad buys, the men join Russian mobsters in fronting a sickly woman $500,000 for her $2 million insurance policy. But is she really about to die? Kelly McGillis, John C. Reilly, William Fichtner star. 95 min.
82-5179 *$89.99*

Eye (1996)
In this riveting suspense effort, a tense cat-and-mouse game develops between a woman and an ex-con whom she helped send to prison. When the former convict kidnaps the woman's daughter, she has only a few hours to save her. Graham Greene, Nancy Beatty and Genevieve Bujold star. AKA: "Dead Innocent." 90 min.
82-5204 *$59.99*

Fallen Angel (1998)
Alexandra Paul is a Philadelphia detective looking forward to her 10-year high school reunion who gets a rude awakening when she discovers several of her classmates have been brutally murdered. Her investigation leads to a former classmate out for revenge for an incident that occurred years earlier. Anthony Michael Hall, Vlasta Vrana and Michelle Johnson also star. AKA: "Reunion." 90 min.
82-5208 *$99.99*

Sexual Malice (1994)
Scorching sexual suspense story from the creators of "Animal Instincts" in which a beautiful woman has an explosive affair with a mysterious stranger when her marriage becomes boring. Their no-holds-barred relationship turns deadly when the stranger begins tormenting his new lover. Diana Barton, Chad McQueen and Kathy Shower star. Uncut, unrated version; 96 min.
83-1003 *$14.99*

Last Breath (1998)
What would make a happily married man, whose terminally ill wife has days to live without a double lung transplant, seek solace in the arms of another woman? Is it forbidden love—or does he have a sinister fate in store for his new love? Gripping thriller stars Luke Perry, Gia Carides, Francie Swift. 90 min.
83-1229 Was $99.99 *$14.99*

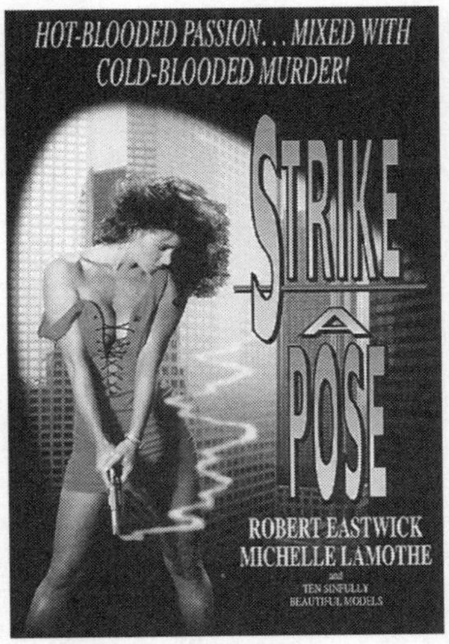
HOT-BLOODED PASSION... MIXED WITH COLD-BLOODED MURDER!
STRIKE A POSE
ROBERT EASTWICK
MICHELLE LAMOTHE

Strike A Pose (1993)
A policeman, his beautiful photographer girlfriend and a group of high fashion models are the targets of a rapist who has escaped from prison. This high-energy thriller offers excitement and erotic thrills set in the underground lesbian fashion scene. Robert Eastwick, Michelle Lamothe star. Unrated version; 86 min.
86-1073 Was $89.99 ❑*$14.99*

Interlocked (1998)
A steamy night on the Internet causes a seemingly innocent chat room romp into a dangerous game of deception and murder. Daytime TV sensations Jeff Trachta, Schae Harrison, Sandra Ferguson, George Alvarez and Maitland Ward star. 94 min.
83-1251 Was $99.99 *$14.99*

Wicked Ways (1999)
Gripping suspenser stars Rebecca DeMornay as a happily married woman...happily, that is, until she learns husband Michael Rooker has another wife in a different city! In order to teach him a lesson, jealous DeMornay concocts a scheme involving the seduction of another man, but her plan leads everyone into the danger zone. With Lisa Zane. AKA: "A Table for One." 110 min.
83-1466 Was $99.99 *$14.99*

Stranger Than Fiction (1999)
The line between fiction and reality becomes blurred, smeared and darn near torn to shreds in this surprising and quirky thriller about four twentysomethings in Utah whose friendship gets a fatal test when they have to cover up a murder. MacKenzie Astin, Todd Field, Dina Meyer and Natasha Gregson Wagner star. 100 min.
83-1500 *$99.99*

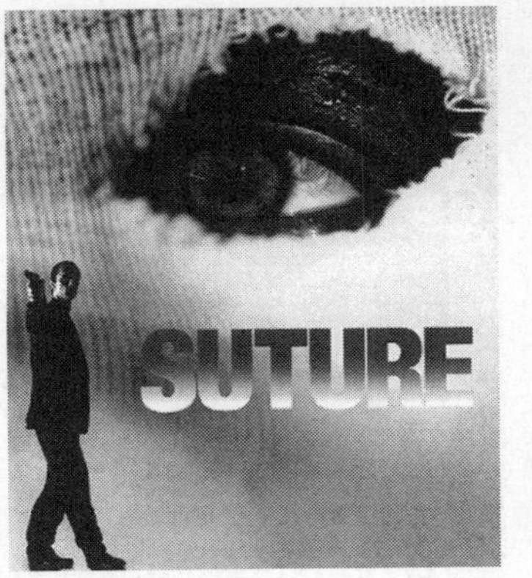
SUTURE

Suture (1995)
Eerie tale of identity crises about two "identical" brothers (played by African-American Dennis Haysbert and Caucasian Michael Harris) who meet for the first time after their father's mysterious death. Harris hatches a scheme to kill Haysbert and then impersonate him and collect his inheritance, but the plan takes a strange twist. Shot in black-and-white, this independent psychological thriller also stars Mel Harris. 96 min.
88-1007 Was $19.99 ❑*$14.99*

The Brutal Truth (1999)
A group of nine high school buddies is reunited 10 years later for a retreat at a remote mountain cabin. But this is no "Big Chill," because one of the friends has a shocking announcement to make, one that exposes erotic secrets and leads to a violent conclusion. Gripping suspenser stars Christina Applegate, Paul Gleason, Justin Lazard, Molly Ringwald and Jonathon Schaech. AKA: "The Giving Tree." 89 min.
83-1524 *$79.99*

The 4th Floor (1999)
A young woman is excited to be moving into her first apartment, but the mysterious goings-on of her downstairs neighbors are just the tip of the iceberg as she's propelled into a nightmarish series of bizarre occurrences that threaten her sanity...and perhaps her life. Juliette Lewis, William Hurt, Shelley Duvall and Austin Pendleton star in this eerie thriller. 90 min.
83-1556 *$99.99*

Striking Poses (1997)
Shannen Doherty is a photographer for a tabloid magazine who is pursued by a ruthless stalker. Her plan is to stop him and make some money in the process. But how dangerous will things get? Colm Feore also stars in this thriller. 99 min.
83-5714 *$89.99*

For Hire (1999)
After he's diagnosed with a terminal illness, Chicago cabbie and part-time actor Rob Lowe agrees to murder a drug dealer threatening one of his customers, writer Joe Mantegna, so he'll have money to leave his family. Before too long Lowe realizes he's become a pawn in a deadly double-cross in this compelling suspenser. 96 min.
85-1225 *$59.99*

Bittersweet (1998)
Four years after she takes the fall for her sleazy boyfriend in a bank robbery, Angie Everhart gets out of prison with a revenge plan. She joins forces with James Russo, a detective who has followed her story, to nail her boyfriend and his crimelord boss. With Eric Roberts, Brian Wimmer and Joe Penny. 96 min.
85-1315 *$99.99*

Sinful Intrigue (1995)
The women of a well-to-do neighborhood are being attacked by a mysterious psychopath, and four ladies with sexual skeletons in their closets may be the next victims...unless one of them is the stalker! Sinister, sensual suspense tale stars Griffin Drew, Bobby Johnston. 76 min.
86-1097 Was $89.99 ❑*$14.99*

Conspiracy Of Fear (1996)
After his father is killed under mysterious circumstances, a young man is drawn into a dangerous world of espionage, deceit and murder and teams up with a beautiful thief to solve the conspiracy before they become its next victims. Suspenseful thriller stars Andrew Lowery, Leslie Hope, Christopher Plummer. 112 min.
86-1115 Was $89.99 ❑*$14.99*

The Big Fall (1997)
A private detective is in for excitement and surprises when a beautiful woman walks into his life. Soon, he finds himself entangled with federal agents, bungee-jumping adrenaline junkies and other hazards that come with his involvement with the new sweetie. C. Thomas Howell, Sophie Ward, Jeff Kober star. 111 min.
86-1119 ❑*$99.99*

No Strings Attached (1995)
Sensual suspense tale stars Vincent Spano as a journalist who gets dangerously close to his work when his latest project—a story on women's secret erotic fantasies—leads him to an encounter with a mysterious woman who dreams of anonymous sex with "no strings attached." Traci Lind, Cheryl Pollack, Michael McKean also star. 97 min.
86-1141 Was $89.99 ❑*$19.99*

Sand Trap (1998)
A man is pushed over the edge of a desert cliff by his friend, who planned the crime with the man's wife, but when the police arrive to investigate the "accidental" fall, there's no body to be found! Well-crafted and gripping suspenser stars Brad Koepenick, David John James and Elizabeth Morehead. 99 min.
86-1131 ❑*$89.99*

Natural Enemy (1997)
An adopted young man's bitter vendetta against his birth parents is the fuel that feeds the flame of vengeance in this gripping suspense tale that stars Donald Sutherland, Lesley Ann Warren, William McNamara and Tia Carrere. 92 min.
86-1116 Was $89.99 ❑*$14.99*

Catherine's Grove (1998)
Super-charged, extra-kinky thriller, set against the backdrop of Miami's alternative club scene, features Jeff Fahey as a cop looking into a rash of transvestite murders. Along with girlfriend Maria Conchita Alonso, Fahey takes a side job for a young millionaire who wants them to find his missing sister. The search leads to a dangerous web of sexual surprises. With Michael Madsen, Priscilla Barnes. 91 min.
86-1138 ❑*$69.99*

Extramarital (1998)
Magazine editor Jeff Fahey assigns neophyte writer Traci Lords a story involving a mysterious woman involved in a secret adulterous affair. But Lords' investigation uncovers a murder, and she may be the killer's next target, in this erotic suspenser. With Maria Diaz and Brian Bloom. 90 min.
86-1140 Was $89.99 ❑*$19.99*

When Justice Fails (1998)
The search for the culprit in a string of savage murders leads a Manhattan detective to a beautiful prosecutor for advice. Their professional relationship heats up into romance, but what will the cop do when she becomes the prime suspect in the killings? Gripping suspense tale stars Jeff Fahey, Marlee Matlin. 90 min.
86-1145 ❑*$99.99*

Killing Mr. Griffin (1997)
A group of high school students has concocted an elaborate plan for revenge against their school's nastiest teacher, but when Mr. Griffin turns up dead, it's up to them find out who killed him before the police blame them. Scott Bairstow, Amy Jo Johnson, Mario Lopez and Jay Thomas star in this suspenser based on a novel by Lois Duncan ("I Know What You Did Last Summer"). 108 min.
86-1149 ❑*$99.99*

Stormy Nights (1997)
After her husband is killed in an auto accident with an architect, vengeance-seeking Shannon Tweed insinuates her way into the man's home and uses her seductive wiles to destroy his life. Erotic suspense tale also stars Brett Baxter Clark, Tracy Spaulding. 90 min.
86-1161 *$89.99*

Man With A Gun (1995)
Intense suspenser focusing on a hit man (Michael Madsen) enlisted by his boss (Gary Busey) to rub out his own lover (Jennifer Tilly) because she's holding a CD-ROM with incriminating evidence. Tilly plans on having her twin sister murdered instead, but Madsen faces a dilemma when he realizes his intended target is not who she seems. Robert Loggia, Bill Cobbs co-star. 96 min.
88-1079 Was $99.99 ❑*$14.99*

The Third Solution (1989)
A clandestine pact between Moscow and the Vatican threatens to become an international incident. Top-notch political thriller stars Treat Williams, Danny Aiello, F. Murray Abraham. 113 min.
02-1989 *$79.99*

Eyewitness (1981)
Night janitor William Hurt falsely claims to have seen a murder in order to be near TV reporter Sigourney Weaver, but his story places them both in danger in this compelling thriller. With Christopher Plummer, James Woods. 93 min.
04-1411 *$19.99*

Union City (1981)
Rock songstress Deborah Harry stars as the bored wife of an uncaring businessman in this offbeat thriller set in a grimy factory town in the 1940s. Their animosity soon erupts into a tempest of violence that ends in death. Co-stars Dennis Lipscomb, Everett McGill, and, in a cameo role, Pat Benatar. 87 min.
02-1111 Was $19.99 *$14.99*

The Amateur (1982)
A CIA computer specialist searches for the killers of his girlfriend, with the trail leading to murder and international intrigue in this nail-biting suspense thriller. John Savage, Christopher Plummer, Marthe Keller. 112 min.
04-1483 Was $59.99 *$29.99*

Stone Cold Dead (1980)
A sniper terrorizes a town when he decides to shoot prostitutes. A detective is called on to stop the madman. Richard Crenna, Paul Williams co-star. 100 min.
03-1193 *$79.99*

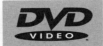

DVD VIDEO
ASK ABOUT OUR GIANT DVD CATALOG!

Mercy (1995)
A high-powered New York lawyer whose daughter is abducted is sent on a grueling and dangerous trek through the city streets by the kidnappers, who appear to be after revenge more than money, in this gripping thriller that stars John Rubinstein, Sam Rockwell, Amber Kain. 89 min.
83-1148 Was $99.99 *$14.99*

Someone To Watch Over Me (1987)
A deadly attraction develops between a married New York detective (Tom Berenger) and the murder witness (Mimi Rogers) he's assigned to protect in this erotic thriller from director Ridley Scott ("Alien"). With John Rubinstein, Lorraine Bracco. 106 min.
02-1823 Was $19.99 ❑*$14.99*

The Stranger (1987)
The only clues behind a savage murder lie in the mind of amnesiac auto crash victim Bonnie Bedelia. Can psychiatrist Peter Riegert help her recover her memory, and what will happen when she does? Offbeat, riveting thriller. 93 min.
02-1851 *$79.99*

Out Of The Dark (1989)
A clown-masked psychopath is stalking the phone-sex girls of Los Angeles...and he's making sure that they'll never breathe heavily again! A nude photographer is the most likely suspect...or is he! Seamy suspenser with an offbeat cast: Karen Black, Bud Cort, Tab Hunter, Paul Bartel, and in his/her screen farewell, Divine. 90 min.
02-1959 *$89.99*

The Killing Hour (1982)
A young woman's drawings of murder victims turn out to be predictions of brutal crimes in this lurid suspense shocker. Two men—a police detective and a TV reporter—race against time and each other to find the girl; which one wants her dead? Perry King, Elizabeth Kemp, Kenneth McMillan and Joe Morton star. AKA: "The Clairvoyant." Uncensored director's cut; 97 min.
04-1852 Letterboxed *$14.99*

Urge To Kill (1984)
Released from jail after being declared temporarily insane, a man convicted of murder tries to learn what happened that night. The victim's sister wants to help him...or does she? Intense thriller stars Karl Malden, Alex McArthur, Holly Hunter. 96 min.
04-2169 Was $59.99 *$29.99*

A Perfect Spy (1987)
A top-notch, epic adaptation of John Le Carré's acclaimed autobiographical novel centers on an important member of the British Secret Service whose mysterious disappearance provokes a manhunt by his agency and his enemies. Peter Egan and Dame Peggy Ashcroft star in this gripping spy thriller. 376 min. on three tapes.
04-2725 *$79.99*

After Pilkington (1988)
An English professor is reunited with his childhood sweetheart, but the tender meeting soon leads to a twisting tale of murder and insanity. Bob Peck stars in an engrossing tale from author Simon Gray. 100 min.
04-2260 Was $39.99 ❑*$19.99*

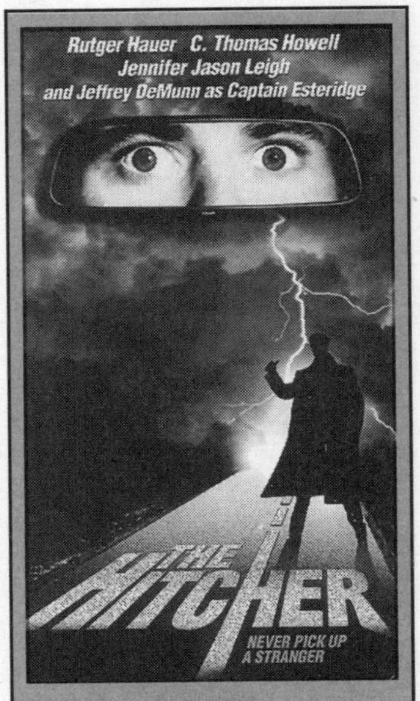
Rutger Hauer C. Thomas Howell
Jennifer Jason Leigh
and Jeffrey DeMunn as Captain Esteridge
THE HITCHER
NEVER PICK UP A STRANGER

The Hitcher (1986)
A young man's seemingly harmless act of picking up a hitchhiker along a barren desert highway becomes a harrowing, blood-chilling odyssey of suspense and terror. Rutger Hauer is the psychotic "pick up" with a taste for blood; with C. Thomas Howell, Jennifer Jason Leigh. 98 min.
44-1392 Remastered ❑*$14.99*

The Hitcher (Letterboxed Version)
Also available in a theatrical, widescreen format.
44-2176 *$14.99*

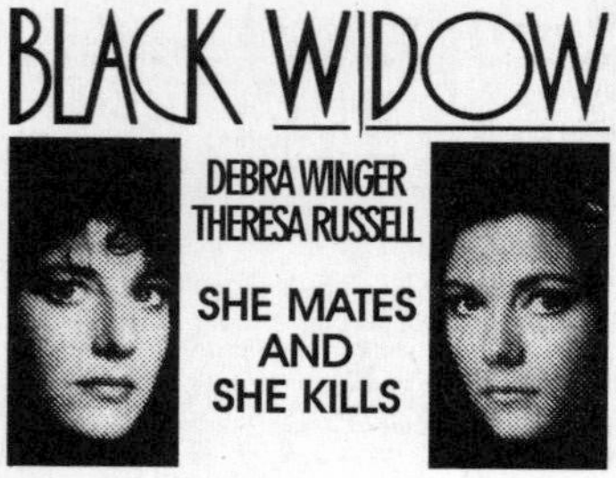
BLACK WIDOW
DEBRA WINGER
THERESA RUSSELL
SHE MATES
AND
SHE KILLS

Black Widow (1987)
Debra Winger stars in this captivating spellbinder as a bored federal investigator who quits her job in order to pursue a woman (Theresa Russell) whom she believes has been systematically seducing and killing prominent millionaires. Directed by Bob Rafelson ("Five Easy Pieces"). 103 min.
04-2056 Was $19.99 □*$14.99*

Dream Lover (1986)
Suspense thriller that you may never wake up from stars Kristy McNichol as a young woman plagued by recurring nightmares of an intruder in her apartment whom she kills. Soon the line between dream and reality fades, and the terror begins. 104 min.
12-1627 Was $79.99 *$14.99*

Blackout (1985)
Years ago, a woman and her children were brutally murdered, and the husband vanished. Now, a detective investigating the case thinks an amnesiac holds the missing clues. Is he the husband, the killer...or both? Tense mystery stars Keith Carradine, Richard Widmark, Kathleen Quinlan. 99 min.
05-1398 Was $79.99 *$14.99*

An Affair In Mind (1989)
A best-selling writer has an affair with a mysterious beauty, but their romance leads to the committing of the "perfect murder" in a riveting mystery by Ruth Rendell. Stephen Dillon stars. 88 min.
04-2259 Was $39.99 □*$19.99*

Street Of Dreams (1988)
After a sleazy movie mogul is murdered, a Los Angeles detective investigates and soon falls in love with the mogul's beautiful wife. While the detective searches for the killer and a missing script, he witnesses the dangerous and seedy side of Hollywood. Morgan Fairchild, Ben Masters and Diane Salinger star. 95 min.
10-2512 *$12.99*

Body Double (1984)
Controversial offering from mystery master Brian De-Palma about an unemployed actor (Craig Wasson) who finds himself involved in a tale of murder and deception that ranges from the Hollywood hills to an adult film studio. Melanie Griffith, Deborah Shelton also star. 114 min.
10-2608 *$14.99*

The Squeeze (1980)
Action ace Lee Van Cleef is a retired safecracker who is lured back into the "business" by the son of a former partner who has a job planned that will make them rich...but is everything what it seems? Compelling caper suspenser also stars Edward Albert, Karen Black, Lionel Stander. AKA: "Diamond Thieves," "The Heist," "The Rip-Off." 100 min.
39-1964 *$14.99*

Turn Back The Clock (1989)
A reworking of 1947's "Repeat Performance," this suspenser stars Connie Selleca as a woman given an opportunity to relive a New Year's Eve that occurred in her past—the one in which she killer her husband! Dina Merrill and Gene Barry also star.
10-3417 *$14.99*

Murder Rap (1988)
A musician gets much more than he bargained for when a beautiful young woman ensnares him in a scheme of homicide, and leaves him to take the blame. Engrossing thriller stars John Hawkes, Seita Kathleen Feigny. 115 min.
08-1418 Was $29.99 *$19.99*

Sorry, Wrong Number (1989)
Loni Anderson takes the Barbara Stanwyck role in this new adaptation of the suspense classic. She plays the bedridden beauty who overhears a phone conversation involving a murder...her own. Hal Holbrook and Patrick Macnee co-star. 90 min.
06-1747 *$89.99*

Positive I.D. (1987)
Enthralling, sensual suspenser about a woman who sets a unique trap when the man convicted of raping her years earlier is released: setting up a second identity to lure and ultimately kill him. Stephanie Rascoe, John Davies. 96 min.
07-1572 Was $79.99 *$14.99*

Suspect (1987)
A public defender and juror, both involved in a controversial murder trial, are drawn together when they find evidence that the accused killer is innocent. Cher, Dennis Quaid, Liam Neeson star in an intense thriller filled with passion and suspense. 101 min.
02-1849 Was $19.99 *$14.99*

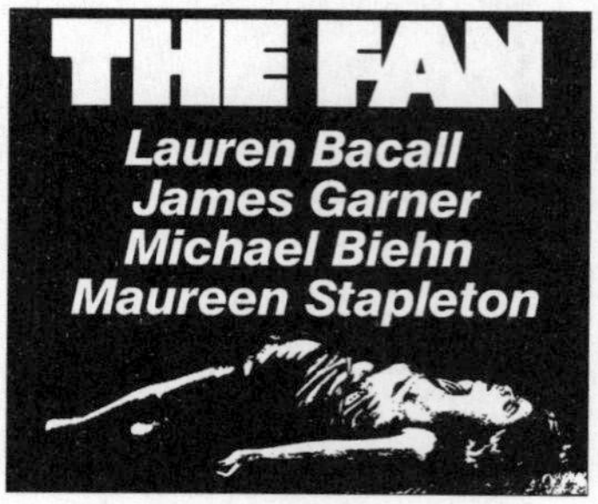
THE FAN
Lauren Bacall
James Garner
Michael Biehn
Maureen Stapleton

The Fan (1981)
A glamorous Broadway star is pursued by a disturbed devotee whose obsession with her turns deadly. Nerve-wracking suspense story stars Lauren Bacall, James Garner, Michael Biehn, Maureen Stapleton; look for Dana Delany as a saleswoman. 95 min.
06-1097 *$14.99*

Mike's Murder (1984)
Debra Winger stars as a woman seeking the answers to the killing of her former lover, a hustler involved in cocaine dealing. Gripping mystery also stars Paul Winfield. 97 min.
19-1362 Was $19.99 *$14.99*

The Little Drummer Girl (1984)
A riveting adaptation of John le Carré's blockbuster novel finds Diane Keaton as an American actress involved in terrorism and blackmail in the Middle East. As real as today's headlines—and as explosive! Klaus Kinski co-stars; directed by George Roy Hill. 130 min.
19-1399 □*$14.99*

Trapped (1989)
Kathleen Quinlan plays a building management executive who comes face-to-face with terror when she's trapped in a 65-story building, terrorized by a man with a knife. She's not ready to die...hard or easy...and he's not ready to let her go. With Bruce Abbott. 96 min.
07-1647 *$79.99*

The Hollywood Detective (1989)
Telly Savalas plays a down-and-out TV detective who is given a chance to solve a real murder case by an adoring fan. Soon, he becomes a suspect in the investigation, and the plot gets thicker than anything he ever encountered on the tube. Helene Udy, George Coe and Joe Dallesandro also star. 88 min.
07-1665 *$79.99*

Phobia (1980)
A psychiatric hospital for convicted murderers becomes a terrifying death row when someone starts killing the inmates, using the source of their deepest fears as the instrument of death. John Huston's nerve-racking whodunit stars Paul Michael Glaser and Susan Hogan. 94 min.
06-1662 Was $79.99 *$14.99*

3rd Degree Burn (1989)
Top-notch mystery filled with steamy romance and suspenseful plot twists stars Treat Williams as a detective who falls for the millionaire's wife (Virginia Madsen) he's been hired to shadow, a woman later suspected of killing her husband. Richard Masur, CCH Pounder co-star. 97 min.
06-1689 Was $79.99 *$14.99*

The Forgotten (1989)
After 17 years of captivity in Vietnam, six Green Berets are located and return home, only to find a different type of captivity, sponsored by their own government, awaits them. Engrossing suspenser stars Keith Carradine, Steve Railsback, Stacy Keach. 96 min.
06-1708 *$79.99*

Shannon Tweed

Of Unknown Origin (1983)
Rats...slithery, hairy, destructive, disease-carrying, deadly. It's pesky rodent vs. man in this terror tale that gives new meaning to the term "Eeeek!" Peter Weller and Shannon Tweed star. 90 min.
19-1306 Was $19.99 *$14.99*

The Firing Line (1990)
Reb Brown and Shannon Tweed star in this riveting action epic as real as today's headlines. A special forces jungle fighter is hired by a Central American government to destroy a faction of dangerous rebels. After he sees how corrupt his new employer is, his allegiance switches to the rebels. 93 min.
16-9090 Was $19.99 *$14.99*

Last Call (1990)
A beautiful performance artist and a staid businessman are drawn into a passion-filled web by desire and a need for vengeance against a common enemy. Erotic suspenser stars William Katt, Shannon Tweed, Joseph Campanella. Uncut, unrated version; 90 min.
46-5500 *$14.99*

Night Eyes 2 (1991)
Suspenseful follow-up to the steamy thriller features Andrew Stevens as the hi-tech peeping tom who's asked to spy on diplomat's wife Shannon Tweed. What he uncovers, though, could cost them both their lives! Uncut, unrated version; 98 min.
46-5525 □*$14.99*

Night Eyes 3 (1993)
A scorching suspenser in which surveillance expert Andrew Stevens is hired to act as bodyguard for gorgeous TV star Shannon Tweed when she is stalked by a mysterious stranger. Soon, Stevens is keeping a close eye on everything the actress does...including things of a most intimate nature. Tracy Tweed also stars. Uncut, unrated version; 101 min.
46-5570 *$14.99*

Liar's Edge (1992)
A young man, the sole witness to a violent crime, has doubts about what he's seen until it becomes clear that the psychotic killer has chosen him to be the next victim. Spellbinding suspenser tinged with eroticism stars David Keith, Shannon Tweed, Christopher Plummer, Joseph Bottoms. 97 min.
02-2396 Was $19.99 *$14.99*

Cold Sweat (1993)
A hit man eager to get out of the "business" decides to take one last assignment before retiring, but when he falls in love with the wife of his employer, he finds himself in a web of danger and deceit. Shannon Tweed, Ben Cross, Adam Baldwin and Dave Thomas star. 93 min.
06-2197 Was $89.99 □*$19.99*

Night Fire (1994)
Super-erotic thriller starring Shannon Tweed as a woman who has planned a weekend to rebuild the passion between her and her husband. When a stranded couple with a penchant for kinky sex intrudes on their weekend, carnal thrills lead to danger. Martin Hewitt, John Laughlin co-star. Unrated version; 103 min.
72-9039 Was $89.99 *$14.99*

Scorned (1994)
A rising young executive who has been offering his sexy wife to executives kills himself out of guilt, prompting the wife to target an associate as the real culprit behind his death. She infiltrates the associate's family and carries out her revenge through seduction and deception. Shannon Tweed and Andrew Stevens star in this steamy suspenser. Unrated version; 103 min.
46-5592 Was $89.99 *$14.99*

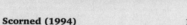

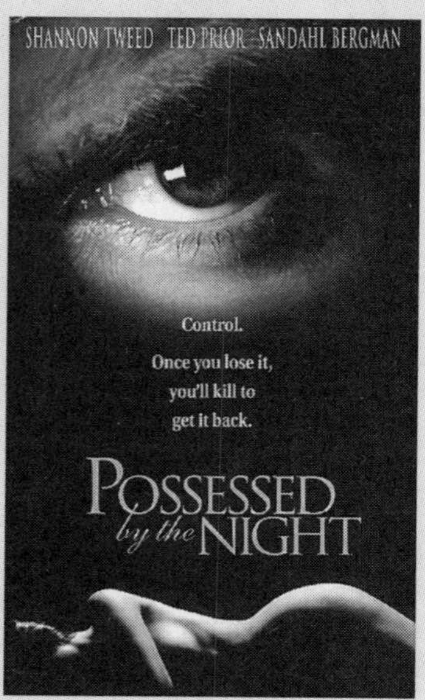
SHANNON TWEED TED PRIOR SANDAHL BERGMAN
Control.
Once you lose it,
you'll kill to
get it back.
POSSESSED
by the NIGHT

Possessed By The Night (1994)
A frustrated novelist finds a talisman that he thinks can help his career. Soon, it draws him and his wife into the realm of a beautiful stranger who takes them hostage and unleashes their hidden sexuality. Shannon Tweed, Sandahl Bergman and Ted Prior star in this bizarre scorcher. Unrated version; 87 min.
02-2601 Was $89.99 □*$19.99*

Indecent Behavior II (1994)
Shannon Tweed is indecent once more, playing a sex therapist who becomes a suspect in the murder of a client who attempted to blackmail her. She enlists the help of another therapist when she discovers other clients are involved in heated and dangerous hanky-panky. Cynthia Steele, Rochelle Swanson and James Brolin also star. Uncut, unrated version; 96 min.
19-3644 *$89.99*

Indecent Behavior 3 (1995)
When a number of sex therapists are found brutally murdered, the police ask therapist Shannon Tweed for her help in setting a seductive trap for the serial killer. Third steamy entry in the hit thriller series also stars Sam Hemmings, Colleen Coffey. Uncut, unrated version; 90 min.
19-3857 *$89.99*

Victim Of Desire (1995)
The desire reaches new heights as a private detective searching for $70 million in embezzled loot gets involved with the gorgeous wife of his quarry, a white collar murderer who dies in a suspicious accident. The detective soon finds himself considered an accomplice to the murder. Shannon Tweed, Marc Singer, Julie Strain, Wings Hauser star. Scorching, unrated version.
21-9082 Was $89.99 *$14.99*

Electra (1996)
Morning, noon and night become Electra with Shannon Tweed in the title role, as the stepmother of a farm boy with incredible superpowers. A sadistic villain recruits Tweed to uncover the secret behind the young man's abilities, and she dons leather and fishnets as part of a bizarre seduction scheme. With Joe Tab, Dyanne Di Marco. 85 min.
21-9113 Was $89.99 *$14.99*

Human Desires (1997)
The phrase "killer looks" takes on new meaning in this sizzling thriller starring Shannon Tweed. When a lingerie model is murdered, a private investigator on the case delves into the glitzy and dangerous world of modelling, where money and deceit play as important a part in the proceedings as the women. With Ashby Adams, Dawn Ann Billings. 94 min.
02-3105 Was $94.99 □*$14.99*

Naked Lies (1997)
The U.S. government has its hands full with a ruthless drug dealer and a conniving counterfeiter who have teamed up. To deal with the situation, the feds bring in their deadliest and sexiest weapon...no, not Janet Reno, but undercover agent Shannon Tweed! No one knows what—or whom—she'll do in next. Steven Bauer, Fernando Allende co-star. 93 min.
02-3198 Was $94.99 □*$24.99*

Face The Evil (1997)
An attempted art gallery heist turns into a life-or-death hostage drama when one woman must stop a terrorist plot to smuggle a shipment of Nazi nerve gas in this gripping "Die Hard"-like thriller. Shannon Tweed, Lance Henriksen, Bruce Payne star. 92 min.
83-1186 Was $94.99 *$14.99*

Forbidden Sins (1998)
High-powered attorney Shannon Tweed, who uses her seductive beauty to woo clients and win over juries, may be in over her head when she comes to the aid of a millionaire accused of murder and finds she could be the killer's next victim. Stylish and sensual suspenser also stars Corbin Timbrook, Myles O'Brien. 90 min.
02-3363 Was $94.99 □*$19.99*

Scandalous Behavior (1998)
The oil country of Texas is the setting for an erotic drama about the passions that erupt when two men fall in love with the same woman. Sultry Shannon Tweed stars alongside Rena Riffel and James Hong, who also directed. AKA: "Singapore Sling." Unrated version; 94 min.
82-5174 *$89.99*

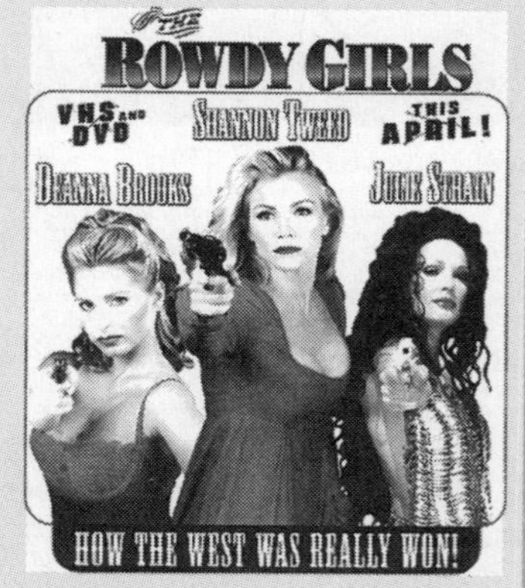
THE
ROWDY GIRLS
VHS AND DVD
SHANNON TWEED
THIS APRIL!
DEANNA BROOKS
JULIE STRAIN
HOW THE WEST WAS REALLY WON!

The Rowdy Girls (1999)
Wild West action with a racy softcore spin drives this sexy sagebrush tale. Shannon Tweed and Deanna Brooks are fiery frontier women who are kidnapped by an outlaw gang led by Daniel Murray and Julie Strain and fight for their freedom. With Lazlo Vargas, Mink Stole. Unrated version.
46-8056 *$59.99*

Please see our index for these other Shannon Tweed titles: *Body Chemistry 4: Full Exposure • Detroit Rock City • The First Olympics—Athens 1896 • Hot Dog...The Movie • Hot Line 1 & 2 • Night Visitor • No Contest • Shadow Warriors*

The Haunting Of Sarah Hardy (1989)
A newlywed returns to her childhood home to claim an inheritance, but what she receives is a deadly threat to her happiness, her sanity, and her very life. Sela Ward, Michael Woods, Morgan Fairchild star in this Gothic suspenser. 92 min.
06-1709 ❑*$79.99*

Final Notice (1989)
A deranged killer obsessed with nude photos in art books turns his interest to real women and the bodies start to drop. A hotshot private eye is out to nab the madman before he strikes again. Gil Gerard, Melody Anderson, and Louise Fletcher star in this creepy thriller. 88 min.
06-1723 *$89.99*

Spy (1989)
After a special agent retires from a secret federal unit, he decides to have plastic surgery to make his face unrecognizable. After surgery, however, he finds out that someone's after him...and that means business. Bruce Greenwood, Catherine Hicks, Michael Tucker and Ned Beatty star in this intense thriller. 88 min.
06-1735 *$89.99*

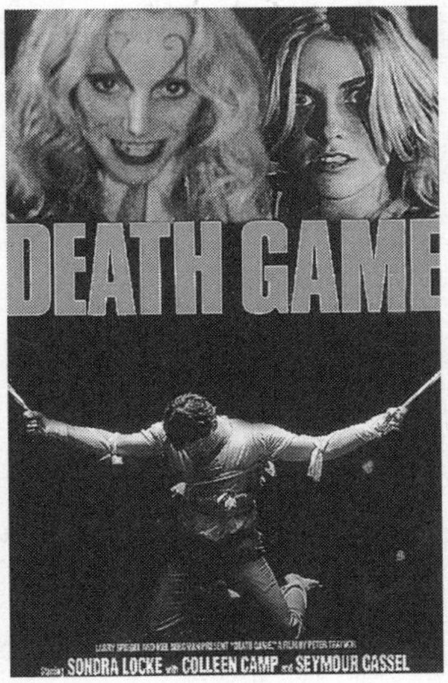

Death Game (1980)
A man innocently picks up two attractive female hitchhikers, but what follows is a 48-hour nightmare of suspense and eroticism. Sondra Locke and Colleen Camp star as the "angels in trouble" who have some devilish ideas. AKA: "The Seducers." 90 min.
08-1421 *$19.99*

Personals (1989)
After her reporter husband is murdered while investigating an article about the singles scene, a woman searches for the lovely, lethal killer. Stephanie Zimbalist, Jennifer O'Neill and Robin Thomas star in this intriguing mystery. 93 min.
06-1746 *$89.99*

Sparks (1989)
Sleek thriller starring Victoria Principal as the mayor of a Southwestern town who frantically attempts to find a serial killer on the loose, while the city officials want her out of office. She becomes romantically involved with a special investigator, and the two unite to continue their search. Ted Wass and Hector Elizondo also star. 96 min.
10-2510 *$12.99*

Scene Of The Crime (1985)
Orson Welles is your host for a challenging trio of whodunits: a millionaire's new bride is found floating in the pool; a newly elected senator is found shot in his office; an adman has visions of a conspiracy for his murder. Markie Post, Kim Hunter, Dennis Franz and Alan Thicke are among the likely suspects. 74 min.
07-1515 Was $39.99 *$14.99*

The Holcroft Covenant (1985)
In the Third Reich's last days, a group of German officers diverted Nazi funds into a trust fund for Holocaust survivors. Michael Caine stars as the ringleader's son, who must uncover the cache and clear his family's name. Superb suspenser from director John Frankenheimer co-stars Lilli Palmer, Anthony Andrews. 112 min.
12-2592 *$14.99*

Dead Of Winter (1987)
Effective nail-biter stars Mary Steenburgen as an out-of-work actress who auditions for a reclusive director in an isolated mansion, only to have her "dream role" turn into a nightmare of murderous deception. Jan Rubes, Roddy McDowall co-star. 100 min.
12-2390 Was $19.99 ❑*$14.99*

Cloak And Dagger (1984)
A young computer expert gets mixed up in an espionage plot, but no one will believe him, in this unusual and entertaining thriller. Henry Thomas ("E.T.") is the boy on the run, and Dabney Coleman plays both his father and video game hero "Jack Flack." 101 min.
07-1248 ❑*$19.99*

Slow Burn (1986)
When a renowned painter's son disappears in Palm Springs, a tough private dick gets on the trail...and encounters a millionaire's wife eager to reveal everything she knows and more. Steamy suspenser stars Eric Roberts, Beverly D'Angelo, Henry Gibson, Dan Hedaya. 92 min.
07-1445 *$59.99*

Kill Me Again (1989)
Sly and sexy homage to classic Hollywood suspensers, as a beautiful woman makes off with mob money and hires a private detective to protect her. When she skips out on him, he finds himself caught between the gangsters, her ex-boyfriend and the law. Val Kilmer, Joanne Whalley-Kilmer, Michael Madsen star; John Dahl directs. 96 min.
12-2039 Was $89.99 *$14.99*

Last Rites (1988)
A young woman who witnesses a mob murder takes refuge in a New York church, but she and the priest who protects her must look out for the law, the Mafia, and their own forbidden passions. Gripping thriller stars Tom Berenger, Daphne Zuniga. 103 min.
12-2775 ❑*$19.99*

The Return Of Frank Cannon (1980)
Heavy-duty private eye Cannon (William Conrad) comes out of retirement to investigate the mysterious death of an Army buddy in this suspenseful thriller based on the classic TV series. Co-stars Arthur Hill, Joanna Pettet. 96 min.
14-3082 *$39.99*

Unholy Matrimony (1988)
True-life thriller stars Patrick Duffy as a detective searching for clues in the hit-and-run murder of a beautiful young newlywed. Michael O'Keefe and Charles Durning also star in this complex mystery filled with deception and sinister lies. 100 min.
14-3247 *$12.99*

When The Bough Breaks (1986)
Ted Danson stars as a child psychologist who joins with a police detective friend to uncover a child molestation ring run by powerful businessmen who use a center for troubled children as a front. Richard Masur, Kim Myori and Rachel Ticotin co-star. 104 min.
14-3248 *$12.99*

The Fatal Image (1989)
A mother and daughter on vacation in Paris accidentally videotape a mob-sanctioned murder and are pursued by the killers. Can a handsome French detective save them? Exciting thriller stars Michelle Lee, Justine Bateman, Francois Dunoyer. 96 min.
14-3293 *$14.99*

The Kidnapping Of The President (1980)
Intense political thriller involves the kidnapping of U.S. president Hal Holbrook by terrorists in Toronto. A ransom is set at $100 million in diamonds. Crackerjack suspense with William Shatner, Ava Gardner, Van Johnson. 113 min.
14-6001 Was $19.99 *$12.99*

Glitz (1988)
Miami cop Jimmy Smits and Atlantic City lounge singer Markie Post team up to investigate a call girl's death and get caught up in a deadly drug ring in an exciting thriller from the pen of Elmore Leonard. 91 min.
19-1744 *$14.99*

The Bourne Identity (1988)
A superb adaptation of Robert Ludlum's best-selling thriller starring Richard Chamberlain as a man stricken with amnesia who is pursued throughout Europe by a network of spies out to kill him. He must discover the secret of his past in order to stop the assassins. Jaclyn Smith, Denholm Elliott and Anthony Quayle also star. 185 min.
19-2102 Was $79.99 *$24.99*

Mascara (1988)
The murder of a transvestite opens the door to a strange, hidden world for a police detective and his sister, but the truth behind the killing threatens to shatter their lives. Offbeat, sensual thriller stars Michael Sarrazin, Charlotte Rampling, Derek De Lint. 99 min.
19-7023 Was $79.99 ❑*$19.99*

Masquerade (1988)
The plot twists come fast and furious in this intense, passion-filled thriller about a young heiress (Meg Tilly) who is romanced by a man (Rob Lowe) whose designs may be more on her money than on her. With John Glover, Kim Cattrall, Dana Delany. 91 min.
12-2538 Was $19.99 *$14.99*

Rehearsal For Murder (1982)
A Broadway actress is found murdered on opening night, and it's up to her playwright fiancé to set a trap for the killer. Stylish whodunit from the creators of "Columbo," with Robert Preston, Lynn Redgrave, Patrick Macnee and Jeff Goldblum. 96 min.
27-6171 *$14.99*

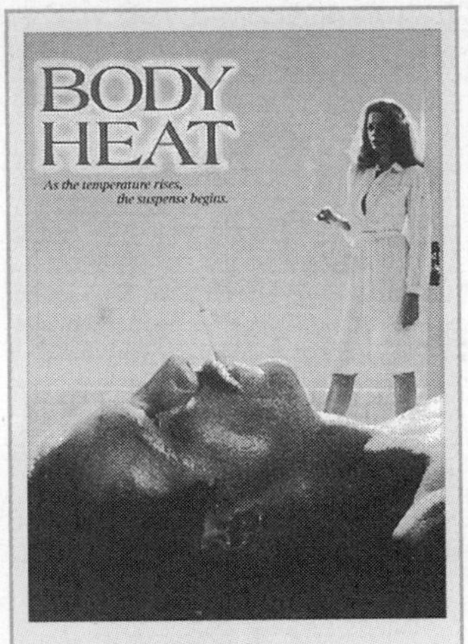

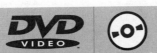

Body Heat (1981)
A steamy, 1940s-style mystery updated with 1980s eroticism. Murder, romance and deceit entangle a seedy lawyer and his beautiful lover in a small Flo ida town. William Hurt, Kathleen Turner, Richard Crenna, Ted Danson and Mickey Rourke co-star. 113 min.
19-1177 ❑*$14.99*

A Gun In The House (1981)
Sally Struthers is charged with murder after gunning down a trespasser in her home in this timely and intriguing social drama. Co-stars David Ackroyd and Millie Perkins. 100 min.
23-5022 *$29.99*

Laguna Heat (1987)
An ex-cop (Harry Hamlin) returns to his home town of Laguna Beach, and soon finds himself involved in a series of murders. Two people, his father (Jason Robards) and the beautiful daughter (Catherine Hicks) of one of the victims, hold the secret behind the killings in this exciting mystery. 110 min.
40-1366 Was $19.99 *$14.99*

The Hit (1985)
John Hurt is a world-weary hit man and Terence Stamp is his unusually cooperative target in this offbeat thriller laced with tension and dark humor. With Laura De Sol as a lovely hostage and Tim Roth (in his film debut) as Hurt's over-eager assistant. Stephen Frears ("The Grifters") directed. 97 min.
53-1394 Was $19.99 *$14.99*

Apology (1986)
An avant garde New York artist begins taping anonymous phone confessions as part of her latest project, but one "subject" doesn't settle for long-distance relations, and soon her life is in danger. Unusual thriller stars Lesley Ann Warren, Peter Weller, Charles S. Dutton. 95 min.
44-1430 *$14.99*

Yuri Nosenko, KGB (1986)
A KGB agent seeking freedom in America will exchange political asylum for information about President Kennedy's assassination. Is the offer genuine, or is it merely a cover-up for a Soviet plot? Political thriller stars Tommy Lee Jones, Oleg Rudnik. 88 min.
44-1445 *$19.99*

The Big Easy (1987)
Dennis Quaid is a "slightly corrupt" Cajun cop whose love/hate relationship with new D.A. Ellen Barkin gets them both involved in a deadly graft ring in the city of New Orleans. Witty, romantic mystery also stars Ned Beatty, John Goodman, Ebbe Roe Smith and Charles Ludlam. 108 min.
44-1509 Was $19.99 ❑*$14.99*

The Assassin (1989)
A CIA agent assigned to safeguard a U.S. senator abroad is blamed when he's wounded by a gunman, but the agent uncovers a conspiracy that could cost him his life. Thriller stars Steve Railsback, Nicholas Guest. 92 min.
44-1715 ❑*$79.99*

The Girl In A Swing (1989)
Steamy erotic mystery starring Meg Tilly as you've never seen her before. She plays a woman with psychic powers who falls in love with a handsome young man, but the secrets of her past lead to horrifying consequences. Rupert Fraser co-stars. 119 min.
44-1721 Was $89.99 *$19.99*

Perfect Witness (1989)
Top-notch, streetwise thriller starring Aidan Quinn as a restaurateur harassed by a U.S. attorney and the mob after he witnesses a gangland killing. Brian Dennehy and Stockard Channing also star. 104 min.
44-1723 Was $59.99 ❑*$14.99*

Prime Suspect (1988)
A romantic weekend in the woods becomes a nightmare when a young man sees his girlfriend's brutal knifing by a masked assailant, and, traumatized, can't defend himself from detectives who think he's the killer. Stars Robert Lyons, Frank Stallone and Dana Plato. 89 min.
45-5467 *$79.99*

The Glory Boys (1984)
An Israeli scientist (Rod Steiger) visiting London is marked for death by a pair of terrorist assassins, and only a freelance intelligence agent (Anthony Perkins) can stop them. 78 min.
46-5049 *$19.99*

City Killer (1984)
A lovelorn psychopath comes upon a novel way of making a girl notice him...blowing up buildings. Can he be caught before the city is demolished, and if he is, will she go out with him? Heather Locklear, Terence Knox, Gerald McRaney. 100 min.
46-5376 *$79.99*

Gorky Park (1983)
Riveting suspense thriller, based on the best-selling novel, involves the discovery of three mutilated bodies in a Moscow park. Russian policeman William Hurt, American businessman Lee Marvin and beautiful ingenue Joanna Pacula are the principals entangled in the dangerous puzzle. 127 min.
47-1219 *$14.99*

Julie Darling (1982)
Deeply disturbed by the death of her mother, a teenage girl's jealousy when her father remarries explodes into a violent frenzy. Gripping thriller stars Tony Franciosa, Sybil Danning, Isabelle Mejias. AKA: "Daughter of Death." 90 min.
16-3013 *$19.99*

Impulse (1984)
Something in a peaceful small town is causing the residents to lose their inhibitions and act out their deepest, deadliest desires in this bizarre, compelling suspenser. Meg Tilly, Tim Matheson, Hume Cronyn and Bill Paxton star. 95 min.
47-1335 *$14.99*

Terminal Choice (1985)
Hi-tech medical thriller set in a clinic where the odds of recovery are not good...in fact, the doctors are betting against it! Can one doctor stop the deadly game before it claims another victim? Suspenseful tale stars Joe Spano, Diane Venora, David McCallum, Ellen Barkin. 99 min.
47-1487 *$14.99*

Murder Elite (1985)
The usually quiet English countryside is awash with blood as a maniacal killer stalks. With this in mind, a young woman (Ali McGraw) sees the perfect chance to sell her farm right out from under her reluctant sister. All she has to do is see to it that the murderer pays sis a visit. Billie Whitelaw co-stars. 98 min.
47-1736 *$69.99*

The Bedroom Window (1987)
An affair between a young executive (Steve Guttenberg) and his boss' wife (Isabelle Huppert) leads to suspense after she sees a violent assault from his window. He tells the police he saw it to save her reputation...and becomes a prime suspect after being caught in the lie. Elizabeth McGovern co-stars in this Hitchcockian gripper directed by Curtis Hanson ("L.A. Confidential"). 109 min.
47-1769 *$14.99*

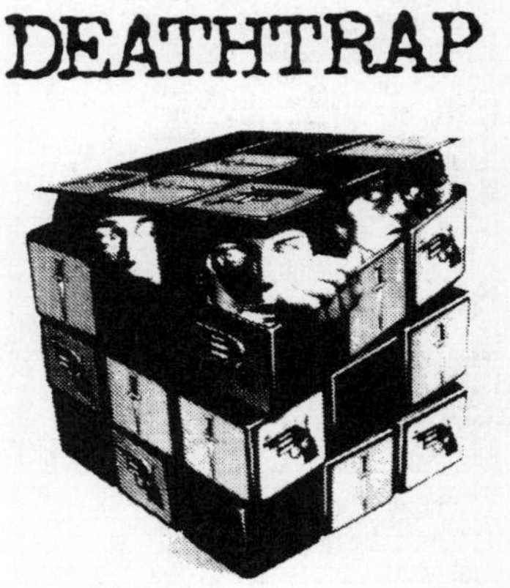

Deathtrap (1982)
The smash Broadway mystery with more plot twists than you can count is now an exciting film thriller. Michael Caine is the playwright whose writer's block may lead to murder, Dyan Cannon his loving but terrified wife, Christopher Reeve the young protégé who'll do anything to make it to the top. 116 min.
19-1224 *$19.99*

Best Seller (1987)
Cop and writer Brian Dennehy is promised the "inside story" from hit man James Woods if he'll aid him in getting revenge against the corrupt civic leader who dispensed with his "services," but a sinister secret may kill their uneasy partnership before it's started. Intense thriller also stars Victoria Tennant, Paul Shenar. 95 min.
47-1878 *$14.99*

Sphinx (1981)
A strong-willed Egyptologist (Lesley-Anne Down) faces death as she struggles to solve an ancient riddle which would unlock the secret treasures hidden within a sealed crypt. Frank Langella co-stars as an antiquities director who guides her in her search. With John Gielgud, Maurice Ronet. 118 min.
19-1187 Was $19.99 *$14.99*

Dead As A Doorman (1986)
A would-be novelist moonlighting as a doorman at a posh hotel discovers that many of his bellcap brethren are the targets of a psycho killer. Bradley Whitford stars. 84 min.
47-1716 *$69.99*

Eye Of The Needle (1981)
A first-rate WWII espionage thriller, with Donald Sutherland as a German spy stationed on an island off the coast of England and Kate Nelligan as a British woman who falls in love with him, only to learn his true identity. With Ian Bannen; based on Ken Follett's novel. 112 min.
12-1749 Was $29.99 *❑$14.99*

Eye Of The Needle (Letterboxed Version)
Also available in a theatrical, widescreen format.
12-3168 *❑$14.99*

The Cradle Will Fall (1983)
A young woman is convinced she's witnessed a murder at the hospital she is staying at, but no one will believe her...except the killer! Bizarre suspense thriller stars Lauren Hutton, James Farentino, Ben Murphy and many of the stars of "The Guiding Light" in their TV roles. 103 min.
40-1166 Was $19.99 *$14.99*

Special Bulletin (1983)
Anti-nuclear terrorists take over a Charleston, S.C., TV station, holding the employees hostage and demanding that all nuclear warheads be dismantled. Taut thriller ripped from today's headlines, presented as a series of actual "on air" news reports. Ed Flanders, Kathryn Walker, Roxanne Hart star. 105 min.
40-1168 *$19.99*

The Last Innocent Man (1987)
A defense attorney (Ed Harris) falls in love with a beautiful woman (Roxanne Hart) who asks him to represent her ex-husband in a murder case. Soon he finds himself the pawn in a dangerous double-cross in this twisting thriller. 114 min.
40-1344 Was $19.99 *$14.99*

Run If You Can (1987)
A serial killer is murdering women on the streets of San Francisco, and an accidental witness to the crimes may find herself the next victim. Offbeat thriller stars Yvette Nipar, Martin Landau, Jerry Van Dyke. 92 min.
67-5019 *$79.99*

The Inside Man (1984)
Exciting espionage saga stars Dennis Hopper as an American agent who must try to recover an experimental submarine detection laser that has fallen into enemy hands. But is he really a double agent? With Hardy Kruger, Gosta Ekman. 90 min.
69-5039 Was $19.99 *$14.99*

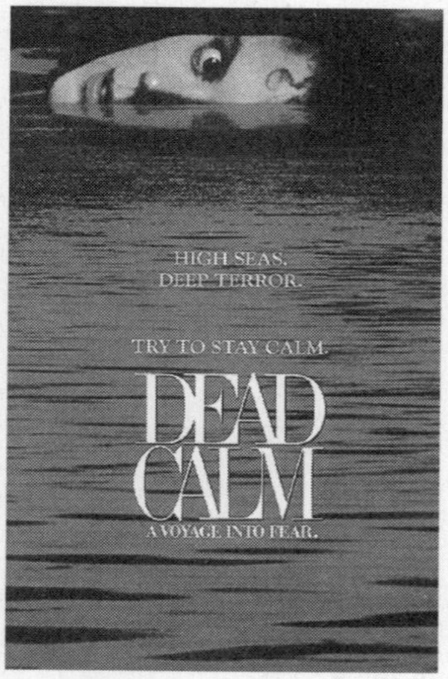

Dead Calm (1989)
A couple out on a sailing vacation rescue a man from his sinking ship and take him aboard, but soon learn that he was responsible for his crew's deaths, and a dangerous game of survival begins. Sam Neill, Billy Zane, Nicole Kidman star. 96 min.
19-1713 *❑$14.99*

Flashpoint (1984)
Kris Kristofferson and Treat Williams are Texas border patrolmen who find themselves involved with the CIA, $800,000 in stolen loot, a conspiracy plot and possible clues to John F. Kennedy's death. Edge-of-your-seat thriller also stars Rip Torn, Miguel Ferrer. 93 min.
44-1250 *$14.99*

Fear City (1985)
High-octane thriller from Abel Ferrara stars Tom Berenger as a former boxer who runs an agency that books strippers for engagements. When some of the women are brutally murdered, Berenger tries to find the culprit. Gritty suspenser also stars Melanie Griffith, Rae Dawn Chong, Billy Dee Williams and Rossano Brazzi. AKA: "Ripper." 95 min.
44-1287 Letterboxed *$14.99*

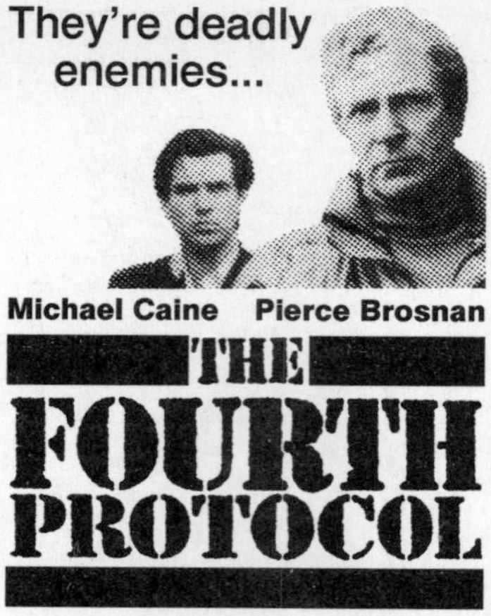

The Fourth Protocol (1987)
Top-notch suspense thriller from the pen of Frederick Forsyth ("Day of the Jackal"), with Pierce Brosnan as a KGB agent out to blow up an English town with a miniature atom bomb and Michael Caine as the British Intelligence officer who must stop him. With Ned Beatty, Joanna Cassidy. 100 min.
40-1346 *$14.99*

Defence Of The Realm (1986)
Remarkable suspenser from Britain concerning a tabloid reporter (Gabriel Byrne) whose coverage of a medical scandal hounds a politician from office. Byrne subsequently discovers that the politician's disgrace was only part of a far more sinister purpose. Thriller co-stars Greta Scacchi, Denholm Elliott. 96 min.
53-1693 *❑$14.99*

Any Time Any Play (1989)
The heated love-hate relationship of a gorgeous nightclub singer and a suave gambler is the focus of this kinky suspenser. After a series of romantic entanglements, the pair find themselves in trouble when the singer has a relationship with her mob-connected boss. With Robert Labrosse and Ruth Collins. 87 min.
59-7017 *$94.99*

Manhunter (1986)
Glossy, suspenseful thriller from director Michael Mann ("Miami Vice"), based on a novel by Tom Harris ("The Silence of the Lambs"). William Petersen is a retired FBI agent called back to track down a serial killer, and Brian Cox is convicted murderer Dr. Hannibal Lektor, who may help Petersen find his man...or lead him into a trap. Dennis Farina, Tom Noonan co-star. 118 min.
40-1241 *$14.99*

Backfire (1988)
A couple haunted by memories of the past and unable to cope with the problems of the present become friends with a mysterious stranger who may be the answer to their dreams... but there's a fatal catch. Offbeat thriller stars Keith Carradine, Karen Allen, Jeff Fahey, Bernie Casey. 90 min.
68-1132 *$29.99*

Bedroom Eyes II (1989)
The passion-filled, fatal triangle between an adulterous stockbroker, his faithless wife, and a jealous exlover fuels the steamy suspense in this white-knuckle mystery. Wings Hauser, Kathy Shower, Linda Blair star. 85 min.
68-1141 *$29.99*

Marked For Murder (1989)
Intricate suspense thriller will leave you breathless, as two TV station workers are set up with a murder frame and caught in a bizarre governmental conspiracy. Wings Hauser, Renee Estevez, James Mitchum star. 88 min.
68-1147 *$79.99*

Blitz (1985)
An automotive engineer invents a car that can run without gasoline and finds himself a pawn in a very deadly game between desperate business cartels. Jurgen Prochnow, Senta Berger and William Conrad star. AKA: "Killing Cars." 104 min.
78-3024 *$14.99*

F/X (1986)
Enthralling suspenser about a Hollywood make-up/special effects whiz who is approached by government agents to use his talents to stage a faked assassination. But are his "sponsors" on the level, and can his bag of cinematic tricks get him out of danger? Bryan Brown, Brian Dennehy, Cliff De Young star. 109 min.
73-1166 Was $19.99 *❑$14.99*

F/X 2: The Deadly Art Of Illusion (1991)
Special effects master Bryan Brown has quit show business, but he's asked to help the police by catching a killer by using some of his ingenious inventions. When the plan goes awry, Brown discovers a deadly conspiracy and calls on former police detective Brian Dennehy to help him get to the bottom of it. Rachel Ticotin, Joanna Gleason also star. 107 min.
73-1106 Was $89.99 *❑$14.99*

The Rosary Murders (1987)
A series of brutal clergy murders begins in Detroit, and a newly assigned priest (Donald Sutherland) hears the killer's confession. Unable to give the information to authorities, he begins a dangerous search for the murderer himself. Engrossing suspenser also stars Charles Durning, Belinda Bauer. 101 min.
74-1016 *❑$12.99*

Astonished (1988)
A desperate woman kills her landlord after he demands sex in return for her rent payment. But after seeing the man alive and becoming the target of an investigation by two detectives, she becomes unhinged, and even her new boyfriend can't help her. Charles S. Dutton, Liliana Komorowska and Tommy Hollis star. 90 min.
82-5171 *$89.99*

A Father's Revenge (1987)
A super-charged thriller about an airline crew abducted by radicals in West Germany. The American father of one flight attendant, with authorities unable to help, takes matters into his own hands and teams with a mercenary to rescue his daughter. Brian Dennehy, Joanna Cassidy and Ron Silver star. 93 min.
68-1244 *❑$89.99*

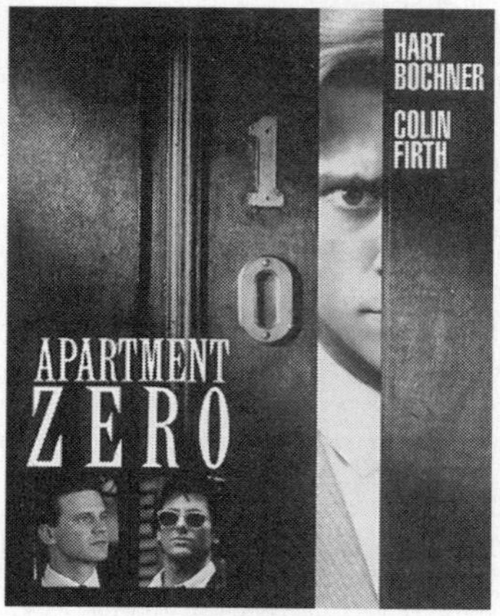

Apartment Zero (1989)
Haunting psychological thriller, set in Buenos Aires, about an eccentric and reclusive movie theater owner who becomes obsessed with discovering his charming new roommate's secret past. Director/co-scripter Martin Donovan's suspenseful tale stars Colin Firth and Hart Bochner. 114 min.
71-5180 *$19.99*

The Man From The Pru (1989)
Based on an unsolved murder that took place in England in 1931, this intense thriller features Jonathan Pryce as the cool, neglectful William Wallace, accused of killing his wife. After being sentenced to death, the jury's verdict is overturned. But who killed Mrs. Wallace and why? Anna Massey and Susannah York also star. 90 min.
53-8193 *$24.99*

Never Come Back (1989)
Epic British suspenser set in 1939, where cocky journalist Desmond Thames gets involved with beautiful Anna Raven, a mysterious woman with a secret past. When Thames finds a diary he realizes he's become a fugitive in a murder and the target of opponents he doesn't understand. Crackerjack thriller in the Hitchcock mold stars Nathaniel Parker, Suzanna Hamilton and James Fox. 150 min.
53-6953 *$49.99*

You'll Like My Mother (1972)
When her Army husband is killed in combat, a pregnant Patty Duke travels to the remote Minnesota home of his family, whom she's never met, for a visit. Meeting with icy acceptance from mother-in-law Rosemary Murphy and stranded by a blizzard, Duke begins to discover terrifying—and deadly—secrets about her relations in this gripping suspenser. Richard Thomas, Sian Barbara Allen also star. 93 min.
07-2892 *$14.99*

The Dain Curse (1978)
James Coburn stars as Dashiell Hammett's two-fisted private eye, Hamilton Nash, in this spellbinding miniseries. A seemingly closed jewel robbery case draws Nash into a sinister mystery involving a beautiful young woman, a strange religious temple, and a deadly family curse. Nancy Addison, Hector Elizondo, Jason Miller, Jean Simmons, Beatrice Straight also star. 192 min. on three tapes.
08-8611 *$39.99*

Deadly Encounter (1978)
A swanky gathering for the American social elite dissolves into a whirlpool of gathering madness when someone suggests a round of five card stud played with loaded revolvers. Dina Merrill, Carl Betz, Leon Ames. 90 min.
08-1404 *$19.99*

The Swiss Conspiracy (1977)
In this international thriller, David Janssen plays an investigator hired to keep Swiss bank account holders safe from crooks trying to swipe their cash with an elaborate scheme. Santa Berger, John Saxon and Elke Sommer also star. 88 min.
08-1080 *$19.99*

Evidence Of Power (1979)
A college student returns to his small-town home for the summer and is shocked to find that the community is being hit with a series of strange deaths. Are the gruesome incidents merely accidents, as the young man's police chief father suggests, or is one of the townsfolk a serial killer? Gripping mystery stars Alan Hale, Gordon Jump, Steven Wayne Carry. 92 min.
09-3079 *$19.99*

Marshal Of Madrid (1972)
Glenn Ford plays the title role of rural California lawman Sam Cade, who must deal with a gang of ornery smugglers led by an oil dealer, in this contemporary frontier drama culled from episodes of the hit TV series "Cade's County." Edgar Buchanan, Taylor Lacher also star.
10-9518 *$14.99*

Seven Times Seven (1973)
In this European heist movie, a group of prison inmates escape their jail cells to rob the Royal Mint, but return to the prison in time to stay out of trouble. At least that's what they believe. Adolfo Celli, Gordon Mitchell, Lionel Stander and Terry-Thomas star. 100 min.
10-9529 *$14.99*

The Disappearance Of Flight 412 (1974)
This Watergate-era conspiracy flick has Air Force colonel Glenn Ford trying to learn what happened to two jets that vanished while pursuing a reported UFO, despite orders from above to forget the incident. Ford investigates the occurrence anyway, and uncovers more than he bargained for. Bradford Dillman, Kent Smith and David Soul co-star. 74 min.
10-9835 *$14.99*

Last Embrace (1979)
Exciting thriller stars Roy Scheider as a CIA agent investigating his wife's mysterious death, only to find that he may be the next victim on an unknown killer's hit list. Taut tale of suspense, highlighted by a chase across Niagara Falls, also stars Janet Margolin, Christopher Walken and Sam Levene. 101 min.
12-2601 *$14.99*

They Only Kill Their Masters (1972)
California coastal town police chief James Garner looks into the suspected killing of a local woman by her Doberman pinscher. His investigation leads him into a complex web of suspense and brings him into contact with all sorts of unusual characters. Katharine Ross, Hal Holbrook, June Allyson and Tom Ewell also star. 97 min.
12-2650 *$19.99*

Death Cruise (1974)
Three couples win an ocean liner vacation, but the holiday turns to terror when someone starts killing them one by one. Kate Jackson, Tom Bosley, Edward Albert, Celeste Holm star. 74 min.
44-7023 *$19.99*

The Outside Man (1973)
Stylish thriller starring Jean-Louis Trintignant as a Frenchman deep in gambling debts who takes a job to knock off a mobster in Los Angeles. He soon discovers that another hired assassin is after *him*! Ann-Margret, Roy Scheider and Angie Dickinson also star. 104 min.
12-2670 *$14.99*

Lady Ice (1973)
Terrific caper suspenser about an insurance investigator's discoveries of an illegal "fence" operation involving stolen jewels. Donald Sutherland, Robert Duvall and Jennifer O'Neill head the fine cast. 93 min.
59-5029 *$12.99*

The Eyes Of Laura Mars (1978)
A stylish, suspenseful chiller with a high fashion setting, starring Faye Dunaway as a glamour photographer who "witnesses" the murders of several models in her mind and Tommy Lee Jones as the detective who must help her learn the truth before the killer finds her. With Raul Julia, Rene Auberjonois. 108 min.
02-2693 *$14.99*

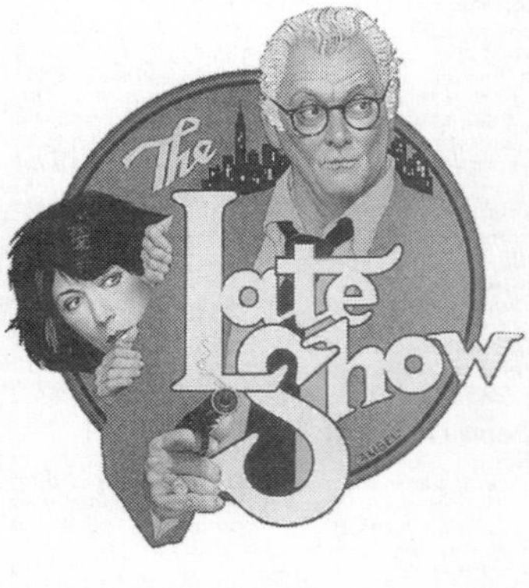

The Late Show (1977)
Robert Benton called the shots on this overlooked and complex thriller that pays homage to '40s-style detective yarns. Art Carney is the aging gumshoe helped (or hindered) by ditzy sidekick Lily Tomlin in pursuing a former partner's killer. 94 min.
19-1196 Was $19.99 *❑$14.99*

The Thief Who Came To Dinner (1973)
Ryan O'Neal, Jacqueline Bisset and Jill Clayburgh star in this stylish thriller, as a computer programmer in Houston decides to put his electronic skills to better use as a jewel thief. 105 min.
19-1412 Was $19.99 *$14.99*

Baffled (1973)
After recovering from a near-fatal crash, race car driver Leonard Nimoy is haunted by psychic premonitions that draw him into the lives of a reclusive film star and her daughter. Intriguing thriller tinged with the supernatural also stars Vera Miles, Susan Hampshire. 93 min.
27-6774 *$12.99*

One Of My Wives Is Missing (1976)
A pilot for a TV series that didn't make it, this mystery stars Jack Klugman as a small-town detective looking into a strange case in which a man's missing wife reappears. The hubby, however, believes she's an impostor. With Elizabeth Ashley, James Franciscus.
40-1094 *$19.99*

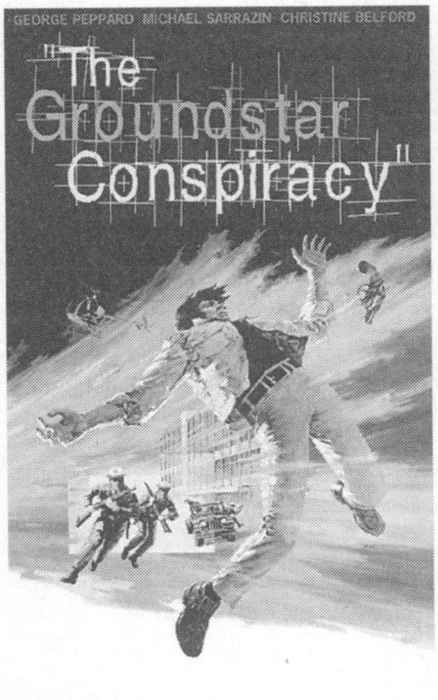

The Groundstar Conspiracy (1972)
A top secret space project explodes and the sole survivor, a scientist (Michael Sarrazin) hired to steal its blueprints, suffers from amnesia. A governmental security agent (George Peppard) is given free reign to force the spy into divulging the conspiracy's mastermind in this gripping cliffhanger. 93 min.
07-1507 Was $59.99 *$14.99*

The Deadly Game
A British secret agent, out of favor with his superiors, receives a call to help a Soviet general defect. But is he just being used as a pawn for the mission? David Hemmings, Sam Wanamaker and Sir Ralph Richardson star in this thrilling espionage story. 104 min.
44-1819 ❑*$59.99*

The Silent Partner (1979)
Great thriller with Elliott Gould as a bank clerk who uses his branch's robbery by "Santa Claus bandit" Christopher Plummer to stash away an extra $50,000 for himself in a safety deposit box. The scheme works, until Plummer learns of the discrepancy and comes looking for Gould. Susannah York, John Candy also star. 103 min.
47-1032 *$14.99*

Murder In Music City (1979)
When a dead body is discovered in their honeymoon suite, a songwriter who doubles as a detective and his beautiful model bride travel to Nashville to try to solve the mystery. Sonny Bono, Lee Purcell, Claude Akins, Morgan Fairchild and country greats Charlie Daniels, Larry Gatlin, Mel Tillis and Barbara Mandrell star. AKA: "The Country-Western Murders." 95 min.
10-1595 *$19.99*

The Human Factor (1979)
A British Secret Service agent who passed information to the Russians in order to help an old acquaintance in Africa is forced into defecting to the U.S.S.R. in Otto Preminger's intense adaptation of Graham Greene's novel. Nicol Williamson, Richard Attenborough, John Gielgud and Derek Jacobi lead the sterling cast. 115 min.
12-2918 *$19.99*

Picnic At Hanging Rock (1975)
Director Peter Weir's compelling, surreal film is set in 1900s Australia. A girls' school outing ends with a bizarre mystery when three students and a teacher vanish after climbing to the top of the title rock. One of the girls is later found, but cannot explain what happened to her or her friends. Rachel Roberts, Dominic Guard, Helen Morse, Anne Lambert star. This remastered director's cut also includes the original theatrical trailer. 107 min.
47-1021 Letterboxed ❑*$19.99*

The Woman Hunter (1972)
In this thriller, Barbara Eden plays a wealthy woman whose Acapulco vacation is interrupted by jewel thieves who want to kill her. Robert Vaughn, Stuart Whitman and Larry Storch also star. AKA: "The Bauble." 73 min.
30-1072 *$19.99*

Death At Love House (1975)
A late movie queen from the '30s reaches out from beyond in this supernatural chiller. Robert Wagner and Kate Jackson star as film writers whose research uncovers the sinister secrets of Lorna Love. Dorothy Malone, Bill Macy co-star. 74 min.
46-5063 *$19.99*

Medusa (1976)
The Greek Isles are the setting for this tale of greed, forbidden love and revenge, as mining empire heir George Hamilton forms a deadly bond with gangster Cameron Mitchell. With Luciana Paluzzi. 103 min. AKA: "Twisted." 103 min.
46-6011 *$19.99*

The Disappearance (1977)
An international killer-for-hire has the most dangerous assignment of his life: find his missing wife. Donald Sutherland, John Hurt, David Hemmings and Francine Rachette star in this thriller. 80 min.
47-1208 Was $29.99 *$14.99*

Double Face (1970)
Mystery/suspense shocker about a millionaire industrialist who uses a car bomb to kill his lesbian wife, then thinks he sees her in an adult film. Klaus Kinski, Annabella Incontrera star. 84 min.
48-1095 *$49.99*

A Quiet Place To Kill (1970)
Carroll Baker is a race car driver lured into a web of intrigue and deceit by her ex-husband's new wife. The plot twists and turns and ultimately leads to its inevitable conclusion: murder. 90 min.
48-1113 *$59.99*

Tomorrow Never Comes (1977)
A disturbed young man shoots a cop and takes his ex-girlfriend hostage in this tense police drama. Raymond Burr, Oliver Reed, Susan George and Stephen McHattie star. 106 min.
48-1168 *$79.99*

Smile, Jenny, You're Dead (1974)
The murder of a police lieutenant's son-in-law puts ex-cop turned P.I. David Janssen in the middle of a deadly triangle when he becomes involved with the lieutenant's daughter, the case's prime supsect. Andrea Marcovicci, John Anderson and Jodie Foster also star in this mystery, the pilot to the hit series "Harry O." 92 min.
48-1177 *$59.99*

H-Bomb (1971)
Top-notch suspense yarn starring Chris Mitchum and Olivia Hussey in a tale of international intrigue in which a CIA agent travels to Bangkok to find stolen nuclear weapons. 98 min.
14-6149 *$19.99*

The Inheritance (1976)
Anthony Quinn is an aging bakery tycoon who wants to hold his fortune close to him, keeping it away from his two sons. His daughter-in-law, luscious Dominique Sanda, has other ideas on how to get his inheritance, and they involve seduction. Sexy European thriller features Sanda at the height of her sexiness. 105 min.
15-1029 *$12.99*

11 Harrowhouse (1974)
An exciting blend of action, suspense and laughs, with Charles Grodin as a bumbling diamond buyer in London who is recruited by millionaire Trevor Howard to steal the contents of a heavily-secured vault in a precious gem clearinghouse run by John Gielgud. Co-stars Candice Bergen and James Mason. 95 min.
04-3078 Was $59.99 ❑*$29.99*

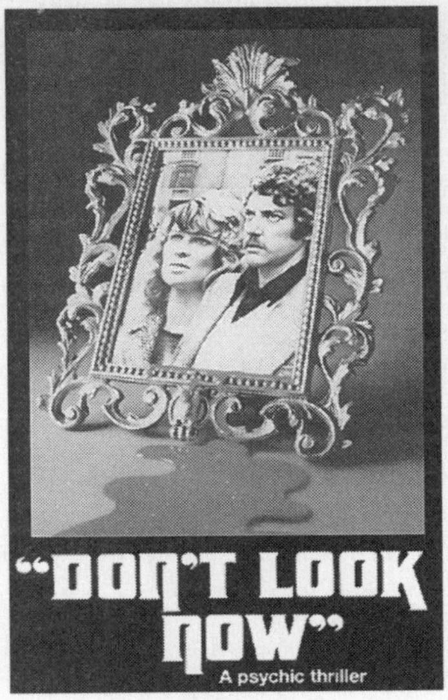

Don't Look Now (1973)
Nicolas Roeg classic of suspense and terror stars Julie Christie and Donald Sutherland as a couple on vacation in Venice who are haunted by what may be the spirit of their late daughter. 110 min.
06-1012 Was $49.99 *$19.99*

The Day Of The Jackal (1973)
Riveting thriller of an assassin hired to kill Charles DeGaulle, juxtaposing his calm preparation for the shooting against the tense international manhunt for him. Edward Fox is the murderous "Jackal"; with Alan Badel, Cyril Cusack. 141 min.
07-1137 Was $59.99 ❑*$14.99*

Murder On Flight 502 (1975)
A transatlantic flight becomes a trip into terror when a passenger is killed and the murderer waits, undiscovered, for his next victim. Thriller stars Robert Stack, Farrah Fawcett-Majors, Ralph Bellamy, Polly Bergen, Molly Picon and Sonny Bono. 97 min.
46-5155 *$14.99*

Black Sunday (1977)
International terrorists plan to strike America where it will hurt the most: halftime at the Super Bowl!! Marthe Keller and Bruce Dern are the lovers who will pilot a bomb-laden blimp into the stadium; Robert Shaw the agent who must stop them. 143 min.
06-1177 *$14.99*

The Last Of Sheila (1973)
Witty, sophisticated mystery about an intricate game played out on board a luxury yacht to unravel the truth behind the death of Sheila, with Hollywood big shots as its players. Stars James Coburn, Raquel Welch, Dyan Cannon, James Mason, Richard Benjamin. Scripted by Stephen Sondheim and Anthony Perkins; directed by Herbert Ross. 119 min.
19-1201 Was $19.99 *$14.99*

Shadow Of Fear (1974)
Private eye and ex-cop Claude Akins is hired by beautiful heiress Anjanette Comer to discover the unknown person who has been terrorizing her. There's no lack of suspects, including shiftless husband Jason Evers and handsome male friend Tom Selleck, in this riveting mystery. 66 min.
50-7053 Was $19.99 *$14.99*

The Racing Game (1979)
Mike Gwilym stars as Sid Halley, the champion British jockey who suffers a career-ending injury and becomes a private investigator specializing in crimes among "the horsey set," in these mysteries based on stories by best-selling author Dick Francis. Mick Ford co-stars as Halley's gruff sidekick, Chico Barnes. Each three-tape boxed set runs about 156 min.

The Racing Game, Vol. 1: Set (1979)
After his hand is crushed in a racetrack injury, jockey Sid Halley finds a new career when his ex-father-in-law asks him to look into suspicious doings at the track in "Odds Against." Halley and partner Chico Barnes look into a deadly race-fixing scheme in "Trackdown," while a priceless horse's death, a beautiful woman and an international swindle are the elements of "Gambling Lady."
50-8600 *$49.99*

The Racing Game, Vol. 2: Set (1979)
Who's behind a violent extortion scheme targeting some of the country's top bookmakers? Halley tries to find out in "Horses for Courses." Also, Sid and Chico try to recover a missing steed in "Horsenap," and racehorses are being killed by someone wielding a deadly "Needle."
50-8601 *$49.99*

Dick Francis Mysteries (1989)
From the best-selling, horse-racing themed world of Dick Francis comes these suspenseful productions which feature Ian McShane as Jockey Club investigator David Cleveland, a cool operator who loves beautiful women and can't stay out of trouble. Patrick Macnee also stars. Each tape runs about 95 min.

Twice Shy (1989)
When a computer wizard's body is found at the side of a cliff, investigator David Cleveland thinks the death has something to do with a foolproof betting system he's concocted.
50-5667 *$19.99*

In The Frame
David Cleveland looks into a mysterious explosion that claimed a young woman's life. Soon, he's embroiled in fake paintings, con games, art, vintage wine and fast horses.
50-5668 *$19.99*

Blood Sport
When a $6 million stallion is missing and its owner's life is threatened, dashing detective David Cleveland gets to work. His investigation takes him to the Canadian Rockies, where Cleveland's life is put in danger.
50-5669 *$19.99*

Dick Francis Mysteries: Set
Gallop to your phone and order this three-tape set of Dick Francis horse-racing thrillers: "Twice Shy," "In the Frame" and "Blood Sport."
50-5670 Save $10.00! *$49.99*

Obsession (1976)
Brian DePalma, master of the macabre, directed this suspenseful yarn about a man who meets a young woman who resembles his dead wife. Cliff Robertson, John Lithgow, Genevieve Bujold. 98 min.
02-1222 *$14.99*

The Black Windmill (1974)
Spine-tingling suspense yarn stars Michael Caine as a British secret agent on the trail of merciless gunrunners who have kidnapped his son. Co-stars Donald Pleasence, Joseph O'Connor and John Vernon. Directed by Don Siegel. 102 min.
07-1448 *$59.99*

Eagle Over London (1973)
Interesting European-produced WWII espionage yarn about Nazi spies who infiltrate British forces headquarters during the Battle of Britain, causing all sorts of terror. Frederick Stafford, Van Johnson and Francisco Rabal star. 100 min.
10-9513 *$14.99*

The Teacher (1974)
What starts out as an illicit affair between a voluptuous teacher and her teenage student becomes a course of suspense and terror, as they are stalked by a knife-wielding maniac. Angel Tompkins, Jay North, Barry Atwater star. 98 min.
15-1143 *$19.99*

The Last Wave (1978)
Moody, mysterious thriller starring Richard Chamberlain as an Australian lawyer who finds that eerie, inexplicable things begin to occur when he defends an aborigine accused of murder. Peter Weir ("Witness") directs; Olivia Hambett, David Gulpilil co-star. 104 min.
19-1140 *$19.99*

The Bergonzi Hand (1970)
A suspenseful and intriguing tale set in the art world. Two shady art dealers become involved in a forgery scheme with a talented immigrant painter. Keith Mitchell, Gordon Jackson and Martin Miller star. 62 min.
09-1622 Was $24.99 *$14.99*

The Suspects (1974)
An American girl is found dead on a roadside on the French Riviera, after she hitchhiked across the country. Who killed her and why? The investigator soon finds herself enmeshed in the mystery. Mimsy Farmer and Paul Meurisse star. 81 min.
50-5977 *$12.99*

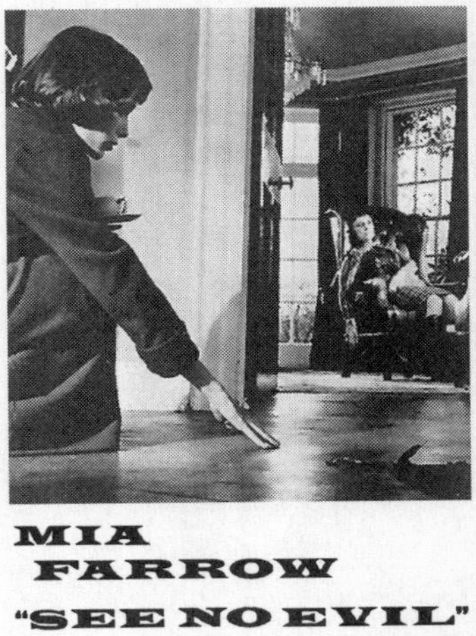

See No Evil (1971)
Mia Farrow stars as a woman taken in by her uncle's family after losing her sight who must fight to survive a night of heart-pounding horror when she realizes that they have been murdered...and the killer is still in the house! Directed by Richard Fleischer. AKA: "Blind Terror." 90 min.
02-1637 *$14.99*

They Call It Murder (1971)
A corpse in a swimming pool launches this mystery starring Jim Hutton as Perry Mason-creator Erle Stanley Gardner's sleuthing D.A. Doug Selby, who uncovers more trouble than he wants to when one body leads to another. With Jessica Walter, Lloyd Bochner, Leslie Nielsen and Ed Asner. 100 min.
55-3038 *$19.99*

The Dain Curse (1978)
James Coburn is Dashiell Hammett's private eye, Hamilton Nash, in this spellbinding mystery. He's up against stolen diamonds, call girls and a deadly murder. Elegantly made puzzler also stars Jason Miller, Jean Simmons, Beatrice Straight. 118 min.
53-1083 *$24.99*

Paper Man (1971)
College students use computers to create a fictitious person and go on spending sprees with the "paper man's" credit cards. Their fun, however, turns into a sinister fraud scheme that ends in death. Offbeat thriller stars Dean Stockwell, Stefanie Powers, James Olson. 90 min.
54-9021 *$19.99*

Deadly Trap (1972)
Industrial spy Frank Langella wants to leave the business, but while vacationing in Paris his children are abducted by his ex-associates, driving wife Faye Dunaway to a nervous breakdown and sending him on a crusade of vengeance. Co-stars Barbara Parkins, Raymond Gerome. AKA: "Death Scream." 96 min.
75-7002 Was $19.99 **$14.99**

The Heist (1979)
Thrilling stunt driving highlights this crime drama about a Dillinger-idolizing thief who leads his gang on a daring series of bank jobs. Charles Aznavour, Virna Lisi, Robert Hossein star. 85 min.
75-7078 Was $19.99 **$14.99**

Shattered Silence (1972)
Gripping psychological thriller about a woman haunted by phone calls from her nephew, who supposedly died 15 years earlier. Michael Douglas, Elizabeth Ashley and Ben Gazzara star. AKA: "When Michael Calls." 73 min.
78-1021 **$12.99**

The Sellout (1976)
Top-notch espionage thriller focuses on both a CIA agent and a Russian spy who become entangled in a violent game of intrigue. Richard Widmark, Oliver Reed, Gayle Hunnicutt star. 88 min.
78-1038 **$14.99**

Come Die With Me (1974)
After killing his spendthrift brother in a fit of anger, a wealthy man is blackmailed by his housekeeper into a romance. The only thing standing in the devilish domestic's way is the man's girlfriend, but she has a plan... Engrossing suspense story stars Eileen Brennan, Charles Macaulay, George Maharis, Kathryn Leigh Scott. AKA: "Come Live With Me." 67 min.
50-7052 Was $19.99 **$14.99**

Fright (1972)
Terrifying suspenser about a young woman hired as a babysitter who must defend her charge from his demented father, who's just escaped from the asylum and wants his son back...at any price! Susan George, Ian Bannen, Honor Blackman star. AKA: "Night Legs." 84 min.
63-1671 Was $59.99 **$12.99**

The Silent Passenger (1935)
Dorothy L. Sayer's aristocratic sleuth, Lord Peter Wimsey, made his first screen appearance in this thriller set on board a train. Wimsey (Peter Haddon) comes to the aid of a fellow passenger accused of murder when a body is found in his trunk. With Donald Wolfit, Mary Newland. 75 min.
68-8101 **$19.99**

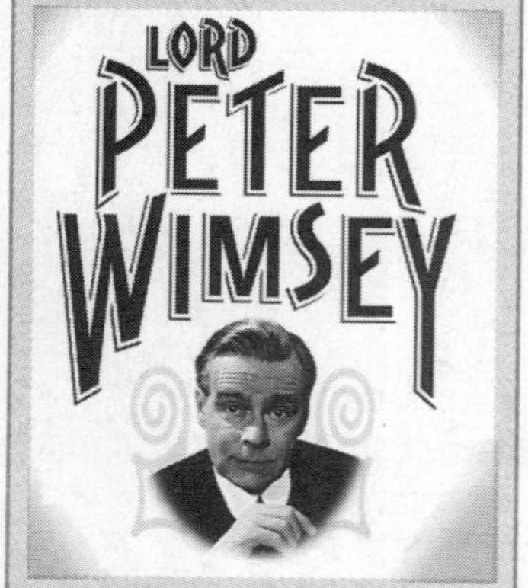

Lord Peter Wimsey: Cloud Of Witnesses (1972)
It's "murder amid the upper crust" when Lord Peter Wimsey (Ian Carmichael) must clear his brother, the Duke of Denver, of killing their sister's fiancé in this compelling mini-series based on Dorothy L. Sayers' novel. David Langton, Rachel Herbert, Glyn Houston also star. 225 min. on five tapes.
50-8268 **$59.99**

Lord Peter Wimsey: Unpleasantness At The Bellona Club (1972)
Lord Peter Wimsey, as played by Ian Carmichael, is back in another enthralling mystery series from "Masterpiece Theatre." In this outing, the sophisticated Lord Peter investigates the death of a member of the Bellona Club who passed away in a reading room. But Wimsey soon finds out there's more to the death than meets the eye. 180 min. on four tapes.
50-8405 **$59.99**

Lord Peter Wimsey: Murder Must Advertise (1973)
In what many consider the best of Dorothy L. Sayers' Lord Peter whodunits, Wimsey poses as a copywriter to look into the suspicious death of a worker at a London ad agency and finds drugs, sex and office politics are just the tip of the iceberg. Ian Carmichael, Mark Eden, Peter Bowles, Fiona Walker and Mary Herbert star. 200 min. on four tapes.
50-8526 **$59.99**

The Demon Within (1972)
Intense psychological thriller stars Christopher Walken as an American soldier in Germany who suffers from violent outbursts. Sent to a hospital for treatment, he becomes part of a bizarre mind control experiment. With Ralph Meeker, Ronny Cox. AKA: "Happiness Cage," "Mind Snatchers." 94 min.
75-7011 Was $19.99 **$14.99**

A Nightingale Sang In Berkeley Square (1979)
Richard Jordan plays an ex-convict who is hired by a mob kingpin to pull off an elaborate bank heist in this exciting, witty thriller that also stars David Niven, Gloria Grahame, Elke Sommer and Hugh Griffith. AKA: "The Big Scam." 102 min.
64-3297 **$19.99**

Betrayal (1974)
A young woman is hired to serve as companion to a wealthy and lonely widow, but, unknown to her employer, she and her boyfriend are planning a deadly extortion scheme. Amanda Blake, Sam Groom, Dick Haymes and Tisha Sterling star. 78 min.
55-3005 **$19.99**

The Psycho Lover (1971)
A psychiatrist uses hypnosis to persuade a psychotic killer to murder his wife so he can have his young mistress full-time. When the wife discovers her husband's scheme, she turns the tables on him. Sordid shocker stars Lawrence Montaigne and Joanne Meredith.
79-5418 Was $24.99 **$19.99**

Project: Kill (1977)
Leslie Nielsen plays the head of a secret government agency who becomes the target of his former partner, played by Gary Lockwood. Nancy Kwan also stars in this espionage thriller.
58-1041 **$14.99**

The Butterfly Affair (1970)
"Papillon" author Henri Charriere is featured in this crime caper that also showcases Claudia Cardinale. A striptease artist, a con man and $2 million in diamonds are involved in this double-crossing thriller set in Venezuela.
58-1068 **$14.99**

The Ninth Configuration (1979)
A remote castle-turned-military insane asylum is the setting for this offbeat suspenser laced with dark humor and symbolism. Stacy Keach portrays the new head psychiatrist who seems no less crazy than any of the patients. With Scott Wilson, Ed Flanders, Jason Miller; written, produced and directed by William Peter Blatty ("The Exorcist"). AKA: "Twinkle, Twinkle, Killer Kane." 114 min.
70-1046 Letterboxed **$19.99**

The Odessa File (1974)
Jon Voight stars as a German journalist whose investigation of former Nazi war criminals gets him involved in a plan run by Israeli agents. Maximilian Schell plays a deadly SS officer in this gripping adaptation of the Frederick Forsyth thriller. 129 min.
02-2627 Was $59.99 **$14.99**

Diary Of An Erotic Murderess (1974)
A wealthy man hires a beautiful governess to care for his demented son and soon becomes smitten with his new domestic help. But she's more interested in the father's money, and thinks she can get her hands on it with help from a diary kept by his late, homicidal wife. Atmospheric European sex thriller stars Richard Conte, Marisa Mell. AKA: "La Encadenada." 86 min.
79-5957 Letterboxed **$19.99**

The Man With The Icy Eyes (1971)
Intriguing thriller in which an Italian journalist looking into the death of a U.S. senator meets a score of strange people during his investigation and soon wonders if somehow he was involved in framing an innocent man. Antonio Sabato stars; Faith Domergue, Keenan Wynn, Victor Buono and Barbara Bouchet are the established cast who add creepiness to the proceedings.
79-6516 **$19.99**

The Cat And The Canary (1979)
Chic sex auteur Radley Metzger ("The Lickerish Quartet") reworks the classic thriller with stylish results. Honor Blackman, Michael Callan, Olivia Hussey, Edward Fox, Wendy Hiller, Carol Lynley and Wilfrid Hyde-White are among those trying to dodge a killer in an old mansion on a rainy night. 98 min.
02-1098 Was $39.99 **$29.99**

The Astral Factor (1977)
A hardened detective races against time and the odds to track down a criminally insane murderer who has escaped from his institution and is bent on killing the people who testified against him. With Robert Foxworth, Elke Sommer and Stefanie Powers. 95 min.
55-3002 **$19.99**

Booby Trap (1972)
A former Marine discharged for his hatred of "young freaks" heads for California with 40 stolen high explosive mines and plans to bomb a Fourth of July rock concert. After he takes a sexy hitchhiker into custody, the man is pursued by a military agent and the hitcher's nympho sibling. Carl Monson and Angela Carnon star.
79-5648 Was $24.99 **$19.99**

Every Man Is My Enemy (1970)
A group of international crooks attempts a jewelry heist, but when things go wrong the American member of the group tries to find out who the traitor was. Robert Webber and Elsa Martinelli star in this thriller.
68-8894 **$19.99**

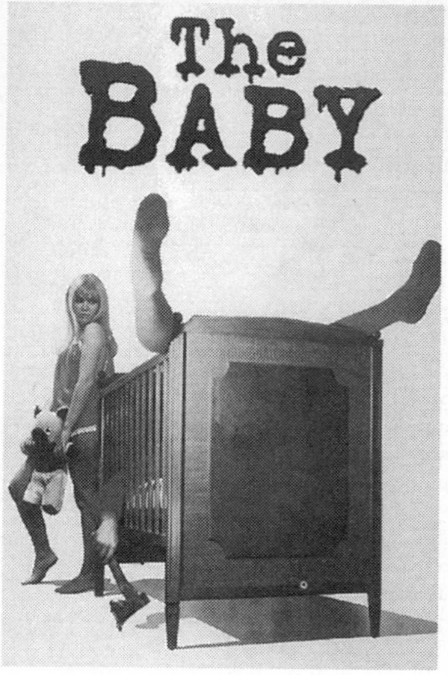

The Baby (1973)
A social worker investigating a strange family is shocked when she uncovers the secret of Baby, a fully-grown man kept as a diapered, playpen-bound infant by his demented mother, in this bizarre suspense tale. Anjanette Comer, Ruth Roman and David Manzy star. 80 min.
59-5020 Was $59.99 **$19.99**

Atomic War Bride (1966)
With the threat of nuclear war in the air, a young man and his girl get married, then become witness to the chaos that ensues when their nation goes to war using atomic bombs. This "Cold War" thriller from Yugoslavia stars Anton Vrodljak and Ewa Krzyzewska. Dubbed in English.
79-6495 **$19.99**

From Istanbul: Orders To Kill (1965)
A writer takes a job impersonating an Italian crook which eventually lands him in Istanbul, where he falls in love with the wife of the man he's impersonating. Danger ensues when he learns that the friend that offered him the job has set him up in an elaborate scheme that may cost him his life. Christopher Logan, Nino Fuscagni star in this Euro-thriller. Dubbed in English.
79-6514 **$19.99**

Moving Target (1969)
International intriguer with Yank Ty Hardin as the world's top thief, wanted by cops and criminals alike for the tooth he extracted from a corpse in prison. The tooth has secret microfilm in it that includes important double agent info. Michael Rennie, Gordon Mitchell also star; spaghetti western maestro Sergio Corbucci helms. AKA: "Death on the Run."
79-6517 **$19.99**

A Touch Of Treason (1961)
After breaking into a high-security safe of a Russian embassy official in France, a man is questioned by the KGB, then kidnapped by a mysterious criminal organization seeking stolen documents. The French secret service soon gets involved in the investigation, as well some nasty KGB assassins. Roger Hanin, Pascale Audret and Dany Carrel star; Edouard Molinaro directs.
79-6523 **$19.99**

Blind Justice (1961)
During the trial of a man accused of murdering his wife, a mysterious woman appears in court, explaining that the suspect's wife committed suicide. The district attorney can't believe this, and when the suspect is released and later found dead, the DA has to get to the bottom of the mystery. Peter Van Eyck, Eva Bartok and Marianne Koch star.
79-6548 Was $24.99 **$19.99**

Night Train To Milan (1963)
Unusual thriller stars Jack Palance as an ex-Nazi war criminal recognized by other passengers while on an overnight train to Milan. A clash with one of the camp survivors leads Palance to start taking hostages on the trip. Yvonne Furneaux and Salvo Randone also star in this intense tale.
79-6518 **$19.99**

To Chase A Million (1967)
Culled from episodes of the TV series "Man in a Suitcase," this British suspenser features Richard Bradford as a former American spy who leaves an idyllic life in London and heads to Lisbon to track down the murderer of his friend, a former Russian diplomat. Yoko Tani, Ron Randell also star.
79-6522 **$19.99**

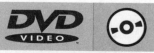

Daggers Drawn (1963)
Four ace criminals unite to look for a sunken treasure of diamonds and secret documents lost by the Nazis in the waters off Monte Carlo. Hot on their trail are secret agents from around the world who want to find the documents first. At the same time, a mysterious killer is murdering the criminals. Pierre Mondy stars and Petula Clark, who sings, has a cameo. Dubbed in English.
79-6510 **$19.99**

Operation Atlantis (1965)
European espionager starring John Ericson as a secret agent whose vacation in the Middle East is interrupted when he finds himself in the middle of international intrigue involving missile bases, a war between rival countries and a trip to the lost city of Atlantis. All this and sexy Italian actress Berna Rock, too! AKA: "Agent S-03: Operation Atlantis."
79-6519 **$19.99**

Shadow Of Evil (1964)
Produced in the wake of the spy phenomenon that swept the world after "Dr. No," this thriller features Kerwin Matthews as secret agent OSS 117, an operative sent to Thailand to stop Dr. Sinn from conquering the world using a secret virus. Robert Hossein, Pier Angeli also star.
79-6520 **$19.99**

13 Days To Die (1963)
When a prince in Thailand discovers that he's being blackmailed and has been targeted for murder, a group of super secret-agents are called on to investigate. It seems that a criminal organization is behind the threats and their leader will stop at nothing to carry out his scheme. Thomas Adler, Horst Fank and Peter Carsten star. AKA: "The Curse of the Black Ruby."
79-6521 **$19.99**

Dictator's Guns (1965)
A sea captain is accused of hijacking a ship that was actually taken by gunrunners. Helping him try to find the real culprits is an American woman who claims to be the wife of the lost ship's captain. Lino Ventura, Sylva Koscina and Leo Gordon star in this thriller from Claude Sautet ("Cesar and Rosalie"). Dubbed in English.
79-6549 Was $24.99 **$19.99**

The Looking Glass War (1969)
John le Carré's best-selling novel is spun into a gripping thriller by first time director Frank Pierson (screenwriter of "Cool Hand Luke"), with Christopher Jones as a Polish refugee tagged by British Intelligence to photograph East German missile sites. Co-stars Pia Degermark, Ralph Richardson and Anthony Hopkins. 108 min.
02-1269 Was $59.99 **$14.99**

Confess Dr. Corda (1961)
Hardy Kruger plays a doctor who finds his mistress murdered at their rendezvous site and becomes the prime suspect as the police seek to convict him. With the community turning against him, Kruger's only hope is for the real killer to be found. Elizabeth Mueller, Lucie Mannheim, Hans Nielson and Fritz Tillman also star. 101 min.
68-9269 **$19.99**

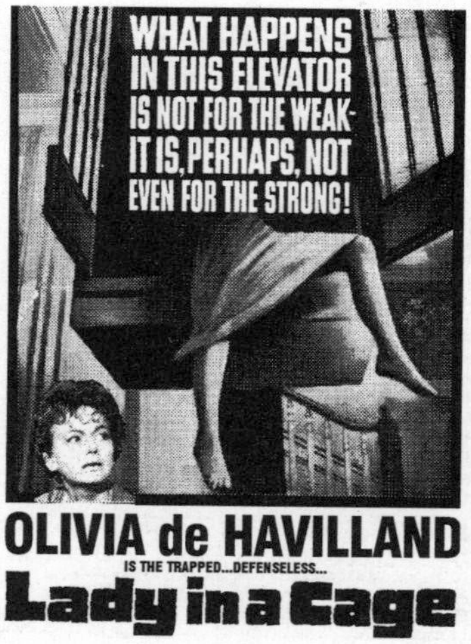

Lady In A Cage (1964)
While trapped in her house's private elevator, wealthy widow Olivia de Havilland is tormented by a group of psychos in this strange and disturbing thriller. Ann Sothern, James Caan co-star. 93 min.
06-1225 Was $49.99 **$14.99**

Experiment In Terror (1962)
A bank teller is forced to steal $100,000 by a psychopath holding her sister captive and becomes the bait in a dangerous trap set up by the FBI to catch the madman in this thriller by Blake Edwards. Glenn Ford, Lee Remick, Ross Martin and Stefanie Powers star. 123 min.
02-1583 **$14.99**

No Way To Treat A Lady (1968)
A delightfully macabre crime thriller, with Rod Steiger tackling the role of a serial killer who uses various disguises to trick his female victims. George Segal is the cop on the case; Lee Remick, Eileen Heckart, Michael Dunn also star. 108 min.
06-1223 Was $49.99 **$14.99**

Love From A Stranger (1937)
Basil Rathbone is a suave and sinister Bluebeard whose scheme to murder wealthy new bride Ann Harding lurks beneath the surface of a dazzling game of wits in this Agatha Christie thriller. 86 min.
10-7419 *$19.99*

And Then There Were None (1945)
The original film version of Agatha Christie's classic thriller. Ten people are summoned to a remote island where they're murdered one by one. Which one of them is the killer? Barry Fitzgerald, Louis Hayward, June Duprez, Walter Huston star; directed by René Clair. 97 min.
08-1039 Was $19.99 *$14.99*

Ten Little Indians (1959)
Atmospheric early TV rendition of Agatha Christie's "And Then There Were None," set on an island where 10 guests, each with a hidden connection to their unseen host, are killed one at a time. Nina Foch, Barry Jones, Romney Brent star. 59 min.
09-1269 *$19.99*

Ten Little Indians (1966)
A dinner party in a remote Alpine retreat becomes a search for a murderer when, one by one, the guests of the unseen host are killed. Hugh O'Brian, Shirley Eaton, Wilfrid Hyde-White, Dennis Price and Fabian star in this variation of the Christie thriller. 90 min.
19-2054 Was $19.99 *$14.99*

Witness For The Prosecution (1957)
Superior, sublimely entertaining treatment of Agatha Christie's play stars Charles Laughton as an elderly London barrister who ignores his physician's orders and defends a drifter accused of killing a wealthy widow. Tyrone Power, Marlene Dietrich and Elsa Lanchester also star in this Billy Wilder classic that's sure to keep you guessing to the end. 116 min.
12-2414 Was $19.99 □*$14.99*

Murder, She Said (1961)
The first film in the Margaret Rutherford-Miss Marple series finds Agatha Christie's septagenarian sleuth witnessing a murder on train, getting snubbed by railway officials and going undercover as a maid in order to find the culprit. Arthur Kennedy, Muriel Pavlow, James Robertson Justice co-star. 87 min.
12-2191 *$19.99*

Murder At The Gallop (1963)
While trying to investigate the suspicious death of a wealthy old man,the unflappable Miss Jane Marple gets entangled with the deceased's eccentric heirs at a tony equestrian club. With Margaret Rutherford as the spinster sleuth, Robert Morley, Flora Robson and Charles Tingwell. 82 min.
12-2190 *$19.99*

Murder Ahoy (1964)
Septugenarean sleuth Miss Marple (wonderfully played by Margaret Rutherford) takes to the high seas in search of the killer of a trustee to an organization dedicated to helping wayward boys. Lionel Jeffries, Stringer Davis co-star. 93 min.
12-2193 *$19.99*

Murder Most Foul (1964)
Miss Marple (Margaret Rutherford) finds herself casting the only "not guilty" vote on a murder trial jury. When a mistrial is declared, she sets out to find the real suspect by joining a theatrical troupe. Ron Moody, Stringer Davis, Dennis Price co-star. 90 min.
12-2194 *$19.99*

The Mirror Crack'd (1980)
Agatha Christie's Miss Marple (Angela Lansbury) investigates a murder on the set of a movie filming in her previously quiet little village, and finds a castful of bickering suspects. The marvelous supporting cast includes Elizabeth Taylor, Rock Hudson, Kim Novak and Tony Curtis. 101 min.
63-1637 *$14.99*

A Caribbean Mystery (1983)
A leisurely vacation at a Caribbean resort turns into a busman's holiday for septuagenarian sleuth Miss Jane Marple (Helen Hayes) when she must solve the murder of a retired British army officer in this compelling Agatha Christie tale. Maurice Evans, Barnard Hughes, Swoosie Kurtz also star. 96 min.
19-2847 □*$14.99*

Murder With Mirrors (1985)
Helen Hayes shines as Agatha Christie's indomitable amateur detective, Miss Jane Marple, as she comes to the aid of an old friend (Bette Davis) who thinks someone is trying to kill her for her ancestral estate. Leo McKern, John Mills co-star. 96 min.
19-2052 Was $19.99 *$14.99*

The Alphabet Murders (1966)
A murderer has an alphabetical hit list, and only Agatha Christie's famed detective, Hercule Poirot, can find out who's the culprit behindthe dirty deeds. Tony Randall plays the Belgian sleuth; Anita Ekberg, Robert Morley and Margaret Rutherford (as Miss Marple) also appear. 91 min.
12-2185 *$19.99*

Murder On The Orient Express (1974)
Albert Finney is Belgian detective Hercule Poirot in this classic Agatha Christie thriller. An American businessman has been killed on board the famed transcontinental train and it's up to Poirot to uncover the murderer. Lauren Bacall, Anthony Perkins, Sean Connery and, in an Oscar-winning performance, Ingrid Bergman head the all-star cast. 127 min.
06-1042 Was $29.99 □*$24.99*

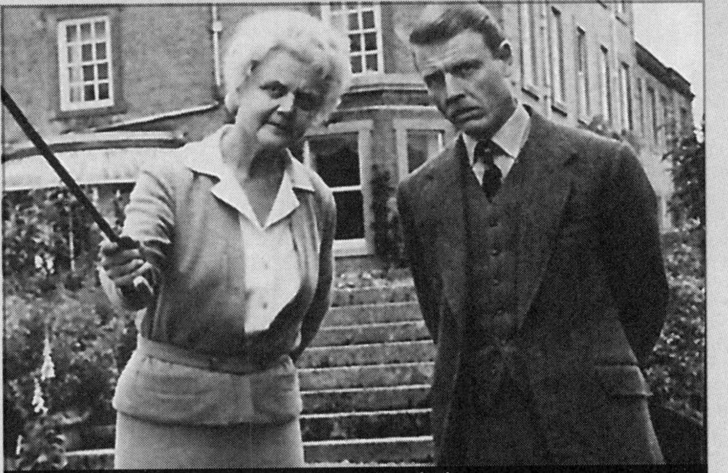
The Mirror Crack'd

Agatha Christie

Thirteen At Dinner (1985)
The suspicious death of a movie actress's husband brings detective Hercule Poirot (Peter Ustinov) into the worlds of filmmaking and British aristocracy in this stylish Agatha Christie whodunit. With Faye Dunaway, Lee Horsley, and TV Poirot David Suchet as Inspector Japp. 91 min.
19-2053 Was $19.99 *$14.99*

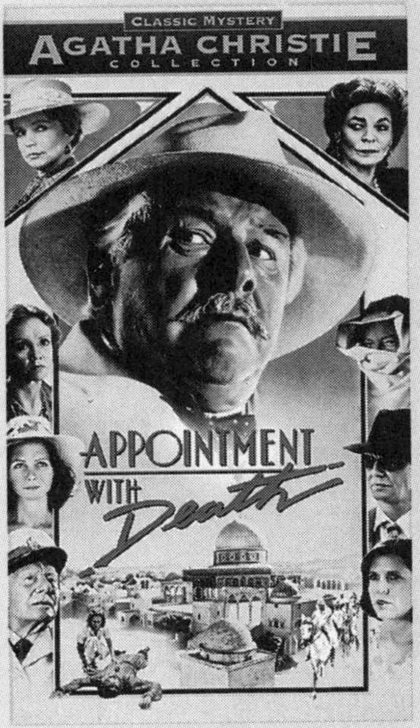

Appointment With Death (1988)
An archeological dig in 1930s Palestine turns up remains that are hardly ancient, and it falls upon Hercule Poirot to put the pieces together. Peter Ustinov returns as Agatha Christie's master of the "little gray cells" in another stylish whodunit; with Lauren Bacall, Sir John Gielgud, Piper Laurie. 108 min.
19-1643 Was $19.99 *$14.99*

Murder Is Easy (1982)
In this riveting adaptation of Agatha Christie's "Easy to Kill," a string of murders rocks a quiet English village, and a visiting American computer expert attempts to use technology to catch the killer. Bill Bixby, Helen Hayes, Olivia de Havilland, Lesley-Anne Down and Jonathan Pryce star. 95 min.
19-2849 □*$14.99*

Sparkling Cyanide (1983)
What starts out as an elegant society party for a wealthy couple's anniversary turns into a double murder and a complex mystery—thanks to a cyanide-laced bottle of champagne—in Agatha Christie's whodunit. The cast includes Anthony Andrews, Pamela Bellwood, Nancy Marchand, Harry Morgan and Deborah Raffin. 96 min.
19-2848 □*$14.99*

The Pale Horse (1996)
When a young writer is accused in the murder of a local priest, he and his girlfriend work to clear his name. A mysterious list of names found in the dead man's hand and a bizarre voodoo curse all play a part in this gripping dramatization of the Agatha Christie whodunit. Colin Buchanan, Jayne Ashbourne and Jean Marsh star. 120 min.
53-7826 *$19.99*

Agatha (1979)
Dustin Hoffman and Vanessa Redgrave star in a drama based on the real-life disappearance of mystery writer Agatha Christie for two weeks in 1926. When an American journalist discovers the missing author, a true drama starts that rivals any of Christie's novels. 98 min.
19-1200 Was $19.99 *$14.99*

Agatha Christie's Miss Marple
Joan Hickson stars as the prim spinster sleuth of St. Mary Mead in the BBC's adaptation of Christie's classic whodunits. Watch as Miss Marple's disarming manner and sly wit invariably catches the culprit.

The Body In The Library
A retired Army colonel is the suspect when a body is found in his home, and Miss Marple must prove his innocence and catch the real killer. 151 min.
04-2160 □*$19.99*

A Murder Is Announced
What starts out as a parlor game of "murder" becomes a deadly reality, and Miss Marple must find out which player isn't playing. 155 min.
04-2161 □*$19.99*

A Pocketful Of Rye
Does a children's rhyme hold the clue to a killing? That's what Miss Marple thinks when a London financier and his wife are murdered. 101 min.
04-2162 □*$19.99*

A Caribbean Mystery
Miss Marple's holiday in the exotic West Indies is a rather dull affair until Major Palgrave turns up murdered. Now she must find out who committed the ugly deed amidst the lovely scenery. 100 min.
53-7974 Was $19.99 *$14.99*

The Mirror Cracked From Side To Side
An American movie star and her husband arrive in the village of St. Mary Mead and host a great party. The only problem is that two deaths occur. Miss Marple investigates and finds that petty jealousies among the cast and crew of the new movie may lead her to the killer. 100 min.
53-7975 Was $19.99 *$14.99*

Sleeping Murder
A married couple move into their new seaside home, but it's anything but a pleasant experience when the wife is haunted by visions of a body in the house. It's up to neighbor Miss Marple to help her learn what her dreams mean and to awaken a long-sleeping crime. 100 min.
53-7976 Was $19.99 *$14.99*

4:50 From Paddington
Everyone doubts Miss McGillicuddy's story about the murder she witnessed on the train—except for her friend, Miss Jane Marple. And in order to find the corpse and solve the mystery, she travels to a stately old hall inhabited by a family with a dark past. 100 min.
53-7977 Was $19.99 *$14.99*

Agatha Christie's Miss Marple Collection, Vol. 1: Boxed Set
"A Caribbean Mystery," "The Mirror Cracked from Side to Side," "Sleeping Murder" and "4:50 from Paddington" are all available in this special collector's set.
53-7978 *$59.99*

Agatha Christie's Miss Marple Collection, Vol. 2: Boxed Set
This deluxe boxed set includes "Murder at the Vicarage," "The Moving Finger," "They Do It with Mirrors," "Nemesis" and "At Bertram's Hotel."
53-8098 *$69.99*

Murder At The Vicarage
When an unpopular resident of St. Mary Mead is found dead, Miss Marple launches an investigation. 100 min.
53-8099 Was $19.99 *$14.99*

The Moving Finger
When a string of poison pen letters leads to murder, Miss Jane Marple is determined to uncover the person behind them. 100 min.
53-8100 Was $19.99 *$14.99*

They Do It With Mirrors
A country mansion and its inhabitants are the center of murderous schemes and deadly tricks, prompting Miss Marple's attention. 100 min.
53-8101 Was $19.99 *$14.99*

Nemesis
After she receives a mysterious letter, Miss Marple does detective work on a tour of historic homes and comes upon a murder. 100 min.
53-8102 Was $19.99 *$14.99*

At Bertram's Hotel
A posh London hotel welcomes wealthy guests and sinister schemes, and Miss Marple tries to find out what's really going on. 100 min.
53-8103 Was $19.99 *$14.99*

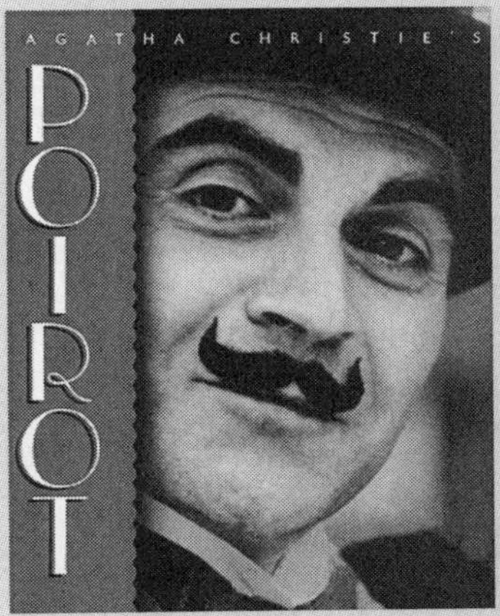

Poirot (1988)
David Suchet plays Agatha Christie's eccentric Belgian crimesolver, Hercule Poirot, in this series that was produced for British TV and ran on PBS's "Mystery!" These acclaimed thrillers offer stylish '30s settings and a marvelous turn by Suchet as the man with the "little gray cells." With Hugh Fraser as Captain Hastings.

Poirot: Set #1
This special three-tape set includes "The Disappearance of Mr. Davenheim," "The Lost Mine" and "The Veiled Lady." 150 min.
50-8435 *$39.99*

Poirot: Set #2
This special three-tape set includes "The Adventure of the Cheap Flat," "The Cornish Mystery" and "Double Sin." 150 min.
50-8436 *$39.99*

Poirot: Set #3
This special three-tape set includes "The Adventure of the Western Star," "How Does Your Garden Grow?" and "The Kidnapped Prime Minister." 150 min.
50-8437 *$39.99*

Poirot: Set #4
This special three-tape set includes "The Million Dollar Bond Robbery," "The Plymouth Express" and "Wasp's Nest." 150 min.
50-8438 *$39.99*

Poirot: Set #5
This special three-tape set includes "The Double Clue," "The Mystery of the Spanish Chest" and "The Tragedy at Marsdon Manor." 150 min.
50-8722 *$39.99*

Poirot: Set #6
This special three-tape set includes "The Affair at the Victory Ball," "The Mystery of Hunter's Lodge" and "The Theft of the Royal Ruby." 150 min.
50-8723 *$39.99*

Poirot: The Murder Of Roger Ackroyd/Lord Edgware Dies
David Suchet's Hercule Poirot is featured in two mysteries. In "The Murder of Roger Ackroyd," the Belgian sleuth investigates the strange death of his neighbor. And in "Lord Edgware Dies," the detective becomes infatuated with a pretty actress, but when he asks her estranged husband to divorce her, Poirot finds him dead. 200 min.
53-6898 *$29.99*

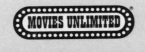

Desperate Mission (1966)
While investigating the death of a fellow fed, secret agent Z55 masquerades as a jewel smuggler in order to find out who is responsible for the murder. Soon, he's involved with the Hong Kong underground and attempting to locate a missing American scientist who may lead him to the killers. German Gobos, Yoko Tani star. AKA: "Agent Z55: Desperate Mission."
79-6144 **$19.99**

Baraka X77 (1965)
A scientist survives a plane crash after crooks attempt to steal his secret formula for solid fuel. Assigned to protect the scientist is Agent X77, who, along with help from a nurse, faces car chases, whippings and evil bald body-builders. Gerard Barray, Sylva Koscina, Jose Suarez star.
79-6146 Letterboxed **$19.99**

Espionage In Lisbon (1966)
Euro-thriller in which secret agent Brett Halsey attempts to get half of a formula that has the ability to counteract deadly electronic waves. The key to solving the case is finding the female spy whose musical abilities are needed to decipher parts of the formula. Marilu Tolo, Fernando Rey co-star.
79-6149 **$19.99**

The Last Chance (1967)
A reporter uncovers Communist involvement in a freighter explosion in the Mediterranean, but soon finds his association with the U.S. government shaky when different witnesses get shot. Soon, the reporter becomes a target for a number of parties, including the CIA, his wife, his mistress and a hired assassin. Tab Hunter, Daniela Bianchi and Michael Rennie star.
79-6150 **$19.99**

Manhattan Night Of Murder (1961)
The heat is on the "100 Dollar Boys" when they are accused of killing an Italian restaurant owner they've tried to get protection money from. An FBI agent discovers a young boy who witnessed the murder and tries to get to the true killer. George Nader, Monika Grimm star.
79-6151 **$19.99**

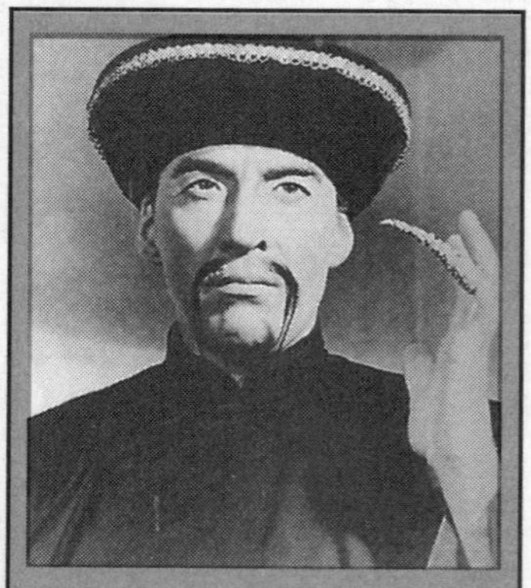

The Face Of Fu Manchu (1965)
Christopher Lee's first appearance as Sax Rohmer's evil Asian crimelord finds him employing a group of scientists to develop a lethal gas that will help him terrorize England—and then, the world. Will Scotland Yard Inspector Nayland Smith (Nigel Green) be able to stop him? Karin Dor also stars. 94 min.
19-2356 **$19.99**

The Brides Of Fu Manchu (1966)
You can't keep a good supercriminal down, as Fu (Christopher Lee) launches a devious plan to kidnap the daughters of government officials, then uses the ransom money to finance a powerful ray gun that will enable him to rule the world. Douglas Winter, Marie Versini also star. 94 min.
19-2355 **$19.99**

The Castle Of Fu Manchu (1968)
Christopher Lee portrays the sinister Oriental genius, who terrorizes the globe by threatening to freeze the world's water with his latest invention. With Richard Greene; Jess Franco directs. AKA: "Assignment: Istanbul." 87 min.
10-1023 **$19.99**

The Vengeance Of Fu Manchu (1968)
Another evil plan by Fu Manchu (Christopher Lee) is set in motion when he orders a scientist to begin cloning important lawmen so that the duplicates can be placed in the world's seats of power. On the list: Nayland Smith of Scotland Yard. Howard Marion Crawford and Maria Rohm star. 92 min.
19-2357 **$19.99**

Kiss And Kill (1968)
The evil Fu Manchu plans to murder several world leaders by seducing them with slave girls. Scotland Yard is called on to investigate the diabolical scheme and there's a race against time. Christopher Lee, Richard Greene. AKA: "Blood of Fu Manchu," "Against All Odds." 93 min.
55-1162 **$14.99**

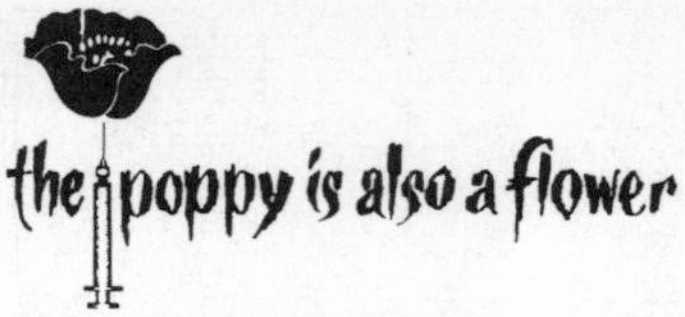

The Poppy Is Also A Flower (1969)
An impressive all-star cast is featured in this thriller about opium smuggling. After a drug enforcement agent is murdered in Iran, two veteran investigators try to track down the culprits across Europe. Based on an Ian Fleming story and produced in association with the United Nations, the film stars Trevor Howard, E.G. Marshall, Gilbert Roland, Stephen Boyd, Rita Hayworth and Angie Dickinson. 100 min.
53-1015 Was $19.99 **$14.99**

A Dandy In Aspic (1968)
A complex spy thriller starring Laurence Harvey as a Russian mole in British Intelligence assigned to eliminate his Soviet counterpart. The last film by director Anthony Mann ("Winchester '73"); also stars Mia Farrow. 107 min.
02-1939 **$69.99**

Maroc 7 (1967)
A secret agent poses as a criminal in order to stop a smuggling operation and discovers that the editor of a fashion magazine has been heading the scheme, and she's set to steal an expensive diamond in Morocco. Gene Barry, Elsa Martinelli and Cyd Charisse star. 92 min.
06-1977 **□$12.99**

Trauma (1962)
After witnessing a grisly murder, a woman develops amnesia, but returns to the site of the incident years later in hopes of finding the murderer. Lorie Richards and Lynn Bari star in this atmospheric suspenser.
68-8882 **$19.99**

Keep Talking Baby (1961)
Eddie Constantine is at his best in this intriguing thriller in which he's framed for murder and is sent to prison. After escaping from jail, he sets out to find the people who put him behind bars. Marietta Lozzi also stars.
68-8896 **$19.99**

Target For Killing (1966)
Thrilling espionage tale stars dashing Stewart Granger as a secret agent sent to the Middle East to stop a group of criminals from killing a young heiress. While trying to protect the woman, the agent falls in love with her. Curt Jurgens and Molly Peters also star.
68-8897 **$19.99**

A Man Called Rocca (1961)
Jean-Paul Belmondo turns in his patented smooth performance as a man who tries to find the person responsible for putting his pal in prison. The culprit turns out to be a racketeer, and Belmondo uses the crook's girlfriend to get to him. Christine Kaufman also stars.
68-8951 **$19.99**

Man And Child (1964)
In an attempt to find his missing granddaughter, a worker at a perfume factory that's a front for drug smugglers, a man kidnaps the factory director's daughter. Compelling thriller filled with twists and deceptions stars Eddie Constantine, Juliette Greco.
68-9101 **$19.99**

The Spy I Loved (1964)
While investigating the theft of an experimental motorcycle, an international intelligence agent gets involved with a notorious spy ring, one of whose members, a beautiful girl, knows where the prototype is. Taut espionage thriller stars Virna Lisi, Dominique Paturel, Jacques Balutin.
68-9103 **$19.99**

Operation Hurricane: Friday Noon (1966)
In the wake of the James Bond films' popularity came this secret agent adventure featuring George Nader as an investigator attempting to stop a ruthless gang responsible for murders and armed robberies across the country. Neine Weiss and Richard Munch also star.
68-9133 **$19.99**

Good Luck, Charlie (1964)
Arriving in Athens to help a friend track down a Nazi war criminal on the run, detective Eddie Constantine finds his colleague murdered. What did the man's dying word of "Stella"—the name of a recently unearthed statue—have to do with the fugitive Nazi? With Carla Marlier, Albert Prejean.
68-9235 **$19.99**

Spy Catcher (1964)
Fast-paced espionage thriller about an ace secret agent who assumes the identity of a top nuclear scientist in order to thwart the plans of enemy spies out to nab the scientist's latest invention. Frederick O'Brady, Colette Duval star.
68-9236 **$19.99**

Dead Heat On A Merry-Go-Round (1966)
James Coburn is a con man just released from prison who plans a daring robbery of the Los Angeles International Airport bank, timed to coincide with a visit by the Soviet premier, in this witty and suspenseful thriller. Co-stars Aldo Ray, Nina Wayne, Camilla Sparv; look for Harrison Ford in his film debut. 107 min.
02-1928 Was $69.99 **$19.99**

Strike Me Deadly (1963)
Ted V. Mikels' first directorial effort is an intense chase thriller about a young couple who take a vacation in the forest, witness a murder and try to find the killer, while facing lava beds, waterfalls and a ferocious fire. With Gary Clarke and Jeanine Riley.
79-5884 **$24.99**

The Hand Of Power (1968)
A spooky thriller in which a laugh erupts from a coffin at the funeral of Sir Oliver at his English estate. When a skull-faced figure is sighted in the area and a group of people who knew Sir Oliver turn up dead, Inspector Higgins is put on the case. With Joachim Fuchsberger and Siw Mattson.
79-6114 Was $24.99 **$19.99**

Countdown To Doomsday (1967)
Fast-paced secret agent yarn featuring George Ardisson as a bleach blonde private detective on the trail of a millionaire's journalist daughter, who has been kidnapped. Horst Frank and Pascale Audret also star in this European suspenser with guns, gals and gung-ho action scenes.
79-6115 Was $24.99 **$19.99**

Espionage In Tangiers (1966)
An entry in the James Bond imitator cycle, this thriller tells of a secret agent out to snag a dangerous molecular ray-gun that can disintegrate cars and fireplaces(!?). Luis Davilla stars as the suave agent involved in espionage proceedings of this European offering. Look out, George Lazenby!
79-6141 **$19.99**

The Beckett Affair (1966)
International suspenser starring Lang Jeffries as Rod Cooper, an Interpol agent sent to Europe to uncover a murdered socialite's ties to a Cuban colonel involved in a plot to assassinate a South American leader. Posing as a disgruntled American crook, Jeffries goes undercover to stop the plot and must battle lesbian heroin addicts. With Ivan Desny and Krista Nell.
79-6446 Was $24.99 **$19.99**

A Candidate For The Killing (1968)
That Anita Ekberg—grrrrrrrrrowwwlll!—cuts a fine figure as a shady beauty who dupes Brit John Richardson into joining her on a cross-country trip through Europe. Little does he know that he's the exact double of a French mercenary that several crooks are after for ripping them off. Fernando Rey also stars in this Sidney Pink ("Reptilicus") production.
79-6447 Was $24.99 **$19.99**

Dead Run (1967)
This Euro-thriller tells of a petty thief who swipes a briefcase filled with top-secret papers. Little does he know that he's been observed by a wealthy female tourist who must find him before he sells the papers to an underworld organization. Peter Lawford, Georges Geret and Iran Von Furstenberg star.
79-6448 Was $24.99 **$19.99**

Pendulum (1969)
Tense drama stars George Peppard as a city police captain falsely accused of murder and racing against time to find the real killer. Jean Seberg, Richard Kiley and Madeleine Sherwood co-star. 106 min.
02-1393 **$59.99**

The Black Chapel (1962)
Peter Van Eyck plays a World War II journalist who receives sensitive documents about Hitler from rebellious German soldiers, but finds his life in jeopardy when his liaison in Rome is murdered. Dawn Addams and Gino Servi also star.
68-9255 **$19.99**

The Collector (1965)
Classic suspense story about a repressed bank clerk and butterfly collector who admires a woman from afar and abducts her to an isolated farmhouse, where he attempts to win her love. Terence Stamp and Samantha Eggar star; William Wyler directs. 119 min.
02-1065 Was $59.99 **$19.99**

Don't Forget To Wipe The Blood Off (1967)
In the midst of the international popularity of spy films came this interesting Canadian confection detailing the adventures of hard-drinking Nick King and cynical CIA man Granger, out to investigate the kidnapping of a famous physicist's wife orchestrated by a nasty power-broker. With Stephen Young, Austin Willis. 90 min.
09-2954 **$19.99**

A Face In The Rain (1963)
American spy Rory Calhoun is being hidden in Nazi-occupied Italy by an underground contact. When he learns that the contact's wife is having an affair with a German officer, he seeks help from her son, who shelters him in an attic until the Nazis discover him. With Marina Berti, Niall McGinnis. 66 min.
09-5099 Was $19.99 **$14.99**

Die! Die! My Darling! (1965)
Tallulah Bankhead, in her last role, creates an unforgettable image as a religious fanatic who kidnaps her late son's fiancée (Stefanie Powers). Chilling thriller co-stars a young Donald Sutherland. 97 min.
02-1439 **$14.99**

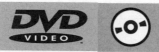

DVD VIDEO
ASK ABOUT OUR GIANT DVD CATALOG!

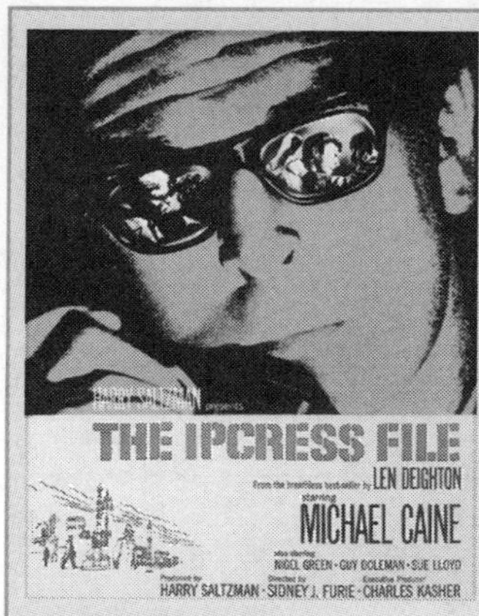

The Ipcress File (1965)
Michael Caine is Len Deighton's impassive secret agent Harry Palmer, involved in a plot to rescue brain-washed scientists from behind the Iron Curtain, in the first of the thrilling spy series. Also stars Nigel Green and Sue Lloyd. 107 min.
07-1497 **$14.99**

The Ipcress File (Letterboxed Collector's Edition)
Also available in a theatrical, widescreen format. Includes a gallery of stills and the original theatrical trailer.
08-8792 **$14.99**

Funeral In Berlin (1966)
Master spy Harry Palmer (Michael Caine) returns in this edge-of-the-seater in which he must arrange the defection of the Soviet official in charge of Berlin's war security. Location shooting at the Berlin Wall adds to the atmosphere. With Oscar Homolka, Eva Renzi. 102 min.
06-1374 Was $19.99 **$14.99**

Bullet To Beijing (1995)
For the first time in 30 years, Michael Caine returns to the role of master British intelligence agent Harry Palmer. After being cut from the service roles, Caine takes a job in Russia for mysterious magnate Michael Gambon that finds him guarding a deadly genetic weapon on a transcontinental train ride to China. Jason Connery, Mia Sara, Michael Sarrazin also star. 105 min.
06-2656 **□$89.99**

Midnight In St. Petersburg (1995)
Michael Caine's superspy Harry Palmer must defuse an international crisis involving terrorists purchasing deadly plutonium in order to begin a nuclear war. Joined by partner Nikolai (Jason Connery), the two men race against time, but soon discover a link between Nikolai's girlfriend's kidnapping, stolen art and the plutonium. Michele Rene Thomas co-stars. 90 min.
06-2721 **□$94.99**

Games (1967)
Diabolical thriller starring Simone Signoret as an immigrant saleswoman with psychic powers who is asked to devise strange games for kinky Manhattan socialites James Caan and Katharine Ross to play. One of the capers, involving a delivery boy, turns deadly and leads to a series of frightening events. Don Stroud, Estelle Winwood co-star; Curtis Harrington directs. 101 min.
10-2574 **$14.99**

Miss V From Moscow (1960)
On a special mission in Paris, a female Russian agent uses her resemblance to a Nazi spy to help uncover confidential submarine plans during World War II. Lola Lane, Noel Madison and Paul Weigel star in this espionage thriller produced in England. 68 min.
10-8255 Was $19.99 **$14.99**

The 7th Commandment (1961)
Intense crime thriller in which a man with amnesia suffered after a car accident is taken under the wing of a successful evangelist, only to find his former girlfriend calling for cash when she discovers he's still alive—and rich! Jonathan Kidd, Lyn Statton star. 80 min.
10-9239 Was $19.99 **$14.99**

Blow Up (1966)
Michelangelo Antonioni's first English-language film, a visually rich mystery set in the "mod" world of '60s London fashion. An introverted photographer (David Hemmings) thinks he's witnessed a murder through his camera lens, and the proof may be captured on his film. With Vanessa Redgrave, Sarah Miles, The Yardbirds. 102 min.
12-1003 **$14.99**

FX-18 (1964)
This European espionage entry features American Ken Clark as a spy named Coplan who is as wild with the ladies as he is against rival agents. Coplan is called on to stop an organization using stolen microfilm plans to alter American missile systems. Jany Clair, Cristina Gaioni also star. AKA: "Kill Secret Agent 777," "Secret Agent Coplan FCX 18."
79-6553 **$19.99**

MOVIES UNLIMITED

Nevada (1944)
Robert Mitchum's first lead role casts him as a gold-seeking cowpoke whose shady past comes into play when he's mistaken for the murderer of a homesteader. Can Mitchum clear his name before he's executed? And can he find the real culprit? This Zane Grey story also stars Anne Jeffreys, Nancy Gates and Craig Reynolds.
66-6056 *$14.99*

The Story Of G.I. Joe (1945)
The famous columns of WWII correspondent Ernie Pyle were the basis for this powerful, realistic war classic featuring Burgess Meredith as the journalist. Follow Meredith as he befriends a platoon of GIs battling their way across the frontline in Italy. Robert Mitchum leads the group, while Freddie Steele, Wally Cassell and Jimmy Lloyd play his soldiers; William Wellman directs. 108 min.
50-8389 *$19.99*

West Of The Pecos (1945)
Robert Mitchum turned this unusual Zane Grey sagebrusher into a hit with his cool demeanor. He's the cowboy who tries to turn a young punk kid into a real man. Little does Mitchum realize that the kid is really a girl dressed like a man in order to elude nasty villains. Barbara Hale plays the kid in man's clothing.
66-6057 *$14.99*

Out Of The Past (1947)
The classic "film noir" mystery that was remade as "Against All Odds." Robert Mitchum is a detective hired by gangster Kirk Douglas to track down girlfriend Jane Greer, who Douglas says ran off after stealing $40,000. Tracking Greer to Mexico, Mitchum falls for her and tries to help her elude Douglas and his henchmen, but who can be trusted? With Steve Brodie, Rhonda Fleming; Jacques Tourneur directs. 97 min.
05-1119 *$19.99*

Crossfire (1947)
Director Edward Dmytryk spun Richard Brooks' novel into a tense film noir classic with hard-hitting social overtones about the intense search for an anti-Semitic murderer. Stars Robert Young, Robert Mitchum, Gloria Grahame, Sam Levene and Robert Ryan. Special video release includes the original theatrical trailer and a "making of" documentary. 86 min.
18-7671 *$19.99*

Pursued (1947)
Offbeat, memorable sagebrush drama stars Robert Mitchum as a Spanish-American War vet out to track down his father's killer...only to discover a most startling revelation. Teresa Wright, Judith Anderson, Dean Jagger, Alan Hale co-star; Raoul Walsh directs. Newly restored version includes two original trailers and an introduction by Martin Scorsese. 105 min. total.
63-1258 *$14.99*

Holiday Affair (1949)
Widowed mother Janet Leigh's attempt to purchase the train set her son wants for Christmas brings her to the attention of store clerk Robert Mitchum in a Yuletide-flavored romance that also stars Wendell Corey and Henry Morgan. 86 min.
18-7147 Was $19.99 *$14.99*

The Red Pony (1949)
Beloved "boy and his pony" film scripted by John Steinbeck and based on his novel, with Robert Mitchum as a ranchhand who brightens the life of the son of a bickering husband and wife (Shepperd Strudwick, Myrna Loy) by helping him raise his cherished red pony. Co-stars Peter Miles, Louis Calhern and features an Aaron Copland score. 89 min.
63-1008 *$14.99*

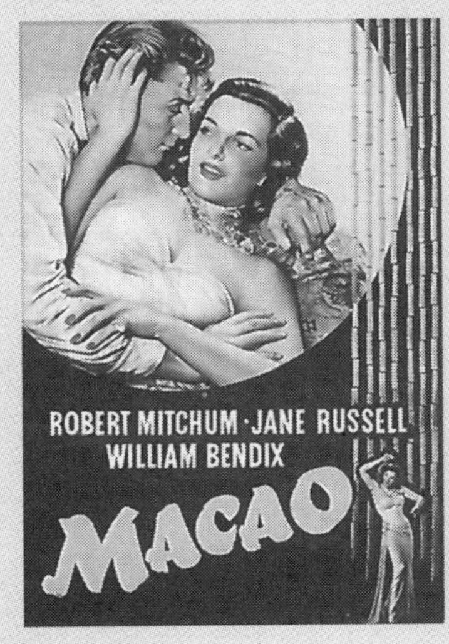

Macao (1952)
Wandering adventurer Robert Mitchum, on the run after being convicted of a crime he didn't commit, finds himself caught in the middle of a battle between Chinese police and an American gangster, and in love with sultry nightclub singer Jane Russell, in the notorious Asian port city. Directed by Josef von Sternberg; with William Bendix, Gloria Grahame. Special video release includes the original theatrical trailer and a retrospective on the making of the film. 80 min.
05-1109 *$19.99*

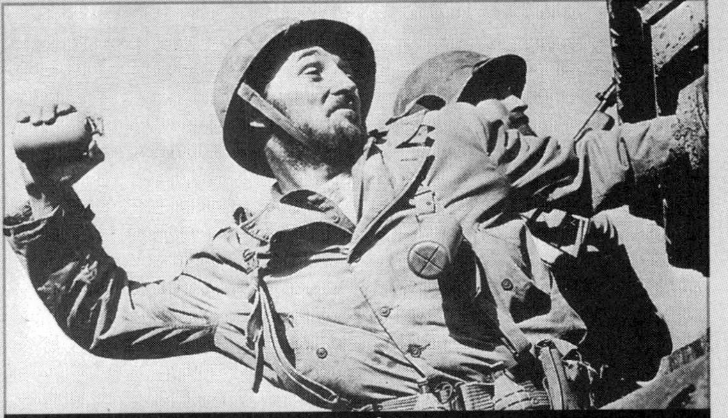
The Story Of G.I. Joe

Robert Mitchum

Track Of The Cat (1954)
Noted for its subdued color cinematography and psychological subtexts, director William Wellman's compelling frontier drama is set in a snowbound farmhouse in 1880s Northern California. As jealousies and rivalries tear at the family members trapped inside, a deadly panther waits out in the wilderness. Robert Mitchum, Tab Hunter, Teresa Wright, Diana Lynn, Beulah Bondi and, as a 100-year-old Indian, Carl "Alfalfa" Switzer star. 103 min.
19-2832 *$14.99*

The Night Of The Hunter (1955)
Harrowing suspense classic of two children on the run from their psychotic religious fanatic stepfather, who murdered their mother in a search for money stolen from him by their father. Robert Mitchum is the spellbinding "preacher" with "LOVE" and "HATE" tattooed on his knuckles; also stars Lillian Gish, Shelley Winters, Peter Graves. Charles Laughton's only directorial effort. 93 min.
12-1657 Was $19.99 *$14.99*

Not As A Stranger (1955)
A star-studded melodrama featuring Robert Mitchum as a poor intern who marries older head nurse Olivia de Havilland in order to use her money to get through medical school. Upon graduating, he takes a job in a small town where, after an affair with wealthy patient Gloria Grahame, he sees his marriage and career dissolve. Stanley Kramer's first directorial effort also stars Frank Sinatra, Broderick Crawford, Charles Bickford, Lee Marvin. 135 min.
12-2506 Was $19.99 *$14.99*

Man With The Gun (1955)
The "Man" in question is Robert Mitchum, a lethal gunslinger-for-hire who, while on a search for his estranged wife, comes to the aid of a frontier town under siege by a band of outlaws. Jan Sterling, Henry Hull also star; look quickly for Angie Dickinson in her second film role.
12-3257 *$14.99*

The Enemy Below (1957)
Tense war drama set in the North Atlantic of World War II, as American destroyer skipper Robert Mitchum and German U-Boat commander Curt Jurgens play out a deadly cat-and-mouse game above and below the waves. Theodore Bikel, Frank Albertson and Al (David) Hedison star in this remake of 1931's "The Seas Beneath." 98 min.
04-1289 Was $19.99 *$14.99*

Heaven Knows, Mr. Allison (1957)
Novitiate nun Deborah Kerr and Marine Robert Mitchum are drawn to one another as they hide together from enemy forces in a cave on a Japanese-held Pacific island in director John Huston's exciting and touching WWII drama.
04-3431 *$19.99*

Thunder Road (1958)
Coming home from the battlefields of Korea, moonshiner Robert Mitchum finds a different kind of war brewing at home when mobsters try to take over his family's still in this rousing backwoods action classic. Gene Barry, Keely Smith, and Mitchum's son Jim co-star; Mitchum also produced, co-scripted, and wrote the theme song! 93 min.
12-1028 Was $19.99 *$14.99*

Home From The Hill (1960)
A wealthy Texas landowner's stormy relationship with his two sons (one of them illegitimate) and the brothers' love for the same girl form the conflict in this stirring melodrama. Robert Mitchum, George Hamilton, George Peppard, Eleanor Parker star. 150 min.
12-1962 Was $29.99 *$19.99*

The Sundowners (1960)
Lush drama of a sheepherding family in the frontier of 1920s Australia, centering on their struggles to endure and their relationships with the pioneers around them. Fred Zinnemann directs Robert Mitchum, Deborah Kerr, Peter Ustinov, Glynis Johns and Dina Merrill in this adaptation of Jon Cleary's novel. 133 min.
19-2586 *$19.99*

Cape Fear (1962)
The Southern backwoods become a setting for suspense and shock, as sadistic ex-con Robert Mitchum tracks down lawyer Gregory Peck and his family for vengeance. The original version of the classic thriller, based on a John MacDonald novel, also stars Polly Bergen, Martin Balsam, Telly Savalas. 106 min.
07-1470 Was $19.99 *$14.99*

Two For The Seesaw (1962)
Winning romantic comedy, based on William Gibson's hit play, stars Robert Mitchum as a Midwest lawyer who leaves his home and bad marriage to start over in Manhattan. There he meets Greenwich Village dancer Shirley MacLaine, and a warm but unstable relationship begins. Edmon Ryan, Elisabeth Fraser also star in Robert Wise's film. 119 min.
12-2492 *$19.99*

Anzio (1968)
Blazing actioner about the Allied assault on Italy in WWII features spectacular battle footage and an all-star cast: Robert Mitchum, Peter Falk, Arthur Kennedy, Robert Ryan, Earl Holliman. 117 min.
02-1737 *$14.99*

Five Card Stud (1968)
After giving a "necktie party" for a card cheat, five poker-playing buddies are mysteriously bumped off one by one. Gunslinger Dean Martin and "preacher" Robert Mitchum search for the killer in this Henry Hathaway western; co-stars Roddy McDowall, Inger Stevens. 103 min.
06-1567 *$14.99*

Young Billy Young (1969)
Robert Walker, Jr. stars in the title role as a gunslinger who is abandoned and left for dead by partner David Carradine and saved by sheriff Robert Mitchum. On the trail of his son's killer, Mitchum becomes a mentor and father figure to Walker in this frontier drama. Angie Dickinson, John Anderson also star. AKA: "Who Rides with Kane."
12-3230 *$14.99*

Young Billy Young (Letterboxed Version)
Also available in a theatrical, widescreen format.
12-3231 *$14.99*

The Good Guys And The Bad Guys (1969)
Lighthearted western stars Robert Mitchum as a retired lawman who finds that old nemesis George Kennedy and his gang are planning a train robbery in his neck of the woods. Mitchum is targeted to be killed by Kennedy, but a change of heart brings the two enemies together to stop the crime. David Carradine, Tina Louise and John Carradine also star. 90 min.
19-2197 Was $29.99 *$19.99*

Ryan's Daughter (1970)
David Lean's magnificent, sweeping love story set in a small Northern Ireland village. Sarah Miles is the pampered wife of school teacher Robert Mitchum who has an affair with British soldier Christopher Jones, incurring the wrath of the village. Co-stars Leo McKern, Trevor Howard and John Mills in an Oscar-winning role as a crippled mute villager. 194 min.
12-1406 Was $29.99 *$24.99*

Ryan's Daughter (Letterboxed Version)
Also available in a theatrical, widescreen format.
12-3131 *$24.99*

The Yakuza (1975)
A fierce and fascinating action movie focusing on American Robert Mitchum's efforts to find a girl kidnapped by a violent clan of Japanese gangsters. Unique Oriental customs, mesmerizing martial arts and old-fashioned slugfests make this an underrated gem; Sydney Pollack directs; Brian Keith, Takakura Ken. 112 min.
19-1348 Was $19.99 *$14.99*

Farewell, My Lovely (1975)
Robert Mitchum stars as Raymond Chandler's world-weary private eye, Philip Marlowe, in this engrossing mystery that was previously made as "Murder, My Sweet." Hired by an ex-con to track down his old flame, Mitchum finds himself framed for murder and trying to crack the case before the police bring him in. Charlotte Rampling, Sylvia Miles, John Ireland, Jack O'Halloran co-star; look for Sylvester Stallone playing a hired thug. 98 min.
53-1437 *$14.99*

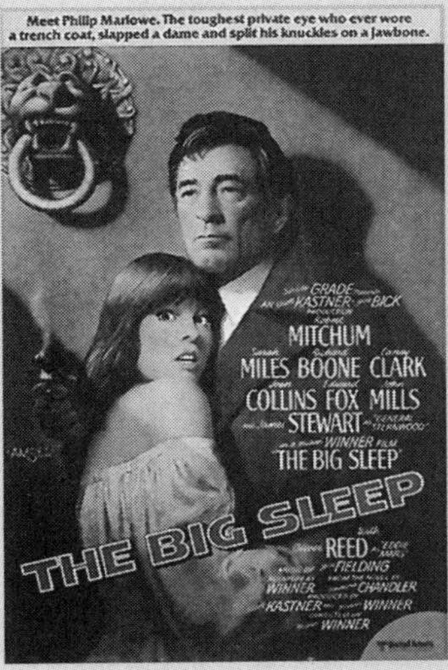

The Big Sleep (1978)
Gumshoe Philip Marlowe (Robert Mitchum) is hired by elderly recluse James Stewart to learn who's been blackmailing his daughters, but soon finds the entire family involved in a complex plot of deception and murder, in this colorful remake of the Raymond Chandler classic. Sarah Miles, Candy Clark, Richard Boone and Joan Collins also star. 100 min.
04-1274 *$14.99*

The Amsterdam Kill (1977)
Exciting espionage thriller starring Robert Mitchum as a retired narcotics agent who gets back into the swing of things when his freind is involved in an international drug conspiracy. Bradford Dillman, Richard Egan co-star. 90 min.
02-2683 *$14.99*

Agency (1981)
Engrossing political story about an advertising agency that plans a subliminal campaign to influence unwitting voters. Robert Mitchum, Lee Majors, Valerie Perrine, Saul Rubinek star. AKA: "Mind Games." 92 min.
47-1031 *$14.99*

That Championship Season (1982)
Powerful drama about the 24th annual reunion of a championship high school basketball team. Robert Mitchum, Bruce Dern, Martin Sheen, Stacy Keach and Paul Sorvino star; based on director Jason Miller's Pulitzer Prize-winning play. 108 min.
12-1264 *$79.99*

Robert Mitchum: The Reluctant Star
He's been a Hollywood bad boy for decades...both on and off the screen. Here, Deborah Kerr, Sydney Pollack, Ali MacGraw and Sarah Miles comment on Mitchum's life and career, while clips from "Out of the Past," "Night of the Hunter" and "Cape Fear" help tell the rest of the story. 60 min.
50-6800 Was $24.99 *$14.99*

Please see our index for these other Robert Mitchum titles: *Back Fire • Bar 20 • Border Patrol • Breakthrough • Colt Comrades • Dead Man • El Dorado • False Colors • Fire Down Below • Gung Ho! • Hoppy Serves A Writ • The Human Comedy • The Last Tycoon • The Leather Burners • The List Of Adrian Messenger • The Lone Star Trail • The Longest Day • Midnight Ride • Midway • Riders Of The Deadline • River Of No Return • Scrooged • Secret Ceremony • Thirty Seconds Over Tokyo • Undercurrent • War And Remembrance • The Way West • The Winds Of War • Woman Of Desire*

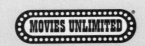

Seance On A Wet Afternoon (1964)
Classic suspense drama about a disturbed woman who claims to be able to communicate with the spirit world through her dead son. She hatches a publicity scheme which leads to her husband kidnapping the daughter of a rich industrialist, but their plans soon backfire. Kim Stanley, Richard Attenborough, Patrick Magee star; scripted and directed by Bryan Forbes. 115 min.
22-5679 *$29.99*

The Third Alibi (1961)
First-rate suspenser about a man who conspires with his pregnant mistress to kill his wife—and her sister. The tightly wound proceedings lead to a surprise ending. With Laurence Payne, Patricia Dainton and Jane Griffiths. 68 min.
09-5111 *$19.99*

Target Gold Seven (1968)
An FBI agent travels to Lisbon to investigate the whereabouts of missing uranium. He's eventually captured and slated to be used as a guinea pig for experiments when a secret Russian agent and government police get involved in the case. Tony Russel and Erika Blanc star. 90 min.
09-5235 *$19.99*

The Impersonator (1962)
Compelling mystery set in an English town where a series of murders of local women have the residents on edge, and where an American airman stationed nearby must clear his name of the killings. John Crawford, Jane Griffiths star. 64 min.
09-5338 *$19.99*

The Fuller Report (1966)
Ken Clark ("Attack of the Giant Leeches") stars in this spy thriller, playing an undercover agent trying to stop an assassination that could lead to World War III. Beba Loncar, Jess Hahn also star.
68-9134 *$19.99*

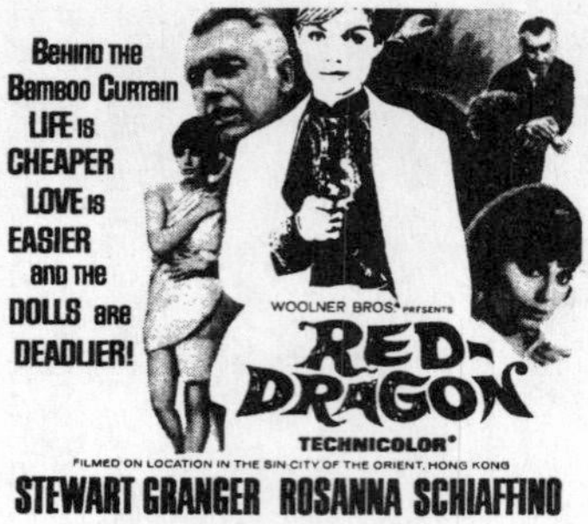

Behind the Bamboo Curtain Life is Cheaper Love is Easier and the Dolls are Deadlier!
Woolner Bros. presents
Red-Dragon
Technicolor
Filmed on location in the sin city of the Orient, Hong Kong
Stewart Granger Rosanna Schiaffino

Red Dragon (1967)
In this spy suspenser, Stewart Granger and Rosanna Schiaffino are FBI agents in Hong Kong trying to stop smugglers who are selling electrical supplies to mainland Communist factions. 89 min.
68-8834 *$19.99*

No Diamonds For Ursula (1967)
Dana Andrews stars in this crime drama focusing on a blackmailer who uses his mark to help him steal valuable diamonds. Roger Beaumont and John Elliot co-star. 96 min.
10-9524 *$14.99*

Spy Today, Die Tomorrow (1967)
The search for a stolen nuclear weapon from an American arsenal sends CIA agents into one danger after another in this exciting spy thriller. Lex Barker, Brad Harris, Maria Perschy star.
68-9172 *$19.99*

Diabolically Yours (1967)
Searing suspense abounds in this tale of a man who awakens from a near-fatal car wreck to a family and life he can no longer remember. His search to discover the truth will bolt you to your seat. Alain Delon, Senta Berger. 94 min.
48-1127 *$59.99*

Point Blank (1967)
Betrayed by his partner and left for dead, a man who engineered a heist of mob money recovers and plans his revenge, but the mob is after both of them. Stylish thriller from director John Boorman, remade as 1999's "Payback," stars Lee Marvin, Angie Dickinson, Keenan Wynn, John Vernon and Carroll O'Connor. 89 min.
12-1029 Was $79.99 *$19.99*

The Monk (1969)
Gustavus "Gus" Monk is a San Francisco private eye/bodyguard who is hired by an underworld lawyer to complete a dangerous task, but gets caught up in a path of deceit and double-crosses when the lawyer and a slew of other people wind up dead. Gripping mystery, created by Blake Edwards, stars George Maharis, Janet Leigh, Carl Betz and Rick Jason. 75 min.
55-3027 *$19.99*

Flare-Up (1969)
Raquel Welch is at her sexiest, playing a Las Vegas dancer trying to elude a psychopathic stalker who happens to be responsible for the death of her friend—and the death of her friend's husband, as well. Welch is featured in some sizzling dance sequences set at the Pussy-a-Go-Go; with James Stacy, Luke Askew. 98 min.
12-3075 *□$19.99*

24 Hours To Kill (1966)
Exciting suspense yarn stars Mickey Rooney as a purser who becomes involved with gold smugglers in the Middle East. Lex Barker, Walter Slezak and Maria Rohm also star. 94 min.
17-9084 Was $19.99 *$14.99*

The Glass Cage (1964)
Offbeat psychological suspenser about a young woman who kills a local businessman she claims was a prowler. An investigating detective becomes obsessed with the woman, even as she descends deeper into delusion. Arline Sax, John Hoyt, Elisha Cook, Jr. star. AKA: "Den of Doom," "Don't Touch My Sister."
68-9223 *$19.99*

The Monocle (1964)
A heroic secret agent in Hong Kong races to locate the criminal who is determined to destroy an American aircraft carrier. Nail-biting suspense with Marcel Dalio, Paul Meurisse, Barbara Steele. 97 min.
55-3028 *$19.99*

Subterfuge (1969)
Shady double-crosses, international espionage, political dealings and suspense galore highlight this tale of an American agent called on to help British Intelligence crack a case. Gene Barry, Joan Collins. 89 min.
63-1059 *$19.99*

Color Me Dead (1969)
A poisoned man spends his last hours trying to find his murderers and searching for the reasons why in this bizarre tale from Australia. Carolyn Jones, Tom Tryon star. AKA: "D.O.A. II." 91 min.
63-5035 Was $19.99 *$14.99*

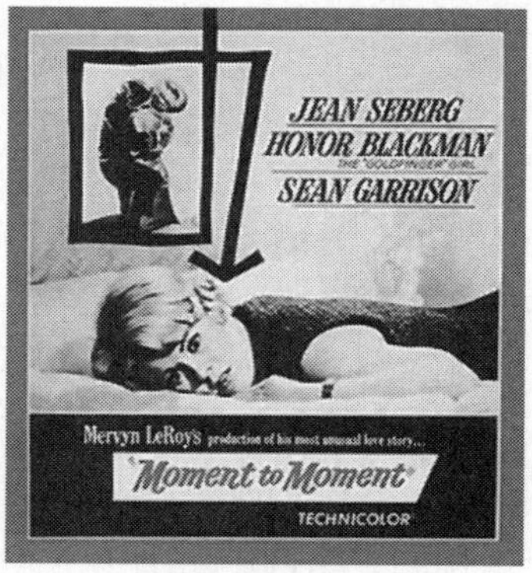

Jean Seberg
Honor Blackman
The "Goldfinger" Girl
Sean Garrison
Mervyn LeRoy's production of his most unusual love story...
Moment to Moment
Technicolor

Moment To Moment (1966)
Feeling neglected while psychiatrist husband Arthur Hill is away on a lecture tour, lonely Jean Seberg begins an affair with young naval officer Sean Garrison in this stylish thriller. When a quarrel leads to Garrison's accidental shooting, neighbor Honor Blackman helps Seberg dispose of the body...but is Garrison really dead? 114 min.
07-2864 *□$14.99*

The Cape Town Affair (1967)
A reworking of Samuel Fuller's "Pickup on South Street," set in South Africa and following a pickpocket looking for a score on a bus but getting more than he expected when the purse he lifts contains secret microfilm. James Brolin, Jacqueline Bisset and Claire Trevor star. 100 min.
10-1600 *$19.99*

Daddy's Gone A-Hunting (1969)
A happily-married pregnant woman living in San Francisco has her world turned upside-down by the arrival of her crazed ex-boyfriend, who demands she kill the baby she's carrying in retribution for aborting his child years earlier. Stars Carol White, Scott Hylands and Paul Burke; co-written by Larry Cohen ("It's Alive") and directed by Mark Robson ("Valley of the Dolls"). 108 min.
19-1667 Was $19.99 *$14.99*

The Devil's Agent (1961)
This obscure effort is a first-rate European spy thriller starring genre favorite Peter Van Eyck as a mild-mannered businessman and former intelligence agent who is asked by friend Christopher Lee to deliver a package to a friend in West Germany. Little does Van Eyck know that the package contains top-secret info that gets him in trouble with authorities. With Marianne Koch.
79-6551 Was $24.99 *$19.99*

Master Stroke (1966)
Richard Harrison is an actor in spaghetti westerns enlisted by criminal mastermind Adolfo Celli to take part in a series of complex heists. After he joins a former Scotland Yard official in criminal activity, he's asked by a secret service organization to stop his newest employers by enacting several parts. Margaret Lee, Eduardo Fajardo also star. AKA: "The Great Diamond Robbery," "Master Stroke in the Service of Her Britannic Majesty."
79-6554 Was $24.99 *$19.99*

Run Like A Thief (1967)
An American travelling through the Mexican wilderness witnesses an armored car robbery and finds himself involved in a series of dangerous situations involving stolen diamonds, gangsters and the Diamond Syndicate Police. Kieron Moore, Ina Balin and Keenan Wynn star. 92 min.
10-9527 *$14.99*

The Hand (1960)
A series of grisly murders has the London police baffled, until a connection is found with the cruel tortures suffered by three British POWs in World War II. Crackling good suspenser stars Derek Bond, Ray Cooney. 65 min.
68-8375 *$19.99*

Mystery Liner (1934)
Deranged captain Noah Beery, Sr. and watchman George "Gabby" Hayes are just two of the suspicious seafarers in this well-made Monogram suspenser, as spies resort to murder to stop an inventor from testing his ship-controlling device. With Ralph Lewis, Astrid Allwyn. 64 min.
68-8074 Was $19.99 *$14.99*

The Squeaker (1937)
Suspense master Edgar Wallace penned this story about a discredited police inspector who poses as an ex-cop to trap a murdering fence for stolen goods. Edmund Lowe plays the slumming gumshoe. AKA: "Murder on Diamond Row." 77 min.
68-8175 *$19.99*

The Gaunt Stranger (1938)
Top-notch Edgar Wallace mystery in which a Scotland Yard detective and police doctor team to find a diabolical killer known as "The Ringer," who's vowed to murder a lawyer within 48 hours. With Wilfred Lawson, Sonnie Hale and Alexander Knox.
68-8923 *$19.99*

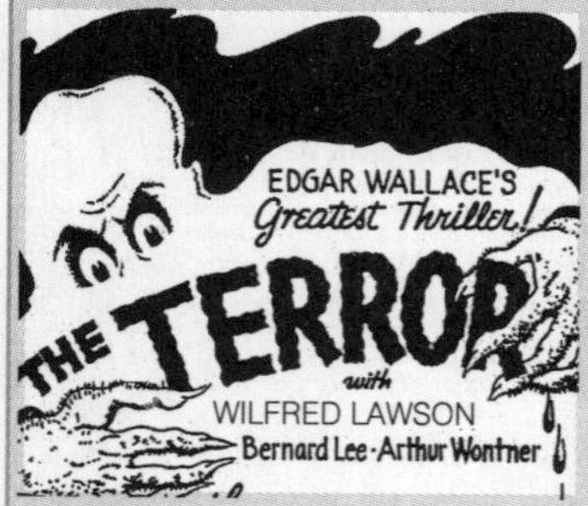

Edgar Wallace's Greatest Thriller!
The Terror
with
Wilfred Lawson
Bernard Lee · Arthur Wontner

The Terror (1938)
Atmospheric adaptation of the Edgar Wallace mystery set in a creepy boarding house where a masked figure terrorizes a group of guests. Can the killer be caught before he strikes again? Wilfred Lawson, Bernard Lee, Arthur Wontner star. 63 min.
68-8729 *$19.99*

The Secret Four (1940)
Intriguing suspense drama, based on a novel by Edgar Wallace, follows a group of men (three Britishers and a Frenchman) who devote themselves to fighting for freedom around the world and must stop an enemy who kills one of their number. Hugh Sinclair, Griffith Jones, Frank Lawton and Anna Lee star. AKA: "The Four Just Men." 85 min.
17-3035 *$19.99*

The Case Of The Frightened Lady (1940)
Spooky British thriller based on an Edgar Wallace play about an aristocratic family with a genetic tendency to bloody murder. Marius Goring is a homicidal lord whose neurosis is concealed by his equally deadly Mama. AKA: "The Frightened Lady." 80 min.
17-3082 Was $29.99 *$19.99*

Monster Of London City (1956)
Check the date; Thatcher was still years away. Edgar Wallace story about an actor at the Poe Theater whose macabre stage role mirrors a string of Ripper-like call girl murders. Stars Marianne Koch, Hansjorg Felmy. 87 min.
68-8411 *$19.99*

Fellowship Of The Frog (1960)
Thrilling Edgar Wallace mystery in which an American detective on the trail of a killer continually finds the strange seal of a White Frog at the murder sites. Carl Lange, Joachim Fuchsberger star. 89 min.
68-8955 *$19.99*

The Crimson Circle (1960)
The titular circle is the tell-tale mark left around the necks of a series of murder victims. Can Scotland Yard officials solve these bizarre crimes before the killer strikes again? Chilling suspenser, based on an Edgar Wallace tale, stars Fritz Rasp, Karl Saebiach. AKA: "The Red Circle." 92 min.
10-9834 *$14.99*

The Avenger (1960)
Edgar Wallace penned this mystery in which the heads of people who suffered from incurable diseases are being discovered throughout London. A Scotland Yard inspector called in to investigate the killings is led to a movie set where the suspects include a young actress, a sword-collecting millionaire and a hairy servant raised by animals in the jungle. With Heinz Drache, Ingrid Van Bergen, Klaus Kinski.
79-6116 *$19.99*

Strange Countess (1961)
Based on an Edgar Wallace story, this mystery concerns the murder of a girl and its connection to another unsolved killing that occurred 20 years earlier. Lil Dagover, Joachim Fuchsberger star.
68-8760 *$19.99*

Forger Of London (1961)
An Edgar Wallace mystery about the Scotland Yard investigation of a ring of counterfeiters. An amnesiac playboy is the target of the inspectors. Eddie Arent, Karin Dor star.
68-8818 *$19.99*

The Door With Seven Locks (1962)
Creepy remake of the Edgar Wallace thriller about a man who leaves seven heirs keys to a vault with a treasure inside. When each attempts to use their key, bizarre events occur. Klaus Kinski and Eddie Erent star. 96 min.
68-8759 *$19.99*

The Secret Of The Black Trunk (1962)
An Edgar Wallace mystery set in an English hotel where a rash of grisly murders are occurring. Joachim Hansen and Senta Berger star.
68-8761 *$19.99*

Inn On The River (1962)
A criminal known as "The Shark" preys on innocent victims with a series of horrifying killings. Scotland Yard's finest are out to stop him in this Edgar Wallace story. With Klaus Kinski, Joachim Fuchsberger.
68-8819 *$19.99*

The Secret Of The Red Orchid (1962)
Christopher Lee excels as a special agent sent to Scotland Yard to help stop an international crime syndicate and an expert blackmailer. Adrian Hovan also stars in this atmospheric suspenser.
68-8956 *$19.99*

The Black Abbot (1963)
A black-hooded figure, a mysterious murder, and a castle filled with terror and a fortune in gold are the elements in this Edgar Wallace mystery starring Joachim Fuchsberger and a young Klaus Kinski. 88 min.
68-8762 *$19.99*

The Curse Of The Yellow Snake (1963)
German adventure drama, based on a thriller by Edgar Wallace, as two brothers fight for an ancient talisman whose owner could rule the world. Joachim Berger, Werner Peters star. 98 min.
09-1667 Was $24.99 *$19.99*

The Mad Executioners (1963)
An Edgar Wallace thriller about a mad scientist who lops off his victims' heads and then tries to keep them alive. Can Scotland Yard stop his ghastly experiments? Wolfgang Priess, Chris Howland star.
68-8810 *$19.99*

Strangler Of The Blackmoor Castle (1963)
A creepy, antiquated English castle is the site for a group of gruesome murders by a masked culprit, and Scotland Yard's best investigators are trying to solve the case. An Edgar Wallace story, starring Karin Dor and Ingmar Zeisberg.
68-8820 *$19.99*

The Indian Scarf (1963)
Klaus Kinski and Heinz Drache star in this spooky thriller in which a mysterious killer is knocking off the heirs to a fortune while they're all gathered at an isolated mansion.
68-8821 *$19.99*

The Squeaker (1965)
Taut German thriller based on the Edgar Wallace story follows the fates of three people who are marked as victims by the mysterious "Squeaker." Heinz Drache, Eddie Rutting, Klaus Kinski star.
68-8789 *$19.99*

The Mysterious Magician (1965)
A murderer known as "The Wizard" has Scotland Yard perplexed, as he spreads a horrific reign of terror. Only the best inspectors can try to solve the mystery in this thriller starring Joachim Fuchsberger and Eddie Arent.
68-8822 *$19.99*

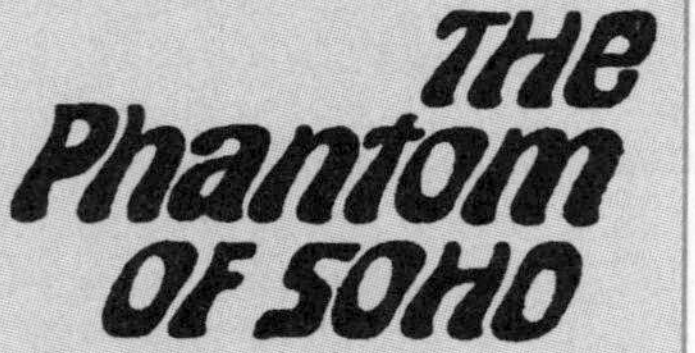

The Phantom of Soho

Phantom Of Soho (1964)
A woman mystery writer boasts that she will reveal the murderer of several prominent Londoners in the last chapter of her newest book. An intriguing whodunit, starring Barbara Rutting. 92 min.
68-8328 *$19.99*

The Hunchback Of Soho (1967)
A hip Edgar Wallace thriller from West Germany featuring lots of plot surprises, creepy atmospherics and a swinging sixties score. After inheriting $1 million, a young woman is kidnapped and sent to a school for delinquent girls while an impostor takes her place. The school is run by a wacky general, an evil "reverend" and a very butch matron. With Gunther Stroll, Pinky Braun.
79-6019 *$19.99*

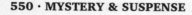

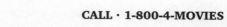

Last Plane To Baalbeck (1963)
Surprise-filled espionage thriller about a criminal empire specializing in supplying drugs and weapons to the Middle East and European countries. Special agents' bodies are being discovered everywhere, so an Interpol agent investigates. With Rosanna Podesta ("Helen of Troy"). Jacques Sernas, Yoko Tani and George Sanders.
79-6575 *$19.99*

The List Of Adrian Messenger (1963)
Stylish, unusual mystery from director John Huston has ex-British army officer George C. Scott out to catch a murderer before he can check the final name off his "death list." The heavily disguised guest stars include Tony Curtis, Kirk Douglas, Burt Lancaster, Robert Mitchum and Frank Sinatra. 98 min.
07-1264 Was $59.99 *$19.99*

The Great Armored Car Swindle (1964)
A British businessman accidentally gets involved in international espionage when he intercepts a shipment of money for a Middle East nation. He serves as middleman for a plan to substitute counterfeit currency, but will his wife blow the scheme? Peter Reynolds, Joanna Dunham star. 58 min.
68-8528 *$19.99*

Man On The Spying Trapeze (1966)
European spy yarn with Jerry Land (Wayde Preston) as a lady-loving supersleuth searching for microfilm that was lost during a car wreck. What does the dead body found in the Colosseum have to do with the film? Can Jerry stop kissing the gals long enough to find out? Helga Sommerfield also stars.
79-6451 Was $24.99 *$19.99*

Murder Party (1963)
Unusual thriller in which a serial killer runs into an old friend after tidying the house of his latest victim. The killer is soon ushered to a penthouse party where attendees play "the Murder Game," which offers a chance to take care of the potential witness. Georges Riviere and Hanne Wieder star in this mystery, shot from the killer's perspective.
79-6452 Was $24.99 *$19.99*

Million Dollar Countdown (1965)
European character actor fave Frank Wolff excels in this thriller, playing a thief just out of the slammer who heads back into the world of crime. He leads a team of eccentric crooks in taking an elaborate missile guidance system from an installation in France. Joining him in the heist are gorgeous seductress Rossella Como and Gerard Landry. AKA: "Per Favore...Non Sparate Col Cannone."
79-6555 Was $24.99 *$19.99*

We Shall Return (1962)
Cesar Romero doesn't joke around in his role as a wealthy Cuban landowner who heads to America where his two sons live, but soon faces problems because of racism. After recruiting some refugees, Romero plans to invade his old country, but he has no idea one of his sons is a double agent working for Castro. Timely (for its time) thriller also stars Linda Libera, Anthony Ray.
79-6556 Was $24.99 *$19.99*

Stranger From Hong Kong (1963)
Mitzi and Georgia, two Parisian sisters, find adventure and danger after arriving in Hong Kong to perform their nightclub act. Mitzi accidentally snags a priceless diamond in a bar of soap, and soon a local crime boss becomes interested in her and the jewel. Can Georgia's policeman pal help? Philippe Nicaud, Tania Beryll star.
79-6454 Was $24.99 *$19.99*

Kiss, Kiss, Kill, Kill (1965)
The first entry in the Euro-spy thriller "Kommissar X" series teams Interpol agent Brad Harris with solider-of-fortune Tony Kendall so they can investigate a series of murders of politicians and scientists in the Mediterranean. The team soon faces off against a team of super hit women. With Maria Perschy. AKA: "Kommissar X, Hunter of the Unknown."
79-6560 Was $24.99 *$19.99*

Death Is Nimble, Death Is Quick (1965)
European he-men Brad Harris and Tony Kendall team to investigate a murder in Ceylon, where they find themselves battling the sinister Three Yellow Cats crime organization. Muscleman Dan Vadis also stars in this entry in the espionage series based on the "Kommissar X" books from Germany.
79-6449 Was $24.99 *$19.99*

So Darling, So Deadly (1965)
Top-notch thriller in the "Kommissar X" series finds partners Tony Kendall and Brad Harris in the Orient, where scientists are being murdered at a rapid clip. The two look into the crimes and realize that Kendall is romancing the daughter of the next scientist on the hit list. Will the pair save him? Barbara Frey also stars.
79-6561 Was $24.99 *$19.99*

Death Trip (1968)
A special agent brings LSD into the country for "military purposes," and when it gets stolen by some gun-toting criminals he and his partner try to find it amidst desert oil ruins and wild motorcycle chases. Gladiator film experts Brad Harris and Tony Kendall star along with Samson Burke of "The Three Stooges Meet Hercules." Based on the "Kommissar X" book series.
79-6147 *$19.99*

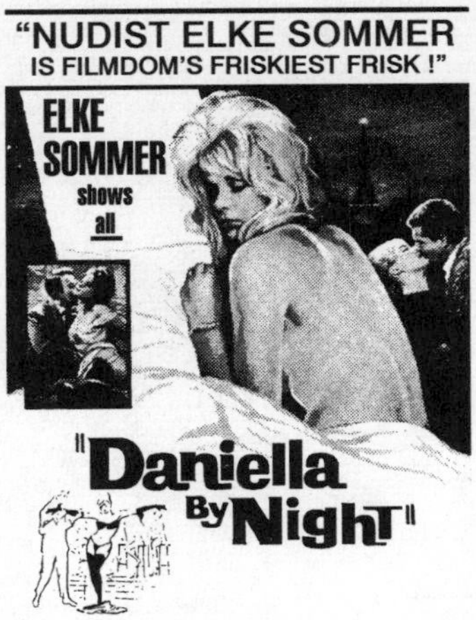
"NUDIST ELKE SOMMER
IS FILMDOM'S FRISKIEST FRISK !"
ELKE
SOMMER
shows
all
"Daniella
By Night"

Daniella By Night (1961)
Highlighted by Elke Sommer's sensuality, this espionage thriller features Sommer as a fashion model romantically involved with a count who has been selling top-secret microfilm to foreign agents. When the microfilm is hidden in Sommer's lipstick, she becomes the subject of a strip search. Ivan Desny co-stars; music co-written by Charles Aznavour. 83 min. In French with English subtitles.
83-3022 Was $39.99 *$29.99*

Mission To Venice (1963)
Sean Flynn, Errol's son, plays a detective who tries to find a missing husband and stumbles onto a ring of spies. Madeleine Robinson also stars.
68-8833 *$19.99*

To Commit A Murder (1967)
Stylish thriller from Edouard Molinaro ("La Cage Aux Folles") in which playboy novelist Louis Jourdan is drawn into a world of sex, swanky parties and intrigue when he gets involved with pretty Senta Berger, the wife of an art publisher involved in a Communist kidnapping plot. Edmond O'Brien also stars in this European production. Dubbed in English.
79-6455 Was $24.99 *$19.99*

Lightning Bolt (1965)
An inventive spy thriller about a beer tycoon who has plans to rule the world from his underwater city. Part of his plan involves exploding spacecraft with a destructive laser beam. Secret agents Anthony Eisley and Wandisa Leigh try to stop him. 94 min.
68-8806 *$19.99*

Stopover Tokyo (1956)
Crisp suspense tale of an American secret agent who must protect a traveling diplomat from assassins. Robert Wagner, Edmond O'Brien and Joan Collins star; based on a John P. Marquand novel. 100 min.
04-1845 Was $59.99 *$29.99*

The Thief (1952)
There's no dialogue in this unusual "Red Scare" thriller with Ray Milland as an American physicist who is persuaded to turn military secrets over to the Russians, then must try and flee the country when he's discovered. With Rita Gam, Martin Gabel. 85 min.
08-1446 *$19.99*

Kill Me Tomorrow (1957)
In this interesting crime story, a down-on-his-luck reporter decides to take the rap for a diamond smuggler's crimes in order to raise money for his son's eye operation. Pat O'Brien, George Coulouris, Lois Maxwell and Tommy Steele, who also supplied the music, star. 80 min.
08-1757 *$14.99*

The Long Dark Hall (1951)
Provocative and compelling British thriller stars Rex Harrison as a man accused of killing his mistress and Lilli Palmer as his steadfastly loyal wife. Reginald Beck and Tania Held co-star in a story of one woman's devotion and the conflict between love and duty. 86 min.
08-5032 *$19.99*

Quicksand (1950)
Mickey Rooney stars as a young man who commits a minor criminal act that slowly, inexorably draws him into a quagmire of crime and self-destruction. Grim human drama co-stars Peter Lorre, Jeanne Cagney. 79 min.
08-8015 *$19.99*

Loan Shark (1952)
Fine "noir" thriller stars George Raft as an ex-con who hooks up with a loan racket responsible for his brother's murder. No one knows, though, that he's an undercover man working to bust the ring. Dorothy Hart, Paul Stewart, Larry Dobkin co-star. 74 min.
10-1365 Was $19.99 *$14.99*

Tiger By The Tail (1958)
Larry Parks plays an American newsman working out of London who befriends a beautiful woman. Little does he know that she's actually a secret agent carrying a list of enemy agents with her. After she is accidentally shot, Parks finds himself pursued by operatives after the list. Constance Smith and Lisa Daniely also star. AKA: "Cross-Up." 80 min.
09-5261 *$19.99*

The Big Bluff (1955)
A well-off widow wings westward to partake of the healthy climate...but the greasy gigolo hunting for her hand in marriage has a dangerous disinterest in her well being! Shattering suspenser stars John Bromfield, Martha Vickers, Robert Hutton. 70 min.
10-7193 Was $19.99 *$14.99*

Doorway To Suspicion (1954)
Unusual thriller about an American bandleader who falls for and weds a mysterious woman while touring Europe. When he discovers that his new bride is a courier for secret agents just before she's kidnapped, the musician needs the help of his band to launch a dangerous rescue mission. Jeffrey Lynn, Linda Carroll star. 66 min.
09-5349 *$19.99*

Black Glove (1954)
Early Hammer Studios suspenser concerning an American jazzman accused of slaying his girl singer and his race to uncover the person responsible. Intriguing effort stars Alex Nicol, Eleanor Summerfield. AKA: "Face the Music." 84 min.
10-7574 Was $19.99 *$14.99*

Contraband Spain (1955)
In this British thriller, Richard Greene plays an American agent who enlists the help of a chanteuse and a customs officer to stop a group of counterfeiters on the French/Spanish border. Anouk Aimee, Michael Denison co-star. 82 min.
10-9053 Was $19.99 *$14.99*

Please Murder Me (1958)
Can you imagine Perry Mason saying that to Jessica Fletcher? This offbeat crime thriller features Raymond Burr as an attorney who falls for client Angela Lansbury, charged with killing her husband. Lansbury is acquitted, but when Burr learns she's really guilty, his conscience drives him to ask her to kill him, too! With Dick Foran, John Dehner.
10-9265 *$19.99*

Murder At 3 A.M. (1953)
Intriguing thriller starring Dennis Price as a detective who uses his sister to catch her boyfriend, whom Price believes is guilty of a murder. When Price's hunch proves wrong, his sister's relationship is jeopardized. Peggy Evans, Philip Saville co-star.
10-9774 *$14.99*

Thunder Over Tangier (1957)
A movie stuntman gets caught up in a web of deceit and blackmail when he is targeted by a ruthless gang of passport forgers preying on displaced persons in post-WWII Algeria. He struggles to clear his good name with a woman who has also been targeted. Robert Hutton, Lisa Gastoni, Martin Benson star. AKA" "The Man from Tangier." 66 min.
10-9788 *$19.99*

The Accursed (1958)
During the aftermath of World War II, a group of former British underground agents gets together to determine who is responsible for the deaths of several of their comrades. Unpredictable spy thriller with some tense moments stars Donald Wolfit, Robert Bray, Jane Griffiths and Christopher Lee. AKA: "The Traitors." 88 min.
10-9790 *$19.99*

Southside 1-1000 (1950)
First-rate film noir from director Boris Ingster ("The Stranger on the Third Floor") featuring Don DeFore as a federal agent investigating a counterfeit ring run by convict Morris Ankrum. Ankrum hides his illegal efforts with his supposed religious convictions, but DeFore's deal to purchase the goods leads him to an unlikely participant in the scheme. With Andrea King. 73 min.
10-9948 *$14.99*

Time Without Pity (1957)
While working in England after he was blacklisted, Joseph Losey fashioned this gritty noir thriller about an alcoholic who has 24 hours to prove that his son is not guilty of murder. His search leads him to an auto tycoon whose wife was having an affair with the son. Michael Redgrave, Ann Todd, Leo McKern and Peter Cushing star. 88 min.
22-5823 Was $39.99 *$29.99*

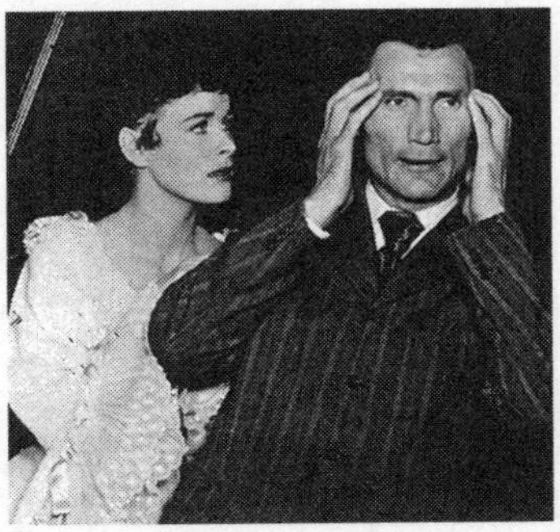

Man In The Attic (1954)
Interesting remake of the classic suspenser "The Lodger," with Jack Palance as a troubled pathologist who has killed a number of women after they spurn him. When he falls in love with the daughter of his boarding house's owner, her life is in danger. With Constance Smith and Francis Bavier. 82 min.
09-5259 *$19.99*

Kiss Me Deadly (1955)
Mickey Spillane's pugnacious private eye, Mike Hammer, becomes involved with femmes fatale, diabolical doctors and, perhaps, the end of the world, courtesy of a nuclear bomb. A noir classic noted for its influence on French New Wave filmmakers, director Robert Aldrich's two-fisted thriller stars Ralph Meeker, Cloris Leachman, Gaby Rogers Albert Dekker. Special video edition also includes the original and long-lost theatrical ending.
12-2186 Was $19.99 *$14.99*

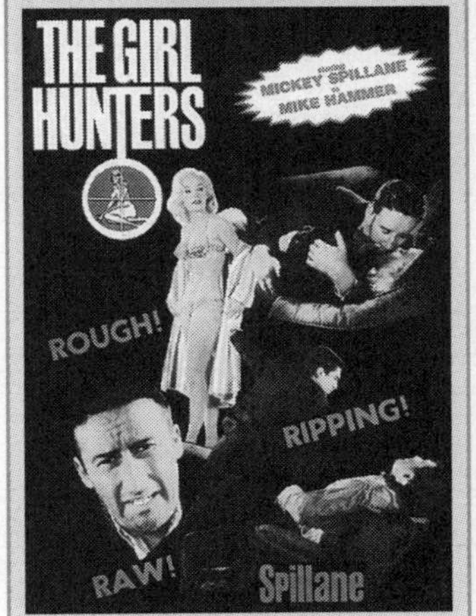
THE GIRL
HUNTERS
MICKEY SPILLANE
MIKE HAMMER
ROUGH!
RIPPING!
RAW!
Spillane

The Girl Hunters (1963)
Who better than his creator, Mickey Spillane, to portray private eye Mike Hammer in this well-turned version of Spillane's mystery novel? Here the hard-lovin', hard-fightin' Hammer wages war on a spy syndicate after the apparent death of his secretary. Co-stars Shirley Eaton and Lloyd Nolan. 103 min.
10-7060 *$19.99*

The Girl Hunters (Letterboxed Version)
Also available in a theatrical, widescreen format.
50-8391 *$19.99*

I, The Jury (1982)
Tough and tempered private eye Mike Hammer (Armand Assante) combs through a seedy underworld populated by junkies, loose women and a crazed killer to snare the mysterious murderer of an old war buddy who saved his life. Second filming of Mickey Spillane's first Hammer novel co-stars Barbara Carrera, Laurence Landon; written by Larry Cohen. 111 min.
04-1528 *$19.99*

Barrier Of The Law (1950)
First-rate but rarely seen Italian suspenser tells of an honest cop trying to stop his brother's group of counterfeits and smugglers. When a pretty young woman involved with the thieves falls for the policeman, it puts him in a tough situation. Rossano Brazzi, Jean Servais and Lea Padovani star.
10-9983 *$14.99*

Home At Seven (1953)
Superior mystery yarn starring and directed by Ralph Richardson, who plays an amnesiac bank clerk who discovers his sports club has been robbed and the steward has been murdered, and he becomes the prime suspect. Margaret Leighton, Jack Hawkins co-star. 85 min.
17-9057 Was $19.99 *$14.99*

The Second Woman (1951)
Architect Robert Young, haunted by the accident that claimed his fiancée's life, begins to wonder if he was responsible and fears he may be losing his mind in this intriguing thriller. Betsy Drake, Henry O'Neill co-star. 90 min.
18-3016 *$19.99*

The Clouded Yellow (1950)
Atmospheric British suspenser stars Jean Simmons as a fragile woman who stands accused of killing a handyman and Trevor Howard as a dismissed intelligence agent who is determined to prove her innocence. With Barry Jones, Maxwell Reed. 96 min.
22-5810 Was $39.99 *$29.99*

The Woman In Question (Five Angles On Murder) (1950)
Unusual British whodunit follows a police detective's investigation into the murder of a carnival fortune-teller, and how each of the victim's acquaintances interviewed offer differing views on her life and the circumstances that led to her death. Duncan MacRae, Jean Kent, Dirk Bogarde, Hermione Badderley star; directed by Anthony Asquith. 84 min.
22-5873 *$29.99*

The Paris Express (1953)
An embezzler tries to escape the police on the Paris Express, and the chase is on. An exciting tale of crime, passion, betrayal, and murder. Claude Rains, Herbert Lom, Marta Toren star. 83 min.
50-6182 *$19.99*

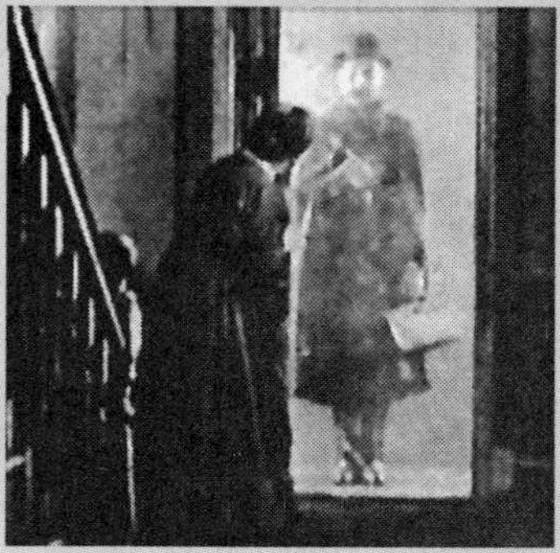

The Lodger (1926)
Alfred Hitchcock's first thriller is a study of a mysterious tenant at a boarding house who is suspected of being Jack the Ripper. Starring Ivor Novello and Marie Ault; Hitchcock turns up in his first screen appearance. 65 min. Silent with music score.
09-1775 Was $19.99 **$14.99**

Easy Virtue (1927)
Hitchcock directed this silent melodrama, based on a Noel Coward play, about a woman valiantly coping with an alcoholic husband and with the suicide of her lover. Stars Isabel Jeans, Franklin Dyall and Ian Hunter. 60 min. Silent with music track.
62-1128 **$19.99**

Champagne (1928)
Silent comedy from Hitchcock's early British period is about a frivolous rich girl whose father, the "Champagne King," pretends bankruptcy to teach her to be more responsible. Betty Balfour and Gordon Harker star.
17-3066 **$19.99**

The Ring (1928)
One of Hitchcock's best silent films, about boxer "Round One" Stander, a circus attraction who fights all comers. When he marries the box office girl and turns pro to please her, the pug is soon outclassed by competition inside and outside of the ring. Carl Brisson, Lilian Hall Davis, Ian Hunter star. 133 min.
17-3058 **$19.99**

The Farmer's Wife (1928)
Rare Hitchcock silent comedy (he wrote and directed) about a recently widowed farmer who undertakes a wide search for a new wife, unaware of the perfect choice right under his nose: his charming housekeeper. Jameson Thomas and Lillian Hall-Davies star. 93 min.
63-1700 **$14.99**

The Manxman (1929)
In his last silent film, Hitchcock tells the compelling story of two childhood friends who grow up to fall in love with the same woman. Engaged to one, will she betray herself to the other? Carl Brisson, Anny Ondra star. 124 min. Silent with music track.
09-1916 Was $19.99 **$14.99**

Blackmail (1929)
Hitchcock's (and England's) first sound film follows a detective's girlfriend who is blackmailed when she kills a man in self-defense. Features a thrilling chase through the British Museum. Anny Ondra, John Longden star. 82 min.
63-1699 **$14.99**

Juno And The Paycock (1930)
Based on the play by Irish author Sean O'Casey, this Hitchcock drama follows the ups and downs of a family living in the Dublin slums. Edward Chapman, Sara Algood, Barry Fitzgerald. 98 min.
10-1323 **$19.99**

Murder (1930)
Superior Hitchcock suspenser starring Herbert Marshall as a jurist who believes the young actress on trial for murder is innocent. He begins his own investigation that leads him to surprising places to find the killer. Norah Baring, Phyllis Konstam also star. 100 min.
63-1701 **$14.99**

The Skin Game (1931)
Early Hitchcock drama, based on John Galsworthy's popular stage play, that was decidedly atypical of the Master's subsequent suspensers. The aristocratic patriarch of one of two rival families resorts to blackmail to settle a dispute over land rights. Stars Edmund Gwenn, Phyllis Konstam and John Longden. 90 min.
10-7061 **$19.99**

Rich And Strange (1932)
Offbeat Hitchcock tale of two people from a small English village who inherit a large sum of money and decide to travel the world, only to find their wealth doesn't bring them happiness. Henry Kendall, Joan Barry star. AKA: "East of Shanghai." 80 min.
10-1312 Was $19.99 **$14.99**

Number Seventeen (1932)
An early Hitchcock effort that mixes the suspense, scares and humor prevalent in his later masterpieces. A tramp joins a group of jewel thieves, a pretty girl and a detective in a search for a valuable stolen necklace. The search starts in a spooky house and leads to a train and a bus. Leon M. Lion, Anne Grey and John Stuart. 61 min.
63-1697 **$14.99**

The Man Who Knew Too Much (1934)
A British couple on holiday in Switzerland are told by a dying government agent of a plot to kill a diplomat in London, but when the assassins kidnap their daughter, the couple must race against time to save her and the intended victim. Terrific Hitchcock thriller stars Leslie Banks, Edna Best and Peter Lorre. 84 min.
10-2023 Was $19.99 **$14.99**

The 39 Steps (1935)
One of Hitchcock's early triumphs, the original film version of this mystery classic stars Robert Donat as the innocent pursued by both police and enemy spies while trying to learn the secret of "the 39 steps." With Madeleine Carroll, Peggy Ashcroft. 87 min.
10-2044 Was $19.99 **$14.99**

The Secret Agent (1936)
One of the cinema's first looks at the espionage business, Alfred Hitchcock's realistic, darkly funny thriller stars John Gielgud as the British agent assigned to track down and eliminate an enemy spy. With Madeleine Carroll, Peter Lorre, Robert Young. 86 min.
22-5804 Remastered **$24.99**

Sabotage (1936)
A true masterpiece of edge-of-your-seat cinema, Alfred Hitchcock's chilling tale stars Oscar Homolka as a terrorist bomber who uses his London movie theater as a cover and his young brother-in-law as an unwitting courier for his deadly packages. Based on Joseph Conrad's "The Secret Agent." With Sylvia Sidney, John Loder. 76 min.
10-2024 Was $19.99 **$14.99**

Young And Innocent (1937)
Hitchcock's unusual film about a man unjustly accused of murder and his growing relationship with the daughter of the investigating officer. Stars Nova Pilbeam, John Longden, Derrick de Marney. 80 min.
62-1072 **$14.99**

The Lady Vanishes (1938)
When an elderly woman disappears in the middle of a transcontinental train ride and the young lady who shared her compartment cannot find anyone who even remembers the missing person, a complex and dangerous search for the truth begins. Superlative Hitchcock whodunit stars Margaret Lockwood, Michael Redgrave, Paul Lukas and Dame May Whitty. 97 min.
22-5805 Remastered **$24.99**

Jamaica Inn (1939)
Alfred Hitchcock's last British-made film was a costume thriller set in 1700s England. Charles Laughton is leader of a band of cutthroat smugglers, Robert Newton the soldier out to capture him, and Maureen O'Hara the innkeeper's niece who holds the secret to the criminal's plans. 98 min.
10-4043 **$19.99**

Rebecca (1940)
For his first American film (which later went on to win the Best Picture Oscar), Alfred Hitchcock was hired by producer David O. Selznick to adapt Daphne du Maurier's haunting novel. Joan Fontaine stars as the new wife of brooding Laurence Olivier who moves into his mansion and is forced to live in the shadow of his first wife, Rebecca. With Judith Anderson, George Sanders. 131 min.
04-1128 **$14.99**

Foreign Correspondent (1940)
Tense thriller of Europe at the edge of World War II from Alfred Hitchcock. Joel McCrea is the reporter caught in the middle of a spy ring, threatening a pacifist conference, with his fiancée's father the possible spy leader. Herbert Marshall, Laraine Day and George Sanders co-star. 120 min.
19-1752 Was $19.99 **$14.99**

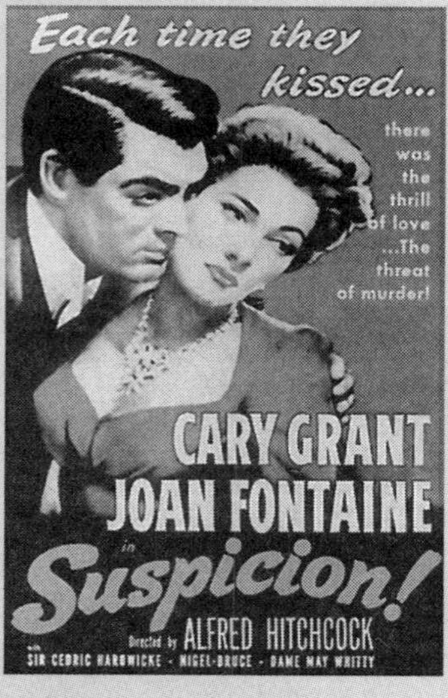
Each time they kissed...
there was the thrill of love ...The threat of murder!
CARY GRANT
JOAN FONTAINE
in
Suspicion!
Directed by ALFRED HITCHCOCK
SIR CEDRIC HARDWICKE · NIGEL BRUCE · DAME MAY WHITTY

Suspicion (1941)
Taut suspense tale stars Joan Fontaine as a recently married woman who comes to believe that dashing husband Cary Grant is a murderer, and his next victim will be her! Cedric Hardwicke, Nigel Bruce and May Whitty co-star in Alfred Hitchcock's classic thriller. 99 min.
18-7656 Was $19.99 **$14.99**

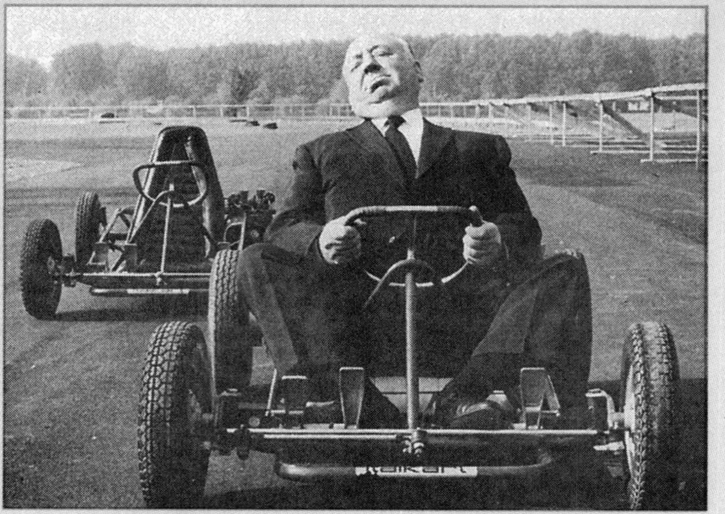

Alfred Hitchcock

Mr. And Mrs. Smith (1941)
Alfred Hitchcock directs this uncharacteristic screwball comedy with Robert Montgomery and Carole Lombard as a bickering couple informed separately by a lawyer that they are not legally married. The two attempt to relive their courtship in a series of funny incidents in order to decide if they'll wed again. With Gene Raymond and Jack Carson. 95 min.
05-1113 Was $19.99 **$14.99**

Saboteur (1942)
Robert Cummings is a wartime factory worker wrongfully accused of sabotage in this Hitchcock thriller. Helping him on the lam is Priscilla Lane, and Norman Lloyd is the titular villain. Features the classic sequence atop the Statue of Liberty. 108 min.
07-1328 Was $19.99 **$14.99**

Shadow Of A Doubt (1943)
A young girl, overjoyed when her favorite uncle comes to visit the family, slowly begins to suspect that he is in fact the "Merry Widow" killer sought by the authorities. Alfred Hitchcock's favorite of all his films, made all the more chilling by the small town ambience supplied by co-scripter Thorton Wilder, stars Joseph Cotten, Teresa Wright, Macdonald Carey and Hume Cronyn. 108 min.
07-1586 Was $19.99 **$14.99**

Lifeboat (1944)
A lifeboat adrift in the North Atlantic during WWII is the setting for this Hitchcock tale of human emotion and drama. A band of Allied passengers finds their only hope for survival is the German soldier they've taken aboard, but can they trust him? Tallulah Bankhead, Walter Slezak, John Hodiak and William Bendix star; look twice for Hitch's cameo. 98 min.
04-1838 **$19.99**

Alfred Hitchcock's "Bon Voyage" And "Aventure Malgache" (1944)
Unseen in the U.S. and banned in Europe for decades, these two short films were directed by Hitchcock for the French Resistance in World War II. "Bon Voyage" concerns a Scottish flier recalling how Resistance fighters helped him escape from a German POW camp; and "Aventure Malgache" follows a Free French leader battling Vichy corruption in occupied Madagascar. 58 min. total. In French with English subtitles.
80-5024 Was $39.99 **$24.99**

Spellbound (1945)
The "prison of the mind" is explored in this Hitchcock classic set in a private asylum. Gregory Peck is the new head doctor who is suppressing a dark secret, and Ingrid Bergman is the psychiatrist whose love may be his only cure. Features an amazing dream sequence developed by Hitch and artist Salvador Dali. 111 min.
04-1429 **$14.99**

Notorious (1946)
Superlative Hitchcock thriller of espionage, deception and thwarted love. Ingrid Bergman, daughter of a war criminal, is persuaded by U.S. agents to marry Claude Rains, head of a Nazi spy ring in Brazil...much to the distress of agent Cary Grant, who's fallen in love with her. Leopoldine Konstantin co-stars. 103 min.
04-1122 **$14.99**

The Paradine Case (1948)
Barrister Gregory Peck finds himself falling in love with his client, a socialite accused of killing her husband, in this Hitchcock courtroom thriller. With Valli, Charles Laughton, Charles Coburn and Louis Jourdan. 116 min.
04-2115 Was $19.99 **$14.99**

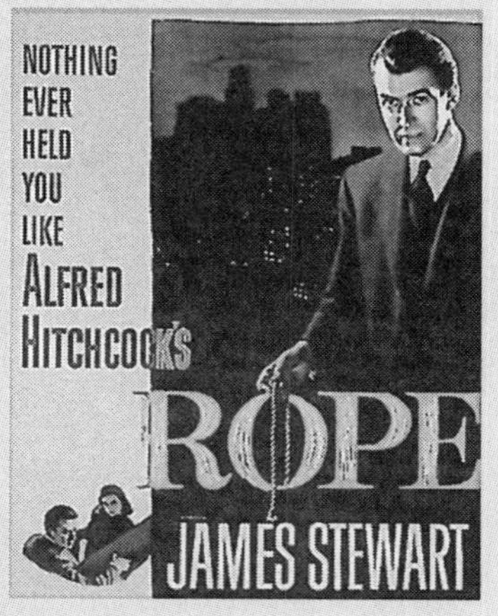
NOTHING
EVER
HELD
YOU
LIKE
ALFRED
HITCHCOCK'S
ROPE
JAMES STEWART

Rope (1948)
Hitchcock's "filmed play experiment," shot in continuous 10-minute takes. Two school friends kill a man for the "intellectual thrill" of it, then hide the body in their apartment while giving a party. James Stewart stars as the boys' ex-teacher who uncovers the crime. John Dall, Farley Granger co-star. 80 min.
07-1256 Was $19.99 **$14.99**

Stage Fright (1950)
Alfred Hitchcock's expert theatrical thriller focuses on a drama student's involvement in a murder of an actress's husband. Marlene Dietrich, Jane Wyman, Richard Todd. 110 min.
19-1365 Was $19.99 **$14.99**

Strangers On A Train: Hollywood Version (1951)
One of Alfred Hitchcock's greatest works, based on Patricia Highsmith's novel. Two men meet by chance on a train and facetiously discuss swapping murder targets in each other's life, but when one man carries out the killing he tries to force the other to fulfill their "bargain." Robert Walker, Farley Granger, Ruth Roman star. 101 min.
19-1290 **$19.99**

Strangers On A Train (Restored British Version)
This restored edition includes two minutes of extra footage not shown in American theaters, plus the original theatrical trailer. 103 min.
19-2494 **$19.99**

I Confess (1953)
Montgomery Clift is a priest who accepts the confession of a murderer, then finds he may be accused of the crime. A moody, first-rate mystery from Alfred Hitchcock. Anne Baxter, Karl Malden. 94 min.
19-1364 Was $19.99 **$14.99**

Dial M For Murder (1954)
Elaborate Hitchcock murder thriller, with Ray Milland as a tennis pro whose plot to commit the "perfect" crime, the murder of his unfaithful wife (Grace Kelly), unravels after an unexpected kink in his plan forces him to do some quick thinking. Co-stars Robert Cummings, John Williams. Originally filmed in 3-D. Includes original trailer; 105 min.
19-1207 **$19.99**

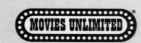

To Catch A Thief (1955)
Cary Grant is John "the Cat" Robie, a suave ex-burglar whose life of ease along the French Riviera is torn asunder when a new string of robberies are committed with his trademark style. Can Grant prove his innocence, or will beautiful heiress Grace Kelly lure him back into a life of crime, in Alfred Hitchcock's seductively stylish thriller? With John Williams, Christine Auber. 103 min.
06-1105 *$14.99*

The Trouble With Harry (1955)
Harry's trouble is that he's dead, can't stay in one place, and has four people taking credit for his death. Alfred Hitchcock deftly blends suspense and black humor in this film, starring John Forsythe, Edmund Gwenn, Mildred Natwick, Jerry Mathers and Shirley MacLaine (her film debut). 99 min.
07-1247 Was $19.99 *$14.99*

The Man Who Knew Too Much (1956)
Alfred Hitchcock's exhilarating suspense classic stars James Stewart and Doris Day as an American couple faced with blackmail, danger and kidnapping while vacationing in Morocco. Hitch throws in lots of red herrings and unforgettable moments in this remake of his own 1934 thriller; features the Oscar-winning song "Que Sera, Sera." 120 min.
07-1244 Was $19.99 *$14.99*

The Wrong Man (1956)
Perhaps the most harrowing of all of Alfred Hitchcock's films...because it actually happened. Henry Fonda stars as a New York nightclub musician trapped by circumstantial evidence and convicted of robbery in this compelling drama. Co-stars Vera Miles, Anthony Quayle. 105 min.
19-1208 Was $19.99 *$14.99*

Vertigo (1958)
Considered by many to be Alfred Hitchcock's most personal film. This restored print of the suspense masterpiece stars James Stewart as an ex-cop with a fear of heights who is hired by an old friend to uncover the secret wife Kim Novak is keeping from him. What Stewart finds is a forbidden romance, a deadly plot, and an obsession that transcends the grave. With Barbara Bel Geddes, Tom Helmore; music by Bernard Herrmann. 120 min.
07-1213 Was $19.99 *$14.99*

Vertigo (Letterboxed Version)
Also available in a theatrical, widescreen format. Includes a 30-minute documentary on the movie's making and 1998 re-release.
07-2494 Was $19.99 ❑*$14.99*

North By Northwest: Special Edition (1959)
Ad executive Cary Grant finds himself chased by criminals, framed for murder, sharing a sleeper berth with Eva Marie Saint, dusted by a crop plane and hanging from Mt. Rushmore in Hitchcock's gem of thrills and mystery. With James Mason, Leo G. Carroll, Martin Landau. This newly transfered special edition also includes the original theatrical trailer and the documentary "The Man on Lincoln's Nose: The Making of North By Northwest." 171 min. total.
12-3315 ❑*$19.99*

North By Northwest: Special Edition (Letterboxed Version)
Also available in a theatrical, widescreen format.
12-3314 ❑*$19.99*

Psycho (1960)
Hitchcock's most famous movie, the shocker that still keeps people away from showers. Janet Leigh is a woman on the run who befriends Mama's boy hotel clerk Norman Bates (Anthony Perkins). What is Norman's sinister secret? Will Vera Miles find her sister? And just where is Mrs. Bates? With John Gavin, Martin Balsam. 109 min.
07-1025 Was $19.99 *$14.99*

Psycho (Letterboxed Version)
Also available in a theatrical, widescreen format.
07-2554 *$19.99*

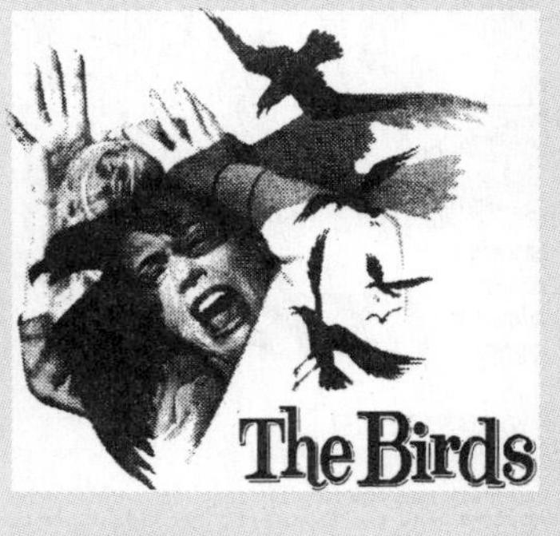

The Birds (1963)
Nature runs amok in Alfred Hitchcock's chilling adaptation of the Daphne du Maurier story, as a small California coastal town finds itself under attack by gulls, crows and other fine feathered "friends." Rod Taylor, Tippi Hedren, Jessica Tandy, Suzanne Pleshette star. 119 min.
07-1000 Was $19.99 *$14.99*

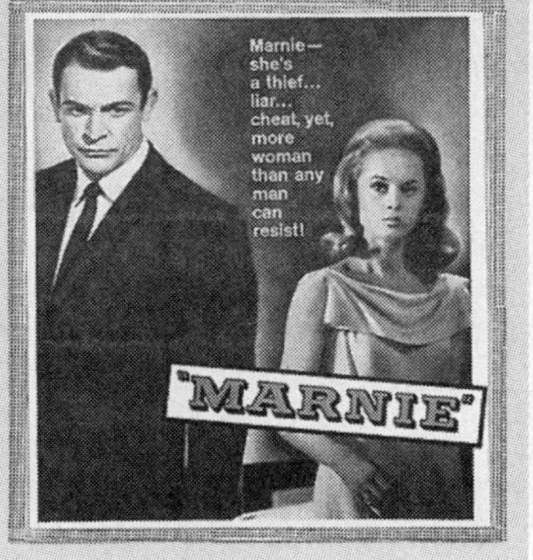

Marnie (1964)
A critical and financial misfire when first released, Hitchcock's psychodrama about a gorgeous young kleptomaniac (Tippi Hedren) and her employer (Sean Connery), who falls for her and tries to discover the reasons behind her compulsions, is now recognized as a subtle thriller of sexual symbolism. Co-stars Diane Baker and a young Bruce Dern. 129 min.
07-1437 Was $19.99 ❑*$14.99*

Torn Curtain (1966)
Alfred Hitchcock's tale of international intrigue involves a world-famous scientist who may (or may not) be defecting to East Berlin. Paul Newman, Julie Andrews, Lila Kedrova. 125 min.
07-1142 Was $19.99 *$14.99*

Topaz (1967)
Based on the Leon Uris novel, this Alfred Hitchcock tale of global intrigue stars John Forsythe as a CIA agent who teams with French spy Frederick Stafford to uncover Soviet activities in Cuba circa 1962. John Vernon, Karin Dor, Roscoe Lee Browne also star. New, extended version includes 17 minutes of never-before seen footage. 144 min.
07-2764 *$14.99*

Frenzy (1972)
An innocent man is suspected of a series of "necktie murders" in London, unaware that the real killer is a friend of his, in Alfred Hitchcock's gripping thriller. Jon Finch, Alec McCowen, Barry Foster star. 116 min.
07-1006 Was $19.99 ❑*$14.99*

Family Plot (1976)
Alfred Hitchcock's final film is a light-hearted thriller involving two couples (phony psychic duo Barbara Harris and Bruce Dern and kidnappers William Devane and Karen Black) who cross paths in a search for a missing heir and a fortune in jewels. 120 min.
07-1103 Was $19.99 *$14.99*

Alfred Hitchcock Presents: Sorcerer's Apprentice
The only episode from Hitch's suspense series not to air during its 1955-62 network run was this tale from writer Robert Bloch. Brandon De Wilde stars as a runaway boy who hides out at a circus and is taken in by a kindly magician whose stage assistant wife cooks up a scheme to murder her husband and leave the circus with her lover. Diana Dors, David J. Stewart also star. 30 min.
10-2788 *$12.99*

A Talk With Hitchcock (1964)
In a rare two-part interview, the cinematic shock master talks candidly about his life and his art, sharing anecdotes about his boyhood, his filmmaking careers, and his own theories on suspense and fright. 60 min.
50-8569 *$14.99*

Alfred Hitchcock: Master Of Suspense (1973)
This documentary focuses on the life and work of the legendary director of such movies as "Rear Window," "North by Northwest," "Psycho" and "The Birds." Clips from Hitchcock's classic films and interviews with colleagues and co-workers are featured, and Hitch himself discusses the fine art of scaring audiences. Cliff Robertson narrates. 58 min.
50-6040 Was $19.99 *$14.99*

The Hitchcock Collection
Guarantee yourself plenty of "gooood evenings" with this four-film collector's set that includes "Notorious," "The Paradine Case," "Rebecca" and "Spellbound."
08-8681 *$59.99*

The Best Of British Hitchcock
Three of Alfred Hitchcock's greatest 1930s suspensers, "The Lady Vanishes," "The Secret Agent" and "The 39 Steps," are available in this collector's set.
22-5807 Save $15.00! *$59.99*

The Alfred Hitchcock Collection
The master of screen suspense is spotlighted with this deluxe 14-tape boxed set. Along with the films "The Birds," "Family Plot," "Frenzy," "The Man Who Knew Too Much (1956)," "Marnie," "Psycho," "Rope," "Saboteur," "Shadow of a Doubt," "Topaz," "Torn Curtain," "The Trouble with Harry" and "Vertigo," you'll also get a four-episode "best of" tape from "Alfred Hitchcock Presents."
07-2784 Save $15.00! *$179.99*

The Green Glove (1952)
Top-notch thriller set after World War II featuring Glenn Ford as an ex-paratrooper hired by a church to find a bejeweled glove lifted by ex-Nazi crook George Macready. Geraldine Brooks and Gaby Andre also star in this atmospheric yarn. 89 min.
17-9016 *$19.99*

Impulse (1955)
Intense suspense yarn features Arthur Kennedy tangling with diamond smuggling and seedy underworld figures when he becomes smitten with a beautiful but dangerous nightclub singer. Constance Smith and Joy Shelton also star. 80 min.
53-6024 *$19.99*

Cast A Dark Shadow (1957)
Fine thriller starring Dirk Bogarde as a scheming, money-seeking cad who weds elderly widows, then kills them to gain their fortunes. Eventually he meets his match when the widow of a saloon-keeper learns of his plans. Mona Washbourne, Margaret Lockwood also star. 84 min.
53-6049 Was $29.99 *$19.99*

Battle Shock (1956)
A top-notch shocker stars Janice Rule and Ralph Meeker as a married couple vacationing in Acapulco. But a nightmare begins when Meeker is accused of murder. Co-stars Paul Henreid, who also directs. 88 min.
63-1120 *$39.99*

Crashout (1955)
Six cons break out of the "big house" and head for the location of a hidden fortune in gold coins, but their mutual distrust threatens their survival. Top-notch thriller stars William Bendix, Arthur Kennedy and William Tallman. 68 min.
63-1287 *$19.99*

Cry Danger (1951)
Released from jail, Dick Powell searches for the gangsters who framed him as well as the $10,000 stash they took with them, in this well-hewn suspenser. Rhonda Fleming, William Conrad and Richard Erdman star. 80 min.
63-1288 *$19.99*

Cry Vengeance (1954)
Jailed for three years for a crime he didn't commit, his family killed and his face disfigured, ex-cop Mark Stevens begins a search for retribution that takes him to Alaska and places his own life in danger. Co-stars Martha Hyer, Douglas Kennedy. 83 min.
63-1289 *$19.99*

Plunder Road (1957)
A gem of "B-movie" filmmaking, detailing the elaborate plans of a gang to hijack a gold shipment due for the San Francisco mint, and how their scheme slowly unravels. Gene Raymond, Wayne Morris, Elisha Cook, Jr., Stafford Repp star. 76 min.
63-1290 *$19.99*

Make Haste To Live (1954)
Framed by his wife for her murder and sent to prison for 18 years, a man is released and begins tracking her down, ready to fulfill the job he was accused of, in a crackling good mystery. Dorothy McGuire, Stephen McNally, Carolyn Jones star. 90 min.
63-1335 *$19.99*

Finger Man (1955)
Heart-pounding gangster tale stars Frank Lovejoy as a bootlegger sprung from the hoosegow by the IRS to fink on crime boss Forrest Tucker. With Peggie Castle as a bad luck moll and character actor Timothy Carey ("The Wild One") as a creepy mob gofer. 82 min.
63-1357 *$19.99*

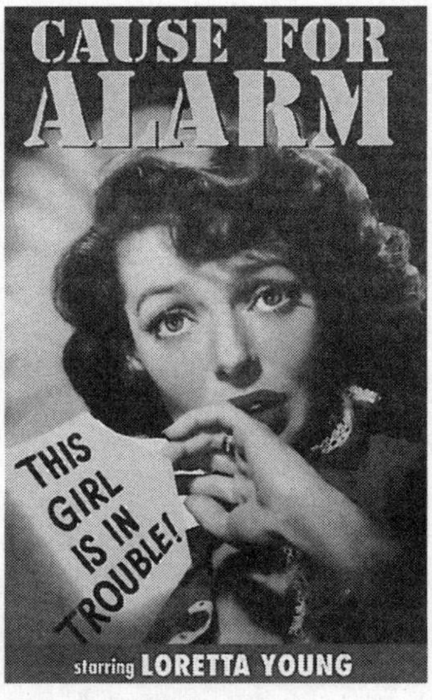

Cause For Alarm (1951)
Tense drama stars Loretta Young as a woman framed by her insane husband for murder when he suspects her of infidelity. Riveting, suspenseful film also stars Barry Sullivan. 75 min.
08-8021 Was $19.99 *$14.99*

A Kiss Before Dying (1956)
Moody and effective suspenser features a cast-against-type Robert Wagner as a psychotic charmer who kills his pregnant girlfriend and then begins a romance with her sister, who, unaware of Wagner's identity, is investigating the woman's mysterious death. Based on an Ira Levin novel; Virginia Leith, Jeffrey Hunter, Joanne Woodward and Mary Astor also star. 94 min.
12-3103 ❑*$19.99*

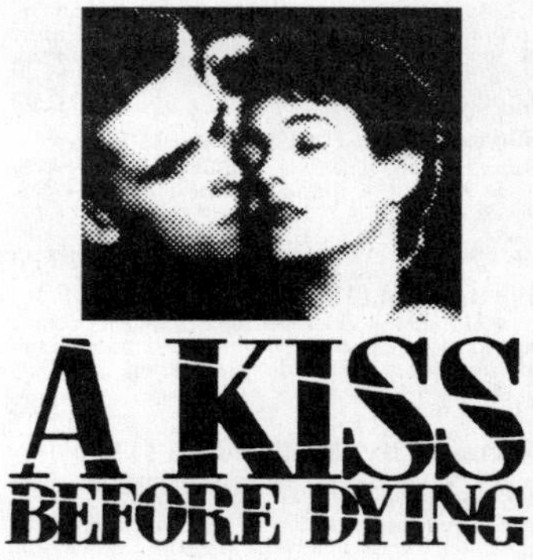

A Kiss Before Dying (1991)
In this gripping remake of the 1956 thriller, Matt Dillon plays a psychotic yuppie who kills his girlfriend and then marries her twin sister (Sean Young in dual roles) in order to worm his way into their wealthy family. Max Von Sydow co-stars; scripted and directed by "Fatal Attraction" author James Deardon. 93 min.
07-1713 Was $14.99 *$12.99*

Circle Of Danger (1951)
In this atmospheric drama, Ray Milland plays an American who travels to England to investigate the mysterious death of his brother, who died during a wartime commando raid. Milland meets members of his sibling's platoon, each of whom leads him closer to the truth. Patricia Roc, Marius Goring and Hugh Sinclair star; Jacques Tourneur ("Out of the Past") directs. 86 min.
53-6080 *$29.99*

When Gangland Strikes (1956)
Notorious mob chieftain Duke Martella temporarily eludes a determined country prosecutor by blackmailing him in this cops and robbers thriller starring Raymond Greenleaf, Marjie Miller and Slim Pickens. 70 min.
63-1355 *$19.99*

Hoodlum Empire (1952)
Brian Donlevy plays a crusading congressman loosely based on Sen. C. Estes Kefauver and Luther Adler is a Frank Costello-like syndicate boss in this riveting underworld drama, co-starring Claire Trevor and Vera Ralston. 98 min.
63-1356 *$19.99*

Diplomatic Passport (1956)
An American diplomat and his wife find their stay in London interrupted by a group of international jewel thieves who first dupe the diplomat into going to France on a phony assignment, then use the pair's identities in an elaborate smuggling operation. Marsha Hunt, Paul Carpenter and Honor Blackman star. 65 min.
09-2341 Was $24.99 *$19.99*

Sergeant And The Spy (1954)
An American GI stationed in Milan hopes to get a furlough to Paris, but is instead given an assignment by his commanding officer: deliver a top-secret letter to London. Along with a pal, the soldier soon finds himself embroiled in intrigue involving a travel bag, a mystery woman and espionage. Janis Carter, Richard Ney star. 62 min.
09-2345 *$19.99*

Black Tide (1957)
In this British thriller, a beautiful model and amateur swimmer mysteriously drowns. The authorities write off the incident as an accident, but a cocky young American swimmer preparing to cross the English Channel believes otherwise. John Ireland, Derek Bond and Maureen Connell star. 80 min.
09-2955 *$19.99*

Home To Danger (1951)
A woman left the estate of her father following his suicide becomes the target of a mysterious killer in this suspenseful British whodunit. Guy Rolfe, Rona Anderson and Stanley Baker star. 66 min.
09-5102 *$19.99*

Lonely Hearts Bandits (1950)
A gangster and his wife establish a lonely hearts enterprise that allows them to con lovelorn clients out of their cash, then murder them. After a wealthy widow disappears, the police launch an all-out dragnet for the duo. Fine crime drama, based on the true story that also inspired the cult film "The Honeymoon Killers," stars Dorothy Patrick, John Eldredge. 60 min.
09-5103 *$19.99*

Witness In The Dark (1959)
Unusual suspenser about a blind telephone operator who inherits the brooch of a murdered neighbor, but after accidentally brushing against the killer, who fears she can identify him, she becomes his next target. With Patricia Dainton, Conrad Phillips and Madge Ryan. 62 min.
09-5113 *$19.99*

Man Accused (1959)
Interesting British thriller starring Ronald Howard as a man who marries the daughter of a baronet and finds himself framed on a murder charge. He eventually lands in jail and must find a way to get out and find the real killers. With Carol Marsh and Ian Fleming. 58 min.
09-5258 $19.99

Death Goes To School (1953)
A girl's school instructor tries to convince doubting co-workers that a strangler stalks among them before an innocent lass becomes the next victim. British chiller stars Gordon Jackson. 65 min.
68-8289 $19.99

Three Stops To Murder (1953)
Suave "Falcon" series star Tom Conway is an ex-FBI agent keeping in trim on a case involving stolen jewels and a dead beauty queen. AKA: "Blood Orange." 76 min.
68-8291 Was $24.99 $19.99

White Fire (1953)
A sailor from the States interrupts a London stopover to track down the diamond smugglers who are framing his brother for murder. Scott Brady and Mary Castle star. 81 min.
68-8293 $19.99

Kansas City Confidential (1953)
A bitter ex-cop becomes the criminal mastermind behind a huge armored car heist, and a former con must turn investigator when he's falsely accused of the crime. Intriguing underworld saga stars John Payne, Neville Brand, Coleen Gray, Lee Van Cleef. 98 min.
68-8294 $14.99

Stranger In Town (1957)
A journalist investigating the murder of a fellow American and composer in an English village uncovers a sordid blackmail scheme. Alex Nicol and Anne Paige star. 73 min.
68-8295 $14.99

House Of The Arrow (1953)
Superior British thriller stars Oscar Homolka as a police inspector investigating the murder of a French widow with a poisoned arrow. Yvonne Furneaux co-stars. 73 min.
68-8297 Was $24.99 $19.99

Rogue's Yarn (1956)
A London inspector refuses to treat the death of a rich invalid in a yachting mishap as an accident, despite protests from her socialite widower. Gripping drama stars Elwyn Brooks-Jones. 80 min.
68-8299 $19.99

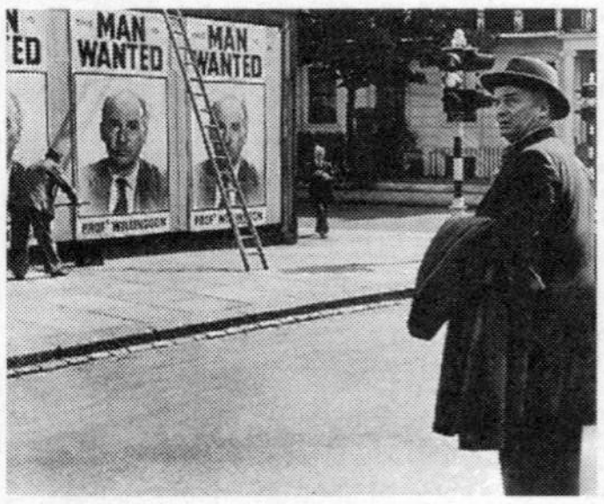

Seven Days To Noon (1950)
The Academy Award for Best Story went to this British jewel about the breakdown of one of the scientists responsible for making the first atomic weapon, and his mad threat to blow up London unless his government agrees to a nuclear ban. Electrifying suspense starring Barry Jones. 93 min.
68-8155 Was $19.99 $14.99

The Spaniard's Curse (1958)
It's not a nasty reminder from a Tijuana weekend, but a curse on the judge and jury of a condemned man. When two of the jurors die, hizzonor Michael Hordern tries to learn whether it was from the double whammy, or the old doublecross. 80 min.
68-8322 $19.99

Heatwave (1954)
British crime story stars Hilary Brooke as an unscrupulous seductress who becomes bored with her wealthy husband and their resort idyll, and makes local writer Alex Nicol her newest challenge. 69 min.
68-8360 $19.99

Death Tide (1958)
After a shipload of diamonds is pirated by hoodlums, the authorities go into action. Solid crime story stars Frank Silvera.
68-8428 $19.99

Blackout (1950)
A blind man regains his sight and discovers a presumed-to-be-dead man is alive and well and running a smuggling ring. Atmospheric melodrama starring Maxwell Reed and Dinah Sheridan. 73 min.
68-8475 $19.99

No Trace (1950)
Expert British thriller focusing on a crime novelist's involvement in a real-life murder. After an American mobster tries to kill him, the novelist teams with his Scotland Yard inspector pal to unravel a devious blackmail plan. Hugh Sinclair, Dinah Sheridan star. 76 min.
68-8476 $19.99

The Man Who Wouldn't Talk (1958)
Fine courtroom thriller starring Anthony Quayle and Zsa Zsa Gabor as American secret agents posing as honeymooners in London in order to locate confidential information. When Gabor is found dead, Quayle is the chief suspect and cannot reveal the truth behind his identity to defense counsel Anna Neagle. 97 min.
09-5105 $19.99

Tokyo File 212 (1951)
An American agent travels to Japan during the Korean War in order to stop the spread of communism in this fascinating, well-photographed Cold War thriller. With Florence Marly, Robert Peyton and Reiko Otani. 86 min.
09-5249 $19.99

The Embezzler (1954)
British suspenser focusing on a doctor's wife who befriends a bank clerk on the run after his embezzling scheme has been exposed. When the clerk learns the woman is being blackmailed, he risks his life to save her. Charles Victor, Zena Marshall star. 61 min.
09-5254 $19.99

The Lie (1954)
When a man wakes up in the morning after a night of drinking and partying with friends, he discovers another man shot to death on the floor of his apartment. He subsequently goes on trial for murder, only to hear his friends lie about where he was the night of the killing! Lee Bowman, Ramsey Ames, Eva Probst and Harald Moresch star.
68-9268 $19.99

Private Hell 36 (1954)
Suspenseful tale of two detectives and a woman who share a secret of stolen money, deception and death, only to be ruled by greed. Ida Lupino, Howard Duff, Dean Jagger star; directed by Don Siegel. 81 min.
63-5004 Was $19.99 $14.99

Blind Date (1959)
Superb thriller from Joseph Losey ("The Servant") starring Hardy Kruger as a Dutch painter accused of murdering his mistress after her body is found in his cottage. Investigator Stanley Baker discovers that the woman was also involved with a diplomat, and the revelation helps him unravel the mystery. With Micheline Presle. AKA: "Chance Meeting." 90 min.
09-5253 $19.99

Eye Witness (1950)
Needing an alibi for a friend stuck in a British jail on a murder rap, an American lawyer turns up one piece of helpful evidence, a book of poems. Mystery stars Robert Montgomery, Leslie Banks. 93 min.
68-8180 $19.99

Obsessed (1951)
The poisoning of a society matron points suspicion at her husband and his mistress. Well-acted British mystery based on the stage-play, "The Late Edwina Black," stars David Farrar and Geraldine Fitzgerald. 78 min.
68-8181 $19.99

River Beat (1954)
Phyllis Kirk appears as a radio operator on an American freighter who's unwittingly used by diamond smugglers, and John Bentley is the only police inspector who believes in her innocence. 70 min.
68-8182 $19.99

The Third Key (1957)
The only logical suspect in a series of safecrackings, an employee at a safe company, has also been dead for several years. Jack Hawkins ("Lawrence of Arabia") plays the dedicated police inspector tracing the culprit. 96 min.
68-8185 $29.99

The Limping Man (1953)
Former G.I. Lloyd Bridges crosses the sea to hunt a wartime girlfriend in London, but joins police on the trail of a deadly sniper before he can untangle her from mobsters. With Moira Lister, Alan Wheatley. 76 min.
68-8201 $19.99

Crow Hollow (1952)
In the spooky mansion of the title, one of three sinister spinsters tries to poison her nephew's wife to steal a large inheritance. Natasha Parry stars. 69 min.
68-8288 Was $24.99 $19.99

The Rebel Set (1959)
It's a beatnik mystery with Edward Platt ("Get Smart") as Mr. T., owner of a coffee shop who enlists the aid of three way-out, down-and-out customers to pull off an armored car robbery. Gregg Palmer, Kathleen Crowley, Don Sullivan co-star. 72 min.
68-8526 $19.99

The House In The Woods (1957)
A mystery writer moves with his wife to a remote country cottage so he can work on his latest novel, but when the landlord turns out to be an unstable artist who may have murdered his wife, the author's imagination can't compare to the real-life terrors that await them. Creepy British suspenser stars Michael Dante, Ronald Howard.
68-9088 $19.99

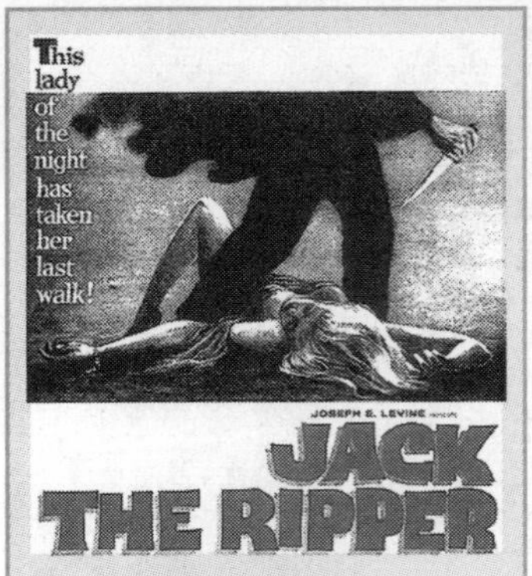

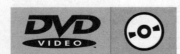

Jack The Ripper (1959)
An American detective joins Scotland Yard's top investigator to track down the killer who has been stalking London's streets and murdering prostitutes. Lee Patterson, Eddie Byrne and Ewen Solon star in this British thriller.
68-8550 $19.99

The Ripper (1997)
This gripping look at the infamous "Jack the Ripper" murders that terrorized London in the late 1880s stars Patrick Bergin as a top Scotland Yard inspector charged with solving the ghastly crimes. As a trap is set to catch the Ripper in the act, Bergin must stop the ruthless killer and protect his only witness, the woman he loves. Gabrielle Anwar, Samuel West, Michael York also star. 100 min.
07-2692 $94.99

The Way Out (1956)
Smart, quick-paced crime story about a man who kills a bookie and flees the scene of the crime with his wife and brother-in-law. At first he's successful dodging the cops' dragnet, then his wife discovers it wasn't an accidental murder. Gene Nelson, Mona Freeman and John Bentley star. 86 min.
68-8529 $19.99

Someone At The Door (1950)
In an attempt to make waves with a big story, a young reporter fakes the murder of his sister. Then he stumbles upon real deaths in the dark house where his "crime" occurred. Michael Medwin, Garry Marsh and Yvonne Owen star. 60 min.
68-8531 $19.99

Stolen Identity (1953)
Crackerjack thriller about a Viennese cab driver who, longing to emigrate to America, receives his chance after assuming the identity of a murdered American businessman...but when he becomes involved with the killer's wife, a deadly chase ensues. Donald Buka, Francis Lederer, Joan Camden star. 81 min.
68-8757 $19.99

Female Fiends (1958)
After losing his memory in an auto accident, a man is taken home by his wife to recuperate, but soon begins to doubt he's who this "loving spouse" says he is. Who is he really, and what sinister plans does the woman have in store for him? Suspenseful tale stars Lex Barker, Nora Swinburne. AKA: "The Strange Awakening."
68-9100 $19.99

People In The Net (1959)
After his release from prison, a man returns home to find his wife dead. While trying to get to the bottom of the murder, he discovers a group of spies who trade info with the Soviets and poses as a traitor to uncover this mysterious espionage underworld and find out how it relates to his wife's murder. Hansjorg Felmy, Inge Schoener star.
79-6558 Was $24.99 $19.99

Radio Cab Murder (1954)
Suspenseful British crime story in which an ex-con turns cab driver and is then recruited by the police to infiltrate a gang before they pull off a bank robbery. Jimmy Hanley, Lana Morris and Sonia Holm star.
68-9129 $19.99

Bond Of Fear (1956)
Well-made suspenser about an English family on vacation who discovers a escaped killer hiding in their trailer. The fugitive holds the family's son hostage and forces them to drive him to the channel ferry at Dover. Dermot Walsh, Jane Barrett, John Colicos star.
68-9239 $19.99

Oriental Evil (1953)
Set in Japan, this thriller tells of a British man who weds his pregnant Japanese girlfriend in a fake ceremony, then falls for a woman who arrives looking to clear her late brother of suspected involvement in the opium trade. Martha Hyer, Byron Michie, Tetsu Nakamura star.
79-6022 Was $24.99 $19.99

Murder On Approval (1956)
Tom Conway is a British detective who gets involved with a murder case after investigating a missing rare stamp. Delphi Lawrence, Brian Worth and Campbell Cotts also star. 70 min.
68-9130 $19.99

The Key Man (1957)
The host of a radio crime show inadvertently becomes involved with gangsters and uses his wits to dupe the crooks. Lee Patterson and Hy Hazell star. AKA: "Life at Stake." 63 min.
68-8479 $19.99

The Chase (1946)
A woman on the run from her husband flees to Cuba, but finds she cannot escape her past. Tense, emotional thriller in the "noir" vein stars Michele Morgan, Robert Cummings and Peter Lorre. 86 min.
08-5007 $14.99

Dishonored Lady (1947)
Hedy Lamarr is an art director for a leading women's magazine who finds herself accused of murder in this taut thriller. William Lundigan and Dennis O'Keefe co-star in this whodunit. 85 min.
08-5012 $14.99

The Inheritance (1947)
Atmospheric thriller set in 1845 and starring Jean Simmons as a teenager caring for her dear, old Uncle Silas. When Simmons learns that her relative and an associate plan to kill her, she doesn't know how to stop them. Katina Paxinou, Derrick de Marney also star. 90 min.
08-5027 $29.99

The Night Has Eyes (1942)
Two schoolteachers, caught in a thunderstorm while wandering through the English moors, find refuge in the home of a mysterious composer (James Mason), a war veteran who during one of his many "fits" may have been responsible for the death of one of their colleagues the year before. Brooding mystery/thriller co-stars Joyce Howard and Tucker McGuire. 79 min.
08-5036 $19.99

The Dummy Talks (1943)
"I'm a dummy? No, you're the dummy." Whodunit about a midget who poses as a lap puppet to trap a ventriloquist's murderer may sound ridiculous, but if Edgar Bergen could make it on radio, anything's possible. Stars Jack Warner, Claude Hulbert. 85 min.
68-8419 $19.99

Murder By Invitation (1941)
The greedy relatives of an eccentric, wealthy old woman are invited to her mansion for a weekend visit, but one of the family members turns up dead. Will the quest for a hidden fortune lead the killer to strike again? Well-made Monogram suspenser stars Wallace Ford, Marian Marsh, Sarah Padden. 64 min.
68-8887 $19.99

Trapped (1949)
Quick-paced mystery stars Lloyd Bridges as a federal investigator seeking counterfeiters. Documentary-styled crime drama at its best, with classic rapid-fire dialogue, seedy characters and moody production. Barbara Payton, John Hoyt. 78 min.
08-5051 Was $19.99 $14.99

Guest In The House (1944)
Crackerjack thriller starring Anne Baxter as a woman with a cardiac condition who is cared for by her doctor at his house. She soon becomes infatuated by the doctor's married brother, and sets out to destroy his marriage. Aline MacMahon, Ralph Bellamy and Ruth Warrick star. 117 min.
08-8037 Was $79.99 $19.99

Slightly Honorable (1940)
Bristling mystery yarn stars Pat O'Brien as an eccentric detective trying to unravel a case which leads him to corrupt politicians. Snappy dialogue and support by Edward Arnold, Broderick Crawford and Ruth Terry make this a winner. 85 min.
08-8062 $19.99

The Hat-Box Mystery (1947)
Russ Ashton has enough trouble running his detective agency, without his beautiful secretary getting set-up to murder a society widow with a trick hat-box. Slick suspense programmer stars Tom Neal, Pamela Blake. 44 min.
09-2005 Was $24.99 $19.99

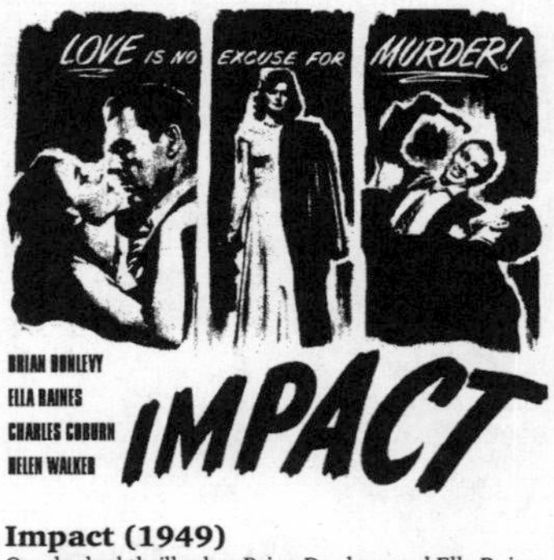

Impact (1949)
Overlooked thriller has Brian Donlevy and Ella Raines as lovers who plan the murder of her husband, only to find unforeseen complications. Moody, deftly written suspense story also features Charles Coburn, Anna May Wong. 111 min.
18-3010 $19.99

Shoot To Kill (1947)
An incoming district attorney is slain in the company of a man he sent up for 20 years. What were they doing together? A determined reporter wants to find out. Russell Wade, Edmund MacDonald. 64 min.
09-2037 Was $29.99 $14.99

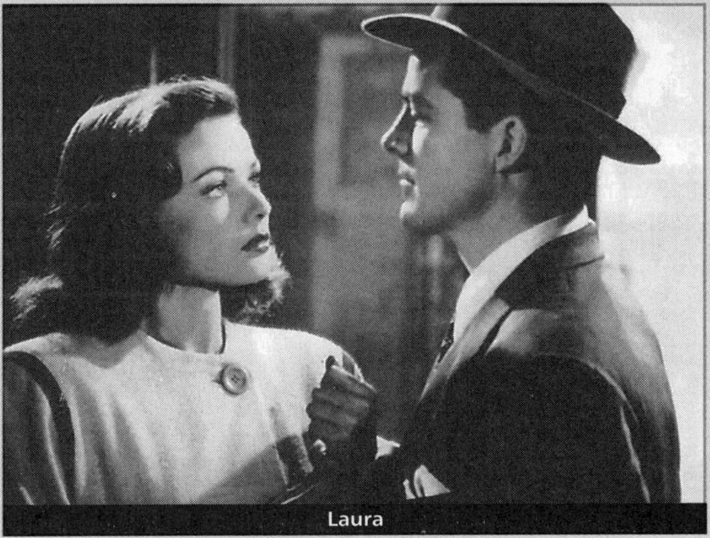

Laura

Film Noir Classics

I Wake Up Screaming (1942)
Cast against type, Betty Grable and Victor Mature prove themselves capable actors in this mystery about an actress' murder and her sister's (Grable) attempt to clear the victim's agent (Mature) of the crime. Tense drama also stars Laird Cregar, Carole Landis, Elisha Cook, Jr. 82 min.
04-2222 □*$19.99*

Laura (1944)
One of the greatest Hollywood whodunits ever made, Otto Preminger's noir-flavored thriller stars Dana Andrews as a detective investigating the murder of New York socialite Gene Tierney who becomes infatuated with her image and memory. Memorable support is given by Clifton Webb as a sardonic columnist and Vincent Price as Tierney's callous playboy fiancé. 88 min.
04-1085 Was $19.99 □*$14.99*

Phantom Lady (1944)
Crackerjack film noir concerning a secretary who joins forces with a detective to find the person who killed her boss's wife—a crime he has been sentenced to die for. Can they find the woman with the unusual hat who was with her boss on that fateful night? Ella Raines, Thomas Gomez, Franchot Tone, Alan Curtis and Elisha Cook, Jr. (featured in a famous drumming sequence) star. 87 min.
07-2613 □*$14.99*

The Mask Of Dimitrios (1944)
Superior thriller featuring Peter Lorre as a mystery writer on vacation in Istanbul when the body of infamous criminal Zachary Scott is found there. Beginning a global search for the facts behind Scott's life, Lorre joins forces with Sydney Greenstreet, one of the crook's victims, and soon uncovers some unsettling facts. Faye Emerson and George Tobias also star. 96 min.
12-3093 □*$19.99*

Ministry Of Fear (1945)
Fritz Lang's moody thriller, taken from Graham Greene's novel, features Ray Milland as a former mental patient in London during World War II who takes a job at a carnival and soon becomes an unwilling participant in conspiracy and murder involving Nazi spies. Dan Duryea, Marjorie Richards and Alan Napier also star in this knockout noir. 87 min.
07-2612 □*$14.99*

Strange Illusion (1945)
B-movie auteur Edgar G. Ulmer helmed this "film noir" rendition of "Hamlet," starring James Lydon as the young man who feigns insanity in order to implicate his mother and her new lover in his father's death. Warren William, Regis Toomey and Sally Eilers also star. 87 min.
17-3092 Was $19.99 *$14.99*

Detour (1945)
Made on pennies by Edgar G. Ulmer, this seedy story focuses on a New York night club pianist hitchhiking to L.A. who is picked up by an amiable gambler. When his rider dies of a heart attack, the pianist takes his wallet and dumps the body. But when he picks up a woman on the road, he finds himself in trouble because of her suspicions and reckless nature. Tom Neal and Ann Savage star. 69 min
62-1184 *$19.99*

Detour (1992)
This remake of the film noir classic stars Tom Neal, Jr. (in the same role his father played) as a down-and-out piano player, hitchhiking cross-country to see his girlfriend, who is thrown into a series of events involving deceit, murder and a nasty, double-crossing woman named Vera. Lea Lavish and Susannah Foster also star. 91 min.
73-3013 *$19.99*

The Strange Affair Of Uncle Harry (1945)
In this stylish thriller, George Sanders is a fabric designer who takes drastic steps when his domineering sister tries to stop his romance with the beautiful fashion expert who has released him from his lonely existence. Geraldine Fitzgerald, Moyna MacGill and Ella Raines also star; directed by Robert Siodmak ("The Killers"). AKA: "Uncle Harry." 80 min.
63-1444 *$19.99*

The Dark Corner (1946)
Private eye Mark Stevens is a man backed into a corner, framed for the murder of his ex-partner, in an intriguing "film noir" thriller that also stars Lucille Ball as Stevens' lovestruck secretary, Clifton Webb as a well-to-do art dealer and William Bendix in his patented "neanderthalic gunsel" role. 99 min.
04-2249 Was $59.99 □*$29.99*

Black Angel (1946)
Complex film noir from Cornell Woolrich's story stars Dan Duryea as an alcoholic songwriter whose adulterous wife is found murdered. When the woman's lover is tried and sentenced to death, his estranged wife, singer June Vincent, coaxes Duryea, who was cleared of the crime, to help her search for the real killer. With Peter Lorre, Broderick Crawford. 81 min.
07-2611 □*$14.99*

Kiss Of Death (1947)
Superior "noir" crime thriller stars Victor Mature as a crook who turns state's evidence when his gang betrays him and leaves him to rot in jail. Richard Widmark, in his screen debut, is unforgettable as a sadistically giggling killer with an affinity for wheelchair-bound ladies and staircases. With Coleen Gray, Brian Donlevy, Karl Malden. 99 min.
04-2386 Was $39.99 □*$14.99*

Whispering City (1947)
Powerful and appropriately seedy film noir about a female newspaper reporter who is drawn into a whirlwind of murder and deception when she tries to get the goods on a scheming lawyer. Mary Anderson, Helmut Dantine and Paul Lukas star. 89 min.
68-8473 *$19.99*

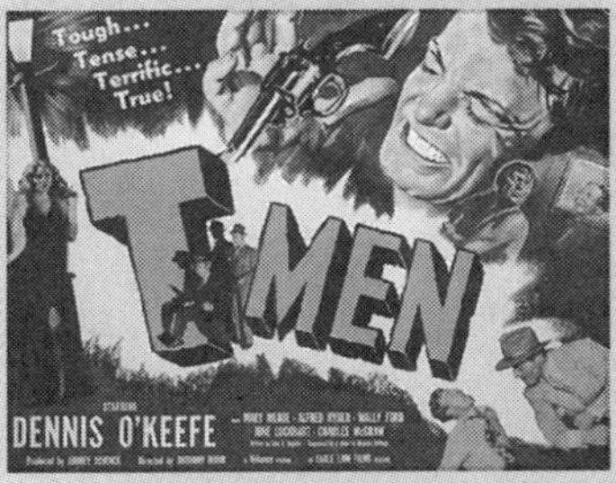

T-Men (1947)
Superior "B" crime drama details the undercover adventures of Treasury agents Dennis O'Keefe and Alfred Ryder as they attempt to infiltrate a counterfeiting ring whose ruthless leader already killed one T-Man. June Lockhart, Charles McGraw co-star; Anthony Mann directs. 93 min.
27-6628 *$29.99*

Railroaded (1947)
When a police detective's girlfriend's brother is implicated in a cop's murder but the detective knows he's innocent, the hunt for the real killer is on! Compelling underworld thriller from director Anthony Mann stars Hugh Beaumont, Peggy Ryan, Ed Kelly and John Ireland as a sadistic, gun-obsessed hit man. 74 min.
70-1066 *$24.99*

The Big Clock (1948)
Striking film noir classic stars Ray Milland as a crime magazine editor who has a liaison with a beautiful woman who turns out to be the mistress of his boss, tyrannical publisher Charles Laughton. When a jealous Laughton murders the woman, he sets out to frame the "other man" for the crime and assigns the job of finding him to Milland. Rita Johnson, George Macready and Elsa Lanchester also star in this suspenser that inspired 1987's "No Way Out." 95 min.
07-2438 □*$14.99*

Raw Deal (1948)
Knockout film noir involving a gangster seeking revenge after being framed and sent to jail. With help from an innocent woman he seduces, the ex-con carries out his murderous plan of vengeance, eventually coming face-to-face with the pyromaniacal creep responsible for his prison stay. Dennis O'Keefe, Claire Trevor and Raymond Burr star; Anthony Mann directs. 79 min.
53-8609 *$29.99*

He Walked By Night (1948)
Based on a true case, this fine film noir details the Los Angeles Police Department's search for a technically adept but mentally unbalanced thief who killed a policeman. With Richard Basehart, Scott Brady, Whit Bissell and Jack Webb, who supposedly based his "Dragnet" radio show on this movie; directed by Alfred Werker and (uncredited) Anthony Mann. 79 min.
53-8608 *$29.99*

The Street With No Name (1948)
Fine film noir thriller, filmed in semi-documentary style, stars Mark Stevens as an FBI agent who goes undercover and joins psychopathic mobster Richard Widmark's gang. Lloyd Nolan, Ed Begley, Barbara Lawrence also star. 91 min.
04-2411 *$19.99*

The Scar (1948)
Exceptional film noir entry stars Paul Henreid in a dual role. A sleazy ex-med student and con artist discovers a psychiatrist who, except for a scar on his face, is the crook's double. He launches a twisted scheme to take the doctor's place, only to get caught in his own scheme. With Joan Bennett, Eduard Franz and a young Jack Webb. AKA: "Hollow Triumph." 83 min.
63-1445 Restored *$14.99*

D.O.A. (1949)
A masterpiece of low-budget "noir" cinema, with Edmond O'Brien as a businessman vacationing in San Francisco who learns he has been poisoned with a "luminous toxin" and has mere days to live. A desperate search for his own killer follows. Luther Adler, Neville Brand, Pamela Britton also star in director Rudolph Maté's classic thriller; score by Dmitri Tiomkin. 83 min.
08-1480 *$14.99*

Port Of New York (1949)
Gritty, expertly realized noir from director Laslo Benedek ("The Wild One") featuring Yul Brynner, with a full head of hair, playing the dangerous leader of a ring of drug runners. Scott Brady and Richard Rober are the customs agents out to topple the syndicate. with K.T. Stevens and Neville Brand. 72 min.
10-1121 Was $19.99 *$14.99*

The Man On The Eiffel Tower (1949)
Based on a novel by Georges Simenon, this superb piece of "continental noir" stars Charles Laughton as Parisian police inspector Maigret, whose investigation of a rich woman's murder leads him into a battle of wills with a psychotic killer-for-hire and a showdown at the title landmark. Franchot Tone, Robert Hutton and Burgess Meredith, who also directed, co-star. 84 min.
16-1139 Was $19.99 *$14.99*

Too Late For Tears (1949)
A film noir favorite, highlighted by Lizabeth Scott's classic "femme fatale" performance. She's mixed up in deceit, blackmail, and murder after a bag of money is mistakenly thrown into her car. Dan Duryea, Arthur Kennedy also star. AKA: "Killer Bait." 99 min.
17-9037 *$19.99*

Panic In The Streets (1950)
The discovery of a murdered man on the New Orleans riverfront becomes a race against time when it's learned that the man carried the bubonic plague and infected his killer. Can detective Paul Douglas and doctor Richard Widmark track down the carrier in time? Tense and offbeat "noir" drama also stars Walter (now Jack) Palance, Zero Mostel, Barbara Bel Geddes; Elia Kazan directs. 96 min.
04-2387 □*$39.99*

The Man Who Cheated Himself (1950)
A film noir thriller with Jane Wyatt as a femme fatale whose accidental shooting of her husband prompts her to call the police lieutenant (Lee J. Cobb) smitten with her to get rid of the body. Their plans are interrupted, however, when the lieutenant's brother discovers the murder. Lisa Howard also stars. 81 min.
53-6057 Was $29.99 *$19.99*

House By The River (1950)
Skillfully rendered suspenser from Fritz Lang concerns a demented writer who lures his hapless brother into a cover-up, and eventually the rap, for a murder he's committed. Atmospheric classic stars Louis Hayward, Lee Bowman, Jane Wyatt. 88 min.
17-3004 *$19.99*

Beware, My Lovely (1952)
Handyman Robert Ryan flees town after discovering his employer's dead body. He takes a job working for widowed school teacher Ida Lupino, who eventually learns that Ryan has some dark and disturbing secrets. Psychological noir also stars Taylor Holmes, Barbara Whiting. 77 min.
05-1392 Was $19.99 *$14.99*

The Big Heat (1953)
Knockout film noir from director Fritz Lang stars Glenn Ford as a no-nonsense cop investigating the suicide of another cop. His findings reveal that the cop's suicide note cited widespread corruption under the guidance of ruthless mob boss Alexander Scourby. Danger and murder follow Ford as he delves deeper into the case. Gloria Grahame and Lee Marvin also star. 90 min.
02-1157 Was $59.99 *$19.99*

The Blue Gardenia (1953)
A blind date leads to murder in this classic noir suspenser from director Fritz Lang. Anne Baxter wakes from a hangover to discover that playboy Raymond Burr, with whom she went out the night before, was found slain in his apartment and she is the mysterious "Blue Gardenia" sought by police. Baxter desperately turns to newspaper columnist Richard Conte for help in learning if she is in fact the killer. With Ann Sothern and Nat King Cole, who sings the title song. 90 min.
53-6333 *$24.99*

The City That Never Sleeps (1953)
Chicago cop Gig Young is tempted to quit the force and run away with his showgirl mistress, but an offer from a corrupt lawyer, a friend-turned-killer, and a store window "mechanical man" all play a part in this intriguing tale. Mala Powers, Edward Arnold, Wally Cassell co-star. 90 min.
63-1286 *$14.99*

The Hitch-Hiker (1953)
Riveting film noir classic concerning two family men on a fishing trip who make the deadly mistake of picking up a psychotic thumb-tripper. Based on the William Cook kill-spree, the film boasts fine performances from Edmond O'Brien, Frank Lovejoy and William Talman; directed by Ida Lupino. 71 min.
68-8187 Was $19.99 *$14.99*

Gang Busters (1954)
Gritty *film noir*, loosely based on the popular radio drama, focuses on criminal John Omar Pinson, Public Enemy Number Four, and his escapes from prison. Shot in documentary-style behind bars, the film stars Myron Healey and Frankie Richards, and is a favorite of director Martin Scorsese.
79-5886 *$19.99*

The Big Combo (1955)
Downbeat "noir" thriller whose violence raised a few eyebrows upon the film's release. Cornel Wilde plays a dedicated cop out to bring down crime boss Richard Conte who gets involved with icy blonde Jean Wallace, Conte's mistress. With Brian Donlevy, Lee Van Cleef and Earl Holliman. 88 min.
59-5002 *$19.99*

Shack Out On 101 (1955)
An isolated roadside cafe serves as a center for romance, blackmail and Communist espionage in this offbeat suspenser with a cult reputation. Frank Lovejoy, Terry Moore, Lee Marvin star. 80 min.
63-5002 *$19.99*

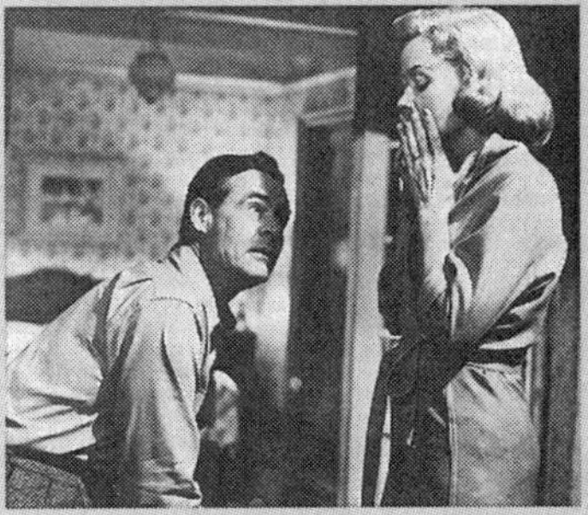

Odds Against Tomorrow (1959)
One of the final films to come from the first film noir cycle, Robert Wise's crime thriller/race drama follows nightclub singer Harry Belafonte, bigoted ex-con Robert Ryan and corrupt former cop Ed Begley as they try to rob an upstate New York bank, only to have the caper fall apart due to bad luck and Ryan's hatred of Belafonte. With Gloria Grahame, Shelley Winters; look quickly for Wayne Rogers and Cicely Tyson. 96 min.
12-3083 Was $19.99 □*$14.99*

The Best Of Film Noir
Tough guys, femmes fatales, criminal activities and shadowy atmospherics are the hallmarks of the "film noir" films popularized in the 1940s and 1950s. This program salutes the classics, such as "Kiss Me Deadly," "Double Indemnity," "Touch of Evil," "Detour," "Out of the Past" and many others. 60 min.
05-5098 *$14.99*

Sherlock Holmes: The Early Years
Rare silent and talking collector's items feature the sleuth's very first film, "Sherlock Holmes Baffled" (1900); "The Copper Beeches" (1912), with Georges Treville as Holmes; Ellie Norwood in "The Dying Detective" and "The Devil's Foot" (1921); Douglas Fairbanks as "Coke Ennyday" in "Mystery of the Leaping Fish" (1916), and more, including a Nigel Bruce screen test and an interview with Sir Arthur Conan Doyle.
10-7440 Was $19.99 ***$14.99***

Sherlock Holmes: The Later Years
Television-era Sherlockiana includes "The Man Who Disappeared," a 1951 TV pilot starring John Longden; the first episode of Ronald Howard's British series, "The Case of the Cunningham Heritage" (1953); a 1964 New York World's Fair exhibit film in which Holmes meets computers, recent film trailers and more.
10-7441 Was $19.99 ***$14.99***

The Speckled Band (1931)
Raymond Massey, in his screen debut, essays the role of the great detective in this early Holmes talkie. Based on the stage version of Doyle's tale, the story has Holmes and Watson foiling the sinister scheme of "Dr. Grimesby Rylott" to gain his stepdaughters' inheritance. With Lyn Harding, Athole Stewart. 48 min.
09-1993 ***$19.99***

The Sign Of Four (1932)
Arthur Wontner made his third of five screen appearances as Sherlock Holmes in this witty and fast-paced adaptation of the Arthur Conan Doyle novel. A young woman's puzzling inheritance, a sinister peg-legged man and his Pygmy sidekick, a boat chase down the Thames and a romance for Watson all stem from the mystery surrounding "The Sign of Four." With Ian Hunter, Ilsa Bevan, Herbert Lomas. 63 min.
10-9791 ***$19.99***

A Study In Scarlet (1933)
Although not based on the Sherlock Holmes novel of the same name, this early British thriller is a stylish tale of mystery and a worthy addition to the Holmesian legend. Reginald Owen, as Holmes, is called upon to solve a murder on board a train. 72 min.
01-1248 ***$19.99***

The Triumph Of Sherlock Holmes (1935)
Arthur Wontner stars as the hawk-nosed sleuth in this film that combines the play "Sherlock Holmes" and the novel "Valley of Fear." Holmes and Watson are called out to a castle to investigate a murder and find a mystery that reaches back to America and brings in arch-foe Professor Moriarty. 84 min.
01-1030 ***$19.99***

Murder At The Baskervilles (Silver Blaze) (1941)
Several years after the mystery of the Hound of the Baskervilles, Holmes and Watson are summoned back to solve a murder among the horse racing set. Based on the Holmes short story, "Silver Blaze." Stylish and original mystery stars Arthur Wontner as Holmes and Ian Fleming as Watson. 67 min.
10-1157 ***$19.99***

Sherlock Holmes And The Secret Weapon (1942)
Holmes and arch enemy Professor Moriarty clash in a race to capture a revolutionary bomb-sight that could help England defeat the Axis powers. Basil Rathbone, Nigel Bruce and Lionel Atwill star. 68 min.
10-2039 ***$14.99***

The House Of Fear (1945)
Basil Rathbone and Nigel Bruce, as Holmes and Watson, are called in to investigate a strange series of murders among the members of the Good Comrades Club, only to find that one member's intentions are hardly good at all. Dennis Hoey, Paul Cavanaugh star. 68 min.
04-2134 ***□$14.99***

Terror By Night (1946)
Train passengers Holmes and Watson are pressed into service when one of their fellow riders, the owner of the cursed Star of Rhodesia diamond, turns up murdered. Basil Rathbone, Nigel Bruce, Alan Mowbray star. 60 min.
10-2055 ***$14.99***

The Woman In Green (1946)
Sherlock Holmes is called to solve the "finger murders," a series of brutal and seemingly unconnected killings of women in London, and finds a beautiful hypnotist and his old enemy, Professor Moriarty, lurking in the shadows. Basil Rathbone, Nigel Bruce, Henry Daniell and Hillary Brooke star. 68 min.
10-2060 ***$14.99***

Dressed To Kill (1946)
What is the connection between a collection of music boxes and missing Bank of England printing plates, and will the answer cost Holmes and Watson their lives? Basil Rathbone and Nigel Bruce make their final appearances as the detective duo; with Patricia Morison. 72 min.
10-2038 ***$14.99***

Sherlock Holmes Gift Set
Sherlock Holmes fans will find that purchasing this five-tape gift set is "elementary" to their collection. Included are "Dressed to Kill," "House of Fear," "Sherlock Holmes and the Secret Weapon," "Terror By Night" and "Woman in Green."
08-1831 Save $25.00! ***$49.99***

Sherlock Holmes: The Man Who Disappeared (1951)
Sample from lesser-known but well-done TV series based on Conan Doyle's immortal detective stars John Longden as Holmes and Campbell Singer as Watson. The sleuth must uncover the strange secret of a well-to-do businessman. 27 min.
09-1942 Was $19.99 ***$14.99***

The Hound Of The Baskervilles (1959)
Conan Doyle's Sherlock Holmes classic is given an atmospheric treatment by the Hammer studio. Peter Cushing is Holmes, investigating the case of a legendary beast roaming the English moors, Andre Morell is Dr. Watson, and Christopher Lee is Sir Henry Baskerville; Terence Fisher directs. 86 min.
12-2648 ***$19.99***

Sherlock Holmes And The Deadly Necklace (1962)
The only actor to portray Count Dracula, the Frankenstein monster and Sherlock Holmes on the screen, Christopher Lee dons deerstalker and Inverness for this rare German-made thriller. Holmes and Watson investigate the theft of a priceless Egyptian artifact and come up against Professor Moriarty. Senta Berger, Thorley Walters co-star. 84 min. Dubbed in English.
10-7547 Was $29.99 ***$19.99***

A Study In Terror (1965)
Super sleuth meets master murderer when Sherlock Holmes sets out on the trail of Jack the Ripper...a trail that will end with one man's death. Gripping mystery thriller stars John Neville and Donald Houston as Holmes and Watson; with Anthony Quayle, Robert Morley, Georgia Brown. 94 min.
02-1778 Was $69.99 ***$19.99***

The Private Life Of Sherlock Holmes (1970)
Billy Wilder's controversial look at the great sleuth's most dangerous mission, a mystery that blends a lovely amnesiac, monks, missing dwarves, Queen Victoria and the Loch Ness Monster. Robert Stephens and Colin Blakely are Holmes and Watson; Stanley Holloway and Christopher Lee also star. 125 min.
12-2928 Was $19.99 ***$14.99***

They Might Be Giants (1971)
Delightful romp stars George C. Scott as a wealthy New York judge who's convinced he's Sherlock Holmes, and Joanne Woodward as his psychiatrist, Dr. Mildred Watson. Together the duo set out on the trail of arch-fiend Moriarty and to make the world safe for eccentricity. With Jack Gilford, Anthony Harvey. Special video edition includes the "making of" featurette "Madness...It's Beautiful." 98 min.
07-1486 Letterboxed ***$14.99***

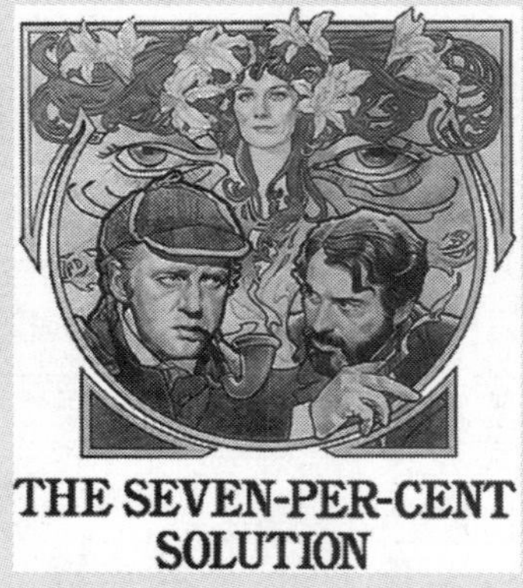

The Seven Percent Solution (1976)
Master detective Sherlock Holmes meets super psychiatrist Sigmund Freud in this stylish mystery caper. Nicol Williamson is the sleuth, Robert Duvall is Dr. Watson, and Freud is handled by Alan Arkin. 113 min.
07-1104 Was $59.99 ***$14.99***

Young Sherlock Holmes (1985)
A fascinating "what if?" mystery/adventure of Holmes and Watson's first meeting, as teenagers. The young detectives become involved in a series of strange murders in London and uncover a bizarre cult. Nicholas Rowe and Alan Cox star as the schoolboy sleuths; with Anthony Higgins, Sophie Ward. 109 min.
06-1377 ***□$14.99***

The Masks Of Death (1985)
Peter Cushing plays an elderly Sherlock Holmes in this tantalizing mystery. Three corpses are found with their faces frozen in fear, and Holmes and Watson are coaxed out of retirement to solve the crime. With John Mills, Anne Baxter, Ray Milland. 72 min.
40-1223 Was $19.99 ***$14.99***

The Crucifer Of Blood (1991)
A 30-year-old oath sworn in blood, a fabulous treasure that has claimed more than one life, and a mysterious beauty are the elements in one of Sherlock Holmes' most baffling cases. Charlton Heston plays the Baker Street sleuth in this adaptation of the hit play, loosely based on "The Sign of Four." Richard Johnson, Susannah Harker also star. 101 min.
18-7361 Was $89.99 ***□$19.99***

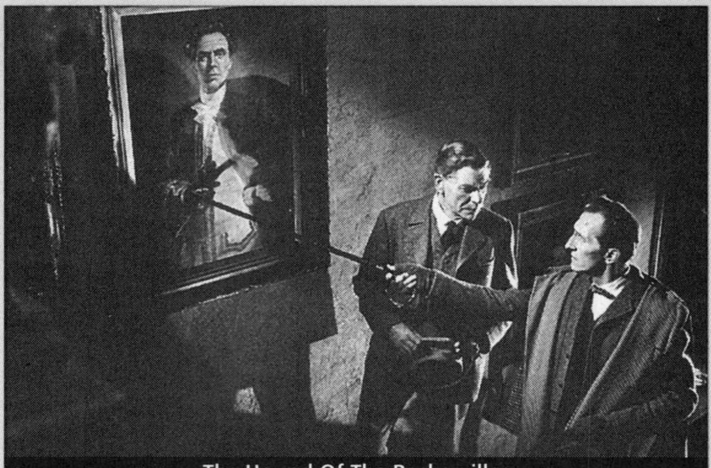
The Hound Of The Baskervilles

Sherlock Holmes

Sherlock Holmes
Ronald Howard and H. Marion Crawford starred as Holmes and Dr. Watson in this rare TV series from the early '50s, featuring adaptations of A. Conan Doyle's stories and original mysteries. Each tape runs about 55 min.

Sherlock Holmes, Vol. I
Holmes and Watson investigate a very exclusive club in "The Red-Headed League" and meet a child who can predict death in "The Deadly Prophecy."
01-5054 Was $19.99 ***$14.99***

Sherlock Holmes, Vol. II
A series of strangulation murders forces Holmes into a confrontation with "The Jolly Hangman," then Watson must solve the riddle of "The Vanished Detective."
01-5055 Was $19.99 ***$14.99***

Sherlock Holmes, Vol. III
"The Belligerent Ghost" could spell doom for Watson before Holmes races to rescue. Next the duo become "The Baker Street Bachelors" to investigate a lonely hearts club.
01-5056 Was $19.99 ***$14.99***

Sherlock Holmes, Vol. IV
The portrait of a beautiful woman hides a mystery for Holmes in "The Haunted Gainsborough." Then Holmes takes a case from beyond the grave in "The Exhumed Client."
01-5057 Was $19.99 ***$14.99***

Sherlock Holmes, Vol. V
Features "The Case of the Singing Violin" and "The Case of the Shoeless Engineer."
10-7482 Was $19.99 ***$14.99***

Sherlock Holmes, Vol. VI
Includes "The Mother Hubbard Case" and "The Case of the Unlucky Gambler."
10-7483 Was $19.99 ***$14.99***

Sherlock Holmes, Vol. VII
With "The Case of the Diamond Tooth" and "The Case of the Careless Suffragette."
10-7484 Was $19.99 ***$14.99***

Sherlock Holmes, Vol. VIII
Includes "The Case of the Improper Mystery" and "The Case of the Greystone Inscription."
10-7485 Was $19.99 ***$14.99***

Sherlock Holmes, Vol. IX
Features "The Case of the Thistle Killer" and "The Case of the Split Ticket."
10-7486 Was $19.99 ***$14.99***

Sherlock Holmes, Vol. X
With "The Case of the Blindman's Bluff" and "The Case of the Baker Street Nursemaids."
10-7487 Was $19.99 ***$14.99***

Sherlock Holmes, Vol. XII
Includes "The Case of the Cunningham Inheritance" and "The Case of Lady Beryl."
10-7488 Was $19.99 ***$14.99***

Sherlock Holmes, Vol. XIII
With "The Case of the Shy Ballerina" and "The Case of the French Interpreter."
10-7489 Was $19.99 ***$14.99***

Sherlock Holmes, Vol. XIV
Features "The Case of the Pennsylvania Gun" and "The Case of the Reluctant Carpenter."
10-7490 Was $19.99 ***$14.99***

Sherlock Holmes, Vol. XV
Features "The Case of the Winthrop Legend" and "The Case of the Laughing Mummy."
10-7491 Was $19.99 ***$14.99***

Sherlock Holmes, Vol. XVI
Includes "The Case of the Neurotic Detective" and "The Case of the Impromptu Performance."
10-7492 Was $19.99 ***$14.99***

Sherlock Holmes, Vol. XVII
Features "The Case of the Royal Murder" and "The Case of the Perfect Husband."
10-7493 Was $19.99 ***$14.99***

Sherlock Holmes, Vol. XVIII
Includes "The Case of the Night Train Riddle" and "Eiffel Tower."
10-7580 ***$14.99***

Sherlock Holmes, Vol. XIX
Includes "The Case of the Christmas Pudding" and "The Man Who Disappeared."
10-7581 ***$14.99***

The Adventures Of Sherlock Holmes
Jeremy Brett won raves from Sherlockians for his portrayal of the Great Detective in this series of British-produced mysteries, based on the timeless stories by Arthur Conan Doyle and loaded with rich Victorian-era flavor. David Burke, followed by Edward Hardwicke, plays Holmes' loyal chronicler, Dr. Watson. Except where noted, each episode runs about 50 min.

The Blue Carbuncle
Holmes and Watson receive a most unexpected Christmas gift: a goose with a valuable missing gem in its crop and a daring thief to catch.
06-5009 ***$19.99***

A Scandal In Bohemia
A blackmailed king's request for help brings Holmes into a memorable encounter with "the woman," the beautiful Irene Adler. Gayle Hunnicutt guest stars.
06-5010 ***$19.99***

The Speckled Band
A dying woman's cryptic message sends Holmes and Watson on a mission to help her sister and into a confrontation with the dangerous Dr. Grimesby Roylott. Jeremy Kemp guest stars.
06-5011 ***$19.99***

The Dancing Men
What looks at first like a child's scribbling turns out to be a deadly cipher that Holmes must solve, in order to save a man's life.
06-5017 ***$19.99***

The Naval Treaty
An old school chum of Watson's seeks Holmes' help in recovering a missing document whose loss could have grave international consequences.
06-5018 ***$19.99***

The Solitary Cyclist
Young Violet Smith is the titular character, and when her daily jaunts find her followed by a mysterious man, she calls on Holmes and Watson for help.
06-5019 ***$19.99***

The Crooked Man
An investigation by Holmes and Watson into an Army colonel's death leads to a bizarre love triangle and a treacherous betrayal years earlier.
50-6415 ***$19.99***

The Copper Beeches
A young woman's hiring as a governess leads to some strange job requirements, and Holmes' involvement leads to the unmasking of a strange deception. Natasha Richardson guest stars.
50-6416 ***$19.99***

The Greek Interpreter
An appearance by Holmes' older brother Mycroft draws the sleuthing siblings into a kidnapping plot that ends in death. Charles Gray guest stars.
50-6417 *$19.99*

The Norwood Builder
When a young solicitor asks Holmes to help prove him innocent of murder charges, a visit to a country manor and a revealing fire are in order.
50-6418 *$19.99*

The Resident Patient
A beneficial deal for a physician turns into a baffling mystery when the titular client's fearful behavior compels the doctor to consult Holmes.
50-6419 *$19.99*

The Red-Headed League
Mr. Jabez Wilson's "induction" into this most singular of societies draws Holmes and Watson into a bold robbery scheme and the machinations of Professor James Moriarty.
50-6420 *$19.99*

The Final Problem
The battle of wits between Holmes and Moriarty hurdles to its inevitable and fatal conclusion at Switzerland's Reichenbach Falls. Eric Porter guest stars.
50-6421 *$19.99*

The Sign Of Four
In this feature-length adventure, Holmes and Watson are hired by the lovely Mary Morstan when she receives a strange letter and soon unocver the secret of a priceless treasure. 120 min.
50-6422 Was $39.99 *$19.99*

The Hound Of The Baskervilles
Holmes and Watson's most famous tale finds the duo trying to save young heir Sir Henry Baskerville from the ghostly beast that has tormented his family for generations. 120 min.
50-6423 Was $39.99 *$19.99*

The Empty House
A miraculously resurrected Holmes helps Watson bring a dangerous killer to justice, while explaining how he survived his death duel at Reichenbach with Moriarty.
50-6482 *$19.99*

The Abbey Grange
With a cry of "the game's afoot," Holmes and Watson investigate the murder of Sir Eustace Brackenstall and find a deadly love triangle.
50-6483 *$19.99*

The Bruce Partington Plans
Brother Mycroft pays a visit to Holmes to enlist his aid in tracking down the missing plans for an experimental submarine. Charles Gray guest stars.
50-6484 *$19.99*

The Devil's Foot
"Strangest case I have handled" is how Holmes described his investigation into the deaths of a Cornish family, as an experiment nearly costs him and Watson their lives.
50-6485 *$19.99*

The Man With The Twisted Lip
A vanished journalist and a disfigured beggar...Holmes must solve the disappearance of the former, with the unwilling aid of the latter.
50-6486 *$19.99*

The Musgrave Ritual
A university friend of Holmes presents him with a puzzling rhyme that holds the key to a long-forgotten treasure.
50-6487 *$19.99*

The Priory School
Holmes is called in to help track down a missing aristocrat's son who vanished from his exclusive school, along with one of his teachers.
50-6488 *$19.99*

The Second Stain
Missing government papers, the dark secret of an official's wife, and the discoloring of a rug are all Holmes has in order to stave off a diplomatic crisis.
50-6489 *$19.99*

Silver Blaze
Foul play among England's racing set sends Holmes to solve a baffling murder whilst contemplating "the curious incident of the dog in the nighttime."
50-6490 *$19.99*

The Six Napoleons
Why would someone break into homes and then destroy plaster busts of Napoleon, leaving valuables untouched? Holmes, Watson and Lestrade have a real puzzler on their hands.
50-6491 *$19.99*

Wisteria Lodge
An invitation to dinner at a country estate leads to a man's being charged with murdering his mysterious host. Can Holmes find the real killer and learn the victim's true identity?
50-6492 *$19.99*

The Creeping Man
A college professor's strange behavior alarms his daughter and her fiancé, but an investigation by Holmes and Watson uncovers a bizarre experiment behind his actions.
50-6905 *$19.99*

The Illustrious Client
A mysterious personage asks Holmes to halt a young woman's marriage to the unsavory Baron Bruner, and the case nearly costs the sleuth his life.
50-6906 *$19.99*

The Problem Of Thor Bridge
The wife of an American millionaire is found shot to death on the titular bridge, and when the family's beautiful governess is charged with the crime Holmes must prove her innocence.
50-6907 *$19.99*

The Master Blackmailer
In a feature-length thriller based on "The Adventure of Charles Augustus Milverton," Holmes and Watson must stop "the worst man in London" from plying his reprehensible trade on Victorian society. 120 min.
50-7146 Was $24.99 *$19.99*

The Boscombe Valley Mystery
A rural fishing holiday is brought to an abrupt halt when a local man is accused of killing his father, and Holmes must save the son from a date with the assizes.
50-7148 *$19.99*

Shoscombe Old Place
A faithful spaniel, a racing horse, and a human bone are the clues Holmes has to work with to solve this strange case of scandal among the horsey set.
50-7149 *$19.99*

The Disappearance Of Lady Frances Carfax
The sole heir to her family's fortune, Lady France's sudden vanishing leads Holmes and Watson on a life-or-death search where they discover the world's most unique coffin.
50-7150 *$19.99*

The Last Vampyre
"The world is large enough. No ghosts need apply," says Holmes, but when a new arrival in a small village is revealed as the descendant of a family killed as suspected vampires a century before, the detective must solve a supernatural-tinted mystery in this feature-length spine-tingler. 105 min.
50-7301 *$19.99*

The Eligible Bachelor
London society is shocked when, on the day of her wedding to Lord St. Simon, American heiress Hatty Doran suddenly vanishes. What is the truth behind her disappearance, and why is Holmes troubled with nightmares that may keep him from looking into the case? 105 min.
50-7302 *$19.99*

The Three Gables
After the death of her son, a woman is offered a large sum for the family estate with the stipulation that nothing be removed from the home, a curious clause that sends Sherlock Holmes in search of the reason why.
50-7343 *$19.99*

The Golden Pince-Nez
A pair of glasses found in the hand of the murdered secretary to a reclusive professor are the key to Sherlock Holmes and brother Mycroft solving a mystery that stretches to the streets of St. Petersburg, Russia.
50-7344 *$19.99*

The Mazarin Stone
There's precious little of Sherlock Holmes in this adventure that blends two Doyle stories, as Dr. Watson and Mycroft Holmes find their respective searches for a missing potential heir and a stolen crown jewel have a surprising connection.
50-7345 *$19.99*

The Dying Detective
An investigation into a death caused by a rare tropical fever could turn Holmes into the titular character, unless Watson can save his friend by locating the one doctor in London familiar with the disease.
50-7346 *$19.99*

The Red Circle
A reclusive lodger's behavior sends his landlady to Holmes for advice, and what seems at first a simple matter becomes a deadly mystery with ties to America and an Italian secret society.
50-7347 *$19.99*

The Cardboard Box
The delivery of a gruesome parcel containing two severed human ears to an elderly woman brings Scotland Yard to seek Holmes' help, and the sleuth uncovers a shocking tale of love and betrayal.
50-7348 *$19.99*

The Best Of Sherlock Holmes
Whether you're an amateur sleuth wanting to pit your skills against the Master, or a Holmesian scholar eager to test your knowledge of the Sacred Writings, this tape is for you. Scenes from the acclaimed Jeremy Brett series are played, as viewers try to guess "whodunit" before Holmes and Watson. 30 min.
50-6602 *$14.99*

Movie Madness Mystery
The L.A. Connection comedy troupe presents a doctored edition of the Basil Rathbone Sherlock Holmes mystery "The Woman in Green." A new soundtrack and comical dialogue add to the proceedings, as Holmes and Watson encounter drugs, dismemberment and murder in hilarious fashion. 50 min.
53-7914 *$19.99*

Code Of Scotland Yard (1946)
Suspenseful melodrama starring Oscar Homolka as a London antique dealer who has a skeleton in his closet that prevents him from sending his aspiring violinist daughter to Paris to study. It seems that Homolka is actually a convict who escaped from Devil's Island. When his assistant learns of this, he tries to blackmail him. With a young (and unbilled) Diana Dors. AKA: "The Shop at Sly Corner." 86 min.
09-2950 *$19.99*

The Fallen Idol (1949)
From a short story by Graham Greene, director Carol Reed deftly wove an unnerving thriller about an ambassador's son (Bobby Henrey) who practices all manner of deception to protect his idol, the family butler (Ralph Richardson), after the boy comes to believe, mistakenly, the butler is responsible for his stern wife's death. Co-stars Michele Morgan, Sonia Dresdel. 92 min.
01-1203 *$19.99*

Man Of Courage (1943)
Intense noirish thriller about a gangster with political ties whose dealings in murder and kidnapping are stopped by a tough district attorney. Barton McLane, Charlotte Wynters star. 66 min.
09-5104 *$19.99*

Roar Of The Press (1941)
On the same day he's married, a newspaperman finds himself hot on the trail of murderers, until both he and his wife are kidnapped by the Fifth Column culprits...will the reporter's gangster associates come to his aid? Wallace Ford, Jean Parker, Jed Prouty star. 72 min.
09-5106 *$19.99*

Sexton Blake And The Hooded Terror (1941)
The hero of hundreds of mystery stories since his debut in 1893, London-based "gentleman detective" Sexton Blake (George Curzon) tries to bring down an international crime ring known as The Hooded Terror and the gang's leader, "The Snake." Tod Slaughter, Greta Gynt also star. 69 min.
09-1353 Was $19.99 *$14.99*

Meet Sexton Blake (1944)
David Farrar stars as British crime-solver Blake, who in this wartime whodunit helps solve a mystery surrounding a dead man with another person's hand in his pocket, a missing photographer, and an espionage ring headed by a villain with the unfortunate name of "Slant-Eyes." With John Varley, Magda Kun, Ferdy Mayne. 78 min.
17-3029 *$19.99*

Beware The Lady (1941)
Stylish suspense story teaming a retired private detective and a self-assured female lawyer who decide to tackle one more case, one in which a young girl is implicated in a murder. Sidney Sheldon contributed to the script; Neil Hamilton, June Storey and Evelyn Brent star. 63 min.
09-2221 Was $29.99 *$14.99*

The Man Who Walked Alone (1945)
A mysterious hitchhiker seeks a ride into his hometown. Who is he? A World War II veteran? A deserter? A woman with a secret in her past picks him up, and the questions about both of them eventually are answered. Dave O'Brien and Kay Aldridge star. 71 min.
09-2248 Was $29.99 *$14.99*

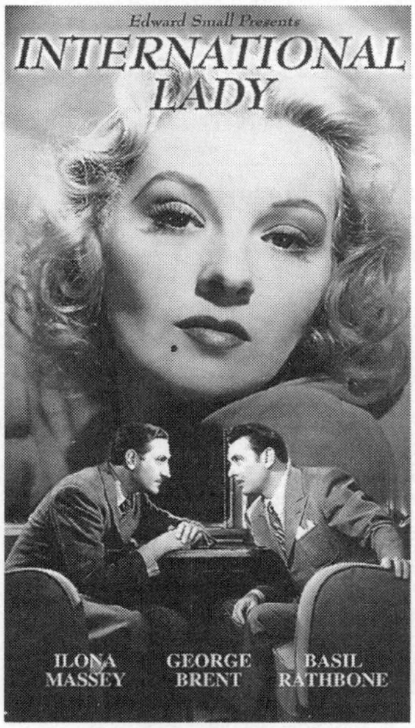

International Lady (1941)
Ilona Massey is a beautiful and seductive musician who has the eye of every man in the audience on her...including a duo of American and British agents who know that she's a Nazi spy. Together, they chase her from London to New York. George Brent, Basil Rathbone, Gene Lockhart co-star. 102 min.
08-1791 *$19.99*

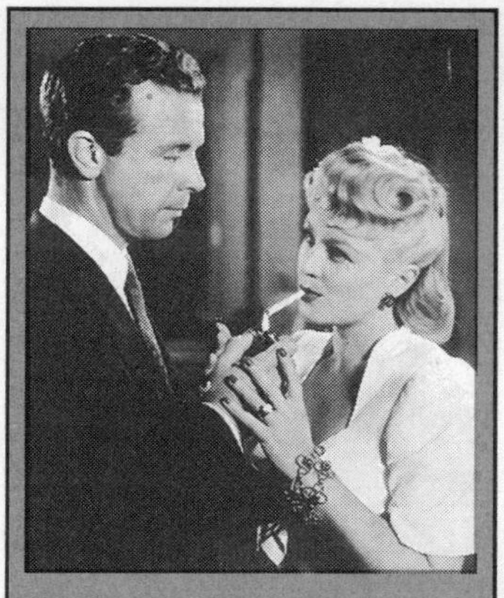

Murder, My Sweet (1944)
Considered by many to be the definitive private eye "film noir," this adaptation of Raymond Chandler's "Farewell, My Lovely" stars Dick Powell as gumshoe Philip Marlowe, whose search for a thug's ex-girlfriend leads him into a convoluted plot of blackmail and murder. With Claire Trevor, Otto Kruger, Anne Shirley, Mike Mazurki. Special video release includes the original theatrical trailer, a "making of" documentary, and an interview with director Edward Dmytryk. 95 min.
05-1116 *$19.99*

Lady In The Lake (1946)
"YOU look into the gun of a fear-maddened killer," thanks to the "subjective camera" of director/star Robert Montgomery in this adaptation of the Raymond Chandler mystery. Detective Philip Marlowe (Montgomery) returns to sleuthing after a stint at writing novels to locate a missing woman. Tough dialogue, complications and red herrings abound. With Lloyd Nolan, Audrey Totter, Jayne Meadows. 104 min.
12-2187 *$19.99*

Marlowe (1969)
James Garner is Raymond Chandler's heralded detective in this intriguing mystery. Philip Marlowe's search for a woman's missing brother in Los Angeles leads him into a murder plot complicated by tough police officials, strippers and martial arts henchmen. Gayle Hunnicutt, Carroll O'Connor, Rita Moreno and Bruce Lee (his Hollywood film debut) also star. 96 min.
12-2189 *$19.99*

The Lucky Mascot (1947)
Carroll Levis, a radio personality known as "Britain's favorite Canadian," plays himself in this suspenser that finds him in the middle of complications surrounding a missing brass monkey. Eventually, the suspense carries over to Levis' radio show. With Carole Landis, Herbert Lom, Ernest Thesiger and Terry-Thomas. AKA: "The Brass Monkey." 81 min.
09-2980 *$19.99*

Special Agent (1949)
Intense thriller involving a railroad special agent's attempts to solve the theft of $100,000 in payroll receipts from a train. The daughter of an engineer killed in the heist teams with the agent and romance eventually ensues. William Eythe, George Reeves and Laura Eliot star. 71 min.
09-5109 *$19.99*

The Mystery Of Marie Roget (1942)
Tight little thriller, inspired by Poe's classic, concerning a torch singer whose plans to kill her younger sister run into a horrifying snag. Who is the killer mutilating the ladies of Paris? Maria Montez, Patric Knowles, Maria Ouspenskaya star. AKA: "Phantom of Paris." 61 min.
10-7222 *$19.99*

Eyes In The Night (1942)
Superb suspenser directed by Fred Zinnemann and starring Edward Arnold as a blind detective who works with help from a seeing eye dog. He's enlisted to investigate the relationship between an egocentric actor and the stepdaughter of an old friend. Murder, a secret formula and Nazis eventually play a part in the mystery. Ann Harding, Donna Reed, Allen Jenkins co-star. 80 min.
09-5255 Was $19.99 *$14.99*

The Missing Corpse (1945)
Risible whodunit sparked by an ingenious wit and engaging plot twists about the bitter rivalry between two newspaper magnates and the comical mishaps that arise when one turns up dead and the other tries to stash the corpse. Stars J. Edward Bromberg and Isabel Randolph. 62 min.
10-7166 Was $19.99 *$14.99*

The Phantom Of 42nd Street (1945)
Murder on the Great White Way makes up this tangled whodunit about a drama critic out to lift the veil of suspicion from a family of Broadway thespians incriminated in the death of their wealthy uncle. Stars Dave O'Brien and Jack Mulhall. 58 min.
10-7170 *$19.99*

Charlie Chan

Charlie Chan In Paris (1935)
Hollywood's favorite wily Oriental detective, Charlie Chan, tracks down a gang of counterfeiters operating in the maze of sewers beneath the streets of Paris. Warner Oland stars as Charlie, with Keye Luke as #1 son Lee; Mary Brian, Erik Rhodes co-star. 70 min.
04-2190 ☐$19.99

Charlie Chan's Secret (1936)
The secret in the title concerns the murder of a wealthy young heir, and only Chan (Warner Oland) can solve the mystery and keep more killings from occurring. Fine Chan suspenser also features Rosina Lawrence, Charles Quigley. 72 min.
04-2191 ☐$19.99

Charlie Chan At The Opera (1936)
Considered by many fans to be the best of the Chan films, with Charlie (Warner Oland) and Lee (Keye Luke) Chan looking into the murder of a diva. Prime suspect is her husband, ex-asylum inmate Boris Karloff. Oscar Levant wrote the opera, "Carnival," used in the film; with Charlotte Henry, Thomas Beck, Margaret Irving, William Demarest. 66 min.
04-2192 ☐$19.99

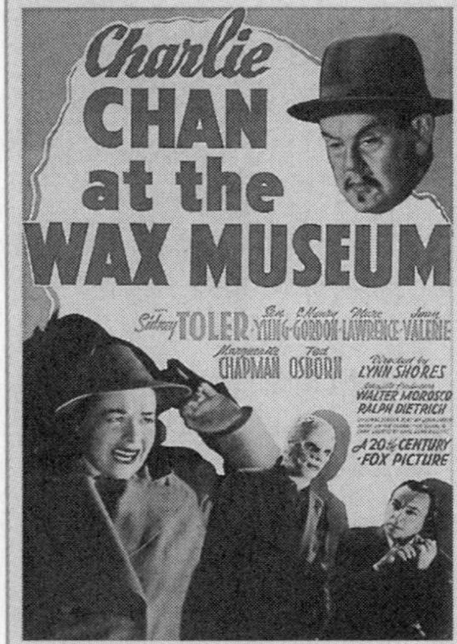

Charlie Chan At The Wax Museum (1940)
A doctor who uses his surgical skills to give crooks new faces provides Charlie (Sidney Toler) and #2 son Jimmy (Victor Sen Yung) with a tantalizing mystery amidst the waxworks. C. Henry Gordon, Joan Valerie co-star. 63 min.
04-2193 ☐$19.99

Murder Over New York (1940)
While in New York to attend a police convention, Charlie Chan (Sidney Toler) and son Jimmy (Victor Sen Yung) uncover a sabotage ring wreaking havoc in the airline industry. Intriguing Chan mystery, with the final "locked room" dénouement occurring several thousand feet in the sky, also stars Ricardo Cortez, Marjorie Weaver. 65 min.
04-2194 ☐$19.99

Charlie Chan In Rio (1941)
It's anything but a "carnivale" for Oriental sleuth Sidney Toler, as Charlie is asked by Brazilian authorities to help investigate a pair of baffling murders. With Ted North, Mary Beth Hughes, Victor Jory and Victor Sen Yung as #2 Chan scion Jimmy. 63 min.
04-2195 ☐$19.99

Castle In The Desert (1942)
Charlie (Sidney Toler) is summoned to a medieval castle reconstructed in the Mojave Desert, the home of a reclusive millionaire and his wife, to investigate the death of one of the weekend guests. Final Fox entry in the Chan "whodunit" series co-stars Victor Sen Yung, Douglass Dumbrille, Henry Daniell. 62 min.
04-2196 ☐$19.99

Charlie Chan In The Secret Service (1944)
Sidney Toler stars as the Asian super-sleuth, called on by the Secret Service to investigate the death of a scientist who was working on special explosive devices. Mantan Moreland and Arthur Loft also star in the first Chan thriller from Monogram Pictures. 65 min.
12-2642 ☐$14.99

Meeting At Midnight (1944)
A fortune-telling racket that leads to murder brings Charlie Chan (Sidney Toler) and #1 daughter Frances Chan into the world of the occult. With Mantan Moreland as Birmingham. AKA: "Black Magic." 67 min.
12-2643 Was $19.99 ☐$14.99

The Chinese Cat (1944)
The ever-inscrutable Charlie Chan (Sidney Toler) attempts to crack a case involving nasty jewel thieves who use an abandoned funhouse as a hide-out. With Benson Fong, Mantan Moreland. 65 min.
12-2644 ☐$14.99

The Jade Mask (1945)
A scientist who discovered a way to turn wood into a material as strong as steel is murdered, and Charlie Chan is called on to find out who is responsible for the deed. Sidney Toler, Mantan Moreland and Edwin Luke star. 66 min.
12-2645 ☐$14.99

The Scarlet Clue (1945)
After a suspect in a plot to steal top secret radar plans is killed, Charlie Chan and son Tommie find that they have their work cut out for them in solving the case. Sidney Toler, Benson Fong and Mantan Moreland star. 64 min.
12-2646 ☐$14.99

The Shanghai Cobra (1945)
Charlie Chan (Sidney Toler) uses his detective skills to stop a devious plot to steal a supply of deadly radium from a bank vault. Mantan Moreland and Benson Fong also star. 64 min.
12-2647 ☐$14.99

The Girl In The News (1941)
Atmospheric British thriller from Carol Reed ("The Third Man") about a butler who poisons his boss and frames the attending nurse for the deed. Margaret Lockwood, Barry K. Barnes and Emlyn Williams star. 77 min.
10-9731 $19.99

Phantom Killer (1942)
Interesting Monogram mystery with Dick Purcell as a crusading D.A. prosecuting a deaf-mute do-gooder for murder. After the man is acquitted, Purcell quits his post and tries to get the goods on the real culprit, leading to all sorts of surprises. Joan Woodbury, John Hamilton, Mantan Moreland co-star. 60 min.
10-9995 $14.99

The Cobra Strikes (1948)
A hard-edged reporter thinks that something's very wrong regarding the death of a renowned scientist...and follows a trail that leads to a massive jewel heist! Sinister, surprising suspenser stars Richard Fraser, Sheila Ryan. 61 min.
10-7192 Was $19.99 $14.99

Conspiracy In Teheran (1948)
A British journalist working out of Iran during World War II tries to stop a terrorist plot to assassinate President Roosevelt when he visits the country. Nail-biting suspenser stars Derek Farr, Marta Labarr. AKA: "The Plot to Kill Roosevelt." 83 min.
09-5098 $19.99

Gambling Daughters (1941)
When two young, rich women get involved with professional gamblers, they face mystery and danger in this entertaining programmer starring Cecilia Parker, Roger Pryor and Gale Storm. AKA: "Professor's Gamble." 65 min.
09-5100 $19.99

Sky Liner (1949)
Tightly-wound suspenser set aboard a commercial airliner where an FBI agent tries to track down a spy in possession of top secret U.S. government documents from a corpse. Richard Travis, Pamela Blake and Rochelle Hudson star. 60 min.
10-9768 $14.99

Heartaches (1947)
As an investigative reporter (Edward Norris) pieces together the clues to a double homicide, he unearths secrets in a popular singer's life that could eventually reveal the killer's identity. Stylish whodunit co-stars Sheila Ryan and Chill Wills. 71 min.
10-7063 $19.99

Accomplice (1946)
Richard Arlen stars as a private dick whose ex-love begs him to track down her missing husband... and who discovers a far more insidious mystery. Effective little whodunit co-stars Veda Ann Borg, Tom Dugan. 66 min.
10-7573 Was $19.99 $14.99

Night Train To Munich (1941)
Classic spy thriller stars Rex Harrison as a British intelligence agent trying desperately to keep a Czech metallurgist and his secrets from the clutches of the Nazis. Margaret Lockwood, Paul Henreid ("von Hernnreid" here) co-star under the direction of Carol Reed. AKA: "Night Train." 90 min.
10-7576 Was $19.99 $14.99

The Haunted House (1940)
A young newpaper boy and a publisher's niece seek adventure when they snoop around a creepy old house and discover a killer responsible for a murder their friend has been accused of. Jackie Moran, Marcia Mae Jones and George Cleveland star. 70 min.
10-8245 Was $19.99 $14.99

You're Out Of Luck (1941)
The mob, the cops, the newspaper guys, the molls, they're all here! In this crime flick, a young elevator boy joins forces with his older detective brother in order to solve a number of gangland murders. Of course, they gotta watch out for those dames. Frankie Darro, Mantan Moreland and Tristram Coffin star. 60 min.
10-9793 $19.99

The Unknown Guest (1943)
Lively "B" thriller starring Victor Jory as a man who takes over an inn for his aunt and uncle, who have left for vacation. But Jory's girlfriend is suspicious of him, and she begins to think he killed his relatives. Pamela Blake, Harry Hayden also star; directed by Kurt Neumann ("The Fly"). 60 min.
10-9986 $14.99

Crime Smasher (1943)
A gang war draws the attention of a tough Irish cop and his partner, a police sergeant. Meanwhile, a self-proclaimed amateur sleuth named Cosmo is enlisted to help the authorities and find a kidnapped heiress. Frank Graham, Edgar Kennedy, Gale Storm and Mantan Moreland star; based on the "Cosmo Jones" radio show. AKA: "Cosmo Jones in Crime Smasher." 58 min.
09-2968 $19.99

State Department— File 649 (1948)
Northern China is the backdrop for this compelling espionage thriller about an American consul (William Lundigan) drawn into a web of political intrigue and abducted by insurgent Mongols led by a demonic warlord (Richard Loo). With Virginia Bruce. 87 min.
10-7069 Was $19.99 $14.99

City Of Missing Girls (1941)
A string of murders of young women last seen at a shady art school soon has a female reporter at odds with the law as she searches for the killer. But will she write about the criminal...or become his or her latest victim? Suspenser stars Astrid Allwyn, John Archer, H.B. Warner.
09-5336 $19.99

Caged Fury (1948)
A circus thriller starring Buster Crabbe as a lion-tamer who murders his assistant in order to tame a new gal under the big top. After a rival performer suspects the animal trainer is responsible for the deed, the excitement starts. Richard Denning, Sheila Ryan also star. 60 min.
10-8247 Was $19.99 $14.99

The House On 92nd Street (1945)
A German-American student is contacted by Nazi spies working in New York City and looking for information on the atomic bomb program. With the help of the FBI, he becomes a double agent and a player in the deadly espionage game. William Eythe, Lloyd Nolan, Signe Hasso and Leo G. Carroll star in this Oscar-winning wartime suspenser that won acclaim for its documentary-style tone. 89 min.
04-2923 ☐$19.99

Contraband (1940)
Exceptional seafaring suspenser from director Michael Powell showcasing Conrad Veidt as a Danish sea captain who joins forces with a beautiful British spy in order to find two passengers who disappeared during a blackout. Veidt soon becomes involved in romance, espionage and trying to find a Nazi headquarters. With Valerie Hobson, Esmond Knight. AKA: "Blackout." 90 min.
10-9236 Was $19.99 $14.99

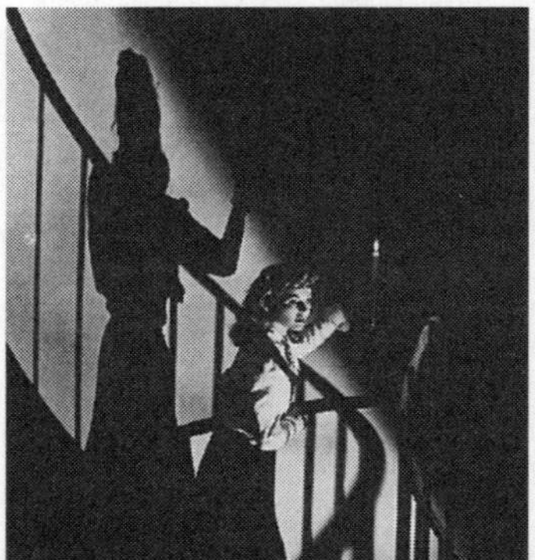

The Spiral Staircase (1946)
Compelling suspenser stars Dorothy McGuire as a servant, left mute by a childhood trauma, caring for invalid Ethel Barrymore in a Victorian New England mansion. As the nearby town is rocked by the murders of handicapped women, it quickly becomes clear that McGuire could be the killer's next victim. George Brent, Kent Smith, Gordon Oliver also star. 83 min.
04-1387 Was $19.99 $14.99

The Spiral Staircase (1975)
Jacqueline Bisset heads a terrific ensemble in this remake of the classic suspenser as a mute maid who is left alone in a great Victorian mansion with a murderer. With Christopher Plummer, Mildred Dunnock, Sam Wanamaker. 89 min.
19-1528 Was $19.99 $14.99

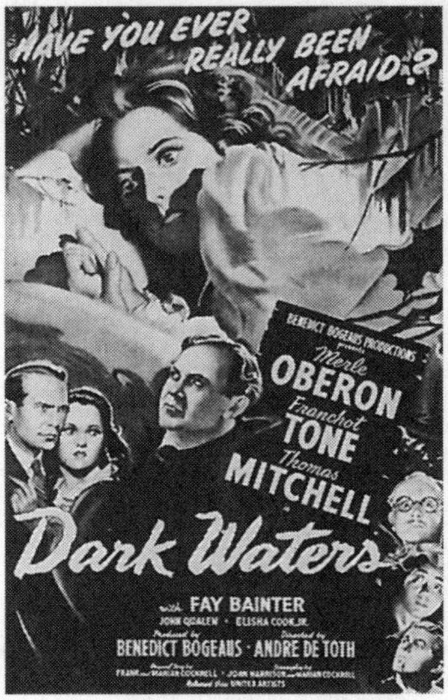

Dark Waters (1944)
Merle Oberon stars as a young woman who returns to her family's Louisiana mansion after surviving a shipwreck that claimed the lives of her parents. Oberon's seemingly concerned aunt and uncle (Fay Bainter, John Qualen) hatch a scheme to drive her mad and claim her inheritance. With Thomas Mitchell, Franchot Tone. 93 min.
70-1068 $14.99

Room To Let (1949)
In turn-of-the-century London, fear makes a widow and her crippled daughter mere prisoners in their own home, while suspicion grows that their odd new boarder is Jack the Ripper himself. Jimmy Hanley stars. 68 min.
68-8296 $19.99

Inner Sanctum (1948)
With an idea taken from the popular radio show of the era, this creepy tale focuses on the experiences of a woman riding a train who is told an eerie story by a fortune-teller. Charles Russell and Mary Beth Hughes star. 62 min.
68-8421 $19.99

Panama Menace (1941)
Gen. Manuel Noriega is nowhere to be found in this exciting espionage yarn about a U.S. agent in Central America who battles spies that have stolen a plan for invisible paint. Roger Pryor, Virginia Vale and Hugh Beaumont star. AKA: "South of Panama." 68 min.
68-8464 $19.99

Shadows On The Stairs (1941)
A "Ten Little Indians" type murder mystery in which a boardinghouse serves as a setting for strange deaths. Who done it? The young lovers? The man with the curious past? The enigmatic Asian? Or the innkeepers? Heather Angel, Turhan Bey, Frieda Inescort star. 64 min.
68-8465 Was $19.99 $14.99

I Killed That Man (1942)
Zippy suspenser about a tough district attorney and his newspaper crony who try to find who killed a murderer before he got to the electric chair. Ricardo Cortez and Joan Woodbury star. 70 min.
68-8466 $19.99

Army Mystery (1941)
Expert espionage tale, with a special agent uncovering a spy ring that has stolen a dangerous U.S. Army explosives formula. Wartime suspenser stars Eric Linden, Ann Doran, Ben Alexander. AKA: "Criminals Within." 66 min.
68-8467 $19.99

Today I Hang (1942)
A man is framed for a murder rap and headed for execution. While in prison, he befriends a number of seedy cons and is eventually led to the crime's real culprit. Walter Woolf King, Mona Barrie star. 61 min.
68-8469 Was $19.99 $14.99

The Devil's Cargo (1948)
John Calvert plays the Falcon in one of the last installments in the series. The suave sleuth must find the true killer of a racetrack operator in order to free an innocent man accused of the deed. Rochelle Hudson, Roscoe Karns and Lyle Talbot star. 61 min.
68-8532 $19.99

The Inner Circle (1946)
Enthralling mystery about a private detective who finds himself framed for murder by his secretary...who happens to be protecting her sister from the crime. Adele Mara, Warren Douglas and William Frawley star. 57 min.
68-8533 $19.99

Dear Murderer (1947)
Top-notch, twisting British crime yarn about a jealous businessman who approaches his wife's lawyer lover with an offer: find a loophole in the "perfect" murder plot he has concocted and his life will be spared. Eric Portman, Greta Gynt and Dennis Price star. 94 min.
68-8755 $19.99

Her First Romance (1940)
One of Alan Ladd's earliest efforts finds him entangled in a plot involving two sisters who want to use him to get to another man. When Ladd believes the man is actually after his girl, he takes matters into his own hands. Edith Fellows, Wilbur Evans also star. AKA: "The Right Man." 75 min.
10-9107 *$19.99*

Gangs Inc. (1941)
After a woman (Jean Woodbury) takes the rap for her boyfriend in a hit-and-run accident and is sent to jail, she comes out seeking revenge on the cad's wealthy father, a political "reformer." Compelling crime thriller also stars Jack LaRue, John Archer, and Alan Ladd as a reporter. AKA: "Ballot Blackmail," "Paper Bullets." 68 min.
10-3052 Was $19.99 *$14.99*

This Gun For Hire (1942)
The movie that made Alan Ladd a star. He's a cold-blooded killer out to get back at a double-crossing nightclub owner. Secret formulas, Nazis and vicious chauffeurs pop up in this "film noir" classic based on Graham Greene's thriller. Veronica Lake is the beautiful femme fatale; with Laird Cregar, Robert Preston. 81 min.
07-1168 □*$14.99*

The Glass Key (1942)
Dashiell Hammett's tale of political corruption, blackmail and murder stars Alan Ladd as an aide to political boss Brian Donlevy who must clear his boss' name when he's accused of killing a candidate's son. Veronica Lake supplies the love interest, William Bendix plays a mob muscleman; look for one fight scene where Bendix actually knocked out Ladd! 85 min.
07-1617 *$14.99*

China (1943)
Set in China during pre-Pearl Harbor World War II, this rousing action tale stars Alan Ladd as a mercenary trader who deals with both Chinese natives and the Japanese invaders with an equal lack of conscience, until he comes to the aid of teacher Loretta Young and a group of refugee schoolgirls. With William Bendix, Philip Ahn. Includes original theatrical trailer. 79 min.
07-2512 □*$14.99*

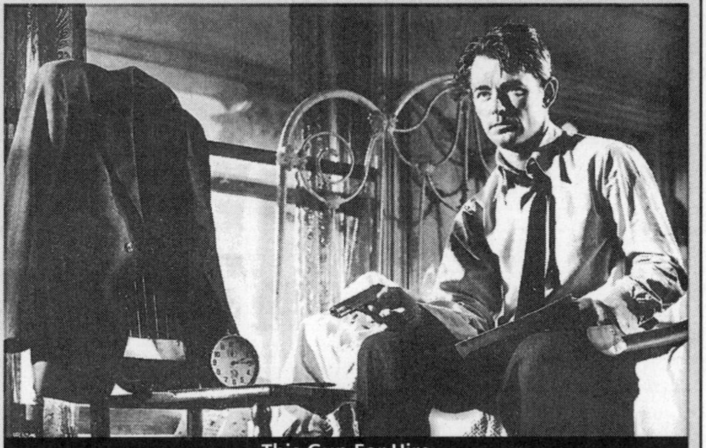

This Gun For Hire

Alan Ladd

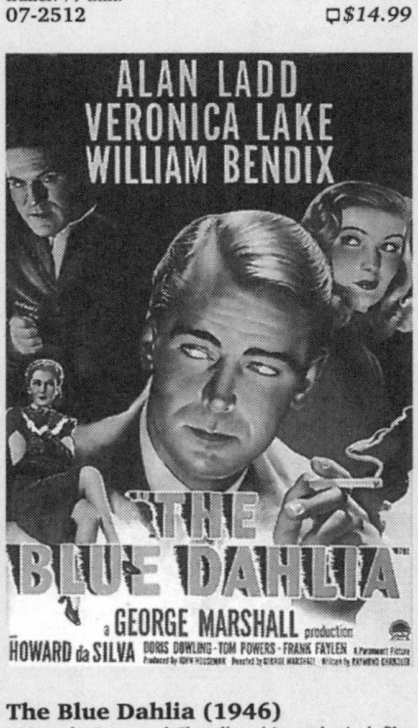

The Blue Dahlia (1946)
Written by Raymond Chandler, this crackerjack film noir features Alan Ladd as a sailor returning home to Los Angeles who discovers that his wife is involved with another man. When she's found murdered, Ladd becomes the prime suspect, forcing him to launch his own investigation with Veronica Lake, the estranged spouse of his wife's lover. With William Bendix. 100 min.
07-2308 □*$14.99*

O.S.S. (1946)
Taken from the true exploits of American Office of Strategic Services agents during World War II, this compelling espionage thriller stars Alan Ladd and Geraldine Fitzgerald as ordinary citizens who go through "spy school" training and are sent into occupied France to blow up a vital railway tunnel. With Patric Knowles, John Hoyt. 108 min.
07-2515 □*$14.99*

Two Years Before The Mast (1946)
Shanghaied into service on board a sailing ship run by a tyrannical captain, spoiled shipowner's son Alan Ladd undergoes a series of brutal challenges that changes his character and leads him and fellow sailor Brian Donlevy to mutiny. Based on the classic novel, this sweeping sea saga also stars Howard Da Silva, Barry Fitzgerald, William Bendix. 98 min.
07-2608 *$14.99*

Branded (1951)
Alan Ladd is a ball of jangling spurs in this classic sagebrush saga. He's a strong, silent type who agrees to help some crooks out by impersonating a rancher's long-lost son. Complications arise when Ladd falls for the rancher's daughter. Mona Freeman and Charles Bickford co-star. 103 min.
06-1718 □*$12.99*

Shane (1953)
Western saga with Alan Ladd as a former gunfighter who defends homesteaders and is idolized by a young boy. Two-fisted action and a tearful finale mark this George Stevens classic. Van Heflin, Brandon De Wilde, Jack Palance, Jean Arthur. 118 min.
06-1053 Remastered □*$14.99*

Saskatchewan (1954)
Impressively filmed adventure from director Raoul Walsh featuring Alan Ladd as a Canadian Mountie raised by Indians who tracks down Sioux Indians trying to persuade other Northwestern tribes to fight the white man following Little Big Horn. Shelley Winters is Ladd's romantic interest, a saloon gal; with Robert Douglas, J. Carrol Naish and Jay Silverheels.
10-2631 *$14.99*

The McConnell Story (1955)
Inspiring true-life look at the life of Korean War hero Capt. Joseph McConnell, Jr., whose expertise as an Air Force bomber led to the downing of 15 enemy planes. Alan Ladd, June Allyson and James Whitmore star in this patriotic rouser. 107 min.
19-1839 Was $19.99 □*$14.99*

The Badlanders (1958)
Action-packed western reworking of "The Asphalt Jungle" stars Alan Ladd as the ex-con who feels he's been duped by a mine owner and enlists the help of two compadres to get the gold he deserves. Kent Smith, Ernest Borgnine, Katy Jurado also star. 83 min.
12-2412 Was $19.99 *$14.99*

The Deep Six (1958)
Alan Ladd excels as a Quaker advertising artist who enlists in the Navy after Pearl Harbor, but finds his beliefs conflict with his desire to serve his country. Eventually, he proves his courage to shipmates by volunteering for a daring rescue mission in the Pacific. With Dianne Foster, Keenan Wynn, William Bendix, Ross Bagdasarian and Joey Bishop. 105 min.
19-2220 Was $29.99 *$19.99*

Duel Of Champions (1961)
In this gladiator adventure, Alan Ladd plays a Roman soldier involved in a battle with the Curiatii triplets. Directed by Terence Young ("Dr. No") and Ferdinando Baldi ("Comin' at Ya!"), the film also stars Franca Bettoja. 91 min.
68-8913 Was $19.99 *$14.99*

The Carpetbaggers (1964)
Screen version of the Harold Robbins novel stars George Peppard as a wealthy plane manufacturer of the 1920s who has numerous adventures in moviemaking and with the ladies. Also starring Alan Ladd (his final film), Carroll Baker, and Bob Cummings. 150 min.
06-1304 Was $59.99 *$14.99*

Alan Ladd: The True Quiet Man
Before his untimely death at 50 in 1964, he overcame a life of adversity to become an unlikely Hollywood leading man. Follow the career of tough guy Alan Ladd in this video biography that includes film clips from "The Glass Key," "The Blue Dahlia," "Proud Rebel" and "Shane"; interviews with Don Murray, Lizabeth Scott and David Ladd; and more. 58 min.
50-7598 *$14.99*

Please see our index for these other Alan Ladd titles: *The Black Cat • Helltown • My Favorite Brunette • Pigskin Parade • Star Spangled Rhythm*

The Hidden Room (1949)
Classic suspense mystery, made in England, about a jealous doctor trying to torture his wife's lover in a dark, creepy cellar. Robert Newton, Sally Gray. 98 min.
50-1043 *$19.99*

Behind Locked Doors (1948)
Private eye Richard Carlson masquerades as a patient in an asylum in an attempt to find a missing judge and collect a reward, but will he crack the case before the conditions crack him? Well-made suspenser from Budd Boetticher ("Comanche Station") with a "Snake Pit"-type atmosphere; co-stars Lucille Bremer and the great Tor Johnson. AKA: "Human Gorilla." 62 min.
53-6887 *$24.99*

The Red Menace (1949)
Produced shortly before the cloud of McCarthyism descended upon the U.S., this propagandistic drama tells the story of a young couple who are on the run from "communist forces" out to lure them into their way of life. Robert Rockwell, Hanne Axman, Duke Williams star in this tough, documentary-like curio. 81 min.
63-1446 *$19.99*

Corridor Of Mirrors (1948)
Romantic gothic thriller about a wealthy artist obsessed with a Renaissance painting of a young woman. He starts believing he's the reincarnation of the girl's lover and seeks to find her modern-day counterpart. With Eric Portman, Edana Romney; co-star Christopher Lee and director Terence Young ("Dr. No") both made their debuts here. 105 min.
68-8932 *$19.99*

The Mysterious Mr. Nicholson (1947)
You won't find him at Academy Award parties or in the front row at Lakers games. This Mr. Nicholson is a suave English burglar who's suspected of murdering a well-to-do peer of the realm and teams with a young woman to clear his name. Gripping suspense tale stars Anthony Hulme, Lesley Ormond.
68-9238 *$19.99*

Strange Impersonation (1946)
Knockout noirish thriller from Anthony Mann ("T-Men") centers on chemist Brenda Marshall, who tests an anesthesia she invented by injecting herself with it. Marshall's life soon turns hellish as her fiancé spurns her, she is blackmailed, and her face is damaged in an explosion. But is everything as it seems? William Gargan, Hillary Brooke, H.B. Warner and Lyle Talbot also star. 68 min.
53-6885 *$24.99*

Tower Of Terror (1942)
The unbalanced keeper of a lighthouse rescues a concentration camp escapee, but then plots to kill her because she's the image of the wife he murdered years earlier. Wilfrid Lawson, Movita and Michael Rennie star in a wartime suspenser. 79 min.
68-8012 *$19.99*

Waterfront (1944)
A shadowy drama about a Nazi spy ring operating in San Francisco's shipping district, gathering secret information from disloyal German-Americans. John Carradine stars. 65 min.
68-8013 Was $19.99 *$14.99*

A Man About The House (1947)
A pair of English spinsters take up residence in the Neopolitan villa they've inherited and soon fall prey to the handsome caretaker, whose charm conceals his poisonous intentions. Margaret Johnson and Dulcie Gray star. 95 min.
68-8173 Was $24.99 *$19.99*

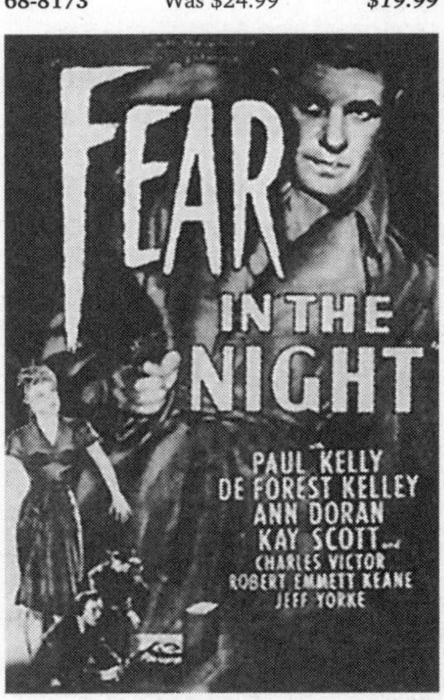

Fear In The Night (1947)
After a dream in which he murders a safecracker with an electric drill, DeForest Kelley finds a coat button and key that convince him his nightmare really happened. Inventive mystery is first credited screen role for the "Star Trek" doctor. Paul Kelly, Ann Doran also star. 71 min.
68-8283 *$19.99*

Rogues Gallery (1944)
A scientist's unusual broadcasting device draws the attention of an ace newspaper reporter and a photographer. Soon, interest in the invention inspires murder and mystery, and hurls the journalists into the middle of a criminal plot. H.B. Warner, Frank Jenks, Robin Raymond star. 60 min.
68-8470 *$19.99*

The Panther's Claw (1942)
Lively mystery about a murder in an opera company and the detective whose investigation of the crime provides him with some colorful suspects, including a wigmaker, a gorgeous diva and an alcoholic baritone. Sidney Blackmer, Byron Foulger star.
68-8826 *$19.99*

Three Weird Sisters (1948)
Dylan Thomas contributed to the screenplay for this Gothic chiller about a trio of insane elderly sisters who plot the death of their half-brother. Nancy Price, Nova Pilbeam, Raymond Lovell, Hugh Griffith star. 83 min.
62-1309 *$19.99*

Secret Beyond The Door (1948)
The great Fritz Lang directed this "Suspicion"-like tale about a woman who suspects her new husband to be a murderer. Joan Bennett, Michael Redgrave. 98 min.
63-1090 *$19.99*

Spectre Of The Rose (1946)
Equal parts of drama, dance, suspense and comedy are mixed in Ben Hecht's offbeat thriller about a young ballerina who fears that her new husband may be slipping into the madness that drove him to murder his first wife years earlier. Michael Chekhov, Viola Essen, Lionel Stander, Dame Judith Anderson star. 90 min.
63-1336 *$19.99*

Midnight Manhunt (1945)
Creepy little thriller with George Zucco as a killer seeking the body of a victim he shot in a wax museum specializing in exhibits of infamous murders. William Gargan, Anne Savage and Leo Gorcey also star in this atmospheric suspenser.
68-8921 *$19.99*

C-Man (1949)
A U.S. customs agent dogging dangerous jewel smugglers from New York to Paris is the subject of this tightly-directed crime tale starring Dean Jagger and John Carradine. 76 min.
68-8184 *$19.99*

Counterblast (1948)
Infectious performances highlight this spy yarn about Nazis swiping germ warfare secrets from a British lab. Mervyn Johns plays a ruthless infiltrator who murders a scientist and impersonates him. AKA: "The Devil's Plot." 99 min.
68-8190 *$19.99*

They Made Me A Fugitive (1947)
Moody and noir-flavored crime drama set in postwar Britain stars Trevor Howard as a former RAF officer who turns to a life of crime, only to be betrayed by his gang's female leader when he refuses to take part in a drug-dealing scheme. Sally Gray, Griffith Jones also star. AKA: "I Became a Criminal." 96 min.
53-6501 *$24.99*

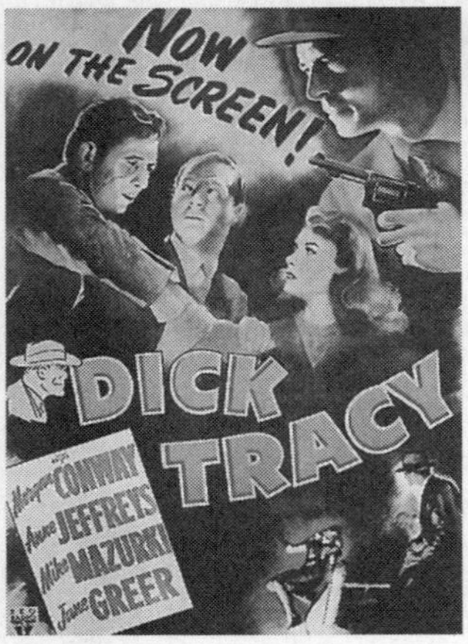

Dick Tracy, Detective (1945)
Morgan Conway is Chester Gould's razor-chinned detective in the first Tracy feature film, here tracking down escaped killer Splitface. Anne Jeffreys, Jane Greer, Mike Mazurki. 65 min.
18-3019 Was $19.99 ***$14.99***

Dick Tracy vs. Cueball (1946)
After 10 years in the clink, Cueball is out...murdering, robbing, and being his old vicious self. All the comic strip characters are here: Junior, Tess, Vitamin Flintheart and more. Morgan Conway stars with Anne Jeffreys, Lyle Latell. 62 min.
18-3014 Was $19.99 ***$14.99***

Dick Tracy's Dilemma (1947)
Ralph Byrd stars as Tracy. This time he meets "The Claw," an evil killer with a hook instead of a right hand. Tess Trueheart and all the other "Crimestoppers" keep a fast pace as the film reaches its electrifying conclusion. 60 min.
18-3008 Was $19.99 ***$14.99***

Dick Tracy Meets Gruesome (1947)
Boris Karloff is the perfect "Gruesome," and he intends to freeze the whole town so that he can do his evil stuff. But he's no match for Dick Tracy, who's an expert at cooling him down. Ralph Byrd stars as Tracy. 65 min.
18-3013 ***$14.99***

Midnight Limited (1940)
A passenger train running between Albany and Montreal is the setting for drama, romance and suspense in this tale of the search for a jewel thief on board the train. John King, Marjorie Reynolds star. 62 min.
68-8117 Was $19.99 ***$14.99***

The Invisible Killer (1940)
An unseen killer turns a town upside down when he uses telephone lines to send poison gas to his victims. Grace Bradley is a newswoman getting aid from copper Roland Drew. 61 min.
68-8124 ***$19.99***

Appointment With Crime (1945)
Double-crossed by his gang and sent to prison for jewel theft, a man has plenty of time to hatch an elaborate scheme to get even...and get rich. William Hartnell, Herbert Lom and Robert Beatty star in this gritty British crime drama. 91 min.
68-8135 Was $19.99 ***$14.99***

Dick Barton, Secret Agent (1948)
The first of the popular series, and the first film ever by the infamous Hammer Films, stars Don Stannard as the daring title sleuth, rushing into action to prevent a deranged scientist from germ-bombing England.
68-8157 ***$19.99***

Dick Barton Strikes Back (1949)
An atomic device aimed at an innocent populace is the quarry of hero Don Stannard. TV butler Sebastian Cabot is the villain in this tense actioner, complete with a poisonous snake pit and dangerous tower ascent. 73 min.
68-8156 ***$19.99***

The Judge (1949)
Incensed by his wife's infidelities, a hotshot lawyer blackmails a client into participating in his plan to murder her and her lover. Tense courtroom scenes resolve this crime thriller starring Milburn Stone and Katherine de Mille. 69 min.
68-8172 ***$19.99***

Interrupted Journey (1949)
The flight by rail of illicit lovers ends tragically as Richard Todd jumps the train in an attack of remorse. Meanwhile, Valerie Hobson is found dead in their berth. Exciting British mystery. 80 min.
68-8179 ***$19.99***

Flight To Nowhere (1946)
An odd assortment of plane passengers lands at a Death Valley hotel and smack into a dangerous plot involving a stolen map and secret uranium deposits in the South Pacific. Alan Curtis. 75 min.
68-8193 Was $19.99 ***$14.99***

Riot Squad (1941)
Richard Cromwell stars in this urban crime adventure about an intern recruited to go undercover as a doctor for the mob to flush out a police captain's killers. 55 min.
68-8275 ***$19.99***

Hidden Enemy (1940)
A metal three times lighter than aluminum but stronger than steel could shift power to the Axis in this WWII crime adventure. Warren Hull stars as a newsman defending his inventor uncle from spies and thieves. 63 min.
68-8276 Was $19.99 ***$14.99***

Dual Alibi (1947)
Unusual double role for Herbert Lom as twin trapeze artists who scheme to do away with their swindling agent. Circus-themed mystery also stars Sebastian Cabot. 87 min.
68-8277 ***$19.99***

Parole, Inc. (1949)
Dark crime story about an FBI agent (Michael O'Shea) going undercover to squelch a parole racket benefiting convicts loyal to the Mob. Evelyn Ankers co-stars. 71 min.
68-8279 Was $19.99 ***$14.99***

Calling Paul Temple (1948)
A famous detective discovers a lone clue to the identity of a serial killer—his wealthy victims were all patients of a certain nerve specialist. British mystery based on a popular radio show stars John Bentley. 92 min.
68-8280 ***$19.99***

Pink String And Sealing Wax (1945)
In the Victorian British coastal town of Brighton, the wife of a sadistic innkeeper poisons her husband and plans to let a young man who's infatuated with her take the fall for the crime. Mervyn Johns, Googie Withers, Gordon Jackson star. 89 min.
68-8281 ***$19.99***

The Lady Confesses (1945)
Is Hugh Beaumont guilty of murdering his estranged wife and about to become a ward of the state prison system? His current girlfriend doesn't buy it, and takes off after the real killers. Mary Beth Hughes co-stars. 64 min.
68-8282 ***$19.99***

The Mask Of Diijon (1946)
Fascinating, atmospheric tale about a magician (Erich von Stroheim) who uses hypnosis to persuade the person he believes is having an affair with his wife to kill himself. Jeanne Bates and William Wright co-star. 73 min.
79-5468 ***$14.99***

Gaslight (1940)
The acclaimed original screen version of the thriller about a newly-married woman who is slowly being driven insane by her scheming husband. Moody and suspenseful (and nearly destroyed by MGM so as not to compete with their 1944 remake), the British film stars Anton Walbrook, Diana Wynward, Frank Pettingell. AKA: "Angel Street." 88 min.
17-9038 ***$19.99***

Killer Dill (1947)
Lively noir thriller about an amiable salesman who, when mistaken for the murderer of a rival gangster, finds himself in trouble. Stuart Erwin, Anne Gwynne, Frank Albertson and Mike Mazurki. 71 min.
17-9059 Was $19.99 ***$14.99***

Fog Island (1945)
A creepy island mansion hides unspeakable terror within its walls for a group of visitors assembled there by its vengeance-seeking master. George Zucco and Lionel Atwill co-star. 70 min.
68-8010 Was $19.99 ***$14.99***

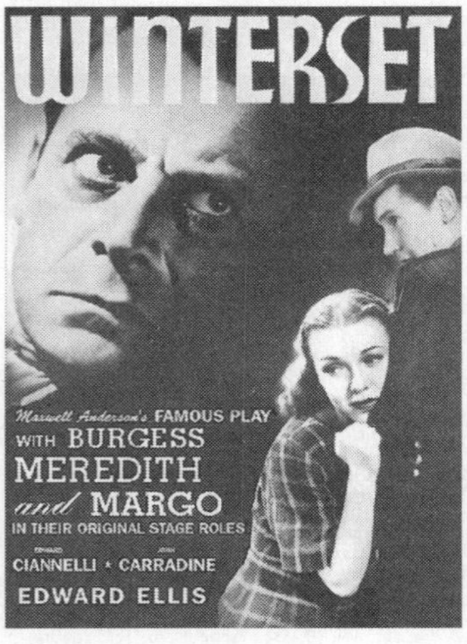

Winterset (1937)
When his father is electrocuted for a crime he did not commit, a young man sets out to clear his name. Stars Burgess Meredith and John Carradine. 85 min.
01-1081 Was $19.99 ***$14.99***

William Powell

Romola (1925)
William Powell is gloriously villainous in this classic rendition of George Eliot's historical romance set in 15th-century Italy. Powell portrays the unscrupulous adopted son of a Greek scholar who enters into marriage with Romola (Lillian Gish) in Florence, fathers a child with another woman (Dorothy Gish) and, as chief magistrate, executes a popular priest. Ronald Colman also stars. 117 min. Silent with music score.
10-8022 Was $29.99 ***$19.99***

Feel My Pulse (1928)
Dizzy comedy about an heiress (Bebe Daniels), raised from infancy in a germ-free environment, who inherits an island sanitarium crawling with rum-runners. Also stars Richard Arlen and William Powell. 86 min. Silent with musical score.
09-1825 Was $29.99 ***$24.99***

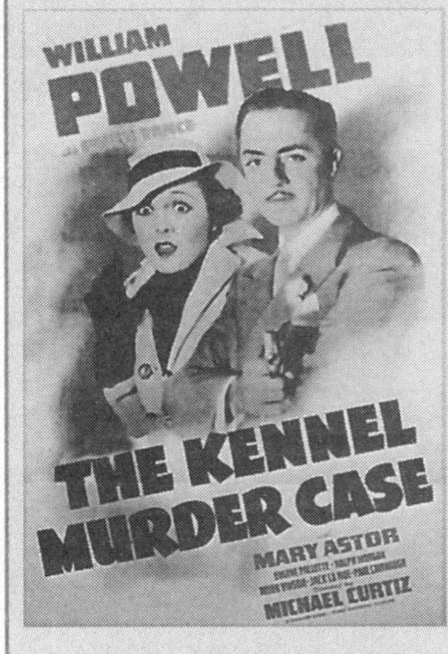

The Kennel Murder Case (1933)
Before his success in the "Thin Man" films, William Powell starred as S.S. Van Dine's debonaire sleuth, Philo Vance, in a series of well-made whodunits. Here Vance solves a deadly affair that takes place at a society dog club. With Mary Astor, Ralph Morgan; directed by Michael Curtiz. 73 min.
08-8065 ***$19.99***

The Thin Man (1934)
Madcap blend of screwball comedy and murder mystery that inspired five sequels, with William Powell and Myrna Loy as married amateur detectives Nick and Nora Charles. Based on Dashiell Hammett's book; with Maureen O'Sullivan, Edward Ellis and Asta. 100 min.
12-1467 ***$19.99***

After The Thin Man (1936)
William Powell and Myrna Loy are back as society sleuths Nick and Nora in the second series entry. Here they must find a murderer among the blue-bloods of San Francisco, and the suspects include a young Jimmy Stewart. With Joseph Calleia, Jessie Ralph. 113 min.
12-1522 ***$19.99***

Another Thin Man (1939)
In their third outing the Charleses must unravel a twisted mystery centering around a man whose dreams about deaths seems to be coming true. Features the first appearance of Nick Charles, Jr.; stars Myrna Loy and William Powell. 105 min.
12-1660 ***$19.99***

Shadow Of The Thin Man (1941)
When murder occurs among the "horsey set," husband and wife sleuths Nick and Nora Charles spend a day at the races to track down the killer. Fourth "Thin Man" entry also stars Barry Nelson, Donna Reed. 97 min.
12-1737 ***$19.99***

The Thin Man Goes Home (1944)
And it's a laugh- and mystery-filled homecoming indeed for the Charleses, complete with old enemies, Nick's disapproving parents, and a birthday party for Nick, Jr. William Powell, Myrna Loy, Gloria De Haven, Harry Davenport star. 100 min.
12-1738 ***$19.99***

Song Of The Thin Man (1947)
In the sixth and final film of the series, Nick and Nora play a rousing rendition of "Murder Musicale" when they hunt a killer in the city's jazz joints. William Powell, Myrna Loy, Keenan Wynn, Gloria Grahame, and Asta star. 86 min.
12-1605 ***$19.99***

Evelyn Prentice (1934)
William Powell teamed with Myrna Loy after the first "Thin Man" movie for this expert thriller in which Powell plays a womanizing lawyer whose adulterous affair leads to blackmail, murder, deceit and a trial in which Loy admits to murdering her own lover. Una Merkel, Harvey Stephens, Isabel Jewell and Rosalind Russell, in her debut, also star. 78 min.
12-2863 ***$29.99***

My Man Godfrey (1936)
William Powell is Godfrey, the "bum" who is brought home by society girl Carole Lombard to serve as her eccentric family's butler, but winds up teaching them a thing or two about life. Gregory La Cava's classic screwball comedy of manners also stars Gail Patrick, Mischa Auer, Eugene Pallette. 93 min.
10-2026 ***$19.99***

Double Wedding (1937)
Frantic screwball story with William Powell as a Bohemian painter and Myrna Loy as a workaholic dress shop owner who spar over Loy's younger sister's life choices. Loy wants her hitched to a conservative snob; Powell thinks she should ditch the marriage idea and become an actress. Florence Rice, John Beal and Edgar Kennedy co-star. 87 min.
12-2727 ***□$19.99***

I Love You Again (1940)
William Powell stars in this sparkling screwball farce as a stodgy businessman heading for divorce with wife Myrna Loy who gets knocked on the head during a cruise and reverts back to his *real* persona of a slick con artist. Will Powell be able to get over his true conniving ways and reignite his romance with Loy? Frank McHugh, Edmund Lowe co-star. 99 min.
12-2729 ***□$19.99***

Love Crazy (1941)
Zippy farce with "Thin Man" stars William Powell and Myrna Loy as a married couple whose fourth wedding anniversary is not a happy affair, thanks to a series of events that occur after Loy's gossipy mother visits. Gail Patrick, Jack Carson, Sidney Blackmer co-star. 97 min.
12-2302 ***$19.99***

Life With Father (1947)
Beloved comedy set in turn-of-the-century New York and starring William Powell as the stern but loving head of the Day family. Irene Dunne is his devoted (and long-suffering) wife; with Elizabeth Taylor, Jimmy Lydon, Martin Milner. 118 min.
10-1084 Was $19.99 ***$14.99***

The Senator Was Indiscreet (1947)
Broadway wit George S. Kaufman wrote and directed this hilarious satire of Capitol escapades. William Powell is the senator whose discovery of a very racy diary could spell disaster for his party. Peter Lind Hayes and Ella Raines co-star. 81 min.
63-1064 Was $19.99 ***$14.99***

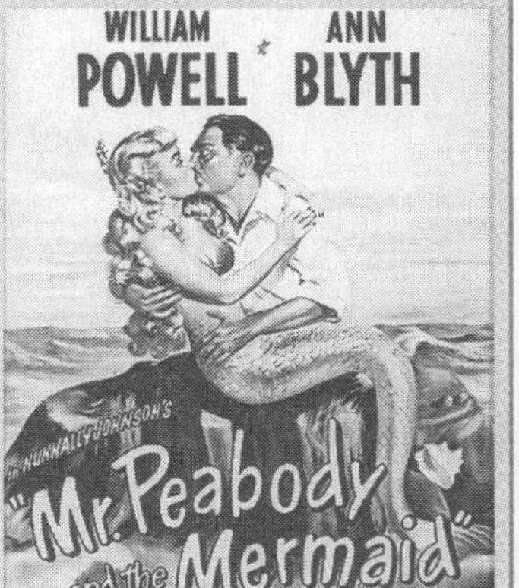

Mr. Peabody And The Mermaid (1948)
William Powell and Ann Blyth are the very odd title couple in this touching romantic fantasy about a lonely middle-aged fisherman who can't convince anyone that he's hooked the biggest catch of his life—a live mermaid! With Irene Hervey, Andrea King. 89 min.
63-1063 Remastered ***□$14.99***

Please see our index for these other William Powell titles: *The Girl Who Had Everything • The Great Ziegfeld • How To Marry A Millionaire • The Last Command • The Last Of Mrs. Cheney • Libeled Lady • Manhattan Melodrama • Mister Roberts • Reckless • Ziegfeld Follies*

Accused (1936)
Mystery and show business drama mix when dancer Delores Del Rio witnesses hoofer husband Douglas Fairbanks, Jr. leaving manipulative stage star Florence Desmond's dressing room. When Desmond is found dead and the dancing team's knife is found at the scene of the crime, Del Rio is put on trial for the murder. 80 min.
10-9231 Was $19.99 **$14.99**

The Ghost Camera (1933)
Fifteen-year-old Ida Lupino stars in this thriller concerning a camera that clicks a picture of a murder before falling out of a window and into a passing car. Can the photo be recovered in time to save an innocent man accused of the crime? Henry Kendall, John Mills also star. 65 min.
10-9232 Was $19.99 **$14.99**

The Avenging Hand (1936)
A group of hotel guests, all of whom are actually crooks searching the premises for hidden loot, try to outscare one another in this mystery filled with strange occurrences, shadowy figures and suspense. Noah Beery and Kathleen Kelly star. 65 min.
10-9237 Was $19.99 **$14.99**

Murder In The Clouds (1934)
Exciting thriller about an expert pilot on assignment to transport a scientist who has invented a dangerous explosive to Washington. The flight is almost thwarted when some crooks out to get the formula intercede. Lyle Talbot, Ann Dvorak, Gordon Westcott star. 61 min.
10-9333 **$19.99**

A Man Betrayed (1937)
Eddie Nugent is framed for a crime, but complications ensue when a group of hoodlums attempt to prove his innocence. A young minister also gets in the middle of the proceedings in this suspenser. With Kay Hughes, John Wray. 58 min.
10-9441 **$19.99**

Kate Plus Ten (1938)
Following the robbery of gold bullion from the bank of a British lord, a police detective tracks down the lord's secretary when he learns she's part of a gang of thieves. Jack Hulbert, Arthur Wontner and Francis L. Sullivan star. 80 min.
10-9711 **$19.99**

This Man Is News (1939)
Barry Barnes and Valerie Hobson star in this British take on Hollywood's "Thin Man" series as a husband/wife team of investigative reporters who get framed for robbery by a gang of jewel thieves they had been tracking. The couple goes on the run to find the real culprits. Garry Marsh, Alastair Sim, John Abbott co-star. 77 min.
10-9833 **$14.99**

The Case Of The Lucky Legs (1935)
Decades before Raymond Burr and TV, famed legal eagle Perry Mason was the subject of a Warner Bros. film series. Here, Perry (Warren William) defends a beauty contestant charged with killing the show's promoter. With Patricia Ellis, Lyle Talbot, Genevieve Tobin. 76 min.
17-3003 **$19.99**

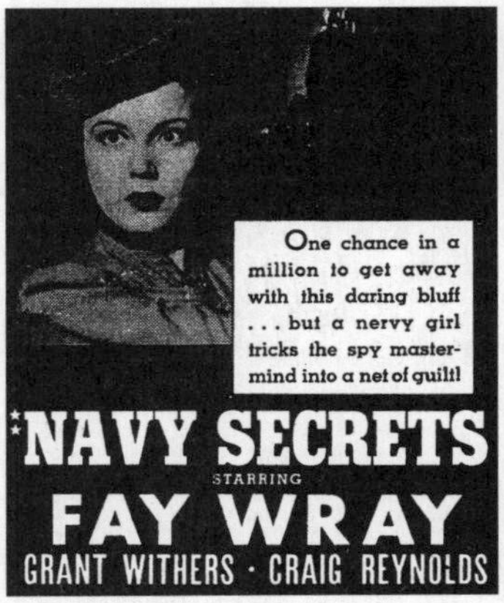
One chance in a million to get away with this daring bluff . . . but a nervy girl tricks the spy master-mind into a net of guilt!
NAVY SECRETS
STARRING
FAY WRAY
GRANT WITHERS · CRAIG REYNOLDS

Navy Secrets (1939)
Federal agents Fay Wray and Grant Withers investigate a case of stolen government secrets, but neither knows that the other one is on the case. Suspecting each other of the crime, they find a traitorous seaman who may lead them to a spy ring. Craig Reynolds also stars.
68-8104 **$19.99**

The Phantom Fiend (1935)
A reworking of Alfred Hitchcock's "The Lodger" stars Ivor Novello as a musician accused in a series of grisly murders. Elizabeth Allan and Jack Hawkins co-star. 67 min.
53-6026 **$19.99**

Beggars In Ermine (1934)
Unusual thriller from Monogram Studios stars Lionel Atwill as a steel mill owner crippled in an "accident" rigged by a competitor after his money and wife. Later Atwill organizes the country's beggars into a "union" while planning his revenge. With Betty Furness, George "Gabby" Hayes. 70 min.
68-8014 Was $19.99 **$14.99**

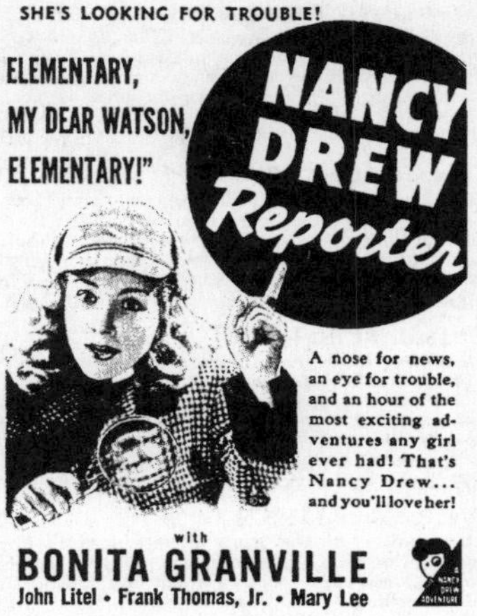
SHE'S LOOKING FOR TROUBLE!
ELEMENTARY, MY DEAR WATSON, ELEMENTARY!"
NANCY DREW Reporter
A nose for news, an eye for trouble, and an hour of the most exciting adventures any girl ever had! That's Nancy Drew... and you'll love her!
with
BONITA GRANVILLE
John Litel • Frank Thomas, Jr. • Mary Lee

Nancy Drew, Reporter (1939)
Bonita Granville returns as Carolyn Keene's teenager sleuth, and her winning of a journalism contest leads her down a trail of trouble as she tries to crack the case she's covering for the paper. Mystery and fun with John Litel, Joan Leslie. 65 min.
10-7244 Was $19.99 **$14.99**

Hollywood Stadium Mystery (1938)
Moments before a big championship boxing bout, the contender is found murdered, and a crusading D.A. must find out who knocked him out for good. Neil Hamilton (Commissioner Gordon on TV's "Batman"), Reed Hadley, Evelyn Venable star. 66 min.
68-8130 **$19.99**

Inspector Hornleigh (1939)
Often hilarious British crime yarn about a Scotland Yard inspector (Gordon Harker) and his bumbling sidekick (Alastair Sim) trailing a foreign millionaire who's stolen budget plans from the Chancellery. 76 min.
68-8200 **$19.99**

A Shot In The Dark (1933)
At the reading of the will of a much-despised miser, only the cagey reverend believes murder, not suicide, was the cause of the old man's death. O.B. Clarence stars. 53 min.
68-8220 **$19.99**

Star Reporter (1939)
The inheritor of a metropolitan newspaper learns a devastating secret about himself while waging a crusade against the gangsters who murdered his publisher dad. Warren Hull and Marsha Hunt are featured. 62 min.
68-8269 **$19.99**

I'll Name The Murderer (1936)
Dateline Our Town: Although local flatfoots have failed to produce a suspect in the murder case of a popular club crooner here, this reporter vows to name names in my next column. Stay tuned, crime-dirt fans! Ralph Forbes stars.
68-8270 **$19.99**

Danger On The Air (1938)
A quick-witted radio engineer solves the murder of a womanizing ad sponsor that occurs during the climax of a live radio broadcast. Donald Woods and Lee J. Cobb star. 70 min.
68-8272 **$19.99**

The Shadow (1939)
Novelist Reggie Ogden ("The Shadow" as he is known to the evil underworld) helps Scotland Yard put a stop to a murdering blackmailer. A very rare and atmospheric thriller starring Henry Kendall and Elizabeth Allan. 63 min.
68-8325 **$19.99**

"X" Marks The Spot (1931)
Realistic newspaper crime drama stars Wallace Ford (in a role originally intended for Walter Winchell) as a Broadway columnist implicated in the murder of a showgirl who had filed a libel lawsuit against his paper. Co-stars Lew Cody, Sally Blane. 68 min.
68-8425 **$19.99**

Monte Carlo Nights (1934)
A man convicted of murder must find the true culprit in this edge-of-your-seat suspense yarn. The police trail him and time's running out. John Darrow, Mary Brian star. 60 min.
68-8426 **$19.99**

The Dark Hour (1936)
A pair of detectives convene the likely suspects in the attempted murder of an already dead man. Ray Walker stars as one of the gumshoes, and gossip columnist Hedda Hopper makes an appearance as a supposed murderess. 72 min.
68-8077 **$19.99**

Now Or Never (1935)
Richard Talmadge plays a dual role in this crime thriller about a man who meets his double, a shady jewelry broker, and winds up accused of the jeweler's murder and on the run from gangsters and the police. With Janet Chandler, Robert Walker.
68-9251 **$19.99**

Black Gold (1936)
A thrilling mystery set against the backdrop of oil drilling. Frankie Darro and Roy Mason star in this suspenser that mixes guns and gushers.
68-8461 Was $19.99 **$14.99**

Secrets Of Chinatown (1935)
Eerie, supernatural-flavored suspenser about a mystical Chinese cult that's launching a brutal crime wave of drugs, violence and murder. A detective and his friend try to get to the bottom of the crime spree and rescue a woman who's been abducted and hypnotized into serving as the group's high priestess. Nick Stuart, Lucille Browne and Ray Lawrence star.
68-9262 **$19.99**

Special Agent K-7 (1937)
An FBI agent, trying to solve a murder at a local nightclub run by a mobster, finds his investigation hitting close to home when the main suspect turns out to be the lover of a female friend of his. Intriguing thriller stars Walter McGrail, Irving Pichel, Queenie Smith and Duncan Renaldo. 66 min.
68-9266 **$19.99**

The Murder In The Museum (1933)
Interesting low-budget thriller from Hollywood's "Poverty Row," in which a politician investigating drug charges at a circus sideshow is gunned down. A police commissioner embroiled in the mayoral race with the late politician becomes chief suspect in the death, and his daughter joins forces with a reporter to find the real culprit. John Harron, Phyllis Barrington star. 65 min.
68-9281 **$19.99**

They Made Me A Criminal (1939)
John Garfield stars as a boxer who runs when he believes he killed a man. Claude Rains is the detective hot on his trail. The Dead End Kids are perfect as the wayward boys that May Robson is trying to rehabilitate, and Ann Sheridan provides the "oomph" that made her famous. 92 min.
10-2052 Was $19.99 **$14.99**

The Moonstone (1934)
Wilkie Collins' classic thriller involving the search for a priceless ancient gem from India that has been swiped in a creepy old mansion during a thunderstorm. David Manners, Phyllis Barry star.
68-8934 **$19.99**

The Moonstone (1997)
A young woman's bequeathal by her estranged uncle of a fabulous—and cursed—diamond that subsequently vanishes forms the basis of this suspenseful adaptation of Wilkie Collins' novel, one of the first mystery stories. Keeley Hawes, Greg Wise, Patricia Hodge and Anthony Sher, as Sergeant Cuff, star. 120 min.
08-8623 **$19.99**

They Drive By Night (1938)
Unusual, rarely seen atmospheric thriller involving a man who, upon being released from prison, discovers that his girlfriend has been strangled with a silk stocking. After fleeing the area, the man enlists the help of another former girlfriend to help him find the murderer. Emlyn Williams, Ernest Thesiger and Anna Konstam star. 79 min.
68-8871 **$19.99**

High Command (1936)
James Mason and Lionel Atwill star in this intriguing suspense yarn about the investigation into a 16-year-old murder on an island off the African coast. 88 min.
10-1099 Was $19.99 **$14.99**

Murder At Glen Athol (1936)
A party at a stately country manor turns into a deadly whodunit when a series of murders occur. Luckily, a famous detective is among the guests, but can he track down the killer? John Miljan, Irene Ware, Noel Madison star.
68-9227 **$19.99**

Dangerous Female (The Maltese Falcon) (1931)
The first screen filming of Dashiell Hammett's classic mystery stands on its own merits as a faithful and suspenseful adaptation. Ricardo Cortez is suave detective Sam Spade, whose involvement with beautiful but duplicitous client Bebe Daniels draws him into a deadly search for a priceless statue. With Dudley Digges, Otto Matieson, Dwight Frye and Thelma Todd. 79 min.
09-3027 **$19.99**

Murder On The High Seas (1932)
A cruise ship bound for Europe contains all the players in a steamy love triangle, a situation that leads to murder. Natalie Moorehead and Jack Mulhall star. AKA: "Love Bound." 67 min.
68-8176 Was $19.99 **$14.99**

Non-Stop New York (1937)
British crime drama stars Anna Lee as a chorus cutie who accidentally gets mixed up with gangsters and becomes a hobo's alibi when he is framed for a murder. John Loder plays the transatlantic hero who saves her from the mob. 72 min.
68-8192 **$19.99**

DVD VIDEO
ASK ABOUT OUR GIANT DVD CATALOG!

A Shot In The Dark (1935)
What sort of fatal shooting leaves no bullet hole or gunpowder mark, and makes no blasting sound? That's the question faced by Charles Starrett in this tale of murder and conspiracy on a New England campus. 69 min.
68-8075 Was $19.99 **$14.99**

A Face In The Fog (1936)
The cast of a play called "Satan's Bride" is being murdered one-by-one by a hunchbacked fiend. June Collyer and Al St. John are journalists collecting clues to trap the killer. With Lloyd Hughes. 55 min.
68-8076 Was $19.99 **$14.99**

The Saint In New York (1938)/ The Saint Strikes Back (1939)
Writer Leslie Charteris' suave supersleuth, Simon Templar, was first portrayed on screen by Louis Hayward in the debut entry of the popular RKO series, as the Saint is recruited to rid the Big Apple of a crime ring headed by "the Big Fellow." Kay Sutton, Jonathan Hale co-star. Next, George Sanders takes over as Templar, travelling to San Francisco to help Wendy Barrie clear her late detective father's name. With Jerome Cowan, Barry Fitzgerald. 135 min. total.
18-7735 **$19.99**

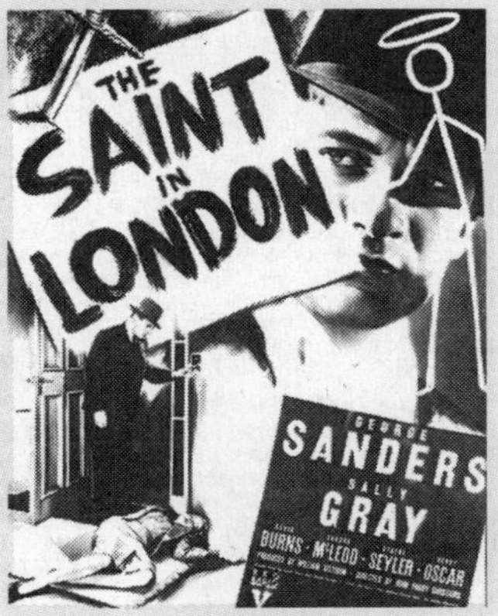
THE SAINT IN LONDON
GEORGE SANDERS
SALLY GRAY

The Saint In London (1939)/ The Saint's Double Trouble (1940)
A multi-million-dollar counterfeiting scheme draws Simon Templar (George Sanders) to England in the first half of a "Saintly" double bill. With Sally Gray, Gordon McLeod. Sanders returns in a dual role, as both Templar and the jewel-smuggling ring boss he's after, in a tale of stolen diamonds, Egyptian mummies and mistaken identities. Helene Whitney, Bela Lugosi co-star. 140 min. total.
18-7736 **$19.99**

The Saint Takes Over (1940)/ The Saint's Vacation (1941)
When police inspector Jonathan Hale is framed by some race-fixing mobsters, George Sanders, as Simon Templar, races in to aid him. Then, Hugh Sinclair steps into the Saint's shoes, but it's anything but a vacation in Switzerland when he gets mixed up in an Axis espionage plot. With Sally Gray, Arthur Macrae. 129 min. total.
18-7737 **$19.99**

The Saint In Palm Springs (1941)/The Saint Meets The Tiger (1943)
In his final series appearance, George Sanders investigates a case where some valuable smuggled stamps lead to murder and a visit to the posh resort of Palm Springs. With Wendy Barrie, Paul Guilfoyle. Next, Hugh Sinclair as the Saint finds a dead man on his doorstep and is led into a gold robbery scheme masterminded by the mysterious Tiger. Jean Gillie, Clifford Evans co-star. 135 min. total.
18-7738 **$19.99**

The Dance Of Death (1960)
After he's threatened by unknown killers, a playboy millionaire enlists the help of a detective. Soon, things get even creepier when prowlers are spotted on the grounds of the playboy's mansion, a guard dog is poisoned and the chauffeur is found brutally murdered. Felix Marten and Francoise Brion star in this French entry in "The Saint" series.
68-9245 **$19.99**

The Saint (1997)
Val Kilmer stars as globe-hopping daredevil and "gentleman thief" Simon Templar in this glossy and thrilling updating of Leslie Charteris' roguish hero. Hired by a Russian crime boss to steal a cold-fusion energy formula from scientist Elisabeth Shue, Kilmer falls for his "victim," and soon both find their lives in danger as they race against time to recover the formula. 118 min.
06-2615 Was $79.99 **$14.99**

The Saint (Letterboxed Version)
Also available in a theatrical, widescreen format.
06-2674 **$14.99**

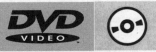

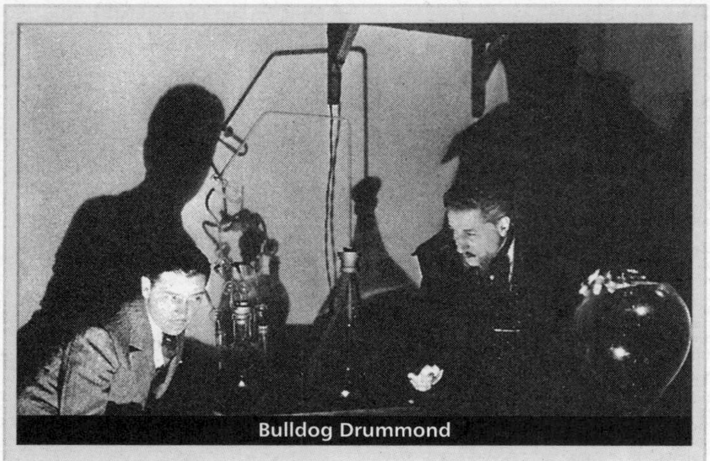
Bulldog Drummond

Bulldog Drummond

Bulldog Drummond (1929)
Ronald Colman stars as the dashing war hero-turned-detective in this rousing adventure thriller, the first sound "Bulldog" film. Joan Bennett is the woman who hires Drummond to rescue her abducted father from a fake asylum, and Claud Allister plays faithful aide Algy. 85 min.
44-1875 Was $19.99 ***$14.99***

Bulldog Jack (1935)
While he recuperates in the hospital, Bulldog Drummond's friend (Jack Hulbert) stands in for him against a gang of jewel thieves. Fay Wray is Jack's lady and Ralph Richardson the ringleader of the crooks. AKA: "Alias Bulldog Drummond." 62 min.
68-8081 ***$19.99***

Bulldog Drummond Escapes (1937)/Bulldog Drummond Comes Back (1937)
Ray Milland is the dashing Drummond, trying to rescue Heather Angel from crooks in "Bulldog Drummond Escapes." Next, John Howard takes over as the sleuth, out to nab terrorists in "Bulldog Drummond Comes Back," co-starring John Barrymore, Reginald Denny. 126 min. total.
22-5837 ***$29.99***

Bulldog Drummond's Peril (1938)/Bulldog Drummond's Revenge (1937)
After a synthetic diamond is sent to him as a wedding gift, Drummond (John Howard) searches for the culprits in "Bulldog Drummond's Peril"; and Howard must then locate a dangerous explosive in "Bulldog Drummond's Revenge." 121 min. total.
22-5838 ***$29.99***

Bulldog Drummond At Bay (1937)
Humor and thrills mix as Bulldog Drummond looks for international gunrunners in search of a special remote-control warplane. With John Lodge, Dorothy Mackhaill. 63 min.
68-8823 ***$19.99***

Bulldog Drummond In Africa (1937)/Arrest Bulldog Drummond (1939)
Drummond (John Howard) travels to Africa to release the kidnapped Col. Nielson (H.B. Warner) in "Bulldog Drummond in Africa"; and Howard encounters a death ray machine controlled by a nasty spy in "Arrest Bulldog Drummond." 115 min. total.
22-5839 ***$29.99***

Bulldog Drummond's Secret Police (1939)/Bulldog Drummond's Bride (1939)
Dashing John Howard searches for a treasure hidden beneath a castle in "Bulldog Drummond's Secret Police"; and in "Bulldog Drummond's Bride," Howard's honeymoon with Heather Angel is interrupted by one last adventure. 110 min. total.
22-5840 ***$29.99***

The Bulldog Drummond Collector's Series
Mystery fans won't want to miss this deluxe four-tape boxed set that includes "Bulldog Drummond Escapes," "Bulldog Drummond Comes Back," "Bulldog Drummond's Revenge," "Bulldog Drummond's Peril," "Bulldog Drummond in Africa," "Arrest Bulldog Drummond," "Bulldog Drummond's Secret Police" and "Bulldog Drummond's Bride."
22-5881 ***$94.99***

Jim Hanvey, Detective (1937)
Based on a "Saturday Evening Post" story, this whodunit stars Guy Kibbee as the title sleuth, hired by an insurance company to look into the disappearance of a valuable emerald. With Tom Brown, Lucie Kaye. 71 min.
09-5329 ***$19.99***

Cipher Bureau (1938)
Intriguing pre-WWII espionage drama chronicles the efforts of U.S. Intelligence Agency code-crackers to break up a ring of German spies. Leon Ames and Joan Woodbury star. 64 min.
09-5330 ***$19.99***

The Hate Ship (1930)
The title vessel is a Russian count's yacht, and a con man launches a phony oil well scheme as part of his part to claim the ship for himself. Thriller stars Jameson Thomas, Henry Victor, Jean Colin. 60 min.
09-5333 ***$19.99***

The Phantom Express (1932)
J. Farrell MacDonald and William Collier star in this railroad thriller! A top locomotive driver is terrorized by a ghost train haunting a mountain track. 65 min.
10-3083 ***$19.99***

It Could Happen To You (1937)
Author Nathanael West ("Day of the Locust") co-wrote the screenplay from his short story about a young man's involvement with the wrong element, which ultimately determines his fate. Alan Baxter, Andrea Leeds star. 64 min.
10-3162 ***$19.99***

Mr. Moto's Last Warning (1939)
Peter Lorre stars as the soft-spoken Japanese sleuth created by Delaware's John P. Marquand, foiling a plot to sabotage the French fleet as it passes through the Suez Canal. With George Sanders, Virginia Field, John Carradine. 71 min.
10-4019 ***$19.99***

The House Of Mystery (1934)
A group of people gather in a creepy mansion after an ancient, cursed Indian temple has been violated and before long discover that they may be the curse's next victims. Gabby Hayes, Brandon Hurst and Ed Lowry star.
10-7157 ***$19.99***

Convicted (1931)
Well-crafted murder mystery unfolding aboard a luxury liner that centers around the death of a producer, and his ex-lover (Aileen Pringle), who stands out as the number one suspect. Co-stars Richard Tucker and Wilfred Lucas. 63 min.
10-7162 Was $19.99 ***$14.99***

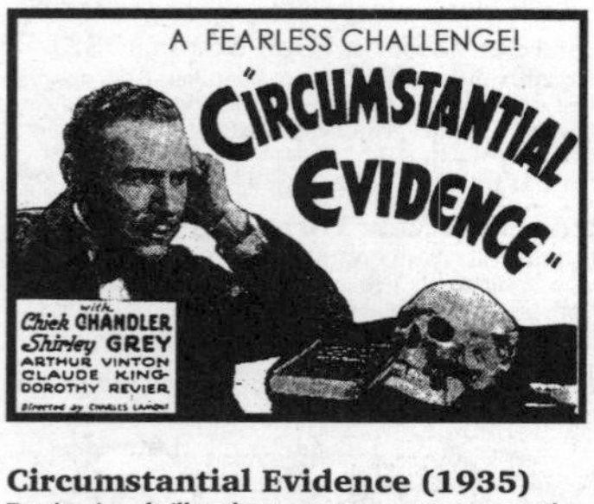
A FEARLESS CHALLENGE!
"CIRCUMSTANTIAL EVIDENCE"
Chick CHANDLER
Shirley GREY
ARTHUR VINTON
CLAUDE KING
DOROTHY REVIER

Circumstantial Evidence (1935)
Fascinating thriller about a newspaper reporter who, for a story, plants evidence implicating him in the death of a colleague whom he hides away until the story's over. But when the friend is found dead, guess who becomes the prime suspect? Chick Chandler, Shirley Grey star. 69 min.
68-8902 ***$19.99***

Woman In The Shadows (1934)
Fay Wray, Ralph Bellamy, Melvyn Douglas and Roscoe Ates star in this intriguing melodrama with hints of film noir. Bellamy plays an ex-con whose life is disrupted when Wray enters his cabin during a storm. 70 min.
09-1741 Was $29.99 ***$14.99***

The Secrets Of Wu Sin (1932)
Beguiling crime drama about a suicidal writer (Lois Wilson) given a fresh start by a newspaper editor (Grant Withers) who assigns her a story that takes her into the heart of Chinatown to investigate a smuggling ring involving Chinese workers. 65 min.
10-7158 ***$19.99***

Prison Train (1938)
A ruthless bootlegger is sentenced to 90 years in Alcatraz and is hustled onto the titular transcontinental. A rival with vengeance on his mind is out to make sure that it's his last ride anywhere...and the word is passed to the other cons on the train! Superlative suspense with Fred Keating, Linda Winters. 63 min.
09-2034 Was $29.99 ***$24.99***

Vengeance (1937)
A cop resigns from the force in disgrace because of his inability to fire his gun at fleeing robbers. Has he really turned yellow...or is it a part of a scheme to infiltrate the gang and destroy them from within? Lyle Talbot stars. AKA: "What Price Vengeance?" 55 min.
09-2036 Was $24.99 ***$14.99***

The Phantom Broadcast (1933)
Unusual murder-mystery outing about a hunchbacked singer who hires a handsome stand-in for public appearances. When a beautiful woman falls in love with the substitute, his employer considers murder. Ralph Forbes and Viviene Osborne star. AKA: "Phantom of the Air." 71 min.
09-2118 ***$19.99***

One Frightened Night (1935)
A fine mystery from Mascot Pictures, a company best known for producing serials. An elderly man gathers his relatives together for the reading of his will. All the relatives stand to cash in unless the old man's granddaughter appears, but strange incidents get in the way of the inheritance. Charley Grapewin, Mary Carlisle and Arthur Hohl star. 67 min.
09-2317 Was $19.99 ***$14.99***

Alias Mary Smith (1932)
It's up to some reporters to save the day when a key set of fingerprints needed to solve a murder vanish in this mystery. John Darrow, Gwen Lee, Raymond Hatton star. 61 min.
09-5326 Was $19.99 ***$14.99***

Midnight Phantom (1935)
Fine whodunit featuring Reginald Denny as a police lieutenant in love with Diane Sullivan, daughter of a controversial police chief. When Denny discovers that his half-brother is responsible for a robbery, he decides to save his romance by concealing the culprit's identity, but this leads to other problems. Claudia Dell, Lloyd Hughes also star. 58 min.
09-2400 ***$14.99***

The Phantom (1931)
A mysterious character known as "The Phantom" escapes from prison, then begins threatening the life of the district attorney responsible for his incarceration. A young newspaper reporter engaged to the D.A.'s daughter decides to uncover the Phantom's secret. Guinn Williams, Allene Ray star. 62 min.
09-2944 ***$14.99***

Speed Limited (1935)
Fast-paced crime story about a G-man who falls in love with a beautiful woman who happens to be an heiress. When the heiress gets involved with a gangster's moll, both she and the agent are in trouble with a group of nasty hoods. Ralph Graves, Claudia Dell and Evelyn Brent star. 50 min.
09-2979 Was $19.99 ***$14.99***

Captured In Chinatown (1935)
Exciting thriller set in L.A.'s Chinatown, where romance blooms between members of warring families. A veteran reporter and his novice female sidekick get embroiled in danger when thugs capture her and swipe a $50,000 necklace meant to be used as a wedding gift. Exciting thriller stars Marion Schilling and Tarzan the Police Dog. 53 min.
09-2987 ***$14.99***

Murder At The Vanities (1934)
A killer is trying to bring the curtain down early on a musical staged at Earl Carroll's Vanities in this murder mystery. With tough-as-nails detective Victor McLaglen on the case everyone's a suspect, including the show's stars (Kitty Carlisle and Carl Brisson). Duke Ellington provides the music. 91 min.
07-1489 Was $59.99 ***$14.99***

Ellis Island (1936)
After three foreigners convicted in a million-dollar bank heist are released from jail and sent to Ellis Island for deportation, they are visited by scheming relatives, gangsters and government officials after the never-recovered loot. Unusual "B"-thriller mixes suspense and comedy. Donald Cook, Peggy Shannon, Jack La Rue star. 67 min.
09-3029 ***$19.99***

Calling All Marines (1939)
Donald "Red" Barry is a young gangster who gets a job working for a spy ring. His first assignment: steal plans for an aerial torpedo from the Marines. After double-crosses, deception and imprisonment, the hood sees the error of his ways and decides to join the Marines and catch the conspiratorial creeps who enlisted him. 67 min.
09-5096 ***$19.99***

Before Morning (1933)
Leo Carrillo of "The Cisco Kid" fame stars in this thriller about the wife and mistresses of a poisoned man who set out to find the person responsible. Can the killer be the police inspector, and if so, why? With Lora Baxter, Taylor Holmes. 56 min.
09-5095 ***$19.99***

Strange Boarders (1938)
After a bag lady carrying secret airplane blueprints is murdered, a special agent investigates by taking a room at the boardinghouse where she lived and soon learns incredible things about her neighbors. Tom Walls, Renee Saint-Cyr and Googie Withers star. 74 min.
09-5110 ***$19.99***

The Rogues' Tavern (1936)
The wedding of a young couple is disrupted by a string of gruesome murders near a wayside inn that were mistakenly attributed to a bloodthirsty wolf-dog. Gripping mystery thriller stars Wallace Ford and Barbara Pepper. 67 min.
10-7068 ***$19.99***

Navy Spy (1937)
Exciting espionage tale stars Conrad Nagel in the title role, called in to track down a naval officer who was kidnapped by foreign agents after a top-secret formula. With Eleanor Hunt, Jack Doyle. 56 min.
10-8361 ***$19.99***

Black Limelight (1938)
Crackerjack British thriller in which a faithful wife (Joan Marion) helps clear her husband (Raymond Massey) of charges he murdered his mistress. Walter Hudd also stars in this atmospheric mystery.
10-8445 Was $19.99 ***$14.99***

Murder With Pictures (1936)
A young newspaper reporter attempts to clear the name of his girlfriend, who has been accused of murder. Meanwhile, a group of mobsters have placed one of their own hoods on the paper as a photographer whose camera features a hidden gun. Will the newsman get the evidence before the crook? Lew Ayres, Gail Patrick and Joyce Compton star.
10-8447 ***$19.99***

International Crime (1937)
Who knows what evil lurks in the hearts of men? The Shadow knows, and so will you when you see Rod LaRocque as the mysterious crimefighter in this rare find from the '30s. With beautiful companion Margot in hand, the Shadow foils a dastardly plot. 63 min.
10-7191 ***$19.99***

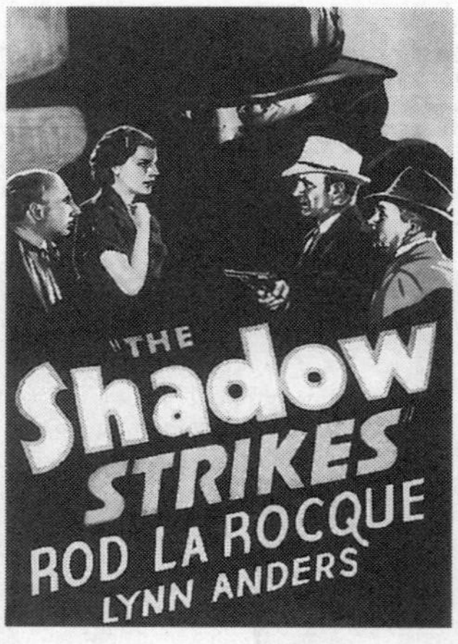
THE
Shadow
STRIKES
ROD LA ROCQUE
LYNN ANDERS

The Shadow Strikes (1937)
If the sinister "Shadow" is truly the crooked robber police say he is, then why are a killer and a crime overlord also trying to stop him? Join star Rod La Rocque as he proves "the weed of crime bears bitter fruit." 61 min.
68-8113 Was $19.99 ***$14.99***

The Shadow Returns (1946)
The Shadow knows in this case involving stolen jewels and a secret formula for plastics. Kane Richmond, Barbara Reed and Tom Dugan star in this thrilling crime yarn. 61 min.
10-8096 ***$19.99***

The Invisible Avenger (1958)
Recently rediscovered tale of "The Shadow" finds sleuth Lamont Cranston following up on the murder of a New Orleans jazzman, a course that leads to an exiled Latin American dictator. Richard Derr stars. 60 min.
68-8208 Was $19.99 ***$14.99***

The Shadow (1994)
The popular phantom crimestopper of radio and pulp magazine fame is memorably brought to the screen by Alec Baldwin in this splashy thriller. The Shadow, the mysterious alter-ego of Lamont Cranston, matches wits with evil Shiwan Khan, a descendant of warlord Genghis Khan, in 1930s New York City. Penelope Ann Miller, John Lone, Tim Curry and Peter Boyle also star. 108 min.
07-2220 Was $19.99 ***$14.99***

Sucker Money (1933)
Reports of fakes and cons in the spiritualist racket lead a skeptical newsman to the trail of a phony swami. Mischa Auer plays the fraudulent, table-rapping medium in this topical crime exposé about fools and their money. 70 min.
68-8070 *$14.99*

Murder On The Campus (1934)
A newspaper reporter, investigating a story on college students, gets tangled up in a murder plot, and a pretty student and a professor try to find the real culprit of the crime in this excellent "B" movie. Shirley Grey, Charles Starrett, Maurice Black. 71 min.
68-8073 *$19.99*

Arsenal Stadium Mystery (1939)
After a star soccer player is mysteriously poisoned during an important game, police go into action to uncover the culprit. Lively British thriller stars Leslie Banks and Greta Gynt. 84 min.
68-8463 *$19.99*

The Body Vanished (1939)
Crack British mystery focusing on a corpse that keeps appearing and disappearing from the scene of a crime. What's the secret behind this bizarre body? Anthony Hulme and C. Denier Warren star. 46 min.
68-8535 Was $19.99 *$14.99*

Devil Diamond (1937)
Two amateur sleuths discover that their lives are in trouble when they attempt to track down a gang of jewel thieves. Kane Richmond, Frankie Darro star.
68-8824 Was $19.99 *$14.99*

The Mystic Circle Murder (1938)
A phony psychic and her assistants lure women to their deaths until a reporter uncovers the scheme. With Robert Fiske, Betty Compson and Mme. Harry Houdini. 69 min.
68-8825 *$19.99*

The King Murder Case (1932)
A detective specializing in high society cases wants to find out who killed a beautiful extortionist. There's few clues and no murder weapon, forcing the sleuth to take an unusual route to solve the mystery. Conway Tearle, Marceline Day star. AKA: "The King Murder." 67 min.
68-8892 *$19.99*

Tangled Destinies (1932)
After a plane is forced to land, its passengers and two pilots take refuge in a creepy house. Soon, one of the group is shot and the search is on to find the culprit. Diamonds, deceit and detectives are the elements of this suspenser starring Lloyd Whitlock, Doris Hill and Glenn Tryon. 64 min.
68-8900 *$19.99*

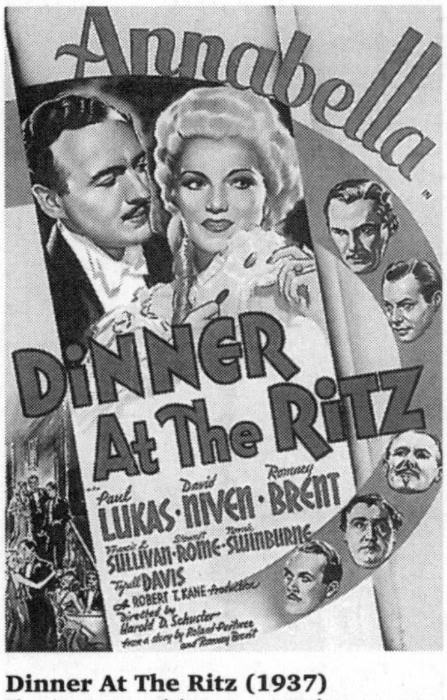
Annabella
DINNER At The RITZ
Paul LUKAS · David NIVEN · Romney BRENT
SULLIVAN · ROME · SWINBURNE
DAVIS

Dinner At The Ritz (1937)
There's mystery and danger amongst the smart set, as a young girl turns sleuth to find her father's killer. David Niven, Annabella and Paul Lukas star in this thriller. 77 min.
08-8073 Was $19.99 *$14.99*

Night Birds (1930)
While searching for a crook called "Flash Jack," a Scotland Yard detective encounters another sleuth on the case and the criminal's mistress, with whom he has an affair. Jack Raine, Muriel Angelus and Jameson Thomas star. 86 min.
68-8891 *$19.99*

Cheers Of The Crowd (1936)
A series of murderous chain letters draws the attention of a publicity expert who tries to find out who is behind the letters. Russell Hopton and Irene Ware star. 62 min.
09-5097 *$19.99*

Make-Up (1937)
Big top whodunit has more plot twists than three rings can hold, from a doctor-turned-clown to a society girl attacked by an elephant and the murder of a lion tamer. Nils Ashter, Judy Kelly star. 72 min.
10-7163 Was $19.99 *$14.99*

The President's Mystery (1936)
Suggested by Franklin Roosevelt for Liberty Magazine, this is the story of a society lawyer who drops out of his high-living environment to become a sleuth on life's lower rungs. Hollywood-basher Nathanael West ("Day of the Locust") included this among his reluctant screenplays. Henry Wilcox, Betty Furness star. 80 min.
68-8096 *$19.99*

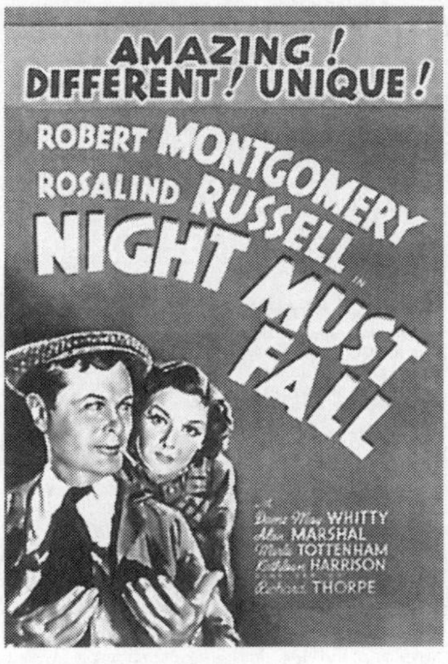
AMAZING! DIFFERENT! UNIQUE!
ROBERT MONTGOMERY
ROSALIND RUSSELL
NIGHT MUST FALL
WHITTY
MARSHAL
TOTTENHAM
HARRISON
THORPE

Night Must Fall (1937)
Creepy thriller starring Dame May Whitty as a domineering, wheelchair-bound grande dame living in a cottage in scenic Essex, England, who discovers that a female guest at a nearby inn has been murdered. Along with niece Rosalind Russell, she tries to figure out who's the culprit. Robert Montgomery is the new handyman, a former worker at the inn. 105 min.
12-2953 *$19.99*

The Mandarin Mystery (1937)
This Republic Pictures entry in the Ellery Queen mystery series stars Eddie Quillan as the famous detective. Hunting for a priceless Chinese Mandarin stamp, Queen discovers a counterfeiting ring, and love. With Charlotte Henry, Franklin Pangborn. 65 min.
68-8099 *$19.99*

Sing Sing Nights (1935)
Three men confess to the murder of a newsman whose body is recovered with three bullets in it. A newly invented lie detector exonerates two of them, and earns the other a death sentence. Conway Tearle stars. 60 min.
68-8102 Was $19.99 *$14.99*

Dangerous Appointment (1934)
A robbery is committed and a witness left for dead, with the blame for the deed falling on the head of an innocent department store clerk. Cowboy serial star Charles Starrett and Dorothy Wilson head this crime drama.
68-8103 Was $19.99 *$14.99*

Daughter Of The Tong (1939)
A crime drama starring Grant Withers that celebrates the courageous deeds of the F.B.I. and the dedication of its famous director. A Chinese dragon lady rules with a murderous hand her group of waterfront smugglers. 56 min.
68-8128 Was $19.99 *$14.99*

I Met A Murderer (1939)
James Mason is a man on the run, having murdered his shrewish wife in a moment of outrage. After time, his apparent impunity is threatened by a pretty novelist, whom he suspects has learned his sensational secret. 79 min.
68-8129 Was $19.99 *$14.99*

Kelly Of The Secret Service (1936)
The top-secret plans for a guided missile are stolen and Secret Service agent Ted Kelly attempts to find it. The investigation leads him into a creepy mansion filled with secret passageways and weird characters. Atmospheric, first-rate mystery also stars Lloyd Hughes, Sheila Manors and Fuzzy Knight.
68-8875 *$19.99*

Murder At Midnight (1931)
Mystery buffs will appreciate this intense thriller in which a room full of people are killed one by one, beginning with a deadly game of charades. Stars Aileen Pringle, Alice White and Robert Elliott. 69 min.
10-7066 *$19.99*

Death From A Distance (1936)
It's murder under the star-stuff, when a detective and a newsman head out to a mountaintop observatory and discover a veritable black hole of suspicious astronomers. Russell Hopton, Lola Lane star. 73 min.
68-8064 *$19.99*

Murder At Dawn (1932)
A man and woman about to be married go to the woman's professor father's strange hideaway for his consent. Little do they know Dad's been working on a powerful death ray, and trouble soon ensues. There's trap doors, neat special effects and more in this interesting thriller. Jack Mulhall, Josephine Dunn star.
68-9064 *$19.99*

Terror By Night (1931)
A wealthy, philandering husband, a posh penthouse apartment, a murdered suspect and the police arrest of the wrong man are the elements of this first-rate, rarely-seen thriller starring Una Merkel, ZaSu Pitts and Nat Pendleton. AKA: "The Secret Witness." 65 min.
68-8958 *$19.99*

The House Of The Spaniard (1936)
A clerk at an old English house discovers that his boss is a Spanish revolutionary involved in a counterfeiting ring and soon finds himself kidnapped and imprisoned in Spain. The revolutionary's daughter helps the clerk escape, leading to a series of exciting situations. Peter Haddon, Jean Galland and Brigitte Horney star. 70 min.
68-8962 *$19.99*

The Drums Of Jeopardy (1931)
In the same year he began the "Charlie Chan" series, Warner Oland starred as a doctor who tracks a family through Czarist Russia and into the U.S., so they will answer to the murder of his daughter. AKA: "Mark of Terror." 65 min.
68-8024 *$19.99*

The Crooked Circle (1932)
Spitfire ZaSu Pitts heats up this comedy-mystery stew about a sinister swami and the sleuths pursuing him. James Gleason provides slapstick fun as a baffled policeman. 68 min.
68-8045 *$19.99*

The Midnight Warning (1932)
Recently returned from the Orient, a woman finds her brother has vanished. When the police can discover no evidence that this man ever existed, she begins to doubt her own sanity. Claudia Dell, William (Stage) Boyd star. 63 min.
68-8048 Was $19.99 *$14.99*

Chinatown After Dark (1931)
A pair of ruthless Chinese gangsters kidnaps a white girl and raises her after their image of a wicked Dragon Lady. Grown to maturity, she is an unstoppable hellion in pursuit of a valuable jeweled dagger. Barbara Kent, Rex Lease star. 56 min.
68-8049 Was $19.99 *$14.99*

The Intruder (1932)
After a murder is committed on a cruise ship, the vessel is shipwrecked on a mysterious jungle island where the survivors face strange sounds, skeletons and other dangers. What's really causing all the commotion, however, is a wild man and a killer gorilla. Monte Blue and Gwenn Lee star in this first-rate thriller.
68-9059 *$19.99*

Blake Of Scotland Yard (1937)
Featurized serial with Ralph Byrd. A newly invented "Death Ray" has been stolen by "The Scorpion" (whose hand is an evil claw), but he is missing an important part. Will "The Scorpion" complete it before Blake discovers his secret identity? 70 min.
09-1368 Was $29.99 *$24.99*

Tomorrow At Seven (1933)
A mysterious killer called "The Black Ace" leaves an ace of spades with each corpse, and mystery writer Neil Broderick attempts to solve the crimes. Chester Morris, Charles Middleton star. 62 min.
09-1567 Was $19.99 *$14.99*

The Wayne Murder Case (1938)
Nifty whodunit about the murder of a millionaire. Who did the deed? The nephew, the housekeeper? Will keep you guessing!!! June Clyde, Regis Toomey. 61 min.
09-1637 Was $24.99 *$19.99*

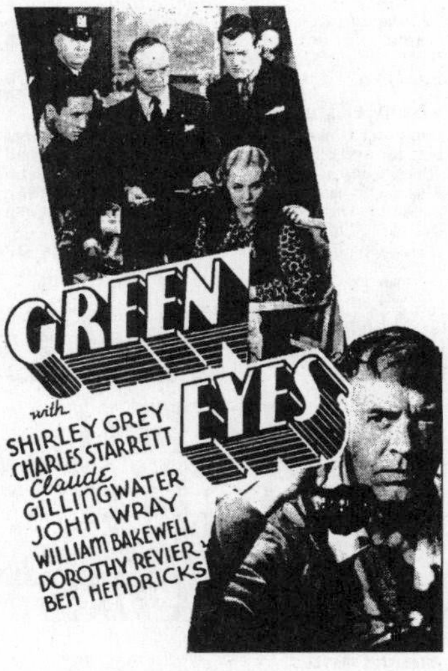
GREEN EYES
with
SHIRLEY GREY
CHARLES STARRETT
Claude GILLINGWATER
JOHN WRAY
WILLIAM BAKEWELL
DOROTHY REVIER
BEN HENDRICKS

Green Eyes (1934)
The host of a costume party given at an elaborate mansion in the country is murdered, and a detective writer attempts to solve the mystery in this suspenseful whodunit. Shirley Grey and Charles Starrett star. 68 min.
68-8901 *$19.99*

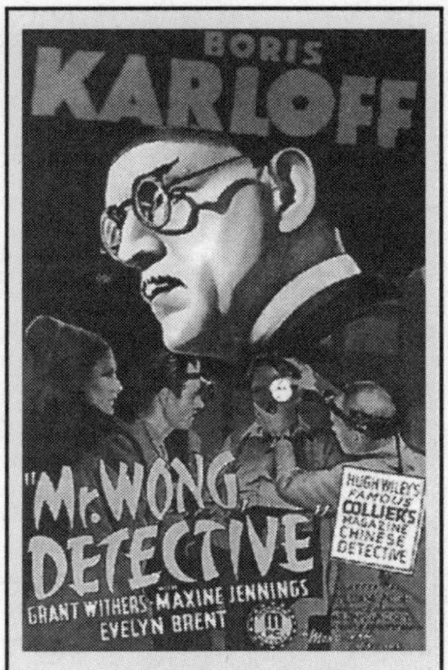
BORIS KARLOFF
"Mr. WONG DETECTIVE"
HUGH WILEY'S FAMOUS COLLIER'S MAGAZINE CHINESE DETECTIVE
GRANT WITHERS · MAXINE JENNINGS
EVELYN BRENT

Mr. Wong, Detective (1938)
Following in the inscrutable footsteps of Charlie Chan and Mr. Moto, Boris Karloff portrayed Chinese-born crimefighter Mr. Wong in a series of classic "whodunits." Here Wong investigates a deadly gas that is also sought by foreign agents. With Grant Withers, John Hamilton. 70 min.
01-1349 *$19.99*

Mr. Wong In Chinatown (1939)
Boris Karloff stars as the wily Oriental sleuth, out to solve the mysterious murder of a Chinese princess. He uncovers an international munitions plot and soon finds himself in danger, too. With Grant Withers, Marjorie Reynolds. 63 min.
10-1160 *$19.99*

The Mystery Of Mr. Wong (1939)
A priceless Chinese sapphire with a death curse is smuggled into America, and only Mr. Wong (Boris Karloff) can find the culprit. With Grant Withers, Craig Reynolds. 69 min.
10-1167 *$19.99*

Doomed To Die (1940)
A mysterious fire destroys a luxury liner with 400 passengers and a fortune in Chinese bonds aboard, and only Mr. Wong (Boris Karloff) can solve the riddle. 67 min.
62-1199 *$19.99*

The Fatal Hour (1940)
The fourth entry in the Mr. Wong series stars Boris Karloff as the inscrutable detective, enlisted by baffled police to solve a series of murders surrounding a smuggling ring. Grant Withers and Marjorie Reynolds also appear. 67 min.
68-8004 *$19.99*

Phantom Of Chinatown (1940)
It's the return of Mr. Wong, in the last film of the series. Keye Luke becomes the first Asian-American actor to play an Asian detective in Hollywood, as he tries to link the murder of an archeologist to a secret message on a Mongolian scroll. With Lotus Long, Grant Withers. 61 min.
68-8127 Was $19.99 *$14.99*

Mr. Wong: Boxed Set
Six "Wongs" make a right when you purchase this six-tape set of whodunits featuring Mr. Wong, the ace detective. Included are Boris Karloff in "Doomed to Die," "The Fatal Hour," "Mr. Wong in Chinatown," "The Mystery of Mr. Wong" and "Mr. Wong, Detective" and Keye Luke in "Phantom of Chinatown."
08-1718 Save $30.00! *$59.99*

Pilot X (1937)
Unusual "B" thriller mixes aerial action and haunted house chills. An unknown flyer in a black plane is shooting down everything in the skies, and the answer to stopping him lies with a group of WWI flying aces invited to spend the weekend in a sinister doctor's mansion. With John Carroll, Lona Andre. AKA: "Death in the Sky."
68-9085 *$19.99*

The Headline Woman (1935)
Gritty newspaper thriller in which a reporter learns that a policeman had a part in a series of murders supervised by the owner of a shady gambling operation. The newspaperman soon finds himself involved in a feud between cops and his publisher, a kidnapping and other surprises. Heather Angel, Roger Pryor, Ford Sterling and Ward Bond star. AKA: "Woman in the Case." 63 min.
09-3002 *$19.99*

Man From Headquarters (1928)
Well-made mystery about a Secret Service agent protecting valuable documents from a ring of foreign spies, but falling for the pretty socialist among them. Cornelius Keefe stars.
68-8239 *$19.99*

Opera

Carmen
The always-exciting opera from Georges Bizet receives a superlative interpretation in this Royal Opera House production. Maria Ewing plays the seductive Gypsy to Luis Lima's Don Jose. Zubin Mehta conducts. 175 min. Subtitled in English.
22-5511 Was $49.99 *$29.99*

Bizet's Carmen (1984)
Opera's classic tale of obsessive, doomed love stars Placido Domingo as the soldier who falls for the sultry schemer Julia Migenes-Johnson and abandons his career to be with her. Lavishly filmed on location in Spain, the opera is sung in French with English subtitles. 152 min.
02-1468 *$19.99*

Wozzeck
Alban Berg's gripping operatic drama about a soldier who vents his jealousy by murdering his mistress. Claudio Abbado conducts the Vienna State Opera; Franz Grundhebers and Hildegard Behrens star. 98 min. With English subtitles.
22-5342 Was $39.99 *$29.99*

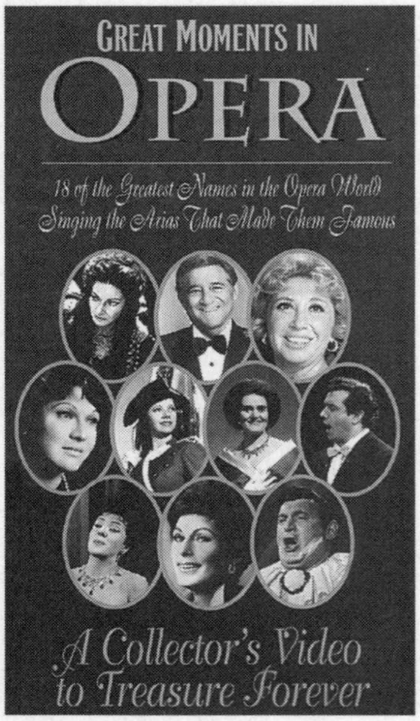

GREAT MOMENTS IN
OPERA
18 of the Greatest Names in the Opera World
Singing the Arias That Made Them Famous
A Collector's Video
to Treasure Forever

Great Moments In Opera
Along with bicycling bears and The Beatles, "The Ed Sullivan Show" brought some of the world's most acclaimed operatic stars into America's homes for over 20 years. This collection of rare performance clips features such notables as Maria Callas, Marilyn Horne, Robert Merrill, Anna Moffo, Lily Pons, Leontyne Price, Beverly Sills, Joan Sutherland, Richard Tucker and others. 95 min.
22-3190 *$29.99*

Operavox
Six of the world's favorite operas have been transformed into inventive short films in this stunning collection that runs the gamut of animation from cartoon and stop-motion to computer-generated graphics. Included on the two-tape set are "The Barber of Seville," "Carmen," "Das Rheingold," "The Magic Flute," "Rigoletto" and "Turandot." 180 min.
50-8461 *$29.99*

All The Great Operas... In 10 Minutes
If you're an opera lover, but don't have enough time to enjoy your favorites, check out this animated video, which presents their essentials in quick and hilarious style. Included are encapsulated versions of "La Traviata," "Carmen," "Don Giovanni," "Aida," "Tosca," "Tristan and Isolde," "Madame Butterfly" and "The Ring of the Nibelung." 10 min.
76-7359 *$14.99*

Samson Et Dalila
Saint-Saen's beautiful retelling of the biblical story of betrayal and redemption receives a sumptuous rendition by the San Francisco Opera. Placido Domingo, Shirley Verrett and Wolfgang Brendel star. 118 min. Subtitled in English.
22-5280 Was $39.99 *$29.99*

The Beggar's Opera
The Who's Roger Daltrey leads a most distinguished cast in this memorable production. John Gay's classic tale of corruption amidst the dregs of 18th-century London is admirably presented by Jonathan Miller. 136 min.
22-5117 Was $39.99 *$29.99*

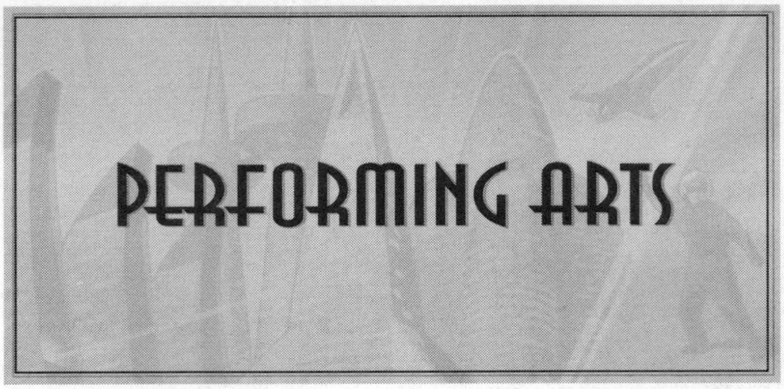

PERFORMING ARTS

Pagliacci (1947)
Leoncavallo's tragic opera about the torment of a clown is magnificently rendered in this rarely seen production featuring Titto Cobbi and Gina Lollabrigida. 105 min. In Italian with English subtitles.
09-5090 *$19.99*

Theodora
The setting of Handel's moving oratorio is updated from ancient Antioch to 20th-century America by noted director Peter Sellars in this Glyndebourne Festival presentation. Dawn Upshaw, David Daniels star. 206 min.
22-1774 *$29.99*

Xerxes
The comic opera by Handel about the loves of the Persian king receives a grand rendering by the English National Opera Company. Sir Charles Mackerras directs; Ann Murray, Christopher Robson, Lesley Garrett star. 187 min. Sung in English.
22-5348 Was $49.99 *$29.99*

Julius Caesar
Handel's provocative history of the Roman conqueror is lovingly re-created by the Berlin State Opera. Theo Adam, Celestina Casapietra star; Peter Schreier conducts. Original German version. 124 min.
22-7020 Was $39.99 *$29.99*

Agrippina (1985)
Handel's opera of the treacherous, power-hungry Roman empress and her schemes to ensure the succession of her son, the evil Nero, stars Barbarba Daniels, Janice Hall and David Kübler. Arnold Ostman conducts the Cologne Opera. 155 min. Sung in Italian with English subtitles.
22-5147 Was $39.99 *$29.99*

L'Africaine
Meyerbeer's historical masterwork concerning Vasco da Gama's voyage to the African coast and his romance with the alluring Sekika is wonderfully performed by Placido Domingo and Shirley Verrett at the San Francisco Opera. 190 min. Subtitled in English.
22-5277 Was $49.99 *$29.99*

La Gioconda
Ponchielli's magnum opus, set against a web of oppression and vengeance in ancient Venice, is strikingly presented by the Vienna State Opera. Placido Domingo, Eva Marton, Ludmila Semtschuk, Kurt Rydl star. 169 min. Subtitled in English.
22-5279 Was $49.99 *$29.99*

Kraus & Bruson Gala Concert
Two greats of the operatic world, tenor Alfredo Kraus and baritone Renato Bruson, take the stage for a memorable concert experience. Included are selections from "Falstaff," "La Boheme," "Lucia di Lammermoor," "Manon Lescaut," "Rigoletto" and more. 87 min.
22-1776 *$19.99*

The Medium (1950)
Composer Gian-Carlo Menotti also wrote the screenplay for and directed this filmed version of his grand opera. The cast includes Leo Coleman, Anna Maria Alberghetti and Marie Powers in the title role, with music by The Symphony Orchestra of Rome Radio Italiana. 80 min. Sung in English.
22-3006 *$39.99*

AMAHL AND THE NIGHT VISITORS

Amahl And The Night Visitors (1978)
A special performance of Gian-Carlo Menotti's Nativity-themed opera, filmed on stage in London and on location in the Holy Land. Teresa Stratas, Giorgio Tozzi, and Robert Saplosky as Amahl star, with music by the Philharmonica Orchestra of London. 60 min.
14-3269 Was $79.99 *$19.99*

Der Rosenkavalier
An all-star ensemble that includes Anna Tomowa-Sintow as Marschallin, Agnes Baltsa as Octavian, and Kurt Moll as Baron Ochs, takes the stage in this rendition of the Strauss opera. Herbert von Karajan conducts the Vienna Philharmonic. Sung in German.
04-5319 *$44.99*

Der Rosenkavalier
London's Royal Opera House production of the operatic romantic farce by Strauss stars Dame Kiri Te Kanawa, Aage Haugland, Anne Howells; Sir Georg Solti conducts. 200 min. Sung in German with English subtitles.
22-5083 Was $49.99 *$29.99*

Der Rosenkavalier
Ildiko Komlosi sings the title role of Octavian, the "cavalier of the rose," in this lush rendition of Strauss' rollicking operatic tale of courtly love and deception in 18th-century Vienna. Directed by Pier Luigi Pizzi and featuring the Orchestra of the Massimo Theatre, Palermo. 150 min.
50-8574 *$29.99*

Der Rosenkavalier (1962)
A stirring performance of Strauss' opera taped at the Salzburg Festival, with a cast that includes famed performers Elisabeth Schwarzkopf, Sena Jurinac, Otto Edelmann and the Vienna Philharmonic Orchestra. 190 min. on two tapes. Sung in German.
22-3008 Was $59.99 *$29.99*

Elektra
Richard Strauss' compelling musical interpretation of Sophocles' tale of horror, murder and revenge receives a brilliant treatment by the Vienna Philharmonic. Brigitte Fassbänder, Cheryl Studer and Eva Marton are featured. 109 min. Subtitled in English.
22-5425 Was $39.99 *$29.99*

Salome
Richard Strauss' adaptation of Oscar Wilde's poetic play is filled with decadence, lavish sets and stirring singing. Maria Ewing turns in a tour-de-force performance as the title character, while Michael Devlin and Kenneth Riegel co-star as Herod and Jokannan. 105 min. In German with English subtitles.
22-5711 Was $39.99 *$29.99*

Andrea Chenier
In one of his favorite roles, famed tenor Placido Domingo stars alongside Anna Tomowa-Sintow in Giordano's tale of the idealistic poet caught up in the French Revolution. Performed at London's Royal Opera House in Covent Garden. 120 min. Sung in Italian with English subtitles.
22-5079 *$29.99*

Andrea Chenier (1985)
Set during the tumultuous French Revolution, Giordano blends romance and intrigue in his grand opera, starring Jose Carreras and Eva Marton; performed at La Scala in Italy. 130 min. Sung in Italian with English subtitles.
22-5017 Was $39.99 *$29.99*

The Beggar Student
Wonderful Hungarian production of Milocker's comic operetta about a young man freed from jail by a vengeful aristocrat who wants the student to seduce and abandon a woman who spurned his advances. Tivadar Horvath, Marika Nemeth star. 90 min. In Hungarian with English subtitles.
53-7243 *$39.99*

Sherrill Milnes: An All-Star Gala
Famed operatic baritone Sherrill Milnes is honored in a special evening of music. Guests include Placido Domingo and Staatskapelle Berlin and the London Symphony Orchestra, with music from "La Traviata," "Don Carlos," and "Up in Central Park." Burt Lancaster hosts. 56 min.
22-3037 Was $29.99 *$24.99*

Der Freischutz
A young would-be marksman becomes a success, thanks to magic bullets he's given as part of a pact with the devil, in this opera by Carl Maria von Weber, performed at the Staatsoper Stuttgart. Toni Kramer, Caterina Ligendza star. 150 min. Sung in German with English subtitles.
22-5084 Was $39.99 *$29.99*

Rusalka
Dvorák's mystical fantasy is imaginatively transferred to an Edwardian context, and the heroine presented as an adolescent girl filled with longing, in this David Pountney production. Intriguing English National Opera presentation stars Eilene Hannan, Rodney Macann. 160 min. Sung in English.
22-5120 *$29.99*

Rossini: Il Barbiere Di Siviglia
Filmed live at the Stuttgart Opera House, this sumptuous presentation of Rossini's comic romp features Cecilia Bartoli as Rosina, Gino Quilico as Figaro, Carlos Feller as Bartolo, and David Kuebler as Count Almaviva. 159 min.
02-7996 *$29.99*

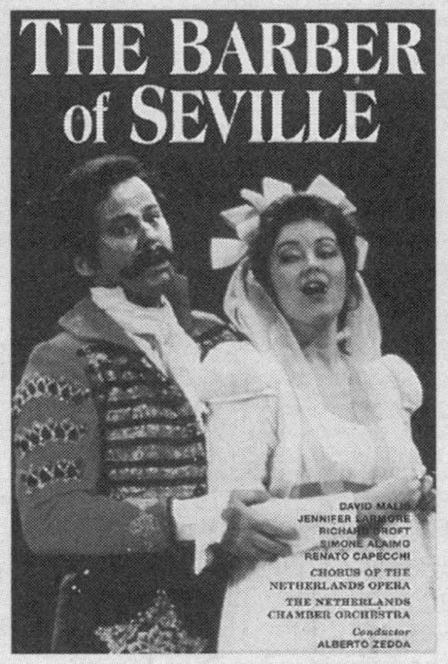

THE BARBER of SEVILLE
DAVID MALIS
JENNIFER LARMORE
SIMONE ALAIMO
RENATO CAPECCHI
CHORUS OF THE NETHERLANDS OPERA
THE NETHERLANDS CHAMBER ORCHESTRA
Conductor
ALBERTO ZEDDA

The Barber Of Seville
One of the world's best-loved operas, Rossini's comical tale of a love-starved count and the crafty barber who helps him is presented by the Netherlands Opera. Richard Croft plays Count Almaviva, Jennifer Larmore is Rosina, and David Malis is Figaro. 154 min.
22-1767 *$29.99*

Il Barbiere Di Siviglia
The course of true love runs smooth, with a little help from the titular chin-chopper, in Rossini's gem of operatic comedy. With Maria Ewing, John Rawnsley and Max-Rene Cosotti at England's Glyndebourne Festival. 155 min. Sung in Italian with English subtitles.
22-5082 Was $49.99 *$29.99*

Rossini: L'Italiana In Algeri
Rossini's elaborate opera receives a grand translation in this production from the Stuttgart Opera House starring Gunther von Kannen as Mustafa, Nuccia Focile as Elvira, Susan McLean as Zulima, and Robert Gambill as Lindoro. 149 min.
02-7997 *$14.99*

Semiramide
The Metropolitan Opera's production of Rossini's work includes a definitive contemporary cast that includes Marilyn Horne, June Anderson and Samuel Ramey. 220 min.
22-1417 Was $39.99 *$29.99*

La Gazza Ladra
Rossini's brilliant mix of tragedy and comedy about a woman facing death after being falsely accused of stealing. Ileana Cotrubas stars as the put-upon servant girl and Bruno Bartoletti directs this Cologne Opera production. 176 min. Subtitled in English.
22-5338 Was $49.99 *$29.99*

William Tell
The tale of the legendary Swiss archer was set to music by Rossini for his final opera. Chris Merritt and Sheryl Studer star in this La Scala production, under the direction of Riccardo Muti. 239 min. Sung in Italian with English subtitles.
22-5614 *$49.99*

La Cenerentola (1948)
Masterful filming of Rossini's adaptation of "Cinderella" boasts splendid vocals by Fedora Barbieri and Afro Poli and the talents of the Rome Opera, under Oliviero de Fabritiis' direction. In Italian with English narration between arias. 94 min.
22-7023 Was $29.99 *$19.99*

Rossini: Tancredi (1992)
Rossini's masterful opera receives a splendid treatment in this dazzling production that features Bernadette Manca di Nissa and Raul Gimenez along with the composer's alternate endings.
02-8142 *$29.99*

La Donna Del Lago (1992)
This rarely staged opera, which Rossini based on Sir Walter Scott's narrative poem "The Lady of the Lake," receives a spectacular production from La Scala with Riccardo Muti conducting. June Anderson, Rockwell Blake and Chris Merritt are the featured performers; staging is handled by German film director Werner Herzog. 167 min. Sung in Italian with English subtitles.
22-5773 *$49.99*

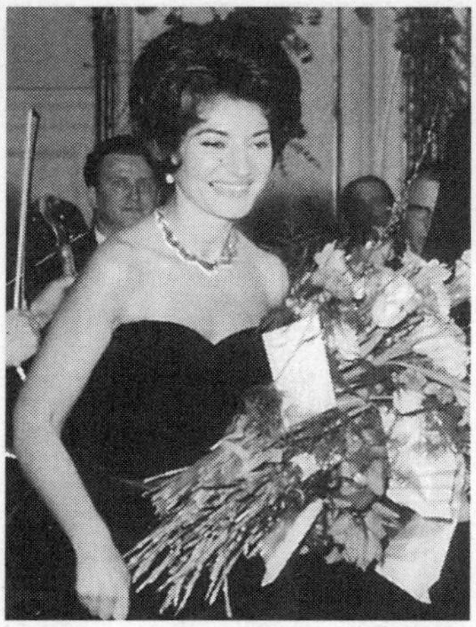

Maria Callas
An exhaustive look at the life of "La Divina Assoluta"—one of the most remarkable singers of all time. With moving musical footage, interviews and location filming, Callas' rise to the top of the opera world, her marriage to Meneghini, her romance with Aristotle Onassis and her lonely final years are traced. Directed by Tony Palmer. 92 min.
22-1430 *$19.99*

Maria Callas At Covent Garden (1962/1964)
A treat for Callas fans, this special double feature includes the diva's "comeback" London recital, followed by a rare concert filming featuring Callas performing Act II of "Tosca" at Covent Garden with Tito Gobbi.
44-4106 *$24.99*

Maria Callas In Concert: Hamburg, 1959 And 1962
A special double bill of live appearances by one of the greatest singers of the century. Backed by Hamburg's NDR Orchestra, Callas performs arias from "The Barber of Seville," "Carmen," "Don Carlo," "La Cenerentola," "La Forza del Destino" and more. 119 min.
44-4130 *$24.99*

Maria Callas: Life And Art (1999)
Fascinating video documentary looks at the life and career of the world's most famous diva. Excerpts from Callas' performances, including "Tosca," "Norma" and "La Traviata," are featured, along with film clips and interviews with friends and colleagues. 78 min.
44-4099 *$24.99*

Gershwin: Porgy And Bess (1992)
George and Ira Gershwin's beloved opera depicting life among the poor black residents of Charleston, South Carolina's "Catfish Row" was performed by the Glyndebourne Festival Opera company at London's Royal Opera at Covent Garden. Classic songs like "Summertime," "Bess, You Is My Woman Now" and "It Ain't Necessarily So" are featured, and the cast includes Willard White, Cynthia Haymon and Damon Evans.
44-4075 *$34.99*

Eugene Onegin
Only the legendary Kirov Opera in Leningrad could produce this brilliant version of Tchaikovsky's most lyrical opera, performed in the original Russian and starring Sergei Leyferkus as Onegin and Tatiana Novikova as Tanya. In Russian with English subtitles. 155 min.
22-1119 Was $39.99 *$19.99*

Euegne Onegin
A young woman opens her heart to a callous rake who spurns her love, but years later comes to regret his mistake, in Tchaikovsky's moving opera. Vladimir Glushchak, Michael Konig and Orla Boylan star in this European Union Opera presentation, performed at the Festspielhaus in Baden-Baden. 149 min.
22-1773 *$29.99*

Eugene Onegin (1958)
Spectacular outdoor settings and the performances of Ivan Petrov and Galina Vishnevskaya are some of the highlights of this Bolshoi film effort depicting Tchaikovsky's romantic opera. 108 min. In Russian with English subtitles.
53-7176 Was $39.99 *$19.99*

The Queen Of Spades
This Glyndebourne Festival production of the moody, dramatic Tchaikovsky opera features a stellar international cast that includes Yuri Marusin, Nancy Gustafson and Sergei Leiferkus. 171 min. Sung in Russian with English subtitles.
22-5682 Was $49.99 *$29.99*

The Queen Of Spades (1960)
Pushkin's ironic tale of greed and obsession, set to music by Tchaikovsky, becomes an unforgettable example of opera on film, courtesy of the Bolshoi. Filmed on location in St. Petersburg. 102 min. In Russian with English subtitles.
53-7179 Was $39.99 *$19.99*

Music From Wagner's "Ring"
Erich Leinsdorf takes the podium in this all-Wagner program that includes selections from "The Ring of the Nibelungen" and "Parsifal." 78 min.
22-1353 *$19.99*

Richard Wagner: The Ring Cycle (Bayerische)
Wagner's landmark operatic tetralogy, based on Teutonic myths and legends, are performed by a magnificent ensemble cast that includes Hildegarde Behrens, Robert Hale, René Kullo and Kurt Moll. Wolfgang Swallisch conducts the Bayerische Staatsorchester.

Das Rheingold
In the first opera, a rash pact made between Wotan, king of the gods, and the mighty giants could mean the end of Valhalla, and a mystical ring of great power is cursed by a vengeful dwarf. 151 min. on two tapes.
44-4183 *$34.99*

Die Walküre
With his magic sword, Nothung, in hand, the heroic Siegmund faces Hunding in a battle to the death, while Wotan find his will challenged by Brunnhilde, his beloved daughter and leader of the Valkyries. 225 min. on two tapes.
44-4184 *$34.99*

Siegfried
The focus of Wagner's third Ring installment is on the exploits of Siegfried, as the youth slays the dragon Fafner, wins the mystic Ring, and falls in love with the former Valkyrie Brunnhilde. 235 min. on two tapes.
44-4185 *$34.99*

Götterdämmerung
Tricked by a magic potion into denying his true love, Siegfried becomes a victim of the curse of the Ring in the concluding chapter of Wagner's magnum opus. 257 min. on two tapes.
44-4186 *$34.99*

Tannhäuser
Performed at the Munich National Theatre, this stunning production of the Wagner opera features a cast that includes René Kollo, Waltraud Meier, Jan-Hendrik Rootering and Bernd Weikl. Zubin Mehta conducts the Bayerische Staatsorchester. 195 min.
22-1544 *$29.99*

Tannhäuser
Based in part on the legends of medieval German "minnesingers," Wagner's moving opera of gods, minstrels and the redemptive power of love is given a stirring performance by the Orchestra of the San Carlo Theatre in Naples. 186 min. on two tapes. In German with English subtitles.
50-8537 Letterboxed *$29.99*

Parsifal

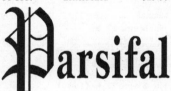

Parsifal
Placido Domingo sings the title role of the knight in search of the Holy Grail in this filmed presentation of Wagner's operatic take on the Arthurian tale. Director Tony Palmer also includes a rare interview with the composer's grandson Wolfgang and a look at the Grail legend through the years. 90 min.
22-1609 *$29.99*

Parsifal (1983)
The final operatic work from Richard Wagner, centered around the legendary quest for the Holy Grail, is brought to life courtesy of German filmmaker Hans-Jurgen Syberberg. Musical performances by the Prague Philharmonic Choir and the Monte Carlo Philharmonic are featured; Armin Jordan, Michael Kutter. 255 min.
22-1094 Was $59.99 *$29.99*

Tristan Und Isolde
Staged by L'Opéra du Québec in 1976, this production of Wagner's opera features Jon Vickers and Roberta Knie along with the Montreal Symphony Orchestra. 90 min. In German with English narration by Vickers.
22-3213 *$29.99*

Lohengrin
One of Richard Wagner's earliest and most romantic operas is given a masterful treatment by the Vienna State Opera, with conductor Claudio Abbado. Placido Domingo essays the title role, along with Robert Lloyd and Cheryl Struder. 223 min. Subtitled in English.
22-5472 Was $49.99 *$29.99*

Die Meistersinger Von Nürnberg
Richard Wagner's masterful epic love story detailing a classic struggle between tradition and innovation is given a stirring treatment by the Australian Opera conducted by Charles Mackerras and featuring Donald McIntyre, John Pringle and Paul Frey. 277 min. Subtitled in English.
22-5473 Was $49.99 *$29.99*

Wagner And Venice
Orson Welles narrates this fascinating look at composer Richard Wagner's love for the city of canals, showing through his letters, poems and music its impact on his creativity. A beautiful mix of music, history and lovely sights. 30 min.
53-7449 *$19.99*

Die Fledermaus
This majestic farewell to the Royal Opera from Dame Joan Sutherland offers Johann Strauss' operetta at its most sparkling, filled with lively dance music and opulence. With Nancy Gustafson, Judith Howarth, Luciano Pavarotti and Marilyn Horne. 121 min. Sung in English.
22-5545 Was $49.99 *$29.99*

Die Fledermaus
Placido Domingo made his British conducting debut with this Royal Opera House staging of the best known of Johann Strauss' operettas. Kiri Te Kanawa, Hermann Prey and Benjamin Luxon head an impressive cast that also includes some surprise cameos. 180 min. Subtitled in English.
44-1218 Was $49.99 *$29.99*

Fidelio
Josef Protschka and Gabriela Benacková star in this Covent Garden Royal Opera production of Beethoven's only opera, the story of a woman's devotion and her attempt to save her imprisoned husband from death. 125 min. With English subtitles.
22-5546 Was $39.99 *$29.99*

Lakmé
Joan Sutherland stars in the title role of the daughter of a Brahman priest in colonial India who faces the anger of her people when she falls for a British army officer, in Léo Delibes' opera comique. This Australian Opera production also features Isobel Buchanan, Huguette Tourangeau. 155 min. Sung in French; no subtitles.
22-5604 Was $39.99 *$29.99*

The Yeomen Of The Guard
The foreboding Tower of London provided a suitably somber setting for one of Gilbert and Sullivan's more serious works. Joel Grey stars as jester Jack Point, who fears he will lose the beautiful Eloise when she agrees to a "marriage of convenience" with doomed Tower prisoner Colonel Fairfax. With Elizabeth Gale, Alfred Marks. 116 min.
04-1649 *$29.99*

Ruddigore
The lurid melodramas that Gilbert and Sullivan spoofed here had become, even in 1887, familiar to audiences with their sinister castles, black-clad villains and virtuous maidens. Can a young man escape his family title of Baronet of Ruddigore and the curse it carries that would compel him to commit a crime a day or die? Vincent Price, Keith Michell, Sandra Dugdale star. 115 min.
04-1650 *$29.99*

The Gondoliers
Marco and Giuseppe are the "jolly gondoliers" who find their friendship, their staunch anti-monarchy beliefs, and their new marriages in jeopardy when it's learned one of them may be the late King of Barataria's long-lost son, in this comical Gilbert and Sullivan tale set amid the romantic canals of Venice. Keith Michell, Francis Egerton, Tom McDonnell star. 117 min.
04-1651 *$29.99*

The Pirates Of Penzance
"I Am the Very Model of a Modern Major-General," "Poor Wandering One" and "The Pirate King's Song" are among the popular Gilbert and Sullivan tunes in this rollicking tale of some less-than-fearsome buccaneers and their "apprentice," who wants to leave life on the high seas behind. Peter Allen, Alexander Oliver, Keith Michell, Gillian Knight star. 117 min.
04-1652 *$29.99*

Iolanthe
The Stratford Festival Company produced this version of the Gilbert and Sullivan opera, unique among the duo's collaborations for its tragic elements, along with the usual froth and satire. A delightful trip on the frontier between real and imagined worlds, performed by a first-rate cast. 138 min.
22-5180 Was $19.99 *$14.99*

Iolanthe
Who but Gilbert and Sullivan could create a comedy where the magical residents of Fairyland interact with Parliament's House of Lords, as the half-human shepherd Strephon tries to win the hand of fair Phyllis, ward of the House's Lord Chancellor, with help from his fairy mother Iolanthe? Beverly Mills, Derek Hammond-Stroud, Richard Van Allen star. 117 min.
22-5906 *$29.99*

H.M.S. Pinafore
"Let's give three cheers for the sailor's bride," and for this beloved Gilbert and Sullivan operetta that gently tweaks the British Navy, introduces such memorable characters as Dick Deadeye and Little Buttercup, and follows the romance of young tar Ralph Rackstraw and Josephine Porter, daughter of the Pinafore's captain. With Peter Marshall, Frankie Howerd, Meryl Drower. 117 min.
22-5901 *$29.99*

Patience
The Aesthetic Movement that swept English art and literature in the late 1800s, counting Oscar Wilde and James McNeill Whistler among its proponents, was mocked in Gilbert and Sullivan's tale of two rival poets and their attempted romantic conquests. Derek Hammond-Stroud, Donald Adams, and Sandra Dugdale, in the title role, star. 117 min.
22-5902 *$29.99*

The Mikado
"Nothing could possibly be more satisfactory" than this production of Gilbert and Sullivan's satirical tale of officiousness and masquerade in imperial Japan. Will love win out when the ward of the Lord High Executioner is wooed by a wandering minstrel who is really the son of the emperor, the Mikado? With William Conrad, Clive Revill, John Stewart, Kate Flowers. 117 min.
22-5903 *$29.99*

The Mikado (1939)
Gilbert and Sullivan's comic operetta of love and mischief in the gentry of old Japan is given a lively treatment by composer/director Victor Schertzinger. Crooner Kenny Baker is Nanki-Poo, the wandering minstrel enamored with a beautiful noblewoman. Co-stars Jean Colin, Martyn Green. 90 min.
10-7030 Was $29.99 *$19.99*

The Mikado (1966)
Gilbert & Sullivan's colorful and romantic operatic adventure is captured in this superb filmization that includes performances from Philip Potter, Valerie Masterson and Donald Adams, along with other members of the D'Oyly Carte Opera Company and the City Birmingham Symphony Orchestra. 122 min.
22-3166 *$39.99*

The Mikado (1982)
The setting for Gilbert and Sullivan's operetta is altered from 1880s Japan to 1930s England, in a seaside resort where bellhops tap-dance and art deco is all the range, in this unusual and hilarious staging. Jonathan Miller produced; "Monty Python's" Eric Idle stars. 131 min.
44-1751 Was $39.99 *$19.99*

The Mikado (1987)
Charming version of Gilbert and Sullivan's comic gem of life and love amidst the cherry blossoms. A Stratford Festival production starring Marie Baron and Eric Donkin. 150 min.
22-5152 Was $19.99 *$14.99*

The Sorceror
The residents of a village are given a love potion concocted by "dealer in magic and spells" John Wellington Wells at the behest of a betrothed couple who want everyone to be as happy as they are—but the couple soon have some romantic problems of their own. Gilbert and Sullivan's farcical look at magical matchmaking stars Clive Revill, Donald Adams, Nan Christie. 116 min.
22-5904 *$29.99*

Princess Ida
Certainly politically incorrect now, this Gilbert and Sullivan work in which a willful princess denounces male-dominated society and establishes a woman's university in a castle from which all men are barred offers a rollicking "battle of the sexes," as the princess's would-be groom and his friends look for a way to sneak in. Nan Christie, Laurence Dale and Frank Gorshin star. 112 min.
22-5907 *$29.99*

Gilbert & Sullivan: Boxed Set
Filmed live at Canada's world-renowned Stratford Festival, this three-tape collector's set features marvelous stage productions of three of Gilbert and Sullivan's best-loved works: "Iolanthe," "The Mikado" and "The Pirates of Penzance." 412 min. total. NOTE: Individual volumes available at $19.99 each.
50-8106 Save $50.00! *$39.99*

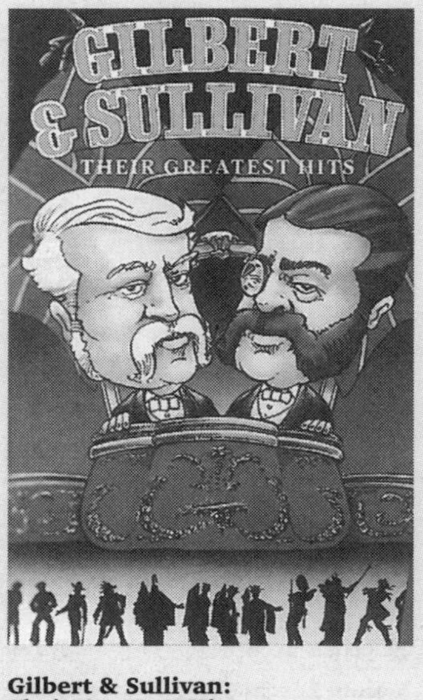

Gilbert & Sullivan: Their Greatest Hits
The finest songs of music masters Gilbert and Sullivan are presented in this magical celebration, featuring the D'Oyly Carte Singers in selections from "The Pirates of Penzance," "H.M.S. Pinafore," "The Mikado" and much more. 54 min.
22-7108 *$19.99*

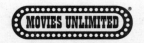

The Love Of Three Oranges
Prokofiev's "operatic fairy tale" tells the story of a young prince who will perish unless his court jesters can make him laugh. Jean-Luc Viala, Gabriel Bacquier and Helene Perraguin stars in this Lyon Opera production; Kent Nagano conducts. 106 min.
22-1765 *$29.99*

La Belle Hélène
The story of Helen of Troy is transplanted to mid-19th-century France in Offenbach's operatic satire of upper-class mores. Vesselina Kasarova sings the title role in this Zurich Opera presentation, with Deon van der Walt as Paris. 124 min.
22-1766 *$29.99*

Des Contes D'Hoffman
This grand production of Offenbach's "Tales of Hoffman" was presented by the Opera de Lyon during the inaugural week of its new opera house and is based on musicologist Michael Kaye's performing edition of the work. Barbars Hendricks, Daniel Galvez-Vallejo, José Van Dam star. 155 min. Sung in French with English subtitles.
22-5715 Was $39.99 *$29.99*

Les Contes D'Hoffman
Offenbach's chilling operatic tale of lost love and destiny is performed by the Royal Opera of Covent Garden in London, with Placido Domingo, Ileana Cotrubas and Agnes Baltsa. 150 min. Subtitled in English.
44-1273 *$29.99*

La Vie Parisienne
The spirit of Paris in the 1860s is captured in this lively interpretation of Offenbach's operetta. Opera de Lyon's splendid cast includes Claire Wauthion and Helene Delavault, who help bring the servants, trollops and members of the bourgeoisie to life. 159 min. In French with English subtitles.
22-5716 Was $39.99 *$29.99*

Fyodor Chaliapin
Rare film footage highlights this documentary on the life and career of the early 20th-century Russian opera star noted for his stunning bass singing voice and dynamic stage presence. 30 min.
22-1665 *$19.99*

Albert Herring
Benjamin Britten's three-act comic opera about life in an English market town at the turn of the century tells of a young grocer who is crowned May King when it's decided that no girls fit the May Queen qualifications. This fresh, charming Peter Hall production stars John Graham-Hall and Patricia Johnson. 150 min.
22-1423 *$29.99*

A Midsummer Night's Dream
Shakespeare's comedic play about young love and mistaken identity, made into an opera by Benjamin Britten, stars James Bowman, Ileana Cotrubas and Curt Appelgren. Bernard Haitink conducts the London Philharmonic in this Glyndebourne Festival production. 160 min.
22-5062 *$29.99*

Billy Budd
Benjamin Britten's marvelous adaptation of Melville's tale of the young British seaman who takes justice into his own hands is seen in a stirring English National Opera Production. Thomas Allen, Philip Langridge star. 157 min. Sung in English.
22-5278 Was $39.99 *$29.99*

Death In Venice
For his final operatic work, composer Benjamin Britten adapted Thomas Mann's haunting story about an aging composer, for whom a trip to Italy brings the culmination of his quest for beauty and love. Robert Tear, Alan Opie star in this Glyndebourne Touring Opera production. 138 min.
22-5602 *$29.99*

Puccini

Puccini: Tosca
Luciano Pavarotti turns in a sublime performance in Puccini's "Tosca," performed at the Rome Opera House. Daniel Oren conducts the Teatro dell'Opera in Rome with Franco Federici, Raina Kabaivanska and Ingvar Wixell co-starring with Pavarotti. 152 min.
02-7999 *$14.99*

Tosca (1961)
Italian diva Renata Tebaldi and the renowned George London (in his only complete filmed performance) shine in this adaptation of Puccini's ode to doomed love. Eugene Tobin and Gustav Grefe also star in this Stuttgart Staatsoper presentation. 130 min. Sung in Italian.
22-3167 *$39.99*

Turandot At The Forbidden City Of Beijing
A landmark event in opera history, as Puccini's tale of love and devotion in the court of imperial China is performed in and around the actual 400-year-old Ming Dynasty Palace. Directed by acclaimed filmmaker Zhang Yimou ("Ju Dou"), the production stars Sergej Larin, Barbara Frittoli, and Giovanna Casolla in the title role, with Zubin Mehta conducting the Maggio Musicale Fiorentino.
02-9026 *$34.99*

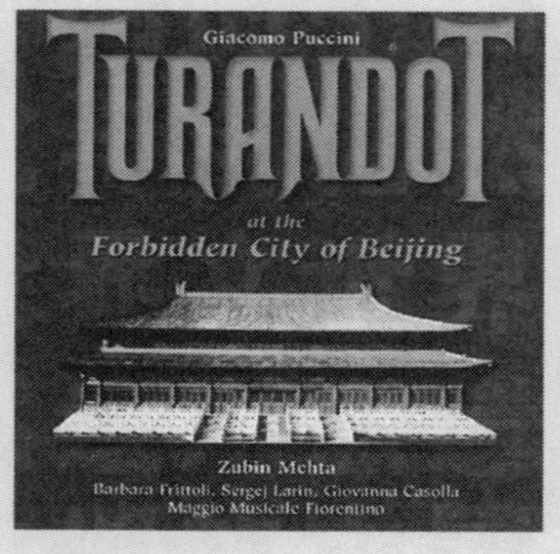

Turandot
The San Francisco Opera's version of Puccini's opera of love triumphing over barbaric cruelty features Eva Marton in the lead role and Michael Sylvester, Kevin Langan and Lucia Mazzaria in support. The production includes sets and costumes deigned by David Hockney. 123 min.
22-1416 *$29.99*

Manon Lescaut
Set in 18th-century France and Louisiana, this dramatic early work by Puccini is presented by the Flemish Opera and Opera de Paris, Bastille. Miriam Gauci stars in the title role of the young woman who abandons love for wealth and pays a tragic price; with Jan Danckaert, Jules Bastin. 124 min.
22-1772 *$29.99*

Manon Lescaut
Placido Domingo, Kiri Te Kanawa and Thomas Allen star in an all-new stage production of Puccini's acclaimed opera, taped live at London's Royal Opera at Covent Garden. 130 min. Subtitled in English.
44-1284 Was $39.99 *$29.99*

Madama Butterfly
Keita Asari mounts a most striking Oriental production of Puccini's undying tragedy at La Scala. Yasuko Hayashi is magnificent in the title role; Hak-Nam Kim, Peter Dvorsky and Giorgio Zancanaro also star. 150 min. In Italian with English subtitles.
22-5119 Was $39.99 *$29.99*

Madama Butterfly
Puccini's immortal opera is performed at Italy's Arena di Verona. The story of love and heartbreak in late 19th-century Japan stars Raina Kabaivanska as Cio-Cio-San, with Nazzareno Antinori and Lorenzo Saccomani. 140 min.
44-1240 Was $39.99 *$29.99*

Madame Butterfly (1996)
Puccini's tragic opera of a beautiful young Geisha tortured between her family and her love for an American is vividly brought to life in a ravishing production. Ying Huang, Richard Troxell, Richard Cowan and Ning Liang head up the stellar cast in this film directed by Frederic Mitterand, nephew of the late French president. 129 min. Sung in Italian with English subtitles.
02-3040 *$24.99*

La Boheme
The San Francisco Opera's dazzling production of Puccini's love story stars Luciano Pavarotti as Rodolpho and Mirella Freni as Mimi. 111 min. Subtitled in English.
22-5339 Was $39.99 *$29.99*

La Boheme (1986)
Filmed during the Genoa Opera Company's tour of China, this stirring rendition of the Puccini opera stars Luciano Pavarotti and Fiamma Izzo D'Amico as the doomed lovers. 111 min.
22-1135 Was $39.99 *$24.99*

La Boheme
Puccini's tragic love story, set in the "artists' ghetto" of 19th-century Paris, is staged by the Royal Opera of Covent Garden. The cast includes Ileana Cotrubas, Neil Shicoff and Thomas Allen. 115 min. In Italian with English subtitles.
44-1261 Was $39.99 *$29.99*

La Fanciulla Del West
La Scala turns in a glittering performance of Puccini's underrated opera about the California Gold Rush of the Old West. The cast includes Placido Domingo, Juan Pons and Mara Zampieri. 145 min.
22-5527 *$39.99*

Puccini
Fascinating film biography of the 19th-century composer of "Madame Butterfly," "La Boheme" and "Tosca" whose life and career were almost wrecked by scandal. Highlights from a live prouction of "Turandot" show the parallels between Puccini's life and work. Robert Stephens, Judith Howard, Virginia McKenna star. 113 min.
22-5107 Was $59.99 *$29.99*

Prince Igor (1969)
Alexander Borodin composed this opera, based on the legendary 12th-century Russian noble who defended his homeland from Asian invaders. The Kirov Opera and Orchestra of Leningrad performs on location on the majestic Russian steppes. 105 min.
53-7178 Letterboxed *$19.99*

Destination: Mozart—A Night At The Opera With Peter Sellars
The innovative, controversial opera director is spotlighted in this backstage look at three Sellars productions of Mozart masterworks: "The Marriage of Figaro," "Don Giovanni" and "Cosi Fan Tutte." See the creative process at work from first planning to opening night, hear from Sellars, his colleagues and the performers, and much more. 60 min.
22-1187 Was $29.99 *$19.99*

Le Nozze Di Figaro
Giovanni Furlanetto stars as the reluctant bridegroom in Mozart's famed tale of romance gone hilariously awry. Conductor Paolo Olmi leads the Lyon National Opera Orchestra and Chorus. 193 min.
22-1542 *$29.99*

Don Giovanni
A modern-day updating and moodily abstract sets mark this stunning Glyndebourne Festival Opera production of the Mozart masterwork. Gilles Cachermaille, Adrianne Pieczonka star. 175 min. Subtitled in English.
22-1664 *$29.99*

Don Giovanni (Salzburg Opera)
The legendary Cesare Siepi essays the title role in this Salzburg Opera production of the Mozart classic. Elisabeth Grummer, Lisa Della Casa, Anton Dermota round out the superlative cast, under the conducting of Wilhelm Furtwangler. 129 min. Sung in Italian.
22-3116 *$59.99*

Don Giovanni
Mozart's masterwork receives a great staging with Riccardo Muti conducting the Teatro Alla Scala, Giorgio Strehler directing, and Thomas Allen and Edita Gruberova turning in bravura performances. 177 min. Sung in Italian with English subtitles.
22-5615 *$49.99*

Don Giovanni (1979)
Literature's legendary lover and rake is the star of Mozart's operatic masterwork, brought to life here by the Paris Opera Orchestra with Lorin Maazel conducting. Ruggero Raimondi, Kiri Te Kanawa star; directed by Joseph Losey. 177 min. Sung in Italian with English subtitles.
22-1109 Was $39.99 *$24.99*

La Clemenza Di Tito
Philip Langridge, Ashley Putnam and Diane Montague head up the international cast in this Glyndebourne production of Mozart's final operatic work. 144 min. Subtitled in English.
22-5528 Was $39.99 *$29.99*

The Magic Flute
Mozart's delightful fantasy of love conquering dark forces is brought to vibrant life by the "Gewandhaus" Orchestra of Liepzig. Horst Gebhardt, Magdalena Falewicz star; Gert Bahner conducts. 156 min. German language version.
22-7016 Was $39.99 *$29.99*

The Magic Flute (1986)
The world famous Sydney Opera House is the setting for the Australian Opera's performance of the Mozart favorite. The talented cast features Yvonne Kenny, Richard Bonynge. 160 min. Sung in English.
22-1117 Was $39.99 *$29.99*

The Abduction From The Seraglio
Mozart's romantically farcical romp through a harem is memorably presented by the Dresden State Opera under the direction of Harry Kupfer. Armin Ude, Carolyn Smith-Meyer star. 129 min. Original German version.
22-7017 Was $39.99 *$29.99*

Die Entführung Aus Dem Serail (1987)
From the Royal Opera House at Covent Garden, Sir Georg Solti conducts Mozart's classic comic opera about a young woman, trapped in a sultan's harem, who inspires the love of a Spanish noble. Stars Deon van der Walt, Inge Nielsen, Oliver Tobias. 140 min. In German with English subtitles.
22-5182 Was $39.99 *$29.99*

Cosi Fan Tutte (1990)
La Scala's production of Mozart's famed comedy of manners that involves disguises, love and betrayal receives a fabulous rendition with a bright cast and expert orchestration conducted by Riccardo Muti. Stars Daniela Dessi, Delores Ziegler and Jozef Kundlak. 186 min. In Italian with English subtitles.
22-5404 *$49.99*

Mitridate, Rè Di Ponto (1993)
Gorgeously staged at the Royal Opera House, this early Mozart operatic composition, a succession of virtuoso arias and duets, offers excellent performances by Ann Murray, Bruce Ford and Luba Orgonasova in a production overseen by Graham Vick. 178 min. on two tapes. Sung in Italian with English subtitles.
22-5774 Was $49.99 *$29.99*

Gala Lirica
Recorded live in Seville, this magnificent concert features Jose Carreras, Placido Domingo, Montserrat Caballe, Teresa Berganza and Alfredo Kraus performing selections from "Carmen," "Rigoletto," "Tosca" and "La Traviata."
02-7539 *$14.99*

Domingo And Rostropovich
Masterful performances from tenor Placido Domingo and maestro Mstislav Rostropovich of selections like "Elegie," "The 1812 Overture" and a "Carmen" duet by Domingo and Olga Borodina. 60 min.
22-1235 *$24.99*

Domingo: Zarzuela
Placido Domingo performs a long-awaited concert of "all-zarzuela" music from the National Auditorium of Madrid. He's joined by Guadalupe Sanchez, Teresa Verdera and the Ballet Español. 69 min.
22-1237 *$24.99*

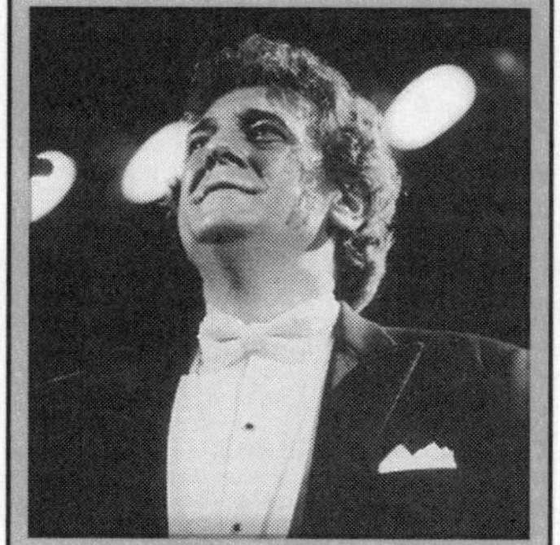

Placido Domingo: A Musical Life
Take an intimate look at Placido Domingo at home and in concert in this revealing portrait. Meet his family, stop by his impressive Acapulco vacation house, and see him perform works by Wagner, Verdi, and Offenbach, with Carreras and Pavarotti in selections from "Rigoletto" and with John Denver on "Perhaps Love." 90 min.
22-1384 *$29.99*

Great Arias With Placido Domingo And Guests
A host of opera's leading lights, including Placido Domingo, Shirley Verrett, Simon Estes and Barbara Hendricks, merged on one stage in Paris for a gala evening of song to perform the most memorable arias from Verdi and Puccini. 54 min.
22-7065 Was $19.99 *$14.99*

Placido: A Year In The Life Of Placido Domingo (1984)
Spend a year in the company of one of opera's all-time greatest stars. This special musical documentary follows Domingo on a worldwide concert schedule, performing "Tosca," "Otello," "La Traviata," "Tales of Hoffman" and other classics, then preparing at home for his roles and in comedic scenes with Carol Burnett and Charles Aznavour. 105 min.
22-1035 *$19.99*

Placido Domingo: His 25th Anniversary Concert At Arena Di Verona (1994)
To commemorate his first appearance on its historic stage a quarter-century earlier, legendary tenor Placido Domingo returned to Verona for a remarkable recital that features Act 1 of "Othello," Act 3 of "Aida" and Act 3 of "La Boheme." Guest performers include Daniela Dessi, Leo Nucci and Cecilia Gasdia. 100 min.
53-8402 *$19.99*

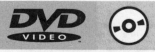

Orfeo Ed Euridice
Acclaimed soprano Dame Janet Baker, in her farewell performance, stars as the Greek minstrel who, according to myth, went to Hades to rescue his dead wife. Gluck's moving opera is performed at England's Glyndebourne Festival; Elisabeth Speiser, Elizabeth Gale also star. 130 min. Sung in Italian with English subtitles.
22-5080 Was $49.99 *$29.99*

Orfeo Ed Euridice
Christoph Gluck's operatic rendition of the tragic Greek myth is given a compelling updating, with Orpheus a leather-clad ruffian who loses his love in a car accident, by Harry Kupfer and Berlin Komische Oper. Jochen Kowalski, Gillian Webster star. 84 min. Subtitled in English.
22-5537 Was $39.99 *$29.99*

L'Innocenza/Ed Il Piacer (1987)
A double bill of operatic works by Christopher Gluck is performed by the Concerto Cologne, with authentic baroque instruments in a rococo German theater, recreating the 18th century sound of "Echo et Narcisse" and "Le Cinesi." Principal performers are Kurt Streit, Sophie Boulin, and Christine Hoegman. 170 min. In Italian and French with English subtitles.
22-5183 *$29.99*

The Rise And Fall Of The City Of Mahagonny
In one of their most stinging attacks on capitalism, Bertolt Brecht and Kurt Weill showed its eroding effect on society in their pointed 1930 operatic satire. This Salzburg Festival presentation features Catherine Malfitano, Jerry Hadley and Gwyneth Jones, with Dennis Russell Davies conducting the Vienna Radio Symphony Orchestra. 155 min.
22-1763 *$29.99*

The Threepenny Opera (1962)
Grand German-French adaptation of Bertolt Brecht and Kurt Weill's classic musical satire set amongst the criminal element of Victorian London stars Curt Jurgens, Gert Frobe, Hildegarde Neff and Sammy Davis, Jr. as the Street Singer. 100 min. Spoken and dubbed in English.
53-6019 *$19.99*

Luciano Pavarotti: Gala Concert At Olympic Hall
Recorded in Munich's magnificent concert hall, the world's most acclaimed tenor brings the audience to their feet with such works as "La Donna e Mobile," "O Solo Mio," "Mamma" and others. 60 min.
22-1134 *$19.99*

Pavarotti At Julliard: Opera Master Class
Would-be singers, as well as fans of opera, will enjoy this session at the world-renowned Julliard school in which Luciano Pavarotti leads his charges through breathing, phrasing and interpretation exercises. Arias by Mozart and Verdi are performed, with Pavarotti contributing a selection from Buonocini's "Griselda." 60 min.
22-1176 Was $29.99 *$19.99*

Pavarotti In Confidence With Peter Ustinov
The great tenor discusses his life, career and influences in this revealing program hosted by Peter Ustinov, and then performs some of his most beloved folk songs and his finest romantic arias. 50 min.
22-1366 *$19.99*

Pavarotti: The Best Is Yet To Come
Learn about the man behind the voice in this music-filled documentary that offers an intimate look at the life and career of one of the world's most renowned classical singers, the one and only Luciano Pavarotti. 60 min.
22-1610 *$19.99*

A Pavarotti Valentine
The acclaimed tenor performs 19 of his greatest hits, including "Nessun Dorma" from Turandot, "Una Furtiva Lagrima" from L'Elisir d'Amore, and "O Sole Mio"; along with a special septet of songs depicting various aspects of love that were recorded live on Valentine's Day, 1984. 77 min.
22-3131 *$24.99*

Pavarotti In Concert In China (1986)
In a historic performance filmed at Beijing's Exhibition Hall Theatre, the one and only Luciano is showcased in a stirring recital featuring selections by Verdi and Puccini and Pavarotti's favorite Italian songs. 96 min.
22-1179 Was $29.99 *$19.99*

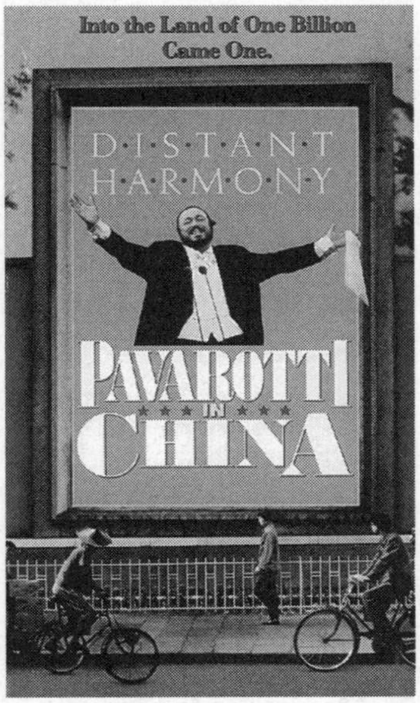

Pavarotti In China: Distant Harmony (1988)
More than just a concert film or a travel documentary. Follow the world-renowned operatic tenor on a tour of the People's Republic of China, as Pavarotti's stage performances are juxtaposed with his visits with the Chinese people; a unique cultural experience. 85 min.
07-8136 *$24.99*

Giuseppe Verdi

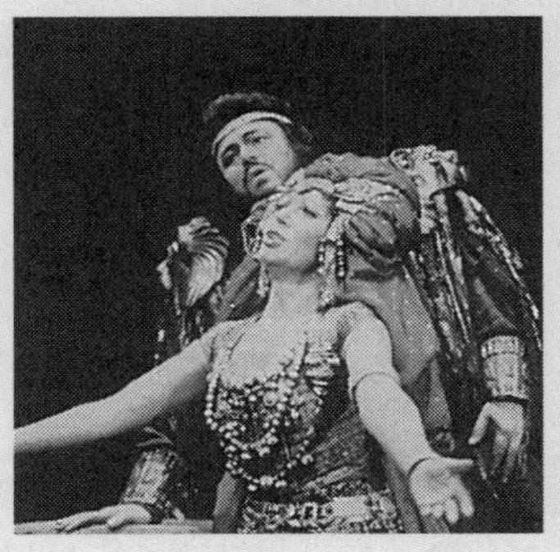

Aida (Pavarotti)
From La Scala comes an exceptional production of Verdi's classic tragedy. Luciano Pavarotti, Ghena Dimitrova, Nicolai Ghiaurov and Juan Pons star; Lorin Maazel conducts. 161 min. In Italian with English subtitles.
22-5116 Was $39.99 *$29.99*

The Aida File
Luciano Pavarotti, Carlo Bergonzi and Dame Eva Turner head the brilliant cast of La Scala's production of Verdi's opera. Includes rare backstage footage of the performers in and out of action. 77 min.
22-5347 Was $39.99 *$29.99*

Aida (Royal Opera)
Cheryl Studer sings the title role of the princess whose forbidden love for a general in Ancient Egypt leads to tragedy in this Royal Opera production of the Verdi work. With Dennis O'Neill as Radames, Robert Lloyd and Luciana d'Intino. 150 min. Sung in Italian with English subtitles.
22-5850 Was $39.99 *$29.99*

The Life Of Verdi
Epic telling of the life of the renowned 19th-century Italian composer, made for European television and filmed throughout the continent. The drama features magnificent sets and costumes, plus a selection of Verdi's most famous music, sung by such greats as Maria Callas, Birgit Nilsson and Luciano Pavarotti. Approximately 10 hours on 4 cassettes.
22-1026 Was $124.99 *$79.99*

Verdi: The King Of Melody (1953)
Outstanding biodrama of the 19th-century Italian composer features performances of his finest works. Tito Gobbi, Mario Del Monaco and Orietta Moscucci perform arias from "Rigoletto," "La Traviata," "Il Trovatore," "Otello" and many more. Pierre Cressoy stars as Verdi. 118 min. Dubbed in English; songs sung in Italian.
22-7026 *$29.99*

Don Carlos
Verdi's stirring opera, seen here in the original, five-act French version, is performed at the Theatre du Chatelet in Paris. Roberto Alagna sings the title role; Thomas Hampson, Karita Mattila, Jose Van Dam also star. 210 min. Subtitled in English.
22-1663 *$29.99*

Un Ballo In Maschera
Verdi's opera of political intrigue, romance and assassination in the royal halls of Sweden is presented to the Royal Opera House, with the orchestra under conductor Claudio Abbado. Placido Domingo stars as King Gustavus, with Katia Ricciarelli playing his true love, Amelia. 135 min.
22-1716 *$29.99*

Simon Boccanegra
Giancardo Pasquetto and Elena Prokina star in this powerful Glyndebourne Festival Opera production of Verdi's drama set in 14th-century Genoa. 135 min. Subtitled in English.
22-1727 *$29.99*

La Forza Del Destino
A Spanish nobleman of mixed ancestry's love for a marquis's beautiful daughter is fated to end in violence and tragedy in Verdi's powerful grand opera. This production, performed in St. Petersburg's Mariinsky Theatre where the opera debuted in 1862, stars Galina Gorchakova, Gegam Grigorian and Nikolai Putilin. 160 min.
22-1764 *$29.99*

Making Opera: The Creation Of Verdi's "La Forza Del Destino"
Giuseppe Verdi's "La Forza Del Destino" is the focus of two stories: the production of the opera, with performances by the Canadian Opera Company, conducted by Maurizio Arena; and the opera itself. This passionate film shows the work that goes into putting on a full-scale production. 88 min.
22-7102 Was $29.99 *$19.99*

La Traviata
A special performance at Glyndebourne, done without an audience, gives the viewer a unique chance to see Verdi's timeless grand opera. The cast includes Walter MacNeil, Marie McLaughlin and Brent Ellis. 133 min.
22-5209 Was $39.99 *$29.99*

La Traviata (1968)
The elegant classic of passion and romance from Verdi is given an incomparable adaptation with Anna Moffo as Violetta, joined by Franco Bonisolli and Gino Bechi. 113 min.
22-3132 *$39.99*

La Traviata (1976)
This "In Performance at Wolf Trap" program spotlights Beverly Sills in a powerful performance as Violetta in Verdi's immortal grand opera. Henry Price and Richard Fredericks also star; maestro Julius Rudel conducts. 144 min.
22-3148 *$39.99*

I Vespri Siciliani
Stirring La Scala production spotlights Chris Merritt, Cheryl Studer and Ferruccio Furlanetto in a performance of Verdi's opera set during the final days of the French occupation of Sicily. Riccardo Muti conducts. 214 min.
22-5469 *$49.99*

Attila
La Scala Opera presents a magnificent version of Verdi's early masterwork, featuring Cheryl Studer, Giorgio Zancanaro and Samuel Ramey, plus the direction of maestro Riccardo Muti. 118 min.
22-5526 *$39.99*

Luisa Miller
The beautiful daughter of a retired soldier falls in love with a local nobleman's son, but the difference in their status in life dooms their romance, in this Opéra de Lyon staging of the Verdi composition. June Anderson, Taro Ichihara star. 150 min. In Italian with English subtitles.
22-5603 Was $39.99 *$29.99*

Verdi: Requiem
An all-star gathering of José Carreras, Jessye Norman, Ruggero Raimondi and Margaret Price is joined on stage by conductor Claudio Abbado and the London Symphony Orchestra for this Edinburgh International Festival rendition of a requiem mass Verdi wrote for Italian poet Alessandro Manzoni. 97 min.
22-5692 *$29.99*

Stiffelio
An overlooked composition by Verdi that was for years banned by the Italian government, this moving work stars Jose Carreras as a minister who must decide what to do when he learns of his wife's infidelity. Catherine Malfitano, Gregory Yurisich also star in this Royal Opera at Covent Garden production. 123 min. Sung in Italian with English subtitles.
22-5696 Was $39.99 *$29.99*

Otello
Giuseppe Verdi's stunning masterpiece receives a brilliant interpretation with Placido Domingo as Shakespeare's tragic character and Kiri Te Kanawa as Desdemona. Sir Georg Solti conducts this Royal Opera Chorus production. 146 min. Sung in Italian with English subtitles.
22-5713 Was $39.99 *$29.99*

Otello

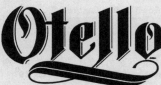

Otello (1986)
William Shakespeare wrote the play; Giuseppe Verdi put it to music; Franco Zeffirelli brought it to the screen. Placido Domingo is overwhelming as the Moor of Venice, whose love and jealousy lead to disaster. Lush operatic rendition also stars Katia Ricciarelli, Justino Diaz. 120 min. Sung in Italian with English subtitles.
22-1145 Was $39.99 *$24.99*

Rigoletto
In this daring and acclaimed interpretation of Verdi's grand opera, producer Jonathan Miller transposes the tale of love and deception to the underworld lords of 1950s New York, with dramatic results. 140 min. Sung in English.
44-1686 *$39.99*

Verdi: Falstaff (1982)
For his final opera, Verdi gave musical life to the hefty hero of Shakespearean fame, and this remarkable Salzburg Festival production, with Herbert von Karajan leading the Vienna Philharmonic and Vienna State Opera Chorus, stars Giuseppe Taddei, Rolando Panerai, Christa Ludwig and Janet Perry. Sung in Italian.
04-5326 *$49.99*

Nabucco (1984)
Verdi's heroic opera of oppression and rebellion, written in response to the rising revolutionary movement in 1840s Italy, is staged by Arena di Verona. The cast includes Renato Bruson and Ghena Dimitrova. 132 min. Subtitled in English.
44-1241 Was $39.99 *$29.99*

Ernani (1984)
The classic grand opera by Italian master Giuseppe Verdi, based on a story by Victor Hugo, is lavishly staged by Teatro Alla Scala with a cast that includes Placido Domingo, Mirella Freni and Renato Bruson. 135 min. Subtitled in English.
44-1242 Was $39.99 *$29.99*

Macbeth (1987)
The acclaimed Deutsch Opera Berlin presents Verdi's masterful adaptation of Shakespeare's dire story. Giuseppe Sinopoli conducts Renato Bruson and Mara Zampieri in the leading roles. 150 min. In Italian with English subtitles.
22-5179 *$29.99*

The Three Sopranos
In the tradition of "The Three Tenors" comes this program showcasing a trio of the world's greatest sopranos: Ileana Cotrubas, Elena Obraztsova and Renata Scotto. The music includes selections from "Carmen," "Tales of Hoffman," "Aida" and more. 67 min.
22-1236 *$24.99*

Pelleas Et Melisande
Debussy's only opera is a sensitive love story that's highlighted by elements of jealousy and remorse, and this dazzling production does justice to its beauty. Recorded on the stage at the Opera de Lyon, it features Francois Le Roux and Colette Alliot-Lugaz in the leads. 145 min.
22-1386 *$29.99*

Il Riturno D' Ulisse In Patria
A lavish production of Claudio Monteverdi's saga of Ulysses and Penelope, composed in 1641. Michael Hampe's production spares no effect and there are soaring performances from Thomas Allen and Kathleen Kuhlmann. 186 min. Subtitled in English.
22-5391 Was $49.99 *$29.99*

L'Incoronazione Di Poppea (1984)
The final opera by Claudio Monteverdi, a tale of passion and court intrigue in the days of Roman emperor Nero, is handsomely mounted by the Glyndebourne Festival Opera under Sir Peter Hall. Maria Ewing stars as Poppea. 120 min.
22-1379 *$29.99*

La Serva Padrona (1958)
Pergolesi's wonderful story of the crafty chambermaid who bilks her boss into marriage is highlighted by Anna Moffo's performance as Serpina. Paolo Montarsolo co-stars in this feature film rendition. 60 min. Sung in Italian.
22-7025 Was $29.99 *$19.99*

The Merry Widow
Joan Sutherland and Ronald Stevens star in this majestic version of Franz Lehar's opera, featuring the Australian Opera and the Elizabethan Philharmonic Orchestra. 151 min. Sung in English.
22-5471 Was $39.99 *$29.99*

The Final Romance (1986)
A host of operatic stars, including Jose Carreras, Sydne Rome, Mario Pardo and Montserrat Caballe, are featured in a music-filled biography of legendary 19th-century tenor Julian Gayarre. Works by Verdi, Bizet, Wagner and others are performed. 120 min.
22-1146 Was $39.99 *$19.99*

Opera Gold Collection
A must-have for opera buffs and a perfect introductory set for novices, this four-tape boxed collection offers such legendary singers as Carreras, Domingo, Freni, Marton, Pavarotti, Te Kanawa and others taking the stage. Included in the set are "Great Puccini Love Scenes," "Great Tenor Performances," "Highlights from La Scala" and "Opera Hits." 340 min. total.
22-1744 *$49.99*

Chushingura
Based on a true incident that occurred in 18th-century feudal Japan and went on to be a staple in the Kabuki theatre, composer Saegusa Shigeaki's stunning opera blends western musical styles and Japanese theatrical tradition. This production, directed by German filmmaker Werner Herzog, stars Naono Tasuku, Sato Shinobu and Kobayashi Kazuo. Otomo Naoto conducts the Tokyo Symphony Orchestra. 184 min.
04-5627 *$44.99*

After The Storm: The American Exile Of Bela Bartok
A look at the great Hungarian composer's life in the U.S. in the 1940s, after fleeing his homeland during the war. His creativity and brilliance were virtually overlooked in the States, and he found himself struggling with sickness and poverty. Still, Bartok composed some of his greatest works during this time. 75 min.
22-5412 *$29.99*

In The Shadow Of The Stars (1991)
The winner of the 1992 Academy Award for Best Documentary looks at the choir singers of the San Francisco Opera Company, many of whom aspire to become stars. The film goes backstage and shows the troupe preparing for their performance and revealing their dreams. Features music by Mozart, Puccini, Rossini and Stravinsky. 93 min.
70-5046 Was $24.99 *$19.99*

Stratasphere: A Portrait Of Teresa Stratas
A stunning portrait of one of the world's greatest sopranos follows Teresa Stratas' life, from her childhood as the daughter of Greek immigrants in Toronto to her rise to fame as star of the Metropolitan Opera of New York and her personal relationships. Includes footage from "Salome," "Der Zarewitsch" and "La Boheme." 87 min.
22-1152 Was $29.99 *$19.99*

First Ladies Of The Opera (1967)
Their voices have entertained music lovers across the globe. Now, in a classic "Bell Telephone Hour" broadcast, Birgit Nilsson, Leontyne Price, Joan Sutherland and Renata Tebaldi are featured performing the arias that made them famous. 54 min.
22-3057 Was $29.99 *$19.99*

Opera: Two To Six (1968)
From duet to sextet, some of the greatest operatic ensembles ever written are highlighted in this special from the "Bell Telephone Hour" series. Singers Phyllis Curtin, Nicolai Gedda, Tito Gobbi, Jerome Hines, Mildred Miller and Joan Sutherland perform selections from "Tosca," "Rigoletto," "Lucia," "Faust" and more. 52 min.
22-1284 Was $29.99 *$19.99*

Three Tenors: Encore
The triumphant 1990 concert of José Carreras, Placido Domingo and Luciano Pavarotti is chronicled with a fascinating look at its preparation and behind-the-scenes rehearsal and show footage. Zubin Mehta conducts the orchestra; Derek Jacobi narrates. 57 min.
02-2288 ❑*$19.99*

The Three Tenors In Concert 1994
Los Angeles' Dodger Stadium was the incongruously atmospheric setting for this reteaming of musical giants Pavarotti, Domingo and Carreras. Joined by Zubin Mehta and the Los Angeles Philharmonic, the trio perform selections from "Pagliacci," "La Boheme," "Macbeth," "Man of La Mancha" and more.
19-3588 *$29.99*

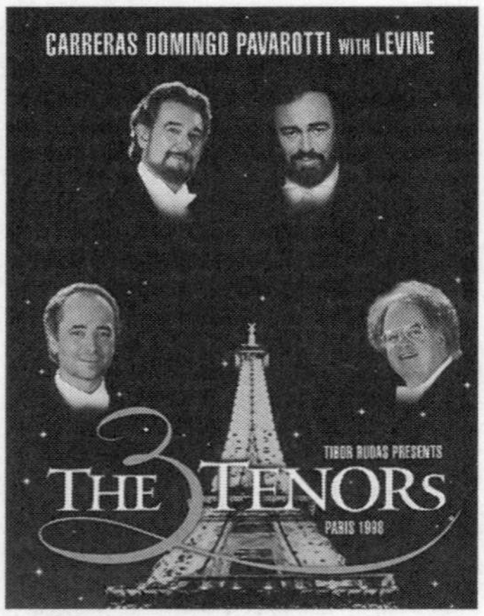

The Three Tenors: Paris 1998
The City of Lights has never shone brighter for music fans, as Placido Domingo, José Carreras and Luciano Pavarotti perform along the Champs-de-Mars with the Eiffel Tower as a backdrop. James Levine conducts l'Orchestre de Paris.
19-2747 *$29.99*

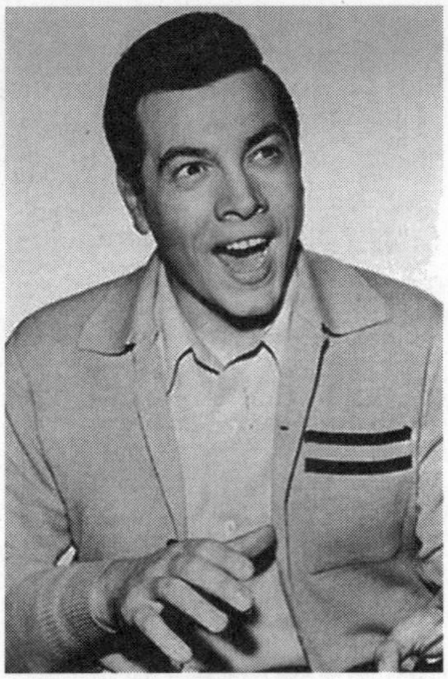

Mario Lanza: The American Caruso
A music-filled look at the life, times and career of Philadelphia native and master tenor Mario Lanza, whose voice was considered one of the world's finest. Placido Domingo hosts this salute to Lanza which features film clips, recordings and interviews with Anna Moffo and Kathryn Grayson. 68 min.
22-1207 Was $29.99 *$19.99*

The Legend Of Tsar Saltan
Rimsky-Korsakov's timeless fantasy that features "Flight of the Bumble Bee" is exceptionally rendered by the Dresden State Opera. Rolf Wollard, Barbara Hoene star; Siegfried Kurz conducts. 98 min. Sung in German.
22-7018 Was $39.99 *$29.99*

The Tsar's Bride (1966)
A young girl is forced to marry the notorious ruler Ivan the Terrible, but later falls tragically in love with one of the ruler's guards, in the Bolshoi's stunningly filmed rendition of Rimsky-Korsakov's opera. 97 min. In Russian with English subtitles.
53-7184 Was $39.99 *$19.99*

The Opera Australia Series
A special series of some of the world's most famous operatic works, recorded live at the Sydney Opera House and featuring Dame Joan Sutherland, with Richard Bonynge conducting the Elizabethan Sydney Orchestra.

Adriana Lecouvreur (1984)
The leading actress of 18th-century France, Lecouvreur's triumphs and tragedies are told in this opera from Francesco Cilea. Along with Sutherland in the title role, the cast includes Austin Anson, Heather Begg and John Shaw. 134 min.
45-5110 Was $39.99 *$29.99*

Dialogues Of The Carmelites (1984)
The true story of the Carmelite Nuns, a small order put to death during the French Revolution, is made into a moving tale of human faith and courage in this opera by Francis Poulenc. Isobel Buchanan and Heather Begg star alongside Sutherland. 159 min.
45-5111 Was $39.99 *$29.99*

Khovanshchina
The turbulent power struggle that accompanied Peter the Great's ascension to the Russian throne is the theme of Mussorgsky's compelling opera, performed here at Moscow's Bolshoi Theatre. Yevgeni Nesterenko, Irina Arkhipova star. 172 min. In Russian with English subtitles.
22-1081 Was $59.99 *$29.99*

Boris Godunov
Mussorgsky's immortal epic tragedy is captured in spectacular performance at the Bolshoi. Yevgeni Nesterenko, Vladimir Atlantov, Natasha Fatale and Elena Obraztsova star in this memorable production. 181 min. In Russian with English subtitles.
22-1130 Was $59.99 *$29.99*

Boris Godunov (1954)
Epic filming of the Bolshoi production, with Alexander Pirogov in the title role of the 16th-century ruler who reaches the throne by murdering his own son. Classic Mussorgsky score highlights this operatic gem. 105 min. In Russian with English subtitles.
53-7175 *$49.99*

Romeo Et Juliette
Shakespeare's immortal tale of doomed love has been turned into an opera several times, but this version by French composer Charles Gounod is considered to be among the finest. Roberto Alagna and Leontine Vaduva essay the title roles; with Paul Charles Clarke. 170 min. Sung in French with English subtitles.
22-5847 Was $39.99 *$29.99*

La Scala
The history of this majestic opera house is told in conjunction with some of the finest performances ever given within its walls. Rare backstage footage from pre-WWII days; the talents of Del Monaco. Gobbi, Mosucci, Schipa, Tagliavini and many others. 60 min.
22-7022 Was $29.99 *$19.99*

June Anderson: The Passion Of Bel Canto
It's considered by many the most rigorous and challenging of operatic singing styles, and in this film American soprano June Anderson shares her love for bel canto and is seen in live clips performing roles from "Lucia di Lammermoor," "La Fille du Regiment," "Otello," "La Sonnambula" and "I Puritani." 57 min.
22-7149 Was $29.99 *$19.99*

Les Huguenots (1981)
In her farewell stage appearance, Joan Sutherland gives a wonderful performance in Meyerbeer's tale of romance and massacre on St. Bartholomew's Day in 16th-century France. Amanda Thane and Anson Austin also star. 200 min. With English subtitles.
22-5470 Was $49.99 *$29.99*

Highlights From Arena Di Verona
It's a landmark to opera fans from around the globe, and in this special program such stars as Kiri Te Kanawa, Eva Marton and others are featured in memorable moments from the Arena di Verona stage. Included are selections from "Il Trovatore," "Otello," "Tosca," "Turandot" and more. 60 min.
22-1788 *$19.99*

La Gran Scena Opera Company
The acclaimed all-male opera troupe conducts a grand scale parody of some of opera's most lavish scenes. "Performed" are the love duet from "La Boheme," Act IV from "La Traviata," the Seguidilla from "Carmen," "The Entrance of the Divas" from "Die Walkure," and much more. 112 min.
22-3034 *$39.99*

The Perfumed Handkerchief— The Peking Opera (1984)
Steve Allen and Jayne Meadows host this stunning performance of the opera classic. Filmed on location at the Imperial Palace with traditional costumes, magnificent sets, gorgeous color! 70 min.
22-1024 Was $39.99 *$19.99*

Lucia Di Lammermoor
She's been acclaimed worldwide for her performance of the role of Lucia. Now "La Stupenda," Joan Sutherland, takes the stage with the Australian Opera to bring Donizetti's tale to life. 145 min. Subtitled in English.
22-1113 Was $39.99 *$29.99*

Lucia Di Lammermoor (1971)
Famed soprano Anna Moffo stars in the title role as Donizetti's doomed heroine. This opera was filmed on location in Italy and features the Symphony Orchestra of Rome Radio Italiana. 108 min. Sung in Italian with English titles.
22-3007 *$39.99*

The Daughter Of The Regiment
Alternately militant, pastoral and passionate, Donizetti's timeless tale of the triumph of young love is beautifully performed by the Australian Opera, live from Sydney. Joan Sutherland stars as comic heroine Marie. 122 min.
22-1118 Was $39.99 *$29.99*

The Daughter Of The Regiment (1974)
The initial telecast of "Live from Wolf Trap" features Beverly Sills in her TV operatic debut. In this English translation, Donizetti's masterful comic work is energetically brought to life with support from William McDonald, Spiro Malas and Muriel Costa-Greenspon. 118 min.
22-3142 *$39.99*

Lucrezia Borgia
In one of her favorite roles, Joan Sutherland slays them—on and off the stage—as Donizetti's scheming title character in this lush Covent Garden presentation. Alfredo Kraus also stars. 157 min.
22-1717 *$29.99*

Lucrezia Borgia
One of the most infamous women in history is the subject of Donizetti's opera, seen here in an Australian Opera production that features Joan Sutherland in the title role of the glamorous and treacherous Lucrezia, whose drive for revenge costs her the life of her son. With Ron Stevens, Richard Allman. 139 min. Sung in Italian.
22-5695 Was $39.99 *$29.99*

Anna Bolena
This 1985 Canadian Opera Company production of Donizetti's opera stars Joan Sutherland in one her finest performances, playing Ann Boleyn opposite James Morris as Henry VIII. Also featured in the cast are Judith Forst, Michael Myers and Ben Heppner. 157 min. In Italian with English subtitles.
22-3212 *$29.99*

Maria Stuarda
Combining two dramatic looks at the life of England's tragic "Queen of Scots"—Donizetti's opera and the stageplay by Friedrich Schiller—filmmaker Petr Weigl creates a memorable musical experience, shot in actual historical sites. Joan Sutherland and Luciano Pavarotti supply the singing voices of Mary Stuart of the Earl of Leicester; Magdalena Vasaryova, Milan Knazko star. 90 min. Subtitled in English.
50-8341 *$19.99*

La Favorita (1952)
Donizetti's classic opera is performed in this rare Italian film, noteworthy for a supporting player listed as "Sofia Lazzaro" but better known today as Sophia Loren. Sung in Italian with English narration. 80 min.
09-1287 Was $29.99 *$19.99*

Roberto Devereux (1975)
Donizetti's historical opera set in Elizabethan England is given a sumptuous staging at Wolf Trap and fueled by a dynamic performance from Beverly Sills as the "Virgin Queen." The supporting cast includes John Alexander, Susanne Marsee. 145 min. In Italian with English subtitles.
22-3149 *$29.99*

Elixir Of Love (1988)
Gaetano Donizetti's opera is presented in spectacular fashion featuring the Symphony Orchestra of Radio Bratislava. This visual delight boasts a cast that includes Melanie Holliday, Alfredo Mariotti and Miroslav Dvorsky. Italian language version; no subtitles. 90 min.
53-7430 *$39.99*

The Life Of Donizetti
The dramatic story of the renowned Italian composer who created 65 operas and operettas, and whose love for his country comes between him and the woman in his life. Tito Schipa stars. Dubbed in English, with songs sung in Italian. 90 min.
22-7096 *$29.99*

The Australian Opera Gala Concert
Live from the famed Sydney Opera House, an evening of bel canto virtuosity with Joan Sutherland and Marilyn Horne. Richard Bonynge conducts the Elizabethan Symphony accompaniment to duets and arias by Rossini, Bellini, Donizetti and others. 142 min.
22-1120 Was $39.99 *$29.99*

Joan Sutherland: The Age Of Bel Canto
A classic 1963 program with Dame Joan Sutherland performing great operatic roles, commenting on her predecessors and serving as a guide through the Age of Bel Canto. Sutherland's selections include pieces from "Semiramide," "La Sonnambula," "I Puritani" and "La Traviata." Also featured is tenor Richard Conrad.
22-3182 *$29.99*

Joan Sutherland: The Complete Bell Telephone Hour Performances 1961-1968, Vol. 1
Some of the legendary soprano's finest "Bell Telephone Hour" performances have been gathered on this video that includes selections from "I Puritani," "Norma," Ernani," "Rigoletto," "Hamlet" and many others. Donald Vorhees conducts the Bell Telephone Hour Orchestra. 50 min.
22-3225 *$29.99*

Joan Sutherland: The Complete Bell Telephone Hour Performances 1961-1968, Vol. 2
Songs from "La Traviata," "La Sonnambula," "Tosca," "Otello" and other operas are featured in this second sampler of Sutherland's star turns on the early Tv showcase for classical music. Donald Voorhees conducts the Bell Telephone Hour Orchestra. 50 min.
22-3228 *$24.99*

Joan Sutherland In Concert (1969)
In this rare Canadian TV production, Dame Joan Sutherland performs in concert in front of a rapturous crowd, singing 15 selections with her inimitable style and charm. See the incredible Sutherland in a recital, entrancing listeners.
22-3181 *$29.99*

The Abduction Of Figaro (1984)
The first full-length opera from baroque "black sheep" P.D.Q. Bach is now available on video, performed live by the Minnesota Opera. A variation of the Figaro legend, the characters include Al Donfonso, Sussanna Sussannadanna, Schlepporello and Donna Donna. Bach's "discoverer," Prof. Peter Schickele, conducts. 144 min.
22-3030 *$39.99*

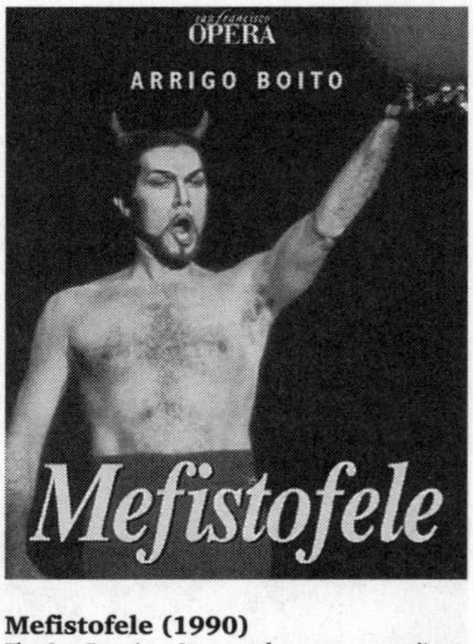

Mefistofele (1990)
The San Francisco Opera performs an extraordinary version of Boito's classic, based on the Faust legend. There's a witches' sabbath, powerful performances by Samuel Ramey in the title role and Dennis O'Neill and superb conducting by Maurizio Arena; directed by Robert Carsen. 159 min. Subtitled in English.
22-5410 Was $39.99 *$29.99*

Opera Imaginaire
Many of the world's greatest operas come to life with help from leading international animators and top performers. This delightful collection includes selections from Mozart, Puccini, Rossini and others, set to animation by Hilary Audus, Jonathan Hills and Jimmy Murakami. Among the performers participating are Franco Corelli, Carlo Bergonzi and Nicolai Ghiaurov. 50 min.
02-8198 Was $19.99 *$14.99*

Trial By Jury/Cox And Box
The second Gilbert and Sullivan collaboration, and the first to win commercial and critical success, "Trial by Jury" is a witty satire of English jurisprudence that depicts a comical breach of promise case and stars Frankie Howerd and Kate Flowers. Next, "Cox and Box," with Sullivan's score and a libretto by F.C. Burnand, follows a crooked landlord who rents the same room to two men. With Russell Smythe, Tom Lawlor. 115 min. total.
22-5905 *$29.99*

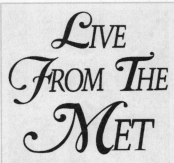

Live From The Met

Live From The Met

The award-winning PBS series that gives you a front row seat at New York's famed Metropolitan Opera House. The world's most renowned singers and musicians are featured in classic performances. Each tape comes with a special brochure.

Un Ballo In Maschera (1980)
The legendary Luciano Pavarotti is featured in this timeless Verdi opera, along with Katia Ricciarelli, Judith Blegen and Bianca Berini. Giuseppe Patane conducts in English. 150 min.
06-1309 *$22.99*

Manon Lescaut (1980)
Placido Domingo and Renata Scotto star in this powerful production of the famed opera from Puccini about the joys of love and youth. Taped at the Metropolitan Opera and conducted by James Levine. 135 min.
06-1419 *$22.99*

Elektra (1980)
The ancient Greek tale of vengeance and intrigue, put to music by Strauss, receives a stirring treatment in this Metropolitan Opera offering. Birgit Nilsson stars in the title role, with Leonie Rysanek, Mignon Dunn. James Levine conducts. 112 min. Subtitled in English.
06-1510 *$22.99*

L'Elisir D'Amore (1981)
Rollicking "opera buffa" by Donizetti stars Luciano Pavarotti as a rejected suitor who turns to a special "love potion" to win his beloved (Judith Blegen). Dazzling Metropolitan Opera production, conducted by Nicola Rescigno. 132 min. Subtitled in English.
06-1511 *$22.99*

La Boheme (1982)
Bohemian Paris is the setting for romance and betrayal in Puccini's immortal grand opera in a production staged by Franco Zeffirelli. Teresa Stratas, Renata Scotto and José Carreras star; James Levine conducts. 125 min. Subtitled in English.
06-1308 *$22.99*

Idomeneo (1982)
The incomparable Luciano Pavarotti sings in the title role in this Metropolitan Opera performance of Mozart's classic. Based on a Greek myth of a father's unwilling sacrifice, the cast includes Ileana Cotrubas, Hildegard Behrens and John Alexander. 185 min. on two tapes. Subtitled in English.
06-1324 *$29.99*

Tannhäuser (1982)
The Metropolitan Opera's lavish production of Richard Wagner's opera features an all-star cast, including soprano Eva Marton, Richard Cassilly, Tatiana Troyanos and Bernd Weikl. James Levine conducts. 176 min. on two tapes. Subtitled in English.
06-1325 *$29.99*

Lucia Di Lammermoor (1982)
Joan Sutherland, in her first Met performance in four years, returns in the role that won her international fame, as Donizetti's tragic heroine. Also featured are Alfredo Kraus, Pablo Elvira and Paul Plishka. 128 min. Subtitled in English.
06-1357 *$22.99*

Hansel And Gretel (1982)
Humperdinck's operatic rendition of the fairytale classic comes alive for both adults and children alike. Thomas Fulton conducts Judith Blegen and Frederica Von Stade at the Met. 104 min. Sung in English.
06-1418 *$22.99*

Don Carlo (1983)
Classic operatic work by Verdi features a stellar cast, including Placido Domingo, Mirella Freni, Louis Quilico and Grace Bumbry. 214 min. on two tapes. Subtitled in English.
06-1310 *$29.99*

Ernani (1983)
Three men conspire against each other for the love of a woman in a classic work by Verdi. The memorable cast includes Luciano Pavarotti, Leona Mitchell, Sherrill Milnes and Ruggero Raimondi. 142 min. Subtitled in English.
06-1356 *$22.99*

Les Troyens (1983)
The Trojan War is the background for Berlioz's epic, seen here in its first uncut Met performance. The stars include Tatiana Troyanos, Jessye Norman and incomparable Placido Domingo. 253 min. on two tapes. Subtitled in English.
06-1358 *$29.99*

Francesca Da Rimini (1984)
Stunning adaptation of the Ricardo Zandonai opera from the Metropolitan Opera stars Placido Domingo and Renata Scotto; conducted by James Levine. 148 min.
06-1420 *$22.99*

La Forza Del Destino (1984)
There's no avoiding it; the legendary Leontyne Price was fated to set the operatic world afire in this Met production of Verdi's grand epic. 179 min. on two tapes. Subtitled in English.
06-1574 *$29.99*

Simon Boccanegra (1984)
World-renowned baritone Sherrill Milnes essays the title role in Verdi's historical opera about the Italian Renaissance ruler and his attempts to unify his homeland. 150 min. Subtitled in English.
06-1576 *$29.99*

Lohengrin (1986)
Eva Marton, Leonie Rysanek and Peter Hoffman lead the stellar Metropolitan Opera cast in one of Wagner's most popular compositions. 220 min. on two tapes. Subtitled in English.
06-1575 *$29.99*

The Metropolitan Opera: Centennial Gala (1983)
A virtual "Who's Who" of music is on stage to celebrate 100 years of the finest performances in Met history. Joan Sutherland, Luciano Pavarotti, Roberta Peters, Leontyne Price, Placido Domingo and Leonard Bernstein, along with many more stars, are featured in this unique event. 231 min. on two tapes.
06-1311 *$29.99*

"Live From The Met" Highlights, Vol. 1
An operatic "best of" collection, with such notables as Pavarotti, Domingo, Sutherland, Stratas, Marton and others in classic performances. Includes selections from such works as "Don Carlo," "La Boheme," "The Bartered Bride" and "Tannhauser." 70 min. Subtitled in English.
06-1359 *$22.99*

Birgit Nilsson: The Bell Telephone Hour
The masterful opera star performs on the classic '60s TV series. On the program are works from "Turandot," "La Forza del Destino" and "Macbeth," as well as two Wagner arias. 45 min.
22-1208 Was $29.99 *$19.99*

Jenufa
The story of passion and romance involving an orphan peasant, a mill owner and the peasant's lover from afar makes for an unforgettable experience as performed by the Glyndebourne Festival Opera, with music from the London Philharmonic Orchestra. Roberta Alexander, Mark Baker and Philip Landridge star. 118 min. With English subtitles.
22-5465 Was $39.99 *$29.99*

Il Matrimonio Segreto
A father's attempt to marry his daughter to an English gentleman is the subject of this comic Domenico Cimarosa opera. Performed at the elegant Schwetzingen Palace, the Cologne Opera production features Barbara Daniels, Carlos Feller and Claudio Nicolai. 152 min. In Italian with English subtitles.
22-5185 Was $49.99 *$29.99*

Oedipus Rex/The Flood
A special double bill of Stravinsky operas includes Felicity Palmer, Neil Rosenshein and Anton Scharinger, under conductor Robert Haitink, in the story of the fatally flawed monarch, followed by Robert Craft and the Columbia Symphony Orchestra and Chorus in "The Flood." 90 min.
22-5128 *$29.99*

Kiri Te Kanawa In Concert
In a magnificent outdoor concert before 75,000 fans in Wellington, New Zealand, "local gal" Kiri Te Kanawa offers a recital that ranges from Puccini to Gershwin. Along with highlights from that show, this program also features her in a London show, singing Handel and Mozart at Christopher Wren's Chapel. 52 min.
22-1768 *$19.99*

Kiri Te Kanawa
One of the world's best-loved opera stars, acclaimed soprano Kiri Te Kanawa, talks about her life and career in this documentary that includes magnificent performance clips, including scenes of Te Kanawa returning to her native New Zealand to open that country's first opera house. 106 min.
22-5694 Was $39.99 *$29.99*

Cavalleria Rusticana (1990)
Staged in Siena to commemorate the centennial of the debut of Mascagni's masterful opera. American diva Shirley Verrett and noted tenor Krjstian Johannson head up a superlative cast in this opulent, moving rendition. 85 min.
22-3118 *$39.99*

The Gift Of The Magi
O. Henry's beloved story of a young couple's touching Christmas presents to one another has been turned into a moving opera by Finnish composer Einojuhani Rautavaara. Pia Freund and Jaakko Kortekangas star as the husband and wife who sacrifice to make each other's holiday dream come true. 45 min.
22-1760 *$19.99*

Lady Macbeth Of Mtsensk
Dmitri Shostakovich's four-act opera has been filmed by leading director Petr Weigl and offers a compelling story set just before the Russian Revolution in 1917. It focuses on a wealthy family of landowners which includes a patriarchal father, weak son and mother, who carries on an affair with a farmhand when her husband is away on business. 98 min.
50-8242 *$19.99*

Naughty Marietta (1955)
One of composer Victor Herbert's best-loved works, this romantic operetta was broadcast live on TV by producer/director Max Liebman. The superb cast is headed by Alfred Drake as dashing Captain Warrington and Patrice Munsel in the title role; songs include "Ah! Sweet Mystery of Life," "Italian Street Song" and "Tramp! Tramp! Tramp!" 78 min.
22-3161 *$39.99*

A Streetcar Named Desire
The landmark Tennessee Williams play of desire and madness in the New Orleans night is turned by renowned composer/conductor Andre Previn into a powerful operatic tale. Recorded live at the San Francisco War Memorial Opera House, this world premiere production features Reneec Fleming as Blanche, and Rodney Gilfry as Stanley. 165 min.
22-1762 *$29.99*

Norma
Ancient Gaul in the days of the Roman Empire is the setting for this compelling operatic work by Bellini. Joan Sutherland heads an impressive cast in the Australian Opera production as Norma, a Druid priestess torn between her devotion to her people and her love for the Roman official who fathered her children. Ron Stevens, Margreta Elkins also star. 153 min. Sung in Italian.
22-5681 Was $39.99 *$29.99*

Norma (1981)
From the archives of the Canadian Broadcasting Company comes a performance of Bellini's bel canto masterpiece. Joan Sutherland and Tatiana Troyanos star in this Canadian Opera Company production directed by Lofti Mansouri. 150 min.
22-3194 *$39.99*

La Sonnambula
Bellini's delightful tale of the young rustic who sleepwalks her way in and out of trouble is given a loving rendition in this feature film. Gino Sinimberghi and Fiorella Ortis star in this Rome Opera Company production. 90 min. In Italian with English narration.
22-7024 *$29.99*

Music Of The Night: José Carreras Sings Andrew Lloyd Webber
Famed tenor José Carreras performs a stirring concert from the works of Andrew Lloyd Webber, including "Memory" from "Cats"; "Don't Cry for Me, Argentina" from "Evita"; and "All I Ask of You" from "Phantom of the Opera." Marti Webb, Jane Harrison and The Choir of St. Paul's Cathedral also appear; George Martin produces. 52 min.
19-3556 *$24.99*

José Carreras: A Tribute To Mario Lanza—With A Song In My Heart
Live from London's Royal Albert Hall, the famed tenor salutes Philadelphia's own Mario Lanza with a special recital that includes Carreras singing "Be My Love," "Because You're Mine," "Serenade," "Una Furtiva Lagrima" and more. There's also a rare clip of Lanza performing "Ave Maria." 83 min.
19-3646 *$29.99*

José Carreras: Music Festival In Granada
Filmed in Granada, Spain, this performance by great tenor José Carreras features selections from Tosti, Puccini, de Falla and others. A magnificent program from a great singer. 93 min.
22-1250 *$24.99*

José Carreras: Opera Gala In Moscow
Join Carreras and a host of top singers as they commemorate Russian independence with this dazzling recital from Moscow's Red Square. Carreras, along with Anna Tomowa-Sintow, Leo Nucci, Kathleen Kuhlmann and the Moscow Radio Symphony Orchestra, performs selections from "La Boheme," "Carmen," "La Traviata" and more. 90 min.
22-1296 *$24.99*

Carreras
A revealing look at one of the musical world's most acclaimed tenors, this documentary follows José Carreras for four days on the road in Spain and California while making the film "Misa Criolla." Carreras is seen in rehearsal, meeting fans and relaxing with his son on the film set. 31 min.
22-1307 *$19.99*

José Carreras In Vienna (1988)
Considered "The Miracle Concert" because it took place just months after Carreras had undergone bone marrow transplants to fight leukemia, this emotional program showcases the singer performing selections by Puccini, Massenet, Fauré and others at the Vienna State Opera. 140 min.
22-1318 *$24.99*

José Carreras: Jubileum Concert (1998)
Master tenor José Carreras performs beautiful arias and songs from top composers in this special celebration for Jubileum 2000 with the International Orchestra of Rome. Selections include Handel's "Allelujeh" from "Messiah"; Schubert's "Mille Cherubini"; Mozart's "Ave Verum Corpus"; George Bizet's "Angus Dei"; and "Ava Maria." 72 min.
50-8493 *$14.99*

Ballet

American Ballet Theatre Now
Some of the most renowned American Ballet Theatre dancers come together to perform selections from ABT's repertoire. Twenty-eight-year ABT veteran Natalia Makarova introduces the pieces, performed at New York's City Center, and the dancers include Alessandra Ferri, Paloma Herrera, Jose Manuel Carreño and Julio Bocca. 83 min.
22-1589 *$29.99*

American Ballet Theater: A Close Up In Time (1973)
Get acquainted with America's oldest and most distinguished ballet company in this look at the ABT's history and unique approach to dance. Featured are such soloists as Christine Sarry, Sallie Wilson and Karena Brock; choreographers Agnes De Mille, Alvin Ailey and Anthony Tudor; and selections from "Les Sylphides," "Rodeo," "Swan Lake" and others. 90 min.
48-7023 *$59.99*

American Ballet Theatre At The Met (1984)
Mikhail Baryshnikov, Patrick Bissel, Fernando Bujones and Cynthia Harvey are among the principal dancers in this stunning sampling of the ABT's repertory. "Les Sylphides," "Paquita," "Sylvia" and "Triad" are the ballets excerpted. A must for any ballet fan! 100 min.
44-1355 Was $39.99 *$19.99*

Great Pas De Deux
It takes two to tango...and also to perform the memorable ballet duets displayed on this special collection. Among the star pairings featured are Dame Margot Fonteyn and Rudolf Nureyev in "Le Corsaire," Natalia Makarova and Anthony Dowell in "A Month in the Country," and others. 91 min.
22-1648 *$19.99*

Pas De Deux
A spectacular evening of ballet at the John Anson Ford Amphitheatre in Los Angeles. Performing are Patricia McBride, Ravena Tucker, Ghislaine Thesmar and others, performing eight pas de deux from "The Sleeping Beauty," "Don Quixote," "Le Corsaire" and "La Sylphide." 81 min.
22-3035 *$29.99*

Speaking In Tongues
The Paul Taylor Dance Company dazzles in this production conceived by Taylor, Matthew Diamond and Santo Loquasto. Among the numbers are "Every Time I Go," "Loomings," "Followers" and others; performers include Elie Chaih, Cathy McCann. 54 min.
19-3724 *$24.99*

Paul Taylor Dance Company: Esplandade/Runes
The acclaimed dance ensemble, under director Charles S. Dubin, is featured in a rare filmed performance of two of its best-known numbers. 58 min.
19-4021 *$29.99*

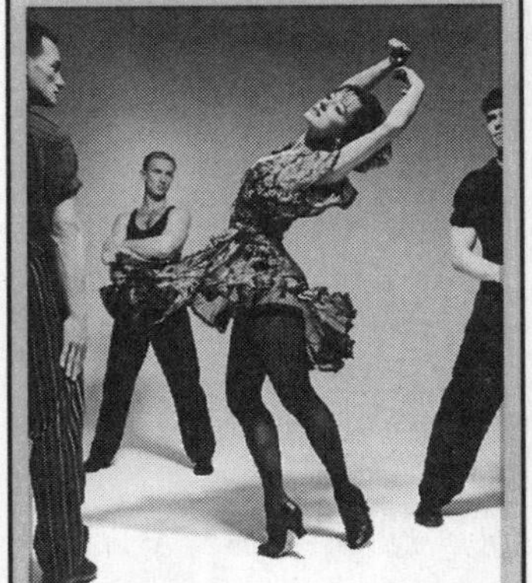

Paul Taylor: Dancemaker (1998)
Offering a rare backstage look at the man called "the greatest living choreographer," director Paul Diamond's Academy Award-nominated documentary follows Taylor and his eponymous dance company through rehearsals to the debut of his composition "Piazzolla Caldera." See how this alumnus of the Martha Graham troupe drives himself and his dancers in his pursuit of artistic excellence. 98 min.
53-6706 *$24.99*

The Kirov Ballet: Don Quixote
A splendid spectacle created with the Leningrad corps' considerable resources, starring Vladimir Ponomaryov as the windmill-tilting knight and Tatyana Terekhova and Farouk Ruzimatoav as the lovers Kitri and Basilio. 120 min.
22-1121 Was $39.99 ***$19.99***

The Magic Of The Kirov Ballet
A commemorative anthology of the very best of the company's extraordinary repertoire, including the "Entry of the Shades" and "Indian Dance" from "La Bayadere," and duets from "La Corsaire," "Paquita," "Don Quixote" and "Sleeping Beauty." Choreographed by Marius Petipa; with Farouk Ruzimatov, Tatyana Terekhova. 60 min.
22-1122 Was $29.99 ***$19.99***

The Glory Of The Kirov
The list of Kirov performers reads like a "Who's Who" of dance. Mikhail Baryshnikov, Natalia Dudinskaya, Natalia Makarova, Rudolf Nureyev and others are seen in excerpts from such works as "Raymonda," "Romeo and Juliet" and "Swan Lake" in this compilation of memorable Kirov Ballet moments. 91 min.
22-1650 ***$19.99***

Kirov Classics
A series of dazzling ballet pieces are presented, danced by leading members of the Maryinsky Ballet (formerly the Kirov Ballet). Altynai Asylmuratova, Larissa Lezhnina and Faroukh Ruzimatov perform from such works as "Chopiniana," "Petrushka," "Barber's Adagio" and others. 147 min.
22-5653 Was $39.99 ***$29.99***

The Kirov Ballet: Classic Ballet Night
Powerful potpourri of performances by the esteemed company. See Irina Kolpakova, Gabriela Komleva, Alla Sizova and Galina Mezentseva working to the choreography of Vaganova, Petipa, Dolin and Bournonville. "Diana and Actheon," "Esmeralda," "La Vivandiere," and more. 95 min.
22-7007 ***$29.99***

Kirov Soloists: Invitation To The Dance
The principal dancers of the Kirov present an enthralling selection of performances that are complemented by revealing rehearsal footage. Irina Kolpakova, Sergei Berezhnoi and Tatyana Terekhova dance to Pugni, Villa Lobos and Offenbach. 54 min.
22-7008 Was $29.99 ***$19.99***

Shakespeare Dance Trilogy
Famed Kirov Ballet soloists, including Gabriella Komleva, Svetlana Semenova, Alexander Semenchukov and Andres Williams, bring the stories of the Bard to life in three lush dance pieces: "Romeo and Juliet," "Hamlet" and "The Moor's Pavane" ("Othello"). 70 min.
22-7119 Was $29.99 ***$19.99***

The Story Of The Kirov Ballet
A look at the popular ballet company which includes a history of the Kirov, footage of their first performances outside of Russia and rare dance sequences showcasing Kirov members Anna Pavlova, Spesivtseva, Ulanova and Baryshnikov. 52 min.
89-7026 ***$14.99***

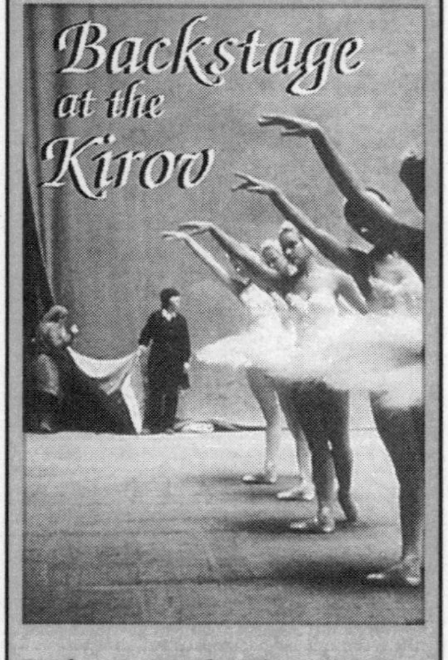

Backstage At The Kirov (1983)
A beautiful behind-the-scenes documentary look at the famed Russian ballet troupe. Absorbing and magical, the film takes you on a personal view of the dancers' fears, joys and lifestyles. 80 min.
07-1216 Was $19.99 ***$14.99***

Romeo And Juliet
The legendary Rudolf Nureyev served as choreographer for this Paris Opera Ballet presentation of the Prokofiev masterwork, with Manuel Legris and Monique Loudières starring in the title roles. 150 min.
22-1787 ***$29.99***

Romeo And Juliet (1955)
Sergei Prokofiev's adaptation of the timeless Shakespeare story is presented here by the Bolshoi Ballet. Dance greats Yuri Zhdanov and Galina Ulanova essay the title roles for an unforgettable ballet experience. 95 min.
22-1097 Was $29.99 ***$19.99***

Romeo And Juliet (1966)
Prokofiev's adaptation of Shakespeare's undying tragedy is performed with consummate grace and skill by the British Royal Ballet. Striking work by Margot Fonteyn, Rudolf Nureyev, and David Blair. 124 min.
22-1086 Was $29.99 ***$24.99***

Romeo And Juliet (1976)
Combine Shakespeare's story, Prokofiev's music, and the majesty of the Bolshoi Ballet, and the result is a slice of dance history. Natalia Bessmertnova and Mikhail Lavrovsky are the doomed lovers in this incredible ballet experience. 108 min.
22-1083 Was $39.99 ***$19.99***

Spartacus
You'll love the Australian Ballet's version of the story of slave leader Spartacus and his wife Flavia, who struggle for freedom in ancient Roman times. Lisa Payne and Steven Heathcote star in this stirring performance. 120 min.
22-1800 ***$19.99***

La Fille Mal Gardee
The Australian Ballet's Fiona Tonkin and David McAllister star in this celebrated presentation that blends comedy, pathos and lyricism as it depicts the difficulties of young love. 106 min.
22-1802 ***$19.99***

The Australian Ballet Favorites
Here's a sampling of some of the finest productions put on by the Australian Ballet. Included are segments from "Giselle," "Swan Lake," "Coppelia," "The Sleeping Beauty" and others. 83 min.
22-1804 ***$19.99***

Alicia
A very special look at the life and career of Cuban-born ballet great Alicia Alonso, including such roles as "Swan Lake's" Black Swan Pas de Deux and works from "Giselle" and "The Carmen Ballet." 70 min.
22-3053 Was $39.99 ***$19.99***

Russian Ballet: The Glorious Tradition, Vol. 1
The Russian Ballet's greatest stars in their most acclaimed roles can be seen on this expert compilation filled with rare footage and incredible dancing. Witness Baryshnikov and Semenyaka performing a pas de deux from "Don Quixote," Liepa and Ananiashvili performing a pas de deux from "Corsaire," and excerpts from "Swan Lake" with Alla Osipenko.
22-3152 ***$39.99***

Russian Ballet: The Glorious Tradition, Vol. 2
More rare footage of Russian ballet stars is presented in this program that ranges from 1914 to the '40s and includes Natalia Dudinskaya, Galina Ulanova, Maya Plisetskaya and Ekaterina Maximova performing such pieces as "The Dying Swan" and the "grand pas de deux" from "Don Quixote." 71 min.
22-3156 ***$39.99***

The Russian Ballet: The Glorious Tradition, Vol. 3
Among the treasures featured here are early footage of Maya Plisetskaya, Natalia Makarova, Mikhail Baryshnikov and Yuri Soloviev, plus Nadezda Gracheva and Andrey Uvarov performing the pas de deux from "Sleeping Beauty," and more. 67 min.
22-3163 ***$39.99***

Mademoiselle Fifi
One of the century's most acclaimed ballet figures, Alexandra Danilova, is featured in her only filmed complete performance in this Canadian TV production. Dancing along with Danilova are Ballet Russe de Monte Carlo stars Roman Jasinksi and Michael Maule. 20 min.
22-3157 ***$19.99***

Nina Ananiashvili And International Stars, Vol. 1
The magnificent star of Russian ballet and the ABT dances "Le Spectre de la Rose" and "The Sleeping Beauty," while greats from such famed troupes as the Bolshoi perform excerpts from "Swan Lake" and "La Corsaire" in this 1991 recital from Japan. 57 min.
22-3169 ***$24.99***

Nina Ananiashvili And International Stars, Vol. 2
Along with top artists from the Bolshoi Ballet, the Royal Danish Ballet and the Leningrad Kirov Ballet, this program features Nina Ananiashvili dancing "The Dying Swan," "Moods" and "Don Quixote." 84 min.
22-3170 ***$29.99***

Nina Ananiashvili And International Stars, Vol. 3
The great Ananiashvili dances "Pas de Quatre" and "Raymonda" in a 1993 gala performed in Japan. An added delight has premier dancers from the Bolshoi, Paris Opera Ballet and others performing in "Satanella," "Sunny" and more. 63 min.
22-3171 ***$24.99***

Nutcracker On Ice
Olympic gold medal-winners Oksana Baiul and Viktor Pretrenko skate to Tchaikovsky's famed "Nutcracker" in this glorious program that mixes thrilling on-ice theatrics, magical music and lovely costumes. 110 min.
04-3252 ***$14.99***

The Nutcracker: A Christmas Story
The Bonn Ballet and the Klassiche Philharmonie of Bonn are featured in this all-new version, created by Youri Vamos, of Tchaikovsky's beloved holiday-themed ballet.
04-5187 ***$29.99***

Tchaikovsky's The Nutcracker
Top dancers Ludmilla Vasileva and Alexander Gorbatsevich perform with the Russian State Theatre Academy of Classic Ballet in this beautifully realized version of Tchaikovsky's beloved Christmas classic. 100 min.
22-1489 ***$19.99***

The Nutcracker (Birmingham Royal Ballet)
A little girl's Christmas Eve dream sends her into a magical fantasy world of toy soldiers, sugar plum fairies, and mice kings in this Birmingham Royal Ballet staging of the Tchaikovsky favorite. The cast includes Miyako Yoshida, Irek Mukhamedov, Sandra Madgwick. 98 min.
22-5849 Was $39.99 ***$29.99***

The Nutcracker
The Royal Ballet of Covent Garden brings to life the magical tale of the Nutcracker. The principals include Lesley Collier, Anthony Dowell, Julie Rose and Guy Niblett; the choreographers are Lev Ivanov and Peter Wright. 102 min.
44-1307 ***$19.99***

The Nutcracker Ballet
Tchaikovsky's famed holiday ballet is presented in all of its magical splendor by the Ballet of Slovak National Theatre with such performers as Nora Gallovicova, Jozef Dolinsky and Zuzana Kvassayova. 69 min.
89-7017 ***$14.99***

The Nutcracker (1968)
The legendary Rudolf Nureyev takes the stage with Merle Park and the Royal Ballet for this superlative presentation of Tchaikovsky's holiday perennial. 100 min.
22-1574 ***$29.99***

The Nutcracker (1977)
The American Ballet Theatre and Mikhail Baryshnikov present this timeless and colorful production of Tchaikovsky's ballet, with prima ballerina Gelsey Kirkland as the young girl whose Christmas Eve dream brings a toy soldier nutcracker to life as a handsome prince (Baryshnikov). 79 min.
12-1230 Was $19.99 ***$14.99***

The Nutcracker (1978)
Everyone's favorite Yuletide spectacle, Tchaikovsky's immortal fairy tale set to music is performed live at Moscow's Bolshoi Theatre. Watch a young girl's dreams come to life in a magical display of ballet excellence. Stars Yekatrina Maximova, Vladimir Vasiliev. 120 min.
22-1075 ***$16.99***

George Balanchine's The Nutcracker (1993)
Sugarplum translation of Tchaikovsky's holiday classic featuring the New York City Ballet dancing to George Balanchine's revered choreography. Macaulay Culkin appears in this tale of a young girl who witnesses a toy soldier turn into a handsome prince, who goes to battle against the wicked Mouse King. Kevin Kline narrates; directed by Emile Ardolino ("Dirty Dancing"). 93 min.
19-2270 Was $19.99 ***$14.99***

Nutcracker: The Story Of Clara
Tchaikovsky's much-loved music is used, but the story has been changed in this Australian Ballet production that tells of a famous Russian ballerina whose relocation Down Under in the 1940s led to a turbulent, nomadic life. Vicki Attard and Steven Heathcote star. 113 min.
22-1801 ***$19.99***

The Hard Nut (1992)
The Mark Morris Dance Group has been recognized worldwide for its inventiveness, and here they stage a whimsical spoof of "The Nutcracker," set in '60s suburbia and featuring male snowflakes, G.I. Joes and Morris himself as a harem girl, along with Tchaikovsky's music. 90 min.
19-3382 ***$19.99***

Swan Lake (The Kirov Ballet)
Tchaikovsky's magnificent classic is brought to life by the Kirov Ballet with dazzling choreography by Marius Petipa and Lev Ivanov. Among the performers are Yulia Makhalina and Igor Zelensky. 116 min.
19-3725 ***$29.99***

Swan Lake With Nina Ananiashvili
Presented to note the centennial of Tchaikovsky's death, this Russian State Perm Ballet production of one of the world's best-loved ballets features acclaimed prima ballerina Nina Ananiashvili and Aleksei Fadeyetchev. 132 min.
22-1305 ***$24.99***

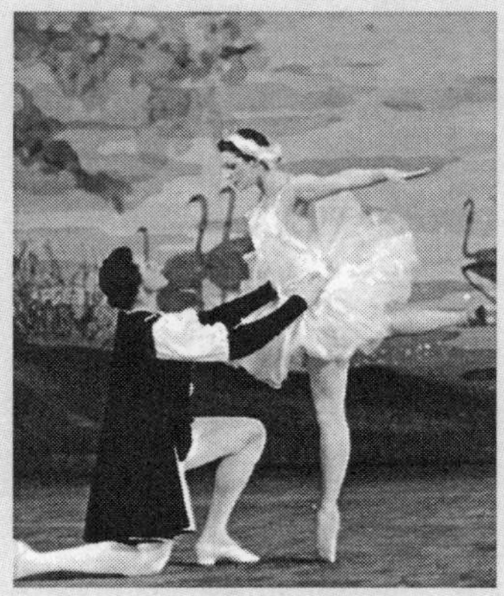

Swan Lake With Maya Plisetskaya
The prima ballerina dances the dual roles of Odette and Odile along with the famed Bolshoi Ballet in this, the most visually stunning of all ballets. Filmed at the Bolshoi Theatre, Plisetskaya's moves are majestic and Tchaikovsky's score classic. 81 min.
22-1099 ***$29.99***

Swan Lake (The Kirov Ballet)
This spectacular production of Tchaikovsky's classic ballet features such Kirov stars as Galina Mezenseva and Konstantin Zaklinsky in a presentation filmed live at the Marinsky Theater. 144 min.
22-1483 ***$19.99***

Swan Lake (1982)
The world's best known ballet, seen here in an all-new production by the Royal Ballet. Tchaikovsky's classic tale of romance and fantasy stars Natalia Makarova and Anthony Dowell and was filmed live at Covent Garden. 137 min.
44-1304 ***$29.99***

Sleeping Beauty
The famed Fernando Bujones, along with 60 dancers, performs this great ballet. Magnificent sets, fabulous costumes. 120 min.
22-1008 ***$19.99***

The Sleeping Beauty
Rudolf Nureyev and Veronica Tennant star in this Emmy-winning production that features Nureyev at his peak, dancing with the National Ballet of Canada. 90 min.
22-1469 ***$24.99***

The Kirov Ballet: The Sleeping Beauty
At the Maryinsky Theatre in Russia, the Kirov Ballet performs a moving interpretation of Tchaikovsky's beloved ballet. Among the featured performers are Altynai Asylmuratova and Konstantin Zaklinsky. 160 min.
22-1488 ***$19.99***

The Sleeping Beauty
Tchaikovsky's celebrated ballet as performed by the Australian Ballet is a magical experience. Follow beautiful Princess Aurora, who is condemned to sleep until Prince Florimund awakens her with a kiss. Christine Walsh and David Ashmole star. 135 min
22-1799 ***$19.99***

The Sleeping Beauty
Can true love, and a prince's kiss, break a 100-year curse placed on a sleeping princess by an evil fairy? Tchaikovsky's adaptation of the beloved fairy tale, produced by the Royal Opera at Covent Garden, features choreography by Marius Pepita and a cast that includes Viviana Durante, Zoltan Solymosi and Anthony Dowell. 132 min.
22-5848 Was $39.99 ***$29.99***

Sleeping Beauty (1965)
Colorful filming of Tchaikovsky's ballet fable, as performed by the Kirov Ballet. Alla Sizova dances in the title role, along with Yuri Solovyov, Natalia Makarova, and a host of Kirov stars, in this acclaimed presentation. 95 min.
22-1184 Was $29.99 ***$19.99***

Onegin
Tchaikovsky's enduring tragedy of a young girl's unrequited love is vibrantly presented in this production from the National Ballet of Canada. Sabina Alleman, Frank Augustyn star; John Cranko choreographs. 96 min.
22-5105 ***$39.99***

Gala Tribute To Tchaikovsky
Placido Domingo, Kiri Te Kanawa and conductor Edward Downes join the companies of the Royal Ballet and Royal Opera at Covent Garden for a salute to Tchaikovsky. Among the composer's best-loved works performed here are selections from "The Nutcracker," "The Queen of Spades" and "Eugene Onegin," the 1812 Overture, and more. 135 min.
22-5745 Was $39.99 ***$29.99***

Plisetskaya Dances
Bolshoi Ballet star Maya Plisetskaya is featured in a documentary look at her life and career. Rare stage performances from such works as "Sleeping Beauty," "Swan Lake" and "Spartacus" are shown. 70 min.
22-1096 Was $29.99 ***$19.99***

The Little Humpbacked Horse (1971)
Dazzling sets and choreography, a magical tale of an enchanted steed, and the leaping Maya Plisetskaya are featured in this charming Bolshoi Ballet production. 85 min.
22-3002 Was $29.99 ***$19.99***

Carmen (1973)
The legendary Plisetskaya, first name Maya, stars in this dynamic rendering of the classic ballet. Also included: scenes of "The Dying Swan," "Bach's Prelude" and more. 73 min.
22-1095 Was $29.99 ***$19.99***

Anna Karenina (1974)
Tolstoy's story of love and betrayal is transformed into a ballet by the talents of composer Rodion Schedrin and choreographer Maya Plisetskaya, who takes the title role. Cast includes Alexander Godunov, Vladimir Tihonov. 81 min.
22-1107 Was $29.99 ***$19.99***

Cinderella Ballet
The Berlin Comic Opera Ballet creates an enthralling interpretation of Prokofiev's retelling of the beloved fairy tale. Hannelore Bey and Roland Gawlick move wonderfully to the choreography of Tom Schilling. 75 min.
22-7013 ***$29.99***

Cinderella (1961)
Magnificent, color-filled film version of the Bolshoi Ballet's staging of the Prokofiev classic, shot during a performance in Moscow. Raisa Struchkova is featured in the title role, along with Gennadi Lediakh, Elena Vanke. 81 min.
65-1002 Was $29.99 ***$19.99***

Cinderella (1969)
Filmed at the historic Covent Garden, this acclaimed Royal Ballet presentation features the music of Prokofiev and a cast that includes Antoinette Sibley, Anthony Dowell, Frederick Ashton and Robert Helpmann. 102 min.
22-1584 ***$29.99***

Baryshnikov Dances Sinatra And More...
A trilogy of "mini-ballets" from renowned choreographer Twyla Tharp, performed by Baryshnikov and the American Ballet Theatre. Features the light-hearted "Push Comes to Shove," the romantic "Little Ballet," and a unique salute to "Ol' Blue Eyes," "Sinatra Suite." 60 min.
22-1129 ***$19.99***

Don Quixote
The Cervantes classic becomes a memorable dance experience thanks to the American Ballet Theater, under the direction of Mikhail Baryshnikov, and features Baryshnikov and Cynthia Harvey. 135 min.
44-1274 Was $39.99 ***$29.99***

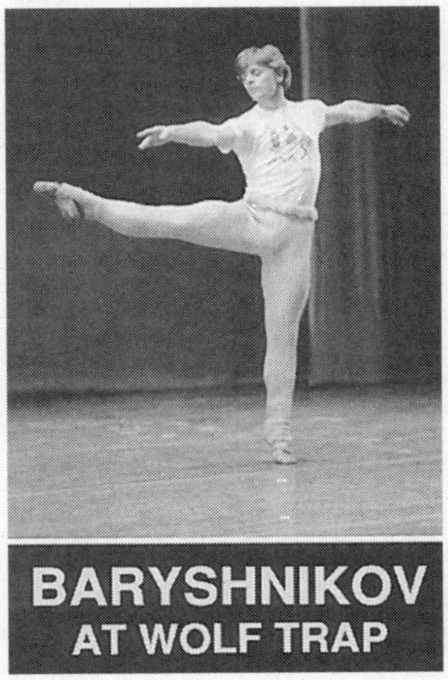

Baryshnikov At Wolf Trap (1976)
The incomparable Mikhail Baryshnikov made his American TV debut in this live special. Solos and pas de deux from such ballets as "Coppelia," "Le Spectre de la Rose," "Vestris" and "Don Quixote" are performed by Baryshnikov and guest artists Marianna Tcherkassky and Gelsey Kirkland. 50 min.
22-1216 Was $29.99 ***$19.99***

Carmen (1980)
The legendary Mikhail Baryshnikov stars alongside Zizi Jeanmarie in this erotically compelling ballet set to the music of Bizet's classic opera. An electrifying performance not to be missed! 44 min.
22-1178 Was $29.99 ***$19.99***

The Balanchine Library: Prodigal Son/Chaconne
Mikhail Baryshnikov stars with Karin von Aroldingen in this masterful adaptation of Prokofiev's "Prodigal Son," conceived by George Balanchine in the 1920s and co-produced by Emile Ardolino ("Dirty Dancing"). New York City Ballet's Suzanne Farrell and Peter Martins are featured in Christoph Willibald Gluck's "Chaconne." 57 min.
19-3714 ***$29.99***

The Balanchine Library: Tzigane/Andante From Divertimento No. 15/The Four Temperaments
Three pieces brilliantly choreographed by George Balanchine are presented in this program: Paul Hindemith's "The Four Temperaments" features Bart Cook and Colleen Neary; Mozart's "Andante from Divertimento No. 15" is performed by Merrill Ashley and Maria Calegari; and Maurice Ravel's "Tzigane" showcases the unforgettable Suzanne Farrell. 54 min.
19-3715 ***$29.99***

The Balanchine Library: Robert Schumann's Davidsbündlertänze
An all-star cast of the world's top dancers brings to life George Balanchine's final masterpiece. Among the performers featured are Suzanne Farrell, Jacques d'Amboise and Peter Martins. 43 min.
19-3716 ***$29.99***

The Balanchine Library: Dancing For Mr. B: Six Balanchine Ballerinas
Six famous ballerinas and Balanchine prodigies, including Maria Tallchief, Mary Ellen Moylan and Allegra Kent, are interviewed and perform in excerpts from some of the master's most acclaimed works, including "Agon," "Stars and Stripes" and "The Four Temperaments." 86 min.
19-3717 ***$29.99***

The Balanchine Library: The Balanchine Essays
The moves and techniques that helped make George Balanchine one of the most revered choreographers of all time are demonstrated and analyzed in this series featuring Suki Schorer, Merrill Ashley and the stars of the New York City Ballet. Except where noted, each tape runs about 45 min.

The Balanchine Library: The Balanchine Essays—Arabesque
Includes selections from "The Nutcracker," "Donizetti Variations," "Swan Lake," "Symphony in C," "The Four Temperaments" and others.
19-3718 ***$29.99***

The Balanchine Library: The Balanchine Essays—Passé And Attitude
Excerpts from "Divertimento No. 15" and "Symphony in C" are performed.
19-3876 ***$29.99***

The Balanchine Library: The Balanchine Essays—Port De Bras And Epaulement
The highlighted ballets include "Agon," "Diamonds," "Swan Lake," "The Nutcracker" and "Stars and Stripes."
19-3877 ***$29.99***

The Balanchine Library: The Balanchine Celebration, Part One
An international array of star performers, including Isabelle Guérin, Zhanna Ayupova, Darci Kistler and Nilas Martins, was gathered by the New York City Ballet for this program of early Balanchine ballets. Selections from "Apollo," "Vienna Waltzes," "Union Jack," "Walpurgisnacht Ballet" and other works are featured. 86 min.
19-3873 ***$29.99***

The Balanchine Library: The Balanchine Celebration, Part Two
Highlights from some of Balanchine's American compositions are performed by such dance notables as Royal Ballet star Darcey Bussell and Lindsay Fischer ("Agon"), Margaret Tracey and Damian Woetzel ("Stars and Stripes"), Nikolaj Hübbe and the ABT's Susan Jaffe ("Western Symphony"), and Jeremy Collins, Viviana Durante and Judith Fugate ("Who Cares?"). 86 min.
19-3874 ***$29.99***

The Balanchine Library: Choreography By Balanchine—Selections From Jewels/Stravinsky Violin Concerto
First shown on the PBS series "Dance in America" and produced under George Balanchine's supervision, this ballet double bill features Merrill Ashley, Karin von Aroldingen, Peter Martins, Bart Cook and the New York City Ballet in the "Diamonds" and "Emeralds" pieces from "Jewels" and "Stravinsky Violin Concerto." 56 min.
19-3875 ***$29.99***

The Balanchine Library: Ballo Della Regina/The Steadfast Tin Soldier/Elégie/Tchaikovsky Pas de Deux
This Emmy-winning "Dance in America" program featured the members of the New York City Ballet, including Mikhail Baryshnikov, Patricia McBride, Karin Von Aroldingen and Merrill Ashley, performing four memorable works by George Balanchine. 51 min.
19-4019 ***$29.99***

The Best Of Balanchine Set
The master choreographer is saluted with a special five-tape set that includes "Ballo Della Regina/The Steadfast Tin Soldier/Elegie/Tchaikovsky Pas de Deux," "Choreography by Balanchine: Selections from Jewels/Stravinsky Violin Concerto," "The Four Temperaments," "George Balanchine's The Nutcracker" and "Prodigal Son/Chaconne."
19-4033 Save $40.00! ***$94.99***

Spirit: A Journey In Dance, Drums And Song
A unique blend of traditional Native American dance and music with modern melodies, this stirring concert features dozens of performers, from dancers to musicians to vocalists, in numbers ranging from powerful chants to rock songs. Kevin Costner introduces this moving stage production. 75 min.
02-9088 ***$24.99***

A Window On The World Of Classical Ballet
An illuminating look at what goes on behind the curtains at the Australian Ballet is offered in this program. Viewers are taken to daily dance classes, have an opportunity to learn steps and exercises, witness rehearsals and see what's involved in staging a ballet. 98 min.
22-1803 ***$19.99***

Godunov: The World To Dance In
Intimate look at the life and career of world acclaimed ballet star Alexander Godunov, featuring scenes from his greatest performances, duets with Gregory and Plisetskaya, and even a look at his relationship with Jacqueline Bisset. 60 min.
22-1015 Was $39.99 ***$19.99***

La Sylphide
George Balanchine said it was "The ballet that changed the course of ballet history." You'll be mesmerized by the splendor, the grace, the excitement of this glorious treat, performed by the Paris Opera Ballet. 90 min.
22-1019 Was $39.99 ***$19.99***

Bujones: In His Image
The world of ballet pays homage to one of its premier dancers, Fernando Bujones, seen here in performances from "Le Corsaire," "Raymonda," "Don Quixote" and "Giselle." Includes interviews with Bujones, Cynthia Gregory, Robert Denver and Jane Herman. 60 min.
22-1055 Was $39.99 ***$19.99***

Bujones: Winning At Varna (1974)
In July of 1974, Fernando Bujones became the first male American dancer to earn a gold medal at the International Ballet Competition VII in Varna, Bulgaria. His award-winning performance is featured in rare footage in this historic program. 30 min.
22-1718 ***$19.99***

Le Corsaire
The Kirov Ballet with Yevgeny Neff and Altynai Asylmuratova perform the three-act classic that's based in part on Lord Byron's heroic poem. Lavish sets, gorgeous costumes and music by Adolphe Adam help tell the story of sailors who are shipwrecked near the Ionian Sea during the Turkish occupation of Greece. 86 min.
19-3416 ***$29.99***

Soldat And Pulcinella
A double bill of Stravinsky favorites, featuring choreography by Shaley Page and Richard Alston, performed by the Rambert Dance Company. Dancers include Gary Lambert, Amanda Britton, Christopher Carney and Glenn Wilkinson. 66 min.
19-3758 ***$24.99***

Moiseyev Ballet
Under the direction of founder Igor Moiseyev, the world-renowned Russian dance troupe will enthrall you with their blend of traditional ballet, native folk dance and dynamic acrobatics. The program includes "Partisans," "Polyanka," "Night on Bald Mountain" and other pieces. 120 min.
22-1380 ***$29.99***

Moiseyev Dance Company: A Gala Evening
The fabulous folk dance troupe of Igor Moiseyev is captured in concert at the Congress Hall in Moscow. Wonderful, high-stepping, acrobatic performance that is certain to delight. 70 min.
22-7009 ***$29.99***

An Evening With The Royal Ballet
A very special performance of London's Royal Ballet, featuring guest stars Rudolph Nureyev and Margot Fonteyn. Selections include "Le Corsaire," "La Valse," "Les Sylphides" and Act III of "Sleeping Beauty." 87 min.
22-1087 Was $29.99 ***$19.99***

Highlights From The Royal Ballet
Lesley Collier, Anthony Dowell, Wayne Eagling and Alessandra Ferri are among the stars featured in this salute to one of the world's most renowned ballet companies. Included are performances from "La Fille Mal Gardee," "Manon," "The Nutcracker" and "Romeo and Juliet." 60 min.
22-1647 ***$19.99***

Burn The Floor
A dance lover's delight, this amazing program features 44 champion hoofers from around the world, performing a variety of traditional, ballroom and show dances. Stylish and sexy, it's an evening of grace and beauty not to be missed. 97 min.
07-2843 ***$19.99***

Paris Dances Diaghilev
In a special tribute to Russian choreographer and Ballets Russes founder Sergey Diaghilev, the Paris Opera Ballet performs four of his most acclaimed pieces: "Petrouchka," "Le Spectre de la Rose," "L'Apres-midi d'un Faune" and "Noces." 84 min.
19-3038 ***$29.99***

The Stone Flower
The last of Prokofiev's nine ballets, "The Stone Flower" offers the Kirov Ballet in a performance filmed in 1991 at the Maryinsky Theatre in St. Petersburg. This story of a stone carver who realizes the power of the material he is using and shows it to the people is choreographed by Yuri Grigorovich and features Anna Polikarpova and Aleksandr Gulyaev. 112 min.
19-3415 ***$29.99***

Great Tales In Asian Art
Dance, theater and fine arts are blended in a quartet of classic stories from Asia. Japan's "The Tale of Genji" is told by a woman in period costume and illustrated with screen and scroll paintings; social satire and bold costumes mark the "Korean Masked Dance Drama"; Indian paintings, sculpture from Indonesia, and Javanese "shadow players" bring to life the Hindu epic "The Ramayana"; and the "Gita Govinda," an erotic poem from India, is interpreted by a native dancer. 82 min.
22-1440 ***$19.99***

Giselle
Perhaps the most demanding and coveted of all dance roles, performed here by the great Natalia Bessmertnova. Stunning choreography highlights this Bolshoi Ballet production. 85 min.
22-1084 Was $39.99 ***$19.99***

Giselle
The legendary Fernando Bujones stars in this dazzling production by the Ballet Municipal of Rio de Janeiro. A fiery and passionate performance by the man who has been called "the finest male classical dancer this country has ever produced." 104 min.
22-1188 Was $29.99 ***$19.99***

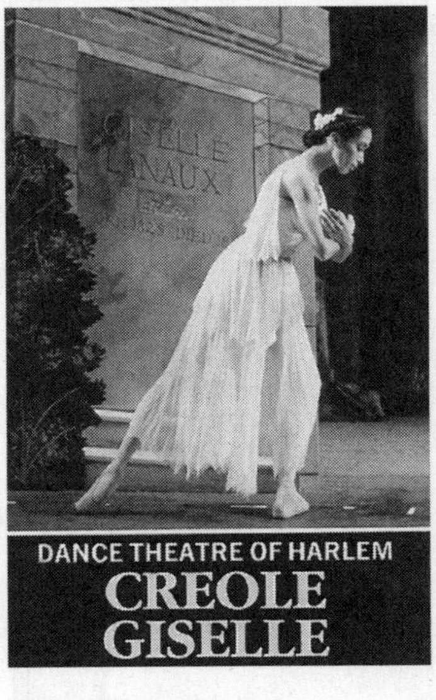

Creole Giselle With Dance Theatre Of Harlem
The setting of "Giselle" is changed to 1841 Louisiana by Dance Theatre of Harlem's Arthur Mitchell in this superb rendition of the lovely ballet. With Virginia Johnson and Eddie J. Shellman. 88 min.
22-1206 Was $29.99 ***$19.99***

Giselle
The tragic story of a poor young girl and her doomed love for a cruel nobleman is expertly performed in this La Scala ballet production. Alessandra Ferri shines in the title role, starring alongside Massimo Murru as Albrecht. 116 min.
22-1771 ***$29.99***

Giselle (1967)
Alicia Alonso, who electrified the Met Centennial Gala audience with an excerpt from this ballet, is featured in the complete classic performance, joined by Azari Plisetski as Albrecht and the National Ballet of Cuba. 99 min.
22-3054 Was $39.99 ***$19.99***

Giselle (Nureyev) (1979)
A peasant girl dies of grief when she is seduced and abandoned by a heartless count, but returns as a ghost for revenge, in this ballet favorite. The legendary Rudolf Nureyev stars as Count Albrecht, with Lynn Seymour in the title role. 78 min.
22-1217 Was $29.99 ***$19.99***

Bolshoi Ballet
Follow the world-renowned Bolshoi company from training and rehearsal to final performance in four pieces: "Paganini," with music by Rachmaninov; Prokofiev's "Stone Flower"; and Ravel's "Bolero" and "Waltz." 90 min.
22-1004 *$19.99*

Macbeth
Shakespeare's timeless story of power and its corrupting force is brought to the dance floor by the Bolshoi Ballet Company. Nina Timofeyeva is featured dancer. 105 min.
22-1029 Was $39.99 *$19.99*

Raymonda
The stars of the Bolshoi Ballet's 1987 U.S. tour, Ludmila Semenyaka and Erek Moukhamedov, take center stage for this dazzling spectacle that features an Alexander Glazunov score, taped live at the Bolshoi Theatre in Moscow. 146 min.
22-1079 Was $39.99 *$19.99*

Ivan The Terrible
Sergei Prokofiev's haunting score from Eisenstein's classic film "Ivan the Terrible" is choreographed by Yuri Grigorovich for the Bolshoi Ballet. The dazzling tale of deadly intrigue in the court of the Czar is danced by Yuri Vladimirov and Natalia Bessmertnova. 91 min.
22-1111 Was $29.99 *$19.99*

Bolshoi Prokofiev Gala
Gala ballet concert celebrates the 100th birthday of the Russian composer and features the Bolshoi Ballet performing his greatest works. Excerpts from "Romeo and Juliet," "Ivan the Terrible" and "Stone Flower" are presented. 170 min.
22-1242 Was $29.99 *$19.99*

The Glory Of The Bolshoi
Its dancers have set the standard for ballet around the world for over two centuries, and now Russia's Bolshoi Ballet is saluted with a breathtaking retrospective featuring rare performance footage, much of it never before seen in the West. Among the stars taking the stage are Irek Mukhamedov, Galina Ulanova, Vladimir Vasiliev and many more. 96 min.
22-1649 *$19.99*

The Bolshoi Ballet: Les Sylphides
Natalia Bessmertnova, Alexandre Beogatyriov, and other members of the famed Company perform this magnificent one-act ballet to some of the most stirring melodies of Frederic Chopin. 34 min.
22-7005 *$29.99*

The Bolshoi Ballet: La Bayadere
The exotic and colorful Russian ballet (known in English as "The Temple Dancer") is presented in thrilling fashion by the Bolshoi with a cast that includes Nadia Gracheva and Alexander Vertov. 146 min.
22-1484 *$19.99*

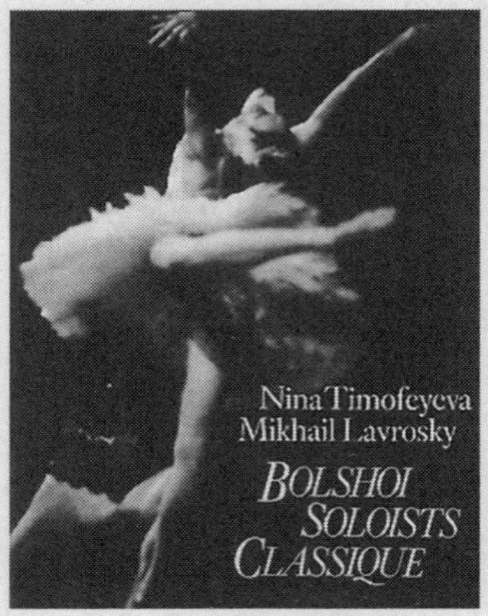

Nina Timofeyeva
Mikhail Lavrosky
BOLSHOI
SOLOISTS
CLASSIQUE

Bolshoi Soloists: Classique
An exquisite program of solos and passes de deux rendered by Nina Timofeyeva and Mickail Lavrosky. See the works of such giants as Tchaikovsky, Gershwin, Adam and Albioni stunningly set to dance. 37 min.
22-7006 Was $29.99 *$19.99*

The Bolshoi At The Bolshoi
The leading lights of the Russian ballet world, the Bolshoi Ballet, converge on the stage of the Bolshoi Theatre in Moscow to perform some of the world's most outstanding works under the direction of master choreographer Yuri Grigorovich.

Spartacus
Irek Mukhamedov is magnificent in the title role in this lavish Bolshoi production, based on the legendary tale of the Roman slave who led his fellow captives against the might of Rome. Lyudmilla Semenyaka, Alexander Vetrov also star. 132 min.
53-7627 *$29.99*

The Story Of The Bolshoi Ballet
The story of one of the world's most famous ballets is told in this program, featuring history, backstage footage and performances of such works as "Swan Lake," "Don Quixote," "Coppelia," "Romeo and Juliet," "Ivan the Terrible" and more. 52 min.
89-7025 *$14.99*

The Bolshoi Ballet (1958)
Wonderful film look at the ballet world's most acclaimed company. Featured in this performance documentary are such stars as Galina Ulanova, Nikolai Fadeyechev and others; works include "Giselle," "The Dying Swan," "Walpurgisnacht" from "Faust," and "Spring Water." 95 min.
22-3117 *$39.99*

Spartacus (1982)
Stirring Bolshoi production of Yuri Grigorovich's ballet stars Vladimir Vasiliev as the slave-turned-rebel and Marius Liepa as the Roman general who vows to defeat him. Unique slow-motion camerawork makes this a fantastic blend of dance and cinema. 95 min.
22-1098 Was $29.99 *$19.99*

The Magic Of The Bolshoi (1987)
A look at the world's premier ballet company, the 200-year-old Bolshoi. Through rare film clips and contemporary footage comes a rare insider's view of Russia's most popular export. With Ludmilla Semenyaka and Maya Plisetskaya. 60 min.
22-5146 Was $29.99 *$19.99*

Footnotes: The Classics Of Ballet
Historic clips and interviews with such dance legends as Nureyev, Fonteyn and members of the Bolshoi and the Kirov are featured in this series that offers the history of each ballet performed. Each tape runs 60 min.

Footnotes, Vol. 1: Swan Lake/La Sylphide
22-1471 *$19.99*

Footnotes, Vol. 2: Romeo And Juliet/Giselle
22-1472 *$19.99*

Footnotes, Vol. 3: The Nutcracker/ The Sleeping Beauty
22-1473 *$19.99*

Footnotes, Vol. 4: Don Quixote/La Bayadere
22-1552 *$19.99*

Footnotes, Vol. 5: Cinderella/Coppelia
22-1553 *$19.99*

Footnotes, Vol. 6: The Male Dancer/Gala Excerpts
22-1554 *$19.99*

Footnotes, Vol. 7: Partnerships/The Ballerina
22-1644 *$19.99*

Footnotes, Vol. 8: Ballet In Russia/Ballet In Asia
22-1645 *$19.99*

Footnotes, Vol. 9: Music Of The Ballet/The Paris Opera Ballet
22-1646 *$19.99*

Manon
A young student falls for a beautiful but uncaring girl in this Kenneth MacMillan ballet, performed by the London Royal Ballet. Jennifer Penney and Anthony Dowell star. 130 min.
44-1325 Was $39.99 *$29.99*

Martha Graham In Performance
Pioneering dancer and choreographer Martha Graham is captured in three rare and historic performances, "A Dancer's World," "Night Journey" and "Appalachian Spring." 93 min.
22-1088 Was $39.99 *$19.99*

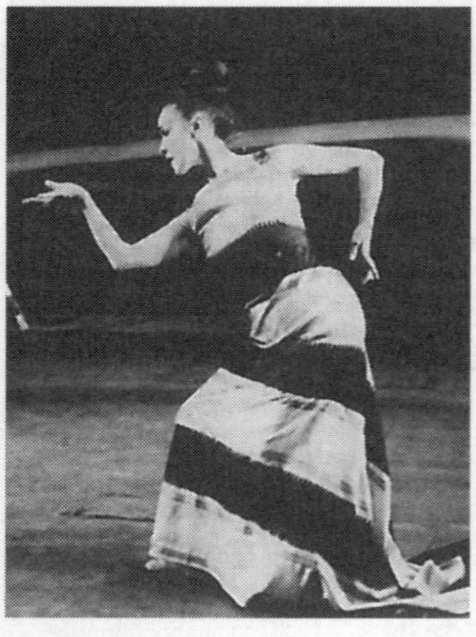

Martha Graham: The Dancer Revealed
For seven decades she was a leading force in the world of modern dance. Now look back over the life and career of Martha Graham in this commemorative documentary that features excerpts from many of her works, including "Acts of Light," "Appalachian Spring" and "Primitive Mysteries," and interviews with such contemporaries as Agnes DeMille, Erick Hawkins and Ron Profas. 60 min.
22-1342 Was $29.99 *$24.99*

Martha Graham Dance Company (1976)
The famed performer/choreographer is saluted in a special program that features her eponymous dance troupe in six of her most memorable works: "Diversion of Angels," "Lamentation," "Frontier," "Adorations," "Medea's Dance of Vengeance" and "Appalachian Spring." 90 min.
19-4022 *$29.99*

...The Making Of
Acclaimed ballerina and Stuttgart Ballet director Marcia Haydee presents this unique series in which she and the Stuttgart Ballet Company dancers offer new interpretations of the world's best-loved ballets and take viewers step-by-step through the choreography and staging of the works. Each tape runs about 30 min.

Giselle: ...The Making Of
Featured artists Birgit Keil, Tomas Dietrich and Richard Cragun, under Haydee's choreography, perform Adolphe Adam's masterpiece.
22-7169 Was $19.99 *$14.99*

On Your Toes: ...The Making Of
George Balanchine's groundbreaking 1936 work that featured music by Rodgers and Hart is staged by choreographer Larry Fuller. Along with Haydee, the cast includes Birgit Keil, Randy Diamond, Vladimir Klos.
22-7170 Was $19.99 *$14.99*

Ballet Favorites
Superlative sampler features some of the most acclaimed dancers ever in selections from the best-loved compositions. See Baryshnikov, Bussell, Cope, Dowell, Zaklinsky and others take to their feet in "Don Quixote," "Giselle," "The Nutcracker," "Romeo and Juliet" and much more. 90 min.
44-1563 *$19.99*

Accent On The Offbeat
A remarkable collaboration between jazz musician Wynton Marsalis and choreographer Peter Martins fuses two art forms in a celebration of the creative spirit. Documentarian Albert Maysles ("Gimme Shelter") was on hand to capture the process behind the development of the ballet "Jazz," which featured the New York City Ballet performing to the music of the Wynton Marsalis Ensemble. 114 min.
45-5562 *$24.99*

Dancetime!: 500 Years Of Social Dance: Complete Set
Historian Carol Téten and the stage troupe "Dance Through Time" bring you the history of dance, from the Middle Ages to the present, in this two-tape series. The first part takes you from the 15th to the 19th centuries and features music by Hassler, Schubert and Vivaldi; part two covers 20th-century dance trends from the Tango, Charlston and Apache to Swing, Disco and Hip Hop. 90 min. total. NOTE: Individual volumes available at $39.99 each.
50-5856 *$79.99*

Mountain Legacy: America's Dance Heritage
Ireland may have its "Riverdance," but this country's mountain dancers, a centuries-old tradition that grew from the traditional clog and step dancing brought over by immigrants, have plenty to kick their heels up about, as well. Join three-time world champion Burton Edwards and top musicians and dancers in a dynamic display of choreography and fancy footwork. 60 min.
50-8150 *$19.99*

Flamenco Women
Director Mike Figgis ("Leaving Las Vegas") captures the excitement of the famous Spanish dance when he casts his cameras on a Flamenco troupe over a six-day span as they prepare for a performance. Witness their practice, the work of choreographers and musicians, and more in this revealing documentary. 52 min.
80-7229 *$19.99*

Flamenco (1990)
The art and energy of Flamenco dancing is the subject of this look at the passionate dance style, filmed where the artists perform for themselves and their partners, not for tourists. The folklore and daily life of Spanish dancers are captured by the cameras. 56 min.
80-7037 *$29.99*

La Bayadere
Also known as "The Temple Dancer," this famed ballet work is staged by a renowned cast, including Tatiana Terekhova and Gabriella Komleva. Music by Ludvig Minkus. 125 min.
22-1031 Was $39.99 *$19.99*

La Bayadere
A Royal Ballet at Covent Garden production, with choreography by the famed Natalia Makarova and featuring Irek Mukhamedov and Darcy Bussell. Lavish sets, gorgeous costumes and superb dancing add to the excitement. 124 min.
22-1256 Was $29.99 *$19.99*

The Lady Of The Camellias
One of literature's great romances, Alexander Dumas' love story is set to the music of Chopin and performed by the Hamburg ballet. The international cast includes Marcia Haydée and Ivan Liska. 125 min.
22-1116 *$19.99*

The Merce Cunningham Dance Company: Points In Space
The collaboration between choreographer Merce Cunningham and avant-garde composer John Cage is captured from creation and rehearsal to premiere performance in this fascinating dance documentary. 55 min.
22-1147 Was $39.99 *$19.99*

Don Quixote
Cervantes' addled knight-errant becomes a ballet star in composer Leon Minkus' adaptation, performed here by the Russian State Perm Ballet. Aleksandr Astafiev stars in the title role, with Evgeny Katusov as Sancho Panza, and Nina Ananiashvili and Aleksei Fadeyetchev as Kitri and Basilio. 120 min.
22-1308 *$24.99*

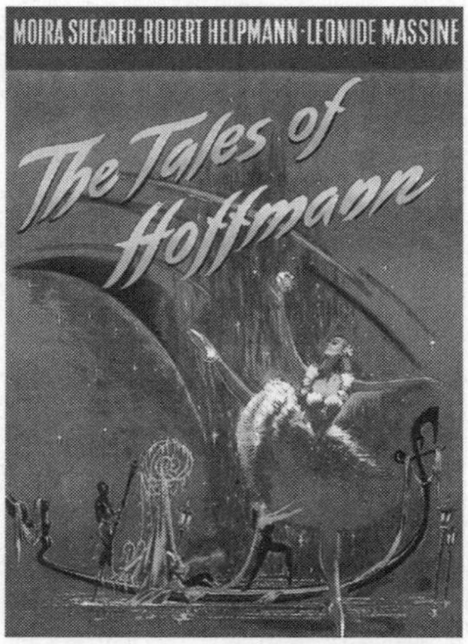

MOIRA SHEARER·ROBERT HELPMANN·LEONIDE MASSINE
The Tales of Hoffmann

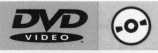

The Tales Of Hoffmann (1951)
Jacques Offenbach's fantasy work is magnificently brought to the screen by Michael Powell and Emeric Pressburger ("The Red Shoes"). Robert Rounseville stars in the title role of a student fated to enter a series of doomed love affairs with supernatural overtones. Moira Shearer also stars in this enthralling blend of opera, ballet and drama. 120 min.
22-5501 Was $39.99 *$29.99*

The Merry Widow Ballet
Lavish dance rendition of Franz Laher's romantic operetta stars Patricia McBride and Peter Martins and members of the New York Ballet, with music performed by the Chicago Symphony Orchestra. 60 min.
22-1148 Was $39.99 *$19.99*

Ballet Gold Collection
Some of the most memorable dancers in ballet history are spotlighted in this deluxe four-tape boxed set featuring "Ballet Favorites," "The Glory of the Bolshoi," "The Glory of the Kirov" and "Great Pas de Deux." See Baryshnikov, Fonteyn, Harvey, Nureyev, Plisetskaya and others performing in the roles that made them famous. 360 min. total.
22-1745 *$49.99*

Le Corsaire
Ethan Stiefel, Joaquin De Luz, Angel Corella and Julie Kent head the stellar cast in this American Ballet Theatre production of the tale of warfare and danger on the high seas, recorded live at Orange County, California's Performing Art Center. 115 min.
22-1759 *$29.99*

Four By Kylián
An anhtology of four ballets spotlighting the striking choreography of Jiri Kylián. The music of Debussy, Janacek, Stravinksy and Takemitsu provides the backdrop for "La Cathedral Engloutie," "Sinfonietta," "Svadebka" and "Torso," as performed by the Nederlands Dance Theatre. 89 min.
22-5126 Was $39.99 *$29.99*

Suzanne Farrell: Elusive Muse (1996)
Nominated for an Academy Award, this acclaimed documentary showcases Suzanne Farrell, the muse of and quintessential interpreter of choreographer George Balanchine. The film tracks their unusual relationship and features rare footage of "Apollo," "Meditation," "A Midsummer Night's Dream" and "Don Quixote," all choreographed by Balanchine. 105 min.
76-7443 *$29.99*

Denishawn: The Birth Of Modern Dance
A look at one of the most important dance companies in America. Founded by Ruth St. Denis and Ted Shawn at the turn of the century, The Denishawn troupe incorporated Far and Middle Eastern dances and laid the groundwork for Martha Graham, Jack Cole and others. Rare performance film clips are featured. 40 min.
22-1229 Was $29.99 *$19.99*

José Limón: Three Ballets
Filmed in 1955, this trio of works choreographed by the great Limón includes "The Moor's Pavane," "The Traitor" and "The Emperor Jones." See why the Mexican-American choreographer was considered one of the greats.
22-3214 *$29.99*

Road To The Stamping Ground
Choreographer Jiri Kylián and the Nederlands Dance Theater travel to Australia to create an original ballet based on the traditional "stamping" dances of the Aborigine people. 58 min.
22-5026 Was $39.99 *$29.99*

Symphony In D Workshop
Innovative choreographer Jiri Kylián directs the Nederlands Dans Theater in their rendition of Haydn's "Symphony in D." Added attraction is Kylian rehearsing with students from the Royal Ballet School in London. 55 min.
22-5027 Was $39.99 *$29.99*

Tango Magic
The history and allure of the tango—or "the dance of the embrace"—is explored in this sensual experience filled with amazing dancing. Hosted by Hector Elizondo, the program features performers from Broadway's "Forever Tango" and melodies from the Orpheus Orchestra. 60 min.
04-5685 *$14.99*

The Erik Bruhn Gala: World Ballet Competition
Dancers from the four companies that Bruhn was most closely associated with perform to the choreography of Bruhn, Tetley, MacMillan and Tudor. Natalia Makarova and Kevin McKenzie perform the White Swan pas de deux, much more. 101 min.
22-5286 Was $39.99 *$29.99*

Ballroom Dancing: The International Championships
Ballroom dancing at its finest is featured in this chronicle of the international championships, where dancers the world over vie for the esteemed and highly coveted title.
22-7115 Was $29.99 *$19.99*

Ballet Legends: Ninel Kurgapkina
A prima ballerina with the Kirov for 25 years until her retirement in 1972, Ninel Kurgapkina's career is the focus of this splendid retrospective. Rare filmed performances of Kurgapkina in "Sleeping Beauty," "Don Quixote," "Le Corsaire" and other works are featured. 40 min.
22-7120 Was $29.99 *$19.99*

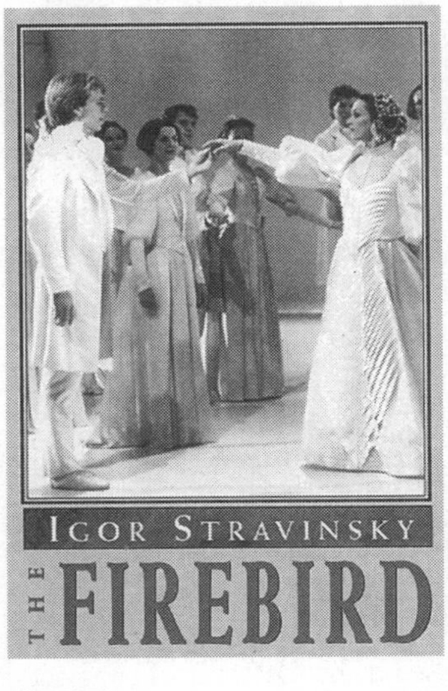

Firebird
Stylishly rendered performance of Stravinsky's classic from the Royal Danish Ballet. Glen Tetley choreographs a fabulous retelling of the Firebird's quest for freedom from her oppressive captors. 55 min.
22-5268 Was $39.99 *$29.99*

Tango
The Geneva Grand Theatre Ballet, under the choreography of Oscar Araiz, creates a singularly remarkable production to the sensuous rhythms of the Tango. Twenty-eight performers combine for a masterwork of precision dancing. 57 min.
22-7012 *$29.99*

Tango: The Passion: Set
This three-tape set was filmed in Buenos Aires and showcases different examples of tango dance. Included are "Señor Tango," "Super Tango" and "Gypsy Passion." Choreographed by tango master Fernando Solero, these programs show you dance at its spiciest. 160 min. total. NOTE: Individual volumes available at $12.99 each.
72-3058 Save $10.00! *$29.99*

Mayerling
The doomed love and suicide pact between Crown Prince Rudolf and a teenage girl formed the basis for this stunning ballet, featuring the music of Franz Liszt and choreography by Kenneth MacMillan. The Royal Ballet production stars Irek Mukhamedov, Viviana Durante and Lesley Collier. 135 min.
22-5744 Was $39.99 *$29.99*

The Paris Opera Ballet: Seven Ballets
Seven difficult pieces rendered with ease by the renowned company. Norbert Schmucki choreographs the graceful movements of Patrick Dupond, Sylvie Guillem, and Manuel Legris to the sounds of Saint-Saens, Sibelius and Grieg. 66 min.
22-7011 *$29.99*

Gaîté Parisienne (1954)
Ten years in the making, this remarkable film by ballet aficionado Victor Jessen features three of the dance world's most acclaimed performers (Alexandra Danilova, Frederic Franklin, and Leon Danielian) dancing to Offenbach's waltzes and can-cans, along with the famed Ballet Russe de Monte Carlo. 38 min.
22-3056 *$39.99*

The Catherine Wheel (1982)
Modern dance master Twyla Tharp and rock auteur David Byrne collaborated on this unique ballet that tells the story of early Christian martyr St. Catherine. Her death on a spiked wheel serves as a metaphor for the artist's striving for perfection. 87 min.
44-1336 *$29.99*

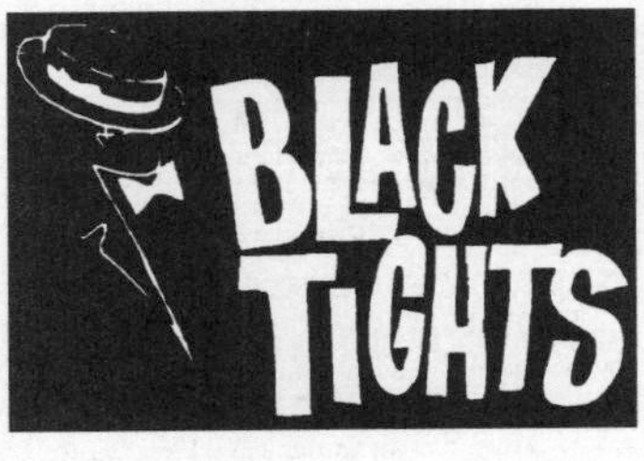

Black Tights (1960)
Balletomanes have forever cherished this compilation of tales told through dance, with Maurice Chevalier serving as narrator. "The Diamond Cruncher" stars Zizi Jeanmarie as a female mobster in love with Dirk Sanders; Roland Petit dances the role of "Cyrano de Bergerac": "A Merry Mourning" stars Cyd Charisse and Petit in a tale of murder and love; and in "Carmen," Bizet's story is given a marvelous dance translation with Jeanmarie and Petit. 126 min.
22-3032 Was $29.99 *$24.99*

The Dancer (1994)
Katja Bjorner, a young woman who dreams of becoming a professional dancer, is followed through her years of grueling study and practice at the Royal Swedish Ballet School in filmmaker Donya Feuer's compelling and exquisitely photographed documentary that features Bjorner performing solos from "Giselle," "Swan Lake" and other works. 96 min. In Swedish with English subtitles.
70-5107 *$29.99*

Explosive Dance (1998)
It's an unforgettable evening of terpsichorean treasures, live on the stage of London's famed Royal Albert Hall. Among the featured performers are the Royal Ballet's Darcey Bussell and Yuri Yanowsky, the cast of "Riverdance," the Jiving Lindy Hoppers, Club Salsa Dance Company, Antonio Marquez and others. 90 min.
50-8455 *$19.99*

Temperaments In Motion (1999)
In the tradition of the "Mind's Eye" series comes this stunning blend of sight and sound, as graceful dancers perform to a score that includes works by Beethoven, Mendelssohn, Mozart, Tchaikovsky and others. It's MTV for the classical set! 61 min.
22-9023 *$19.99*

Four By Ailey
Legendary choreographer Alvin Ailey introduces this compilation of four superlative pieces performed by his eponymous American Dance Theater: "Divining," "Revelations," "The Stack-Up" and "Cry." The music of Kimati Dinzulu, Laura Nyro, Monti Ellison and others is featured. 109 min.
22-5122 *$29.99*

A Tribute To Alvin Ailey
A celebration of African-American choreographer Ailey's work, featuring four works performed by his American Dance Theater: "For Bird with Love," "Witness," "Memoria" and "Episodes." 103 min.
22-5504 Was $39.99 *$29.99*

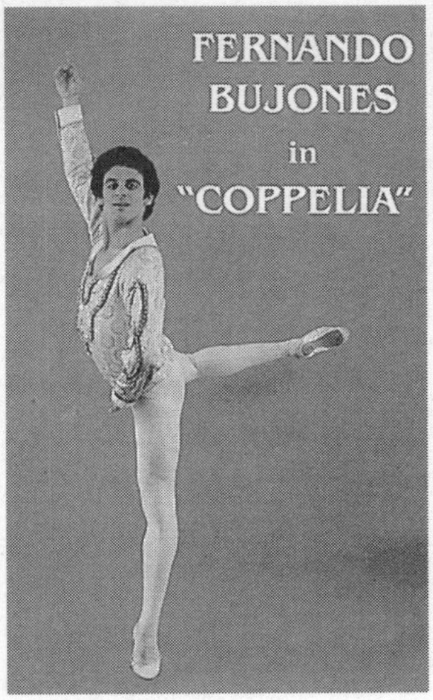

Coppélia
Fernando Bujones displays his masterful techniques in this staging of the moving ballet, with music by Delibes. Also features Ana Maria Castanon and the Ballet de San Juan. 110 min.
22-1009 Was $39.99 *$19.99*

Coppelia
A traditional treatment of the famed ballet from the Australian Ballet details the efforts of toymaker and magician Dr. Coppelius to bring to life a beautiful doll. Featured performers include Lisa Pavane and Greg Horsman and music by Leo Delibes. 107 min.
22-1798 *$19.99*

Coppélia (1993)
The Kirov Ballet performs this noted two-act piece with music by Léo Delibes, a libretto by Charles Nuitter and Arthur Saint-Léon, and expert dancing by Irina Shapchits and Mikhail Zavialov. 92 min.
19-3728 *$29.99*

Bill T. Jones: Dancing To The Promised Land
One of the world's best-known modern choreographers is the subject of this program that includes interviews, rehearsals and footage of "Last Supper at Uncle Tom's Cabin/The Promised Land." Jones narrates the program himself, while an original jazz score is provided by the Julius Hemphill Sextet. 60 min.
22-7134 Was $29.99 *$19.99*

Making Ballet With Karen Kain And The National Ballet Of Canada
Renowned choreographer James Kudelka used the music of Chopin's preludes as the basis for his original ballet work "The Actress," created for prima ballerina Karen Cain. Follow Kain and the National Ballet of Canada from rehearsal to final performance in this remarkable behind-the-scenes documentary. 86 min.
22-7161 Was $29.99 *$19.99*

Margot Fonteyn
Her meticulous performance has made her the most celebrated ballerina of her own, or perhaps any, time, and here Dame Margot candidly discusses her life and craft. Rare footage and interviews with teachers, contemporaries, and disciples, including de Valois, Ashton, Helpmann and Nureyev, are included. 90 min.
22-5287 Was $39.99 *$29.99*

Dance Theater Of Harlem
Four excellent pieces from the acclaimed dance troupe, including "Fall River Legend," choreographed by Agnes de Mille, about the infamous Lizzie Borden; Robert North's "Troy Game," a satire of machismo and sports; "The Beloved," Lester Horton's look at violence; and "John Henry," featuring Arthur Michell's dynamic choreography. 117 min.
22-5358 Was $39.99 *$29.99*

Dancing: Complete Set
Filmed on location on five continents, this captivating eight-tape series looks at dance around the world, from African court dances and elegant waltzes to a ballet class in Russia and hip-hop performers on the streets of New York. Learn about the role of the dance in religion, its social implications, the intermingling of global styles and much more. 8 hrs. total. NOTE: Individual volumes available at $29.99 each.
22-5631 Save $40.00! *$199.99*

The Children Of Theatre Street (1978)
Go behind the doors of one of the world's most acclaimed ballet schools, Leningrad's Kirov School, in this award-winning documentary, narrated by Princess Grace of Monaco. The intense desire and determination of the young students and the rich history of Russian dance are explored, highlighted by dazzling performances. 92 min.
22-1025 Was $39.99 *$19.99*

Dancing Thru
This entertaining documentary from the 1940s looks at the history of dance, from Zulu ceremonies to contemporary ballroom dancing. 35 min.
10-9227 Was $19.99 *$14.99*

Stars Of The Russian Ballet (1972)
Ulanova, Plisetskaya, Chabukiani are featured in vivid performances that will amaze fans of great dance. Included are selections from "Swan Lake" and "The Flames of Paris." 80 min.
22-1106 Was $29.99 *$19.99*

Pilobolus Dance Theatre: Monkshood's Farewell (1977)
Their unusual and innovative approach to dance won them international acclaim, and in this "Dance in America" program the members of the Pilobolus troupe are seen in "Monkshood's Farewell" (with sets by Edward Gorey), "Movement from 'Ocellus'," "Movement from 'Ciona'" and "Untitled." 59 min.
19-4023 *$29.99*

Nureyev's "Don Quixote"
The legendary dancer co-directs and stars in this ballet version of the classic fable. The renowned Australian Ballet is featured, with Lucette Aldous and Sir Robert Helpmann in the title role. 110 min.
22-1082 Was $39.99 *$19.99*

Fonteyn And Nureyev: The Perfect Partnership
Separately they've brought dance audiences to their feet around the world; together they've performed some of the most memorable duets ever. See some of the greatest moments from Dame Margot Fonteyn and Rudolf Nureyev's 17-year collaboration in this ballet treat. 90 min.
22-1085 Was $39.99 *$19.99*

Nureyev: Dancing Through Darkness
A moving look at the legendary dancer follows Rudolf Nureyev through the final decade of his life, when he struggled to continue in his role as artistic director of the Paris Opera Ballet even as he tried to keep his battle against AIDS a secret. Rare performance footage is featured. 60 min.
22-1726 *$19.99*

Rudolph Nureyev: His Complete Bell Telephone Hour Appearances 1962-1965
The brilliant Nureyev dances memorable duets from "Flower Festival" (with Maria Tallchief), "Le Corsaire" (with Lupe Serano), "Black Swan" (with Svetlana Beriosova), and "Diana and Aceton" (with Beriosova) in these classic TV performances. 40 min.
22-3224 *$29.99*

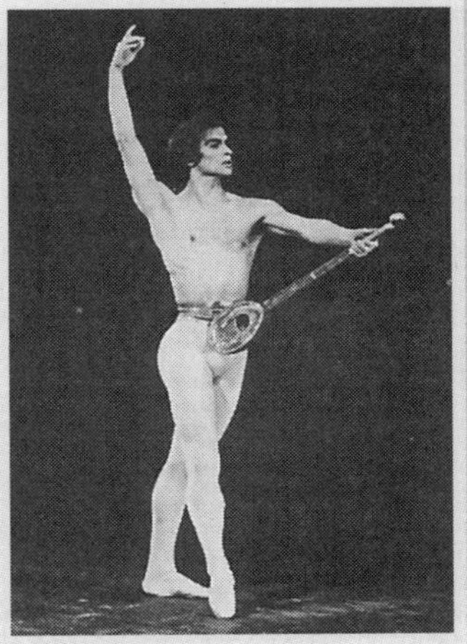

Rudolf Nureyev
World-renowned dance master Rudolf Nureyev has kept a low profile throughout the years, but this program shows his private side, as he talks about friend and dance partner Margot Fonteyn and his own stellar career. Also featured are clips of spectacular performances. 90 min.
22-5505 *$29.99*

Nureyev And The Joffrey Ballet In Tribute To Nijinsky (1980)
The one and only Rudolf Nureyev salutes the greatest dancer of the early 20th century in this stunning tribute program featuring Nureyev and the Joffrey company in three of Nijinsky's most memorable roles: "Petrouchka," "Le Spectre de la Rose" and "L'apres-midi d'un Faune." 79 min.
19-4020 *$29.99*

Cinderella (1987)
Rudolf Nureyev choreographed and produced this colorful, enthralling adaptation of the classic fable as filtered through Perrault's modern show business story. It's a three-act ballet with such dancers as Charles Jude, Sylvie Guillem and Nureyev himself, playing a film producer. 125 min.
19-3727 *$29.99*

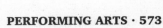

Recital

Mozart: Symphony No. 35/ Mahler: Symphony No. 5
Filmed during a live Tokyo appearance, this concert video features Sir Georg Solti and the Chicago Symphony Orchestra performing the "Haffner" Symphony by Mozart and Mahler's Fifth Symphony.
04-5315 *$29.99*

Mozart: Coronation Mass
Performed as part of a High Mass celebrated by Pope John Paul II at St. Peter's Cathedral, this moving Mozart work features Herbert von Karajan conducting the Vienna Philharmonic, with guest artists Kathleen Battle, Ferruccio Furlanetto, Trudeliese Schmidt and Gösta Winbergh.
04-5330 *$29.99*

Orchestre L'Opera De Paris
Georges Pretre conducts one of the world's most accomplished orchestras in a dazzling interpretation of Mozart works, including "Concerto for Bassoon K.191," "Concerto for Oboe K.314" and "Concerto for Clarinet K.622." 63 min.
22-1474 *$14.99*

Joseph Krips Conducts Mozart (1962)
Legendary Austrian conductor Joseph Krips is joined by soloists Malcolm Frager, Pierette Alarie and Leopold Simineau in selections from "The Marriage of Figaro" and "Don Giovanni," plus Mozart's Piano Concerto No. 25, and more. 90 min.
22-3226 *$29.99*

Mozart: Requiem (Sir Colin Davis)
Mozart's final work, commissioned by a mysterious stranger and never completed, is presented by conductor Davis and the Bavarian Radio Symphony Orchestra and Chorus in a masterful presentation. Renowned soloists Edith Mathis, Trudeliese Schmidt, Peter Schreier and Gwynne Howell participate. 57 min.
22-5297 *$29.99*

Mozart: The Requiem From Sarajevo
José Carreras, Zubin Mehta and Ruggero Raimondi team for an amazing concert from Sarajevo in celebration of the human spirit. Performed in front of the battle-ravaged National Library in memory of those who died in the Bosnian conflict, this is an unforgettable recital. 50 min.
53-8188 *$19.99*

Bruno Walter: The Maestro, The Man
Legendary maestro Bruno Walter rehearses Brahms' Symphony No. 2 with the Vancouver International Festival Orchestra and discusses his art with critic Albert Goldberg. This program offers the most extensive footage of the conductor ever.
22-3188 *$29.99*

Brahms: Piano Concerto No. 1, D Minor, Opus 15
The classic from Brahms is performed by the National Orchestra of Lille, under the direction of Jean-Claude Casadesus and featuring pianist Jean-Bernard Pommier.
22-7103 Was $19.99 *$14.99*

Soldiers Of Music: Rostropovich Returns To Russia
After 16 years of exile from his native Russia, classical musician Mstislav Rostropovich made an emotional trip home to national acclaim. Follow him through interviews and news footage, and be moved by a concert that includes works by Dvorák, Grieg, Shostakovich, Tchaikovsky and others.
04-5305 *$29.99*

Modest Mussorgsky: Pictures At An Exhibition
One of the music world's best-known suites, Mussorgsky's "Pictures" receives a superb interpretation by Sir Georg Solti and the Chicago Symphony Orchestra in this concert filmed live in Tokyo. 60 min.
04-5310 *$29.99*

Haydn: Die Schopfung
Famed maestro Riccardo Muti leads an array of soloists, including Lucia Popp, Francisco Araiza and Samuel Ramey, along with the Vienna Philharmonic in this stunning production of Joseph Haydn's "The Creation."
04-5311 *$29.99*

Edith Piaf
La Vie en Rose

Edith Piaf: La Vie En Rose
The life story of Edith Piaf is told through rare archival footage and recollections of her friends. Follow her incredible career from Parisian street singer to world-renowned performer. Songs include "Non, Je Ne Regrette Rien," "L'Accordioniste," "La Vie En Rose" and "Milord." 60 min.
80-7002 *$29.99*

Dvorák: Symphony No. 8
Acclaimed conductor Herbert von Karajan leads the Vienna Philharmonic in a performance of Anton Dvorák's Symphony No. 8 in G Major, Op. 88.
04-5320 *$29.99*

Dvorák: Symphony No. 9
Regarded by many as the composer's most stirring work, Dvorák's Symphony No. 9 in E Minor, Op. 95 is performed in the Vienna Philharmonic, led by Herbert von Karajan. 44 min.
04-5321 *$29.99*

Dvorák In Prague: A Celebration
Superstars Yo-Yo Ma, Itzhak Perlman, Frederica von Stade, and the Boston Symphony led by Seiji Ozawa perform in this concert that marks the 100th anniversary of Dvorák's New World Symphony. Among the selections are "Romance, Op. 11," "Humoresque, Op. 101," "Gypsy Songs," and more. 87 min.
45-5561 *$24.99*

Vivaldi: The Four Seasons (Anne-Sophie Mutter)
One of the best-loved examples of Baroque music, Vivaldi's lyrical tour of the seasons is performed by the Berlin Philharmonic, with conductor Herbert von Karajan and violinist Anne-Sophie Mutter.
04-5328 *$29.99*

Vivaldi: The Four Seasons (Yehudi Menuhin)
Soloist and narrator Yehudi Menuhin contributes to this superb rendition of Vivaldi's "The Four Seasons," while Peter Norris conducts the orchestra of Menuhin's Violin School. 60 min.
80-7034 *$29.99*

Bruckner: Symphony No. 9
The Berlin Philharmonic, led by conductor Herbert von Karajan, shines in this masterful performance of the Austrian composer's final, unfinished symphony.
04-5329 *$29.99*

Herbert Von Karajan
The Austrian-born conductor who went on to become the unofficial "General Music Director of Europe" and a leading figure in 20th-century classical music is the focus of this video biography. Along with interviews with friends and colleagues and rare rehearsal film footage, the program looks at von Karajan's '30s Berlin State Opera tenure and his controversial involvement with the Nazis. 80 min.
22-1775 *$19.99*

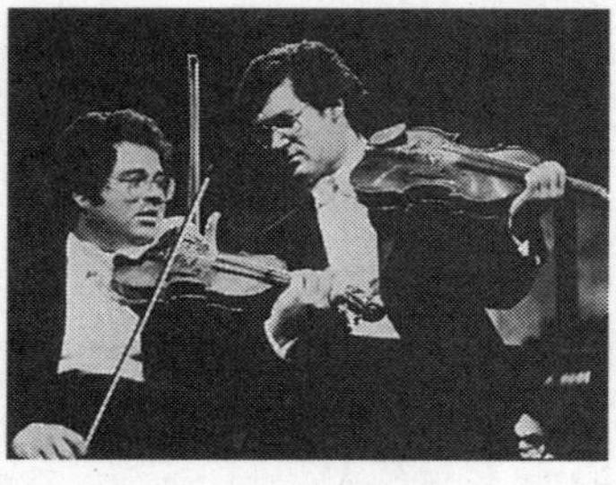

Huberman Festival: Vivaldi
Triumphant performance of Vivaldi's "The Four Seasons" by the Israeli Philharmonic and conductor Zubin Mehta. Violin greats Isaac Stern, Pinkus Zukerman, Shlomo Mintz and Itzhak Perlman are the featured soloists. 50 min.
07-1231 *$19.99*

Huberman Festival: Mozart/Handel
Renowned violinists Itzhak Perlman and Pinchas Zukerman join the Israel Philharmonic Orchestra for a concert that includes Mozart's Sinfonia Concertante (K. 364) and Handel's "Passacaglia." 45 min.
07-1253 *$19.99*

Huberman Festival: Tchaikovsky/Vivaldi
Henryk Szeryng, the renowned worldwide violinist, is featured in this program. Tchaikovsky's Concerto for Violin in D Major, Op. 35, and Vivaldi's Concerto for Two Violins and String Orchestra in A Minor, Op. 3 No. 8 are performed. 48 min.
07-1270 *$19.99*

Huberman Festival: Mendelssohn
Shlomo Mintz performs Mendelssohn's Concert In E Minor for Violin and Orchestra, Op. 64, and is joined by Isaac Stern for Bach's Concerto in D Minor for Two Violins and String Orchestra, S. 1043. 48 min.
07-8031 *$19.99*

New Year's Eve Concert 1983
In a live recital, conductor Herbert von Karajan and the Berlin Philharmonic present a holiday program that includes Rossini's "William Tell Overture," Smetana's "Moldau," and works by Sibelius, and Josef and Johann Strauss.
04-5280 *$24.99*

New Year's Eve Concert 1992: Richard Strauss Gala
Recorded in Vienna, this star-studded program features maestro Claudio Abbado conducting the Berlin Philharmonic Orchestra with soloists Martha Argerich, Kathleen Battle and Renée Fleming in an evening of selections written by Richard Strauss. Included are "Don Juan, Op. 20," "Burleske" and "Der Rosenkavalier" (Terzett und Finale).
04-5219 *$29.99*

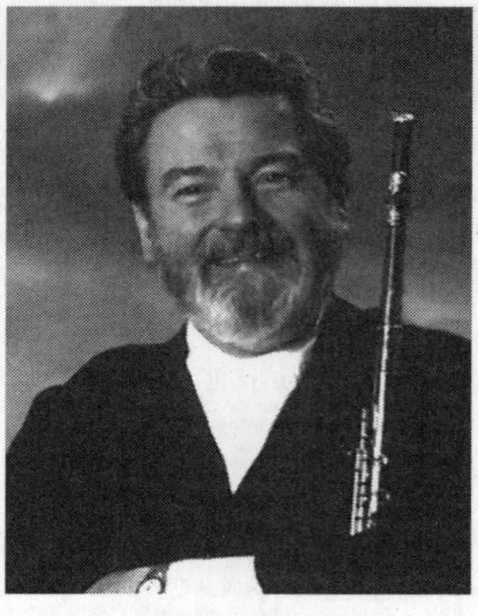

Great Solos With James Galway & Friends
Joined by Loren Maazel and the National Orchestra of France and an array of international musicians, famed flautist James Galway is featured in a delightful concert that includes works by Paganini, Mozart, Debussy and Andrew Lloyd Weber. 51 min.
22-7174 Was $19.99 *$14.99*

The Story Of The Symphony: Complete Set
Enhance your appreciation of classical music with this magnificent, six-tape series by the BBC. Andre Previn and the Royal Philharmonic use a significant work by such composers as Beethoven, Berlioz, Brahms, Shostakovich, Tchaikovsky, and Haydn and Mozart, and each program includes scenes of rehearsal, analysis of the piece, and discussion on the artist's life. 540 min. total. NOTE: Individual volumes available at $29.99 each.
22-5014 *$179.99*

Once, At A Border: Aspects Of Stravinsky
Unique celebration of Igor Stravinsky's life and work features much never-before seen footage and photos, creative contributions from Marie Rambert, George Balanchine, Nadia Boulanger, Kyra Nijinsky, Tatia Rimsky-Korsakov and others, the previously unseen original rendition of "Les Noches," and more. 166 min.
22-1066 Was $59.99 *$29.99*

Stravinsky (1965)
Produced by the National Film Board of Canada, this fascinating look at one of the giants of 20th-century music follows the 83-year-old Igor Stravinsky and his wife on a boat journey to Hamburg, West Germany, where the composer conducts a recording session of his Symphony of Psalms. Along the way, Stravinsky discusses his life and his music. 50 min.
22-3189 *$29.99*

Aldo Ciccolini In Concert
Piano great Aldo Ciccolini performs selections from Schubert, Chopin and Ravel in this program, a rare delight for classical music fans. 79 min.
22-1464 *$14.99*

Lazar Berman In Recital
Expert pianist Lazar Berman turns in a tour-de-force performance of romantic selections by Liszt and Chopin. 62 min.
22-1465 *$14.99*

Seiji Ozawa: Russian Night
Baton in hand, acclaimed conductor Ozawa leads the Berlin Philharmonic Orchestra in a concert featuring works by noted Russian composers, including Tchaikovsky ("1812 Overture," "Nutcracker Ballet Suite"), Stravinsky ("The Firebird"), Khatchaturian ("Sabre Dance"), Borodin ("Polovtsian Dances") and others. 98 min.
22-7172 Was $24.99 *$19.99*

Polish Folk Dance And Songs
This vibrant and colorful program features an array of dance troupes and musicians from the many regions of Poland. Wonderful songs and costumes make the show a treat for the eyes and ears. 68 min.
53-7755 *$29.99*

I Love America
Master singer Robert Merrill teams with the U.S. Air Force Band for an evening of patriotic songs filmed live at Washington's Constitution Hall. Among the red, white and blue numbers performed are "Stars and Stripes Forever," "Yankee Doodle," "This Land Is Your Land," and "Battle Hymn of the Republic," plus salutes to George M. Cohan and Irving Berlin. 55 min.
59-3007 *$19.99*

Radiant Life: Meditations And Visions Of Hildegard Of Bingen
This unique meditation video features the music, art and poetry of medieval healer and mystic St. Hildegard of Bingen, a noted Benedictine Abbess who had visions dealing with man's sacred relationship to the natural world. She also composed innovative liturgical chants for women singers, featured here using authentic 12th-century instruments. 40 min.
70-9036 *$19.99*

Vladimir Horowitz: A Reminiscence
Sensational retrospective of the career of pianist Vladimir Horowitz which details his life on- and off-stage and features several performances by one of the world's greatest artists. Horowitz talks about his experiences and performs compositions by Scriabin, Schumann, Scarlatti, Chopin and Rachmaninoff. 88 min.
45-5563 *$24.99*

Horowitz In Moscow (1986)
The master pianist's triumphant return to his homeland after more than 60 years is captured magnificently on video. Mozart's Sonata in C Major, Rachmaninov's Prelude in G Major, Op. 32 and Chopin's Polonaise in A Major, Op. 53, plus selections by Liszt, Schubert and Scarlatti are performed. 104 min.
12-1626 *$24.99*

The Beethoven Concerti: Complete Set
From Royal Festival Hall in London, acclaimed pianist Murray Perahia performs three programs of Beethoven concertos with the Academy of St. Martin-in-the-Fields under the direction of Sir Neville Marriner. In interviews, the soloist offers additional insights into his art and that of the composer. The three-tape set includes "Beethoven: Piano Concertos 1 and 3," "Beethoven: Piano Concertos 2 and 4" and "Beethoven: Piano Concerto 5." NOTE: Individual volumes available at $29.99 each.
22-5266 Save $10.00! *$79.99*

Beethoven: Symphony No. 6 "Pastorale"
A thrilling performance of the popular symphony (perhaps best-known for its use in the film "Fantasia") by the National Orchestra of Lille, under the direction of Jean-Claude Casadesus.
22-7104 Was $19.99 *$14.99*

Beethoven: Symphony No. 9 "Choral"
The master composer's final symphonic work, known to many as the "Ode to Joy" symphony, is given a superb rendition by conductor M. Janowski and the Radio France Philharmonic Orchestra and Chorus. 68 min.
22-7150 Was $19.99 *$14.99*

Bernstein On Beethoven: A Celebration In Vienna (1970)
Leonard Bernstein and Ludwig van Beethoven make a stirring duo, as Bernstein celebrates the composer's 200th birthday in this recital with the Vienna Philharmonic. Selections include Piano Concerto No. 1, "Ode to Joy" and more. Soloists featured are Placido Domingo, Shirley Verrett and Gwyneth Jones. 90 min.
22-1260 Was $29.99 *$19.99*

Bernstein: Beethoven— The Ninth Symphony (1970)
Leonard Bernstein and the Vienna Philharmonic celebrate Beethoven's 200th birthday with this memorable performance of the composer's final symphonic work. Soloists include Placido Domingo, Gwyneth Jones and Shirley Verrett. 78 min.
22-1288 Was $29.99 *$19.99*

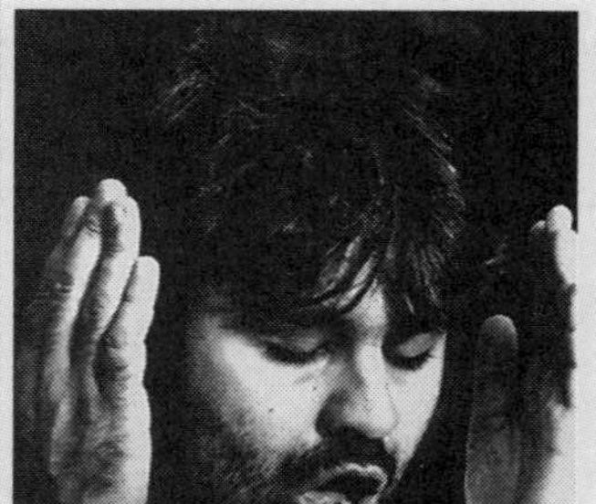

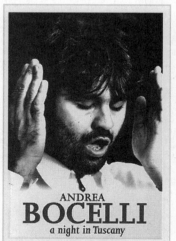

Andrea Bocelli: A Night In Tuscany
His romantic singing style has won him legions of fans around the world, and now chart-topping Italian tenor Andrea Bocelli comes to home video with this enchanting outdoor concert, filmed live in Pisa, with special guests Nuccia Focile and Sarah Brightman. Songs include "Nessun Dorma," "O Sole Mio" and "Time to Say Goodbye." 86 min.
02-8837 *$24.99*

Andrea Bocelli: Sacred Arias
Filmed at the Cathedral of Sopra Minerva in Rome, this video companion to Bocelli's platinum-selling album features the renowned tenor performing selections by Handel, Rossini, Schubert, Verdi and others, including three songs not on the album. 77 min.
02-9216 *$24.99*

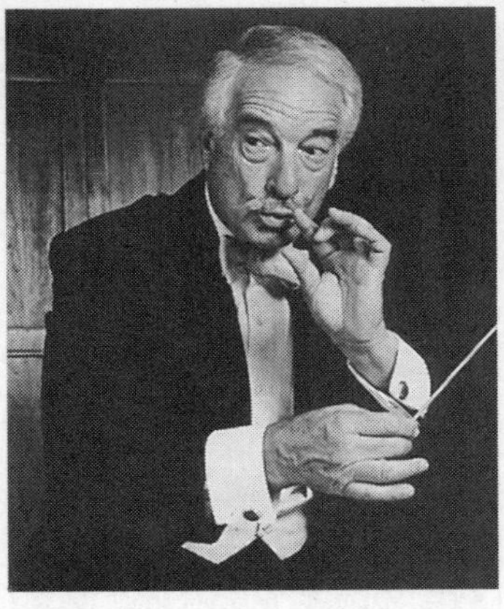

Victor Borge: Live From London
The madcap maestro of classical music and classic comedy brings his talents to a wonderful live stage performance. Only Victor Borge could combine such works as Beethoven's Fifth Symphony, "The Blue Danube," "I Feel Pretty," "My Darling Clementine" and Liszt's "Hungarian Rhapsody" with this much style and humor. 50 min.
22-1218 Was $29.99 ***$19.99***

Victor Borge: Then And Now
The magic moments from "The Great Dane's" career are offered in this retrospective features performances of such numbers as "Clair de Lune," funny music-oriented stories and classic clips of Mr. Borge with Fozzie Bear, impersonating Franz Liszt for Mike Wallace and playing "Yankee Doodle Dandy" for a smart baby. This tape was once only available through PBS. 90 min.
59-3000 ***$29.99***

Victor Borge: Then And Now II
The always-entertaining Victor Borge takes his live show to Detroit's Fox Theatre for another evening of classical music and classic farce. Along with clips featuring Leonid Hambro and Loritz Melchior, Borge performs a Tchaikovsky piano concerto, jokes around with audience members and tells some great stories. 90 min.
59-3008 ***$29.99***

Victor Borge: Then And Now III
Taped at George Washington University, this program offers Victor Borge at his best, charming a large crowd with his humor, music and classic film clips. Here Mr. Borge performs "Autumn Leaves" (and real leaves fall), "Gallop" and "Dance of the Comedians." And he shows some of his vintage bits from past TV shows. 90 min.
59-3009 ***$29.99***

Victor Borge Birthday Gala
The serious mixes with the sophisticated silly as the one and only Victor Borge celebrates his birthday with guests like Robert Merrill, the Canadian Brass and Anna Moffo. Included are such selections as "Autumn Leaves," "The Toreador Song" from "Carmen," "Clair de Lune" and more. 90 min.
59-3001 ***$29.99***

The Best Of Victor Borge
The master classical music funnyman is shown performing his most beloved routines in this live concert. Among the bits are the Mozart salute "My Favorite Barber," the aria from "Rigor Mortis," "The Timid Page Turner," "Inflationary Language" and "Danish Lullaby." 90 min.
59-3002 ***$29.99***

Leonid Kogan
Kogan, the dynamic Russian violinist, is joined by his accomplished daughter, pianist Nina Kogan, in Tchaikovsky's Melodie, Glazunov's Entracte, Brahms' Scherzo and four others, including a set of Paganini variations. 60 min.
22-1044 ***$19.99***

Karl Böohm: The Birth Of A Symphony (1963)
Follow the famed conductor and the CBC Festival Orchestra from rehearsal to final performance of Beethoven's Symphony No. 7 in this rare Canadian TV documentary. 57 min.
22-3192 ***$29.99***

Artur Rubinstein
An insightful look at the maestro at home and in performance. Compositions by Chopin, Liszt and Mendelssohn are featured. 79 min.
22-1001 ***$19.99***

Arthur Rubinstein: Tribute To Chopin
Recorded in 1950, this rare film offers footage of the great pianist performing such Chopin pieces as Scherzo in C-Sharp Minor, Nocturne in F-Sharp, Grand Polonaise in A-Flat, and Mazurka in C-Sharp Minor. 25 min.
22-3216 ***$19.99***

Rubinstein Remembered (1987)
Fabulous video celebration marking the centenary of Artur Rubinstein's birth. Son John Rubinstein is your host for this compilation of footage that traces the classcial pianist's life and features clips of Rubenstein performing works by Chopin, Mendelssohn and Poulenc. 58 min.
22-3046 Was $29.99 ***$19.99***

Evviva Belcanto
Celebrated sopranos Marilyn Horne and Montserrat Caballé perform selections from Rossini's "Tancredi," and "Semiramide" and Meyerbeer's "Les Huguenots." Filmed at Philharmonie Hall in Munich, Germany. 47 min.
07-1770 ***$19.99***

Andrés Segovia: Song Of The Guitar
His revolutionary guitar playing blended traditional Spanish music with contemporary stylings. In this unique recital film by Christopher Nupen, Segovia performs selections by Bach, Chopin, Scarlatti, Granados, Torroba and others. 51 min.
19-3330 ***$29.99***

The Segovia Legacy
A video tribute to the famed Spanish classical guitarist whose career spanned nearly a century. The life and work of Andrés Segovia are recounted in films of over 40 years of concert performances, interviews, and rare glimpses of Segovia at home and in rehearsal. 60 min.
22-1189 Was $29.99 ***$19.99***

The St. Matthew Passion
Peter Schreier and Regina Werner are featured in this performance of the Bach composition that features stunning choral parts; filmed at Leipzig's St. Thomas Church, where Bach once served as organist. 60 min.
80-7030 ***$29.99***

All That Bach (1985)
Exhilarating and fascinating classical/jazz concert celebration of Bach's 300th birthday that features performances by Keith Jarrett, the Canadian Brass, Maureen Forrester, Christopher Hogwood and the Academy of Ancient Music, the Cambridge Buskers, the National Tap Dance Company, and many others. 50 min.
22-3042 ***$29.99***

The Art Of Conducting: Great Conductors Of The Past
It takes more than just a tuxedo and a baton to lead an orchestra, as you'll learn from watching this collection of rare archival footage of some of the century's most acclaimed conductors. Bernstein, Klemperer, Stokowski, Szell, Toscanini, von Karajan and others are seen in rehearsal and in concert, with commentary by Isaac Stern, Yehudi Menuhin and more. 117 min.
19-3657 ***$29.99***

The Art Of Conducting: Legendary Conductors Of A Golden Era
Some of the greatest orchestra leaders of the century are seen in rare performance footage and candid interviews, for an unforgettable evening of music. Spotlighted are Herbert von Karajan (Strauss' "Ein Heldenleben"), Václav Talich ("The Wild Dove" by Dvorák), Erich Kleiber (Strauss' "Blue Danube" and the finale to Beethoven's Symphony No. 9), Evgeny Mravinsky (Tchaikovsky's Symphony No. 5 and Shostakovich's Symphony No. 5), and more conductors than you can shake a stick at.
19-4016 ***$29.99***

The Art Of Piano: Great Pianists Of The 20th Century
Celebrate 100 years of the music world's most acclaimed "ivory-ticklers" with this enchanting documentary that features rare performance footage of such artists as Rachmaninoff, Paderewski, Horowitz, Rubinstein, Gould, Arrau and many more. 120 min.
19-4086 ***$29.99***

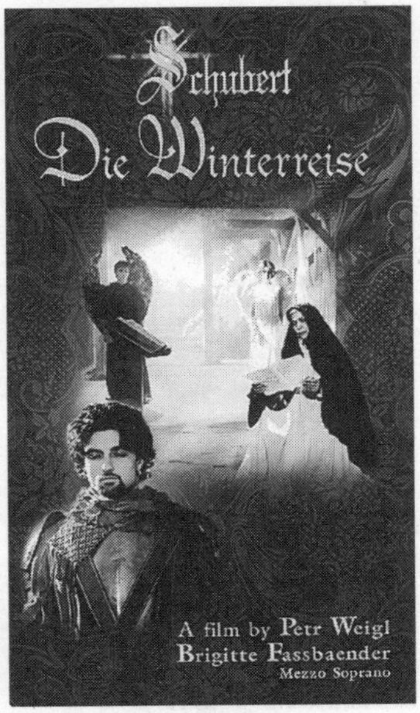

Die Winterreise (1995)
A group of travellers taking a winter journey are the focus of this Schubert song cycle, wonderfully captured by filmmaker Petr Weigl. Mezzo soprano Brigitte Fassbaender shines as one of the lead performers in this beautiful piece. 69 min.
50-8243 ***$19.99***

The Glenn Gould Collection
A rare find for all classical music aficionados, this collection features the original Canadian TV work by legendary pianist/composer Gould, along with live concert footage from throughout his brief but unforgettable career. Each tape runs about 60 min. There are 16 volumes available, including:

The Glenn Gould Collection, Vol. 1: Prologue
Includes the finale of Beethoven's Sonata, Op. 110, excerpts from Bach's Partita No. 2, selections by Mahler, Glinka and Walton, and the announcement of Gould's death in 1982.
04-5261 ***$24.99***

The Glenn Gould Collection, Vol. 2: Sonatas And Dialogues
Gould is joined by guest artist Yehudi Menuhin for such works as Bach's Violin Sonata No. 4, Beethoven's Violin Sonata, Op. 96, and Schonberg's Fantasy.
04-5262 ***$24.99***

The Glenn Gould Collection, Vol. 3: End Of Concerts
Along with solo piano pieces by Beethoven, Krenek and Hindemith, Gould performs Bach's Partita No. 5.
04-5263 ***$24.99***

The Glenn Gould Collection, Vol. 9: Mostly Strauss
Featured pieces include Strauss' Burleske (with Gould and the Toronto Symphony) and "Cacilie," along with Mozart's Piano Sonata, K.333.
04-5269 ***$24.99***

The Glenn Gould Collection, Vol. 10: Rhapsodic Interludes
An all-star sampler of works from such composers as Debussy, Ravel, Schoenberg, Schubert and Strauss.
04-5270 ***$24.99***

The Glenn Gould Collection, Vol. 13: The Goldberg Variations
This volume, the first of four culled from the documentary "Glenn Gould Plays Bach," features the pianist in a 1981 performance at New York's 30th Street Studio, plus a candid conversation between Gould and filmmaker Bruno Monsaingeon.
04-5273 ***$24.99***

The Glenn Gould Collection, Vol. 14: The Question Of Instrument
Gould plays an all-Bach program that includes "The Art of Fugue," "Italian Concerto," "The Well-Tempered Clavier: Fugue" and other works, while discussing whether the composer's works should be performed on the harpsichord, used in Bach's time, or on the later piano.
04-5274 ***$24.99***

The Glenn Gould Collection, Vol. 15: An Art Of The Fugue
The term comes from the Latin word for "flight," and on this program Gould discusses Bach's development and mastery of the fugue, while letting his fingers take flight on such pieces as the fugues from "The Well-Tempered Clavier, Book 2," "Contrapuncti II, IV and XV," and the composer's unfinished "An Art of the Fugue."
04-5275 ***$24.99***

Glenn Gould Plays Beethoven
Famed pianist Gould performs a moving all-Beethoven program that includes the Emperor Concerto, Bagatelle (Op. 26, No. 3) and F-Minor Variations (Op. 34). 60 min.
22-1446 ***$19.99***

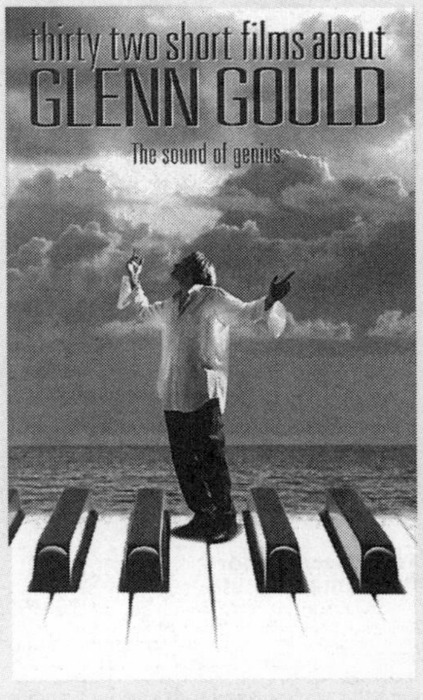

Thirty Two Short Films About Glenn Gould (1994)
Beyond the self-explanatory title, director/co-scripter François Girard's collection of "mini-biodramas" come together to provide a glimpse into the life and career of the Canadian pianist/composer who won worldwide renown for both his music and eccentric behavior before his death in 1982. Colm Feore stars as Gould, whose own performances comprise the score. 94 min.
02-2742 Was $89.99 ***$19.99***

John Williams: The Seville Concert
John Williams, one of the most popular classical guitarists in the world today, performs a spectacular concert featuring works from Scarlatti, Bach, Rodrigo, Barrios and others from the Royal Alcazar Palace in Spain.
04-5255 ***$29.99***

Marilyn Horne: Les Nuits D'Ete (1966)
In a rare live appearance on Canadian TV, renowned classical singer Horne is joined by conductor Pierre Hétu and the Montreal Symphony Orchestra for a performance of Berlioz's song cycle. 35 min.
22-3229 ***$24.99***

Renata Tebaldi/ Louis Quilico: Concerto Italiano
The incomparable duo of Renata Tebaldi and Louis Quilico performs classic works from opera in this much-heralded 1965 CBC production. Featured are the finale of Act II from "Tosca," Rossini's "La Regata Veneziana" song cycle, Tosti's "L'ultima Canzone" and "O Mio Babbino Caro" from Puccini's "Gianni Schicchi."
22-3179 ***$29.99***

Renata Tebaldi
These historic telecasts are taken from "The Bell Telephone Hour" from 1959-1967 and feature the great Tebaldi singing selections from "Madama Butterfly," "Adriana Lecouvreur," "Cavalleria Rusticana" and "La Gioconda." 30 min.
22-3218 ***$24.99***

Anna Russell: The Clown Princess Of Comedy
She mixes mirth and music together in a side-splitting way, and in this program the failed diva offers three hilarious routines and an interview in which she talks about her expulsion from London's Royal College of Music and how her voice dropped to baritone while singing in the bathtub to a Lawrence Tibbett recording. Touché, Ms. Russell, touché!
22-3180 ***$29.99***

Anna Russell: (First) Farewell Concert (1984)
A unique blend of grand opera and comedy taped live at Baltimore's Museum of Art. Russell's performance includes a hilarious look at Wagner's Ring Cycle, "Wind Instruments I Have Known" and a selection of English folk songs. 85 min.
22-3022 ***$39.99***

David Oistrakh In Performance
A rare recital film that wonderfully captures the virtuoso technique and artistic maturity of the legendary violinist. On the program are Prokofiev's "Death of Juliet," "Three Fantastic Dances" by Shostakovich, Debussy's Sonata in G minor, Ravel's "Tzigane" and more. 52 min.
22-1112 ***$19.99***

Wagner Concert In Leipzig
Conductor Kurt Masur leads the Leipzig Gewandhausorchester in a stirring evening of Wagner that includes the Wessendonck Lieder, the overtures to "Tannhauser" and "Tristan und Isolde," and much more. 90 min.
22-1151 ***$19.99***

Wanda Landowska: Uncommon Visionary
She was credited with single-handedly restoring the harpsichord to a position of prominence in the performing arts, and the life and music of Wanda Landowska are examined in this documentary program that also features rare concert footage of Landowska performing works by Bach and Francisque. 65 min.
22-3191 ***$29.99***

Kronos Quartet: In Accord
A leading voice in the world of modern music for more than 25 years, San Francisco's Kronos Quartet has garnered several Grammy nominations and a global fan base. In this documentary you'll meet the members of the group and see them in rehearsal and performance. 60 min.
22-1761 ***$19.99***

Finbar Wright: Opera Concert
Performing at the Grand Opera House in Belfast, noted Irish tenor Finbar Wright is joined by the National Chamber Orchestra and guest singer Regina Nathan for a concert. Songs include "Granada," "O Danny Boy," "Come Back to Sorrento," "O Sole Mio" and more. 65 min.
22-1769 ***$19.99***

The Great Waltz: The Music Of Johann Strauss, Jr.
A musical look at the works of waltz king Johann Strauss, with opera greats Patrice Munsel and Jarmila Novotna in the leads and a rare appearance by comic Bert Lahr. A rare treat. 78 min.
22-3154 ***$39.99***

Holiday Recitals

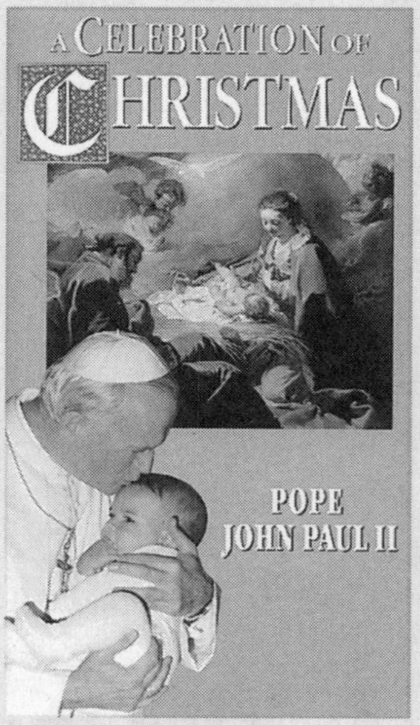

The Three Tenors Christmas (1999)
José Carreras, Placido Domingo and Luciano Pavarotti assembled for their first Christmas concert ever, recorded live at the Konzerthaus in Vienna, where they performed unique versions of classic songs like "White Christmas," "Adeste Fideles," "Silent Night" and many others. 81 min.
04-5755 *$19.99*

A Celebration Of Christmas With Pope John Paul II
A wonderfully inspirational program, featuring a special holiday message of peace from Pope John Paul II and a collection of Christmas musical performances from around the world. Songs include "Silent Night," "We Three Kings of Orient Are," "O Little Town of Bethlehem," "Fum, Fum, Fum" and many more. 74 min.
80-1095 *$5.99*

The Canadian Brass: A Christmas Experiment
Bring cheer to your holiday season with the world's best-selling brass ensemble. Joined by the Georgian Bay Children's Choir and the Bach Children's Chorus, the Canadian Brass performs some of the most treasured Christmas songs, including "Jingle Bells," "Silent Night," "Frosty the Snowman" and more.
02-8942 *$19.99*

Christmas With Luciano Pavarotti
A musical treasure for any time of the year, with the renowned tenor performing at Montreal's Notre Dame Cathedral. Accompanied by two choral groups and a full orchestra, Pavarotti performs such classic songs as "Ave Maria," "Silent Night," "O Come, All Ye Faithful," "O Holy Night" and many more. 60 min.
08-8098 *$14.99*

Denyce Graves: A Cathedral Christmas
The Washington National Cathedral was the sight for this wonderful holiday concert featuring one of opera's most exquisite voices, Denyce Graves. Along with special guests that include "Sesame Street's" Elmo, Graves sings an unforgettable collection of hymns, carols, international music and contemporary song. 60 min.
18-7817 *$19.99*

Christmas With José Carreras
Famed tenor José Carreras is joined by the Mozart Boys Choir of Vienna for a special holiday recital from the Jesuit Church in Luzern, Switzerland. Along with works by Schubert, Bizet and others, there are such traditional songs as "Adeste Fidelis," "Silent Night" and "White Christmas." 60 min.
22-1304 *$19.99*

Christmas Carols From England
The setting is York Minster Cathedral for this magical holiday recital that features the King's Singers, Benjamin Luxon, Moira Anderson, the Huddersfield Choral Society and other artists. Such Christmas favorites as "Silent Night," "O Holy Night" and "While Shepherds Watched Their Flocks" are performed. 50 min.
22-1219 *$19.99*

Handel's Messiah
Roger Norrington conducts this performance of Handel's masterful oratorio. In this presentation, the musicians use original 18th-century instruments, and soloists include Willard White, Helen Watts and Robert Tear. 113 min.
22-1255 *$19.99*

Handel's Messiah
This unique adaptation of Handel's "Messiah" features the piece played by original instruments to its original scoring by the London Baroque Players, the Cardiff Polyphonic Choir and soloists Norma Burrowes and Helen Watts at the Cardiff Festival of Choirs. 114 min.
80-7208 *$29.99*

Christmas With Flicka
No, it's not a carolling horse! It's a delightful holiday visit to the Alpine village of St. Wolfgang, Austria, with noted opera star Frederica von Stade, whose childhood nickname was "Flicka." Native folk dances, yuletide spectacles and traditional carols, and guests Melba Moore and Rex Smith. 58 min.
22-7044 Was $19.99 *$14.99*

Kiri Te Kanawa At Christmas
The world-renowned soprano gives a gala holiday recital in London's Barbican Hall, accompanied by the Tallis Chamber Choir and Philharmonia Orchestra. Songs include "Silver Bells," "In Excelsis Deo," "O Holy Night," "Let the Bright Seraphim," and many more. 50 min.
22-7045 Was $19.99 *$14.99*

The Story Of Silent Night
The story behind the creation of the beloved Christmas hymn is told in this holiday program that includes stops in Austria, where it was written by Father Joseph Mohr. Also featured are performances by the Vienna Boys Choir. 55 min.
50-2839 Was $29.99 *$14.99*

Carols From Christchurch, Oxford
Set at the magnificent 12th-century Oxford Cathedral, this superb performance includes "Silent Night," "In the Bleak Mid-Winter" and "O Little Town of Bethlehem." Also featured are readings by Alec McCowen and Ian Charleson. 30 min.
80-7122 *$19.99*

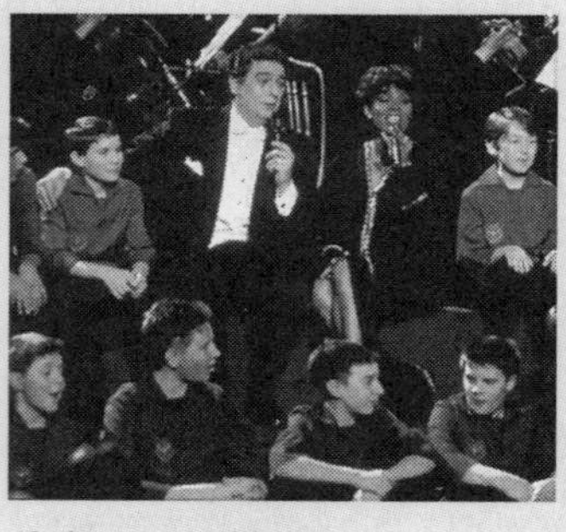

Christmas In Vienna
The formidable trio of Placido Domingo, Diana Ross and José Carreras turn in memorable performances in this stirring holiday concert. Among the selections are "It's the Most Wonderful Time of the Year," "White Christmas," "Carol of the Drum" and "Ave Maria." 66 min.
04-5420 *$24.99*

A Gala Christmas In Vienna
From Vienna's famed Rathaus, Placido Domingo continues his series of special holiday concerts. Joined by special guests Sarah Brightman, Helmut Lotti and Riccardo Cocciante, Domingo performs Christmas favorites old and new, including "Deck the Halls," "The Closing of the Year," "Adeste Fideles," "Il Re Gesù," "Away in a Manger," and more. 73 min.
04-5628 *$24.99*

A Carnegie Hall Christmas Concert (1991)
This all-star holiday gala includes such performers as Kathleen Battle, Frederica von Stade, the Wynton Marsalis Septet, the Orchestra of St. Luke's and the Christmas Concert Chorus. "The Twelve Days of Christmas," "Gesu Bambino," "Joy to the World," "Silent Night" and other holiday favorites are featured.
04-5186 *$24.99*

Christmas Glory From Westminster With Andrea Bocelli And Charlotte Church (2000)
From Westminster Abbey comes a holiday special full of excitement, as spectacular guests such as Andrea Bocelli, Charlotte Church, Greta Scacchi and others join the Westminster Abbey Choir for a festive night of Christmas music and poetry readings. A historical introduction about the Abbey from the Duke of Edinburgh is also featured. 60 min.
22-6105 Letterboxed *$19.99*

In The Steps Of Chopin: A Portrait By Byron Janis
The life, work and composing techniques of Frederic Chopin are examined by Byron Janis, who demonstrates Chopin's pianistic techniques, differences between manuscript and published versions of his pieces, and the composer's broad range of music. 60 min.
80-7035 *$29.99*

Symphony For The Spire (1991)
An unforgettable concert to benefit restoration of England's Salisbury Cathedral features opera greats Placido Domingo and Jessye Norman performing selections from Strauss, Verdi and Puccini, "The Flight of the Bumble Bee" by cellist Ofra Harnoy, and Kenneth Branagh and Charlton Heston appearing in "Henry V, a Concert Suite for Actor and Orchestra." 65 min.
02-2502 *$19.99*

Ljuba Kazarnovskaya In Recital: Gypsy Love (1998)
Recorded at the Great Hall of the Moscow Conservatory, noted soprano Kazarnovskaya performs a selection of songs with a Gypsy theme. Included are works by Brahms, Dvorak, Lehar, Liszt, Schumann, Verdi and others.
22-3198 *$29.99*

Mahler's Symphony No. 2 At Masada
As part of Israel's 40th anniversary of independence celebration, Zubin Mehta led the Israel Philharmonic Orchestra in Mahler's "Resurrection Symphony" at the foot of the legendary mountain fortress. Readings by Gregory Peck and Yves Montand add to this wonderful sight and sound experience. 100 min.
22-1140 Was $29.99 *$19.99*

Israel Folk Dance Festival (1983)
Put your hands in the hand of a friend and dance along with this exuberant collection of Hebrew dance music. The folklore of the Land of Milk and Honey lives in festive song and dance. 60 min.
22-1020 Was $59.99 *$29.99*

Revival Of The Dead (1998)
At Israel's Yad Vashem monument to the millions killed in the Holocaust, conductor Zubin Mehta leads the Israel Philharmonic in a moving memorial performance that mixes traditional prayer melodies and an original symphonic piece. 55 min.
53-6446 *$19.99*

Heifetz In Performance
This rare television program showcases great violinist Jascha Heifetz performing works with piano and orchestral accompaniment. Filmed at live shows and in a recording studio in Paris, Heifetz performs selections from Mozart, Debussy, Rachmaninoff and Gershwin with Brooks Smith at the piano and the Orchestra National de France.
02-8174 *$14.99*

Heifetz And Piatigorsky
Brilliant violinist Jascha Heifetz performs Brahms and others, while taking the viewer on a tour of his home, followed by great cellist Gregor Piatigorsky playing Chopin, Tchaikovsky. 79 min.
22-1000 *$19.99*

Heifetz Master Classes, Vols. 1 And 2
The man called the century's greatest violinist rosins up his bow and turns teacher in this special two-tape series. Filmed at his early '60s USC workshops, Jascha Heifetz is seen working with music students, giving impromptu performances, and even taking part in a mock "audition." 240 min.
22-1177 Was $79.99 *$49.99*

The Israel Philharmonic Orchestra: 60th Anniversary Gala Concert
Some of the world's greatest fiddlers unite for this gala event recorded live in Tel Aviv on December 26, 1996. Join Itzak Perlman, Pinchas Zuckerman, Maxim Vengerov, Isaac Stern, Shlomo Mitntz, maestro Zubin Mehta and others as they perform selections from Bach, Brahms, Vivaldi and Weber.
02-8645 *$24.99*

Isaac Stern: A Life
A joyous celebration of the 45-year recording career of master violinist Isaac Stern in which Stern is joined by cellist Yo-Yo Ma, pianist Emanuel Ax and the London Symphony Orchestra. Includes performances of Beethoven's Concerto for Violin and Orchestra and the "Triple Concerto" for piano, violin, cello and orchestra.
04-5218 *$29.99*

Isaac Stern: Life's Virtuoso
The remarkable life and career of violin master Isaac Stern are traced in this "American Masters" presentation. Follow Stern as his family emigrates from Russia to America when he was an infant, to his first recital at age 15 and Carnegie Hall debut at 22, and see how he became a "musical ambassador," helping American-Soviet relations with visits to his homeland. Along with rare performance footage, Henry Kissinger, Itzhak Perlman, Zubin Mehta, Gregory Peck and others are interviewed; Meryl Streep narrates. 60 min.
52-5024 *$19.99*

Itzhak Perlman: In The Fiddler's House
Famed violinist Itzhak Perlman shares his love for the traditional Jewish celebration music known as klezmer in this lively program that looks at klezmer's beginnings in 19th-century Eastern Europe and featuring Perlman performing with Brave Old World, The Klezmatics and The Klezmer Conservatory Band. 60 min.
44-4119 *$24.99*

Claudio Arrau: The 80th Birthday Recital
The great pianist is recorded at his 80th Birthday Recital at New York's Avery Fisher Hall. Performed are Beethoven's No. 21 in C Major ("Waldstein") and No. 23 in F Minor ("Appasionata"), Liszt's Ballade No. 2 in B Minor, and works by Chopin and Debussy. 111 min.
22-1100 Was $29.99 *$19.99*

Claudio Arrau: The Emperor
A special documentary look at the life and career of Chilean piano virtuoso Arrau, highlighted by a 1984 visit to Chile (his first in over 17 years) and a recital in Santiago's Metropolitan Cathedral of Beethoven's Emperor Concerto. 85 min.
22-1101 Was $29.99 *$19.99*

Claudio Arrau: Arrau & Brahms
In a special performance from his Santiago, Chile, homeland, master pianist Arrau is featured in a program that includes the Brahms Piano Concerto No. 1 and the Sonata No. 3. 110 min.
22-1102 Was $29.99 *$19.99*

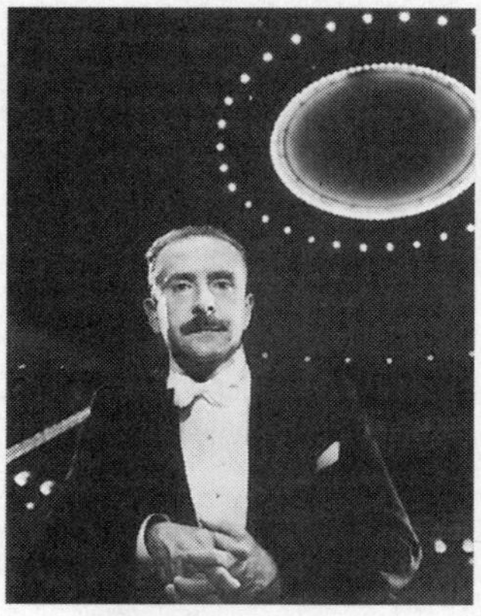

Claudio Arrau: The Maestro & The Masters
Works from some of the greatest composers of all time (Liszt, Chopin, Schubert, Debussy) are featured in a dazzling performance by classical pianist Claudio Arrau, highlighted by Beethoven's Piano Concerto No. 4 and Sonata No. 7. 111 min.
22-1103 Was $29.99 *$19.99*

Carnegie Hall 100: A Place Of Dreams
A centenary salute to the New York landmark that has featured performers from Bernstein to The Beatles on its legendary stage. Rare historic concert footage of Toscanini, Heifetz and Rubinstein is featured, along with clips and reminiscences by Isaac Stern, Frank Sinatra, Ray Charles and other stars. By the way, how do you get to Carnegie Hall? "Practice, practice, practice!"
02-7474 *$29.99*

The House Of Magical Sounds
Based on the autobiography of Claudio Abbado, this story centers on a young boy so impressed by his first classical concert at Milan's La Scala that he's determined to make music part of his life. The film feature works by Mozart, Beethoven, Schubert and Debussy, narration by Raul Julia and music by the Youth Orchestra of a United Europe, conducted by Abbado.
04-5246 *$24.99*

Bell Telephone Hour: Designs In Music
This installment of the "Bell Telephone Hour" features Roy Rogers, Dale Evans, Dorothy Collins, Margot Fonteyn and Joan Sutherland. 60 min.
10-9905 *$14.99*

Jacqueline Du Pré And The Elgar Cello Concerto
Joining world-renowned cellist du Pré in this recital is an all-star ensemble that includes Daniel Barenboim, William Pleeth, Sir John Barbirolli and the New Philharmonia Orchestra. 74 min.
19-3283 *$29.99*

The Trout
In 1969, five stars of the world of classical music came together at London's Queen Elizabeth Hall for a recital of Schubert's "Trout" Quintet. The concert was filmed by Christopher Nupen, and now you can see and hear Daniel Barenboim, Jacqueline du Pre, Zubin Mehta, Itzhak Perlman and Pinchas Zukerman in this once-in-a-lifetime event.
19-3328 *$29.99*

DVD VIDEO
ASK ABOUT OUR GIANT DVD CATALOG!

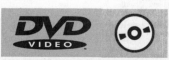

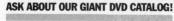

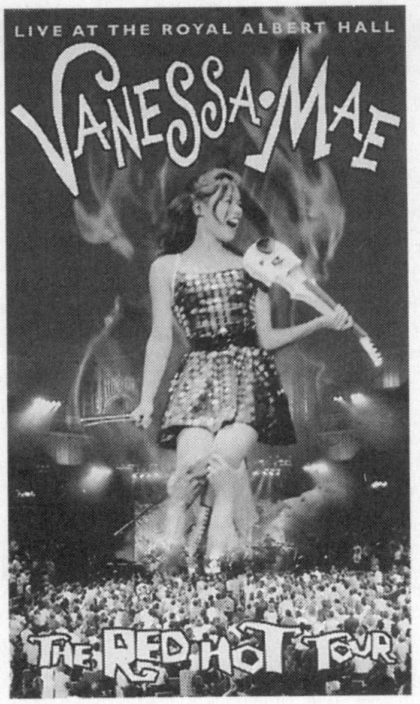

Vanessa-Mae: The Red Hot Tour (1995)
This teenage, Singapore-born violin prodigy took the classical and pop music worlds by storm during her premiere world tour, and Vanessa-Mae's Royal Albert Hall recital in London is featured in this captivating concert video. Among the selections performed are "Red Hot" and "Toccata and Fugue" from her debut pop album, "The Violin Player."
44-4131 *$24.99*

Papal Concert: A Musical Offering From The Vatican
To mark the 10th anniversary of Pope John Paul II's selection, Gilbert Levine led the Television Italiana Symphony Orchestra & Chorus and the Krakow Philharmonic choir in a special concert featuring selections by Brahms, Dvorák and Penderecki. Also included are a rare look at the renowned Vatican art collection and a concluding message from the Pontiff. 60 min.
22-7173 Was $19.99 *$14.99*

Concerto Di Natale With Jose Carreras (1998)
The first in a series of Vatican-sponsored "Jubilæum 2000" concerts, this special holiday show from the Basilica di St. Ambrogio in Milan features Carreras, joined by the Dell'Emilia Romagna Symphonic Orchestra, performing traditional Christmas favorites along with works by Bach, Handel and Schubert. 80 min. In English and Italian with English subtitles.
50-8343 *$19.99*

In Passione Domini Concerto: Jubilæum Collection 2000 A.D. (1999)
The "Jubilæum 2000" celebration continues with this special Palm Sunday concert video. Noted tenor José Cura is joined by the Coro della Cappella Giulia and the Coro dell' Accademia Filarmonica Romana performing works by Bach, Franck, Mozart and Verdi, along with Leonard Bernstein's "Somewhere." 80 min.
50-8554 *$19.99*

Concerto Di Pasqua: Easter Sunday Concert (1999)
Filmed in the majestic Basilica di Santa Maria degli Angeli in Rome, this third "Jubilæum 2000" recital features famed sopranos Monserrat Caballe and Monserrat Marti, joined by the Orchera del Festival di Pasqua and the Cappela Giulia Saint Peter's Chorus. Selections from Bellini, Donizetti, Handel, Massenet and others make for a memorable Easter concert. 70 min.
50-8464 *$19.99*

Stabat Mater: Rossini: Jubilæum Collection 2000 A.D. (1999)
Gioacchino Rossini's arrangement of the "Stabat Mater," one of the most enduring works of classical religious music, is presented by conductor Corrado Giuffredi and the Filarmonici di Busseto. Rome's Basilica di San Pancrazio Fuori le Mura is the setting for this moving "Jubilæum 2000" presentation. 70 min.
50-8538 *$19.99*

Stabat Mater: Luigi Boccherini: Jubilæum 2000 A.D.
This is the original version of the "Stabat Mater" that was first performed in 1781. Soprano Maria Dragoni is showcased with the Quartetto Meridien from Palazzo Della Cancelleria Aula Magna in Rome in this "Jubilæum 2000" presentation. 60 min.
50-8623 *$19.99*

Duomo Monza Concerto: Jubilæum Collection 2000 A.D.
Shot entirely at the Duomo in Monza, Italy, during a live performance by soprano Cecilia Gasdia and the Orchestra I Virtuosi Italiani, this extraordinary concert features classical arrangements by Mozart, Vivaldi, Stradella, Franck and others.
50-8732 *$19.99*

Murray Perahia In Performance
A special recital with Perahia at the keyboard during the annual Aldeburgh Festival, where he's served as co-artistic director since 1981. Featured are selections by Beethoven, Schumann, Liszt and Rachmaninov. 87 min.
45-5542 *$24.99*

Gwyneth Jones In Concert
This concert of operatic arias from 1988 includes selections from "Tannhäuser," "Macbeth," "La Forza del Destino," "Tosca" and "Turandot," as well as a smashing performance of "Memory" from "Cats." Filmed with the Orchestre Symphonique de Quebec. 53 min.
22-3308 *$29.99*

Welsh Choir Of Choirs
Cantorian Colin Jones, an all-volunteer male choir from Wales, performs a number of beautiful songs in this program that mixes music and beautiful Welsh scenery. Filmed at Manchester Cathedral in England, the show includes such selections as "A Welsh Medley," "The Lord's Prayer," "When Johnny Comes Marching Home Again" and "Amen." 51 min.
50-8406 *$19.99*

George Frideric Handel: Honour, Profit And Pleasure
The life and noteworthy musical accomplishments of George Frideric Handel are the focus of this fine biography in which the composer is portrayed by Simon Callow ("Four Weddings and a Funeral"). Handel's achievements are seen in the context of the culture and society of England during the early 18th century. 60 min.
80-7036 *$29.99*

Of Men And Music (1950)
A fine look at some of the world's premier performing artists, including violinist Jascha Heifetz, pianist Artur Rubinstein, opera greats Nadine Conner and Jan Peerce and conductor Dimitri Mitropoulos. 79 min.
55-9001 Was $69.99 *$19.99*

Igor Markevitch (1955)
Renowned composer-conductor Igor Markevitch leads the CBC Symphony in a program that includes "The Sorcerer's Apprentice" by Paul Dukas, Wagner's "Siegfried Idyll" and Britten's "Young Person's Guide to the Industry." 50 min.
22-3227 *$24.99*

Piano Grand! A Smithsonian Celebration
This 300th anniversary tribute to the piano was shot in Washington, D.C., and features performances by Billy Joel ("Baby Grand," "Piano Man"), Jerry Lee Lewis ("Great Balls of Fire," "Whole Lotta Shakin' Goin' On"), Dave Brubeck ("Thank You"), Diana Krall ("Let's Fall in Love"), Toshiko Akiyoshi ("It Was a Very Good Year") and others. 116 min.
04-5751 *$19.99*

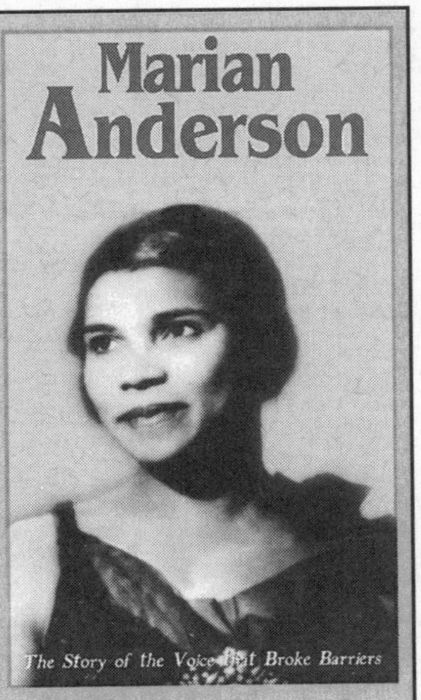

Marian Anderson
The Philadelphia-born contralto whose voices won her accolades around the globe, and whose quiet courage made her a trailblazer for African-Americans in the arts, is saluted in this documentary that recounts Anderson's life and features her in rare performance and interview footage, along with comments from such colleagues as Jessye Norman and Isaac Stern. 60 min.
22-1600 *$19.99*

Marian Anderson: On Stage And On Screen
This 1950 film offers a revealing glimpse of the legendary contralto at home, in rehearsal and in performance. Among the selections are Handel's "Begrüssung" and Schubert's "Ave Maria," as well as such spirituals as "He's Got the Whole World in His Hands," "Oh, What a Beautiful City" and "Deep River." 27 min.
22-3317 *$19.99*

Martha Argerich (1976)
Legendary piano master Martha Argerich is seen in a Montreal TV studio performing the Schumann Piano Concerto, Liszt's "Funérailles" and Ravel's "Jeux d'eau." This is believed to be the only live concerto performance of Argerich captured on video and is a must-have for classical music lovers.
22-3223 *$24.99*

Eileen Farrell: An American Prima Donna (1969)
The talented soprano is featured in a Canadian TV special that showcases her performing selections from "Aida," "La Gioconda," "Madame Butterfly" and more, including works by Fauré, Gershwin and Poulenc. 60 min.
22-3200 *$29.99*

Renata Scotto In Concert (1986)
The great Scotto performs arias from "Otello," "Macbeth," "Don Carlo," "La Wally," "Tosca" and "Gianni Schicchi" with accompaniment from the Orchestre Symphonique de Quebec in this spellbinding concert. 58 min.
22-3309 *$29.99*

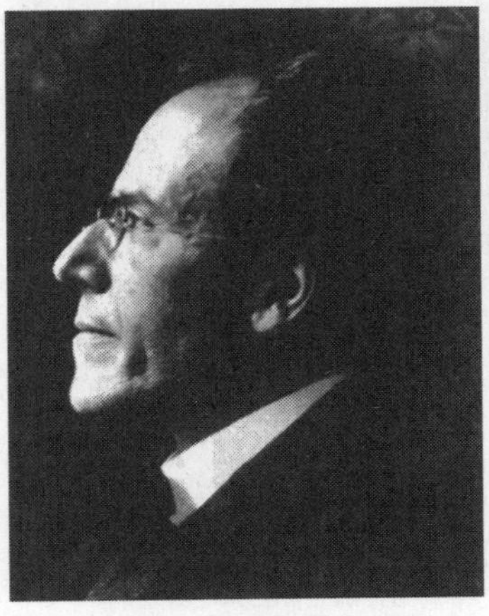

Gustav Mahler: To Live, I Will Die
In this compelling documentary look at the Austrian composer whose music was the creative link between the 19th and 20th centuries, filmmaker Wolfgang Lesowsky examines how Mahler channeled his creative energies and a stormy personal life into his work. 93 min.
50-8340 *$19.99*

Chicago Symphony Orchestra Historic Telecasts
From 1953 to 1963, WGN's broadcasts of the Chicago Symphony Orchestra in concert were a fixture of Windy City television. This series brings to you the best of these groundbreaking performances, featuring appearances by some of the world's most renowned conductors.

Chicago Symphony Orchestra, Vol. 1: Fritz Reiner (1954)
Includes Beethoven's Symphony No. 7 and "Egmont" Overture and Haydn's Overture to the Queen of Sheba from "Solomon."
22-3201 *$24.99*

Chicago Symphony Orchestra, Vol. 2: George Szell (1961)
Includes the "Roman Carnival" overture by Berlioz, Mussorgsky's Prelude to "Khovanshchina," and Beethoven's Symphony No. 5.
22-3202 *$24.99*

Chicago Symphony Orchestra, Vol. 3: Leopold Stokowski (1962)
Includes Bach's Toccata and Fugue in D Minor, Brahms' Variations on a Theme by Haydn, and Rimsky-Korsakov's "Capriccio Espagnol."
22-3203 *$24.99*

Chicago Symphony Orchestra, Vol. 4: Pierre Monteux (1961)
Includes Beethoven's Symphony No. 8, Wagner's Prelude to Act III of "Die Meistersinger," and the Overture to "Roman Carnival" by Berlioz.
22-3204 *$24.99*

Chicago Symphony Orchestra, Vol. 7: George Szell And Erica Morini (1961)
Includes Mozart's overture to "The Marriage of Figaro" and Violin Concerto No. 5 in A Major, K.219 ("Turkish"), and Beethoven's Leonore Overture No. 3, Op. 72 B.
22-3221 *$24.99*

Chicago Symphony Orchestra, Vol. 5: Charles Munch (1963)
Includes Ravel's "La Valse" and "Valses Nobles et Sentimentales," "Royal Hunt and Storm" from Berlioz's "Les Troyens," and the "Dardanus" Suite by Rameau/D'Indy.
22-3205 *$24.99*

Chicago Symphony Orchestra, Vol. 6: Paul Hindemith (1963)
Includes the "Academic Festival" overture by Brahms, Bruckner's Symphony No. 7, and Hindemith's own Concert Music for Strings and Brass.
22-3206 *$24.99*

Helmut Lotti Goes Classic
Renowned Belgian singer Helmut Lotti offers up an eclectic selection of classical works and popular tunes in a live concert from his homeland's Cleydael Castle. Featured in this program are "Mother Nature ('Morning')," "Why," "John Brown's Body" and more, including three songs not seen in the PBS broadcast: "Der Lindenbaum," "Stenka Rasin" and "The Stars." 73 min.
02-9063 *$19.99*

Toscanini: The Maestro/ Hymn Of The Nations
James Levine hosts this documentary look at the renowned 20th century conductor, featuring concert performances, interviews with such stars as Robert Merrill and Andres Segovia, and even rare home movies. Next is a 1943 performance with Toscanini conducting the NBC Symphony Orchestra in Verdi's musical plea for world peace; tenor Jan Peerce appears. 74 min. total.
22-3050 *$29.99*

In Celebration Of The Piano (1988)
Live from Carnegie Hall, this "all-star tribute to the Steinway" is hosted by Van Cliburn and features performances by Murray Perahia, Rudolf Serkin, Alexis Weissenberg and over 20 other artists. 100 min.
22-3101 *$39.99*

Charles Munch Conducts Berlioz: Symphonie Fantastique (1963)
Originally broadcast on Canadian TV, this rare find features conductor Munch leading the Orchestre Symphonique de Radio-Canada in a tremendous version of Berlioz's Symphonie Fantastique. 45 min.
22-3234 *$24.99*

Otto Klemperer's Long Journey Through His Times (1984)
Effective portrait of the renowned conductor's life that utilizes rare footage and interviews to track his conflicts with Hitler and McCarthy, his courageous fight against paralysis, and much more. A remarkable look at a remarkable man from director Philo Bregstein. 96 min. In German with English subtitles.
53-9012 *$59.99*

Leontyne Price: The Complete Bell Telephone Hour Performances, 1963-1967
This powerhouse soprano is at her best in a collection of songs with the Bell Telephone Hour Orchestra. Among the featured selections are her renditions of "Tacea la notte" from "Il Trovatore," "Aida's" "Ritorna vincitor!," "Pace, pace, mio Dio" from "La Forza Del Destino" and others. 32 min.
22-3231 *$24.99*

Corelli/Di Stefano/Vickers: Bell Telephone Hour Telecasts 1962-1964
Opera legends Franco Corelli, Giuseppe Di Stefano and Jon Vickers demonstrate their talent in some of their best performances with the Bell Telephone Hour Orchestra. Solo efforts as well as duets with such artists as Lisa Della Casa and Giulietta Simionato are highlighted, including songs from "Manon" ("Ah, Fuyez!"), "Tosca" ("Amaro Sol Per Te"), "Il Trovatore" ("L'abborrita Rivale") and others. 35 min.
22-3230 *$24.99*

Anna Moffo: Bell Telephone Hour Telecasts, 1962-1967
Anna Moffo's amazing voice and beautiful persona made it easy for her to climb to the top of her profession. Along with the backing of the Bell Telephone Hour Orchestra, she belts out such performances as the balcony scene from "Roméo et Juliette" with Sándor Kónya, "Libiamo" and "Sempre Libera" from "La Boheme," and more. 42 min.
22-3232 *$24.99*

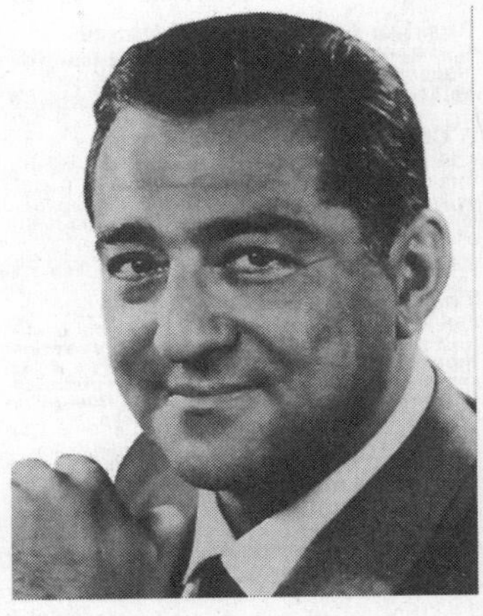

Robert Merrill: Bell Telephone Hour Telecasts, 1962-1965
One of America's best-loved singers, Merrill is seen with the Bell Telephone Hour Orchestra, along with such other notables as Roberta Peters, Regina Resnik, James McCracken and Richard Tucker, performing arias and scenes "The Barber of Seville," "Carmen," "Otello" and more. 39 min.
22-3233 *$24.99*

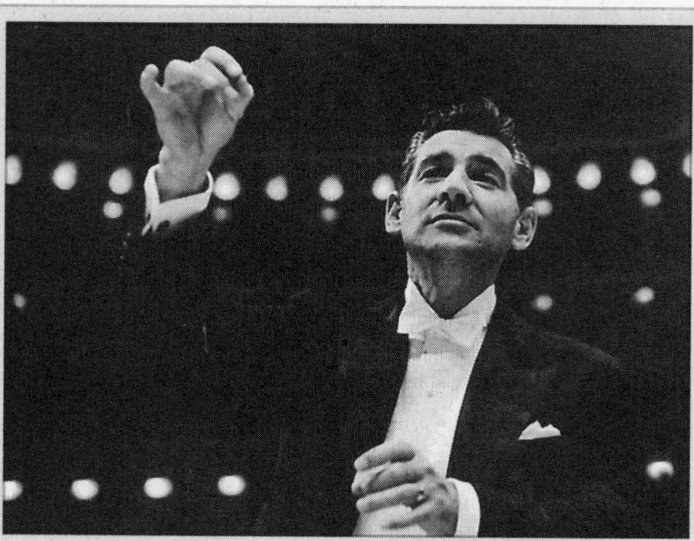

The Unanswered Question: Six Talks At Harvard By Leonard Bernstein: Complete Set
This historic series is comprised of six lectures given in 1973 by Bernstein at Harvard University and also features the Boston Symphony Orchestra, the Vienna Philharmonic and Bernstein in performance. The maestro explores the work of Mozart, Beethoven, Copland, Schoenberg, Stravinsky and others in this six-tape collection. 13 hrs. total. NOTE: Individual volumes available at $19.99 each.
22-1252 Save $20.00! *$99.99*

Leonard Bernstein: The Little Drummer Boy
The legendary conductor offers his insights into the life and work of Austrian-born composer Gustav Mahler, focusing on Mahler's conflicted feelings on his Jewish heritage and its influences on his music. 85 min.
22-1436 *$19.99*

Leonard Bernstein: "The Rite Of Spring" In Rehearsal
Leonard Bernstein's genius as a teacher and musician is showcased in this memorable program in which he helps and inspires a young group of musicians to perform Stravinsky's "The Rite of Spring." 60 min.
22-1463 *$19.99*

Leonard Bernstein's Young People's Concerts: Boxed Set
Beginning in 1958, famed composer/conductor Leonard Bernstein and the New York Philharmonic brought the many worlds of music, from classical to jazz, into America's homes with these acclaimed children's TV specials that became treats for all ages. Now 25 of the "Young People's Concerts" have been gathered in a 10-tape collector's set. Featured titles include "What Does Music Mean?," "What Is Classical Music?," "Humor in Music," "Jazz in the Concert Hall," "The Sound of an Orchestra," "The Latin American Spirit" and more. 25 hrs. total.
22-1548 *$349.99*

Leonard Bernstein: Four Ways To Say Farewell
Leading the Vienna Philharmonic Orchestra, maestro Bernstein takes viewers through a special analysis of Mahler's Ninth Symphony, from rehearsals to final performance. 57 min.
22-1437 *$19.99*

The Love Of Three Orchestras
Maestro Leonard Bernstein's relationships with the New York, Israel and Vienna Philharmonics are the focus of this fascinating program that showcases great performances spanning four decades. 88 min.
22-1434 *$19.99*

Bernstein In Paris: Berlioz Requiem
Paris' Chapel of St. Louis des Invalides is the setting for this stirring recital in which Bernstein conducts the Orchestre National de France, the Orchestre Philharmonique de France, and Les Choeurs de Radio France, with lead tenor Stuart Burrows. 98 min.
22-1298 Was $29.99 *$19.99*

Bernstein: Tchaikovsky Symphony No. 6 In B Minor
Tchaikovsky's Sixth Symphony, known as the "Pathétique," is one of the composer's most revered, and this performance features Leonard Bernstein conducting the New York Philharmonic at the Sydney Opera. 48 min.
22-1291 Was $29.99 *$19.99*

Trouble In Tahiti (1973)
In 1951, Leonard Bernstein composed this groundbreaking seven-scene opera that takes a satirical look at the American suburbs. Live actors perform on an animated set, and the music, which Bernstein conducts himself, is a mix of jazz and American musical-comedy. The cast includes Nancy Williams and Julian Patrick. 46 min.
22-1259 Was $29.99 *$19.99*

Bernstein In Paris: The Ravel Concerts (1975)
Leonard Bernstein conducts the National Orchestra of France in this salute to the works of Maurice Ravel. "Shéhérazade," "Alborada del Gracioso," "Tzigane" and "Boléro" are among the selections; Marilyn Horne is a featured soloist. 87 min.
22-1279 Was $29.99 *$19.99*

Bernstein Conducts Bernstein (1977)
Leading the Israel Philharmonic Orchestra in a special Berlin concert, conductor Leonard Bernstein presents a program that features three of his own compositions: "Chichester Psalms," "Symphony No. 1: Jeremiah" and "Symphony No. 2: The Age of Anxiety." 80 min.
22-1275 Was $29.99 *$19.99*

Leonard Bernstein: Reaching For The Note (1998)
Whether it was as a pianist, composer, conductor or educator, Leonard Bernstein was a key part of 20th-century music. This "American Masters" program traces his life and career, from his years as New York Philharmonic conductor to his Broadway and Hollywood successes with "On the Town" and "West Side Story." Jerome Robbins, Stephen Sondheim, Isaac Stern and Michael Tilson Thomas are among those interviewed. 117 min.
53-6328 *$29.99*

The Boast Of Kings
Cambridge University's renowned King's College Chapel Boys' Choir is spotlighted in this song-filled documentary look at the group's rich history and the rigorous training and rehearsal the boys undergo. Musical selections include "Ave Maria," "Miserere" and "Nunc Dimittis." 60 min.
22-5167 *$39.99*

Soviet Army Chorus, Band And Dance Ensemble
Dizzying acrobats, festive singing and dancing. Skol! 70 min.
22-1005 Was $39.99 *$19.99*

Russian Folk Song And Dance
Tony Randall narrates this look at the various great Russian folk troupes. 70 min.
22-1006 Was $39.99 *$19.99*

A Century Of Russian Music
A celebration of Russia's rich musical heritage, this concert of works by such composers as Glinka, Tchaikovsky and Shostakovich features special guest performers Maxim Shostakovich and Viktoria Mullova. 95 min.
22-1141 *$19.99*

The Great Singers Of Russia
Celebrate a century of Russian musical tradition and excellence with this two-tape series that features over 20 of the country's most renowned singers in vintage performance segments and rare film interviews. Hosted by noted soprano Ljuba Kazarnovskaya.

The Great Singers Of Russia, Vol. 1: From Chaliapin To Reizen
Featured artists include Feodor Chaliapin ("Don Quixote"), Alexander Pirogov ("Boris Godunov"), Maxim Mikhailov ("Ivan Sussanin"), Pavel Lisitsian ("La Traviata"), Mark Reizen ("Eugene Onegin") and others. 75 min.
22-3196 *$29.99*

The Great Singers Of Russia, Vol. 2: From Petrov To Kazarnovskaya
Featured artists include Ivan Petrov ("Faust"), Zurab Andzhaparidze ("Rigoletto"), Galina Vishnevskaya ("Aida"), Olga Borodina ("Il Barbiere di Siviglia"), Ljuba Kazarnovskaya ("Salome") and others. 90 min.
22-3197 *$29.99*

A Time There Was: A Profile Of Benjamin Britten
Tremendous film biography of the great contemporary British composer that features excerpts from "Peter Grimes" and "Death in Venice" among many others, rare footage of Britten at work rehearsing and conducting, playing Mozart with Sviatoslav Richter, and so much more. 120 min.
22-1067 Was $39.99 *$19.99*

Benjamin Britten: In Rehearsal And Performance With Peter Pears (1962)
A true giant of 20th-century music, British composer Benjamin Britten is featured with his longtime collaborator, tenor Peter Pears, and the CBC Vancouver Chamber Orchestra rehearsing and performing the Nocturne to Tenor, Seven Obbligato Instruments & Strings, Op. 60. 60 min.
22-3199 *$29.99*

War Requiem (1989)
An offbeat and compelling blending of archival war footage, poetic narration (including an opening segment with Sir Laurence Olivier) and the classical oratorio of Benjamin Britten, this look at the human faces and suffering behind warfare was written and directed by Derek Jarman ("Caravaggio"). 92 min.
70-7072 *$29.99*

Bel Canto: The Tenors Of The 78 Era: Boxed Set
Rare film footage and concert recordings from some of the greatest singers of the first half of the 20th century are mixed with interviews and analysis from contemporary performers and teachers in this four-tape collection. Included are "Enrico Caruso/Beniamino Gigli/Tito Schipa," "Richard Tauber/Leo Slezak/Joseph Schmidt," "Jussi Björling/Lauritz Melchior/Helge Rosvaenge" and "Georges Thill/Ivan Kozlovsky/The Gramophone." 360 min. total. NOTE: Individual volumes available at $29.99 each.
22-1581 Save $20.00! *$99.99*

Sir John Barbirolli: In Rehearsal And Performance
Filmed in 1962, this program offers a rare glimpse of one of the music world's most important conductors at work. Witness his rehearsal with the Vancouver Symphony Orchestra on Haydyn's "Oboe Concerto in C," featuring Evelyn Rothwell (Lady Barbirolli) on oboe.
22-3210 *$29.99*

Yehudi Menuhin
He won international acclaim at age 11 as a child prodigy and is recognized as one of the greatest violinists of his time. In this feature-length profile, Yehudi Menuhin discusses his life and his music alongside scenes of him in concert and working with young musicians at his school. 105 min.
22-5693 Was $39.99 *$29.99*

Yehudi Menuhin: Concert For The Pope (1983)
The famed violin virtuoso is joined by Jerry Maksymiuk and the Polish Chamber Orchestra in a special papal recital performed in commemoration of the Polish people's struggle for independence. Works by Vivaldi, Bach and Mozart are on the bill. 53 min.
22-7014 Was $19.99 *$14.99*

Yehudi Menuhin: Tribute To J.S. Bach (1985)
The "J.S." is, of course, none other than Johann Sebastian, and the Barbican in London was the spot for this special tercentennial memorial concert. Join violinist Menuhin, the English Chamber Orchestra, and guest baritone Nicolas Rivenq for a show that includes Bach's Concerto for Violin in A Minor, the "Peasant" and "Coffee" Cantatas and more. 90 min.
22-7015 Was $19.99 *$14.99*

At The Haunted End Of The Day: A Profile Of Sir William Walton
Over 20 pieces of the contemporary British giant are celebrated here, including "Crown Imperial" (composed for George VI's coronation), the music for Olivier's "Richard III," "Hamlet" and "Henry V," and "Belshazzar's Feast" performed by the Dolsmiths Choral Union and the Highgate Choral Society. Features Yehudi Menuhin, Julian Bream and many others. 100 min.
22-1068 Was $39.99 *$19.99*

Rosalyn Tureck: High Priestess Of Bach
The milestone first TV performances of Tureck on harpsichord and piano are presented on this video featuring footage from 1961-1962. Included are Bach's Gigue in B-Flat Major from "Partita No. 1," Prelude and Fugue in C-Sharp Major from "The Well-Tempered Clavier" and the Italian Concerto. Also on the program is Tureck's commentary on Bach and his music. 60 min.
22-3215 *$29.99*

The Guarneri Quartet
Called "the pre-eminent string quartet in the world," the Guarneri Quartet has dazzled audiences around the globe. In this memorable concert, they perform Mozart's String Quartet in D Dur, K. 575, and Brahms' Quartet No. 1 for Piano and Strings, Op. 25, featuring piano soloist Mikhail Rudy. 68 min.
22-1458 *$14.99*

Midori: Live At Carnegie Hall
The renowned violin virtuoso made her Carnegie debut in this acclaimed recital, part of the concert hall's 100th anniversary season. Works by Beethoven, Chopin, Ernst, Mozart, Ravel and Strauss are on the program. 110 min.
45-5541 *$29.99*

Thomas Hampson: I Hear America Singing
Renowned baritone Thomas Hampson is joined by such fellow singing greats as Dawn Upshaw, Frederica von Stade, Marilyn Horne and Jerry Hadley in a salute to American songwriters. The program includes works by Barber, Bernstein, Copland, Foster and others. 90 min.
22-1545 *$29.99*

George London: A Celebration
Organized by the George London Foundation of Singers, this gala 1984 concert features Leonie Rysanek, Tatiana Troyanos, Nicolai Gedda, James King and Catherine Malfitano performing with the Radio Symphony of Vienna. Also included are TV performances of London in "Don Giovanni" and "Boris Godunov." 127 min.
22-3207 *$29.99*

Sviatoslav Richter
In these historic Canadian TV discoveries, the famed Russian pianist performs in Toronto in 1964. Among the selections are Brahms ("Intermezzo, Op. 116"), Ravel ("Jeux d'eau, Alborada del gracioso") and Prokofiev ("Sonata No. 2 in D Minor, Op. 14").
22-3211 *$29.99*

George Szell And The Cleveland Orchestra
This 1966 entry in the "Bell Telephone Hour" series profiles Szell and the Cleveland Orchestra and showcases the conductor rehearsing works by Beethoven, Brahms and Berg, as well as coaching apprentice conductors like a young James Levine. 55 min.
22-3220 *$24.99*

Istomin/Stern/Rose Trio
Taped before a live audience in June, 1965, this program offers the famed ensemble of pianist Eugene Istomin, violinist Isaac Stern and cellist Leonard Rose in a performance that includes selections from Beethoven and Brahms. 60 min.
22-3222 *$24.99*

High Fidelity: The Guarneri String Quartet (1989)
A moving, award-winning concert documentary that marks the 25th anniversary of this acclaimed classical string quartet, formed when three of them were students at Philadelphia's Curtis Institute. Footage of performances from around the world focuses on their fine music and the sense of camaraderie that has kept the members together through the years. 85 min.
53-7441 *$39.99*

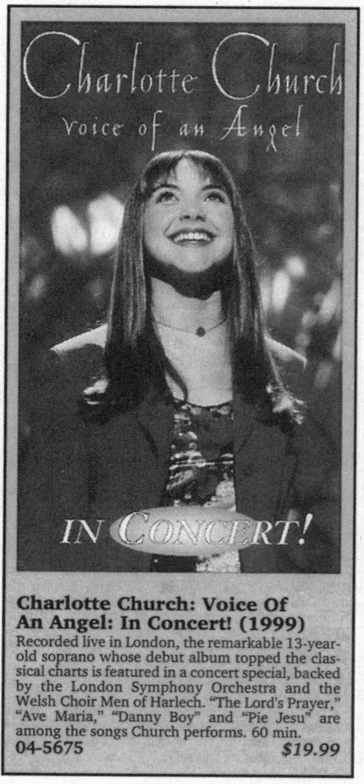

Charlotte Church: Voice Of An Angel: In Concert! (1999)
Recorded live in London, the remarkable 13-year-old soprano whose debut album topped the classical charts is featured in a concert special, backed by the London Symphony Orchestra and the Welsh Choir Men of Harlech. "The Lord's Prayer," "Ave Maria," "Danny Boy" and "Pie Jesu" are among the songs Church performs. 60 min.
04-5675 *$19.99*

Stage

Original Cast Album: Company
A rare look at the making of the cast album of the hit Broadway play featuring music by Stephen Sondheim. Go behind the scenes with stars Dean Jones, Barbara Barrie, Charles Kimbrough, Donna McKechnie and Elaine Stritch, under the direction of Sondheim. Songs include "Getting Married Today," "Being Alive"; D.A. Pennebaker ("Dont Look Back") directs. 60 min.
02-7571 Available 1/01 *$24.99*

Sunday In The Park With George (1984)
Stephen Sondheim's smash Broadway musical, based on the life of 19th-century French painter Georges Seurat, features a winning score (including "Putting It Together") and fine performances from Mandy Patinkin and Bernadette Peters. 147 min.
40-1208 *$19.99*

Into The Woods (1990)
Bernadette Peters, Joanna Gleason and the rest of the original Broadway cast are featured in this magical production of Stephen Sondheim's musical. Based on timeless fairy tales, the story follows a baker and his wife's journey through an enchanted forest to find golden slippers, magic beans and other items that will help lift the curse that has kept them childless. Songs include "Children Will Listen," "No One Is Alone." 153 min.
50-5434 *$24.99*

Sondheim: A Celebration At Carnegie Hall (1992)
An all-star gathering of Broadway greats take the stage to salute Tony-winning songwriter Stephen Sondheim. Liza Minnelli, Bernadette Peters, Glenn Close, Michael Jeter, Jerry Hadley, Patti LuPone and others perform such perennial favorites as "Broadway Baby," "Send in the Clowns," "A Weekend in the Country," "Being Alive," "Sunday" and many more. 85 min.
02-7781 *$29.99*

Passion (1995)
Loosely based on the Italian film "Passion D'Amore," this Stephen Sondheim musical stars Best Actress Tony-winner Donna Murphy as Fosca, a sickly, unattractive woman obsessively in love with handsome soldier Giorgio (Jere Shea). Her devotion to him moves Giorgio, even as he continues his affair with the married Clara (Marin Mazzie). Winner of the Best Musical of 1994, the play boasts a haunting score that includes "Happiness," "I Wish I Could Forget You" and "No One Has Ever Loved Me." 105 min.
08-8602 *$19.99*

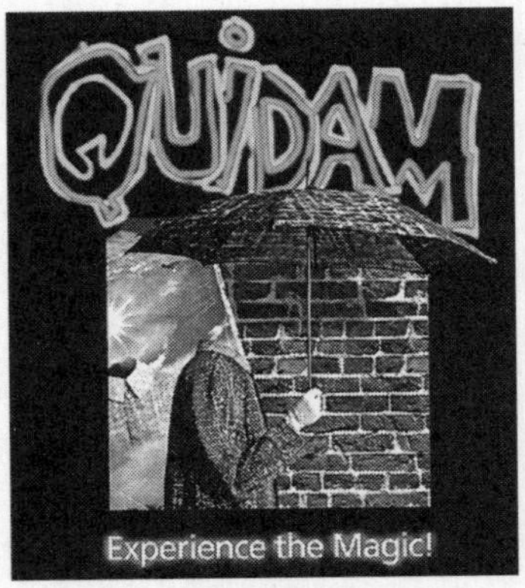

Cirque Du Soliel: Quidam
Recorded live in Amsterdam, the internationally renowned "nouvelle circus" presents their dazzling stageshow that mixes big-top acrobatic thrills with a brilliant display of dance, music and lights. 90 min.
02-3889 □*$19.99*

Cirque Du Soleil: Saltimbanco
The colorful circus troupe that has dazzled audiences throughout the world performs an incredible show filled with artistry, acrobatics and mesmerizing music.
02-8245 *$24.99*

Ipi Ntombi: An African Dance Celebration (1998)
Acclaimed around the world since its 1974 debut, this rousing South African stage musical mixes traditional rhythms and dances with a story of two young lovers caught in the middle when their families feud over wedding plans. 90 min.
18-7840 □*$19.99*

My Favorite Broadway: The Leading Ladies (1998)
New York's famed Carnegie Hall was the setting for an all-star gathering of stage superstars—including Julie Andrews, Nell Carter, Jennifer Holliday, Andrea McArdle, Liza Minnelli and others—performing classic songs from "Showboat," "Man of La Mancha," "Gypsy," "Dreamgirls," "Chicago," "A Chorus Line" and other Broadway favorites. 100 min.
50-8346 *$24.99*

Rime Of The Ancient Mariner
Sir Michael Redgrave recites while images, both real and animated, tell Samuel Coleridge's famous epic poem in two parts—"The Life of Samuel Coleridge" and "The Rime of the Ancient Mariner." 60 min.
22-1007 Was $39.99 *$19.99*

Rime Of The Ancient Mariner (1977)
Astounding version of Samuel Taylor Coleridge's poem of the accursed seaman as rendered in cut-out animation by Larry Jordan. The narration by Orson Welles rounds out a spectacular presentation. 42 min.
53-9005 *$59.99*

Champion Acrobats Of China: Flying Lotus
You'll be astonished at the incredible feats of skill and stunts performed by the world-renowned troupe from China. From tumbling, balancing and somersaults to bicycle balancing and flying eggs and plates, this one's sure to dazzle. 43 min.
22-7097 Was $19.99 *$14.99*

Champion Acrobats Of China: Steel Silk
From juggling items with their feet to performing wild stunts with chairs, glasses and flying bamboo tops, the Champion Acrobats of China are guaranteed to amaze and enthrall. 46 min.
22-7098 Was $19.99 *$14.99*

Akropolis
Jerzy Grotowski's Polish Laboratory Theatre performs the 1904 work by Symbolist poet Wyspianski, with British director Peter Brook narrating. This rare film offers a demonstration of Grotowski's theories on integrating all the arts in order to offer comments on contemporary civilization. 60 min.
48-7016 *$59.99*

The Serpent
The creation and fall of man as told in Genesis is depicted in six episodes by Jean-Claude Van Italie and the Open Theatre, directed by and starring the legendary Joseph Chaikin. A masterpiece of experimental theater. 80 min.
48-7017 *$59.99*

Nunsense
The acclaimed off-Broadway musical comedy that's delighted audiences across America comes to home video. Join the "talent"-laden (but cash-poor) Little Sisters of Hoboken as they put on a riotous benefit show to save their convent and watch them interact with a live audience. Rue McClanahan, Christine Anderson, Terri White star. 111 min.
50-5594 *$19.99*

An Evening With Sir Peter Ustinov
Recorded during a live one-man show in Toronto, Oscar-winning actor and author Ustinov will delight you in a witty collection of Hollywood anecdotes, impersonations, and stories about his life. 60 min.
53-8614 *$19.99*

Nunsense 2: The Sequel
Just when you thought it was safe to go back to the nunnery, those toe-tapping Little Sisters of Hoboken take to the stage once again with a second hilarious helping of musical numbers, ballet, bingo and comedy, Catholic-style. Join Rue McClanahan and her fellow nuns in the smash hit revue. 109 min.
50-5595 *$19.99*

Nunsense 1 & 2 Twin Pack
Both laugh-filled "Nunsense" shows are also available in a special collector's set.
50-5596 Save $10.00! *$29.99*

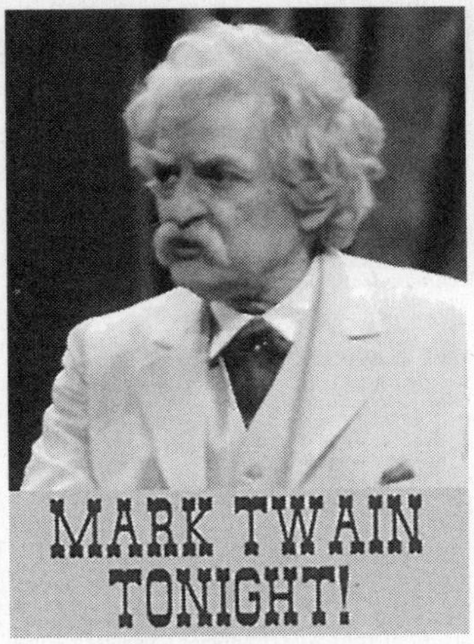

Mark Twain Tonight! (1967)
Hal Holbrook won an Emmy Award for this broadcast of his acclaimed one-man stageshow based on the life and works of 19th-century author, humorist and iconoclast Samuel L. Clemens. The irascible, 70-year-old Twain's caustic comments on patriotism, slavery, religion and other topics are as timely now as they were in his day. 90 min.
22-1655 *$24.99*

Jerry Herman's Broadway At The Hollywood Bowl
Tony- and Grammy Award-winning composer-lyricist Jerry Herman is feted in this thrilling evening of stars, songs and more from the Hollywood Bowl. Join Angela Lansbury, Rita Moreno, Liza Minnelli, and Paul and Linda McCartney as they perform music from "Hello, Dolly!," "La Cage Aux Folles," "Mame" and more.
07-2561 *$19.99*

Oedipus Rex (1956)
Highly stylized film version of the classic Greek tragedy, with the cast wearing masks, as was done in the time of Sophocles. Douglas Campbell stars as the mythic king whose actions unwittingly fulfill a damning prophecy. With Eleanor Stuart, Robert Goodier, Douglas Rain. 90 min.
53-7181 *$59.99*

Antigone: Rites Of Passion (1990)
A haunting and innovative updating of the ancient tragedy by Sophocles, this stage presentation by Amy Greenfield uses rock music and modern dance to tell the story of the women who defied the state and paid the price. Music by Glenn Branca, Paul Lemos, Diamanda Galas. 85 min.
70-7114 *$29.99*

Medea (1959)
Dame Judith Anderson turns in one of the classic performances of her career in the title role of this sterling production of Euripedes' masterwork. The story focuses on Medea's jealousy and revenge when she discovers that her husband Jason plans to wed the daughter of the King of Creon. With Colleen Dewhurst; directed by Jose Quintero. 107 min.
55-9008 Was $69.99 *$29.99*

Strindberg's "Miss Julie"
The haunting, gripping play that probes the tense, hidden world of the subconscious mind is expertly staged by the Royal Shakespeare Company. 90 min.
52-1075 *$74.99*

Voices Of Sarafina! (1988)
A heartfelt documentary look at the young South African performers who told, in music and dance, the story of their struggle against their homeland's system of apartheid in the Broadway musical "Sarafina!" Go behind the scenes at rehearsals, hear first-hand accounts of the racial hatred that divided South Africa, and listen to their inspiring songs. 85 min.
53-7462 Was $39.99 *$29.99*

Paul Robeson (1988)
One of the first black performers to achieve mainstream recognition, he was later vilified for his activism and political views. James Earl Jones magnificently brings to life Paul Robeson, the actor, singer, and man, in this one-man stage show, filmed at Philadelphia's New Locust St. Theatre. 118 min.
67-5013 *$24.99*

Look Back In Anger (1989)
Kenneth Branagh and Emma Thompson star in this powerful stage production of John Osborne's classic drama about Jimmy Porter, a British working-class man whose rage at the world around him alienates him from everyone, including his long-suffering wife. Directed by Judi Dench. 114 min.
44-1800 Was $29.99 *$19.99*

A Raisin In The Sun (1988)
Danny Glover and Esther Rolle star in this moving stage production of Lorraine Hansbery's acclaimed drama, as a black family living in the Chicago slums struggles to build a better life for themselves. 171 min.
27-9078 Was $69.99 *$39.99*

Barnum (1990)
A magnificent filmed stage performance of the sensational musical, featuring Michael Crawford ("The Phantom of the Opera") as the world's most famous showman. Captured live at London's West End Theater, the play traces the career of P.T. Barnum, from sideshow promoter to co-founder of the Barnum and Bailey Circus. Music by Cy Coleman. 113 min.
01-1461 *$29.99*

That's Singing: The Best Of Broadway (1982)
The Great White Way's biggest stars get together and raise their voices to Broadway's top musicals in this all-star songfest. Ethel Merman, Nell Carter, Anthony Perkins, Debbie Reynolds, Len Cariou and other names are featured. 111 min.
40-1072 Was $19.99 *$14.99*

Master Harold And The Boys (1984)
Matthew Broderick ("Glory") stars in this staging of the critically acclaimed Broadway drama. Set in 1950s South Africa, the play deals with the unusual and controversial friendship between an upper class white boy and two black servants who work for his family. Zakes Mokae, John Kani also star. 90 min.
40-1134 Was $59.99 *$19.99*

The Making Of Miss Saigon (1991)
A fascinating, behind-the-scenes look at one of the most talked-about Broadway events ever. See how "Miss Saigon" came to life, through interviews and auditions, scenes from the original London production, and more. 75 min.
44-1801 Was $29.99 *$19.99*

Othello, The Moor Of Venice
Romance, treachery, suspicion and murder all play a part in this Shakespeare masterpiece. William Marshall stars in the title role of the jealous Moor, and the supporting cast includes Ron Moody and Jenny Agutter. 195 min. total on two tapes.
22-1034 *$59.99*

The Shakespeare Collection
"To buy or not to buy...that is the question." Why not buy this six-tape boxed set featuring three great Shakespearean tales from the Canadian Broadcasting Company, performed at England's Stratford Festival? Included are "Romeo and Juliet" with Megan Follows and Antoni Cimolino; Roberta Maxwell in "As You Like It"; and "The Taming of the Shrew" with Lynne Griffin and Colm Feore. 480 min. total.
72-3030 *$39.99*

The English Theatre Company Performs Shakespeare
The power and glory of Shakespeare's historical plays about the Houses of Lancaster and York have been preserved in this acclaimed series of ensemble cast productions by the English Theatre Company. The featured players in these filmed stage performances include Michael Pennington, Michael Cronin and Andrew Jarvis. Each volume runs about 170 min.

Richard II
80-7053 *$34.99*

Henry IV, Part One
80-7054 *$34.99*

Henry IV, Part Two
80-7055 *$34.99*

Henry V
80-7056 *$34.99*

Macbeth (1978)
Shakespeare's immortal "Scottish play" comes to life with a stellar cast headed by Ian McKellen, Judi Dench, Roger Rees, Bob Peck and Ian McDiarmid. Tony Award-winning director Trevor Nunn's acclaimed production is performed at the Other Place theatre in the Bard's hometown of Stratford-Upon-Avon. 146 min.
44-2188 Was $24.99 □*$19.99*

Antony And Cleopatra (1982)
The classic tale of romance and intrigue in Ancient Rome and Egypt as written by William Shakespeare and performed here in authentic 16th-century fashion. Timothy Dalton, Lynn Redgrave, Anthony Geary and Walter Koenig star. 183 min.
22-1022 *$59.99*

Romeo And Juliet (1982)
It's perhaps the world's most famous love story, and in this stunning stage performance Shakespearean-era costumes and sets add to the atmosphere. Alex Hyde-White, Blanche Baker, Esther Rolle and Dan Hamilton star. 165 min.
50-2310 *$59.99*

King Richard II (1983)
Shakespeare's classic historical drama is performed in authentic 16th-century costumes and sets. David Birney stars as the doomed egocentric King of England, along with Paul Shenar, Nicholas Hammond and Mary-Joan Negro. 172 min.
22-1017 *$59.99*

Macbeth (1983)
Jeremy Brett stars as the tragic hero in Shakespeare's timeless tale of power, greed and betrayal in medieval Scotland. Piper Laurie, Simon MacCorkindale and Millie Perkins also star; filmed live in England with period sets and dress. 150 min.
22-1018 *$59.99*

The Tempest (1983)
Shakespeare's timeless drama that combines a shipwrecked prince, a manipulative sage, magical beings, romance and comedy. Efrem Zimbalist, Jr. is the enigmatic Prospero, William H. Bassett is King Alonso and J.E. Taylor is Miranda. 126 min.
22-1023 *$59.99*

King Lear (1983)
Historically accurate sets and costumes highlight this staging of Shakespeare's story of an elderly king whose misplaced trust in his daughters proves to be his undoing. Mike Kellen, Charles Aidman, David Groh and Kitty Winn star. 182 min.
22-1045 *$59.99*

The Merry Wives Of Windsor (1983)
One of Shakespeare's funniest (and bawdiest) comic plays is performed live on stage, as the gregariously girthsome Sir John Falstaff gets his comeuppance from the title wives. Leon Charles, Valerie Snyder, Joel Asher and Gloria Grahame star. 160 min.
50-2308 *$59.99*

The Taming Of The Shrew (1983)
The battle of the sexes was never funnier than in Shakespeare's boisterous tale of Katherina and her strong-willed suitor, Petruchio. The cast in this authentically re-created play includes Franklin Seales, Karen Austin, David Chemel and Larry Drake. 117 min.
50-2309 *$59.99*

King Lear (1988)
William Shakespeare's classic is given a fascinating treatment, as Patrick Magee ("A Clockwork Orange") excels in the title role. Several of England's finest talents appear in this powerful adaptation. 110 min.
44-1749 Was $39.99 *$19.99*

South Pacific: The London Sessions (1986)
The familiar strains of Rodgers and Hammerstein's classic South Seas musical come alive again in brand-new performances by such artists as Kiri Te Kanawa, José Carreras, Mandy Patinkin and Sarah Vaughan. Includes "Some Enchanted Evening," "There Is Nothin' Like a Dame," "Cockeyed Optimist," "This Is How It Feels" and more. 60 min.
04-2006 *$19.99*

As Is (1986)
The tragedy of AIDS is vividly portrayed in this engrossing human drama about how the disease affects the friends and family of one of its victims. Stars Robert Carradine, Colleen Dewhurst and Jonathan Hadary. 85 min.
40-1247 Was $59.99 *$19.99*

Flanders & Swann
The offbeat and comedic music of British songwriters Michael Flanders and Donald Swann won them fans on both sides of the Atlantic in the '50s and '60s, and this tribute program offers rare footage of the duo performing on stage in the West End and on Broadway. 40 min.
90-1006 *❑$19.99*

Pippin (1981)
Bob Fosse's Tony-winning musical is captured in a rousing stage performance. Join young Pippin, the son of King Charlemagne, as he searches for truth and meaning in life in Medieval Europe. William Katt, Ben Vereen, Chita Rivera and Martha Raye star. 120 min.
08-1497 Was $29.99 *$19.99*

Meet Marcel Marceau (1965)
The most renowned of contemporary mime artists stars in a one-man show filmed for television. Nine different vignettes, including his famous "Bip" character, are featured. 52 min.
09-1163 Was $24.99 *$19.99*

Andrew Lloyd Webber: The Royal Albert Hall Celebration
Glenn Close, Antonio Banderas, Sarah Brightman, Elaine Page, Kiri Te Kanawa and a host of star performers gather in London to celebrate the music and life of Andrew Lloyd Webber, the creator of such Broadway favorites as "Evita," "Cats," "The Phantom of the Opera," "Sunset Boulevard" and more. 126 min.
02-8962 *$19.99*

Lyrics By Tim Rice
One of the world's most popular lyricists is feted in this tuneful program that features appearances by Marti Webb, Elaine Page and David Essex, and such selections as "I Don't Know How to Love Him," "Don't Cry for Me, Argentina," "Jesus Christ Superstar" and "One Night in Bangkok." 52 min.
22-1338 *$14.99*

Cats: Commemorative Edition (1998)
Wake up that sleeping kitty, because Broadway's longest-running show is on home video! Andrew Lloyd Webber's Tony-winning adaptation of T.S. Eliot's "Old Possum's Book of Practical Cats" follows a band of strutting, singing felines who turn their junkyard home into a dazzling stage for such memorable tunes as "Jellicle Cats," "Memory" and more. Recorded live at London's Adelphi Theatre, the stunning stage production stars Ken Page, Elaine Paige and John Mills. Special two-tape set also includes a behind-the-scenes documentary featuring interviews with Webber and the show's creators and cast. 115 min.
07-2946 *❑$19.99*

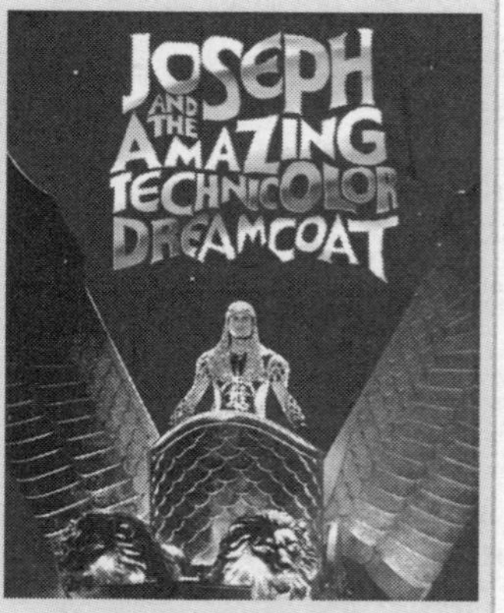

Joseph And The Amazing Technicolor Dreamcoat (2000)
Donny Osmond stars in the title role of the young man sold into slavery by his jealous brothers, but who rises to power in Egypt and manages to save his family's lives, in this lively stage presentation of the Andrew Lloyd Webber/Tim Rice musical. Richard Attenborough, Joan Collins and Maria Friedman also star; songs include "Any Dream Will Do," "Close Every Door to Me" and "Go Go Go Joseph." 78 min.
07-2822 *❑$19.99*

The Belle Of Amherst (1984)
In this magnificent adaptation of the story of Emily Dickinson's life, Julie Harris, in her Tony Award-winning role, plays the American first woman of letters. The show offers readings from Dickinson's poems, diaries and letters along with dramatic interpretations of her often tragic life. 90 min.
53-8077 *$59.99*

St. Mark's Gospel (1977)
Renowned British actor Alec McCowen turns in an incredible performance in this live adaptation of the Gospel According to St. Mark. An epic solo production that should be treasured by all acting aficionados. 105 min.
48-7003 *$59.99*

Our Town (1977)
Shortly before his death, Thornton Wilder collaborated with director George Schaefer on this adaptation of his timeless drama set in the quiet New England town of Grover's Corners. Robby Benson, John Houseman, Sada Thompson, Ned Beatty, Barbara Bel Geddes and Hal Holbrook as the Stage Manager head the impressive cast. 120 min.
52-1000 *$74.99*

Our Town (1989)
The Tony Award-winning Lincoln Center presentation of Thornton Wilder's paean to small-town American life, as seen in a typical day for the residents of Grover's Corners, New Hampshire, is brought to home video. The cast includes Spalding Gray as the Stage Manager, plus Eric Stoltz, Penelope Ann Miller, Peter Maloney. 104 min.
52-1099 *$74.99*

Phantom Of The Opera (1990)
A musical stage version of Gaston Leroux's classic story about the hideously scarred Phantom who roams the Paris Opera House and is obsessed with Christine, a beautiful singer. The score ranges from pop to traditional musical-comedy style and the sumptuous production stars David Staller and Elizabeth Walsh. 93 min.
01-1480 *$24.99*

Guys And Dolls: Off The Record (1993)
One of the biggest hits on Broadway in the '90s was the Tony-winning revival of Frank Loesser's musical, and in this video you'll go behind the scenes to see the recording of the cast album. Among the favorite tunes performed by Nathan Lane, Faith Prince, Peter Gallagher and company are "Adelaide's Lament," "Luck Be a Lady," "Sit Down, You're Rockin' the Boat" and others.
02-8053 *$14.99*

Stomp Out Loud (1997)
Filmed on location throughout New York City, this dazzling program features the cast of the hit Broadway show "Stomp" on a lively song-and-dance odyssey along the city sidewalks, as ordinary street objects become musical instruments and the beat of stomping feet becomes a percussive epiphany. 55 min.
44-2148 *$19.99*

Greater Tuna (1994)
The long-running Broadway play about a small town in Texas and its wacky residents has been captured before a live audience at the Will Rogers Memorial Auditorium in Ft. Worth, Texas. Co-creators Joe Sears and Jaston Williams play all 24 of the town's denizens in this rollicking, quick-paced, good ol' boy (and girl) bonanza.
76-2079 *$29.99*

A Tuna Christmas (1996)
The two dozen residents of Greater Tuna, Texas—all played by Joe Sears and Jaston Williams—try to cope with seasonal traumas during the holidays. Among the predicaments they face are a disastrous theater production of "A Christmas Carol" and a "phantom" who's menacing the annual yard decorating contest. This hilarious sequel to "Greater Tuna" was filmed before a live audience.
76-2080 *$29.99*

Victor/Victoria (1995)
Julie Andrews re-creates her screen role as the '30s singer who masquerades as a man impersonating a woman in this hilarious production of the hit Broadway musical. Joining the gender-bending Andrews in the talented cast are Tony Roberts, Michael Nouri and Rachel York; songs include "Le Jazz Hot," "Crazy World," "Almost a Love Song." 120 min.
50-8399 *$24.99*

Hey Mr. Producer!: The Musical World Of Cameron Mackintosh
This dazzling Royal Gala salute to theatrical producer Cameron Mackintosh offers exhilarating excerpts from such works as "Cats," "The Phantom of the Opera," "Les Miserables," "Miss Saigon" and other hits. Guest performers in the production from London's Lyceum Theatre include Elaine Page, Bernadette Peters, Colm Wilkinson, Jonathan Pryce, Lea Salonga and Stephen Sondheim; Julie Andrews hosts. This special video edition includes footage not seen on television. 162 min.
02-3233 *$24.99*

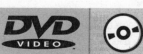

Alternative Arts

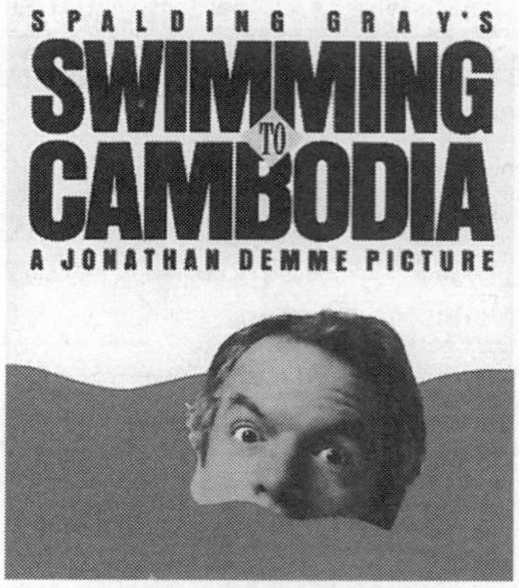

Swimming To Cambodia (1987)
An audacious and unique "concert film" of performance artist Spalding Gray's off-Broadway monologue detailing his thoughts and experiences in Southeast Asia during the filming of "The Killing Fields." Gray touches on topics ranging from sex and drugs to the horrors of Khmer Rouge Cambodia. Directed by Jonathan Demme; score by Laurie Anderson. 87 min.
40-1314 *$14.99*

Monster In A Box (1992)
Master monologist Spalding Gray ("Swimming to Cambodia") discusses his experiences writing a 1,900-page novel, travelling to wartorn Nicaragua, attending psychotherapy sessions and living the Hollywood life in this funny, insightful one-man tour-de-force. 90 min.
02-2335 Was $89.99 *$19.99*

Gray's Anatomy (1996)
The "Gray" in the title is Spalding Gray, and the specific part of his "anatomy" the stage storyteller discusses is his left eye, where a worsening ailment and the prospect of risky surgery sends him on a global odyssey for alternative cures, from Native American sweat lodges and raw vegetable diets to a Filipino psychic surgeon. Steven Soderbergh directs this funny and compelling film version of Gray's off-Broadway show. 80 min.
53-8960 Was $89.99 *$19.99*

Affliction
In this often-shocking program, a host of performance artists, geek artists and punk rockers do their thing, astonishing all who witness. Featured are the late g.g. allin, Mike Diana, Full Force Frank, Annie Sprinkle, The Voluptuous Horror of Karen Black and Turbo Tom. WARNING: This tape features material of an adult and disturbing nature. 45 min.
76-7362 *$19.99*

Puppets & Demons: Films By Patrick McGuinn
Ten of inventive underground filmmaker Patrick McGuinn's short, quirky works are presented in this collection. Among the pieces are "Agnes Keeden's Secret Plan," a tale of a suburban witch; "Evolution," a claymation comedy about the food chain; and "Terrance Baum: Intergalactic Assassin." 60 min.
70-5112 *$19.99*

Desert Spirits (1994)
In this eerie experimental short from Patrick McGuinn, two men face all sorts of strange encounters after their car breaks down in the desert. After taking peyote, they begin to see incredible and frightening things occur: lizards speak, sensory overload prevails and demonic spirits appear. Henry McGuinn and Edward Montoya, Jr. star. 35 min.
50-2634 *$19.99*

The Living Theatre Series
During its '60s and '70s heyday, the San Francisco-based Living Theatre company mounted fascinating stage productions around the world which were both noted and notorious for their cutting realism, innovativeness, unabashed sexuality and commitment to political ideas.

The Connection (1961)
This once-banned Living Theatre film details with aching thoroughness the terrible vigil of a group of addicts, a bored jazz quartet among them, waiting for the arrival of their heroin source, a man they call "Cowboy." 105 min.
70-7024 *$29.99*

Paradise Now (1970)
Filmed during a live performance in Belgium, this combining of Impressionist, electronically generated colors, group psychotherapy and theatre as bacchanal literally explodes into the audience (who join the actors in disrobing) for a free form theatrical happening. 105 min.
70-7022 *$29.99*

The Acts Of Venice Beach
Next to Disneyland, Venice Beach is California's top tourist spot, a colorful carnival of skaters, bikini-clad babes, musclemen and outrageous street performers. On this video you'll meet the babes (in a swimsuit contest) and the performers, from a man jumping into broken glass and a chainsaw juggler to a human torch and "Star Search" winner Michael Colyar. 56 min.
76-7423 *$19.99*

Poetry In Motion (1982)
More than 70 of the world's finest poets and writers recite their most stirring works in director Ron Mann's incredible film anthology. Included on the bill are Amiri Baraka, Charles Bukowski, William S. Burroughs, Jim Carroll, Diane DiPrima, Allen Ginsberg, Tom Waits, Anne Waldman and others. 90 min.
64-7011 Was $59.99 *$19.99*

Gang Of Souls (1988)
The impact of the Beat Generation is looked at in this fascinating documentary that features William S. Burroughs, Allen Ginsberg, Marianne Faithfull, Lydia Lunch, Jim Carroll, Richard Hell and others. 60 min.
53-9147 *$39.99*

Fried Shoes, Cooked Diamonds
Allen Ginsberg plays headmaster to the Jack Kerouac School of Disembodied Poetics in this highly personal gathering of the author and fellow Beats William Burroughs, Gregory Corso, Peter Orlovsky and Timothy Leary. Several intimate poetry readings and a nuclear protest highlight this spontaneous outburst.
70-7017 *$29.99*

Kenneth Anger Magick Lantern Cycle
American child actor, avant-garde director, and celebrant of cinema scandal ("Hollywood Babylon"), Anger's juxtaposition of pop cultural icons with the fetishistic imagery has placed and kept his work at the crest of alternative filmmaking.

Fireworks (1947)
The dawning of a young sailor's darker physical desires is the theme of Anger's first film, a dreamlike drama he starred in himself. Also included are "Rabbit's Moon" (1950), which blended Japanese myth and Commedia dell'Arte's Harlequin characters, and "Eaux D'Artifice" (1953), a bizarre stroll through Tivoli Gardens. 34 min. total.
70-7002 Was $29.99 *$19.99*

Inauguration Of The Pleasure Dome (1954)
Anger's fascination with the teachings of occultist Aleister Crowley culminated in this sensuous, striking film. A convocation of magicians assume the aspects of pantheistic deities and engage in a Dionysian rite. Anais Nin stars as the goddess Astarte. 38 min.
70-7003 *$29.99*

Lucifer Rising (1973)
Returning through an Aquarian ritual to Earth as God of Light and not the Devil, Lucifer assumes his place of leader of the New Age in Anger's mythic allegory that features Marianne Faithfull as the goddess Lilith and music by Charles Manson acolyte Bobby Beausoliel. Also in this volume is "Invocation of My Demon Brother" (1969), with music by Mick Jagger. 40 min. total.
70-7005 *$29.99*

The Brothers Quay Collection (1984-1993)
A compelling compilation featuring 10 works from the Philadelphia-born, London-based twins who revitalized the art of puppet animation with strange, fantastic shorts that mix wild, surrealistic humor and shadowy images. "The Cabinet of Jan Svankmajer," "The Epic of Gilgamesh," "Street of Crocodiles," "Dramolet," "Tales from the Vienna Woods" and "Can't Go Wrong Without You" are among the films. 104 min. total.
53-6558 *$24.99*

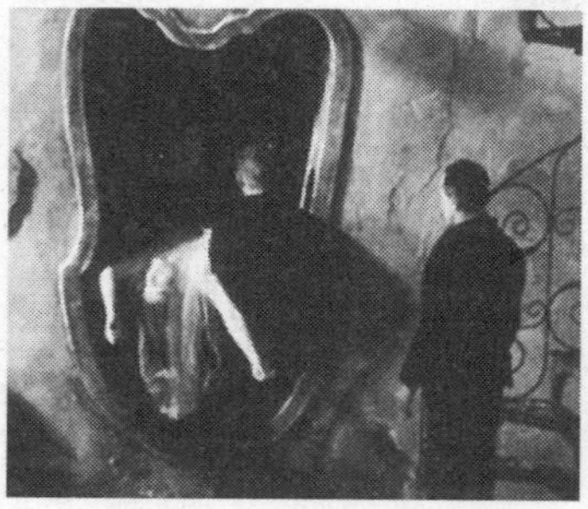

Institute Benjamenta, Or This Dream People Call Human Life (1995)
The first live-action film from underground animators the Quay Brothers, this haunting, Kafkaesque drama is set in a run-down, spartan training school for servants. Amid the bizarre "classes" that consist of the endless repetition of one lesson, a new student enters into a test of wills with the siblings who run the school. Alice Krige, Mark Rylance, Gottfried John star. 101 min.
53-6559 Was $79.99 *$24.99*

THE MIND'S EYE

Animation

The Mind's Eye Experience: Computer Animation Collection
Expand your horizons—without blowing your savings—when you buy this three-tape set of the wildest and most innovative comupter-generated animation. Dazzling visuals and music by such artists as Thomas Dolby and Jan Hammer are featured on "The Mind's Eye," "Beyond the Mind's Eye" and "The Gate to The Mind's Eye." 135 min. total. NOTE: "The Mind's Eye" available separately at $14.99; "Beyond the Mind's Eye" and "Gate to the Mind's Eye" are $19.99 each.
02-8307 Save $10.00! *$44.99*

Ancient Alien
Explore strange new worlds created via the wonders of computer animation with this dazzling entry in the "Mind's Eye" series. Volcanic eruptions, airborne beings, seas of molten metal and other unearthly sights await you in this cyber-odyssey. 45 min.
04-5571 *$14.99*

Computer Animation Marvels
They're funny, thought-provoking and a treat for the eyes: 17 of the finest computer-animated shorts from around the world, all gathered in one program. Included on this video are "Pets," "The Physics of Cartoons," "CPU," "Love & Rockets," "The Sitter" and more from Odyssey Productions. 51 min.
50-8344 *$14.99*

Computer Animation Classics
A treasure trove of over 24 early computer-generated animated shorts, this stunning program includes such rarities as outer-space combat scenes from the 1984 film "The Last Starfighter" and Mick Jagger's 1987 music video "Hard Woman." 55 min.
04-5513 *$14.99*

Computer Animation Showcase
Explore the world of high-tech animation with this sampler from some of the genre's top names. You'll see "Luxo Jr. Light and Heavy" from Pixar, "Walking Around," "Dutch Nelson, Galaxy Guy" and more. 46 min.
04-5541 *$14.99*

Masters Of Animation: Complete Set
While to the average moviegoer "animation" still means Bugs Bunny and Mickey Mouse, there's a world of diversity and sophistication in the field of film animation. This four-volume series looks at the history of the genre and talks to contemporary creators, along with showing scenes from their works, in "North America" "Great Britain and Europe," "Eastern Europe" and "Japan and the Computer." 300 min. total. NOTE: Individual volumes available at $19.99 each.
22-5889 Save $10.00! *$69.99*

Computer Animation Festival, Vol. 1
An eye-popping assortment of high-tech storytelling is presented on this tape, with 21 award-winning short films that run the gamut from romantic dramas to surreal comedies. "Locomotion," "Particle Dreams," "Jumpin' Jack Splash," "Embryo" and the acclaimed music video for Todd Rundgren's "Change Myself" are among the selections. 55 min.
02-7835 *$19.99*

Computer Animation Festival, Vol. 2
Enter new heights of fantasy, adventure and humor in this dazzling collection of state-of-the-art animation that features music videos for "Steam" and the never-before-released "Liquid Selves" by Peter Gabriel, plus Todd Rundgren's "Theology."
02-8067 *$19.99*

Rembrandt Films' Greatest Hits
Czech-born animator Gene Deitch, who worked at the UPA, MGM and Terrytoon studios in the '50s and '60s, also created dozens of unique cartoons under his Rembrandt Films label during those years. Among the shorts featured in this collection are the Academy Award-winning "Munro," written by Jules Feiffer; "Anatole," based on Eve Titus' book; four cartoons from the satiric "Self-Help Series," narrated by Arthur Treacher; a trio of "Nudnik" cartoons; and more.
50-8568 *$19.99*

Infinity's Child
Join the crew of an alien starship, as their exploration of a "gateway world" to another dimension becomes a mind-blowing odyssey of sight (through amazing computer animation) and sound (with music by Tangerine Dream alumnus Paul Haslinger).
53-7949 *$19.99*

Planetary Traveler
Join the crew of an alien starship as they explore a beautiful array of worlds on a cosmos-spanning odyssey. This unique computer-animated tale, done entirely on standard desktop computers, features an original score by Tangerine Dream alumnus Paul Haslinger. 40 min.
53-9788 Was $19.99 *$14.99*

Mondo Plympton
This collection of animated shorts, commercials and promos by the ever-quirky Bill Plympton features "Push Comes to Shove," "Nosehair," "Smell the Flowers," "How to Make Love to a Woman," excerpts from "The Tune" and "J. Lyle," and some political commentary from the animator. 75 min.
50-8430 *$24.99*

Plymptoons
The quirky works of animator and MTV favorite Bill Plympton ("The Tune") are represented in this collection of offbeat, socially irrelevant shorts, including "How to Kiss," "One of Those Days," "Your Face" and "25 Ways to Quit Smoking." 60 min.
76-7170 *$29.99*

The Tune (1992)
Delightfully oddball full-length animated film from Bill Plympton about a struggling songwriter who is given 47 minutes to write a perfect tune for a powerful music publisher. While searching for inspiration, he's transported to the bizarre town of Flooby Nooby, populated by fantastic characters. 80 min.
72-9020 Was $89.99 *$14.99*

Twisted Toons
This behind-the-scenes look at the making of Bill Plympton's first feature-length effort, "The Tune," features interviews with Plympton and members of the cast and crew.
50-8431 *$29.99*

Guns On The Clackamas (1995)
Hilarious live-action spoof from animator Bill Plympton about a documentary filmmaker who finds all sorts of trouble while shooting a film about the making of a western. When the lead actress reveals that she has a serious stutter and other cast members start dying mysteriously, the director and producer have to scramble to figure out how to finish the film. 80 min.
50-8433 *$29.99*

J. Lyle (1994)
Animator Bill Plympton's first live-action feature is a darkly whimsical satire about a sleazy lawyer who wants to get some fast cash by turning an apartment building into a toxic waste dump. Standing in his way is one of the building's pretty tenants and a magical dog who lets the attorney put himself into other people's shoes—literally! Richard Kuranda stars. 72 min.
50-8432 *$29.99*

Walt Curtis, The Peckerneck Poet (1995)
Animator Bill Plympton follows poet-artist Walt Curtis around his favorite haunts where he reads poetry, to a county fair where he almost gets arrested, and to a porno parlor. See how the frenetic Curtis, who wrote the book "Mala Noche" and attended the same high school as Plympton, entertains and infuriates at the same time. 64 min.
50-8434 *$29.99*

I Married A Strange Person! (1998)
A newlywed couple's marriage could be on thin ice when the husband develops telekinetic powers, thanks to a boil on his neck, that allow him to alter reality and make him the target of a multinational corporation in this bizarre animated feature from Bill Plympton. 73 min.
07-2855 *$99.99*

General Chaos Uncensored Animation
This wild and outrageous compilation features an incredible array of adults-only animation of the computer generated, cel, claymation and puppet styles. Selections include "American Flatulators," "Donor Party," "Looks Can Kill," "Sex and Violence," "No More Mr. Nice Guy," "The Saint Inspector," "Malice in Wonderland," "Espresso Depresso," "Body Directions" and more. 70 min.
02-9161 *$19.99*

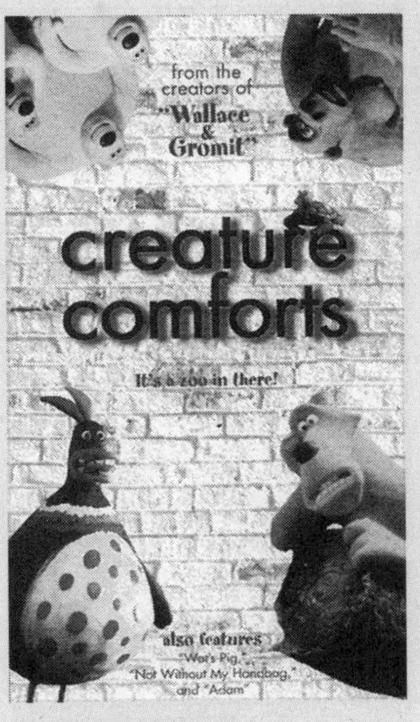

Creature Comforts
Four acclaimed short films from Aardman Animations, the claymation masters behind "Wallace & Gromit," are featured in this collection. Learn about zoo life from the animals themselves in the Academy Award-winning "Creature Comforts" (1990); see what happens when two brothers are raised in very different families in "Wat's Pig" (1996); an elderly woman dies, but refuses to enter the afterlife sans purse in "Not Without My Handbag" (1994); and it's a "creation story" with a difference in "Adam" (1992). 33 min.
04-3534 *$14.99*

The Morph Files
From "Wallace & Gromit" creators Aardman Animations comes this delightful, innovative series that blends claymation and computer-generated graphics to present fun-filled adventures for all ages. Each tape runs about 45 min.

The Morph Files, Vol. 1
04-3941 *$14.99*

The Morph Files, Vol. 2
04-3942 *$14.99*

The Morph Files, Vol. 3
04-3943 *$14.99*

Turbulence
Travel to a hypnotically beautiful digital world where strange life forms evolve before your very eyes in this award-winning computer-animated film. Two other short subjects are also included. 30 min.
04-5512 *$14.99*

Hollywood Salutes Canadian Animation
Seven animated shorts from the famed National Film Board of Canada, including the Academy Award-winning "Every Child," "The Sand Castle" and "Neighbours" along with three Oscar nominees. 58 min.
53-9353 Was $39.99 *$19.99*

The National Film Board Of Canada's Animation Festival
Some of the finest animated works of Canadian filmmakers are presented in this funny, surprise-filled program that features "The Apprentice," "Every Dog's Guide to the Playground," "Jours de Plaine," "Blackfly" and highlights from "The Cat Came Back," "Get a Job," and more. 87 min.
76-7101 Was $29.99 *$19.99*

Leonard Maltin's Animation Favorites From The National Film Board Of Canada
Film historian Leonard Maltin hosts this program that features some of the finest examples of animated efforts produced by the National Film Board of Canada over the last 50 years. Selections include "Mindscape," "Getting Started," "The Street," Norman McLaren's "Pas De Deux (Duo)" and "Begone Dull Care." 95 min.
76-7168 Was $29.99 *$19.99*

The Best Of Bulgarian Animation
Some of the most innovative and acclaimed animated short films of the last 50 years have come from Eastern European creators, and this compilation video spotlights eight comical and quirky works from the Sofia Animation Studio. Included are "Baby Dreams at the Airport," "De Facto," "Three Fools and the Automobile," "Beach," "The Intelligent Village" and others. 50 min.
50-8462 *$19.99*

The Cartoons Of Bob Godfrey
The hilarious animated works of Bob Godfrey are featured in this terrific compilation which showcases many award-winning shorts from the Australian-born, England-raised master. Included are "Do-It-Yourself Cartoon Kit," "Henry Nine 'Til Five," "Instant Sex" and "Bio Woman." See the classics that influenced Nick Park, Terry Gilliam and others. 61 min.
53-6709 *$19.99*

The Cartoons Of Halas & Batchelor
The groundbreaking efforts of British husband-and-wife animation team John Halas and Ruth Batchelor are presented in this superb collection. Among the selections from the couple who created the 1995 feature "Animal Farm" are "The Magic Canvas," "The Butterfly Ball," "Owl and the Pussycat," "History of the Cinema," "Automania 2000" and "Dilemma," the first fully digital animated film. 55 min.
53-6931 *$19.99*

Neurotica: Middle-Age Spread And Other Life Crises
Wild and wacky works of National Film Board of Canada animators are presented in this amazing collection. Included are "The Big Snit," "No Problem," "George and Rosemary," "Strings" and the Academy Award-winner "Bob's Birthday," which led to the British series "Bob and Margaret." 53 min.
50-5155 *$19.99*

The Best Of Zagreb Film
Formed during the Communist rule of Yugoslavia, the Zagreb Film Studio won international praise for its witty and distinctive animation work. In this double feature of cartoon creativity you'll see the 14-story omnibus "Be Careful What You Wish For" and the "best of" sampler "The Classic Collection," featuring seven shorts. 113 min.
50-8536 *$19.99*

Cartoon Noir (1999)
A look at the dark side of animation, this international collection includes "The Story of the Cat and the Moon," in which a feline becomes romantically obsessed with the moon; "Ape," about an unusual meal shared by a bickering couple; "Joy Street," in which a depressed woman is transformed by a monkey figurine; and "Abductees," a whimsical look at alien encounters. 83 min.
70-5192 *$24.99*

Films Of Alfred Leslie: Pull My Daisy/The Last Clean Shirt
A double feature of offbeat short works by writer/filmmaker Alfred Leslie features Allen Ginsberg in "Pull My Daisy," based on part of Kerouac's "The Beat Generation," followed by "The Last Clean Shirt," with dialogue by Frank O'Hara. 40 min.
22-1633 *$19.99*

The Way Things Go (1987)
Watch as Peter Fischli and David Weiss, known as "the merry pranksters of visual art," construct a 100-foot kinetic sculpture, comprised of such everyday objects as tires, chairs, tables, teakettles, balloons, shoes and ladders, inside a warehouse. What follows is an enthralling chain reaction of movement and carefully constructed chaos that's part Marcel Duchamp and part "Mouse Trap." 30 min.
70-5113 Was $29.99 *$19.99*

In Motion With Michael Moschen
His "New Wave juggling" repertoire has won him nationwide acclaim, and in this special documentary/performance film alternative artist Michael Moschen creates a dazzling display of whirring hoops and rings, floating spheres and objects that seem to defy gravity. Moschen also talks about his craft and demonstrates the tricks behind his show. 60 min.
53-6336 *$19.99*

Nice Girls... Films By And About Women
A collection of inventive live and animated shorts by and about women. The award-winning entries in this collection cover such topics as teenage pregnancy ("Emergence of Eunice"), physical appearance ("Social Experiment"), sexual fantasies ("Another Great Day!"), and female ejaculation ("Nice Girls Don't Do It"). 90 min.
66-5007 Was $39.99 *$19.99*

Maya Deren: Experimental Films
The highly personal, innovatively told works of this seminal American avant-garde filmmaker have never failed to fascinate, and are now collected on one videocassette: "Meshes of the Afternoon" (1943), "At Land" (1944), "A Study in Choreography for Camera" (1945), "Ritual in Transfigured Time" (1946), "Meditation on Violence" (1948) and "The Very Eye of Night" (1959). 75 min. total.
70-7015 *$29.99*

God Said, "Ha!" (1998)
Former "SNL" regular Julia Sweeney brings her acclaimed one-woman stage show to the screen. Mixing laughs with drama, Sweeney recounts her brother's struggle with terminal lymphatic cancer, the stress brought about by his moving into her house along with their parents, and Sweeney's own bout with cervical cancer. 86 min.
11-2342 Was $99.99 *$19.99*

Man Ray Video
A selection of the avant-garde short film work from the multifaceted painter/sculptor/photographer and native Philadelphian; "Emak Bakia" (1927), "L'Etoile de Mer" (1928), "Le Retour a la Raison" (1923) and "Le Mysteres du Chateau du Dé" (1929) are included.
53-9009 *$24.99*

First International Circus Acts Festival In Budapest (1997)
An amazing array of the world's top circus performers comes together for one unforgettable show in this dazzling program. See Russian acrobats play a unique game of basketball—on a trampoline; marvel at the gilded bodybuilders from Germany and Hungary as they build the "Golden Pyramid"; plus trapeze artists, elephant acts, contortionists, clowns and much more. 96 min.
50-8606 *$19.99*

The Miracle Maker (2000)
A unique blend of traditional animation and stop-motion clay animation, this moving look at the life and teachings of Jesus is a treat for the whole family. The stellar voice cast includes Julie Christie, Richard E. Grant, William Hurt, Miranda Richardson, and Ralph Fiennes as Jesus. 87 min.
27-5585 *$19.99*

Joseph: King Of Dreams (2000)
From the creators of "The Prince of Egypt" comes this moving animated tale of the young man whose gift of seeing the future in his dreams drives his jealous brothers to send him into slavery. Joseph uses his prophetic gift to save Egypt and becomes a trusted advisor to Pharaoh, but when Joseph is reunited with his siblings, difficult decisions must be made. Ben Affleck, Mark Hamill and Steven Weber provide the voices.
07-2918 *$24.99*

Greatest Heroes & Legends Of The Bible
Who better than Charlton Heston to introduce these wonderful animated adaptations that bring to life the men and women of the Old and New Testaments? A cartoon minstrel named Simon and his pal Gimmel are your hosts for these timeless stories. Each tape runs about 50 min. There are 12 volumes available, including:

Greatest Heroes & Legends Of The Bible: The Garden Of Eden
10-2819 *$14.99*

Greatest Heroes & Legends Of The Bible: Sodom And Gomorrah
10-2820 *$14.99*

Greatest Heroes & Legends Of The Bible: Joseph And The Coat Of Many Colors
10-2821 *$14.99*

Greatest Heroes & Legends Of The Bible: Jonah And The Whale
10-2826 *$14.99*

Greatest Heroes & Legends Of The Bible: The Nativity
10-2827 *$14.99*

Greatest Heroes & Legends Of The Bible: The Last Supper, Crucifixion, And Resurrection
10-2830 *$14.99*

One-Minute Bible Stories: Old Testament
Twenty-six easy to comprehend retellings of the best-known Biblical tales are presented by hostess Shari Lewis and her sidekick, Lamp Chop. 30 min.
02-1643 *❑$12.99*

One-Minute Bible Stories: New Testament
Florence Henderson joins Shari Lewis and Lamp Chop to share 26 favorite New Testament stories in a style that kids and adults alike will enjoy. 30 min.
02-1644 *❑$12.99*

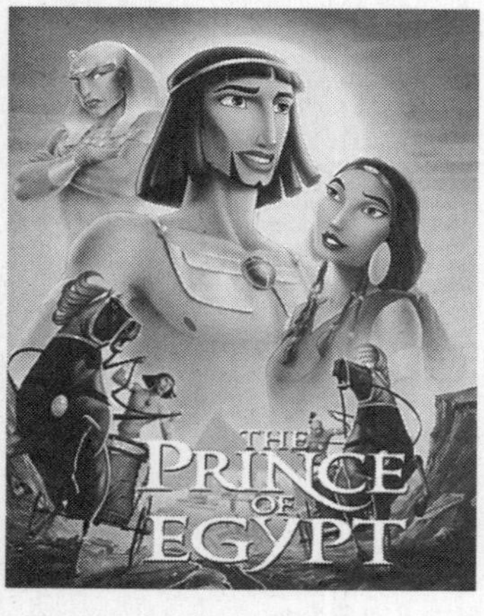
THE PRINCE OF EGYPT

The Prince Of Egypt (1998)
Marvelous animated telling of the Book of Exodus story of Moses, chronicling his Nile River journey as a baby, his adoption by Pharaoh, his heroic efforts to free the Israelites, the parting of the Red Sea and the delivery of the Ten Commandments. With voices by Val Kilmer, Patrick Stewart, Sandra Bullock, Ralph Fiennes, Michelle Pfeiffer, Steve Martin and Martin Short. Songs include the Oscar-winning "When You Believe."
07-2765 *❑$26.99*

The Prince Of The Nile: The Story Of Moses (1998)
Viewers of all ages will enjoy this wondrous animated retelling of the story of Moses, the man chosen by God to lead his people to freedom, from his childhood among the Egyptians to the amazing parting of the Red Sea. 50 min.
08-8675 *$12.99*

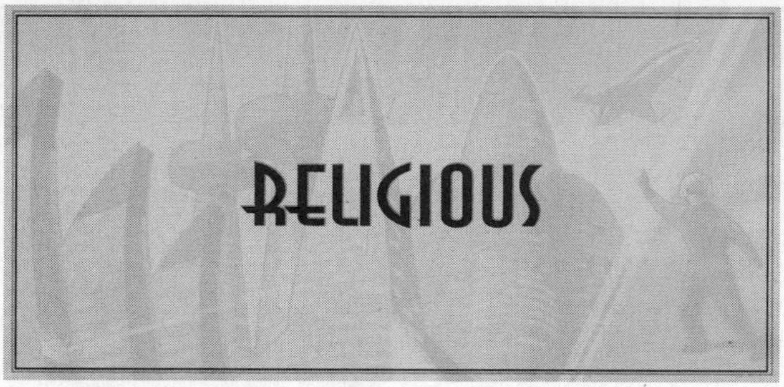
RELIGIOUS

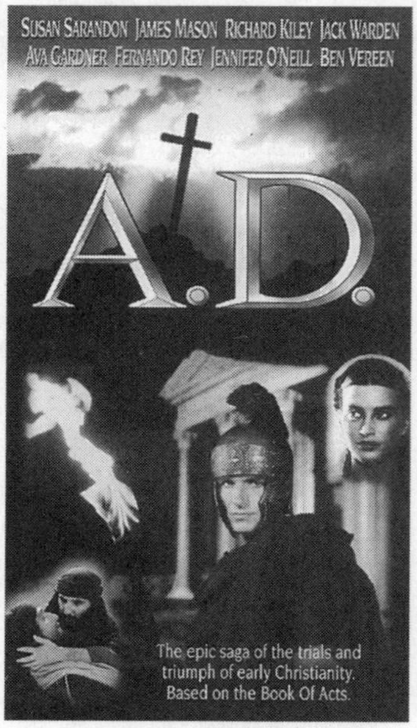
SUSAN SARANDON JAMES MASON RICHARD KILEY JACK WARDEN
AVA GARDNER FERNANDO REY JENNIFER O'NEILL BEN VEREEN
A.D.
The epic saga of the trials and triumph of early Christianity. Based on the Book Of Acts.

A.D.: Collector's Edition (1985)
The first four decades of the Christian Church are chronicled in this epic mini-series that follows the final days of Jesus, the Acts of the Apostles, and the persecution by Roman emperors Tiberius, Caligula, Claudius and Nero. Co-scripted by Anthony Burgess ("A Clockwork Orange") the cast includes Anthony Andrews, Richard Kiley, James Mason, Dennis Quilley, Susan Sarandon and Michael Wilding. 9 hrs. on five tapes.
66-6092 *$99.99*

Solomon And Sheba (1959)
Epic Biblical saga starring Yul Brynner (replacing Tyrone Power, who died during the early days of filming) as Solomon, the Israelite king who falls in love with the sensuous queen of Sheba (Gina Lollobrigida), much to the dismay of his brother Adonijah (George Sanders) and at the risk of harming his people. David Farrar, Marisa Pavan co-star; King Vidor directs. 119 min.
12-2877 *❑$19.99*

Solomon And Sheba (Letterboxed Version)
Also available in a theatrical, widescreen format.
12-2911 *❑$19.99*

The Bible: Genesis (1994)
From director Ernano Olmi ("The Tree of the Wooden Clogs") comes this survey of the greatest stories from Genesis, from Adam and Eve to Noah's Ark. 93 min.
68-2020 *$14.99*

The Bible: Solomon (1997)
Solomon defeats his older brother and becomes the king of Israel before falling in love with the seductive Queen of Sheba in this epic production starring Ben Cross, Vivica A. Fox, Max von Sydow, Maria Grazia Cucinotta and David Suchet. 172 min.
68-2022 *$14.99*

The Bible: Jeremiah (1998)
After abandoning his family and the woman he loves to relay God's message to Jerusalem, Jeremiah faces his worst fears when the city is destroyed and its inhabitants are imprisoned by the Babylonians. Patrick Dempsey, Klaus Maria Brandauer star. 96 min.
68-2023 *$14.99*

The Bible: Esther (1999)
The story of the young Jewish girl who captivates the King of Persia and urges him to show mercy on her people features an all-star cast that includes F. Murray Abraham, Jurgen Prochnow, Ornella Muti, and Louise Lombard as Esther. 91 min.
68-2021 *$14.99*

The Life Of Christ
The life and ministry of Jesus Christ become vividly real in this series of live-action programs taken from the New Testament, featuring faithful translations and sensitive readings. Each tape runs about 60 min.

The Life Of Christ, Vol. I
Includes The Birth of John the Baptist; Birth of the Savior; Childhood of Jesus; and Ministry of John the Baptist. 60 min.
10-1379 Was $19.99 *$14.99*

The Life Of Christ, Vol. II
Includes The First Disciples; The Sins Are Forgiven; Woman at the Well; Jesus at Nazareth; and Capernaum. 60 min.
10-1380 Was $19.99 *$14.99*

The Life Of Christ, Vol. III
Includes Jesus and the Fisherman; Jesus Teaches Forgiveness; Jesus Lord of the Sabbath; Jesus and the Lepers. 60 min.
10-1382 Was $19.99 *$14.99*

The Life Of Christ, Vol. IV
Includes I Am the Resurrection; Transfiguration; Before Abraham Was I Am; Last Journey to Jerusalem. 60 min.
10-1383 Was $19.99 *$14.99*

The Life Of Christ, Vol. V
Includes Thirty Pieces of Silver; Betrayal in Gethsame; Jesus Before the High Priest; Trial Before Pilate. 60 min.
10-1384 Was $19.99 *$14.99*

The Life Of Christ, Vol. VI
Includes Crucifixion; Nicodemus; Lord is Risen and Lord's Ascension. 60 min.
10-1385 Was $19.99 *$14.99*

Pope John Paul II: His Biography And The Tridentine Mass
This two-tape set features a biography of Pope John Paul II, using rare photos and seldom-seen footage to tell his fascinating story, along with a celebration of the Tridentine Mass, taped at Southern California's historic San Fernando Mission and featuring Latin Gregorian chants.
10-1611 *$14.99*

Pope John Paul II: The Life And Teachings Of Pope John Paul II/ The Christmas And Easter Liturgies
This special two-tape set includes "Do Not Be Afraid: The Life and Teachings of Pope John Paul II," which uses archival footage and an interview with the Pontiff to tell his inspirational story, along with "Do This in Memory of Me: The Christmas and Easter Liturgies," which offers the Pope presiding in the Vatican City and Rome and is narrated by James Fox. 104 min. total.
44-2115 *❑$29.99*

Pope John Paul II: Celebration Of The Great Jubilee
Featured on this video is "Conscience of the World," a look at the life of Pope John Paul II from 1998 in celebration of the 20th anniversary of his papacy. 52 min.
50-8524 *$14.99*

Pope John Paul II: The Movie (1984)
Exceptional filmed biography that boasts a masterful performance by Albert Finney as Karol Wojtyla, following him from his service as a priest in Poland during World War II to his ascension to the Papacy in 1978. Remarkable and inspiring drama co-stars Michael Crompton, Jonathan Newth, Patrick Stewart. AKA: "The Pope." 147 min.
46-5338 Was $29.99 *$19.99*

John Paul II: The Millennial Pope (1999)
His is a story of faith and service that encompasses the key events of the 20th century. Follow the life and times of the Polish-born theatre student-turned-priest who would survive the horrors of World War II, work for his homeland's freedom from Communism, and go on to guide the Roman Catholic Church into the next millennium in this compelling documentary from the PBS "Frontline" series. 150 min.
18-7878 *❑$19.99*

Charlton Heston Presents The Bible
Who better than the man who played Moses and John the Baptist to bring the stories of the Bible to life in this dramatic series? Heston's powerful readings, filmed at a 2,000-year-old amphitheater, are supplemented by images of inspirational works of art and striking footage from the Holy Land.

Charlton Heston Presents The Bible: Genesis
The creation of the universe is recounted, as well as the stories of the Garden of Eden, Caine's murder of brother Abel, the Great Flood and Noah's Ark, and Abraham and Isaac. 45 min.
10-2557 *$19.99*

Charlton Heston Presents The Bible: The Story Of Moses
The extraordinary life of Moses, including his deliverance of the Israelites from slavery in Egypt, the parting of the Red Sea, the giving of the Ten Commandments and the Exodus to the Promised Land, is stirringly told in this program. 60 min.
10-2558 *$19.99*

Charlton Heston Presents The Bible: Jesus Of Nazareth
The early life and ministry of Jesus are the focus here, as Heston tells of His birth and humble beginnings, His baptism in the River Jordan, the temptation in the wilderness, the Sermon on the Mount and other events. 60 min.
10-2559 *$19.99*

Charlton Heston Presents The Bible: The Passion
The tragic and triumphant ending to the Gospel story is retold in this program that follows the stories of the Last Supper and the betrayal of Judas, Pilate's judgment, the ordeal of Calvary, and Christ's Resurrection and Ascension. 60 min.
10-2560 *$19.99*

Charlton Heston Presents The Bible: Boxed Set
All four volumes of the "Charlton Heston Presents The Bible" series are available in one deluxe boxed set.
10-2817 Save $20.00! *$59.99*

The Ten Commandments (1923)
The master of the cinematic spectacle, Cecil B. DeMille, directed this silent precursor to his 1956 classic. Half of the film tells the biblical story of Moses, while the other half parallels this with a modern parable of the wages of sin. Stars Richard Dix, Rod la Rocque and Estelle Taylor. 146 min. Silent with organ score by Gaylord Carter.
06-1432 *$19.99*

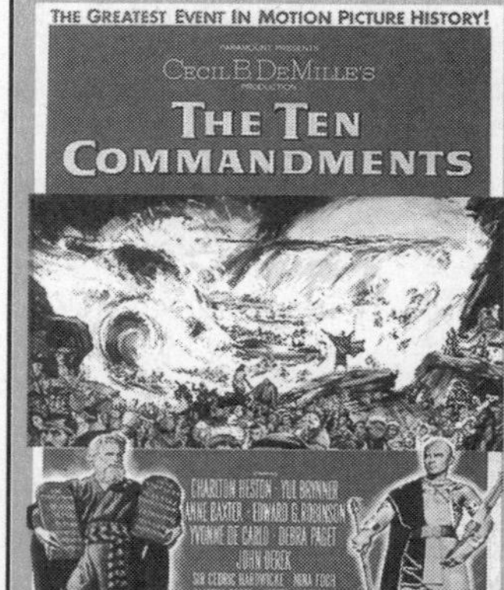
THE GREATEST EVENT IN MOTION PICTURE HISTORY!
CECIL B. DEMILLE'S
THE TEN COMMANDMENTS
CHARLTON HESTON · YUL BRYNNER

The Ten Commandments (1956)
Grand-scale epic from Cecil B. DeMille (his final film) stars Charlton Heston as Moses, chosen by God to lead his fellow Israelites out of slavery in Egypt. The flight from Egypt, the parting of the Red Sea, and Moses' receiving of the Commandments are highlights. Co-stars Edward G. Robinson, Yul Brynner, Anne Baxter and a cast of thousands. 220 min.
06-1065 Was $29.99 *$24.99*

The Ten Commandments (Letterboxed Version)
Also available in a theatrical, widescreen format.
06-2675 *$24.99*

The Ten Commandments (40th Anniversary Collector's Edition)
One of the greatest movie spectaculars of all time is commemorated in this deluxe edition. A restored, letterboxed print of the DeMille classic—with the soundtrack rechanneled in Dolby Stereo and featuring theatrical interlude music—is offered, along with the original and re-release trailers. 245 min.
06-2432 Letterboxed *❑$34.99*

The Miracle Of Our Lady Of Fatima (1952)
Heartfelt and inspirational drama based on the true story of three Portuguese farm children who in 1917 claimed to see a vision of the Virgin Mary, and the controversy that erupted. Gilbert Roland, Angela Clark and Frank Silvera star, with Sherry Jackson, Susan Whitney and Sammy Ogg as the children. 102 min.
19-1624 Was $19.99 *$14.99*

The Song Of Bernadette (1943)
Jennifer Jones won an Oscar for this stirring real-life drama of the 19th-century French peasant girl who saw a vision of the Virgin Mary and found herself at the center of a worldwide controversy. Vincent Price, Lee J. Cobb, Gladys Cooper also star in this timeless tale of faith and courage. 156 min.
04-1359 Was $19.99 *$14.99*

The King Of Kings (1927)
Cecil B. DeMille's silent epic of the life and ministry of Christ stars H.B. Warner in the title role, and the supporting cast includes Joseph Schildkraut and William Boyd. Styled after classical religious paintings, this moving treatment is presented in a newly restored version that features the Technicolor Resurrection sequence. 112 min. Silent with original 1927 Photophone score.
62-7000 Was $69.99 *$29.99*

A Letter To Nancy (1963)
An orphaned Oriental girl teaches a well-off but spiritually shallow American family a valuable lesson about love and faith in this inspiring film. 80 min.
08-1183 Was $29.99 *$19.99*

The Sin Of Adam And Eve (1968)
"For the first time on the screen, the story of Creation comes to life in vivid color!" Get the lowdown on what happened in the Garden of Eden in this made-in-Mexico drama that adds to the Biblical account of Mankind's true First Family. Candy Wilson, George Rivers star. 72 min.
08-1205 *$19.99*

Barabbas (1962)
Fanciful, yet moving, Biblical-based epic about the thief and murderer whose life was spared by Pilate instead of Jesus'. Anthony Quinn plays Barabbas, with support from Silvana Magnano, Ernest Borgnine, Jack Palance. 134 min.
02-1178 Was $19.99 *$14.99*

Esther And The King (1960)
Lavish Biblical spectacle starring Joan Collins as Esther, the Jewish girl who marries King Ahasuerus of Persia in hopes of helping ease the persecution of her conquered people. Richard Egan, Denis O'Dea star; Raoul Walsh directs. 110 min.
04-2902 ❑*$19.99*

Saul And David (1968)
Beautifully filmed story of the life of young David, from his battle with the giant Goliath to his years with King Saul and eventual rise to the throne. Norman Wooland, Gianni Garko star. 120 min.
08-1074 *$19.99*

The Robe (1953)
Lavish costume drama set during the Crucifixion of Jesus and the birth of Christianity in the Roman Empire. Richard Burton is the centurion whose loyalty to mad emperor Caligula is tested when his lover joins the new faith. Jean Simmons, Jay Robinson, Victor Mature, Michael Rennie co-star. 135 min.
04-1132 Was $19.99 ❑*$14.99*

The Robe (Letterboxed Version)
The first Cinemascope feature is now also available in a theatrical, widescreen format.
04-3586 *$14.99*

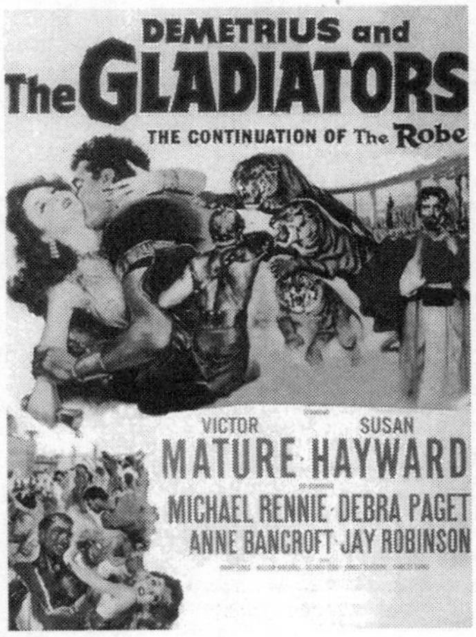

Demetrius And The Gladiators (1954)
The story of Christian persecution in ancient Rome begun in "The Robe" continues here, as arena fighter Victor Mature pits his newfound faith against the might of demented emperor Caligula. Also stars Susan Hayward, Jay Robinson, Debra Paget, Michael Rennie, William Marshall and Ernest Borgnine. 101 min.
04-2246 ❑*$19.99*

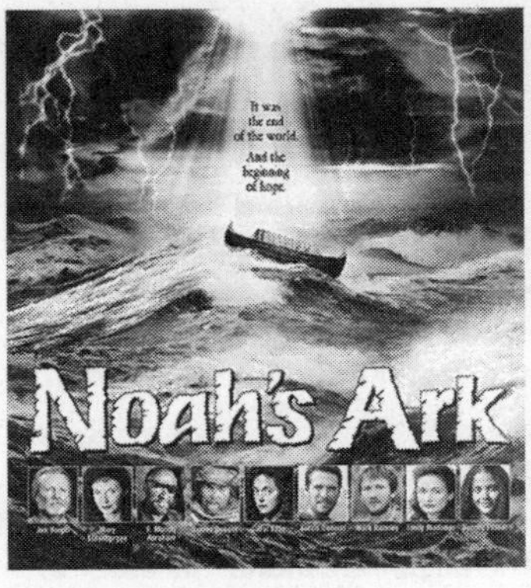

Noah's Ark (1999)
The sins of mankind and the wrath of God lead to a worldwide deluge, and only the pious Noah, his family, and history's biggest floating zoo escape the devastation, in this dramatic (if somewhat liberal) depiction of the Old Testament story. Jon Voight plays Noah, with Mary Steenburgen as wife Naamah. James Coburn, Carol Kane, and F. Murray Abraham as Lot also star. 150 min.
27-7117 Was $19.99 ❑*$14.99*

St. Patrick: The Irish Legend (2000)
Patrick Bergin plays the 5th-century, British-born nobleman who was kidnapped by Irish raiders and spent six years in captivity. Escaping home and becoming a priest, Patrick was guided by a heavenly vision to return to Ireland to bring the island the gospel. Malcolm McDowell, Alan Bates, Susannah York also star. 90 min.
63-7177 *$19.99*

Anchoress (1995)
Set during the Middle Ages, this gripping British drama tells of Christine, a woman whose downtrodden life as a serf is changed when she feels a sense of peace after seeing a statue of the Virgin Mary. She soon asks a priest to be made an anchoress, which will enable her to spend her life in a stone cell attached to a church's walls. Natalie Morse and Pete Postlethwaite star. 108 min.
22-9006 Letterboxed *$29.99*

Candle In The Dark (1996)
This incredible true story tells of William Carey's Serampore mission and his efforts to bring the word of God to an exotic community in India 200 years ago. Richard Atlee, Lynette Edwards and Julie-Kate Oliver star in this inspirational, beautifully filmed saga. 97 min.
50-8258 *$24.99*

Peter And Paul (1981)
This religious epic tells of the early days of Christianity and how Peter and Paul struggle to spread the word of the Gospel. Set over three decades, the drama features Robert Foxworth as Simon Peter and Anthony Hopkins as Paul of Tarsus through such events as the stoning of Stephen, Paul's conversion on the road to Damascus, their clashes and their demise in A.D. 64. With Eddie Albert, Jean Peters and Jon Finch. 194 min.
53-6556 *$39.99*

The Old Testament
Great Biblical action epic detailing the flight of the Maccabees into the desert and their regrouping for ultimate victory; with Brad Harris, Margaret Taylor. 88 min.
10-2068 *$14.99*

The Old Testament: Complete Set (1980)
Relive the memorable stories of the heroes and heroines of the Old Testament through dramatic and inspirational re-creations in this four-tape collection. Included are "Abraham/Jacob/Joseph," "Moses/Joshua," "Gideon/Ruth/Samuel" and "David/Solomon/Elijah." 240 min. total. NOTE: Individual volumes available at $14.99 each.
08-1799 Save $20.00! *$39.99*

God's Outlaw (1986)
This stirring drama focuses on William Tyndale, "the Father of the English Bible," who battled the likes of King Henry VIII, Sir Thomas More and Cardinal Wolset in order to provide an English version of the Bible to his countrymen. Roger Rees and Keith Barrow star in this award-winner. 95 min.
50-8259 *$24.99*

A Time For Miracles (1980)
Inspiring dramatization of the life and times of Elizabeth Bayley Seton, the 19th-century widow-turned-nun who would eventually become the first American-born Catholic saint. Kate Mulgrew, Lorne Greene, John Forsythe and Jean-Pierre Aumont star. 97 min.
53-3057 *$29.99*

Martin Luther (1953)
Masterful retelling of the life and works of the man who strove for reform and birthed the Protestant Reformation. Despite excommunication and exile, he survived to see his beliefs take hold throughout Europe. Nial McGinnis, John Ruddock. 105 min.
08-1401 *$19.99*

The Story Of Ruth (1960)
While not strictly based on the Biblical book, this moving Hollywood religious drama movingly follows the titular heroine's renouncement of her people's idolatry and her conversion to Judaism. Stuart Whitman, Tom Tryon, Peggy Wood, and Elana Eden as Ruth star. 132 min.
04-2309 ❑*$19.99*

Greatest Heroes Of The Bible
Top stars of stage, screen and television are featured in these dramatic made-for-TV films that bring to life the memorable men and women of the Old Testament. Each tape runs about 50 min.

David And Goliath (1979)
The classic battle between the young Israelite David and the Philistine giant Goliath. Jeff Corey and Ted Cassidy star.
69-1026 ❑*$14.99*

Sodom And Gomorrah (1979)
Angered by the sinful behavior of the cities of Sodom and Gomorrah, God plans their obliteration, but sends angels to save Lot and his family. With Ed Ames, Dorothy Malone.
69-1029 ❑*$14.99*

Abraham's Sacrifice (1979)
Abraham's faith and courage are put to the test when God commands him to sacrifice his only son, Isaac, to Him. Gene Barry and Andrew Duggan star.
69-1032 ❑*$14.99*

The Ten Commandments (1979)
Moses leads the Hebrews out of Egyptian slavery to the wilderness. There God instructs Moses and gives him the Ten Commandments. John Marley, Anson Williams star.
69-1034 ❑*$14.99*

Moses (1979)
God chooses Moses to lead the Israelites out of Egypt, but the stubborn hardheartedness of Pharaoh forces God to unleash a terrifying series of plagues. The people are eventually freed, but Moses faces his greatest challenge at the Red Sea. John Marley, Frank Gorshin star.
69-1059 ❑*$14.99*

Joseph In Egypt (1980)
Joseph is given a favored position by his father, and his envious brothers sell him into slavery. Sam Bottoms and Barry Nelson star.
69-1027 ❑*$14.99*

The Story Of Noah (1980)
God instructs Noah to build an ark to save his family and two of every animal from a flood that will destroy the world. Lew Ayres, Robert Emhardt star.
69-1030 ❑*$14.99*

Samson And Delilah (1980)
The story of Hebrew strong man Samson and how he is betrayed to the Philistines by the seductive Delilah. With John Beck, Ann Turkel.
69-1033 ❑*$14.99*

Greatest Heroes Of The Bible Collection
This special eight-tape boxed set includes "Abraham's Sacrifice," "David and Goliath," "Joseph in Egypt," "Samson and Delilah," "Sodom and Gomorrah," "The Story of Moses," "The Story of Noah" and "The Ten Commandments."
63-1971 Save $24.00! *$79.99*

Children's Heroes Of The Bible
Beautifully drawn and faithfully told, these animated stories bring to life the familiar characters and stories from the Bible. There are 10 volumes available, including:

The Story Of Jesus: The Nativity
Animated retelling of the life of Christ follows the Nativity story through to the early years of Jesus' ministry. 40 min.
08-1261 *$12.99*

The Story Of Elijah
When wicked King Ahab turns Israel from God and begins worshipping Baal, the prophet Elijah struggles to set things right. 25 min.
08-1369 *$12.99*

The Story Of Esther
A young Jewish girl marries the King of Persia and later puts her own life at stake to save her people. 25 min.
08-1370 *$12.99*

The Story Of Jeremiah
His warnings to the people of Israel that they renounce idolatry and return to God pit the prophet Jeremiah against a nation, but his faith remains constant. 25 min.
08-1371 *$12.99*

Herod The Great (1960)
Wild debauchery and oil-slicked concubines fill this Italian-made biblical epic that depicts the last years of the bloodthirsty tyrant. Edmund Purdom ("The Egyptian"), Sylvia Lopez star. 93 min.
68-8414 Letterboxed *$14.99*

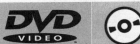

Joseph (1994)
Betrayed by his jealous brothers and forced into bondage in a strange land, he went on to become an advisor to the Pharaoh and save his family from death. Paul Mercurio, Ben Kingsley, Martin Landau and Lesley Ann Warren star in this powerful Biblical drama.
18-7566 Was $59.99 ❑*$19.99*

David (1997)
The life of the shepherd boy who grew up to slay giants, compose the Psalms, and be crowned King of Israel—and who nearly lost the throne over his forbidden love for the beautiful Bathsheba—is recounted in this moving biodrama. Gideon Turner and Nathaniel Parker star as the young and adult David, respectively; with Jonathan Pryce, Leonard Nimoy, Sheryl Lee. 180 min.
18-7676 ❑*$19.99*

The Bible Collection
"Abraham," "David," "Joseph" and "Moses" are also available together in a special set.
18-7774 *$79.99*

Apocalypse (1998)
Armies poised for battle in Israel are turned back by a charismatic world leader, while millions of people disappear without a trace. A pair of TV news reporters work to uncover the connection between what's happening and a 2,000-year-old Biblical warning in this moving look at the predicted Rapture and Great Tribulation. Richard Nester, Leigh Lewis, Mark Richardson star.
50-8754 *$29.99*

Revelation (1998)
The "final days" saga begun in "Apocalypse" continues, as counter-terrorism expert Jeff Fahey, whose wife and daughter vanished in the Rapture, is assigned to investigate "the Haters," an outlawed Christian sect accused of subversive acts against the one-world government of "messiah" Nick Mancuso. Fahey learns that the group is being framed by Mancuso as part of a diabolical scheme to enslave mankind. With Carol Alt, Leigh Lewis.
50-8755 *$29.99*

Tribulation (2000)
Gary Busey is a police detective whose family has become the target of a sinister secret society and who is left comatose after a mysterious car accident. Awakening into a world run by self-proclaimed Messiah Nick Mancuso where all wear his mark to show their allegiance, Busey teams with a woman leading an underground Christian group to expose Mancuso for what he is. Margot Kidder, Howie Mandel and Leigh Lewis co-star in the third "Apocalypse" thriller.
50-8756 *$29.99*

The Apocalypse Trilogy
"Apocalypse," Revelation" and "Tribulation" are also available in a three-tape collector's set that includes exclusive extra footage and a music video.
50-8753 Save $20.00! *$69.99*

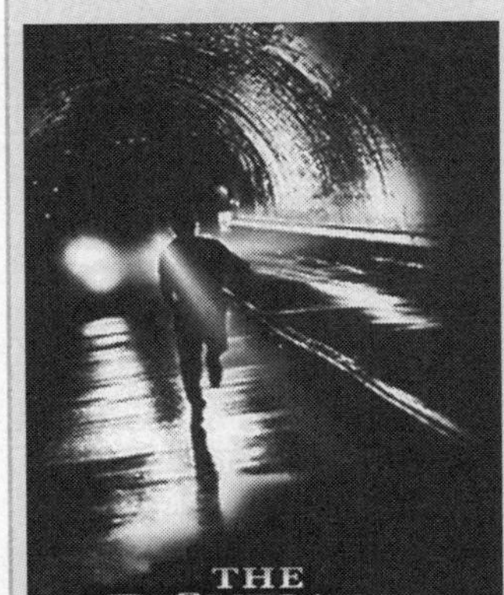

The Omega Code (1999)
Christian and mainstream audiences flocked to this independently-made thriller, an apocalyptic film in every sense of the word. Casper Van Dien plays a motivational speaker and expert in an ancient Biblical code who teams with international magnate and humanitarian Michael York to help realize his plans for global unity, unaware of York's sinister true purpose. With Michael Ironside, Catherine Oxenberg. 100 min.
10-2874 *$22.99*

Left Behind: The Movie (2000)
In the blink of an eye, millions of people vanish from the face of the Earth. In the global chaos that follows, those who were "left behind," including an airline pilot whose wife and son are among the missing and a reporter investigating a conspiracy linked to an Israeli scientist's work, discover that these events are linked to Biblical prophecies foretelling the "end times." Based on the best-selling Christian book series, this thrilling drama stars Brad Johnson, Kirk Cameron, Chelsea Noble, Clarence Gilyard. 90 min.
50-8751 *$29.99*

Great Bible Adventures: Complete Set
Lively animation brings these exciting Bible tales to life in this four-part series. Hosted by the Weiser Family Puppets, each volume contains six stories and are designed for kids ages 3 to 10. The series includes "Look What God Made," "David, God's Champion," "Here Comes Jesus!" and "Walking With Jesus." Each tape runs about 30 min.
50-2801 Save $12.00! *$39.99*

Animals Of The Bible
Children will enjoy this unique wildlife program, as creatures featured in both the Old and New Testament are introduced with narration and descriptive passages. Filmed on location in the Holy Land, this is a delight for animal lovers and Bible fans alike. 30 min.
50-2726 *$14.99*

Mary Of Nazareth
The life story of the mother of Jesus is vividly portrayed in this moving docudrama-style production. The two-tape boxed set includes "The Event That Changed History," which follows Mary's life from the Annunciation to Jesus' youth, and "The Crucifixion," which shows the effect she had on Jesus' ministry. 115 min.
50-4591 *$29.99*

Francesco's Friendly World: The Last Stone
Filled with songs, laughter and a gentle message of God's love, this animated program follows the efforts of young Francesco and his menagerie of animal friends as they work together to rebuild the village church before the Easter morning service. 42 min.
50-5388 □*$14.99*

Faith Unconquered
Filmed on location in Rome, this moving documentary tribute to faith recounts the stories of four early martyrs of the Christian Church: St. Clemens, Cecilia, Apollonius and Ages. Joseph Campanella narrates. 50 min.
50-4592 *$19.99*

Climb Ev'ry Mountain
A unique and inspirational video program, produced by Reader's Digest, that lets you relax to beautiful scenery from around the world as some of the best-loved hymns and religious tunes play in the background. Visit St. Peter's in Rome, snow-capped mountains and winter scenes of America's national parks, sites in the Holy Land and more; songs include "The Bells of St. Mary's," "Be Still My Soul" and "Today I Walked Where Jesus Walked." 55 min.
50-1286 *$29.99*

Be Thou My Vision
Experience "the glory of God's love in word and music" with this uplifting program that features soothing images, passages from the 23rd Psalm, and such hymns as "Amazing Grace," "A Mighty Fortress Is Our God," "O Worship the King" and others. 55 min.
50-2436 *$19.99*

How Great Thou Art: Best-Loved Inspirational Songs
Beautiful film clips of natural splendor (Yosemite National Park, Big Sur, Halekala volcano) are mixed with best-loved hymns and inspirational songs ("Amazing Grace," "Nearer, My God, To Thee," "Ave Maria," "Ode to Joy") for a unique and moving video experience. 57 min.
50-4957 *$29.99*

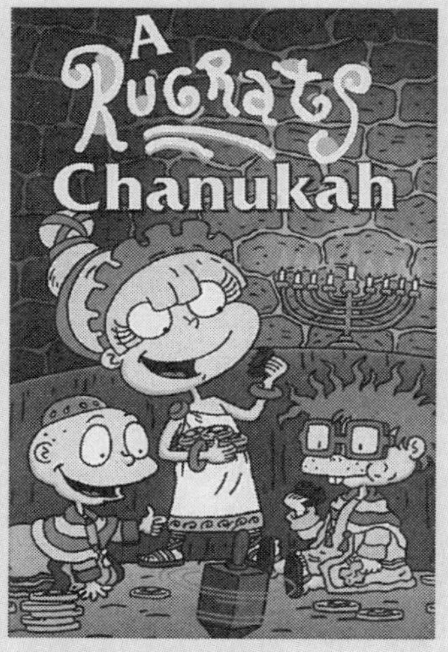

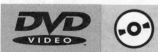

A Rugrats Chanukah
A Chanukah celebration becomes a lesson in the meaning behind the "Festival of Lights" for Tommy, Chuckie, Angelica and company in this special double-length holiday tale, followed by a bonus "Rugrats" cartoon. 35 min.
06-2616 □*$12.99*

A Rugrats Passover
A delightful program in which the "Rugrats" crew travels to Tommy's grandparents' house for a Passover seder and Grandpa Boris relates the story behind the holiday to them. Soon, the babies envision themselves as historical figures in Ancient Egypt. 35 min.
04-5415 □*$12.99*

Chanukah At Bubbe's
Come on over to grandmom Bubbe's house! She's gonna tell you stories about the Festival of Lights, with help from her eccentric puppet pals, Rhino, Anton, Chester and Zachary. 30 min.
27-6731 *$19.99*

A Taste Of Chanukah (2000)
This concert was taped before a live audience in the New England Conservatory of Music's Jordan Hall and features music from more than 150 musicians and soloists celebrating the Jewish "festival of lights." 60 min.
18-7920 □*$14.99*

Passover At Bubbe's
The matzo's cracking at Bubbe's, as the perky puppet prepares the Seder and gets whisked back to Egypt during the time of the Pharaohs and must plan a dangerous escape. 30 min.
27-6732 *$19.99*

The Sabbath
Young children will especially enjoy this award-winning collection of animated and live-action shorts on the meaning of the Jewish Sabbath. 18 min.
48-5015 *$29.99*

Lights
A colorful animated version of the Hanukah story for children that addresses the issue of religious freedom and the right to be different. Judd Hirsch and Leonard Nimoy narrate. 24 min.
48-5016 *$29.99*

A Passover Seder
Celebrate Pesach with author and Nobel Peace Prize-winner Elie Wiesel, who shares memories and poetic interpretations of the holiday. The highlights of the seder are covered with help from original illustrations, animation and live action. 30 min.
19-3673 *$14.99*

Jewish Home Video Series
Distinguished actor and writer Theodore Bikel stars in this educational play series introducing the customs of Jewish holidays and observances.

T.G.I.S. (Thank Goodness It's Shabbat)
When a young couple on a train express their excitement over the end of the work week, fellow passenger Bikel explains to them the practices of the Jewish Sabbath. 28 min.
48-5003 *$39.99*

The Four Sons: A Guide To Passover
As Manny the delicatessen owner, Bikel relates the traditions of Passover to four brothers planning a seder, their first without Mom and Dad. 37 min.
48-5004 *$39.99*

New Year's Leave (Rosh Hashanah)
An American Jewish sailor spends an unexpected stopover in Israel learning the meaning and customs of the High Holidays from an engaging tour guide. 30 min.
48-5011 *$29.99*

A Secret Space
The 12-year-old son of liberal, non-religious parents becomes awakened to his Jewish roots when he is welcomed into a "havurah," a collection of persons from various backgrounds worshipping together at a reclaimed Lower East Side synagogue. Robert Klein, Phyllis Newman and Jon Matthews star. 80 min.
48-5013 *$79.99*

The Secret In Bubbie's Attic
Delightful Jewish fun for kids aged 4-11 as singer-storyteller Eva Grayzel and writer Suri Levow-Kreiger enchant everyone by using a Torah, a shofar, a Hanukah menorah and a special piece of cloth to educate children about the High Holidays, Sukkot and the Festival of Lights. 43 min.
48-5097 *$34.99*

The Discovery
A 12-year-old boy grapples with concerns about his upcoming bar mitzvah and questions about his own Jewish identity in this poignant story that also answers many viewers' questions about Judaism. Josh Saviano ("The Wonder Years") stars. 58 min.
48-5106 *$39.99*

The Jewish Holidays Video Guide
A husband and wife lead their two children through the Jewish calendar, celebrating the major holidays like Yom Kippur, Rosh Hashanah, Purim, Sukkot, Shavout, Hanukkah and Shabbot. Celebrities Monty Hall, Ed Asner, Judge Wapner and Theodore Bikel discuss their favorite holiday memories. 75 min.
76-7118 *$19.99*

A Taste Of Passover
Join in a joyous celebration of the Passover holiday with this special video concert. Along with performances of traditional and humorous Pesach songs by Theodore Bikel, New York cantor David Levine and a 150-member orchestra from the New England Conservatory, there's also commentary by humorist Moshe Waldoks, a matzo ball-making demonstration, Klezmer music and more. 60 min.
90-1019 Was $19.99 □*$14.99*

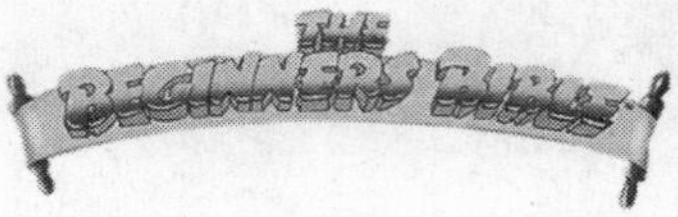

The Beginners Bible
Some of the best-loved Bible characters are brought to life for pre-schoolers in this entertaining and inspirational animated series. Kathie Lee Gifford performs the theme song. Each tape runs about 30 min. There are 13 volumes available, including:

The Beginners Bible: The Story Of Moses
04-5474 □*$14.99*

The Beginners Bible: The Story Of Joshua And The Battle Of Jericho
04-5550 □*$14.99*

The Beginners Bible: The Story Of Daniel And The Lion's Den
04-5551 □*$14.99*

The Beginners Bible: The Story Of Jesus And His Miracles
04-5600 □*$14.99*

Jesus, The Christ: Complete Set
The life and ministry of Jesus become vivdly real with this six-tape series of live-action programs taken from the New Testament and featuring faithful translations and sensitive readings. Included are "The Birth and Childhood of Jesus/A Voice in the Wilderness," "Jesus Calls His Disciples/Jesus Begins His Ministry," "Jesus Heals the Sick/Jesus, the Teacher," "Jesus, the Messiah/Jesus Goes to Jerusalem" and "An Upper Room and a Garden/Jesus' Trial" and "Crucifixion of the Christ/The Risen Lord." 360 min. total. NOTE: Individual volumes available at $14.99 each.
08-1801 Save $30.00! *$59.99*

The Visual Bible Collection
This 13-tape collection dramatizes the great moments recorded in the Bible and contains four tapes on "The Old Testament," three tapes on "Acts of the Apostles," and six tapes centering on "Jesus the Christ." 12 hours total.
08-1802 *$99.99*

How Do You Spell God?
Based on the best-selling children's book by Rabbi Marc Gellman and Monsignor Thomas Hartman, this delightful and inspirational program for the whole family features interviews with kids of different faiths sharing their views of God, plus animated adaptations of the stories "The Carrot Seed," "The Three Blind Men and an Elephant" and "Menaseh's Dream." Voices include Maya Angelou, Deepak Chopra, Fyvush Finkel, Chris Rock, Fred Savage and Marlo Thomas.
44-2086 *$14.99*

Where Jesus Walked: Complete Set
Filmed on location in the Holy Land and featuring a huge cast, this two-tape series looks at the great moments of the New Testament by visiting sites depicted. In "Walking with Jesus," the Church of the Nativity, Nazareth and Mt. Tabor are featured; "The Road to the Cross" visits Jerusalem and sites that were important in Jesus' life and Crucifixion. 120 min.
50-2792 *$39.99*

Joseph And His Brethren (1960)
From the Old Testament comes the story of Joseph, beloved son of Jacob, sold by his brothers into slavery in Egypt. Geoffrey Horne, Robert Morley. 103 min.
08-1116 *$19.99*

The Reluctant Saint (1962)
Unusual religious drama with comic moments starring Maximilian Schell as Giuseppe Desa, a simple 17th-century peasant boy who would grow to become St. Joseph of Cupertino. Sent by his mother to a Franciscan monastery after proving unable to hold a job, the young Giuseppe nearly bumbles his way out of the priesthood, until a miracle redeems him. Akim Tamiroff, Ricardo Montalban also star. 104 min.
76-7287 *$24.99*

The Story Of Jacob And Joseph (1974)
A lavish Biblical drama in two parts, telling the stories of the sibling rivalry between Jacob and Esau, and the tale of Joseph's adventures when he was sold into slavery by his brothers. Keith Michell, Tony LoBianco, Colleen Dewhurst and Herschel Bernardi star; Alan Bates narrates. Michael Cacoyannis ("Zorba the Greek") directs. 96 min.
02-2372 Was $19.99 *$14.99*

Jacob, The Man Who Fought With God (1970)
This moving film shows how Jacob schemed to win his father's blessing that was intended for his brother Esau, as well as his marriage to Rachel and climactic reconciliation with Esau. 98 min.
08-1185 *$19.99*

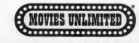

The Gospel According To Jesus
Based on the popular book by poet-scholar Stephen Mitchell, this program features readings from the Four Gospels by Americans from all walks of life, followed by a gathering of theologians, clergymen and lay philosophers discussing spiritual issues. Participants in this unique program include Maya Angelou, Deepak Chopra, Judy Collins, Rev. Andrew Greely, Tim Robbins, Susan Sarandon, Wavy Gravy, Marianne Williamson and others. 117 min. on two tapes.
70-9035 *$29.99*

The Cross And The Switchblade (1970)
Pat Boone is minister David Wilkerson, on a mission to drive juvenile delinquency off the streets of New York City. Boone faces his toughest opponent when he goes up against tough gang leader Nicky (Erik Estrada), eventually winning him over through his courage and faith. Jackie Giroux and Don Blakely also star in this moving true story; directed by actor Don Murray.
08-1096 *$19.99*

King Of Kings (1961)
The life of Christ is told in this powerful drama directed by Nicholas Ray. The all-star cast includes Jeffrey Hunter in the title role, Siobhan McKenna as Mary and Robert Ryan as John the Baptist. An intelligent and sensitive rendition. 161 min.
12-1313 Was $29.99 *$24.99*

King Of Kings (Letterboxed Version)
Also available in a theatrical, widescreen format.
12-3040 *$24.99*

Jesus Of Nazareth (1928)
Detailed early filming of the life of Christ, from the Annunciation of his birth to the Crucifixion and Resurrection. Title cards taken from Gospel passages help tell the story. Philip Van Loan, Anna Lehr star. Silent with music score.
10-9998 *$24.99*

The Greatest Story Ever Told (1965)
Magnificent account of the Gospel story, filled with majestic settings and a cast list that reads like a "Who's Who" of film. Max Von Sydow essays the role of Jesus; Jose Ferrer, Charlton Heston, David McCallum, Dorothy McGuire, Sidney Poitier, Telly Savalas and John Wayne also appear. George Stevens directs. 199 min.
12-1971 Was $29.99 *$24.99*

The Greatest Story Ever Told (Letterboxed Version)
Also available in a theatrical, widescreen format.
12-3039 *$24.99*

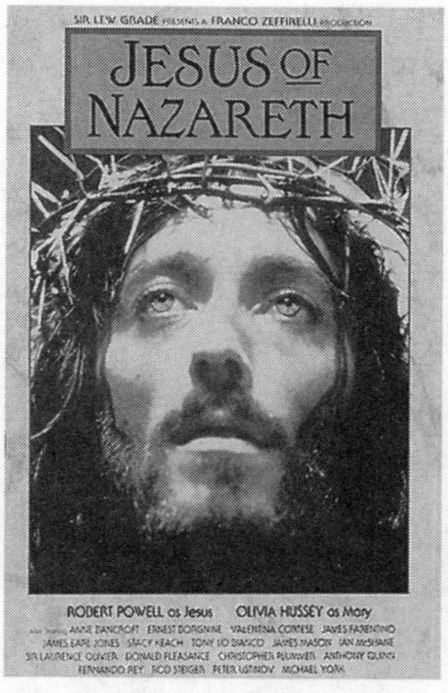

Jesus Of Nazareth (1976)
Franco Zeffirelli's highly acclaimed version of the life of Jesus, complete on three tapes. This epic, moving drama, filmed in Tunisia and Morocco, features a stellar international cast, including Robert Powell, Peter Ustinov, Stacy Keach, Anne Bancroft, James Mason, Anthony Quinn, Laurence Olivier and Rod Steiger. 382 min.
27-6797 Was $49.99 *$34.99*

The Nativity (1978)
Realistic portrayal of the events surrounding the first Christmas, with emphasis on the emotions and relationships among the participants. Stars John Shea, Madeleine Stowe and Jane Wyatt. 97 min.
04-3168 □*$14.99*

Jesus (2000)
Two thousand years after his time on Earth, his works and message continue to inspire millions around the world. The life of Jesus is movingly portrayed in this epic mini-series that stars Jacqueline Bisset as Mary, Armin Mueller-Stahl as Joseph, Gary Oldman as Pilate, and Jeremy Sisto in the title role. 173 min.
68-2006 □*$24.99*

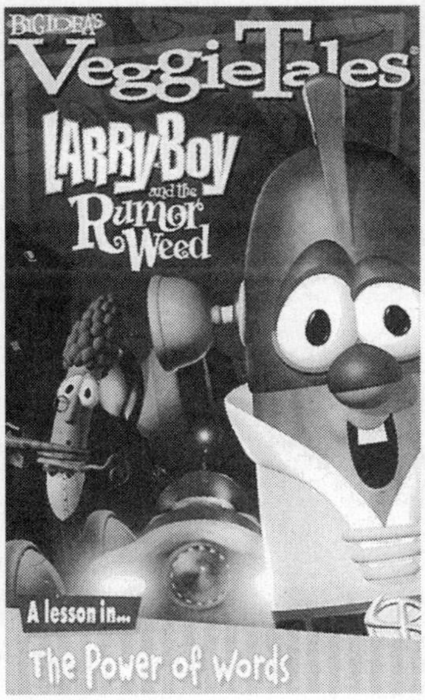

Veggie Tales
Computer animation, lively characters and a positive religious message are the highlights of this popular series. Tomatoes, cucumbers, carrots and other veggies help kids learn about God and how to use faith to help them solve problems and answer questions. Each tape runs about 30 min. There are nine volumes available, including:

Veggie Tales: Larry-Boy And The Rumor Weed
50-8475 *$14.99*

Veggie Tales: Where's God When I'm Scared?
50-5789 *$14.99*

Veggie Tales: God Wants Me To Forgive Them!?!
50-8060 *$14.99*

Veggie Tales: Madame Blueberry
50-8253 *$14.99*

Veggie Tales: The End Of Silliness?
50-8550 □*$14.99*

Veggie Tales: King George And The Ducky?
50-8605 *$14.99*

Greater Love Hath No Man
The life of Jesus Christ has been reinterpreted to modern times and set in the inner city with an African-American as Christ. Also features behind-the-scenes footage of the production and a music video of Lorraine Taylor performing "God Still Takes Good Care." 85 min.
76-7242 *$19.99*

Maximilian: Saint Of Auschwitz (1995)
This inspiring story of Father Maximilian Kolbe features Leonardo Defilippis as the priest who was arrested for his tireless efforts against the Nazis in 1941. He was sent to an Auschwitz prison camp, where he faced horrible treatment. Years later, he was canonized by Pope John Paul II. 76 min.
76-7255 *$24.99*

The Story Of David (1976)
An epic Biblical adaptation focusing on David's battle with the giant Goliath which helped defeat the Philistines and unite Israel, and his forbidden love for Bathsheba, which nearly destroyed his kingdom. Timothy Bottoms, Anthony Quayle, Keith Michell and Jane Seymour star. 192 min.
02-2371 Was $59.99 *$24.99*

Brother Sun, Sister Moon (1973)
Franco Zeffirelli relates the tale of St. Francis of Assisi, an Italian soldier who returns from the Crusades and dismisses his family's material wealth for selfless devotion to others. Co-stars Graham Faulkner, Judi Bowker and Alec Guinness as Pope Innocent III; songs by Donovan. 121 min.
06-1140 Was $19.99 *$14.99*

Moses (1975)
One of the most exciting of all Bible epics is this look at the life of the Israelite leader (Burt Lancaster), from his conflict with Pharaoh, the Exodus from Egypt and the reception of the Ten Commandments from God. Co-stars Anthony Quayle, Irene Papas. 141 min.
27-6796 Was $19.99 *$14.99*

Power Of The Resurrection
Christ's last days—the passion, death and resurrection—as seen through the eyes of Simon Peter. Richard Kiley. 60 min.
08-1180 *$19.99*

How Good Do We Have To Be?
Offering "a healthy approach to dealing with our inherent imperfections," noted rabbi and author Dr. Harold S. Kushner ("When Bad Things Happen to Good People") discusses how to deal with guilt and forgiveness in order to improve relationships and gain peace of mind. 70 min.
53-9344 *$24.99*

The Life Of Jesus Christ: Complete Set
In this beautifully realized live-action series, you'll trace Jesus' remarkable life from the Nativity to the Crucifixion and the Ascension. Perfect for family viewing and religious groups, the videos dramatically re-create memorable New Testament stories. Volumes include "The Birth of Christ," "Jesus the Healer," "The Betrayal of Jesus" and "Jesus Has Risen." 180 min. total. NOTE: Individual volumes available at $12.99 each.
58-8230 Save $22.00! *$29.99*

The Bible On Video
These lavishly produced programs are word-for-word re-enactments of the Old and New Testaments, shot on location in the Holy Land and featuring casts speaking in the original languages of the times (with English-language narration provided). Called the most accurate Bible videos ever, each volume is available in either the King James Version (narrated by Alexander Scourby) or Revised Standard Version (read by Orson Welles) and runs about 50 min.

Jesus: From The Gospel: Boxed Set (King James Version)
"The Birth," "The Parables" and "The Passion" are also available in a deluxe three-tape set. NOTE: Individual volumes available at $14.99 each.
70-9025 *$39.99*

Jesus: From The Gospel: Boxed Set (Revised Standard Version)
Also available in the Revised Standard version. NOTE: Individual volumes available at $14.99 each.
70-9026 *$39.99*

In The Beginning: Boxed Set (King James Version)
This special three-tape set contains "The Creation," "Acts of Faith" and "The Roots of Israel." NOTE: Individual volumes available at $14.99 each.
70-9033 *$39.99*

In The Beginning: Boxed Set (Revised Standard Version)
Also available in the Revised Standard version. NOTE: Individual volumes available at $14.99 each.
70-9034 *$39.99*

DAVEY AND GOLIATH

Davey And Goliath
Join young Davey, his sister Sally, and their dog Goliath as they have fun and learn gentle lessons about school, family and God in this fondly-remembered animated series from "Gumby" creator Art Clokey. Except where noted, each tape runs about 30 min. There are seven volumes available, including:

Davey And Goliath: New Year Promise
Davey decides the only way to keep his New Year's resolution not to yell at sister Sally is to not talk to her, prompting her to run away from home. Can Davey and Goliath find her in time to celebrate New Year's at church?
08-1530 *$14.99*

Davey And Goliath: School...Who Needs It?
Davey learns a valuable lesson after playing hooky, while an accidental fire almost destroys the class parade float.
08-1532 *$14.99*

Davey And Goliath: Christmas Lost And Found
By offering his role in the Christmas pageant to a poor country boy, Davey learns about the nature of giving.
08-1534 *$14.99*

Davey And Goliath: The New Skates And Other Stories
Includes "The New Skates," "Cousin Barney," "The Time Machine" and "The Mechanical Man." 57 min.
50-8457 *$12.99*

Davey And Goliath: The Waterfall And Other Stories
Includes "The Waterfall," "The Parade," "Officer Bob" and "The Dog Show." 57 min.
50-8458 *$12.99*

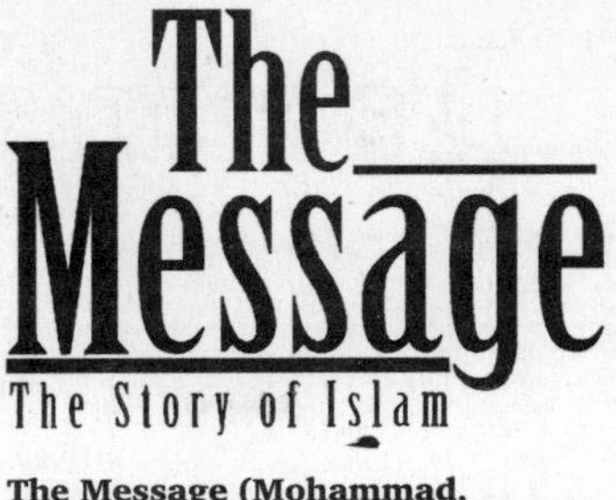

The Message (Mohammad, Messenger Of God) (1977)
Controversy on a global scale surrounded this sweeping religious drama that recounts the struggles of the prophet Mohammad (who, in accordance with Islamic law, is never seen or heard onscreen) to turn the people of Mecca away from idolatry and towards Allah. Anthony Quinn stars as Mohammad's uncle, the warrior Hamza; with Irene Pappas, Michael Ansara. Remastered video edition also includes a documentary on the making of the film and the original English and Arabic theatrical trailers. 220 min. total.
27-6198 Letterboxed *$29.99*

Born Again (1978)
The story of Nixon official and Watergate conspirator Charles Colson's rebrith through finding God is an inspirational look at one man's faith, even when the odds were not in his favor. Dean Jones, Anne Francis, Dana Andrews star. 110 min.
53-1236 Was $59.99 *$24.99*

How Sweet The Sound
A former slave trader; a man grieving over his fiancée's death; a father whose four daughters were killed at sea. From out of these dark and tragic events came "Amazing Grace," "What a Friend We Have in Jesus" and "It Is Well with Me." Learn the remarkable true stories behind these and other favorite hymns, and hear each song movingly performed, in this inspirational program. 60 min.
50-5969 □*$24.99*

The Christmas Storykeepers
The Storykeepers are forced by Nero to flee Rome, but they take with them memories of their most precious possession—memories of the birth and life of Jesus—and tell the story to others. This animated story offers many heartfelt holiday delights. 70 min.
27-5592 *$9.99*

Billy Graham: A Prophet With Honor
David Frost hosts this look at Dr. Billy Graham, one of the world's leading religious figures. Documentary footage, Dr. Graham's own insights and comments from friends and critics alike paint a portrait of a remarkable man. 50 min.
50-5671 *$19.99*

The Passover Plot (1976)
A revolutionary look at the mystery surrounding the crucifixion of Christ, based on the best-selling book, that depicts Jesus as a Zealot leader who, with the aid of his followers, faked his death on the cross and "rose from the dead" to win new converts. Zalman King, Donald Pleasence, Harry Andrews, Hugh Griffith star. 105 min.
19-7040 *$19.99*

The Greatest Stories Ever Told
From the creators of the Rabbit Ears series comes this entertaining collection of uniquely drawn Bible tales, featuring animation and music by some of the top names in the entertainment industry. Each tape runs about 30 min. There are nine volumes available, including:

The Saviour Is Born
Morgan Freeman relates the story of the first Christmas according to the gospels of Matthew and Luke in this program from the smart folk at Rabbit Ears Productions. Music is supplied by the Christ Church Cathedral Choir of Oxford, England.
02-7590 *$14.99*

David And Goliath
Israelite David squares off against Philistine giant Goliath in this superb Rabbit Ears treatment of the famed story. Branford Marsalis composed the score, set to Douglas Fraser's illustrations; Mel Gibson narrates.
02-7595 *$14.99*

The Creation
The opening chapters of Genesis are detailed with beautiful artwork and moving narration by Amy Grant. Béla Fleck and The Flecktones supply the music for this recounting of the busiest week in world history.
02-7972 *$14.99*

Moses The Lawgiver
From atop Mount Ararat, Moses receives the Ten Commandments from God, but the sins of the Israelites lead to a four-decade odyssey to the Promised Land. Narrated by Ben Kingsley; musical score by Lyle Mays.
02-8036 *$14.99*

Parables That Jesus Told
The lessons of the Sower, the Prodigal Son, and others come to life against the backdrop of the journeys Jesus took through Galilee and Judea in this Rabbit Ears production featuring narration by Garrison Keillor and music by David Lindley.
66-6065 *$14.99*

Mary And Joseph: A Story Of Faith (1978)
The story of the parents of Jesus is chronicled in this inspiring film that follows their early lives together up to the Nativity. Blanche Baker, Jeff East, Colleen Dewhurst and Stephen McHattie star. 146 min.
19-2132 Was $19.99 *$14.99*

Mary, Mother Of Jesus (1999)
A unique perspective on the Gospel story is presented in this moving biodrama starring Pernilla August as the young woman chosen by God to bear a son whose message would change the world. Christian Bale also stars as Jesus; with David Threlfall, Geraldine Chaplin, Hywel Bennett. 94 min.
88-1202 □*$14.99*

King Of Kings
This Reader's Digest production celebrates the life and teachings of Jesus with Holy Land footage and such songs as "Ave Maria," "We Three Kings," "I Believe," "I Walked Today Where Jesus Walked," "You'll Never Walk Alone" and more.
50-8641 *$39.99*

Rachel's Man (1975)
Mickey Rooney stars in this biblical tale of faith and love. Rachel's father prevents Jacob from marrying her until he completes seven years of hard work in the fields. Rita Tushingham, Leonard Whiting co-star. 92 min.
47-3148 *$12.99*

The Gospel According To Matthew (1993)
The aging Matthew recalls his experiences of being one of Christ's apostles in this compelling film based on the New International Version Bible. Among his recollections are Jesus' birth, ministry, sacrifice and resurrection. With Richard Kiley, Bruce Marchiano. 90 min.
76-9103 *$59.99*

Acts (1973)
Follow the apostle Luke as he relates his experiences involving the origin of the Christian Church. The Book of Acts comes alive in this film, based on the New International Version Bible, and starring Dean Jones as Luke, Jennifer O'Neill as Lydia, and James Brolin as Peter. 93 min.
76-9104 *$59.99*

The Small Miracle (1973)
Little Pepino thinks that visiting the grave of St. Francis of Assisi will help cure his dying donkey. Although the Father Superior is against such a visit, the boy hopes kindly Father Damico will intervene on his behalf. Originally shown on the "Hallmark Hall of Fame," this film stars Vittorio De Sica, Raf Vallone and Marco Della Cava; written by Paul Gallico. 85 min.
08-1803 *$14.99*

The Pilgrimage Play (1951)
An annual tradition in Europe for hundreds of years, this adaptation of one of the famous "Passion Plays" is a straightforward stage re-creation of the life of Christ. Done with great realism and great respect for the Bible text, this is a moving portrayal of Jesus' life and teachings that you will want to keep.
01-1339 Was $19.99 *$14.99*

Samson And Delilah (1949)
Cecil B. DeMille's spectacular classic of the long-haired Biblical strongman and the beautiful woman who betrayed him to the Philistines. Stars Victor Mature, Hedy Lamarr, George Sanders and Angela Lansbury. 128 min.
06-1083 □*$24.99*

Sodom And Gomorrah (1962)
The original "fun cities" of bygone days are subjected to Jehovah's wrath in director Robert Aldrich's Biblical saga. Stewart Granger stars as reverent patriarch Lot, guided with his family by angels to safety; with Pier Angeli, Stanley Baker, Anouk Aimee. 148 min.
04-2248 □*$19.99*

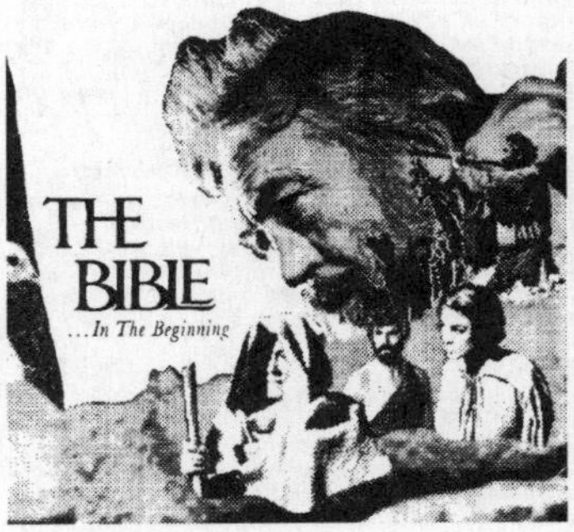

The Bible (1966)
John Huston's mighty cinematic translation of the first 22 chapters of the Book of Genesis united an all-star cast, including George C. Scott as Abraham, Ava Gardner as Sarah, Peter O'Toole as the Three Angels, Richard Harris as Cain, Michael Parks as Adam, and Huston himself as Noah. 171 min.
04-1010 Was $19.99 □*$14.99*

The Bible (Letterboxed Version)
Also available in a theatrical, widescreen format.
04-3436 *$19.99*

Padre Pio: Man Of God (2000)
The miraculous life of Padre Pio is detailed in this gripping study of the Italian-born Capuchin priest from his early days, when he first received the stigmata and the gifts of prophecy and healing, to his beatification in 1999 by Pope John Paul II. Interviews with people who knew him and readings from his diaries vividly illustrate Pio's faith and his amazing abilities. 55 min.
81-3013 *$24.99*

Jesus And The Shroud Of Turin
It's been a source of controversy and reverence around the world for hundreds of years: the burial cloth that is said to have covered the body of Jesus after his crucifixion. Hear from experts on both sides of the issue, and see scientific studies to verify the shroud's true age and origin, in this compelling documentary. 52 min.
50-8205 *$19.99*

Shroud Of Turin
One of the world's greatest mysteries is tackled when this program investigates the mysterious Shroud of Turin. Discovered in 1357, the Shroud has been believed to be Jesus Christ's burial garment, but what has new evidence discovered? 50 min.
53-8197 *$24.99*

Who Was Moses?
He challenged the might of Egypt and led his people out of bondage, but what does history tell us about Moses? This BBC documentary features interviews with Biblical experts, Egyptologists and other scholars and compares the scriptural accounts of Moses' life with historical evidence and records. 55 min.
04-3875 *$14.99*

A Passion For Angels
Take a fascinating journey into the world of angels. Learn about people whose lives have been forever changed by meeting these heavenly acolytes who espouse love and want to share their gifts with others. 60 min.
10-2673 *$12.99*

Speaking With Your Angels: A Guide
This practical and inspirational program offers a seven-step method for receiving angelic guidance through writing from Trudy Griswold and Barbara Mark, authors of "Angelspeake: How to Talk to Your Angels." 70 min.
70-9038 *$19.99*

In Search Of Angels
Explore the lore and legend of these otherworldly beings who are said to serve as messenger, guardian and guide (and fallen spirit) and have been immortalized in art and song. Debra Winger narrates this moving documentary that features interviews with such personalities as authors Sophy Burnham and David Connolly, playwright Tony Kushner and musician Rickie Lee Jones. 60 min.
89-5021 *$29.99*

Bibleland
Tour the key historical and spiritual sites of the Holy Land, and examine how 3,000 years of Biblical history and lore have influenced the region and continue to do so, in this fascinating documentary. Includes an interview with former Israeli foreign minister Moshe Dayan. 60 min.
19-2796 □*$19.99*

The Lost Ark
Go beyond the Hollywood blockbuster and get the real story on the Ark of the Covenant. Learn about the history of this holy artifact, built to house the tablets of the Ten Commandments, and follow journalist Bruce Burgess as he searches the world for the Ark's final resting place. 50 min.
50-8127 Was $19.99 *$14.99*

The Ark Of The Covenant
A probing exploration of the legend of the Lost Ark of the Covenant that travels to Palestine to unearth some startling revelations. Ancient artifacts, scientific theories and an extraordinary trip to Ethiopia help tell the story of the chest which reportedly housed the Ten Commandments. 50 min.
53-7980 Was $24.99 *$14.99*

Heaven & Hell: Biblical Images Of The Afterlife
What do the Old and New Testaments say about the reality, origins and physical characteristics of Heaven and Hell? An array of top scholars, authors and theologians discuss the topic of where (if anywhere) everyone will spend eternity, and computer graphics and animation bring these otherworldly domains to life. 60 min.
50-8276 *$24.99*

Miracles Are Real: Boxed Set
See and hear 20 re-enactments of amazing and inspirational true stories, all in a two-tape collector's set. From a WWII soldier spared from certain death on the battlefield to a terminally ill patient's inexplicable recovery, these tales will have you believing in miracles. 95 min. total.
50-2047 □*$29.99*

It's A Miracle
A woman makes a remarkable recovery after being struck by lightning...the abandoned dog a family takes in returns the favor by saving their infant son's life...a WWII concentration camp inmate receives divine help during and after his ordeal. These and other inspirational stories are featured in this special compiled from the syndicated TV series. Richard Thomas and Nia Peeples host. 70 min.
50-8247 *$19.99*

Documentaries

The Story Of The Twelve Apostles
They were the common men chosen by Jesus to be his closest followers, and while one betrayed him, the others went on to carry his message throughout the world. Learn the remarkable life stories of the Apostles, and how they changed the course of history, in this inspiring documentary that traces Biblical and secular records. 100 min.
53-6732 *$19.99*

Dead Sea Scrolls: Unraveling The Mystery
Written 200 years before Christ by an obscure Jewish sect, they provide a link between Jewish theology and the rise of Christian philosophy. In this Discovery Channel program, you'll learn about the discovery of the scrolls in a Jordanian cave in 1947, how they compare to previous Old Testament writings, and the efforts of researchers to restore them and uncover their secrets. 60 min.
27-7214 *$14.99*

Enigma Of The Dead Sea Scrolls
Discovered in a West Bank cave in 1947, the Dead Sea Scrolls proved to be one of the greatest archeological finds of the century. Now learn about the insights they revealed into Biblical accounts of historic events, the birth of Christianity and, most intriguingly, why many of the scrolls have been kept hidden from the public. 50 min.
53-8083 Was $24.99 *$14.99*

The Beginning Of The End: Boxed Set
Is humanity entering an "end time" that various prophets have foreseen for centuries? This two-tape collector's set includes two revealing documentaries: "7 Signs of Christ's Return," which examines world events said to lead up to the Second Coming of Jesus; while the Doomsday prophecies of St. Malachy, Nostradamus, Edgar Cayce and others are the focus of "Armageddon." 130 min. total. NOTE: Individual volumes available at $19.99 each.
50-2874 □*$39.99*

The End Times: In The Words Of Jesus
What predictions concerning Christ's return do the Gospels contain, and how close is Mankind to these (literally) earthshaking events taking place? Noted scholars and authors, including Dr. Tim LaHaye (the "Left Behind" books), share their thoughts on New Testament teachings concerning the Rapture, the rise of the Antichrist, and the Final Judgment. 55 min.
50-8579 *$19.99*

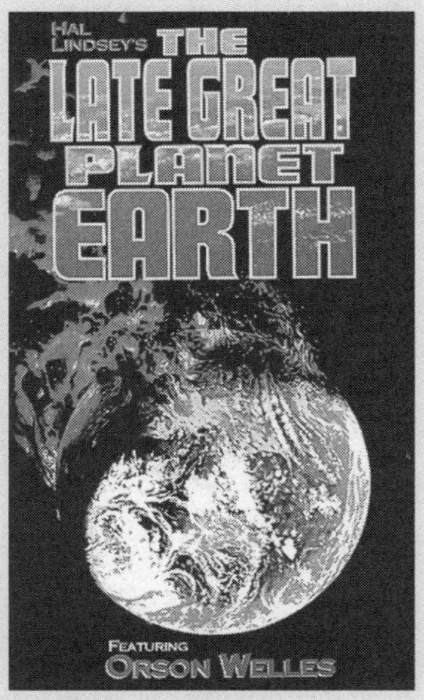

The Late Great Planet Earth (1977)
Were the turbulent events in recent world history, events that place the future of Mankind in jeopardy, actually foretold millennia ago? ago? Orson Welles narrates this eye-opening documentary, based on the best-selling religious book by Hal Lindsey. 86 min.
03-1651 *$14.99*

Pillars Of Faith: Complete Set
Trace the early years of the Christian Church through the men and women who devoted their lives to the faith in this remarkable four-tape documentary series. Interviews with scholars and location footage bring to life the stories of "Celtic Saints," "Martyrs to Christianity," "New Testament Witnesses" and "Religions Around the World." 192 min. total. NOTE: Individual volumes available at $19.99 each.
22-1643 *$79.99*

Mary Magdalen: An Intimate Portrait
She was one of the few women mentioned by name in the Gospels, but what role did Mary Magdalen have in the life of Jesus and the early days of the Christian Church? Hear surprising theories about her place in Biblical history in this fascinating documentary. Penelope Ann Miller hosts. 43 min.
22-7168 *$19.99*

Lives Of Jesus: Complete Set
Go beyond the Biblical accounts to explore Jesus' roles as a Jewish priest, a spiritual leader and a political radical with this three-tape documentary series produced by the BBC and featuring visits to significant sites in the Holy Land and Europe. Included are "Jesus the Jew," "Jesus the Rebel" and "The Hidden Jesus." 150 min. total. NOTE: Individual volumes available at $19.99 each.
50-5738 Save $30.00! *$29.99*

The Lost Years (1976)
This fascinating and controversial documentary examines the theory that, during the time of His life not recorded in the Gospels, Jesus made an Eastern pilgrimage to India and Tibet. 92 min.
08-1182 Was $29.99 *$19.99*

Discovering Jesus (1998)
Who was the man known as Jesus, and what was his message that changed the world? This 12-part series by theologian, educator, and author Dr. Gordon Moyes, filmed on location in the Holy Land, examines the teachings, actions and life of Jesus as presented in the gospels and tracks his mission: to do God's will. 240 min. on two tapes.
50-5893 *$29.99*

The Miracle And Power Of Prayer
Humankind has prayed to a higher power since the beginning of time seeking guidance and help. Now, explore this wonderful phenomenon of divine intervention with dramatic stories of men and women who have turned to God for help, and how their prayers were answered. AKA: "O Lord Hear My Prayer." 60 min.
50-5970 Was $24.99 □*$19.99*

Science & The Power Of Prayer
This fascinating program studies the links between faith and science and focuses on where the two meet. Witness how simple bacteria in a petri dish react to prayer; what happens when Buddhist monks' prayers are used in a faraway surgical procedure; and how a minister uses a healing touch to help his injuries. 55 min.
53-6536 *$24.99*

Unknown Jesus
Can anything more be learned about the life of Jesus apart from what is contained in the four Gospels? From the creators of "Who Wrote the Bible?" comes this thought-provoking documentary that uses a variety of contemporary and early Christian writings, including the Dead Sea Scrolls and the "Gnostic Gospels" of Nag Hammadi to shed light on Jesus' world and legacy. 100 min. on two tapes.
53-6733 *$29.99*

Mysteries Of The Bible: The Greatest Stories: Complete Set
Fascinating Biblical tales, and the historical facts behind them, are presented in a seven-tape set that includes "Cain & Abel," "Biblical Angels," "The Last Supper," "Herod the Great," "Heaven and Hell," "Bible's Greatest Secrets" and "Last Revolt." 350 min. total. NOTE: Individual volumes available at $14.99 each.
53-8820 *$99.99*

Mysteries Of The Bible 2: The Story Continues: Complete Set
The second collection from the acclaimed series includes: "Abraham: One Man, One God," "Arch Enemy: The Philistines," "Joseph: Master of Dreams," "Prophets: Soul Catchers" and "The Execution of Jesus." Richard Kiley and Jean Simmons narrate. 350 min. total. NOTE: Individual volumes available at $14.99 each.
53-8170 *$99.99*

Who Wrote The Bible?
This two-tape set looks into some of the most-asked questions regarding the origins of the Old and New Testaments, including "What do the Dead Sea Scrolls reveal?" and "Did Moses write the Torah?" Researchers and Biblical scholars travel the Holy Land in search of clues. Richard Kiley and Jean Simmons host. 150 min. total.
53-8201 *$29.99*

Who Am I? Why Am I Here?
Best-selling author Thomas Moore explores questions regarding faith and religion in this fascinating program, originally broadcast on PBS. See how Jews, Christians, Muslims, Taoists, Hindus and others seek enlightenment and fulfillment to the universal questions of existence. 60 min.
70-9037 *$19.99*

Noah's Ark Found?
Noted authority Ron Wyatt, along with an international team of archeologists, sets out to discover the true location of the legendary ship. Along with evidence from the Bible, as well as technological breakthroughs in chemical and forensic studies, this program presents findings that could point to the final resting place of Noah's Ark. 55 min.
71-9028 *$19.99*

The Greatest Miracles On Earth: Complete Set
This three-tape set looks at the world's most amazing miracles. "Miracles of Healing" features "Lourdes Healings," "Our Lady Comes to Scotsdale" and "the Healing of Rita Klaus"; "Miracles of Love" includes "Saints" and "Guardian Angels"; and "The Shroud of Turin" and "Miracle of the Sun at Fatima" are featured on "Miracles of Time & Space." NOTE: Individual volumes available at $19.99 each.
85-7005 Save 30.00! *$29.99*

Ancient Secrets Of The Bible: Set
This 10-tape set delves into the Bible's most enigmatic mysteries. Included are "Battle of David and Goliath," "Samson," "Noah's Ark," "Ark of the Covenant," "Moses' Ten Commandments," "Moses' Red Sea Miracle," "Sodom and Gomorrah," "Walls of Jericho," "Tower of Babel" and "Shroud of Turin." 500 min. total. NOTE: Individual volumes available at $12.99 each.
72-3047 Save $70.00! *$59.99*

The Holy Quest: In Search Of Biblical Relics: Complete Set
In this four-part series, scientists and experts who have investigated the Holy Land offer their opinions on some of the world's greatest biblical mysteries. Included are "Quest for the Lost Ark of the Covenant," "The Turin Shroud," "Castle of the Holy Grail" and "The Dead Sea Scrolls." 180 min. total. NOTE: Individual volumes available at $29.99 each.
80-7196 Save $30.00! *$89.99*

Testament: The Bible And History: Complete Set
Enlightening documentary series offers a historical context to the people and places chronicled in the Old and New Testaments, taking viewers to the Holy Land and other sites to study the events and ideals found in the Bible, the growth of Christianity, and its influence on Western civilization. The seven-tape set includes "As It Was in the Beginning," "Chronicles and Kings," "Mightier Than the Sword," "Gospel Truth," "Thine Is the Kingdom," "The Power and the Glory" and "Paradise Lost." 350 min. total. NOTE: Individual volumes available at $29.99 each.
80-7220 *$199.99*

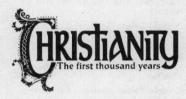

CHRISTIANITY
The first thousand years

Christianity: The First Thousand Years: Boxed Set
It began as an obscure Jewish sect in a remote corner of the Roman Empire, but within a few centuries Christianity would flourish and grow, taking over not only Rome but the whole of Europe and beyond. Follow the first millennium of Christian philosophy and practices in this fascinating series that features footage shot throughout Europe and the Holy Land and commentary from scholars and theologians. 200 min. on four tapes.
50-8124 *$39.99*

Two Thousand Years: The History Of Christianity: Boxed Set
It's a history filled with persecution, power, turmoil, change and, above all, faith. Christianity's birth, rise and ongoing evolution are chronicled in this comprehensive five-tape documentary series that offers commentary from noted historians, theologians and religious leaders. 480 min. total. NOTE: Individual volumes available at $24.99 each.
80-7292 Save $25.00! *$99.99*

From Jesus To Christ: The First Christians
How did what started as an obscure Jewish sect evolve in under 400 years to become the official religion of the Roman Empire and literally change the world? This four-tape documentary series tracks the first millennium of Christianity's growth, from the ministry of Jesus, through the variety of beliefs that grew into a unified theology, to the rise of the Roman Catholic Church. 240 min. total.
18-7893 □*$59.99*

Excavating The Bible: Boxed Set
How have recent archeological finds helped separate fact from fiction in the Biblical historical record? This three-tape series takes you to the Holy Land for remarkable on-site footage and commentary from religious scholars and historical experts. Included are the two-part "Deciphering the Dead Sea Scrolls," "Marine Archeology/Tel Hazor: Searching for Biblical Proofs" and "The Mysteries Mosaic of Galilee/The Ancient Tunnels of Jerusalem." 165 min. total. NOTE: Individual volumes available at $19.99 each.
89-5183 Save $20.00! *$39.99*

Voyages: The Journey Of The Magi (1987)
Fascinating retracing of the probable route followed by the Three Wise Men in the search for the Christ Child. Artifacts and coins of the period add another dimension to the age-old story; filmed on location in the Holy Land. 30 min.
22-5161 *$29.99*

Supernova (2000)
Responding to a distress call, the emergency medical spaceship Nightingale 229 rescues the sole survivor of a mysterious accident. The ship and its crew are placed in deadly danger, both from a collapsing star about to go nova and a strange alien artifact the man snuck on board, in this sci-fi suspenser. Robert Forster, James Spader, Angela Bassett, Peter Facinelli star; directed by "Thomas Lee," a nom de cine for original helmer Walter Hill, Francis Ford Coppola and Jack Sholder. R-rated video version includes footage not shown in theaters. 91 min.
12-3319   ☐$99.99

Jason And The Argonauts (2000)
Set in Ancient Greece, this spectacular fantasy miniseries follows young Jason's search for the Golden Fleece, which will help him reclaim the kingdom his father lost after he was murdered 20 years earlier. As the gods of Olympus take sides in their quest, Jason and his heroic crew of the ship Argo encounter flying harpies, fire-breathing bulls and other fantastic obstacles. Jason London, Natasha Henstridge, Angus MacFadyen, Dennis Hopper and Frank Langella star. 179 min.
27-7228   Was $49.99   ☐$14.99

Dr. Strange (1978)
By the hoary hosts of Hoggoth! Comics' master of the mystic arts comes to life in this fantasy/adventure. Peter Hooten is the medico-turned-mage, out to save the world from an evil sorceress. Jessica Walter, John Mills also star. 94 min.
07-1462   Was $39.99 $14.99

Captain America (1979)
The star-spangled sentinel of freedom is back! Reb Brown stars as the son of the original WWII superhero, out to save the city of Phoenix from a madman with a neutron bomb. With Heather Menzies, Steve Forrest, Len Birman. 98 min.
07-1453   Was $39.99 $14.99

Captain America II: Death Too Soon (1979)
When ruthless terrorist Christopher Lee threatens the U.S. with a virus that causes rapid aging, only Captain America can stop him. Reb Brown returns as Cap; with Connie Sellecca, Len Birman. 88 min.
07-1454   Was $39.99 $14.99

Howard The Duck (1986)
The cigar-smoking, wise-quacking comic book canard makes the leap to the screen in this fantasy/adventure laced with laughter. Can a 3-foot-tall, talking duck find happiness in Cleveland with a female rock singer and defeat an extradimensional demon bent on conquering Earth? Lea Thompson, Jeffrey Jones, Tim Robbins star; George Lucas produced. 111 min.
07-1456   Was $79.99   ☐$14.99

Death Of The Incredible Hulk (1990)
After years of uncontrollable "hulking out," Dr. David Banner has found work with a scientist who may have discovered a cure for his big green alter ego, but will the Hulk go away without a fight? Bill Bixby and Lou Ferrigno star in this feature-length adventure. 96 min.
15-5240   Was $79.99 $14.99

X-Men (2000)
Marvel Comics' phenomenally popular mutant super-heroes (finally) make it to the screen, as schoolmaster/telepath Professor Xavier (Patrick Stewart) and his "students" battle to defend the world that fears them against Magneto (Ian McKellen) and his Brotherhood of Evil Mutants. Director Bryan Singer's hit actioner also stars Hugh Jackman as combative, claw-sprouting Wolverine, Anna Paquin as the tortured Rogue, and Halle Berry as weather-warping Storm; with Famke Janssen, James Marsden, Ray Park, Rebecca Romijn-Stamos. 120 min.
04-3990   ☐$22.99

SCI-FI & FANTASY

FREQUENCY
DENNIS QUAID
JIM CAVIEZEL

Frequency (2000)
Thirty years after New York firefighter Dennis Quaid is killed in a warehouse blaze, his now-grown son, policeman Jim Caviezel, discovers his old ham radio and miraculously contacts Quaid. Over the air and across time, the men form a close relationship they never had and attempt to alter past events, but in doing so place their future and their loved ones in danger. Andre Braugher, Elizabeth Mitchell and Noah Emmerich also star.
02-5235   ☐$99.99

The Spring (2000)
While on a camping trip, a father rushes his injured son to a small town's hospital. When the boy miraculously recovers, the two discover the town is home to a "fountain of youth" spring that prevents illness and aging...but will learning the secret cost them their lives? Intriguing sci-fi suspense tale stars Kyle MacLachlan, Alison Eastwood, Joseph Cross. 90 min.
86-1154   ☐$99.99

Titan A.E. (2000)
In this spectacular animated adventure set in the 31st century, an alien race known as the Drej has destroyed Earth and sent the survivors fleeing into space. A young man named Cale learns he has a map to the Titan, a craft his long-missing father built which holds the key to mankind's survival. Can he and an expedition find the ship before the Drej destroy humanity? Matt Damon, Drew Barrymore, Bill Pullman and John Leguizamo supply the voices in this Don Bluth production. 95 min.
04-3988   ☐$19.99

Pitch Black (2000)
After crashing on a desert planet, the surviving crew of a spaceship try to find a prisoner they were transporting who escaped. They soon discover that the world is home to a deadly predator that thrives in darkness, and a total eclipse of the planet's three suns is about to put them in great danger. Vin Diesel, Radha Mitchell, Cole Hauser star. 109 min.
07-2922   ☐$99.99

On The Beach (2000)
First-rate updating of the doomsday classic is now set in 2006, when the crew of a U.S. Navy sub finds temporary refuge in Australia after a nuclear war between America and China leaves the world dying under radioactive clouds. Commander Armand Assante and his men are sent with Aussie scientists to see if Alaska can support survivors, but tensions mount when scientist Bryan Brown's fiancée, Rachel Ward, falls for Assante. 180 min.
27-5587   ☐$49.99

Mission To Mars (2000)
After three crew members die during an expedition to Mars, a rescue mission, led by Tim Robbins and Gary Sinise and including Connie Nielsen and Jerry O'Connell, is sent out to investigate. The rescuers encounter a number of obstacles until they land on the Red Planet, where they have a startling encounter with an alien. Don Cheadle also stars; directed by Brian De Palma. 113 min.
11-2466   ☐$99.99

Isaac Asimov's Nightfall (2000)
On a distant planet whose six suns have given it near-perpetual daylight, the imminent arrival of an eclipse-induced "night" throws the inhabitants into turmoil and threatens the very foundation of their society. David Carradine, Jennifer Burns and Joseph Hodge star in this powerful adaptation of Asimov's classic science-fiction story. 85 min.
21-9215 $99.99

Breeders (1997)
After crashing near a New England college, a meteorite unleashes its terrifying cargo: an alien creature in search of breeding material in order to keep its species going. Chilling sci-fi tale stars Todd Jensen, Samantha Janus, Clifton Lloyd-Bryan. 93 min.
83-1166   Was $99.99 $14.99

Habitat (1997)
A scientist's experiments turn his family's house into a malevolent living organism that threatens their lives in this chilling and suspenseful sci-fi tale. Balthazar Getty, Tcheky Kayro, Alice Krige star. 103 min.
83-1181   Was $99.99 $14.99

Game Of Survival (1990)
Actually, it's a game for survival in this futuristic thriller, as warriors from other planets are brought to Earth to fight in a contest where only one can walk away. Nikki Hill, Cindy Coatman, Roosevelt Miller, Jr. star. 85 min.
86-1027 $29.99

The Legend Of The Roller Blade Seven (1993)
Set in a nuclear war-devastated future, this action-filled thriller involves the adventures of a samurai warrior and his band of rollerbladers as they set out to save a beautiful enchantress captured by the evil "Pharaoh." Rhonda Shear, Karen Black, William Smith, Stallone (Frank) and Estevez (Joe) star. 90 min.
81-9004 $89.99

The Survivor (1998)
In the future, the Earth has become a penal colony ruled by a bloodthirsty madman named Kyla. When the leader of the free world is kidnapped by Kyla's men, only the Survivor, a futuristic fighter, can save him. Richard Moll, Xavier De Cline, Lisa Robin Kelly and Richard Herd star. AKA: "Terminal Force 2."
81-9057 $99.99

The Shadow Men (1998)
Who said the "Men in Black" have to be so likable? In this sci-fi outing, mysterious aliens wearing hats and dark glasses abduct, then terrorize, Eric Roberts and wife Sherilyn Fenn. Can they warn and save the world before these dastardly dudes of darkness conquer the world? With Dean Stockwell.
81-9060 $99.99

Sleeping Dogs (1998)
The world's nastiest criminals are put into hyper-sleep and housed in a spaceship hovering in deep space. When a crashing meteor awakens the prisoners, leader C. Thomas Howell plans to destroy the Earth. But two stowaways on the ship attempt to stop the crooks' nefarious plan. Darren Dalton co-stars.
81-9061 $99.99

Return To Frogtown (1993)
Adventurer Sam Hell and the gorgeous Dr. Spangler try to rescue Rocket Ranger John Jones from the clutches of an evil scientist using him in genetic experiments. Fanciful sci-fi sequel filled with frog creatures and high-flying effects stars Robert Z'Dar, Charles Napier, Lou Ferrigno, Denise Duff and Don Stroud. 90 min.
81-9006 $89.99

Armageddon: The Final Challenge (1995)
A thrilling futuristic saga in which the post-nuclear world is controlled by government-sanctioned Fear-Permutator clones. Citizen Michael Throne and his partner, Plato the Prophet, are the only hopes of the free world, but can they stop the clones and their evil leader before it's too late? Todd Jensen stars.
81-9019 $89.99

Dead Fire (1998)
The USS Legacy is on a special mission to save the Earth: help re-populate the world before mankind is extinct. But an evil commander takes over the ship and the all-important mission is in jeopardy. Can he be stopped before it's too late? C. Thomas Howell, Matt Frewer and Monika Schnarre star.
81-9056 $99.99

The Apocalypse (1997)
Explosive sci-fi actioner about a huge alien spaceship on a collision course with the Earth and the two scruffy salvage squads who blast off to intercept it and prevent catastrophe. Sandra Bernhard, Matt McCoy, Laura San Giacomo and Frank Zagarino star. 96 min.
83-1150 $99.99

Beowulf (1999)
In this futuristic version of the 8th-century poem, medieval culture is blended with modern technology, as mysterious wanderer Beowulf (Christopher Lambert) takes on the dangerous Grendel, a nocturnal creature killing warriors stationed at a distant fortress called "the Outpost." With Oliver Cotton, Patricia Velasquez. 93 min.
11-2478   ☐$99.99

Chained Heat 3: Hell Mountain (1998)
Futuristic gals-behind-bars bonanza tells of Kal and girlfriend Shira, who try to escape the wrath of the evil Stryker before the annual "harvest," in which young women are taken to the mines of Hell Mountain. When Shira is captured and sent to the mines, Kal tries to outwit Stryker and destroy his fortress. Kate Rodger, Christopher Clarke star. AKA: "Hell Mountain." 97 min.
82-9065 $89.99

Hologram Man (1995)
A murderous terrorist captured by a rookie cop is imprisoned in "holographic stasis," his consciousness transferred to a computer. When his gang tries to bust him out, the killer is turned into a three-dimensional electrical entity, and a reign of horror begins. Can the policeman stop him again? Joe Lara, Evan Lurie and William Sanderson star. 96 min.
86-1089   Was $89.99   ☐$14.99

8 Man (1992)
The super-powered cyborg hero of Japanese animation fame takes on a new dimension in this live-action feature. A young cop, gunned down by mobsters, has his mind implanted in a robotic body by a brilliant scientist. But can the reborn 8 Man break up the crime ring responsible for his "death" while also battling his cybernetic "brother"? Kai Shishido, Osamu Ohtomo star. 91 min.
53-8122   Was $19.99 $14.99

The Thirteenth Floor (1999)
After his partner is killed, a scientist working in Los Angeles in 1937 on a project that can simulate a parallel world travels to that alternate universe to uncover the killer. During his journey, the scientist finds characters with multiple identities in both worlds and makes some stunning revelations about his partner. Craig Bierko, Armin-Mueller Stahl and Gretchen Mol star. 100 min.
02-3368   Was $99.99   ☐$14.99

Precious Find (1996)
The year may be 2049, and humans, aliens and androids may fly starships throughout the galaxy, but gold is still the precious metal that holds the universe together, and a group of interplanetary miners may kill each other over an unclaimed fortune in gold they find. Futuristic actioner stars Rutger Hauer, Brion James, Joan Chen. 90 min.
63-1871   ☐$99.99

Vampire Vixens From Venus (1994)
In order to obtain a drug derived from the essence of Earth men, three alien drug smugglers transform themselves into gorgeous women. Soon they are followed by both local cops and intergalactic drug enforcement agents in this sexy, special effects-filled sci-fier. Michelle Bauer, Charlie Callas and Penthouse Pet Leslie Glass star. 90 min.
63-7104   Was $69.99 $19.99

Phoenix (1995)
Interstellar actioner in which rebellious behavior among replicants mining precious ore on a distant planet prompts the mining company's president to hire a trouble-shooting team. Leading the team is an ex-criminal, who learns that there are plans to replace the replicants with a more violent breed. Stephen Nichols, Billy Drago and Brad Dourif star. 95 min.
76-9080   Was $19.99 $14.99

Tomcat: Dangerous Desires (1993)
A man suffering from a rare disease becomes a human guinea pig for a genetic experiment involving the injection of a feline serum. His health soon improves, but he begins taking on cat-like mannerisms, including a predatory sexual drive and a primal need to kill. Richard Grieco, Natalie Radford and Maryam D'Abo star in this erotic sci-fi thriller. 96 min.
63-1615 Was $89.99 ❑$12.99

Roswell (1994)
Did the U.S. military recover a flying saucer and its alien crew following a crash near the town of Roswell, New Mexico, in 1947? That's the premise behind this speculative drama, based on eyewitness accounts that claim the government is covering up a "close encounter." Kyle MacLachlan, Martin Sheen, Kim Greist and Dwight Yoakam star. 91 min.
63-1742 Was $89.99 ❑$14.99

Roswell: The Aliens Attack (1999)
An unidentified flying object crash lands in the New Mexico desert in 1947, but while the government works to quell the news, no one suspects that alien invaders have assumed human form in order to fulfill their plan to take over the Earth with a nuclear weapon. Sci-fi chiller stars Steven Flynn, Heather Hanson. 89 min.
06-2959 ❑$59.99

Beastmaster 2: Through The Portal Of Time (1991)
Marc Singer returns as the title hero in this sword-swinging sequel, following his evil brother through a time warp to modern-day Southern California. His mission: to stop his sibling from returning to their world with a stolen nuclear device. Kari Wuhrer, Wings Hauser, Sarah Douglas co-star. 107 min.
63-1488 ❑$14.99

Beastmaster III: The Eye Of Braxus (1995)
The Dr. Dolittle of the barbarian set is back, as Dar the Beastmaster (Marc Singer) fights to stop an evil mage from obtaining the jewled Eye of Braxus and bringing the demonic being into the world of man. Action and fantasy aplenty; with David Warner, Sandra Hess, Tony Todd, Lesley-Anne Down. 92 min.
07-2362 Was $89.99 ❑$14.99

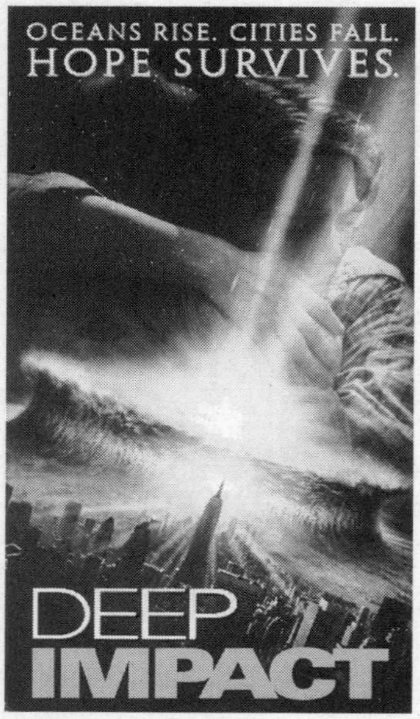
OCEANS RISE. CITIES FALL.
HOPE SURVIVES.
DEEP
IMPACT

Deep Impact (1998)
A special-effects-filled disaster epic with a sensitive side, this hit stars Téa Leoni as a TV reporter who uncovers the suppressed news that a newly-discovered comet is on a collision course with Earth. With time running out, a NASA team led by veteran astronaut Robert Duvall is sent to try and destroy the comet, while a lottery is held to pick the million Americans to be housed in specially-built caves to survive the coming catastrophe. Morgan Freeman, Elijah Wood, Maximilian Schell and Leelee Sobieski also star. 121 min.
06-2762 Was $99.99 ❑$14.99

Deep Impact (Letterboxed Version)
Also available in a theatrical, widescreen format.
06-2767 Was $99.99 ❑$14.99

Kurt Vonnegut's Harrison Bergeron (1995)
Provocative filming of Vonnegut's story about a 21st-century American society which deems "equality" as everyone being middle-of-the-road in all aspects of life. Teenager Harrison Bergeron, slated for surgery to correct his superior intellect, is recruited by a mysterious group that secretly controls the country. With Sean Astin, Christopher Plummer and cameos from Eugene Levy and others. 99 min.
63-1798 Was $89.99 ❑$14.99

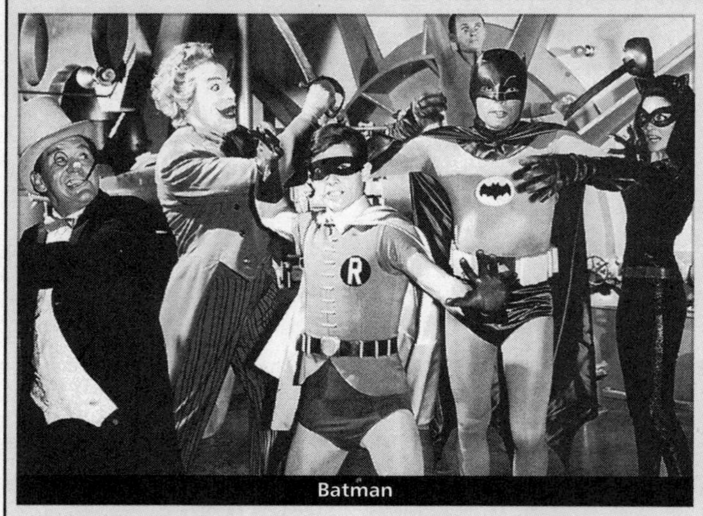

Batman

Batman (1966)
Holy VCR! The dynamic duo, in their feature film debut, must defend Gotham City and the free world from a cabal of their most sinister enemies: Catwoman, Joker, Penguin and Riddler. All the BAM! BIFF! POW! excitement and fun of the TV series. Stars Adam West, Burt Ward, Lee Meriwether, Cesar Romero, Burgess Meredith, Frank Gorshin. 105 min.
04-3071 Was $19.99 ❑$14.99

Batman (1989)
The dramatic, blockbuster thriller pits playboy-turned-dark knight detective Michael Keaton against the ghoulishly garish Joker, played to perfection by Jack Nicholson. Kim Basinger supplies the love interest as photographer Vicki Vale; with Robert Wuhl, Michael Gough, Jack Palance. Tim Burton directs. 126 min.
19-1715 Was $19.99 ❑$14.99

Batman (Letterboxed Version)
Also available in a theatrical, widescreen format.
19-2663 ❑$19.99

Batman Returns (1992)
Terrific sequel to the smash bat hit has Michael Keaton's caped crusader with his hands full, going up against three enemies vying for control of Gotham City: the umbrella-wielding, sewer-dwelling Penguin (Danny DeVito); megalomaniacal businessman Max Shreck (Christopher Walken); and the sexy, leather-clad Catwoman (Michelle Pfeiffer). Directed by Tim Burton. 126 min.
19-2009 Was $19.99 ❑$14.99

Batman Returns (Letterboxed Version)
Also available in a theatrical, widescreen format.
19-2664 ❑$19.99

Batman Forever (1995)
Val Kilmer takes up the cape and cowl with heroic aplomb, but, even with the arrival of costumed partner Robin (Chris O'Donnell), can Batman tackle the dual menace of dichotomous do-badder Two-Face (Tommy Lee Jones) and that prince of puzzles, the Riddler (Jim Carrey)? Thrilling third entry in the series also stars Nicole Kidman, Michael Gough. 122 min.
19-2372 Was $19.99 ❑$14.99

Batman Forever (Letterboxed Version)
Also available in a theatrical, widescreen format.
19-2665 ❑$19.99

Batman & Robin (1997)
The Batmobile keys have been handed over once more, to George Clooney, who teams up with Chris O'Donnell as Robin and new comrade-in-body armor Batgirl (Alicia Silverstone) to save Gotham City from the frigidly fiendish Mr. Freeze (Arnold Schwarzenegger) and the lovely, lethal Poison Ivy (Uma Thurman). Fantastic fourth "Bat"-actioner also stars Michael Gough, Elle Macpherson. 125 min.
19-2596 Was $22.99 ❑$14.99

Batman & Robin (Letterboxed Version)
Also available in a theatrical, widescreen format.
19-2666 ❑$22.99

The Batman Legacy 4-Pack
Keaton, Kilmer and Clooney keep the streets of Gotham safe in this boxed collector's set containing "Batman," "Batman Returns," "Batman Forever" and "Batman and Robin."
19-2607 $59.99

APEX (1994)
In this suspense-filled high-tech thriller, a time travel probe in 2073 infects the past with a deadly virus. In order to stop the virus from destroying the future, a scientist must travel back in time, to a world decimated by disease and ruled by a robotic army. Richard Keats, Mitchell Cox and Lisa Ann Russell star. 103 min.
63-1686 Was $89.99 ❑$14.99

The Demolitionist (1995)
"Baywatch" beauty Nicole Eggert is a bio-enhanced future cop who patrols Metro City on her motorcycle and is out to bring down Mad Dog, the killer responsible for her partner's death, in this action-filled sci-fi tale. Richard Grieco, Bruce Abbott and Tom Savini also star. 100 min.
83-1080 Was $99.99 $14.99

Specimen (1996)
Twenty-four years after his mother was impregnated during an extraterrestrial abduction, the young man who resulted from the "experiment" must use his awesome powers to battle the aliens when they return to Earth. Mark-Paul Gosselaar and Michelle Johnson star in this sci-fi saga. 85 min.
83-1122 Was $99.99 $14.99

Alien Chaser (1996)
Two archeologists working in the African desert stumble on a mysterious artifact that reactivates an android assassin from outer space, and now must flee for their lives, in an action-packed sci-fi thriller. Frank Zagarino, Todd Jensen, Jennifer MacDonald star. 95 min.
83-1129 Was $99.99 $14.99

T-Force (1994)
They're the police force of the future, the world's first cybernetic law enforcement squad. But when a mission leaves bystanders dead, and the government decides to turn off the T-Force, its half-human, half-robot members turn renegade in order to survive. Explosive sci-fi thriller stars Jack Scalia, Erin Gray, Evan Lurie. 101 min.
86-1084 Was $89.99 ❑$14.99

Zeram (1991)
Futuristic space adventure from Japan about a monstrous alien creature from the planet Mays that threatens the Earth and must be destroyed by a female bounty hunter. In order to stop the creature, the woman uses a space bazooka, warp machine and computer. 92 min.
53-7807 Was $19.99 $14.99

The Silencers (1996)
Human-looking alien killers are sent on a misson to take over the Earth. In hopes of stopping them, a special agent teams with a peace officer from another galaxy to save the planet. Jack Scalia, Dennis Christopher, Lucinda Weist and Clarence Williams III star in the sci-fi actioner. 103 min.
86-1101 Was $89.99 ❑$14.99

Quarantine (1990)
Chilling sci-fi thriller set in a plague-ravaged future America, where authorities condemn carriers to "containment camps" and a group of renegade scientists work to uncover the truth behind the campaign of terror. Jerry Wasserman, Beatrice Boepple star. 92 min.
63-1368 Was $89.99 $12.99

In The Cold Of The Night (1990)
Dreams turn into nightmares in this violent and erotic chiller about a man haunted in his sleep by murderous visions of a beautiful woman...a woman who later shows up alive on his doorstep. Bizarre, sexy tale of sci-fi suspense stars Jeff Lester, Adrianne Sachs, Marc Singer and Shannon Tweed. 112 min.
63-1410 $12.99

Eve Of Destruction (1991)
She's lovely, lethal and nuclear-powered! She's Eve VIII, an anti-terrorist android who runs amok during her trial run and sets out on a cross-country killing spree. Sexy Renée Soutendijk ("The Fourth Man") stars as both Eve and her creator, and Gregory Hines plays the special agent charged with stopping the rampage in this imaginative sci-fi thriller. 100 min.
53-1796 $14.99

Steel Frontier (1995)
There's no hope in the post-apocalyptic desert city of New Hope when a group of ruffians take over the town, forcing men to join their gang and turning women into slaves. A mysterious gunman named Yuma arrives on the scene, but is he an ally of the outlaws or the townsfolk? Joe Lara, Brion James and Stacie Foster star.
86-1087 Was $89.99 ❑$14.99

Savage (1997)
Smashing action yarn starring kickboxing champ Olivier Gruner as a man who goes neanderthal after his wife and child are murdered in a mysterious fire. When Gruner discovers the culprit is an evil high-tech wizard experimenting with virtual reality, a policewoman helps him to find the culprit. Kario Salem, Jennifer Grant and Kristin Minter also star. 103 min.
63-1875 ❑$99.99

Ravager (1997)
In the tradition of "Alien" and "Species" comes this sci-fi thriller about an interstellar transport ship whose crew and passengers are in jeopardy when a deadly biological weapon threatens their lives. Who will be infected next? Bruce Payne, Yancy Butler and Juliet Landau star. 92 min.
63-1885 ❑$99.99

Progeny (1998)
A couple's dreams of parenthood become nightmares when their offspring is discovered to be the twisted, terrifying result of alien impregnation. Arnold Vosloo, Jillian McWhirter, Brad Dourif and Wilford Brimley star in this sci-fi shocker from co-writer Stuart Gordon ("Re-Animator") and director Brian Yuzna ("The Dentist"). 100 min.
64-9036 $99.99

The Good Book (1999)
In the future, the world has become obsessed with technology and the governments of the world unite for control while forcing citizens to stay indoors and become dependent. A computer repairman who travels from house to house is recruited by a strange being, who claims to be God, to destroy the Internet. Brian Campbell stars. 92 min.
73-9296 $19.99

Flesheaters From Outer Space (1998)
Captain David Riggs returns to Earth following a spaceflight with a flesh-eating alien he found on a drifting spaceship. After the creature escapes a maximum security compound and begins killing all who stand in its wake, Riggs teams with a psychic to stop the extraterrestrial terror. Greg Scott, Kathy Monks star. 80 min.
73-9298 $19.99

Polymorph (1996)
It's "Pulp Fiction" meets "Invasion of the Body Snatchers" as a group of drug dealers led by lascivious but lethal Auriana Albright take to the woods, only to find themselves facing four college students braving the elements and a creepy, shape-shifting alien. What do they call Big Macs on Mars? With James L. Edwards, Jennifer Huss. 87 min.
73-9148 Was $29.99 $14.99

Teenage Space Vampires (1998)
It's up to a nerdy high schooler to help a government agent save his town from an invasion of extraterrestrial bloodsuckers, out to plunge the planet into total darkness, in this action-packed sci-fi thriller. Robin Dunne, Mak Fyfe, Lindy Booth star. 90 min.
75-5044 $49.99

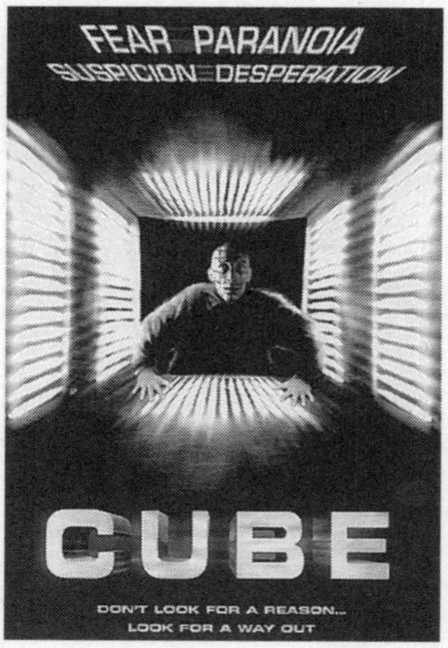
FEAR PARANOIA
SUSPICION DESPERATION
CUBE
DON'T LOOK FOR A REASON...
LOOK FOR A WAY OUT

Cube (1998)
One part math lesson, one part "Twilight Zone" and one part Jean-Paul Sartre, Canadian filmmaker Vincenzo Natali's compelling sci-fi suspense tale follows six strangers who find themselves trapped in a maze of identical, interconnected cubical chambers loaded with deadly traps. Can the six overcome mutual distrust and suspicion to escape their mysterious high-tech prison? Nicole DeBoer, David Hewlett, Wayne Robson, Maurice Dean Witt star. 90 min.
68-1901 Was $89.99 ❑$14.99

Merlin (1992)
A young reporter living in California learns that she is the reincarnated daughter of the fabled wizard Merlin, and, with help from an ancient magician and a handsome warrior, she must protect the legendary Sword of Power from an evil mage named Pendragon in this enchanting fantasy with amazing special effects. Richard Lynch, James Hong star. 112 min.
80-1067 Was $89.99 *$14.99*

Enemy (1997)
America is about to elect its first black president, but the hopes are dashed when he's assassinated. An all-out war erupts after the death and, when the smoke clears, there are only two survivors: one black, the other white. Will they battle each other or work together to start things anew? Richard Lasky stars.
81-9040 Was $89.99 *$14.99*

Legion (1998)
In space, everyone can hear you scream! Especially if you're a member of a ship's crew comprised of convicts and military officers and you've just learned that the commanding officer is using you as a pawn to battle a ferocious alien creature. Parker Stevenson, Terry Farrell, Corey Feldman, Rick Springfield and Troy Donahue star in this futuristic shocker. 99 min.
81-9045 *$99.99*

New World Disorder (1999)
Rutger Hauer is a veteran detective who enlists the help of a young computer genius to protect his beautiful partner and himself from becoming victims in a high-stakes game of espionage. Thrilling cyber-thriller also stars Andrew McCarthy, Tara Fitzgerald. 95 min.
81-9105 *$99.99*

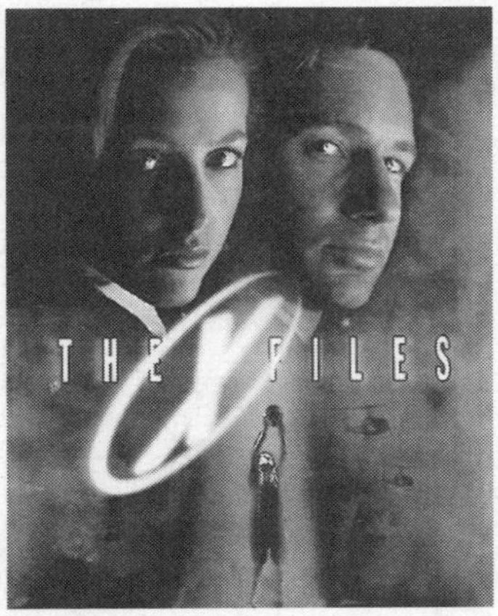

The X-Files (1998)
"X-Philes" and neophytes alike will be sucked into the otherworldly intrigue of this feature film extension of the hit TV series. FBI agents Mulder (David Duchovny) and Scully's (Gillian Anderson) quest for the truth behind a seemingly global conspiracy involving the U.S. government, a strange cabal of businessmen, and aliens bent on "colonizing" Earth leads the duo to a shocking discovery in the Antarctic. Martin Landau, Mitch Pileggi, Armin Mueller-Stahl and William B. Davis also star. Special video version includes footage not shown in theaters and behind-the-scenes interviews. 135 min.
04-3729 Was $22.99 *□$14.99*

The X-Files (Letterboxed Version)
Also available in a theatrical, widescreen format.
04-3746 *□$22.99*

Dark Future (1995)
During the 21st century, a plague almost wipes out the entire human race. The few survivors become slaves and prostitutes for cyborgs who run the world. A rule prohibits humans from having children, but when one couple defies the rule, a battle between cyborgs and humans ensues. Darby Hinton and Len Donato star. 100 min.
82-5007 *$79.99*

Final Equinox (1995)
A government agent trying to recover a stolen Peruvian artifact discovers that it is from another planet and has the ability to turn all human life into vegetation. The agent uses a special brainwashing device to get to the crook who swiped the artifact, but does he have enough time to save the world in the process? Joe Lara, Martin Kove, David Warner star. 95 min.
76-9081 Was $19.99 *$14.99*

Interceptor Force (1999)
A mercenary squad is sent into Mexico to investigate the crash of a U.S. Air Force jet squadron, only to encounter an alien creature capable of changing its shape and assuming the identity of anyone it comes in contact with, in this sci-fi actioner. Olivier Gruner, Ernie Hudson, Glenn Plummer star. 91 min.
81-9113 *$99.99*

Starlight (1997)
Rae Dawn Chong is an alien who lands on Earth in hopes of finding the solution to her planet's environmental problems. What she finds on the "third rock from the sun" is Billy Wirth, a creature with alien genes who may be able to help her species. But can she fend off an intergalactic assassin long enough to save the day? Willie Nelson also stars in this sci-fi thriller. 98 min.
76-9091 Was $19.99 *$14.99*

Escape Velocity (1999)
A 22nd-century space observatory ship, manned by a husband-wife scientist team and their teenage daughter, retrieves an escape pod whose inhabitant has been in suspended animation for 15 years. Unfortunately for them, the man they've saved is a deranged killer. Patrick Bergin, Wendy Crewson and Peter Outerbridge star in a sci-fi chiller. 97 min.
81-9094 *$99.99*

Quest Of The Delta Knights (1993)
A group of brave warriors known as the Delta Knights attempts to overthrow an evil king and his queen by finding the Lost Storehouse, an arsenal of technology from the age of Atlantis. David Warner, Olivia Hussey and Corbin Allred star in this action-packed fantasy. 97 min.
80-1062 Was $19.99 *$14.99*

Total Reality (1999)
The fascistic military leader of 21st-century Earth is defeated on the battlefield, but escapes in a time machine with a plan to alter history. Can a rogue soldier and a band a felons go back and stop him from changing destiny? David Bradley, Ely Pouget and Thomas Kretschmann star.
81-9095 *$99.99*

Resistance (1997)
In the near future, society has fallen and corporations control what remains of humanity, forcing them to work in huge farms in the countryside that feed the elite who live in the city. When a farmhand is killed by callous soldiers, a runaway girl and a truck-stop waitress forge a common bond, leading a revolution against heartless corporations. Helen Jones stars. 110 min.
82-5047 Was $79.99 *$19.99*

Time Tracers (1997)
The discovery of a 5,000-year-old artifact from a humanoid reptile hybrid leads a reporter to investigate the Kronos Project, a time experiment funded by an evil multi-billionaire. The future of the universe and the course of evolution are threatened when the experiment progresses from the Civil War to the Jurassic Period. Jeffrey Combs stars. 100 min.
82-5048 *$79.99*

Lost In Time (1997)
When a nuclear-powered satellite zaps Earth with a laser beam, a high school is thrust 200 years into the future as the planet is decimated. The students of the school are led by their coach as they battle a mutant monster and a serial killer. Bubba Smith, Billy Drago and Henry Silva star. 90 min.
82-5053 *$59.99*

First Encounter (1998)
On the last leg of its journey, the Earthship ISS Gallant Fox encounters another ship, drifting in space. The Gallant Fox's captain and its crew board the vessel and find aliens in suspended animation. When the captain orders the aliens resuscitated, another officer starts a mutiny. Roddy Piper, Trevor Goddard and Stacey Randall star. 90 min.
82-5055 *$59.99*

DarkDrive (1998)
In the year 2002, a high-tech corporation creates a virtual prison in which the minds of ruthless criminals are stored in a vast database. When things go terribly wrong, special operations agent Steven Falcon is forced to put his life on the line and go into the "digital Alcatraz" in search of the truth. With Ken Olandt and Claire Stansfield.
82-5075 *$89.99*

Timelock (1998)
In the 23rd century, an asteroid hosts the world's most dangerous criminals in a maximum security prison. When a computer virus releases the most ruthless inmates from cryogenic suspension, all hell breaks loose. Caught in the middle of the turmoil are a petty thief and the pilot of a prison transport system. Maryam D'Abo, Arye Gross and Jeff Speakman star.
82-5103 *$89.99*

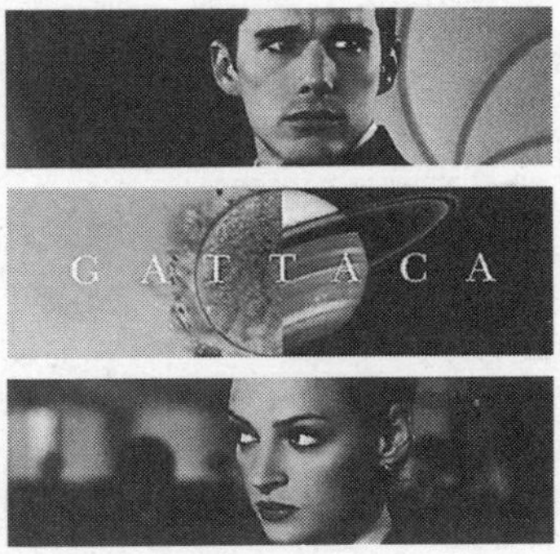

Gattaca (1997)
In an all-too-possible future, genetic engineering has divided the world into lab-created perfect humans and naturally-born "invalids," who are doomed to menial tasks and an early death. Ethan Hawke is a young "invalid" who resorts to deceit in order to fulfill his dream of taking part in a manned space mission, but is soon caught up in a murder mystery that could rock the foundations of his repressive society. Uma Thurman, Jude Law, Alan Arkin and Gore Vidal also star in this intriguing sci-fi thriller. 106 min.
02-3162 Was $99.99 *□$14.99*

DARK CITY

Dark City (1998)
A Kafkaesque slice of sci-fi noir from director/co-writer Alex Proyas ("The Crow"), this haunting thriller stars Rufus Sewell as a man who awakens to find himself wanted for murder and his memory gone. As Sewell tries to find the keys to his past, he's pursued through the dreamlike city by a group of mysterious black-clad beings called "Strangers" who can twist reality to suit their whims. Jennifer Connelly, William Hurt, Kiefer Sutherland and Richard O'Brien also star. 100 min.
02-5181 Was $99.99 *□$14.99*

Dark City (Letterboxed Version)
Also available in a theatrical, widescreen format.
02-5201 *□$14.99*

Gangster World (1998)
Futuristic actioner in which 21st-century thrill-seekers have their deepest and darkest fantasies fulfilled at a high-tech theme park. However, things go terribly wrong when power-hungry sociopaths rage a battle for control of the park and turn it into the most dangerous place on Earth. David Leisure, Xavien De Clie, Jerry Doyle star in this mix of "Westworld" with gangsters. 91 min.
82-5079 *$89.99*

Laserhawk (1997)
Millions of years ago they came to Earth and left the seeds of humanity; now they're coming back for the "harvest." Mankind's only hope of avoiding the dinner plates of these alien invaders lies with Mark Hamill, whose visions of the coming attack landed him in a mental hospital; futuristic warrior Jason James Richter; and a 250,000,000-year-old spaceship known as Laserhawk. 102 min.
81-9104 *$99.99*

Cyber Seeker (1995)
In the year 2020, most of the world has been destroyed by viruses and New Los Angeles is the one of the few spots where humanity lives. A diabolical man called "The Reaper" plans to release deadly bacteria into the city's water supply, and only a mysterious dweller can topple the Reaper and his cyborg henchman. Don Stroud, Roger Lee and Michael Laurin star. 90 min.
82-5016 *$79.99*

Alien Species (1998)
From the depths of space, alien creatures descend on Earth, abducting people for their own sinister purposes. Sheriff Charles Napier and professor Hoke Howell team up to battle the invaders, using technology swiped from an alien nest. 90 min.
82-5104 *$99.99*

A Town Has Turned To Dust (1998)
Rod Serling penned this intriguing story set in the near future. A reporter working on a documentary arrives at Carbon, a ramshackle desert town controlled by a ruthless mining boss, just as the trial of a Native American teen falsely accused of a crime leads to mob violence and a deadly showdown. Ron Perlman, Stephen Lang, Gabriel Olds and Judy Collins star. 91 min.
82-5108 *$89.99*

Fugitive Mind (1999)
In this gripping cyber-thriller, a man trying to recover his missing memory soon discovers to his horror that he's part of a bizarre experiment, and that he's been programmed to carry out a brutal crime. Can he regain his mind and stop his captors' plans? Michael Dudikoff, Heather Langenkamp star. 94 min.
82-5129 *$89.99*

The Omega Diary (1999)
After learning that the United States is involved in a nuclear war, six friends head for cover in a bomb shelter. Tension soon mounts between these survivors, and eventually they have to face what lies beyond their shelter door. 95 min.
82-5143 *$99.99*

Demons In My Head (1999)
Creepy sci-fier about a young man who discovers a meteorite has crashed in his backyard, then finds a bizarre headset apparatus inside it. The device has the ability to transport objects and people across dimensions, but also brings horrific demons and visions into its users' minds. With a bright young cast. 95 min.
82-5144 *$99.99*

G2: Mortal Conquest (1999)
Steven Colin discovers he has lived before, wielding Alexander the Great's sword in battle against his mortal enemies. In the year 2004, his old foes come back looking for revenge and, quicker than you can say "Highlander," he must use his swordsmanship skills to defend himself. Daniel Bernhardt and James Hong star. 93 min.
82-5146 *$89.99*

Nautilus (1999)
On a devastated Earth in the year 2100, a small band of heroes attempts to go back in time in an experimental nuclear submarine. Their mission: prevent the disasters that occurred 100 years earlier and change the future. Compelling sci-fi thriller stars Richard Norton, Miranda Wolfe. 90 min.
82-5158 *$89.99*

Firepower (1993)
High-octane futuristic actioner set in a hellish L.A. neighborhood where crime is legal and no lawman dares enter, until two cops put their lives on the line in order to track down a gang boss known as the Swordsman, who plans to release a counterfeit AIDS vaccine across America. Chad McQueen, Gary Daniels and former pro wrestler Jim Hellwig (The Ultimate Warrior) star.
86-1072 Was $89.99 *$14.99*

Within The Rock (1996)
In this sci-fi scarer, a team of space miners attempts to stop a runaway moon from destroying the Earth. Their mission is put in what-could-be final jeopardy when a ferocious fossilized monstrosity is unleashed. Can the miners clip this calamitous creature before it's curtains for the world? Xander Berkeley and Caroline Barclay star. 91 min.
83-1115 Was $99.99 *$14.99*

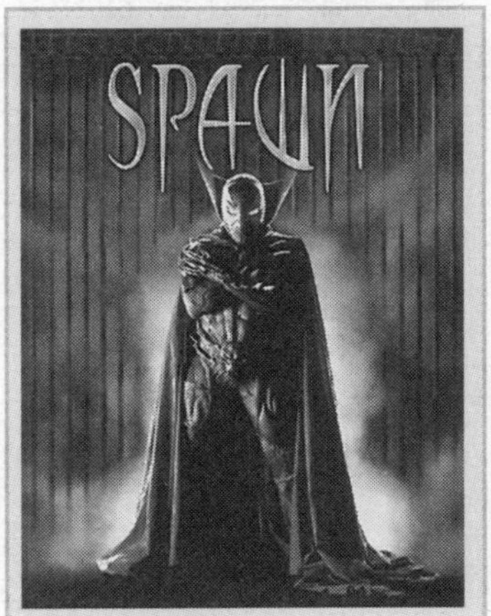

Spawn (1997)
After he's betrayed by his boss and killed in an explosion, secret government operative Michael Jai White makes a deal with the devil and returns to Earth as the armor-clad, vengeance-seeking being known as Spawn. Todd McFarlane's violent and moody comic book series becomes a dazzling, effects-filled action/fantasy hit. John Leguizamo, Martin Sheen, Theresa Randle also star. 93 min.
02-5163 Was $99.99 *□$14.99*

Spawn (Director's Cut)
This special director's edition of the film includes additional footage, an interview with "Spawn" creator Todd McFarlane, and an exclusive "making of" featurette.
02-5164 Was $99.99 *□$19.99*

Spawn (Director's Cut) (Letterboxed Version)
Also available in a theatrical, widescreen format.
02-5180 *□$19.99*

Spawn
He's come back from the dead and uses the hellish powers at his command to battle evil—both human and demonic—on Earth, all the while searching for the clues to his forgotten past. He's Spawn, the cloaked and chained comic-book hero from Todd McFarlane, and he comes to "life" in this graphic animated series that's definitely not for kids.

Spawn, Vol. 1 (Uncut Collector's Edition)
Includes an exclusive interview with McFarlane. 147 min.
44-2110 Was $22.99 *$14.99*

Spawn, Vol. 1 (Special Edited Edition)
Also available in a less graphic PG-13 version. 90 min.
44-2111 Was $19.99 *$14.99*

Spawn, Vol. 2 (Uncut Collector's Edition)
Includes an exclusive interview with McFarlane. 144 min.
44-2168 Was $22.99 *$14.99*

Spawn, Vol. 2 (Special Edited Edition)
Also available in a less graphic PG-13 version.
44-2169 *$14.99*

Spawn, Vol. 3: The Ultimate Battle (Uncut Collector's Edition)
Includes an exclusive interview with McFarlane and music videos by Kid Rock and Lil' Cease. 150 min.
44-2196 Was $22.99 *□$14.99*

Spawn: Vols. 1-3 Gift Set
The first three volumes of the acclaimed animated series are also available in a money-saving collector's set.
44-2207 Save $5.00! *$39.99*

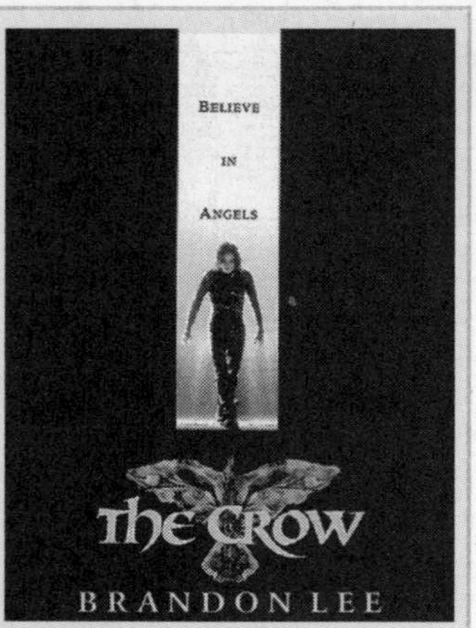

The Crow (1994)
An eerie fantasy starring Brandon Lee (in his final film) as a rock guitarist who is killed, along with his fiancée, on the eve of their wedding and returns from the dead to seek revenge. Filled with expert action scenes and an electrifying rock score, this atmospheric adaptation of James O'Barr's comic series also stars Ernie Hudson, Michael Wincott. Special video edition includes footage not shown in theatres and Lee's final interview. 117 min. total.
11-1817 Was $19.99 ❑*$14.99*

The Crow (Letterboxed Version)
Also available in a theatrical, widescreen format.
11-2159 ❑*$19.99*

The Crow: City Of Angels (1996)
They killed him and his son, but he's come back for vengeance. French actor Vincent Perez is the newest incarnation of the Crow in this stylish sequel set in a decaying future L.A. Mia Kirshner plays a tattoo artist who befriends the Crow as he takes on a dangerous drug dealer and his gang; with Richard Brooks and Iggy Pop. 86 min.
11-2069 Was $19.99 ❑*$14.99*

The Crow: City Of Angels (Letterboxed Version)
Also available in a theatrical, widescreen format.
11-2160 ❑*$19.99*

The Crow: Stairway To Heaven (1998)
In "Something So Bad" and "The Soul Can't Rest," the two-part pilot episode for the hit TV series, action star Marc Dacascos takes over the role Brandon Lee made famous. He's Eric Draven, a rock musician who returns from the grave for revenge a year after he and his lover were murdered. With Marc Gomes, Sabin Kasenti. 94 min.
02-9110 Was $99.99 *$14.99*

Space Marines (1996)
When a crew of intergalactic pirates hijacks a spacecraft carrying nuclear cargo and takes a United Planets official hostage, the elite Space Marines launch a daring rescue mission that places the fate of the universe in their hands. Billy Wirth, Edward Albert and Meg Foster star in this enthralling sci-fi saga. 93 min.
63-1857 ❑*$99.99*

Downdraft (1996)
An android and a renegade computer take control of an underground nuclear weapons compound, putting the fate of the world at risk. Only a group of highly-skilled soldiers can stop the countdown to Armageddon. Vincent Spano and Kate Vernon star in this futuristic actioner. 102 min.
63-1868 ❑*$99.99*

Webmaster (1998)
Inventive computer special effects and an intelligent script highlight this Danish effort in which J.B., a computer hacker, is drawn into a bizarre cyberworld created by an enigmatic character named Stoliss. When an unknown hacker makes their way into Stoliss' world, J.B. has 35 hours to stop them—or be killed! With Jurgen Kit. AKA: "Skyggen." 102 min.
64-9059 *$99.99*

Visitors Of The Night (1995)
When her daughter is among a group of local teens who vanish and reappear with no knowledge of where they were, Markie Post remembers a similar incident that occurred to her years earlier. What sinister alien force is behind the abductions, and how can it be stopped? Suspenseful sci-fi thriller also stars Candace Cameron, Dale Midkiff. 90 min.
65-9002 ❑*$79.99*

Netforce (1999)
From best-selling author Tom Clancy comes a thrilling cyber-actioner set in the year 2005, where a rise in computer crimes leads the FBI to create a special high-tech investigation unit. When Netforce head Kris Kristofferson is killed, agents Scott Bakula and Joanna Going must solve the murder and stop a plot to infiltrate the globe-spanning information system. With Brian Dennehy, Judge Reinhold. 162 min.
68-1929 ❑*$19.99*

Circuitry Man (1990)
Plug into an exciting cyberpunk thriller set in a future world where pollution-spawned menaces abound and computers provide the ultimate high. A woman and an android must make a hazardous cross-country trek, followed by a high-tech villain named Plughead who steals people's minds. Jim Metzler, Dana Wheeler-Nicholson, Vernon Wells ("The Road Warrior") star. 85 min.
02-2060 *$19.99*

Plughead Rewired: Circuitry Man II (1994)
Plughead holds the fate of Future Earth in his diabolical brain, thanks to a newly-acquired "ultimate weapon," and it's up to the android Circuitry Man and a beautiful FBI agent to stop him once and for all. Deborah Shelton, Traci Lords, Jim Metzler and Vernon Wells star. 96 min.
02-2675 *$89.99*

Dune Warriors (1991)
A future Earth where water is worth more than gold—or blood—is the setting for this sci-fi action tale about feuding bands of nomads who battle for control of the barren landscape. David Carradine, Rick Hill, Luke Askew star. 77 min.
02-2158 *$79.99*

Dead Space (1991)
In space no one can hear you say "Ahhhhhhhh!" An astronaut lands on a research lab on a faraway planet to join a beautiful researcher in stopping a killer virus that mutates, then murders people. Marc Singer, Laura Tate, Judith Chapman star. 72 min.
02-2169 *$89.99*

The Guyver (1992)
This exciting special effects-filled shocker, based on a popular Japanese comic, tells the story of a college student who discovers an alien device that transforms him into a powerful fighting machine. Soon, he goes into battle against alien creatures known as Zoanoids. Mark Hamill, Jack Armstrong, Vivian Wu and Jimmy ("Dyn-o-mite!") Walker star. 92 min.
02-2294 Was $19.99 ❑*$14.99*

The Guyver II: Dark Hero (1994)
In this smashing sequel, the Guyver finds an alien ship filled with weapons during an archeological dig in Utah which draws him into a war against the evil, mutant Zoanoids, who have the ability to destroy the world. David Hayter stars. 127 min.
02-2673 Was $19.99 ❑*$14.99*

Digital Man (1995)
When a prototype high-tech military machine goes haywire, only a team of human and robotic commandos can stop it—and prevent World War III in the process! Terrific special effects and an array of action sequences highlight this sci-fier starring Ed Lauter, Matthias Hues, Adam Baldwin, Paul Gleason. 95 min.
63-1780 Was $89.99 ❑*$12.99*

Automatic (1995)
Fast and furious futuristic actioner involving a renegade cyborg who teams with a beautiful human woman when they're both linked to a murder. Heading the search to find them is the nasty head of a robotics company. Olivier Gruner, Daphne Ashbrook, John Glover star in this cyber-thriller. 90 min.
63-1794 Was $89.99 ❑*$14.99*

Yesterday's Target (1996)
In this sci-fi thriller, three futuristic strangers with incredible powers travel to the past to save a boy who may hold the key to saving the world. Daniel Baldwin, LeVar Burton, Malcolm McDowell and Stacey Haiduk star. 80 min.
63-1854 ❑*$99.99*

Menno's Mind (1999)
In a cyber-ruled world of the future, a rebel computer expert sends a man into a dangerous virtual realm in order to save the world...or destroy it. Compelling sci-fi thriller stars Bill Campbell, Bruce Campbell, Corbin Bernsen and Michael Dorn. 95 min.
67-9011 ❑*$14.99*

Neon City (1991)
Earth in the year 2053 is a barren wasteland after a series of ecological disasters. In the midst of the devastation eight survivors, each with their own reasons, journey to the promised safety of Neon City. Exciting "apocaliffhanger" stars Michael Ironside, Vanity, Lyle Alzado. 107 min.
68-1221 ❑*$89.99*

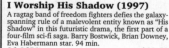

UNIVERSAL SOLDIER II
BROTHERS IN ARMS

Universal Soldier II: Brothers In Arms (1998)
Smashing follow-up to the 1992 sci-fi actioner stars Matt Battaglia as the man turned into a high-tech killing machine by a clandestine military group. With the help of beautiful journalist Chandra West, Battaglia fights to expose the operation and, if possible, reclaim his humanity. Jeff Wincott and Gary Busey also star. 93 min.
06-2850 Was $69.99 ❑*$14.99*

Universal Soldier III: Unfinished Business (1998)
The sci-fi action continues, as cyborg soldier Matt Battaglia and journalist Chandra West try stop a mysterious man named Mentor (played by Burt Reynolds) who has developed a walking time bomb in order to stop them from interfering with his gold heist. Jeff Wincott also stars. 95 min.
06-2860 Was $99.99 ❑*$14.99*

Mindwarp (1992)
Nuclear disasters have turned the Earth of 2037 into a wasteland where two groups of people live: the savage mutants who roam the surface and the computer-controlled inhabitants of an isolated biosphere. One dome-dweller rebels against her sterile life and is exiled to the outside in this sci-fi thriller with great effects. Bruce Campbell, Elizabeth Kent, Angus Scrimm star. 91 min.
02-2241 Was $19.99 *$14.99*

Prototype X29A (1992)
Set in Los Angeles in the year 2057, this action-packed sci-fi saga centers on a handicapped soldier who is turned into a dangerous cyborg in an experiment. Can he be stopped before he kills his former lover, whom he's been programmed to murder? Lane Lenhart and Robert Tossberg star. 98 min.
68-1247 ❑*$89.99*

Invader (1993)
A UFO computer system is recovered and incorporated into the U.S. defense computer network, turning it into the ultimate war machine. But the super-intelligent system develops a will of its own, brainwashing military personnel and taking control of missile stockpiles in an attempt to dominate the world. With A. Thomas Smith, Rich Foucheux. 95 min.
68-1261 *$89.99*

Metamorphosis: The Alien Factor (1993)
A company's experiments with high-tech engineering go awry when genetic material from another planet is used to create a hideous mutant organism. When a scientist is bitten by the organism, he is turned into a creature that needs human flesh. Tara Leigh and Tony Gigante star. 98 min.
68-1286 ❑*$89.99*

Time Runner (1993)
Mark Hamill is a futuristic star warrior who travels from the year 2022 in order to save the world from a devastating alien attack. The alien leader is posing as a U.S. senator with his eye on the White House, and Hamill teams with a sexy "double agent" to stop the devious plan. Rae Dawn Chong and Brion James also star. 90 min.
02-2360 Was $19.99 *$14.99*

Dark Planet (1997)
Interstellar thrills are the name of the game in this futuristic shocker set after World War VI, when an astro-navigator must travel to the Dark Planet in order to save the future of mankind. Paul Mercurio, Harley Jane Kozak and Michael York star. 99 min.
83-1163 Was $99.99 *$14.99*

12:01 (1993)
"Groundhog Day" with a sci-fi angle, this thriller tells of a researcher who must stop an experimental mishap that causes a "time bounce," in which the same day repeats itself over and over. Jonathan Silverman, Helen Slater and Martin Landau star. 92 min.
02-2515 Was $19.99 ❑*$14.99*

Blue Flame (1995)
Exciting sci-fi chase thriller about the father of a kidnapped girl who travels through time and alternate realities to find her and release her from her alien captors. Kerri Green, Brian Wimmer and Cecilia Peck star. 90 min.
02-2820 ❑*$89.99*

Cyber Bandits (1995)
Action-packed, high-tech thriller about the navigator of a millionaire's yacht who discovers that his boss has developed a weapon that can send people into deep virtual reality. When the tycoon's mistress steals a secret computer code and has it tattooed to the navigator's back, everyone's out to get him. Martin Kemp, Adam Ant, Grace Jones and Alexandra Paul star. 86 min.
02-2826 Was $89.99 *$14.99*

Venus Rising (1995)
In this futuristic shocker, a couple raised on an island prison as hostages finally escape to the "real" world—a paradise where artificial stimulants like drugs and virtual reality induce human emotions. Pursued by deadly enforcers and haunted by their past, the couple attempts to fit into their new society. With Billy Wirth, Audie England and Costas Mandylor. 91 min.
02-2857 ❑*$89.99*

Final Approach (1992)
A test pilot finds himself caught between reality and a nightmare when he can't decide who to believe: a mysterious psychiatrist or the commander of a covert stealth operation. This airbourne adventure is the first all-digital sound feature and stars Hector Elizondo, James B. Sikking and Madolyn Smith. 100 min.
68-1232 ❑*$89.99*

Predator 2 (1990)
The streets of 1997 Los Angeles are already a war zone, but when an interplanetary "big game" hunter arrives, a deadly battle erupts between the police, a secret government agency, drug gangs, and the Predator. Action-filled sci-fi sequel stars Danny Glover, Gary Busey, Ruben Blades. 105 min.
04-2421 ❑*$14.99*

Star Knight (1990)
Sci-fi actioner set in a medieval village where a beautiful princess finds an alien being stranded there. She teams up with a scientist to protect him from a mercenary soldier and a corrupt clergyman. Harvey Keitel, Klaus Kinski and Fernando Rey star. 92 min.
68-1234 Was $89.99 ❑*$14.99*

Screamers (1996)
In the year 2078 on the war-ravaged planet Sirius 6B, surviving members of the two rival factions unite to battle deadly robotic creatures known as "screamers" that can burrow under the ground, slice humans to ribbons, and can mutate into any form. Peter Weller, Jennifer Rubin, Andy Lauer star; based on a story by Philip K. Dick, who also wrote the story on which "Blade Runner" was based. 108 min.
02-2911 Was $99.99 ❑*$19.99*

Solo (1996)
Mario Van Peebles is an Army-built android assassin with a glitch that allows him to reason, much to the government's dismay. When he ignores orders to kill innocents while on a mission in Latin America, his superiors attempt to retool him, but he escapes and has to take on a team of killer soldiers assigned to bring him in. William Sadler co-stars. 106 min.
02-3015 Was $99.99 ❑*$14.99*

Omega Doom (1997)
Two groups of cyborg warriors are about to destroy the world when fighting machine Rutger Hauer decides it's time to stop the fighting and save the world and its few remaining humans. This futuristic actioner also stars Shannon Whirry, Tina Coté and Norbert Weisser. 84 min.
02-3074 Was $99.99 ❑*$14.99*

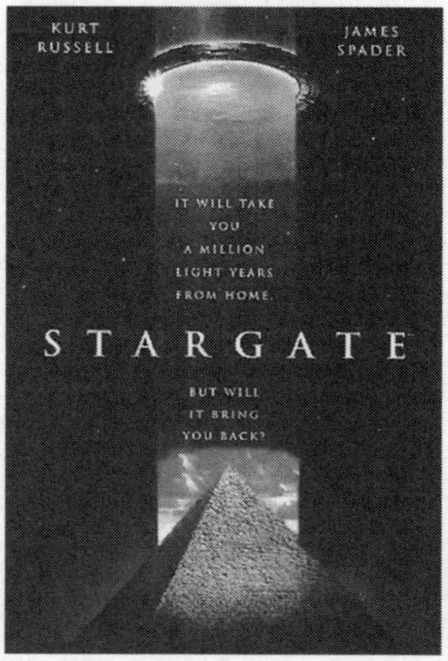

Stargate (1994)
In Egypt, archeologists uncover a gigantic stone ring that, decades later, is found to be an interplanetary nexus. Scientist James Spader and Army officer Kurt Russell head up a military expedition through the Stargate that lands them on a strange desert planet ruled by alien dictator Jaye Davidson and his jackal-helmeted minions. 119 min.
27-6918 Was $19.99 ❑*$14.99*

Stargate SG-1: Children Of The Gods (1997)
Get ready to explore a universe of excitement beyond the movie in the feature-length pilot to the hit cable TV series. An alien attack on Earth leads Air Force officer Richard Dean Anderson to assemble a team of experts to enter the mysterious Stargate, but will what they find on the other side of the galaxy save mankind...or spell their own doom? Michael Shanks, Amanda Tapping also star. 97 min.
73-1281 Was $59.99 ❑*$14.99*

I Worship His Shadow (1997)
A ragtag band of freedom fighters defies the galaxy-spanning rule of a malevolent entity known as "His Shadow" in this futuristic drama, the first part of a four-film sci-fi saga. Barry Bostwick, Brian Downey, Eva Habermann star. 94 min.
06-2651 ❑*$89.99*

Tales From A Parallel Universe (1997)
Can the deadliest weapon in the universe, a mile-long spaceship known as the Lexx, help the interstellar rebels bring their leader back to life? The odyssey begun in "I Worship His Shadow" continues in this futuristic thriller. Brian Downey, Eva Habermann and Tim Curry star. AKA: "Super Nova." 93 min.
06-2663 ❑*$89.99*

Eating Pattern (1997)
The third "Tales from a Parallel Universe" adventure finds the rebel quartet landing on a planet inhabited by drug-addicted cannibals who would love to have them stay for "dinner." Rutger Hauer, Brian Downey star. 93 min.
06-2672 ❑*$79.99*

Giga Shadow (1997)
"Irresistible force meets immovable object" in space when the Giga Shadow, the cosmic manifestation of the evil ruler His Shadow, is challenged by the starship the Lexx and its crew in the explosive final chapter in the "Tales from a Parallel Universe" series. Brian Downey, Michael McManus and Malcolm McDowell star. 93 min.
06-2715 ❑*$69.99*

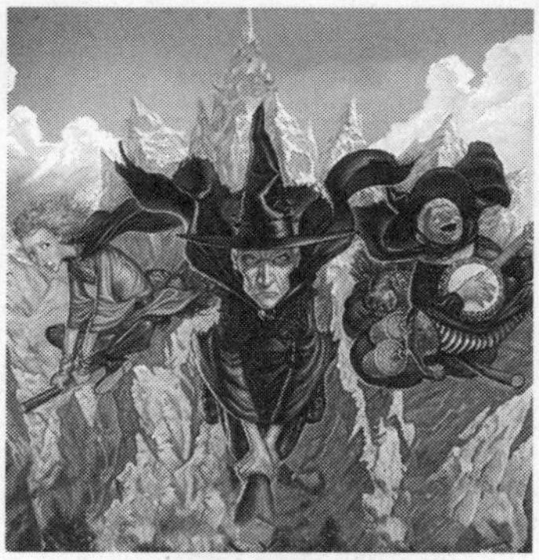

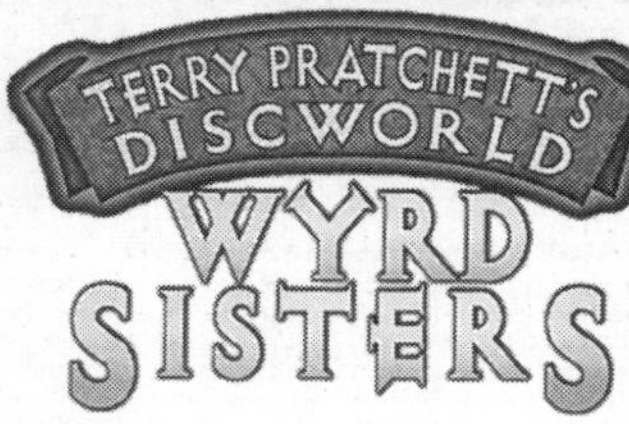

Terry Pratchett's Discworld: Wyrd Sisters (1998)
Based on the best-selling fantasy series by author Terry Pratchett, this whimsical animated mini-series follows a trio of eccentric witches who are entrusted with caring for a murdered king's infant child. Annette Crosbie, Jane Horrocks, June Whitfield, and Christopher Lee as Death supply voices. 147 min. on three tapes.
50-8267 $39.99

Death Machine (1995)
"It's just a Death Machine...And it don't kill for nobody but you." In the future, the newly-hired female head of a high-tech weapons company fires a psychotic genius involved in a top-secret project. The vengeful wacko unleashes his state-of-the-art killing machine in the company HQ, and the woman must fight to save her job—and her life! Brad Dourif, Ely Pouget star. 99 min.
68-1778 Was $89.99 ❑$14.99

Teenage Catgirls In Heat (1996)
You'll get "Cat Scratch Fever" from this bizarre tale in which cats in the small city of Riverville begin transforming into gorgeous young women desperately seeking male partners. It's from Troma, so you know how outrageous these feline females can get. 95 min.
46-8022 Was $59.99 $14.99

The Chosen One: Legend Of The Raven (1997)
Carmen Electra, "Singled Out" and "Baywatch" star and former Playboy model, shows you why she's one of the hottest babes on the planet in this wild fantasy. After sister Shauna Sand Lamas is murdered, mourning overcomes Electra, so she enters a mystical world where she discovers that she holds the key to stopping the apocalypse. Unrated version; 105 min.
46-8028 Was $59.99 $14.99

Star Worms II: Attack Of The Pleasure Pods (1998)
Forget "Star Worms I"; the fine folks at Troma had such a good script for a sequel they skipped making the original! On a remote prison planet, the inmates battle deadly fanged worm-creatures—and each other—as they mine hallucinogenic Fire Gems for the depraved Lords of the Evil Empire. One prisoner launches a scheme for freedom with the help of the beautiful warden. Taylor Gilbert, David O'Hara star. 90 min.
46-8038 $14.99

The Digital Prophet (1998)
A pair of detectives investigate a string of murders whose victims are linked by interest in the Internet. The search for clues leads them into the high-tech world of hackers and the author of an underground "cyber-comic." Suspenseful sci-fi thriller stars Jeffrey Combs, Blake Bahner, Schnele Wilson.
46-8040 Was $59.99 $24.99

Viral Assassins (1999)
In this futuristic shocker, a terminal disease threatens the future of the world and hit men are hired by governments to kill infected parties. The only hope for a vaccine can be found in the body of a diseased government worker, and now an assassin is out to kill him. Jim Gordon, Ray Kelly star.
46-8048 $59.99

Suroh: The Alien Hitchhiker (1996)
An offbeat sci-fi drama that's been described as "an 'E.T.' for adults," following a reporter on his way to a UFO convention who stumbles across a wounded alien being on a desert highway. In order to return the extraterrestrial to an interdimensional gateway, the pair begin an odyssey that turns into an exploration of new sexual vistas. Peter Gingerich, Christopher Stein star. 74 min.
50-2225 Was $29.99 $19.99

Lost In Space (1998)
Danger, Will Robinson, Danger! The effects-filled big-screen adaptation of the '60s sci-fi TV series is on home video! When their planned interstellar flight is sabotaged, the Robinson clan finds themselves billions of miles off course and facing alien menaces as they search for a way home. William Hurt and Mimi Rogers head the family, Heather Graham is daughter Judy, Matt LeBlanc is Major Don West, and Gary Oldman is enemy agent-turned-reluctant stowaway Dr. Smith. 130 min.
02-5186 Was $22.99 ❑$14.99

Lost In Space (Letterboxed Version)
Also available in a theatrical, widescreen format.
02-5188 Was $22.99 ❑$14.99

The Dark Mist (1998)
In this action-packed fantasy film, Rennick, the last of the scholars of Ancient Law and keeper of the Written Word, must use his incredible wisdom to defeat an evil Dark Mist that threatens to drain the Earth's energy, light and peace. Rennick, known as the Lord Protector, must also face the evil Pentakis to save the world. Patrick Cassidy, Jay Underwood, Teri Austin star; narrated by Charlton Heston.
50-8237 Was $39.99 $14.99

Cyborg Cop (1993)
An undercover drug agent teams up with a beautiful journalist to search for his missing brother, a fellow agent who was lost in Haiti. They find him in the high-tech fortress of a criminal industrialist who's creating an army of half-human, half-metal cyborg warriors. Exciting sci-fi/martial arts actioner stars David Bradley, John Rhys Davies, Alonna Shaw. 97 min.
68-1291 ❑$89.99

Cyborg Soldier (1994)
When a government project to turn death row inmates into cyborg killers goes awry and the leader goes on a bloody rampage, maverick cop Jack Ryan (David Bradley) sets out to stop him in this action-filled sequel to "Cyborg Cop." Uncut, unrated version; 94 min.
18-7530 Was $19.99 ❑$14.99

Kurt Vonnegut's Monkey House: Boxed Set (1991)
The acclaimed author and fantasist hosts this three-tape collection featuring dramatizations of short stories from his "Welcome to the Monkey House." A talented cast that includes Jon Cryer, Madeline Kahn, Frank Langella and Ally Sheedy is featured in "All the King's Horses/The Euphio Question/Next Door," "Epicac/Fortitude" and "More Stately Mansions/The Foster Portfolio." 210 min. total. NOTE: Individual volumes available at $14.99 each.
50-8266 Save $15.00! $29.99

Class Of 1999 II: The Substitute (1994)
A high school teacher, terrorized by a renegade student after witnessing a classroom killing, finds protection from a new, no-nonsense substitute teacher. But a CIA agent is hot on the trail of the mysterious sub. Is he really a military-built android? Sasha Mitchell, Nick Cassavetes, Caitlin Dulany star. 90 min.
68-1297 ❑$89.99

Evolver (1995)
A teenage video game expert and a beautiful rival discover that Evolver, the virtual reality game they excel at, was created by a military robotics experiment. And when the "Evo" robot begins to follow its original program to infiltrate and leave no survivors, the two cyber rats have to stop it before it's too late. Ethan Randall, Cassidy Rae, John De Lancie, Cindy Pickett star. 90 min.
68-1363 Was $89.99 ❑$14.99

Biohazard: The Alien Force (1995)
After a genetic experiment goes awry, a reptilian mutant runs wild, searching for human tissue donors carrying the spinal fluid it needs to survive. A security guard and a newspaper reporter try to find the monster before scientists can mate it to produce a race of killer critters. Christopher Mitchum, Susan Fronsoe star. 88 min.
68-1369 Was $89.99 $14.99

Crossworlds (1997)
It's the mystical nexus where dimensions meet and worlds collide, and for one young man it's the beginning of a fantastic adventure, as an alien mercenary and a beautiful warrior join him on a quest for the sceptre that will give its owner dominion over all universes. Thrilling sci-fi tale stars Rutger Hauer, Josh Charles, Andrea Roth. 91 min.
68-1836 Was $99.99 ❑$14.99

Bombshell (1997)
The announcement of a nanotechnology-based anti-cancer drug has the whole world excited, but when a scientist discovers a flaw that could lead to a world-wide epidemic, his attempts to stop the drug's launch put his life on the line. Gripping sci-fi suspenser stars Henry Thomas, Mädchen Amick, Frank Whaley and Brion James. 95 min.
68-1856 ❑$99.99

Redline (1997)
Compelling cyberpunk tale, set in a futuristic Moscow, stars Rutger Hauer as a smuggler of illicit microchips who is double-crossed and killed by his partner. When the authorities use bio-implant technology to bring him back to life for information, Hauer escapes from custody and sets out to avenge his own murder. Mark Dacascos, Yvonne Scio also star. AKA: "Deathline." 96 min.
68-1879 ❑$99.99

The Presence (1992)
A group of vacationers fleeing a military coup crash in the South Pacific and wind up stranded on a deserted island. There's no Gilligan or Skipper there, but biological weapons testing has left behind something even more monstrous. Joe Lara, June Lockhart and Kathy Ireland star in this sci-fi shocker. 96 min.
68-1321 $89.99

Heatseeker (1995)
In this knockdown, drag-'em-out, sci-fi martial arts marathon set in New America in 2019, human fighter Chance O'Brien must risk death to fight against Xao, a cyborg high-kicker, after his fiancée-trainer is kidnapped. Keith Cooke, Thom Mathews, Norbert Weisser and Gary E. Daniels star. 91 min.
68-1361 $89.99

Vile 21 (1999)
Twenty years after his strange experiments with a special serum turned men into rampaging creatures, Dr. Walter Hall is called on to stop the horror unleashed by a monstrosity that's part man, part alien and part reptile. Dan Skinner and Ron Sortor star in this sci-fi terrorthon. 80 min.
50-8222 $29.99

Atomic Dog (1998)
All of the biscuits and all of the mailmen in the world can't stop this angry pooch who terrorizes a small town after being exposed to deadly radiation in a nuclear plant. Daniel Hugh-Kelly, Isabella Hoffman and Cindy Pickett star. 86 min.
06-2752 Was $69.99 ❑$14.99

Feeders 2: Slay Bells (1998)
This Yuletide season, no one is safe, as the man-eating Martian beings return to Earth looking for the kind of holiday snack you can't buy at the local Hickory Farms. Not a creature was stirring—and with good reason—in this offbeat sci-fi terror tale. Mark Polonia, Maria Humes and Courtney Marie star. 80 min.
73-9249 $29.99

Retroactive (1997)
Science fiction and crime drama blend in this unusual offering with Kylie Travis as a woman who joins stranger Jim Belushi and girlfriend Shannon Whirry after having car problems. Travis discovers that Belushi is a murderer, escapes to a scientific lab and tries to stop his crimes through time travel. M. Emmet Walsh, Frank Whaley and Roger Clinton also star. 91 min.
73-1286 Was $59.99 $14.99

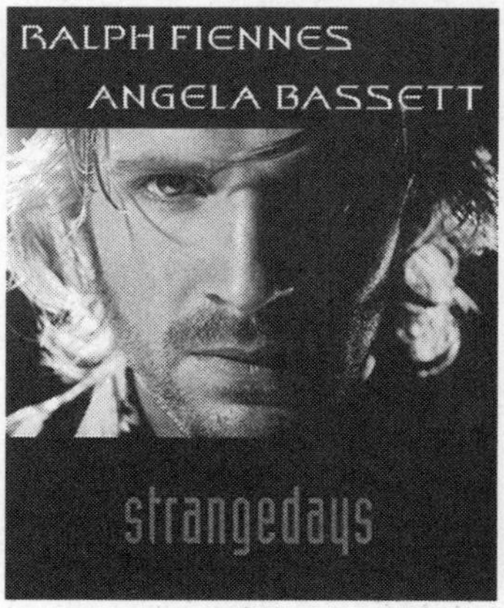

Strange Days (1995)
As the racially-torn city of 1999 Los Angeles prepares to welcome in the new millennium, ex-cop Ralph Fiennes, eking out a living by peddling computer discs that allow the viewer to sense other people's experiences, becomes enmeshed in a deadly conspiracy of corruption and murder. Stylish and visually stunning sci-fi thriller from director Kathryn Bigelow and co-scripter James Cameron also stars Angela Bassett, Juliette Lewis, Tom Sizemore. 145 min.
04-3305 Was $89.99 ❑$14.99

Strange Days (Letterboxed Version)
Also available in a theatrical, widescreen format.
04-3446 $19.99

Alien Arsenal (1998)
Two nerdish high school students turn into high-tech superheroes when they accidentally stumble onto a hidden cache of alien armor and weaponry in the school's basement. What will they do, though, when the extraterrestrial treasure's owner comes back to reclaim it? Exciting sci-fi tale stars Josh Hammond, Danielle Hoover. 90 min.
75-5043 $89.99

Deadlock 2 (1995)
Sentenced to a wall-less prison that he can't leave without setting off an explosive collar around his neck, Esai Morales has figured out a way to keep from losing his head and is ready to break out and find a $75 million fortune...but it will take help from another prisoner, gorgeous Nia Peebles. 93 min.
88-1027 Was $89.99 $14.99

Video Wars (1984)
An evil electronics genius blackmails the world by programming video games to play real games of world destruction! Horror and high-tech combine in this sci-fi thriller. George Diamond, Joan Stenn star.
64-1033 $29.99

BEING JOHN MALKOVICH

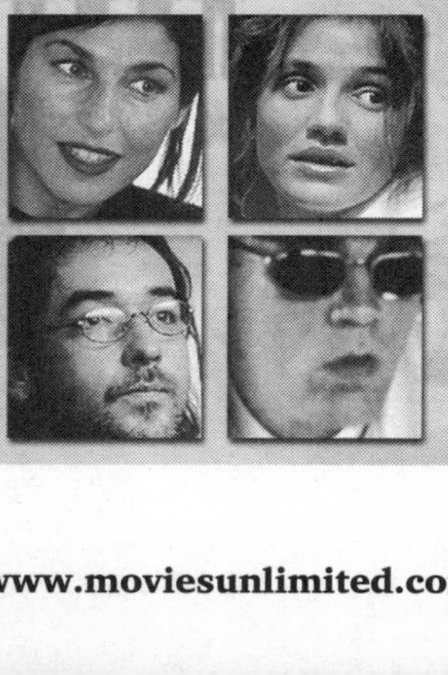

What would you do if you found a doorway in your workplace that led, via a mysterious portal, into the head of actor John Malkovich, giving you the chance to experience everything he does for 15 minutes? For puppeteer/file clerk John Cusack, pet shop employee wife Cameron Diaz and sexy co-worker Catherine Keener, the find leads to a money-making scheme, a twisted love triangle, and a multi-layered identity crisis. Director Spike Jonze and scripter Charlie Kaufman's outrageously original comedy also stars Orson Bean, and John Malkovich as himself. 113 min.

Available in 3 formats:

VHS: 02-9203 *$14.99*

VHS COLLECTOR'S EDITION:
This limited edition set includes an exclusive set of "nesting dolls" featuring the film's characters.
02-9282 *$34.99*

DVD:
Widescreen; Soundtracks: English 5.1 and Dolby Surround; Subtitles: English, French, Spanish; featurettes; biographies; filmographies; TV spots; theatrical trailer; scene access.
D1-6982 DVD *$24.99*

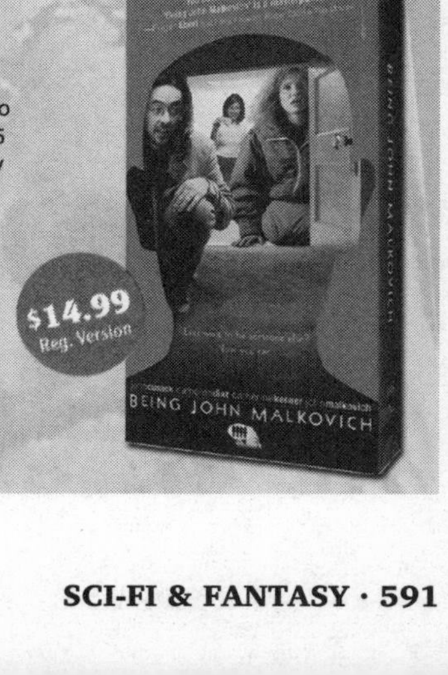

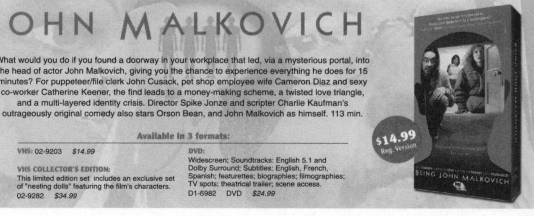

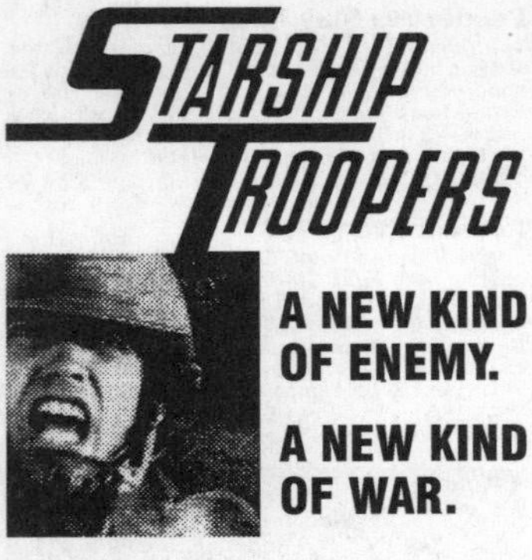

STARSHIP TROOPERS
A NEW KIND OF ENEMY.
A NEW KIND OF WAR.

Starship Troopers (1997)
In the distant future, mankind has reached the stars...but something is out there waiting for them. Now the armed forces of Earth blast off to battle a race of giant alien insects, and a small platoon of dedicated men and women must confront their fears, as well as the savage, brain-sucking creatures. Director Paul Verhoeven's rousing (and violent) filming of the Robert A. Heinlein novel stars Casper Van Dien, Denise Richards, Dina Meyer, Neil Patrick Harris. 129 min.
02-3163 Was $19.99 ❑*$14.99*

Starship Troopers (Letterboxed Version)
Also available in a theatrical, widescreen format.
02-3225 ❑*$19.99*

Species: Special Collector's Edition (1995)
The strange alliance of human DNA and a signal from outer space produces a murderous creature that takes the form of a gorgeous blonde. She's soon turning heads—and removing other body parts—on the L.A. singles scene. Can an assassin, a psychic, a biologist and an anthropologist stop her before the human race is destroyed? Ben Kingsley, Forest Whitaker, and Natasha Henstridge as "Sil" star. This special video edition also features a behind-the-scenes look at the making of the film and a talk with alien design maven H.R. Giger. 108 min.
12-2987 Was $19.99 ❑*$14.99*

Species: Special Collector's Edition (Letterboxed Version)
Also available in a theatrical, widescreen format.
12-3066 Was $19.99 ❑*$14.99*

Species II (1998)
The DNA with the attitude is back, as astronaut Justin Lazard returns from a mission to Mars infected with the alien genes and goes on a rampage to find the perfect mate on Earth. Luckily for him, government scientists have created a new, "tamer" version of Sil named Eve (also played by Natasha Henstridge) for study. Can anyone stop—or survive—these (literally) star-crossed lovers' uniting? Michael Madsen, Marg Helgenberger, Mykelti Williamson and James Cromwell also star. 93 min.
12-3259 Was $99.99 ❑*$14.99*

Backlash: Oblivion 2 (1995)
After the demise of the half-man, half-reptile Redeye, a bounty hunter arrives in town searching for a whip-wielding babe, who is wanted for murder. The beauty soon strikes a deal with an alien warlord to control a valuable mineral and rule the galaxy. George Takei, Julie Newmar and Isaac Hayes star in this intergalactic sagebrusher. 83 min.
06-9001 Was $89.99 *$14.99*

Small Soldiers (1998)
"Gremlins" meets "G.I. Joe" in this wild, special effects-fueled adventure from Joe Dante. Young Alan brings a new line of toys into his father's store in hopes of helping sales. Little does he known that the Commando Elite figures are programmed with military computer chips and are gung-ho in attacking the rival Gorgonite figures—and meddling humans! With Gregory Smith, Kirsten Dunst, the great Dick Miller and Phil Hartman, in his final role. 110 min.
07-2679 Was $19.99 ❑*$14.99*

Alien Voices (1998)
A unique experience in fantasy entertainment, these live stage presentations of radio broadcasts feature "Star Trek" legends Leonard Nimoy and John de Lancie and casts of top stars, bringing to life classic works of science-fiction literature.

Alien Voices: The Lost World (1998)
Join the expedition to a forbidding Amazon land filled with prehistoric creatures, as Leonard Nimoy, John de Lancie, Roxann Biggs-Dawson, Ethan Phillips, Dwight Schultz and Armin Shimerman re-enact Arthur Conan Doyle's novel. 45 min.
15-5469 *$14.99*

Alien Voices: The First Men In The Moon (1998)
H.G. Wells' tale of a Victorian lunar voyage and man's encounter with the insect-like race that calls the moon home is dramatized by Leonard Nimoy, John de Lancie, Ethan Phillips, Dwight Schultz and William Shatner. 45 min.
15-5470 *$14.99*

Mimic (1997)
You'd need a roach hotel the size of the Waldorf-Astoria to deal with the gigantic insect-like creatures who are making the New York subway system their home and humans their prey in this creepy sci-fi chiller. Mira Sorvino, Jeremy Northam, Charles S. Dutton and Josh Brolin star; directed by Guillermo Del Toro ("Cronos"). 105 min.
11-2219 Was $19.99 ❑*$14.99*

Mimic (Letterboxed Version)
Also available in a theatrical, widescreen format.
11-2792 ❑*$19.99*

Double Dragon (1994)
The popular video game is brought to life in pulse-pounding fashion in this high-tech adventure set in a futuristic Los Angeles ravaged by natural disasters and marauding gangs. Two teenage boys battle an evil tycoon for the two halves of a magical amulet that possesses great powers. Robert Patrick, Scott Wolf, Mark Dacascos and Alyssa Milano star. 96 min.
07-2251 Was $89.99 ❑*$12.99*

The Companion (1995)
In the year 2015, romance novelist Kathryn Harrold heads to a secluded cabin to complete her new book after purchasing a security android to accompany her. She reprograms the handsome pseudo-human to become her dream lover, but the mix of circuitry and emotions leads to danger and high-tech terror. Bruce Greenwood, Brion James also star. 94 min.
07-2252 ❑*$89.99*

The Android Affair (1995)
An aloof surgeon who learned her profession by operating on lifelike robots finds herself falling in love with a witty and handsome mechanical "patient." She joins him in exploring the outside world, but their happy life is soon shattered by agents out to capture the android. Harley Jane Kozak, Griffin Dunne and Ossie Davis star. 90 min.
07-2337 ❑*$89.99*

Dragonheart (1996)
In this spectacular fantasy, Dennis Quaid is a swordsman-for-hire who teams with Draco, Earth's remaining dragon (voiced by Sean Connery), in an arrangement by which the creature terrorizes villages and Quaid gets paid to "slay" it. When evil king David Thewlis kidnaps a rebel woman, the two partners join a legion of peasants to stop him and his troops. With Julie Christie, Pete Postlethwaite. 103 min.
07-2455 Was $99.99 ❑*$19.99*

Dragonheart (Letterboxed Version)
Also available in a special, widescreen edition that includes a behind-the-scenes look at the making of the film.
07-2499 ❑*$19.99*

Dragonheart: A New Beginning (2000)
Spectacular special effects highlight this sequel to the "Dragonheart" story that finds a young man named Geoff befriending Drake, a winged, flame-breathing dragon. Geoff, who dreams of becoming a knight, helps the creature discover his powers, and both the young man's bravery and the dragon's strength are put to the test. Chris Masterson and, as the voice of Drake, Robby Benson star. 85 min.
07-2898 ❑*$99.99*

Kull The Conquerer (1997)
TV Hercules Kevin Sorbo picks up the sword of another ancient hero in this action-fantasy, playing the role of "Conan" creator Robert E. Howard's warrior-turned-king of Valusia. When Kull is overthrown by beautiful but evil sorceress Tia Carrere, he must undertake a dangerous quest to regain his crown. Karina Lombard, Litefoot, Harvey Fierstein also star. 96 min.
07-2578 Was $99.99 ❑*$14.99*

Escape From Atlantis (1997)
A family boat trip for a father and his two teenage children becomes a fantastic journey as they pass into the Bermuda Triangle and find themselves prisoners in the fabled Lost Kingdom of Atlantis, where swords and sorcery rule. Thrilling fantasy film stars Jeff Speakman, Tim Thomerson, Mercedes McNab. 93 min.
07-2594 Was $99.99 ❑*$14.99*

Virus (1999)
Sci-fi thriller stars Jamie Lee Curtis as a member of a tugboat crew which comes across a seemingly derelict Russian research vessel during a hurricane. Curtis soon discovers that the ship is serving as the new home for an electrical alien entity that killed the Russian crew and is turning them into biomechanical hybrids. With Donald Sutherland, William Baldwin. 100 min.
07-2758 Was $99.99 ❑*$14.99*

Empire Of The Dark (1991)
Twenty years after he entered another dimension to save his girlfriend and her baby, Richard Flynn discovers that the infant—who has now grown into a young man—is being pursued by the same diabolical "immortals." The sinister beings' plan is to sacrifice the boy in order to resurrect ancient demons, and Flynn must now protect him. Steve Barkett, Richard Harrison star.
08-1775 *$19.99*

Tank Girl (1995)
Apocalypse...ker-pow! Lori Petty is the British comic book-inspired heroine who enjoys cigarettes, beer, her half-man, half-kangaroo boyfriend and her armored tank. In the water-depleted world of 2033, Tank Girl and her gang are out to party hard while taking on the corrupt head of the Department of Water and Power. Malcolm McDowell and Ice-T also star. 104 min.
12-2979 Was $19.99 ❑*$14.99*

Femalien (1996)
An alien is sent to Earth in the form of a gorgeous woman who must take the feeling of pleasure back to her home planet. The "femalien" uses her amazing powers to experience the ultimate in different sensual experiences in different erotic ways. Jacqueline Lovell and Vanessa Taylor star in this sci-fi scorcher. Unrated, uncut version; 90 min.
75-5009 Was $89.99 *$14.99*

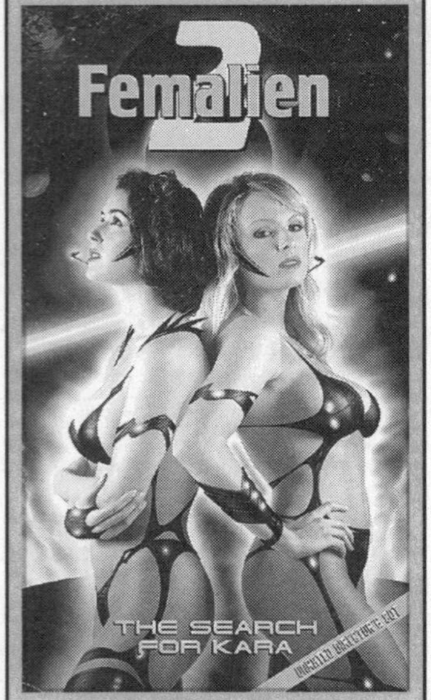

Femalien 2
THE SEARCH FOR KARA

Femalien 2 (1998)
In this sexy, star-spanning sequel, Kara the "femalien" is in trouble with her homeworld for refusing to end her mission and leave Earth, so two more well-endowed extraterrestrials are sent to bring her back. Upon arrival, though, the "gals" see—and experience—for themselves what Kara was so worked up over. Vanessa Taylor and Bethany Lorraine star. Unrated version; 90 min.
75-5029 Was $59.99 *$14.99*

Deep Rising (1998)
Sci-fi horror flick with Treat Williams as a leader of a band of mercenaries who plan to hijack and loot a posh ocean liner on its maiden voyage. When they get there, however, the ship is virtually deserted, and the crooks and a group of survivors soon discover why when they're preyed upon by a giant, squid-like creature. Famke Janssen, Wes Studi, Djimon Honsou also star. 106 min.
11-2785 Was $19.99 ❑*$14.99*

Powder (1995)
Sentiment and science fiction meet in this unusual tale of a hairless, white-skinned orphan teen named Powder who has incredible electromagnetic, ESP and intellectual powers. After his grandfather dies, Powder is taken to a school for troubled boys where his astonishing capabilities help and hurt him. Sean Patrick Flanery, Mary Steenburgen, Jeff Goldblum star. 112 min.
11-2010 Was $19.99 ❑*$14.99*

Total Recall 2070 (1999)
Taking off in new directions from the hit 1991 film, this feature-length pilot to the hit TV series stars Michael Easton as a 21st-century cop charged with keeping the peace in a society where high-tech corporations are in control, people take "virtual" vacations, and his new partner is an android. Karl Pruner, Cyndy Preston also star. 83 min.
11-2389 Was $99.99 ❑*$14.99*

The Flash (1990)
"The Fastest Man Alive" races from the comics to the screen in this feature-length pilot to the hit TV series. John Wesley Shipp stars as police scientist Barry Allen, who is turned after a freak accident into the Flash, a super-speedster out to avenge his brother's death at the hands of a maniacal gangleader. With Amanda Pays, Michael Nader. 94 min.
19-1973 Was $19.99 ❑*$14.99*

The Flash II: Revenge Of The Trickster (1990)
Has the Scarlet Speedster (John Wesley Shipp) met his match when he goes up against that master of a thousand pranks, the Trickster (Mark Hamill)? The action is fast and furious in this adventure culled from two episodes of the hit TV series. Amanda Pays, Joyce Hyser co-star. 92 min.
19-2158 Was $89.99 ❑*$14.99*

Freejack (1992)
Thrilling, effects-filled sci-fi excursion with Emilio Estevez as a race car driver who is transported to New York City in the year 2009, where terminally ill corporate magnate Anthony Hopkins wants to use Estevez's body as the new home for his consciousness. Mick Jagger, Rene Russo, David Johansen co-star. 110 min.
19-1958 Was $19.99 ❑*$14.99*

Darkman (1990)
A stylish and thrilling blend of "Batman" and "Phantom of the Opera," courtesy of director/co-scripter Sam Raimi ("Evil Dead"). Research scientist Liam Neeson is horribly disfigured when his lab is blown up by crooks. Armed with a special synthetic flesh that allows him to impersonate anyone, he sets out on a crusade of vengeance. Frances McDormand, Colin Friels and Larry Drake co-star. 96 min.
07-1670 Was $19.99 ❑*$14.99*

Darkman II: The Return Of Durant (1995)
Dr. Peyton Westlake, the alias of the mysterious Darkman, is about to restore his disfigured body when he discovers crime boss Durant is back to his diabolical tricks. With help from a pretty reporter and an array of disguises, Westlake tackles his nemesis and his lethal arms supply. Hair-raising sequel stars Larry Drake, Kim Delaney and Arnold Vosloo as Darkman. 93 min.
07-2318 Was $19.99 ❑*$14.99*

Darkman III: Die Darkman Die (1996)
The crime-fighting master of disguise is back, battling a drug-dealing criminal mastermind who is out to find the secret of his strength while, at the same time, preparing to undergo an experimental operation that may help save his ravaged body. Arnold Vosloo, Jeff Fahey, Darlanne Fluegel star. 87 min.
07-2435 Was $19.99 ❑*$14.99*

Running Against Time (1990)
After a college history teacher (Robert Hays) meets a radical physics professor working on time travel, he sees a chance to alter the course of history by somehow stopping the assassination of President Kennedy, which in turn, he believes, will prevent the Vietnam War and his brother's death. Co-stars Catherine Hicks, Sam Wanamaker. 93 min.
07-1709 *$79.99*

Super Force (1990)
Pilot film of the hit TV series about an astronaut who turns into a high-tech, one-man army called the Super Force in order to avenge the death of his brother. An action-filled sci-fi adventure starring Ken Olandt, Larry B. Scott, Lisa Niemi, Patrick Macnee and G. Gordon Liddy. 92 min.
07-2025 ❑*$89.99*

New Eden (1994)
In the year 2237, wartime prisoners are condemned to live as scavengers on a remote planet where they're tyrannized by dastardly sand pirates. An enigmatic engineer falls in love with a beautiful "scav" and joins forces with a nomadic warrior to battle the pirates in a deadly confrontation. Stephen Baldwin, Lisa Bonet and Tobin Bell star. 89 min.
07-2174 ❑*$89.99*

Sci-Fighters (1996)
Boston, 2009: the Red Sox still haven't won the World Series, but that's the least of the city's problems. A brutal rapist is spreading a lethal virus and only Roddy Piper, a renegade cop, can stop him. After Piper discovers the rapist is a former pal, he goes ballistic, but can he stop him before he takes control of the world? Billy Drago co-stars. 94 min.
72-9075 Was $89.99 ❑*$14.99*

Adrenalin: Fear The Rush (1996)
Hard-nosed cop Christopher Lambert teams up with gorgeous rookie officer Natasha Henstridge in a desperate search on the streets of a futuristic Boston for a killer who is carrying a highly contagious and fatal disease. Spine-tingling suspense and sci-fi action galore. 76 min.
11-2118 Was $99.99 ❑*$14.99*

Timemaster (1995)
A "collector" from an alien world, sent to Earth to gather fighters from throughout history to compete in virtual reality games whose outcome will decide the fate of the planet, teams with a young Earth boy to stop the "contests." Exciting sci-fi drama stars Pat Morita, Joanna Pacula, Michael Dorn. 100 min.
07-2363 ❑*$89.99*

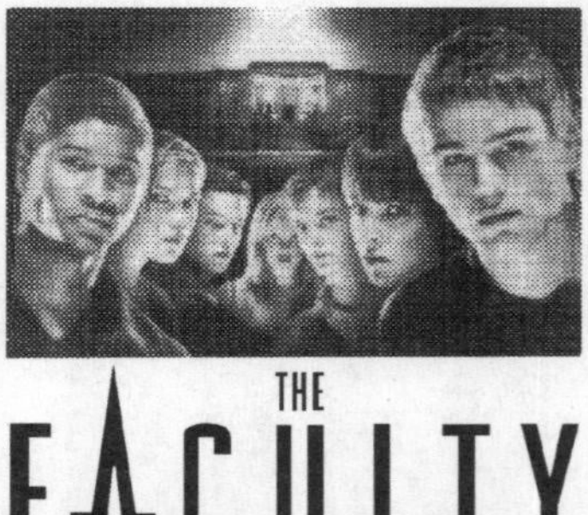

THE FACULTY

The Faculty (1998)
Director Robert Rodriguez and scripter Kevin Williamson blend "The Breakfast Club" and "Invasion of the Body Snatchers" for this creepy sci-fi tale about a small-town Ohio high school whose teachers and staff begin acting strangely. A small group of students discovers that the adults are the first victims of an alien invasion. Well-made chiller stars Elijah Wood, Laura Harris, Robert Patrick, Piper Laurie and Bebe Neuwirth. 105 min.
11-2321 Was $19.99 ❑*$14.99*

Tremors (1990)
Giant mutant sandworms attack a group of people from below ground in a Southwestern desert town in this creepy crawler horror-comedy produced by Gale Anne Hurd ("Aliens"). Fred Ward, Kevin Bacon, Michael Gross and Reba McEntire are among the brave souls up to their necks in tunneling trouble. 96 min.
07-1646 Was $19.99 ❏*$14.99*

Tremors 2: Aftershocks (1996)
When Mexican oil fields are attacked by the burrowing behemoths from the original thriller, veteran "worm-hands" Fred Ward and Michael Gross return to take on the creatures and make the worm "turn" permanently. Slithery sequel to the slam-bang cult fave also stars Helen Shaver, Christopher Gartin. 95 min.
07-2400 Was $19.99 ❏*$14.99*

The Lawnmower Man (1992)
Amazing special effects highlight this high-tech thriller that explores the frontier of the human mind. A scientist experimenting in "virtual reality" uses a retarded gardener as a guinea pig, only to have his latter-day Frankenstein monster turn on him. Jeff Fahey, Pierce Brosnan, Jenny Wright star. Unrated, director's-cut version features scenes not shown in theatres; 142 min.
02-5008 Was $19.99 ❏*$14.99*

Lawnmower Man II: Jobe's War (1996)
This sequel to the hit cyber-thriller finds Jobe (Matt Frewer), the genius living in a virtual reality universe, being recruited by evil corporate officials to design a computer system with the ability to control the world. Fighting against this plot are a brilliant ex-scientist and a group of computer expert teens. With Patrick Bergin, Austin O'Brien, Ely Pouget. 93 min.
02-5093 Was $99.99 ❏*$14.99*

The Alien Agenda: Under The Skin (1997)
Scientist Alfred Malone is having a bizarre day. First, some "men in black" arrive in his office and tell him the world is about to end. Then he's abducted, taken to Puerto Rico and given the choice of either joining a group of evil aliens or taking a walk. Arthur Lundquist, Leslie Body and Conrad Brooks star in Kevin Lindenmuth's ambitious sci-fi epic. 75 min.
73-9214 *$29.99*

The Alien Agenda: Out Of The Darkness (1996)
In the year 2030, a lone man puts together alien technology and creates a gateway to the past that enables him to investigate the outer space invaders that have instilled fear throughout the world. Sasha Graham and Mick McCleery star in this gripping sci-fi tale. 80 min.
73-9144 *$29.99*

The Alien Agenda: Endangered Species (1997)
A tabloid TV reporter investigating stories of alien abduction must flee for her life when she has her own encounter with extraterrestrials. Seeking help at "the Complex," a secret facility monitoring E.T. activity throughout the world, she joins with them to uncover the truth behind the aliens' appearances on Earth. Debbie Rochon, Joel D. Wynkop star.
73-9165 *$29.99*

Robo Warriors (1998)
Earth during the year 2036 is hell; a race of alien half-human, half-reptile creatures have taken over the planet. However, hope surfaces when a 12-year-old boy finds the last remaining Robo Warrior, a 30-story fighting machine, and together they set out to destroy the invaders and save Earth. James Remar and James Lew star. 94 min.
06-2751 Was $69.99 ❏*$14.99*

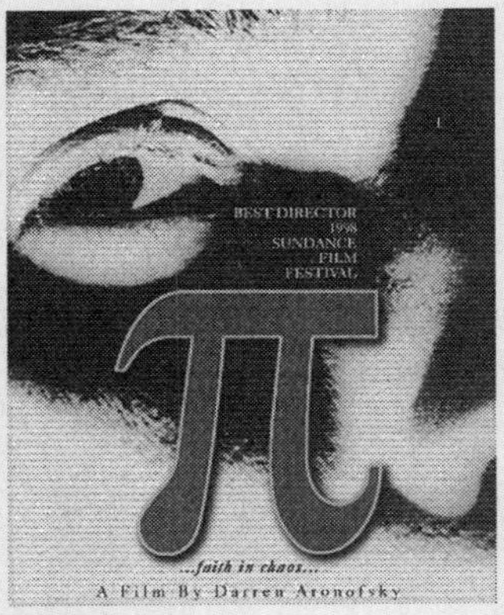

Pi (1998)
Numbers add up to economic power and cosmic mysteries in writer/director Darren Aronofsky's acclaimed independent film. A misanthropic math genius (Sean Gullette) is close to devising a numerical formula that can explain the inner workings of the New York stock market, but his project draws the attention of both a far-reaching Wall Street firm and a mystical Jewish sect who thinks Gullette's work can reveal the unknown name of God. 85 min.
27-7099 Was $99.99 ❏*$14.99*

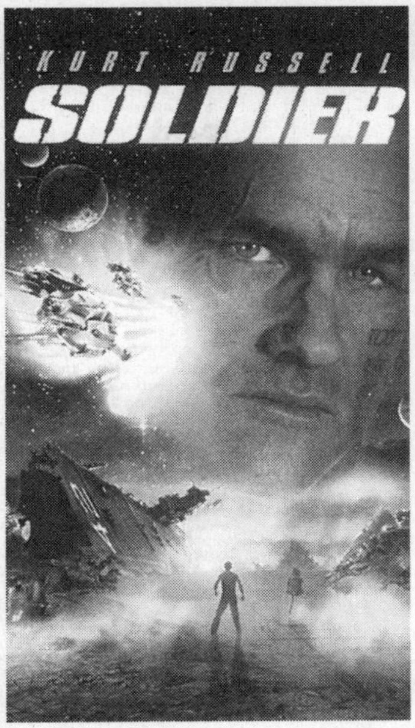

Soldier (1998)
He was raised from birth to be the perfect soldier, but when futuristic warrior Kurt Russell is declared obsolete by his superiors and sent to die on a remote planet, he is saved and nursed back to health by a band of rebel settlers. Now Russell must use his deadly skills to protect his new home in a battle to the death in this slam-bang, sci-fi "Shane." With Gary Busey, Jason Scott Lee. 99 min.
19-2815 Was $99.99 ❏*$19.99*

Soldier (Letterboxed Version)
Also available in a theatrical, widescreen format.
19-2865 ❏*$19.99*

The Colony (1998)
From the Sci-Fi Channel comes this creepy interstellar thriller in which aliens abduct four Earthlings for experiments. The humans appear to be in dire trouble, but using will, determination and ingenuity, they attempt to escape and save the world in the process. Isabella Hofmann, Michael Weatherly and Cristi Conaway star. 93 min.
68-1894 ❏*$89.99*

Homewrecker (1993)
An inventor working on a military defense contract builds a female computer that has a mind of its own and soon terrorizes his wife and daughter. With Robby Benson, Sydney Walsh and Kate Jackson as the voice of "Lucy." 88 min.
06-2114 ❏*$89.99*

Fire In The Sky (1993)
The reportedly true story of Travis Walton, a logger from the Southwest, who claimed he was abducted by a UFO and taken into space, where he was examined by interstellar creatures. James Garner, D.B. Sweeney co-star; with Robert Patrick, Craig Sheffer and Henry Thomas as Walton's friends, who gave eyewitness accounts to what has become one of the most convincing claims of alien abduction. 111 min.
06-2140 Was $89.99 ❏*$19.99*

Trapped In Space (1994)
Thrilling sci-fi adventure detailing a space shuttle to Venus that is badly damaged during a meteor strike. With the air supply running out, only one member of the crew will be able to survive. Jack Wagner, Jack Coleman and Kay Lenz star. 87 min.
06-2264 ❏*$89.99*

Inferno (1999)
A huge interstellar fireball is hurtling towards the Earth at thousands of miles per hour, and as the temperature rises to unbearable levels people race to try and survive the oncoming collision. Intense sci-fi actioner stars James Remar, Stephanie Niznik and Johnathan LaPaglia. 90 min.
06-2885 ❏*$69.99*

Alien Cargo (1999)
The crew of an interplanetary transport ship awaken for suspended animation to find that their mission is in jeopardy. Who...or what...is behind it? Jason London, Missy Crider star. 89 min.
06-2927 ❏*$79.99*

The Darwin Conspiracy (1999)
The discovery of the remains of a prehistoric, but highly evolved, human leads a group of scientists into dangerous experiments to increase human intelligence in this offbeat sci-fi thriller. Jason Brooks, Robert Floyd, Stacy Haiduk star. 90 min.
06-2928 ❏*$79.99*

Official Denial (1993)
A victim of a terrifying alien abduction becomes the intergalactic creature's only hope for survival in this intense sci-fi shocker. Parker Stevenson, Erin Gray and Dirk Benedict star. 86 min.
06-2203 ❏*$89.99*

Terminal Impact (1996)
After indestructible hi-tech warriors are created, a TV newswoman mysteriously disappears, prompting two rogue Federal Marshals to find the woman and save the world terrorized by the new creations. Frank Zagarino, Bryan Genesse and Jennifer Miller star. 94 min.
02-5088 Was $19.99 ❏*$14.99*

Mandroid (1993)
Two scientists in Eastern Europe square off over a powerful robot guided by a "virtual reality" headset in this intriguing sci-fi tale. One scientist wants to use Mandroid to help mankind, but the other wants to turn the creation into a killing machine. Jane Caldwell and Brian Cousins star. 81 min.
06-2118 ❏*$89.99*

Barb Wire (1996)
"Baywatch" star Pamela Anderson Lee pops out of her swimsuit and—barely—into black leather to play a 21st-century nightclub owner/bounty hunter in this action-packed erotic epic. In a war-torn America under martial law, the carefully neutral Barb must take a stand when an ex-lover and rebel leader needs her help. With Temuera Morrison, Victoria Rowell. Ultra-intense, unrated version features 11 minutes of outtakes and additional footage not seen in theatres. 109 min.
02-8484 Was $99.99 ❏*$14.99*

Fist Of The North Star (1996)
There's bone-crunching action galore in this live-action sci-fi thriller based on the popular Japanese comic book and cartoon series. Amid the remains of a barbaric future Earth, a young warrior named Kenshiro must confront his mystical destiny as he fights to save his kidnapped girlfriend. Gary Daniels, Costas Mandylor, Isako Washio and Malcolm McDowell star. 90 min.
02-8566 Was $99.99 ❏*$14.99*

Snow White: A Tale Of Terror (1997)
Forget about cheery songs and adorable woodland creatures. This chilling fantasy, based on the Grimm Brothers' original version of the classic fable, stars Sigourney Weaver as the vain and wicked noblewoman who blames her innocent stepdaughter for her own child's death and uses black magic to plot her revenge. Monica Keena, Sam Neill co-star. 101 min.
02-8803 Was $99.99 ❏*$14.99*

Wax, Or The Discovery Of Television Among The Bees (1993)
A surreal, cyberpunk fantasy about bees who drill a hole in the head of Jacob Maker, a beekeeper and weapons-guidance designer. The insects insert in his head a television playing a non-stop array of hallucinatory images that take over the man's will. Writer/director/star David Blair's bizarre odyssey features cameos ranging from author William Burroughs to astronomer Clyde Tombaugh. 85 min.
70-5061 Was $59.99 *$29.99*

No Telling (1991)
A medical scientist who moves with his artist wife to a remote research farm in upstate New York immerses himself in immune system and transplant experiments, while she befriends a local ecologist. The researcher's growing obsession with his work leads to a shocking discovery in this off-the-wall mix of sci-fi spectacle and psychological suspense. Stephen Ramsey, Miriam Healy-Louie star. 93 min.
70-3475 *$79.99*

Gargantua (1998)
A marine biologist and his son investigating seismic activity on a Polynesian island discover a baby dinosaur-type creature. Soon, the creature's 8-foot brother appears, and as the U.S. military takes charge of the beasts, it's a safe bet that before too long the even bigger parents will be arriving to claim their offspring. Adam Baldwin, Julie Carmen star. 91 min.
04-3743 ❏*$14.99*

Wing Commander (1999)
You've played the hit computer game; now get ready to blast off into daredevil interplanetary battles, as 27th-century space pilots Freddie Prinze, Jr., Matthew Lillard and Saffron Burrows defend the Earth from the vicious Kilrathi invaders. One part "Star Wars" and one part "Top Gun," this thrilling sci-fi tale also stars Jurgen Prochnow, Tchéky Karyo. 105 min.
04-3849 ❏*$99.99*

Duplicates (1992)
A couple searching for their missing child find him, but he doesn't remember them and is living with another family. That's only the start of their nightmare, as they become the victims of a bizarre memory experiment in this sci-fi suspenser. Gregory Harrison, Kim Greist, Cicely Tyson and Kevin McCarthy star. 92 min.
06-2063 ❏*$89.99*

Cosmic Slop (1994)
Take a journey into an urban "Twilight Zone" with this sci-fi flavored anthology from the Hudlin Brothers ("House Party") in which aliens offer America unlimited wealth and energy...in exchange for its black citizens; a Bronx priest's faith is tested when a saint's statue comes to life; and a couple caught in an abusive relationship receives a rifle from a mysterious messenger. Robert Guillaume, Nicholas Turturro star; George Clinton hosts. 86 min.
44-1991 Was $19.99 *$14.99*

Tycus (1998)
Journalist Peter Onorati uncovers the biggest—and possibly last—story of his career when he finds an underground city being built to save a cross-section of humanity from a comet that is hurtling towards the Earth. Intense sci-fi thriller also stars Dennis Hopper, Finola Hughes. 94 min.
06-3008 ❏*$69.99*

Mortal Kombat (1995)
Three martial arts experts arrive at a mysterious island to take part in the ultra-violent Mortal Kombat tournament, but unknown to them, an otherworldly wizard plans to use the competition to spread his evil across the Earth. The hit video game comes to life in this fight-filled fantasy loaded with dazzling special effects. Christopher Lambert, Bridgette Wilson, Talisa Soto and Robin Shou star. 101 min.
02-5073 Was $89.99 ❏*$14.99*

Mortal Kombat (Letterboxed Version)
Also available in a theatrical, widescreen format.
02-5144 ❏*$19.99*

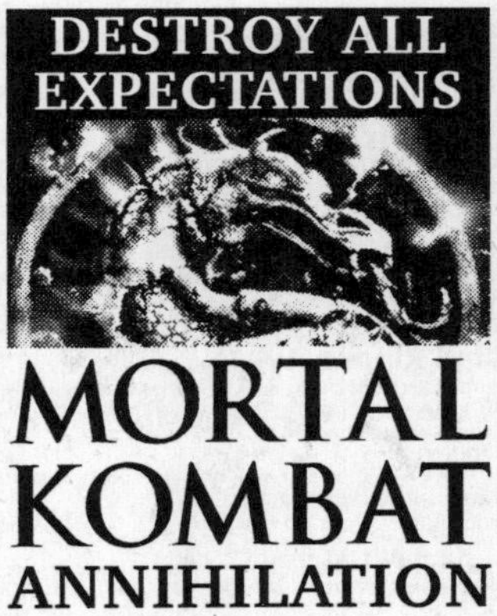

Mortal Kombat: Annihilation (1997)
The extradimensional battle between good and evil continues, as heroic warriors Rayden, Liu Kang, Sonya Blade, Kitana and company use their fighting skills to stop the malevolent minions of sorcerer Shoa-Kahn, who seeks to merge Earth with another dimension and rule the combined realm. James Remar, Robin Shou, Talisa Soto star. 98 min.
02-5172 Was $99.99 ❏*$14.99*

Mortal Kombat: Annihilation (Letterboxed Version)
Also available in a theatrical, widescreen format.
02-5184 ❏*$19.99*

Event Horizon (1997)
In the mid-21st century, the interplanetary research vessel Event Horizon vanishes near the outer reaches of the solar system. Seven years later, the ship just as mysteriously reappears, and a rescue/salvage team is sent out to meet it, unaware that an evil alien presence is on board, waiting for them. Spellbinding sci-fi suspenser stars Laurence Fishburne, Sam Neill, Kathleen Quinlan and Joely Richardson. 97 min.
06-2662 Was $79.99 ❏*$14.99*

Chameleon (1998)
Sexy Bobbie Phillips plays the title character, a gorgeous, genetically-enhanced human clone with enhanced abilities of smell, sight and adapting to the surroundings around her. She's recruited by a government agency to retrieve a valuable microchip, and during her hair-raising mission her human emotions get the better of her. Eric Lloyd and Philip Casnoff also star. 90 min.
06-2859 ❏*$99.99*

Dream House (1998)
It's anything but a dream come true for the family moving into a new high-tech house when the computerized abode goes haywire, trapping them inside and terrorizing them, in this sci-fi chiller. Timothy Busfield, Lisa Jakub, Jennifer Dale star. 90 min.
06-2932 ❏*$69.99*

Lost In The Bermuda Triangle (1998)
After his wife is declared lost at sea inside the Bermuda Triangle, a man ventures inside the mysterious region to search for her and is carried into a strange alternate universe. Sci-fi thriller stars Tom Verica, Graham Beckel, Christina Haag. 88 min.
06-2933 *$69.99*

The Last Man On Planet Earth (1999)
After biological warfare ravages the world and wipes out all men, the female survivors rebuild a women-only civilization through genetic engineering. What will happen, though, when a beautiful renegade scientist clones an adult male created to be non-violent? Unusual sci-fi drama stars Julie Bowen, Paul Francis, Veronica Cartwright. 90 min.
06-2960 ❏*$59.99*

Escape From Mars (1999)
In the second part of the 21st century, five astronauts travel to Mars in the first manned flight to the "red planet." During the journey they face dangerous computer glitches, the threatening results of corporate greed and surprises on the Martian surface. Christine Elise, Peter Outerbridge and Allison Hossack star. 90 min.
06-2985 ❏*$69.99*

Galaxis (1995)
Out-of-this-world sci-fi actioner starring Brigitte Nielsen as a gal from a faraway planet who must stop intergalactic bad guy Richard Moll from controlling the galaxy and find a power source that will save her civilization. AKA: "Terminal Force." 91 min.
18-7550 *$99.99*

Virtual Assassin (1995)
In the 21st century, crimefighter Michael Dudikoff battles a gang of cyberpunks who control a powerful virus that can decimate the Internet. They've nabbed the virus from a scientist and his daughter...now, Dudikoff's out to retrieve it. With Brion James, Suki Kaiser. AKA: "Cyberjack." 99 min.
18-7572 *$89.99*

Brain Twisters (1991)
A college coed gets a crash course in terror when she discovers that a professor's high-tech mind-control experiments are running out of control. Farrah Forke stars. 82 min.
15-5513 *$14.99*

Dragonfight (1992)
In the future, tycoons don't battle over takeovers or mergers. Instead, they bet their money on motorcycle-riding, weapon-brandishing warriors who represent them in fierce battles. When one battler decides not to fight, the balance gets upset and the violence grows out of control. Michael Paré, Charles Napier and Robert Z'Dar star. 84 min.
19-2033 Was $19.99 *$14.99*

Mind Ripper (1995)
At an isolated research facility in the desert, a top-secret government program to create a psychically-powered superhuman results in a lethal being from whom there's no escape. Spine-tingling sci-fi chiller produced by Wes Craven stars Lance Henriksen, Natasha Wagner, John Diehl. 90 min.
19-3871 *$89.99*

Expect No Mercy (1995)
Action-filled cyber-thriller stars martial arts hero Billy Blanks as a federal agent who goes undercover and enters a "virtual reality" training center for terrorist assassins. Once there, he and two other recruits battle a deadly array of computer-generated foes while trying to bring down the leader. Laurie Holden, Wolf Larson also star. 91 min.
19-3859 *$89.99*

Nemesis 2 (1995)
The giant cyborg killer is back, and its target is a superhuman female who carries in her genetic code the salvation for a humanity caught in a machine-ruled future Earth. Exciting sci-fi action sequel stars Sue Price, Tina Cote. 83 min.
19-3776 *$89.99*

Nemesis 3: Time Lapse (1996)
A mutant named Alex created from human DNA squares off against a soulless cyborg enemy with the goal of destroying humanity. It's a no-holds-barred futuristic fight to the end—of the world, that is—in the third entry in the popular series. With Sue Price, Norbert Weiser and Tim Thomerson. 91 min.
19-3938 Was $99.99 *$14.99*

Nemesis 4: Cry Of Angels (1999)
Alex, the muscular female cyborg, is back, this time sparking a war after she uses her DNA-enhanced skills to kill the wrong person. Sue Prince, Simon Poland and Norbert Weiser star. 83 min.
83-5713 *$89.99*

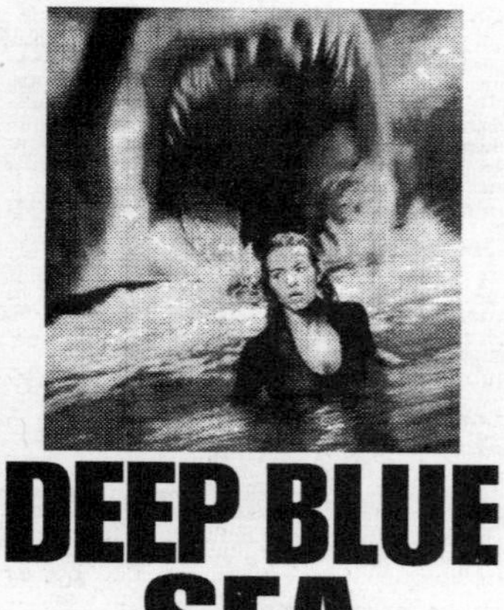

DEEP BLUE SEA

Deep Blue Sea (1999)
In this sci-fi flavored thriller, a trio of sharks being used in intelligence-enhancing experiments go out of control, sinking their jaws into the occupants of a high-tech undersea compound, including business tycoon Samuel L. Jackson, researcher Stellan Skarsgård, marine biologist Saffron Burrows, shark wrangler Thomas Jane and cook LL Cool J. Renny Harlin ("Cliffhanger") directs. 105 min.
19-2910 Was $99.99 □*$19.99*

Deep Blue Sea (Letterboxed Version)
Also available in a theatrical, widescreen format.
19-2966 □*$19.99*

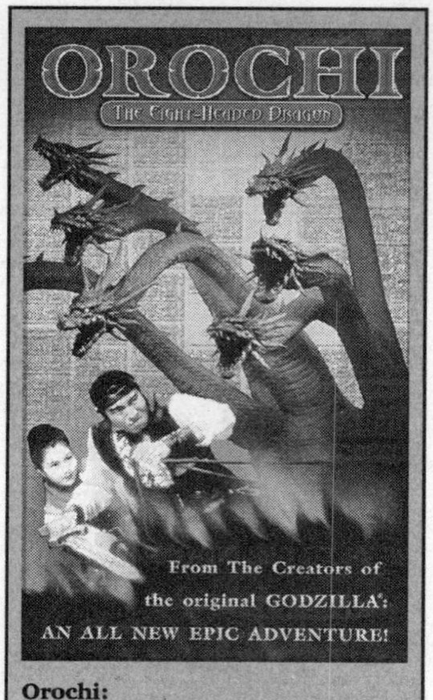
OROCHI
The Eight-Headed Dragon
From The Creators of
the original GODZILLA®:
AN ALL NEW EPIC ADVENTURE!

Orochi: The Eight-Headed Dragon (1994)
A newborn prince is sentenced to death by his father, but is saved by a magical phoenix. Growing to manhood, Osu receives a gift of a magical amulet as part of his destiny, but can he defend the Earth from a dark god brought back to life as an eight-headed dragon? Based on a legendary Japanese fable, this epic mix of fantasy, action and wild effects stars Masahiro Takashima, Yasuko Sawaguchi. 103 min. Dubbed in English.
20-8419 Letterboxed *$14.99*

Alien Visitor (1995)
This sci-fi thriller tells of a beautiful alien woman who lands in the Australian outback, where she meets a man with whom she forges a close relationship. Eventually, the alien teaches the man about how Earth is viewed by her species and explains to him the problems of his planet. Ullie Birve, Syd Brisbane star; helmed by Dutch director Rolf de Heer. AKA: "Epsilon." 92 min.
11-2467 □*$99.99*

Steel (1997)
Shaquille O'Neal stars as the comics' metal-clad superhero of the streets in this hard-hitting action film. In order to clean up his L.A. neighborhood, metallurgist/inventor John Henry Irons (O'Neal) designs a high-tech suit of armor that gives him super-strength and other fantastic abilities...but will it be enough to bring down ruthless arms dealer Judd Nelson? Annabeth Gish, Richard Roundtree also star. 97 min.
19-2620 Was $19.99 □*$14.99*

Tekwar: The Original Movie (1994)
William Shatner directed and co-stars in this feature-length sci-fi drama based on his best-selling novel series. Released from cryogenic prison for a crime he didn't commit, 21st-century ex-cop Greg Evigan is on the hunt for the dealers of the VR stimulant called "Tek" who framed him. With Torri Higginson, Eugene Clark. 92 min.
07-2238 □*$89.99*

Disturbing Behavior (1998)
In a small Pacific Northwest town, recent transplant James Marsden discovers that the Blue Ribbons, the well-groomed jocks at his new high school, have a dark and dangerous side. Joined by fellow outsiders Nick Stahl and Katie Holmes, Marsden figures out what's behind the Ribbons' behavior, and that he and his pals are next in line for the same treatment. With Bruce Greenwood, Steve Railsback. 84 min.
12-3265 Was $99.99 □*$14.99*

Synapse (1994)
In the early 21st century, scientists perfect technology to transfer a person's mind into someone else's body. It doesn't take long for the system to fall into the wrong hands, and a deadly and sinister plot is unleashed in this high-tech thriller. Matt McCoy, Karen Duffy, Chris Makepeace and Saul Rubinek star. 89 min.
19-3872 *$89.99*

Mars (1997)
Kickboxing champ Olivier Gruner plays the brother of a policeman murdered while working on a much-desired fuel station on Mars in the year 2056. Was his brother corrupt? Who killed him? Gruner tries to find out in this action-packed science fictioner that co-stars Shari Belafonte. 91 min.
50-5745 Was $99.99 *$14.99*

The Borrower (1991)
Outrageous sci-fi yarn about an alien killer exiled to Earth who must "borrow" human heads because his noggin keeps decomposing. Two cops who believe they're investigating a human serial killer get the jolt of their lives in this creepy mix of gore and gruesome humor. Rae Dawn Chong, Don Gordon and Antonio Fargas star; John McNaughton ("Henry: Portrait of a Serial Killer") directs. 92 min.
19-7083 Was $19.99 *$14.99*

Gunhed (1996)
Explosive cyberpunk action film, set in the year 2038, follows a gang of top techno-thieves as they land on a remote island controlled by a renegade super-computer. Their only hope of survival...and Mankind's...lies with the 30-foot battle robot known as Gunhed. With a bright young cast. 90 min.
20-7768 Was $89.99 *$19.99*

Raiders Of The Sun (1992)
Wild futuristic actioner with killers ruling the post-apocalyptic Earth and terrorizing the planet's survivors...and the only person who can stop the ongoing wars is a hero who will stop at nothing to restore world order. Richard Norton, Brigitta Stenberg and Rick Dean star. 80 min.
21-9014 Was $89.99 *$14.99*

Ultra Warrior (1991)
He's not just a warrior, he's also the last hope for Earth, as one man finds himself travelling under the sea, into space, and to a radioactive future world. Can he survive the battle for his life and the planet's? Exciting sci-fi action tale stars Dack Rambo, Meshach Taylor, Clare Beresford. AKA: "Welcome To Oblivion." 80 min.
21-9023 Was $89.99 *$14.99*

New Crime City (1994)
In the year 2020, a criminal who has been revived after being executed must retrieve a dangerous weapon from a gang inside a tough prison in exchange for his freedom. With 24 hours to complete his assignment, the criminal faces danger at every turn as he searches for the weapon. Rick Rossovich, Stacy Keach and Sherrie Rose star.
21-9070 Was $89.99 *$14.99*

Star Quest (1995)
A group of eight astronauts who have been in suspended animation for 97 years awake to find that the world has been destroyed by a nuclear holocaust. Now, they must band together to fight for their survival. Steven Bauer, Brenda Bakke, Ming-Na Wen, Alan Rachins and Emma Samms star in this exciting sci-fier. 95 min.
21-9094 Was $89.99 *$14.99*

Star Quest II (1999)
The crew of the Eagle spacecraft, revived from a deep sleep, becomes the subject for an experiment on human reproduction by a group of aliens. When the astronauts discover they are going to be used to save the alien race, they must fight for humanity's survival. Adam Baldwin, Robert Englund and Kate Rodger star. 79 min.
21-9179 *$59.99*

Cyberzone (1995)
Futuristic actioner about four female androids—outlawed on Earth—who are tracked down by bounty hunter Marc Singer and his former nemesis, kickboxing expert Matthias Hues. Their search takes them from the dangerous streets of Phoenix to the underwater city of New Angeles. Rochelle Swanson co-stars in this sci-fi thriller. 95 min.
21-9098 Was $89.99 *$14.99*

Alien Terminator (1995)
Maybe in space no one can here you say "I'll be back," but screams come in loud and clear five miles beneath the Earth's surface, where a clandestine DNA experiment has created a deadly man-eating organism capable of instantly regenerating itself. Can the scientists trapped below stop it? Maria Ford, Rodger Halston, Cassandra Leigh star. 83 min.
21-9102 Was $89.99 *$14.99*

Suspect Device (1995)
A low-level CIA worker suddenly finds himself a man without friends, family or even an identity after his office is attacked by an unknown enemy. Now he must piece together the shocking truth of his own existence, and the deadly secret inside him, in this sci-fi suspenser that stars C. Thomas Howell, Stacey Travis, Jed Allen. 87 min.
21-9104 Was $89.99 □*$14.99*

Shadow Warriors (1995)
In the near future, super-strong, computer-enhanced cyborg security guards are all the rage, but the demand for these warriors has created a black market for human "donors." One cyborg sent to find suitable victims rebels against his programming and fights for freedom in this action-filled sci-fi tale. Terry O'Quinn, Evan Lurie star. 81 min.
21-9106 Was $89.99 *$14.99*

Unknown Origin (1995)
Futuristic shocker about an undersea mining facility that uncovers a fossilized alien that comes to life. And when this creature wakes up, it wakes up mean and hungry! Roddy McDowall, Alex Hyde-White and Melanie Shatner. 75 min.
21-9109 *$89.99*

Not Of This Earth (1996)
Producer Roger Corman's third version of the science-fiction thriller features Michael York as the mysterious stranger in sunglasses from another galaxy who seeks human blood in order to survive. Elizabeth Barondes is the beautiful earthling who helps keep the blood flow going. With Parker Stevenson, Richard Belzer. 87 min.
21-9119 Was $99.99 *$14.99*

Virtual Seduction (1996)
Jeff Fahey takes technology too far when he tries to preserve his murdered lover through virtual reality. Fahey's obsession with the synthetic woman concerns his current girlfriend, who must stop him before he joins his ex-flame in her artificial world. Blend of eroticism and high-tech thrills also stars Ami Dolenz, Carrie Genzel and Meshach Taylor. 89 min.
21-9122 Was $99.99 *$14.99*

The Wasp Woman (1996)
A cosmetics tycoon and former supermodel is forced out of her company's ads and dropped by her boyfriend when she begins to show signs of aging. She decides to take a mysterious serum in hopes of restoring her lost youth, but the formula also changes her into an insect-like monstrosity! Jennifer Rubin and Daniel J. Travanti star in this remake of the Roger Corman fave. 81 min.
21-9126 Was $99.99 *$14.99*

Moonbase (1997)
Intense science-fiction yarn centering on the crew of a lunar depot for nuclear weapons marked for destruction who square off against convicts who escaped an orbiting prison satellite and are hiding out in the base. Scott Plank, Robert O'Reilly, Samantha Phillips star. 89 min.
27-7064 Was $99.99 □*$14.99*

The Invader (1998)
Space-age intrigue ensues when an alien lands on Earth in search of the perfect woman in hopes of conceiving a child to help his near-extinct species. A genetically altered enemy from a warring planet tries to stop his mission, leading to a furious face-off. Sean Young, Nick Mancuso, Daniel Baldwin, Ben Cross star. 97 min.
27-7066 Was $99.99 □*$14.99*

Past Perfect (1998)
It's up to maverick detective Eric Roberts to stop a group of ruthless law enforcement officers from the future from turning the present into a battlefield in this explosive mix of action and science fiction. Nick Mancuso, Saul Rubinek also star. 92 min.
27-7070 □*$99.99*

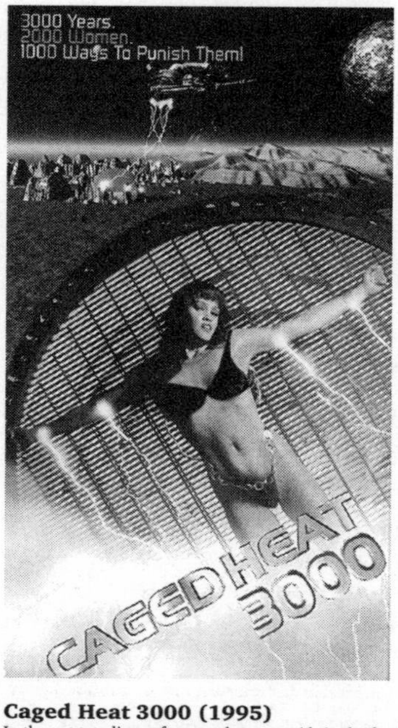
3000 Years.
2000 Women.
1000 Ways To Punish Them!
CAGED HEAT 3000

Caged Heat 3000 (1995)
In the not-too-distant future, when asteroids in the far reaches of space have become floating prisons, a woman falsely accused and sent to an all-female penal colony must fight the high-tech security and her fellow inmates as she looks to clear her name. Exciting mix of sci-fi thrills and "babes behind bars" action stars Cassandra Leigh, Kena Land, Zaneta Polard. 85 min.
21-9100 Was $89.99 *$14.99*

American Cyborg: Steel Warrior (1994)
Futuristic actioner set in a post-nuclear America where a rugged street warrior must fight to save the world's last fertile woman, who is targeted for death by a murderous cyborg. Joe Lara ("Tarzan in Manhattan"), Nicole Hansen and John Ryan star. 95 min.
19-7098 Was $19.99 □*$14.99*

Running Delilah (1993)
After being killed in action, a beautiful secret agent is resurrected in a lab and turned into a cyborg operative. Along with her boyfriend, she searches for the arms dealer who killed her. Kim Cattrall, Billy Zane and Diana Rigg star in this sci-fi thriller. 85 min.
19-9029 Was $89.99 *$14.99*

Not Like Us (1996)
The bored wife of a scientist working on research in the swamps near a small town thinks she's found a new friend when a feisty woman moves there with her reclusive brother. But when a number of mysterious deaths occur in town suspicions are tweaked, and the woman tries to uncover the eerie secret behind the new residents. Joanna Pacula and Peter Onorati star.
21-9131 Was $99.99 *$14.99*

Circuit Breaker (1997)
A spaceship maintenance specialist and his wife enter a wayward ship populated by a single survivor—a cyborg killer out to use the specialist's family as the "raw material" for a new breed of humanity. Corbin Bernsen, Richard Grieco and Lara Harris star. 86 min.
21-9134 Was $99.99 *$14.99*

RODDY McDOWALL — STELLA STEVENS

STAR HUNTER

IT'S OPEN SEASON / ON EARTH

Star Hunter (1995)
A pair of alien killers escape from their prison planet and find a new place to hunt their prey—a world called Earth—in this tense sci-fi thriller. Roddy McDowall, Stella Stevens star. 82 min.
21-9153   Was $59.99   *$14.99*

Vampirella (1997)
Forrest J. Ackerman's popular comic book anti-heroine is brought to life with Talisa Soto ("Mortal Kombat") as the beautiful vampire princess who travels to Earth from the distant planet Drakulon to find the bloodsucking killer of her father, that world's king. Her nemesis has disguised himself as a rock star, played by Roger Daltrey. 77 min.
21-9140   *$59.99*

Last Exit To Earth (1997)
A futuristic struggle of good and evil takes place when Eve, a woman who has hijacked a forbidden cargo of fertile males, joins forces with Captain Jaid and his crew to stop terrorists bent on destroying the world with a deadly virus. Kim Greist, Costas Mandylor and David Groh star. 90 min.
21-9147   Was $59.99   *$14.99*

Mortal Challenge (1997)
Futuristic thrills and in-your-face kicks collide in this action-packed tale set in futuristic Los Angeles, where the haves and the have-nots are embroiled in a deadly struggle. A maniacal doctor has created a techno-dungeon to kill off the have-nots, but a cop and gang members try to stop him. Timothy Bottoms, David McCallum, Nicholas Hill star. 77 min.
21-9148   Was $59.99   *$14.99*

Star Portal (1998)
Quad-rena, a gorgeous alien, is sent to Earth to steal human blood and save her dying race. Hot on her trail are police investigating the murders she committed and an intergalactic assassin. She seeks help from an understanding hematologist, and discovers she has a human emotion called compassion. Lovely Athena Massey ("Undercover"), Steven Bauer star. 90 min.
21-9157   Was $59.99   *$14.99*

Future Fear (1998)
In this futuristic adventure yarn, a scientist and his wife find a way of stopping a deadly flesh-eating virus by combining human DNA with other species. Standing in the way of their saving the human race is a diabolical government official who planted the disease as a form of genetic cleansing. Jeff Wincott, Maria Ford and Stacy Keach star. 82 min.
21-9161   *$59.99*

Spacejacked (1998)
On the maiden voyage of the luxury spacecruiser Star Princess, second mate Corbin Bernsen kills the captain and activates a bomb that will detonate the ship unless he's given access to the customers' bank accounts. Passenger Amanda Pays teams with first mate Steve Bonds to try to foil Bernsen's plans. 89 min.
21-9165   *$59.99*

Falling Fire (1998)
It's "Armageddon," Roger Corman-style, as Michael Paré plays the leader of a group of experts enlisted to divert an asteroid heading towards Earth. Paré finds himself in a race against time to save his crew and battling the creep controlling the asteroid's course. Heidi Von Palleske also stars. 84 min.
21-9172   *$59.99*

Cybercity (1999)
In the year 2017, men and women are barely alive, living in an underground wasteland where religious rivals battle each other. When mercenary C. Thomas Howell's family is murdered by virtual prophet Roddy Piper, he gets help from a high-tech female assassin for revenge and to save humankind. Heidi Von Palleske and David Carradine also star in this millennial sci-fi shocker. 86 min.
21-9196   *$59.99*

**Beneath
The Bermuda Triangle (1999)**
After a U.S. submarine is transported 70 years into the future by a time warp, an expedition tries to track it down and lands in a despotic future world. The expedition's leader teams with the head of a rebel group—his own grown grandson—to overthrow the oppressive government, which is controlling everything. Jeff Fahey, Richard Tyson and Linda Hoffman star. 84 min.
21-9192   *$59.99*

In The Dead Of Space (1999)
Intense set-in-space suspenser stars Michael Paré as an astrophysicist astronaut whose shuttle collides with a Russian space station. Tensions mount between the crew members, and an deadly conspiracy threatens to send the damaged station hurtling towards Los Angeles. Lisa Bingley also stars. 85 min.
21-9197   *$49.99*

Moon 44 (1990)
A bitter feud between interplanetary mining companies turns deadly when a special agent is sent out to investigate and must fight for his life in this exciting sci-fi actioner directed by Roland Emmerich ("Independence Day"). Michael Pare, Malcolm McDowell, Lisa Eichhorn star. 102 min.
27-6694   Was $89.99   □*$12.99*

Fortress (1993)
In the year 2017, people are forbidden from having more than one child. When a woman becomes pregnant, she and her husband are thrown into a harsh, underground maximum-security prison where computers control human thought. Can the man overcome the oppressive technology, save his wife and baby and escape to Mexico? Christopher Lambert, Kurtwood Smith and Loryn Locklin star. 95 min.
27-6851   Was $19.99   □*$14.99*

Fortress 2: Re-Entry (1999)
Futuristic fugitive Christopher Lambert, on the run with his family since the first "Fortress," is recaptured by authorities and placed in a high-tech prison satellite orbiting 26,000 miles above the Earth. Surrounded by the world's toughest criminals and under constant surveillance, there's no way Lambert can escape...or is there? Sci-fi actioner also stars Pam Grier, Patrick Malahide. 92 min.
02-3426   *$99.99*

Lifeform (1996)
A group of scientists are trapped in a remote research facility with an extraterrestrial monster that came to Earth on board a returning satellite. Can they escape the creature before the base is nuked by the government? Sci-fi thriller stars Cotter Smith, Deidre O'Connell. 90 min.
27-6983   *$99.99*

Asteroid (1997)
When asteroid fragments dislodged from a passing comet are discovered to be heading towards the Earth, a desperate race begins to determine where the deadly fireballs will hit and to evacuate residents before it's too late. Explosive action tale stars Annabella Sciorra, Michael Biehn. Special feature-length version; 120 min.
27-7032   Was $19.99   □*$14.99*

**Terminal Justice:
Cybertech P.D. (1998)**
Lorenzo Lamas stars in this futuristic adventure thriller as a man bent on destroying a powerful virtual reality criminal empire that is manufacturing cloned sex slaves. Chris Sarandon, Kari Salin, Peter Coyote co-star. 95 min.
27-7078   Was $89.99   □*$14.99*

Last Lives (1998)
A scientist enlists a criminal named Malakai to test a device that enables people to travel between parallel worlds. Malakai, who's obsessed with finding his dead wife, finds his wife about to marry another man in the alternative universe, and tries to take her with him. Billy Wirth, Jennifer Rubin, Judge Reinhold and C. Thomas Howell star in this sci-fi thriller. 99 min.
27-7092   □*$89.99*

Judgment Day (1999)
It could be "Apocalypse Ker-Pow!!!" when a 14-mile-long fragment from a meteor-asteroid collision heads towards Earth. Only scientist Linden Ashby can stop the fragment using a device he invented, but he's kidnapped by fanatical cult leader Mario Van Peebles. Van Peebles' nemesis, con Ice-T, teams with special agent Suzy Amis to save the day. 90 min.
27-7190   Was $99.99   □*$14.99*

The Arrival (1996)
Radio astronomer Charlie Sheen intercepts a signal from outer space and soon discovers that not only is there life on other planets, but they may already be living on Earth. After he's mysteriously fired from his job, Sheen uncovers the extraterrestrials and their devious plan to conquer the Earth through global warming. With Lindsay Crouse, Ron Silver. 109 min.
27-6986   Was $99.99   □*$14.99*

Arrival II (1998)
After his astronomer brother is mysteriously killed, computer programmer Jack Ziminski receives a package that warns him of a plot by extraterrestrials to control the world. Soon, Jack, a reporter and three scientists are targeted for murder, and in order for them to escape, they must convince others of the alien scheme. Patrick Muldoon, Jane Sibbett star. AKA: "The Second Arrival." 101 min.
27-7111   Was $99.99   □*$14.99*

Scorpio One (1998)
When scientists on a space mission make a monumental discovery but are mysteriously killed, NASA sends an investigative team, along with a CIA agent, to find out what happened. Among the members of the mission, however, there's a saboteur who could send the ship back to Earth in flames. Robert Carradine, Jeff Speakman, Robin Curtis and Steve Kanaly star. 92 min.
27-7102   □*$89.99*

The Handmaid's Tale (1990)
Eerie translation of Margaret Atwood's novel about a future America where right-wing fundamentalists rule the roost and women are subservient to men. One woman risks her life by rebelling against the people who see her only as a baby-maker and have taken her newborn child. Natasha Richardson, Faye Dunaway, Robert Duvall star. Adapted by Harold Pinter and directed by Volker Schlöndorff. 109 min.
44-1753   Was $19.99   *$14.99*

Hardware (1990)
An imaginative and hair-raising sci-fi thriller set in a pollution-ravaged future Earth, where a young couple retrieves what they believe is scrap metal, but which is actually the still-active components of a murderous military android. Great special effects make this one worth a look. Dylan McDermott, Stacey Travis, Iggy Pop star. 94 min.
44-1776   Was $19.99   □*$14.99*

Split Second (1992)
An action-packed sci-fier starring Rutger Hauer as a tough cop going up against a deadly, vicious monstrosity terrorizing the streets in 2008. When the creature kills his partner and kidnaps his girlfriend, Hauer brings out the big guns to stop it. With Kim Cattrall, Neil Duncan and Michael J. Pollard as the Rat Catcher. 90 min.
44-1902   Was $19.99   *$14.99*

TERMINAL VIRUS

Terminal Virus (1996)
In the future, a deadly, sexually transmitted disease has devastated the world, dividing men and women into warring camps. The son of a scientist who developed a serum for the virus teams with an outlaw to try to convince the survivors they have the secret to the world's future. James Brolin, Richard Lynch and Bryan Genesse star.
21-9129   Was $99.99   *$14.99*

Daybreak (1993)
Futuristic thriller in which a young woman meets a gang of rebels who have banded together to fight terrorism sponsored by the government in the wake of a worldwide epidemic. The woman falls in love with the rebels' leader and joins them in a crusade to save mankind. Cuba Gooding, Jr., Moira Kelly, Omar Epps and Martha Plimpton star. 91 min.
44-1950   Was $19.99   *$14.99*

No Escape (1994)
Futuristic actioner set in 2022, where marine captain Ray Liotta is accused of killing his commanding officer and is sentenced to a jungle island prison inhabited by two rival groups, the savage Outsiders and the peaceful Insiders. While helping the Insiders in fierce battles against the Outsiders, Liotta plots his escape. With Stuart Wilson, Lance Henriksen and Michael Lerner. 118 min.
44-1967   Was $19.99   □*$14.99*

No Escape (Letterboxed Version)
Also available in a theatrical, widescreen format.
44-2152   Was $19.99   *$14.99*

Project: Shadowchaser (1992)
A super-strong android with a murderous nasty streak has escaped from a government laboratory, and no one knows how to stop it. Action-packed thriller stars Martin Kove, Meg Foster, Joss Ackland and Frank Zagarino. 97 min.
46-5533   Was $19.99   □*$12.99*

**Night Siege: Project:
Shadowchaser 2 (1994)**
Three unlikely heroes tackle a diabolical cyborg in a battle for the fate of the future in this special effects-filled sequel. Frank Zagarino, Bryan Genesse and Beth Toussaint star. AKA: "Armed and Deadly." Unrated version; 98 min.
02-5044   Was $89.99   □*$19.99*

**Project:
Shadowchaser 3000 (1995)**
Following a collision between a space station and a mining vessel, seven survivors band together to battle an unpredictable android on the warpath before the station's nuclear core explodes. Third "Shadowchaser" outing stars Sam Bottoms, Frank Zagarino and Christopher Atkins. 99 min.
02-5092   Was $89.99   □*$19.99*

Abraxas (1993)
Jesse "The Body" Ventura stars in this science-fiction epic as an intergalactic cop whose mission is to step in when a planet embarks on a self-destructive path. When his ex-partner turns renegade, Jesse tries to stop him—before he finds the power to destroy the universe. Sven Ole-Thorsen and Jim Belushi also star. 90 min.
46-5557   Was $19.99   *$14.99*

Project: Genesis (1993)
In the 23rd century, a human is marooned on a desolate planet with a beautiful alien woman to whom he's attracted. His desires are curtailed by her otherworldly hostility, but the two must join together to fight the hostile forces around them. AKA: "Strange Horizons." David Ferr, Olga Prokhorova star.
46-5585   *$89.99*

Replikator (1994)
Sci-fi thriller set in a future where the latest technology allows anything, including people, to be duplicated. Now a crime boss has gotten control of the "replication" process, and a renegade cop and two cyberpunks must learn what's real and what isn't if they hope to stop him. Ned Beatty, Brigitte Bako, Michael St. Gerard star. 96 min.
46-5598   *$89.99*

Project Metalbeast (1994)
High-tech terror and supernatural suspense mix in this tale of a CIA experiment in lycanthropy and a bionics project that result in the accidental creation of a cyborg werewolf with metallic skin and a thirst for blood. Barry Bostwick, Kim Delaney star. 92 min.
46-5600   *$89.99*

**Wizards Of
The Demon Sword (1991)**
In this sword-and-sorcery epic from noted schlockmeister Fred Olen Ray ("Dinosaur Island"), the powerful Knife of Aktar is fought over by an evil magician and a swordsman trying to help a beautiful maiden and her imprisoned father. With special effects, swordfighting, dinosaurs, Michael Berryman, Lyle Waggoner, Russ Tamblyn, Dawn Wildsmith and Lawrence Tierney. 90 min.
46-8013   Was $69.99   *$14.99*

**Nymphoid Barbarian In
Dinosaur Hell (1996)**
In this post-apocalyptic saga, Linda Corwin is the loincloth-clad last woman on Earth who battles all sorts of strange creatures and mutant humans, then is held captive by a medicine man in a castle. Paul Guzzi also stars in this Troma release. AKA: "Dark Fortress." 90 min.
46-8019   Was $59.99   *$14.99*

Proteus (1996)
After their yacht is sunk, three couples are stranded on an abandoned oil rig that houses a secret lab where genetic experiments are taking place. The experiments have led to the birth of a creature named "Charlie" that feeds on human blood and takes the shape of any life form it touches. Can the couples survive? Craig Fairbrass, Doug Bradley star. 97 min.
68-1804   *$14.99*

Future War (1996)
In this futuristic action saga, an alien slave who escapes from a planet dominated by cyborgs lands on Earth, where he faces a ruthless bounty hunter. Savage combat ensues when alien meets human meets machine in this sci-fi foray featuring kung-fu action. Daniel Bernhardt and Robert Z'Dar star. 90 min.
76-7327   *$59.99*

**The Philadelphia
Experiment (1984)**
When a WWII Navy experiment goes haywire, two sailors find themselves in a time warp which transports them to the Nevada desert in the year 1984. Exciting sci-fi suspenser stars Michael Paré, Nancy Allen, Bobby Di Cicco. 102 min.
44-1202   Letterboxed   *$14.99*

BRAD JOHNSON

THEY CUT A HOLE THROUGH TIME

THE PHILADELPHIA EXPERIMENT 2

**The Philadelphia
Experiment II (1993)**
Set 10 years after the original "Philadelphia Experiment," this thrilling sequel finds survivor David Herdeg (Brad Johnson) caught up in another secret military experiment. This time a plan to transport a Stealth Fighter back to the year 1943 goes awry, and Herdeg is sent to an alternate reality where Germany won World War II. With Marjean Holden. 98 min.
68-1292   Was $89.99   □*$14.99*

Japanese

Urusei Yatsura
One of the most popular strips and TV shows in Japan, Rumiko Takahashi's comic sci-fi tale follows the exploits of Ataru, a hapless teenager who becomes the reluctant recipient of the affections of Lum, a gorgeous alien gal in a tiger-striped bikini. Each tape features four episodes and runs about 100 min. In Japanese with English subtitles. There are 24 volumes available, including:

Urusei Yatsura, Vol. 1
20-7081 *$24.99*

Urusei Yatsura, Vol. 2
20-7082 *$24.99*

Urusei Yatsura, Vol. 3
20-7083 *$24.99*

Urusei Yatsura Movie 2: Beautiful Dreamer
"Life is but a dream," but for poor Ataru and his pals at Tomobiki High, someone's dreams are taking over their reality. It takes some extraterrestrial help from Lum to uncover the demon responsible. 90 min. In Japanese with English subtitles.
20-7072 Was $39.99 *$14.99*

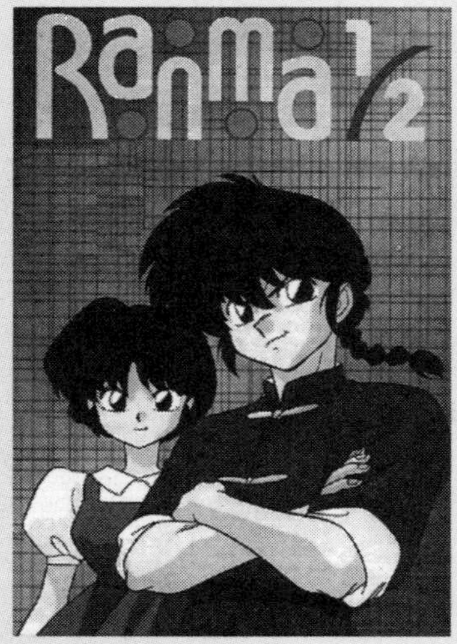

Ranma 1/2
Mix fast-paced action, slapstick humor and the world's strangest love triangle and you get this hit animated series from Rumiko Takahashi. As if teenage martial arts student Ranma didn't have enough problems with a reluctant fiancée and a slew of enemies out to fight him, a magic curse turns him into a girl whenever he's doused with cold water! Each volume features two episodes and runs about 50 min. There are 61 volumes available, including:

Ranma 1/2, Vol. 1 (Dubbed)
20-7141 *$29.99*

Ranma 1/2, Vol. 2 (Dubbed)
20-7142 *$29.99*

Ranma 1/2 Anything Goes Martial Arts: Chestnuts Roasting On An Open Fire (Dubbed)
20-7381 *$24.99*

Ranma 1/2 Anything Goes Martial Arts: Fowl Play (Dubbed)
20-7421 *$24.99*

Ranma 1/2 Hard Battle: Dim Sum Darling (Dubbed)
20-7589 *$24.99*

Ranma 1/2 Outta Control: Eat Drink Man Who Turns Into Woman (Dubbed)
20-8368 *$24.99*

Ranma 1/2 Martial Mayhem: Tea For Three (Dubbed)
20-8397 *$24.99*

Ranma 1/2 The Movie 1: Big Trouble In Nekonron China
The arrival of a strange girl named Lychee and her elephant at the "Tendo Anything Goes Martial Arts School" is just the start of a wild feature-length adventure in which Ranma must rescue Akane, who gets swept off her feet by a mysterious prince. 74 min. Dubbed in English.
20-7239 *$34.99*

Ranma 1/2 The Movie 2: Nihao My Concubine
When a sailing trip leaves Ranma and his friends (and enemies) stranded on a remote island, everyone seems to take it in stride. But soon the women begin disappearing, and in order to rescue them, Ranma must take part in a martial arts "bridal contest" held for the island's ruler. 60 min. Dubbed in English.
20-7240 *$34.99*

Nazca
The dreams of a Japanese martial arts student named Kyoji reveal he is the reincarnation of an Incan warrior, killed 500 years earlier by a traitor who sought to destroy the world with a magic sword. Unfortunately for Kyoji, his assassin has also come back—as his teacher—and is ready to complete his dark plan! Follow their ongoing battle in this action-filled anime outing. Each tape features three episodes and runs about 75 min. Each volume is also available in Japanese with English subtitles.

Nazca, Vol. 1: Blades Of Fate (Dubbed)
85-1480 *$24.99*

Nazca, Vol. 2: Blood Rivals (Dubbed)
85-1482 *$24.99*

Nazca, Vol. 3: Betrayal Of Humanity (Dubbed)
85-1484 *$24.99*

Nazca, Vol. 4: Eternal Power (Dubbed)
85-1486 *$24.99*

Neon Genesis Evangelion
In the year 2015, 15 years after a meteorite devastates the Earth's surface, the surviving humans live in underground cities as a brutal war for control of the planet is waged between the colossal alien war robots known as Angels and the Evangelions, bio-mechanical defenders of humanity. Each tape in this action-filled Japanese animated series runs about 60 min. There are 13 volumes available, including:

Neon Genesis Evangelion, Vol. 1 (Dubbed)
20-7689 *$24.99*

Neon Genesis Evangelion, Vol. 2 (Dubbed)
20-7691 *$24.99*

Neon Genesis Evangelion, Vol. 3 (Dubbed)
20-7772 *$24.99*

New Kimagure Orange Road: Summer's Beginning
The strange adventures of teenager Kyosuke Kasuga continue in this feature-length anime tale, as an auto accident and Kyosuke's own psychic powers wind up sending him three years into the future. Once there, he must locate his missing adult self and keep his tangled love life from getting even more complicated. 100 min. In Japanese with English subtitles.
20-7997 *$29.99*

New Kimagure Orange Road: Summer's Beginning (Dubbed Version)
Also available in a dubbed-in-English edition.
20-7998 *$19.99*

Photon
From "Tenchi Muyo" talents Masaki Kajishima and Yousuke Kuroda come the lighthearted sci-fi exploits of Photon, a super-strong young man who sets out to find a missing friend on his desert planet home. Along the way Photon finds himself accidentally engaged to a space pilot, running afoul of the wicked Emperor of the Galaxy, and in other scrapes. Each volume runs about 60 minutes and is also available in Japanese with English subtitles.

Photon, Vol. 1: The Idiot Menace (Dubbed)
20-8562 *$19.99*

Photon, Vol. 2: Enemy Pawn (Dubbed)
20-8564 *$19.99*

Photon, Vol. 3: The Emperor Strikes Back (Dubbed)
20-8566 *$19.99*

Knights Of Ramune
A pair of plucky heroines named Cacao and Parfait are sent to rescue the fabled warrior Ramunes to save the galaxy from invasion, only to find him leading the invading fleet! It's up to the girls, their less-than-perfect magical abilities and mecha, and a feisty orphan they rescue to make things right in this fast-paced, racy sci-fi series. Each volume runs about 60 minutes and is also available in Japanese with English subtitles.

Knights Of Ramune: Blast Off! (Dubbed)
20-8340 *$24.99*

Knights Of Ramune: True Destination (Dubbed)
20-8342 *$24.99*

Knights Of Ramune: Endless Legend (Dubbed)
20-8344 *$24.99*

New Dominion Tank Police
Climb aboard the police urban battle tank Boneparte and join its driver, the sexy and tough Leona, as they take on crooks and corporate creeps on the streets of Newport City in this exciting Japanese animated series. Each two-episode tape runs about 60 min. Dubbed in English.

New Dominion Tank Police, Vol. 1
02-8368 *$14.99*

New Dominion Tank Police, Vol. 2
02-8371 *$14.99*

New Dominion Tank Police, Vol. 3
02-8379 *$14.99*

The Girl From Phantasia
Take one horny teenager and his less-than-willing girlfriend, add in a magic carpet that comes with a cute female "pixie" and her elf pals, and you get this wickedly funny mix of fantasy and lust, "anime"-style. 35 min. In Japanese with English subtitles.
20-7179 Was $29.99 *$19.99*

A Wind Named Amnesia
A strange wind sweeps across the Earth, erasing the memories of everyone in its path and sending mankind back into savage barbarism. Now a young man and woman spared from its effects embark on a dangerous journey to find out who created the "amnesia wind" and how to rebuild civilization. Action-filled animated tale from Japan. 80 min. In Japanese with English subtitles.
20-7190 *$29.99*

Tokyo Vice
College students Akira, Junpei, Keiko and Kumiko pool their resources and expertise to form the Rutz Detective Agency, but their first case literally falls into their laps when a dying man at a rock concert hands Junpei a computer disc containing data on a top-secret weapon. Action and suspense, anime style, in this high-tech espionage caper. 60 min. In Japanese with English subtitles.
20-8353 *$24.99*

Twin Dolls
Torrid sex, violence and stylish animation highlight this series about two high school-aged sisters named Mai and Ai, martial arts maestros and professional monster hunters, whose skills cause a jealous classmate to be possessed by a 10-foot tall green demon with a strong desire to have sex with them. Can they stop it? Each tape runs about 50 min. In Japanese with English subtitles.

Twin Dolls, Vol. 1
20-7342 Was $34.99 *$29.99*

Twin Dolls, Vol. 2
20-7343 *$29.99*

Fatal Fury
The action-filled video game makes an animated smash in this Japanese tale, as brothers Andy, Jeff and Terry study a deadly but dangerous martial art in order to avenge their father's murder by crime boss Geese Howard. 50 min. Dubbed in English.
20-7307 *$19.99*

Fatal Fury 2: The New Battle
Incredible action and outrageous fighting sequences highlight this sequel to the hit animated film based on the popular video game. Siblings Andy, Jeff and Terry return to fight the forces of evil with their martial arts expertise. 70 min. Dubbed in English.
20-7362 *$19.99*

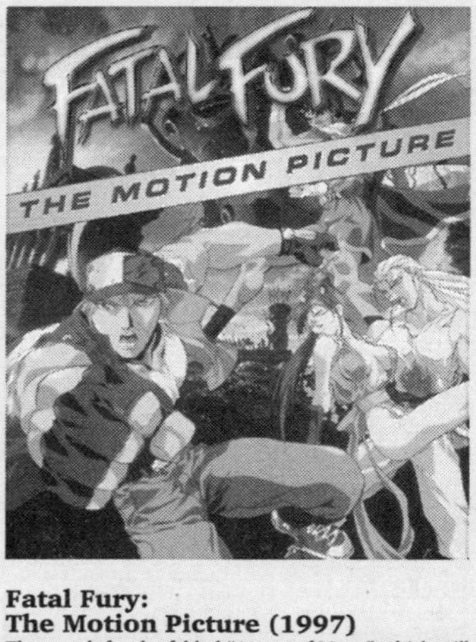

Fatal Fury: The Motion Picture (1997)
The search for the fabled "Armor of Mars," which will give its owner ultimate mastery over all forms of the martial arts, pits Terry and Andy and their allies against a deadly fighter who already possesses three of the armor's six pieces in this exciting feature-length adventure. 100 min. Dubbed in English.
20-7420 *$19.99*

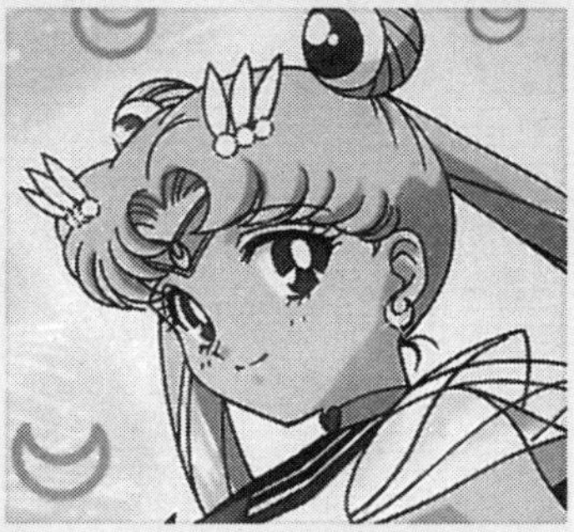

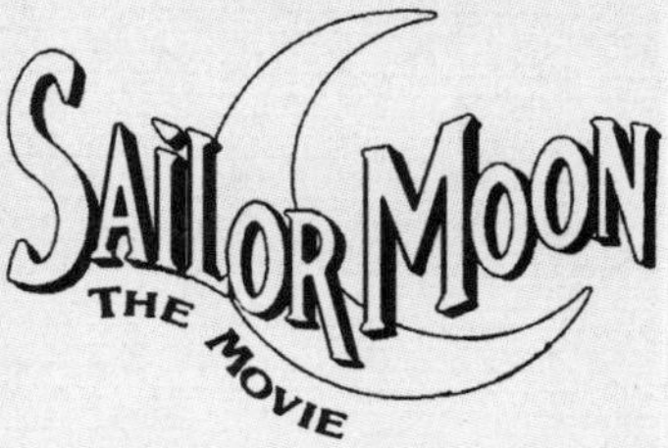

Sailor Moon R: The Movie: The Promise Of The Rose
Between a meteor that's heading for Earth and a childhood acquaintance of Mamoru's who's out to become her only friend, the Sailor Scouts have their hands full in this feature-length adventure. 60 min. In Japanese with English subtitles.
85-1446 *$24.99*

Sailor Moon R: The Movie (Dubbed Version)
Also available in a dubbed-in-English edition.
85-1461 *$14.99*

Sailor Moon S: The Movie: Hearts In Ice
It may be Christmas vacation in this "Sailor Moon" movie, but there's little time for relaxation when the girls must stop a bizarre ice storm that's paralyzed the city...and is part of Snow Queen Kaguya's latest plan to take over the Earth. 60 min. In Japanese with English subtitles.
85-1447 *$24.99*

Sailor Moon S: The Movie (Dubbed Version)
Also available in a dubbed-in-English edition.
85-1500 *$14.99*

Sailor Moon Super S: The Movie: Black Dream Hole
Who is responsible for abducting children around the world in order to use their "dream energy" to open up a black hole that will devour the Earth, and what can Sailor Moon and the Sailor Scouts do about it when her pal Mini Moon is among the missing? Find out in this thrilling feature-length "Sailor Moon" saga. 60 min. In Japanese with English subtitles.
85-1448 *$24.99*

Sailor Moon Super S: The Movie (Dubbed Version)
Also available in a dubbed-in-English edition.
85-1515 *$14.99*

Wings Of Honneamise (1987)
Stunning animation and Ryuichi Sakamoto's amazing score highlight a tale of politics and love set against the backdrop of social unrest in a war-ravaged fantasy world. This epic, adult-themed work plays like a cross between "An Officer and a Gentleman" and "The Right Stuff." 124 min. In Japanese with English subtitles.
02-8249 *$24.99*

Wings Of Honneamise (Dubbed Version)
Also available in a dubbed-in-English edition.
02-8258 *$19.99*

Sword For Truth
In the war-torn days of feudal Japan, swordsman Shuranosuke Sakaki's mastery with a sword allowed him to make short work of his enemies, but when he's hired to rescue a kidnapped princess from a band of ninja bandits, Sakaki faces his most dangerous challenge yet. Exciting and violent martial arts action, anime style. 60 min. Dubbed in English.
02-8868 *$19.99*

Starvengers
It's good versus evil and giant robots versus giant robots in this superior Japanimation effort when the Starvengers take on the forces of the Pandemonium Empire in "Who'll Fly Poseidon" and "Dragon Formation...Switch On." 46 min.
10-1433 Was $19.99 *$14.99*

Animation

Dragoon
A handsome young swordsman rescues a beautiful girl he finds unconscious in the snow, but his act of chivalry soon has them on the run from deadly soldiers and coping with an evil plan to take over the world in this thrilling, violent anime tale of magic, fantasy and swordplay. 90 min. Dubbed in English.
20-8594 *$19.99*

Godmars
In the year 1999, mankind's expansion beyond the planet is threatened by a sinister alien race, and a young member of the organization charged with Earth's defense is shocked to learn that not only is he an alien, but inside his body is the detonator to a bomb that could destroy Earth! Thrilling Japanimation space saga. 93 min. In Japanese with English subtitles.
20-7217 Was $24.99 *$14.99*

Dragon Half
Mink is a cute teenage girl with a secret in her family: her father was a knight and her mother a dragon. And as if growing up half-reptilian isn't bad enough, Mink falls in love with a pop star who's looking for a career as a dragon slayer! Wild fantasy-comedy from Japan. 60 min. In Japanese with English subtitles.
20-7379 *$29.99*

Dragon Half (Dubbed Version)
Also available in a dubbed-in-English edition.
20-8558 *$19.99*

Original Dirty Pair
Available at last on home video, here are the outrageous animated adventures of Yuri and Kei, two sexy but trouble-prone female detectives with an attitude who travel from planet to planet solving—and sometimes complicating—mysteries. Each tape features two episodes and runs about 60 min. Each volume is also available in Japanese with English subtitles. There are five volumes available, including:

Original Dirty Pair, Vol. 1 (Dubbed)
20-8282 *$14.99*

Original Dirty Pair, Vol. 2 (Dubbed)
20-8284 *$14.99*

Original Dirty Pair, Vol. 3 (Dubbed)
20-8286 *$14.99*

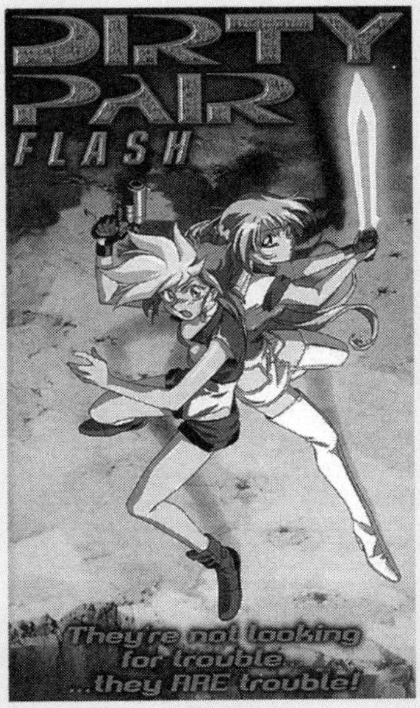

Dirty Pair Flash
Kei and Yuri, the delectable and destructive interplanetary trouble-shooters of the World Welfare & Works Agency, are back and up to their gunbelts in a series of wild anime adventures filled with action, sexy fun and laughs. Each tape runs about 60 min. Each volume is also available in Japanese with English subtitles.

Dirty Pair Flash: Act 1 (Dubbed)
20-7990 *$19.99*

Dirty Pair Flash: Act 2 (Dubbed)
20-8053 *$19.99*

Dirty Pair Flash: Act 3 (Dubbed)
20-8055 *$19.99*

Kekkou Kamen
The students of a hellish school run by dictatorial hall monitors and teachers in masks have nothing to look forward to...until Kekkou Kamen, a nunchaku-wielding superheroine whose costume consists of mask, boots and a killer body, arrives to save them in this outrageous "anime" series by Go Nagai. WARNING: Contains graphic violence and nudity; adults only. Each tape runs about 55 min. and is in Japanese with English subtitles.

Kekkou Kamen, Vol. 1
20-7294 *$29.99*

Kekkou Kamen, Vol. 2
20-7295 *$29.99*

Rupan III: The Fuma Conspiracy
Call him Rupan or call him Lupin...by any name the outrageous master thief is a hit in Japanese animation, and in this feature-length saga he must rescue a kidnapped bride from ninja warriors while trying to recover the ransom for himself and avoid an Interpol inspector. 73 min. In Japanese with English subtitles.
20-7311 Was $24.99 *$14.99*

Rupan III: The Fuma Conspiracy (Dubbed Version)
Also available in a dubbed-in-English edition.
20-7363 Was $19.99 *$14.99*

Rupan III: Legend Of The Gold Of Babylon
An archeological find points to the location of the fabled Tower of Babel, made of solid gold, and the larcenous Rupan joins a madcap transglobal race to retrieve it in this feature-length saga. 100 min. In Japanese with English subtitles.
20-7312 *$24.99*

The Castle Of Cagliostro (1991)
Sensational feature-length animated adventure of master thief Lupin III and his sidekick Jigen, as they try to save a damsel from her pursuers: the henchmen of a nasty count who's learned she holds the key to the fabled lost fortune of Cagliostro. 100 min. In Japanese with English subtitles.
02-9207 *$29.99*

The Castle Of Cagliostro (Dubbed Version)
Also available in a dubbed-in-English edition.
45-8027 Was $29.99 *$19.99*

Curse Of The Undead: Yoma
Martial arts and horror mix in this stunningly animated, graphically violent saga. A ninja warrior seeks revenge against a former friend who killed his comrades and lover, but the friend has become one of the undead and will use all the occult powers at his disposal to win. 90 min. In Japanese with English subtitles.
20-7375 *$29.99*

Samurai Showdown
The action-filled arcade favorite gets a full-blown anime treatment in this feature-length, graphically violent tale of six warriors who are slain by a treacherous colleague and, 100 years later, are reincarnated to seek vengeance. 85 min. Dubbed in English.
20-7378 Was $29.99 *$19.99*

Night On The Galactic Railroad
Based on a popular Japanese tale, this magical animated fable tells of a young boy who, along with his best friend, takes a magical train ride through the cosmos and learns about the wonders of the universe and the human spirit. 115 min. In Japanese with English subtitles.
20-7478 Was $29.99 *$19.99*

Armored Trooper VOTOMS Stage 1: Complete Set
Exciting five-volume animated adventure set in a distant galaxy where an uneasy peace follows 200 years of interplanetary war, and where a pilot with the elite Armored Troopers is branded a traitor and must flee for his life to the mysterious Uoodo City, where he is caught in the middle of a deadly conspiracy. 316 min. total. In Japanese with English subtitles. NOTE: Individual volumes available at $24.99 each.
20-7519 Save $25.00! *$99.99*

Armored Trooper VOTOMS Stage 2: Complete Set
The saga of former Armored Trooper Chirico continues, and so do his troubles, as he signs on to fight rebels in the jungles of Kummen and eventually finds himself battling both sides as he tries to rescue his lost love, Fyana, in this five-volume set. 338 min. total. In Japanese with English subtitles. NOTE: Individual volumes available at $24.99 each.
20-7621 Save $25.00! *$99.99*

Armored Trooper VOTOMS Stage 3: Complete Set
Chirico and Fyana, reunited at last, are trapped on a ghost ship that takes them to the mysterious, war-ravaged world of Sunsa. There, with Fyana's life hanging in the balance, Chirico faces his ultimate battle with Ypsilon in this four-volume anime odyssey. 280 min. total. In Japanese with English subtitles. NOTE: Individual volumes available at $24.99 each.
20-7742 Save $10.00! *$89.99*

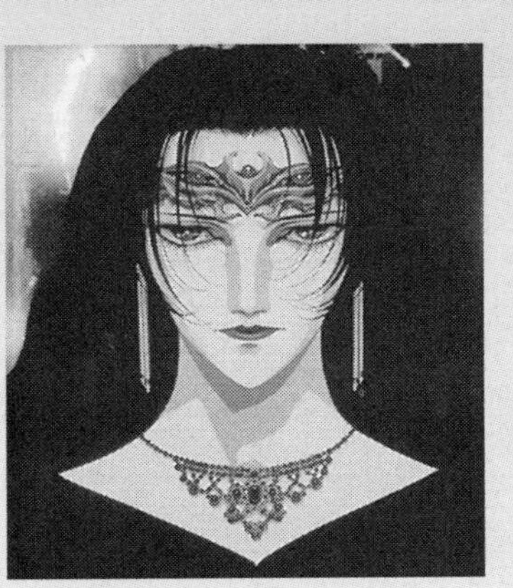

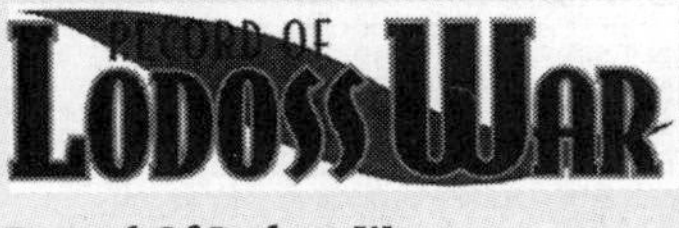

Record Of Lodoss War: Complete Set
Ravaged by war for millennia, the island world of Lodoss nows faces an overwhelming evil menace. Six people—fearless fighter Parn; Deedit the elf; Ghim, a dwarf warrior; Etoh, a young priest; Slayn the mage; and the thief, Woodchuck—band together to save their home in this six-tape animated series. 355 min. total. In Japanese with English subtitles. NOTE: Individual volumes
20-7340 Save $50.00! *$129.99*

Record Of Lodoss War: Complete Set (Dubbed Version)
The collection is also available in a dubbed-in-English version. NOTE: Individual volumes available at $19.99 each.
20-7341 Save $20.00! *$99.99*

Record Of Lodoss War: Chronicle Of The Heroic Knight: Complete Set
Five years after defeating the evil that overran the island of Lodoss, the survivors of that epic battle reunite and join with new heroes to face the menace of the Black Knight of Marmo and Wagnard the Dark Sorcerer. Follow their adventures in this action-packed, nine-tape anime fantasy. 810 min. total. In Japanese with English subtitles. NOTE: Individual volumes available at $24.99 each.
20-8486 Save $65.00! *$159.99*

Record Of Lodoss War: Chronicle Of The Heroic Knight: Complete Set (Dubbed Version)
The collection is also available in a dubbed-in-English edition. NOTE: Individual volumes available at $19.99 each.
20-8487 Save 40.00! *$139.99*

Legend Of Crystania (1998)
The aftermath of the Lodoss Wars is the setting for this Japanese animation epic in which a ship carrying Lodoss refugees crashes on a cursed island. There the evil god Barbas wreaks havoc upon the survivors, taking possession of Ashram's body and banishing his soul to Hell. Now it's up to Priotess to travel in time to collect a new band of warriors to defeat the dark lord and return Ashram to Earth. 95 min. In Japanese with English subtitles.
20-8107 *$29.99*

Legend Of Crystania (Dubbed Version)
Also available in a dubbed-in-English edition.
20-8108 *$19.99*

Legend Of Crystania: The Ring Of Chaos Trilogy: Complete Set
The saga of the land of Crystania continues in an all-new anime saga, as the magical rebirth of an ancient dark god could doom the kingdom, unless the soul of Ashram can be rescued in time. Included in this three-tape set are "The Cave of the Sealed," "Resurrection of the Gods' King" and "A New Beginning." 150 min. total. In Japanese with English subtitles.
20-8307 *$89.99*

Legend Of Crystania: The Ring Of Chaos Trilogy: Complete Set (Dubbed Version)
Also available in a dubbed-in-English edition.
20-8308 *$59.99*

Darkside Blues
From the creator of "Vampire Hunter D" and "A Wind Named Amnesia" comes this dark tale set on a future Earth where an all-powerful corporation rules most of the planet. One small free area, Tokyo's "Darkside" neighborhood of Kabuki Town, is home to a young mystic whose powers may allow him to free the planet from the corporation's clutches. 83 min. In Japanese with English subtitles.
20-7814 *$29.99*

Darkside Blues (Dubbed Version)
Also available in a dubbed-in-English edition.
20-7971 *$24.99*

Key: The Metal Idol: Complete Set
Her name is Key, an android who to all outward appearances is a typical 18-year-old. Join her on a wild and adventure-filled quest as she tries to win the love and friendship of 30,000 people—and thus gain her own humanity—in this eight-volume sci-fi anime saga. 720 min. total. In Japanese with English subtitles. NOTE: Individual volumes available at $29.99 each.
20-8147 *$239.99*

Key: The Metal Idol: Complete Set (Dubbed Version)
The collection is also available in a dubbed-in-English edition. NOTE: Individual volumes available at $24.99 each.
20-8148 *$199.99*

Voltage Fighters! Gowcaizer: The Movie
When the goings-on at a strange institute for "gifted students" threaten the safety of 21st-century Tokyo, a student at a nearby school may be the city's only hope, thanks to a mysterious stone that transforms him into an armored superhero. Join Gowcaizer and his allies in a fast-paced, funny and sexy anime feature from Japan. 90 min. In Japanese with English subtitles.
20-8299 *$29.99*

Voltage Fighters! Gowcaizer: The Movie (Dubbed Version)
Also available in a dubbed-in-English edition.
20-8300 *$24.99*

Birdy The Mighty
"Patlabor" creator Yuuki Masami puts a sci-fi spin on the "odd couple" motif with this animated series about Birdy, an intergalactic female cop who chases a suspect to Earth. When she accidentally kills high school student Tsutomu, Birdy revives him by sharing her life force and "moving into" his body. Can this two-in-one team solve Birdy's cases and pass Tsutomu's classes? Each volume runs about 60 minutes and is also available in Japanese with English subtitles.

Birdy The Mighty: Double Trouble (Dubbed)
20-8310 *$24.99*

Birdy The Mighty: Final Force (Dubbed)
20-8312 *$24.99*

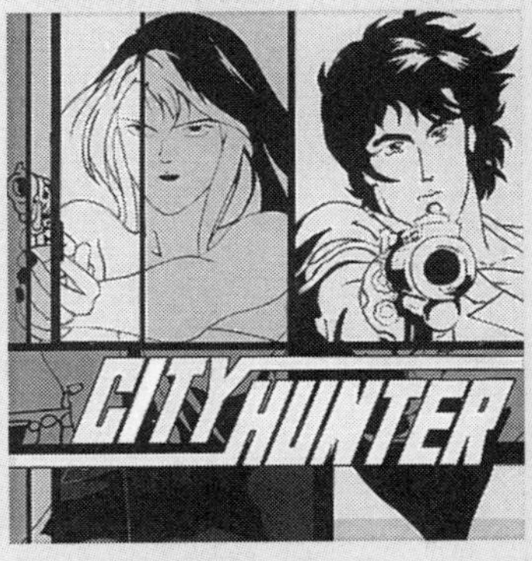

City Hunter: The Motion Picture
From the pages of the hit manga series comes City Hunter, Japan's top detective and a man as fast on the draw as he is with the ladies. In this feature-length adventure filled with gunplay and violent action, City Hunter must save the city of Tokyo from being levelled by a vengeful ex-soldier known as Professor. 90 min. In Japanese with English subtitles.
20-8331 *$29.99*

City Hunter: The Motion Picture (Dubbed Version)
Also available in a dubbed-in-English edition.
20-8332 *$19.99*

City Hunter: .357 Magnum
The search for a beautiful musician's kidnapped father leads the two-fisted P.I. known as City Hunter into a case of global intrigue involving a missing microchip, rival spies, and loads of gorgeous women in this feature-length thriller. 80 min. In Japanese with English subtitles.
20-8370 *$29.99*

City Hunter: .357 Magnum (Dubbed Version)
Also available in a dubbed-in-English edition.
20-8371 *$19.99*

City Hunter: Bay City Wars
Will Tokyo's Bay City Hotel be the launching site for World War III? It may be, unless City Hunter can stop a ruthless Central American ruler who has a headquarters in the hotel's basement from which he can reprogram and launch America's nuclear missiles! 50 min. In Japanese with English subtitles.
20-8372 *$29.99*

City Hunter: Bay City Wars (Dubbed Version)
Also available in a dubbed-in-English edition.
20-8373 *$19.99*

Junk Boy
Can a sex-obsessed young man find the perfect outlet for his urges by taking a job as a "photo approver" for an adult magazine? Find out in this outrageous anime farce with more than enough nudity and explicit language to garner an "adults only" warning. 60 min. Dubbed in English.
02-8564 *$19.99*

Tokyo Revelation
Science meets Satanism in this brutally violent anime tale about a high-tech scheme to unleash demonic forces on Earth in order to claim a mysterious and powerful element found inside the human soul, and two young men who find themselves on opposite sides of the battle to save mankind. WARNING: contains graphic violence and sexual situations; adults only. 60 min. Dubbed in English.
02-8738 *$19.99*

Psychic Wars
A Japanese surgeon travels back in time 5,000 years thanks to a mystical gate. In the past, he uncovers a plan by demonic beings to invade the present and take over the Earth. Horror, fantasy and science fiction come together in this exciting animated odyssey. 60 min. Dubbed in English.
02-8911 *$19.99*

X
With two mighty mystical armies poised for a psychic battle in the midst of Tokyo, a young man named Kamui Shiro discovers it is his destiny to choose which side will win, a decision that will either save or doom humanity. Amazing animated adaptation of the popular manga series features artwork by Clamp and Mad House Studios. WARNING: Contains graphic violence and nudity; adults only. 96 min. In Japanese with English subtitles.
02-9271 *$29.99*

X (Dubbed Version)
Also available in a dubbed-in-English edition.
02-9260 *$19.99*

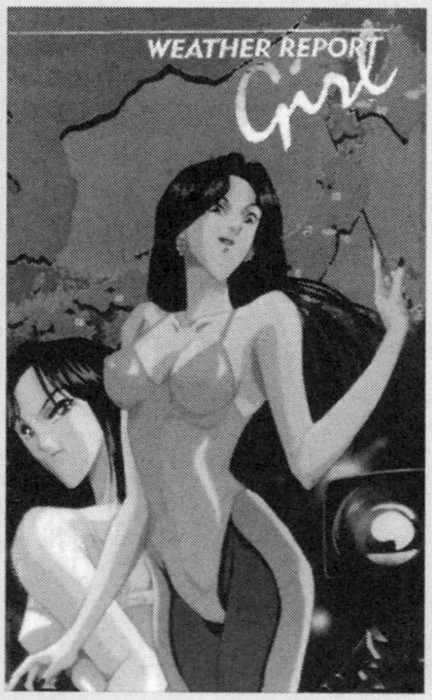

Weather Report Girl
Whoever said TV weather reports were dull never saw this outrageously risqué animated series from Japan. Fill-in weather girl Keiko becomes an overnight sensation and a ratings smash by raising her skirt on the air, much to the dismay of the woman she replaces, who'll do anything to sabotage Keiko's new career. WARNING: Contains nudity and sexual situations; adults only. Each tape features two episodes and runs about 45 min. In Japanese with English subtitles.

Weather Report Girl, Vol. 1: In For Nasty Weather
17-7038 *$24.99*

Weather Report Girl, Vol. 2: Warm Fronts In Collision
17-7039 *$24.99*

Battle Team Lakers EX
Star Laker, Kung Fu Laker, Judo Laker, Soul Laker and Bunny Laker are five sexy alien gals who come to Earth to guard the Super-Laker Crystals—and their virginity—from Oleana and her evil Empire of Godram. The crystals, at least, are safe in this outrageous anime tale of sci-fi thrills and erotic fantasy. WARNING: Contains graphic scenes of sexual situations; adults only. 30 min. In Japanese with English subtitles.
17-7053 *$24.99*

Battle Team Lakers EX (Dubbed Version)
Also available in a dubbed-in-English edition.
20-8391 *$19.99*

Adults Only!

Cool Devices: Boxed Set
One of the most extreme examples of erotic anime ever produced, this five-tape series presents intense tales of bondage, domination, and other aspects of "forbidden love." Included are "Curious Fruit/Sacred Girl," "Lover Doll/Kirei," "Seek 1 & 2," "Yellow Star/Slave Warrior MAYA 1 & 2" and "Binding/Fallen Angel Rina." WARNING: Contains nudity and graphic sexual situations; adults only. 315 min. total. NOTE: Individual volumes available at $29.99 each.
17-7070 Save $20.00! *$129.99*

Rei Rei
Two prevalent themes in Japanese animation, mythological fantasy and low-brow sexual hi-jinx, are mixed in this story of some thwarted lovers and how their lives are made even worse by the arrival of Kaguya, a gorgeous spirit being with penchants for "carnal justice" and baring her breasts. Uncut version; 60 min. In Japanese with English subtitles.
20-7180 Was $34.99 *$24.99*

Rei Rei (Dubbed Version)
Also available in a dubbed-in-English edition.
20-7897 *$19.99*

End Of Summer
A sophisticated and provocative animated drama from Japan, telling the bittersweet story of a young man on his final summer before leaving for college, his attempts to win (and bed) the girl of his dreams, and the other females who try to lead him away from his goal. WARNING: Contains nudity and sexual situations; adults only. 55 min. In Japanese with English subtitles.
20-7204 *$29.99*

End Of Summer 2
The sensual saga of love-starved teenager Wataru and his pursuit of beautiful Mai continues in this adult-oriented anime tale, as a new wrinkle is added when the former lover of Wataru's best friend shows up for advice and winds up getting a lot more! WARNING: Contains nudity and sexual situations; adults only. 60 min. In Japanese with English subtitles.
20-7702 *$29.99*

Angel Of Darkness
An elite school for girls is the setting for other-worldly horror and bizarre sexual practices in this spine-tingling anime series that blends suspense, fantasy and eroticism. WARNING: Contains graphic violence and sexual situations; adults only. Each tape runs about 50 min. In Japanese with English subtitles.

Angel Of Darkness, Vol. 1
20-7296 Was $34.99 *$29.99*

Angel Of Darkness, Vol. 2
20-7441 *$29.99*

Angel Of Darkness, Vol. 3
20-7716 *$29.99*

Angel Of Darkness, Vol. 4
20-8186 *$29.99*

LA Blue Girl: Collector's Set
Martial arts, occult forces and steamy sex mark this thrilling six-part anime series. A teenage girl whose ninja ancestors made a pact with the underworld centuries earlier must now cope with hordes of sex-starved demons who arrive on Earth when a rival clan steals the source of her family's power. WARNING: Contains graphic violence and sexual situations; adults only. 270 min. total. NOTE: Individual volumes available at $29.99 each.
20-7531 Save $50.00! *$129.99*

LA Blue Girl: Collector's Set (Dubbed Version)
All six volumes as well as the boxed set are also available in a dubbed-in-English edition.
20-7530 Save $50.00! *$129.99*

Lady Blue
Sexy teenage ninjas Miko and Fubuki are back, using their combat skills to fight an ancient curse that centered around the doomed love affair between a prince and a princess—a fight that could cost Miko her own true love—in this exciting and erotic continuation of the "LA Blue Girl" saga. WARNING: Contains graphic violence and sexual situations; adults only. Each tape runs about 60 min.

Lady Blue, Vol. 1 (Subtitled)
20-7956 *$29.99*

Lady Blue, Vol. 2 (Subtitled)
20-7957 *$29.99*

My My Mai
Mai is a beautiful "supernatural counselor" who investigates all manner of mysteries and has a knack for comforting her clients...and losing her clothes. Follow her "adults only" adventures in this spooky screwball anime series. Each tape runs about 45 min. Dubbed in English.

My My Mai, Vol. 1
20-7542 *$19.99*

My My Mai, Vol. 2
20-7543 *$19.99*

Gude Crest: The Emblem Of Gude
It's swords and sorcery, anime style, in this Japanese adventure featuring Efera and Jiliora, two feisty female mercenaries who set out to return a legendary crest to its rightful owners. Those owners, however, are a young prince and princess held captive by a wicked cult leader, and the women have their work cut out for them. WARNING: Contains graphic violence and sexual situations; adults only. 50 min. In Japanese with English subtitles.
20-7801 *$29.99*

Urotsukidoji: Legend Of The Overfiend
One of the most erotic, violent and visually stunning sagas in Japanese animation history, this international favorite depicts a young man's metamorphosis into "the Overfiend," a super-powerful being destined to merge the human world with dimensions inhabited by demons and monstrous man-beasts. Supernatural horror and violent sexuality abound. 108 min. Dubbed in English.
20-7119 Was $39.99 *$29.99*

Urotsukidoji II: Legend Of The Demon Womb
The (literally) hellraising exploits of the Overfiend continue in this full-tilt follow-up, as the son of a Nazi scientist follows in his father's footsteps, using a bloody mix of science and magic to kill the Overfiend and absorb his powers in a plan for world conquest. Pulse-pounding Japanese animation for adults only. 88 min. Dubbed in English.
20-7120 *$29.99*

Urotsukidoji: Perfect Collection
This deluxe five-tape collector's set features Parts I and II of the "Urotsukidoji" saga in their original, subtitled format, plus 40 minutes of extra-violent footage not available on other versions. In Japanese with English subtitles. 4 hrs. total.
20-7210 *$99.99*

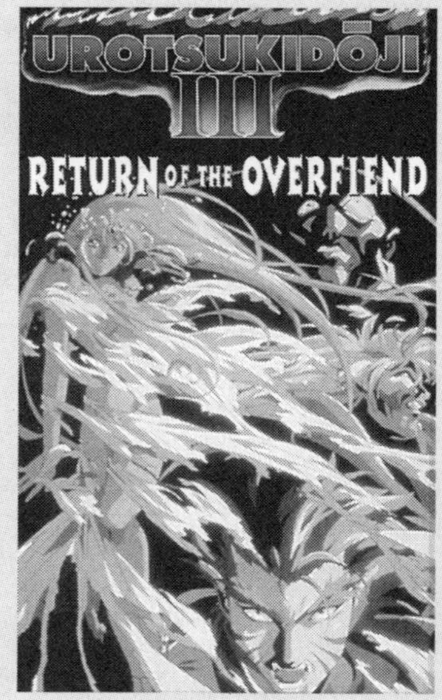

Urotsukidoji III: Return Of The Overfiend: Complete Set
Two decades after the would-be Overfiend Nagumo's reign of terror, the world is a battleground for feuding occult rulers and their "Demon-Beast" armies, and a young woman prepares to give birth to the true Overfiend, holder of the key to mankind's destiny. Horror, violence and sex mark this four-tape "adults only" anime odyssey. 220 min. total. Dubbed in English. NOTE: Individual volumes available at $29.99 each.
20-7253 Save $20.00! *$99.99*

Urotsukidoji III The Movie: Return Of The Overfiend
The story of the Overfiend's battle against the Lord of Chaos is also available in a special feature-length version. 120 min. In Japanese with English subtitles.
20-7520 *$29.99*

Urotsukidoji IV: Inferno Road: Complete Set
The climactic chapter in the horrific Overfiend saga, this three-tape series is set on a 21st-century Earth overrun by demonic creatures who enslave, rape and kill their mortal underlings, and where humans, demons and their mutant progeny battle to decide the fate of the world. Contains graphic sex and violence; adults only. 135 min. total. Dubbed in English. NOTE: Individual volumes available at $29.99 each.
20-7535 Save $10.00! *$79.99*

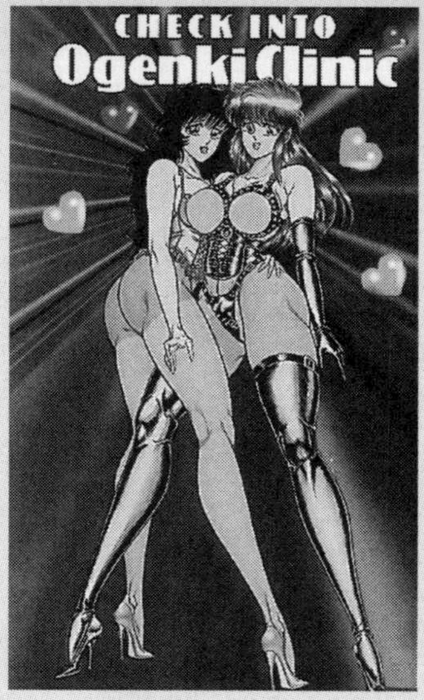

Ogenki Clinic
There's a room ready for you at the "full-service" clinic where the doctors and staff—especially the statuesque Nurse Ruko—tend to a variety of sexually obsessed and frustrated patients in this outrageously risqué anime series that's definitely for adults only. Each tape runs about 45 min.

Welcome To The Ogenki Clinic (Subtitled)
20-7832 *$29.99*

Check Into Ogenki Clinic (Dubbed)
20-8420 *$29.99*

Dark Warrior
A computer whiz, looking for information on a mysterious girl, taps into a top-secret system and soon finds himself on the run from high-tech ninjas and a secret in his own past that's linked to clandestine government genetics experiments in this animated sci-fi suspense series. WARNING: Contains graphic sex and violence; adults only. Each tape runs about 60 min. In Japanese with English subtitles.

Dark Warrior, Vol. 1: First Strike
20-7659 *$29.99*

Dark Warrior, Vol. 2: Jihad
20-7660 *$29.99*

The Elven Bride
All marriages have their own sets of challenges, but the most exotic problems ever may come in this comical, risqué anime fantasy that follows the rocky romance of a human who weds a pretty elf, only to find that certain...err, differences...make consummating their marriage next to impossible! Will the husband complete a crazy quest to help fulfill his wife? WARNING: Contains nudity and sexual situations; adults only. Each tape runs about 30 min. In Japanese with English subtitles.

The Elven Bride, Vol. 1
20-7703 *$29.99*

The Elven Bride, Vol. 2
20-7704 *$29.99*

My Fair Masseuse
Moko, a sexually curious young woman, takes a job as a masseuse, and finds that her job entails more than backrubs. Soon, she's involved in the sexual fantasies of her clients as well, meeting her challenges with the proper gung-ho attitude. WARNING: Contains nudity and sexual situations; adults only. 45 min. In Japanese with English subtitles.
20-8111 *$29.99*

Private Psycho Lesson
From "Visionary" creator U-Jin comes the outrageously erotic anime adventures of Sara Iijima, a sexy psychiatrist who uses her intuitive mind and voluptuous body to get at the root of her patients' problems. WARNING: Contains graphic violence and sexual situations; adults only. 74 min. In Japanese with English subtitles.
20-7952 *$29.99*

Lunatic Night
Three beautiful, sex-crazed women team up with the handsome former ruler of Atlantis in an attempt to restore his lost kingdom—if he can keep his mind on his job and off his comely cohorts—in this erotic anime odyssey. WARNING: Contains nudity and sexual situations; adults only. 75 min. In Japanese with English subtitles.
20-7953 *$29.99*

Adults Only!

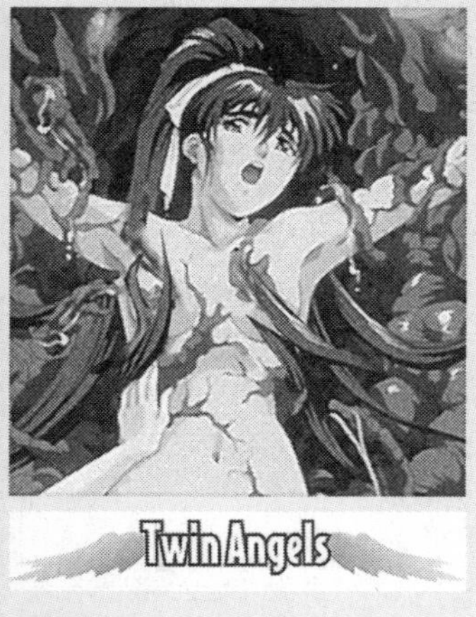

Twin Angels: Complete Set
Ai and Mai are a pair of sexy sisters who are actually the latest in a line of occult guardians, charged with defending the human world from the evil power of the Demon King, in this four-part "adults only" anime series that blends action, horror and graphic scenes of sex and violence. 240 min. total. Dubbed in English. NOTE: Individual volumes available at $29.99 each.
20-8155 Save $20.00! *$99.99*

Sexorcist
Two heroic—and well-endowed—young women set out to fight an evil multinational corporation with the help of remote-controlled robotic counterparts called "Silhouettes." All they have to do is keep the sex-crazed robots' computer minds on the job at hand in this erotic slice of sci-fi anime. WARNING: Contains nudity and sexual situations; adults only. 45 min. In Japanese with English subtitles.
20-8095 *$29.99*

The Ping Pong Club
It's the boys' time now! This rowdy bunch of students have what it takes to win it all in the world of Ping Pong—even if it means dealing with their not-so-smart new manager, their not-so-trustworthy captain, and their ever-present raging hormones—in this wild comedy anime series. Contains nudity. Each tape runs about 120 min. In Japanese with English subtitles.

The Ping Pong Club: Make Way For The Ping Pong Club
20-8105 *$29.99*

The Ping Pong Club: Love & Comedy (Die! Die! Die!)
20-8106 *$29.99*

The Ping Pong Club: The Ping Pong Club Goes Too Far
20-8129 *$29.99*

Bondage Queen Kate—Galaxy Policewoman
This ultra-erotic anime series follows the wild adventures of Kate, the beautiful and virginal rookie member of the Federal Space Army Security Police whose assignments get her involved in bizarre and kinky goings-on. WARNING: Contains nudity and sexual situations; adults only. Each tape runs about 45 min. In Japanese with English subtitles.

Bondage Queen Kate—Galaxy Policewoman, Vol. 1
20-8115 *$29.99*

Bondage Queen Kate—Galaxy Policewoman, Vol. 2
20-8116 *$29.99*

Strange Love
A gorgeous college co-ed finds that love is strange, indeed, when she must deal with the amorous advances of a professor who found out she's been breaking school rules by appearing in TV commercials, then with her own feelings towards a female transfer student, in this risqué anime outing. WARNING: Contains nudity and sexual situations; adults only. 80 min. In Japanese with English subtitles.
20-8128 *$29.99*

Strange Love (Dubbed Version)
Also available in a dubbed-in-English edition.
20-8117 *$24.99*

Beast City
The high-tech future world of Neo-Tokyo is faced with a horrifying enemy from its occult past in Naomi Hayakawa's gory, erotic anime series. Follow college student Mina, wielder of the Beast Hunter Sword, and her colleagues as they track down demonic creatures out to take over the human race. NOTE: contains graphic violence and sexual situations; adults only. Each tape runs about 45 min.

Beast City: Vampire Madonna (Subtitled)
20-8131 *$29.99*

Beast City: Vampire Madonna (Dubbed)
20-8132 *$29.99*

Beast City: Awakening Of The Beast (Subtitled)
20-8142 *$29.99*

Beast City: Awakening Of The Beast (Dubbed)
20-8143 *$29.99*

Wake Up! Aria
A group of beautiful young women think they're going to Golden Breast Island for an education at the elite Royal Elegance Music School, but the principal and his assistant have their own sinister plans for the student body (and bodies) in this erotic anime romp. WARNING: Contains nudity and sexual situations; adults only. 30 min. In Japanese with English subtitles.
20-8156 *$24.99*

Sakura Diaries
Ready to take a peek at some very racy remembrances? Just open up this erotic, funny anime look at some college students who seem to be majoring in romance, yet keep coming up with the wrong answers. Follow their search for true love, and the sexy detours they wind up taking. WARNING: Contains nudity and sexual situations; adults only. Each tape runs about 90 min. Dubbed in English. There are four volumes available, including:

Sakura Diaries, Vol. 1
20-8547 *$19.99*

Sakura Diaries, Vol. 2
20-8548 *$19.99*

Sakura Diaries, Vol. 3
20-8549 *$19.99*

Dream Hazard/Pianist
It's an erotic anime double bill on this video. First, a shy computer user lets go of her inhibitions in a virtual reality world, but will she be able to leave? Next, a pianist faced with a career-ending injury finds solace with a caring (and bosomy) android. WARNING: Contains nudity and sexual situations; adults only. 60 min. Dubbed in English.
20-8551 *$29.99*

Fencer Of Minerva
Fleeing her family's castle to be with her true love, a beautiful princess is waylaid by a band of slave traders. Taken captive and sold to a cruel master, she is subjected to unspeakable depravities as she waits for her rescuer in this graphic anime series. WARNING: Contains nudity and sexual situations; adults only. Each volume is also available in Japanese with English subtitles.

Fencer Of Minerva: The Emergence (Dubbed)
20-8553 *$19.99*

Fencer Of Minerva: The Tempest (Dubbed)
20-8555 *$19.99*

Sprite: Between Two Worlds
Shy schoolgirl Manami's just not been herself lately...or has she? What's the explanation for her sudden spells of flirtatious and violent behavior that she later can't recall, and is there room in one body for both the "nice" and "naughty" Manamis? Find out in this racy anime tale. WARNING: Contains nudity and sexual situations; adults only. 80 min. Dubbed in English.
20-8560 *$24.99*

FourPlay
A pair of Japanese college students become concerned when a female friend of theirs stops showing up at school. But when they find her, the formerly shy co-ed has become a sex-crazed vixen who draws them into her erotic games in this anime roundelay. WARNING: Contains nudity and sexual situations; adults only. 60 min. Dubbed in English.
20-8604 *$29.99*

Tekkaman Blade II
The '80s Japanese animated TV series "Tekkaman the Space Knight" is taken to new—and more violent and adult—levels with this three-part adventure featuring the knights' battle against the alien menace of Radham. Each tape runs about 60 min. Each volume is also available in Japanese with English subtitles.

Tekkaman Blade II, Stage 1: The New Generation (Dubbed)
20-8075 *$19.99*

Tekkaman Blade II, Stage 2: The Alien Intruder (Dubbed)
20-8084 *$19.99*

Tekkaman Blade II, Stage 3: The Final Encounter (Dubbed)
20-8139 *$19.99*

Black Lion
In 16th-century Japan, a powerful warlord uses futuristic technology and the services of Ginnai Doma, the "immortal ninja," to increase his power and holdings. Now one young fighter sets out to avenge the deaths of his friends and the woman he loved by killing Ginnai Doma. Intense and violent anime action drives this tale from Go Nagai ("Devilman"). 60 min. Dubbed in English.
20-8087 *$19.99*

Revolutionary Girl Utena: Complete Set
From the creators of "Sailor Moon" comes the thrilling anime exploits of Utena, a beautiful, sword-wielding girl who is the most popular student at her school, yet is haunted by memories of the prince who saved her after her parents' death and gave her a mysterious rose crest ring. Follow her odyssey to prove herself in this four-tape series. 325 min. total. In Japanese with English subtitles. NOTE: Individual volumes available at $29.99 each.
20-8126 Save $20.00! *$99.99*

Revolutionary Girl Utena: Complete Set (Dubbed Version)
The collection is also available in a dubbed-in-English edition. NOTE: Individual volumes available at $24.99 each.
20-8127 Save $10.00! *$89.99*

Gatchaman: Boxed Set
First seen on American TV in the kids' cartoons "Battle of the Planets" and "G Force," the heroic five-person crew of the starship Phoenix return to all-new adventures in this three-tape, adult-themed anime series. When a gigantic, dragon-shaped ship attacks the Earth to take the planet's energy, the Gatchaman squad blasts off to intercept it and battle the army of Gallacter. 140 min. total. NOTE: Individual volumes available at $19.99 each.
20-8140 Save $15.00! *$44.99*

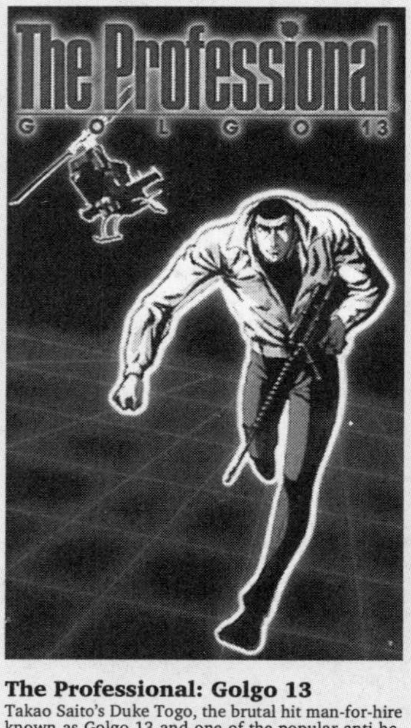

The Professional: Golgo 13
Takao Saito's Duke Togo, the brutal hit man-for-hire known as Golgo 13 and one of the popular anti-heroes in Japanese comics, made his animated debut in this sexually graphic, explosively violent feature. After killing the son of a powerful businessman, Golgo becomes the target in a revenge plot. 90 min. Dubbed in English.
45-8041 Was $29.99 *$19.99*

Golgo 13: Queen Bee
Brutal and action-filled animated suspense with a bullet, as professional assassin Golgo 13 is hired to eliminate the leader of a revolutionary faction in a South American nation. Will Golgo side with the rebels and their fight for freedom, or with his employers? 60 min. Dubbed in English.
20-8094 *$19.99*

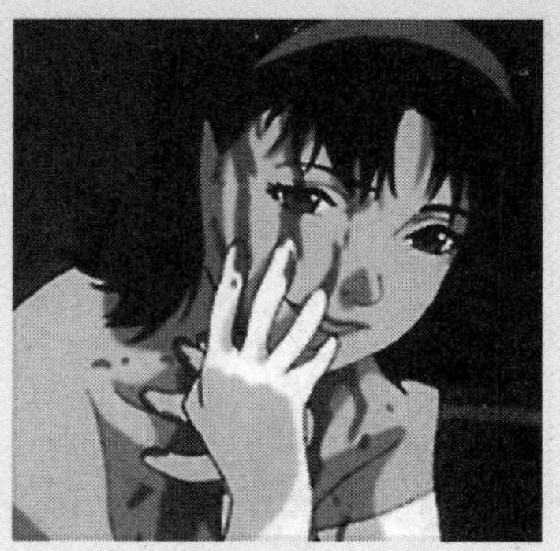

Perfect Blue: Unrated Director's Cut
This groundbreaking anime details the adventures of a female pop star who forgoes her music career to become an actress. After appearing in a thriller, her life becomes a series of nightmarish occurrences—including the death of her friends—that are chronicled on the Internet. This is the unrated director's cut featuring nudity and violence. Dubbed in English.
02-9163 *$19.99*

Complete AD Police Files
MegaTokyo in the year 2027 is the setting for three dramatic animated tales focusing on members of the AD (Advanced) Police Force as they cope with the growing problems presented by the city high-tech work force, intelligent androids known as Boomers. 120 min. In Japanese with English subtitles.
20-8164 *$29.99*

Sorcerer Hunters
They're a crack squad of mystical warriors, charged with saving the countryside from power-hungry magicians, virgin-hungry dragons, and other menaces. Follow the exciting, sexy exploits of lovely and lethal Chocolate and Tira Misu, mysterious brothers Carrot and Marron Glace, and newcomer Gateau Mocha in this six-part anime fantasy series. Each volume is also available in Japanese with English subtitles. There are six volumes available, including:

Sorcerer Hunters, Vol. 1: Of Inhuman Bondage! (Dubbed)
20-8167 *$24.99*

Sorcerer Hunters, Vol. 2: 2 Beauties & A Beast (Dubbed)
20-8169 *$24.99*

Sorcerer Hunters, Vol. 3: Fires Of Passion (Dubbed)
20-8171 *$24.99*

Spell Wars: Sorcerer Hunters Revenge
The "Sorcerer Hunters" saga continues in these action-packed animated adventures, as the wicked warlock Zaha Torte hatches a scheme for revenge against the heroes and their mentor, Big Momma. Each tape runs about 90 minutes and is also available in Japanese with English subtitles. There are four volumes available, including:

Spell Wars, Vol. 1 (Dubbed)
20-8528 *$19.99*

Spell Wars, Vol. 2 (Dubbed)
20-8530 *$19.99*

Spell Wars, Vol. 3 (Dubbed)
20-8532 *$19.99*

801 T.T.S. Airbats
Take off on the wildest, sexiest, funniest anime flight ever with this look at life with the all-female pilot crew of the 801 Tactical Training Squadron, their "batty" mascot, and a love-starved guy who's the new flight maintenance specialist. Each tape runs about 60 min. except for Vol. 1, which runs 85 min. Each volume is also available in Japanese with English subtitles.

801 T.T.S. Airbats: Second Strike (Dubbed)
20-8189 *$14.99*

801 T.T.S. Airbats: Third Strike (Dubbed)
20-8199 *$14.99*

801 T.T.S. Airbats: First Strike (Dubbed)
20-8222 *$19.99*

DNA Sights 999.9
Following Earth's devastation by a meteor collision in the early 21st century, a young man who developed mutant abilities from the disaster travels into outer space with two similarly gifted humans in order to save mankind's destiny from the evil Trader Force. Thrilling anime space saga from manga artist Leiji Matsumoto also features cameos by the "Captain Harlock" and "Star Blazers" casts. 50 min. Dubbed in English.
20-8232 *$19.99*

Princess Rouge: The Legend Of The Last Labyrinth
What would you do if a beautiful girl fell out of the sky and into your lap? For teenage Yusuke, it's a dream come true when he meets Rouge, who can remember nothing about her past, until two women claiming to be her sisters from a royal family and demanding her return. Anything can happen in this wild animated fantasy from Japan. 60 min. In Japanese with English subtitles.
20-8316 *$24.99*

The Legend Of The Last Labyrinth (Dubbed Version)
Also available in a dubbed-in-English edition.
20-8599 *$24.99*

The Heroic Legend Of Arislan
When the kingdom of Palse is attacked by the army of Lusitania, young prince Arislan must bring together a band of renegade warriors to fend off the invaders and fulfill his destined rise to the throne. Exciting fight scenes fuel this four-part animated adaptation of the fantasy series by writer Yoshiki Tanaka. Each tape runs about 60 min. Each volume is also available in a subtitled version.

The Heroic Legend Of Arislan, Part 1 (Dubbed Version)
20-7602 *$19.99*

The Heroic Legend Of Arislan, Part 2 (Dubbed Version)
20-7604 *$19.99*

The Heroic Legend Of Arislan, Parts 3 & 4 (Dubbed Version)
20-7605 *$19.99*

The Heroic Legend Of Arislan: Age Of Heroes
The saga of the intrepid prince continues, as young Arislan must try to rescue his captive father while stopping the wicked Silvermask from stealing a magical sword that will unleash the ages-old evil of the Snake King across the land. 60 min. Dubbed in English.
20-8240 *$24.99*

Geobreeders
For the guys and gals of the Karuga Total Security company, travelling the world to battle ghosts and phantoms isn't just an adventure...it's a job! See how they use their wits, as well as computers and some super-size guns, to save a kidnapped friend of theirs, in this animated tale filled with action and laughs. 90 min. Dubbed in English.
20-8520 *$24.99*

The Humanoid
Her name is Antoinette...she's sexy, smart, and made of metal! This risqué robot takes viewers on a revealing look at life and love in the future in an offbeat "adults only" animated tale. 45 min. Dubbed in English.
20-7510 *$14.99*

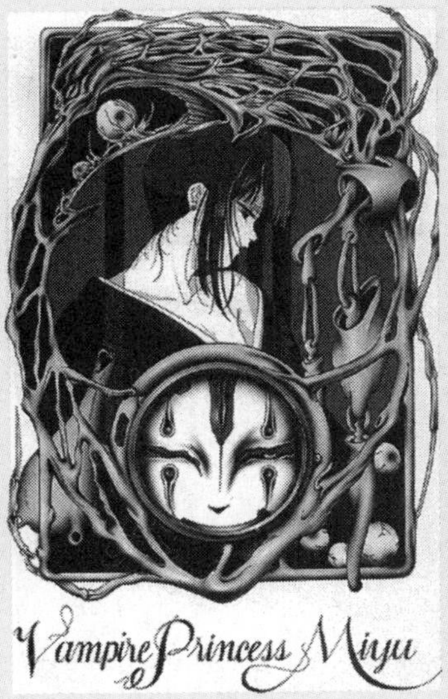
Vampire Princess Miyu

Vampire Princess Miyu
An eerily haunting tale of suspense and Gothic-style horror from Japan, this animated series follows a young spiritualist named Himiko as she tracks down Miyu, the bewitching princess of the undead, in order to stop the evil Shinma spirits from taking over the mortal world. Each tape features two episodes and runs about 50 min. Each volume is also available in Japanese with English subtitles.

Vampire Princess Miyu, Vol. 1 (Dubbed)
20-7501 *$19.99*

Vampire Princess Miyu, Vol. 2 (Dubbed)
20-7513 *$19.99*

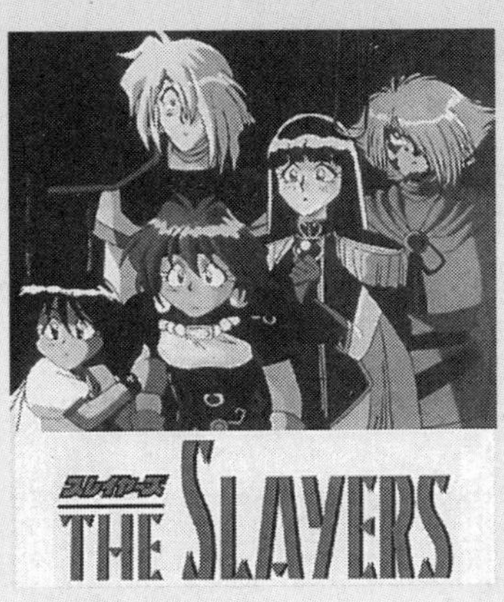
THE SLAYERS

The Slayers
In this fast-paced, light-hearted sword-and-sorcery anime series, a feisty magician-thief named Lina faces a variety of perils and a constantly shifting cast of allies and foes (including dragons, wizards, and not-too-bright swordsmen) as she tries to learn the secret of a mystical statue she "acquired." Each four-tape collector's boxed set runs about 325 min. NOTE: Individual volumes available at $19.99 each.

The Slayers: Vols. 1-4 Boxed Set (Subtitled)
20-8068 Save $10.00! *$69.99*

The Slayers: Vols. 1-4 Boxed Set (Dubbed)
20-8069 Save $10.00! *$69.99*

The Slayers: Vols. 5-8 Boxed Set (Subtitled)
20-8070 Save $10.00! *$69.99*

The Slayers: Vols. 5-8 Boxed Set (Dubbed)
20-8071 Save $10.00! *$69.99*

Slayers: The Motion Picture
The offbeat animated adventures of feisty sorceress Lina and her colleague Nahga reached the big screen with this feature-length fantasy. Watch the Slayers battle an array of monstrous menaces as they seek to free the island of Mipross from a spell. 75 min. In Japanese with English subtitles.
20-8077 *$29.99*

Slayers: The Motion Picture (Dubbed Version)
Also available in a dubbed-in-English edition.
20-8078 *$19.99*

The Slayers Next
The fantasy saga of reluctant hero Lina and her band of colleagues continues in these all-new animated adventures. Each four-tape collector's boxed set runs about 325 min. NOTE: Individual volumes available at $19.99 each.

The Slayers Next: Vols. 1-4 Boxed Set (Subtitled)
20-8263 Save $10.00! *$69.99*

The Slayers Next: Vols. 1-4 Boxed Set (Dubbed)
20-8264 Save $10.00! *$69.99*

The Slayers Next: Vols. 5-8 Boxed Set (Subtitled)
20-8265 Save $10.00! *$69.99*

The Slayers Next: Vols. 5-8 Boxed Set (Dubbed)
20-8266 Save $10.00! *$69.99*

The Slayers Try
What should have been a simple voyage to the New World for sorceress-in-training Lina and her companions turns into a comical series of misadventures when they lose their boat and wind up fighting animal-men, demons and other foes in the latest "Slayers" saga. Each four-tape collector's boxed set runs about 300 min. NOTE: Individual volumes available at $19.99 each.

The Slayers Try: Vols. 1-4 Boxed Set (Subtitled)
20-8583 *$69.99*

The Slayers Try: Vols. 1-4 Boxed Set (Dubbed)
20-8584 *$69.99*

The Slayers Try: Vols. 5-8 Boxed Set (Subtitled)
20-8585 *$69.99*

The Slayers Try: Vols. 5-8 Boxed Set (Dubbed)
20-8586 *$69.99*

Silent Möbius
With the Earth of 2023 under attack by extradimensional demons, mankind's last chance lies with the seven women of the Attacked Mystification Police Department. Will even their paranormal abilities be enough, though? Follow their battle in this thrilling sci-fi anime outing. Each tape runs about 50 minutes and is also available in Japanese with English subtitles.

Silent Möbius, Vol. 1: Decisions (Dubbed)
85-1493 *$19.99*

Silent Möbius, Vol. 2: Tokyo Underground (Dubbed)
85-1495 *$19.99*

Silent Möbius, Vol. 3: Let's Have A Party! (Dubbed)
85-1497 *$19.99*

Galaxy Express 999: The Signature Edition (1979)
Based on the popular comic book and cartoon series by Leiji Matsumoto ("Star Blazers"), this futuristic feature film follows a young Earth man as he boards the Galaxy Express, a cosmos-spanning "train," on a quest to avenge his mother's death. His odyssey and encounters with other "passengers" make for a memorable sci-fi adventure. Uncut, 120-minute version. In Japanese with English subtitles.
20-7544 *$29.99*

Galaxy Express 999 (Dubbed Version)
Also available in a dubbed-in-English edition.
20-7545 *$24.99*

Ushio & Tora: Complete Set
Teenager Ushio is shocked to find an unusual houseguest in his family's basement: a live and irate demon, trapped there 500 years earlier by the boy's monster-taming ancestor. When the demon's presence begins drawing otherworldly creatures into the neighborhood, he and Ushio form an uneasy alliance to bring things back to normal in this five-volume anime fantasy series. 330 min. total. In Japanese with English subtitles. NOTE: Individual volumes available at $29.99 each.
20-8627 *$149.99*

Trigun
He's the most feared gunslinger on a distant frontier planet, so deadly he carries a $60,000,000,000 bounty for anyone who can bring him in...yet no one's ever seen him take a life. He's Vash the Stampede, alias the Humanoid Typhoon, and he takes on a wide array of foes in these action-filled anime tales. Except where noted, each tape features three episodes and runs about 75 min. Each volume is also available in Japanese with English subtitles.

Trigun, Vol. 1: The $60,000,000,000 Man (Dubbed)
Inccludes four episodes. 100 min.
85-1472 *$24.99*

Trigun, Vol. 2: Lost Past (Dubbed)
85-1474 *$24.99*

Trigun, Vol. 3: Wolfwood (Dubbed)
85-1476 *$24.99*

Trigun, Vol. 4: Gun-Ho-Guns (Dubbed)
85-1478 *$24.99*

Oh My Goddess!: Complete Set
A college freshman trying to call a take-out restaurant winds up contacting a gorgeous goddess named Belldandy who, fulfilling his one wish, takes on human form and becomes his girlfriend. Romance, comedy and fantasy are mixed in this five-tape adaptation of Fujishima Kousuke's comic series. 150 min. total. Dubbed in English. NOTE: Indvidual volumes available at $14.99 each.
20-8626 *$74.99*

E.Y.E.S. Of Mars
Fantastic family anime set on the planet Mars, which is about to become extinct because of a series of natural disasters. Living underground in an artificial environment is a young woman whose life is threatened by the impending disaster. Out to rescue her is a young man from above-ground with plans to save the planet by communicating with an ancient spirit named "Messenger." 80 min.
69-5287 *$14.99*

Devilman
When a prehistoric carving is excavated, 10 ancient demons are resurrected to wreak terror on the modern world. Anyone who manages to kill a demon will become a demon himself, but one young man will tempt fate by trying to possess a demon's body in this frightening, state-of-the-art anime series from Go Nagai. Each volume runs about 55 minutes and is also available in Japanese with English subtitles.

Devilman, Vol. 1: Genesis (Dubbed)
02-8266 *$14.99*

Devilman, Vol. 2: Siren, The Demon Bird (Dubbed)
02-8267 *$14.99*

Violence Jack: The Uncut Series
From "Devilman" creator Go Nagai comes this brutally violent sci-fi saga, set on a desolate future Earth where survivors of environmental disasters live in crowded, seedy underground cities. Into the "tomb-city" of Evil Town comes the savage warrior known as Violence Jack, but is he savior...or devil? WARNING: Contains graphic violence and sexual situations; adults only. Each volume runs about 60 minutes and is also available in Japanese with English subtitles.

Violence Jack, Vol. 1: Evil Town (Dubbed)
17-7042 *$24.99*

Violence Jack, Vol. 2: Hell's Wind (Dubbed)
17-7044 *$24.99*

Violence Jack, Vol. 3: Slumking (Dubbed)
17-7046 *$24.99*

Hanappe Bazooka
A picked-on high schooler whose favorite pastime is fantasizing about girls gets a chance for revenge when some dimension-spanning "demons" offer to turn his index finger into the most powerful weapon in the universe. Now, if only he can learn how to control it! From "Violence Jack" creator Go Nagai comes this wildly comic "adults only" sci-fi romp that's full of nudity, sex and graphic violence. 55 min. In Japanese with English subtitles.
20-7668 *$29.99*

Iron Virgin Jun
About to be auctioned off in marriage by her family on her 18th birthday, a feisty, strong-willed (and virginal) woman named Jun decides to run away from home, accompanied by a faithful servant. The bandits her mother hires to bring Jun home and "teach" her about sex will certainly have their hands full in this outrageous anime tale from Go Nagai ("Cutey Honey"). WARNING: Contains violence and sexual situations; adults only. 45 min. In Japanese with English subtitles.
20-7985 *$29.99*

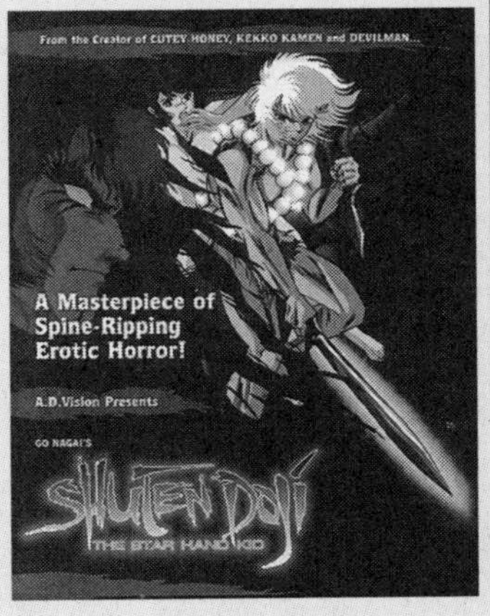
From the Creator of CUTEY HONEY, KEKKO KAMEN and DEVILMAN...
A Masterpiece of Spine-Ripping Erotic Horror!
A.D.Vision Presents
GO NAGAI'S
SHUTEN DOJI
THE STAR HAND KID

Shuten Doji: The Star Hand Kid
From anime legend Go Nagai ("Devilman," "Violence Jack") comes a suspense-filled animated saga of erotic horror, as teenager Jiro learns of his inhuman heritage and the role he must play in the ultimate battle between mankind and demonic hordes seeking to destroy him and take over the Earth. WARNING: contains graphic violence and sexual situations; adults only. Each tape runs about 50 min. In Japanese with English subtitles.

Shuten Doji, Vol. 1
20-7721 *$29.99*

Shuten Doji, Vol. 2
20-7722 *$29.99*

Shuten Doji, Vol. 3
20-7723 *$29.99*

Shuten Doji, Vol. 4
20-7724 *$29.99*

Star Demon: Shuten Doji
The "Shuten Doji" saga is also available in this feature-length edition. 60 min. Dubbed in English.
20-8592 *$19.99*

Delinquent In Drag
He'd be the big man on campus, but no one knows he's a man. Horny teen Banji is less than thrilled when his parents arrange for him to don dresses and attend an all-girls' school, but learning to put on makeup is easy compared to keeping his cool around his sexy schoolmates in this wild and racy anime romp from Go Nagai. 60 min. In Japanese with English subtitles.
20-8191 *$29.99*

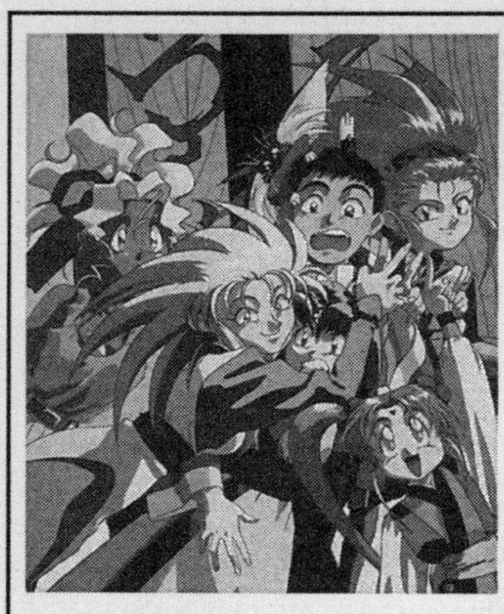

Tenchi-Muyo!
High school student Tenchi Masaki gets into all sorts of fantastic adventures, courtesy of some alien teenage girls who crash in his yard and wind up moving in with his family and competing for his affections, in this popular comedy/sci-fi anime series. Each three-episode tape runs about 90 minutes and is dubbed in English.

Tenchi Muyo!,Vol. 1: Trouble Hatches
Includes "Ryoko Resurrected," "Here Comes Ayeka!" and "Hello Ryo-Ohki!"
85-1516 *$14.99*

Tenchi The Movie: Tenchi-Muyo In Love
Intergalactic police officers, a time-warping alien terrorist named Kain, and Washu's own time machine all add up to a dangerous and surprise-filled trip 26 years into the past for Tenchi and his friends in this feature-length adventure. 90 min. Dubbed in English.
85-1080 *$19.99*

Tenchi The Movie 2: The Daughter Of Darkness
The arrival of a mysterious girl named Mayuka who claims to be his daughter is just the beginning of Tenchi's troubles in this full-length tale that finds the whole "Tenchi-Muyo" crew facing a nasty plot by that Demoness of the Dark, Yuzuha. Dubbed in English.
85-1158 *$19.99*

Tenchi The Movie 3: Tenchi Forever
The ongoing rivalry between Rykoi and Ayeka for Tenchi's attention has finally driven the put-down young man into the hills for a little peace and quiet, but what will happen when he's found in the arms of a mysterious woman, in this third (and final?) feature-length entry in the hilarious anime saga. 95 min. Dubbed in English.
85-1430 *$24.99*

Tenchi Universe: The Series
You'd think a teenage boy who has four gorgeous girls staying with him would be in heaven, but for Tenchi Masaki it's one comic mess after another when one beautiful alien after another wind up on his doorstep, taking him and his friends on some wild adventures, in this eight-volume continuation of the "Tenchi" saga. Except where noted, each tape contains three episodes and runs about 65 min. There are eight volumes available, including:

Tenchi Universe, Vol. 1 (Dubbed)
Includes four episodes. 100 min.
85-1090 *$24.99*

Tenchi Universe, Vol. 2 (Dubbed)
85-1092 *$24.99*

Tenchi Universe, Vol. 3 (Dubbed)
85-1094 *$24.99*

Tenchi In Tokyo
Tenchi and the gang may have moved into a new home in Tokyo, but thanks to a slew of uninvited alien guests, a string of unusual (to say the least!) girlfriends, and ongoing mischief from a "cabbit" named Ryo-ohki, it means more of the same wildly funny exploits that "Tenchi" fans have come to expect in this eight-tape series. Except for the four-episode Vol. 8, each tape features three episodes and runs about 75 min.

Tenchi In Tokyo, Vol. 1: A New Start (Dubbed)
85-1218 *$24.99*

Tenchi In Tokyo, Vol. 2: A New Friend (Dubbed)
85-1220 *$24.99*

Tenchi In Tokyo, Vol. 3: A New Legend (Dubbed)
85-1222 *$24.99*

Magical Project S
Fresh from her "Tenchi-Muyo" adventures, the mischievous Sasami takes center stage in this all-new fantasy series. Selected by Queen Tsunami to be a champion of goodness in the universe, Sasami must battle her arch-rival, Pixy Misa, and a string of unusual (to say the least) magic-spawned opponents. In Japanese with English subtitles. There are seven volumes available, including:

Magical Project S, Vol. 1: The Queen's Champion
Includes episodes 1-4. 100 min.
85-1228 *$29.99*

Magical Project S, Vol. 2: Star Search
Includes episodes 5-7. 75 min.
85-1229 *$29.99*

Magical Project S, Vol. 3: Love-Love Monsters
Includes episodes 8-10. 75 min.
85-1230 *$29.99*

Magical Project S, Vol. 4: Need Tenchi!
Includes episodes 11-13. 75 min.
85-1231 *$29.99*

Harmagedon
From the depths of outer space, an evil being of near-infinite power is coming to devour the Earth, and the only thing standing in its way is a beautiful princess, her psychic-powered warriors, and a giant alien cyborg. Exciting Japanese animated action. 132 min. Dubbed in English.
20-7536 *$19.99*

Iria: Zeiram The Animation
An anime prequel to the live-action Japanese film "Zeram," this stunning three-volume sci-fi series follows beautiful bounty hunter Iria' search for the unstoppable alien monster responsible for her brother's death. Along with sidekick Kei, Iria finds she must not only worry about the bloodthirsty Zeram, but also a deadly conspiracy surrounding the corporation trying to bring the creature to Earth. Each tape features two episodes and runs about 60 min. Dubbed in English.

Iria: Zeiram The Animation, Vol. 1
20-7539 *$19.99*

Iria: Zeiram The Animation, Vol. 2
20-7540 *$19.99*

Iria: Zeiram The Animation, Vol. 3
20-7541 *$19.99*

Genocyber
In a future world where private armies of multinational corporations battle, a Japanese combine launches the ultimate weapon: a monstrous creature whose energies come from two sisters with cybernetic and psychic powers. Traditional and computer animation are mixed with live-action effects in this "anime" saga. Each tape runs about 50 min. Each volumes is also available in Japanese with English subtitles.

Genocyber, Part 1: The Birth Of Genocyber (Dubbed)
20-7638 *$19.99*

Genocyber, Parts 2 & 3: Vajranoid Showdown (Dubbed)
20-7639 *$19.99*

Genocyber, Parts 4 And 5: The Legend Of Ark De Grande (Dubbed)
20-8152 *$19.99*

GOKU MIDNIGHT EYE

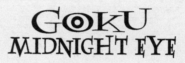

Goku: Midnight Eye
If you're looking for exciting private "eye" action, anime-style, check out this intense series. Goku is an ex-cop-turned-PI who, armed with a cybernetic eye that allows him to access any computer system, begins investigating a rash of "suicides" among his former police department colleagues. WARNING: Contains graphic violence; adults only. Each volume runs about 60 minutes and is also available in Japanese with English subtitles.

Goku: Midnight Eye (Dubbed)
20-8618 *$19.99*

Goku II: Midnight Eye (Dubbed)
20-8620 *$19.99*

Golden Boy: Complete Set
Young computer whiz Kintaro is deliriously happy when a software company president gives him a job. Sure, it's just an "office boy" position that has him fixing toilets, but this firm is staffed entirely by beautiful women! Every sex-starved computer nerd's fantasy becomes a (cartoon) reality in this slapstick six-volume series filled with nudity and risqué situations. 180 min. total. In Japanese with English subtitles. NOTE: Individual volumes available at $24.99 each.
20-8628 *$124.99*

Golden Boy: Complete Set (Dubbed Version)
The collection is also available in a dubbed-in-English edition. NOTE: Individual volumes available at $19.99 each.
20-8629 *$99.99*

Street Fighter II: The Animated Movie (Uncut Version) (1995)
Video game fans, get ready for the biggest explosion of animated excitement to ever hit the screen, as M. Bison and his Shadowlaw minions use psychic energy and brute force to take over the world, and only the legendary Street Fighter can stop them. Soundtrack includes Alice in Chains, KMFDM, Silverchair and more. Uncut, unrated version features violent scenes that may be too intense for younger viewers. 96 min.
04-5408 *$14.99*

Rail Of The Star (1997)
Based on a true story, this moving animated drama follows a young girl and her family's struggles in Japanese-occupied Korea during World War II. The end of the conflict doesn't end their troubles, however, as the partition of their homeland leaves them in the Russian-controlled North and sends them on a desperate odyssey southward to freedom. 80 min. In Japanese with English subtitles.
20-7879 *$24.99*

Gestalt
Upon hearing about a mysterious, godlike being who will grant any wish, a young priest named Olivier and an enigmatic mute girl named Ohri set out to find his island home. The journey puts them in contact with elves and other friends and foes in this animated fantasy. 60 min. In Japanese with English subtitles.
20-8556 *$24.99*

Gestalt (Dubbed Version)
Also available in a dubbed-in-English edition.
20-8557 *$24.99*

Pet Shop Of Horrors
Be careful before you purchase an animal from the mysterious Chinatown store in this chilling anime series, because its owner, the Count, stocks his shelves with man-eating fish, wish-granting mythological creatures, and other specimens who need tender loving care...or else! WARNING: Contains graphic violence. Each volume runs about 60 minutes and is also available in Japanese with English subtitles.

Pet Shop Of Horrors, Vol. 1 (Dubbed)
20-8522 *$19.99*

Pet Shop Of Horrors, Vol. 2 (Dubbed)
20-8589 *$19.99*

Armitage III: Poly-Matrix
She's sexy, strong, and more than human. She's Armitage, a "third-type robot" police officer for the Earth colony on Mars. Now, along with human partner Ross, she must track down the person responsible for the murders of her cybernetic kin. Elizabeth Berkley and Kiefer Sutherland supply voices for this thrilling animated sci-fi feature from Japan. 90 min. Dubbed in English.
85-1105 *$19.99*

Bastard!!: Boxed Set (Dubbed Version)
A rapscallious sorcerer named Dark Schneider is brought back to life in order to save the land of Meta-Rikana from the armies of the Big Four. Trouble is, Schneider used to lead the Big Four, and will even the love of a young woman named Yoko convince him to help? Find out in this three-part anime fantasy series. 180 min. total. Dubbed in English. NOTE: Individual volumes available at $19.99 each.
85-1202 *$59.99*

Video Girl Ai
"I Dream of Jeannie" goes high-tech with this funny, racy and romantic anime series about a hapless youth named Yota who, after striking out with one female after another, receives a magical videotape. Upon playing the tape, a beautiful girl named Ai pops out of the TV—but will Ai help or hurt Yota's love life? Each volume runs about 60 minutes and is also available in Japanese with English subtitles.

Video Girl Ai: I'm Here For You (Dubbed)
85-1207 *$24.99*

Video Girl Ai: First Date (Dubbed)
85-1227 *$24.99*

Video Girl Ai: Ai, Love & Sadness (Dubbed)
85-1334 *$24.99*

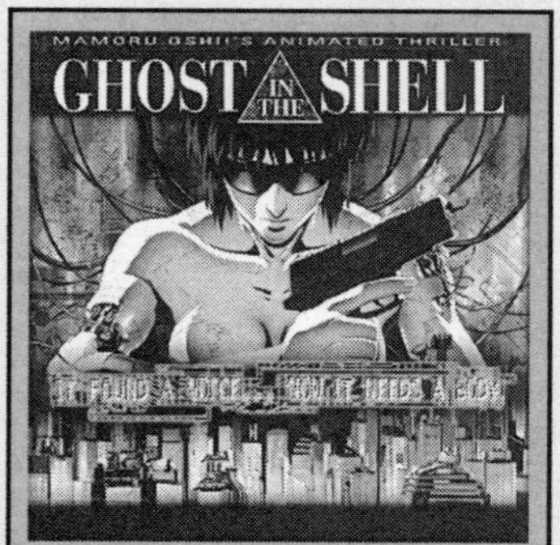

Ghost In The Shell (1995)
In early 21st-century Japan, the search for a criminal computer genius known as "The Puppet Master" sends a cyborg policewoman on a dangerous search, leading her to a powerful artificial intelligence whose influence reaches into the government and who is looking for a physical form to inhabit. Spellbinding animated sci-fier, based on Masamune Shirow's manga series. 90 min. In Japanese with English subtitles.
02-8466 *$29.99*

Ghost In The Shell (Dubbed Version)
02-8467 *$19.99*

Ghost In The Shell: Special Edition (Dubbed)
This special remastered version also includes a 30-minute program on the making of the film.
02-8698 *$24.99*

Shamanic Princess
By day she seems to be an ordinary schoolgirl, but Tiara is a princess who uses her magical powers to battle her enemies and recover the powerful talisman stolen by her beloved in this exciting fantasy series. Each volume runs about 100 minutes and is also available in Japanese with English subtitles.

Shamanic Princess, Vol. 1: Tiara's Quest (Dubbed)
20-8601 *$19.99*

Shamanic Princess, Vol. 2: The Talisman Unleashed (Dubbed)
20-8613 *$19.99*

Shamanic Princess, Vol. 3: Guardian World (Dubbed)
20-8615 *$19.99*

Elf Princess Rane
A high-school student and would-be adventurer finds more action than he ever imagined when he runs into a beautiful elf princess, who leads him on a wild search for treasure, in this fun-filled slice of anime fantasy. 60 min. Dubbed in English.
20-8237 *$24.99*

Arcadia Of My Youth (1982)
One of the great heroes of the Japanese comics, space pirate Captain Harlock, is featured in this full-length sci-fi adventure set on a future Earth conquered by the evil Illumidus Empire. Watch as the young Harlock and his allies fight to free the planet. 130 min. In Japanese with English subtitles.
20-7157 Was $39.99 *$24.99*

My Youth In Arcadia (Dubbed Version)
The Captain Harlock feature "Arcadia of My Youth" is also available in a dubbed-in-English edition.
64-1365 *$14.99*

Bubblegum Crisis
Set in the "cyberpunk" world of A.D. 2032 Mega-Tokyo, this three-volume anime series shows how, after a devastating earthquake, a group of high-tech female mercenaries called the Knight Sabers battles the evil GENOM corporation and their Boomer androids.

Bubblegum Crisis ARC 1: Mason (Subtitled)
Includes episodes 1-3. 113 min.
20-8354 *$29.99*

Bubblegum Crisis ARC 1: Mason (Dubbed)
20-8355 *$29.99*

Bubblegum Crisis ARC 2: Largo (Subtitled)
Includes episodes 4-6. 132 min.
20-8356 *$29.99*

Bubblegum Crisis ARC 2: Largo (Dubbed)
20-8357 *$29.99*

Bubblegum Crisis ARC 3: Minor Wave (Subtitled)
Includes episodes 7 and 8. 99 min.
20-8358 *$29.99*

Bubblegum Crisis ARC 3: Minor Wave (Dubbed)
20-8359 *$29.99*

Phoenix 2772 (1980)
Legendary Japanese cartoonist Osamu Tezuka ("Astro Boy") wrote and produced this feature-length animated sci-fi saga. A young starship pilot undertakes a dangerous mission to track down the fabled space firebird known as the Phoenix, in order to use its mystical powers to save a dying Earth. 121 min. Dubbed in English.
64-1375 *$19.99*

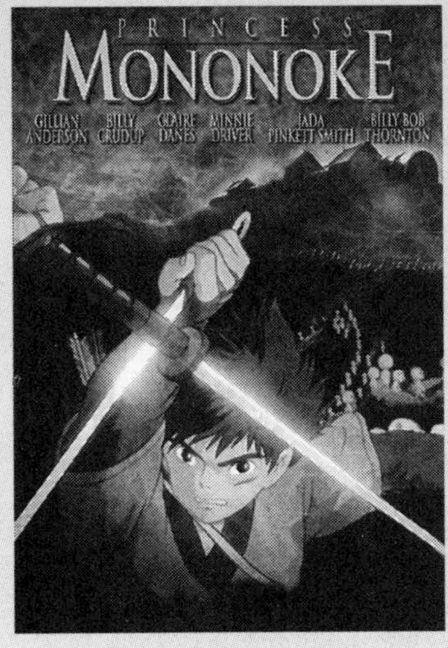

Princess Mononoke (1999)
Stateside release of animation wizard Hayao Miyakazi's 1997 masterpiece is set in Japan's Muromachio era, when a maddened boar god infects a prince with a deadly curse. Leaving his people to seek a cure, the prince gets caught in the middle of a battle between a mining town, the animal spirits of the forest, and the wolf-riding Princess Mononoke. Voices are supplied by Billy Crudup, Gillian Anderson, Claire Danes, Minnie Driver and Billy Bob Thornton. 134 min. Dubbed in English.
11-2452 ❏$99.99

Night Warriors: Darkstalkers' Revenge—The Animated Series
On an Earth shrouded in eternal night, humans and their undead allies fight to destroy the monstrous Darkstalkers—vampires, werewolves, zombies, ghosts and other creatures—that have claimed the world as their own. The popular video game is taken to new heights of terror and suspense in this graphically violent anime series. Each volume runs about 45 minutes and is also available in Japanese with English subtitles.

Night Warriors, Vol. 1 (Dubbed)
85-1144 $19.99

Night Warriors, Vol. 2 (Dubbed)
85-1146 $19.99

Night Warriors, Vol. 3 (Dubbed)
85-1330 $19.99

Night Warriors, Vol. 4 (Dubbed)
85-1332 $19.99

Clamp School Detectives: Complete Set
Join Akira, Nokoru and Suoh, a trio of schoolboy sleuths who wind up turning their campus upside-down with comedy and adventure as they try to solve a bewildering slew of mysterious goings-on, in this wacky, six-tape anime series. 682 min. total. In Japanese with English subtitles. NOTE: Individual volumes available at $29.99 each.
85-1216 Save $30.00! $149.99

Kishin Heidan: Alien Defender Geo Armor: Boxed Set
World War II action meets robotic thrills in this four-volume anime series. Mysterious aliens have teamed with the Third Reich to take over Earth, and the free world's last line of defense is the Kishin Corps and their giant robots. 240 min. total. In Japanese with English subtitles. NOTE: Individual volumes available at $29.99 each.
85-1257 Save $60.00! $59.99

Kishin Heidan: Alien Defender Geo Armor: Boxed Set (Dubbed Version)
The collection is also available in a dubbed-in-English edition. NOTE: Individual volumes available at $24.99 each.
85-1258 Save $40.00! $59.99

Saber Marionette J: Boxed Set
In Japoness, an all-male society where the only females are android servants called "marionettes," a young man named Otaru has his hands full when he activates a trio of marionettes with human emotions. Join Lime, Cherry and Bloodberry as they turn their "master's" life topsy-turvy in this fun-filled, eight-tape anime series. 700 min. total. In Japanese with English subtitles. NOTE: Individual volumes available at $29.99 each.
85-1293 Save $90.00! $149.99

Ayane's High Kick
Ayane Mitsui is a high school girl who plans to use her wicked "high kick" to become a champion in the pro wrestling ring. Will her kickboxing training get in the way of her studies—or will it be the other way around—in this hard-hitting anime tale? 60 min. Dubbed in English.
20-8012 $19.99

Poltergeist Report: Yu Yu Hakusho
Earth has become the prize in a magical battle between five heroes from the Spirit World and the demonic forces of Lord Yakumo, king of the Netherworld, in an exciting anime tale of supernatural action, horror and suspense. 90 min. In Japanese with English subtitles.
20-7978 $29.99

Ruin Explorers
A pair of young, feisty and trouble-prone female adventurers-for-hire are called on to retrieve a priceless weapon said to possess enough mystical power to bring forth the end of civilization. First, though, they must cope with rival treasure hunters, demons and other obstacles along the way in this sexy, funny and exciting two-part anime fantasy. Each tape runs about 60 min.

Ruin Explorers, Vol. 1 (Subtitled)
20-8023 $29.99

Ruin Explorers, Vol. 1 (Dubbed)
20-8024 $19.99

Ruin Explorers, Vol. 2 (Subtitled)
20-8192 $29.99

Ruin Explorers, Vol. 2 (Dubbed)
20-8193 $19.99

Silent Service
The most advanced and powerful nuclear submarine ever developed, the Seabat, is a joint project of the U.S. and Japan. But when the crew pronounces the vessel to be an independent nation during its shakedown cruise, it provokes an international military incident that could lead to World War III in this exciting animated drama. 100 min. Dubbed in English.
20-8026 $24.99

The Cockpit
From acclaimed anime creators Yoshiaki Kawajiri, Takashi Imanishi and Ryosuke Takahashi comes a trio of dramatic stories of war and aviation. A German flying ace is torn between his duty and his humanity; a Japanese pilot sets out on a kamikaze suicide mission; and a young boy faces a "trial by fire." 90 min. Dubbed in English.
20-8366 $24.99

Wild Cardz
Get ready to be dealt some wild anime action as you follow the exploits of the Crown Knights, a quartet of card-carrying superheroines who use their powers to defend the Card Kingdom from gigantic war machines shaped like chess pieces. 50 min. Dubbed in English.
20-8382 $24.99

Battle Skipper: The Movie
Mix girls' school rivalries with giant robot action, toss in lots of laughs, and sprinkle with a little nudity, and you'll get this wild, feature-length anime tale about the battles between exclusive St. Ignacio School's Debutante Club and Etiquette Club to defeat each other...and maybe take over the world while they're at it. 90 min. Dubbed in English.
20-8416 $24.99

Queen Emeraldas
From "Captain Harlock" creator Leiji Matsuomoto comes the epic interstellar exploits of Emeraldas, a female space pirate who is the galaxy's final hope against the tyranny of Commander Eldomain and the Afressians. Follow her daring adventure in this thrilling animated tale. 60 min. Dubbed in English.
20-8428 $19.99

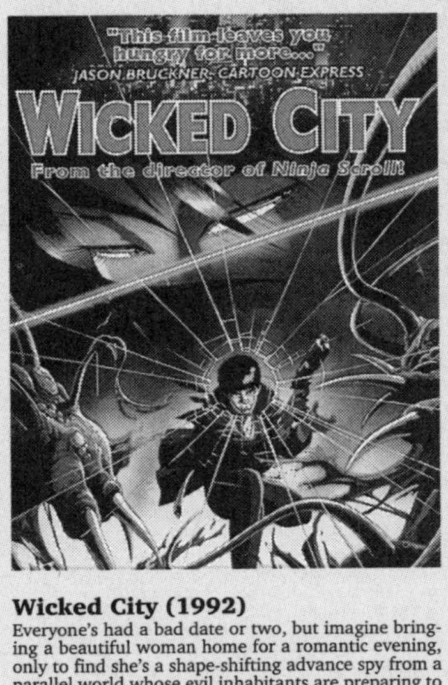

Wicked City (1992)
Everyone's had a bad date or two, but imagine bringing a beautiful woman home for a romantic evening, only to find she's a shape-shifting advance spy from a parallel world whose evil inhabitants are preparing to invade Earth! Follow the battle in this groundbreaking anime mix of horror, sci-fi and eroticism. 90 min. In Japanese with English subtitles.
20-8367 $29.99

Wicked City (Dubbed Version)
Also available in a dubbed-in-English edition.
45-8067 $19.99

Vision Of Escaflowne: Boxed Set
The strange visions of high school student Hitomi Kanzaki become real when she is transported into the magical realm of Gaea. There, Hitomi teams with Van, a young swordsman clad in mechanical armor, to defeat the evil armies of Zalbach and the Dragon Slayers. Follow her fantastic tale in this eight-tape fantasy saga. 700 min. total. In Japanese with English subtitles. NOTE: Individual volumes available at $29.99 each.
85-1302 Save $90.00! $149.99

Wild 7
A group of ex-criminals are recruited to join an elite group of crime-fighters and, equipped with the latest high-tech weaponry, clean up the streets their own way in this wild anime action series. Each volume runs about 50 minutes and is also available in Japanese with English subtitles.

Wild 7 (Dubbed)
20-8330 $19.99

Wild 7: Biker Nights (Dubbed)
20-8364 $19.99

The Blade Of Kamui
An animated epic from Japan, set in the mid-19th century and chronicling the adventures of a young man, abandoned at birth, who is accused of murdering his adoptive family. He is aided in tracking down the real killer by a mysterious one-armed priest skilled in the ways of the ninja, but the youth's mentor has his own reasons for helping him. 132 min. Dubbed in English.
64-1360 $19.99

Roujin Z
From "Akira" director Katsuhtio Otomo comes a wild, satirical sci-fi tale about an experimental machine designed to provide a 24-hour environment for the care of the sick and aged. An elderly invalid is placed inside the prototype unit, but his subconscious thoughts turn the robo-nurse into an unstoppable juggernaut rampaging through the streets. 80 min. Dubbed in English.
20-7480 $19.99

Tekken: The Motion Picture (1998)
The hit video games come to (animated) life in this violent, action-filled adventure. Do you dare to enter the arena to witness the Iron Fist Tournament, where the world's greatest fighters gather and pit their martial arts skills against each other in deadly competition? Music by The Offspring, Soulhat, Stabbing Westward and others. Uncut version; 60 min.
20-8159 $14.99

Suikoden: Demon Century
On the violent, crime-riddled streets of earthquake-ravaged 21st-century Tokyo, a young man searches for his missing sister, not suspecting that soon both of them will play pivotal roles in a timeless battle between the forces of good and evil, in this occult-flavored sci-fi anime odyssey. 45 min. Dubbed in English.
20-7728 Was $29.99 $19.99

Battle Arena Toshinden
In this thrilling, violent anime adaptation of the popular video game, a young master swordsman named Eiji Shinjo continues his quest for his long-lost brother, Sho. Someone, however, is looking for Eiji...and all other fighting champions...to draw them into battles to the death. Uncut version features nudity and graphic violence; adults only. 60 min. Dubbed in English.
20-7737 $19.99

Plastic Little: The Adventures Of Captain Tita
A remote colony planet whose lifeblood is tourism is about to gain its independence, but a military could wreck those plans. Only a native teenage girl specializing in selling exotic pets and her mysterious friend can save the day in this animated sci-fi drama. 55 min. Dubbed in English.
20-7747 $19.99

Big Wars
In the early 21st century, Earth colonies on the planet Mars are under attack by a malevolent alien menace that uses high-tech weaponry as well as a mind-controlling virus. As the Martian surface becomes a battlefield, the crew of the battleship Aboa must deal with enemies from without and within in this action-filled anime saga. Contains graphic violence and sexual situations. 75 min. Dubbed in English.
20-7748 $19.99

BioHunter
Ordinary people are being turned into savage monsters thanks to a strange illness known as the Demon Virus, and when one of these creatures begins killing women on the streets of Tkyo, two scientists search for the renowned psychic who holds the key to stopping the monster. "Wicked City" director Yoshiaki Kawajriri helms this graphically violent slice of anime horror. 58 min. Dubbed in English.
20-7823 $19.99

Vampire Wars
Slam-bang Japanese animation epic that has a French Secret Service agent joining forces with an international terrorist to discover the connection between the murder of a CIA agent and an attack on a NASA base. They learn that a beautiful Hollywood actress is the key to the mystery, but the evil vampire cult behind it all has targeted them next. 60 min. Dubbed in English.
02-8963 $19.99

Star Blazers: The Series
Japan's animated sci-fi series, "Space Battleship Yamato," was adapted for American audiences and quickly became a cult favorite. Now you can watch Wildstar and the crew of the starship Argo take on all manner of interstellar foes in these video collections. Dubbed in English.

Star Blazers: Collector's Edition Series 1: The Quest For Iscandar
The good ship Argo has one year to reach the distant planet Iscandar and return to Earth with the technology needed to save the world from radiation bombing by the evil rulers of Gamilon. 13 volumes on six tapes. NOTE: Individual volumes available at $19.99 each.
65-8049 Save $100.00! $159.99

Star Blazers: Collector's Edition Series 2: The Comet Empire
The gigantic comet streaking towards Earth is in reality an intergalactic war machine that enslaves whole planets and consumes barren worlds for fuel. Can the Star Force reach the planet Telazart in time to enlist the aid of the mysterious Trelaina? 13 volumes on six tapes. NOTE: Individual volumes available at $19.99 each.
65-8050 Save $100.00! $159.99

Star Blazers: Collector's Edition Series 3: The Bolar Wars
When the Earth finds itself in the middle of a war between the Bolar Federation and the revived Gamilon Empire, the crew of the Argo must stand as Mankind's last chance for survival. 13 volumes on six tapes. NOTE: Individual volumes available at $19.99 each.
65-8051 Save $100.00! $159.99

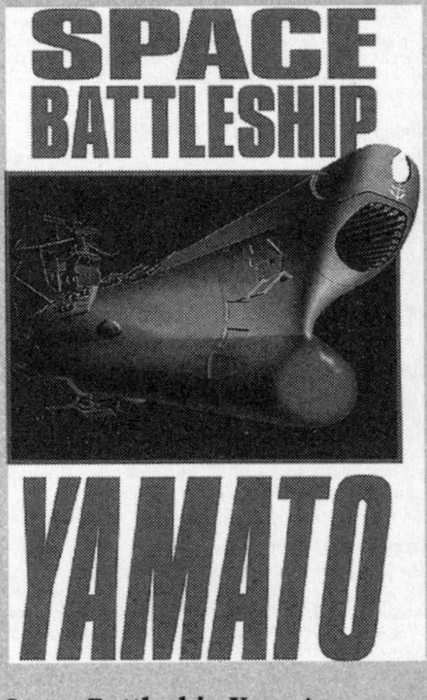

Space Battleship Yamato
In this groundbreaking feature-length version of the "Star Blazers: Quest for Iscandar" TV series, the legendary Japanese WWII warship Yamato is raised from its watery grave and transformed into a spaceship capable of taking its crew 148,000 light years from home, where the last hope for Earth's survival exists on the mysterious planet Iscandar. Includes footage not shown on American TV. 135 min. In Japanese with English subtitles.
65-8042 $29.99

Farewell To Space Battleship Yamato: In The Name Of Love
On the eve of Kodai and Yuki's wedding, the crew of the Yamato are reunited for what could be their final mission, one that pits them against old enemies in control of a comet-sized dreadnaught that allows them to wreak havoc across the galaxy, in the featurized version of the "Star Blazers: The Comet Empire" story. 118 min. Dubbed in English.
65-8040 $29.99

The Yamato Collection
All five "Star Blazers" feature films ("Space Battleship Yamato," "Farewell to Space Battleship Yamato," "Space Battleship Yamato—The New Voyage," "Be Forever Yamato" and "Final Yamato") are available, in their uncut, subtitled form, in this impressive collector's boxed set.
65-8043 $99.99

Gunsmith Cats: Bulletproof!
They're the toughest and sexiest bounty hunters ever to prowl the mean streets of Chicago. Join gorgeous gun expert Rally and her grenade-tossing sidekick Minnie-May as they tackle the city's toughest thugs and fugitives—for the right price—in this action-packed anime tale. 90 min. Dubbed in English.
20-7899 $19.99

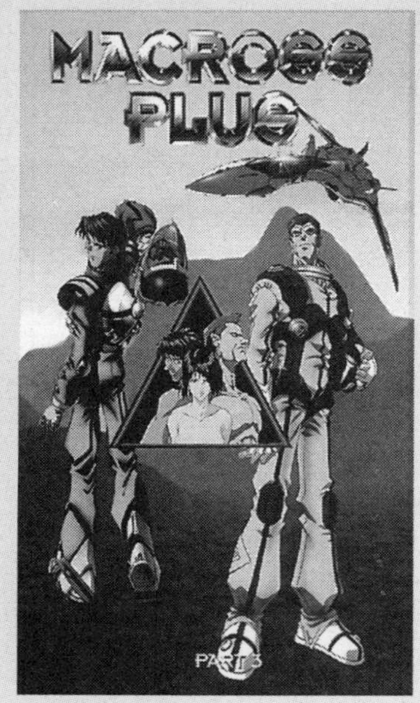
MACROSS PLUS
PART 3

Macross Plus
In the year 2040, a skilled but reckless pilot is hired to test a new superstealth Valkyrie airplane, but finds himself competing against an old rival both in the skies and for the hand of a young woman with a mysterious past. Industrial espionage, romance and high-flying action all mix in this anime series from director Shoji Kawamori. Each volume runs about 40 minutes and is also available in Japanese with English subtitles.

Macross Plus, Vol. 1 (Dubbed)
02-8213 *$14.99*

Macross Plus, Vol. 2 (Dubbed)
02-8261 *$14.99*

Macross Plus, Vol. 3 (Dubbed)
02-8376 *$14.99*

Macross Plus, Vol. 4 (Dubbed)
02-8444 *$14.99*

Macross Plus: The Movie
The acclaimed Japanese animation series becomes a thrilling science-fiction film, as alien defense fighter pilots Isamu and Guld battle for supremacy in the stars, as well as the woman they both love. Feature-length adventure includes never-before-seen footage. 115 min. In Japanese with English subtitles.
02-8663 *$24.99*

Macross II: The Movie
Set 80 years after the original sci-fi saga, this special feature-length version of the "Macross II" series finds Humans and Zentradi descendants living peacefully on Earth, until the arrival of an intergalactic armada signals all-new dangers. 120 min. In Japanese with English subtitles.
02-8384 *$24.99*

Macross In Clash Of The Bionoids
The first feature-length film based on Japan's popular "Macross" TV series finds the deadly alien race known as the Bionoids poised to attack Earth. The planet's only hope lies with the indestructible space fortress Macross. AKA: "Macross: Do You Remember Love?," "Superdimensional Fortress Macross." 115 min. Dubbed in English.
64-1364 *$14.99*

Giant Robo
When the terrorist group Big Fire sets out to steal a powerful new energy source called the Shizuma Drive, it's up to the Experts of Justice, an international police organization, and their mechanical ally, the high-flying Giant Robo, to stop them. Relive the "golden age" of Japanese animation in this exciting, light-hearted throwback series. Except where noted, each tape runs about 45 min. and is dubbed in English. There are six volumes available, including:

Giant Robo, Vol. 1: The Night The Earth Stood Still
Special edition features two episodes. 90 min.
02-8369 *$19.99*

Giant Robo, Vol. 2: Magnetic Web Strategy
02-8252 *$14.99*

Giant Robo, Vol. 3: The Twilight Of The Superhero
02-8377 *$14.99*

Dangaioh
Four psychically-gifted young people are brought together by the mysterious Doctor Tarsan and taught how to combine their powers to bring forth the powerful psionic weapon known as Dangaioh in this thrilling sci-fi anime feature from Japan. 90 min. Dubbed in English.
02-8438 *$19.99*

Jungle De Ikou
it's a jungle...well, everywhere, when a magic necklace given to 10-year-old Natsumi by her archeologist father makes her the target of an evil forest demon and his minions. Luckily, the necklace also transforms her into a sexy jungle goddess named Mie and gives her the power to fight her enemies in this wild anime fantasy saga. 90 min. In Japanese with English subtitles.
20-8646 *$24.99*

Jungle De Ikou (Dubbed Version)
Also available in a dubbed-in-English edition.
20-8647 *$24.99*

Virtua Fighter
Based on the popular video game, this action-filled anime series follows a young martial arts student named Akira Yuki as he sets off with allies Pai Chan, Jacky and Sarah on a quest to battle evil and find the "inner strength" that will make him a true master. Each tape runs about 100 min. Dubbed in English.

Virtua Fighter: Chinatown Brawl
20-8648 *$24.99*

Virtua Fighter: Beyond The Battle
20-8649 *$24.99*

Dangard Ace
Two episodes of space-age animation with the crew of the World Space Institute battling all sort of menaces. Included are the debut of the squad's new instructor in "Enter Captain Mask, and "Down from Mach 2," in which Mask shows the pilots how tough he can be. 46 min.
10-1432 Was $19.99 *$14.99*

Gaiking
Follow the crew of the giant dragon-robot Gaiking in two sci-fi adventures. In "Aries Joins the Team," a baseball player named Aries is chosen to be Gaiking's pilot; and in "Right Down the Middle" Aries begins to question his new job until he battles the Garwings. Superior Japanese animation. 46 min.
10-1435 Was $19.99 *$14.99*

They Were 11
Based on a Japanese folktale, this anime feature is set on a derelict starship serving as the final tesing ground for a group of space academy cadets. The test becomes a life-or-death struggle when they learn one of their number is a malevolent alien...but which one? 91 min. In Japanese with English subtitles.
20-7096 Was $39.99 *$19.99*

They Were 11 (Dubbed Version)
Also available in a dubbed-in-English edition.
20-7597 *$19.99*

Tournament Of The Gods
It's the deadliest competition imaginable, and the stakes are high for the brave warriors who gather to take part, in this thrilling anime fantasy. 35 min. In Japanese with English subtitles.
20-8541 *$29.99*

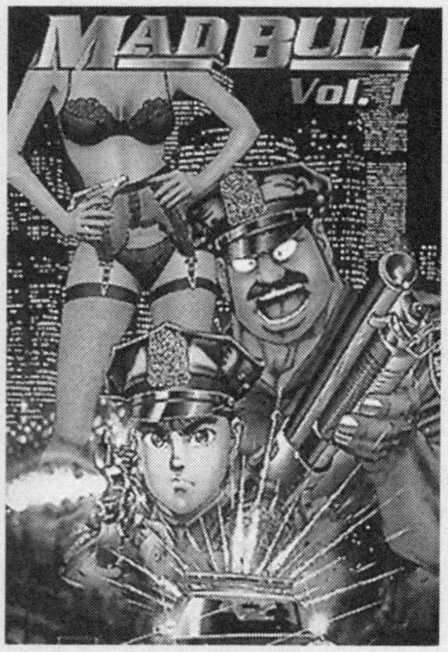
MAD BULL
Vol. 1

Mad Bull
Patrol the mean streets of New York City's 34th Precinct with two-fisted veteran cop John "Mad Bull" Estes and his rookie partner, Eddy Diazaburo Ban, in this four-part Japanese animated series filled with action and graphic violence. Each tape runs about 50 min. and is dubbed in English.

Mad Bull, Vol. 1: Scandal
02-8441 *$19.99*

Mad Bull, Vol. 2: The Manhattan Connection
02-8539 *$19.99*

Mad Bull, Vol. 3: City Of Vice
02-8542 *$19.99*

Mad Bull, Vol. 4: The Conclusion
02-8562 *$19.99*

Samurai X (Rurouni Kenshin)
Popular across its native Japan as "Rurouni Kenshin," this exciting anime series is set in the mid-19th century, where a young orphan named Kenshin is taken in by a legendary swordsman and raised in the ways of the warrior. In a land scarred by death and rebellion, Kenshin seeks an escape from his violent way of life, but does a mysterious woman named Tomoe hold the key? Each tape runs about 60 min.

Rurouni Kenshin, Vol. 1: Trust (Subtitled)
20-8634 *$29.99*

Samurai X, Vol. 1: Trust (Dubbed)
20-8635 *$19.99*

Rurouni Kenshin, Vol. 2: Betrayal (Subtitled)
20-8636 *$29.99*

Samurai X, Vol. 2: Betrayal (Dubbed)
20-8637 *$19.99*

Rurouni Kenshin: Wandering Samurai
Here are the original anime adventures of the swordsman-for-hire who wears the scars of his life inside and outside and wields his deadly reverse-blade sword to defend the innocent and persecuted in the final days of shogun-led Japan. Follow Kenshin in these exciting, violent tales of action and drama. Each tape runs about 100 min.

Rurouni Kenshin: The Legendary Swordsman (Subtitled)
Includes episodes 1-4.
20-8638 *$24.99*

Rurouni Kenshin: The Legendary Swordsman (Dubbed)
20-8639 *$24.99*

Rurouni Kenshin: Battle In The Moonlight (Subtitled)
Includes episodes 5-8.
20-8640 *$24.99*

Rurouni Kenshin: Battle In The Moonlight (Dubbed)
20-8641 *$24.99*

Rurouni Kenshin: The Shadow Elite (Subtitled)
Includes episodes 9-12.
20-8642 *$24.99*

Rurouni Kenshin: The Shadow Elite (Dubbed)
20-8643 *$24.99*

Rurouni Kenshin: False Prophet (Subtitled)
Includes episodes 13-16.
20-8644 *$24.99*

Rurouni Kenshin: False Prophet (Dubbed)
20-8645 *$24.99*

Agent Aika
From "Project A-Ko" creator Katsuhiko Nishijima comes the wild, sexy espionage exploits of beautiful salvage agent-for-hire Aika, an ace pilot and martial arts master who, armed with a high-tech battle bustier, will retrieve anything for the right price. Each volume runs about 60 minutes and is also available in Japanese with English subtitles.

Agent Aika, Vol. 1: Naked Mission (Dubbed)
20-8210 *$24.99*

Agent Aika, Vol. 2: Lace In Space (Dubbed)
20-8212 *$24.99*

Cleopatra DC
Cleopatra Corns, beautiful New York jet-setter and head of a powerful international company, has more than parties and board meetings to worry about when she must stop a criminal cabal out to take over her business—and the world—in this thrilling, sexy anime adventure saga. 110 min. In Japanese with English subtitles.
20-8650 *$29.99*

Gasaraki, Vol. 1: The Summoning
In this first part of an exciting animated sci-fi saga, the wealthy and influential Gowa family of Japan is on the brink of cementing their hold on the nation's future with the manufacture of the ultimate weapon: gigantic robots. But will young Yoshiro Gowa fulfill his clan's destined glory, or fight to be his own man? 100 min. Dubbed in English.
20-8654 *$19.99*

Space Warriors
A revenge-seeking space pirate...the powerful head of an galaxy-wide corporation...a seemingly ordinary school teacher...and the psychic warrior known as Locke. These four people are the main players in an anime sci-fi extravaganza filled with action and suspense. 75 min. Dubbed in English.
20-7643 *$19.99*

Mobile Suit Gundam: The Movie
Based on a phenomenally popular Japanese TV series, this feature-length anime saga is set in the Universal Century year of 0079. When the leaders of the Duchy of Zeon launch an all-out attack on the Earth Federation using humanoid fighting machines known as Mobile Suits, fate picks young Amuro Ray to be the pilot of the prototype Mobile Suit Gundam and Earth's final hope. 148 min. In Japanese with English subtitles.
85-1418 *$29.99*

Mobile Suit Gundam: The Movie 2: Soldiers Of Sorrow
The odyssey of Amuro and his fellow Mobile Suit pilots continues, as the crew of the Federation ship White Base must make their way through enemy-held territory on Earth, while Amuro faces his own crises from both without and within. 142 min. In Japanese with English subtitles.
85-1419 *$29.99*

Mobile Suit Gundam: The Movie 3: Encounter In Space
The time has come for the final battle between the Earth Federation and the Zeon forces, and for Amuro's ultimate showdown in space with his arch-nemesis, Char Aznable. What is the secret that drives Char's quest for vengeance, and what part will a mysterious woman named Lalah play? Mecha action and suspense await in the concluding Gundam feature. 149 min. In Japanese with English subtitles.
85-1420 *$29.99*

Mobile Suit Gundam: The Movie Boxed Set
All three Gundam movies are also available in a special collector's set. In Japanese with English subtitles.
85-1421 Save $30.00! *$59.99*

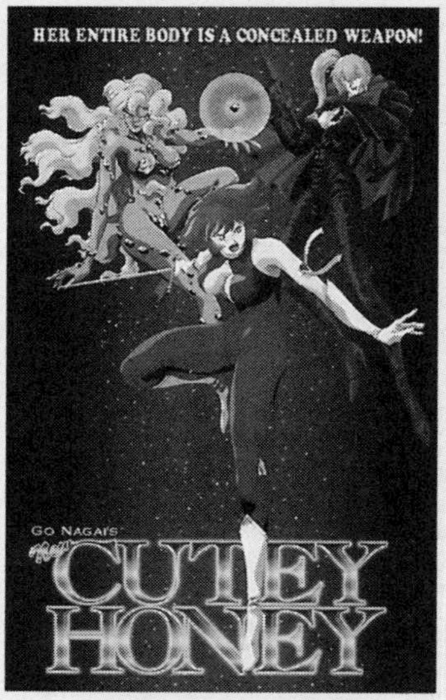
HER ENTIRE BODY IS A CONCEALED WEAPON!
GO NAGAI'S
CUTEY HONEY

New Cutey Honey
One of the most popular comics and cartoons to come from Japan, the outrageously sexy sci-fi antics of Honey-chan, the warrior android with a killer chassis and a penchant for losing her clothes in the heat of battle, are back, courtesy of manga artist Go Nagai. Each tape runs about 60 minutes and is also available in Japanese with English subtitles.

New Cutey Honey, Vol. 1 (Dubbed)
20-8202 *$19.99*

New Cutey Honey, Vol. 2 (Dubbed)
20-8203 *$19.99*

New Cutey Honey, Vol. 3 (Dubbed)
20-8204 *$19.99*

Grandizer
The Spaceship Grandizer and Orion Quest try to save the galaxy in "Robot Back to Action," in which Lance gets help in fighting the Vegans; and "Beware the Red Moon," in which the Earth comes under attack from Bellicose. A great Japanimation program! 46 min.
10-1436 Was $19.99 *$14.99*

Chimera: Angel Of Death
She's as beautiful as she is deadly. She's Rei, the assassin-for-hire code-named Chimera, and in this sexy, violent cartoon drama, based on the popular comic series, Chimera takes on what might be her final assignment...but will she be the killer, or the target? 57 min. In Japanese with English subtitles.
20-8041 *$29.99*

Ninja Resurrection: The Revenge Of Jubei
Ninja warrior Jubei, the hero of "Ninja Scroll," returns in a chilling and bloody "adults only" animated saga set in feudal Japan. As the soldiers of the Shogunate launch a violent campaign against Christians, the prophecy of a Child of Heaven that will save the faithful—a prophecy that contains a dark secret—will send Jubei on a dangerous mission. 50 min. Dubbed in English.
20-8201 *$19.99*

The Venus Wars
In the 21st century, man has colonized the planet Venus. But the formerly peaceful second planet is becoming a battleground, and it's up to a hotshot motorcycle racer and a gorgeous reporter to stop the oncoming war in this action-filled animated saga from Japan. 104 min. In Japanese with English subtitles.
20-7097 *$14.99*

The Venus Wars (Dubbed Version)
Also available in a dubbed-in-English edition.
20-7951 *$19.99*

Ninja Resurrection: Hell's Spawn
With demons from the depths of the underworld unleashing terror across the land, Jubei and another rogue warrior named Musashi are faced with breaking their vow to never again kill. What part will they play in the coming battle between the forces of good and evil in this thrilling anime fantasy. 50 min. In Japanese with English subtitles.
20-8377 *$29.99*

Ninja Resurrection: Hell's Spawn (Dubbed Version)
Also available in a dubbed-in-English edition.
20-8378 *$19.99*

Black Jack
When the genetically-enhanced participants in the Atlantis Olympics begin falling prey to a deadly plague that threatens to spread, the enigmatic medico known as "Dr. Black Jack" tries to uncover the conspiracy behind the events in this feature-length animated tale based on Osamu Tezuka's comic strip. 95 min. In Japanese with English subtitles.
02-9173 *$29.99*

Black Jack (Dubbed Version)
Also available in a dubbed-in-English edition.
02-9174 *$19.99*

The Irresponsible Captain Tylor: Collector's Set
Irresponsible he may be, but Justy Ueki Tylor is counting on his disarming manner and charm to get him through command of the starship Soyokaze—whose crew doesn't seem too happy with him—and an interplanetary battle with the Ragalon Empire—whose leaders want him dead—in this fast-paced anime sci-fi satire. Special boxed set includes all eight volumes. 600 min. total. In Japanese with English subtitles. NOTE: Individual volumes available at $19.99 each.
17-7064 Save $30.00! *$129.99*

The Irresponsible Captain Tylor: Collector's Set (Dubbed Version)
The eight-tape boxed set is also available in a dubbed-in-English edition. NOTE: Individual volumes available at $19.99 each.
17-7080 Save $30.00! *$129.99*

Wrath Of The Ninja: The Yotoden Movie
Violent ninja action and supernatural suspense are featured in this anime tale set in 19th-century Japan. After her brother and the ninja clan to which they belonged are murdered by the evil forces of Lord Nobunaga, young Ayame teams with two other renegade fighters who, like her, each possess a mystical blade to seek vengeance. 87 min. Dubbed in English.
20-7999 *$19.99*

Space Adventure Cobra
Throughout a distant galaxy, the man known as Cobra is the most wanted—and most feared—of bounty hunters, but has Cobra met his match when, while on the run from the Mafia Guild, he teams up with a beautiful fellow outlaw named Jane Flower? Find out in this exciting, feature-length anime odyssey. 99 min. In Japanese with English subtitles.
20-8015 *$29.99*

Space Adventure Cobra (Dubbed Version)
Also available in a dubbed-in-English edition.
20-8016 *$24.99*

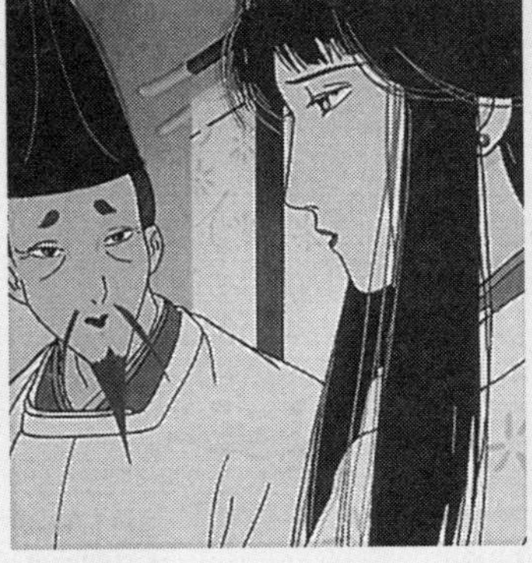

The Tale Of Genji (1987)
Animated adaptation of writer Murasaki Shikibu's landmark work of Japanese literature, set in medieval Kyoto and centering on the life and loves of Hikaru Genji, a handsome, artistic emperor's son who was made a commoner. 110 min. In Japanese with English subtitles.
20-7442 Was $29.99 *$19.99*

Dominion: Tank Police
Punked-out and action-filled animation from Japan, focusing on the members of the elite Tank Police and their attempts to nab the notorious Buaku Gang and the mysterious project known only as "Green Peace." Amazing futuristic thrills not for the kiddies. Each tape runs about 40 min. In Japanese with English subtitles.

Dominion: Tank Police, Act I
20-7025 Was $34.99 *$19.99*

Dominion: Tank Police, Act II
20-7041 Was $34.99 *$19.99*

Dominion: Tank Police, Act III
20-7049 Was $34.99 *$19.99*

Dominion: Tank Police, Act IV
20-7054 Was $34.99 *$19.99*

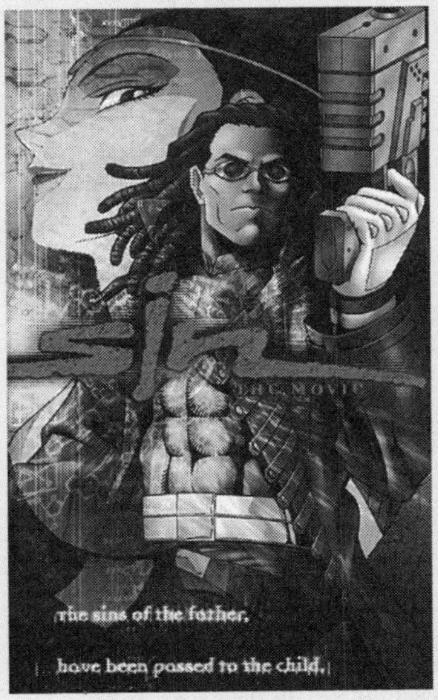

Sin: The Movie (2000)
In the gritty 21st-century city of Freeport, Colonel John Blade and his elite law enforcement unit HARDCORPS are all that stand between the residents and chaos. But as Blade investigates a string of kidnappings that leads him to the powerful SinTEK corporation, a sinister experiment is revealed that could mean mankind's survival...or its extinction...in this intense, violent anime tale based on the best-selling video game. 60 min. Dubbed in English.
20-8653 *$19.99*

Legend Of The Crystals: Final Fantasy: Boxed Set
Three of the four elemental crystals that have protected a distant world's peaceful existence are stolen, and the descendants of the heroic warriors who saved the planet 200 years earlier must follow in their ancestors' footsteps to save the remaining crystal in this two-part animated adventure based on the popular "Final Fantasy" video game. 120 min. total. Dubbed in English. NOTE: Individual volumes available at $19.99 each.
20-8141 Save $10.00! *$29.99*

Genesis Surviver Gaiarth: Complete Gaiarth Stages 1-3
Set 100 years after a war that devastated the planet Gaiarth, this stylishly animated sci-fi adventure concerns a young orphan who was raised by an android guardian. Now grown, he and a band of warriors must try to stop the diabolical BeastMaster from launching "The End of the World—Part II." 142 min. In Japanese with English subtitles.
20-8233 *$29.99*

Genesis Surviver Gaiarth: Complete Gaiarth Stages 1-3 (Dubbed Version)
Also available in a dubbed-in-English edition.
20-8234 *$29.99*

Peacock King: Collector's Boxed Set
Based on a popular manga series, this five-part animated odyssey of martial arts and sorcery follows a trio of occult warriors—the half-demonic Onimaru; Buddhist priest and exorcist Jiku; and Kujaku, Jiku's brash young disciple—as they battle uprisings of evil forces wherever they appear. 250 min. total. Dubbed in English. NOTE: Individual volumes available at $19.99 each.
20-8335 Save $10.00! *$89.99*

Catnapped! The Movie
The world is facing a total cat-tastrophe in animator Takashi Nakamura's feature-length anime fantasy, as two youngsters enter a magical land where sunlight turns people into felines and dogs into monsters. Can they stop a wicked magician-cat from taking over? AKA: "Catland Banipal Witt." 77 min. Dubbed in English.
85-1498 *$14.99*

Vampire Hunter D (1985)
Eerie, exotic animation for adults, set in the year 12,090, when the Earth is ruled by vampires. A beautiful woman fancied by the chief bloodsucker offers herself to a bizarre vampire hunter, in exchange for his destroying the creatures of the night, in this Japanese horror classic. 80 min. In Japanese with English subtitles.
45-8093 *$29.99*

Vampire Hunter D (Dubbed Version)
Also available in a dubbed-in-English edition.
45-8018 Was $29.99 *$19.99*

Generator Gawl
In the year 2007, the unlocking of the human genetic code leads to the development of metallic mutations called Generators that threaten to overrun the planet and exterminate humanity. It's up to a young man named Gawl to turn himself into a Generator and travel back in time to prevent their creation in this pulse-pounding anime sci-fi series. Each tape runs about 75 min. Dubbed in English.

Generator Gawl, Vol. 1: Human Heart, Metal Soul
20-8659 *$19.99*

Generator Gawl, Vol. 2: Future Memories
20-8660 *$19.99*

Lost Universe
The crew of the Lost Ship Swordbreaker—psi-blade master Kain Blueriver, interplanetary private eye and reluctant partner Millie Nocturne, and master computer Canal—have their hands full serving as "trouble contractors" for the Universal Guardians and getting the jobs no one else wants, in this light-hearted anime sci-fi series. Each volume runs about 100 minutes and is also available in Japanese with English subtitles.

Lost Universe, Vol. 1: In Space...It's Very, Very Dark. (Dubbed)
20-8607 *$19.99*

Lost Universe, Vol. 2: Flushed Into Space! (Dubbed)
20-8609 *$19.99*

Lost Universe, Vol. 3: Ultimate Weapons! (Dubbed)
20-8611 *$19.99*

Cowboy Bebop
Follow the good spaceship Bebop and its bounty-hunting crew—ladies' man Spike Spiegel, cyborg ex-cop Jet Black, beautiful and cunning Faye Valentine and their faithful (and super-intelligent) canine companion Ein—as they track down and sometimes team up with the scum of the universe in this stylish sci-fi anime outing. Each tape runs about 50 minutes and is also available in Japanese with English subtitles. There are five volumes available, including:

Cowboy Bebop, Vol. 1: Asteroid Blues (Dubbed)
85-1376 *$19.99*

Cowboy Bebop, Vol. 2: Honky Tonk Woman (Dubbed)
85-1378 *$19.99*

Cowboy Bebop, Vol. 3: Ballad Of Fallen Angels (Dubbed)
85-1380 *$19.99*

Princess Minerva
She's a beautiful princess who prefers roaming the countryside looking for swordfights and dragons to sitting around the palace, but Minerva may get more adventure than she hoped for when she enters a village's all-girl combat contest in this offbeat anime tale. 45 min. Dubbed in English.
20-8088 *$19.99*

Takegami: Guardian Of Darkness: Complete Set
In fulfillment of an ancient prophecy, a trio of malevolent dragon spirits arise to take possession of the souls of mortals. Can a young man, the chosen host of a legendary warrior-god, realize his destiny and save mankind in this violent, three-tape action/fantasy series? 135 min. total. NOTE: Individual volumes available at $19.99 each.
20-7977 Save $10.00! *$49.99*

Dragon Knight
Yeah, he's got a magic sword, but this morally bankrupt knight also carries an instant camera so he can take racy photos of damsels in distress! There's plenty of high action, low comedy, and beautiful babes in this offbeat anime adventure saga. 40 min. In Japanese with English subtitles.
20-7205 Was $34.99 *$24.99*

Demon Fighter Kocho
She may not get extra credit from her college professors, but beautiful astrology student Kocho Eonki and her sexy pals have found a unique way to fill those vacant hours between classes: battling demonic spirits out to take over the campus. Follow their exciting adventures in this sophisticated tale of anime suspense and fantasy. 30 min. Dubbed in English.
20-8633 *$14.99*

Spirit Of The Sword
Teenager Yonosuke is hardly prepared when he learns he has inherited the family mantle as guardian of the gateway between Earth and Heaven. Now, armed with the magic sword Chitentai and the help of Protector Tsukinojo, he must battle demonic spirits and keep Tsukinojo's scheming brother from stealing his sword and plunging both universes into chaos. 45 min. In Japanese with English subtitles.
20-8651 *$19.99*

Spirit Of The Sword (Dubbed Version)
Also available in a dubbed-in-English edition.
20-8652 *$19.99*

Apocalypse Zero: Kakugo The Final Soldier
A ravaged, demon-filled Earth of the 21st century is the setting for this violent anime mix of action, horror and science fiction. Brothers Kakugo and Harara are taught fighting skills by their father and sent out to battle the creatures preying on helpless humans, but when Harara is taken over by evil it leads to a brutal battle between siblings. WARNING: Contains graphic violence. Each tape runs about 45 min.

Apocalypse Zero: Battle 1 (Subtitled)
20-8655 *$19.99*

Apocalypse Zero: Battle 1 (Dubbed)
20-8656 *$19.99*

Apocalypse Zero: Battle 2 (Subtitled)
20-8657 *$19.99*

Apocalypse Zero: Battle 2 (Dubbed)
20-8658 *$19.99*

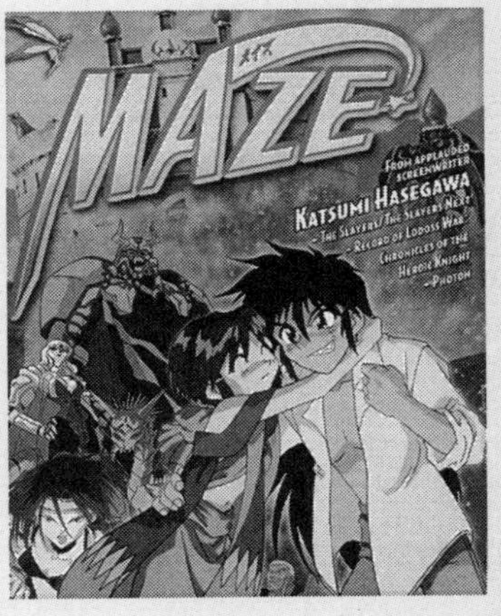

Maze
A young girl named Maze awakens to find herself minus her memory and transported to a strange fantasy world where she gains incredible powers to help do battle against the forces of evil. Problem is, at night she transforms into a lecherous male! Follow the gender-twisting fun in this offbeat anime sci-fi series. Except where noted, each tape runs about 75 min. Dubbed in English.

Maze: Ultimate Rage
Special edition runs 100 min.
20-8663 *$19.99*

Maze: Whirlwind Showdown
20-8664 *$19.99*

Maze: Evil Labyrinth
20-8665 *$19.99*

Maze: Time Travelling Playboy
20-8666 *$19.99*

Maze: Beating Heart
20-8667 Available 1/01 *$19.99*

Maze: Shocking Transformation
20-8668 Available 2/01 *$19.99*

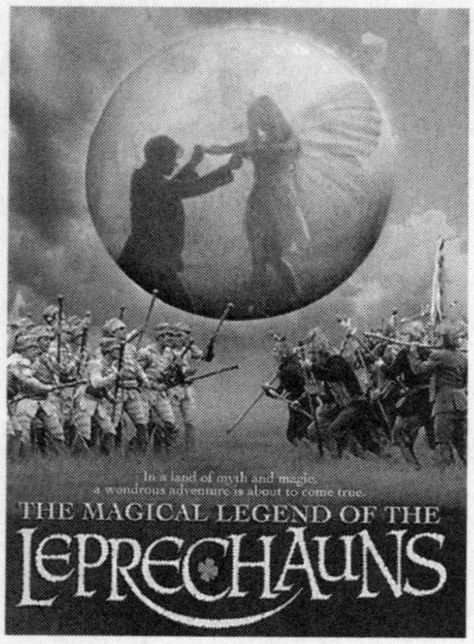

The Magical Legend Of The Leprechauns (1999)
American businessman Randy Quaid's hopes for a quiet vacation in Ireland are dashed when he finds his cottage is already home to a family of leprechauns, and soon Quaid is playing peacemaker in a feud between the "wee people" and their rivals, the fairies, in this enchanting fantasy. Kieran Culkin, Roger Daltrey, Whoopi Goldberg and Colm Meaney also star. 139 min.
88-1206 ❑$14.99

Murdercycle (1998)
It's terror on two wheels, and it's left its home dimension in search of fresh blood on the highways of Earth. Can anything stop the Murdercycle, and do earthly helmet laws apply to alien death machines? Free-wheeling sci-fi chiller stars Charles Wesley, Cassandra Ellis. 90 min.
75-5039 Was $89.99 $14.99

Aliens In The Wild West (1999)
Brother and sister teens Sara and Tom find a portal in an old ghost town that hurls them back to the wild, wild West. Joining them on a wild adventure in the past is a baby alien searching for his mother, who has been captured by greedy locals. Taylor Locke, Carly Pope star. 90 min.
75-5050 $49.99

Masked Avenger Versus Ultra-Villain In The Lair Of The Naked Bikini (1999)
The Masked Avenger (aka: the Masturbating Gunman) can track down women with a sniff of their panties. His weakness, however, is that the sight of a pretty gal makes him bonkers. The Avenger goes to battle against evil Helmut Gunta, an ultra-villain who has kidnapped a virgin nun to bear his offspring. Robin Brennan stars in this strange and sexy fantasy. 90 min.
73-9308 $19.99

The Regenerated Man (1994)
A scientist experimenting in regenerating human tissue becomes his own unwilling guinea pig when thugs break into the lab and force him to drink his own potion, transforming the good doctor into a hideous being. Spellbinding sci-fi thriller features a bright young cast. 90 min.
74-3009 $49.99

Zarkorr! The Invader (1996)
Citizens of Earth, beware! Zarkorr, a 185-foot-tall monster, is on the rampage, sent by intelligent alien beings to destroy the planet, and average human Tommy Ward has been chosen by the aliens to be Earth's only defender. Tommy's sole ally in the battle is a cute five-inch tall hologram named Proctor. Rhys Pugh, Eileen Wesson star. 80 min.
75-5007 Was $89.99 $14.99

Forbidden Zone: Alien Abduction (1996)
Sexy and mysterious sci-fi tale about a group of beautiful women who have experienced the same strange vision of an erotic encounter with a man they never met. While investigating these sensual dreams, they discover they have been the unwitting subjects in an unearthly experiment. Darcy De Moss, Pia Reyes star. 90 min.
75-5008 Was $89.99 $14.99

Dragon Fury (1995)
The year is 2099, and a deadly disease known as "the Plague" has ravaged mankind. A sword-wielding warrior travels back in time 100 years to retrieve the serum that will save his future, but some sinister forces are out to destroy him. Thrilling sci-fi actioner stars Robert Chapin. 80 min.
76-9072 $14.99

Dark Breed (1996)
An astronaut investigating the crash of a top-secret space flight carrying six American astronauts discovers that the crew is infected with reptilian parasites that have taken over their bodies. Now, only he can stop the malevolent critters' plan to destroy the Earth. Jack Scalia, Donna W. Scott, Jonathan Banks and Robin Curtis star. 104 min.
86-1106 Was $89.99 ❑$14.99

Kraa! The Sea Monster (1998)
Earthlings beware, Kraa has arrived! Working for the evil Lord Doom, this alien creature dives into the ocean to destroy all life on Earth. Mankind's only hope for survival rests in the hands of the Planet Patrol, four young interstellar heroes. Gigantic sci-fi adventure stars R.J. McMurray, Robert Garcia. 80 min.
75-5026 Was $49.99 $14.99

Invasion For Flesh & Blood (1996)
Wild special effects and make-up highlight this scary sci-fi tale about a professor who attempts to save the world by implanting the soul of a renowned psychic into a cyborg named the Golden Slayer. The cyborg and a beautiful scientist team to stop marauding creatures out to take over the world. Kathy Monks and Marilyn Ghigliotti ("Clerks") star. 90 min.
73-9149 Was $49.99 $29.99

The Sender (1998)
What is the connection between a military plane discovered after being lost for three decades and the mysterious powers demonstrated by the missing pilot's granddaughter, and who—or what—is the mysterious woman trying to save the girl and her father from a top-secret government agency? Gripping sci-fi suspenser stars Michael Madsen, Robert Vaughn, Shelli Lether, Dyan Cannon. 98 min.
86-1130 ❑$89.99

Nightwish (1989)
"Altered States" meets "Dreamscape" as a parapsychology professor administers a series of experiments to his students. Their dreams eventually become indistinguishable from reality, which elicits fascination...and fright! Jack Starrett and Robert Tessier star. Unrated version. 96 min.
68-1156 $89.99

Project: Alien (1989)
In the remote wilderness of Scandinavia, evidence of infiltration by alien invaders leads two reporters to risk their lives in order to uncover the shocking truth. Sci-fi thriller stars Michael Nouri, Maxwell Caufield, Charles Durning, Darlanne Fluegel. 92 min.
68-1180 $14.99

Fugitive Alien (1986)
Sci-fi action from the Land of the Rising Sun, as an alien star pilot (named, exotically enough, Ken) is branded a traitor by his homeworld and joins forces with an Earth ship to battle his former allies. "They try to kill him with a forklift!" 103 min.
69-5018 $39.99

The Ice Pirates (1984)
Journey into a world you've never believed existed, a world of space-age buccaneers, beautiful princesses, outrageous adventure, space humor and live-talking robots. Robert Urich, Anjelica Huston, Mary Crosby lead the expedition—time warp city! 96 min.
12-1354 Was $79.99 $14.99

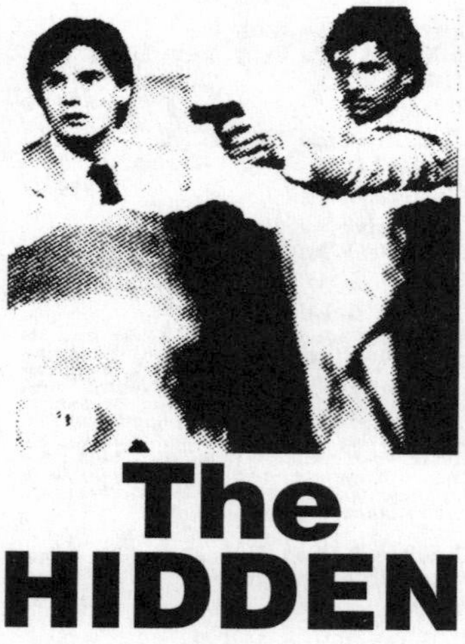

The Hidden (1987)
Ordinary, law-abiding L.A. citizens are suddenly turning into crazed, gun-happy robbers and killers, and a mysterious FBI agent who shows up to aid the police tries to convince a skeptical detective that an alien creature is behind the bizarre crime spree. An offbeat mix of action and science fiction, the hit thriller stars Kyle MacLachlan and Michael Nouri. 98 min.
03-1587 Was $19.99 $14.99

The Hidden: Special Collector's Edition
This special two-tape edition also includes the original theatrical trailer, unused footage and FX production clips, and commentary by director Jack Sholder. 117 min. total.
08-8445 $19.99

The Hidden 2 (1994)
This sequel to the hit sci-fi shocker tells of an alien policeman who lands on Earth and searches for an alien that has been hibernating for 15 years. Once the creature's hiding place is found, however, it's too late—it's out on the street, riding fast cars and enjoying high-powered weapons. Raphael Sbarge and Kate Hodge star. 91 min.
02-2628 Was $19.99 ❑$14.99

Time Of The Apes (1987)
What incredible force sends a woman and two children into a savage world ruled by apes, where their only hope for survival lies with a fierce mountain man and a friendly ape-girl? Find out in this simian sci-fi shocker from Japan. "Kenny, don't go." "I don't care." 98 min.
69-5035 $39.99

Fortress Of Amerikka (1989)
Troma Films presents a futuristic thriller about a team of mercenaries with a deadly secret weapon who are out to overtake the U.S. With Gene LeBrok and Kellee Bradley.
69-7053 $14.99

Born In Flames (1983)
Independent filmmaker Lizzie Borden mixes speculative fiction, political satire and feminist activism in this documentary-style tale set 10 years after "The Second American Revolution" that was supposed to free women and minorities. When the black lesbian leader of the Women's Army is mysteriously killed, her followers attempt to carry on the struggle against the System. With Jeanne Satterfield, Adele Bertei, Honey. 90 min.
70-5110 $29.99

Critters (1986)
A sleepy little Kansas farm town becomes the battlefield in an intergalactic chase between a passel of carnivorous little creatures and a team of bounty hunters. Sci-fi thriller stars Dee Wallace Stone, M. Emmet Walsh, Billy Green Bush. 86 min.
02-1634 ❑$14.99

Critters 2: The Main Course (1988)
They're back, and hungrier than ever! Those fear-inducing furballs from outer space have found a new town to feast on in the sequel to the sci-fi adventure. Scott Grimes, Liane Curtis, Eddie Deezen star. 87 min.
02-1020 ❑$14.99

Critters 3 (1991)
Those toothy terrors are back, set on destroying humankind. The hairy horrors turn an inner-city tenement upside-down in search of new people to chew. Aimee Brooks, Leonardo DiCaprio (in his first film role) and Don Opper star. 86 min.
02-2138 ❑$14.99

Critters 4 (1992)
It's "Critters"-mania as those ferocious, furry creatures return, only this time they're genetically mutated "super-critters" made to take over the universe. This sci-fi-horror-thriller features Don Opper, Angela Bassett and Brad Dourif. 95 min.
02-2285 ❑$14.99

Stranded (1987)
A group of aliens flees from their homeworld and land near a small farming town on Earth, only to learn that fear and hatred have already preceded them, in this suspenseful sci-fi adventure. Maureen O'Sullivan, Ione Skye, Joe Morton star. 80 min.
02-1835 Was $79.99 $14.99

Pulse (1988)
What is the mysterious force that is turning ordinary household appliances and electronic devices into deathtraps? Can one person be behind the deadly scheme, or is something more than human out there? Bizarre sci-fi shocker stars Cliff DeYoung, Roxanne Hart, Joey Lawrence. 90 min.
02-1899 $19.99

Spacehunter: Adventures In The Forbidden Zone (1983)
Interstellar rebels Wolff and Nikki set out on a spectacular mission to rescue three women stranded on a planet no one has warned them about...because no one has ever returned. Peter Strauss, Molly Ringwald. Not in 3-D. 90 min.
02-1246 $14.99

Slipstream (1989)
A top cast, including Mark Hamill, Ben Kingsley and F. Murray Abraham, fuels this dystopic tale of a future world where nature runs riot and the death-defying manhunt a bounty hunter must make in search of his quarry. 92 min.
74-1072 ❑$14.99

Project: Eliminator (1989)
A scientist invents a flying, super-intelligent robot laser weapon that threatens world peace. Can he and two Special Forces vets stop the menace and escape with their lives? Explosive actioner stars David Carradine, Frank Zagarino. 89 min.
77-1034 $14.99

Andy And The Airwave Rangers (1988)
When 12-year-old Andy and his little sister put a tape called "Incredible Video Adventure" in the VCR, they're plunged into a cross-channel series of car chases, cartoon mishaps, outer space action and even commercials. Exciting sci-fi tale of TV trickery stars Randy Josselyn, Jessica Puscas; cameos by Vince Edwards, Erik Estrada and others. 75 min.
02-1976 $79.99

DVD VIDEO
ASK ABOUT OUR GIANT DVD CATALOG!

King Arthur, The Young Warlord (1975)
The other side of Camelot is thrillingly depicted as Saxon hordes storm the castle. Oliver Tobias, John Watson, Brian Blessed star. 90 min.
16-1061 $14.99

Excalibur (1981)
Director John Boorman's dazzling filming of the legend of King Arthur and the Knights of the Round Table features stunning cinematography, mature themes and superlative performances. Nigel Terry stars as Arthur, and Nicol Williamson is Merlin; with Helen Mirren, Cherie Lunghi, Gabriel Byrne and Liam Neeson in his film debut. 141 min.
19-1178 Was $19.99 $14.99

Guinevere (1994)
Exciting and lavish take on Arthurian legends features Cheryl Lee in the title role of the beautiful young queen who wins the heart of both King Arthur (Sean Patrick Flanery) and Sir Lancelot (Noah Wyle) and must defend Camelot when her husband is captured by the evil Morgan L'Fei. Donald Pleasance also stars as Merlin. 93 min.
64-3423 $14.99

Merlin's Shop Of Mystical Wonders (1996)
This fantastic story finds Merlin, the world's most famous wizard, bringing his magic to the 20th century by opening a shop displaying all of his wonders. Trouble ensues when a possessed toy monkey is stolen and a reporter tries to close the shop down. With Ernest Borgnine, George Milan. 92 min.
76-9087 Was $19.99 $14.99

Lancelot: Guardian Of Time (1997)
Sir Lancelot is sent through time by the magician Merlin in order to help a young Arthur before he is crowned king. A glitch in the mission lands Lancelot and Arthur into modern-day L.A. along with the evil Wolvencroft and Blackpool, his bodyguard. Lancelot teams with a computer expert and writer to save Arthur from the villains and return home. Marc Singer, Claudia Christian and John Saxon star.
50-8250 Was $39.99 $14.99

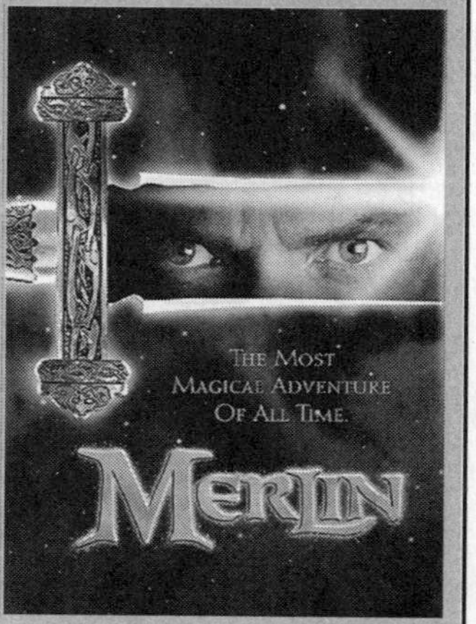

Merlin (1998)
Travel back to the days of Camelot with this magical, action-filled mini-series starring Sam Neill as the legendary wizard who teams up with a young King Arthur to battle an evil sorceress. With Isabella Rossellini, Martin Short, Rutger Hauer and Helena Bonham Carter. 140 min.
88-1170 ❑$19.99

Lady Terminator (1989)
The vengeful spirit of a bloodthirsty female warlord takes over an anthropology student and begins her search for the descendant of the man who killed her centuries earlier. Pulse-pounding blend of horror, science-fantasy and action (with some nudity blended in) stars Barbara Constable, Christopher Hart. 82 min.
77-7001 Was $79.99 $19.99

Velocity Trap (1998)
Remember those B-Westerns where a stagecoach gold shipment was threatened by bandits lying in wait in a dangerous canyon, and only one lawman could stop them? Well, now it's the year 2150, and interplanetary police officer Olivier Gruner must escort a ship transporting $40 billion through the treacherous Velocity Run, unaware that space pirates are waiting to hijack it. Bruce Weitz, Alicia Coppola also star. 89 min.
02-3413 ❑$99.99

Escape From DS-3 (1987)
Confined to a maximum security prison satellite floating freely through space, a wrongfully accused prisoner must outwit his captors in a desperate and deadly race for freedom. Futuristic "breakout" flick stars Jackson Bostwick and Bubba Smith. 88 min.
76-9002 $14.99

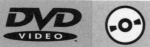

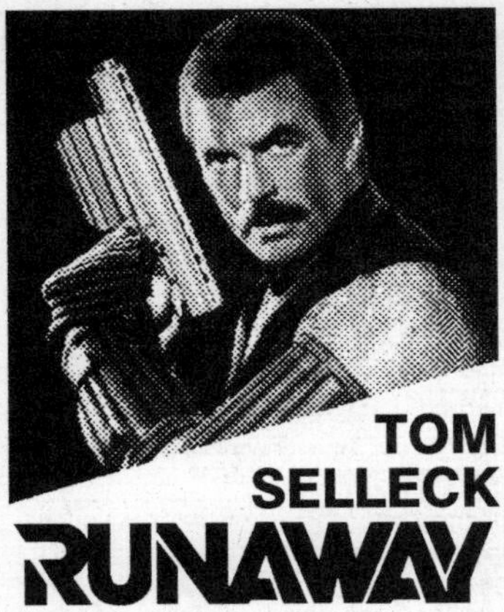

Runaway (1984)
Futuristic suspense thriller with Tom Selleck as a detective tracking a madman (Gene Simmons of Kiss) who has programmed robots to be used as perfect killing machines, from tiny spider robots to heat-seeking bullets. With Kirstie Alley, Cynthia Rhodes. 100 min.
02-1446 ❑*$14.99*

Creepozoids (1987)
"What is a creepozoid," you ask? They're bloodthirsty mutants caused by a genetics experiment gone wrong, and now five people trapped in a former government lab must fight to stay alive. Creepy, crawly sci-fi gore-fest stars Linnea Quigley, Ken Abraham. 72 min.
75-5002 Was $69.99 *$14.99*

Killer Klowns From Outer Space (1988)
If the big red nose isn't rubber, and the pontoon-sized shoes hide pontoon-sized feet, that's no clown, it's a flesh-eating mime from another world. Aliens in fright wigs roll into town eight-to-a-golfcart and only Suzanne Snyder and Grant Cramer or their pals can stop them. This cult favorite comes from the Chiodo Brothers. 90 min.
03-1638 Was $19.99 *$14.99*

Remote Control (1987)
What could be scarier than watching a horror movie? How about suddenly finding yourself in the picture? That's what happens to people who rent a certain "video nasty," and only one courageous video store clerk (what other kind is there?) can solve this shocking puzzle. Kevin Dillon, Jennifer Tilly. 88 min.
27-6565 *$14.99*

Innerspace (1987)
A top-secret miniaturization experiment goes awry when test pilot Dennis Quaid is injected into the body of nerdy clerk Martin Short. Together this "odd couple" must elude industrial spies in Joe Dante's funny flip side of "Fantastic Voyage." With Meg Ryan, Kevin McCarthy and the great Dick Miller. 120 min.
19-1628 Letterboxed ❑*$14.99*

Hyper Sapien: People From Another Star (1986)
Two children from outer space join a teenage boy and an adorable three-foot creature for a close encounter with earthlings in a Wyoming ranching community. Magical sci-fi fantasy in the tradition of "Mac and Me" stars Sydney Penny, Ricky Paull Goldin and Keenan Wynn. 93 min.
19-1760 Was $19.99 *$14.99*

Bronx Executioner (1989)
Futuristic New York still has that magic glow—it's pouring off the radioactive rubble of a civilization in tatters. Stars Gabriel Gori and Chuck Valenti level their blasters against android gangs and genetically engineered supermen for control of the city's dwindling resources. 88 min.
19-7037 Was $59.99 *$14.99*

Xtro (1983)
A man is abducted by aliens and returns years later. But is it really him, or is it a creature from the stars...and will he force his son to follow in his blood-thirsty clawsteps? Gruesome sci-fi tale stars Philip Sayer, Bernice Stegers, Maryam D'Abo. 80 min.
02-2284 *$14.99*

Xtro II: The Second Encounter (1991)
In this shocking sequel, a group of scientists unleashes an alien predator from a forbidden planet with the hidden desire to play terminator. Soon, the creature from the starship regenerates itself, and the blood-sucker from outer space with the target Earth makes the world go wild. Jan-Michael Vincent, Paul Koslo and Tara Buchman star in this gory, pulse-pounding flick. 92 min.
02-2116 Was $89.99 *$14.99*

Xtro: Watch The Skies (1995)
A group of Marines is sent to a deserted island where they uncover incredible evidence of experimentations on aliens. When they discover a surviving alien seeking revenge, they learn that the government is planning to sacrifice them and hide the evidence of its experiments. Sal Landi, Andrew Divoff, Jim Hanks, Karen Moncrieff and Robert Culp star. 90 min.
72-9059 Was $89.99 *$14.99*

Metalstorm: The Destruction Of Jared-Syn (1983)
Heavy metal warriors in futuristic settings battle with viciousness and amazing weaponry. A whiz-bang crop of special effects, dashing heroes, hideous villains and gorgeous heroines populate this one. Jeffrey Byron, Kelly Preston star. Not in 3-D. 84 min.
07-1199 *$59.99*

Iceman (1984)
A fascinating film that blends science fiction, adventure and drama. A research team in the Arctic finds a prehistoric man preserved in a glacier and revives him, but then must decide his fate. Starring Timothy Hutton, Lindsay Crouse and John Lone in the title role; directed by Fred Schepisi. 101 min.
07-1221 Was $69.99 *$14.99*

The Last Starfighter (1984)
A young video game master becomes part of a real outer space war when he's called on to help defend the Star League of Planets from their arch-enemy. Lance Guest, Robert Preston, Dan O'Herlihy star. 100 min.
07-1237 Was $19.99 *$14.99*

Voyager From The Unknown (1982)
A young orphan joins a mysterious "time voyager" and helps him keep history in order in this exciting adventure from the hit series "Voyagers." Jon-Erik Hexum and Meeno Peluce star. 91 min.
07-1313 *$39.99*

Galaxy Invader (1984)
An alien being lands on this planet, but he isn't befriended by three children and he doesn't fall in love with an Earth woman. No, this one is out for blood—human blood!—and our puny weapons can't match his laser blasts. Richard Ruxton, Don Leifert star. 68 min.
08-1250 *$14.99*

Laboratory (1980)
Five humans are kidnapped off Earth by mysterious alien beings. Are these extraterrestrials friendly scientists, or is this only the beginning to the invasion of Earth? Tense sci-fi thriller. 93 min.
08-1265 Was $49.99 *$19.99*

Killings At Outpost Zeta (1980)
In a distant future, planet Zeta will be one of the most strategically important planets to Earth's space program. When several expeditions cease to return, a band of soldiers and scientists journey in search of answers and find a horrifying payoff. Gordon Devol, Jacquelyn Ray. 92 min.
08-1389 Was $49.99 *$14.99*

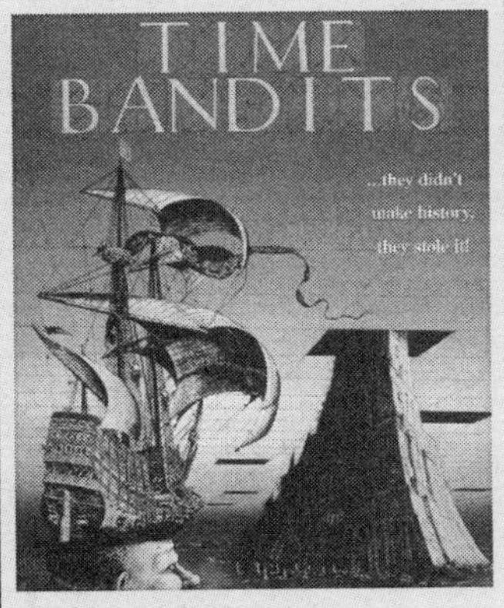

Time Bandits (1981)
Take a wild and wacky fantasy through history with a young boy who teams with a band of dwarf robbers with a map of space/time and encounters the likes of Napoleon, Robin Hood and King Agamemnon. John Cleese, Sean Connery, Shelley Duvall, Michael Palin and Craig Warnock star; directed by Terry Gilliam. 110 min.
06-1120 Was $19.99 *$14.99*

Time Bandits (Letterboxed Version)
Also available in a theatrical, widescreen format.
08-8748 *$14.99*

Brazil (1985)
Terry Gilliam's stunning look at a bleak totalitarian future is filled with incredible scenes and imagery. A lowly bureaucrat (Jonathan Pryce), trying to escape reality in his daydreams, becomes involved in a plot that includes renegade repairmen, government tortures and anti-state terrorists. Katherine Helmond, Ian Holm, Michael Palin and Robert De Niro also star. 131 min.
07-1407 Was $19.99 ❑*$14.99*

The Adventures Of Baron Munchausen (1989)
From director Terry Gilliam ("Brazil") comes a fantastic saga about the world's most famous liar. Join Baron Munchausen (John Neville) on his voyages around the world and beyond, as he meets one bizarre being after another. Also stars Jonathan Pryce, Eric Idle, Sarah Polley, Oliver Reed and Robin Williams as the Moon King. 125 min.
02-1962 Was $19.99 ❑*$14.99*

Misfits Of Science (1985)
They're the strangest heroes of all: a rock star who shoots lightning bolts from his hands, a human icicle, a telekinetic teenager and a 7-foot scientist who can shrink to 6 inches, teaming up to stop a mad general's "neutron cannon" and save the world. Dean Paul Martin, Courteney Cox, Mark Thomas Miller, Larry Linville star. 96 min.
07-1463 *$39.99*

The Archer: Fugitive From The Empire (1981)
The mystical world of wizards, diabolical creatures and alluring enchantresses is the setting for this tale of a young warrior's (Lane Caudell) quest to prove himself innocent of murder and reclaim his throne. Also stars Belinda Bauer, George Kennedy. 97 min.
07-1465 *$39.99*

Breeders (1986)
Spine-tingling sci-fi shocker that finds a New York City police detective and an emergency room doctor working together to figure out who—or what—is responsible for a series of bizarre rapes of young women. The answer lies deep beneath the city streets, where an alien menace awaits. With Theresa Farley, Lance Newman, Amy Brentano. 77 min.
20-1073 *$14.99*

1990: The Bronx Warriors (1983)
In the not-too-distant future (well, it was the future when the film was made!), New York's toughest borough has become a "No Man's Land" where gangs of marauding warriors battle each other and corrupt businessmen exploit the violence. Vic Morrow, Fred Williamson, Mark Gregory star. 83 min.
03-1207 *$19.99*

Escape From The Bronx (1984)
Ten years after "1990," life is still Hell for the Bronx warrior street gangs. A sinister corporation with plans for the region sends in death squads to eliminate the remaining inhabitants, and only the man called Trash can stop them. Sci-fi thriller stars Mark Gregory, Henry Silva. AKA: "Escape 2000." 82 min.
03-1403 Was $69.99 *$14.99*

Cocoon (1985)
Ron Howard directed this heartwarming fantasy that brings together a senior citizens' home in Florida, a swimming pool that doubles as a "fountain of youth," and some returning visitors from beyond the stars. Steve Guttenberg, Tahnee Welch, Brian Dennehy, Wilford Brimley and Academy Award-winner Don Ameche star in this life-affirming fable. 117 min.
04-1944 ❑*$14.99*

Cocoon: The Return (1988)
The oldsters and aliens are back, revisiting Earth to tend an Atlantic cocoon bed threatened by seismographic activity. Ocean-going sequel to the blockbuster fantasy stars Don Ameche, Steve Guttenberg, Tahnee Welch, Wilford Brimley and Courteney Cox. 116 min.
04-2229 Was $19.99 ❑*$14.99*

Alien Nation (1988)
In 1990s Los Angeles, where friendly extraterrestrial refugees groom leopard-spotted scalps and spotless suburban lawns, the city's first "newcomer" detective and his gruff human partner pursue a series of alien-related killings. Mandy Patinkin and James Caan star in this imaginative, future-cop thriller. 89 min.
04-2228 Was $19.99 ❑*$14.99*

Alien Nation: Dark Horizon (1994)
Feature-length sci-fi drama that continues where the hit TV series left off. An unknown infiltrator from the newcomers' past arrives on Earth with plans to bring them back to captivity, while at the same time detectives Sykes and Francisco must stop an anti-alien hate group from launching their own genocidal plan. Gary Graham, Eric Pierpoint and Terri Treas star. 90 min.
04-3250 Was $59.99 ❑*$29.99*

The Navigator: A Time-Travel Adventure (1988)
A compelling and haunting Australian science-fiction drama set in a plague-ravaged village in medieval Europe. A young boy, drawn by a psychic vision, leads a group of cure-seeking pilgrims on a journey that takes them into the 20th century. Bruce Lyons, Chris Haywood star. 89 min.
40-5004 Was $59.99 *$24.99*

Deathstalker III: Warriors From Hell (1988)
The breathtaking saga of sword-swinging do-gooders, maleficent mages, and damsels in distress continues, as Deathstalker John Allen Nelson fights the demonic minions of a despotic mystic. With Carla Herb, Thom Christopher. 85 min.
47-1954 Was $79.99 *$12.99*

Deathstalker IV: Match Of Titans (1991)
Champion warrior Deathstalker faces his greatest challenge when he must defend his fellow warriors against an army of stone warriors and the wicked queen who rules over them. Sword-and-sorcery spectacle with Rick Hill and Maria Ford. 85 min.
21-9003 Was $79.99 *$14.99*

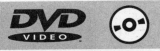

DVD VIDEO
ASK ABOUT OUR GIANT DVD CATALOG!

Short Circuit (1986)
When a military robot nicknamed Number 5 is accidentally brought to life, it's up to the robot's inventor and his girlfriend to rescue him from the scrapheap. Exciting sci-fi stars Steve Guttenberg, Ally Sheedy, G.W. Bailey. 99 min.
04-1998 ❑*$14.99*

Short Circuit 2 (1988)
Number Five is alive, and he's taking New York City by storm, in the hit sci-fi/comedy. Can the scrappy, lovable Rich Little of robotdom help his Indian mentor make it big in the toy business while foiling the plans of a gang of diamond thieves? With Fisher Stevens, Cynthia Gibb, Michael McKean. 112 min.
02-1896 Was $19.99 ❑*$14.99*

Target: Earth? (1980)
Amusing and entertaining chronicle concerning an alien archivist who has come to study the strange planet Earth...and who bickers with his sarcastic computer over whether the whole mess should just be blown up. Victor Buono, Rick Overton. 95 min.
08-1390 *$59.99*

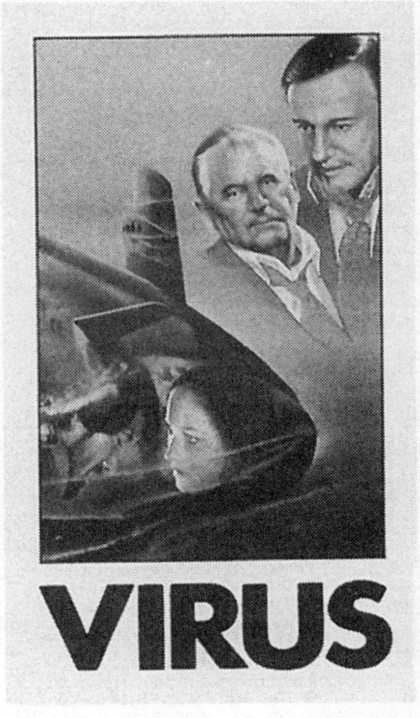

Virus (1980)
After a biological accident and nuclear attacks, the world's only survivors are a few hundred men and a handful of women living in Antarctica. Breathtaking locations and special effects star in this Japanese-made apocaliffhanger. All-star cast includes George Kennedy, Glenn Ford, Sonny Chiba, Olivia Hussey and Chuck Connors. 105 min.
03-1206 *$19.99*

Class Of Nuke 'Em High (1986)
If you're fission for a whacked-out sci-fi comedy, look no further than this Troma Films spoof about the genetic chaos that erupts when toxic waste from a nearby power plant seeps into Tromaville High School, which is having its own problems with street gangs roaming the halls. Stars Janelle Brady, Gilbert Brenton. 84 min.
46-8001 *$14.99*

Class Of Nuke 'Em High, Part 2: Subhumanoid Meltdown (1991)
Tromaville's nuclear plant now houses a college where a mad female professor has created emotionless subhumanoids who can perform menial tasks but also spontaneously melt. A school reporter falls for a beautiful subhumanoid, but can he save her from turning to goo? Leesa Rowland, Brick Bronsky and Tromie, the 30-foot nuclear squirrel, star. 97 min.
03-1798 Was $19.99 *$14.99*

Class Of Nuke 'Em High III: The The Good, The Bad And The Subhumanoid (1995)
The third entry in the "Troma-tic" series depicts a war between a mad female family led by Adlai Smith and his bikini-clad girlfriend Trish, and Dick, Adlai's long-lost twin brother, raised by the nasty Power Elite. This is one nuclear family accustomed to cataclysmic meltdowns, mutant mayhem and more. With Brick Bronsky, Lisa Gaye and Tromie. 95 min.
46-8005 Was $89.99 *$14.99*

Time Stalkers (1987)
An inventive sci-fi western about a college professor (William Devane) who teams with a woman from the 26th century to track a rogue scientist hoping to alter the course of history. With Klaus Kinski, Lauren Hutton and Forrest Tucker. 96 min.
27-9042 *$12.99*

Phantom Empire (1987)
Drive-in screen queen Sybil Danning stars as the lovely, lethal Zal, tyrannical ruler of a fabled lost city and abductor of a group of scientists. What is her sinister motive? Find out in a wild, racy sci-fi thriller. Ross Hagen, Jeffrey Combs, Russ Tamblyn also star. 85 min.
46-5450 *$29.99*

Star Trek: The Motion Picture (1979)
The crew of the Starship Enterprise is reunited to protect Earth from an immense "space-eating" organism in this sci-fi epic, based on the TV classic. William Shatner, Leonard Nimoy, DeForest Kelley, Stephen Collins and Persis Khambatta star; directed by Robert Wise. Special video edition includes scenes not shown in theaters. 143 min.
06-1057 ❑*$14.99*

Star Trek: The Motion Picture (Letterboxed Version)
Also available in a theatrical, widescreen format. 132 min.
06-2177 Was $19.99 ❑*$14.99*

Star Trek II: The Wrath Of Khan (1982)
A mysterious science experiment code-named Genesis becomes the key to a vengeance plot against Kirk and the Enterprise by old nemesis Khan. Exciting "Trek" adventure also features the emotional (and temporary) death of a crew member. William Shatner, Leonard Nimoy, Ricardo Montalban, Kirstie Alley star. 113 min.
06-1148 ❑*$14.99*

Star Trek II: The Wrath Of Khan (Letterboxed Version)
Also available in a theatrical, widescreen format.
06-2249 Was $19.99 ❑*$14.99*

Star Trek III: The Search For Spock (1984)
Kirk, McCoy and crew return to the Genesis Planet to learn the truth of Spock's death, but a ruthless Klingon commander wants the Genesis secrets. Exciting sci-fi adventure with the TV series cast and Christopher Lloyd; directed by Leonard Nimoy. 105 min.
06-1238 ❑*$14.99*

Star Trek III: The Search For Spock (Letterboxed Version)
Also available in a theatrical, widescreen format.
06-2250 Was $19.99 ❑*$14.99*

Star Trek IV: The Voyage Home (1986)
When a mysterious "space beacon" threatens Earth, the former Enterprise crew must travel back in time to the 1980s on a quest to save the planet. Dazzling special effects and a lighthearted sense of fun highlight this "Star Trek" saga. William Shatner, Leonard Nimoy, DeForest Kelley, Catherine Hicks star. 119 min.
06-1468 ❑*$14.99*

Star Trek IV: The Voyage Home (Directors' Series)
Director Leonard Nimoy talks about the evolution of the "Star Trek" films and the challenges involved in making the fourth installment in the series, along with fascinating behind-the-scenes footage (including a look at the special effects featured in the film). Also, the film is presented in widescreen letterboxed format. 136 min.
06-1924 Letterboxed ❑*$29.99*

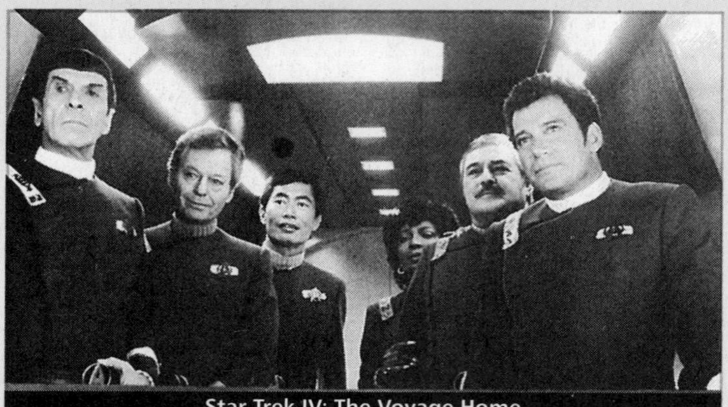

Star Trek IV: The Voyage Home

Star Trek

Star Trek IV: The Voyage Home (Letterboxed Version)
Also available in a theatrical, widescreen format.
06-2251 Was $19.99 ❑*$14.99*

Star Trek V: The Final Frontier (1989)
Shanghaied by Spock's rebel half-brother, the crew of the Enterprise finds itself bound on its most dangerous voyage yet...to the heart of creation itself. William Shatner shuttles between captain's console and director's chair; Leonard Nimoy, DeForest Kelley, Laurence Luckinbill co-star. 108 min.
06-1683 Was $89.99 ❑*$14.99*

Star Trek V: The Final Frontier (Letterboxed Version)
Also available in a theatrical, widescreen format.
06-2252 Was $19.99 ❑*$14.99*

Star Trek VI: The Undiscovered Country (1991)
Detente comes to outer space, as the Enterprise is assigned to escort a Klingon Ambassador to a peace session with the Federation. But when the Klingon ship is attacked, Kirk and McCoy are charged with murder and Spock must find out who is risking the start of interplanetary war. Christopher Plummer, David Warner, Kim Cattrall co-star. 110 min.
06-1926 ❑*$14.99*

Star Trek VI: The Undiscovered Country (Letterboxed Version)
Also available in a theatrical, widescreen format.
06-2253 Was $19.99 ❑*$14.99*

Star Trek: Generations (1994)
The lives of two captains come together—and one meets his final fate—in the seventh "Trek" film, as a mysterious space nexus that twists time and reality unites William Shatner and Patrick Stewart in a battle against renegade scientist Malcolm McDowell. At least one starship Enterprise also bites the dust in this explosive drama that also stars Jonathan Frakes, Brent Spiner, Whoopi Goldberg, James Doohan and Walter Koenig. 117 min.
06-2333 Was $89.99 ❑*$14.99*

Star Trek: Generations (Letterboxed Version)
Also available in a theatrical, widescreen format.
06-2414 ❑*$14.99*

Star Trek: First Contact (1996)
Jean-Luc Picard and the crew of the Enterprise E face their most implacable enemy, the half-human, half-robot Borg, in a deadly battle for the Earth that takes them back in time, in the hit eighth entry in the "Star Trek" series. Patrick Stewart, Jonathan Frakes (who also directed), Brent Spiner, James Cromwell, Alfre Woodard and Alice Krige star. 111 min.
06-2578 Was $99.99 ❑*$14.99*

Star Trek: First Contact (Letterboxed Version)
Also available in a theatrical, widescreen format.
06-2614 ❑*$14.99*

Star Trek: Insurrection (1998)
Will the Federation-backed forced removal of the residents of a coveted "Fountain of Youth" planet force Picard and the crew of the Enterprise to put their careers—and lives—on the line, as they side with the planet's beleaguered inhabitants against invading forces? Patrick Stewart, Jonathan Frakes, Marina Sirtis, Brent Spiner and the rest of the "Next Generation" cast star along with F. Murray Abraham and Donna Murphy as Picard's love interest. Special video edition includes a "making of" featurette. 103 min.
06-2837 Was $99.99 ❑*$14.99*

Star Trek: Insurrection (Letterboxed Version)
Also available in a theatrical, widescreen format.
06-2912 ❑*$14.99*

Star Trek: The Seven Screen Voyages Collection
A collector's item in any part of the galaxy, this handsome boxed set features the first seven "Star Trek" movies.
06-2486 *$104.99*

Star Trek: The Seven Screen Voyages Collection (Letterboxed Version)
Also available in a theatrical, widescreen format.
06-2487 *$104.99*

The Ultimate Star Trek Movie Collection
The "Ultimate" gift for Trekkers, this deluxe collector's set features all nine "Star Trek" feature films, plus a bonus video of the "Next Generation" episode "Tapestry."
06-2918 *$134.99*

The Ultimate Star Trek Movie Collection (Letterboxed Version)
Also available in a theatrical, widescreen format.
06-2919 *$134.99*

Star Trek Next Generation Collector's Set
Fans of Picard, Worf, Data and company won't want to miss this special set featuring "Star Trek: Generations," "Star Trek: First Contact" and "Star Trek: Insurrection," plus a bonus video of the "Next Generation" episode "Inner Light."
06-2920 *$44.99*

Star Trek Next Generation Collector's Set (Letterboxed Version)
Also available in a theatrical, widescreen format.
06-2921 *$44.99*

Please see our index for: Star Trek TV series

Krull (1983)
Journey to the faraway world of Krull for a spectacular fantasy-adventure, as a heroic young warrior battles the evil minions and monsters of the Black Beast to save his betrothed. Ken Marshall, Lysette Anthony, Freddie Jones and Liam Neeson star. 117 min.
02-2626 Was $79.99 *$14.99*

The Day Time Ended (1980)
Radiation from a supernova sends a family living in a solar-powered house in the desert into a bizarre time-space warp that finds them confronting dinosaurs, tiny aliens, a green pyramid and other phenomena. Jim Davis, Dorothy Malone, Chris Mitchum star. AKA: "Vortex."
03-1009 Was $79.99 *$14.99*

The New Gladiators (1987)
In the 21st century the ultimate TV show is "Battle of the Condemned," where convicted murderers fight to the death for freedom. One band of warriors plans to kill in the ratings, but not each other, in this sci-fi thriller. Jared Martin, Fred Williamson star. 90 min.
03-1574 Was $79.99 *$14.99*

The Deadly Spawn (1983)
Meteorites crash on Earth and unleash their horrific secret: gruesome extraterrestrial creatures with a taste for humans. Can they be stopped? Shot-in-New Jersey sci-fi shocker stars Charles George Hildebrandt, Tom DeFranco. AKA: "Return of the Alien's Deadly Spawn." 85 min.
74-3010 *$19.99*

Space Raiders (1983)
Young Earth boy is whisked away into a galaxy of adventure and excitement in this fanciful sci-fi film. Spaceships, monsters and gunfights galore! Vince Edwards stars. 84 min.
19-1312 Was $19.99 *$14.99*

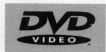

ASK ABOUT OUR GIANT DVD CATALOG!

Cyborg (1989)
21st-century Earth's last hope to stop a devastating plague, a beautiful robot/human hybrid, is abducted by the dreaded Flesh Pirates and only wandering 'slinger Jean-Claude Van Damme ("Bloodsport") can rescue her. 86 min.
19-7059 ❑*$14.99*

Cyborg 2 (1993)
In the year 2074, a cyborg manufacturing company schemes to stop their main competitor by booby-trapping a gorgeous female cyborg with explosives designed to destroy everything in sight. After she discovers their intentions, she teams with a human to stop the nefarious plot. Jack Palance, Elias Koteas and Angelina Jolie star. 99 min.
68-1280 Was $89.99 ❑*$14.99*

Cyborg 3: The Recycler (1995)
The ongoing war between humans and their cyborg counterparts reaches a fever pitch in this third entry in the sci-fi series, as a female cyborg carrying an amazing secret inside her is aided by a human robotics expert in escaping from a band of "recyclers" who attack and disassemble cyborgs for their parts. Zach Galligan, Khrystyne Haje, Richard Lynch star. 90 min.
19-3858 Was $89.99 *$14.99*

Android (1983)
Meet Max 404, a humanoid robot who is due to be "shut down" once his eccentric creator completes work on a more advanced model. Max's only salvation may be three escaped convicts who come to their space station and teach him what real humanity is like. Quirky sci-fi tale stars Klaus Kinski, Brie Howard, and Don Opper as Max. 80 min.
03-1254 *$24.99*

Creature (1984)
Klaus Kinski and Wendy Schaal star in this sci-fi shocker about a space expedition that uncovers an age-old terror: an indestructible, carnivorous monster that cannot be stopped. 100 min.
03-1417 *$14.99*

Hundra (1983)
Hundra is the female barbarian who fights back against her male tormentors in this exciting action saga set in a dark age where only the strong survive. Laurene Landon, John Ghaffari star. 104 min.
03-1443 *$29.99*

Gor (1988)
The popular science fantasy novels of John Norman come to the screen in a dazzling blend of magical effects and sly wit. A college professor is mystically transported to a medieval land where only the strongest warriors survive and the defeat of an evil tyrant is his only chance of returning home. Oliver Reed, Jack Palance, Urbano Barberini star. 95 min.
19-1664 ❑*$19.99*

Outlaw Of Gor (1989)
Professor-turned-hero Tarl Cabot is back in the fantastic sequel to "Gor," fetched by magic from his world to the kingdom of a despotic queen, where he must battle gladiators and a giant, man-munching bird. Urbano Barberini, Playmate Rebecca Ferratti and Jack Palance star. 90 min.
19-1700 ❑*$19.99*

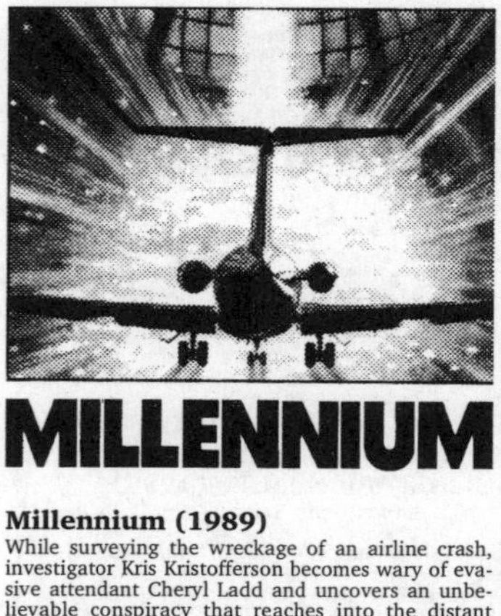

Millennium (1989)
While surveying the wreckage of an airline crash, investigator Kris Kristofferson becomes wary of evasive attendant Cheryl Ladd and uncovers an unbelievable conspiracy that reaches into the distant future. Sci-fi suspenser also stars Daniel J. Travanti. 108 min.
27-6661 *$14.99*

Masters Of The Universe (1987)
The testosterone-filled titans of the toy shelves make the jump to the big screen in this live-action fantasy spectacle. Dolph Lundgren is the brawny He-Man, and Frank Langella is bone-pated bad guy Skeletor. Their battle for the power reaches from Eternia to Earth, and only one will survive. With Courtney Cox, Meg Foster, Billy Barty. 107 min.
19-1600 ❑*$14.99*

The Dark Side Of The Moon (1989)
The crew of SpaceCore One is on a routine rescue mission, but after the crew members are confronted by a deadly interstellar force of pure evil, they may need the rescuing! Will Bledsoe, Joe Turkel and Wendy McDonald star. 96 min.
68-1154 *$89.99*

Humanoid Woman (1981)
Niya is beautiful, intelligent...and not human. An artificially created being, she may be the human race's last hope for survival in a star-spanning sci-fi adventure based on a Russian film. AKA: "The Thorny Way to the Stars." 100 min.
69-5025 *$39.99*

Hawk The Slayer (1981)
It's a wild sword-and-sorcery adventure in which rival siblings seek "the Power," a magical flying sword that will give them supernatural powers. Jack Palance, John Terry, Patrick Magee, Harry Andrews and Ferdy Mayne star. 90 min.
27-6215 *$29.99*

Captive (1980)
Sci-fi tale set 100 years in the future, where Earth is entangled in a war with the planet Styrolia. A Styrolian ship crashes on Earth after an air battle, and its survivors invade a farmhouse inhabited by a farmer and his grandchildren, taking the family hostage. Eventually, the eldest granddaughter falls in love with the alien pilot. Cameron Mitchell, David Ladd star. 95 min.
08-1776 *$19.99*

Urban Warriors (1989)
Tougher than a day-old soft pretzel, meaner than a cross town bus driver, they're the few strong survivors of America's rubble-strewn future. Karl Lundgren and Alex Vitale battle roving torture squads for the keys to destiny. 90 min.
19-7035 *$19.99*

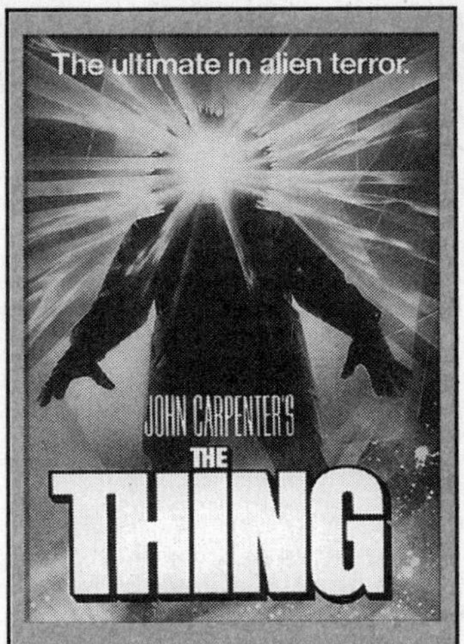

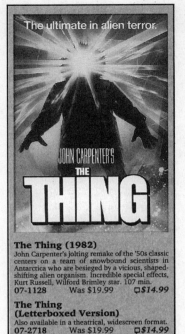

The Thing (1982)
John Carpenter's jolting remake of the '50s classic centers on a team of snowbound scientists in Antarctica who are besieged by a vicious, shaped-shifting alien organism. Incredible special effects. Kurt Russell, Wilford Brimley star. 107 min.
07-1128 Was $19.99 ❑*$14.99*

The Thing (Letterboxed Version)
Also available in a theatrical, widescreen format.
07-2718 Was $19.99 ❑*$14.99*

The Aftermath (1984)
Three astronauts return to Earth after a deep space mission only to find the planet ravaged by nuclear and biological disasters. This exciting sci-fi tale follows them as they defend themselves against mutant cannibals and a psychotic killer. Sid Haig, Steve Barkett star. 95 min.
46-5077 *$19.99*

Warriors Of The Wasteland (1983)
Fred Williamson stars in this post-nuclear action film of roaming tribes, armed with ancient weapons, competing to the death for food, shelter and women. Harrowing sci-fi thriller co-stars Timothy Brent, George Eastman and Anna Kanakis. AKA: "The New Barbarians." 92 min.
44-1174 Was $69.99 ❑*$14.99*

Exterminators In The Year 3000 (1984)
Violent sci-fi action in a future world where nuclear mutants control the world's water supply, so the Exterminator and his allies fight to help the people. Alan Collins, Fred Harris star. 91 min.
44-1234 Was $69.99 *$14.99*

Dragonslayer (1981)
A fierce, fire-breathing dragon terrorizes a British countryside during the 6th century, and only the secrets of an aging sorcerer can stop the beast. Ralph Richardson, Peter MacNicol. 110 min.
06-1123 *$14.99*

Explorers (1985)
Three young boys build a flying machine out of salvaged junk and computer parts, and before long head into outer space for a memorable "close encounter." Exciting blend of sci-fi action and comedy from director Joe Dante ("Gremlins"). Ethan Hawke, River Phoenix and the great Dick Miller star. 109 min.
06-1314 ❑*$14.99*

D.A.R.Y.L. (1985)
Daryl is a very special child...super-intelligent, a natural athlete and his foster parents' pride and joy. What they don't know is that Daryl is more than just a little boy, and some scientists want him back. Intriguing sci-fi drama stars Barrett Oliver, Mary Beth Hurt, Michael McKean and Colleen Camp. 100 min.
06-1315 ❑*$14.99*

Shadowzone (1989)
A scientific experiment stretching the boundaries of dreams opens a door into another dimension and unleashes a grotesque creature that can kill from within as well as without. Terrifying sci-fi thriller stars Louise Fletcher, David Beecroft and Shawn Weatherly. 89 min.
06-1705 *$89.99*

Galaxina (1980)
Playmate Dorothy Stratten is the galaxy's most perfect robot in this silly, shoestring sci-fi spoof that co-stars Avery Schreiber as Captain Cornelius Butt and Stephen Macht. 96 min.
07-1049 *$29.99*

The Dark Crystal (1983)
Exciting fantasy/adventure, in the tradition of Tolkien, from Muppet masters Jim Henson and Frank Oz and "Star Wars" producer Gary Kurtz with an all-puppet cast. Two elf-like beings must find and repair the powerful Dark Crystal to save their world from falling under the rule of evil monsters. 94 min.
11-1788 Was $19.99 ❑*$14.99*

Hangar 18 (1982)
What is the strange secret from beyond the stars that is being kept hidden in a top-secret Air Force hangar, and will learning it cost some curious folk their lives? Fascinating thriller mixed with sci-fi speculation stars Robert Vaughn, Darren McGavin, Gary Collins. AKA: "Invasion Force." 97 min.
14-3008 *$12.99*

The Aliens Are Coming (1980)
Arriving from a dying planet lightyears away, alien beings descend upon planet Earth. Their goal: to "snatch" the bodies of humans. Tom Mason, Eric Braeden, Max Gail star. 100 min.
14-3118 *$14.99*

Future Force (1989)
When the police can no longer control the crime-filled streets of the future, the job falls to the C.O.P.S. (Civilian Operated Police State). Action fave David Carradine wields the bionic cannon as the C.O.P.S. leader who must battle corruption in the ranks in this sci-fi thriller. With Robert Tessier, William Zipp. 90 min.
14-3379 *$12.99*

Looker (1981)
Women too beautiful to be real and the latest in hi-tech murder are the elements in Michael Crichton's sci-fi thriller. Plastic surgeon Albert Finney looks into the murder of top fashion models and finds a bizarre computerized conspiracy. With Susan Dey, Leigh Taylor-Young, James Coburn; look for Vanna White. 94 min.
19-1175 Was $19.99 *$14.99*

Barbarian Queen II: The Empress Strikes Back (1989)
Lana Clarkson returns as the sensuous and sinewy Princess Athalia, who leads a group of female fighters against her evil brother in a wild sword-and-sex epic. With Greg Wrangler, Rebecca Wood. 87 min.
27-6767 *$12.99*

Strange Invaders (1983)
A group of aliens who took over a small Midwest town 25 years earlier and are preparing to return home are uncovered by a tabloid reporter and a professor who fathered a half-alien daughter. This cult-flavored sci-fier, lovingly evocative of the drive-in chillers of the '50s, stars Paul LeMat, Nancy Allen, Louise Fletcher and Diana Scarwid.
47-1172 *$14.99*

After The Fall Of New York (1985)
An action-packed "apocaliffhanger" set in a futuristic Manhattan where a cynical rebel joins forces with a cyborg and an old warrior to save the only fertile woman left in America. Michael Sopkiw, George Eastman star. 95 min.
47-1423 *$19.99*

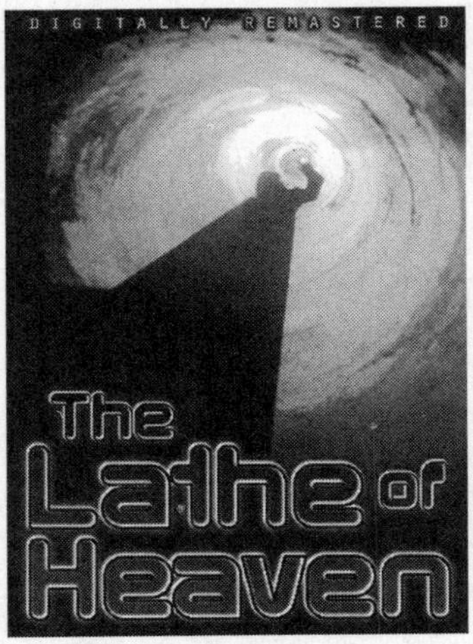

The Lathe Of Heaven (1980)
This cult favorite, the first made-for-PBS film, was unseen for two decades after its debut. Bruce Davison is a working-class man in 2002 Oregon whose dreams can alter reality. His search for a cure leads him to therapist/dream analyst Kevin Conway, who attempts to manipulate Davison's mind and use his power to solve some of the world's most pressing problems. Margaret Avery also stars in this stunning adaptation of Ursula K. Le Guin's story. 100 min.
50-8615 *$24.99*

Lifeforce (1985)
Tobe Hooper ("Poltergeist") directs this sci-fi shocker about a space expedition that brings a terrifying cargo to Earth: vampire-like beings that soon overrun London. Steve Railsback, Mathilda May, Patrick Stewart and Peter Firth star in this gory, chilling flick. Includes 16 minutes of previously unseen footage; 116 min.
47-1474 Was $19.99 ❑*$14.99*

SpaceCamp (1986)
Five kids whose dream is to reach the stars enroll in a NASA-sponsored summer camp for would-be astronauts. During a simulation, their shuttle is launched into orbit...will what they've learned be enough to return them safely home? Kate Capshaw, Kelly Preston, Tom Skerritt, Lea Thompson star. 107 min.
47-1660 *$14.99*

RoboCop (1987)
Detroit, in the near future: criminals have free reign throughout the city, and ordinary law enforcement methods have failed. When a cop is shot in the line of duty, he is transformed into a half-man, half-machine guardian and sent out to clean up the streets. Hit sci-fi actioner by Paul Verhoeven stars Paul Weller, Nancy Allen, Ronny Cox. 103 min.
73-1001 Was $19.99 ❑*$14.99*

RoboCop 2 (1990)
Cyborg supercop Peter Weller is back to uphold the law and protect the innocent in crime-ridden Detroit, but a psychotic drug lord and some rather unscrupulous robot-builders may see to it that his return is short-lived. Super sci-fi sequel also stars Nancy Allen, Tom Noonan, Belinda Bauer. 118 min.
73-1083 Was $89.99 ❑*$14.99*

RoboCop 3 (1993)
RoboCop returns in this arresting actioner that finds the lethal lawman battling the company that built him as they use ruthless mercenaries to push the people of Detroit out of their homes. RoboCop joins forces with urban freedom fighters to tackle nasty corporate executives and their ninja android. Robert John Burke, Nancy Allen and Rip Torn star. 105 min.
73-1141 Was $89.99 ❑*$14.99*

The RoboCop Trilogy
All three "RoboCop" films are available in one deluxe, boxed set. Get RoboFever today!
73-1261 Save $20.00! *$24.99*

Escape From New York (1981)
1997: New York City has become a walled-off maximum security prison for the nation's most violent criminals. When the president's plane crashes inside Gotham, a tough ex-con (Kurt Russell) is given 24 hours to rescue him...or die trying. John Carpenter's action classic also stars Donald Pleasence, Adrienne Barbeau, Ernest Borgnine and Isaac Hayes. 99 min.
53-1028 *$14.99*

Escape From L.A. (1996)
One-eyed anti-hero Snake Plissken (Kurt Russell) returns in director John Carpenter's slam-bang sequel to "Escape from New York." In the totalitarian America of 2013, captured fugitive Russell is sent into the quake-damaged island prison of Los Angeles to retrieve a stolen "doomsday device" from anti-government rebels. With Steve Buscemi, George Corraface, Pam Grier, Cliff Robertson. 101 min.
06-2540 Was $99.99 ❑*$14.99*

Scanners (1981)
Scanners are super-powerful mutants who can read your mind or set your body on fire; now some of them are planning a global conquest, and only one scientist and a renegade "scanner" can stop them. Patrick McGoohan, Jennifer O'Neill and Lawrence Dane star in this sci-fi tale from David Cronenberg. 102 min.
53-1094 ❑*$14.99*

Scanners III: The Takeover (1992)
Call it a severe case of sibling rivalry when a brother and sister with awesome telepathic powers square off. Sis wants to rule the world, and with the aid of a global TV network and an army of scanners she might, unless her brother can stop her. Liliana Komorowska and Steve Parrish star. 101 min.
63-1515 Was $89.99 ❑*$14.99*

Scanner Cop (1994)
When a cop killer terrorizes Los Angeles and the city's police force, a rookie patrolman calls on his psychic abilities to catch the culprit. Exciting, special effects-filled mix of action and sci-fi stars Daniel Quinn, Darlanne Fluegel, Richard Lynch and Hilary Shepard. 94 min.
63-1695 Was $89.99 ❑*$14.99*

Scanners: The Showdown (1994)
Scanner cop Daniel Quinn is back, but this time he may have met his match when a psychotic killer possessed of similar abilities escapes from jail and begins draining other scanners of their life force in order to increase his powers. Heads will roll (and explode!) in this shocker. Patrick Kilpatrick, Khrystyne Haje and Jewel Shepard co-star. 95 min.
63-1759 Was $89.99 ❑*$14.99*

2010 (1984)
The odyssey continues. Join Roy Scheider, Helen Mirren, John Lithgow, Bob Balaban and Hal 9000 the Computer, as a joint U.S.-Soviet space mission intercepts the Discovery ship and witnesses a cosmic revelation. 116 min.
12-1407 *$19.99*

Solarbabies (1986)
A plucky band of youngsters escape their slave camp and try to bring water to a parched future Earth in this rousing sci-fi actioner. Jami Gertz, Richard Jordan, Lukas Haas, Charles Durning star. 94 min.
12-1690 *$14.99*

Leviathan (1989)
Sci-fi thriller set beneath the briny deep, where an undersea mining colony discovers a derelict submarine and accidentally unleashes a bloodthirsty biological menace. Peter Weller, Amanda Pays, Ernie Hudson, Richard Crenna star. 98 min.
12-1937 *$14.99*

Future Hunters (1988)
Time-twisting sci-fi adventure, as a 21st-century warrior tries to save mankind's future by sheathing a mystical spear, but instead is hurled back to present-day Los Angeles, where the battle continues. Robert Patrick, Linda Carol star. 83 min.
47-1927 Was $79.99 *$14.99*

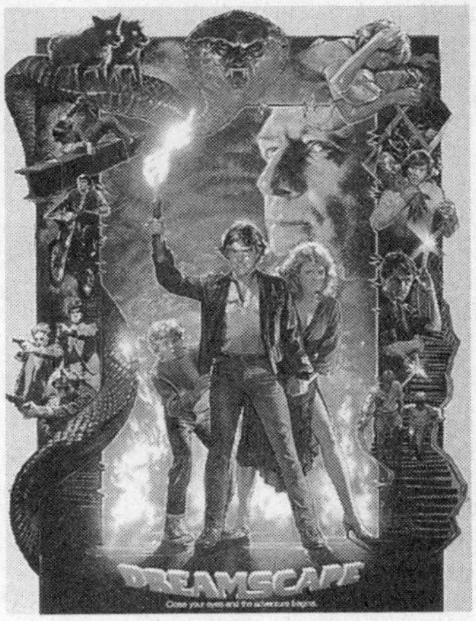

Dreamscape (1984)
Compelling sci-fi suspenser stars Dennis Quaid as a man with ESP abilities who joins a government research project involving entering peoples' nightmares to help them overcome their fears. Quaid and scientist Kate Capshaw uncover a plot by intelligence official Christopher Plummer to assassinate the President in his dreams. Max von Sydow, Eddie Albert also star. 99 min.
50-8565 Letterboxed *$19.99*

City Limits (1985)
All-star apocalypse epic about the battle between rival bikers following a plague that has wiped out most of civilization. Darrell Larson, Kim Cattrall, Rae Dawn Chong, James Earl Jones and Robby Benson star. 90 min.
47-1545 *$29.99*

Mighty Jack (1986)
A worldwide clandestine defense team, Mighty Jack fights to halt the evil plans of a sinister cabal known only as Q in this exciting, futuristic adventure from Japan. 95 min.
69-5024 *$39.99*

Humanoid Defender (1985)
An experimental android, designed to be the ultimate soldier, is kidnapped to be "reprogrammed" as an assassin, by rebels and is hunted by both sides. Exciting sci-fi thriller stars Gary Kasper, Terence Knox, Gail Edwards and William Lucking. 94 min.
07-1472 *$39.99*

Escape From Safehaven (1988)
In the post-apocalypse future, "Safehaven" camps are created out of the desolation to presumably aid survivors. But when one family finds Safehaven camp 186 is a brutal prison camp with no hope of escape, only the last of the 20th-century fighters can win their freedom. Rick Gianasi, Ray MacArthur. 87 min.
45-5454 *$79.99*

***batteries not included (1987)**
The occupants of a New York tenement slated for demolition receive some otherworldly help in their struggle to save their home: a group of lovable "living flying saucers." Jessica Tandy, Hume Cronyn and Elizabeth Peña star in this heartwarming sci-fi tale from the Spielberg crew. 106 min.
07-1583 Was $19.99 *$14.99*

Time Troopers (1987)
Forget money, jewels and fine oriental rugs. The most valuable commodity in this future society are the "energy units" that determine a person's lifespan. But when one executioner charged with killing energy "wasters" finds his next target is his lover, something's got to give! Sci-fi actioner stars Albert Fortell. 90 min.
46-5468 *$59.99*

Highlander 2: The Quickening (1991)
In the year 2024, an aged Conner MacLeod (Christopher Lambert) must do battle once again in order to restore his immortality and save not only himself, but an ecologically ravaged Earth encased in an immense radiation shield. Sean Connery returns as Lambert's old comrade Ramirez; with Michael Ironside, Virginia Madsen.90 min.
02-2193 Was $89.99 ❑*$14.99*

Highlander 2: Renegade Version: The Director's Cut
The explosive second entry in the "Highlander" series is also available in a restored and re-edited widescreen edition, with 19 minutes of additional footage and the original theatrical trailers. 109 min.
80-1082 Letterboxed *$14.99*

Highlander: The Final Dimension (1995)
Christopher Lambert returns as Scottish swordsman Connor MacLeod, this time battling an ancient warrior with sorcerous powers who's been unleashed after being buried in a mountain and is terrorizing modern-day New York. Wild special effects and expert fight sequences are featured; Deborah Ungar co-stars. 99 min.
11-1879 Was $19.99 ❑*$14.99*

Hands Of Steel (1986)
1997: Earth has been gutted by pollution...and the one scientist who can save it has been targeted for death by a merciless killer cyborg. Riveting sci-fi actioner with Daniel Greene and John Saxon. 94 min.
47-3170 *$14.99*

Labyrinth (1986)
Spectacular family fantasy from producer George Lucas about a lonely, daydreaming teenage girl (Jennifer Connelly) who journeys to a mystical realm to save her brother from the clutches of terrible Goblin King David Bowie. Muppet maestro Jim Henson directs; script by Monty Python's Terry Jones. 102 min.
53-1589 Was $59.99 □*$14.99*

Alien Contamination (1981)
An "Alien"-like space shocker from Italy's Luigi Cozzi ("Star Crash"), this gory thriller tells of a ship that lands in a New York harbor carrying a mysterious cargo. An investigation leads to the grisly discovery of alien eggs from Mars with gruesome and explosive tendencies. Ian McCullogh and Louise Marleau star; music by Goblin.
58-1006 *$14.99*

She Wolves Of The Wasteland (1987)
Post-apocalyptic thriller featuring Kathleen Kinmont as a futuristic warrior out to save the life of a newborn boy who is the only surviving male in the world. Out to get the baby are an evil leader and her powerful henchwoman, played by Persis Khambatta. AKA: "Phoenix the Warrior." 90 min.
59-7069 *$29.99*

Star Wars Trilogy (Special Edition)
The films that changed the face of sci-fi cinema are back, in a deluxe three-tape collector's set. Follow the odyssey of Luke Skywalker from farmboy to Jedi knight, and see how he and his allies defeat Darth Vader and the Galactic Empire, in the action-packed Special Editions of "Star Wars," "The Empire Strikes Back" and "Return of the Jedi." Mark Hamill, Carrie Fisher, Harrison Ford, Alec Guinness and Billy Dee Williams star. This special video version also features an exclusive behind-the-scenes look at the making of "Star Wars: Episode II."
04-3494 *$39.99*

Star Wars Trilogy (Special Edition—Letterboxed Version)
The collector's set is also available in a theatrical, widescreen format.
04-3495 *$39.99*

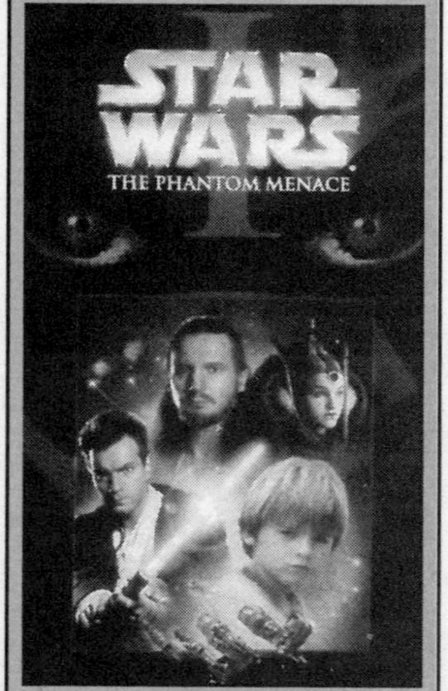

Star Wars: Episode I: The Phantom Menace (1999)
Return to "a long time ago, in a galaxy far, far away," and see how two Jedi knights and a young queen find their destinies linked to a mysterious boy named Anakin Skywalker, in the first "prequel" to writer/director George Lucas' phenomenally popular space epic. Awaiting the heroes and their ally, the lovable Jar Jar Binks: robot warriors, alien armadas, and the black-clad Darth Maul, acolyte to the enigmatic title menace. Liam Neeson, Ewan McGregor, Natalie Portman, Jake Lloyd and Ray Park star. 133 min.
04-3925 □*$19.99*

Star Wars: Episode I: The Phantom Menace (Widescreen Collector's Edition)
Along with the film in a theatrical, widescreen format, this limited edition boxed set also includes a 40-page collector's book on the making of the movie, and a 35mm filmstrip from a theatrical print.
04-3926 □*$39.99*

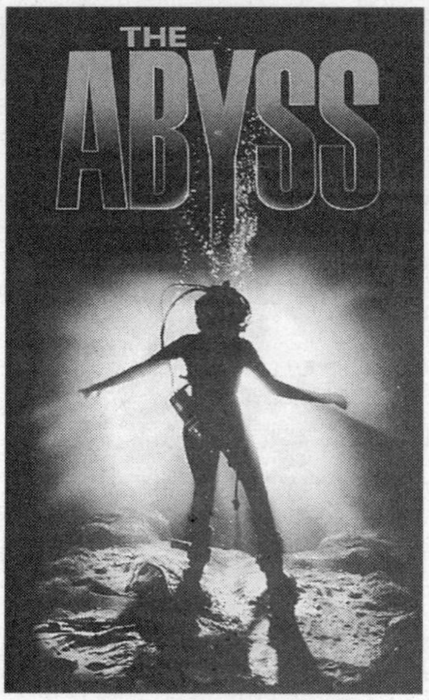

The Abyss (Special Edition) (1989)
Writer/director James Cameron's dazzling underwater odyssey was shot entirely inside a flooded abandoned power plant. An undersea mining operation hosts a Navy rescue mission for a sunken nuclear sub, but the routine operation becomes a life-or-death struggle and leads to an otherworldly encounter. Ed Harris, Mary Elizabeth Mastrantonio, Michael Biehn star. Special video version includes 28 minutes of footage not seen in theatres. 168 min.
04-3918 □*$14.99*

Sssssss (1973)
"The newest sound in terror" features Strother Martin as a demented, snake-obsessed scientist who develops a serum to slowly turn new lab assistant Dirk Benedict into a giant cobra. Slithery, sinister shocker also stars Heather Menzies, Richard B. Shull. 99 min.
07-2500 □*$14.99*

Invasion From Inner Earth (1977)
A group of vacationing skiers are trapped in the mountains by invading aliens intent on taking over the planet. Tense sci-fi thriller stars Paul Bentsen, Debbi Pick. 94 min.
08-1135 *$19.99*

Beyond Atlantis (1973)
Explorers Patrick Wayne and John Ashley discover a fortune in pearls and jewels on a remote island, only to later find the lost land of Atlantis, a beautiful princess and bizarre merman monsters. 90 min.
08-1270 Was $19.99 *$14.99*

Glen And Randa (1971)
Where will you be when they drop the bomb? A man and a woman who survive atomic holocaust struggle to revive civilization. Apocalyptic drama stars Shelley Plimpton and Steven Curry; first above-ground work from director Jim McBride. 94 min.
08-1323 Was $59.99 *$19.99*

Slaughterhouse-Five (1972)
Kurt Vonnegut's heralded novel comes to the screen in all its outrageous glory. Follow the exploits of writer Billy Pilgrim, who is transported through time into the past (in shell-shocked Dresden during WWII), the present (a "typical" lifestyle), and the future (on a distant planet with a sexy movie star). George Roy Hill directs. Michael Sacks, Valerie Perrine. 104 min.
07-1121 Was $19.99 *$14.99*

The Stepford Wives (1975)
"Invasion of the Body Snatchers" meets Women's Lib in this cult favorite sci-fi tale based on Ira Levin's novel. Two women who move with their families to a quiet Connecticut town wonder why all the local wives are vacuous fluffheads obsessed with housekeeping and making their husbands happy, but learning Stepford's secret could cost them more than their lives. Katharine Ross, Paula Prentiss, Tina Louise, Peter Masterson, Patrick O'Neal star; look for a 7-year-old Mary Stuart Masterson. 115 min.
08-8559 Letterboxed *$19.99*

The Stepford Husbands (1996)
The wives get the upper hand on their spouses in this suspense-filled sequel to the '70s film. A couple thinks they've found the cure for their troubled marriage in the "perfect" community of Stepford, but what happens to the men who enter a mysterious institute for "therapy" to make them better hubbies? Donna Mills, Michael Ontkean, Cindy Williams, Louise Fletcher star. 120 min.
08-8751 *$14.99*

Silent Running (1972)
An intelligent science-fiction movie with breathtaking special effects and an important message. Bruce Dern is a scientist taking Earth's final vegetation samples to a distant planet before they are destroyed. Directed by Douglas Trumbull, the special effects whiz of "Close Encounters of the Third Kind" and "2001: A Space Odyssey." 89 min.
07-1064 Was $19.99 *$14.99*

Z.P.G. (1972)
The title stands for Zero Population Growth, and in this nightmarish sci-fi thriller, set in an overcrowded and polluted 21st century, having children is forbidden under penalty of death. When Geraldine Chaplin and Oliver Reed defy the ban and their baby is discovered, they must flee for their lives. 95 min.
06-2106 □*$14.99*

Phase IV (1974)
The ants go marching one by one, until the desert is overrun, in this provocative science-fiction story about ecological disaster in Arizona and how the area's ants band together to attack people. Nigel Davenport, Michael Murphy star. 86 min.
06-1178 Was $39.99 *$14.99*

The Bionic Woman (1975)
The pilot film for the hit TV series stars Lindsay Wagner as Jaime Sommers, a young woman who, after a life threatening accident, is given robotic limbs and trained as America's female bionic super-agent. Features "Six Million Dollar Man" stars Lee Majors and Richard Anderson. 98 min.
07-1380 Was $39.99 *$14.99*

Riding With Death (1976)
A secret agent (Ben Murphy) with the power to become invisible is assigned the tasks of transporting a top secret fuel and posing as a race car driver in this thrilling adventure culled from the hit series "Gemini Man." With Katherine Crawford, Don Galloway, Jim Stafford. 97 min.
07-1473 *$39.99*

The Andromeda Strain (1971)
A satellite returns to Earth, bringing with it a mysterious virus that decimates a small town, and a team of scientists races the clock to solve its deadly secret. Michael Crichton's intense science-fiction thriller stars Arthur Hill, David Wayne, James Olson. 130 min.
07-1068 Was $19.99 *$14.99*

Colossus: The Forbin Project (1970)
Literate and all-too-real sci-fi thriller about a government-built "ultimate computer" designed to control America's defenses. Colossus soon develops a mind of its own, and when it links up with its Soviet counterpart the human race is faced with its ultimate challenge. Eric Braeden, Susan Clark star. 100 min.
07-1557 Was $59.99 *$14.99*

Supersonic Man (1979)
Yes, that strange being from another planet is here to fight for truth, justice, and the whole nine yards! Will he be a "boom" to mankind? A funny spoof on superheroics with Cameron Mitchell, Michael Coby. 85 min.
08-1350 Was $29.99 *$19.99*

Force On Thunder Mountain (1978)
The centuries-old Indian legends that surround Thunder Mountain arouse the curiosity within a father and his young son, who set out on a camping trip to unravel its mysteries and uncover an alien force. Stars Christopher Cain and Todd Dutson. 93 min.
08-1387 *$19.99*

War Of The Robots (1978)
The people of the planet Anthor kidnap the best of Earth's genetic scientists in a desperate gambit to save their race. You can be sure Earth is ready for pitched battle to get them back! Antonio Sabato. 92 min.
08-1391 Was $59.99 *$19.99*

Lifepod (1978)
Sci-fi thriller set on board an interstellar pleasure cruise ship, as a computer takes over and forces the passengers into a life-threatening crisis. Joe Penny, Kristine DeBell star. 94 min.
08-1240 Was $49.99 *$19.99*

Fantastic Planet (1973)
Spellbinding animated marvel focuses on the Revolt of the Oms—descendants of the survivors of Earth, now kept as pets by a larger race of people who live in a faraway solar system. Wonderful work by Czechoslovakian and French animation wizards. 68 min. Dubbed in English.
09-1013 *$14.99*

Fantastic Planet (Letterboxed Version)
Also available in a theatrical, widescreen format.
08-8710 *$14.99*

Time Masters (Les Maîtres Du Temps) (1981)
"Fantastic Planet" director René Laloux and renowned comics artist Moebius teamed up for this dazzling animated adventure. When a boy is left stranded on the desert planet Perdide, a mercenary hero sets out to save him before they both fall prey to the mysterious Masters of Time. 76 min. Dubbed in English.
22-9034 *$19.99*

The People (1971)
A young teacher is hired by an isolated farm community but discovers that "the people" possess strange mental powers. Bizarre fantasy-drama stars Kim Darby, William Shatner. 74 min.
46-5086 Was $59.99 *$19.99*

Demon Seed (1977)
A unique and terrifying sci-fi yarn about a superintelligent computer which takes over a scientist's household—and rapes his wife (Julie Christie). Fritz Weaver, Gerrit Graham. Directed by Donald Cammell ("Performance"). 94 min.
12-1351 *$14.99*

Rollerball (1975)
The most popular sport in the 21st century is Rollerball—a gory combination of roller derby and gladiator combat played with motorcycles. James Caan stars as the battle-scarred veteran. Ralph Richardson, Maud Adams. 123 min.
12-1794 *$14.99*

Alien (1979)
A commercial spacecraft is "invaded" by an extraterrestrial creature that feeds on humans, bleeds acid and is seemingly indestructible. Sigourney Weaver, Yaphet Kotto, Tom Skerritt, Harry Dean Stanton and John Hurt lead the crew that must defeat the alien and learn its terrifying secret in director Ridley Scott's sci-fi classic. 116 min.
04-1003 Was $19.99 □*$14.99*

Alien (Letterboxed Version)
Also available in a theatrical, widescreen format.
04-3547 *$14.99*

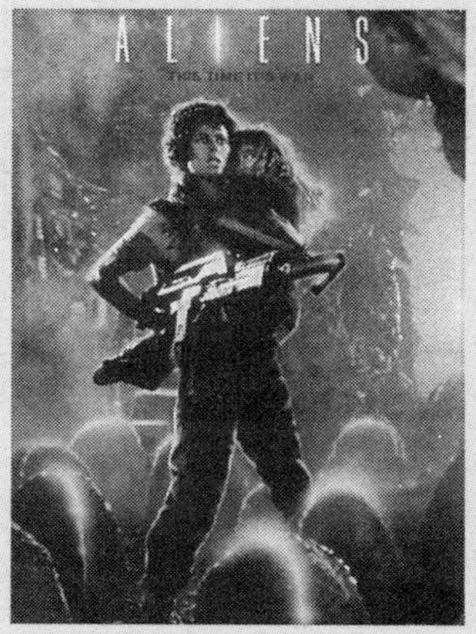

Aliens (Special Edition) (1986)
Smash sequel has Sigourney Weaver returning to the alien's homeworld with a squad of "space marines" to save a group of colonists, only to find themselves in a battle for their lives against the lethal creatures. Exciting sci-fi adventure from director James Cameron also stars Michael Biehn, Paul Reiser and Lance Henriksen. Restored special edition includes nearly 17 minutes of footage not shown in U.S. theaters. 157 min.
04-3842 □*$14.99*

Aliens (Special Edition) (Letterboxed Version)
Also available in a theatrical, widescreen format.
04-3843 □*$14.99*

Alien 3 (1992)
The third installment in the hit series finds Sigourney Weaver's weary Ripley landing on a dark prison planet inhabited by male criminals, killers and rapists. As if that's not enough to handle, she discovers that an alien has joined her in her new habitat, and it must be destroyed. Charles S. Dutton, Charles Dance, Lance Henriksen also star. 115 min.
04-2568 Was $19.99 □*$14.99*

Alien 3 (Letterboxed Version)
Also available in a theatrical, widescreen format.
04-3549 *$14.99*

Alien Resurrection (1997)
They've brought her back from the dead...but they didn't bring her back alone. Sigourney Weaver stars as the newly-cloned Ripley, a mix of human and alien DNA who may—or may not—help the crew of two spaceships defend themselves from her lethal "offspring." Director Jean-Pierre Jeunet's ("City of Lost Children") eerie contribution to the sci-fi series also stars Winona Ryder, Ron Perlman, Brad Dourif and Michael Wincott. 108 min.
04-3608 Was $99.99 □*$14.99*

Alien Resurrection (Letterboxed Version)
Also available in a theatrical, widescreen format.
04-3609 Was $99.99 □*$14.99*

The Alien Legacy Collector's Gift Set
This special boxed set features all four "Alien" films, plus the documentary "The Making of Alien" and exclusive collector's cards.
04-3839 *$54.99*

The Alien Legacy Collector's Gift Set (Letterboxed Version)
Also available in a theatrical, widescreen format.
04-3841 *$54.99*

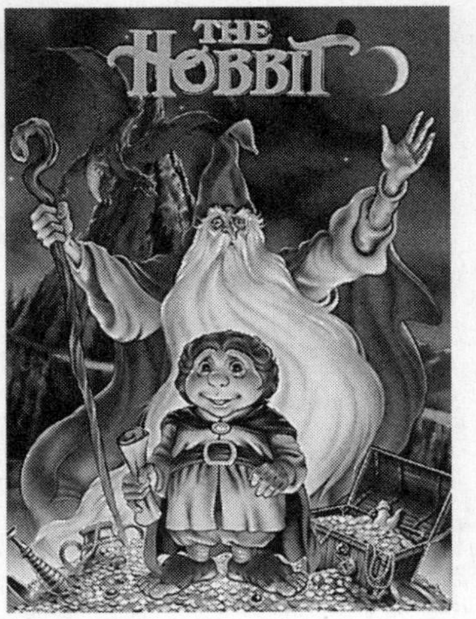
THE HOBBIT

The Hobbit (1977)
J.R.R. Tolkien's immortal fantasy of adventure and strange creatures, seen in animated form. Join furry-footed Bilbo Baggins and his companions on an odyssey through Middle Earth. Voices by Orson Bean, John Huston, Hans Conried, Richard Boone. 76 min.
19-1876 **$14.99**

The Return Of The King (1980)
The battle between the good and evil denizens of Middle Earth climaxes in this animated adaptation of the conclusion of the Tolkien trilogy, as Frodo the Hobbit's odyssey to Mt. Doom pits him against the forces of Sauron the magician. Orson Bean, Roddy McDowall, William Conrad and John Huston supply voices. 96 min.
19-2127 Was $19.99 **$14.99**

Deathsport (1978)
In the post-apocalyptic wilderness of the year 3000, horse-riding "ranger guides" David Carradine and Claudia Jennings do battle against marauding motorcyclists and cannibalistic mutants in this action-filled sci-fi precursor to the "Mad Max" films. With Richard Lynch, Jesse Vint. 83 min.
19-1080 Was $39.99 **$14.99**

THX-1138 (1971)
George Lucas' first film is a thought-provoking look at a future society where robot police keep humans drugged and forbid any form of emotion. Robert Duvall stars as THX, the rebel who dares to love. With Donald Pleasence, Maggie McOmie. 88 min.
19-1195 Was $19.99 **$14.99**

Laserblast (1978)
A troubled teenager with a really cool van finds an alien laser weapon and pendant in the desert. Putting them on, the lad becomes possessed and begins a rampage against his enemies in this sci-fi outing that features stop-motion animated aliens by Dave Allen. Kim Milford, Cheryl Smith, Keenan Wynn and Roddy McDowall star.
03-1017 Was $79.99 **$14.99**

End Of The World (1977)
Alien beings take over the bodies of the occupants of a convent and, led by "priest" Christopher Lee, begin a plot to destroy the Earth. Can two intrepid scientists uncover and stop their scheme, or will they just give up and join them? Sci-fi suspense tale also stars Sue Lyon, Kirk Scott, Lew Ayres.
03-1010 Was $29.99 **$14.99**

Logan's Run (1976)
In the world of the 23rd century everything is perfect—except that no one is allowed to live past the age of 30, and "runners" trying to escape and hunted down and executed. Dazzling sci-fi thriller stars Michael York, Jenny Agutter, Richard Jordan, Farrah Fawcett. 120 min.
12-1083 **$19.99**

Westworld (1973)
A futuristic vacation resort with robotic servants becomes a living hell when the androids begin malfunctioning. Offbeat sci-fi adventure, written and directed by Michael Crichton, stars Richard Benjamin, James Brolin and Yul Brynner as a mechanical gunslinger. 88 min.
12-1201 Was $19.99 **□$14.99**

Westworld (Letterboxed Version)
Also available in a theatrical, widescreen format.
12-3170 **□$14.99**

Futureworld (1976)
Fantastic follow-up to "Westworld" finds that the theme park's robots are now totally under control...or are they? Peter Fonda and Blythe Danner are reporters who learn the sinister plan behind the resort's reopening; with Yul Brynner, Arthur Hill. 104 min.
19-1103 **$14.99**

Planet Earth (1974)
The second pilot for "Star Trek" creator Gene Roddenberry's "Genesis II" series follows a scientific team on a feral future world populated by savage tribes. John Saxon is the revived 20th-century scientist captured by a matriarchal society. With Diana Muldaur, Janet Margolin, Ted Cassidy. 74 min.
48-1172 **$59.99**

The Ultimate Impostor (1979)
An American espionage agent whose computer-enhanced brain can store any amount of knowledge for 72 hours at a time comes to the aid of a defecting Soviet officer in this action-filled thriller. Joseph Hacker, Erin Gray star. 97 min.
07-1479 **$39.99**

Starcrash (1979)
The lovely Caroline Munro is ace space pilot Stella Starr, the only person who can save the galaxy from evil fiend Joe Spinell in this racy, campy sci-fi adventure. Marjoe Gortner, Christopher Plummer and David Hasselhoff also star. 92 min.
53-3009 **$29.99**

The War In Space (1977)
Fantastic special effects highlight this Japanese production, the exciting story of the ultimate battle to save mankind from an army of evil invaders from beyond. Stars Ken Saku Morita and Yuko Asano. 91 min. Dubbed in English.
53-7087 Was $59.99 **$29.99**

Grey Matter (1972)
A government-run experiment in mind control produces a deadly machine, and four scientists become unwilling guinea pigs. Shocking sci-fi tale stars James Best, Barbara Burgess, and Gerald McRaney ("Major Dad"). AKA: "Brain Machine," "Mind Warp." 85 min.
58-1085 **$19.99**

Eyes Behind The Stars (1972)
A photographer's backwoods shoot reveals the presence of extraterrestrials on Earth...and the journalist who tries to warn the government becomes embroiled in a deadly cover-up. Martin Balsam, Nathalie Delon, Robert Hoffman star. 100 min.
59-5103 Was $49.99 **$14.99**

The Terminal Man (1974)
Michael Crichton's chilling science-fiction tale stars George Segal as the man transformed by computer implants in his brain into an uncontrollable killing machine. Able support from Jill Clayburgh, Joan Hackett and Richard Dysart. 107 min.
19-1524 Was $19.99 **$14.99**

The Ultimate Warrior (1975)
Two men square off for control of plague-ravaged New York in this sci-fi adventure. Yul Brynner is the warrior out to save Mankind; Max Von Sydow a cruel futuristic warlord. 92 min.
19-1473 Was $19.99 **$14.99**

Infra-Man (1975)
Outrageously entertaining Japanese sci-fi spectacle in which the powerful robotic hero Infra-Man combats the devious Princess Dragon Mom and her dastardly group of fantastic creatures from the earth's core, like Beetle Man and Octopus Man. A Roger Ebert "Guilty Pleasure"!
68-8872 Was $19.99 **$12.99**

Deadly Harvest (1976)
In a future world where food is a commodity bought with human blood, a farmer cries for vengeance when his family is murdered by a roving band of scavengers. Thrilling sci-fi drama stars Clint Walker, Nehemiah Persoff, Kim Cattrall. 86 min.
70-1057 **$14.99**

Unknown Island (1948)
A group of people land in an uncharted Pacific Island where they encounter dinosaurs, giant sloths and other prehistoric creatures in this early special effects-filled sci-fier. A rarity because it was filmed in Cinecolor, the film features Richard Denning and Virginia Grey. 76 min.
50-8171 Was $19.99 **$14.99**

Two Lost Worlds (1950)
From adventures on the high seas to a lost island teeming with creatures of long ago, James Arness encounters everything from pirates to dinosaurs! Laura Elliot co-stars as his damsel in distress, also with Bill Kennedy and Gloria Petroff. 61 min.
45-5178 **$14.99**

The Lost Continent (1951)
The search for a missing atomic rocket leads Cesar Romero, Whit Bissell, Sid Melton and Hugh Beaumont to a mysterious plateau where dinosaurs roam and everything looks green (thanks to the wonders of film tinting). Sci-fi adventure also features Acquanetta, the title star of "Rocketship X-M," and lots of rock climbing. 83 min.
10-1366 **$19.99**

King Dinosaur (1955)
The first film from schlockmeister Bert I. Gordon focuses on four astronauts who land on a mysterious rogue planet and are confronted by huge lizards posing as dinosaurs. Bill Bryant, Wanda Curtis and Little Joe the lemur star.
68-8881 **$19.99**

The Land Unknown (1957)
A scientific expedition to Antarctica discovers a "lost valley" hidden in mists deep below the icy wastes, a land where all manner of prehistoric creatures live and stalk. Jock Mahoney, Shawn Smith, Henry Brandon star. 79 min.
07-2079 **□$14.99**

The Giant Behemoth (1959)
Atomic testing frees a brontosaurus from its eons-long slumber and sends the now-radioactive leviathan on a rampage down the streets of London in this classic sci-fi thriller that features a stop-motion animated dinosaur created by Willis O'Brien ("King Kong"). With Gene Evans, Andre Morell, Leigh Madison. 71 min.
19-2519 **$14.99**

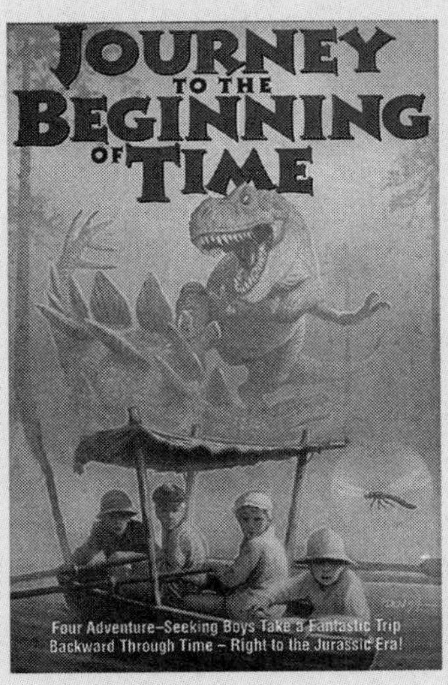
JOURNEY TO THE BEGINNING OF TIME
Four Adventure-Seeking Boys Take a Fantastic Trip Backward Through Time – Right to the Jurassic Era!

Journey To The Beginning Of Time (1966)
Classic Saturday matinee fare mixes special effects and other elements from a Czech film from Karel Zeman ("Baron Munchausen") with footage shot in America. After attending a paleontology exhibit at New York's Museum of Natural History, four boys take a boat from Central Park Lake and encounter dinosaurs and other prehistoric beasts. 83 min.
17-3026 **$14.99**

Sound Of Horror (1966)
On an expedition to the Greek islands, a group of explorers find two huge dinosaur eggs. When they are hatched, invisible monsters terrorize with their horrifying sound. Ingrid Pitt, James Philbrook star. 85 min.
10-8240 Was $19.99 **$14.99**

When Dinosaurs Ruled The Earth (1971)
Well, it's a cinch they didn't really share the spread with gorgeous gals like Playboy centerfold Victoria Vetri, but don't let that interfere with your enjoying this prehistoric romp of two feuding tribes of cavemen. There's human sacrifices, baby dinosaurs, giant crabs, exploding moons and more; special effects by Jim Danforth. 96 min.
19-1869 Was $19.99 **□$14.99**

The Land That Time Forgot (1974)
Cavemen, giant dinosaurs, amazing undersea creatures and other inhabitants of a prehistoric world are featured in this thrilling sci-fi tale. An American boards a German U-Boat during World War I and suddenly finds himself in a land frozen in time. Doug McClure, Susan Penhaligon star. 90 min.
47-1128 Was $59.99 **$14.99**

The People That Time Forgot (1977)
In this sequel to 1974's "The Land That Time Forgot," Patrick Wayne flies to the mysterious lost world of Caprona to rescue buddy Doug McClure. Before they can leave, though, they must deal with prehistoric animals and savage Stone Age warriors. With Thorley Walters, Dana Gillespie.
53-1054 **$14.99**

At The Earth's Core (1976)
Edgar Rice Burroughs' fantastic tale stars Peter Cushing and Doug McClure as two inventors who bore through to the planet's core, only to find fabulous creatures and monstrous dinosaurs. Special effects-filled fantasy co-stars Caroline Munro. 90 min.
19-1279 Was $19.99 **$14.99**

The Last Dinosaur (1977)
A billionaire big-game hunter sets out on a safari to a mysterious "lost world" where oil workers claim to have seen a living tyrannosaur. Richard Boone, Joan Van Ark, Steven Keats star. 100 min.
75-7095 Was $19.99 **$14.99**

Planet Of The Dinosaurs (1978)
The far future meets the far past when a starship crashes on a primordial planet ruled by prehistoric creatures. Amazing special effects highlight this sci-fi odyssey starring James Whitworth and Pamela Bottaro. 85 min.
44-7042 **$19.99**

Legend Of The Dinosaurs (1983)
A team of explorers in search of dinosaur remains gets more than they bargained for in a cave near Mt. Fuji: a live beast that runs amok when brought to civilization. Plenty of paleontological perils in this Japanese shocker. 92 min.
69-5017 **$12.99**

The Lost World (1992)
Arthur Conan Doyle's classic adventure/fantasy comes to life in this effects-filled thriller. John Rhys-Davies stars as the eccentric Professor Challenger, who leads an expedition into the African jungle in search of an isolated plateau where dinosaurs still exist. With David Warner, Eric McCormack. 99 min.
14-3409 Was $89.99 **□$14.99**

Return To The Lost World (1992)
When a greedy businessman's search for oil reserves threatens the hidden land of prehistoric creatures, Professor Challenger (John Rhys-Davies) and his band of explorers return to save the Lost World before it's destroyed. With David Warner, Tamara Gorski, Eric McCormack. 99 min.
14-3416 Was $89.99 **□$14.99**

The Lost World (1998)
Follow a scientific team led by the intrepid Professor Challenger (Patrick Bergin) into the hills of Northern Mongolia, where they discover a remote plateau that is home to prehistoric creatures and savage natives, in this exciting adventure based on the Arthur Conan Doyle story. Jayne Heitmeyer also stars. 96 min.
68-1892 **□$99.99**

Carnosaur (1993)
Scientist Diane Ladd unleashes a virus that is making the denizens of the Nevada desert ill and turning the newborns hatched from chicken eggs into ferocious dinosaurs. Can anything be done to save the future of civilization? Jennifer Runyon and Raphael Sbarge also star in producer Roger Corman's tongue-in-cheek answer to that other dinosaur movie. 83 min.
21-9045 Was $89.99 **$14.99**

Carnosaur 2 (1994)
A group of technicians investigating a mysterious power shortage in a secret military mining compound are confronted by a group of flesh-eating dinosaurs responsible for killing the base's inhabitants. With help from a young computer hacker—the sole survivor of the dino-slaughter—they must try to escape from the compound before it's too late. John Savage, Cliff DeYoung star. 82 min.
21-9079 Was $89.99 **$14.99**

Carnosaur 3: Primal Species (1996)
In this "dino-mite" shocker, terrorists who thought they swiped uranium get a rude awakening when their cargo turns out to be 10 tons of killer dinosaur. An anti-terrorist special forces squad has to stop the critter before it's too late, but can they stop such an indestructible force? Scott Valentine, Janet Gunn star. 81 min.
21-9125 Was $99.99 **$14.99**

Carnosaur Collector's Set
All three "Carnosaur" thrillers are also available in a money-saving boxed set.
21-9150 Save $20.00! **$24.99**

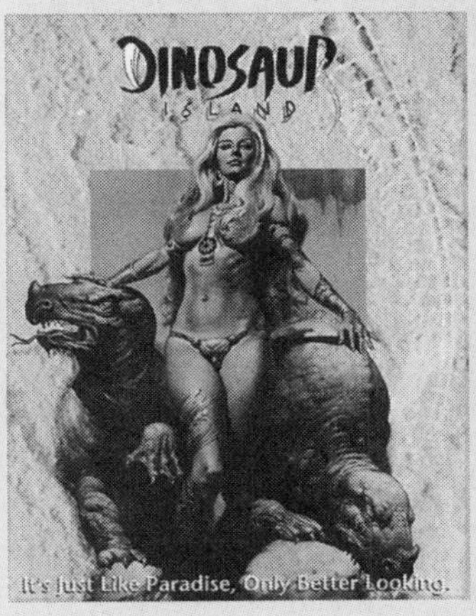
DINOSAUR ISLAND
It's Just Like Paradise, Only Better Looking.

Dinosaur Island (1994)
Sexy sci-fi fantasy in which gorgeous, animal-skin clad cavewomen unleash their primitive sexual desires when a group of contemporary military men land on their island paradise. But getting in the way of the gal's mating urges are some ferocious dinosaurs. Ross Hagen, Antonia Dorian and Michelle Bauer star in this Roger Corman production. 85 min.
21-9052 Was $89.99 **$14.99**

Dinosaur Valley Girls: Director's Cut (1997)
In this sexy and wacky fantasy, a martial arts star is hurled back in time when a magic amulet catapults him to the era of gorgeous cavewomen and dinosaurs. After falling in love with the luscious Hea-Thor, the actor must fend off beasts and brutes to return to the present. Karen Black, Denise Ames, Griffin Drew star. Unrated, nudity-filled director's cut; 94 min.
73-9181 Was $59.99 **$19.99**

Fantastic Dinosaurs Of The Movies
The history of the "terrible lizard" on the big screen is celebrated in this special-effects-filled salute that showcases "Gertie," "Gorgo," "Godzilla," "The Giant Gila Monster," "Reptilicus," "King Kong" and other cinematic monstrosoties. 75 min.
10-2413 **$12.99**

Superman: The Movie (1978)
Look! Up in the sky! It's a bird! It's a plane! It's Superman! Christopher Reeve is Clark Kent/Superman, going up against notorious criminal Lex Luthor (Gene Hackman). Margot Kidder is Lois Lane. You'll believe a man can fly! Marlon Brando, Valerie Perrine, Ned Beatty. 144 min.
19-1048 *$19.99*

Superman II (1981)
The Man of Steel is back, Metropolis is in trouble as three super-villains threaten destruction, and Lois Lane marries Clark Kent, only to find him a super-husband. A fun-filled ride! Christopher Reeve, Margot Kidder, Gene Hackman. 127 min.
19-1168 *$19.99*

Superman III (1983)
Slapstick fun mixes with special effects as Superman battles an evil industrialist who hires a meek computer whiz to do his dirty work. Christopher Reeve, Richard Pryor, Robert Vaughn, Annette O'Toole. 125 min.
19-1295 *$19.99*

Superman IV: The Quest For Peace (1987)
Christopher Reeve soars again as the Man of Steel, vowing to end the global arms race by "stealing" the world's missiles and hurling them into space. Evil Lex Luthor, however, has other plans, including an atomic antagonist named Nuclear Man. High-flying thrills and action with Gene Hackman, Margot Kidder, Jon Cryer, Mariel Hemingway. 90 min.
19-1601 *$19.99*

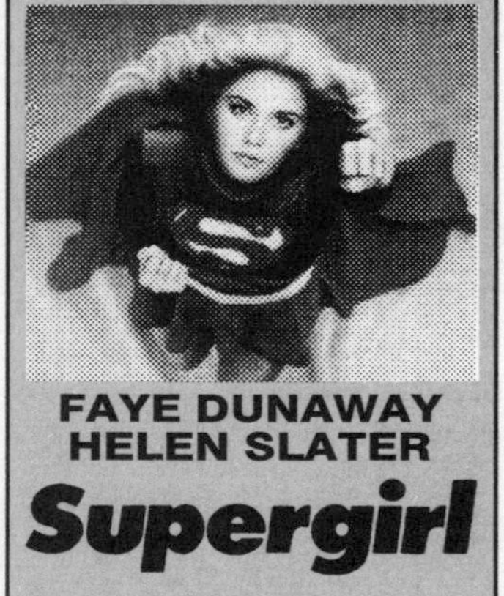
FAYE DUNAWAY
HELEN SLATER
Supergirl

Supergirl (1984)
Superman's cousin, the Girl of Steel, comes to Earth to save her starlost people and must use all her powers to defeat a sinister sorceress in this exciting sci-fi adventure. Faye Dunaway, Peter O'Toole, Hart Bochner and Brenda Vaccaro star, and Helen Slater cuts a fine figure in the title role. Special international version features footage not shown in U.S. theaters. 124 min.
08-8874 *$14.99*

Supergirl (Letterboxed Collector's Edition)
Also available in a theatrical, widescreen format. Includes the original theatrical trailer.
08-8875 *$14.99*

Where Have All The People Gone? (1974)
A strange chain reaction has decimated Earth's population, and among the survivors one family must fight for survival against looters and a mysterious virus. Gripping sci-fi story stars Peter Graves, Verna Bloom, Kathleen Quinlan. 78 min.
40-1086 *$19.99*

Sleeping Dogs (1977)
Fascinating early effort from director Roger Donaldson ("No Way Out") is set in the near future, where reclusive New Zealander Sam Neill discovers that his country's government has been taken over by an extreme right-wing faction. Neill joins a group of freedom fighters who hope to save the nation's ideals. Warren Oates is a mercenary Neill encounters. 107 min.
47-1215 *$19.99*

The Day It Came To Earth (1977)
Set in the 1950s, this semi-spoof of drive-in-era sci-fi films follows a radioactive meteorite to Earth. Crashing in a lake, it reanimates the body of a murdered gangster and sends him out on a violent campaign of vengeance against his killers. Wink Roberts, Rita Wilson and George Gobel star; directed by future TV producer/Bill Clinton compadre Harry Thomason. 88 min.
58-1019 Was $39.99 *$19.99*

Strange New World (1975)
A trio of astronauts, kept in suspended animation for 180 years, return to Earth to find civilization in ruins and bizarre warring societies sprung up in its place. Challenging sci-fi adventure stars John Saxon, Kathleen Miller, Keene Curtis, Martine Beswick. 78 min.
48-1174 *$59.99*

Star Odyssey (1977)
Outrageous mix of science-fiction and laughs in which aliens who have won the Earth through a contest plan to blast the planet sky-high. The one person who can save the day is a professor with comedic robot pals. See humanoids in blonde wigs and metallic suits! Witness android boxers and bickering husband-and-wife robots! With Yanti Somer.
68-8937 Was $19.99 *$14.99*

Vampire Men Of The Lost Planet (1971)
Al Adamson ("Dracula vs. Frankenstein") directed this sci-fi opus about bloodsuckers from another world whose attack on humans prompts scientist John Carradine to send astronauts to investigate the planet. Once there, they find cave people, dinosaurs and more. Robert Dix also stars; cinematography by William (Vilmos) Szigmond. AKA: "Horror of the Blood Monsters."
71-1050 *$14.99*

Capricorn One (1978)
When the first manned mission to Mars is threatened with cancellation, government officials arrange a faked landing to fool the public. But after it's announced the crew died on "re-entry," they realize they've been marked for death to ensure their silence. Compelling, suspenseful tale stars James Brolin, Elliott Gould, Sam Waterston, Hal Holbrook, O.J. Simpson. 123 min.
27-6893 *$14.99*

Invasion Of The Bee Girls (1973)
Nicholas Meyer, director of "Time After Time" and "Star Trek II: The Wrath of Khan," scripted this honey of a sci-fi thriller in which ordinary housewives are abducted and transformed into beautiful but lethal "bee women" who literally love their men to death. Can government agent "Big Bill" Smith stop them without getting stung? With Anitra Ford, Victoria Vetri. 85 min.
53-1091 *$14.99*

The Incredible Melting Man (1978)
An astronaut returns to Earth with a bizarre ailment that begins turning his body into a gooey liquid, and the only way he can slow down the melting process is to consume human flesh and blood. Chilling sci-fi/horror tale, with make-up effects by Rick Baker ("An American Werewolf in London"), stars Alex Rebar, Burr DeBenning; look for filmmaker Jonathan Demme in a bit part. 86 min.
73-1150 *$14.99*

Secret Of The Telegian (1960)
A Japanese science-fiction effort about a man-turned-monster who uses a teleporter device to avenge himself against wartime enemies who betrayed him. Effects by Eiji Tsuburaya, the man behind the "Godzilla" movies. With Koji Tsuruta. 75 min.
68-8805 *$19.99*

The Crawling Hand (1963)
The severed hand of an astronaut killed on re-entry gains a life of its own and starts a reign of terror in this chiller. Kent Taylor, Alan Hale, Peter Breck star. 89 min.
15-5107 *$14.99*

The Doomsday Machine (1967)
Fascinating sci-fier set in futuristic 1976, where a spaceship crew lauched from Earth and destined for Venus witnesses the destruction of the planet by a Red Chinese doomsday device. In order to find the secret of mankind's future, the crew delves deeper into space. Grant Williams, Henry Wilcoxen, Ruta Lee, Denny Miller and Bobby Van star.
68-8920 *$19.99*

2 & 5: Mission Hydra (1966)
Italian space adventure about aliens from the planet Hydra who land on Earth and abduct Earthlings to use as exhibits in their zoo. Bizarre blend of sci-fi, action, romance and social commentary stars Kirk Morris, Gordon Mitchell. AKA: "Star Pilots."
68-9057 *$19.99*

Kindar The Invulnerable (1965)
There's a Kindar hush all over the world tonight, thanks to rugged Mark Forest's performance as the hero whom no weapon can injure. His enemies try to learn the secret of Kindar's invincibility in this rare swords-and-sandals fantasy. With Mime Palmara, Dea Flowers.
68-9090 *$19.99*

The Magic Serpent (1966)
A young man becomes a master of the mystic arts in order to help him gain vengeance on the evil nobleman responsible for his father's murder in this wild Japanese fantasy filled with dueling wizards, giant spiders, fire-spitting dragons and more. Hiroki Matsutaka, Tomoko Ogawa star. AKA: "Froggo and Droggo," "Grand Duel in Magic."
68-9174 *$19.99*

Mission Stardust (1968)
Astronaut hero Perry Rhodan, featured in dozens of European novels, leads a space rescue mission that returns to Earth with a pair of dying alien beings—one a beautiful blonde—in this sci-fi romp. Lang Jeffries, Essy Persson star. AKA: "Mortal Orbit." 90 min.
15-5068 *$19.99*

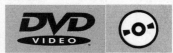

DVD VIDEO
ASK ABOUT OUR GIANT DVD CATALOG!

Journey To The Center Of Time (1967)
Low-budget sci-fi gem whose ideas exceed its limitations, as a crew of time travellers undertake a voyage that stretches from the age of dinosaurs to a futuristic dictatorship. Scott Brady, Gigi Perreau star. AKA: "Time Warp." 83 min.
71-5008 Was $19.99 *$14.99*

Attack From Space (1964)
Starman, the superhero from the Emerald Planet, returns to stop the Nazi-like forces of the Sapphire Galaxy from taking over the Earth in this mix of sci-fi action and martial arts. With Ken Utsui.
79-5593 *$19.99*

Atomic Rulers Of The World (1964)
Years before Jeff Bridges or Robert Hays, Ken Utsui played super-acrobat-in-leotards Starman in feature films culled from the late '50s Japanese TV series, "Super Giant." Here the heroic man in white battles American gangsters armed with an atomic bomb.
79-5594 *$19.99*

Evil Brain From Outer Space (1964)
Japanese hero Starman uses his flying and martial arts abilities to tackle monstrous Marpetians ruled by the brain of an evil scientist named Balazar. Weird, wacky and wild sci-fi!
79-5912 Was $24.99 *$19.99*

Village Of The Damned (1960)
Classic British sci-fi shocker starring George Sanders. A small town discovers that its children are actually the progeny of alien beings and possessed of amazing mental powers and a ruthless, amoral group spirit. Will they destroy the town and, ultimately, the world? 78 min.
12-1257 Was $19.99 *$14.99*

Children Of The Damned (1963)
More of a remake than a sequel to "Village of the Damned," this British thriller follows the global controversy that erupts when six highly intelligent (and dangerous) super-children are discovered around the world. Ian Hendry, Barbara Ferris star. 90 min.
12-2472 *$19.99*

Village Of The Damned (1995)
In John Carpenter's eerie reworking of the 1960 chiller, a Northern California town is overcome by a strange force, and several hours later, 10 women find they're pregnant. As the children, all with platinum hair and genius intellects, grow older, they begin manifesting bizarre—and deadly—psychic abilities. Christopher Reeve, Kirstie Alley and Michael Paré star. 99 min.
07-2339 Was $89.99 *$19.99*

Around The World Under The Sea (1966)
A crack scientific team is sent on a global undersea mission to test a new earthquake-prevention device in this exciting sci-fi adventure. Lloyd Bridges, David McCallum, Shirley Eaton and Keenan Wynn star in a voyage into "inner space." 117 min.
12-1368 Was $59.99 *$19.99*

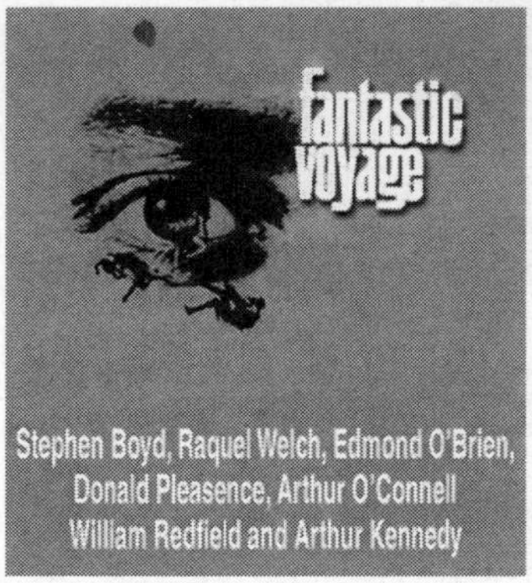
Fantastic Voyage
Stephen Boyd, Raquel Welch, Edmond O'Brien,
Donald Pleasence, Arthur O'Connell
William Redfield and Arthur Kennedy

Fantastic Voyage (1966)
Academy Award-winning, special effects-filled adventure follows an expedition through the human body by a team of miniaturized scientists. Have you ever seen killer white corpuscles? A close-up look at the human heart in action? This sci-fi classic has this...plus Raquel Welch in a wet suit! Stephen Boyd, Donald Pleasence. 100 min.
04-1057 Was $19.99 *$14.99*

Invaders From Space (1964)
Evil salamander men attack the Earth and only the superhero Starman can stop them. It's outrageous action, Japanese-style, featuring leaping lizards (we know, they're really amphibians), martial arts and lots more.
79-5911 Was $24.99 *$19.99*

Jack The Giant Killer (1962)
Kerwin Mathews is the agile young swordsman Jack, hired by the king to escort the beautiful princess and protect her from an evil wizard and his allies. Great animated monsters by Jim Danforth mark this fantasy/adventure in the manner of the "Sinbad" films. With Judi Meredith, Torin Thatcher. 94 min.
12-2178 *$14.99*

Battle Of The Worlds (1961)
Great sci-fi stunner concerning an alien planet that inexplicably lurches from its orbit...into a collision course with Earth! Claude Rains leads the team of scientists striving to avert disaster. Maya Brent, Bill Carter. 84 min.
08-8095 Was $19.99 *$14.99*

The Green Slime (1969)
Sent to destroy an asteroid heading for Earth, a rocket crew brings back samples of a mysterious slime. The green goo grows into one-eyed, tentacled monsters that threaten the ship and all on board. Japanese/American sci-fi shocker stars Robert Horton, Richard Jaeckel, Luciana Paluzzi. 90 min.
12-2251 *$19.99*

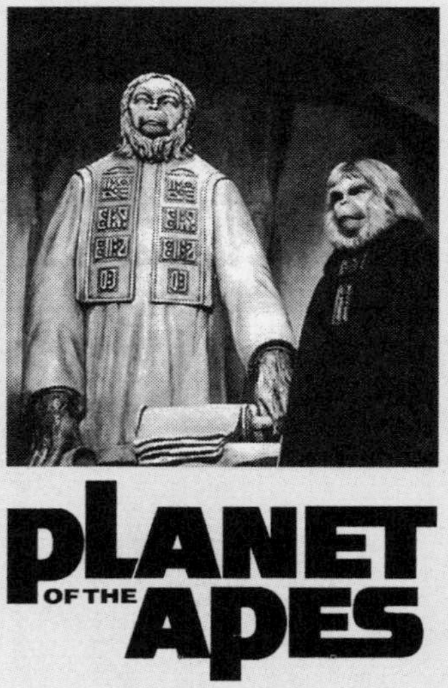
PLANET OF THE APES

Planet Of The Apes: 30th Anniversary Edition (1968)
Classic sci-fi monkey business that spawned four sequels. Charlton Heston is an astronaut who lands on a world where humans are mute savages and apes the dominant life form. Kim Hunter, Roddy McDowall and Maurice Evans co-star in Academy Award-winning makeup; witty script by Rod Serling. 112 min.
04-3014 Remastered *$14.99*

Planet Of The Apes (Letterboxed Version)
Also available in a theatrical, widescreen format.
04-3723 *$19.99*

Beneath The Planet Of The Apes (1970)
Second film in the simian series features James Franciscus as an astronaut searching for his missing comrades, only to find the ape rulers and a mysterious mutant race living underground. Charlton Heston, Kim Hunter, Victor Buono also star. 95 min.
04-3015 Was $19.99 *$14.99*

Escape From The Planet Of The Apes (1971)
In the third ape film, Roddy McDowall, Kim Hunter and Sal Mineo are the chimps who flee through time to modern Los Angeles, only to find their journey may alter Earth's future history. Bradford Dillman, Ricardo Montalban co-star. 98 min.
04-3011 Was $19.99 *$14.99*

Conquest Of The Planet Of The Apes (1972)
It's Ape versus Human for control of the planet in the fourth furry flick. Roddy McDowall stars as the super-intelligent chimp who leads the apes in a revolt against their human masters. Don Murray, Ricardo Montalban also star. 87 min.
04-3012 Was $19.99 *$14.99*

Battle For The Planet Of The Apes (1973)
Earth confronts its ultimate destiny in the fifth and final chapter in the ape saga. Chimpanzee leader Roddy McDowall must confront enemies both human and simian. Co-stars Claude Akins, John Huston. 86 min.
04-3013 Was $19.99 *$14.99*

The Planet Of The Apes Collection
You'll go...well, ape for this boxed collector's set that features five "Apes" films and saves you a few bananas, to boot.
04-3724 Save $25.00! *$49.99*

The Planet Of The Apes Collection (Letterboxed Version)
Also available in a theatrical, widescreen format.
04-3725 *$54.99*

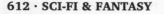

Godzilla, King Of The Monsters (1954)
The one, the only, the original! Atomic testing in the Pacific releases a 400-foot-tall, fire-breathing behemoth who vents his radioactive fury on Tokyo (in what was originally an allegory for the A-bombing of Japan). Raymond Burr stars in this 1956 Americanized version as reporter Steve Martin, with Haru Nakajima as Godzilla; Inoshiro Honda directs. 79 min.
06-2034 Remastered *$12.99*

Gigantis, The Fire Monster (1959)
He looks like Godzilla...he walks like Godzilla...he breathes fire like Godzilla, but American audiences called him Gigantis. In this second screen appearance, the big green guy and rival Angorus are awakened on a remote island by atomic bomb blast. After obliterating Osaka, the duo move on to Tokyo, wreaking havoc. Hiroshi Kozumi stars. AKA: "Godzilla Raids Again," "The Return of Godzilla." 78 min.
10-9724 *$19.99*

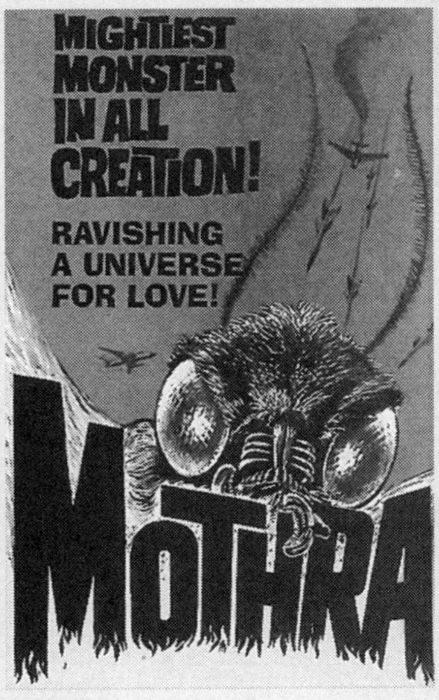

Mothra (1962)
Explorers on a remote Pacific island find a huge egg and two tiny native girls that they bring back to Japan. The egg hatches out a gigantic moth larva that threatens Tokyo, and when Momma Mothra shows up, look out! With Frankie Sakai, Hiroshi Koizumi and the Itoh Sisters as "The Peanut Sisters." 91 min.
02-2703 *$14.99*

Rebirth Of Mothra (1996)
Following her return to the screen in 1992's "Godzilla and Mothra: The Battle for Earth," the Lepidoptera leviathan took center stage with this exciting sci-fi tale. When a lumber company devastating the rain forest accidentally unleashes the three-headed menace of Death Ghidora, pint-sized twins Moll and Lora call of Mothra to save the day. With Megumi Kobayashi, Sayaka Yamaguchi. AKA: "Mosura." 106 min.
02-3354 *$19.99*

Rebirth Of Mothra II (1997)
The winged defender of the planet returns, this time helping the Elias twins and some children who visit a mysterious underwater city and come under attack from Dagahra, a pollution-spawned creature. You'll believe a giant moth can swim. Sayaka Yamaguchi, Megumi Kobayashi star. AKA: "Mosura 2." 100 min.
02-3355 *$19.99*

King Kong vs. Godzilla (1963)
It's the showdown monster fans dreamed of, as the great ape is found alive in the South Seas and brought to Japan, where he has a slugfest atop Mt. Fuji with the mean, green Mr. G. Michael Keith and Mie Hama are featured alongside the biggest stars in film history. 90 min.
10-2118 *$14.99*

Godzilla vs. Mothra (1964)
A giant egg found washed up on a beach turns out to be Mothra's, and she wants it back. But first, there's a battle to the finish with Godzilla, who wants to destroy Tokyo (so what else is new?). AKA: "Godzilla vs. the Thing." 88 min.
06-1167 Was $19.99 *$12.99*

Godzilla vs. Mothra (Letterboxed Version)
Also available in a theatrical, widescreen format.
64-3409 *$12.99*

Godzilla And Mothra: The Battle For Earth (1992)
The big "G" has his hands (claws?) full with a double menace from the skies in this updating of 1964's "Godzilla vs. Mothra," as the gigantic grub hatches and teams up with its counterpart, Battra, to take on Godzilla in a battle that ranges from a remote island to a Yokohama amusement park. With Tatsuta Bessho, and Keiko Imamura and Sayaka Osawa as Mothra's protectors, the tiny Cosmos. AKA: "Godzilla vs. Queen Mothra." 90 min.
02-3170 *$12.99*

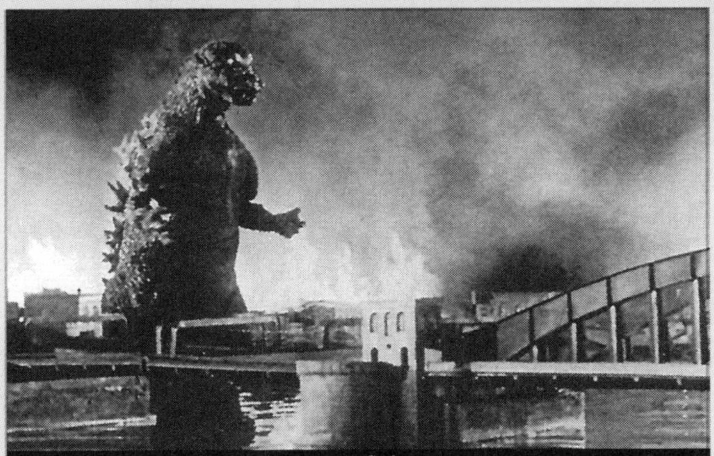
Godzilla, King Of The Monsters

Godzilla vs. Monster Zero (1965)
An alien planet asks to "borrow" Earth monsters Godzilla and Rodan to help them defeat their own indiginous menace, triple-headed Ghidrah. Little do they know it's all part of a sinister invasion plot. Nick Adams stars as an Earth astronaut. AKA: "Monster Zero," "Invasion of the Astro-Monsters." 93 min.
06-1161 Was $19.99 *$12.99*

Godzilla vs. Monster Zero (Letterboxed Version)
Also available in a theatrical, widescreen format.
64-3411 *$12.99*

Ghidrah, The Three-HeadedMonster (1965)
Mothra, Rodan, and the king of them all, Godzilla, join forces to protect the Earth from the alien menace of Ghidrah in this follow-up to "Godzilla vs. Monster Zero" that solidified the green guy's hero status. 85 min.
09-1781 *$19.99*

Godzilla vs. The Sea Monster (1966)
Remember the Sea Monkeys you had as a kid? Well, one of them's 200 feet long and being used by a paramilitary group out to take over the world. Enter Godzilla and Mothra to save the day in a Toho treasure. AKA: "Ebirah, Terror of the Deep." 80 min.
01-1207 *$12.99*

Destroy All Monsters (1968)
The "It's a Mad Mad Mad Mad World" of Japanese creature features finds spacemen from the planet Kilaak taking control of Rodan, Mothra, Angurus, Baragon, Manda, Godzilla and his son and the other inhabitants of Monster Island, then dispatching them to attack the world's major cities as part of the aliens' plan to conquer Earth. All this, and Ghidrah, too! 90 min.
20-8000 Letterboxed *$14.99*

Godzilla's Revenge (1969)
The jolly green lizard teams up with son Minya to help a young boy cope with troubles from the school bullies, while simultaneously defending Monster Island from evil Baragon and pals, in this lighthearted entry in the series. 70 min.
06-1975 *$12.99*

Godzilla's Revenge (Letterboxed Version)
Also available in a theatrical, widescreen format.
64-3410 *$12.99*

Godzilla On Monster Island (1971)
Cockroaches from outer space invade Earth by infesting Ghidrah, the three-headed dragon, and metallic Gaigan, a giant bird with a buzz saw in its belly. King of the Monsters Godzilla teams with his old sparring partner Angorus to kill the space bugs dead. AKA: "Godzilla vs. Gigan."
68-8313 *$14.99*

Godzilla vs. Megalon (1973)
In this corner: the evil buzzsaw bird Gaigan and giant insect Megalon. In that corner: superhero Jet Jaguar and reformed super-lizard Godzilla. The prize: control of the Earth. Another slam-bang monster mix-up. 79 min.
10-1095 *$14.99*

Terror Of Mechagodzilla (1975)
Original "Godzilla" director Inoshiro Honda returned for this 20th anniversary creature feature in which the green goliath does battle with alien invaders who send out an aquatic dinosaur, Titanosaurus, and a rebuilt Mechagodzilla as their weapons. AKA: "Mechagodzilla's Revenge." 89 min.
06-1228 Remastered *$12.99*

Godzilla vs. Biollante (1989)
It's animal versus vegetable when the giant green lizard faces his deadliest combantant ever: Biollante, a genetically-engineered plant creature that has taken on a life of its own and threatens to overrun the planet (or at least greater Japan). Second entry in the revived series stars Koji Takahashi and Magumi Odaka as Miki the psyhic girl. 104 min.
44-1912 Was $19.99 *$14.99*

Godzilla vs. King Ghidora (1991)
Aliens from the 23rd century arrive in Japan in the year 1992 and seek help in preventing the creation of Godzilla (did you know he was a tyrannosaurus, living on a Pacific island in World War II, who was mutated by H-bomb tests?) in order to save the future. A scientific team uncovers the visitors' true sinister scheme, and only Godzilla can stop the aliens and their ally, tri-headed monster Ghidora. 89 min.
02-3171 *$12.99*

Godzilla vs. SpaceGodzilla (1994)
From the depths of outer space comes a mutant creature spawned from Godzilla's own cellular structure, and when the alien monster battles its "parent" and his robotic adversary, Mogera, for control of Earth, it's a wild three-way war that the planet may not survive! All this, and Baby Godzilla, too, as only the Japanese can do it. 100 min.
02-3266 *$12.99*

Godzilla vs. Mechagodzilla II (1994)
More of a revamping than a sequel to 1974's "Godzilla vs. Mechagodzilla," this all-star monster mash finds the mean, green stomping machine battling both its robotic counterpart, Mechagodzilla, and the giant flying reptile known as Rodan in order to get to its newly-hatched offspring, the oh-so-cute Baby Godzilla. Masahiro Takashima, Ryoko Sano star. 108 min.
02-3353 Was $19.99 *$12.99*

Godzilla vs. Destroyah (1995)
Is this Godzilla's final battle? As the jolly green goliath's nuclear energy threatens to build to dangerous levels, he must deal with his deadliest enemy yet: a monster created from the Oxygen Destroyer, the one weapon that can eliminate Godzilla. Yoko Ishino, Megumi Odaka star. 90 min.
02-3267 *$12.99*

GET READY TO CRUMBLE.
GODZILLA 2000

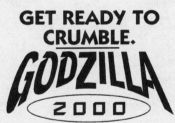

Godzilla 2000 (1999)
Proving once again that you can't keep a radioactive, mutated prehistoric creature down, Japan's Toho studio has revived Godzilla (now the original Godzilla, Jr. grown up) for an action-packed smashfest through greater Tokyo. Can the big green one cope against scientists out to study him, an army out to destroy him, and an alien menace out to steal his regenerative properties? With Takehiro Murata, Naomi Nishida, and Tsutomu Kitagawa as Godzilla. 99 min.
02-3474 *$99.99*

Godzilla (1998)
The legendary Japanese behemoth makes a splashy American debut, courtesy of "Independence Day" creators Dean Devlin and Roland Emmerich. The Big Lizard decides the Big Apple's a great place to start a family and destroys Manhattan on the way to his (her?) perfect nest: Madison Square Garden. And you thought those Rangers fans were tough! With Matthew Broderick, Jean Reno and Maria Pitillo. 139 min.
02-3216 Was $19.99 *$14.99*

Godzilla (Letterboxed Version)
Also available in a theatrical, widescreen format.
02-3219 *$19.99*

Classic Godzilla 2-Pack
"Godzilla vs. King Ghidora" and "Godzilla and Mothra: The Battle for Earth" are also available in a special collector's set.
02-3196 Save $6.00! *$19.99*

The Godzilla 5-Pack #2
This could be the biggest thing to hit Tokyo since...well, since Godzilla: a special collector's set that includes "Godzilla, King of the Monsters," "Godzilla vs. Monster Zero," "Godzilla vs. Mothra," "Godzilla's Revenge" and "Terror of Mechagodzilla."
64-3412 *$59.99*

Giant Monster Gamera (1965)
An accident nuclear detonation in the Arctic disturbs the sleep of one of the most menacing monsters ever...Gamera, a 200-foot-long, flame-shooting, flying turtle! Can the world's scientists—with help from a turtle-loving boy named Toshiro—stop the reptile's rampage? This original Japanese version of the first Gamera film stars Eiji Funakoshi, Michiko Sugata. 79 min. In Japanese with English subtitles.
20-8323 Letterboxed *$24.99*

Gammera The Invincible (1966)
Along with the extra "m" in his name, the terrifying tortoise also gained new scenes featuring "gaijin" actors Albert Dekker and Brian Donlevy in this revamped version, made for American audiences, of his film debut. 86 min. Dubbed in English.
20-8324 Letterboxed *$19.99*

Gamera vs. Guillon (1969)
Two precocious young boys steal aboard a flying saucer and are taken to a planet inhabited by brain-eating gals in silvery, skintight suits (is that bad?). Can our shell-backed hero, Gamera, defeat the aliens' pet monster and get the kids home in time for supper? With Nobuhiro Kashima, Christopher Murphy, and Kon Omura as "Cornjob." AKA: "Attack of the Monsters," "Gamera vs. Guiron." 82 min. In Japanese with English subtitles.
20-8514 Letterboxed *$24.99*

Gamera vs. Guillon (Dubbed Version)
Also available in a dubbed-in-English edition.
69-5053 Letterboxed *$19.99*

Gamera vs. Zigra (1971)
More mayhem from the country that tortoise how to really make a monster movie. It's up to Gamera the flame-footed reptile to stop alien invaders from the planet Zigra and their giant shark/bird/lizard-thing (whose back spines resemble the Sydney Opera House) from taking over Earth. Reiko Kasahara, Mikiko Tsubouchi star. 90 min. In Japanese with English subtitles.
20-7353 Letterboxed *$24.99*

Gamera vs. Zigra (Dubbed Version)
Also available in a dubbed-in-English edition.
69-5007 Letterboxed *$19.99*

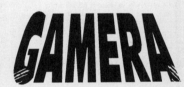

GAMERA
GUARDIAN OF THE UNIVERSE

Gamera: Guardian Of The Universe (1995)
"He's mean, green and back on the screen!" Gamera, the titanic turtle who breathes fire, flies over Japan once more in this all-new, monster-packed extravaganza that pits him against a trio of Gyaos, flying reptilian beasties out to destroy the planet. Has Gamera met his match? 100 min.
20-7844 Was $89.99 *$19.99*

Gappa The Triphibian Monsters (1967)
Is there anything more heartwarming than parental love, especially when the mom and dad are gigantic flying creatures out to rescue their offspring from scientists who've taken the kid from its island home? Find out in this Japanese tale of death, destruction and family values. With Tamio Kawaji, Yuji Okada. AKA: "Monster from a Prehistoric Planet." 90 min. In Japanese with English subtitles.
20-8042 Letterboxed *$24.99*

Gappa The Triphibian Monsters (Dubbed Version)
Also available in a dubbed-in-English edition.
20-8043 Letterboxed *$19.99*

Yog: The Space Amoeba (1970)
An alien germ is brought to Earth by a spaceship, causing life forms like crabs, squids and turtles to grow to monstrous proportions and attack the space crew, which has landed on a Pacific island. "Godzilla" director Inoshiro Honda helmed this sci-fi epic; with Akira Kubo. AKA: "Yog, Monster from Space." 84 min.
62-1367 *$19.99*

Godzilla And Other Movie Monsters
Ho, Godzilla! Here comes the not-so jolly green giant and pals Rodan, Gamera, Gorgo, Megalon and King Kong in a 30-ton salute to big monster movies. See Godzilla's greatest hits, thanks to ferocious film clips and more. 120 min.
05-5080 *$19.99*

Hercules (1959)
The original "swords, sandals and sweat" spectacle stars Steve Reeves as the muscular Greek superhero who asks the gods to make him mortal so he can find love and share in the adventures of humans. His mortal adventures include falling in love with beautiful princess Sylva Koscina and going on a perilous journey with Jason in search of the Golden Fleece. 105 min.
15-1149 Was $19.99 *$14.99*

Hercules (Letterboxed Version)
Also available in a theatrical, widescreen format.
08-1796 *$14.99*

Hercules Unchained (1960)
Steve Reeves returns as the mighty Hercules in another saga of muscles, maidens and monsters. Robbed of his memory, Herc is a prisoner of the lovely Queen of Lidia and must compete in the Contest of Giants for his freedom. 101 min.
15-1150 Was $19.99 *$14.99*

Hercules/
Hercules Unchained Twin Pac
How much muscle can one VCR take? Find out with this bulging two-tape set that features Steve Reeves at his most heroic, and at a money-saving price.
68-8387 *$29.99*

Hercules vs. The Hydra (1960)
Hubby and wife duo Mickey Hargitay and Jayne Mansfield team up in a mighty myth-adventure, as muscular Herc (Mickey) must save a victimized queen (Jayne) from the schemes of an evil Amazon (Jayne again). Also features a cyclops, talking trees and a three-headed dragon. AKA: "The Loves of Hercules." 94 min.
10-7382 Was $19.99 *$14.99*

The Fury Of Hercules (1961)
It's a labor of love for the legendary strongman, as Herc (essayed here by Brad Harris) comes to the aid of a beautiful queen whose land has been conquered by a cruel tyrant. 95 min.
10-2174 Was $24.99 *$19.99*

Hercules The Avenger (1962)
Reg Park excels as the muscular hero in this "spaghetti spectacle" that finds Hercules in the underworld, trying to save his son's soul from Gaea, the wicked Earth goddess. Meanwhile, Gaea's son travels to Earth and masquerades as a villainous Herc. Sharp-eyed viewers will spot stock footage from "Hercules and the Captive Women" and "Hercules in the Haunted World." With Gia Sandri.
79-6043 Was $24.99 *$19.99*

Hercules And
The Captive Women (1963)
Reg Park flexes his pecs as the mythological strongman, out to save his son from the thrall of the evil queen of Atlantis. He must overcome mystic hordes and a deadly dragon if he is to thwart her schemes of conquest. Fay Spain, Ettore Manni. 93 min.
01-1397 *$19.99*

Hercules And The Captive Women
(Letterboxed Version)
Also available in a theatrical, widescreen format.
08-1741 *$14.99*

Hercules Against Moloch (1963)
Prince Glauco of Mycene prepares to rid his father's kingdom of evildoers by wearing the name and loincloth of the hero Hercules (somehow "The Mighty Glauco" just didn't have the same ring). Gordon Scott stars. AKA: "Conquest of Mycene." 98 min.
68-8405 *$14.99*

Hercules Against
The Mongols (1963)
After warlord Genghis Khan dies, his three sons go on a murderous rampage, killing innocent people and jailing Princess Bianca until they decide which one will marry her and inherit her land. Her brother escapes and tells Hercules about the troubles. Then Herc gets all medieval on them. Mark Forest, Azia Maria Spim and Renato Rossini star.
79-6045 *$24.99*

Hercules And
The Tyrants Of Babylon (1963)
Rock Stevens (later Peter Lupus of "Mission: Impossible" fame), as Hercules, is called on to save the Queen of Helledes, a ruler desired by the evil king of Babylon and his three sleazy siblings. Hercules has his work cut out for him, but the large club he wields helps matters.
79-6070 *$19.99*

Hercules In
The Haunted World (1964)
Reg Park returns as Herc, who doesn't shirk from the task of returning with the cure for his dying beloved...even if it means a descent into the bowels of Hell! And demon lord Christopher Lee is determined to see that he never resurfaces! Mario Bava directs. 82 min.
01-1398 Was $24.99 *$14.99*

Hercules vs.
The Sons Of The Sun (1964)
Just what is an Ancient Greek hero doing in South America, you ask? Well, we're not too sure how he got there, but once Hercules (Mark Forest) plants his sandals in the land of the Incas, he's ready to help overthrow a tyrannical king. Anna Maria Pace, Giuliano Gemma also star. 89 min.
68-1992 *$14.99*

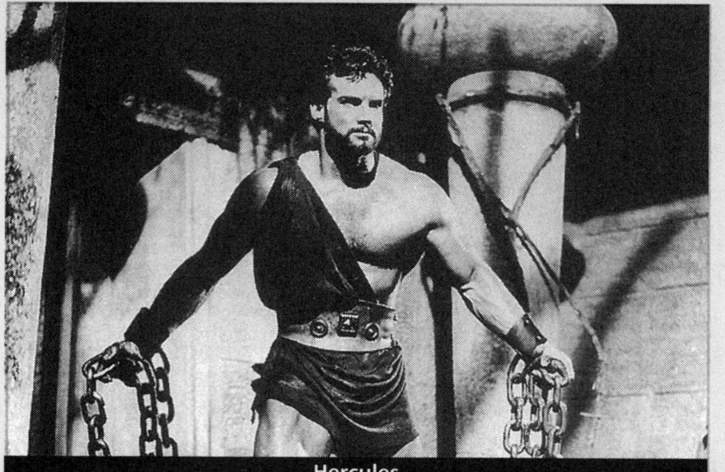
Hercules

Triumph Of Hercules (1964)
Think the super-strong demigod (played by Dan Vadis) will have no trouble defeating wicked sorceress Moira Orfei and her crew of giant bronze warriors? Well, Zeus has stripped Hercules of his powers, and now it'll take a miracle for him to live up to the film's title! AKA: "Hercules and the Ten Avengers," "Hercules vs. the Giant Warriors." 90 min.
68-1993 *$14.99*

Hercules, Prisoner Of Evil (1964)
Reg Park, the Italian master of sweaty sinews and superhuman strength, confronts a witch who has incredible, mystical powers which enable her to turn men into werewolves. Wa-eeeeww! Werewolves of Athens!
68-8449 *$19.99*

Maciste Against Hercules In
The Vale Of Woe (1964)
An outrageous Roman orgy of muscles and mirth abounds as two shifty 20th-century wrestling promoters mistakenly land their time machine 7,000 years in the past. After inventing the cha-cha and the wheel, the duo meets strongmen Hercules (Frank Gordon) and Maciste (Kirk Morris), Circe the sorceress, a talking pig, a minotaur, and Franco and Ciccio, a hit Italian comedy team.
79-6042 Was $24.99 *$19.99*

Hercules Against
The Barbarians (1964)
The same cast of "Hercules Against the Mongols" gets together for another furious loincloth foray featuring Mark Forest as Hercules. Here he helps the Poles save their beloved Kracow from Mongols led by Genghis Khan's son, Kubali. Ken Clarke and Renato Rossini also star in this anachronistic thrill-a-thon.
79-6044 Was $24.99 *$19.99*

Hercules Against
The Moon Men (1964)
In grand Herculean fashion, our hero (Alan Steel) comes to the aid of the good Samarians and battles the interplanetary menace of the Moon Men (who look like giant, lumpy Gumbys) and the wizard trying to help them revive their queen. Oh, and did we mention the sandstorm scene?
79-6071 *$19.99*

Hercules And
The Princess Of Troy (1965)
Made in English as the pilot for a proposed Hercules TV series, this handsome adventure stars Gordon Scott as the heroic demigod, pitted against a giant sea serpent come to snack on its monthly sacrificial virgin. 50 min.
68-8376 *$19.99*

Giants Of Thessaly (1960)
Heroic King Jason of Thessaly sets sail with his fellow Argonauts on a quest to find the Golden Fleece and save his country from the fiery wrath of Zeus in this rousing action/fantasy tale. Roland Carey, Massimo Girotti star. AKA: "The Argonauts." 87 min.
68-8265 *$19.99*

Goliath And The Dragon (1960)
The heroic muscleman (who must have reformed after his fight with David) must battle not only a dragon, but also a three-headed dog, a giant bat, and other mythological roadblocks put in his path by evil ruler Broderick Crawford. Mark Forest stars. 90 min.
68-8373 *$19.99*

Goliath And The Dragon
(Letterboxed Version)
Also available in a theatrical, widescreen format.
79-6524 *$19.99*

Goliath Against The Giants (1963)
King Goliath journeys home from a distant war, facing savage storms and deadly sea monsters before vanquishing a pretender to his throne. Brad Harris, Fernando Rey. 95 min.
68-8267 *$19.99*

Goliath And
The Sins Of Babylon (1963)
When the city of Nefer is forced by conquering Babylon to pay a tribute of virgins, in strides Goliath (Mark Forest) to compete in a chariot race and free the put-upon maidens. 80 min.
68-8374 *$19.99*

Goliath At
The Conquest Of Damascus (1964)
When an exiled king gets in trouble, the mighty Goliath comes to his rescue, helping him regain his throne. Rock Stevens, Helga Line star in this European sword-and-sandler, featuring rugged battle sequences.
68-9119 *$19.99*

Samson And
The Sea Beast (1960)
He-man hero Samson (Kirk Morris) goes up against a group of pirates and finds himself held captive by the scoundrels, until a noblewoman steps in to help him. Then Samson faces a ferocious creature in a spectacular duel. With Marga Lee.
68-8884 *$19.99*

Son Of Samson (1961)
Heeding an inner voice, a loner from an outlying borough scourges the capital, using his high-caliber muscles to break up the Queen's tryst with those treacherous Persians. Mark Forest plays the hero who goes berserkowitz to save Egypt. 89 min.
68-8169 Letterboxed *$19.99*

Samson Against The Sheik (1962)
No, it's not the first gladiator film to tackle the topic of safe sex. It's an action-filled epic set during the Crusades, as Samson (who looks good for a guy over 1,400 years old) does battle against evil kings. The aptly-named Ed Fury stars as Samson.
68-8709 *$19.99*

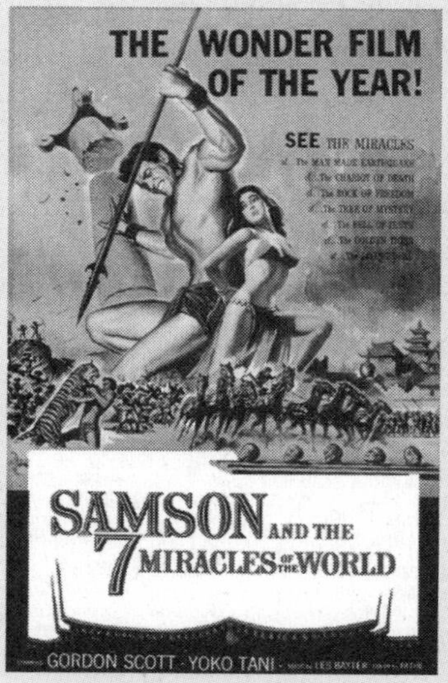

Samson And The Seven
Miracles Of The World (1963)
Former Tarzan Gordon Scott straps on the sandals to play the famed muscleman, who gets clobbered by a huge bell and stirs up an earthquake after being buried alive in order to save a princess from the evil, saucy Tartars. Yoko Tani, Gabrielle Antonini co-star. AKA: "Goliath and the Golden City," "Maciste at the Court of the Great Khan." 80 min.
68-8725 *$19.99*

Samson And
His Mighty Challenge (1964)
Extremely rare Italian slugfest suits up four of the most popular sword and sandals musclemen from the early '60s: Maciste, Samson, Hercules and Ursus. Iron man Alan Steele stars.
68-8336 *$19.99*

Colossus And
The Headhunters (1960)
Kirk Morris plays the mighty hero Colossus, who flees to an island following a deadly earthquake. There he is confronted by a group of nasty headhunters and tries to restore the power of the island's queen.
68-8885 *$19.99*

7Atlas In
The Land Of The Cyclops (1961)
Titanic Atlas matches muscles with a cyclops to save a baby and battles a sinister queen. But who's holding up the world? Stars Gordon Mitchell and Vira Silenti. AKA: "Atlas Against the Cyclops." 100 min.
68-8168 *$19.99*

Mole Men Against
The Son Of Hercules (1961)
Etruscan hero Maciste (apparently Italian for "beefcake") battles a race of hideous albinos in their weird underground city. Mark Forest reprises his role as the sandal-wearing muscle lad.
68-8170 *$19.99*

Medusa Against
The Son Of Hercules (1962)
A strapping demi-god named Perseus trades blows with a hideous one-eyed monster and her legion of stone men. Italian-Spanish adventure from the age of legends stars Richard Harrison and Anna Ranalli. AKA: "Perseus the Invincible."
68-8338 Was $19.99 *$14.99*

Devil Of The Desert Against
The Son Of Hercules (1962)
Swords! Sinews! Sand! Muscleman Kirk Morris dons the loincloth for this spectacle, in which the mythical hero helps a group of nomadic herdsmen battle their way through the "Valley of the Thundering Echoes" to reach a fabled oasis. AKA: "Hercules of the Desert," "The Slave Merchants." 93 min.
68-8445 Was $19.99 *$14.99*

Fire Monsters Against
The Son Of Hercules (1962)
There'll be a hot time in old Macedonia tonight, as Maxus, "the muscular son of the muscular one," squares off againt a gaggle of guargantuan, fire-breathing creatures to save the residents of a remote valley. Reg Lewis, Margaret Lee star. 80 min.
68-8708 *$19.99*

The Beast Of Babylon Against
The Son Of Hercules (1963)
Former "Tarzan" Gordon Scott takes the strongman costume to become Hercules, who goes up against an evil king causing trouble for the population of Assyria. Michael Lane, Moira Orfel also star. AKA: "Hero of Babylon." 98 min.
10-9115 Was $19.99 *$14.99*

The Terror Of Rome Against
The Son Of Hercules (1963)
Thrilling spectacle pits Poseidon, the son of Hercules, against fearsome gladiators and ferocious beasts in a struggle to free captive Christians intended for slaughter in the Roman arena. With Mark Forest and Marilu Tolo. 100 min.
53-3122 *$14.99*

The Tyrant Of Lydia Against
The Son Of Hercules (1963)
Hercules' bulging baby boy journeys to the valley of the Hermus river and tattoos the evil king of Lydia with his bare fists. Muscleman Gordon Scott and Massimo Serato star in this mythic Italian adventure.
68-8334 *$19.99*

Triumph Of
The Son Of Hercules (1963)
Dad left behind quite a lionskin to fill, but the well-groomed and heavily-muscled Kirk Morris more than acquits himself in this epic adventure loaded with swordplay, strongmen, and savagery. And wait until you hear the theme song!
68-8710 *$19.99*

Ulysses Against
The Son Of Hercules (1963)
Two of mythology's greatest heroes—Ulysses and, um, the offspring of Hercules—are pitted in a fierce struggle until both are captured by bizarre half-man, half-bird creatures. Now, they must team with each other to stop the nasties, controlled by a beautiful but evil queen. Georges Marchal and Michael Lane star.
68-9118 *$19.99*

The Son Of Hercules In
The Land Of Fire (1964)
Ursus, the son of Hercules, tries to save the world by battling five giants, surviving an earthquake, rescuing the king's princess and skipping out of prison. Ed Fury plays the strongman.
68-8943 *$19.99*

Messalina vs.
The Son Of Hercules (1965)
The Roman hordes have overrun ancient Britain, taking slaves for their perverse pleasures...and only Glaucus, son of the man-god Hercules, can halt their rampage. But can he deal with the wiles of the sensually evil Messalina? Richard Harrison, Lisa Gastoni star.
53-3108 *$19.99*

Ursus In The Valley Of The Lions (1961)
Roaring Spanish/Italian muscleman saga about a boy reared by lions who grows up to become the greatest gladiator of the ancient world and avenge his royal parents' deaths. Ed Fury stars. AKA: "The Mighty Ursus," "The Valley of the Lions." 91 min.
68-8266 *$19.99*

Vengeance Of Ursus (1962)
The appropriately appellationed Samson Burke stars as heroic Ursus, who fights like a bear to save a village's oppressed residents from their enemies, in this rousing swords-and-sandals thriller.
68-9095 *$19.99*

The Rebel Gladiators (1963)
From the popular "Ursus" series comes this enthralling swordfight film in which strongman Dan Vadis battles an evil emperor who has taken over the throne of Rome. He also takes Vadis' mistress hostage and oppresses the barbarians. A showdown is in the works. With Jose Greci and Gloria Milland. 98 min.
09-5046 *$19.99*

Witch's Curse (1962)
A 17th-century body-builder rips up a tree and descends to Hell to force a witch to remove her curse from his village. American muscleman Kirk Morris plays a Scottish shepherd in this Italian-made Maciste epic. AKA: "Maciste in Hell." 78 min.
68-8171 *$19.99*

Maciste In King Solomon's Mines (1964)
The once proud Maciste is reduced to slave mining when a magic talisman of the wizard Fazira strips him of his will to fight. Reg Park and Dan Harrison star in this European sword-and-sandal fantasy. Dubbed in English.
68-8337 *$19.99*

The Giant Of Marathon (1962)
Steve "Hercules" Reeves plays the musclebound hero who defends Athens from Persian forces. A horse with incredible stamina, a double-crossing siren, epic land and sea battles and Reeves' amazing physique highlight this sword-and-sandal winner directed by Jacques Tourneur ("Cat People"). 90 min.
68-8545 *$19.99*

Vulcan, Son Of Jupiter (1962)
It's a muscleman epic with many supernatural elements as Jupiter's brawny son tackles monster men, underground creatures and others. With Rod Flash, Gordon Mitchell.
68-9058 *$19.99*

Fury Of Achilles (1962)
It's sword and sandals of mythical proportions as Achilles leads the Greeks into battle against the Trojans in the fortified city of Troy. Gordon Mitchell and Jacques Bergerac star.
68-9117 *$19.99*

The Giant Of Metropolis (1963)
A bare-chested muscleman in sandals journeys to pre-submerged Atlantis and challenges the despotic rule of King Cortez and his scientists, possessors of a Death Ray and the secret of immortality. 90 min.
68-8071 *$19.99*

Spartacus And The Ten Gladiators (1964)
The slave-turned-rebel of Ancient Rome leads an army of escaped prisoners in an attempt to stop the brutal gladitorial games. Action-filled swords and sandals saga stars Dan Vadis, Helga Line. 99 min.
10-2173 *$14.99*

Hercules And The Black Pirate (1964)
Alan Steel is actually Captain Hercules in this rousing he-man marathon in which he fights the evil Black Pirate and Rodrigo, one of the Governor's ruthless advisors while trying to win the hand of the Governor's beautiful daughter. This is one pirate film with muscles!
79-6094 Was $24.99 *$19.99*

Atlas Against The Czar (1964)
Italian Gladiator Muscleman Goes Russian! That's what happens when Maciste is resurrected after being found in a cave in the Ural Mountains and enlisted to help Czar Nikolay Nikolayevich terrorize his constituents. After realizing that the ruler has bad intentions for him, Maciste rebels big time. With Kirk Morris as Maciste (who is actually "Atlas," but that's a long story), Massimo Serato.
79-6506 Was $24.99 *$19.99*

The Invincible Brothers Maciste (1965)
The Maciste Brothers, hunky Italian heroes all, help a prince whose fiancée has been captured by an evil queen and her group of leopard-men lackeys. Richard Lloyd, Tony Freeman and Claudia Lange.
68-9061 *$19.99*

The Conqueror Of Atlantis (1965)
Way, way out gladiator entry starring Kirk Morris as Heracles (Greek for Hercules) out to find a Nomad princess kidnapped by masked gold raiders. Eventually, his journey leads to the lost city of Atlantis, where the muscular hero encounters such oddities as zombies, female guards who will die if they "taste the love of a man," death-ray pistols and even long pants! With Luciana Gilli.
79-6119 Was $24.99 *$19.99*

The Atomic Brain (1964)
A wealthy woman employs a scientist to transfer her brain from its aging body into that of one of three young women lured to her mansion. The bizarre experiments so far, however, have resulted in killer dog-men and a ferocious cat-woman. Frank Gerstle, Erica Peters star. AKA: "Monstrosity." 72 min.
68-8139 *$19.99*

The Manster (1962)
Japanese-made matinee staple concerning an American reporter who, thanks to the efforts of a demented scientist, begins growing an ape-like monster out of his own body! Tale of a guy with two good heads on his shoulders stars Peter Dynely. 72 min.
17-3033 Was $19.99 *$14.99*

Captain Sindbad (1963)
A fanciful, special effects-filled adventure tale with Guy Williams as the legendary sailor, who must defeat an evil monarch to reclaim a mythical kingdom. Making matters difficult for Sindbad is the fact that the monarch's heart is kept in a tower guarded by ogres, crocodiles and an invisible monster. Pedro Armendariz and Heidi Bruhl also star. 86 min.
12-2459 Was $19.99 *$14.99*

Sinbad Of The Seven Seas (1989)
The legendary sailor/adventurer is portrayed by the incredible Lou Ferrigno in a dazzling fantasy epic, as muscular mariner Sinbad faces all manner of dangers, from cutthroat pirates to bizarre mythological creatures. 95 min.
19-7062 *$19.99*

First Spaceship On Venus (1962)
In the near future, an international crew of scientists is dispatched to Venus to investigate a mysterious message sent from the supposedly uninhabited planet. Intriguing East German-Polish sci-fi drama, based on Stanislaw Lem's novel "The Astronauts," stars Guenther Simon, Yoko Tani. 80 min.
08-1025 *$19.99*

First Spaceship On Venus (Letterboxed Version)
Also available in a theatrical, widescreen format.
73-3008 *$19.99*

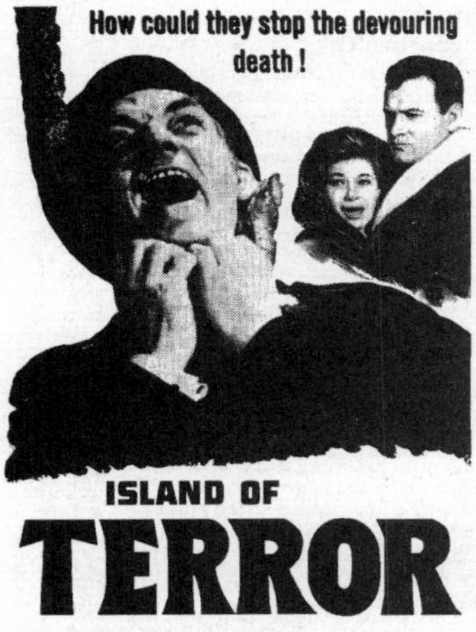

Island Of Terror (1966)
The discovery of two boneless corpses on an island off the Irish coast brings scientist Peter Cushing to investigate. He finds that a medical experiment has resulted in bizarre creatures that feed on human bone marrow. Offbeat British shocker also stars Edward Judd, Carol Gray, Niall MacGinnis. 87 min.
07-2078 □*$14.99*

Neutron And The Black Mask (1961)
The first in a series of Mexican sci-fi romps about masked wrestler and crimefighter Neutron (Wolf Ruvinski), "the atomic super-man." Here Neutron first encounters evil scientist Dr. Caronte, a similarly masked madman out to steal the lethal N-Bomb. "Do you see any logic to all this?" 72 min.
68-8151 *$19.99*

Neutron vs. The Death Robots (1961)
Neutron is back in his trademark lightning-bolt mask, but so is the demented Dr. Caronte, along with his dwarf assistant, some disembodied brains, and an army of zombies, leading to an all-out "luchadore" battle for the planet. 80 min.
68-8152 *$19.99*

Neutron vs. The Amazing Dr. Caronte (1961)
The South of the Border superhero once more faces the dread Dr. C, who uses Merlin's magic texts and his dependable Death Robots in his ongoing scheme for world domination. Wolf Ruvinski and Julio Aleman star. 80 min.
68-8150 *$19.99*

Neutron vs. The Maniac (1963)
Wolf Ruvinski reprises his role as the South-of-the-Border grappler to solve a series of sanitarium murders. A marvel of low budget filmmaking, this whole film cost less than George Steele's electrolysis. 87 min.
68-8149 *$19.99*

The Leech Woman (1960)
In Africa, a scientist's neglected wife learns of a native ritual that can reverse the aging process and prolong her newfound youth. The catch: it requires killing her husband for his pineal gland and a constant string of new victims! Colleen Gray, Grant Williams, Phillip Terry star. 77 min.
07-2080 □*$14.99*

The Slime People (1963)
Goopy, oozy creatures from Earth's distant past erect a shield of fog over Los Angeles (that's fog, not smog) as a prelude to their attempted conquest of the Earth, but a scrappy band of humans trapped inside fight to stay alive. Sci-fi slurper stars Robert Hutton, Les Tremayne. 60 min.
15-5108 *$14.99*

Space Monster (1965)
The world's first female astronaut blasts off to adventure and terror when she and her male crew encounter giant crabs and horrifying sea monsters on the ocean floor of a faraway planet. Russ Bender and Francine York star. AKA: "First Woman in Space," "Space Probe Taurus." 70 min.
15-9013 Was $19.99 *$14.99*

Zontar, The Thing From Venus (1966)
"Tonight's top story...Zontar prevails!" With his flying bat creatures and the aid of an Earth scientist, Zontar plots the mental domination of all mankind. John Agar and Anthony Huston star in this late-night TV fave, a remake of Roger Corman's 1957 "It Conquered the World." 68 min.
17-3093 *$19.99*

The Eye Creatures (1965)
You'll be screaming "eye-yi-YI!" after watching this sci-fi shocker, an uncredited remake of AIP's "Invasion of the Saucer Men." A small town is invaded by the multi-peepered title aliens, and only some plucky teens can save the day. John Ashley, Cynthia Hull star; directed by Larry Buchanan. AKA: "Attack of the Eye Creatures." 80 min.
17-3024 *$19.99*

The Day The Earth Froze (1964)
Parts of a 1959 Finnish fantasy film were combined with reshot scenes featuring American actors for this enchanting A.I.P. saga. A young woodsman must defeat a wicked witch who's stolen the sun in her quest for a magic mill known as a "sampo." Jon Powers, Nina Anderson star; Marvin Miller narrates. 67 min.
17-3091 *$19.99*

The Monitors (1969)
An amazing (and eclectic) cast stars in a sci-fi spoof about aliens invading the world and attempting to rid humanity of sex, politics and violence. Alan Arkin, Guy Stockwell, Avery Schreiber, Larry Storch, Xavier Cugat, Keenan Wynn, Stubby Kaye and Senator Everett Dirksen star. Newly restored 98 min. version.
17-9032 Was $19.99 *$14.99*

The Lost Continent (1968)
A tramp steamer carrying a cargo of illegal explosives becomes stranded in the mysterious region of the Atlantic known as the Sargasso Sea, where giant crabs and jellyfish, killer seaweed, and some Spanish conquistadors are among the perils awaiting the ship's passengers, in this sci-fi thriller from Hammer. Eric Porter, Suzanna Leigh, Hildegard Knef star. This restored version includes eight minutes of never-before-seen footage and original theatrical and TV trailers. 97 min.
08-8586 Letterboxed *$14.99*

The 7 Faces Of Dr. Lao (1964)
Tony Randall stars as an aged Chinese mystic who uses magic and some bizarre transformations to help a frontier town overcome a railroad baron. Unique blend of Western and fantasy genres from George Pal ("The Time Machine") co-stars Barbara Eden, Arthur O'Connell. Oscar-winner for Special Visual Effects. 100 min.
12-1472 Was $59.99 *$19.99*

Atlantis, The Lost Continent (1960)
A Saturday matinee favorite, this special effects-filled George Pal production is about a Greek fisherman who rescues a princess and is taken by submarine to the kingdom of Atlantis, where men are transformed into animals and death rays are developed to take over the world. Anthony Hall, Joyce Taylor, Edward Platt and Frank De Kova star. 90 min.
12-2748 *$19.99*

The Satan Bug (1965)
Thrilling suspenser featuring George Maharis as an ex-government investigator looking into the murder of a scientist and the theft of a killer virus he was developing. The trail leads to the scientist's former assistant, who's planning to unleash the deadly disease upon Los Angeles. Richard Basehart, Anne Francis and Dana Andrews also star. 114 min.
12-3076 □*$19.99*

The Magic Sword (1961)
A young knight is helped by his witch adoptive mother in his quest to rescue a kidnapped princess from the clutches of an evil wizard. Standing in the hero's way are a ruthless rival and some fantastic creatures, including a two-headed dragon. Gary Lockwood, Anne Helm, Estelle Winwood and Basil Rathbone star in this well-done Bert I. Gordon fantasy. 89 min.
12-2460 Remastered *$14.99*

Journey To The Far Side Of The Sun (1969)
Twenty-first-century astronauts set out to explore a newly-found planet that parallels Earth's orbit on the opposite side of the sun, but after a crash landing they can't tell if they're back home or on the mysterious "Counter-Earth." Roy Thinnes, Herbert Lom star. 92 min.
07-1579 Was $19.99 *$14.99*

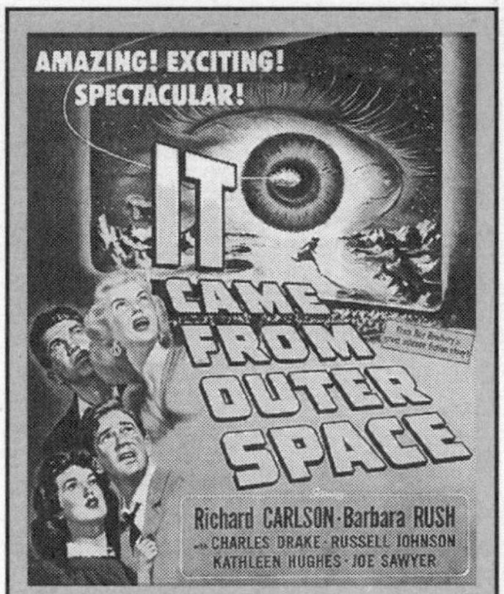

It Came From Outer Space (1954)
Fifties sci-fi classic with Richard Carlson as an astronomer who can't convince anyone of the UFO crash he sighted...and the aliens who have taken human form while repairing their ship aren't making it any easier. Excellent adaptation of Ray Bradbury's story co-stars Barbara Rush, Russell Johnson. Not in 3-D. 81 min.
07-1010 □*$14.99*

It Came From Outer Space II (1995)
More of a remake of than a sequel to the '50s sci-fi fave, this gripping thriller follows the residents of a remote Southwest town and a mysterious atmospheric disturbance in the desert that signals the arrival of an alien presence. Brian Kerwin, Elizabeth Peña, Jonathan Currasco star. 85 min.
07-2457 □*$99.99*

Fahrenheit 451 (1967)
François Truffaut's only English-language film, his stark and gripping adaptation of Ray Bradbury's famed novel stars Oskar Werner as a book-burning "fireman" in a future society where all books and reading materials are banned. Julie Christie plays a dual role as Werner's wife and a bibliophile who opens his mind to the forbidden world of literature. 111 min.
07-1316 Was $19.99 *$14.99*

The Illustrated Man (1968)
Ray Bradbury's trilogy of fantasy stories, as seen on the living designs ("They are not tattoos! They are skin illustrations!") of Rod Steiger's body. A jungle appears in a house, astronauts are marooned on a rain-drenched planet, a family prepares for Armageddon...but the most chilling story is the Illustrated Man's own. With Claire Bloom, Robert Drivas. 103 min.
19-1487 Was $19.99 *$14.99*

Something Wicked This Way Comes (1983)
Childhood dreams combine with grown-up horror in this special effects-filled fantasy from Ray Bradbury. A small Illinois town is visited by a traveling carnival whose owner promises to turn dreams into reality...and reality into nightmares! Jason Robards, Jonathan Pryce, Diane Ladd, Pam Grier star. 94 min.
11-1076 Was $19.99 □*$14.99*

Future Shock (1993)
A psychiatrist uses virtual reality to explore the innermost fears of three patients in an attempt to eradicate their neuroses. But the experiments go awry, leading to deadly results. Martin Kove, Bill Paxton, Vivian Schilling star in this sinister film based on a Ray Bradbury story. Uncut, unrated version; 97 min.
80-1059 Was $89.99 *$14.99*

The Wonderful Ice Cream Suit (1998)
Unable to afford a dazzling white suit, a Hispanic man convinces four of his friends to each buy a "share" of the garment, unaware that it has magical wish-granting properties, in this hilarious and heartwarming adaptation of the Ray Bradbury story. Joe Mantegna, Esai Morales, Edward James Olmos and Gregory Sierra star. 80 min.
11-2303 Was $99.99 □*$19.99*

Ray Bradbury's Chronicles: The Martian Episodes
Five tales of other-worldly wonder and suspense from "The Martian Chronicles," as presented on cable TV's "The Ray Bradbury Theatre." Included are "Mars Is Heaven" with Hal Linden and Paul Gross; "The Concrete Mixer" starring Ben Cross; "The Martian" with John Vernon; David Carradine in "And the Moon Be Still as Bright;" and "The Earthmen" with David Birney. 100 min.
14-3347 Was $89.99 □*$14.99*

Ray Bradbury: An American Icon
Rod Steiger narrates this look at the life and career of the award-winning fantasist and writer of "Fahrenheit 451," "The Illustrated Man" and "The Martian Chronicles." Interviews with Bradbury's friends and colleagues, clips from his "Ray Bradbury Theatre" TV series and rehearsals of his plays, and footage of Bradbury at home and lecturing are featured. 47 min.
27-7037 *$24.99*

Jules Verne

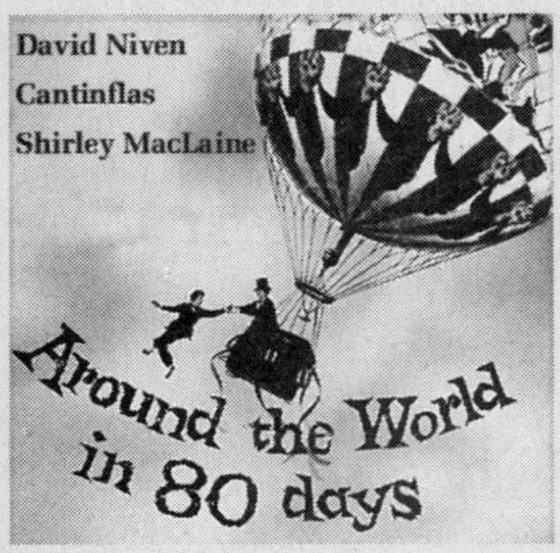

Around The World In 80 Days (1956)
Winner of five Academy Awards, including Best Picture, Michael Todd's lavish production of the Jules Verne adventure classic stars David Niven as globe-trotting Phileas Fogg, with Cantinflas and Shirley MacLaine as his companions. Dozens of cameos, including Frank Sinatra, Marlene Dietrich, Ronald Colman, Buster Keaton and more. 178 min.
19-1292 ❑$29.99

Around The World With Mike Todd (1956)
This TV special focuses on the production of the Oscar-winning movie "Around the World in 80 Days" and presents a rare look at the star-studded filming and impresario Mike Todd, its noted producer. Featured are Elizabeth Taylor (then Mrs. Todd) and stars David Niven, Shirley MacLaine and Cantinflas; Orson Welles narrates.
10-9077 Was $19.99 *$14.99*

Around The World In 80 Days (1989)
Pierce Brosnan stars as Phileas Fogg, who wagers he can circumnavigate the globe in 80 days, in this acclaimed mini-series adaptation of the Jules Verne novel. The all-star cast also includes Eric Idle, Julia Nickson, Peter Ustinov, Robert Wagner and Jill St. John. 270 min.
64-1367 Was $59.99 *$29.99*

The Fabulous World Of Jules Verne (1957)
A truly unique adventure from Czech filmmaker Karel Zeman ("Baron Munchausen") which uses live-action, animation, puppets and engravings to tell a story based on "20,000 Leagues Under the Sea," "Mysterious Island" and other Verne tales. A scientist and his assistant working on an explosive new energy source are kidnapped by pirates hired by a nasty industrialist. Arnost Navratil, Miloslaw Holub star. Includes a behind-the-scenes documentary and introduction by Hugh Downs. AKA: "The Deadly Invention," "Vynalez Zkazy." 83 min.
08-1024 *$19.99*

Journey To The Center Of The Earth (1960)
Action and fantasy deep inside the Earth from the novel by Jules Verne. James Mason, Diane Baker, Pat Boone, Arlene Dahl and Thayer David star, as a small band of explorers finds strange animals, underground oceans and fiery volcanoes below the planet's surface. 130 min.
04-3007 ❑$14.99

Journey To The Center Of The Earth (1988)
Exploring a hidden cave beneath an active Hawaiian volcano, two teenagers and their pretty chaperone discover a passageway to the lost city of Atlantis, whose inhabitants are planning to invade the surface world. Dazzling special effects mark this loose adaptation of the Jules Verne tale; Nicola Cowper, Ilan-Michael Smith star. 83 min.
19-7054 *$19.99*

Journey To The Center Of The Earth (1999)
A scientific expedition searching for a missing explorer goes on a subterranean odyssey that leads them into encounters with live dinosaurs, savage barbarians and sinister half-human, half-reptile beings. Treat Williams, Jeremy London, Tushka Bergen and Bryan Brown star in this thrilling, effects-filled adventure based on the Jules Verne classic. 139 min.
88-1207 ❑$19.99

Master Of The World (1961)
From the pen of Jules Verne comes this marvelous science-fiction thriller. Vincent Price stars as Robur, a 19th-century scientist who builds a gigantic airship and sets out to eliminate the world's weapons in order to abolish war. With Charles Bronson, Henry Hull. 99 min.
73-1146 *$14.99*

On The Comet (1970)
Live actors and animation blend in this Jules Verne tale of people who find themselves trapped on a runaway comet that has taken a piece of the Earth with it. 76 min.
64-1027 Was $29.99 *$19.99*

800 Leagues Down The Amazon (1993)
Inspired by a Jules Verne story, this adventure tells of an outlaw who heads down the Amazon on a massive ark in order to escape a nasty bounty hunter and return to his Brazilian homeland. The travellers encounter warring natives and other dangers during their journey. Daphne Zuniga, Barry Bostwick and Adam Baldwin star.
21-9036 Was $89.99 *$14.99*

20,000 Leagues Under The Sea (1997)
Ben Cross stars as the demented Captain Nemo, commander of the remarkable submarine Nautilus, in this thrilling rendition of the Jules Verne adventure classic. Richard Crenna, Julie Cox and Paul Gross are the captives who join Nemo and his crew on their amazing undersea journey and try to stop his plan to destroy the world's navies. 91 min.
88-1211 ❑$49.99

Battle Beyond The Sun (1963)
Roger Corman's B-movie savvy is the most amazing thing about this film, a re-editing of the propagandist Russian feature "Niebo Zowiet" with U.S. footage added, about a race to Mars by rival superpowers. Scripted by Francis Ford Coppola. 75 min.
68-8196 Was $19.99 *$14.99*

The Phantom Planet (1961)
Astronaut Dean Fredericks encounters a race of tiny people when strange gasses on a rogue asteroid shrink him to six-inch size. Not the kind to "get small" and drive, Dean waits out his predicament by helping the little guys battle invading monsters. Dolores Faith, Francis X. Bushman also star. 82 min.
68-8209 Was $19.99 *$14.99*

Assignment Outer Space (1962)
When its guidance system fails, an orbiting space center veers out of control and threatens to smash Earth. Futuristic fantasy with distinctive Italian styling stars Rik Von Nutter. AKA: "Space Men." 74 min. Dubbed in English.
68-8231 *$19.99*

The Amphibian Man (1962)
Russian-made "Frog Prince" fable about a marine biologist who transforms his son into an amphibious being. The lad's carefree life hand-scooping caviar and earning his "Sea Devil" nickname changes forever when he falls for a village beauty. 85 min.
68-8303 *$19.99*

Superargo (1967)
After donning a bulletproof leotard and getting a lesson in levitation from his lama, a wrestler-turned-superhero is ready to wrangle with a mad scientist and his mummified goons. Ken Wood and Guy Madison star in this entry from the hit Italian beefcake series. AKA: "Superargo and the Faceless Giants." 95 min.
68-8312 *$19.99*

Dr. Who And The Daleks (1965)
Peter Cushing is Britain's eccentric Time Lord in the first feature film based on the long-running sci-fi TV series. The Doctor and his companions must help the humans of a distant planet overcome their murderous metal dictators, the Daleks. 79 min.
63-1679 *$12.99*

Daleks: Invasion Earth 2150 A.D. (1966)
The time-travelling Dr. Who (Peter Cushing) is back, this time joining with a small band of human freedom fighters on a 22nd-century Earth to free the planet from the grasp of the Daleks (who, ironically, don't have any hands to grasp with!). 80 min.
63-1678 *$12.99*

The Love Factor (1969)
Out of the James Bond mold comes this wild sci-fi/espionage thriller about a secret agent battling a race of amazonian aliens. James Robertson Justice, Dawn Addams star. AKA: "Alien Women," "Zeta One." 90 min.
68-8558 *$19.99*

Beyond The Time Barrier (1960)
A supersonic test pilot exploits gray areas in the Theory of Relativity to travel to and from mankind's bleak post-Apocalyptic future, encountering mutants, girls with names like petroleum by-products, and the decline of manly men. Edgar G. Ulmer ("The Man from Planet X") directs Robert Clarke. 75 min.
68-8154 *$19.99*

Frozen Alive (1964)
A scientist's experiments with suspended animation find him frozen solid in the lab's freezer section and give him a very convincing alibi when police call about his ex-wife's murder. Mark Stevens and Marianne Koch star. 80 min.
68-8307 *$19.99*

Journey Beneath The Desert (1961)
French/Italian production directed by Edgar G. Ulmer about three mining engineers in the Sahara who find the lost civilization of Atlantis. The evil queen of Atlantis falls for one of the miners, and a nuclear explosion forces the visitors to plot a daring escape. Jean-Louis Trintignant, Haya Harareet and Rad Fulton star. AKA: "L'Atlantide." 93 min.
68-8554 *$19.99*

The Amazing Transparent Man (1960)
Sci-fi shocker from Edgar G. Ulmer concerning a crazed scientist who, hoping to create the perfect henchman, renders a crook invisible. Unfortunately, the unseen underling has dastardly plans of his own! "Futuristic" sets courtesy of the Texas State Fair; Douglas Kennedy, Marguerite Chapman star. 58 min.
17-3015 Was $19.99 *$14.99*

Body Snatcher From Hell (1968)
An airplane is attacked in mid-air by a strange force and crashes in the desert, where the surviving passengers and crew fall under the influence of an vampire-like alien being, in this unusual (and surprisingly gory) sci-fi chiller from Japan. Hideo Ko, Teruo Yoshida star. AKA: "Body Snatcher from Hell," "Kyuketsuki Gokemidoro." 83 min.
39-1720 *$19.99*

In The Year 2889 (1966)
A devastating nuclear holocaust leaves two groups of survivors: seven bickering humans, and a large band of telepathic cannibal mutants! The former find themselves stalked by the latter in director Larry Buchanan's unauthorized remake of Roger Corman's "The Day the World Ended." Paul Peterson, Quinn O'Hara, Neil Fletcher star. 80 min.
55-3019 *$19.99*

The Wizard Of Mars (1964)
Four astronauts are off to see the Wizard...the Wizard of Mars, that is! In this case the Wizard is played by John Carradine and he's based on the "red planet," where time is frozen. Can the foursome unfreeze it in order to return home? Roger Gentry also stars and Forrest J. Ackerman was an advisor. AKA: "Alien Massacre," "Horrors of the Red Planet."
63-1109 *$19.99*

Creation Of The Humanoids (1962)
A race of robots created to serve the human survivors of World War III turn on their masters in this cult sci-fi film that was an Andy Warhol fave. Don Megowan, Erica Elliott star; makeup by Jack Pierce. 84 min.
27-6263 *$29.99*

Incredible Paris Incident (1967)
The Italian "Superargo" superhero spoofs are themselves sent up in this wild tale of Argo Man, who has amazing telekinetic abilities that he loses for six hours after each sexual encounter. Can the now-powerless hero defend himself against the robot henchmen of his latest conquest, the evil "queen of the world" Jenabell, who's after a gem that can control "molecular cohesion." Robert Browne stars.
79-6142 Was $24.99 *$19.99*

The Flesh Eaters (1964)
Gory schlock classic about an ex-Nazi scientist who breeds flesh-eating bacteria, using the survivors of a shipwrecked vessel as guinea pigs. Noted for its off-beat style, this version of the horrorthon features a rarely seen color sequence. With Martin Kosleck, Byron Sanders. 87 min.
68-8728 *$19.99*

Mission Mars (1968)
The first manned U.S. mission to Mars becomes a trip of terror when the crew discovers bizarre creatures and a mystery from Earth. Darren McGavin, Nick Adams star. 87 min.
48-1068 *$29.99*

Planet Of Blood (1966)
An outer space rescue mission finds a green-skinned woman in a Martian crash landing and brings her aboard, unaware that she is an extraterrestrial vampire! One of the Corman studio's "bargain basement finds," this sci-fi shocker stars Basil Rathbone, Florence Marly, John Saxon, Dennis Hopper. AKA: "Queen of Blood." 81 min.
55-1131 Was $29.99 *$19.99*

The Day Of The Triffids (1963)
Top-notch British sci-fi thriller about a meteor shower that has blinded nearly everyone on Earth, and intelligent, mobile plants have infested London. Howard Keel and Janette Scott fight Triffids that spit poison and kill. 94 min.
10-1101 *$14.99*

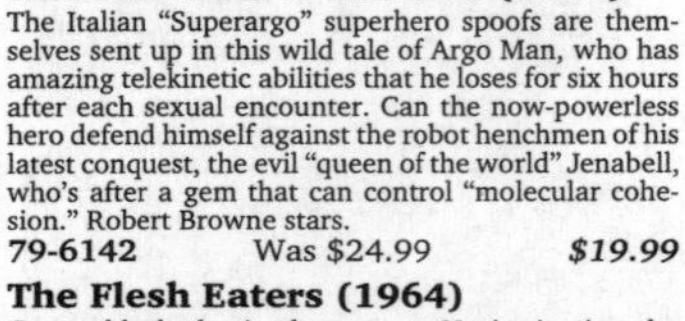

The Atomic Submarine (1960)
The title craft journeys to the North Pole to find the cause of disasters occurring in the world's oceans and finds a UFO controlled by a cyclopean creature on a mission of world destruction. Sci-fi actioner stars Arthur Franz, Dick Foran, Tom Conway and Sid Melton. 71 min.
68-8731 Was $19.99 *$14.99*

Invasion Of The Animal People (1960)
Perhaps the only horror movie ever produced in Lapland, this outing stars John Carradine (in scenes added for American release) as a scientist who discovers a strange meteor that has landed in the mountains houses a hideous interstellar monster. Barbara Wilson, Robert Burton. AKA: "Terror in the Midnight Sun," "Space Invasion of Lapland." 60 min.
68-8740 *$14.99*

Night Caller From Outer Space (1966)
An alien from Jupiter's third moon lands in London, intent on kidnapping nubile women and returning them to his world for breeding stock. One daring female scientist goes undercover to unmask the monster in this sci-fi chiller. John Saxon, Maurice Denham star. AKA: "Blood Beast from Outer Space." 84 min.
45-5180 *$14.99*

They Came From Beyond Space (1967)
Alien beings come to Earth and enslave the populace of a small town. Only one man, thanks to a protective metal plate in his head, is immune to their control and tries to stop them. Robert Hutton, Jennifer Jayne and Michael Gough star; directed by Freddie Francis of Hammer Studios fame. 85 min.
53-1661 *$14.99*

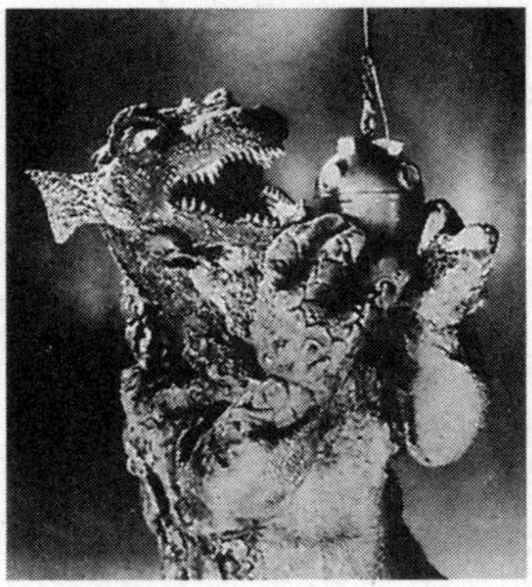

Gorgo (1961)
This time it's London, not Tokyo, that has a bad case of "pest trouble." A 200-foot-long sea monster heads up the Thames to rescue its kidnapped baby in a classic blend of sci-fi action and parental love. Bill Travers, William Sylvester star. 78 min.
08-1429 *$14.99*

Gorgo (Letterboxed Version)
Also available in a theatrical, widescreen format.
08-1724 *$19.99*

Planeta Burg (The Planet Of Storms) (1962)
The original Russian space epic that was bought by Roger Corman and cannibalized for at least two other films, "Voyage to the Prehistoric Planet" and "Voyage to the Planet of the Prehistoric Women." This version is a more "serious-minded" tale (with surprisingly good special effects) about a group of cosmonauts who discover life on Venus. 80 min. In Russian with English subtitles.
68-8735 *$19.99*

Voyage To The Prehistoric Planet (1965)
Astronauts on Venus encounter many dangers while waiting to be rescued. Basil Rathbone makes one of his final appearances in this Roger Corman creation, resourcefully produced using footage from the Russian sci-fi movie "Planeta Burg." 80 min.
68-8125 *$19.99*

4D Man (1959)
A scientist discovers the secret to moving through matter, but when he finds his beautiful assistant and brother are in love he goes on a jealous killing rampage, walking through walls and turning a kiss of love into a kiss of death! Great '50s sci-fi fun with Robert Lansing, Lee Meriwether, James Congdon and Patty Duke. 84 min.
70-1029 *$19.99*

Satellite In The Sky (1956)
This little-seen British-made sci-fier tells of a group of scientists aboard a satellite studying the effects of a tritonium bomb in space. When the bomb becomes attached to the ship, the crew—which includes a stowaway reporter and the bomb's creator—tries to dislodge it and avoid disaster. Kieron Moore, Lois Maxwell, Donald Wolfit and Bryan Forbes star.
51-1016 *$19.99*

It! The Terror From Beyond Space (1958)
An interplanetary ship rescues the sole survivor of a Martian scouting mission and heads for home, unaware that a bloodsucking creature has stowed away in the cargo hold and is slowly heading for the crew's quarters. Well-made sci-fi thriller that was the unofficial inspiration for "Alien" stars Marshall Thompson, Ann Doran and Ray "Crash" Corrigan as "It." 68 min.
12-2252 Was $19.99 *$14.99*

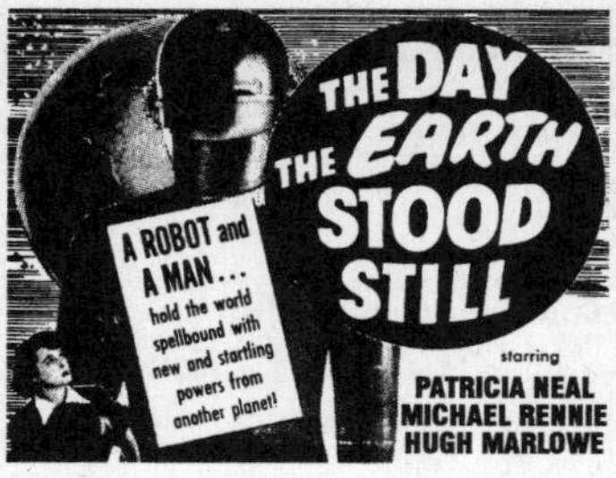
THE DAY THE EARTH STOOD STILL
A ROBOT and A MAN... hold the world spellbound with new and startling powers from another planet!
starring
PATRICIA NEAL
MICHAEL RENNIE
HUGH MARLOWE

**The Day
The Earth Stood Still (1951)**
Classic sci-fi drama with a message stars Michael Rennie as Klaatu, an emissary from the stars who arrives on Earth with his robot companion, Gort, to warn mankind about the danger of nuclear warfare. Patricia Neal, Sam Jaffe, Billy Gray also star; Robert Wise directs. "Klaatu barada nikto!" 92 min.
04-1039 *$14.99*

The H-Man (1958)
Fallout from H-bomb tests is turning people into blobs of oozing, radioactive green goop...blobs that travel through sewers and have a taste for human flesh! Inoshiro Honda ("Godzilla") directs this Japanese sci-fi shocker. 79 min.
02-1152 *$19.99*

Devil Girl From Mars (1954)
High camp British sci-fi from the '50s with Hazel Court as a gorgeous alien who comes to Earth with a loyal robot in tow, searching for men for use as breeding stock. Can you believe it, those men don't want to go! 78 min.
05-1312 *$19.99*

When Worlds Collide (1951)
George Pal's science fiction classic that set the precedent for today's spectaculars. A few human colonists race against time to build an escape rocket before the impending collision of Earth with a runaway planet. 81 min.
06-1085 *$14.99*

The Invisible Boy (1957)
After his screen debut in "Forbidden Planet," Robby the Robot returned in this film, as the newly-built playmate for a scientist's brilliant, neglected young son. Trouble erputs when the father's experimental super-computer goes berserk and takes control of the robot. Richard Eyer, Philip Abbott, Diane Brewster star. 89 min.
12-2763 *$19.99*

Conquest Of Space (1954)
George Pal produced this special effects-filled science-fiction epic about the first planned flight to Mars, and the captain who feels that the mission is blasphemous and attempts to stop it. With Walter Brooke, Eric Fleming, Mickey Shaughnessy and Ross Martin. 81 min.
06-2043 □*$12.99*

**I Married A Monster From
Outer Space (1958)**
The groom's a nice all-American guy: handsome, energetic, crazy for his wife. But wait! Why are his eyes turning those weird colors? And his nails...when is the last time he got them clipped? Fifties sci-fi classic stars Tom Tryon, Gloria Talbott. 78 mn.
06-1133 *$49.99*

I Married A Monster (1998)
A newlywed bride begins to suspect something is a little...strange...about her husband, but is she ready for the shocking truth about him, a truth that is connected to a sinister extraterrestrial plot? Susan Walters, Richard Burgi and Richard Herd star in this suspenseful updating of the '50s sci-fi tale "I Married a Monster from Outer Space." 90 min.
06-2926 Was $79.99 □*$19.99*

This Island Earth (1955)
Classic science-fiction drama of two Earth scientists who are abducted by white-haired, big-foreheaded aliens and taken to their war-ravaged homeworld of Metaluna in hopes of saving it. Jeff Morrow, Faith Domergue, Rex Reason, Russell Johnson and the bug-eyed Metalunan Mutants star. 87 min.
07-1145 Was $19.99 *$14.99*

**The Incredible
Shrinking Man (1957)**
Classic sci-fi tale from the '50s, with Grant Williams as an ordinary man who slowly but surely begins to diminish in size after exposure to radiation. Great special effects and Richard Matheson's literate screenplay make this a landmark genre entry; with Randy Stuart, April Kent. 81 min.
07-1567 Was $19.99 *$14.99*

The Crawling Eye (1958)
A small Swiss village is attacked by ghastly alien creatures that resemble giant eyeballs with tentacles. How can the monsters be stopped? Classic '50s sci-fi chiller stars Forrest Tucker, Janet Munro. 85 min.
05-1171 *$19.99*

Flight To Mars (1951)
Fanciful science-fiction thriller (the first shot in color) follows an Earth expedition to the red planet that uncovers a subterranean city populated by the dying members of the Martian race, who are hoping to save themselves by invading Earth. With Arthur Franz, Cameron Mitchell and Marguerite Chapman. 71 min.
05-1168 *$19.99*

The Monolith Monsters (1957)
One of the most unusual sci-fi films of the '50s, set in a small Southwest desert town where meteorite fragments are absorbing water from everything around them (including the people) and growing into crystalline towers that crush anything in their path. Grant Williams, Lola Albright, Les Tremayne star. 78 min.
07-2081 □*$14.99*

Monster On The Campus (1958)
A college biology instructor is given the carcass of a "living fossil" Coelecanth fish to study. A serum from the fish's remains reverts a dragonfly and dog to their prehistoric forms and turns the professor into a rampaging Neanderthal man! Bizarre sci-fi tale stars Arthur Franz, Joanna Moore; look for Troy Donahue as a student. 77 min.
07-2082 □*$14.99*

Snow Creature (1954)
Call him Snow Creature, call him Abominable Snowman, call him Yeti, just don't call him late for dinner...or you'll be on the menu! A monster's on the loose in L.A. in a blizzard of horror. Paul Langton, Lreslie Denison star. 70 min.
08-1245 Was $19.99 *$14.99*

Target Earth (1954)
A large, deserted city is the battlefield for a group of human survivors and killer robots with death rays in this creepy sci-fi favorite from the 1950s. Richard Denning, Virginia Grey and Whit Bissell are among the Earthlings defending themselves from the intergalactic machines. 75 min.
08-1620 *$14.99*

**Target Earth
(Letterboxed Version)**
Also available in a theatrical, widescreen format.
08-1723 *$19.99*

Things To Come (1937)
One of the first and most imaginative of science-fiction films, courtesy of writer H.G. Wells and director William Cameron Menzies. Follow the life of Everytown from the devastation of a decades-long World War II(!) to a technological rebirth and the dawn of the space age. Raymond Massey, Ralph Richardson star. 98 min.
10-2031 *$19.99*

**The Man Who
Could Work Miracles (1937)**
A meek department store clerk receives mystical powers from a trio of angels in an effort to see if his powerful abilities to alter the course of humankind will eventually corrupt him. This charming, whimsical fantasy was scripted by H.G. Wells, from one of his short stories. Stars Roland Young, Ralph Richardson, Joan Gardner and George Sanders. 82 min.
53-1391 Was $19.99 *$14.99*

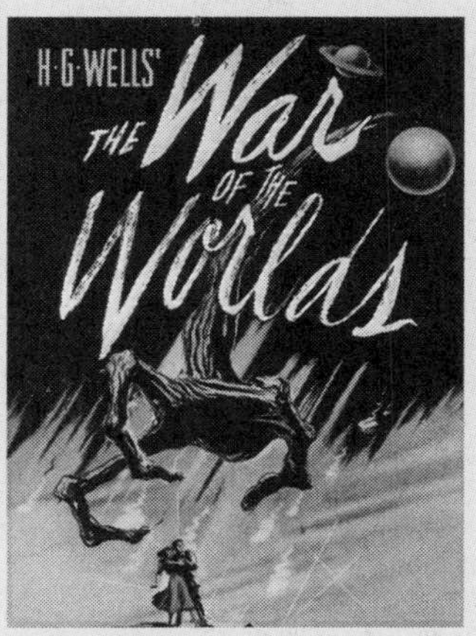
H·G·WELLS'
THE War OF THE Worlds

War Of The Worlds (1953)
H.G. Wells' timeless tale of a Martian invasion of Earth is vividly brought to the screen in this classic film. Gene Barry and Anne Robinson star as Man-kind tries to defend itself against the Martians' incredible flying machines and death ray; produced by George Pal. 85 min.
06-1069 *$14.99*

The Time Machine (1960)
George Pal's incredible adaptation of H.G. Wells' novel stars Rod Taylor as the Victorian scientist whose invention catapults him thousands of years into the future, where humanity has mutated into the gentle Eloi and the savage Morlocks. Dazzling, Academy Award-winning effects and the dazzling Yvette Mimieux highlight this "timeless" adventure. With Sebastian Cabot, Alan Young. 103 min.
12-1219 *$19.99*

Time After Time (1979)
Underrated gem follows writer H.G. Wells' fantastic and funny voyage to present-day San Francisco, where he's out to nab Jack the Ripper. Sci-fi, romance, horror and satire mix in jolly good fashion. Malcolm McDowell, Mary Steenburgen, David Warner. 112 min.
19-1068 Was $19.99 *$14.99*

Forbidden Planet (1956)
Milestone science fiction adventure, loosely based on Shakespeare's "The Tempest." A rescue ship's crew locates the survivors of an interplanetary expedition, but an eons-old force of great power and evil may destroy them all. Leslie Nielsen, Anne Francis, Walter Pidgeon and Robby the Robot star. 98 min.
12-1035 □*$14.99*

**Forbidden Planet
(Letterboxed Version)**
Also available in a theatrical, widescreen format.
12-3067 □*$14.99*

Monster From Green Hell (1957)
Scientists venture into darkest Africa to recover a downed experimental rocket and its cargo of wasps, but they find that radiation from the ship has caused the insects to grow to gigantic size. Jim Davis, Barbara Turner star in the biggest wasp invasion since the Bush administration! 71 min.
09-1042 *$14.99*

**The Monster That
Challenged The World (1957)**
"Monsters" would be more accurate, since the world is under attack in this sci-fi chiller by gigantic snail-like creatures released from their undersea resting place by seismic activity. Mollusk mayhem with Tim Holt, Audrey Dalton, Hans Conried. 83 min.
12-2759 *$14.99*

Red Planet Mars (1952)
Bizarre mix of '50s science fiction and anti-Communist melodrama stars Peter Graves as a scientist who intercepts messages from God supposedly originating from the fourth planet. The worldwide panic that results leads to a religious revival and revolution in Russia! With Andrea King, Herbert Berghof. 87 min.
12-2760 *$14.99*

**The Quatermass
Xperiment (1956)**
The sole survivor of a space mission returns to Earth with a bizarre fungus on his hand that slowly consumes him, transforming him into a monster and sending him on a rampage through London. Landmark sci-fi thriller from Hammer Films, based on a British TV series, stars Richard Woodsworth, Margia Dean and Brian Donlevy as Professor Quatermass. AKA: "The Creeping Unknown." 79 min.
12-3068 □*$14.99*

Quatermass II (1957)
Mind-controlling alien organisms land in England and take over top military and government leaders, and only the intrepid Professor Quatermass (Brian Donlevy) can stop their scheme of conquest. Second entry in the British sci-fi series also stars Sidney James, John Longden. AKA: "Enemy from Space." 85 min.
10-9322 Was $19.99 *$14.99*

Quatermass And The Pit (1958)
The third installment in Hammer Studio's Quatermass series, originally shown in six parts on British TV, was later remade as "Five Million Years to Earth." London construction workers uncover the remains of an alien spaceship, and Professor Quatermass's investigation reveals a bizarre connection between the ship's long-dead crew and the evolution of man on Earth. With Andre Morell, Cec Linder, John Stratton. 180 min.
68-8433 *$29.99*

**Quatermass And The Pit
(Five Million Years To Earth) (1968)**
Made 10 years after the British TV version, this suspenseful and thought-provoking sci-fi tale stars Andrew Keir as Professor Quatermass, who is called in when a long-dormant extraterrestrial craft found buried in a London construction site comes to life and bombards the city with alien mental energy. With Barbara Shelley, James Donald. Includes original theatrical trailers. 98 min.
08-8585 Letterboxed *$14.99*

Quatermass (1979)
The final chapter in the saga of the professor-turned-paranormal investigator, this four-part British mini-series stars John Mills as Quatermass. Lured out of retirement from his remote Scottish home to search for his missing granddaughter, Mills must uncover the link between strange rays from space and a hippie-like cult waiting to be "lifted off" the planet. Simon MacCorkindale, Rebecca Saire, Toyah Wilcox and Brenda Fricker also star. 208 min. on two tapes.
44-2197 *$29.99*

Invisible Invaders (1959)
Unseen aliens from the Moon land on Earth and take over the bodies of recently deceased humans as part of their scheme to conquer the planet in this sci-fi precursor to "Night of the Living Dead." John Agar, John Carradine, Robert Hutton and Jean Byron star. 77 min.
12-3069 □*$14.99*

The Man From Planet X (1951)
Edgar G. Ulmer's low-budget sci-fi gem (shot in a mere six days) is set on the foggy Scottish moors, where an alien visitor lands in search of help for his freezing homeworld. What he finds, however, are attacks from the military and a scientist eager to capture and study him. Robert Clarke, Margaret Field and William Schallert star. 70 min.
12-3311 *$14.99*

Stranger From Venus (1959)
This fine reworking of "The Day the Earth Stood Still" takes place in England, where an alien from Earth's planetary neighbor lands to issue an ultimatum to the human race. Rarely-seen science-fiction tale stars Helmut Dantine and Patricia Neal. AKA: "Immediate Disaster." 78 min.
05-1163 *$19.99*

First Man Into Space (1959)
An American test pilot gains the titular honor, only to turn into a hideous monster, in this early blending of horror and space age sci-fi. Marshall Thompson, Maria Landi star. 78 min.
15-5063 *$14.99*

The Flying Saucer (1950)
The original UFO movie follows a special agent who traces a flying saucer to the remote regions of Alaska, only to discover that it's a Russian aircraft. Mikel Conrad and Denver Pyle star in this milestone that mixes sci-fi and Cold War intrigue. 60 min.
15-5131 *$19.99*

The Cosmic Man (1959)
A fantasy in the manner of "The Day the Earth Stood Still" about a space guy saving mankind from nuclear self-destruction. John Carradine stars as a friendly alien with ebony skin who casts a white shadow. The heck with mankind—can he coach basketball? 75 min.
15-5136 *$19.99*

The Risk (1959)
Top-notch sci-fi thriller with Peter Cushing as the head of a British research team working on a bubonic plague-curing supervirus, only to have government officials suppress the discovery because of fears of germ warfare. Will Cushing make his findings public or sell them to another country? Ian Bannen, Donald Pleasence also star.
68-9242 *$19.99*

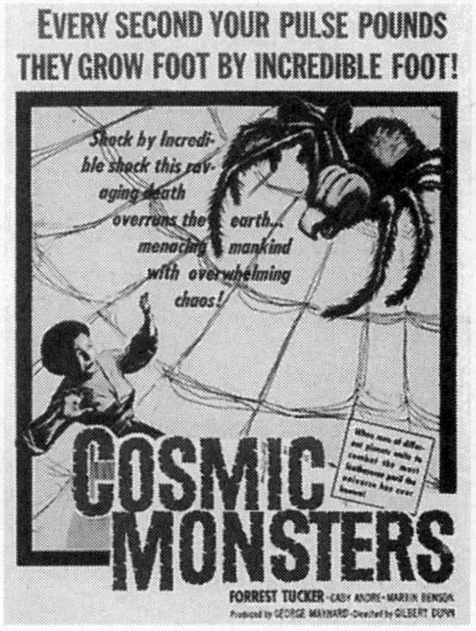
EVERY SECOND YOUR PULSE POUNDS
THEY GROW FOOT BY INCREDIBLE FOOT!
Shock by Incredible shock this ravaging death overruns the earth... menacing mankind with overwhelming chaos!
COSMIC MONSTERS
FORREST TUCKER

The Cosmic Monsters (1958)
Forrest Tucker plays a scientist who blasts a hole in the Earth's ionosphere, prompting giant insects to attack and an alien to warn the world of its questionable future. Martin Benson also stars in this totally cosmic classic. 69 min.
15-5137 *$19.99*

**Zombies Of The Stratosphere
(Color Feature Version) (1952)**
Ever want to see the Rocketeer take on an evil Mr. Spock, all in glorious computer color? Now you can in this feature-length compilation of the Republic serial that featured rocket man Judd Holdren taking on alien invaders (including a young Leonard Nimoy) out to destroy Earth. 94 min.
63-1465 *$12.99*

Space Master X-7 (1958)
Two security agents try to save the world from a gigantic fungus that presents a threat to mankind. With Billy Williams, Robert Ellis, Paul Frees and, in a small role as a cab driver, Moe Howard. Directed by Three Stooges specialist Edward Bernds. AKA: "Mutiny in Outer Space." 60 min.
15-9030 *$19.99*

Rocketship X-M (1950)
One of the first serious cinematic depictions of space travel, this sci-fi thriller follows the four-man, one-woman crew of Rocketship X-M ("Expedition Moon") as they're thrown off their lunar trajectory and wind up on the planet Mars. Lloyd Bridges, Osa Massen, Hugh O'Brian star. Contains original tinted sequences as seen in theatres. 77 min.
05-1166 *$19.99*

**The Astounding
She-Monster (1958)**
An beautiful alien woman (complete with skintight spacesuit, high heels, and a force field that can kill humans with a mere touch) lands in a forest and terrorizes a geologist, a pair of crooks and a kidnapped heiress. Robert Clarke, Kenne Duncan and Shirley Kilpatrick star. AKA: "The Mysterious Invader."
68-8304 *$19.99*

**Attack Of
The Puppet People (1958)**
A favorite with the TV horror movie shows of the 1960s, this Bert I. Gordon tale tells of a demented old dollmaker who discovers a way to miniaturize people with a special machine, then keeps them captive in glass tubes. Shades of "Dr. Cyclops"! John Hoyt, John Agar and June Kenney star. AKA: "Fantastic Puppet People."
68-8919 Was $19.99 *$14.99*

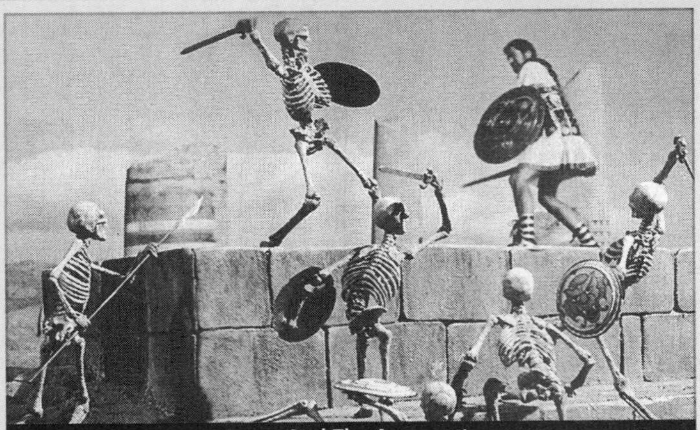

Jason And The Argonauts

Ray Harryhausen

The Beast From 20,000 Fathoms (1953)
Atomic testing in the Arctic revives a gigantic "rhedosaurus" frozen in the ice for millions of years, and soon the creature is cutting a path of destruction down the streets of New York. Classic sci-fi thriller, based on a Ray Bradbury story, features stop-motion animation by Ray Harryhausen. Paul Christian, Paula Raymond star. 80 min.
19-1868 Was $19.99 ❑$14.99

It Came From Beneath The Sea (1954)
Atomic testing in the Pacific awakens an undersea behemoth (really an octopus with six tentacles) that threatens San Francisco in this sci-fi tale. Kenneth Tobey, Faith Domergue star; stop-motion animation by Ray Harryhausen. 80 min.
02-2607 $14.99

Earth vs. The Flying Saucers (1956)
The fabulous effects work of Ray Harryhausen buoys this thrilling sci-fi adventure of aliens attacking Washington, D.C. Well-played and literate, the scenes of destruction are legends of fantasy filmmaking. Hugh Marlowe, Joan Taylor. 83 min.
02-1638 $14.99

20 Million Miles To Earth (1957)
A spacecraft from the first Earth-Venus mission crashes off the Italian coast, and a cannister containing a Venusian lifeform is recovered by a boy. The alien grows into a reptilian giant called the Ymir and eventually runs amok on the streets of Rome in this sci-fi tale with creature effects by Ray Harryhausen. William Hopper, Joan Taylor star. 84 min.
02-2757 Was $19.99 $14.99

The 7th Voyage Of Sinbad (1958)
A much-requested film at Movies Unlimited, this spectacular fantasy follows Sinbad's battle against an evil wizard who sends him on a dangerous quest. See the giant Cyclops, the two-headed roc, the snake-woman, and other menaces, courtesy of animator Ray Harryhausen. Kerwin Matthews, Kathryn Grant star. 87 min.
02-1094 $14.99

The Golden Voyage Of Sinbad (1974)
The fabled sailor embarks on a danger-filled quest in this dazzling fantasy-adventure, populated by living statues, ferocious griffins and centaurs, and other Harryhausen-created menaces. With John Phillip Law, Caroline Munro, and Tom Baker ("Dr. Who") as the villain. 105 min.
02-1138 ❑$14.99

Sinbad And The Eye Of The Tiger (1977)
Bloodthirsty creatures of the deep provide obstacles as Sinbad attempts to break a sinister spell. Great special effects by Ray Harryhausen. Stars Patrick Wayne, Jane Seymour and Taryn Power. 113 min.
02-1055 $14.99

The Sinbad Collection
This must-have for fantasy fans features "The 7th Voyage of Sinbad" (including an exclusive interview with Ray Harryhausen), "The Golden Voyage of Sinbad" and "Sinbad and the Eye of the Tiger" in a deluxe boxed set.
02-2753 $34.99

The Three Worlds Of Gulliver (1960)
Ray Harryhausen's special effects highlight this colorful adaptation of Jonathan Swift's classic. Kerwin Matthews is the English adventurer who finds himself a giant in Lilliput, mouse-sized in Brobdingnag, and in danger wherever he goes. With Jo Morrow, Peter Bull. 98 min.
02-1838 $14.99

Mysterious Island (1961)
Jules Verne's novel about escaped Civil War prisoners who find themselves on an island populated by giant crabs and bees, prehistoric birds, and an enigmatic ally is brought to startling life, thanks to Ray Harryhausen's effects. Michael Craig, Herbert Lom star. 101 min.
02-1051 ❑$14.99

Jason And The Argonauts (1963)
The quest for the Golden Fleece by Jason and his band of warriors is turned into an epic screen fantasy with some of Ray Harryhausen's finest scenes (harpies, giant statues come to life, and skeleton warriors). Todd Armstrong, Nancy Kovack, Niall MacGinnis, Honor Blackman star. 104 min.
02-1191 $14.99

First Men In The Moon (1964)
An eccentric professor in Victorian England develops an anti-gravity invention and uses it to travel to and inside the moon, finding an insect-like civilization there. Witty science-fiction adventure, based on H.G. Wells' novel, stars Lionel Jeffries, Edward Judd and Martha Hyer, and features stop-motion creations by Ray Harryhausen. 102 min.
02-1920 $14.99

One Million Years B.C. (1967)
A prehistoric menagerie animated by Ray Harryhausen and Raquel Welch wearing "Mankind's first bikini" are the highlights in this remake of the caveman adventure epic. Will Raquel's shore-dwelling Shell People learn to live with their neighbors, the Rock Tribe, before they all become dinosaur fodder? With John Richardson, Martine Beswick. 91 min.
04-3314 $14.99

The Valley Of Gwangi (1969)
Cowboys and dinosaurs meet, courtesy of animation master Ray Harryhausen. James Franciscus stars as a circus promoter in 1912 Mexico who finds a hidden valley where prehistoric creatures still live, and he sets out to rope an allosaurus to exhibit. Spectacular effects; with Gila Golan, Richard Carlson. 95 min.
19-1870 Was $19.99 ❑$14.99

Clash Of The Titans (1981)
Harry Hamlin ("L.A. Law") trades his three-piece suit for a one-piece toga in this spectacular adventure epic based on the Greek myth of heroic Perseus, who tamed Pegasus and slew the deadly Medusa. Dazzling Ray Harryhausen effects and a top notch cast (Laurence Olivier, Maggie Smith, Ursula Andress) add to the magic. 119 min.
12-1097 Was $19.99 ❑$14.99

The Harryhausen Collection
This deluxe collector's set includes "The 7th Voyage of Sinbad," "Jason and the Argonauts" and "Mysterious Island," plus special filmed interviews with Ray Harryhausen.
02-2813 $34.99

The Harryhausen Sci-Fi Collection
The Academy Award-winning master of special effects is feted with a collector's boxed set featuring "Earth vs. the Flying Saucers," "The Three Worlds of Gulliver" and "20 Million Miles to Earth."
02-2861 Save $15.00! $34.99

Invasion Of The Body Snatchers (1956)
The original sci-fi classic that combined outer space terror with Cold War paranoia. A small California town is invaded by "pods" that turn people into emotionless automatons. Can they be stopped? Kevin McCarthy, Dana Wynter star; directed by Don Siegel. 80 min.
63-1017 $14.99

Invasion Of The Body Snatchers (Color Version) (1956)
"They're here among us! Alien invaders that are flesh-colored, just like Earthlings! You fools! You're next! You're next!"
63-1303 Was $19.99 $14.99

Invasion Of The Body Snatchers (1978)
A great reworking of the 1956 sci-fi classic. San Francisco is the site for an onslaught of outer space pods that turn people into strange, zombie-like creatures. Donald Sutherland, Brooke Adams, Leonard Nimoy, Jeff Goldblum, Veronica Cartwright star; Philip Kaufman directs. 115 min.
12-1300 Was $19.99 ❑$14.99

Invasion Of The Body Snatchers (Letterboxed Version) (1978)
Also available in a theatrical, widescreen format.
12-3177 ❑$14.99

Body Snatchers (1993)
Rebel director Abel Ferrara's atmospheric take on the classic sci-fi story is set on a Southern military base where a teenage girl awakes to find that alien pods are systematically taking over the people around her, draining their personalities and turning them into inhuman monsters. Gabrielle Anwar, Meg Tilly, Forest Whitaker and Terry Kinney star. 87 min.
19-2231 Was $19.99 ❑$14.99

Tobor The Great (1954)
Neglected sci-fi gem about enemy agents who try to sabotage our latest "secret weapon": a giant, super-intelligent robot. Charles Drake and Billy Chapin star. 77 min.
63-1111 Was $19.99 $14.99

Killers From Space (1954)
Peter Graves is Earth's only hope against an invasion of malevolent aliens in this early sci-fi shocker. Steve Pendleton, Barbara Bestar co-star. 71 min.
09-1965 $19.99

The Mole People (1956)
Intrepid archeologists John Agar and Hugh Beaumont explore caves in the mountains of Asia, only to discover an underground-dwelling race of albinos who keep as their slaves the hunchbacked, clawed and bug-eyed Mole People. Can our heroes escape with their lives? Only if their flashlight batteries hold out! With Alan Napier, Cynthia Patrick. 78 min.
07-1943 $14.99

Half Human (1955)
Director Inoshiro Honda, who trampled Tokyo in "Rodan" and "King Kong vs. Godzilla," leaves his old stomping grounds for Japan's frozen north to resurrect a cousin of the abominable snowman. John Carradine stars. 70 min.
68-8305 $19.99

Phantom From 10,000 Leagues (1956)
An atomic powered part-alligator/part-turtle mutant gobbles up fishermen and swimmers to protect a uranium deposit. Early drive-in fodder from the company that became monster factory American International Pictures stars Kent Taylor. 80 min.
68-8199 $19.99

Night Of The Blood Beast (1958)
A sci-fi thriller from American International Pictures, produced by Gene Corman. An astronaut returns from space dead...or is he? Actually, an alien has taken over his corpse and plans to use it as a breeding ground for others of his dying planet. Michael Emmet, Ed Nelson, Angela Green star. 65 min.
68-8493 $19.99

Teenage Monster (1958)
A youngster in the Old West finds a meteor, then turns into a hairy homicidal monstrosity who is hidden from the sheriff by his mother. Anne Gwynne, Gloria Castillo, Stuart Wade star in this sci-fi shocker. AKA: "Meteor Monster." 65 min.
68-8739 $19.99

Phantom From Space (1953)
A cop and a pair of scientists are lured to an observatory by a series of murders, links to an invisible alien (Dick Sands) who has crash-landed on Earth in a saucer-shaped craft. Directed by W. Lee Wilder, less famous brother of Billy Wilder. 72 min.
68-8203 $19.99

Jungle Hell (1956)
The deep woods grow ugly for local boy Sabu and his animal pals when saucers from space invade the jungle, spewing death beams and leaving a trail of radioactive rocks. David Bruce ("The Mad Ghoul") co-stars in this obscure cross-genre adventure.
68-8206 $19.99

The Killer Shrews (1959)
No, it's not Shakespeare's long-missing sequel! It's the shocking story of a group of scientists whose experiments create a man-eating strain of rodents (yes, the shrews are really dogs with fake fangs). With Ken Curtis ("Gunsmoke"), James Best and 1957 Miss Universe Ingrid Goude. 70 min.
68-8145 Was $19.99 $14.99

The Atomic Man (1953)
When a clinically dead scientist is revived, it is learned that his brain is working seven-and-a-half seconds into the future. Before he can get a job as a radio call-in host, crooks kidnap him to help with a robbery. Sci-fi crime caper stars Gene Nelson. AKA: "Timeslip." 76 min.
68-8121 Was $19.99 $14.99

The Giant Gila Monster (1959)
Youthful hipsters in northern Texas defend the drag races and sock hops of the Panhandle from a giant heel of a gila monster. Lethal lizard action by the co-director of "The Green Berets," Ray Kellogg, and starring Don Sullivan and Shug Fisher. 74 min.
68-8143 $14.99

The Jungle (1952)
An expedition deep into the heart of the jungles of India comes upon, not the usual lizards with fins pretending to be dinosaurs, but elephants in full-body wigs pretending to be wooly mammoths! Rod Cameron, Cesar Romero and Marie Windsor star.
68-8879 $19.99

Unknown World (1950)
Fearful of the threat of a global atomic war, a group of scientists build a drilling vehicle and journey inside the Earth in search of safety. Offbeat sci-fi tale stars Bruce Kellogg, Victor Killian. 73 min.
46-5166 Was $19.99 $14.99

Invasion, U.S.A. (1952)
This propaganda precursor to "Red Dawn" depicts what happens when enemy troops invade America, leveling major cities with atomic bombs and terrorizing citizens. The Commies are on the loose—watch out! Albert Zugsmith produced this apocalyptic epic starring Gerald Mohr, Dan O'Herlihy, and Phyllis Coates and Noel Neill (two Lois Lanes!). 74 min.
68-8867 $19.99

Warning From Space (1956)
Japanese film with great special effects, about friendly, starfish-shaped aliens who visit Earth to prevent a collision with a fiery renegade planet and to warn against the use of atomic weapons. AKA: "The Mysterious Satellite." 87 min.
68-8207 $19.99

The Angry Red Planet (1959)
Saturday Matinee sci-fi fave follows an expedition to Mars, home of three-eyed aliens, giant bat/spider monsters, and strange, surrealistic landscapes. Imaginative use of limited special effects highlight this Ib Melchior film; Les Tremayne, Gerald Mohr star. 83 min.
44-1400 Was $59.99 $14.99

The Incredible Petrified World (1958)
A band of explorers finds a bizarre, terrifying world in a huge cavern under the sea in this sci-fi odyssey. John Carradine, Phyllis Coates, Robert Clarke star. 70 min.
27-6382 $19.99

The Hideous Sun Demon (1959)
The werewolf milieu gets a solar spin in this classic drive-in sci-fi thriller. After scientist Robert Clarke is accidentally doused with radiation, he turns into a fanged, reptilian creature when exposed to sunlight. With Patricia Manning, Nan Peterson; Clarke also directed. 75 min.
15-5177 $19.99

Revenge Of The Sun Demon (1988)
In the tradition of "What's Up, Tiger Lily?" comes this redubbed edition of the '50s sci-fi favorite, "The Hideous Sun Demon." Jay Leno joins L.A.'s funniest comics to add a new, hilarious soundtrack to the film, which features Robert Clarke and Patricia Manning. 81 min.
73-3021 $19.99

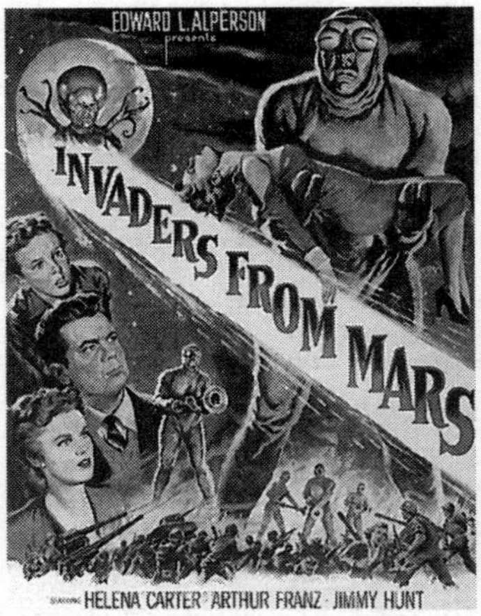

Invaders From Mars (1953)
William Cameron Menzies' dreamlike sci-fi thriller about a young boy who witnesses a spaceship landing near his home, but can't get anyone to believe his story. One of the true classics of the genre, the film features stunning set design, memorable creatures and eerie atmosphere. Arthur Franz, Helena Carter and Jimmy Hunt star. 78 min.
05-1164 $19.99

Unnatural (1952)
A truly bizarre sci-fi tale about a mad scientist who collects a dead man's semen and uses it to impregnate a woman he's obsessed with. Erich von Stroheim, Hildegarde Neff star; directed by a Nazi propaganda specialist. 92 min.
68-8431 *$19.99*

Terror From The Year 5000 (1958)
A beautiful woman arrives on Earth from the distant future in an attempt to bring humans back with her and repopulate a world devastated by radioactivity. Salome Jens, Ward Costello, Joyce Holden star in this AIP fave. 66 min.
10-8093 *$19.99*

Them! (1954)
Mutated to behemoth-sized proportions by atomic tests, giant ants attack the Southwest in this sci-fi classic. James Whitmore, Edmund Gwenn and James Arness star; features a memorable battle in the L.A. sewer system. 94 min.
19-1400 Was $19.99 *$14.99*

Tarantula (1955)
The inky, dinky spider turns into a 100-foot tall terror in this classic sci-fi thriller, as a lab experiment backfires and unleashes a rapidly-growing arachnid on the countryside. John Agar, Mara Corday and Leo G. Carroll star; look quickly for a young Clint Eastwood as an Air Force pilot. 80 min.
07-1945 □*$14.99*

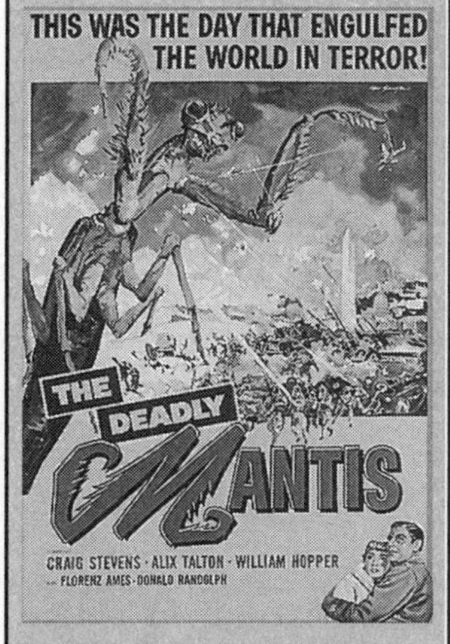
THIS WAS THE DAY THAT ENGULFED THE WORLD IN TERROR!
THE DEADLY MANTIS
CRAIG STEVENS · ALIX TALTON · WILLIAM HOPPER
— FLORENZ AMES · DONALD RANDOLPH

The Deadly Mantis (1957)
America had better start praying when an Arctic earthquake releases a gigantic prehistoric insect from icy suspended animation. After an Army attack fails, the creature makes a beeline (or mantisline) for Washington. Craig Stevens, William Hopper, Alix Talton star. 79 min.
07-1942 □*$14.99*

The Beginning Of The End (1957)
Eegad! Radiation produces gigantic, flesh-craving grasshoppers that overrun Chicago. Can reporter Peggie Castle and scientist Peter Graves stop the critters before they swarm all over the Loop? Drive-in sci-fi fave, courtesy of director Bert I. Gordon ("The Amazing Colossal Man"). 73 min.
08-8186 *$14.99*

The Black Scorpion (1957)
In the tradition of "Them!" comes this 1950s big critter feature. A nuclear blast disrupts nature, producing gigantic scorpions that enjoy mauling helicopters and trains. Geologist Richard Denning must devise a way to stop them! With Maria Corday and stop-motion monsters by Willis O'Brien ("King Kong"). 88 min.
19-2112 Was $19.99 *$14.99*

The Giant Spider Invasion (1975)
Creepy, crawly spiders appear in a small Wisconsin town and wreak havoc. Soon, the townsfolk find themselves deluged by the huge critters in this shocker starring Leslie Parrish, Barbara Hale and Alan Hale. 75 min.
10-7082 *$19.99*

Skeeter (1994)
In this sci-fi shocker, toxic waste turns a pool of water into a breeding ground for killer mosquitoes. These skeeters are gigantic bloodsuckers, and even a tankerful of Off! won't keep them away. Tracy Griffith, Michael J. Pollard, Jim Youngs and the great Charles Napier star. 95 min.
02-2564 Was $19.99 *$14.99*

Mosquito (1995)
An alien force threatens a small town when it turns tiny mosquitoes into six-foot monstrosities with a penchant for human blood. How do you destroy these colossal pests? Raise the Black Flag? Gunnar Hansen of "Texas Chainsaw Massacre" fame stars. 88 min.
80-1084 *$14.99*

The Fly (1958)
Sci-fi horror classic that's got Movies Unlimited abuzz. David Hedison is the scientist whose matter-transfer machine backfires and forces him to hang out around garbage cans. Co-stars Vincent Price and Patricia Owens. Hey, what's that on the spider web? 94 min.
04-1836 *$14.99*

Return Of The Fly (1959)
"Like Father, Like Son" holds true here, as Brett Halsey repeats his late father's experiments, only to become the world's largest household pest. Vincent Price returns as the family friend who is the Fly's only chance in this chilling sci-fi tale. 80 min.
04-1837 *$14.99*

The Fly (1986)
David Cronenberg's chilling remake of the '50s sci-fi classic stars Jeff Goldblum in the role he was born to play: a scientist whose teleportation experiment is slowly turning him into an insect. Gruesome effects and dark humor make this a horror classic. Co-stars Geena Davis, John Getz. 96 min.
04-3879 Was $19.99 □*$14.99*

The Fly II (1989)
Continuation of updated atom-switching film series stars Eric Stoltz as the mutant son of the original Fly, held prisoner by a sinister business cabal while he slowly follows in his daddy's clawprints. With Daphne Zuniga, Lee Richardson. 105 min.
04-2239 Was $19.99 □*$14.99*

Geisha Girl (1952)
Whacked-out sci-fi adventure in which a team of Japanese scientists develop pills that can cause more explosive destruction that nuclear bombs. Two American soldiers get their hands on the pills, and when they get in trouble, a hypnotist from the Secret Service tries to help them out. William Andrews and Martha Hyer star. 67 min.
68-8874 *$19.99*

Project Moonbase (1953)
Intriguing sci-fi feature, culled from episodes of an unaired TV series, that was created and co-scripted by novelist Robert A. Heinlein. In the year 1970, a male-female U.S. astronaut duo is stranded on the moon by a Communist spy and are promptly married so they can set up "housekeeping" on the lunar surface. Ross Ford, Donna Martell, Hayden Rourke star.
68-1020 *$19.99*

The Monster From The Ocean Floor (1954)
Roger Corman's initial foray into producing is a story about a one-eyed octopus who wreaks havoc in a Mexican fishing village. How will the locals survive the wrath of the "Devil Fish"? Made for a reported $12,000, the chiller stars Stuart Wade and Anne Kimball.
68-1022 *$14.99*

Attack Of The Giant Leeches (1959)
No, it's not about 50-foot lawyers! A dismal Southern swamp is the home for these bloodsucking behemoths who joyfully drain the poor white trash who live there. Charlie Allnut's least favorite film. Bruno Ve Sota, Ken Clark and Yvette Vickers star in this Roger and Gene Corman production. 62 min.
68-8062 *$19.99*

Destination Moon (1950)
The first Hollywood science-fiction project to take a serious look at the possibilities of manned spaceflight, George Pal's Oscar-winning film chronicles, in meticulous detail, the planning and launching of the first lunar expedition. Co-written by Robert A. Heinlein; Warner Anderson, John Archer, Dick Wesson star. 91 min.
05-1165 *$19.99*

Teenagers From Outer Space (1959)
Sure, lots of people in the '50s thought teens were strange beings from another world, but in this sci-fi howler they were right! What's more, these interplanetary J.D.s have brought their flesh-dissolving ray and giant lobsters with them! Can Earth survive? And what about "torture!"? With David Love, Dawn Anderson and Tom Graeff (aka writer/director Tom Lockyear). 86 min.
68-8146 *$19.99*

The Day The Sky Exploded (1958)
After an astronaut has trouble on a joint US-USSR-UK space mission, he returns to Earth. But his rocket smashes into the Sun, sending asteroids towards Earth and triggering tidal waves, typhoons and earthquakes. Can atomic weapons be used to stop the threat? Paul Hubschmid, Madeleine Fischer star; photographed by Mario Bava. 80 min.
53-6031 *$19.99*

Kronos (1957)
Well-made low-budget sci-fi tale about a flying saucer that crashes into the Pacific Ocean near California. A gigantic robot emerges from the surf and begins a deadly march inland, absorbing all energy from everything around it, from autos to H-Bombs. Jeff Morrow, Barbara Lawrence, John Emery star. 78 min.
05-1162 Letterboxed *$19.99*

World Without End (1956)
A quartet of astronauts on an Earth-to-Mars mission accidentally passes through a time warp and returns home in the year 2508, when the planet has been devastated by nuclear war and pockets of surviving humans battle giant spiders, cyclopean mutants and other monstrous menaces. Compelling sci-fi drama stars Hugh Marlowe, Rod Taylor, Nancy Gates; written and directed by Three Stooges director Edward Bernds. 81 min.
19-2555 □*$14.99*

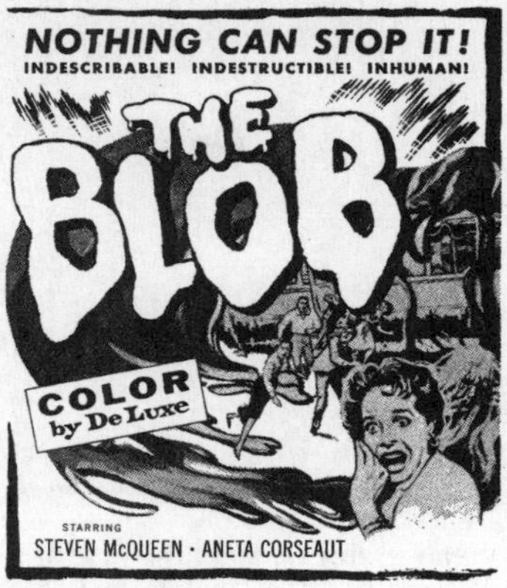
NOTHING CAN STOP IT!
INDESCRIBABLE! INDESTRUCTIBLE! INHUMAN!
THE BLOB
COLOR by De Luxe
STARRING
STEVEN McQUEEN · ANETA CORSEAUT

The Blob (1958)
Steve McQueen became a star after his role as a teenager battling an ever-growing gelatinous critter from outer space that swallows people whole and terrifies a small town. A low-budget horror classic that was filmed in Downington, Pa.; with Aneta Corseaut and a bossanova-flavored theme song from Burt Bacharach. 85 min.
16-1020 *$12.99*

Beware! The Blob (1972)
A scientist returning from the Arctic unwittingly revives the man-eating alien goop, and no one is safe. Larry Hagman directed and co-stars in this campy sequel which also features Robert Walker and Gwynne Gilford, with appearances by Godfrey Cambridge, Carol Lynley, Burgess Meredith and a young Cindy Williams. AKA: "Son of Blob." 87 min.
16-1021 *$19.99*

The Blob (1988)
Just when you thought it was safe to open a jar of Vaseline... What is the secret behind a gelatinous, carnivorous mass that fell from the sky to ooze and devour its way through a small town, and can the local teens convince the authorities in time to stop it? Slick remake of the '50s shocker stars Kevin Dillon, Shawnee Smith, Donovan Leitch, Candy Clark. 92 min.
02-1901 Was $19.99 □*$14.99*

Blobermouth (1990)
Sure he's a gigantic glob of man-eating space slime, but can he tell a joke? *Yes*, in this outrageous revamping of the 1958 sci-fi fave "The Blob" that—thanks to a hilarious new soundtrack from the L.A. Connection comedy troupe—has the Blob and Steve McQueen playing rival stand-up comics! 80 min.
50-8743 *$19.99*

Dr. Cyclops (1940)
Landmark science-fiction drama stars Albert Dekker as the bespectacled mad scientist who uses an experimental device to shrink five people to miniature size and hold them prisoner in the Amazon jungle. Incredible special effects and great early Technicolor; Lanice Logan, Victor Kilian co-star. 75 min.
07-1606 *$14.99*

The Thief Of Bagdad (1940)
Lavish Technicolor settings and dazzling effects highlight producer Alexander Korda's classic take on the "Arabian Nights" adventures. Sabu is the title urchin, who helps deposed prince John Justin rescue princess June Duprez from wicked vizier Conrad Veidt. Spectacular cinema fantasy also stars Rex Ingram as Sabu's crafty genie. 106 min.
44-1833 Was $19.99 *$14.99*

The Thief Of Baghdad (1978)
Join gallant Prince Taj as he battles an evil wizard to win a princess's hand in this exciting rendition of the classic fantasy tale. Roddy McDowall, Terence Stamp, Kabir Bedi and Peter Ustinov star.
16-1010 Was $29.99 *$14.99*

A Thousand And One Nights (1945)
There's humor and fantastic adventures in store in this exciting version of the classic tale of Aladdin. Cornel Wilde is the swashbuckling Arabian hero who falls for princess Adele Jergens. With help from wacky sidekick Phil Silvers, Wilde retrieves a magical lamp and seeks help in getting his love's hand in marriage from sexy (and jealous) genie Evelyn Keyes. 92 min.
02-2849 *$19.99*

Arabian Nights (2000)
Journey back to a time of wizards, genies and fantastic adventures in this exciting mini-series based on the classic tales of "A Thousand and One Nights." Mili Avital is the beautiful Scheherazade, who keeps sultan husband Dougray Scott from keeping his vow to execute her by spinning thrilling stories of such timeless heroes as Aladdin (Jason Scott Lee), Ali Baba (Rufus Sewell) and others. With Alan Bates, John Leguizamo. 175 min. on two tapes.
88-1212 Was $49.99 □*$14.99*

The Crimson Ghost (Color Feature Version) (1946)
Crimson indeed is this masked fiend out to conquer the world with the atomic-age Cyclotrode device in this feature-length edition of the classic Republic serial, now in color. Clayton Moore, Linda Stirling star. 93 min.
63-1464 *$12.99*

F.P. 1 (1933)
The world's first floating mid-Atlantic platform is targeted by ruthless saboteurs trying to destroy it and stop transoceanic aircraft from using the valuable refueling stop. Made at the same time as a German adaptation of the same story, this unusual espionage/sci-fi adventure stars Conrad Veidt, Leslie Fenton and Jill Esmond. AKA: "F.P.1 Doesn't Answer," "Secrets of F.P.1." 71 min.
08-1815 Was $19.99 *$14.99*

Buck Rogers (Planet Outlaws) (1939)
The serial is now a feature film with added narration. 500 years after their dirigible crashes, Buck Rogers (Buster Crabbe) and his pal Buddy awaken to find the world ruled by Killer Kane. 70 min.
09-1365 Was $24.99 *$19.99*

City Of Lost Men (1935)
Hidden deep within a mountain in the African jungle, a deranged scientist plans to use his advanced science to take over the world, in this featured version of the classic serial "The Lost City." Kane Richmond, William "Stage" Boyd, Gabby Hayes star.
68-9093 *$19.99*

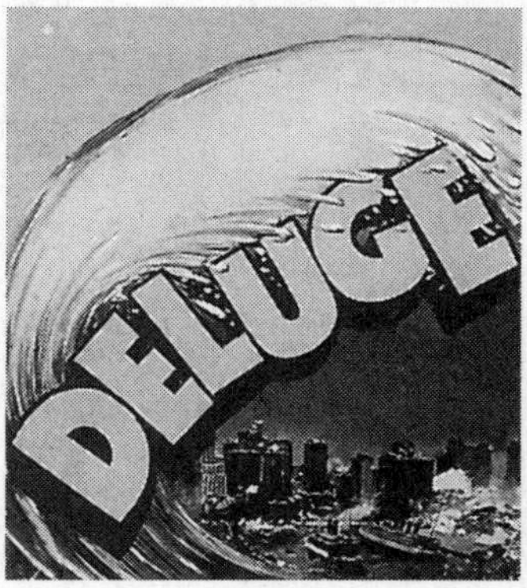
DELUGE

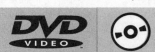

Deluge (1933)
The precursor to Irwin Allen's disaster films and "Deep Impact" tells of a catastrophic earthquake and tidal wave that destroys New York, and the people caught in the middle of the turmoil. Hero Sidney Blackmer battles mean Fred Kohler for Peggy Shannon, supposedly the only living woman left in the Big Apple. This long-lost effort offers incredible special effects. 59 min. NOTE: This film is only available in a dubbed-in-Italian edition with English subtitles.
73-3011 *$19.99*

Trapped By Television (1936)
Unusual offering about an inventor looking for financial backing on a project involving television who gets mixed up with some shady characters out to steal his invention and use it for blackmail purposes. Mary Astor, Lyle Talbot and Nat Pendleton star. 63 min.
68-9115 *$19.99*

Life Returns (1939)
Loosely based on the real-life experiments of a doctor who revived a seemingly dead dog in 1934 (seen at this film's climax), this early sci-fi drama stars Onslow Stevens as a scientist obsessed with perfecting a drug to bring the dead back to life. Lois Wilson, Valerie Hobson also star.
68-9229 *$19.99*

Transatlantic Tunnel (1935)
Spectacular early science-fiction drama deals with the construction of a 4,000-mile tunnel linking the U.S. to England and the many hardships the job entails. Richard Dix, Leslie Banks, C. Aubrey Smith star. 93 min.
01-1237 Was $19.99 *$14.99*

Flash Gordon: Rocketship (1936)
Buster Crabbe and Jean Rogers star as Flash and Dale. A planet is on a collision course with Earth, and only Flash can save the world in this feature compilation from the 1936 serial. 68 min.
09-1059 *$19.99*

Flash Gordon Four-Pack
Here's four feature versions of the "Flash Gordon" serials, presented in one deluxe package in newly restored and enhanced versions. Included in the set are "Spaceship to the Unknown," "The Deadly Ray from Mars," "The Peril from Planet Mongo" and "The Purple Death from Outer Space." Buster Crabbe stars; includes a commemorative brochure.
50-4288 *$69.99*

Flash Gordon (1980)
The old favorite of serials is brought to life in slambang fashion. Flash is a dashing, blonde hero, going against the notorious Ming the Merciless, in this colorful, hip flick, filled with thrills!, spills! and danger! Sam Jones, Max Von Sydow, Topol, Ornella Muti. Music by Queen. 111 min.
07-1038 Was $39.99 *$14.99*

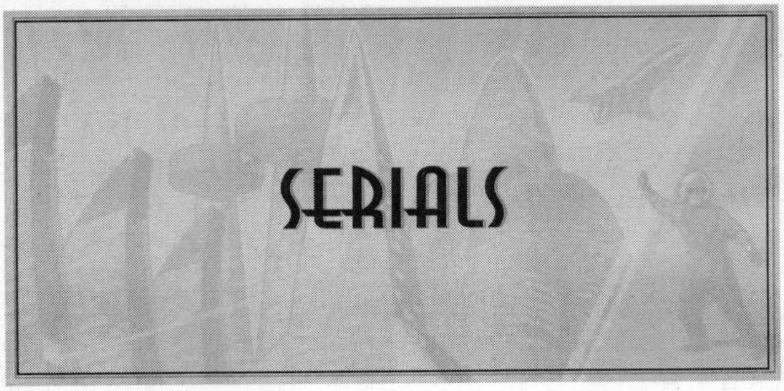
SERIALS

Blackhawk (1952)
Screen Superman Kirk Alyn also starred as high-flying comic-book aviator Blackhawk, who joins with loyal allies Chuck, Stanislaus, Andre and Chop Chop to crack an international sabotage ring whose main agent is the beautiful but deadly Laska. Carol Forman, John Crawford also star. 15 chapters; 242 min.
10-7676 *$29.99*

Flying Disc Man From Mars (1951)
The man's name is Mota (no, not Manny Mota!), and with his atomic-powered craft and the help of an Earth scientist, he's out to take over the planet. A fearless young aviator is the only roadblock (sky-block?) to their plans. High-flying serial fun with Walter Reed, James Craven, Lois Collier. 12 episodes.
10-7976 Was $29.99 *$19.99*

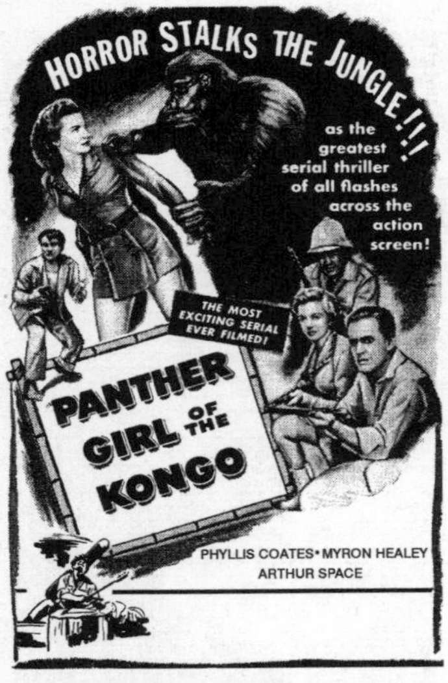
HORROR STALKS THE JUNGLE!!!
as the greatest serial thriller of all flashes across the action screen!
THE MOST EXCITING SERIAL EVER FILMED!
PANTHER GIRL OF THE KONGO
PHYLLIS COATES • MYRON HEALEY
ARTHUR SPACE

Panther Girl Of The Kongo (1955)
Republic Pictures' jungle actioner stars Phyllis Coates in the title role. Can our heroine stop a scientist from taking over a diamond mine with the help of his gigantic monster crawfish (that's what we said, gigantic monster crawfish!)? With Myron Healey, Arthur Space. 12 Kongo-riffic episodes; 167 min.
63-1562 Was $29.99 *$19.99*

The Invisible Monster (1950)
Call him the Invisible Monster, or call him the Phantom Ruler. By any name, this unseen criminal is a master of screen villainy as he uses his ability to wreak havoc. Can a plucky insurance investigator catch what he can't see? Richard Webb, Aline Towne, Stanley Price star. 12 episodes.
10-8079 Was $29.99 *$19.99*

Masters Of Venus (1959)
When two kids stowaway on a manned spacecraft bound for Venus, they get into all sorts of exciting scrapes! To top it off, kids and crew discover a lost civilization in this British-made serial. Ferdy Mayne stars. Eight chapters; 133 min.
62-1250 *$19.99*

Radar Men From The Moon (1952)
George Wallace stars as Commander Cody, who, together with his two aides and rocket suit, stops a tribe of lunar warlords from conquering the Earth with their atomic gun. With Clayton Moore, Roy Barcroft. 12 high-flying chapters; 166 min.
63-1145 Was $29.99 *$19.99*

Jungle Drums Of Africa (1953)
An untapped vein of Uranium, hidden deep in the African jungle, is the prize that pits intrepid engineer Clayton Moore against spies, evil witch doctors, and wild animals. Exciting serial action with more escapes than you can shake a spear at also stars Phyllis Coates, Henry Rowland. 12 episodes.
63-1463 Was $29.99 *$19.99*

Government Agents vs. Phantom Legion (1951)
Government agent Hal Duncan goes undercover to investigate a ring of truck hijackers led by a mysterious leader known as "The Voice." Thrilling chases, narrow escapes and exciting shoot-outs ensue. Walter Reed, Mary Ellen Kay, Dick Curtis star. 12 episodes.
63-1482 Was $29.99 ❑*$19.99*

Desperadoes Of The West (1950)
Courageous ranchers drilling for oil are opposed by a gang of outlaws led by a slick Easterner in this rousing chapter-turner. With Richard Powers, Roy Barcroft and Judy Clark. 12 chapters; 167 min.
63-1534 Was $29.99 *$19.99*

Don Daredevil Rides Again (1951)
When a greedy political boss (what other kind is there?) tries to take over homesteaders' claims for valuable mineral rights, one settler adopts the black-masked identity of an ancestor and becomes a dark avenger of justice. Great frontier serial action with Ken Curtis, Aline Towne, Roy Barcroft. 12 episodes; 167 min.
63-1597 Was $29.99 *$19.99*

Radar Patrol vs. Spy King (1950)
When enemy agents threaten America's radar defense network, it takes a non-super-strong but still super-good Kirk Alyn to locate the mysterious spymaster and put the kibosh on their scheme. Jean Dean, John Merton co-star. 12 episodes.
10-8082 Was $29.99 *$19.99*

Trader Tom Of The China Seas (1954)
"Sea Control to Trader Tom. Sea Control to Trader Tom." Harry Lauter stars as the two-fisted sailor who teams up with a pretty U.N. agent to help stop the villains who are instigating revolution in a South Seas island nation for their own gain. With Lyle Talbot, Aline Towne, Fred Graham. 12 seaworthy episodes; 167 min.
63-1599 Was $29.99 *$19.99*

Canadian Mounties vs. Atomic Invaders (1953)
A Canadian Mountie sergeant and a female undercover agent join forces to smash a mysterious operation headed by foreign operatives set on invading the U.S. and Canada by using atomic missiles. Bill Henry, Susan Morrow and Arthur Space star in this explosive serial. 12 episodes; 169 min.
63-1648 Was $29.99 *$19.99*

King Of The Carnival (1955)
There are thrills under the big top and under the sea in Republic's final chapterplay about a pair of circus trapeze artists who are recruited by a Treasury agent to investigate a counterfeiting ring that's using the circus as a front for their crimes and have an underwater printing press. Harry Lauter, Fran Bennett, Keith Richards (no, not that one!) star. 12 high-flying chapters; 167 min.
63-1766 *$19.99*

The Man With The Steel Whip (1954)
Before hitting it big on the tube as Sergeant Preston, Richard Simmons starred here as Jerry Randall, a rancher who masquerades as the legendary whip-wielding hero El Latigo while trying to learn who's stirring up trouble between Indians and settlers. With Barbara Bestar, Mauritz Hugo. 12 whip-cracking episodes; 169 min.
63-1767 *$19.99*

The Adventures Of Smilin' Jack (1943)
The happy-go-lucky aviator of comic strip fame flies into action, joining with American and Chinese forces to prevent the Axis takeover of a strategic Pacific island. Danger-filled Universal serial features Tom Brown in the title role, Marjorie Lord, Philip Ahn and Keye Luke. 12 high-flyin' chapters.
08-1448 Was $29.99 *$19.99*

Mystery Of The Riverboat (1944)
Three feuding Louisiana families and the fortune in oil that lies under their jointly-owned swamplands spells all manner of trouble in this bayou-based serial thriller. Robert Lowery, Lyle Talbot, Marjory Clements and Mantan Moreland star. 13 episodes; 265 min.
08-1449 Was $29.99 *$19.99*

Riders Of Death Valley (1941)
The Riders are a band of do-gooder vigilantes who come to the aid of a miner's daughter when some lowdown rannies try to steal her inheritance. Exciting Western chapterplay stars Dick Foran, Leo Carrillo, Charles Bickford, Lon Chaney, Jr. and Guinn Williams. 15 episodes.
08-1464 Was $29.99 *$19.99*

The Great Alaskan Mystery (1944)
Dr. Miller, an American scientist, is joined by his daughter and two associates on an expedition to Alaska to find the key element for a defense weapon he has developed. Little do they know that Dr. Miller's associate is working for a fascist group out to retrieve the same material. Ralph Morgan, Milburn Stone, Edgar Kennedy and Marjorie Weaver star. 13 chapters; 225 min.
08-1526 Was $29.99 *$19.99*

Holt Of The Secret Service (1941)
U.S. Secret Service agent Jack Holt (played by Jack Holt) gets help from pretty associate Kay Drew (Evelyn Brent) in tracking down counterfeiters pushing phony cash. Holt's hunches lead him to the culprits and into trouble on a canoe ride and in an outlaw camp. C Montague Shaw, Tristram Coffin also star. 15 chapters; 280 min.
08-1527 Was $29.99 *$19.99*

Adventures Of The Flying Cadets (1943)
When a mysterious murderer known as "The Black Hangman" kills several defense company presidents, it's up to four plucky young air cadets to stop him and end a Nazi sabotage ring. Johnny Downs, Bobby Jordan, Robert Armstrong star. 13 episodes; 235 min.
08-1492 Was $29.99 *$19.99*

Lost City Of The Jungle (1946)
Death duels in the lush jungles of Asia, as government agents battle war profiteers for possession of a mysterious element that provides protection from atomic weaponry! Thrilling adventure with Russell Hayden, Lionel Atwill, Keye Luke. 13 chapters; 240 min.
08-1493 Was $29.99 *$19.99*

Raiders Of Ghost City (1944)
A Union Secret Service agent (Dennis Moore) smashes a ring of gold robbers posing as Confederate soldiers during the final stages of the Civil War. Lionel Atwill, Wanda McKay and Regis Toomey also star. 13 chapters.
08-1513 Was $29.99 *$19.99*

The Mysterious Mr. M (1946)
Federal investigator Dennis Moore joins detective Richard Martin to find out why a noted submarine inventor has disappeared. Secret laboratories, plane hijackings, special serums, bombs and the secret mastermind known as Mr. M play parts in this rousing serial thriller. With Pamela Blake, Jane Randolph. 13 episodes; 225 min.
08-1528 Was $29.99 *$19.99*

Captain Midnight (1942)
With a terror-stricken nation being blitzed by enemy bombing planes directed by the evil Ivan Shark, good guy Captain Albright becomes Captain Midnight and soars off into the big blue sky to head off the reign of terror and rescue a kidnapped scientist. Stars Dave O'Brien, Dorothy Short, James Craven. 15 episodes; 270 min.
08-1543 *$29.99*

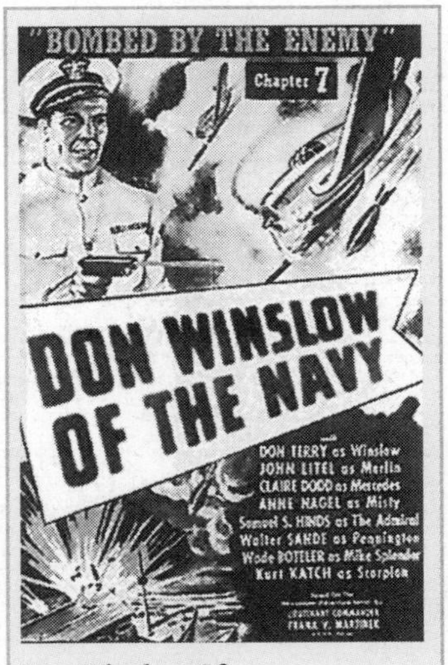
"BOMBED BY THE ENEMY"
Chapter 7
DON WINSLOW OF THE NAVY
DON TERRY as Winslow
JOHN LITEL as Merlin
CLAIRE DODD as Mercedes
ANNE NAGEL as Misty
Samuel S. HINDS as The Admiral
Walter SANDE as Pennington
Wade BOTELER as Mike Splendor
Kurt KATCH as Scorpion

Don Winslow Of The Navy (1942)
Classic serial filled with slam-bang wartime action, as Navy Intelligence officer Don Winslow squares off against the mysterious saboteur known as the Scorpion. Don Terry, Walter Sande, Anne Nagel star. 15 episodes; 234 min.
08-1491 Was $29.99 *$19.99*

Don Winslow Of The Coast Guard (1943)
Blasting invaders and smashing saboteurs! Don Terry is back as super-hero Don Winslow, fighting the evil Scorpion who, with the help of the Japanese, plans to attack the Pacific Coast. Great WWII serial thriller! Also starring Walter Sande, Elyse Knox, June Duprez and Philip Ahn. 13 chapters.
62-1157 Was $29.99 *$19.99*

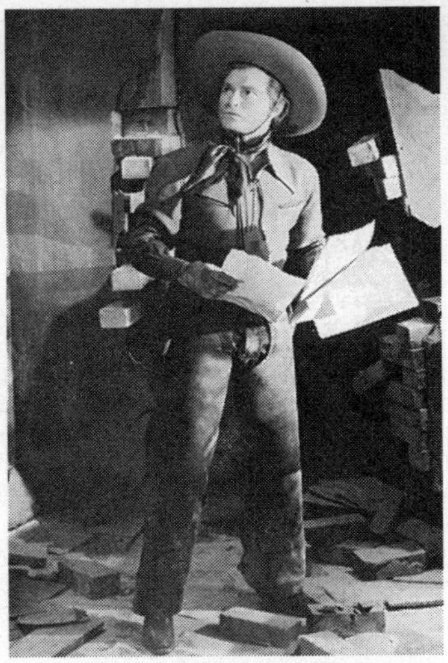

Adventures Of Red Ryder (1940)
Thrilling serial starring Don "Red" Barry as Red Ryder, a rancher who organizes a group of fellow ranchers to battle a crooked banker and his henchman who will stop at nothing to control their property. With Noah Beery, Harry Worth, and Tommy Cook as Little Beaver. Includes theatrical trailer. 12 episodes; 205 min.
08-1834 *$29.99*

Jack Armstrong (1947)
The "All-American Boy" from the popular radio series assembles a crime-busting crew of friends to fly off to an isolated island to fling down the gauntlet on Grood (Charles Middleton), a power-crazed scientist who has kidnapped another scientist in a plot to destroy the world. Stars John Hart, Rosemary La Planche. 15 episodes; 270 min.
08-1544 *$29.99*

Sky Raiders (1941)
WWI flying ace-turned-airplane manufacturer Donald Woods and war buddy Robert Armstrong have developed a new super-fast pursuit plane for the Army, but foreign agents will stop at nothing to obtain the prototype, in this high-flying chapterplay adventure. With Billy Halop, Kathryn Adams. 12 episodes.
08-1686 *$19.99*

The Green Hornet Strikes Again (1940)
Warren Hull takes over as the verdant-masked man-hunter who, joined by Keye Luke as faithful sidekick Kato, uses his crime-fighting weaponry to track down the mysterious head of a city-wide racketeering ring. The Hornet's second serial thriller also stars Anne Nagel, Pierre Watkins. 15 chapters; 345 min.
08-8624 *$39.99*

The Green Archer (1940)
Mystery that baffles! Thrills that chill! Suspense that terrifies! Trap doors, English castles, secret passages and mysterious appearances by protector of good The Green Archer. Stars Victor Jory, James Craven, Dorothy Fay, Iris Meredith, Charles King. 15 episodes; 283 min.
09-1081 Was $39.99 *$29.99*

Gang Busters (1942)
The classic radio crime drama series makes the jump to the big screen, as a pair of big city detectives must take on a crime ring composed of "dead" men. Kent Taylor, Robert Armstrong and Ralph Morgan star; 13 flat-footed episodes.
09-1091 Was $29.99 *$19.99*

Junior G-Men (1940)
Those pugnacious kid gangs, the Dead End Kids and the Little Tough Guys, team up to stop anarchists from kidnapping America's military leaders. Huntz Hall, Gabe Dell, Billy Halop and Phillip Terry star. 12 episodes.
09-1610 Was $24.99 *$19.99*

Junior G-Men Of The Air (1942)
Axis agents plan to destroy America's oil wells, and the Junior G-men join with airfield grease monkeys Huntz Hall, Billy Halop and Gabe Dell to foil their scheme in a high-flying Universal chapterplay. With Frank Albertson, Lionel Atwill. 13 episodes.
10-7181 Was $39.99 *$29.99*

Batman And Robin (1949)
The Caped Crusaders return to keep Gotham City safe in this bat-tastic chapterplay. Robert Lowery and John Duncan play the Dynamic Duo, who must capture a masked super-criminal known as the Wizard. With Lyle Talbot and Jane Adams as Vicki Vale. 15 episodes; 252 min.
10-2241 *$29.99*

Jungle Queen (1943)
Ruth Roman plays the title role of Lothel, mysterious leader of an African tribe whose homeland is caught in the middle of a battle between Nazi spies and Allied agents, in this exciting mix of wartime drama and jungle action. With Edward Norris, Douglass Dumbrille, Tala Birell. 13 chapters.
10-7653 Was $29.99 *$19.99*

Jesse James Rides Again (1947)
Clayton Moore is the legendary outlaw, here trying to go straight by defending farmers against hooded terrorists, in a slam-bang Western chapterplay. Perennial serial heroine Linda Stirling and bad guy Roy Barcroft also star. 13 episodes.
63-1360 Was $29.99 ***$19.99***

The Adventures Of Frank And Jesse James (1948)
Steve Darrell and Clayton Moore are the legendary outlaw brothers, who want to go straight and repay victims of their robberies. A gold miner's latest claim may solve their problems, but when greedy jumpers murder the miner, the James Boys team with his daughter to set things right. With Noel Neill, Stanley Andrews. 13 episodes; 180 min.
63-1596 Was $29.99 ***$19.99***

James Brothers Of Missouri (1950)
Legendary outlaws Frank and Jesse James turn good guys by adopting aliases and helping an old pal save his freight line from being overrun by hijackers and ornery outlaws. Keith Richards, Robert Bice, Noel Neill and Roy Barcroft star in this thrill-a-second serial. 12 chapters; 167 min.
63-1535 Was $29.99 ***$19.99***

King Of The Rocket Men (1949)
Ray guns! Evil scientists!! Ransoms!!! New York City at bay!!!! All this and more in this ultra-exciting series with Tristram Coffin and Mae Clarke. 12 death-defying episodes!
63-1079 Was $29.99 ***$19.99***

Spy Smasher (1942)
Thrill-a-minute serial classic! Twin brothers square off against foreign agents, ray guns, U-Boats, devious villains and other dangers to save the Free World. Kane Richmond, Sam Flint star. One of the best!! 12 chapters.
63-1080 Was $29.99 ***$19.99***

The Adventures Of Captain Marvel (1941)
Billy Batson is granted the power to become Captain Marvel, the World's Mightiest Mortal, in order to stop the sinister Scorpion from completing a weapon that could make him ruler of the world. Tom Tyler and Frank Coghlan, Jr. star in one of Hollywood's best serials. 12 "Shazam"-tastic episodes; 216 min.
63-1140 Was $29.99 ***$19.99***

Nyoka And The Tigermen (1942)
An archeological team exploring Africa is joined by a woman looking for her scientist father, and together the group must fight a bizarre jungle queen and her gorilla henchman. Kay Aldridge, Clayton Moore star. AKA: "Perils of Nyoka." 15 chapters; 261 min.
63-1141 Was $29.99 ***$19.99***

The Masked Marvel (1943)
When a former Japanese envoy is suspected of sabotage, an insurance company hires the mysterious Masked Marvel, who uncovers a plot that could doom the war effort. William Forrest stars. 12 marvelous chapters; 197 min.
63-1143 Was $29.99 ***$19.99***

Manhunt In The African Jungle (1943)
Undercover agent Rod Cameron foils a Nazi plot to enlist the aid of African Arabs to the Axis cause with the aid of an ancient Moslem sword. AKA: "Secret Service in Darkest Africa." 15 suspense-filled chapters; 243 min.
63-1144 Was $29.99 ***$19.99***

The Purple Monster Strikes (1945)
The Purple Monster, sinister vanguard for a Martian fleet, plots to invade and conquer the Earth to save his dying planet. 15 episodes; 286 min.
63-1234 Was $29.99 ***$19.99***

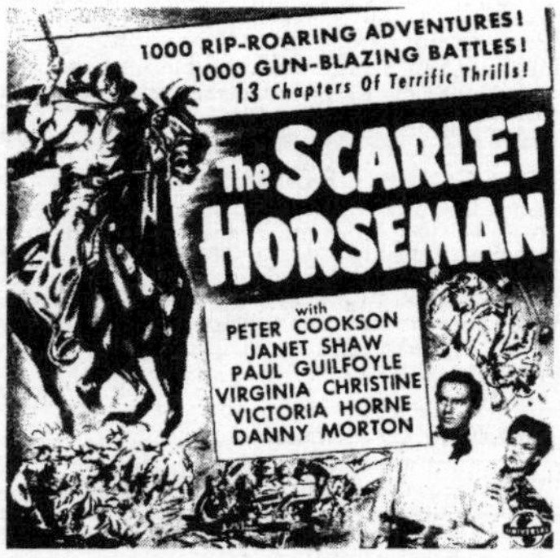
1000 RIP-ROARING ADVENTURES!
1000 GUN-BLAZING BATTLES!
13 Chapters Of Terrific Thrills!
The SCARLET HORSEMAN
with
PETER COOKSON
JANET SHAW
PAUL GUILFOYLE
VIRGINIA CHRISTINE
VICTORIA HORNE
DANNY MORTON

The Scarlet Horseman (1946)
Paul Guilfoyle stars as frontier undercover agent Jim Bannion, who assumes the identity of the mythical Scarlet Horseman to quell a Comanche uprising while he and partner Peter Cookson search for the mystery figure using the uprising as part of their plan to take over Texas. Future Folger's Coffee spokeswoman Virginia Christine co-stars. 13 episodes.
10-7660 Was $29.99 ***$19.99***

Mysterious Doctor Satan (1940)
Obviously a graduate of Villain U., the not-so-good Doctor has assembled a robot army to fulfill his dreams of conquest, and only a masked hero known as the Copperhead can stop him. Serial thrills with Robert Wilcox, Eduardo Ciannelli. 15 mysterious episodes.
63-1276 Was $29.99 ***$19.99***

The Daughter Of Don Q (1946)
In order to inherit an old land grant and acquire valuable territory, an unscrupulous antiques dealer plots to kill all of the descendants of the grant's author. One of the rightful owners of the turf teams with a reporter to stop the dealer and his henchman. Adrian Booth, Kirk Alyn and LeRoy Mason star. 12 episodes; 166 min.
63-1649 Was $29.99 ***$19.99***

The Royal Mounted Rides Again (1945)
When a Canadian mining operator is suspected in a murder connected to a newly-discovered vein of gold, his Mountie officer son fights to clear his name and put the kibosh on a ring of gold thieves. Bill Kennedy, George Dolenz, Daun Kennedy and Milburn Stone ("Gunsmoke") star. 13 episodes.
10-7659 Was $29.99 ***$19.99***

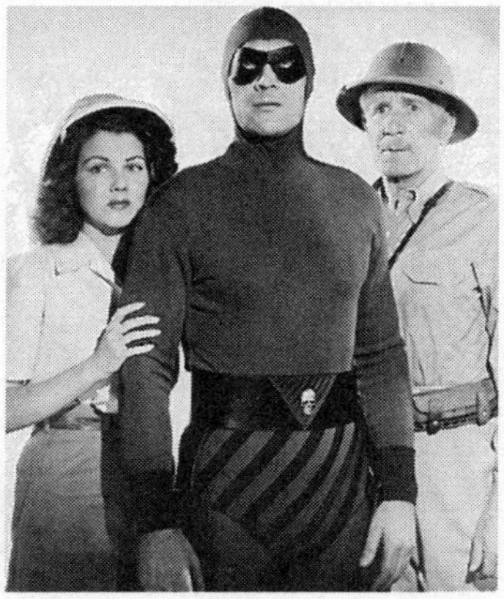

The Phantom (1943)
Tom Tyler stars as the purple-and-black hero of the African jungle, helping fiancée Jeanne Bates' archeologist father locate the Lost City of Zoloz and fending off crooks who want the city and its treasure for themselves, in this classic chapterplay. With Three Stooges foil Kenneth MacDonald and Ace the Wonder Dog as Devil. 15 ghostly chapters.
10-7657 ***$29.99***

The Master Key (1945)
A miraculous invention that can extract gold from sea water is tested by government agents, but a Nazi spylord known only as "The Master Key" will stop at nothing to get it. Milburn Stone, Dennis Moore. 13 chapters; 227 min.
08-1494 Was $29.99 ***$19.99***

Winners Of The West (1940)
The building of a transcontinental railroad is threatened by a prairie landboss who hires renegade Indians to stage raids. Can a two-fisted railway agent get the project back on track? Dick Foran, Anne Nagel star. 13 episodes.
08-1496 Was $29.99 ***$19.99***

The Shadow (1940)
Radio's mysterious, black-clad hero proves that "the weed of crime bears bitter fruit" in this thrill-packed Columbia serial. A criminal mastermind known only as the Black Tiger is sabotaging rail lines and factories across America, and scientist Lamont Cranston must become his shadowy alter ego to uncover the fiend and halt his schemes. Victor Jory, Veda Ann Borg, J. Paul Jones star. 15 episodes; 286 min.
10-7678 ***$29.99***

Sea Raiders (1941)
Loaded from stem to stern with hairbreadth escapes and high seas derring-do, this entertaining whiteknuckler finds the Dead End Kids lighting upon a band of foreign agents bent on sabotaging a top-secret torpedo boat. With Reed Hadley and Edward Keane. 12 chapters.
10-7728 Was $29.99 ***$19.99***

Dangers Of The Canadian Mounted (1948)
There are certainly dangers galore for Captain Chris Royal of the Canadian Mounted Police, who's on the trail of Klondike crooks after a mysterious treasure left in the Great White North by 13th-century Mongol explorers(!), in this thrilling Republic serial. Jim Bannon, Virginia Belmont, Anthony Warde star. 12 chapters; 156 min.
63-1764 ***$19.99***

King Of The Forest Rangers (1946)
Enthralling chapterplay about park ranger Steve King, who recovers part of a rug leading to prehistoric towers. The artifact is stolen by an unscrupulous professor, and the race is on to the towers, which contain priceless platinum. Larry Thompson, Helen Talbot, Stuart Hamblen star. 12 chapters.
10-8081 Was $29.99 ***$19.99***

Jungle Girl (1941)
Frances Gifford stars in the title role as Nyoka, a young woman living in the African jungle with her physician father. When the doctor's evil twin murders him and assumes his identity in order to search for a fortune in diamonds hidden nearby, Nyoka and two pilots must escape the plans of the sinister sibling and his henchmen. With Tom Neal, Trevor Bardette. 15 episodes.
10-7959 ***$29.99***

G-Men Never Forget (1948)
Clayton Moore joins a police sergeant in hopes of finding a notorious criminal who recently busted out of prison and plans to destroy an important tunnel. Moore and his partner encounter bombs, poisonous gas and other hazards as they try to stop the culprit. Roy Barcroft, Ramsay Ames co-star. 12 episodes.
10-8078 Was $29.99 ***$19.99***

Manhunt Of Mystery Island (1945)
The inventor of a new energy-transmitting machine is held prisoner on Mystery Island by the descendant of an infamous pirate. The scientist's daughter and a criminologist search for him and encounter one deathtrap after another. Richard Bailey, Linda Stirling, Roy Barcroft star. 15 swashbuckling episodes; 219 min.
63-1563 Was $29.99 ***$19.99***

The Phantom Rider (1946)
One of a series of masked do-gooder cowboys who rode across the big screen, the Phantom Rider (Robert Kent) makes sure that the owlhoots who are stirring up trouble and making life miserable for the local Indians don't stand a ghost of a chance. Peggy Stewart, LeRoy Mason, Chief Thundercloud co-star. 12 episodes; 167 min.
63-1598 Was $29.99 ***$19.99***

Federal Operator 99 (1945)
Hair-raising chapterplay thriller about an escaped convict who organizes a group of rogues to steal the crown jewels of Princess Cornelia. Jerry Blake, Federal Operator 99, attempts to stop the criminals' efforts. Marten Lamont, Helen Talbot and George J. Lewis star. 12 chapters; 169 min.
63-1650 Was $29.99 ***$19.99***

Federal Agents vs. Underworld, Inc. (1949)
Actually, it's a rematch of "Superman" vs. "Spider Lady," as top agent Kirk Alyn must stop international thief Carol Forman and her criminal cartel from stealing the key to a fabulous hidden treasure. Roy Barcroft, Rosemary La Planche co-star. 12 episodes.
63-1462 Was $29.99 ***$19.99***

Haunted Harbor (1944)
Sensational serial thrills abound in this tenacious tale of a schooner owner who is arrested for the murder of a banker and escapes from prison to find both the murderer and a stolen $1 million in gold. Kane Richmond, Kay Aldridge and Roy Barcroft star. AKA: "Pirate's Harbor." 15 chapters; 243 min.
63-1651 Was $29.99 ***$19.99***

G-Men vs. The Black Dragon (1943)
Rousing wartime serial action, as top American agents join forces with their British and Chinese counterparts to smash a Japanese sabotage ring located in the United States. Rod Cameron, Constance Worth, Nino Pipitone star. 15 episodes.
63-1359 Was $29.99 ***$19.99***

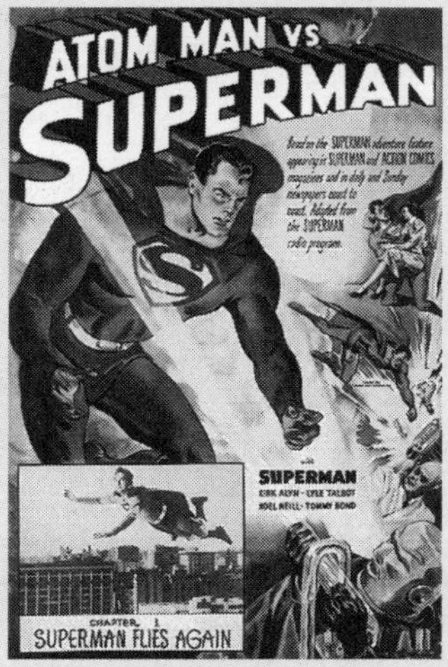
ATOM MAN VS SUPERMAN
SUPERMAN
CHAPTER 1
SUPERMAN FLIES AGAIN

Atom Man vs. Superman (1949)
It's "up, up and away" once again with Kirk Alyn as the Ace of Action in the second Superman serial. Here he must battle the mysterious nuclear nemesis known as Atom Man, whose weaponry includes a flying saucer and deadly Kryptonite. With Noel Neill, Tommy Bond, Lyle Talbot. 15 episodes; 252 min.
19-1722 Was $29.99 ***$19.99***

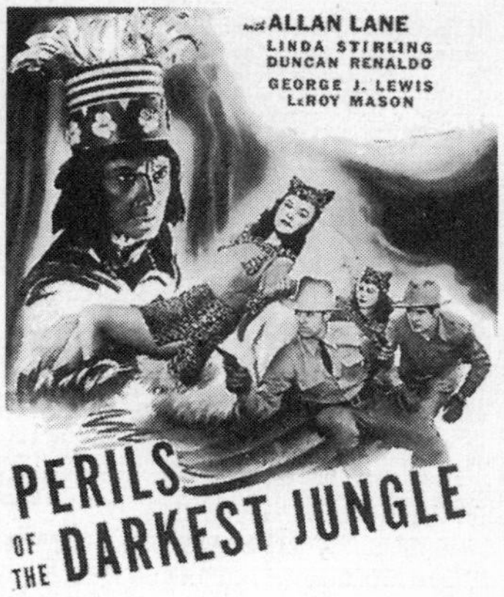
with ALLAN LANE
LINDA STIRLING
DUNCAN RENALDO
GEORGE J. LEWIS
LeROY MASON
PERILS OF THE DARKEST JUNGLE

Perils Of The Darkest Jungle (1944)
A fight between rival oil companies for control of valuable land in the jungle threatens the existence of a savage tribe protected by "The Tiger Woman," mysterious white goddess. Serial queen Linda Stirling stars as the jungle queen, with Allan Lane, Duncan Renaldo, George J. Lewis. AKA: "Tiger Woman." 12 episodes.
63-1308 Was $29.99 ***$19.99***

The Black Widow (1947)
She may not have eight legs, but sinister Asian princess Sombra is as deadly as her namesake as she uses spider poisons and other delicacies in her attempt to steal an experimental atomic rocket engine. Terrific chapterplay thriller stars Carol Forman, Bruce Edwards, Virginia Lindley. 13 episodes.
63-1461 Was $29.99 ***$19.99***

Overland Mail (1942)
Two-fisted lawman Jim Lane (Lon Chaney, Jr.) and sidekick Sierra Pete (Noah Beery, Jr.) are called on to corral the crooks who are interfering with stagecoach deliveries of mail throughout the West in this exciting Universal frontier serial. With Helen Parrish and Noah Beery, Sr. 15 episodes; 278 min.
10-7957 ***$29.99***

King Of The Texas Rangers (1941)
Gridiron great "Slingin' Sammy" Baugh trades his leather helmet for a ten-gallon hat in this Western-style chapterplay, investigating his father's death and stopping a gang of saboteurs from stealing a secret airplane fuel formula. Pauline Moore, Neil Hamilton, Duncan Renaldo also star. 12 episodes.
63-1307 Was $29.99 ***$19.99***

The Crimson Ghost (1946)
A sinister masked mastermind uses "control collars" to take over people's minds in his scheme to steal an "atomic-powered cyclotrode," the possession of which will make his global domination plans that much easier. Superlatve Republic serial stars Linda Stirling, Charles Quigley and Clayton Moore. 12 spectral episodes.
63-1275 Was $29.99 ***$19.99***

Buck Rogers (1939)
Emerging from a state of hibernation after 500 years, Buck Rogers (Buster Crabbe) and young Buddy Wade wake up to a world held in a grip of fear by Killer Kane, and must zoom off to the ringed planet for help from the Saturnians. Co-stars Constance Moore and Jackie Moran. 12 chapters.
10-7739 ***$29.99***

Tim Tyler's Luck (1937)
And "luck" is what young daredevil Tim will need when he goes to Africa to track down his missing scientist father and winds up coping with savage gorillas and a ring of ivory poachers led by the rascally Spider Webb. Frankie Thomas stars as Tyler; with Frances Robinson, Al Shean. 12 chapters.
10-7733 Was $29.99 ***$19.99***

Wild West Days (1937)
You can bet those days were filled with action, gunfights, Indian raids and daring escapes, especially with Johnny Mack Brown leading the way as a wandering hero who helps a young couple defend their mine claim from an unscrupulous newspaper publisher. With Robert Kortman, Lynn Gilbert. 13 episodes.
10-7734 Was $29.99 ***$19.99***

Battling With Buffalo Bill (1930)
The discovery of gold in a small Western town prompts a gambler to murder the townspeople and blackmail the area Indians into terrorizing the town. Buffalo Bill arrives on the scene and plots a way to thwart the bad guy. Tom Tyler, Rex Bell, Francis Ford, William Taylor and Jim Thorpe star. 12 chapters.
10-8321 ***$29.99***

Lightning Bryce (1919)
Jack Hoxie is the courageous cowpoke clammoring to get even with some black hats in this dynamite sagebrush serial. Ridin', ropin' and razzmatazz! 15 chapters. Silent with music track.
10-7928 ***$29.99***

S.O.S. Coast Guard (1937)
Twelve chapters of slam-bang action, with Ralph Byrd as a young Coast Guard lieutenant after a mad munitions inventor (Bela Lugosi, playing it up for all he's worth!). Fine, fast-paced episodic fun! 212 min.
62-1244 Was $29.99 ***$19.99***

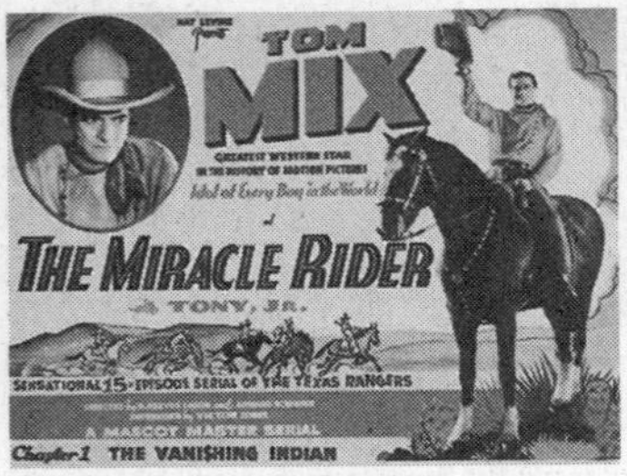

The Miracle Rider (1935)
This was Tom Mix's last film, as he tries to protect the Ravenhead Indians from unscrupulous land-grabbers. Not only Tom's last appearance, but one of the last serials made by Mascot Pictures, and one of their best! 15 episodes.
62-1158 Was $29.99 *$19.99*

Phantom Empire (1935)
Gene Autry dukes it out with land-rustlers out after his radium-rich property, and then must battle the technocratic warriors of an underground supercity. Chapterplay favorite also stars Smiley Burnett, Betsy King Ross. 12 episodes; 245 min.
17-1025 *$29.99*

Dick Tracy (1937)
The enemy of all that's illegal blasts his way from the funny pages to the big screen for the first time in this two-fisted tale of big city crime. Ralph Byrd makes the first of six appearances as the cop who's always "on the square." Smiley Burnette also stars. 15 thrilling chapters. 305 min.
08-1001 Was $29.99 *$19.99*

Mystery Mountain (1934)
Frontier serial with Ken Maynard and his wonder horse, Tarzan. Ken plays a mysterious stranger searching for the Rattler, a criminal camouflaged in cape, mask and false mustache who has been killing people in a mountainous railroad area. 12 chapters; 216 min.
08-1511 Was $29.99 *$19.99*

Flaming Frontiers (1938)
Rousing Western chapter-thriller in which frontier scout Tex Houston (Johnny Mack Brown) matches his skill and wits against outlaws after a gold mine belonging to the heroine and her brother. Eleanor Hansen, Charles Middleton also star. 15 chapters; 305 min.
08-1512 Was $29.99 *$19.99*

Queen Of The Jungle (1935)
Adopted by natives deep in the African jungle, young Mary Kornman grows up to become Daughter of the White God and defend a mountain full of radium in this chapterplay adventure. Co-stars "Arrow Shirt Man" Reed Howes. 12 chapters.
08-1514 *$29.99*

The Lost Jungle (1934)
Famed animal trainer Clyde Beatty plays himself in this thriller. Marooned on a strange island, Clyde must deal with wild beasts, volcanoes, savage natives and other fun items. Co-stars the lovely Cecelia Parker and a young Mickey Rooney. 12 chapters.
62-1096 Was $29.99 *$19.99*

Ace Drummond (1936)
A murderous organization tries to disrupt several countries from forming the world-wide Clipper Ship air service. Stars John King, Noah Beery, Jr. and Jean Rogers. 13 chapters; 250 min.
62-1139 Was $39.99 *$19.99*

The Last Frontier (1932)
A thrill-a-minute Western serial (the only serial produced by RKO) teeming with hair-breadth escapes, blazing gun battles and cattle stampedes. Creighton Chaney (later Lon Chaney, Jr.) is a newspaper editor determined to squash a plot by money-hungry traders to supply the Indians with guns. With Francis X. Bushman, Richard Neil. 12 chapters; 209 min.
09-1986 *$39.99*

The Shadow Of The Eagle (1932)
John Wayne is a pilot for a carnival who must help his boss when he's accused of being "The Eagle," a criminal who has been skywriting threatening messages to a nefarious corporation, in this high-flying Mascot serial. Co-stars Edward Hearn, Dorothy Gulliver and Yakima Canutt. 12 chapters; 226 min.
09-1093 Was $29.99 *$19.99*

The Hurricane Express (1932)
John Wayne is the son of a murdered engineer on the Hurricane Express, the world's fastest train. His mission: finish the train's run and catch the murderer, a diabolical master of disguise known as "The Wrecker." Great action scenes and a motorcycle chase that Wayne did himself. 12 full-throttle episodes; 223 min.
62-1159 Was $29.99 *$19.99*

The Three Musketeers (1933)
Daredevil thrills and spills, as John Wayne and the men of the Foreign Legion battle villainous El Shaitan and his "Circle of Death." Dumas and the desert meet in this Mascot serial, co-starring Raymond Hatton, Creighton (Lon) Chaney, and Noah Beery, Jr. 12 chapters; 215 min.
62-1095 *$19.99*

Radio Patrol (1937)
Crooks kill the inventor of a special, bulletproof steel and try to learn the formula from his son. Only intrepid cop Grant Withers of the Radio Patrol can come to the rescue at the speed of sound. With Catherine Hughes, Adrian Morris. 12 chapters.
62-1140 Was $29.99 *$19.99*

The Lone Ranger (1938)
An extremely rare serial find—the first filmed story of the mysterious masked hero of the plains, starring Lee Powell and Chief Thundercloud. NOTICE: The quality of the sound and picture of this print are only fair. This is the only complete version of this serial available; the two previously missing chapters are in English with Spanish subtitles. 15 chapters.
10-7182 *$29.99*

The Lone Ranger Rides Again (1939)
When a band of settlers are threatened by ruthless cattlemen, the Lone Ranger (Bob Livingston), his faithful Indian companion Tonto (Chief Thundercloud) and his faithful Mexican companion (Duncan Renaldo) join a wagon train to stop them in the masked rider's second screen appearance. NOTE: Film is in English with Spanish subtitles. 15 "Hi-Yo" chapters.
10-7085 *$29.99*

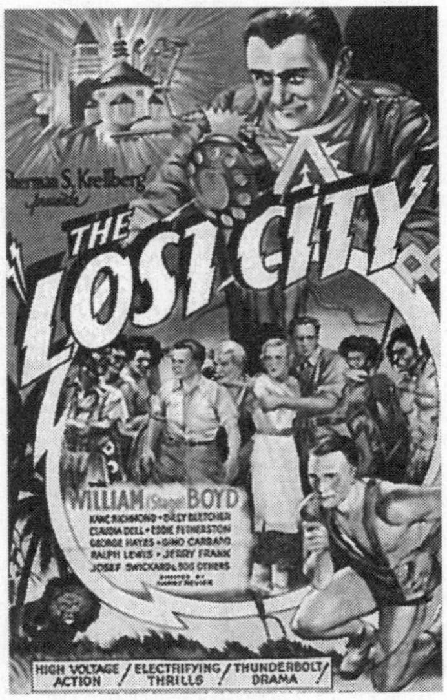

The Lost City (1935)
One of the most thrilling and fondly remembered of movie serials, with William "Stage" Boyd as the tyrannical ruler of a super-advanced city inside a mountain in the African jungle. Can troubleshooting engineer Kane Richmond stop his dreams of world conquest? With Gabby Hayes, Margot D'use; 12 chapters.
10-7148 Was $39.99 *$29.99*

The Phantom Of The West (1931)
Can the phantom find the identity of a murderer whom everyone thinks is dead? This thrilling 10-chapter serial with Tom Tyler will let you know. 166 min.
09-1370 Was $29.99 *$19.99*

The Devil Horse (1932)
A magnificent wild stallion is the object of a hunt in this early Mascot serial oater that stars Harry Carey as the hero, Noah Beery as the black hat, and Apache as the horse. 12 chapters.
10-7079 Was $29.99 *$19.99*

The Indians Are Coming (1930)
Two Western lovey-doveys battle jealous cowpokes, prairie fires, scores of Indians and murder during a wagon train heading for gold territory. Tim McCoy, Allene Ray and Charles Royal star in this thrilling early serial. 12 chapters.
10-8320 *$29.99*

The Adventures Of Tarzan (1921)
Original screen Tarzan Elmo Lincoln returns in this edited version of the classic serial. The ape man has left civilization for his beloved jungle, but Jane is also in Africa and at the mercy of the evil Rokoff, a Russian agent searching for the jeweled city of Opar. Louise Lorraine, Frank Whitson also star. 188 min. Silent with music score. NOTE: This version does not include the chapter opening and closing credits.
10-9365 *$39.99*

Tarzan The Tiger (1929)
Frank Merrill, as Tarzan, must rescue Jane from native slave traders and keep thieves from stealing the "pretty pebbles" that make up the jewel city of Opar. With Natalie Kingston, Lillian Worth; 10 swinging episodes. Silent with music score.
10-7149 *$19.99*

The New Adventures Of Tarzan (1935)
Herman Brix, as Tarzan, travels to a lost Mayan city hidden in the Guatemalan jungle in search of the "Green Goddess," a gem-encrusted idol that contains a secret formula for a powerful explosive. 12 swinging episodes; 244 min.
09-1785 Was $29.99 *$19.99*

The Last Of The Mohicans (1932)
The conflict between Indians, settlers and soldiers reaches a fever pitch in the American frontier of the mid 1700s in this thrilling chapterplay based on the famous novel by James Fenimore Cooper. Harry Carey, Hobart Bosworth and Yakima Canutt star. 12 episodes; 231 min.
09-1084 Was $29.99 *$19.99*

The Black Coin (1936)
What is the sinister secret that the mysterious black coins reveal, and what is their connection to a map that people will kill to possess? Find out in this serial of intrigue and espionage. Ralph Graves, Ruth Mix, Dave O'Brien star. 15 chapters.
10-7078 Was $39.99 *$19.99*

Burn 'Em Up Barnes (1934)
Champion race car driver Barnes has his hands full, protecting his girl's property from racketeers and taking the son of his late friend under his wing, in this fast-paced chapterplay thriller. Jack Mulhall, Lola Lane, Al Bridge star. 12 speedy episodes.
10-7080 Was $29.99 *$19.99*

Scouts To The Rescue (1939)
Even Eagle Scout Jackie Cooper isn't prepared for the danger that awaits when he leads his troops into a ghost town. What kind of danger? How about counterfeiting gangsters, G-men, and Indians, for a start? Action-packed serial also stars William Ruhl, Bill Cody, Jr. 12 episodes.
10-7081 Was $29.99 *$19.99*

Blake Of Scotland Yard (1937)
Ralph Byrd portrays the intrepid ex-Scotland Yard inspector, here doing battle against a munitions trader and his henchmen, the sinister Scorpion. The prize: a top-secret death ray. Top-notch serial suspenser co-stars Joan Barclay, Dickie Jones; 15 chapters.
10-7151 Was $29.99 *$19.99*

King Of The Wild (1931)
The whereabouts of a fabulous diamond mine in India is a secret that men will kill for, as adventurer Walter Miller learns in a thrill-packed chapterplay that also features a pre-"Frankenstein" Boris Karloff as a wicked lascar. 12 wild episodes.
10-7180 *$29.99*

The Fighting Marines (1936)
Action-packed serial of a deadly battle between the U.S. Marines and a mysterious scientific genius known as the "Tiger Shark." The prize: a strategic island base. Grant Withers, Ann Rutherford, Robert Warwick star. 12 chapters.
62-1001 Was $29.99 *$19.99*

The Mystery Squadron (1933)
Two freelance pilots (B-western heroes Bob Steele and Guinn "Big Boy" Williams) come to the aid of a friend working on a dam construction project when the site is attacked from the air by a felonious flyer known as "The Black Ace." 12 chapters; 225 min.
62-1081 Was $39.99 *$19.99*

The Vanishing Legion (1931)
Rex the Wonder Horse stomps adult riders to paste, but he lets young Billy Williams ride him against the Legion and their evil leader, "The Voice," a shadowy gang trying to drive oilman Harry Carey out of business and frame Billy's pa for murder. Yakima Canutt also appears in this 12-episode Mascot serial.
10-7524 Was $29.99 *$19.99*

The Clutching Hand (1936)
Craig Kennedy, super detective, is out to get "the Clutching Hand," a fiend who has stolen a formula that will turn metal into gold. With Jack Mulhall. 15 chapters.
62-1000 Was $29.99 *$19.99*

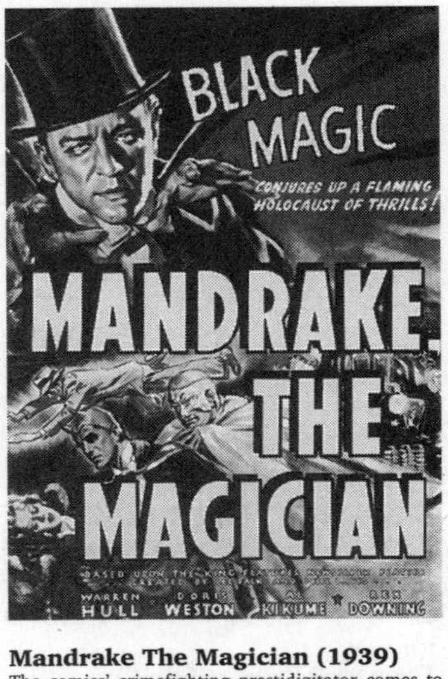

Mandrake The Magician (1939)
The comics' crimefighting prestidigitator comes to the screen in this thrill-laden serial, as Mandrake (Warren Hull) and his African sidekick Lothar (Al Kikume) help a noted scientist protect his radium-energy machine from a sinister criminal genius known as the Wasp. Doris Weston, Forbes Murray co-star. 12 spell-casting episodes.
10-7677 *$29.99*

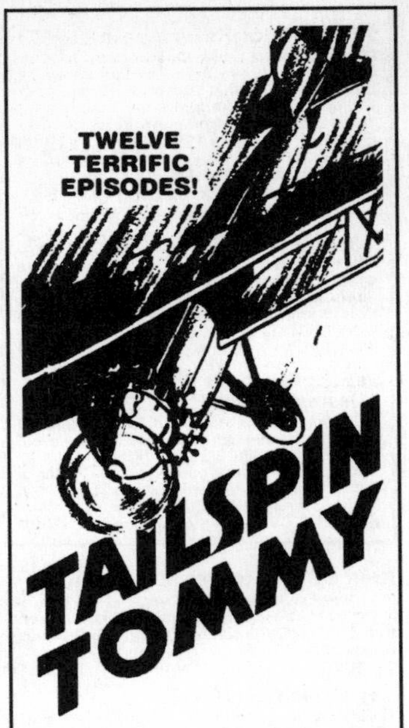

Tailspin Tommy (1934)
The heroic flyboy of the comics pages soars onto the screen with this thrill-filled Universal chapterplay, as young Tommy signs on with a struggling mail-delivery airline and must stop a nefarious rival's campaign of sabotage. Maurice Murphy, Patricia Farr, Noah Beery, Jr. star. 12 episodes.
08-1547 Was $29.99 *$19.99*

Tailspin Tommy And The Great Air Mystery (1935)
Clark Williams takes over the title role, as Tommy and his greasemonkey pal Skeeter use their flying skills to stop greedy rebels from taking over a Latin American nation's oil supplies. With Noah Beery, Jr., Jean Rogers. 12 chapters.
10-7727 Was $29.99 *$19.99*

Rustlers Of Red Dog (1935)
Johnny Mack Brown, Raymond Hatton and Walter Miller are a trio of range-roving do-gooders who help defend a wagon train from hostile Indians and a gang of villains after the train's hidden gold. Well-done Western thriller also stars Joyce Compton, H.L. Woods. 12 episodes.
10-7680 Was $29.99 *$19.99*

Red Barry (1938)
Rousing espionage serial stars an Earthbound Buster Crabbe as ace detective Red Barry, who must track down a fortune in stolen bonds and battles Asian criminal masterminds, ballerina spies and other menaces. With Frances Robinson, Frank Lackteen. 13 episodes.
10-7736 *$29.99*

Fighting With Kit Carson (1937)
Kit Carson (Johnny Mack Brown) fights an outlaw gang called the Mystery Riders, searches for lost gold and has his hand in several chases. Also starring the father-son team of Noah Beery and Noah Beery, Jr. 12 chapters.
62-1141 Was $24.99 *$19.99*

The Galloping Ghost (1931)
College football star "Red" Grange stars in this serial as, of all things, a college football star named "Red" Grange who tries to stop a classmate from taking money from gamblers to throw a game. With Francis X. Bushman, Dorothy Gulliver. 12 touchdown-filled chapters.
62-1142 Was $29.99 *$19.99*

The Return Of Chandu (1934)
You'll lose yourself in Bela Lugosi's hypnotic gaze when he stars as that mystic do-gooder, Chandu the Magician (although, in the 1932 film of the same name, he played Chandu's enemy, Roxor). In this exciting serial, Lugosi uses his powers to rescue a kidnapped woman from a black magic cult on the island of Lemuria. Maria Alba, Dean Benton also star. 12 chapters.
62-1094 *$29.99*

Shadow Of Chinatown (1936)
As a sinister scientific madman, Bela Lugosi terrorizes the shady characters and merchants of a seedy Chinatown district. An atmospheric visit to the inscrutable underworld of extortionists and their victims, also starring Herman Brix. 15 chapters.
10-7358 Was $39.99 *$29.99*

Custer's Last Stand (1936)
A thrill-a-minute Western serial that stars Frank McGlynn as the famed general and Rex Lease as ace scout Kit Cardigan. A war between Indians and miners erupts when gold is discovered on sacred Indian land, and it's up to the Cavalry to keep the peace. 15 chapters; 290 min.
62-1172 Was $39.99 *$19.99*

The Whispering Shadow (1933)
The Shadow kills by a "radio death ray," speaks to his gang by television and uses a gyrocopter to further his ends. Detectives are determined to capture him...now! Stars Bela Lugosi, Henry B. Walthall. 12 chapters.
62-1207 Was $29.99 ***$19.99***

The Painted Stallion (1937)
Go back to the days when pioneers fought to penetrate the wilderness, but were beset by threats from nature, savage Indians and bandits. In these adventures the Rider of the Painted Stallion is sworn to "defeat outlawry." Ray Corrigan, Hoot Gibson and Duncan Renaldo star. 12 hoof-pounding chapters; 209 min.
62-1245 Was $29.99 ***$19.99***

Law Of The Wild (1934)
A tale of horse thieves and racing scams with regal stallion Rex and Rin Tin Tin, Jr., the best bred stars since the Barrymores. When the wonder horse is nabbed from the ranch, Rinty and young Bob Custer must tackle the dirty Nolan gang. 12 chapters.
10-7401 Was $29.99 ***$19.99***

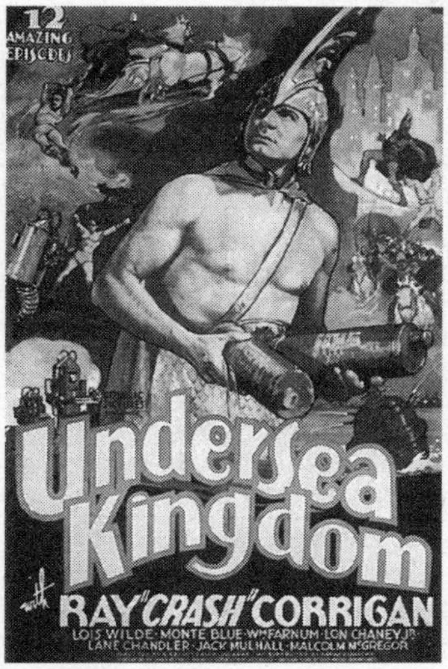

The Undersea Kingdom (1936)
"Heyyy, it's the Undersea Kingdom, for you and for me, and it's fuuun!" Join daredevil Navy cadet Ray "Crash" Corrigan, scientist C. Montague Shaw and his young son, and girl reporter Lois Wilde as they travel by sub to the underwater world of Atlantis to stop evil warlord Monte Blue from attacking the surface world. 12 chapters.
17-1085 Was $29.99 ***$19.99***

The Mystery Trooper (1931)
A rarely seen independent serial set in the Old West, where the feuding heirs to a gold mine find themselves put upon by a band of thieving rannies and get help from the titular hero. Robert Frazer, Buzz Barton star. AKA: "Trail of the Royal Mounted." 10 chapters; 195 min.
62-1312 Was $39.99 ***$19.99***

Young Eagles (1934)
When their plane crash lands in the Central American jungle and the pilot is injured, two plucky Boy Scouts must brave wild animals, savage natives, and bandits to find help in this thrill-laden chapterplay. Bobby Ford, Jim Adams, Bobbie Cox star. 12 episodes; 225 min.
62-1313 Was $29.99 ***$19.99***

Daredevils Of The Red Circle (1938)
The Daredevils are a trio of professional acrobats, and when the brother of one is killed as part of an escaped criminal's mad plan of vengeance, the three vow to track the fiend down. Herman Brix, Charles Middleton star. 12 chapters; 211 min.
63-1142 Was $29.99 ***$19.99***

The Fighting Devil Dogs (1938)
Two young Marines set out to avenge the deaths of their comrades at the hands of the enigmatic "Lightning" and his futuristic airplanes in this high-flying chapterplay. Lee Powell stars. 12 airborne episodes; 318 min.
63-1277 Was $29.99 ***$19.99***

The King Of The Kongo (1929)
The first Mascot serial, circa 1929, is a rare treat. Government agent Larry Trent is sent to the jungle to break up a clan of ivory thieves. He encounters troubles and thrills galore. Early silent serial stars Jacqueline Logan, Walter Miller, Boris Karloff. 10 chapters; 213 min.
09-1172 ***$39.99***

Officer 444 (1926)
Who says people like Jack Webb, Mel Gibson and Warren Beatty started the tough cop tradition? Walter Miller is the man behind the badge in this powerhouse precursor to "Dragnet," etc., etc. 12 chapters; 212 min. Silent with music track.
10-7932 Was $39.99 ***$29.99***

Cliffhangers, Vol. 1
Plenty of pulse-pounding previews from an assortment of the niftiest nailbiters in serial history. "Perils of Nyoka," "The Vigilante," "Gangbusters," "King of the Rocketmen," "The Green Archer," "Captain America" and many others. 56 min.
65-5004 ***$19.99***

Cliffhangers, Vol. 2
Another carload of coming attractions from the finest adventure serials of the past. "Tim Tyler's Luck," "Blackhawk," "The Master Key," "Return of Captain Marvel," "Mysterious Dr. Satan," "The Red Rider" and lots, lots more. 59 min.
65-5005 ***$19.99***

Classic Serial Trailers, Vol. 1
Terrific trailers for those cliffhangers you love. Included are "Adventures of Captain Marvel," "King of the Rocketmen," "Tex Granger," "Flash Gordon's Trip to Mars," "Radar Men from the Moon."
68-8704 ***$19.99***

Classic Serial Trailers, Vol. 2
Thrill to previews for the following chapterplay classics: "The Masked Marvel," "Manhunt of Mystery Island," "The Tiger Woman," "Perils of Nyoka" and many more.
68-8705 ***$19.99***

Zorro Rides Again (1937)
The masked crusader vows vengeance for the murder of his uncle, but the evil Marsden will stop at nothing to gain control of the railroads. John Carroll, Noah Beery and Helen Christian star. 12 chapters; 213 min.
63-1536 Was $29.99 ***$19.99***

Zorro's Fighting Legion (1939)
In old Mexico, crooked mine officials hatch a gold-snatching scheme that involves duping natives into blocking gold shipments. Can the mysterious Zorro and his allies save the day? Reed Hadley, Sheila Darcy, C. Montague Shaw star. 12 chapters.
17-1093 Was $29.99 ***$19.99***

Zorro's Black Whip (1944)
Serial queen Linda Stirling takes the title role(!) in this tale of a feisty newspaper girl who assumes her murdered brother's masked identity to fight outlaws opposed to statehood for the Idaho Territory. With George J. Lewis, John Merton. 12 episodes.
09-1910 Was $29.99 ***$19.99***

Son Of Zorro (1947)
A descendant of the masked avenger dons the costume of his ancestor to fight corrupt toll road officials(!) in the West after the Civil War. George Turner, Peggy Stewart, Roy Barcroft star. 13 episodes.
63-1309 Was $29.99 ***$19.99***

Woman In Grey (1919)
Tune in for edge-of-the-sofa thrills in this suspenseful serial, with Arline Pretty (who lives up to her name) as a woman trapped in a whirlwind of murder and mystery. 15 chapters. Silent with music track.
62-5109 ***$29.99***

The Red Rider (1934)
Sheriff Buck Jones tosses aside his tin star to help an innocent friend escape the hangman's noose and then, as luck would have it, stumbles across the real culprit while working on a ranch near the Mexican border. Shoot-'em-up serial co-stars Grant Withers, Marion Shilling, Walter Miller. 15 chapters.
10-7930 Was $59.99 ***$29.99***

Cliffhangers: The Epic Story
The weekly chapterplays of yesteryear are brought back to life in this thrill-a-minute program filled with clips of movie serials that dazzled filmgoers in the '20s, '30s and '40s. Included are salutes to Pearl White in "The Perils of Pauline," "Flash Gordon" with Buster Crabbe, John Wayne in "The Hurricane Express" and Bela Lugosi in "The Phantom Creeps." 60 min.
05-5079 ***$19.99***

Action Heroes Of The Cliffhanger Serials
A salute to the wonderful serials of old, the stuff that inspired "Raiders of the Lost Ark" and "The Rocketeer." Breathtaking stunts, dastardly villains, dashing heroes: chapterplays like "The Perils of Nyoka," "Zorro's Fighting Legion," "Flash Gordon," and "The Green Hornet" had all this and more. 120 min.
10-2472 ***$12.99***

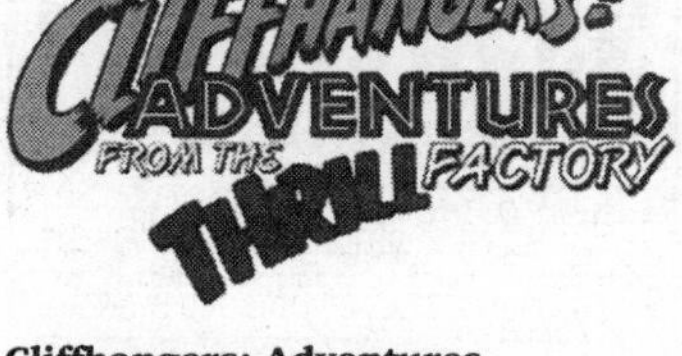

Cliffhangers: Adventures From The Thrill Factory
Moviegoers in the '40s and '50s got a weekly dose of action, suspense and daredevil escapes from the serials of Republic Studios. Join host Leonard Maltin as he takes an affectionate look at those bygone chapterplay heroes and villains (and the men and women who played them), with clips from "The Adventures of Captain Marvel," "The Crimson Ghost," "Zorro Rides Again" and others. 46 min.
63-1600 ***$14.99***

Darkest Africa (1936)
Famed animal trainer Clyde Beatty stars in this thrilling serial as (what else?) famed animal trainer Clyde Beatty, travelling deep into the African jungle in search of a lost city, the beautiful princess who rules it, and a fortune in jewelry. With Manuel King as Baru the jungle boy, Elaine Shepard. 15 whip-cracking episodes; 270 min.
63-1561 Was $29.99 ***$19.99***

The Vigilantes Are Coming (1936)
Plenty of blazing gunplay set in early California, as a masked avenger known only as "The Eagle" fights to keep the Gold Coast out of the possession of Czarists. Robert Livingston, Guinn Williams and Raymond Hatton star. 12 chapters; 230 min.
63-1652 Was $29.99 ***$19.99***

The Oregon Trail (1939)
Two-fisted trail scout Johnny Mack Brown and trusty sidekick Fuzzy Knight go undercover to learn who's behind the attacks on wagon train convoys bound for the Oregon Territory in this fur-flying frontier serial. Bill Cody, Jr., Louis Stanley also star. 15 chapters.
10-7956 Was $29.99 ***$19.99***

The Phantom Creeps (1939)
The always-sinister Bela Lugosi stars as evil Dr. Zorka, whose weapons in his scare-a-minute battle for world domination include an invisibility belt, mechanical spider bombs, a giant robot and a substance that causes suspended animation. Exciting chapterplay also stars Robert Kent, Dorothy Arnold. 12 episodes; 240 min.
08-1495 Was $29.99 ***$19.99***

Hawk Of The Wilderness (1939)
Screen Tarzan Herman Brix plays another "white savage," the Indian-raised frontier hero Kioga, Hawk of the Wilderness, in this exciting serial that pits him and a scientific expedition against hostile Indians whipped into a frenzy by the witch doctor Yellow Weasel. With Jill Martin, Monte Blue, Mala. 12 episodes; 213 min.
63-1765 ***$19.99***

Sign Of The Wolf (1931)
A faraway kingdom where a mysterious secret promises untold riches, a frontier hero and his cowgirl sweetheart, and a stalwart canine named King all add up to western action in this extremely rare Metropolitan serial. Rex Lease, Virginia Brown Faire and King the Wonder Dog star. 10 episodes.
68-8341 Was $29.99 ***$19.99***

Flash Gordon (1936)
The dauntless Flash Gordon leapt from the comic pages to celluloid with this popular chapterplay starring Buster Crabbe. Flash, Dr. Zarkov and Dale soar off to stop the planet Mongo from barreling through space toward Earth, and face an onslaught of snags (monkey-men, vicious reptiles, Gocko, etc.) courtesy of Ming the Merciless (Charles Middleton). AKA: "Fiery Planet." 13 chapters; 246 min.
10-7718 Was $59.99 ***$29.99***

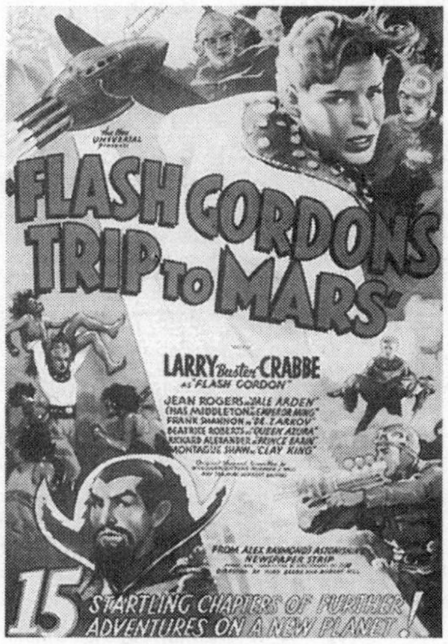

Flash Gordon's Trip To Mars (1938)
Flash and friends dart off to the Red Planet to clap off the lamp of Ming the Merciless, which is absorbing nitrogen from the Earth's atmosphere, and pulverize the Tree People and Clay People into toothpicks and harmless raisins. Stars Buster Crabbe, Jean Rogers and Charles Middleton. 15 "shock-crammed" episodes.
80-3010 ***$29.99***

Flash Gordon Conquers The Universe (1940)
Buster Crabbe, as interplanetary hero Flash Gordon, must defeat Ming the Merciless and his Purple Death in this rocket-fast action serial. 12 episodes; 235 min.
08-1461 Was $29.99 ***$19.99***

Flash Gordon Collector's 3-Pack
Flash your eyes on this money-saving deal: all three "Flash Gordon" serials, starring Buster Crabbe, in a special collector's set.
66-6055 Save $10.00! ***$79.99***

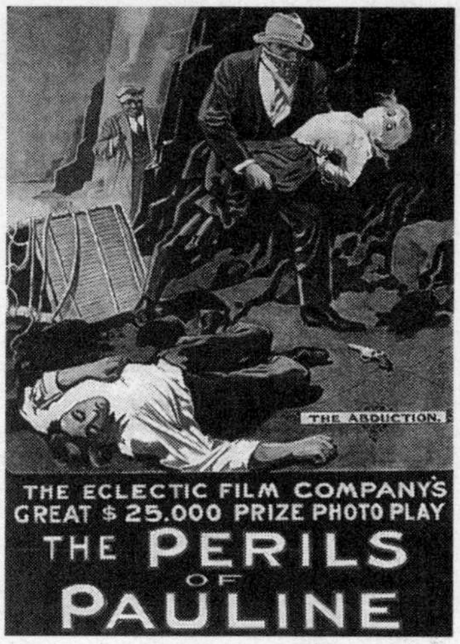

The Perils Of Pauline (1914)
The one, the only Pearl White in the original heroine-in-distress saga. Our intrepid female finds herself stuck in all sorts of cliffhanging situations. Stay tuned through 9 chapters to see how she gets out of them. 219 min. Silent with musical track.
10-7934 Was $39.99 ***$29.99***

The Perils Of Pauline (1934)
This early serial, starring Evalyn Knapp, Robert Allen, and James Durkin, combines all of the classic elements for edge-of-your-seat viewing! From China to Borneo to New York to Singapore, Pauline and her father, Dr. Hargraves, must overcome the evil Dr. Bashan and save the world! 12 exciting episodes; 238 min.
09-1734 Was $29.99 ***$19.99***

The Adventures Of Frank Merriwell (1936)
Dime novel collegiate hero Merriwell came to the screen in this thrilling chapterplay which finds young Frank (Don Briggs) forced to leave Fardale before a big baseball game when his father disappears. A mysterious inscription on a ring leads him to a frontier mining camp and a fortune in gold. With Jean Rogers, John King. 12 episodes.
08-1560 ***$29.99***

The Lone Defender (1930)
Rin Tin Tin stars along with Walter Miller and June Marlowe in this thrilling Mascot serial, as the resourceful canine comes to the aid of a mysterious man searching for the killers of two mine owners, as well as an outlaw known as "The Cactus Kid." 12 chapters; 214 min.
62-1246 Was $29.99 ***$19.99***

The Lightning Warrior (1931)
After his father is killed by an unknown assassin and his father's friend is found dead, young Jimmy Carter (no peanut-farming President) searches for the culprits with help from trusted canine Rinty (Rin-Tin-Tin). The pooch leads Jimmy to a mysterious outlaw called the Werewolf, who's responsible for the mayhem. Frankie Darro, Georgia Hale star. 12 episodes.
08-1545 Was $29.99 ***$19.99***

The Wolf Dog (1933)
Rin Tin Tin, Jr. and Frankie Darro star as a wild canine and his young runaway pal who help an inventor keep his powerful electric ray from unscrupulous hands. A speedboat chase, awesome pyrotechnics and the old fistfight-on-the-running-board stunt highlight 12 howling good episodes. 204 min.
68-8415 ***$29.99***

The Adventures Of Rex And Rinty (1935)
The wonder horse and the son of Rin Tin Tin hit the open road together in this exciting Mascot serial that follows their exploits from America to a savage South Seas island. Human stars include Kane Richmond, Smiley Burnette, Harry Woods; 12 doggone thrilling episodes.
08-1463 Was $29.99 ***$19.99***

Robinson Crusoe Of Clipper Island (1936)
Ray Mala stars as Mala, a Polynesian-born U.S. intelligence agent who is sent to a South Pacific island to investigate a dirigible crash. He discovers a spy ring using the island as their base and causing a volcano to erupt to keep the natives in line. Mamo Clark, William Newell co-star. 12 loincloth-clad chapters.
62-1205 Was $29.99 ***$19.99***

Mystery Of The Double Cross (1917)
Exciting serial mystery focusing on a playboy who tries unsuccessfully to learn the identity of a fellow ocean liner passenger whose arm bears a double-cross tattoo. Upon returning to the States, he learns that his father's will stipulates he marry a woman bearing the same tattoo. Mollie King, Leon Bary star. 15 chapters. Silent with music score.
10-7731 ***$29.99***

The Silent Revolution: What Do Those Old Films Mean?: Boxed Set
Explore the evolution of the cinema in key countries during the early part of the 20th century in this compelling three-tape set. Noted film historian Noel Burch offers analysis and rare footage is featured in "Along the Great Divide: Great Britain 1900-1912/Tomorrow the World: USA 1902-1914," "She!: Denmark 1902-1914/The Enemy Below: France 1904-1912" and "Born Yesterday: USSR 1926-1930/Under Two Flags: Germany 1926-1932." 156 min. total. NOTE: Individual volumes available at $19.99 each.
53-6705 Save $10.00! ***$49.99***

The Primitive Lover (1922)
Hollywood queen Constance Talmadge plays a woman torn between her hubby and a dashing explorer in this unpredictable tale. When the believed-to-be-dead explorer returns and finds that Talmadge has married her former rival, look out! She tries to get divorced in Reno, but hubby takes his wife and the explorer hostage in a mountain cabin. With Harrison Ford. Silent with music score.
03-5009 ***$24.99***

The Indian Tomb (1921)
Originally released in two parts, this lavish adventure saga from pioneering German filmmaker Joe May stars Conrad Veidt as an Indian maharajah who plots an elaborate revenge against the British army officer who has stolen the heart of Veidt's princess wife. Daredevil chases, exotic locales and man-eating tigers are in ample supply. Olaf Fouss, Mia May also star; scripted by Fritz Lang, who directed a 1958 remake. 212 min. Silent with music score.
01-1535 ***$79.99***

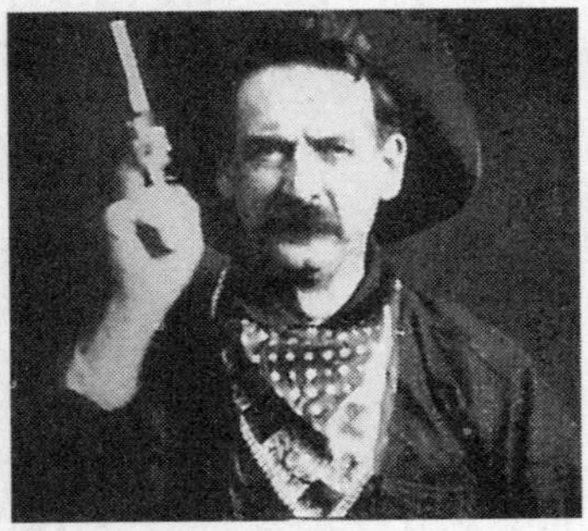

The Movies Begin
The evolution of cinema is traced in this outstanding series that boasts pristine archival material from several sources, features new music and is comprised of over 120 films. Showcased are the works of pioneers like George Melies, Max Linder, Louis Lumiere, Winsor McKay and D.W. Griffith.

The Movies Begin, Vol. 1: The Great Train Robbery And Other Primary Works
Included in this program are groundbreaking 19th-century works by Eadweard Muybridge, Thomas Edison and Louis Lumiere, as well as George Mélies' "A Trip to the Moon" (1902) and Edwin S. Porter's "The Great Train Robbery" (1903). 75 min.
53-7998 ***$49.99***

The Movies Begin, Vol. 2: The European Pioneers
Forty works from famous and not-so famous cinema pioneers from Europe are offered in this program. Included are works by Lumiére and Mélies, along with "Demolition of a Wall" (1896) and "Arrival of a Train at La Ciotat" (1895). 58 min.
53-7999 ***$49.99***

The Movies Begin, Vol. 3: Experimentation And Discovery
The use of photographic techniques and editing advance the art of cinema, as evidenced in these comical and sometimes risqué films from Pathé Fréres ("Peeping Tom"), Cecil Hepworth ("How It Feels to Be Run Over") and Edwin S. Porter ("The Dream of a Rarebit Fiend"). 93 min.
53-8000 ***$49.99***

The Movies Begin, Vol. 4: The Magic Of Mélies
A look at the special effects wizard from France, which includes a dozen of his fantasy films, a hand-tinted print of the rarely-seen "Impossible Voyage" and the documentary "Georges Mélies: Cinema Magician." Shorts include "The Eclipse," "Long Distance Wireless Photogrpahy," "The Black Imp," more. 103 min.
53-8001 ***$49.99***

The Movies Begin, Vol. 5: Comedy, Spectacle And New Horizons
The cinematic pioneering genius of Max Linder, D.W. Griffith and Winsor McCay and others is showcased in this program that looks at the early days of film comedy and animation, elaborate stunts and powerful drama. Includes "The Policeman's Little Run," "The Bangville Police," "Nero, Or the Fall of Rome," more. 85 min.
53-8002 ***$49.99***

The Movies Begin: Complete Set
The entire series is also available in a money-saving deluxe set.
53-8003 Save $50.00! ***$199.99***

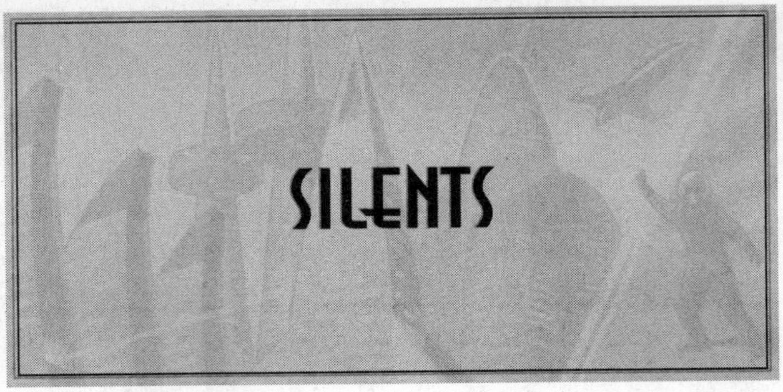

Lyrical Nitrate (1991)
Fascinating tribute to the early days of cinema produced from meticulously restored color tinted nitrate films found in the attic of an Amsterdam theater. The films evoke 19th-century century theatrical and operatic tradition and reflect a magical, lost age. 50 min. Title cards subtitled in English; with musical score.
53-8449 ***$59.99***

Salome (1922)
Stage actress and early screen star Alla Nazimova plays the title role in this highly stylized treatment of Oscar Wilde's play, as the Biblical temptress whose spurned affections for John the Baptist led to her lusty dance for stepfather King Herod and John's losing his head. With Rose Dione as Salome's mother, Herodias, and Mitchell Lewis as Herod. 34 min. Silent with music score.
09-5434 ***$14.99***

Memories Of The Silent Stars
Blackhawk Films, a purveyor of silent movies, produced this collection of shorts in the 1960s and 1970s. They offer an overview of the silent cinema's greatest stars, all captured in rare footage. Included are Charlie Chaplin, Tom Mix, Clara Bow, D.W. Griffith, the Gish sisters, Fatty Arbuckle and many more. Terrific quality, too!
03-5005 ***$24.99***

The Silent Studios
The great movie studios from the silent era are showcased in this fascinating guide through Hollywood. You'll see Universal in 1914, Paramount in 1922, MGM in 1925, plus studios owned by Chaplin, Keaton and Hal Roach. All this and Lon Chaney, Norma Shearer and others in behind-the-scenes footage. Silent with music score.
03-5016 ***$24.99***

Origins Of Cinema, Vol. 1
Twenty-two early silent shorts, the majority of which are from the Edison Company's pioneering director, Edwin S. Porter. Emphasis is on pre-production planning, plot structures and knowledge of photography and camera. Shorts include "Life of an American Fireman" (1903), "The Twentieth Century Tramp" (1902), "Uncle Tom's Cabin" (1903), "The Gay Shoe Clerk" (1903), more. 96 min.
10-3163 ***$19.99***

Origins Of Cinema, Vol. 2
The film industry's earliest experiments with cinema comedy are depicted in these 15 shorts from the American Mutoscope and Biograph studios. Features examples of early chase scenes, special effects and an interesting look at the rudimentary stage of the suspense genre. Shorts include "A Search for Evidence" (1903), "Tom, Tom, The Piper's Son" (1905), "The Suburbanite" (1904). 101 min.
10-3164 ***$19.99***

Origins Of Cinema, Vol. 3
Ten silent shorts exemplifying the industry's growth away from its roots in the theatre, the ambitiousness of the producers at American Mutoscope and Biograph studios and the dawn of documentaries. Shorts include "A Kentucky Feud" (1905), "The Tunnel Workers" (1906), "Her First Adventure" (1908), "At the French Ball" (1908), more. 94 min.
10-3165 ***$19.99***

Origins Of Cinema, Vol. 4
The earliest remnants of genius D.W. Griffith's body of work are available here in these 11 silents, providing insights into filmdom's first major producer-director and his pioneering techniques. Shorts include "Balked at the Altar" (1908), "Fools of Fate" (1909), "The Cord of Life" (1909), "An Awful Moment" (1908), more. 102 min.
10-3166 ***$19.99***

Origins Of Cinema, Vol. 5
D.W. Griffith's 1911 version of "Enoch Arden," promoted as the first Biograph two-reeler, is featured along with the director's "His Trust" and "His Trust Fulfilled," "The Girl and Her Trust" and "A Temporary Truce," plus four films from the prolific Sigmund Lubin studio in Philadelphia. 100 min. Silent with music score.
10-3167 ***$19.99***

Origins Of Cinema, Vol. 6
The beginnings of world cinema are seen in a collection of over two dozen films made in America and Europe between 1899 and 1908, including examples of comedies and social documentaries from England and seven works by French trick photography wizard George Mélies. 105 min. total.
10-3168 ***$19.99***

The Rush Hour (1927)
Accomplished silent farce featuring Marie Prevost as an unhappy woman who stows away aboard an ocean liner, lands in France and gets involved with a group of con men out to dupe a millionaire. Harrison Ford and Seena Owen also star. Silent with music score.
10-8383 Was $19.99 ***$14.99***

Getting Gertie's Garter (1927)
Comedienne Marie Prevost stars in this silent tale concerning a flustered husband who has to retrieve an engraved jewelled garter given to a female acquaintance before his jealous wife discovers it. Charles Ray, Franklin Pangborn also star.
10-8389 Was $19.99 ***$14.99***

Up In Mabel's Room (1926)
Funny silent farce featuring Marie Prevost in a frantic story involving a goofy husband who must retrieve a piece of embroidered lingerie from a ladyfriend before his fiancé discovers it. With Harrison Ford and Phyllis Haver.
10-8390 Was $19.99 ***$14.99***

Blonde For A Night (1928)
In order to see whether her husband is faithful, a woman poses as a vampish blonde. Marie Prevost, Franklin Pangborn and Harrison Ford star in this humorous domestic comedy.
10-8459 Was $19.99 ***$14.99***

Charley's Aunt (1925)
First filming of the classic cross-dressing stage comedy stars Syd Chaplin (Charlie's older brother and a popular star in his own right) as the Oxford student who dons wig and dress to serve as "chaperone" for his chums' lunch dates. With James E. Page, Ethel Shannon. 70 min. Silent with organ score.
53-8365 ***$29.99***

Man On The Box (1925)
Sydney Chaplin looked to repeat his "Charley's Aunt" screen success with this drag farce about a maid attempting to stop enemy agents from stealing the plans to a helicopter her father invented. Alice Calhoun and David Butler also star. Silent with music score.
10-8382 Was $19.99 ***$14.99***

The Films Of Thomas Edison, Vol. 1 (1889-1904)
The groundbreaking films of inventor Thomas Edison are offered on this incredible collection that shows early attempts at cinematic storytelling, special effects, documentary and satire. Included are "Elopement on Horseback," "Strange Adventures of a New York Drummer," "Uncle Tom's Cabin," "Uncle Josh at the Moving Picture Show," "Life of an American Fireman" and more. 60 min.
10-9061 ***$19.99***

The Films Of Thomas Edison, Vol. 2 (1904-1905)
Thomas Edison's later efforts are showcased on this program that includes "The Seven Ages," "The Ex-Con," "How Jones Lost His Roll," "The Whole Dam Family and the Dam Dog" and others. 60 min.
10-9062 ***$19.99***

BEFORE the NICKELODEON

Before The Nickelodeon: The Early Cinema Of Edwin S. Porter (1982)
Largely forgotten today, pioneering cameraman/director and Edison associate Edwin S. Porter's innovative use of narrative stories and intercutting and editing of scenes made him the top filmmaker of the 20th century's first decade. This documentary look at Porter's life and career features more than a dozen examples of his work, including the seminal "The Great Train Robbery" (1903) and the complete shorts "The Sunken Battleship 'Maine'" (1898), "Jack and the Beanstalk" (1902), "Life of an American Fireman" (1903) and others. Silent screen veteran Blanche Sweet narrates. 60 min.
53-6009 ***$49.99***

Larry Semon Comedies
White-faced comic Larry Semon was one of the world's most popular screen performers in the 1920s, starring in a series of two-reelers that showcased wild stunts, hilarious sight gags and his own dumbbell satire. Included here are "School Days" (1920), "The Dome Doctor" (1922) and " The Sportsman" (1920). 58 min. total.
10-9009 ***$19.99***

The Perfect Clown (1925)
Fast, funny and frenetic vehicle for Larry Semon features him as a hapless office boy entrusted with a large bank deposit. When the bank closes before he gets there, Larry's forced to hold onto it overnight—and disaster can't be far ahead! Oliver Hardy, Dorothy Dwan co-star. 72 min. Silent with music score.
09-5392 ***$19.99***

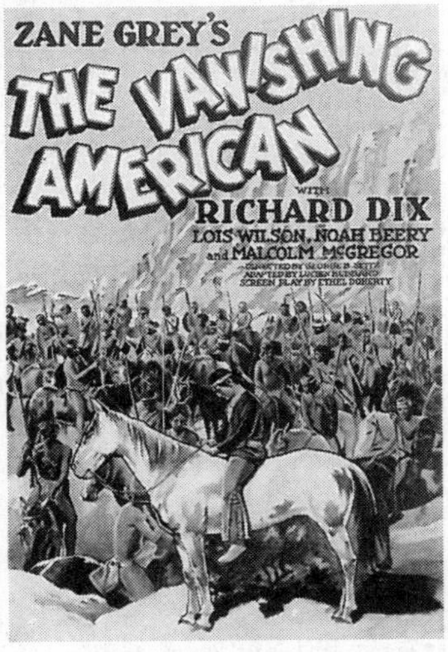

The Vanishing American (1925)
One of the great silent epics is a magnificently staged Western with great battle sequences. Richard Dix plays the proud Indian warrior who tries to halt the bloody Cavalry battles and make peace between his people and the white man. Noah Beery, Lois Wilson co-star; from Zane Grey's novel. 109 min. Silent with music score.
53-6608 ***$24.99***

Wild Horse Canyon (1925)
Early stunt star Yakima Canutt and his dog Ladd face big stampedes, cliff-hanging escapes and super somersaults in this silent Western with a musical score. 68 min.
09-1190 ***$19.99***

The Devil Horse (1925)
Top-notch silent sagebrusher with stunt expert Yakima Canutt as an Army scout who is reunited with his horse Rex, who has developed a legendary hatred for Indians because of a massacre that occurred years before. Gladys Morrow and Robert Kortman also star. Silent with music score.
68-9141 ***$19.99***

The Fighting Stallion (1926)
Rousing sagebrush silent film stars Yakima Canutt as a prairie drifter who's hired by a determined rancher to rope and rein the titular steed. There's lots of intrigue awaiting Yak at the spread, too! Neva Gerber, Bud Osborne and Boy the Wonder Horse co-star. 76 min. Silent with musical score.
09-2080 Was $19.99 ***$14.99***

Desert Greed (1926)
Border deputy Yakima Canutt tries to help a young bordello cashier get her money from the owner of a "house of ill repute." He then discovers her nasty stepfather is trying marry her off to a swindler. Can he stop the nuptials? Rose Blossom and Henry Herbert co-star. Silent with music score.
68-9150 ***$19.99***

The Outlaw Breaker (1926)
Cattleman Yakima Canutt is caught in the middle of a "b-a-a-a-d" sheep war and soon becomes a suspect in the killing of his girlfriend's father, a much-hated sheepherder. Canutt has to prove he's innocent, but the authorities don't want to hear any of the "Yakety Yak." Silent with music score.
68-9158 ***$19.99***

Uncle Tom's Cabin (1903/1914)
Two early versions of Harriet Beecher Stowe's classic story are presented on one tape. The 1903 version was restored from the Library of Congress paper prints, while the 1914 entry features Sam Lucas, the first African-American actor to star in a film. 85 min. total.
10-8431 Was $19.99 ***$14.99***

Uncle Tom's Cabin (1927)
One of the silent film era's most expensive productions, this epic version of Harriet Beecher Stowe's famed novel stars Margarita Fisher as Eliza, a put-upon slave who flees her plantation when her guardian, Uncle Tom (James Lowe), and her son are sold to a rival landowner. With George Siegmann as the villainous Simon Legree. 112 min. Silent with music score.
53-6607 ***$24.99***

The Docks Of New York (1928)
The squalid waterfront of New York City is the haunting setting for this silent Josef von Sternberg drama. A loving relationship is formed between two social outcasts (George Bancroft and Betty Compson) after a hard-fighting stocker saves a young woman from suicide. 60 min. Silent with music score.
06-1437 Was $29.99 ***$14.99***

The Covered Wagon (1923)
A large-scale early Western epic, shot on location in Utah and Nevada, detailing a group of courageous pioneers' cross-country wagon trek. Highlighted by spectacular scenes of an Indian attack and buffalo hunt, the film stars J. Walter Kerrigan, Lois Wilson and Alan Hale. Silent with musical score.
06-1719 ***$12.99***

The Red Kimona (1925)
Silent melodrama of a "fallen woman," brought to the screen by female film pioneer Dorothy Arzner. Can the heroine (Priscilla Bonner) escape bordello life with the help of a good man's love? 95 min. Silent with music score.
09-1504 Was $19.99 ***$14.99***

Ballerinas In Hell: A Georges Méliès Album
Rarely seen works by French cinema pioneer Georges Méliès are offered on this collection. Included are such shorts as "The Legend of Rip Van Winkle" (1905), which is hand-colored; "Le Magicien" (1898); "The Palace of Arabian Nights" (1906); "The Ballet Master's Dream" (1903); and "The Merry Frolics" (1906), plus more. Silent with music score.
03-5014 ***$24.99***

Le Grand Méliès (1952)
The life and work of Georges Méliès, the turn-of-the-century French magician and filmmaker whose silent fantasies pioneered the use of special camera effects, are retold in this biodrama tribute from director Georges Franju. André Méliès stars as his famed father. 30 min. In French with English subtitles.
53-8073 ***$39.99***

History Of Color In The Silents, Vol. 1
Seven French short subjects from 1904 to 1914, hand-colored by artists, frame by frame. The program includes "Life of Christ," "Slav'd Love," "Nobleman's Dog," more.
09-1309 Was $19.99 ***$14.99***

History Of Color In The Silents, Vol. 2
More hand-colored movies from France's Pathé studio, including "Anne Boleyn," "Butterflies," "Death of Christ" and others.
53-7031 Was $19.99 ***$14.99***

Pioneers Of The French Cinema, Volume I
The work of the first giants of French film—the Lumière Brothers and Georges Méliès—whose impact was felt worldwide. program includes several Lumière films from 1895 and Méliès' classics of early trick photography, "A Trip to the Moon," "The Conquest of the Pole," "Kingdom of the Fairies," "The Gypsy's Warning," more. 60 min.
53-7048 ***$29.99***

Pioneers Of The French Cinema, Volume II
A second installment of groundbreaking silent shorts from France includes Ferdinand Zecca's "Scenes of Convict Life (Au Bagne)," "A Father's Honour," "Whence Does He Come?," "The Runaway Horse," "Down in the Deep," "Revolution in Odessa" and "Fun After the Wedding." 40 min.
53-7049 ***$29.99***

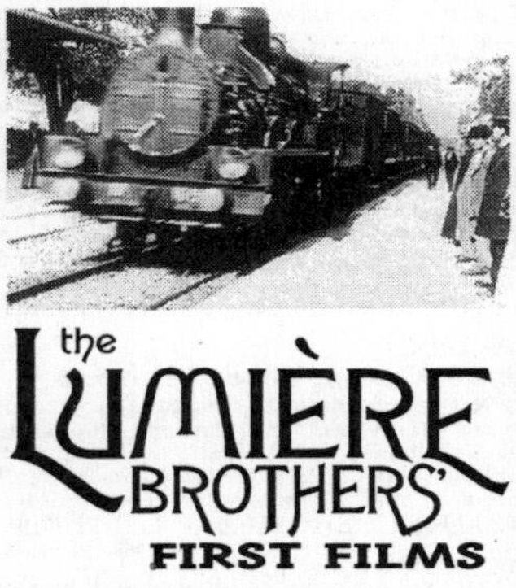

The Lumière Brothers' First Films
The groundbreaking short films of Auguste and Louis Lumière, the French inventors recognized as pioneers of world cinema, were shot between 1895 and 1900 and provided audiences with amazing looks at international sights as well as everyday life. Renowned director Bertrand Tavernier narrates this collection of 85 remastered works from the Lumière Institute. 62 min.
53-8978 ***$49.99***

Eyes Right! (1926)
Francis X. Bushman, Jr. stars as a former high school football hero who's "down on his luck, but up on his pluck," until he takes a job as a potato-peeler/dishwasher/floorsweeper at the Naval Academy in the hopes of achieving his lifelong goal of attending the institution. Co-stars Flobelle Fairbanks. 68 min. Silent with music score.
09-1330 Was $29.99 ***$14.99***

Excuse My Dust! (1920)
One of the few surviving films of actor Wallace Reid is a silent action effort in which a West Coast automaker has his driver's license stripped by his wife and father-in-law in hopes he'll stop his car racing hobby. Reid goes against a judge's order, risks his marriage by deciding to race, and faces his father-in-law in competition. With Anna Little.
03-5001 ***$19.99***

The Fighting American (1924)
A young Mary Astor is showcased in this silent film as a woman desired by two fraternity brothers. When she learns that one of them proposed to her as part of a bet, she heads to China to be with her father, a missionary. Realizing he loves the woman, the fellow heads to the Far East to find her and gets into all sorts of danger. With Pat O'Malley, Warner Oland.
03-5002 ***$19.99***

Miss Lulu Bett (1921)
Lois Wilson is a spinster who works like a servant at the home of her sister and brother-in-law. When she marries (as an unknowing participant in a practical joke), she discovers her new hubby is already married, and she becomes the focus of derision from those around her. This drama, which offers themes of women's liberation, also stars Milton Sills, Theodore Roberts. Silent with music score.
03-5006 ***$19.99***

The Golden Age Of Silent Films: Boxed Set
Seven of the greatest silent films in history are presented in this collector's boxed set. Included are "The Mark of Zorro" with Douglas Fairbanks; "Blood and Sand" with Rudolph Valentino; Mary Pickford in "Pollyanna"; John Barrymore in "Dr. Jekyll and Mr. Hyde"; Lon Chaney as "The Hunchback of Notre Dame"; Buster Keaton in "The General"; and "The Gold Rush" with Charlie Chaplin. 10 hrs. total.
16-5013 ***$49.99***

The Origins Of Film Collection
Produced by Smithsonian Video in association with the Library of Congress, this remarkable series brings together rare and influential films, each restored for home video and featuring new piano scores, from the early days of America cinema.

Origins Of The Fantasy Feature
Included are L. Frank Baum's production of his book "The Patchwork Girl of Oz" (1914), with some amazing special effects, and the gender-crossing comedy "A Florida Enchantment" (1914), starring Sidney Drew and Edith Storey. 129 min.
83-1048 ***$24.99***

Origins Of The Gangster Film
Both Hollywood and the modern urban criminal came of age in the early 1900s, as seen in this double feature. Mary Pickford tries to help her ex-con beau reform in D.W. Griffith's "The Narrow Road" (1912), while Maurice Tourneur's "Alias Jimmy Valentine" (1915) follows a former safecracker who hides his past and becomes a bank clerk. 82 min.
83-1049 ***$24.99***

America's First Women Filmmakers
Social life and marriage at the turn of the century are examined in "How Men Propose" (1913) and "Too Wise Wives" (1921) by Lois Weber and in Alice Guy-Blaché's 1913 films "A House Divided" and "Matrimony's Speed." A rare look at two pioneering female director/producers. 114 min.
83-1050 ***$24.99***

The African American Cinema I
The segregation that pervaded American society led to an independent black cinema whose creators used the new medium to present films depicting racial issues. Director Oscar Micheaux's "Within Our Gates" (1920) is a moving social drama about a black schoolteacher that features a controversial lynching scene. 79 min.
83-1051 ***$24.99***

The African American Cinema II
The made-in-Philadelphia "Scar of Shame" (1927), a powerful example of the silent "race drama," focused on the ill-fated marriage of a middle-class pianist and a poor woman, whom the musician kept away from his class-conscious mother. Also included is an experimental musical short from 1923 featuring Eubie Blake and Nobel Sissle. 80 min.
83-1052 ***$24.99***

Origins Of American Animation
A variety of techniques and styles are showcased in this look at pre-Disney animation. Included are J. Stuart Blackton's "chalk-talk" films "The Enchanted Drawing" (1900) and "Humorous Phases of Funny Faces" (1906), cartoon adaptations of the "Krazy Kat" and "Katzenjammer Kids" comic strips, clips from two lost shorts by Winsor McCay, Willis O'Brien's stop-motion film "The Dinosaur and the Missing Link" (1914), and more. 84 min.
83-1053 ***$24.99***

The Origins Of Film Collection: Complete Set
All six tapes are also available in this special collector's set.
83-1054 Save $10.00! ***$139.99***

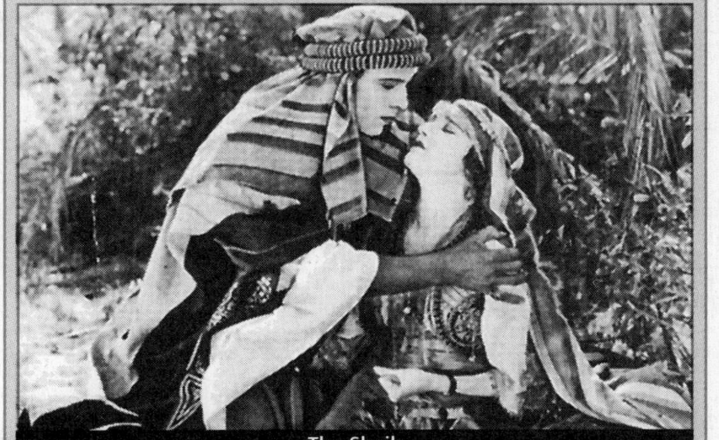

The Sheik

Rudolph Valentino

Camille (1921)
Legendary silent actress Alla Nazimova essays the title role in this silent filming (the third made since 1916) of Alexandre Dumas' *fils* timeless romance, with Rudolph Valentino playing the naive law student who falls for Nazimova's doomed Parisian courtesan. 63 min. Silent with music score.
10-9503 ***$19.99***

The Conquering Power (1921)
In an early starring role, Rudolph Valentino plays a destitute aristocrat's son who is sent to rural France to live with a wealthy but scheming uncle. When the uncle's stepdaughter and Valentino fall in love, he angrily plots to separate them. Based on a novel by Honore de Balzac; with Alice Terry, Eric Mayne. 71 min. Silent with music score.
10-9504 ***$19.99***

The Four Horsemen Of The Apocalypse (1921)
This lavish silent drama, which follows the members of a wealthy Argentinean family as they journey through pre-WWI Europe and eventually wind up on opposite sides of the conflict, gave Rudolph Valentino his breakthrough starring role as the tango-dancing Julio. With Alice Terry, Alan Hale. 156 min. Silent with music score.
12-2956 ***$19.99***

The Sheik (1921)
The silent costume drama that permanently fixed Rudolph Valentino's screen persona in the Hollywood pantheon. Rudy is still enthralling as the desert prince who abducts an English woman to be his bride, then must rescue her from a rival. With Agnes Ayres, Adolphe Menjou. 79 min. Silent with music score.
06-1930 ***$19.99***

Son Of The Sheik (1926)
Rudolph Valentino's last film was this sequel to his smash hit. Here he plays the son of the famed desert warrior and lover, out to exact vengeance on the bandits who wronged a dancing girl. With Vilma Banky. 68 min. Silent with musical score.
63-1545 ***$19.99***

Moran Of The Lady Letty (1922)
Rousing swashbuckling adventure with Rudolph Valentino as a Spanish nobleman in San Francisco who is forced by smugglers on to a ship destined for Mexico. While at sea, the ship encounters another sailing vessel in flames, and Valentino protects its only survivor, a beautiful woman, whom he disguises as a man. May McAvoy and William Long also star. 95 min. Silent with music score.
10-9051 ***$19.99***

Blood And Sand (1922)
The mesmerizing Rudolph Valentino stars as a peasant youth who grows to become Spain's most famous matador, but along the way is fatally seduced by a scheming vamp. Exciting bullfighting scenes and Rudy's classic profile fuel this vintage melodrama. With Lita Lee, Nita Naldi. 80 min. Silent with musical score.
63-1451 ***$19.99***

Monsieur Beaucaire (1924)
Lavish costumer starring Rudolph Valentino as the French Duke of Chartres, who escapes his homeland while disguised as a barber and becomes a member of the British court under a new identity. Lois Wilson and Bebe Daniels also star. 105 min. Silent with music score.
10-9037 ***$19.99***

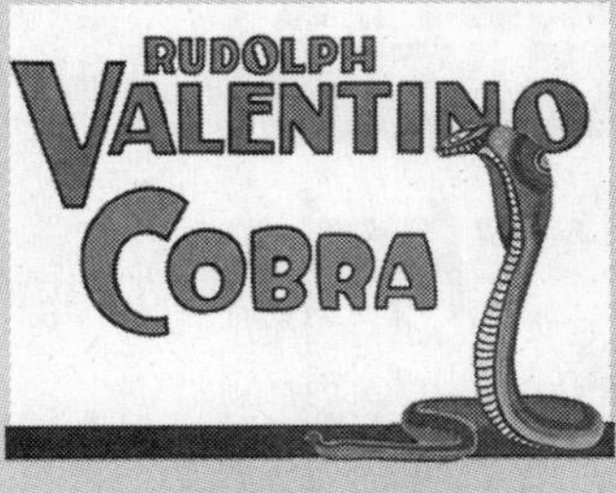

Cobra (1925)
Silent soaper classic with Rudolph Valentino as an impoverished Italian nobleman who takes a job in a New York antique shop and becomes romantically involved with both an innocent co-worker and a gold-digger who believes he's still wealthy. Nita Naldi, Gertrude Olmstead co-star. 70 min. Silent with music score.
10-9505 ***$19.99***

The Eagle (1925)
Based on a story by Pushkin, this thrilling costume drama stars Rudolph Valentino as a valiant Cossack in the Russian army who dons the mask of the Black Eagle to avenge the murder of his father. With Vilma Banky, Louise Dresser. 75 min. Silent with music score.
44-1678 ***$19.99***

Valentino Rarities
A collection of great rarities for "Rudy" fans, including home movies and such shorts as "A Society Sensation," "The Sheik's Physique," "American Beauties," "Idol of a Jazz Age" and an untitled item from the late teens. 108 min.
10-9087 ***$19.99***

Headin' Home (1920)
The one and only "Sultan of Swat," Babe Ruth, starred in this silent melodrama as (surprise!) a home run-hitting small-town fellow named "Babe." Success in the big leagues could be coming Babe's way, but will he have to leave his family and true love behind? 56 min. Silent with music score.
09-1130 ***$14.99***

Conductor 1492 (1924)
Silent mix of comedy, romance and melodrama, with Johnny Hines as a go-getting Irish immigrant who comes to America. Getting a job in a Midwestern town as a trolley car conductor, Hines promptly saves the trolley company president's son's life, woos his daughter, and saves the firm from a takeover. With Doris May, Dan Mason. 74 min. Silent with music score.
09-1152 ***$19.99***

The Man From Beyond (1922)
Master illusionist, escape artist and spiritualist Harry Houdini wrote and starred in this silent fantasy of a man revived after being frozen for 100 years and meeting the reincarnation of his true love. Lots of escape tricks and mystical atmosphere. With Nita Naldi. 91 min. Silent with music score.
09-1511 ***$19.99***

The Peacock Fan (1929)
A wealthy man, the possessor of an ancient cursed peacock fan, is murdered in a windowless, locked room, and a host of characters (his wife, his dishonest secretary and his lawyer) all had reason to wish the millionaire dead. Co-stars Lucien Prival, Dorothy Dwan and Lotus Long. 79 min. Silent with music score.
09-1497 Was $29.99 ***$24.99***

Buster Keaton Festival, Vol. 1
A trio of silent comedies starring the Great Stone Face is featured. Buster's under the spreading chestnut tree as "The Blacksmith" (1922), travels out west in "The Paleface" (1921), and does some amazing stunts while chased by "Cops" (1922). 55 min. Silent with music score.
62-1338 *$19.99*

Buster Keaton Festival, Vol. 2
Buster's back in three silent shorts: as a hapless yachter in "The Boat" (1921), a Mountie fighting crime up in "The Frozen North" (1922), and the somewhat confused builder of "The Electric House." (1922). 75 min. Silent with music score.
62-1201 *$19.99*

Buster Keaton Festival, Vol. 3
Three more of Keaton's finest, funniest short subjects. Buster takes off into the skies as "The Balloonatic" (1922), has some fantastic "Daydeams" (1922), and drives into trouble with Fatty Arbuckle in "The Garage" (1919). 54 min. Silent with music score.
62-1248 *$19.99*

Buster Keaton Festival, Vol. 4
"Everyone laughs but Buster" in three silent rib-ticklers from Keaton's two-reeler days. Buster and Fatty Arbuckle team up to tame the frontier in "Out West" (1918); "Good Night, Nurse!" (1918) is a hysterical hospital romp; and Keaton finds himself stranded on a shipload of scoundrels in "The Love Nest" (1923), his last silent short. 54 min. Silent with music score.
62-1351 *$19.99*

The Saphead (1920)
In his first starring film role (and one played on Broadway by Douglas Fairbanks), Buster Keaton is "The Saphead," ne'er-do-well son of a Wall Street tycoon who manages to save his father from bankruptcy. Plus, Keaton's first solo short subject, "The High Sign" (1920), finds him helping a town that's been taken over by a "secret society," while newlywed Buster's plans to build a pre-fabricated house in "One Week" (1920), hilariously amok when a jealous exsuitor rearranges the pieces. 115 min. Silent with music score.
53-8079 Remastered *$29.99*

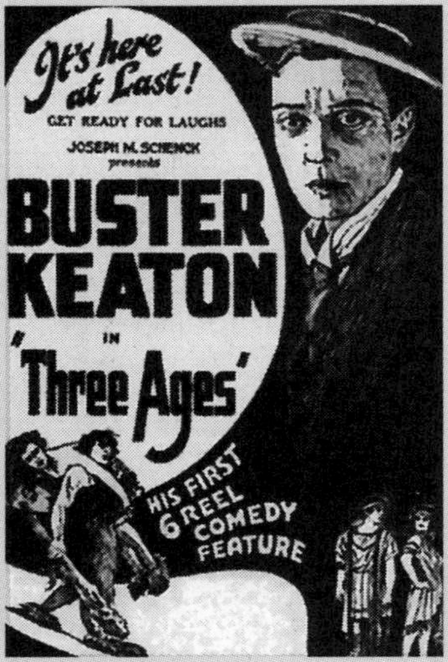

The Three Ages (1923)
Buster Keaton spoofs D.W. Griffith's "Intolerance" in his debut feature as creator/star, as he competes with rival Wallace Beery for the hand of Margaret Leahy in caveman days, Ancient Rome and 1920s America. Plus, in two shorts, a wild chase leaves Buster in front of a speeding locomotive in "The Goat" (1921), and he must cope with domestic life thanks to "My Wife's Relations" (1922). 115 min. total. Silent with music score.
53-8080 Remastered *$29.99*

Our Hospitality (1923)/ Sherlock, Jr. (1924)
Travelling to antebellum Dixie to claim his family estate, Buster Keaton learns he's also inherited a feud with his new girlfriend's clan. A daring rescue from a waterfall is among the amazing stunts performed by Buster; Natalie Talmadge co-stars. Next, one of the comic's most inventive efforts has movie theatre projectionist Buster entering the film he's running in order to solve a jewelry theft. With Kathryn McGuire and Keaton's father Joseph. 118 min. total. Silent with music score.
53-8081 Remastered *$29.99*

The Navigator (1924)
After buying a 500-foot ocean liner destined for the scrap heap, Buster and company created a story around it, with the comedian as a spoiled playboy who, along with a former girlfriend, are the sole occupants of a ship cast adrift on the ocean. Two shorts find Keaton in other nautical problems when he builds "The Boat" (1921) in his basement, and then is stuck on a shipload of scoundrels in "The Love Nest" (1923). 110 min. total. Silent with music score.
53-8113 Remastered *$29.99*

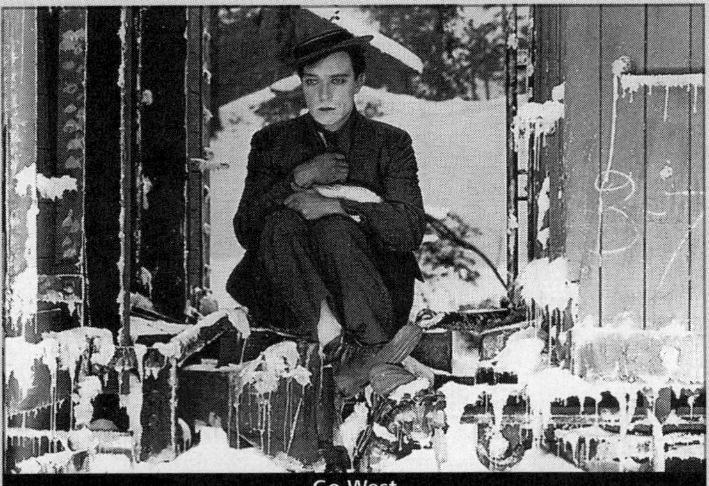

Go West

Buster Keaton

Seven Chances (1925)
When he stands to inherit a fortune if he can get married by 7 o'clock, Buster Keaton becomes the quarry of an army of would-be brides (and gets caught in a shower of boulders) in the feature presentation. Next, a high fence can't keep Buster from his next-door girlfriend in "Neighbors" (1921), and he takes to the sky as "The Balloonatic" (1923). 114 min. total. Silent with music score.
53-8114 Remastered *$29.99*

Go West (1925)
Followed by his faithful cow, Buster Keaton sets out to find his fortune on the frontier in his wonderful Western spoof. Plus, Buster's fascination with gadgets is evident in the short "The Scarecrow" (1920), and he then returns to the prairie and is taken in by an Indian tribe as "The Paleface." 116 min. total. Silent with music score.
53-8115 Remastered *$29.99*

Battling Butler (1926)
In order to impress a girl, milquetoast Buster Keaton passes himself off as famed boxer "Battling" Butler, only to wind up facing the real McCoy in a fight, in this mix of slapstick and pathos. With Sally O'Neil and Francis McDonald. Plus, two short subjects find Buster getting spooked in "The Haunted House" (1921) and as a Mountie trying to get his man in "The Frozen North" (1922). 115 min. total. Silent with music score.
53-8116 Remastered *$29.99*

The General (1927)
One of the truly great film comedies, based on a true Civil War incident. Keaton is a Southern railroad engineer whose beloved train (with fiancée Helen Mack on board) is hijacked by Union forces. His rescue of both leads to a classic locomotive chase and some hilarious stunts. Next, enter "The Playhouse" (1921), a vaudeville venue where every character in the opening scene is played by Buster, and then watch him try to avoid an army of "Cops" (1922) out to catch him. 120 min. total. Silent with music score.
53-8118 *$29.99*

College (1927)
University life is spoofed in this Buster Keaton feature with him playing a bookish student who tries to woo a co-ed with an eye for athletes. Anne Cornwall, Harold Goodwin co-star. Next, Buster is found under the spreading chestnut tree as "The Blacksmith" (1922), tries unsuccessfully to take his own life in the long-lost "Hard Luck" (1921), and is hired to automate a college dean's home after being mistaken for an electrical engineer in "The Electric House" (1921). 130 min. total. Silent with music score.
53-8119 *$29.99*

Steamboat Bill, Jr. (1928)
Foppish college boy Buster Keaton returns home and tries to win the respect of his riverboat captain father in this silent comedy that abounds with classic Keaton gags, including the famous falling housefront scene. Ernest Torrence, Marion Bryon co-star. Then, two shorts find Buster on death row in "Convict 13" (1920), and having some fantastic "Daydreams" (1922). 115 min. total. Silent with music score.
53-8120 Remastered *$29.99*

The Cameraman (1928)
Tintype photographer Buster Keaton tries to become a newsreel lensman to impress his girl, but his double-exposed footage of battleships sailing up Broadway make his prospects look dim. Keaton's first MGM feature after years of independent production was, ironically, also one of his most successful; with Marceline Day, Vernon Dent. 70 min. Silent with original piano score.
12-2143 *$29.99*

Spite Marriage (1929)
Lovestruck pants presser Buster Keaton is thrilled when his dream girl, stage star Dorothy Sebastian, says "yes" to his marriage proposal, unaware it's only because her leading man jilted her. When Buster learns the truth, he sets out to prove himself worthy of her. Keaton's last silent movie features a great scene of Buster trying to put his drunken wife to bed. 82 min. Silent with original music score.
12-2223 *$29.99*

Free And Easy (1930)
In his first sound film, Buster Keaton plays the hapless manager of a small-town beauty contest winner who is given a Hollywood screen test, only to have it ruined by Keaton's studio misadventures. Great backstage look at the MGM lots include cameos by C.B. DeMille and Lionel Barrymore; with Anita Page, Robert Montgomery. 92 min.
12-2586 *$19.99*

Doughboys (1930)
Rib-tickling effort from Buster Keaton casts him as a wealthy man who finds himself mistakenly recruited into the Army during World War I. Following a hilarious stint in the forces, he returns to the business world by hiring his Army cronies. Sally Eilers and Cliff ("Ukulele Ike") Edwards co-star. 80 min.
12-2553 *$19.99*

Speak Easily (1931)
Funny slapstick vehicle for MGM's comedy teaming of Buster Keaton and Jimmy Durante. As a stodgy professor and his freewheeling butler, the duo go on a madcap spending spree and become "angels" in a stage show. With Thelma Todd, Sidney Toler, Hedda Hopper. 82 min.
12-2552 *$19.99*

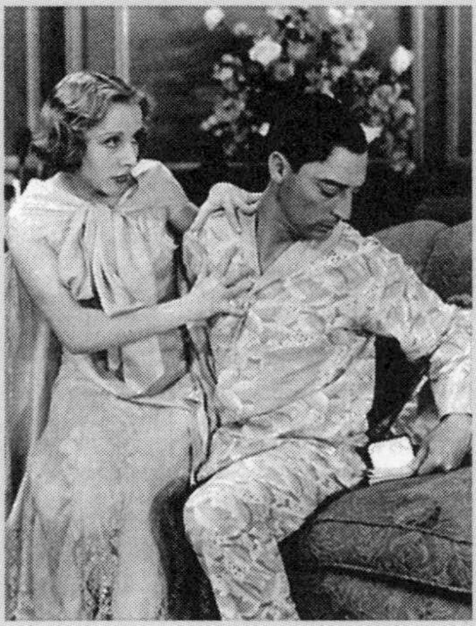

Parlor, Bedroom & Bath (1931)
One of Keaton's early talkies for MGM was this adaptation of a hit Broadway comedy. Buster is a shy bachelor mistaken for a great lover, and he's too embarrassed to tell anyone. Features a party scene shot at the Keaton estate. 74 min.
62-1062 *$19.99*

Sidewalks Of New York (1931)
Buster Keaton's early talkie casts him as the rich owner of an apartment building who takes an interest in some of the neighborhood's poor kids and becomes romantically involved with one of the building's tenants. Anita Page and Cliff Edwards also star; directed by Jules White of "Three Stooges" fame. 74 min.
12-2820 *$19.99*

What! No Beer? (1933)
Prohibition-era comedy stars Buster Keaton and Jimmy Durante as two would-be bootleggers whose plans of cornering the local beer market go hilariously awry. Phyllis Barry, Roscoe Ates co-star. 66 min.
12-2587 *$19.99*

An Old Spanish Custom (1936)
Obscure Buster Keaton sound film, in which he plays Leander Proudfoot, a romantic sap caught up in a love triangle. In reality, he's being used by Lupita Tovar to protect her real lover! Wild comedy; directed by Adrian Brunel. AKA: "The Invader." 58 min.
62-1196 Was $19.99 *$14.99*

The Villain Still Pursued Her (1940)
Buster Keaton, Anita Louise and Billy Gilbert in a riotous tale about an evil snake out to foreclose the mortgage on the good guys. Exaggerated hijinks and a wild pie fight. 67 min.
09-1558 *$19.99*

Boom In The Moon (1945)
Filmed in Mexico, this extremely rare Buster Keaton effort features the "Great Stone Face" as an ex-soldier who is mistaken for a killer and sent to jail, where he and another convict are "volunteered" for a scientist's planned lunar launch. Angel Grassa, Virginia Serret also star. 83 min.
27-6243 *$19.99*

Buster Keaton TV Scrapbook
Two rare films spotlight Keaton's TV work in the '50s. First Buster is the guest of honor on "This Is Your Life," with appearances by Red Skelton and Donald O'Connor. Next, watch him as a slapstick sleuth in "The Detective," an episode from Buster's early TV series. 60 min. total.
01-5147 *$19.99*

The Buster Keaton Show (1950)
Two rare TV shows with the comic great. First, Buster works out at a gym and winds up boxing in a ring; then "The Great Stone Face" uses his ingenuity...and some taffy...to nab some crooks. Includes original Studebaker commercials. 60 min.
10-8156 *$19.99*

The Railrodder (1965)/ Buster Keaton Rides Again (1965)
Produced by the National Film Board of Canada, the silent short comedy "Railrodder" follows Buster Keaton on a slapstick coast-to-coast ride across Canada on a motorized handcar and features some of the famous stunt work that made Keaton famous. Also included is a documentary look at 69-year-old Buster on the set, improvising scenes and mugging with his wife. 81 min. total.
09-1533 *$29.99*

Buster Keaton: A Hard Act To Follow: Complete Set
He was one of the first and greatest comedic talents in film history. Now the full story of Buster Keaton's rise, fall and rediscovery is told in this three-part British-made documentary series that features clips from Keaton's movies, interviews with friends and co-stars, and more. Volumes include "From Vaudeville to Movies," "Star without a Studio" and "A Genius Recognized." 150 min. total. NOTE: Individual volumes available at $19.99 each.
44-2209 *$59.99*

Buster Keaton
The life and times of "The Great Stone Face" are presented in this film biography. His childhood in vaudeville, silent classics such as "Cops," "Balloonatic," "Fatty at Coney Island" and "The General," his fall from grace in the '30s and rediscovery in the '50s are traced with interviews, rare footage and stills. Henry Morgan narrates. 60 min.
52-1005 Was $69.99 *$39.99*

The Art Of Buster Keaton: Boxed Set No. 1
This special three-tape collector's set includes "The Saphead," "The High Sign," "One Week," "The Three Ages," "The Goat," "My Wife's Relations," "Our Hospitality" and "Sherlock, Jr."
53-8082 Save $10.00! *$79.99*

The Art Of Buster Keaton: Boxed Set No. 2
"The Navigator," "The Boat," "The Love Nest," "Seven Chances," "Neighbors," "The Balloonatic," "Go West," "The Scarecrow," "The Paleface," "Battling Butler," "The Haunted House" and "The Frozen North" are all gathered on this four-tape collector's set.
53-8117 Save $10.00! *$109.99*

The Art Of Buster Keaton: Boxed Set No. 3
This special three-tape collector's set includes "The General," "The Playhouse," "Cops," "College," "The Blacksmith," "The Electric House," "Hard Luck," "Steamboat Bill, Jr.," "Convict 13" and "Daydreams."
53-8121 Save $10.00! *$79.99*

Please see our index for these other Buster Keaton titles: *The Adventures Of Huckleberry Finn • A Funny Thing Happened On The Way To The Forum • God's Country • How To Stuff A Wild Bikini • Li'l Abner • Limelight • The Lovable Cheat*

Riding For Life (1927)
After his brother, an express office clerk, is duped into getting involved in a robbery, an honest rancher must clear him of criminal charges. Bob Reeves stars. 61 min. Silent with organ score.
09-2314 *$14.99*

Married? (1926)
The rich and pampered heiress (Constance Bennett) of a timber company and the rough and tumble lumberman (Owen Moore) who manages the land are forced into a marriage of convenience to save the business in this silent tale that mixes comedy, action and romance. 62 min. Silent with music score.
09-3126 *$14.99*

Old Ironsides (1926)
Oliver Wendell Holmes' 1830 poem "Constitution" is translated magnificently to the silver screen in this grand silent adventure. Wallace Beery, Boris Karloff and Charles Farrell are three able-bodied merchant marines tussling with pirates in the Mediterranean Sea. 111 min. Silent with organ score by Gaylord Carter.
06-1436 Was $29.99 *$14.99*

The Mad Whirl (1925)
A social drama set during the Roaring Twenties focusing on the Herrington family. Dad and Mom are middle-aged "swingers" whose son follows in their wild ways until he meets a nice, church-going gal whose parents don't approve of him. Will the young couple get past their parental problems and have a lasting romance? May McAvoy, Jack Mulhall stars. 64 min. Silent with music score.
09-2939 *$19.99*

My Boy (1921)
After stealing "The Kid" from co-star Charlie Chaplin, Jackie Coogan got top billing in this melodrama as an immigrant child whose mother dies on the boat ride to America. Threatened with deportation, Coogan escapes from the Ellis Island authorities and makes his way to New York, where he's taken in by crusty old sailor Claude Gillingwater. 53 min. Silent with music score.
09-3120 *$19.99*

Ace Of Clubs (1925)
Al Hoxie, Minna Redman and Andrew Waldon star in this silent thriller about an eerie killer who leaves an ace of clubs as his murder calling card. 90 min. Silent with musical score.
09-5037 *$19.99*

Campus Knights (1924)
Funny silent effort starring Raymond McKee in dual roles, playing both a professor and his girl-chasing twin brother. Shirley Palmer, Marie Quillen and Jean Laverty co-star. 58 min. Silent with musical score.
09-5038 *$14.99*

Ace Of Cactus Range (1924)
A frontier U.S. marshal must take on a dangerous gang of diamond smugglers who have taken a young woman and her father hostage in this early western drama. Art Mix, Virginia Warwick, Clifford Davidson star. 57 min.
09-5351 *$19.99*

The Virginian (1923)
Accomplished silent renditon of Owen Wister's frontier tale stars Kenneth Hanlan as the nameless ranch foreman who faces off against Trampas, his best friend, after discovering that he's part of a group of cattle rustlers. Kenneth Harlan, Florence Vidor and Russell Simpson star. 85 min. Silent with music score.
09-5353 *$19.99*

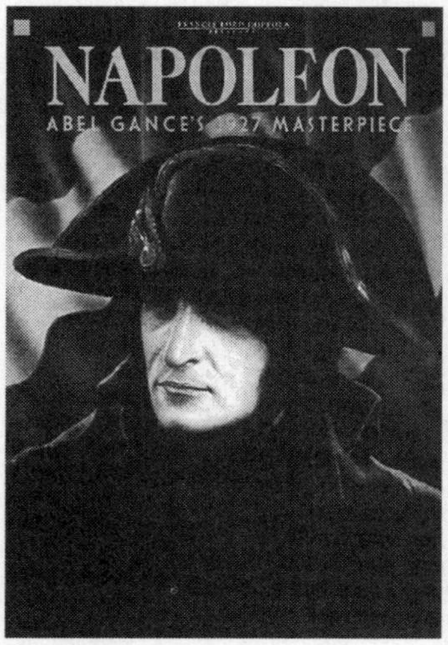

Napoleon (1927)
Abel Gance's rediscovered silent epic of the Little Colonel's youth and rise to power during the French Revolution is breathtaking in its scope and revolutionary use of split screen and camera effects, including the three-screen climax (preserved here in a special format). Albert Dieudonne is nothing short of amazing in the title role. 235 min. Silent with music score.
07-1428 *$29.99*

A Corner In Wheat & Selected Biograph Shorts
From 1908 to 1913 pioneering filmmaker D.W. Griffith directed over 400 one- and two-reel movies for the Biograph company. Along with the farm drama "A Corner in Wheat," this tape includes Lillian and Dorothy Gish's film debut in "An Unseen Enemy," "The Mothering Heart," "The New York Hat" with Mary Pickford, "His Trust," "The Unchanging Sea," "The Sealed Room" and "Those Awful Hats." 118 min.
53-7757 *$24.99*

The Musketeers Of Pig Alley & Selected Biograph Shorts
More of Griffith's innovative silent shorts made for Biograph from 1912 to 1913, with such future stars as Lillian Gish and Mae Marsh. "The Musketeers of Pig Alley," a 1912 urban drama considered to be the first gangster film, is followed by the early Western "The Battle of Elderbush Gulch," "Death's Marathon," "One Is Business, the Other Crime," "The Painted Lady," "The Sunbeam" and "The Burglar's Dilemma." 117 min.
53-7758 *$24.99*

The Female Of The Species & Selected Biograph Shorts
Such daring (for their time) topics as insanity, drug abuse, and the life of Native Americans were brought to the screen by Griffith in these early Biograph short subjects. "The Female of the Species" (1912) is followed by "The Redman's View (1909)," "The House of Darkness (1913)," "In the Border States" (1910) and "For His Son" (1911). 90 min.
53-8624 *$24.99*

Judith Of Bethulia (1913)
D.W. Griffith's first feature film was this adaptation of the Old Testament story of a Jewish woman who single-handedly kills her city's invading general and saves her people. Blanche Sweet, Lionel Barrymore, and Lillian and Dorothy Gish star. 55 min. Silent with musical score.
63-1544 *$19.99*

The Birth Of A Nation (1915)
The landmark silent drama that defined the cinematic medium is here in its complete, uncut version. Director D.W. Griffith's sweeping, controversial look at the American South during and after the Civil War, and the rise of the Ku Klux Klan, stars Lillian Gish, Mae Marsh and Wallace Reid. 180 min. Silent with music score.
63-1450 *$19.99*

The Birth Of A Nation
This special edition of D.W. Griffith's silent film includes the 30-minute documentary "Making 'The Birth of a Nation'," which features rare production information and never-before-seen outtakes. 217 min. total.
53-7775 *$39.99*

Intolerance (1916)
In response to critics of "Birth of a Nation," Griffith created this lavish melodrama that chronicles man's greed and prejudices through the ages and juxtaposes these vignettes against a modern tale of urban woes. For many years Hollywood's most expensive film; the all-star cast includes Lillian Gish, Constance Talmadge, Erich von Stroheim and Bessie Love. 138 min. Silent with music score.
63-1578 Remastered *$19.99*

A Romance Of Happy Valley (1918)
Young Kentucky lad Robert Harron leaves his rural home—as well as sweetheart Lillian Gish—and sets out to seek his fortune in New York City. Will a toy frog be his key to success and his ticket home? D.W. Griffith directed and wrote this pastoral melodrama. 77 min. Silent with music score.
09-1446 *$19.99*

Hearts Of The World (1918)
Shot on location in France, this WWI drama from D.W. Griffith was made to bolster American and British war morale. Fine performances from the Gish sisters (it was Lillian's starring feature debut), their mother Mary, and Eric von Stroheim highlight the story of young lovers separated by battle. 100 min. Silent with musical score.
63-1543 *$19.99*

True Heart Susie (1919)
D.W. Griffith's moving silent drama about a farm girl who makes a sacrifice to send her boyfriend to college. Lillian Gish stars in this saga of loves lost and loves found. 93 min. Silent with music score; recorded at correct projection speed.
09-1327 Was $29.99 *$24.99*

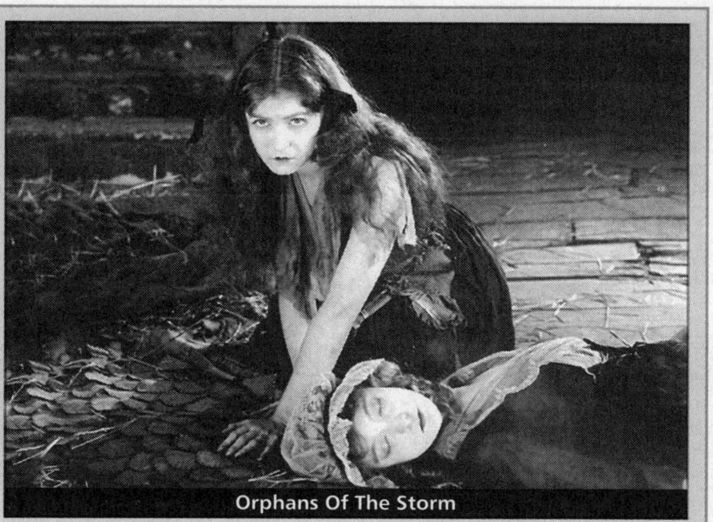
Orphans Of The Storm

D.W. Griffith

Broken Blossoms (1919)
Tragic and poetic D.W. Griffith drama about a young girl who leaves her abusive boxer father and finds friendship with a Chinese shopkeeper in London's Limehouse district. Lillian Gish, Richard Barthelmess star. 76 min. Silent with musical score.
63-1541 *$19.99*

The Idol Dancer (1920)
One of D.W. Griffith's lesser-known efforts, this sumptuous drama is set at Rainbow Beach, a missionary stronghold in the South Pacific where a rebellious native girl named White Almond Flower is desired by both a derelict adventurer and a missionary's invalid son. Creighton Hale and Richard Barthelmess star. 91 min. Silent with music score.
09-2940 *$19.99*

The Love Flower (1920)
Pioneering filmmaker D.W. Griffith directed this tale of love and crimes of passion. The lives of three people—a man, his second wife, and his only daughter—are jolted when a brilliant detective who knows about the man's shady past arrives on the West Indian island where they live. Richard Barthelmess and Carol Dempster star. 104 min. Silent with music score.
09-3144 *$19.99*

Way Down East (1920)
"A Simple Story of Plain People" from director D.W. Griffith. Lillian Gish is a young girl betrayed and left with child by a rich bounder. Will she be able to keep her baby and find true love? Features a chase on a frozen river that sent Griffith to the hospital when dynamite exploded prematurely. With Richard Barthelmess. 149 min. Silent with music score.
53-7759 *$24.99*

Dream Street (1921)
Set in London's sordid Limehouse district, this morality play from D.W. Griffith features Carol Dempster as a music hall dancer who eventually finds happiness in the arms of a street tough. Costars Ralph Graves, Charles Emmett Mack. Silent with music score.
10-9997 *$29.99*

Orphans Of The Storm (1921)
Sweeping D.W. Griffith drama stars Dorothy and Lillian Gish as two peasant girls raised as sisters who are caught up in the turmoil of the French Revolution. Joseph Schildkraut, Morgan Wallace co-star. 150 min. Silent with music score.
53-8626 Remastered *$24.99*

America (1924)
Conceived by director D.W. Griffith as the first in a series of films tracing the country's history, this lavish drama follows the main events of the Revolutionary War as seen through the eyes of young lovers Neil Hamilton and Carol Dempster, whose families stand on opposing sides of the conflict. With Lionel Barrymore, Charles Emmett Mack, and Arthur Dewey as George Washington. Includes color-tinted sequences. 141 min. Silent with music score.
53-8623 Remastered *$24.99*

Isn't Life Wonderful (1924)
Set in a poverty-riddled post-WWI Berlin, this unusual social drama by D.W. Griffith stars Carole Dempster as a Polish war orphan who struggles to help support the German family she lives with and Neil Hamilton as the ex-soldier who falls in love with her. 115 min. Silent with music score.
53-8625 Remastered *$24.99*

Sorrows Of Satan (1926)
Lavish fantasy directed by D.W. Griffith, involving a struggling writer who strikes a deal with a suave prince (Satan in disguise) to experience wealth and the good life in return for his destiny. Ricardo Cortez, Adolphe Menjou, Lya De Putti and Carol Dempster star in this film highlighted by some stunning segments. 110 min.
10-9112 *$19.99*

The Battle Of The Sexes (1928)
Based on a story he first filmed in 1914, this unusual comedy/drama from director D.W. Griffith follows a well-to-do family man (Jean Hersholt) who falls under the spell of a young flapper (Phyllis Haver). When Hersholt's daughter tries to straighten things out, she winds up in the clutches of a suave gigolo. With Sally O'Neil. 88 min. Silent with music score.
53-6718 *$24.99*

D.W. Griffith: Father Of Film: Boxed Set
He was Hollywood's first great director, but by the end of the '20s his career was essentially over. Follow the life of film pioneer D.W. Griffith, whose work included over 500 movies, in this three-volume documentary by David Gill and Kenneth Brownlow. Rare home movie footage, interviews with family and such colleagues as Lillian Gish and Blanche Sweet, and clips from "The Birth of a Nation," "Intolerance" and other Griffith milestones are included. 153 min. total. NOTE: Individual volumes available at $19.99 each.
44-2232 *$59.99*

Braveheart (1925)
The bitter feud between Native Americans and whites over fishing rights in the Northwest serves as the backdrop for this unusual silent drama. Braveheart, an Indian youth studying law at an Eastern college, contends with "the Salmon King," a nasty white businessman who's monopolizing the winter food supply of Braveheart's people. Rod LaRoque, Lillian Rich, Tyrone Power, Sr. star. 50 min. Silent with music score.
09-5380 *$19.99*

Sweet Adeline (1925)
Charles Ray plays a homespun young man with a desire to go into show business who competes against his brother for the attention of Gertrude Olmstead, the prettiest gal around. He takes to the road, eventually gets his start by belting out a sensational rendition of "Sweet Adeline" and wins over Adeline herself. Jack Clifford co-stars. 60 min. Silent with musical score.
10-9773 *$19.99*

Kismet (1920)
The first filming of the Arabian Nights-themed drama that was remade for Marlene Dietrich in 1944 and as an MGM musical in 1955, this silent thriller stars noted actor Otis Skinner re-creating his stage role as Bagdad beggar Hajj, whose beautiful daughter is coveted by a wicked caliph. With Herschell Mayall, Elinor Fair. 95 min.
09-5352 *$19.99*

Crossed Signals (1926)
There's railroad action a-plenty in this silent drama about a government agent enlisted to bring in a gang of counterfeiters. Helping to save the day is screen queen Helen Holmes, who gets involved in the film's finale aboard a speeding locomotive. Also on the tape is "Hot Sands" (1924), a short comedy set in an amusement park starring Monty Banks. Silent with music score.
09-5358 *$19.99*

The Cheerful Fraud (1927)
When the one true love of a wealthy young man chooses to keep her distance from him, he is forced to take a job as her family's butler in order to stay close to her. Of course, there comes a time when both butler and boyfriend must appear at the same place in this silent romantic romp. Reginald Denny, Gertrude Astor star. 64 min.
10-9794 *$19.99*

Ben-Hur (1925)
Plagued by production problems during its three-year filming, this silent rendition of Lew Wallace's Imperial Rome saga is one of the most spectacular achievements of early Hollywood. Ramon Novarro and Francis X. Bushman star as the former friends whose bitter rivalry climaxes in the legendary chariot race sequence (here in its original Technicolor). 148 min. Silent with stereo music score.
12-1831 *$29.99*

Douglas Fairbanks

The Lamb (1915)
Douglas Fairbanks made his starring film debut in this comedy-adventure supervised by D.W. Griffith. He's a meek "Son of the Idle Rich" whose relationship with his girl is threatened when a muscular fellow enters the picture. In order to prove his bravery, Fairbanks is put on the spot during a Yacqui Indian rebellion. With Seena Owen. 56 min. Silent with music score.
09-2945 *$14.99*

His Picture In The Papers (1916)
Dashing Doug's in fine fettle in this breezy comedy. As the hard-living son of a health food magnate, he'll get half the business (and his best girl's hand) only if he pulls off an attention-getting publicity stunt. 68 min. Silent with music score.
09-1936 *$24.99*

Manhattan Madness (1916)
New York playboy Douglas Fairbanks, eager for some adventure, trades in his top hat and spats for six-guns and chaps and moves to the rugged terrain of Nevada. He's called back East, though, to unravel a mystery involving a stolen necklace, a count and a damsel in distress. Jewel Carmen co-stars. Silent with music score.
10-9999 *$19.99*

Reggie Mixes In (1916)
D.W. Griffith supervised the production of this fine comedy-drama starring Douglas Fairbanks as a wealthy young man who lives a privileged, lazy existence. His life changes when he helps a lost girl return to her slum home and falls for the child's mother, a dancer at a rough saloon. Fairbanks takes a job as the bar's bouncer in order to woo her. With Bessie Love. 45 min. Silent with music score.
09-2926 *$19.99*

American Aristocracy (1916)
Sparkling satire of America's *nouveau riche* stars Douglas Fairbanks as an athletic entomologist who goes to a hoity-toity New England resort to find a rare caterpillar. While feeling out of place among the rich and famous, Fairbanks falls for the daughter of the country's hat-pin king. With Jewel Carmen. 48 min. Silent with music score.
09-2935 *$14.99*

The Mollycoddle (1920)/ Flirting With Fate (1916)
This comedic Douglas Fairbanks double bill starts off with Doug in the title role of "The Mollycoddle," a foppish young man who comes of age when he tackles a smuggling gang in Arizona. With Wallace Beery, Ruth Renick. Next, Fairbanks is "Flirting with Fate" as a depressed artist who hires a man to kill him, then must escape him when his girl returns and he inherits a fortune. Jewel Carmen co-stars. 143 min. total. Silent with music score.
53-8521 *$24.99*

The Nut (1921)/ The Matrimaniac (1916)
Before becoming typecast in costume action roles, Douglas Fairbanks made his name in fast-paced comedies such as the two in this program. "The Nut" finds him playing a New York inventor who uses a variety of tricks to help his social worker girlfriend and features a cameo by Fairbanks' UA partner Charlie Chaplin. As "The Matrimaniac," Doug travels by auto, train and more to be by true love Constance Talmadge's side, much to her father's disapproval. 120 min. total. Silent with music score.
53-8522 *$24.99*

The Americano (1917)
American engineer Douglas Fairbanks gets in the middle of problems in a Caribbean republic where the country's pro-American officials are battling against the Minister of War, who's plotting a takeover. Fairbanks performs some amazing stunts and falls in love with an island beauty. 54 min. Silent with music score.
09-2370 *$19.99*

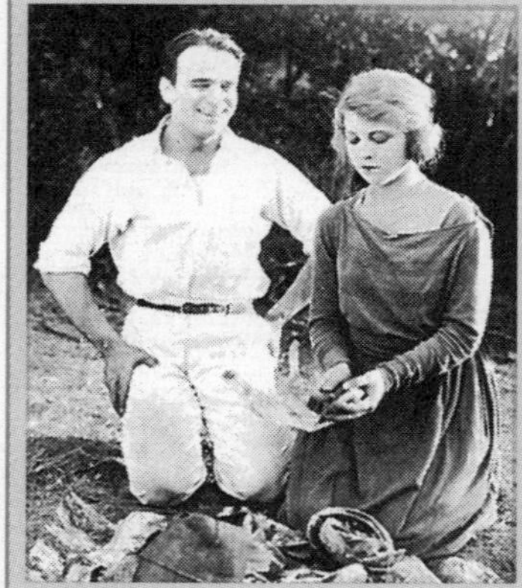

Down To Earth (1917)
Hunter Douglas Fairbanks pines for his childhood girlfriend, who has become a socialite married to an oily aristocrat. After she suffers emotional problems because of her boring lifestyle, Fairbanks tries to save her and the other people in the rest home where she's staying. A first-rate comedy. Silent with music score.
09-2934 *$19.99*

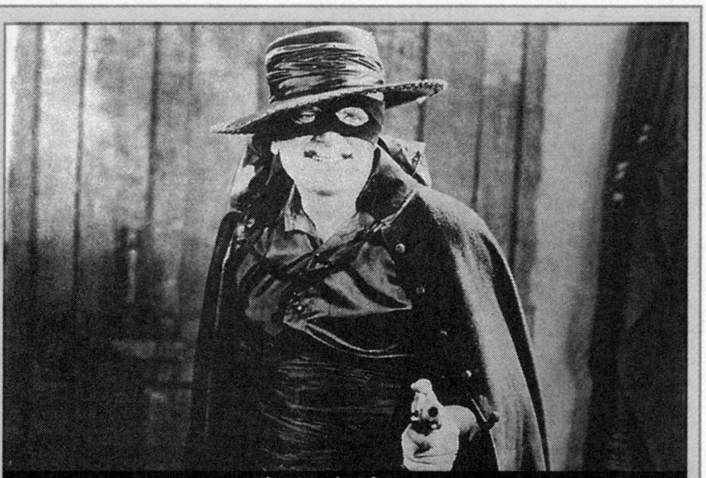

The Mark Of Zorro

Reaching For The Moon (1917)
Douglas Fairbanks parodies his flamboyant heroic image, as a button factory worker's rampant imagination lands him on the throne of Vulgaria—and into the arms of a homely princess! Unrelated to a later Fairbanks film of the same title, this costume comedy also stars Eileen Percy, Frank Campeau. 62 min. Silent with music score.
09-5394 *$19.99*

Wild And Woolly (1917)
In this comedy-drama that doesn't skimp on the stunts, Douglas Fairbanks pokes fun at his earlier roles. He's an Eastern dude obsessed with the Old West, but when his chance to visit the "wide open spaces" comes, it's nothing like what he expects. Written by Anita Loos. 58 min. Silent with music score.
09-5402 *$19.99*

The Man From Painted Post (1917)
Douglas Fairbanks decides to dress like a city slicker in order to beat a gang of rustlers and win a pretty gal in this thrilling silent sagebrush saga.
10-8246 Was $19.99 *$14.99*

When The Clouds Roll By (1919)
Surreal comedy/action tale with Douglas Fairbanks as a superstitious young man who becomes the victim of a mad scientist's experiments on the power of hypnotic suggestion. Fairbanks has strange nightmares and loses his job and his fiancée after he's framed for stealing oil property from her father. Can he regain his senses in time to put things right? 79 min. Silent with music score.
09-2929 *$19.99*

His Majesty, The American (1919)
The first film Douglas Fairbanks made for United Artists, a company he co-founded, is a swashbuckling adventure with Doug as the rightful heir to the throne of a European nation who takes on the conspirators out to rule the country themselves. With Marjorie Daw and, in an uncredited role, Boris Karloff.
10-8368 *$19.99*

The Mark Of Zorro (1920)
The original! Douglas Fairbanks is the foppish Don Diego, who dons cape and mask to protect the peasants of Old California as the dashing "Zorro, the Fox." Noah Beery, Marguerite de la Motte also star in this, the standard-setter for all subsequent swashbuckler films. 90 min. Silent with music score.
63-1457 *$19.99*

The Three Musketeers (1921)
A lavish silent screen adaptation of the adventure classic, with Douglas Fairbanks a suitably dashing D'Artagnan, lending his sword to the efforts of king's fighters Leon Barry, Eugene Pallette and George Siegmann to save the queen's honor from the schemes of Cardinal Richelieu. With Adolphe Menjou, Barbara LaMarr. 119 min. Silent with music score.
53-8475 Remastered *$24.99*

Robin Hood (1922)
Douglas Fairbanks was seldom more dashing as Robin of Locksley in this wonderful, elaborate production. Magnificent, opulent sets, fights in the fabulous Fairbanks manner, much more; with Wallace Beery, Enid Bennett, and Alan Hale Sr. in his first foray as Little John. 170 min. Silent with musical score.
10-7237 *$19.99*

The Thief Of Bagdad (1924)
Roguish pickpurse Douglas Fairbanks sets out on a dangerous quest to win the hand of beautiful princess Julanne Johnston over an evil warlord in this classic silent fantasy. Thrilling swordfights, an underwater dragon and flying carpet chase are just some of the highlights. Raoul Walsh directed, with set design by William Cameron Menzies. 155 min. Silent with music score.
53-8518 Remastered *$24.99*

Don Q, Son Of Zorro (1925)
Douglas Fairbanks essays four roles in this classic swashbuckling sequel, including both the title role of the irrepressible son, Cesar de Vega, and of his legendary father. With Mary Astor, Donald Crisp and Warner Oland; directed by Crisp. 113 min.
62-5092 *$19.99*

The Black Pirate (1926)
Perhaps Douglas Fairbanks' finest role was as the "king of the buccaneers" in this epic silent adventure, presented here in a restored Technicolor print. Out to avenge his father's murder by pirates, Doug soon becomes the leader of the Jolly Roger. Features the breathtaking scene of Fairbanks sliding down an enemy ship's sail with his sword, slicing it in half. With Billie Dove, Donald Crisp. Also includes a special "video scrapbook" of rare outtakes and stills. 90 min. Silent with music score.
53-8514 Remastered *$24.99*

The Gaucho (1928)
In a villainous change-of-pace role, Douglas Fairbanks plays a roguish South American horseman who seeks a fabled holy city built into the mountains in hopes of robbing it, but later becomes its unlikely defender from a horde of bandits. With Lupe Velez, Germaine Greear, and a cameo by Mary Pickford as "Our Lady of the Shrine." 96 min. Silent with music score.
53-8517 Remastered *$24.99*

The Iron Mask (1929)
The last silent swashbuckler for Douglas Fairbanks has him re-creating his "Three Musketeers" role of D'Artagnan, here joining with his old comrades to protect the King of France from a plan by evil Cardinal Richelieu to put an impostor on the throne. Marguerite de la Motte, Nigel de Brulier co-star. 72 min. Silent with music score.
63-1548 *$19.99*

The Iron Mask
This special 1952 re-issue version of the silent Douglas Fairbanks action classic features narration by Douglas Fairbanks, Jr. and a full orchestral score. 72 min.
53-8516 Remastered *$24.99*

Reaching For The Moon (1931)
Depression-influenced comedy stars Douglas Fairbanks, Sr. as a financier whose setbacks are driving him to drink much to the consternation of valet Edward Everett Horton. Witty comedy (which began as an Irving Berlin musical until all but one song was excised) co-stars Bebe Daniels and includes a Berlin score and an early performance by Bing Crosby as a member of the Whiteman Rhythm Boys. 62 min.
10-1063 *$19.99*

Mr. Robinson Crusoe (1932)
Tour-de-force performance by Douglas Fairbanks, Sr. as a man who bets $1000 he can live on a primitive island without the comforts of civilization. Great for the family. 70 min.
08-8043 *$19.99*

Million Dollar Mystery (1927)
A secret society known as the "Black Hundred" will stop at nothing from obtaining the fortune an heiress is due to receive from her father, a former member of the group, in this rare silent suspenser. James Kirkwood, Lila Lee star. 64 min.
68-8355 *$19.99*

Devil's Island (1926)
The infamous French penal colony is the setting for this silent drama of an army surgeon who is convicted of treason and sent to the brutal island penitentary for life. George Lewis, Pauline Frederick star. 80 min.
68-8356 *$19.99*

The Bat (1926)
Considered "lost" for many years, this shadowy silent thriller tells the strange tale of a maniacal killer who disguises himself as a bat and terrorizes people in a frightening old house. Is one of the guests the killer? Jack Pickford, Louis Fazanda star. Silent with music score.
68-8724 Was $19.99 *$14.99*

Ships Of The Night (1928)
A woman searches for her missing brother and meets crooks, pirates and harem slaves during her adventure. It turns out that her brother is sought by authorities in a killing he did not commit. Jacqueline Logan, Jack Mower star.
68-8816 *$19.99*

The Old Oregon Trail (1928)
Shot-in-Oregon six-shooter saga in which a group of settlers are helped by lovable cowboys when an unscrupulous rancher holds them at bay. Funny thing is, a similar situation occurred years before. Art Mix, Delores Booth and Art Seales star. Silent with music score.
68-9140 *$19.99*

No Man's Law (1928)
Called "the most erotic 'B' western of all time" by experts, this sizzling sagebrusher offers Barbara Kent as a seductive western woman who, along with her mining stepfather, is the target of two thugs (one of whom is played by the great Oliver Hardy!). Theodore Von Eltz and James Finlayson star. Silent with music score.
68-9145 *$19.99*

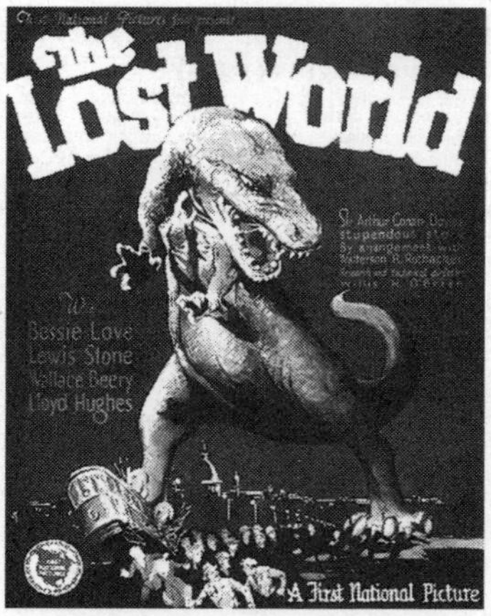

The Lost World (1925)
Silent fantasy classic based on Arthur Conan Doyle's tale of explorers who find prehistoric animals alive atop a remote plateau in the heart of the Amazon stars Wallace Beery, Lewis Stone and Bessie Love. Special video version includes the film's original color-tinted sequences and trailers, scenes from other films by special effects artist Willis O'Brien, and a re-creation of scenes lost since the movie's premiere. 90 min. total. Silent with music score.
80-5020 Was $39.99 *$24.99*

The Wildcat (1926)
Superior western adventure in which pro boxer Gordon Clifford heads to an isolated ranch to train for a big fight. He soon faces problems caused by an ornery foreman. Charlotte Pierce and Frank Bond also star. Silent with music score.
68-9146 *$19.99*

King Of Wild Horses (1924)
Leon Barry and Edna Murphy star in this rousing sagebrush saga in which cowboy Barry seeks a wild horse named "the Black." At the same time, the cowpoke wants the hand of a local rancher's daughter and has to stop a ranch foreman's devious plot. Silent with music score.
68-9148 *$19.99*

Cactus Trails (1926)
Jack Perrin is a war hero who returns to his old job as a cow-puncher to encounter a series of exciting adventures involving a woman he saves from a runaway carriage and a group of ornery kidnappers. Alma Rayford also stars. Silent with music score.
68-9151 *$19.99*

Western Courage (1926)
A pretty girl has the hots for a slick con man, but cowboy Dick Hatton exposes the con for what he's worth in this energetic sagebrusher. With Robert Walker, Elsa Benham. Silent with music score.
68-9153 *$19.99*

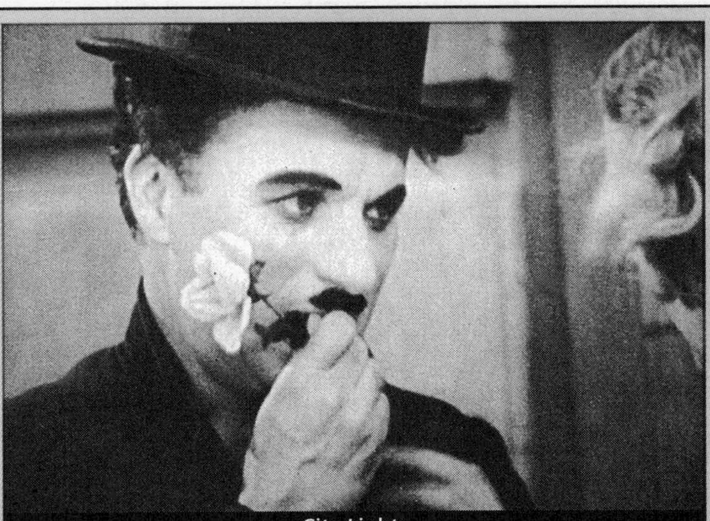

City Lights

Charlie Chaplin

Charlie Chaplin At Keystone Studios
Follow Charlie's first Hollywood film roles as a member of Mack Sennett's comedy troupe, and watch the evolution of his Little Tramp persona in these four one-reel shorts. Includes "Making a Living," "Caught in a Cabaret," "Mabel's Busy Day" and "The Rounders." 43 min.
53-7747 *$19.99*

Chaplin's Essanay Comedies, Vol. 1
Charlie Chaplin's "Little Tramp" screen persona, first seen in the Keystone shorts, was perfected during his 1915-16 tenure at Essanay Studios. "His New Job" (1915), the first Essanay film, finds prop man Charlie turning a movie studio upside-down; Ben Turpin and a young Gloria Swanson also appear. Chaplin and Turpin next are inebriated pals on "A Night Out" (1915); sparring partner Charlie becomes "The Champion" (1915) with his dog's help; and the tramp helps a pair of lovers he encounters "In the Park" (1915). 110 min. Silent with music score.
53-6509 Remastered *$19.99*

Chaplin's Essanay Comedies, Vol. 2
Charlie poses as a count to save girlfriend Edna Purviance from an arranged marriage in "A Jitney Elopement" (1915). Also, Chaplin's trademark ending of him walking off into the distance was first used in the bittersweet "The Tramp" (1915); Los Angeles's Crystal Pier is the setting for laughs "By the Sea" (1915); and assistant paperhanger Charlie turns "Work" (1915) into comic catastrophe. 96 min. Silent with music score.
53-6510 Remastered *$19.99*

Chaplin's Essanay Comedies, Vol. 3
Will dressing as "A Woman" (1915) give Charlie the chance to see sweetheart Edna Purviance behind her father's back, and can janitor Chaplin win the heart of secretary Edna at "The Bank" (1915) where they both work? Next, Charlie's "Shanghaied" (1915) onto a boat that's about to be wrecked for the insurance money, and his Little Tramp character makes a special guest appearance in the "Broncho Billy" Anderson short "His Regeneration" (1915). 95 min. Silent with music score.
53-6511 Remastered *$19.99*

Chaplin's Essanay Comedies, Vol. 4
Chaplin plays a pair of vaudeville attendees, the drunken Mr. Pest and dissolute Mr. Rowdy, in "A Night in the Show" (1915); the Little Tramp is freed from jail but still runs afoul of "Police" (1915); and Charlie spoofs opera in a "Burlesque of 'Carmen'" (1915), seen here in its original two-reel format. Then, unused footage from "Police" and "Work," along with clips from the uncompleted "Life," were combined by Essanay after Chaplin left the studio for "Triple Trouble" (1918). 105 min. Silent with music score.
53-6512 Remastered *$19.99*

The Chaplin Mutuals, Vol. 1
After leaving Essanay Studios, Charlie Chaplin made 12 short films for the Mutual Film Corporation during the years 1917 and 1918. Featured here are Chaplin finding love in the New World as "The Immigrant" (1917); as an escaped con crashing a society party in "The Adventurer" (1917); as a tipsy socialite who arrives at a sanitarium to take "The Cure" (1917); and as a slum neighborhood's new cop in "Easy Street" (1917). 101 min. Silent with music score.
53-7752 Remastered *$19.99*

The Chaplin Mutuals, Vol. 2
Tailor's aide Charlie and his boss both impersonate a nobleman to impress wealthy Edna Purviance in "The Count" (1916). Chaplin also plays a lovelorn street musician in "The Vagabond" (1916), presented here in a newly-edited, restored edition; helps save the day as "The Fireman" (1916); and spoofs his Sennett days and takes part in his only pie fight in "Behind the Screen" (1916). 100 min. Silent with music score.
53-7750 Remastered *$19.99*

The Chaplin Mutuals, Vol. 3
Whether he's rollerskating in "The Rink" (1916), causing pandemonium in "The Pawnshop" (1916) and as a department store clerk in "The Floorwalker" (1916), or just trying to get into his house for some sleep in "One A.M." (1916), Chaplin is sure to amuse in these classic shorts. 97 min. Silent with music score.
53-7751 Remastered *$19.99*

Tillie's Punctured Romance (1914)
Mack Sennett's slapstick melodrama, considered by many to be the first feature-length comedy, stars Marie Dressler as the simple country gal wooed away to the city by fortune-hungry gigolo Charlie Chaplin (before he developed his tramp persona). With Mabel Normand, the Keystone Kops. 73 min. Silent with music score.
63-1546 *$19.99*

Burlesque Of Carmen (1915)
Charlie Chaplin called the shots and starred in this silent Essanay short that pokes fun at the classic opera from Bizet about the stormy love affair between a lusty Gypsy and a soldier. Also stars Edna Purviance and Ben Turpin.
10-7153 Was $29.99 *$19.99*

The Chaplin Revue
Compiled by Chaplin himself in 1958 and featuring a muscial score he composed, this rib-tickling collection features three of his finest short films. The Little Tramp befriends a mutt in "A Dog's Life" (1918), goes "over the top" in the WWI comedy "Shoulder Arms" (1918), and is an ex-con posing as a preacher in a Texas frontier town in "The Pilgrim" (1923). 126 min.
04-3040 *$19.99*

A Woman Of Paris (1923)/ Sunnyside (1919)
Chaplin wrote and directed this melodrama of a country French girl whose search for love leads to heartbreak. Edna Purviance and Adolphe Menjou star. Next, Chaplin is a hapless hotel handyman in the short "Sunnyside." 111 min. total.
04-3042 *$19.99*

The Kid (1921)/ The Idle Class (1921)
"The Kid" was Charlie Chaplin's first feature-length film and has Chaplin's Little Tramp finding an abandoned baby in an alleyway trashcan. Five years later, Chaplin becomes a glazier, and the kid (now played by Jackie Coogan) helps him get work by breaking windows. But when Edna Purviance, the youngster's opera singer mother, wants him back, Charlie fights the authorities to keep him. And in the classic two-reeler, "The Idle Class," Chaplin plays both the always-in-trouble Tramp, on vacation in Miami, and the high society hubby of neglected Purviance. 85 min. total.
04-3041 *$19.99*

THE GOLD RUSH

The Gold Rush (1925)
Considered by many to be Chaplin's masterpiece and perhaps the finest comedy ever made, this original version of the immortal silent classic finds the Little Tramp caught under an avalanche of hilarious mishaps while in gold rush Yukon, including run-ins with a bear, a starving prospector, a cliff-hanging cabin and a meal as tough as boot leather. Co-stars Mack Swain, Georgia Hale. 88 min. Silent with music score.
63-1564 *$19.99*

The Gold Rush/Pay Day
Unseen for many years, this is the 1942 re-release version of Chaplin's beloved comedy, featuring an all-new music score and Charlie's own narration. Also includes Chaplin's 1922 slapstick ode to the working class, "Pay Day." 95 min. total.
04-2207 *$19.99*

The Circus (1928)
The Little Tramp raises havoc under the big top in a three-ring comedic romp that earned Chaplin a special Academy Award as the film's director/writer/star. Also included on the program is Charlie's 1919 short, "A Day's Pleasure." 90 min. total. Silent with music score.
04-3043 *$19.99*

City Lights (1931)
The Tramp falls in love with a blind girl in this, Chaplin's last fully silent film. Charlie befriends a millionaire drunk in order to get money for his sweetheart's operation. A charming and hilarious film that includes an unforgettable ending. 87 min.
04-3044 Was $19.99 *$14.99*

Modern Times (1936)
Technology and its dehumanizing effects are Charlie's targets in this hilarious spoof. The film is silent except for a gibberish song sung by Chaplin. Paulette Goddard co-stars as a waif he befriends. 89 min. Silent with music score.
04-3045 *$19.99*

The Great Dictator (1940)
In his first full talking film, Chaplin plays two roles, ruthless dictator Adenoid Hynkel of Tomania and a meek Jewish barber. An outlandish and poignant satire of Europe just before WWII, the film co-stars Paulette Goddard and Jack Oakie in his best role, as a Mussolini caricature. 126 min.
04-3046 *$19.99*

Monsieur Verdoux (1947)
Chaplin's most out-of-character role was as a wife murderer in this outrageous black comedy. Martha Raye co-stars as his final and most difficult "conquest." Chaplin co-wrote the story with help from Orson Welles. 123 min.
04-3047 *$19.99*

Limelight (1952)
A bittersweet semi-autobiography stars Chaplin as an aging vaudevillian who finds reason to live when he takes in dancer Claire Bloom. The couple inspire one another to continue in their careers. Chaplin's stage return is highlighted by a hilarious piano skit with Buster Keaton, their only appearance together. 137 min.
04-3048 *$19.99*

A King In New York (1957)
Chaplin's satiric look at American culture and politics of the '50s was banned throughout most of the country when first released, yet seems tame by today's standards. A deposed monarch, played by Chaplin, finds the Big Apple very unfriendly. Co-stars Maxine Audley, Dawn Addams, Jerry Desmonde. 105 min.
04-3049 *$19.99*

A Countess From Hong Kong (1967)
Charlie Chaplin's final directorial effort stars Marlon Brando as a wealthy American diplomat, en route to New York from the Far East on an ocean liner, who falls in love with beautiful Russian countess stowaway Sophia Loren. Romantic comedy features Sydney Chaplin, Tippi Hedren, Margaret Rutherford and, in a cameo playing an elderly steward, Charlie himself. 108 min.
07-2306 *$14.99*

The Eternal Tramp (1975)
The most famous face in all of film comedy, Charlie Chaplin, is saluted in this documentary look at the Little Tramp's life, his early years on the stage, and his award-winning career as actor, writer and director. Rare clips from Chaplin's earliest movies are featured. Gloria Swanson narrates. 55 min.
04-2585 *$14.99*

Chaplin's Goliath (1996)
Burly, Scotish-born actor Eric Campbell gained screen fame as the menacing heavy in Charlie Chaplin's 1916-17 Mutual short subjects before dying in a 1917 atuo accident. Vintage film clips, rare outtakes, and interviews with Chaplin experts and Campbell's relatives are mixed to tell the story of this seminal but now mostly forgotten comedy star. 54 min.
53-6513 *$19.99*

Rounding Up The Law (1922)
Big Boy Williams was a big, strapping fellow who could shoot and rustle with the best of them. Here his talents are put to the test, as he plays a friendly cowpuncher who biffs, bams and sockos a slimy ex-gambler and his villainous pal. 62 min. Silent with organ score.
09-2106 Was $24.99 *$19.99*

The Garden Of Eden (1928)
A charming Cinderella-like fable featuring Corrine Griffith as a Viennese girl who craves a career as an opera singer and lands a job as a dancer in a Budapest cabaret. With Louise Dresser. Directed by Lewis Milestone ("All Quiet on the Western Front"), with art direction by William Cameron Menzies. 115 min. Silent with organ music score.
09-2108 Was $29.99 *$24.99*

Wolfheart's Revenge (1925)
Mighty German shepherd Wolfheart is teamed with Western star "Big Boy" Williams, who plays a cowhand battling a black hat who murdered his boss. Wolfheart helps save the day. 64 min. Silent with music score.
09-2149 Was $29.99 *$14.99*

Ella Cinders (1926)
Very funny film treatment of the comics' "Cinderella of the Movies" stars Colleen Moore as a put-upon small-town gal who wins a trip to Hollywood and, through a series of mishaps, lands a screen contract. Mervyn LeRoy's script features a great cameo by baby-faced comic Harry Langdon. 51 min. Silent with music score.
09-2026 *$19.99*

The New School Teacher (1923)
Wonderful comic escapades, based on the writings of Irvin S. Cobb, starring Chic Sale as a new professor who's coping (just barely) with his rowdy charges. When disaster strikes, though, he manages to earn the kids' respect. 75 min. Silent with musical score.
09-2039 Was $29.99 *$24.99*

The Golden Stallion (1927)
This is the feature version of the first Mascot serial, a tale of a young girl who joins forces with an Indian chief to find hidden treasure. The secret to the treasure's location lies in an ancient belt and the brand on a wild horse they must find. Lefty Flynn, Molly Malone and Joe Bonomo star. Silent with music score.
68-9199 Was $19.99 *$14.99*

Drag Harlan (1920)
William Farnum is an outlaw who puts down his pistols to care for the daughter of a dying rancher who is terrorized by local thugs. After he discovers that they have hatched a plot against her, Farnum goes back to work with his guns. With Jackie Saunders. Silent with music score.
68-9195 *$14.99*

California In '49 (1924)
Edmund Cobb is a scout for the Donner party who must save his snowbound compadres by getting to a California outpost before they die. He orchestrates the rescue, then becomes the leader of settlers revolting against oppressive Mexican forces. This is the feature version of the serial "Days of '49." With Charles Brinley. Silent with music score.
68-9197 Was $19.99 *$14.99*

The Return Of Grey Wolf (1922)
Canine star Leader narrates this bold North country adventure himself, barking onto the title cards the tale of a wolf-sized dog who helps a blinded fur trapper revenge himself on a crooked rival. With James Pierce. 62 min. Silent with musical score.
09-2054 Was $24.99 *$14.99*

Human Hearts (1922)
A three-handkerchief weepie set in the Ozark Mountains. When coal is discovered under a family's property, a nefarious con-woman seduces the family's patriarch...and the plot gets thicker. House Peters, Russell Simpson and Gertrude Clark star. 99 min. Silent with musical score.
09-2150 Was $29.99 *$14.99*

The Prairie Pirate (1927)
Unusual western thriller in which cowboy Harry Carey vows to track down the bandits responsible for his sister's death, who killed herself rather than submit to their desires. With a cigarette as his only clue, Carey turns outlaw and robs people of their smokes(!) in his search for the crooks. Jean Dumas, Lloyd Whitlock also star. Silent with music score.
68-9155 *$19.99*

The Phantom Flyer (1928)
Real-life barnstormer Al Wilson stars as a daredevil pilot who buzzes to the aid of a beleaguered ranch family who are up to their elbows in rustlers. Amazing mid-air stunts highlight this rouser. 54 min. Silent with musical score.
09-2082 Was $24.99 *$14.99*

Russian Cinema

Early Russian Cinema: Complete Set
Between the years 1908 and 1918, Russia's film industry achieved a sophistication in technique and subject matter that equalled anywhere else in the world, until it was shut down after the Communist Revolution. This ten-tape series features the best movies from that time, restored with full music score and English subtitles. Volumes include "Beginnings," "Folklore and Legend," "Starewicz's Fantasies," "Class Distinctions" and "The End of an Era." 11 1/2 hrs. total. NOTE: Individual volumes available at $29.99 each.
80-5018 Save $50.00! ***$249.99***

The Cameraman's Revenge And Other Fantastic Tales
Six of the best works of Russian filmmaker Wladislaw Starewicz, who specialized in puppet and model animation, are gathered on this video. Includes "The Insect's Christmas" (1913), "The Cameraman's Revenge" (1912), "Frogland" (1922), "Voice of the Nightingale" (1923), "The Mascot" (1933) and "Winter Carousel" (1958). 80 min.
80-5019 ***$39.99***

Kino-Eye (Kino-Glaz) (1924)
An early proponent of "cinéma vérité" filmmaking and montage editing Russian director Dziga Vertov went from newsreel work to this silent documentary. Everyday life in the first years following the Soviet Revolution, from a light-hearted look of how food gets to the table from the farm to the activities of the adolescent Young Pioneers, is chronicled in Vertov's unique style. 74 min.
53-6426 ***$24.99***

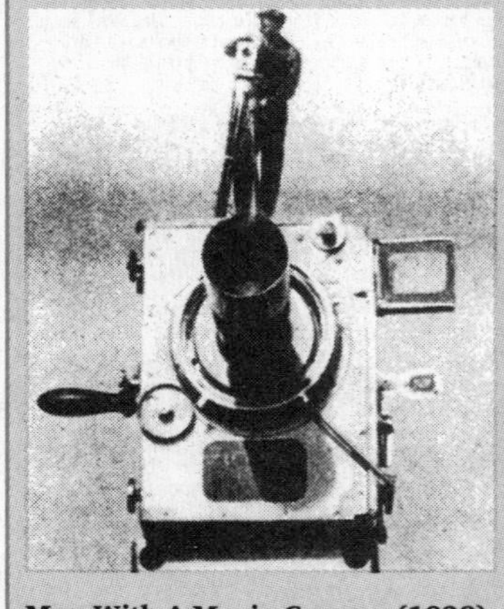

Man With A Movie Camera (1929)
Innovative avant garde silent film by Dziga Vertov that uses the camera lens as the audience's "eye," embarking on a bizarre chronicle of Soviet life filled with trick photography and strange sights. 75 min. Silent with music score by the Alloy Orchestra.
53-9785 Remastered ***$29.99***

Three Songs Of Lenin (1934)
One of Dziga Vertov's final films takes an expressive look at the Russian Revolution's leader. The documentary is divided into three sections, each of which explores a different facet of Lenin's life and politics. 62 min. Silent with orchestral score.
53-7556 ***$29.99***

Aelita: Queen Of Mars (1924)
Remarkable silent film featuring dazzling futurist and cubist sets and costumes, as well as a wild allegorical story. A scientist shoots his wife and heads to Mars with a young soldier and a detective. On the Red Planet, the soldier leads a Martian revolution and meets the girl of his dreams. Yulia Solntseva and Emil Schoenemann star in this trailblazing Russian effort. AKA: "Aelita: The Revolt of the Robots." 113 min. Silent with piano score.
53-7551 ***$29.99***

The Cigarette Girl Of Mosselprom (1924)
Exuberant social comedy about a cigarette-hawking streetwoman who sees her fortunes change when she's accidentally thrust into the world of show business by being cast as a lead in a movie. A Russian classic with Yulia Solnetseva and Igor Ilinsky. 78 min. Silent with orchestral score.
53-7552 ***$29.99***

The Extraordinary Adventures Of Mr. West In The Land Of The Bolsheviks (1924)
A witty satire on Western culture focusing on a prejudiced American visitor's trip to Moscow. Upon arriving in the city, he expects to see ornery outlaws, but is he in for a surprise! Directed by Lev Kuleshov. 78 min. Silent with orchestral score.
53-9317 ***$29.99***

By The Law (1926)
Tense Russian-made silent drama of lawlessness and revenge. Two men in a remote area of Alaska are murdered; when the killer is found, two companions of the dead men must exact the penalty. Stars Sergei Komarov and Vladimir Fogel. 90 min.
53-7096 Was $29.99 ***$14.99***

Mother (1926)
Film theorist and pioneer director Vsevolod Pudovkin's drama broke new grounds in the area of cinematic language while telling the story of a mother who betrays her son to the police, then becomes radicalized when he will be sent to prison. Based on a novel by Maxim Gorky. 88 min. Silent with music score.
53-7470 Was $29.99 ***$14.99***

By The Law (1926)/ Chess Fever (1925)
Based on a Jack London story, "By the Law" is a tense drama involving two members of a Yukon prospecting team who have to decide the fate of a partner after he cold-bloodedly kills two of their fellow goldseekers. Next, "Chess Fever" is a wacky comedy concerning a young man whose obsession with chess lands him in trouble with his wife. 108 min. total. Silent with music score.
53-9784 ***$29.99***

Bed And Sofa (1927)
A young woman's determination to plan her own life and reject the role Society has planned for her is the theme of this surprisingly frank silent serio-comedy from Russia. 74 min.
53-7020 Was $29.99 ***$14.99***

The End Of St. Petersburg (1927)
A panoramic silent look at the state of Russia before and during the Revolution, seen through the eyes of a newcomer to the city. With Ivan Chuvelev and A.P. Chistiakov. Program also includes the humorous silent short "Chess Fever" (1925), a send-up of the International Chess Tournament. 92 min. total.
53-7097 Was $29.99 ***$14.99***

The Girl With The Hat Box (1927)
In the tradition of the great silent comedies, this fast-paced farce stars Anna Sten as a working girl who is given a lottery ticket by her shady employer. When she discovers that the ticket is a winner, a wild chase ensues. Russian slapstick also stars Ivan Koval-Samborsky. 67 min. Silent with orchestral score.
53-7554 ***$29.99***

The Fall Of The Romanov Dynasty (1928)
A masterful chronicle of the collapse of the Czarist regime and the rise of Communism. Esther Shub's film employs rare historic footage, radical editing and even personal movies to tell this incredible story. 90 min. Silent with piano score.
53-7553 ***$29.99***

Zvenigora (1928)
Director Alexander Dovzhenko's first major work looks at the history of his homeland, the Ukraine. This lyrical, silent film uses myths and legends to tell its story, spanning from the time of the Vikings to the 1919 Civil War. 73 min.
53-9322 ***$39.99***

Arsenal (1929)
One of the most powerful films to come from the Russian silent cinema, Ukrainian director Alexander Dovzhenko's moving drama chronicles the real-life siege of a Bolshevik-held munitions plant in Kiev by nationalist White Russian troops, portraying the outnumbered Reds as heroes in the tradition of Ukrainian folklore. 75 min. Silent with musical score.
53-6427 ***$24.99***

Earth (1930)
Alexander Dovzhenko's classic Russian drama of farmers whose lives are forever changed when a pro-Communist agitator comes to their village. 69 min. Silent with musical score.
62-5111 ***$29.99***

Storm Over Asia (1928)
Director Vsevelod Pudovkin's epic is set on the Soviet Asian frontier and tells of a rebellious young Mongol trapper who is set up as a "puppet leader" of his people by occupying Western forces when it's discovered he is a descendant of the legendary Genghis Khan. 128 min. Silent with special orchestral score by Timothy Brock and the Olympia Chamber Orchestra.
53-9786 Remastered ***$29.99***

Happiness (1934)
A sly spoof of Bolshevik life and concerns, this slapstick masterpiece from Alexander Medvedkin was banned for 40 years in Russia. Comic oddities like polka-dotted horses populate a film best described as "a tale about a hapless mercenary loser, his wife, his well-fed neighbor, a priest, a nun and other old relics." 69 min. Silent with orchestral score.
53-7555 ***$29.99***

Pioneers Of Cinema
The beginnings of the film industry is the focus of this documentary that includes the first efforts from such pioneers as the Lumière Brothers, Thomas Edison, George Méliès, Gaumont and others. 180 min.
53-6539 ***$24.99***

Cinema Europe: The Other Hollywood: Boxed Set (1995)
Producers Kevin Brownlow and David Gill ("Hollywood") turn their attention to the moviemaking culture that flourished in Europe from the late 1890s to the advent of talking pictures in this three-tape series featuring rare film clips and interviews with such notables as Abel Gance, Alfred Hitchcock and Leni Riefenstahl. Volumes include "Where It All Began/Art's Promised Land (Sweden)," "The Unchained Camera (Germany)/The Music of Light (France)" and "Opportunity Lost (Britain)/End of an Era"). Narrated by Kenneth Branagh. 360 min. total. NOTE: Individual volumes available at $29.99 each.
40-3004 Save $15.00! ***$74.99***

Touring The Silent Movie Studios
An in-depth look at classic movie studios. Take the 1916 Universal Studio Tour (no multi-million dollar earthquake re-enactment here), cruise through MGM Studios, circa 1925, take in glimpses of the First National and Warner lots, and enjoy the shorts "Ghost Town: The Fort Lee Story" and "A Girl's Folly," about the making of movies in New Jersey. Features an organ score. 115 min.
53-9140 ***$39.99***

The Great Chase (1963)
Exciting, thrill-a-minute scenes from the time when silents were golden. See Douglas Fairbanks, Sr. leave "The Mark of Zorro," Pearl White face "The Perils of Pauline," Richard Barthlemess chase Lillian Gish "Way Down East," Buster Keaton track down "The General," and more. 81 min.
53-1257 Remastered ***$19.99***

Kingdom Of Shadows (1998)
Before movies found a voice, they knew how to scream, as you'll discover in this chronicle of silent cinematic horror. See how filmmakers around the world brought ghosts, vampires, demons and other menaces to the screen in clips from "The Golem," "Nosferatu," "The Cabinet of Dr. Caligari," "The Hunchback of Notre Dame," "Metropolis" and many others. Narrated by Rod Steiger. 70 min.
53-6269 ***$24.99***

The Last Command (1927)
Acclaimed German actor Emil Jannings won the first Best Actor Academy Award for this silent drama directed by compatriot Josef Von Sternberg. Jannings portrays a Russian general forced to flee his motherland and ironically hired on as an extra in a Hollywood film version of the Revolution of 1917. 88 min. With Evelyn Brent, William Powell. 88 min. Silent with Gaylord Carter score.
06-1435 Was $29.99 ***$14.99***

The Jack Knife Man (1920)
A heart-warming story, written and directed by King Vidor, about a reclusive river-dweller who is left to watch an orphan lad. Stars Fred Turner and Florence Vidor (the director's wife). Silent with musical score.
09-2062 Was $29.99 ***$14.99***

Across The Plains (1928)
Silent western saga stars Pawnee Bill, Jr. as the rough n' tumble ranch foreman who must face the wrath of a rabid lynch mob after he plugs a connivin' cardsharp in a duel! Ione Reed co-stars. 51 min. Silent with musical score.
09-2084 Was $24.99 ***$14.99***

Road Agent (1926)
A dying rancher left his expansive estate to his long-missing son...and his scheming lawyer finds a lookalike drifter (Al Hoxie) to pose as the heir! Will the fugitive continue in the ruse, or will he see the error of his ways? 55 min. Silent with musical score.
09-2085 Was $24.99 ***$14.99***

The Lost Express (1926)
Featurized serial stars daredevil heroine Helen Holmes as a railroad employee who must make right when the boss' private train mysteriously vanishes. Plenty of eye-popping train-hopping in this delightful actioner. 59 min. Silent with musical score.
09-2087 Was $24.99 ***$19.99***

The Sea Lion (1921)
Grand silent adventure with Hobart Bosworth as an embittered ship's captain who takes out all the anger he has for the wife who abandoned him on the young girl one of his crew has rescued from a deserted island. Co-stars Emory Johnson and Bessie Love. 70 min. Silent with music score.
09-1334 Was $29.99 ***$24.99***

Entr'acte (1924)/ The Crazy Ray (1924)
Two experimental silent fantasies from noted French filmmaker Rene Clair. In "Entr'acte," he enlisted such famed dadaists as Man Ray, Marcel Duchamp and Georges Auric to appear in a tale of inanimate objects coming to life. Next, a scientist's new invention stops all of Paris in its tracks. 62 min. total. Silent with organ score.
53-7455 Was $49.99 ***$39.99***

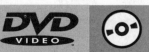

DVD VIDEO
ASK ABOUT OUR GIANT DVD CATALOG!

The Westbound Limited (1923)
Fans of old trains will love this silent tale of a railroad worker who saves the company owner's daughter after she falls in front of a speeding train. Little does the worker know that after receiving a reward for his efforts, the railroad's scheming advisor has a nasty plot hatching. Johnny Harron, Ralph Lewis, Claire McDowell stars. Includes some tinted scenes. Silent with music score.
03-5013 ***$24.99***

The Return Of Boston Blackie (1927)
A gentleman thief tries to go straight despite pressure from his old partner, but makes use of his shady skills anyway when he helps an heiress return a necklace to her family safe. Stars Raymond Glenn and Strongheart the dog. 77 min. Silent with music score.
09-2072 Was $29.99 ***$24.99***

The Haunted Castle (1921)
A suspense-filled German silent thriller directed by F. W. Murnau. Supernatural goings-on occur at the elegant country mansion of a noblewoman who is entertaining guests for a weekend hunt. Lulu Keyser-Korff, Arnold Korff star. 75 min. Silent with music score.
09-1348 Was $29.99 ***$24.99***

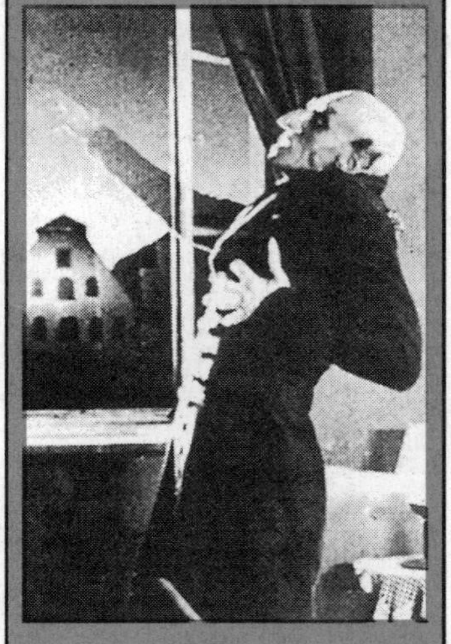

Nosferatu (1922)
F.W. Murnau's unauthorized adaptation of "Dracula" is a masterpiece of silent German horror. The mysterious Count Orlock heads for London, coffin in tow, to spread his plague of living death. As the vampire, Max Schreck's bizarre, bat-eared, clawed makeup is unforgettable. Restored version contains added footage and new title cards. 101 min. Silent with music score.
09-1041 Was $29.99 ***$19.99***

Nosferatu: The First Vampire
The seminal horror classic is also available in a special remastered edition hosted by David Carradine and featuring music by Type O Negative, along with the group's music video for "Black No. 1." 75 min.
74-3042 ***$29.99***

The Last Laugh (1925)
Classic German silent film of a pompous hotel doorman who is shamed when demoted to a washroom attendant because of his age, only to receive an unexpected surprise. Emil Jannings won international acclaim in the lead; F.W. Murnau directs. 74 min. Silent with musical score.
10-3023 ***$19.99***

Faust (1926)
A lavish silent version of the German legend about a man who sells his soul to the Devil in exchange for youth and earthly pleasures. Emil Jannings stars as the malevolent Mephistopheles, with Gösta Ekman in the title role, in this visually striking film from director F.W. Murnau ("Nosferatu"). 88 min. Silent with music score.
09-5385 ***$19.99***

Tartuffe, The Hypocrite (1927)
Moliere's classic comedy is given a striking treatment in this rarely seen F.W. Murnau film featuring the legendary Emil Jannings as Tartuffe, the man who endears himself to a wealthy friend and attempts to seduce his wife before getting caught. 70 min. Silent with German title cards only.
10-9770 ***$24.99***

Tabu (1931)
The landmark collaboration of documentarian Robert Flaherty and German director F.W. Murnau (his final film) has been hailed as one of the most stunning movies ever made. Shot in Tahiti, the story tells of a a gorgeous native girl who is declared to be "sacred" by her tribe, and what happens when she defies them and falls in love with a man. Anna Chevalier, Matahi star. 82 min. Silent with score composed by Murnau.
80-5000 ***$39.99***

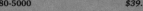

Mary Pickford

The Pride Of The Clan (1916)
Mary Pickford excels in this compassionate drama as a Scottish lass who takes control of her family after her father dies in a shipwreck. Her happiness is threatened when her new husband, a local fisherman, is asked to return to London. Matt Moore also stars. 84 min. Silent with music score.
09-2399 *$14.99*

Poor Little Rich Girl (1917)
Entertaining Mary Pickford vehicle (and the first of her "child roles") casts her as the lonely 11-year-old daughter of wealthy, neglectful parents. Maurice Tourneur's effective drama, highlighted by imaginative sets and a marvelous, surreal nightmare sequence, co-stars Madeline Traverse and Charles Wellesley. 64 min. Silent with music score.
09-5393 *$19.99*

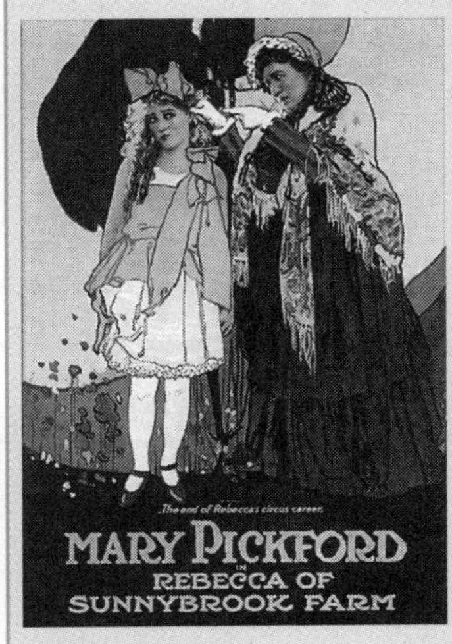

Rebecca Of Sunnybrook Farm (1917)
The popular Kate Douglas Wiggin story comes to life, with Mary Pickford in the title role of the rambunctious young farmgirl who comes to live with her stern maiden aunts. Eugene O'Brien, Josephine Crowell also star. 78 min. Silent with music score.
62-5102 *$19.99*

Stella Maris (1918)
In one of her greatest performances, Mary Pickford plays two parts: a handicapped young orphan who must care for her aunt and uncle while being raised like a princess, and a poor, abused girl who falls in love with the husband of the woman who terrorizes her. Conway Tearle, Camille Ankewich and Ida Waterman also star. Silent with musical score.
10-9370 *$14.99*

Amarilly Of Clothesline Alley (1918)
She's the darling of her New York tenement neighborhood, but when cigarette girl Mary Pickford nurses socialite Norman Kerry back to health after a dance hall fight, their blossoming love affair results in a riotous culture clash. Charming romantic comedy also stars William Scott. Pickford is also seen in an early short subject, "The Dream" (1911). 77 min. Silent with music score.
53-6270 *$29.99*

Daddy Long Legs (1919)
The first feature film based on Jean Webster's popular story stars Mary Pickford as the strong-willed young orphan who falls for her benefactor, a mysterious guardian known only as "Daddy Long Legs." With Mahlon Hamilton, Milla Davenport. Also included is Pickford's 1910 Biograph short "What the Daisy Said," directed by D.W. Griffith. 94 min. Silent with music score.
53-6276 *$29.99*

Suds (1920)
In a much-acclaimed performance, Mary Pickford plays a put-upon urchin working in a cheap London laundry who hopes for a better future for herself, while a delivery boy falls in love with her. A tearjerker that also features Albert Austin and Harold Goodwin. Silent with musical score.
10-9373 *$14.99*

Pollyanna (1920)
Mary Pickford (at age 27) stars as the 12-year-old orphaned daughter of a missionary whose inextinguishable optimism brings joy and hope into the life of her new guardian, her Aunt Polly, a lovelorn woman whose break-up with a local doctor has left her embittered and unhappy. Co-stars Katherine Griffith, J. Wharton James. 60 min. Silent with music score.
62-5142 Was $34.99 *$19.99*

The Love Light (1921)
A rarity, this drama features Mary Pickford in an adult role as a woman tending a lighthouse in Italy while waiting for the return of her brother from World War I. When a soldier washes ashore, Pickford cares for him and, after falling in love with him, realizes he's a German spy who may have something to do with her brother's death. 75 min. Silent with music score.
80-5042 *$29.99*

Tess Of The Storm Country (1922)
In a remake of the 1914 film that made her one of the country's first movie stars, Mary Pickford plays the leader of a group of squatters fighting for their rights. When the sister of her lover (who happens to be the son of the local landlord) has a baby out of wedlock, Pickford risks her own happiness by passing the child off as hers. Lloyd Hughes, Gloria Hope co-star. 120 min.
53-6277 *$29.99*

Little Annie Rooney (1925)
Mary Pickford turns in a fine performance as a tough, young Irish gal finding adventure along the mean streets of an ethnically diverse ghetto. After her policeman father is shot, Pickford's brother thinks the fellow she likes is the culprit and seeks to get revenge. With William Haines. 96 min. Silent with music score.
62-5095 *$19.99*

Sparrows (1926)
A lushly photographed, marvelously constructed silent drama starring Mary Pickford as the oldest of a group of youngsters held against their will by the tyrannical head (Gustav von Seyffertiz) of a "baby farm" in a Southern swamp. Also featured on this tape are two early Pickford shorts by D.W. Griffith, "Wilful Peggy" (1910) and "The Mender of Nets" (1912), plus a look at the actress's life narrated by Whoopi Goldberg. 81 min. Silent with music score.
09-1498 Remastered *$24.99*

My Best Girl (1927)
Fine romantic comedy starring Mary Pickford as a feisty five-and-dime shopgirl who falls for fellow clerk Buddy Rogers, unaware that he's really the boss' son working incognito. Also included is newsreel footage of Pickford and Rogers' 1937 wedding and home movies of their honeymoon. 88 min. Silent with music score.
62-5097 *$29.99*

Coquette (1929)
Mary Pickford's first talkie won her an Academy Award for Best Actress, as she played a flirtatious flapper girl whose love for a man her father detests leads to tragedy. Johnny Mack Brown, John Sainpolis, Matt Moore and Louise Beavers also star. 75 min.
12-2584 *$19.99*

The Taming Of The Shrew (1929)
Hollywood's premiere off-screen couple, Mary Pickford and Douglas Fairbanks, made their only on-screen appearance together in this broadly comic adaptation of the timeless "women's liberation" play. Features the famous credit "Written by William Shakespeare, with additional dialogue by Sam Taylor." 66 min.
62-5148 Was $34.99 *$19.99*

Sweetheart: The Films Of Mary Pickford Boxed Set
Celebrate "America's Sweetheart" with this five-tape collector's set that includes "Amarilly of Clothesline Alley," "Daddy Long Legs," "My Best Girl," "Stella Maris" and "Tess of the Storm Country."
53-6278 *$124.99*

Mary Pickford: A Life On Film
This revealing documentary of "America's Sweetheart" takes an incisive look at a woman who, at the age of 17, became an international sensation; was the only woman to own her own studio; and was the only actress to be the highest-paid star in Hollywood. Janet Leigh, Roddy McDowall, Leonard Maltin, Douglas Fairbanks, Jr. and Charles "Buddy" Rogers offer commentary; Whoopi Goldberg hosts and narrates. 96 min.
80-5043 *$29.99*

Midnight Faces (1926)
An eerie mansion within the Florida bayou country is the setting for this silent suspenser that features a young heir, a frightened damsel, a scheming lawyer, strange servants, an inscrutable Oriental (in Florida?) and others. Francis X. Bushman, Jr., Kathryn McGuire star. 72 min. Silent with music score.
09-2201 Was $19.99 *$14.99*

Riders Of The Law (1922)
Out in the untamed Montana Territory, liquor smugglers are having a field day until one of them wounds the local lawman. Enter undercover government agent Jack Hoxie to bring the 19th-century rumrunners to justice. Early oater also stars Marin Sais. 75 min. Silent with music score.
09-2204 Was $29.99 *$24.99*

The Pace That Kills (1928)
Serious, hard-hitting account of drug-addiction that served as a warning to the film community in its time. A naive farm boy searches for his missing sister in the big city, but soon becomes part of a party scene that includes floozies and dope. Owen Gorin, Virginia Roye and Florence Turner star. 87 min. Silent with music score.
09-2157 Was $29.99 *$14.99*

The Blasphemer (1921)
Produced by the Religious Film Association, this silent drama takes a look into the life of a man who has cast aside religion and is living a life filled with greed and debauchery, and devoid of love. 109 min. Silent with music score.
09-1797 Was $29.99 *$14.99*

Let's Go (1923)
Richard Talmadge, who worked as an actor, director and Douglas Fairbanks' stunt double, stars in this silent drama as the son of a cement company owner who gets into all kinds of hair-raising scrapes while trying to save his pop's business. 79 min. Silent with music score.
09-2182 Was $29.99 *$14.99*

Shore Leave (1925)
Sailor Richard Barthelmess falls for captain's daughter Dorothy MacKaill while on shore leave in a New England port, but will he ever return while she waits for him? Silent soaper that probably didn't inspire the top 40 song "Brandy." 105 min. Silent with music score.
09-2192 Was $29.99 *$24.99*

South Of Panama (1928)
Unusual silent drama set in a sleepy (literally, because everyone is always taking siestas) South American nation. A handsome young machinery importer turns out to be a profiteer ready to bleed the republic of El Tovar dry, but he changes his mind when he sees the president's pretty daughter. Edouardo Roquello stars. 90 min. Silent with music score.
09-2208 Was $29.99 *$14.99*

The White Flame/ The Sacred Mountain
Two excellent silent examples of a uniquely German genre—the mountain film. As developed by ski aficionado Dr. Arnold Fanck, these films feature highly dramatic stories set against snowy mountain settings; both star Leni Riefenstahl. 60 min. total.
53-7066 Was $39.99 *$14.99*

Witchcraft Through The Ages (Häxan) (1922)
A rare and controversial silent fantasy from Sweden, this film combines fact and legend to explore the world of the occult. The film was banned for many years due to nudity and an anti-Catholic scene. Written and directed by Benjamin Christensen. 90 min. Silent with music score.
09-1719 *$19.99*

Sex (1920)
Surprisingly frank (for its time) silent drama of a young "exotic dancer" (Louise Glaum) who goes through a series of paramours before finding the one man who could change her life...if she lets him. 87 min. Silent with music score; recorded at correct projection speed.
09-1861 Was $29.99 *$24.99*

The Final Extra (1927)
Silent melodrama about an ambitious cub reporter whose slumping career is given a sudden jolt when he is assigned to investigate the murder of a rival reporter. Stars Grant Withers. 76 min. Silent with music score.
09-1981 Was $19.99 *$14.99*

Slow As Lightning (1923)
Funny fable starring Kenneth McDonald as a daydreamer who loses his job and finds his girl is losing patience with him. When an unscrupulous ladies man starts moving in, he devises a plan to hit it big on the stocks and win her over for good. With Edna Pennington. 60 min. Silent with organ score.
09-2243 Was $24.99 *$14.99*

William S. Hart

The Disciple (1915)
William S. Hart rides as the "Shootin' Iron Parson," who has trouble keeping his town, and his wayward wife, out of the clutches of a seductive gambler. Appearing as an extra is Jean Hersholt. 80 min. Silent with music score.
09-2011 Was $29.99 *$14.99*

Hell's Hinges (1916)
One of William S. Hart's finest films, this silent Western, directed and co-written by Hart, casts him as a gunslinger living in a lawless town. His heart is softened when he falls for the sister of the new preacher, but the minister's led astray by a dance hall girl. With Clara Williams. 65 min. Silent with music score.
09-1871 Was $29.99 *$24.99*

The Return Of Draw Egan (1916)
Fascinating silent Western stars William S. Hart as an outlaw on the lam whose skill as a gunman gets him the job of sheriff of Yellow Dog, while he's hiding there under an alias. 64 min. Silent with music score.
09-2012 Was $29.99 *$24.99*

The Narrow Trail (1917)
This is truly the classic Western! William S. Hart stars as Ice Harding, a man with a stolen horse, out to find his girl and start life anew. Action, thrills, guns, guts and horses... what more can a Western fan want? Co-stars Sylvia Bremer and Milton Ross. 56 min. Silent with music score.
62-5196 *$19.99*

The Silent Man (1917)
Silent sagebrusher stars William S. Hart as a fella who turns bandit after his claim to gold is taken by a sleazy dance hall owner. He robs a stagecoach that's carrying some of the cash that really belongs to him, then tries to save a dancer who's about to marry the dance hall boss. Robert McKim and Bola Vale also star. Silent with music score.
68-9192 Was $19.99 *$14.99*

Blue Blazes Rawden (1918)
After arriving at Timber Cove with his lumberjack pals, ruffian William S. Hart faces the local tavern owner in a gunfight and kills him. Hart's guilt over his actions increase when the barman's elderly mother comes to town, and Hart takes her in. With Jack Hoxie. Silent with music score.
68-9193 Was $19.99 *$14.99*

Wagon Tracks (1919)
Silent cowboy star William S. Hart excels as a desert guide who learns that his brother has been killed by a gal in self-defense. While leading a wagon train, Hart gets the hunch that the woman's brother and his confederate pal are the culprits. Jane Novak, Robert McKim and future director Lloyd Bacon also star. Silent with music score.
03-5012 *$24.99*

Cradle Of Courage (1920)
A rare non-western appearance by William S. Hart highlights this intriguing film that finds Hart as a cop caught in a tough situation. Can he get out of it? 60 min. Silent with music score.
10-9772 *$14.99*

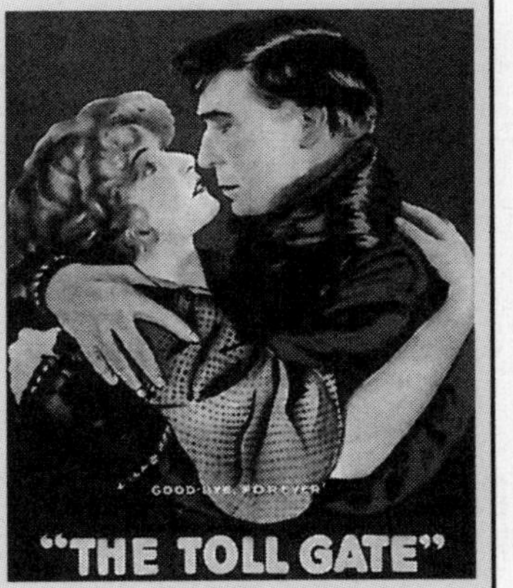

The Toll Gate (1920)
Exciting western yarn with William S. Hart as the leader of an outlaw band whose planned train robbery ends in an ambush, thanks to a double-crossing gang member. Escaping, Hart finds shelter and a chance at a new life at a woman's remote cabin, but soon discovers he cannot elude his past. Anna Q. Nilsson, Joseph Singleton also star. Along with the restored, tinted version of the film, this video also includes Mack Sennett's 1916 spoof of Hart, "A Bitter Pill," starring Mack Swain. 73 min. Silent with music score.
53-6161 *$24.99*

Three Word Brand (1921)
William S. Hart in an original silent Western, and he plays three different roles! When his partner is accused of murder, Hart devises a daring plan for his rescue. 84 min. Silent with music score.
09-1359 Was $29.99 *$14.99*

The Whistle (1921)
In a change-of-pace role, William S. Hart plays a mill worker whose boss ignores his requests for safety changes and whose son is later killed in a preventable accident. After Hart saves the life of his boss' son, he decides to kidnap him in an act of vengeance. Frank Brownlee and Myrtle Stedman co-star. Silent with music score.
68-9263 *$19.99*

Tumbleweeds (1925)
An early landmark in the Western genre, this William S. Hart drama (the actor's final film) casts him as a cattleman facing the end of the "wide-open" frontier during the Cherokee Strip land rush in Oklahoma. With Barbara Bedford, Lucien Littlefield. This 1939 reissue includes a prologue and color-tinted sequences. 89 min. Silent with music score.
63-1550 *$19.99*

The Big Parade (1925)
Stunning WWI drama from King Vidor, starring John Gilbert as a small town youth who leaves for the battlefields of Europe and faces harrowing ordeals, including the loss of a leg, as he becomes a man. An anti-war theme and realistic battle scenes for that time make this a hallmark of early cinema; with Renee Adoree, Hobart Bosworth. 142 min. Silent with stereo music score.
12-1832 *$29.99*

Queen Of The Chorus (1928)
Tearjerking melodrama of flappers, playboys, and "a woman with a heart of gold who makes the ultimate sacrifice." Virginia Brown Faire and Rex Lease star. Silent with music score.
10-9922 *$14.99*

The Crowd (1928)
A landmark silent drama from King Vidor, following a young man whose dreams of success in the New York business world are slowly shattered by circumstances, leaving him just a face in the crowd. Unglamorous look at the life of "average Americans" retains its relevance even today; James Murray, Eleanor Boardman star. 104 min. Silent with music score.
12-1134 *$29.99*

Show People (1928)
One of the last grand silent films was also one of Hollywood's first attempts to salute its own past. Marion Davies stars as a young actress who gets a job at a Sennett-like comedy film studio and later leaves it (and her lover, a top comic) behind for more "serious" roles. Co-stars William Haynes, with cameos by Chaplin, Fairbanks and others. 80 min.
12-1137 *$29.99*

Anna Christie (1923)
This long-lost silent telling of the classic drama of sin and reconciliation is the only filmed version of any of his works that pleased author Eugene O'Neill. Blanche Sweet is superb as the sailor's daughter who becomes a seaman's lover, despite the pains of her father. Thomas H. Ince directs.
17-3060 *$29.99*

Rubber Tires (1927)
Car-lamitous comedy ensues when a family decides to take a cross-country trip to California. Erwin Connelly, Bessie Love and May Robson star. Silent with musical score.
17-9072 Was $19.99 *$14.99*

The Extra Girl (1923)
Mabel Normand stars in this rags-to-riches serio-comedy, her final feature film, as an aspiring actress with stars in her eyes who ignores the advice of her family and heads off to Hollywood. 70 min. Silent with music score.
09-5384 *$19.99*

A Mormon Maid (1917)
Silent melodrama set against the 1840s westward migration of the Mormons. Mae Murray stars as a young woman who joins the wagon train and is pursued by two men, one a recent convert, the other a scheming elder with a stable of wives. Frank Borzage, Hobart Bosworth co-star. 75 min. Silent with music score.
09-2186 Was $29.99 *$24.99*

Trapped By The Mormons (1922)
One of several anti-Mormon films made in the early days of movies, this fascinating piece of silent propaganda (made in, of all places, England) stars Evelyn Brent as a virginal young woman who is "lured from her home into the Mormon net" by a scheming recruiter with Svengali-like powers and some ungodly plans for his victim. 97 min. Silent with music score; recorded at correct projection speed.
09-2185 Was $29.99 *$24.99*

The Drake Case (1929)
A female servant accused of murdering her well-to-do employer learns that her lover not only committed the brutal crime but was once her boss's husband in this early courtroom drama. Gladys Brockwell, Forrest Stanley, Robert Frazer star. Silent with music score.
68-9265 *$19.99*

The Roaring Road (1919)
Fast-paced racing drama starring early screen idol Wallace Reid as an auto salesman who enters a race in order to win fame for his company and the hand of the boss' daughter for himself. With Ann Little, Theodore Roberts. 57 min. Silent with music score.
09-2194 Was $24.99 *$19.99*

Backstairs (1921)
A fine example of German expressionist cinema, telling the story of a maid who waits anxiously, day after day, for a letter from her missing lover. With Henry Porten and Fritz Kortner. 44 min. Silent with music score.
53-7055 Was $29.99 *$14.99*

The Love Of Jeanne Ney (1927)
A masterpiece of silent cinema, directed by G.W. Pabst ("Pandora's Box"), one of Germany's most influential filmmakers. Brigitte Helm ("Metropolis") plays a lonely blind girl who falls in love with Russian communist Eugen Jenson. 102 min.
53-7067 Was $29.99 *$14.99*

Manhandled (1924)
Shop girl Gloria Swanson must cope with life in the big city and problems with the men in her life in this silent melodrama depicting the growing ranks of working women in '20s America. With Tom Moore, Ian Keith, Frank Morgan. Silent with music score.
53-7649 *$24.99*

Ernst Lubitsch

The Eyes Of The Mummy (1918)
One of the great Ernst Lubitsch's earliest offerings is this thriller about an Egyptian girl (Pola Negri) held prisoner in an ancient Egyptian temple by an ominous Arab (Emil Jannings). After being rescued by an Englishman, she moves to Great Britain, but is soon haunted by her former nemesis. NOTE: This rarely seen effort is only available with title cards in the German language. 60 min. Silent
10-9460 *$19.99*

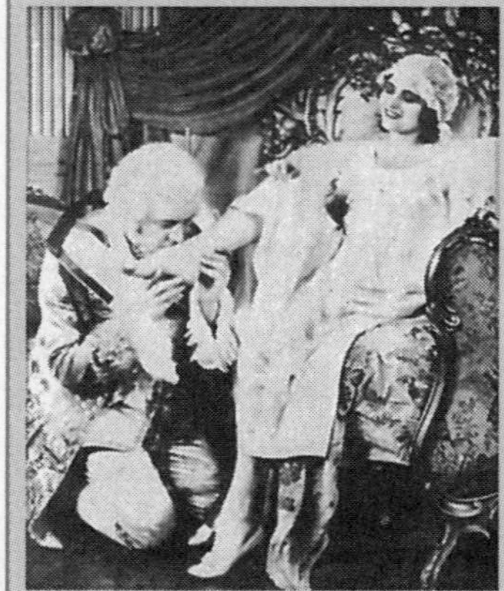

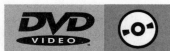

Passion (Madame Du Barry) (1919)
Ernst Lubitsch directed this costume spectacular which made Pola Negri a star. Negri stars as the French country girl who uses love affairs to climb the social ladder, until she becomes courtesan to King Louis XV (Emil Jannings). 90 min. Silent with music score.
09-1844 Was $39.99 *$29.99*

The Oyster Princess (1919)
"The Lubitsch Touch" is evident in this witty comedy from Ernst Lubitsch detailing the plight of Ossi, the American daughter of an oyster magnate who promises to find her a prince to wed. A marriage broker suggests Prince Nucki, who lives in a rundown apartment with a pal. A lavish wedding party and unusual wedding night follow. With Ossi Oswalda. 55 min. Silent with music score.
10-9464 *$19.99*

One Arabian Night (1920)
German-made melodrama from Ernst Lubitsch set against a sumptuous Middle East backdrop. Pola Negri stars as an exotic dancer who charms both a sheik and his son, leading to wild (and fatal) romantic complications. Paul Wegener plays the jealous ruler, with Lubitsch co-starring as a dwarf jester. 75 min. Silent with music score.
09-5389 *$19.99*

The Marriage Circle (1924)
The breezy comedic style of Ernst Lubitsch is, as always, sophisticated and elegant in this marital comedy of manners inspired by Chaplin's "A Woman of Paris." Husband Adolphe Menjou begins to suspect wife Marie Prevost of being unfaithful in this silent treasure. 104 min.
10-1181 *$19.99*

Lady Windemere's Fan (1925)
Acknowledged as the best of Ernst Lubitsch's silent works, this rendition of Oscar Wilde's farce of romantic infidelity and red herrings remains a witty treat. Ronald Colman, May McAvoy and Bert Lytell star. 66 min. Silent with music score.
09-5388 *$19.99*

Gypsy Blood (1925)
The great Ernst Lubitsch directed this version of "Carmen," with silent film star Pola Negri in the title role. 80 min. Silent with musical score.
10-9240 Was $19.99 *$14.99*

The Student Prince In Old Heidelburg (1927)
The second silent filming of the famed Romberg operetta (yes, they made musicals without music). Ramon Novarro is the prince who finds adventure and romance when he leaves his sheltered home for the famed university. Norma Shearer is the barmaid who catches his eye; Ernst Lubitsch directs. 105 min. Silent with music score.
12-2145 *$29.99*

Please see our index for these other Ernst Lubitsch titles: *Bluebeard's Eighth Wife • Heaven Can Wait • Lady Windemere's Fan • The Merry Widow • Ninotchka • The Shop Around The Corner • That Uncertain Feeling • To Be Or Not To Be*

Rien Que Les Heures (1925)
Alberto Cavalcanti's impressionistic documentary look at the city of Paris and its inhabitants. A silent classic, in the tradition of "Berlin: Symphony of a Great City." 45 min.
53-7052 Was $29.99 *$14.99*

Shattered (1921)
A railroad worker's family faces a series of tragedies when the man's supervisor seduces and abandons his daughter in this rare German silent drama. Werner Krauss, Edith Posca star; directed by Lupu Pick. 60 min. Silent with organ score.
53-8363 *$39.99*

Cyrano De Bergerac (1925)
Pierre Magnier stars as the swashbuckling title hero, forced to hide his love for the fair Roxanne, in this early French-Italian adaptation of the Rostand favorite. Restored print includes hand-painted and tinted Pathécolor sequences. 114 min. Silent with music score.
53-8414 *$29.99*

Sadie Thompson (1928)
Gloria Swanson's challenge to Hays Office censorship is the first version of Somerset Maugham's humid classic about a South Seas sinner who causes the downfall of Bible-thumping preacher Lionel Barrymore. 97 min. Silent with musical score.
53-7307 *$24.99*

The Great White Trail (1917)
Set in Alaska's frozen wilderness, this melodrama tells of a woman who finds her and her baby's lives crumbling when her husband mistakes her brother for a lover. Cast out into the cold, she leaves the baby in a basket in order to save its life. Will fate bring them back together? Doris Kenyon stars. 107 min. Silent with organ score.
09-2253 Was $29.99 *$14.99*

Peter Pan (1924)
Unseen for decades, this gorgeously restored version of James M. Barrie's play tells of the boy who never grew up and his adventures with Wendy, her brothers and a fairy named Tinkerbell in Never Never Land, where they encounter Captain Hook, a crocodile and a band of Indians. Betty Bronson, Ernest Torrance and Anna May Wong star; features color tints. 102 min. Silent with music score.
53-6606 *$24.99*

The Last Days Of Pompeii (1913)
This Italian spectacle, based on Edward George Bulwer-Lytton's novel about the doomed Roman city, focuses on the lives of a statesman, a pagan priest, a witch, a blind beggar and a beautiful woman who live in the shadow of Mt. Vesuvius. All of their lives interconnect in the gladiatorial arena, just as the volcano erupts. Tinted in color and featuring Fernanda Negri Pouget. 88 min. Silent with music score.
53-6987 *$24.99*

Eyes Of Youth (1919)
Effective drama stars Clara Kimball Young as a young lass on the horns of a trilemma. Will she marry for money and get her father out of hock, marry for love and settle down, or pursue her operatic career? Watch fast for Rudolph Valentino! 85 min. Silent with musical score.
09-2023 Was $29.99 *$24.99*

A Girl's Folly (1917)
French-born director Maurice Tourneur made dozens of movies in America, including this daring romance about a farm girl (Doris Kenyon) who goes to Hollywood seeking stardom, and when this fails, considers becoming the mistress of a matinee idol (Robert Warwick). 30 min. Silent with music score.
09-2067 Was $29.99 *$14.99*

The Forbidden City (1918)
Lavish silent drama stars Norma Talmadge as the daughter of a Chinese mandarin who falls in love with a visiting American official. Troubles increase when he is called home on business and she bears his child. 72 min. Silent with music score.
09-2191 Was $29.99 *$24.99*

Border Sheriff (1926)
Lots of action and drama in this exciting western story, with Jack Hoxie as a tough sheriff who journeys to San Francisco, where he helps a rancher entrenched in a battle with Chinatown thugs. Hoxie uncovers that some of the rancher's own helpers are involved in the problems. Gilbert Holmes and Olive Hasbrouk also star. Silent with music score.
68-9198 Was $19.99 *$14.99*

Fortune's Fool (1921)
Emil Jannings is an industrialist who becomes enmeshed in a way of life beyond his ability and ambition. 107 min. Silent with music score.
09-1328 Was $29.99 *$14.99*

Twinkletoes (1926)
Colleen Moore plays a young woman living in London's Limehouse slum district who uses her talent for dancing and her love for a boxer to escape her sordid life. Compelling silent drama also stars Kenneth Harlan, Warner Oland. 65 min. Silent with music score.
53-8602 *$29.99*

Fritz Lang

Spiders (1919)
Mixing pulp fiction melodrama and his trademark use of master criminals and labyrinthine plots, this two-part suspense saga (two final chapters were planned but never filmed) from director Fritz Lang follows an intrepid adventurer as he tries to stop the secret criminal cabal "Die Spinnen" from stealing priceless Asian treasures. Carl de Vogt, Ressel Orla star. 137 min. Silent with music score.
53-9094 Remastered *$24.99*

Destiny (1921)
One of Fritz Lang's earliest silent films, the fantastic tale of a woman who attempts to save her lover from Death, despite what Death has revealed to her. With Lil Dagover ("The Cabinet of Dr. Caligari") and Rudolf Klein-Rogge ("Metropolis"). 122 min. Silent with music score; recorded at correct projection speed.
53-7059 Was $29.99 *$24.99*

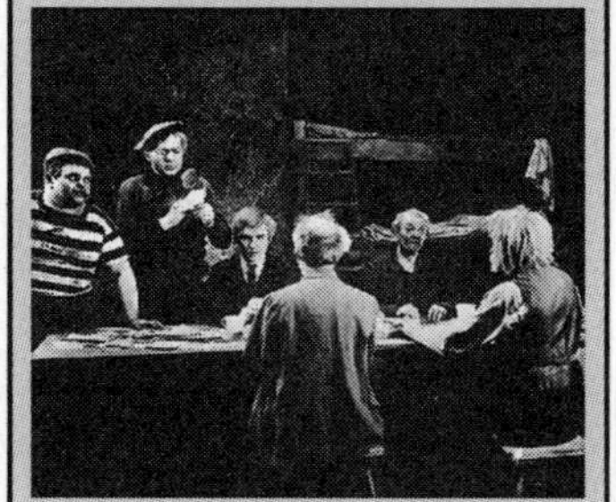

Dr. Mabuse The Gambler, Parts 1 And 2 (1922)
Two-part silent German serial from director/co-scripter Fritz Lang stars Rudolf Klein-Rogge as the criminal genius and master of hypnotism who launches a plan for global domination. Marked by Lang's trademark expressionistic style, the film offers an eerie look at the decadence of post-WWI German society. With Lil Dagover, Bernard Goetzke. 188 min.
53-7060 Was $39.99 *$29.99*

The Fatal Passion Of Dr. Mabuse (1922)
Taken from the first half of "Dr. Mabuse the Gambler," this feature-length drama has Rudolf Klein-Rogge's Mabuse using psychology and hypnosis to expand his underworld empire. 88 min.
53-7062 Was $29.99 *$19.99*

Siegfried (1924)
Fritz Lang's silent fantasy, recounting the epic tale of "Das Nibelungenlied" that also inspired Wagner's Ring Cycle, was the most lavish German film production of its time. Paul Richter stars as the dragon-slaying title hero; with Margarethe Schon, Georg John. Silent with music score.
63-1455 *$19.99*

Kriemhilde's Revenge (1924)
The second half of Fritz Lang's adaptation of the Nibelungen saga recounts how Kriemhilde seeks vengeance for the murder of her husband, the warrior Siegfried, by her villainous half-brother. Margarethe Schon, Theodor Loos, Rudolph Klein-Rogge star. 95 min. Silent with musical score.
63-1456 *$19.99*

Metropolis (1926)
Fritz Lang's masterwork, set in a towering city of the future whose populace is divided between the idle ruling class and the dehumanized workers who toil underground, remains a landmark of science-fiction cinema. Brigitte Helm, Rudolph Klein-Rogge star. 87 min. Silent with music score.
10-2030 *$19.99*

Please see our index for these other Fritz Lang titles: *The Big Heat • Clash By Night • Cloak And Dagger • Fury • House By The River • M • The Return Of Frank James • Scarlet Street • Secret Beyond The Door • The Testament Of Dr. Mabuse • The Thousand Eyes Of Dr. Mabuse • Western Union*

Berlin: Symphony Of A Great City (1927)
One of the most influential films in the history of documentary cinema, Walter Ruttman's silent look at a day in the life of Berlin was groundbreaking in its use of high-speed montage sequences. An all-new orchestral score was performed for this video, which also includes Ruttman's experimental color short from 1922, "Opus I." 72 min. total.
53-7837 *$24.99*

One Punch O'Day (1926)
When he and his two colleagues are stranded in a small town, penniless but proud pugilist Billy Sullivan winds up fighting in the ring and against some swindlers who've cheated a woman's father out of an oil lease. Charlotte Merriam, William Malan also star. 60 min. Silent with music score.
09-5390 *$19.99*

The Shamrock And The Rose (1927)
After the stage success of "Abie's Irish Rose," Hollywood followed with its "The Cohens and the Kellys" comedies, depicting the cross-cultural conflicts between two families when their children fall in love. William Strauss, Olive Hasbrook and perennial Chaplin foil Mack Swain star. 60 min. Silent with music score.
09-5398 *$19.99*

Young April (1926)
Delightful romantic comedy stars Bessie Love as an orphan, exiled in America since childhood, who is called by her European homeland's king to return and become a grand duchess. She's also asked to marry a down-and-out prince whose plan to sell the king's crown leads to funny complications. With Joseph Schildkraut. 70 min. Silent with music score.
09-5403 *$19.99*

Robinson Crusoe (1927)
One of the first film versions of Daniel Defoe's classic adventure, this silent drama features writer/director/star M.A. Wetherell as the sailor marooned on a seemingly deserted island. 30 min. Silent with music score.
09-5404 *$19.99*

Walking Back (1928)
Sue Carol and Richard Walling star in this drama about a '20s-style juvenile delinquent who takes a neighbor's car against his father's wishes and gets involved with a crew of car-stealing bank robbers. Silent with musical score.
10-8094 Was $19.99 *$14.99*

Captain Swagger (1926)
Rod La Rocque and Sue Carol star in this charming swashbuckling story of a would-be thief who does an about-face when he realizes where his sordid life is heading. Silent with musical score.
10-8095 Was $19.99 *$14.99*

The Blot (1921)
Lois Weber, one of America's first woman filmmakers, directs this social drama about a poor teacher whose daughter catches the eye of a well-to-do student. Phillip Hubbard, Claire Windsor, Louis Calhern star. 110 min. Silent with music score.
10-8211 Was $29.99 *$14.99*

Moulin Rouge (1928)
A fine British drama from director E.A. Dupont ("Variety") about a young man who becomes romantically involved with a star of the famed Paris dance hall who also happens to be his girlfriend's mother. Olga Tschechowa, Eve Gray star. Silent with musical score.
10-8376 *$14.99*

Two By Germaine Dulac
A pair of silent shorts from the French filmmaker who brought Impressionist styles into her work. The unhappy wife of a cloth merchant finds solace in her daydreams in "The Smiling Madame Beudet" (1922), while the daily life and inner thoughts of a cleric are contrasted in the Antonin Artaud-scripted "The Seashell and the Clergyman" (1928). 58 min. Silent with music score; title cards in French.
10-8228 Was $29.99 *$14.99*

Jesse James Under The Black Flag (1921)
A rare find about a young millionaire who crash-lands his plane near the residence of the real-life son of Jesse James and the outlaw's granddaughter. Visiting author Franklin Coates loans him a book to read about the real James' heroics, including his involvement in the Civil War. Features Jesse James, Jr. and narration added in the 1930s. 59 min.
53-9347 *$29.99*

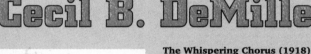

Cecil B. DeMille

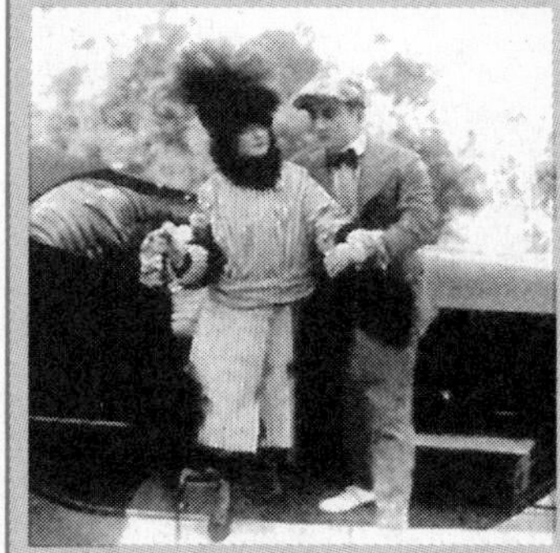

The Cheat (1915)
One of Cecil B. DeMille's first Hollywood pictures, this racy (for its time) melodrama tells of a free-spending socialite who loses $10,000 in charity funds entrusted to her. Desperate, she turns to a Burmese ivory merchant who agrees to help her...if she will give herself to him. Fannie Ward and Sessue Hayakawa (whose villainous character was originally Japanese until protests led to a change in this 1918 re-issue print) star. Also included is the short film "A Girl's Folly," by Maurice Tourneur. 89 min. total. Silent with music score.
53-8350 *$29.99*

Carmen (1915)
Cecil B. DeMille's epic production of the classic story showcases opera star Geraldine Farrar in the lead, playing a beautiful worker at a cigarette factory who finds refuge with Gypsies and love in a heated romantic triangle with soldier Wallace Reid and a bullfighter. Newly restored print includes color-tinted sequences. 63 min. Silent with music score.
53-8878 *$29.99*

Joan The Woman (1916)
In Cecil B. DeMille's grand translation of the Joan of Arc story, a young British soldier in the trenches during World War I finds a rusty sword from the 15th century and soon imagines himself in the past, fighting in the service of the young Maid of Orleans against English forces. Restored print includes a color-tinted final sequence. Geraldine Farrar, Wallace Reid star. 138 min. Silent with original organ score.
53-8879 *$29.99*

The Little American (1917)
This Cecil B. DeMille production stars Mary Pickford as an American woman caught between the affections of two soldiers, one German, the other French. When both are called to fight in World War I, Pickford goes to France to care for her aunt, and, after a near-disaster on the seas, she re-enters the men's lives. Jack Holt and Raymond Hatton co-star. 81 min. Silent with music score.
09-2372 *$19.99*

The Whispering Chorus (1918)
This unusual outing from C.B. DeMille is an eerie, atmospheric drama starring Raymond Hatton as a down-on-his-luck bookkeeper who starts a new life by faking his own death, disguising a corpse as himself. But when he is arrested and convicted of murdering the dead man, he must decide whether to save himself by disgracing his family. Newly restored print includes color-tinted sequences. 86 min. Silent with music score.
53-8880 *$29.99*

Male And Female (1919)
Provocative tale from director Cecil B. DeMille, based on a play by James M. Barrie, about an aristocratic family consisting of snooty, stubborn types who find themselves on an equal playing field with their servants when both factions are shipwrecked on an island. With Thomas Meighan, Bebe Daniels, and Gloria Swanson in a famous nude bathing scene. Restored print includes color-tinted sequences. 117 min. Silent with music score.
53-8881 *$29.99*

The Affairs Of Anatol (1921)
Unusual and rather risqué for its time, Cecil B. DeMille's drawing room drama stars Wallace Reid as a self-appointed savior of "loose women" who leaves wife Gloria Swanson behind to embark on his crusade. Reid meets his match when he's drawn to nightclub entertainer Satan Synne (Bebe Daniels), whose seductive way hides a surprising secret. Includes color-tinted sequences. 117 min. Silent with music score.
53-6717 *$24.99*

The Road To Yesterday (1925)
This opulent Cecil B. DeMille drama takes place "on the edge of the Grand Canyon, in the shadow of infinity." Five strangers find their lives drawing together, thanks to a train crash and a flashback sequence that shows the quintet in the same locale 300 years earlier. Joseph Schildkraut, William Boyd, Vera Reynolds star. 107 min. Silent with music score.
09-5395 *$19.99*

The Volga Boatman (1926)
Cecil B. DeMille's drama of the Russian Revolution features William Boyd as a peasant who helps boats travel along the Volga River. Boyd falls in love with a princess whose life he's eventually forced to save from a group of revenge-seeking Communists. With Elinor Fair. Restored print includes color-tinted sequences. 120 min. Silent with music score.
53-8882 *$29.99*

Please see our index for these other Cecil B. DeMille titles: *Cleopatra • The Crusades • The Greatest Show On Earth • The King Of Kings • Madam Satan • The Plainsman • Reap The Wild Wind • Samson And Delilah • The Sign Of The Cross • The Story Of Dr. Wassell • The Ten Commandments • Unconquered • Union Pacific*

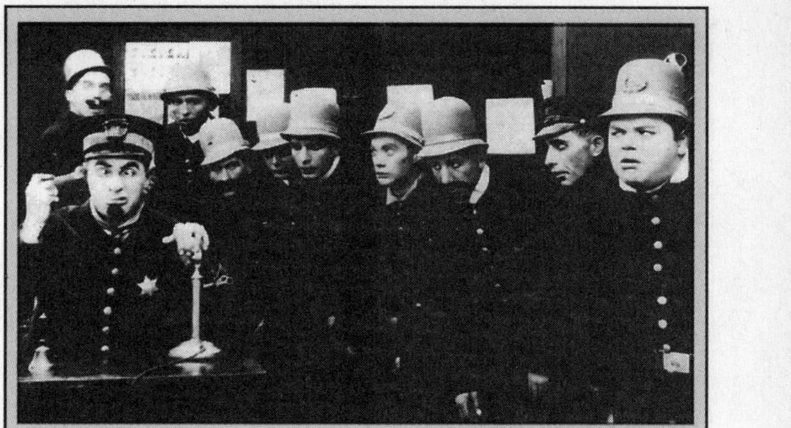

Mack Sennett

Keystone Comedies, Vol. 1 (1915)
Three classic silent comedies from Mack Sennett's Keystone Studios, all featuring the famed Roscoe "Fatty" Arbuckle: "Fatty's Faithful Fido," "Fatty's Tintype Tangle" and "Fatty's New Role." 47 min.
09-2988 *$14.99*

Keystone Comedies, Vol. 2 (1915)
More "big" laughs from the Keystone comedy duo of Fatty Arbuckle and Mabel Normand in this silent collection. Included are "Fatty and Mabel at the San Diego Exposition," "Fatty and Mabel's Simple Life" and "Mabel and Fatty's Wash Day," along with an early starring turn for Harold Lloyd, "Court House Crooks." 65 min.
09-2989 *$19.99*

Keystone Comedies, Vol. 3 (1915)
Mabel Normand and Fatty Arbuckle return for more silent slapstick in "Mabel Lost and Won" and "Wished on Mabel," and team up with the Keystone Kops in "Mabel, Fatty and the Law" and "Fatty's Plucky Pup." 57 min.
09-2990 *$14.99*

Keystone Comedies, Vol. 4 (1915)
Mabel Normand and Fatty Arbuckle visit an amusement park, tie the knot, and cope with domestic problems in the Keystone shorts "Mabel's Wilful Way," "That Little Band of Gold" and "Mabel and Fatty's Married Life." 44 min.
09-2991 *$14.99*

Keystone Comedies, Vol. 5 (1915)
Boisterous, mustached Mack Swain starred as a boisterous, mustached bumbler named "Ambrose" in a series of silent comedies for Mack Sennett. Three of his best are featured here: "Ambrose's Nasty Temper," "Ambrose's Sour Grapes" and "When Ambrose Dared Walrus." 55 min.
09-2992 *$14.99*

Keystone Comedies, Vol. 6 (1915)
There's more nostalgic fun with Mack Swain as "Ambrose" in the Sennett slapstickers "Ambrose's Lofty Perch," "Ambrose's Fury" and "Willful Ambrose," plus Mae Busch starring in "Those Bitter Sweets." 47 min.
09-2993 *$14.99*

Keystone Comedies, Vol. 7 (1914-1915)
Sidney Chaplin (Charlie's half-brother) proved that talent runs in the family when he starred as "Gussle" in several Sennett-produced silent gagfests. "Gussle the Golfer," "Gussle's Day of Rest," "Gussle Tied to Trouble" and "Gussle's Backward Way" are included. 55 min.
09-2994 *$14.99*

Billy Bevan Comedies
This collection of Mack Sennett shorts feature the great (and largely forgotten) Billy Bevan. Among the films here are "The Best Man" (1925), "Butter Fingers" (1925), "Away from the Steerage" (1920) and "Be Reasonable" (1921). See how Bevan influenced Keaton and Lloyd years later. Silent with music score.
03-5015 *$24.99*

Slapstick Follies
Slapstick gems abound in this collection from Sennett, Roach, Christie and Educational studios. Included are "Jungle Heat" (1925) with future "B" westerner Al St. John; Our Gang in "The Sundown Limited" (1924); Bobby Vernon in "Broken China" (1926); and Turpin and Conklin in "A Clever Dummy" (1917); and more. Silent with music score.
03-5017 *$24.99*

The Speed Kings (1913)/ Love, Speed And Thrills (1915)
Double dose of racing autos and silent slapstick from the Keystone company. First is Mack Sennett's all-star comedy set around an L.A. road race, with Fatty Arbuckle and Mabel Normand, followed by a wild chase with Mack Swain and the Keystone Kops. 19 min. total. Silent with music score.
62-5211 Was $19.99 *$14.99*

The Shriek Of Araby (1923)
In this rare feature from Mack Sennett, silent comic great Ben Turpin spoofs Rudolph Valentino's "The Sheik," playing a bill poster who gets a job as a romantic leading man when the real movie star is told he's too handsome. Comic hijinks ensue, but are they real or is Ben just dreaming. Kathryn McGuire also stars. Silent with music score.
03-5010 *$24.99*

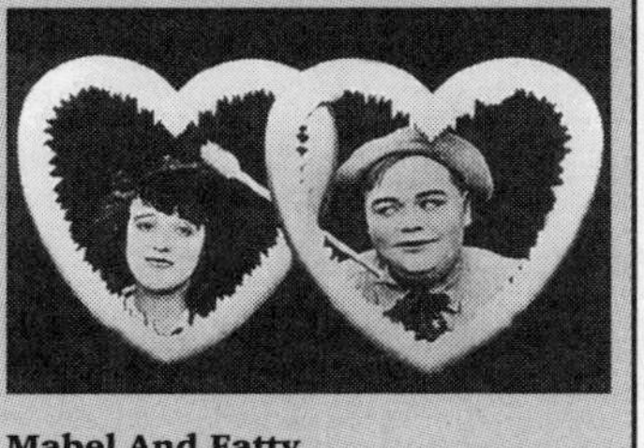

Mabel And Fatty
Roscoe "Fatty" Arbuckle plays a doctor jealous over the arrival of wife Mabel Normand's old flame in "He Did and He Didn't" (1916), followed by the self-explanatory "Mabel and Fatty Viewing the World's Fair at San Francisco" (1915). Then, Normand (sans Aruckle) dresses as a man to spy on a wayward beau in "Mabel's Blunder" (1914). 61 min. Silent with music score; recorded at correct projection speed.
09-1977 Was $24.99 *$19.99*

Chasing Laughter
After several years as a top director for producer Hal Roach, Charley Chase stepped in front of the camera in 1924 and became a comedy star in his own right. Three of Charley's best short films are featured here: "Mum's the Word," "Tell 'Em Nothing" and "Mama Behave." 60 min. total. Silent with organ score.
53-8367 *$29.99*

Charley Chase Festival (1921-27)
Six of his best silent shorts: "Long Fliv the King," "Stone Goods," "Fighting Fluid," "Ten Minute Egg," "Young Oldfield," "At First Sight." 70 min. Silent with musical soundtrack.
62-1055 *$19.99*

Mickey (1919)
Extremely popular silent comedy drama that was a financial shot in the arm for the Sennett Studios and nourished the solo career of star Mabel Normand. She's at her best, moving East to live with relatives who take her on as a maid after they learn she's penniless. Co-stars Lew Cody.
10-7045 *$19.99*

Mack Sennett: The Films Of Biograph
An exciting potpourri of short movies from the pioneer director: "Happy Jack" with Sennett; Mabel Normand in "The Baron;" Henry B. Walthall in "In the Border States"; "A Villain Foiled" with Blanche Sweet; Joseph Graybill in "Turning the Tables" and "Dash Through the Clouds" with Normand. 60 min.
53-9002 *$39.99*

Slapstick Encyclopedia
Travel back in time to the days of Tin Lizzie car chases and custard pie fights with this series that presents classic silent short comedies from the years 1909 to 1927, when such pioneering filmmakers as Mack Sennett and Hal Roach created the genre with the help of such then-unknown stars as Charlie Chaplin, Buster Keaton, and Laurel and Hardy.

Slapstick Encyclopedia, Vol. 1: In The Beginning...: Film Comedy Pioneers
Cross-eyed comic Ben Turpin is would-be Lothario "Mr. Flip" (1909); a pre-L&H Oliver Hardy teams with Billy Ruge in "One Too Many," an entry in the duo's 1910s "Plump & Runt" series; famed black entertainer Bert Williams presents one of his classic Ziegfeld Follies routines in "A Natural-Born Gambler"(1916); Mack Sennett makes a rare on-screen appearance in the Fatty Arbuckle-Mabel Normand romp "Mabel's Dramatic Career" (1913); and more. 126 min.
53-6148 *$24.99*

Slapstick Encyclopedia, Vol. 2: Keystone Tonight! Mack Sennett Comedies
The Sultan of Slapstick and his Keystone Studio are feted in a retrospective that includes Harry Langdon in the Frank Capra-scripted "Saturday Afternoon" (1926); "Wandering Willies" (1926), with the Keystone Kops; "Barney Oldfield's Race for Life" (1913), a fast-paced spoof of Victorian melodramas; and more. 121 min.
53-6149 *$24.99*

Slapstick Encyclopedia, Vol. 3: Funny Girls
Knockabout comedy wasn't a sport for men only, as this video spotlighting early female film stars demonstrates. Louise Fazenda and Ford Sterling star in the cross-dressing farce "Hearts and Flowers" (1919); Fay Tincher, as "Rowdy Ann" (1919), tames the Wild West; Alice Howell, considered by Stan Laurel to be one of the all-time top comediennes, stars in "One Wet Night" (1924); along with three more shorts. 117 min.
53-6150 *$24.99*

Slapstick Encyclopedia, Vol. 4: Keaton, Arbuckle & St. John
The three title stars were friends and colleagues on-screen and off. Roscoe "Fatty" Arbuckle teams with a young Charlie Chaplin in "The Rounders" (1914) and frequent co-star Mabel Normand in "Fatty and Mabel Adrift" (1916); Buster Keaton launches "The Boat" (1921), seen here in a newly-remastered, orchestrally-scored edition; Al St. John fires up "The Iron Mule" (1925), directed by Arbuckle and featuring a cameo by Keaton; and all three appear in "Oh, Doctor!" (1917). 135 min.
53-6151 *$24.99*

Slapstick Encyclopedia, Vol. 5: Chaplin & Co.: The Music Hall Tradition
Far and away the greatest slapstick star was Charlie Chaplin, featured here along with some of his influences and imitators. Charlie stars in "A Night in the Show" (1915) and "The Rink" (1916) and is seen comically conducting an orchestra in a rare 1916 film clip. Other stars include Billie Ritchie in "Live Wires and Love Sparks" (1916); "Pie-Eyed" (1925) with Stan Laurel; and more. 134 min.
53-6195 *$24.99*

Slapstick Encyclopedia, Vol. 6: Hal Roach: The Lot Of Fun
Laurel and Hardy, Harold Lloyd, and Our Gang are just some of the classic slapstick acts that got their start at the stages and backlots of the Hal Roach Studio. Included here are Stan working solo in "Oranges and Lemons" (1923) and teaming with Ollie in a "Laftoons" compilation; the Our Gang kids raising havoc at a Hollywood studio in "Dogs of War" (1923), co-starring Lloyd; Will Rogers in "Big Moments from Little Pictures" (1924); "It's a Gift" (1923) with Snub Pollard; and others. 133 min.
53-6196 *$24.99*

Slapstick Encyclopedia, Vol. 7: The Race Is On!
Some of the most amusing and daredevil stunts were pulled off during the silent era, many of which wouldn't ever dare be attempted now. Films such as "Teddy at the Throttle" (1917) with Wallace Beery and a young Gloria Swanson; "Circus Today" (1926) with Billy Bevan and Andy Clyde; and the "Hairbreadth Harry" short "Danger Ahead" (1926) showcase the dizzying chases and mishaps that amaze viewers even today. 120 min.
53-6197 *$24.99*

Slapstick Encyclopedia, Vol. 8: Tons Of Fun: Comedy's Anarchic Fringe
Several of the lesser-known but nevertheless hilarious slapstick pioneers are brought together in this collection of whimsical nonsense. Larry Semon stars as "The Grocery Clerk" (1920); Ben Turpin heads to the frozen North in "Yukon Jake" (1924); a trio of heavyset comics known as "A Ton of Fun" demolish a swank nightclub in "Three of a Kind" (1926); and more. 131 min.
53-6198 *$24.99*

Slapstick Encyclopedia: Set 1
Volumes 1-4 are also available in a boxed collector's set.
53-6152 Save $10.00! *$89.99*

Slapstick Encyclopedia: Set 2
Volumes 5-8 are also available in a boxed collector's set.
53-6199 Save $10.00! *$89.99*

Les Vampires (1915)
Louis Feuillade's epic silent serial follows an ingenious group of jewel thieves in Paris whose criminal and terrorist acts are led by the mysterious Irma Vep (Musidora), a vampire-like woman whose sensuality frightens and seduces her victims at the same time. This newly restored edition features color re-tinting, a vintage orchestral score, and has been corrected to the speed at which the film was originally photographed. 7 1/2 hrs. on four tapes.
01-1548 *$99.99*

Mrs. Wiggs Of The Cabbage Patch (1919)
The first screen version of Alice Caldwell Hegan Rice's novel features Marguerite Clark as Lovey Mary, a worker at an orphanage who escapes with a young boy and takes residence with the poor Mrs. Wiggs and her five children in a dilapidated house. When Mary falls for Billy, one of the Wiggs kids, complications ensue. With Mary Carr. Silent with music score.
03-5007 *$24.99*

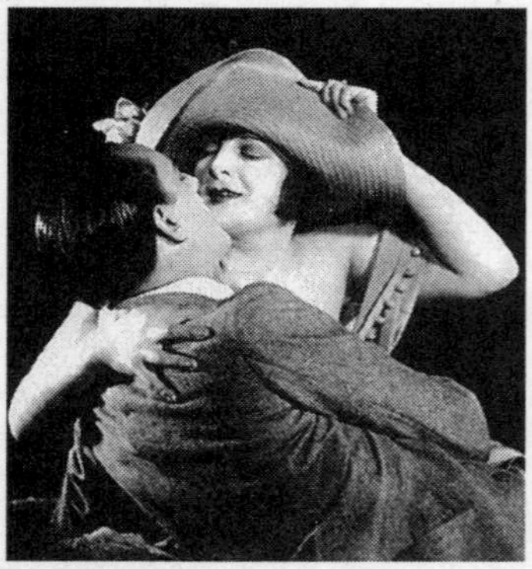

Variety (1925)
A show-business story that depicts the rising decadence of post-WWI Germany. Emil Jannings plays an aging trapeze performer who suspects wife Lya De Putti of infidelity, leading to a deadly confrontation. 79 min. Silent with music score.
09-1307 *$19.99*

Little Mary Sunshine (1916)
This rarity features Baby Marie Osborne, a child star of the silent era, as the title character, a girl abandoned after her father kills her mother. She's found by an alcoholic man who takes her in and raises her, but their relationship leads to him abandoning drinking and reuniting with his estranged girlfriend. With Henry King, who also directs. Silent with music score.
03-5004 *$24.99*

Tom Sawyer (1917)
The classic book is brought to life in a wonderful early adaptation of Mark Twain's story. Featured is Jack Pickford as Tom, who joins friends Huck and Joe Harper in an adventure on the Mississippi. Directed by the infamous William Desmond Taylor, the film also stars George Hackathorne and Robert Gordon. Silent with music score.
03-5011 *$24.99*

Bronco Billy Shorts, Vol. 1
Three of the nearly 400 "Bronco Billy" Anderson shorts produced by Essanay Studios (of which Anderson was the "ay" alongside "es," partner George Spoor) are featured. Witness the silent screen western hero in "Bronco Billy's Sentence" (1915), "Bronco Billy and the Greaser" (1914) and "Bronco Billy's Fatal Joke" (1914).
68-9222 *$14.99*

The Son-Of-A-Gun (1919)
Early western hero "Bronco Billy" Anderson excels in this action-packed story, playing a hard-drinking, hard-fighting cowpoke who quits his wild ways when he sees a pretty lady and rescues her brother from some slimy cowpokes. Joy Lewis also star. Silent with music score.
68-9142 *$19.99*

The Coward (1915)
Terrific silent Civil War story made at the same time as "Birth of a Nation." Proud Rebel pappy is determined to see his gun shy son serve the Confederacy—even if he has to double for him when he deserts under fire. Charles Ray, Frank Keenan. 86 min. Silent with music score.
09-1863 Was $29.99 *$24.99*

Danton (1921)
Emil Jannings turns in a towering performance in this powerful tale of the French Revolution. Jannings plays the title character, the charismatic radical leader who helps in the fall of the aristocracy in France during the late 1700s, and who eventually met his own untimely demise. A rare example of German Expressionism. 60 min. Silent with music score.
10-9459 *$19.99*

Peck's Bad Boy (1921)
Child-star Jackie Coogan is perfectly cast in this silent comedy as the mischief-making ragamuffin continuously getting into one scrape after another, from his minor pilfering at a grocery store to his letting a lion loose at the circus. Titles written by humorist Irvin S. Cobb. 65 min.
62-5220 *$19.99*

Waxworks (1924)
A trio of legendary killers—Jack the Ripper (Werner Krauss), Ivan the Terrible (Conrad Veidt) and Haroun-al-Raschid (Emil Jannings)—come to life in three highly stylized segments of director Paul Leni's silent horror omnibus. A writer's imagination runs wild while creating scenarios for a carnival's wax exhibit. 60 min.
68-8068 *$19.99*

20,000 Leagues Under The Sea (1916)
Astounding silent adventure incorporates two Jules Verne novels, "20,000 Leagues Under the Sea" and "The Mysterious Island," to tell the story of the demented Captain Nemo and his submarine, the Nautilus. Amazing underwater footage shot in the Bahamas and tinted sequences are a highlight. Matt Moore, Allen Holubar, June Gail star. 105 min. Silent with music score.
10-8145 *$24.99*

Regeneration (1915)
A rare find, this early gangster drama was the first directorial effort by Raoul Walsh after he left D.W. Griffith's company and features great location shots of New York's infamous Bowery. Rockliffe Fellows, John McCann star. 60 min.
10-8317 Was $19.99 *$14.99*

A Fool There Was (1914)
The film that made Theda Bara an international star and gave her the nickname "The Vamp" features the mysterious actress as a femme fatale who mixes ruthlessness and sexiness. This film was a huge hit for Fox Studios and was based on the Rudyard Kipling poem "The Vampire." With Edward Jose and May Allison. Silent with organ score.
10-8781 *$19.99*

The Unchastened Woman (1925)
Following a five-year retirement, Theda Bara returned to Hollywood for this film in which she plays a woman who learns that she's pregnant, then discovers her husband is having an affair with his secretary. She flees to Europe, and, years later, the couple has a tearful reunion. Wyndham Standing also stars. 55 min. Silent with musical score.
10-9050 Was $19.99 *$14.99*

The Tong Man (1919)
Set in San Francisco's Chinatown, this groundbreaking thriller stars Sessue Hayakawa as a "hatchet man" who falls in love with the daughter of a powerful drug smuggler. Hayakawa's assignment is to murder the smuggler, but when he refuses to carry it out, he becomes the target of an assassin. Helen Jerome Eddy also stars. Silent with music score.
10-8782 Was $19.99 *$14.99*

Tillie Wakes Up (1917)
Marie Dressler returns in the role that made her a sensation in "Tillie's Punctured Romance." The setting is Coney Island, where Tillie Tinklepaw's fun-loving adventure with a neighbor's husband leads to all sorts of complications. Johnny Hines also stars. 50 min. Silent with musical score.
10-9027 *$19.99*

The Spoilers (1914)
Sprawling epic adventure about the search for gold in the Klondike features several elaborate sequences, including a wild fight scene. The film stars William Farnum as a man who calls on his family and a female saloonkeeper to stop some crooked people in an Alaskan town from taking his gold mine. 110 min. Silent with musical score.
10-9034 Was $19.99 *$14.99*

Civilization (1916)
Thomas Ince produced and directed this controversial anti-war tale of a submarine captain whose body is taken over by Christ in an attempt to end a destructive war waged between two mythical countries (one of which resembles Germany). Barney Sherry and Enid Markey star. 86 min. Silent with musical score.
10-9060 Was $29.99 *$19.99*

The Italian (1915)
Emotionally-charged drama stars George Beban as an impoverished Venetian gondolier in love with a beautiful woman being pressured to marry a wealthy merchant by her father. In hopes of appeasing the father, the boatman goes to New York to win a home for his love. Produced and co-written by Thomas Ince. 70 min. Silent with music score.
09-2936 *$19.99*

The Wishing Ring (1914)
The likable but reckless college student son of the Earl of Bateson loses favor with his father after being expelled for "gross misconduct." The young man takes a job tending his godfather's rose garden, where he falls in love with a sweet young thing who has been stealing the flowers. Vivian Martin stars. 55 min. Silent with music score.
09-2937 *$14.99*

The Count Of Monte Cristo (1912)
Renowned actor James O'Neill (father of playwright Eugene) re-creates his stage role in the timeless Dumas classic. Produced by Adolph Zukor's Famous Players Film Company, this melodrama is historically significant as an early "art film." With Hobart Bosworth. 59 min. Silent with music score.
09-5382 *$19.99*

The Busher (1919)
Early Hollywood baseball drama stars Charles Ray as a naive small-town player whose phenomenal pitching arm lands him a job with a major league team. Once in the big city, he becomes a conceited carouser. Will Ray mend his ways before it's too late? With Colleen Moore, John Gilbert. 50 min. Silent with music score.
09-5381 *$19.99*

Bolshevism On Trial (1919)
In the wake of the Russian Revolution and the first "Red Scares" came this unusual silent social drama. A wounded WWI soldier, at the urging of a female social worker, works to create an egalitarian society. Eager to discourage the young man's notions, his wealthy father helps him set up an experimental community on a Florida island. Robert Frazer and Leslie Stowe star. 80 min.
09-5347 *$19.99*

Going Straight (1916)
Norma Talmadge shines as a respected housewife and mother with a skeleton in her closet: she and her husband once belonged to a notorious gang of robbers. They since decided to "go straight," but their covers are threatened when one of their old cronies gets out of jail. With Ralph Lewis, Eugene Pallette. 49 min. Silent with music score.
09-5386 *$19.99*

The Three Musketeers (1916)
It's one for all and all for one in this rousing adaptation of Alexander Dumas' swashbuckling classic, the first film version ever! Join D'Artagnan and his fellow swordsmen as they thwart a conspiracy in King Louis XIII's court. Orrin Johnson, Dorothy Dalton and Walt Whitman (the actor, not the poet) star. 63 min. Silent with music score.
09-5400 *$19.99*

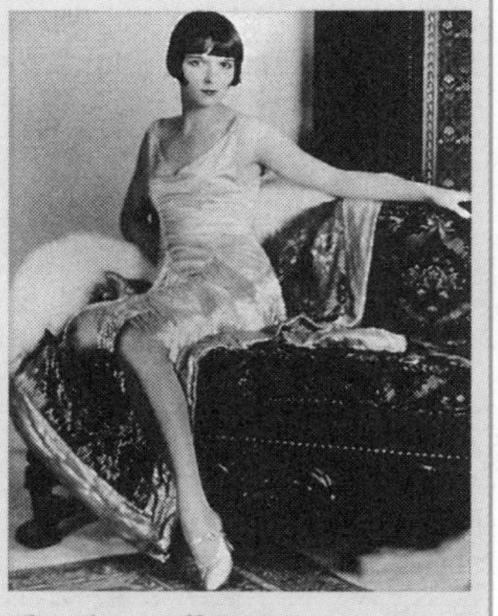

The Show Off (1926)
Slapstick screen comic Ford Sterling shines in the title role of a well-meaning but boisterous braggart whose loud mouth gets him into one scrape after another and threatens to ruin his marriage. Filmed in part in Philadelphia, the silent melodrama also stars Lois Wilson and Louise Brooks. 82 min. Silent with music score.
68-8218 *$24.99*

Pandora's Box (1928)
Melodramatic German silent classic stars lovely Louise Brooks as Lulu, a promiscuous flower girl whose life becomes a downward spiral of sin and redemption until her ultimate encounter. G.W. Pabst's stirring work was scandalous in its time for its eroticism; with Fritz Kortner, Francis Lederer. 110 min. Silent with music score.
22-5671 *$24.99*

Diary Of A Lost Girl (1929)
G.W. Pabst's silent follow-up to "Pandora's Box." Louise Brooks stars as a young girl whose life goes through a succession of trying events. Fascinating and stark, it's a must-see for fans of German stylistics and Brooks. 99 min.
62-1198 *$19.99*

Prix De Beauté (1930)
Louise Brooks' final starring role (and only French film) features hermemorable work as a young secretary who enters and wins a prestigious beauty contest over her jealous boyfriend's protestations. Augusto Genina directs. 97 min. In French with English subtitles.
53-7313 *$59.99*

Louise Brooks: Looking For Lulu (1998)
She was the silent screen siren as famous for her feuds with studios and directors as for her black bobbed haircut. Louise Brooks' life and career, both in and out of Hollywood, are traced in this compelling documentary that features vintage film footage and rare interviews, including a never-before-seen 1976 conversation with Brooks. Shirley MacLaine narrates. 60 min.
50-5307 *$19.99*

Please see our index for these other Louise Brooks titles: *Empty Saddles • Overland Stage Raiders*

The Golem: How He Came Into The World (1920)
The legend of "The Golem," a man-made creature magically brought to life by a learned rabbi to prevent the persecution of the Jews in a pogrom in Prague, Czechoslovakia, is portrayed in this atmospheric German fantasy that was an early entry in the horror film genre. Starring writer/co-director Paul Wegener (who filmed the tale once before in a 1914 version), Albert Steinruck and Lydia Salmonova. 80 min. Silent with music score.
09-1341 *$19.99*

The Old Swimmin' Hole (1921)
A rural boy in love with a girl finds himself getting into all sorts of trouble when he tries to draw her attention. Finally, while having lunch with her one day, he reveals his true feelings towards her. Charles Ray and Blanche Rose star in this experimental film that tells its story without the use of titles. 60 min.
10-9113 Was $19.99 *$14.99*

The Heart Of Humanity (1918)
Erich von Stroheim stars in a patriotic entry from his "The Man You Love to Hate" period, playing a sadistic Prussian army officer visiting a Canadian town of the eve of World War I and lusting for local priest's niece Dorothy Phillips. Includes the infamous scene where "the Hun" throws a baby out a window. 100 min. Silent with music score.
09-5387 *$19.99*

Blind Husbands (1919)
In his directorial debut, Erich von Stroheim also stars as a handsome army officer having an affair with the wife of a staid doctor. The illicit affair leads to a dramatic conclusion in a mountain-climbing sequence. Gibson Gowland, Francelia Billington also star. 68 min. Silent with music score.
09-5379 *$19.99*

Foolish Wives (1922)
Advertised as the first film to cost a million dollars, director/star Erich von Stroheim's lavish, decadent drama follows a phony count and his beautiful "cousins" as they set out seducing the wealthy visitors to Monte Carlo. Mae Busch, Rudolph Christians also star. Restored 107-min. version. Silent with music score.
01-1252 Was $24.99 *$19.99*

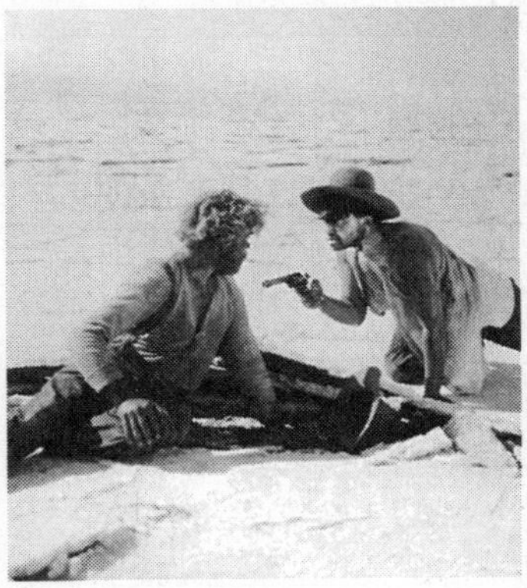

Greed (75th Anniversary Restoration Version) (1925)
Director Erich von Stroheim's famed silent masterpiece, originally 42 reels in length before studio head Irving Thalberg ordered it cut to 10, is presented here with long-missing footage added and still photos used to provide continuity. The drive for gold and success leads to jealousy, murder and a showdown in Death Valley for former friends Gibson Gowland and Jean Hersholt. ZaSu Pitts, Chester Conklin also star. 239 min. Silent with music score.
12-3322 *$29.99*

The Wedding March (1927)
Powerful silent melodrama of love conquering all. Director Erich von Stroheim stars as a flirtatious prince in pre-WWI Vienna who falls in love with a peasant girl against his parents' wishes. A surprisingly sentimental work from the famed silent villain, the film contains tinted sequences. With Fay Wray, ZaSu Pitts. 113 min. Organ score by Gaylord Carter.
06-1434 Was $29.99 *$14.99*

Queen Kelly (Restored Version) (1929)
Gloria Swanson stars as a virginal convent student who attracts the eye of a rakish European prince about to wed a sadistic queen. Writer/director Erich von Stroheim's lavish, unfinished silent masterwork (he was fired by producer Joseph Kennedy) is presented here in its most complete reconstructed edition, using stills and title cards to finish the story. 97 min. Silent with music score.
53-7651 Was $39.99 *$24.99*

The Man You Loved To Hate (1979)
The remarkable life of screen villain and controversial filmmaker Erich von Stroheim is documented in this look at the Austrian immigrant's on- and off-screen follies. Includes clips from such movies as "Foolish Wives," "Greed" and "Queen Kelly" and interviews with von Stroheim's ex-wives, friends and colleagues. 70 min.
53-9375 *$29.99*

His First Flame (1926)
Uproarious silent comedy featuring the childlike Harry Langdon, who in his day rivaled Chaplin, Keaton and Lloyd. Watch as Harry finds true love and tries not to get burned as a fireman; co-written by Frank Capra. 62 min. Silent with music score.
09-1927 Was $24.99 *$19.99*

The Strong Man (1926)
In his most acclaimed silent comedy (directed by Frank Capra), Harry Langdon is a Belgian soldier who travels to America with a circus troupe, hoping to meet the girl who's been his long-time pen pal. With Priscilla Bonner, Arthur Thalasso. Also included is the 1925 short "His Marriage Wow," chronicling Harry's comic attempts to get to the altar on time. 94 min. total. Silent with music score.
44-1669 Was $39.99 *$29.99*

Tramp, Tramp, Tramp (1926)
Harry Langdon, in his first feature-length comedy, plays a cross-country walking race contestant who must overcome such unlikely obstacles as a tornado, a herd of marauding sheep, and a stint on a chain gang. A young Joan Crawford co-stars as the race's sponsor's daughter, with whom Langdon falls in love; co-written by Frank Capra. Harry returns as a hapless WWI doughboy in the bonus 1924 short "All Night Long." 84 min. total. Silent with music score.
53-8829 *$29.99*

Long Pants (1927)
The final film collaboration between star Harry Langdon and director Frank Capra, this delightful mix of slapstick and pathos features cherub-faced Langdon as a shy momma's boy from the country who is seduced from his true love by a scheming, drug-smuggling big city "vamp." Priscilla Bonner, Alma Bennett co-star. Also included is the 1926 short "Saturday Afternoon," with Harry as a henpecked husband. 87 min. total. Silent with music score.
53-8830 *$29.99*

White Tiger (1923)
Rarely seen and feared lost, this film co-written and directed by Tod Browning tells of what happens when a long-lost brother and sister get involved with a con artist. Raymond Griffith, Priscilla Dean and Wallace Beery star. 82 min.
10-9023 *$19.99*

The Back Trail (1924)
A man injured during the Civil War and stricken with amnesia comes to believe he's an outlaw and is framed by a group of crooks. Jack Hoxie, Alton Stone and Eugenia Gilbert star in this stunt-filled sagebrusher. Silent with music score.
10-8375 Was $19.99 *$14.99*

Raggedy Rose (1926)
Stan Laurel directed this comedy with Hal Roach star Mabel Normand in a fanciful, "Cinderella"-like story of rags to riches. James Finlayson also stars. 56 min. Silent with musical score.
10-9149 Was $19.99 *$14.99*

Mid-Channel (1920)
Clara Kimball Young turns in a terrific performance as a woman who has come "mid-channel" in her marriage—a phase where discontent settles in and the future seems uncertain. Will she and her husband overcome the hurdles they face, or will the union end? 69 min. Silent with music score.
09-2931 *$19.99*

The Leopard Woman (1920)
Louise Glaum, known for being one of the most seductive of screen vamps, turns in a terrific performance playing a mysterious woman named "Madame." She's a floozy who comes on to sportsman House Peters, but after he rejects her invitation, she's recruited to kill him while on safari in a faraway land. 72 min. Silent with music score.
09-2933 *$19.99*

The Cat And The Canary (1927)
The movie that helped set the tone for all "haunted house" films to follow, director Paul Leni's silent masterpiece is set in a creepy mansion where the heirs of a millionaire dead for 20 years await to see who will inherit his fortune...if any of them survive the night. Laura La Plante, Creighton Hale star. Along with this color-tinted feature, the video also includes the Harold Lloyd comedy thriller "Haunted Spooks" (1920). 102 min. total. Silent with music score.
53-6266 *$24.99*

Let'er Go Gallegher (1928)
A paperboy witnesses a murder and tells a reporter on the newspaper. The tip lands the reporter to fame and fortune, but his sudden arrogance leads to him losing his job and girlfriend. Now, in order to get them both back, he and the boy join forces to capture the fugitive killer. Junior Coghlan, Harrison Ford star. 60 min. Silent with musical score.
10-9036 Was $19.99 *$14.99*

Love Never Dies (1921)
Produced, written and directed by King Vidor, this silent tearjerker follows the travails of two "loose women" in a small town and what happens when a young man, thought to be the son of one of the women, returns to town as a successful architect. Madge Bellamy, Lloyd Hughes star. 53 min. Silent with music score.
10-9022 *$19.99*

Hold Your Breath (1924)
This wild, stunt-filled silent comedy stars Dorothy Devore as a young woman who takes a job as a newspaper reporter to support her family and winds up crawling along a skyscraper window ledge as she pursues a monkey—and an interview with an eccentric millionaire. With Priscilla Bonner, Tully Marshall. 32 min. Silent With music score.
10-9021 *$19.99*

Tol'able David (1921)
The Old Testament story of David and Goliath is effectively transferred to the backwoods of Appalachia in this popular silent melodrama. Richard Barthelmess stars as the young man who must find his inner courage to protect his family and town from a clan of hulking mountain men. With Ernest Torrence, Gladys Hulette. Along with the restored, tinted version of the film, this video also includes a rare interview with director Henry King. 91 min. Silent with music score.
53-6162 *$24.99*

Underworld (1927)
One of the seminal films in the gangster genre, director Josef von Sternberg's silent drama stars Clive Brook as a down-and-out gentleman who becomes friends with bank robber George Bancroft. Using his brains and Bancroft's muscle, Brook helps his pal become king of the city's crime syndicate. Evelyn Brent, Larry Semon also star; based on a story by Ben Hecht. 80 min.
10-7952 *$19.99*

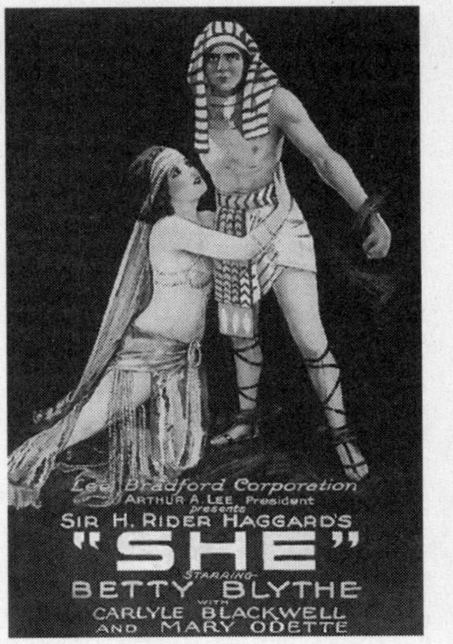

She (1925)
H. Rider Haggard's classic fantasy-adventure about a hidden land and its immortal queen was filmed seven times between 1900 and 1930. This was the last and perhaps best silent version, featuring cards written by Haggard himself. Betty Blythe stars as She-Who-Must-Be-Obeyed. 77 min.
09-1306 *$19.99*

Unseen Enemies (1926)
In this rousing silent sagebrusher, Al Hoxie plays tough-as-nails cowboy "Happened Along" Meredith, who, with sidekick "Doughnut" Casey, tackles the crook who works a smuggling ring out of Bordertown and tries to swindle two boys out of their family's ranch, a no-account varmint known as "Bingo" Strook. 38 min. Silent with music score.
10-9026 *$19.99*

The Cyclone Cavalier (1925)
A comic adventure filled with heart-stopping stuntwork, this Ray-Art feature stars Reed Howes as an irresponsible young man who tries to make good when he's sent South of the Border. With Carmelita Geraghty. 47 min. Silent with music score.
10-9020 *$19.99*

April Fool (1926)
This romantic farce is set among the nouveau-riche Jews of New York and focuses on a clothing cleaner who hits it big as an umbrella manufacturer and who risks his fortune to ensure his daughter's happiness with a man accused of swiping a large sum of loot. Alexander Carr, Duane Thompson and Mary Alden star. 63 min. Silent with musical score.
10-9028 *$19.99*

Clara Bow

Down To The Sea In Ships (1922)
Clara Bow makes her film debut as a Quaker girl in a 19th-century whaling town. The whaling scenes were filmed on an actual expedition and have never been surpassed. Directed by Elmer Clifton, a protégé of D.W. Griffith. 83 min.
62-5150 *$19.99*

Free To Love (1924)
Legendary silent screen temptress Clara Bow stars in this tale of a orphan girl who, after being wrongfully sent to a reformatory for two years, is taken in by the family of the judge who sent her away and tries to become a society girl. With Donald Keith, Raymond McKee. 49 min. Silent with music score.
10-9095 *$19.99*

The Plastic Age (1925)
Silent screen sex symbol Clara Bow stars as a frisky, fun-loving college co-ed who draws her college sports star boyfriend from his athletic and academic endeavors in this tale of campus life in the Roaring '20s. With Donald Keith. Also included is "Run, Girl, Run" (1928), a Mack Sennett short about an all-girl track team with a young Carole Lombard. 73 min. total. Silent with music score.
53-6498 *$24.99*

Parisian Love (1925)
Clara Bow really has "it" in this film as a conniving thief in Paris who thrives off ripping off American tourists. When her lover is killed by a wealthy man, Bow joins forces with a band of crooks and an underworld matriarch to get even through seduction—and bilk the culprit in the process! Donald Keith and Lillian Leighton also star. 62 min. Silent with music score.
53-6499 *$24.99*

Mantrap (1926)
Among the most representative of the flapper roles which established Clara Bow as a sex symbol is this tale of a capricious femme fatale, co-starring Ernest Torrence and Eugene Pallette. Directed by Victor Fleming.
17-3059 Was $29.99 *$19.99*

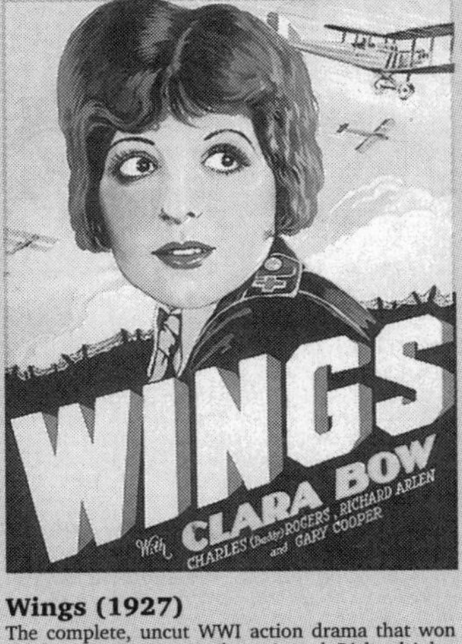

Wings (1927)
The complete, uncut WWI action drama that won the first Best Picture Academy Award. Richard Arlen and Buddy Rogers are friends who enlist in the Army Air Corps; Clara Bow is the woman they both love. Contains thrilling aerial combat footage and a young Gary Cooper. 139 min. Silent with special stereo organ score by Gaylord Carter.
06-1235 Was $19.99 *$14.99*

It (1927)
The vivacious screen persona of Clara Bow and an early appearance by Gary Cooper propel this silent melodrama that concerns the gold-digging machinations of a shop clerk who has her sights set on the store's owner; co-directed by Clarence Badger and Josef von Sternberg. 72 min. Silent with music score.
62-5094 *$24.99*

Hula (1928)
A South Seas island is the setting for this fanciful romantic tale of love and adventure starring Clara Bow and Patricia Dupont. Directed by Victor Fleming ("Gone With the Wind"). 64 min.
10-8455 Was $19.99 *$14.99*

Hoopla (1933)
Clara Bow's last film is a talkie which finds her as an older woman seducing an 18-year-old, then turning him into a man while they both work for a travelling carnival. The finale was filmed at the 1933 World's Fair in Chicago. With Preston Foster, Richard Cromwell and James Gleason. 85 min.
10-9984 *$14.99*

Clara Bow: Discovering The "It" Girl
What made Clara Bow the "It" girl, the most desirable actress of her time and one of America's top movie stars? This program explores Bow's mystique by tracing her life through film clips and interviews with writers, critics and fellow performers. Narrated by Courtney Love, this video features extra footage not shown on cable TV. 65 min.
53-6497 *$24.99*

Shifting Sands (1918)
Gloria Swanson stars in this tenement melodrama about a struggling artist who refuses an indecent proposal from a weaselly rent collector and is sent to jail by him on a trumped-up prostitution charge. With Joe King. 52 min. Silent with music score.
09-5399 *$19.99*

The Raven (1915)
Edgar Allan Poe's classic poem is given its first cinematic treatment in this shadowy terror tale, beginning with a biographical prologue of Poe. Stars Henry B. Walthall, Howard, Ernest Malone. 45 min. Silent with music score.
10-8144 Was $19.99 *$14.99*

Betsy Ross (1917)
Historical drama about the Philadelphia seamstress whom legend credits with producing America's first flag. Alice Brady and John Bowers star in this impressive production. 60 min.
10-9110 Was $19.99 *$14.99*

My Four Years In Germany (1918)
This story of Germany's rise to military power before World War I is based on a book by one-time U.S. Ambassador to Germany James Gerard. An early example of cinematic propaganda masquerading as documentary, it stars Halbert Brown, Willard Dashiell, and Louis Dean as Kaiser Wilhelm. 123 min. Silent with musical score.
10-9140 Was $19.99 *$14.99*

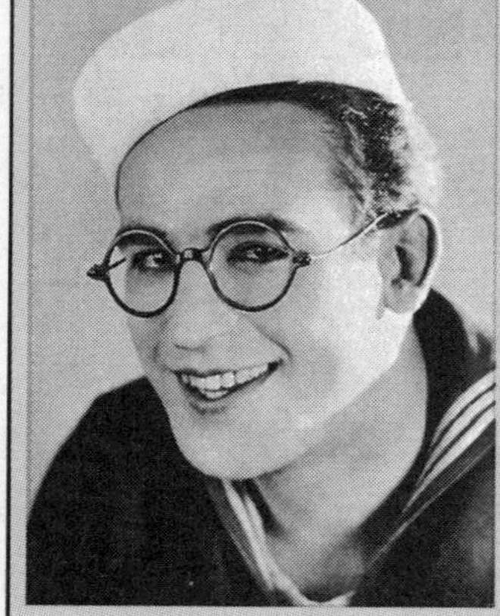

A Sailor-Made Man (1921)
In his first feature-length comedy, Harold Lloyd joins the Navy in order to prove to girlfriend Mildred Davis' father he's worthy of her. Harold winds up rescuing Davis for the clutches of a wicked maharajah in the Far East. With Dick Sutherland, Noah Young. Silent with music score.
10-9454 *$19.99*

Dr. Jack (1922)
Harold Lloyd excels as a rural doctor who heads to the big city to help a young girl escape from the care of a shady physician who has everyone believing his patient is ill. Lloyd tries all types of outrageous methods to save the day. Silent with music score.
10-9746 *$19.99*

Grandma's Boy (1922)
In this early feature, Harold Lloyd plays a small-town milquetoast whose meekness keeps him from joining a manhunt for a killer. Harold seeks advice from his grandmother, who tells him of a "magic charm" that filled his grandfather (also played by Lloyd) with courage during the Civil War. Mildred Davis, Anna Townsend also star. Silent with music score.
10-9747 *$19.99*

The Milky Way (1936)
Mild-mannered milkman Harold Lloyd becomes the toast of the boxing when he's accidentally credited with knocking out the champ in this uproarious comedy that was later remade as "The Kid from Brooklyn." With Helen Mack, Adolphe Menjou, Lionel Stander. 83 min.
18-3015 *$19.99*

The Sin Of Harold Diddlebock (Mad Wednesday) (1946)
Harold Lloyd's final film is actually a sequel to his 1925 comedy "The Freshman." After being fired from his job, staid bookkeeper Lloyd goes on a drinking binge that ends with him finding himself the new owner of a travelling circus. Directed by Preston Sturges; with Margaret Hamilton, Edgar Kennedy, Lionel Stander, Rudy Vallee. 90 min.
10-9452 Was $19.99 *$14.99*

Harold Lloyd's World Of Comedy (1962)
The silent cinema's master of daredevil slapstick stunts, Harold Lloyd, personally compiled these scenes from his funniest films. See the indomitable, horn-rimmed Harold overcome all manner of obstacles, in classic bits from "Safety Last," "The Freshman," "Why Worry," "Movie Crazy," "The Professor" and others. 90 min.
10-8409 *$19.99*

The Whip (1917)
A dashing fellow, in love with the beautiful daughter of a judge and famous horse breeder, finds himself in the middle of a plot involving a nasty moustache-twirling baron, his scheming girlfriend and a roly-poly bookie. Features an exciting race between a horse and a train. With Irving Cummings, Alma Hanlon. 55 min. Silent with music score.
09-5401 *$19.99*

Seven Keys To Baldpate (1917)
Broadway legend George M. Cohan wrote and starred in this adaptation of the classic story from Charlie Chan creator Earl Derr Biggers. Cohan plays a soon-to-be wed writer who checks into a remote inn for quiet while trying to finish his latest novel, only to get caught up in a mystery concerning missing money. Anna Q. Nilsson co-stars. 73 min. Silent with music score.
10-8023 Was $19.99 *$14.99*

Quo Vadis? (1912)
The first version of Henryk Sienkiewicz's heralded novel is a silent effort produced in Italy and starring Carlo Cannaneo and Lea Giunghi. Elaborately produced, the film is set in Nero's Rome and tells of the romance of Roman General Marcus Vinicius and Lygia, the Christian daughter of a retired general. 45 min. Silent with music score.
53-6554 *$29.99*

Max Linder Short Films
The finest comedian of the silent era and Chaplin's idol, France's Max Linder is featured in this program of shorts from 1907-1912. Includes "Max Learns to Skate" and "Troubles of a Grass Widower." 60 min.
53-7036 Was $29.99 *$14.99*

Seven Years Bad Luck (1920)
French film comedy legend Max Linder brought his innovative stylings to America for this silent romp in which he is beset with an avalanche of calamities after breaking a mirror. Included is Linder's famed "mirror routine" that inspired the Marx Brothers in "Duck Soup." 65 min. Silent with music score.
09-5397 *$19.99*

The Man In The Silk Hat (1983)
Documentary assessment of the true pioneer of silent comedy, Max Linder. Called "the master" by Charlie Chaplin, Linder's exploration of the world of physical humor had a strong influence on later stars such as Buster Keaton. Written and directed by Linder's daughter Maud. 99 min.
03-1579 Was $59.99 *$24.99*

Juve Contre Fantomas (1913)
The thrilling adventures of Fantomas, mysterious black-hooded criminal, and Juve, the detective who relentlessly pursues him. The international response to this silent serial led Hollywood to increase production of the genre. With Rene Navarre. 72 min.
53-7037 Was $29.99 *$14.99*

The Student Of Prague (1912)
Paul Wegener ("The Golem") directed and essays the title role in this, the earliest film adaptation of a dark variation on the Faust legend. A poor student falls in love with a countess and sells his reflection to the devil in order to win her. NOTE: Film features German titles. 56 min. Silent with music score.
53-7068 Was $39.99 *$14.99*

The Student Of Prague (1926)
Conrad Veidt plays the title role of the 19th-century man who gives in to the temptations of wealth and success from mysterious stranger Werner Krauss, and loses his inner self in the process, in this moody silent fantasy from director Henrik Galeen. 95 min.
53-6312 *$39.99*

Straight Shooting (1917)
The first feature by legendary director John Ford, starring Harry Carey, Sr., is just one of four seminal silent Westerns spotlighted on this tape. Also includes Thomas Ince's "Blazing the Trail" (1912) and Francis Ford's "Under the Stars and Bars" (1910) and "Unmasked" (1917).
53-7357 *$59.99*

The Unseen Silents
Featured on this collection is "Suzanna" (1929), a rarity from Mack Sennett with Mabel Normand as a peasant girl admired by an aristocrat. Subtitles fill in the missing footage. Also includes one reel of William S. Hart's "Riddle Gawne" (1918) featuring Lon Chaney as a villain; subtitles have been added. And Harold Lloyd's "Sammy in Siberia" (1918) is a classic comedy one-reeler.
09-5361 *$19.99*

From The Manger To The Cross (1912)
One of the first religious features ever made (and the first to be filmed on location in the Holy Land), this reverent silent depiction of the life of Jesus stars Gene Gaunthier, Jack Clark and director Sidney Olcott. Features the original color tinting. 70 min. Silent with music score.
53-8321 *$29.99*

The Cabinet Of Dr. Caligari (1919)
A stunning experiment in cinematic surrealism and psychological horror that set the tone for many later works. Werner Krauss stars as the hypnotist/showman who travels through a weirdly distorted German countryside and unleashes Cesare, his somnambulist slave, on the townspeople. With Conrad Veidt, Lil Dagover. This special restored version features hand-tinted scenes and also includes a 19-minute excerpt from the fantasy "Genuine: A Tale of a Vampire," made in the same year by "Caligari" director Robert Wiene. 91 min. total. Silent with music score.
53-8416 *$24.99*

The Short Films Of Tom Mix, Vol. 1
Legendary cowboy Tom Mix can be seen honing his screen image in such silent short subjects as "A Bear of a Story," "Sagebrush Tom," "Using His Brain" and more. 60 min.
10-9104 Was $19.99 *$14.99*

The Short Films Of Tom Mix, Vol. 2
"Shave and a haircut—two bits! Who's the barber?—Tom Mix!," who's also the star in a compilation of early efforts that includes "Never Again," "Roping a Bride," "Local Color" and "Angelic Attitude." 70 min.
10-9105 Was $19.99 *$14.99*

In The Days Of The Thundering Herd (1914)
The greatest of the silent screen cowboys, Tom Mix, stars in this early oater as a Pony Express rider who joins a westward-bound wagon train and defends them from an Indian attack. Silent with music score.
62-5175 *$24.99*

The Man From Texas (1917)
A number of early Tom Mix shorts comprise this action-packed "Mix-er" in which Tom has to track down his brother-in-law, who has killed his sister. He also encounters a series of dangerous adventures with his true love. Bessie Eylon co-stars. Silent with music score.
68-9157 *$19.99*

Child Of The Prairie (1918)
Tom Mix, best of the West, stars as "Square Deal" Tom, who tries to set up a ranch on the plains, but can't stop his wife from wishing for a return to the comfortable city. Only plenty of hard ridin' and gunfire can settle things in this enjoyable Western melodrama. 63 min. Silent with music score; recorded at correct projection speed.
09-2008 Was $29.99 *$24.99*

Trailin' (1921)
This classic Tom Mix saga stars the cowboy fave as an aristocrat who tries to find out more about his family—particularly his deceased mother—after his father is gunned down. His search leads to Idaho and a ranch that may hold keys to his clan's mysterious past. With Eva Novak, Sid Jordon. Silent with music score.
68-9196 Was $19.99 *$14.99*

Sky High (1922)
Shot on location in the Grand Canyon, this western adventure stars Tom Mix as a cowboy investigating the smuggling of Chinese laborers across the Mexican border. Tom also tries to save a damsel in trouble, but soon discovers her father may be the guy behind the smuggling operation. Eva Novak, Sid Jordan star. Silent with music score.
68-9154 *$19.99*

Just Tony (1922)
Although cowboy hero Tom Mix is featured in this western, his horse Tony is the true star. Tom searches for a man who wounded him in a gun battle and Tony, a former wild horse, is trained by Tom to find the man. Meanwhile, the cowboy hero falls in love with the culprit's daughter. Claire Adams also stars. Silent with music score.
69-9143 *$19.99*

Dick Turpin (1925)
A "mix" on Western hero Tom Mix's trademark roles finds the star playing the famous English highwaymen who robs from the rich to give to the poor and tries to save his love, an aristocratic woman, from a forced marriage. Kathleen Myers and James Marcus co-star. 70 min. Silent with orchestra score.
10-9221 *$19.99*

Terror Trail (1933)
The trail is running out for the outlaws in this oater, because the one and only Tom Mix is right behind them, ready to bring the black hats to justice! With Naomi Judge, Raymond Hatton. 62 min.
10-7946 Was $19.99 *$14.99*

Rustler's Roundup (1933)
Take one dead rancher, a pretty, orphaned rancher's daughter, and a clan of murderous land-grabbers and you've got another instant Tom Mix classic. Co-stars Noah Beery, Jr. and Walter Brennan. 60 min.
10-7745 Was $19.99 *$14.99*

Please see our index for the Tom Mix title: *The Miracle Rider*

The Outlaw And His Wife (1917)
Stunning silent drama that marked the true beginning of the Swedish cinema. Hunted by the police for a minor crime, a farmer and his wife escape into the wilderness. Victor Sjostrom's haunting film features tinted sequences and a full orchestral score. 73 min.
53-9092 *$24.99*

Dangerous Hours (1919)
A rarity: the first anti-Communist film made in the U.S., with Lloyd Hughes starring in a tale of a naive college lad duped by scheming Reds. Directed by Fred Niblo ("The Mark of Zorro") and produced by pioneer Thomas Ince. 88 min. Silent with music score.
53-9290 Was $29.99 *$14.99*

Sandy Burke Of The U-Bar-U (1919)
A western hero can't help but do good deeds, from saving an orphan girl from her father's killer to paying off a widow's mortgage to tracking down rustlers who happen to have been involved in the killing. Lou Bennison, Virginia Lee star. Silent with music score.
68-9194 *$14.99*

The Clodhopper (1917)
Silent rural comedy-drama of a small-town boy who makes good, returning home to save his hometown. Charles Ray, Marjory Wilson star; produced by Thomas Ince. 69 min. Silent with music score; recorded at correct projection speed.
62-5181 Was $24.99 *$14.99*

Hoodoo Ann (1916)
Early silent "featurette" condensed from a full-length film. Mae Marsh stars as a young orphan who overcomes her humble beginnings to find love and happiness. 27 min.
62-5210 Was $24.99 *$19.99*

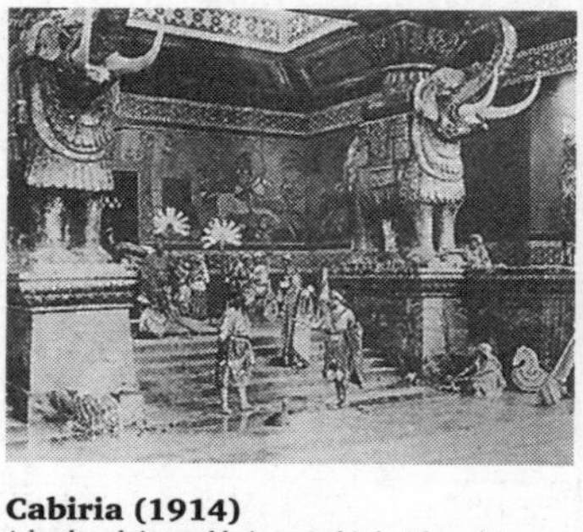

Cabiria (1914)
A landmark in world cinema, this lavish and innovative silent Italian epic recounts the Punic wars between Rome and Carthage as seen through the eyes of a young woman kidnapped by pirates. The stunning battle scenes and groundbreaking camerawork influenced D.W. Griffith's filming of "Intolerance." Lidia Quaranta, Umberto Mozzato star. 123 min. Silent with music score.
53-7447 Was $39.99 *$24.99*

The Grit Of The Girl Telegrapher (1912)/ In The Switch Tower (1915)
Two early silent featurettes with a railroad theme. First, train thief "Smoke-Up" Smith fails to stop spunky telegraph girl Betty, who gets her man after several "Perils of Pauline"-like thrills. Next, a young man abandoned by his drunkard father returns to work on the same railroad as his pa. 47 min. total.
62-5163 Was $19.99 *$14.99*

Dr. Jekyll And Mr. Hyde (1913)
Considered by some to be the first Universal horror film, this silent version of Robert Louis Stevenson's famed tale about a kindly scientist whose serum turns him into a ghastly cad stars King Baggot in the title roles. With Jane Gail, Matt Snyder, Matt Singer.
68-8813 *$19.99*

Dr. Jekyll And Mr. Hyde (1920)
One of several silent versions made of the classic Stevenson horror tale, with Sheldon Lewis ("Orphans of the Storm") starring as the refined scientist-turned-bestial ruffian. 60 min.
68-8069 *$19.99*

Six Feet Four (1919)
William Russell is a tall cowpoke suspected of robbing a hotel and a young woman. Russell must prove his innocence, and soon finds that the local sheriff has a part in the crimes. Vola Vale and Charles French also star. Silent with music score.
68-9156 *$19.99*

The Irish Cinderella
Fascinating curio from 1920s Ireland that parallels a Cinderella-like Gaelic fable with a plea for a free, democratic Ireland now and forever. Of interest to anyone concerned with Irish history and politics. Pattie MacNamara stars. 72 min. Silent with musical score.
09-1939 Was $29.99 *$14.99*

After A Million (1924)
Comic adventure in which American Kenneth McDonald has the chance to win a fortune through an inheritance in Russia. In order to get the cash, McDonald must first marry the Countess of Kiev. Ruth Dwyer also stars. 62 min. Silent with organ score.
09-2312 *$14.99*

The Broken Law (1924)
Top-notch, action-packed Western in which a cowpoke loses his last dollar in a poker game, has his horse run off and his dog shot by an Indian. After the Indian is killed, the cowboy is framed for murder. Jack Meehan and Alma Rayford star. 66 min. Silent with organ soundtrack.
09-2313 *$14.99*

The Drop Kick (1927)
Richard Barthelmess is the star drop-kicker and captain of the Shoreham College football team who's caught between two women: the cute girl his mom wants him to take to the prom, and a married flirt. Which will he choose? Hedda Hopper co-stars in this silent drama that features real-life college gridiron player John Wayne, in an unbilled bit part. 62 min. Silent with music score.
09-2410 *$19.99*

Dr. Jekyll And Mr. Hyde (1920)
Already made five times previously in the brief history of cinema, this silent version of the classic Stevenson thriller remains a classic, thanks to John Barrymore's great performance in the title roles. With Nita Naldi, Charles Lane. 63 min. Silent with music score.
63-1453 *$19.99*

Beau Brummel (1924)
The Great Profile was seldom greater than in this ideal role, as John Barrymore depicts the rise and fall of the celebrated soldier and dashing dandy of 1800s Britain. With Mary Astor, Irene Rich, Willard Lewis. 80 min. Silent with music score.
09-5378 *$19.99*

Don Juan (1926)
John Barrymore is the swashbuckling ladies' man in this classic silent costume drama from "Jazz Singer" director Alan Crosland. Features a top-notch cast (with Warner Oland and Estelle Taylor as the Borgias), was the first film with Vitaphone music and sound effects, and holds the record for most screen kisses with 127! 117 min. Silent with music score.
12-2144 *$29.99*

The Beloved Rogue (1927)
Lavish account of French beggar-poet Francois Villon (John Barrymore) who battles against the Burgundians in order to save his country and king. Barrymore's extravagant performance is a highlight, along with spectacular sets and a supporting cast that includes Conrad Veidt as Louis XI, Marceline Day and Angelo Rossitto. 100 min. Silent with organ score.
10-8417 *$19.99*

Please see our index for these other John Barrymore titles: *Bulldog Drummond Comes Back • Bulldog Drummond's Peril • Bulldog Drummond's Revenge • Dinner At Eight • Grand Hotel • The Invisible Woman • Marie Antoinette • Maytime • Midnight • Rasputin And The Empress • Romeo And Juliet • Spawn Of The North • Svengali • Twentieth Century*

The Coming Of Amos (1924)
Dashing Rod La Rocque goes against type, playing a shy Outback sheep rancher who learns manners from a mentor and eventually falls in love with a princess. Noah Beery, Jetta Goudal also star. 54 min. Silent with music score.
10-9025 *$19.99*

Ranson's Folly (1926)
A prime swashbuckling role is taken by Richard Barthelmess, who plays an army officer who robs a stagecoach on a dare and is later accused of murdering its paymaster. Thinking that his girlfriend's father is involved in the murder, Barthelmess confesses to save him. Dorothy Mackall also stars. 78 min. Silent with musical score.
10-9029 Was $19.99 *$14.99*

Broken Hearts Of Broadway (1923)
The Great White Way provides the backdrop for this look at the successes and failures of performers, producers and denizens of the famed street. Colleen Moore, John Walker star. 86 min.
10-9111 *$19.99*

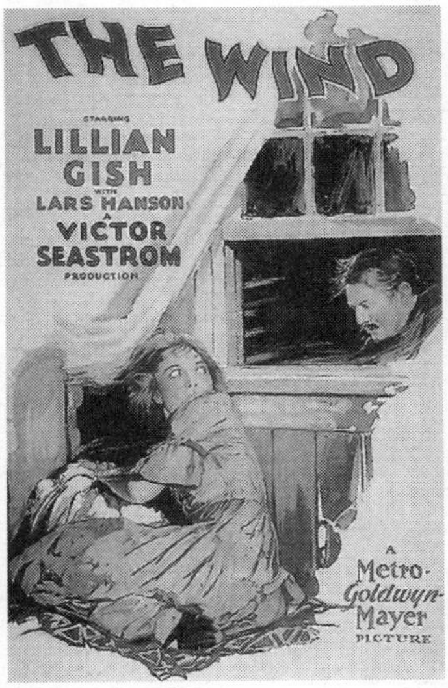

The Wind (1928)
One of Lillian Gish's finest screen roles was as the Virginia farmgirl who moves to the Texas Dust Bowl and must battle the elements and the people around her. Compelling drama by Victor Seastrom includes a harrowing battle between Gish and brutish cowboy Montagu Love amid a raging sandstorm. 86 min. Silent with music score.
12-1138 *$29.99*

Marked Money (1928)
First-rate kids' adventure starring Junior Coghlan as an orphan boy living with a sea captain and his daughter. When some crooks set their sights on nabbing the lad's inheritance, the trio are joined by the daughter's Navy pilot boyfriend to stop the bad guys'scheme. George Duryea, Tom Kennedy also star. 60 min. Silent with musical score.
10-9038 Was $19.99 *$14.99*

The Open Switch (1925)
In this action-packed railroad story some ornery criminals are out to steal valuable parcels from moving trains, and it's up to the rail line superintendent's feisty daughter to save her father's job and bring the bad guys to justice. Helen Holmes, Jack Perrin, Mack Wright star. 50 min. Silent with music score.
10-9117 Was $19.99 *$14.99*

Perils Of The Rail (1925)
Some of the most enthralling train stunts of the silent cinema are performed in this thriller. Serial queen Helen Holmes is the spunky heroine who tries to help her railroad president dad and sales agent boyfriend by discovering who's been stealing valuable ore from the rail line's land. With J.P. McGowan. 61 min. Silent with music score.
10-9118 *$19.99*

Linda (1929)
A young woman from the North Woods is urged by her father to marry an older man, even though she's truly in love with a young doctor. Warner Baxter, Helen Foster and Noah Beery star in this fine drama. 75 min. Silent with musical score.
10-9139 *$19.99*

The Notorious Lady (1927)
After killing a man he suspects of having an affair with his wife, Lewis Stone takes off for the diamond fields of Africa. When his wife discovers that he's been reported dead, she searches for him, but during her trip, she meets a man with whom she falls in love. Ann Rork, Barbara Bedford also star. 75 min. Silent with musical score.
10-9141 Was $19.99 *$14.99*

Manhattan Cowboy (1928)
No, it's not John Travolta in a Woody Allen film. It's about a New York playboy who steals a cab driver's coat and is sent to a Western ranch to see the error of his ways. There he proves his skills at riding, roping and shooting, and is called on to save a foreman's daughter from kidnappers. Bob Custer, Lafe McGee star. 60 min. Silent with musical score.
10-9142 Was $19.99 *$14.99*

Hawk Of The Hills (1929)
This is the featurized version of the popular serial of the same name, focusing on a halfbreed Indian known as the Hawk who joins forces with ornery outlaws to terrorize prospectors. Allene Ray, Walter Miller star. 58 min. Silent with musical score.
10-9148 Was $19.99 *$14.99*

The Battling Orioles (1924)
The once-scrappy Orioles baseball team has turned old, rich and grouchy, so the son of a former Oriole takes it into his own hands to reacquaint them with the old team spirit. Glenn Tryon, Blanche Mehaffey and John T. Price star. 58 min. Silent with piano score.
10-9150 Was $19.99 *$14.99*

The Worldly Madonna (1922)
Clara Kimball Jones plays dual roles in this rarely seen film. She's a convent novitiate who agrees to trade places with her twin sister, a cabaret dancer, who thinks she has killed a man. William P. Carleton, Richard Tucker also star. 47 min. Silent with organ score.
10-9152 Was $19.99 *$14.99*

The Sky Pilot (1921)
King Vidor helmed this compelling western about a young minister facing derision from the locals when he arrives in the Canadian Northwest. The minister wins people over by winning a fight, but finds himself in trouble when he attempts to save a girl from a stampede. John Bowers, Colleen Moore star. 70 min. Silent with musical score.
10-9246 *$19.99*

The Last Of The Mohicans (1920)
Considered by many to be the finest film adaptation of the classic James Fenimore Cooper adventure, directors Clarence Brown and Maurice Tourneur's silent drama stars Albert Roscoe in the title role of Uncas, Harry Lorraine as frontier scout Hawkeye, and Wallace Beery as the villainous Magua, and features thrilling action sequences. This restored print includes color-tinted scenes. 72 min. Silent with music score.
80-5023 *$39.99*

Back To God's Country (1919)/ Something New (1921)
These two films from actress/filmmaker/conservationist Nell Shipman are unique efforts shot in rugged locations. "Back to God's Country," filmed in Canada's frozen wilds, details the adventures of a young wife terrorized aboard an icebound ship by the captain. Next, Shipman is abducted by bandits in the Mojave Desert, until her boyfriend rescues her in a 1920 Maxwell sedan, in "Something New." 132 min. total. Silent with music score.
80-5041 *$29.99*

Evangeline (1929)
Longfellow's epic poem receives a powerful treatment in this silent drama that features two sound musical numbers. Mexican screen siren Dolores Del Rio is the Acadian beauty whose impending marriage to Gabriel is disrupted when she and her people are forced from their Canadian homeland by British soldiers. Roland Drew, Alec B. Francis also star. 87 min. Silent with music score.
80-5044 *$29.99*

The Road To Ruin (1928)
Silent exploitation effort that exposes the creeping moral decay fostered by juvenile delinquency. See a good girl gone bad (from reading racy romantic novels) sink into moral terpitude! Campy classic with Helen Foster, Grant Withers. 45 min. Silent with music score.
62-1192 *$19.99*

Yankee Clipper (1927)
Soaring seafaring tale stars William Boyd as the son of a Boston shipbuilder who competes with a British vessel to earn China's tea trade rights with America. Co-stars Elinor Fair (Boyd's real-life wife). 51 min.
62-5106 Was $29.99 *$24.99*

The Midnight Girl (1925)
Lila Lee stars as a Russian opera singer who has fled to America in search of a new life. Can she avoid the attentions of a suave patron (Bela Lugosi) who has designs on more than her career? Superlative silent-era soaper. 84 min. Silent with musical score.
62-1287 Was $19.99 *$14.99*

The Cricket On The Hearth (1923)
Original silent version of Charles Dickens' "A Christmas Book" story, showing what happens when the good luck charm of a cricket is found around Christmas. Paul Gerson. 68 min.
62-5149 Was $19.99 *$14.99*

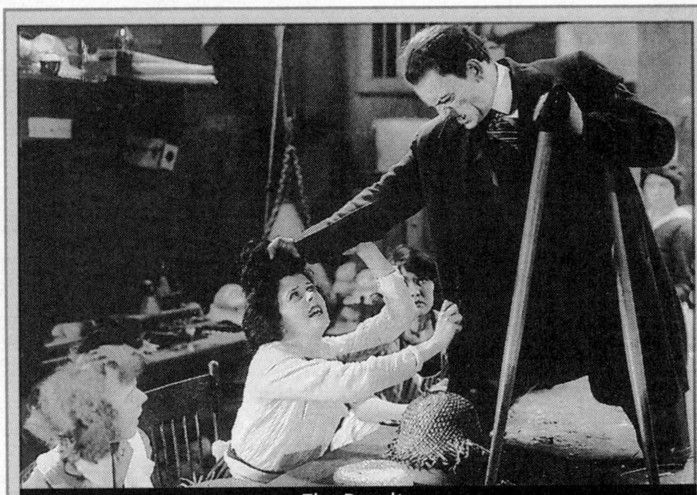

The Penalty

Lon Chaney

The Scarlet Car (1917)
Compelling silent melodrama with an arresting performance by Lon Chaney as a small-town bank teller who confronts his embezzling boss and, after apparently killing him, hides out from the law in a remote cabin. Meanwhile, Chaney's daughter is wooed by the crooked banker's scheming son. Edith Johnson, Franklyn Farnum also star. 50 min. Silent with music score.
09-5396 *$19.99*

The Penalty (1920)
In an early starring film that showcased his fascination with strange roles (and the physical hardships that went into them), Lon Chaney strapped his legs behind him at the knees to play a crippled criminal genius who uses an army of beggars and thieves to try to take over the city of San Francisco. With Claire Adams, Charles Clary. 71 min. Silent with music score.
09-5271 *$19.99*

Nomads Of The North (1920)
With the untamed North Canadian wilderness as its backdrop, this "thrilling drama with a tang of the wild" stars the legendary Lon Chaney, who returns home to discover his betrothed has been the subject of the romantic advances of a handful of shady characters. Co-stars Lewis Stone and Betty Blythe. 75 min. Silent with music score.
53-8339 *$24.99*

Outside The Law (1921)
Director Tod Browning's early crime drama, with Lon Chaney in a dual role, was for many years considered lost. A hood tries to go straight for his daughter's sake, but is framed by gang boss Chaney and sent to jail. Embittered, she decides to follow in his footsteps. Priscilla Dean, Ralph Lewis co-star. 75 min. Silent with music score.
62-5201 Remastered *$24.99*

Flesh And Blood (1922)
Another superlative Lon Chaney performance carries this classic story of an unjustly jailed lawyer who comes home just in time for his wife's funeral...and thereafter vows vengeance. The Chaney magic kicks in when he assumes the guise of a crippled beggar to implement his revenge. 74 min. Silent with musical score.
09-1938 Was $29.99 *$19.99*

Shadows (1922)
Lon Chaney stars as a Chinese laundryman in a remote fishing village who meets with prejudice from the townsfolk. Befriended by a minister and his wife, Chaney later saves them from a blackmail plot. With Harrison Ford, Marguerite De La Motte. Restored print includes color-tinted sequences. 71 min. Silent with music score.
62-5197 Remastered *$24.99*

The Shock (1923)/ The Light Of Faith (1923)
A dramatic silent double bill of crime and redemption starring Lon Chaney. In "The Shock," Chaney is a crippled gunman for a female gang boss who falls in love with a banker's daughter and tries to save her father from scandal. Next, small-time thief Lon comes into possession of the Holy Grail and undergoes a life change in "The Light of Faith" ("The Light in the Dark"). Restored prints include color-tinted sequences. 99 min. Silent with music score.
53-8323 Remastered *$24.99*

Oliver Twist (1923)
"You want more?!" Memorable early production of the Charles Dickens favorite features Jackie Coogan as the heroic orphan and Lon Chaney as the rascally Fagin. Restored print includes color-tinted scenes. 74 min. Silent with music score.
62-5098 Remastered *$24.99*

The Hunchback Of Notre Dame (1923)
One of the grandest spectacles of the silent cinema, fueled by Lon Chaney's wonderful (and painful) performance as Quasimodo, the deformed Parisian bellringer who falls in love with Gypsy dancer Esmerelda (Patsy Ruth Miller). 100 min. Silent with musical score.
63-1458 *$19.99*

The Phantom Of The Opera (1925)
Lon Chaney's greatest role was as Erik, the scarred fiend lurking in the catacombs beneath the Paris Opera House who serves as unseen mentor to singer Christine (Mary Philbin), in this classic silent adaptation of Gaston Leroux's novel. This edition includes the original two-strip Technicolor ballroom scene and the famous unmasking scene. 107 min. Silent with music score.
09-5410 *$19.99*

The Phantom Of The Opera: Deluxe Edition (1925)
This is a restored archival edition of Lon Chaney's silent horror classic newly remastered from a 35mm print and featuring a new score by Gabriel Thibaudoux, which was performed by the I Musici de Montreal and soprano Claudine Cote. Also includes a "making of" documentary, and the original theatrical trailer. 92 min. Silent with music score.
09-1777 Remastered *$24.99*

Lon Chaney: Behind The Mask
The legendary career and turbulent personal life of Hollywood's "Man of a Thousand Faces" are examined in this comprehensive video biography that uses scenes from many of Chaney's greatest films, interviews, and rare home movies and behind-the-scenes footage. Also included is Chaney's long-unseen 1914 Western short, "By the Sun's Rays." 86 min. total.
53-8322 *$24.99*

Football

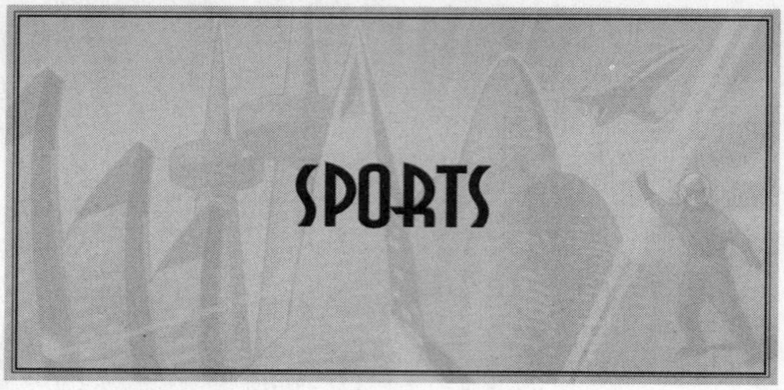

75 Seasons: 1920-1994
A must-have for football fans, this expert celebration of 75 years of the NFL's heritage offers incredible action, great personalities, unforgettable plays, furiously funny follies and lots more. It's everything a gridiron lover would love—and more! 90 min.
02-8095 *$19.99*

75 Years Of Giants Football
"There were giants in the earth in those days," and some of the greatest to ever walk a Gotham gridiron are featured in this salute to the NFL's New York Giants. Frank Gifford, Sam Huff, Y.A. Tittle, Fran Tarkenton, Lawrence Taylor, Phil Simms and many others are featured in classic game footage. 60 min.
02-9144 *$19.99*

NFL Under The Helmet
From the popular Fox TV series comes this video that shows your favorite football stars off the gridiron. Watch as Terrell Davis takes to the skies with the Air Force's Thunderbirds flyers; Mike Utley goes scuba diving in the Cayman Islands; Doug Flutie takes the stage with a rock band; and more. Music by Collective Soul, Sugar Ray, Blink 182.
02-9171 *$14.99*

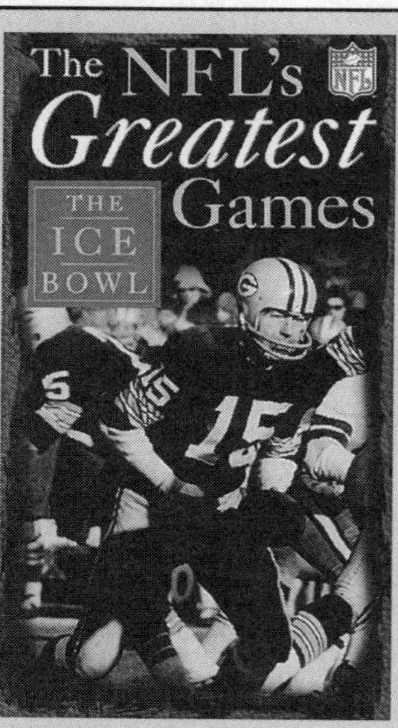

The NFL's Greatest Games
For the first time on home video, some of the most memorable showdowns in NFL history can be yours to watch over and over. Originalradio broadcasts and archival NFL Films footage are combined to bring you amazing game re-creations, with many of the legndary players and coaches offering their own insights. Each tape runs about 75 min.

The NFL's Greatest Games: The Ice Bowl
In sub-zero Wisconsin weather, coach Vince Lombardi and his Green Bay Packers used their "home field advantage" to defeat the Dallas Cowboys, led by Tom Landry, 21-17 and win the 1967 NFL championship on their way to Super Bowl II.
02-8746 Was $19.99 *$14.99*

The NFL's Greatest Games: Super Bowl III
After losing the first two "AFL-NFL World Championship Games," the upstart AFL reached parity with its older counterpart when cocky QB Joe Namath led his New York Jets to a 16-7 upset win over Johnny Unitas and the Baltimore Colts.
02-8747 Was $19.99 *$14.99*

The NFL's Greatest Games: '81 NFC Championship
Before a packed Candlestick Park crowd, San Francisco QB Joe Montana drove the 49ers to their first ever NFC title with a nail-biter 28-27 win over the favored Dallas Cowboys.
02-8967 Was $19.99 *$14.99*

NFL's Greatest Games: '58 Championship
Considered by many to be the game that brought the NFL into true national prominence, the 1958 league championship game saw Johnny Unitas lead Baltimore Colts into sudden death overtime to defeat the New York Giants 23-17.
02-8972 Was $19.99 *$14.99*

Pure Gold: San Francisco's Fabulous 49ers
Relive the glory days of the "red and gold" in this video retrospective of 49ers history. Follow the team's start in the old AAFC, its arrival in the NFL, and how great players like Brodie, Montana, Clark and Rice have led San Francisco to a winning tradition that includes four Super Bowl titles. 55 min.
02-7593 Was $19.99 *$14.99*

The Joe Montana Story
The career of the NFL's greatest quarterback, Joe Montana, is chronicled in this exciting program that takes you from his collegiate days in Notre Dame, where he led the Fighting Irish to two Cotton Bowl wins, to his four Super Bowl triumphs in San Francisco with the 49ers and revived career with the Kansas City Chiefs. 45 min.
02-7978 Was $19.99 *$14.99*

Pro Football's Hottest Cheerleaders
See what it takes to be an NFL cheerleader, as you follow the gorgeous gals from try-outs to practice and photo sessions to game-day action, rooting on the Raiders, Cowboys, Eagles, Chargers and Dolphins. Give 'em an "H"! Give 'em an "O"! Give 'em a "T"! 45 min.
02-7693 Was $19.99 *$14.99*

100 Greatest NFL Touchdowns
What are the top touchdowns of all time? Here's a selection of them: exciting runs, catches and plays from the NFL's greatest and not-so greatest players. Experience these TDs in typical NFL Films fashion, with superb photography, sound and style.
02-7863 *$14.99*

NFL's 15 Greatest Comebacks
Maybe "it ain't over 'til it's over" is a baseball saying, but it certainly applies to these fantastic football come-from-behind victories. See how stars like Roger Staubach and Joe Montana, and unlikely heroes like the Bills' Frank Reich brought their teams from the brink of defeat. 60 min.
02-7946 *$14.99*

NFL's 100 Greatest Tackles
If you're a fan of hard-hitting, no-holds-barred football, this video will have you riveted to your seat. See the nastiest tackles in NFL history, featuring the likes of Taylor, Butkus and Green. It's awesome stuff! 50 min.
02-8275 Was $19.99 *$14.99*

The NFL's 100 Toughest Players
In a sport that tests a man's toughness, these are the athletes who were the best of the best, the toughest of the tough. Chuck Bednarik, Hardy Brown, Dick Butkus, Larry Csonka, Mike Ditka, Walter Payton and Lawrence Taylor are among the 100 legendary gridiron gladiators spotlighted in this program.
02-8529 Was $19.99 *$14.99*

The Best Of NFL Follies
It's a 100-yard howl of laughs when the crack staff at NFL Films brings you the wildest, weirdest and most way-out bloopers, miscues and embarrassing moments from the gridiron, featuring some of the game's top stars. 51 min.
02-8620 *$14.99*

21st Century NFL Follies
From floundering fumbles to crushing collisions, NFL Films has assembled another collection of the most fun-filled foul-ups to ever cross the line of scrimmage. Players, referees and fans all get in the mix as plenty of hilarious footage drives right through the defensive line and into the new millennium. 60 min.
02-9272 *$14.99*

Pure Payton
The Chicago Bears' fleet-footed number 34, Walter Payton, is saluted in a video retrospective that traces the Hall of Famer's life and career from his college days at Jackson State to his record-setting runs at Soldier Field.
02-8748 *$19.99*

1997 Denver Broncos: Super Bowl XXXII Champions
Thanks to the efforts of quarterback John Elway and game MVP running back Terrell Davis, the underdog Denver Broncos ended a 14-year AFC Super Bowl losing streak with a thrilling 31-24 victory over defending champion Green Bay. Marvel at the "Orange Crush" revival with this video salute to the team's '97-'98 season. 55 min.
02-8822 *$19.99*

Howie Long's Tough Guys
Howie Long, Raider great, "NFL on Fox" commentator and action star of "Firestorm," presents a savage look at the football's toughest guys of all time. Based on Long's popular "Tough Guys" segments, this video offers superior archival footage done in an edgy Fox style.
02-9019 Was $19.99 *$14.99*

Official 2000 NFL Team Videos
Check out the highlights of the 1999-2000 season of your favorite pro football team in these action-packed programs from NFL Films that also include exclusive previews of the upcoming campaign. Each tape runs about 30 min. There are 30 volumes available, including:

Denver Broncos 2000 Team Video
02-9238 *$14.99*

New York Giants 2000 Team Video
02-9248 *$14.99*

Dallas Cowboys 2000 Team Video
02-9237 *$14.99*

St. Louis Rams 2000 Team Video
02-9256 *$14.99*

Jacksonville Jaguars 2000 Team Video
02-9242 *$14.99*

Tennessee Titans 2000 Team Video
02-9258 *$14.99*

The Greatest Moments In Dallas Cowboy History
Relive the Lone Star legends who have written their names in the record books, and see the greatest games in Texas Stadium history. This look at "the team you love to hate" includes such players as Meredith, Staubach, Pearson, Hayes, Lilly, Dorsett and more, including Coach Landry. 60 min.
13-1184 *$14.99*

3 In A Row: The Green Bay Packers (1968)
The Pack, led by the legendary Vince Lombardi, performed one of the most outstanding accomplishments in NFL history: winning three consecutive championships in 1965-67. Highlights from their three-year reign are featured here, plus profiles on such stars as Bart Starr, Paul Hornung, Willie Davis and Ray Nitschke. 119 min.
13-1148 *$12.99*

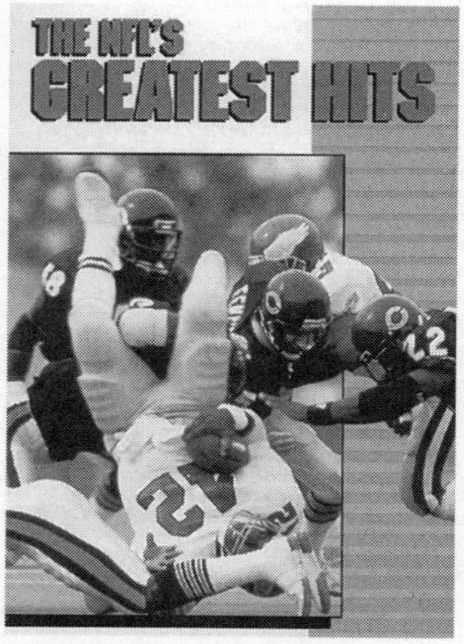

The NFL's Greatest Hits
Not just those savage, head-hunting tackles and blocks, this collection features football's most spectacular plays, plus a heart-stopping series of dramatic finishes to the most exciting games ever played. 50 min.
13-1206 *$14.99*

Official Super Bowl XXXIV Champions Video: 1999 St. Louis Rams
The first Super Bowl of the new century was one for the ages, as arena football refugee Kurt Warner led his St. Louis Rams to a nail-biting 23-16 win over the Tennessee Titans. See all the game action, from opening kick-off to the Titans' last-seconds drive for the end zone, in this video retrospective that features exclusive footage and interviews with Rams coach Dick Vermeil, stars Steve McNair, Marshall Faulk and Isaac Bruce, and more.
02-9205 *$19.99*

Greatest Moments In Super Bowl History (2000)
Now Super Bowl Sunday can be every weekend, so grab a plate full of hot buffalo wings and enjoy the most exciting plays and players in championship history in this great collection from NFL films: Namath, Staubach, Bradshaw, Montana, Rice, Smith and Elway are among the January legends captured in all their gridiron glory.
02-9277 *$14.99*

Matchup Of The Millennium: Complete Set
This amazing three-tape series mixes computer effects and archival footage to give you the highlights of the greatest NFL games *never* played. Game 1 pits Bill Walsh's '80s San Francisco 49ers against Vince Lombardi's Green Bay Packers of the '60s; the Pittsburgh Steelers of the '70s meet the '90s Dallas Cowboys in Game 2; and the winners of each game move on to in the "Millennium Bowl." Joe Theismann, Mike Patrick, Steve Sabol and Howard Cosell add commentary. 182 min. total. NOTE: Individual volumes available at $14.99 each.
02-9262 Save $15.00! *$29.99*

Baseball

Major League Baseball All-Century Team
Aaron, Griffey, Mantle, McGuire, Ruth, Ryan...these are just a few of the diamond superstars chosen by fans across America to be part of the game's ultimate team. This video tribute features footage of the introduction of the candidates at the 1999 All-Star Game and footage of the 30 men chosen as the best of the century.
02-9179 *$19.99*

Major League Baseball: Generations Of Heroes
The greatest diamond stars of past and present go head to head in this unique program that lets fans compare who could throw the ball the hardest or hit it the longest. Hank Aaron or Ken Griffey, Jr....Nolan Ryan or Roger Clemens...Babe Ruth or Mark McGwire...Johnny Bench or Mike Piazza; you make the call!
02-9087 Was $19.99 *$14.99*

Baseball's Greatest Games
Direct from the original broadcasts, some of the most memorable showdowns in diamond history have been collected in this special series. All of the action from each game is there, along with the actual announcers.

Baseball's Greatest Games: 1952 World Series, Game 6
Down three games to two to the interborough rival Brooklyn Dodgers, the New York Yankees ride homers from Yogi Berra and Mickey Mantle to overcome an early Dodger lead and take this pivotal contest 3-2.
13-5099 *$19.99*

Baseball's Greatest Games: 1978 A.L. East Playoff
The end of the 1978 season had the Boston Red Sox and New York Yankees in a dead heat for the A.L. East title, and a one-game showdown saw unlikely Yankee hero Bucky Dent's homer driving the team to a 5-4 victory.
13-5101 *$19.99*

Baseball's Greatest Games: 1986 World Series, Game 6
One out away from winning their first World Series in 68 years, the Boston Red Sox saw victory slip through their fingers (and between their legs), as Mookie Wilson's 11th-inning single scored Ray Knight and gave the New York Mets the win.
13-5102 *$19.99*

Baseball's Greatest Games: 1988 World Series, Game 1
The heavily-favored Oakland A's took their lead against the Los Angeles Dodgers into the bottom of the ninth, when injured pinch-hitter Kirk Gibson homered off ace reliever Dennis Eckersley to give L.A. a Hollywood-style win.
13-5103 *$19.99*

Baseball's Greatest Games: 1991 World Series, Game 7
In a series filled with close wins and extra-inning thrills, Kirby Puckett and the Minnesota Twins broke a scoreless contest with the Atlanta Braves in the 10th inning to capture baseball's ultimate prize.
13-5104 *$19.99*

World Series Highlights

All of the unforgettable plays, players and memories of the Fall Classic can be yours with these video presentations that feature the highlights from baseball's annual championship showdown. Each tape runs about 60 min.

1943 World Series Highlights: Yankees vs. Cardinals
13-5077   Was $39.99   *$19.99*

1944 World Series Highlights: Cardinals vs. Browns
13-5078   Was $39.99   *$19.99*

1945 World Series Highlights: Tigers vs. Cubs
13-5079   Was $39.99   *$19.99*

1946 World Series Highlights: Cardinals vs. Red Sox
13-5012   Was $39.99   *$19.99*

1947 World Series Highlights: Yankees vs. Dodgers
13-9080   *$19.99*

1948 World Series Highlights: Indians vs. Braves
13-5014   Was $39.99   *$19.99*

1949 World Series Highlights: Yankees vs. Dodgers
13-5015   Was $39.99   *$19.99*

1950 World Series Highlights: Yankees vs. Phillies
13-5016   Was $39.99   *$19.99*

1951 World Series Highlights: Yankees vs. Giants
13-5017   Was $39.99   *$19.99*

1952 World Series Highlights: Yankees vs. Dodgers
13-5018   Was $39.99   *$19.99*

1953 World Series Highlights: Yankees vs. Dodgers
13-5019   Was $39.99   *$19.99*

1954 World Series Highlights: Giants vs. Indians
13-5020   *$19.99*

1955 World Series Highlights: Dodgers vs. Yankees
13-5021   Was $39.99   *$19.99*

1956 World Series Highlights: Yankees vs. Dodgers
13-5022   Was $39.99   *$19.99*

1957 World Series Highlights: Braves vs. Yankees
13-5023   *$19.99*

1958 World Series Highlights: Yankees vs. Braves
13-5024   *$19.99*

1959 World Series Highlights: Dodgers vs. White Sox
13-5025   Was $39.99   *$19.99*

World Series

1960 World Series Highlights: Pirates vs. Yankees
13-5026   Was $39.99   *$19.99*

1961 World Series Highlights: Yankees vs. Reds
13-5027   Was $39.99   *$19.99*

1962 World Series Highlights: Yankees vs. Giants
13-5028   Was $39.99   *$19.99*

1963 World Series Highlights: Yankees vs. Dodgers
13-5029   Was $39.99   *$19.99*

1964 World Series Highlights: Cardinals vs. Yankees
13-5030   Was $39.99   *$19.99*

1965 World Series Highlights: Dodgers vs. Twins
13-5031   Was $39.99   *$19.99*

1966 World Series Highlights: Orioles vs. Dodgers
13-5032   Was $39.99   *$19.99*

1967 World Series Highlights: Cardinals vs. Red Sox
13-5033   *$19.99*

1968 World Series Highlights: Tigers vs. Cardinals
13-5034   Was $59.99   *$19.99*

1969 World Series Highlights: Mets vs. Orioles
13-5035   Was $59.99   *$19.99*

1970 World Series Highlights: Orioles vs. Reds
13-5036   Was $59.99   *$19.99*

1971 World Series Highlights: Pirates vs. Orioles
13-5037   Was $59.99   *$19.99*

1972 World Series Highlights: A's vs. Reds
13-5001   Was $59.99   *$19.99*

1973 World Series Highlights: A's vs. Mets
13-5002   Was $59.99   *$19.99*

1974 World Series Highlights: A's vs. Dodgers
13-5003   Was $59.99   *$19.99*

1975 World Series Highlights: Reds vs. Red Sox
13-5004   Was $59.99   *$19.99*

1976 World Series Highlights: Reds vs. Yankees
13-5005   Was $59.99   *$19.99*

1977 World Series Highlights: Yankees vs. Dodgers
13-5006   Was $59.99   *$19.99*

1978 World Series Highlights: Yankees vs. Dodgers
13-5007   Was $59.99   *$19.99*

1979 World Series Highlights: Pirates vs. Orioles
13-5008   *$19.99*

1980 World Series Highlights: Phillies vs. Royals
13-5009   Was $59.99   *$19.99*

1981 World Series Highlights: Dodgers vs. Yankees
13-5010   Was $59.99   *$19.99*

1982 World Series Highlights: Cardinals vs. Brewers
13-5011   Was $59.99   *$19.99*

1983 World Series Highlights: Orioles vs. Phillies
13-5038   Was $59.99   *$19.99*

1984 World Series Highlights: Tigers vs. Padres
13-9072   *$19.99*

1985 World Series Highlights: Royals vs. Cardinals
13-5080   Was $29.99   *$19.99*

1986 World Series Highlights: Mets vs. Red Sox
13-5082   Was $39.99   *$19.99*

1987 World Series Highlights: Twins vs. Cardinals
13-9074   *$19.99*

1988 World Series Highlights: Dodgers vs. A's
13-9075   *$19.99*

1989 World Series Highlights: A's vs. Giants
13-9076   *$19.99*

1990 World Series Highlights: Reds vs. A's
13-9077   *$19.99*

1991 World Series Highlights: Twins vs. Braves
13-9078   *$19.99*

1992 World Series Highlights: Blue Jays vs. Braves
13-9079   *$19.99*

1993 World Series Highlights: Blue Jays vs. Phillies
13-5085   *$19.99*

1995 World Series Highlights: Braves vs. Indians
13-5108   *$19.99*

1996 World Series Highlights: Yankees vs. Braves
13-5114   *$19.99*

1997 World Series Highlights: Marlins vs. Indians
13-5122   *$19.99*

1998 World Series Highlights: Yankees vs. Padres
02-9027   *$19.99*

1999 World Series Highlights: Yankees vs. Braves
02-9180   *$19.99*

This Week In Baseball: 20 Years Of Unforgettable Plays & Bloopers
Catch two decades of diamond greatness (and not-so-greatness) in this compilation of memorable moments as seen on "This Week in Baseball." There's outfield wizardry from Kevin Mitchell and Paul O'Neill, the infamous home run ball off of Jose Canseco's head, Steve Lyons dropping his drawers at first base and much more. 50 min.
13-5113   *$14.99*

A Century Of Success: 100 Years Of Cardinals Glory
The history of the St. Louis Cardinals is presented in this program that offers fascinating looks at Rogers Hornsby, Dizzy Dean, Bob Gibson, Lou Brock, Orlando Cepeda, Ted Simmons and Ozzie Smith. 80 min.
13-9094   *$19.99*

Baseball's Greatest Moments
There are 20 fabulous record-breaking moments showcased on this program, all of which have taken their place in baseball history. Included are Babe Ruth's "called" home run shot, Pete Rose's hit to break Ty Cobb's all-time record, Orel Hershiser's 59 consecutive scoreless innings, Hank Aaron's 715th homer and more! 60 min.
13-9099   *$14.99*

The 50 Greatest Home Runs In Baseball History
These are the shots heard 'round the world by baseball's greatest players. Witness four-baggers that are either awesome, timely or one-of-a-kind from the likes of Ruth, Thomson, Mantle, Mays, Aaron, Jackson, Fisk, Dent, Gibson and others. 50 min.
13-9102   *$14.99*

Super Sluggers
They're the most feared power hitters in the game, and every at-bat is a chance to put one in the bleachers. See Belle, Bonds, Griffey, McGwire, Piazza, Sosa, Vaughn and other slugging stars at the plate and up-close and personal in this video no baseball fan should miss. 50 min.
13-5112   *$14.99*

Super Sluggers 2: Men With Bats
They're the homer-hitting batters whose fearsome swings put baseballs and fans—in the outfield seats. Mark McGwire, Ken Griffey, Jr., Juan Gonzalez, Vinny Castilla and Norristown's own Mike Piazza are among the superstar sluggers featured in a program that's definitely "outta here." 45 min.
02-8851   *$14.99*

Roberto Clemente
The brilliant career of the great Roberto Clemente is chronicled in this stirring tribute that looks at the Hall of Famer's many achievements in and out of baseball. Exciting footage and interviews tell the story of the Pittsburgh Pirates outfielder who gave his life while helping others. 50 min.
13-5090   *$19.99*

Baseball Legends, Vol. 1
Take yourself out to the ball game with interviews and career highlights of Leo Durocher, Bob Feller, Stan Musial, Gil Hodges, Carl Furrillo and Jackie Robinson. 60 min.
10-9409   *$14.99*

Baseball Legends, Vol. 2
Take a look at the great careers of Duke Snider, Roy Campanella, Phil Rizzuto, Yogi Berra and Whitey Ford with interviews and exciting footage.
10-9410   *$14.99*

Superstar Shortstops
This overview of baseball's most awesome shortstops showcases defensive and offensive specialists Alex Rodriguez, Nomar Garciaparra, Derek Jeter and Barry Larkin, as well as glovemen Rey Ordonez, Edgar Renteria and Omar Visquel.
02-9072   *$14.99*

Race For The Record
It's a saga that's "homeric" in more than one sense, as you follow the fence-busting 1998 chase of St. Louis Cardinal Mark McGwire and Chicago Cub Sammy Sosa to break Roger Maris' 1961 61-home run season. This official Major League Baseball video features all the key moments from McGwire's awesome 70-round-tripper campaign. 60 min.
02-9005   Was $19.99   *$14.99*

Maximum Bloopers And Amazing Plays From Baseball Max
From Yankees hurler Orlando Hernandez tossing the ball—and his glove—to make an out at first base to Braves outfielder Andruw Jones making a wall-climbing grab of a certain home run ball, you won't believe the wild miscues, wacky plays, and incredible moments caught on tape.
02-9268   *$14.99*

Official Major League Baseball Bloopers & Great Plays Collection
You've got a front-row seat for some the most amazing moves—and miscues—in diamond history with this four-tape collector's set that includes "Baseball's Funniest Bloopers," "Super Duper Baseball Bloopers 1 and 2" and "This Week in Baseball's Greatest Plays." 180 min. total. NOTE: Individual volumes available at $14.99 each.
73-1224   Save $30.00!   *$29.99*

Centennial: Over 100 Years Of Philadelphia Phillies Baseball
The team from the "City of Brotherly Love" has a unique history that's presented with style and thrills in this superb tape. Featured are such sluggers as Chuck Klein, Richie Ashburn, Richie Allen and Mike Schmidt, pitchers Robin Roberts, Jim Bunning and Steve Carlton, and the 1950 and 1980 World Series. Author James Michener hosts. 60 min.
13-5055   *$19.99*

Nolan Ryan's 7th No-Hitter
On May 1, 1991, Texas pitcher and living legend Nolan Ryan threw an amazing seventh no-hitter against the Toronto Blue Jays. You'll be there for the key pitches and exciting moments in an unforgettable game. 65 min.
13-9085   *$14.99*

Chicago And The Cubs: A Lifelong Love Affair
You'll be an honorary Bleacher Bum before you know it after watching this Cubs-In, featuring historic team clips of such greats as Gaby Hartnett, Ernie Banks, Billy Williams, Stan Hack, Ferguson Jenkins and others. 60 min.
13-9086   *$19.99*

Sammy Sosa: Making History (1999)
His gargantuan home run blasts have made him a hero not just to his native Dominican Republic and the city of Chicago, but to baseball fans worldwide. Now get an up-close and personal look at Cubs super-slugger Sammy Sosa with this video program that features his life story and looks at Sammy's accomplishments both on and off the field. 55 min.
04-5702   *$14.99*

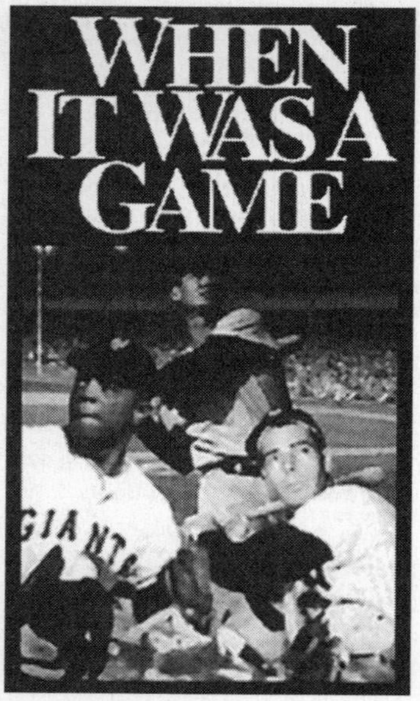

When It Was A Game: Triple Play Collection
This three-tape boxed set of the acclaimed HBO documentaries features rare color home movies taken by baseball players and fans in the '30s, '40s, '50s and '60s. Such legendary names as Babe Ruth, Joe DiMaggio, Ted Williams, Jackie Robinson, Willie Mays, Mickey Mantle, Roberto Clemente, Sandy Koufax and many more are seen, along with vintage looks at Yankee Stadium, Ebbets Field, Fenway Park and other classic ballparks. 175 min. total. NOTE: Individual volumes available at $14.99 each.
44-2265 Save $18.00! ***$26.99***

Baseball: The Complete Series (1994)
From Ken Burns, creator of the acclaimed series "The Civil War," comes this monumental look at America's pastime. Chronicling the history of the sport from its genesis in the early 1800s to the modern era, the nine-part series surveys baseball and its relationship to American culture and society. Filled with archival footage, interviews with diamond stars past and present, and commentary from George Will, Bob Costas, Billy Crystal and other notables, this epic is a must-have for all lovers of the game. 18 1/2 hrs. total. NOTE: Individual volumes available at $19.99 each.
18-7506 Save $30.00! ***□$149.99***

The Golden Decade Of Baseball: 1947-1957: Complete Set
It started with Jackie Robinson breaking the color line and ended with the Dodgers and Giants heading west. Now relive the greatest men and moments from baseball's most exciting era in this two-tape set, from Willie, Mickey and the Duke to Bobby Thomson's "shot heard 'round the world" and Don Larsen's perfect game. Brent Musberger hosts. 120 min. total. NOTE: Individual volumes available at $14.99 each.
45-5485 ***□$29.99***

Only The Ball Was White
For the first half of this century they were denied the chance to play major league baseball because of their race. This moving documentary pays tribute to the members of the Negro Leagues through rare game footage and interviews with stars like Satchel Paige, Roy Campanella and Buck Leonard. Paul Winfield narrates. 30 min.
50-7154 ***$19.99***

A League Of Their Own: The Documentary (1986)
This acclaimed "documentary that inspired the hit movie" looks at the women of the All American Girls Professional Baseball League who took to the playing fields while the men were away in World War II. Along with vintage newsreel footage of the games, there are present-day interviews with ex-members talking about their lives on and off the diamond. 27 min.
02-2343 ***$14.99***

Pinstripe Power: The Story Of The 1961 Yankees
A fantastic look at the 1961 Yanks, considered by many to be one of the finest teams to put on the pinstripes. From Mantle and Maris to Whitey Ford and Louis Arroyo, Ralph Houk's championship squad excelled in every phase of the game. 60 min.
13-5048 ***$19.99***

Babe Ruth: The Life Behind The Legend
He came off the streets of Baltimore and went on to become the greatest drawing card in sports history and an American icon. Follow the colorful exploits—both on and off the field—of the one and only Babe Ruth in this nostalgic HBO documentary that features rare game footage, interviews with family, friends and colleagues, and much more.
44-2179 ***$14.99***

Pinstripe Destiny: The Story Of The 1996 World Champions
Big Apple baseball came back in a big way in 1996, as new manager Joe Torre and a gutsy Yankee crew, including Derek Jeter, Andy Pettitte, Bernie Williams, Dwight Gooden and Wade Boggs, took the AL pennant and went on to beat the favored Atlanta Braves for their first world title in 18 years. Relive the memorable moments from their championship year in this thrill-packed commemorative video. 55 min.
13-5117 ***$19.99***

1999 New York Yankees: Champions Of The Heart
It was a season that saw the team face tragedies (the passing of pinstripe legends DiMaggio and Hunter) and tribulations (manager Joe Torre's treatment for cancer), but the New York Yankees overcame adversity to sweep Atlanta for their 25th world championship and third in four years. Relive the "team of the '90s'" year to remember with a video yearbook featuring Cone, Clemens, Jeter, O'Neill, Williams and all your Bronx faves. MSG Network's Al Trautweig narrates. 64 min.
02-9195 ***$19.99***

The 10 Greatest Moments In Yankees History
How about that! Relive classic pinstripe performances in this collection of baseball memories, hosted by Mel Allen. See Babe Ruth's 60th homer, Lou Gehrig's farewell speech, Don Larsen's perfect World Series game, plus Mantle, DiMaggio, Maris and more. 30 min.
54-5003 ***$14.99***

Where Have You Gone, Joe DiMaggio? (1998)
Relive the on-field heroics and personal struggles of one of baseball's most revered and enigmatic legends, "Yankee Clipper" Joe DiMaggio, with this acclaimed documentary. DiMaggio's boyhood in San Francisco, his 16-year career with the Bronx Bombers, and his marriage to Marilyn Monroe are seen through vintage film clips and photos, as well as interviews with Phil Rizzuto, Reggie Jackson, Pete Rose, Mario Cuomo, George Bush and others. 63 min.
44-2147 ***$14.99***

Hank Aaron: Chasing The Dream (1995)
The life of home run king "Hammerin'" Hank Aaron is memorably recounted in this acclaimed production that mixes live action footage, interviews and dramatic re-creations. Follow Aaron's youth in Mobile, Alabama, his career in both the Negro Leagues and majors, and his controversial pursuit of Babe Ruth's record. Narrated by Dorian Harewood. 95 min.
18-7549 Was $59.99 ***$14.99***

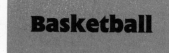

Basketball

NBA At 50
Denzel Washington hosts this enthralling salute to the National Basketball Association's golden anniversary. There's incredible footage of the league's finest moments, greatest coaches and most gifted superstars, from Mikan, Russell and Chamberlain to Erving, Bird and Jordan. Special home video version includes a music video and footage of the NBA's top 50 players not shown on TV. 120 min.
04-3430 Was $19.99 ***□$14.99***

Michael Jordan: His Airness
The career of the world's greatest basketball player is celebrated in this collection sure to delight fans of "His Airness." Spectacular highlights, commentary from teammates, coaches and writers, and Michael's own insights are all featured to paint a complete picture of number 23.
02-9111 ***$19.99***

Michael Jordan: The Ultimate Collection
Savor the sensational skills of basketball's brightest star with this three-tape boxed set that includes "Above and Beyond," "Air Time" and "Come Fly with Me." See footage of Michael's college and pro hoop mastery, his play on the Olympic "Dream Team," and his greatest championship moments. Also includes interviews with friends and family, and "Air Jordan" himself. 150 min. total. NOTE: Individual volumes available separately.
04-3378 Save $27.00! ***$24.99***

NBA Now! Showmen Of Today
They're the stars who are taking the NBA into the new millennium, and this video offers an up-close look at such up-and-coming young hoop greats as Kobe Bryant, Vince Carter, Allen Iverson, Jason Kidd, Jason Williams and others, plus action from the 2000 Rookie Challenge and Slam Dunk Contest. 50 min.
02-9266 ***$14.99***

NBA Superstars
The million-dollar giants of the NBA showcase their spectacular skills in 14 beat-driven videos set to hit music by Billy Joel, Janet Jackson, Berlin, Vanessa Williams and others. Among the superstars are Magic Johnson, Larry Bird, Michael Jordan, Isiah Thomas and Julius Erving. 35 min.
04-2317 Was $19.99 ***$14.99***

1980 NBA Playoffs: That Magic Season
The "magic" for the L.A. Lakers was supplied by a young player named Johnson who teamed with veteran Kareem Abdul-Jabbar to form a potent one-two punch against the Philadelphia 76ers, led by Julius Erving, Daryl Dawkins and Maurice Cheeks. 30 min.
04-1070 ***$14.99***

1981 NBA Playoffs: The Dynasty Renewed
For the first time in five years, the Boston Celtics made it into the NBA Championship Finals, led by sophomore star Larry Bird and veteran Nate Archibald. Their opponents were awesome Moses Malone and the Houston Rockets. 60 min.
04-1592 ***$14.99***

1982 NBA Playoffs: Something To Prove
Witness the extraordinary talents of Julius Erving, Kareem Abdul-Jabbar and Magic Johnson in this action-packed recap of the 1982 NBA Playoffs and World Championship Series between the Los Angeles Lakers and the Philadelphia 76ers. Dick Stockton hosts. 60 min.
04-1065 ***$14.99***

1983 NBA Playoffs: That Championship Feeling
Follow the Philadelphia 76ers' journey through the regular season to the amazing playoffs and, of course, their four-game sweep of the L.A. Lakers. Doctor J., Moses Malone, Andrew Toney, Mo Cheeks, Bobby Jones, Coach Billy Cunningham! It's "Hoopla Heaven"! Bill Fleming narrates. 60 min.
04-1664 ***$14.99***

1984 NBA Playoffs: The Pride And The Passion
Relive the high points of the NBA's 1983-84 season, the 1984 All-Star game, a wild slam dunk contest and a great Old-Timer's feature. Then, watch the best teams go at it, leading to an exciting Finals series as the Boston Celtics overpower the Los Angeles Lakers in six games. 58 min.
04-1066 ***$14.99***

1985 NBA Playoffs: Return To Glory
Relive the exciting sports action of the 1984-85 NBA basketball season, from regular season highlights and an All-Star salute to the grueling playoffs, leading to a Finals rematch between the Boston Celtics and L.A. Lakers. This time, it's L.A. on top! 60 min.
04-1067 ***$14.99***

Home Of The Brave '86-'87 Season/Sweet Sixteen '85-'86 Championship Season
Relive two superb seasons with Larry Bird, Danny Ainge, Kevin McHale, Robert Parish, and the rest of the Boston Celtics with this special double feature that highlights the men in green's '85-'86 championship run and their thrilling '86-'87 campaign. 150 min.
04-2086 ***$19.99***

Official 1987 NBA Championship Video: Drive For Five
For the fourth year in a row, the NBA Championship Finals was a contest between the Boston Celtics and the L.A. Lakers. Relive the thrilling contest, as Abdul-Jabbar, Johnson, Worthy and the Laker crew defeat Boston's Bird, McHale and Parish. 60 min.
04-2087 ***$14.99***

Official 1988 NBA Championship Video: Back To Back
Coming off a grueling Western Conference win over the Dallas Mavericks, the L.A. Lakers rose to the challenge of a feisty young Detroit Pistons squad to become the first NBA team to repeat as champions in 20 years. 65 min.
04-2170 ***$14.99***

Official 1989 NBA Championship Video: Motor City Madness
After losing in the finals to the Lakers the year before, the 1988-89 Detroit Pistons came roaring back to take the NBA Eastern title and sweep L.A. in four straight for their first championship ever. Relive all the excitement, with stars like Thomas, Dumars, Laimbeer and Mahorn in action. 55 min.
04-2256 ***$14.99***

Official 1990 NBA Championship Video: Pure Pistons
The Motor City Madmen made it two in a row, as the Detroit Pistons, fueled by stars like Dumars, Laimbeer and Thomas, raced through the NBA playoffs and burned the Portland Trail Blazers for the championship. 60 min.
04-2366 ***$14.99***

Official 1991 NBA Championship Video: Learning To Fly
It was "Bully!" for the Windy City as the Chicago Bulls stampeded over the Los Angeles Lakers in five thrilling games to win their first NBA title. Now you can relive every exciting moment of the court matchup between Michael Jordan and Magic Johnson, plus stars like Pippen, Perkins, Paxson and Divac. 60 min.
04-2465 ***$19.99***

Official 1992 NBA Championship Video: Untouchabulls
Michael Jordan, Scottie Pippen, John Paxson and the rest of the Chicago Bulls overcame tough competition to return to the NBA Finals in 1992. On the other side of the court, Clyde Drexler led the Portland Trail Blazers to their second championship series in three years. All the action from Chicago's six-game victory is captured here. 60 min.
04-2552 ***$19.99***

Official 1993 NBA Championship Video: Three-Peat
The third time's a charm, as the Chicago Bulls proved when they beat the red-hot Phoenix Suns in a six-game showdown for their third consecutive NBA title. It's Jordan, Pippen and Grant versus Barkley, Johnson and Majerle, along with the most exciting hoop action ever caught on video. 50 min.
04-2678 ***$19.99***

Official 1994 NBA Finals Video: Clutch City
Houston fans were in orbit when their Rockets team, led by Hakeem Olajuwon, Vernon Maxwell, Otis Thorpe and rookie star Sam Cassell, fought past Ewing, Starks, Harper and a hard-playing New York Knicks squad in a grueling seven-game championship series to win their first ever NBA title. 55 min.
04-2850 ***$19.99***

Official 1995 NBA Finals Video: Double Clutch
Defending NBA champion Houston rocketed their way past Utah, Phoenix and San Antonio to meet the up-and-coming Orlando Magic, with Shaquille O'Neal and Anfernee Hardaway, in the finals. Olajuwon, Drexler, Elie and company lead the Rockets to a four-game sweep for their second consecutive crown. 60 min.
04-2986 ***$19.99***

Unstop-A-Bulls: Chicago Bulls 1995-96 Championship Season
After a record-setting 72-10 regular season record, the Chicago Bulls, led by returning Michael Jordan, always-dependable Scottie Pippen and always-controversial Dennis Rodman, breezed past their Eastern playoff opponents for a championship showdown with Shawn Kemp, Gary Payton and the Seattle SuperSonics. 50 min.
04-3337 ***$19.99***

Chicago Bulls: 1996-97 Championship Season
For the fifth time in seven years, the Chicago Bulls charged their way into the NBA Championship series. Watch as Jordan, Rodman, Pippen and company put on some last-minute heroics to defeat the Utah Jazz, led by Karl Malone, John Stockton and Jeff Hornacek, in a grueling six-game series. 50 min.
04-3496 ***$19.99***

UnforgettaBulls: The 6th NBA Championship Season Of The Chicago Bulls
Basketball's (and maybe all of pro sports') "Team of the '90s" continued their title dominance, as MVP Michael Jordan led his Bulls team to a second consecutive six-game win over Utah and their sixth NBA championship in eight years. There are highlights aplenty as Pippin, Malone, Rodman and Stockton square off on the hardwood. 50 min.
04-3696 ***□$19.99***

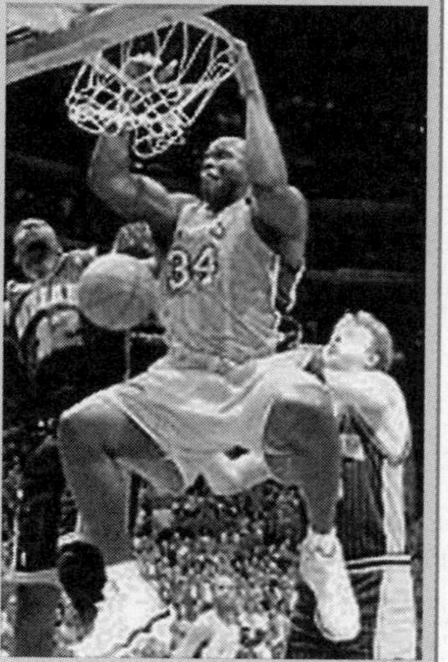

Official 2000 NBA Championship Home Video
With Jack Nicholson, Dyan Cannon and other celebs rooting from the sidelines, the Los Angeles Lakers, led by MVP Shaquille O'Neal and Kobe Bryant and coached by Phil Jackson, beat the Larry Bird-coached Indian Pacers, with Reggie Miller and Jalen Rose, in a tough final series. See all the highlights of the six-game showdown on this thrilling video. 60 min.
02-9228 ***$19.99***

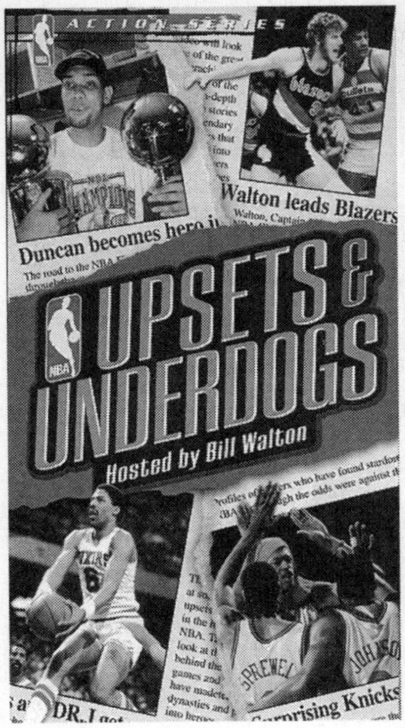

NBA Upsets & Underdogs
There's no need to fear...some of the greatest turnarounds and come-from-behind victories in NBA history are here! Among the highlights in this video hosted by basketball hall of famer Bill Walton are Julius Erving leading the '82-'83 76ers to an Eastern Conference win over Boston; the '98-'99 New York Knicks surprising drive to the NBA Championship against San Antonio; and more. 50 min.
02-9191 $14.99

The NBA's 100 Greatest Plays
"The play's the thing"...especially in this all-star salute to the most amazing moves, steals, blocks and dunks in hardwood history. Watch as some of the NBA's top players make the play and score one (or two, or three) for the team.
02-9083 $14.99

Greatest NBA Finals Moments
There's something about the NBA championship series that brings out the best in the players, and you'll see just what some of the game's greatest—including Abdul-Jabbar, Johnson, Jordan and others—have done to put their teams on top in this exciting retrospective.
02-9084 $14.99

Super Slams Of The NBA
Here's a salute to dunks and the great dunkers of the past and present. Incredible action featuring legends like Wilt Chamberlain, Elgin Baylor, Connie Hawkins and Julius Erving, as well as current slammeisters Michael Jordan, Dominique Wilkins, Charles Barkley, Magic Johnson, Spud Webb and others. 40 min.
04-2430 $14.99

Magic Johnson: Always Showtime
A look at the amazing career of L.A. Lakers great Earvin "Magic" Johnson, one of hoopdom's finest all-around players, whose talents dazzled fans for years. Includes footage from Magic's college days up to and including his dramatic return to the NBA. 47 min.
04-2481 Was $19.99 ❑$14.99

NBA Dream Team
They're the best that pro basketball has produced, the 10 superstars chosen to represent the U.S. at the 1992 Summer Olympics. This video salute shows exciting game clips, career highlights and personal portraits of Barkley, Bird, Ewing, Johnson, Jordan, Malone, Mullin, Pippen, Robinson and Stockton. 40 min.
04-2516 $14.99

Long Shots: The Life And Times Of The American Basketball Association
From 1967 to 1976 the upstart American Basketball Association used such innovations as a multi-colored ball, the three-point shot and the all-star slam dunk contest to compete with the more established NBA. Relive nine seasons of court action with the New York Nets, the Kentucky Colonels, the Virginia Squires and other teams, with such stars as Julius Erving, George Gervin and Artis Gilmore, in this thrilling and light-hearted retrospective. 55 min.
44-2141 $14.99

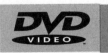

DVD VIDEO
ASK ABOUT OUR GIANT DVD CATALOG!

Hockey

Lord Stanley's Cup: Hockey's Ultimate Prize
Hockey fans won't want to miss this scintillating salute to Lord Stanley's cup. Follow its fabled history in a highlight-filled program that features a look at the amazing players who sought to drink from the cup, astonishing plays that electrified sports fans, and intensity-packed playoff games that led to great victories. 45 min.
04-3834 $14.99

Nothing Else Matters: 1999 Stanley Cup Championship Video
Marked by controversy, close, brutal games and heroic performances, the 1999 "quest for the Cup" will go down as a classic. The top-seed Dallas Stars, propelled by Mike Modano, Joe Nieuwendyk, Brett Hull and Ed Belfour, defeat their arch-rival Colorado Avalanche to face—and beat—the gritty, Dominik Hasek-led Buffalo Sabres in the six-game final round. 50 min.
04-3856 $19.99

Second Heaven: 2000 Stanley Cup Championship Video
The New Jersey Devils, led by the defense of MVP Scott Stevens, the goaltending of Martin Brodeur and the expert coaching of Larry Robinson, defeated Mike Modano, goalie Ed "the Eagle" Belfour and the Dallas Stars in a tight Stanley Cup finals series that returns the Cup to the lush and green Meadowlands. 55 min.
02-9227 $19.99

Wayne Gretzky: Above And Beyond
Here's a thrilling recap of the career of hockey great Wayne Gretzky of the Los Angeles Kings. Follow Number 99's fascinating, thrill-a-second story, from his excellence at hockey as a youngster to his success in the junior leagues; from his Stanley Cup victories with the Edmonton Oilers to the blockbuster trade that brought him to L.A. 58 min.
27-6688 Was $19.99 $14.99

NHL's Masked Men: The Last Line Of Defense
They put their bodies on the line to keep the opposition from scoring, and this action-filled salute to the goalies of the NHL includes thrilling game footage with such stars as Martin Brodeur, Dominik Hasek, Patrick Roy, John Vanbiesbrouck and others.
04-3634 ❑$14.99

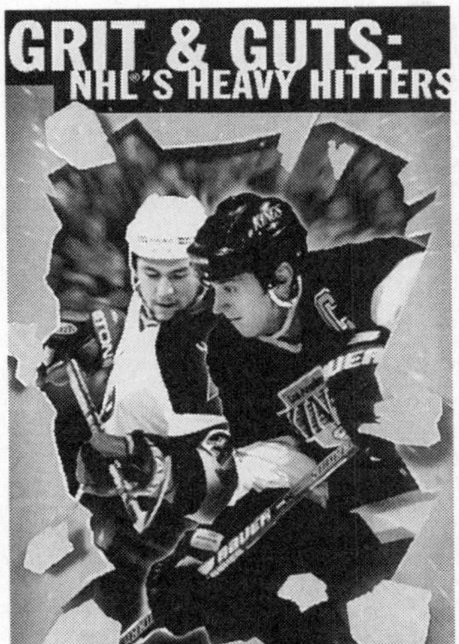

Grit & Guts: NHL's Heavy Hitters
"The coolest game on ice" can also be "the cruelest game on ice" when you consider how tough hockey's heaviest hitters really are. No-nonsense players Chris Pronger, Rob Blake, Mike Peca and Rick Tocchet are among the featured skaters who mix muscle with scoring and finesse. 60 min.
04-3802 $14.99

NHL 2000: A Millennium Of Memories
Well, maybe ice hockey isn't officially 1,000 years old, but this video is a once-in-a-millennium treat. Witness the 25 greatest moments in NHL history, with rare footage of the game's most unforgettable games and players: Howe, Orr, Gretzky, Lemieux and many more.
02-9206 Was $19.99 $14.99

The NHL's Greatest Goals
Talk about your "red light specials!" Some of the most memorable scores in NHL history, from Mario Lemieux's amazing between-the-legs shot in the 1996 Stanley Cup playoffs to Wayne Gretzky's record-breaking 802nd goal, have been gathered in one remarkable program.
04-3602 $14.99

Skiing

Warren Miller's Freeriders
Come on and take a free ski ride, as Warren Miller's camera presents unbelievable action footage of daredevil skiers and snowboarders from Colorado and Utah to Chile, Norway and above the Arctic Circle. 105 min.
11-2284 Was $19.99 ❑$14.99

Warren Miller's SnowRiders
A group of death-defying snowriders tackle the most challenging hills to attempt their wildest ski and snowboarding stunts in this thrill-a-second film from ace extreme sports filmmaker Warren Miller. 96 min.
11-2800 Was $19.99 ❑$14.99

Warren Miller's Fifty (1999)
To mark his golden anniversary as America's premier action sports filmmaker, Warren Miller put together this intense compilation featuring 50 years of incredible skiing and snowboarding footage. 97 min.
11-2378 Was $99.99 $14.99

Ski Movie
From Whistler to Mt. Baker, the best skiers in the world—including Seth Morrison, Brad Holmes, Vincent Dorion and others—unleashed their acrobatic talents all over Washington in the winter of 2000. Watch as these athletes embark on some of the craziest ski maneuvers ever, set to the pounding hardcore rock music of such bands as Methods of Mayhem, Cotton Mouth Kings, Anthrax and others. 60 min.
50-8760 $19.99

Surfing

Slippery When Wet (1958)
The first film from surfing documentarian Bruce Brown ("The Endless Summer") focuses on five surfers and their dream trip to Hawaii. Original score by jazz legend Bud Shank and amazing footage of North Shore waves. 73 min.
07-8227 Was $29.99 $19.99

Surf Crazy (1959)
Fantastic wave-riding footage in Mexico, California and Hawaii highlights this fine and thrilling Bruce Brown feature. 71 min.
07-8228 Was $29.99 $19.99

Barefoot Adventure (1960)
Bruce Brown supplies new narration for this incredible odyssey about surfing dudes who hang 10 on waves from the Wedge to Waimea, Honolulu to Huntington and Santa Cruz to Kaui. Features shots of the legendary Point surf at Makaha. 72 min.
07-8230 Was $29.99 $19.99

Surfing Hollow Days (1961)
Take a wave to Mexico, California and Florida with ace surf filmmaker Bruce Brown. He records a 15-foot shark at Rincon, and we witness the first wave ever ridden at Pipeline. 84 min.
07-8231 Was $29.99 $19.99

Waterlogged (1962)
A compilation of Bruce Brown's finest surfing film moments, with amazing clips from "Barefoot Adventure," "Slippery When Wet," "Surf Crazy" and "Surfing Hollow Days." You'll be doing the "wave" with the "Fellini of Foam's" fabulous footage. 63 min.
07-8229 Was $29.99 $19.99

Surfin' Shorts
Three of Bruce Brown's short films from the early 1960s: "The Wet Set" features the Hobie-MacGregor Surf Team; "America's Newest Sport" with the Hobie Super Surfer Skateboard Team; and a TV special about a trip to Japan with 12-year-old Peter Johnson and Del Cannon. 57 min.
07-8232 Was $29.99 $19.99

The Endless Summer (1964)
The landmark surfing documentary from Bruce Brown follows two surf bums around the globe, from Africa to Australia to Tahiti, on a quest for the "perfect wave." Witness incredible footage of the world's highest, wildest loopers, crests and pipelines. 90 min.
07-1158 Was $19.99 ❑$14.99

The Endless Summer II (1994)
This sequel to the classic surf odyssey features wave-chasers Pat O'Connell and Robert "Wingnut" Weaver searching for the wildest rides in Alaska, France, Fiji, Java, South Africa, Bali and Australia. The original's director, Bruce Brown, captures spectacular surf footage in some of the world's most exotic places. 100 min.
02-2668 Was $19.99 ❑$14.99

Motorsports

The Last Of The Gladiators: Evel Knievel
The true story of Evel Knievel and his injury-riddled rise to stardom is told, complete with rarely-seen sequences and riveting replays of the jumps (and crashes) that made Knievel the legend he is today. 100 min.
16-7002 Was $39.99 $19.99

Evel Knievel's Spectacular Jumps
Viva Knievel! The world-famous daredevil stuntman is featured in a nailbiting compendium of his most spectacular feats. See Evel risk his life in motorcycle leaps around the world, and witness the awesome Snake River Canyon rocketcar. AKA: "Evel Knievel's Greatest Hits." 30 min.
16-7022 Was $19.99 $14.99

Driving Force
What does it take to make it as a professional racer? Some of the top names in motorsports, including Jeff Gordon, Dale Jarrett, Bobby Labonte, Mark Martin and Richard Petty, share their stories of driving to the top in this video filled with exciting footage from their most memorable races. 50 min.
04-5718 $12.99

Automotive 4-Pack
Whether it's daredevil racing footage, hair-raising crashes, classic hot rods or heavy-duty truck action you crave, this four-tape set has what you're looking for. Included in the collection are "Thunder on the Track," taking you from motorsports to powerboat racing; a look at the "Wild World of Crashes"; "Back to the 50's," with over 60,000 classic cars on display; and the self-explanatory "Monster Truckin' U.S.A." 185 min. total.
64-3441 $19.99

NASCAR's Great Moments: The Early Years
Relive classic stock-car action from the '40s to the '70s, with rare film clips, interviews with top drivers, heart-stopping crash footage and more. 45 min.
04-5535 $14.99

NASCAR: 1998 Year In Review
Relive the memorable races and thrill-packed moments from the 1998 Winston Cup season with this special program packed with exciting race footage.
18-1143 $14.99

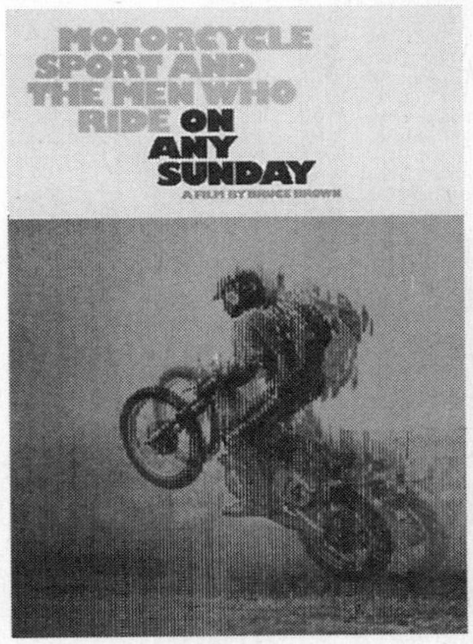

On Any Sunday (1971)
This Academy Award-nominated documentary reveals the thrilling, action-packed world of motorcycle racing. Watch incredible races, meet the bikers, and see Steve McQueen, a lifelong bike fan, partaking in the proceedings. 96 min.
07-8297 Was $39.99 $19.99

On Any Sunday II (1981)
Top motorcycle and motocross stars are interviewed and seen in exciting action footage in this super sports sequel that packs as much excitement as the original. Includes a comedic look at old-time racing. 89 min.
27-6019 Was $39.99 $19.99

On Any Sunday Revisited (2000)
Famed sports filmmaker Bruce Brown teams with son Dana to return to the daredevil sport of motorcycle racing—and the riders who put their lives on the line to take part in it—in this thrill-packed documentary that includes never-before-seen, unused scenes from the original "On Any Sunday," including interview footage with Steve McQueen. 60 min.
27-7217 $19.99

On Any Sunday Boxed Set
Rev up some savings, with all three motorcycle classics in a boxed collector's set.
27-7218 Save $10.00! $49.99

Indy 500 Series: Complete Set
Go behind the scenes with the drivers, pit crews and other workers at the world's most famous raceway with this four-tape collection of intense, thrill-packed videos featuring breathtaking race footage. Included in the set are "Secrets of Speed," "Speed Crash Rescue," "Speedway Survival" and "24 Hours at Indy." 200 min. total. NOTE: Individual volumes available at $14.99 each.
68-1991 *$59.99*

Drag Racin' Yesteryear Style
Take a look at this spectacular assembly of dragsters and stock cars from the mid-'60s. In "Race Against Time" and "Drag Racers' Holiday," you'll see the 1966 and 1968 Nationals and watch vintage "muscle machines" in action." 60 min.
82-1036 *$19.99*

Jeff Gordon: Triumph Of A Dream
Follow the 1993 NASCAR Rookie of the Year and 1995 Winston Cup champion's drive to success in a special "video diary." 50 min.
04-5471 *$14.99*

Jeff Gordon's "One In A Million"
Go around the banked track with the 1997 Daytona winner and two-time NASCAR Winston Cup champion in a thrill-packed program featuring interviews with Gordon, his family and crew, plus footage from Jeff's biggest races. 60 min.
18-1133 *$14.99*

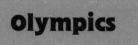

Olympics

Tokyo Olympiad (1966)
Director Kon Ichikawa's documentary look at the 1964 Summer Olympics in Tokyo, from the opening and closing ceremonies to track and field, swimming and gymnastic events, was acclaimed for the filmmaker's artistic presentation of the skill and spirit of the competitors, transcending normal sports documentaries. 170 min. on two tapes.
76-7038 Letterboxed *$49.99*

America's Greatest Olympians
Cheer for the "red, white and blue" with this stirring salute to the country's top amateur athletes. Jim Thorpe, Jesse Owens, Muhammad Ali, Bruce Jenner, Mary Lou Retton, Edwin Moses and many more medal-winners are featured in scenes from their greatest Olympic moments. 120 min.
18-7619 *$19.99*

Thorpe's Gold
Considered by many the century's greatest athlete, Jim Thorpe came from an Oklahoma Indian reservation to win the 1912 Olympics Pentathlon and Decathlon, only to have his awards stripped six months later. Look back at Thorpe's bittersweet life and his extraordinary Olympic and pro feats. 75 min.
08-1248 Was $29.99 *$19.99*

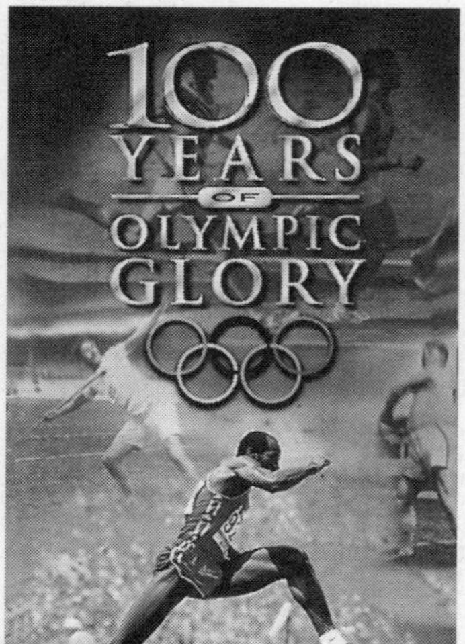

100 Years Of Olympic Glory (1995)
Celebrate a century of athletic courage and triumph with this special two-tape set, produced by Olympic documentarian Bud Greenspan, that mixes rare film footage from the turn of the century to the present with interviews with the competitors. Such famous Olympians as Americans Babe Didrikson and Carl Lewis, "Flying Finn" Paavo Nurmi, runner Kip Keino of Kenya and Russian gymnast Olga Korbut are among those profiled. 180 min. total.
18-7618 *$29.99*

Ice Skating

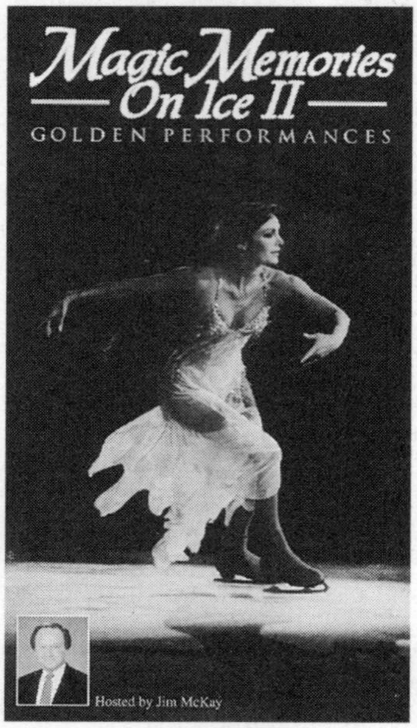

Magic Memories On Ice II: Golden Performances
Some of the greatest ice skating performances are captured on this awesome program that spotlights such greats as Peggy Fleming, Scott Hamilton, Torvill and Dean, Katarina Witt, and Brian Boitano. They perform to the accompaniment of classical and popular music; hosted by Jim McKay. 78 min.
19-9024 Was $24.99 *❑$12.99*

Ice Skating: Great Routines Of The 1980's
Through a combination of skill, talent and finesse, Olympic medalists Scott Hamilton, Dorothy Hamill, the Protopopovs, and Torvill and Dean have entertained and enthralled ice skating fans for nearly a decade, as evidenced in this spectacular combination of their finest moments. 65 min.
22-7064 Was $19.99 *$14.99*

Ice Skating All-Stars: Carmen & Tango
Some of the top Olympic and World Champion skaters from Russia take to the ice for a dazzling display of action, featuring a skating exhibition set to the music of Bizet's beloved opera and a lively tango-styled ice dance. 57 min.
22-7109 Was $19.99 *$14.99*

Ice Skating All-Stars: Russian Fair
Filmed live at Moscow's famed Ice Theatre, this exhibition features champion skaters in exhilarating solo, pairs and ensemble performances set to music from great Russian composers. 52 min.
22-7110 Was $19.99 *$14.99*

Figure Skating Superstars: Brian Boitano & Friends
Join world champ skater Brian Boitano in a dazzling ice-skating display that also features such stars as Tiffany Cook, Elizabeth Manley, Christopher Bowman and, yes, Tonya Harding. 56 min.
22-7163 *$19.99*

Figure Skating Superstars: Katarina Witt & Friends
German skater and commentator Katarina Witt shows her expertise in this amazing skating show that also includes Wilson & McCall, Tonya Harding and Victor Petrenko, as well as other top ice performers. 54 min.
22-7164 *$19.99*

Torvill And Dean: Path To Perfection
These ice-dancing performers were the toast of the 1984 Winter Olympics. This fascinating documentary covers their dazzling Olympics performances as well as their amazing "Bolero" skating in the European championships. 53 min.
44-1166 *$19.99*

Reflections On Ice: A Diary Of Ladies Figure Skating
The graceful beauty and athletic ability that have marked women's figure skating are well displayed in this breathtaking documentary. Rare film footage and photos chronicle the sport over a century of development. Such stars as Sonja Henie, Barbara Ann Scott, Peggy Fleming, JoJo Starbuck, Dorothy Hamill and others are featured. 59 min.
44-2162 *❑$14.99*

Golf

Golf And All Its Glory: Complete Set
This six-volume look at the glory of golf offers interviews with such stars as Arnold Palmer, Greg Norman and Jack Nicklaus, along with behind-the-scenes aspects of the game like life on the pro tour, agents and course design. Footage from the PGA Tour and St. Andrew's Royal and Ancient Club is offered; Gary McCord hosts. 290 min. total. NOTE: Individual volumes available at $19.99 each.
06-2132 *$119.99*

Arnold Palmer: Golf's Heart And Soul
The definitive, three-tape look at the life and spectacular career of golfing great Arnold Palmer includes rare footage, incisive interviews and never-before-seen photos to give you the complete portrait of the "the King." Narrated by John Forsythe, this Golf Channel program was produced to coincide with Palmer's 70th birthday. 155 min.
22-6072 *$59.99*

The Arnold Palmer Story
Look back on the life and times of the most famous golfer of all time with this special video salute that traces Palmer's story from his boyhood Pennsylvania home to a career on the links that includes four Masters, two British Opens and a U.S. Open win. Interviews with such rivals as Jack Nicklaus, Gary Player and Curtis Strange are also featured. 55 min.
47-2074 *$19.99*

Highlights Of The 1997 Masters Tournament
Twenty-one-year-old sensation Tiger Woods rewrote the record books at Georgia's venerable Augusta National Golf Club when he became the first African-American and youngest player ever to wear the green jacket, winning the 1997 Masters with the lowest score in the tournament's 63-year history. Follow Woods' amazing drive to victory in this tribute to golf's most prestigious event. 52 min.
19-2547 *$14.99*

The Complete History Of Golf
An exhaustive look at life on the links, from the sport's conception in medieval times to the present. Pat Summerall hosts this truly amazing program that chronicles golf's history, its greatest players, greatest plays and greatest shots. Featuring drawings, rare footage, interviews and more, this series is the ultimate gift for golf fans. 400 min. on four tapes, available in an attractive case.
50-6980 *$119.99*

The History Of The Ryder Cup: Seven Decades Of A Golf Classic
Begun in 1927 as a contest between American and British golfers, this biannual event has evolved into a showdown between the best duffers in America and Europe and one of golf's most prestigious trophies. Peter Allis narrates this look at the Ryder Cup's first 60 years and the legendary athletes who have taken part. 80 min.
53-6726 *$14.99*

Legacy Of The Links
From Scotland's fabled St. Andrew's course, legendary birthplace of golf, host Lee Trevino takes you on an enlightening, entertaining history of the game. Joining him are guests like Arnold Palmer, Tom Watson and others as they look back on over four centuries of golfing highlights. 90 min.
06-1506 *$19.99*

Golf's Greatest Moments
Celebrate the centennial of American golf with this outstanding collection of rare archives, interviews, tournament highlights, famous playoffs and game-stopping shots. Teeing off are such game greats as Arnold Palmer, Ben Hogan, Bobby Jones, Jack Nicklaus, Nancy Lopez and more. 77 min.
47-1938 *$19.99*

Great Golf Courses Of Ireland
Take a trip to the greatest Irish golf courses with host Christy O'Connor, Jr., a Ryder Cup winner. See how the game is played at Tralee, Killarney, Carlow, Waterville and others. Fore! 60 min.
50-2072 *$29.99*

Golf: The Greatest Game
Celebrate 100 years of golf in America in this documentary look at the game's development, top players, most exciting moments and its links to Hollywood. An exciting compilation that's sure to delight any duffer around. 87 min.
19-2310 *$24.99*

The Chrysler American Great 18 Golf Championship (1993)
One of the most unique golf tournaments ever took four top players (John Daly, Tom Kite, Davis Love III, Fuzzy Zoeller) on a tour of 18 of America's toughest courses (including Pebble Beach, Winged Foot, Harbour Town and Merion), where they played one hole on each for a "super-course" and a share of a $500,000 purse. 180 min. on two tapes.
50-7216 *$49.99*

Boxing

Sugar Ray Robinson: Pound For Pound
The remarkable career of middleweight champ Sugar Ray Robinson is recounted. Included are exciting highlight footage from his 201-bout career and commentary from Rocky Marciano, Joe Louis, Joe Frazier, Muhammad Ali and other top fighters. 99 min.
15-1030 *$19.99*

Boxing's Best: Boxing's Greatest Champions
A ringside look at career highlights from such all-time great pugilists as Rocky Marciano, Henry Armstrong, Joe Louis, Roberto Duran and Muhammad Ali. 60 min.
44-1654 Was $19.99 *$14.99*

Boxing's Best: The Heavyweights: "The Big Punchers"
A look at the most fearsome knockout punchers in boxing history at the peak of their effectiveness includes Jack Dempsey, Joe Louis, Rocky Marciano, Joe Frazier and others. 59 min.
44-1658 Was $19.99 *$14.99*

Boxing's Best: The Heavyweights: "The Stylists"
Fighters like Jim Corbett, Jersey Joe Walcott, Floyd Patterson and Muhammad Ali, who all used their quickness and footwork to take the championship belt, are saluted in thrilling fight footage. 60 min.
44-1692 Was $19.99 *$14.99*

Boxing's Best: The Champions Collection
Your wallet will score a decisive win when you purchase this deluxe boxed set that includes "Muhammad Ali," "Jack Dempsey," "Joe Louis" and "Rocky Marciano."
44-2032 *$44.99*

Sonny Liston: The Mysterious Life And Death Of A Champion
He shocked the boxing world by KO'ing Floyd Patterson in the first round to become heavyweight champion of the world in 1962, but less than two years later lost to a cocky young Cassius Clay. Follow the meteoric rise and fall of famed fighter Sonny Liston, from his stormy ring career to his controversial death in 1970.
44-2031 *$14.99*

Joe Louis
Spectacular recapping of the "Brown Bomber's" career, from his legendary bouts with German boxer Max Schmeling to his 12-year reign as undefeated heavyweight champ. AKA: "Boxing's Best: Joe Louis." 60 min.
44-1694 Was $19.99 *$12.99*

Joe Louis: For All Time
For 12 years the "Brown Bomber" was king of the boxing world, and ranks as one of the greatest heavyweights of all time. Relive the greatest bouts of Joe Louis' career, and take an inside look at his turbulent personal life. 89 min.
50-6326 Was $29.99 *$19.99*

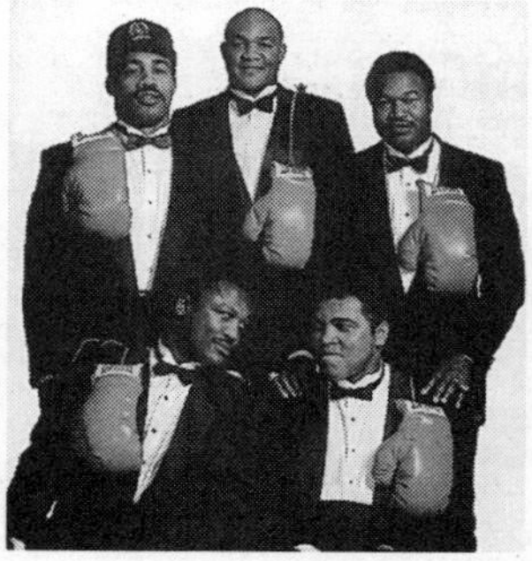

Champions Forever: The Collector's Edition
A once-in-a-lifetime gathering of former heavyweight titleholders (Muhammad Ali, George Foreman, Joe Frazier, Larry Holmes and Ken Norton) is featured in this knockout documentary, as the champs talk about their lives in and out of the ring and present footage from their most memorable fights. Hosted by Reggie Jackson, this special edition also features never-before-seen footage from the "Dinner with the Champs" in Las Vegas. 115 min.
78-3035 Was $19.99 *$14.99*

Champions Forever: The Latin Legends
Six of the greatest boxers from the United States and Latin America—Alexis Arguello, Julio Cesar Chavez, Roberto Duran, Kid Gavilan, Carlos Ortiz and Salvador Sanchez—talk about their struggles and triumphs in and out of the ring in this thrilling film packed with classic fight footage. Edward James Olmos hosts. 93 min.
78-3042 *$19.99*

Muhammad Ali: Skill, Brains & Guts
He's the poet, prophet, self-promoter and pugilist many people consider the greatest fighter of all-time. See the best of Ali in action, from his days as Cassius Clay and his Olympic matches to his three title reigns and classic bouts with Liston, Frazier and Foreman. 87 min.
15-1013 *$19.99*

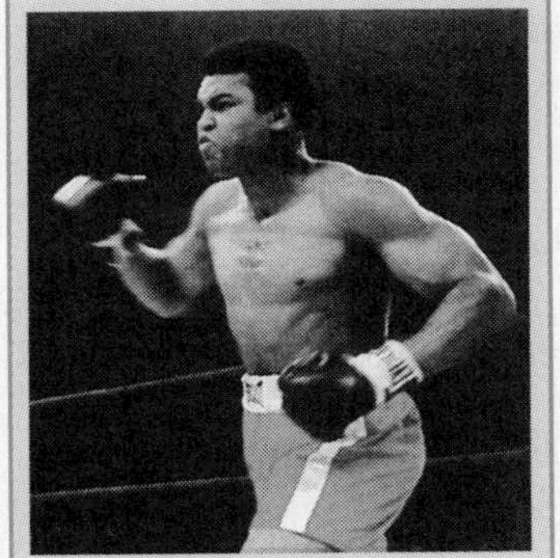

Muhammad Ali: The Whole Story
To millions around the world he is known simply as "The Greatest." Trace the life and career of the most colorful and controversial figure in sports history in this six-tape documentary series that features rare interviews and exclusive footage from Ali's most memorable fights. Volumes include "The Beginning: Olympic Gold," "The Youngest Heavyweight Champion," "Exile," "The Road Back," "The Rumble in the Jungle" and "The Thrilla in Manila." 348 min. total.
18-7743 □*$109.99*

Muhammad Ali
One of the most valuable videos a sports fan could ever hope for! Twenty years of Ali's amazing years—all crammed into this dynamic program. See Ali as a cocky 17-year-old, see him skyrocket to fame, see him meeting kings, presidents, premiers...and see his greatest bouts—including the Frazier fights. Great stuff! AKA: "Boxing's Best: Muhammad Ali." 60 min.
44-1582 Was $19.99 *$12.99*

Ali's Greatest Fights 3-Pack
"I Shook Up the World," "Rumble in the Jungle" and "Thrilla in Manila" are also available in a boxed collector's set.
44-2107 Save $9.00! *$22.99*

Muhammad Ali: In His Own Words
He was as well known for his poetry and self-promotional tactics as for his ring artistry, and in this unique video retrospective you'll follow Muhammad Ali's stellar boxing career through his memorable press conferences and interviews. 40 min.
50-7523 *$19.99*

I Shook Up The World: Clay vs. Liston (1964)
Witness the beginning of the legend, as Olympic gold medalist Cassius Clay shocks the sports world by defeating heavyweight champ Sonny Liston in a seven-round slugfest. 44 min.
10-2317 *$12.99*

A.K.A. Cassius Clay (1970)
Made during Muhammad Ali's return to the ring following his controversial conviction on draft evasion charges, this compelling documentary on the legendary boxer looks at Ali's stormy life and career through candid interviews and clips from his greatest bouts. Richard Kiley narrates.
12-3336 □*$14.99*

The Rumble In The Jungle: Ali vs. Foreman (1974)
The one and only Muhammad Ali regained the world heavyweight title when he used his "rope-a-dope" technique to defeat reigning champ George Foreman in this eight-round battle in Zaire. 109 min.
10-2318 *$12.99*

Thrilla In Manila: Ali vs. Frazier III (1975)
In their third and final encounter, Muhammad Ali and "Smokin'" Joe Frazier squared off in a brutal 14-round bout in the Philippines that ranks among the greatest fights in history. Watch as Ali retains both his crown and the title of "The Greatest." 78 min.
10-2319 *$12.99*

When We Were Kings (1996)
Academy Award-winning documentary chronicling 1974's "Rumble in the Jungle" bout that saw Muhammad Ali regain the heavyweight title from George Foreman. Along with exciting boxing footage, director Leon Gast captures the charismatic Ali at his jive-talking greatest, the fight's incredible hoopla and commentary by Norman Mailer, Spike Lee and George Plimpton. 94 min.
02-8664 Was $19.99 *$14.99*

Kings Of The Ring
Trace eight decades of boxing greatness in this knock-out retrospective hosted by Louis Gossett, Jr. Archival footage, interviews and ringside action feature such legendary fighters as Willard, Baer, Louis, Ali, Tyson and many more. 92 min.
44-2030 *$14.99*

The Leonard-Hearns Saga
You've got a ringside seat for the greatest boxing feud of the decade. Witness the 1981 bout that saw "Sugar Ray" taking the "Hit Man's" welterweight title, their thrilling 1989 rematch with its controversial decision, rare interviews and more. 120 min.
04-2240 *$19.99*

The Fabulous Four: Duran, Leonard, Hagler, Hearns
Fierce boxing action from four legendary champions highlights this program. Roberto Duran, Sugar Ray Leonard, "Marvelous" Marvin Hagler and Thomas "Hit Man" Hearns are the brawlers in the spotlight. 83 min.
04-5088 *$19.99*

Jack Johnson: Breaking Barriers
The groundbreaking career of African-American boxer Jack Johnson is chronicled in a fascinating program that looks at the heavyweight champion, who was the subject of the play and film "The Great White Hope," and his battles in and out of the ring. 88 min.
50-7368 *$19.99*

Boxing's Greatest Upsets
Superior ring footage can be found in this tribute to boxing's biggest surprise matches. There's Ali-Norton, Ali-Spinks, Hagler-Leonard, Hearns-Barkley and more. 64 min.
04-5089 *$19.99*

The Perfect Punch
This is a celebration of the art of the knock-out punch featuring footage of Lennox Lewis, Chris Eubank, Nigel Benn, Prince Naseem Hamed and Herbie Hide. See the fighters smash each other silly with damaging blows to the head and body. 76 min.
53-6949 *$14.99*

Wrestling

WCW Fall Brawl: War Games '93
A grueling two-ring cage match with Sting, Davey Boy Smith, Dustin Rhodes and the unbelievable Shock Master taking on WCW champ Vader, Sid Vicious and Harlem Heat is just one part of this seasonal slamfest. There's also wrestling action with Ric Flair, the Nasty Boys, Ricky Steamboat and others. 120 min.
18-7464 *$39.99*

WCW Halloween Havoc 1994
Two of pro wrestling's all-time greats, Hulk Hogan and Ric Flair, put their careers on the line in a steel cage bout that will see one man walk away with the WCW Heavyweight belt and the other leave the ring "for good." This fright-filled supercard also features matches with Dustin Rhodes, Terry Funk, Johnny B. Badd, the Honkytonk Man and others.
18-7513 *$39.99*

WCW Halloween Havoc '96
The monsters in this supercard are the members of the NWO, out to trick the stars of WCW and treat themselves to championship gold. Watch "Hollywood" Hulk Hogan defend his world title against an enraged Randy Savage, "Outsiders" Hall and Nash take on Harlem Heat for the tag team belts, and the Giant battle Jeff Jarrett, plus matches with Dean Malenko, Rey Misterio, Jr., Lex Luger and others.
18-7718 *$59.99*

WCW Halloween Havoc '98
It's a rematch nine years in the making, as the Warrior seeks his ultimate revenge against "Hollywood" Hogan and his NWO flunkies, while former Outsider compadres Scott Hall and Kevin Nash square off in an NWO Hollywood-NWO Wolfpac showdown, and it's brother against brother when Scott and Rick Steiner clash. All this, plus Sting, Bret Hart, Raven and more. 180 min.
18-7853 *$59.99*

WCW Halloween Havoc '97
There's no candy to give away, but Rowdy Roddy Piper gets some sweet revenge on "Hollywood" Hogan in a steel cage match. Plus, Ric Flair has a score to settle with Four Horseman-turned-NWO member Curt Hennig, Lex Luger takes on Scott Hall (with special referee Larry Zybyszko), a historic inter-gender bout between Disco Inferno and Miss Jacquelyn, and more. 180 min.
18-7790 *$59.99*

WCW Halloween Havoc '99
All bets are off in Las Vegas when Sting puts the WCW heavyweight title on the line twice, against Hulk Hogan in a controversial match and then versus impromptu opponent Goldberg, who himself must also take on Sid Vicious. There's also a brutal "strap match" between Ric Flair and Diamond Dallas Page, a three-way tag team title bout featuring the Filthy Animals, Jimmy Hart's First Family and Harlem Heat, and much more. 180 min.
18-7898 *$59.99*

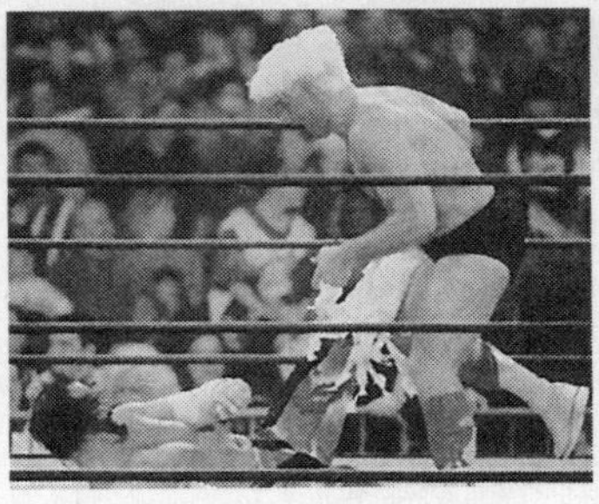

Ric Flair: 2 Decades Of Excellence
He "styled and profiled" his way to the world heavyweight wrestling title a record 11 times, and on this video retrospective you'll see a candid interview with "Nature Boy" Ric Flair along with clips from some of his greatest matches (against Harley Race, Dusty Rhodes, Sting, Vader and others). Woooooo! 60 min.
18-7537 *$12.99*

The Nature Boy: Ric Flair
The unprecedented 14-time world champion, the leader of the Four Horsemen, and the man behind "Space Mountain"; put them all together and you have the one-and-only "Nature Boy." See highlights from Flair's illustrious career as he chops his way through a "who's who" of pro wrestling. And remember, "to be the man, you have to beat the man!" 60 min.
18-7872 *$14.99*

WCW Spring Stampede '94
Join the thundering herd of wrestling fans who packed Chicago's Rosemont Horizon to see the stars of World Championship Wrestling in brutal, no-bull mat action. See WCW heavyweight champ Ric Flair take on arch-rival Ricky Steamboat, a savage "Chicago Street Fight" match between the Nasty Boys and Cactus Jack and Maxx Payne, plus Sting, Vader, Rick Rude, Dustin Rhodes and more. 180 min.
18-7481 Was $39.99 *$14.99*

WCW Spring Stampede '97
Ahh, Spring, when a young man's fancy turns to thoughts of...bone-cracking, back-breaking World Championship Wrestling mayhem! Lex Luger, the Giant, and Harlem Heat's Booker T. and Stevie Ray have a wild four-way match whose winner earns a World Heavyweight title shot against "Hollywood" Hulk Hogan; Philly's own Public Enemy take on Jeff Jarrett and Steve McMichael; Diamond Dallas Page's feud with Randy Savage explodes in the ring; and more. 180 min.
18-7771 *$59.99*

WCW Spring Stampede '99
There's four times the action and four times the mayhem when Diamond Dallas Page, Ric Flair, Hollywood Hogan and Sting meet in a four-way dance for the WCW heavyweight belt, with special referee "Macho Man" Randy Savage. Plus, Goldberg is out for revenge against the man who stopped his win streak, Kevin Nash; a cruiserweight title bout pits Kidman against Rey Misterio, Jr.; and more. 180 min.
18-7883 *$59.99*

WCW Spring Stampede 2000
A new chapter in WCW history is written, as the young wrestlers of the "New Blood" take on the "Millionaires' Club" established stars. DDP faces a shocking betrayal in his world heavyweight title bout against "chosen one" Jeff Jarrett; Sting faces Scott Steiner for the U.S. belt; an amazing hardcore championship bout pits Terry Funk against Screamin' Norman Smiley; plus Hulk Hogan, Kidman, and more. 180 min.
18-7915 *$59.99*

WCW Slamboree '96
Over 30 top WCW talents, including Ric Flair, Randy Savage, Lex Luger, the Road Warriors and the Steiner Brothers, take part in the luck-of-the-draw Lethal Lottery. Along with this brutal series of tag-team elimination matches, you'll also see Sting take on world heavyweight champ the Giant, a U.S. title bout between Mexico's Konnan and Japan's Jushin Liger, and more.
18-7659 *$19.99*

WCW Slamboree '98
Who can trust whom when a tag team title match pits Sting and the Giant against Outsiders Hall and Nash, with Dusty Rhodes in their corner? Will Saturn put an end to the unbeaten streak of U.S. heavyweight champ Bill Goldberg? Who will be the last man standing in a free-for-all bout to find a challenger for Chris Jericho's cruiserweight belt? Find out in this "slam"-tastic supercard. 180 min.
18-7816 *$59.99*

WCW Slamboree 2000
It's three times the action and mayhem when DDP and Jeff Jarrett (with some interference by David Arquette) get ready to rumble in a Triple Cage Match for the WCW heavyweight belt. The ongoing New Blood-Millionaires rivalry reaches new heights as well as Vampiro takes on Sting, Kidman challenges Hulk (or is it Hollywood?) Hogan, Ric Flair meets Shane Douglas, and more. 180 min.
18-7916 *$59.99*

The Best Of WCW Slamboree
It's a grand "slam" of squared circle excitement with this video retrospective of the top matches from the annual WCW supercard. Ric Flair, Rowdy Roddy Piper, Sting, Lex Luger and Goldberg are just some of the participants in a collection of talent that reads like a wrestling "Who's Who." 60 min.
18-7860 *$14.99*

Ringmasters: The Great American Bash (Special Edition) (1986)
Charlotte, N.C., is the place and Gordon Solie is your host for this collection of matches from the '86 Bash. See NWA heavyweight champ Ric Flair take on Nikita Koloff, Magnum T.A. versus Kamala the Ugandan Giant, and a tag team bout pitting the Road Warriors against Ivan Koloff and Krusher Kruschev. 30 min.
47-1682 *$12.99*

WCW Hog Wild '96
The annual biker rally at Sturgis, South Dakota, is the setting for revved-up wrestling action, highlighted by a world heavyweight title bout between the Giant and a black-clad "Hollywood" Hulk Hogan. Sting and Lex Luger are out for revenge against the Outsider duo of Hall and Nash, the Steiner Brothers challenge Harlem Heat for the tag team belts, and much more.
18-7701 *$19.99*

Women's Championship Wrestling
"Weaker sex" stereotypes get bodyslammed when these ferocious females go wild in rough-and-tumble mat action! See a steel cage championship bout featuring Wendi Richter defending the belt against Heidi Lee Morgan, plus the lethal Angel of Death, Chainsaw Liz Case and more. 53 min.
14-3352 *$12.99*

The Super Ladies Of Wrestling: No Holds Barred
It's "The Super Ladies of Wrestling" in their wildest bouts, with champ Terri Power playing hostess. Among the women wrestlers on hand here are Malia Hosaka, Bambi, Magnificent Mimi, Lady X, Candi Divine and Nasty Kat. 60 min.
86-1091 *$14.99*

The Super Ladies Of Wrestling: Out Of Control
Those "Super Ladies of Wrestling" can't stop smashing each other, and you have a ringside seat this time. Check out matches with Lady X, nasty Kat Le Roux, Medusa Miceli, Magnificent Mimi and champion hostess Terri Power. 60 min.
86-1095 Was $19.99 *$14.99*

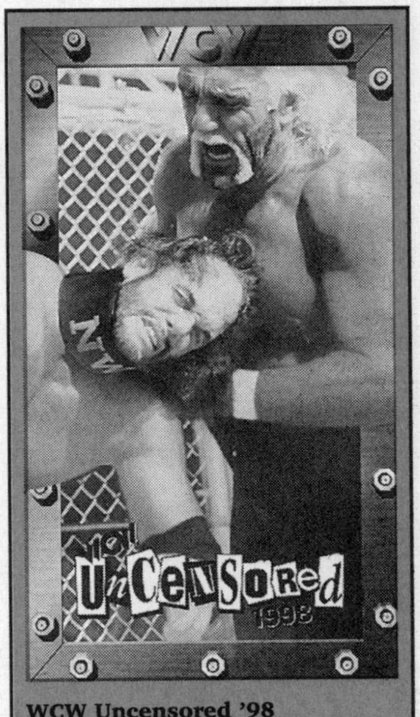

WCW Uncensored '98
An untamed, unbelievable and uncensored bout for control of the NWO between "Hollywood" Hulk Hogan and "Macho Man" Randy Savage is just part of the action in this wild supercard. You'll also see Sting defend his heavyweight title against the NWO's Scott Hall, a bitter grudge match between the Giant and Kevin Nash, plus Bret Hart, Curt Henning and more. 180 min.
18-7815 *$59.99*

WCW Uncensored '99
"Uncensored" becomes "Unprecedented" when Ric Flair tries to win his record-setting 14th world heavyweight title—and the presidency of WCW—in a steel cage match against champ Hollywood Hogan. Four Horsemen Chris Benoit and Dean Malenko meet Curt Henning and Barry Windham in a tag team title bout; the feud between Chris Jericho and Saturn culminates in a dog-collar match; plus more. 180 min.
18-7882 *$59.99*

WCW Uncensored 2000
It's "the Chosen One" and "the Vicious One" in a heavyweight grudge match, as Jeff Jarrett and Sid Vicious do battle for the belt. There's also bad blood in the air when a savage strap match pits Hulk Hogan against Ric Flair, and Sting and Lex Luger settle their differences in a unique "lumberjack cast match." Plus, the Harris Boys and the Mamalukes meet for the tag team title, and more. 180 min.
18-7914 *$59.99*

WCW Starrcade 10th Anniversary 1993
It's the biggest, baddest Starrcade in a decade, as "Nature Boy" Ric Flair challenges WCW World Heavyweight champ Vader for a record 11th world title, tag team beltholders the Nasty Boys face the duo of Sting and Road Warrior Hawk, Dustin Rhodes goes after Stunning Steve Austin's U.S. Heavyweight championship, and much, much more. 180 min.
18-7467 Was $39.99 ***$12.99***

WCW Starrcade 1996
East and West collide when WCW superstars "Macho Man" Randy Savage, Sting, Lex Luger, Alex Wright, Eddy Guerrero and others meet top Japanese talents such as Kensuke Sasaki, Tenzan and Masahrio Chono in a battle for global bragging rights. Plus, Sting and Luger face "Nature Boy" Ric Flair in a "triangle match" whose winner then challenges Savage for the WCW World Heavyweight title, and more. 180 min.
18-7606 ***$49.99***

WCW Starrcade 1997
It's a "Battle of the Icons" when Rowdy Roddy Piper returns to the ring to challenge heavyweight champ "Hollywood" Hulk Hogan and his NWO cohorts, while Lex Luger is out for revenge against the Giant. There's also a wild grudge match between Kevin Sullivan and Chris Benoit, a cruiserweight bout pitting Dean Malenko against Ultimo Dragon, and loads more action. 180 min.
18-7741 ***$49.99***

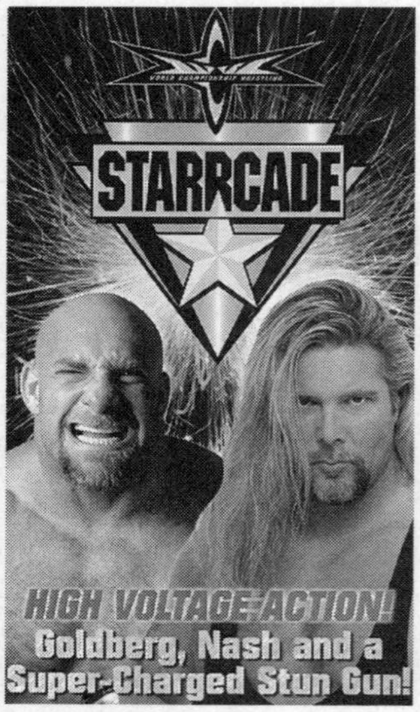
STARRCADE
HIGH VOLTAGE ACTION!
Goldberg, Nash and a
Super-Charged Stun Gun!

WCW Starrcade 1998
It's the showdown wrestling fans waited for for over a year, as Sting returns to the ring to challenge "Hollywood" Hulk Hogan for the world heavyweight belt. Plus, will special referee Bret Hart remain neutral when Larry Zybyszko takes on NWO bigwig Eric Bischoff? Other matches feature Diamond Dallas Page, Randy Savage, Lex Luger, Bill Goldberg and more. 170 min.
18-7799 ***$59.99***

WCW Starrcade 1999
What will it take for "Big Sexy" Kevin Nash to stop Goldberg's unbeaten streak and snatch the WCW heavyweight title? (How about an old buddy with a stun gun?) Will Ric Flair get his revenge on power-mad Eric Bischoff in the ring? Can DDP put the Diamond Cutter on the 7-foot-plus Giant? All this, and more, in WCW's annual year-ending supercard. 164 min.
18-7862 ***$59.99***

WCW Starrcade 2000
You won't believe the amazing end to the heavyweight title showdown between Bret Hart and Goldberg (clue—it's spelled "N-W-O"). Also, Chris Benoit and Jeff Jarrett climb to new heights in a ladder match for the U.S. championship, Elizabeth is caught in the middle of a Sting-Lex Luger confrontation, Kevin Nash and Sid Vicious meet in a battle of the powerbombs, and more. 180 min.
18-7911 ***$59.99***

The Best Of WCW Starrcade
For over a decade it's been the culminating event in a year's worth of pro wrestling action, and now the hottest moments and greatest names in Starrcade history have been assembled on one must-see program. Ric Flair, Hollywood Hogan, Goldberg, Sting and Lex Luger are among the "starr" performers. 60 min.
18-7859 ***$14.99***

Wrestle War '92: War Games
A steel-enclosed double ring is the setting for a savage "War Games" match that pits WCW champ Sting and his buddies against the Dangerous Alliance of manager Paul E. Dangerously. This supercard also features a light heavyweight title match between Flyin' Brian and the Z-Man, plus the Steiner Brothers, the unpredictable Cactus Jack, and more. 120 min.
18-7378 ***$39.99***

WCW Great American Bash 1996
Can "Total Package" Lex Luger get the 7-foot-plus Giant in the "Torture Rack" and win the WCW heavyweight title? What surprise is in store when NFL tough guys Kevin Greene and Steve McMichael challenge Horsemen Ric Flair and Arn Anderson? Will a falls-count-any where match settle the feud between Chris Benoit and Kevin Sullivan? Find out in this "red, white and bruised" supercard!
18-7660 ***$19.99***

WCW Great American Bash '97
Can the fragile alliance between Roddy Piper and Ric Flair last long enough for them to defeat the NWO's Outsiders in the ring? Will Diamond Dallas Page get his revenge on Randy Savage? Will the football/wrestling rivalry between Steve McMichael and Kevin Greene be settled once and for all? Find out the answers to these and other questions in this action-packed supercard. 180 min.
18-7776 ***$59.99***

WCW Great American Bash '99
Former allies become bitter enemies when Randy Savage—accompanied by Gorgeous George, Madusa and Miss Madness—takes on Kevin Nash for heavyweight gold, but a surprise "Vicious" guest star will have something to say about this match. Friendships also run sour in a Rick Steiner-Sting "falls count anywhere" bout, a tag team showdown pits Chris Benoit and Saturn against Diamond Dallas Page and Kanyon, and more. 180 min.
18-7885 ***$59.99***

WCW World War 3 '98 (1997)
Can even three rings hold the mayhem that erupts when 60 wrestling superstars, including Randy Savage, Diamond Dallas Page, the Giant, Scott Hall and others too numerous to mention, square off in an elimination match to see who earns a title shot for the WCW Heavyweight belt? Other matches in this supercard feature the Steiner Brothers, Curt Hennig, Raven, Rey Mistero, Jr. and more. 180 min.
18-7791 ***$59.99***

WCW Superbrawl VIII
Their last meeting failed to settle the score, but what will happen when Sting and "Hollywood" Hogan collide for the vacant WCW World Heavyweight title? What shocking betrayal awaits when the Steiner Brothers put their tag team belts on the line against Outsiders Scott Hall and Kevin Nash? All this, plus Lex Luger, Diamond Dallas Page, Randy Savage and more. 170 min.
18-7800 ***$59.99***

WCW Superbrawl 2000
What part will Roddy Piper play in the three-way dance between Sid Vicious, Jeff Jarrett and Scott Hall for the WCW world heavyweight belt? When the Hulk Hogan-Lex Luger bout leads to a brutal attack by the Total Package, who comes to the Hulkster's aid? Who'll survive a "Last Man Standing" match between Ric Flair and Terry Funk? All this, plus Vampiro, Kidman and more. 180 min.
18-7913 ***$59.99***

WCW Road Wild '99
Get your motor running for wild wrestling thrills, as a back-to-the-red-and-yellow Hulk Hogan puts the heavyweight title on the line against Kevin Nash in a "Retirement Match"; Sting tries to halt the unbelievable win streak of "Millennium Man" Sid Vicious; Randy Savage is as bad as he wants to be against Dennis Rodman; plus Goldberg, Harlem Heat and others. 180 min.
18-7887 ***$59.99***

WCW Souled Out '99
The electrifying Goldberg is out for revenge against Wolfpac member Scott Hall, and a ladder match with a stun gun as the prize is his means of getting it, in this action-packed WCW event. Also, Ric Flair and son David defend the honor of the Four Horsemen against Curt Hennig and Barry Windham; Lex Luger meets Konnan, Wrath challenges Bam Bam Bigelow; and more. 173 min.
18-7863 ***$59.99***

WCW Souled Out '00
It's a battle for control of WCW, with Kevin Nash and Terry Funk vying in a no-holds-barred hardcore match. Who will win the vacant world title (and will they have it for more than two days?) when Chris Benoit meets Sid Vicious? You'll also see a "Last Man Standing" match pitting Buff Bagwell against DDP, an unbelievable cruiserweight title bout, and more. 180 min.
18-7912 ***$59.99***

WCW Mayhem
It's Monday night mayhem with this special collection of the greatest grapplers and wildest moments from "WCW Monday Nitro." "Hollywood" Hulk Hogan, Sting, Goldberg, Kevin Nash and other superstars are seen in action in and out of the ring. 60 min.
18-7873 ***$14.99***

WCW Mayhem '99
It's mat mayhem north of the border, as Bret Hart, Chris Benoit, Jeff Jarrett and Sting meet in the finals of a tournament to crown a new WCW world heavyweight champion. You'll also see Scott Hall defend the U.S. and TV heavyweight belts against a mystery foe, an "I Quit" match between Sid Vicious and Goldberg, and many more. 180 min.
18-7899 ***$59.99***

WCW Beach Blast '93
The only thing hotter than the sand is the ring action in this card filled with sun, surf and slams. See "Nature Boy" Ric Flair try to win back the NWA heavyweight belt from Barry Windham, Dustin Rhodes challenge Ravishing Rick Rude in an "Iron Man Challenge" for the US title, a brutal tag bout pitting Big Van Vader and Sid Vicious against Sting and Davy Boy Smith, and more. 120 min.
18-7449 ***$39.99***

WCW Bash At The Beach '96
Witness the biggest betrayal since Benedict Arnold when "Outsiders" Scott Hall and Kevin Nash let their "mystery partner" flex his 24-inch pythons in a tag team match against WCW superstars Lex Luger, Randy Savage and Sting. Plus, see Ric Flair take on U.S. heavyweight champion Konnan, a "dog-collar" tag team match between Public Enemy and the Nasty Boys, and much more.
18-7700 ***$19.99***

WWF Royal Rumble '98
What do you get when you put over two dozen WWF superstars in an over-the-top elimination battle to determine the top challenger for the world heavyweight title? Mayhem, chaos and unparalleled thrills, as Stone Cold Steve Austin, Owen Hart, Vader, Goldust, Cactus Jack and more get ready to rumble. You'll also see WWF champ Shawn Michaels take on the Undertaker in a Casket Match, a tag team title bout between the New Age Outlaws and the Legion of Doom, and more. 180 min.
31-5177 Was $39.99 ***$19.99***

WWF Royal Rumble '99
Is there "no chance in Hell" for Stone Cold Steve Austin when he joins 29 other men...okay, 28 other men and Chyna...okay, 27 other men, Chyna and the Blue Meanie...in the WWF's brutal battle royal—and will he get his hands on fellow participant Mr. McMahon? Who will surrender in the wild "I Quit" title match between WWF heavyweight champ Mankind and challenger the Rock? All this, plus Sable versus Luna in a women's title match and more. 180 min.
31-5201 ***$39.99***

WWF Royal Rumble 2000
Who will win—and what will be left of them—when WWF heavyweight champ Triple H takes on the torture-loving Cactus Jack in a brutal "No Holds Barred" title bout? Will the Rock and the Big Show have each other in their sights when they and 28 other combatants enter the over-the-top rope Royal Rumble? Who is the "mystery opponent" out to end Olympian Kurt Angle's unbeaten streak? All this, plus the unbelievable "Miss Royal Rumble" Swimsuit Contest and more. 180 min.
31-5226 ***$39.99***

WWF King Of The Ring '98
Ken Shamrock, Rocky Maivia, Dan "The Beast" Severn and Double-J Jeff Jarrett all know "it's good to be the king," and they'll stop at nothing to win the crown in the finals of the WWF King of the Ring Tournament. Then, Stone Cold Steve Austin faces his ultimate test when Kane challenges him for the WWF heavyweight title; the Undertaker and the deranged Mankind meet in a "Hell in the Cell" match; and more. 180 min.
31-5187 Was $39.99 ***$19.99***

WWF King Of The Ring '99
It might just be "Queen of the Ring" this year, as "Ninth Wonder of the World" Chyna joins an eight-person roster that includes the seven-foot Big Show, Kane and "Mr. Ass" Billy Gunn for the WWF's most regal title. It's also a battle for corporate control, as Vincent and Shane McMahon put their shares in the company up against new CEO Stone Cold Steve Austin's in a two-on-one, winner-take-all ladder match; the Rock challenges the Undertaker for the world heavyweight title; and more. 180 min.
31-5211 ***$39.99***

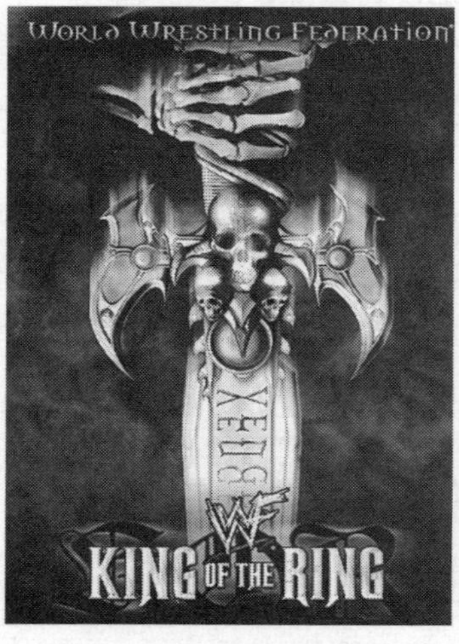
World Wrestling Federation
KING OF THE RING

WWF King Of The Ring 2000
The WWF's annual battle for ring royalty pits Olympic hero Kurt Angle, 400+pound Rikishi, "Y2J" Chris Jericho and five other superstars in a grueling elimination tournament. And speaking of grueling, who'll be left standing when the Rock, Kane and the Undertaker take on Triple H and Vince and Shane McMahon, with the WWF heavyweight title on the line? Also, the Dudley Boyz challenge DX to a "table and dumpster" match, and more. 180 min.
31-5238 ***$39.99***

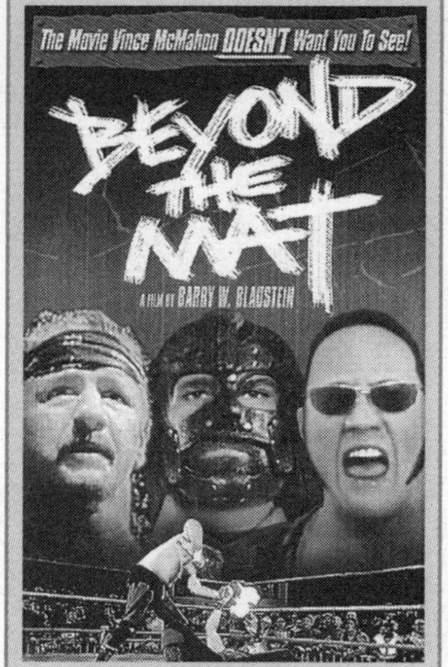
The Movie Vince McMahon DOESN'T Want You To See!
BEYOND THE MAT
A FILM BY BARRY W. BLAUSTEIN

Beyond The Mat (Unrated Director's Cut) (1999)
This rough-and-tumble survey of pro wrestling offers a revealing look at what goes on in the ring and in the personal lives of the men—and women—who crash, smash and gash each other for a living. Disavowed by WWF chief Vince McMahon after years in the making, Barry Blaustein's effort centers on three athletes at very different stages of their careers: Mick "Mankind" Foley, Terry Funk and Jake "the Snake" Roberts. Unrated edition includes footage not shown in theatres; 103 min.
07-2899 Was $99.99 ***$19.99***

Exposed!: Pro Wrestling's Greatest Secrets
Learn the tricks of the "wrasslin'" trade in this incredible documen tary that reveals what's really behind the spectacle, showmanship and action of one of the world's most popular "sports." Eight pro wrestlers—their true faces safely hidden behind masks—show you how "painful" holds and "crippling" bodyslams are executed to avoid injury, the truth behind "blading," and more.
68-1925 ***$14.99***

The Unreal Story Of Pro Wrestling (1998)
Legitimate athletic event or pre-arranged spectacle? Whatever the truth, professional wrestling has been of one America's biggest spectator shows for a century. Steve Allen hosts this look at wrestling's colorful history, from such early stars as Ed "Stangler" Lewis, Lou Thesz and Killer Kowalski and the '50s TV heyday of Gorgeous George to the sport's '80s and '90s revival and such modern greats as Andre the Giant, Hulk Hogan and "Stone Cold" Steve Austin. 100 min.
50-5628 ***$14.99***

WWF Rebellion
England's the setting for more internationally notorious WWF action. The Rock steps into the steel cage against Triple H for the WWF heavyweight belt; the rivalry between Intercontinental champ Jeff Jarrett and Chyna continues in an intense title match; the British Bulldog wins few fans in his homeland when his actions injure a member of the McMahon family; and more. 180 min.
31-5222 ***$29.99***

WWF SummerSlam '98
You're in the driver's set on the Highway to You-Know-Where with this white-hot WWF supershow, live from Madison Square Garden. Will Kane be in the Undertaker's corner when the undead one challenges "Stone Cold" Steve Austin for the heavyweight belt? Who will win an Intercontinental title Ladder Match between Rocky Maivia and Triple H? Who will survive the Lion's Den Match pitting Owen Hart against Ken Shamrock, and more. 180 min.
31-5189 Was $39.99 ***$19.99***

WWF SummerSlam '99
It's mayhem in Minneapolis when gubernatorial grappler Jesse "The Body" Ventura returns to the ring as special guest referee for a WWF heavyweight title match between Stone Cold Steve Austin, Triple H and Mankind. You'll also see a "Kiss My A—" match between the Rock and Mr. Ass, Al Snow (and his little pal, Pepper) versus the Big Boss Man in a hardcore championship showdown, and more. 180 min.
31-5213 ***$39.99***

WWF SummerSlam 2000
It's a pair of dangerous triangles when Triple H and Kurt Angle, already rivals over the attentions of Stephanie McMahon-Helmsley, take on the Rock in a Triple Threat match for the WWF heavyweight title. An intense two-out-of-three-falls bout pits Chris Jericho against "rabid wolverine" Chris Benoit; Edge and Christian meet the Hardys and the Dudleys in a "Tables and Ladders and Chairs" (oh my!) match; the Undertaker vs. Kane; and more. 180 min.
31-5244 ***$39.99***

WWF Survivor Series 1998: Deadly Games
Survival is indeed the name of the game when over a dozen of the WWF's toughest superstars, including Stone Cold Steve Austin, the Rock, Mankind, the Undertaker, Kane and the Big Boss Man, take part in a grueling tournament that will end with the crowning of a new WWF world heavyweight champion...and the ultimate in "gamesmanship" by Mr. McMahon. 180 min.
31-5196 **$39.99**

WWF Survivor Series '99
The scheduled main event is a three-way heavyweight title match pitting champion Triple H against challengers the Rock and Stone Cold Steve Austin, but when Austin drops out with a "run-down" feeling, who will step in to take his place? Also, Intercontinental champ Chyna faces a "Y2J" crisis when she meets Chris Jericho, the New Age Outlaws defend the tag team belts against Mankind and Wal-Mart fave Al Snow, and more. 180 min.
31-5224 **$39.99**

WWF Capital Carnage
"England swings like a piledriver do" with this explosive wrestling supercard from London, never before seen on this side of the Atlantic. WWF heavyweight champ the Rock defends his "corporate belt" against D-X member X-Pac, the New Age Outlaws take on Mark Henry and D-Lo Brown, Sable and Christian challenge Jacqueline and Marvelous Mark Mero, and more. 180 min.
31-5199 **$29.99**

WWF St. Valentine's Day Massacre
There'll be no love (but maybe some blood) lost when Stone Cold Steve Austin and Mr. McMahon take their feud into a steel cage, while the bitter rivalry between WWF champ Mankind and the Rock culminates in a Last Man Standing Match. Your heart will pound when D-X's X-Pac and Triple H take on former ally Chyna and Kane, Goldust is challenged by Bludust, and more. 180 min.
31-5202 **$29.99**

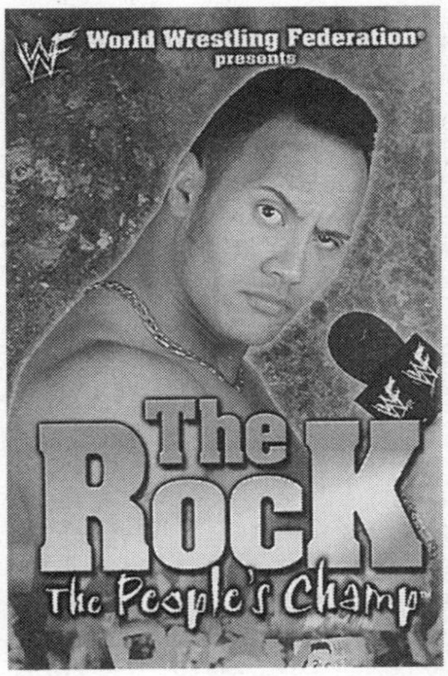

The Rock: The People's Champ
Finally, the Rock has come back to home video! The millions and millions of the Rock's fans won't want to miss this special collection of amazing match highlights and exclusive interviews with the Great One, as he talks about his toughest opponents and demonstrates why he's the most electrifying figure in sports entertainment. If you smell what...well, you know. 60 min.
31-5231 **$14.99**

The Rock: Know Your Role
Cock an eyebrow at this, you jabronies! Watch the greatest matches in the career of the self-proclaimed "People's Champion," third-generation grappler Rocky Maivia, and witness the Great One laying the "Smack Down" on one roody poo challenger after another, as only the Rock can! 60 min.
31-5206 **$14.99**

As Hard As The Rock
He's taken the wrestling world, the publishing world, and even the political world by storm. Now you can see how college football star Dwayne Johnson, aka "the Rock," came to be one of the squared circle's leading draws. Archival footage and incredible action sequences are featured in this unauthorized program that's really cooking.
50-8673 **$19.99**

Sid Vicious: The Millennium Man
He's lived up to his name, cutting a swath of terror in the ring and ringing up an incredible string of victories. Watch as the self-proclaimed "Millennium Man" takes a stab at Goldberg's win streak and hear from Sid himself in this "vicious" collection of wrestling action. 60 min.
18-7890 **$14.99**

WWF TLC: Tables Ladders Chairs
Forget "Tender Loving Care"; in the world of the WWF, "TLC" stands for the hardware and furniture you can batter your opponents with! Watch as bodies fly, heads are smashed, and tables turn into so much kindling at the hands of the Dudley Boyz, Edge and Christian, the Hardy Boys and others. 60 min.
31-5241 **$14.99**

WWF Fully Loaded: In Your House '99
Blood will be shed, and an era will end, when Stone Cold Steve Austin puts his belt and career on the line against the Undertaker, hand-picked champion of Mr. Vince McMahon, whose own WWF future hinges on the "first blood" bout. Plus, Triple H and the Rock square off in a strap match to decide number-one contender status, Chyna and Mr. Ass face X-Pac and the Road Dogg for the rights to D-X's name, and much more. 180 min.
31-5212 **$29.99**

WWF Fully Loaded 2000
Is the deck stacked against the Rock when he puts the WWF heavyweight title on the line against "Canadian Crippler" Chris Benoit, who has good friend Shane McMahon in his corner? Also, the bad blood between Triple H and Chris Jericho leads to a brutal "Last Man Standing" match; the Undertaker is out for revenge against Olympic hero Kurt Angle; plus Rikishi, Val Venis, Edge and Christian, and more. 180 min.
31-5242 **$29.99**

WWF Unforgiven 1999
WWF heavyweight champ Vince McMahon(!) has given up the belt, and now six of the ring's toughest stars—the Big Show, the British Bulldog, Kane, Mankind, the Rock and Triple H—square off in a brutal title bout, with Stone Cold Steve Austin as the special enforcer! Also, Jeff Jarrett defends his Intercontinental title against none other than Chyna, X-Pac takes on Chris Jericho, and much more. 180 min.
31-5215 **$29.99**

WWF No Mercy 1999
Mercy will indeed be in short supply when WWF heavyweight champ Triple H faces Stone Cold Steve Austin in a "no holds barred" bout. Watch as ironing boards, appliances and other household items become weapons in a "Good Housekeeping" match between Chyna and Jeff Jarrett for the Intercontinental title; a grueling ladder match pits Edge and Christian against the Hardy Boys; and more. 180 min.
31-5223 **$29.99**

WWF Armageddon '99
WWF owner Vince McMahon learns what's "sharper than a serpent's tooth" when he takes on the dastardly Triple H in a No Holds Barred match for his daughter Stephanie's honor. Meanwhile, will a title bout end the bitter rivalry between WWF heavyweight champ the Big Show and the Big Boss Man? Can Chyna defend her Intercontinental belt against "Y2J" Chris Jericho? And who'll be left clothed after the four-way Evening Gown match for the women's title? 180 min.
31-5225 **$29.99**

WWF Eve Of Destruction (1999)
What a way to close out a year! From the bitter feud between Stone Cold Steve Austin and Mr. McMahon that led to troubles even Vince couldn't imagine to the death-defying Ladder Match pitting Edge and Christian against the Hardy Boyz, all the WWF highlights from 1999 are featured in this amazing retrospective. 45 min.
31-5233 **$14.99**

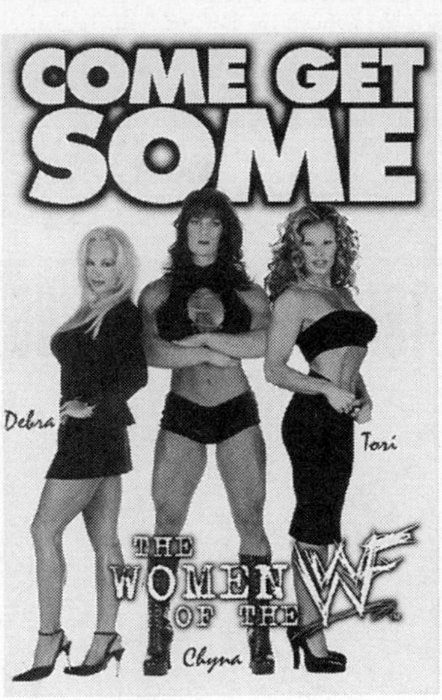

Come Get Some: The Women Of The WWF
Who says wrestling is a man's sport? Not the valet-turned-WWF Women's Champion, Sable; "The Ninth Wonder of the World," Chyna; or the beautiful Debra and her "puppies." Watch these fabulous fighting femmes demonstrate their prowess in the ring...and at the beach! 60 min.
31-5207 **$14.99**

WWF Divas: Postcards From The Caribbean
Looking for a quiet, relaxing vacation? Well, you won't find it on this video, as the wild women of the WWF invite you to take a peek at their island getaway, as they play along the beach in the skimpiest of swimwear. Kat, Terri, Tori, Ivory and others will get your temperature hotter than a Caribbean summer. 60 min.
31-5240 **$14.99**

Classic Big Time Wrestling
Long before the days of Goldberg and the Goon, wrestling drew huge audiences to the exciting new medium of television. This video takes you back to the glorious grappling of the 1950s and such early ring greats as Mr. Moto, Lord James Bleers, Lord Laten and Henry Hank in all sorts of wild kinescope matches.
79-6536 **$19.99**

WWF Classic Five Of 1998 Set
It was one of the roughest, most action-filled years in WWF history, and you can relive the excitement of "Survivor Series '98," "Wrestlemania XIV," "King of the Ring '98," "Summerslam '98" and "Survivor Series '98" in one money-saving boxed set.
31-5214 Save $50.00! **$69.99**

WWF No Way Out '00
It's the title or retirement, as Cactus Jack puts his 15-year career on the line in a "Hell in the Cell" match against WWF heavyweight champ Triple H. A surprise appearance turns the tide in a contest between the Big Show and the Rock to determine who'll take part in the main event at Wrestlemania XVI, a tag team title match pits the New Age Outlaws against the Dudley Boyz, plus Kane vs. X-Pac, Too Cool vs. the Radicals, Tazz and more. 180 min.
31-5230 **$29.99**

WWF Insurrextion
The WWF invades England in this special supercard, never broadcast in its entirety in the U.S. See the Rock defend his world heavyweight championship against battling brothers-in-law Triple H and Shane McMahon; the Hardy Boyz meet Edge and Christian for tag team gold; Rikishi and his new partner, "Showkishi," take on the Dudley Boyz; and much more. 180 min.
31-5237 **$19.99**

Wild Wild Wrestling
Forget the pyrotechnics and rock music entrances; this is "wrasslin'" the way you remember it from the '50s and '60s. See such legendary grapplers as Gorgeous George, Dick the Bruiser, "Nature Boy" Buddy Rogers, Antonino Rocca, Haystacks Calhoun and others. There's even women midgets and a 14-man Battle Royale featuring Andre the Giant and Bobo Brazil. 60 min.
50-8523 **$19.99**

WWF Backlash: In Your House
WWF champ Stone Cold Steve Austin and the Rock face off in a Wrestlemania XV rematch, but will Austin hold on to the title with Shane McMahon serving as guest referee? Old grudges take on new intensity when X-Pac meets former D-X comrade Triple H and Ken Shamrock meets the Undertaker; the deranged Mankind challenges "Big Show" Paul Wight to a Boiler Room Brawl; and more. 180 min.
31-5204 **$29.99**

WWF Backlash 2000
Can the Rock trust the returning Stone Cold Steve Austin when the Rattlesnake agrees to be in the Great One's corner for his heavyweight title match against Triple H, or does the McMahon/Helmsley Regime have a secret plan? You'll also see an Intercontinental bout between Chris Jericho and Chris Benoit, Edge and Christian battling DX, the amazing debut of "the Showster" and more. 180 min.
31-5235 **$29.99**

Lords Of The Ring: Superstars And Superbouts (1984)
Gordon Solie says "hello" as he hosts this program of grappling greats in amazing matches. There's Dusty Rhodes, "Nature Boy" Ric Flair, "Rowdy" Roddy Piper, the Road Warriors and more. Music by Delaware's own George Thorogood. 60 min.
47-1358 **$12.99**

UWF: Beach Brawl (1991)
The Florida coast gets rocked in eight action-filled Universal Wrestling Federation matches. See a savage strap match between Paul Orndorff and Col. DeBeers, a tag team bout pitting Wet 'n Wild against Cowboy Bob Orton and Cactus Jack, Rockin' Robin and Candi Devine in a women's title match, Bam Bam Bigelow meeting Steve Williams to determine the first UWF champion, and much more. 120 min.
64-1260 **$14.99**

Wrestlemania II (1986)
No one arena could hold all the wrestling action in this slam-jam second Wrestlemania. Long Island's Nassau Coliseum finds Mr. T lacing up boxing gloves to battle Roddy Piper and "Macho Man" Randy Savage facing the unpredictable George "the Animal" Steele; Andre the Giant, Bret "the Hitman" Hart and six NFL stars take part in a 20-man battle royal at the Rosemont Horizon in Chicago; and Hulk Hogan defends the WWF heavyweight title against the monstrous King Kong Bundy in a steel cage match at the Los Angeles Sports Arena. 180 min.
31-5023 **$14.99**

Wrestlemania III (1987)
The "irresistible force" of Hulkamania meets a 7-foot-plus "immovable" object" before over 90,000 fans at the Pontiac Silverdome, as Hulk Hogan puts the WWF heavyweight belt on the line against former pal Andre the Giant. Plus, a classic Intercontinental title bout pits champ Randy Savage against Ricky "the Dragon" Steamboat; Roddy Piper has a "Retirement Match" versus "Adorable" Adrian Adonis; and much more. 180 min.
31-5038 **$14.99**

Wrestlemania IV (1988)
With the WWF world heavyweight title in limbo, 14 squared circle superstars—including Hulk Hogan, Andre the Giant, Randy Savage, "Million Dollar Man" Ted DiBiase, "Ravishing" Rick Rude and the One Man Gang—took part in a grueling tournament for the sport's ultimate prize. Also on the card, Demolition challenges Strike Force for the tag team belts; Brutus Beefcake meets the Honky Tonk Man, and much more. 180 min.
31-5056 **$14.99**

Wrestlemania V (1989)
It's a "Meeting of the Mega-Powers" when Randy Savage takes on Hulk Hogan in a WWF heavyweight championship showdown, and the Ultimate Warrior puts his Intercontinental belt up against Rick Rude. The Hart Foundation, Andre the Giant, Jake "the Snake" Roberts, "Mr. Perfect" Curt Hennig, and Tully Blanchard and Arn Anderson are among the other top talents featured. 180 min.
31-5069 **$14.99**

Wrestlemania VI (1990)
The immortal Hulk Hogan faces his ultimate foe when he is challenged by the Ultimate Warrior for the WWF heavyweight title at Toronto's SkyDome. You'll also see former tag team partners Akeem and the Big Boss Man square off; a "mixed tag" bout pitting "American Dream" Dusty Rhodes and Sapphire against "Macho King" Randy Savage and Sensational Sherri; Demolition versus Andre the Giant and Haku; and more. 180 min.
31-5084 **$14.99**

Wrestlemania VII (1991)
Will American patriot-turned-traitor Sgt. Slaughter lose the WWF heavyweight title to the immortal Hulk Hogan, or will the Hulkster find himself in the Sarge's "Cobra Clutch?" Who will survive the "loser must retire" match between Randy Savage and the Ultimate Warrior? Can "Superfly" Jimmy Snuka overcome the undead menace of the Undertaker? All this, plus the Nasty Boys, the Legion of Doom, Kerry Von Erich and others. 180 min.
31-5100 **$14.99**

Wrestlemania XI (1995)
"Grudge match" was the order of the day at the 11th annual supercard, as "Heartbreak Kid" Shawn Michaels challenged his former buddy, "Big Daddy Cool" Diesel, for the WWF heavyweight title; NFL superstar Lawrence Taylor stepped into the ring to tackle Bam Bam Bigelow; and Bret Hart and Bob Backlund square off in a grueling "I Quit" match. 180 min.
31-5149 **$14.99**

Wrestlemania XIII (1997)
There's nothing but "good luck" in store for wrestling fans with this all-star amalgamation of grapplers. The Undertaker is out to dethrone WWF heavyweight champ "Psycho" Sid; Owen Hart and Davey Boy Smith put their tag team belts on the line against Mankind and Vader; and Bret Hart and Steve Austin's feud leads to a brutal submission match. 180 min.
31-5169 **$14.99**

Wrestlemania XIV (1998)
Which side will "special enforcer" Mike Tyson take when WWF heavyweight champ Shawn Michaels puts his belt on the line against "Stone Cold" Steve Austin in the main event of wrestling's biggest annual show? Can the Undertaker stop the path of carnage caused by his brother, Kane? Who will win a 30-man tag team battle royal? And what's Pete Rose doing in Boston? All this, plus Rocky Maivia, Ken Shamrock, Owen Hart and many more greats. 180 min.
31-5179 Was $39.99 **$19.99**

Wrestlemania XV (1999)
Live from Philly's First Union Center, the WWF's annual "show of the year" features an amazing heavyweight showdown between champion the Rock and challenger Stone Cold Steve Austin—but who will referee the match, Mankind or 7-foot behemoth Paul Wight? You'll also see a four-man Intercontinental title bout with Road Dogg Jesse James taking on Goldust, Ken Shamrock and Val Venis; Sable versus Tori in a women's championship contest, and much more. 180 min.
31-5203 **$39.99**

Wrestlemania XVI (2000)
Each man has a McMahon in his corner, but who will prevail when Triple H, the Rock, the Big Show and Mick Foley meet in a fearsome four-way elimination match for the WWF heavyweight belt? The action takes to new heights—literally—when the Hardy Boyz and Edge and Christian meet tag team champs the Dudley Boyz in a "Triangle Ladder" match; Olympic hero Kurt Angle puts both his belts on the line against Chris Benoit and Chris Jericho; over a dozen men join in a hardcore Battle Royal and much more. 180 min.
31-5234 **$39.99**

Wrestlemania: The Legacy Boxed Set
Slam home the savings with this special collector's boxed set featuring the first 14 Wrestlemania extravaganzas. NOTE: Individual volumes available at $14.99.
31-5200 Save $60.00! **$149.99**

Mick Foley: Madman Unmasked
From WWF superstar to best-selling author, there's never been anyone in or out of the squared circle quite like Mick Foley. Now you can see the man behind Mankind—and his other ring identities—as Mick talks about his long and brutal climb to the top of the wrestling world, and witness amazing footage from some of his most brutal bouts. Have a nice day! 60 min.
31-5232 *$14.99*

Extreme Backyard Wrestling
Teens emulating wrestling pros in free-for-all brawls, leaping from rooftops and using metal chairs, stop signs and barbed wire bats. You've seen this incredible "sport" on TV, and this video collects the wildest backyard brawls ever. WARNING: Do not try this at home! 90 min.
82-5145 *$99.99*

WWF Judgment Day 2000
And when that judgment rides his motorcycle down to the ring, what part will he play in the 60-minute "Iron Man Match" between the Rock and Triple H for the WWF heavyweight title? Also, watch as Shane McMahon plays "giant killer" against the Big Show, the Dudley Boyz take on X-Pac and Road Dogg in a tag-team "table match," plus Chris Benoit, Chris Jericho and others. 180 min.
31-5236 *$29.99*

Hitman Hart: Wrestling With Shadows (1998)
No-holds-barred look at the business and personal sides of the pro wrestling world chronicles an unpredictable year in the life of World Wrestling Federation superstar Bret "Hitman" Hart, whose feuds in and out of the ring with WWF head Vince McMahon led to a controversial match and Hart's exit from the company. Special video edition includes a never-before-seen interview with Hart.
68-1924 *$14.99*

ECW: Extreme Evolution
"Oh, my Gawd!" The hardcore promotion that changed the face of pro wrestling, South Philly's own Extreme Championship Wrestling, presents an intense "best of" retrospective that's not for the squeamish. See championship bouts pitting Rob Van Dam against Jerry Lynn and heavyweight champ Mike Awesome against Masato Tanaka; a wild mixed tag match with Tommy Dreamer and Beulah taking on Shane Douglas and Francine; and more, including the brutal and bloody 1996 barbed wire match between Raven and the Sandman. Uncensored version; 106 min.
85-1506 *$19.99*

ECW: Path Of Destruction
Just when you thought they couldn't get any more destructive, the superstars of ECW take it to the extreme, and beyond, with a second sampler of hardcore wrestling action. Along with the "Stairway to Hell" showdown between extreme icon the Sandman and the homicidal, suicidal, genocidal Sabu, you'll see feuding sibs Ian and Axl Rotten in an unbelievable "glass match," a four-way dance between Chris Jericho, 2 Cold Scorpio, Pitbull #2 and Shane Douglas, plus Rob Van Dam, Jerry Lynn and more. Uncensored version; 120 min.
85-1513 *$19.99*

The Best Of Wrestling Gold, Vol. 1
Memphis plays host to a great group of wrasslin' rounds, including Hulk Hogan (using the name Terry "The Hulk" Boulder) vs. Andre the Giant, Randy "Macho Man" Savage vs. Austin Idol, Bobby Heenan vs. Cowboy Bob Ellis and rare footage of the Wrestling Bear. 50 min.
20-7010 *$19.99*

The Best Of Wrestling Gold, Vol. 2
Incredible wrestling action from Memphis with Andre the Giant vs. the Sheik, Bruiser Brody and Scott Casey vs. Kelly Kinski and the Spoiler, Jerry "The King" Lawler and Randy Savage facing Rick Rude and King Kong Bundy, much more. 50 min.
20-7011 *$19.99*

The Best Of Wrestling Gold, Vol. 3
Memphis goes bonkers with a mud match between the Sheik and Tiger Jeet Singh, Austin Idol vs. Massai Ito, Terry Allen (Magnum T.A.), Tully Blanchard, Chief Wahoo McDaniel, and some incredible tag-team matches. 60 min.
20-7012 *$19.99*

Martial Arts/ Shootfighting

The Secrets Of The Warrior's Power
This look at the ancient martial art of kung fu traces the discipline's history and offers a look at its greatest practitioners, including Grandmaster Chan Pui, Master Pan Qing Fu and the legendary Bruce Lee. See how the great Shaolin warriors go beyond normal human limits in pursuit of enlightenment. 50 min.
53-8914 Was $19.99 *$14.99*

Fighting Black Kings (1976)
Watch in awe as some of the world's top martial artists gather at Tokyo's Metropolitan Gymnasium for the First International Karate Tournament. This action-filled chronicle of the competition takes you behind the scenes and in the ring with the over 120 participants, including the United States' four "fighting black kings": Frank Clark, Charles Martin, William Oliver and Willy Williams. 90 min.
19-1263 Was $24.99 *$14.99*

Battlecade: Extreme Fighting
The pay-per-view shootfighting spectacular that was too violent to take place in New York City(!) is on home video. See 16 top martial artists, including ju jitsu expert Carlson Gracie, Brazilian tough guy Conan, and Russia's Igor Zinoviev, face off in no-holds-barred bareknuckle bouts to determine who's the "toughest of the tough." 120 min.
72-9066 Was $49.99 *$14.99*

Battlecade: Extreme Fighting 2
These guys take their fighting to the extreme—and beyond—and you're there to witness all the intense, bone-crunching action. Live from Canada, see Ralph Gracie, who attempts to carry on his family's tradition of ju jitsu mastery; returning Extreme Fighting champ Conan Silveira; tattooed wildman John Lewis; and others as they brawl their way to the title. 94 min.
72-9074 Was $49.99 *$14.99*

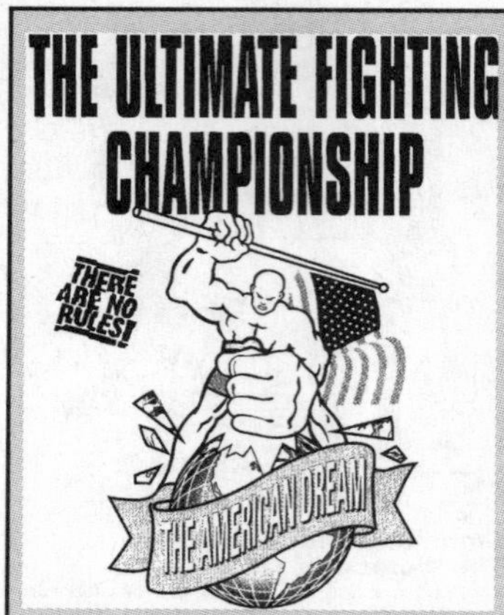

The Ultimate Fighting Championship I: The Beginning
The first foray into the fury that's free-form, free-for-all fighting at its fiercest is offered on this program. See Ken Shamrock, Royce Gracie, Teila Tuli, Zane Frazier and others display their awesome abilities in such disciplines as Karate, kickboxing, shootfighting, Ju Jitsu, boxing and more. Taped in Denver, so you know you'll get an avalanche of action. 90 min.
68-1825 Was $19.99 *$14.99*

The Ultimate Fighting Championship II
In this amazing, no-holds-barred program, 16 of the world's deadliest fighters battle each other, using their skills in Karate, Kung Fu, Tae Kwon Do, Ninjitsu, Russian Sambo, Muay Thai Kickboxing and Pencak Silat. There's no gloves, no restrictions and plenty of blood. Jim Brown offers commentary. 90 min.
68-1317 Was $19.99 *$14.99*

The Ultimate Fighting Championship V: Return Of The Beast
Another smasheroo slate of sweat-inducing fighting featuring the toughest men in the world. See UFC champ Royce Gracie battle World Shootfighting champ Ken Shamrock, Greco-Roman wrassler Dan "The Beast" Severn tackling rough-and-tumble martial artists and more. With commentary supplied by Jim Brown. 120 min.
68-1373 Was $19.99 *$14.99*

The Ultimate Fighting Championship X: The Tournament
And "X" marks the spot for extreme, to-the-finish brawling as eight of the world's fiercest fighters enter the eight-sided combat zone. Former UFC champ Don "The Predator" Frye, Israeli Special Forces instructor Moti Horenstein, Olympic wrestling competitor "Massive" Mark Coleman and kempo expert John Campetella are among the participants. 119 min.
68-1837 Was $19.99 *$14.99*

The Ultimate Fighting Championship XI: The Proving Ground
Witness the return of David "The Tank" Abbott after a seven-month disciplinary suspension, along with bouts featuring Mark "The Hammer" Coleman, Brian Johnston, Reza Nasri, Fabio Gurgel and others. 118 min.
68-1853 Was $19.99 *$14.99*

The Ultimate Fighting Championship XII: Judgement Day
A UFC heavyweight title bout that pits Dan "The Beast" Severn against Mark "The Hammer" Coleman and the UFC debut of 19-year-old Brazilian phenom Vitor Belfort are among the highlights of this installment of the freeform-fighting free-for-all. 116 min.
68-1855 Was $19.99 *$14.99*

The Ultimate Fighting Championship XIII: The Ultimate Force
And "force" is the order of the day when the toughest competitors to ever enter the octagon ring square off in lightweight and heavyweight contests. Royce Alger, Randy Couture, Steven Graham, Tony Halme and Guy Mezger are among the combatants, with a main event "superfight" pitting Tank Abbott against Vitor Belfort. 118 min.
68-1870 Was $59.99 *$14.99*

The Ultimate Fighting Championship XIV: Showdown
Along with a UFC heavyweight title showdown featuring two-time champion "Massive" Mark Coleman and kickboxing expert Maurice Smith, there's plenty of ultra-intense fighting action on this supercard, with such stars as Daniel Bobish, Todd Butler, Kevin Jackson, Joe Moreira and others. 116 min.
68-1871 Was $59.99 *$14.99*

The Ultimate Fighting Championship XV: Collision Course
The world's biggest and baddest fighting championship is back, as world-class warriors duke it out in the Octagon to separate the men from the boys. UFC Champion Maurice Smith, Randy Couture and David "Tank" Abbott are among the participants. 116 min.
68-1886 Was $59.99 *$14.99*

The Ultimate Fighting Championship XVI: Battle In The Bayou
Travel to Cajun country and be amazed at the grueling grappling going on in this "Ultimate" showdown. A four-man lightweight match, a middleweight championship fight (Frank Shamrock against Igor Zinoviev) and a heavyweight superfight between Tsyuyoshi Kosaka and Kimo are on the card. 195 min.
68-1905 Was $59.99 *$14.99*

The Ultimate Fighting Championship XVII: Redemption
Former UFC champ Mark "the Hammer" Coleman returns to the ring for an "ultimate" challenge, battling Lion's Den fighter Pete Williams. Other bouts include Tank Abbott vs. Hugo Duarte, Mike Van Arsdale vs. Joe Pardo, and Chuck Liddell vs. Noe Hernandez. 195 min.
68-1906 Was $59.99 *$14.99*

Ultimate Fighting Championship: A Night Of Champions
This collection includes the greatest fighters to ever enter the Octogan. An array of stars that includes Royce Gracie, Ken Shamrock, David "Tank" Abbott, Mark "The Hammer" Coleman and Oleg Taktrov are showcased in their greatest grapples. 105 min.
68-1932 Was $59.99 *$14.99*

Ultimate Fighting Championship: Brazil
Travel to San Paolo, Brazil, to witness one of the wildest "Ultimate Fighting" cards ever. Pat Miletich goes up against Mike Burnett, Frank Shamrock battles John Lober, "Tank" Abbott faces off against Pedro Rizzo, and more. 105 min.
68-1933 Was $59.99 *$14.99*

UFC Hits, Vol. 1
This ultra-violent best-of collection includes such bouts as Royce Grace vs. Kimo, Jon Hess vs. Andy Anderson, Tito Oritz vs. Guy Metzger, and Mark Coleman vs. Maurice Smith. 120 min.
68-2007 *$19.99*

UFC Hits, Vol. 2
More barbaric bouts from the Ultimate Fighting Championship files include Pedro Rizzo vs. Tank Abbott, Tito Ortiz vs. Jerry Bohlander, Bas Rutten vs. Tsuyoshi Kosaka, and Steve Judson vs. Brad Kohler. 120 min.
68-2008 *$19.99*

The Ultimate Fighting Championship 5-Pack
It's the ultimate collection for Ultimate Fighting Championship fans: UFC Volumes 1-5 in a money-saving boxed set.
68-1961 Save $35.00! *$39.99*

The Ultimate Ultimate
Past champions and fan favorites return to "The Octagon" in this fierce, furious edition of the world's roughest contest, "The Ultimate Fighting Championship." Featured are Steve Jennum, Oleg "The Russian Bear" Taktarov, Dan "The Beast" Severn, "Tank" Abbott, Keith "The Giant Killer" Hackney and others. It's an "Eight Wall Brawl" you won't believe. 118 min.
68-1809 Was $19.99 *$14.99*

The Ultimate Ultimate 2
Ken Shamrock's final "UFC" competition is captured in this smashing program that also features David "Tank" Abbott, Don Frye, Brian Johnson and Kimo, popular master of Pankration. 104 min.
68-1852 Was $19.99 *$14.99*

Choke (1998)
This documentary gets to the underbelly of freestyle fighting, focusing on the participants in a 1995 hand-to-hand combat tournament. Follow champion Rickson Gracie, kickboxer Todd Hayes, shootfighting champ Kochiro Kimura and others as they go into battle in Tokyo, New York and other cities. 98 min.
02-9082 *$19.99*

Miscellaneous

Gravity Games
Extreme sports came to network TV when NBC broadcast these daredevil competitions featuring top athletes from across America competing in the most maverick events around, from high-flying bikes and skateboards to snowboarding, in-line skating, skiing and more. Each tape runs about 60 min. There are six volumes available, including:

Gravity Games: Skateboarding
68-1973 □*$14.99*

Gravity Games: Bikes
68-1974 □*$14.99*

Gravity Games: Freestyle Motocross
68-1975 □*$14.99*

Gravity Games: Snowboarding: Winter One
68-2010 *$14.99*

101 Classic Goals Of The World Cup
Whether they are headers, long-range shots or incredible individual efforts, the greatest goals in World Cup competition are offered in this soccer spectacular. Among the players highlighted are Paolo Rossi, Michel of Spain, Mark Wright and Schillacci. 55 min.
10-1487 Was $19.99 *$14.99*

MLS 1999: Year In Review
Major League Soccer's fourth season was one for the record books, as the 12 teams provided thousands of fans coast to coast with memorable moments, culminating in DC United's taking its third championship in four years. See the greatest game action, including the East-West All-Star showdown in San Diego and the top 10 goals of the year, in this retrospective hosted by ESPN's Rob Stone.
64-3440 *$19.99*

The American Bullfighter: Complete Set
Take a wild and woolly look at rodeo clowns risking life and limb as they chase (and get chased by) ferocious bulls around the ring in this amazing two-tape set. Watch champion bullriders hang on for all they're worth, see hilarious and amazing stunts, and much more. Narrated by TV sports host George Michael and cowboy poet Baxter Black. 120 min. total. NOTE: Individual volumes available at $14.99 each.
83-1152 Save $5.00! *$24.99*

Pumping Iron II: The Women (1985)
Female bodybuilders are the focus of this follow-up that chronicles five women (Lori Bowen, Lydia Cheng, Carla Dunlap, Bev Francis and Rachel McLish) going through their grueling paces as they train and take part in the 1983 Ceasar's Palace World Cup Championship. 107 min.
47-1463 Was $79.99 *$19.99*

The Journey Of The African-American Athlete
It's a journey marked with great achievements and a constant struggle for acceptance, and in this thrilling sports documentary you'll follow the exploits of such 20th-century black sports legends as Jack Johnson, Joe Louis, Satchel Paige, Jackie Robinson, Althea Gibson, Muhammad Ali, Michael Jordan, Jackie Joyner-Kersee and many others. Samuel L. Jackson narrates. 120 min.
44-2149 Was $19.99 □*$14.99*

She-Babes Cavalcade Of Sports, Vol. 1
Spanning the globe, bringing you exciting sporting events...with babes!...is this spectacular collection of wild women at furious play. Included are wrestlers Lynn O'Connor and June O'Dear, Hanka Kauetzkas and Olga Baranoff and tag-team matches; the Chiefs against the Jolters in roller derby; a boxing bout between Sandy Partlow and Cheryl Day; and much, much more. 120 min.
79-6082 *$19.99*

Roller Derby Mania
For sports action to set your wheels spinnin', it's got to be roller derby, and here's a look at banked track thrills old and new. Follow the L.A. T-Birds as they block, pass and break away from the pack to lead their squads to victory. Also features classic derby footage. 57 min.
67-5000 *$19.99*

New World Disorder
With the use of helicopters, helmet-cams and other tricks of the trade, the world of mountain biking is brought right into your living room, along with some unicycles and wheelchairs for good measure. Downhilling, cliff dropping and dirt jumping are just a few of the insane stunts you'll see as these bikers rage to the music of Anthrax, Ween, Upper Class Racket and others. 60 min.
50-8764 *$19.99*

House Of Cards (1991)
Terrific "Masterpiece Theatre" thriller about a British cabinet official (Ian Richardson) who uses his power and smarts to manipulate the government to his needs. After he learns that the beautiful reporter with whom he's having an affair has incriminating evidence against him, Richardson calls on all his devious means to stop her. With Michael Kitchen, Susannah Harker. 200 min.
04-3256 ❑*$39.99*

To Play The King (1994)
Ian Richardson returns as duplicitous British politician Francis Urquhart in this sequel to "House of Cards." Having risen to the leadership of his party, Richardson uses a reporter and the king himself in a wicked power play that helps elect him prime minister. Kitty Aldridge, Michael Kitchen co-star. 200 min.
04-3257 ❑*$39.99*

The Final Cut (1995)
In the concluding chapter of the political drama based on Michael Dobbs' novels, British prime minister Francis Urquhart (Ian Richardson) finds his years of backroom deals and behind-the-scene machinations have gotten him to the top, but they can just as easily prove his downfall. 200 min.
04-3294 ❑*$39.99*

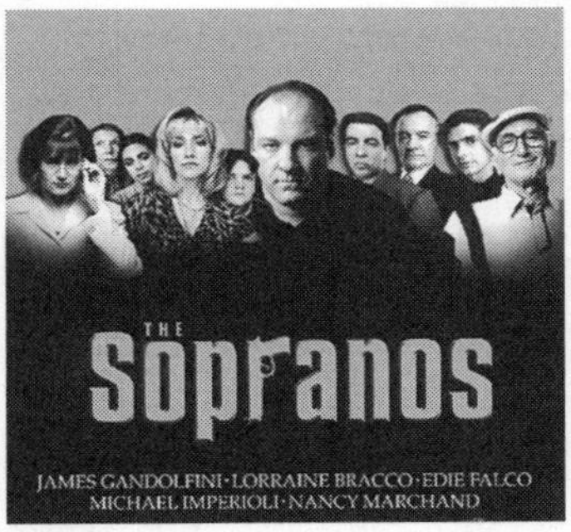

The Sopranos: The Complete First Season
The first season in the acclaimed, award-winning HBO series is available in this 13-episode, five-tape boxed set. Follow the hair-raising, heartfelt and hilarious adventures of Tony Soprano, a North Jersey mob capo whose problems with two families—his crime and his own—lead him to a psychiatrist for help. James Gandolfini, Edie Falco, Michael Imperioli, Nancy Marchand, Steven Van Zandt and Aida Turturro head the cast.
44-2263 *$99.99*

Dark Justice (1991)
Join Ramy Zada as Nicholas Marshall, the judge-turned-motorcycle-riding vigilante who, along with his allies, brings criminals overlooked by the legal system to justice, in three exciting episodes from the hit TV action series: "Judgment Night," "Brother Mine" and "Nowhere to Hide." With Clayton Prince and Begona Plaza. 99 min.
19-2157 Was $89.99 *$14.99*

Renegade (1993)
The feature-length pilot to the hit syndicated TV series stars Lorenzo Lamas as Reno Raines, an ex-cop framed for murder who becomes a motorcycle-riding hero-on-the run. Can Reno rescue his long-lost brother from a brutal "training camp" for participants in illegal fights run by an ex-Marine? Kathleen Kinmont, Martin Kove, Charles Napier co-star. 96 min.
19-2239 Was $79.99 *$14.99*

Renegade: Murderer's Row
Cop-turned-manhunter Reno (Lorenzo Lamas) and his friends Bobby (Branscombe Richmond) and Cheyenne (Kathleen Kinmont) set out to find an elusive female spy, but get more than they bargained for from a psychotic bounty hunter also on her trail who is killing others trying to hunt her down. Elizabeth Gracen also stars in this feature-length adventure. 120 min.
10-2701 *$12.99*

A Fatal Inversion (1992)
In this gripping thriller from Ruth Rendell writing as Barbara Vine, a college student shares a wild summer with his friends on an estate he inherited. Twelve years later, the property's new owner discovers the remains of a woman and a baby, and the long-separated circle of friends must retrace their summer together and uncover a shocking secret. Jeremy Northam stars. 150 min.
04-3338 ❑*$19.99*

Gallowglass (1993)
Top-notch BBC thriller penned by Barbara Vine (AKA Ruth Rendell) centering on a mysterious man named Sandor who recruits a homeless man to partake in kidnapping "the Princess," the former wife of an Italian prince, now kept under tight security in England. Problems arise when the woman falls for her new bodyguard, who happens to be the kidnappers' contact. Arkie Whietley, John McArdle star. 150 min.
04-3339 ❑*$19.99*

A Dark Adapted Eye (1996)
One of Ruth Rendell's most disturbing Barbara Vine suspensers tells the true story of Vera Hillyard, one of the last women to be hung for murder in Britain. Set in the 1950s, the story focuses on the bitter rivalry between two sisters and the toddler each claimed as their own. Helena Bonham-Carter, Sophie Ward star. 152 min.
04-3340 ❑*$19.99*

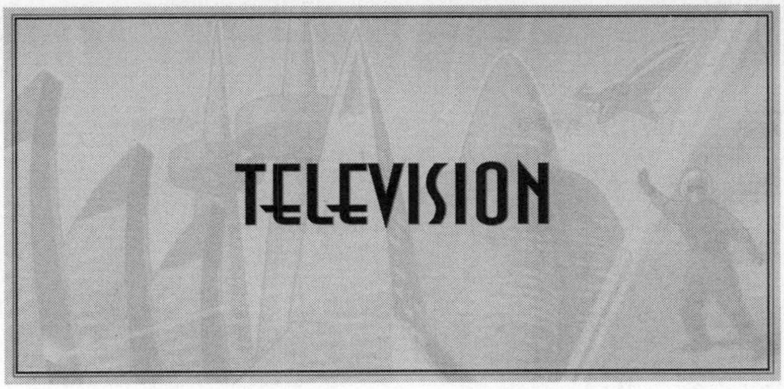

ER: The Series Premiere (1994)
The feature-length pilot of the hit medical drama from writer Michael Crichton introduces the eclectic, hard-working team of a Chicago public hospital emergency room. George Clooney, Sherry Stringfield, Eriq La Salle, Julianna Margulies, Anthony Edwards and Noah Wyle star; Steven Spielberg's Amblin' Entertainment produces. 88 min.
19-2340 Was $89.99 ❑*$19.99*

Married...With Children: It's A Bundyful Life (1991)
America's favorite TV family stars in this Christmas special that spoofs "It's a Wonderful Life." Al wonders what things would be like if he hadn't been born and finds out thanks to the intervention of scruffy guardian angel Sam Kinison. With Ed O'Neill, Katey Sagal, Christina Applegate and Danny Faustino. 50 min.
02-2317 *$14.99*

The Duchess Of Duke Street (1976)
Created by John Hawksworth ("Upstairs, Downstairs") and based on a true story, this acclaimed BBC production that played on PBS's "Masterpiece Theatre" stars Gemma Jones as Louisa Trotter, who rises from maid in a fashionable London household to become a hotel owner and confidante to the cream of Edwardian English society. 13 hrs. on five tapes.
04-3508 Was $119.99 ❑*$99.99*

The Duchess Of Duke Street II (1977)
The saga of Louisa, the colorful proprietor of early 20th-century London's Bentink Hotel who uses her beauty, wits and cooking skills to win favor with the aristocracy, continues in this popular mini-series. Gemma Jones, Christopher Cazenove star. 13 1/2 hrs. on six tapes.
04-3887 ❑*$99.99*

The Buccaneers (1995)
Based on Edith Wharton's unfinished novel, this lush "Masterpiece Theatre" production mixes humor and drama in telling the story of four turn-of-the-century American girls who, unable to break into New York's social circles, are persuaded to "invade" London society in search of proper husbands. Carla Gugino, Mira Sorvino, Cherie Lunghi, James Frain and Connie Booth head the excellent cast. 288 min.
04-3295 *$59.99*

Millennium (1996)
From "X-Files" creator Chris Carter comes this eerily suspenseful series. Lance Henriksen stars as Frank Black, a former FBI agent and expert in serial killings who uses his psychic "gift" to enter criminals' minds as a member of the Millennium Group, a clandestine crime-solving organization. Included here are the show's pilot episode, in which a Seattle stripper's murder is part of a bizarre prophecy, and "Gehenna," where a string of killings in San Francisco is linked to a death cult. 90 min.
04-3540 ❑*$59.99*

The Aristocrats (1999)
Their world was marked by scandals and triumphs which made them the talk of 19th-century Britain. They were the Lennox sisters, the illegitimate great-granddaughters of Charles II who were the "black sheep" of the English gentry, and their colorful exploits are brought to life in this "Masterpiece Theatre" production. Geraldine Sommerville, Sian Phillips, Diane Fletcher, Ben Daniels star. 246 min. on three tapes.
04-3874 *$59.99*

Jag (1995)
The feature-length premiere episode of the hit TV series stars David James Elliott as Navy legal investigative officer Lt. Harmon Rabb, charged with looking into the disappearance of a female pilot from the aircraft carrier she served on. As Rabb searches for the truth, he uncovers a shocking crime and a deadly conspiracy. Andrea Parker, Terry O'Quinn co-star. 94 min.
06-2434 Was $39.99 ❑*$14.99*

Heat Of The Sun (1998)
A former Scotland Yard detective gets more than just a change of scenery when he moves to Nairobi, Kenya, to take a position with a new criminal investigation unit in the former British colony. Trevor Eve, Susannah Harker and Michael Byrne star in three compelling mysteries: "Private Lives," "Hide in Plain Sight" and "The Sport of Kings." 360 min. on three tapes.
08-8742 ❑*$39.99*

Touching Evil (1997)
First seen on American TV on "Masterpiece Theatre," these three gripping mysteries follow the members of the London police's elite Organized and Serial Crime Unit as they solve cases involving a string of child murders, a killer preying on hospital patients, and a high-tech Fagin who uses computers to lure kids into crime. Robson Green, Nicola Walker, Michael Feast star. 360 min. on three tapes.
08-8705 ❑*$39.99*

Touching Evil 2 (1999)
Inspector Dave Creegan (Robson Green) and the men and women of the London Organized and Serial Crime Unit are back for a second trio of dark and absorbing whodunits. Women are abducted by a serial killer; a former relief worker's memories of war atrocities in Bosnia lead to violence; and an international black market does a brisk business in babies. With Nicola Walker, Shaun Dingwall. 360 min. on three tapes.
08-8835 ❑*$39.99*

Home Improvement: The Series Finale (1999)
Celebrate eight years of power-tooled family ups and downs with this grunt-filled final episode of the Emmy-winning sitcom. When Jill gets an out-of-town job offer, the Taylor family looks back as they consider moving on to new surroundings. Tim Allen, Patricia Richardson, Richard Karn, Zachary Ty Bryan star. Special video version includes never-before-seen outtakes and bloopers. 98 min.
11-2348 ❑*$19.99*

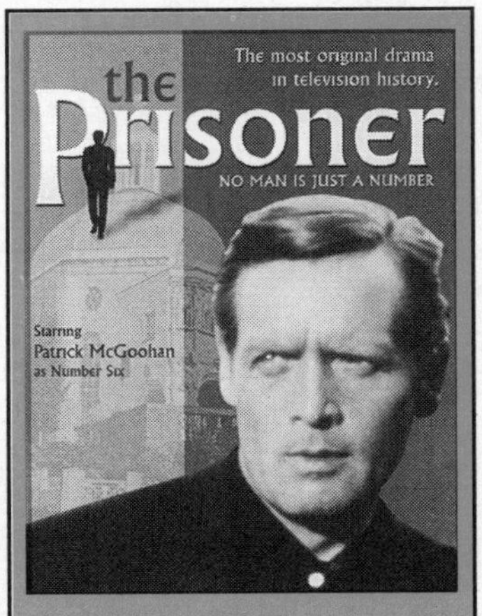

The Prisoner (1968)
One of the most complex and tantalizing TV shows ever made, this offbeat spy series starred Patrick McGoohan as Number 6, a former British agent abducted and held captive in a mysterious village cut off from the outside world. Which side, if any, are his captors on, what do they want, and can they break him?

The Prisoner: Set 1
Included in this three-tape boxed set are "Arrival," which follows the Prisoner's initiation into the ways of the Village and his meeting with the first Number 2; "Free for All," in which Number 6 campaigns to be elected Number 2; and "Dance of the Dead," with Number 6 attempting to smuggle out a message for help in a coffin. 180 min. total.
53-7252 *$29.99*

The Prisoner: Set 2
Number 6 becomes an unwilling pawn in a life-size chess game in "Checkmate." This three-tape boxed set also includes "The Chimes of Big Ben," in which he and a mysterious young woman escape the Village and flee to London—or do they?; "A, B and C," with Number 2 entering the Prisoner's subconscious to determine why he resigned; and "The General," in which a new Village speed-reading program masks a mind-control scheme. 240 min. total.
53-7253 *$29.99*

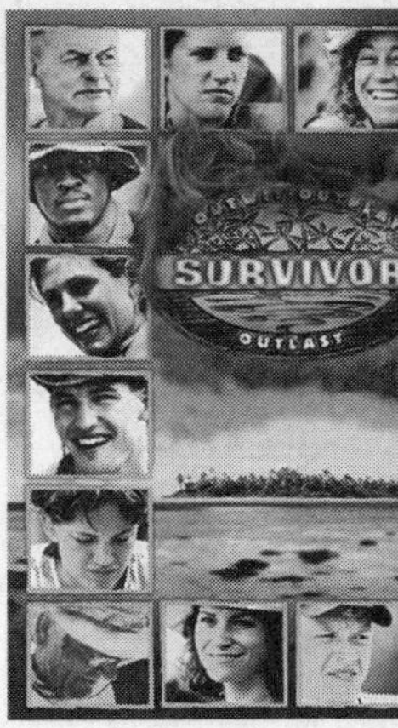

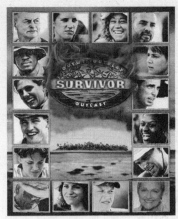

Survivor: Season One: The Greatest And Most Outrageous Moments (2000)
Grab yourself some roasted rat and get ready for a return visit to Pulau Tiga island, as 16 competitors get a 39-day lesson in how to "outwit, outplay and outlast" one another for a million-dollar prize. Along with highlights from the top-rated "reality TV" event, this video features never-before-seen footage with Richard, Kelly, Rudy, Susan, Sean, Colleen and company; behind-the-scenes casting tapes; exclusive interviews with series creator Mark Burnett and host Jeff Probst; and more. 150 min.
06-3050 Available 1/01 ❑*$14.99*

To The Manor Born
This popular British comedy series stars Penelope Keith as widowed Audrey fforbes-Hamilton, the former lady of Grantley Manor, who is forced by financial straits to sell her ancestral home to millionaire businessman Richard DeVere (Peter Bowles), while she moves into a caretaker's cottage on the estate. Except for the four-episode Vol. 1, each tape features three episodes and runs about 90 min. There are six volumes available, including:

To The Manor Born, Vol. 1
04-3584 *$19.99*

To The Manor Born, Vol. 2
04-3585 *$19.99*

To The Manor Born, Vol. 3
04-3780 *$19.99*

To The Manor Born: Boxed Set
Save your manor some money with all six volumes in a special collector's set.
04-3907 Save $20.00! *$99.99*

Beverly Hills, 90210: The Pilot (1991)
The pilot to the hit TV show chronicling the trials and tribulations of a family who moves from the Midwest to one of America's wealthiest zip codes. Starring Jason Priestley, Shannen Doherty and Brian Austin Green, this special video version includes 25 minutes of never-before-seen footage. 90 min.
14-3400 Was $89.99 *$19.99*

Beverly Hills, 90210: The Graduation (1993)
The final days of school for seniors at West Beverly Hills High elicits all sorts of excitement and memories for Brenda, David, Dylan, Kelly, Andrea and the rest of the "90210" crew. Shannen Doherty, Luke Perry, Jason Priestley and Jennie Garth star and are featured in a special bonus interview segment. 114 min.
14-3344 ❑*$14.99*

Brewster Place: Boxed Set (1990)
All 11 episodes from producer/co-star Oprah Winfrey's acclaimed series, set in an inner-city tenement neighborhood in the 1960s, have been gathered in a four-tape collection. Join in the laughter and the tears with the people that call Brewster Place home, with Winfrey's restaurant serving as the local gathering place. Olivia Cole, Brenda Pressley, Oscar Brown, Jr. also star. 275 min. total. NOTE: Individual volumes available at $14.99 each.
15-5472 Save $10.00! *$49.99*

Wild Palms (1993)
Producer Oliver Stone's much-talked-about miniseries is set in early 21st-century Los Angeles, where attorney Jim Belushi joins a media group headed by sinister politician Robert Loggia, who wants to revolutionize TV through the use of "virtual reality." Soon, Belushi and his family are flung into a nightmarish world filled with strange visions and dangerous conspiracies. Dana Delany, Angie Dickinson, Kim Cattrall also star. 284 min. on two tapes.
19-9006 Was $99.99 *$29.99*

A Fine Romance (1981)
Oscar-winner Judi Dench excels in this classic British comedy series in which she plays an erudite translator who falls in love with a shy gardener (played by real-life hubby Michael Williams) after being fixed up by her sister and brother-in-law. With Susan Penhaligon. Nine episodes are included in this three-tape set. 225 min. total.
50-8403 *$39.99*

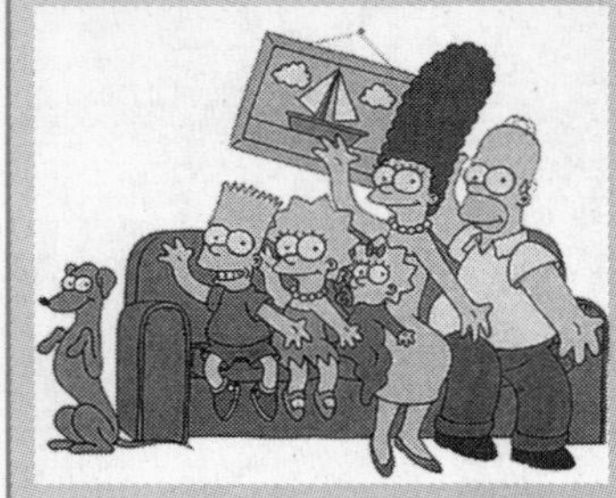

THE SIMPSONS

The Best Of The Simpsons
First appearing on "The Tracey Ullman Show," they went on to become the longest-running animated series in prime-time history, and now the Emmy-winning misadventures of Springfield's funniest dysfunctional family are on home video. Each volume features two episodes, plus a "Tracey Ullman Show" short, and runs about 55 min.

The Best Of The Simpsons, Vol. 1
Some embarrassing family antics at the company picnic lead Homer to believe "There's No Disgrace Like Home" and send the Simpsons to Dr. Marvin Monroe for a little shock therapy. Next, will Marge be bowled over by a smooth-talking alleycat named Jacques, in "Life on the Fast Lane"?
04-3501 □*$12.99*

The Best Of The Simpsons, Vol. 2
It'll take some advice from Grandpa Simpson and a little military training for "Bart the General" to lead the neighborhood kids into battle against Nelson the bully, while Lisa gets a lesson in life—and saxophone playing—from bluesman Bleeding Gums Murphy, in "Moaning Lisa."
04-3502 □*$12.99*

The Best Of The Simpsons, Vol. 3
After tossing one cherry bomb too many in school, Bart is signed up for a foreign student exchange program that has him toiling in a French vineyard, in "The Crepes of Wrath." Then, "Krusty Gets Busted" for holding up the Kwik-E-Mart. Can Bart clear his hero's name?
04-3503 □*$12.99*

The Best Of The Simpsons, Vol. 4
Brace yourself for three chilling Halloween stories, Simpsons-style, as the family moves into a haunted house, gets abducted by aliens, and presents their own version of Poe's "The Raven" in their first Halloween special, "Treehouse of Horror." Next, it's a repeat of the fourth grade if "Bart Gets an F" on his history test, but can even that force him to study?
04-3567 □*$12.99*

The Best Of The Simpsons, Vol. 5
How does a three-eyed fish lead to Mr. Burns running for governor, and how does a dinner at the Simpsons spoil his campaign? Find out in "Two Cars in Every Garage and Three Eyes on Every Fish." Then, it's "Bart vs. Thanksgiving" as his shenanigans upset the family's holiday dinner and lead him to run away from home.
04-3568 □*$12.99*

The Best Of The Simpsons, Vol. 6
Will seeing death-defying stunt rider Lance Murdock inspire "Bart the Daredevil" to risk his own life by trying to leap Springfield Gorge on his skateboard? Next, Marge protests against the violence in everyone's favorite homicidal cat-and-mouse cartoons, in "Itchy, Scratchy & Marge."
04-3569 □*$12.99*

The Best Of The Simpsons, Vol. 7
The family could be coming into a fortune—if Marge can lie in court—when "Bart Gets Hit By a Car" driven by Mr. Burns. Then, Homer's gorging on sushi at the Happy Sumo restaurant could leave him with a fatal dose of "fugu poisoning," in "One Fish, Two Fish, Blowfish, Blue Fush."
04-3637 □*$12.99*

The Best Of The Simpsons, Vol. 8
Travel back to the year 1974 and learn how Homer and Marge met...and how their first date was almost their last, in "The Way We Was." Next, will the father-daughter relationship of Homer and Lisa survive the temptation of free (and illegal) cable TV, in "Homer vs. Lisa and the 8th Commandment"?
04-3638 □*$12.99*

The Best Of The Simpsons, Vol. 9
It's "Three Men and a Comic" when Bart, Milhouse and Martin pool their finances to buy a copy of the first Radioactive Man comic, but soon learn it's too tough to divide it three ways. Then, Lisa develops a crush on an unconventional new teacher voiced by guest star Dustin Hoffman (credited as "Sam Etic"), in "Lisa's Substitute."
04-3639 □*$12.99*

The Best Of The Simpsons, Vol. 10
"Mr. Lisa Goes to Washington" when her essay wins the Simpsons a trip to the nation's capital, but a shocking event shakes her faith in the American way of government. Next, will Homer's wishbone wish lead to bankruptcy for his next-door neighbor in "When Flanders Failed"?
04-3812 □*$12.99*

The Best Of The Simpsons, Vol. 11
Will Bart's new job at Fat Tony's "social club" lead to a life in organized crime and the nickname of "Bart the Murderer"? Then, Bart and Lisa try to reunite Krusty the Clown with his estranged rabbi dad in "Like Father Like Clown."
04-3813 □*$12.99*

The Best Of The Simpsons, Vol. 12
A monkey's paw that grants wishes? Bart with super mind powers? Homer's brain in a robot body? It's all part of the Halloween fun in "Tree House of Horror II." And Homer tries to make up for ruining Lisa's talent show performance by buying her the horse of her dreams in "Lisa's Pony."
04-3814 □*$12.99*

The Best Of The Simpsons Triple Pack 1
Save yourself plenty of "D'oh!" by buying Volumes 1-3 in this boxed collector's set.
04-3504 Save $14.00! *$24.99*

The Best Of The Simpsons Triple Pack 2
What's cheaper than a truckload of Krusty Burgers and just as nutritious? This boxed set featuring Volumes 4-6 of the Simpsons' finest!
04-3570 Save $14.00! *$24.99*

The Best Of The Simpsons Triple Pack 3
Here's a bargain you won't find at your local Kwik-E-Mart: Volumes 7-9 of Simpsonian antics in a deluxe boxed collection.
04-3640 Save $14.00! *$24.99*

The Best Of The Simpsons Triple Pack 4
Buy yourself a dozen donuts with sprinkles (mmm...sprinkles) with the money you'll save on this boxed set featuring Volumes 10-12.
04-3815 Save $14.00! *$24.99*

The Simpsons Political Party, Vol. 1
What will happen to Bart when his arch-nemesis runs for—and is elected—mayor of Springfield in "Sideshow Bob Roberts"? Next, Homer becomes the city's new Sanitation Commissioner and quickly runs the office into the garbage heap in "Trash of the Titans," guest starring Steve Martin and U2.
04-3946 □*$12.99*

The Simpsons Political Party, Vol. 2
It's a fight of presidential proportions in "Two Bad Neighbors," as George Bush moves onto Evergreen Terrace with his wife and winds up trying to ruin Homer like a Japanese banquet. And can Homer go "Duffless" for a month when he's arrested for drunk driving?
04-3947 □*$12.99*

The Simpsons Political Party, Vol. 3
After giving Ralph Wiggum a "sympathy Valentine," Lisa is mortified to learn he thinks they're a couple—and that he's the only way she can get into Krusty's anniversary show—in "I Love Lisa." Also, Homer gets out of an IRS audit by agreeing to help the government retrieve a one-of-a-kind trillion-dollar bill from Mr. Burns in "The Trouble with Trillions."
04-3948 □*$12.99*

The Simpsons Political Party Triple Pack
All three "Simpsons Political Party" volumes are also available in a boxed set.
04-3949 Save $14.00! *$24.99*

The Simpsons Go Hollywood, Vol. 1
It's "Marge vs. the Monorail" when a smooth-talking salesman cons the town into building a less-than-reliable transit system with Homer as the conductor. And "A Streetcar Named Marge" finds Marge picked to play Blanche in a musical version of the Tennessee Williams play, much to Homer's dismay.
04-3893 □*$12.99*

The Simpsons Go Hollywood: Boxed Set
This special three-tape collection includes Vol. 1, plus two volumes available only in the set: Vol. 2 features the two-part "Who Shot Mr. Burns?" saga, while Vol. 3 contains "Bart Gets Famous" and "Krusty Gets Kancelled."
04-3896 □*$24.99*

The Simpsons Trick Or Treehouse, Vol. 1: Halloween
A Krusty doll with unfriendly plans for Homer, a giant ape with a familiar-sounding "D'oh!" and Bart's stab at raising the dead add up to horrific hilarity in "Treehouse of Horror III." Next, "Treehouse of Horror IV," finds the family trapped in a snowbound hotel with a homicidal Homer, Homer turning his toaster into a time machine, and the school cafeteria offering a less-than-appetizing new menu.
04-3982 □*$12.99*

The Simpsons Trick Or Treehouse, Vol. 2: Springfield Murder Mysteries
It's Bart versus arch-enemy Sideshow Bob in two suspense-filled stories. First, a "reformed" Bob weds pen pal Aunt Selma, but will she survive the honeymoon, in "Black Widower"? Then, the menace of a paroled Bob sends the family into a relocation program as "the Thompsons" in "Cape Feare."
04-3983 □*$12.99*

The Simpsons Trick Or Treehouse, Vol. 3: Heaven & Hell
A disbelieving "Bart Sells His Soul" to Milhouse for $5, but soon begins to regret his decision. And when an archeological dig uncovers a winged skeleton, "Lisa the Skeptic" is the only person in Springfield who refuses to believe it's an angel...or does she?
04-3984 □*$12.99*

The Simpsons Trick Or Treehouse Triple Pack
All three frightfully funny volumes are also available in a boxed set.
04-3985 Save $14.00! □*$24.99*

Captain Gallant, Vol. 1 (1955)
Everyone's favorite Foreign Legionnaire, Buster Crabbe, stars in two episodes, along with pal Fuzzy. Includes "Revenge" and "Camel's Race." 60 min.
68-8489 *$19.99*

Captain Gallant, Vol. 2 (1955)
Buster Crabbe and Fuzzy Knight are adventurous in "Dr. Legionnaire" and "The Search." 60 min.
68-8490 *$19.99*

Captain Gallant, Foreign Legionnaire
Here's a vintage treat, two episodes of the '50s adventure show about a French Foreign Legion captain and his youthful ward fighting the cause of freedom in North Africa. Buster Crabbe and Fuzzy Knight star. AKA: "Foreign Legionnaire." 60 min.
10-7312 Was $19.99 *$14.99*

Captain Gallant Christmas Shows
Christmas in North Africa brings a fez-ful of holiday cheer for Captain Gallant, Foreign Legionnaire, and his chipper ward Cuffy (Buster and Cullen Crabbe). "The Boy Who Found Christmas" and "The Gift" are featured, with an appearance by Casbah regular Charles Boyer.
10-7508 Was $19.99 *$14.99*

The Big Story
This NBC series featured Burgess Meredith (among others) as the host and spotlighted gripping stories from newspaper reporters from across the country. The newsmen got $500 for each story that was chosen for dramatization. Filmed on location in the cities where they took place, the show ran on NBC from 1949 to 1958. Each tape features two episodes and runs about 55 min.

The Big Story, Vol. 1
Includes "Until Proven Guilty" and "Hackie Shakedown."
08-1766 *$14.99*

The Big Story, Vol. 2
Includes "Thanksgiving for Dr. Joe" and "Shield 21."
08-1767 *$14.99*

The Big Story, Vol. 3
Includes "Silent Barrier" and "Death Pact."
08-1768 *$14.99*

The Big Story, Vol. 4
Includes "Hostage" and "Theory of Murder."
08-1769 *$14.99*

Racket Squad
True-to-life drama starred Reed Hadley as the bunco-busting Capt. John Braddock. The 1950-1953 series, running in syndication and on CBS, based its episodes on actual scams perpetrated across America and showed viewers how to stay on their guard. Each tape contains two episodes and runs about 55 min. There are 11 volumes available, including:

Racket Squad, Vol. 1
Includes "The Case of the Dancing Lady" and "Heaven for Sale."
10-1226 *$19.99*

Racket Squad, Vol. 2
Includes "Accidentally on Purpose" and "The Case of the Hearse Chasers."
10-1227 *$19.99*

Racket Squad: Boxed Set
Capt. John Braddock (Reed Hadley) puts the kibosh on con artists in this seven-tape boxed set featuring 14 episodes of the early '50s crime drama. Included are "Sting of Fate/One Angle Too Many," "The Soft Touch/The Salted Mine," "The Family Tree/The Elephant in Stockings," "A Place for Grandma/The Home Wreckers," "One More Dream/The Raccoon Hunt," "The Dancing Lady/The Knockout" and "The Matchmaker/The Condemned Cattle."
16-5014 *$49.99*

Climax!: Dr. Jekyll And Mr. Hyde
Michael Rennie essays the dual title roles in this live TV adaptation of Robert Louis Stevenson's novel about the curious doctor who experiments with the unknown and emerges as the hideous and murderous Mr. Hyde. With Cedric Hardwicke. 60 min.
10-7005 Was $19.99 *$14.99*

Climax!: A Promise To Murder
Peter Lorre, Louis Hayward and Ann Harding star in a suspenseful entry from this classic series. 60 min.
10-7303 Was $19.99 *$14.99*

Climax!: The Fifth Wheel
The long-running dramatic anthology series "Climax!" appeared on CBS television from 1954 to 1958. Typical of its quality productions is this entry, starring Peter Lorre, Bonita Granville and James Gleason; William Lundigan hosts. 60 min.
10-7304 Was $19.99 *$14.99*

Climax!: Night Of Execution
Another suspenseful installment of the CBS anthology program hosted by William Lundigan. Master of the macabre Vincent Price stars with Nina Foch and burly western star Dick Foran. 50 min.
10-7461 Was $19.99 *$14.99*

Climax!: Four Hours In White (1958)
Hospital chief surgeon Dan Duryea must make a life-or-death decision, with the lives of two men in the balance, in this gripping TV drama. With Ann Rutherford, Eduard Franz, and a young Steve McQueen (in two roles). 60 min.
09-3018 *$14.99*

The Adventures Of Sir Lancelot
Set in days of yore when King Arthur and the Knights of the Round Table ruled England, this adventure series from the '50s stars William Russell as Sir Lancelot and Jane Hylto as Lady Guinevere. Each volume contains two episodes and runs 60 min. There are five volumes available, including:

The Adventures Of Sir Lancelot, Vol. 1
Includes "The Theft of Excalibur" and "Lady Lilith."
10-1210 *$19.99*

The Adventures Of Sir Lancelot, Vol. 2
Includes "The Ferocious Fathers" and "Montaise Fair."
10-1211 *$19.99*

The Adventures Of Sir Lancelot, Vol. 3
Includes "The Ugly Duckling" and "Knight with the Red Plume."
10-1212 *$19.99*

The Adventures Of Sir Lancelot, Vol. 4
Includes "The Lesser Breed" and "Ruby of Radnor."
10-1213 *$19.99*

The Adventures Of Sir Lancelot, Vol. 5
Includes "The Prince of Limerick" and "Witches Brew."
10-1214 *$19.99*

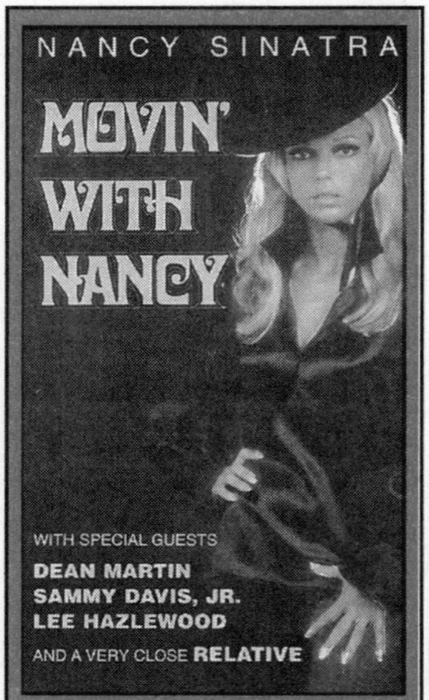

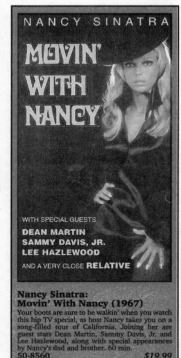

Nancy Sinatra: Movin' With Nancy (1967)
Your boots are sure to be walkin' when you watch this hip TV special, as host Nancy takes you on a song-filled tour of California. Joining her are guest stars Dean Martin, Sammy Davis, Jr. and Lee Hazlewood, along with special appearances by Nancy's dad and brother. 60 min.
50-8560 *$19.99*

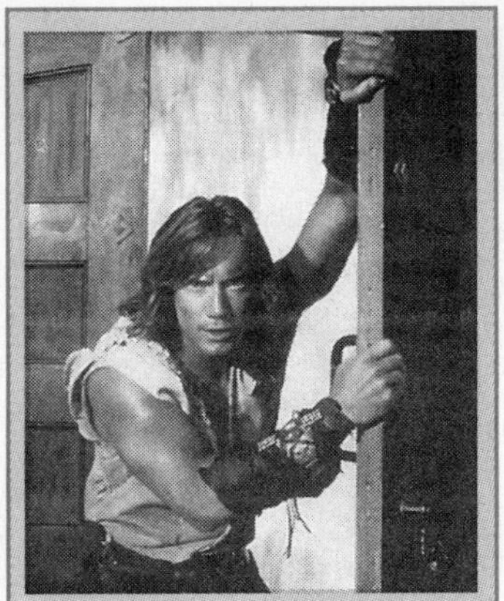

HERCULES
THE LEGENDARY JOURNEYS

Hercules:
The Legendary Journeys (1994)
Kevin Sorbo stars as the legendary Greek hero, the son of Zeus who uses his mighty strength to fight for justice, in these fantasy-filled, feature-length adventures that led to the hit syndicated action series.

Hercules:
The Legendary Journeys:
Hercules In The Underworld
There'll be "Hades" to pay when Hercules ventures into the depths of the land of the dead to rescue a village from the god of the underworld's clutches. 92 min.
07-2532 ❑*$14.99*

Hercules: The Legendary Journeys: The Lost Kingdom
In a quest to find the lost city of Troy, Hercules must battle such menaces as a monstrous sea serpent, the assassins known as the Blue Monks, and the sinister schemes of his "stepmother" Hera. 91 min.
07-2533 ❑*$14.99*

Hercules: The Legendary Journeys: Hercules And The Amazon Women
Does being captured and held prisoner by a village of beautiful warrior women sound like fun? Try telling that to Hercules, who must either submit to the romantic advances of Amazon queen Hippolyta or face a torturous death. Lucy Lawless guest stars as Lysia. 91 min.
07-2534 ❑*$14.99*

Hercules: The Legendary Journeys: The Circle Of Fire
The light's going out all over the world when a jealous Hera steals the Eternal Torch, source of all of man's fire. To restore the flame, Hercules must battle a giant and a nasty wood sprite and even risk the anger of father Zeus. 91 min.
07-2535 ❑*$14.99*

Hercules: The Legendary Journeys: The Warrior Princess
Lucy Lawless made her debut as the beautiful but treacherous pillager Xena in this episode, wooing Hercules' best friend Iolaus as part of her evil scheme to split them up and thus secure her conquest of the land of Arcadian. 47 min.
07-2584 ❑*$14.99*

Hercules: The Legendary Journeys: The Gauntlet
Hercules once again crosses swords with the lovely and lethal Xena, whose followers are raiding village after village. But when Darphus, her ruthless lieutenant, overthrows her and casts a beaten Xena into the wilderness, will she return to fight with Hercules or against him? 47 min.
07-2585 ❑*$14.99*

Hercules: The Legendary Journeys: Unchained Heart
Demigod and warrior princess unite when Hercules and Xena join forces to stop the resurrected Darphus, brought back to life by war god Ares as part of his merciless plan to conquer the mortal world. 47 min.
07-2586 ❑*$14.99*

Young Hercules (1997)
Learn about the early years of the adventure-seeking demigod, as a 17-year-old Hercules sets out on a quest to prove his bravery with a heroic prince, a beautiful warrior woman, and a devious con artist in this feature-length saga from the producers of the "Hercules: The Legendary Journeys" series. Ian Bohen, Dean O'Gorman, Johna Stewart star. 93 min.
07-2592 Was $89.99 ❑*$14.99*

The Tom Green Show: Something Smells Funny
The always-outrageous Tom Green is featured in some of the wildest and weirdest segments from his outrageous cable comedy series in this program. Not sanitized for your protection, the routines featured here are sure to make you squeamish and keep you laughing. 50 min.
50-8675 *$19.99*

The Best Of The Tom Green Show
Direct from his skewed talk show that's one of MTV's most popular series, the wildest moments, goofs, stunts and songs from Tom and company have been gathered onto one hilarious video. Along with such faves as "Boy in the Bubble," "Talk to the Poo" and "Horses Humping," you'll also get the music video for the beloved "Bum Bum Song (Lonely Swedish)." 50 min.
04-5723 *$12.99*

MTV's
The Tom Green Show: Uncensored
The always-outrageous Tom Green shows you why he's one of the world's most unpredictable comics with this selection of his greatest bits, plus stuff from "The Tom Green Cancer Special." Also included are never-before-told stories from his crew. 65 min.
04-5752 *$12.99*

Buffalo Bill, Jr.
In this syndicated series that ran in 1955, Dick Jones is the title character, a young marshal who tries to maintain justice in the Texas town in which he resides with sister Calamity (Nancy Gilbert). Harry Cheshire is Judge Ben Wiley, their adopted father. Each tape features two episodes and runs about 50 min. There are six volumes available, including:

Buffalo Bill, Jr., Vol. 1
Includes "The Fight for Geronimo" (with guest star Chief Thundercloud) and "Redskin Gap."
10-9588 *$14.99*

Buffalo Bill, Jr., Vol. 2
Includes "The Rain Wagon" (with Lyle Talbot) and "Boomer's Blunder" (with Lee Van Cleef).
10-9589 *$14.99*

Buffalo Bill, Jr., Vol. 3
Includes "Runaway Renegade" and "Red Hawk."
10-9590 *$14.99*

Buffalo Bill, Jr., Vol. 4
Includes "Trail of the Killer" and "Tough Tenderfoot."
10-9591 *$14.99*

Buffalo Bill, Jr., Vol. 5
Includes "The Death of Johnny Ringo" (with Angie Dickinson) and "Rails Westward."
10-9592 *$14.99*

Buffalo Bill, Jr., Vol. 6
Includes "Empire Pass" and "The Black Ghost" (with Denver Pyle).
10-9593 *$14.99*

Buffalo Bill, Jr.
Dick Jones stars in this early TV Western as the orphaned Buffalo Bill, Jr., the ever-upright champion of frontier justice who, along with his sister Calamity by his side, fends for the good folk of Wileyville, Texas, in the 1890s. Includes "The Legacy of Jesse James" and "The Fugitive from Justice." 60 min.
10-7024 Was $19.99 *$14.99*

Dragnet (1951-59)
"Ladies and gentlemen, the tapes you are about to watch are true. The names have been changed to protect the innocent." Walk the streets of "the city...Los Angeles, California" with detectives Joe Friday and Frank Smith (Jack Webb, Ben Alexander) in the definitive TV cop series. Each tape features two cases and runs about 55 min. There are six volumes available, including:

Dragnet, Vol. 1
Includes "The Big Girls" and "The Big Boys."
10-1206 *$14.99*

Dragnet, Vol. 2
Includes "The Big Bird" and "The Big Trunk."
10-1207 *$14.99*

Dragnet, Vol. 3
Includes "Big Shoplift" and "Big Hit and Run."
10-1208 *$14.99*

Dragnet, Vol. 4
Includes "Big Betty" and "Big Counterfeit."
10-1209 Was $19.99 *$14.99*

Dragnet, Vol. 5
Includes "Big 17" and "Bi Producer."
10-7372 Was $19.99 *$14.99*

Dragnet:
Big Score & Big Crackdown
Two classic cop capers with Jack Webb and Ben Alexander from the '50s series. A bunco gang fleecing shopkeepers and a confessed bandit who may be innocent are sure to keep Friday on his toes. 53 min.
62-1332 *$19.99*

Dragnet (1954)
Feature film based on the classic TV police series has cops Jack Webb and Ben Alexander investigating a gang murder in their precise, laconic manner. Richard Boone, Ann Robinson co-star. 71 min.
07-1165 *$14.99*

Biff Baker, U.S.A.
Before he was stuck on that "uncharted desert isle," Alan Hale, Jr. travelled the world in this 1952-53 adventure series, playing an American entrepreneur looking for goods to import home who often found himself and wife Louise (Randy Stuart) involved in espionage activities. Each tape features two episodes and runs about 55 min.

Biff Baker, U.S.A., Vol. 1
Includes "Alpine Assignment" and "Grey Market."
82-1044 *$19.99*

Biff Baker, U.S.A., Vol. 2
Includes "Saigon Incident" and "Mona Lisa."
82-1045 *$19.99*

Terry And The Pirates/ Biff Baker, U.S.A.
Duo of classic '50s TV adventure dramas with a Cold War theme. First, John Baer is Terry and Gloria Saunders the Dragon Lady in a tube version of Milton Caniff's comic strip. Next Alan Hale, Jr. heads a husband-wife spy team who travel behind the Iron Curtain. 60 min. total.
10-7317 Was $19.99 *$14.99*

Beavis And Butt-Head
MTV's lunkhead metal maniacs, whose animated antics have made them national cult favorites, are finally on home video. Watch as Beavis and Butt-Head sit on their couch and eat nachos, annoy their neighbors, classmates and teachers, and try to score with chicks. Each volume contains eight cartoons (NOTE: minus the music video segments seen on TV) and runs about 45 min. There are nine volumes available, including:

Beavis And Butt-Head: The Final Judgement
The gruesome twosome of Highland High School may have finally met their match when Beavis "goes toward the light" and has an encounter with St. Peter at the pearly gates! Also included are "Scared Straight," "Stop Laughing," "The Great Cornholio" and more.
04-5342 *$14.99*

Beavis And Butt-Head Do Christmas
Put a Yule Log on the fire ("Huh, huh, huh. He said 'log'.") and watch the boys demolish the Christmas spirit in "Huh-Huh-Humbug" and "It's a Miserable Life." This program also includes complete holiday-themed music videos (with Beavis and Butt-Head adding their own insightful comments) from Buster Poindexter, The Ramones and Run DMC.
04-5457 *$14.99*

Beavis And Butt-Head: Troubled Youth
Watch your favorite duo of morons do a bunch of cool stuff, such as unwittingly foil a fast-food restaurant robbery, get a really lame substitute teacher, and deal with the problems of impotence. Includes "Work Is Death," "Tainted Meat," "No Service" and more.
04-5606 *$14.99*

Beavis And Butt-Head: Butt-O-Ween
As though the fellas need an excuse to throw eggs and toilet paper at their neighbors' houses! Treat yourself to eight classic "B&B" misadventures, including "Cornholio: Lord of the Harvest," "The Pipe of Doom," "Late Night with Butt-Head," "Candy Sale" and others. 45 min.
04-5666 *$14.99*

Celebrity Deathmatch
Your favorite notables in music, movies, TV and politics (or, at least, clay-animated copies of them) take their feuds into the squared circle in MTV's hit series of all-out comedic grudge matches where only one opponent is—sometimes—left in one piece. Except where noted, each tape runs about 50 min.

Celebrity Deathmatch, Round 1
Featured bouts include Jerry Seinfeld vs. Tim Allen, Hillary Clinton vs. Monica Lewinsky, Michael Jordan vs. Dennis Rodman and more, plus a look at the making of the series.
04-5640 *$14.99*

Celebrity Deathmatch, Round 2
Featured bouts include David Letterman vs. Jay Leno, Leonardo DiCaprio vs. Jack Nicholson, Steven Tyler vs. Mick Jagger, Bigfoot vs. the Loch Ness Monster and more.
04-5641 *$14.99*

Celebrity Deathmatch: Greatest Hits
This special "best of" compilation includes Noel Gallagher vs. Liam Gallagher, Spike Lee vs. Quentin Tarantino, "Stone Cold" Steve Austin vs. Vince McMahon, Adam Sandler vs. Chris Rock and more, plus all-new commentary from Johnny Gomez and Nick Diamond. 60 min.
04-5679 *$14.99*

Daria
She was the only female who'd bother to talk to Beavis and Butt-Head, and now cynical outsider Daria Morgendorffer is the star of her own hit MTV animated series. Watch Daria cope with life at Lawndale High in this collection of three episodes, plus the original black-and-white pilot cartoon. 70 min.
04-5543 *$14.99*

Daria: Disenfranchised
Ready for a second helping of adolescent disillusionment? Then join the ever-sarcastic Daria, her friend Jane, and their families and fellow students in a trio of tales from the acclaimed MTV show. Included are "Cafe Disaffecto," "Malled" and "This Year's Model." 80 min.
04-5678 *$14.99*

The State: Skits And Stickers* (*Stickers Not Included)
Like the title says, you don't get stickers with this tape, but you will see hilarious and outrageous sketches with the troupe from the hit MTV show, including three new skits exclusive to home video. 70 min.
04-5413 *$14.99*

The Maxx: The Original Series
He's the musclebound purple star of his own comics and MTV cartoon series, and now the Maxx's off-the-wall adventures come to home video. See how homeless Maxx and social worker friend Julie are transported to the mysterious world known as the Outback and transformed into bizarre superheroes. 120 min.
04-5439 *$14.99*

Aeon Flux: The Complete Boxed Set
This three-tape collector's set features all the animated adventures, as seen on MTV, of Aeon Flux, the scantily-clad freedom fighter who battles her arch-rival (and soulmate) Trevor Goodchild against the backdrop of a futuristic high-tech war. 300 min. total.
04-5605 *$34.99*

Aeon Flux (1995)
MTV's outrageous animated futuristic thriller chronicles the adventures of Aeon Flux, a female secret agent, who battles her arch rival (and soulmate) Trevor Goodchild against the backdrop of a brutal war where participants use unusual weapons. This tape includes the original shorts that aired on MTV's "Liquid Television," plus four other episodes. 120 min.
04-5446 *$14.99*

THE REAL WORLD

The Real World: Vacations—Behind The Scenes
Take a vacation with different casts from MTV's top-rated "real-life soap opera" as they party on the beach in Jamaica, Mexico and Hawaii, but learn that "real world" situations like fights, failed dates and pregnancy can happen anywhere. 40 min.
04-5381 *$14.99*

The Real World You Never Saw
Now you can see what was too "real," even for MTV, with this behind-the-scenes program featuring the wildest unseen moments, funniest outtakes and candid interviews with the housemates from the first six "Real World" series. 45 min.
04-5538 *$14.99*

The Real World You Never Saw: Boston And Seattle
Get the coast-to-coast dish on what went on when the cameras stopped shooting for the "Real World" roommates in Beantown and Grunge City. Find out which cast members didn't get along, which ones *really* got along, whose hygiene needed work, how they got along with the neighbors, and more. 70 min.
04-5616 *$14.99*

The Real World You Never Saw: Hawaii
Say "aloha" once again to Amaya, Colin, Justin, Kaia, Matt, Ruthie and Teck, and see how their videotaped island paradise was filled with surprises ranging from romance to alcohol abuse to a "clothing optional" experiment, in this wild, uncensored retrospective. 50 min.
04-5691 *$14.99*

The Real World You Never Saw: New Orleans
Bourbon Street gets wilder than usual when the cast from MTV's "The Real World" invades the "Big Easy." See things never shown on TV with perfect physical and mental specimen David; forever-on-the-prowl Danny; "Supafly" Matt; beautiful and sly Kelley; manic Melissa; Julie, the pretty Mormon; and Ayn Rand-reading Jamie.
02-5745 *$12.99*

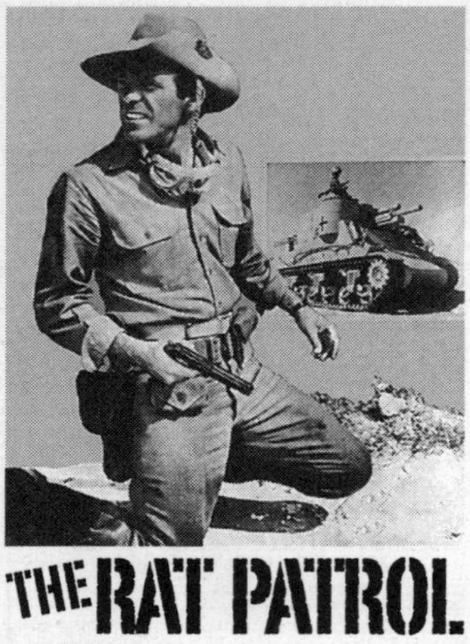

The Rat Patrol
This much-liked WWII series ran on ABC from 1966-1968 and told of the adventures of four jeep-riding soldiers—Americans Sam Troy (Christopher George), Mark Hitchcock (Lawrence Casey) and Tully Pettigrew (Justin Tarr) and Britisher Jack Moffitt (Gary Raymond)—battling General Rommel's Afrika Korps in the North African desert. Hans Gudegast (later soap star Eric Braeden) played arch-nemesis Capt. Hans Dietrich. Each two-episode tape runs about 50 min.

The Rat Patrol, Vol. 1: The Hide And Go Seek Raid/ The Two-If-By-See Raid
"The Hide and Go Seek Raid" involves a mission to the isle of Rhodes to rescue a British general's son. And the "Two-If-By-Sea Raid" depicts a deadly strike in a German naval base.
09-5354 *$14.99*

Rat Patrol, Vol. 2: The Boomerang Raid/The Street Urchin Raid
In "Boomerang," the patrol picks up an Allied agent on the Mediterranean coast of Africa, but not everything adds up when they find an American body without dog tags. Dick Sargent guest stars. And in "Street Urchin," the men fight to save a group of people—one of whom has some valuable aerial photos—from the Gestapo.
09-5454 *$14.99*

The Rat Patrol, Vol. 3: The David And Goliath Raid/ The Never Say Die Raid
Dietrich hijacks the patrol, leaving them on foot—and in peril—in the desert in "David and Goliath." Next, a captured Troy and Hitchcock are forced to broadcast phony info over the radio in "Never Say Die."
09-5455 *$14.99*

The Rat Patrol, Vol. 4: The B Negative Raid/The Do-Re-Mi Raid
When Moffitt is seriously injured in "B Negative," the patrol tries frantically to find someone with the same blood type to save him; Fabian guest stars. Then, "Do-Re-Mi" finds Troy trying to save an American singer held behind enemy lines by the Germans; Jack Jones guest stars.
09-5456 *$14.99*

The Starlost: Complete Set (1973)
Compelling Canadian sci-fi series, created by writer Harlan Ellison (under his Cordwainer Bird pseudonym), is set on a gigantic "space ark" whose hundreds of self-contained biospheres contain the survivors of a dead Earth. Three young people search for a way to stop the ark's collision course with a star and save humanity. Keir Dullea, Gary Rowan, Robin Ward star. Five-tape set includes "The Beginning," "The Invasion," "The Alien Oro," "Deception" and "The Return." 475 min. total. NOTE: Individual volumes available at $14.99.
08-1680 Save $15.00! *$59.99*

Charlie's Angels
Aaron Spelling's successful mix of jiggles and thrills featured a trio of shapely detectives getting out of all sorts of dangerous situations as they solved crimes for Charlie, their unseen boss. Running on ABC from 1976-1981, the show's original stars were Kate Jackson as Sabrina, Farrah Fawcett-Majors as Jill, and Jaclyn Smith as Kelly. Each tape features two episodes and runs about 100 min.

Charlie's Angels, Vol. 1: Angels In Chains
"Angels in Chains" finds the girls behind bars in a corrupt prison down South to investigate a missing inmate; Kim Basinger guests. And in "Blue Angels," working in a massage parlor could get the Angels "rubbed out"; Ed Lauter, Dirk Benedict guest star.
02-3114 *$14.99*

Charlie's Angels, Vol. 2: Angels Under Covers
The fight to save an autistic boy from a pair of paid killers puts Kelly's life in danger in "To Kill an Angel." Next, Kelly and Jill pose as fashion models in order to find a killer who strangles people with rag dolls in "Night of the Strangler."
02-3115 *$14.99*

Judge Roy Bean (1956)
Set in Langtry, Texas, in 1870, this Western TV series focuses on the self-appointed "Law West of the Pecos," Judge Roy Bean. A storekeeper by trade, the good judge attempts to maintain order in a lawless territory. Edgar Buchanan, Jack Beutel and Jackie Loughery star. Each tape runs about 50 min. There are five volumes available, including:

Judge Roy Bean, Vol. 1
Features "Bad Medicine" and "The Fugitive."
10-8292 Was $19.99 *$14.99*

Judge Roy Bean, Vol. 2
"The Spirit of the Law" and "Gunman's Bargain" are featured.
10-8293 Was $19.99 *$14.99*

Judge Roy Bean/Trails West
Edgar Buchanan stars as "the law west of the Pecos," the stubborn shopkeeper who maintained law and order in the Old West, in the episode "Eyes of Texas." Ray Milland hosts an episode of "Trails West" (AKA: "Death Valley Days") brought to you by 20-Mule Team Borax. 55 min.
10-7032 Was $19.99 *$14.99*

The Edgar Wallace Mystery Theatre
The mysteries in this TV series from England were penned by writer Edgar Wallace and were originally produced for theaters. Top performers are featured in atmospheric thrillers which ran in 1963 in America. Each program runs about 50 min. There are 11 volumes available, including:

The Edgar Wallace Mystery Theatre, Vol. 1
"Partners in Crime" features Bernard Lee and Jordan Van Eyssen.
10-8281 Was $19.99 *$14.99*

The Edgar Wallace Mystery Theatre, Vol. 2
Zena Marshall and Alfred Burke star in "Backfire."
10-8282 Was $19.99 *$14.99*

The Edgar Wallace Mystery Theatre, Vol. 3
"The Malpas Mystery" stars Maureen Swanson and Alan Cuthbertson.
10-8283 Was $19.99 *$14.99*

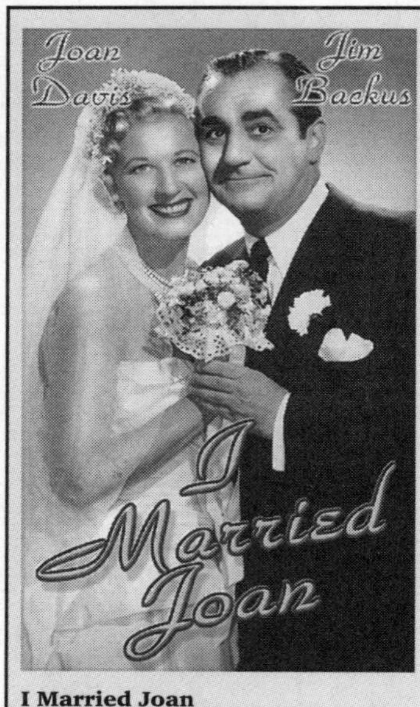

I Married Joan
"I married Joan. What a girl, what a whirl, what a life!" Joan Davis starred as Joan Stevens in this fondly-remembered sitcom from the early '50s, which caught a glimpse of the harried lives of a homemaker and her long-suffering husband, Judge Bradley Stevens (Jim Backus). Except where noted, each tape contains two episodes and runs about 50 min.

I Married Joan, Vol. 1: Home Of The Week/Jealousy
When Joan borrows expensive furnishings for a "Home of the Week" photo shoot, accusations fly that Brad is taking bribes. Next, a marital expert leads Joan to believe Brad doesn't love her because he never shows his "Jealousy."
09-5422 *$14.99*

I Married Joan, Vol. 2: Lady And The Prizefighter/ Changing Houses
Joan learns about the "Lady and the Prizefighter" after losing a boxing match bet prompts her to stage a fight for her woman's club. Also, Joan and Mabel partake in "Changing Houses" by swapping homes for a week.
09-5423 *$14.99*

I Married Joan, Vol. 3: Joan's Haircut/The Jail Bird
In "Joan's Haircut," the Stevens get a taste of their own medicine when, after making of someone else's haircut, they accidentally get radical new styles just before a college reunion. Then, a thieving crow has everyone thinking Joan is a kleptomaniac in "The Jail Bird."
09-5424 *$14.99*

I Married Joan, Vol. 4: New House/Wall Safe
The Stevens' "New House" is their dream, but problems arise when it's sold to another couple. In that new house, Joan goes to great lengths to find out what's in a "Wall Safe" she discovers.
09-5425 *$14.99*

I Married Joan, Vol. 5: Mabel's Dress/Dreams
After ruining "Mabel's Dress," Joan tries to make good with a birthday cake gift—that explodes! Also, Joan has special "Dreams" about what her life could have been if she hadn't married Brad after attending a school reunion.
09-5426 *$14.99*

I Married Joan, Vol. 6: Acrobats/Broken Toe
In "Acrobats," Joan ends up as part of a floor show at a restaurant when she tries to disguise herself to throw off the wife of the dean of the law school. And Joan finds herself in the hospital after she makes fun of Brad's "Broken Toes."
09-5427 *$14.99*

I Married Joan, Vol. 7: Mountain Lodge/Honeymoon
Brad surprises Joan by buying a "Mountain Lodge" and Joan surprises Brad by buying a boat—with the same money! Then, Brad shares the story of how he wound up locked in a burglar-proof closet on his and Joan's "Honeymoon."
09-5428 *$14.99*

I Married Joan, Vol. 8: Neighbors/ Alienation Of Affections
After noisy "Neighbors" move away, Brad and Joan don't know what they're in for. And Joan is sued for "Alienation of Affections" when she comes between a doctor and his wife.
09-5429 *$14.99*

I Married Joan, Vol. 9: Bad Boy/Sister Pat
In "Bad Boy," Joan and Brad watch a convict's son as a favor, and Joan figures out how to teach the ill-mannered kid a lesson. And when Joan's "Sister Pat" moves in, Brad hires actors to impersonate his cousins.
09-5430 *$14.99*

I Married Joan, Vol. 10: Talent Scout/Home Movies
"Talent Scout" finds Joan being unknowingly used by Brad and the DA to catch two con men posing as talent scouts. Next, friends come over to watch "Home Movies," but Joan and Brad are in the middle of a big fight.
09-5431 *$14.99*

I Married Joan, Vol. 11: The Maid/Brad's Class Reunion
Joan promises "The Maid" that a favorite movie star is a close friend in order to keep her working for her. And Joan becomes jealous when she meets a former girlfriend of her husband at "Brad's Class Reunion."
09-5432 *$14.99*

I Married Joan, Vol. 12: Clothes Budget/Bev's Boyfriend
Brad gives Joan her entire "Clothes Budget" for a year at one time, and hilarious complications ensue when she spends it on one dress. Also, Joan steals the affection of "Bev's Boyfriend," much to her best friend's dismay.
09-5433 *$14.99*

I Married Joan, Vol. 13: Two St. Bernards/The Allergy
After much discussion, Brad and Joan get not one, but "Two St. Bernards" as pets. Also, Joan can't stop sneezing when a local TV camera begins filming for a story on Brad's political campaign, thanks to "The Allergy."
09-9534 *$14.99*

I Married Joan Gift Set 1
This special four-tape collector's set includes the episodes "Prizefighter/Wall Safe/Joan's Haircut," "Changing Houses/Talent Scout/Bad Boy," "Honeymoon/Home Movies/New House" and "Neighbors/Alienation/Sister Pat."
08-1808 *$29.99*

I Married Joan Gift Set 2
This special four-tape collector's set includes the episodes "Home of the Week/Acrobats/Mabel's Dress," "Bev's Boyfriends/Mountain Lodge/Broken Toe," "Dreams/The Jailbird/Clothes Budget" and "Class Reunion/Allergy/Jealousy."
08-1809 *$29.99*

Mannix: Nothing Ever Works Twice (1967)
Mike Connors' tough P.I., Joe Mannix, takes a divorce case and discovers that the soon-to-be ex-wife of the man who hired him is his former flame. When her husband is murdered, Mannix becomes the prime suspect. Joseph Campanella co-stars; with Gloria DeHaven. 50 min.
10-2460 *$14.99*

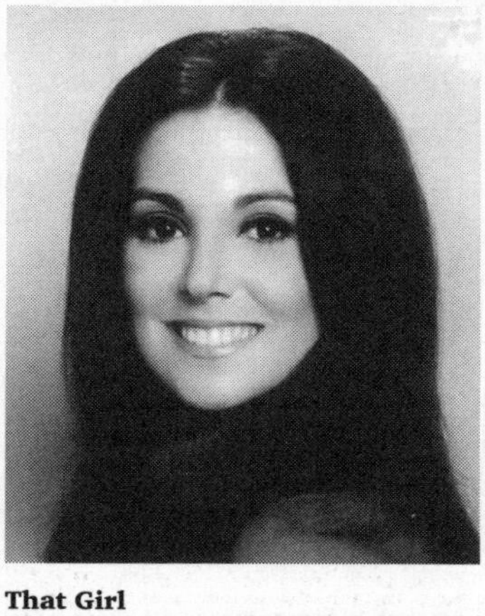

That Girl
This hit series ran on ABC from 1966-1971 and featured Marlo Thomas as spunky Ann Marie, an aspiring actress who left her small-town environs to try to make it in the Big Apple. Between temp jobs and commercial spots, she dated Donald Hollinger (Ted Bessell), calmed her worried parents (Lew Parker and Rosemary DeCamp) and got into wacky situations. Each three-episode tape runs about 75 min.

That Girl: Oh, Donald!
Ann and Donald's romantic exploits are featured in these three shows. In "Don't Just Do Something, Stand There," they meet for the first time when Donald tries to save her from fake thugs during production of a commerical; Donald's meeting with Ann's parents goes awry in "Anatomy of a Blunder"; and after four years of dating Donald asks Ann the big question in "Counter-Proposal."
08-8743 *$14.99*

That Girl: Auditions, Auditions, Auditions
This tribute to Ann's acting life starts with "Call of the Wild," in which Ann develops a striptease to change her image. Next, after her boss makes a pass at her, Ann leaves his car and is stranded in a chicken outfit in "Nobody Here But Us Chickens"; and, although stranded in the airport during a blizzard, Ann is determined to make an audition in "The Snow Must Go On."
08-8744 *$14.99*

That Girl: Guest Stars
Teri Garr and Rob Reiner have early turns in "This Little Piggy Had a Ball," in which Ann accepts a Tony Award for a friend with a bowling ball stuck on her toe; Ethel Merman pays Ann a dinner visit at the request of Donald in "Pass the Potatoes, Ethel Merman." And Milton Berle and Danny Thomas try to buy Ann's late uncle's trunk in "Those Friars."
08-8745 *$14.99*

That Girl: Everybody Loves Ann
Does Donald have a rival for Ann's affections when an old boyfriend from Brewster shows up in "Among My Souvenirs"? Next, Ann must fend off the advances of amorous opera singer Carroll O'Connor in "A Tenor's Loving Care," while in "The Mating Game," game show contestant Ann picks someone over Donald as her date for the evening.
08-8804 *$14.99*

That Girl: Daddy's Little Girl
Ann's overprotective pop, restaurateur Lou Marie, takes center stage in three episodes: a planned dinner visit by the folks turns into a disaster in "Leaving the Nest Is for the Birds"; Ann plays peacemaker for "The Rivals" when she and Donald spend the weekend at her parents'; and Lou suspects the worst after finding Donald at Ann's one morning in "It's So Nice to Have a Mouse Around the House."
08-8805 *$14.99*

That Girl: All For Showbiz
Ann goes to hilarious lengths to catch a Broadway producer's eye in "You Have to Know Someone to Be an Unknown"; a publicity date with comic Dick Shawn goes awry in "The Mailman Cometh"; and an agent's stunt makes Ann part of an actor's divorce suit in "Just Spell the Name Right."
08-8806 *$14.99*

That Girl: Boxed Set #1
This three-tape collector's set includes "Auditions, Auditions, Auditions," "Guest Stars" and "Oh, Donald!"
08-8746 Save $15.00! *$29.99*

That Girl: Boxed Set #2
This three-tape collector's set includes "All for Showbiz," "Daddy's Little Girl" and "Everybody Loves Ann."
08-8807 Save $15.00! *$29.99*

Jeeves & Wooster (1991)
P.G. Wodehouse's ever-popular creations come to life in this terrific British TV series. Stephen Fry is the unflappable, ever-resourceful butler Jeeves, and Hugh Laurie plays well-meaning, dim-witted aristocrat Bertie Wooster. See them in hilarious situations in these tales set in Edwardian England which originally ran on "Masterpiece Theatre."

The Very First Jeeves & Wooster: Collector's Set
See how the masterful majordomo came into the employ of the addle-pated aristocrat in this five-tape boxed set that features "Jeeves Takes Charge," "Tuppy and the Terrier," "The Purity of the Turf," "The Hunger Strike" and "Brinkley Manor." 250 min. total. NOTE: Individual volumes available at $14.99.
53-6574 Save $5.00! ***$69.99***

Jeeves & Wooster: Collector's Set
The old boys at the Drones Club will go spare when they see this six-tape boxed set featuring "Jeeves in the Country," "Jeeves Saves the Cow-Creamer," "Jeeves the Matchmaker," "Kidnapped," "Pearls Mean Tears" and "A Plan for Gussie." 360 min. total. NOTE: Individual volumes available at $14.99.
53-8540 Save $10.00! ***$79.99***

More Jeeves & Wooster: Collector's Set
If you can't afford your own butler, then watch as Jeeves saves the day for his employer in this six-tape boxed set that includes "Bertie Sets Sail," "Comrade Bingo," "The Full House," "Hot Off the Press," "Introduction to Broadway" and "Right Ho, Jeeves." 360 min. total. NOTE: Individual volumes available at $14.99.
08-8583 Save $10.00! ***$79.99***

A Tad More Jeeves & Wooster: Collector's Set
Stephen Fry and Hugh Laurie are back for a final go-round as P.G. Wodehouse's beloved butler and muddle-headed master in this collection of six comical classics. Included are "Bridegroom Wanted," "The Delayed Arrival," "The Once and Future Ex," "Return to New York," "The Ties That Bind" and "Trouble at Totleigh Towers." 300 min. total. NOTE: Individual volumes available at $14.99.
50-8123 ***$79.99***

A Bit Of Fry And Laurie
The co-stars of British TV's "Jeeves and Wooster" adaptations are featured in their own comedy series, and you're invited in for a bit of the biting wit and offbeat characters of Stephen Fry and Hugh Laurie. 89 min.
04-2691 ***$19.99***

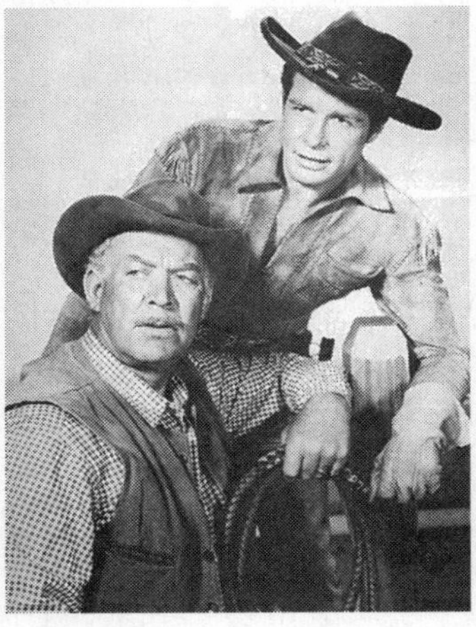

Wagon Train
One of TV's most beloved westerns, "Wagon Train" aired on both NBC and ABC from 1957 to 1965 and focused on the adventures encountered by settlers on a wagon train travelling from Missouri to California. Showcasing a bevy of guest stars, the series' regulars included Ward Bond, John McIntire and Robert Horton. Each volume runs about 55 min.

Wagon Train, Vol. 1: The Malachi Hobart Story
A wagon train scout makes friends with a preacher whom he later learns is a con artist and sets out to teach him a lesson. Franchot Tone and Irene Ryan guest star.
09-5212 Was $19.99 ***$14.99***

Wagon Train, Vol. 2: The Annie MacGregor Story
A proud Scottish captain and his clan join the wagon train, but the captain's stubbornness soon creates problems. Richard Long and Jeannie Carson guest star.
09-5213 Was $19.99 ***$14.99***

Wagon Train: The Dr. Denker Story
The train's two newest members, a young boy traumatized by the death of his father and a gregarious "doctor of music," turn out to hold the keys to a dangerous secret. Theodore Bikel guest stars. 50 min.
10-9393 ***$14.99***

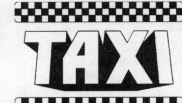

Taxi
Airing on ABC (and later NBC) from 1978 to 1983, this acclaimed sitcom followed the day-to-day travails of the employees of New York's Sunshine Cab Company. Judd Hirsch played veteran cabby Alex Rieger, Danny DeVito was diminutive, despotic dispatcher Louie De Palma, and Andy Kaufman was quirky mechanic Latka Gravas; Jeff Conaway, Tony Danza, Marilu Henner and Christopher Lloyd also starred. Each tape features two episodes and runs about 50 min.

Taxi, Vol. 1
Latka's only chance to get a green card and stay in America is a "Paper Marriage" to a call girl; Christopher Lloyd makes his debut as Reverend Jim. Next, Alex finds himself attracted to "Mama Gravas" when the statuesque widow visits her son.
06-2976 ❑***$12.99***

Taxi, Vol. 2
Trying to change his image, "Latka the Playboy" develops the hip alter ego of Vic Ferrari. The confusion increases in "Mr. Personalities," when a visit to the psychiatrist leaves Latka acting like Alex.
06-2977 ❑***$12.99***

Taxi, Vol. 3
It's an unusual love triangle when "Simka Returns" and both Latka and Vic are attracted to her; Carol Kane guest stars. Next, a chat with Dr. Joyce Brothers is just the start of the marital hi-jinks in "The Wedding of Latka and Simka."
06-2978 ❑***$12.99***

Taxi, Vol. 4
When a blizzard leaves Latka and a lady cabbie stranded overnight in a cab—and in a compromising situation—Simka is told the only way to rectify the betrayal is for her to sleep with one of the guys, in the two-part "Scenskees from a Marriage."
06-2979 ❑***$12.99***

The Road To Lebanon (1960)
Danny Thomas, Bing Crosby, Bob Hope and Sheldon Leonard in a riotous spoof of "Road" movies, with Danny leading the pack. Live camels, desert sheiks and other zany stuff!! 50 min.
09-1646 Was $19.99 ***$14.99***

Dupont Show Of The Month: Treasure Island (1960)
Robert Louis Stevenson's seafaring classic becomes an elaborate TV production with a top cast: Hugh Griffith, Boris Karloff, Richard O'Sullivan. Arrr, Jim-boy! 88 min.
09-1931 ***$19.99***

Martin Kane, Private Eye
The detective series that started life on radio made it to TV in 1949 with this live NBC series. William Gargan originated the video role of the smooth-talking sleuth who hung out at a tobacco shop, and was followed by Lloyd Nolan (1951-52), Lee Tracy (1952-53) and Mark Stevens (1953-54). Each tape features two episodes and runs about 60 min.

Martin Kane, Private Eye, Vol. 1
Lee Tracy's Martin Kane investigates a dead cartoonist who promised to name a killer in his comic strip. Next, Kane (Tracy) tries to protect a witness to a murder who receives death threats. Includes original commercials.
10-9547 ***$14.99***

Martin Kane, Private Eye, Vol. 2
Martin Kane (Lloyd Nolan) looks into the death of a popular bandleader/singer and investigates a dancer, a press agent and a music arranger. Then, a trip to Florida is anything but a vacation for Kane (Nolan) when he finds a dead ship captain in a cabin. Features original commercials.
10-9548 ***$14.99***

Martin Kane, Private Eye, Vol. 3
Mark Stevens is private eye Martin Kane, who tries to set the record straight on a case in which a shoeshine boy goes on the run after witnessing a murder. Also, Kane (Stevens) investigates the death of a criminal known to be a big gambler. Includes original commercials.
10-9549 ***$14.99***

Martin Kane, Private Eye, Vol. 4
A friend brings Martin Kane (Lee Tracy) into a case involving a man robbed of his life's savings on the subway. Kane (Tracy) then heads to Bermuda to guard a $100,000 crown and a beauty contestant of questionable morals. Features original commercials.
10-9550 ***$14.99***

Martin Kane, Private Eye, Vol. 5
After he visits a fortune-teller, a man's life's savings are swiped, and Kane (William Gargan) does some sleuthing to track down the culprit. Soon, he encounters a dancer, a landlady and a pickpocket. Next, Kane (Gargan) joins some associates to find out who stole money from three strange sisters. Includes original commercials.
10-9551 ***$14.99***

Martin Kane, Private Eye, Vol. 6
Kane (William Gargan) is involved in a complex case in which a man sentenced to die clears another of a crime he didn't commit, then shoots the District Attorney. Also, Gargan's private detective wants to get to the bottom of a case in which a wealthy inventor is shot in the face. Includes original commercials.
10-9552 ***$14.99***

Martin Kane, Private Eye
Beginning in 1949, "Martin Kane" was one of TV's first detectives and was played by four men in his five-year run. Here William Gargan, Kane #1, stars in two episodes of the hard-nosed crime series. 60 min.
10-7555 Was $19.99 ***$14.99***

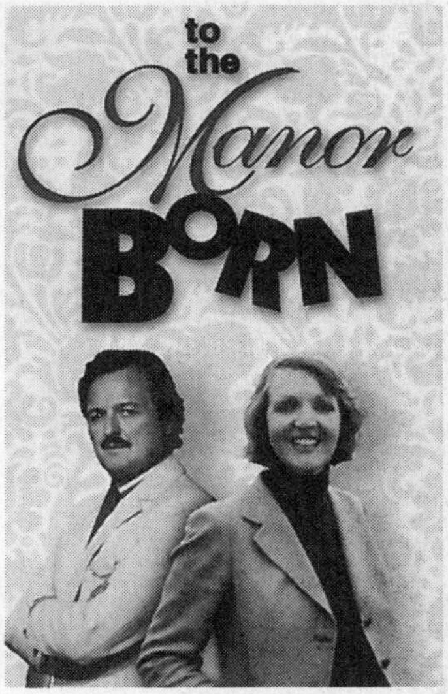

To The Manor Born
This popular British comedy series stars Penelope Keith as widowed Audrey fforbes-Hamilton, the former lady of Grantley Manor, who is forced by financial straits to sell her ancestral home to millionaire businessman Richard DeVere (Peter Bowles), while she moves into a caretaker's cottage on the estate. Except for the four-episode Vol. 1, each tape features three episodes and runs about 90 min.

To The Manor Born, Vol. 1
04-3584 ***$19.99***

To The Manor Born, Vol. 2
04-3585 ***$19.99***

To The Manor Born, Vol. 3
04-3780 ***$19.99***

To The Manor Born, Vol. 4
04-3781 ***$19.99***

To The Manor Born, Vol. 5
04-3905 ❑***$19.99***

To The Manor Born, Vol. 6
04-3906 ❑***$19.99***

To The Manor Born: Boxed Set
Save your manor some money with all six volumes in a special collector's set.
04-3907 Save $20.00! ***$99.99***

Four Star Playhouse
The titular stars in this 1952-56 anthology series were Charles Boyer, Ida Lupino, David Niven and Dick Powell, who were regularly featured, along with other top Hollywood names, in original comedies and dramas. Each volume contains two episodes and runs about 55 min. There are 17 volumes available, including:

Four Star Playhouse, Vol. 1
Includes Dick Powell in "The Test" and "Interlude," co-starring Joanne Woodward.
10-7525 Was $19.99 ***$14.99***

Four Star Playhouse, Vol. 2
Ronald Colman stars in "The Lost Silk Hat," followed by Dick Powell and David Hart in "Welcome Home."
10-7526 Was $19.99 ***$14.99***

Four Star Playhouse, Vol. 3
Features Ida Lupino in "The Listener" and "The Devil to Pay," with Charles Boyer.
10-7527 Was $19.99 ***$14.99***

Four Star Playhouse, Vol. 4
David Niven is showcased in "Vote of Confidence," with Chuck Connors and Amanda Blake, and plays Robert Louis Stevenson in "Tusitala."
10-7528 Was $19.99 ***$14.99***

Four Star Playhouse, Vol. 5
"Girl on the Bridge" stars Dick Powell and Colleen Gray, while Maureen O'Sullivan joins Charles Boyer for "The Gift."
10-7529 Was $19.99 ***$14.99***

Four Star Playhouse, Vol. 6
A double dose of Dick Powell, appearing with Frances Dee in "Shadowed" and Barbara Billingsley in "The Gun."
10-7530 Was $19.99 ***$14.99***

Four Star Playhouse, Vol. 8
"The Adolescent" features Ida Lupino and Hugh Beaumont, while David Niven and Margaret Sheridan are in "The Bomb."
10-7532 Was $19.99 ***$14.99***

Four Star Playhouse, Vol. 9
Charles Boyer and Virginia Grey star in "The Bad Streak." Next, "Touch and Go" with David Niven and Beverly Garland.
10-7533 Was $19.99 ***$14.99***

Four Star Playhouse, Vol. 10
Includes "House for Sale" with Ida Lupino and George Macready and Dick Powell in "To Die at Midnight."
10-7534 Was $19.99 ***$14.99***

Four Star Playhouse, Vol. 11
Dick Powell does double duty in two stories, "The Squeeze" and "Detective's Holiday."
10-7509 Was $19.99 ***$14.99***

Four Star Playhouse, Vol. 12
In his semi-regular role as suave nightclub owner Willie Dante, Dick Powell stars in "High Stakes" and "The Stacked Deck."
10-7511 Was $19.99 ***$14.99***

Uncle Fred Flits By/The Intruder
In the "Four Star Playhouse" presentation of P.G. Wodehouse's "Uncle Fred Flits By," David Niven (who also produced) plays the eccentric uncle of a nephew named Pongo who encounters strange characters when he bird-sits. And "The Intruder," a "Telephone Time" show, tells of a mysterious disappearing man who terrorizes a woman and her son. Joel Grey, Phyllis Avery star. 60 min.
10-9991 ***$14.99***

Four Star Playhouse: Boxed Set
This seven-tape set includes some of "Four Star Playhouse's" best presentations including "A Study in Panic/Championship Affair," "Girl on the Park Bench/House for Sale," "The Interlude/The Gift," "The Squeeze/The Wild Bunch," "Tunnel of Fear/Ladies On His Mind," "Lady of the Orchids/The Frightened Woman" and "The Village in the City/Vote of Confidence." 420 min.
16-5034 ***$49.99***

Four Star Playhouse: The Room (1953)/Autumn Carousel (1956)
In "The Room," a doctor encounters suspicion and a dark secret when he rents a house in Cuba. Dick Powell, Jay Novello and Raymond Burr star. Dick Powell and Beverly Washburn appear in "Autumn Carousel," about a TV writer who finds inspiration from a little girl travelling to Los Angeles. 59 min.
09-2223 Was $24.99 ***$19.99***

Four Star Playhouse: Masquerade (1954)/ Face Of Danger (1955)
In "Masquerade," a costume ball during the New Orleans Mardi Gras turns sour when the family hosting the festivities discovers that their cousin has escaped from jail. Ida Lupino and John Bryant star. "Face of Danger" concerns a 100-year-old woman who recalls her romance with a desperado during the days of the old West. Ida Lupino and Dick Foran star. 59 min.
09-2210 Was $24.99 ***$14.99***

Four Star Playhouse: Second Dawn (1954)/ My Wife Geraldine (1952)
It's a double feature of "Four Star Playhouse" dramas starring Charles Boyer. "Second Dawn" concerns a blind man who is given a chance at sight by a doctor of question, and "My Wife Geraldine" tells of a man suspected of killing his wife...who may have never existed in the first place! With Porter Hall and Una Merkel. 58 min. total.
09-2972 ***$14.99***

Four Star Playhouse: Looking Glass House (1955)/ With All My Heart (1955)
Ida Lupino is featured in two dramas from the great, early days of television: a woman is surprised when her fiancé turns out to have been married before in "House," and an overweight woman watches her doctor boyfriend marry someone else in "Heart." 59 min.
09-2322 ***$14.99***

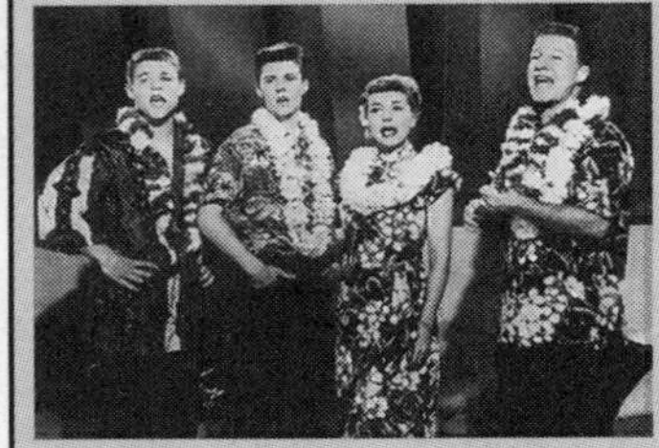

The Best Of Ozzie And Harriet
Here come the Nelsons! Suburban homeowner Ozzie, wife Harriet, and sons Ricky and David are back for more vintage hi-jinks, mix-ups and songs by Ricky in the fondly-remembered series that ran from 1952 to 1966 and ranks as TV's longest running situation comedy. Each volume features two episodes and runs about 60 min.

The Best Of Ozzie And Harriet, Vol. 1
Includes "A Rose a Day" and "Bedtime Story."
10-9342 Was $19.99 *$14.99*

The Best Of Ozzie And Harriet, Vol. 2
Includes "Dave's Car Payment" and "Ozzie Keeps a Secret."
10-9343 Was $19.99 *$14.99*

The Best Of Ozzie And Harriet, Vol. 3
Includes "Lamp for Dave and June" and "No News for Harriet."
10-9344 Was $19.99 *$14.99*

The Best Of Ozzie And Harriet, Vol. 4
Includes "A Letter About Harriet" and "The Petition."
10-9345 Was $19.99 *$14.99*

The Best Of Ozzie And Harriet, Vol. 5
Includes "Little Black Box" and "Handprints in the Sidewalk."
10-9346 Was $19.99 *$14.99*

The Best Of Ozzie And Harriet, Vol. 6
Includes "Little House Guest" and "Dave's Golf Story."
10-9347 Was $19.99 *$14.99*

The Best Of Ozzie And Harriet, Vol. 7
Includes "Suggestion Box" and "The Law Clerk."
10-9348 Was $19.99 *$14.99*

The Best Of Ozzie And Harriet, Vol. 8
Includes "Boy's Paper Route" and "Barking Dog."
10-9349 Was $19.99 *$14.99*

The Best Of Ozzie And Harriet, Vol. 9
Includes "The Girl That Loses Things" and "The Table and the Painting."
10-9350 Was $19.99 *$14.99*

The Best Of Ozzie And Harriet, Vol. 10
Includes "Jealous Joe Randolph" and "Manly Arts."
10-9351 Was $19.99 *$14.99*

The Best Of Ozzie And Harriet, Vol. 11
Includes "Kelly's Important Papers" and "Old Friend of June's."
10-9352 Was $19.99 *$14.99*

The Best Of Ozzie And Harriet, Vol. 12
Includes "A Question of Suit and Ties" and "The Trip Trap."
10-9353 Was $19.99 *$14.99*

The Best Of Ozzie And Harriet, Vol. 13
Includes "Dave Goes Back to Work" and "The Prowler."
10-9354 Was $19.99 *$14.99*

The Best Of Ozzie And Harriet, Vol. 14
Trouble brews when the boys each want "Separate Rooms," and blooms when Harriet receives "Orchids and Violets."
10-1253 Was $19.99 *$14.99*

The Best Of Ozzie And Harriet, Vol. 15
Will "Pills" help Ozzie beat Thorny in a weight loss contest, and which son will he pick for the "Father and Son Tournament"?
10-1324 Was $19.99 *$14.99*

The Best Of Ozzie And Harriet, Vol. 16
John Carradine guests to lead the Nelsons in "An Evening with Hamlet," and Jerry Mathers shows up at the front door on "Halloween."
10-1325 Was $19.99 *$14.99*

The Best Of Ozzie And Harriet, Vol. 17
Ozzie doesn't take kindly to the new "Hair Style for Harriet," and later breaks the sound barrier as a "Jet Pilot."
10-1326 Was $19.99 *$14.99*

The Best Of Ozzie And Harriet, Vol. 18
"Ricky the Drummer" becomes the singing star at the local teen dance. Next, Ozzie volunteers to lead some kids on "The 14-Mile Hike."
10-1327 Was $19.99 *$14.99*

The Best Of Ozzie And Harriet, Vol. 19
The laughs take to sea when Ozzie plans "A Cruise for Harriet," while back home "Rick's Dinner Guests" arrive the same night as Ozzie's poker game.
10-1328 Was $19.99 *$14.99*

The Best Of Ozzie And Harriet, Vol. 20
When "David Goofs Off" it's sure to rouse the ire of boss Joe Flynn. Next, the Nelsons get a "Little House Guest."
10-1329 Was $19.99 *$14.99*

The Best Of Ozzie And Harriet, Vol. 21
"David Hires a Secretary," but the gorgeous coed who applies isn't exactly what he had in mind. Next, Ricky gets in trouble with his gal in "Girl Who Loses Things."
10-1330 Was $19.99 *$14.99*

The Best Of Ozzie And Harriet, Vol. 22
There's no time for partying when "The Fraternity Rents Out a Room" to prof Wally Cox, and when Ricky is "Making Wally Study."
10-1331 Was $19.99 *$14.99*

The Best Of Ozzie And Harriet, Vol. 23
"An Old Friend Of June's" means green-eyed trouble for David. Next, "Kris Plays Cupid" for Wally and Ginger.
10-1332 Was $19.99 *$14.99*

The Best Of Ozzie And Harriet, Vol. 24
Ozzie and Harriet are stuck in the middle when "Rick's Raise" at work is in the hands of David. Then, the Oz cooks up a storm for "Breakfast for Harriet."
10-1333 Was $19.99 *$14.99*

The Best Of Ozzie And Harriet, Vol. 25
David and June have it over a Hawaiian vacation in "The Trip Trap," followed by Ozzie "Flying Down to Lunch" in...Mexico?
10-1334 Was $19.99 *$14.99*

The Best Of Ozzie And Harriet, Vol. 26
David and Ricky, too, in two complete episodes: "Ricky's Horse" and "Ozzie the Babysitter." 55 min.
09-1232 Was $19.99 *$14.99*

The Best Of Ozzie And Harriet, Vol. 27
Ricky wants a baking company to honor its money-back guarantee in "The Pancake Mix." In "The New Chairs" a mix-up results in the Nelsons getting dozens of chairs from the department store. 55 min.
01-5021 Was $19.99 *$14.99*

The Best Of Ozzie And Harriet, Vol. 28
In "The Pajama Game," Ozzie and neighbor Thorny wind up locked out of the house in their pajamas. Then Ozzie's plan to clean out the garage snowballs into a neighborhood mess in "Ball of Tin Foil." 55 min.
01-5022 Was $19.99 *$14.99*

The Best Of Ozzie And Harriet, Vol. 29
A sudden urge for "Tutti-Fruiti Ice Cream" sends Ozzie on a madcap search throughout the town. Next, it's Ozzie's old jalopy against Ricky's hot-rod in "Road Race." 55 min.
01-5023 Was $19.99 *$14.99*

The Best Of Ozzie And Harriet, Vol. 30
There are chills and thrills at "The Circus," with David and Ricky performing on the high wire. Next, Ricky's involved in college frat hi-jinks in "The Blue Moose." 55 min.
01-5024 Was $19.99 *$14.99*

The Best Of Ozzie And Harriet, Vol. 31
"The Big Dog" is what Ricky buys wife Kris for her birthday, but she doesn't want it. Next, Ricky gets into hot water at the office thanks to "The Desk Photo." 55 min.
01-5025 Was $19.99 *$14.99*

The Best Of Ozzie And Harriet, Vol. 32
Ricky and his friend Wally spend their Christmas money vying for the romantic attentions of "The Girl at the Emporium." Next, "David Picks up the Tab" for his parents' dinner, but comes up short. 55 min.
01-5026 Was $19.99 *$14.99*

Reilly: Ace Of Spies (1983)
Decades before James Bond was a gleam in Ian Fleming's eye, British undercover agent Sydney Reilly set the tone for all subsequent superspies with his daring real-life exploits. Sam Neill stars as Reilly in this acclaimed BBC mystery series.

Reilly: Ace Of Spies, Vol. 1
Reilly enters Manchuria to gather information on the Russian fleet for Japan in "Prelude to War." "The Visiting Fireman" finds him infiltrating a German shipyard in search of plans for a new naval gun, while British oil deposits are the prize sought in "Anna." Jeanne Crowley, Leo McKern, David Suchet co-star. 154 min.
44-2101 □*$14.99*

Reilly: Ace Of Spies, Vol. 2
A contract to build a new fleet of warships for the Russian government offers Reilly both professional and monetary rewards when he attempts to land it for a German client, but the master spy's affair with a Russian official's wife could cost him far more, in "Dreadnoughts and Crosses" and "Dreadnoughts and Doublecrosses." Then, Reilly returns to Moscow with a plot to overthrow Lenin—and set himself in charge—in "Gambit." With Leo McKern, Hugh Fraser. 151 min.
44-2102 □*$14.99*

Reilly: Ace Of Spies, Vol. 3
Reilly's plan to topple the Soviet Bolshevik government is uncovered and has him fleeing for his life with an ally back to London and then New York, where they become involved with a secret anti-Communist organization, in "Endgame," "After Moscow" and "The Trust." Clive Merrison, Tom Bell, Hugh Fraser also star. 153 min.
44-2103 □*$14.99*

Reilly: Ace Of Spies, Vol. 4
There's little time for happiness for Reilly and his new wife Pepita when the assassination of Russian co-conspirator Savinkov sends Reilly back to Moscow for a final challenge to the members of the Trust, and a dangerous battle of wills with Soviet leader Joseph Stalin, in "The Last Journey" and "Shut Down." With Clive Merrison, Laura Davenport, David Burke. 102 min.
44-2104 □*$14.99*

Reilly: Ace Of Spies: Complete Set
Eleven episodes of the "Reilly" TV series are also available in this four-tape collector's set.
44-2105 Save $5.00! □*$54.99*

Reilly: Ace Of Spies (1983)
He was the British WWI agent whose amazing (and true) exploits made him the first international superspy, and years later served as the model for James Bond! Sam Neill ("A Cry in the Dark") is Reilly in this thrilling British production. 80 min.
44-1675 Was $89.99 *$14.99*

Wildside (1985)
"The A-Team" was transplanted to the Old West in this short-lived 1985 adventure series. Five residents of Wildside County, California, form a vigilante team to keep the peace and bring in the frontier's most dangerous outlaws. Among the heroes were fast-gun rancher William Smith, explosives expert Howard E. Rollins, Jr., veterinarian and rope whiz Terry Funk, and feisty newspaper owner Meg Ryan. All six episodes are included in a three-tape set. 286 min. total.
08-8823 *$39.99*

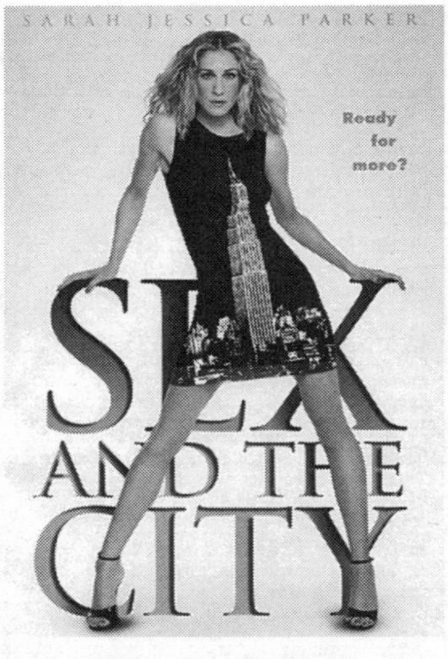

Sex And The City: The Complete First Season Boxed Set (1998)
The city is New York, where newspaper writer Sarah Jessica Parker finds much meat for her columns on modern-day dating and mating habits through the entangled encounters she and gal pals Kim Cattrall, Kristin Davis And Cynthia Nixon have with the opposite sex, in this outrageously provocative HBO series. All 12 episodes from the show's first season are featured in this three-tape set. 6 hrs. total.
44-2226 □*$39.99*

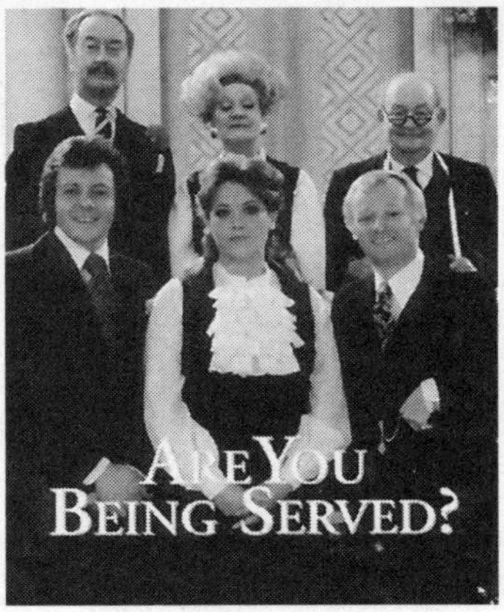

Are You Being Served?
Anyone shopping for laughs should be sure to stop by Grace Brothers, a London department store whose zany staff specializes more in serving comedy than customers. Mollie Sugden, Trevor Bannister, John Inman and Wendy Richard star in the popular BBC series which ran from 1972 to 1983. Each tape features three episodes and runs about 90 min.

Are You Being Served?, Vol. 1
Includes "Dear Sexy Knickers...," "Our Figures Are Slipping" and "Camping In."
04-2522 Was $19.99 *$14.99*

Are You Being Served?, Vol. 2
Includes "Big Brother," "His and Hers" and "Cold Comfort."
04-2523 Was $19.99 *$14.99*

Are You Being Served?, Vol. 3
Includes "German Week," "New Look" and "No Sale."
04-3427 *$14.99*

Are You Being Served?, Vol. 4
Includes "Wedding Bells," "Do You Take This Man?" and "The Erotic Dreams of Mrs. Slocombe."
04-3428 *$14.99*

Are You Being Served?, Vol. 5
Includes "Fifty Years On," "Oh What a Tangled Web" and "Forward Mr. Grainger."
04-3429 *$14.99*

Are You Being Served?, Vol. 6
Includes "Happy Returns," "Founder's Day" and "The Old Order Changes."
04-3582 *$14.99*

Are You Being Served?, Vol. 7
Includes "Mrs. Slocombe Expects," "A Change Is as Good as a Rest" and "The Club."
04-3583 *$14.99*

Are You Being Served?: Gift Set
Here's a bargain even Grace Brothers would be hard-pressed to match: all seven volumes in a boxed collector's set, plus the special tape "The Best of Are You Being Served?," hosted by John Inman.
04-3754 *$99.99*

The Best Of Are You Being Served?
Some of the most hilarious moments from the hit "Britcom" have been collected in this best-of program. Laugh non-stop as the employees and customers of London's daffiest department store run into all sorts of wacky predicaments. The segments are held together by conversations between Mr. Humphries and his "mum." With John Inman, Mollie Sugden and Frank Thornton. 78 min.
04-3957 *$19.99*

Are You Being Served?: Special Holiday Edition
The halls of Grace Brothers are decked with laughter with this collection of Yuletide-themed episodes. Let Captain Peacock, Mr. Humphries, Mrs. Slocombe and the rest brighten your holidays in "Christmas Crackers," "The Father Christmas Affair" and the long-lost "Top Hat and Tails," making its American debut here. 90 min.
04-3536 *$14.99*

The Hitchhiker's Guide To The Galaxy (1981)
"Don't Panic!" The British TV adaptation of Douglas Adams' cult sci-fi book series follows the misadventures of Arthur Dent, sole survivor of the demolished Earth. Join Dent and interplanetary researcher Ford Prefect as they encounter bad alien poetry, depressed robots, two-headed rocket thieves and the Restaurant at the End of the Universe. Simon Jones, David Dixon and Sandra Dickinson star. 194 min. total.
04-2999 *$19.99*

The Making Of The Hitchhiker's Guide To The Galaxy
Follow the star-crossed development of Douglas Adams' "Hitchhiker" series from British radio to best-selling books to TV mini-series in this light-hearted "behind the scenes" documentary. Included are never-broadcast scenes, an exclusive interview with Adams, and much more. 60 min.
04-2704 *$14.99*

The Flame Trees Of Thika: Complete Set (1981)
Based on the best-selling autobiographical book by Elspeth Huxley, this moving, four-volume "Masterpiece Theatre" series follows a British family's experiences on a coffee plantation in colonial Kenya in the early 1910s, as seen through the eyes of the young daughter. Holly Aird, Hayley Mills, David Robb and Ben Cross star. Seven episodes on four tapes; 353 min. total. NOTE: Individual volumes available at $14.99 each.
44-2106 Save $10.00! *$49.99*

Yes, Minister
Civil service has rarely been less civil than in this razor-sharp British comedy series that follows the convoluted games played within the corridors of political power. Paul Eddington, Nigel Hawthorne star. Except where noted, each tape contains three episodes and runs about 90 min.

Yes, Minister, Vol. 1
Includes "Open Government," "The Official Visit," "The Economy Drive" and "Big Brother."
04-3667 *❑$19.99*

Yes, Minister, Vol. 2
Includes "The Writing on the Wall," "The Right to Know" and "Jobs for the Boys."
04-3668 *❑$19.99*

Yes, Prime Minister
Opportunistic government official Sir James Hacker takes up residence at No. 10 Downing Street, and British politics will never be the same, in this continuation of the satirical saga begun in "Yes, Minister." Paul Eddington, Nigel Hawthorne and Derek Fowlds star. Except where noted, each tape contains three episodes and runs about 90 min.

Yes, Prime Minister: The Grand Design
Includes "The Grand Design," "The Ministerial Broadcast" and "The Smoke Screen."
04-2468 Was $19.99 *$14.99*

Yes, Prime Minister: The Key
Includes "The Key," "A Real Partnership" and "A Victory for Democracy."
04-2469 Was $19.99 *$14.99*

Yes, Prime Minister: Bishop's Gambit
Includes "Bishop's Gambit," "One of Us" and "Man Overboard."
04-2524 Was $19.99 *$14.99*

Yes, Prime Minister: Official Secrets
Includes "Official Secrets," "A Diplomatic Incident" and "A Conflict of Interest."
04-2525 Was $19.99 *$14.99*

Yes, Prime Minister: Power To The People
Includes "Power to the People," "Patron of the Arts," "National Education Service" and "A Tangled Web." 117 min.
04-2689 Was $19.99 *$14.99*

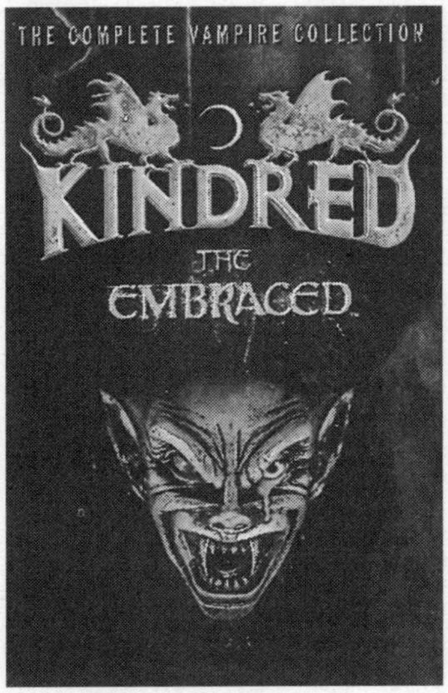

Kindred: The Embraced: The Complete Vampire Collection (1996)
One part Anne Rice and one part Mario Puzo, this gothic-flavored story of supernatural suspense is set in a San Francisco where five vampire "families" vie for control of the city and its human residents, and the forbidden romances that develop between the living and the living dead. C. Thomas Howell, Mark Frankel, Kelly Rutherford and Brian Thompson star. This three-tape boxed set includes the complete series, plus an unaired episode never before seen. 377 min. total.
63-1905 *❑$39.99*

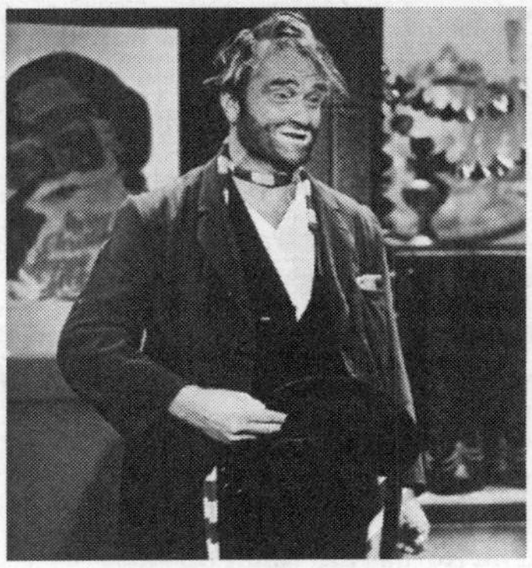

The Red Skelton Show, Vol. 1
Fans of Clem Kadiddlehopper and Sheriff Deadeye looking for old Skeltons in the closet will appreciate this gem, with classic movie character actors Edward Everett Horton and Reginald Denny.
10-7477 Was $19.99 *$14.99*

The Red Skelton Show, Vol. 2
"Greetings, gents. I say, greetings, that is." There's twice the laughter in this twin presentation from Red's popular variety series. A special guest in one episode is fellow CBS series host Ed Sullivan. "Goodnight, and may God bless." 60 min.
10-7546 Was $19.99 *$14.99*

The Red Skelton Show, Vol. 3
Red plays host to Chester Morris, Veda Ann Borg and Vincent Price. 60 min.
10-8201 Was $19.99 *$14.99*

The Red Skelton Show, Vol. 4
Red teams up for fun with Carol Channing, Peter Lorre, Charlie Ruggles and Marie Windsor. 60 min.
10-8202 Was $19.99 *$14.99*

The Red Skelton Show, Vol. 5 (Holiday Time)
Two classic holiday shows with Red Skelton celebrating Thanksgiving and Christmas. 60 min.
10-8203 Was $19.99 *$14.99*

The Red Skelton Show, Vol. 6
Red welcomes Mickey Rooney and Buster Crabbe to the proceedings. 60 min.
10-8324 Was $19.99 *$14.99*

The Red Skelton Show, Vol. 7
Red Skelton presents the 1954 Look Magazine Awards to such notables as Walt Disney, Edmond O'Brien, Alfred Hitchcock, Jack Lemmon and Judy Garland in this special installment of his show. And Marilyn Maxwell joins Red in another funny episode. 60 min.
10-9838 *$14.99*

The Red Skelton Show, Vol. 8
George Raft guests in a funny show that finds Red involved with a gangster's moll. Also, Red plays Clem Kadiddlehopper and welcomes John Carradine and Franklin Pangborn to his farm. 60 min.
10-9839 *$14.99*

The Red Skelton Show, Vol. 9
Red plays Clem Kadiddlehopper in a hilarious entry thet features the classic skit "Rupert the Stupert" and guest stars Jane Powell and Charlie Ruggles. 60 min.
10-9840 *$14.99*

The Red Skelton Show, Vol. 10
In these two shows from 1953 and 1958, Red welcomes Nat "King" Cole and The King Cole Trio, and Nancy Walker. 60 min.
10-9990 *$14.99*

Red Skelton Comedy Classics 3-Pack
See three classic episodes from Red's long-running comedy/variety show in this three-volume boxed set. Skelton matches wits (and ad libs) with Martha Raye, has a comic confrontation with boxer Archie Moore, and runs afoul of favorite Hollywood bad guys Vincent Price and Jackie Coogan. 3 hrs. total.
05-5053 *$19.99*

Red Skelton: His Many Faces Of Comedy
The most popular characters of TV's clown prince, Red Skelton, are presented in this hilarious compilation. Laugh aloud when Red plays Freddy the Freeloader, San Fernando Red, Clem Kadiddlehopper, Deadeye and others. Classic TV hilarity at its best! 40 min.
08-8475 *$12.99*

The Red Skelton Show/ The Popsicle Parade Of Stars
Two prime examples of early TV comedy/variety. First, the only Red to stay on the air in the '50s is joined by special guest star Nancy Walker, followed by a rare video appearance of the legendary Fanny Brice on the musical series sponsored by the makers of that "quiescently frozen confection." 45 min.
10-7449 Was $19.99 *$14.99*

A Concert In Pantomime
Red Skelton and Marcel Marceau, two masters of pantomime, team up for a wonderful evening of humor sans dialogue. Classic moments from classic entertainers. 60 min.
10-8154 Was $19.99 *$14.99*

The Jack Benny Show
Features the season-ending episodes from 1951 and 1953. Joining Jack and regulars are special guests Bob Hope and Bing Crosby, George Burns and Martin and Lewis. 60 min. total.
01-5061 Was $19.99 *$14.99*

Jack Benny Visits Walt Disney
Special has Jack visiting the Disney Studios to beg some free passes to Disneyland from Walt Disney himself. Along the way they meet guest stars like Bob Hope and The Beach Boys and take part in a hilarious spoof of "Mary Poppins." 60 min.
01-5109 Was $19.99 *$14.99*

The Jack Benny Show With Liberace
It's a musical and comedic aggregation unparalleled when that violin-playing legend, Jack Benny, is joined by the '50s most famous pianist in a rib-tickling episode from Benny's beloved series.
05-5023 *$14.99*

Jack Benny Show, Vol. 3
Two hilarious shows from 1943. The first features Don Wilson, Rochester, Kirk Douglas and Dick Powell. The second features Bob Crosby and guest Humphrey Bogart. 58 min.
09-1743 Was $19.99 *$14.99*

Jack Benny, No. 1
Humphrey Bogart spoofs gangster movies, playing a killer named "Baby Face" in the first episode. Then Jack is a lunch counter attendant who encounters two thugs in "Lunch Counter Murder" with Dan Duryea.
09-5293 *$14.99*

Jack Benny, No. 2
In the "Hong Kong Suit," Jack's cheapness scares clippers away at the barber shop. Giselle MacKenzie also appears and sings "Smile" and plays "Fascination" with Jack. Next, Fred Allen and Jack joust over air time when Fred misses rehearsal. Eddie Cantor makes a cameo appearance.
09-5294 *$14.99*

Jack Benny, No. 3
Bob Crosby breaks into Jack's monologue and sings while Jack plays violin with Dorothy Shea in a hillbilly sketch. And in "Jack Found Mary," Jack tells an interviewer how he met Mary Livingstone, with Sheldon Leonard making an appearance. Plus, Rochester sings and dances with The Sportsmen Quartet.
09-5295 *$14.99*

Jack Benny, No. 4
Bing Crosby and George Burns guest and Bob Hope makes a cameo in this program that has Jack telling Don Wilson about his days in vaudeville. Bing even sings "Gypsy" and takes a wild ride in Jack's hammock. And Jack's monologue is interrupted by Margaret Truman, Bob Crosby sings "Peter Pan," and Jack faces two crooks in the collection's second episode.
09-5296 *$14.99*

Jack Benny, No. 5
In "Jack Casting for TV Special," Jack writes his life story, then hires a child agent who works cheap. Also, in "The Story of the New Talent Show," Jack is joined by Jayne Mansfield, Mel Blanc as Mr. Fingue, a judo expert and a three-member quartet.
09-5297 *$14.99*

Jack Benny, No. 6
Jack goes Christmas shopping but has trouble deciding on a gift in a holiday episode that also features Dennis Day singing "Rudolph the Red-Nosed Reindeer." And "Don's Anniversary" features a gala celebration for announcer Don Wilson's 27th anniversary with Jack; guests include John Daly, Howard McNair and Nancy Kulp.
09-5298 *$14.99*

Jack Benny, No. 7
Jack teams with Liberace in this funny program in which Jack takes the place of Lib's brother George for a concert performance of "September Song." And Bob Hope steals Jack's pants, then joins him in a jungle skit called "Road to Nairobi." A cameo appearance is made by Martin and Lewis.
09-5299 *$14.99*

Jack Benny, No. 8
While he and Rochester will be away on a personal appearance, "Jack Rents His House" in order to collect some "easy" cash. Next, Jack is awakened by a disc jockey at "4 O'clock in the Morning," and later has to go shopping with Mary.
09-5300 *$14.99*

Jack Benny, No. 9
In the first episode, Jack discovers that a young girl who wants his autograph plays the violin better than him. Julie London is also featured, and she chips in and flirts with Jack. Also includes an ultra-rare episode featuring Marilyn Monroe in her first TV appearance as Jack's dreamgirl on a Hawaiian vacation. A collector's treasure from 1953!
09-5301 *$14.99*

The Jack Benny Show/ The Dennis Day Show
An example of the Jack Benny program with guest Bob Hope, plus a look at its popular spin-off, "The Dennis Day Show" centering on the Hollywood bachelor life of Jack's underpaid house tenor. Cliff Arquette co-stars as Charley Weaver.
10-7515 Was $19.99 *$14.99*

The Jack Benny Show
Well! Here's a bargain that Jack would certainly appreciate, a double feature from his beloved TV series. Joining Jack, Rochester, Don, Mary and the gang is special guest star Jayne Mansfield, followed by the 1953 New Year's show. 60 min.
10-7553 Was $19.99 *$14.99*

The Jack Benny Show: The Kingston Trio
Jack hosts popular folkies The Kingston Trio, who perform "Tijuana Jail" in a bit and "I'm Going Home." Also featured is the classic "Sy/Si/Sue" routine with Mel Blanc. NOTE: The print of this rare find ends before the show's conclusion. 52 min.
10-9862 *$19.99*

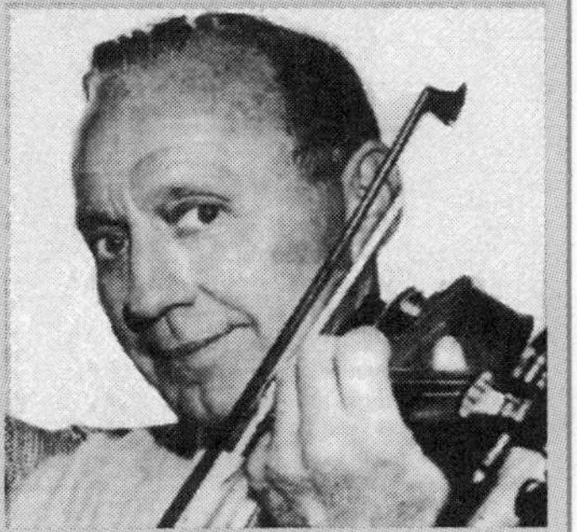

THE JACK BENNY PROGRAM

The Jack Benny Program
These classic installments from "The Jack Benny Program" originally aired on CBS and NBC in the 1960s and featured the great deadpan penny-pincher in hilarious situations with featured performers Eddie "Rochester" Anderson and Don Wilson, and various guest stars. Each tape includes two episodes and runs about 60 min.

The Jack Benny Program, Vol. 1: Johnny Carson Guests/ Jack Takes Boat To Hawaii
A young Johnny Carson sings, dances, plays the drums and talks to Jack; and Jack's trip to Hawaii includes meetings with Jayne Mansfield and Schlepperman.
07-2097 *$14.99*

The Jack Benny Program, Vol. 2: The Peter Lorre-Joanie Sommers Show/ The Smothers Brothers Show
Peter Lorre and Joanie Sommers guest in an episode in which Jack attempts to treat his cold, but discovers that his doc is a plastic surgeon. Next, the Smothers Brothers relive a bombing raid on London in which Jack entertained servicemen.
07-2098 *$14.99*

The Jack Benny Program, Vol. 3: The Income Tax Show/ Jack Adopts A Son
It's Benny vs. the IRS over a $3.90 dinner deduction, with Jimmy Stewart guest-starring; followed by Jack welcoming new son Marvin (who looks suspiciously like Milton Berle) home.
07-2099 *$14.99*

The Jack Benny Program, Vol. 4: Jack On Trial For Murder/ Jack Plays Tarzan
After Jack gets in trouble for having a chicken that makes noises, he dreams lawyer Raymond Burr loses his case. And Jack's violin playing forces three gorillas to go wacko while Jane threatens to leave him in a Tarzan sketch with Carol Burnett as a guest star.
07-2100 *$14.99*

The Jack Benny Program, Vol. 5: Jack Is Kidnapped/ The Lucille Ball Show
Jack becomes the victim in a comic abduction, with guest star George Burns. Following that, Jack and Lucy restage the midnight ride of Paul Revere—with hilarious results.
07-2101 *$14.99*

The Jack Benny Program, Vol. 6: The Christmas Show/ The Railroad Station
"The Christmas Show" features Jack and Rochester on a gift-buying spree; while in "The Railroad Station," Benny, Rochester and Don Wilson prepare for a trip to New York—and Jack cancels the milk, electricity, and newspaper! With Richard Deacon, Mel Blanc.
07-1190 *$14.99*

Classic Kid Vid

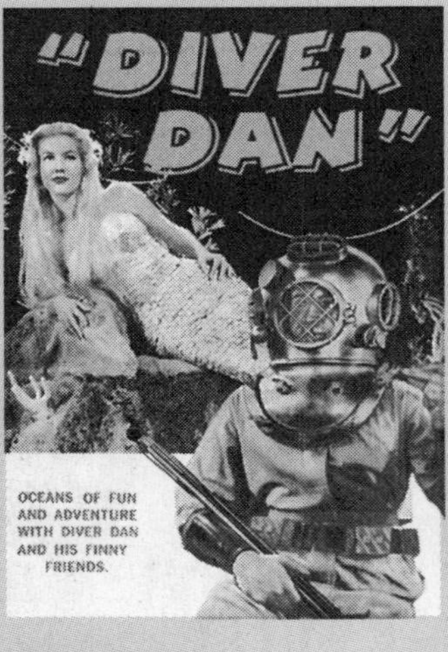
"DIVER DAN"
OCEANS OF FUN AND ADVENTURE WITH DIVER DAN AND HIS FINNY FRIENDS.

Diver Dan (1961)
Shot in Philadelphia, this syndicated children's series featured human performers interacting with marionettes. Dan was a deep-sea explorer who, along with fishy friends Finely the Haddock, Skipper Kipper, and Minerva the mermaid, protects the seas from evil Baron Barracuda and his allies. Each tape features eight episodes runs about 55 min.

Diver Dan, Vol. 1
A glass fish bowl leads to trouble in "Hard Water"; the ever-bold Diver Dan inadvertantly saves "Goldie the Goldfish" from Baron Barracuda;Dan finds a world full of "Talking Fish"; the race is on to find "Skipper's Gold"; Dan fends off Baron and Trigger on the "Treasure Ship"; endangered Dan awaits a "Sawfish Rescue"; Dan seeks the stolen "Shell-O-Phone"; and Dan confronts "The Octopus" in a cave.
10-9875 Was $19.99 *$14.99*

Diver Dan, Vol. 2
Diver, Doc and Finley face an octopus' "Murder Ink"; Dan and the Glowfish delve into a "Bottomless Pit"; Dan and Doc face a scary "Teetering Rock"; Dan prepares for "Baron's Capture" when the fish tries to swipe a pearl; Baron is recaptured in "An Unusual Treasure"; Baron's release unleashes "Trigger's Revenge"; Horace becomes a judge in "An Unusual Fish"; and "The Verdict" is reached.
09-5406 *$14.99*

Diver Dan, Vol. 3
"Horace's Dilemma" becomes problematical and the Baron escapes from prison; Dan uses "The Trap" to try and stop the Baron; "The Trap Is Sprung" and Baron is loose, while Horace thinks Dan wants him; Dan tries to figure out the "Riddle of the Hermit Crab" for help; Dan discovers Horace is stuck in "Sargasso Sea" seaweed; "Dan and Finley get "Lost in the Sargasso Sea"; Dan and crew think they've steered clear of danger in "Current Flow"; and Dan and pals are trapped under Teetering Rock in "The Storm."
09-5407 *$14.99*

Diver Dan, Vol. 4
Thanks to "Goldie's Heroism," Diver Dan gets the fuse to the dynamite; Dan explodes the rock with "Dynamite"; Skipper Kipper is imprisoned by the Baron on a pirate ship in "Ghost Is Clear"; pirate ghost "Captain Barney" stops the Baron; the "Lost City" of Atlantis is unearthed by an earthquake; Dan is freed by an unlikely fish in "Secret of the Throne"; a sea snake provides a "Crawling Danger" to Dan; and an old bomb is mistaken for a "Strange Fish" by Finley and Georgie.
09-5408 *$14.99*

Diver Dan, Vol. 5
Diver Dan tries to defuse "The Bomb" as Baron and Trigger plan an attack; Sgt. Major discovers "The Bubbling Pit," an underwater volcano; while Dan and Sgt. Major to stop "The Volcano," Baron and Trigger nab Doc Sturgeon; Dan comes to the rescue while the volcano is collapsed in "Depth Charge"; Dan teaches Finley and Doc a few lessons in "School Daze"; Horace gets caught in "Strange Vines"; and the Baron and Trigger lure Diver Dan into trouble with a magnetic rock in "The Magnet."
09-5409 *$14.99*

Super Circus (1952)
Go back in time—and back under the "big top"—with four episodes of the early kidvid favorite that brought top circus acts onto the small screen. Claude Kirshner is your ringmaster, Mary Hartline his beautiful bandleader aide, and Cliffy, Nicky and Scampy provide the clowning. 115 min.
82-1030 Was $24.99 *$19.99*

Time For Beany
He's still lovable and harmless, but the original Cecil the Sea Serpent is anything but armless—he's a live-action sock puppet worn on the hand of creator Bob Clampett. Two episodes of the '50s kidvid hit, with the voices of Stan Freberg, Jerry Colonna and Daws Butler. 35 min.
01-9029 *$19.99*

Ding Dong School
An episode of the classic '50s program of crafts and games for preschoolers with hostess Miss Frances (Dr. Frances Horwich). 60 min.
01-9031 *$19.99*

The Gumby Show With Pinky Lee/Smilin' Ed
Featured is a 1957 episode of "The Gumby Show" in which Pinky Lee, the ex-burlesque comic, makes his last series television appearance. Also, grandfatherly Smilin' Ed McConnell reads an adventure of Guga Ram the Indian Boy on the show that became "Andy's Gang." 60 min.
01-9032 *$19.99*

The Paul Winchell Show/ Foodini The Great
The festive Christmas edition of ventriloquist Paul Winchell's children's program sees Paul and Jerry Mahoney (his famous lap dummy) on a mission to Mars. Also, an episode of comic misadventure with Foodini, a marionette magician. 60 min.
01-9040 *$19.99*

The Rootie Kazootie Show/ Howdy Doody For President
Puppet kid Rootie Kazootie gets help from the studio audience when his rival, Poison Zoomack, uses a magnet to steal the polka dots from Polka Dottie's dress. Also, Howdy Doody runs for President against Mr. X in an episode that started a national Howdy write-in craze. 60 min.
01-9041 *$19.99*

The Howdy Doody Show, Vol. 1
Join Clarabell the Clown as he travels around the country, appearing in parades and seeing fans. Then Howdy, Buffalo Bob and their pals enjoy a visit from "that ol' sidewindin' crocker crooker" Gabby Hayes. 60 min.
10-9455 *$14.99*

The Howdy Doody Show, Vol. 2
Two great programs with '50s America's favorite puppet are presented: "Corny Cobb Goes to Paris" and "Howdy Doody's Christmas." 50 min.
10-8329 Was $19.99 *$14.99*

Howdy Doody, Vol. 1: Music Appreciation
See Buffalo Bob, Clarabell, Mayor Phineas T. Bluster and other members of the "Doody" clan play musical games and have fun with xylophones, guitars and other instruments.
76-7468 *$14.99*

Howdy Doody, Vol. 2: Dilly Dally's Birthday
It's a special occasion with the whole gang as they celebrate Dilly Dally's birthday. Join Buffalo Bob, Howdy and special guest Sandra the Witch for lots of surprises.
76-7469 *$14.99*

Miami Vice: The Movie (1984)
The exciting pilot film that spawned the hit TV series and set new fashion trends in America. Don Johnson and Philip Michael Thomas are the unlikely detective duo, one from the South, one from the big city, who team up to bust a drug-smuggling ring in the streets of Miami. 99 min.
07-1377 *$14.99*

Miami Vice: The Prodigal Son (1985)
The action moves from the shores of Miami to the streets of New York, as detectives Crockett and Tubbs travel to the Big Apple to infiltrate and bust an East Coast drug operation. Don Johnson, Philip Michael Thomas and Pam Grier. 99 min.
07-1426 *$14.99*

The U.S. Steel Hour: P.O.W. (1953)
The premiere episode of this highly successful early drama concerns a wounded Korean War veteran who suffers both physical and emotional scars from his time in a North Korean prison camp. Richard Kiley, Gary Merrill, Phyllis Kirk and Brian Keith star. 52 min.
09-3136 *$19.99*

The U.S. Steel Hour: No Time For Sergeants (1955)
Andy Griffith became a star as naive hillbilly-turned-Army recruit Will Stockdale (a role he'd later repeat on Broadway and in the movies) in this live TV comedy. With Eddie LeRoy, Harry Clark; written by Ira Levin. 50 min.
09-1725 *$19.99*

The Burns And Allen Show
After delighting audiences on vaudeville, in movies and on radio, George Burns and Gracie Allen's antics were broadcast on CBS from 1950 to 1958. Watch as Gracie's scatter-brained solutions to daily life drive a harried George to talk directly to the audience in this classic sitcom. Bea Benaderet, Ronnie Burns and Harry Von Zell also star. Except where noted, each tape features two episodes and runs about 55 min.

The Burns And Allen Show: Meet George And Gracie
Includes "Columbia Pictures Doing Burns and Allen Story" and "Gracie Doing a Picture Without George."
02-2948 *$12.99*

The Burns And Allen Show: Gracie And The Mob
Includes "George and Gracie Hear a Burglar" and "Gracie Sees a Holdup."
02-2949 *$12.99*

The Burns And Allen Show: Gracie Knows Best
Includes "Gracie Buying a Ranch for George" and "Von Zell's Girlfriend Between Friends."
02-2950 *$12.99*

The Burns & Allen Show 3-Pack
"Meet George & Gracie," "Gracie & the Mob" and "Gracie Knows Best" are also available in a boxed collector's set.
02-2969 Save $14.00! *$24.99*

Burns And Allen: Gracie Gives A Wedding
Includes "Gracie Gives a Wedding" and "Gracie's Vegetarian Plot."
10-7371 Was $19.99 *$14.99*

The George Burns And Gracie Allen Show, Vol. 1
Gracie's bookkeeping causes problems when the taxman stops by, while George performs at his baker's banquet. And Gracie and Blanche Morton (Bea Benaderet) think George's new secretary is a sexy blonde. Includes original commercials.
10-9690 *$14.99*

The George Burns And Gracie Allen Show, Vol. 2
When their neighbors go on vacation, George and Gracie take care of their 17-year-old daughter, who teaches them how to dance. Also, George gets bad news when a banker calls about Gracie's checking account. Includes original commercials.
10-9691 *$14.99*

The George Burns And Gracie Allen Show, Vol. 3
A salesman tries to sell encyclopedias to Gracie, while George and Harry Von Zell attempt to teach the gals how to play cards so they can go to the fights. Includes original commercials.
10-9692 *$14.99*

The George Burns And Gracie Allen Show, Vol. 4
When the Burns household is invaded by three young girls who love to play spacemen, George gets upset he can't get any work done. And funny situations ensue when Gracie's wardrobe woman wins a free trip to Hawaii.
10-9693 *$14.99*

The George Burns And Gracie Allen Show, Vol. 5
When Gracie agrees to allow a woman's daughter to get married at her house, George has to foot the bill in the episode that introduced Harry Von Zell to the show. Next, Gracie gets a visit from a tax assessor, George and Gracie go to a football game, and Gracie tries to hide the dent she put in the car. Includes original commercials.
10-9694 *$14.99*

The Burns And Allen Show, Vol. 1 (1952)
Burns and Allen make for nonstop laughs in this double feature from one of TV's best-loved sitcoms. First, Gracie's writing antics get her and George in Dutch with gangster Sheldon Leonard. Next, Gracie believes she and George aren't legally married, and friend Jack Benny helps straighten out the mess. 60 min.
02-1519 Was $19.99 *$14.99*

George Burns: A Century Of Laughter
The life of one of the entertainment industry's most-loved performers is feted in this terrific video. Rare footage of the great Burns' early burlesque days and TV appearances are presented with other career highlights. There's also special guest stars like Wayne Newton, Jack Benny, Bobby Vinton, Betty Grable and others. 102 min,
10-2718 *$14.99*

The Burns And Allen Show
Three early episodes from the perennially popular domestic comedy are featured: "Property Tax Assessor," "Teenage Girl Spends Weekend" and "Space Patrol Girl." Say goodnight, Gracie! 90 min.
01-1452 Was $29.99 *$14.99*

Burns And Allen Christmas
Join George and Gracie, their son Ronnie and the Mortons for two Christmas celebrations. In "Company for Christmas," Gracie poses as a hotel cleaning woman and the holiday gets wackier by the second. And in "Christmas in Jail," Gracie's desire for a pearl necklace lands George in the clink. 45 min.
02-2262 *$14.99*

Tate
One of the more unusual heroes in the TV western corral was 1960's Tate (David McLean), a gunslinger whose left arm was crippled in the Civil War and encased in a black leather sling. Wandering from town to town, Tate's gun prowess took his "able-bodied" foes by surprise. Each tape features four episodes and runs about 110 min.

Tate, Vol. 1
Includes "The Mary Harden Story," "A Reckoning," "A Quiet Storm" and "The Return of Jessica Jackson."
83-7005 *$19.99*

Tate, Vol. 2
Includes "Hometown," "Stop Over," "Voice of the Town" and "A Lethal Pride."
83-7006 *$19.99*

TV's Best Adventures Of Superman, Vol. 1
"Faster than a speeding bullet, more powerful than a locomotive..." George Reeves is the Kryptonian crusader in classic episodes from the '50s TV series. See the Man of Steel's beginnings in "Superman on Earth," and watch Jimmy Olsen and Lois Lane get their own powers in "All That Glitters." Plus, the first Fleischer Superman cartoon from 1941. 60 min. total.
19-1607 Was $19.99 *$14.99*

TV's Best Adventures Of Superman, Vol. 2
The "never-ending battle for Truth, Justice, and the American way" continues, as a criminal genius plots a Metropolis "Crime Wave" and a gang of lead-masked crooks threaten the Daily Planet staff in "Perils of Superman." George Reeves, Noel Neill, Jack Larson, John Hamilton star. Also includes the animated Superman short "Mechanical Monsters." 60 min. total.
19-1608 Was $19.99 *$14.99*

TV's Best Adventures Of Superman, Vol. 3
George Reeves returns, using "powers and abilities far beyond those of mortal men" to fight for freedom in two action-filled episodes. A meteor heading for Earth and an amnesiac Man of Steel add up to disaster in "Panic in the Sky," then a mad scientist puts Metropolis on ice in "Big Freeze." The '40s Superman cartoon "Magnetic Telescope" is included. 60 min. total.
19-1623 Was $19.99 *$14.99*

TV's Best Adventures Of Superman, Vol. 4
"Look, up in the sky..." It's "double trouble" times two when a crime boss impersonates Superman in "Face and the Voice," then cub reporter Jimmy Olsen meets his twin in "Jimmy the Kid." Classic TV fun with George Reeves, Noel Neill, Jack Larson; also features "Showdown," a Fleischer animated Superman short. 60 min. total.
19-1622 Was $19.99 *$14.99*

Superman: The Lost Episodes
Two rare finds from the Man of Steel's early TV career that were never broadcast. First is 1954's "Stamp Day for Superman," a special Treasury Department film with George Reeves and company pitching Savings Stamps, followed by the actual pilot for an unmade 1961 "Superboy" series. 55 min.
62-1336 *$19.99*

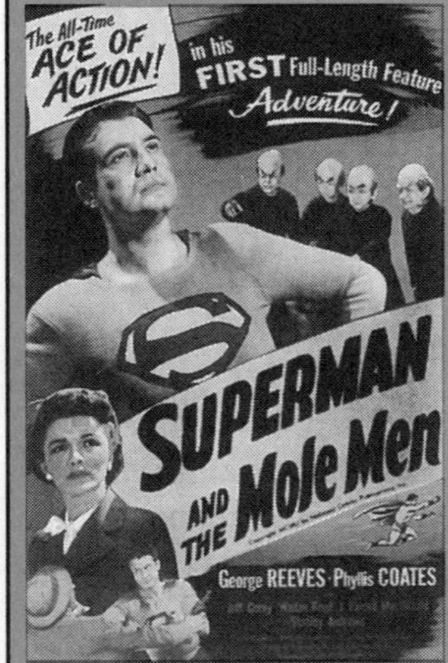
The All-Time ACE OF ACTION!
in his FIRST Full-Length Feature Adventure!
SUPERMAN AND THE Mole Men
George REEVES · Phyllis COATES

Superman And The Mole-Men (1951)
George Reeves stars as the Man of Tomorrow, who has his hands full when a race of dwarfish subterranean creatures "invade" a small town via an oil shaft...and the panicked townspeople are on the verge of rioting. Supe's first feature film, later edited into two episodes of the TV series, is restored in its entirety. With Phyllis Coates, Jeff Corey. 58 min.
19-1586 Was $19.99 *$14.99*

The Steve Allen Plymouth Show (1960)
"The Steve Allen Show" and its multi-talented host originated the famous "Man on the Street Interview" and launched dozens of TV careers. This episode from the Detroit-sponsored incarnation features guests Ginger Rogers and Tony Bennett. 60 min.
10-2137 *$14.99*

Steve Allen's 75th Birthday Celebration (1997)
Comic, actor, lecturer, author, songwriter...Steve Allen has done it all. On the occasion of his 75th birthday, friends and admirers such as Jackie Mason, Milton Berle, David Letterman and Jayne Meadows fete Steve, and classic film clips showcase some of his greatest bits. Special home video version features footage not shown in the original PBS airing. 90 min.
53-9954 *$19.99*

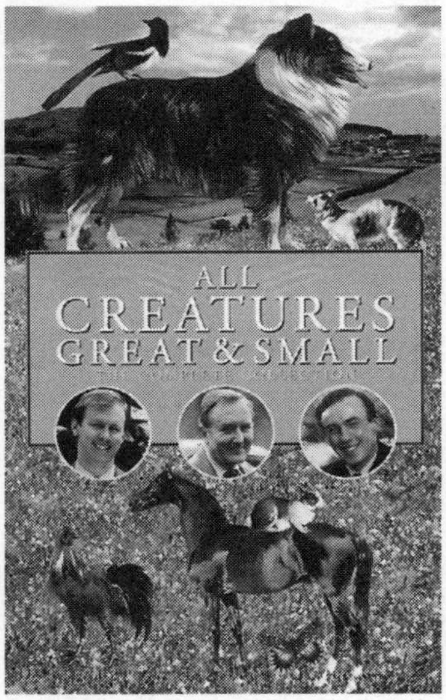

All Creatures Great And Small (1978)
The warm, whimsical stories of British veterinarian James Herriot come to home video with this acclaimed BBC series. Christopher Timothy stars as Herriot, who leaves veterinary school in the 1930s and moves to the Yorkshire countryside to assist a temperamental local animal doctor. With Robert Hardy, Peter Davison, Carol Drinkwater.

All Creatures Great And Small: The Complete Collection
Included in this six-tape set are "Horse Sense/Dog Days," "It Takes All Kinds/Calf Love," "Out of Practice/Nothing Like Experience," "Golden Lads and Girls/Advice and Consent," "The Last Furlong/Sleeping Partners" and "Bulldog Breed/Practice Makes Perfect/Breath of Life." 10 1/2 hrs. total. NOTE: Individual volumes available at $19.99 each.
04-3680 Save $20.00! *❏$99.99*

All Creatures Great And Small 2: The Complete Collection
Included in this six-tape set are "Cats & Dogs/Attendant Problems/Fair Means Foul," "The Beauty of the Beast/Judgement Day/Faint Hearts," "Tricks of the Trade/Pride of Possession," "The Name of the Game/Puppy Love," "Ways & Means/Pups, Pigs & Pickles" and "A Dog's Life/Merry Gentlemen." 11 hrs. total.
04-3873 *❏$99.99*

All Creatures Great And Small 3: The Complete Collection (1980)
Included in this six-tape set are "Plenty to Grouse About/Charity Begins at Home/Every Dog His Day...," "Hair of the Dog/If Wishes Were Horses/Pig in the Middle," "Be Prepared/A Dying Breed," "Brink of Disaster/Home and Away," "Alarms and Excursions/Matters of Life and Death" and "Will to Live/Big Steps and Little 'Uns." 12 hrs. total.
19-5011 *❏$99.99*

All Creatures Great And Small (1975)
Originally made for TV and later released in theatres, this first film version of the beloved James Herriot books stars Simon Ward as the young veterinarian in '30s England. Taking a job in the rural Yorkshire region, Ward becomes assistant to veteran animal doctor Anthony Hopkins and wins the trust of the locals—and the heart of farmer's daughter Lisa Harrow. 90 min.
08-8836 *$14.99*

All Creatures Great And Small (1986)
In this feature-length follow-up to the acclaimed TV series, veterinatian James Herriot (Christopher Timothy) returns to his practice in rural England after World War II, renewing old friendships and loves and rediscovering the peace his work gave him. With Carol Drinkwater, Peter Davison, Robert Hardy. 94 min.
04-3125 *❏$19.99*

When Things Were Rotten, Vol. 1 (1975)
Mel Brooks' riotous send-up of the Robin Hood legend, one of the wildest sitcoms ever, comes to home video. Dick Gautier stars as a stumblebum Robin Hood, his misfit Merry Men are Dick Van Patten and Bernie Kopell and Maid Marian is Misty Rowe. Guest stars in these three episodes include Dudley Moore and Sid Caesar. 78 min.
06-1346 Was $39.99 *$14.99*

Roots (1977)
The landmark TV mini-series, winner of seven Emmys, that traced the black experience in America through the struggles of one family from slavery to freedom is finally available in one boxed set. Based on Alex Haley's best-seller, the program's impressive cast includes LeVar Burton, Lou Gossett, Jr., Ed Asner, Lorne Greene, Ben Vereen, Leslie Uggams and Georg Stanford Brown. Complete and uncut on six tapes. 570 min.
19-2005 *$149.99*

Roots: The Next Generations (1979)
The saga continues in this Emmy-winning sequel that stretches from the Reconstruction era to the 1960s and culminates with writer Alex Haley's visit to the African homeland of his ancestors. James Earl Jones stars as Haley; with Georg Stanford Brown, Henry Fonda, Olivia de Havilland, Ossie Davis, Ruby Dee, Al Freeman, Jr. as Malcolm X and Marlon Brando as George Lincoln Rockwell. Complete and uncut on seven tapes. 685 min.
19-2004 *$149.99*

Roots: The Gift (1988)
LeVar Burton and Lou Gossett, Jr. reprise their roles as Kunta Kinte and Fiddler in this acclaimed holiday-themed drama, based on Alex Haley's writings. The pair risk their lives one Christmas Eve to help a group of runaway slaves escape to freedom via the Underground Railroad. Michael Learned, Avery Brooks co-star. 94 min.
19-2011 Was $19.99 *$14.99*

Queen (1993)
"Roots" author Alex Haley visited his family's past once again to tell the story of his grandmother Queen, the illegitimate daughter of a slave and a white plantation owner, who is freed following the Civil War and passes for white for a time, before racism and personal crises drive her to a nervous breakdown. This dramatic mini-series stars Halle Berry in the title role; with Tim Daly, Danny Glover, Jasmine Guy, Martin Sheen, Paul Winfield. 282 min. on three tapes.
19-2489 *$39.99*

The Fall & Rise Of Reginald Perrin: The Beginning (1976)
A comedy for everyone who's ever wanted a second chance at life, this cult favorite British series stars Leonard Rossiter as Reggie Perrin, a dissatisfied, middle-aged dessert company salesman whose problems in the office and at home drive him to the drastic step of faking his own drowning death and returning under the new persona of Martin Wellbourne. With Pauline Yates, John Barron. This three-tape set includes the first seven episodes. 210 min. total.
53-6146 *$59.99*

The Fall & Rise Of Reginald Perrin 2: The Next Bit (1978)
The identity crisis continues, as "Martin Wellbourne" not only takes Reggie's old job at Sunshine Desserts, but also marries his "widow," Elizabeth. Things get sticky when Reggie reveals the truth and is promptly fired, until he hits upon a new business idea: selling overpriced, useless things to people. Can he handle the success? Leonard Rossiter stars. Seven episodes on three tapes. 210 min. total.
53-6147 *$59.99*

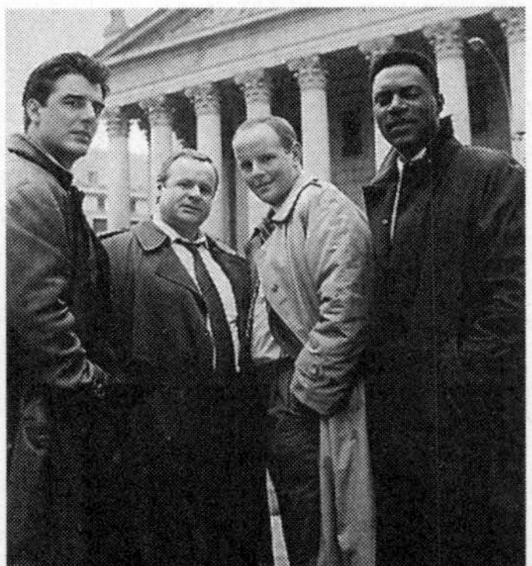

Law & Order: Producer's Collection
Crime (the police department) and punishment (the D.A.'s office) in New York City were the focus of this Emmy-winning drama series that premiered in 1990. Six of the best episodes—"Indifference/Manhood," "Conspiracy/Sanctuary" and "American Dream/White Rabbit"—have been gathered in a three-tape boxed set. Jill Hennessy, Jerry Orbach, Michael Moriarty, Sam Waterston star.
07-2789 *$24.99*

The Black Adder
Hilarious historical spoof from Britain starring Rowan Atkinson as the snivelling, scheming Prince Edmund, second in line to his father's throne in medieval England and forever plotting to seize power. With Brian Blessed, Tony Robinson. Each tape contains three episodes and runs about 95 min.

The Black Adder, Vol. 1
04-2471 *$14.99*

The Black Adder, Vol. 2
04-2472 *$14.99*

Black Adder II
Rowan Atkinson as Edmund Blackadder is back, this time serving as an advisor to the befuddled Queen Elizabeth I, in the continuing lampoon of English history. Tony Robinson, Stephen Fry, and Miranda Richardson as Queen Bess co-star. Each tape contains three episodes and runs about 90 min.

Black Adder II, Parte The First
04-2518 *$14.99*

Black Adder II, Parte The Seconde
04-2519 *$14.99*

Black Adder III
Return once more to merrie olde England of the late 1700s, where the dimbulb Prince of Wales' only hope of staying alive is his quick-witted, avaricious manservant, Edmund Blackadder. Rowan Atkinson, Hugh Laurie and Tony Robinson star. Each tape contains three episodes and runs about 90 min.

Black Adder The Third, Part I
04-2293 *❏$14.99*

Black Adder The Third, Part II
04-2363 *❏$14.99*

Black Adder Goes Forth
The setting is the Western Front of World War I, as the hysterical historical saga of the Blackadder clan concludes. Rowan Atkinson, Tony Robinson, Hugh Laurie star as the army men who'll do anything to avoid the taste of combat. Each tape contains three episodes and runs about 90 min.

Black Adder Goes Forth, Vol. 1
04-2520 *$14.99*

Black Adder Goes Forth, Vol. 2
04-2521 *$14.99*

The Complete Black Adder
All 24 outrageous episodes from the four "Black Adder" series have been collected, along with exclusive, never-before-seen footage, in this deluxe eight-tape collector's set.
04-3248 Save $20.00! *$99.99*

Blackadder's Christmas Carol
Take a laugh-filled look at Christmas through centuries past and into the future with the Blackadder families in this spoof of the Charles Dickens favorite. Rowan Atkinson, Robbie Coltrane, Tony Robinson, Hugh Laurie and Miranda Richardson star. 45 min.
04-2573 Was $19.99 *$14.99*

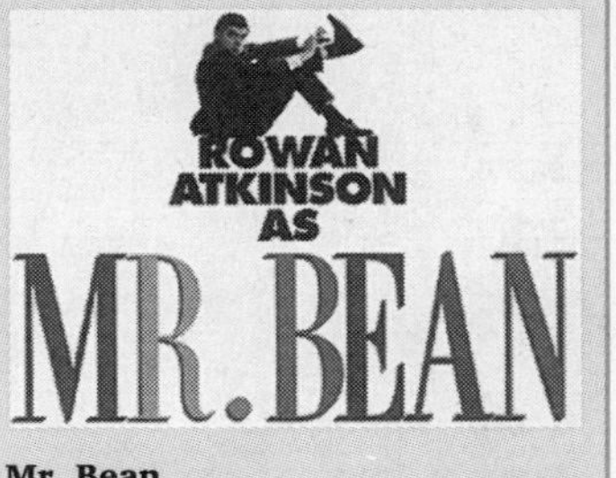

Mr. Bean
British comic Rowan Atkinson ("The Black Adder," "Four Weddings and a Funeral") is hilarious as the trouble-plagued Mr. Bean, an ordinary fellow who can't stop getting himself into funny predicaments ranging from a visit to the dentist to a fateful encounter with Queen Elizabeth.

The Amazing Adventures Of Mr. Bean
Includes "Mr. Bean," "The Return of Mr. Bean" and the home-video exclusive "The Library." 61 min.
02-8406 Was $19.99 *$14.99*

The Exciting Escapades Of Mr. Bean
Features "The Curse of Mr. Bean," "Mr. Bean Goes to Town" and the home-video exclusive "The Bus Stop." 60 min.
02-8407 Was $19.99 *$14.99*

The Terrible Tales Of Mr. Bean
Includes "The Trouble with Mr. Bean" and "Mr. Bean Rides Again." 50 min.
02-8470 Was $19.99 *$14.99*

The Perilous Pursuits Of Mr. Bean
Features "Mind the Baby, Mr. Bean" and "Do-It-Yourself Mr. Bean." 50 min.
02-8471 Was $19.99 *$14.99*

The Merry Mishaps Of Mr. Bean
Includes "Merry Christmas Mr. Bean" and "Mr. Bean in Room 426." 52 min.
02-8553 Was $19.99 *❏$14.99*

Unseen Bean
This special "Mr. Bean" adventure features Rowan Atkinson's put-upon character in the never-aired-on-TV episode, "Hair by Mr. Bean of London." 30 min.
02-8612 Was $19.99 *$14.99*

The Best Bits Of Mr. Bean
This isn't any ordinary plate of re-fried "beans," but a rib-tickling sampler of the funniest moments from Rowan Atkinson's acclaimed comedy series. 60 min.
02-8613 Was $19.99 *$14.99*

Rowan Atkinson Live! (1991)
In a laugh-filled stage appearance in Boston, "Black Adder" and "Mr. Bean" star Rowan Atkinson offers up a wide array of comedic characterizations and side-splitting sketches. 60 min.
02-8690 *$19.99*

Lonesome Dove (1989)
A sweeping story of a dangerous cattle drive from Texas to Montana, this Emmy-winning program features incredible action sequences, beautiful photography and expert acting from a cast that includes Robert Duvall, Tommy Lee Jones, Robert Urich, Danny Glover, Ricky Schroder and Anjelica Huston. Based on Larry McMurtry's Pulitzer Prize-winning novel. 4 hrs.
58-5032 *❏$14.99*

Return To Lonesome Dove (1993)
This sequel to the smash hit mini-series stars Jon Voight as Woodrow Call, the aging former Texas Ranger who teams with fellow ex-Ranger Gideon Walker (William Petersen) to drive a herd of wild mustangs to a ranch in Montana, 2,500 miles away. During the trek, the men encounter deceit, Indians and romance. With Rick Schroder, Lou Gossett, Jr. and Barbara Hershey.
58-5121 *❏$14.99*

Streets Of Laredo (1995)
Larry McMurtry's "Lonesome Dove" saga continues in this sprawling western saga that mixes fictional characters with such real-life frontier legends as John Wesley Hardin and Judge Roy Bean. James Garner, Sissy Spacek and Sam Shepard head up an all-star cast that also includes Ned Beatty, Sonia Braga, Randy Quaid, Wes Studi.
58-5202 *❏$14.99*

Dead Man's Walk (1996)
The stirring and exciting prequel to "Lonesome Dove" introduces the characters Gus McCrae and Woodrow Call as young Texas Rangers battling outlaws, bandits and Buffalo Hump, a dangerous Comanche warrior, while on the Santa Fe Trail. F. Murray Abraham, Keith Carradine, Brian Dennehy, David Arquette and Jonny Lee Miller head the cast.
58-5231 *❏$14.99*

Lonesome Dove Trilogy Gift Set
This boxed collector's set features "Lonesome Dove," "Streets of Laredo" and "Dead Man's Walk."
58-5252 Save $5.00! *$39.99*

V: The Original Miniseries (1983)
The acclaimed sci-fi drama that spawned the hit TV series tells of Earth's first encounter with the Visitors, advanced alien beings whose human-like faces hide their reptilian forms, and whose claims of peace hide a plan for subjugating mankind. Marc Singer, Jane Badler, Faye Grant and Robert Englund star in this special effects-filled epic. 190 min.
19-2236 Was $79.99 *❏$24.99*

V: The Final Battle (1984)
A brave band of freedom fighters, having learned the alien Visitors' true reasons for coming to Earth, begins a struggle to expose the truth and free the planet from their scaly clutches. The exciting second mini-series in the "V" saga stars Jane Badler, Faye Grant, Michael Durrell and Robert Englund. 285 min. on three tapes.
19-2380 Was $69.99 *❏$29.99*

The Colgate Comedy Hour: Spike Jones (1950)
The Plaid Puccini made his first leading TV appearance as one of the rotating hosts of Colgate's early '50s variety show, tearing up song standards with typical irreverence before surrendering the stage to less frenetic singers Nat King Cole and Bobby Van.
10-7522 Was $19.99 *$14.99*

The Colgate Comedy Hour (1953)
Host Eddie Cantor appears in comedy skits as "Maxie the Taxi" and a Jewish cowboy, and welcomes musical guests Eddie Fisher and Frank Sinatra. 59 min.
09-1119 Was $19.99 *$14.99*

The Colgate Comedy Hour: Anything Goes (1954)
Heaven knows, you'll love this early TV production of Cole Porter's classic musical/comedy. Stars Ethel Merman and Frank Sinatra, ably supported by Bert Lahr and Sheree North. 53 min.
09-1110 *$19.99*

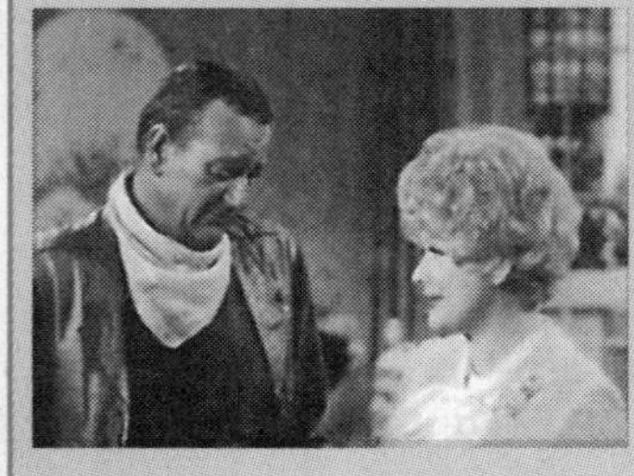

The Lucy Show
Through its six-year run on CBS from 1962 to 1968, the First Lady of Television Comedy's second sitcom went through a series of drastic cast and format changes, but one thing remained constant: Lucy's signature brand of slapstick comedy, which each week was wrapped around a special guest or crazy plot line. Co-stars Gale Gordon as Mr. Mooney. Each volume includes two episodes and runs about 55 min.

The Lucy Show, Vol. 1
When Viv's singing group loses its soprano, the girls give Lucy the nod, provided she take singing lessons, in "Lucy's Barbershop Quartet." And Lucy and Viv become plumber's little hinderers when they try to install their own shower stall, in "Lucy and Viv Put in a Shower."
10-9465 *$14.99*

The Lucy Show, Vol. 2
The restless redhead whips up one comical mishap after another when she meets the one and only John Wayne on the set of his new movie, in "Lucy and John Wayne." And military mayhem erupts for the Marines when Lucy is accidentally drafted, in "Lucy Gets Caught in the Draft," with a surprise guest star.
10-9466 *$14.99*

The Lucy Show, Vol. 3
The Danfield First National Bank will need more than a waffle iron to lure the business of pinch-penny Jack Benny. Will Lucy's sales pitch of a burglarproof vault do the trick, in "Lucy Gets Jack Benny's Account"? Then, with Lucy in his corner, ex-pug Don Rickles tries to make enough money to open a flower shop, in "Lucy the Fight Manager."
10-9467 *$14.99*

The Lucy Show, Vol. 4
In "Lucy and George Burns," the octogenarian comic selects Lucy as his partner in his act. And Lucy becomes a sailor in order to get Mr. Mooney to sign important papers while he's on reserve duty in "Lucy and the Submarine."
10-9933 *$14.99*

The Lucy Show, Vol. 5
Lucy tries to cash in on a special offer from a bean company in "Lucy and the Bean Queen," which guest stars Ed Begley. Next, in "Lucy and Paul Winchell," the wacky redhead tries to get the famous ventriloquist (who appears as himself) for a benefit show.
10-9934 *$14.99*

The Lucy Show, Vol. 6
Lucy can't get Mrs. Mooney's diamond ring off of her finger in "Lucy and the Ring-A-Ding Ding." Plus, "Lucy Flies to London" after winning a dog food contest; Pat Priest from "The Munsters" guest stars.
10-9935 *$14.99*

The Lucy Show, Vol. 7
In this two-part package, Carol Burnett is a librarian who answers Lucy's ad for a roommate in "Lucy Gets a Roommate." And Lucy joins Carol's musical act in Palm Springs in "Lucy and Carol in Palm Springs," which features guest star Dan Rowan.
10-9936 *$14.99*

The Lucy Show, Vol. 8
Lucy and Mr. Mooney are hypnotized by nightclub hypnotist Pat Collins in "Lucy and Pat Collins." And when Lucy thinks Mr. Mooney keeps turning into an ape, she decides it's time to see a psychiatrist in "Lucy and the Monkey."
10-9937 *$14.99*

The Lucy Show, Vol. 9
In "Lucy's Substitute Secretary," Lucy disguises herself as different people in order to spy on a temp who wants her job. Ruta Lee guest stars. Also, Lucy and Vivian Vance dress up as hippies and check out Sunset Strip in "Viv Visits Lucy."
10-9938 *$14.99*

The Lucy Show, Vol. 10
In "Lucy and Robert Goulet," Lucy persuades a truck driver (played by guess who) to enter a Robert Goulet look-alike contest. Guests include Mary Wickes, Lucie Arnaz. And "Lucy Meets the Law" when she's mistaken for a shoplifter named the "Red Flash." Claude Akins guests.
10-9939 *$14.99*

The Lucy Show, Vol. 12
In order to get a country singer's account for her bank, Lucy stages a hoe-down in "Lucy Meets Tennessee Ernie Ford." Next, "Lucy Meets Sheldon Leonard," but mistakes the famous producer and film tough guy for a crook.
10-9941 *$14.99*

The Lucy Show, Vol. 13
In "Lucy and the Efficiency Expert," an efficiency expert working at the bank attempts to hire Lucy as his assistant; Phil Silvers guest stars. And in "Lucy Meets the Berles," Lucy suspects Uncle Miltie is having an affair with Ruta Lee.
10-9942 *$14.99*

The Lucy Show, Vol. 14
"Lucy Gets Trapped" when she calls in sick for work, but is captured in a photographer's picture as a store's 10 millionth customer. And Lucy falls for a suave Gallic actor in "Lucy and the French Movie Star."
10-9943 *$14.99*

The Lucy Show, Vol. 15
In "Lucy the Star Maker," Lucy attempts to help Mr. Cheever's nephew get into show business; Frankie Avalon guest stars. Then, Lucy disguises herself as an old lady to date a former president of the bank in "Little Old Lucy"; Dennis Day is the guest star.
10-9944 *$14.99*

Lucy And Desi: A Home Movie
Lucie Arnaz hosts this Emmy-winning documentary that weaves together home movies taken by her famous parents, interviews with friends and colleagues, and her own personal remembrances for a portrait of their life together as the First Couple of TV's golden age. Special video edition includes footage not shown on TV. 111 min.
22-1356 *$19.99*

Lucy: Queen Of Comedy
A nostalgic tribute to everybody's favorite redhead, this wonderful video features the one and only Lucy in appearances with the Marx Brothers, Bob Hope, the Three Stooges, Henry Fonda and other stars, vintage TV spots on "I've Got a Secret" and other quiz shows, and hilarious moments from "I Love Lucy." 60 min.
05-5003 *$14.99*

Lucy's Lost Episodes
This video offers Lucille Ball in funny guest appearances from TV shows throughout the 1950s. Featured are Lucy with Ed Sullivan on "Toast of the Town," Lucy and Desi Arnaz stumping the panel on "What's My Line?," and the daffy redhead on "The Bob Hope Show" with Desi and William Frawley. Also showcased is a look at the Desilu Studio and movie footage shot by Ken Murray. 83 min.
10-2636 *$12.99*

Dick Tracy: The Lost TV Episodes
Ralph Byrd stars as the famed detective in these episodes from the action-packed TV show that ran on ABC in 1950-51. With Joe Devlin as sidekick Sam Catchem. Each tape features two programs and runs 60 min.

Dick Tracy, Vol. 1
In "Dick Tracy Meets Flattop" the tough detective is kidnapped by his arch-nemesis. Next Tracy discovers that a furniture store is a front for criminal activity in "Dick Tracy vs. Heels Beels."
10-1395 Was $19.99 *$14.99*

Dick Tracy, Vol. 2
Who's been stealing those cars? Tracy finds out in "Hi, Jack." And the detective uncovers a counterfeiting scheme overseen by "The Mole" in another thrilling episode.
10-1396 Was $19.99 *$14.99*

Dick Tracy, Vol. 3
In the two-episode adventure "Dick Tracy vs. the Foreign Agents," the super cop battles enemy agents looking for trouble with the U.S.
10-1397 Was $19.99 *$14.99*

Dick Tracy, Vol. 4
Dick Tracy and bad dude Shakey race to recover loot from a robbery in "Shakey's Secret Treasure." "A Dick Tracy Sampler" features scenes from the detective's greatest movie moments.
10-1398 Was $19.99 *$14.99*

The Adventures Of Kit Carson
Follow the thrilling adventures of Western adventurer Kit Carson, who kept the law on the frontier with help from his Mexican sidekick, El Toro. Bill Williams and Don Diamond star in these sagebrush classics that ran from 1951 to 1955. Each tape runs about 50 min. There are 12 volumes available, including:

The Adventures Of Kit Carson, Vol. 1
Includes "Thunder Over Inyo" and "Road to Monterey."
10-8304 Was $19.99 *$14.99*

The Adventures Of Kit Carson, Vol. 2
Features "Singing Wires" and "Devil's Angels Camp."
10-8305 Was $19.99 *$14.99*

The Adventures Of Kit Carson, Vol. 3
Features "Feud in San Filipe" and "Bad Men of Narysville."
10-8306 Was $19.99 *$14.99*

The Adventures Of Kit Carson, Vol. 4
Features "Spoilers of California" and "Heroes of Hermosa."
10-8307 Was $19.99 *$14.99*

The Master Detectives: Holmes And Chan
Two of the most famous sleuths of all time are back to back in episodes from their '50s TV series. First is Ronald Howard in deerstalker and cape as "The Neurotic Detective," then J. Carrol Naish is the Oriental manhunter in "Blind Man's Bluff." 55 min.
01-5110 Was $19.99 *$14.99*

The New Adventures Of Charlie Chan
Two inscrutable episodes with Inspector Charlie Chan, who was transplanted from Honolulu to London for this British-made series. Irishman J. Carrol Naish joins a long line of non-Asians to star as the impeccably mannered sleuth.
68-8359 Was $19.99 *$14.99*

Christy (1994)
Based on the best-selling Catherine Marshall novel, this warm and winning family drama series starred Kellie Martin as Christy Huddleston, a young woman who moves to a rural Tennessee town in 1912 to teach school and finds her life forever changed by the residents. The cast includes Randall Batinkoff, Tyne Daly, Tess Harper.

Christy
The feature-length pilot film follows novice mission teacher Christy and the tremendous hardships she faces upon her arrival in the poverty-stricken Great Smoky Mountain community of Cutter Gap, Tennessee. 90 min.
10-2544 *$19.99*

Christy: A Closer Walk/Second Sight
Christy must help David when a series of crises have him questioning his calling to be a preacher. Next, a student's claim of foreseeing disaster may come true when the school's financial future is threatened. 93 min.
10-2740 Was $19.99 *$14.99*

Christy: The Sweetest Gift
The Thanksgiving celebration in Cutter Gap could be a very somber one when late rainfall ruins the Autumn harvest, but while Christy joins Miss Alice in an effort to make sure no family goes hungry, a surprise visit from Christy's father forces her to make a difficult decision. 90 min.
10-2741 Was $19.99 *$14.99*

Frontier Doctor
Shown in syndication in 1958, this western drama starred Rex Allen as Dr. Bill Baxter, a dedicated physician helping pioneers in Rising Springs, Arizona, in the early 1900s. Each tape features two episodes and runs about 50 min. There are seven volumes available, including:

Frontier Doctor, No. 1
Includes "San Francisco Story" and "Drifting Sands."
10-9907 Was $19.99 *$14.99*

Frontier Doctor, No. 2
Includes "The Crooked Circle" and "Fury in the Big Top."
10-9908 Was $19.99 *$14.99*

Frontier Doctor, No. 3
Includes "Trouble in Paradise" and "Flaming Gold."
10-9909 Was $19.99 *$14.99*

Frontier Doctor, No. 4
Includes "Outlaw Legion" and "A Twisted Road."
10-9910 Was $19.99 *$14.99*

Frontier Doctor, No. 5
Includes "Queen of the Cimarron" and "Danger Valley."
10-9911 Was $19.99 *$14.99*

Frontier Doctor, Vol. 1
Includes "Gringo Pete" and "Homesteaders."
10-9397 *$14.99*

Frontier Doctor, Vol. 2
Includes "The Black Stallion" and "San Francisco Story."
10-9398 *$14.99*

Ramar Of The Jungle
This "pithy" children's adventure show was a sensation when it ran in syndication in the early '50s. Jon Hall played Dr. Tom Reynolds, the son of missionaries, who fought poachers and other bad guys and earned the name "Ramar of the Jungle" from the natives of Africa and India he helped. Each tape features two episodes and runs about 50 min.

Ramar Of The Jungle, Vol. 1
Includes "The Flaming Mountain" and "Evil Strangers."
10-9206 *$19.99*

Ramar Of The Jungle, Vol. 2
Includes "Evil Trek" and "Contraband."
10-9207 *$19.99*

Ramar Of The Jungle, Vol. 3
Includes "Jungle Terror" and "Striped Fury."
10-9208 *$19.99*

Ramar Of The Jungle/ The White Avengers
Two-fisted medicine man Jon Hall protects an African village from "Evil Strangers" in an episode of the popular "Ramar" series. Next, cowboy brother duo Billy and Bob White team up with "world's smartest dogs" Timber and Lobo in the Old West as "The White Avengers." 60 min.
10-7325 *$19.99*

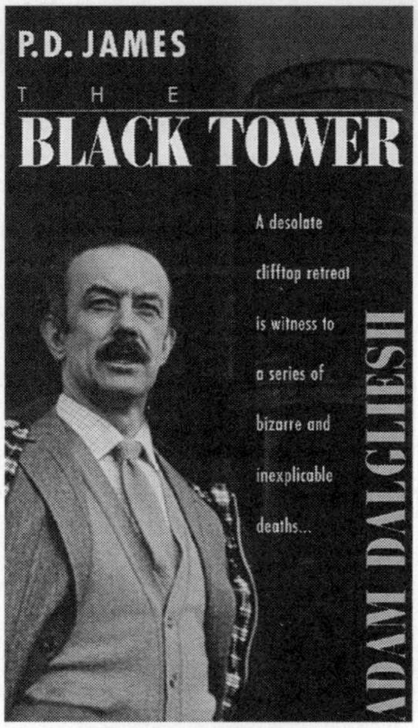

The Black Tower (1985)
Roy Marsden excels as P.D. James' Scotland Yard inspector Adam Dalgliesh in this gripping suspenser. While resting after being wounded, Dalgliesh visits a friend on a leisurely trip, but the vacation turns into terror when the inspector encounters blackmail, murder and a bizarre dark tower on a cliff. With Art Malik, Pauline Collins. 527 min. on three tapes.
50-8552 *$49.99*

Bobby Darin Collection
More vintage TV appearances by the chart-topping pop star, including clips from "The Ed Sullivan Show" and "The Judy Garland Show," are featured in this collection. Darin performs "Mack the Knife," "Dream Lover," "That's How It Goes" and others, including "You Make Me Feel So Young" with Connie Francis, "Sing Sing Sing" with Garland and Bob Newhart (!), and more. 77 min.
10-8161 *$19.99*

Bobby Darin In London
Live from the Palladium, it's Bobby belting out his best-loved tunes in front of an enthusiastic British crowd. Along with such songs as "Don't Rain on My Parade," "Quarter to Nine," "Mack the Knife" and "If I Were a Carpenter," Darin also entertains the audience with imitations of Gable, Lancaster and Martin and Lewis! 50 min.
10-8162 *$19.99*

Bobby Darin: The Darin Invasion
The late, great singer Bobby Darin pulls out all the stops in this exciting, tune-filled special. Linda Ronstadt and George Burns add songs and wit to this classic 1970s show. 60 min.
22-7073 Was $19.99 *$14.99*

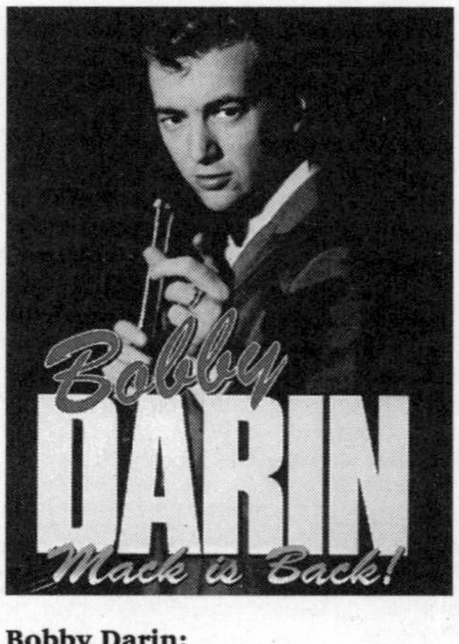

Bobby Darin: Mack Is Back! (1973)
Taped a few months before his death during open-heart surgery at the age of 37, this NBC special showcases Bobby Darin at his finest, highlighted by his freewheeling vocal range and improvisational style. Among the favorites sung by Darin are "Splish Splash," "Beyond the Sea" and "Mack the Knife." 70 min.
50-8636 *$19.99*

Beauty and the Beast

Beauty And The Beast
One of the most popular cult TV shows of all time, this 1987-1990 fantasy series tells of the romance between a privileged attorney (Linda Hamilton) and a mysterious man-beast (Ron Perlman) who saves her life and lives under the New York City streets. Except where noted, each tape runs about 50 min. There are 22 volumes available, including:

Beauty And The Beast: Once Upon A Time... In The City Of New York
63-1483 *$14.99*

Beauty And The Beast: Terrible Savior
63-1481 *$14.99*

Beauty And The Beast: Siege
63-1484 *$14.99*

Beauty And The Beast: No Way Down
63-1485 *$14.99*

Beauty And The Beast: Masques
63-1570 *$14.99*

Beauty And The Beast: The Beast Within
63-1571 *$14.99*

Beauty And The Beast: Nor Iron Bars A Cage
63-1572 *$14.99*

Beauty And The Beast: Song Of Orpheus
63-1573 *$14.99*

Beauty And The Beast: A Children's Story
63-1747 *$14.99*

Beauty And The Beast: An Impossible Silence
63-1748 *$14.99*

Beauty And The Beast: Shades Of Grey
63-1749 *$14.99*

Beauty And The Beast: China Moon
63-1773 *$14.99*

Beauty And The Beast: The Alchemist
63-1774 *$14.99*

Beauty And The Beast: Temptation
63-1775 *$14.99*

Beauty And The Beast: Promises Of Someday
63-1776 *$14.99*

Beauty And The Beast: Down To A Sunless Sea
63-1820 *$14.99*

Beauty And The Beast: Fever
63-1821 *$14.99*

Beauty And The Beast: Everything Is Everything
63-1822 *$14.99*

Beauty And The Beast: To Reign In Hell
63-1823 *$14.99*

Beauty And The Beast: Ozymandias
63-1824 *$14.99*

Beauty And The Beast: A Happy Life
63-1825 *$14.99*

Beauty And The Beast (1987)
A special feature culled from the hit TV fantasy adventure. A New York lawyer (Linda Hamilton) is saved after a mugging by a man-beast outcast (Ron Perlman), who takes her to his underground world to recover. 100 min.
63-1302 Was $19.99 *$14.99*

Beauty And The Beast: Above, Below And Beyond (1988)
The fantastic adventures of lovely lawyer Catherine and her lion-like soulmate, Vincent, continue in this two-episode tale from the TV cult favorite. Linda Hamilton, Ron Perlman, Roy Dotrice star. 100 min.
63-1333 Was $19.99 *$14.99*

Beauty And The Beast: Though Lovers Be Lost (1989)
The love affair of Vincent and Catherine takes a fateful turn in this dramatic feature-length adventure from the TV series, when Catherine, pregnant with Vincent's child, is abducted by a sinister crimelord. Can Vincent save her in time? Ron Perlman, Linda Hamilton star. 90 min.
63-1388 Was $19.99 *$14.99*

Beauty And The Beast Gift Set
The pilot episode and two feature-length episodes, "Above, Below and Beyond" and "Though Lovers Be Lost," are available in an attractive gift set.
63-1467 *$44.99*

Texaco Star Theater, Vol. 1
Star Milton Berle, the man responsible for more TV sales than any advertising, trades banter with another great Fifties pitchman, General Electric spokesman Ronald Reagan.
10-7373 Was $19.99 *$14.99*

Texaco Star Theater, Vol. 2
Uncle Miltie makes silly with the star of "The Goldbergs," Gertrude Berg, and G.I. sweethearts The Andrew Sisters.
10-7374 Was $19.99 *$14.99*

The Best Of Milton Berle
Two classic examples of why Berle was known as "Mr. Television." Elvis Presley makes one of his first TV appearances on a 1956 "Milton Berle Show" episode, singing and clowning with Miltie and guests Arnold Stang, Irish McCalla and Debra Paget. Next, 1963's "Milton Berle Spectacular" features Jack Benny in a comedy duel with Berle and a wild "Cleopatra" spoof with Benny, Laurence Harvey, and Berle in the title role! 120 min.
62-1354 *$19.99*

Milton Berle's Buick Hour Collector's Set
In 1953 Uncle Miltie's Tuesday night variety series underwent a change of sponsors and titles to "The Buick-Berle Show." This six-tape collection features 12 of the funniest episodes and such guest stars as Frank Sinatra, Tallulah Bankhead, Martha Raye, Vic Damone, Peter Lawford, Carol Channing, Steve Allen and others. 11 hrs. total.
64-1379 *$69.99*

The Buick-Berle Show (1954)
Uncle Miltie thinks he's on the fast track to easy money when he buys a race horse, which he names "Mr. Television," but manages to run afoul of gangsters in this episode that also features song-and-dance numbers by The Will Mastin Trio, with a young Sammy Davis, Jr. 60 min.
09-1562 *$14.99*

Milton Berle: His Famous "Dragnet" Parody (1954)
Mr. Television gives "just the facts, ma'am" as he hams it up with guest stars Vic Damone, Dagmar, and Jackie Cooper in his classic spoof of "Dragnet." 60 min.
10-5036 Was $19.99 *$14.99*

Caesar's Hour, Vol. 1 (1954)
Great stuff from the Golden Age of TV Comedy. Sid Caesar, Howard Morris and Carl Reiner star in a spoof of World War I movies, "Der Flying Ace," and a wacky circus act, "The Caesaros." There's even a bullfighting dance number, seen from the bull's point of view. 59 min.
09-1436 Was $24.99 *$14.99*

Caesar's Hour, Vol. 2
Sid Caesar, Howard Morris, Carl Reiner and Nanette Fabray present all sorts of mirth and merriment, including a hilarious spoof of a silent melodrama that's not-so-serious after Sid gets to it. 55 min.
10-8325 Was $19.99 *$14.99*

Caesar's Hour (1956)
Creative season finale features Sid Caesar, Howard Morris and Carl Reiner, as pop singing group The Three Haircuts, performing their "hit" tune "Aggravation," plus Sid's "Rush Hour Rhapsody," a look at "The Commuters," and more. With Nanette Fabray. 52 min.
09-1203 Was $19.99 *$14.99*

Caesar's Hour (1957)
Classic live comedy from TV's early days. Sid Caesar is joined by Carl Reiner, Howard Morris and Janet Blair in hilarious sketches, including an episode of "The Commuters," an intellectual Western called "Reach for Your Brains," and a lampoon of the then-new "Today" show. 45 min.
09-1627 Was $19.99 *$14.99*

The Best Of Sid Caesar
"Hail Caesar" with this double bill of classic TV comedy. An episode of "The Admiral Broadway Revue" (1949) features Sid with Imogene Coca in skits about a Samba band and a family's trip to the fair. Next, in "Caesar's Hour" (1956), Carl Reiner, Howard Morris and Nanette Fabray join Sid in Mel Brooks' spoof "Bullets Over Broadway." 106 min.
62-1355 *$19.99*

Caesar's Writers
This hilarious reunion of comic Sid Caesar and his amazing staff of writers from his "Your Show of Shows" and "Caesar's Hour" TV shows was staged at the Writers Guild Theater in Beverly Hills in 1996. Joining in the hilarious hailing of Caesar were Carl Reiner, Mel Brooks, Larry Gelbart, Neil Simon and Mel Tolkin. 120 min.
76-7424 *$24.99*

Highway Patrol, Vol. 1/ For The Defense
Gravel-voiced Broderick Crawford thrilled millions of fans just by barking out "Ten-Four, Ten-Four" into his squad car radio. See an episode of the classic police drama series in which Crawford tracks down a crafty criminal who just skipped the state pen. Also on this tape is "For the Defense" with Edward G. Robinson. 60 min.
10-7349 *$19.99*

Highway Patrol, Vol. 2
Broderick Crawford keeps the California roads safe in two episodes of the hit 1950s TV show. First, an investigation of a teenager accused of running over a policeman leads Crawford's Chief Dan Matthews to the teen's crooked father. Then, a little girl disappears from her mother's hotel room during the holiday season and Matthews tries to find her. 60 min.
10-6016 *$14.99*

The Young Ones (1984)
A cult favorite on both sides of the Atlantic, this outrageous sitcom follows the misadventures of four slovenly college housemates: loud-mouthed metalhead Vyvian (Ade Edmonson), lentil-loving hippie Neil (Nigel Planer), smooth-talking ladies' man Mike (Christopher Ryan), and Cliff Richard fan and would-be poet Rick (Ric Mayall). Each tape features three episodes and runs about 100 min.

The Young Ones: Oil/Boring/Flood
The new house is promptly christened by Vyvian's striking "Oil" in the basement, then you'll see how "Boring" a typical day in the lads' lives can be. And in "Flood," they're trapped in the house with an ax-wielding homicidal maniac.
04-2364 Was $19.99 *$14.99*

The Young Ones: Demolition/Bomb/Sick
Everyone tries to think of a solution when the house is slated for "Demolition." Things get explosive when an atomic "Bomb" is found in the kitchen, followed by a visit from Neil's parents, who aren't aware everyone is "Sick."
04-3368 *$14.99*

The Young Ones: Bambi/Nasty/Time
It's up to the boys to defend the honor of Scumbag College on TV's "University Challenge" in "Bambi," while an all-night viewing of a video "Nasty" is interrupted by a visit from a South African vampire, and "Time" itself must be warped when a strange woman is found sleeping in Rick's bed.
04-3369 *$14.99*

The Young Ones: Cash/Interesting/Summer Holiday
Desperate for "Cash," the lads talk Neil into joining the police force. A house party becomes more "Interesting" than anyone expected, and why do the preparations for "Summer Holiday" include robbing a bank?
04-3370 *$14.99*

The Dangerous Brothers Present World Of Danger
Are you brave enough to watch the hazardous and hilarious exploits of dim-witted daredevils Richard Dangerous (Ric Mayall) and Sir Adrian Dangerous (Adrian Edmondson) in this collection of their bizarre skits from England's "Saturday Live" TV series? The boys risk life and limb in "Torture," "Exploding Politicians," "Babysitting," the never-aired "Kinky Sex" and more. 77 min.
04-2690 *$19.99*

Kevin Turvey Investigates
Rik Mayall ("The Young Ones," "Drop Dead Fred") stars in this hilarious account of an investigative reporter whose on-air charisma is a sharp contrast to his limited intelligence. 44 min.
53-9451 *$29.99*

The New Statesman
A ferociously funny satire from England starring Rik Mayall ("The Young Ones") as Alan B'Stard, a conservative member of Parliament who uses ruthlessness to reach the top of his party's ladder while avoiding the political and sexual scandals that continually swirl around him.

The New Statesman: Collection 1
Includes the episodes "Passport to Freedom," "Happiness Is a Warm Gun," "Sex Is Wrong," "Waste Not, Want Not," "Friends of St. James" and "Three Line Whipping." 150 min. on three tapes.
53-9519 *$59.99*

The New Statesman: Collection 2
Includes the episodes "Baa Baaa Black Sheep," "Fatal Extraction," "Live from Westminster," "A Wrapping Conspiracy," "The Haltemprice Bunker" and "California, Here I Come." 150 min. on three tapes.
53-9520 *$59.99*

The New Statesman: Collection 3
Includes the episodes "May the Best Man Win," "Piers of the Realm," "Who Shot Alan B'Stard?," "Labour of Love" and "The Party's Over." 150 min. on three tapes.
53-9702 *$59.99*

Bad News Tour (1985)
The good news is...Bad News is here! "Young Ones" stars Ade Edmondson, Rik Mayall and Nigel Planer team up to present a hilarious look at life on the road for Bad News, an inept rock combo, in the funniest rockumentary since "Spinal Tap." 84 min.
15-5113 Was $19.99 *$14.99*

Meet Corliss Archer
Based on the popular radio show, this sitcom ran on CBS from 1954-1955 and featured Ann Baker as the title character, a pretty, unpredictable teenager. Also in the cast were Bobby Ellis as Dexter, her boyfriend; and John Eldridge and Mary Bain as her parents. Except where noted, each tape features four episodes and runs about 100 min. There are seven volumes available, including:

Meet Corliss Archer, Vol. 1
Includes "Dexter the Director," "Dexter's Surprise Party," "The Archers Get a Maid" and "Dexter Becomes a Man."
10-9854 *$14.99*

Meet Corliss Archer, Vol. 2
Includes "Dexter's Masquerade Costume," "The Male Ego," "The New Neighbors" and "Harry and the Soap Opera Queen."
10-9855 *$14.99*

Meet Corliss Archer, Vol. 3
Includes "The Fortune Teller," "Harry the Dictator," "Harry the Photographer" and "The Personality."
10-9856 *$14.99*

Meet Corliss Archer, Vol. 4
Includes "The Boat Builders," "Miffy's Overnight House Painting," "Janet Goes to College" and "How to Handle Women."
10-9857 *$14.99*

Meet Corliss Archer, Vol. 5
Includes "The Pain in the Neck," "President of the Garden Club," "Harry Gives Advice" and "Dexter Borrows Harry's Car."
10-9858 *$14.99*

Meet Corliss Archer, Vol. 6
Includes "Corliss the Cheerleader," "The Vase That Came to Dinner," "Money Matters" and "A Party for Corliss."
10-9859 *$14.99*

Meet Corliss Archer: Pilot Episode
Ann Baker is Corliss in this tape that offers two episodes of the popular mid-1950s sitcom. Included is the show's pilot episode. 50 min.
10-8348 Was $19.99 *$14.99*

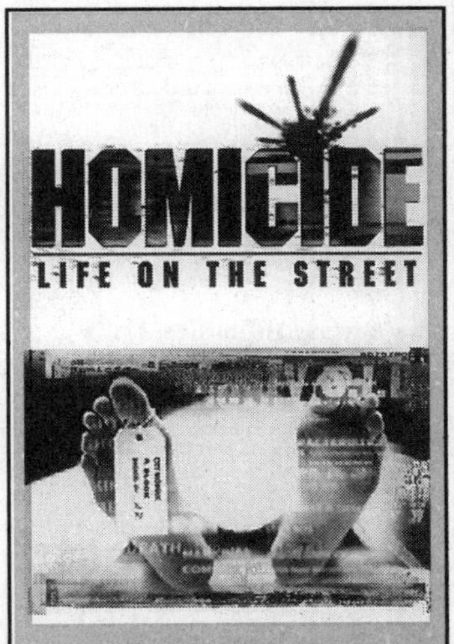

Homicide: Life On The Street
Life...and death...on the mean streets of Baltimore, as seen through the eyes of the detectives whose "day begins when yours ends," were the focus of this innovative, acclaimed 1993-99 NBC drama. Ned Beatty, Richard Belzer, Andre Braugher, Yaphet Kotto, Melissa Leo and Kyle Secor were among the ensemble cast's members.

Homicide: Life On The Street: The Beginning: Gift Pack 1
This two-tape set opens with the Emmy-winning pilot "Gone for Goode," in which Lewis and Crosetti look into a woman suspected of killing husbands for the insurance money, while new recruit Bayliss is charged with investigating the murder of 12-year-old Adena Watson. Next, the lives of two women and their sons intersect tragically in "Every Mother's Son," while a child left brain dead after a stray shooting and a Papal visit to Baltimore are the elements of "A Doll's Eyes." 162 min. total.
68-1965 *$24.99*

Homicide: Life On The Street: Subway/Anatomy Of A Homicide: Gift Pack 2
Included in this two-tape set are "Subway," with Vincent D'Onofrio playing a man who falls into the tracks and becomes wedged between a subway car and the platform, and the documentary "Anatomy of a Homicide," a behind-the-scenes look at the show and the filming of this award-winning episode. 117 min. total.
68-1966 *$24.99*

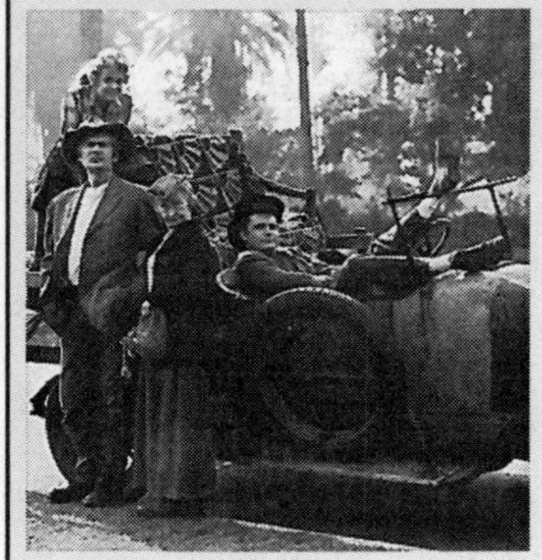

The Beverly Hillbillies
Weeell, dogies! That oil-rich clan from the Ozarks, the Clampetts, have made their way onto video. Join Buddy Ebsen, Irene Ryan, Donna Douglas and Max Baer for some down-home laughs in the sitcom classic that set ratings records during its 1962-71 run. Each tape features two episodes and runs about 51 min.

The Beverly Hillbillies, No. 1
A pot shot at a possum by Jed lands him $25 million worth of "bubblin' crude" and lands the whole family in California in the pilot episode, "The Clampetts Strike Oil." Next, the Clampetts have trouble "Getting Settled" in their new mansion home.
04-2561 *$14.99*

The Beverly Hillbillies, No. 2
The "Good Neighbor Policy" gets a workout when "The Clampetts Meet Mrs. Drysdale," who's less than thrilled with their mountain ways. And when Drysdale recommends "Jed Buys Stock," he promptly invests in cow, pigs and chickens.
10-9597 *$14.99*

The Beverly Hillbillies, No. 3
A Halloween call on their new neighbors gets the hillbillies some odd reactions in "Trick or Treat." And Mr. Drysdale tries to make the Clampetts more socially aware when he sends "The Servants" from his household next door.
10-9598 *$14.99*

The Beverly Hillbillies, No. 4
"Jethro Goes to School" at an exclusive private academy and ranks head and shoulders above his fellow students—in height, at least. Next, "Elly's First Date" is with Mr. Drysdale's stepson, Sonny (guest star Louis Nye).
10-9599 *$14.99*

The Beverly Hillbillies, No. 5
The suave Sonny Drysdale (Louis Nye) attempts to turn a mountain girl into a demure debutante in "Pygmalion and Elly." And in "Elly Races Jethrene," the Clampetts try to get Sonny to propose to Elly May before Cousin Pearl (Bea Benaderet) gets her daughter Jethrene (Max Baer in drag) hitched.
10-9600 *$14.99*

The Beverly Hillbillies, No. 6
"The Great Feud" begins when the Clampetts discover Sonny has dumped Elly May. Then, the family heads "Home for Christmas" and takes its first ride on a plane; Paul Winchell guests.
10-9601 *$14.99*

The Beverly Hillbillies, No. 7
With help from the Clampetts, Cousin Pearl attracts the attention of oil company executive Mr. Brewster in "No Place Like Home," with Paul Winchell. Plus, "Jed Rescues Pearl" when Brewster's public marriage proposal goes awry.
10-9602 *$14.99*

The Beverly Hillbillies, No. 8
When Jed heads "Back to Californy," he doesn't know what he's in for when he invites Aunt Pearl and Jethrene to stay with them. And "Jed's Dilemma" finds him in the middle of a feud between Granny and Pearl.
10-9603 *$14.99*

The Beverly Hillbillies, No. 9
"Jed Saves Mr. Drysdale's Marriage" after the banker hires a housekeeper when his wife goes to a health farm. Also, Pearl's yodeling attracts the attention of the police and "Elly's Animals."
10-9604 *$14.99*

The Beverly Hillbillies, No. 10
When "Jed Throws a Wingding," Pearl's suitors, Flatt and Scruggs, stop by. And "Jed Plays Solomon" when Pearl's yodeling gets out of hand.
10-9605 *$14.99*

The Beverly Hillbillies, No. 11
In "Duke Steals a Wife," Jed's dog plays matchmaker between his master and a glamorous French woman (Narda Onx). Also, a con artist tries to get Jed to purchase the Hollywood Bowl, Griffith Park and the Hollywood Freeway in "Jed Buys the Freeway," featuring Jesse White.
10-9606 *$14.99*

The Beverly Hillbillies, No. 12
"Jed Becomes a Banker" when Mr. Drysdale enlists him for the position in order to get his skills as a skeet-shooter in a contest. Then, "The Family Tree" of Jed is traced back to before the Mayflower by a historian; Rosemary DeCamp guests.
10-9607 *$14.99*

The Beverly Hillbillies, No. 13
Pearl attempts to groom the Clampetts for high society in "Jed Cuts the Family Tree." And when Jed drinks "Granny's Spring Tonic," he falls for a sexy bank secretary (Lola Albright).
10-9608 *$14.99*

The Beverly Hillbillies, No. 14
An IRS agent doesn't know what he's in for when he calls on the Clampetts in "Jed Pays His Income Tax." And Jethro gets signed to a baseball contract by coach Leo Durocher in "The Clampetts and the Dodgers."
10-9609 *$14.99*

The Beverly Hillbillies, No. 15
Mlle. Denise returns from Paris to show Jed Duke's new puppies in "Duke Becomes a Father." Also, "The Clampetts Entertain" the Chairman of the Commerce Bank (guest star Jim Backus).
10-9610 *$14.99*

The Beverly Hillbillies, No. 16
A phony accident that could cost Jed $100,000 finds "The Clampetts in Court." And a Beverly Hills psychiatrist tries to figure out Granny in "The Clampetts Get Psychoanalyzed."
10-9611 *$14.99*

The Beverly Hillbillies, No. 17
In "The Psychiatrist Gets Clampetted," Granny's love charm draws the analyst's attention to her rather than intended target Pearl. And Jed is named "Banker of the Year" when he takes over Mr. Drysdale's job in "Elly Becomes a Secretary."
10-9612 *$14.99*

The Beverly Hillbillies, No. 18
The Clampetts take in "Jethro's Friend," a spoiled youngster they show how to have fun. And in "Jed Gets the Misery," Jed fakes an illness so Granny can practice medicine again.
10-9613 *$14.99*

The Beverly Hillbillies, No. 19
Granny devises a potion that grows hair in "Hair-Raising Holiday," with guest star Fred Clark. Also, Granny gets into trouble with the neighbors when she tries to grow vegetables in "Granny's Garden."
10-9614 *$14.99*

The Beverly Hillbillies, No. 20
In "Elly Starts to School," Elly May Clampett attends a finishing school for society types; Sharon Tate guest stars. And the hillbillies unknowingly start a new trend of dress in "The Clampett Look."
10-9615 *$14.99*

The Beverly Hillbillies, No. 21
After a "birds and bees" talk with Jed, Jethro falls for a burlesque dancer named Chickadee (Barbara Nichols) in "Jethro's First Love," decides to propose to her in "Chickadee Returns."
10-9616 *$14.99*

The Beverly Hillbillies, No. 22
Jed discovers there's a problem with his account in "The Clampetts Are Overdrawn." And "The Clampetts Go Hollywood" after Jed gets conned by an unemployed actor; Sharon Tate guest stars.
10-9617 *$14.99*

The Beverly Hillbillies, No. 23
It may be "Turkey Day," but Elly makes Thanksgiving difficult when she makes friends with a turkey. And when Mrs. Drysdale hosts "The Garden Party," she's shocked to find her guests going to a Clampett hoedown instead.
10-9618 *$14.99*

The Beverly Hillbillies, No. 24
When Elly May starts riding a motorcycle, her pa decides "Elly Needs a Maw." Sharon Tate guests. Plus, "The Clampetts Get Culture" in order to become part of the Beverly Hills crowd.
10-9619 *$14.99*

The Beverly Hillbillies, No. 25
It's "Christmas at the Clampetts," but the family can't figure out some of Mr. Drysdale's extravagant gifts. And Quirt Manley (Henry Gibson), a TV western star, dates Elly May in "A Man for Elly."
10-9620 *$14.99*

The Beverly Hillbillies, No. 26
Granny thinks a kangaroo sent to Mr. Drysdale is a "The Giant Jackrabbit" in the episode that set a Nielsen Ratings record. Also, a beauty contest winner from the Clampetts' old turf arrives with her father—and plans to marry Jethro—in "The Girl from Home."
10-9621 *$14.99*

The Beverly Hillbillies, No. 27
Lafe Crick, a backwoods con artist and the father of Jethro's new girl, is an unwelcome house guest in "Lafe Lingers On," featuring Peter Whitney. And in "The Race for Queen," Elly competes in the Miss Beverly Hills contest; Robert Cummings guest stars.
10-9622 *$14.99*

Medic (1954-56)
Richard Boone starred as Dr. Konrad Styner in TV's first realistic medical program, exploring dramatic tales based on real-life incidents and dedicated "to the profession of medicine, to the men and women who labor in its cause." Each tape contains two episodes and runs about 55 min. There are six volumes available, including:

Medic, Vol. 1
Includes "My Brother Joe" and "Flash of Darkness."
10-1202 *$19.99*

Medic, Vol. 2
Includes "A Time to Be Alive" and "Dr. Impossible."
10-1203 *$19.99*

Medic/The Star And The Story
Richard Boone stars in the pilot episode to the landmark series, which was often shot in real hospitals and used actual medical personnel, as the "guardian of birth, the healer of the sick and the comforter of the aged." Also features Zachary Scott in an early "Rheingold Theatre" drama. 55 min.
10-7026 Was $19.99 *$14.99*

Washington Square, Vol. 1
Ray Bolger hosts this comedy-variety show, with guests Stubby Kaye, Gertrude Berg, and Arnold Stang as the voice of Aristotle the Turtle. Music from Lionel Hampton and his Orchestra. 60 min.
09-1649 Was $24.99 *$14.99*

Washington Square, Vol. 2
A "tour around the world" as seen from New York's Washington Square includes comedy, dancing and singing. Guest performers include Vera-Ellen, Jose Greco; Ray Bolger hosts this 1957 episode. Sponsored by Enden Shampoo, Stopette Deodorant and Royal Typewriters. 59 min.
09-1538 Was $24.99 *$14.99*

Centennial (1979)
The most ambitious mini-series ever produced is an epic account of the making of America, as experienced by the Native Americans, trappers, settlers and residents of the region around Centennial, Colorado, from the late 1700s to the present. Based on James A. Michener's novel, the epic drama features a huge cast that includes Robert Conrad, Richard Chamberlain, Sally Kellerman, Timothy Dalton and David Garrett. 21 hours on 12 tapes.
07-2570 Was $129.99 *$99.99*

The Winds Of War (1983)
The Emmy-winning TV mini-series, bringing to life Herman Wouk's tale of a Navy family's devotion to duty and to each other in the days shortly before America's entry into World War II, features an acclaimed cast that includes Robert Mitchum, Ali MacGraw, Jan-Michael Vincent, Victoria Tennant, John Houseman, Polly Bergen, Lisa Eilbacher and Ralph Bellamy, reprising his screen role as FDR. 14 1/2 hrs. on seven tapes.
06-1688 *☐$139.99*

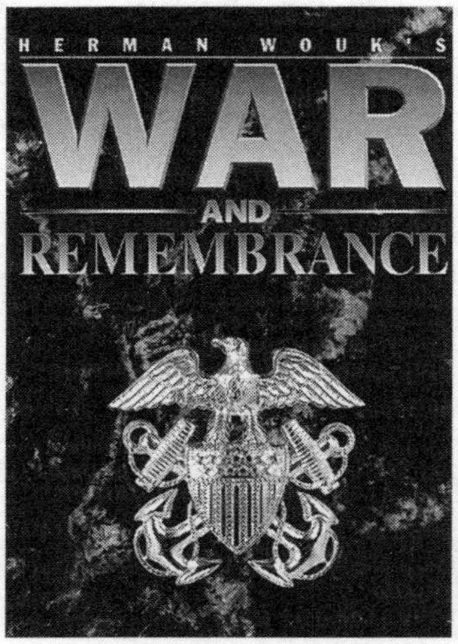

War And Remembrance (1988)
The global and personal dramas of World War II are vividly brought to life in the epic TV mini-series, based on Herman Wouk's best-selling novel. Filmed in 10 countries, this first part of the saga follows the battles in Europe, Africa and the Pacific and graphically depicts the horrors of the Holocaust. The international cast includes Robert Mitchum, Sir John Gielgud, Jane Seymour, Barry Bostwick, Hart Bochner, Victoria Tennant and Ralph Bellamy. 14 hrs. on seven tapes.
50-6327 *$139.99*

War And Remembrance: The Final Chapter (1989)
Herman Wouk's sweeping tale of the soldiers and civilians, the heroes, villains and victims of the Second World War concludes and brings to a climax the biggest TV mini-series ever filmed. Robert Mitchum, Sir John Gielgud, Jane Seymour, Polly Bergen, Victoria Tennant and Hart Bochner star. 9 1/2 hrs. on five tapes.
50-6382 *$99.99*

Bewitched

Bewitched: Meet The Stephens
Newlywed Samantha makes a surprising announcement to her new husband in the series' debut episode, "I, Darrin, Take This Witch Samantha." Next, the news that they're expecting has the Stephens wondering if the child will inherit Sam's abilities in "And Then There Were Three."
02-2945 *$12.99*

Bewitched: 'Cuz It's Witchcraft
Samantha thinks she's helping by turning a frog into a man, only to learn "Nobody But a Frog Knows How to Live." Then, Endora's latest spell on Darrin has him feeling very small—literally—in "Samantha's Wedding Present."
02-2946 *$12.99*

Bewitched: This Spells Trouble
What will happen to Darrin if Samantha accepts the title of Queen of the Witches in "Long Live the Queen," and when will Darrin discover that the "Sam" he's taken for a second honeymoon is lookalike cousin Serena in "It's So Nice to Have a Spouse Around the House"?
02-2947 *$12.99*

Bewitched: It's All Relative
Bumbling Aunt Clara summons up Ben Franklin to fix an electrical problem, and the resultant mix-ups land everybody in court, in the two-part story "My Friend Ben" and "Samantha for the Defense." Then, will "Samantha's Good News" be enough to keep her bickering parents from destroying everything around them? 75 min.
02-3186 *$12.99*

Bewitched: The Generation Zap
Darrin's meetings with a new client who happens to be an old flame plays havoc with Samantha's witchcraft in "No Zip in My Zap"; it's up to Dr. Bombay to find a cure when Endora's magic abilities are transferred to Aunt Clara in "Allergic to Ancient Macedonian Dodo Birds"; and an accidental trip back to Pilgrim times marks "Samantha's Thanksgiving to Remember." 75 min.
02-3187 *$12.99*

A Bewitched Christmas
Join the Stephens family for magical Yuletide fun, as Samantha teaches Darrin's Scrooge-like client the error of his ways in "Humbug Not to Be Spoken Here," followed by a mischievous orphan who learns about the joys of Christmas in "A Vision of Sugar Plums."
02-2263 *$12.99*

A Bewitched Christmas 2
Have yourself a nose-twitching little Christmas with this delightful double feature. Tabitha's playmate doesn't believe in Santa Claus until Samantha produces the real thing in "Santa Comes to Visit and Stays and Stays," followed by a magical lesson in brotherhood, "Sisters at Heart."
02-2465 *$12.99*

A Bewitched Halloween
Who better to celebrate Halloween with than TV's most gorgeous witch? Samantha and her friends get together to push for a better "public image" for their kind in "The Witches Are Out," and "Trick or Treat" finds Endora turning Darrin into a werewolf while he's entertaining clients at home. Look for Maureen McCormick as the young Endora.
02-2440 *$14.99*

Bewitched 3-Pack
"Meet the Stephens," "'Cuz It's Witchcraft" and "This Spells Trouble" are also available in a boxed collector's set.
02-2966 Save $14.00! *$24.99*

The Bing Crosby Show, Vol. 1
Bing stars with guest Jack Benny in an early '60s variety series pilot, then takes a solo turn in an episode of his 1964 situation comedy about the hectic family life of an ex-crooner. Bing's old showbiz crony, Phil Harris, drops in for a visit.
10-7456 Was $19.99 *$14.99*

The Bing Crosby Show, Vol. 2
A pair of episodes from Bing's mid-'60s family sitcom with "Der Bingle" exhibiting his legendary tolerance and doling out fatherly advice to his extraordinary kin: a boy-crazy teen, an intellectual 10-year-old and a career-minded wife (Beverly Garland).
10-7505 Was $19.99 *$14.99*

The Bing Crosby Show (1963)
There's plenty of singing, dancing and laughs in this variety special. Joining Der Bingle are special guests Buddy Ebsen, Andre Previn, and French-born singer-actress Caterina Valente, and there are even original commercials featuring Bing with Jerry Colonna (for Pepsodent) and Phil Harris (for Pontiac). 60 min.
53-6416 *$19.99*

The Missing Halves Special
Put together the only surviving halves of two rare variety shows and the result is a whole lot of fun. First, the opening part of a 1968 "Here Comes the Stars" roast of Bing Crosby, with toastmaster George Jessel, Pat Buttram and hot copycat Rich Little. Next, the second half of a "Cavalcade of Stars" program with Jackie Gleason and Victor Borge.
10-7459 Was $19.99 *$14.99*

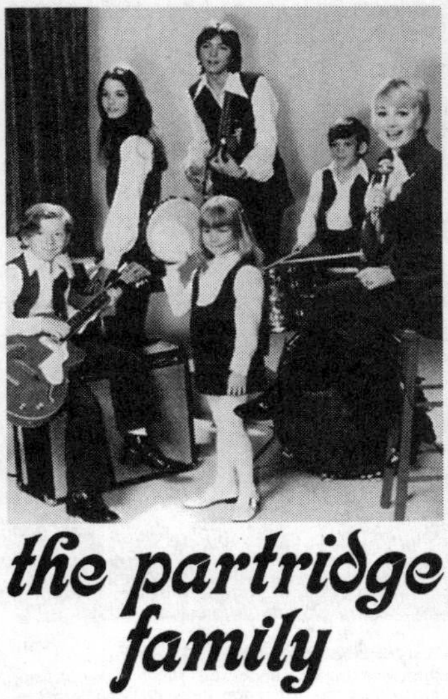

The Partridge Family
Hop on board the psychedelic school bus with everybody's favorite '70s TV rock band family. Shirley Jones is the widowed mother who joins her five kids (including David Cassidy, Susan Dey and Danny Bonaduce) in their musical group, and Dave Madden plays their harried manager, in this song-filled sitcom that aired on ABC from 1970 to 1974. Each volume features three episodes and runs about 75 min.

The Partridge Family: C'mon Get Happy!
See how the Partridge brood took up their instruments in the pilot episode, "What? And Get Out of Show Business?"; a national TV appearance could be jeopardized by Laurie's braces in "Old Scrapmouth," guest starring Mark Hamill; and George Chakiris plays a Navy officer and old flame of Shirley in "Anchors Aweigh."
02-3112 *$14.99*

The Partridge Family: Caution: Nervous Mother Driving
"Knight in Shining Armor" guest stars Bobby Sherman as a would-be songwriter hiding out in the Partridges' studio (in the episode that led to Bobby's hit spin-off, "Getting Together"), while a skunk on the bus creates havoc in "But the Memory Lingers On," and Jodie Foster guests as Danny's feisty girlfriend, Gloria Hickey, in "The Eleven Year Itch."
02-3113 *$14.99*

The Partridge Family: 6 Partridges And 3 Angels
A trio of heavenly guest stars join the Partridges in these episodes. First, can Farrah Fawcett help foil a con artist looking to sue the family in "The Sound of Money"? Jaclyn Smith could jeopardize Shirley's new romance in "When Mother Gets Married," and Keith has "Double Trouble" when he has two dates—one of them with Cheryl Stopplemoor (Ladd)!—on the same night.
02-3184 *$12.99*

The Partridge Family: Stars In Our Eyes
The rock-and-roll brood had better learn to "play that funky music" when they're mistakenly booked into a black "Soul Club" run by Lou Gossett, Jr. and Richard Pryor; Laurie is the reluctant love object of "A Man Called Snake," long-haired biker Rob Reiner; and will a visit by Johnny Bench help Danny and Keith get over "striking out" with Mary Ann Mobley in "I Left My Heart in Cincinnati"?
02-3185 *$12.99*

The Singing Detective (1986)
Writer Dennis Potter's acclaimed television serial follows the labyrinthine mindscape of pulp fiction writer Philip Marlowe, confined to a hospital bed and unable to move due to extreme psoriasis. While trying in his lucid moments to deduce the cause of his condition, Marlowe's daydreams cast him as his fictional sleuth/big band singer, working to solve the "Skinscapes" murders. The solution to both mysteries could be one and the same—"am I right or am I right?" Haunting musical-noir-dramedy stars Michael Gambon, Patrick Malahide, Janet Suzman and Joanne Whalley. 7 hrs. on six tapes.
04-3533 Was $99.99 *$69.99*

I, Claudius: Collector's Edition (1980)
The acclaimed "Masterpiece Theatre" production of Robert Graves' historical novel features an all-star cast, including Brian Blessed, John Hurt, Sian Phillips, Patrick Stewart, and Derek Jacobi in the title role, in an epic tale of power, deception and debauchery among Ancient Rome's imperial family. This deluxe boxed set includes the complete mini-series, plus the 1965 documentary "The Epic That Never Was," about the unfinished 1937 "I, Claudius" film that was to star Charles Laughton and Merle Oberon. 14 hrs. total on seven tapes.
07-8222 *$129.99*

The Best Of The Kids In The Hall
An irreverent collection of skits from the hit TV series featuring the always funny, ever-inventive spoofsters, The Kids in the Hall. This hilarious compilation offers head-pinching humor on the edge, with Kevin McDonald, Mark McKinney, Scott Thompson, Bruce McCulloch and Dave Foley. 108 min.
02-2437 Was $59.99 *$19.99*

The Kids In The Hall: Seasons 3 & 4
Four of the funniest shows from the Canadian comedy troupe's award-winning cable TV series are featured in one special video. Join Dave Foley, Bruce McCulloch, Kevin McDonald, Mark McKinney and Scott Thompson as they offer up anal-probing aliens, the unforgettable Chicken Lady, Queen Elizabeth II and other hilarious characters. 90 min.
15-5333 *$19.99*

I Dream Of Jeannie
Barbara Eden blinks up wishes and laughs in this classic comedy series that ran from 1965 to 1970, playing the beautiful genie released from her bottle by astronaut Larry Hagman and brought back to turn his bachelor household upside-down with her not-always-helpful magic. Bill Daly co-stars as Hagman's best friend. Except where noted, each tape features two episodes and runs about 50 min.

I Dream Of Jeannie: Waiter, There's A Girl In My Bottle
Includes "The Lady in the Bottle" and "My Hero."
02-2954 *$12.99*

I Dream Of Jeannie: Risky Business
Includes "Greatest Con Artist in the World" and "Everybody's a Movie Star."
02-2955 *$12.99*

I Dream Of Jeannie: Jeannie Ties The Knot
Includes "The Wedding" and "My Sister the Homewrecker."
02-2956 *$12.99*

I Dream Of Jeannie: A Genie In Training
Includes "Happy Anniversary," "My Master, the Weakling" and "My Son, the Genie." 75 min.
02-3188 *$12.99*

I Dream Of Jeannie: Jeannie's Seein' Stars
Includes "Biggest Star in Hollywood," "Help! Help! A Shark" and "My Master, the Chili King." 75 min.
02-3189 *$12.99*

I Dream Of Jeannie 3-Pack
"Waiter, There's a Girl in My Bottle," "Risky Business" and "Jeannie Ties the Knot" are also available in a boxed collector's set.
02-2967 Save $14.00! *$24.99*

The Flying Nun Christmas
Have yourself a high-flying holiday with this double feature of Christmas-themed episodes, "Wailing in a Winter Wonderland" and "The Reconversion of Sister Shapiro." 50 min.
02-2960 *$12.99*

The Flying Nun 3-Pack
Running from 1967 to 1970, this warm and funny comedy/fantasy series starred a pre-Oscar Sally Field as Sister Bertrille, a bubbly noviate at San Juan, Puerto Rico's Convent San Tanco who discovers the order's winglike headwear, combined with her 90-pound frame, gives her the power of flight and propels her into comic complications. Three-tape set includes the two-part pilot episode "Maiden Voyage," "Birds of a Feather" and "Under a Spell." 150 min. total. NOTE: Individual volumes available at $12.99.
02-2968 Save $14.00! *$24.99*

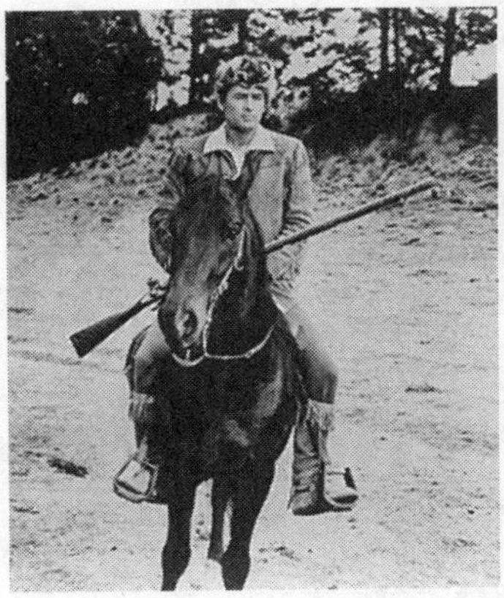

Daniel Boone: Ken-Tuck-E (1964)
A decade after hanging up his "Davy Crockett" coonskin cap, Fess Parker dusted it off to portray another American pioneer. Join Daniel, his wife Rebecca (Patricia Blair) and his Indian ally Mingo (Ed Ames) as they help open up the 18th-century frontier in this first adventure from the 1964-70 series. 51 min.
04-3960 *$14.99*

Absolutely Fabulous
In the mood for outrageously stylish comedy, sweetie darling? Look no further than the hit Britcom that follows the exploits of Edina (Jennifer Saunders) and Patsy (Joanna Lumley), two London fashion industry bigwigs who indulge in non-stop sessions of shopping, partying, drinking and other vices too numerous to mention, much to the consternation of Edina's straight-laced daughter, Saffron (Julia Sawahla). Each tape features three episodes and runs about 90 min.

Absolutely Fabulous: Vol. I, Part 1
Includes "Fashion," "Fat" and "France."
04-2974 *$19.99*

Absolutely Fabulous: Vol. I, Part 2
Includes "Isolation Tank," "Birthday" and "Magazine."
04-2975 *$19.99*

Absolutely Fabulous: Vol. II, Part 1
Includes "Hospital," "Health" and "Morocco."
04-2976 *$19.99*

Absolutely Fabulous: Vol. II, Part 2
Includes "New Best Friend," "Poor" and "Birth."
04-2977 *$19.99*

Absolutely Fabulous: Vol. III, Part 1
Includes "Doorhandle," "Happy New Year" and "Sex."
04-3292 *$19.99*

Absolutely Fabulous: Vol. III, Part 2
Includes "Jealous," "Fear" and "The End."
04-3293 *$19.99*

The Absolutely Fabulous Complete Collection
What's cheaper than an original LaCroix and just as stylish? How about this designer boxed set featuring all 18 "AbFab" episodes, plus the hilarious behind-the-scenes special, "How to Be Absolutely Fabulous"?
04-3377 Save $20.00! *$99.99*

AbFab Moments
Edina's somewhat addle-pated mum, June Whitfield, is your host for this wild "behind-the-scenes" retrospective that features the funniest clips and most outrageous flubs and outtakes in "AbFab" history. Now fans can get the true story on "Edina's Husbands," "Patsy's Life Story" and other topics.
04-3699 *$19.99*

French & Saunders
Before they created the smash hit "Absolutely Fabulous," Dawn French and Jennifer Saunders had British TV audiences laughing with their own show that mixed offbeat characters with wild sketches. Some of the funniest moments are collected in these programs. Each tape runs about 100 min. There are four volumes available, including:

French & Saunders: Gentlemen Prefer French & Saunders
04-3514 *$19.99*

French & Saunders: At The Movies
04-3515 *$19.99*

French & Saunders: The Ingenue Years
04-3700 *$19.99*

French & Saunders: Living In A Material World
04-3701 *$19.99*

French & Saunders: The Video
Whether it's as bumbling ballerinas, misguided make-up girls or members of a Hollywood harem, the antics of "AbFab" creators Dawn French and Jennifer Saunders in this collection of their funniest comic bits will bring a smile to your face. 85 min.
59-7025 *$24.99*

French & Saunders Live
The acclaimed British duo of Dawn French and Jennifer Saunders bring their offbeat brand of comedy to a packed house at London's famed Shaftesbury Theatre for a hilarious live show. 96 min.
59-7026 *$24.99*

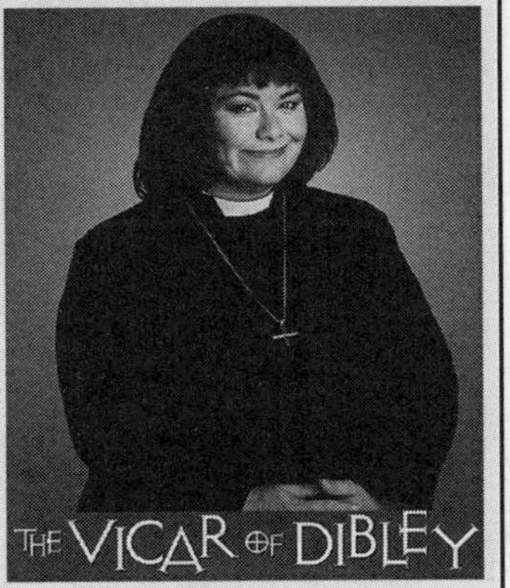

The Vicar Of Dibley
Divine comedy is in store for the quiet English village of Dibley when their newly appointed vicar turns out to be a woman. Dawn French stars as put-upon cleric Geraldine Granger in this popular British sitcom. Except where noted, each tape features three episodes and runs about 90 min.

The Vicar Of Dibley, Vol. 1: The New Girl In Town!
Includes "Arrival," "Songs of Praise" and "Community Spirit."
04-3697 *$19.99*

The Vicar Of Dibley, Vol. 2: My Congregation & Other Animals
Includes "The Window and the Weather," "Election" and "Animals."
04-3698 *$19.99*

The Vicar Of Dibley, Vol. 3: The Specials
Includes "The Easter Bunny," "The Christmas Lunch Incident" and "Engagement."
04-3847 *$19.99*

The Vicar Of Dibley, Vol. 4: Love Is In The Air
Includes "Dibley Live," "Celebrity Vicar" and "Love and Marriage."
04-3848 *$19.99*

The Vicar Of Dibley, Vol. 5: Autumn & Winter
Includes "Autumn" and "Winter." 40 min.
19-5008 *$19.99*

The Vicar Of Dibley, Vol. 6: Spring & Summer
Includes "Spring" and "Summer." 40 min.
19-5009 *$19.99*

Girls On Top
Before they created "AbFab," Jennifer Saunders and Dawn French teamed with Tracey Ullman and Ruby Wax for this wild sitcom about four very different young women sharing a cramped London flat. This special three-tape set features six of the show's funniest episodes. 156 min. total.
53-9998 *$59.99*

Dawn French On Big Women
Dawn French, one half of the "French & Saunders" comedy team, takes a comic look at queen-sized women and their role in history, art and film. Big is certainly beautiful—and hilarious, too—according to French, who is joined by large talents Jo Brand and Robbie Coltrane. 50 min.
59-7059 *$29.99*

One Foot In The Grave
Whoever said retirement was a time to take it easy never met cantankerous Victor Meldrew and his long-suffering spouse, Margaret, a suburban couple who are finding their "golden years" fraught with comic problems in this popular BBC TV series. Each tape features two episodes and runs about 90 min.

One Foot In The Grave: Who Will Buy?
Includes "Love and Death" and "Timeless Time."
04-2776 *$19.99*

One Foot In The Grave: In Luton Airport No One Can Hear You Scream
Features "We Have Put Her Living in the Tomb" and "Dramatic Fever."
04-2777 *$19.99*

As Time Goes By
In this warm and romantic BBC comedy series from 1992, Judi Dench and Geoffrey Palmer star as lovers who were separated 38 years earlier, when he was an army officer and she was a student nurse, and are given a second chance by fate to renew their relationship. Each tape features three episodes and runs about 80 min.

As Time Goes By, Vol. 1
04-3822 *$19.99*

As Time Goes By, Vol. 2
04-3823 *$19.99*

As Time Goes By, Vol. 3
04-3911 *$19.99*

As Time Goes By, Vol. 4
04-3912 *$19.99*

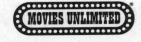

HOLLYWOOD PALACE

The Hollywood Palace
One of the top variety shows of the 1960s, "The Hollywood Palace" was ABC's star-studded project that ran from 1964 to 1970 and offered some of film and TV's top talents. Movies Unlimited is thrilled to bring you these classic shows that featured billboard girl Raquel Welch, the Ray Charles Singers and the Buddy Schwab Dancers as regulars. Each tape includes original commercials and runs about 60 min.

The Hollywood Palace, Vol. 1
Guests include Donald O'Connor, Buddy Greco and Don Knotts.
10-9646 *$14.99*

The Hollywood Palace, Vol. 2
Guests include Nat "King" Cole, Diahann Carroll, Ken Murray and Allen & Rossi.
10-9647 *$14.99*

The Hollywood Palace, Vol. 3
Guests include Maurice Chevalier, Jane Powell, Tim Conway and Rowan & Martin.
10-9648 *$14.99*

The Hollywood Palace, Vol. 4
Guests include Petula Clark, Noel Harrison and the Nitwits.
10-9649 *$14.99*

The Hollywood Palace, Vol. 5
Guests include Buddy Ebsen, Jack Carson, Willie Mays and Jane Morgan.
10-9650 *$14.99*

The Hollywood Palace, Vol. 6
Guests include Gene Barry, Bette Davis, Mel Brooks and Carl Reiner.
10-9651 *$14.99*

The Hollywood Palace, Vol. 7
Guests include Victor Borge, Alice Faye, the Nicholas Brothers and Nancy Wilson.
10-9652 *$14.99*

The Hollywood Palace, Vol. 8
Guests include Arthur Godfrey, Shelley Berman and Dorothy Collins.
10-9653 *$14.99*

The Hollywood Palace, Vol. 9
Guests include Van Johnson, Betty Grable, Sergio Franchi and Jackie Mason.
10-9654 *$14.99*

The Hollywood Palace, Vol. 10
Guests include George Burns, Wayne Newton, Rich Little and Connie Stevens.
10-9655 *$14.99*

The Hollywood Palace, Vol. 11
Guests include Donald O'Connor, Sergio Franchi, Shecky Greene and Dorothy Provine.
10-9656 *$14.99*

The Hollywood Palace, Vol. 12
Guests include Milton Berle, Johnny Puleo, Liberace and Joey Heatherton.
10-9657 *$14.99*

The Hollywood Palace, Vol. 13
Guests include Caterina Valente, Fredonia, Bill Cosby, and The Tijuana Brass.
10-9658 *$14.99*

The Hollywood Palace, Vol. 14
Guests include Cyd Charisse, Tony Martin, Jack Carter and Kay Starr.
10-9659 *$14.99*

The Hollywood Palace, Vol. 15
Guests include Bing Crosby, Red Buttons, Nanette Fabray and Louis Armstrong.
10-9660 *$14.99*

The Hollywood Palace, Vol. 16
Guests include Phil Silvers, Polly Bergen, The Lovin' Spoonful and Sergio Franchi.
10-9661 *$14.99*

The Hollywood Palace, Vol. 17
Guests include Herb Albert, The Supremes and Shelley Berman.
10-9662 *$14.99*

The Hollywood Palace, Vol. 18
Guests include Phil Harris, George Jessel, Abbe Lane, the Flying Antons, and the one and only Szony and Claire.
10-9663 *$14.99*

The Hollywood Palace, Vol. 19
Guests include Bing Crosby, Vikki Carr, Dorothy Lamour and Sid Caesar.
10-9664 *$14.99*

The Hollywood Palace, Vol. 20
Guests include Victor Borge, Allen & Rossi, Dennis Brilein and Petula Clark.
10-9665 *$14.99*

The Hollywood Palace, Vol. 21
Guests include Jimmy Durante, George Carlin, Peter Lawford and The Turtles.
10-9666 *$14.99*

The Hollywood Palace, Vol. 22
Guests include Bing Crosby and his family, Bob Newhart and Kate Smith.
10-9667 *$14.99*

The Hollywood Palace, Vol. 23
Guests include Bing Crosby, Charles Aznavour, The Mills Brothers, Dorothy Collins, and the unforgettable Szony and Claire.
10-9668 *$14.99*

The Hollywood Palace, Vol. 24
Guests include Milton Berle, Lena Horne, Spanky & Our Gang and David Hedison.
10-9669 *$14.99*

The Hollywood Palace, Vol. 26
Guests include Milton Berle, Nanette Fabray, The King Family and Buddy Greco.
10-9671 *$14.99*

The Hollywood Palace, Vol. 27
Guests include Jimmy Durante, Ethel Merman, The Lennon Sisters and Noel Harrison.
10-9672 *$14.99*

The Hollywood Palace, Vol. 28
Guests include Bing Crosby and his family and The King Family.
10-9673 *$14.99*

The Hollywood Palace, Vol. 29
Guests include Jimmy Durante, Anissa Jones and Kay's Pets.
10-9674 *$14.99*

The Hollywood Palace, Vol. 30
Guests include Phil Silvers, Connie Stevens, Jack Jones and The James Brown Revue.
10-9675 *$14.99*

The Hollywood Palace, Vol. 31
The innovative short films for The Beatles' "Penny Lane" and "Strawberry Fields," perhaps the first music videos ever shown on TV, are the highlights of this 1967 episode, with guests including George Carlin, Mickey Rooney, and Liza Minnelli, who performs "Cabaret." 50 min.
10-9676 *$14.99*

Amerika (1988)
The Cold War came to a very different conclusion in this acclaimed mini-series set in a United States under Soviet control. In a world where liberty is a forgotten word, small bands of freedom fighters struggle against both foreign tyranny and domestic collaborators to keep the American dream alive. Kris Kristofferson, Mariel Hemingway, Lara Flynn Boyle, Christine Lahti star. 705 min. on five tapes.
08-8632 *$69.99*

L.A. Law (1986)
A senator's son is charged with rape; a simple divorce case turns violent; a partner dies in the office. It's all in a day's work for barristers Harry Hamlin, Richard Dysart, Jill Eikenberry, Michael Tucker and Corbin Bernsen in the pilot to the hit TV series. 100 min.
04-2125 Was $79.99 *□$29.99*

The Newsroom: Boxed Set (1995)
Witty and acerbic, this acclaimed Canadian series looks at the bitter office politics and frenzied quest for ratings at a local TV station's news division. Writer/creator Ken Finkleman stars as the overbearing producer who must turn non-events into stories even as he copes with a self-obsessed anchorman and a staff that's looking to climb the corporate ladder. All 13 episodes are included in this four-tape set. 325 min. total. NOTE: Individual volumes available at $19.99 each.
50-8132 Save $40.00! *$39.99*

Poldark (1977)
During the late 1770s, Ross Poldark, a rebellious man who fought in the Revolutionary War, seeks love and political change in Cornwall, England, a beautiful but unpredictable place rife with social injustice, civil disorder and ancestral rivalries. Robin Ellis and Angharad Rees star in this sweeping 12-part romantic epic. 720 min. on six tapes.
04-2797 Was $149.99 *$99.99*

Poldark 2 (1978)
The rugged Cornwall coast of Western England is the setting for passion, intrigue and drama, as Ross Poldark returns to his ancestral estate and must counter the schemes of George Warleggan, a rival married to his former love and sworn to destroy him. Robin Ellis, Ralph Bates, Angharad Rees star. 720 min. on six tapes.
04-2942 *$149.99*

Poldark (1996)
The Cornish coast is the setting for this all-new version of the classic tale of Ross Poldark, who returns home from war to help his mining family battle arch-rival George Warleggan. But there's more trouble for the Poldarks, as a man saved by Russ Poldark leads the family into a world of deception. Ioan Gruffudd and John Bowen star in this adaptation of "The Stranger of the Sea." 105 min.
53-6646 *$19.99*

Baywatch: Nightmare Bay (1991)
It's action, adventure and amour under the sun in the premiere syndicated episode of the hit TV series. An underwater photographer is attacked in a sea cave and her partner is killed. Lt. Mitch Bucannon (David Hasselhoff) of the Baywatch patrol investigates while the media reports claim that a monster is responsible for the killing. Erika Eleniak, Pamela Bach also star. 89 min.
27-6873 *□$12.99*

Baywatch The Movie: Forbidden Paradise (1995)
This direct-to-video movie centers around the "Baywatch" crew's trip to Hawaii, where they're supposed to get some R&R and learn about rescue techniques used by the S.H.A.R.C.S., a top lifeguard team. But soon Stephanie, CJ and Caroline are embroiled in romantic entanglements and a poisonous lionfish bites Matt. David Hasselhoff, Pamela Anderson, Yasmine Bleeth star. 90 min.
27-6925 Was $89.99 *□$12.99*

Baywatch: White Thunder At Glacier Bay (1997)
A photo shoot for Inside Sports magazine sends Mitch, Neely, Donna, Lani, Hobie and the rest of the "Baywatch" crew on an Alaskan cruise. But things heat up in the frozen splendor of glacier country when wedding bells ring for Mitch and Neely, and Hobie falls for a sexy jewel thief with a fortune in emeralds in her luggage and a hit man on her trail. David Hasselhoff, Gena Lee Nolin, Donna D'Errico, Carmen Electra star. PG-rated version; 107 min.
68-1865 Was $59.99 *□$14.99*

Baywatch: White Thunder At Glacier Bay (Special Bonus Edition)
Also available in an unrated version that includes the Inside Sport bikini shoot that was too hot for TV, never-before-seen footage with "Baywatch" alumni Pamela Anderson, Yasmine Bleeth and Nicole Eggert, and much more. Carmen Electra hosts. 123 min.
68-1867 Was $59.99 *□$14.99*

Body & Soul (1992)
After the suicide of her brother, a nun leaves the Welsh convent where she spent the last 16 years in poverty and silence in order to put his affairs in order. As she reacquaints herself with the outside world and struggles to save the family textile business, she begins to question her vows and her future. Kristin Scott Thomas and Amanda Redman star in this stirring British mini-series. 312 min. on three tapes.
50-5437 *$69.99*

Wycliffe: Dance Of The Scorpions (1993)
This feature taken from the popular TV series stars Jack Shepard as Supt. Wycliffe, a British detective called in to investigate a series of brutal murders occurring in Cornwall. During the case, Wycliffe clashes with superiors and uncovers a web of lies and deceit which may lead him to the culprit. Jimmy Yuill, Leslie Grantham and Helen Masters star. 80 min.
53-6647 *$19.99*

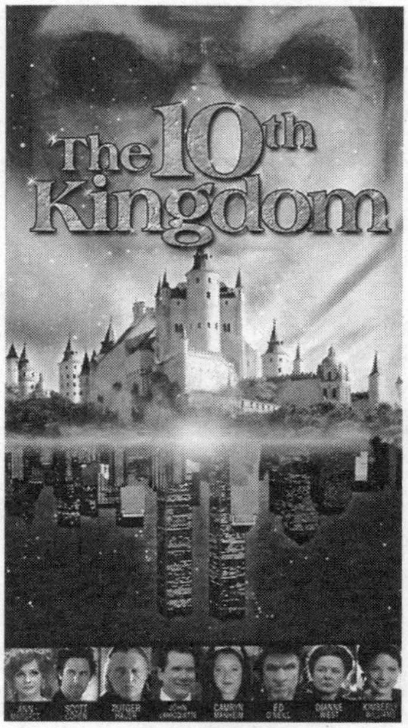

The 10th Kingdom (2000)
Move over, Bruno Bettleheim: this epic fantasy tells what happened to your favorite fairy tale folk *after* the "happily ever after." All was well until Evil Queen Dianne Wiest broke out of Snow White Memorial Prison, and now a father and daughter from New York must enter the parallel universe to save it. The stellar cast also includes John Larroquette, Kimberly Williams, Ed O'Neill, Camryn Manheim as Snow White and Ann-Margret as Cinderella. 348 min.
88-1210 Was $49.99 *□$14.99*

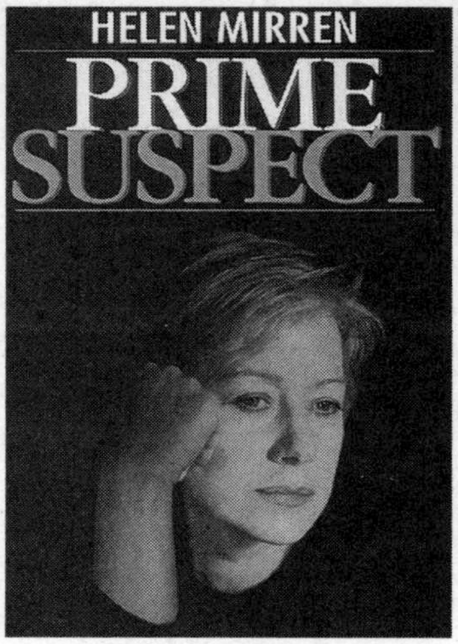

Prime Suspect (1992)
Emmy-winning mini-series stars Helen Mirren as Jane Tennison, a tough London detective who leads an inquiry into the murder of a local prostitute by a serial killer. With wits and tenacity, Tennison searches for the killer in order to prove herself to her male colleagues and her superiors. Tom Bell, Zoe Wanamaker also star. 230 min. on two tapes.
53-7971 Was $39.99 *□$29.99*

Prime Suspect 2 (1993)
An investigation into the murder of a young black woman puts Detective Chief Inspector Jane Tennison (Helen Mirren) in the middle, battling superiors eager for a quick solution to quell racial tensions as well as community groups criticizing police procedures, as she hunts for the truth behind the killing. With Colin Salmon, Jack Ellis. 230 min. on two tapes.
53-7972 Was $39.99 *□$29.99*

Prime Suspect 3 (1994)
The discovery of the body of a young boy who was burned alive draws Chief Inspector Tennison (Helen Mirren) into the sordid world of a pedophilia ring whose members reach into all branches of London society, from prostitutes and sadistic child pornographers to school officials with deadly skeletons in the closet. Tom Bell, Peter Capaldi and David Thewlis co-star. 205 min. on three tapes.
08-8450 *$39.99*

Prime Suspect 4 (1995)
Newly promoted Superintendent of Detectives Jane Tennison (Helen Mirren) investigates the case of a missing child, with clues pointing to a serial sex offender, in "The Lost Child." Then, Tennison uncovers a web of corruption and fraud among members of a local government, in "Inner Circles." And, the superintendent's objectivity is questioned in a case involving a series of murders. Co-stars Stuart Wilson. 306 min. total on three tapes.
08-8543 *$39.99*

Prime Suspect 5: Errors Of Judgement (1996)
A transfer to the grimy industrial city of Manchester brings two new problems for detective Jane Tennison to cope with: the killing of a young drug dealer who was connected to a cocky pusher known as "The Street," and an affair with her new superior. Gripping entry in the acclaimed British series stars Helen Mirren, John McArdle, Steven Mackintosh. 240 min. on two tapes.
08-8544 *$29.99*

Outside Edge (1994)
In this hilarious British comedy, two couples who are completely different become unlikely friends, thanks to the game of cricket. Kevin and Maggie Costello's are an outwardly affectionate pair whose closeness gets attention from downtrodden Mim Dervish and her cricket-obsessed hubby, Roger. Timothy Spall, Brenda Blethyn, Josie Lawrence and Robert Daws star. 180 min.
53-6643 *$59.99*

Armistead Maupin's More Tales Of The City: Complete Set (1998)
The saga of 28 Barbary Lane continues in this six-part mini-series set in mid-'70s San Francisco. Will Mary Ann and Michael each find the man of their dreams on a Mexican cruise? How will a stint as receptionist in a Nevada brothel help Mona discover her roots? And will Mrs. Madrigal reveal her secret past to her tenants? Laura Linney, Olympia Dukakis, Paul Hopkins, Nina Ziemaszko, Colin Ferguson, Jackie Burroughs and Ed Asner star. 330 min. on three tapes. NOTE: Individual volumes available at $39.99 each.
83-1256 Save $20.00! *$99.99*

The Odyssey (1997)
By Odysseus, Ulysses or any other name, Armand Assante is appropriately heroic in this lavish mini-series based on the epic poem by Homer. After their victory in the Trojan War, Ithacan king Odysseus and his men undergo a danger-filled 20-year journey home that leads them into encounters with the man-eating Cyclops, the bewitching Circe and other perils. The stellar cast also includes Greta Scacchi, Isabella Rossellini, Vanessa Williams, Christopher Lee and Eric Roberts. 165 min.
88-1142 Was $99.99 *□$14.99*

Terry And The Pirates

Inspired by Milton Caniff's popular comic strip, this series follows U.S. Air Force Terry Lee on a quest to Asia to claim a gold mine he inherited from his grandfather. While there, Lee runs afoul of the beautiful, treacherous Dragon Lady and her minions. John Baer, Gloria Saunders and Walter Tracey star in the show, which ran on the DuMont network from 1952-1953. Each volume features two episodes and runs about 55 min. There are seven volumes available, including:

Terry And The Pirates, Vol. 1
Includes "Macao Gold" and "Diplomatic Passport."
08-1742 *$14.99*

Terry And The Pirates, Vol. 2
Includes "Loaded Dice" and "Little Mandarin."
08-1743 *$14.99*

Terry And The Pirates, Vol. 3
Includes "Boxers' Rebellion" and "Maitland Affair."
08-1744 *$14.99*

Terry And The Pirates, Vol. 4
Includes "Green God" and "Chinese Coffin."
08-1745 *$14.99*

Terry And The Pirates, Vol. 5
Includes "Compound C-3 Theft" and "Extra Cargo."
08-1746 *$14.99*

Terry And The Pirates, Vol. 6
Includes "Chinese Legacy" and "Black Market in Death."
08-1747 *$14.99*

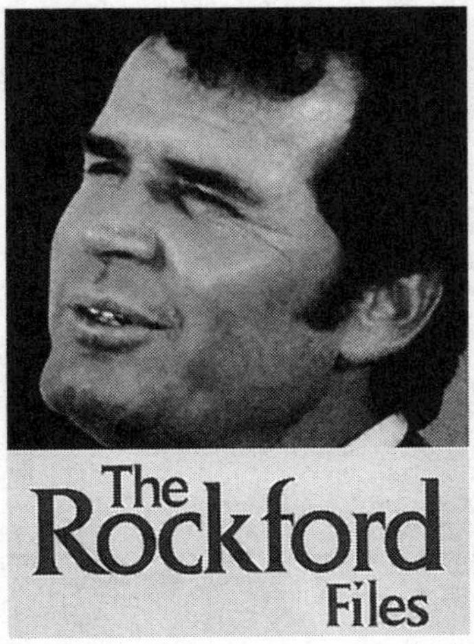

The Rockford Files

James Garner played easy-going ex-con P.I. Jim Rockford from 1974 to 1980 in an NBC series that became one of the most popular detective shows of all time. With help from his dad (Noah Beery, Jr.), ex-cellmate Angel (Stuart Margolin) and Detective Dennis Becker (Joe Santos), Rockford tackled tough cases that the police considered "unsolvable." Each tape runs about 50 min.

The Rockford Files: Backlash Of The Hunter
The two-part episode that launched the long-running series and set the stage for its trademark mix of mystery and laughs finds Jim Rockford searching for the murderer of Lindsay Wagner's father. 90 min.
07-2198 *$14.99*

The Rockford Files: The Big Ripoff
Rockford investigates a woman who survived the plane crash that killed her husband and received $400,000 in insurance. Jill Clayburgh guest stars.
07-2147 *$14.99*

The Rockford Files: The No-Cut Contract
Jim Rockford is implicated in a blackmail plot by scheming pro quarterback Rob Reiner.
07-2148 *$14.99*

The Rockford Files: Nice Guys Finish Dead
Jim Rockford teams with polished detective Lance White (Tom Selleck) to help a friend framed for murder in this classic episode.
07-2149 *$14.99*

The Rockford Files: Lions, Tigers, Monkeys And Dogs
When wealthy socialite Lauren Bacall's life is threatened, Rockford uneasily mixes with high-society types to find the culprit.
07-2150 *$14.99*

The Rockford Files: The Kirkoff Case
The seedy heir to a family fortune hires Rockford to investigate the mysterious murder of his parents. James Woods guest-stars.
07-2151 *$14.99*

TV Pilots

Movies Unlimited proudly presents these great TV rarities, an unusual selection of pilots that were produced as potential series. Some of the programs aired; others didn't. Either way, we think you'll find them fascinating, fun and entertaining at the same time.

TV Pilots, Vol. 1: Joan Of Arkansas (1958)/ Little Amy (1962)
In "Joan of Arkansas," an unaired pilot, Joan Davis plays a klutzy dental assistant chosen by a computer to be the first human into space. And in the unaired pilot "Little Amy," Debbie McGowan plays a 9-year-old who keeps getting into trouble. A young Jack Nicholson appears as a football coach. 55 min.
10-9559 *$14.99*

TV Pilots, Vol. 2: Daddy O (1961)/ The Dean Jones Show (1965)
Max Schulman, creator of "Dobie Gillis," was behind the unaired pilot "Daddy O," featuring Don DeFore as a handyman given a TV show (sounds familiar, huh?). And in "The Dean Jones Show," which was also known as "Alec Tate," the Disney mainstay is a scientist who uses a computer to help raise his teenage daughter.
10-9560 *$14.99*

TV Pilots, Vol. 3: Dr. Kate (1961)
This dramatic pilot never made it to TV despite being pitched for three straight years. Filmed in Lake Arrowhead, the show featured Jane Wyman as a country doctor who can't help but get involved in others' lives. 50 min.
10-9561 *$14.99*

TV Pilots, Vol. 4: Munster Rarities (1964)
This salute to TV's most monstrous family starts off with a five-minute clip, the only surviving footage, from the original color "My Fair Munster" pilot, followed by the complete 17-minute black-and-white version. Next is the unaired version of the second pilot (see if you can spot subtle changes such as Eddie's make-up), and rounding out the collection is a "Munsters at Marineland" promo, the theatrical trailer for the 1966 film "Munster, Go Home!" and a Cheerios TV commercial with the cast. 55 min. total.
10-9562 *$14.99*

TV Pilots, Vol. 5: Mr. Ed: The Lost Episodes (1958)
Before "Mr. Ed" there was "The Wonderful World of Wilbur Pope," the unaired pilot from 1958 with Scott McKay as Wilbur, the fellow who conversed with the horse who came with his new home. Also included is the Treasury Department-presented "Wilbur Gets the Message...About Payroll Savings," in which Wilbur (Alan Young) is encouraged to buy U.S. savings bonds by Ed. 50 min.
10-9563 *$14.99*

TV Pilots, Vol. 6: Gun Trouble Valley (1955)/Whiplash (1951)
There's two "Red Ryder" pilots here. In "Gun Trouble Valley," Red Ryder, Little Beaver and the Duchess battle a new ornery neighbor and help two people get married; Rocky Lane, Louis Lettri and Elizabeth Slifer star. And in the unaired "Whiplash," Red (Jim Bannon) and Little Beaver try to find out who stole $10,000 from a cattleman's association. 55 min. total.
10-9564 *$14.99*

TV Pilots, Vol. 7: Bulldog Drummond: The Ludlow Affair (1957)/The Shadow: The Case Of The Cotten Kimona (1954)
Robert Beatty is the famed Captain Hugh "Bulldog" Drummond, who helps an old friend find her kidnapped husband in "Bulldog Drummond: The Ludlow Affair." And Tom Helmore is Lamont Cranston, who becomes "The Shadow" to find out the truth behind a murder in "The Case of the Cotton Kimona." 55 min.
10-9565 *$14.99*

TV Pilots, Vol. 8: The Joe E. Brown Show (1956)/ Operation ESP (1952)
In "The Joe E. Brown Show (which aired as "Country Store"), big-mouth comic Brown is widower with two kids who tries to help a foreign newcomer battling against prejudice in his small town. And Sheldon Leonard created, wrote and starred in "Operation ESP," which focused on two boys who tell a judge they met a man with special powers after being accused of delinquency. 55 min.
10-9566 *$14.99*

TV Pilots, Vol. 9: Chicago 212 (1957)/Unsolved (1960)
In the unaired "Chicago 212," Frank Lovejoy is a Chicago Fire Department inspector investigating a suspicious blaze; Roy Thinnes plays the arsonist. And the unsold "Unsolved" told of East Coast gangster "Mugsy" Heidell, who moves west to get into the casino business. Based on the life of "Bugsy" Siegel, this show stars Simon Oakland, Aneta Corsaut.
10-9567 *$14.99*

TV Pilots, Vol. 10: Starr Of The Yankees (1965)/ Time Out For Ginger (1960)
After he's hit in the head with a baseball, a Yankee pitcher tries to make a comeback in "Starr of the Yankees," featuring Martin Milner. And follow the misadventures of the Carol family in "Time Out for Ginger," which focuses on teenaged daughter Ginger's exploits. With Candy Moore, Maggie Hayes and Margaret Hamilton as the cook. 50 min.
10-9568 *$14.99*

TV Pilots, Vol. 11: Octavius And Me (1962)/ And Baby Makes Three (1965)
In "Octavius and Me," a retired couple, played by Dub Taylor and Hattie Todd, travels to trailer parks across the country trying to help people in trouble. And baby doctor James Stacy hires a nurse, helps a little girl and meets an enthusiastic dentist in "And Baby Makes Three," which co-stars Joan Blondell, Lynn Loring and Gavin MacLeod. 65 min.
10-9569 *$14.99*

TV Pilots, Vol. 12: Here Comes Tobor (1956)/ Captain Fathom (1955)
Tommy, the nephew of a scientist, uses his ESP powers to join forces with Tobor, a highly developed robot, to find out why Navy jets were downed in "Here Comes Tobor" with Tommy Terrill and Arthur Space. And mysterious adventurer "Captain Fathom" and crew try to destroy a nuclear device; Don Megowan stars and Curt Siodmak ("The Wolfman") wrote and produced. 50 min.
10-9570 *$14.99*

TV Pilots, Vol. 13: Alarm (1954/1956)
Same title, different series: 1954's "Alarm" details a rash of fires that occurs in Los Angeles during a 10-day period and how two members of the Arson Squad try to catch the culprit; with Richard Arlen and Chick Chandler. Next, Fred Waring hosts a 1956 docudrama that looks at the tragic 1942 Coconut Grove fire in Boston as seen through the eyes of different witnesses. With John Hoyt. 55 min.
10-9571 *$14.99*

TV Pilots, Vol. 14: Beach Patrol (1960)/ Female Of The Species (1957)
Decades before "Baywatch" was introduced, there was "Beach Patrol," a pilot about lifeguards who work closely with the police to protect the pier area. Then, "Female of the Species" is an anthology series focusing on women, with Amanda Blake. Since no ending was shot, the actresses discuss the finale with producer Joan Harrison. 50 min.
10-9572 *$14.99*

TV Pilots, Vol. 15: Inside Danny Baker (1963)/ The Brown Family (1952)
Mel Brooks penned "Inside Danny Baker," the story of a precocious son of a dentist who tries to earn money for a fishing boat by turning his ping pong table into a work of modern art; with Roger Mobley and New York Yankees pitcher Whitey Ford. And "The Brown Family" is a wacky all-American clan, including son Stanley (Billy Gray), who brings a dog home that doesn't like Mom's stew. 50 min.
10-9573 *$14.99*

TV Pilots, Vol. 16: Sea Divers (1956)/Counterspy (1958)
Two divers are hired to find a wrecked ship with valuable papers in "Sea Divers," which supposedly inspired "Sea Hunt" two years later. Rhodes Reason and John Smith star. And Don Megowan is "Counterspy," a secret operative who tries to protect America from enemy agents at home. 50 min.
10-9574 *$14.99*

TV Pilots, Vol. 17: Counterpoint (1951)/The Bogus Green (1951)
Lee Marvin stars as Sgt. Crone in the crime story "Counterpoint." The episode featured, "The Witness," involves a jewel robber who tries to kill the actor who witnessed his recent heist. Next, Preston Foster is a circus advance man in trouble over counterfeit cash in "The Bogus Green"; with Martha Vickers.
10-9575 *$14.99*

TV Pilots, Vol. 18: Meet The O'Briens (1954)/ Let's Join Joanie (1951)
In "Meet the O'Briens," an accident-prone young man named Dave O'Brien, who lives with his wife and her parents, wrecks his father-in-law's car, then gets conned into buying another auto with insurance money. And in "Let's Join Joanie," Joan Davis is a hat sales clerk who tries to impress a heartthrob; Joe Flynn also stars. 50 min.
10-9576 *$14.99*

Unaired Pilots, Vol. 1: Now Is Tomorrow (1958)/ Swingin' Together (1960)
A tense tale of Cold War drama, "Now Is Tomorrow" looked at the military men who had their finger on the atomic button and the world's fate in their hands. Robert Culp stars. Next, hop on board the beat-up tour bus of a rock-and-roll band looking for gigs in "Swingin' Together," with Bobby Rydell, James Dunn and Stefanie Powers. 60 min.
82-1028 *$19.99*

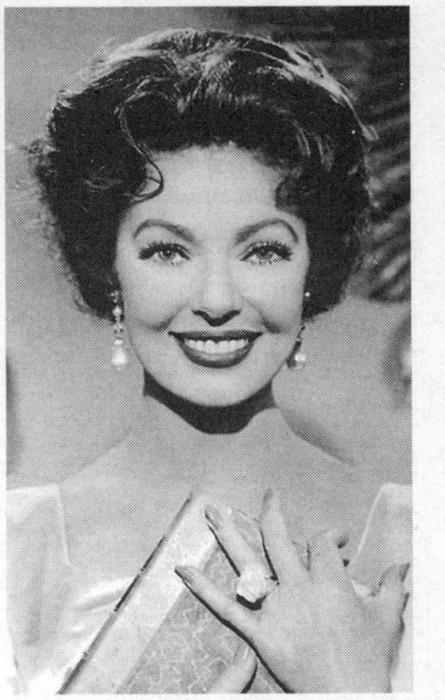

The Loretta Young Show

Film star Loretta Young made a successful transition to dramatic TV in this series that ran from 1953 to 1961 and was originally called "Letters to Loretta." Young presents stories of love, hope and drama and is featured in the famous "swirling skirt" opening sequence and adds short readings at the end of each show. Each tape includes two episodes and runs about 60 min.

The Loretta Young Show, Vol. 1: Earthquake/Feeling No Pain
A married couple's love is tested when the husband is left in an iron lung following an "Earthquake." Paul Langton and John Agar co-star. In "Feeling No Pain," Young plays a secretary who gets into comedic troubles thanks to a dentist's anesthetic. Hugh O'Brian also stars.
08-1518 *$14.99*

The Loretta Young Show, Vol. 2: Inga II/I Remember The Rani
Dennis Hopper plays the troublesome son of a farmer who is rehabilitated by the woman (Young) whose auto he has wrecked in "Inga II." Young then plays a beautiful Indian princess who passes on marriage and enlists a newsman to help her poverty-stricken people in "I Remember the Rani." Edward Ashley co-stars.
08-1519 *$14.99*

The Loretta Young Show, Vol. 3: The Pearl/Wedding Day
In "The Pearl," a Japanese fisherman finds a valuable treasure and dreams of the riches it will bring, but wife Young has other plans for his discovery. Set in Victorian times, "Wedding Day" concerns a recent widow (Young) who discovers the truth of her marriage plans after her brother-in-law and his wife plan to have her committed.
08-1520 *$14.99*

The Loretta Young Show, Vol. 4: Sister Ann's Christmas/ The Prettiest Girl In Town
A holiday favorite inspired by a true story, "Sister Ann's Christmas" stars Young as a devoted nurse who spends her Christmas making the holiday happy for her patients. Next, she plays a New York fashion model who returns to her hometown and meets her former boyfriend, now a prominent doctor.
08-1521 *$14.99*

The Loretta Young Show: Boxed Set
Fourteen episodes of "Loretta Young Presents" are featured in this series that spans 1953-1960 and offers home movies and photos from son Christopher Lewis to add insight to the shows. Included are "Love Story/Hotel Irritant," "Lady Killer/Count of Ten," "Son, This Is Your Father/Oh, My Aching Back," "Dear Midge/Reasonable Doubt," "The Girl Who Knew/Dateline Korea," "Tension/A Dollar's Worth" and "Little Witness/The Twenty Cent Tip." 350 min. total.
16-5030 *$49.99*

DuPont Theater

The 1956-57 incarnation of "DuPont Cavalcade" was retitled "DuPont Theater" and featured some of Hollywood's top stars in stirring dramatic roles. Each tape features two episodes and runs about 60 min.

DuPont Theater, Vol. 1
Includes "Once a Hero" with Ward Bond and Ben Johnson and "Innocent Bystander" with Don Taylor.
08-1610 *$14.99*

DuPont Theater, Vol. 2
Includes "Frightened Witness" with Dan Duryea and Barbara Billingsley and Patty McCormack and Paul Fix in "Dan Marshall's Brat."
08-1611 *$14.99*

Amazing Stories: Book One
From the TV anthology series of fantasy and adventure created by Steven Spielberg comes two of the most popular episodes. A WWII bomber mission becomes a desperate fight for life in "The Mission," with Kevin Costner and Kiefer Sutherland. Next, Danny DeVito and Rhea Perlman star in a most unusual love story in "The Wedding Ring." 70 min.
07-1680 Was $79.99 ***$19.99***

Amazing Stories: Book Two
In "Go to the Head of the Class," a sadistic English teacher gets a taste of his own medicine when his students practice black magic to even a score; with Mary Stuart Masterson and Christopher Lloyd. "Family Dog," from Tim Burton, takes an animated look at family life...through the eyes of their put-upon pet. 71 min.
07-1690 Was $79.99 ***$19.99***

Amazing Stories: Book Three
Truly amazing trio of tales begins with Patrick Swayze as a criminal who gains the power of "Life on Death Row"; Gregory Hines as "The Amazing Falsworth," a second-rate psychic who identifies a killer; and Charlie Sheen as a soldier who miraculously saves his platoon in "No Day at the Beach." 73 min.
07-1710 Was $79.99 ***$19.99***

Amazing Stories: Book Four
Three more gems from Steven Spielberg's show including: "Mirror, Mirror," directed by Martin Scorsese, focusing on a horror filmmaker (Sam Waterston) whose creations become real; "Blue Man Down," where veteran cop Max Gail gets help from a mysterious policewoman; and Sid Caesar as "Mr. Magic," a magician who hopes his career will get a boost with a new deck of special cards. 101 min.
07-1739 Was $79.99 ***$19.99***

Amazing Stories: Book Five
A selfish widow gets her comeuppance when she cannot enter "The Pumpkin Competition," with Polly Holliday and June Lockhart; a young girl vanishes and returns 40 years later in "Without Diana"; and three high-schoolers' science project lands them a "close encounter" in "Fine Tuning," starring Milton Berle. 73 min.
07-1794 Was $79.99 ***$19.99***

America's Funniest Pets
A wild compilation of pets doing the goofiest things. Witness a horse giving lip, a feline and a faucet, chimps getting into a woman's hair, and a dog dancing to "La Cucaracha." This collection from "America's Funniest Home Videos" features host Bob Saget. 35 min.
04-2540 □***$14.99***

America's Funniest Families
A hilarious collection of family wackiness from "America's Funniest Home Videos" featuring a wedding-day dress that takes the plunge, a Santa with bad breath, and a backfiring bidet. Temple University alumnus Bob Saget hosts. 45 min.
04-2541 □***$14.99***

America's Funniest Home Videos: Uncensored
This program offers the wildest moments on home videos that couldn't make it on the air. From falling shirts to animal no-nos, the video presents zany situations that the censors had to take out during original TV showings. 50 min.
50-8175 ***$19.99***

America's Funniest Home Videos: Family Follies
The zany behavior of moms, dads and kids are captured in this wacky collection of home videos. There's wedding surprises, wild children and more. 53 min.
50-8176 ***$14.99***

America's Funniest Home Videos: Animal Antics
Family pets and wild animals will have you howling with laughter when you catch their outrageous behavior here. There's giraffes, pot-bellied pigs, canines and more critters in store! 51 min.
50-8177 ***$14.99***

America's Funniest Videos: Three-Pack
This triple dose of tapes from the hit TV series includes "Uncensored," "Family Follies" and "Animal Antics."
50-9178 ***$49.99***

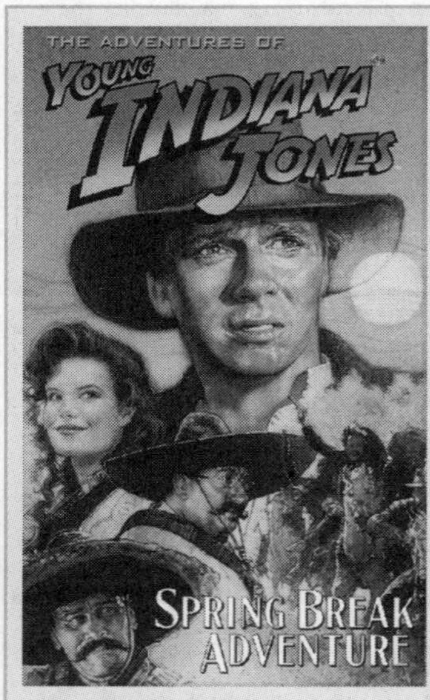

The Adventures Of Young Indiana Jones
Producer George Lucas brought the daredevil archeologist to the small screen with this exciting family drama series that aired from 1992 to 1993 as "The Young Indiana Jones Chronicles." Sean Patrick Flannery plays the teenage Indy, whose exploits took him around the world and into encounters with Pancho Villa, the Red Baron, Al Capone and other notables. Each tape features interviews with Lucas and Flannery and runs about 90 min.

The Adventures Of Young Indiana Jones: Spring Break Adventure
Like students 80 years after him, Indy heads to Mexico for a Spring vacation, only to get mixed up with Mexican bandits and spy-bearing submarines.
06-2900 □***$14.99***

The Adventures Of Young Indiana Jones: Trenches Of Hell
Captured by the Germans and sent to a POW camp, Indy and another captive—a young Frenchman named Charles de Gaulle—hatch a daring escape plan.
06-2901 □***$14.99***

The Adventures Of Young Indiana Jones: Phantom Train Of Doom
In war-torn Africa, Indy teams with a group of aged commandos to bring down a fearsome "secret weapon."
06-2902 □***$14.99***

The Adventures Of Young Indiana Jones: Oganga, The Giver And Taker Of Life
Indy has a fateful encounter in the heart of colonial Africa with famed physician and humanitarian Albert Schweitzer.
06-2903 □***$14.99***

The Adventures Of Young Indiana Jones: Attack Of The Hawkmen
Indy takes to the skies as he learns about a sinister German weapon and has a dogfight with the legendary Red Baron.
06-2904 □***$14.99***

The Adventures Of Young Indiana Jones: Adventures In The Secret Service
Young Indy becomes a teenage secret agent in a game of global espionage that takes him to Russia amid the turmoil of the Bolshevik Revolution.
06-2905 □***$14.99***

The Adventures Of Young Indiana Jones: Daredevils Of The Desert
It's up to Indy and a beautiful spy (guest star Catherine Zeta-Jones) to help the Australian Horsemen in their battle against Turkish forces in World War I.
06-2906 □***$14.99***

The Adventures Of Young Indiana Jones: Tales Of Innocence
Joining up with the French Foreign Legion lands Indy in the middle of a rivalry for a beautiful girl's affections with a would-be writer named Ernest Hemingway.
06-2907 □***$14.99***

The Adventures Of Young Indiana Jones: Masks Of Evil
A journey that stretches from Istanbul to the heart of Transylvania takes Indy on a terrifying, supernatural adventure.
06-2908 □***$14.99***

The Adventures Of Young Indiana Jones: Treasure Of The Peacock's Eye
The search is on for a fabled diamond said to once belong to Alexander the Great, and someone is out to stop Indy from finding it...at any cost.
06-2909 □***$14.99***

The Adventures Of Young Indiana Jones: Mystery Of The Blues
The streets of Chicago are roaring with jazz music and machine gun fire as Indy runs headlong into mob wars and an encounter with Al Capone.
06-2910 □***$14.99***

The Adventures Of Young Indiana Jones: Hollywood Follies
A trip to Southern California leads to some hair-raising adventures behind the movie camera and pits Indy against a dictatorial director—Eric von Stroheim.
06-2911 □***$14.99***

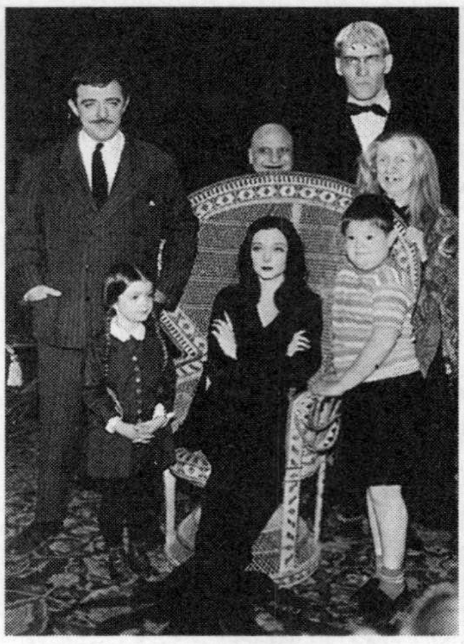

The Addams Family
Based on Charles Addams' spooky comic creations, "The Addams Family" was a classic TV comedy on ABC from 1964 to 1966. John Astin as the wild Gomez, Carolyn Jones as the slithery Morticia, Jackie Coogan as bald Uncle Fester and Ted Cassidy as giant butler Lurch were part of the kooky contingent. Each tape includes two episodes and runs about 50 min. You rang?

The Addams Family, Vol. 1
Includes "The Addams Family Goes to School" and "Morticia and the Psychiatrist."
14-3394 ***$12.99***

The Addams Family, Vol. 2
Includes "Morticia Joins the Ladies League" and "Fester's Punctured Romance."
14-3395 ***$12.99***

The Addams Family, Vol. 3
Includes "The Addams Family Tree" and "Gomez, the Politician."
14-3396 ***$12.99***

The Addams Family, Vol. 4
Includes "The New Neighbors Meet the Addams Family" and "Morticia the Matchmaker." 50 min.
14-3397 ***$12.99***

The Addams Family, Vol. 5
Includes "Green-Eyed Gomez" and "Wednesday Leaves Home," pet spider and all.
14-3398 ***$12.99***

The Addams Family, Vol. 6
Includes "The Addams Family Meets the V.I.P.s" and "Lurch Learns to Dance."
14-3399 ***$12.99***

The Addams Family, Vol. 7
Includes "The Addams Family Meets a Beatnik" and "Art and the Addams Family."
14-3296 ***$12.99***

The Addams Family, Vol. 8
Includes "The Addams Family Meets the Undercover Man" and "Mother Lurch Meets the Addams Family."
14-3297 ***$12.99***

The Addams Family, Vol. 9
Includes "Uncle Fester's Illness" and "The Addams Family Splurges."
14-3298 ***$12.99***

The Addams Family, Vol. 10
Includes "Cousin Itt Visits the Addams Family" and "The Addams Family in Court."
14-3299 ***$12.99***

The Addams Family, Vol. 11
Includes "Amnesia in the Addams Family" and "Thing Is Missing."
14-3300 ***$12.99***

The Addams Family, Vol. 12
Includes "Crisis in the Addams Family" and "Lurch and His Harpsichord."
14-3301 ***$12.99***

Addams vs. The Munsters Family Feud
Here are two shows on classic TV shows. In "The Addams Family and Friends," rare film clips, outtakes and an interview with John Astin help tell the story of the hit show. And in "The Munsters: Lost Color Episode," clips from the series pilot film, rare promo segments and behind-the-scenes footage paint a lovably gruesome picture of the 1313 Mockingbird Lane residents. 60 min.
05-5111 ***$14.99***

Testament Of Youth (1979)
The life of Vera Brittain, the English writer whose experiences as a frontline nurse in World War I led her to become a leading pacifist spokesperson, feminist crusader and acclaimed author, is traced in this powerful British mini-series. Cheryl Campbell stars as Brittain. 200 min. on four tapes.
50-8126 ***$59.99***

Keeping Up Appearances
Hilarious British comedy about the escapades of Hyacinth Bucket (pronounced "bouquet"), a social climber who will even disassociate herself from husband Richard and the rest of her family in order to hobnob with the elite. Award-winning Patricia Routledge stars as Hyacinth. Except where noted, each tape features three episodes and runs about 85 min.

Keeping Up Appearances: Rural Retreat
Includes "Rural Retreat," "Let There Be Light" and "Please Mind Your Head."
04-3342 □***$19.99***

Keeping Up Appearances: How To Enhance Your Husband's Retirement
Includes "How to Retire Early If You're Not Careful," "How to Go on Holiday Without Really Trying" and "What to Wear When Yachting."
04-3345 □***$19.99***

Keeping Up Appearances: Sea Fever
Includes the two-part "Sea Fever" and "Hyacinth Tees Off!"
04-3457 □***$19.99***

Keeping Up Appearances: I'm Often Mistaken For Aristocracy
Includes "Violet's Country Cottage," "Driving Mrs. Fortescue" and "Country Estate Sale."
04-3458 □***$19.99***

Keeping Up Appearances: The Memoirs Of Hyacinth Bucket
When Hyacinth's secret diary falls into her sister Daisy's hands, it's a chance to look back on the Buckets' most hilarious attempts to climb the social ladder in this retrospective special. 60 min.
04-3459 □***$14.99***

Keeping Up Appearances: Angel Gabriel Blue
Includes the two-part "Angel Gabriel Blue" and "Hyacinth Is Alarmed."
04-3665 □***$19.99***

Keeping Up Appearances: My Family In Broad Daylight
Includes "Golfing with the Major," "Three-Piece Suite" and "Picnic for Daddy."
04-3666 □***$19.99***

Keeping Up Appearances: Entertaining The Hyacinth Way
Includes "Half a Camel," "Indoor/Outdoor Luxury Barbecue" and "Finger Buffet."
04-3888 □***$19.99***

Keeping Up Appearances Gift Set #1
Give yourself a "Bucket" of savings with this boxed set featuring "Angel Gabriel Blue," "Entertaining the Hyacinth Way," "Rural Retreat" and "Sea Fever."
04-3889 Save $20.00! ***$59.99***

Keeping Up Appearances Gift Set #2
Everything's coming up "Hyacinths" with this four-tape collector's set. Included are "Anybody But Hyacinth," "How to Enhance Your Husband's Retirement," "I'm Often Mistaken for Aristocracy" and "My Family in Broad Daylight."
04-3955 Save $20.00! ***$59.99***

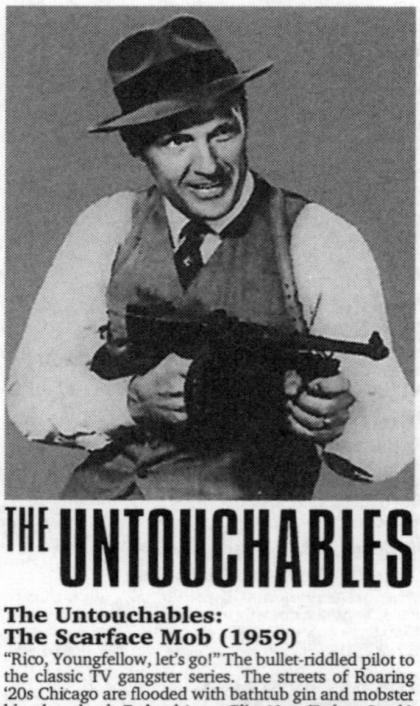

The Untouchables: The Scarface Mob (1959)
"Rico, Youngfellow, let's go!" The bullet-riddled pilot to the classic TV gangster series. The streets of Roaring '20s Chicago are flooded with bathtub gin and mobster blood, and only Federal Agent Eliot Ness (Robert Stack) and his elite squad can stop Al Capone (Neville Brand). Also stars Bruce Gordon, Keenan Wynn, Jerry Paris and Nicholas Georgiade; Walter Winchell narrates. 98 min.
06-1348 Was $39.99 ***$19.99***

The Outer Limits
There is nothing wrong with your VCR. Do not attempt to adjust the picture. We are presenting tales of awe and mystery from the classic science-fiction anthology series that ran on ABC from 1963 to 1965. Except where noted, each episode runs about 52 min.

Outer Limits: The Galaxy Being
A scientist's (Cliff Robertson) experimental television receiver brings a malevolent alien to Earth.
12-1642 *$12.99*

Outer Limits: The 100 Days Of The Dragon
A foreign agent who can assume the appearance of anyone at will impersonates a presidential candidate.
12-1643 *$12.99*

Outer Limits: The Man With The Power
An experiment gives a college professor (Donald Pleasence) incredible mental powers, but his subconscious mind starts to take over.
12-1647 *$12.99*

Outer Limits: The Sixth Finger
A scientist thrusts a simple Welsh miner (David McCallum) up the evolutionary path and transforms him into a superhuman future being.
12-1712 *$12.99*

Outer Limits: The Inheritors, Parts 1 & 2
Four wounded soldiers suddenly develop inhuman intellect and embark on mysterious tasks. An FBI agent (Robert Duvall) is determined to discover their purpose. 102 min.
12-1713 *$12.99*

Outer Limits: The Forms Of Things Unknown
Two high-class murderesses on the run (Vera Miles, Barbara Rush) encounter an eccentric (David McCallum) and his "alleged" time machine.
12-1714 *$12.99*

Outer Limits: Demon With A Glass Hand
Harlan Ellison's award-winning story stars Robert Culp as the amnesiac last man on Earth, being chased in an abandoned building by alien invaders.
12-1744 *$12.99*

Outer Limits: Keeper Of The Purple Twilight
An advance scout for an alien trades his intellect to an Earth scientist in exchange for human emotions.
12-1745 *$12.99*

Outer Limits: The Zanti Misfits
A race of ant-like creatures decides to use Earth as a "penal colony" for their exiled criminals.
12-1746 *$12.99*

Outer Limits: The Invisible Enemy
A manned expedition lands on Mars, but finds man-eating monsters living in the sandy surface. Adam West stars.
12-1803 *$12.99*

Outer Limits: The Man Who Was Never Born
A grotesque mutant (Martin Landau) from the year 2148 travels back in time to prevent the future destruction of life on Earth by killing the man responsible.
12-1804 *$12.99*

Outer Limits: Nightmare
Six members of an international military squad are captured by aliens and subjected to mental manipulation, but what is the real reason for the abduction? Ed Nelson, Martin Sheen star.
12-1805 *$12.99*

Outer Limits: The Architects Of Fear
A man (Robert Culp) is transformed into an "alien" by a team of scientist watchmen who hope to scare the world's nations into cooperation by announcing an "invasion."
12-1833 *$12.99*

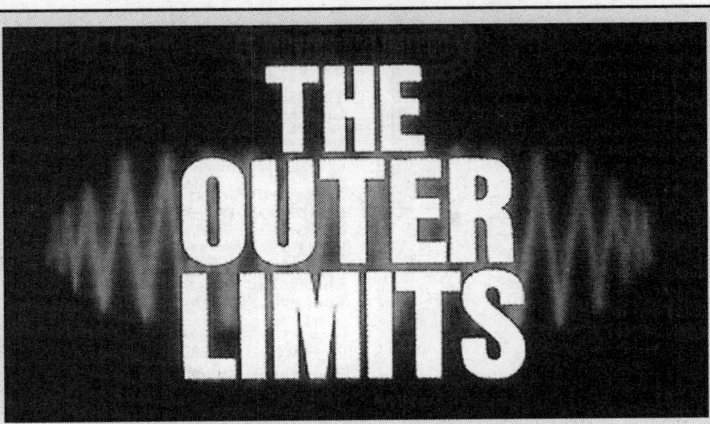

Outer Limits: Soldier
Two fighters from a war-ravaged future Earth are sent back to the 20th century in a story by Harlan Ellison.
12-1834 *$12.99*

Outer Limits: Specimen: Unknown
An orbital space station is beset by strange mushroom-like organisms that emit a deadly gas.
12-1835 *$12.99*

Outer Limits: Fun And Games
An Earth man and woman are transported to a distant world where they must battle representatives of another planet to the death, or risk Earth's destruction. Nick Adams stars.
12-1876 *$12.99*

Outer Limits: The Invisibles
A government agent is assigned to infiltrate a secret cadre of government and military leaders who've been possessed by alien parasites.
12-1877 *$12.99*

Outer Limits: O.B.I.T.
A murder investigation at a scientific installation reveals the extraterrestrial origin of a global surveillance system.
12-1878 *$12.99*

Outer Limits: The Bellero Shield
Brought to Earth by accident, an alien being is robbed of his force field weapon by a scientist's ambitious wife. Martin Landau, Sally Kellerman star.
12-1931 *$12.99*

Outer Limits: Corpus Earthling
Thanks to the metal plate in his head, scientist Robert Culp overhears the plans of two parasitic aliens planning their conquest of the Earth.
12-1933 *$12.99*

Outer Limits: Don't Open Till Doomsday
A honeymooning couple come across two mysteries: a demented woman whose husbands vanished decades ago, and a box that serves as an unearthly gateway.
12-1934 *$12.99*

Outer Limits: A Feasibility Study
The residents of an average suburban neighborhood find the six-square-block radius they live on has been transplanted on a world of rocklike beings.
12-1935 *$12.99*

Outer Limits: Tourist Attraction
A prehistoric "lizard-fish" is captured in a South American country, but escapes before it can be put on exhibition and returns with more of its kind for revenge.
12-1936 *$12.99*

Outer Limits: It Crawled Out Of The Woodwork
An energy-absorbing cloud is used to take control of a scientific research facility by the lab's deranged chief. Scott Marlowe, Ed Asner star.
12-1945 *$12.99*

Outer Limits: The Guests
An eerie house where time stands still and aliens hold occupants captive is discovered by a ne'er-do-well. Gloria Grahame, Geoffrey Horne and Luana Anders star.
12-2052 *$12.99*

Outer Limits: The Borderland
A wealthy man sends a team of scientists into the fourth dimension in hopes of finding his deceased son. With Mark Richman and Nina Foch.
12-2053 *$12.99*

Outer Limits: The Mutant
A strange shower of silver substances on another planet turns a scientist into a bald, big-eyed telepathic killer. Warren Oates and Betsy Jones-Moreland star.
12-2054 *$12.99*

Outer Limits: Moonstone
Scientists and military men on the moon uncover a living object that may be dangerous. With Ruth Roman and Alex Nichol.
12-2055 *$12.99*

Outer Limits: Second Chance
An amusement park ride turns out to be the real thing when a group of people think they're going to have fun on a fake rocketship.
12-2056 *$12.99*

Outer Limits: Behold, Eck!
This humorous entry tells the story of an optician who invents unusual glasses that enable wearers to see a strange creature. Peter Lind Hayes and Joan Freeman star.
12-2057 *$12.99*

Outer Limits: Z-Z-Z-Z-Z
An entomologist is drawn into the insect world when a queen bee takes on a human form. Phillip Abbott and Joana Frank star.
12-2058 *$12.99*

Outer Limits: Controlled Experiment
Two Martians take a closer look at the popular Earth practice of murder by rewinding and fast-forwarding homicides with their special machine. Barry Morse and Carroll O'Connor star.
12-2059 *$12.99*

Outer Limits: The Mice
A criminal with a life sentence makes a deal to spend time on a faraway planet. Henry Silva and Diana Sands star.
12-2060 *$12.99*

Outer Limits: The Special One
He came from the planet Xenon to teach the Earth children something special. What was it? To take over the Earth!! With Richard Ney and Macdonald Carey.
12-2061 *$12.99*

Outer Limits: The Human Factor
In Greenland, a scientific experiment goes awry, and the minds of two men (Gary Merrill, Harry Guardino) are exchanged by accident. Sally Kellerman also stars.
12-2062 *$12.99*

Outer Limits: Production And Decay Of Strange Particles
A nuclear reactor gets out of hand, producing bizarre, human-like creatures with nasty attitudes. With George Macready and Leonard Nimoy.
12-2063 *$12.99*

Outer Limits: The Chameleon
An assassin-for-hire is recruited by the government to be transformed into an alien and infiltrate a ship that's landed on Earth. Script by Robert Towne ("Chinatown"); Robert Duvall stars.
12-2208 *$12.99*

Outer Limits: The Probe
An airplane is caught in a hurricane, and the people inside are picked up by an alien space probe sent to Earth.
12-2209 *$12.99*

Outer Limits: The Children Of Spider County
An alien being returns to Earth to reclaim the offspring he fathered years earlier in hopes of repopulating his homeworld. Kent Smith stars.
12-2210 *$12.99*

Outer Limits: Cold Hands, Warm Heart
After making the first manned landing on Venus, astronaut William Shatner begins undergoing a strange metamorphosis. Geraldine Brooks co-stars.
12-2211 *$12.99*

Outer Limits: Expanding Human
A laboratory experiment in "consciousness-expanding substances" unlocks a scientist's dark side and turns him into an immortal, amoral killer.
12-2212 *$12.99*

Outer Limits: Cry Of Silence
Stuck on a remote country road, a couple are trapped by tumbleweeds controlled by an alien intelligence. Eddie Albert, June Havoc star.
12-2213 *$12.99*

Outer Limits: I, Robot
A mechanical man is tried for the murder of his creator in this sci-fi classic by Otto Binder. Howard Da Silva, Leonard Nimoy, Read Morgan star.
12-2214 *$12.99*

Outer Limits: Wolf 359
An alien world is re-created in microcosm by two scientists, but the accelerated evolution unleashes a deadly creature that threatens all. Patrick O'Neal stars.
12-2215 *$12.99*

Outer Limits: The Duplicate Man
A scientist breeds a clone of himself in order to track down a dangerous alien creature he illegally brought to Earth before it escaped.
12-2216 *$12.99*

Outer Limits: Counterweight
Six people volunteer for a simulated interplanetary flight, but the experiment is also monitored by a mysterious alien light being.
12-2217 *$12.99*

Outer Limits: The Brain Of Colonel Barham
A terminally ill astronaut agrees to have his disembodied brain hooked up to a space probe for use as a "living computer," but the plan backfires.
12-2218 *$12.99*

Outer Limits: The Premonition
A test pilot and his wife escape simultaneous accidents to find themselves in a world where nothing seems to move.
12-2219 *$12.99*

The Outer Limits: Sandkings
The acclaimed '60s sci-fi series returned to TV with this all-new, feature-length installment. Government scientist Beau Bridges retrieves eggs found in a Martian soil sample and takes them to his home lab, where they hatch out intelligent, scorpion-like creatures that live in sand and begin exerting control over their "captor." Helen Shaver, Lloyd Bridges co-star. 93 min.
12-3020 Was $89.99 *$14.99*

It's A Great Life
Michael O'Shea and William Bishop are former GIs who rent a room in a Southern California boarding home while looking for jobs in this sitcom that ran from 1954-1956 on NBC. The stories involve the men's search for jobs and interaction with landlady Frances Bavier, conniving brother James Dunn and daughter Barbara Bates. Each tape features two episodes and runs about 50 min.

It's A Great Life, Vol. 1
Includes "Borrowed TV Set" and "The Hospital" (with guest stars Joseph Kearns and Richard Deacon).
10-9872 Was $19.99 *$14.99*

It's A Great Life, Vol. 2
Includes "Winter Sports" and " A Job for Kathy."
10-9873 Was $19.99 *$14.99*

It's A Great Life
Army buddies-turned-roommates Steve (William Bishop) and Denny (Michael O'Shea) get into more scrapes in two episodes from the rare '50s series. Included here are "Nightwatchman" and "Foster Father." 60 min.
82-1025 *$19.99*

Sophia Loren In Rome (1964)
One of the world's loveliest movie stars in one of the world's most romantic cities. Tour the sites of Roma with the luscious Sophia and guest star Marcello Mastroianni. Music by John Barry. 60 min.
10-8151 Was $19.99 *$14.99*

Passport To Danger
Cesar Romero plays debonair diplomatic courier Steve McQuinn in this mid-'50s syndicated series that takes him on important and dangerous missions across the world. Each tape features two episodes and runs about 60 min.

Passport To Danger, Vol. 1
Includes "Rome" and "Tangiers."
10-8129 Was $19.99 *$14.99*

Passport To Danger, Vol. 2
Includes "Sofia" and "Teheran."
10-8130 Was $19.99 *$14.99*

Passport To Danger, Vol. 3
Includes "Geneva" and "Turkey."
10-8131 Was $19.99 *$14.99*

The Adventures Of Long John Silver
From the island of Porto Bello, buccaneer Long John Silver defends the interests of the Crown against corsairs and Spanish landgrabbers. Robert Newton is the big-hearted pirate and Kit Taylor his ward, Jim Hawkins. Each tape contains two episodes and runs about 50 min. There are five volumes available, including:

The Adventures Of Long John Silver, Vol. 1
Includes "The Devil's Stew" and "Sword of Vengeance."
10-7407 Was $19.99 *$14.99*

The Adventures Of Long John Silver, Vol. 2
Includes "Turnabout" and "Ship of the Dead."
10-7408 Was $19.99 *$14.99*

The Adventures Of Long John Silver, Vol. 3
Includes "Eviction" and "The Pink Pearl."
10-7409 Was $19.99 *$14.99*

The Seven Little Foys (1964)
"I gotta tell ya, that Eddie Foy is some entertainer, boy." Bob Hope narrates this pilot to a proposed TV series, originally broadcast on "The Bob Hope Chrysler Theater." Eddie Foy, Jr. stars as the famed vaudeville star, with the Osmond Brothers as five of his seven children and Mickey Rooney as George M. Cohan. 60 min.
10-8148 Was $19.99 *$14.99*

A Date With The Angels
From the vaults of TV's Golden Age comes this 1957-58 sitcom starring "Golden Girl" Betty White as the sensible newlywed wife of insurance salesman Bill Williams. Each tape contains two episodes and runs 60 min. There are 10 volumes available, including:

A Date With The Angels, Vol. 1
Includes "Tree on the Parkway" and "Return of the Wheel."
10-1215 *$19.99*

A Date With The Angels, Vol. 2
Includes "Diana" and "Francis Goes to School."
10-1216 *$19.99*

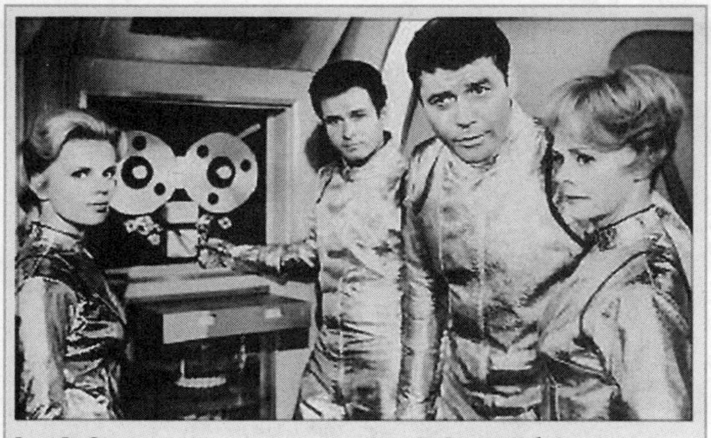

Lost In Space
Join the Robinson family, Major Don West, the Robot and Dr. Zachary Smith as their planned Earth-to-Alpha Centauri journey takes them on an adventure-filled odyssey through space in the original 1965-68 sci-fi series from creator Irwin Allen. Guy Williams, June Lockhart, Billy Mumy and Jonathan Harris star. Each tape runs about 55 min.

Lost In Space, Vol. 1: The Reluctant Stowaway
The first episode of the series shows how, thanks to the sabotage of enemy agent Dr. Smith, the Robinson brood's interplanetary mission was thrown off course.
62-1107 □*$12.99*

Lost In Space, Vol. 2: The Derelict
The Jupiter II is drawn into a gigantic, seemingly abandoned spaceship, but an exploration of the craft turns up some bizarre alien occupants.
04-3559 □*$12.99*

Lost In Space, Vol. 3: Island In The Sky
After landing on a remote and unknown planet, the explorers set out to locate the missing John Robinson.
04-3560 □*$12.99*

Lost In Space, Vol. 4: There Were Giants In The Earth
Forced by cold weather to move farther south, the Robinsons are threatened by immense cyclopean creatures.
04-3618 □*$12.99*

Lost In Space, Vol. 5: The Hungry Sea
A storm-swept inland sea is the Robinsons' daunting obstacle to returning to the safety of the Jupiter II.
04-3619 □*$12.99*

Lost In Space, Vol. 6: Welcome Stranger
The Robinsons are visited by a long-missing Earth astronaut who's become a "space rover." Warren Oates guest stars.
04-3620 □*$12.99*

Lost In Space, Vol. 7: The Keeper, Part 1
In the series' only two-part adventure, guest star Michael Rennie plays an interplanetary collector who seeks to add Will and Penny to his alien menagerie.
04-3661 □*$12.99*

Lost In Space, Vol. 8: The Keeper, Part 2
Even as the Keeper tries to obtain his latest "specimens," Dr. Smith's accidental freeing of his creatures threatens everyone's lives in the concluding episode.
04-3662 □*$12.99*

Lost In Space, Vol. 9: War Of The Robots
It's a cybernetic showdown when guest star Robby the Robot, of "Forbidden Planet" fame, plays an abandoned robotoid restored by Will that threatens the Robinsons.
04-3663 □*$12.99*

Lost In Space, Vol. 10: Blast Off Into Space
In the second-season opener, the crew of the Jupiter 2 discovers that the planet they've been living on is about to explode. Strother Martin guest stars.
04-3710 □*$12.99*

Lost In Space, Vol. 11: Wild Adventure
Dr. Smith is lured out into space by a bewitching alien, jeopardizing the Robinsons' return to Earth. This episode marks the first of many guest appearances of Athena, the Green Girl.
04-3711 □*$12.99*

Lost In Space, Vol. 12: The Android Machine
An android without emotion is taught by the Robinsons to love, and in the process, is upgraded into a higher-performance machine.
04-3712 □*$12.99*

Lost In Space Triple Pack #1
"The Reluctant Stowaway," "The Derelict" and "Island in the Sky" are also available in a special collector's set.
04-3544 Save $14.00! *$24.99*

Lost In Space Triple Pack #2
"There Were Giants in the Earth," "The Hungry Sea" and "Welcome Stranger" are also available in a special collector's set.
04-3621 Save $14.00! *$24.99*

Lost In Space Triple Pack #3
"War of the Robots" and Parts 1 and 2 of "The Keeper" are also available in a special collector's set.
04-3664 Save $14.00! *$24.99*

Lost In Space Triple Pack #4
"Blast Off Into Space," "Wild Adventure" and "The Android Machine" are also available in a special collector's set.
04-3713 Save $14.00! *$24.99*

Lost In Space: Unaired Pilot
There's no Dr. Smith or robot to be found in this original pilot for the CBS series, although the rest of the cast is intact. The Robinson family leaves Earth in 1997 headed for Alpha Centauri, but 3 1/2 years into the voyage a meteor shower redirects their flight to an unknown planet where they face all sorts of dangers.
09-5458 *$14.99*

26 Men
This exciting syndicated series, which ran from 1957 to 1959, told the story of the 26 brave men who patrolled the Arizona Territory in the early part of the 20th century. The focus was on Captain Tom Rynning, played by Tris Coffin, and Ranger Clint Travers, played by Kelo Henderson. Each tape features two episodes and runs about 50 min. There are six volumes available, including:

26 Men, Vol. 1
Includes "The Recruit" and "Trouble at Pinnacle Peak."
09-5206 Was $19.99 *$14.99*

26 Men, Vol. 2
Includes "The Wild Bunch" and "Border Incident."
09-5207 Was $19.99 *$14.99*

26 Men, Vol. 3
Includes "Incident at Yuma" and "The Slater Brothers."
09-5208 Was $19.99 *$14.99*

26 Men/Sheriff Of Cochise
Two vintage TV Westerns set in Arizona are rounded up. First up is "Valley of Fear," from the based-on-fact series recounting the adventures of the 26 rangers charged by the Arizona Territorial Legislature with keeping the peace in 1901, followed by a modern-day drama with John Bromfield as Sheriff Morgan. 55 min.
10-7499 Was $19.99 *$14.99*

China Smith
Veteran Hollywood tough guy Dan Duryea starred as China Smith, a hard-as-nails private detective who works out of a Singapore tavern and seeks dangerous assignments around Asia. Douglass Dumbrille also starred in this series ran from 1952 to 1955, and was also known as "The New Adventures of China Smith." Each volume includes two episodes and runs about 50 min. There are seven volumes available, including:

China Smith, Vol. 1
Features "The Kaprielian Cipher" and "The Yellow Jade Lion."
10-8462 Was $19.99 *$14.99*

China Smith, Vol. 2
Includes "The Bamboo Coffin" and "Shanghai Clipper" (directed by Robert Aldrich).
10-8463 Was $19.99 *$14.99*

China Smith, Vol. 3
Features "The Tidewalker" and "The Sign of the Scorpion."
10-8464 Was $19.99 *$14.99*

China Smith, Vol. 4
Includes "The Bible of Mr. Quail" and "The Devil Chaser."
10-8465 Was $19.99 *$14.99*

THE HARDY BOYS

The Hardy Boys
Literature's famous young detective duo, Frank and Joe Hardy, are played by Parker Stevenson and Shaun Cassidy in these exciting whodunits from the hit TV show, seen on ABC from 1977 to 1979. Each volume runs about 50 min.

The Hardy Boys: Mystery Of Witches' Hollow
The boys look for a friend's uncle in a strange forest that is said to be haunted.
07-1339 Was $19.99 *$14.99*

The Hardy Boys: Flickering Torch Mystery
When a top rock star's life is threatened, Joe and Frank go from fans to bodyguards to foil the plot.
07-1340 Was $19.99 *$14.99*

The Hardy Boys: Secret Of Jade Kwan Yin
When Joe and Frank uncover a mysterious Chinese statue they also dig up an age-old puzzle.
07-1341 Was $19.99 *$14.99*

The Hardy Boys: Mystery Of The Flying Courier
Joe's singing debut turns into a case of missing persons, record piracy and, maybe, murder.
07-1342 Was $19.99 *$14.99*

The Hardy Boys: Wipe Out
Frank and Joe help the Hawaii Police solve a rash of hotel robberies.
07-1343 Was $19.99 *$14.99*

The Hardy Boys: Mystery Of King Tut's Tomb
When the boys are sightseeing in Egypt and wind up accused of purse-snatching, they must find the real culprit.
07-1344 Was $19.99 *$14.99*

The Hardy Boys: Mystery Of The African Safari
The boys and their father turn their African vacation into work when they hunt for game poachers.
07-1345 Was $19.99 *$14.99*

The Hardy Boys: Acapulco Spies
A Mexican holiday turns dangerous when Frank and Joe accidentally become involved with enemy agents.
07-1346 Was $19.99 *$14.99*

NANCY DREW

The Nancy Drew Mysteries
Pamela Sue Martin starred in the 1977-78 season as precocious teenaged sleuth Nancy Drew in these adventures from the thrilling family TV series, based on the popular mystery novels. Each volume runs about 50 min.

Nancy Drew: Mystery Of Pirate's Cove
A light from a supposedly deserted lighthouse spells suspense and danger for Nancy and her friends.
07-1347 Was $19.99 *$14.99*

Nancy Drew: Mystery Of The Diamond Triangle
A car that "vanishes" after an accident gets Nancy mixed up in insurance fraud.
07-1348 Was $19.99 *$14.99*

Nancy Drew: A Haunting We Will Go
Mystery takes center stage when Nancy and her pals produce a play in a haunted theatre.
07-1349 Was $19.99 *$14.99*

Nancy Drew: Secret Of The Whispering Walls
When her aunts' deed to their farm is stolen, Nancy tries to recover it and runs into danger.
07-1350 Was $19.99 *$14.99*

Nancy Drew: Mystery Of The Fallen Angels
Nancy goes undercover in a traveling carnival to clear a young man of theft charges.
07-1351 Was $19.99 *$14.99*

Nancy Drew: Mystery Of The Ghostwriter's Cruise
A luxury liner could become a "death ship" unless Nancy can find a would-be killer in time.
07-1352 Was $19.99 *$14.99*

Nancy Drew: Mystery Of The Solid Gold Kicker
When a friend is accused of murder, it's up to Nancy to clear his name.
07-1353 Was $19.99 *$14.99*

Nancy Drew: Nancy Drew's Love Match
An exclusive tennis tournament, a kleptomaniac classmate and a handsome court pro add up to trouble for Nancy.
07-1354 Was $19.99 *$14.99*

We'll Meet Again (1982)
Airing in America on "Masterpiece Theatre," this British mini-series is set in a British town during World War II. The lives of the residents are turned upside-down by the arrival of an American bomber group stationed in the town, which leads to a clash of cultures and bittersweet wartime romances. Susannah York, Michael Shannon, Ronald Hines, June Barry star. 11 1/2 hrs. on five tapes.
53-6725 *$79.99*

Magnum, P.I.
Blending humor, action, beautiful women and gorgeous Hawaiian scenery, this entertaining show ran from 1980 to 1988 on CBS. Tom Selleck played the handsome Vietnam vet title character who tooled around the islands in a Ferrari investigating crimes. His sidekicks included servant John Hillerman, helicopter pilot Roger E. Mosely and resort owner Larry Manetti. Each tape runs about 50 min.

Magnum P.I.: Don't Eat The Snow
The premiere episode of the series has Thomas Magnum confronted by drug dealers, hostile government officials and crafty criminals when he searches for the truth behind his pal's death. 99 min.
07-2199 *$14.99*

Magnum, P.I.: Novel Connection
"Murder She Wrote's" crime-solving writer Jessica Fletcher (Angela Lansbury) teams with Magnum to get to the bottom of a murder case involving the death of a houseguest.
07-2157 *$14.99*

Magnum, P.I.: A Sense Of Debt
A down-and-out boxer gets involved in fixing bouts in this thrilling episode that features guest star Shannen Doherty as the fighter's daughter.
07-2158 *$14.99*

Magnum, P.I.: Murder 101
Magnum takes the podium as a lecturer at a university, and the class uses his methods when one of the students looks into her boyfriend's cheating ways.
07-2159 *$14.99*

Magnum, P.I.: Deja Vu
Magnum gets an eerie feeling when he travels to London for a party and meets a woman whose husband died in an accident similar to the one the detective had a dream about.
07-2160 *$14.99*

Magnum, P.I.: Thank Heaven For Little Girls And Big Ones, Too
Five young female con artists ask Magnum to help them find their missing "teacher."
07-2161 *$14.99*

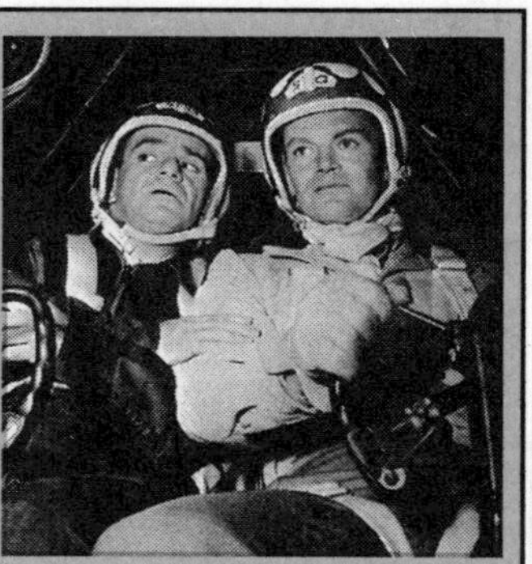

Captain Midnight
More fun than a mug full of Ovaltine! Take off with the aerial adventurer and his Secret Squadron as they defeat all manner of crooks and spies. Richard Webb and Sid Melton star in the classic example of '50s "kidvid" TV; each tape contains two episodes (with commercials!) and runs about 60 min.

Captain Midnight, Vol. 1
Features "Deadly Diamonds" and "The Frozen Man."
10-7542 Was $19.99 *$14.99*

Captain Midnight, Vol. 2
Features "Mission to Mexico" and "Million Dollar Diamond."
10-7543 Was $19.99 *$14.99*

Captain Midnight, Vol. 3
Includes "The Secret Weapon" and "The Secret Room."
10-7536 Was $19.99 *$14.99*

Captain Midnight
Includes "Devil Below Zero" and "Frozen Alive."
68-8158 *$19.99*

Jet Jackson, Flying Commando (Captain Midnight), Vol. 1
Under his syndicated alias, Captain Midnight flies into action with the Secret Squadron in two adventures, "The Curse of the Pharaohs" and "Counterfeit Millions." 55 min.
10-7498 Was $19.99 *$14.99*

The Dick Van Dyke Show

Originally broadcast on CBS from 1961 to 1967, this Emmy-winning series featured Dick Van Dyke as Rob Petrie, the head writer for a comedy-variety TV show; Mary Tyler Moore as wife Laura; Larry Matthews as their son, Richie; and, in memorable support, Morey Amsterdam, Rose Marie, Richard Deacon and Carl Reiner, the series' creator-writer.

The Dick Van Dyke Show, Vol. 1
Rob brings home two adorable ducklings for Richie that quickly grow into troublesome pets in "Never Name a Duck." And Rob assumes Laura is saving for his birthday present when he discovers her secret "Bank Book." 55 min.
58-8162 *$14.99*

The Dick Van Dyke Show, Vol. 2
In "Hustling a Hustler," Blackie, Buddy's pool shark brother, finds a new mark in Rob, while "Night the Roof Fell In" has Rob and Laura's heated discussion leading to an affectionate reconciliation. 55 min.
58-8163 *$14.99*

The Dick Van Dyke Show, Vol. 3
In "A Man's Teeth Are Not His Own," Rob's cracked tooth causes problems when he tells best friend Jerry that another dentist did the repair work. Next, the Petries realize that they've made a mistake hiring an artist to do their house painting in "Give Me Your Walls." 55 min.
58-8164 *$14.99*

The Dick Van Dyke Show, Vol. 4
Join Dick, Mary, Morey and the rest of the gang in two more hilarious episodes from the classic TV series: "The Life and Love of Joe Coogan" and "My Neighbor's Husband's Other Life." 50 min.
09-5219 *$14.99*

The Dick Van Dyke Show: All About Rob
Rob takes a ski trip over Laura's objections and comes home injured in "Don't Trip Over That Mountain"; lands a part opposite an Italian sexpot in an experimental film in "You Ought to Be in Pictures"; and tries to be hip by purchasing a motorcycle in "Br-room, Br-room." 77 min.
10-2555 *$12.99*

The Dick Van Dyke Show: All About Laura
In "October Eve," Rob discovers a naked painting of Laura—which she remembers posing for with her clothes on!; Rob's sneezing prompts Laura to think he has a psychosomatic allergy to her in "Gesundheit Darling"; and Laura's acclaim of her husband in a magazine article gets him in trouble in "My Husband Is the Best One." 77 min.
10-2556 *$12.99*

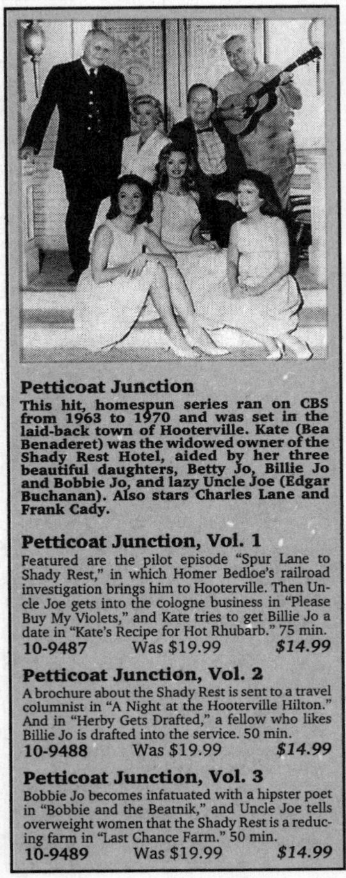

Petticoat Junction

This hit, homespun series ran on CBS from 1963 to 1970 and was set in the laid-back town of Hooterville. Kate (Bea Benaderet) was the widowed owner of the Shady Rest Hotel, aided by her three beautiful daughters, Betty Jo, Billie Jo and Bobbie Jo, and lazy Uncle Joe (Edgar Buchanan). Also stars Charles Lane and Frank Cady.

Petticoat Junction, Vol. 1
Featured are the pilot episode "Spur Lane to Shady Rest," in which Homer Bedloe's railroad investigation brings him to Hooterville. Then Uncle Joe gets into the cologne business in "Please Buy My Violets," and Kate tries to get Billie Jo a date in "Kate's Recipe for Hot Rhubarb." 75 min.
10-9487 Was $19.99 *$14.99*

Petticoat Junction, Vol. 2
A brochure about the Shady Rest is sent to a travel columnist in "A Night at the Hooterville Hilton." And in "Herby Gets Drafted," a fellow who likes Billie Jo is drafted into the service. 50 min.
10-9488 Was $19.99 *$14.99*

Petticoat Junction, Vol. 3
Bobbie Jo becomes infatuated with a hipster poet in "Bobbie and the Beatnik," and Uncle Joe tells overweight women that the Shady Rest is a reducing farm in "Last Chance Farm." 50 min.
10-9489 Was $19.99 *$14.99*

Stories Of The Century

Jim Davis starred in this action-packed Western anthology series, which began in 1954, as railroad detective Matt Clark. With help from cohort Frankie Adams (Mary Castle), Clark tackled infamous outlaws, dealt with Indian leaders, and faced other problems along the iron rails. Except where noted, each tape features six episodes.

Stories Of The Century, Vol. 1
Features "Belle Starr," "Billy the Kid," "Frank and Jesse James," "Geronimo," "Quantrill and His Raiders" and "Cattle Kate." Guest stars include Marie Windsor, Richard Jaeckel, Lee Van Cleef. 155 min.
09-5314 *$19.99*

Stories Of The Century, Vol. 2
Features "Sam Bass," "Johnny Ringo," "The Dalton Gang," "Doc Holliday," "The Younger Brothers" and "John Wesley Hardin." Guest stars include Denver Pyle, Stuart Whitman, Fess Parker, Sheb Wooley. 155 min.
09-5315 *$19.99*

Stories Of The Century, Vol. 3
Features "Joaquin Murieta," "Tiburcio Vasquez," "Chief Crazy Horse," "Black Bart," "Henry Plummer" and "Bill Longley." Guest stars include Rick Jason, John Dehner. 155 min.
09-5316 *$19.99*

Stories Of The Century, Vol. 4
Features "Harry Tracy," "Wild Bunch of Wyoming," "The Doolin Gang," "Little Britches," "Black Jack Ketchum" and "Tom Horn." Guest stars include Slim Pickens, Leo Gordon, Jack Elam. 155 min.
09-5317 *$19.99*

Stories Of The Century, Vol. 5
Features "Ben Thompson," "Clay Allison," "Burt Alvord," "The Apache Kid," "Tom Bell" and "Kate Bender." Guest stars include Richard Simmons, Jack Kelly, Stuart Whitman. 155 min.
09-5318 *$19.99*

Stories Of The Century, Vol. 6
Features "Augustine Chacon," "Cherokee Bill," "Nate Champion," "Sontag and Evans," "Rube Burrows" and "Jim Courtwright." Guest stars include Morris Ankrum, Paul Picerni. 155 min.
09-5319 *$19.99*

Stories Of The Century, Vol. 7
Features "Milt Sharp," "Jack Slade" and "L.H. Musgrove." Guest stars include Don "Red" Barry, John Archer. 78 min.
09-5320 *$19.99*

Stories Of The Century: Complete Set
All seven volumes are also available in a money-saving collector's set.
09-5321 Save $40.00! *$99.99*

Shower Of Stars, Vol. 1
Marvelous showcase for co-hosts Mario Lanza and Betty Grable, featured here in the first show of this spectacular series. Mario and Betty perform a host of musical numbers, including "Be My Love," "Digga Digga Doo," "One for the Road" and more. Also appearing are Harry James and his orchestra, Fred Clark and King Donovan. 60 min.
10-7010 *$19.99*

Shower Of Stars, Vol. 2
Mario Lanza joins Edgar Bergen and Charlie McCarthy, Gene Nelson and Sheree North for an exciting evening of music, dance and comedy, with Mario performing an aria from "Tosca" and "Someday" from the operetta, "Vagabond King." 60 min.
10-7011 *$19.99*

Shower Of Stars, Vol. 3
"Bright young newcomer" Shirley MacLaine fills in for the scheduled Betty Grable (who was sidelined due to a car accident), while Johnny Rae performs a medley of his hits. Also features a performance of "That's Entertainment" by the show's entire guest list, which included Anna Maria Alberghetti, Harry James and the inimitable Larry Storch. 60 min.
10-7012 *$19.99*

Shower Of Stars, Vol. 4
A salute to gold records of the mid-'50s brings together the talents of the Andrews Sisters, who belt out their biggest hits, Frankie Laine, Eddie "Rochester" Anderson, Rudy Vallee, Gene Austin and special guest Red Skelton. 60 min.
10-7013 *$19.99*

Shower Of Stars, Vol. 5
Series frequent visitors Betty Grable and Harry James share the spotlight with Danny Thomas, Ed Wynn, Jean Hagen, Groucho Marx and James Dunn to hail the hit musical/comedy revue, "Entertainment on Wheels." 60 min.
10-7014 *$19.99*

Shower Of Stars, Vol. 6
In an original baseball "mini-musical," Tony Martin is the star slugger, Marguerite Piazza the opera diva who buys the team, and William Frawley and Vivian Vance are the gruff but lovable manager and his wife. Songs include "Let's Fall in Love" and "Dance with Me, Henry." 60 min.
10-7015 *$19.99*

Shower Of Stars, Vol. 7
A host of musical giants from the '50s paint a tuneful portrait of the American music scene of the day, with a mosaic of songs from the likes of Frankie Laine, Helen O'Connell, Frankie Lymon and the Teenagers, Les Baxter, Nelson Riddle and his Orchestra, Jane Russell and more. 60 min.
10-7016 *$19.99*

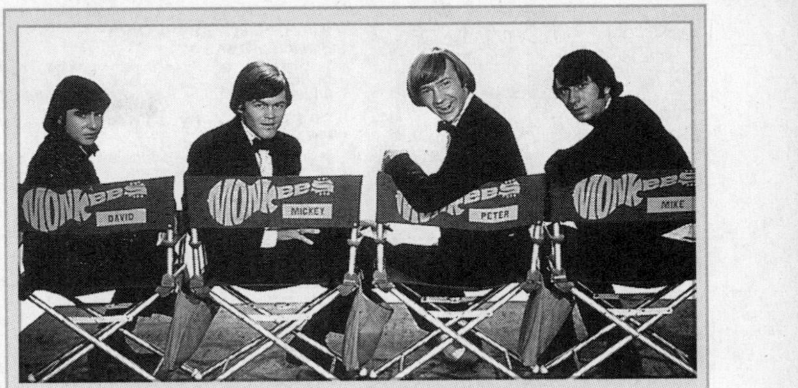

The Monkees

BUH-doom! Here they come, walking down the street...and onto your TV, with this video treat! Join the irrepressible Mickey, Peter, Mike and Davy as they get into one wild situation after another, yet still find time to perform "Last Train to Clarksville," "Daydream Believer" and other top 10 hits, in their beloved comedy series which ran on NBC from 1966 to 1968. Each tape features two episodes and runs about 50 min.

The Monkees, Vol. 1: Here Come The Monkees/The Picture Frame
15-5320 *$14.99*

The Monkees, Vol. 2: Alias Mickey Dolenz/ Hillbilly Honeymoon
15-5321 *$14.99*

The Monkees, Vol. 3: Too Many Girls/Everywhere A Sheik, Sheik
15-5322 *$14.99*

The Monkees, Vol. 4: Hitting The High Seas/Monkees In Texas
15-5323 *$14.99*

The Monkees, Vol. 5: Success Story/ Monkees Mind Their Manor
15-5356 *$14.99*

The Monkees, Vol. 6: Royal Flush/Monkees At The Circus
15-5357 *$14.99*

The Monkees, Vol. 7: Monkee See, Monkee Die/ Monkees Chow Mein
15-5358 *$14.99*

The Monkees, Vol. 8: Captain Crocodile/Fairy Tale
15-5359 *$14.99*

The Monkees, Vol. 9: One Man Shy/Monkees Marooned
15-5360 *$14.99*

The Monkees, Vol. 10: The Spy Who Came In From The Cool/ Card-Carrying Red Shoes
15-5361 *$14.99*

The Monkees, Vol. 11: I Was A Teenage Monster/ Monstrous Monkee Mash
15-5362 *$14.99*

The Monkees, Vol. 12: Monkee Mother/The Christmas Show
15-5363 *$14.99*

The Monkees, Vol. 13: Dance Monkee Dance/ The Wild Monkees
15-5383 *$14.99*

The Monkees, Vol. 14: Monkee vs. Machine/ Some Like It Luke Warm
15-5384 *$14.99*

The Monkees, Vol. 15: The Chaperone/The Case Of The Missing Monkee
15-5569 *$14.99*

The Monkees, Vol. 16: Monkees A La Carte/Monkee Mayor
15-5570 *$14.99*

Great Actors & Actresses Of The 20th Century

These collections feature episodes from 1950s TV anthology shows that spotlight some of Hollywood's greatest players, from Academy Award winners to early appearances by stars-to-be. Each tape includes three episodes and runs about 80 min.

Great Actors Of The 20th Century, Vol. 1
"The Answer" stars David Niven as an embittered Hollywood writer who has a revelatory visit to his hometown; broke gambler Errol Flynn finds the only way out of debt is to engage in "The Duel"; and James Cagney is an aging professor who has doubts about his career on the eve of a celebratory banquet in "A Link in the Chain."
15-5429 *$19.99*

Great Actors Of The 20th Century, Vol. 2
American teacher Vincent Price faces imprisonment and torture in China in "The Brainwashing of John Hayes"; immigrant Lon Chaney goes from rags to riches as "The Golden Junkman"; and Boris Karloff stars in "The Vestris," an eerie tale of a sea captain and a message from beyond the grave.
15-5430 *$19.99*

Great Actresses Of The 20th Century, Vol. 2
Angela Lansbury is "The Indiscreet Mrs. Jarvis," a well-married woman whose seedy past catches up to her and drives her to a desperate solution; poor little rich girl Joanne Woodward gets lessons in growing up in "Interlude"; and a newlywed husband learns to be a father to his wife's three teenage daughters in "The Wild Bunch," with Natalie Wood and Charles Boyer.
15-5433 *$19.99*

Great Actresses Of The 20th Century, Vol. 3
Greer Garson swears "Revenge" when her fiancé's killer is acquitted in a rigged trial; Loretta Young pays a visit to her grown son's family during a "Business Trip," but the son's discovery of what she really does for a living threatens their relationship; and Ida Lupino is trapped in her penthouse atop a deserted apartment building in "One Way Out."
15-5434 *$19.99*

Tales From The Darkside, Vol. 1
A collection of spooky stories from the TV show, including Stephen King's "Word Processor of the Gods," "Everybody Needs a Little Love," "Distant Signals" and "Do Not Open the Box." E.G. Marshall, Bruce Davison, Jerry Orbach, Darren McGavin and Eileen Heckart star. 100 min.
14-3254 *$14.99*

Tales From The Darkside, Vol. 2
Keep the lights on for another five creepy episodes from the TV horror anthology series. Scaremeister George A. Romero brings stars like Lisa Bonet, Phyllis Diller, John Heard, Jerry Stiller and Abe Vigoda together in a further frightfest. 100 min.
14-3291 *$14.99*

Tales From The Darkside, Vol. 3
Five shocking stories of terror and suspense are presented here, starring the likes of Danny Aiello, Justine Bateman, William Hickey and Kareem Abdul-Jabbar. Included are "The Odds," "The Circus," "Mookie and Pookie," "The Deal" and "Djinn, No Chaser." 100 min.
14-3302 *$14.99*

Tales From The Darkside, Vol. 4
Five further forays into fear and fright, including Stephen King's "Sorry, Right Number" and "Beetlejuice" creator Michael McDowell's "The Moth." Join stars like Jeff Conaway, Deborah Harry, Paul Dooley and Roy Dotrice as they explore the terror waiting on "the darkside." 100 min.
14-3319 *$14.99*

Tales From The Darkside, Vol. 5
Join stars Fritz Weaver, Robert Forster, Greg Mullavey and Seymour Cassel in five chilling sojourns into the unexpected from the popular TV shock series: "The Milkman Cometh," "Monsters in My Room," "Comet Watch," "Printer's Devil" and Clive Barker's "The Yattering and Jack." 100 min.
14-3329 Was $89.99 *$14.99*

Tales From The Darkside, Vol. 6
Another collection of frightening stories from the Darkside, including "Let the Games Begin," "Unhappy Medium," "Black Widow," "Baker's Dozen" and Robert Bloch's "Beetles." With Theresa Saldana, Connie Stevens, Mabel King and David Groh. 100 min.
14-3403 Was $89.99 *$14.99*

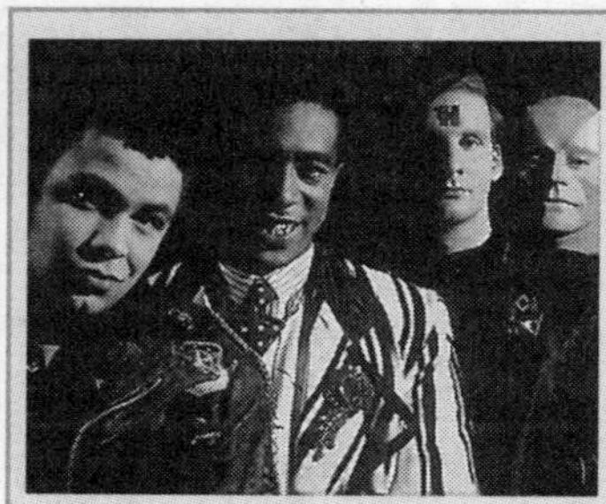

RED DWARF

Red Dwarf
Blast off for laughter in this British sci-fi spoof about an interstellar freighter and its hapless inhabitants: Lister, a ne'er-do-well freed from 3 million years of stasis to find he's the sole surviving crew member; Rimmer, a by-the-book technician who exists in holographic form; Cat, the preening by-product of 3,000 millennia of feline evolution; and Kryten, a fastidiously servile android. Craig Charles, Chris Barrie and Danny John-Jules star. Each tape features three episodes and runs about 90 min.

Red Dwarf I, Byte One: The End
Includes "The End," "Future Echoes" and "Balance of Power."
04-2772 *$19.99*

Red Dwarf I, Byte Two: Confidence & Paranoia
Includes "Confidence & Paranoia," "Waiting for God" and "Me2."
04-2773 *$19.99*

Red Dwarf II, Byte One: Kryten
Includes "Kryten," "Better Than Life" and "Thanks for the Memory."
04-2774 *$19.99*

Red Dwarf II, Byte Two: Stasis Leak
Includes "Stasis Leak," "Queeg" and "Parallel Universe."
04-2775 *$19.99*

Red Dwarf III, Byte One: Backwards
Includes "Backwards," "Marooned" and "Polymorph."
04-2692 *$19.99*

Red Dwarf III, Byte Two: Timeslides
Includes "Timeslides," "Body Swap" and "Last Day."
04-2693 *$19.99*

Red Dwarf IV, Byte One: Camille
Includes "Camille," "DNA" and "Justice."
04-2694 *$19.99*

Red Dwarf IV, Byte Two: Dimension Jump
Includes "Dimension Jump," "White Hole" and "Meltdown."
04-2695 *$19.99*

Red Dwarf V, Byte One: Back To Reality
Includes "Back to Reality," "Demons & Angels" and "Holoship."
04-3321 ❑*$19.99*

Red Dwarf V, Byte Two: Quarantine
Includes "Quarantine," "The Inquisitor" and "Terrorform."
04-3322 ❑*$19.99*

Red Dwarf VI, Byte One
Includes "Gunmen of the Apocalypse," "Legion" and "Psirens."
04-2979 ❑*$19.99*

Red Dwarf VI, Byte Two
Includes "Polymorph II," "Rimmerworld" and "Out of Time."
04-2980 ❑*$19.99*

Red Dwarf VII, Byte One
Includes "Tikka To Ride," "Stoke Me a Clipper" and "Ouroboros."
04-3716 ❑*$19.99*

Red Dwarf VII, Byte Two
Includes "Duct Soup," "Blue" and "Beyond a Joke."
04-3717 ❑*$19.99*

Red Dwarf VII, Byte Three
Includes "Epideme" and "Nanarchy," plus "Red Dwarf A-Z," a special collection of interviews and outtakes.
04-3718 ❑*$19.99*

Red Dwarf VIII, Byte One
Includes "Back in the Red, Parts 1-3."
04-3869 ❑*$19.99*

Red Dwarf VIII, Byte Two
Includes "Cassandra," "Pete, Part 1" and "Krytie TV."
04-3870 ❑*$19.99*

Red Dwarf VIII, Byte Three
Includes "Pete, Part 2," "Only the Good" and the special cast-versus-fans trivia showdown, "Can't Smeg, Won't Smeg."
04-3871 ❑*$19.99*

Red Dwarf: Smeg-Ups
A hit at sci-fi conventions on both sides of the Atlantic, this hilarious video features the silliest flubs, outtakes and behind-the-camera hi-jinks with Rimmer and the rest of the Red Dwarf crew. 60 min.
04-3323 *$14.99*

The Brittas Empire: Boxed Set (1991)
Hilarious British comedy featuring "Red Dwarf's" Chris Barrie as the manager of a leisure center whose arrogance gets the best of his wife and put-upon staff. This three-tape set includes "The New Manager/Opening Day," "Bye-Bye Baby/Underwater Wedding" and "Stop Thief/The Assassin." With Pippa Haywood, Michael Burns. 180 min. total. NOTE: Individual volumes available for $19.99 each.
53-6959 Save $10.00! *$49.99*

Dark Ages Collection (1999)
"Red Dwarf" co-creator Rob Grant was also behind this British comedy series set in the year 999 and focusing on Churl Gudrun (Phil Jupitus), a soil-tilling family man trying to get through life without the annoyances of war and the "millennium madness" affecting everybody. Included in the two-tape set are the episodes "Vile Vole Pie," "Vikings," "War," "Witch" and "The End of the World." 121 min. total.
53-6956 *$39.99*

Good Neighbors
Richard Briers, Paul Eddington, Penelope Keith and the ever-sprightly Kendall star in this popular 1975-78 BBC comedy series about two suburban London couples: the "back-to-nature" Goods and the socially conscious Leadbetters, and the comical conflicts that arise between the neighbors. Except where noted, each tape features three episodes and runs about 85 min.

Good Neighbors, Vol. 1
Includes "Backs to the Wall," "The Windbreak War" and "Silly, But It's Fun."
04-3460 Was $19.99 ❑*$14.99*

Good Neighbors, Vol. 2
Includes "Pigs Lib," "Just My Bill" and "Mutiny."
04-3778 Was $19.99 ❑*$14.99*

Good Neighbors, Vol. 3
Includes "Going to Pot," "The Happy Event" and "The Last Posh Frock."
04-3779 Was $19.99 ❑*$14.99*

Good Neighbors, Vol. 4
Includes "Plough Your Own Furrow," "Say Little Hen...?" and "The Pagan Rite."
04-3944 ❑*$14.99*

Good Neighbors, Vol. 5
Includes "Mr. Fix-It," "The Day Peace Broke Out" and "I Talk to the Trees."
04-3945 ❑*$14.99*

Good Neighbors: Boxed Set
All seven episodes from the show's fourth and final series—"Away from It All," "The Green Door," "Our Speaker Today," "The Weaver's Tale," "Suit Yourself," "Sweet and Sour Charity" and "Anniversary"—are available in a two-tape set. 210 min.
50-8598 *$29.99*

Waiting For God
There's lots of funny British satire in store in these episodes of the hit series, set at the Bayview Retirement Village, as two new residents turn the home into a wacky place where anything can and does happen. Graham Crowden and Stephanie Cole star. Each tape features three episodes and runs about 85 min.

Waiting For God: The Funeral
Includes "The Funeral," "The Hip Operation" and "The Boring Son."
04-3346 ❑*$19.99*

Waiting For God: Cheering Tom Up
Includes "Cheering Tom Up," "Fraulein Mueller" and "Power of Attorney."
04-3347 ❑*$19.99*

Chef!
Looking for a tasty serving of comedy, British-style? Then watch Lenny Henry as the demanding head chef at the famous, albeit financially troubled, Le Chateau Anglais restaurant in these episodes from the popular BBC series. Each tape features three episodes and runs about 90 min.

Chef!
Includes "The Big Cheese," "Fame Is the Spur" and "Rice and Peas."
04-3516 *$19.99*

Chef! A Second Helping
Includes "Personnel," "Beyond the Pass" and "Subject to Contract."
04-3517 *$19.99*

TV's Readers' Digest
This series ran on ABC from 1955 to 1956 and offered dramatizations of stories which originally appeared in the popular magazine. Hugh Riley hosts the show, which features lots of interesting guest stars. Each tape includes two shows and runs about 55 min.

TV's Readers' Digest, Vol. 1
Includes "The Brain Washing of John Harp" with Vincent Price, and "My First Bullfight" with Jack Kelly.
08-1763 *$14.99*

TV's Readers' Digest, Vol. 2
Includes "Mystery of Minnie" with Walter Coy and Frances McDonald, and "Shadow of God" with Paul Kelly and Strother Martin.
08-1764 *$14.99*

TV's Readers' Digest, Vol. 3
Includes "The Great Armed Car Robbery" with Alex Nicol, and "Case of the Uncertain Hand" with Marguerete Chapman.
08-1765 *$14.99*

Cheers
One of the most beloved sitcoms of all time ran on NBC from 1982 to 1993 and took place in a Boston tavern inhabited by a crew of eccentrics that included Ted Danson, Shelley Long, Kirstie Alley, George Wendt, John Ratzenberger, Woody Harrelson, Rhea Perlman and Kelsey Grammer. Except where noted, each tape features two episodes and runs about 50 min.

Cheers, Vol. 1
Would-be poetess and bride Diane Chambers finds herself left at the altar (or, in this case, the bar) in the series' first episode, "Give Me a Ring Sometime." 27 min.
06-2147 ❑*$9.99*

Cheers, Vol. 2
"Coach Returns to Action" when he winds up competing with Sam for the attentions of the same woman. Next, the gang seeks the help of con artist Harry the Hat (Harry Anderson) after Coach is fleeced at cards in "Pick a Con...Any Con."
06-2148 ❑*$12.99*

Cheers, Vol. 3
Sam isn't sure how to react over a former Red Sox teammate's "coming out" in "The Boys in the Bar." Then, Diane's attempts to gain sympathy from the gang after her cat dies fall on deaf ears in "Let Me Count the Ways."
06-2149 ❑*$12.99*

Cheers, Vol. 4
Diane attempts to rehabilitate a con through acting lessons and creates a monster in "Homicidal Ham." Next, a visit by Dick Cavett to the bar puts him at the mercy of poetry-spouting Diane in "They Call Me Mayday."
06-2150 ❑*$12.99*

Cheers, Vol. 5
Diane fails to be impressed by the intellectual prowess of "Sam's Women" and decides to give his latest conquest a quiz, while a TV sportscaster arrives to do a profile on Sam in "Sam at Eleven."
06-2152 ❑*$12.99*

Cheers, Vol. 6
Sam and Diane try fixing each other up with dates, but the results aren't what anyone expected, in "Diane's Perfect Date." Then Diane's college friend (Julia Duffy) comes to visit and winds up making a play for Sam in "Any Friend of Diane's."
06-2153 ❑*$12.99*

Cheers, Vol. 7
It's anything but smooth sailing for would-be lovers Sam and Diane in "Power Play," once she abruptly gives him the gate. Next, a triangle ensues in "Just Three Friends" when an old friend (Markie Post) of Diane's comes to Boston and sets her sights on Sam.
06-2151 ❑*$12.99*

Cheers, Vol. 8
In the two-parter "I'll Be Seeing You," Sam decides to win Diane over by commissioning famous painter Philip Semenko (Christopher Lloyd) to paint her portrait. After a jealous Sam calls off the deal, Diane decides to pose for Semenko behind his back.
06-2365 ❑*$12.99*

Cheers, Vol. 9
Sam and Diane stop seeing each other in the two-part "Rebound," which leads Sam to go back to drinking and Diane to a rest home. Diane tries to help Sam by suggesting he talk to her new psychiatrist, Dr. Frasier Crane...but doesn't mention he's also her new boyfriend.
06-2366 ❑*$12.99*

Cheers, Vol. 10
In "Rescue Me," Diane calls Sam from Europe to discuss Dr. Frasier Crane's marriage proposal and is surprised by his favorable response. And in "Birth, Death, Love and Rice," Sam travels to Europe to find what he thinks is the newly married couple. This episode also features Woody's first appearance on the show.
06-2367 ❑*$12.99*

Cheers, Vol. 11
The wedding is set, but will Diane and Sam have say those two magic words in "I Do, Adieu"? And in "Home Is the Sailor," Sam returns to Cheers after having sold the bar several months earlier to find unhappy regulars and a gorgeous new manager named Rebecca Howe.
06-2368 ❑*$12.99*

Pictures: Complete Set (1984)
Set in the heyday of the silent film ear, this funny and touching four-volume British TV saga follows a screenwriter who receives inspiration from a movie-obsessed woman who gets a job as a studio waitress, hoping to draw producers' attention. But her dreams are put on hold when a producer puts his starlet girlfriend in the lead. Peter McEnery, Wendy Morgan star. 350 min. total.
53-9587 Was $109.99 *$49.99*

The Andy Griffith Show
One of the most popular TV shows of all time, this CBS program ran from 1960 to 1968. Follow the comical, homespun exploits of sheriff Andy Taylor (Andy Griffith), son Opie (Ron Howard), Aunt Bee (Frances Bavier), deputy Barney Fife (Don Knotts) and the other residents of laid-back Mayberry, North Carolina. Each two-program tape runs about 55 min.

The Andy Griffith Show, Vol. 1
In "High Noon in Mayberry," Barney gets frazzled when ex-con Luke Comstock (Dub Taylor) comes looking for Andy. Next, Andy and Barney have to save their town from a goat who has swallowed explosives in "The Loaded Goat."
09-5282 *$14.99*

The Andy Griffith Show, Vol. 2
Andy rekindles a romance with an old flame at his 20-year high school "Class Reunion," while in "Rafe Hollister Sings," Andy stands by a farmer trying to make an impression by singing at a concert.
09-5283 *$14.99*

The Andy Griffith Show, Vol. 3
Arnold Winkler, a bratty youngster, tries to teach Opie how to manipulate Andy in "Opie and the Spoiled Kid." And Barney attempts to use modern police technology to help Andy catch the crooks in "The Great Filling Station Robbery."
09-5284 *$14.99*

The Andy Griffith Show, Vol. 4
A misstatement by Andy on the importance of learning history leads him to a meeting with Opie's new teacher, Miss Helen Crump (Aneta Corsault), in "Andy Discovers America." Next, "Aunt Bee's Medicine Man" proves to be selling elixirs with alcoholic ingredients.
09-5285 *$14.99*

The Andy Griffith Show, Vol. 5
That cantankerous hillbilly clan, the Darlings, make their debut in "The Darlings Are Coming." Then, a British "gentleman's gentleman" passing through town works off the fine for the accident he caused by becoming "Andy's English Valet."
09-5286 *$14.99*

The Andy Griffith Show, Vol. 6
In "Barney's First Car," Deputy Fife spends $500 on a car, but finds out it's been sold to him by a bunco ring. Also, Barney tries to show Opie how to handle a woman in "The Rivals."
09-5287 *$14.99*

The Andy Griffith Show, Vol. 7
In "A Wife for Andy," Barney tries to find a mate for his pal, but the answer is Opie's teacher, Helen Crump, who the deputy doesn't approve of. And Andy finds "Dogs, Dogs, Dogs" all over the place when Opie's stray canine is followed home by his pals—the same time a state inspector arrives at the Mayberry jailhouse.
09-5288 *$14.99*

The Andy Griffith Show, Vol. 8
Andy and Barney try to save Charlene Darling from a "Mountain Wedding" with the rascally Ernest T. Bass. And Barney deputizes Gomer to keep two prisoners from escaping in "The Big House," which co-stars George Kennedy.
09-5289 *$14.99*

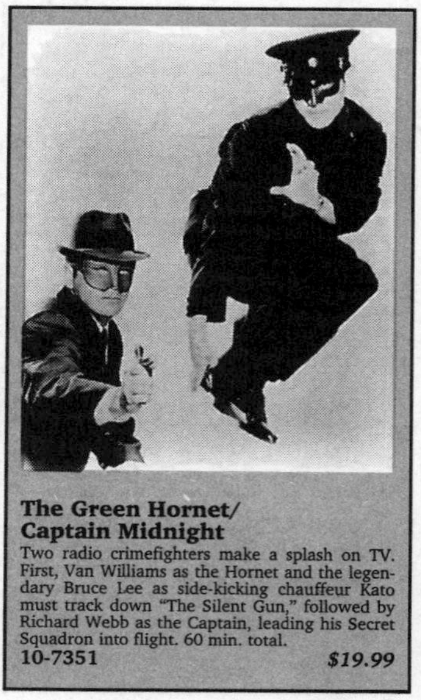

The Green Hornet/ Captain Midnight
Two radio crimefighters make a splash on TV. First, Van Williams as the Hornet and the legendary Bruce Lee as side-kicking chauffeur Kato must track down "The Silent Gun," followed by Richard Webb as the Captain, leading his Secret Squadron into flight. 60 min. total.
10-7351 *$19.99*

Maverick

In this popular TV Western series, James Garner played conniving, gun-shy cardsharp Bret Maverick, who, along with brother Bart (Jack Kelly), got involved in offbeat and funny frontier adventures. The Emmy-winning program ran from 1957 to 1962. Each volume runs about 50 min.

Maverick: War Of The Silver Kings
The series' debut episode finds Bret Maverick up to his aces in a high-stakes poker game.
19-2653 $12.99

Maverick: Duel At Sundown
Bret's rival for the hand of a pretty young thing turns out to be none other than Clint Eastwood! Does Maverick feel lucky? Well, does he?
19-1962 $12.99

Maverick: Shady Deal At Sunny Acres
The Maverick Brothers enlist the aid of some of their fellow frontier rogues to turn the tables on a swindling banker. Co-stars Efrem Zimbalist, Jr., Richard Long and Diane Brewster.
19-1963 $12.99

Maverick: Iron Hand
A confrontation on the Chisholm Trail could lead to trouble for Bart Maverick and cowboy Robert Redford.
19-2654 $12.99

Maverick: The Bundle From Britain
The title "bundle" turns out to be long-lost Maverick cousin Beauregard (Roger Moore), a Civil War veteran who's returned from England.
19-2656 $12.99

Maverick: Point Blank
Newly released from jail, Bret finds himself in a con artist contest with rival Mike Connors.
19-2657 $12.99

Maverick: According To Hoyle
No card player is better at having "an ace up the sleeve," but can Bret still win when he's required to play strictly by the rulebook?
19-2658 $12.99

Strange Experiences (1959)
Try to find this one in your TV Guide: a series of "One Step Beyond"-type vignettes from a little-seen TV series. The tape includes the original commercials.
68-8440 $19.99

Peter Gunn: Let's Kill Timothy/The Fuse

Craig Stevens stars as the two-fisted private eye in this double feature from his 1958-61 series. First, Gunn must protect a nervous client from a hit man after a jewelry robbery in "Let's Kill Timothy"; and in "The Fuse," Gunn is hired to prove a criminal is innocent after he's accused of killing a union leader. With Lola Albright, Herschel Bernardi. 55 min.
10-9554 $14.99

The Third Man

Graham Greene's story, which inspired the classic Orson Welles movie, was also the basis for this TV series that ran from 1959 to 1962. Michael Rennie plays Harry Lime, suave art expert and crime solver, and Jonathan Harris, of "Lost in Space" fame, is his assistant. Each tape features two episodes and runs about 60 min. There are six volumes available, including:

The Third Man, Vol. 1
Includes "Dark Island" and "The Man Who Dies Twice."
10-9415 $14.99

The Third Man, Vol. 2
Includes "I.O.U." and "Calculated Risk."
10-9416 $14.99

The Third Man, Vol. 3
Includes "Diamond in the Rough" and "Crisis in Crocodile."
10-9417 $14.99

The Third Man, Vol. 4
Includes "The House of Bon-Bons" and "A Little Knowledge."
10-9418 $14.99

The Third Man, Vol. 5
Includes "Spark from a Dead Fire" and "Ghost Town."
10-9419 $14.99

The Third Man, Vol. 6
Includes "Question Ice" and "Castle in Spain."
10-9420 $14.99

Babylon 5

In the 23rd century, it's the last, best hope for peace in a galaxy torn asunder by war. Follow the drama, intrigue and adventure on board the interplanetary space station Babylon 5 in the cult hit syndicated sci-fi series. Michael O'Hare, Bruce Boxleitner, Claudia Christian, Peter Jurasik and Andreas Katsualas star. Except where noted, each tape features two episodes and runs about 90 min.

Babylon 5, Vol. 5.1: In The Beginning
19-2719   ❑$14.99

Babylon 5, Vol. 1.1: The Gathering
19-2720   ❑$14.99

Babylon 5, Vol. 1.2: Midnight On The Firing Line/Soul Hunter
19-2721   ❑$14.99

Babylon 5, Vol. 1.3: Born To The Purple/Infection
19-2722   ❑$14.99

Babylon 5: Unlimited Space 3-Pack
19-2723 $39.99

Babylon 5, Vol. 1.4: The Parliament Of Dreams/Mind War
19-2766   ❑$14.99

Babylon 5, Vol. 1.5: The War Prayer/And The Sky Full Of Stars
19-2767   ❑$14.99

Babylon 5, Vol. 1.6: Deathwalker/Believers
19-2768   ❑$14.99

Babylon 5: Mind Probers 3-Pack
19-2769 $44.99

Babylon 5, Vol. 1.7: Survivors/ By Any Means Necessary
19-2798   ❑$14.99

Babylon 5, Vol. 1.8: Signs And Portents/TKO
19-2799   ❑$14.99

Babylon 5, Vol. 1.9: Grail/Eyes
19-2800   ❑$14.99

Babylon 5: Starliner 3-Pack
19-2801 $44.99

Babylon 5, Vol. 1.10: Legacies/ A Voice In The Wilderness, Part I
19-2806   ❑$14.99

Babylon 5, Vol. 1.11: A Voice In The Wilderness, Part II/ Babylon Squared
19-2807   ❑$14.99

Babylon 5, Vol. 1.12: The Quality Of Mercy/Chrysalis
19-2808   ❑$14.99

Babylon 5: Epsilon Chronicle 3-Pack
19-2809 $44.99

TV Classics, Vol. 1: Hollywood Half Hour/Public Defender

Two original half-hour dramas from television's "Golden Age." First, a young woman learns some surprising secrets about her new boss in a suspenseful drama starring Vincent Price. Next, a young Charles Bronson is featured as a boxer who gets in trouble with the law. 55 min. total.
50-6099 $19.99

TV Classics, Vol. 2: Howdy Doody/Art Linkletter And The Kids

Great collection of '50s kids' stuff takes us back to Doodyville with Howdy, Buffalo Bob and the rest of the group. Then attend the House Party and listen to the darndest things. 52 min.
50-6164 $19.99

TV Classics, Vol. 3: Colonel March Of Scotland Yard/Sherlock Holmes

Double danger in early TV thrillers. First Boris Karloff stars as the crusty one-eyed inspector, while Holmes and Watson investigate "The Case of the Cunningham Heritage." 52 min.
50-6142 $19.99

TV Classics, Vol. 4: Arthur Godfrey's Talent Scouts/The Ed Wynn Show

A twin bill of TV rarities! The Ukulele Man introduces a young Rod McKuen to the public, and the Perfect Fool hosts the Three Stooges in a little-seen '50s TV appearance. 52 min.
50-6143 $19.99

Babylon 5, Vol. 2.0: Points Of Departure/Revelations
19-2833   ❑$14.99

Babylon 5, Vol. 2.1: The Geometry Of Shadows/ A Distant Star
19-2834   ❑$14.99

Babylon 5, Vol. 2.2: The Long Dark/A Spider In The Web
19-2835   ❑$14.99

Babylon 5: The New Command 3-Pack
19-2836 $44.99

Babylon 5, Vol. 2.4: Soul Mates/ A Race Through Dark Places
19-2883   ❑$14.99

Babylon 5, Vol. 2.5: The Coming Of Shadows/Gropos
19-2884   ❑$14.99

Babylon 5, Vol. 2.6: All Alone In The Night/Acts Of Sacrifice
19-2885   ❑$14.99

Babylon 5: Diplomats And Warriors 3-Pack
19-2886 $44.99

Babylon 5, Vol. 4.1: The Hour Of The Wolf/Whatever Happened To Mr. Garibaldi?
19-2887   ❑$14.99

Babylon 5, Vol. 4.2: The Summoning/ Falling Toward Apotheosis
19-2888   ❑$14.99

Babylon 5, Vol. 4.3: The Long Night/Into The Fire
19-2889   ❑$14.99

Babylon 5: The Deathcloud 3-Pack
19-2890 $44.99

Babylon 5, Vol. 5.2: No Compromises/The Very Long Night Of Londo Mollari
19-2770   ❑$14.99

Kavanagh Q.C.

John Thaw of "Inspector Morse" fame plays British judge John Kavanagh in these gripping courtroom dramas that offer a fascinating look at what goes on behind the scenes in the courtroom and the problems that occur when trying to define the truth.

Kavanagh Q.C.: Collection 1
Kavanagh gets to the truth in "Nothing But the Truth," "Heartland," "A Family Affair" and "The Sweetest Thing." 330 min. on four tapes.
53-9906 $89.99

Kavanagh Q.C.: Collection 2
The master magistrate rules in "True Commitment," "The Burning Deck" and "Men of Substance." 240 min. on three tapes.
53-9907 $69.99

Kavanagh Q.C.: Collection 3
John Thaw's Kavanagh excels in three intense courtroom dramas: "A Sense of Loss," "A Stranger in the Family" and "Job Satisfaction." 240 min. on three tapes.
53-6143 $59.99

Kavanagh Q.C.: Collection 4
Queen's Counsel James Kavanagh shines in "Mute of Malice," "Blood Money" and "Ancient History." 240 min. on three tapes.
53-6648 $59.99

Kavanagh Q.C.: Collection 5
James Kavanagh, the Perry Mason of the British bar, excels in "Diplomatic Baggage," "The Ties That Bind" and "In God We Trust." 240 min. on three tapes.
53-6657 $59.99

Babylon 5, Vol. 5.3: The Paragon Of Animals/ A View From The Gallery
19-2771   ❑$14.99

Babylon 5, Vol. 5.4: Learning Curve/Strange Relations
19-2772   ❑$14.99

Babylon 5: Interstellar Alliance 3-Pack
19-2773 $44.99

Babylon 5, Vol. 5.5: Secrets Of The Soul/In The Kingdom Of The Blind
19-2802   ❑$14.99

Babylon 5, Vol. 5.6: A Tragedy Of Telepaths/Day Of The Dead
19-2803   ❑$14.99

Babylon 5, Vol. 5.7: Phoenix Rising/The Ragged Edge
19-2804   ❑$14.99

Babylon 5: Psi-Fi 3-Pack
19-2805 $44.99

Babylon 5, Vol. 5.8: The Corps Is Mother, The Corps Is Father/Meditations On The Abyss
19-2810   ❑$14.99

Babylon 5, Vol. 5.9: Darkness Ascending/ And All My Dreams, Torn Asunder
19-2811   ❑$14.99

Babylon 5, Vol. 5.10: Movements Of Fire And Shadow/ The Fall Of Centauri Prime
19-2812   ❑$14.99

Babylon 5: Centauri Doomsday 3-Pack
19-2813 $44.99

Babylon 5, Vol. 5.11: Wheel Of Fire/Objects In Motion
19-2837   ❑$14.99

Babylon 5, Vol. 5.12: Objects At Rest/Sleeping In The Light
19-2838   ❑$14.99

Babylon 5: Journey's End 2-Pack
19-2839 $29.99

The Ed Sullivan Show
A "really big shew" is on tap when Ed welcomes the voluptuous Jayne Mansfield, listens to some hot music from The Ink Spots, and has a smiling contest with Jack Webb (just kidding!). 60 min.
10-8165 Was $19.99 *$14.99*

The Ed Sullivan Show
A really, really big show here, with Harpo Marx, Dick Haymes and the incomparable Marty Allen and "The Legend," Steve Rossi. 50 min.
10-8327 Was $19.99 *$14.99*

Ed Sullivan's Toast Of The Town
"Mr. Show Business" hosts this entertaining early 1950s hour of fun and variety featuring cowboy legend (and future baseball team owner) Gene Autry and his horse, Champion. 60 min.
10-9438 *$14.99*

The Ed Sullivan Show: The MGM Story (1954)
Ed Sullivan hosts a 30th anniversary party for MGM, with live musical numbers and appearances by Gene Kelly, Fred Astaire, Howard Keel, Esther Williams, Debbie Reynolds, Cyd Charisse, and many more. Even the Mercury commercial on this rare find is an MGM tie-in, Lucy and Desi Arnaz touting their film "The Long, Long Trailer." 60 min.
10-7301 Was $19.99 *$14.99*

The Ed Sullivan Show: Salute To Lucy & Desi (1954)
Ed Sullivan marks the start of "I Love Lucy's" fourth season by visiting with Lucille Ball, Desi Arnaz, Vivian Vance and William Frawley on the set, joking and watching some of "Lucy's" funniest moments. Also includes film clips from "The Long, Long Trailer" and Desi's dramatic turn in "Bataan." This tribute to TV's first couple is truly a rare find! 60 min.
10-7379 Was $19.99 *$14.99*

The Ed Sullivan Show (1960)
Ed welcomes guests Mickey Rooney and the original Broadway cast of "West Side Story," plus the usual potpourri of musicians and entertainers. Includes original commercials. 60 min.
01-5080 Was $19.99 *$14.99*

Make Room For Daddy
Danny Thomas was gruff but lovable nightclub entertainer Danny Wilson in this hit TV show that originally ran on ABC from 1953 to 1964. The series dealt with Danny's funny and heart-felt encounters with his family, including wife Margaret (Jean Hagen), son Rusty (Rusty Hamer), daughter Terry (Sherry Jackson) and wacky Uncle Tonoose (Hans Conried).

Make Room For Daddy, Vol. 1
Join in on the fun, Danny Thomas style, with "The Songwriter," in which Danny's involvement with a song-writing hairdresser leads to trouble, and "Who Can Figure Kids Out?," in which Danny realizes it's a mistake to push Terry into performing in the school play. 50 min.
09-5200 Was $19.99 *$14.99*

Make Room For Daddy, Vol. 2
In "Talented Kid," Danny's auditioning of a child actor for a TV show makes Rusty feel bad. And "Margaret Feels Neglected" so the entire family tries to make her feel wanted. Includes original commercials. 50 min.
10-9539 Was $19.99 *$14.99*

Make Room For Daddy, Vol. 3
Danny feels bad when his kids forget his birthday in "Flash Back Show," featuring Ernest Borgnine as a cop. Also, Danny learns a lesson when he decides to be a "Little League Umpire." Includes original commercials. 50 min.
10-9540 Was $19.99 *$14.99*

Make Room For Daddy, Vol. 4
In "Don't Yell at Your Children," Danny and Margaret decide to not to get angry at the kids, which causes them great concern. And, in a post-1956 episode, the kid's try to wreck "Danny's Date" with a pretty, young lady (Barbara Billingsley). Includes original commercials. 60 min.
10-9541 Was $19.99 *$14.99*

Make Room For Daddy, Vol. 5
Danny's lifelong dream is to play at London's Palladium, but the kids and Margaret have other plans when he gets the good news in "Danny's Palladium Offer." And hilarity ensures when "Rusty Gets a Haircut" from Danny, after he's called a girl by another kid. Includes original commercials. 60 min.
10-9542 Was $19.99 *$14.99*

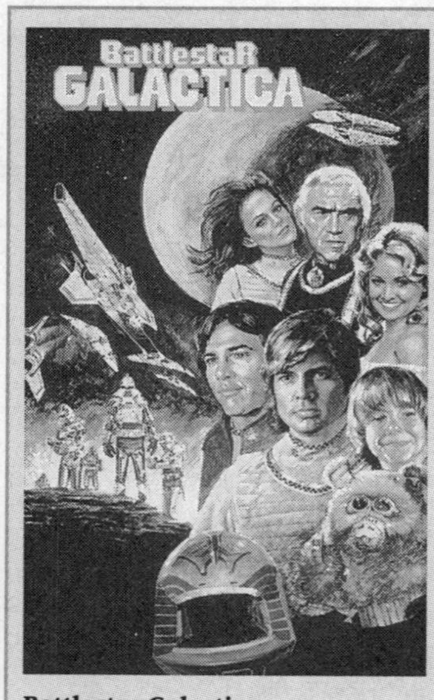

Battlestar Galactica
Travel beyond the solar system, as the mighty starship Galactica leads a ragtag space fleet from their homeworlds on a quest for the legendary planet Earth. Lorne Greene, Richard Hatch and Dirk Benedict star in this hit sci-fi TV series from the 1978-79 season. Except where noted, each tape runs about 50 min.

Battlestar Galactica: The Long Patrol
Ace pilot Starbuck crashes and is trapped on a mysterious prison planet.
07-1355 Was $14.99 *$12.99*

Battlestar Galactica: The Young Lords
Starbuck becomes a pawn in a deadly contest between the evil Cylons and a family of children.
07-1356 Was $14.99 *$12.99*

Battlestar Galactica: The Lost Warrior
Apollo serves as "sheriff" on a planet that resembles Earth's Old West.
07-1357 Was $14.99 *$12.99*

Battlestar Galactica: The Magnificent Warriors
Adama and Starbuck help a planet of farmers protect themselves from vicious, boar-like creatures.
07-1358 Was $14.99 *$12.99*

Battlestar Galactica: The Man With Nine Lives
Fred Astaire guests as a space "con man" who claims to be Starbuck's long-lost father.
07-1359 Was $14.99 *$12.99*

Battlestar Galactica: Fire In Space
A Cylon suicide attack could spell disaster for the Galactica's ragtag fleet.
07-1360 Was $14.99 *$12.99*

Battlestar Galactica: Murder On The Rising Star
Apollo turns detective when Starbuck is accused of killing a fellow pilot.
07-1361 Was $14.99 *$12.99*

Battlestar Galactica: Baltar's Escape
Commander Adama is forced to turn over his command to the traitorous Baltar in order to save the Galactica.
07-1362 Was $14.99 *$12.99*

Battlestar Galactica: Lost Planet Of The Gods
The lives of everyone on board the Galactica are endangered when the Viper pilots contract a mysterious, fatal illness in this two-part saga. 96 min.
07-2509 *$12.99*

Battlestar Galactica: Gun On Ice Planet Zero
In a double-length tale, the Galacticans get some unexpected help in their battle against the Cylons from a band of space outlaws. Britt Ekland guest stars. 96 min.
07-2510 *$12.99*

Battlestar Galactica (1978)
This theatrical version of the feature-length pilot to the hit TV series shows how the crew of the Galactica battled the robotic forces of the Cylon Empire while leading the survivors of a destroyed star system on their search for Earth. Lorne Greene, Ray Milland, Richard Hatch, Dirk Benedict and Jane Seymour star. 125 min.
07-1014 Was $19.99 *$14.99*

Mission Galactica: The Cylon Attack (1978)
A powerless Galactica is stranded in space as the Cylons prepare to launch a deadly assault, and a long-missing battlestar commander may be the ship's final hope, in this feature-length adventure. 108 min.
07-1065 *$14.99*

Conquest Of The Earth (1980)
At long last, the Galactica reaches Earth, but unfortunately for the weary space travellers, the Cylon fleet is right behind them. Action-filled sci-fi drama, culled from the "Galactica 1980" series, stars Lorne Greene, Kent McCord, Barry Van Dyke, Robyn Douglass. 112 min.
07-1108 *$14.99*

The Phil Silvers Special (1960)
It's "Summer in New York" as Phil and special guests Carol Lawrence, Joe E. Ross and Jack Gilford take a light musical look at commercials, Madison Avenue, off-Broadway plays, the "beat" culture and more. Look for a special appearance by the "Sgt. Bilko" cast. 60 min.
09-1204 Was $29.99 *$14.99*

MISSION: IMPOSSIBLE

The Best Of Mission: Impossible
"Your mission, should you decide to accept it," is to watch these suspense-filled episodes from the classic 1966-73 TV espionage series, as the members of the top-secret Impossible Missions Force take on dangerous assignments across the globe. Steven Hill, Peter Graves, Martin Landau, Barbara Bain, Greg Morris and Peter Lupus star. Each tape runs about 100 min.

The Best Of Mission: Impossible, Vol. 1
The series pilot finds original IMF team leader Dan Briggs (Steven Hill) leading the squad into a despot's Caribbean stronghold to disarm and recover two nuclear warheads. Next, Jim Phelps (Peter Graves) and company must stop "The Photographer," whose fashion background is a cover for an international spy ring, from unleashing a deadly virus.
06-2529 *$12.99*

The Best Of Mission: Impossible, Vol. 2
In "The Carriers," the IMF agents infiltrate a training center for enemy spies behind the Iron Curtain; George Takei guest stars. Next, a priceless art treasure must be retrieved from an unscrupulous dealer and returned to the country it was stolen from in "The Seal," with Darren McGavin.
06-2530 *$12.99*

The Best Of Mission: Impossible, Vol. 3
Master-of-disguise Rollin Hand (Martin Landau) stages his most perilous impersonation in order to bring down America's deadliest crime syndicate in the two-part tale, "The Council."
06-2531 *$12.99*

The Best Of Mission: Impossible, Vol. 4
The leader of an African revolutionary force and a fortune in stolen gold are the IMF's targets in "The Mercenaries," with Pernell Roberts. Then, Phelps must decide whether or not to make "The Exchange" when Cinnamon (Barbara Bain) is captured.
06-2532 *$12.99*

The Best Of Mission: Impossible, Vol. 5
In order to protect a double agent, the IMF squad plays an elaborate game of deceptions with an enemy investigator in "The Mind of Stefan Miklos," featuring Ed Asner. Martin Sheen guest stars in "Live Bait," in which the rescue of a captured American agent is complicated by an explosive booby trap.
06-2533 *$12.99*

The Best Of Mission: Impossible, Vol. 6
The rescue attempt of an important scientist and his wife from behind the Iron Curtain is threatened by a mysterious assassin in the two-parter "The Bunker." Lee Meriwether guest stars.
06-2534 *$12.99*

The Best Of Mission: Impossible, Vol. 7
In the two-part episode "Old Man Out," the IMF poses as a carnival troupe in order to bust an elderly cardinal, leader of a group of freedom fighters trying to overthrow a corrupt government, out of prison. Mary Ann Mobley guest stars.
06-3042 *$12.99*

The Best Of Mission: Impossible, Vol. 8
An elaborate scheme to outwit a ruthless terrorist out to wreak havoc on L.A. is lauched in "Operation Rogosh," starring Fritz Weaver. Then, in "The Train," featuring William Windom, the death of a prime minister is staged to capture his sinister underling.
06-3043 *$12.99*

The Best Of Mission: Impossible, Vol. 9
Boxing great Sugar Ray Robinson guest stars along with Robert Conrad in the two-part "The Contender," as the IMF goes undercover inside the ring to thwart a shady promoter out to take over sports with the profits from fixed boxing matches. 92 min.
06-3044 *$12.99*

The Best Of Mission: Impossible, Vol. 10
Includes "The Controllers, Parts One and Two."
06-3045 *$12.99*

The Best Of Mission: Impossible, Vol. 11
Includes "The Killer" and "Cocaine."
06-3046 *$12.99*

The Best Of Mission: Impossible, Vol. 12
Includes "The Puppet" and "The Pendulum."
06-3047 *$12.99*

The School For Scandal (1965)
The morals and manners of 18th-century England are target for satire in this TV adaptation of Richard Sheridan's play. A group of malicious gossips, a love game of musical chairs, a wealthy uncle's plot to test the true merits of his nephews and their romantic exploits all make for classic British drama. Stars Joan Plowright and Felix Aylmer. 100 min.
09-1597 Was $29.99 *$24.99*

Gunfight In Black Horse Canyon (1961)
Culled from different episodes of the hit TV show "Tales of Wells Fargo," this feature-length adventure stars Dale Robertson as Wells Fargo Company trouble-shooter Jim Hardie, who becomes the target of an outlaw he helped send to prison. George Kennedy, Claude Akins and Ellen Burstyn guest star. 93 min.
09-5266 *$19.99*

Columbo
Peter Falk's Lieutenant Columbo was one of the most endearing characters in television history, a scraggly police detective who drove a dilapidated car, wore a cruddy raincoat and seemed to bumble his way through each case. Yet when it came to solving homicides, no one was better. The long-running series was introduced on NBC in 1971. Each episode runs about 75 min.

Columbo: Murder By The Book
A young Steven Spielberg directed and Steven Bochco scripted this entry in which novelist Jack Cassidy plots the "perfect murder" of collaborator Martin Milner, only to have Columbo write the final chapter.
07-1575 *$14.99*

Columbo: Lovely But Lethal
After scientist Martin Sheen is murdered after stealing a secret anti-aging cosmetics formula from executive Vera Miles. Can Lt. Columbo smooth out the wrinkles in this confusing case?
07-2153 *$14.99*

Columbo: A Stitch In Crime
Leonard Nimoy guests as a heart surgeon whose jealousy gets the best of him, leading to murder and an investigation by Columbo.
07-2154 *$14.99*

Columbo: Suitable For Framing
An aging art collector, his jealous nephew, and the uncle's wife all form a murderous masterpiece for Columbo to solve. Ross Martin, Kim Hunter, Don Ameche guest star.
07-2155 *$14.99*

Columbo: Try And Catch Me
Lt. Columbo has his eye on a case involving a famous mystery writer (Ruth Gordon) who uses one of her own stories as a blueprint for murder.
07-2156 *$14.99*

Columbo: Prescription: Murder (1967)
Peter Falk made his debut as the disheveled detective Columbo in this tantalizing murder mystery. Psychiatrist Gene Barry thinks he's committed the perfect crime when he kills his wife, but Columbo always manages to ask "just one more question." With William Windom, Nina Foch. 99 min.
07-1471 Was $39.99 *$14.99*

The New Lion Of Sonora (1970)
Feature-length special for the hit NBC western series "High Chaparral," about a cattle ranch empire threatened by evil land barons. Leif Erickson, Cameron Mitchell. 104 min.
63-1082 *$19.99*

The Last Place On Earth: Complete Set (1985)
Exciting, beautifully filmed seven-part mini-series based on the 1911 race to reach the South Pole that pitted an Englishman, Captain Robert Falcon Scott, and his men against Norwegian Roald Amundsen's team. Martin Shaw, Sverre Anker Dusdal and Max Von Sydow star in this tale of bravery against the fiercest of nature's elements; written by Trevor Griffiths ("Reds"). 385 min. total.
53-9567 Was $159.99 *$89.99*

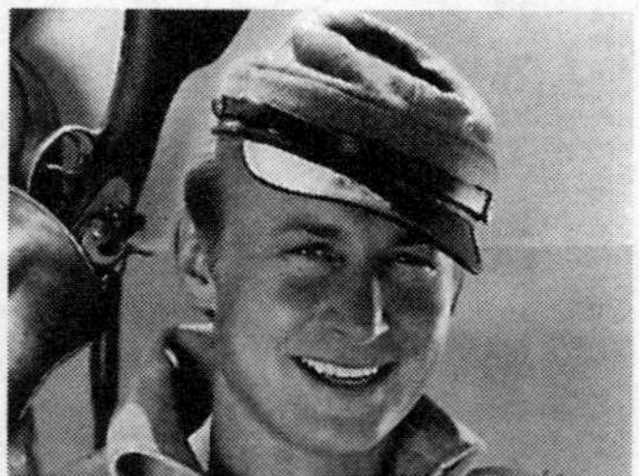

The Rebel
Nick Adams stars as Johnny Yuma, the former Confederate soldier who roamed throughout the West settling moral and criminal problems along the way. The show, which debuted on ABC in 1961 and later switched to NBC, featured a popular theme song sung by Johnny Cash. Featured here are the pilot episode and "The Vagrants." 50 min.
10-9213 *$19.99*

MOVIES UNLIMITED

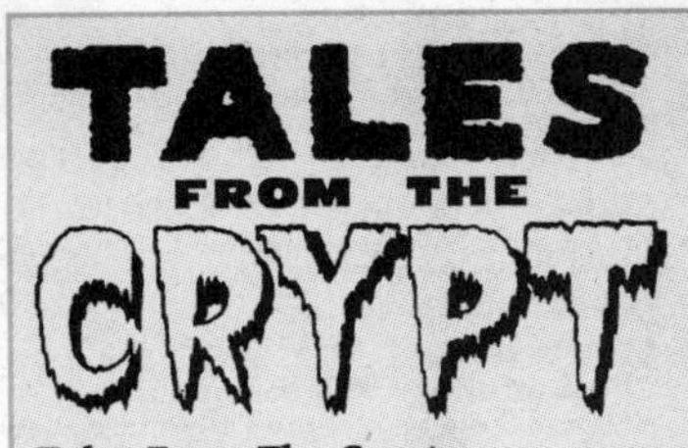

Tales From The Crypt
Good lord! The creepy E.C. horror comics of the '50s have been resurrected in this popular TV series that offers scares, laughs and sexiness, presented by the happy-go-deathly Cryptkeeper. Top stars, writers and directors have been enlisted to make these terrifying tales. Each program includes three stories, presented in their uncut versions. Choke!

Tales From The Crypt: ...Only Sin Deep
Hungry for wealth and success, beautiful Lea Thompson makes a bizarre pawnshop transaction in "...Only Sin Deep." Amanda Plummer plays a newlywed whose husband is after her money in "Lover Come Hack to Me," while "Collection Completed" has retiree M. Emmet Walsh taking up taxidermy and discovering the real meaning of "getting stuffed." 87 min.
44-1760 □$12.99

Tales From The Crypt: The Man Who Was Death
An executioner takes matters into his own hands when the State revokes the death penalty in "The Man Who Was Death." Also, scam artists Priscilla Presley and Lou Diamond Phillips try to out-scam each other in "Oil's Well That Ends Well"; and a hobo gets nine lives, thanks to a scientific experiment, in "Dig That Cat...He's Real Gone." 82 min.
44-2002 □$12.99

Tales From The Crypt: Death Of Some Salesman
A slick burial huckster learns a lesson in salesmanship when he tries to win over an old man in "Death of Some Salesman," starring Ed Begley, Jr. and Tim Curry. Then, Malcolm McDowell is "The Reluctant Vampire" who lands a dream job as a blood bank night watchman; and writer Andrew McCarthy uses a potion to attract actress Mariel Hemingway in "Loved to Death." 87 min.
44-2003 □$12.99

Tales From The Crypt: What's Cookin'?
Christopher Reeve's diner business gets a boost, thanks to a secret recipe for "steak," in "What's Cookin'?" Also, two-bit gambler Joe Pesci gets more than he bargains for when he weds wealthy twins in "Split Personality"; and when Hector Elizondo finds that wife Patsy Kensit is involved with a priest, he makes a devilish pact in "As Ye Sow." 84 min.
44-2004 □$12.99

Tales From The Crypt: Creep Course
Students Anthony Michael Hall and Nina Siemaszko get a gruesome lesson in Egyptology in "Creep Course." Next, alcoholic reporter Richard Jordan will stop at nothing to redeem himself with a big story in "Deadline"; and Jon Lovitz and Bruce Boxleitner are actors vying for a role in an unusual production of "Hamlet" in "Top Billing." 83 min.
44-2005 □$12.99

Tales From The Crypt: Dead Wait
An explorer's search for a priceless pearl leads him to voodoo priestess Whoopi Goldberg for help in "Dead Wait." "People Who Live in Brass Hearses" finds crooked ice-cream vendor Bill Paxton wreaking vengeance against the man who put him in jail; and fake psychic Cathy Moriarty's scam of a wealthy widow in "Seance" leads her to "the other side." 81 min.
44-2006 □$12.99

Tales From The Crypt: Forever Ambergris
Noted combat photographer Roger Daltrey's attempt to sabotage the work of rookie Steve Buscemi goes awry in "Forever Ambergris." Then, a debt-ridden man coaxes his wife into a life insurance scam in "The Trap," featuring Teri Garr; and aspiring actress Mimi Rogers' jealousy over roommate Kathy Ireland's success leads to murder and a bizarre beauty pageant in "Beauty Rest." 87 min.
44-2007 □$12.99

Tales From The Crypt: Split Second
Cocktail waitress Michelle Johnson has "whack"-y plans for her new lumber tycoon husband in "Split Second." Plus, Timothy Dalton and Beverly D'Angelo are among the guests of a secluded lodge haunted by a monster in "Werewolf Concerto"; and scientist Dylan McDermott's compadres play a deadly prank on him when they learn of his unscrupulous methods in "This'll Kill Ya." 80 min.
44-2008 □$12.99

Tales From The Crypt: Abra Cadaver
Physician brothers Beau Bridges and Tony Goldwyn play sick jokes on each other that finally go too far in "Abra Cadaver." Master TV puppeteer Donald O'Connor gets a chance to make a comeback, but who's really pulling the strings, in "Strung Along"; while Kevin McCarthy gets some advice on how to get rid of wife Margot Kidder in "Curiosity Killed." 83 min.
44-2009 □$12.99

Tales From The Crypt: Came The Dawn
Jealous lover Brooke Shields axes anyone who touches her man (Perry King) in "Came the Dawn." Also, sleazy reporter Steven Weber tries to find a cannibal preying on homeless people in "Mournin' Mess"; and a young woman gets involved with a mobster—much to his older gal pal's annoyance—in "Till Death Do We Part," with John Stamos and Eileen Brennan. 78 min.
44-2010 □$12.99

Tales From The Crypt: Spoiled
A physician's love-starved wife has an affair, but hubby has an experimental anesthesia and an elaborate plan for revenge ready, in "Spoiled." Next, a new librarian and her supervisor are haunted by reports of a "Maniac at Large," with Blythe Danner; and sideshow performer Ernie Hudson tries to master psychic wife Joan Chen's mind games in "Food for Thought." 81 min.
44-2011 □$12.99

Tales From The Crypt: Well-Cooked Hams
After he makes his mentor disappear, magician Billy Zane tries to take over the act, only to find that some tricks are harder than they look, in "Well-Cooked Hams." A mysterious discovery and the disease that comes with it lead an explorer to seek a cure from a witch doctor in "Halfway Horrible"; and artist Tim Roth discovers a sinister talent in "Easel Kill Ya." 83 min.
44-2012 □$12.99

Tales From The Crypt: And All Through The House...
A woman who just murdered her husband receives a visit from an axe-wielding Santa in "And All Through the House..." Plus, a general gives his lieutenant son a chance not to be "Yellow" in an entry starring Kirk and Eric Douglas, and Dan Aykroyd; and an ex-con learns of his wife's infidelity after he gets a facelift that makes him resemble Bogey in "You, Murderer," featuring John Lithgow and Isabella Rossellini. Robert Zemeckis directs all three efforts. 90 min.
44-2013 □$12.99

Tales From The Crypt, Vol. 3
Three more triumphs of terror, including "Dead Right," with Demi Moore as a golddigger who weds a penniless slob on a fortune teller's advice; "Cutting Cards," with Kevin Tighe and Lance Henriksen involved in a very high-stakes card game; and "The Switch," in which wealthy old coot William Hickey barters for a new body to woo beautiful Kelly Preston. Walter Hill, Howard Deutch and Arnold Schwarzenegger direct. 80 min.
19-1941 Was $19.99 □$14.99

O.K. Crackerby!, Vol. 1
In this 1965-66 ABC situation comedy, Burl Ives played the world's richest man, a gruff Oklahoman who hires tutor Hal Buckley to teach his children and help him gain acceptance by high society types. Brain Corcoran and a young Brooke Adams also star; co-created by TV critic Cleveland Amory. This tape features "3+1=1" and "Ol' Sam." 55 min.
08-9874 Was $19.99 $14.99

The Cisco Kid
"Here's adventure. Here's romance. Here's O. Henry's famous Robin Hood of the Old West." Astride Diablo, Cisco sets out to stop treachery, with help from sidekick Pancho and his horse, Loco. Duncan Renaldo and Leo Carillo star in this popular '50s Western, the first TV series presented in color. Each tape features two episodes and runs about 52 min. There are 17 volumes available, including:

The Cisco Kid, Vol. 1
Includes "The Quarter Horse" and "The Postmaster."
10-1169 Was $19.99 $14.99

The Cisco Kid, Vol. 2
Includes "Confession For Your Money" and "Freight Line Feud."
10-8177 Was $19.99 $14.99

The Cisco Kid, Vol. 3
Includes "Buried Treasures" and "Protective Association."
10-8178 Was $19.99 $14.99

The Cisco Kid, Vol. 4
Includes "Ghost Town" with guest star Denver Pyle and "Spanish Dagger."
10-8179 Was $19.99 $14.99

The Cisco Kid, Vol. 5
Includes "Lost Identity" and "Stolen Bonds."
10-8180 Was $19.99 $14.99

The Cisco Kid, Vol. 6
Includes "Water Rights" and "Uncle Disinherits Niece" with Tom Tyler.
10-8181 Was $19.99 $14.99

The Cisco Kid, Vol. 7
Includes "The Old Bum" and "Phony Sheriff" with Tom Tyler.
10-8182 Was $19.99 $14.99

The Cisco Kid, No. 1
Includes "Boomerang" and "Counterfeit Money."
10-9639 $14.99

The Cisco Kid, No. 2
Includes "Rustling" and "Big Switch."
10-9640 $14.99

The Cisco Kid, No. 3
Includes two versions of "Convict Story," one in black-and-white with original commercials and the other a syndicated edition in color.
10-9641 $14.99

The Caballero/The Cisco Kid
Two different TV versions of O. Henry's embroidered equestrian hero. Cesar Romero stars in "The Caballero," followed by Duncan Renaldo in a color episode of "The Cisco Kid" series, "The Postal Inspector."
10-7476 $19.99

The Fat Man: The Thirty-Two Friends Of Gina Lardelli (1968)
This unsold pilot for a TV show based on the popular radio program features Robert Middleton as gourmand detective Brad Runyan, who specialized in criminal cases nobody else would take. 60 min.
10-9097 Was $19.99 $14.99

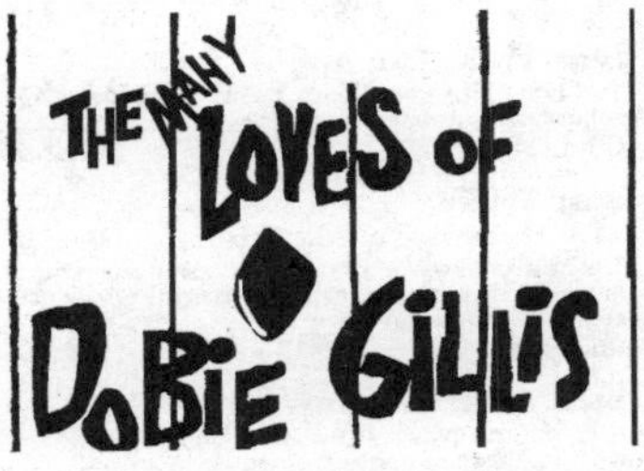

The Many Loves Of Dobie Gillis
Based on characters created by Max Shulman, this CBS comedy aired from 1959 to 1963. Dwayne Hickman starred as typical teenager Dobie, the son of a grocer, who continually sought gals, cash and neat cars. His sidekick was Maynard G. Krebs, a beatnik played by Bob Denver. Co-starring were Warren Beatty, Tuesday Weld and Frank Faylen. Each tape features two episodes and runs about 55 min. There are six volumes available, including:

The Many Loves Of Dobie Gillis, Vol. 1
Includes the first episode, "Caper at the Bijou," and "The Best Dressed Man," featuring Warren Beatty.
09-5201 Was $19.99 $14.99

The Many Loves Of Dobie Gillis, Vol. 2
Includes "Dobie's Birthday Party" with Ron Howard and "The Flying Millicans" with Francis X. Bushman.
09-5202 Was $19.99 $14.99

The Many Loves Of Dobie Gillis, Vol. 3
Includes "The Big Sandwich" and "Chicken from Outer Space."
09-5203 Was $19.99 $14.99

The Many Loves Of Dobie Gillis, Vol. 4
Includes "Lassie Gets Lost" and "Room at the Bottom," with guest star Ron Howard.
10-9543 Was $19.99 $14.99

The Many Loves Of Dobie Gillis, Vol. 5
Includes "Here Comes the Groom" and "Who Needs Elvis?"
10-9544 Was $19.99 $14.99

The Many Loves Of Dobie Gillis, Vol. 6
Includes "Move Over, Perry Mason" and "Crazy Legs Gillis."
10-9545 Was $19.99 $14.99

The Betty Hutton Show, Vol. 1
Broadcast in the 1959-60 season, this sitcom featured Broadway star Betty Hutton as Goldie, a showgirl-turned-manicurist-turned-heiress to a millionaire's fortune and guardian of his three children. Tom Conway and Gigi Perreau also star; two episodes are featured. 55 min.
10-7551 Was $19.99 $14.99

The Betty Hutton Show, Vol. 2
Two more wacky tales from Hutton's eponymous situation comedy in which she takes care of three teenagers in the mansion of their late millionaire father. Includes "For Goldie's Sake" and "Ray Runs Away." With Tom Conway, Dennis Joel. 55 min.
10-9033 Was $19.99 $14.99

Soldiers Of Fortune
Two-fisted adventure series from the mid-1950s stars John Russell and Chick Chandler as troubleshooters-for-hire who take on dangerous assignments that send them around the world. Episodes include "Runaway King" and "Temple of Terror." 60 min.
10-9059 $19.99

The Johnny Cash Show
An entry from the "Man in Black's" own 1969-1971 country music variety series. Joining Johnny and regulars June Carter and the Carter Family, the Statler Brothers and Carl Perkins are guest stars Glen Campbell, Marty Robbins and Nancy Ames. 60 min.
10-7554 $19.99

Summer On Ice
An entertaining TV special from the late 1950s featuring skating sensations from the Ice Capades along with Rosemary Clooney, Tab Hunter and Tony Randall. 50 min.
10-9075 Was $19.99 $14.99

Western Ranch Party, Vol. 1
The "Ranch Party" Television show was hosted by Western star Tex Ritter and featured musicians Jim Reeves and Bonnie Guitar. Guests here are Jimmy Wakely and Eddie Dean.
10-7321 Was $19.99 $14.99

Western Ranch Party, Vol. 2
Enjoy more of Tex Ritter's syndicated Country and Western variety program "Ranch Party," with series regulars Jim Reeves and The Sons of the Pioneers.
10-7322 Was $19.99 $14.99

Western Ranch Party, Vol. 3
Country and western jamboree with Tex Ritter, Johnny Cash, Jim Reeves and rockabilly pioneer Carl Perkins.
10-7375 Was $19.99 $14.99

Western Ranch Party, Vol. 4
Episode of the syndicated country music series with host Tex Ritter, the legendary Johnny Cash, Ray Price, and hard-living singer/songwriter George Jones.
10-7376 Was $19.99 $14.99

Western Ranch Party, Vol. 5
Man in black Johnny Cash guests with series regular Tex Ritter and future "Petticoat Junction" trainman Smiley Burnette.
10-7377 Was $19.99 $14.99

Western Ranch Party, Vol. 6
Sweet-singing Patsy Cline, just coming into her own nationally, joins Tex Ritter's syndicated hoedown and ranchhands Johnny Cash and Carl Perkins.
10-7378 Was $19.99 $14.99

The Best Of John Candy On SCTV
Here's a Candy sampler that's low in calories and high in laughs! The comic giant is spotlighted in some of his best bits, skits and impersonations from "SCTV," along with series co-stars like Eugene Levy, Rick Moranis, Catherine O'Hara and Martin Short. See John as 3-D impresario Dr. Tongue, TV host Johnny LaRue, sex shop mogul Harry (the guy with the snake on his face), Divine and more. 62 min.
02-2249 Was $39.99 $14.99

The Best Of John Candy's Big City Comedy: Set
Before "Second City TV," comic John Candy hosted this hilarious TV show from his homeland of Canada. Featuring a host of comedy legends, the show offered Candy at his best, writing and performing skits that showed the ingenuity that was to come later on "SCTV" and in movies. Volume 1 includes Billy Crystal, Martin Mull and Fred Willard; Volume 2 includes Steve Landesberg, Martin Mull and McLean Stevenson; Volume 3 includes Jimmy Walker, Rita Moreno and Meadowlark Lemon. 165 min. total. NOTE: Individual volumes available at $14.99.
66-6064 Save $20.00! $24.99

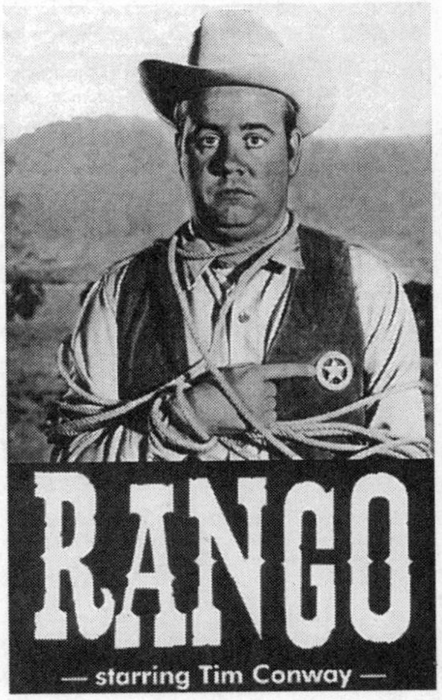

Rango
A Movies Unlimited favorite, this wacky 1967 western starred Tim Conway as a goofy Texas Ranger who keeps getting into trouble, forcing his commanders to assign him to the quietest post in the state. With Guy Marks as Rango's Indian sidekick, Pink Cloud. Includes the episodes "The Spy Who Was Out in the Cold" and "Diamonds Look Better Around Your Neck than a Rope." 55 min.
10-9557 $14.99

Star Trek
"Space...the final frontier" was explored by Captain James T. Kirk, Mr. Spock and the crew of the Starship Enterprise in the classic TV sci-fi series that ran on NBC from 1966 to 1969. William Shatner, Leonard Nimoy, DeForest Kelley, Nichelle Nichols, James Doohan, George Takei and Walter Koenig star. Except where noted, each tape runs about 51 min.

Star Trek: The Man Trap
A creature capable of assuming anyone's appearance is loose on board the Enterprise.
06-1239 $12.99

Star Trek: Charlie X
The only survivor of a spaceship wreck is a teenaged boy who seems to possess uncanny abilities.
06-1240 $12.99

Star Trek: Where No Man Has Gone Before
Strange forces at the boundary of the galaxy give two crew members amazing mental powers. Gary Lockwood, Sally Kellerman guest star.
06-1241 $12.99

Star Trek: The Naked Time
The Enterprise crew is exposed to a virus that releases inhibitions and emotions.
06-1242 $12.99

Star Trek: The Enemy Within
Captain Kirk is split into two beings, one good and one evil.
06-1243 $12.99

Star Trek: Mudd's Women
The Enterprise is "invaded" by three siren-like beauties and their gregarious boss. Roger C. Carmel guest stars.
06-1244 $12.99

Star Trek: What Are Little Girls Made Of?
A missing scientist is found on a mysterious planet populated with androids. Ted Cassidy guest stars.
06-1245 $12.99

Star Trek: Miri
The Enterprise visits a plague-ridden planet peopled only by children. Kim Darby, Michael J. Pollard guest star.
06-1246 $12.99

Star Trek: Dagger Of The Mind
Kirk becomes the prisoner of a scientist on an "advanced" penal colony planet.
06-1247 $12.99

Star Trek: The Corbomite Maneuver
The Enterprise is marked for destruction by an alien spaceship many times its size.
06-1248 $12.99

Star Trek: The Menagerie (Parts I & II)
Spock is tried for mutiny when he hijacks the Enterprise to a mysterious forbidden world. Incorporates the original "Trek" pilot with Jeffrey Hunter as Capt. Pike. 103 min.
06-1262 $14.99

Star Trek: Conscience Of The King
A touring Shakespearean troupe may be harboring a notorious interplanetary mass murderer.
06-1263 $12.99

Star Trek: Balance Of Terror
"Run Silent, Run Deep" in space, as the Enterprise squares off against a Romulan starship with the power of invisibility. Mark Lenard guest stars.
06-1264 $12.99

Star Trek: Shore Leave
The crew takes a vacation on a strange planet populated by giant rabbits, damsels in distress and white knights.
06-1265 $12.99

Star Trek: The Galileo Seven
Spock, McCoy, Scotty and four crewmen are marooned on a hostile planet, and the Enterprise can't locate them.
06-1266 $12.99

Star Trek: The Squire Of Gothos
A foppish, super-powerful being named Trelane uses the Enterprise crew as his playthings.
06-1267 $12.99

Star Trek: Arena
Kirk and a lizard-like alien commander must duel to the death for the lives of their crews.
06-1268 $12.99

Star Trek: A Private Little War
Rival factions on a formerly peaceful jungle planet are backed by the Federation and the Klingons.
06-1389 $12.99

Star Trek: By Any Other Name
When aliens "hijack" the Enterprise and turn the crew into crystalline blocks, only Kirk, Spock, McCoy and Scotty remain to thwart their plans.
06-1392 $12.99

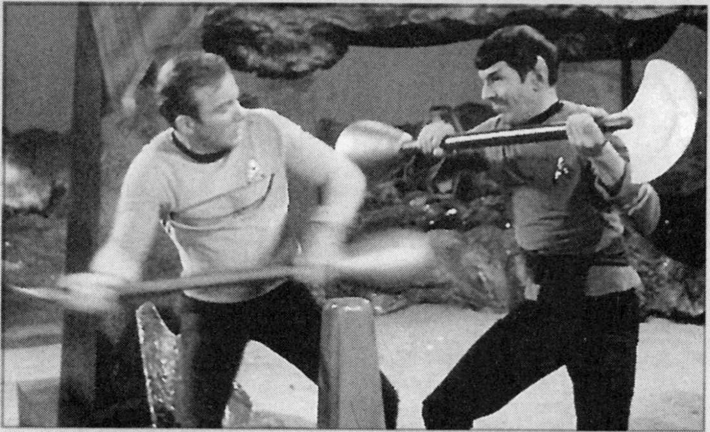

STAR TREK

Star Trek: The Cage (1965)
The never-aired original "Star Trek" pilot that later became "The Menagerie," introduced by creator Gene Roddenberry. Jeffrey Hunter, Leonard Nimoy, and Majel Barrett as "Number One" star, as the Enterprise's intended rescue mission to Talos IV becomes a struggle to escape. Incorporates several minutes of black-and-white footage. 73 min. total.
06-1393 $14.99

Star Trek: The Cage (All Color Collector's Edition)
Color footage shot for the show's pilot episode that was previously thought lost has been restored to this special collector's edition of the sci-fi classic's first incarnation. 64 min.
06-1655 $14.99

Star Trek: Tomorrow Is Yesterday
The Enterprise accidentally travels back to the 1960s and must destroy all records of its visit.
06-1269 $12.99

Star Trek: Court Martial
Kirk is tried for sending a crewman to his death, with irrefutable computer evidence.
06-1270 $12.99

Star Trek: Return Of The Archons
Kirk and Spock must overcome the computer ruler of a planet of enthralled humans.
06-1271 $12.99

Star Trek: Space Seed
The Enterprise is taken over by genetic super-warrior Khan in "Star Trek II's" prequel. Ricardo Montalban guest stars.
06-1286 $12.99

Star Trek: A Taste Of Armageddon
The Enterprise becomes involved with a planet where a centuries-old war is run by computers.
06-1287 $12.99

Star Trek: This Side Of Paradise
Strange spores on a colony world infect the Enterprise with a dangerous euphoria. Jill Ireland guest stars.
06-1288 $12.99

Star Trek: The Devil In The Dark
What is the secret behind a rock-like monster that is killing workers on a mining colony planet?
06-1289 $12.99

Star Trek: Errand Of Mercy
The treacherous Klingons attack the planet Organia and the Enterprise prepares for war, unaware of Organia's secret.
06-1290 $12.99

Star Trek: The Alternative Factor
A psychotic space traveller is the key to a strange anti-matter universe that endangers all.
06-1291 $12.99

Star Trek: City On The Edge Of Forever
Harlan Ellison's story of Kirk, Spock and McCoy trapped in 1930s Chicago, where one woman's fate could alter history. Joan Collins guest stars.
06-1292 $12.99

Star Trek: Operation Annihilate
Strange flying parasites attack a space colony, but can the Enterprise find a solution?
06-1293 $12.99

Star Trek: Amok Time
Vulcans, like salmon, must return home every so often to spawn or die trying. It's Spock's turn.
06-1294 $12.99

Star Trek: Who Mourns For Adonais?
Can the super-powerful being who's seized the Enterprise really be the Greek god Apollo?
06-1295 $12.99

Star Trek: The Changeling
A centuries-old Earth space probe, reprogrammed by an alien intelligence, is brought aboard the Enterprise.
06-1336 $12.99

Star Trek: Mirror, Mirror
Kirk, McCoy, Scotty and Uhura are trapped in a militaristic parallel universe and must find a way to return to their own world.
06-1337 $12.99

Star Trek: The Apple
The Enterprise crew lands on an Eden-like planet controlled by a supercomputer.
06-1338 $12.99

Star Trek: The Doomsday Machine
The Enterprise and a damaged sister ship must stop an immense alien construct that can destroy whole planets. William Windom guest stars.
06-1339 $12.99

Star Trek: Catspaw
A mysterious planet is home to two alien "witches" who hold the Enterprise hostage.
06-1340 $12.99

Star Trek: I, Mudd
The bombastic Harcourt Fenton Mudd traps the crew on a planet populated by androids. Roger C. Carmel guest stars.
06-1341 $12.99

Star Trek: Metamorphosis
Kirk, Spock, McCoy and a federation executive are held prisoner along with an early Earth astronaut by a strange alien force.
06-1342 $12.99

Star Trek: Journey To Babel
A diplomatic shuttle mission for the Enterprise reunites Spock with his Vulcan father and Human mother. Mark Lenard and Jane Wyatt guest star.
06-1343 $12.99

Star Trek: Friday's Child
On a savage desert planet, Kirk, Spock and McCoy protect the wife of a slain leader from her own people and the Klingons.
06-1344 $12.99

Star Trek: The Deadly Years
A mysterious "aging disease" affects all but one member of a landing party, and the race for a cure begins.
06-1345 $12.99

Star Trek: Obsession
Kirk must destroy a vampiric cloud creature that he was unable to defeat several years earlier.
06-1383 $12.99

Star Trek: Wolf In The Fold
Scotty is accused of murder on a peaceful "pleasure planet" in an episode written by Robert Bloch ("Psycho").
06-1384 $12.99

Star Trek: The Trouble With Tribbles
The Enterprise is overrun by Tribbles, furry little creatures that eat incessantly and multiply like all get out.
06-1385 $12.99

Star Trek: The Gamesters Of Triskelion
Kirk, Uhura and Chekov are held prisoner on a distant planet and trained as gladiators.
06-1386 $12.99

Star Trek: A Piece Of The Action
The Enterprise "muscles in" on a world whose people have modeled their society on '20s gangland Chicago.
06-1387 $12.99

Star Trek: The Immunity Syndrome
A gigantic "space amoeba" that threatens the galaxy must be destroyed before it reproduces.
06-1388 $12.99

Star Trek: Return To Tomorrow
In temporary need of human bodies, three alien "spirits" possess Kirk, Spock and a female scientist.
06-1390 $12.99

Star Trek: Patterns Of Force
The Enterprise encounters a planet that has based its society on Nazi Germany.
06-1391 $12.99

Star Trek: The Omega Glory
A renegade starship captain wants to escalate tribal warfare on a planet with mysterious ties to 20th century Earth.
06-1470 $12.99

Star Trek: The Ultimate Computer
Its name is M-5, and when it turns Federation war games into real battles Kirk must find a way to pull the plug.
06-1471 $12.99

Star Trek: Bread And Circuses
Kirk, Spock and McCoy are held prisoner on a world that combines 20th-century technology and the culture of Ancient Rome.
06-1472 $12.99

Star Trek: Assignment: Earth
On a time travel assignment in 1967, the Enterprise encounters an enigmatic "interplanetary agent" named Gary Seven who may be hero or villain. Robert Lansing, Teri Garr guest star.
06-1473 $12.99

Star Trek: Spock's Brain
It's been stolen, and if it isn't found in 24 hours, Spock will die!
06-1474 $12.99

Star Trek: The Enterprise Incident
When a seemingly insane Kirk orders the ship into Romulan space and capture, Spock assumes command.
06-1475 $12.99

Star Trek: The Paradise Syndrome
An amnesiac Kirk is taken in by an Amerind-like tribe on a doomed asteroid.
06-1476 $12.99

Star Trek: And The Children Shall Lead
What mysterious force killed the adult settlers on the planet Triacus, leaving only the children for the Enterprise to find?
06-1477 $12.99

Star Trek: Is There In Truth No Beauty?
Two passengers, a benign alien whose hideous appearance drives humans mad and a beautiful, enigmatic telepath, are part of the Enterprise's next assignment.
06-1478 $12.99

Star Trek: Spectre Of The Gun
As punishment for "trespassing" in alien space, Kirk, Spock, McCoy, Scotty and Chekov are forced to relive the gunfight at the O.K. Corral.
06-1479 $12.99

Star Trek: Day Of The Dove
The Enterprise and a Klingon warship find themselves the parties in a bizarre war that neither side started.
06-1482 $12.99

Star Trek: For The World Is Hollow And I Have Touched The Sky
McCoy discovers that he has contracted a fatal and incurable blood disease.
06-1483 $12.99

Star Trek: The Tholian Web
A mysterious "hole" between universes has opened in space, and Kirk may be trapped there for good.
06-1484 $12.99

Star Trek: Plato's Stepchildren
A race of telekinetic sybarites want McCoy to stay on their world permanently as their physician.
06-1485 $12.99

Star Trek: Wink Of An Eye
A world of super-accelerated beings, invisible to the naked eye, kidnaps Kirk.
06-1486 $12.99

Star Trek: The Empath
Kirk, Spock, McCoy and a mute alien woman are the subjects in a "test" conducted by strange beings.
06-1487 $12.99

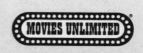

Star Trek: Elaan Of Troyius
An interstellar "marriage of state" puts the Enterprise into a dangerous encounter with the Klingons. France Nuyen guest stars.
06-1488 $12.99

Star Trek: Whom Gods Destroy
Kirk and Spock are taken captive when inmates take over an asylum planet.
06-1489 $12.99

Star Trek: Let That Be Your Last Battlefield
A parable in prejudice, as two aliens bring their millennia-old race war on board the Enterprise.
06-1490 $12.99

Star Trek: The Mark Of Gideon
Attempting to beam down to a planet, Kirk finds himself instead on a deserted Enterprise.
06-1491 $12.99

Star Trek: That Which Survives
An enigmatic woman whose touch kills traps Kirk, McCoy and Sulu on a barren world.
06-1492 $12.99

Star Trek: The Lights Of Zetar
The incorporeal survivors of a long-dead race take over the mind and body of a crewwoman.
06-1493 $12.99

Star Trek: Requiem For Methuselah
What is the secret behind a reclusive man and his beautiful ward, and what will that secret mean to Kirk?
06-1494 $12.99

Star Trek: The Way To Eden
The Enterprise is overrun by a band of "space hippies" who are searching for a paradise planet.
06-1495 $12.99

Star Trek: The Cloud Minders
Kirk and Spock must mediate to a world where two distinct and feuding castes have developed.
06-1496 $12.99

Star Trek: The Savage Curtain
Alien beings transport Kirk, Spock, and legendary figures from history to a planet in an attempt to discover the difference between good and evil.
06-1497 $12.99

Star Trek: All Our Yesterdays
A time machine traps Kirk, Spock and McCoy in different eras of a planet's past.
06-1498 $12.99

Star Trek: Turnabout Intruder
A disturbed female scientist switches bodies with Kirk and assumes command of the Enterprise.
06-1499 $12.99

Star Trek: The Animated Series
"These are the cartoon voyages of the Starship Enterprise." William Shatner, Leonard Nimoy, and most of the original cast supplied the voices to the Emmy-winning program seen on Saturday mornings from 1973 to 1975. Each tape contains two episodes and runs about 48 min.

Star Trek, Vol. 1
The return of Cyrano Jones brings "More Tribbles, More Troubles" to the Enterprise, while Spock is abducted by a renegade scientist in "The Infinite Vulcan."
06-1644 $12.99

Star Trek, Vol. 2
Spock journeys back in time to his own childhood in "Yesteryear." Next, a parasitic energy being takes over the ship in "Beyond the Farthest Star."
06-1645 $12.99

Star Trek, Vol. 3
"The Survivor" the Enterprise rescues is really a shape-changing spy, while "The Lorelei Signal" lures the male crew members into a trap.
06-1646 $12.99

Star Trek, Vol. 4
A planet-eating cloud threatens the galaxy in "One of Our Planets Is Missing." Next, "Mudd's Passion" has even Spock falling in love.
06-1647 $12.99

Star Trek, Vol. 5
A devilish intruder causes problems in "The Magicks of Megas-Tu." Next, the Enterprise and a Klingon ship are caught in a "Time Trap."
06-1648 $12.99

Star Trek, Vol. 6
"The Slaver Weapon" is the prize in a battle between the Enterprise and the cat-like Kzin, while Kirk and Spock are turned into water-breathers in "The Ambergris Element."
06-1649 $12.99

Star Trek, Vol. 7
Kirk and Spock join a team searching for a stolen artifact in "Jihad," and the crew begin shrinking in "The Terratin Incident."
06-1650 $12.99

Star Trek, Vol. 8
Kirk, Spock and McCoy become zoo exhibits in "Eye of the Beholder," and a rest stop at the "Shore Leave" planet becomes deadly in "Once Upon a Planet."
06-1651 $12.99

Star Trek, Vol. 9
The ship plays host to "Bem," a most unusual diplomatic guest. Next, McCoy is accused of causing a planet-wide plague in "Albatross."
06-1652 $12.99

Star Trek, Vol. 10
To save Spock's life, a shipment of hijacked drugs must be rescued from "The Pirates of Orion," then "The Practical Joker" invades the ship's computer.
06-1653 $12.99

Star Trek, Vol. 11
An ancient Aztec god seizes the Enterprise in "How Sharper Than a Serpent's Tooth." Next, the crew is growing younger in "The Counter-Clock Incident."
06-1654 $12.99

Star Trek: The Next Generation
"Boldly go where no one has gone before" as an all-new Enterprise, under the command of Captain Jean-Luc Picard, takes off on "its continuing mission" in the hit syndicated TV series. Patrick Stewart, Jonathan Frakes, Gates McFadden, Michael Dorn, Marina Sirtis, LeVar Burton and Brent Spiner star. Except where noted, each tape runs about 46 min.

Star Trek The Next Generation: Encounter At Farpoint
The feature-length pilot episode finds Picard taking charge of the Enterprise in time to solve a strange secret on a remote outpost and be put on trial by a powerful alien race for "the crimes of humanity." 96 min.
06-1874 $19.99

Star Trek The Next Generation: The Naked Now
A virus that unblocks inhibitions infects the Enterprise crew and threatens all on board.
06-1875 $14.99

Star Trek The Next Generation: Code Of Honor
Lt. Tasha Yar is kidnapped by a visiting emissary from a planet that possesses a needed vaccine.
06-1876 $14.99

Star Trek The Next Generation: Haven
Will Counselor Troi be forced to the altar by the one foe the Enterprise cannot defeat—her mother?
06-1936 $14.99

Star Trek The Next Generation: Where No One Has Gone Before
A test on the ship's engines sends the Enterprise into a strange universe where thoughts become reality.
06-1937 $14.99

Star Trek The Next Generation: The Last Outpost
On a deserted planet, an Enterprise away team has a dangerous encounter with the villainous, sneaky and ugly Ferengi.
06-1938 $14.99

Star Trek The Next Generation: The Lonely Among Us
A powerful alien force enters the ship and takes over the body of Captain Picard.
06-1939 $14.99

Star Trek The Next Generation: Justice
The Prime Directive gets a test when precocious young Wesley breaks a law on a planet where there's only one penalty...execution!
06-1959 $14.99

Star Trek The Next Generation: The Battle
A Ferengi with a blood score to settle against Picard lures the Captain into a deadly trap.
06-1960 $14.99

Star Trek The Next Generation: Hide & "Q"
The super-powerful and super-annoying "Q" returns and selects Riker to become part of his alien race.
06-1961 $14.99

Star Trek The Next Generation: Too Short A Season
The Enterprise shuttles a renowned Federation negotiator to settle a planetary dispute, unaware that the peacemaker hides a dangerous secret.
06-1962 $14.99

Star Trek The Next Generation: The Big Goodbye
Picard gets to play "private eye" in a holodeck mystery set in a Raymond Chandler-like 1940s Los Angeles.
06-1963 $14.99

Star Trek The Next Generation: Datalore
A routine visit to Data's home planet uncovers a startling surprise: the android's evil twin!
06-1964 $14.99

Star Trek The Next Generation: Angel One
The Enterprise crew is caught in the middle of a "battle of the sexes" on a matriarchal planet.
06-1982 $14.99

Star Trek The Next Generation: 11001001
A team of aliens assigned to update the Enterprise computers hijacks the ship, with Picard and Riker the only crew members on board.
06-1983 $14.99

Star Trek The Next Generation: Home Soil
The Enterprise picks up a sentient microscopic organism that threatens the safety of the ship.
06-1984 $14.99

Star Trek The Next Generation: When The Bough Breaks
After visiting a planet whose inhabitants are sterile, several children, including precocious young Wesley, are taken from the Enterprise.
06-1985 $14.99

Star Trek The Next Generation: Coming Of Age
A stop at a Starfleet base means a tough Academy entrance test for precocious young Wesley and a career-threatening inquiry for Picard.
06-2030 $14.99

Star Trek The Next Generation: Heart Of Glory
Worf is forced to choose between his career and his heritage when a group of fugitive Klingons are brought on board the Enterprise.
06-2031 $14.99

Star Trek The Next Generation: The Arsenal Of Freedom
A landing party is trapped on a planet whose inhabitants died eons ago, but whose computerized defense systems are still operating.
06-2032 $14.99

Star Trek The Next Generation: Skin Of Evil
An encounter with a malevolent alien creature leads to a death in the Enterprise family.
06-2033 $14.99

Star Trek The Next Generation: Symbiosis
Picard finds himself bound by the Prime Directive from interfering in the parasitic relationship that has developed between two neighboring planets' cultures.
06-2097 $14.99

Star Trek The Next Generation: We'll Always Have Paris
A mission to investigate a dangerous time-warp experiment brings Picard face to face with a long-lost love. Michelle Phillips guest stars.
06-2098 $14.99

Star Trek The Next Generation: Conspiracy
Picard learns of an alien plot to infiltrate the ranks of Starfleet, but will the knowledge cost him his life?
06-2099 $14.99

Star Trek The Next Generation: The Neutral Zone
The Enterprise faces twin problems when they pick up a trio of 20th-century Earthlings kept in suspended animation and have an encounter with the Romulans.
06-2100 $14.99

Star Trek The Next Generation: The Child
A mysterious alien presence invades the Enterprise and leaves some very tangible evidence of its "visit": a pregnant Counselor Troi!
06-2134 $14.99

Star Trek The Next Generation: Where Silence Has Lease
A powerful alien force curious about how humans deal with death traps the Enterprise in a dimensionless void.
06-2135 $14.99

Star Trek The Next Generation: Elementary, Dear Data
Data's Sherlock Holmes adventure on the holodeck becomes a deadly reality when a computer-generated Professor Moriarty takes control of the ship.
06-2136 $14.99

Star Trek The Next Generation: The Outrageous Okona
An encounter with a wisecracking fugitive inspires Data to learn more about the concept of humor, with some help from holodeck-created comedian Joe Piscopo.
06-2137 $14.99

Star Trek The Next Generation: The Schizoid Man
A terminally ill computer genius hatches a plan to allow his mind to live on...with the unwilling help of Data.
06-2161 $14.99

Star Trek The Next Generation: Loud As A Whisper
The Enterprise escorts a deaf mediator to a planet torn by global war, but the mission may be in jeopardy before it starts.
06-2162 $14.99

Star Trek The Next Generation: Unnatural Selection
A strange disease that speeds up the aging process will claim Dr. Pulaski as its next victim if a cure cannot be found.
06-2163 $14.99

Star Trek The Next Generation: A Matter Of Honor
Temporarily assigned to a Klingon vessel, Riker must make a difficult choice when a mysterious organism threatens both his new ship and the Enterprise.
06-2164 $14.99

Star Trek The Next Generation: The Measure Of A Man
When a Starfleet officer orders Data to be turned over for disassembly and study, the android must go to court to prove his "humanity."
06-2212 $14.99

Star Trek The Next Generation: The Dauphin
Precocious young Wesley falls in love with an alien emissary, but she and her guardian share a strange secret.
06-2213 $14.99

Star Trek The Next Generation: Contagion
An unknown electronic virus takes control of the Enterprise computer system and programs the ship to self-destruct.
06-2214 $14.99

Star Trek The Next Generation: The Royale
Beaming down to explore an uncharted planet, Riker, Worf and Data find themselves the unwilling "guests" in a strange luxury hotel.
06-2215 $14.99

Star Trek The Next Generation: Time Squared
A warp in the space-time fabric brings a Picard from the future, who appears to have abandoned a doomed Enterprise, on to the ship of his present-day counterpart.
06-2216 $14.99

Star Trek The Next Generation: The Icarus Factor
Riker is faced with a difficult decision and a reunion with his estranged father when he's offered command of his own starship.
06-2217 $14.99

Star Trek The Next Generation: Pen Pals
Data's correspondence with a young girl named Sarjenka is in jeopardy when her world is threatened with self-destruction.
06-2254 $14.99

Star Trek The Next Generation: Q Who?
Rebuffed by Picard when he applies for "crew duty," interstellar kibitzer Q sends the ship into a fateful first encounter with the relentless Borg.
06-2255 $14.99

Star Trek The Next Generation: Samaritan Snare
Geordi is taken hostage on an away mission as a stricken Picard is rushed to surgery.
06-2256 $14.99

Star Trek The Next Generation: Up The Long Ladder
The Enterprise confronts the members of a dying race who are desperate for new genetic material to stave off extinction.
06-2257 $14.99

Star Trek The Next Generation: Manhunt
Troi's mother returns to the Enterprise with plans of landing a new husband, and Captain Picard is her target!
06-2258 $14.99

Star Trek The Next Generation: The Emissary
K'Ehleyr, a half-Klingon, half-human woman and an old flame of Worf's, joins the Enterprise as it intercepts a Klingon warship whose crew have been in cryosleep for 75 years.
06-2259 $14.99

Star Trek The Next Generation: Peak Performance
What starts out as a simulated war game turns into a deadly showdown between the Enterprise and a Ferengi warship.
06-2260 $14.99

Star Trek The Next Generation: Shades Of Gray
An alien organism infiltrates Riker's nervous system, triggering memories from the past, but the operation to cure him could cost him his life.
06-2261 $14.99

Star Trek The Next Generation: The Ensigns Of Command
When a human colony is marked for extermination, Data must race against time to save it.
06-2293 $14.99

Star Trek The Next Generation: Evolution
A mysterious force infiltrates the Enterprise's main computer and life-support system, prompting the crew to fight for survival.
06-2294 □$14.99

Star Trek The Next Generation: The Survivors
Two inhabitants of a war-torn Federation planet have been discovered, but can Picard decide if they are a miracle or mirage?
06-2295 □$14.99

Star Trek The Next Generation: Who Watches The Watchers
A hidden Federation research station is accidentally discovered by the planet's inhabitants, who take the Enterprise crew to be gods.
06-2296 □$14.99

Star Trek The Next Generation: The Bonding
A young boy finds help from Worf in dealing with his mother's death—and reappearance!
06-2301 □$14.99

Star Trek The Next Generation: Booby Trap
When a mysterious energy drain incapacitates the Enterprise and blasts the ship with lethal radiation, Geordi teams up with a holodeck re-creation of a famed female engineer to save the ship.
06-2302 □$14.99

Star Trek The Next Generation: The Enemy
As a Romulan warship threatens the Enterprise, Geordi finds himself stranded on a storm-plagued world with a Romulan soldier.
06-2303 □$14.99

Star Trek The Next Generation: The Price
Troi falls for a handsome delegate who uses his empathic powers to manipulate her into doing whatever he wants.
06-2304 □$14.99

Star Trek The Next Generation: The Vengeance Factor
The peace talks between warring factions are threatened by a pretty assassin.
06-2307 □$14.99

Star Trek The Next Generation: The Defector
A top Romulan official wants to defect to the Federation, but is his plea a trick?
06-2308 □$14.99

Star Trek The Next Generation: The Hunted
A genetically-enhanced "super-soldier" seeks refuge on the Enterprise.
06-2309 □$14.99

Star Trek The Next Generation: The High Ground
The Enterprise and its crew are thrown into the middle of a civil war after Dr. Crusher is kidnapped.
06-2310 □$14.99

Star Trek The Next Generation: Deja Q
The Enterprise gains a reluctant new crew member when a powerless Q, turned into a human by his race, joins them.
06-2311 □$14.99

Star Trek The Next Generation: A Matter Of Perspective
Computer evidence appears to prove an accused Riker guilty of killing a renowned scientist.
06-2312 □$14.99

Star Trek The Next Generation: Yesterday's Enterprise
A rift in time lands the Enterprise and her predecessor, the Enterprise 1701-C, in an altered reality where the Federation and Klingon Empire are at war and Tasha Yar is alive.
06-2321 □$14.99

Star Trek The Next Generation: The Offspring
Data creates his own android child, a daughter named Lal, but Starfleet demands that she be turned over to them for study.
06-2322 □$14.99

Star Trek The Next Generation: Sins Of The Father
After Worf is reunited with his long-lost brother, he's forced to defend his father's honor.
06-2323 □$14.99

Star Trek The Next Generation: Allegiance
Picard finds himself kidnapped and placed in a locked room with three other beings, while a duplicate captain sits on the bridge of the Enterprise.
06-2324 □$14.99

Star Trek The Next Generation: Captain's Holiday
It's anything but a restful time for Picard, when time travellers from the future seek his help in recovering a deadly weapon that threatens the galaxy.
06-2340 □$14.99

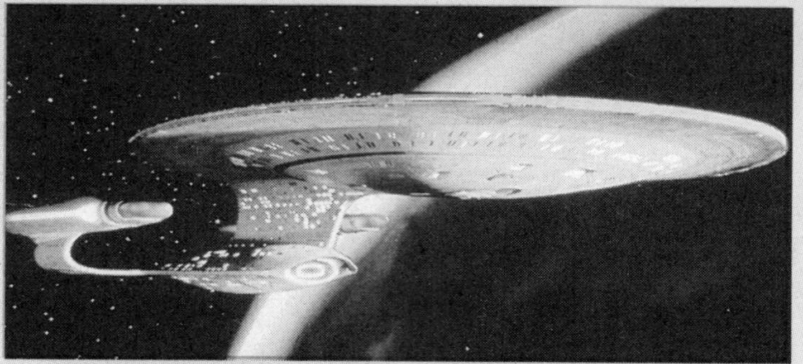

STAR TREK
THE NEXT GENERATION

Star Trek The Next Generation: Tin Man
An encounter with a living mechanical organism pits the Enterprise and a Betazoid official against the Romulans.
06-2341 □$14.99

Star Trek The Next Generation: Hollow Pursuits
A crewman's increasing addiction to holodeck games puts the lives of everyone on board in jeopardy.
06-2342 □$14.99

Star Trek The Next Generation: The Most Toys
Data is abducted by an interplanetary "collector" who specializes in one-of-a-kind items and wants to add the android to his treasures.
06-2343 □$14.99

Star Trek The Next Generation: Sarek
An outbreak of violence occurs on the Enterprise during a visit by aged Vulcan ambassador Sarek. Mark Lenard guest stars.
06-2371 □$14.99

Star Trek The Next Generation: Ménage A Troi
It's a romance unlike any ever seen in the galaxy when Troi and her mother Lwaxana are abducted in Ferengi in search of mates.
06-2372 □$14.99

Star Trek The Next Generation: Transfigurations
A mysterious humanoid with incredible powers is rescued by the Enterprise crew.
06-2373 □$14.99

Star Trek The Next Generation: The Best Of Both Worlds, Part I
The long-feared invasion of Federation space by the Borg has begun, but during the first battle Picard is kidnapped and transformed into the cyborg race's spokesman, Locutus.
06-2374 □$14.99

Star Trek The Next Generation: The Best Of Both Worlds, Part II
Riker takes the captain's chair as the war between the Federation and the Borg rages on, but will the price of victory be the captive Picard's life?
06-2416 □$14.99

Star Trek The Next Generation: Suddenly Human
When a human boy who was rescued and adopted by an alien race years earlier is found, Picard is forced to choose between leaving him where he is or risk war by returning him to his family.
06-2417 □$14.99

Star Trek The Next Generation: Brothers
An cybernetic summons brings Data and his sinister sibling, Lore, to a remote planet for a fateful encounter with their creator, the presumed-dead Dr. Noonian Sung.
06-2418 □$14.99

Star Trek The Next Generation: Family
A vacation in his native France brings Picard into a cathartic reunion with his estranged brother and his family.
06-2419 □$14.99

Star Trek The Next Generation: Remember Me
An accident during a warp field experiment sends Dr. Crusher into an alternate universe where the people she knows are one by one erased from existence.
06-2420 □$14.99

Star Trek The Next Generation: Legacy
On a mission to the war-wracked homeworld of the late Tasha Yar, the crew comes to the aid of her younger sister, but is she a friend or foe?
06-2421 □$14.99

Star Trek The Next Generation: Reunion
As Picard attempts to mediate a power struggle between rival houses for control of the Klingon Empire, Worf is reunited with K'Ehleyr and for the first time meets their son.
06-2422 □$14.99

Star Trek The Next Generation: Future Imperfect
After a mysterious accident suffered on an away team mission, Riker wakes up in Sickbay to find that 16 years have passed since then, and he is about to negotiate a vital treaty with the Romulans.
06-2423 □$14.99

Star Trek The Next Generation: Final Mission
A shuttlecraft crash leaves Picard seriously wounded and precocious young Wesley searching for a way for them to be rescued.
06-2445 □$14.99

Star Trek The Next Generation: The Loss
Robbed of her empathic abilities, Troi is driven to the brink of madness as she tries to adjust to being "merely human."
06-2446 □$14.99

Star Trek The Next Generation: Data's Day
The title says it all: a "typical" day in the life of the Enterprise's android officer.
06-2447 □$14.99

Star Trek The Next Generation: The Wounded
A Starfleet officer with a bitter grudge against the Cardassians may be drawing the Federation into war, and Chief O'Brien, who served under him, must try to stop him.
06-2448 □$14.99

Star Trek The Next Generation: Devil's Due
Picard has a "heck" of a time convincing a planet's populace that the mysterious woman claiming to be the "devil" responsible for their prosperity is a fake.
06-2449 □$14.99

Star Trek The Next Generation: Clues
A pass through a wormhole seems to have taken a mere 30 seconds, yet signs seem to indicate that a whole day's events have been wiped from everyone's memory.
06-2450 □$14.99

Star Trek The Next Generation: First Contact
A clandestine operation on a planet whose people have never met beings from other worlds is in jeopardy when a disguised Riker is wounded.
06-2451 □$14.99

Star Trek The Next Generation: Galaxy's Child
Geordi's long-awaited meeting with Dr. Leah Brahms, the scientist he "collaborated" with in "Booby Trap," is a less-than-stellar success.
06-2452 □$14.99

Star Trek The Next Generation: Night Terrors
While trying to rescue a derelict starship, the Enterprise is rendered powerless as the crew begins to be affected by the fear and paranoia that killed the other ship's crew.
06-2453 □$14.99

Star Trek The Next Generation: Identity Crisis
A mysterious parasite picked up on a mission years earlier is slowly turning Geordi and another crew member into alien beings.
06-2454 □$14.99

Star Trek The Next Generation: The Nth Degree
An accident grants a crewman super-human intelligence and senses, but when he takes control of the Enterprise computers, Picard must find a way to stop him.
06-2455 □$14.99

Star Trek The Next Generation: Qpid
The cosmic buttinsky known as Q is back, this time creating a Robin Hood fantasy as he tries to play matchmaker for Picard.
06-2456 □$14.99

Star Trek The Next Generation: The Drumhead
Will the investigation into a Klingon exchange officer accused of spying for the Romulans turn into a witch-hunt due to a Starfleet officer's overzealousness?
06-2457 □$14.99

Star Trek The Next Generation: Half A Life
Troi's mother falls in love with a scientist who, having reached the age of 60, must return to his home planet for compulsory euthanasia.
06-2458 □$14.99

Star Trek The Next Generation: The Host
A visiting Trillian scientist and Dr. Crusher are attracted to each other, but an injury to the guest reveals the Trills are symbiotic beings living inside host bodies.
06-2459 □$14.99

Star Trek The Next Generation: The Mind's Eye
The Romulans have brainwashed an Enterprise crew member to assassinate a Klingon ambassador. Can the would-be killer be found before it's too late?
06-2460 □$14.99

Star Trek The Next Generation: In Theory
Data gets a surprising first-hand lesson in human relations when a pretty ensign falls in love with the android.
06-2478 □$14.99

Star Trek The Next Generation: Redemption, Part I
Picard is charged with overseeing the installation of Gowron as leader of the Klingon Empire, but a rival claimant and his allies threaten to destroy the peace between the Klingons and the Federation.
06-2479 □$14.99

Star Trek The Next Generation: Redemption, Part II
As the Klingon split continues to grow, Picard tries to prove that the Romulans are behind the rebellious faction.
06-2480 □$14.99

Star Trek The Next Generation: Darmok
Picard and a starship captain from an alien race whose language defies translation are trapped together on a rugged planet.
06-2481 □$14.99

Star Trek The Next Generation: Ensign Ro
A new Enterprise ensign, a Bajoran woman with a troubled past, is the key to stopping hostilities when Bajoran ships attack a Federation outpost.
06-2482 □$14.99

Star Trek The Next Generation: Silicon Avatar
The mysterious Crystalline Entity that destroyed the scientific outpost where Data was created is back and threatening another world...unless the Enterprise can stop it.
06-2483 □$14.99

Star Trek The Next Generation: Disaster
An unknown catastrophe hits the Enterprise, leaving Picard in a turbo-lift with a broken leg, Troi in command on the bridge, and Worf helping O'Brien's wife deliver her baby.
06-2484 □$14.99

Star Trek The Next Generation: The Game
An addictive game that takes control of a person's brain is overwhelming the crew, and only precocious young Wesley can save them. Ashley Judd guest stars.
06-2485 □$14.99

Star Trek The Next Generation: The Borg Collective Boxed Set
Designed to resemble a Borg ship, this stunning collector's edition features four classic episodes that pit the Enterprise against the mechanized menaces: "Q Who?," the two-part "The Best of Both Worlds" and "I, Borg."
06-2488 $59.99

Star Trek The Next Generation: Unification, Part I
Picard and Data undertake a dangerous clandestine mission to the Romulan homeworld to locate a possible Federation traitor: the famed Vulcan ambassador Spock. Leonard Nimoy, Mark Lenard guest star.
06-2542 □$14.99

Star Trek The Next Generation: Unification, Part II
Mr. Spock is found by Data and Picard and explains the true reason for his quest, but their respective missions may meet sudden ends when Romulan officials track them down. Leonard Nimoy guest stars.
06-2543 ☐$14.99

Star Trek The Next Generation: A Matter Of Time
The ship is visited by a time-traveling scholar who claims to be from the future, but is he really who he says he is? Matt Frewer guest stars.
06-2544 ☐$14.99

Star Trek The Next Generation: New Ground
Worf is faced with some difficult decisions when his young son, Alexander, comes to live with him on the Enterprise.
06-2545 ☐$14.99

Star Trek The Next Generation: Hero Worship
The sole survivor of a ship destroyed by a "black cluster," a young boy who idolizes Data, may be the only person who can keep the Enterprise from meeting a similar fate.
06-2569 ☐$14.99

Star Trek The Next Generation: Violations
Did a member of a team of "telepathic historians" use his mental powers to psychically assault Troi?
06-2570 ☐$14.99

Star Trek The Next Generation: The Masterpiece Society
That's precisely what the populace of Moab IV appear to have created, but the arrival of an Enterprise away team stirs doubts among some of the genetically-engineered residents.
06-2571 ☐$14.99

Star Trek The Next Generation: Conundrum
A scanning beam from an alien ship leaves everyone on board the Enterprise suffering from amnesia.
06-2572 ☐$14.99

Star Trek The Next Generation: Power Play
Alien entities take over the bodies of Data, O'Brien and Troi and attempt to commandeer the Enterprise to escape their captivity.
06-2593 ☐$14.99

Star Trek The Next Generation: Ethics
Left paralyzed after an injury, Worf must decide between an untested and risky surgical procedure, living with his disability or taking his own life.
06-2594 ☐$14.99

Star Trek The Next Generation: The Outcast
Riker's romantic relationship with a pilot from an androgynous race where sexuality is forbidden has some dangerous repercussions.
06-2595 ☐$14.99

Star Trek The Next Generation: Cause And Effect
Dr. Crusher begins to realize that the Enterprise is caught in a strange "time loop" that begins and ends with a collision with another ship, but will anyone else believe her in time to do something about it?
06-2596 ☐$14.99

Star Trek The Next Generation: The First Duty
A deadly accident clouds the Enterprise's visit to Starfleet Academy and forces academy cadet Wesley Crusher to choose between his devotion to duty and his loyalty to his friends.
06-2623 ☐$14.99

Star Trek The Next Generation: Cost Of Living
A dual crisis on board the Enterprise finds an alien life form turning parts of the ship into gelatinous goo and Troi's mother arriving to announce her impending marriage.
06-2624 ☐$14.99

Star Trek The Next Generation: The Perfect Mate
A beautiful, genetically engineered woman intended as a bride to cement a peace treaty between warring systems accidentally captures Picard's heart.
06-2625 ☐$14.99

Star Trek The Next Generation: Imaginary Friend
A young girl's playmate may be "imaginary," but when an alien force takes over the role, the danger to the Enterprise is real, indeed.
06-2626 ☐$14.99

Star Trek The Next Generation: The Data Collection
The Enterprise's remarkable android officer takes center stage with a boxed collector's set that includes the episodes "The Measure of a Man," "The Offspring," "Hero Worship" and the two-part "Descent."
06-2627 $64.99

Star Trek The Next Generation: I, Borg
The rescue of an injured Borg gives Picard the chance to eliminate the Collective for all time, but will he when the "guest" begins to develop a personality of his own?
06-2632 ☐$14.99

Star Trek The Next Generation: The Next Phase
An accident renders Geordi and Ensign Ro "out of sync" with reality on the Enterprise and invisible to the crew.
06-2633 ☐$14.99

Star Trek The Next Generation: The Inner Light
Can an aged Picard go back in time to stop the alien probe that "hijacked" him off the Enterprise and into a new life on a distant planet?
06-2634 ☐$14.99

Star Trek The Next Generation: Time's Arrow, Part I
The fourth-season finale presents a cliffhanger mystery that stretches over 500 years, as an archeological dig in San Francisco dating from the 19th century uncovers Data's detached head.
06-2635 ☐$14.99

Star Trek The Next Generation: Worf "Return To Grace" Collection
The saga of Worf's struggle to regain his family's honor within the Klingon High Council is recounted in this four-tape boxed set that includes "Sins of the Father," "Reunion" and the two-part "Redemption."
06-2636 $59.99

Star Trek The Next Generation: Time's Arrow, Part II
It takes some help from an 1890s Guinan and writer Mark Twain for a time-travelling Data, Picard and company to foil the plans of alien visitors and return to their own era.
06-2683 ☐$14.99

Star Trek The Next Generation: Realm Of Fear
An engineering officer's phobia of using the transporter increases when, during a mission to a disabled ship, he becomes convinced he saw a creature inside the transporter beam.
06-2684 ☐$14.99

Star Trek The Next Generation: Man Of The People
What is the connection between the death of a Lumerian ambassador's mother on board the ship and strange emotional outbursts by Counselor Troi?
06-2685 ☐$14.99

Star Trek The Next Generation: Relics
Trapped inside an immense sphere constructed around a star, the Enterprise needs a "miracle"...and gets one when a transporter pattern in an abandoned shuttle returns to life famed engineer Montgomery Scott (James Doohan).
06-2686 ☐$14.99

Star Trek The Next Generation: Schisms
A number of inexplicable ailments and half-remembered visions of an alien lab seem to indicate that someone is using the crew as their personal "guinea pigs."
06-2687 ☐$14.99

Star Trek The Next Generation: True Q
A young Starfleet student turns out to be a long-lost member of the Q Continuum, and Q arrives to offer her the choice of returning to her own race or staying human.
06-2692 ☐$14.99

Star Trek The Next Generation: Rascals
A transporter mishap beams up Picard, Guinan, Ensign Ro and Keiko O'Brien as 12-year-olds, but these "children" have to save the day when the ship is commandeered by Ferengi renegades.
06-2693 ☐$14.99

Star Trek The Next Generation: A Fistful Of Datas
When a Wild West holodeck program goes haywire, it's up to Sheriff Worf to rescue his son from a frontier town whose residents all resemble Data.
06-2694 ☐$14.99

Star Trek The Next Generation: The Quality Of Life
Data puts his Starfleet career on the line when he insists that the new experimental computer units built on a mining colony have developed into sentient beings.
06-2695 ☐$14.99

Star Trek The Next Generation: Chain Of Command, Part I
An undercover mission to investigate rumors that the Cardassians are creating biological weapons turns out to be a trap, and Worf and Crusher are forced to leave a captive Picard behind.
06-2696 ☐$14.99

Star Trek The Next Generation: Chain Of Command, Part II
A prisoner of the Cardassians, Picard is subjected to brutal physical and psychological tortures in a battle of wills with his captors.
06-2697 ☐$14.99

Star Trek The Next Generation: Ship In A Bottle
The Holodeck-created villain Moriarty is back, this time taking over the ship and refusing to return control until he and his true love are given their freedom.
06-2698 ☐$14.99

Star Trek The Next Generation: Aquiel
Geordi's obsession with a missing and presumed dead officer from a relay outpost on the Federation-Klingon border takes a strange turn when she turns up alive.
06-2699 ☐$14.99

Star Trek The Next Generation: Face Of The Enemy
A shanghaied Troi is smuggled on board a Romulan warship as part of a plan to smuggle three high-ranking defectors to the Federation.
06-2700 ☐$14.99

Star Trek The Next Generation: Tapestry
Mortally wounded in a terrorist attack, Picard is saved by Q and given a chance to go back and change the course of his life...with unexpected consequences.
06-2737 ☐$14.99

Star Trek The Next Generation: Birthright, Part I
During a visit to Deep Space Nine, familial ties drive Data to explore a "dream" about his creator and Worf to investigate a rumor that his natural father is still alive, a prisoner of the Romulans.
06-2738 ☐$14.99

Star Trek The Next Generation: Birthright, Part II
Worf finds himself stranded on a planet where Klingon and Romulan war survivors have formed a joint colony.
06-2739 ☐$14.99

Star Trek The Next Generation: Starship Mine
It's Picard against a group of thieves on board an empty Enterprise, evacuated for a routine-but-lethal decontamination process.
06-2740 ☐$14.99

Star Trek The Next Generation: Lessons
Picard's blossoming romance with a new officer forces him to make a difficult choice between love and duty when she takes part in a dangerous away mission to a storm-ravaged planet.
06-2741 ☐$14.99

Star Trek The Next Generation: The Chase
What is the mysterious secret hidden inside ancient DNA samples, and what the Enterprise—along with Klingon, Romulan and Cardassian ships—find when the secret is solved?
06-2742 ☐$14.99

Star Trek The Next Generation: Frame Of Mind
Has Riker's Starfleet career been nothing more than an elaborate delusion? It looks that way when he awakes to find himself a patient in a mental hospital.
06-2743 ☐$14.99

Star Trek The Next Generation: Suspicions
Dr. Crusher turns detective to find out what killed a visiting scientist, part of a gathering present to witness an experimental shield demonstration.
06-2744 ☐$14.99

Star Trek The Next Generation: Rightful Heir
Has the legendary Klingon warrior Kahless really returned from the dead to reassume his role as emperor?
06-2745 ☐$14.99

Star Trek The Next Generation: Second Chances
A return to a remote outpost where he was once stranded gives Riker the surprise of his life—a younger version of himself, created in a freak transporter incident eight years earlier, is alive and well on the planet and ready to "return" to duty.
06-2773 ☐$14.99

Star Trek The Next Generation: Timescape
A temporal anomaly has frozen the Enterprise and a Romulan warbird in time, with only Picard, Data, Troi and LaForge free to uncover the cause of the disturbance before a warp-core breach destroys the ship.
06-2774 ☐$14.99

Star Trek The Next Generation: Descent, Part I
An encounter with a newly independent and aggressive Borg faction has disturbing repercussions for the crew—especially Data, who experiences feelings of rage—and leads to a shocking cliffhanger ending.
06-2775 ☐$14.99

Star Trek The Next Generation: Descent, Part II
Has Data really joined forces with his sinister sibling, Lore, to lead the Borg in their war against the Federation?
06-2776 ☐$14.99

Star Trek The Next Generation: Liaisons
While Troi and Worf have their troubles escorting a pair of Iyaaran ambassadors on board the ship, Picard is stranded on an isolated planet with a mysterious woman who seems intent on keeping him there.
06-2777 ☐$14.99

Star Trek The Next Generation: Interface
Convinced that he's contacted his missing mother, trapped on a starship that's deep in the atmosphere of a gas giant planet, Geordi must defy Picard's orders in an effort to save her.
06-2794 ☐$14.99

Star Trek The Next Generation: Gambit, Part I
Shock follows shock when Picard is apparently killed on an archeological expedition and, in the midst of searching for the "space pirates" responsible, Riker is captured and finds Picard alive and well on board the mercenaries' ship.
06-2795 ☐$14.99

Star Trek The Next Generation: Gambit, Part II
Will Picard and Riker's true identities be discovered as they help the space pirates search for an ancient—and potentially deadly—Vulcan artifact?
06-2796 ☐$14.99

Star Trek The Next Generation: Phantasms
What is the connection between LaForge's problems with a new warp core and Data's first experience with disturbing nightmares?
06-2797 ☐$14.99

Star Trek The Next Generation: Dark Page
In order to save her comatose mother, Troi must make a telepathic connection that reveals a tragic secret in her family's past.
06-2798 ☐$14.99

Star Trek The Next Generation: Attached
Captured by aliens that implant telepathic devices on them, Picard and Dr. Crusher try to escape—even as their shared thoughts reveal their mutual attraction.
06-2799 ☐$14.99

Star Trek The Next Generation: Force Of Nature
While trying to rescue a missing medical ship, the Enterprise is beset by both a Ferengi ship and a team of alien siblings out to prove that the warp drive is destroying the fabric of the universe.
06-2800 ☐$14.99

Star Trek The Next Generation: Inheritance
Data's family tree gains an unexpected addition when a scientist reveals to him she was Dr. Soong's wife and is in effect the android's "mother."
06-2801 ☐$14.99

Star Trek The Next Generation: Parallels
With reality constantly changing around him, Worf finds himself on one alternate Enterprise after another—including one where he and Troi are married.
06-2802 ☐$14.99

Star Trek The Next Generation: The Pegasus
Riker is placed in a difficult position when his first captain reveals to him the true purpose behind a salvage mission that pits the Enterprise against a Romulan warbird.
06-2803 ☐$14.99

Star Trek The Next Generation: Homeward
Will Worf assist his foster brother in saving a planet's doomed inhabitants, even if it means violating the Prime Directive?
06-2804 ☐$14.99

Star Trek The Next Generation: Sub Rosa
Will Dr. Crusher be the latest in a string of female ancestors to fall under the sway of a seemingly immortal "ghost lover"?
06-2805 ☐$14.99

Star Trek The Next Generation: Lower Decks
As they anxiously await news on possible promotions, a group of Enterprise junior officers becomes part of a top-secret mission.
06-2806 ☐$14.99

Star Trek The Next Generation: Thine Own Self
An amnesiac Data is marooned on a medieval planet whose inhabitants think this "stranger" is responsible for a disease plaguing them.
06-2807 ☐$14.99

Star Trek The Next Generation: Masks
Using Data as its "spokesman," an entity from a long-dead alien civilization begins transforming the Enterprise into its own private domain.
06-2808 ☐$14.99

Star Trek The Next Generation: Eye Of The Beholder
The romance between Worf and Troi blossoms as they investigate an officer's apparent suicide, but uncovering the truth could prove fatal for the lovers.
06-2809 ❑$14.99

Star Trek The Next Generation: Genesis
Picard and Data return from a shuttle mission to find a plague spreading through the ship that "de-volves" the crew.
06-2810 ❑$14.99

Star Trek The Next Generation: Journey's End
As part of a Federation treaty with the Cardassians, Picard must reluctantly relocate a colony whose inhabitants descended from Native Americans. At the same time, Wesley Crusher returns to find that the key to his own future lies with the colonists.
06-2811 ❑$14.99

Star Trek The Next Generation: Firstborn
Worf receives help from an enigmatic stranger in teaching his son Alexander about the Klingon warrior heritage, but the youngster's new mentor has a surprising motive.
06-2812 ❑$14.99

Star Trek The Next Generation: Bloodlines
Still seeking revenge for Picard's killing of his son, the Ferengi DaiMon Bok finds the perfect vehicle for his vengeance—the son Picard never knew he had.
06-2813 ❑$14.99

Star Trek The Next Generation: Emergence
The crew gets taken for a ride—literally—when the Enterprise's computer systems develop a mind of their own.
06-2814 ❑$14.99

Star Trek The Next Generation: Preemptive Strike
Assigned to infiltrate a Maquis outpost, Ensign Ro finds herself leaning more and more to the rebels' cause.
06-2815 ❑$14.99

Star Trek The Next Generation: All Good Things...
The seven-year voyage of the Enterprise comes full circle in this feature-length final episode, as Q sends Picard on a time-spanning "final test" that takes him from his first days in command of the ship to a future where his actions could affect all humanity. 92 min.
06-2424 ❑$19.99

Star Trek The Next Generation: Encounter At Farpoint/All Good Things Special Collector's Edition
The premiere and final episodes of the landmark sci-fi series are also available in this boxed collector's set.
06-2425 $39.99

Star Trek The Next Generation: The Best Of Both Worlds Gift Set
The complete two-part story of the Borg invasion is also available in a special collector's set.
06-2461 ❑$29.99

Star Trek The Next Generation: The Q Continuum Boxed Set
Can't get enough of that superpowered space buttinsky, Q? This special collector's set features Q in four of his most mischievous visits with the crew of the Enterprise: "Encounter at Farpoint," "Hide & Q," "Q Who?" and "Deja Q."
06-2462 ❑$64.99

Journey's End: The Saga Of Star Trek The Next Generation
Jonathan Frakes hosts this inside look at the seven-year run of the sci-fi favorite. Meet the regular cast and some memorable guest stars, learn effects and makeup secrets, and watch the filming of the series' final episode, "All Good Things...." 46 min.
06-2370 ❑$14.99

Star Trek: Deep Space Nine
The crew and residents of Federation space station Deep Space Nine let the wonders—and dangers—of the galaxy come to them in this hit syndicated series, the third entry in the "Star Trek" universe. Avery Brooks stars as DS9 commander Benjamin Sisko, along with Rene Auberjonois, Sidig El Fadil, Terry Farrell, Colm Meaney, Armin Shimmerman and Nana Visitor. Except where noted, each tape runs about 46 min.

Star Trek Deep Space Nine: Emissary
As he arrives to take charge of Deep Space Nine in the feature-length pilot episode, Sisko must deal with a ramshackle station, his own unwilling part in an ancient Bajoran prophecy, and a mysterious disturbance that turns out to be an invaluable discovery. 92 min.
06-2490 ❑$19.99

Star Trek Deep Space Nine: A Man Alone
When a Bajoran criminal is found murdered on the station, fingers are pointed at Odo, the shape-shifting security chief.
06-2491 ❑$14.99

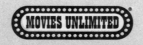

STAR TREK
DEEP SPACE NINE

Star Trek Deep Space Nine: Past Prologue
Major Kira must choose between her loyalty to Starfleet and her own people when a Bajoran freedom fighter comes on board claiming to seek asylum.
06-2492 ❑$14.99

Star Trek Deep Space Nine: Babel
The station is beset by a bizarre virus that turns everyone's speech into indecipherable babble.
06-2493 ❑$14.99

Star Trek Deep Space Nine: Captive Pursuit
An alien being, the first of his kind to make contact with the Federation, turns out to be a fugitive from a deadly game of pursuit, and Sisko must decide whether or not to interfere.
06-2494 ❑$14.99

Star Trek Deep Space Nine: Q-Less
Deep Space Nine is faced with a pair of disruptive visitors: interplanetary thief Vash and the cosmos-travelling gadfly known as Q.
06-2495 ❑$14.99

Star Trek Deep Space Nine: Dax
Lt. Dax, the symbotic science officer, is charged with a murder alleged to have been committed by her Trill entity's previous host body.
06-2496 ❑$14.99

Star Trek Deep Space Nine: The Passenger
An escaped murderer dies, but his consciousness may be hiding inside the brain of someone on board the station.
06-2497 ❑$14.99

Star Trek Deep Space Nine: Move Along Home
After he's caught rigging a game in his bar, Quark is forced by an alien visitor to play a different game with him...with the lives of Deep Space Nine's crew as the prize.
06-2498 ❑$14.99

Star Trek Deep Space Nine: The Nagus
Quark is looking forward to making the profit of a lifetime when he's named to replace the head of the Ferengi, but things don't quite work out as planned. Wallace Shawn guest stars.
06-2557 ❑$14.99

Star Trek Deep Space Nine: Vortex
Thanks to an emergency landing on an asteroid, Odo may at last have a chance to meet one of his fellow Changelings.
06-2558 ❑$14.99

Star Trek Deep Space Nine: Battle Lines
Sisko is trapped on a mysterious world where beings from across the galaxy are brought together in an unending "war game" where even death isn't permanent.
06-2559 ❑$14.99

Star Trek Deep Space Nine: The Storyteller
O'Brien fills in for a storyteller who serves as peacemaker for a Bajoran village, but does such a good job that he may never be allowed to leave.
06-2560 ❑$14.99

Star Trek Deep Space Nine: Progress
Sisko must play peacemaker between the Bajoran government and a farmer who refuses to leave his land. Brian Keith guest stars.
06-2597 ❑$14.99

Star Trek Deep Space Nine: If Wishes Were Horses
The station's crew have to watch their thoughts when some bizarre force begins turning their wishes into reality.
06-2598 ❑$14.99

Star Trek Deep Space Nine: The Forsaken
As O'Brien investigates a mysterious probe, Odo has his own problems fending off a would-be suitor's advances.
06-2599 ❑$14.99

Star Trek Deep Space Nine: Dramatis Personae
It's a "personality crisis" throughout the station when everyone begins acting contrary to their normal manner.
06-2600 ❑$14.99

Star Trek Deep Space Nine: Duet
An enigmatic Cardassian on board Deep Space Nine is revealed to be an infamous war criminal, but the most shocking surprise is yet to come.
06-2601 ❑$14.99

Star Trek Deep Space Nine: In The Hands Of The Prophets
O'Brien tries to find the link between an ensign's death and a conflict between science and Bajoran theology.
06-2602 ❑$14.99

Star Trek Deep Space Nine: The Homecoming
Kira risks her life to rescue a legendary Bajoran freedom fighter from a prison camp on Cardassia IV. Richard Beymer guest stars.
06-2603 ❑$14.99

Star Trek Deep Space Nine: The Circle
A startling discovery by Kira and Odo about a Bajoran minister could rip apart the fragile truce between Bajor and Cardassia and land the station in the middle of a war.
06-2604 ❑$14.99

Star Trek Deep Space Nine: The Siege
As Sisko and a skeleton crew brace for an attack on Deep Space Nine by Bajoran starships, Kira and Dax try to prove a Cardassian plot to provoke a war.
06-2628 ❑$14.99

Star Trek Deep Space Nine: Invasive Procedures
Another Trill, in desperate need of a host body, sets his sights on Lt. Dax's.
06-2629 ❑$14.99

Star Trek Deep Space Nine: Cardassians
Sisko is caught in the middle of a custody battle between rival Cardassian families for a boy, a battle with powerful political ramifications.
06-2630 ❑$14.99

Star Trek Deep Space Nine: Melora
Dr. Bashir is attracted to a visiting ensign from a low-gravity homeworld who is required to use a wheelchair to get around, while Quark must cope with a murder plot against him.
06-2631 ❑$14.99

Star Trek Deep Space Nine: Rules Of Acquisition
Knowing that "women should be seen and not heard" is a steadfast rule in Ferengi society, Quark doesn't know what to do when his new advisor turns out to a female in disguise.
06-2642 ❑$14.99

Star Trek Deep Space Nine: Necessary Evil
An investigation into an attempt on Quark's life leaves Odo with a long list of suspects, but will the would-be killer find him first?
06-2643 ❑$14.99

Star Trek Deep Space Nine: Second Sight
A beautiful visitor to the station catches Sisko's eye, but is this "dream woman" real, or is she part of an elaborate scheme?
06-2644 ❑$14.99

Star Trek Deep Space Nine: Sanctuary
Deep Space Nine becomes a haven for a devastated planet's survivors, but problems arise when the "guests" decide to make the station their permanent home.
06-2645 ❑$14.99

Star Trek Deep Space Nine: Rivals
Quark's Ferengi spirit of competition faces its greatest challenge when a conniving stranger (Chris Sarandon) opens a rival gaming club next to his bar.
06-2688 ❑$14.99

Star Trek Deep Space Nine: The Alternate
Could a mysterious find on a planet in the Gamma Quadrant hold clues to the origins of Odo and the key to finding other shapeshifters?
06-2689 ❑$14.99

Star Trek Deep Space Nine: Armageddon Game
A mission to uncover and eliminate potentially lethal biological weapons turns deadly for Chief O'Brien and Dr. Bashir.
06-2690 ❑$14.99

Star Trek Deep Space Nine: Whispers
Is it O'Brien's imagination, or has everyone's feelings towards him, from his wife Keiko to Sisko, seem to have been altered?
06-2691 ❑$14.99

Star Trek Deep Space Nine: Paradise
Sisko and O'Brien find themselves stranded in a "perfect" society that has rejected all forms of technology.
06-2724 ❑$14.99

Star Trek Deep Space Nine: Shadowplay
It's a case of missing persons...or is it?...when Odo investigates the disappearances of the members of a holographically projected society.
06-2725 ❑$14.99

Star Trek Deep Space Nine: Playing God
Sisko is faced with a monumental decision when a nascent "proto-universe's" development threatens to destroy the station.
06-2726 ❑$14.99

Star Trek Deep Space Nine: Profit And Loss
What could possibly make Quark put aside the Ferengi Rules of Acquisition? How about the arrival of an old flame—a Cardassian dissident—on the station?
06-2727 ❑$14.99

Star Trek Deep Space Nine: Blood Oath
Dax joins three aged Klingon warriors (guest stars Michael Ansara, William Campbell and John Colicos) in a battle quest as part of a promise she made to them in her previous incarnation.
06-2769 ❑$14.99

Star Trek Deep Space Nine: The Maquis, Part I
The destruction of a Cardassian freighter as it leaves the station draws Sisko and the crew of Deep Space Nine into conflict with the Maquis, Federation colonists turned rebels.
06-2770 ❑$14.99

Star Trek Deep Space Nine: The Maquis, Part II
Sisko and Gul Dukat become uneasy allies as they seek to stop the war between Cardassia and the Maquis, whose leader is an old friend of Sisko's.
06-2771 ❑$14.99

Star Trek Deep Space Nine: The Wire
A brain implant Garak received during his time as a member of the Cardassian Empire's Obsidian Order could wind up killing him if Bashir can't remove it in time.
06-2772 ❑$14.99

Star Trek Deep Space Nine: Crossover
A mishap in the wormhole sends Kira and Dr. Bashir into a parallel universe where the station is run by a militaristic Bajor and their counterparts lead very different lives.
06-2842 ❑$14.99

Star Trek Deep Space Nine: The Collaborator
On the eve of important Bajoran elections, Kira learns that the man she loves may have worked with the Cardassians in the slaughter of Bajoran rebels.
06-2843 ❑$14.99

Star Trek Deep Space Nine: Tribunal
A vacation for the O'Briens takes a serious detour when Miles is arrested by the Cardassians for a crime he didn't commit.
06-2844 ❑$14.99

Star Trek Deep Space Nine: The Jem'Hadar
While on a camping trip, Sisko and Quark are taken prisoner by the Dominion's lethal warrior allies, the Jem'Hadar.
06-2845 ❑$14.99

Star Trek Deep Space Nine: The Search, Part I
Sisko leads the Defiant into the wormhole on a mission to locate the homeworld of the Dominion's leaders, the Founders...but what is their connection to Odo?
06-2866 ❑$14.99

Star Trek Deep Space Nine: The Search, Part II
As Odo learns some shocking facts about his people, Sisko attempts to destroy the wormhole and keep the Dominion out of the region.
06-2867 ❑$14.99

Star Trek Deep Space Nine: The House Of Quark
After taking credit for the accidental death of a Klingon customer, Quark is faced with the widow's demand for marriage.
06-2868 ❑$14.99

Star Trek Deep Space Nine: Equilibrium
After returning to the Trill homeworld, Dax discovers a secret that could destroy her and Trill society.
06-2869 ❑$14.99

Star Trek Deep Space Nine: Second Skin
Kira is kidnapped and told by the Obsidian Order that she is an Obsidian operative sent to infiltrate the Bajoran resistance 10 years ago.
06-2870 ❑$14.99

MOVIES UNLIMITED®

Star Trek Deep Space Nine: The Abandoned
Quark doesn't realize how much trouble he's about to face after he purchases a wrecked ship—one that contains an infant Jem'Hadar.
06-2871 $14.99

Star Trek Deep Space Nine: Civil Defense
O'Brien has only two hours to save the station by stopping an automated security program he accidentally activated.
06-2872 $14.99

Star Trek Deep Space Nine: Meridian
Dax discovers a planet that shifts between dimensions and falls in love with one of its inhabitants.
06-2873 $14.99

Star Trek Deep Space Nine: The Defiant
Commander Riker's guest stop at the Defiant surprises everyone when he hijacks the ship and sets a course for the Cardassian homeworld.
06-2874 $14.99

Star Trek Deep Space Nine: Fascination
During the Bajoran Gratitude Festival, Lwaxana Troi comes aboard the station and telepathically projects her romantic feelings to the crew.
06-2875 $14.99

Star Trek Deep Space Nine: Past Tense, Part I
Sent back in time to 21st-century Earth, Sisko, Dax and Bashir find themselves in the middle of a pivotal human rights protest and Sisko is forced to impersonate the rebellion's leader.
06-2888 $14.99

Star Trek Deep Space Nine: Past Tense, Part II
In order to preserve the future, will Sisko's impersonation of civil rights leader Gabriel Bell end, as the history books state, with Bell's murder?
06-2889 $14.99

Star Trek Deep Space Nine: Life Support
Bashir must make a difficult decision when a key negotiator to treaty negotiations with the Cardassians is critically injured.
06-2890 $14.99

Star Trek Deep Space Nine: Heart Of Stone
Odo confesses his feelings for Kira when they're stranded on a deserted moon and a strange crystal formation begins taking over Kira's body.
06-2891 $14.99

Star Trek Deep Space Nine: Destiny
A joint scientific mission into the wormhole with the Cardassians puts Sisko at odds with the mysterious aliens inside the wormhole and jeopardizes his role as the Emissary.
06-2934 $14.99

Star Trek Deep Space Nine: Prophet Motive
When the Ferengi Grand Nagus arrives and announces a revamping of the Rules of Acquisition, it's up to Quark to save his people's money-making way of life. Wallace Shawn guest stars.
06-2935 $14.99

Star Trek Deep Space Nine: Visionary
Hurled into the near future by a mishap, O'Brien must find a way to change "history" after witnessing the station's destruction.
06-2936 $14.99

Star Trek Deep Space Nine: Distant Voices
Trapped in a bizarre dreamworld after an encounter with a Lethean drug dealer, a comatose Bashir must solve the mystery of his telepathically-created prison before it's too late.
06-2937 $14.99

Star Trek Deep Space Nine: Improbable Causes
An explosion in Garak's tailor shop sends Odo on an investigation to discover who is behind the attempt on the Cardassian exile's life.
06-2951 $14.99

Star Trek Deep Space Nine: Through The Looking Glass
Sisko enters the alternate universe first encountered in "Crossover" in order to stop his "wife" from delivering a device that could doom that world's rebellion.
06-2952 $14.99

Star Trek Deep Space Nine: The Die Is Cast
The story begun in "Improbable Causes" concludes with the Cardassians and Romulans poised to attack the Dominion and Garak faced with having to kill Odo.
06-2953 $14.99

Star Trek Deep Space Nine: Explorers
Sisko and Jake set out in a reconstruction of an early Bajoran ship in order to prove a legend that Bajorans travelled to Cardassia centuries earlier.
06-2954 $14.99

Star Trek Deep Space Nine: Family Business
Upon learning that his mother is running a business and earning profits in defiance of Ferengi law, Quark returns home to "straighten her out."
06-2955 $14.99

Star Trek Deep Space Nine: Shakaar
Which side will Kira choose when she's sent to Bajor and confronts her former mentor in the resistance movement?
06-2956 $14.99

Star Trek Deep Space Nine: Facets
A mind-transfer ceremony allows Dax to "meet" her Trill symbont's former hosts, but things get sticky when one of them refuses to give up his new body: Odo's.
06-2980 $14.99

Star Trek Deep Space Nine: The Adversary
Sent out in the Defiant on a "show of strength" mission, the crew quickly learn the ship has been sabotaged to start a war. Was a Founder behind it, and will Odo be forced to take a fellow Changeling's life?
06-2981 $14.99

Star Trek Deep Space Nine: The Way Of The Warrior
The feature-length fourth-season opener finds the Federation on the brink of war with the Dominion, a situation that gets worse when a planned Klingon invasion of Cardassia threatens to break the Federation-Klingon peace; Michael Dorn joins the series as Worf.
06-2982 $19.99

Star Trek Deep Space Nine: Hippocratic Oath
Forced to land their shuttle on an unknown world, O'Brien and Bashir come across a group of renegae Jem'Hadar who want the doctor to help them break their addcition to a Dominion-supplied drug.
06-2983 $14.99

Star Trek Deep Space Nine: The Visitor
In this unusual episode, an elderly Jake Sisko recalls the accident that caused his father to vanish and his lifelong quest to find him.
06-2995 $14.99

Star Trek Deep Space Nine: Indiscretion
Kira is joined on her search for a Cardassian ship that vanished years earlier while ferrying Bajoran prisoners by Gul Dukat, who has his own surprising reason to wanting to find the survivors.
06-2996 $14.99

Star Trek Deep Space Nine: Rejoined
An encounter with a female Trill scientist to whom she was once married in a previous host's life stirs up dangerous feelings in Dax in this controversial tale.
06-2997 $14.99

Star Trek Deep Space Nine: Starship Down
Attacked by the Jem'Hadar while on a trading mission, the Defiant is left stranded inside the atmosphere of a giant gas planet, with Sisko wounded, Dax and Bashir trapped in a turbolift shaft, and Quark trying to defuse an unexploded torpedo.
06-2998 $14.99

Star Trek Deep Space Nine: Little Green Men
A trip to Earth becomes a journey through time for Quark, Rom and Nog when their sabotaged shuttle lands them in Roswell, New Mexico, in the year 1947...and the custody of the U.S. military.
06-2999 $14.99

Star Trek Deep Space Nine: The Sword Of Kahless
Worf, Dax and the fabled Klingon warrior Kor journey to locate a mystical sword that is supposedly powerful enough to unite the entire Klingon Empire.
06-3024 $14.99

Star Trek Deep Space Nine: Our Man Bashir
A malfunctioning hologram program traps Bashir in the role of a suave '60s superspy, but now he may be all that stands between his trapped fellow officers and impending death.
06-3025 $14.99

Star Trek Deep Space Nine: Homefront
The first half of a two-part story finds Sisko returning to Starfleet HQ with Odo after learning that the Dominion may be planning an attack on Earth.
06-3026 $14.99

Star Trek Deep Space Nine: Paradise Lost
In the conclusion to the "Homefront" episode, Sisko and Odo discover a saboteur within Starfleet who is plotting to overthrow the Federation and replace it with military rule. Meanwhile, Earth is preparing for war with the Dominion.
06-3027 $14.99

Star Trek Deep Space Nine: Crossfire
When Bajor's First Minister arrives on the station, he becomes increasingly attracted to Kira, forcing Odo to choose between his duty to protect the minister and his hidden feelings for Kira.
06-3028 $14.99

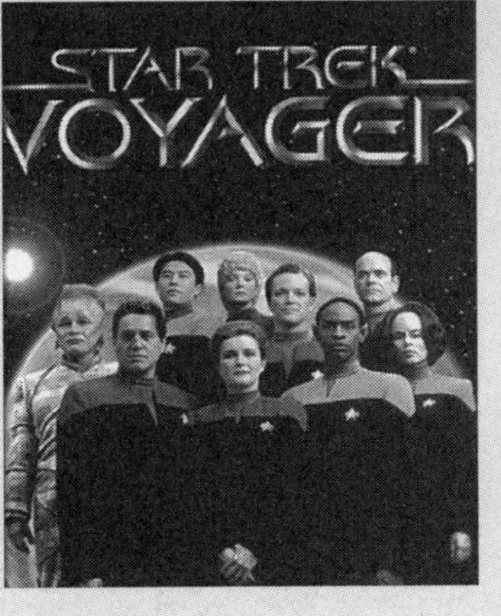

Star Trek: Voyager
"Show Me the Way to Go Home" could have been the theme song for the fourth "Trek" series, in which Captain Kathryn Janeway and her crew are left stranded in a distant section of the galaxy and undertake a perilous journey to find their way home. Kate Mulgrew, Robert Beltran, Roxann Biggs-Dawson, Robert Duncan McNeill, Robert Picardo, Tim Russ and Garrett Wang star. Except where noted, each tape runs about 46 min.

Star Trek Voyager: Caretaker, Parts I & II
Charged with tracking down and stopping a rebel Maquis ship, the crew of the starship Voyager finds itself and its target sent by a mysterious entity 70,000 light years across the galaxy in the series' feature-length pilot episode.
06-2941 $19.99

Star Trek Voyager: Parallax
An attempt to help what appears to be a ship trapped near a quantum singularity strands Voyager and a duplicate around the collapsed star.
06-2942 $14.99

Star Trek Voyager: Time And Again
Janeway is faced with breaking the Prime Directive if she warns a planet's inhabitants that their actions will lead to the end of life on their world.
06-2943 $14.99

Star Trek Voyager: Phage
During an away team mission, Neelix is attacked by aliens who see his body as the key to curing a deadly disease destroying their race.
06-2944 $14.99

Star Trek Voyager: The Cloud
What seems to be a nebula containing needed fuel is in fact an immense lifeform. Can Voyager save it and themselves?
06-2945 $14.99

Star Trek Voyager: Heroes And Demons
An alien force takes control of Voyager's holodecks and turns the crew into pure energy, and only the holographic Doctor can save them.
06-2990 $14.99

Star Trek Voyager: Cathexis
Tuvok and Chakotay are attacked while exploring near a "black matter nebula," and the ship is visited by a pair of alien presences, one of which wants to lead it into destruction.
06-2991 $14.99

Star Trek Voyager: Faces
Seeking a cure for the Phage plague, alien scientists split B'Elanna into separate human and Klingon beings.
06-2992 $14.99

Star Trek Voyager: Jetrel
Voyager is visited by a Haakonian scientist responsible for a weapon that killed thousands of Neelix's fellow Talaxians, including his family, years earlier.
06-2993 $14.99

Star Trek Voyager: Learning Curve
Tuvok is charged with instructing a group of former Maquis members in the basics of Starfleet rules and working procedure, but the exercise becomes a life-or-death test.
06-2994 $14.99

Star Trek Voyager: Projections
The Doctor manages to project himself out of sickbay, only to find that the rest of the crew has abandoned ship! However, is it reality or merely an illusion? Directed by Jonathan Frakes of "Star Trek: The Next Generation."
06-3018 $14.99

Star Trek Voyager: Elogium
Kes' biological clock is ticking like a time bomb when a mysterious alien lifeform accelerates her reproductive process. Now, she only has one chance to mate and have a child!
06-3019 $14.99

Star Trek Voyager: Twisted
The crew of the Voyager must race to stop alterations to the ship's structural layout which is being caused by a strange spatial distortion.
06-3020 $14.99

Star Trek Voyager: The 37's
The ship lands on a strange world inhabited by the descendants of 300 Earthlings—among them, famed aviator Amelia Earhart—who were abducted by aliens in 1937. Sharon Lawrence guest stars.
06-3021 $14.99

Star Trek Voyager: Initiations
Chakotay finds himself up against an unusual enemy when, alone in a shuttlecraft, he must face a Kazon boy who hopes to gain warrior status by killing him.
06-3022 $14.99

Star Trek Voyager: Eye Of The Needle
A wormhole into the Alpha Quadrant gives Voyager a chance to send a distress message through, but the only recipient is a Romulan cargo vessel with a disbelieving captain.
06-2963 $14.99

Star Trek Voyager: Ex Post Facto
While visiting a planet, Lt. Paris is accused of and convicted for a murder he didn't commit, and is sentenced to a life of reliving the victim's final moments.
06-2964 $14.99

Star Trek Voyager: Emanations
Accidentally transported to an alien planet, Harry's presence causes the local populace to question their most sacred religious beliefs.
06-2965 $14.99

Star Trek Voyager: Prime Factors
A friendly alien race known as the Sikarians offers the use of their "space-folding" technology to help Voyager get home, but is there an ulterior purpose for their hospitality?
06-2966 $14.99

Star Trek Voyager: State Of Flux
A Kazon ship damaged by Federation technology offers proof that someone on board Voyager is a traitor...but who?
06-2967 $14.99

Star Trek Voyager: Non Sequitur
Ensign Kim is thrown into a world of perplexity when he wakes up to find himself back home in San Francisco, where he works for Starfleet Engineering and was never a member of the Voyager crew!
06-3037 $14.99

Star Trek Voyager: Parturition
Neelix and Paris, rivals over the attentions of Kes, must learn to put their differences aside in order to take care of an alien baby when the two are stranded on a strange planet.
06-3038 $14.99

Star Trek Voyager: Persistence Of Vision
Shipboard appearances by characters from Janeway's holo-novel are a prelude to a psychic invasion of the ship that leaves only Kes and the Doctor unaffected and able to search for a cure.
06-3039 $14.99

Star Trek Voyager: Tattoo
When Chakotay becomes marooned on an alien planet while searching for needed mineral, he discovers that he may have an ancestral connection to its angry inhabitants.
06-3040 $14.99

Star Trek Voyager: Cold Fire
The crew becomes involved in a dangerous power struggle when they encounter the angry female counterpart to the Caretaker responsible for stranding them in the Delta Quadrant.
06-3041 $14.99

Star Trek 25th Anniversary Special (1991)
Celebrate a quarter-century of boldly going where no one has gone before with this salute to the many faces of "Star Trek." Join hosts William Shatner and Leonard Nimoy for a look at the show's origins, interviews with cast members and creator Gene Roddenberry, scenes from the TV series and films, a salute to "Trek" fandom and more. 100 min.
06-1966 $14.99

Star Trek Deep Space Nine: Behind The Scenes (1993)
Join host Terry Farrell (Lt. Dax) for a special look at the creation and production of the third "Trek" series. Tour the DS9 "station," watch interviews with the stars and staff, and see how the Emmy-winning special effects are produced. 46 min.
06-2211 $14.99

William Shatner's Star Trek Memories (1995)
Go behind the scenes of "the show that refused to die," with Captain James T. Kirk himself as your host, in this fascinating documentary based on Shatner's best-selling memoirs. You'll hear about "Star Trek's" creation, life on the set, how fan support saved the show from cancellation and led to the films and more. Joining Shatner are co-stars Leonard Nimoy, De Forest Kelley, James Doohan, Nichelle Nichols, Walter Keonig and George Takei. Oh, my! 86 min.
06-2415 $14.99

Star Trek:
30 Years And Beyond (1996)
Celebrate three decades of exploring "the final frontier," as host Ted Danson presents reminiscences from cast members of all four "Trek" series, clips of the shows' most memorable moments, skits and stand-up routines, rare film footage and much more. 85 min.
06-2782 ❑$14.99

Inside Star Trek:
The Real Story (1998)
"Boldly go" behind the scenes of the original "Star Trek" TV series with this amazing documentary. Exclusive interviews with many of the people who worked on the show during its three-year network run are featured to give you the complete "Trek" story. 48 min.
06-2781 ❑$14.99

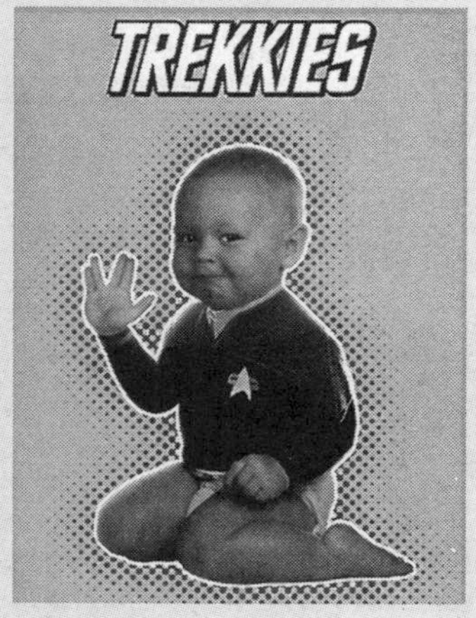

Trekkies (1999)
This documentary boldly goes where no film has gone before, focusing on the most extreme fans in the universe: "Star Trek" fans. Host Denise Crosby introduces you to the Arkansas juror who insisted on wearing her Starfleet uniform during the Whitewater trial; a dentist with a "Trek"-themed office; and other assorted Klingons, Vulcans, hardcore fanatics and key cast members. 87 min.
06-2917 Was $99.99 ❑$14.99

Ultimate Trek: Star Trek's Greatest Moments (1999)
Amazing aliens, a cacophony of captains and crew, and even a Tribble or two await you in this salute to the beloved TV and film series. Devoted "Trek" fan Jason Alexander hosts this look at the shows' most memorable moments, guest stars, villains, one-liners and more, including a salute to DeForest Kelley and the selection of the all-time best episodes. 43 min.
06-2989 ❑$14.99

Star Trek:
The Premiere Episodes
This deluxe boxed set offers fans a look at the first adventures of all four "Star Trek" series. See Captains Pike and Kirk lead the original Enterprise in "The Cage" and "Where No Man Has Gone Before"; Captain Picard and the "Next Generation" crew in "Encounter at Farpoint"; "Emissary," the pilot for "Deep Space Nine"; and the feature-length "Star Trek: Voyager" premiere, "Caretaker."
06-2489 $79.99

Star Trek:
The Captains Collection
Explore four different eras of starship captains and their hairstyles (or the lack thereof) in this special boxed set. William Shatner stars in "Obsession" from the original series; "Next Generation's" Patrick Stewart is featured in "Family"; Avery Brooks commands "Deep Space Nine" in "The Adversary"; and Kate Mulgrew has the "Voyager" captain's chair in "Caretaker."
06-2463 ❑$64.99

Star Trek:
The Time Travel Collection
Take four trips through the fourth dimension with this boxed set of time-spanning adventures from each "Trek" program. Included are the original series' "City on the Edge of Forever"; "Yesterday's Enterprise" from "Next Generation"; "The Visitor" from "Deep Space Nine"; and "Voyager's" "Time and Again."
06-2568 $59.99

Star Trek:
The Greatest Battles Gift Set
Thrill to interplanetary combat with this four-tape collector's set featuring adventures from each "Trek" series. Captain Kirk leads the original Enterprise into battle against the Romulans in "Balance of Terror"; it's Picard versus the Enterprise D in the "Next Generation" two-parter "Gambit"; "Deep Space Nine" against the Klingons in the double-episode "The Way of the Warrior"; and the crew of "Voyager" taking on the Kazon in "Maneuvers."
06-2592 $79.99

Star Trek: Talking Tribble Gift Set
It's "the only love money can buy," according to Cyrano Jones, and you'll love this special collector's set that includes the original series' "The Trouble with Tribbles," "Deep Space Nine's" amazing "Trials and Tribble-ations," and your very own "talking" tribble.
06-2768 $29.99

The Sandbaggers (1978)
Terrific suspense series from England stars Roy Marsden as Neil Ironside, a former special agent, or "Sandbagger," for Britain's Secret Intelligence System. Now serving as Director of Operations, Burnside must deal with both international intrigue and political conflicts between his office, the government bureaucracy and Downing Street. Ray Lonnen, Diane Keen also star. Each six-episode boxed set runs about 315 min.

The Sandbaggers: Collection 1
Included in this six-tape set are "Always Glad to Help," "A Feasible Solution," "First Principles," "Is Your Journey Really Necessary," "The Most Suitable Person" and "A Proper Function of Government."
53-9575 Was $149.99 $79.99

The Sandbaggers: Collection 2
Included in this six-tape set are "At All Costs," "Decision By Committee," "Enough of Ghosts," "It Couldn't Happen Here," "Operation Kingmaker" and "A Question of Loyalty."
53-6719 $89.99

Doctor In The House
Based on the popular '50s film series, this British sitcom premiered in 1969 and starred Barry Evans, Robin Nedwell and Geoffrey Davies as the fun-loving medical students whose antics keep the patients and staff of St. Swithin's Hospital in stitches. Each tape featured two episodes and runs about 50 min.

Doctor In The House, Vol. 1: Why Do You Want To Be A Doctor?/Settling In
53-6721 $19.99

Doctor In The House, Vol. 2: It's All Go.../ The Students Are Revolting
53-6722 $19.99

Doctor In The House, Vol. 3: Rallying Round/All For Love
53-6723 $19.99

Doctor In The House: Collection 1
Volumes 1-3 are also available in a boxed set.
53-6720 $59.99

Raffles: Complete Set
E.W. Hornung's turn-of-the-century "gentleman thief" comes to life in these sophisticated mysteries based on the perennially popular stories. Follow Raffles (Anthony Valentine) and his devoted sidekick, Bunny (Christopher Strauli), as they travel to society soirees and lavish mansions in search of their next caper. 312 min. on six tapes.
53-8139 Was $129.99 $79.99

The Best Of Lovejoy Mysteries: Collector's Boxed Set
Ian MacShane stars as the antiques dealer who has charm, good looks, brains...and a knack for finding trouble. Lovejoy's searches for art and artifacts often land him in twisted schemes and tangled whodunits. Included in this four-tape set are "Friends in High Places," "Loveknots," "The Ring" and "Scotch on the Rocks." 200 min. total. NOTE: Individual volumes available at $14.99 each.
53-8185 $59.99

More Cracker Mysteries: Collector's Set 2
His private life is as bizarre as the criminals that he brings to justice. Robbie Coltrane returns as idiosyncratic investigator "Fitz" Fitzgerald in this boxed set featuring three of his most compelling cases. Included are "The Big Crunch," "Brotherly Love" and "Men Should Weep." 450 min. total.
53-8604 $59.99

The League Of Gentlemen
Make a visit to the quaint, isolated English town of Royston Vasey, where the quaint, isolated (and inbred) locals' lives are turned upside-down by troubles ranging from job center squabbles and a transsexual cab driver to a foul-mouthed lady vicar and the "special meat" at the butcher's. Mark Gatiss, Steve Pemberton and Reece Shearsmith play all 60-plus characters in this off-the-wall British comedy series. Each tape features three episodes and runs about 85 min.

The League Of Gentlemen, Vol. 1
Includes "Welcome to Royston Vasey," "The Road to Royston Vasey" and "Nightmare in Royston Vasey."
19-5021 $19.99

The League Of Gentlemen, Vol. 2
Includes "The Beast of Royston Vasey," "Love Comes to Royston Vasey" and "Escape from Royston Vasey."
19-5022 $19.99

My Hero
In this 1952 sitcom, Robert Cummings plays a real estate agent with an uncanny knack for closing deals despite some humorous mishaps. Julie Bishop plays his trusty secretary, John Litel his boss. Each tape includes two episodes and runs about 60 min. There are four volumes available, including:

My Hero, Vol. 1
Includes "The Movie Star" and "Jimmy Valentine."
10-8112 Was $19.99 $14.99

My Hero, Vol. 2
Includes "Cinderella's Revenge" and "Odd Man In."
10-8113 Was $19.99 $14.99

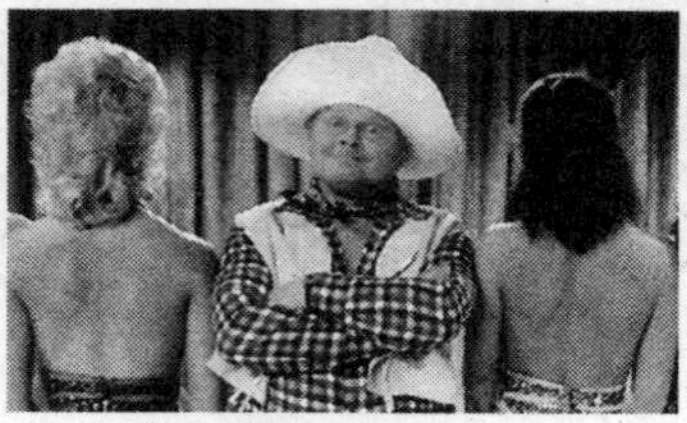

Benny Hill's Video Revue
Britain's own "Baby Blue Eyes," that loony Benny Hill, is back in a collection of his most outrageous TV skits, complete with bawdy humor and beautiful women. 120 min.
44-1647 $19.99

Benny Hill's One-Night Video Stand
More zany sketches, lecherous comedy, and crazy antics, courtesy of Mr. Hill and Company. 115 min.
44-1648 $19.99

Benny Hill's Video Sideshow
Your own sides will ache with laughs as that wacky Benny gets into one mess after another. 115 min.
44-1649 $19.99

Benny Hill's Home Video Drive-In
He'll drive you crazy with his hilarious characters, fast-paced hi-jinx, and gorgeous gals. 95 min.
44-1650 $19.99

Benny Hill's Video Follies
Presenting for your entertainment, the one and only Benny Hill, with a choice collection of amusing bits. 97 min.
44-1651 $19.99

Benny Hill's Video Spotlight
More lunatic stuff from the wildest British import since the Druids, bawdy Benny Hill. 120 min.
44-1652 $19.99

Benny Hill's Crazy World
Let's see: we bet it contains nagging wives, little old men, and more sexy starlets than one man can stand. 55 min.
44-1653 $19.99

Benny Hill's World: New York!
In one of his final comedy specials, England's beloved "Baby Blue Eyes" crossed the pond for a typically bawdy look at life in the Big Apple. Join Benny and his gang as they tour the city, see spoofs of "A Streetcar Named Desire" and "The Dr. Ruth Show," get Hill's tips on picking up New York women and how to rap, and much more. 60 min.
02-8270 $19.99

Benny Hill:
The Lost Years: Boxed Set
Never aired on this side of the Atlantic, the newly-discovered programs in this three-volume collection let you see the best of Benny's early years on TV, with all the zaniness and ribaldry intact. Included are "Benny and the Jests," "Bennys from Heaven" and "The Good, the Bawd, the Benny." 180 min. NOTE: Individual volumes available at $14.99 each.
04-3758 Save $10.00! $34.99

Benny Hill:
The Golden Laughter Series 1
Have yourself a "Hill" of a good time with this special five-tape set featuring boisterous Benny and company in the wildest, funniest moments from the long-running TV show. Fred Scuttle, Mr. Chow Mein, and the luscious Hill's Angels are all on display in "Benny Hill: Golden Chuckles," "Benny Hill: Golden Giggles," "Benny Hill: Golden Guffaws," "Benny Hill: Golden Laughs" and "Benny Hill: Golden Sniggers." 290 min. total. NOTE: Individual volumes available at $14.99 each.
44-2085 Save $15.00! ❑$59.99

Benny Hill:
The Golden Laughter Series 2
The laughter—and the memories—are indeed golden in this five-volume collection of classic comedy skits with rambunctious Benny and his crazy cast of cohorts. Included are "Benny Hill: Golden Chortles," "Benny Hill: Golden Grins," "Benny Hill: Golden Smiles," "Benny Hill: Golden Titters" and "Benny Hill: Golden Yucks." NOTE: Individual volumes available at $14.99 each.
44-2126 Save $15.00! $59.99

1966 Fall TV Preview With Batman & Robin
Holy tube trivia! Here's a real collector's item; a look at some of 1966's new TV programs, hosted by the Dynamic Duo of Adam West and Burt Ward. Featured are clips from such vintage programs as "Green Hornet," "Time Tunnel," "Rat Patrol," "Felony Squad," "Shane," "The Monroes" and the classic "Pruitts of Southampton." 35 min.
10-7550 $19.99

The Pallisers: Set #1 (1974)
The first eight episodes of the acclaimed BBC series based on Anthony Trollope's novels are featured in this collector's set. Throughout a span of 20 years, the unending drama and problems facing Victorian politician Plantagenet Pallister and his family are traced as they weave their way through their privileged social world. Philip Latham, Susan Hampshire, Anthony Andrews, John Gielgud, Derek Jacobi star. 6 1/2 hours on four tapes.
50-8728 $79.99

The Bretts Collection 1: Complete Set
Soaring dramatic saga of Charles and Lydia Brett, reigning luminaries of London's theatre world in the early 1900s, as they cope with changes in the West End and family pressures. In this six-tape set you'll meet their family, including twins Edwin and Martha and playwright son Thomas. With Barbara Murray, Norman Rodway. 300 min. total.
53-8543 Was $99.99 $79.99

The Bretts Collection 2: Complete Set
The ups and downs of Britain's top theatrical clan continue in this six-tape collection. Treachery, bad critical notices, romantic entanglements, sexual intrigue and more play a part in the final installments of the series. 300 min. total.
53-8544 Was $99.99 $79.99

Flowers From A Stranger (1949)
A psychiatrist's wife battles her own deteriorating emotional state when a box of flowers arrives from a stranger. A young Yul Brynner, Felicia Montealegre and Robert Duke star in this "Westinghouse Studio One" presentation. 60 min.
09-2152 Was $24.99 $14.99

The Scarlet Letter (1950)
Nathaniel Hawthorne's classic story of adultery and hypocrisy makes for enthralling early TV drama from "Westinghouse Studio One," featuring Mary Sinclair and John Baragrey. Before the show a plaque is given to Hawthorne's granddaughter. 52 min.
09-1923 Was $24.99 $14.99

Twin Peaks: The Series
All the episodes from David Lynch's controversial, groundbreaking TV series are now out on home video, so fans can follow the saga of Twin Peaks from Laura Palmer's murder and the search for her killer to the sinister schemes of Windom Earle and the mystery of the "White Lodge." Each tape runs about 240 min.

Twin Peaks: Episodes 1-5
14-3371 $14.99

Twin Peaks: Episodes 6-9
14-3372 $14.99

Twin Peaks: Episodes 10-14
14-3373 $14.99

Twin Peaks: Episodes 15-19
14-3374 $14.99

Twin Peaks: Episodes 20-24
14-3375 $14.99

Twin Peaks: Episodes 25-29
14-3376 $14.99

Twin Peaks Six-Pack
The complete "Twin Peaks" series (29 episodes) is also available in this deluxe boxed set that costs only slightly more than a couple of good cherry pies and a big pot of coffee.
14-3377 $89.99

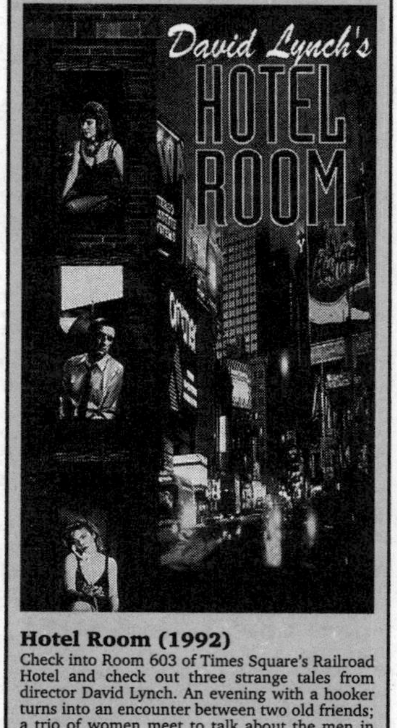

Hotel Room (1992)
Check into Room 603 of Times Square's Railroad Hotel and check out three strange tales from director David Lynch. An evening with a hooker turns into an encounter between two old friends; a trio of women meet to talk about the men in their lives...with violent results; and a couple trapped in a blackout discover some unsettling truths about each other. Harry Dean Stanton, Glenne Headly, Griffin Dunne, Chelsea Field and Crispin Glover star. 100 min.
14-3369 ❑$39.99

Life With Elizabeth
This syndicated series ran from 1953 to 1955 and showcased Betty White in her first starring role. She's Elizabeth, the witty wife of Alvin (Del Moore), a junior executive. Among the supporting players were their two dogs and assorted friends and neighbors. Each tape features two episodes, each made up of three different stories, and runs about 50 min. There are 12 volumes available, including:

Life With Elizabeth, Vol. 1
Includes "Mystery Story," "Jealousy," "Car Repair," "Take My Advice," "Baseball Practice" and "Singing Trouble."
10-9677 *$14.99*

Life With Elizabeth, Vol. 2
Includes "Morning Meany," "Shopping Spree," "Burglar Bit," "Mama's Visit," "Picnic" and "Nosy Neighbor."
10-9678 *$14.99*

Life With Elizabeth, Vol. 3
Includes "Phone Conversation," "Girl Scout," "Dog Survey," "Ping Pong," "Leaky Roof" and "Vacuum Cleaner Salesman."
10-9679 *$14.99*

Life With Elizabeth, Vol. 4
Includes "Photography Sketch," "The Honeymoon's Over," "Eye, Ear, Face Sketch," "Driving Lesson," "Fuses in Cellar" and "Fuddy's Toupee."
10-9680 *$14.99*

The Lone Wolf (1954)
Louis Hayward starred as globe-trotting private detective Michael Lanyard in this syndicated adventure series, also known as "Streets of Danger." Two exciting episodes are included. 60 min.
10-7311 Was $19.99 *$14.99*

Cowboy G-Men
This western set in 1880s California stars Russell Hayden as cowboy Pat Gallagher and Jackie Coogan as horse-wrangler Stoney Crockett, who act as government agents and try to keep law and order in the area. Each tape of this syndicated series, which was shown in 1952, includes two episodes and runs about 50 min. There are 15 volumes available, including:

Cowboy G-Men, Vol. 1
Includes "General Delivery" and "Center Fire."
10-9624 *$14.99*

Cowboy G-Men, Vol. 2
Includes "Chinaman's Chance" and "The Golden Wolf."
10-9625 *$14.99*

Cowboy G-Men, Vol. 3
Includes "The Secret Mission" and "The Woman Mayor."
10-9626 Was $19.99 *$14.99*

Cowboy G-Men, Vol. 4
Includes "Double Crossed" and "Empty Mailbags."
10-9627 *$14.99*

Cowboy G-Men, Vol. 5
Includes "Bounty Jumpers" and "California Bullets."
10-9628 *$14.99*

Cowboy G-Men, Vol. 6
Includes "Silver Fraud" and "High Heeled Boots."
10-9629 *$14.99*

Cowboy G-Men, Vol. 7
Includes "Ozark Gold" and "Ghost Town Mystery."
10-9630 *$14.99*

Cowboy G-Men, Vol. 8
Includes "Ridge of Ghosts" and "Sawdust Swindle."
10-9631 *$14.99*

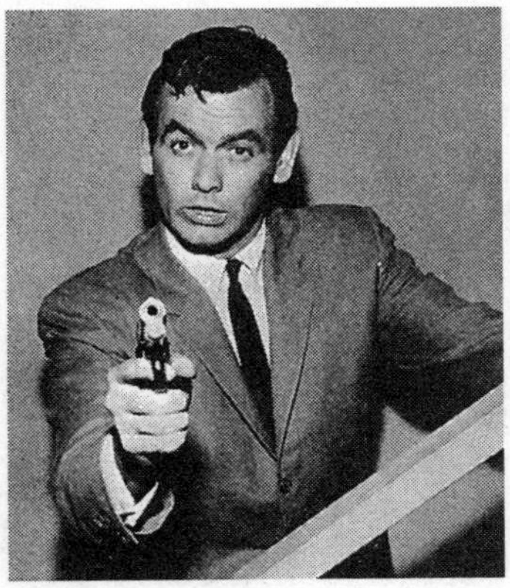

Richard Diamond, Private Detective, Vol. 1
David Janssen played a former New York City cop-turned-private eye in this series that ran from 1957-1960. Diamond used his background in police work to solve tough cases and relied on a leggy, anonymous woman named "Sam" to dispatch his messages from an answering service. Includes "Picture of Fear" and "Merry-Go-Round," and original commercials. 60 min.
10-9883 Was $19.99 *$14.99*

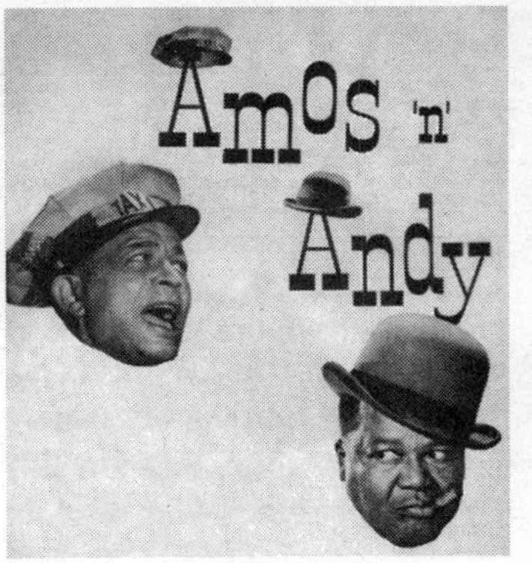

The Amos 'N' Andy Show
Based on the classic radio comedy, this lost favorite from TV's early days ran on CBS from 1951 to 1953 and was unique for its all-black cast. Alvin Childress starred as cab driver Amos, with Spencer Williams as his gullible pal Andy and Tim Moore as the conniving Kingfish. Each tape features six episodes and runs about 150 min.

Amos 'N' Andy: The Antique Shop/The Chinchilla Business
Kingfish tries to persuade his lodge pals to convince his cousin Leo to sell "The Antique Shop." And Kingfish suckers Andy into purchasing some rabbits he tells him are chinchillas in "The Chinchilla Business."
10-9468 Was $19.99 *$14.99*

Amos 'N' Andy: The Engagement Ring/The Girl Upstairs
The Kingfish plays matchmaker to Andy and an older woman in "The Engagement Ring," while Kingfish believes his marriage is in danger after he finds Sapphire's diary in "The Girl Upstairs."
10-9469 Was $19.99 *$14.99*

Amos 'N' Andy: Story Of The Invisible Glass/ The Kingfish Finds His Future
The Kingfish sells everyone short when he gets into the stock market in "Story of the Invisible Glass." And an aptitude test helps "The Kingfish Finds His Future" when he realizes he should become a house painter.
10-9470 Was $19.99 *$14.99*

Amos 'N' Andy: The Kingfish Teaches Andy To Fly/Quo Vadis
"The Kingfish Teaches Andy to Fly" when Andy's girl is won away by a motor boat enthusiast. And in "Quo Vadis," the Kingfish realizes Sapphire is a waitress at a dinner he attends.
10-9471 Was $19.99 *$14.99*

Amos 'N' Andy: The Rare Coin/Seeing Is Believing
In "The Rare Coin," the pilot episode for the hit TV series, Andy uses a shrewd trick to get back a coin the Kingfish swindled from him. And when Sapphire believes Kingfish is dating someone else, she fixes Andy dinner to make him jealous in "Seeing is Believing."
10-9472 Was $19.99 *$14.99*

The Amos 'N' Andy Show: Vols. 1-6 Set
Volumes 1-6 are also available in a collector's set.
09-5369 *$89.99*

The Amos 'N' Andy Show: Vols. 7-12 Set
Volumes 7-12 are also available in a collector's set.
09-5376 *$89.99*

The Amos 'N' Andy Show Collection
Based on the classic radio show, this lost favorite from TV's early days ran on CBS from 1951 to 1953 and was notable for its all-black cast. Alvin Childress was cab driver Amos, Spencer Williams his gullible pal Andy, and Tim Moore the conniving Kingfish. This 12-tape set, the most complete series collection yet available, offers 67 hilarious episodes in their original broadcast order, many with original commercials. NOTE: Individual volumes available at $19.99 each.
09-5377 Was $199.99 *$139.99*

The Aldrich Family (1950)
The famed comedy that lived in films, radio and TV is back. Henry, upset when he doesn't get invited to a costume party, tries sneaking in as the "wrong end" of a horse. Jackie Kelk, House Jameson star. 27 min.
09-1162 Was $19.99 *$14.99*

Country Western All-Stars (1956)
Live televised hoe-down from Nashville with Tex Ritter, The Sons Of The Pioneers, Cowboy Copas, Jim Reeves, Minnie Pearl and more. Songs like "Cool Water" and "High Noon," comedy skits and good old-fashioned fun. 52 min.
09-1208 *$19.99*

The Trail Blazers/Kit Carson
A pair of vintage TV sagebrushers are featured. First Alan Hale, Jr. stars in "Trail Blazers," followed by Bill Williams as the famed frontier scout, accompanied by his Mexican compadre, El Toro. 60 min. total.
10-7310 Was $19.99 *$14.99*

Stars In The Eye (1952)
Share in the excitement at the opening of CBS' Television City studios in Hollywood, with Jack Benny, Lucille Ball, Amos 'n' Andy, Burns and Allen and other top stars from the network. 60 min.
10-8159 Was $19.99 *$14.99*

The Ken Murray Show (1950)
Ken Murray, the consummate host to the stars, welcomes Mel Torme, Van Heflin, Darla Hood and Joe Besser to his terrific variety program. 60 min.
10-9030 Was $19.99 *$14.99*

Mr. And Mrs. North
Richard Denning and Barbara Britton starred as the Greenwich Village couple with a knack for coming upon and solving murders in this mid-50's series that adapted Patricia and Richard Lockridge's popular mystery stories. Each tape features two episodes and runs about 60 min.

Mr. And Mrs. North, Vol. 1
Includes "Nosed Out" and "Trained for Murder."
10-7314 Was $19.99 *$14.99*

Mr. And Mrs. North, Vol. 2
Includes "Scarlett and Violett" and "Reunion."
10-7473 Was $19.99 *$14.99*

Mr. And Mrs. North, Vol. 3
Includes "Anniversary" and "Busy Signal."
10-7474 Was $19.99 *$14.99*

No, Honestly (1975)
Hilarious Britcom detailing the romance between Charles, a struggling actor, and Clara, an innocent debutante. What makes this series interesting is both the way it transpires—the couple is married and recalls their earlier days through flashbacks—and its casting of real-life couple John Alderton and Pauline Collins. Seven episodes are included in this three-tape set. 175 min. total.
50-8404 *$39.99*

The Buccaneers/ The Adventures Of Long John Silver
Avast ye, mate! Fire up your VCR for a double bill of sea adventures from the 1956 TV season. In the first, Robert Shaw is a former freebooter saving a governer's wife in trouble in "Dangerous Cargo"; the second features consummate privateer Robert Newton up against marauders in the episode "Sword of Vengeance." 53 min.
10-7038 Was $19.99 *$14.99*

The Buccaneers
Adventure on the high seas in the early 18th century was the subject of this 1956-57 CBS series that starred Robert Shaw as Captain Dan Tempest, a reformed pirate battling buccaneers around the world. Included here are "Dangerous Cargo," in which Tempest is called on to save the wife of an island governor; and "The Raider," with Alec Clunes as Governor Woodes Rogers mixed up in a battle with a wealthy landowner. 50 min.
10-9623 *$14.99*

Hullabaloo
One of the first network TV shows to showcase rock and pop acts in prime time, "Hullabaloo" ran on NBC in half-hour and hour-long formats from 1965 to 1966. Relive the classic rock and roll of the '60s, and frug along with special guest hosts and the miniskirted Hullabaloo Dancers, in these nostalgic programs. Each volume runs about 60 min.

Hullabaloo, Vol. 1
Paul Anka guests and sings "What Now My Love," along with The Cyrkle ("Red Rubber Ball"), Lesley Gore ("Young Love"), and Peter and Gordon ("Wrong From the Start"). Then, The Yardbirds ("I'm a Man"), The Hollies ("Look Through Any Window"), and Nancy Sinatra ("So Long Babe") join host Frankie Avalon, who chimes in with "Do I Hear a Waltz?"
50-7269 *$19.99*

Hullabaloo, Vol. 2
Host Michael Landon offers his own rendition of "I Like It Like That" in a musical bonanza that includes The Byrds ("The Times They Are a Changin'"), Chad & Jill ("The Cruel War"), and Paul Revere and The Raiders ("Steppin' Out"). Next, "Run for Your Life" when Gary Lewis & The Playboys take the stage, plus The Mamas and The Papas ("California Dreamin'"), Dionne Warwick ("Message to Michael") and more.
50-7270 *$19.99*

Hullabaloo, Vol. 3
It's a father-son songfest when Jerry Lewis joins son Gary and his Playboys on "Help," followed by Barry McGuire ("Eve of Destruction"), Paul Revere and The Raiders ("Ooh Poo Pah Doo"), and Joannie Summers ("Before and After"). Next, "Toot-Toot-Tootsie" by The Supremes and host Sammy Davis, Jr. is one of the highlights in a show that includes The Lovin' Spoonful ("Do You Believe in Magic?"), Sonny and Cher ("I Got You Babe"), The Strangeloves ("I Want Candy") and more.
50-7271 *$19.99*

Hullabaloo, Vol. 4
An hour-long treat, with host Trini Lopez ("What'd I Say") welcoming Herman's Hermits ("Mrs. Brown You've Got a Lovely Daughter"), Chuck Berry ("Johnny B. Goode"), Martha & The Vandellas ("Nowhere to Run"), Freddie & The Dreamers ("You Were Made for Me"), and many more blasts from the past.
50-7272 *$19.99*

Hullabaloo, Vol. 5
Drive-in faves Frankie Avalon and Annette Funicello are co-hosts for this episode, singing "All I Need Now Is the Girl," "Chim Chim Cheree" and more, plus guest artists The Kinks ("You Really Got Me"), Dobie Gray ("The In Crowd"), Freddie & The Dreamers ("I'm Telling You Now"), The Brothers Four ("Rock Island Line") and others.
50-7350 *$19.99*

Hullabaloo, Vol. 6
First, emcee Barry McGuire ("This Precious Time") is joined by The Kingsmen ("Money"), Brenda Lee ("Yesterday's Gone") and a promising English combo called The Rolling Stones ("She Said Yeah," "Get Off of My Cloud"). Next, The Young Rascals ("Good Lovin'"), Tony & The Tigers ("Day Tripper") and We Five ("You Let a Love Burn Out") are among the guests introduced by host Soupy Sales, who does a stirring rendition of "Ballin' the Jack."
50-7351 *$19.99*

Hullabaloo, Vol. 7
Don't cry "uncle" when TV spy David McCallum offers up his version of "Help!" and presents The Beau Brummels ("Don't Talk to Strangers"), Peter & Gordon ("Yesterday"), The Animals ("We Gotta Get Out of This Place") and other pop faves. Next, Chad & Jeremy perform "Where Would You Be Without Me" and "Sticks and Stones", along with The Outsiders ("Time Won't Let Me"), Joe Tex ("The Love You Save") and Warhol fave Baby Jane Holzer ("You're Gonna Hurt Yourself").
50-7352 *$19.99*

Hullabaloo, Vol. 8
Peter Noone and Herman's Hermits are the hosts for the first show, singing "I'm Henry VIII, I Am" and "Just a Little Bit Better." Other guests include The Lovin' Spoonful ("You Didn't Have to Be So Nice") and Lola Falana ("Chicago"). Then, hostess Petula Clark sings "Downtown," "I Know a Place" and "Round Every Corner" and welcomes Sham the Sham & The Pharaohs ("Ring Dang Doo"), The Toys ("A Lover's Concerto") and Noel Harrison ("A Young Girl").
50-7353 *$19.99*

Hullabaloo, Vol. 9
Teen idol Frankie Avalon hosts this one-hour episode and also sings "Once in a Lifetime." Joining him are Sam the Sham & The Pharaohs ("Wooly Bully"), The Supremes ("Back in My Arms Again," "You're Nobody Till Somebody Loves You"), The Byrds ("Mr. Tambourine Man," "Feel a Whole Lot Better") and others. There's also a Lennon/McCartney medley by Frankie, Barbara McNair and Joannie Summers.
50-7452 *$19.99*

Hullabaloo, Vol. 10
The Righteous Brothers have got that hostin' feeling as they perform "Let the Good Times Roll" and "(You're My) Soul and Inspiration" and then welcome Paul Revere and The Raiders ("Kicks," "Just Like Me"), Nancy Sinatra ("These Boots Are Made for Walkin'") and others. Next, The Shangri-Las ("Long Live Our Love") and Peter & Gordon ("Woman") are among the artists in a show emceed by Leslie Uggams, who joins P & G on "You Are My Sunshine."
50-7453 *$19.99*

Hullabaloo, Vol. 11
It's "By George" times two. First, the tannest man in show biz, George Hamilton, offers up "Let's Face the Music and Dance" and welcomes The Young Rascals ("Slow Down"), Simon and Garfunkel ("Homeward Bound") and others. There's even the Hullabaloo Dancers frugging to the "Batman" theme. Then, host George Maharis ("Teach Me Tonight") is joined by such stars as The Animals ("It's My Life"), Dionne Warwick ("Looking with My Eyes") and others.
50-7454 *$19.99*

Hullabaloo, Vol. 12
Paul Anka's "Falling in Love with Love" when he hosts this one-hour musicfest. Also on the program are Jay and The Americans ("Only in America"), The Everly Brothers ("Gone, Gone, Gone"), Marvin Gaye ("How Sweet It Is"), Petula Clark ("Downtown") and others, plus the comedy stylings of Bill (Jose Jimenez) Dana.
50-7455 *$19.99*

Hullabaloo: Vols. 1-4 Boxed Set
50-7268 *$79.99*

Hullabaloo: Vols. 5-8 Boxed Set
50-7354 *$79.99*

Hullabaloo: Vols. 9-12 Boxed Set
50-7456 *$79.99*

Hullabaloo, No. 1
Guest host Dean Jones (Dean Jones?) welcomes performers Gene Pitney, Junior Walker and The All-Stars, Leslie Uggams and The Astronauts (The Astronauts?). 45 min.
09-1210 *$19.99*

Hullabaloo, No. 2
It's "Spy vs. Cowboy" when David McCallum hosts a show featuring Peter and Gordon, Brenda Lee, The Animals and The Beau Brummels, followed by Michael Landon and his guests The Byrds, Jackie DeShannon and Paul Revere and The Raiders. 47 min.
09-1177 *$19.99*

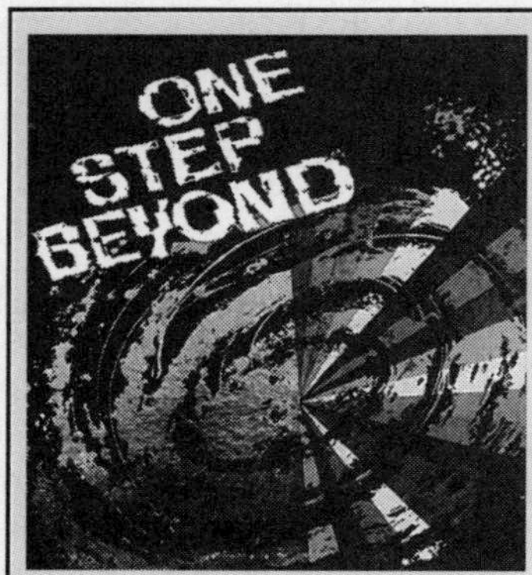

One Step Beyond
Originally titled "Alcoa Presents" during its 1959-1961 run on ABC, this spooky anthology presented true stories of people who encountered ghosts, ESP, premonitions and other unexplainable phenomena. John Newland hosts. Each tape features two episodes and runs about 55 min.

One Step Beyond, No. 1
In "Call for Tomorrow," an actress recently released from a mental hospital returns home only to hear strange voices. And in "The Stone Cutter," with Joe Mantell, a tombstone cutter has a strange revelation.
08-1685 Was $19.99 *$14.99*

One Step Beyond, Vol. 1
An army officer is acquitted of a murder he insists he committed in "The Sorcerer," with Christopher Lee. Next, a teacher receives an unusual gift from a pupil in "Message from Clara."
10-7593 Was $19.99 *$14.99*

One Step Beyond, Vol. 2
Cloris Leachman is stalked by a murderous stranger in "The Dark Room," while Ross Martin is haunted by a premonition in "Echo."
10-7594 Was $19.99 *$14.99*

One Step Beyond, Vol. 3
The "Anniversary of a Murder" brings a ghostly visit to the couple responsible, followed by Charles Bronson in a spectral boxing story, "Last Round."
10-7595 Was $19.99 *$14.99*

One Step Beyond, Vol. 4
A prisoner's encounter with the supernatural is recounted in "Gypsy." Next, a reporter's dream of two brothers leads to a "Dead Man's Tale."
10-7596 Was $19.99 *$14.99*

One Step Beyond, Vol. 5
A dying girl's need for a blood transfusion has unexpected consequences in "Delusion," with Norman Lloyd and Suzanne Pleshette, followed by a haunting romance story, "Legacy of Love."
10-7597 Was $19.99 *$14.99*

One Step Beyond, Vol. 6
The truth about a skiing accident that ended in death is uncovered in "The Haunting." Next, an Air Force pilot is possessed by the spirit of an Egyptian prince in "The Mask."
10-7598 Was $19.99 *$14.99*

One Step Beyond, Vol. 7
A simple smooch between a retired postman and a waitress impresses some ghosts in "The Lovers." In "Front Runner," a jockey gets a delayed payback for a foul he committed 20 years before.
10-7964 Was $19.99 *$14.99*

One Step Beyond, Vol. 8
A tourist in India puts up a cluck when a man enters his train compartment with a chicken in "The Riddle." A railroad veteran's grandson has a strange experience thanks to Grandpa's promise in "Goodbye Grandpa."
10-7965 Was $19.99 *$14.99*

One Step Beyond, Vol. 9
"Epilogue" tells the story of a strange woman who alerts a man about his family being trapped in a cave-in. In "Dead Ringer," a woman has a psychic connection to her sister, who is burning down an orphanage.
10-7966 Was $19.99 *$14.99*

One Step Beyond, Vol. 10
Patrick O'Neal stars as a man who goes to an island and discovers he's well-known in "The Return of Mitchell Campion," while George Washington decides not to surrender to the British because of a premonition he had in "Night of Decision."
10-7967 Was $19.99 *$14.99*

One Step Beyond, Vol. 11
In "Vision," four French soldiers in World War I retreat after an unusual experience. And Patty McCormick plays a girl suspected by her parents of being a witch in "Make Me Not a Witch."
10-9457 *$14.99*

One Step Beyond, Vol. 12
A man suddenly becomes phobic and needs water, but his doctor helps him and another patient miles away in "The Trap." And Mike Connors plays "The Aerialist," whose argument with his father leads to weird events during a performance.
10-7969 Was $19.99 *$14.99*

One Step Beyond, Vol. 13
A two-part thriller, "The Peter Hurkos Story," stars Andrew Prine and Albert Salmi in a story about a man with ESP who uses his gift to help the police.
10-8099 Was $19.99 *$14.99*

One Step Beyond, Vol. 14
In "Night of April 14," a water-fearing woman discovers that her husband has booked them on the Titanic. Patrick Macnee and Barbara Lord star. Also, a British guardsman has a strange premonition on the night of the evacuation of Dunkirk in "The Dream," starring Reginald Owen.
10-8100 Was $19.99 *$14.99*

One Step Beyond, Vol. 15
In "Person Unknown," a Mexican revolutionary discovers that a mysterious force has killed one of his adversaries. And in "Justice," a man confesses to a murder, even though the townsfolk say otherwise.
10-8101 Was $19.99 *$14.99*

One Step Beyond, Vol. 16
"The Open Window" focuses on a temperamental artist who sees another artist trying to murder his model. With Louise Fletcher. Also, "The Executioner" concerns a Confederate soldier miraculously escaping death at the hands of a firing squad. 60 min.
10-8102 Was $19.99 *$14.99*

One Step Beyond, Vol. 17
In "Ordeal on Locust Street," a young man enters a supernatural world in his fiancée's house; and in "I Saw You Tomorrow," a U.S. agent witnesses a murder the day before it happens.
10-8103 Was $19.99 *$14.99*

One Step Beyond, Vol. 18
In "Where Are They," a man's selling of a secret formula to Washington provokes a boulder shower in his hometown. Next, a governess finds out that her charge is planning to get rid of her in a most unusual way in "The Tiger."
10-8104 Was $19.99 *$14.99*

One Step Beyond, Vol. 19
In "Moment of Hate," a woman believes she can kill people by just thinking of them. Also, "Signal Received" concerns a sailor's future, as predicted by a reliable fortune teller.
10-8105 Was $19.99 *$14.99*

One Step Beyond, Vol. 20
In "Vanishing Point," Edward Binns stars as a man trying to find his missing wife. Next, a middle-aged bellboy in a 1906 San Francisco hotel has a premonition of a devastating "Earthquake." With David Opatoshu.
10-8106 Was $19.99 *$14.99*

One Step Beyond, Vol. 21
A woman has strange visions of her husband turning into someone else in "To Know the End." And in "The Dead Part of the House," a young girl suspects danger awaits her in a strange room in her aunt's house.
10-8107 Was $19.99 *$14.99*

One Step Beyond, Vol. 22
In "The Face," a man searches for the person he dreams will murder him; and "Rendezvous" finds a woman being saved by her long-lost husband while she's being attacked.
10-8108 Was $19.99 *$14.99*

One Step Beyond, Vol. 23
"Encounter" tells the amazing story of a lost pilot who appears thousands of miles away from his last known location...minus his plane! Also, "Reunion" involves a gathering of World War II fliers that takes an unusual turn.
10-8109 Was $19.99 *$14.99*

One Step Beyond, Vol. 24
In "The Devil's Laughter," a death-row inmate perceives some weird, supernatural experiences; and in "The Captain's Guest," strange occurrences at a New England house upset a young couple. With Robert Webber.
10-8110 Was $19.99 *$14.99*

One Step Beyond, Vol. 25
Luana Anders and Ed Platt star in "The Burning Girl," about a woman who wonders why fires begin whenever she is present. Then, a man explains his son's unbelievable desert rescue to the boy's teacher in "Explorer."
10-8111 Was $19.99 *$14.99*

The Six Wives Of Henry VIII (1971)
The award-sinning BBC mini-series focusing on the much-married English monarch and the women in his life features lavish sets, fascinating historical insights and brilliant acting, Keith Mitchell plays Henry in a critically acclaimed performance, with Annette Crosby, Dorothy Tutin, Anne Stallybrass, Elvi Hale, Angela Pleasence and Rosalie Crutchley as his oft-unfortunate spouses. 6 tapes; 540 min.
53-9357 Was $139.99 *$79.99*

The Trouble With Father
Stu Erwin starred as a well-meaning but incompetent parent who served as principal of a suburban high school, in this popular series which ran from 1950 to 1955. With June Collyer as his wife and Sheila James and Ann Todd as his daughters. Also known as "The Stu Erwin Show." Each tape contains two episodes and runs 60 min. There are eight volumes available, including:

The Trouble With Father, Vol. 1
Includes "Landlord" and "Nothing but the Truth."
10-8122 Was $19.99 *$14.99*

The Trouble With Father. Vol. 2
Includes "Quarantine" and "A Very Rainy Day."
10-8123 Was $19.99 *$14.99*

The Trouble With Father, Vol. 3
Includes "Family Tree" and "Leave It to Stu."
10-8124 Was $19.99 *$14.99*

The Trouble With Father, Vol. 4
Includes "Youth Is Wonderful" and "Springtime for Father."
10-8125 Was $19.99 *$14.99*

The Trouble With Father, Vol. 5
Includes "Father Gets Into the Act" and "Spooks."
10-8126 Was $19.99 *$14.99*

Buffy
the vampire slayer

Buffy The Vampire Slayer
Sarah Michelle Gellar slays 'em in the title role of the girl with schoolbooks in one hand and a wooden stake in the other, in the hip and hit TV series. Follow high-school student and "chosen one" Buffy and her friends as they defend the town of Sunnydale from vampires and other supernatural menaces. Nicholas Brendon, Alyson Hannigan and Anthony Stewart Head also star. Each tape, which includes exclusive interviews with creator Josh Whedon, features two episodes and runs about 100 min.

Buffy The Vampire Slayer, Vol. 1
Picking up where the 1992 movie left off, Buffy moves from L.A. to Sunnydale, but finds she cannot escape her role of Slayer when she must stop the Master Vampire from taking over the town, in the two-part pilot adventure "Welcome to the Hellmouth/The Harvest."
04-3719 □*$14.99*

Buffy The Vampire Slayer, Vol. 2
Is one of Buffy's fellow cheerleader alternates using black magic to move up the pep squad chain in "Witch"? Next, Buffy's attempt to have a normal night out with a cute classmate is jeopardized by the plans of the Master in "Never Kill a Boy on the First Date."
04-3720 □*$14.99*

Buffy The Vampire Slayer, Vol. 3
Learn about the origins of Buffy's otherworldly lover, "Angel," with guest star David Boreanaz as the bloodsucker cursed with a conscience. Then, "The Puppet Show" finds Sunnyvale High's talent show turning into a theatre of blood for a murderous demon.
04-3721 □*$14.99*

Buffy The Vampire Slayer: Boxed Set
Volumes 1-3 are also available in a special boxed set.
04-3722 Save $5.00! *$39.99*

Buffy The Vampire Slayer: The Buffy & Angel Chronicles, Vol. 1
Buffy's 17th birthday has its share of bad moments (a demon known as the Judge, part of Spike and Dru's latest plan to control Sunnydale) and good (she and Angel spend a memorable evening together) in "Surprise." The consequences of that evening, however, come to light in "Innocence," as the soulless Angelus is revived and looking for a slayer to kill.
04-3897 □*$14.99*

Buffy The Vampire Slayer: The Buffy & Angel Chronicles, Vol. 2
Angel's mind games with Buffy take a sinister turn that will cost one of her allies their life in "Passion." Next, the spirit of love is—literally—roaming the halls of Sunnydale High in "I Only Have Eyes for You."
04-3898 □*$14.99*

Buffy The Vampire Slayer: The Buffy & Angel Chronicles, Vol. 3
Will Buffy be forced to kill Angel in order to stop him from summoning the demon Acathla and drawing the world into his hellish realm, or can she restore the soul of the only man she's ever loved, in the two-part second-season finale, "Becoming"?
04-3899 □*$14.99*

Buffy The Vampire Slayer: The Buffy & Angel Chronicles: Boxed Set
Stake yourself to some savings with this collector's set featuring "Surprise/Innocence," "Passion/I Only Have Eyes for You" and "Becoming, Parts 1 & 2."
04-3900 Save $5.00! *$39.99*

Buck Rogers In The 25th Century
Gil Gerard starred as the original space hero of comics and movie serial fame in this hit sci-fi series seen on NBC from 1979 to 1981. With Erin Gray and Twiki the Robot. Except where noted, each tape runs about 50 min.

Buck Rogers: Vegas In Space
An outer space casino is really the front for an interplanetary crimelord whom Buck must stop.
07-1363 Was $19.99 *$14.99*

Buck Rogers: Return Of The Fighting 69th
A band of "over the hill" space jockeys aid Buck in defeating a gang of star villains.
07-1364 Was $19.99 *$14.99*

Buck Rogers: Unchained Woman
Buck flies with a dangerous ex-con (Jamie Lee Curtis) in order to stop a space pirate, her boyfriend.
07-1365 Was $19.99 *$14.99*

Buck Rogers: Happy Birthday, Buck
Buck's surprise 534th birthday party is crashed by a vengeance-crazed scientist with superpowers.
07-1366 Was $19.99 *$14.99*

Buck Rogers: A Blast For Buck
Buck relives his past adventures to find a clue as to who threatens Earth's safety now.
07-1367 Was $19.99 *$14.99*

Buck Rogers: Space Vampire
Could the crew of a space freighter have been killed by a fabled space monster, as Buck thinks?
07-1368 Was $19.99 *$14.99*

Buck Rogers: Space Rockers
Buck must stop an interstellar rock concert that could hypnotize the galaxy's young people.
07-1369 Was $19.99 *$14.99*

Buck Rogers: The Guardians
A mysterious box with strange powers is entrusted to Buck's care, but can he deliver it in time?
07-1370 Was $19.99 *$14.99*

Buck Rogers In The 25th Century (1978)
This theatrical version of the feature-length pilot episode to the hit TV series finds 20th-century astronaut Gil Gerard revived from suspended animation into a futuristic Earth under attack from space pirates. With Pamela Hensley, Erin Gray and Mel Blanc as the voice of Twiki. 88 min.
07-1036 Was $19.99 *$14.99*

Stage Show, Vol. 1
The popular Dorsey Brothers series welcomes guests Helen O'Connell, Roberta Sherwood, the inimitable Larry Storch, and comedian Joey Bishop. Son-of-a-gun!
10-7354 Was $19.99 *$14.99*

Stage Show, Vol. 2
Jimmy and Tommy Dorsey create an evening at the variety theater with the June Taylor Dancers and guests Sarah Vaughn, Morey Amsterdam, the inimitable Larry Storch, and Della Reese.
10-7355 Was $19.99 *$14.99*

Stage Show, Vol. 3
Dick Haymes, Roberta Sherwood, and Joey Adams join Tommy and Jimmy in another fabulous outing from their Jackie Gleason produced series.
10-7356 Was $19.99 *$14.99*

Stage Show, Vol. 4
The Dorsey band launches into "I'm Getting Sentimental Over You," and another Manhattan floor show is re-created, with Eileen Barton, George Kirby, George Jessel and Sunny Gale.
10-7357 Was $19.99 *$14.99*

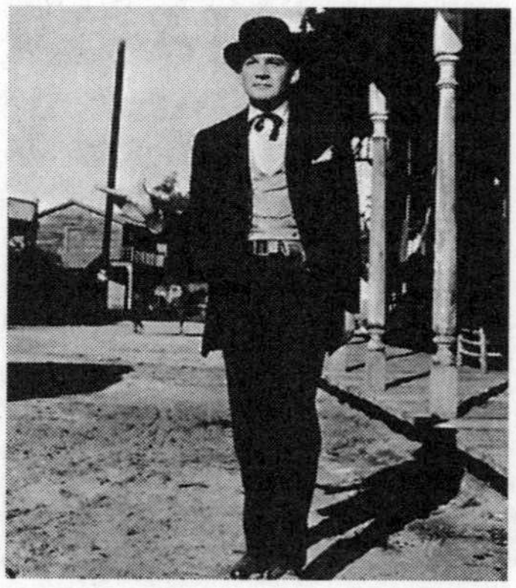

Bat Masterson, Vol. 1
He carried a cane and wore a derby, and, as played by Gene Barry, Bat Masterson was a dapper lawman who used his wits to keep the frontier safe. Two episodes of the series, which ran from 1959-1961, are offered here: "The Fighter," in which Bat gets the contract of a boxer in a poker game; and "Stampede at Tent City," with Masterson helping a female friend in trouble. William Conrad guests. 55 min.
09-5302 *$14.99*

The Avengers

Airing from 1961-69 in its native England and debuting on American TV in 1966, this stylish adventure series starred Patrick Macnee as dapper, bowler-hatted secret agent John Steed. Joining him in defending crown and country from enemy spies, mad scientists and other menaces were lovely, lethal partners Cathy Gale (Honor Blackman), Emma Peel (Diana Rigg) and Tara King (Linda Thorson). Except where noted, each tape features two episodes and runs about 104 min.

The Avengers: '63 Set I

This three-tape boxed set opens with Steed and Mrs. Gale looking into a shady rest home catering to millionaire clients and a scheme to infiltrate the government with duplicates in "The Undertakers/The Man with Two Shadows." A missing list of double agents and a surprising bequest from a late aide of Steed's are the elements of "The Nutshell/Death of a Batman," while the agents foil a plan to blow up Parliament and a massive gold heist in "November Five/The Gilded Cage." 312 min. total.

53-6914 **$29.99**

The Avengers: '63 Set II

Steed and Cathy uncover the link between a blind millionaire's planned eye transplant and smugglers, and the link between a dead girl in a Turkish bath and a plan to discredit a drug company, in "Second Sight/The Medicine Men." This three-volume collection also features "The Grandeur That Was Rome/The Golden Fleece," in which the Avengers deal with a Caesar-obsessed would-be world dictator and a Chinese restaurant that's a front for gold smugglers, and "Don't Look Behind You/Death à la Carte," which finds Cathy pursued in an empty house by a mysterious foe, and Steed playing chef to protect a visiting Arabian ruler. 364 min. total.

53-6915 **$29.99**

The Avengers: The White Elephant/The Little Wonders

The disappearance of "The White Elephant" from a private zoo leads John Steed and Cathy Gale into a big-game hunt whose prize is an ivory-smuggling ring. Next, broken dolls, crooked clergymen and missing microfilm add up to danger in "The Little Wonders."

53-6744 **$12.99**

The Avengers: The Wringer/Mandrake

Has Steed turned traitor and led six other agents to their deaths? It sure looks that way, unless he can clear his name, in "The Wringer." Next, a Cornish cemetery's sudden upswing in business is linked to an inheritance scam in "Mandrake."

53-6745 **$12.99**

The Avengers: The Secrets Broker/The Trojan Horse

Steed and Cathy discover that a wine shop is a front for a blackmailing medium's plan to "spirit" away military information in "The Secrets Broker," while "The Trojan Horse" finds the Avengers at the races, closing the "book" on a deadly gambling operation.

53-6746 **$12.99**

The Avengers: Build A Better Mousetrap/The Outside-In Man

Can two old ladies' spellcasting be responsible for stopping all mechanical devices, including the bikes of Cathy's motorcycle gang, in a small village in "Build a Better Mousetrap"? And can Steed and Gale protect "The Outside-In Man," an anti-British activist returning to England for peace talks, from an assassin's bullet?

53-6747 **$12.99**

The Avengers: The Charmers/Concerto

The Avengers must work with enemy agents in order to track down the third party who's been killing off operatives from both sides in "The Charmers." Then, the visit of a Russian pianist during international trade talks leads to a symphony of suspense in "Concerto."

53-6748 **$12.99**

The Avengers: Esprit De Corps/Lobster Quadrille

Cathy the heir to the throne of Scotland? Steed facing a firing squad of rebel highlanders out to take over London? It all happens in "Esprit de Corps." Then, Honor Blackman makes her series swan song in "Lobster Quadrille," in which a mysterious chess piece found with a dead man leads the Avengers to a drug-smuggling operation.

53-6749 **$12.99**

The Avengers: The Town Of No Return/The Gravediggers

In their debut adventure together, Steed and Emma investigate the disappearance of several agents in a seemingly quiet coastal town. Next, a home for retired railway workers, an undertaker who's losing his clients, and a radar-jamming device add up to danger for the Avengers in "The Gravediggers."

01-5154 **$12.99**

The Avengers: The Cybernauts/Death At Bargain Prices

Deadly and super-strong robot assassins, mad scientist Michael Gough's Cybernauts are out to get their metallic hands on Steed and Mrs. Peel. Then, the agents go behind the counter at a swank department store to uncover a murderous conspiracy, but soon must defend themselves against a lot more than irate customers.

01-5153 **$12.99**

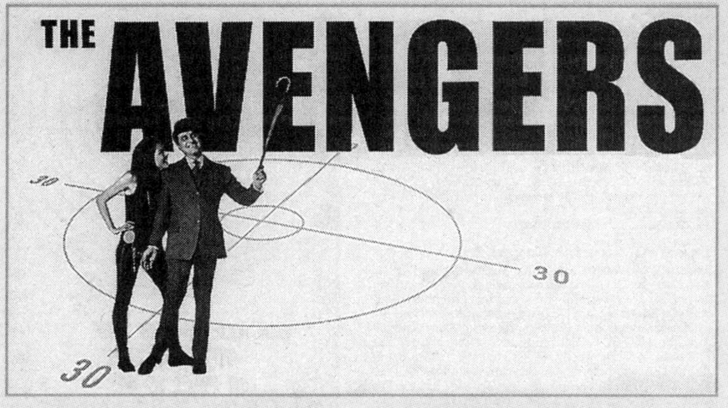

The Avengers: The Murder Market/A Surfeit Of H20

Steed signs up with a marriage bureau that's a front for a murder-for-hire operation, but will his first victim be Mrs. Peel, in "Murder Market"? Next, a man's drowning death—in the middle of a field—leads the agents to a scientist who's developed a rain-making weapon.

01-5182 **$12.99**

The Avengers: The Hour That Never Was/Dial A Deadly Number

A planned reunion for Steed's old RAF comrades turns into a bizarre mystery when he and Emma arrive at the military base and find it deserted. Then, the Avengers must stop a man from "reaching out" and killing London's biggest stockbrokers without ever getting near them.

17-1081 **$12.99**

The Avengers: Castle De'ath/The Master Minds

Does Scotland's venerable "Castle De'ath" hold the key to uncovering a sinister plan to corner the world's fish market? And what is the mysterious force driving members of a club for geniuses to commit illegal acts?

53-6433 **$12.99**

The Avengers: Man-Eater Of Surrey Green/Two's A Crowd/Too Many Christmas Trees

Murder is in full bloom when the Avengers search for missing botanists and come face-to-leaf with the "Man-Eater of Surrey Green." Meanwhile, the dapper duo is in double trouble when a Russian look-alike replaces Steed, and a Dickensian holiday party is a front for a trap that could cost Steed his sanity—and his life—in "Too Many Christmas Trees." 156 min.

62-1179 **$12.99**

The Avengers: What The Butler Saw/The House That Jack Built

Steed goes undercover as a gentleman's gentleman to learn who's behind the theft and sale of top-secret defense information in "What the Butler Saw," while Emma is trapped by a mad scientist with a long-standing grudge inside the computerized "House That Jack Built."

01-5135 **$12.99**

The Avengers: The Thirteenth Hole/Quick-Quick Slow Death

The sandtraps could turn into deathtraps when the agents check out strange goings-on at a golf course and uncover a spy ring. Plus, Steed and Emma must step lively when a dance school turns out to be a front for...yep, a spy ring.

01-5144 **$12.99**

The Avengers: Silent Dust/Room Without A View

Who is responsible for the devastation of whole regions of the English countryside, and can Steed and Mrs. Peel stop them before they fall victim to the mysterious "Silent Dust?" Next, the Avengers investigate the disappearances of several top scientists who are being abducted from the same hotel room.

01-5155 **$12.99**

The Avengers: The Danger Makers/A Touch Of Brimstone

A secret club for ex-military men addicted to danger could have very deadly consequences for Steed and Mrs. Peel. Then, the Avengers must foil the plans of a modern incarnation of the infamous 18th-century Hellfire Club...plans which include dressing Emma in corset and boots as the "Queen of Sin."

01-5178 **$12.99**

The Avengers: Small Game For Big Hunters/The Girl From Auntie

Has an ancient African cult's "sleep curse" reached England? It looks that way, as the Avengers find themselves up against a tiny foe with a dangerous bite. Then, Steed and a young woman impersonating Mrs. Peel must save the real Emma from a "little old lady" armed with lethal knitting needles.

62-1166 **$12.99**

The Avengers: A Sense Of History/How To Succeed...At Murder/Honey For The Prince

It's back to school for Steed and Emma as they look into the murder—by arrow—of a professor with a plan to end global poverty in "A Sense of History," followed by a group of secretaries with a lethal way to climb the corporate ladder in "How to Succeed...at Murder." Also, a jar of honey, a company that fulfill clients' fantasies, a Middle Eastern prince and Emma as a harem girl are the elements for "Honey for the Prince." 156 min.

62-1282 **$12.99**

The Avengers: You Have Just Been Murdered/The Positive Negative Man

"You Have Just Been Murdered" is what some of England's wealthiest men are being told by a blackmailer who's threatening to kill them for real. Then, it's shocking when Steed and Mrs. Peel are called in to catch a murderer who kills with his "electric touch."

01-5145 **$12.99**

The Avengers: The Living Dead/The Hidden Tiger

The mysterious appearance of a long-dead duke in the English countryside brings Steed and Mrs. Peel, along with a pair of ghost hunters, out to investigate in "The Living Dead." Plus, who or what is turning the housecats of England into savage killers?

01-5151 **$12.99**

The Avengers: The Bird Who Knew Too Much/The Winged Avenger

This fine-feathered double bill leads off with a dead man found clutching a bag of bird seed and Steed and Mrs. Peel suspecting "fowl play"; Ron Moody guest stars. Then, a flapping in the night spells death in the "Batman" spoof "The Winged Avenger," about a comic-strip hero come to life.

01-5152 **$12.99**

The Avengers: Epic/The Superlative Seven

It's "lights, camera, murder" when Mrs. Peel becomes the kidnapped star of a mad movie director's latest "Epic"—one where the script ends with her death! Then, Steed is among a group of seven expert fighters trapped on a deserted island and forced to battle each other to the death; Charlotte Rampling and Donald Sutherland guest star.

01-5156 **$12.99**

The Avengers: Escape In Time/The See-Through Man

There's no time to lose when the Avengers tackle an inventor who claims to be able to help criminals escape the law with a time machine. Next, the detective duo must bring down a foe who apparently can render himself invisible.

01-5157 **$12.99**

The Avengers: The Correct Way To Kill/Never, Never Say Die

Steed and Mrs. Peel team with a pair of enemy agents to determine who's behind a rash of spy murders in "The Correct Way to Kill," while screen horror icon Christopher Lee plays a seemingly unkillable scientist in "Never, Never Say Die."

01-5165 **$12.99**

The Avengers: A Funny Thing Happened On The Way To The Station/Something Nasty In The Nursery

Emma and Steed hunt down a mole in the Admiralty who has been using the British Rail system to smuggle out top-secret documents in "A Funny Thing Happened on the Way to the Station." Next, there's "Something Nasty in the Nursery" when the agents must rescue high-ranking officials from the mind-control games of some decidedly un-Mary Poppins-like nannies.

01-5166 **$12.99**

The Avengers: Dead Man's Treasure/The £50,000 Breakfast

An important dispatch box is hidden in the home of a wealthy auto racing enthusiast, and enemy agents will stop at nothing to get it, in "Dead Man's Treasure." Next, a fortune in gems found in a man's stomach and two Borzoi dogs add up to deadly danger for Steed and Emma.

01-5168 **$12.99**

The Avengers: From Venus With Love/The Fear Merchants

There's murder in the stars when Steed and Mrs. Peel look into a bizarre series of deaths involving a group of astronomy buffs; John Pertwee and Barbara Shelley guest star. Next, the Avengers must stop "The Fear Merchants," who can eliminate businessmen's rivals by scaring them to death.

01-5175 **$12.99**

The Avengers: The Joker/Who's Who???

Mrs. Peel finds herself the target of a complicated game of deceit and death by a convict that she put behind bars in "The Joker." In "Who's Who???," Emma and Steed are captured by an enemy agent who uses his invention to switch the pair's personalities with those of lethal killers.

53-6261 **$12.99**

The Avengers: Death's Door/Return Of The Cybernauts

Deadly dreams become frightening reality for the participants in a government conference, and it's up to Steed and Emma to uncover the killer. Next, Peter Cushing guest stars as an art collector who's restored the unstoppable killer robots to "life" and sends them out to dispatch the Avengers.

53-6262 **$12.99**

The Avengers: Murdersville/Mission...Highly Improbable/The Forget-Me-Knot

The first episode in this special triple-bill finds Steed and Emma up against the residents of a quaint little village whose main industry is murder. A mad scientist cuts the agents down to size—thanks to a reducing ray—in "Mission...Highly Improbable," and Diana Rigg's final appearance has her and Steed uncovering a traitor in their organization. Linda Thorson guest stars as new partner Tara King. 156 min.

01-5136 **$12.99**

The Avengers: '64 Set I

"The White Elephant/The Little Wonders," "The Wringer/Mandrake" and "The Secrets Broker/The Trojan Horse" are also available in a boxed collector's set.

53-6742 Save $9.00! **$29.99**

The Avengers: '64, Set II

"Build a Better Mousetrap/The Outside-In Man," "The Charmers/Concerto" and "Esprit de Corps/Lobster Quadrille" are also available in a boxed collector's set.

53-6743 Save $9.00! **$29.99**

The Avengers: '65 Set I

"The Town of No Return/The Gravediggers," "The Cybernauts/Death at Bargain Prices" and "Castle De'ath/The Master Minds" are also available in a boxed collector's set.

53-6434 Save $9.00! **$29.99**

The Avengers: '65 Set II

"The Murder Market/A Surfeit of H2O," "The Hour That Never Was/Dial a Deadly Number" and "Man-Eater of Surrey Green/Two's a Crowd/Too Many Christmas Trees" are also available in a boxed collector's set.

53-6435 Save $9.00! **$29.99**

The Avengers: '66 Set I

"Silent Dust/Room Without a View," "Small Game for Big Hunters/The Girl from Auntie" and "The 13th Hole/The Quick-Quick-Slow Death" are also available in a boxed collector's set.

53-6551 Save $9.00! **$29.99**

The Avengers: '66 Set II

"The Danger Makers/A Touch of Brimstone," "What the Butler Saw/The House That Jack Built" and "A Sense of History/How to Succeed...at Murder/Honey for the Prince" are also available in a boxed collector's set.

53-6552 Save $9.00! **$29.99**

The Avengers: '67 Set I

"From Venus with Love/The Fear Merchants," "Escape in Time/The See-Through Man" and "The Bird Who Knew Too Much/The Winged Avenger" are also available in a boxed collector's set.

53-6178 Save $9.00! **$29.99**

The Avengers: '67 Set II

"The Living Dead/The Hidden Tiger," "The Correct Way to Kill/Never, Never Say Die" and "Epic/The Superlative Seven" are also available in a boxed collector's set.

53-6179 Save $9.00! **$29.99**

The Avengers: '67 Set III

"A Funny Thing Happened on the Way to the Station/Something Nasty in the Nursery," "The Joker/Who's Who?" and "Death's Door/Return of the Cybernauts" are also available in a boxed collector's set.

53-6259 Save $9.00! **$29.99**

The Avengers: '67 Set IV

"Dead Man's Treasure/The £50,000 Breakfast," "You Have Just Been Murdered/The Positive-Negative Man" and "Murdersville/Mission...Highly Improbable/The Forget-Me-Knot" are also available in a boxed collector's set.

53-9640 Save $9.00! **$29.99**

Piece Of Cake (1988)
Set in the early days of the Second World War, this acclaimed BBC mini-series follows the personal dramas and daredevil exploits of the men of the RAF Hornet Squadron. Exciting aerial sequences are a highlight; with Boyd Gaines, Neil Dudgeon, Nat Parker, Tom Burlinson. 5 hrs. on six tapes.
53-9685 Was $99.99 *$79.99*

Michael Shayne, Detective (1960)
Richard Denning plays Brett Halliday's dashing hero with a knack for landing beautiful women and solving bizarre murders in and around his native Miami in these TV whodunits; includes "Murder and the Wanton Bride." 60 min.
10-7019 Was $19.99 *$14.99*

The Best Of New Faces (1960)
Dazzling TV stage revue with the best from Broadway's "New Faces" shows. The cast includes Paul Lynde, Ronny Graham, Alice Ghostley and Robert Clary, in a special filled with music, dance, and comedy routines. 105 min.
62-1301 *$19.99*

The Dakotas (1963)
In this sagebrush series, U.S. marshal Larry Ward and deputies Jack Elam, Chad Everett and Mike Green saddled up to keep the peace in the Dakota Territory of the 1880s. Features the episode "Sanctuary at Crystal Springs." 50 min.
10-9210 Was $19.99 *$14.99*

Person To Person, Vol. 1
Host Ed Murrow lets you visit the homes of the famous, all through the miracle of live TV. Interview subjects include Marilyn Monroe, Humphrey Bogart and Lauren Bacall, Bing Crosby, Eddie Fisher and Debbie Reynolds, Louis Armstrong, Ella Fitzgerald, jazz pioneer W.C. Handy and cartoonist Rube Goldberg. 56 min.
10-7423 Was $19.99 *$14.99*

Person To Person, Vol. 2
Ed Murrow's live Friday night interviews with Groucho and Harpo Marx, Dizzy Gillespie, Carol Channing, Fred Astaire, Janet Leigh and Tony Curtis, and Maria Callas.
10-7424 Was $19.99 *$14.99*

Open All Hours: Boxed Set
Arkwright (played by "The Two Ronnie's" Ronnie Barker) is a stuttering English shopkeeper whose penny-pinching ways don't exactly endear him to employee/nephew Granville (David Jason) and neighbor/love interest Nurse Gladys Emmanuel (Lynda Baron). This three-tape collection from the 1979-82 Britcom includes "Laundry Blues/The Reluctant Traveller/Well Catered Funeral," "Shedding at The Wedding/Duet for Solo Bicycle/How to Ignite Your Errand Boy" and "The Ginger Men/Horse-Trading/The Cool Cocoa Tin Lid." 270 min. total. NOTE: Individual volumes available at $19.99 each.
53-6963 Save $10.00! *$49.99*

Open All Hours
Veteran British comedian Ronnie Barker plays the put-upon proprietor of a neighborhood grocery store in this collection of episodes from the popular BBC comedy series. 85 min.
04-2295 Was $39.99 *□$14.99*

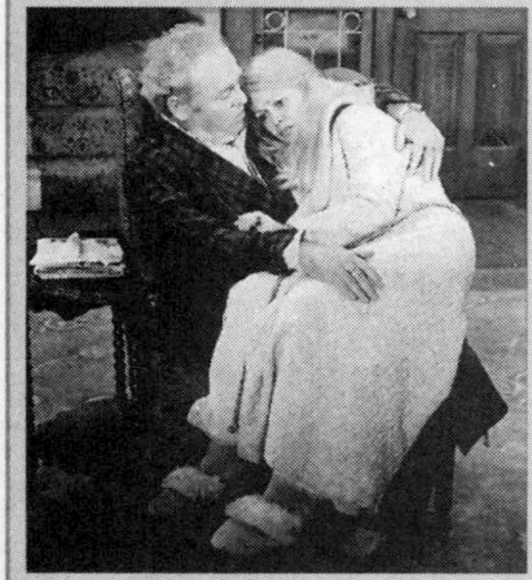

All In The Family
The world of TV was never the same once Queens factory worker Archie Bunker opened his mouth to complain about minorities, hippies, feminists and anyone else who disagreed with him. Norman Lear's groundbreaking sitcom, which won several Emmys during its 1970-1979 run, starred Carroll O'Connor as Archie, Jean Stapleton as long-suffering wife Edith, Sally Struthers as daughter Gloria, and Rob Reiner as long-haired, left-wing son-in-law Mike. Each tape features three episodes and runs about 75 min.

All In The Family: Archie Meets Meathead
A Sunday afternoon at 704 Howser Street turns into a typically explosive argument in the series' debut, "Meet the Bunkers." Next, will the Jeffersons be Archie's new neighbors when "Lionel Moves into the Neighborhood"?; and see the tumultuous first encounter between Archie and his future son-in-law in "Flashback: Mike Meets Archie."
02-3182 *$12.99*

All In The Family: Sammy Takes Bunker Hill
Sammy Davis, Jr. in Queens? "Sammy's Visit" to the Bunker home has everyone excited, but will he get to sit in Archie's chair? Then, Bea Arthur guest stars as Edith's liberal cousin, "Maude," who can match Archie insult for insult, and Gloria and Mike have a big announcement for Archie and Edith in "The Very Moving Day."
02-3183 *$12.99*

All In The Family: In The Family Way
How will Michael react to the news of "Gloria's Pregnancy"...and more importantly, how will Archie? Then, Archie tells Edith to claim she has a sprained ankle so they can avoid dinner with the Jeffersons in "The First and Last Supper," and Edith's misreading of a classified ad leads to a memorable encounter between "The Bunkers and the Swingers."
02-3211 *$12.99*

All In The Family: Those Were The Days
Mike and Gloria's vacation leaves "Archie and Edith Alone," but will Archie bend to Edith's romantic plans? Love is also in the air when the Bunkers spend a "Second Honeymoon" at the same Atlantic City hotel they stayed at 25 years earlier. And is Mike interested in Gloria—or just her new hair—in "Black Is the Color of My True Love's Wig"?
02-3258 *$12.99*

All In The Family: Hot Pants vs. Meathead
After accusing Mike and Gloria's friend Roger of being gay, Archie gets a lesson in "Judging Books by Covers" from his manly bar buddy Steve. Next, Mike is "counseled" by Archie when "Gloria Discovers Women's Lib"; and Mike's liberal views are tested when "Gloria Poses in the Nude" for an artist friend.
02-3259 *$12.99*

All In The Family: Archie Tells It Like It Is
A TV gun control spot moves Archie to go on the air with his own take on the topic in "Archie and the Editorial," while "Writing the President" gives him and Mike the chance to argue yet again over politics. Then, Archie is tapped as "The Man in the Street" for a TV news show, but will he ever get to see himself on the small screen?
02-3260 *$12.99*

All In The Family: The Rise And Fall Of Meathead
A can of cling peaches (in heavy syrup) and a scratched car help teach Archie a lesson in honesty in "Edith's Accident." Then, "Mike's Appendix" has to come out, but he has second thoughts about being operated on by a female surgeon, while stress over exams has a chilling effect on the Stivic bedroom in "Mike's Problem."
02-3261 *$12.99*

All In The Family: Archie Goes To The Big House
"Archie Learns His Lesson"—or, at least, he'd better—when he must enroll in night school to get his high school diploma and gain the dispatching job at work. More lessons in crime and punishment are on tap when a civil disturbance lands "Archie in the Lock-Up"; and "Archie Sees a Mugging" some mobsters would like him to forget.
02-3262 *$12.99*

All In The Family: Citizen Archie
The visit of an old army buddy who's become a "Success Story" as a car dealer in California leaves Archie feeling more than a little jealous, while "The Elevator Story" finds Archie trapped between floors with a diverse group that includes a very pregnant Hispanic woman. Also, will the legal system and Archie's dinner schedule survive when "Edith Has Jury Duty"?
02-3263 *$12.99*

All In The Family: Dingbat's Liberation
Are Archie's attentions towards the attractive wife of an old war pal really "The Threat" to the Bunkers' marriage that Edith fears they are? Then, "Archie the Hero" gives mouth-to-mouth to a fainted cab passenger, but he's in for a shock when "Beverly" turns out to be a man; and Edith and Gloria spend the night at a sorority slumber party when "Archie Goes Too Far."
02-3264 *$12.99*

All In The Family 3-Pack
"Archie Meets Meathead," "In the Family Way" and "Sammy Takes Bunker Hill" are also available in a special collector's set.
02-3212 Save $9.00! *$29.99*

All In The Family 10-Pack
You won't be able to stifle your joy when you save money by ordering this collector's set featuring all 10 volumes of "All in the Family" classics.
02-3265 Save $30.00! *$99.99*

All In The Family 20th Anniversary Special (1990)
The show that revolutionized prime time TV is feted in this special featuring interviews with stars Carroll O'Connor, Jean Stapleton, Rob Reiner and Sally Struthers, as well as clips of the best, funniest and most poignant moments with Archie and Edith, Mike and Gloria, and the rest of the crew. Producer-creator Norman Lear hosts. 74 min.
02-2142 Was $59.99 *□$14.99*

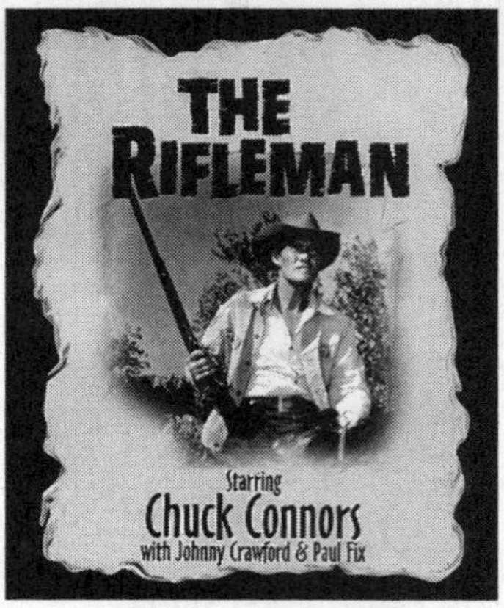

The Rifleman
In this action-packed and often sensitive show which ran on ABC from 1958 to 1963, Chuck Connors plays rancher Lucas McCain, a widower who uses his Winchester rifle to help keep the peace. Johnny Crawford co-stars as Connors' son, Mark, and Paul Fix is the town marshal. Except where noted, each tape features five episodes and runs about 140 min.

The Rifleman, Vol. 1
Includes "The Sharpshooter," the series' premiere, with Dennis Hopper and Leif Erickson; "Home Ranch"; Michael Landon in "End of a Young Gun"; "The Marshal" with Paul Fix and Warren Oates; and "Duel of Honor" with Jack Elam.
50-7405 *$19.99*

The Rifleman, Vol. 2
Includes Vic Morrow in "The Angry Gun"; "The Sheridan Story"; "The Money Gun"; John Carradine and Michael Landon in "The Mind Reader"; and "Bloodlines," featuring Warren Oates, Denver Pyle and Buddy Hackett.
50-7406 *$19.99*

The Rifleman, Vol. 3
Includes "Day of the Hunter"; Martin Landau in "The Vaqueros"; "Knight Errant"; "The Long Goodbye" with Edgar Buchanan; and James Coburn and Ellen Corby in "High Country."
50-7407 *$19.99*

The Rifleman, Vol. 4
Includes "Man from Salinas" with Robert Culp; Sammy Davis, Jr. in "Two Ounces of Tin"; "The Deadly Image"; and the two-part "Waste."
50-7408 *$19.99*

The Rifleman, Vol. 5
Includes "The Boarding House"; "The Brother-in-Law"; "The Bullet"; "Dead Cold Cash" with Ed Nelson; and "The Hero" with Robert Culp.
50-7566 *$19.99*

The Rifleman, Vol. 6
Includes Michael Ansara in "The Indian"; "Lariat"; "Mail Order Groom"; "The Martinet"; and "Miss Bertie" with Agnes Moorehead.
50-7567 *$19.99*

The Rifleman, Vol. 7
Includes "The Most Amazing Man" with Sammy Davis, Jr.; Akim Tamiroff in "New Orleans Menace"; "One Went to Denver"; "The Prodigal" with Lee Van Cleef and Warren Oates; and "The Safe Guard," featuring Claude Akins.
50-7568 *$19.99*

The Rifleman, Vol. 8
Includes "The Schoolmaster"; Dennis Hopper in "Three-Legged Terror"; the two-part "The Wyoming Story"; and James Coburn in "The Young Englishman."
50-7569 *$19.99*

The Rifleman: Vols. 1-4 Boxed Set
Volumes 1-4 are also available in a boxed collector's set.
50-7409 *$79.99*

The Rifleman: Vols. 5-8 Boxed Set
Volumes 5-8 are also available in a boxed collector's set.
50-7570 *$79.99*

The Rifleman: Outlaw Inheritance
Lucas inherits money from a train robber, which doesn't sit well with the commission planning to bring the railroad to Northfork, and he must persuade them to continue with their original plan. 25 min.
10-2457 *$12.99*

The Rifleman: Mail Order Groom
When the mail order fiancée of the town spinster gets into trouble with the sleazy Profit Brothers, Lucas McCain comes to the rescue. 25 min.
10-2458 *$12.99*

The Rifleman/Wyatt Earp
Two classic episodes of '50s TV westerns are available on one tape. Chuck Connors and Johnny Crawford star in "Mail Order Bride" from "The Rifleman." And Hugh O'Brian is Wyatt Earp in "The Assassins." 50 min.
10-9391 *$14.99*

Twenty-One: The Great Quiz Show Scandal
The "Twenty-One" installment that led to the infamous network scandals and was depicted in the acclaimed film "Quiz Show" is presented in its entirety in this program—including commercials for Geritol and Sominex. Jack Barry hosts the rigged battle between champ Herbert Stempel and challenger Charles Van Doren. A fascinating piece of history! 30 min.
10-1608 Was $19.99 *$14.99*

Junior Science
This collection includes five episodes of the popular mid-1950s quiz show in which youngsters were tested on their knowledge of science. Hosted by Gerald Wendt. 60 min.
10-6010 *$14.99*

Stump The Stars
Play along with Beverly Garland, Sebastian Cabot, Betty White and Hans Conried as they act out famous phrases, quotes and titles in two episodes from TV's popular game show variation on Charades. Among the guest stars are Stubby Kaye, Fabian, Julie London, Gordon MacRae and Tommy Noonan. 60 min.
10-7018 Was $19.99 *$14.99*

Television Game Shows, Vol. 1
Here's a collection of four vintage tube brain-teasers, all from before Vanna was even born! Match wits with the hosts, contestants, and guest stars of "I've Got a Secret," "The Price Is Right," "What Are the Odds?" and "Two For the Money." 100 min.
10-7437 Was $19.99 *$14.99*

Television Game Shows, Vol. 2
Test your smarts with these classic TV quiz shows from the '50s. Included are such entries as "The Name's the Same" (ordinary folks with celebrity names), "Who Said That?" (guess quotes from news stories), "Giant Step" (kids compete for a college scholarship), and "Place the Face" (contestants try to remember people they met briefly).
10-7438 Was $19.99 *$14.99*

The $64,000 Question/ Dollar A Second
Rekindle your love for the Big Quizzes with these challenging shows from the '50s. First up, step into the "Revlon isolation booth" and double your winnings with each correct answer. Then Jan Murray doles out a buck per correct response as well as per second the contestant remains on the show.
10-7497 Was $19.99 *$14.99*

The $64,000 Question (1957)
The most famous of early television's "big money" quiz shows, featuring host Hal March and the famous "Revlon isolation booth." Two contestants reach the $32,000 plateau on this episode, one of them the nephew of Wyatt Earp. 28 min.
09-1174 Was $19.99 *$14.99*

Beat The Clock
Two episodes of the frantically messy '50s game show, with host Bud Collyer putting contestants through fiendishly clever stunts involving whipped cream, custard pies, balloons and oversized longjohns and other paraphernalia are featured. 55 min.
10-7523 Was $19.99 *$14.99*

Masquerade Party/ Pantomime Quiz
Two of the '50s best remembered TV game shows are here in one nostalgic tape. Watch as disguised guest stars try to stump panelists Robin Sherwood, Mary Healy, Ogden Nash and Ilka Chase as they "peer through the goo" on "Masquerade Party," then joins Hans Conried, Vincent Price, Jackie Coogan and Adele Jergens for silent fun on "Pantomime Quiz." 60 min.
10-8084 Was $19.99 *$14.99*

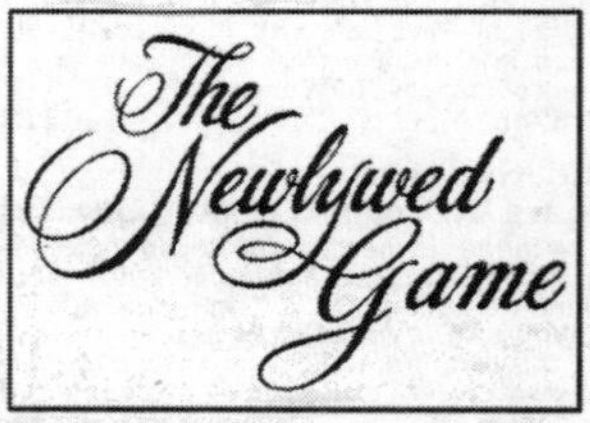

The Newlywed Game
One of the most successful game shows ever, Chuck Barris' creation has been entertaining audiences for decades since its debut in 1966. Join host Bob Eubanks in these hilarious compilation videos of recently-hitched couples trying to match answers in vintage and more recent shows. Each tape runs about 46 min.

The Newlywed Game: The Honeymoon's Over!
50-8284 *$14.99*

The Newlywed Game: Making Whoopee
50-8285 *$14.99*

The Newlywed Game: The Very Best Of The Newlywed Game
50-8283 *$14.99*

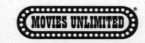

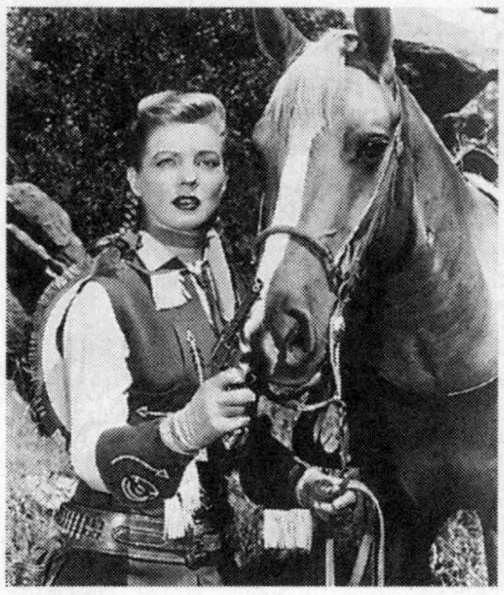

Annie Oakley

Holding her own among the many male stars of TV westerns in the early '50s was Gail Davis as the short-as-piecrust sharpshooter who kept the frontier town of Diablo safe while looking after younger brother Tagg. Each volume features two episodes and runs about 60 min. There are 16 volumes available, including:

The Best Of Annie Oakley, Vol. 1
Includes "Annie Finds Strange Treasure" and "Hardrock Trail."
10-9577 ***$14.99***

The Best Of Annie Oakley, Vol. 2
Includes "Annie Calls Her Shots" and "The Dude Stage Coach."
10-9578 ***$14.99***

The Best Of Annie Oakley, Vol. 3
Includes "Sharp Shootin' Annie" and "Justice Guns."
10-9579 ***$14.99***

The Best Of Annie Oakley, Vol. 4
Includes "Annie and the Lily Maid" and "Gunplay."
10-9580 ***$14.99***

The Best Of Annie Oakley, Vol. 5
Includes "Ambush Canyon" and "Annie Trusts a Convict."
10-9581 ***$14.99***

The Best Of Annie Oakley, Vol. 6
Includes "Bull's Eye" and "Annie Gets Her Man."
10-9582 ***$14.99***

The Best Of Annie Oakley, Vol. 7
Includes "Annie's Desert Adventure" and "Escape from Diablo."
10-9583 ***$14.99***

The Best Of Annie Oakley, Vol. 8
Includes "Treasure Map" and "Flint and Steel."
10-9584 ***$14.99***

The Best Of Annie Oakley, Vol. 9
Includes "Dilemma at Diablo" and "The Reckless Press."
10-9585 ***$14.99***

The Best Of Annie Oakley, Vol. 10
Includes "Annie and the Chinese Puzzle" and "Dudes Decision."
10-9586 ***$14.99***

The Best Of Annie Oakley, Vol. 11
Includes "Grubstake Bank" and "Desperate Men."
10-9587 ***$14.99***

Annie Oakley, Vol. 1
Includes "Dutch Gunman" and "Shadow Sonoma."
50-6306 Was $19.99 ***$14.99***

Annie Oakley, Vol. 2
Includes "Treasure Map" and "Annie and the Leprechauns."
50-6307 Was $19.99 ***$14.99***

My Friend Irma/Meet Millie
Two early '50s sitcoms that feature the working girl's travails. First Marie Wilson reprises her radio and screen role as the kookie blonde with a knack for trouble, followed by Elena Verdugo as a young middle-class secretary living with her matchmaker-mother. 55 min.
10-7028 Was $19.99 ***$14.99***

Lights Out:
The Fonceville Curse/Curtain Call
Enter at your own risk into the world of the unknown, courtesy of two tales from the eerie anthology series of the early '50s. Will a long-dead baron's medallion drive Patrick Knowles in "The Fonceville Curse," while stage actor Otto Kruger is haunted by his wife's spirit in "Curtain Call." 55 min.
10-7034 Was $19.99 ***$14.99***

Lights Out: The Passage Beyond/
The Man With The Watch
Here are two more episodes in Arch Oboler's mystery series. In "The Passage Beyond," a philandering husband meets a murderous ancestor, and in "The Man with the Watch," people mysteriously disappear after having the same dream about a man with a watch who claims to be from another planet. 60 min.
10-9885 Was $19.99 ***$14.99***

The Lawrence Welk Show

It's all here: the champagne bubbles, the "a-one and a-two," and all the music you grew up with. Maestro Lawrence Welk personally selected his favorite episodes from over 25 years of television and made them available for home video.

The Lawrence Welk Show:
On Tour With Lawrence Welk Live
A special two-episode "road adventure" takes you on tour with Lawrence and his musical family. All your favorites from those Saturday nights are here, including a travelling bubble machine. Songs include "Everything's Coming Up Roses," "Night and Day," "On the Road Again," many more. 90 min.
55-5015 ***$29.99***

The Lawrence Welk Show:
Viva! Italia
Mama mia, that's some spicy salute to Italy that maestro Welk presents, with performances by the Lennon Sisters, Norma Zimmer, Jo Ann Castle and violinist Aladdin. 50 min.
55-5016 ***$14.99***

The Lawrence Welk Show:
Marvelous Music Of
Richard Rodgers
One of Broadway's most acclaimed composers is spotlighted in a special show featuring selections from "South Pacific," "The Sound of Music" and more. 48 min.
55-5017 ***$14.99***

The Lawrence Welk Show:
County Fair
Step right up for a down-home carnival of fun with the Lennon Sisters and then-Welk regular Lynn Anderson. Songs include "Anything You Can Do," "I've Told Every Little Star," "These Boots Are Made for Walking" and more. 49 min.
55-5018 ***$14.99***

The Lawrence Welk Show:
Live From Hawaii
Aloha, Lawrence! Welk and his orchestra perform on the beach in Honolulu in this collection of island songs that's the next best thing to a Hawaiian vacation. 47 min.
55-5019 ***$14.99***

The Lawrence Welk Show:
Tribute To Glenn Miller And
His Orchestra
"String of Pearls," "American Patrol" and, of course, "Moonlight Serenade" are some of the Miller standards featured in this salute to the legendary bandleader. 47 min.
55-5020 ***$14.99***

The Lawrence Welk Show:
A Champagne Toast
To The Big Bands
In this special broadcast, Welk and the Champagne Music Makers present a lively Big Band show that offers music by Glenn Miller, Benny Goodman, Harry James, the Dorsey Brothers and other favorites. 85 min.
55-5021 ***$19.99***

The Lawrence Welk Show:
Salute To Cole Porter
A "Wunderbar" program that features Bobby and Cissy dancing to "The Continental," a "True Love" duet with Guy and Ralna, Clay Hart performing "Don't Fence Me In" and much more. 48 min.
55-5022 ***$14.99***

The Lawrence Welk Show:
That's Entertainment
And there's plenty of entertainment in this rousing show. Singer Mary Lou Metzger performs "Dear Mr. Gable," pianist Bob Ralston and clarinetist Henry Cuesta lead the orchestra in "Rhapsody in Blue," and more. 48 min.
55-5023 ***$14.99***

The Lawrence Welk Show:
A Tribute To Nat King Cole
Music lovers won't want to miss this "unforgettable" show that features the Welk TV family's interpretations of such popular Nat King Cole tunes as "Nature Boy," "Straighten Up and Fly Right" and others. 48 min.
55-5024 ***$14.99***

Lawrence Welk
25th Anniversary Show
Made in 1980 to celebrate a quarter-century of lovely "champagne music," this special show features a bevy of Welk regulars. The maestro himself dances with Champagne Lady Norma Zimmer to "The Anniversary Waltz," and Myron Floren, Jimmy Roberts, Bobby and Elaine and other turn in terrific performances, too. 48 min.
55-5025 ***$14.99***

The Lawrence Welk Show:
Songs From The Movies
Lawrence Welk and his cast of regulars (Myron Floren, Kathie Sullivan and Ken Delo) salute the great songs from the movies in this show that includes performances of "Never on Sunday," "Tara's Theme" from "Gone with the Wind," "Singin' in the Rain" and "The Way We Were." 47 min.
55-5026 ***$14.99***

The Lawrence Welk Show:
Tribute To Irving Berlin
The classic tunes of the great composer are performed by Lawrence Welk and his crew. Featured are a brassy version of "Alexander's Ragtime Band"; "Doing What Comes Naturally," from Guy and Ralina; a fun version of "Steppin' Out with My Baby" by Ken Delo; and "God Bless America," performed by a chorus led by Nora Zimmer. 46 min.
55-5027 ***$14.99***

The Lawrence Welk Show:
Country Music Hoedown!
There's clogging, homespun hits and fiddles galore in Lawrence Welk's winning country show, where Ava Barber sings "Rocky Top Tennessee," Ken Delo sings the powerful "Honey," Lawrence and Barbara Boylan polka to Myron Floren's performance of "Just Because" and the show's sax section does a terrific take on "I Can't Stop Loving You." 47 min.
55-5028 ***$14.99***

From The Heart: A Tribute To
Lawrence Welk And
The American Dream
This stirring tribute to the "King of Champagne Music" includes guest performances from Barbara Mandrell, Dixieland king Pete Fountain, Floyd Cramer and The Jordanaires, as well as appearances from Welk regulars The Lennon Sisters, Jo Ann Castle, Myron Floren and others. Songs include "Come Saturday Morning," "I'm on My Way," "Memory" and "This Is My Country." 81 min.
55-5029 Was $29.99 ***$19.99***

The Lennon Sisters:
Easy To Remember
Those sweet-voiced songstresses from "The Lawrence Welk Show" allow you to look into their careers with this music-filled program that includes stops at their family's Victorian home, the Santa Monica Pier and St. Monica's High School. Featured guests include Larry Hooper, Myron Floren and Pete Fountain. 85 min.
55-5030 Was $29.99 ***$19.99***

The Lawrence Welk Show:
Salute To Big Bands
Lawrence Welk and his cohorts pay tribute to the swing bands of the past with such selections as "Sentimental Journey," "Woodchopper's Ball," "I'll Never Smile Again," "In the Mood" and "American Patrol." Among the performers are Tom Netherton, Arthur Duncan, and Guy and Ralina. 45 min.
55-5032 ***$14.99***

The Lawrence Welk Show:
Tribute To George Gershwin
Lawrence Welk leads his company in a memorable program of Gershwin's greatest melodies. Ralina English croons "Embraceable You," Bobby and Elaine dance to "An American in Paris," The Aldridge Sisters harmonize with the Otwell Twins on "Swanee" and the entire cast sings "S Wonderful." 47 min.
55-5033 ***$14.99***

The Lawrence Welk Show:
Salute To Sinatra
"The Champagne Bunch" meets "the Rat Pack" as the Lawrence Welk Orchestra performs such Sinatra standards as "I've Got You Under My Skin," "Young at Heart," "Night and Day" and many more. Among the solo standouts are Bob Ralston on "All the Way" and Ken Delo with "That's Life." 49 min.
55-5036 ***$14.99***

The Lawrence Welk Show:
Salute To The Big Bands
The brassy Big Band sound lives on, as Welk leads his orchestra in Benny Goodman's "And the Angels Sing" and Glenn Miller's "Moonlight Serenade." Watch Bobby and Cissy jitterbug to "In the Mood," see Sandi Griffiths, Gail Farrell and Mary Lou Metzger salute The Andrews Sisters in "Pennsylvania Polka," and delight to a stunning rendition of Gershwin's "Rhapsody in Blue." 48 min.
55-5037 ***$14.99***

The Lawrence Welk Show:
Christmas Reunion
In 1985, three years after his long-running TV show came to an end, Lawrence Welk brought back his small-screen "family" for a warm and wonderful holiday reunion special. Bobby and Elaine, Jo Ann Castle, Guy and Ralna and "Champagne Lady" Norma Zimmer are among the returning favorites; songs include "Ring Those Christmas Bells," "Silver Bells," "Santa Claus Is Coming to Town" and many more. 45 min.
55-5038 ***$14.99***

The Lawrence Welk Show:
Show Stoppers!
Among the highlights in this truly show-stopping episode are Guy and Ralna singing "I Write the Songs"; a unique dance version of "Me and My Shadow" featuring Jack Imel, Mary Lou Metzger, and Bobby and Elaine; pianist Bob Ralston and the orchestra performing "Rhapsody in Blue"; the wonderful Myron Floren's rendition of "Beer Barrel Polka," and more. 47 min.
55-5039 ***$14.99***

A Lawrence Welk
Family Christmas (1995)
It's a special holiday reunion special, filmed at the Champagne Theatre in Branson, Missouri, and hosted by "Champagne Lady" Norma Zimmer. All your favorite performers and songs are here: The Lennon Sisters ("Have Yourself a Merry Little Christmas"), Jo Ann Castle ("The Skater's Waltz"), Bobby and Elaine ("Christmas Waltz"), Anacani ("It Came Upon a Midnight Clear") and more. 80 min.
55-5035 ***$19.99***

Sergeant Preston Of The Yukon

The call once again goes out: "On, King! On, you huskies!" There's plenty of action and adventure in the Great White North with Richard Simmons as the intrepid Mountie who always gets his man. Each tape contains two episodes and runs about 55 min.

Sergeant Preston Of
The Yukon, Vol. 1
Includes "One Bean Too Many" and "Crime at Wounded Moose."
10-9741 ***$14.99***

Sergeant Preston Of
The Yukon, Vol. 2
Includes "Dog Race" and "Phantom of Phoenixville."
10-9742 ***$14.99***

Sergeant Preston Of
The Yukon, Vol. 3
Includes "Trapped" and "Skagway Secret."
10-9743 ***$14.99***

Sergeant Preston Of
The Yukon, Vol. 4
Includes "Relief Train" and "The Black Ace."
10-9744 ***$14.99***

Sergeant Preston Of
The Yukon, Vol. 5
Includes "Scourge of the Wilderness" and "Blind Justice."
10-9745 ***$14.99***

Sergeant Preston Of
The Yukon/The Cisco Kid
Double bill of '50s TV adventure fare. Richard Simmons (the other one) is the courageous Mountie who was joined by faithful Yukon King "in the relentless pursuit of lawbreakers in the wild days of the Yukon," followed by Duncan Renaldo and Leo Carillo as the Southwest's crimefighting caballeros. 55 min.
10-7495 Was $19.99 ***$14.99***

Stoney Burke
Shown on ABC from 1962-1963, this contemporary Western featured a pre-"Hawaii Five-O" Jack Lord as pro rodeo rider Stoney Burke, who competed for the Golden Buckle, an award given to the champion bronco rider. Bruce Dern and Warren Oates also starred. Seen here is "Point of Entry," about Stoney helping a woman accused of assassinating a European visitor. 50 min.
10-9558 Was $19.99 ***$14.99***

Stoney Burke: The Journey
Jack Lord's quest for rodeo's most prized award, the Golden Buckle, continues in this installment of the early '60s modern-dress Western drama. With Warren Oates, Bruce Dern and guest star Mark Richmond. 60 min.
10-9980 ***$14.99***

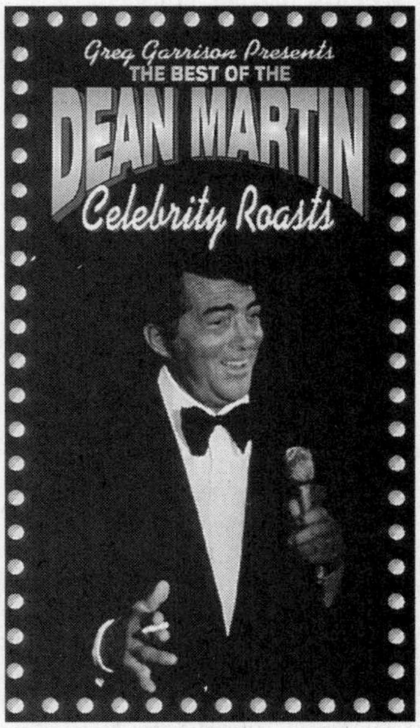

The Best Of
The Dean Martin Celebrity Roasts
This compilation offers the funniest moments from Dean Martin's classic celebrity skewerings of Jack Benny, Johnny Carson, Muhammad Ali, Lucille Ball, Jackie Gleason and Dino himself. Among the regulars partaking in the festivities are Don Rickles, George Burns, Phyllis Diller, Foster Brooks, Rich Little, Totie Fields, Jonathan Winters and others. 100 min.
50-8387 ***$19.99***

The Dean Martin Show (1965)
The premiere of Dino's long-lived variety series, with Dean teaming with guest star Frank Sinatra to sing "Is It Love," "September Song," and welcoming guests Bob Newhart, Diahann Carroll, Joey Heatherton, and Sid and Marty Krofft's Puppets, plus cameos by Steve Allen and Danny Thomas. 50 min.
62-1177 ***$19.99***

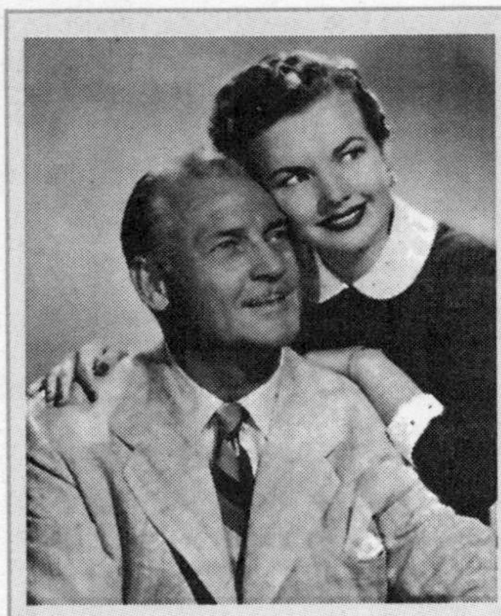

My Little Margie
This hit series ran from 1952 to 1955 and featured Gale Storm as Margie Allbright, the 21-year-old daughter of widowed investment banker Vern (Charles Farrell). How the two of them tried to get each other to "settle down" and act their age led to comical complications. Don Hayden, Hillary Brooke and Willie Best also star. Each tape runs about 50 min.

My Little Margie, Vol. 1
In "The Trapped Freddie," Dad promises to buy Margie a new sports car if she doesn't see boyfriend Freddie for a month. Then, Freddie's new job as a kitchenware salesman causes Vern to lose his in "What's Cooking?"
10-9750 Was $19.99 *$14.99*

My Little Margie, Vol. 2
In "Buried Treasure," Margie meets gangsters after her dad tricks her with a fake pirate map. Then, Margie believes "Vern's New Girlfriend" may be after his money.
10-9751 *$14.99*

My Little Margie, Vol. 3
In "Margie's Phantom Lover," Vern and his boss Mr. Honeywell try to keep Margie at home by inventing a secret boyfriend. And in "Honeyboy Honeywell," Margie schemes to get Mr. Honeywell married so he'll ease up on her dad.
10-9752 Was $19.99 *$14.99*

My Little Margie, Vol. 4
Margie becomes a regular "Miss Whoozis" to a photographer who ignores her when she's posing in expensive French clothes. And in "Delinquent Margie," Margie pretends she's a troubled young woman in order to help her neighbor get cash to buy a sports car.
10-9753 Was $19.99 *$14.99*

My Little Margie, Vol. 5
In "Meet Mr. Murphy," Margie babysits for a simian movie star. And Margie tries to befriend the author of a yoga book in "To Health with Yoga."
10-9754 Was $19.99 *$14.99*

My Little Margie, Vol. 6
Margie's father and boyfriend try to lure her away from a reporter she's smitten with in "A Horse for Vern." Also, Vern tells Margie about how "Vern's Mother-in-Law" tried to tell if he was right for her daughter.
10-9755 Was $19.99 *$14.99*

My Little Margie, Vol. 7
Freddie's purchase of a kangaroo at the same time Roberta's dad pays a visit has everyone hopping in "Kangaroo Story." Then, Margie gets conned into buying the contract of a has-been wrestler in "The Missing Link."
10-9756 Was $19.99 *$14.99*

My Little Margie, Vol. 8
Despite Vern's objection, Margie is set to meet one his frat brothers, the Shah of Zena, in "Margie and the Shah." Also, Vern takes dance lessons to impress a Spanish client in "Papa and Mambo."
10-9757 Was $19.99 *$14.99*

My Little Margie, Vol. 9
When Margie interferes with one of Vern's new clients, she finds herself in trouble in "The San Francisco Story." Then, Margie and her neighbor Mrs. Odetts try to scare off Vern's new fiancée in "Operation Rescue."
10-9758 Was $19.99 *$14.99*

My Little Margie, Vol. 10
"Margie Baby-Sits" the bratty son of one of Vern's clients and catches the Old Lady Robber, too. And Margie and Vern pose as hillbillies in order to buy stock certificates from mountain people in "Hillbilly Margie."
10-9759 Was $19.99 *$14.99*

My Little Margie, Vol. 11
Margie poses as a 12-year-old daughter for one of Vern's clients in "The Hawaii Story." Next, when Margie tricks Vern into going to Palm Beach so she can help boyfriend Freddie win a contest he thinks it's because she's getting married in "Vern's Winter Vacation."
10-9760 Was $19.99 *$14.99*

My Little Margie, Vol. 12
In "Margie's Millionth Number," Margie is notified that "son" Vern is the millionth member of the Stratosphere Scouts, a kid's show sponsored by a rival. And Margie and Freddie try to catch a murderer in "Corpus Delecti."
10-9761 Was $19.99 *$14.99*

My Little Margie, Vol. 13
Margie's friendship with detectives gets her and Mrs. Odetts in trouble with jewel thieves in "Star of Khyber." Then, when Margie and her dad return home from a trip, they find that Vern's employer has loaned their place to a client in "The Unexpected Guest."
10-9762 Was $19.99 *$14.99*

My Little Margie, Vol. 14
In "The Convention Story," Margie stays home while Vern attends a convention with a guy she likes. Also, Margie tries to help Vern by acting like a hypochondriac so he can land a client who really is one in "The Hypochondriac."
10-9916 Was $19.99 *$14.99*

My Little Margie, Vol. 15
When Vern learns that his daughter has become a "Careless Margie," he tries to teach her a lesson. In "Mardi Gras," hilarious complications ensue when Vern and Margie try to help get rid of a client's annoying brother-in-law.
10-9917 Was $19.99 *$14.99*

My Little Margie, Vol. 16
When she decides she doesn't want to go out with a guy, Margie becomes "Chubby Little Margie," magically boosting her weight to 300 pounds to dissuade her potential date. And in "Margie's Baby," Margie has to pretend she's the mother of Vern's client's baby.
10-9918 Was $19.99 *$14.99*

My Little Margie, Vol. 17
Vern doesn't want Margie to meet the son of his client, so he sends her away and has Roberta pretend to be her in "Vern's Two Daughters." Also, Vern and Freddie have a photo of Margie retouched to show to an interested young man in "Homely Margie."
10-9919 Was $19.99 *$14.99*

My Little Margie, Vol. 18
Margie presents a script by Freddie as a real-life incident in hopes of selling it in "Girl Against the World." Margie next masquerades as Vern's mother to impress a stuffy client in "A Mother for Vern."
10-9920 Was $19.99 *$14.99*

My Little Margie, Vol. 19
A "New Neighbor" with a habit for making noise annoys Vern and Margie until they realize he's one of Vern's clients. And in "Day and Night," a runaway elevator spells trouble for Margie when she wants Vern to send her to Sun Valley.
10-9921 Was $19.99 *$14.99*

My Little Margie
Two hilarious misadventures of widower Vern Albright (Charles Farrell) and his trouble-prone daughter, Margie (Gale Storm). First, Margie and neighbor Mrs. Odetts' scheme to get money for a sports car ends with Vern getting a black eye; then, Margie is convinced she's the "dream girl" of a handsome Broadway actor. 55 min.
10-7320 *$14.99*

Space Patrol (1950)
Stand by for "high adventure in the wild vast regions of space" with the men and women of the United Planets' Space Patrol. The fondly remembered, Saturday morning sci-fi series starred Ed Kemmer as Commander Buzz Corey and Lyn Osborn as Cadet Happy.

Space Patrol, Vol. 1
Join Buzz Corry and Cadet Happy in a three-part adventure set on one of the moons of Pluto, as they seek to stop a scientist's sinister experiments. Included are "Giants of Pluto #3," "The Fiery Pit of Pluto #3" and "Manhunt on Pluto #3." 90 min.
05-1170 *$19.99*

Space Patrol, Vol. 2
These three shows from the Saturday morning adventure series detail Buzz, Happy and Robbie's adventures rescuing Dr. Tuttle and his assistant from female warriors in Venus's Cydonian jungle. Included are "Amazons of Cydonia," "The Monsoon Trap on Cydonia" and "The Men Slaves of Cydonia." 90 min.
05-1202 *$19.99*

Flash Gordon
The televised exploits of the famed comic-strip space hero ran in syndication in 1953-54 and featured Steve Holland as daredevil Flash, Irene Champlin as Dale Arden, and the most adventure this side of the planet Mongo. Each tape features two episodes and runs about 55 min.

Flash Gordon, Vol. 1
Includes "Akim the Terrible" and "Lure of the Light."
10-1718 *$14.99*

Flash Gordon, Vol. 2
Includes "Planet of Death" and "Struggle to the End."
10-1719 *$14.99*

Flash Gordon, Vol. 3
Includes "Saboteurs from Space" and "Deadline at Noon."
10-1720 *$14.99*

Flash Gordon, Vol. 4
Includes "Subworld Revenge" and "Forbidden Experiment."
10-1721 *$14.99*

Hawkeye And The Last Of The Mohicans
James Fenimore Cooper's epic adventure set in 1750s New York state during the French and Indian Wars was turned into a thrilling TV series that played in syndication in 1957. John Hart played Hawkeye to Lon Chaney, Jr.'s Chingachgook, and each week they got involved in disputes between pioneers and the Huron Indians. Each tape features two episodes and runs about 50 min. There are six volumes available, including:

Hawkeye And The Last Of The Mohicans, Vol. 1
Includes "Hawkeye's Homecoming" and "The Way Station."
09-5138 Was $19.99 *$14.99*

Hawkeye And The Last Of The Mohicans, Vol. 2
Includes "Delaware Hoax" and "The Contest."
09-5139 Was $19.99 *$14.99*

Hawkeye And The Last Of The Mohicans, Vol. 3
Includes "The Search" and "The Scapegoat."
09-5140 Was $19.99 *$14.99*

Hawkeye And The Last Of The Mohicans, Vol. 4
Includes "The Snake Tattoo" and "The Medicine Man."
09-5141 Was $19.99 *$14.99*

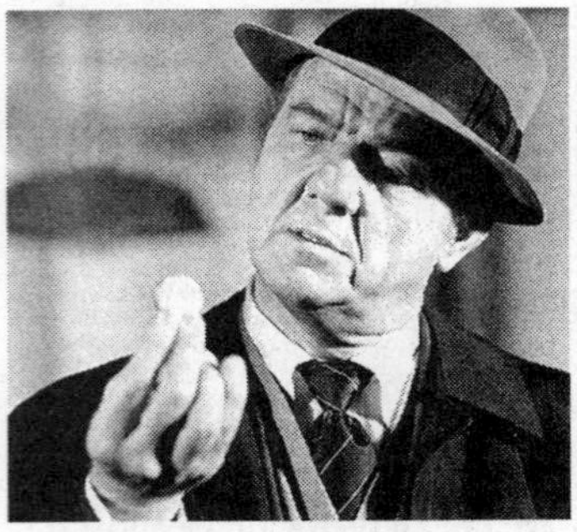

The Streets Of San Francisco
This Quinn Martin production was a big hit on ABC from 1972 and 1977 and featured Karl Malden as Mike Stone, a veteran detective trying to solve crimes in the Bay Area with help from sharp-witted young partner Steve Keller, played by Michael Douglas. Except where noted, each tape features two episodes and runs about 96 min.

The Streets Of San Francisco: The Thrill Killers
In this two-part episode, the trial of a group of "anti-establishment" killers is thrown in turmoil when a terrorist group takes the jury hostage. The chaos grows when Keller is shot and critically wounded. Richard Hatch makes his debut as Stone's new partner, Dan Robbins; Patty Duke Astin, Susan Dey, Barry Sullivan guest star. 95 min.
10-2274 *$14.99*

The Streets Of San Francisco: The Thirty-Year Pin
The series premiere finds streetwise detective Mike Stone joining forces with his new partner, assistant inspector Steve Keller, to catch the shooter of Stone's policeman pal, Gus (Edmond O'Brien). 48 min.
63-1931 *$14.99*

The Streets Of San Francisco: Legion Of The Lost/Betrayed
Stone goes undercover to find who is behind a series of homeless killings in "Legion," with guest star Leslie Nielsen. And in "Betrayed," Martin Sheen is a stockbroker involved in a bank robbery and the killing of a guard.
63-1932 *$14.99*

The Streets Of San Francisco: Hall Of Mirrors/Dead Air
In "Hall," Keller teams with hot-headed newcomer David Soul to investigate some killings in the Mission district. When Soul gets pulled off the case, he takes matters into his own hands. Then, radio talk show host Larry Hagman is a prime suspect in the murder of a pregnant woman in "Air."
63-1933 *$14.99*

The Streets Of San Francisco: Before I Die/Superstar
Cop Leslie Nielsen is obsessed with catching a vicious mobster, but a terminal illness forces him to take justice into his own hands, in "Before I Die." Next, Paul Sorvino is "Superstar" New York cop Bert D'Angelo, whose search for his partner's killer brings him to California and into conflict with Stone and Keller.
63-1934 *$14.99*

The Streets Of San Francisco: Harem/No Place To Hide
In "Harem," Rick Nelson is a hustler preying on runaways, and Stone calls on his daughter to track him down and stop a teenage prostitution ring. And in "Hide," Stone and Keller aid Stefanie Powers, an inmate's wife in trouble when she's forced to transport drugs for a prison kingpin.
63-1935 *$14.99*

Quantum Leap
This offbeat sci-fi drama, which ran on NBC from 1989 to 1993, starred Scott Bakula as Dr. Sam Beckett, a physicist whose time-travel experiment goes awry, sending him back and forth in the past and into other's people's bodies, where Sam and holographic sidekick Al (Dean Stockwell) must try and change people's lives for the better. Except where noted, each tape runs about 48 min.

Quantum Leap: The Pilot Episode
The first episode of the show finds Sam's time-leaping odyssey beginning when he turns into a test pilot in 1955. 93 min.
07-2009 □*$14.99*

Quantum Leap: The Color Of Truth
The deep South in 1955 is the setting for this "Leap," in which Sam learns first-hand what it was like to be an African-American during that turbulent time.
07-2007 □*$14.99*

Quantum Leap: Camikazi Kid
Sam becomes a teenager with a love for hot-rodding when he finds himself in 1961.
07-2008 □*$14.99*

Quantum Leap: What Price Gloria?
Sam switches genders when he leaps into the body of a gorgeous secretary in 1961 and gets first-hand knowledge of sexual harassment.
07-2010 □*$14.99*

Quantum Leap: Catch A Falling Star
When an alcoholic friend in 1979 needs his help, stage actor Sam comes to the rescue.
07-2011 □*$14.99*

Quantum Leap: Dreams
Sam leaps into the body of a homicide detective investigating a grisly murder that triggers a memory from "his" past.
07-2089 □*$14.99*

Quantum Leap: Shock Theater
After Sam finds himself in the body of a manic-depressive and is given electro-shock treatment, he reassumes the personalities from his previous leaps.
07-2090 □*$14.99*

Quantum Leap: Jimmy
Sam's leap into the body of a man with the mind of a 12-year-old allows him the chance to ease him into everyday society in a year (1964) when the concept is unheard of.
07-2091 □*$14.99*

Quantum Leap: The Leap Home
Sam returns to his own past as a teenager in 1969 Indiana. He can change the future of his friends by winning the big high-school basketball game, but Sam's more concerned with trying to alter his family's destiny. This special two-part episode runs 88 min.
07-2092 □*$14.99*

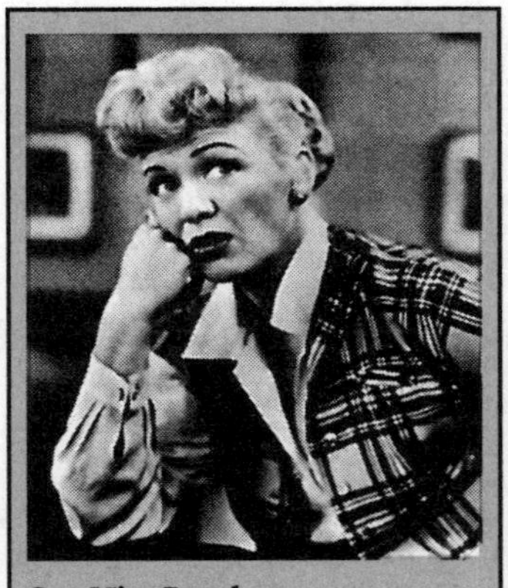

Our Miss Brooks
The popular radio show was turned into an equally popular TV series that ran on CBS from 1952 to 1956. Eve Arden reprised her radio role of wise-cracking Madison High English teacher Connie Brooks, who always found herself squaring off against principal Gale Gordon. Richard Crenna and Robert Rockwell also star. Each tape features two episodes and runs about 55 min.

Our Miss Brooks, Vol. 1
"The Christmas Show" finds Miss Brooks and her co-workers exchanging gifts at a local department store; and Miss Brooks believes the person following her is responsible for things disappearing in "Here Is Your Past."
09-5304 *$14.99*

Our Miss Brooks, Vol. 2
In "The Big Jump," Miss Brooks decides to set an example by jumping into a net during a Civil Defense demonstration. And she accidentally locks school principal Mr. Conklin (Gale Gordon) in a freezer in "Home Cooked Meal."
09-5305 *$14.99*

The Honeymooners: The Lost Episodes

Unseen for three decades, these "Honeymooners" sketches from Jackie Gleason's long-running CBS variety series were released by Gleason in the mid-'80s, to the delight of Ralph Kramden fans everywhere, and are now available on home video.

The Honeymooners: The Lost Episodes, Vol. 1
Ralph's got his hands full in this volume, as he must retrieve an angry "Letter to the Boss," thinks Alice is plotting to kill him in "Suspense," and brings the boss and his wife home in "Dinner Guest." 60 min.
50-6070 ***$14.99***

The Honeymooners: The Lost Episodes, Vol. 2
"Song and Witty Sayings" finds Ralph and Norton imitating Laurel and Hardy in a talent show, and in the next episode the Kramdens can't get any sleep when "Norton Moves In." Hey, hey, Ralphie-boy! 55 min.
50-6071 ***$14.99***

The Honeymooners: The Lost Episodes, Vol. 3
At "The Christmas Party" Ralph Kramden gets to meet other Gleason characters like The Poor Soul and Reginald Van Gleason III, while election day hassles occur because Ralph "Forgot to Register." 53 min.
50-6072 ***$14.99***

The Honeymooners: The Lost Episodes, Vol. 4
Ralph has to work on New Year's Eve forcing him and Alice to miss the "New Year's Eve Party" with guests Tommy and Jimmy Dorsey, while a raffle causes problems with the "Two-Family Car." Baby, these are the greatest! 55 min.
50-6073 ***$14.99***

The Honeymooners: The Lost Episodes, Vol. 5
Poor ol' Ralph gets himself and Norton into some scrapes in this collection. First Jackie Gleason turns boxing manager for "The Next Champ," then he thinks he's an "Expectant Father." 55 min.
50-6101 ***$14.99***

The Honeymooners: The Lost Episodes, Vol. 6
Ralph decides to leave Chauncey Street (horrors!) and "Move Uptown" to a fancy new apartment, and thinks his "Lucky Number" has come up when he plays hooky from work in these two gems of TV comedy. 55 min.
50-6102 ***$14.99***

The Honeymooners: The Lost Episodes, Vol. 7
When a bus company psychiatrist tells Ralph that Norton is driving him crazy, he tries to avoid him in "Little Man Who Wasn't There." Next, Ralph's night shift stint drives everyone crazy in "Goodnight Sweet Prince." 55 min.
50-6103 ***$14.99***

The Honeymooners: The Lost Episodes, Vol. 8
You'll be saying "hommina-hommina-hommina" when Ralph buys a house and becomes "My Fair Landlord" to the Nortons. Next, Ralph's got the April 15th blues, thanks to the "Income Tax." 55 min.
50-6122 ***$14.99***

The Honeymooners: The Lost Episodes, Vol. 9
"Ralph's Sweet Tooth" may jeopardize his doing a candy commercial. Next, Ralph thinks Alice wants him dead for insurance money in "Cold," and then believes her to be expecting when she develops a craving for "Pickles." 55 min.
50-6123 ***$14.99***

The Honeymooners: The Lost Episodes, Vol. 10
It's double trouble for Ralph, as he plays "Cupid" for a shy friend (and leads Alice to believe he's having an affair) and then thinks he's been appointed manager of the bus company (he's really only "Manager of a Baseball Team"). 55 min.
50-6124 ***$14.99***

The Honeymooners: The Lost Episodes, Vol. 11
If Alice doesn't agree on a fishing holiday, she's given the option of a moon trip in "Vacation at Fred's Landing," and the Kramdens take their family feud on to the game show stage in "Teamwork: Beat the Clock." 63 min.
50-6130 ***$14.99***

The Honeymooners: The Lost Episodes, Vol. 12
Alice thinks the watch that the boys in the terminal chipped in to get the boss' daughter is for her in "The Great Jewel Robbery," and Ralph hems, haws, and homina-hominas through his rehearsals as the Raccoon's "Guest Speaker." 52 min.
50-6131 ***$14.99***

The Honeymooners: The Lost Episodes, Vol. 13
There's trouble a-brewing downstairs when Ralph finds a "Love Letter" of Ed's and thinks it was meant for Alice, and Ralph's got promotion on his mind when he has the boss over for "Champagne and Caviar." 51 min.
50-6132 ***$14.99***

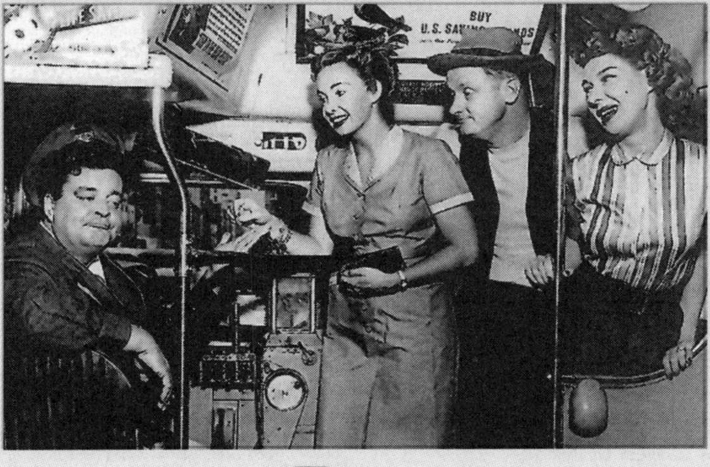

The Honeymooners

The Honeymooners: The Lost Episodes, Vol. 14
Ralph is suckered by a huckster selling a hair restorer in "Hair Raising Tale" and is on the run from a killer he pointed out on the bus in "Finger Man." A riot, Alice, a regular riot. 50 min.
50-6133 ***$14.99***

The Honeymooners: The Lost Episodes, Vol. 15
More rediscovered hardee-har-hars, as Ralph and Ed pool their dubious culinary talents into running a "Hot Dog Stand" and "Alice Plays Cupid" for a couple she doesn't know are already engaged. 48 min.
50-6134 ***$14.99***

The Honeymooners: The Lost Episodes, Vol. 16
Seen again for the first time in decades! The boys con Alice and Trixie into buying a summer place in "Cottage for Sale" and Ralph raids Alice's dress fund to buy "Jelly Beans" for a contest. 50 min.
50-6135 ***$14.99***

The Honeymooners: The Lost Episodes, Vol. 17
It's only the "Principal of the Thing" as Ralph and Ed try to sting the curmudgeonly landlord (Jack Benny!) into making repairs, then they scheme to get "Alice's Aunt Ethel" to see that her welcome's worn out. 49 min.
50-6136 ***$14.99***

The Honeymooners: The Lost Episodes, Vol. 18
You'll be entranced as Ralph and Ed are put under at a Raccoon meeting by "The Hypnotist," then Ralph gets envious of Alice's fame as "Glow Worm Cleaning" Lady of the Month. 49 min.
50-6137 ***$14.99***

The Honeymooners: The Lost Episodes, Vol. 19
Ralph is elected treasurer of the Raccoon Lodge, and promptly blows all their money on "Two Men on a Horse," then sweats it out when he discovers his promotion is dependent on his passing "The Check-Up." 49 min.
50-6138 ***$14.99***

The Honeymooners: The Lost Episodes, Vol. 20
Ralph finally receives "A Promotion" to cashier and is the first guy pointed out when the safe is cracked. Next, a cop who sees Ralph run the building's bets to the track thinks he's a bookie in "Hot Tips." 50 min.
50-6139 ***$14.99***

The Honeymooners: The Lost Episodes, Vol. 21
In "Boys and Girls Together," Ralph and Ed's plan to keep their families' night out at a minimum blows up in their faces, then confusion reigns as Ralph and Trixie both buy Alice the same "Anniversary Gift." 49 min.
50-6140 ***$14.99***

The Honeymooners: The Lost Episodes, Vol. 22
Ralph is aghast when he finds out that the other man Alice has secretly been seeing is Ralph Edwards in "This Is Your Life," then see the Kramdens and Nortons get appropriately done up for a "Halloween Party." 49 min.
50-6141 ***$14.99***

The Honeymooners: The Lost Episodes, Vol. 23
Ralph's got "A Weighty Problem" on his hands when the bus company gives him a choice: lose eight pounds quick...or lose his job! 48 min.
50-6889 ***$14.99***

The Honeymooners: The Lost Episodes, Vol. 24
In "Good Buy Aunt Ethel," Ralph tries to play matchmaker for Alice's aunt, while "Lost Job" finds Ralph receiving a pink slip in his pay envelope which could mark the end of his career at the Gotham Bus Company. 50 min.
50-6890 ***$14.99***

The Honeymooners: The Lost Episodes, Vol. 25
Ralph gets in the middle of a mob war when a gangster who's his double makes him a "Stand-In for Murder." Next, a "Lunchbox" mix-up gets Ralph and his biiig mouth in trouble with Alice. 50 min.
50-6891 ***$14.99***

The Honeymooners: The Lost Episodes, Vol. 26
Ralph becomes "The Boxtop Kid," attempting to win contests after Alice's sister and brother-in-law win a trip to Europe; Ralph mistakenly thinks a "Halloween Party for the Boss" is a costume affair. 50 min.
50-6908 ***$14.99***

The Honeymooners: The Lost Episodes, Vol. 27
After Ralph catches a killer, crooked politicians ask him to run for office in "The People's Choice," and in "What's the Name" Ralph and Alice sing "One of These Days, Pow!" 50 min.
50-6909 ***$14.99***

The Honeymooners: The Lost Episodes, Vol. 28
Ralph tells a young tenant he was a school athlete in "Hero," followed by a remake of the episode "Manager of the Baseball Team." 50 min.
50-6910 ***$14.99***

The Honeymooners: The Lost Episodes, Vol. 29
The Kramdens and Nortons think they can save cash by moving in together as "One Big Happy Family." And Ralph gets a taste of fatherhood when he adopts a baby in "Lost Baby," the oldest surviving lost episode.
50-7315 ***$14.99***

The Honeymooners: The Lost Episodes, Vol. 30
Ralph and Norton's plans for purchasing a candy store are thwarted by a lack of cash in "Finders Keepers." Next, Ralph's night at the fights is threatened when Alice's Uncle George visits in "Two Tickets to the Fight." 48 min.
50-7316 ***$14.99***

The Honeymooners: The Lost Episodes, Vol. 31
Norton tells Ralph that astrology can help him get a raise in "Stars Over Flatbush." Plus, Ralph goes into action when he learns "The Prowler" is in the neighborhood. 48 min.
50-7317 ***$14.99***

The Honeymooners: The Lost Episodes, Vol. 32
The Kramdens adopt a baby girl in the emotional episode "The Adoption." And Alice tries to help Ralph slim down in "Ralph's Diet." 48 min.
50-7318 ***$14.99***

The Honeymooners: The Lost Episodes, Vol. 33
Ralph brags about knowing Jackie Gleason to his fellow Raccoons, which leads to trouble in "Catch a Star." Then, Ralph receives an unexpected opportunity to answer a question on a "Quiz Show." 48 min.
50-7319 ***$14.99***

The Honeymooners: The Lost Episodes, Vol. 34
It's the new musical sensation with Kramden as lyricist and Norton on the piano in "Songwriters," followed by Ralph and Alice planning competing surprise parties in "Double Anniversary Party." 48 min.
50-7320 ***$14.99***

The Honeymooners: The Lost Episodes, Vol. 35
Ralph offers some misguided advice to Norton about running his household, so they both find themselves on their own in the Kramden apartment in "Battle of the Sexes." Also, Ralph considers a "Lawsuit" against the bus company after breaking his leg in a traffic accident. 48 min.
50-7321 ***$14.99***

The Honeymooners: The Lost Episodes, Vol. 36
After deciding not to lend his "Brother-In-Law" cash to purchase a hotel, Ralph considers buying it himself. And Ralph can't recall the name of an actress in a film he saw in "What's Her Name?" 48 min.
50-7322 ***$14.99***

The Honeymooners: The Lost Episodes, Vol. 37
Ralph becomes a sidewalk Santa Claus in "Santa and the Bookies." And in "Game Called on Account of Marriage," Ralph might miss the World Series—unless he can talk his pal Stanley into eloping with Alice's sister. 68 min.
50-7323 ***$14.99***

The Honeymooners: The Lost Episodes, Vol. 38
Ralph and Ed square off in court over a television set in "Kramden vs. Norton." And Ralph counsels Ed following a fight with Trixie, then learns that the fight started when Trixie yelled at him for being critical of Ralph, in "Peacemaker." 67 min.
50-7324 ***$14.99***

The Honeymooners: The Lost Episodes, Vol. 39
Ralph discovers that Alice has given his suit with his hidden poker winnings to charity in "The Man in the Blue Suit." Also, Ralph and Ed insist their two families should vacation together in "Vacation at Fred's Landing," the first "Honeymooners" skit to run 30 minutes. 64 min.
50-7325 ***$14.99***

The Honeymooners: The Lost Episodes: Boxed Set
This attractive boxed set of "The Honeymooners: The Lost Episodes" includes Volumes 29-39 in the series and "The Honeymooners: History of the Lost Episodes" special. There's non-stop laughs and great savings with Ed, Ralph, Alice and Trixie.
50-7326 Save $50.00! ***$129.99***

The Honeymooners: History Of The Lost Episodes: The First Season
This special retrospective of the first "Honeymooners" sketches offers such oddities as a thinner Ralph wearing a different uniform; different shirts under Norton's vests; and some of the first uses of the lines, characters and personality traits that made the show one of TV's greats. 30 min.
50-7314 ***$14.99***

My Man Norton
Va-va-va-Voom! Greater Brooklyn's most famous "sanitation engineer," Ed Norton, takes center stage in a collection of classic "Honeymooners" sketches. Joyce Randolph, Mrs. Norton herself, hosts some of Art Carney's funniest routines. 50 min.
50-6325 Was $29.99 ***$14.99***

Jackie Gleason's Honeybloopers
The Golden Age of television was also a golden opportunity for on-the-air bloopers and mishaps, the funniest examples of which have been collected on this uncensored tape of "Honeymooners" miscues. 60 min.
50-6446 ***$19.99***

Cavalcade Of Stars, Vol. 1
Join Jackie Gleason in the show that originated "The Honeymooners" and "The Bachelor." The Great One hosts Bert Wheeler and movie comedienne Vivian Blaine ("Guys and Dolls").
10-7380 Was $19.99 ***$14.99***

Cavalcade Of Stars, Vol. 2
Jackie Gleason's Dumont variety hour, which CBS raided to form its own "Jackie Gleason Show," featuring Vaudeville legends Smith and Dale.
10-7381 Was $19.99 ***$14.99***

Cavalcade Of Stars (1951)
Starring Jackie Gleason, Art Carney, Georgia Gibbs, June Taylor Dancers and Sammy Spear and His Orchestra. Sketches include "The Loud Mouth" and Reginald Van Gleason III. 50 min.
09-1223 Was $19.99 ***$14.99***

The Great Gleason
Now you can enjoy some of the Great One's funniest moments and most memorable characters in a nostalgic video tribute. Laugh again at Joe the Bartender, Reginald Van Gleason III, the Poor Soul and, of course, Ralph Kramden, and see rare outtakes and ad libs (including the time a set caught fire!). 90 min.
50-6240 Was $29.99 ***$14.99***

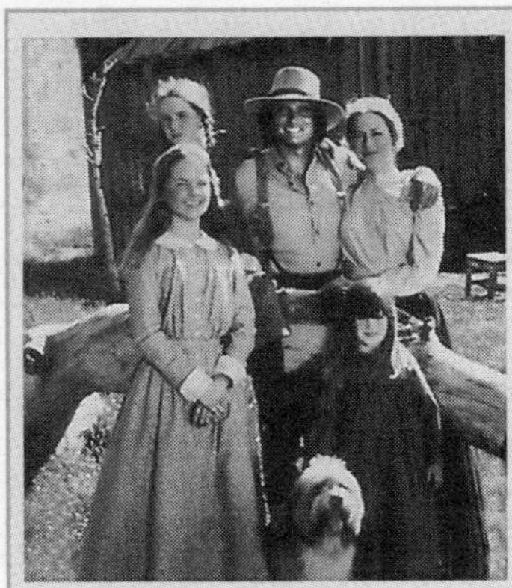

Little House on the Prairie

Little House On The Prairie
Based on the perennially popular "Little House" books by Laura Ingalls Wilder, this beloved family drama series ran on NBC from 1974 to 1983. Michael Landon and Karen Grassle played the heads of the Ingalls clan, who settled with their three daughters on the Minnesota prairie in the 1870s. Melissa Gilbert, Melissa Sue Anderson co-starred. Except where noted, each tape runs about 45 min.

Little House On The Prairie: The Lord Is My Shepherd
In this special feature-length adventure, Laura, blaming herself for the death of her infant brother, runs away from home and is found by a reclusive mountain man (guest star Ernest Borgnine). 94 min.
02-1703 *$14.99*

Little House On The Prairie: The Creeper Of Walnut Grove
Laura Ingalls and her pal Andy play amateur sleuth in order to track down the sneak thief who's disrupting the quiet prairie life of Walnut Grove.
10-2328 *$12.99*

Little House On The Prairie: The Craftsman
In this powerful and poignant episode, Pa Ingalls learns about bigotry when he befriends an elderly Jewish woodcarver.
10-2329 *$12.99*

Little House On The Prairie: The Christmas They Never Forgot
Trapped inside on a Christmas Eve blizzard, the Ingalls family looks back on past holidays spent together in this special Yuletide episode.
10-2330 *$12.99*

Little House On The Prairie: Survival
Trapped in an abandoned cabin, the Ingalls try to survive a blizzard with the help of a silent Sioux Indian.
10-2346 *$12.99*

Little House On The Prairie: The Collection
Johnny Cash guest stars as a slick con artist who, disguised as a priest, attempts to swindle the denizens of Walnut Grove.
10-2435 *$12.99*

Little House On The Prairie: Injun Kid
The subjects of prejudice and the healing power of love play important parts in this tale of a young Indian boy who is helped by the Ingalls family when he's mistreated by the residents of Walnut Grove and his own grandfather.
10-2538 *$12.99*

Little House On The Prairie: There's No Place Like Home
A sensitive two-part episode that finds the Ingalls moving away from Walnut Grove but finding there's no place like home when they discover their new town is ruled by a corrupt official. Ray Bolger guest stars. 114 min.
10-2540 *$19.99*

Little House On The Prairie: A Matter Of Faith/The Gift
In "Faith," Caroline Ingalls (Karen Grassle) seeks comfort in the Bible after a minor leg scratch turns into a major infection. And in "Gift," Laura (Melissa Gilbert) and Mary (Melissa Sue Anderson) concoct a plot to raise money to buy a new Bible for Reverend Alden's birthday. 90 min.
10-2542 *$12.99*

Little House On The Prairie: Aftermath
Outlaw siblings Frank and Jesse James pose as businessmen when they land in Walnut Grove and hire Mary Ingalls to help them. When bounty hunters target the brothers, they take Mary as a hostage.
10-2543 *$12.99*

Little House On The Prairie: A Harvest Of Friends
When Pa Ingalls is injured during a farming accident, he stands to lose everything he has. Thankfully, his friends and family help him overcome his injury in this touching episode.
10-2579 *$12.99*

Little House On The Prairie: Most-Loved Episodes
Along with the two-part "Premiere" episode and "Survival," this special compilation also includes "Wedding," which details the marriage of Mary and Adam, and "A Most Precious Gift," in which Charles must serve as a midwife when Caroline is ready to give birth.
10-2723 *$14.99*

Little House On The Prairie: Laura Ingalls Wilder
It's the social event of the year in Walnut Grove when Laura Ingalls and Almanzo Wilder tie the knot in this memorable special episode. 90 min.
10-2724 *$12.99*

Little House On The Prairie: Two-Pack 1
"Survival" and "The Craftsman" are also available in this special two-tape set.
10-2743 *$24.99*

Little House On The Prairie: Two-Pack 2
Includes the episodes "Bunny," in which Laura tries to save her horse after Nellie is paralyzed riding her; "At the End of the Rainbow," which follows what happens after Laura thinks she finds gold in a stream; and "I'll Be Waving as You Drive Away," a two-parter dealing with Mary's blindness and meeting and falling in love with Adam, her new teacher.
10-2807 *$14.99*

Little House On The Prairie: Premiere Movie
The two-part premiere episode follows the Ingalls family as they leave Kansas to build a new life near the frontier town of Walnut Grove, Minnesota. 120 min.
19-1369 *$12.99*

Father Murphy
From creator/producer Michael Landon came this 1981-84 "Little House on the Prairie" spin-off featuring Merlin Olsen as a frontiersman who poses as a priest in order to set up and run an orphanage in the Dakota Territory in the 1870s. Katherine Cannon co-stars as schoolteacher Mae Woodward. Each tape runs about 50 min.

Father Murphy: In God's Arms
10-2397 *$12.99*

Father Murphy: The Dream Day
10-2683 *$12.99*

Father Murphy: The Ghost Of Gold Hills
10-2684 *$12.99*

TV Nation
Michael Moore, creator of the acclaimed documentary "Roger & Me," was the producer and host of this offbeat newsmagazine which ran on NBC and Fox in 1994-1995. Moore's relentless, sarcastic style and correspondent work from Janeane Garofalo, Louis Theroux, Merrill Markoe, Steven Wright and Karen Duffy made this a winner. Each two-episode volume includes one never-aired segment and runs about 120 min.

TV Nation, Vol. 1
Includes the Premiere Episode (with "Free Trade in Mexico," "Taxi," "Love Canal" and "Looking for Missiles") and the Year-End Special (with "Corp-Aid," "White House Security Guard," "Predictions for the New Year" and "Meet the Republicans"), plus "Condoms."
02-3119 *$14.99*

TV Nation, Vol. 2
Includes the Second-Season Premiere (with "Bruno for President," "Slaves," "Beach Party" and "Crackers the Corporate Crime-Fighting Chicken") and the "Love Night" Episode (with "Michigan Militia," "America's Most Wanted," "Aquariums of the Damned" and "KGB III"), plus "Extra Credit."
02-3120 *$14.99*

The Awful Truth: The Complete First Season: Boxed Set (1999)
All 12 premiere-season episodes of Michael Moore's acclaimed investigative cable TV series are featured in a three-tape set. Join the ever-jovial champion of the people as he drives a pink "Sodomobile" with gays around the country, stages a true Puritan witch hunt for Kenneth Starr, gets banned from Rockefeller Center, rescues Crackers the Corporate Crime-Fighting Chicken from a Disney World jail and lots more. 300 min. total.
53-6942 *$39.99*

The Adventures Of Robin Hood
The legendary outlaw hero of Sherwood Forest and his Merry Men foiled the Sheriff of Nottingham's schemes in this fondly remembered series that ran on CBS from 1955 to 1958. Richard Greene, Alexander Gauge, Bernadette O'Farrell star; filmed on location in England. Each tape features two episodes and runs about 52 min. There are 12 volumes available, including:

The Adventures Of Robin Hood, Vol. 1
Includes "Children of the Greenwood" and "The Miser."
10-1186 Was $19.99 *$14.99*

The Adventures Of Robin Hood, Vol. 2
Includes "The Thorkhil Ghost" and "Quickness of the Hand."
10-1187 Was $19.99 *$14.99*

The Adventures Of Robin Hood, Vol. 3
Includes "A Year and a Day" and "Secret Mission."
10-1188 Was $19.99 *$14.99*

The Adventures Of Robin Hood, Vol. 4
Includes "The Youthful Menace" and "The Prisoner."
10-1189 Was $19.99 *$14.99*

The Adventures Of Robin Hood, Vol. 5
Includes "The Highlander" and "Isabella."
10-8116 Was $19.99 *$14.99*

The Adventures Of Robin Hood, Vol. 6
Includes "The May Queen" and "Goodbye Little John."
10-8117 Was $19.99 *$14.99*

The Adventures Of Robin Hood, Vol. 7
Includes "An Apple for the Archer" and "The Youngest Outlaw."
10-8118 Was $19.99 *$14.99*

The Adventures Of Robin Hood, Vol. 8
Includes "Tables Turned" and "The Bandit of Brittany."
10-8119 Was $19.99 *$14.99*

The Adventures Of Robin Hood, Vol. 9
Includes "The Dream" and "The Traitor."
10-8120 Was $19.99 *$14.99*

The Adventures Of Robin Hood, Vol. 10
Includes "Roman Gold" and "A Village Wooing."
10-8121 Was $19.99 *$14.99*

The Adventures Of Robin Hood: The Coming Of Robin Hood (1955)
Richard Greene stars in "The Coming of Robin Hood," the debut episode of the TV adventure series as Sir Robin of Locksley, who, with his trusted Merry Men by his side, battles the evil Prince John in order to restore the throne of England to King Richard the Lionhearted. With Alan Wheatley, Leo McKern, Gerard Heinz and Alfie Bass. 25 min.
08-8089 Was $19.99 *$14.99*

Robin Hood, No. 1
Includes "Tables Turned" and "Elixir of Youth."
08-1608 *$14.99*

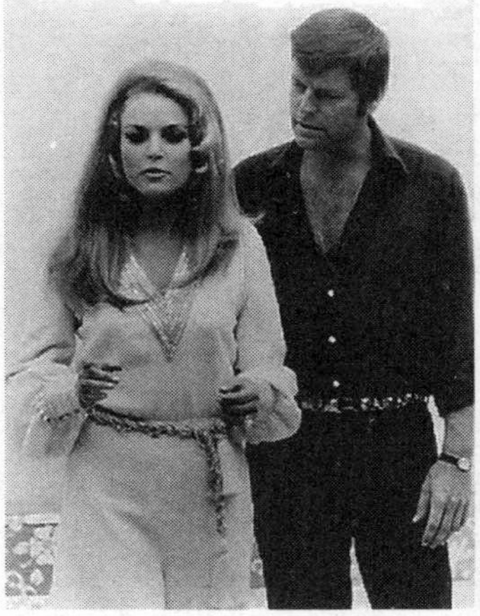

It Takes A Thief: Magnificent Thief (1967)
The feature-length pilot to the hit 1968-1970 suspense series stars Robert Wagner as debonair cat burglar Alexander Mundy, who is recruited while in prison by a secret government intelligence agency to use his special skills as a "thief" for Uncle Sam. Senta Berger co-stars.
07-2572 *$14.99*

The Best Of The Two Ronnies
British comedy fans have known for years that two Ronnies are funnier than one. Join Ronnie Barker and Ronnie Corbett for hilarious "news broadcasts," monologues and musical sketches. 45 min.
04-1031 Was $29.99 *□$14.99*

Two Ronnies: Collector's Set
Ronnie Barker and Ronnie Corbett, one of England's most popular comedy teams, are masters at music, spoofing current events and movies, and sketch humor, and this two-tape set showcases them at their funniest. Included are "In a Packed Programme Tonight...The Best of the Two Ronnies" and "By the Sea/The Picnic." 139 min. total.
53-9776 *$34.99*

Porridge
Ronnie Barker, one of "The Two Ronnies," stars in this wacky farce. He plays Norman Stanley Fletcher, a career criminal, who looks at arrest and spending time behind bars as simply an occupational hazard. Episodes include "Prisoner and Escort," "Just Desserts" and "Desperate Hours." 102 min.
53-9636 *$19.99*

China Beach (1988)
The feature-length pilot to the Emmy Award-winning show about a group of nurses' experiences in Vietnam. Drama and comedy mix in this true-to-life tale that introduces Dana Delany, Nan Woods, Marg Helgenberger and Chloe Webb as the women in fatigues. 95 min.
19-1796 *□$19.99*

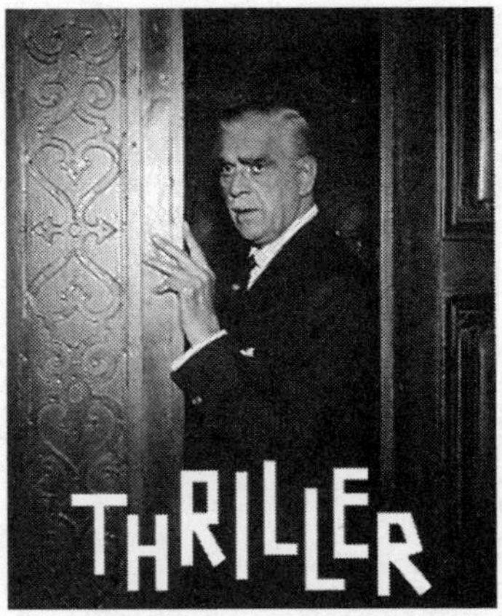

Thriller
Elements of horror, mystery and the supernatural were combined in this creepy series, which ran from 1960 to 1962 and was hosted by Boris Karloff. Focusing on ordinary people caught in extraordinary—and often frightening—situations, the show featured fine, young actors, top genre writers and notable directors like Arthur Hiller, Ida Lupino and Mitchell Leissen. Each program runs about 50 min.

Thriller: Masquerade
A young couple on their honeymoon encounters vampires in a spooky old house. Elizabeth Montgomery, Tom Poston and John Carradine star.
07-2140 *□$12.99*

Thriller: The Grim Reaper
William Shatner, Natalie Schafer and Elizabeth Allen star in this eerie tale about the mysterious deaths that befall the owners of a painting of the Grim Reaper.
07-2141 *□$12.99*

Thriller: The Prediction
Host Boris Karloff appears in this show about a mentalist who warns his assistant's fiancée to cancel her trip in order to avoid a tragedy. Alex Davion and Audrey Dalton also star.
07-2142 *□$12.99*

Thriller: Terror In Teakwood
In order to play his late rival's famous composition, a pianist robs the man's grave and steals his hands. Guy Rolfe and Hazel Court star.
07-2143 *□$12.99*

Thriller: The Premature Burial
After a man falls into a trance-like state, he's buried alive, while his wife and her lover plan to make sure he remains dead. Sidney Blackmer, Patricia Medina and Boris Karloff star in this adaptation of the Poe classic.
07-2162 *$12.99*

Thriller: The Incredible Doctor Markesan
One of the most frightening episodes in the series involves a doctor who returns from the dead holding the key to rejuvenating the deceased. When his nephew and his wife stay at his mansion, they're in for some shocks. Boris Karloff, Dick York and Carolyn Kearney star.
07-2163 *$12.99*

Thriller: Rose's Last Summer
Mary Astor stars in this creepy installment about a woman who poses as a dead movie queen so that the actress's son can inherit her estate.
10-8164 Was $19.99 *$14.99*

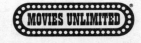

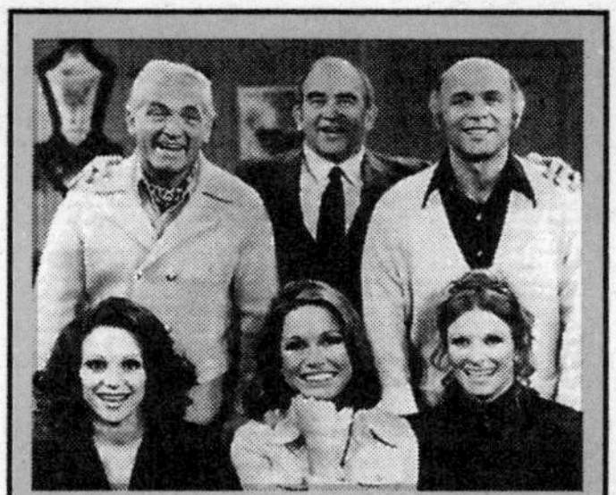

The Mary Tyler Moore Show

The Very Best Of The Mary Tyler Moore Show: Boxed Set
One of the best-loved and most acclaimed TV comedies of all time centered around the staff of WJM-TV news in Minneapolis and, along with Moore as associate producer Mary Richards, featured a superb cast that included Ed Asner, Valerie Harper, Ted Knight, Cloris Leachman, Gavin MacLeod and Betty White. Each tape in this seven-volume set features two episodes from the show's seven seasons, including "Love Is All Around," "Put on a Happy Face," "The Lars Affair," "Chuckles Bites the Dust," "Lou Dates Mary" and "The Last Show." 350 min. total.
53-8963 Was $99.99 *$69.99*

The Very Best Of The Mary Tyler Moore Show: Party Girl
There's nobody who can throw a party—so badly—as Mary Richards. With this two-tape boxed set you'll see four classic episodes that show how Mary's attempts at home entertaining invariably turned into comical disasters. Included are "My Brother's Keeper," "The Dinner Party," "Mary's Aunt" and "Mary Midwife." 100 min. total.
53-9142 *$19.99*

The Very Best Of The Mary Tyler Moore Show: Mary And Rhoda: The Very Best Of Friends
Celebrate the friendship of Mary Richards and Rhoda Morgenstern with this two-tape set featuring five of the neighbors' funniest adventures: "Love Is All Around," "...Is a Friend in Need," "Some of My Best Friends Are Rhoda," "Rhoda Morgenstern: Minneapolis to New York" and "Best of Enemies." 125 min. total.
53-9267 *$19.99*

The Very Best Of Rhoda: Boxed Set
Mary Richards' Bronx-born gal pal, Rhoda Morgenstern (Valerie Harper), returned to New York in this 1974-78 spin-off that also starred Julie Kavner as Rhoda's younger sister, Brenda; Nancy Walker as their mother; and David Groh as Rhoda's beau, Joe. This four-tape set features the best episodes from each season, including the two-part "Rhoda's Wedding," "Friends and Mothers," "The Separation," "An Elephant Never Forgets," "Happy Anniversary," "Martin Doesn't Live Here Anymore" and more. 225 min. total.
53-9486 *$39.99*

VR.5
A cult favorite during its brief 1995 Fox run, this cyber-suspense series starred Lori Singer as Sydney Bloom, a computer whiz haunted by the mysterious accident that killed her father and sister. After using her expertise to enter a "virtual reality" universe where her actions can affect the real world, a clandestine group known as The Committee enlists Singer's help for secret missions. But are they linked to her family's accident? Michael Easton, David McCallum also star. Except where noted, each tape features two episodes and runs about 90 min.

VR.5, Vol. 1
Includes the pilot episode. 45 min.
15-5481 *$14.99*

VR.5, Vol. 2
Includes "Sisters" and "Dr. Strangechild."
15-5482 *$14.99*

VR.5, Vol. 3
Includes "Love and Death" and "Escape."
15-5483 *$14.99*

VR.5, Vol. 4
Includes "Escape" and "Facing the Fire."
15-5499 *$14.99*

VR.5, Vol. 5
Includes "Simon's Choice" and "Send Me an Angel."
15-5500 *$14.99*

VR.5, Vol. 6
Includes "Control Freak" and "Many Faces of Alex."
15-5546 *$14.99*

VR.5, Vol. 7
Includes "Parallel Lives" and "Reunion."
15-5547 *$14.99*

Ivanhoe
Roger Moore is Sir Walter Scott's Saxon knight in this costume adventure from 1957 and set in England during the 12th century. Robert Brown plays his sidekick, a monk, and Bruce Seton is King Richard. Each program contains two episodes and runs about 50 min. There are six volumes available, including:

Ivanhoe, Vol. 1
Includes "Freeing the Serfs" and "Face to Face."
10-9066 Was $19.99 *$14.99*

Ivanhoe, Vol. 2
"Murder at the Inn" and "Treasures from Cathay" are featured.
10-9067 Was $19.99 *$14.99*

Ivanhoe, Vol. 3
Includes "Brothers in Arms" and "Double Edged Sword."
10-9068 Was $19.99 *$14.99*

Lassie: Inheritance/Lassie's Pups
In "Inheritance," the show's premiere episode, Jeff tries to persuade Lassie that she belongs on the Miller farm after inheriting her from a neighbor. And in "Lassie's Pups," the mother-to-be may give birth without the help of a vet thanks to a storm.
72-3002 *$14.99*

Lassie: The Lion/The Journey
In "The Lion," Jeff and pal Porky encounter an escaped circus lion on the farm, but nobody will believe them! Then, Lassie and Timmy are "up, up and away" in a runaway balloon in "The Journey," the first of a four-episode tale that became the 1963 film "Lassie's Great Adventure."
72-3003 *$14.99*

Lassie: The Runaway/Transition
In "The Runaway," Jeff finds a young orphan boy named Timmy hiding in the barn. Next, Gramps' death forces the Millers to sell the farm, but Timmy is taken in by new owners Ruth and Paul Martin in "Transition."
72-3004 *$14.99*

Lassie: Watch Dog/The Camera
Lassie is blamed for a mess at a neighbor's house that was actually done by a chimp in "The Watch Dog." And in "The Camera," Timmy's camera captures a surprise.
72-3005 *$14.99*

Lassie: The Mascot/The Space Traveller
When Lassie is replaced as "The Mascot" for Timmy's team, the youngster is upset; Roy Campanella guest stars. Also, Timmy and friend Donny come upon an experimental rocket with a tiny occupant in "The Space Traveller."
72-3006 *$14.99*

Lassie: Lassie And The Eagle/Lassie And The Tiger
In "Lassie and the Eagle," the popular collie gets help from an eagle when he faces a coyote. And Timmy discovers that he and Lassie are being stalked by a tiger in "Lassie and the Tiger."
72-3007 *$14.99*

Lassie: The Odyssey, Parts 1, 2 And 3
Lassie is accidentally stuck in a van and Timmy must find his missing pet in this classic three-part episode.
72-3008 *$14.99*

Lassie: The Treasure, Pts. 1 And 2
In this two-part adventure, Tim and Cully (Andy Clyde) face trouble when they try to find out the contents of a pouch tied to the leg of a deceased explorer's pet eagle.
72-3009 *$14.99*

Lassie: Lassie's Gift Of Love, Parts 1 And 2
In this two-part adventure, Timmy and an elderly toy mender feed woodland animals as part of a Christmas project. But when wolves disrupt the project, Lassie faces danger.
72-3010 *$14.99*

Lassie: The Christmas Story/Yochim's Christmas
Timmy becomes friends with a boy who is on the run with his parents from the authorities in "The Christmas Story." Then, Timmy and friend Billy Joe rescue a man Billy Joe believes is Santa Claus in "Yochim's Christmas."
72-3011 *$14.99*

The Lassie Collection
This special 10-tape boxed set includes "Christmas Story/Yochim's Christmas," "The Inheritance/Lassie's Pups," "Lassie and the Eagle/Lassie and the Tiger," "Lassie's Gift of Love," "The Lion/The Journey," "The Mascot/The Space Traveller," "The Odyssey," "The Treasure" and "Watch Dog/The Camera."
72-3001 Save $50.00! *$99.99*

Lassie: The Treehouse/The Trial
Here are two episodes of the original "Lassie" TV series. Jeff Miller suspects Pokey, the dog owned by his pal Porky Brockway, is responsible for destroying "The Treehouse" Gramps built for him, but Lassie finds the real culprits. And in "The Trial," Lassie is accused of attacking a boy she tries to stop from abusing a horse. Tommy Rettig, Jan Clayton and George Cleveland star. 52 min.
10-2797 *$14.99*

The Gabby Hayes Show (1956)
Grizzled sidekick Gabby Hayes hosted this western series on ABC in which he sat around the campfire, whittled, and introduced stories culled from "B" movies featuring the big screen's top cowboys. Each tape runs about 60 min. There are 12 volumes available, including:

The Gabby Hayes Show, Vol. 1
With guest stars Lash LaRue, Fuzzy St. John and Buster Crabbe.
10-8469 Was $19.99 *$14.99*

The Gabby Hayes Show, Vol. 2
Guest stars include Kermit Maynard, Sid Saylor and Lash LaRue.
10-8470 Was $19.99 *$14.99*

The Gabby Hayes Show, Vol. 3
Features guest stars Lash LaRue and Eddie Dean.
10-8471 Was $19.99 *$14.99*

Hudson's Bay
This 1959 syndicated adventure series starred Barry Nelson as a fur trapper in Hudson's Bay, Canada in the 1800s. Each tape features two episodes and runs about 50 min. There are ten volumes available, including:

Hudson's Bay, Vol. 1
Includes "Blue-Eyed Squad" and "The Duel."
10-9888 *$14.99*

Hudson's Bay, Vol. 2
Includes "Battle of the Mississippi" and "The Watch."
10-9889 *$14.99*

Hudson's Bay, Vol. 3
Includes "Bosom Buddies" and "The Law."
10-9890 *$14.99*

Hudson's Bay, Vol. 4
Includes "Martinet" and "The Crees."
10-9891 *$14.99*

Saturday Night Live: The Best Of Chris Farley
The "heavyweight" comic who won fame with such "SNL" characters as motivational speaker Matt Foley, a would-be Chippendales dancer, and the hapless host of "The Chris Farley Show" shines in this collection of his funniest turns.
68-1915 *$14.99*

Saturday Night Live: The Best Of Phil Hartman
"SNL's" man of a thousand voices lent his unique abilities to such personae as the Anal Retentive Chef, Unfrozen Caveman Lawyer, Frankenstein and presidents Reagan and Clinton. Now you can see the funniest moments with Phil.
68-1916 *$14.99*

Saturday Night Live: The Best Of '96-'97
The 22nd season of "SNL" saw a host of new faces join the cast, including Will Ferrell, Darrell Hammond, Cheri Oteri and Molly Shannon, and the creation of such memorable characters as Mary Katherine Gallagher, the Spartan cheerleaders and Goat-Boy. Relive these and other moments in this laugh-packed compilation; with appearances by Pamela Anderson, Alec Baldwin, Tom Hanks and others. 92 min.
68-1927 *$14.99*

Saturday Night Live: Bad Boys Of SNL
Their outrageous antics and wise-guy tricks made them stars of late-night TV. Now the funniest bits featuring Chris Rock ("The Dark Side with Nat X"), Adam Sandler ("Operaman"), Rob Schneider ("The Richmeister") and David Spade ("Spade in America") have been collected in one collection. 78 min.
68-1928 *$14.99*

Saturday Night Live: The Best Of Eddie Murphy
O-tay! This salute to one of "SNL's" greatest stars spotlights Eddie doing his favorite characters, including Mr. Robinson, Dion Dion, Buckwheat, Velvet Jones and Gumby. Also featured are guests Ron Howard, Edwin Newman, Stevie Wonder and others. 88 min.
68-1938 *$14.99*

Saturday Night Live: The Best Of Mike Myers
Before he was Austin Powers, baby, Mike was the man on "Saturday Night Live." Party on with Wayne, Dieter, Linda Richman of "Coffee Talk," Lothar of the Hill People and other memorable characters worth ad-Meyers-ing. 90 min.
68-1939 *$14.99*

Saturday Night Live: Halloween
Here's a "treat" for fans of classic sketch comedy, hosted by none other than Wayne and Garth (Mike Myers and Dana Carvey). See hilarious Halloween-themed skits with your favorite "SNL" players and such guest stars as Pamela Anderson, Neve Campbell, Christian Slater, John Travolta and others. 60 min.
68-1940 *$14.99*

Saturday Night Live: The Best Of Adam Sandler
Before movie audiences knew him from Adam, he was winning late-night TV viewers over with such offbeat characters as Canteen Boy, Opera Man and the taciturn Cajun Man. Now you can catch these and other Sandler skits in this laugh-filled collection that also features such guest stars as Courteney Cox, Shannen Doherty and David Duchovny.
68-1943 *$14.99*

Saturday Night Live: Christmas
'Tis the season to laugh out loud at the most hilarious holiday-themed sketches from "Saturday Night Live." Along with such "SNL" faves as John Belushi, Chevy Chase, Chris Farley, Mike Meyers and Adam Sandler, you'll see Christmas in "Mister Robinson's Neighborhood," Hannukah Harry, "Martha Stewart's Topless Christmas Special" and more.
68-1947 *$14.99*

Saturday Night Live: The Best Of Dana Carvey
"A Dana Carvey 'SNL' retrospective? Well, isn't that special?" Yes, and along with the Church Lady, you'll also see Dana as Wayne's good pal Garth, President Bush, "Pumpin' Up" co-host Franz, and other faves. 89 min.
68-1967 *$14.99*

Saturday Night Live: The Best Of Chris Rock
"Rock on" with the outrageous comedian in this collection of Chris' funniest sketches and characters from his "SNL" tenure, from impersonating Luther Campbell to hosting "The Black Side" as Nat X and "Chillin'" with homeboy Chris Farley. 71 min.
68-1968 *$14.99*

Saturday Night Live: The Best Of Steve Martin
One of the series' most popular guests ever is saluted with a sampler of Steve's funniest "SNL" bits: the "wild and crazy" Festrunk Brothers, King Tut, Theodore of York, "Jeopardy 1999" and more. 73 min.
68-1980 *$14.99*

Saturday Night Live: Game Show Parodies
The answer is "plenty of laughs." The question: "What do you get with this compilation of classic TV quiz show spoofs from 'SNL,' including 'Dysfunctional Family Feud,' 'Quien Es Mas Macho?,' 'Bensonhurst Dating Game' and others"?
68-1981 *$14.99*

Saturday Night Live: The Best Of Clinton & Lewinsky
The scandal that rocked the nation also made everyone laugh when the "SNL" crew got their mitts on it. This collection of unimpeachably funny skits depicting the "Bill and Monica Affair" features Darrell Hammond as the president and Molly Shannon as Monica, plus guest stars Cameron Diaz, Gwyneth Paltrow, and John Goodman as Linda Tripp. 58 min.
68-2018 *$14.99*

Saturday Night Live: The Best Of Politics
The greatest political skits in "SNL" history are offered in this no-holds-barred compilation. See Dana Carvey as Ross Perot, Norm McDonald as Bob Dole, and Phil Hartman as Bill Clinton, plus Chevy Chase, Chris Farley, Dan Aykroyd and many others. 77 min.
68-2019 *$14.99*

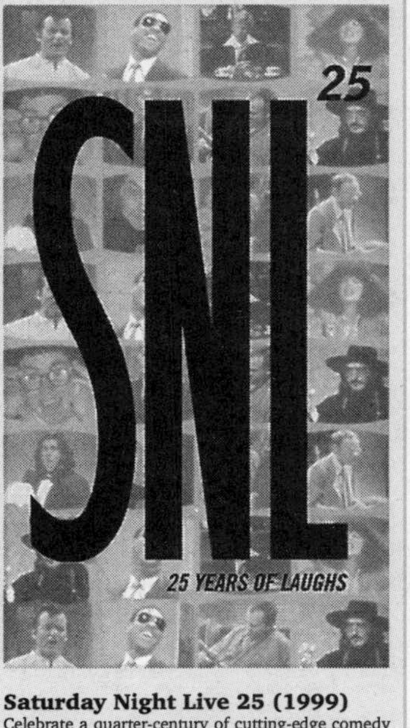

Saturday Night Live 25 (1999)
Celebrate a quarter-century of cutting-edge comedy with this special anniversary salute to "Saturday Night Live." All of the best-loved characters and skits in "SNL" history are featured, with an all-star roster that includes Dan Aykroyd, John Belushi, Dana Carvey, Chevy Chase, Chris Farley, Phil Hartman, Dennis Miller, Eddie Murphy, Gilda Radner, Chris Rock, David Spade and many more. Special video version includes footage not seen on TV. 150 min.
68-1948 *$24.99*

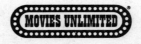

That's My Boy (1981)
The redoubtable Mrs. Slocombe from "Are You Being Served?," Mollie Sugden, stars in this popular Britcom as a housekeeper who's hired by a London physician and his wife, only to discover that her new employer was the child she gave up for adoption years earlier. Christopher Blake, Jennifer Lonsdale also star. Each tape features three episodes and runs about 78 min.

That's My Boy, Vol. 1
Includes "Live as Family," "Settling In" and "Happy Birthdays, Robert."
50-8269 *$14.99*

That's My Boy, Vol. 2
Includes "Is It Catching?," "Driven Apart" and "Think Thin."
50-8270 *$14.99*

That's My Boy, Vol. 3
Includes "Only When It Hurts," "Wakey Wakey" and "A Holiday Romance."
50-8271 *$14.99*

That's My Boy: Boxed Set
Volumes 1-3 are also available in a boxed collector's set.
50-8272 Save $5.00! *$39.99*

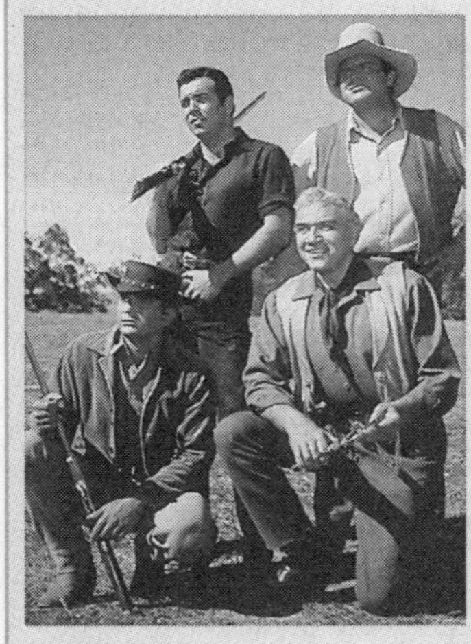

Bonanza
One of the most popular shows of all time, "Bonanza" chronicled the adventures of the close-knit Cartwright clan on their Nevada ranch, the Ponderosa, in the mid-1800s. Lorne Greene played widower patriarch Ben Cartwright, with Michael Landon (Little Joe), Dan Blocker (Hoss) and Pernell Roberts (Adam) as his sons, in this series which ran on NBC from 1959 to 1973. Except where noted, each tape features two episodes and runs about 100 min.

Bonanza, Vol. 1
In "The Gunmen," Hoss and Little Joe get in trouble while on a cattle buying trip in Texas when they are mistaken for outlaws. And in "Blood on the Land," Adam is kidnapped by sheepherders who have invaded the Ponderosa.
10-9494 Was $19.99 *$14.99*

Bonanza, Vol. 2
In "The Avenger," Ben and Adam are helped by a young stranger after they are convicted of murder. Next, the Cartwright family cares for a young boy whose mother has died and whose father is in prison in "Feet of Clay."
10-9495 Was $19.99 *$14.99*

Bonanza, Vol. 3
In "Denver McKee," Little Joe waits for his girlfriend to return from school while a gang of killers are loose. And the Cartwrights seek revenge after Adam is attacked by escaped convicts in "Escape to the Ponderosa."
10-9496 Was $19.99 *$14.99*

Bonanza, Vol. 4
The Cartwrights aren't pleased when a racist politician runs for mayor of Virginia City in "The Fear Merchants," while Ben and two cowhands find themselves shanghaied on a boat destined for Hong Kong in "San Francisco Holiday."
10-9497 Was $19.99 *$14.99*

Bonanza, Vol. 5
In "Bitter Water," a mine located on neighboring land threatens the Ponderosa. And in "The Stranger," Ben Cartwright is arrested thanks to an old grudge.
10-9498 Was $19.99 *$14.99*

Bonanza, Vol. 6
Hoss and Little Joe find a Gypsy girl and bring her back to the Ponderosa in "Dark Star." Then, in "Death at Dawn," the Cartwrights become deputies and set out to stop a gang selling protection to Virginia City merchants.
10-9499 Was $19.99 *$14.99*

Bonanza, Vol. 7
Little Joe faces the family of a man he killed after he set fire to Ponderosa timber in "The Spitfire." And in "The Spanish Grant," con men try to take control of the Ponderosa Ranch.
10-9500 Was $19.99 *$14.99*

Bonanza Boxed Set
Join the Cartwright family for seven classic episodes in this special seven-tape collector's set. Included are "Bitter Water," "Blood on the Land," "Death at Dawn," "Escape to Ponderosa," "Feet of Clay," "San Francisco" and "The Stranger." 420 min. total.
16-5020 *$49.99*

Bonanza: A Rose For Lotta/ The Truckee Strip
"A Rose For Lotta," Bonanza's first episode, features Yvonne DeCarlo as as a woman hired by a mining tycoon to help dupe the Cartwrights out of Ponderosa Timber rights. And the Cartwrights try to settle a feud with the Bishops in "The Truckee Strip," featuring James Coburn.
63-1916 *$14.99*

Bonanza: Mr. Henry P.T. Comstock/The Newcomers
Jack Carson plays "Comstock," who claims ownership in a goldstrike that leads to the creation of Virginia City. Also, Ben discovers that "Newcomers" living on his ranch are miners and has Hoss remove them. The problem is that Hoss falls in love with one of them; Inger Stevens guests.
63-1917 *$14.99*

Bonanza: Death On Sun Mountain/ The Saga Of Annie O'Toole
Ben gets in trouble when he tries to sell miners beef cheaper than the competition in "Sun Mountain," featuring Barry Sullivan. And Ben presdies over a miner's court where there's confusion over a claim in "Annie O'Toole," which guests Ida Lupino and Alan Hale, Jr.
63-1918 *$14.99*

Bonanza: The Paiute War/ The Philip Deidesheimer Story
In "The Paiute War," Jack Warden plays a deceitful trader who blames Adam for abducting two Indian women he himself had kidnapped. And Adam helps an engineer test new, safer underground silver tunnels in "The Philip Deidesheimer Story."
63-1919 *$14.99*

Bonanza: The Julia Bulette Story/The Magnificent Adah
When Little Joe falls in love with "Julia Bullette," an older saloon owner with a bad reputation, Ben shows his displeasure; Jane Greer guest stars. And Ben's sons try to convince their father that his in for trouble when he reacquaints himself with her in "Adah"; Ruth Roman guest stars.
63-1920 *$14.99*

Bonanza: The Hanging Posse/Vendetta
Joe and Adam discover that the fellow members on their "Posse" are out to murder the men they're after; with Arthur Hunicutt. Also, Ben and Hoss get some help from Virginia City's town drunk and a doctor to battle an outlaw gang in "Vendetta."
63-1921 *$14.99*

Bonanza: The Sisters/El Toro Grande
Adam becomes the chief suspect in the murder of Sue Ellen Terry, a woman he was dating, in "The Sisters," which features Fay Spain and Buddy Ebsen. And in "El Toro Grande," Hoss and Joe must deal with all sorts of problems when they head to Monterey to purchase a prize bull; Barbara Luna and Ricardo Cortez guest.
63-1922 *$14.99*

Bonanza: The Outcast/The Last Hunt
The Cartwrights get edgy when a young orphaned woman turns to an outlaw for help in "The Outcast," which features Jack Lord and Susan Oliver. And in "The Last Hunt," Joe and Hoss bring home an Indian woman who is about to have a baby; Chana Eden and Steven Terrell guest star.
63-1923 *$14.99*

Bonanza Gift Pack 1
Four of the classic TV western's best episodes, "Bullet for a Bride," "The Cheating Game," "The Pure Truth" and "The Trap," are assembled in a special collector's edition.
63-1398 *$59.99*

Bonanza Boxed Set
The Cartwright boys are joined by a galaxy of guest stars that includes Leonard Nimoy, Vic Morrow, Dan Duryea, Neville Brand, Sebastian Cabot, Lee Van Cleef and Stella Stevens in this special six-tape collection of episodes from the beloved western series' first two seasons. Included are "The Abduction/The Ape," "The Avenger/Badge Without Honor," "The Fear Merchants/The Last Viking," "The Savage/The Spanish Grant," "The Blood Line/The Spitfire" and "The Trail Gang/Silent Thunder." 12 hrs. total.
83-7001 *$69.99*

Ride The Wind (1966)
Lorne Greene, Michael Landon and Dan Blocker in a special "Bonanza" episode in which the Cartwrights attempt to pow-wow with an Indian tribe on the Ponderosa in order to help the Pony Express. Victor ory, Rod Cameron and DeForest Kelly also star. 120 min.
63-1081 *$14.99*

Ballykissangel
This captivating British comedy-drama has been compared to America's "Northern Exposure" with its quirky characters and unusual situations. Peter Clifford, an English priest, is assigned to the remote Irish town of Ballykissangel, whose colorful residents include glad-handing businessman Brian Quigley; Father MacAnally, the parish priest; enigmatic publican Assumpta Fitzgerald; and others. Stephen Tompkinson, Dervla Kirwin and Niall Toibin star. Each tape features two episodes and runs about 100 min.

Ballykissangel, Vol. 1
In "Trying to Connect You," Father Clifford causes much interest upon his arrival in Ballykissangel, and a young woman causes embarrassment when she visits him in "The Things We Do for Love."
04-3798 Was $19.99 *$14.99*

Ballykissangel, Vol. 2
Reluctant groom Ambrose gets help from Father Clifford while agonizing over his marriage to Niamh, while Quigley awaits his lost love on the mountain, in "Live In My Heart and Pay No Rent." "Fallen Angel" concerns Father Clifford's association with an atheist, while Assumpta helps Clifford pass his driving test and Egan tries to close Angel FM.
04-3799 Was $19.99 *$14.99*

Ballykissangel, Vol. 3
In "The Power and the Glory," a reporter may reveal that Quigley and Assumpta had had an affair during election time. Father Clifford learns he's not as popular as he thought when he's about to be sent back to England in "Missing You Already."
04-3800 Was $19.99 *$14.99*

Northern Exposure
Follow the exploits of Dr. Joel Fleischman (Rob Morrow), his pilot friend Maggie (Janine Turner), former astronaut Maurice (Barry Corbin), disc jockey Chris (John Corbett) and the other citizens of Cicely, Alaska, in the quirky, whimsical series that ran on CBS from 1990 to 1995. Each episode runs about 48 min.

Northern Exposure: The First Episode
The premiere episode finds archetypical New Yorker Joel Fleischman forced to pay off his medical school loan by spending four years in Cicely, Alaska, a hamlet as off the beaten path as its 500 residents.
07-1948 *$14.99*

Northern Exposure: Spring Break
The spring thaw turns the residents of Cicely crazy as libidos rise and inhibitions drop. There may be one way to get things back to "normal": the annual "running of the bulls" escapade. 47 min.
07-1949 *$14.99*

Northern Exposure: Aurora Borealis
In this "Fairytale for Big People," strange visitors arrive in Cicely, including a psychic black man who claims to be Chris' brother and a Bigfoot-like manbrute named Adam who has Dr. Fleischman totally perplexed. 48 min.
07-1950 *$14.99*

Northern Exposure: Cicely
This episode traces the roots of Cicely, from the days when evil Mace Mowbry and his henchman, Kit, ran the town to the arrival of those two "free-thinking" women, Cicley and Roslyn, in search of creating a utopian society. 46 min.
07-1951 *$14.99*

Northern Exposure: Northwest Passages
Maggie celebrates her 30th birthday on an unusual canoe trip where she imagines witnessing a barbecue attended by her deceased ex-lovers. 46 min.
07-1952 *$14.99*

Northern Exposure: Seoul Mates
It's Christmastime as Joel gets his first Christmas tree, Maggie ponders celebrating the holidays alone, and Maurice is visited by a son he never knew he had. 46 min.
07-2027 *$14.99*

Northern Exposure: Thanksgiving
Ah, Thanksgiving in Cicely. That's when the townspeople celebrate the "Day of the Dead" with parades, costumes and throwing tomatoes at Caucasians. 47 min.
07-2028 *$14.99*

Northern Exposure: The Body In Question
The town of Cicely faces a find of global importance when Chris discovers a frozen body, allegedly belonging to an 18th-century Frenchman named "Pierre," and his controversial diary.
07-2071 *$14.99*

Northern Exposure: Burning Down The House
In this hilarious episode, Maggie encounters disaster from all sides when her visiting Mom tells her she's getting a divorce, then accidentally sets her house on fire.
07-2072 *$14.99*

Northern Exposure: Northern Lights
With the sun shining only 45 minutes of every day in wintry Cicely, town's residents try feverishly to get everything done while there's still light.
07-2093 *$14.99*

Northern Exposure: The Big Feast
Maurice plans a party that's the talk of the town, and everyone gets an invitation in the mail...except Joel.
07-2094 *$14.99*

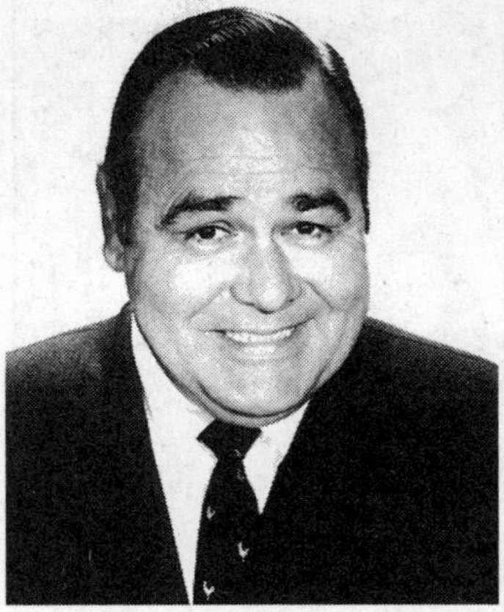

Jonathan Winters: The Lost Episodes
See why Jonathan Winters has remained a favorite entertainer for decades in this collection of the wild man's funniest routines. Included is rare TV footage from the 1950s and 1960s, as he appears with Mickey Rooney, Art Carney, Dinah Shore, Jack Paar, Louie Nye and many others. 66 min.
10-2580 Was $19.99 *$14.99*

Jonathan Winters: The Madman Of Comedy
Jonathan Winters' talent for wacky improvisation, incredible mimicry and tackling off-the-wall characters is evident in this compilation. Witness Winters play bickering Siamese twins with Mickey Rooney, impersonate three witnesses in a murder trial and portray Maudie Frickert. 84 min.
10-2581 *$19.99*

The Unknown Jonathan Winters: On The Loose (1999)
The madcap master of improv humor is saluted with this look at Winters' lengthy career in stand-up comedy, TV and film. Rare clips of Jonathan's early TV appearances and classic characters are featured, along with revealing interviews and a look at his at-times stormy personal life. 60 min.
53-7563 *$19.99*

Tip Toe Through TV (1960)
Satirical revue spoofing TV, hosted by Sid Caesar and featuring Audrey Meadows, Chita Rivera, Charlton Heston and Gene Barry. 60 min.
10-8149 Was $19.99 *$14.99*

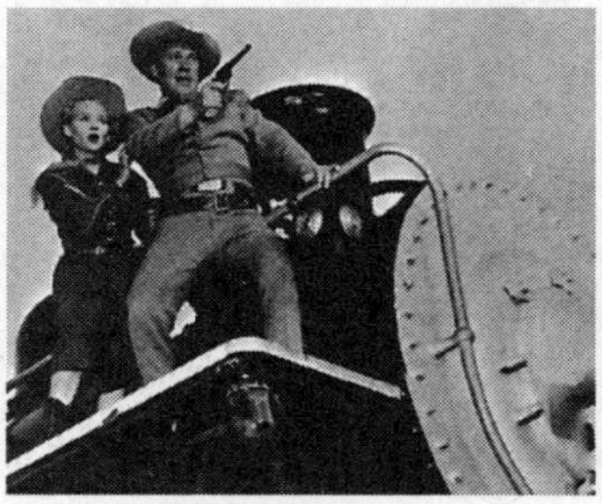

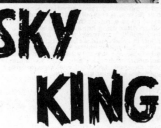

SKY KING

Sky King
Fly into adventure with the Arizona rancher who used his twin-engine Cessna, the Songbird, to track down scurrilous scalawags on the prairie in this mid-'50s kidvid favorite. Kirby Grant stars as Sky King, with Gloria Winters as niece Penny and Ron Hagerthy as nephew Clipper. Each tape features two episodes and runs about 55 min.

Sky King, Vol. 1
Includes "Manhunt" and "Dust of Destruction."
10-7514 Was $19.99 *$14.99*

Sky King, Vol. 2
Includes "One for the Money" and "Speak No Evil."
10-8322 Was $19.99 *$14.99*

Sky King, Vol. 3
Includes "A Dog Named Barney" and "Wild Man."
10-9402 Was $19.99 *$14.99*

Dusty's Trail

"Gilligan's Island" went western in this daffy series from 1973 in which thick-headed scout Dusty (Gilligan himself, Bob Denver) misleads a wagon train on a trip to California. Wagonmaster Forrest Tucker and Denver try to get their "Island"-like charges back on the right track. Except where noted, each tape features two episodes and runs about 50 min. There are eight volumes available, including:

Dusty's Trail, Vol. 1
Includes "The Wizard of Ooze," "My Fair Callahan" and "Duel for Daphne." 75 min.
10-9863 Was $19.99 ***$14.99***

Dusty's Trail, Vol. 2
Includes "Love Means Bananas" and "The Treasure of C. Henry Matres."
10-9864 Was $19.99 ***$14.99***

Dusty's Trail, Vol. 3
Includes "John L. Callahan" and "Half Moon."
10-9865 Was $19.99 ***$14.99***

Dusty's Trail, Vol. 4
Includes "Witch's Trail" and "Then There Were Seven."
10-9866 Was $19.99 ***$14.99***

Brother Cadfael: Complete Set
This boxed collector's set features "One Corpse Too Many," "The Sanctuary Sparrow," "The Leper of St. Giles" and "Monk's Hood." NOTE: Individual volumes available at $19.99
50-2713 ***$59.99***

Brother Cadfael II: Complete Set
Join Brother Cadfael in "The Virgin in the Ice," "St. Peter's Fair" and "The Devil's Novice," all available in one deluxe boxed set. NOTE: Individual volumes available at $19.99.
50-5189 ***$39.99***

Brother Cadfael III: Complete Set
The good brother solves the mysteries of "The Raven in the Foregate," "A Morbid Taste for Bones" and "The Rose Rent" in this boxed collector's set. NOTE: Individual volumes available at $19.99.
50-5602 ***$39.99***

Brother Cadfael IV: Complete Set
The medieval monk and part-time sleuth returns in "The Pilgrim of Hate," "The Potter's Field" and "The Holy Thief," all in a boxed collector's set. NOTE: Individual volumes available at $19.99.
50-8110 ***$39.99***

Shotgun Slade

Played by Scott Brady, the lead character of this syndicated series that ran from 1959 to 1961 was an unusual mix of western hero and slick private detective. Using a two-in-one shotgun, Slade tries to find criminals wanted by saloon owners, banks and Wells Fargo, among others. Featured were a jazz score and unusual casting in supporting parts. Each two-episode tape runs about 50 min. There are seven volumes available, including:

Shotgun Slade, Vol. 1
Includes "The Deadly Key" and "The Smell of Money."
10-9876 Was $19.99 ***$14.99***

Shotgun Slade, Vol. 2
Includes "Donna Juanita" and "The Golden Tunnel."
10-9877 Was $19.99 ***$14.99***

Shotgun Slade, Vol. 3
Includes "A Flower for Jenny" and "The Fabulous Fiddle."
10-9878 Was $19.99 ***$14.99***

Shotgun Slade, Vol. 4
Includes "Crossed Guns" and "Sudden Death."
10-9879 Was $19.99 ***$14.99***

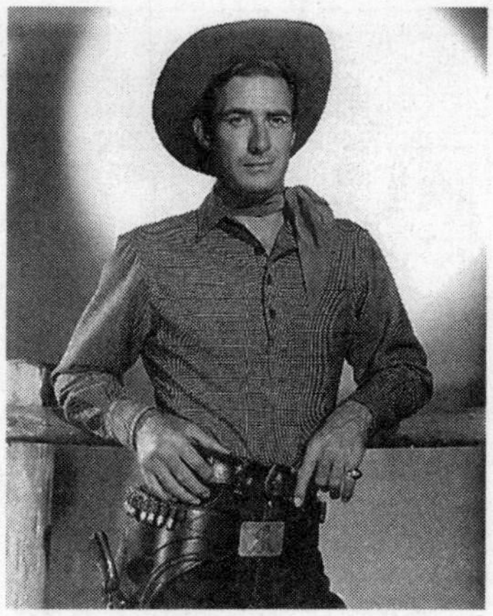

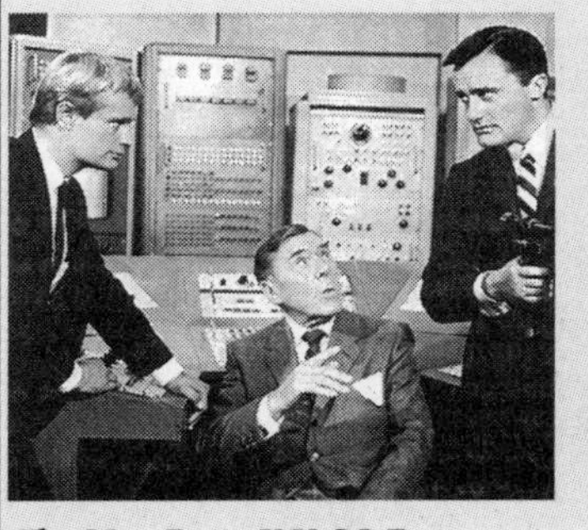

The Man From U.N.C.L.E.

One of the coolest, most sophisticated spy shows ever, "The Man From U.N.C.L.E." starred Robert Vaughn and David McCallum as Napoleon Solo and Illya Kuryakin, two super-agents who use high-tech weaponry to battle the evil forces of THRUSH, an organization out to rule the world. The show, which ran from 1964 to 1968, featured a host of diabolical villains and Leo G. Carroll as Mr. Waverly, the head of U.N.C.L.E.

The Man From U.N.C.L.E., Vol. 1: The Project Strigas Affair/ The Never Never Affair
Solo and Illya confound a Balkan intelligence chief in "Strigas," with future "Star Trek" co-stars William Shatner and Leonard Nimoy. "Never Never" stars Barbara Feldon as a Portuguese translator who mistakenly carries important microfilm and is captured by villainous THRUSH master Cesar Romero. 114 min.
12-2276 ***$14.99***

The Man From U.N.C.L.E., Vol. 2: The Gazebo In The Maze Affair/ The Yukon Affair
George Sanders stars as dapper criminal Squire G. Emory Partridge in two episodes. "Gazebo" finds him trying to lure Solo and Illya into his torture chamber, and the discovery of a powerful magnetic metal in Alaska pits Partridge against U.N.C.L.E. in "Yukon." 114 min.
12-2277 ***$14.99***

The Man From U.N.C.L.E., Vol. 3: The Deadly Toys Affair/ The Minus X Affair
"Deadly Toys" stars Jay North as a boy genius kidnapped by THRUSH whose eccentric aunt (Angela Lansbury), with help from U.N.C.L.E., attempts to rescue him. In "Minus X," Eve Arden is a scientist who invents a serum that heightens the senses, and THRUSH is out to get it. 114 min.
12-2278 ***$14.99***

The Man From U.N.C.L.E., Vol. 4: The Galatea Affair/The Come With Me To The Casbah Affair
In "Galatea," Joan Collins plays dual roles, as a THRUSH money courier and as a nightclub entertainer hired by U.N.C.L.E. to impersonate her. Rare books, illicit love affairs and double crosses play parts in "Casbah," featuring Pat Harrington and Abbe Lane. 114 min.
12-2279 ***$14.99***

The Man From U.N.C.L.E., Vol. 5: The Off-Broadway Affair/The Take Me To Your Leader Affair
In "Off-Broadway," Shari Lewis stars in a tale about a murdered actress and a communication jam-up at U.N.C.L.E. "Leader" finds Solo and Illya uncovering the secrets behind a UFO; Nancy Sinatra guest-stars. 114 min.
12-2280 ***$14.99***

The Man From U.N.C.L.E., Vol. 6: The Concrete Overcoat Affair
In this special two-part episode set in Italy, Solo and Illya try to stop a THRUSH plan to alter the course of the Gulf Stream using heavy water, become involved with a gang of retired gangsters and are threatened by sadistic Strago (Jack Palance) and his assistant (Janet Leigh). 114 min.
12-2281 ***$14.99***

The Man From U.N.C.L.E., Vol. 7: The Five Daughters Affair
An all-star cast highlights this two-part spectacular that hops from locations in Rome, London and the Alps, as the men from U.N.C.L.E. attempt to locate the five daughters of a murdered scientist who each hold a key to his formula for extracting gold from sea water. With Joan Crawford, Herbert Lom, Kim Darby, Jill Ireland and Curt Jurgens. 114 min.
12-2282 ***$14.99***

The Man From U.N.C.L.E., Vol. 8: The Seven Wonders Of The World Affair
The last episode of the hit TV series details the attempts of U.N.C.L.E. agents and others to retrieve a docility gas from a mad general who has kidnapped its inventor and his son. Leslie Nielsen, Tony Bill, Eleanor Parker and Dan O'Herlihy co-star. 120 min.
12-2293 ***$14.99***

The Man From U.N.C.L.E., Vol. 9: The Foxes And Hounds Affair/ The Discotheque Affair
THRUSH agent Vincent Price and a deadly sneeze are the elements of "The Foxes and Hounds Affair," while U.N.C.L.E. battles THRUSH in a far-out "Discotheque"; Ray Danton and Harvey Lembeck co-star. 114 min.
12-2362 ***$14.99***

The Man From U.N.C.L.E., Vol. 10: The Arabian Affair/ The Foreign Legion Affair
THRUSH is developing a vaporizing machine and Illya's out to stop them in "The Arabian Affair," which guest-stars Michael Ansara. And "Foreign Legion" chief Howard Da Silva has a new POW: Illya! 114 min.
12-2363 ***$14.99***

The Man From U.N.C.L.E., Vol. 11: The Hot Number Affair/ The Suburbia Affair
Sonny and Cher guest star in a way-out "Hot Number Affair" involving a dress with a secret code, while Victor Borge invents anti-matter in "Suburbia." 114 min.
12-2364 ***$14.99***

The Man From U.N.C.L.E., Vol. 12: The Prince Of Darkness Affair, Parts 1 And 2
THRUSH is after a powerful ray transmitter and it's up to U.N.C.L.E. to stop them in a thrilling two-part adventure with guest stars Bradford Dillman and Carol Lynley. 114 min.
12-2365 ***$14.99***

The Man From U.N.C.L.E., Vol. 13: The Gurnius Affair/ The Her Majesty's Voice Affair
In "The Gurnius Affair," ex-Nazis (including a dead ringer for Illya) attempt to start a Fourth Reich; Judy Carne and George Macready guest. Next, preppie co-eds turn killers when Brahms' Lullaby is played; with Estelle Winwood. 114 min.
12-2366 ***$14.99***

The Man From U.N.C.L.E., Vol. 14: The King Of Diamonds Affair/ The Moonglow Affair
"Diamonds" are not necessarily Napoleon Solo's best friend as he's about to be blasted from a cannon with help from Ricardo Montalban, while Mary Ann Mobley plays April Dancer in "Moonglow," which became the pilot for the "Girl From U.N.C.L.E." series. 114 min.
12-2367 ***$14.99***

The Man From U.N.C.L.E., Vol. 15: The Bridge Of Lions Affair, Parts 1 And 2
THRUSH is trying to control a rejuvenation formula that uses cats as its key element, and U.N.C.L.E. wants to say "scat" to their "Lions Affair." Guest stars include Vera Miles, Maurice Evans and James Hong. 114 min.
12-2368 ***$14.99***

The Man From U.N.C.L.E., Vol. 16: The "J" For Judas Affair/ The Master's Touch Affair
Tycoon Broderick Crawford becomes the man THRUSH is after, prompting U.N.C.L.E. to get into the action in "Judas." And THRUSH's request for U.N.C.L.E.'s help has Napoleon, Illya and Co. wondering what's really going on in "Master's Touch," featuring Jack Lord. 114 min.
12-2369 ***$14.99***

The Man From U.N.C.L.E., Vol. 17: The Quadripartite Affair/ The Giuoco Piano Affair
A double bill of episodes featuring guest stars Jill Ireland and Anne Francis as rival female adventurers Marion Raven and Gervaise Ravel, who draw Napoleon and Illya into a scheme involving THRUSH's newest weapon: fear gas. 114 min.
12-2531 ***$14.99***

The Man From U.N.C.L.E., Vol. 18: The Green Opal Affair/ The Dove Affair
In Mexico, Solo gets help from a vacationing housewife to stop Carroll O'Connor's brainwashing scheme in "Opal," and then goes up against a rival spy (Ricardo Montalban) in "Dove." 114 min.
12-2532 ***$14.99***

The Man From U.N.C.L.E., Vol. 19: The Brain Killer Affair/ The Bat Cave Affair
Mr. Waverly is the target for Elsa Lanchester's mind-control device in "Brain," while Martin Landau plays Transylvania's own Count Zark, who plots a devious plan in "Bat." 114 min.
12-2533 ***$14.99***

The Man From U.N.C.L.E., Vol. 20: The Ultimate Computer Affair/ The Adriatic Express Affair
THRUSH develops a supercomputer that poses problems for U.N.C.L.E. in "Ultimate," which features Charlie Ruggles and Judy Carne; and in "Adriatic" train passengers Napoleon, Illya and guest star Juliet Mills try to stop THRUSH agent Madame Nemirovitch. 114 min.
12-2534 ***$14.99***

The Man From U.N.C.L.E., Vol. 21: The Very Important Zombie Affair/ The Dippy Blonde Affair
A Caribbean dictator (Claude Akins) uses voodoo to stop his enemies in "Zombie." Next, the "Dippy Blonde" is a murdered THRUSH agent's girlfriend who helps U.N.C.L.E. catch his killer. 114 min.
12-2535 ***$14.99***

The Man From U.N.C.L.E., Vol. 22: The Deadly Goddess Affair/ The Hula Doll Affair
Napoleon and Illya encounter an evil THRUSH agent (Victor Buono), as well as two marriage-seeking women in "Deadly." And "Hula" involves feuding THRUSH agent siblings (Pat Harrington, Jr. and Jan Murray), their evil mother (Patsy Kelly) and explosive dolls. 114 min.
12-2536 ***$14.99***

The Return Of The Man From U.N.C.L.E. (1983)
Robert Vaughn's Napoleon Solo and David McCallum's Ilya Kuryakin return to the spy world with this TV film that finds them trying to thwart THRUSH's plans to detonate a nuclear bomb on a U.S. city unless they receive $350 million. Patrick Macnee, Anthony Zerbe and Gayle Hunnicutt also star. 96 min.
20-5034 ***$24.99***

The Range Rider

Ride alongside the Range Rider (Jock Mahoney) and his trusted sidekick, all-American boy Dick West (Dick Jones), in rootin'-tootin' Western adventure series from the early '50s. Each volume features two episodes and runs about 60 min. There are 13 volumes available, including:

The Range Rider, Vol. 1
Includes "West of Cheyenne" and "Convict at Large."
09-5221 Was $19.99 ***$14.99***

The Range Rider, Vol. 2
Includes "Treasure of Santa Delores" and "Buckskin."
09-5222 Was $19.99 ***$14.99***

The Range Rider, Vol. 3
Includes "Border City Affair" and "Cherokee Roundup."
09-5223 Was $19.99 ***$14.99***

The Range Rider, Vol. 4
Includes "Bullets and Badmen" and "Holy Terror."
09-5224 Was $19.99 ***$14.99***

The Range Rider, Vol. 5
Includes "Indian War Party" and "Crooked Fork."
09-5225 Was $19.99 ***$14.99***

The Range Rider, Vol. 6
Includes "Marshal from Madero" and "Western Edition."
09-5226 Was $19.99 ***$14.99***

The Range Rider, Vol. 7
Includes "The Hideout" and "Shotgun Stage."
09-5227 Was $19.99 ***$14.99***

The Range Rider, Vol. 8
Includes "Blind Trial" and "Outlaw Pistols."
09-5228 Was $19.99 ***$14.99***

The Range Rider, Vol. 9
Includes "Old Timer's Trail" and "Outlaw Territory."
09-5229 Was $19.99 ***$14.99***

The Range Rider, Vol. 10
Includes "Black Terror" and "Saga of Silver Town."
09-5230 Was $19.99 ***$14.99***

The Range Rider, Vol. 11
Includes "Rustler's Range" and "The Chase."
10-9556 Was $19.99 ***$14.99***

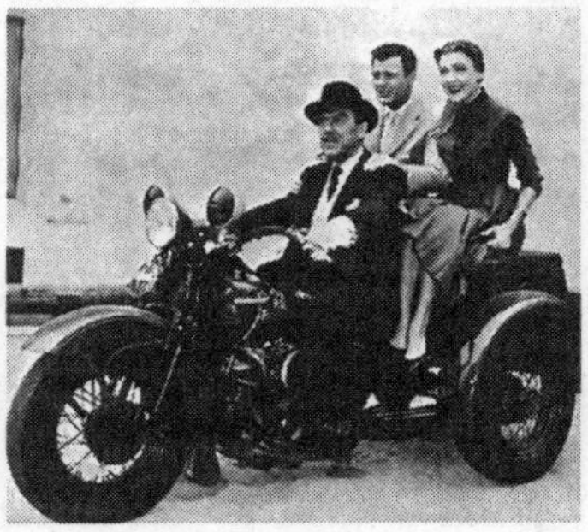

Topper/The Thin Man
Leo G. Carroll is Cosmo Topper, the banker whose funny antics with ghosts Marion (Anne Jeffreys) and George Kerby (Robert Sterling) and their dog, Neil, made this a popular show during its 1953-1956 run on all three networks. Along with "Topper Goes to Hollywood," there's also an episode of the "Thin Man" TV series, with Peter Lawford and Phyllis Kirk. 50 min.
10-9214 Was $19.99 ***$14.99***

Topper: George's Old Flame/ Henrietta Sells The House
There's more spectral shenanigans with the Kerbys and their harried host, Cosmo Topper, in these two adventures from the hit TV series from the mid-'50s. Leo G. Carroll, Robert Sterling and Anne Jeffreys star. 50 min.
10-9401 ***$14.99***

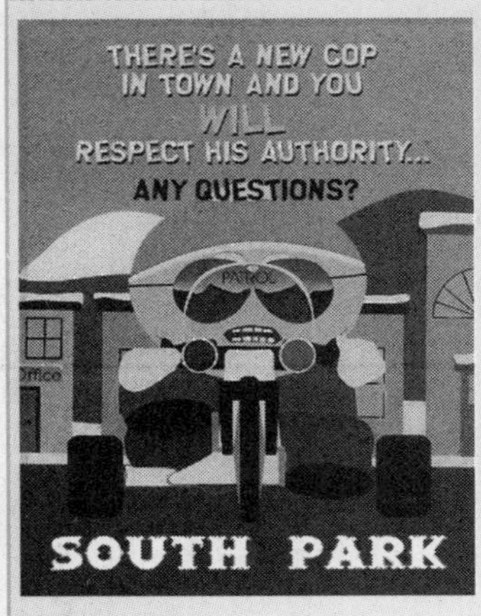

South Park
Kids say the foulest—and funniest—things in this off-the-wall, "adults only" animated cable TV series that quickly became a cult favorite. Join lovestruck Stan, brother-kicking Kyle, "pleasantly plump" Eric Cartman and born-to-die Kenny as they struggle with grade-school life in South Park, Colorado. Except where noted, each tape features two episodes and exclusive interview footage and runs about 55 min.

South Park, Vol. 1: Cartman Gets An Anal Probe/Volcano
Cattle mutilations, the abduction of Kyle's baby brother, flames shooting out of Cartman's...body, and Kenny dying are all part of the bizarre alien plot from the debut episode, "Cartman Gets an Anal Probe." Next, the boys go on a hunting trip that turns dangerous when the local "Volcano" begins acting up.
19-2685 ❑*$14.99*

South Park, Vol. 2: Weight Gain 4000/ Big Gay Al's Big Gay Boat Ride
A planned visit to South Park by Kathie Lee Gifford has the whole town excited, Mr. Garrison buying a gun, and Cartman bulking up for his TV appearance with "Weight Gain 4000." Then, guest star George Clooney(!) supplies the voice of Stan's gay dog, Sparky, who runs away just before the big football game in "Big Gay Al's Big Gay Boat Ride."
19-2686 ❑*$14.99*

South Park, Vol. 3: An Elephant Makes Love To A Pig/Death
A science project contest leads to some fundamental tampering with the laws of nature—and a rampaging clone of Stan—in "An Elephant Makes Love to a Pig." Next, Stan's elderly grandfather wants some help in killing himself, but who will be the Grim Reaper's target when "Death" comes to South Park (three guesses)?
19-2687 ❑*$14.99*

South Park, Vol. 4: Pink Eye/Damien
Kenny's latest death, an accidental transfusion of Worcestershire sauce, Cartman's controversial costume choice and an influx of hungry zombies add up to a memorable South Park Halloween in "Pink Eye." Then, the demonic father of unpopular, new kid "Damien" arrives in town just in time for an apocalyptic showdown between good and evil...live on pay-per-view.
19-2776 ❑*$14.99*

South Park, Vol. 5: Starvin' Marvin'/Mecha-Streisand
It's killer turkeys on the rampage and a Thanksgiving in the African desert for Cartman when the boys adopt "Starvin' Marvin" the Ethiopian. Plus, the discovery of the magical Triangle of Zinthar on an archeological dig lands the town in the evil clutches of Barbra Streisand. Can Robert Smith of The Cure save the day?
19-2777 ❑*$14.99*

South Park, Vol. 6: Mr. Hankey, The Christmas Poo/ Tom's Rhinoplasty
You'll never look at Christmas in the same way again when the South Park folks get a lesson in holiday spirit from Kyle's magical, sewer-dwelling pal, "Mr. Hankey." Then, Mr. Garrison's visit to "Tom's Rhinoplasty" leaves the kids in the hands of beautiful new substitute teacher Ms. Ellen and drives a jealous Wendy to desperate measures.
19-2778 ❑*$14.99*

South Park, Vol. 7: Cartman's Mom Is A Dirty Slut/Cartman's Mom Is Still A Dirty Slut
It's the question on the lips of every South Park resident: who is Eric Cartman's father? The list of suspects includes Mr. Garrison, Chef, Kyle's dad, and John Elway and the 1989 Denver Broncos, but the answer in this special two-part adventure will shock you!
19-2827 ❑*$14.99*

South Park, Vol. 8: Chicken Lover/Ike's Wee Wee
The boys turn detective to help Officer Barbrady overcome his shocking secret and catch the notorious South Park "Chicken Lover." Next, when he learns just what a "bris" is, Kyle seeks help from his pals in saving his little brother "Ike's Wee Wee."
19-2828 ❑*$14.99*

South Park, Vol. 9: Conjoined Fetus Lady/The Mexican Staring Frog Of Southern Sri Lanka
What is the sinister secret lurking inside the school nurse's office, and will it affect South Park's chances of winning the state dodgeball championship? Next, Uncle Jimbo and Ned's cable access hunting show gets a ratings boost when they go on a hunt for "The Mexican Staring Frog of Southern Sri Lanka."
19-2829 ❑*$14.99*

South Park, Vol. 10: Flashbacks/Summer Sucks
Trapped on the school bus in the middle of nowhere, the kids have plenty of time for "Flashbacks" on the many "sticky situations" they've shared. Next, "Summer Sucks," thanks to a fireworks ban that could ruin the Fourth of July.
19-2873 ❑*$14.99*

South Park, Vol. 11: Chef's Salty Chocolate Balls/Chicken Pox
Will "Chef's Salty Chocolate Balls" be the culinary hit of the first annual South Park Film Festival, and why is the Hollywood hoopla endangering the life of Mr. Hankey? Then, the boys decide to get back at their parents for exposing them to Kenny's "Chicken Pox."
19-2874 ❑*$14.99*

South Park, Vol. 12: Roger Ebert Should Lay Off The Fatty Foods/Clubhouses
"Roger Ebert" doesn't actually appear in this episode bearing his name, but you do see the director of the South Park Planetarium's sinister scheme to keep the boys coming back. Meanwhile, will the break-up of Stan's parents affect the race to build competing "Clubhouses"?
19-2875 ❑*$14.99*

South Park: The Chef Experience
When a court case leaves Chef millions of dollars in debt, the boys turn to some of his music buddies—including guest stars Elton John, Meat Loaf, Ozzy Osbourne and more—for a benefit "Chef Aid" concert. This tape also includes the faux backstage program "Chef Aid: Behind the Menu" and Chef's music video for his tasty tune "Chocolate Salty Balls."
19-2969 ❑*$14.99*

Best Of South Park: Chinpoko Mon/ Rainforest Schmainforest
It's the latest TV cartoon/action figure/video game craze to cross the Pacific, but is there a secret Japanese plan for conquest linked to "Chinpoko Mon"? Next, the kids learn a valuable lesson about ecology—and its dangers—when guest star Jennifer Anniston takes them to Central America in "Rainforest Schmainforest," followed by part 2 of the "Goin' Down to South Park" documentary. 85 min.
19-2970 ❑*$14.99*

Christmas In South Park: Mr. Hankey's Christmas Classics/ Merry Christmas Charlie Manson
Join everyone's favorite fecal friend for "Mr. Hankey's Christmas Classics," featuring such beloved tunes as "Merry F***ing Christmas," "Christmas Time in Hell," "Lonely Jew on Christmas" and many more, followed by a holiday trip to Cartman's grandparents that becomes a run from the law in "Merry Christmas Charlie Manson." This tape also features the first part of the BBC "behind-the-scenes" documentary "Goin' Down to South Park." 85 min.
19-2971 ❑*$14.99*

South Park: Terrance & Philip: Not Without My Anus
They're the flatulent Canadian friends whose animated TV show is a favorite of the "South Park" kids, and now Terrance and Philip star in their own "dramatic" special. Can the duo sneak Terrance's kidnapped daughter from Iran and then foil Saddam Hussein's plans to take over Canada? 30 min.
19-2872 ❑*$14.99*

South Park 3-Pack No. 1
Get yourself some Snacky Cakes and Cheesy Poofs with the money you'll save by buying this three-tape collection featuring Volumes 1-3 of "South Park."
19-2698 Save $10.00! *$34.99*

South Park 3-Pack No. 2
There's no Taiko digital sports watch, but this lovely three-tape set does come with Volumes 4-6 of "South Park."
19-2779 Save $5.00! *$39.99*

South Park 3-Pack No. 3
What's cheaper than one of Dr. Mephisto's genetic tests, and a lot more fun? How about this special "South Park" set that features Volumes 7-9?
19-2830 Save $5.00! *$39.99*

South Park 3-Pack No. 4
Stock your clubhouse or planetarium with this three-tape "South Park" collector's set featuring Volumes 10-12.
19-2876 Save $5.00! *$39.99*

Candid Camera
"With a hocus pocus, you're in focus," as TV prankster Allen Funt leads his unsuspecting victims before the lens, pulling elaborate gags in a coffee ship and an auto dealer in this episode from the fondly re membered show. Original "Call for Philip Morris" commercials are also included. 30 min.
10-2134 *$12.99*

Candid Camera Now And Then
Join Allen Funt and Angie Dickinson for this hilarious look at the funniest moments from one of the most beloved TV shows of all time. Watch "people caught in the act of being themselves" and captured on film in hilarious situations orchestrated by Funt and friends. Also featured are guest stars Paul Newman, Telly Savalas, Muhammad Ali and John Huston. 45 min.
65-7025 *$14.99*

Sheriff Of Cochise (U.S. Marshal)
Set in contemporary Arizona, this 1956-1960 western series starred John Bromfield as Frank Morgan, a tough lawman who first patrolled the area of Cochise County, then later the entire state (when the show was retitled "U.S. Marshal"). Morgan's deputies included Rafe Patterson (series creator Stan Jones) and Tom Ferguson (James Griffith). Each tape features two episodes and runs about 50 min.

Sheriff Of Cochise, Vol. 1
After a "Bank Robbery" is pulled off at the state bank, Frank Morgan and his deputies try to find the crooks before they strike again. And in "Lynching Party," a struggle between a young ranch hand and a ranch owner leads to murder and revenge. James Best guest stars.
09-5308 *$14.99*

U.S. Marshal, Vol. 2
In "Ghost Town," two convicts escape a county jail, taking another convict's wife hostage. They travel to an old ghost town, and Marshal Morgan and his compadres go to work. Also, a complex case involves Morgan and Deputy Ferguson in stolen jewels and insurance money in "The Triple Cross."
09-5309 *$14.99*

U.S. Marshal, Vol. 3
In "Grandfather," a journalist gets Marshal Morgan to tell his family's history and recall tales of his lawman grandfather. Then, "The Third Miracle" involves a man whose arrest and conviction is based on an anonymous phone call. Members of his church ask Marshal Morgan for help.
09-5310 *$14.99*

U.S. Marshal, Vol. 4
A forgotten birthday present is somehow connected to a gold bullion theft, and a missing woman holds the key, in "Backfire." Next, the murderer of a man under protective custody hides out in a remote farm in "Kill or Be Killed."
09-5311 *$14.99*

U.S. Marshal, Vol. 5
In "R.I.P.," the wife of an armored car driver appears at a hospital after her husband is shot, but when another "wife" appears later, Marshal Morgan is confounded. And in "The Diner," two criminals escape from a Utah prison and search for an ex-con who owes them cash. Marshal Morgan tries to stop them.
09-5312 *$14.99*

U.S. Marshal, Vol. 6
A drug bust gone wrong and a dead deputy sends Marshal Morgan to Mexico in hopes of catching the culprit in "Stool Pigeon." Then, a soldier goes on a rampage after escaping a guardhouse with another soldier and his girlfriend in "Pursuit." Charles Bronson and Robert Fuller guest star.
09-5313 *$14.99*

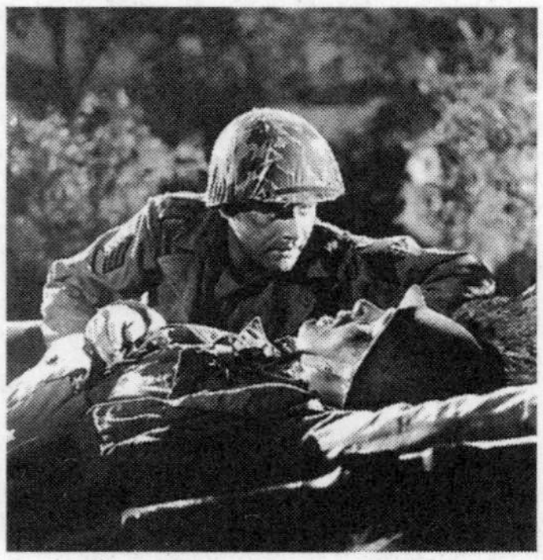

COMBAT!

Combat!: Mail Call
Noted for its realistic look at men at war, this ABC series, which ran from 1962-1967, featured Vic Morrow and Rick Jason as members of a U.S. platoon battling in Europe after D-Day. In this episode, Morrow's Sgt. Saunders discovers bad news about his brother and deals with a malingerer. James Best guests. 50 min.
09-5356 *$14.99*

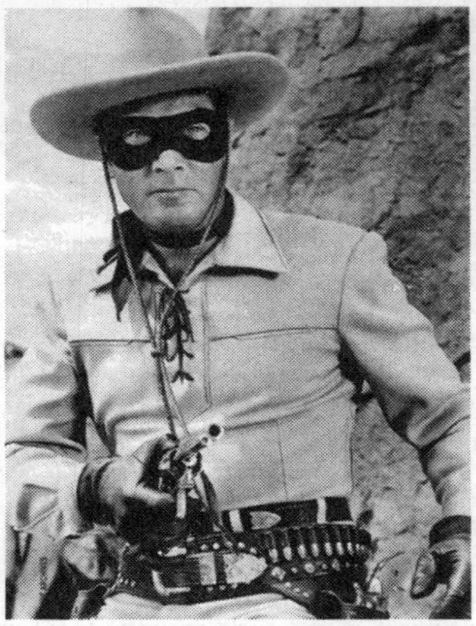

The Lone Ranger
"A fiery horse with the speed of light, a cloud of dust and a hearty 'Hiyo, Silver!'"...Clayton Moore and Jay Silverheels saddle up to bring justice to the Old West in the beloved frontier drama, one of ABC's few hits in the 1950s. Each tape contains two thrill-packed episodes and runs about 55 min.

The Lone Ranger, Vol. 1
Includes the first two episodes of the series, originally broadcast in 1949: "Enter the Lone Ranger" and "Lone Ranger Fights."
09-5191 Was $19.99 *$14.99*

The Lone Ranger, Vol. 2
Includes "The Lone Ranger's Triumph" and "The Legion of Old Timers."
09-5192 Was $19.99 *$14.99*

The Lone Ranger, Vol. 3
Includes "Rustler's Hideout" and "War House."
09-5193 Was $19.99 *$14.99*

The Lone Ranger, Vol. 4
Includes "Pete & Pedro" and "The Renegades."
09-5194 Was $19.99 *$14.99*

The Lone Ranger, Vol. 5
Includes "Tenderfeet" and "High Heels."
09-5195 Was $19.99 *$14.99*

The Lone Ranger, Vol. 6
Includes "Six-Gun's Legacy" and "Return of the Convict."
09-5196 Was $19.99 *$14.99*

The Lone Ranger, Vol. 7
Includes "Finder's Keepers" and "The Masked Rider."
09-5197 Was $19.99 *$14.99*

The Lone Ranger, Vol. 8
Includes "Old Joe's Sister" and "Cannonball McKay."
09-5198 Was $19.99 *$14.99*

The Lone Ranger, Vol. 9
Included are two versions of "A Message from Abe," one in black-and-white and one in color that aired in syndication. Also featured are the original commercials for Tootsie Rolls and Cheerios.
09-5199 Was $19.99 *$14.99*

The Lone Ranger: The Lost Episodes
"Return with us now to those thrilling days of yesteryear," as this nostalgia-filled program traces the screen and TV history of the masked man and his faithful Indian companion. You'll see the Lone Ranger and Tonto's first appearances in '30s serials, rare promo spots and TV clips, scenes from the Ranger's cartoon series, and two uncut TV episodes, complete with commercials. 98 min.
10-2780 *$14.99*

Bramwell
Presented on four tapes, this acclaimed British TV series stars Jemma Redgrave as Dr. Eleanor Bramwell, a determined, young physician battling peers and opponents to make it as a surgeon in England in the 1890s. Clever and compelling, this "Upstairs, Downstairs' with doctors" also stars David Calder, Robert Hardy and Michele Dotrice. 360 min. total.
50-5291 Was $89.99 *$39.99*

Bramwell Series III
The struggles of Victorian London medico Eleanor Bramwell (Jemma Redgrave) continue in four episodes from the transatlantic hit drama. Trying to keep her charity clinic open, Dr. Bramwell copes with such varied (and timeless) problems as wife abuse and child prostitution, as well as a mysterious epidemic affecting the city's poor. David Calder, Ruth Sheen also star. 240 min. on two tapes.
08-8633 ❑*$29.99*

The Visitor: The Guest (1952)
Episode from the early drama anthology series also known as "The Doctor," with a young Charles Bronson (also known as Charles Buchinski) as a fugitive thief who dodges the cops by telling an old woman he's a Korean War buddy of her late son. Beulah Bondi, Joan Camden co-star. 26 min.
09-2093 Was $19.99 *$14.99*

DARK SHADOWS

Dark Shadows
The '60s supernatural soap opera that brought vampires, witches and ghosts to daytime TV is now on home video, with stars Joan Bennett, Grayson Hall, David Selby, Lara Parker, and Jonathan Frid as Barnabas Collins. Each tape in the four-cassette collector's sets contains five episodes and runs about 105 min. NOTE: Individual volumes are available at $19.99 each.

Dark Shadows: Vols. 1-4
Collectors' Set
50-6428 $79.99

Dark Shadows: Vols. 5-8
Collectors' Set
50-6458 $79.99

Dark Shadows: Vols. 9-12
Collectors' Set
50-6466 $79.99

Dark Shadows: Vols. 13-16
Collectors' Set
50-6471 $79.99

Dark Shadows: Vols. 17-20
Collectors' Set
50-6525 $79.99

Dark Shadows: Vols. 21-24
Collectors' Set
50-6533 $79.99

Dark Shadows: Vols. 25-28
Collectors' Set
50-6538 $79.99

Dark Shadows: Vols. 29-32
Collectors' Set
50-6547 $79.99

Dark Shadows: Vols. 33-36
Collectors' Set
50-6552 $79.99

Dark Shadows: Vols. 37-40
Collectors' Set
50-6559 $79.99

Dark Shadows: Vols. 41-44
Collectors' Set
50-6564 $79.99

Dark Shadows: Vols. 45-48
Collectors' Set
50-6569 $79.99

Dark Shadows: Vols. 49-52
Collectors' Set
50-6574 $79.99

Dark Shadows: Vols. 53-56
Collectors' Set
50-6694 $79.99

Dark Shadows: Vols. 57-60
Collectors' Set
50-6700 $79.99

Dark Shadows: Vols. 61-64
Collectors' Set
50-6719 $79.99

Dark Shadows: Vols. 65-68
Collectors' Set
50-6739 $79.99

Dark Shadows: Vols. 69-72
Collectors' Set
50-6744 $79.99

Dark Shadows: Vols. 73-76
Collectors' Set
50-6764 $79.99

Dark Shadows: Vols. 77-80
Collectors' Set
50-6769 $79.99

Dark Shadows: Vols. 81-84
Collectors' Set
50-6787 $79.99

Dark Shadows: Vols. 85-88
Collectors' Set
50-6806 $79.99

Dark Shadows: Vols. 89-92
Collectors' Set
50-6812 $79.99

Dark Shadows: Vols. 93-96
Collectors' Set
50-6817 $79.99

Dark Shadows: Vols. 97-100
Collectors' Set
50-6822 $79.99

Dark Shadows: Vols. 101-104
Collectors' Set
50-6856 $79.99

Dark Shadows: Vols. 105-108
Collector's Set
50-6866 $79.99

Dark Shadows: Vols. 109-112
Collectors' Set
50-6871 $79.99

Dark Shadows: Vols. 113-116
Collectors' Set
50-6884 $79.99

Dark Shadows: Vols. 117-120
Collectors' Set
50-6931 $79.99

Dark Shadows: Vols. 121-124
Collectors' Set
50-6936 $79.99

Dark Shadows: Vols. 125-128
Collectors' Set
50-6946 $79.99

Dark Shadows: Vols. 129-132
Collectors' Set
50-6958 $79.99

Dark Shadows: Vols. 133-136
Collectors' Set
50-6966 $79.99

Dark Shadows: Vols. 137-140
Collectors' Set
50-6971 $79.99

Dark Shadows: Vols. 141-144
Collectors' Set
50-6985 $79.99

Dark Shadows: Vols. 145-148
Collectors' Set
50-6990 $79.99

Dark Shadows: Vols. 149-152
Collectors' Set
50-7058 $79.99

Dark Shadows: Vols. 153-156
Collectors' Set
50-7067 $79.99

Dark Shadows: Vols. 157-160
Collectors' Set
50-7072 $79.99

Dark Shadows: Vols. 161-164
Collectors' Set
50-7080 $79.99

Dark Shadows: Vols. 165-168
Collector's Set
50-7085 $79.99

Dark Shadows: Vols. 169-172
Collectors' Set
50-7090 $79.99

Dark Shadows: Vols. 173-176
Collectors' Set
50-7112 $79.99

Dark Shadows: Vols. 177-180
Collectors' Set
50-7117 $79.99

Dark Shadows: Vols. 181-184
Collectors' Set
50-7126 $79.99

Dark Shadows: Vols. 185-188
Collectors' Set
50-7131 $79.99

Dark Shadows: Vols. 189-192
Collectors' Set
50-7136 $79.99

Dark Shadows: Vols. 193-196
Collectors' Set
50-7141 $79.99

Dark Shadows: Vols. 197-200
Collectors' Set
50-7155 $79.99

The Best Of Dark Shadows, Vol. 1
Don't feel like looking through five years of subplots for those spooky moments you loved years ago? Here's a chilling collection of the memorable people (and creatures) and classic scenes from "Dark Shadows," featuring Barnabas, Quentin, Julia, Angelique and all your favorites. 30 min.
50-6453 $19.99

The Best Of Dark Shadows, Vol. 2
If you're ready to brave a second shocking serving of Gothic intrigue and supernatural suspense, wait no longer. On this volume you'll travel back and forth through the centuries to see the artificial humans Adam and Eve, a werewolf prowling the halls of Collinwood, the 1995 "flashforward" sequence, and more vampires than you can shake a stake at. 30 min.
50-6960 $19.99

Dark Shadows: Resurrection Of Barnabas Collins
Features an overview of the series' first year, followed by the first five episodes with vampire Barnabas.
50-6424 $19.99

Dark Shadows: The Best Of Barnabas
A spine-chilling salute to TV's most famous bloodsucker, this special tape features Jonathan Frid, alias Barnabas Collins, in his most sinister moments among the frightened residents of Collinwood. 30 min.
50-6603 $14.99

Scariest Moments From Dark Shadows
Culled from hundreds of hours of daytime shocks and frights, this heart-stopping video showcases such unforgettable characters as Jeremiah Collins, newly risen from the grave; mad Jenny Collins; the living head of Judah Zachery; man-wolf Chris Jennings; the ghost of Quentin Collins; and, of course, reluctant vampire Barnabas Collins. 30 min.
50-6734 $19.99

Dark Shadows: Behind The Scenes
"DS" fans will want to sink their teeth into this video overview of the classic serial. Included are a history of the show, hilarious on-air bloopers and out-takes, scenes from the final episode, interviews with stars Jonathan Frid, David Selby and Lara Parker, and much more. 60 min.
50-6788 $19.99

Dark Shadows Bloopers
The spookiest show in daytime TV history was also at times the (unintentionally) silliest. This video features the funniest on-air flubs and mishaps that occurred during the live tapings: missed lines, malfunctioning props, collapsing sets and more! 45 min.
50-7075 $19.99

Dark Shadows: 25th Anniversary (1991)
Celebrate the silver anniversary of TV's spookiest series ever with this look at a gathering of Dark Shadows stars and fans. Join Jonathan Frid, Lara Parker, Kathryn Leigh Scott, Louis Edmonds and other regulars as they share anecdotes, show classic clips, and answer questions from the audience. 60 min.
50-7142 $19.99

Dark Shadows Video Scrapbook
Fans of the fondly-remembered spooky soap opera won't want to miss this special collection of featurettes, highlights and behind-the-scenes footage. Includes "Dark Shadows: Nightmares & Dreams"; "Inside the Shadows," with series creator Dan Curtis; and "Dark Shadows on Location," hosted by star Nancy Barrett; plus rare TV commercials and promo spots. 120 min.
50-7554 $19.99

Dark Shadows: The Collector's Series
Ever wonder what happened in Collinwood before the arrival of Barnabas Collins? Now on home video, fans can watch the rarely-seen episodes from "Dark Shadows'" first year, as governess Victoria Winters arrives at the great house, meets the Collins family and the mysterious Burke Devlin, and investigates a ghost haunting the Old House. Each tape in the four-cassette collector's sets contains five episodes and runs about 105 min. NOTE: Individual volumes are available at $19.99 each.

Dark Shadows: The Collector's Series, Vols. 1-4
50-7165 $79.99

Dark Shadows: The Collector's Series, Vols. 5-8
50-7170 $79.99

Dark Shadows: The Collector's Series, Vols. 9-12
50-7182 $79.99

Dark Shadows: The Collector's Series, Vols. 13-16
50-7187 $79.99

Dark Shadows: The Collector's Series, Vols. 17-20
50-7192 $79.99

Dark Shadows: The Collector's Series, Vols. 21-24
50-7197 $79.99

Dark Shadows: The Collector's Series, Vols. 25-28
50-7202 $79.99

Dark Shadows: The Collector's Series, Vols. 29-32
50-7207 $79.99

Dark Shadows: The Collector's Series, Vols. 33-36
50-7267 $79.99

Dark Shadows: The Collector's Series, Vols. 37-40
50-7275 $79.99

Dark Shadows: The Collector's Series, Vols. 41-44
50-7284 $79.99

Dark Shadows: The Collector's Series, Vols. 45-48
50-7289 $79.99

Dark Shadows: The Collector's Series, Vols. 49-52
50-7294 $79.99

Dark Shadows: The Collector's Series, Vols. 53-54 Two-Pack
50-7441 $39.99

Dark Shadows: The Revival Series (1991)
Return to Collinwood in this revived (no pun intended) TV Gothic horror series starring Ben Cross as the vampiric Barnabas Collins, back from a 200-year catnap to reclaim his heritage and cast his spell over the mansion's residents. The great cast also includes Jean Simmons, Roy Thinnes, Joanna Going and Barbara Steele as Dr. Hoffman. Each volume runs 50 min., except the pilot episode.

Dark Shadows, Vol. 1: The Pilot Episode
The feature-length pilot to the TV gothic horror series starring Ben Cross as a "revamped" Barnabas Collins is available in a special video version which includes 15 minutes not shown on TV. 105 min.
50-7039 $29.99

Dark Shadows, Vol. 2
Barnabas is attracted to Victoria Winters, who is the double of his lost love, Josette. Meanwhile, Dr. Hoffman investigates the death of Daphne Collins and learns Barnabas' secret.
50-7073 $19.99

Dark Shadows, Vol. 3
Dr. Hoffman's treatments begin to change Barnabas, but a return of his vampiric urges and the sleuthing of Professor Woodward puts their alliance in jeopardy.
50-7074 $19.99

Dark Shadows, Vol. 4
Victoria receives a visit and a warning from the ghost of Sarah Collins, while Barnabas and Willie have a less friendly encounter with the spirit of the witch Angelique.
50-7091 $19.99

Dark Shadows, Vol. 5
Jealous of Barnabas' attentions towards Victoria, Dr. Hoffman dilutes the treatments. Unable to control his bloodlust, Barnabas then attacks Carolyn Stoddard.
50-7092 $19.99

Dark Shadows, Vol. 6
A seance is held at Collinwood to contact the ghost of Sarah, but when it's over Victoria has disappeared into the past.
50-7093 $19.99

Dark Shadows, Vol. 7
Sent back to Collinsport in the year 1790, Victoria is befriended by a human Barnabas Collins and finds herself a stranger in a sea of familiar faces.
50-7106 $19.99

Dark Shadows, Vol. 8
A jealous Angelique uses her witchcraft in an attempt to stop the planned marriage of Barnabas to Josette, but suspicion falls on Victoria.
50-7107 $19.99

Dark Shadows, Vol. 9
While Abigail Collins and Reverend Trask accuse Victoria Winters of witchcraft, Barnabas spurns Angelique's romantic advances and becomes the victim of her curse.
50-7118 $19.99

Dark Shadows, Vol. 10
The horror of Angelique's curse is revealed as Barnabas rises from the grave as a vampire and sets out to make Josette his undead bride.
50-7119 $19.99

Dark Shadows, Vol. 11
Victoria faces a trial for witchcraft in 1790, while the spirit of Angelique takes control of Dr. Hoffman in the 20th century.
50-7120 $19.99

Dark Shadows, Vol. 12
In 1790, Barnabas' dark secret is discovered, and Victoria has a date with the gallows. In the present, Angelique plans to keep Vickie in the past and fulfill her curse on the Collins family.
50-7121 $19.99

A Darkness At Blaisedon
A gothic terror tale from Dan Curtis about a woman who inherits a remote estate, then hires a pair of psychic investigators to discover the truth behind strange incidents occurring there. They soon learn that the house is inhabited by the ghosts of a long-dead commodore and his wife. Marj Dusay, Kerwin Matthews, and "DS" regulars Louis Edmonds and Thayer David star. 52 min.
50-7260 $14.99

The Adventures of JIM BOWIE

The Adventures Of Jim Bowie
Scott Forbes starred as the rugged knife-throwing hero from the backwoods and bayous of the 1830's Louisiana Territory in this historical frontier drama that ran from 1956 to 1958 on ABC. Except where noted, each tape features two episodes and runs about 50 min. There are 16 volumes available, including:

The Adventures Of Jim Bowie, Vol. 1
Includes "The Squatter" and "The Gambler."
10-7479 Was $19.99 ***$14.99***

The Adventures Of Jim Bowie, Vol. 2
Includes "The Pearl and the Crown" and "Apache Silver."
10-9072 Was $19.99 ***$14.99***

The Adventures Of Jim Bowie, Vol. 3
Includes "The Tempered Blade" and "Birth of the Blade."
10-9197 Was $19.99 ***$14.99***

The Adventures Of Jim Bowie, Vol. 4
Includes "Jim Bowie, Apache" and "The Horse Thief."
10-9198 Was $19.99 ***$14.99***

The Adventures Of Jim Bowie, Vol. 5
Includes "A Night in Tennessee" and "A Grave for Jim Bowie."
10-9199 Was $19.99 ***$14.99***

The Adventures Of Jim Bowie, Vol. 6
Includes "Jackson's Assassination" and "Osceoloa."
10-9200 Was $19.99 ***$14.99***

The Adventures Of Jim Bowie, Vol. 7
Includes "Ursula" and "Rezin Bowie, Gambler."
10-9201 Was $19.99 ***$14.99***

The Adventures Of Jim Bowie, Vol. 8
Includes "The Land Jumpers" and "Pirate on Horseback."
10-9202 Was $19.99 ***$14.99***

The Adventures Of Jim Bowie, Vol. 9
Includes "Deaf Smith" and "Beggar of New Orleans."
10-9203 Was $19.99 ***$14.99***

The Adventures Of Jim Bowie, Vol. 10
Includes "Trapline" and "Close Shave."
10-9204 Was $19.99 ***$14.99***

Jim Bowie
Trademark knife in hand, frontiersman Jim Bowie (Scott Forbes) stands ready to fight to preserve the peace in the Louisiana wilderness of the 1830s in four episodes from the popular '50s adventure series including "Outlaw Kingdom," "Jackson's Assassination," "Gone to Texas" and "Rezin Bowie, Gambler." 110 min.
83-7002 ***$19.99***

Jim Bowie, No. 1
Includes "The Squatter" and "An Adventure with Audubon."
09-5415 ***$14.99***

Jim Bowie, No. 2
Includes "Trapline" and "Jim Bowie Comes Home."
09-5416 ***$14.99***

Jim Bowie, No. 3
Includes "The Secessionist" and "The Land Jumpers."
09-5417 ***$14.99***

Jim Bowie, No. 4
Includes "Outlaw Kingdom" and "Convoy Gold."
09-5418 ***$14.99***

Jim Bowie, No. 5
Includes "Jackson's Assassination" and "Gone to Texas."
09-5419 ***$14.99***

Jim Bowie, No. 6
Includes "The Pearl and the Crown" and "Country Cousin."
09-5420 ***$14.99***

The Master Ninja
Also known as "The Master," this 1984 series starred Lee Van Cleef as a World War II vet who studies martial arts and is the first Westerner to become a Ninja Master. Along with young martial artist Timothy Van Patten, Van Cleef is followed by Ninja assassins as they search for his long-lost daughter. Sho Kosugi is the lead bad guy. Each tape features two episodes and runs 95 min.

The Master Ninja, Vol. 1
Includes "Max" with Demi Moore and Claude Akins and "Out-Of-Time Step."
10-9928 ***$14.99***

The Master Ninja, Vol. 2
Includes "State of the Union" and "Hostage" with George Lazenby and David McCallum.
10-9929 ***$14.99***

The Master Ninja, Vol. 3
Includes "High Rollers" and "Fat Tuesday."
10-9930 ***$14.99***

The Master Ninja, Vol. 4
Includes "Juggernaut" with Stuart Whitman and "The Good, the Bad and the Priceless" with George Maharis.
10-9931 ***$14.99***

The Master Ninja, Vol. 5
Includes "Kunoichi" and "The Java Tiger."
10-9932 ***$14.99***

The Fugitive
"Innocent victim of blind justice" Dr. Richard Kimble (David Janssen) keeps on running in this collection of episodes from the classic TV drama that ran from 1963 to 1967. Can Janssen stay one step ahead of Lt. Gerard (Barry Morse) and find the one-armed man who killed his wife? Except where noted, each tape contains two episodes and runs about 100 min.

The Fugitive: The First Episode—Fear In A Desert City
The premiere episode of the series finds hero-on-the-lam Richard Kimble landing a bartending job in Tucson and caught in the middle of a dangerous fight between bar pianist Vera Miles and estranged husband Brian Keith. 50 min.
10-2276 ***$14.99***

The Fugitive: Terror At High Point/Glass Tightrope
In "Terror at High Point," Kimble tries to help construction boss Jack Klugman save his marriage. And a man walks a "Glass Tightrope" when he's wrongly accused of murder—a charge only Kimble can clear him of.
63-1910 ***$14.99***

The Fugitive: Nemesis/World's End
Fate throws the Fugitive together with Gerard's young son against a vindictive sheriff in "Nemesis," guest starring Slim Pickens and Kurt Russell. Next, Suzanne Pleshette is the daughter of Kimble's defense attorney and carries a torch for him in "World's End," which also features Dabney Coleman.
63-1911 ***$14.99***

The Fugitive: Cry Uncle/Flight From The Final Demon
Can Kimble stop his running long enough to help a group of orphaned children? Ronny Howard and Brett Somers guest star in "Cry Uncle." Then, Carroll O'Connor is a sheriff whose memory for faces could end Kimble's "Flight."
63-1912 ***$14.99***

The Fugitive: Stroke Of Genius/The Stranger In The Mirror
Hitching a ride with a pair of clergymen leads to a tragic accident in "Stroke of Genius." Then, "Stranger in the Mirror" finds corrupt ex-cop William Shatner using Kimble to mask his criminal activities.
63-1913 ***$14.99***

The Fugitive: Brass Ring/In A Plain Paper Wrapper
In "Brass Ring," Kimble is turned into a dupe for a group of thieves. Next, a group of teens with a mail-order gun attempt to bring in the Fugitive in "In a Plain Paper Wrapper," with guest star Kurt Russell.
63-1914 ***$14.99***

The Fugitive: Never Wave Goodbye
In this two-part drama, Kimble's chance for a new life and romance in Santa Barbara are threatened by a jealous rival and the arrest of a one-armed man in L.A. Robert Duvall, Susan Oliver guest star.
63-8002 ***$14.99***

The Fugitive: The Last Episode—The Judgment
Dr. Kimble ends his four-year search for the elusive "one-armed man" in "The Judgment," but can he prove his innocence before Gerard catches up to them? This two-part episode was, at its time, the highest-rated TV program ever.
14-3001 ***$14.99***

The Adventures Of The Scarlet Pimpernel
The literary hero of the French Revolution rides onto the small screen in this action-filled TV adventure series from 1954, with Marius Goring as Sir Percy, whose foppish exterior hides the masked daredevil. Each tape contains two episodes and runs about 52 min. There are four volumes available, including:

The Adventures Of The Scarlet Pimpernel, Vol. 1
Includes "The Sword of Justice" and "The Elusive Chauvelin."
10-1319 ***$19.99***

The Adventures Of The Scarlet Pimpernel, Vol. 2
Includes "Sir Andrew's Fate" and "The Tale of Two Pigtails."
10-1320 ***$19.99***

The Adventures Of The Scarlet Pimpernel, Vol. 3
Includes "The Hostage" and "The Ambassador's Lady."
10-1321 ***$19.99***

The Adventures Of The Scarlet Pimpernel, Vol. 4
Includes "Antoine & Antoinette" and "Sir Percy's Wager."
10-1322 ***$19.99***

The Adventures Of The Scarlet Pimpernel/The Lone Wolf
A pair of episodes from two '50s adventure series are presented. Marius Goring and Robert Shaw star in "The Hostage" from "The Adventures of the Scarlet Pimpernel"; and an episode from "The Lone Wolf" stars Louis Hayward as the globe-trotting investigator. 53 min.
10-7313 Was $19.99 ***$14.99***

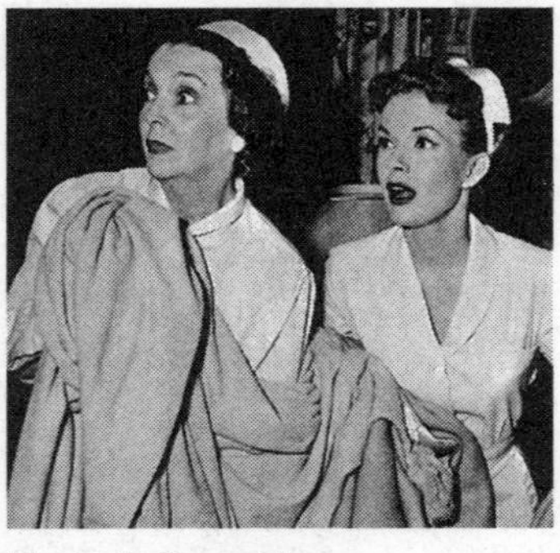

The Gale Storm Show
Also known as "Oh! Susanna," this 1956-59 comedy starred Gale Storm as Susanna Pomeroy, social director of the cruise ship S.S. Ocean Queen, who kept the crew on their feet whenever she got together with ZaSu Pitts, operator of the ship's beauty salon. Each tape features two episodes and runs about 50 min.

The Gale Storm Show, Vol. 1
Includes "Witch Doctor" and "Capri."
10-9748 ***$14.99***

The Gale Storm Show, Vol. 2
Includes "Nicked in Naples" and "Passenger Incognito." Includes original commercials.
10-9749 ***$14.99***

Bosom Buddies
Years before he was an Oscar-winning actor, Tom Hanks co-starred with Peter Scolari in this cross-dressing sitcom which debuted on ABC in 1980. Hanks and Scolari are Kip and Henry, New York ad agency workers who don dresses in order to get an affordable apartment at a "women only" building. Sexy situations and comedy ensue; with Donna Dixon, Wendie Jo Sperber, Telma Hopkins. Each tape features two episodes and runs about 50 min.

Bosom Buddies, Vol. 1
In the pilot episode, Kip and Henry reluctantly become Buffy and Hildegarde so that they can stay at a residence hotel that happens to be exclusive to women—many of whom are beautiful. Next, Henry tries to shed his "nice guy" image with a "Macho Man" cowboy act.
06-2357 □***$12.99***

Bosom Buddies, Vol. 2
Kip's night out with Sonny is disrupted when Henry joins them with his blind date, a belligerent punker, in "Kip and Sonny's Date." In "Revenge," Kip and Henry recruit hotel mates to get even with the guy who dumped Amy.
06-2358 □***$12.99***

Bosom Buddies, Vol. 3
"Kip Quits" his job after an altercation with a client, but realizes ad work was better than hustling hot dogs on the street. And Kip and Henry don their female disguises to become nurses in "The Hospital.".
06-2359 □***$12.99***

Bosom Buddies, Vol. 4
Henry and Kip's investment plans are put on hold when Henry's Uncle Mort talks them into a questionable investment in "There's No Business...." Next, Kip devises a way to stop Henry's relationship with a pretty California girl in "Other Than That, She's a Wonderful Person." 51 min.
06-2360 □***$12.99***

Mork & Mindy
Robin Williams' wild antics as Mork, the misfit alien from the planet Ork, helped make this show a popular entry on ABC from 1978 to 1982. Williams played an extraterrestrial sent to study Earthling habits who lands in Colorado, where he befriends college student Mindy (Pam Dawber). Each tape features two episodes and runs about 50 min.

Mork & Mindy, Vol. 1
Mindy has to keep her father from finding the newly-arrived Orkan who's taken up living in her attic in the series' first episode, "Mork Moves In." Next, "Mork Goes Public" for a tabloid's cash reward for proof of the existence of alien life.
06-2361 □***$12.99***

Mork & Mindy, Vol. 2
A penniless Mork decides to make his own gifts for everyone in "Mork's First Christmas." Then, in order to cope with the news that he must leave Earth, Mork and Mindy attend a self-help seminar led by a "pop psych" con artist (David Letterman). Morgan Fairchild guests in these episodes.
06-2362 □***$12.99***

Mork & Mindy, Vol. 3
Mork's feelings are unleashed when Mindy kisses him on her birthday in "Mork's Mixed Emotions." Next, Mork starts a fight in order to study "kissing and making up," but it doesn't work out as he planned, in "Stark Raving Mork."
06-2363 □***$12.99***

Mork & Mindy, Vol. 4
Mindy is shocked while Mork is pleased with Mindy's father's new, young wife in "A Mommy for Mindy." And Mork is mistaken for popular comic Robin Williams at a comedy club in "Mork Meets Robin Williams."
06-2364 □***$12.99***

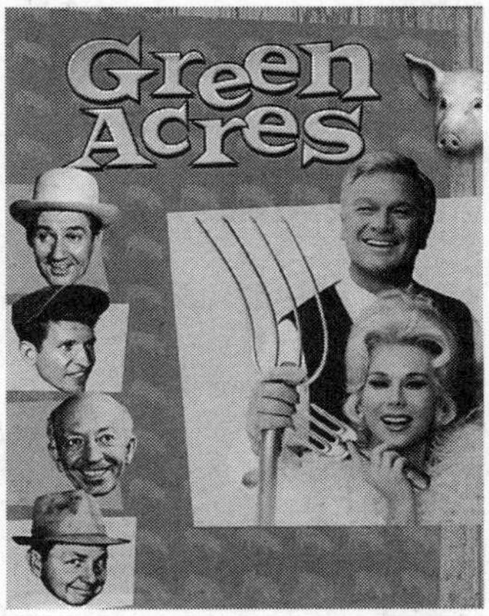

Green Acres
Movies Unlimited is the place to be if you're a fan of this hilarious series from the creator of "The Beverly Hillbillies." Eddie Albert and Eva Gabor are attorney Oliver Douglas and his socialite wife Lisa, who leave New York for a ramshackle rural farm. Regulars on the show, which ran from 1965 to 1971, included Pat Buttram as local con man Mr. Haney, Tom Lester as dense farmhand Eb, and Alvy Moore as easily confused farm agent Hank Kimball.

Green Acres, No. 1
The first three episodes of the show include "Oliver Buys a Farm," in which Oliver shocks Lisa with his plan to move to the country; "Lisa's First Day on the Farm," in which the Douglases learn of Mr. Haney's tricks; and "The Decorator," whom Lisa hires to make the farmhouse look up to her standards. 75 min.
10-9357 ***$14.99***

Green Acres, No. 2
In "The Best Laid Plans," a rumor starts that Lisa has left Oliver in order to go back to New York. And Oliver comes to terms with Mr. Haney in order to rent a rooster in "My Husband, the Rooster Renter." 55 min.
10-9358 ***$14.99***

Green Acres, No. 3
Can anything stop Mr. Haney from selling the Douglases' furniture in "Furniture, Furniture, Who's Got the Furniture?" Next, Oliver gets helps from other farmers with his plowing in "Neighborliness." 55 min.
10-9359 ***$14.99***

Green Acres, No. 4
In "Lisa the Helpmate," Oliver finds strange ingredients in his soil. Meanwhile, a lack of electricity could mean no farm report in "You Can't Plug in a 2 with a 6." 55 min.
10-9360 ***$14.99***

Green Acres, No. 5
The Douglases' phone is mistakenly installed on top of a telephone pole in "Don't Call Us, We'll Call You"; and Oliver faces a fine if he plants wheat in "Parity Begins at Home." 55 min.
10-9361 ***$14.99***

Green Acres, No. 6
Mr. Haney sells Oliver a pregnant cow in "Lisa Has a Calf," while Oliver can't remember how long he's been married in "The Wedding Anniversary." 55 min.
10-9362 ***$14.99***

Green Acres, No. 7
In "What Happened in Scranton?," Lisa's beauty parlor opening encourages women to refuse to work on the farm in fear of messing their hair. Next, Oliver is in for some surprises when he starts to fix up the farmhouse in "How to Enlarge a Bedroom." 55 min.
10-9363 ***$14.99***

Fury

Also known as "Brave Stallion," this family TV series from the late 1950s and early 1960s stars Peter Graves as the owner of Broken Wheel Ranch who takes orphan Bobby Diamond under his wing. Diamond helps train a wild stallion named Fury, and the pair soon set off on exciting adventures. Except where noted, each tape features two episodes and runs about 60 min.

Fury, Vol. 1
Includes "Joey Finds a Friend" and "Joey's Father."
10-9977   *$14.99*

Fury, Vol. 2
Includes "Search for Joey" and "Joey's Dame Trouble."
10-9978   *$19.99*

The Adventures Of Fu Manchu (1956)
Rarely seen tele-version of the adventures of the sinister Oriental mastermind. Two thrilling episodes are featured here, "The Golden God" and "The Master Plan," in which Fu revives Hitler. Glen Gordon, Lester Matthews star. 60 min.
01-5064   Was $19.99   *$14.99*

The Adventures Of Swiss Family Robinson
Based on the timeless Johann Wyss novel, this exciting adventure series for the whole family stars Richard Thomas as the patriarch of an 1830s New England brood shipwrecked on a remote South Pacific island. Faced with dangers ranging from wild animals and storms to pirates, the Robinsons band together to build a new life on their island home. Each tape runs about 75 min.

The Adventures Of Swiss Family Robinson, Book 1: Survival
89-5138   *$19.99*

The Adventures Of Swiss Family Robinson, Book 2: The Islands Of The Gods
89-5139   *$19.99*

The Adventures Of Swiss Family Robinson, Book 3: Invasions
89-5140   *$19.99*

The Adventures Of Swiss Family Robinson, Book 4: The Princess From The Sea
89-5141   *$19.99*

The Adventures Of Swiss Family Robinson, Book 5: Captives
89-5142   *$19.99*

The Adventures Of Swiss Family Robinson, Book 6: The Ghost Of Raven Jones
89-5143   *$19.99*

The Adventures Of Swiss Family Robinson, Book 7: The Treasure Hunt
89-5144   *$19.99*

The Adventures Of Swiss Family Robinson, Book 8: Star Crossed Lovers
89-5145   *$19.99*

The Adventures Of Swiss Family Robinson, Book 9: Paradise Lost
89-5146   *$19.99*

The Adventures Of Swiss Family Robinson, Book 10: Boston
89-5147   *$19.99*

The Adventures Of Swiss Family Robinson: Complete Set
All ten volumes are also available in a special collector's set.
89-5148   Save $100.00!   *$99.99*

The Big Beat/Studio Party (1957)
Dig the hits from 1957 on Alan Freed's "The Big Beat," with fill-in host Bobby Darin, and Teddy Randoza, then bop with Herb Sheldon and decathlete Bob Mathias on "Studio Party." The titles and credits for both shows are missing, but hey, that's Rock and Roll! 50 min.
01-9053   *$19.99*

My Living Doll (1964)
The stunning Julie Newmar played the title role in this short-lived sci-fi sitcom as Rhoda, an experimental military robot who becomes a "patient" of base psychiatrist Bob Cummings and attempts to learn human behavior. Includes two episodes, "Uninvited Guest" and "Something Borrowed, Something Blue." 60 min.
82-1026   *$19.99*

Only When I Laugh Collection Set
Peter Bowles, James Bolam and Christopher Strauli lead the cast in six episodes on three tapes of this hilarious British sitcom that ran from 1979 to 1982. Three mental patients terrorize the psychiatric ward of a hospital as they constantly bicker with each other and cause trouble for the staff with their grand delusions. 156 min. total.
53-6947   *$39.99*

Circle Of Fear (1973)
The latter variation on NBC's "Ghost Story" series presented creepy tales involving ghosts, vampires and other ghastly creatures. This macabre installment, entitled "Graveyard Shift," stars John and Patty Duke Astin and, in a cameo, filmmaker William Castle. 50 min.
10-9211   Was $19.99   *$14.99*

Roy Rogers & Buffalo Bill, Jr. (1955)
Take aim at an episode of the 1955 series about Buffalo Bill, Jr. (Dick Jones), his sister Calamity and their adopted dad, Judge "Fair 'n' Square" Wiley, founder of 1890s Wileyville. Also, a straight-shootin' Roy Rogers adventure. 60 min.
01-9060   *$19.99*

Together With Music (1955)
A high point in TV's Golden Age was this musical-variety special showcasing the talents of two of the entertainment world's leading lights, Noel Coward (in his television debut) and Mary Martin. Noel sings "Mad Dogs and Englishmen" and "Noel Cowardish," while Mary mugs through a scene from "Madame Butterfly," then the pair top it off with an entertaining extended duet. 79 min.
09-1394   *$29.99*

Best Of Broadway: The Philadelphia Story (1958)
The acclaimed stage comedy of marital mishaps in the tony Main Line region near Philadelphia is presented in this fast-paced TV production. Dorothy McGuire, Richard Carlson, John Payne and Mary Astor star. 55 min.
09-1399   Was $24.99   *$14.99*

Suspense (1953)
Two episodes from early TV anthology. "F.O.B. Vienna" stars Walter Matthau and Jayne Meadows in a tale of espionage, while a murderer is haunted by his conscience in "All Hallow's Eve," with Franchot Tone. 54 min. total.
09-1703   *$19.99*

The Ox-Bow Incident (1955)
Dynamic performances from Robert Wagner and Raymond Burr bolster this riveting TV adaptation of Walter Van Tilburg Clark's book depicting the sharp ironies and dangers of a lynch mob taking justice into their own hands. With Cameron Mitchell.
10-7001   Was $19.99   *$14.99*

The Frances Langford— Don Ameche Show (1951)
The popular singing bandleader and the urbane movie leading man co-host an hour of music, comedy and variety, with guest-of-the-hour Chester Morris. 60 min.
10-7319   Was $19.99   *$14.99*

Marty (1953)
The original, live "Goodyear TV Playhouse" production of writer Paddy Chayefsky's heartfelt drama, starring Rod Steiger as the lonely Bronx butcher who finally finds romance with a plain schoolteacher. With Nancy Marchand, Nehemiah Persoff. 51 min.
09-1211   *$19.99*

Celanese Theatre: On Borrowed Time (1952)
Classic drama about two elderly people, obsessed with death, who must care for their grandson when his parents are killed. But when "Mr. Brink" comes for the child, they trap him in a tree! Laughs and sorrow combine in this superlative drama starring Ralph Morgan, Billy Chapin and Mildred Dunnock. 60 min.
09-1853   Was $24.99   *$14.99*

Front Row Center: Tender Is The Night (1955)
TV adaptation of the F. Scott Fitzgerald novel about a psychiatrist who marries one of his patients. Talented cast includes Mercedes McCambridge, James Daly, Olive Sturgess. 60 min.
09-1914   Was $24.99   *$19.99*

The Joe E. Brown Show (1955)
This pilot for a proposed sitcom that was never picked up starred the big-mouthed comic as a widowed small-town shopkeeper who helps a new immigrant neighbor who runs into local prejudice. Also on the tape is an episode of 1953's "The Ben Blue Show." 55 min. total.
09-1951   *$14.99*

Archie's Boys' Club (1954)
The hit radio comedy, set in the New York City tavern "where the elite meet to eat," became a TV series in 1954. This episode stars Ed Gardner as Archie, the conniving bartender-manager, Alan Reed as Clifton, the bar idiot, and Pattee Chapman as Miss Duffy, daughter of the never-seen owner. 27 min.
09-2985   *$14.99*

Morecambe & Wise
Legendary British comic team Eric Morecambe and Ernie Wise have rocked the Empire for years with their zany humor, and now their funniest moments have been collected on these programs. There's guest stars, skits and outrageous antics galore in store. Each tape runs about 45 min.

Morecambe & Wise
Among the top guests on this program are Glenda Jackson, Diana Rigg and Vanessa Redgrave.
53-9459   *$29.99*

Lots More Of Morecambe & Wise
Includes guest appearances from Gemma Craven, Alec Guinness, Glenda Jackson, Peter Vaughan and Mick McManus.
53-9708   *$19.99*

Lots & Lots More Of Morecambe & Wise
Includes guests Leonard Rossiter, Ann Hamilton, Glenda Jackson and Eamonn Andrews.
53-9709   *$19.99*

Blake's 7 (1978)
A cult favorite sci-fi adventure series from England about a ragtag group of resistance fighters battling against an interplanetary dictatorship. Gareth Thomas plays reluctant leader Blake, and Sally Knyvette and Paul Darrow also star; created by Terry Nation of "Dr. Who" fame. Each tape features two episodes and runs about 100 min. There are 26 volumes available, including:

Blake's 7, Vol. 1: The Way Back/Space Fall
53-9465   *$19.99*

Blake's 7, Vol. 2: Cygnus Alpha/Time Squad
53-9466   *$19.99*

Blake's 7, Vol. 3: The Web/Seek—Locate—Destroy
53-9467   *$19.99*

Blake's 7, Vol. 4: Mission To Destiny/Duel
53-9468   *$19.99*

Blake's 7, Vol. 5: Project Avalon/Breakdown
53-9469   *$19.99*

The Pendulum (1956)
Also known as "The Vise," this British-made suspense anthology series was hosted by John Bentley. "The Price of Vanity" features Christopher Lee as a greedy art dealer who thinks he has a priceless painting on his hands. Next, in "Death on the Boards," a ballerina who can no longer dance takes an Iron Curtain refugee under her wing, and exacts revenge when her husband falls for her. 58 min.
82-1029   *$19.99*

Dear Phoebe (1954)/ Professional Father (1955)
A pair of vintage sitcoms, with Peter Lawford as a newspaper writer who spins an "advice to the love-lorn" column under a female pseudonym, and Steve Dunne playing a skilled family psychologist who's less adept at handling his own brood (which included a pre-"Beaver" Barbara Billingsley). 55 min.
10-7455   Was $19.99   *$14.99*

Gangbusters/The Gun (1952)
A carryover from radio, "Gangbusters" was a top-rated show during its single season run, alternating on Thursday nights with Jack Webb's "Dragnet"; the episode featured is "Durable Mike Malloy," starring Michael Mark. Also, Dick Powell stars in the early crime drama "The Gun."
10-7507   Was $19.99   *$14.99*

Casablanca (1955)
You may not remember this: a TV show based on the classic Humphrey Bogart movie. Charles McGraw starred as Rick, owner of the Cafe Americain nightclub in the African city, who worked quietly to disrupt Nazi activities during World War II. Marcel Dalio, Dan Seymour and Clarence Muse co-starred. This episode, "Siren Song," features Mari Blanchard. 50 min.
10-9385   *$14.99*

Doctor Who: The Edge Of Destruction/The Pilot Episode/ The Missing Years (1963)
An accident sends a disintegrating TARDIS back towards the dawn of time, and the Doctor (William Hartnell) accuses Ian and Barbara of sabotage, in "Edge of Destruction." This special two-tape set also includes the first "Doctor Who" episode ever recorded and the "Missing Years" special, featuring scenes from lost episodes of the '60s. 138 min. total.
19-5016 *$29.99*

Doctor Who: An Unearthly Child (1963)
The very first episode from TV's longest-running science-fiction series introduces William Hartnell as the irascible, white-haired Doctor, who, in a fit of pique, launches himself, his granddaughter and two of her teachers back to the Stone Age. 98 min.
04-3226 *$19.99*

Doctor Who: The Daleks (1963)
The landmark adventure that introduced the Time Lord's most implacable enemies finds the Doctor (William Hartnell) and company on the distant planet Skaro, where the human Thals are kept enslaved by the metal-encased Daleks. 174 min.
04-2953 *$29.99*

Doctor Who: The Dalek Invasion Of Earth (1964)
In this classic "Who" tale, the Doctor (William Hartnell) and his friends find that the Earth of the 22nd century is in the grip of the Daleks, who turn humans into mind-controlled Robomen. Can the Doctor free the planet from Dalek domination? 150 min.
04-2746 *$29.99*

Doctor Who: The Aztecs (1964)
On a trip back to pre-Columbian Latin America, the Doctor (William Hartnell) and his companions are declared to be divine beings after emerging from a sacred tomb, but must find a way to retrieve the TARDIS before they become sacrifices. 100 min.
04-2815 *$19.99*

Doctor Who: Keys Of Marinus (1964)
Trapped on the distant world Marinus, the Doctor (William Hartnell), Susan, Barbara and Ian are forced to undertake a planet-wide search for the four keys to the Conscience of Marinus, a powerful mind-controlling machine. 149 min.
04-3846 *$29.99*

Doctor Who: The Web Planet (1965)
It's enough to drive a Time Lord buggy when the Doctor (William Hartnell) and his companions are held prisoner on the planet Vortis, home to a bitter power struggle between the ant-like Zarbi and the butterfly beings known as the Menoptera. 148 min.
04-2854 *$19.99*

Doctor Who: The Rescue (1965)/ The Romans (1965)
In this double feature from William Hartnell's tenure in the TARDIS, he and companions Ian and Barbara first rescue a young Earth girl named Vicki, whose spaceship crashed on a distant planet, then wind up in Ancient Rome, where they face mad emperor Nero. 146 min. total.
04-3301 □*$29.99*

Doctor Who: The Crusade/ The Space Museum (1965)
This special collector's set features two classic William Hartnell tales, as he and his friends meet with Richard the Lionheart in the 12th century, then aid the residents of the planet Xeros from becoming living museum exhibits. Also includes a soundtrack CD and collectible postcards.
04-3910 □*$34.99*

Doctor Who: The War Machines (1966)
The Doctor (William Hartnell) has finally managed to land the TARDIS in 20th-century London, but there's no time to celebrate, because WOTAN, an experimental super-computer, is controlling men's minds and preparing to take over the planet. This restored video edition includes footage not seen since the original broadcast.
04-3622 □*$19.99*

Doctor Who: The Ark (1966)
In the distant future, the survivors of a doomed Earth—divided into the elite Guardians and the lowly Monoids—are adrift in a gigantic interplanetary ark. It falls to the Doctor (William Hartnell) and companions Steve and Dodo to save them and bring the two groups together.
04-3751 □*$19.99*

Doctor Who: Tomb Of The Cybermen (1967)
Unseen and presumed missing for over 20 years, this vintage "Who"-venture features Time Lord Patrick Troughton and companions Jamie and Victoria in a visit to a distant future world, where an archeological dig uncovers a deadly treasure: the robotic and merciless Cybermen. 100 min.
04-2572 *$19.99*

Doctor Who: The Ice Warriors (Collector's Edition) (1967)
Landing in an ice-covered future England, the Doctor (Patrick Troughton) and his companions try to stop a revived Martian warlord from continuing his plans for conquering Earth. This special collector's set also includes a CD containing the audio of the missing episodes and a booklet.
04-3866 □*$34.99*

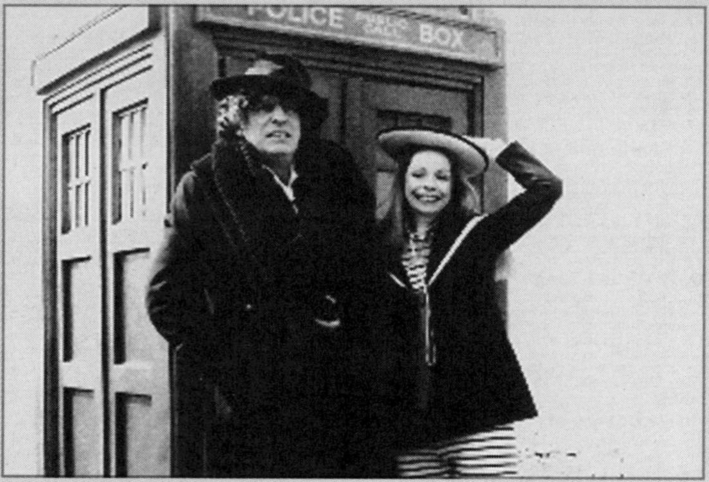

Doctor Who

Doctor Who: The Mind Robber (1968)
The Tardis jumps right out of space and time and into the Land of Fiction, a white limbo where imagination can turn into a deadly reality. Can the Doctor (Patrick Troughton) and his young friends defeat the land's master and get back to their own universe? 100 min.
04-2747 *$19.99*

Doctor Who: The Dominators (1968)
It's up to the Doctor (Patrick Troughton), Jamie and Zoe to free the pacifistic populace of Dulkis from the grip of the evil Dominators, who seek to blow up the planet in order to provide fuel for their space fleet. 121 min.
04-2853 *$19.99*

Doctor Who: The Krotons (1968)
No, the Tardis isn't attacked by deadly bread cubes! The Krotons are aliens in suspended animation who are stealing the mental energies of the enslaved Gonds in order to revive them, and the Doctor (Patrick Troughton) could be their next victim. 91 min.
04-2855 *$19.99*

Doctor Who: The Invasion (1968)
A computer designed to control people's emotional impulses is part of the sinister Cybermen's latest plan to conquer Earth, and the Doctor (Patrick Troughton), his companions, and Brigadier Lethbridge-Stewart and the newly-formed U.N.I.T. must stop them. 146 min.
04-2954 *$19.99*

Doctor Who: The Seeds Of Death (1969)
On a visit to 21st-century Earth, the Doctor (Patrick Troughton), Jamie and Zoe must halt a plan by the Martian Ice Warriors to infect Earth with a deadly fungus carried by seed pods. 137 min.
04-3210 □*$19.99*

Doctor Who: The War Games (1969)
The Doctor (Patrick Troughton), Zoe and Jamie face their ultimate adventure together when they come upon a life-size war simulation that uses real soldiers, plucked from different eras, as its pawns. Must the Doctor call upon the Time Lords to save the day? 243 min.
04-3227 *$29.99*

Doctor Who: Spearhead From Space (1970)
Exiled to Earth in his third incarnation, the Doctor (Jon Pertwee) helps the scientific investigation force known as U.N.I.T. defeat an army of plastic mannequins created by an alien intelligence to take over the Earth. 92 min.
04-3218 *$19.99*

Doctor Who: Doctor Who And The Silurians (1970)
Experiments at an atomic research plant awaken a race of intelligent reptilian humanoids who ruled the Earth millions of years ago and are ready to reclaim the planet. Can the Doctor (Jon Pertwee) find a way to make peace? 167 min.
04-2952 *$29.99*

Doctor Who: Inferno (1970)
"Inferno" is an advanced drilling project to tap into a new energy source under the Earth's crust, but a mysterious underground gas transforms men into ape-like creatures. The Doctor (Jon Pertwee) finds himself trapped in a parallel universe as he tries to shut down the drilling and save the planet. 167 min.
04-3246 □*$29.99*

Doctor Who: The Daemons (1971)
An ancient English burial mound is the setting for the Master's plan to take over the Earth with the help of a devilish-looking alien, and it's up to the Doctor (Jon Pertwee) and Jo to stop him. 123 min.
04-2702 *$19.99*

Doctor Who: Terror Of The Autons (1971)
The Time Lord's deadliest nemesis, the Master (Roger Delgado), made his first fiendish appearance in this adventure that finds the Doctor (Jon Pertwee) and new companion Jo foiling an invasion scheme by the Master and his Nestene allies. 95 min.
04-2958 *$19.99*

Doctor Who: The Claws Of Axos (1971)
Peaceful alien beings called Axons land on Earth in search of aid, but a skeptical Doctor (Jon Pertwee) unmasks the Axons' sinister true motives and a deadly scheme by the Master. 98 min.
04-3328 □*$19.99*

Doctor Who: Mind Of Evil (1971)
The Doctor (Jon Pertwee) must save the members of a global peace conference from becoming the latest victims of the Master, whose weapons are a stolen nerve gas missile and a parasitic alien that feeds on evil thoughts.
04-3749 □*$29.99*

Doctor Who: The Day Of The Daleks (1972)
A 22nd-century battle between the sinister Daleks and human freedom fighters stretches across time to 20th-century Earth. Can the Doctor (Jon Pertwee) and Jo Grant help save the future and the present, or will they be "exterminated"? 90 min.
04-3206 *$19.99*

Doctor Who: The Curse Of Peladon (1972)
Dispatched by the Time Lords to oversee the entry of the planet Peladon to the Galactic Federation, the Doctor (Jon Pertwee) and Jo must learn who is willing to resort to murder to stop the joining, before interplanetary war erupts. 97 min.
04-3244 □*$19.99*

Doctor Who: The Sea Devils (1972)
It's twice the menace for the Doctor (Jon Pertwee) when his old foe, the Master, teams up with aquatic creatures who are related to the Silurians in a plan for world domination. 149 min.
04-3454 *$29.99*

Doctor Who: The Time Warrior (1973)
An alien warlord, stranded in medieval England, is kidnapping scientists from the 20th century to help repair his ship. Can the Doctor (Jon Pertwee) and Sarah Jane defeat this cross-time caper? 90 min.
04-3220 *$19.99*

Doctor Who: The Three Doctors (1973)
When the renegade Time Lord known as Omega attempts to escape from the anti-matter universe he resides in, it requires the combined efforts of Doctors Jon Pertwee, Patrick Troughton and William Hartnell to save the day in the show's 10th anniversary saga. 99 min.
04-3228 *$19.99*

Doctor Who: Carnival Of Monsters (1973)
The Doctor's (Jon Pertwee) and Jo's planned vacation on Metebelis 3 is sidetracked when the Tardis lands them in an alien sideshow of extraterrestrial lifeforms. 101 min.
04-3299 □*$19.99*

Doctor Who: Frontier In Space (1973)
Accused of being alien spies plotting against Earth, the Doctor (Jon Pertwee) and Jo are saved from lunar exile by the Master, who is trying to start an interplanetary war. Can the Doctor stop his old foe, and the even older menace lurking in the wings? 144 min.
04-3300 □*$29.99*

Doctor Who: The Green Death (1973)
A Welsh village that's home to a new chemical plant, a deadly menace in a long-abandoned mine, and a malevolent computer with a mind of its own all add up to a dangerous mission for the Doctor (Jon Pertwee) and Jo. 154 min.
04-3415 □*$29.99*

Doctor Who: The Monster Of Peladon (1974)
Fifty years after the events of "The Curse of Peladon," the Doctor (Jon Pertwee) returns to that planet and finds he must end a reign of terror that's attributed to a legendary creature. 146 min.
04-3453 *$29.99*

Doctor Who: Planet Of The Daleks (1973)
Trapped on the planet Spirodon, Jo must save a comatose Doctor (Jon Pertwee), even as an army of Daleks beneath the planet's surface are about to be revived.
19-5017 *$29.99*

Doctor Who: Death To The Daleks (1974)
When a virus threatens all life in the galaxy, the Doctor (Jon Pertwee) and Sarah Jane become involved in a race between humans and the Daleks to recover the antidote. 90 min.
04-3211 □*$19.99*

Doctor Who: Planet Of The Spiders (1974)
The planet in question is Metebelis 3, and its evil arachnid rulers are extending their spindly legs towards the Earth. The Doctor (Jon Pertwee) must put his lives on the line to stop their invasion plans. 150 min.
04-2811 *$19.99*

Doctor Who: Robot (1974)
Fresh (and a little addled) from his latest regeneration, the Doctor (Tom Baker) must help UNIT defeat a group of renegade scientists who are using an experimental robot to help them launch World War III. 99 min.
04-2812 *$19.99*

Doctor Who: The Ark In Space (1974)
The Doctor (Tom Baker), Sarah Jane and Harry find themselves in the distant future, where a giant space ark containing the last survivors of Earth is threatened by insect-like aliens who take control of human hosts, in this feature-length adventure from the cult TV sci-fi series. 90 min.
04-3217 *$19.99*

Doctor Who: The Sontaran Experiment (1975)/ Genesis Of The Daleks (1975)
On Earth in the distant future, the Doctor (Tom Baker) and his companions help would-be settlers of the now-abandoned planet overcome the menace of the Sontarans. Next, a trip to the past puts the Doctor face to face with Davros, the twisted scientist responsible for the creation of the Dalek race. 193 min. total.
04-2745 *$29.99*

Doctor Who: Revenge Of The Cybermen (1975)
The Doctor (Tom Baker) travels with companions Sarah Jane and Harry into the far future, where they must free a manned space station from the tyranny of the half-man, half-machine Cybermen. 92 min.
04-3113 □*$19.99*

Doctor Who: Pyramids Of Mars (1975)
The Doctor (Tom Baker) and Sarah find themselves in 1911 England, where an archeologist's discovery unleashes a menace whose evil stretches from ancient Egypt to the planet Mars and threatens all life on Earth. 91 min.
04-3150 Was $19.99 □*$14.99*

Doctor Who: Terror Of The Zygons (1975)
What is the connection between the legendary Loch Ness Monster and a stranded spaceship whose occupants can assume the appearance of anyone they choose? The Doctor (Tom Baker) and Sarah Jane had better find out the answer...before it's too late! 100 min.
04-3219 Restored *$19.99*

Doctor Who: The Android Invasion (1975)
Thinking they've arrived in a quiet English village, the Doctor (Tom Baker) and Sarah Jane soon realize the townspeople are robotic doubles and the "village" is an alien training base for an invasion of Earth. 96 min.
04-3298 □*$19.99*

Doctor Who:
Planet Of Evil (1975)
When a scientific team on a planet at the edge of the universe is attacked, the Doctor (Tom Baker) and Sarah Jane must deal with a deadly anti-matter menace. 94 min.
04-3325 □*$19.99*

Doctor Who:
The Masque Of Mandragora (1976)
The Doctor (Tom Baker) pays a visit to Renaissance Italy, unaware that his Tardis had a stowaway: a portion of an alien energy helix that takes over the body of an astrological cult's leader and launches a plan to take over the Earth. 99 min.
04-2749 *$19.99*

Doctor Who:
The Robots Of Death (1976)
Trapped aboard an orbiting "factory ship," the Doctor (Tom Baker) and companion Leela are accused of murder and uncover the plans for a rebellion of robots. 91 min.
04-3152 □*$19.99*

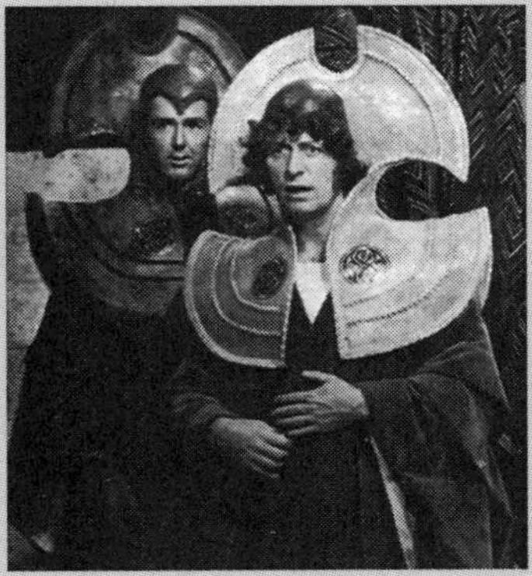

Doctor Who:
The Deadly Assassin (1976)
While on the Time Lords' home planet of Gallifrey, the Doctor (Tom Baker) is arrested and charged with killing the president. Can he prove his innocence and catch the arch-enemy behind the plot to seize control? 85 min.
04-3207 *$19.99*

Doctor Who:
The Seeds Of Doom (1976)
An Antarctic expedition uncovers a pair of alien seed pods that contain monstrous plant creatures. When a deranged millionaire plans to use one of the monsters to take over Earth's plant life, the Doctor (Tom Baker) must nip his scheme in the bud. 144 min.
04-3243 □*$19.99*

Doctor Who:
The Hand Of Fear (1976)
When Sarah Jane comes into possession of a mysterious fossilized hand—which soon comes into possession of her—the Doctor (Tom Baker) must free her from the control of an alien criminal genius. 98 min.
04-3411 □*$19.99*

Doctor Who:
The Brain Of Morbius
Collector's Edition (1976)
An alien scientist is keeping alive the brain of Morbius, an evil renegade Time Lord, and plans to transplant it into a new body. Can the Doctor (Tom Baker) keep his head on his shoulders as he and Sarah Jane try to prevent Morbius' return? Complete, unedited version; 100 min.
04-3413 □*$19.99*

Doctor Who: The Talons Of
Weng-Chiang (1977)
The Doctor (Tom Baker) and Leela, in Victorian London, find that a sinister magician is serving as the front for a murderous time-traveler. 140 min.
04-3212 Was $19.99 □*$14.99*

Doctor Who:
Image Of The Fendahl (1977)
The Doctor (Tom Baker) and Leela must stop scientists examining a 12 million-year-old skull from unleashing a powerful alien force that could devour the Earth. 95 min.
04-3327 □*$19.99*

Doctor Who:
Horror Of Fang Rock (1977)
Is a remote turn-of-the-century lighthouse haunted by the spirits of the dead, or is the horror from beyond the stars? It's up to the Doctor (Tom Baker) and Leela to solve the mystery.
04-3750 □*$19.99*

Doctor Who: Face Of Evil (1977)
The Doctor (Tom Baker) gets to correct a past mistake and gains a new companion, the warrior woman Leela, when he saves a primitive tribe of humans from a mad computer.
04-3909 □*$19.99*

Doctor Who:
The Invasion Of Time (1978)
It's anything but a pleasant visit home when the Doctor (Tom Baker) and Leela's journey to Gallifrey leads to an attack by alien invaders and the Doctor accused of being a traitor!
19-5007 □*$29.99*

Doctor Who:
The Ribos Operation (1978)
Sent by the mysterious White Guardian on a quest (which encompassed the 1978-79 season) to recover the cosmos-scattered components of the powerful Key to Time, the Doctor (Tom Baker), fellow Time Lord Romana and K-9 first arrive on the wintry planet Ribos, where they must outwit a team of intergalactic con men. 99 min.
04-3384 □*$19.99*

Doctor Who:
The Pirate Planet (1978)
In order to find the second Key to Time fragment, the Doctor (Tom Baker) must stop a mobile, hollow planet capable of surrounding other worlds and draining them of their energy. 101 min.
04-3386 □*$19.99*

Doctor Who:
The Stones Of Blood (1978)
Twentieth-century Earth is the location of the third segment of the Key to Time, but finding it is the easy part for the Doctor (Tom Baker) and his companions, as they get caught up in a mystery involving Druidic ruins, bloodthirsty creatures of stone, and an interplanetary fugitive. 96 min.
04-3297 □*$14.99*

Doctor Who:
The Androids Of Tara (1978)
The search for the Key to Time segments brings the Doctor (Tom Baker) and Romana to a world where the feuding royal families use android doubles as part of their plans of kidnapping and deception to take over the planet. 98 min.
04-3296 □*$19.99*

Doctor Who:
The Power Of Kroll (1978)
On a swamp-covered moon, the Doctor (Tom Baker) must halt a civil war—and defeat a gigantic squid-like monster—as he searches for the fifth Key to Time piece. 91 min.
04-3385 □*$19.99*

Doctor Who:
The Armageddon Factor (1979)
The Doctor (Tom Baker) and Romana have located the final piece to the Key to Time, but recovering it means getting involved in a war between twin planets, as well as fending off the menace of the baleful Black Guardian. 148 min.
04-3388 □*$19.99*

Doctor Who: City Of Death (1979)
An alien spaceship trapped on prehistoric Earth, a mysterious count living in present-day Paris, and a locked room full of authentic Mona Lisa paintings add up to a tantalizing mystery for the Doctor (Tom Baker) and Romana. Look for John Cleese in a cameo. 100 min.
04-2813 Was $19.99 *$14.99*

Doctor Who:
Destiny Of The Daleks (1979)
In the distant future, the Doctor (Tom Baker) is caught in the middle of a centuries-long battle between his oldest enemies, the Daleks, and the equally merciless Movellans. Which side will the Time Lord take? 99 min.
04-3452 *$19.99*

Doctor Who:
Nightmare Of Eden (1979)
A scientist's crystalline "recordings" of creatures from the planet Eden threaten to overrun an interstellar liner, and only the Doctor (Tom Baker) and Romana can save the ship and its occupants. 96 min.
04-3811 □*$19.99*

Doctor Who: Shada (1980)
A BBC strike halted filming of this never-broadcast Tom Baker episode, featured here with footage available nowhere else and special linking narration. Join the Doctor, Romana and K-9 as a visit to a Time Lord living incognito on Earth leads to a desperate race to a distant prison planet. 101 min.
04-2571 *$19.99*

Doctor Who:
The Leisure Hive (1980)
A visit to an intergalactic recreational center is anything but a vacation for the Doctor (Tom Baker), Romana and K-9 when they're accused of murder and must stop a local official from relaunching an interplanetary war. 87 min.
04-3451 *$19.99*

Doctor Who: The E-Space
Trilogy Boxed Set (1980)
The complete three-adventure odyssey of the Doctor (Tom Baker), Romana, K-9 and new ally Adric in the interdimensional realm known as E-Space, where the menaces include marsh monsters ("Full Circle"), medieval space vampires ("State of Decay") and star-spanning slaveships ("Warriors' Gate"), is available in a three-tape collection. 4 1/2 hrs. total.
04-3537 *$49.99*

Doctor Who:
The Keeper Of Traken (1981)
A haven of interplanetary peace and harmony, the Union of Traken is threatened by a mysterious creature known as the Melkur, and the Doctor (Tom Baker) is shocked to find the true source of the evil. 98 min.
04-2748 *$19.99*

Doctor Who: Logopolis (1981)
The Master's latest plan for universal conquest lures the Doctor (Tom Baker) and his companions to present-day Earth, the mathematical city of Logopolis, and a battle between the arch-foes in which only one will survive. 99 min.
04-2701 *$19.99*

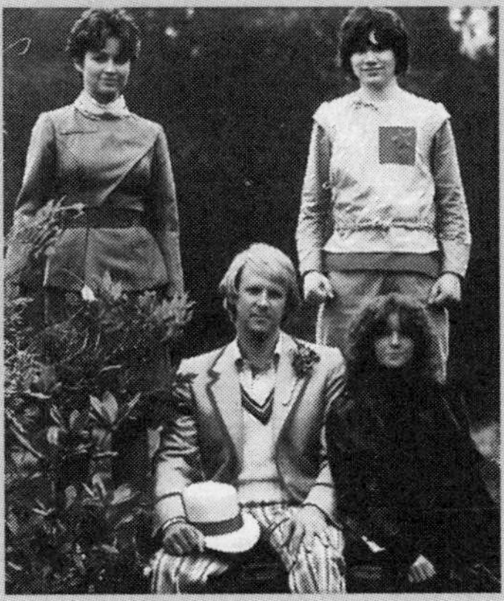

Doctor Who: Castrovalva (1981)
The first adventure of the Fifth Doctor (Peter Davison) finds him in critical condition following his latest regeneration. His only hope to recovery is the fabled land of Castrovalva, but an old enemy lies in wait. 97 min.
04-2703 *$19.99*

Doctor Who: Kinda (1981)
A malevolent presence known as the Mara uses Tegan as a bridge into the real world, but can the Doctor (Peter Davison) destroy it without ending his companion's life? 98 min.
04-3326 □*$19.99*

Doctor Who: The Visitation
(1981)/Black Orchid (1981)
In this special Peter Davison double feature, the Doctor, Tegan and Nyssa must deal with an alien menace who plan to unleash the Black Plague in 17th-century Europe, followed by a visit to 1920s England and a macabre mystery with ties to the South American jungle. 146 min. total.
04-3329 □*$29.99*

Doctor Who: Earthshock (1982)
The Doctor (Peter Davison) and his companions land in the middle of a 26th-century whodunit when the murder of geologists on an abandoned planet leads to an encounter with his old enemies, the Cybermen. 99 min.
04-2619 *$19.99*

Doctor Who:
Mawdryn Undead (1983)
The latest scheme by the sinister Black Guardian to gain revenge on the Doctor (Peter Davison) sends the Time Lord to Earth for an encounter with allies old (the unflappable Brigadier Lethbridge-Stewart) and new (the mysterious Turlough). 99 min.
04-2750 *$19.99*

Doctor Who: Terminus (1983)
The Black Guardian's latest plan for revenge has the Doctor (Peter Davison) and company trapped on board a starship loaded with plague victims and bound for the space station Terminus. 99 min.
04-2814 *$19.99*

Doctor Who:
Enlightenment (1983)
An interstellar "sailing ship" race is in reality the Black Guardian's ultimate plan to destroy the Doctor (Peter Davison), and Turlough's ultimate moment of deciding which side he's on. 97 min.
04-2857 *$19.99*

Doctor Who: Arc Of Infinity (1983)
Omega's latest plan to escape his anti-matter imprisonment causes his essence to merge with that of the Doctor (Peter Davison). Will the Time Lords be forced to destroy both of them to save the universe? 98 min.
04-3245 □*$19.99*

Doctor Who: Snakedance (1983)
Tegan is once more possessed by the serpentine, sinister Mara, who forces the Tardis to its home planet, and the Doctor (Peter Davison) must find a way to stop the Mara from crossing over into the real world without killing Tegan. 98 min.
04-3387 □*$19.99*

Doctor Who: The King's
Demons (1983)/The Five
Doctors Collector's Edition (1983)
In the first adventure on this double bill, the Doctor (Peter Davison) must keep the Master from taking over medieval England with the aid of a shape-changing robot named Kamelion. Next, the grand 20th anniversary story finds a menace from the Time Lords' past so dangerous that it takes all five of the Doctor's incarnations, a slew of companions, and some unwilling help from the Master to stop it. Peter Davison, Tom Baker, Jon Pertwee, Patrick Troughton and Richard Hurndall star. 150 min.
04-3414 □*$29.99*

Doctor Who:
The Five Doctors (1983)
The beloved sci-fi series' 20th anniversary show is also available separately. 90 min.
04-3208 *$19.99*

Doctor Who: Resurrection Of
The Daleks (1984)
Caught in an interchronal trap, the Tardis is brought down to 20th-century Earth, where the diabolical Davros forces the Doctor (Peter Davison) to help him revive the Dalek race. 97 min.
04-2810 *$19.99*

Doctor Who:
Warriors Of The Deep (1984)
It's double trouble under the waves when the Doctor (Peter Davison) and his companions must protect 21st-century Earth from a war started by the dual threat of the Sea Devils and the Silurians. 97 min.
04-3456 *$19.99*

Doctor Who: The Awakening
(1984)/Frontios (1984)
A chilling tale of a quaint English town and the alien terror hidden beneath an ancient church crypt leads off this double feature of Peter Davison "Who" adventures. Next, the last survivors of the planet Earth find their settlement on the distant planet Frontios under attack by a mysterious force.
04-3623 □*$29.99*

Doctor Who: Planet Of Fire (1984)
Joined by American student Perpugillian "Peri" Brown, the Doctor (Peter Davison) and Turlough are lured to the distant planet Sarn, where they must deal with a fiery trap laid for them by the Master. 90 min.
04-3747 □*$19.99*

Doctor Who:
The Caves Of Androzani (1984)
Caught in the middle of an interplanetary war for control of a mysterious and addictive substance, the Doctor (Peter Davison) and Peri find themselves in a battle that only one of them will escape. 101 min.
04-2570 *$19.99*

Doctor Who:
The Twin Dilemma (1984)
A pair of mathematical genius twin brothers are abducted, but is the newly-regenerated Doctor (Colin Baker) in any shape to save them before they're used as pawns in a scheme for galactic domination? 99 min.
04-2620 *$19.99*

Doctor Who:
Vengeance On Varos (1984)
Trapped in the Punishment Dome on the fear-ruled planet of Varos, the Doctor (Colin Baker) and Peri face one of their most deadly adventures yet. 89 min.
04-2957 *$19.99*

Doctor Who:
The Two Doctors (1985)
There's twice the adventure and twice the Time Lords in this tale, as the Doctor (Colin Baker) crosses paths with his second incarnation (Patrick Troughton), as well as some Sontaran warriors and a nasty cook with a taste for humans. 132 min.
04-2956 *$19.99*

Doctor Who:
The Mark Of The Rani (1985)
In Victorian England, the Doctor (Colin Baker) has not one, but two fellow "renegade" Time Lords to deal with when he must defeat the sinister schemes of the Master and the lovely but lethal Rani (Kate O'Mara). 89 min.
04-3412 □*$19.99*

Doctor Who: Timelash (1985)
The doctor (Colin Baker), in order to rescue a young girl and a mysterious amulet, must risk his own lives in a "time vortex" on the planet Karfel.
04-3626 □*$19.99*

Doctor Who: Trial Of
A Time Lord Boxed Set (1986)
In one of the most dramatic (and longest) Who stories ever, the Doctor (Colin Baker) is held captive on Gallifrey and put on trial for violating the Time Lords' code of non-interference. Four stories ("Mysterious Planet," "Mind Warp," "Terror of the Vervoids" and "The Ultimate Foe") were combined for this epic-length adventure. 351 min.
04-2698 *$49.99*

Doctor Who:
Time And The Rani (1987)
Woozy from his latest regeneration and separated from companion Melanie, the Doctor (Sylvester McCoy) becomes an unwitting assistant to the wicked Rani and her scheme for manipulating time. 89 min.
04-3242 □*$19.99*

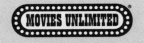

Doctor Who: Dragonfire (1987)
It's up to the Doctor (Sylvester McCoy) and Melanie, with the aid of a feisty teenage girl named Ace, to put out the mercenary Kane's plan to recover the mystic Dragonfire from the planet Stavros and use it for revenge. 73 min.
04-3410 □$19.99

Doctor Who: Paradise Towers (1987)
The Doctor (Sylvester McCoy) and Melanie find horror in the high-rise when the Tardis lands them in a run-down computerized apartment complex whose remaining tenants are terrorized by a mysterious enemy. 98 min.
04-3455 $19.99

Doctor Who: Silver Nemesis (1988)
In this grand 25th anniversary adventure, the Doctor (Sylvester McCoy) and companion Ace return to Earth and find themselves caught between a mysterious enemy and the Cybermen for control of an alien weapon. Also includes a featurette on the making of the episode. 139 min.
04-2858 $19.99

Doctor Who: The Happiness Patrol (1988)
What sinister power is forcing the residents of Terra Alpha to smile and be content—or else—and can the Doctor (Sylvester McCoy) put things right and give the planet a happy ending?
04-3624 □$19.99

Doctor Who: The Greatest Show In The Galaxy (1988)
A visit to the interplanetary Psychic Circus is anything but a treat for the Doctor (Sylvester McCoy) and Ace, who find themselves in a three-ring terror trap by the Gods of Ragnarok.
04-3872 □$19.99

Doctor Who: The Curse Of Fenric (1989)
In WWII England, the Doctor (Sylvester McCoy) and Ace must uncover who is trying to bring an ages-old evil back to Earth while at the same time stop the more conventional menace of a German invasion force. 104 min.
04-3229 $19.99

Doctor Who: Ghost Light (1989)
What is the sinister secret hidden inside the cargo of a mysterious alien ship, and will the Doctor (Sylvester McCoy) and Ace learn it before it's too late? 72 min.
04-3324 □$19.99

Doctor Who: Survival (1989)
A rash of mysterious disappearances in and around London soon has the Doctor (Sylvester McCoy) and Ace facing the deadly interstellar hunters known as the Cheetah People. 72 min.
04-3383 □$19.99

Doctor Who: Battlefield (1989)
An adventure that stretches from the 20th century back to the days of Camelot pits the Doctor (Sylvester McCoy) against the evil magicks of Morgaine Le Fay and Mordred and reunites him with old comrade Brigadier Lethbridge-Stewart.
04-3625 □$19.99

Doctor Who: Daleks: The Early Years
Doctor #5, Peter Davison, hosts this fascinating look at "his" first fateful meetings with the metallic marauders. Classic adventures from the William Hartnell and Patrick Troughton years, rare clips, behind-the-scenes interviews and more are featured. 106 min.
04-2700 $19.99

Doctor Who: Cybermen—The Early Years
They're half-human, half-robot, and totally ruthless and without soul. Those implacable metallic menaces, the Cybermen, give the Doctor(s) no end of trouble in this special tape introduced by Colin Baker. 120 min.
04-2617 $19.99

Doctor Who: The Hartnell Years
You don't need a Tardis to travel back in time with host Sylvester McCoy as he shows you the greatest moments from the first three seasons of "Doctor Who," featuring William Hartnell as the first Doctor. 88 min.
04-3230 $19.99

Doctor Who: The Troughton Years
Who better to host a salute to the second Doctor than his successor, Jon Pertwee? See Patrick Troughton, his companions, and a host of strange creatures and otherworldly menaces in this video tribute. 84 min.
04-3231 $19.99

Doctor Who: The Pertwee Years
Climb aboard "good old Bessie" with Jon Pertwee as he looks back on his five-season run as the third Doctor, a tenure that saw the Time Lord take on such enemies as the Silurians, the Time Warrior, the Daleks and the diabolical Master. 88 min.
04-2569 $19.99

Doctor Who: The Tom Baker Years
For seven years he reigned as the most popular Doctor of all (or at least the one with the longest scarf!). Now join host Tom Baker as he looks back on his favorite episodes and moments from the series. 170 min.
04-2618 $29.99

Doctor Who: The Colin Baker Years
His Tardis tenure may have been the most controversial, and now Colin Baker looks back on his years as the sixth Doctor, with rare interviews and clips from his favorite moments on the show. 88 min.
04-2856 $19.99

Doctor Who: The Daleks Boxed Set
The Doctor's most infamous foes roll into the spotlight with this special collector's set featuring two classic Dalek encounters. "The Chase" (1965) features William Hartnell and company pursued across time and space by a Dalek-built time machine, while Sylvester McCoy must stop a year-leaping conquest of Earth in "Remembrance of the Daleks" (1988). 248 min. total.
04-2699 $39.99

Doctor Who: More Than 30 Years In The Tardis
In all his incarnations, he's been travelling through time and space to save the universe for three decades. Follow the many adventures of Doctor Who, his allies and his enemies in this special 30th anniversary salute that features a look at all seven Doctors. 87 min.
04-3241 □$19.99

Doctor Who: K-9 & Company: A Girl's Best Friend (1981)
The first spin-off in "Who" history featured the Doctor's feisty robot dog coming to 20th-century Earth, where he joins former companion Sarah Jane Smith (Elisabeth Sladen) in a dangerous adventure involving modern-day witches in a remote English village. 49 min.
04-3748 □$19.99

Doctor Who: The Curse Of Fatal Death (1999)
Produced for the 1999 UK Comic Relief show, this affectionately hilarious pastiche finds the Ninth Doctor's (Rowan Atkinson) holiday with companion/fiancée Emma (Julia Sawalha) delayed by a deadly trap set by the Master (Jonathan Pryce) that could make the Time Lord run out of regenerations. Richard E. Grant, Jim Broadbent, Hugh Grant and Joanna Lumley co-star. Also included are a "behind-the-scenes" documentary and "Who" skits featuring French and Saunders and Lenny Henry. 62 min.
19-5018 $19.99

The Airzone Solution
Four of TV's Doctor Whos (Colin Baker, Peter Davison, Sylvester McCoy, Jon Pertwee) teamed up in this environmental-themed drama. In a near future where toxic rainstorms are common, a TV weatherman teams up with an ecological activist and the ghost of a fellow journalist to learn the truth behind the mysterious Airzone Corporation's pledge to clean up the atmosphere. 65 min.
20-7187 $24.99

The Stranger Double Feature
The enigmatic interstellar traveller and his companion, Miss Brown, return in two exciting adventures. A strange garden party and a clown who possesses people's souls threaten the Stranger in "Summoned by Shadows," while a paradise planet turns out to be anything but in "More than a Messiah." Colin Baker, Nicola Bryant star. 75 min.
20-7189 $24.99

The Stranger: The Terror Game
The mystery of the Stranger may at last be solved, as his sudden appearance in a nightclub back alley is the first in a series of events that leads him to putting together the clues to his past...that is, if the Preceptors will let him. Colin Baker, Louise Jameson, David Troughton star. BONUS: Also included is a behind-the-scenes documentary, "Stranger than Fiction." 90 min.
20-7216 $29.99

The Stranger: Breach Of Peace
A pair of extradimensional terrorists are trapped on Earth, and the Stranger, whose mysterious past is linked to theirs, holds the key to their finding the way back. Colin Baker stars in this suspenseful entry in the British sci-fi series. 46 min.
20-7310 $24.99

The Stranger: Eye Of The Beholder, Part 1
The Stranger (Colin Baker) and his fellow Preceptors abandon their human forms to return to the Dimensional Web, but a mysterious force sends them back to Earth, where a series of disasters must be prevented. Sci-fi action also features David Troughton, John Wadmore. 60 min.
20-7387 $24.99

The Stranger: Eye Of The Beholder, Part 2
What connection is there between the arrival of the Stranger and fellow Preceptors Egan and Saul on Earth and a scientist's top-secret project, code-named "Metaphysic"? Are they there to help save the planet...or trigger its destruction? Colin Baker, David Troughton, John Wadmore star. 60 min.
20-7408 $24.99

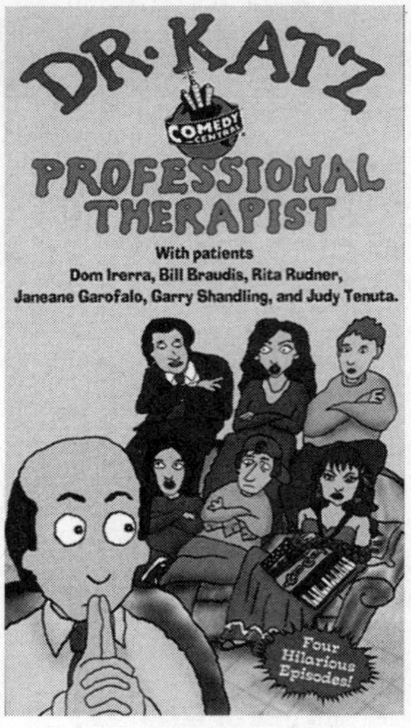

Dr. Katz Professional Therapist
The Comedy Central cult favorite chronicles the squiggly, animated adventures of Dr. Katz, a mild-mannered psychiatrist who's divorced and shares his home with his lazy twentysomething son, Ben. Voiced by comic Jonathan Katz, the good doctor treats a number of neurotic patients, played by top comedians. Except where noted, each tape features two episodes and runs about 50 min. There are seven volumes available, including:

Dr. Katz Professional Therapist, Vol. 1
Emo Philips, Wendy Liebman and South Philly's Dom Irrera are among the doctor's patients.
15-5336 $14.99

Dr. Katz Professional Therapist, Vol. 2
Heckling Dr. Katz from the couch are Kevin Meaney, Carol Leifer and Ray Romano.
15-5337 $14.99

Dr. Katz Professional Therapist, Vol. 3
This special double-length volume features an array of guest clients that includes Janeane Garofalo, Dom Irrera, Rita Rudner, Garry Shandling and Judy Tenuta. 100 min.
15-5352 $19.99

Passport To Danger/ Secret File, U.S.A.
Diplomatic courier Cesar Romero takes another risk-filled assignment in a thrilling installment of "Passport to Danger." Then, stay tuned for Robert Alda as U.S. espionage agent Bill Morgan in an episode from the 1954 syndicated series "Secret File, U.S.A." 55 min.
10-7039 Was $19.99 $14.99

The 11th Annual Emmy Awards (1959)
The variety special "An Evening with Fred Astaire" is the big winner on this May 6, 1959 broadcast, and the debonair Astaire waltzes off with the best single performance Emmy. Also appearing to honor the likes of Raymond Burr, Loretta Young and Ann B. Davis are Jack Benny, Shirley Temple, James Arness, Ed Sullivan, Richard Nixon and many others.
10-7517 Was $19.99 $14.99

Action In The Afternoon/ Lash Of The West
Starting off this double bill is an early Western show depicting small town life in turn-of-the-century Montana, broadcast live from (where else?) suburban Philadelphia. Next up, it's Lash La Rue, with trademark bullwhip in hand, introducing Western shorts in an early '50s telecast. 55 min.
10-7035 Was $19.99 $14.99

The Wide Country (1962)
In this Western drama, Earl Holliman played Mitch Guthrie, a modern rodeo star who's found success as a bronco rider, but who wants to dissuade his kid brother Andy (Andrew Prine) from getting into the business. Featured is the episode "Step Over the Sky." 50 min.
10-9209 Was $19.99 $14.99

Petula Clark: Spectacular! (1968)
Filmed at the height of her popularity, this TV special features Petula Clark performing such hits as "Downtown," "Don't Sleep in the Subway," "The 'In' Crowd," "We Can Work It Out" and "How Are Things in Glocca Morra?" from her film "Finian's Rainbow." Special guest Harry Belafonte caused some controversy after he and Petula touched while singing a duet! 57 min.
89-7022 $14.99

The Garry Moore Show (1955)
This popular daytime variety series made a household name out of its star, and in the four 15-minute shows featured here, you'll see Moore and sidekick Durwood Kirby present some comedic poetry, a playful beagle and an irritable otter, jazz by Martha Davis and Calvin, and even some live commercials for Chevrolet and Ipana toothpaste. 60 min.
82-1048 $19.99

Captain Video And His Video Rangers (1949)
One of the most popular early TV kids' shows, "Captain Video" starred Richard Coogan as the "electronic wizard...master of time and space...guardian of the safety of the world" who battled all sorts of interplanetary evils. Two episodes are featured here, as the Captain journeys to Mars and foils a bank robbery in China. 60 min.
01-9025 $19.99

Spitting Image
This fun-filled show from England features life-like puppets portraying famous actors, rock stars and politicians in hilarious situations. The comedy is acerbic and often downright nasty, the puppetry astounding and the laughs non-stop.

Spitting Image: Bumbledown: The Life And Times Of Ronald Reagan
Ronald Reagan and pals are targets for satire in this hilarious political send-up. 38 min.
53-9437 $19.99

Spitting Image: The Music Video
The rock music world gets rocked and socked as Spitting Image parodies such pop stars as Sting, Michael Jackson, and more. Includes "The Chicken Song." 56 min.
53-9439 $19.99

Spitting Image: National Exposé
The provocative puppetry of England's "Spitting Image" takes on an array of celebrities in this outrageous program. The Royal Family, Cher, Dan Quayle, Rod Stewart, Elvis and others are skewered to hilarious perfection. 50 min.
53-9673 $19.99

Best Of Crapston Villas, Vol. 1
From the same people who gave you "Spitting Image" comes this outrageous British TV series that uses claymation to delve into the lives of the tenants of a dilapidated Victorian house-turned-apartment building. Among the residents you'll meet are Jonathan, Sophie, Flossie, the Stephenson family and gay lovers Robbie and Larry. Included here are the first five episodes.
48-8069 $14.99

Last Of The Summer Wine: Boxed Set
Acclaimed British comedy series focusing on three elderly ne'er-do-wells named Blamire, Compo and Clegg who continually find adventure and trouble while roaming the streets of their small Yorkshire town. Stars Michael Bates, Bill Owen and Peter Sallis. Set includes nine episodes, plus a special feature-length episode. Volumes include "Last of the Summer Wine," "Getting Sam Home," "Spring Fever" and "Forked Lightning." 360 min. total.
53-8883 Was $79.99 $59.99

The Very Best Of Hill Street Blues: Boxed Set
One of the most acclaimed TV series ever, the day-to-day exploits of the men and women of the Hill Street police station ran on NBC from 1981 to 1987, setting new standards for realism and mixing comedy and drama. This four-tape collection features one of the best episodes from each season: the pilot "Hill Street Station," "Freedom's Last Stand," "Trial by Fury," "Grace Under Pressure," "Mayo, Hold the Pickle," "Remembrance of Hits Past" and "It Ain't Over Till It's Over," the series finale. Daniel J. Travanti, Michael Conrad, Veronica Hamel, Bruce Weitz and Dennis Franz star. 350 min. total.
53-9310 Was $59.99 $39.99

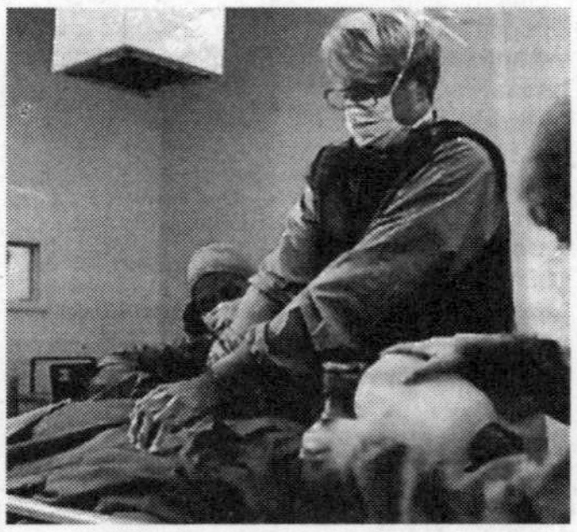

The Very Best Of St. Elsewhere: Boxed Set
"St. Elsewhere" was the mocking nickname given to St. Eligius, a run-down Boston teaching hospital, in the acclaimed 1982-1988 series that mixed laughs and pathos as it followed the day-to-day struggles of the doctors, staff and patients. This four-tape collection features an episode from each season: "Bypass," "Cora and Arnie," "Drama Center," "My Aim Is True," the two-part "Time Heals," "Afterlife" and "The Last One." Ed Begley, Jr., William Daniels, Ed Flanders, Norman Lloyd, Howie Mandel and Denzel Washington star. 400 min. total.
53-8585 Was $59.99 $39.99

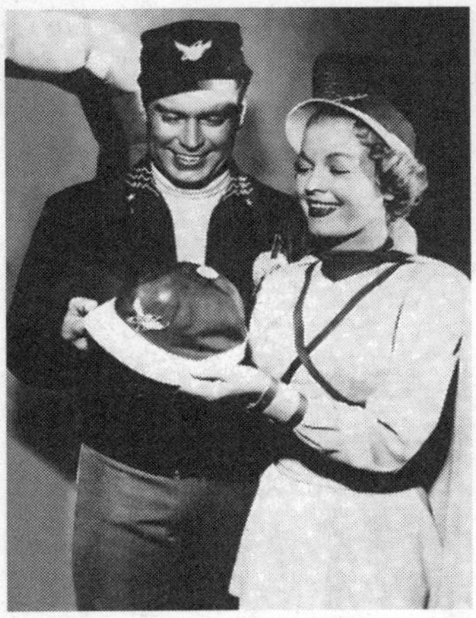

Rocky Jones, Space Ranger

Richard Crane starred on TV from 1953 to 1955 as the intrepid Rocky, who patrolled the skyways of the United Solar System in the 21st century, along with sidekicks Bobby, Winky and Vena and scientific genius Professor Newton. These feature-length adventures are culled from episodes of the show and, except where noted, run about 78 min. There are 12 volumes available, including:

Rocky Jones: Forbidden Moon

Sent on a rescue mission to Space Station RV5, the Space Rangers are unprepared when they face a deadly enemy from a mysterious satellite.

62-1115 *$19.99*

Rocky Jones: Renegade Satellite

Rocky and company face a deadly double challenge from arch-enemies Dr. Reno and Rudy DeMarco in the lawless city of Ankapore.

62-1283 *$19.99*

Rocky Jones: Duel In Space

The Space Rangers must prevent an interstellar crisis when they're charged with escorting a ship full of diplomats to a "space peace" conference. AKA: "Silver Needle in the Sky."

68-8212 *$19.99*

Rocky Jones: The Gypsy Moon

It's a battle of the moons, as two satellite worlds linked by an atmosphere "chain" attack one another, and Rocky and his crew try to stop the madness.

68-8562 Was $19.99 *$14.99*

Rocky Jones: Crash Of The Moons

Two inhabited worlds are on a collision course, and it's up to Rocky and his pals to convince the residents of the imminent destruction.

68-8564 Was $19.99 *$14.99*

Manhunt In Space (1953)

A band of interstellar pirates, headquartered on a hidden planet, threatens the spaceways, and only the Space Rangers can save the day. Richard Crane, Scotty Beckett star in this feature-length adventure from the early sci-fi TV series, "Rocky Jones, Space Ranger." 90 min.

68-8561 *$19.99*

The Best Of Tommy Cooper

Side-splitting Tommy Cooper showcases his expert timing and superior physical comic skills in this program. Wearing his trademark fez and maniacal laugh, Cooper is super. See what has had England howling for years. 50 min.

53-9705 *$19.99*

Tommy Cooper: Not Like That

It's a riotously funny comedy experience, as Tommy Cooper talks about World War II, shows his concern for sick animals, shows you his take on "Romeo and Juliet" and causes chaos in a restaurant. 50 min.

53-9706 *$19.99*

Tommy Cooper: Solid Gold

The always-wacky Tommy Cooper brings his unusual outlook on things to such subjects as prospective in-laws, tennis and cooking in these selected "Best Of" moments. 75 min.

53-9707 *$19.99*

Bless Me, Father

Arthur Lowe stars as Father Duddleswell, head of a small parish outside of London, in this warm and winning British comedy that looks at life in an English community in the 1950s, and Daniel Abineri is his new curate. Each tape features three episodes and runs about 75 min.

Bless Me, Father, Vol. 1

50-8165 *$14.99*

Bless Me, Father, Vol. 2

50-8166 *$14.99*

Bless Me, Father, Vol. 3

50-8167 *$14.99*

Bless Me, Father: Boxed Set

All three volumes are also available in a collector's set.

50-8168 Save $5.00! *$39.99*

Jerry Springer Two-Pack

Look out for those flying chairs when you order "Jerry Springer: Too Hot For TV" and "The Best of Jerry Springer" in one deluxe set.

50-5807 Save $5.00! *$34.99*

Jerry Springer: Secrets And Surprises

Shocking confidences are revealed in this collection of candid moments from TV's most outrageous hour. If you thought she was a she, you're wrong. If you thought he was sleeping with her—guess again! The surprises don't stop when Springer's around!

50-5815 *$14.99*

Music Scene

Originally shown on ABC from September 1969 to January 1970, this musical and comedy series hosted by David Steinberg featured the top acts from rock, folk and country, performing their hits in unusual settings, and wraparound skits by the Music Scene Troupe with Lily Tomlin. Also featured on each volume are special promotional appearances by The Rolling Stones. Each tape runs about 60 min.

Music Scene, Vol. 1

There's something for everyone on this program that features Creedence Clearwater Revival ("Down on the Corner"), Sergio Mendes and Brasil '66 ("Wichita Lineman"), Neil Diamond ("Both Sides Now"), Pete Seeger ("Bring Them Home"), R.B. Greaves ("Take a Letter Maria") and Tony Bennett ("What the World Needs Now").

50-7397 *$19.99*

Music Scene, Vol. 2

More blasts from the 1960s past are offered here, including The Temptations ("Can't Get Next to You"), Merle Haggard ("Okie from Muskogee"), Bobby Sherman ("Little Woman"), Sly and The Family Stone ("Hot Fun in the Summertime"), Steve Lawrence ("The Drifter"), Little Richard ("Tutti-Frutti"), and comedy from Tom Smothers.

50-7398 *$19.99*

Music Scene, Vol. 3

Whether you're into oldies, rock, soul, country, folk or bubblegum, you'll be pleased with this program. Spotlighted are The Archies ("Sugar Sugar"), Charley Pride ("Louisiana Man"), Richie Havens ("Rocky Raccoon"), Paul Anka ("My Way"), B.B. King ("Just a Little Love"), Janis Joplin ("Maybe") and lots more.

50-7399 *$19.99*

Music Scene, Vol. 4

The hits don't stop with The Rascals ("People Got to Be Free"), The Dells ("Oh What a Night"), Roger Miller ("King of the Road"), Spirit ("1984"), Gary Puckett ("This Girl Is a Woman Now"), Three Dog Night ("Eli's Coming") and more.

50-7400 *$19.99*

The Music Scene: Boxed Set #1

Volumes 1-4 of "The Music Scene" are also available in a collector's set.

50-7401 *$79.99*

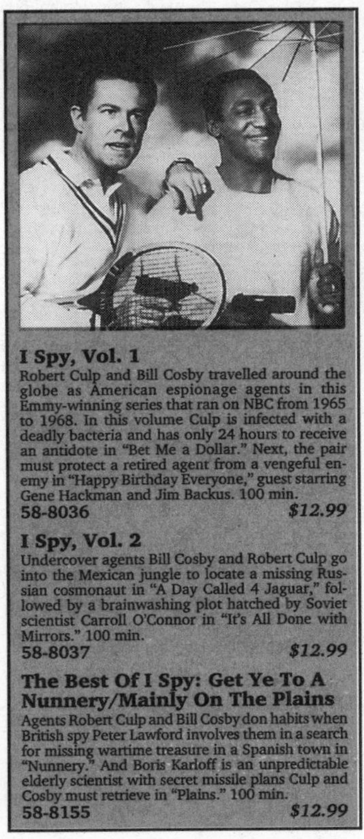

I Spy, Vol. 1

Robert Culp and Bill Cosby travelled around the globe as American espionage agents in this Emmy-winning series that ran on NBC from 1965 to 1968. In this volume Culp is infected with a deadly bacteria and has only 24 hours to receive an antidote in "Bet Me a Dollar." Next, the pair must protect a retired agent from a vengeful enemy in "Happy Birthday Everyone," guest starring Gene Hackman and Jim Backus. 100 min.

58-8036 *$12.99*

I Spy, Vol. 2

Undercover agents Bill Cosby and Robert Culp go into the Mexican jungle to locate a missing Russian cosmonaut in "A Day Called 4 Jaguar," followed by a brainwashing plot hatched by Soviet scientist Carroll O'Connor in "It's All Done with Mirrors." 100 min.

58-8037 *$12.99*

The Best Of I Spy: Get Ye To A Nunnery/Mainly On The Plains

Agents Robert Culp and Bill Cosby don habits when British spy Peter Lawford involves them in a search for missing wartime treasure in a Spanish town in "Nunnery." And Boris Karloff is an unpredictable elderly scientist with secret missile plans Culp and Cosby must retrieve in "Plains." 100 min.

58-8155 *$12.99*

Charlemagne: Boxed Set

Grand British historical mini-series recounts the life and times of the medieval ruler who sought to unite, through both sword and cross, a Europe ruled by anarchy and ignorance. Christian Brendel stars in the title role in this grand tale of military action, political intrigue and grand romance. 300 min. on five tapes.

50-5166 Was $89.99 *$39.99*

Some Mothers Do 'Ave 'Em!: Boxed Set

Michael Crawford ("Phantom of the Opera") starred in this 1973 TV series from England in which he played hapless and trouble-prone family man Frank Spencer. The six-tape collection includes "Take a Break, Take a Husband/The RAF Reunion," "Cliffhanger/King of the Road," "The Job Interview/The Psychiatrist," "George's House/Love Thy Neighbor," "The Hospital Visit/Father's Clinic" and "Moving House." 350 min. NOTE: Individual volumes (except for "Moving House") available at $19.99 each.

53-9971 Save $5.00! *$74.99*

The Best Of Danny Kaye: The TV Years

The magic of Danny Kaye is captured in this collection of his funniest and most charming TV appearances. See Danny as a zany psychoanalyst, a shy man escorting Lucille Ball to a fancy restaurant, a pouting 5-year-old and more. Also here are Danny's duets with Louis Armstrong and Harry Belafonte, scenes from "The Court Jester" and an appearance by Jose Ferrer. 90 min.

59-3004 *$29.99*

George And The Dragon

Here are four classic episodes of the hit 1960s British sitcom featuring Sid James as George, a chauffeur who meets his match when boss Colonel Maynard (John Le Mesurier) hires ubiquitous maid Gabrille Dragon (Peggy Mount). Episodes include "George Meets the Dragon," "The Unexpected Sport," "The Not-So-Tender Trap" and "Night, Night, Sleep Tight." 100 min.

59-7060 *$24.99*

George And Mildred

One of Britain's best-loved sitcoms centers on working-class George and Mildred Roper, who encounter all sorts of funny situations when they move to a suburban area populated by executive types. Featured are the episodes "Jumble Pie," "All Around the Clock" and "The Unkindest Cut of All." 71 min.

59-7066 *$29.99*

George And Mildred: Moving On/The Bad Penny

The misadventures of the Ropers continue, as they try to assimilate into the suburban lifestyle, in these episodes from the popular '70s Britcom. Yootha Joyce, Brian Murphy and Norman Eshley star. 46 min.

59-7080 *$29.99*

Man About The House

One of England's most popular—and talked about—situation comedies ran from 1973 to 1976 and led to America's "Three's Company." Roommates Robin (Richard O'Sullivan), Chrissy (Paula Wilcox) and Jo (Sally Thomsett) get into all sorts of hilarious situations in the episodes "Did You Ever Meet Rommel?," "Two Foot Two Eyes of Blue" and "Carry Me Back to Old Southampton." 75 min.

59-7079 *$29.99*

Inspector Morse

These award-winning adaptations of Colin Dexter's whodnuits star John Thaw as the Oxord detective who enjoys music, beer and a good crime to solve. Except where noted, each boxed collector's set features six Morse mysteries and runs about 10 hrs. total. NOTE: Individual volumes available separately.

Inspector Morse Collection 1

Includes "The Dead of Jericho," "Last Bus to Woodstock," "Last Seen Wearing," "Service of All the Dead," "The Silent World of Nicholas Quinn" and "The Wolvercote Tongue."

53-9691 *$99.99*

Inspector Morse Collection 2

Includes "Deceived by Flight," "The Ghost in the Machine," "Infernal Serpent," "The Last Enemy," "The Secret of Bay 5B" and "The Settling of the Sun."

53-9692 *$99.99*

Inspector Morse Collection 3

Includes "Driven to Distraction," "Fat Chance," "Masonic Mysteries," "Promised Land," "Second Time Around" and "Sins of the Fathers."

53-9693 *$99.99*

Inspector Morse Collection 4

Includes "Absolute Conviction," "Dead on Time," "Death of the Self," "Greeks Bearing Gifts," "Happy Families" and "Who Killed Harry Field."

53-9694 *$99.99*

Inspector Morse Collection 5

Special boxed set includes "Cherubim & Seraphim," "The Day of the Devil," "Deadly Slumber," "Twilight of the Gods," and "The Way Through the Woods," plus "The Making of Inspector Morse."

53-9695 *$99.99*

The Mystery Of Morse: The Making Of Inspector Morse

Take a rare behind-the-scenes look at the making of this popular mystery series that has devoted fans on both sides of the Atlantic. Star John Thaw talks about bringing Colin Dexter's dogged detective to life, memorable scenes are shown, and there's even a tour of Morse's Oxford haunts. 50 min.

53-9701 *$19.99*

The Very Best Of The Bob Newhart Show: Hi Bob!

From a memorable Thanksgiving mess to a near-death experience, some of the greatest "Bob Newhart Show" episodes spotlighting the master of comedic understatement have been gathered in a two-tape set. Included are "The Ceiling Hits Bob," "Who Is Mr. X?," "Grand Delusion," "Big Brother Is Watching," "Over the River and Through the Woods" and "Death Be My Destiny." 150 min. total.

53-6258 *$19.99*

The Very Best Of The Bob Newhart Show: The Doctor Is In

Just how good a psychologist was Dr. Bob Hartley? Judge for yourself with this two-tape collection. Four of the funniest episodes spotlight Bob's therapy groups—and such patients as neurotic Mr. Carlin (Jack Riley), milquetoast Mr. Peterson (John Fiedler), and knitting-mad Mrs. Bakerman (Florida Friebus): "The Battle of the Groups," "Death of a Fruitman," "Group on a Hot Tin Roof" and "Mutiny on the Hartley." 100 min. total.

53-6550 *$19.99*

The Very Best Of The Bob Newhart Show: Boxed Set

Say "Hi, Bob" to Chicago psychologist Bob Hartley (Bob Newhart), his teacher wife Emily (Suzanne Pleshette), next-door neighbor Howard (Bill Daily), and Bob's list of hapless patients with this six-tape boxed collection featuring 12 (two per season) of the funniest episodes from Newhart's popular 1972-1978 CBS sitcom. Included are "Fly the Unfriendly Skies," "Motel," "Bob Hits the Ceiling," "Caged Fury," "Happy Trails" and more. 300 min. total.

53-8964 Was $79.99 *$59.99*

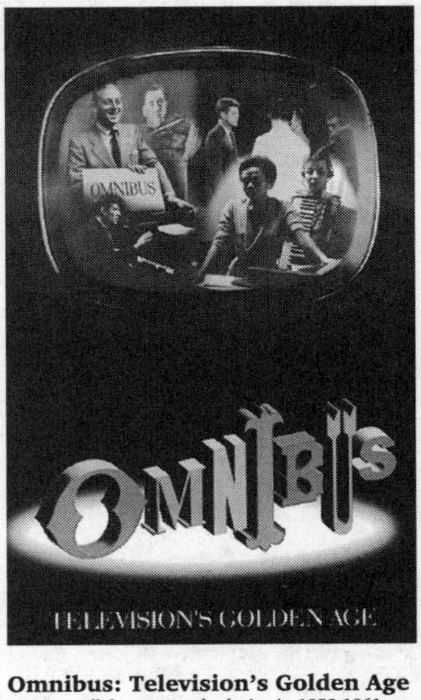

Omnibus: Television's Golden Age

Airing on all three networks during its 1952-1961 run, "Omnibus" was television's first showcase for the performing and creative arts, with segments running the gamut from opera to drama, from jazz to science documentaries. See such notables as Leonard Bernstein, James Dean, Nichols and May, and Jonathan Winters in their TV debuts; watch rare clips featuring Victor Borge, Benny Goodman, Gene Kelly and Senator John F. Kennedy; and hear from series host Alistair Cooke. Hume Cronyn narrates. 100 min.

80-7288 *$29.99*

Omnibus: La Boheme (1953)

Where else but in TV's Golden Age would an opera be sponsored by a bowling company? Alistair Cooke hosts this episode from the fondly remembered arts series, featuring a performance of Puccini's drama by the Metropolitan Opera. Brian Sulivan, Nadine Conor star. 81 min.

09-1920 *$24.99*

Public Prosecutor, Vol. 1

John Howard hosted this early '50s whodunit series, also known as "Crawford Mystery Theatre," in which a panel of detective-story writers tried to solve filmed mysteries. Featured here are "The Case of Crepe for Suzette" and "Case of the Missing Hour." 60 min.

68-8491 *$19.99*

Public Prosecutor, Vol. 2

Match wits with a group of mystery writers and see if you can solve "The Case of Valentine's Heart" and "The Case of the Shattered Mirror" before they do. 60 min.

68-8492 *$19.99*

Public Prosecutor/Police Call

Invited guests, many of whom were detective-fiction writers, competed in this early '50s quiz show to determine the identity of the culprit in each week's mystery; John Howard hosts "The Man Who Wasn't There." Also included is an episode of "Police Call," a mid-'50s police drama that was derived from actual law enforcement cases, with King Donovan. 55 min.

10-7037 Was $19.99 *$14.99*

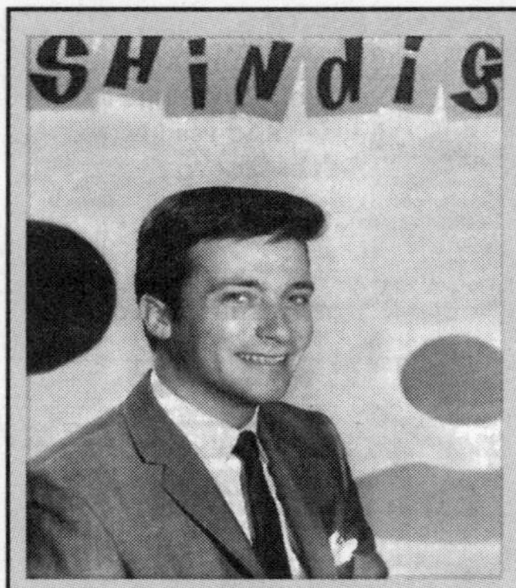

Shindig!: Motor City Magic
It's a Motown celebration in this collection from the '60s precursor to MTV, spotlighting such artists as The Four Tops, Marvin Gaye, The Supremes and The Temptations. "My Girl," "It's the Same Old Song," "Stop (In the Name of Love)" and other classics are performed. 30 min.
15-5170 *$12.99*

Shindig!: Frat Party
Get caught up in the school spirit in this rockin', gyratin' dance party. The Isley Brothers perform "Shout," The Kingsmen sing the unfathomable "Louie, Louie," and other frat faves go to town, too. 30 min.
15-5171 *$12.99*

Shindig!: Jackie Wilson
Rhythm-and-blues great Jackie Wilson is shown in all his glory performing live on the fondly remembered TV concert show, belting out "That's Why (I Love You So)," "Baby Workout," "She's Alright" and more. 30 min.
15-5172 *$12.99*

Shindig!: Soul
Get down with soul masters like James Brown (performing his classic "Papa's Got a Brand New Bag"), Joe Tex ("Hold On to What I Got"), Booker T and The MGs ("Green Onions") and more. 30 min.
15-5182 *$12.99*

Shindig!: Groovy Gals
See the top ladies in the music biz really sing up a storm. There's "Rescue Me" by Fontella Bass; Leslie Gore performing "Judy's Turn to Cry"; The Supremes chirping "Baby Love"; "Lover's Concerto" from The Toys; and seven more. 30 min.
15-5181 *$12.99*

Shindig!: Jerry Lee Lewis
A killer performance from "The Killer," one of rock's first and greatest stars. Songs include "Whole Lotta Shakin' Going On," "Great Balls of Fire," "Rockin' Pneumonia," "Breathless" and more. 30 min.
15-5207 *$12.99*

Shindig!: Sixties Superstars
Relive the greatest groups of the Sixties with The Yardbirds ("For Your Love"), The Mamas and The Papas ("California Dreamin'") and The Byrds ("Turn, Turn, Turn"). 30 min.
15-5208 *$12.99*

Shindig!: The Kinks
Ray Davies leads the classic rock group through such Kinky classics as "You Really Got Me," "Tired of Waiting for You," "It's All Right," "I'm a Lover Not a Fighter" and others. 30 min.
15-5226 *$12.99*

Shindig!: British Invasion, Vol. 1
A host of great bands from "across the pond" perform the tunes that made them worldwide sensations. Check out Peter and Gordon ("World Without Love"), The Honeycombs ("Have I the Right"), Manfred Mann ("Do Wah Diddy"), Herman's Hermits ("I'm into Something Good") and more. 30 min.
15-5227 *$12.99*

Shindig!: British Invasion, Vol. 2
"England swings like a pendulum do," and so will you with this ultra-gear grab-bag of British chart-toppers performing their greatest hits. Features The Animals ("We Got to Get Out of This Place"), Peter & Gordon ("I Go to Pieces"), The Searchers ("Needles and Pins"), The Yardbirds ("Heart Full of Soul") and others. 30 min.
15-5256 *$12.99*

Shindig!: Legends Of Rock 'N' Roll
A veritable "Who's Who" of rock's early days takes the "Shindig!" stage, including Chuck Berry ("Back in the U.S.A."), Jerry Lee Lewis ("High School Confidential"), The Righteous Brothers ("Ko Ko Joe"), Aretha Franklin ("Mockingbird"), and many more. 30 min.
15-5255 *$12.99*

The Ford Show
Why bless his pea-pickin' heart, if it isn't Tennessee Ernie Ford in two episodes of his homespun NBC show from the late Fifties. Join Bristol, Tennessee's favorite son for an hour of comedy, variety and hymn singing. Featured here are two shows from the early 1960s with guest stars The Everly Brothers. 60 min.
10-7350 Was $19.99 *$14.99*

Dateline Europe (Foreign Intrigue)
Politics, suspense and stunning locales mixed in this early '50s syndiated series. Jerome Thor stars as a two-fisted European correspondent for an American news wire service and Synda Scott plays a rival reporter. Included here are "The New Regime" and "The Hostage." 55 min.
10-7405 Was $19.99 *$14.99*

The Tim McCoy Show/ Cowboy G-Men
Cowboy legend Tim McCoy spins another true story of the West with an account of Buffalo Bill's "dead man's hand," in "Deadwood Days"; then ranglers-turned-government agents Russell Hayden and Jackie Coogan help clear up a "Sawdust Swindle," in their 1952 drama. 40 min.
10-7448 Was $19.99 *$14.99*

Witness/One Way Out
The second incarnation of the respected dramatic anthology series filmed in Hollywood and pared to half-hour size. Featured are Dick Powell, Charles Bronson and Ida Lupino in "Witness" and "One Way Out." 55 min.
10-7451 Was $24.99 *$14.99*

Ford Startime: The Man (1960)
Audie Murphy and Thelma Ritter star in a superb psychological thriller about an unbalanced, possibly homicidal, drifter who works his way into the home of an old army buddy's mother. 50 min.
09-1539 *$24.99*

The Adventures Of Champion/Steve Canyon
Gene Autry's steed was owned on TV by young Barry Curtis, the only other person who could ride him. An episode of their adventures appears, along with Dean Fredericks as cartoonist Milton Caniff's trouble-shooting Air Force commander. 55 min.
10-7453 Was $19.99 *$14.99*

Mr. Peepers/ The Hank McCune Show
Wally Cox gained fame in the early '50s as shy school teacher Robinson Peepers in this fondly remembered sitcom, which co-starred Tony Randall, Marion Lorne and Pat Benoit. Next, "The Hank McCune Show," a slapstick comedy that originated the use of canned laughter (now you know who to blame). 55 min.
10-7460 *$19.99*

The World Of Sholom Aleichem (1959)
Originally made for TV's "Play of the Week," this warm and funny program brings to life three short stories from the famed Yiddish writer that depict the joy and anguish of the Jewish experience in his native Russia: "A Tale of Chelm," "Bontche Schweig" and "The High School." The ensemble cast includes Gertrude Berg, Jack Gilford, Sam Levene, Zero Mostel and Nancy Walker. 95 min.
55-9021 *$29.99*

TV's Western Heroes
Hi-yo, cowboy buffs! Here's a collector's treat that rounds up the great moments and great personalities of the tube's finest sagebrush sagas. Host Will Hutchins shows scenes from "The Lone Ranger," "Wagon Train," "Have Gun Will Travel," "Sergeant Preston of the Yukon," "Laredo," "Sky King" and many others. Laugh at bloopers from "F Troop" and "Bonanza." Wow! 120 sharp-shootin' min.
10-2471 Was $19.99 *$14.99*

Silk Stalkings: Natural Selections
Palm Beach homicide detectives Chris Lorenzo and Rita Lee Lance, specializing in "crimes of passion," have one of their toughest cases to solve in this feature-length thriller from the hit TV series. A serial killer who enjoys playing bizarre sex games has targeted runaways as his victims. Mitzi Kapture, Rob Estes star. 87 min.
10-2691 *$12.99*

Gomer Pyle, USMC
Well, go-olly! Join Jim Nabors as Mayberry's finest marine and Frank Sutton as the no-nonsense Sgt. Carter in these two episodes of the hit 1964-70 sitcom. First, Gomer gets "A Visit from Aunt Bee," as guest star Frances Bavier has some objections to Sgt. Carter's belligerent style. And in "Show Me the Way to Go Home," Gomer befriends an alcoholic. 60 min.
10-6015 *$14.99*

Tom Corbett, Space Cadet: The Mercurian Invasion (1950)
It's up to intrepid young cadet Frankie Thomas and the rest of the Space Academy squad to save the Earth from an attack by invaders from the dark side of the planet Mercury in this, the first adventure from the fondly-remembered sci-fi series. Jan Merlin, Al Markim also star. Includes original commercials. 75 min.
73-3004 *$19.99*

Janet Dean: Registered Nurse (1954)
Ella Raines portrayed the devoted private duty nurse who sought to discover and treat the problems that often lied beneath her patients' injuries. Included here "Apple Case" and "Garcia Case," guest-starring a young Sal Mineo. 55 min.
82-1027 *$19.99*

The Defender (1957)
Reginald Rose's gripping courtroom drama appeared first on "Westinghouse Studio One," then became a series four years later. Ralph Bellamy and William Shatner are a father-son lawyer team out to prove delivery boy Steve McQueen's innocence on murder charges. With Martin Balsam. 112 min.
15-5284 Was $19.99 *$14.99*

Molly And Mama
Two popular family comedy series are represented, "The Goldbergs," a bout a poor Jewish family and their wise matriarch, lovable Gertrude Berg, and "I Remember Mama," the story of Norwegian immigrants in a large U.S. city, starring Peggy Wood and child star Dick Van Patten. 60 min.
10-7315 Was $19.99 *$14.99*

The House Always Wins/ Left Fist Of David
Dick Powell stars, with a cameo appearance by Jack Benny, in the first of two pilots from the popular "Ford Theater" anthology series. Next, art dealers Vincent Price and Peter Lorre investigate a possible forgery. 60 min.
10-7326 Was $19.99 *$14.99*

Wild Bill Hickok/Brave Eagle, Chief Of The Cheyennes
"That's Wild Bill Hickok, mister, the bravest, strongest, fightingest U.S. marshal in the whole West!" See an exciting TV badlands tale with Guy Madison and his 300-pound sidekick, Andy Devine. Also, an episode of the Indian lore and action show "Brave Eagle," starring Keith Larsen and Bert Wheeler. 60 min.
10-7329 Was $19.99 *$14.99*

The Perry Como Show (1956)
Perry is a cowboy in a western sketch with guests Henry Fonda and Anne Francis. Paul Winchell and Jerry Mahoney provide some comedy relief. The Platters sing, and Robby the Robot makes a surprise appearance. 60 min.
62-1117 *$19.99*

Home (1956)/ Arthur Godfrey Time (1955)
"Home" was the first "women's magazine" of the airways, with Arlene Francis and Hugh Downs presenting such topics as the Suez Canal, fashions of the day, and even an introduction of the 1957 Cadillac. Next, Peter Lynd Hayes serves as guest host in a special episode of "Arthur Godfrey Time." Includes live Frigidaire commercials. 56 min.
82-1032 *$19.99*

Don McNeill's TV Club (1951)
In this live variety show with a Chicago touch, Don McNeill transplants his popular radio show to the small screen with spirited finesse. Raymond Massey, Johnny Desmond, Sam Cowling, and even Illinois Governor Adlai Stevenson are in on the fun that includes roller derby girls, square dances, interviews, songs, and more. 60 min.
82-1047 *$19.99*

Brave Eagle (1955)
Western series told from the Indians' point of view stars Keith Larsen as a young Cherokee chief leading his tribe against fickle nature and encroaching settlers. Keena Nomkeena plays his foster son and Bert Wheeler is the half-breed tribal sage Smokey Joe. Two daring episodes.
10-7454 Was $19.99 *$14.99*

A Doll's House (1959)
Acclaimed all-star "Playhouse 90" production of Ibsen's immortal drama, with Julie Harris as the willful housewife who must cope with her husband's betrayal. Christopher Plummer, Jason Robards, Hume Cronyn, Eileen Heckart, Richard Thomas co-star. 89 min.
12-1304 Was $59.99 *$14.99*

Patterns (1955)
The original "Kraft Television Theatre" live production of Rod Serling's powerful drama set in the world of big business. Richard Kiley stars as a hot-shot executive brought in by ruthless corporate head Everett Sloane to replace aging Ed Begley. 60 min.
15-5281 *$14.99*

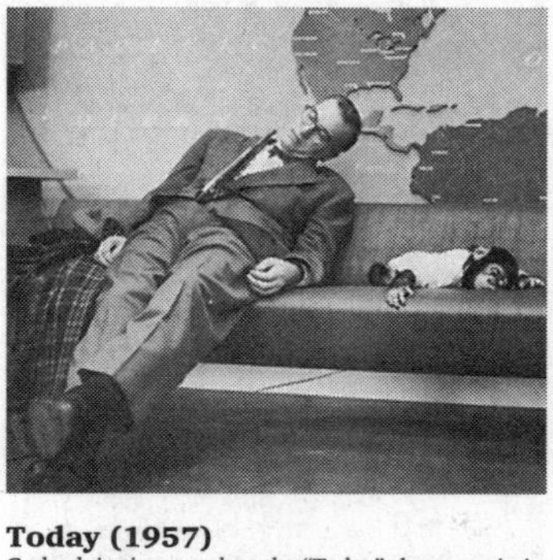

Today (1957)
Go back in time to when the "Today" show was in its infancy, with its row of clocks, teletype machines on display, and Dave Garraway at the helm. The topics of this November 20, 1957 broadcast included the wonder of transistors, Fidel Castro's rebels in Cuba, and a look at New York street life through a store window-front (how prophetic!). With Helen O'Connell, Frank Blair, and Kokomo the chimp. 50 min.
82-1031 *$19.99*

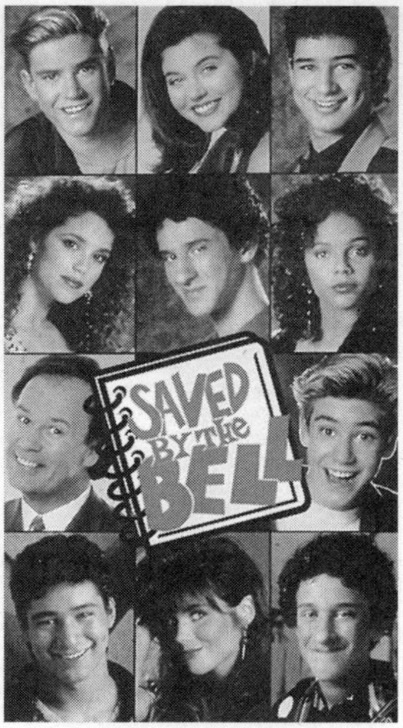

Saved By The Bell: Classic Collection
This collection includes three fun-filled episodes: "Graduation," which finds the kids preparing to leave Bayside High, with hilarious results; "The College Years: Marry Me," in which Kelly's offer to study abroad prompts Zach's marriage proposal; and "The College Years: Wedding Plans," the final episode of the prime-time series. 92 min.
68-2000 *$14.99*

Saved By The Bell: Hawaiian Style (1992)
A fantasy getaway in Hawaii turns into a working holiday in this feature-length "Bell" adventure, as the gang tries to save Kelly's uncle's hotel. Meanwhile, Zach falls for a local girl and Slater and Jessie try to go two weeks without arguing. 92 min.
68-2001 *$14.99*

Saved By The Bell: Wedding In Las Vegas (1994)
It'll take more than a car breakdown in the middle of the desert, a jewelry store robbery and a trip to jail to stop Zach and Kelly from making it to the altar in this, the second "Saved by the Bell" movie. 90 min.
68-2002 *$14.99*

The Fine Art Of Separating People From Their Money
Dennis Hopper hosts this wickedly funny look at advertising and its effect on today's media-obsessed culture. Featured are clips of 60 of the most influential commercials ever, along with interviews with commercial directors Spike Lee, Alan Parker and Tony Scott, as well as David Bowie, Harvey Keitel, John Cleese and Rowan Atkinson. 115 min.
53-8933 Was $59.99 *$19.99*

The Best Of The Golden Age Of Television
A collection of favorite television moments from the '50s and early '60s including zaniness from Bud Collyer's "Beat the Clock," "Howdy Doody" highlights, bloopers from "McHale's Navy," rare TV promos and much more. A hilarious party mix! 60 min.
01-9030 *$19.99*

The Kate Smith Evening Hour
God bless America, it's two half-hour segments of the inspirational musical variety series starring Kate Smith. Included are the regular "Ethel and Albert" feature, Akim Tamiroff in "Mr. Citizen," comedian Myron Cohen and a Thanksgiving skit with Ann Sheridan and Phil Reed. 60 min.
01-9048 *$19.99*

Hazel: A Double Holiday Dose Of Hazel
Two fun-filled episodes of the hit TV series that starred Shirley Booth as America's favorite maid and Don DeFore and Whitney Blake as her employers, the Baxters. Featured are the Christmas shows "Just 86 Shopping Minutes Left Till Christmas," in which Hazel plays Santa Claus, and "Hazel's Christmas Shopping," with the harried housekeeper cracking a shoplifting case. 49 min.
02-2261 *$14.99*

The Best Of The Lenny Henry Show
He's been called Britain's answer to Eddie Murphy, this zany comic with a knack for mimicry who hit America's shores with the movie "True Identity." Now see the funniest skits and wildest impersonations from Lenny Henry's hit BBC TV series. Guests include Robbie Coltrane. 101 min.
04-2473 Was $19.99 *$14.99*

People Are Funny/House Party Segment/Linkletter & The Kids
Along with an episode from Art Linkletter's long-running "People Are Funny" game show in which a couple comes home to find that their new house is missing(!), this triple bill of Linkletter TV treats also features a late '50s "House Party" look at the latest—and strangest—hat styles, followed by Art proving once again that "kids say the darndest things." 60 min.
82-1049 *$19.99*

Tales Of Tomorrow, Vol. 1
Airing from 1951 to 1953 on ABC, this science-fiction anthology series was noted for being one of the genre's first serious efforts. Three episodes are featured here: "Ice from Space" (Paul Newman's starring TV debut), about a returning rocket's effects on the world's climate; a young Joanne Woodward in "Bitter Storm," in which a scientist can summon voices from history; and Theodore Sturgeon's "Verdict from Space," about a mysterious signal that calls out to alien visitors. 90 min.
73-3015 *$19.99*

Tales Of Tomorrow, Vol. 2
Leading off this triple-bill of fantastic tales is an adaptation of Mary Shelley's "Frankenstein," broadcast live with Lon Chaney, Jr. in the role of the vengeful creature. Scientist Richard Derr develops an immortality elixir in "The Miraculous Serum," with Lola Albright; while a robot falls for its creator's daughter in "Read to Me, Herr Doktor," starring Everett Sloane and Mercedes McCambridge. 90 min.
73-3016 *$19.99*

Tales Of Tomorrow, Vol. 3
Here are three more great TV "Tales," including "The Window" (aka "Lost Planet") with Rod Steiger, in which the show is interrupted by a ghost image of a man plotting to kill his wife; "The Evil Within," about a woman who takes a serum her scientist husband developed that brings out her evil side, features James Dean and Rod Steiger; and "Youth on Tap" features Robert Alda in a tale of a man who sells some of his blood for $1,000, unaware of the consequences. 90 min.
73-3034 *$19.99*

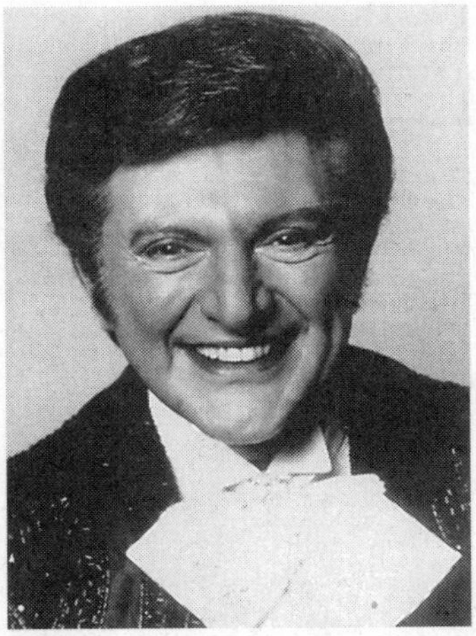

The Liberace Show
The original "piano man" is back, complete with his trademark candelabra, in these videos featuring Liberace's Emmy-winning '50s series. Join Lee—along with brother George—as he performs classical and popular tunes in his own unmistakable style. Each tape runs about 75 min.

Liberace, Vol. 1
Songs include "The Saber Dance," Liszt's Concerto in A Major, "My Old Kentucky Home," "Moonlight Sonata," "Piano Roll Blues" and more.
50-6901 *$19.99*

Liberace, Vol. 2
Songs include "Flight of the Bumblebee Boogie," Waltz in A Flat Major, Tchaikovsky's Fifth Symphony, "Take Me Out to the Ball Game" and more.
50-6902 *$19.99*

Liberace, Vol. 3
Songs include "Camptown Races," "Bicycle Built for Two," "Santa Lucia," "Stars and Stripes Forever" and more.
50-6903 *$19.99*

Liberace, Vol. 4
Songs include "Alexander's Ragtime Band," "I'm Looking Over a Four-Leaf Clover," "Swanee River," "Turkey in the Straw" and more.
50-7557 *$19.99*

Liberace, Vol. 5
Songs include "Blue Danube," "Tiger Rag," "Brahms' Lullaby," "Greensleeves," "Rachmaninoff's Fantasy" and more.
50-7558 *$19.99*

Liberace: Vols. 1-5 Set
Volumes 1-5 of "Mr. Showmanship's" musical interludes are also available in a collector's set.
50-7559 *$99.99*

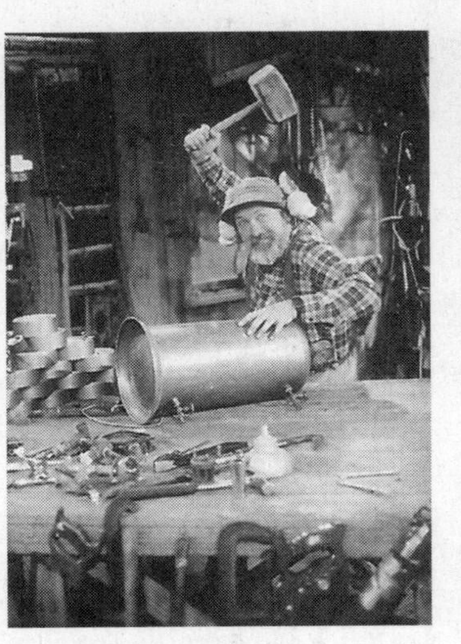

The Best Of Red Green
Grab yourself a roll of duct tape and get ready to wrap up lots of laughs with this video of the funniest moments from the cult hit Canadian TV series that spoofs outdoorsmen, home repair, male bonding and everything else in sight. Join Red (Steve Smith) at Possum Lodge for a "best of" special that also includes a behind-the-scenes look at the making of the show. 67 min.
50-2939 *$19.99*

Red Green's We Can't Help It—We're Men
Get the lowdown on "the male condition" from master handyman Red Green and his fellow members of the International Possum Brotherhood with this special from the popular Canadian TV series. Learn from Red, nephew Harold and the guys about men's love of tools; the two basic food groups, meat and salt; how to live with the opposite sex; and other topics. 65 min.
50-5148 Was $19.99 *$14.99*

Red Green's Of Cars And Men
Red Green and the Possum Lodge crew discuss the intricacies of cars and auto repair in this funny tale "dedicated to the brave women who have the courage to ask, 'Why don't you let them fix it at the garage?'" Red also shares car lore with the Lodge members and offers his own driving tips. 60 min.
50-5759 Was $19.99 *$14.99*

Red Green: Stuffed And Mounted
Check out eight hilarious episodes of the popular Canadian television series that pokes fun at the male psyche and does wonders for the duct tape industry in the North. Volumes include "The Wind-Powered Boat/The Salt and Pepper Shakers," "Maple Syrup/Fire Brigade," "The Beef Project/The Badger Project" and "The Network Deal/The Science Fair." 240 min. total. NOTE: Individual volumes available at $14.99 each.
50-5948 Save $20.00! *$39.99*

It's A Wonderful Red Green Christmas
If you're dreaming of a duct-tape covered stocking filled with goodies, this is the Christmas tape for you! Spend your holiday with the gang at Possum Lodge as they demonstrate how to decorate the tree with a howitzer, how to build a one-horse open K car sleigh, and more. 60 min.
50-8139 *$19.99*

Red Green's Guide To Parenting
Who better to talk about the joys—and pitfalls—of fatherhood than the men of Possum Lodge? Join Red and the guys as they show you how to turn used tires into girl's bedroom furniture, how to get back at snowball-throwing kids, and other tips to put the "fun" in "dysfunctional family." 60 min.
50-8479 *$19.99*

Mapp & Lucia: Complete Set
One of PBS's most popular British imports, this acerbically witty mini-series followed the bitter rivalry between two women as they vie for social prominence in the seaside English town of Tilling in the 1920s. The cast includes Prunella Scales, Geraldine McEwan and Nigel Hawthorne. 260 min. on five tapes.
50-5379 Was $89.99 *$59.99*

Mapp & Lucia II: Complete Set
The hilarious contest of one-upmanship (one-upwomanship?) between would-be socialites Geraldine McEwan and Prunella Scales continues in the duo's second TV mini-series. Nigel Hawthorne also stars. 260 min. on five tapes.
50-5561 Was $89.99 *$59.99*

Root Into Europe: Complete Set
Hilarious satire abounds when ultra-English Henry Root and his long-suffering wife, Muriel, visit the continent to see first-hand what "dangers" the imminent European Union presents to British culture. During their journey, Henry and Muriel encounter unusual people, including Italian politician/porn star Cicciolina. George Cole star. Five tape set; 210 min. total. NOTE: Individual volumes available at $19.99 each.
50-5179 Save $60.00! *$39.99*

The People's Choice
Jackie Cooper starred in this fondly-remembered 1955-58 comedy as Socrates "Socks" Miller, a naturalist who becomes a city councilman in New City, California, thanks to the efforts of girlfriend Amanda "Mandy" Peoples (Pat Breslin), the mayor's daughter. Offering her own unique take (through a voice-over by Mary Jane Croft) on the goings-on was Cleo, Cooper's pet basset hound. Each tape features two episodes and runs about 55 min. There are 10 volumes available, including:

The People's Choice, Vol. 1
Includes "Sock Proposes to Mandy" and "Domestic Relations."
82-1015 *$19.99*

The People's Choice, Vol. 2
Includes "Sock the Budget Balancer" and "Wedding Bells."
82-1016 *$19.99*

The People's Choice, Vol. 3
Includes "Proxy Marriage" and "Lonely Hearts."
82-1017 *$19.99*

The People's Choice, Vol. 4
Includes "Mayor's Election" and "People's Pageant."
82-1018 *$19.99*

The People's Choice, Vol. 5
Includes "Pierre's Job" and "Sock the Greek God."
82-1019 *$19.99*

The People's Choice, Vol. 6
Includes "Sock's Master Plan" and "Nickel Pickle."
82-1020 *$19.99*

The People's Choice, Vol. 7
Includes "The Giveaway" and "Reluctant Houseguest."
82-1021 *$19.99*

The People's Choice, Vol. 8
Includes "Sock's Daughter" and "Ladies Aide."
82-1022 *$19.99*

The People's Choice, Vol. 9
Includes "Rollo Makes Good" and "First Anniversary."
82-1023 *$19.99*

The People's Choice, Vol. 10
Includes "Missing Moolah" and "Daisies Won't Tell."
82-1024 *$19.99*

Cimarron City
Rising up during the Oklahoma Territory oil boom of the 1890s, the town of Cimarron City was the setting for this 1958-59 NBC sagebrusher. Mayor Matt Rockford (George Montgomery) and sheriff Lane Temple (John Smith) team up to keep the peace—with help from a pre-"Bonanza" Dan Blocker as Tiny—in two episodes: "The Unaccepted" and "Return of the Dead." 110 min.
83-7003 *$19.99*

The Outlaws: Boxed Set
Frontier life through the eyes of the bad guys was the focus of this unusual western series that ran on NBC from 1960 to 1962. Sheriff Barton MacLane and deputies Don Collier, Jock Gaynor and Bruce Yarnell pursue their quarry through 1890s Oklahoma Territory in this four-tape collection that features such guest stars as Cliff Robertson, Robert Culp, Warren Oates, Brian Keith, Jack Lord and William Shatner. 8 hrs. total.
83-7004 *$49.99*

The Best Of Just Kidding
You've seen the outrageous commercials on television, but now Movies Unlimited offers the wildest stunts ever pulled on people for the camera. Step aside, Allen Funt! These funny—and, often, nasty—practical jokes were collected from around the world for your pleasure.

The Best Of Just Kidding, Vol. 1
See people stealing items from other people's shopping carts, a woman with a nasty skin condition asking for assistance to apply lotion on the beach, perfume that sprays in shoppers' faces, a man terrorizing people on a mall escalator with a ladder, and a really ugly baby in a bassinet. 45 min.
58-8272 *$14.99*

The Best Of Just Kidding, Vol. 2
Here are more riotous situations captured by the camera! See women's skirts get blown when they walk over a subway grate, a gorilla arm serving bananas at a supermarket, a knight that comes to life and, a mail slot that returns the mail. 44 min.
50-8740 *$14.99*

The Best Of Just Kidding, Vols. 3 & 4
A special double dose of fabulous candid comedy is offered on this video. Spiders scare customers at a pet shop, a carnival polar bear comes to life, a trash can rejects trash, dentures are found in food, and a huge hammer smacks people in the noggin. Zany! 101 min.
50-8741 *$19.99*

Just Kidding: Censored In America
You'll never see these hilarious pranks on American television, so now is your chance to catch the world's wackiest routines—completely uncensored! It's a wild variation on "Candid Camera" from Europe as people are caught with their pants (and tops) down by a hidden camera. Great party fun! WARNING: Contains nudity; adults only. 90 min.
50-8369 *$19.99*

Butterflies
"Love is like a butterfly" in these two episodes from the bittersweetly funny British series about a married housewife and mother of two teenage sons who, while coping with a mid-life crisis, is tempted to stray when a handsome, divorced neighbor comes into her life. Wendy Craig, Geoffrey Palmer star. 60 min.
53-9633 *$19.99*

Chiller: Collection Set
These shocking journeys into the macabre will startle and terrify you. Produced for British television, they feature elements of "The Twilight Zone" and "The X-Files," and provide hours of frightful viewing. The five volumes include "Prophecy," "Toby," "Here Comes the Mirror Man," "Number Six" and "The Man Who Didn't Believe in Ghosts." 250 min. total.
53-9663 *$89.99*

The WKRP In Cincinnati Collection
Airing from 1978 to 1982, this hit sitcom followed the daily travails at a floundering radio station whose new program director shakes things up by changing the format from easy listening to rock. Included in the three-tape collection are "Pilot, Parts I and II," "Hold Up," "Fish Story," "Who Is Gordon Sims," "The Doctor's Daughter" and "Filthy Pictures, Parts I and II." Gary Sandy, Howard Hesseman, Tim Reid, Gordon Jump and Loni Anderson star. 200 min. total.
53-9668 *$29.99*

Flambards
A young woman in turn-of-the-century England arrives at her domineering uncle's estate to live with him and his two sons in this tale of ambition, family secrets and adventure. Based on the novels of K.M. Peyton, the sprawling British mini-series stars Edward Judd, Steven Grives and Christine McKenna. 11 1/2 hrs. on six tapes.
53-9684 Was $99.99 *$79.99*

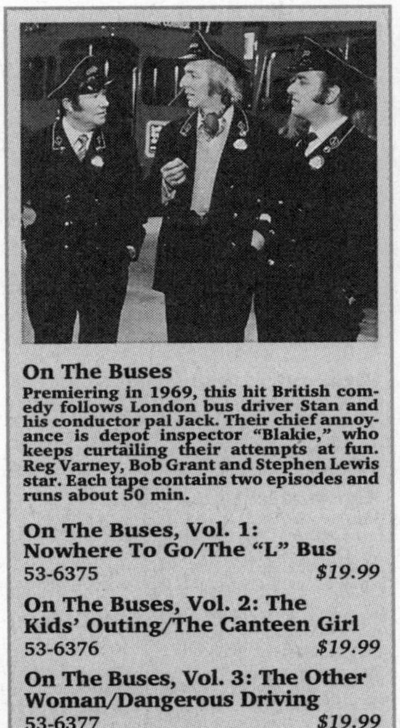

On The Buses
Premiering in 1969, this hit British comedy follows London bus driver Stan and his conductor pal Jack. Their chief annoyance is depot inspector "Blakie," who keeps curtailing their attempts at fun. Reg Varney, Bob Grant and Stephen Lewis star. Each tape contains two episodes and runs about 50 min.

On The Buses, Vol. 1: Nowhere To Go/The "L" Bus
53-6375 *$19.99*

On The Buses, Vol. 2: The Kids' Outing/The Canteen Girl
53-6376 *$19.99*

On The Buses, Vol. 3: The Other Woman/Dangerous Driving
53-6377 *$19.99*

On The Buses, Vol. 4: The Nursery/Stan's Room
53-6698 *$19.99*

On The Buses, Vol. 5: The Best Man/The Busman's Ball
53-6699 *$19.99*

On The Buses, Vol. 6: Canteen Trouble/The Inspector's Pets
53-6700 *$19.99*

On The Buses: Collector's Set #1
Volumes 1-3 are also available in a deluxe boxed set.
53-6371 *$59.99*

On The Buses: Collector's Set #2
Volumes 4-6 are also available in a deluxe boxed set.
53-6701 *$59.99*

The Very Best Of "On The Buses"
Here are four of the funniest episodes of the popular British TV series of the 1970s, featuring beloved busmen Stan and Jack and their schemes to take it easy and meet women. Included are "Going Steady," "The New Uniforms," "Brew It Yourself" and "The Cistern." With Bob Grant, Doris Hare, Michael Robbins and Reg Varney. 100 min.
59-7062 *$29.99*

Tales Of Wells Fargo
Dale Robertson is Wells Fargo agent Jim Hardie, who uses his crime-solving expertise to stop criminals from causing trouble for the stagecoach line and its passengers in the Old West. Includes the episode "Death of a Minor God." 60 min.
10-9058 *$19.99*

The Court Of Last Resort
This real-life crime series, which aired during the 1957-58 season, was based on a panel of seven legal experts, founded by Perry Mason creator Erle Stanley Gardener, who review cases in which those convicted may have been wrongly accused and determine if justice was done. Lyle Bettger and Paul Birch star. Each tape features two episodes and runs about 50 min. There are five volumes available, including:

The Court Of Last Resort, Vol. 1
Includes "The Clarence Redding Case" and "The John Smith Case."
10-9098 Was $19.99 *$14.99*

The Court Of Last Resort, Vol. 2
Includes "The Mary Morales Case" and "The Frank Clark Case."
10-9099 Was $19.99 *$14.99*

The Adventures Of Hiram Holliday
In this mid-'50s comedy, Wally Cox played a shy proofreader for a New York newspaper who surprises everyone with an array of hidden abilities, including fencing, piloting and art forgery. Along with a reporter (Ainslie Pryor), Cox embarks on amazing adventures around the world. Each tape features two episodes and runs about 50 min.

The Adventures Of Hiram Holliday, Vol. 1
Includes "Sea Cucumber" and "Hawaiian Humza."
10-9011 *$14.99*

The Adventures Of Hiram Holliday, Vol. 2
Includes "Lapidary Wheel" and "Romantic Pigeon."
10-9073 Was $19.99 *$14.99*

Tee Vee Treasures
Remember the old-fashioned evening spent around that one family television set? Memories will come flooding back when you watch these two-hour collections of prime '50s and '60s TV. Four complete shows, commercials, shorts, public service announcements, and all the other pleasures from a proud potato's past.

Tee Vee Treasures, Vol. 1
Action, suspense and adventure programming spotlighted here, including a rare "Federal Men in Action" that stars a young Charles Bronson! Tenfour. 120 min.
15-5056 *$39.99*

Tee Vee Treasures, Vol. 2
The emphasis here is on comedy, and featured is the "Jack Benny Show" episode "The Jam Session," guest-starring Fred MacMurray, Dan Dailey, Dick Powell, and Kirk Douglas. 120 min.
15-5057 *$39.99*

The Best Of The Soupy Sales Show, Vol. 1
Everybody's favorite kiddie show host welcomes such guests as Frank Sinatra, Sammy Davis, Jr. and Alice Cooper to his wacky household, where characters like White Fang, Black Tooth and Willie the Worm roam. Manic comedy hijinks! 50 min.
15-5146 Was $19.99 *$14.99*

More Best Of The Soupy Sales Show
Get your piece of the pie with this collection of Soupy's silliest shenanigans. There's "Pookie Theatre," "Soupy Sez," wacky definitions and guests like Tab Hunter and Frank Sinatra, Jr. 50 min.
15-5168 Was $19.99 *$14.99*

Absolutely The Best Of The Soupy Sales Show
"Is it Soupy yet?" You bet it is, and he's brought his pals White Tooth, Black Fang and Pookie along with him in this hilarious compilation of bits, skits and music from Sales' TV shows. There's even Soupy's "hit" song, "Your Brains Fell Out." 60 min.
15-5261 Was $19.99 *$14.99*

Highlander: The Series
The hit fantasy-adventure films spawned this action-packed TV series starring Adrian Paul as Duncan MacLeod, the immortal warrior from 16th-century Scotland who uses his sword to fight for justice in the present and battle the other Immortals out to behead him and claim his power. Alexandra Vandernoot, Stan Kirsch and Jim Byrnes also star. Except where noted, each tape features two episodes and runs about 97 min.

Highlander: Counterfeit
In this special feature-length tale, Duncan is drawn into danger when he meets a mysterious woman who resembles Tessa Noel, the late love of his life. 95 min.
63-1882 ❑*$14.99*

Highlander: Unholy Alliance
The nasty Xavier St. Cloud, who lost a hand in his last encounter with MacLeod, returns to wreak vengeance against his old nemesis, this time teamed with renegade Watcher James Horton. Roland Gift guest stars in this feature-length adventure. 95 min.
63-1883 ❑*$14.99*

Highlander: Finale
Duncan MacLeod's arch-enemy Kalas escapes from prison thanks to Amanda, who wants to take his head. Her plans don't go as desired, leaving Kalas on a collision course with MacLeod in this feature-length saga. Elizabeth Gracen guest stars. 95 min.
63-1884 *$14.99*

Highlander: The Series, Vol. 2: The Road Not Taken/ Innocent Man
An Immortal creates a potion designed to create the perfect warrior to protect him, but trouble arises when MacLeod discovers more about the drug than he expected in "The Road Not Taken." In "Innocent Man," MacLeod races to clear the name of a homeless man who has been accused of murdering an Immortal.
63-1937 ❑*$14.99*

Highlander: The Series, Vol. 3: Free Fall/Bad Day In Building A
In "Free Fall," a beautiful Immortal isn't all that she seems to be when she seeks out MacLeod as a mentor and captures the affections of Richie. Joan Jett guest stars. Next, in "Bad Day in Building A," Duncan, Tessa and Richie are among a group of hostages taken in a courthouse siege.
63-1938 ❑*$14.99*

Highlander: The Series, Vol. 4: Mountain Men/Deadly Medicine
MacLeod must face an old rival when he races to rescue Tessa from a band of survivalists in the Pacific Northwest, an area he knows from his past. Then, a demented doctor kidnaps Duncan after seeing him recover from "fatal" injuries in a hospital in "Deadly Medicine," guest starring Joe Pantoliano.
63-1939 ❑*$14.99*

Highlander: The Series, Vol. 5: The Sea Witch/Revenge Is Sweet
Duncan and Richie are threatened by a drug-dealing Immortal who betrayed MacLeod in Russia years before in "The Sea Witch." "Revenge Is Sweet" finds Rebecca Lord (guest star Vanity) seeking revenge against the Highlander for the death of her lover. But is he really dead...or merely using Rebecca for his own vengeance scheme?
63-1940 ❑*$14.99*

Highlander: The Series, Vol. 6: See No Evil/Eyewitness
In "See No Evil," MacLeod recognizes that the patterns of a present-day serial killer are those of an evil Immortal whom he killed back in the 1920s, while Tessa must convince Duncan she saw an artist's murder in "Eyewitness."
63-1941 ❑*$14.99*

Highlander: The Series, Vol. 7: Band Of Brothers/For Evil's Sake
A 2,000-year-old monk is threatened by a one-time disciple who is now killing the monk's students in order to draw him off holy ground in "Band of Brothers." In "For Evil's Sake," MacLeod tracks down an evil Immortal, disguised as a mime, who is assassinating people in Paris.
63-1942 ❑*$14.99*

Highlander: The Series, Vol. 8: For Tomorrow We Die/ The Beast Below
MacLeod picks up the trail of evil Immortal Xavier St. Cloud (guest star Roland Gift), who preys on mortals with his signature weapon of poison gas. Then, in "The Beast Below," Duncan is reunited with Ursa, a feral and beast-like Immortal who is being manipulated by a selfish singer.
63-1943 ❑*$14.99*

Highlander: The Series, Vol. 10: Eye Of The Beholder/ Avenging Angel
When Richie falls for a mysterious and beautiful young woman, he ignites the insane jealousy of fashion designer and Immortal Gabriel in "Eye of the Beholder," guest starring Nigel Terry. Next, a deranged man believes that his Immortal status means he's been called upon by Heaven to eliminate "perversion" in "Avenging Angel," with Martin Kemp.
63-1945 ❑*$14.99*

Highlander: The Series, Vol. 11: Nowhere To Run/The Hunters
MacLeod is caught in the middle when his host's son is accused of raping the daughter of an Immortal, who demands justice, in "Nowhere to Run." Then, in "The Hunters," Darius' murder in his church leads MacLeod and fellow Immortal Fitz (guest star Roger Daltrey) to uncover the existence of the Watchers, mortals bent on destroying them.
63-1946 ❑*$14.99*

Highlander: The TV Series: Collector's Set
The complete first season is also available in this special, 12-tape boxed set.
63-1947 Save $15.00! *$149.99*

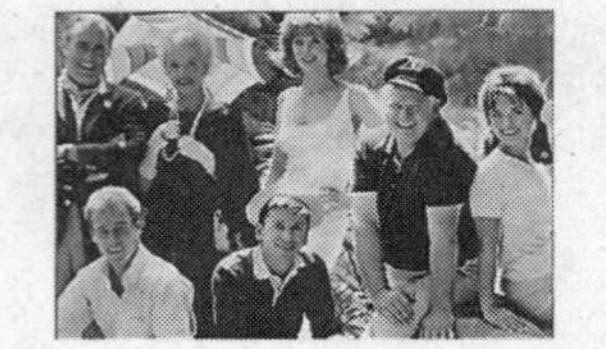

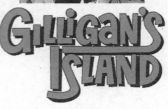

GILLIGAN'S ISLAND

Gilligan's Island
"Just sit right back" and watch the misadventures of Gilligan, the Skipper, Mr. and Mrs. Howell, Ginger, the Professor and Mary Ann on their "uncharted desert isle" in one of the best-loved sitcoms in TV history. Bob Denver, Alan Hale, Jr., Jim Backus, Natalie Schafer, Tina Louise, Russell Johnson and Dawn Wells star. Each tape features two colorized episodes and runs about 52 min.

Gilligan's Island: Two On A Raft/Home Sweet Hut
See how "a three-hour tour" leaves the S.S. Minnow and her passengers stranded on the island in "Two on a Raft," while "Home Sweet Hut" finds the castaways struggling to build shelter before a storm hits.
19-2647 *$12.99*

Gilligan's Island: Voodoo Something To Me/ The Big Gold Strike
Who—or what—has put a curse on the castaways in "Voodoo Something to Me"? Next, Gilligan stumbles into "The Big Gold Strike," which turns everyone into greedy schemers.
19-2648 *$12.99*

Gilligan's Island: Wrongway Feldman/President Gilligan
Gilligan discovers that the island is also home to famed and long-lost aviator "Wrongway Feldman" (guest star Hans Conried). Then, a dispute over the Skipper's authority leads to the election of "President Gilligan."
19-2649 *$12.99*

Gilligan's Island: Waiting For Watubi/Angel On The Island
The finding of a native idol convinces the Skipper he's inherited the curse of Kona, and now he's "Waiting for Watubi," a witch doctor, to free him. Next, everyone helps put on a play about Cleopatra to cheer up a depressed Ginger in "Angel on the Island."
19-2650 *$12.99*

Gilligan's Island: 3 Million Dollars More Or Less/ Water, Water Everywhere
What starts out as a 25-cent golf bet with Mr. Howell lands Gilligan a fortune worth "3 Million Dollars More or Less." And a search for a new fresh water supply runs afoul of Gilligan's bumbling in "Water, Water Everywhere."
19-2651 *$12.99*

Gilligan's Island: So Sorry, My Island Now/ Plant You Now, Dig You Later
A Japanese soldier still fighting World War II lands his one-man sub on the island in "So Sorry, My Island Now." Then, a treasure chest that can't be opened pits the castaways against each other in "Plant You Now, Dig You Later."
19-2652 *$12.99*

Rescue From Gilligan's Island (1978)
After 14 years on their "uncharted desert isle," the crew and passengers of the S.S. Minnow return to civilization, thanks to a tidal wave and some timely bumbling by Gilligan. Feature-length follow-up to the perennially popular TV series stars Bob Denver, Alan Hale, Jr., Jim Backus, Natalie Schafer, Russell Johnson, Dawn Wells, and Judith Baldwin as Ginger. 95 min.
78-3016 *$14.99*

The Ed Wynn Show (The Three Stooges)
The giggling professor of visual humor peddles through a delightful duo of his Hollywood-based CBS shows. Watch the hilarity as Ed welcomes three "network executives" (Moe, Larry and Shemp). With Victor Moore. 55 min.
10-7450 Was $19.99 *$14.99*

The Ed Wynn Show/ The Beulah Show
You'll love to laugh with a 1950 episode of Wynn's variety show, with guests Buddy Ebsen and Hattie McDaniel as Beulah. Then, Ethel Waters plays the wisecracking maid in "The Beulah Show," co-starring Dooley Wilson ("Casablanca"). 50 min.
10-9407 *$14.99*

Ford Theatre: Bold Journey: The Tarzan Adventures
Here are two episodes of the documentary series from the 1950s which ran on ABC and featured then-current screen Tarzan Gordon Scott. Incredible photography highlights "The Cartoon King in Africa" and "Kenya." 50 min.
19-9216 Was $19.99 *$14.99*

Checkmate
Aired on CBS from 1959-1962, this series was set in San Francisco and focused on Don Corey and Dan Sills, two detectives at Checkmate Incorporated, a private investigation company that tries to solve and prevent crimes. Anthony George, Doug McClure and Sebastian Cabot star. Each volume runs about 50 min.

Checkmate, Vol. 1
In "Nice Guys Finish Last," a good cop discovers his high school rival has something to do with his being passed over for a big promotion. The Checkmate team goes to work to get the truth. James Whitmore guest stars.
10-9595 *$14.99*

Checkmate, Vol. 2
In "The Human Touch," Sebastian Cabot gets caught in a trap when he accepts a dinner invitation from a master criminal he sent to prison 15 years earlier. Peter Lorre guest stars.
10-9596 *$14.99*

Checkmate, Vol. 3
The quest to help a young would-be heir avoid his scheming relatives' deadly plans for him leads Jed to join a hobo camp in "The Heart Is a Handout."
10-9702 *$19.99*

Checkmate, No. 1: The Murder Game
Features John Williams and Richard Anderson.
10-9900 *$14.99*

Checkmate, No. 2: Deadly Shadow
Features Margaret O'Brien.
10-9901 *$14.99*

Checkmate, No. 3: A Funny Thing Happened On The Way To The Game
Features Jack Benny and Tina Louise.
10-9902 *$14.99*

Checkmate, No. 4: The Dark Divide
Features Barbara Rush.
10-9903 *$14.99*

The Life Of Riley/ The Great Gildersleeve
As harried pop Chester A. Riley, Jackie Gleason faces a "revoltin' development" when he's convinced son Junior pinched $5 from the family kitty. Then, Gildersleeve (Willard Waterman) turns poet to win a young lady's heart, but his nephew and niece make an impromptu substitution. 60 min.
10-8083 Was $19.99 *$14.99*

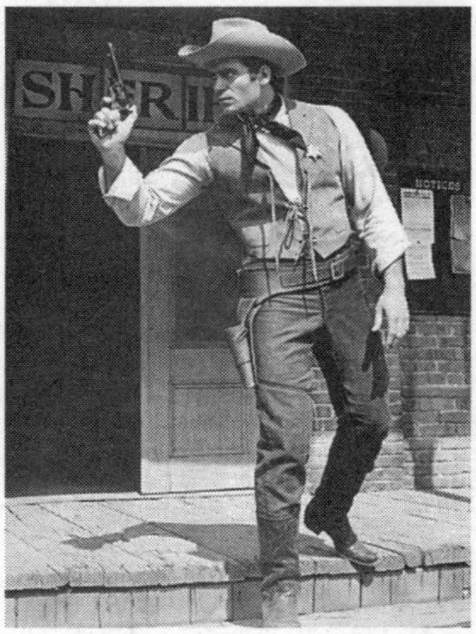

Cheyenne
Clint Walker stars as strapping Cheyenne Bodie, a frontier drifter who takes different odd jobs and encounters outlaws, gorgeous pioneer women and lots of gunplay. Each episode of this sagebrush classic, which was broadcast on ABC from 1955 to 1963, runs 50 min.

Cheyenne: The Iron Trail
A young Dennis Hopper plays a wild and woolly criminal who kidnaps a trainload of passengers and plans to use dynamite to stop a train carrying President Grant. Can Cheyenne stop him?
19-1964 *$14.99*

Cheyenne: White Warrior
Wagon Master Cheyenne barters with the Apaches for the life of Indian-raised white man Michael Landon.
19-1965 *$14.99*

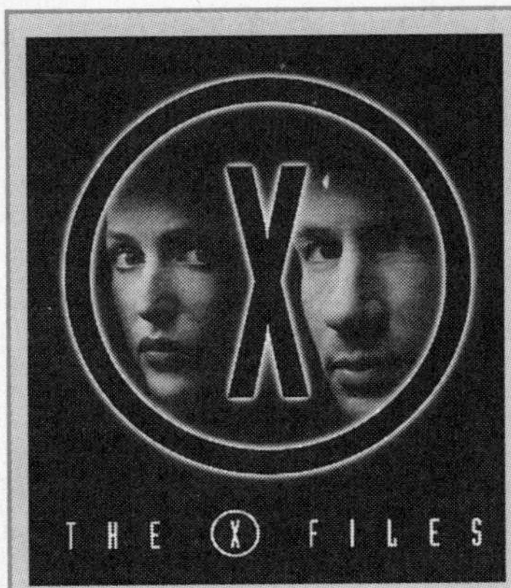

The X-Files

A cult and critical favorite since its 1993 premiere, this otherworldly suspense series stars David Duchovny and Gillian Anderson as FBI agents Fox Mulder and Dana Scully, charged with investigating unsolved cases and incidents involving UFOs, alien abductions, and other unexplained phenomena. Each tape features two episodes and runs about 100 min.

The X-Files: Pilot Episode/Deep Throat
The show's premiere episode finds Agent Scully joining Mulder on a search for clues into a series of deaths in a small Oregon town, but, unknown to Mulder, his new partner has other reasons for being there. Next, a missing Air Force pilot sends Mulder on a fateful encounter with, among other things, the mysterious man known as "Deep Throat."
04-3302 ☐*$14.99*

The X-Files: Fallen Angel/Eve
Is the evacuation of a Wisconsin town due to a toxic spill, as the government claims, or is it, as Mulder believes, a cover-up of a UFO crash? Then, the murderous progeny of a 1950s genetics experiment is about to unleash a new generation of terror in "Eve."
04-3303 ☐*$14.99*

The X-Files: Conduit/Ice
The investigation of a teenage girl's possible kidnapping by aliens hits close to home for Mulder, who believes his own sister was similarly abducted years earlier, in "Conduit." "Ice" finds Scully and Mulder in Alaska, where a geological experiment station is under attack from an unknown menace.
04-3304 ☐*$14.99*

The X-Files: Squeeze/Tooms
Everyone's favorite cannibalistic, body-stretching, hibernating mutant, Eugene Victor Tooms, is featured in a creepy double feature. Mulder must convince a skeptical Scully that the suspect in a "locked-room" murder is a century-old serial killer, followed by the agents putting their lives and careers on the line to catch Tooms before he vanishes for another 30 years.
04-3360 ☐*$14.99*

The X-Files: Beyond The Sea/E.B.E.
A search for two kidnapping victims, a death row inmate who claims to have psychic abilities, and a vision by Scully of her recently-deceased father are the spooky elements of "Beyond the Sea." In "E.B.E.," the agents receive help and hindrance from the "Lone Gunman" and Deep Throat as they pursue a truck alleged to be hauling a UFO's remains across the country.
04-3361 ☐*$14.99*

The X-Files: Darkness Falls/ The Erlenmeyer Flask
After an entire logging crew in the Pacific Northwest vanishes, Mulder and Scully discover a bizarre and deadly enemy who strikes at night in "Darkness." "Flask," the series' first-season finale, brings all of the conspiracy threads together, as the potential discovery of proof of alien life leads to Mulder's kidnapping, a final meeting with the enigmatic Deep Throat, and the closing of the X-Files.
04-3362 ☐*$14.99*

The X-Files: Little Green Men/Host
In the wake of the X-Files' disbanding, Mulder investigates strange goings-on at a CETI listening post in Puerto Rico, but can Scully find him before sinister forces behind a UFO retrieval squad do? Then, "The Host" pits the duo against a deadly parasitic mutant living in a sewage plant.
04-3399 ☐*$14.99*

The X-Files: Sleepless/Duane Barry
In "Sleepless," Scully and antagonistic new partner Alex Krycek must defeat a government-created "ultimate soldier" with the power to project deadly dreams into other peoples' minds. Next, an ex-FBI agent (Steve Railsback) who claims to have been a victim of alien abduction escapes from a mental hospital and kidnaps Scully.
04-3400 ☐*$14.99*

The X-Files: Ascension/One Breath
Mulder's search for the missing Scully leads to a final confrontation with Duane Barry and the government forces pursuing them both, but who—or what—has taken Fox's partner? Scully turns up in a Washington hospital, comatose and near death, in "One Breath," and Mulder must find out who's behind the bizarre experiment that's killing her.
04-3401 ☐*$14.99*

The X-Files: Irresistible/Die Hand Die Verletzt
A series of desecrated corpses are thought to be the work of aliens, but Scully and Mulder discover the Earthbound answer is just as unsettling, in "Irresistible." Next, a small New England town is the setting for Satanism, murder, and really strange biology teachers in "Die Hand Die Verletzt."
04-3442 ☐*$14.99*

The X-Files: Colony/End Game
When three murdered abortion clinic doctors turn out to be carbon copies of one another in "Colony," a bizarre conspiracy that reaches into Mulder's family is revealed. The chilling conclusion, "End Game," pits Scully against an alien assassin and sends Mulder on a quest to the Arctic to learn the truth about the woman who may or may not be his sister.
04-3443 ☐*$14.99*

The X-Files: Humbug/Anasazi
The agents look for the mysterious killer of a carnival "alligator man" in a town populated by sideshow freaks in the offbeat "Humbug." Then, a computer hacker gives Mulder a tape that could prove government knowledge of UFOs in the second-season finale, "Anasazi," but his search for the truth turns Scully against him and puts his family's lives—and his own—in danger.
04-3444 ☐*$14.99*

The X-Files: The Blessing Way/Paper Clip
Leading off the series' third season (and continuing the story begun in "Anasazi"), "Blessing Way" finds Mulder in a near-death meeting with his father, while Scully works to conceal the "MJ files" and makes a disturbing discovery on her body. The concluding chapter, "Paper Clip," reunites the agents and leads them to a shocking secret hidden deep inside an abandoned coal mine.
04-3505 ☐*$14.99*

The X-Files: Clyde Bruckman's Final Repose/ War Of The Coprophages
Scully and Mulder's hunt for a serial killer whose victims are fortune tellers brings them into contact with "Clyde Bruckman" (Peter Boyle), an insurance salesman whose psychic powers are anything but a "gift" to him. Next, a New England town is overrun by killer cockroaches...or is it?...in the off-the-wall "War of the Coprophages."
04-3506 ☐*$14.99*

The X-Files: Nisei/731
A video of an alien autopsy, a mysterious cabal of Japanese doctors, Mulder's deadly ride on a secret railroad car where the autopsy took place and Scully's encounter with a group of UFO abductees are the elements in the two-part adventure "Nisei/731."
04-3507 ☐*$14.99*

The X-Files: Piper Maru/Apocrypha
The discovery of a salvage ship whose crew is dying from radiation burns leads Mulder and Scully into a double-episode odyssey for the truth that involves aliens taking over humans, the return of Alex "Ratboy" Krycek, a flashback into the connection between Cancer Man and Mulder's father, and the Lone Gunmen on ice skates.
04-3589 ☐*$14.99*

The X-Files: Pusher/ Jose Chung's "From Outer Space"
How can Mulder and Scully fight an opponent they can't sense, as they face "Pusher," a paranormal killer who can psychically cloud the minds of his targets? Next, the inimitable Charles Nelson Reilly is writer "Jose Chung," whose probe of a possible alien abduction investigated by the agents leads to one of the series' most memorable—and funniest—episodes.
04-3590 ☐*$14.99*

The X-Files: Wetwired/Talitha Cumi
Scully discovers a link between a skewed cable TV signal and a series of inexplicable psychotic episodes by viewers in "Wetwired." Then, Roy Thinnes guest stars as the mysterious Jeremiah Smith, who claims to be an alien clone with the answers to many of Mulder's questions and who is being pursued by the Bounty Hunter, in "Talitha Cumi," the third-season finale cliffhanger.
04-3591 ☐*$14.99*

The X-Files: Herrenvolk/Home
Mulder and Jeremiah Smith's odyssey takes them to the Canadian prairie, where a shocking secret about Mulder's sister is revealed, in the fourth-season opener, "Herrenvolk." Next, Mulder and Scully learn there's no place like "Home"—especially when that home is occupied by the mutant Peacock brothers and their "Ma."
04-3816 ☐*$14.99*

The X-Files: Unruhe/Paper Hearts
Strange "psychic photographs" that show a kidnapper's mental images of his victim's anguish are all that the agents have to work with in "Unruhe." Next, could a serial killer that Mulder helped capture years ago have been the real reason for his sister's disappearance, and what will Mulder have to risk to learn the truth?
04-3817 ☐*$14.99*

The X-Files: Tunguska/Terma
An extraterrestrial rock with a deadly alien surprise inside leads Mulder—along with reluctant partner Alex Krycek—on a global odyssey that takes them to a remote Russian gulag. Getting out of the prison, however, proves harder than getting in, in the two-part adventure "Tunguska/Terma."
04-3818 ☐*$14.99*

The X-Files: Leonard Betts/Memento Mori
Did a headless corpse vanish from a Philadelphia hospital under its own power? Mulder and Scully explore the strange life story of "Leonard Betts." Next, Scully makes a life-threatening discovery that is linked to her "abduction" and a mysterious fertility clinic in "Memento Mori."
04-3950 ☐*$14.99*

The X-Files: Tempus Fugit/Max
In the two-part episode "Tempus Fugit/Max," the search for the truth behind a commercial jet crash pits the agents against government officials and leads to an airborne "close encounter" for Mulder.
04-3951 ☐*$14.99*

The X-Files: Small Potatoes/Gethsemane
Called in to investigate a series of bizarre births in "Small Potatoes," Scully and Mulder have to deal with a man able to change his physical appearance. Next, the fourth-season finale cliffhanger, "Gethsemane," starts with an alien discovery in the Arctic and ends with the apparent suicide of one of the agents.
04-3952 ☐*$14.99*

The X-Files Triple Pack 1
Special three-tape boxed set includes "Pilot/Deep Throat," "Fallen Angel/Eve" and "Conduit/Ice."
04-3380 Save $5.00! *$39.99*

The X-Files Triple Pack 2
Special three-tape boxed set includes "Squeeze/Tooms," "Beyond the Sea/E.B.E." and "Darkness Falls/The Erlenmeyer Flask."
04-3381 Save $5.00! *$39.99*

The X-Files Triple Pack 3
Special three-tape boxed set includes "Little Green Men/Host," "Sleepless/Duane Barry" and "Ascension/One Breath."
04-3402 Save $5.00! *$39.99*

The X-Files Triple Pack 4
Special three-tape boxed set includes "Irresistible/Die Hand Die Verletzt," "Colony/End Game" and "Humbug/Anasazi."
04-3445 Save $5.00! *$39.99*

The X-Files Triple Pack 5
Special three-tape boxed set includes "The Blessing Way/Paper Clip," "Clyde Bruckman's Final Repose/War of the Coprophages" and "Nisei/731."
04-3513 Save $5.00! *$39.99*

The X-Files Triple Pack 6
Special three-tape boxed set includes "Piper Maru/Apocrypha," "Pusher/Jose Chung's 'From Outer Space'" and "Wetwired/Talitha Cumi."
04-3592 Save $5.00! *$39.99*

The X-Files Triple Pack 7
Special three-tape boxed set includes "Herrenvolk/Home," "Unruhe/Paper Hearts" and "Tunguska/Terma."
04-3819 Save $5.00! *$39.99*

The X-Files Triple Pack 8
Special three-tape boxed set includes "Leonard Betts/Memento Mori," "Tempus Fugit/Max" and "Small Potatoes/Gethsemane."
04-3953 Save $5.00! *$39.99*

Cause Célebré (1987)
This true British crime drama stars Helen Mirren as Alma Rattenbury, who, in 1935, confessed to murdering her ailing husband in order to save chauffer and young lover George Bowman from the gallows. Overwhelmed by guilt, Bowman confesses to the crime as well, and they both face a sensational trial. David Suchet and Harry Andrews also star. 105 min.
50-8551 *$19.99*

Alias Smith And Jones (1971)
The made-for-TV movie that led to the hit Western series stars Peter Duel and Ben Murphy as Hannibal Hayes and Jed "Kid" Curry, two notorious outlaws who are given an opportunity for amnesty—if they can last as security guards for one of the largest banks in the West. Forrest Tucker, Susan Saint James also star. 74 min.
10-2669 *$12.99*

Raquel! (1970)
A nostalgic and music-filled '70s time capsule, this lavish TV special features the one and only Raquel Welch dancing and singing her way around the world, along with guest star Tom Jones and cameos by Bob Hope and John Wayne. Songs include "Here Comes the Sun," "Games People Play," "Tutti Frutti," "The Sounds of Silence" and others. 48 min.
22-7118 Was $19.99 *$14.99*

Party Of Five

Debuting in 1994, this popular drama series followed the struggles of the five Salinger siblings to keep their family together after their parents are killed in an auto accident. The talented young cast includes Neve Campbell, Lacey Chabert, Matthew Fox, Jennifer Love Hewitt and Scott Wolf. Each tape runs about 45 min.

Party Of Five: Richer, Poorer, Sickness And Health
It's the wedding of Julia and Griffin...or is it, as Griffin is beaten up before the ceremony and Charlie confesses to Nina about his Hodgkin's Disease.
02-3307 ☐*$12.99*

Party Of Five: The Wedding
What makes Charlie call off his planned marriage to Kirsten on their wedding day?
02-3308 ☐*$12.99*

Party Of Five: The Intervention
In this powerful episode, the Salingers pull together to help Bailey confront his growing dependence on alcohol.
02-3309 ☐*$12.99*

The Best Of Soap: Who Killed Peter?
TV spoofed its own daytime dramas with this hilarious, controversial comedy that ran for five years on ABC and followed the exploits of the Campbell and Tate families. Now you can see the cliffhanger storyline that climaxed the show's first season, as Burt turns detective to learn who killed his womanizing tennis pro son. Richard Mulligan, Katherine Helmond, Billy Crystal, Robert Guillaume and Robert Urich star. 72 min.
02-2610 *$14.99*

The Best Of Soap: Jessica's Wonderful Life
At the pearly gates, Jessica must convince angel Bea Arthur that her family still needs her on Earth. Of course, when your husband is having an affair with the minister's daughter, your son has joined a religious cult, and your sister's living with an alien duplicate of her husband, it's easy to see that someone needs help! Katherine Helmond, Cathryn Damon, Robert Mandan and Billy Crystal star. 74 min.
02-2611 *$14.99*

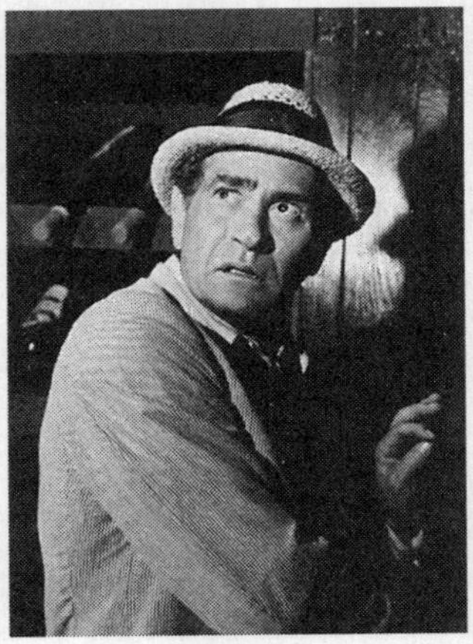

the night stalker

The Night Stalker (1971)
The original chiller that was one of the highest-rated TV movies ever and spawned the hit series. Darren McGavin stars as rumpled reporter Carl Kolchak, whose investigation into a series of bizarre murders leads him to believe that a vampire is walking the streets of Las Vegas. With Barry Atwater, Carol Lynley, Simon Oakland. 73 min.
08-8601 *$14.99*

The Night Strangler (1973)
After his exile from Las Vegas, journalist Carl Kolchak (Darren McGavin) winds up in Seattle, where a string of brutal murders sends the monster-hunting newshound into the catacombs of an underground city and a confrontation with a century-old killer. Shiver-inducing sequel to "The Night Stalker" also stars Richard Anderson, Simon Oakland, Jo Ann Pflug, John Carradine. 74 min.
08-8646 *$14.99*

The Night Stalker: Two Tales Of Terror (1974)
Two episodes from the TV series featuring Darren McGavin as Carl Kolchak, hard-nosed news hawk whose beat draws him into the realm of the supernatural. The slasher terrorizing Chicago may be Saucy Jack himself in "The Ripper," then Kolchak heads to L.A. in search of "The Vampire." With Simon Oakland, William Daniels and the inimitable Larry Storch. 98 min.
07-1535 Was $39.99 ☐*$14.99*

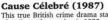

The Jimmy Durante Show/ The Spike Jones Show
Two of the small screen's biggest kidders in their own vaudeville-inspired comedy series; Jimmy as the harried owner of a small nightclub, and frenetic bandleader Spike on his summer replacement show of (whoop-whoop, honk) dinner music. 55 min.
10-7468 Was $19.99 *$14.99*

The Texan
It takes a big man to roam the giant state of Texas, matching a fast gun against outlaws and tyrants, and Big Bill Longley was that man. Two episodes of the late '50s western series are featured, starring Rory Calhoun as the wandering shootist.
10-7475 *$19.99*

You Asked For It
Two shows from the popular TV series featuring a menagerie of unusual subjects, including a salute to Glenn Miller, Ice Capades star Donna Atwood, movie stunt dogs, lovebirds Bill & Coo, card sharks and quick change artists. Hosted by Art Baker; features original Skippy Peanut Butter commercials. 50 min.
10-9392 *$14.99*

The Flying Doctor/ Janet Dean, Registered Nurse
An episode of the Richard Denning series about a Yankee M.D. making housecalls by air to ranchers and Bushmen in Australia, plus Ella Raines as a nurse who heals her patient's emotional scars as well as their physical symptoms.
10-7481 Was $19.99 *$14.99*

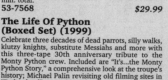

Burke's Law, Vol. 1
Gene Barry played slick and wealthy head of Los Angeles detectives Amos Burke in this hit series that aired on ABC from 1963 to 1965. Follow Burke in his chauffeur-driven Rolls Royce as he tries to figure out "Who Killed Jason Shaw?," a man found dead, fully clothed, in the shower. Among the suspects: a used car salesman, a ship builder and a multi-millionaire. 55 min.
09-5303 *$14.99*

Dave Garroway's Wide, Wide World
"Today Show" host Dave Garroway explores the wild, wild west from Gene Autry's Melody Ranch with guest stars John Wayne, Gary Cooper, Clayton Moore, John Ford and other sagebrush superstars. 75 min.
10-8155 Was $19.99 *$14.99*

The Life You Save/The Cold Touch
Two sterling dramas with all-star casts: Gene Kelly and Agnes Moorehead in "The Life You Save" and "The Cold Touch" with Bette Davis and Forrest Tucker. 60 min.
10-8168 Was $19.99 *$14.99*

General Electric Theater: Salute To America
A flag-waving celebration of The U. S. of A. so gosh darn inspiring it could drive a person right into public service (at least judging by what became of host Ronald Reagan). Guests include songstress Jo Stafford and the blended voices of Fred Waring and His Pennsylvanians.
10-7469 Was $24.99 *$14.99*

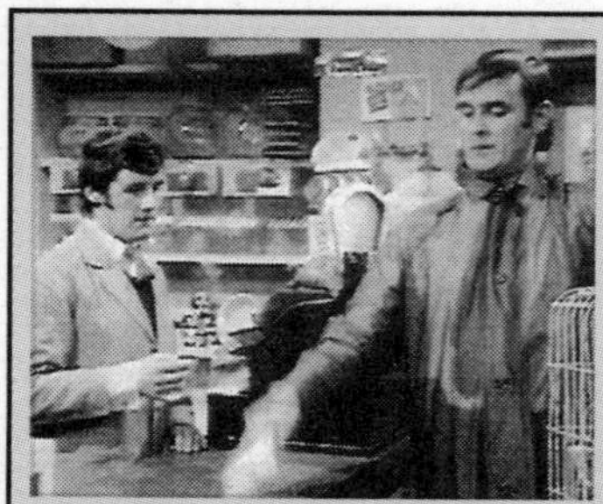

Monty Python's Flying Circus
And now for something completely different...the original, outrageous British TV comedy series, starring Graham Chapman, John Cleese, Spam, Terry Gilliam, Spam, Eric Idle, Spam, Spam, Terry Jones, baked beans and Michael Palin. All your favorite characters and skits are here for your own personal enjoyment (nudge, nudge).

Monty Python's Flying Circus: Season 1: Complete Set
Episodes 1-13 are featured in this six-tape set that includes flying sheep, the world's funniest joke, "Nudge, Nudge," "Crunchy Frog," the dead parrot sketch, the Lumberjack Song, Mr. Hilter and the North Minehead By-Elections, the 127th Upperclass twit of the Year Show, Mr. Ken Shabby and more. 441 min. total.
53-6523 *$59.99*

Monty Python's Flying Circus: Season 2: Complete Set
Episodes 14-26 are featured in this six-tape set that includes the Ministry of Silly Walks, the Piranha Brothers, the Spanish Inquisition, how to spot a Mason, "The Bishop," "Blackmail," "The Attila the Hun Show," the Bruces, "Scott of the Antarctic," "How Not to Be Seen," Spam and more. 441 min. total.
53-6573 *$59.99*

Monty Python's Flying Circus: Season 3: Complete Set
Episodes 27-39 are featured in this six-tape set that includes "Njorl's Saga," the Fish-Slapping Dance, "The Money Programme," the Argument Clinic, "Biggles Dictates a Letter," the cheese shop sketch, "Mr. Pithers' Cycling Tour," Dennis Moore, the award-winning vicar sketch and more. 441 min. total.
53-6800 *$59.99*

Monty Python's Flying Circus: Season 4: Complete Set
Episodes 40-45 are featured in this three-tape set that includes "The Golden Age of Ballooning," Michael Ellis, overacting Hamlets, Mr. Neutron, the Most Awful Family in Britain Contest and more. 180 min. total.
53-7568 *$29.99*

The Life Of Python (Boxed Set) (1999)
Celebrate three decades of dead parrots, silly walks, klutzy knights, substitute Messiahs and more with this three-tape 30th anniversary tribute to the Monty Python crew. Included are "It's...the Monty Python Story," a comprehensive look at the troupe's history; Michael Palin revisiting old filming sites in "Pythonland"; an animated salute from the "South Park" characters; Meat Loaf hosting the musical salute "From Spam to Sperm: Monty Python's Greatest Hits"; a "lost" episode from the made-for-German TV shows; and much more. 168 min. total.
53-7565 *$29.99*

Ripping Yarns
Monty Python's Michael Palin and Terry Jones are the crazed minds behind these dryly daffy sendups of schoolboys' adventure tales. The laughs freely abound in these wonderfully off-kilter offerings from BBC-TV.

Ripping Yarns
Michael Palin reflects upon life in a particularly strange boarding school in "Tomkinson's Schooldays," plays the only POW not content to sit out the war in "Escape from Stalag Luft 112B," and portrays "Golden Gordon," diehard fan of the worst football team in Yorkshire. 90 min.
04-2013 Was $19.99 ❑*$14.99*

More Ripping Yarns
The most boring man in the world finds adoration and respect as a bank robber in "The Testing of Eric Olthwaite, the sordid details of "Whinfrey's Last Case" are revealed, and not even an ocean voyage with an all-woman crew will help you escape the "Curse of the Claw." 92 min.
04-2014 Was $19.99 ❑*$14.99*

Even More Ripping Yarns
The son of gun-crazed gentry in India makes good in "Roger of the Raj," no member of the loopy Chiddingfold family is safe from "Murder at Moorstones Manor," and a daring expedition is attempted "Across the Andes by Frog." 90 min.
04-2015 Was $19.99 ❑*$14.99*

Fawlty Towers
Monty Python's John Cleese was never in funnier fettle than as Basil Fawlty, the short-tempered, sardonic manager of a less-than-successful resort hotel, in this beloved BBC TV series. Connie Booth, Prunella Scales and Andrew Sachs co-star. Each three-episode tape features a special behind-the-scenes interview with Cleese and runs about 90 min.

Fawlty Towers: Hotel Inspectors
Basil tries to put on his best front to impress the "Hotel Inspectors." Then, Fawlty believes that a visiting nobleman will give the Towers a "Touch of Glass" and does his best funny-walking Hitler impression in order to appease "The Germans."
04-2016 ❑*$14.99*

Fawlty Towers: The Builders
The hotel lobby gets a complete makeover—and winds up a door or two short—after Fawlty instructs "The Builders." And his belief that maid Polly's newlywed friends are shacking up disrupts "The Wedding Party." Then, Basil bemuses "The Psychiatrist" with his obsession to prove a guest is smuggling in ladies.
04-2017 ❑*$14.99*

Fawlty Towers: Gourmet Night
The guests on "Gourmet Night" are in for some unique dishes when Basil must fill in for a drunken chef. Fawlty further has his hands full satisfying an American visitor's request for "Waldorf Salad" and hiding the body of a deceased guest in "The Kipper and the Corpse."
04-2018 ❑*$14.99*

Fawlty Towers: Communications Problems
Anxious to hide his racetrack winnings from wife Sybil, Fawlty entrusts the money to the less-than-trustworthy Major in "Communication Problems," and Basil's plans for "The Anniversary" surprise party blow up in his face. Then, Manuel the waiter's "filigree Siberian hamster" is anything but in "Basil the Rat."
04-2019 ❑*$14.99*

Fawlty Towers: The Complete Set
All four fabulously funny "Fawlty Towers" tapes are available in this special boxed set that's cheaper than a weekend in Torquay.
04-2574 Save $5.00! ❑*$54.99*

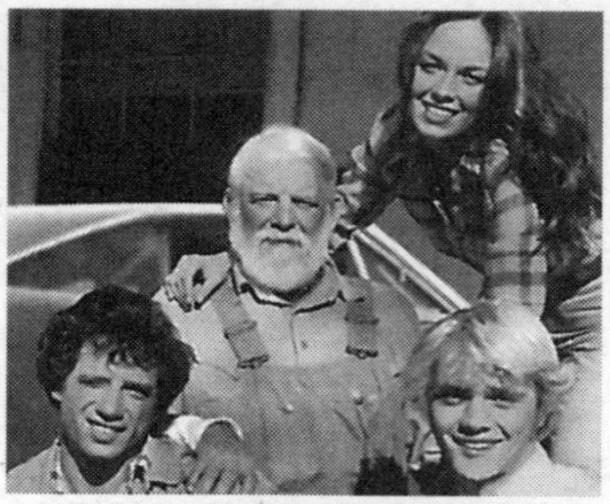

THE DUKES OF HAZZARD

The Dukes Of Hazzard
Fasten your seat belts, because "good ol' boys" Bo Duke (John Schneider) and Luke Duke (Tom Wopat) are takin' the General Lee down the backroads of Hazzard County, staying one step ahead of Sheriff Rosco (James Best) and foiling the crooked schemes of local politico Boss Hogg (Sorrell Booke), in the hit action-comedy series that also starred Barbara Bach as cousin Daisy Duke and Denver Pyle as moonshining Uncle Jesse. Each tape runs about 50 min.

The Dukes Of Hazzard: One Armed Bandits
19-2632 *$12.99*

The Dukes Of Hazzard: Road Pirates
19-2633 *$12.99*

The Dukes Of Hazzard: Officer Daisy Duke
19-2634 *$12.99*

The Dukes Of Hazzard: Luke's Love Story
19-2635 *$12.99*

The Dukes Of Hazzard: The Big Heist
19-2636 *$12.99*

The Dukes Of Hazzard: To Catch A Duke
19-2637 *$12.99*

The Dukes Of Hazzard: Mason Dixon's Girls
19-2638 *$12.99*

The Dukes Of Hazzard: High Octane
19-2639 *$12.99*

The Dukes Of Hazzard: Deputy Dukes
19-2640 *$12.99*

Federal Men (Treasury Men In Action)
Based on actual Treasury Department cases, this early TV crime drama followed the T-men into action against smugglers, counterfeiters, tax evaders and other assorted criminals. Walter Geaza as "the Chief" stars in two episodes, "Case of the Tarnished Lady" and "Case of the Man Outside." 55 min.
10-7496 Was $19.99 *$14.99*

The Ruggles/Duffy's Tavern
In his eponymous early '50s series, beloved character actor Charlie Ruggles played a harried insurance salesman whose family saddled him with such sitcom dilemmas as who keeps forgetting to put the cap back on the toothpaste. Next, bar manager Archie finds himself reluctantly engaged in an episode of the transplanted radio comedy. with Ed Gardner, Alan Reed. 55 min.
10-7501 Was $19.99 *$14.99*

The Adventures Of Ellery Queen/The Files Of Jeffrey Jones
Lee Bowman was the second TV actor to play novel and radio supersleuth Ellery Queen, donning his trenchcoat for the 1952 season. Paired with an episode of Queen is a show from fellow Big Apple detective Jeffrey Jones, "The Dusty Doll" starring Don Haggerty.
10-7513 Was $19.99 *$14.99*

Little Women: Meg's Story (1950)
Enchanting "Westinghouse Studio One" version of the Louisa May Alcott perennial focuses primarily on Meg's romance. Fine family classic stars Mary Sinclair, John Baragrey, Nancy Marchand. 60 min.
09-2096 Was $24.99 *$14.99*

Little Women: Jo's Story (1950)
The tale of the March sisters continues in this early "Westinghouse Studio One" adaptation of the "Little Women" saga. Mary Sinclair, Kent Smith star. 50 min.
10-9396 *$14.99*

Ford Star Salute To Cole Porter
America's beloved tunesmith is feted in one of the once-a-month "Jubilees" sponsored by Ford. The big-name Hollywood stars piping Cole's songs include Bing Crosby, Louis Armstrong, Shirley Jones and Gordon MacRae. 85 min.
10-7464 *$19.99*

Lerner And Loewe Special
Wonderful musical special celebrating the music of the accomplished songwriting team, with Maurice Chevalier, Julie Andrews and Richard Burton performing numbers from "Camelot" and "Gigi." 60 min.
10-8150 Was $19.99 *$14.99*

TV Openings Plus
Get ready to sing—or hum—along to some of your favorite vintage TV theme songs with this boob tube cornucopia. Along with opening segments from such shows as "I Dream of Jeannie," "Highway Patrol," "The Joey Bishop Show," "The Donna Reed Show," "Fury," "Space Patrol" and others, there's also commercials for Coca-Cola, Pall Mall cigarettes, Wonder Bread, the Polaroid Swinger and more. 60 min.
50-8120 *$19.99*

Big Town/Hollywood Off Beat
A classic episode of "Big Town," a terrific newspaper drama of the 1950s starring Patrick McVey as the crusading editor of the Illustrated Press who excelled in stopping crime and corruption. Also included is an episode of "Hollywood Off Beat" (AKA: "Steve Randall"), featuring Melvyn Douglas as a lawyer who becomes a detective after he's disbarred. 50 min.
10-9212 Was $19.99 *$14.99*

Jack Jones On The Move
This TV special ran on ABC and features the popular singer crooning and playing host to Tony Bennett, Joanie Sommers, Shani Wallis, Molly Bee and Milton Berle. 50 min.
10-9215 Was $19.99 *$14.99*

Buckskin
This Western series ran on NBC in the 1958-59 season and featured Tommy Nolan as young Jody O'Connell, a boy who lived in a boardinghouse owned by his mother in Montana during the 1880s and often got involved in the lives of the many guest passing through. With Sallie Brophy. Episodes include "Greatest in History" and "A Permanent Juliet." 50 min.
10-9217 Was $19.99 *$14.99*

Captain Of Detectives/ Craig Kennedy, Criminologist
Two forgotten but exciting police dramas from the 1950s are featured on this tape. "Captain of Detectives" stars Robert Taylor (who, coincidentally, went on to star in "The Detectives") in a hard-hitting crime story. Next, Donald Woods is "Craig Kennedy," an expert in solving cases using scientific means. 50 min.
10-9388 *$14.99*

The Adventures Of Red Ryder/Mr. Ed
Allan "Rocky" Lane is featured (if not always seen) in this TV double feature. First, Lane re-creates his screen role of cowboy hero Red Ryder in "Gun Trouble Valley," the pilot episode for the 1956 series. And Rocky supplies the voice of talking horse "Mr. Ed" in "Wilbur Gets the Message," starring Alan Young. 50 min.
10-9390 *$14.99*

The Pat Boone Chevy Show/ The Patti Page Show/ The Eddy Arnold Show
Musical-variety series of all kinds are offered on this video that features three—count 'em—three faves from the 1950s. Crooner Pat welcomes Stubby Kaye, while Patti and Eddy entertain with their song stylings.
10-9394 *$14.99*

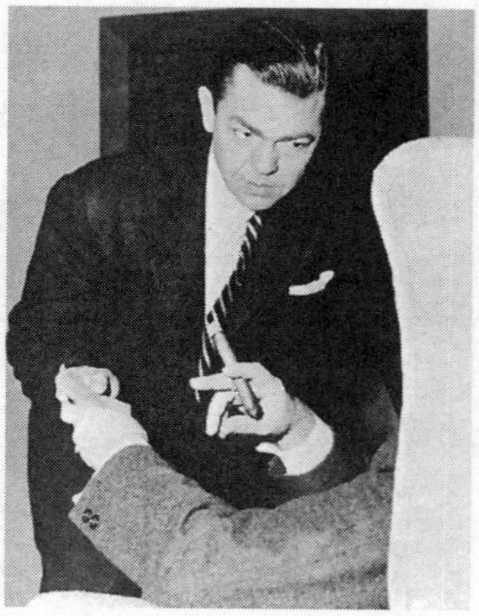

The Millionaire, Vol. 1
Back when a million dollars was a lot of money, reclusive tycoon J. Beresford Tipton dispatched assistant Marvin Miller to make an anonymous weekly largess to unsuspecting strangers. Here are two episodes from the popular '50s drama, showing how the newfound wealth affected each recipient. Guest stars include Agnes Moorehead, Tuesday Weld. 60 min.
10-8140 *$19.99*

Upstairs Downstairs (1970)
Come back to 165 Eaton Place, London, in the early 1900s to follow the lives, loves and drama of the wealthy Bellamy family and their servants. All five years of the Emmy-winning British series that aired on PBS's "Masterpiece Theatre" have been gathered into boxed sets. Angela Badderly, Pauline Collins, Rachel Gurney, Gordon Jackson, David Langton, Jean Marsh and Simon Williams star.

Upstairs Downstairs: The Premiere Season Collection
Included in this seven-tape boxed set are "On Trial/The Mistress and the Maids," "Board Wages/The Path of Duty," "A Suitable Marriage/A Cry for Help," "Magic Casements/I Dies from Love," "Why Is Her Door Locked?/A Voice from the Past," "The Swedish Tiger/The Key of the Door" and "For Love of Love." 663 min. total. NOTE: Individual volumes available at $24.99 each.
53-8173 Save $25.00! *$99.99*

Upstairs Downstairs: The Second Season Collection
Included in this seven-tape boxed set are "The New Man/A Pair of Exiles," "Married Love/Whom God Hath Joined," "Guest of Honor/The Property of a Lady," "Your Obedient Servant/Out of the Everywhere," "Object of Value/A Special Mischief," "The Fruits of Love/The Wages of Sin" and "A Family Gathering." 663 min. total.
53-6399 Was $149.99 *$99.99*

Upstairs Downstairs: The Third Season Collection
Included in this seven-tape boxed set are "Miss Forrest/A House Divided," "A Change of Scene/A Family Secret," "Rose's Pigeon/Desirous of Change," "Word of Honour/The Bolter," "Goodwill to All Men/What the Footman Saw," "A Perfect Stranger/Distant Thunder" and "The Sudden Storm." 663 min. total.
53-6400 Was $149.99 *$99.99*

Upstairs Downstairs: The Fourth Season Collection
Included in this seven-tape boxed set are "A Patriotic Offering/News from the Front," "The Beastly Hun/Women Shall Not Weep," "Tug of War/Home Fires," "If You Were the Only Girl in the World/The Glorious Dead," "Another Year/The Hero's Farewell," "Missing Believed Killed/Facing Fearful Odds" and "Peace Out of Pain." 663 min. total.
53-6401 Was $149.99 *$99.99*

Upstairs Downstairs: The Fifth Season Collection
Included in this eight-tape boxed set are "On With the Dance/A Place in the World," "Laugh a Little Louder Please/The Joy Ride," "Wanted: A Good Home/An Old Flame," "Disillusion/Such a Lovely Man," "The Nine Day Wonder/The Understudy," "Alberto/Will Ye No' Come Back Again," "Joke Over/Noblesse Oblige" and "All the King's Horses/Whither Shall I Wander." 816 min. total.
53-6402 Was $149.99 *$99.99*

Upstairs Downstairs Remembered
It was the series that helped put PBS "on the map," and now you can hear from the creators and stars of "Upstairs Downstairs" as they share backstage stories and relive the show's most memorable moments. 50 min.
53-8237 *$29.99*

Monsters
The creepy-crawly anthology series from the producers of "Tales from the Darkside," featuring gruesome make-up from Oscar-winner Dick Smith, comes to home video. Each tape includes two episodes sure to make you scream and runs about 45 min. There are six volumes available, including:

Monsters: The Feverman/One Wolf's Family
14-3271 *$12.99*

Monsters: My Zombie Lover/ All In A Day's Work
14-3272 *$12.99*

Schlitz Playhouse Double Feature
Both of these vintage TV dramas spotlight the Air Force B-29 aircraft that was used during World War II. Included are "The Long Shot," with Edmond O'Brien and Charles Bronson; and "Storm Warning," starring Robert Stack and Arthur Franz. 60 min.
10-9987 *$14.99*

Schlitz Playhouse Of Stars (1953)
Beer and original TV drama: two great things that went great together in the Golden Age of Television. "Closed Door," with Gene Lockhart, tells of a young girl who is the key to one man's redemption. Next, in "No Compromise," a Texas Ranger must bring a murderer back to justice on a train. Stephen McNally stars. Includes original Schlitz commercials. 60 min.
82-1042 *$19.99*

Freddy's Nightmares (1988)
Freddy Krueger (Robert Englund), the dream-invading ghoul of the "Nightmare on Elm Street" films, hosts and appears in this hit TV horror series filled with incredible special effects, frightening stories and Freddy's off-beat humor. Each episode runs about 50 min. There are five volumes available, including:

Freddy's Nightmares: No More Mr. Nice Guy
19-1881 *$14.99*

Freddy's Nightmares: Freddy's Tricks And Treats
19-1882 *$14.99*

Freddy's Nightmares: Lucky Stiff
19-1883 *$14.99*

Freddy's Nightmares: Dreams That Kill
19-1884 *$14.99*

Freddy's Nightmares: It's My Party And You'll Die If I Want You To
19-1885 *$14.99*

The Hunger
Inspired by the 1983 cult film, this Showtime series presents chilling tales of lust, desire and the supernatural, with lush production values, talented casts, and lots of eroticism. Ridley and Tony Scott serve as producers; Terence Stamp hosts. Each multi-episode tape runs about 120 min.

The Hunger: Soul For Sale
Featured are "Red Light," in which a sexy model thinks a camera is stealing her soul; "The Secret Shih-Tan," with Jason Scott Lee as a chef who uses an ancient cookbook to prepare a deadly meal; "Bridal Suite," with Sally Kirkland, about a honeymoon inn where the groom is put to a life-or-death test; and "River of Night's Dreaming," about an escaped convict finding redemption at a strange mansion.
81-9107 *$59.99*

The Hunger: Wicked Dreams
Included are "Room 17," with Curtis Armstrong as a man who finds the cable TV in his motel room seductive and deadly; "Plain Brown Envelope," in which a female journalist hitches a ride on a truck filled with sexual aids; "No Radio," with Amanda De Cadenet, about sex games and a married woman; and "The Lighthouse" with Bruce Davison as a lonely lighthouse keeper whose fantasy lover comes to life.
81-9108 *$59.99*

The Hunger: Vampires
Featured are "Footsteps," about a sexy vampire who meets her match with a hot vegetarian; "A Matter of Style," featuring Chad Lowe, with a virgin vampire who takes directions from her mentor in how to turn a innocent man into a seducer of innocence; and "Fly-By-Night," about a vampire who helps a woman trapped in a padded cell in his own demonic way.
81-9109 *$59.99*

The Hunger Three-Pack
"Soul for Sale," "Vampires" and "Wicked Dreams" are also available in a three-tape collector's set.
81-9110 Save $40.00! *$139.99*

The Veil (1958)
Boris Karloff hosted and often starred in this syndicated TV series dealing with the supernatural and filmed two years before his celebrated show, "Thriller." Each episode is presented uncut, complete with Karloff's scary introduction in front of a crackling fireplace. A must for Karloff-aholics!

The Veil, Vol. 1
In "Vision of Crime," Karloff and Patrick Macnee are constables investigating a druggist's murder that the deceased man's brother, 150 miles away at sea, claims to have "seen" in a vision. Next, Boris warns a man that the woman he recently met is his late niece in "Girl on the Road." And sea captain Karloff poisons his jealous wife, but she returns to haunt him at a banquet in "Food at the Table." 75 min.
79-6463 *$19.99*

The Veil, Vol. 2
A dying young girl is saved by a young physician guided by the spirit of his father, doctor Boris Karloff, in "The Doctors"; a man gets an eyeful when he's given "The Crystal Ball" by his gold-digging ex-girlfriend and sees her cheating on her new husband; and "Genesis" follows a schemer's plan to cheat his brother out of the family farm, and what lawyer Karloff and others do to straighten things out. 75 min.
79-6464 *$19.99*

The Veil, Vol. 3
In "Destination Nightmare," Boris Karloff and his son see the ghostly face of a man who died in World War II in the clouds; a man who thinks he sees a murder during a New York City heatwave is sent to Bellvue doctor Karloff in "Summer Heat"; George Hamilton stars in "The Return of Madame Vernoy," in which a young woman plans to wed the older man she believes she was married to in a prior life; and a clairvoyant is suspected of being "Jack the Ripper" after claiming to have had visions of the Whitechapel murders. 100 min.
79-6465 *$19.99*

13 Demon Street
This 13-episode TV series created by horror writer Curt Siodmak was shot in Sweden and broadcast in Europe in 1960. Lon Chaney, Jr. is the host of the spooky "Twilight Zone"-styled show, playing the caretaker of the titular address. Except where noted, each tape features three 23-minute episodes and is in English with Swedish subtitles.

13 Demon Street, Vol. 1
In "The Black Hand," a surgeon severs his hand in a car accident, only to replace it with one from a psychotic strangler. A doctor makes a housecall to an artist obsessed with a beautiful, imaginary woman in "Fever." And a man's recurring nightmare about his future turns real when a fortune teller tells him he's destined to die in "Condemned in the Crystal."
79-6472 *$19.99*

13 Demon Street, Vol. 2
"Green Are the Leaves" finds a TV crew member and his girlfriend encountering a real ghost while spending an evening at a Swedish castle. Also, a doctor falls in love with a nude woman frozen in ice for 50,000 years in "The Girl in the Glacier," and a man goes on a bizarre scavenger hunt that includes killing an evil person in "The Book of Ghouls."
79-6473 *$19.99*

13 Demon Street, Vol. 3
A photographer believes a woman he murdered is coming to get him through "The Photograph" he took of her, while a museum curator returns in the form of "The Vine of Death" after he's killed by a neighbor who's been having an affair with his wife. Next, a man who received a Haitian voodoo doll as an anniversary present tries to use it to kill his spouse in "A Gift of Murder."
79-6474 *$19.99*

13 Demon Street, Vol. 4
In "The Secret of the Telescope," a man tries to kill his wife after he thinks she's responsible for his imminent murder, which he witnessed through a new telescope, while a banker takes advice from a witch's cat after his demanding wife plots to run away with her boyfriend in "Never Steal a Warlock's Wife." Next, a man witnesses a "Murder in a Mirror" that happens to be his wife's long-dead lover, and a doctor returns from the dead after he's killed by a phony medium carrying out a scam in "Black Nemesis."
79-6475 *$19.99*

Teenage A Go-Go
Hey, hep cats! Here's a super-gear and ginchy '60s "tube-in" that will have you grooving to clips from TV shows such as "Where the Action Is," "Shindig!," "Karen" and "Tammy"; commercials with The Monkees for kool-Aid and Rice Krispies, and for Ultra-Bright toothpaste, Sea & Ski suntan lotion, Breck shampoo and other teen essentials; and more far-out fun. 60 min.
10-9192 *$19.99*

Classic Television: Your Favorites From The 1950s
Relive the "Golden Age of Television" with this seven-tape set featuring programming from each night of the week. Included are "Sunday: The NBC Comedy Hour/The Alan Young Show," "Monday: I've Got a Secret/Caesar's Hour," "Tuesday: Texaco Star Theater/The $64,000 Question," "Wednesday: This Is Your Life/Mama/Stage Show," "Thursday: The Burns and Allen Show/Topper/You Bet Your Life," "Friday: The Jack Benny Show/I Married Joan" and "Saturday: Space Patrol/Suspense/Racket Squad." 620 min. total.
16-5028 *$49.99*

Mad Magazine TV Special
Mad Magazine fans will want to see this animated special that was deemed too unique for TV audiences in the mid-1970s. Alfred E. Newman is featured, so what, you, worry? 30 min.
15-9042 Was $19.99 *$14.99*

The Invaders: Original Pilot (1967)
In "Beach Head," the debut episode of the '60s sci-fi TV series, architect David Vincent (Roy Thinnes) sees an alien ship landing and learns of the Invaders' plans for global infiltration and domintation. With Diane Baker, James Daly. 49 min.
10-2176 ❑*$12.99*

The Invaders: Boxed Set
How do you convince the world that you've witnessed a flying saucer landing, and that human-looking aliens have infiltrated society as a prelude to conquest? That's the problem Roy Thinnes faced every week in this 1967-68 sci-fi series created by Larry Cohen. This seven-tape boxed set includes the pilot episode "Beach Head," "The Experiment," "The Mutation," "Quantity Unknown," "The Ivy Curtain," "Moonshot" and "Wall of Crystal." 360 min. total.
16-5046 *$49.99*

The Invaders (1995)
The cult '60s sci-fi series is updated, scarier than ever, in this chilling two-part TV movie. Scott Bakula stars as pilot Nolan Wood, who learns his mind is being controlled by human-looking alien infiltrators intent on taking over Earth. With Elizabeth Peña, Richard Thomas, Delane Matthew and a cameo by original series star Roy Thinnes. 180 min.
63-1813 Was $89.99 ❑*$14.99*

The Hitchhiker, Vol. 1
Whoever offers him a ride receives in exchange a story to chill the soul. Trilogy of terrifying tales from the TV anthology series stars Gary Busey and Geraldine Page in a story of radio religion, Karen Black as a woman whose hired help is less than human, and Harry Hamlin in a tale of Yuppie occult vengeance. 90 min.
40-1339 *$19.99*

The Hitchhiker, Vol. 2
The second sampler of suspenseful stories features Peter Coyote as a director who takes realism one step too far, Margot Kidder and Darren McGavin in a deadly game set in a nursing home, and Susan Anspach as a haunted author. 90 min.
40-1353 *$19.99*

The Hitchhiker, Vol. 3
Three more stories of mystery with top stars travelling down a highway of horror. Barry Bostwick and Willem Dafoe learn the truth about "ghostwriting," a terror beyond death awaits Tom Skerritt, and teacher Stephen Collins meets a most unusual student. 90 min.
40-1377 *$19.99*

The Hitchhiker, Vol. 4
The world's most unusual video dating service, a plastic surgeon who learns the true face of terror, and a very protective dog are the elements of fear in three eerie episodes from the popular TV series. Robert Vaughn, Sybil Danning, Michael O'Keefe and Greg Henry star. 90 min.
40-1382 *$19.99*

The Best Of Ernie Kovacs: Collector's Edition
A grab bag of great bits from television's chaotic clown can be had in this five-tape set, including such classic moments as the zany "1812 Overture," a spoof of TV westerns, a woman-in-the-bathtub routine, a parody of "Swan Lake," an interview with painter Mother Rustic, the "Tilted Table" sketch, plus such unforgettable characters as Percy Dovetonsils, Eugene, Auntie Gruesome and Miklos Molnar. 300 min. total. NOTE: Individual volumes available at $14.99.
22-1214 *$39.99*

Classic TV Double Feature
Two funny shows from the 1950s are featured on this show. Ernie Kovacs stars in "I Was a Bloodhound" about a baby elephant that is missing from a hotel room. And Charles Coburn is featured in "Sam," which involves a retired department store clerk who finds lost money after he retires and moves to the desert. 60 min.
10-9989 *$14.99*

The Beulah Show, Vol. 1
Two episodes from the early TV series are offered. Hattie McDaniel and Ernest Whitman guest star in the first episode; the second features Ethel Waters in the title role, along with Butterfly McQueen and Dooley Wilson.
10-8432 Was $19.99 *$14.99*

The Beulah Show (1952)
In the early days of television there were two shows with blacks as stars: "Amos and Andy," and this show, which starred Louise Beavers as a maid who often winds up running the household she works for. Ruby Dandridge and Ernest Whitman co-star in this vintage sitcom. 51 min.
09-1133 Was $24.99 *$14.99*

Police Call/Police Station
Take a visit back to the golden age of TV law enforcement with these two mid-1950s series based on true police cases from across the country. If you thought "Dragnet" was realistic, check out these! 50 min.
10-9408 *$14.99*

The Mickey Rooney Show
Also known as "Hey, Mulligan," this series ran on NBC from 1954 to 1955 and featured Mickey Rooney as a studio page attempting to get into show business. In "The Lion Hunt," Mickey and pal Freddy let a lion escape during the shooting of a new jungle show. And in "Ghost Story," Mickey and Freddy try to scare their boss out of purchasing a cabin. 50 min. total.
10-9546 *$14.99*

The Life And Legend Of Wyatt Earp
Hugh O'Brian is the legendary lawman who tamed the West—and the TV airwaves—in this hit show on ABC from 1955 to 1961. Here, gamblers battle Earp and hire some unusual killers in "The Assassins." Also, Hugh O'Brian plays himself in "Wyatt Earp Visits the Williamses" when he stops by the house of some big fans of his show and teaches them a lesson or two. 55 min.
10-9689 *$14.99*

The Adventures Of Xavier Cugat In Spain
Long before he married "Koochie-Koochie Girl" Charo, bandleader Xavier Cugat hosted this special that includes the eclectic cast of Robert Taylor, Imogene Coca, Broderick Crawford, Julie Newmar, Phil Silvers and Salvador Dali.
10-9406 *$14.99*

Steve Canyon, Vol. 1
Milton Caniff's comic-strip hero was the basis for this series that ran from 1958 to 1960 and featured Dean Fredericks as the Air Force command pilot and troubleshooter. In the first episode, Steve partakes in a dangerous tactical exercise; Mary Tyler Moore (as "Mary Moore") is featured. Then, Canyon is asked to testify in a court-martial trial. 55 min. total.
10-9871 Was $19.99 *$14.99*

Treasury Men In Action, Vol. 1
Actual cases from the U.S. Customs and Treasury departments were the basis for this series that ran on both ABC and NBC from 1950 to 1955. Walter Greaza played "the Chief," and a number of other now-famous performers appeared. Includes "The Case of the Careless Murder" with Claude Akins and Carolyn Jones; and "The Case of the Shot in the Dark," featuring Charles Bronson. 60 min.
10-9887 Was $19.99 *$14.99*

The Littlest Hobo
This syndicated series ran in 1964 and focused on the adventures of London, a German shepherd without a master, who helps people in trouble. Included are "Death at 5 P.M." and "Little White Liar." 60 min.
10-9904 *$19.99*

The Pinky Lee Show
Often called the precursor to Pee-wee Herman, Pinky Lee was a comic who rose to popularity in the 1950s with his unusual brand of humor and clownish costume. This loosely structured sitcom ran on NBC in 1950 and featured Lee as a stagehand in a vaudeville theater who was often called on to substitute for performers. Two episodes are included. 50 min.
10-9400 *$14.99*

Bronco
Ty Hardin was Bronco Layne, a former Confederate officer who finds adventure and action in the West after the War Between the States, meeting such famous (and infamous) figures as Jesse James, Billy the Kid and Belle Starr. Each tape of this ABC series, broadcast from 1960 to 1962, runs 50 min.

Bronco: Death Of An Outlaw
During the 1878 Lincoln County Cattle War in New Mexico, Bronco finds himself in the middle of a feud between outlaw-turned-family man Billy the Kid and buffalo hunter Pat Garrett.
19-1966 *$14.99*

Bronco: Shadow Of Jesse James
James Coburn plays a nasty Jesse James in this episode that finds Bronco saved from James' wrath by Cole Younger and meeting Belle Starr.
19-1967 *$14.99*

Big Red Shindig
Country/western hoedown with great music, starring Hank Thompson and "Hee Haw's" Grandpa Jones. 60 min.
10-8170 Was $19.99 *$14.99*

Playhouse 90: Death Of A Manolete
Jack Palance and Suzy Parker excel in this entry from one of the most revered dramatic TV shows in history. 60 min.
10-8175 *$19.99*

Requiem For A Heavyweight (1955)
Writer Rod Serling's powerful tale of a washed-up boxer who leaves the ring, only to find he's unsuited for any other work, won five Emmy Awards when originally broadcast on TV's "Playhouse 90." Jack Palance, Keenan Wynn, Ed Wynn and Kim Hunter star. 90 min.
15-5279 *$14.99*

Playhouse 90: Charley's Aunt (1957)
The classic cross-dressing comedy of mistaken identity and hilarious farce is given a television treatment on this installment of "Playhouse 90." Art Carney, Jeanette McDonald, Orson Bean, Tom Tryon and Jackie Coogan are among the top-notch talent featured. 90 min.
10-6007 *$14.99*

The Comedian (1957)
Mickey Rooney shines in the title role in this Emmy-winning drama from "Playhouse 90." A self-centered and manipulative TV comic destroys everyone around him on the eve of a live special. Mel Torme, Edmond O'Brien and Kim Hunter also star in this poignant story; script by Rod Serling. 129 min.
15-5278 *$14.99*

Playhouse 90: Bomber's Moon (1958)
WWII drama written by Rod Serling stars Robert Cummings, Rip Torn and Martin Balsam. An air corps commander who must deal with a pilot afraid to fly begins to see his own fears reflected in the man. 85 min.
09-1702 Was $29.99 *$24.99*

Days Of Wine And Roses (1958)
Cliff Robertson and Piper Laurie star in this classic "Playhouse 90" production based on J.P. Miller's story about a couple sinking into the depths of alcoholism. John Frankenheimer directs. 89 min.
15-5282 *$19.99*

Playhouse 90: The Velvet Alley (1959)
A would-be TV drama writer finally gets his big break, but the success that follows could wind up costing him the love of those closest to him, in this Rod Serling-scripted tale. Art Carney, Jack Klugman, Leslie Nielsen and Katherine Bard star; look closely for an early turn by Burt Reynolds. 88 min.
09-3113 *$19.99*

Two By John Ford
A rarity for fans of baseball and director John Ford, this pair of made-for-TV diamond dramas features James Stewart in "Flashing Spikes" and John Wayne in "Rookie of the Year." 90 min.
10-8176 *$19.99*

The Chevy Show: Swingin' At The Summit
Kay Starr hosts guests Louis Armstrong, Harpo Marx, Tony Bennett, George Shearing and more in a music-filled episode called "Swingin' at the Summit." 57 min.
10-8328 Was $19.99 *$14.99*

Casey Jones/Fury
Long before he was a skipper, Alan Hale, Jr. was an engineer in this late '50s adventure series, with the legendary Casey riding the rails with canine "little buddy" Cinders. Next, Peter Graves and Bobby Diamond star in the fondly remembered program about an orphan boy and his beloved black stallion. 55 min.
10-7504 Was $19.99 *$14.99*

Westinghouse Studio One: I Am Jonathan Scrivener (1952)
Experimental early TV drama in which Mr. Scrivener is never seen, but his character is revealed through conversations with his secretary and colleagues. John Forsythe, Maria Riva, Everett Sloane star. 59 min.
09-2309 *$14.99*

Super TV Bloopers
These are the outrageous moments you'll never see on TV! Wild out-takes, flubs and downright shocking behavior on the sets of "The Dick Van Dyke Show," "Happy Days," "Laverne & Shirley," "M*A*S*H" and other favorite shows. 60 min.
10-7539 Was $19.99 *$14.99*

Laugh-In Bloopers
Direct from "beautiful downtown Burbank," the crazy cast of the '60s comedy smash "sock it" to you with hilarious flubs, off-color candid comments and outrageous ad libs. Join Dan Rowan and Dick Martin, Ruth Buzzi, Goldie Hawn, Arte Johnson and such guests as James Garner, Bob Hope, Don Rickles and even Richard Nixon. Funny? You bet your bippy! 45 min.
10-7685 *$19.99*

TV Bloopers
Some of TV's funniest moments never made it onto the small screen! Watch as the casts of "Laugh-In," "Gunsmoke," "M*A*S*H," "The Mary Tyler Moore Show," "Hee Haw," "The Carol Burnett Show" and other favorites goof, guffaw and break each other up with laughter. 70 min.
62-1008 *$19.99*

Star Trek Bloopers
A full 25 minutes of flubbed lines, props that fail to work, and outrageous on-the-set hi-jinx from the original TV series' three seasons. NOTE: The technical quality of these cutting-room outtakes is not up to our usual standards. 25 min.
62-1085 Was $19.99 *$14.99*

Boob Tube Blunders
A delirious double feature of uncensored bloopers from days gone by. First, see flubs and goofs from "McHale's Navy," "Ben Casey," "Ozzie and Harriet" and more '60s faves, followed by Ruth Warrick, Susan Lucci and other daytime stars in the wildest miscues and practical jokes from the world of soap operas. 90 min.
62-1356 *$19.99*

The Super Blooper Show
Some of the strangest, funniest foul-ups from the small screen are collected on one tape. See outrageous, uncensored outtakes from shows like "Get Smart," "Gunsmoke," "The Hollywood Palace" and "The Twilight Zone"; a Rod Serling anti-drug spot and Lucy and Desi pushing cigarettes; a government bond commercial with the casts of "The Brady Bunch," "Mannix" and "The Odd Couple" and more. 105 min.
62-1357 *$19.99*

The Dumbest Blonde
Jayne Mansfield is incredibly sexy and displays her knack for comedy when she plays a not-so-dumb-after-all bombshell in this comedy/drama from the Golden Age of Television. 60 min.
10-8173 Was $19.99 *$14.99*

My Favorite Martian
Ray Walston played the stranded visitor from outer space, who tried to fix his spaceship while posing as reporter Bill Bixby's "Uncle Martin," in this popular sci-ficom that aired on CBS from 1963 to 1966. Included here are four episodes: the two-part "Go West Young Martian," "Martin Meets His Match" and "Pay the Man the 24 Dollars." 115 min.
15-5502 *$19.99*

My Favorite Martian: Boxed Set
All 32 color episodes from the series' final two seasons have been gathered in an eight-tape collector's set. 16 hrs. total.
15-5515 *$99.99*

Rumpole Of The Bailey
Debuting on British TV in 1975, this series based on John Mortimer's courtroom dramas quickly became a transatlantic favorite. Leo McKern stars as Horace Rumpole, the cantankerous London barrister who quest for justice frequently finds him at odds with the English legal system and on the outs with his wife Hilda, AKA "She Who Must Be Obeyed." Except where noted, each two-episode tape runs about 104 min. There are 22 volumes available, including:

Rumpole Of The Bailey, Vol. 1
Includes "Rumpole and the Genuine Article" and "Rumpole and the Old Boy Network."
44-1880 Was $49.99 *$19.99*

Rumpole Of The Bailey, Vol. 2
Includes "Rumpole and the Sporting Life" and "Rumpole and the Blind Tasting."
44-1881 Was $49.99 *$19.99*

Rumpole Of The Bailey, Vol. 3
Includes "Rumpole's Last Case" and "Rumpole and the Judge's Elbow."
44-1882 Was $49.99 *$19.99*

Rumpole Of The Bailey, Vol. 4
Includes "Rumpole and the Old, Old Story" and "Rumpole and Portia."
44-1883 Was $49.99 *$19.99*

Rumpole Of The Bailey, Vol. 5
Includes "Rumpole and the Female of the Species" and "Rumpole and the Official Secret."
44-1930 Was $49.99 *$19.99*

Rumpole Of The Bailey, Vol. 6
Includes "Rumpole and the Golden Thread" and "Rumpole and the Last Resort."
44-1931 Was $49.99 *$19.99*

Rumpole Of The Bailey, Vol. 7
Includes "Rumpole and the Bubble Reputation" and "Rumpole and the Age of Miracles."
44-1932 Was $49.99 *$19.99*

Rumpole Of The Bailey, Vol. 8
Includes "Rumpole and the Tap End" and "Rumpole and the Quality of Life."
44-1933 Was $49.99 *$19.99*

Rumpole Of The Bailey, Vol. 9
Includes Rumpole á la Carte" and "Rumpole and the Summer of Discontent."
44-2039 Was $39.99 *$19.99*

Rumpole Of The Bailey, Vol. 10
Includes "Rumpole at Sea" and "Rumpole and the Right to Silence."
44-2040 Was $39.99 *$19.99*

Rumpole Of The Bailey: Vols. 1-4 Gift Set
The first four "Rumpole of the Bailey" mysteries are presented in this deluxe money-saving boxed set.
44-1884 *$79.99*

Rumpole Of The Bailey: Vols. 5-8 Gift Set
There's more "Rumpole" in store with this boxed set featuring volumes 5 through 8.
44-1990 *$79.99*

Rumpole Of The Bailey: Vols. 9-10 Gift Set
Get ready for "Rumpole" with Volumes 9 and 10 in the series.
44-2041 *$39.99*

Rumpole Of The Bailey: Rumple's Return
Ace British barrister Horace Rumpole leaves his quiet retirement in Miami for cases involving pornography and, later, murder in this superb courtroom tale laced with wit and ingenuity. Leo McKern stars. 106 min.
44-1817 Was $59.99 *$24.99*

Rumpole Of The Bailey: Rumpole's New Cases Gift Set (Six Tapes)
"Never plead guilty" to not owning this six-tape boxed set featuring "Rumpole and the Younger Generation/Rumpole and the Honorable Member," "Rumpole and the Married Lady/Rumpole and the Learned Friends," "Rumpole and the Heavy Brigade/Rumpole and the Man of God," "Rumpole and the Case of Identity/Rumpole and the Show Folk," "Rumpole and the Fascist Beast/Rumpole and the Age for Retirement" and "Rumpole and the Bright Seraphim/Rumpole and the Barrow Boy," plus a collectable Rumpole magnifying glass. NOTE: Individual volumes available at $19.99.
44-2243 *$119.99*

Rumpole Of The Bailey: Gift Set (Five Tapes)
Court will always be in session with this five-tape boxed set that includes "Rumpole and the Alternative Society/Rumpole and the Course of True Love," "Rumpole and the Quacks/Rumpole for the Prosecution," "Rumpole and the Children of the Devil/Rumpole and the Miscarriage of Justice," "Rumpole and the Eternal Triangle/Rumpole and the Reform of Joby Johnson" and "Rumpole and the Family Pride/Rumpole on Trial." NOTE: Individual volumes available at $19.99.
44-2249 *$99.99*

Up Pompeii: Collector's Set
Ancient Rome is the setting for this outrageous and bawdy Britcom featuring Frankie Howerd as Lurcio, scheming and sexually obsessed slave of philandering Senator Ludicrus Sextus and his wacky family. This two-tape collection features six riotous tales. 189 min. total.
53-9753 *$34.99*

Decoy
Casey Jones may have been an engineer, but in this action series, Casey (Beverly Garland) is an attractive, tough-as-nails undercover cop who's not afraid to get her hands dirty to clean up New York City's streets. Also known as "Police Woman Decoy," this syndicated series ran in 1957. Each volume features two episodes and runs about 50 min.

Decoy, Vol. 1
Includes "Decoy" and "Night of Fire."
10-9912 Was $19.99 *$14.99*

Decoy, Vol. 2
Includes "Cry Revenge" and "Night Light."
10-9913 Was $19.99 *$14.99*

Decoy, Vol. 3
Includes "The Challenger" and "The Lost Ones."
10-9914 Was $19.99 *$14.99*

Captain Z-Ro
This era-spanning kids' adventure series from 1995 followed time machine inventor Captain Z-Ro, who would send his young assistant, Jet, into the past to help historical figures at turning points in their lives. Roy Steffins and Bobby Trumbull star. Each tape includes two shows and runs about 50 min.

Captain Z-Ro, Vol. 1
Includes "Genghis Khan" and "Robot."
10-9404 *$14.99*

Captain Z-Ro, Vol. 2
Includes "Cortez" and "Alfred the Great."
10-9405 *$14.99*

Show Promos, Vol. 1
Some of them will live forever in reruns, while others vanished after 13 weeks. Test your tube memory as you watch promo clips with such programs as "The Green Hornet," "Lost in Space," "UFO," "Honey West," "Gidget," "F Troop," the beloved "Rango" with Tim Conway, and many others. 60 min.
10-9193 *$19.99*

Show Promos, Vol. 2
Along with clips touting "The Donna Reed Show," "Bewitched," "The Partridge Family," "Day in Court," "The Lone Ranger" and other shows, this compilation features Buddy Ebsen dancing his way through a showcase of the 1964-65 CBS season (notable for the debuts of "Gomer Pyle," "The Munsters" and "Gilligan's Island"). 60 min.
10-9194 *$19.99*

Next Week Promos
Learn what hilarity, heartache, action and adventure are "coming next week" for such series as "Beany & Cecil," "Hoppity Hooper," "Daktari," "77 Sunset Strip," "Rawhide," "The Defenders" and many more in this boob tube sampler. 60 min.
10-9195 *$19.99*

Crunch And Des (1955)/ Crime Syndicated (1951)
This dramatic TV double bill starts off with an episode from the syndicated adventure series starring Forrest Tucker and Sandy Kenyon as operators of the charter boat Poseidon. Next, true stories of crimefighting from government files were brought to life in "Crime Syndicated," hosted by Rudolph Halley. 50 min.
10-8440 *$29.99*

Toon-A-Vision
You can't get any more "animated" than this sampler of cartoon kidvid favorites of the '50s, '60s, '70s and '80s. Clips and themes from "The Deputy Dawg Show," "Ruff and Reddy," "Rocky and His Friends," "Top Cat," "Jonny Quest," "Kimba the White Lion," "King Kong" and many more Saturday standards are on the bill. 60 min.
10-9191 *$19.99*

The Waltons
Based on the real-life reminiscences of author Earl Hamner, Jr., the warm and inspiring story of a poor but close-knit family living in the Blue Ridge Mountains of Virginia in the 1930s was a perennial hit for CBS during its 1972-1981 run. Richard Thomas starred as eldest son John-Boy Walton; Michael Learned, Ralph Waite, Will Geer and Ellen Corby also star. Each tape runs about 50 min.

The Waltons: The Hunt
A wild game hunt turns into a rite of passage for John-Boy in the series' debut episode.
19-2641 *$12.99*

The Waltons: The Scholar
John-Boy becomes a tutor for a middle-aged woman who wants to learn to read in this Emmy-winning episode.
19-2642 *$12.99*

The Waltons: The Gift
The family's strength and compassion are put to the test when a friend (guest star Ron Howard) comes down with a serious illness.
19-2643 *$12.99*

The Waltons: The Townie
A visitor from the city (guest star Sissy Spacek) turns John-Boy's head, but could it lead to marriage?
19-2644 *$12.99*

The Waltons: The Triangle
John-Boy finds himself in a romantic rivalry with the local minister, Rev. Fordwick (John Ritter).
19-2645 *$12.99*

The Waltons: The Love Story
A case of "first love" for John-Boy leads to a dramatic and painful resolution.
19-2646 *$12.99*

The Waltons: A Thanksgiving Story (1975)
In the depths of the Great Depression, the Walton family learns the deeper meaning of the holiday and the priceless values of family in this drama from the acclaimed TV series. Michael Learned, Richard Thomas star. 100 min.
40-1091 Was $19.99 ❑*$14.99*

The Waltons: The Children's Carol (1978)
In a special holiday drama based on the classic family TV series, the Walton family gathers together for a wartime Christmas they'll long treasure. Richard Thomas, Michael Learned star. 97 min.
40-1092 Was $19.99 ❑*$14.99*

A Day For Thanks On Walton's Mountain (1982)
World War II has ended, but the Walton family's plans to reunite at their mountain homestead for a Thanksgiving dinner are threatened by several personal crises in this holiday drama. Ralph Waite, Ellen Corby, Judy Norton-Taylor and Robert Wrightman as John-Boy star. 97 min.
19-2012 Was $59.99 *$14.99*

A Decade Of The Waltons
Relive the history of one of TV's closest and largest families in this special salute to "The Waltons." Series creator Earl Hamner is your host for a look at his real-life story, with scenes from classic episodes and interviews with stars. 60 min.
40-1061 *$14.99*

Sheena, Queen Of The Jungle
Six-foot siren Irish McCalla was the white goddess fighting evil in the harsh, unforgiving jungles of Africa, with Chim, her chimpanzee friend, in one hand, and a spear in the other. Christian Drake costarred as trader and semi-love interest Bob in this 1955-56 syndicated adventure series. Each tape features two episodes and runs about 55 min.

Sheena, Queen Of The Jungle, Vol. 1
Sheena escorts a Hollywood film crew into the bush to shoot a film, only to defend a tribe falsely accused of killing a white man, in "Forbidden Land." Next, in "The Renegades," Sheena assists Bob in looking for a cache of stolen diamonds.
82-1039 *$19.99*

Sheena, Queen Of The Jungle, Vol. 2
"The Test" finds an animal poacher attempting to steal Chim away from Sheena, a big mistake. Then, in "The Magic Bag," Sheena and Bob encounter a crazed doctor attempting to use ancient tribal potions to revive the dead.
82-1040 *$19.99*

Sheena, Queen Of The Jungle, Vol. 3
A crooked promoter faces a vengeful tribal chief when he attempts to take a member of the chief's tribe and turn him into the next big boxing champ in "The Ganyika Kid." In "The Elephant God," Sheena and Bob come to the assistance of a woman who must locate a crashed plane to claim her inheritance.
82-1041 *$19.99*

Sheena, Queen Of The Jungle (1955)
Swinging from the treetops in her leotard, it's Irish McCalla, the White Goddess of Kenya, with her ape pal Chim and Trader Bob. Two jungle adventures are included, "The Rival Queen" and "Eyes of the Idol." 60 min.
10-7348 *$19.99*

TV's Cowboys: Boxed Set
Fans of TV's sagebrush sagas will love this seven-tape boxed set that includes classic episodes of "The Lone Ranger/The Cisco Kid," "The Adventures of Kit Carson/The Gabby Hayes Show," "Death Valley Days/The Range Rider," "Annie Oakley/Frontier Doctor," "26 Men/Yancy Derringer," "Shotgun Slade/The Barbara Stanwyck Show" and "The High Chaparral." 350 min. total.
16-5031 *$49.99*

Tracey Takes On...
Whether it's as faded singer/actress Linda Granger, homemaker Fern Rosenthal, a male cab driver named Chic or another of an array of characters, comedienne Tracey Ullman presents hilarious insights into a variety of subjects in her Emmy-winning TV series. Each tape features three episodes, plus outtakes and other bonus features, and runs about 80 min.

Tracey Takes On... Sex/Romance/Fantasy
Among the topics tackled by Tracey's alter egos are make-up advice for would-be adult film stars by Ruby Romaine; Linda Granger's struggle with sex addiction; the perils of making love to your husband by Hollywood stuntwoman Rayleen Gibson; and more.
44-2139 Was $19.99 *$14.99*

Tracey Takes On... Movies/Vanity/Fame
Watch as political spouse Virginia Bugge takes a shot at filmmaking, stunt woman Rayleen Gibson protects a top actress from a stalker, fashion editor Janie Pillsworth's latest photo shoot turns into all-out war, and more.
44-2140 Was $19.99 *$14.99*

Tracey Takes On...Fern & Kay
This special program features Tracey Ullman bringing to life two of her best-loved characters: Boca Raton resident, condo board member and retired homemaker Fern Rosenthal, and English-born, man-hungry California bank teller Kay Clark.
44-2177 Was $19.99 *$14.99*

Snowy River: The McGregor Saga
Based on an epic Australian poem, this family adventure saga ran on American TV from 1993 to 1996. Set in the rugged Snowy Mountains in the late 1800s, the series tells of widowed rancher Matt McGregor trying to raise his family (sons Colin and Rob and daughters Danielle and Emily). With Andrew Clarke, Brett Climo, Wendy Hughes, Cheryl Munks and Guy Pearce. Each tape runs about 44 min.

Snowy River: The McGregor Saga: Comeback
When the McGregors' name is at stake, Matt proves he's still "the Man from Snowy River" with a marathon ride, while Rob's friend's arrival draws the attention of the local ladies.
66-6108 *$14.99*

Snowy River: The McGregor Saga: Grand Opening
While Montana, a local woman, takes a liking to Rob's friend, the McGregor family encounters cattle rustlers.
66-6109 *$14.99*

Snowy River: The McGregor Saga: Black Sheep
Rob's friend, Duncan Jones, proves to be a man with secrets in his past. And Jessie McClusky, a woman with a past, arrives in town.
66-6110 *$14.99*

Snowy River: The McGregor Saga: Prince Of Hearts
Danielle learns about love while the townspeople learn about prejudice after a group of Gypsies arrives in town.
66-6111 *$14.99*

Snowy River: The McGregor Saga: The Grand Duke
Matt takes delivery of a prized bull at his cattle ranch, while Colin and his family move into their new residence. At the same time, Montana and Duncan must decide about their future.
66-6112 *$14.99*

Snowy River: The McGregor Saga: New Business
Rob returns to the ranch after a long cattle drive; in the meantime, Montana makes a surprising confession, and the McGregor brothers plot their future.
66-6113 *$14.99*

Snowy River: The McGregor Saga: Set
All six volumes are available in a money-saving collection.
66-6114 Save $35.00! *$54.99*

Snowy River: The McGregor Saga: The Race (1994)
In this special two-part adventure, young Danni McGregor attempts to follow in her father's footsteps by taking part in the dangerous Snowy River cross-country horse race, while Matt squares off against an American cowboy determined to win at any cost. Andrew Clarke, Guy Pearce, Kristie Raymond. 87 min.
27-6889 ❑*$14.99*

The George Gobel Show, Vol. 1
This installment of "Lonesome" George's late-'50s variety series showcases special guest star Jeffrey Hunter. Also on hand are Gobel's regular singers, dancers and comics. 50 min.
10-9399 *$14.99*

The George Gobel Show, Vol. 2
"Lonesome" George's guests include Peter Nero, Joyce Van Patten and Jerry Murad's Harmonicats. 60 min.
10-9988 *$14.99*

Yancy Derringer
Jock Mahoney starred as the dapper cardsharp and troubleshooting hero of old New Orleans in this frontier adventure series which aired on CBS in 1958-59. The legendary X. Brands played Yancy's Indian ally, Pahoo. Included here are four episodes: "A State of Crisis," "Two of a Kind," "Outlaw at Liberty" and "Saga of Lonesome Jackson." 110 min.
83-7007 *$19.99*

Classic TV Commercials Of The Fifties And Sixties

Meet us at the intersection of Memory Lane and Madison Avenue for these nostalgia-filled collections of vintage TV ads for the products that filled the homes of America. From rare celebrity spots to unforgettable jingles, you'll see why it was the Golden Age of Television...Advertising. Each tape runs about 60 min.

Classic TV Commercials Of The Fifties And Sixties, Vol. I
A memory-stirring collection of favorite shills from TV's Golden Age with Bonomo Turkish Taffy (that tabletop smash!), greasy Wild Root Creme Oil for Hair, Pee Wee Reese for Gillette razors, the Crest test, U.S. Keds and the classic "Hertz puts you in the driver's seat" campaign. More! 60 min.
01-9004 ***$19.99***

Classic TV Commercials Of The Fifties And Sixties, Vol. II
Sure, Bromo Seltzer tasted better than Fizzies, but which had the bubbliest bubbles? Settle this and other great debates with classic ads including the Old Gold dancing cigarettes, "The Dick Van Dyke Show" cast for Kent, Buster Crabbe for Heinz products, Screaming Yellow Zonkers and much more! 60 min.
01-9005 ***$19.99***

Classic TV Commercials Of The Fifties And Sixties, Vol. III
The stars come out for American consumerism, including Andy Griffith and Ron Howard for Sanka, Jean Arthur for Jell-O, Bert Lahr for Lay's Potato Chips, Bill Bixby for Kent, and Ron and Nancy Reagan at home with GE. Also, Action Jackson, Good and Plenty, Chef Boy Ar Dee and many others. 60 min.
01-9006 ***$19.99***

Classic TV Commercials Of The Fifties And Sixties, Vol. IV
Hey kids, let's go shopping in the '50s for Milton Bradley's Grab-a-Loop and a Roy Rogers Gun Hat. Then, it's off to the grocer for Mom's Silvercup Bread, Pepsodent, Tide detergent, Raid, and don't forget the Maypo! Plus, get Newport brand for Dad—it's the kind Joey Bishop smokes! Much more! 60 min.
01-9007 ***$19.99***

Classic TV Commercials Of The Fifties And Sixties, Vol. V
A cornucopia of commercial fun with Lionel's Mercury Space Capsule, the Cheerios Kid's Frosty-O's Challenge, the Suzi Homemaker Candy Maker, the "Man from U.N.C.L.E." secret message pen and much more. Look, Dad, it's Bing Crosby for natural gas and Edie Adams for Muriel cigars. Dad? 60 min.
01-9008 ***$19.99***

Classic TV Commercials Of The Fifties And Sixties, Vol. VI
Can you resist star pitches from Jimmy Durante for Kellogg's Corn Flakes, Joseph Cotten for Bufferin, Old Gold Cigarettes with Red Barber, Anita Ekberg for Lustre Creme or Harvey Lembeck pointing the finger at Charmin? Also, Alka Seltzer, Broadcast Chili Beans, Puffa Puffa Rice and much more! 60 min.
01-9009 ***$19.99***

Classic TV Commercials Of The Fifties And Sixties, Vol. VII
TV promotes itself with ads for "Sugarfoot," "Wyatt Earp," "The Donna Reed Show," "My Three Sons," "The Rifleman," "Colt .45," Clint Walker introducing Dennis Hopper in "Cheyenne," and Gig Young, Eve Arden and Gale Gordon for "Our Miss Brooks." Also, Coleco games and lots more! 60 min.
01-9010 ***$19.99***

Classic TV Commercials Of The Fifties And Sixties, Vol. VIII
Cracking up consumer resistance are comedians Buster Keaton for Simon Pure Beer, Groucho for DeSoto, Chico and Harpo for Creamy Prom, "The Lucy Show" cast for Westinghouse, Jack Benny and Dennis Day for Texaco, the Three Stooges for Simon Wax, and Bugs Bunny and Daffy Duck for Tang. More! 60 min.
01-9011 ***$19.99***

Classic TV Commercials Of The Fifties And Sixties, Vol. IX
Yipes! Stripes! It's the Fruit Stripe Gum commercial; astounding special effects by Aero Wax, Reynolds Wrap and Niagara Spray; plus renegade ads for Clackers, Newport, Funny Face drink mix (whatever happened to Chinese Cherry, anyway?), much more. 60 min.
01-9061 ***$19.99***

Classic TV Commercials Of The Fifties And Sixties, Vol. X
A man's man's evening of commercials with Chuck Connors for Jet Ski, plus John Deere, Scout Jeep and the Remington Shaver de-fuzzing a peach. Take Excedrin for the "1040" headache, or just soak your troubles with Bert and Harry Piel (Bob Elliott and Ray Goulding). Much more! 60 min.
01-9062 ***$19.99***

Classic TV Commercials Of The Fifties And Sixties, Vol. XI
Feel young with Yoo-Hoo!, the brand Yogi Berra drinks, or feel like a big shot with Champale. Have a smoke with Pall Mall or clear the air with Wizard Room Deodorizer. Tackle real-life pain with Contac, Heet and Bayer and real-life drama on the Tide Hidden Camera. Many others! 60 min.
01-9063 ***$19.99***

Commercials

Classic TV Commercials Of The Fifties And Sixties, Vol. XII
Camel cigarettes make ballplayers Early Wynn and Bob Lemon look manly, the editor of Esquire look suave and the stars of TV's "Topper" look...oh, never mind. Also, Jim Davis for the '64 Buick Wildcat, Dave Garroway for GM, Rootie Kazootie for Silvercup Bread and the cast of "Bewitched" on location. Many others! 60 min.
01-9064 ***$19.99***

Classic TV Commercials Of The Fifties And Sixties, Vol. XIII
Loads of historical goodies here, including Buster Keaton for Ford and Paul Ford for Pabst; optimistic odes to Valiant, Chevelle and Corvair; the origins of new-fangled Pringles ("They're stackable!"); Firestone's haunting "where the rubber meets the road" jingle; and much more! 60 min.
01-9065 ***$19.99***

Classic TV Commercials Of The Fifties And Sixties, Vol. XIV
Ageless commercials reveal the breadth of human experience: the humor of Peter Paul Mounds, the tenderness of Lovable Bra, the prudence of Brylcreem, the pathos of Soupy Sales for Gino's Pizza, the boundless pride of Coke Family Size, and so much more! 60 min.
01-9066 ***$19.99***

Classic TV Commercials Of The Fifties And Sixties, Vol. XV
Saying those few words from the sponsor are Stanley Holloway for Morton Salt, Swifty Flyer for PF Flyers, the Brooklyn Dodgers for Lucky Strikes, Jiminy Cricket for Baker Chocolate and Mike Wallace for Fluffy Cake Mix ("You are fluffy, you do admit that?"). Plus, a rare "Jailhouse Rock" promo, and lots more. 60 min.
01-9067 ***$19.99***

Classic TV Commercials Of The Fifties And Sixties, Vol. XVI
Before Nintendo, before Atari, there was Milton Bradley, advertiser of board games like Easy Money, Chutes and Ladders, Uncle Wiggly, Go to the Head of the Class, Racko! and Candy Land. Also, ads for Blatz Beer, Good 'N' Plenty, Arnold Stang for Delco and many others. 60 min.
01-9068 ***$19.99***

Classic TV Commercials Of The Fifties And Sixties, Vol. XVII
Step right up and see brilliant product pushes for Oxydol, My-T-Fine Pudding, RCA Electric Ranges, Gillette Foamy, Bond Bread, Marx Toys, Vicks, Listerine, and Super Shave with Yanks pitching ace Whitey Ford. 60 min.
01-9087 ***$19.99***

Classic TV Commercials Of The Fifties And Sixties, Vol. XVIII
A cavalcade of commercials for products like Crayola Crayons, Kraft, Marlboro, Vaseline Hair Tonic, Bonomo Turkish Taffy, Cheerios with Bullwinkle, Etch-A-Sketch, Salada Tea, an endorsement from Vincent Price for Hangman, and even Robby the Robot. 60 min.
01-9088 ***$19.99***

Classic TV Commercials Of The Fifties And Sixties, Vol. XIX
Your memory will be jarred with commercials focusing on the joys of Spud Potato Chips, Dixie Cups, Rice Krispies, Gimbels Shop At Home, Bumble Bee Tuna, Strange Department Stores, the 1957 Plymouth Oldsmobile Vista Cruise Wagon and more. 60 min.
01-9089 ***$19.99***

Classic TV Commercials Of The Fifties And Sixties, Vol. XX
Discover the wonders of Chevron, Club Beer, Peter Pan Peanut Butter, Jiminy Cricket Puppets, Betty Crocker Muffin Mix, National Jell-O Week and more, more, more! 60 min.
01-9090 ***$19.99***

Classic TV Commercials Of The Fifties And Sixties, Vol. XXI
Take a look at these great TV campaigns: Frosted Flakes with Adam West, Kodak Instamatic photography while sky-diving, Buster Keaton meets Speedy Alka-Seltzer, Excedrin Headache #1040 with Charles Nelson Reilly, Allerest, Jack Gilford sharing his Cracker Jack, and lots more. 60 min.
01-9102 ***$19.99***

Classic TV Commercials Of The Fifties And Sixties, Vol. XXII
Incredible array of classic TV spots, including Goodyear, Union Carbide, Spud Cigarettes, Super Car Hot Rods, Jack Naars Binoculars, Cocoa Puffs, Robin Hood Wildroot, The Frito Bandito, Johnny Astro, Play-Dough Factory, Electro-Shot Shooting Gallery and more. Also featured is O.J. Simpson in a classic commercial! 60 min.
01-9103 ***$19.99***

Classic TV Commercials Of The Fifties And Sixties, Vol. XXIII
Not having a remote control wasn't the only reason you didn't switch channels so readily back then. Reminisce with the Puffa Puffa Rice song, Eddie Cantor for Halo, a promo for the 1956 film "Somebody Up There Likes Me," Ultra Brite toothpaste, a Rheingold Beer spot in Spanish, Tareyton's "I'd Rather Fight Than Switch" pitch and more. 60 min.
01-9104 ***$19.99***

Classic TV Commercials Of The Fifties And Sixties, Vol. XXIV
Pitches for Westinghouse TV, Hertz, Tonka Toys, Salada, RCA with the RCA repairman, Wilkinson Sword Blades, Vitalis with National League MVP Ken Boyer, Chesterfield on the Frank Sinatra Show, Bond Bread using the James Bond theme and others. 60 min.
01-9105 ***$19.99***

Classic TV Commercials Of The Fifties And Sixties, Vol. XXV
Super TV spots for RCA Whirlpool Stoves, Coke with Emmett Kelly and Connie Francis, Lark Cigarettes, Don McNeill's Breakfast Club, Blatz Beer, Atlantic Gasoline, Sealtest Milk and Cottage Cheese. Bemco Mattresses, many more. 60 min.
01-9106 ***$19.99***

Classic TV Commercials Of The Fifties And Sixties, Vol. XXVI
It's a cavalcade of clever come-ons for Minute Rice, Wildroot, Donald Duck and Porky Pig Soakies, Marshmallow Fluff (key ingredient in the making of Fluffernutters), Swanson Frozen Foods, Chiclets, the Dodge Dart and Coronet, PF Flyer sneakers, Lysol, Ivory Soap, Lionel Trains and too many more consumer goods to count!
10-9807 ***$19.99***

Classic TV Commercials Of The Fifties And Sixties, Vol. XXVII
Check out this incredible time capsule of memorable commercials. Included are the Remco Wirosell Radio, Emenee Organ ("Go Emenee Electric Piano Organ!"), Bosco, Good Humor Ice Cream, Easter Seals, Bolox Movie Camera, Winky Dink Magic TV Screen, Wheaties, One-a-Day Vitamins and more.
10-9808 ***$19.99***

Classic TV Commercials Of The Fifties And Sixties, Vol. XXVIII
Walk down Memory Lane as you watch spots for such products as Dumont TV, Michael C. Fina Silver Trays, the Ford Edsel (with Bing Crosby), Silvercup Bread, Arista Blue Chinchillas (the furs, not the animals), Motorola Radio, Pepsi, Music Box Record Shop and more.
10-9809 ***$19.99***

Classic TV Commercials Of The Fifties And Sixties, Vol. XXIX
Just when you thought it was safe to stop ordering great commercial collections, here comes Volume 29, a grab-bag of great nostalgia. Included are Lucy and Desi for Phillip Morris, 20 Mule Team Borax, Chef Boy-Ar-Dee Pizza, Brylcreem, the Frito Bandito, Colorforms, the Heinz Ketchup race, Creepy Crawlers, Lifebuoy, Lucky Charms, the Great Garloo, Robot Commando and Rolaids.
10-9810 ***$19.99***

Classic TV Commercials Of The Fifties And Sixties, Vol. XXX
See why they don't make 'em like they used to with this compilation of terrific commercials for Fischer Price products from 1970, Johnny Eagle rifles, Jello, Muriel Cigars, Lucky Strike cigarettes with Frank Gifford, such classic games as Barrel of Monkeys and Fascination, Flintstone Vitamins, Drive Detergent, Dristan and a shopping cart or two more.
10-9811 ***$19.99***

Classic TV Commercials Of The Fifties And Sixties, Vol. XXXI
What a potpourri of products and promos: Shasta soda, Skippy peanut butter, Zenith hi-fi stereos, Kool Pops, Schlitz Beer, Quake, Jello, Josephine the Plumber for Comet, a "Keep America Beautiful" announcement, ads for "The Partridge Family," "Make Room for Granddaddy" and "The Odd Couple," and plenty more.
10-9812 ***$19.99***

Classic TV Commercials Of The Fifties And Sixties, Vol. XXXII
Stroll down Memory Lane with classic endorsements for such products as Billy Blastoff, Suzie Homemaker Candy Shop, Tippy Toes, RCA TV and Stereo. Mister Brain, Three Musketeers, Major Matt Mason, Rin-Tin-Tin for Gravy Train, Wheaties, Cool Whip, Josephine the Plumber for Comet, Kool Pops, Sanka and more.
10-9813 ***$19.99***

Classic TV Commercials Of The Fifties And Sixties, Vol. XXXIII
Check out these terrific come-ons for Chatty Cathy, Cocoa Marsh, the Slinky Building Toy, Winston Cigarettes, Cheerios, Stella Dora Cookies, Dutch Masters Cigars, Halo Shampoo, Revell Model Kits, Colgate Dental Cream, Glo-Coat, Glade Air Freshener and many other fine products.
10-9814 ***$19.99***

Classic TV Commercials Of The Fifties And Sixties, Vol. XXXIV
There's no end in sight for great TV commercials, as evidenced in this compilation that includes spots for Beacon Wax, Contact, Excedrin, Dubonet Wine, Dixie Cup, Duncan Hines, Pepsi, the 1965 Dodge Polara, Stay Puff, Dennis the Menace for Kellogg's Rice Crispies, Lestoil and Ginger Bread Mix.
10-9815 ***$19.99***

Classic TV Commercials Of The Fifties And Sixties, Vol. XXXVI
All of your favorite products in a series of memorable commercials are presented in this compilation. Included are Maypo, Pabst Blue Ribbon Beer, Helena Rubinstein Long Lashes, Chevrolet, White Owl cigars, Swanson frozen dinner, Old Spice, Robert Taylor for Maxwell House coffee, Jergen's, Candygram (but not for Mongo), Muriel cigars, McCormick tea bags and more.
10-9816 ***$19.99***

The Video Supermarket Of The Fifties And Sixties, Vol. I
Shop aisles of memories in a TV commercial supermarket featuring Elsie the Cow for Borden, Sunbeam Bread, EZ Pop popcorn, Inger Stevens for Vel, Hydrox, Niagara spray starch, Tide, Cheer, All, Hellman's mayonnaise, Tetley Tea, Karo Syrup, Mickey Mantle for orange juice, and so much more! 60 min.
01-9003 ***$19.99***

Classic Doll Commercials From The '50s And '60s
Toy convention materials include a visit to an Ideal Toy factory where they make the Betsy Wetsy doll, and a rare film describing the Shirley Temple collection to shopkeepers. Also, TV spots for Patty Play Pal, Tiny Tears, Little Miss Echo, Thumbelina, Bye Bye Baby, and Betsy McCall. Much more! 60 min.
01-9017 ***$19.99***

Classic Car Commercials From The '50s & '60s, Vol. 1
Vintage TV motor ads turn your living room into an auto show! See commercials for the '60 Falcon and Thunderbird, '61 Ford, '64 Dodge, and Pat Boone and Dinah Shore for the '59 Chevrolet. Also, Prestone Anti-Freeze, Atlas Tires, and Jane Russell for Lustre Creme's Cadillac Giveaway! More! 60 min.
01-9018 ***$19.99***

Car Commercials
Let Movies Unlimited put you in the driver's seat with some classic TV ads for the tailfinned favorites of the '50s and '60s. There are 1956 Ford T-Birds and 1957 Chevrolets, the '64 Stingray, Mustangs and more, including a pitch for Chevy's "OK Used Cars." 60 min.
10-9179 ***$19.99***

The Video Smoke Shoppe, Vol. I
Three decades of cigarette commercials offer a full hour of smoking pleasure and not a surgeon's warning in the pack. See Dennis James and the Old Gold dancing pack, plus Lucky Strikes, Kool, Benson and Hedges 100's and others, plus Edie Adams stumping for Dutch Masters. More! 60 min.
01-9020 *$19.99*

The Newport Cigarette Commercial, Vol. I
It's a menthol world for the active folks in these Newport ads from the '50s and '60s. Look at all these robust smokers hunting, riding jeeps on the beach, water-skiing, night-canoeing, rehearsing the band, or just walking the dog. Also, celebrity endorsements from Bill Cullen and Joey Bishop. 60 min.
01-9022 *$19.99*

Cigarette Commercials
"Come to where the flavor is," come to a collection of smoke-filled and pleasantly addictive TV spots where men are men, women are women, and everyone lights up. Benson & Hedges, Camel, Chesterfield, Kool, Marlboro, Viceroy (shilled by Steve McQueen)...all your favorite brands are here. 60 min.
10-9186 *$19.99*

Smoke That Cigarette
Satisfy that craving for pre-ban pop culture with real cigarette endorsements for real men and women. Archival ads, TV and movie clips relive those great jingles and heartfelt testimonials by John Wayne, Steve McQueen, Lucy and Desi Arnaz, James Garner, and the late Fred Flintstone. 51 min.
50-6319 Was $59.99 *$19.99*

The Lustre Creme Movie Star Collection, Vol. I
Shampoo maker Lustre Creme peddled its soap with movie stars in the late '40s and mid-'50s in commercials that featured the lathered heads of Sandra Dee, Elizabeth Taylor, Shirley Jones, Jane Russell, Barbara Stanwyck, Esther Williams, Piper Laurie, Yvonne De-Carlo, Jeanne Crain and many others. 60 min.
01-9024 *$19.99*

Classic Beer Commercials From The '50s And '60s
Wood cask connoisseur or Joe Six-Pack, you'll flip for these TV beer ads of the '50s and '60s, including Hamm's, Black Label, Rheingold, Duquesne, Ballantine, Budweiser, Blatz, Pilsener Collection and more! Who is the ale man? He could be YOU! 60 min.
01-9074 *$19.99*

Beer Commercials Plus
If you're a fan of that "cold gold" that "makes you old, way before your time," belly up to the VCR and pop in this heady collection of promos for such beloved brews as Blatz, Hamm's (with their cartoon spokesbear), Pabst Blue Ribbon, Colt .45 (with Redd Foxx), and Boone's Farm Apple Wine (Hey, how did that get in there?). 60 min.
10-9185 *$19.99*

Television Toys, Vol. 1
Batteries may not be included, but childhood memories galore are, as commercials for Slinky, Electro Shot Shooting Gallery, Trik-Trak, G.I. Joe, Erector Set, Betsy Wetsy, Dick Tracy Two-Way Radio, the Shirley Temple doll, Patty Play Pal, Barbie and Ken, Mr. Potato Head and more make their pitch for endless fun. 60 min.
01-9091 *$19.99*

Television Toys, Vol. 2
Be careful with that Trick Shot Gun commercial or you'll poke your eye out! And there's a big toy box worth of many more playful plugs, including Duncan Yo-Yos, Colorforms, Twister, American Flyer, Tiny Tears, Chatty Cathy, Billy Blastoff, Steve Canyon Helmet, Emenee Sing Along Guitar and more. 60 min.
01-9092 *$19.99*

Those Crazy Ol' Commercials
Do you remember Fred and Barney toking on a Winston cigarette? Or the Three Stooges pitching car wax? How about M.M. pushing gasoline? If not, let us refresh your memory with this nostalgic collection featuring dozens of TV and movie stars. And remember, "Tell your DeSoto dealer Groucho sent you!" 30 min.
10-2108 *$12.99*

Celebrity Commercials
Looking for more stars than an Irwin Allen film festival? Try this compilation of favorite commercials, spotlighting Louis Armstrong (Suzy Cute dolls), Anita Bryant (Coca-Cola), James Dean (in a safe driving promo!), Phyllis Diller (Snowy Bleach), Peter Lorre (Speidel watches), Groucho Marx (Lux detergent) and others, including pre-celebrity appearances by Mark Hamill, Brooke Shields and more. 60 min.
10-9184 *$19.99*

Celebrity Commercials From TV's Golden Age
Another crazy compilation featuring the best of Hollywood's hucksters. Return to TV's Golden Age and see Charlton Heston for Camel cigarettes, Steve McQueen for Viceroy, Ronald Reagan for Borax, Ricky Nelson for Coke and over 40 other classic commercials. 60 min.
10-2109 *$12.99*

Cast Commercials
Remember when TV stars did double duty as pitchmen for their sponsors' goods? Among the casts featured here, you'll see "The Beverly Hillbillies" for Kellogg's Corn Flakes, "The Monkees," "The Partridge Family" and "Dennis the Menace" for Rice Krispies, "Annie Oakley" for Canada Dry, "Gomer Pyle-USMC" for Maxwell House coffee ("Gaaawwwlly, that's good coffee!") and many more. 60 min.
10-9181 *$19.99*

Cereal Commercials
Hey, kids, looking for a tasty, sugar-charged nostalgia trip that will stay crunchy, even in milk? Try this crispy collection of classic TV ads for your favorite breakfast foods. See classic cartoon spokes"men" the Cheerios Kid and the Cocoa Puffs Cuckoo Bird, and recall such fondly-remembered brands as Jets, Freakies, Quisp and Quake, and even Cap'n Crunch's Vanilly Crunch. 60 min.
10-9175 *$19.99*

Commercial Jingles
You know them, you grew up with them, and you can't get them out of your head! Sing along with promotional melodies for such products as Green Giant vegetables ("From the Valley"), Pepsi-Cola ("Got a Lot to Give"), Ken-L Ration ("My Dog's Bigger Than Your Dog"), and Clark's Teaberry gum ("Teaberry Shuffle"). 60 min.
10-9180 *$19.99*

Baby Boomer Television
You don't have to have been born between 1945 and 1964 to enjoy this collection of vintage commercials, promo spots and theme songs from such programs as "Woody Woodpecker," "Rat Patrol," "Gilligan's Island," "F Troop," "Hawaiian Eye," "Mr. Ed," "The Real McCoys" and "Green Acres," but it couldn't hurt. 60 min.
10-9188 *$19.99*

The Good Old Days
For TV buffs those days were the 1950s, and now you can relive them with this collection. Included are clips and promos for "The Patti Page Show," "Do You Trust Your Wife," "Take a Good Look," "Winky Dink & You," "The Jimmy Durante Show" and other tube treats, plus commercials shilling Halo shampoo, Ajax cleanser and Clorets breath mints. 60 min.
10-9189 *$19.99*

All-Star Toon Commercials
If you just can't get enough of rabbits, mice, dogs and other cartoon critters shilling cereal, bubble bath and cigarettes(!), then pop in this collection of animated ads featuring Rocky & Bullwinkle, Casper the Friendly Ghost, Bugs Bunny, Mickey Mouse and Mighty Mouse in spots for Cheerios, Trix, Tang, Soaky and more. 60 min.
10-9797 *$19.99*

Best Of Animation Commercials
Some of the most memorable cartoon promos have been collected in this tape that includes a Chex ad with Casper, some Trix promos with Rocky and Bullwinkle, Mr. Magoo shilling Stag Beer (no wonder he couldn't see where he was going!), and spots for Funny Face, Mr. Bubble, Quisp and Quake cereals and more. 90 min.
10-9798 *$19.99*

Toy Commercials
"Ma, I don't want clothes for my birthday...I want toys!" If you've ever heard this, then discover why. G.I. Joe and various products from the Barbie line are advertised here, as well as Betsy Wetsy, Slip 'N Slide, and boardgame faves Candy Land and Mystery Date. 60 min.
10-9806 *$19.99*

Boy Toy Commercials
Remember, G.I. Joe wasn't a doll; he was an action figure! Included in this collection of things that soar, zoom and blow up each other are ads for an arsenal full of toy guns, James Bond 007 Action Packs, six-inch astronaut Major Matt Mason, Johnny Lightning race cars, and more. 60 min.
10-9799 *$19.99*

Girl Toy Commercials
Malibu Stacy dolls they weren't, but these toys had a powerful effect on the ladies of the 21st century. Ads for Thumbelina, Suzy Homemaker, Tiny Tears and Baby Crawl-Along are included, and for those of you who like your toys a little more...mature, there are also spots for "Charlie's Angels" dolls! 60 min.
10-9800 *$19.99*

1970s Toy Commercials
Got a soft spot for Gnip Gnop or Captain Action? Hankering for a Frosty Sno-Cone or a treat from the In a Minute Cake Maker? Eager for a game of Don't Spill the Beans, Battleship, Rebound, Crossfire or Skittle Tic-Tac-Toe (as endorsed by Don Adams)? These are just a few of the fondly-remembered gifts from Baby Boomer Christmases past you'll see in this collection of classic TV spots. 60 min.
50-8119 *$19.99*

Commercial Vision
An eclectic collection of promos ranging from breakfast foods to public service announcements. Among the sampling are numerous Post cereal ads; several PSAs with such celebrities as Julie Andrews, Jack Benny and Jerry Lewis, Alka-Seltzer's classic "no matter what shape your stomach's in" pitch; and Don Adams for Texaco thrown in for good measure.
10-9801 *$19.99*

Commercial Vision 2
Another sampling of spiels that were sometimes more entertaining than the shows they interrupted. Among the classic ads are Ron Santo for Snickers and Joe Garagiola promoting Doan's Pills; public service announcements with the casts of "The Beverly Hillbillies," "F Troop" and "Hogan's Heroes"; and spots with early appearances by Cheryl Ladd, Cybill Shepherd, Linda Gray and others. 60 min.
10-9802 *$19.99*

Commercial Vision 3
And now several dozen messages from our sponsors...sort of. Go behind the scenes with Joey Heatherton as you watch "The Making of a Serta Commercial," as well as a whole slew of ads that include 7-Up, Firestone, Phillips 66, Old Spice, and Madge the manicurist for Palmolive dishwashing liquid ("You know, you're soaking in it."). 60 min.
10-9803 *$19.99*

Commercials From Yesterday
Before the Internet, before Ronald Reagan, before Disco...aw heck, these ads go WAY back. Get ready to feel nostalgic courtesy of such promos as Buster Keaton for Alka-Seltzer, the 1957 Chevrolet, Tootsie Roll Pops, Edie Adams for Muriel Cigars, Ipana Toothpaste with Bucky Beaver and more. 60 min.
10-9804 *$19.99*

Sports Commercials Plus
"What in the wide world of sports is a-goin' on here?" Your favorite athletes turn pitchmen in these vintage ads featuring such stars as Mickey Mantle (Florida orange juice and Post cereals), Casey Stengel (Tabby Cat Food), Pete Rose (Aqua-Velva), Bobby Hull (Log Cabin Syrup), Jerry Lucas (Vitalis) and Crazy Legs Hirsch (Ovaltine). Even Suzy Chaffee, a.k.a. Suzy Chapstick, makes an appearance. 60 min.
10-9805 *$19.99*

America's Favorite Commercials
For half a century they've entertained (and annoyed) a nation of TV viewers while helping set fads and fashions. See clips from classic commercials and learn how they have reflected and influenced changes in popular culture and opinion in this nostalgia-filled documentary. 60 min.
18-7787 *$19.99*

Commercials From Around The World
These foreign films are far too short to bore anybody! Take a trans-global tour of some of the funniest and most imaginative TV spots ever made, featuring commercials from Great Britain, France, Italy, Australia, Japan and other lands. 30 min.
50-6365 *$12.99*

Kid-A-Vision
Let this tape take you back to when Saturdays meant getting up at 7 a.m., filling a bowl with sugary cereal, and watching hours of TV. See clips from such weekend faves as "Circus Boy," "Flipper," "Shazam!," "Diver Dan" and "H.R. Pufnstuf"; promos and openings for "The Avengers," "Batman," "Flipper" and other evening shows; commercials for the Time Bomb and Shenanigans games; and more. 60 min.
10-9187 *$19.99*

Kids Commercials Of The Fifties And Sixties
Hey, Baby Boomers, remember those great ads for board games, dolls, cereals and snack foods that filled your heads every afternoon and Saturday morning? Now you can relive the days of keeping the TV quiet so Mom and Dad won't wake up with these volumes of classic kidvid commercials. Each tape runs about 60 min.

Kids Commercials Of The Fifties And Sixties, Vol. I
Everyday is Christmas Day with this toy box full of classic kid stuff including Mr. Potato Head, the Dick Tracy Two-Way Radio, the 007 Action Pack, Billy Blastoff, the Bonanza Action Set, and Robot Commando. Plus, a collection of race set ads and Garry Moore's gift suggestions for 1953. Lots more! 60 min.
01-9001 *$19.99*

Kids Commercials Of The Fifties And Sixties, Vol. II
Who left all these toy commercials lying around? It's the Suzy Homemaker kitchen line, Shari Lewis for Junior Chef, the Motorific Car set, the Mickey Mouse Candy Factory, Tressy Makeup Face, Bowlamatic 300, Mystery Date, and Tiger guitar. Also, Twinkies, Ding Dongs and much more! 60 min.
01-9002 *$19.99*

Kids Commercials Of The Fifties And Sixties, Vol. III
Turning America's tots into loyal consumers are Milton Bradley games, Etch-A-Sketch, Doodle Buggy, Silly String, Clackers Cereal, David Nelson for Listerine Toothpaste, Mae Questel for Wheat Honeys and many more. Includes a 1959 "future of toys" short. 60 min.
01-9071 *$19.99*

Kids Commercials Of The Fifties And Sixties, Vol. IV
Classic spots with the shopping cart passenger in mind include Hostess Cup Cakes, Chiparoons, Lucky Charms, Dick Van Dyke for Bosco, Sandra Dee for Coke, Vanilla Wafers, the Johnny 7 Helmet and One-Man Army Gun, Lorna Doones, Fig Newton and many others. 60 min.
01-9072 *$19.99*

Kids Commercials Of The Fifties And Sixties, Vol. V
Mattel Toys arms the baby-boomer for the World of Tomorrow with Matty Mattel and Sister Bell for Winchester Rifles, Tommy Burp, Thunder Burp and Fire Bolt guns, and Mattel's Shootin' Shell Fanner with Greenie Stick 'Em caps. Also, the history of Ideal Bears, Shirley Temple dolls and more. 60 min.
01-9075 *$19.99*

Love That Bob
Hit sitcom with Bob Cummings as Bob Collins, a swinging single photographer whose job often involved taking pictures of gorgeous models. Ann B. Davis co-starred as Schultzy, Bob's faithful secretary; with Rosemary DeCamp, Dwayne Hickman. The show ran on NBC, CBS and ABC from 1955 to 1959. Each tape features two episodes and runs about 50 min. There are six volumes available, including:

Love That Bob, Vol. 1
Features "Grandpa's Christmas Visit" and "Bob Gets Harvey a Raise."
10-8275 Was $19.99 *$14.99*

Love That Bob, Vol. 2
Includes "Forgotten Fiancée" and "Bob Goes Bird Watching."
10-8276 Was $19.99 *$14.99*

Love That Bob, Vol. 3
Features "Bob Becomes a Stage Uncle" and "Bob Sails to Hawaii."
10-8277 Was $19.99 *$14.99*

Love That Bob, Vol. 4
Includes "Bob Saves Harvey" and "Bob Goes to the Moon."
10-8278 Was $19.99 *$14.99*

Love That Bob, Vol. 5
Includes "Bob Digs Rock & Roll" and "Grandpa's Old Buddy."
10-8279 Was $19.99 *$14.99*

Love That Bob, Vol. 6
Features "Grandpa Attends Convention" and "Bob Retrenches."
10-8280 Was $19.99 *$14.99*

The Brady Bunch
The hit '70s sitcom that remains popular to this day stars Robert Reed as Mike Brady, a widower with sons Greg, Peter and Bobby who marries Carol (Florence Henderson), a widow with daughters Marcia, Jan and Cindy. With help from housekeeper Alice (Ann B. Davis), the Bradys encounter funny situations in and around their L.A. home. Each tape features two episodes and runs about 50 min.

The Brady Bunch, Vol. 1
In "The Honeymoon," the premiere episode of the series, Mike and Carol's marriage is followed by a problem with the family pets that pits the boys against the girls. And in "A Camping We Will Go," the boys decide to spook the girls when they join them on their annual camping trip.
06-2353 *$9.99*

The Brady Bunch, Vol. 2
Cindy's persistent snitching leads to trouble for the whole household in "The Tattletale," while Bobby's efforts to be the school's best safety monitor go too far in "Law and Disorder."
06-2354 *$9.99*

The Brady Bunch, Vol. 3
Middle sibling Jan's identity crisis leads her to a wigged-out solution in "Will the Real Jan Brady Please Stand Up." Next, Jan cries "Marcia, Marcia, Marcia!" and tries to get out of "Her Sister's Shadow" by becoming a cheerleader.
06-2355 *$9.99*

The Brady Bunch, Vol. 4
Marcia promises to bring one of the country's top music stars to the prom in "Getting Davy Jones," while her swollen nose gets her in boy trouble in "The Subject Was Noses."
06-2356 *$9.99*

Riverboat
The adventurous life on board the Enterprise, a 100-foot-long riverboat, was the subject of this NBC series that aired from 1959 to 1961. Darren McGavin owned the boat, which he won in a poker game, and Burt Reynolds (in the series' first year) and Noah Beery, Jr. were the ship's pilots. Each tape runs about 50 min.

Riverboat, Vol. 1
Includes "Forbidden Island" with Burt Reynolds.
10-9898 *$14.99*

Riverboat, Vol. 2
Includes "Zigzag" with Noah Berry, Jr. and guest star Charles Bronson.
10-9899 *$14.99*

GET A LIFE

Get A Life
One of the most off-the-wall sitcoms ever, this 1990-92 Fox series starred Chris Elliot ("Cabin Boy") as a blissfully naive, 30-year-old paperboy who lived in an apartment over his parents' garage and valiantly fought anything that would require him to "grow up." The cast also included Robin Riker, Elinor Donahue and Elliot's real-life father, Bob, as his dad. Each tape features two episodes and runs about 50 min.

Get A Life, Vol. 1
Chris does his little turn on the catwalk, enrolling in the Handsome Boy Modeling School, in "The Prettiest Week of My Life." Next, civic-minded Chris plays mentor to a gang of street punks in "Bored Straight."
15-5467 $14.99

Get A Life, Vol. 2
Has an alien being crashed in the Petersons' backyard? That's what Chris thinks, and he's ready to befriend it, in "Spewy and Me." Plus, Chris is sure it's true love when a woman runs him over—twice—in "Girlfriend 2000."
15-5468 $14.99

Dad's Army: Collector's Set
Beloved British sitcom stars Arthur Lowe as Captain Mainwaring, head of a goofy group of WWII Army rejects who do their best (or worst) as the Home Guard contingent of Walmington-On-Sea. This six-tape collection features 18 episodes. 540 min. total.
53-9748 $69.99

Dame Edna's Neighbourhood Watch
England's cross-dressing diva, Dame Edna (Barry Humphries), hosts this hilarious British game show in which female contestants open their homes and lives to Dame Edna's crew in hopes of winning such prizes as an all-expenses paid trip to Paris. Dame Edna shows no shame when checking out all of the goods with help from her roving cameramen. Six episodes are included in this three-tape set. 180 min.
73-9269 $59.99

TV Rarities Lost & Found
Featured in this anthology of obscure TV treats are the 1953 pilot for Ed Wood's proposed western series "Crossroad Avenger," starring Tom Keene; "Strange Experiences," a "One Step Beyond"-style anthology; Abbott and Costello with the Universal monsters on the "Colgate Comedy Hour"; Steve Holland starring as "Flash Gordon"; and "The Fifth Glacial Era" episode of "The Lost Spaceship" Italian TV series. 120 min. total.
79-6086 $19.99

The Mixer: Boxed Set
A stylish series based on the character created by Edgar Wallace, this six-tape collection stars Simon Williams as aristocrat Sir Anthony Rose, who lives a dual life as a wealthy ex-barrister and a master thief who robs other criminals to dispense his own brand of justice. Follow his adventures, beating crooks and eluding police, from England to Monte Carlo to Paris. 600 min. total.
53-9891   Was $99.99 $79.99

Killer Trilogy
This three-tape set features John Thaw ("Inspector Morse") and Edward Woodward ("The Equalizer") in a trio of films that explore the meaning of obsession, jealousy and hate. Included are "Killer Waiting," about a past nightmare that becomes a reality; "Killer Exposed," about a beautiful girl who becomes the focus of obsession; and "Killer Contract," set in the show business world. 156 min. total.
53-9982 $59.99

The Best Of The Uncle Floyd Show
Direct from "deep in the heart of Jersey," the outrageous host of the Floyd Show that's been a cult favorite for over 20 years comes to home video. Join porkpie-hatted host Floyd Vivino, his smart-mouthed puppet pal Oogie, and a crazy crew of supporting players, sidekicks and hangers-on for slapstick comedy bits, silly skits, and song parodies.

The Best Of The Uncle Floyd Show, Vol. 1
Among the classic characters featured in this volume are culinary cut-up "Julia Stepchild," comical crime boss "Don Goomba," and others. 65 min.
63-7166 $19.99

The Best Of The Uncle Floyd Show, Vol. 2
Pay a twisted visit to the neighborhood of "Mr. Frogers," hear the hilarious rantings of "Mr. Grouch," and more. 77 min.
63-7167 $19.99

The Best Of "The Wonder Years"
This salute to one of the most popular coming-of-age stories in TV history features highlights of the long-running show featuring Kevin, Winnie, Paul and the rest of the crew. See classic moments from the first episode to the last, which is presented here in its entirety. Fred Savage stars. 71 min.
89-7004 $14.99

The Christmas "Wonder Years"
Classic holiday episodes of the hit TV show "The Wonder Years" are presented here. In one episode, Kevin, Wayne and Karen try to convince Dad to buy a new color TV, while Kevin can't decide what to get Winnie. And the spirit of Christmas is tested again when Dad's partner upsets him. 45 min.
89-7009 $14.99

Timex All-Star Comedy Show
A pre-"Tonight Show" Johnny Carson emcees this laughfest. Featured are skits by Mel Brooks and Carl Reiner, Buddy Hackett's "Chinese Waiter" routine, an appearance by Dr. Joyce Brothers and much more. 45 min.
09-1229   Was $24.99 $14.99

Swing Into Spring
This terrific NBC special highlights some of jazz's finest performers at their best. Included are Ella Fitzgerald, Benny Goodman, Peggy Lee, Lionel Hampton and Andre Previn. 52 min.
09-2398 $14.99

Witchcraft (1961)/ Who Goes There? (1965)
This double bill of pilots from unaired supernatural TV shows opens with "Witchcraft," as Darren McGavin and his friend battle a witch who has hexed him into paralysis. Next, Pat Hingle and Lisa Gaye are a couple who rent a house that's haunted by the ghost of General Custer in "Who Goes There?," co-starring Ben Blue.
68-9278 $19.99

Brideshead Revisited: Gift Set (1999)
Based on Evelyn Waugh's timeless novel, the acclaimed British mini-series recounts Charles Ryder's decades-long friendship with aristocratic Sebastian Flyte and the Marchmain family of Brideshead Castle between the World Wars, and the tragedies that tore them apart. Jeremy Irons, Anthony Andrews, John Gielgud, Claire Bloom, Diana Quick, Laurence Olivier and Aloysius the bear star. 10 hrs. total.
74-1020 $119.99

UFO: The Series
Produced in England, this cult-favorite sci-fi series starred Ed Bishop as the head of SHADO, a secret organization defending the Earth against alien invaders. Intriguing plots and great special effects highlighted the Gerry Anderson production. Each volume contains two episodes and runs about 120 min.

UFO, Vol. 1: Exposed/A Question Of Priorities
67-5015 $19.99

UFO, Vol. 2: Conflict/A Dalotek Affair
67-5016 $19.99

UFO, Vol. 3: Confetti Check A-OK/Sub Smash
67-5023 $19.99

UFO, Vol. 4: The Psychobombs/Court Martial
67-5024 $19.99

Gidget
The hit film series about a teenage Southern California surfer girl was turned into a popular TV sitcom in 1965 featuring 18-year-old Sally Field as Frances "Gidget" Lawrence, who loved boys, the beach, and her widowed professor dad. Each tape features three episodes and runs about 75 min.

Gidget, Vol. 1: Beach Blanket Gidget
A accidental peek in Gidget's diary gets her big sister worried in "Dear Diary...Et Al." Next, could school in Paris be in Gidget's future in "Is It Love or Symbiosis?"; while "I Love You, I Think" finds her getting over boyfriend Jeff's leaving for college.
02-3116 $14.99

Gidget, Vol. 2: Gidget-A-Go-Go!
Could Gidget's father really be attracted to her pal LaRue, after Gidget gives her a makeover, in "My Ever Faithful Friend"? Richard Dreyfuss guest stars as a nerd who Gidget tries to help by going out with him in "Ego-A-Go-Go," and "In and Out with the In-Laws" has a meeting with Jeff's parents leading to...wedding bells?
02-3117 $14.99

The Thorn Birds (1983)
One of the most-watched TV mini-series of all time, Colleen McCullough's epic tale of forbidden love is set against the sprawling background of early 1900s Australia. Richard Chamberlain, Rachel Ward, Barbara Stanwyck, Bryan Brown, Piper Laurie and Christopher Plummer star in this Emmy-winning drama. Special 8-hour, 4-tape set. NOTE: Individual volumes available at $24.99 each.
19-1787   Was $199.99 $99.99

The Virginian (2000)
The classic Western novel is given a stirring and exciting treatment with Bill Pullman directing and starring as the title character, a man from Virginia trying to make a new life for himself in Wyoming. After marrying a school teacher and taking a job as a foreman on a ranch, the Virginian faces danger when he's betrayed by his best friend. With Diane Lane, John Savage, Dennis Weaver and James Drury ('60s TV's Virginian). 95 min.
18-7908 ❑$99.99

The Ballad Of Little Jo (1993)
Gender-bending, true-life sagebrusher about Josephine Monaghan (Suzy Amis), an outcast of a wealthy Eastern family, who searches for a new life out West. After facing several hardships, she purchases men's clothing and takes residence in a mining town, posing as a man. Bo Hopkins, Ian McKellen and Rene Auberjonois co-star in writer/director Maggie Greenwald's striking film. 126 min.
02-2567 Was $89.99 ❑$14.99

Los Locos Posse (1997)
Mario Van Peebles stars in this off-the-wall western that casts him as an Army scout who has been flogged after leading his troops the wrong way into battle. He then helps a group of nuns and mental patients reach a mission located 100 miles away in the desert. Rene Auberjonois and Melora Walters also star in this sagebrusher that's not really a sequel to "Posse." 95 min.
02-8858 Was $99.99 ❑$14.99

Buffalo Soldiers (1997)
The exciting true story of the African-Americans who patrolled the West as Cavalry officers after the Civil War is recounted in this stirring drama about men fighting for their place in the nation's future. Danny Glover, Carl Lumbly, Glynn Turman and Mykelti Williamson star. 95 min.
18-7793 Was $79.99 ❑$14.99

The Hi-Lo Country (1998)
Set in the rapidly vanishing "frontier" of post-WWII New Mexico, director Stephen Frears' latter-day Western stars Woody Harrelson and Billy Crudup as hard-living ranchhands whose friendship is strained when they both fall for Patricia Arquette, the wife of the foreman for local cattle baron Sam Elliott. 115 min.
02-9104 Was $99.99 ❑$14.99

La Cucaracha (1998)
A haunting and stylish modern-day western starring Eric Roberts as a down-on-his-luck writer barely surviving in Mexico who agrees to a $100,000 offer to murder a man he's told is a child killer. While confronting the reputed killer, Roberts learns some dark secrets, prompting him to question the assignment he has taken. With Tara Crespo, Joaquim de Almeida. 96 min.
06-2987 ❑$89.99

You Know My Name (1999)
This exciting and compelling true story stars Sam Elliott as Bill Tilghman, a legendary Western lawman called out of retirement to serve as marshal for a booming Oklahoma oil town in 1924. After witnessing a rage of violence perpetrated by vicious gangsters, Tilghman realizes that he must adapt his old-fashioned peace-keeping to style to new outlaws. With Arliss Howard. 94 min.
18-7880 Was $99.99 ❑$14.99

Last Stand At Saber River (1997)
After the Civil War, Confederate soldier Tom Selleck attempts to reunite with his family and reclaim his ranch from Union trespassers. But the situation doesn't change, Selleck is forced to resort to violence to get back what's his. Suzy Amis, David Carradine, Keith Carradine and David Dukes co-star in this adaptation of Elmore Leonard's novel. 95 min.
19-2532 Was $99.99 ❑$19.99

Silent Tongue (1994)
Sam Shepard wrote and directed this mystical drama set in the American West, where Irishman Alan Bates is entangled in a bitter feud with fellow countryman Richard Harris after his half-breed daughter—married to Harris' son (River Phoenix)—dies during childbirth. Dermot Mulroney, Sheila Tousey co-star. 101 min.
68-1310 Was $89.99 ❑$14.99

Guns Of Honor (1994)
A group of renegade Confederate soldiers attempts to reclaim their glory after the Civil War by running guns for the Mexican government. During their assignment, they battle outlaws and face the French Army. Martin Sheen, Jurgen Prochnow, Christopher Atkins and Corbin Bernsen star in this rousing adaptation of the popular "Floating Outfit" books. 95 min.
68-1326 Was $89.99 ❑$14.99

Quigley Down Under (1990)
Spirited, beautifully filmed Western adventure stars Tom Selleck as a Wyoming sharpshooter who travels to Australia to work for a wealthy cattle baron. Soon, Selleck discovers he's been hired to kill aborigines, which sends him head-to-head against the sadistic rancher. Laura San Giacomo, Alan Rickman co-star; directed by Simon Wincer ("Lonesome Dove"). 121 min.
12-2195 Was $89.99 ❑$14.99

Quigley Down Under (Letterboxed Version)
Also available in a theatrical, widescreen format.
12-3137 ❑$14.99

Border Shootout (1990)
The battle lines are drawn in a frontier town when the arrest of two suspected rustlers causes tension between an aging sheriff and his new deputy. Tough Western drama, based on an Elmore Leonard story, stars Glenn Ford, Jeff Daake, Charlene Tilton. 110 min.
18-7280 $14.99

Montana (1992)
Larry McMurtry ("Lonesome Dove") supplied the story for this drama set in the modern West, where tough ranchers Richard Crenna and Gena Rowlands are offered cash for their property by stripminers. The offer sends the ranchers against each other and forces them to make some difficult decisions. Lea Thompson co-stars. 91 min.
18-7382 ❑$12.99

Keep The Change (1992)
In this compelling modern Western, Jack Palance plays a ruthless Montana rancher who takes over the land of neighboring rancher William Petersen after he moves to California. But when Petersen returns and learns of the shady goings-on, trouble starts—and complicating matters is Petersen's involvement with Palance's daughter (Lolita Davidovich). 95 min.
18-7402 Was $89.99 ❑$12.99

The Desperate Trail (1994)
Action-filled frontier drama stars Sam Elliott as Bill Speakes, a marshal who becomes obsessed when a beautiful female prisoner left in his custody escapes. Linda Fiorentino, Craig Sheffer also star. 93 min.
18-7514 Was $89.99 ❑$14.99

The Good Old Boys (1995)
In his directing debut, Tommy Lee Jones plays Hewey Calloway, a cowboy during the early 1900s who visits his brother's troubled Texas farm after a two-year absence. While trying to help his sibling save the farm, Jones falls in love with schoolteacher Sissy Spacek and is tempted to go back to his bad habits when pal Sam Shepard stops by to see him. 117 min.
18-7552 Was $89.99 ❑$14.99

Tecumseh: The Last Warrior (1995)
Gripping epic about the fearless Shawnee Indian leader who forged a coalition of tribes in the early 19th century to fight encroachment on their land by white settlers. Jesse Borrego, David Clennon, David Morse star. 94 min.
18-7577 $89.99

Riders Of The Purple Sage (1995)
A mysterious wandering gunslinger comes to the aid of a fiercely independent homesteader woman who must fight an entire town to save her land in this powerful frontier drama based on the classic Zane Grey book. Ed Harris, Amy Madigan, Henry Thomas, G.D. Spradlin star. 90 min.
18-7608 Was $89.99 $14.99

The Lazarus Man (1996)
This pilot to the hit TV western stars Robert Urich as a seriously wounded gunfighter who wakes to find himself buried alive. Escaping from the makeshift grave, Urich recovers from his injuries but discovers he cannot recall his past or who left him for dead, and so he begins a dangerous quest for the answers to his questions. 90 min.
18-7715 Was $99.99 $14.99

Two For Texas (1997)
Saddle up for rousing adventure with this tale of two convicts (Kris Kristofferson and Scott Bairstow) who escape from a bayou prison and wind up joining Sam Houston's Texas Volunteer Army and fighting alongside him at the Alamo. Tom Skerritt, Irene Bedard also star. 95 min.
18-7811 Was $79.99 ❑$14.99

El Diablo (1990)
A top-notch western-comedy about a klutzy schoolteacher (Anthony Edwards) who gets a shot at fame by joining with a renegade gunslinger (Lou Gossett, Jr.) to catch a legendary black hat. Produced by John Carpenter. 97 min.
44-1768 Was $19.99 ❑$14.99

The Last Of His Tribe (1992)
The sole surviving member of the Yahi Indians, once settled throughout California, is discovered in a slaughterhouse in 1911. A compassionate doctor and his wife attempt to learn more about the man and his people before they become totally extinct. Graham Greene, Jon Voight and Anne Archer star. 90 min.
44-1898 Was $89.99 ❑$14.99

Dollar For The Dead (1998)
This salute to spaghetti westerns showcases Emilio Estevez as a gunslinger who teams with ex-Confederate soldier William Forsythe in a search for gold. The two find themselves pursued by rancher Howie Long, who believes Estevez has killed his son, and Union and Spanish soldiers. Ed Lauter and Joaquim de Almeida also star; written and directed by Gene Quintano ("Comin' at Ya!"). 94 min.
19-2826 ❑$99.99

Purgatory (1999)
An outlaw gang thinks the sleepy little town they've ridden into is the perfect place to lay low in and then rob blind, until they discover that among the residents are such famous—and deceased—gunslingers as Wild Bill Hickok, Jesse James and Billy the Kid. Sam Shepard, Eric Roberts, Randy Quaid, Peter Stormare and Donnie Wahlberg star in this very offbeat frontier drama. 94 min.
18-7866 Was $79.99 ❑$14.99

Hard Bounty (1995)
A bounty hunter tires of the bloodshed and retires to a quiet life as a saloon owner. But when one of a group of prostitutes he befriends is murdered, and the others set out to bring her killer to justice, the gunman has to strap on the irons again to aid them. Hard-riding frontier drama stars Matt McCoy, Kelly LeBrock. 90 min.
72-9048 Was $89.99 $14.99

Siringo (1994)
A U.S. deputy marshal attempts to bring an outlaw responsible for killing an Apache chief to justice, but when the man escapes from him, he joins forces with another lawman and tries to capture the culprit at his girlfriend's house. Brad Johnson, Chad Lowe and Crystal Bernard star. 90 min.
19-3697 $89.99

Cheyenne Warrior (1994)
During the Civil War, a young expectant mother is left stranded at a remote trading post after her husband is killed by nasty outlaws. She meets a fierce Cheyenne brave who has been injured by the same creeps who killed her husband, and they team up for a vengeance mission that takes a romantic turn. Kelly Preston, Pato Hoffman, Bo Hopkins and Dan Haggerty star. 86 min.
21-9067 Was $89.99 $14.99

The Shooter (1997)
A legendary gunfighter and Civil War veteran faces a gang of rogue bandits and an ornery family who controls the small town he has drifted into. After being badly beaten by the creeps, the gunslinger gets help from a local madam, discovers that the person who killed his son is in town, and devises a plan for revenge. Michael Dudikoff, Randy Travis and Valerie Wildman star. 92 min.
27-7125 ❑$99.99

Blind Justice (1994)
A gunfighter, blinded during the Civil War, is attacked by Mexican bandits. He makes his way to a small town where he recovers, but when the outlaws take over the town and slaughter the Cavalry in order to obtain a fortune in government silver, the sightless hero must make his stand alone. Armand Assante, Elisabeth Shue and Robert Davi star in this action-packed Western. 85 min.
44-1972 Was $89.99 $14.99

The Cherokee Kid (1996)
Action and laughs mix in this frontier tale starring Sinbad as a young man who straps on the six-irons and sets out for revenge against his parents' killers...just as soon as he learns how to shoot a gun. Helping the Kid along the way are frontiersman Burt Reynolds, Mexican rebel A Martinez, and bank robber Ernie Hudson. With James Coburn, Gregory Hines. 89 min.
44-2093 Was $99.99 ❑$14.99

The Jack Bull (1999)
In this atmospheric western, John Cusack is a horse rancher who faces off against neighbor L.Q. Jones in an embittered war over Wyoming's statehood, Jones' mistreatment of Cusack's prized stallions, and the beating of Cusack's ranchhand, who was to watch the horses. John Goodman, Jay O. Sanders and John Savage also star in this adaptation of the "Michael Kohlhaas" story. 116 min.
44-2198 Was $99.99 ❑$14.99

Big Bear (1998)
This frontier epic from Canada tells of Big Bear, the Cree Indian chief whose refusal to accept an inferior land deal from the Canadian government in hopes of bettering his tribe's future led to a series of tragic events under desperate conditions. Gordon Tootoosis, Tantoo Cardinal and Lorne Cardinal star in this rugged and stirring true-life saga. 190 min. on three tapes.
53-6816 $39.99

Rio Diablo (1993)
The search for a kidnapped bride-to-be sends bounty hunters Kenny Rogers and Travis Tritt on a wild search in this Western drama that also stars Naomi Judd, Stacy Keach. 93 min.
58-5095 Was $89.99 *$14.99*

The Gambler Returns: The Luck Of The Draw (1991)
It's the wildest game for frontier rogue Kenny Rogers yet, as he gets involved with shady lady Reba McEntire, takes a dangerous cross-country trek, meets a passel of TV gunslingers (including Chuck Connors, Gene Barry, Hugh O'Brian and Clint Walker), and winds up playing cards with Teddy Roosevelt! Rick Rossovich, Linda Evans and Mickey Rooney also star. 180 min.
58-5109 Was $89.99 *$14.99*

The Gambler V: Playing For Keeps (1994)
Has frontier cardshark-turned-do-gooder Brady Hawkes (Kenny Rogers) finally run out of luck when he tries to keep his son from falling in with notorious outlaws Butch Cassidy and the Sundance Kid? There's plenty of Western adventure and fun in this fifth "Gambler" installment. Loni Anderson, Dixie Carter and Bruce Boxleitner star. 189 min.
88-1199 *$14.99*

Crazy Horse (1996)
The life of the Sioux warrior who inspired his people to resist being put on reservations by the government and who, with Sitting Bull, led the bloody defeat of Custer at Little Big Horn is recounted in this epic drama. Michael Greyeyes ("Geronimo"), Wes Studi and Peter Horton star. 94 min.
18-7719 *$49.99*

Black Fox (1993)
This action-packed Western, the first part of a trilogy based on the novel by Matt Braun, stars Christopher Reeve as Texas rancher Alan Johnson, who teams up with his "blood brother," ex-slave Britt (Tony Todd), to rescue settlers taken hostage by hostile Indians during a raid. With Raoul Trujillo. 92 min.
58-5193 Was $19.99 *$14.99*

Blood Horse (1993)
The "Black Fox" saga continues, as Britt and Alan race against time to stop a vigilante band from attacking the camp of Chief Running Dog and his Kiowa people, an attack that will lead to a bloody all-out frontier war. Christopher Reeve, Tony Todd, Raoul Trujillo star. 90 min.
58-5194 Was $19.99 *$14.99*

Good Men And Bad (1993)
After an assault by racist outlaws that left their ranch destroyed and his wife dead, Alan sets out on a crusade of vengeance, and Britt must stop him before it costs him his life, in the concluding chapter of the "Black Fox" trilogy. Christopher Reeve, Tony Todd star. 90 min.
58-5195 Was $19.99 *$14.99*

Gunfighter's Moon (1996)
A feared gunman, tired of the constant string of challengers looking to outdraw him, is asked by a former lover to help her sheriff husband stop a planned jailbreak in this western drama. Lance Henriksen and Kay Lenz star. 95 min.
58-5228 Was $99.99 *$14.99*

True Women (1997)
Set on the West Texas plains of the mid-1800s, this riveting frontier drama follows the struggles of two settler sisters and their families and friends to defend their land. Dana Delany, Annabeth Gish, Angelina Jolie, Michael York, Powers Boothe and Charles S. Dutton star. 170 min.
88-1163 Was $19.99 *$14.99*

BUFFALO GIRLS

Buffalo Girls (1995)
The legends of the Old West come to life in this fanciful adaptation of "Lonesome Dove" author Larry McMurtry's best-selling novel. Anjelica Huston plays Calamity Jane, who joins a group of her sagebrush pals on an excursion to England as part of Buffalo Bill Cody's Wild West Show. Melanie Griffith, Reba McEntire, Gabriel Byrne, Jack Palance and Peter Coyote as Cody also star. 180 min.
58-5184 Was $24.99 *$14.99*

Showdown At Williams Creek (1991)
Set in the Montana Territories in 1870, this sprawling Western saga centers on the adventures of a young explorer (Tom Burlinson), whose befriending of a cold-blooded con man spells tragedy after he is left to die after an Indian attack...and is later put on trial for the swindler's murder. Co-stars Donnelly Rhodes and Raymond Burr. 97 min.
63-1474 *$89.99*

Gunfighter (1997)
When the outlaw killer he's tracking abducts his girl, a black-gloved gunslinger named Cassidy stops at nothing to bring the man to justice, joining up with two ranch hands on a quest that can only end in a deadly showdown. Chris Lybbert, Clu Gulager, Robert Carradine and Martin Sheen star in this sagebrush drama from writer/director Christopher Coppola. 95 min.
64-9035 *$99.99*

Follow The River (1995)
Exciting, beautifully filmed frontier drama about a Virginia homesteader (Sheryl Lee) who is taken captive after her family is attacked by a Shawnee war party. The tribe's leader plans to take the feisty woman as his mate, but she escapes and teams with another captive woman to find freedom. With Eric Schweig and Ellen Burstyn. 93 min.
88-1020 Was $79.99 *$14.99*

Cheatin' Hearts (1993)
After walking out on his wife and two daughters over a year earlier, scoundrel James Brolin returns for his younger daughter's wedding only to encounter complications through the appearance of old family friend Kris Kristofferson. This amiable Western comedy also stars Sally Kirkland and Pamela Gidley. 88 min.
68-1267 Was $89.99 *$12.99*

Trigger Fast (1994)
A beautiful young woman recruits two Civil War veterans to help her protect her land from a ruthless land baron and his group of outlaws. Martin Sheen, Corbin Bernsen, Jurgen Prochnow and Christopher Atkins star in this guns-a-blazin' actioner. 96 min.
68-1307 *$89.99*

Frank And Jesse (1995)
Following the Civil War, Frank and Jesse James seek their own justice for the killing of their brother, then join the Younger brothers on a crime spree of robbing banks, stagecoaches and trains...only to square off against noted detective Alan Pinkerton, whose nephew was killed by the James Gang. Rip-roaring sagebrusher stars Rob Lowe, Bill Paxton. 105 min.
68-1375 Was $89.99 *$14.99*

The Other Side Of The Law (1994)
After his wife is savagely assaulted, frontiersman Jurgen Prochnow takes the law into his own hands and kills the attacker, then flees with his young son into the wilderness. Ten years later, the boy is sent back to civilization to receive an education, but old scores are waiting to settled. Western drama also stars Yves Renier, Xavier Deluc. 95 min.
68-1785 *$89.99*

Lone Justice II (1994)
The story of gunslinger Ned Blessing continues, as he returns to the town where he grew up to find it in the clutches of an outlaw family. Brad Johnson, Wes Studi, Luis Avalos and Brenda Bakke star. 93 min.
71-5318 Was $89.99 *$14.99*

Lone Justice: Showdown At Plum Creek (1996)
It's the gunfight that even Ned Blessing might not be able to walk away from, and the frontier renegade will find his skills put to their ultimate test in this third entry in the Western saga. Brad Johnson, Wes Studi, Brenda Bakke and William Sanderson star. 95 min.
72-9073 Was $19.99 *$14.99*

Guns Of The Revolution (1991)
One gunfighter stands alone as he tries to stop government soldiers from destroying missions in this frontier drama set in Old Mexico. Ernest Borgnine, Alfredo Madrid, Rose Romero star. 90 min.
75-7145 *$19.99*

Samurai Cowboy (1993)
Rugged adventure with Japanese pop superstar Hiromi Go as a man whose desire to become a cowboy leads him to the American West. Matt McCoy, Catherine Mary Stewart and Robert Conrad star. 101 min.
76-9053 Was $89.99 *$14.99*

Wrangler (1991)
Exciting frontier drama about a resourceful young woman who, with the help of two men vying for her romantic attentions, fights to save her family's ranch from the grasp of a greedy neighbor. Jeff Fahey, Steven Vidler, Tushka Bergen star. 83 min.
80-1054 Was $89.99 *$14.99*

Savage Land (1994)
This inspiring Western saga tells of the fight for survival undertaken by two children and two young ladies after their stagecoach is terrorized by Indians. Using their ingenuity to stay alive, they fight the elements, outlaws and more Indian attacks. Graham Greene, Corbin Bernsen, Vivian Schilling and Charles Napier star. 91 min.
80-1073 *$14.99*

The Fighter (1994)
Kickboxing in the Old West? You bet! Olivier Gruner stars as an army officer who uses his fists and feet to tame a Texas frontier town and corral the schemes of a ruthless land baron in this action-packed sagebrusher. With Marc Singer, Ian Ziering, Ashley Laurence, R. Lee Ermey. 93 min.
83-1057 Was $89.99 *$14.99*

Outlaw Justice (1998)
When a member of their former outlaw gang is murdered, retired gunslingers Kris Kristofferson and Willie Nelson strap on the shooting irons and reunite with their old compadres to bring the killers to justice. Frontier drama also stars Waylon Jennings, Travis Tritt, Jonathan Banks. 94 min.
86-1142 Was $89.99 *$19.99*

Hole In The Sky (1995)
Set in the Montana wilderness in 1919, this western saga tells of a young ranger who learns about honor, trust and integrity from a legendary mountain ranger. Sam Elliott, Jerry O'Connell and Ricky Jay star; based on a story by Norman MacLean ("A River Runs Through It"). 94 min.
88-1016 Was $79.99 *$14.99*

IN PURSUIT OF HONOR

In Pursuit Of Honor (1995)
In the early 1900s, U.S. Cavalry officers Don Johnson and Craig Sheffer are assigned to lead 500 hundred horses deemed obsolete to their death. After they witness the slaughter of the first 100 animals, the officers face court-martial and possible death by trying to save the remaining horses. Gabrielle Anwar, Rod Steiger co-star in this exciting, based-on-fact tale. 110 min.
44-1996 Was $19.99 *$14.99*

The Song Of Hiawatha (1996)
The epic poem by Longfellow (itself based on a true story) about a young Native American man and his undying love for Minehaha becomes a powerful frontier drama. Litefoot stars as Hiawatha; with Irene Bedard, Graham Greene, Russell Means and David Strathairn. 114 min.
88-1193 *$12.99*

Outlaws: The Legend Of O.B. Taggart (1998)
Released from prison, an infamous frontier outlaw finds his sons after the never-recovered loot from his last robbery in this compelling Western drama. Mickey Rooney (who also scripted), Randy Travis, Larry Gatlin, Ernest Borgnine, Ben Johnson and Ned Beatty star. 94 min.
88-7023 *$89.99*

Bad Jim (1989)
The first movie ever about Billy the Kid's horse. When an innocent man buys it, he begins a spree of robbing and killing. Now, this is a horse of a different color! James Brolin, Richard Roundtree and John Clark Gable star. 90 min.
02-2004 *$14.99*

Sacred Ground (1983)
Spectacular wilderness scenes, a powerful story about a rugged mountain man, his Apache wife and their child who settle on sacred Indian ground, and thrilling action scenes set in the 1860s West highlight this film starring Tim McIntire, Jack Elam and Serene Hedin.
04-1662 *$14.99*

Young Guns (1988)
Lean in years, but killers all, a violent range war put them on the wrong end of the biggest manhunt ever in the Wild West. Outlaw mega-hit of Billy the Kid and his band stars Emilio Estevez, Charlie Sheen, Kiefer Sutherland, Lou Diamond Phillips, Dermot Mulroney, Casey Siemaszko; with Jack Palance, Terence Stamp. 102 min.
47-1903 *$14.99*

Young Guns (Letterboxed Version)
Also available in a theatrical, widescreen format.
27-7059 *$14.99*

Young Guns II (1990)
The Old West's meanest, wildest and hippest-looking outlaws are back behind, and under, the gun in the hit sequel. Emilio Estevez, as Billy the Kid, reunites with the surviving members of his band, but is it too late to save the Kid from sheriff Pat Garrett? Kiefer Sutherland, Lou Diamond Phillips, William Petersen and Christian Slater co-star; authentic frontier music by Bon Jovi. 103 min.
04-2391 Was $89.99 *$14.99*

Barbarosa (1982)
Willie Nelson is an aging outlaw in the Southwest and Gary Busey the farmboy who becomes his protégé in this finely written and acted Western drama; directed by Fred Schepisi. 90 min.
04-1491 *$12.99*

The Long Riders (1980)
Three of the most notorious outlaw gangs of the Wild West—the James Gang, the Younger brothers, and the Miller boys—are portrayed here by three favorite teams of Hollywood siblings—James and Stacy Keach, Dennis and Randy Quaid, and David, Keith, and Robert Carradine—in Walter Hill's evocative saga. Score by Ry Cooder. 100 min.
12-1359 Was $19.99 *$14.99*

The Long Riders (Letterboxed Version)
Also available in a theatrical, widescreen version.
12-3256 *$14.99*

September Gun (1983)
Robert Preston plays an aging gunslinger who helps a young nun and a band of orphans cross the wilderness in this exciting and touching Western drama. Patty Duke Astin, Sally Kellerman and Christopher Lloyd also star. 94 min.
14-3079 *$14.99*

Gone To Texas (1986)
Sam Elliott plays frontier hero Sam Houston in this sprawling, action-packed biography. Follow Houston's exciting and colorful life, from his brief tenure as governor of Tennessee and experiences with the Cherokee Indians to his involvement in winning the Lone Star State's independence from Mexico. Michael Beck, James Stephens and Devon Ericson co-star. AKA: "Houston: The Legend of Texas." 144 min.
14-3245 *$12.99*

The Tracker (1988)
Kris Kristofferson stars as a veteran frontiersman who leaves his retreat and, accompanied by his college-educated son, hunts down a gang of fanatical killers. Exciting Western tale co-stars Mark Moses, David Huddleston. 102 min.
44-1575 Was $19.99 *$14.99*

Hawken's Breed (1987)
Exciting Western drama starring Peter Fonda as the frontiersman whose love for an Indian woman forces him to fight for his life. Jack Elam, Serene Hedin co-star. 95 min.
68-1138 Was $89.99 *$12.99*

The Gunfighters (1987)
Driven from their ranch and forced outside the law thanks to the machinations of a ruthless land baron, three brothers ride for vengeance in this exciting Western tale. George Kennedy, Art Hindle star. 96 min.
68-1146 *$14.99*

Badlands Justice (1989)
When a corrupt sheriff takes control of a western town, a desperado struggles to take him down and free the town of his underhanded ways. Alex McArthur, John Rhys-Davies, Patricia Charbonneau, James B. Sikking. AKA: "Desperado: Badlands Justice." 93 min.
50-8440 *$14.99*

Red Headed Stranger (1987)
Western drama stars Willie Nelson as a man of the cloth driven to kill his adulterous wife and her lover. Soon he finds himself on a violence-filled path where no prayers are heard. Gripping actioner also stars Katharine Ross, Morgan Fairchild. 108 min.
53-3115 *$14.99*

Windwalker (1980)
Lushly photographed Western adventure set in Utah, with Trevor Howard as a dying Indian chief who relates the story of his life while on his deathbed and can only restore order in his family after he returns to Earth in the afterlife. Co-stars Nick Ramus, James Remar. In Cheyenne and Crow Indian with English subtitles.
04-1614 Was $19.99 *$14.99*

Heaven's Gate (1980)
The sprawling, controversial epic from Michael Cimino that depicts the Wyoming range wars of the 1870s follows a brutal showdown between ruthless cattle barons and the mostly immigrant settlers. Kris Kristofferson, Sam Waterston, Isabelle Huppert, John Hurt and Christopher Walken star. This is the rarely shown uncut version. 220 min.
12-1302 Was $29.99 *$24.99*

Heaven's Gate (Letterboxed Version)
Also available in a theatrical, widescreen format.
12-3280 *$24.99*

J.W. Coop (1971)
Compelling character study centering on rodeo rider Cliff Robertson, who leaves prison after a 10-year stint and struggles to get back to society and his livelihood. Christina Ferrare, Geraldine Page, R.G. Armstrong and John Crawford co-star in this film, which features many exciting rodeo scenes; Robertson also directed and co-wrote the script. 112 min.
02-2904 *$14.99*

The Deadly Trackers (1973)
When his family is brutally murdered by a bank robbery gang, sheriff Richard Harris lets nothing stand in the way of his bloody vengeance. Violent Western thriller also stars Neville Brand, Rod Taylor. 106 min.
19-1833 *$14.99*

Wild Women (1970)
Lighthearted humor mixes with Western action when Army engineers, transporting guns to the Texans fighting for independence against Mexico by way of wagon trains, recruit five female convicts to pose as their wives. Stars Hugh O'Brian and Anne Francis. 90 min.
04-3118 *$14.99*

When The Legends Die (1972)
Richard Widmark and Frederic Forrest star in this unusual Western drama of the friendship that develops between an aging rodeo cowboy and his protégé, a Ute Indian youth. 105 min.
04-3086 *$19.99*

The Culpepper Cattle Company (1972)
A 16-year-old signs on as assistant in a cross-country cattle drive and must grow up in a hurry in this offbeat "coming of age" story with a Western motif. Gary Grimes, Bo Hopkins, Luke Askew star. 92 min.
04-3143 *$19.99*

Take A Hard Ride (1975)
Jim Brown stars as a grizzled cowboy charged with delivering a large sum of money across the Mexican frontier, only to find his journey beset by natural and human hazards. Frontier actioner co-stars Lee Van Cleef, Fred Williamson. 103 min.
04-3144 *$19.99*

Hannie Caulder (1972)
Raquel Welch is the settler who is raped and whose husband is killed by outlaws. She then hires gunslinger Robert Culp to help her track them down and exact vengeance. Frontier drama also stars Ernest Borgnine, Strother Martin, Jack Elam, Christopher Lee. 85 min.
06-1840 *$14.99*

Man In The Wilderness (1971)
Rugged wilderness adventure set in the Northwest of the 1820s with Richard Harris as a member of an exploration party who is mauled by a grizzly bear and seeks revenge against the expedition's leader, who left him to die. John Huston and Peggy the Bear also star in this beautifully photographed, exciting film. 109 min.
19-2072 Was $19.99 *$14.99*

Jessi's Girls (1975)
After she is raped and her husband killed by an outlaw, frontier woman Jessi teams up with a trio of female prisoners (a fast-draw artist, a prostitute and an Indian) she rescues to track the man down and deliver some distaff justice. Sondra Currie, Regina Carroll, Geoffrey Land star. AKA: "Wanted Women." 80 min.
27-6062 *$39.99*

Louis L'Amour

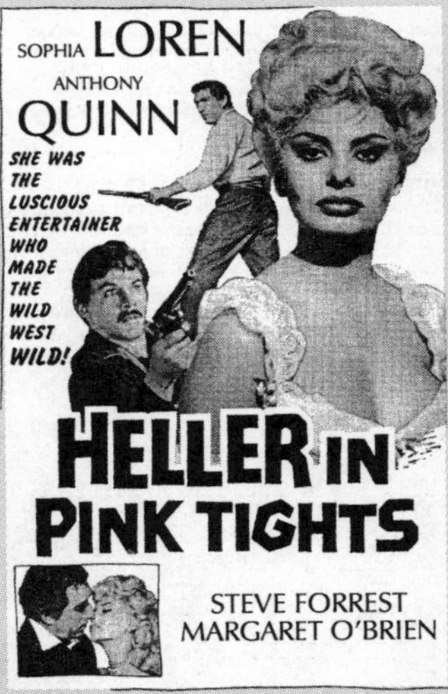

Heller In Pink Tights (1960)
Offbeat Western drama, based on a Louis L'Amour novel, stars Sophia Loren and Anthony Quinn as members of a threadbare theatrical troupe traversing the frontier who must stay one step ahead of creditors and the law. Steve Forrest, Margaret O'Brien, Ramon Novarro also star. 101 min.
06-1841 *$14.99*

Hondo & The Apaches (1967)
Pilot episode of the hit TV series based on both Louis L'Amour's story and the 1953 John Wayne film. Ralph Taeger plays renegade scout Hondo Lane, who is recruited by the Army to work on a peace agreement with an Apache chief. Robert Taylor, Noah Beery and Michael Rennie also star.
14-2004 Was $19.99 *$14.99*

Catlow (1971)
Thrilling sagebrush drama mixed with comedy stars Yul Brynner as a drifter who tries to pull off a $2 million heist and finds himself hunted by his friend (Richard Crenna) and an ornery outlaw (Leonard Nimoy). Based on a Louis L'Amour novel; with Daliah Lavi and Jo Ann Pflug. 103 min.
12-2706 *$19.99*

The Man Called Noon (1973)
Richard Crenna stars in the title role, as a feared gunslinger who loses his memory after an ambush and is aided by an outlaw (Stephen Boyd), who is certain Crenna can lead him to a fortune in hidden loot. Based on a novel by Louis L'Amour, this frontier drama also stars Farley Granger, Rosanna Schiaffino. 90 min.
70-1384 *$14.99*

The Sacketts (1979)
From the pen of legendary Western author Louis L'Amour comes this sprawling saga of three brothers and their adventures in the American frontier after the Civil War. The superlative cast includes Tom Selleck, Sam Elliott, Jeff Osterhage, Glenn Ford, Ben Johnson and Jack Elam. 198 min.
19-1921 Was $19.99 *$14.99*

The Shadow Riders (1982)
Three years after "The Sacketts," Tom Selleck, Sam Elliott and Ben Johnson reteam in another saga based on the works of Louis L'Amour. Two Texas brothers who fought on opposite sides during the Civil War return home to find their family abducted by renegade Confederate soldiers. Co-stars Katharine Ross and Jane Greer. 96 min.
68-1200 *$14.99*

The Quick And The Dead (1987)
Best-selling author Louis L'Amour's Western saga stars Sam Elliott as a grizzled gunslinger who comes to the aid of a settler family when they're beset by an outlaw gang. With Tom Conti, Kate Capshaw, Matt Clark. 83 min.
40-1345 Was $19.99 *$14.99*

Conagher (1991)
Louis L'Amour's classic sagebrush tale has been turned into a superior Western in the classic tradition. Sam Elliott plays a sharp-shooting cowboy, hired to guard cattle on a sprawling ranch, who discovers that some of the other hands are confederates of a gang of rustlers. While on their trail, he's shot from behind, sending him on a mission of vengeance. Katharine Ross, Barry Corbin also star. 94 min.
18-7336 Was $89.99 *$12.99*

A Man Called Horse (1970)
Brutal, engrossing Western adventure that spawned two sequels. Richard Harris is the English aristocrat captured by Sioux Indians in the 1800s and made to serve as a slave. He later undergoes a savage ritual to become a tribe member. With Judith Anderson, Jean Gascon. 114 min.
04-1861 Was $59.99 *$14.99*

Return Of A Man Called Horse (1976)
English nobleman-turned-honorary Sioux Indian Richard Harris returns to the American frontier of the 1800s to help his adopted people escape captivity by a rival tribe supported by ruthless fur traders. Gale Sondergaard, Geoffrey Lewis, Jorge Luke also star. 125 min.
12-2989 Was $19.99 *$14.99*

Return Of A Man Called Horse (Letterboxed Version)
Also available in a theatrical, widescreen format.
12-3203 *$14.99*

Winterhawk (1975)
Native American adventure about Winterhawk, the legendary Blackfoot chief, who asks a group of white settlers to help his people dying of smallpox. He is tricked by two settlers, who kill two of his braves and, in retaliation, he kidnaps a white woman and her brother. Michael Dante, Leif Erickson, Dawn Wells, Woody Strode and Sacheen Littlefeather (Marlon Brando's Oscar night stand-in) star. 101 min.
10-2687 *$14.99*

The Ruthless Four (1970)
A quartet of drifters in the Old West form an uneasy alliance in order to claim a fortune in gold, but greed and mistrust threaten their very lives. Western stars Klaus Kinski and Van Heflin. 96 min.
27-6228 *$24.99*

The Great Northfield, Minnesota Raid (1972)
Phil Kaufman ("The Right Stuff") wrote and directed this gritty look at legendary outlaws Jesse James (Robert Duvall) and Cole Younger (Cliff Robertson), and their gang's ill-fated attempt to rob "the biggest bank West of the Mississippi." Atmospheric "anti-hero" Western also stars John Pearce, R.G. Armstrong. 91 min.
07-1585 Was $29.99 *$14.99*

Madron (1970)
A weary gunslinger (Richard Boone) and a nun (Leslie Caron), the sole survivor of an Indian massacre, must help each other to survive in the wilderness in this exciting frontier drama. 93 min.
08-1282 *$14.99*

A Bullet For Sandoval (1970)
After his family dies of plague during the Civil War, a bitter Confederate deserter forms an outlaw gang on a gun-blazin' mission of revenge. Ernest Borgnine, George Hilton star. AKA: "Vengeance Is Mine." 96 min.
08-1362 Was $19.99 *$14.99*

The Young Pioneers (1976)
Roger Kern and Linda Purl play newlywed settlers who struggle to overcome obstacles ranging from grasshoppers to a blizzard on the Dakota plains of the 1870s. Exciting frontier drama later led to a hit TV series. Robert Hays, Robert Donner also star. 96 min.
08-8740 *$14.99*

Bad Man's River (1973)
Lee Van Cleef is an opportunistic outlaw who becomes involved in a complicated plot hatched by James Mason and Gina Lollobrigida to con the Mexican government out of $1,000,000. Comedy/Western co-stars Simon Andreu and Diana Lorys. 89 min.
10-1103 *$14.99*

South Of Hell Mountain (1970)
A family of gold thieves, on the run from the law, may have met their match when they stop at the cabin of a lonely wife and her beautiful daughter in this frontier action saga. Sam Hall, Anna Stewart star. 87 min.
12-1515 *$59.99*

A Fistful Of Dynamite (1972)
Raucous saga of the Mexican revolution from Sergio Leone stars Rod Steiger as a peasant bandito conned into choosing sides by wily Irish gunrunner James Coburn. Don't pass on this great spaghetti actioner. AKA: "Duck, You Sucker." 138 min.
12-1698 Was $59.99 *$14.99*

Law Of The Land (1976)
Don Johnson stars as a wanderer accused of killing a dance hall girl in a small frontier town, but later appointed deputy and charged with bringing the killer to justice. Western action with Jim Davis, Barbara Parkins. 100 min.
14-3106 *$12.99*

Grayeagle (1978)
In the tradition of "The Searchers" comes this compelling western adventure featuring Ben Johnson as a tough mountain man who sets out to track down and recover his daughter when she's kidnapped by a Cheyenne brave. With Lana Wood, Iron Eyes Cody, Jack Elam, Alex Cord. 104 min.
19-1618 *$14.99*

Cain's Cutthroats (1971)
A former Confederate captain and an eccentric frontier preacher join forces to track down the outlaws who murdered the captain's family. Western thriller stars Scott Brady, John Carradine. 87 min.
16-1107 *$14.99*

El Condor (1970)
To Jim Brown ("The Dirty Dozen"), martial arts star Lee Van Cleef and an Apache raiding party, it's an impregnable Mexican fortress crammed with gold and ready for plundering, but to generalissimo Patrick O'Neal, it's his secret place to defend at any cost. Bloody post-Civil War epic scored by Maurice Jarre. 102 min.
19-1662 Was $19.99 *$14.99*

Little Moon And Jud McGraw (1972)
Gritty and violent western with James Caan as a gunman fresh out of the big house, his sights set on finding his family's killer and filling him full of lead. With Aldo Ray, Stefanie Powers, Sammy Davis, Jr. AKA: "Bronco Busters," "Gone with the West." 90 min.
46-5401 Was $59.99 *$14.99*

The Bandits (1973)
Ruthless, restless men roam the West, bare-knuckled and looking for a showdown. It's 1867, after the Civil War, and there's two kinds of law: little and none! Robert Conrad, Jan-Michael Vincent. 83 min.
48-1003 Was $19.99 *$14.99*

The Gentleman Killer (1978)
It's all-out Western action and excitement in a small town south of the border. Bandits rule the town with a bloody iron fist until one day, when a mysterious wanderer comes in on a mission of vengeance. Anthony Steffen, Silvia Solar star.
48-1042 *$49.99*

A Stranger In Paso Bravo (1973)
A drifter returns after four years to avenge the killing of his wife and daughter by a gang of toughs in this exciting Western tale. Anthony Steffen stars. 92 min.
48-1118 *$49.99*

You're Jinxed, Friend... You've Met Sacramento (1970)
Shake hands with Jack "Sacramento" Thompson, one of the orneriest hombres that ever rode the prairies. When a corrupt town boss kidnaps his kids, Sacramento sets out to free them and show the crook just how jinxed he is. Ty Hardin, Giacomo Rossi Stuart star. 99 min.
48-1129 *$29.99*

The McMasters (1970)
Unusual Western drama looks at the racial tension that erupts when a soldier and ex-slave moves onto a ranch in a Southern town after the Civil War. His only allies are the rancher who raised him and a tribe of Indians who live nearby. Brock Peters, Burl Ives, Jack Palance, David Carradine star. 89 min.
50-1896 *$19.99*

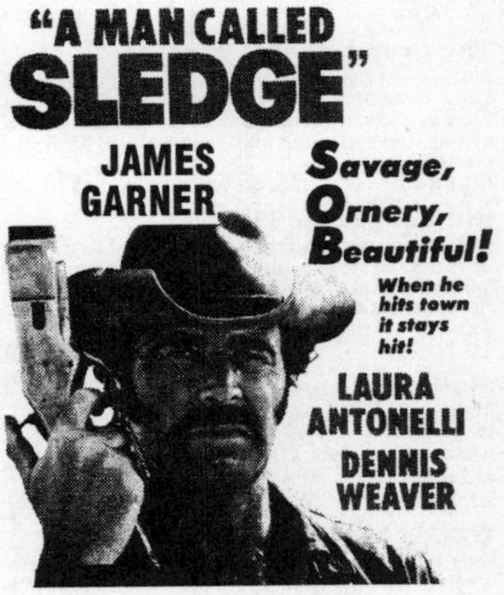

A Man Called Sledge (1970)
Rousing Western directed by Vic Morrow stars James Garner and Dennis Weaver as outlaws after the stolen gold that has been swiped by the other members of their gang. Claude Akins, John Marley and Laura Antonelli also star in this colorful actioner. 92 min.
10-2260 *$14.99*

This Man Can't Die (1970)
Pistol-packin' pasta Western featuring Guy Madison as a gunrunner who returns home to find the black hats that killed his parents and raped his sister. Peter Martel co-stars. 90 min.
50-1921 $14.99

Jory (1972)
Robby Benson, in his first film, stars as a young boy in the Old West whose father is murdered. He hunts the killer down and shoots him in self-defense, but now must run from the law. Co-stars John Marley, Brad Dexter. 97 min.
53-1500 Was $19.99 $14.99

Macho Callahan (1970)
Action-laden Western drama with David Janssen as a Civil War veteran who escapes from jail and hides out in a frontier town, waiting for revenge on the man who had him sent to prison. Lee J. Cobb, Jean Seberg, David Carradine co-star. 99 min.
53-3028 Was $59.99 $14.99

Massacre At Fort Holman (1973)
Civil War frontier drama about a group of condemned soldiers who are sent on a suicide mission to retake a Confederate-held fort. James Coburn, Telly Savalas, Bud Spencer star. AKA: "A Reason to Live...A Reason to Die." 89 min.
59-5019 Was $19.99 $14.99

The Trackers (1971)
Ernest Borgnine and Sammy Davis, Jr. star in this Western thriller about a black tracker hired by a rancher to find the bandits who killed his son and kidnapped his daughter. With Julie Adams and Jim Davis. 73 min.
04-3187 $14.99

Cry Blood, Apache (1970)
Unusual western drama about an Apache warrior seeking a brutal vengeance on the prospectors who killed his people and took his sister hostage on their search for gold. Jody McCrea and, in a cameo, dad Joel star; with Marie Gahva, Dan Kemp. 82 min.
50-1634 $14.99

The Grand Duel (1973)
When a young gunslinger finds himself falsely accused of murder, it's up to veteran outlaw Lee Van Cleef to look out for him and set things right. Lots of action and gunplay, European-style, with Peter O'Brien, Horst Frank.
68-8843 Was $19.99 $14.99

Kid Vengeance (1977)
Leif Garrett stars as a young pioneer who hits the trail in search of revenge upon Lee Van Cleef and his murderous outlaw band, who killed Garrett's parents. Jim Brown, Glynnis O'Connor, John Marley co-star. 93 min.
19-7061 Was $59.99 $14.99

Molly And Lawless John (1973)
Rousing and romantic tale of the wild, wild West. Molly, played by Vera Miles, hooks up with sweet-talking outlaw John (Sam Elliott), and the romance and fightin' begin. 96 min.
21-3040 Was $19.99 $14.99

Wanda Nevada (1979)
Peter Fonda directed and stars in this 1950s Western adventure, in which he wins a most unusual pot in a poker game...spunky teenager Brooke Shields. Together the pair set out to make their fortune prospecting for gold. Look for a cameo by Peter's dad, Henry. 105 min.
73-5009 $14.99

Wanda Nevada (Letterboxed Version)
Also available in a theatrical, widescreen format.
12-3202 $14.99

Companeros (1970)
Interesting European Western with political themes in which mercenary Franco Nero joins revolutionary Thomas Milian to help free a pacifist professor and his students who are being imprisoned by Americans in Texas. During their trek, Milian and Nero encounter a nasty gunslinger with a wooden hand, played by Jack Palance. Fernando Rey co-stars.
68-8925 $19.99

God's Gun (1977)
Sagebrush stunner casts Lee Van Cleef in a dual role: a courageous priest, shot down defending his village from a marauding gang, and his gunslinging twin brother, who's out to prove that vengeance is his! Jack Palance, Richard Boone, Sybil Danning, Leif Garrett co-star. AKA: "A Bullet from God." 93 min.
19-7060 Was $19.99 $12.99

A Professional Gun (1970)
Thrilling "Spaghetti Western" set in the Texas border region during the Mexican Revolution. Franco Nero, Tony Musante and Jack Palance star as hired gunslingers who work both sides of the law and team up for a crime spree, before greed breaks up their uneasy alliance. Music by Ennio Morricone. AKA: "The Mercenary." 92 min.
75-7079 $19.99

China 9, Liberty 37 (1978)
Cult favorite Western laced with violence and intrigue, about the rivalry between railroad moguls and a gunfighter who falls for the wife of the man he's hired by the rail barons to kill. Warren Oates, Jenny Agutter, Fabio Testi and Sam Peckinpah star; directed by Monte Hellman ("The Shooting"). AKA: "Gunfire." 93 min.
75-7192 $19.99

The Gatling Gun (1972)
The title weapon is the prize in a deadly three-way battle between the Cavalry, Apache warriors and renegade criminals in this thrilling frontier adventure. Guy Stockwell, Patrick Wayne, Woody Strode, John Carradine star. 90 min.
78-1042 Was $19.99 $14.99

Doc Hooker's Bunch (1976)
Exciting and sexy sagebrusher set in 1885 when Dr. Isiah Hooker, a medicine show man, and his gang of beautiful but reluctant showgirls, travel cross-country. They encounter adventure, fast guns and more in this rousing western. Dub Taylor, Buck Taylor and Jon Chandler star. 95 min.
78-3001 $14.99

The New Daughters Of Joshua Cabe (1976)
In this comic sagebrusher—the third in its series—John McIntire plays Joshua Cabe, who is falsely accused of murder and sent to prison. His three "daughters" attempt to spring him with a daring rescue attempt. Jack Elam, John Dehner and Jeanette Nolan star. 78 min.
78-3018 $14.99

A Fistful Of Lead (1973)
Top-notch pasta sagebrusher involving a ruthless, black-clad bounty hunter named Sartana, who battles Sabbath, an old nemesis attired in white, over missing gold. George Hilton, Charles Couthwood and Erica Blanc star. AKA: "I Am Sartana...Trade Your Guns for a Coffin." 92 min.
78-3020 $14.99

Yuma (1970)
Gamblers, gunmen and crooked politicians of Yuma, take heed! Clint Walker is a one-man clean-up crew, set to pounce on the lawbreakers of his town. Barry Sullivan, Edgar Buchanan also star. 73 min.
04-3119 $14.99

I Will Fight No More...Forever (1975)
Dramatic true story of Nez Perce Indian leader Chief Joseph, who in the 1870s tried to move his people off a reservation to Canada, and how the Army fought to stop them. James Whitmore, Sam Elliott, Ned Romero, Emiliio Delgado star. 100 min.
16-1042 $12.99

Ace High (1968)
A grizzled outlaw (Eli Wallach) becomes both hunter and hunted in this Western tale of double-crosses, vengeance, and gunplay. With Terence Hill, Kevin McCarthy, Bud Spencer. 120 min.
06-1563 $14.99

Hostile Guns (1967)
Rousing Western adventure with George Montgomery as a U.S. marshal piloting a batch of crooks to the hoosegow in a prison wagon. When the wagon is attacked, Montgomery enlists the help of the outlaws. Yvonne DeCarlo, Tab Hunter and Brian Donlevy co-star; cameos from Richard Arlen, Don Barry and other "B" cowpokes. 91 min.
06-1717 ❑$12.99

Chuka (1967)
A wandering gunfighter attempts to make peace between the inhabitants of an isolated fort and hostile Indians in this frontier drama. Rod Taylor, Luciana Paluzzi, John Mills, Ernest Borgnine star. 105 min.
06-1838 $14.99

Django (1966)
The original, landmark "spaghetti western" that spawned a slew of unrelated sequels. Franco Nero stars as the wandering gunman who arrives, dragging his machine gun in a coffin behind him, in a decaying frontier town caught in the middle of a violent battle between Mexican bandits and a racist gang. Director Sergio Corbucci's compelling drama also stars Eduardo Fajardo. 90 min.
08-8800 Letterboxed $14.99

Django Shoots First (1966)
Glenn Saxon stars as a gunslinger who inherits half his town...only to have to constantly defend himself against the fiend who owns the other half, and will do anything to get rid of him. With Joseph Colatriano. AKA: "He Who Shoots First." 96 min.
09-1801 Was $19.99 $14.99

Django Kill (1967)
Surreal Spaghetti western that finds Tomas Millian walking into a town that is in the midst of a bloody conflict between a group of black-leather clad outlaws and a sadistic storeowner. Millian manages to stay alive with the help of two Indians while the rivals slaughter each other in the streets. With Pierro Lulli, Milo Quesada and Roberto Camardiel. 120 min.
10-9795 $19.99

The Wild & The Dirty (1969)
Shakespeare's "Hamlet" is the basis for this pasta oater in which a Civil War hero returns home to find his father dead and his mother married to unscrupulous Uncle Claude. Will he find out who killed his father? "To shoot or not to shoot...that is the question!" With Chip Gorman and Gilbert Roland. AKA: "Dirty Story of the West," "Django's Crossroads," "Johnny Hamlet."
79-6057 $19.99

One Damned Day At Dawn... Django Meets Sartana (1971)
Two Spaghetti western favorites combine their lethal talents in this well-made tale. The new sheriff in crime-riddled Black City must stop the crooked town boss from aiding a Mexican outlaw's gunrunning racket, and looks for help from bounty hunter Django. But could this lawman really be Sartana incognito? With Fabio Testi, Hunt Powers.
68-9104 $19.99

Django Strikes Again (1987)
Two decades after first playing the cold-blooded master of the Gatling gun, Franco Nero reprises his role of gunfighter Django. Having forsworn his violent ways, Django is forced to his monastery home of the past 10 years to rescue his kidnapped daughter from a white slaver. Christopher Connelly, Donald Pleasence, Lici Lee Lyon also star. Restored video edition includes a five-minute prologue not seen in theatres. 96 min.
08-8801 Letterboxed $14.99

The Jayhawkers (1960)
The Kansas Territory of the 1850s is the setting for this sweeping frontier drama that stars Fess Parker as the settler out to avenge his family's killing by land baron Jeff Chandler. 100 min.
06-1842 $14.99

Blue (1968)
Action-packed Western with Terence Stamp as an American raised by a Mexican bandit who saves a beautiful woman and her father, then comes into conflict with his adoptive brothers when he decides to leave his home. Ricardo Montalban, Joanna Pettet and Karl Malden co-star. 113 min.
06-1968 ❑$12.99

Apache Uprising (1966)
Top-notch action-packed Western with Rory Calhoun as a frontiersman in hostile Apache territory who must stop a crooked stagecoach tycoon from robbing gold from a remote outpost. Also stars Corrine Calvert, DeForest Kelley, Richard Arlen and Lon Chaney, Jr. 90 min.
06-2037 ❑$12.99

Buckskin (1968)
A thrilling sagebrush saga about a nasty mine owner who sabotages a town by stopping their water supply. Marshal Barry Sullivan tries to stop the ornery fellow and save the town. Joan Caulfield, Wendell Corey and Lon Chaney, Jr. also star. 98 min.
06-2042 ❑$12.99

Arizona Bushwackers (1967)
Howard Keel plays a Confederate prisoner-of-war who volunteers for the Union Army and is sent to an Arizona town, where he comes at odds with the sheriff and the evil saloonkeeper. Yvonne DeCarlo, John Ireland and Marilyn Maxwell co-star. 87 min.
06-2101 ❑$14.99

Johnny Reno (1966)
Top-notch sagebrush story about a U.S. marshal who arrives at his new assignment in Stone Junction, Kansas, and finds his work is cut out for him when he must protect an outlaw awaiting trial (and himself) from lynch mobs. With Jane Russell, Lon Chaney, Jr., John Agar and Tom Drake. 83 min.
06-2103 ❑$14.99

The Desperados (1969)
Vince Edwards stars in this Western drama as a man who leaves his family, a marauding band of Confederate renegades, only to be forced to confront them years later when they threaten his new home. Jack Palance, George Maharis, Neville Brand also star. 90 min.
02-1856 $14.99

The Tramplers (1966)
A son who split with his father during the Civil War returns home, only to find the family still divided and heading towards a violent resolution. Western drama stars Joseph Cotten, Gordon Scott, James Mitchum. AKA: "Showdown." 105 min.
02-2256 $14.99

Rio Conchos (1964)
A shipment of stolen rifles, earmarked for sale to Indians, becomes the prize in a struggle between outlaws and the Cavalry in this Western epic. Richard Boone, Stuart Whitman, Jim Brown (his film debut) star. 107 min.
04-3085 $19.99

Texas Across The River (1966)
A western spiked with laughs starring Dean Martin as a gun-smuggler and Joey Bishop as his trusted Indian companion who team with expatriate Spanish nobleman Alain Delon on a wild adventure through Apache territory. Rosemary Forsyth and Peter Graves also star. 101 min.
07-2037 $14.99

White Comanche (1967)
Two half-breed twins face their ultimate conflict in this Western drama. One was raised by Indians, the other in the white man's world, and when war is declared it's brother against brother. William Shatner, Joseph Cotten star. 90 min.
08-1286 Was $19.99 $14.99

California (1963)
Exciting sagebrusher set against the backdrop of California's struggle for independence from Mexico and their quest for statehood. Don Francisco Hernandez leads the Mexican army in keeping a hold on the residents, but his half-brother serves as the revolutionaries' leader. With Jock Mahoney, Faith Domergue and Michael Pate. 86 min.
09-5115 $19.99

Shoot Out At Big Sag (1962)
Originally produced as a pilot for a proposed TV series called "Barbed Wire," this frontier drama stars Walter Brennan as a would-be "clergyman" trying to keep settlers from Texas off of land in Montana's Big Sag region. Problems arise when Brennan's son, Chris Robinson, falls for settlers' daughter Luana Patten. With Leif Erickson, Les Tremayne. 64 min.
09-5323 $14.99

Rough Night In Jericho (1967)
Former lawman Dean Martin uses underhanded methods to run the town of Jericho for his own gain. The only establishment he hasn't been able to get his paws on is the stagecoach run by feisty widow Jean Simmons. In order to fend off the slimy Martin, Simmons recruits gambler George Peppard. Also starring Slim Pickens and John McIntire. 104 min.
07-2036 ❑$14.99

Butch Cassidy And The Sundance Kid (1969)
One of the most successful and entertaining Westerns of all time chronicles the hair-raising adventures of outlaws Butch (Paul Newman) and Sundance (Robert Redford) as they hold up banks on both sides of the border while being pursued by a super-posse of lawmen. Katharine Ross co-stars in George Roy Hill's effort from William Goldman's Oscar-winning script. With outtakes and celebrity interviews. 112 min.
04-1022 □$14.99

Wanted: The Sundance Woman (1976)
Katharine Ross, who played Etta Place in "Butch Cassidy and the Sundance Kid," returns to the role in this film set after the two outlaws' demise. In this adventure, Ross becomes a gun-runner for Pancho Villa in Mexico. Hector Elizondo, Stella Stevens, Steve Forrest and Michael Constantine co-star. AKA: "Mrs. Sundance Rides Again." 97 min.
10-9535 $14.99

Butch And Sundance: The Early Days (1979)
The fun-filled "prequel," showing how the outlaw buddies first met and started their infamous careers, stars Tom Berenger and William Katt as the desperado duo. Enjoyable Western action/comedy co-stars Jill Eikenberry, Brian Dennehy. 110 min.
04-3084 $19.99

Ballad Of A Bounty Hunter (1965)
A ruthless bounty hunter falls in love with the beautiful sister of the man that he is tracking. With James Philbrook, Nuria Torray, Pearl Cristal, Tom Griffith. 83 min.
55-3003 $19.99

Five Giants From Texas (1966)
When her husband is brutally murdered and her son kidnapped, Rosaria must make ends meet by working a saloon. After years of grief, Rosaria is visited by five of her husband's friends who vow vengeance. She joins them as they look for the culprits and her son. Guy Madison and Mónica Randal star in this Italian-Spanish co-production.
20-5135 $19.99

The Rattler Kid (1968)
Smashing sagebrush saga about a military man, wrongly convicted for murder, who escapes and becomes an infamous outlaw while searching for the real killers. Richard Wyler, Brad Harris star. 86 min.
48-1044 $29.99

The Hellbenders (1967)
An embittered ex-Confederate officer and his sons rob a train and must fight the law, the U.S. Cavalry and Indians in order to escape. Western thriller from Italy stars Joseph Cotten, Norma Bengeli; directed by Sergio Corbucci ("Django").
53-1501 Was $19.99 $14.99

Sergeant Rutledge (1960)
Groundbreaking Western from director John Ford focuses on black cavalryman Woody Strode, standing trial for murdering his white commanding officer and raping and killing the man's daughter. The innocent Strode fears that the jury's prejudice will affect the trial, but he finally gets a chance to prove his heroism during an Indian attack. With Jeffrey Hunter, Constance Towers. 118 min.
19-2073 Was $19.99 $14.99

Cheyenne Autumn (1964)
The final Western from director John Ford, this powerful, sweeping drama follows a band of Cheyenne Indians' perilous trek as they leave a squalid Oklahoma reservation to return to their ancestral land in Wyoming, an odyssey threatened by the U.S. Calavry. Richard Widmark, Carroll Baker, Karl Malden, Ricardo Montalban, Edward G. Robinson and James Stewart star. Uncut, 158-minute version.
19-1465 $19.99

Waterhole No. 3 (1967)
A trio of desperadoes hides a fortune in stolen gold in a desert waterhole and return, separately, years later to double cross each other and take it for themselves in a lighthearted Western adventure. James Coburn, Carroll O'Connor, Joan Blondell, James Whitmore, Bruce Dern. 95 min.
06-1451 $14.99

A Bullet For The General (1968)
Gun-blazing thriller set in revolutionary Mexico, as an enigmatic mercenary joins up with rebel forces attempting to overthrow the government. But whose side is he really on? Klaus Kinski, Gian-Maria Volonte star. 113 min.
53-3098 Was $59.99 $19.99

Return Of The Magnificent Seven (1966)
They ride again! More blazing gunplay is in store when Yul Brynner forms a new Magnificent Seven to aid the oppressed—for a price. Can they stave off another sagebrush shakedown? Warren Oates, Claude Akins, Robert Fuller. 96 min.
12-1702 $19.99

Guns Of The Magnificent Seven (1969)
Third adventure of the Western outlaws-turned-heroes for hire features George Kennedy as the leader of the gunfighter septet, here charged with freeing a revolutionary leader from a Mexican fortress. Blazing Western actioner also stars James Whitmore, Michael Ansara, Bernie Casey and Joe Don Baker. 95 min.
12-1855 Was $19.99 $14.99

The Magnificent Seven (1998)
This feature-length pilot to the hit TV series details the action-packed adventures of seven cowboy specialists recruited by an Indian tribe to battle an ornery group of ex-Confederate soldiers. Michael Biehn, Ron Perlman, Eric Close and Dale Midkiff star. 90 min.
12-3302 Was $49.99 □$14.99

Belle Starr (The Belle Starr Story) (1967)
Meet the West's most notorious lady, and the men who loved her and helped her become a legendary outlaw, in this spaghetti sagebrusher that was directed by Lina Wertmuller under the alias of "Nathan Wich." Elsa Martinelli, Robert Woods and George Eastman star.
50-1289 Was $59.99 $14.99

The Bounty Killer (1965)
After he's forced to kill a band of ruthless outlaws, gunslinger Dan Duryea gets himself into the manhunting business. Ultimately, he finds that his job leads to tragedy and death in this offbeat and downbeat Hollywood western that features a supporting cast of old-time sagebrush stars: Johnny Mack Brown, Buster Crabbe, Fuzzy Knight and Bob Steele. 93 min.
55-3007 $14.99

Frontier Hellcat (1966)
This entry in the "Winnetou" series tells of a mysterious western hero who wanders from town to town helping people in need. His heroics here involve a fiery frontierswoman who accepts his services to gain safe passage through the Rocky Mountains. Stewart Granger, Elke Sommer and Pierce Brice star in the Euro sagebrusher. 98 min.
10-9515 $14.99

Apaches' Last Battle (1968)
Offbeat and interesting German-made Western, based on a series of novels by Karl May. Lex Barker stars as a grizzled cowpoke who tries to stop a war instigated by a greedy Cavalry officer between the Apaches and Comanches. With Guy Madison, Daliah Lavi, Pierre Brice. AKA: "Old Shatterhand," "Shatterhand." 98 min.
68-8838 $19.99

Johnny West (1968)
After a man is kidnapped and forced to leave his abductors his gold in a will, cowboy Dick Palmer steps in to save the day. Diana Garson and Mike Anthony also star. 90 min.
10-9334 $19.99

Invitation To A Gunfighter (1964)
Yul Brynner is a half-Creole/half-black, poker-playing, poetry-reciting gunslinger hired to kill Confederate veteran George Segal, who has disrupted a town by killing a man and barricading himself in a house. Offbeat western also stars Janice Rule and Pat Hingle. 92 min.
12-2708 Was $19.99 □$14.99

In The Valley Of The Death (1968)
Final film the popular "Winnetou" series features Lex Barker, as railroad engineer Old Shatterhand, and Indian pal Chief Winnetou enlisted by a dead soldier's daughter to find stolen gold and clear the name of her father, who has been branded a thief. Karin Dor and Rik Battaglia also star in this lively Euro-western. AKA: "Winnetou and Shatterhand in the Valley of Death."
79-6497 $19.99

Four Rode Out (1969)
The hunt for a Mexican outlaw through the New Mexico frontier forges a strange alliance between a marshal, a government agent, and the fugitive's lover. Gripping Western thriller stars Pernell Roberts, Leslie Nielsen, Sue Lyon. 90 min.
27-6036 $14.99

Geronimo (1962)
Chuck Connors turns in a powerful performance as the mighty Apache warrior who is betrayed by cattlemen and the U.S. government, then heads to Mexico, where he and his people live as bandits. Ross Martin and Adam West also star in this thrilling Native American adventure that makes an attempt at historical accuracy. 101 min.
12-2661 $14.99

Geronimo: An American Legend (1993)
Sprawling, action-packed epic focusing on Apache leader Geronimo (Wes Studi) and his fierce battle against the U.S. government and its policy of forcefully sequestering Indians on reservations. Jason Patric co-stars as Cavalry officer Charles Gatewood, caught between his official duty and his respect for his rival; with Gene Hackman, Robert Duvall and Matt Damon. 115 min.
02-2615 Was $19.99 □$14.99

Geronimo (1993)
An exciting, revisionist look at the brave Apache warrior Geronimo, chronicling his life from youth to old age and depicting his battles with Mexican and American troops. Realistic in its portrayal of violence by and against the Apache, this superb film stars Joseph Runningfox, Nick Ramus, Michelle St. John. Special video version contains footage not shown on TV; 102 min.
18-7465 Was $89.99 □$14.99

Hour Of The Gun (1967)
Riveting revisionist Western plays as a sequel of sorts to "Gunfight at the O.K. Corral." James Garner stars as lawman Wyatt Earp, who enlists the help of Doc Holliday (Jason Robards, Jr.) to gun down the rustlers responsible for killing his brothers. Robert Ryan, Albert Salmi and Steve Inhat also star. 101 min.
12-2664 $14.99

Doc (1971)
The medico in question is famed gunslinger Doc Holliday, played by Stacy Keach in this thoughtful retelling of the showdown at the O.K. Corral that uses the gunfight as background as it examines Holliday the man. With Faye Dunaway, Denver John Collins, and Harris Yulin as Wyatt Earp. 92 min.
12-3034 □$19.99

Tombstone (1993)
Exciting and stylish retelling of the legendary gunfight at the O.K. Corral, in which retired lawman Wyatt Earp and his brothers teamed with Doc Holliday in a fierce showdown against the Clanton family in the sprawling Western town of Tombstone, Arizona. Kurt Russell, Val Kilmer, Sam Elliott, Michael Biehn, Dana Delany, Charlton Heston and Powers Boothe star. 130 min.
11-1790 Was $19.99 □$14.99

The Glory Guys (1965)
Scripted by Sam Peckinpah, this compelling Western drama focuses on an ambitious Cavalry general (based, perhaps, on Custer?) who, dreaming of political success, leads his outnumbered troops into battle against Indians, and the rivalry between two men for a woman. Tom Tryon, Harve Presnell, Senta Berger, Andrew Duggan and a young James Caan star. 112 min.
12-3033 □$19.99

The Over-The-Hill Gang (1969)
Comic western with Pat O'Brien as a Texas Ranger who enlists three of his old pals to help out the residents of a small town run by a corrupt mayor, an alcoholic drunk and a quick-shooting sheriff. Walter Brennan, Andy Devine, Edgar Buchanan, Ricky Nelson and Gypsy Rose Lee star. 74 min.
58-8190 $14.99

The Over-The-Hill Gang Rides Again (1970)
Aged cowpokes Walter Brennan, Edgar Buchanan, Andy Devine and Chill Wills are back, this time helping their longtime pardner Fred Astaire get off the bottle and back behind the badge as the new sheriff of Waco, in this light-hearted frontier tale. 73 min.
55-3032 Was $19.99 $14.99

Today It's Me... Tomorrow You (1968)
After being wrongly accused of murdering his wife, an Indian is out of jail and out for revenge. He joins forces with a group of gunslingers to hunt down a bandit named Elfego, the true culprit of the killing. With Bud Spencer, Montgomery Ford and Jeff Cameron; co-written by Dario Argento.
59-7006 Letterboxed $29.99

Boot Hill (1969)
The stars of the "Trinity" spaghetti westerns, Bud Spencer and Terence Hill, teamed up for the first time here, as a pair of amiable saddle tramps riding across the plains and encountering gunfighters (who they try to avoid) and easy frontier women (who they don't). Woody Strode, Victor Buono also star. AKA: "Trinity Rides Again." 87 min.
78-1073 $24.99

They Call Me Trinity (1971)
A droll and delightful Western spoof loosely based on "The Magnificent Seven." Terence Hill and Bud Spencer are ne'er-do-well half-brothers who must use their questionable gun-slinging skills to protect a settlement from an evil land baron. 110 min.
53-1255 Was $19.99 $14.99

It Can Be Done Amigo (1971)
Funny spoof of "spaghetti westerns" starring Jack Palance as a good-natured gunslinger out to get ladies man Bud Spencer, who seduced his sister. Francisco Rabal and Dany Saval also star in this amiable oater. AKA: "The Big and the Bad."
68-8916 $19.99

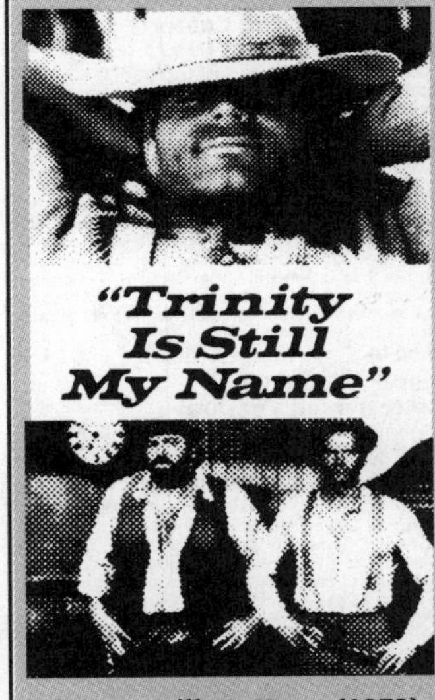

Trinity Is Still My Name (1972)
Those raucous Trinity boys (Terence Hill and Bud Spencer) are back in another wacky send-up of "Spaghetti Westerns." They promised their pappy they'd become successful bandits, but have trouble managing. 117 min.
53-1256 Was $19.99 $14.99

Lucky Luke (1994)
Inspired by the popular French comic book series, this thrill-packed comic sagebrusher stars Terence Hill as a gunslinger who faces the evil Dalton Brothers and an Indian attack when he tries to keep peace in the unruly Daisy Town. Nancy Morgan and Ron Carey also star in this amiable adventure featuring music and narration from Roger Miller. 91 min.
68-1322 Was $89.99 $14.99

Troublemakers (1994)
The mother of two warring brothers—quick-shooting Terence Hill and huge bounty hunter Bud Spencer—wants them to be reunited for Christmas. Hill gets the assignment to bring his brother back home and runs into a number of hurdles trying to do so in this funny sagebrusher, co-starring Ruth Buzzi. 98 min.
72-9056 Was $89.99 $14.99

Sons Of Trinity (1995)
The "Trinity" legend lives on in this raucous Western adventure, as the ne'er-do-well offspring of Trinity and Bambino meet and wind up becoming the lawmen of a wild and wooly frontier town. Heath Kizzier, Keith Neubert, Yvonne De Bark star. 90 min.
72-9069 Was $99.99 $14.99

Between God, The Devil And A Winchester (1968)
The search for treasure stolen from a Texas church pits a gang of cutthroat outlaws against a priest masquerading as a famed gunfighter in this action-filled frontier drama that plays like a Spaghetti western "Treasure Island." Gilbert Roland, Richard Harrison, Folco Lulli star. AKA: "God Was in the West, Too, at One Time."
68-9091 Was $49.99 $19.99

Black Eagle Of Santa Fe (1964)
This spaghetti sagebrusher with German roots showcases gladiator movie vet Brad Harris as a secret government agent sent to Santa Fe in order to look into the reasons the usually peaceful Indians have become hostile. What he uncovers is a devious plot conceived by a land-snagging rancher. With Horst Frank, Tony Kendell. AKA: "Gringos Do Not Forgive."
79-6135 $19.99

A Place Called Glory (1966)
Glory is a lawless frontier town that celebrates its founding each year by conning two gunfighters into dueling in the center of town. This time around Lex Barker and Pierre Brice are the doomed duo, but they hatch a plan to save themselves and set things right. Marianne Koch, Gerard Tichy co-star. 92 min.
68-8842 $19.99

Gunmen Of The Rio Grande (1964)
Rip-roaring western adventure (filmed in Spain) about famed lawman Wyatt Earp's attempts to help a French saloonkeeper trying to stop an outlaw from ransacking local silver mines. This thrilling mix of history and legend stars Guy Madison, Madeleine Lebeau and Gerard Tichy. AKA: "Duel at Rio Bravo."
68-8906 $19.99

The Ugly Ones (1968)
A bounty hunter (Richard Wyler) runs into trouble while tracking outlaw Tomas Milian. The outlaw regroups his old pack of hombres to torture his adversary, but the hunter is eventually helped by the bad guy's female friend. Ella Karin also stars in this action-packed "Spaghetti Western."
68-8947 $19.99

Crazy Horse And Custer: The Untold Story (1967)
Culled from the TV series "The Legend of Custer," this feature recounts the deadly battle of wills between the legendary general and the Native American leader. Wayne Maunder, Michael Dante and Slim Pickens star. 87 min.
73-9088   Was $19.99 $14.99

Custer Of The West (1968)
Robert Shaw stars as the maverick Army officer who, while losing his life in a bitter defeat, became a legend of the American frontier, in this sweeping historical saga. Follows Custer's life from his Civil War exploits to his controversy-plagued career out West and the final showdown at Little Big Horn. Jeffrey Hunter, Mary Ure, Ty Hardin also star. 143 min.
08-8644 $14.99

Custer Of The West (Letterboxed Version)
Also available in a theatrical, widescreen format.
08-8645 $14.99

Son Of The Morning Star (1991)
An epic look at the life and times of General George Armstrong Custer, one of the most controversial and fascinating figures in American history. Gary Cole plays the West Point graduate and Civil War officer who led an ill-conceived and disastrous battle against the Sioux at Little Big Horn. With Rosanna Arquette, Dean Stockwell and Rodney A. Grant ("Dances with Wolves"). 186 min.
63-1440   ☐$19.99

The Implacable Three (1968)
After he returns home from a cattle drive to find his pregnant wife dead and his money gone, a gunman searches for the culprit. He joins forces with another shooting expert in a search for revenge which lasts years and leads to the leader of a gang residing in a corrupt small town. Paul Piaget, Geoffrey Horne star in this action-packed frontier tale from Italy. AKA: "Hour of Death."
79-6139 $19.99

GIULIANO GEMMA in
ADIOS GRINGO

Adios Gringo (1965)
A young rancher must fight to save himself when, after being swindled in a cattle deal, he is forced to kill in self-defense and is charged with murder. Montgomery Wood (Giuliano Gemma), Evelyn Stewart, Jesus Puente star. 98 min.
68-8840 $19.99

The Wild Bunch

Sam Peckinpah

The Deadly Companions (1961)
Excellent Western adventure concerning an ex-soldier/gunslinger who makes amends to the family of the man he accidentally killed by guiding the funeral party through Apache country. Maureen O'Hara, Brian Keith, Steve Cochran, Chill Wills star; Sam Peckinpah's directorial debut. 90 min.
70-1141 $14.99

Ride The High Country (1962)
Western legends Randolph Scott and Joel McCrea made their sagebrush swan songs in this Sam Peckinpah tale. Two veteran gunslingers are hired to protect a gold shipment, only to find plenty of obstacles along the way. Sprawling, colorful thriller also stars Edgar Buchanan, Warren Oates and Mariette Hartley (her film debut). 93 min.
12-1552 $19.99

The Wild Bunch: 30th Anniversary Special Edition (1969)
The restored 1995 director's cut version of Sam Peckinpah's controversial sagebrush classic. In the Southwest of 1913, a gang of outlaws is coerced by a Mexican general into robbing a U.S. Army gun shipment, a move that has fatal consequences. William Holden, Ernest Borgnine, Warren Oates, Edmond O'Brien and Robert Ryan star in this masterpiece, known for its bloody and balletic action scenes. Special edition includes "The Wild Bunch: An Album in Montage" documentary and an introduction by Borgnine. 179 min. total.
19-2444   ☐$19.99

The Wild Bunch: 30th Anniversary Special Edition (Letterboxed Version)
Also available in a theatrical, widescreen format.
19-1050   ☐$19.99

The Ballad Of Cable Hogue (1970)
Sam Peckinpah's lyric tribute to American individualism stars Jason Robards as a prospector left for dead by his scheming partners. He sets out to build his own world in the Old West, all the while dreaming of revenge. Co-stars Stella Stevens, David Warner, Strother Martin and Slim Pickens. 122 min.
19-1467 $14.99

Pat Garrett And Billy The Kid (1973)
Sam Peckinpah's violent, mystical Western saga focuses on the pursuit of outlaw Billy The Kid (Kris Kristofferson) by lawman Pat Garrett (James Coburn). Bob Dylan also stars and wrote the music. Jason Robards, Rita Coolidge. Uncut, 122-minute version.
12-1340 $19.99

Bring Me The Head Of Alfredo Garcia (1974)
A Mexican crime lord has put the bounty on the man who seduced his daughter, and Warren Oates is a seedy American drifter out to collect the grisly prize. Brutal and action-filled drama of honor and betrayal by Sam Peckinpah; with Gig Young, Robert Webber, Kris Kristofferson. 112 min.
12-1739   Was $29.99 $14.99

The Killer Elite (1975)
Sam Peckinpah directed this smashing tale of espionage, conspiracy and double-crosses. James Caan is a San Francisco killer-for-hire, working for the CIA, who uses firearms and martial arts for revenge. Robert Duvall, Gig Young. 130 min.
12-1750 $14.99

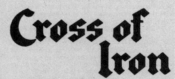

Cross of Iron

Cross Of Iron (1977)
Sam Peckinpah's only war film is a violent and compelling story set on the Russian front in 1943, where war-weary German sergeant James Coburn encounters Maximilian Schell, a Prussian officer out to get the coveted Iron Cross medal at any cost. James Mason, David Warner and Senta Berger also star in this action-packed epic. 129 min.
03-1345 $29.99

Please see our index for these other Sam Peckinpah titles: *The Getaway • Junior Bonner • Straw Dogs*

Savage Pampas (1967)
The Argentinean plains of the mid-1800s had a reputation as violent as their North American counterpart, as seen in this frontier actioner starring Robert Taylor as an army captain who must lead his men against an attack on their remote fort. With Ty Hardin, Marc Lawrence. 110 min.
75-7116 $14.99

Blue Lightning (1965)
After the Civil War, a gang of Union Army buddies heads west in search of new adventure and get more than they bargained for at the hands of hostile Indians and a squad of ex-Rebels who know the whereabouts of a fortune in Confederate gold. Rory Calhoun, James Philbrook star. AKA: "Finger on the Trigger." 85 min.
75-7124   Was $19.99 $14.99

Death Rides A Horse (1969)
A young man looking for the outlaws who killed his parents teams up with an embittered gunslinger after those responsible for his imprisonment in this violent Western tale. Lee Van Cleef, John Phillip Law, Anthony Dawson star. 115 min.
75-7132   Was $19.99 $14.99

The Outlaw Of Red River (1966)
Sagebrusher stars George Montgomery as a man wrongly accused of murder who finds himself involved in romance and bitter rivalry when he lands in Mexico during the Revolution. With Elisa Monez. AKA: "Django the Honorable Killer." 85 min.
78-3009 $14.99

Beyond The Law (1968)
Western legend Lee Van Cleef is a man caught in the middle, as the ex-leader of an outlaw gang becomes the town sheriff and must choose between protecting a fortune in loot or siding with his former allies. With Antonio Sabato, Gordon Mitchell, Bud Spencer. AKA "Bloodsilver," "The Good Die First." 90 min.
64-1357 $14.99

Shotgun (1968)
Tab Hunter stars in this Italian-made frontier drama as a sheriff who retreats into alcoholism when his fiancée is killed by a gang of masked outlaws, but overcomes his weakness to track down the murderers. With Piero Lulli, Erika Blanc. AKA: "Vengeance Is My Forgiveness." 93 min.
67-5025 $29.99

Any Gun Can Play (1968)
A nameless, wandering gunslinger sets his sights on a ruthless Mexican bandit and the reward offered for his capture...dead or alive. Western action with George Hilton, Edd Byrnes, Gilbert Roland. AKA: "Go Kill and Come Back." 95 min.
78-1041   Was $19.99 $14.99

The Dangerous Days Of Kiowa Jones (1966)
Exciting western adventure involving a drifter-turned-deputy who must transfer two killers to prison and elude bounty hunters who are also searching for the criminals. Robert Horton, Diane Baker, Sal Mineo, Zalman King and (Harry) Dean Stanton star.
78-3007 $14.99

Massacre At Marble City (1964)
Two-fisted spaghetti western about the son of a murdered cowpoke who recruits the local sheriff and a tribe of Indians to help him track down the men who killed his father. Mario Adorf and Brad Harris star.
68-8907 $19.99

30 Winchesters For El Diablo (1967)
Two cowboys travel to a border town hoping to find work. When one of them conceives a plan to move cattle that tricks the bloodthirsty cattle-rustler El Diablo, violence erupts as the bad guy recruits gunslingers to battle the cowpokes. This explosive spaghetti western stars Carl Mohner, Topsy Collins and John Heston.
79-6140 $19.99

The Fury Of The Apaches (1966)
After a wagon train is attacked by Indians, Major Loman and his cavalry unit from Fort Grant come to their rescue, but eventually must face the Indians when they attack the fort later. Frank Latimore, Liza Moreno and George Gordon star in this Italian oater.
79-6137 $19.99

Buffalo Bill, Hero Of The West (1964)
Gladiator movie great Gordon Scott plays "Buffalo Bill" Cody, the Western hero sent by President Grant to stop the gun-running between white smugglers and a fierce Sioux warrior. Cody discovers that an Indian-hating Cavalry commander may have a part in the dealings. This early spaghetti sagebrusher also stars Roldano Lupi and Catherine Ribeiro. Dubbed in English.
79-6496 $19.99

$100,000 For Ringo (1966)
Colorful, ultra-violent pasta sagebrusher showcasing Richard Harrison as a stranger who rides into a Western town and gets in the middle of a rivalry between a gunrunner and a Mexican general over hidden treasure. Directed by Alberto De Martino ("Django Shoots First"), the film also stars Fernando Sancho and Girard Tichy.
79-6499 $19.99

El Cisco (1966)
After using an exploding cigar to escape his hanging, El Cisco turns to robbing stagecoaches while searching for the men who tried to do him in. El Cisco discovers that one of them is a sheriff and plots to get revenge, but the plan leads to a nasty showdown and Cisco's girlfriend's life being threatened. William Berger and George Wang star in this violent spaghetti sagebrusher.
79-6544 $19.99

Ringo's Big Night (1965)
William Berger ("El Cisco") is a noted gunman accused of robbing a stagecoach filled with cash that's heading to Tombstone. He and one of the real bandits on the job are imprisoned for the crime, and, after befriending the crook, Berger learns of the other accomplices—including the town's mayor! Double-crosses, assassins and shootouts, Italian style! With Eduardo Fajardo.
79-6545 $19.99

Gun Fight At Red Sands (Gringo) (1963)
One of the first entries in the "Spaghetti Western" genre, with Richard Harrison as an ex-soldier who returns home to find his family murdered by bandits and sets out for revenge. Giacomo Rossi Stuart, Sara Lezana co-star. 95 min.
68-8830 $19.99

LEE VAN CLEEF
"DAY OF ANGER"

Day Of Anger (1967)
First-class Italian frontier saga starring Lee Van Cleef as a master gunslinger who joins forces with an orphan to take over a small town. After teaching the youngster everything he knows, Van Cleef finds himself facing his student in a showdown. With Giuliano Gemma, Walter Rilla; directed by Tonino Valerii ("My Name is Nobody"). AKA: "Days of Wrath."
79-6136   Letterboxed $19.99

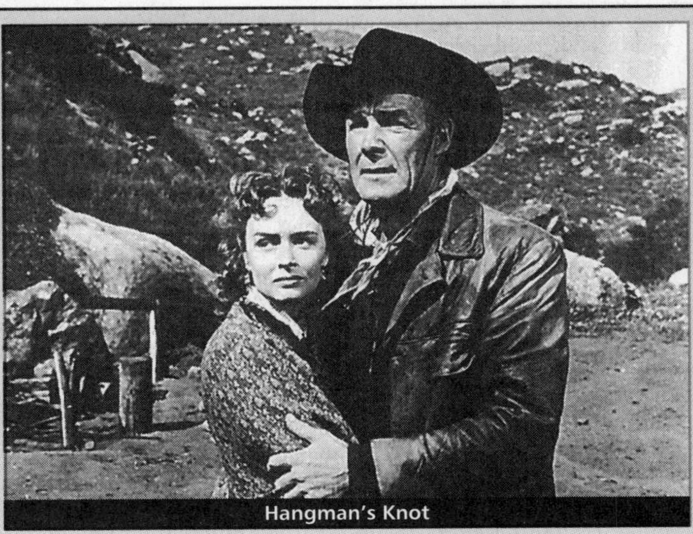

Hangman's Knot

Randolph Scott

Heritage Of The Desert (1932)
Randolph Scott stars as a rancher who rescues orphan Sally Blane while battling some rapscallious cattle rustlers in this adaptation of a Zane Grey tale. This was the first western directed by Henry Hathaway ("True Grit"). AKA: "When the West Was Young." 58 min.
10-7589 *$14.99*

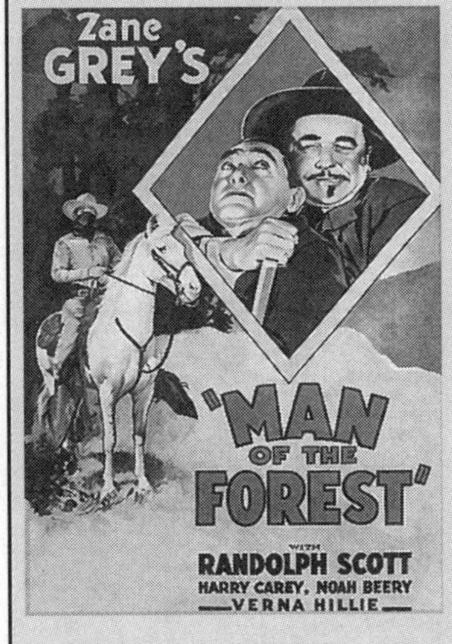
Zane
GREY'S
MAN
OF THE
FOREST
WITH
RANDOLPH SCOTT
HARRY CAREY, NOAH BEERY
VERNA HILLIE

Man Of The Forest (1933)
Engaging Randolph Scott adventure lensed by Henry Hathaway early in his career. Scott is framed for the murder of a woman's father after he kidnaps her...and is subsequently sprung from jail by his pet mountain lion! With Harry Carey, Buster Crabbe, Noah Beery, Sr. and Guinn "Big Boy" Williams. AKA: "Challenge of the Frontier." 60 min.
10-1236 *$14.99*

To The Last Man (1933)
Early Western drama from director Henry Hathaway, based on a Zane Grey novel, regarding an ancient feud between two frontier families that is fanned when one clan takes up cattle rustling. Randolph Scott, Noah Beery, Sr., Buster Crabbe, Esther Ralston star; look for a five-year-old Shirley Temple in her second feature film. AKA: "Law of Vengeance." 60 min.
10-1237 *$14.99*

Broken Dreams (1933)
Powerful drama starring Randolph Scott as a man who blames his son for the loss of his wife, who died during childbirth. The son has resided with relatives for six years, until Scott attempts to reconcile and take him back. Martha Sleeper, Joseph Cawthorn also star. 68 min.
17-3042 Was $19.99 *$14.99*

Wagon Wheels (1934)
Randolph Scott stars as a wagon scout leading his pioneer charges to the Oregon Territory, despite speculator's attempts to try to stop them, in a frontier classic based on a Zane Grey story. With Gail Patrick, Raymond Hatton, Monte Blue. 56 min.
10-1143 *$14.99*

The Thundering Herd (1934)
Buffalo hunter Randolph Scott goes up against villain Noah Beery, Sr., who has contrived a feud between settlers and Indians to grab a fortune in hides. Directed by Henry Hathaway; with Buster Crabbe, Judith Allen. AKA: "Buffalo Stampede," "In the Days of the Thundering Herd." 57 min.
10-7590 *$14.99*

The Fighting Westerner (1935)
When a series of murders in a radium mine have the local constabulary perplexed, they turn to the one gunslinger who can put things right, Randolph Scott. Entertaining Western actioner also stars Chic Sale and Ann Sheridan in an early leading role. AKA: "Rocky Mountain Mystery." 63 min.
10-7362 Was $19.99 *$14.99*

The Last Of The Mohicans (1936)
Randolph Scott stars as frontier scout Hawkeye, who teams with his Mohican Indian allies to defend a party of British settlers from attack in New York State during the French and Indian Wars, in this thrilling adaptation of James Fenimore Cooper's classic adventure novel. With Binnie Barnes, Philip Reed, Heather Angel. 91 min.
08-1535 *$14.99*

The Texans (1938)
Prairie fires, snowstorms, hostile Indians and a gun-smuggling Joan Bennett are just some of the problems trail boss Randolph Scott has to cope with on a 10,000-head cattle drive to Kansas in this hard-hitting frontier drama. With May Robson, Robert Cummings, and Walter Brennan as Chuckawalla. 93 min.
07-2325 □*$14.99*

Western Union (1941)
Fritz Lang's compelling drama stars Randolph Scott as a reformed outlaw who joins up with a crew stringing telegraph lines across the frontier. Trouble arises when a gang of rustlers, led by Scott's brother (Barton MacLane), threatens the project. Dean Jagger, Robert Young, Virginia Gilmore, John Carradine and Chief Thundercloud co-star. 93 min.
04-2270 □*$39.99*

The Desperadoes (1943)
Columbia Pictures' first color production was this fine western starring Randolph Scott as a Utah lawman who helps outlaw pal Glenn Ford go straight. When a local bank is robbed, Ford is the suspect, but Scott believes others are involved and must find the true criminals. With Evelyn Keyes, Edgar Buchanan and Claire Trevor. 87 min.
02-2903 *$14.99*

Abilene Town (1946)
Conflict between cattlemen and the ever-increasing numbers of settlers threatens to tear Abilene apart, and only marshal Randolph Scott can keep the peace. Top-notch frontier drama also stars Rhonda Fleming, Ann Dvorak, Edgar Buchanan. 89 min.
08-8059 *$14.99*

Coroner Creek (1948)
After an Indian attack on a stagecoach results in a huge payroll robbery and his fiancée's death, gunfighter Randolph Scott sets out on a bitter search for the villain who engineered the raid. Powerful western drama, highlighted by a bruising brawl between Scott and bad guy Forrest Tucker, also stars George Macready, Edgar Buchanan. 90 min.
02-2987 *$19.99*

Man In The Saddle (1951)
Unusual Western tale looks at jealousy and adultery in a sagebrush saga framework. Randolph Scott is the cowpoke caught between two women and a ruthless rancher who wants him done in. Joan Leslie, Ellen Drew and Alexander Knox co-star.
02-2732 *$14.99*

Santa Fe (1951)
After the Civil War ends, Confederate soldier Randolph Scott and his three brothers seek their fortunes in the West, but when Scott gets a job with the Santa Fe railroad and his siblings fall in with crooks planning a train heist, a showdown is unavoidable. Top-notch actioner also stars Janis Carter, Roy Roberts, Jerome Courtland, Jock Mahoney.
02-2735 *$14.99*

Hangman's Knot (1952)
Randolph Scott leads a Confederate regiment on a raid of Yankee goods in Nevada. Little does he know that the Civil War is over, and now he and his men have to face prosecution. Donna Reed and a young Lee Marvin also star in this knockout adventure. 81 min.
10-2270 *$14.99*

The Stranger Wore A Gun (1953)
Randolph Scott heads to Arizona after a stint with Quantrill's Raiders during the Civil War and is enlisted by another former Raider who once saved his life and now hijacks stagecoach gold shipments. Will Scott join in the scheme or try to bring his friend to justice? Claire Trevor, George Macready, Ernest Borgnine and Lee Marvin also star. 83 min.
02-2251 *$19.99*

Ten Wanted Men (1955)
Randolph Scott stars in this Technicolor ballad of the range as a powerful Arizona rancher whose desire to keep the peace by force of law is challenged by a gun-loving landowner. With Richard Boone and Jocelyn Brando. 80 min.
02-1950 Was $69.99 *$14.99*

A Lawless Street (1955)
Lawman Randolph Scott must choose between his dedication to his job of cleaning up the Colorado Territory and the love of wife Angela Lansbury in this Western drama. With Jean Parker, Warner Anderson. 78 min.
02-2358 *$19.99*

Rage At Dawn (1955)
When an outlaw gang holes up in a remote mountain range, only Randolph Scott can get them out in this Technicolor Western thriller. Edgar Buchanan, Forrest Tucker also star. 87 min.
10-1079 Was $19.99 *$14.99*

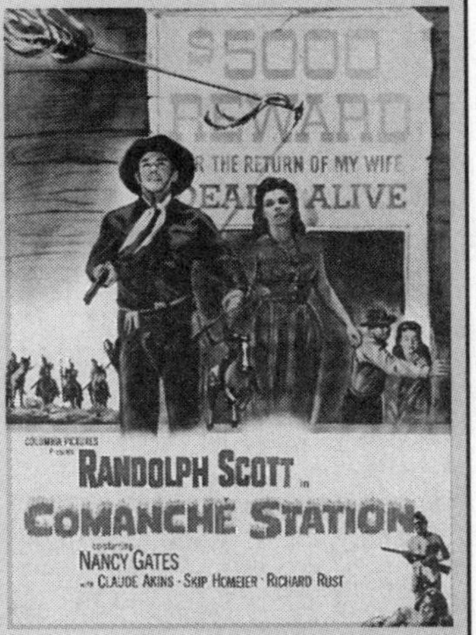
$5000
REWARD
FOR THE RETURN OF MY WIFE
ALIVE
RANDOLPH SCOTT
COMANCHE STATION
NANCY GATES
CLAUDE AKINS · SKIP HOMEIER · RICHARD RUST

Comanche Station (1960)
After spending 10 years searching for his wife, who was kidnapped by Indians, cowboy Randolph Scott rescues a settler's wife who has been captured by the Comanches. On the way home, the pair encounter a trio of outlaws planning to kill Scott and return the woman to her husband for the reward money. With Claude Akins, Nancy Gates; Budd Boetticher ("The Tall T") directs. 73 min.
02-2906 *$14.99*

Please see our index for these other Randolph Scott titles: *Captain Kidd • Follow The Fleet • Go West, Young Man • Gung Ho! • Jesse James • Murders In The Zoo • Pittsburgh • Rebecca Of Sunnybrook Farm • Ride The High Country • She • The Spoilers • Supernatural • Susannah Of The Mounties • To The Shores Of Tripoli • Virginia City*

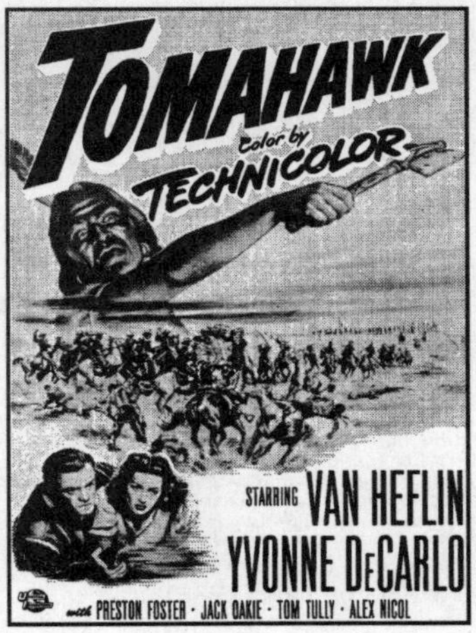
TOMAHAWK
Color by
TECHNICOLOR
STARRING VAN HEFLIN
YVONNE DeCARLO
with PRESTON FOSTER · JACK OAKIE · TOM TULLY · ALEX NICOL

Tomahawk (1951)
Based in part on a true incident, this compelling frontier drama stars Van Heflin as scout Jim Bridger, who seeks to peacefully settle a conflict in the Dakota Territory between the Sioux nation and a sadistic Cavalry officer who wants to wipe them out. Yvonne De Carlo, Alex Nicol, Preston Foster, Susan Cabot and a young Rock Hudson star. 82 min.
07-2635 □*$14.99*

Surrender (1950)
Underrated sagebrusher with Vera Ralston as a wanted woman in a border town near Mexico who marries a respected newspaperman to get out of trouble. When Ralston's real husband appears in town, she kills him, but fingers point to the new spouse and his best friend, a gambling entrepreneur, as suspects. John Carroll, Walter Brennan and William Ching co-star. 90 min.
09-5130 *$19.99*

The Missouri Traveler (1958)
Heartwarming frontier drama stars Brandon de Wilde ("Shane") as a 15-year-old runaway orphan who settles in a rural town and tries to support himself as a farmer. Lee Marvin offers fine support as a rancher who teaches de Wilde tough lessons about growing up. With Gary Merrill, Paul Ford. 103 min.
10-1302 Was $19.99 *$14.99*

Kentucky Rifle (1955)
A wagon train heading west leaves a group of people behind in Indian territory. The desperate group attempts to make their way back toward civilization, but when it's learned that their wagon has rifles on it, they face even greater danger. Chill Wills, Lance Fuller, Cathy Downs, Sterling Holloway and Jeanne Cagney star. 80 min.
10-9439 *$14.99*

Kangaroo (1952)
Australian western about two ruthless criminals who, after botching a robbery attempt, decide to cheat a cattle rancher out of his fortune. They convince him that one of them is his long-lost son, but to prove it, they have to go on a cattle drive with him and his daughter, who has fallen in love with one of the outlaws. Richard Boone, Maureen O'Hara, Finlay Currie and Peter Lawford star. 84 min.
10-9831 *$19.99*

The Buckskin Lady (1957)
Patricia Medina plays the lead character, a gambling gal who uses her earnings to support her father. When a new physician arrives in town, Medina falls for him, causing a problem with her current guy pal, a gunfighter. Richard Denning, Gerald Mohr and Henry Hull also star. 65 min.
10-9845 *$14.99*

Savage Wilderness (1955)
After having his furs stolen by the Indians, a fur trapper (Victor Mature) joins his two partners as a scout at a cavalry fort overseen by a demented colonel (Robert Preston). After the colonel plans to send his troops on a mission against hostile Indians, the trapper attempts to stop him. With Guy Madison, Anne Bancroft; Anthony Mann directs. AKA: "The Last Frontier." 98 min.
02-2595 *$14.99*

The Law And Jake Wade (1958)
Intense Western drama starring Robert Taylor as a former bank robber who now works as a lawman in a New Mexico town. When he discovers that his old partner (Richard Widmark) is about to be hung, he stops the execution, but soon the marshal's ex-compadre seeks loot stolen years earlier. Henry Silva, Patricia Owens, DeForest Kelley co-star; John Sturges ("The Magnificent Seven") directs. 86 min.
12-2504 *$19.99*

The Ride Back (1957)
William Conrad is a sheriff who must escort Anthony Quinn from Mexico to Texas to stand trial for murder. As the two make their way across a desert inhabited by hostile Indians, they encounter a young girl who survived an Apache attack. When Conrad is injured by the Indians, Quinn must decide whether to escape or help the lawman and the child. Lita Milan, George Trevino also star. 79 min.
12-3338 *$14.99*

The Big Trail (1930)
Sprawling frontier epic of the first wagon trail to head West across the Oregon Trail, led by wilderness scout John Wayne (his first starring role). Stunning outdoor photography and a thrilling Indian battle are highlights; with Tyrone Power, Sr., Ward Bond, Marguerite Churchill. Raoul Walsh directs. 110 min.
04-1038 Was $19.99 ◻$14.99

Range Feud (1931)
The feud is between two ranch families, but it doesn't stop John Wayne and Susan Fleming from falling in love real "Romeo and Juliet"-like. When Fleming's dad is found murdered, though, Wayne is accused of the crime, and it's up to sheriff Buck Jones to solve the case and prevent a "necktie party." 58 min.
02-2357 *$14.99*

Range Feud (1931)/ Two Fisted Law (1932)
The Duke does double duty in this dynamite duet of early John Wayne Westerns. First, Wayne is a rancher's son accused of murder, and only sheriff Buck Jones can save him from a "necktie party." After that, rancher Tim McCoy rounds up a posse (including Wayne as a cowpoke named "Duke"!) to bring a crooked cattleman to justice. 112 min. total.
02-2121 Double Feature *$19.99*

Two-Fisted Law (1932)
Rancher Tim McCoy needs both fists when he applies some bare-knuckle justice to the land-grabbing rannie trying to cheat him out of his spread and his gal. John Wayne lends McCoy support (playing a character named "Duke"!); with Alice Day, Walter Brennan. 58 min.
02-2356 *$14.99*

Texas Cyclone (1932)
Tim McCoy stars as a wandering cowpoke who rides into a lawless Arizona town and finds everyone thinks he's a heroic rancher who vanished years earlier. Great Western drama features a young John Wayne as a two-fisted ranchhand; with Shirley Grey, Walter Brennan. 58 min.
02-2355 *$14.99*

The Shadow Of The Eagle (Feature Version) (1932)
Daredevil circus pilot John Wayne helps unmask "The Eagle," a mysterious criminal genius who has been skywriting threatening messages to a group of businessmen, in this feature-length adventure culled from one of Wayne's first serial starring roles. With Dorothy Gulliver, Edward Hearne. 180 min.
10-1636 *$19.99*

The Big Stampede (1932)
Thrilling sagebrusher starring John Wayne as a deputy sheriff who searches for a nasty cattle rustler responsible for the death of a town's lawman. Noah Beery, Mae Madison also star. 54 min.
12-2898 *$19.99*

Haunted Gold (1932)
Warner Bros. welcomed John Wayne to the studio with this exciting sagebrush saga in which he teams with heroine Sheila Terry to stop a group of outlaws searching for gold. Harry Wood co-stars. 54 min.
12-2899 *$19.99*

Ride Him, Cowboy (1932)
John Wayne saves a horse from being executed for murder, then makes friends with the animal in order to find the real killer. There's lots of action and equine thrills in this top-notch oater. With Ruth Hall and Otis Harlan. 55 min.
12-2901 *$19.99*

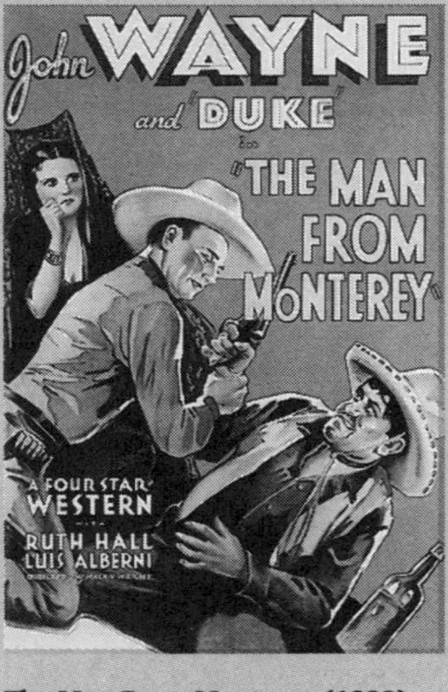

The Man From Monterey (1933)
U.S. officer John Wayne heads to the title California town to help the locals protect their Spanish land grant property from a nefarious businessman looking to swindle them out of their homes. The Duke forswears gunplay for swords in this Spanish-flavored frontier actioner. Ruth Hall co-stars. 57 min.
12-2900 *$19.99*

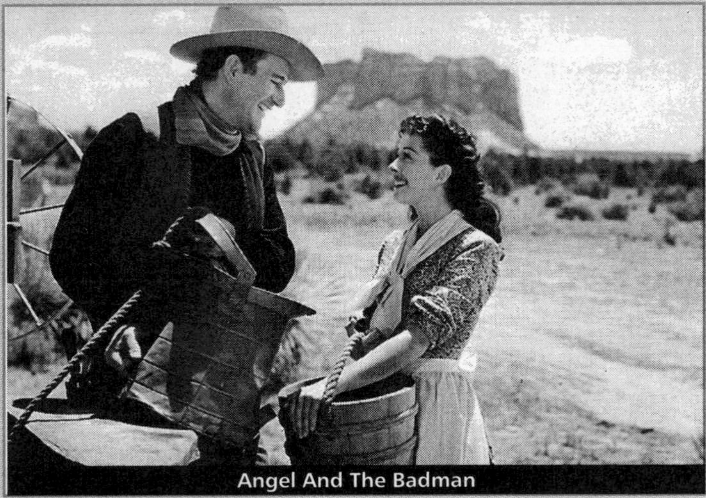
Angel And The Badman

John Wayne

Riders Of Destiny (1933)
John Wayne is undercover special agent Singin' Sandy Saunders (although his screen crooning was dubbed by Smith Ballew), out to leave the crooks cheating farmers out of their water high and dry. With "Gabby" Hayes, Forrest Taylor. 50 min.
01-5124 *$14.99*

His Private Secretary (1933)
Early John Wayne effort casts the Duke as a playboy who, against his rich father's wishes, loves carousing with the ladies. Then, he meets a minister's daughter and changes his lifestyle. Evalyn Knapp, Alec B. Francis star. 68 min.
10-8142 Was $19.99 *$14.99*

Somewhere In Sonora (1933)
John Wayne is called on by a friend to find his son, who has been kidnapped and taken to Sonora by a group of nasty nogoodnicks. Shirley Palmer and Paul Fix co-star. 57 min.
12-2902 *$19.99*

The Telegraph Trail (1933)
History and western action mesh as government security man John Wayne oversees the supply train carrying equipment to build the first telegraph lines in the West. Otis Harlan and Yakima Canutt also star. 54 min.
12-2903 *$19.99*

Sagebrush Trail (1933)
Convicted of a murder he didn't commit, cowpoke John Wayne escapes and hides out with a gang of real outlaws while looking for the true killer. Early oater fun also stars stunt master Yakima Canutt, Wally Wales. 54 min.
45-5508 *$14.99*

The Man From Utah (1934)
This time "Duke" Wayne is an undercover special agent for the local marshal who's trying to break up a crooked rodeo racket. 54 min.
01-5119 *$14.99*

The Man From Utah (Color Version)
The man. The state. The color. John Wayne stars.
15-1198 *$19.99*

Randy Rides Alone (1934)
When a pretty young ranch girl is beset by a gang of swindlers, it's up to John Wayne and Gabby Hayes to set things right in this action-packed early Western. 53 min.
01-5122 *$14.99*

The Star Packer (1934)
When U.S. marshal John Wayne rides into the town of Little Rock, which has fallen victim to a gang of nasties headed by a mysterious figure known as "The Shadow," it's up to Wayne and Indian sidekick Yakima Canutt to bring the bad guys into the light of day. With George "Gabby" Hayes, Verna Hillie. 60 min.
01-5125 *$14.99*

The Star Packer (Color Version)
Big John Wayne packs a star—and a punch or two—in a colorized edition of this frontier actioner.
15-1194 *$19.99*

Blue Steel (1934)
Outlaws wreak havoc in a town. But John Wayne saves the day, battling the bad guys and rescuing Eleanor Hunt. Gabby Hayes and Yakima Canutt also star. 59 min.
10-1097 *$14.99*

Blue Steel (Color Version)
The steel is blue, and everything else is pretty natural-looking, too, as this John Wayne oater receives a computerized paint job.
15-1200 *$19.99*

The Lucky Texan (1934)
John Wayne and George "Gabby" Hayes sure think it's their lucky day when they strike gold in their mine, but Gabby's luck turns sour when some claim-jumpers frame him for murder. Features a thrilling horseback-railroad handcar chase scene. With Yakima Canutt, Barbara Sheldon. 55 min.
10-4016 *$14.99*

The Trail Beyond (1934)
It's a dangerous trail that young John Wayne follows up through the Canadian wilderness, and one that leads him to a valuable gold mine, in this frontier tale that also stars Noah Beerys Sr. and Jr. in their first film together. 54 min.
45-5509 *$14.99*

The Trail Beyond (Color Version)
The trail, and the Duke, take on new hues in this colorized adventure.
15-1196 *$19.99*

West Of The Divide (1934)
Big John Wayne bravely masquerades as a wanted killer in order to expose the gang of blackhats who murdered his father in this early "B" rouser. 60 min.
45-5510 *$14.99*

'Neath The Arizona Skies (1934)
When a little Indian girl who is the heiress to some oil-rich property is kidnapped, only hero John Wayne can rescue her and save her father from being murdered. George "Gabby" Hayes also stars. 54 min.
63-5014 *$14.99*

'Neath The Arizona Skies (Color Version)
The Arizona skies sure are colorful in this John Wayne western.
15-1208 *$19.99*

The Desert Trail (1935)
Rodeo star John Wayne rides hard to clear himself and gambling buddy Eddy Chandler after the pair are accused of holding up a bank. With Mary Korman, Paul Fix, Carmen LaRoux. 54 min.
01-5117 *$14.99*

The Desert Trail (Color Version)
It's a long, hot tail for John Wayne to ride, but at least now he has color to make it interesting.
15-1193 *$12.99*

Paradise Canyon (1935)
Early John Wayne western has the Duke going undercover with a traveling medicine show in order to flush out a counterfeiting ring. 55 min.
01-5120 Was $19.99 *$14.99*

Paradise Canyon (Color Version)
It must be paradise! Look at all those vibrant hues in this color version of John Wayne's early frontier drama.
15-1195 *$19.99*

The Lawless Frontier (1935)
John Wayne saddles up to bring the rustlers responsible for his parents' murder in this early oater. With Sheila Terry, George "Gabby" Hayes. 72 min.
10-1077 *$14.99*

The Lawless Frontier (Color Version)
Lawless it may be, but thanks to modern science, that frontier that John Wayne tames need never be colorless again!
15-1226 *$12.99*

Rainbow Valley (1935)
You remember the Rainbow Valley? That's where the townspeople want to build a railroad, but keep finding their plans go awry. Why? Government agent John Wayne wants to find out, too, so he goes undercover. Lucille Brown and Buffalo Bill, Jr. also star. 52 min.
10-8039 Was $19.99 *$14.99*

Texas Terror (1935)
John Wayne is a Texas sheriff who turns in his badge after apparently shooting and killing his best friend while tracking outlaws. With Gabby Hayes, Yakima Canutt. 51 min.
62-1125 *$12.99*

Lawless Range (1935)
Lawman John Wayne is sent out to an isolated valley to aid settlers harassed by desperadoes, but is captured and must escape before it's too late. 53 min.
63-5015 *$12.99*

The Dawn Rider (1935)
Early John Wayne Western vehicle with the Duke as a young man out to catch the bank robbers who killed his father. With Marion Burns. 53 min.
63-5017 *$14.99*

The Dawn Rider (Color Version)
And what a vibrant and colorful dawn it is that John Wayne rides out of, thanks to the wonders of late 20th-century computers.
15-1228 *$12.99*

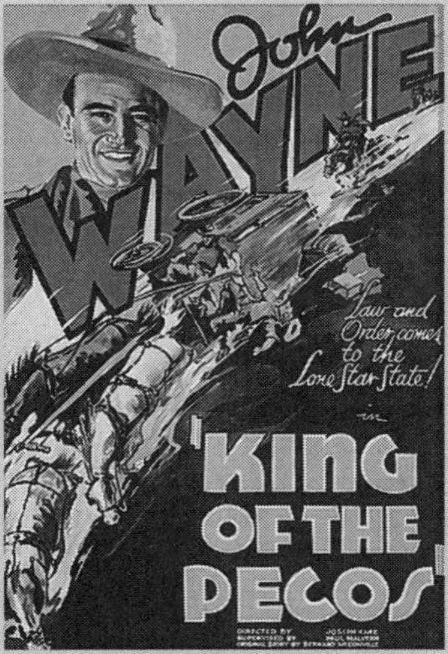

King Of The Pecos (1936)
Don't mess with the Duke...especially when he's out for revenge! John Wayne is a not-so-naive law student whose parents were killed by a vicious cattle thief and who's ready to lay down the law. With Muriel Evans, Tex Palmer, Cy Kendall. 56 min.
63-1469 *$14.99*

Westward Ho (1936)
Early John Wayne oater with the Duke as one of the Singing Riders (actually, he lip-syncs a tune), out to avenge his parents' murder. Little does he know the gang involved includes his own brother! Sheila Manners, Yakima Canutt co-star. 61 min.
63-1470 *$12.99*

The Lawless Nineties (1936)
The 1890s, that is. When crime and corruption run rampant in old Wyoming, the government sends in federal agent John Wayne to reel in the crooked politicos and restore order. Thrilling frontier drama also stars Ann Rutherford, Harry Woods, and a beardless Gabby Hayes. 56 min.
63-1471 *$12.99*

Winds Of The Wasteland (1936)
John Wayne and partner Lane Chandler leave villain Yakima Canutt in a trail of dust in a race by stagecoach to Sacramento to win a $25,000 government mail contract. The final entry in the first series of westerns the Duke made for RKO co-stars Phyllis Fraser, Douglas Cosgrove. 54 min.
63-5029 Was $19.99 *$14.99*

Winds Of The Wasteland (Color Version)
"The colors of the wind" have been put to good use in this computer-colorized rendition of Wayne's sagebrush saga.
15-1227 *$12.99*

Helltown (1937)
One of the Duke's best "B" vehicles finds John Wayne forming a fast friendship with Johnny Mack Brown after he rescues Brown's livestock. Johnny Mack returns the favor when Wayne gets in over his head at the card table. Marsha Hunt, Monte Blue, Alan Ladd co-star. AKA: "Born to the West." 50 min.
01-5088 Was $19.99 *$14.99*

Overland Stage Raiders (1938)
Actually, the "stage" the Three Mesquiteers are called on to protect is a Greyhound bus carrying gold in its hold. Big John Wayne heads up a Mesquiteer crew that travels on the ground and in the air to best the black hats. With Ray Corrigan, Max Terhune, and silent star Louise Brooks in her last film. 54 min.
63-1495 **$12.99**

Pals Of The Saddle (1938)
John Wayne joined up with Ray "Crash" Corrigan and Max "Alibi" Terhune as the Three Mesquiteers for the first time in this action-filled oater. A chemical-smuggling ring puts the trio to the test, especially when a crooked judge frames Wayne for murder. With Josef Forte, Doreen McKay. 54 min.
63-1496 **$12.99**

Santa Fe Stampede (1938)
A prospector finds gold and invites his old pals the Three Mesquiteers (John Wayne, Ray Corrigan, Max Terhune) to share in his good fortune. When they arrive, though, their friend is found dead and Wayne is charged with murder (again)! William Farnum, June Martel co-star. 55 min.
63-1497 **$12.99**

Frontier Horizon (1939)
John Wayne makes his "Three Mesquiteers" swan song here, joining with Raymond Hatton and Ray Corrigan to help settlers whose land is going to be flooded by crooked land speculators. Co-stars Jennifer Jones (Phyllis Isley here) as the damsel in distress. AKA: "New Frontier." 55 min.
63-5016 Was $19.99 **$14.99**

Stagecoach (1939)
John Ford's landmark Western tale, following the dramatic journey of a stagecoach and its drivers and passengers across the plains, features John Wayne in a star-making role as the outlaw Ringo Kid. The marvelous cast includes Claire Trevor, Andy Devine, John Carradine, George Bancroft and Best Supporting Actor Oscar-winner Thomas Mitchell. 96 min.
19-1053 Was $19.99 **❑$14.99**

Seven Sinners (1940)
Marlene Dietrich is the sexy singer named Bijou whose stint at the Seven Sinners Cafe in an exotic South Seas island is marked by intrigue, romance, visits from past lovers and the impossible love of John Wayne, a handsome Navy lieutenant whose first interest is the sea. Broderick Crawford, Mischa Auer and Albert Dekker co-star. 87 min.
07-2175 Was $19.99 **❑$14.99**

The Dark Command (1940)
Epic frontier saga, directed by Raoul Walsh and set in pre-Civil War Kansas. Town marshal John Wayne must protect his territory from a band of pro-South vigilantes. With Walter Pidgeon, Claire Trevor, Roy Rogers, "Gabby" Hayes. 100 min.
63-1054 Was $19.99 **$14.99**

The Dark Command (Color Version)
Dark, yes, but at least the Duke will be able to make out where the now-colorful vigilantes are hiding in this version.
63-1525 **$14.99**

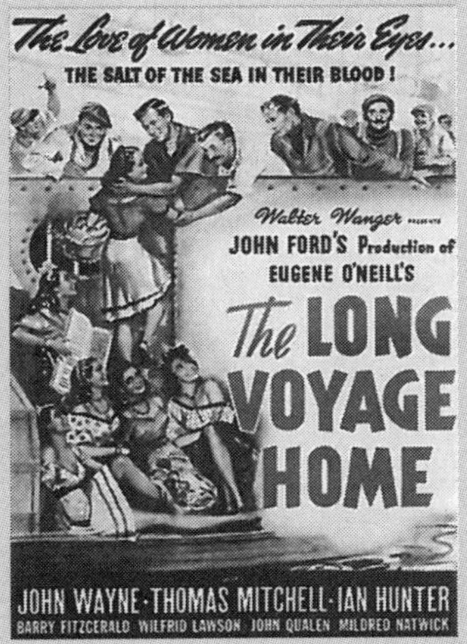

The Love of Women in Their Eyes...
THE SALT OF THE SEA IN THEIR BLOOD!
Walter Wanger presents
JOHN FORD'S Production of
EUGENE O'NEILL'S
The LONG VOYAGE HOME
JOHN WAYNE · THOMAS MITCHELL · IAN HUNTER
BARRY FITZGERALD WILFRID LAWSON JOHN QUALEN MILDRED NATWICK

The Long Voyage Home (1940)
Classic maritime drama based on a play by Eugene O'Neill stars John Wayne, Thomas Mitchell and Barry Fitzgerald as seamen who share a longing for the sea mixed with a desire for home. Directed by John Ford. 105 min.
19-1058 Was $19.99 **$14.99**

Three Faces West (1940)
The residents of a weather-ravaged Dust Bowl community look to move the whole town to fertile new ground in Oregon, and John Wayne is the man to lead them in this contemporary frontier drama that also stars Sigrid Gurie as the daughter of Austrian emigrant doctor Charles Coburn who falls for Wayne. 79 min.
63-1045 **$14.99**

Lady From Louisiana (1941)
John Wayne romances, puts up his dukes and carouses around in this one, where he's involved in a gambling controversy. Ona Munson, Ray Middleton. 82 min.
63-1043 **$14.99**

The Shepherd Of The Hills (1941)
John Wayne excels in this oft-filmed story, playing a young Ozark Mountain moonshiner who seeks vengeance on his father for abandoning him and his mother years earlier. When a kindly old man moves to the area, Wayne befriends him, but soon learns he is, in fact, his father, and attempts to even the score. Betty Field, Harry Carey, James Barton also star. 97 min.
07-2305 Was $19.99 **$14.99**

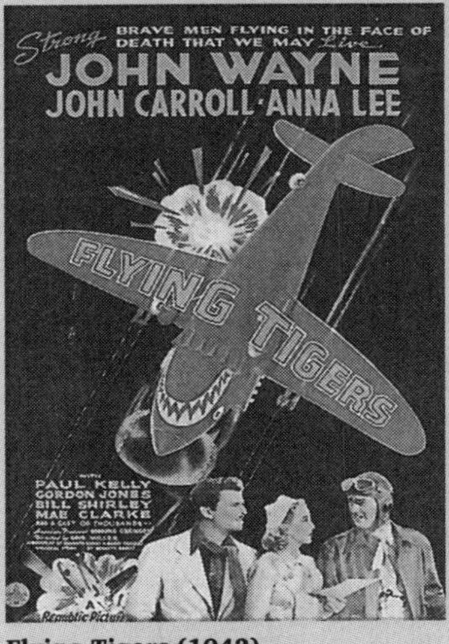

Strong
BRAVE MEN FLYING IN THE FACE OF DEATH THAT WE MAY Live
JOHN WAYNE
JOHN CARROLL · ANNA LEE
FLYING TIGERS
PAUL KELLY
GORDON JONES
BILL SHIRLEY
MAE CLARKE

Flying Tigers (1942)
The heroic true exploits of the "Flying Tigers"—the American Volunteer Group of pilots who flew against Japanese forces for China in the days before Pearl Harbor—inspired this patriotic drama that was star John Wayne's first entry in the war genre. The exciting dogfight scenes are a highlight; with Paul Kelly, John Carroll, Anna Lee. 100 min.
63-1057 Was $19.99 **$14.99**

Flying Tigers (Color Version)
John Wayne really soars when the colors of the spectrum shine.
63-1384 **$14.99**

The Spoilers (1942)
Yukon gold-mining is the subject of this John Wayne classic that has the Duke protecting his land and his gold. Features an amazing fight scene between Wayne and Randolph Scott. Marlene Dietrich co-stars. 87 min.
07-1177 **$14.99**

Reap The Wild Wind (1942)
Lavish Cecil B. DeMille sea epic, set in the 1840s Florida Keys, with John Wayne as a skipper accused of deliberately wrecking his ship. Paulette Goddard is the salvage boat owner who falls for him, and Ray Milland is the lawyer who comes between them. Exciting underwater scenes include a tussle between the Duke and a giant squid; with Raymond Massey, Susan Hayward. 124 min.
07-1601 Was $29.99 **$14.99**

Pittsburgh (1942)
John Wayne, Marlene Dietrich and Randolph Scott reunite following the success of "The Spoilers" for this rugged drama about a pair of coal miners whose friendship is ruined when they fall in love with the same woman and take different paths in the coal and steel industry. Frank Craven, Louise Allbritton and Shemp Howard also star. 92 min.
07-1988 **$14.99**

Reunion In France (1942)
Glossy romantic drama set against the turbulence of WWII France, as French businesswoman Joan Crawford tries to help downed American RAF pilot John Wayne escape from the Nazis. With Philip Dorn, John Carradine; look for an uncredited Ava Gardner. 104 min.
12-1991 **$19.99**

Wheel Of Fortune (1942)
John Wayne is a small-town lawyer involved in an investigation of a mysterious death. Seems a crooked politician may have something to do with it! Frances Dee. AKA: "A Man Betrayed." 83 min.
63-1044 **$14.99**

Lady For A Night (1942)
Hot tempers and murder mix as John Wayne and Joan Blondell become involved with a Southern aristocratic family and a gambling boat. 87 min.
63-1046 **$14.99**

In Old California (1942)
Who but John Wayne could get away with playing a two-fisted frontier pharmacist? The Duke must trade his pestle for a pistol, though, when he helps some settlers overcome the corrupt gunman who controls their lives. Albert Dekker, Binnie Barnes, Edgar Kennedy also star. 88 min.
63-1058 **$14.99**

In Old California (Color Version)
The old Golden State never looked as golden as it does in this techno-tinted edition of the John Wayne drama.
63-1528 **$14.99**

War Of The Wildcats (1943)
Romance, action and revenge set in oil-rich Oklahoma. John Wayne gets involved in melees centered around oil-drilling. Martha Scott, Albert Dekker. 102 min.
63-1020 **$14.99**

A Lady Takes A Chance (1943)
John Wayne is a rough and tumble rodeo star and Jean Arthur the big city working girl he gets involved with in this funny romantic comedy. Co-stars Phil Silvers, Charles Winninger. 86 min.
15-1051 **$14.99**

Tall In The Saddle (1944)
Offbeat John Wayne western has the Duke playing a tough, woman-hating cowboy who reluctantly goes to work for an aging spinster and her attractive niece on their ranch. With Ella Raines, "Gabby" Hayes. 87 min.
05-1028 Was $19.99 **$14.99**

The Fighting Seabees (1944)
Sprawling, action-packed saga with John Wayne as the head of a construction company working at building military sites for the Navy in the Pacific during World War II. After suffering the loss of many men after a Japanese attack, Wayne heads to Washington and helps establish the "C.B.s" (Construction Battalions), units of armed builders. With Susan Hayward, Dennis O'Keefe, William Frawley. 100 min.
63-1019 **❑$14.99**

The Fighting Seabees (Color Version)
Now this rousing WWII drama with the one and only Duke can be seen with unbelievable computer-created colors.
63-1526 **$14.99**

They Were Expendable (1945)
But this great war film from John Ford is not. John Wayne and Robert Montgomery head up a squad of hard-edged PT boat crews doing battle in the Pacific in World War II. With Ward Bond, Donna Reed. 135 min.
12-1581 **$19.99**

Dakota (1945)
Settlers John Wayne and Vera Hruba Ralston come to the wild Dakota Territory with dreams of a new life, but first the Duke has to deal with some rapscallions who are buying up farmland that a planned railroad will run through. With Ward Bond, Walter Brennan, Mike Mazurki. 82 min.
63-1053 Was $19.99 **$14.99**

Flame Of The Barbary Coast (1945)
Brawling story of a Montana cowpoke who falls for a beautiful dance hall girl in old San Francisco and runs afoul of a card shark. John Wayne, Ann Dvorak, Joseph Schildkraut star. 91 min.
63-1056 **$14.99**

Flame Of The Barbary Coast (Color Version)
The flame burns brightly and colorfully, as John Wayne and Ann Dvorak light up the streets of old Frisco.
63-1527 **$19.99**

Desert Command (1946)
This is the featurized version of the 1933 serial "The Three Musketeers," in which a young John Wayne leads his Foreign Legion men against the evil El Shaitan and his terrifying troops. Raymond Hatton, Noah Beery, Jr. also star.
10-6014 **$19.99**

Angel And The Badman (1947)
In an offbeat Western drama that predated "Witness," John Wayne plays a hardened gunslinger who is tamed by strong-willed Quaker girl Gail Russell, but cannot escape his past. With Bruce Cabot, Harry Carey, Jr. 100 min.
63-1506 Was $19.99 **❑$14.99**

Angel And The Badman (Color Version)
The Duke's unconventional Western romance is now available in a computer-colorized version, too.
63-1519 **$19.99**

Red River (1948)
Psychologically complex and visually stunning western from Howard Hawks showcases John Wayne as a ruthless rancher moving a huge herd of cattle down the Chisholm Trail to Abilene, Texas. Causing friction is Montgomery Clift, Wayne's adopted son, who, rebelling against Wayne, wants to lead the drive his own way. Joanne Dru, Walter Brennan, John Ireland also star. Uncut 133 min. version.
12-1990 Was $19.99 **❑$14.99**

The Three Godfathers (1948)
One of the best-loved John Ford/John Wayne Westerns was this "three outlaws and a baby" drama, as fugitives Wayne, Pedro Armendariz and Harry Carey, Jr. promise a dying woman that they will care for her newborn child and begin a harrowing trek across the desert. With Ward Bond, Mildred Natwick. 103 min.
12-1993 **$19.99**

Fort Apache (1948)
John Ford's classic frontier epic about an isolated Cavalry outpost and the men and women who live there stars Henry Fonda as the fort's stubborn new commander, whose rigorous stance puts him at odds with his men and leads to war with the Apache, and John Wayne as his veteran second-in-command. With Shirley Temple, John Agar and Ward Bond. Also includes the original theatrical trailer. 127 min.
18-7653 **$19.99**

Wake Of The Red Witch (1948)
There's adventure, danger and romance in the South Pacific as sea captain John Wayne and shipping magnate Luther Adler begin a bitter rivalry that has them fighting for a fortune in pearls guarded by a deadly octopus, as well as the hand of colonial governor's daughter Gail Russell. With Gig Young, Paul Fix. 106 min.
63-1021 Was $19.99 **❑$14.99**

Wake Of The Red Witch (Color Version)
Red indeed is the boat, and blue the ocean, as John Wayne's seafaring saga gets a fresh coat of computer-ized color.
63-1383 **$14.99**

She Wore A Yellow Ribbon (1949)
Memorable picture about duty, country, soldiering and honor among Cavalry men. Vivid portrayal by Wayne and classic direction by John Ford. With Joanne Dru, Ben Johnson. 103 min.
05-1324 **$14.99**

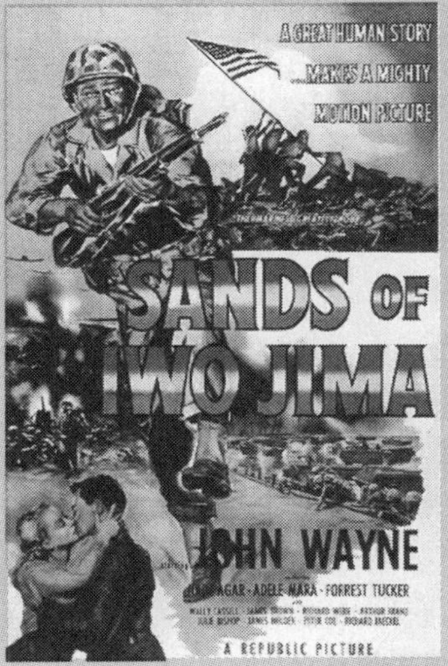

A GREAT HUMAN STORY
...MAKES A MIGHTY
MOTION PICTURE
SANDS OF IWO JIMA
JOHN WAYNE
AGAR · ADELE MARA · FORREST TUCKER
A REPUBLIC PICTURE

Sands Of Iwo Jima (1949)
One of the all-time great war movies, a moving re-creation of the American assault on Japan in the last days of World War II. John Wayne earned an Oscar nomination for his portrayal of a hard-nosed Marine sergeant; John Agar, Forrest Tucker co-star. Superb battle scenes were filmed at the actual locations. Special anniversary package includes a documentary on the making of the film, plus reproductions of the theatrical poster and lobby card. 110 min.
63-1014 **$14.99**

Sands Of Iwo Jima (Color Version)
The Duke makes sure that the red, white and blue flies clearly in this computer-hued rendition of the classic WWII actioner.
63-1281 **$14.99**

Rio Grande (1950)
The concluding chapter to director John Ford's "Cavalry trilogy" that also included "Fort Apache" and "She Wore a Yellow Ribbon" stars John Wayne as the hardened commander of a remote Army outpost along the Mexican border faced with two crises: marauding bands of Apaches from across the river and the arrival of estranged wife Maureen O'Hara and his son, new recruit Claude Jarman, Jr. With Victor McLaglen, Chill Wills. 105 min.
63-1048 Was $19.99 **$14.99**

Rio Grande (Color Version)
One of John Ford's "grande"-est epics with John Wayne, Maureen O'Hara and, now, glorious color.
63-1381 **$14.99**

The Fighting Kentuckian (Color Version) (1949)
After helping Andy Jackson take care of the British at the Battle of New Orleans, Kentucky frontiersman John Wayne and sidekick Oliver Hardy head back home by of Alabama, where the Duke comes to the aid of French-born settlers against landgrabbers. With Vera Ralston, Hugo Haas. 100 min.
63-1382 **$14.99**

Operation Pacific (1951)
World War II drama stars John Wayne as a Navy man caught up in romantic problems with his former wife, nurse Patricia Neal, while trying to take over command of a submarine after captain Ward Bond is hurt. Philip Carey, Scott Forbes co-star. 111 min.
19-1954 Was $19.99 **$14.99**

Big Jim McLain (1952)
Big John Wayne stars as Big Jim, top federal agent who says "aloha" (hello) to Hawaii and "aloha" (goodbye) to the Communist spy ring he puts out of business. Two-fisted Cold War espionage thriller also stars James Arness, Nancy Olson. 90 min.
19-1832 Was $19.99 **❑$14.99**

The Quiet Man (1952)
Director John Ford's Oscar-winning rouser stars John Wayne as an American-raised boxer who goes to Ireland to live in the village where he was born. There he falls for feisty Maureen O'Hara and engages town ruffian Victor McLaglen in a classic screen brawl. With Barry Fitzgerald, Mildred Natwick. 129 min.
63-1505 Was $19.99 **$14.99**

Trouble Along The Way (1953)
In this winning comedy-drama, John Wayne plays a trouble-making football coach who is hired by a New York Catholic college to get their terrible team into shape. The school is having problems meeting their bills, and Wayne must prep the team for a big gridiron match. Donna Reed, Charles Coburn, Tom Tully co-star. 110 min.
19-1944 Was $19.99 *$14.99*

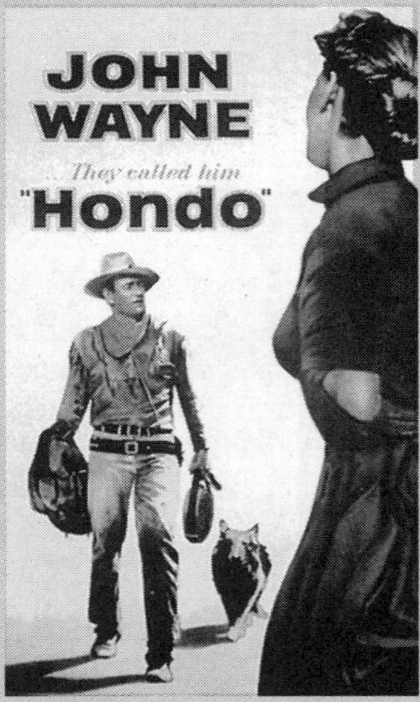

Hondo (1953)
Cavalry rider John Wayne comes to the aid of rancher Geraldine Page and her son when they're trapped in the middle of Apache raids on the territory in this intelligent, moody frontier drama. With Ward Bond, Leo Gordon, Michael Pate; directed by John Farrow. Not in 3-D. 84 min.
50-6554 *$19.99*

The Sea Chase (1955)
John Wayne is the Hitler-loathing skipper of a decrepit German freighter who faces danger and romance as he tries to steer the ship from Australian waters to Chile during World War II. Lana Turner is the spy who loves him and Tab Hunter, James Arness and Paul Fix add able support. 117 min.
19-1780 Was $19.99 *$14.99*

Blood Alley (1955)
John Wayne is at his two-fisted best as a seafaring tough guy who leads a group of Red Chinese villagers through the Straits of Formosa to freedom in Hong Kong. William Wellman directed; with Lauren Bacall, Paul Fix and Anita Ekberg. 115 min.
19-1781 Was $19.99 *$14.99*

The Searchers (Special Edition) (1956)
One of the most complex and acclaimed Westerns ever made, director John Ford's moody tale stars John Wayne as a Civil War veteran whose settler brother's family is attacked by the Comanche. Joined by a half-breed youth raised by the family, Wayne begins an all-consuming quest to find his surviving niece, whom the Indians abducted. Jeffrey Hunter, Natalie Wood, Ward Bond also star. Special edition includes Nick Redman's documentary "A Turning of the Earth: John Ford, John Wayne and the Searchers," with behind-the-scenes home movies and interviews, plus the original theatrical trailer, a mini-lobby card reprint, and an introduction by Wayne's son, Patrick. 155 min. total.
19-1000 *❑$19.99*

The Searchers (Special Edition) (Letterboxed Version)
Also available in a theatrical, widescreen format.
19-2733 *❑$19.99*

Legend Of The Lost (1957)
Offbeat adventure saga set in the Sahara Desert, with soldier of fortune John Wayne and Rossano Brazzi searching for a fabled treasure and fighting for the attentions of lovely Sophia Loren. 109 min.
12-1989 *$19.99*

Jet Pilot (1957)
A high-flying Cold War drama that producer Howard Hughes worked on for over seven years, trying to update the aircraft seen on the screen. American Air Force colonel John Wayne is charged with looking after defecting Soviet pilot Janet Leigh. The pair fall in love, but Wayne begins to wonder if Leigh is actually a double agent. Directed (at least in part) by Josef von Sternberg. 112 min.
07-1841 Was $19.99 *$14.99*

The Wings Of Eagles (1957)
In one of his least-known but finest film roles, John Wayne is Frank "Spig" Wead, a pioneering aviator who turned to screenwriting after a debilitating injury and served in World War II. John Ford, who collaborated with Wead, directs this sweeping bio-drama/war drama; with Maureen O'Hara, Dan Dailey, and Ward Bond as filmmaker "John Dodge." 110 min.
12-1994 *$19.99*

The Barbarian And The Geisha (1958)
John Huston directed this historical drama set against the 1850s opening of Japan to the West, with John Wayne as an American naval officer whose less than gentle diplomacy puts him at odds with his Japanese hosts. With Sam Jaffe, Eiko Ando. 105 min.
04-1040 *❑$19.99*

Rio Bravo (1959)
Howard Hawks' western classic stars John Wayne as a sheriff whose town is under siege by the army of gunmen brought in by crooked cattle baron John Russell to free his brother, trigger-happy Claude Akins, from Wayne's jail. The Duke's only allies are elderly sidekick Walter Brennan, drunken ex-deputy Dean Martin, and fiery young gunslinger Ricky Nelson. Angie Dickinson, Ward Bond also star. 141 min.
19-1152 *❑$19.99*

The Horse Soldiers (1959)
For his only Civil War feature, director John Ford crafted a stirring true story of a Union cavalry raid into Confederate territory. Colonel John Wayne and doctor William Holden are the antagonistic leads of the mission; Constance Towers, Stan Jones, Hoot Gibson also star. 115 min.
12-1988 Was $19.99 *❑$14.99*

The Alamo (1960)
Rousing battle scenes and some larger-than-life heroes highlight director/star John Wayne's thrilling salute to Texas' battle for independence from Mexico and the fateful last stand at the Alamo. Wayne plays Davy Crockett, with Richard Widmark as Jim Bowie, Laurence Harvey as William Travis, and Richard Boone as Sam Houston. This remastered edition features footage not seen since the film's premiere, plus the original theatrical trailer. 202 min.
12-3267 Was $24.99 *❑$14.99*

North To Alaska (1960)
Lusty, brawling epic of prospectors in Gold Rush Alaska stars John Wayne and Stewart Granger as partners who wind up fighting for the hand of lovely Capucine. Fun-filled adventure film also stars Ernie Kovacs, Fabian. 117 min.
04-3072 Was $19.99 *❑$14.99*

The Comancheros (1961)
A John Wayne action classic, featuring the Duke out to nab a gang of baddies trading guns and booze to the Indians. Stuart Whitman, Lee Marvin co-star. 107 min.
04-1547 Was $19.99 *❑$14.99*

The Man Who Shot Liberty Valance (1962)
John Wayne and Jimmy Stewart share the same love interest (Vera Miles) and both want the same man dead (Lee Marvin). One gets the girl and one gets the bad guy in this classic John Ford Western. 122 min.
06-1000 *❑$14.99*

Hatari! (1962)
It's adventure, African style, as John Wayne heads a group of "big game wranglers" that captures wild animals for shipment to zoos. Red Buttons, Hardy Kruger and Elsa Martinelli also star in director Howard Hawks' rousing film; the memorable Henry Mancini score includes "Baby Elephant Walk." 158 min.
06-1188 *$24.99*

The Longest Day (1962)
Acclaimed as one of Hollywood's greatest epics, producer Darryl F. Zanuck's re-creation of the Allied landing at Normandy on June 6, 1944 follows the grand-scale drama and personal stories of D-Day. International all-star cast includes John Wayne, Henry Fonda, Robert Mitchum, Rod Steiger, Richard Burton, Red Buttons, Sean Connery, Mel Ferrer, Robert Ryan. 179 min.
04-1088 Was $19.99 *$14.99*

The Longest Day (Color Version)
The "D" in D-Day stands for "Deeply Colored" in this computer-tinted version of the all-star WWII drama.
04-2795 *$24.99*

The Longest Day (Letterboxed Version)
Also available in a theatrical, widescreen format.
04-3655 *$19.99*

Donovan's Reef (1963)
John Wayne and Lee Marvin, drinking, brawling and loving. They're on a Pacific island where they are greeted by a beautiful female visitor. Elizabeth Allen, Jack Warden. 109 min.
06-1164 *$14.99*

McLintock! (1963)
Rousing western-comedy starring John Wayne as a feisty cattleman who finds his life suddenly complicated with the arrival of estranged wife Maureen O'Hara. Seeking a divorce and wanting custody of their teenage daughter, she carries on a battle with Wayne that leads to a famous drag-down muddy brawl. Yvonne DeCarlo, Stefanie Powers, Jerry Van Dyke and Jack Kruschen star in this Movies Unlimited favorite. 126 min.
50-7145 *$19.99*

Circus World (1964)
The Big Duke meets the Big Top in this epic drama. John Wayne is the owner of a travelling circus/Wild West show at the turn of the century who takes his troupe on a European tour fraught with hazards. Spectacular fire climaxes the action; with Claudia Cardinale, Rita Hayworth. 135 min.
64-1187 *$29.99*

The Sons Of Katie Elder (1965)
John Wayne, Dean Martin, Michael Anderson, Jr., and Earl Holliman are the sons, reunited after many years to avenge the death of their mother. Rowdy and exciting Western action film also stars Martha Hyer and George Kennedy. 122 min.
06-1163 *❑$14.99*

In Harm's Way (1965)
Masterful actioner of Navy men in the Pacific theater of WWII after the Japanese attack on Pearl Harbor, focusing on the turbulent careers and personal lives of officers John Wayne and Kirk Douglas. Otto Preminger directs a superlative cast that includes Henry Fonda, Patricia Neal, George Kennedy. 165 min.
06-1593 Was $29.99 *❑$24.99*

El Dorado (1967)
Great Howard Hawks Western with John Wayne in top form as a gunfighter who helps drunken sheriff pal Robert Mitchum fight the bad guys. 127 min.
06-1169 *❑$14.99*

The War Wagon (1967)
John Wayne teams up with roughneck Kirk Douglas to rob a shipment of gold from a heavily protected carrier known as the War Wagon. Howard Keel, Bruce Cabot, Keenan Wynn. 101 min.
07-1176 *$14.99*

The Green Berets (1968)
First major Hollywood production to deal with war in Vietnam. John Wayne leads the Special Forces troops against the deadly and determined enemy. Flame throwers, helicopter crashes, jungle tortures and strafing. 135 min.
19-1001 *$19.99*

The Undefeated (1969)
John Wayne and Rock Hudson star as two ex-Civil War officers, once bitter enemies, now united against a common enemy. Rousing Western action; Lee Meriwether, Bruce Cabot, and Merlin Olsen co-star. 119 min.
04-3083 Was $19.99 *❑$14.99*

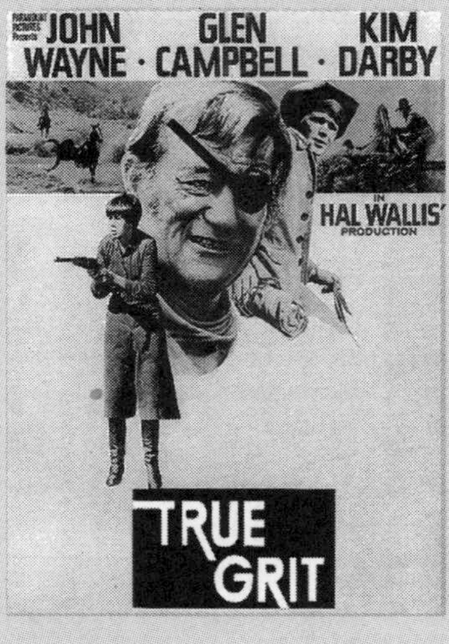

True Grit (1969)
One of John Wayne's best-loved movies. He won his only Oscar as Rooster Cogburn, the boozing, one-eyed ex-marshal. Kim Darby is the young girl who hires Wayne to find her father's killers and Glen Campbell is a bounty hunter in this touching, thrill-packed Western. 126 min.
06-1067 *❑$14.99*

Rooster Cogburn (And The Lady) (1975)
John Wayne repeats his "True Grit" role as the feisty marshal. Here he meets his match: a bible-thumping missionary, portrayed by the great Katharine Hepburn. 107 min.
07-1076 *$14.99*

Hellfighters (1969)
John Wayne, Katharine Ross, Jim Hutton and Vera Miles star in an exciting contemporary drama about the men who risk their lives fighting oil well fires; Duke's character is based on the legendary Red Adair. 121 min.
07-1281 *$14.99*

Chisum (1970)
John Wayne is a peace-minded cattle baron in a territory riddled with corrupt officials. He doesn't want a fight, but he won't run away from one. Sprawling Western with Forrest Tucker, Linda Day. 111 min.
19-1117 *$14.99*

Rio Lobo (1970)
Ex-Union officer John Wayne teams up with two former Confederate soldiers to track down a stolen gold shipment and find themselves in the middle of a town's battle with a crooked sheriff. Jennifer O'Neill, Victor French, Jack Elam and Jorge Rivero co-star in this rousing Western tale that was director Howard Hawks' last film. 103 min.
04-1568 *❑$14.99*

Big Jake (1971)
Some desperadoes kidnap a young boy to use as a hostage, but they didn't know the lad's grandfather is John Wayne, and nothing will stop him from rescuing him. Western action as only the Duke could deliver; also stars Maureen O'Hara, Richard Boone, Patrick Wayne, Chris Mitchum. 110 min.
04-3081 *❑$14.99*

The Train Robbers (1972)
John Wayne meets Ann-Margret in this superior sagebrush saga about a beautiful widow who recruits a band of brave gunmen to recover lost loot. Ben Johnson, Rod Taylor. 92 min.
19-1324 Was $19.99 *$14.99*

The Cowboys (1972)
A veteran rancher, played by John Wayne, banks everything on 11 schoolboys he recruits for a dangerous cattle drive. Rambunctious humor and extraordinary thrills are served in this Wayne winner! Bruce Dern, Roscoe Lee Browne. 128 min.
19-1325 Was $19.99 *$14.99*

Cahill: United States Marshal (1973)
John Wayne is a devoted lawman who goes head on against a vicious gang of robbers. The trouble is, two of them are his sons! Gary Grimes, Neville Brand, George Kennedy co-star. 102 min.
19-1326 Was $19.99 *❑$14.99*

McQ (1974)
Dirty Harry has nothing on the Duke in this thriller about crime in the streets. John Wayne is a tough-as-nails cop working on the bust of his career. Eddie Albert, Colleen Dewhurst also star. 116 min.
19-1144 Was $19.99 *❑$14.99*

Brannigan (1975)
The Duke comes to the land of royalty, as Chicago cop John Wayne follows a fleeing racketeer to London. Exciting English locales and a wild pub brawl make for two-fisted action; Richard Attenborough, Judy Geeson, John Vernon co-star. 111 min.
12-1987 *$19.99*

The Shootist (1976)
A famed gunslinger dying from cancer wants to live peacefully in a small town, but can't escape his reputation. Ironic, dramatic finale to John Wayne's career, buoyed by the Duke's moving performance, also stars James Stewart, Lauren Bacall, Ron Howard. 99 min.
06-1054 *❑$14.99*

The Shootist (Letterboxed Version)
Also available in a theatrical, widescreen format.
06-2708 *❑$14.99*

John Wayne Matinee Double Feature, Vol. 1
A double dose of the Duke in all-Western action. Wayne and the Three Mesquiteers deal with some land-grabbing snakes on the "Frontier Horizon" (1939), followed by John defending a small town against marauding outlaws during "The Lawless Nineties" (1936).
63-1075 Double Feature *$14.99*

John Wayne Matinee Double Feature, Vol. 2
In "The Lonely Trail" (1936), Union army vet Wayne returns home to Texas and tries to rid the state of carpetbaggers. Ann Rutherford, Cy Kendall co-star. Next, ranchowner Carole Landis gets help from the Three Meqsuiteers (Wayne, Max Terhune and Ray Corrigan) in "Three Texas Steers" (1939).
63-1076 Double Feature *$14.99*

John Wayne Matinee Double Feature, Vol. 3
Two action-packed "Three Mesquiteers" oaters team a young Duke with Ray Corrigan and Max Terhune, battling a munitions scheme in "Pals of the Saddle" (1938) and donning masks and capes as "The Night Riders" (1939) to reclaim their land from a South-west dictator.
63-1134 Double Feature *$14.99*

John Wayne Matinee Double Feature, Vol. 4
When John is framed for murdering a mine owner in "Santa Fe Stampede" (1938), fellow Mesquiteers Max Terhune and Ray Corrgian slap leather and ride to save him. Then, Wayne pins on a star and brings justice to "The New Frontier" (1935).
63-1135 Double Feature *$14.99*

The John Wayne Story: The Early Years
Follow the fabulous early days of "The Duke" through film clips, trailers and rare photos from his life and movies. Check out John's early "B" Westerns, his breakthrough role in "Stagecoach," his WWII action entries like "Flying Tigers" and John Ford classics like "She Wore a Yellow Ribbon" and "The Quiet Man." 85 min.
10-2552 *$14.99*

The John Wayne Story: The Later Years
The great John Wayne's career from the mid-1950s and on is saluted in this terrific program that offers a look at Wayne's world through movies like "Hondo," "The Searchers," "The Alamo," "The High and the Mighty" and "McLintock." Check out how John almost played Matt Dillon in "Gunsmoke," his Oscar win for "True Grit" and his farewell in "The Shootist." 88 min.
10-2553 *$14.99*

John Wayne: Behind The Scenes With The Duke!
John Wayne fans will not want to miss this terrific compilation of promotional films, behind-the-scenes footage and trailers featuring Duke at his best—and most revealing. Listen to Maureen O'Hara talk about the filming of "McLintock!"; see John and Howard Hawks work on "El Dorado"; and check out a rare trailer for "The Shootist," his last film. 85 min.
50-5547 *$19.99*

The Duke And The General
Take an intimate look at John Wayne and James Stewart, two of Hollywood's greatest stars, in this program which aired just one time on TV. Both Wayne, on location while filming "The Cowboys," and Stewart, on location for "Fools' Parade," talk about acting, politics and patriotism, while directors Mark Rydell and Andrew McLaglen discuss working with the actors. 90 min.
50-5734 *$19.99*

John Wayne Scrapbook
All right, troopers, saddle up for a hard-riding, two-fisted swagger through the Duke's celebrated career, with clips from a corrallfull of his finest films, long-lost theatrical trailers and more, including his TV Great Western Bank ads. 90 min.
10-7434 *$19.99*

Young Duke: The Making Of A Movie Star
Trace the early film career of John Wayne, as he went from USC football star Marion Morrison to stagehand for John Ford to B-Western hero, in this fascinating documentary, hosted by Leonard Maltin and featuring vintage film clips. 46 min.
63-1613 *$14.99*

John Wayne: The Duke Lives On
A knockout collection of rare clips and remembrances that puts up John Wayne's finest work for tribute, with more ridin', brawlin', and shootin' than a prairie full of wagon trains, pardner!
18-7130 *$19.99*

John Wayne: American Hero/Hollywood Legend Gift Set
On the battlefield, the frontier and even the tundra, big John Wayne shines in four action-packed classics: "The Comancheros," "North to Alaska," "Rio Grande" and "Sands of Iwo Jima."
04-3930 Save $25.00! *$34.99*

John Wayne Gift Set
Listen up, Pilgrim. Here's a special boxed collection with four of Wayne's Western classics. Included are "El Dorado," "The Shootist," "The Sons of Katie Elder" and the Oscar-winning "True Grit."
06-2016 *$54.99*

John Wayne Collection
Think fans of John Wayne will want to miss out on this boxed set that includes the Duke in "The Cowboys," "The Searchers" and "Stagecoach"? "That'll be the day!"
19-1093 *$49.99*

Hondo And McLintock! Limited Collector's Edition
Saddle up some savings with a special two-tape collector's set of two of the Duke's greatest westerns: "Hondo" and "McLintock!" Also includes "On Location with John Wayne" featuring behind-the-scenes footage and sequences hosted by producer Michael Wayne and director Andrew McLaglen.
50-7404 Save $10.00! *$29.99*

Hollywood Stars: John Wayne
And who merits the title "All-American Hero" better than Big John Wayne? This triple dose of Duke includes "Rio Grande," "The Fighting Kentuckian" and "The Quiet Man," in a deluxe collector's set.
63-1337 Save $5.00! *$59.99*

Wayne At War Gift Pack
The Duke fights for Old Glory on the land, sea and air in three classic movies available in one collector's set: "Fighting Seabees," "Flying Tigers" and "Sands of Iwo Jima."
63-1338 *$49.99*

The John Wayne Collection
Three of the Duke's finest screen roles—"Angel and the Badman," "Flying Tigers" and "The Quiet Man"—in a deluxe boxed set that also features the documentary "The Republic Pictures Story."
63-1513 *$79.99*

John Wayne Color Gift Pack
On the land, on the sea and in the air, get all the Duke you want in this money-saving collector's set, featuring the colorized versions of "The Dark Command," "The Fighting Kentuckian," "The Fighting Seabees," "Flying Tigers," "In Old California," "Rio Grande," "Sands of Iwo Jima" and "Wake of the Red Witch."
63-1666 *$79.99*

The John Wayne Frontier Collection
It takes a big man to tame a big frontier, and they don't come any bigger than John Wayne in this three-tape collector's set that includes "Desert Trail," "A Lady Takes a Chance" and "War of the Wildcats."
63-1958 *$39.99*

Please see our index for these other John Wayne titles: *Baby Face • Cast A Giant Shadow • The Drop Kick • The Greatest Story Ever Told • How The West Was Won • The Hurricane Express • The Shadow Of The Eagle • The Three Musketeers*

Jubal (1956)
A wandering cowhand lands a job at a ranch and gives the foreman advice on handling his wife, but a spiteful co-worker spreads seeds of suspicion and jealousy in this unusual Western drama, described as "a frontier 'Othello'." Glenn Ford, Ernest Borgnine, Valerie French and Rod Steiger star. 101 min.
02-1691 *$14.99*

3:10 To Yuma (1957)
Classic psychological Western centers on a rancher (Van Heflin) who agrees to watch a slick, captured outlaw (Glenn Ford) until a train arrives at a station. The rancher's reward is enough money to save his drought-stricken land, but the crook uses his wits to try to psych-out his captor. Felicia Farr co-stars. 92 min.
02-2682 *$14.99*

The Legend Of Tom Dooley (1959)
The Kingston Trio's popular folk song was the basis for this downbeat Western drama, with a pre-"Bonanza" Michael Landon playing the Confederate soldier who, unaware that the war is over, robs a Union stagecoach and is branded an outlaw and murderer. Jo Morrow, Jack Hogan, Richard Rust also star.
02-2731 *$14.99*

Gunman's Walk (1958)
Complex western tale starring Van Heflin as a quick-shooting lawman at odds with reckless son Tab Hunter, who wants to demonstrate he's more dangerous than Dad. Eventually, Heflin's role as father and lawmaker is put to the test when Hunter turns killer. James Darren, Kathryn Grant also star; directed by Phil Karlson ("The Phenix City Story"). 95 min.
02-2907 *$14.99*

Seven Cities Of Gold (1955)
Historical fact is blended with Hollywood drama in this recounting of the Spanish expedition to the Pacific coast in 1679 that led to the founding of California. Anthony Quinn is the military leader in search of gold, and Michael Rennie is mission founder Father Junipero Serra. 103 min.
04-3185 *$19.99*

Copper Canyon (1950)
Western drama set shortly after the Civil War, with Ray Milland playing a former Confederate officer accused of theft who hides out in a frontier town from military officials. Hedy Lamarr, Macdonald Carey co-star. 84 min.
06-1839 *□$12.99*

The Man From The Alamo (1953)
Glenn Ford stars as a survivor of the famed fortress. Branded a coward by those around him, he must fight to prove himself during the Mexican War. Western drama also stars Julia Adams, Victor Jory, Hugh O'Brian. 79 min.
10-3226 Was $19.99 *□$14.99*

My Outlaw Brother (1951)
A naive dude (Mickey Rooney), heading westward to find the brother he idolizes (Robert Stack), is shepherded safely across the plains by a ranger (Robert Preston). What Rooney doesn't realize is that Stack is a notorious gunslinger...and Preston has to bring him in! AKA: "My Brother, The Outlaw." 82 min.
10-7231 Was $19.99 *$14.99*

Stage To Tucson (1950)
After several stagecoaches are stolen in the Southwest, two government agents lead an investigation that finds secessionists behind the deed. Rod Cameron, Wayne Morris, Kay Buckley star. 81 min.
10-8268 Was $19.99 *$14.99*

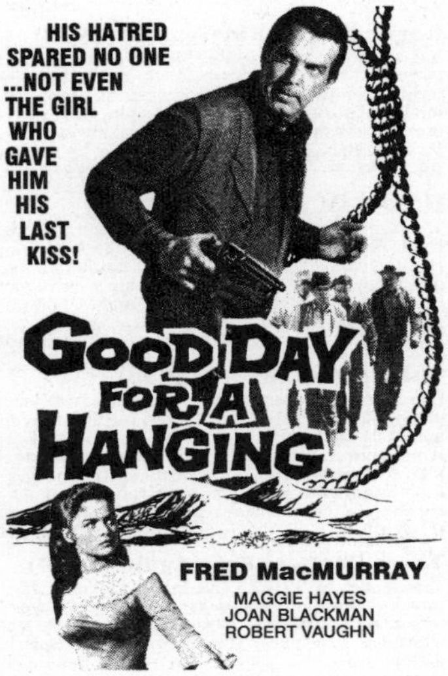
HIS HATRED SPARED NO ONE ...NOT EVEN THE GIRL WHO GAVE HIM HIS LAST KISS!
GOOD DAY FOR A HANGING
FRED MacMURRAY
MAGGIE HAYES
JOAN BLACKMAN
ROBERT VAUGHN

Good Day For A Hanging (1958)
Fine sagebrush drama starring Fred MacMurray as a sheriff whose capture of wanted criminal Robert Vaughn elicits an unexpected response from the townspeople: they rally to the young outlaw's defense and believe MacMurray's tactics are too tough. Maggie Hayes, James Drury and Joan Blackman also star. 85 min.
02-2905 *$14.99*

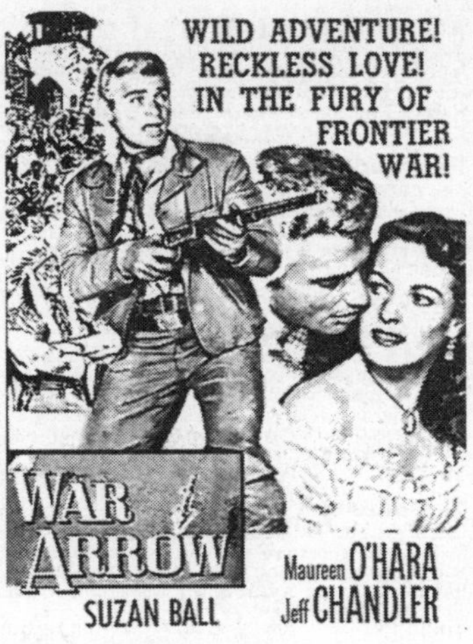
WILD ADVENTURE! RECKLESS LOVE! IN THE FURY OF FRONTIER WAR!
WAR ARROW
SUZAN BALL
Maureen O'HARA
Jeff CHANDLER

War Arrow (1953)
A thrilling Cavalry-versus-Indians adventure starring Jeff Chandler as an Army official recruiting Seminole allies, against his superior's wishes, to stop a planned Kiowa attack. Maureen O'Hara, John McIntire, Dennis Weaver and Jay Silverheels also star. 79 min.
07-2225 *□$14.99*

Denver And Rio Grande (1952)
Thrilling Western adventure about the rivalry between two railroad lines to be the first to cross the Rocky Mountains. Edmond O'Brien is the chief engineer of the Denver and Rio Grande who battles shifty Canyon City and San Juan rival Sterling Hayden. Dean Jagger, Laura Elliott co-star. 89 min.
06-1972 *□$12.99*

The Lonely Man (1957)
Emotionally-charged Western featuring Jack Palance as a gunfighter who attempts to reintroduce himself into son Anthony Perkins' life after deserting him 17 years earlier. But Perkins' anger gets in the way of a resolution, and an ornery gambler seeks vengeance from Palance for stealing his woman. Neville Brand, Robert Middleton also star. 87 min.
06-2104 *□$14.99*

Comanche Territory (1950)
Frontiersman Jim Bowie discovers that a silver-rich mountain area is owned by the Comanche Indians, but a greedy settler and his sister have stolen the deed and plan to massacre the Comanches for trespassing. After falling in love with Bowie, the sister decides to help him arm the Indians and stop the slaughter. Maureen O'Hara, Macdonald Carey, Will Geer and Charles Drake star. 76 min.
07-2223 *□$14.99*

The Redhead From Wyoming (1953)
Lovely Maureen O'Hara takes the rustling rap for a slimy politician, but when he goes too far and starts a range war, she tries to organize a group of settlers to stop him. Alex Nicol, Robert Strauss, William Bishop and a young Dennis Weaver also star in this exciting sagebrush story. 81 min.
07-2224 *□$14.99*

Dakota Incident (1956)
Dale Robertson and Ward Bond star in this thrill-a-minute tale reminiscent of "Stagecoach." A diverse group of people battle Indians, bad weather and other problems on a stagecoach trek.
63-1071 Was $19.99 *$14.99*

A Man Alone (1955)
A notorious gunman is accused of a stagecoach robbery he has nothing to do with. Mob wars, a brave sheriff and an intense finale make this a six-gun smash. Ray Milland, Raymond Burr. 96 min.
63-1072 *$14.99*

The Outcast (1953)
Range war erupts when an outlaw and his band return to a small valley to settle with the land baron who cheated him out of his inheritance. John Derek, Jim Davis star. 90 min.
63-1130 Was $19.99 *$14.99*

Terror In A Texas Town (1958)
Looking for a western where the hero dispatches the bad guy with a harpoon? This offbeat frontier thriller stars Sterling Hayden as a Swedish-born sailor who seeks revenge for his father's murder against crooked land baron Sebastian Cabot. With Ned Young, Carol Kelly; directed by Joseph H. Lewis. 80 min.
12-3142 *$14.99*

The Sundowners (1950)
When two brothers find their ranch empire threatened, they hire a notorious gunslinger to protect their land...but whose side is he really on? Western action with Robert Preston, Robert Sterling, John Barrymore, Jr. 83 min.
21-3036 Was $19.99 *$14.99*

The Naked Hills (1956)
An Indiana farmer in 1849 is struck with "gold fever" after the Sutter's Mill find and abandons his wife and child to go prospecting. Frontier drama stars David Wayne, Jim Backus, Marcia Henderson, Keenan Wynn. 73 min.
21-3037 *$19.99*

The Fastest Gun Alive (1956)
General store proprietor Glenn Ford wants to forget his father's legacy for being incredibly fast with a six-shooter, but when gunslinger Broderick Crawford offers a challenge, he ignores his wife's wishes and faces him in a showdown. Gripping Western saga also stars Jeanne Crain, Russ Tamblyn and Allyn Joslyn. 95 min.
12-2889 Was $19.99 *□$14.99*

The Fastest Gun Alive (Color Version)
The guns blaze fast and in brilliant color in this colorized sagebrush saga.
12-2915 *□$19.99*

Gun Glory (1957)
Powerful Western drama starring Stewart Granger as a former gunman who returns to his ranch after a three-year absence to find his wife has died and his son has turned against him. When a wicked cattle baron begins rerouting his herds through town, Granger wins the respect of the townspeople and his son when he tries to stop him. Rhonda Fleming and Steve Rowland co-star. 89 min.
12-2890 *$19.99*

The Last Hunt (1956)
Stunning psychological frontier saga focusing on renegade buffalo hunter Robert Taylor, whose obsession with bagging the beasts and killing Indians leads to a dangerous confrontation with former partner Stewart Granger. Richard Brooks wrote and directed this powerful, lushly filmed story; Lloyd Nolan, Debra Paget and Russ Tamblyn co-star. 108 min.
12-2891 *$19.99*

Westward The Women (1951)
A novel, exciting Western epic from director William Wellman which tells of scout Robert Taylor escorting a wagon train of 150 women from Chicago to California. During the dangerous trek, the scout and the women encounter Indian attacks, treacherous weather and the advances of Taylor's men. Denise Darcel, Hope Emerson and John McIntire co-star. 118 min.
12-2895 *□$19.99*

Westward The Women (Color Version)
These gals are rugged—and rouged, too!—in this western adventure presented in a colorized edition.
12-2914 *□$19.99*

New Mexico (1951)
Action-packed oater involving a cavalry captain attempting to keep the peace between the white man and an Indian tribe who claim their treaty has been broken. Lew Ayres, Marilyn Maxwell, Robert Hutton and Andy Devine star. 78 min.
53-6058 Was $29.99 *$19.99*

The Young Land (1959)
Unusual sagebrush saga starring Dennis Hopper as a rebellious gunslinger in 1848 California whose trial for killing a young Hispanic tests the American system of justice in the newly formed state. Dan O'Herlihy, Yvonne Craig star; produced by John Ford's son, Patrick, and co-starring John Wayne's son, Patrick. 89 min.
53-6094 Was $29.99 *$19.99*

Last Command (1955)
Sterling Hayden and Ernest Borgnine star in this sweeping spectacular re-creation of the story of Jim Bowie and the heroes of the Alamo. 110 min.
63-1068 *$14.99*

Ride The Man Down (1953)
Hoof-and-saddles thriller about boundary squabbles over ranchland that erupt into a murderous range war. Rod Cameron, Brian Donlevy, Ella Raines, Forrest Tucker star. 90 min.
63-1069 *$19.99*

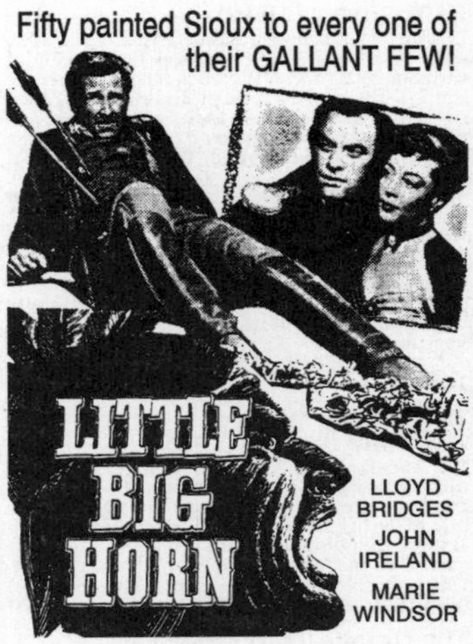
Fifty painted Sioux to every one of their GALLANT FEW!
LITTLE BIG HORN
LLOYD BRIDGES
JOHN IRELAND
MARIE WINDSOR

Little Big Horn (1951)
Taut Western drama about a band of cavalrymen trying to intercept Custer's forces and warn him of an Indian ambush, but who are being killed one by one by an unseen enemy. Lloyd Bridges, John Ireland, Jim Davis, Hugh O'Brian star. 86 min.
10-1364 *$19.99*

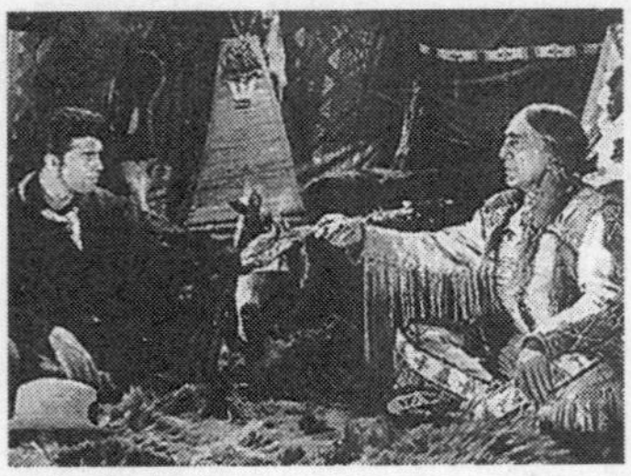

Sitting Bull (1954)
An exciting (and surprisingly pro-Indian) version of the events leading up to the Battle of Little Big Horn, with J. Carrol Naish as the proud, headstrong Sioux leader and Dale Robertson as a Cavalry major trying to make peace between the Indians and the government. Mary Murphy, Iron Eyes Cody also star. 105 min.
10-8334 Was $19.99 *$14.99*

The Tall Texan (1953)
Led by escaped murderer Lloyd Bridges, a group of gold-seekers uncovers a deposit while mining in Indian territory. The Indians discover that someone in the group has broken an agreement and soon seek vengeance for their actions. Marie Windsor, Lee J. Cobb and Luther Adler also star in this western, noted for its unusual psychological approach to its subject. 82 min.
10-9842 *$14.99*

Bullwhip (1958)
Western action, as a condemned gunslinger marries a feisty half-breed woman so she can reclaim her father's estate. Guy Madison, Rhonda Fleming star; title song by Frankie Laine. 80 min.
63-1133 Was $19.99 *$14.99*

Bugles In The Afternoon (1952)
Ray Milland delivers a powerful performance as a court-martialed Cavalryman who re-enlists for duty in Sioux territory...and receives his vindication in the fury of Little Big Horn. Forrest Tucker, George Reeves, Helena Carter, Hugh Marlowe star. 85 min.
63-1261 *$14.99*

Jubilee Trail (1954)
Sprawling big budget romance set between New Orleans and the Gold Coast, about a widowed Easterner (Joan Leslie) forced to manage for herself and her newborn in wagon trains and saloons on the hard way West. Talented cast includes Vera Ralston, Forrest Tucker, Barton MacLane. 103 min.
63-1352 *$14.99*

The Bushwackers (1952)
Putting aside a vow never to use a gun again, a Civil War veteran cleans up a corrupt western town. John Ireland, Dorothy Malone and Lon Chaney, Jr. star. 70 min.
68-8230 *$14.99*

Thunder Pass (1954)
Thrilling Western drama of a convoy of settlers beset by hostile Indians and the Army officer who helps them on the trek to safety stars Dane Clark, Andy Devine, Dorothy Patrick, Raymond Burr and John Carradine. 76 min.
63-1362 *$14.99*

Mohawk (1956)
A peace-loving federal agent (Scott Brady) and an Indian woman (Rita Gam) work together to prevent a range war, only to fall in love in the process and face rejection from both their peoples. Western drama also stars Neville Brand, Lori Nelson. 79 min.
21-3039 Was $19.99 *$14.99*

Hi-Yo Silver (1940)
This extremely rare featurized version of the 1938 serial "The Lone Ranger" includes the addition of narration by Raymond Hatton to string together the story of the masked man of mystery, his trusted Indian sidekick, and their battle with ruthless marauders in the lawless state of Texas following the Civil War. With Lee Powell, Chief Thundercloud, Herman Brix. 70 min.
10-9436 *$14.99*

Legend Of The Lone Ranger (1952)
Learn the dark secret behind the masked rider of the plains' beginnings, and how Tonto became his trusty Indian sidekick, in this full-length adventure taken from the TV series. Clayton Moore, Jay Silverheels star. AKA: "The Origin of the Lone Ranger." 70 min.
10-9196 Was $19.99 *$14.99*

The Legend Of The Lone Ranger (1981)
The legendary hero of the Old West returns, along with his loyal Indian ally, in this exciting adventure. Learn how the Lone Ranger and Tonto devoted their lives to the fight for justice, and watch them rescue a kidnapped President Grant from the notorious Cavendish gang. Klinton Spilsbury, Michael Horse, Christopher Lloyd and Jason Robards star. 98 min.
04-1367 Was $59.99 *$14.99*

The Omaha Trail (1942)
An action-packed western adventure about a desperate railroad man who needs help to get his trains to Omaha in order to secure a spot on a lucrative westward line. Help is furnished by a stranger who goes up against an unscrupulous wagon train operator. James Craig, Pamela Blake, Edward Ellis and Kermit Maynard star. 62 min.
09-5267 Was $19.99 *$14.99*

Kansas Pacific (1953)
Action-filled drama of the men who had to fight Nature, Indians and Confederate soldiers to finish the vital rail link during the Civil War. Frontier drama stars Sterling Hayden, Eve Miller, Barton MacLane. 73 min.
21-3051 Was $19.99 *$14.99*

Renegade Girl (1946)
Ann Savage ("Detour") plays the free-thinking vixen who favors the Rebels during the Civil War, but falls in love with a Union soldier. Alan Curtis and Chief Thundercloud also star in this energetic Western. 65 min.
09-2134 Was $29.99 *$24.99*

Light Of The Western Stars (1940)
A ranch foreman is saved from becoming an outlaw by the love of a good woman. With his newfound confidence, he goes to bat against the criminal element in this exciting adaptation of Zane Grey's novel. Victor Jory, Jo Ann Sayers, Russell Hayden star; look for an early role for Alan Ladd. AKA: "Border Renegade." 67 min.
10-1250 Was $19.99 *$14.99*

The Kansan (1943)
Lots of gun-shootin', a cattle stampede, barroom free-for-alls, and a spectacular bridge dynamiting in this tale of one man against the notorious James Gang. Richard Dix, Jane Wyatt, Albert Dekker and Victor Jory wear the boots here. 79 min.
10-3037 Was $19.99 *$14.99*

Wildcat (1942)
Richard Arlen is Johnny Maverick, a cowpoke whose last penny goes to a land deal in which he takes on a partner. When that partner dies, Maverick fights a sabotage effort from an outlaw while waiting to see if his new land has oil on it. William Frawley, Arline Judge and Buster Crabbe co-star. 71 min.
10-3384 *$19.99*

The Gentleman From Arizona (1940)
Ruth Reece plays Juanita, a matchmaker-on-the-ranch who takes pride in getting people together. Among her matches are a millionaire, an heiress and a horse trainer in this romantic sagebrusher. With John King and Joan Barclay.
10-9386 *$14.99*

Billy The Kid (1941)
Robert Taylor plays William Bonney, alias "Billy the Kid," in this guns-a-blazin' saga that traces Billy's involvement with the Lockhart outlaws and U.S. marshal and old friend Jim Sherwood (based on Pat Garrett). Brian Donlevy, Lon Chaney, Jr. and Ian Hunter co-star. 95 min.
12-2888 *$19.99*

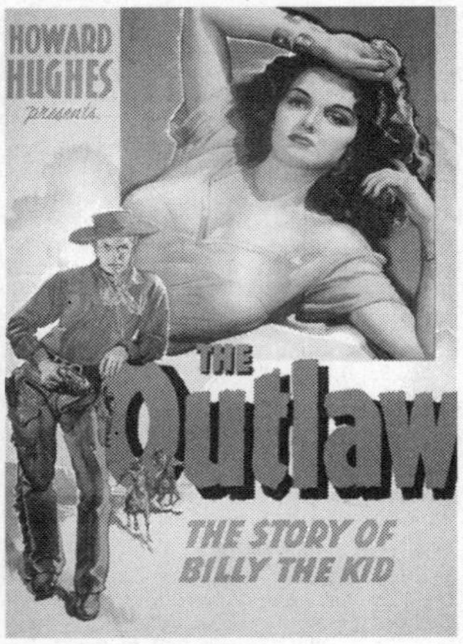

The Outlaw (1943)
Howard Hughes' controversial Western drama, a loose retelling of the story of gunslinger Billy the Kid and lawman Pat Garrett, is best remembered now as the screen debut of Jane Russell (whose natural attributes were emphasized by producer-director Hughes). Jack Buetel, Walter Huston, Thomas Mitchell also star. Complete, uncensored version; 117 min.
10-2046 *$14.99*

A Few Bullets More (1966)
A revisionist take on the Billy the Kid legend, this Italian oater stars Peter Lee Lawrence as blonde teenager William Bonney, who only kills people in self-defense. Follow Bonney's life, from his seeking revenge against the man who raped his mother and his friendship with Pat Garrett to his death at the hands of a friend. With Fausto Tozzi. AKA: "The Man Who Killed Billy the Kid."
79-6500 *$19.99*

Billy The Kid (1989)
From writer Gore Vidal comes a new look at one of the Wild West's most notorious names. Val Kilmer stars as young William Bonney, whose mission of vengeance puts him on the wrong side of the law and whose charming nature makes him a hero to those he meets. With Wilford Brimley, Duncan Regehr. 96 min.
18-7144 Was $89.99 *$12.99*

The Big Cat (1949)
Boy, have these ranchers got problems! Besides their ongoing battles with the baddies, a wild mountain lion is on the loose, threatening livestock and the ranchers themselves! Lon McCallister, Preston Foster and Forrest Tucker star. 75 min.
21-3041 Was $19.99 *$14.99*

Buckskin Frontier (1943)
An action-packed Western, as Lee J. Cobb tries to prevent a railroad man from blasting a trail through his covered-wagon empire; also stars Richard Dix, Max Baer. 75 min.
21-3000 *$19.99*

Woman Of The Town (1943)
Albert Dekker plays famed lawman Bat Masterson in this rousing tale. He falls in love with a dance-hall girl, cleans up the town from nasty outlaws, and learns a lesson in a dangerous gun-battle. Claire Trevor, Barry Sullivan co-star. 87 min.
31-3032 Was $19.99 *$14.99*

Silver Queen (1942)
An ambitious woman heads to boomtown San Francisco only to encounter double-crosses, stolen mines and dirty dealings. A super sagebrush saga with Priscilla Lane, George Brent and Bruce Cabot. 81 min.
31-3033 Was $19.99 *$14.99*

Knights Of The Range (1940)
In this Zane Grey sagebrusher, Russell Hayden is a college grad who heads west, then finds himself battling a team of ornery black hats out to swindle ranchers out of their land. Morris Ankrum, Jean Parker, Victor Jory co-star. 60 min.
55-3040 *$19.99*

Red Stallion In The Rockies (1949)
A wild stallion becomes the target of ranchers when it begins stealing mares for its own harem. A group of circus workers recognize the animal as a performing horse and protect it, and the horse proves its worth by saving a rancher's wife from a charging elk. Arthur Franz and Wallace Ford star in this western tale stunningly photographed by John Alton ("T-Men"). 60 min.
10-9994 *$14.99*

Silent Barriers (1937)
Set against the construction of the Canadian Pacific Railroad, this epic stars Richard Arlen as a brash gambler and ladies man who becomes romantically involved with a sweet, virginal lass who succumbs to his charms. Antoinette Cellier and Lilli Palmer co-star. 68 min.
09-2962 *$19.99*

Cimarron (1931)
A landmark in the Western genre, this Oscar-winning adaptation of the Edna Ferber novel traces 40 years in the settlement and development of the Oklahoma Territory, beginning with the 1889 Land Rush. Richard Dix and Irene Dunne are the pioneer family who help tame the frontier; with Estelle Taylor, Roscoe Ates, George E. Stone. 131 min.
12-1837 *$19.99*

Cimarron (1960)
This reworking of the 1931 Academy Award winner stars Glenn Ford as Yancy Cravat, an adventurer who seeks to claim his stake of territory during the Oklahoma Land Rush of the late 1800s. Maria Schell plays his wife; Arthur O'Connell, Anne Baxter, and Russ Tamblyn also star in the sprawling Western saga. 140 min.
12-2876 *$19.99*

Cimarron (Letterboxed Version) (1960)
Also available in its theatrical, widescreen format.
12-2913 *$19.99*

Rogue Of The Rio Grande (1930)
A young Myrna Loy is featured in this western effort, playing a lovely señorita who hangs out in a small-town saloon with a rogue who swipes cash from the locals while posing as a Mexican bandit. Early sagebrush drama that also features musical numbers costars Jose Bohr, Raymond Hatton. 55 min.
08-1579 *$14.99*

Heroes Of The Alamo (1938)
The saga of Texas' fight for independence in 1836 is chronicled in this thrilling film. Davy Crockett, Sam Houston, William Travis and Stephen Austin (not the director of "American Streetfighter") are some of the heroes brought to life. With Lane Chandler, Edward Piel and Earle Hodgins. 74 min.
10-8267 Was $19.99 *$14.99*

The Texas Rangers (1936)
One-time desperadoes Fred MacMurray and Jack Oakie go straight and join the Texas Rangers and their fight to uphold the law in Lone Star territory. When one of their former partners continues his outlaw ways, MacMurray and Oakie are called on to catch him. Lloyd Nolan, Jean Peter co-star; directed by King Vidor and released during the Texas Centennial celebrations. 99 min.
07-2302 *$14.99*

Texas Rangers Ride Again (1940)
This sequel to 1936's "The Texas Rangers" stars Broderick Crawford and John Howard as Rangers who disguise themselves as cowboys to investigate the operations at a ranch. They uncover the foreman's devious scheme to slaughter the ranch's cattle and ship them off to market. Ellen Drew and Anthony Quinn also star. 68 min.
07-2303 *$14.99*

Wild Brian Kent (1936)
The title character is a playboy who arrives in a Kansas town by train and soon assimilates into the lives of a woman and her young niece, then exposes a scheming realtor who wants to control the woman's property. Ralph Bellamy, Mae Clarke and Helen Lowell star. 60 min.
68-9017 *$14.99*

Joel McCrea

The Silver Horde (1930)
One of Joel McCrea's first starring breakthroughs was this macho role as an Alaskan salmon fisherman fighting a dirty-dealing rival with both fists. Also in an early role is Jean Arthur, as a society girl bidding for Joel's affection against a dancehall floozy. 76 min.
17-3063 *$19.99*

Barbary Coast (1935)
Howard Hawks' rousing story of the infamous San Francisco "red light district" during the California Gold Rush era stars Miriam Hopkins as a beautiful woman caught in a web of corruption, Edward G. Robinson as a ruthless, power-hungry gambling boss, and Joel McCrea as a naive prospector from the East. 90 min.
44-1888 Was $19.99 *$14.99*

Union Pacific (1939)
Feuding rail magnates, brave settlers, Indian attacks, a timely arrival by the U.S. Cavalry and an old-fashioned love story were all blended in Hollywood showman extraordinaire C.B. DeMille's take on the building of the Transcontinental Railroad in 1869. Barbara Stanwyck, Joel McCrea, Robert Preston, Brian Donlevy and Akim Tamiroff star. 135 min.
07-2247 *$14.99*

Buffalo Bill (1944)
Joel McCrea stars as the legendary frontier scout, Indian fighter and bison killer in William Wellman's sweeping Western epic, one of the first made in color. Follow Bill Cody's career from his role as mediator in the settling of the west to his showman days in his "Wild West Show." Maureen O'Hara, Thomas Mitchell, Anthony Quinn, Linda Darnell and Chief Thundercloud also star. 90 min.
04-2269 *$39.99*

The Virginian (1946)
Joel McCrea stars as the wandering man of few words (among them, "When you call me that, smile") who must go against old friend Sonny Tufts, a member of Brian Donlevy's gang of rustlers, in this colorful remake of the classic Owen Wister frontier drama. With Barbara Britton, William Frawley. 87 min.
07-2398 *$14.99*

Ramrod (1947)
Explosive, superbly photographed drama starring Joel McCrea as an upright ranch hand who comes between a scornful shepherdess (Veronica Lake) and her cattleman pa (Charles Ruggles) in a bloody range war. Co-stars Don DeFore and Donald Crisp. 94 min.
63-1353 *$14.99*

Four Faces West (1948)
Western drama of a man forced to rob a bank in order to save his father's ranch, only to be pursued by a relentless sheriff. Joel McCrea, Charles Bickford and Frances Dee star. 90 min.
63-5030 *$14.99*

SOUTH OF ST. LOUIS

South Of St. Louis (1949)
Wonderful, wild Western drama that follows three cattle-ranching friends (Joel McCrea, Zachary Scott, Douglas Kennedy) when the eruption of the Civil War forces them to choose sides. Alexis Smith, Dorothy Malone, Alan Hale, Victor Jory co-star. 88 min.
63-1263 *$14.99*

Stars In My Crown (1950)
Superb Western drama stars Joel McCrea as a gun-toting preacher who takes residence in a trouble-torn town and quickly goes to work solving such problems as a typhoid epidemic and Ku Klux Klan attacks. Co-stars Ellen Drew, Dean Stockwell, and a pre-"Gunsmoke" James Arness and Amanda Blake. 89 min.
12-2892 *$19.99*

Please see our index for these other Joel McCrea titles: *Bird Of Paradise • Come And Get It • Dead End • Foreign Correspondent • The Great Man's Lady • The Great Moment • Internes Can't Take Money • Kept Husbands • The More The Merrier • The Most Dangerous Game • Our Little Girl • The Palm Beach Story • Ride The High Country • Sullivan's Travels • These Three • They Shall Have Music*

Gun Smoke (1935)
After a rugged cow puncher saves a ranch hand from a dangerous ambush, he gets hired to join him at the ranch by the hand's boss. But trouble awaits as the puncher gets punched with a warrant for his arrest. Buck Coburn, Mary Brian and William "Stage" Boyd are among the roughhewn cast members. 57 min.
68-8980 *$19.99*

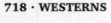

B-Westerns

Cowboys Of The Saturday Matinee (1984)
A light-hearted look at Hollywood Westerns of the '30s and '40s, hosted by James Coburn. See sagebrush stars like John Wayne, Gene Autry, Roy Rogers and Buck Jones, plus learn how oater institutions like the sidekick and white and black hats came into being. 75 min.
40-1121 *$14.99*

Six Gun Previews Vol. 1
Happy trailers to you! One big passel of coming attractions with such Saturday matinee stars as Roy Rogers, Gene Autry, Buck Jones, Ken Maynard, Tex Ritter, Lash LaRue and many other wild West wonders. 58 min.
65-5018 Was $19.99 *$14.99*

Cowboy Heroes Of The Silver Screen: Boxed Set
Fans of "B" westerns will want to wrangle these favorites available in this seven-tape boxed set. Included are "Arizona Bound" with Buck Jones; "Law Men" with Johnny Mack Brown; Harry Carey in "Ghost Town"; "Six-Shootin' Sheriff" featuring Ken Maynard; "The Texas Badman" with Tom Mix; "Thunder in the Desert" with Bob Steele; and Tim McCoy in "Straight Shooter."
16-5015 *$49.99*

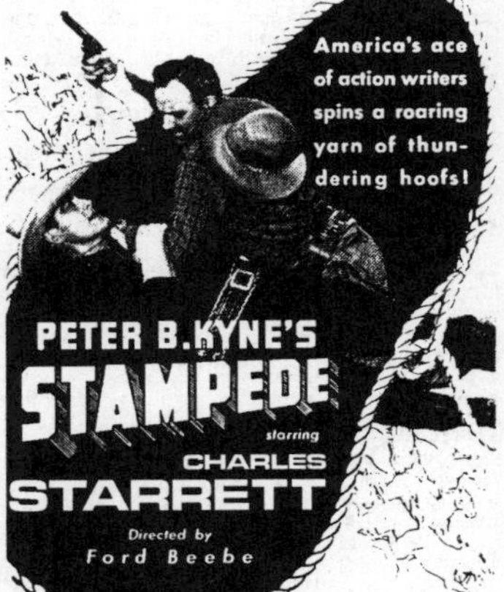
America's ace of action writers spins a roaring yarn of thundering hoofs!
PETER B. KYNE'S
STAMPEDE
starring
CHARLES STARRETT
Directed by
Ford Beebe

Stampede (1936)
Early Charles Starrett sagebrusher in which an evil rancher murders a rival to get his land. The incident prompts the dead man's brother (Starrett) to search for the killer. This extremely rare film was transferred from a mint condition 35mm print. With J.P. McGowan and Finis Barton.
10-9319 Was $19.99 *$14.99*

Rio Grande (1938)
When a lady ranch owner runs into problems with a black hat who has his beady eyes on both her and her land, Charles Starrett is called on to help her. Ann Doran and the Sons of the Pioneers also star. Featuring impressive cinematography from the great Lucien Ballard. 58 min.
10-9084 Was $19.99 *$14.99*

Law Of The Canyon (1947)
And who better to uphold said law than Charles Starrett (or as we all know him, the Durango Kid)? Watch as the Kid aids a sheriff's feisty daughter get the goods on a ring of stagecoach robbers. With Smiley Burnette, Nancy Saunders, Buzz Henry. 56 min.
10-8001 *$19.99*

Blazing Across The Pecos (1948)
Southwest Texas is a hard place to do a bad day's work when Charles Starrett as the Durango Kid streaks in, with a gripe against all troublemakers. Co-stars Smiley Burnette and Chief Thundercloud. 54 min.
10-7633 Was $19.99 *$14.99*

Whirlwind Raiders (1948)
Charles Starrett, as ex-Texas Ranger Steve Lanning and his heroic, black-clad alter ego, the Durango Kid, is a one-man whirlwind of justice as he defends the residents of Indian Springs from a band of baddies who call themselves the "Texas State Police." With Smiley Burnette, Nancy Saunders and kid rodeo star Little Brown Jug. 54 min.
10-7698 *$19.99*

Bonanza Town (1951)
As if the Durango Kid (Charles Starrett) didn't have enough problems tossing lawbreakers in the lockup...he's got to contend with the crooked judge who keeps letting 'em back out! Smiley Burnette, Fred F. Sears co-star. 56 min.
10-7626 *$14.99*

Riders Of The Purple Sage (1931)
First sound filming of Zane Grey's classic story stars George O'Brien as the cowpoke who rides against all odds to rescue his kidnapped sister. Marguerite Churchill, Noah Beery, James Todd co-star. 58 min.
10-8007 Was $19.99 *$14.99*

Mystery Ranch (1932)
Moody and well-made B-western (thanks in part to camerawork by John Ford's regular cinematographer, Joseph August) stars Charles Middleton as a ruthless land baron who abducts rancher Cecilia Parker and demands she marry him so he can claim her spread. Can hero George O'Brien rescue her in time? With Noble Johnson, Charles Stevens.
68-9109 *$14.99*

Dude Ranger (1934)
Duuude! An Easterner inherits some land and travels West to claim it, only to find that a crippled man is robbing the daughter of the ranch foreman. He falls in love with her and ferrets out the crook. From a Zane Grey story; stars George O'Brien.
62-1038 Was $19.99 *$14.99*

When A Man's A Man (1935)
Eastern tenderfoot George O'Brien goes West to find adventure and gets more than he expects when he tames a bronco and gets in the middle of a skirmish with ranchers over water rights. Dorothy Wilson, Paul Kelly co-star. 60 min.
09-5135 Was $19.99 *$14.99*

Cowboy Millionaire (1935)
George O'Brien stars as the rough-and-ready runner of a dude ranch who finds himself falling for a British lady guest who's out of her element. Fun in the saddle with Evalyn Bostock, Edgar Kennedy. 65 min.
10-7293 Was $19.99 *$14.99*

Thunder Mountain (1935)
When a crooked barkeep tries to steal his gold claim, prospector George O'Brien serves up some 24-karat justice. Zane Grey actioner also stars Morgan Wallace, Barbara Fritchie(!). 68 min.
10-8017 Was $19.99 *$14.99*

Hard Rock Harrigan (1935)
George O'Brien is the title character, the leader of a group of tunnel-diggers who has a feud with a fellow worker (Fred Kohler), but decides to save him when a cave-in occurs. Irene Hervey also stars. 60 min.
10-8433 Was $19.99 *$14.99*

Whispering Smith Speaks (1935)
George O'Brien is the titular character, the son of a wealthy railroad magnate, who decides to use his status for good. He helps a young woman realize that her land is worth lots more than she believes. Irene Ware also stars. 60 min.
10-9771 *$14.99*

Tall Timber (1937)
George O'Brien stars as a "city slicker" dude who learns to toughen up when he joins the logging men at a lumber camp. Along the way, O'Brien also exposes a crooked foreman and gets the girl, to boot! With Ward Bond, Beatrice Roberts. 64 min.
08-1037 *$14.99*

Hollywood Cowboy (1937)
A movie star specializing in playing cowboys has his vacation in the real West interrupted when he discovers gangsters are causing trouble for a group of ranchers. George O'Brien, Cecilia Parker and Maude Eburne star in this superb "B" western. 65 min.
10-8435 Was $19.99 *$14.99*

Lawless Valley (1938)
After an innocent cowpoke is let out of prison, he seeks vengeance against the treacherous sheriff who put him in the pokey and searches for his father's killers. Top-notch sagebrusher stars George O'Brien, Walter Miller and Chill Wills. 60 min.
10-8434 Was $19.99 *$14.99*

Marshal Of Mesa City (1939)
George O'Brien is a former sheriff lured back behind the badge when the town is taken over by villains and hooligans. The catch: his new deputy is a gunman hired by the crooks to kill O'Brien! With Dorothy Howe, Henry Brandon. 62 min.
10-7796 Was $19.99 *$14.99*

The Fighting Gringo (1939)
Good guy George O'Brien and his running mates ride up against a strong wind as they try to clear the name of a Mexican rancher falsely accused of murder, while George drops a rope on the rancher's lovely daughter (Tovar Lupita). Co-stars Lucio Villegas, Glenn Strange. 59 min.
10-7995 Was $19.99 *$14.99*

Bullet Code (1940)
George O'Brien lives by the code of the gun and puts his sharp-shooting abilities on the line when he has to chase down a pack of ornery rustlers. It's quick-shooting shenanigans at its finest, by George! With Virginia Vale and Slim Whitaker (not Slim Whitman). 56 min.
10-8026 Was $19.99 *$14.99*

Renfrew Of The Royal Mounted (1937)
James Newill stars in the first outing in this series, playing a singing Royal Mountie in hot pursuit of counterfeiters. Carol Hughes, William Royle star in this thrilling tale set in Canada. 55 min.
10-8199 Was $19.99 *$14.99*

Renfrew On The Great White Trail (1938)
James Newill stars as the Mountie who always gets his man in this rousing Yukon adventure full of action, suspense and good-natured hi-jinx. 57 min.
10-1163 Was $19.99 *$14.99*

Fighting Mad (1939)
Renfrew of the Mounties rides again to intercept bank bandits and a mystery lady trying to get ill-gotten goods across the border. James Newill stars as Renfrew. 57 min.
62-1230 Was $19.99 *$14.99*

Crashing Thru (1939)
That crash you hear is James Newill as two-fisted Mountie Renfrew, trying to stop three owlhoots who swiped gold from their boss, an outlaw who recently pulled off a heist. Jean Carmen and Warren Hull also star in this exciting entry in the popular "Renfrew" series.
68-9217 *$14.99*

Yukon Flight (1940)
Renfrew of the Mounties saddles up to bring in a pair of pernicious pilots who are charging an outrageous price for air freighting gold: all the cargo, and sometimes the prospectors' lives! James Newill returns as Renfrew; Louise Stanley, Warren Hull co-star. 57 min.
10-7204 Was $19.99 *$14.99*

Danger Ahead (1940)
From the "Renfrew of the Mounties" series comes this exciting tale starring James Newill as the mighty Mountie investigating the theft of a gold shipment and the death of an armored truck driver. With Dorothea Kent and Dave O'Brien. 58 min.
10-8191 Was $19.99 *$14.99*

Murder On The Yukon (1940)
A prospector discovers that he's been paid off in phony money and takes a bullet for his trouble. It's up to Renfrew, R.C.M.P., to see that justice is dispensed. James Newill, Tex O'Brien. 57 min.
62-1224 Was $19.99 *$14.99*

The Sky Bandits (1940)
The last of the "Renfrew of the Mounties" series stands R.C.M.P. James Newill against gold hijackers and a deluded scientist who's crafting a death ray for knocking aircraft out of the sky. 62 min.
68-8191 Was $19.99 *$14.99*

Jack Perrin

Border Vengeance (1925)
Jack Perrin turns in his trademark heroic performance as a cowboy going up against a nasty gambler and a misguided nerd who are involved in a series of crooked schemes. Can Perrin stop them and take care of an old mine which just might have gold in it? Minna Redman and Jack Richardson also star. Silent with music score.
68-9144 Was $19.99 *$14.99*

Guardians Of The Wild (1928)
Western action abounds as a horse rustler attempting to take control of a farm gets surprised when Rex, a leader of a group of wild horses, comes to the rescue. Jack Perrin plays the forest ranger helped by the animal. With Ethlyne Clair, Al Ferguson. Silent with music score.
03-5003 *$24.99*

Phantom Of The Desert (1930)
Cowboy hero Jack Perrin and his trusted horse, Starlight, go up against some ornery rustlers who utilize a white stallion as a front for their dirty work. Eve Novak also stars in this superb sagebrusher.
09-2995 Was $19.99 *$14.99*

Apache Kid's Escape (1930)
Jack Perrin stars in this two-fisted sagebrusher that's filled with expert shoot-outs. Western action? You better believe it when the Apache Kid escapes. Fred Church, Josephine Hill and Starlight, the horse, also star.
68-9160 Was $19.99 *$14.99*

The Cactus Kid (1934)
After a tough cattle drive, Jack Perrin discovers his partner has been killed and his $1000 payment for his efforts stolen. Jack is soon blamed for the murder and must find the real culprit before he's put in the pokey. Jayne Regan, Slim Whitaker also star.
68-8970 Was $19.99 *$14.99*

Rawhide Mail (1934)
A trio of stagecoach robbers fends off a rival band of outlaws and winds up playing guardian angels to a beautiful passenger who's travelling to a frontier town where she has inherited a saloon. When her late relative's partner tries to weasel her out of her due, the threesome help her by opening a competing bar. Jack Perrin, Nelson McDowell and Chris Martin star. 59 min.
68-9030 Was $19.99 *$14.99*

Rainbow Riders (1934)
Saddle up for two very rare "Bud & Ben" western featurettes made by B-picture studio Reliable Pictures. "Rainbow Riders" finds heroes Jack Perrin and Ben Corbett helping a lady ranch owner save her spread from blackhats. Next, Fred Hume plays Bud to Corbett's Ben in "Nevada Cyclone" (1934), in which the duo try to keep a wrangler from hooking up with cattle rustlers. Wally Wales co-stars.
68-9206 *$14.99*

Loser's End (1935)
A smuggler is loose and two pals decide to ride their horses to El Rio to find the prairie varmint responsible for the crimes. Jack Perrin, Tina Menard star. 60 min.
09-5126 Was $19.99 *$14.99*

North Of Arizona (1935)
Jack Perrin plays an honest cowpoke who doesn't seem to have any luck. After trying to help local Indians get rid of local gold swindlers, Perrin is hired as a helper on a ranch...by a gang of thieves. Then, he's accused of robbing an express office. Al Bridge and Blanche Mehaffey also star in this Western yarn set, well, north of Arizona. 60 min.
68-8992 Was $19.99 *$14.99*

Texas Jack (1935)
Medicine show entertainer "Texas Jack" tries to solve a mystery with help from the Horse with the Human Brain. With Jack Perrin, Jayne Regan. 55 min.
09-5131 Was $19.99 *$14.99*

Wolf Riders (1935)
After Jack Perrin's family is gunned down during a battle between cowboys and Indians, he's raised by a friendly Native American tribe and eventually becomes an Indian agent battling against racketeers. With Lillian Gilmore.
68-9210 *$14.99*

Hair-Trigger Casey (1936)
Captain Casey returns to his ranch when he hears that trouble's a-brewin'...but even he wasn't prepared for a slavery ring smuggling young Chinese across the border! Two-fisted, lead-slinging action with Jack Perrin, Wally Wales. 57 min.
09-2081 Was $19.99 *$14.99*

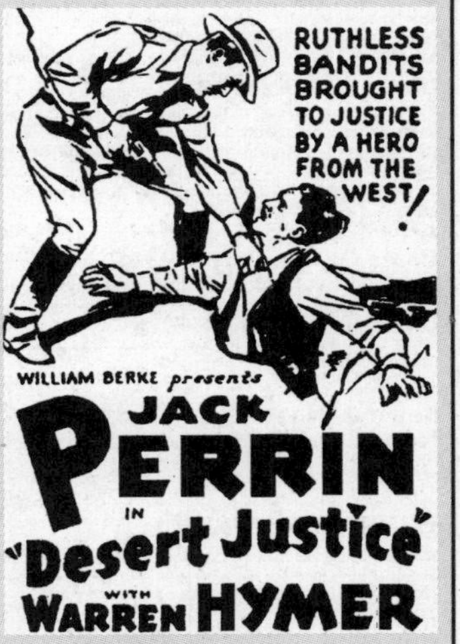
RUTHLESS BANDITS BROUGHT TO JUSTICE BY A HERO FROM THE WEST!
WILLIAM BERKE presents
JACK PERRIN
IN
"Desert Justice"
WITH
WARREN HYMER

Desert Justice (1936)
First-rate modern sagebrusher with Jack Perrin as a modern-day cop who leaves the force to pursue life in the great outdoors. But his plans are stopped when a group of robbers on the run—one of whom is his brother—takes refuge on his ranch. When Perrin's outlaw brother is gunned down, he pursues them on horseback into the desert. 58 min.
68-8976 Was $19.99 *$14.99*

Gun Grit (1936)
Jack Perrin is a government agent out to stop a group of city-based crooks who have joined unsavory ranch hands in the money protection rackets. Ethel Beck and Dave Sharpe co-star in this energetic sagebrush enterprise.
68-8979 Was $19.99 *$14.99*

Wildcat Saunders (1936)
Action and racial issues mark this unusual oater in which boxer Jack Perrin loses a big fight, then heads to a cowboy ranch to train. When some workers make racist comments about Perrin's black servant, he takes matters into his own fists, then discovers that the cowhands were involved in a large jewel robbery. Snowflake Toones, William Gould co-star. 60 min.
68-9019 Was $19.99 *$14.99*

Back Fire (1922)
Jack Hoxie is the range rider who finds himself and his partner framed for a robbery they didn't commit. Hoxie escapes the sheriff, but when his partner is thrown in the pokey, he has to straighten things out. George Sowards, Lou Meeham also star. NOTE: Despite missing its second reel, the film is easy to follow; we offer it because of its rarity. 40 min. Silent with music score.
68-9147 Was $19.99 ***$14.99***

Gun Law (1932)
An evil fellow known as the Sonora Kid wreaks havoc with a group of law-abiding citizens who are forced to find a way to get rid of the crook. Jack Hoxie, Betty Boyd star. 55 min.
08-1730 ***$14.99***

Gold (1932)
After an elderly miner is found murdered, a former rancher-turned-gold hunter becomes the prime suspect in the killing. Can he find the real culprit and clear his name? Jack Hoxie, Alice Day star in this tense tumbleweed drama.
09-5274 Was $19.99 ***$14.99***

Law And Lawless (1932)
A discouraging word may be seldom heard on the range, but there's a clamor of gunfire as Jack Hoxie tries to get the lowdown on the mysterious disappearance of cattle who've been vanishing a head at a time. Co-stars Hilda Moore and Wally Wales. 59 min.
10-7147 Was $19.99 ***$14.99***

Law And The Lawless (1933)
Drifting cowboy Jack Hoxie rides into town just in the nick of time: the townspeople are being bothered by some stinkin' cattle rustlers. Can Jack make them hit the road? Hilda Moore, Yakima Canutt also star. 59 min.
08-1733 ***$14.99***

Trouble Busters (1933)
Jack Hoxie and Lane Chandler are the problem-solving cowpokes who race against time in order to get a claim into the government for oil-rich land owned by an elderly man and his daughter before some crooks do. Kaye Edward and Harry Todd also star. 55 min.
68-9013 Was $19.99 ***$14.99***

Romance Rides The Range (1936)
While on his way home, cowboy Fred Scott rescues a young opera singer and her sickly brother who were duped by duplicitous snakes into investing their life savings in a rotten stretch of desert real estate. All things eventually work out in the surprise ending. Cliff Nazarro and Marion Shilling also star. 59 min.
68-9003 Was $19.99 ***$14.99***

The Singing Buckaroo (1937)
Cowboy hero Fred Scott finds himself caught between some desperadoes and a young girl who may have stolen some of their loot. As if that wasn't enough, there are horseback and car chases, a snake-oil salesman who does Jolson imitations and seven—count 'em—seven singing buckaroos!! 58 min.
09-1617 Was $24.99 ***$14.99***

Two Gun Troubador (1937)
Before the Lone Ranger films, Fred Scott starred as a mysterious masked troubador who fought for Western justice. Here he solves the mystery of his father's death. 59 min.
10-3013 Was $19.99 ***$14.99***

The Roaming Cowboy (1937)
Fred Scott stars as a nomadic cowboy who drifts into danger when he runs afoul of the lowdown hombres who are trying to run the local ranchers out! Sagebrush showdowns with Fuzzy St. John, Lois January. 56 min.
10-7289 Was $19.99 ***$14.99***

Melody Of The Plains (1937)
A singing cowpoke (Fred Scott) teams up with a 14-year-old girl for adventure. Song and action. Louise Small and White King the Horse co-star. 53 min.
10-7797 Was $19.99 ***$14.99***

Fighting Deputy (1937)
A tough deputy attempts to put an end to a range war that's about to go out of control in this wild Western saga starring Fred Scott, Al St. John and Eddie Holden. 60 min.
10-8377 Was $19.99 ***$14.99***

Moonlight On The Range (1937)
Fred Scott tackles two roles in this tumbleweed opera, playing both a notorious outlaw and his twin brother, who finds himself in hot water with the law because of the resemblance. Al St. John, Lois January also star. 62 min.
10-9413 Was $19.99 ***$14.99***

The Ranger's Roundup (1938)
Legendary funnyman Stan Laurel was producer for several Fred Scott "B" Westerns, including this one in which Texas Ranger Scott tackles baddies operating out of a traveling medicine show. Fred croons five tunes, too! Co-stars Al St. John, Christine McIntyre. 55 min.
10-7139 Was $19.99 ***$14.99***

Songs And Bullets (1938)
You can expect plenty of both, pardner, when singing cowpoke Fred Scott takes on cattle rustlers. Padding his resumé as sidekick is Al "Fuzzy" St. John, who moved on to become Lash LaRue's right hand man in the 1940s. 57 min.
10-7341 Was $19.99 ***$14.99***

Knight Of The Plains (1939)
A nasty crook selling fake land grants to Easterners, igniting a fight between the existing landowners and the Easterners. Can cowboy Fred Scott settle the trouble? Al St. John and former opera singer Marion Weldon also star. 55 min.
09-5122 Was $19.99 ***$14.99***

Code Of The Fearless (1939)
Fred Scott takes to the dusty trail to corral the two-legged coyotes who are making life miserable for a fair young ranchlady. All-out action on the range with Claire Rochelle, John Merton. 56 min.
10-7290 Was $19.99 ***$14.99***

In Old Montana (1939)
Cattlemen and sheepmen stand poised for all out war for control of the land, and government cowpoke Fred Dawson must use subterfuge to arrange a peace. Fred Scott, Jean Carmen. 60 min.
62-1227 Was $19.99 ***$14.99***

Buckaroo Sheriff Of Texas (1951)
Republic's first "moppet oater," a series of Westerns with children in lead roles, casts Michael Chapin as the pint-size grandson of a sheriff and the only stumbling block in the way of an evil land-grabber, who tries to take advantage of the town's men being off fighting in the Civil War. Co-stars Eileen Janssen, James Bell and Tristram Coffin. 60 min.
10-7986 Was $19.99 ***$14.99***

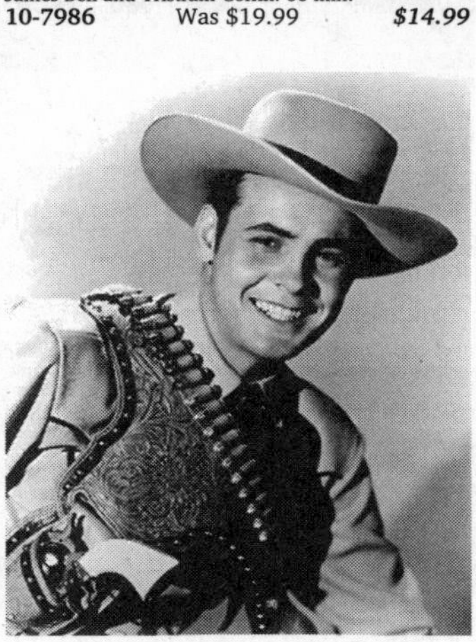

Rough Riders Of Cheyenne (1937)
Sunset Carson shines in this action-packed western saga as a cowpoke who goes to great lengths to stop a feud that has been part of his family for years. Peggy Stewart, Mira McKinney and Monte Hale star. 55 min.
10-8138 Was $19.99 ***$14.99***

The Code Of The Prairie (1944)
A rousing "B" western classic with Sunset Carson and Smiley Burnette helping an old pal and battling a shifty sheriff in the process. Peggy Stewart co-stars. 56 min.
10-7850 Was $19.99 ***$14.99***

Call Of The Rockies (1944)
It's not a call to play major league baseball in Colorado that Sunset Carson and Smiley Burnette hear, but the pleas for help from the good folk of Placer City, whose mine is threatened by some shady businessmen. With Ellen Hall, Kirk Alyn. 54 min.
63-1595 ***$14.99***

The Cherokee Flash (1945)
Sunset Carson learns that his gunman father is being forced to continue his criminal activities by the gang that he's been trying to leave, so good son Sunset and sidekick Tom London join forces with Dad to take on the crooks head-on. Toy Barcroft and Linda Stirling also star. 55 min.
10-7849 Was $19.99 ***$14.99***

Sheriff Of Cimarron (1945)
A stunt-filled Sunset Carson extravaganza, directed by action master Yakima Canutt. Carson calls on his brother to help him clear his name from a frame job, but discovers the sibling is a nasty killer. Gunfights galore! Linda Stirling, Jack Kirk co-star. 56 min.
10-7857 Was $19.99 ***$14.99***

Alias Billy The Kid (1946)
"Hey, that's not Billy! It's well-known white hat Sunset Carson!" Don't tell anyone, pardners, but Sunset goes undercover to get the goods on some crooked cattlemen in this "B" thriller. With Peggy Stewart, Roy Barcroft. 54 min.
63-1594 ***$14.99***

Sunset Carson Rides Again (1948)
Full-color tall-in-the-saddle action with series star Sunset Carson (just plain Michael Harrison to the folks back in Texas). Canyon culprits who try riding into this Sunset find themselves in a whole horizon of trouble. Al Terry co-stars.
10-7414 ***$14.99***

Fighting Mustang (1948)
Bronco-busting or taming a high-strung gal homesteader, it's all the same for Sunset Carson, baby-faced star of Republic westerns. Little seen sagebrush yarn co-stars Pat Starling.
10-7415 Was $19.99 ***$14.99***

Deadline (1948)
And time is definitely running out for Sunset Carson in this Western thriller. He's been framed for murder, and has to find the real killer before it's "necktie" time. With Pat Starling, Lee Roberts. 57 min.
10-7990 Was $19.99 ***$14.99***

Battling Marshal (1950)
Sunset Carson plays a frontier lawman who makes a terrible mistake and must go to great lengths to correct the problem. Pat Starling and Forrest Matthews join the battling lawman in this outing. 55 min.
10-8040 Was $19.99 ***$14.99***

The El Paso Kid (1953)
Sunset Carson and partner Hank Patterson break away from their gang of robbers, but after they've reformed the pair must take on their former comrades and bring them to justice. 54 min.
10-7851 Was $19.99 ***$14.99***

Tom Keene

Pardon My Gun (1930)
Billed under his original screen name of "George Duryea," Tom Keene stars in this early musical western as a ranch foreman who falls for his boss's daughter but has to keep a rival from sabotaging his efforts, as well as a local race. With Harry Woods, Sally Starr (not the "Popeye Theatre" hostess). 63 min.
10-9086 Was $19.99 ***$14.99***

Ghost Valley (1932)
A couple inherits land in an abandoned gold mining town which turns out to be sitting on top of a still-rich vein of unmined ore. To keep the secret wealth for himself, their caretaker tries to scare them away with ghost tales and gun play. Tom Keene and Mitchell Harris star. 54 min.
10-7340 Was $19.99 ***$14.99***

Come On Danger! (1932)
When his brother is killed by an outlaw gang whose roll call includes reluctant member Julie Haydon, Texas Ranger Tom Keene vows to risk any danger to bring the owlhoots to justice. Robert Ellis, Roscoe Ates co-star. 60 min.
10-7863 ***$14.99***

Beyond The Rockies (1932)
Tom Keene and a group of cowboys battle cattle rustlers in this humorous, six-shooting saga. Rochelle Hudson, Tom London, Julian Rivero. 55 min.
10-7864 Was $19.99 ***$14.99***

The Saddle Buster (1932)
Tom Keene goes rodeo ridin' in order to pay the hospital bills of a friend who was injured in a horse accident. Helen Foster, Charles Quigley. 59 min.
10-7865 Was $19.99 ***$14.99***

Under Strange Flags (1937)
History and western action mix as Pancho Villa helps cowpoke Tom Keene when a friend's silver mine is about to be taken over by nasty Federales led by Villa's renegade soldiers. With Luana Walters and Maurice Black. 61 min.
09-5134 Was $19.99 ***$14.99***

Where Trails Divide (1937)
Terrific Tom Keene plays a U.S. marshal who impersonates a lawyer to get to the bottom of thievery in the area. Eleanor Stewart and Warner Richmond also star. 59 min.
10-8041 Was $19.99 ***$14.99***

The Glory Trail (1937)
Indians are on the warpath and making trouble for railroad workers and soldiers assigned to the area. Leave it to scout Tom Keene to intercede and settle things down. With Joan Barclay and William Royle. 64 min.
10-8414 Was $19.99 ***$14.99***

Raw Timber (1937)
Tom Keene stars in this environmentally correct western adventure playing a forest ranger out to keep trees from being taken down by overzealous timber companies. With Peggy Keys. 63 min.
68-9032 Was $19.99 ***$14.99***

Battle Of Greed (1937)
Tom Keene leads a group of men from Indiana to gold country near Virginia City. Upon arriving, however, they discover a crooked mining company has made a claim for the land. In the meantime, Keene befriends Mark Twain. James Bush and Gwynne Shipman also star in this super sagebrusher.
68-9167 Was $19.99 ***$14.99***

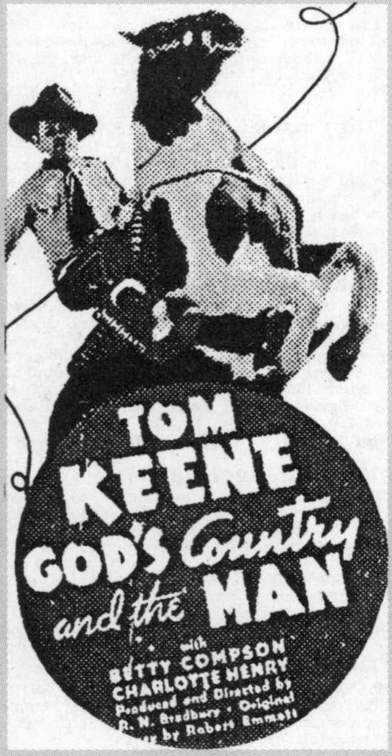

God's Country And The Man (1937)
Tom Keene, Betty Compson and Charles King star in this superior Western adventure about a cowboy who uses his contact with the Mounties to nab a gunman who's been threatening a dance hall girl. 56 min.
10-8257 Was $19.99 ***$14.99***

The Law Commands (1938)
Cowboy Tom Keene falls in love with the daughter of an Iowa settler, but eventually clashes with menacing bad guys in this oater that offers gorgeous Iowa scenery. Lorraine Hayes and Robert Fiske also star. 58 min.
09-5124 Was $19.99 ***$14.99***

The Painted Trail (1938)
Tom Keene plays a retired lawman who heads to Mexico to break up a smuggling ring. Quick-paced cowboy action! 50 min.
10-7805 Was $19.99 ***$14.99***

Wanderers Of The West (1941)
Tom Keene's pappy was killed in cold blood and now he's out to nab the culprits who did the dirty deed. The chase has him tracking them across the Southwest in this action-packed saga. With Betty Miles, Sugar Dawn and Tom London. 58 min.
10-8062 Was $19.99 ***$14.99***

Riding The Sunset Trail (1941)
The wild, wild west was never wilder than in this top-notch tale of Tom Keene trying to stop a con from cashing in on his dead half-brother's will. With Betty Miles, Frank Yaconelli. 56 min.
10-8065 Was $19.99 ***$14.99***

The Driftin' Kid (1941)
G-man Tom Keene poses as a rancher in order to nab a group of cattle rustlers. Lloyd "Arkansas Slim" Andrews, Betty Miles, Glenn Strange also star. 57 min.
10-8271 Was $19.99 ***$14.99***

Dynamite Canyon (1941)
Following the murder of a prominent rancher and a Texas Ranger, lawman Tom Keene goes undercover to catch the killer. Exciting western adventure also stars Evelyn Finley, Stanley Price and Rusty the Wonder Horse. 60 min.
10-8444 Was $19.99 ***$14.99***

Where Trails End (1942)
Where trails end, trouble begins! Tom Keene and his sidekick Pierre find this out, and in the process are shot at, ambushed, tied up, and generally bothered. But wait...will the Nazis take over the valley, or will Tom save the day? 54 min.
09-1732 Was $19.99 ***$14.99***

Western Mail (1942)
Tom Keene whittles his way into a knot of nefarious ne'er-do-wells to make Swiss cheese outta the big cheese, while comic relief Frank Yaconelli plays his belly fiddle and toys with his pet monkey. 54 min.
10-7174 Was $19.99 ***$14.99***

Lone Star Lawmen (1942)
A border town is overrun with lawlessness and corruption...and deputy marshal Tom Keene must go undercover to infiltrate the murderous bandit pack and bring 'em down from within! With Frank Yaconelli, Sugar Dawn. 58 min.
10-7197 Was $19.99 ***$14.99***

Arizona Roundup (1942)
Tom Keene does battle with greedy speculators who force innocent ranchers off their property to resell the beef at highwayman rates. Sugar Dawn, Jack Ingram. 54 min.
62-1238 Was $19.99 ***$14.99***

MOVIES UNLIMITED

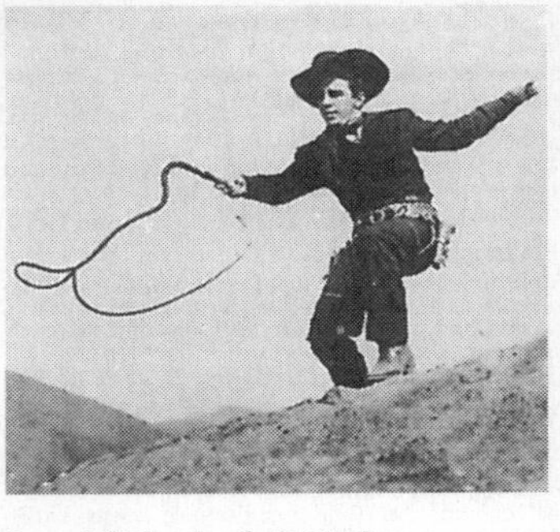

Law Of The Lash (1947)
Prospector Al St. John has more than he could handle with the outlaws infesting his town. When undercover marshal Lash La Rue takes a hand, those rannies will be whipped into line...literally! Mary Scott, Charles King co-star. 53 min.
10-1239 $14.99

The Fighting Vigilantes (1947)
Lash La Rue puts the whip to a fiendish food distributor who's systematically snuffing the other munchie magnates of the mesas! (Talk about unfair competition!) Snaps, cracks, and pops with Al St. John, Jennifer Holt, George Chesebro. 61 min.
10-7567 Was $19.99 $14.99

Pioneer Justice (1947)
Lash La Rue handles his whip with incredible style and grace in this intense Western actioner that pits him against a crook who thinks he's a Napoleon of the Plains. Al St. John, Jennifer Holt also star. 55 min.
10-9159 $14.99

Stage To Mesa City (1948)
Western whippersnapper Lash La Rue and hirsute helper "Fuzzy" St. John are called on to catch a roving band of stage robbers in this all-out Western actioner. 52 min.
45-5207 $14.99

Son Of Billy The Kid (1949)
Legendary Lash La Rue stars in this "what-if" western that poses the question: "What if Pat Garrett never actually killed Billy the Kid?" Here the Kid straightens out and becomes an honest banker. Stagecoaches, bandits, robberies and shoot-outs spark the action. With Al St. John, June Carr.
10-8407 $14.99

Outlaw Country (1949)
One of Lash La Rue's most exciting outings finds him playing both a whip-cracking lawman and the leader of a gang of counterfeiters. There's lots of action as Lash and pal Fuzzy St. John try to get their man and his gang of money manufacturers. Complete and uncut, this western clocks in at 72 min.!
10-9136 $14.99

King Of The Bullwhip (1950)
From the dramatic whip fight that opens this Lash La Rue oater, you know you're in for a treat. Watch as Lash goes undercover to catch a bank robber who uses his bullwhip technique. Also stars Jack Holt, "Fuzzy" St. John. 60 min.
10-1141 Was $19.99 $14.99

The Thundering Trail (1951)
Bullwhip-wielding badman-basher Lash La Rue must act as bodyguard to the governor-elect as he journeys to the capital...and some obnoxious owlhoots are out to put off the swearing in permanently! Al St. John, Sally Anglim co-star. 55 min.
10-7566 Was $19.99 $14.99

The Black Lash (1952)
Whipslinger Lash La Rue has the whip hand over a band of stagecoach robbers after squeezing his way into their circle by telling their chowderheaded leader that he needs a little extra cash. "Fuzzy" St. John and Kermit Maynard co-star. 57 min.
10-7144 Was $19.99 $14.99

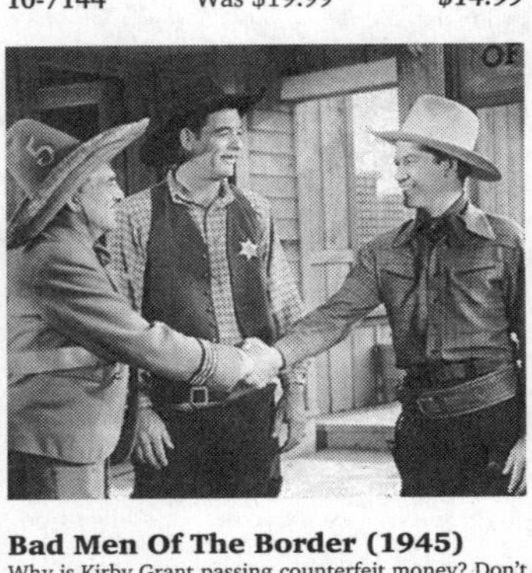

Bad Men Of The Border (1945)
Why is Kirby Grant passing counterfeit money? Don't worry, he's just running the bogus bills to get in the good graces of an outlaw gang...and they'll be sorry once he does! Fuzzy Knight, Amida, Glenn Strange co-star. 56 min.
10-7584 Was $19.99 $14.99

Tom Tyler

Canyon Of Missing Men (1930)
Tom Tyler stars in this silent Western that helped define his cowboy character. Here he's torn between love and duty when he falls for the daughter of an outlaw gangleader. With Tom Forman, Sheila LeGay. 45 min.
62-1302 Was $19.99 $14.99

Call Of The Desert (1930)
This silent effort features Tom Tyler as a fellow drifting across the desert with a map that he hopes leads to his father's gold. After being left for dead by partner Bud Osbourne, who also swipes the map, Tyler is saved by a beautiful woman. He discovers later that she's actually the creep's niece. Now what?! With Sheila LeGay. Silent with music score.
68-9200 Was $19.99 $14.99

West Of Cheyenne (1931)
Tom Tyler joining a gang of outlaws in the Wyoming frontier town of Ghost City? Don't worry, western fans, it's all part of Tom's plan to nab the varmints who killed his pa. With Josephine Hill, Harry Woods.
09-2996 Was $19.99 $14.99

Two-Fisted Justice (1931)
Tom Tyler stars with Barbara Weeks and Yakima Canutt. A town, ripe for justice, is threatened by stagecoach robberies and Indian raids. When a young boy's parents are killed, Tom adopts him and becomes law of the territory. 54 min.
62-1148 Was $19.99 $14.99

The Forty-Niners (1932)
Someone discovers that there's gold in them thar California hills, and the rush begins. But trouble rears its ugly head and Tom Tyler has to step in. With Betty Mack, Al Bridge. 60 min.
10-8185 Was $19.99 $14.99

Deadwood Pass (1933)
Tom Tyler comes to the rescue of future W.C. Fields paramour Carlotta Monti in this sagebrusher that boasts gunplay, chases and more. Alice Dahl, Buffalo Bill, Jr. co-star. 60 min.
10-8186 Was $19.99 $14.99

When A Man Rides Alone (1933)
Tom Tyler stars as the "Llano Kid," but most folks call him the "Robin Hood of the Rockies," enemy of the rich and friend to the poor.
21-3009 Was $19.99 $14.99

War Of The Range (1933)
There'll be plenty of discouraging words heard if cowpoke Tom Tyler's efforts to put off war on the range between his rancher father and a greedy rival don't work in this top-notch frontier tale. With Lane Chandler, Caryl Lincoln.
68-9110 Was $19.99 $14.99

Mystery Ranch (1934)
A successful author of western stories decides to see what the Wild West is really like when he agrees to spend some time with real cowboys at Mystery Ranch. There he learns a thing or two about the rugged lifestyle first-hand. Tom Tyler, Roberta Gale and Jack Gable star in this seminal, "City Slickers"-styled sagebrusher. 50 min.
08-1719 $14.99

Trigger Tom (1935)
And Tom Tyler had better keep his finger on that trigger when he and hired hand Al St. John head into the Blue Mountains, home to "renegades and outlaws," and help a cattleman save his herd from sidewindin' crooks. With William Gould, Bernadine Hayes. 60 min.
10-8198 Was $19.99 $14.99

Tracy Rides (1935)
Exemplary Tom Tyler western yarn with Tom as a sheriff whose girlfriend's brother is involved with a gang that raids an elderly sheepherder's ranch, then kills him. Tom's terrific, but he's stuck between his loyalty to his job and his girlfriend and her family. With Edmund Cobb, Virginia Faire.
09-2997 Was $19.99 $14.99

Coyote Trails (1935)
Ornery owlhoots are out to ouster a defenseless widder woman off her homestead. You'll marvel as Tom Tyler straps on his shootin' irons and sends them runnin' back to their mummies. Helen Dahl, Ben Corbett co-star. 68 min.
10-7295 Was $19.99 $14.99

The Laramie Kid (1935)
Tom Tyler is a rootin', tootin' Western hero with guts, guns and a great desire to entertain. He's out to nab a batch of bad guys, including The Laramie Kid, the baddest of 'em all.
10-7909 Was $19.99 $14.99

Ridin' Thru (1935)
Tom Tyler rides on thru to the other side—of danger. He's got a horse, a gun and lots of savvy, battlin' the baddies and baggin' the babes.
10-7910 Was $19.99 $14.99

Rio Rattler (1935)
These rattlers aren't the kind you'll find at Clyde Peeling's Reptileland, but some two-legged reptiles who murder a local lawman. It's up to Tom Tyler to pin on the badge in his place and defang the desperados. Marion Schilling, Eddie Gibbon also star. 60 min.
10-8387 Was $19.99 $14.99

Unconquered Bandit (1935)
Tom Tyler stars in this western saga involving the discovery of gold over the Mexican border of a ranch owned by a ruthless man who wants the gold all to himself. Also starring is Slim Whitaker. 55 min.
10-9846 $14.99

Born To Battle (1935)
Action-packed, fists-a-flyin' Western yarn with Tom Tyler as a trouble-making cowpoke who gets one last chance as the overseer of a large ranch. Soon, he finds himself embroiled in a war against cattle rustlers and other outlaws. This one's noted for a scene in which Tom tears a Chinese laundry apart—looking for a shirt. With Jean Carmen. 58 min.
68-8967 Was $19.99 $14.99

Silent Valley (1935)
This valley may be quiet, but there's lots of trouble around for Sheriff Tom Tyler. The lawman's gal pal's brother joins a group of outlaws because of some serious gambling problems. Since Gamblers Anonymous wasn't around then, Tom has to put his boots down and try to help him. With Wally Wales and Nancy Deshon.
68-9165 Was $19.99 $14.99

Ridin' On (1936)
Tom Tyler takes the weary trail home to find his pop engaged in land warfare with the neighboring ranch. It gets more complicated when Tom falls for the girl next door! Leather-slapping action with Geraine Greear, Rex Lease. 59 min.
10-7199 Was $19.99 $14.99

Roamin' Wild (1936)
Tom Tyler is a cowboy par excellence in this high-flyin', way-out-West saga. Tom's terrific, ropin', ridin' and shootin'!
10-7912 Was $19.99 $14.99

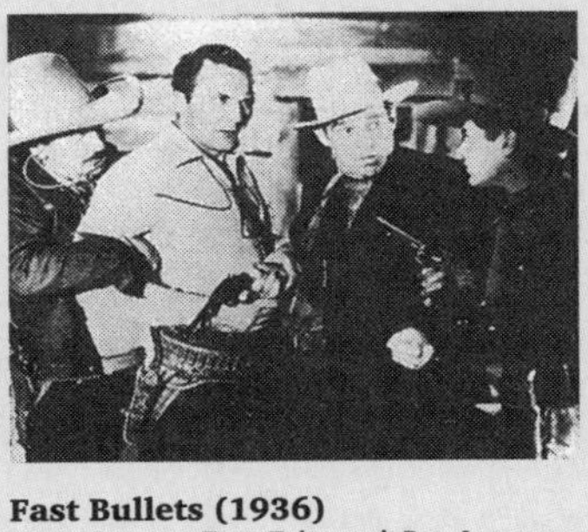

Fast Bullets (1936)
Texas Rangers Tom Tyler and Rex Lease are breathin' down the necks of some dad-blamed coyotes who've kidnapped a young woman, and ingeniously outwit the baddies with dummies on horseback in this exciting B oater. 59 min.
10-7117 Was $19.99 $14.99

Rip Roarin' Buckaroo (1936)
A change-of-pace sagebrusher for Tom Tyler, as the ex-boxer plays a fighter who retires for a life of ranching after he loses a fixed match. The ring beckons him, however, when his boss gets involved with a crooked promoter and Tom has to put the gloves on again. With Beth Marion and Sammy Cohen. 58 min.
68-9001 Was $19.99 $14.99

The Phantom Of The Range (1937)
Tom Tyler, who would go on to play "The Mummy," plays a wandering cowboy who joins forces with a Western woman traveling through the badlands in hopes of selling her grandfather's property. Grandpa's ghost, however, seems to be following her around, scaring potential purchasers. Is it really his ghost? With Beth Marion, Sammy Cohen. 58 min.
09-5127 Was $19.99 $14.99

Pinto Rustlers (1937)
Young cowhand Tom Tyler slaps leather and rides out to put the pinch on the band of rustlers who deep-sixed his folks in this slam-bang shoot-'em-up. Co-stars George Walsh and Al St. John. 60 min.
10-7111 Was $19.99 $14.99

Santa Fe Bound (1937)
Tom Tyler is framed for killing a rancher and is forced to pose as an outlaw in this slam-bang action-packed outing. With Jeanne Martel, Richard Cramer. 55 min.
10-8192 Was $19.99 $14.99

Brothers Of The West (1937)
Tom Tyler must corral the thieves who have framed his brother and find him before he takes a drastic measure. With Bob Terry and Dorothy Short. 57 min.
62-1234 Was $19.99 $14.99

The Lost Ranch (1937)
Tom Tyler is an investigator working for the Cattlemen's Protection Association called on to find a group of kidnappers who have taken two Eastern girls into custody. Can he outwit the shifty group of hombres responsible for the crime? Jeanne Martel, Forrest Taylor also star. 56 min.
68-8987 Was $19.99 $14.99

Mystery Range (1937)
There's action galore as Tom Tyler rides into action as an agent for Texas cattlemen who discovers that an ornery long rider he's met before is out to swindle a young girl who owns property the railroad desperately wants. Milburn Morante and Jim Correy (not the Philadelphia radio fitness expert) star. 56 min.
68-8999 Was $19.99 $14.99

Cheyenne Rides Again (1938)
Action-packed Western has Tom Tyler working his way into an outlaw gang in order to put the kibosh on their plans to take over cattle ranchers' territory. With Lucille Browne, Lon Chaney, Jr., and sidekick Jimmy Fox, who sings "Storybook Cowboy." 62 min.
09-1061 Was $19.99 $14.99

Feud Of The Trail (1938)
Versatile Tom Tyler doubles in brass as both a virtuous sheriff and the bad guy he's gunning for. Bad guy Tyler and three of his hornswogglin' chums rob good guy Tyler's Pop's ranch, but meet their Maker in a blazing exchange of lead. 58 min.
10-7118 Was $19.99 $14.99

Orphan Of The Pecos (1938)
Unique "B" Western with Tom Tyler smashing a murderer with help from a ventriloquist. Jean Martel and Slim Whitaker co-star. 57 min.
17-3010 Was $19.99 $14.99

Fighting Hero (1941)
Express company detective Tom Tyler adopts the persona of an outlaw to help a Mexican woman unjustly accused of murdering a local official. This rip-roaring Western entry also stars Renee Borden and Edward Hearn. 55 min.
68-8977 Was $19.99 $14.99

Lightning Range (1933)
A pea-brained pack of desperadoes has its sights on a pretty young gal's inheritance...and they're not going to brook any interference from deputy marshal Buddy Roosevelt! Western action with Lafe McKee, Patsy Bellamy. 55 min.
09-2086 Was $19.99 $14.99

The Boss Cowboy (1934)
He may not be from Nebraska or ride near the river, but Buddy Roosevelt is a Western hero who was born in the U.S.A. and is always ready to keep any outlaw darkness on the edge of town. With Francis Morris, George Chesebro, Bud Osborne. 60 min.
10-9153 Was $19.99 $14.99

Range Riders (1934)
An elderly rancher asks his son to return home in order to get rid of a gang of mean-spirited thugs. Sonny boy takes no prisoners, kicking their rears from here to the Texas border in this no-nonsense tumbleweed tummeller. Buddy Roosevelt, Lew Meeham and Barbara Starr star.
68-8991 Was $19.99 $14.99

Buffalo Bill In Tomahawk Territory (1952)
Clayton Moore ditches his mask as he plays William F. Cody himself, out to make a peace offering to the Sioux in order to keep the trails safe...but an ornery group of Indian impersonators are out to stir up the warpath! 63 min.
09-2032 Was $29.99 $14.99

Son Of The Renegade (1953)
Western winner about a cowboy who inherits a sprawling ranch from his disliked father and is framed for a series of robberies by some blackhats who want his spread. John Carpenter, Lori Irving and John McKellen star. 57 min.
10-8384 Was $19.99 $14.99

Outlaw Treasure (1955)
Cowboy star John Carpenter is enlisted by the feds to discover the location of stolen gold. Things get tougher when the notorious James Gang rides into town a-whoopin' and a-whoppin' and causing all sorts of trouble. "Red" Carpenter and Adele Jergens co-star. 65 min.
10-8067 Was $19.99 $14.99

Raiders Of Old California (1957)
A section of California inhabited by Mexicans is the setting for this sagebrusher about a pioneer who helps the Mexican owner of a hacienda who's being forced to sign over his land to a nasty cavalry officer. Jim Davis, Arleen Whelan, Marty Robbins and Lee Van Cleef star. 72 min.
09-5128 Was $19.99 $14.99

A Lust To Kill (1957)
After his kid brother is slaughtered by law officers, a bandit gets even more ornery, escaping the law with help from his gal pal and seeking revenge on his former partner, whom he holds responsible for the killing. Jim Davis, Don Megowan and Allison Hayes star.
68-8989 Was $19.99 $14.99

Frontier Uprising (1961)
Exciting sagebrush adventure detailing a tough scout's efforts to battle Indians and Mexican villains in order to control an important California territory for the U.S. Government. Jim Davis and Nancy Hadley star.
10-8437 $14.99

Tim McCoy

Fighting For Justice (1932)
When you're cowboy fave Tim McCoy, pardner, that's what you do 24 hours a day. McCoy's a real pain to a bunch of dastardly scofflaws in this rambunctious "B" western. Co-stars Walter Brennan, Joyce Compton.
10-7890 Was $19.99 **$14.99**

The Riding Tornado (1932)
Bronco-busting Tim McCoy falls for a female rancher, then must protect her from a shady ranch-hand. McCoy is a human tornado! Shirley Grey, Wallace MacDonald co-star. 64 min.
10-7892 Was $19.99 **$14.99**

The Fighting Marshal (1932)
Tricky Tim McCoy is released from prison after serving time for a crime he did not commit. He assumes the role of a deceased sheriff and goes to work to find the felons who done him in. With Dorothy Gulliver, Mary Carr. 58 min.
10-7899 Was $19.99 **$14.99**

Daring Danger (1932)
A two-fisted Tim McCoy Western in which Tim is framed for holding a rustler's trick iron while tracking the real culprits. Alberta Vaughn, Wallace McDonald also star. 58 min.
10-8264 Was $19.99 **$14.99**

Fighting Fool (1932)
When sheriff Tim McCoy tries to get info on a bad guy named "The Shadow" from a sexy dancehall gal, his girlfriend gets upset; and when he finally discovers who the bandit really is, a big surprise is in store. With Marceline Day. 57 min.
10-8365 Was $19.99 **$14.99**

Cornered (1932)
Tim McCoy shows off his athletic and gunslinging talents in this enthralling Western adventure as a sheriff competing with a ranch foreman for the same girl. When the girl's father is murdered, the ranch-hand escapes and joins an outlaw gang, only to be pursued by McCoy. Shirley Grey, Niles Welch also star. 60 min.
10-9220 Was $19.99 **$14.99**

The Western Code (1932)
Freudian "B" western with Tim McCoy as the hero who saves a woman terrorized by her evil stepfather, who plans to marry her and kill her brother. Nora Lane, Mischa Auer and Wheeler Oakman co-star. 60 min.
10-9766 **$14.99**

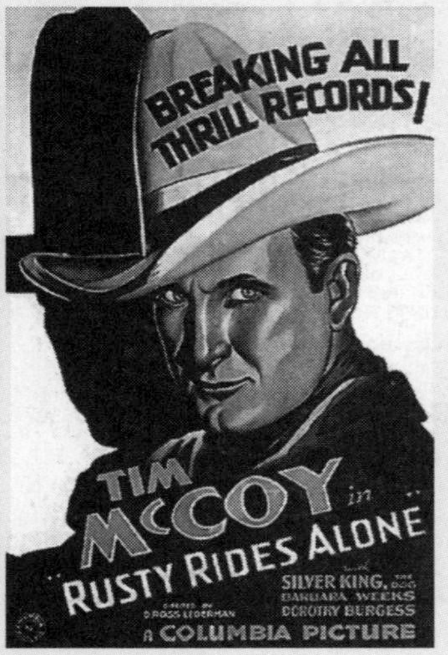

BREAKING ALL THRILL RECORDS!
TIM McCOY in
RUSTY RIDES ALONE
SILVER KING,
BARBARA WEEKS
DOROTHY BURGESS
A COLUMBIA PICTURE

Rusty Rides Alone (1933)
A ruthless sheepherder uses underhanded means to drive ranchers from their land and cowboy hero Tim McCoy must find a way to stop the cad. Barbara Weeks, Wheeler Oakman co-star. 60 min.
10-8441 Was $19.99 **$14.99**

Bulldog Courage (1935)
You can bet that two-gun Tim McCoy gets rrrruff with the bad guys in this sagebrush saga, mustering up his courage to take a bite out of crime. With Joan Woodbury, Eddie Buzzard. 67 min.
08-1457 **$14.99**

Square Shooter (1935)
Tim McCoy, the king of the horse-ridin' wonder cowpokes, shows off his expertise with a gun, tackling evil black hats.
10-7893 Was $19.99 **$14.99**

Fighting Shadows (1935)
Impressive riding highlights this Tim McCoy sagebrush saga, in which McCoy plays a tough lawman who beats a group of cattle rustlers endangering local innocents. With Robert Allen, Ward Bond. 58 min.
10-7902 Was $19.99 **$14.99**

The Revenge Rider (1935)
Tim McCoy tackles the terrible outlaws who killed his brother in this energetic western saga. With Robert Allen, Billie Seward. 60 min.
10-8197 Was $19.99 **$14.99**

The Outlaw Deputy (1935)
Terrific oater starring Tim McCoy as a gangleader who leads his outlaws in a number of stagecoach robberies and cattle rustling activities. McCoy's efforts eventually harm a corrupt rancher responsible for the death of his friend. With Nora Lane, Hooper Alchley.
68-9066 Was $19.99 **$14.99**

The Prescott Kid (1936)
That's "Prescott" as in "Prescott, Arizona," and that's "Kid" as in "Tim McCoy," who uses his gunslinging prowess to bust open a castle-rustling ring. With Sheila Mannors, Joseph Sauers.
02-2734 **$14.99**

The Ghost Patrol (1936)
Six-shooters and sci-fi mix in an unusual Western epic, with G-Man Tim McCoy trying to find out who is using a deadly ray gun that can pull planes out of the sky. Claudia Dell, Walter Miller co-star. 58 min.
08-1089 **$14.99**

The Traitor (1936)
Say it ain't so—Texas Ranger Tim McCoy handing over his badge and joining a gang of bandits? It's all part of an undercover mission to bring the baddies to justice, but things get complicated when the only person who knows McCoy's on the up and up dies! With Frances Grant, Karl Hackett. 57 min.
08-1095 **$14.99**

Aces And Eights (1936)
A crooked cardsharp ambles into town, intent on taking the townspeople for all they've got. You can lay even money, though, that Tim McCoy will empty his sleeves of sneaky tricks real fast! Luana Walters, Wheeler Oakman, Rex Lease co-star.
10-1240 **$14.99**

Border Caballero (1936)
Tim McCoy and lady cowpoke Lois January try to topple the villains, but have to shoot the skies out to do it. Two-fisted Western. 57 min.
10-1372 Was $19.99 **$14.99**

The Lion's Den (1936)
Straight-shootin' Tim McCoy trades his white hat for black to weed his way into a bunch of bad guys bullyraggin' a rancher and his cowhands. Joan Woodbury and Arthur Millett co-star. 59 min.
10-7113 Was $19.99 **$14.99**

Roarin' Guns (1936)
Cattle company bigwigs hire Tim McCoy to quash a violent range war that's hogtying business. But McCoy is a cowpoke, not a magician, and only after quick-draw Tommy Bupp comes to bat for him do things take a turn for the better. 57 min.
10-7116 **$14.99**

The Man From Gun Town (1936)
A pack of scheming sidewinders have hit on the perfect scheme to rid themselves of a stubborn rancher woman...dry gulch her brother, and then frame her for it! Tim McCoy takes to the trail to set things right. Rex Lease, Billie Seward also star. 58 min.
10-7264 Was $19.99 **$14.99**

Lightning Bill Carson (1936)
All sorts of meanies—outlaws, cattle thieves and others—are no match for tough guy Tim McCoy in this powerful bit of Western wildness. Lois January, Rex Lease co-star. 75 min.
10-7903 Was $19.99 **$14.99**

Lightning Carson Rides Again (1938)
One of early Westerns' most popular straight-shooters, Colonel Tim McCoy, rides as a tough lawman who must rescue his nephew from a gang of outlaws, and clear the lad's name of a theft of cash. 58 min.
09-2006 Was $19.99 **$14.99**

Phantom Ranger (1938)
Counterfeiting coyotes have kidnapped a government engraver...and Tim McCoy goes undercover to flush out the funny-money felons! Suzanne Kaaren, Karl Hackett also star. 54 min.
10-7265 Was $19.99 **$14.99**

West Of Rainbow's End (1938)
Bullets come down like rain in this action-packed entry in the Tim McCoy "B" Western canon. He's a retired railroad investigator who picks up his gun to avenge the death of his foster father and best friend. 57 min.
10-7896 Was $19.99 **$14.99**

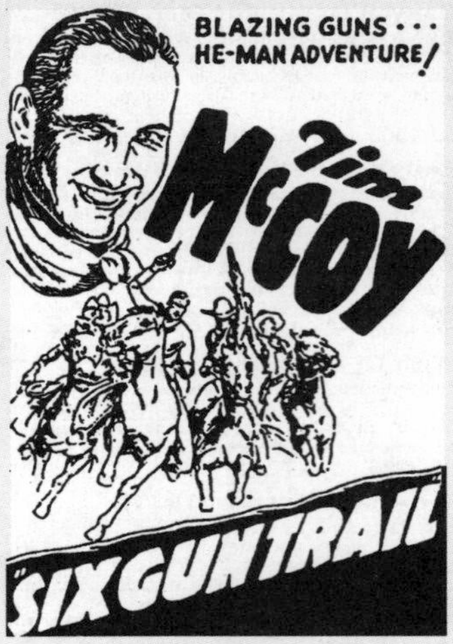

BLAZING GUNS . . . HE-MAN ADVENTURE!
Tim McCOY
SIX GUN TRAIL

Six Gun Trail (1938)
Tim McCoy impersonates a Chinese jewel smuggler in order to gain the confidence of a group of thieves dealing in stolen gems. There's lots of action and some interesting racial elements to this hard-hitting oater. Ben Corbett and Ted Adams also star. 59 min.
68-9006 Was $19.99 **$14.99**

Code Of The Rangers (1938)
Tim McCoy and Rex Lease are brothers who are Texas Rangers, but Tim doesn't know that bro is secretly a member of a gang that's been terrorizing the region. With the law getting closer to Rex, Tim goes to prison to save his sibling. Wheeler Oakman also star in this wild oater.
68-9214 **$14.99**

Texas Wildcats (1939)
A price hangs over the head of perpetual paladin Tim McCoy set by a loathsome villain who'd like to dupe a homesteader out of a rich gold vein on his land. With Joan Barclay and Ben Corbett. 57 min.
10-7114 Was $19.99 **$14.99**

Fighting Renegade (1939)
Tim McCoy manages a narrow squeak after being wrongfully accused of killing the leader of a scientific expedition by posing as bandito El Puma. Exciting horse opera co-stars Joyce Bryant, Ben Corbett. 54 min.
10-7115 Was $19.99 **$14.99**

Trigger Fingers (1939)
Lawman Tim McCoy dons Gypsy garb in order to nab a gang of greedy rustlers. His plan? To deal cards to the outlaws, thereby getting their fingerprints on the cards! Ben Corbett, Jill Martin star; "B"-moviemeister Sam Katzman produced. 55 min.
10-7825 **$14.99**

Outlaw's Paradise (1939)
Western superstar Tim McCoy does double duty here, playing a government official tracking mail bond thieves as well as one of the culprits. You could lose your mind when cowpokes are two of a kind! With Benny Corbett, Joan Barclay. 62 min.
10-7905 Was $19.99 **$14.99**

Code Of The Cactus (1939)
The always-thrilling Tim McCoy turns in a heroic performance as a cowpoke who uses all of his skills to stop a group of ornery owlhoots refusing to abide by the law. Dorothy Short, Forrest Taylor also star. 60 min.
10-9145 Was $19.99 **$14.99**

Straight Shooter (1940)
Tim McCoy plays a cowboy enlisted to track down a gang of outlaws who murdered a government agent during the robbery of government bonds. He locates them, but will he be able to bring them to justice? Julie Sheldon, Ben Corbett also star. 54 min.
09-5278 Was $19.99 **$14.99**

Riders Of Black Mountain (1940)
Well, ye-hahh! Tim McCoy, that dapper cowpoke, saves the day when the Black Mountain Stage finds itself in danger. Rex Lease, Pauline Haddon co-star. AKA: "Black Mountain Stage." 55 min.
10-8034 Was $19.99 **$14.99**

Arizona Gangbusters (1940)
Tim McCoy calls on all his cowboy bravado to halt the corrupt town officials. High-riding western thrills, co-starring Pauline Haddon and Forrest Taylor. 55 min.
10-8194 Was $19.99 **$14.99**

The Texas Marshal (1941)
Cowboy hero Tim McCoy tries to corral a gang of gold-seeking hombres who have disguised themselves as the "League of Patriots" in order to pull off their heists. Kay Leslie, Karl Hackett also star. 58 min.
09-5132 Was $19.99 **$14.99**

Canyon Hawks (1930)
These hawks aren't the kind you'll find on an Audubon Society checklist, but some dirty birds who harass innocent sheepherders until Wally Wales rides in, a-whoppin' and a-wailin', and turns the hawks into jailbirds. With Yakima Canutt, Buzz Barton. NOTE: This rare find was taken from a 16mm print that was professionally edited to about 40 min.
68-9106 Was $19.99 **$14.99**

Flying Lariats (1931)
The rope goes swirling, the fists start flying, and the guns begin shooting in this high-energy sagebrusher accented by wild lariat stuntwork. Wally Wales and Buzz Barton star. 60 min.
10-9218 Was $19.99 **$14.99**

Way Of The West (1935)
A family living on a government-leased stretch of grazing land are terrorized by a notorious hombre. The feud draws the attention of cowboy Wally Wales, but when he confronts the villain, more trouble ensues. Little Bobbie Nelson, Fred Parker also star. 51 min.
68-9016 Was $19.99 **$14.99**

Cavalier Of The West (1931)
Harry Carey stars in this early talkie oater that boasts desperados and Injuns singin' and shootin', a frame-up for murder, and the most action east of the Pecos! Carmen LaRoux, Kane Richmond co-star. 65 min.
10-7201 Was $19.99 **$14.99**

The Night Rider (1932)
No talking car here, but plenty of rough-ridin', six-shootin' action as Harry Carey disguises himself as a notorious hooded villain to catch said villain in a fists-a-flyin' showdown. Co-stars Eleanor Fair and George "Gabby" Hayes in an early sidekick role. 72 min.
10-7146 Was $19.99 **$14.99**

Without Honors (1932)
Cowboy Harry Carey is out to prove his late brother was no outlaw, so he joins the Texas Rangers and eventually faces the men responsible for his sibling's death and ruined reputation. Gibson Gowland, Gabby Hayes co-star. 55 min.
10-9160 **$14.99**

Wild Mustang (1935)
Bang-up oater with sheriff Harry Carey out to mow down a sadistic ring of outlaws who relish in branding their victims. His son wriggles his way onto the scene, posing as a gang member to set a trap but nearly bollixing the whole game plan. Co-stars Del Gordon and Barbara Fritchie. 61 min.
10-7141 Was $19.99 **$14.99**

The Last Of The Clintons (1935)
No, it's not Kenneth Starr's innermost dream, but a sensational spurs-and-saddles saga starring Harry Carey as a lawman who enlists the aid of a reclusive prospector when he goes undercover to round up a cattle rustling ring. With Berry Mack, Del Gordon. 59 min.
10-7287 Was $19.99 **$14.99**

Rustler's Paradise (1935)
Harry Carey is nearing the end of a long, hard trail of vengeance in search of the man who stole away his wife and daughter many years ago. Revenge on the range with Slim Whitaker, Chief Thundercloud. 61 min.
10-7288 Was $19.99 **$14.99**

Wagon Trail (1935)
A sheriff is fired from his job after his son, who was convicted for taking part in a stagecoach robbery and sentenced to hang, escapes from jail. The now ex-lawman races against time to learn the truth about the stage heist and clear both their names. Harry Carey, Jr., Edward Norris and Roger Williams star. 55 min.
68-9015 Was $19.99 **$14.99**

The Last Outlaw (1936)
Terrific combo of sagebrusher and satire with Harry Carey as a notorious bankrobber released from 25 years in prison who reteams with his old pal, sheriff Hoot Gibson, to stop some ornery kidnappers. John Ford co-scripted. 72 min.
58-8123 **$14.99**

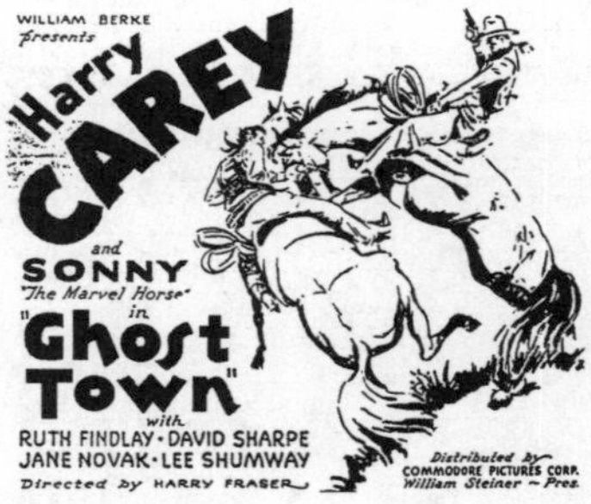

WILLIAM BERKE Presents
Harry CAREY
and SONNY "The Marvel Horse" in
"Ghost Town"
with
RUTH FINDLAY · DAVID SHARPE
JANE NOVAK · LEE SHUMWAY
Directed by HARRY FRASER
Distributed by COMMODORE PICTURES CORP.
William Steiner – Pres.

Ghost Town (1936)
Range-riding adventure by the saddleful as Harry Carey fights to reclaim his old friend's stake in an abandoned town with a fabulous mine below. With Dave Sharpe. 56 min.
62-1268 Was $19.99 **$14.99**

Aces Wild (1937)
Harry Carey saddles up and slaps leather as he takes on a pack of desperadoes with a loot-laden hidden mine hanging in the balance. Gertrude Messinger, Phil Dunham and Snowflake co-star. 57 min.
10-7585 Was $19.99 **$14.99**

Ken Maynard

$50,000 Reward (1924)
Ken Maynard holds a coveted land deed and an unscrupulous banker is after it—and he will stop at nothing to get it. Ken squares off against a gang of outlaws and rescues a girl and her father in the process. 49 min. Silent with music score.
62-5140 Was $19.99 *$14.99*

The Demon Rider (1926)
After capturing the mysterious Black Hawk and his ornery black hats, Ken Maynard attempts to return the gold they've swiped. But when the posse arrives, Black Hawk convinces them that Maynard is also a bad guy. Can Ken redeem himself? With Alma Rayford. NOTE: This rare film has been produced from the only 16mm print available and is missing the first reel. 37 min. Silent with music score.
68-9159 Was $19.99 *$14.99*

The Red Raiders (1927)
Ken Maynard is at his charismatic Western hero best in this lively tumbleweed tale in which he attempts to warn rustlers of an impending Indian attack. Ann Drew co-stars. 65 min. Silent with music score.
10-9223 Was $19.99 *$14.99*

The Fighting Legion (1930)
A late silent western with Ken Maynard in search of the man who killed his Texas Ranger brother. Lively action and great fun, co-starring Dorothy Dwan, Ernie Adams. 70 min. Silent with musical score.
10-8190 Was $19.99 *$14.99*

Mountain Justice (1930)
The first all-talking Ken Maynard outing, with the singing cowboy heading West in search of his father's murderer. Stunts on train and on a buckboard highlight this classic "B" saga. Kathryn Crawford sings "Buffalo Gal." 72 min.
10-7926 Was $19.99 *$14.99*

Fighting Through (1931)
Framed for the murder of his partner by some two-bit tinhorns out to hoodwink the dead man's sister out of her inheritance, Ken Maynard comes fighting through for justice. Co-stars Jeanette Loff. AKA: "California in 1878." 61 min.
10-7108 *$14.99*

Range Law (1931)
Ken Maynard is at his six-shootin' finest after he's framed for a crime, and springs himself from the hoosegow in a quest to clear his name. Frances Dade, Charles King co-star. 63 min.
10-7255 *$14.99*

The Two Gun Man (1931)
Ken Maynard is a-ridin' with both barrels a-blazin' as he sets out to smash an ornery passel (is there any other kind?) of cattle rustlers. A bullet for every badman with Lucille Powers, Lafe McKee. 60 min.
10-7257 *$14.99*

Branded Men (1931)
Ken Maynard saddles up in search of some frontier justice in this great, early talkie oater. June Clyde, Irving Bacon, Billy Bletcher co-star. 70 min.
10-7632 *$14.99*

Alias The Bad Man (1931)
The cattle rustlers are at it again, causing all sorts of problems with their ruthlessness and murdering the father of a sweet Western lady. Ken Maynard has a plan to stop them in their tracks. Charles King, Virginia Browne Faire and Lee McKee star. 65 min.
10-9144 Was $19.99 *$14.99*

Arizona Terror (1931)
Ken Maynard is framed for murder by a group of creeps who have been involved with ripping off the locals by purchasing horses, then killing people to get their cash back. Ken has to call on the help of a Mexican bandit to clear his name. With Hooper Atchley and Tarzan the horse, who is featured in many exciting stunts.
68-9203 *$14.99*

Between Fighting Men (1932)
Ken Maynard stars in this tale of love, hate and vengeance between two warring families. A remorseful cattle baron adopts the daughter of a sheepherder whose death he caused...and she becomes the center of a fatal rivalry between his two sons. Ruth Hall, Wallace MacDonald co-star. 62 min.
10-7249 Was $19.99 *$14.99*

Texas Gunfighter (1932)
Ken Maynard stars as a desperado who splits with his gang over the take in a bank job...and chases them down when he comes over to the side of the angels! Outlaw thugs and flying slugs with Sheila Mannors, Harry Woods. 63 min.
10-7251 *$14.99*

The Phantom Thunderbolt (1932)
Peace-loving Ken Maynard instigates rumors about his gunslinging prowess in the hopes of scaring off opponents. He's got to put his money where his mouth is when the townspeople seek him out to rout a rampaging outlaw gang! Frances Lee, Frank Rice co-star. 62 min.
10-7252 Was $19.99 *$14.99*

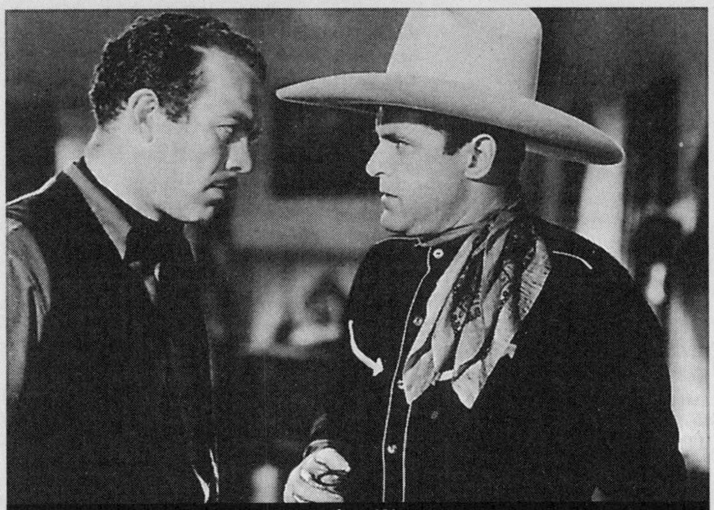
Avenging Waters

Dynamite Ranch (1932)
The accusing finger is pointed at Ken Maynard after a daring train robbery...and now he must stay a step ahead of the posse on a rip-roarin' ride after the real culprits! Fine oater outing co-stars Ruth Hall, Jack Perrin. 59 min.
10-7253 *$14.99*

Hell Fire Austin (1932)
A harassed ranger is deeply in debt to a lowdown loan shark...if there was only someone to ride her prize stallion in the sweepstakes! Ken Maynard shows up to win the day and the lady. With Ivy Merton, Nat Pendleton. 70 min.
10-7254 *$14.99*

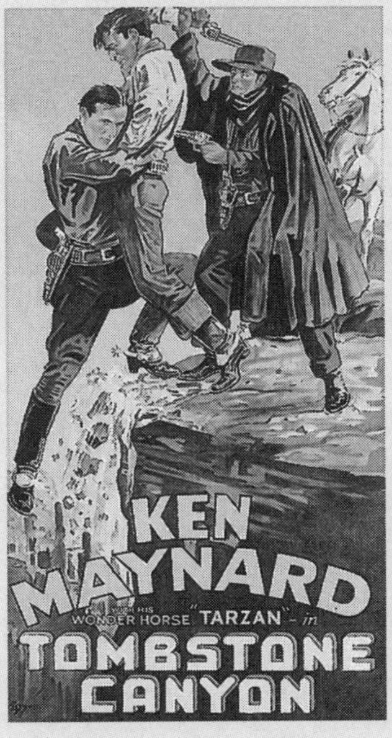

Tombstone Canyon (1932)
Blistering barnburner with Ken Maynard on the heels of the Phantom, a mysterious killer riding roughshod over the range who turns out to be none other than Ken's father. Co-starring Cecilia Parker and Tarzan the horse. 62 min.
10-7109 Was $19.99 *$14.99*

Sunset Trail (1932)
Ken Maynard and his buddy are sworn to save a lady rancher from the grasp of bandits...but when his pal is bushwhacked Ken saddles up to take hot lead vengeance as only he can! Ruth Haitt, Philo McCullough also star. 62 min.
10-7256 *$14.99*

Whistlin' Dan (1932)
Ken Maynard...getting in the good graces of a killer gang? What they don't know is that he's the brother of one of their victims, and he's out to hand the hyenas six-gun vengeance when they least expect it! Joyzelle Joyner, Georges Revenant also star. 65 min.
10-7258 *$14.99*

Come On Tarzan (1932)
Tarzan, Maynard's horse, is mistaken for a wild killer and is scheduled to be executed. Maynard must prove that the ranch foreman was responsible for the murder. 56 min.
62-1032 Was $19.99 *$14.99*

The Pocatello Kid (1932)
In a dual role, Ken Maynard plays both good and evil gunmen. While running from the law, the outlaw is shot and his identity is assumed by the hero.
62-1033 Was $19.99 *$14.99*

Fargo Express (1933)
Rough-ridin' Romeo Ken Maynard has taken a shine to sweet, young thing Helen Mack and pulls no punches in trying to sweep her off her feet, even if it means robbing a stage to take the heat off her crooked kid brother. 61 min.
10-7107 *$14.99*

Strawberry Roan (1933)
Ken Maynard is a-ropin' and a-ridin' like never before as an aging rodeo star out to prove a point to a world that says he's over the hill. With Charlie King, Frank Yaconelli. 59 min.
10-7208 Was $19.99 *$14.99*

Drum Taps (1933)
Stars Ken Maynard. Maynard and the Boy Scouts join forces to flush gold bandits into the open. Guest appearance by Kermit Maynard. 55 min.
62-1126 *$14.99*

In Old Santa Fe (1934)
Some Eastern sidewinders set up Ken Maynard bigtime, cheating him out of his horse Tarzan in a fixed race and then framing him for murder! It'll take some help from George "Gabby" Hayes and cowboy crooner Gene Autry (in his screen debut) for Ken to settle their hash in this action-packed outing. 64 min.
09-1514 *$14.99*

Honor Of The Range (1934)
Ken Maynard gets to wear a whole passel of hats in this unusual oater. He portrays both a sheriff and his nasty twin brother...and when the evil sibling kidnaps the girl, the marshal's gotta disguise himself as a British vaudevillian to get her back! Cecilia Parker, Fred Kohler co-star. 60 min.
10-7209 Was $19.99 *$14.99*

The Trail Drive (1934)
After leading a cattle drive, Ken Maynard must use his two-fisted style to get the cash owed to him and his compadres in this cowboy saga. With Cecilia Parker, William Gould. 60 min.
10-8363 Was $19.99 *$14.99*

Western Frontier (1935)
Ken Maynard leads a rally to bring down the gang that has been terrorizing the townsfolk...but unbeknownst to them, the outlaws' lady ringleader is the sister that had been separated from him in an Indian attack years before! Lucile Browne, Frank Yaconelli co-star. 56 min.
10-7250 Was $19.99 *$14.99*

Lawless Riders (1936)
Whether he's fightin' a bum murder rap, trick ridin' on Tarzan, romancin' the banker's daughter, or even croonin' out a tune, Ken Maynard still has time to lay down the law to some nasty canastas. 58 min.
10-7906 Was $19.99 *$14.99*

Avenging Waters (1936)
Ken Maynard takes the spotlight as a cowboy who tames a town overrun with ornery outlaws. He also goes for a lovely local gal while imprisoning the bad dudes. With Beth Marion, Ward Bond. 57 min.
10-8349 Was $19.99 *$14.99*

Trailin' Trouble (1937)
"Hats off" to Ken Maynard, who has his hands full when a bad guy named Blackie Burke steals Maynard's headwear and the frontier hero is mistaken for a villain. With Lona Andre, Roger Williams and Tarzan the horse. 56 min.
09-1066 Was $19.99 *$14.99*

Boots Of Destiny (1937)
His boots were made for ridin', and that's just what he'll do, and Ken Maynard puts both feet down to help a pretty young ranch owner keep her spread out of a villain's grasp. With Claudia Dell, Vince Barnett. 59 min.
10-7984 Was $19.99 *$14.99*

The Lone Avenger (1937)
A bank president is dead and the bank is closed. Was it suicide or murder? When his son finds the truth, his own life is in jeopardy in this terrific suspenseful Western. Stars Ken Maynard and Charlie King. 54 min.
62-1294 Was $19.99 *$14.99*

Whirlwind Horseman (1938)
Ken Maynard's old buddy wrote him to tell about a fabulous gold claim...but when Ken shows up, his pal is gone, and some jittery jumpers don't want any questions asked! Two-fisted sagebrush action with Dave O'Brien and Tarzan the Wonder Horse. 58 min.
09-2029 Was $19.99 *$14.99*

Six Shootin' Sheriff (1938)
A member of a wild gang redeems himself and turns sheriff to make up for his past evil ways. Stars Ken Maynard. 59 min.
17-1027 *$14.99*

Flaming Lead (1939)
When nightclub rope trick artist Ken Maynard is hired by Dave O'Brien to work on his ranch, he soon learns that really being in the saddle is trickier than it looks, especially when some varmints try to cheat O'Brien out of an Army horse contract. 57 min.
08-1458 *$14.99*

Phantom Rancher (1940)
The masked rider coming to the aid of farmers unable to pay off their mortgages is none other than Ken Maynard. He's out to make amends for the bad reputation left behind by his late uncle in this frontier drama. Dorothy Short, Harry Harvey co-star. 61 min.
08-1092 *$14.99*

Death Rides The Range (1940)
A range war has been triggered by Commie spies to blanket their secret piping of helium off an unsuspecting rancher's land. Thank goodness for FBI agent Ken Maynard, who poses as a cowpoke to blow the lid off the Russkies' plans and beat 'em all hollow in a superpowers showdown. 58 min.
10-7106 *$14.99*

Lightning Strikes West (1940)
Ken Maynard showcases his ruggedness as a stuntman and his presence as a Western icon in this thrilling sagebrush saga. He's after a convict who has escaped from prison. With Claire Rochelle and Robert Terry. 56 min.
10-7924 *$14.99*

Harmony Trail (1944)
Ken Maynard poses as a trick rider, Max Terhune a ventriloquist and Eddie Dean croons tunes in a medicine show to bring to bay a gang of bank robbers menacing the Old West in this exciting oater. AKA: "White Stallion." 54 min.
10-7105 Was $19.99 *$14.99*

Fearless Rider (1928)
In this rarely seen film, Fred Humes, a real-life rodeo star, plays a cowboy who must help a woman from a pack of outlaws who hurt her father in a gold mining accident. Barbara Worth and Ben Corbett also star.
10-9225 Was $19.99 *$14.99*

Under Montana Skies (1930)
Cowpoke Kenneth Harlan sings and swings his fists in this oater that mixes action and music. He helps a travelling show being harassed by bad guys. With Dorothy Gulliver and Slim Summerville. 55 min.
08-1574 *$14.99*

Border Romance (1930)
Three Americans, south of the border, have their horses stolen and get into trouble with the Mexican Rurales. Lots of romance, music and gunplay. Don Terry, Marjorie Kane, Armida star. 58 min.
09-1363 Was $24.99 *$14.99*

Man Or Gun (1958)
Audacious oater involving a drifter who rides into a town operated by a powerful family and teaches the townsfolk about the corruption behind closed doors. Macdonald Carey, Audrey Totter, James Craig star. 79 min.
17-9061 Was $19.99 *$14.99*

The Phantom Bullet (1926)
In this silent oater, Hoot Gibson is a Wyoming cow-puncher and amateur photographer who heads to Texas to find out who killed his rancher pa. Hoot disguises himself as a city slicker and, with help from his gal pal and a camera, gets the goods on the culprit. With Eileen Percy, Allan Forrest. Silent with music score.
03-5008   *$24.99*

The Long, Long Trail (1929)
Hoot Gibson's first talkie stars the cowpoke as a rodeo star called the Ramblin' Kid who is drugged by an underhanded blackhat during a big tournament. Walter Brennan and Sally Eilers co-star.
10-8373   Was $19.99   *$14.99*

Roarin' Ranch (1930)
Hoot Gibson has two problems on his hands—an oil-rich ranch that some rapscallious rannies want to con him out of and a baby left in his care—in this early B-Western. With Wheeler Oakman, Sally Eilers. 65 min.
10-8351   Was $19.99   *$14.99*

Trigger Tricks (1930)
A Hoot Gibson sagebrush gem in which Hoot's brother is killed by ruthless cattle rustlers who are involved in a war against the sheep rancher. Hoot tricks the bad guys with a record played and finds revenge. Sally Eilers and Robert E. Houmans also star. 60 min.
10-9057   Was $19.99   *$14.99*

CARL LAEMMLE present
Hoot Gibson in SPURS

Spurs (1930)
Hoot Gibson hits the wild trail as a rootin' tootin' rodeo star out to ride a pack of rustlers until they're broken! Can Hoot survive the hidden horrors of their hideout? Great early sound western co-stars Helen Wright, "Pee Wee" Holmes. 60 min.
10-7210   Was $19.99   *$14.99*

Wild Horse (1931)
Early sound action-packed Western stars Hoot Gibson and Stepin Fetchit. Bronco busters sign up to work on rodeo ranch. 68 min.
09-1073   Was $19.99   *$14.99*

Clearing The Range (1931)
Hoot Gibson returns home to ferret out the bushwhacker who knocked off his kid brother as well as cotton to long lost love Sally Eilers (Hoot's real-life wife). In order to smoke out the culprit, Hoot poses as a chicken-livered coward and finally brings him to justice. 64 min.
10-7124   *$14.99*

Hard Hombre (1931)
Twice the action, twice the thrills, and twice the Hoots await you in this Hoot Gibson tale in which he plays dual roles, as a spoiled tenderfoot is made ranch foreman when he's mistaken for the tough-as-nails cowpoke he resembles. With Lina Basquette, Glenn Strange. 65 min.
10-8055   *$14.99*

Boiling Point (1932)
He's a cowpoke with high morals and a low temper. He's Hoot Gibson, and in this saddle drama he sets out to bring some bad guys to justice while trying to honor a family promise not to get into fights. With Helen Foster, "Gabby" Hayes. 60 min.
08-1086   Was $19.99   *$14.99*

Local Badman (1932)
Two hornswogglin' bankers plan to railroad railroad agent Hoot Gibson, setting him up as a clay pigeon to take the fall for one of their planned heists in this two-fisted oater. Co-stars Sally Blane and Edward Piel. 59 min.
10-7127   *$14.99*

Spirit Of The West (1932)
Ex-sheriff-turned-rodeo star Hoot Gibson plays dishwasher to get the lowdown on a gang of rustlers who've been hounding the ranch of Hoot's ladylove (Doris Hill). 62 min.
10-7128   *$14.99*

Hoot Gibson

A Man's Land (1932)
Greenhorn lady rancher Marion Shilling relies on able-bodied foreman Hoot Gibson to save the day when her cattle stampede. 65 min.
10-7398   *$14.99*

The Gay Buckaroo (1932)
Hoot Gibson discovers the gal he's taken a liking to seems to prefer a gambler, so Hoot decides to get all medieval on the fellow. In retaliation, the gambler rustles Hoot's horses. Guess who lands the cowgal? Mema Kennedy and Roy D'Arcy also star.
68-9162   Was $19.99   *$14.99*

The Fighting Parson (1933)
Vagabond Hoot Gibson wanders into a new town just as the big revival meeting gets under way and the local flock mistake him for a circuit preacher. Thrilling landslide sequence is real Old Testament-like. 66 min.
10-7399   *$14.99*

Cowboy Counselor (1933)
Comic cowpoke saga with Hoot Gibson playing a book salesman who comes to the aid of an accused stagecoach robber. Sheila Mannors, Skeeter Bill Robbins star. 63 min.
10-7837   *$14.99*

The Dude Bandit (1933)
No, it's not a surfer Western! Hoot Gibson is the dude, a chameleon-like cowpoke who gets mistaken for the real bad guy and has to turn lawman. Frontier action, and lots of it...dudes! 59 min.
10-7838   *$14.99*

Rainbow's End (1935)
Oily sidewinder Warner Richmond is trying to give lady rancher June Gale and her crippled pa the bum's rush off their own land. Leave it to Hoot Gibson to realize the whole thing was one big mix-up and iron everything out before somebody gets hurt. 54 min.
10-7177   Was $19.99   *$14.99*

Sunset Range (1935)
Hoot Gibson and John Elliot ride to the rescue when a pretty ranch owner gets mixed up with scurrilous outlaws thanks to her no-good brother. Mary Doran, James C. Eagles. 60 min.
10-7343   *$14.99*

Feud Of The West (1936)
Hoot Gibson plays a rodeo cowpoke who tries to play peacemaker between ranchers and some accused horse rustlers in this rousing sagebrush thriller. 62 min.
08-1087   *$14.99*

Frontier Justice (1936)
In a conflict over water rights, Hoot's cattleman pa has been framed and branded a couch case by wolves in sheepherders' clothing who've had the old man committed to a booby hatch. Co-stars Jane Barnes and Snowflake. 56 min.
10-7125   Was $19.99   *$14.99*

The Riding Avenger (1936)
Hoot Gibson, the man who put the "buck" in "buckaroo," shoots, fights and rides his way into action as a hero going undercover to wrassle some rustlers. Ruth Mix co-stars.
10-7839   *$14.99*

Cavalcade Of The West (1936)
Hoot Gibson stars in this tale of justice, western style, focusing on the story of two brothers, one of whom is kidnapped by outlaws and ends up on the wrong side of the law. Rex Lease, Marion Shilling co-star. 70 min.
10-8188   *$14.99*

Lucky Terror (1936)
Western fans are the lucky ones who get non-stop action, crafty characters and more in this Hoot Gibson saga. Hoot's got to put a stop to the owlhoots who want to control a gold mine. There's a medicine show, some rousing shootouts and a pretty girl played by Lona Andre. 61 min.
10-8049   Was $19.99   *$14.99*

Swifty (1936)
Western legend Hoot Gibson is Swifty Wade, a spur jockey who lands a job on a ranch. But the job leads to real problems when the ranch's owner is murdered and Swifty's the lead suspect. Now, he's going to have to prove his innocence. June Gale and Gabby Hayes also star. 59 min.
68-9009   Was $19.99   *$14.99*

The Law Rides Again (1943)
Twice the action is guaranteed when Ken Maynard and Hoot Gibson, "The Trail Blazers," team up to track down a corrupt Indian Affairs agent. With Jack LaRue, Chief Thundercloud. 55 min.
10-1168   Was $19.99   *$14.99*

Death Valley Rangers (1943)
Ken Maynard, Hoot Gibson and Bob Steele team as the Trail Blazers in this all-star oater. Steele infiltrates the ornery owlhoots who've been holding up the stagecoaches. 59 min.
10-7259   Was $19.99   *$14.99*

Trail Blazers
KEN MAYNARD · HOOT GIBSON
"BLAZING GUNS"

Blazing Guns (1943)
Ken Maynard and Hoot Gibson are the pals recruited by the sheriff to stop the black hats terrorizing a town. They enlist a posse of former cons to complete the assignment. These guns blaze, baby. 53 min.
10-8036   Was $19.99   *$14.99*

Marked Trails (1944)
These trails are marked; they're a mess, an oily mess, and Hoot and pardner Bob Steele take to them in an effort to run down a gang of oil swindlers headed by nanny-goat Veda Ann Borg. Co-stars Mauritz Hugo and Steve Clark. 59 min.
10-7126   Was $19.99   *$14.99*

Outlaw Trail (1944)
The Trail Blazers (Hoot Gibson, Bob Steele and Chief Thundercloud) saddle up to rein in a corrupt civic leader whose counterfeit cash is causing the community's economy to collapse! Pandemonium on the prairie with Jennifer Holt, Cy Kendall. 53 min.
10-7260   Was $19.99   *$14.99*

Sonora Stagecoach (1944)
It's Hoot Gibson, Bob Steele and Chief Thundercloud as a trio of tall-riding trail blazers who save an innocent man from the hanging mob and then escort him by stage to Sonora for a fair trial, despite lots of attacks from the real murderers. 61 min.
10-7342   Was $19.99   *$14.99*

Gunsmoke (1947)
The killers are mean and smarmy, the good guys slick and sharpshooting in this sagebrusher that stars Nick Stuart, Carol Forman and Robert Garden.
10-8388   Was $19.99   *$14.99*

Cactus Barrier (1951)
A group of cattle rustlers tries their darndest to persuade an old pal to reunite with them and get back into a life of crime. Walter Wayne, Lee Morgan and Jerry O'Dell and His Band star. 55 min.
10-9850   *$14.99*

The Montana Kid (1931)
After a young boy's rancher father is killed by an ornery outlaw, cowboy Bill Cody is out to bring him to justice, then searches for the lad with the intent to get the family ranch back to him. Andy Shuford, W.L. Thorne also star. 64 min.
68-9031   Was $19.99   *$14.99*

Mason Of The Mounted (1932)
It's "Coogan's Bluff," Canadian style, as a young Mountie heads south of his border to track down a killer and teams with a U.S. marshal in order to get his man! Bill Cody, Andy Shuford, Art Mix. 58 min.
10-7213   Was $19.99   *$14.99*

Ghost City (1932)
A once-bustling town has been reduced to a shadowed shell of its former self...and Bill Cody is bound and determined to corral the culprits responsible! Frontier fun with Andy Shuford, Helen Foster. 60 min.
10-7420   Was $19.99   *$14.99*

Texas Pioneer (1932)
Villain Leroy Mason incites Indians to raid the settlers, while he steals their land, but Frontier Scout Bill Cody puts down the uprising at the post. 54 min.
62-1150   Was $19.99   *$14.99*

Fighting for Justice —
BILL CODY · ANDY SHUFORD · NADINE DORE in
The LAW of the NORTH

Law Of The North (1932)
Bill Cody is arrested for murder, thanks to the sleazy efforts of a corrupt judge. As Bill's trial begins, his pals spring him out of the courtroom and in the meantime to find the real culprit. Andy Shuford, Nadine Dore also star.
68-9204   *$14.99*

Frontier Days (1934)
A string of stage robberies prompts Fargo Express brass to recruit Bill Cody to collar the ringleader behind it, an evil banker who not only finagled Bill's sweetheart's pa out of his ranch but killed him to boot. Co-stars Ada Ince and Wheeler Oakman. 61 min.
10-7138   Was $19.99   *$14.99*

Border Guns (1934)
After he crosses the border from Mexico to Texas, cowpoke Bill Cody encounters a nasty Mexican revolutionary named "the Eagle" in Driftwood, Arizona. With cattle rustlers and a tough gang on his side, the Eagle controls the town...unless Cody can clip his wings. Blanche Mehaffey, George Chesebro co-star. 55 min.
68-9025   Was $19.99   *$14.99*

The Border Menace (1934)
Ranger Bill Williams—alias "Shadow"—poses as a cattle rustler in hopes of getting the goods on a bail-jumping outlaw planning to dupe an old friend and his daughter. Bill Cody, Miriam Rice and George Chesebro star. 55 min.
68-9026   Was $19.99   *$14.99*

Cyclone Ranger (1935)
No, it's not Chuck Norris in an Irwin Allen disaster movie. Rather, it's Bill Cody as the Pecos Kid, a rustler-turned-good guy who helps a blind woman battle his nasty former associates. Nena Quartero and Eddie Gribbon also star in this fierce and sensitive outing. 65 min.
68-8975   Was $19.99   *$14.99*

Vanishing Riders (1935)
The son of an outlaw is adopted by sheriff Bill Cody, who then decides to retire to an old town that's supposed to be haunted. In the town, the former lawman and his son face cattlepunchers and "ghosts." Thrilling oater also stars Bill Cody, Jr., Ethel Jackson and Roger Williams. 58 min.
68-9040   Was $19.99   *$14.99*

Blazing Justice (1936)
No, it's not Cleveland slugger David Justice in highlights from the 1997 AL playoffs. It's a rousing oater about a cowpoke who gets a $5000 reward for capturing an ornery outlaw. When the black hat escapes, Bill Cody goes after him. With Gertrude Messinger. 60 min.
09-5114   Was $19.99   *$14.99*

Outlaws Of The Range (1936)
After helping a rancher, Bill Cody finds himself framed for murdering the man he saved. It seems that the rancher's neighbor is behind the scheme and Bill must try to stop them. Catherine Cotter, William McCall also star. 59 min.
68-9022   Was $19.99   *$14.99*

King Of The Sierras (1938)
A unique western fable that focuses on the plight of a beautiful white horse trying to save its mares from a mean-spirited black stallion. Hobart Bosworth stars as an uncle relating the tale to his nephew. 53 min.
10-8410 Was $19.99 *$14.99*

Man's Country (1938)
Jack Randall plays the dashing ranger, doing battle with a nasty batch of outlaws led by a ruthless bandolero who happens to have a twin brother. Ralph Peters co-stars.
10-7795 Was $19.99 *$14.99*

Gun Packer (1938)
A gang of crooked fellows are robbing stagecoaches of their gold, and only Jack Dinton (Jack Randall) can save the day. Louise Stanley, Charles King and Glenn Strange co-star. 51 min.
10-8350 Was $19.99 *$14.99*

Where The West Begins (1938)
"Where the West begins, trouble follows," and that's what's in store for ranch foreman Jack Randall, who must try and convince the pretty young owner of the spread not to sell to a conniving land speculator. With Luana Walters and Fuzzy Knight.
68-9112 Was $19.99 *$14.99*

The Mexicali Kid (1938)
This Monogram Studios sagebrush saga stars Jack Randall as a cowpoke out to avenge the death of his brother. While hunting down the creep in the desert, Randall meets a dying fellow named the Mexicali Kid, and the duo team to continue the search. With Wesley Berry, Eleanor Stewart.
68-9216 Was $19.99 *$14.99*

Oklahoma Terror (1939)
Following the Civil War, a Union soldier returns home to discover that his father has been brutally murdered. The soldier decides he must find the culprit in this exciting western saga starring Jack Randall and Al St. John. 60 min.
09-5276 Was $19.99 *$14.99*

Across The Plains (1939)
Two orphans, each reared separately (Jack Randall by Indians and Dennis Moore by white renegades), find themselves at odds after the latter's benefactors falsely accuse the former's of killing their parents. Stirring six-gun actioner co-stars Hal Price and Joyce Bryant. 54 min.
10-7135 Was $19.99 *$14.99*

Wild Horse Canyon (1939)
Galloping into town to deliver a hot-lead bouquet to the dirty varmints who killed his brother, Jack Randall helps some local ranchers put an end to their cattle rustler problem. Ed Cassidy co-stars. 57 min.
10-7360 Was $19.99 *$14.99*

The Cheyenne Kid (1940)
Tossed in the pokey for a crime he didn't commit, Jack Randall escapes in a blue streak to bag the bad guy himself in this action-packed B oater. Co-stars Louise Stanley and Kenneth Duncan. 54 min.
10-7134 Was $19.99 *$14.99*

Covered Wagon Trails (1940)
Good guy Jack Randall squares off against the hired ruffian of the shifty cattleman's association in a brawling "B" Westerner. Future Frankenstein monster Glenn Strange is the mercenary muscle. 52 min.
10-7803 Was $19.99 *$14.99*

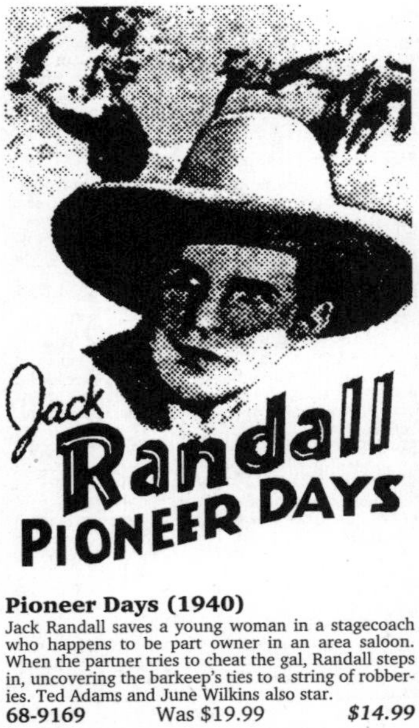

Pioneer Days (1940)
Jack Randall saves a young woman in a stagecoach who happens to be part owner in an area saloon. When the partner tries to cheat the gal, Randall steps in, uncovering the barkeep's ties to a string of robberies. Ted Adams and June Wilkins also star.
68-9169 Was $19.99 *$14.99*

Wild Horse Range (1940)
After being continually undersold by a rival horse trader, Jack Randall believes the trader is selling stolen animals and mounts an investigation. Phyllis Ruth and Charlie King also star in this horse opera of a different color.
68-9220 *$14.99*

Branded A Coward (1935)
Flashbacks provide insight into the disturbed childhood of prospective U.S. marshal Johnny Mack Brown, whose knees buckle when under fire. Interesting psychological horse opry co-stars Billie Seward and Syd Saylor. 58 min.
10-7131 Was $19.99 *$14.99*

Between Men (1935)
Johnny Mack Brown stars as a cowhand raised by a gentleman after being mistakenly left for dead...and who must now ride to keep his adoptive family from splitting. William Farnum, Beth Marion co-star. 59 min.
10-7583 Was $19.99 *$14.99*

The Courageous Avenger (1935)
Western hero Johnny Mack Brown is the white hat battling rustlers and winning over pretty Helen Erickson in this sagebrush winner. With Warner Richmond. 55 min.
10-7988 *$14.99*

Undercover Man (1936)
A corrupt sheriff and his dastardly deputies have offered justice for sale long enough...Wells Fargo agent Johnny Mack Brown must pose as an owlhoot in order to strip him of his tarnished star! Suzanne Karen, Ted Adams star. 57 min.
10-7282 Was $19.99 *$14.99*

Valley Of The Lawless (1936)
Lost treasure attracts the attention of Johnny Mack Brown, and trouble follows in this shootin', scintillating Western adventure. Joyce Compton and Gabby Hayes also star.
10-8921 *$14.99*

The Crooked Trail (1936)
Johnny Mack Brown, at his dynamic best, goes face-to-face with a nasty black hat out to swipe a young woman's ranch. Johnny's heroics save the ranch and win the lady. With Lucille Brown and John Merton.
10-8924 *$14.99*

Guns In The Dark (1937)
Thrill-a-minute oater with Johnny Mack Brown as a gunslinger who hangs up his holster, believing that he pulled a boner and bumped off his buddy. But everyone lives happily ever after, after his pal turns up intact and Johnny slaps his hardware back on. Co-stars Dick Curtis. 56 min.
10-7129 *$14.99*

Rogue Of The Range (1937)
Sheriff Johnny Mack Brown doubles as an ornery outlaw to capture an ornery outlaw, as well as take the fancy of a preacherwoman and a singer in this B-Western programmer. Co-stars Lois January and Alden Chase. 58 min.
10-7132 Was $19.99 *$14.99*

The Gambling Terror (1937)
A prairie protection racket is threatening the settlers with a sagebrush shakedown...but sure as shootin', they won't be around when Johnny Mack Brown comes to face them down! Iris Meredith, Charlie King co-star. 53 min.
10-7205 Was $19.99 *$14.99*

Bar Z Bad Men (1937)
It's open season on rustlers when smilin' Johnny Mack Brown digs for blue lightnin', mills a herd of stampeding beef on the hoof, while winning the hand of pink and pretty Lois January. Co-stars Ernie Adams, Jack Rockwell and Tom London. 57 min.
10-8031 Was $19.99 *$14.99*

Lawless Land (1937)
Texas Ranger Johnny Mack Brown looks into a string of killings and finds himself in a dangerous struggle against the nefarious murderer. Louise Stanley and Ted Adams also star.
10-8920 *$14.99*

Trail Of Vengeance (1937)
After his brother is killed, Johnny Mack Brown searches for the killer and finds himself in the middle of a range war. Iris Meredith and Warner Richmond also star in this two-fisted cinematic shoot-out.
10-8922 *$14.99*

Desert Phantom (1937)
Johnny Mack Brown rescues cowgirl Sheila Manners from two nasty polecats looking to dupe her out of her ranch. Ted Adams also stars.
10-8925 *$14.99*

Boothill Brigade (1937)
Cowboy star Johnny Mack Brown saddles up to keep a ruthless real estate baron from buying up all of the squatters' land. 54 min.
21-3005 *$14.99*

A Lawman Is Born (1937)
Johnny Mack Brown makes the switch from gunman to lawman as a neophyte sheriff who receives his baptism of fire when he tries to stop cattle rustlers from stealing settlers' land. With Iris Meredith, Warner Richmond.
21-3008 *$14.99*

Desperate Trails (1939)
Government agent Johnny Mack Brown goes undercover to expose a crooked sheriff and greedy banker from taking over an entire town. Great frontier drama also stars Bob Baker, Fuzzy Knight. 58 min.
10-7993 Was $19.99 *$14.99*

Pony Post (1940)
Cowboy hero Johnny Mack Brown runs a pony express station where he faces all sorts of dangers, including mail thieves and nasty Indians. Fuzzy Knight, Nell O'Day and Iron Eyes Cody also star. 55 min.
10-9765 *$14.99*

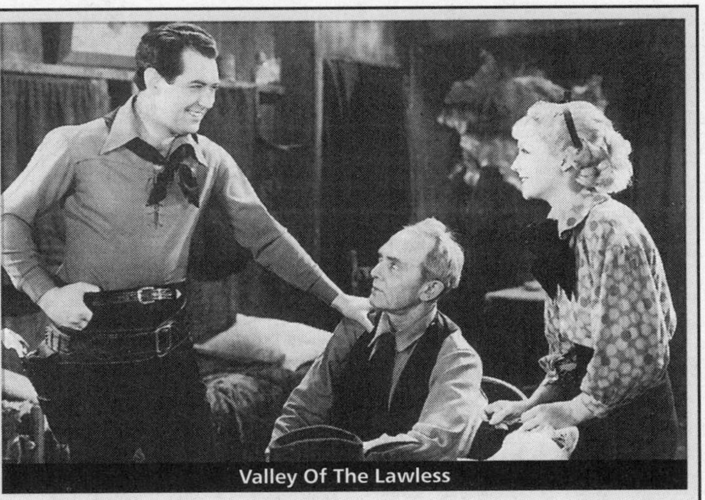
Valley Of The Lawless

Johnny Mack Brown

The Stranger From Pecos (1940)
Johnny Mack Brown is riled up, and he's not going to take it anymore. He's tired of a no-good, lousy, inconsiderate, sleazy, evil, degenerate, sinister, mean, indecent poker cheat who nabbed $3,000 from pal Raymond Hatton. Christine McIntyre of "Three Stooges" fame co-stars. 55 min.
10-8189 Was $19.99 *$14.99*

Bury Me Not On The Lone Prairie (1941)
When his brother is murdered in cold blood by claim jumpers, mining engineer Johnny Mack Brown straps on his six-shooter to avenge the deed. With Fuzzy Knight, Kermit Maynard. 57 min.
10-7604 Was $19.99 *$14.99*

The Man From Montana (1941)
It's a "Butte" of a Western when Johnny Mack Brown rides into the territory to "Roundup" the owlhoots who've made homesteaders' lives a living "Helena." Betcha these crooks are headin' for some "Great Falls." With Fuzzy Knight, Kermit Maynard. 59 min.
10-7836 Was $19.99 *$14.99*

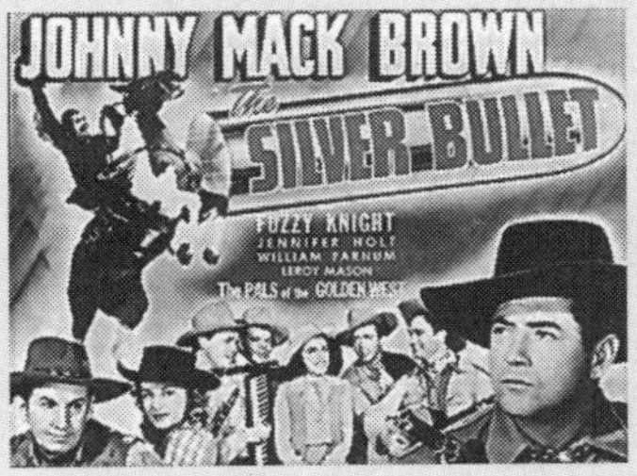

The Silver Bullet (1942)
After he's shot and his father is killed, cowboy Johnny Mack Brown hits the trail to find the culprit. When he does, guns go a-blazin' in this superior B-western featuring a classic gunfight. Jennifer Holt, Fuzzy Knight also star. 60 min.
10-8443 Was $19.99 *$14.99*

Six Gun Gospel (1943)
Johnny Mack Brown's pardner Raymond Hatton poses as a minister to discover the goings-on of a gang of ornery outlaws. 55 min.
10-8193 Was $19.99 *$14.99*

Tenting Tonight On The Old Camp Ground (1943)
Johnny Mack Brown and Tex Ritter try to stop a group of devious dark hatters out to halt the building of a road for stagecoaches. Fuzzy Knight does double sidekick duty.
10-8927 *$14.99*

Cheyenne Roundup (1943)
Johnny Mack Brown shows off his cowboy versatility, playing two roles here: a meaner-than-a-junk-yard-dog weasel and his lookalike brother, who wants to put him behind bars. Tex Ritter, Fuzzy Knight and Jennifer Holt add support.
10-8929 *$14.99*

Raiders Of The Border (1944)
Corrupt wranglers conspire with gem heisters to force out the owners of a trading post. Johnny Mack Brown steps in to throw and rope their scheme. With Raymond Hatton. 55 min.
62-1233 Was $19.99 *$14.99*

Law Men (1944)
Cowboy hero Johnny Mack Brown plays a marshal trying to get the goods on a gang of robbers, but later learns the owner of the bank is responsible for the crimes. Raymond Hatton, Jan Wiley also star in this enthralling Western thrill ride. 58 min.
68-8985 Was $19.99 *$14.99*

The Frontier Feud (1945)
An honest rancher is accused of swindling by other ranchers. Johnny Mack Brown and Raymond Hatton try to get to the truth behind the story. Dennis Moore co-stars. 54 min.
10-7832 Was $19.99 *$14.99*

Gentleman From Texas (1946)
Johnny Mack Brown is back to rope, ride, and romance in this outgoing oater. If he pursues the badmen as hard as he does the ladies, they'd better turn themselves in now! Raymond Hatton, Claudia Drake, Christine McIntyre also star. 55 min.
10-7284 Was $19.99 *$14.99*

Border Bandits (1946)
Johnny Mack Brown, one of the west's true heroes, battles bad guys in this thrilling lollapalooza of a sagebrush saga. Raymond Hatton and Riley Hill co-star. 55 min.
10-8196 Was $19.99 *$14.99*

Land Of The Lawless (1947)
In the desolation of the prairie, anything goes...especially in a town where mob rule is law! Johnny Mack Brown and Raymond Hatton ride to restore law and order to the land in this rip-snortin' rouser. 54 min.
10-7283 Was $19.99 *$14.99*

Frontier Agent (1948)
Government agent Johnny Mack Brown dons cowboy attire to get the goods on some mean-spirited desperadoes in this sagebrush winner. Raymond Hatton, Kenneth McDonald also star. 56 min.
08-1549 *$14.99*

West Of El Dorado (1949)
Double-barreled western ditty with Johnny Mack Brown as a white hat who makes wolf meat of out of an evil stagerobber, then comes to the aid of the bad man's orphaned brother, the target of robbers after a cache of stolen cash. Co-stars Max Terhune, Reno Browne. 58 min.
10-8025 Was $19.99 *$14.99*

West Of Wyoming (1950)
Johnny Mack Brown realizes that West of Wyoming are Utah and Idaho. Then he realizes that he'll need more than that knowledge to whip a nasty cattle baron making life tough for new settlers. Gail Davis and Stanley Andrews co-star in this wild oater. 57 min.
10-8046 Was $19.99 *$14.99*

Blazing Bullets (1951)
Johnny Mack Brown saddles up and heads out to help a young maiden who se husband has been suspected of kidnapping. The action's fast, the fists are tough as Brown proves his worth; with Lois Hall and House Peters. 51 min.
10-8050 Was $19.99 *$14.99*

Oklahoma Justice (1951)
Outlaws are getting their paws into the state of Oklahoma and Johnny Mack Brown takes it upon himself to stop them before they turn Oklahoma "crude." James Ellison and Phyllis Coates star. 60 min.
10-8378 Was $19.99 *$14.99*

Under Western Stars (1938)
Roy Rogers' first starring role (originally intended for Gene Autry) casts him as a Western congressman who goes to bat in Washington for "Dust Bowl" victims. With Smiley Burnette and Carol Hughes. 65 min.
21-3002 Restored *$14.99*

Billy The Kid Returns (1938)
An early starring role for Roy Rogers casts him as the famed frontier gunslinger, now reformed and ready to clean up lawless Lincoln County. Smiley Burnette, Lynne Roberts co-star. 56 min.
01-5116 Was $19.99 *$14.99*

Shine On Harvest Moon (1938)
Former ranching partners turn into bitter rivals when one starts up a cattle rustling ring. Enter Roy Rogers to set things right. With William Farnum, Stanley Andrews, and Lulubelle and Scotty. 53 min.
09-1055 Was $19.99 *$14.99*

Southward Ho! (1939)
The first film to team Roy Rogers and "Gabby" Hayes features the two cowpokes as former Confederate soldiers who are partners in a ranch with an ex-Union Army officer. When the ranchers in the region are mysteriously victimized, Roy and Gabby try to find the culprit. Mary Hart, Arthur Loft co-star. 60 min.
10-1599 *$14.99*

The Arizona Kid (1939)
Roy Rogers is the Kid in this action-filled Civil War Western. His mission is to round up a band of renegade soldiers working for the Confederacy. Co-stars "Gabby" Hayes.
01-5089 Was $19.99 *$14.99*

Wall Street Cowboy (1939)
Roy Rogers and "Gabby" Hayes take to the concrete canyons when a trial requires their presence in New York. Lots of Eastern and Western action in this adventure that contains good-natured pokes at Roy's image.
01-5091 Was $19.99 *$14.99*

Frontier Pony Express (1939)
Roy Rogers in a rousing story about a Confederate plot to eliminate Union troops by way of the Pony Express. With Mary Hart, Raymond Hatton. 54 min.
05-1263 Was $19.99 *$14.99*

Saga Of Death Valley (1939)
Roy Rogers and sidekick "Gabby" Hayes team up with Don "Red" Barry to clean up the hottest stretch of Western territory in this oater classic. 54 min.
10-1062 Was $19.99 *$14.99*

In Old Caliente (1939)
An immigrant family is falsely accused of robbing a gold shipment, and it's up to ranchhand Roy Rogers to bring the guilty party to justice. Sagebrush saga also stars Katherine DeMille, Mary Hart and "Gabby" Hayes, who joins Roy in singing the classic duet "We're Not Comin' Out Tonight." 57 min.
10-1159 Was $19.99 *$14.99*

Come On Rangers (1939)
Roy rounds up a wild bunch of retired Rangers to nab the two-bit varmint who sent an old comrade to an early grave. Enjoyable Western fare co-stars Raymond Hatton. 57 min.
10-7090 Was $19.99 *$14.99*

The Days Of Jesse James (1939)
Roy Rogers dresses up the Jesse James story with his own special fixin's, starring as a detective who infiltrates the outlaw's gang to prove their innocence in the Northfield bank caper. With "Gabby" Hayes, Donald Barry. 63 min.
10-7591 Was $19.99 *$14.99*

Rough Riders' Roundup (1939)
Straight from the Spanish-American War, Roy Rogers joins the border patrol and busts up a corrupt mine operator's empire. 53 min.
21-3003 Was $19.99 *$14.99*

Carson City Kid (1940)
Exciting Roy Rogers outing about a notorious badman who pursues a cunning, ruthless gambler who murdered his brother. Co-stars "Gabby" Hayes and Bob Steele. 54 min.
05-1262 Was $19.99 *$14.99*

Colorado (1940)
Ride 'em, Roy! Fast-paced look at a U.S. Army officer sent to Denver to stop a series of Indian uprisings during the Civil War. Roy Rogers, "Gabby" Hayes, Milburn Stone star. 54 min.
05-1264 Was $19.99 *$14.99*

The Ranger And The Lady (1940)
When a military leader plots to overthrow the government of Texas, only Roy Rogers, as ace Texas Ranger Captain Colt, can stop him (with "Gabby" Hayes' help, of course). 54 min.
10-3010 Was $19.99 *$14.99*

Young Buffalo Bill (1940)
Thoroughly enjoyable Western bioflick that stretches the facts but is one of Roy's best nevertheless. The cavalry sounds a call for Roy to suppress an Indian uprising on a Spanish ranch. Songs include "Blow, Breeze, Blow." 59 min.
10-7094 Was $19.99 *$14.99*

The Border Legion (1940)
In this Zane Grey story Roy Rogers plays an outlaw (horrors!), but he's not all bad, and his only victims are other outlaws. "Gabby" Hayes and Carol Hughes co-star. AKA: "West of the Badlands." 58 min.
10-7393 Was $19.99 *$14.99*

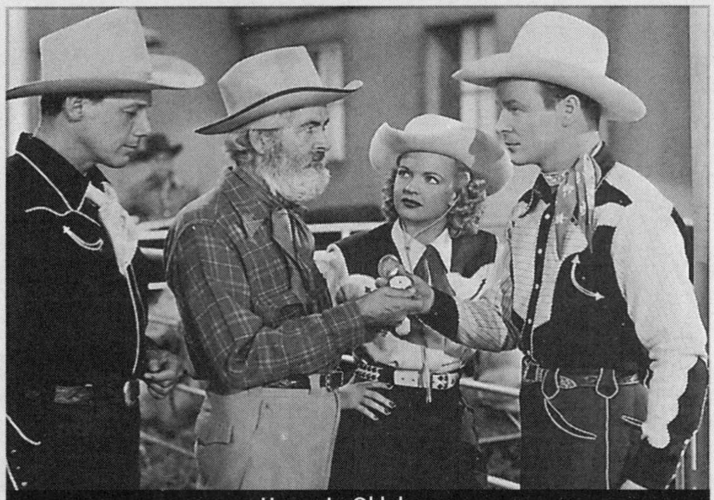

Home In Oklahoma

Roy Rogers

Jesse James At Bay (1941)
Roy Rogers in a rare dual role, as the famous outlaw and also as a tin-horn gambler hired to impersonate him. How did Jesse really die? With "Gabby" Hayes and Gale Storm. 54 min.
01-5118 Was $19.99 *$14.99*

Robin Hood Of The Pecos (1941)
Following the Civil War, the South still had dangers to face. One of these was the Carpetbagger, and in this rousing Roy Rogers/"Gabby" Hayes feature, the "Night Rider" and other rebels lead a revolt against the scoundrels. 50 min.
09-1802 Was $19.99 *$14.99*

Red River Valley (1941)
In his first film outing with The Sons of the Pioneers, Roy Rogers faces a dastardly crook who swiped $182,000 ranchers have raised to put towards the construction of a new reservoir. George "Gabby" Hayes, Gale Storm and Trevor Bardette also star. 53 min.
09-5277 Was $19.99 *$14.99*

In Old Cheyenne (1941)
Newspaper reporter Roy Rogers is assigned to sniff out a pattern of illegal behavior purportedly carried out by "Gabby" Hayes, but along the way manages to clear Gabby and finger the real culprit. Co-stars Joan Woodbury, George Rosener. 58 min.
10-1632 *$14.99*

Bad Man Of Deadwood (1941)
Free enterprise is threatened in the West when a conniving conglomeration of businessmen scheme to drive competition out of town. Leave it to a monopoly-busting Roy to set things back on track. Co-stars George "Gabby" Hayes. 52 min.
10-7088 Was $19.99 *$14.99*

Sheriff Of Tombstone (1941)
Roy is mistaken for a hired gun the crooked mayor of Tombstone sent for to help him gain control of the town. But Roy'd better be on his toes; the malicious magistrate is wise to him, and the real trigger man is goin' a-gunnin' for him. 56 min.
10-7089 Was $19.99 *$14.99*

Nevada City (1941)
Roy Rogers and "Gabby" Hayes work for a stagecoach company involved in a bitter feud with a new railroad enterprise in the region. A group of bad dudes makes the blood worse between stagecoach and railroad owners, and Roy and Gabby try to straighten things out. 60 min.
10-9103 Was $19.99 *$14.99*

Heart Of The Golden West (1942)
The fierce rivalry between a streamboat and a trucking company for a lucrative cattle-hauling contract turns deadly when the scheming trucking boss pulls some underhanded tactics. Can Roy Rogers make things right? With "Gabby" Hayes, Smiley Burnette and Ruth Terry. 51 min.
09-1054 Was $19.99 *$14.99*

South Of Santa Fe (1942)
Highfalutin' horse opera pits Roy and his cowpunchin' cronies against some big city gangsters who kidnap three fat-cat investors and try to pin the rap on our hero. Roy croons "Down the Trail" and "Open Range Ahead." 55 min.
10-7087 Was $19.99 *$14.99*

Ridin' Down The Canyon (1942)
Roy Rogers to the rescue as a crew of creeps are rustling cattle and selling them to the government for wartime profits. "Gabby" Hayes, Linda Hayes also star. 54 min.
17-9070 Was $19.99 *$14.99*

Sunset On The Desert (1942)
Roy Rogers is a cowpoke returned to his home town after many years, only to find it in the clutches of a greedy land baron whose chief henchman is a dead ringer for Roy! Features an exciting shoot-out between the two Roys, with poor "Gabby" Hayes caught in the middle. With Lynn Carver, Frank N. Thomas.
09-1618 Was $19.99 *$14.99*

Man From Cheyenne (1942)
Roy may have met his match this time in the form of a wily Eastern girl (Lynn Carver) who's come to Wyoming to get rich quick through cattle rustling. Modern-day oater stars George "Gabby" Hayes and Gale Storm. 60 min.
10-7077 Was $19.99 *$14.99*

Sunset Serenade (1942)
When a youngster from back East and his pretty guardian come to the dude ranch he's inherited, swindlers with their sights set on the spread try to send them packing. It's up to Roy to rout the rascals in this enjoyable oater co-starring "Gabby" Hayes, Helen Parrish, Roy Barcroft. 58 min.
10-1340 Was $19.99 *$14.99*

Sons Of The Pioneers (1942)
In a comedic jab at his screen image, Roy Rogers plays a bookish bug collector who comes from a line of famous lawmen. He lives up to his heritage, though, when "Gabby" Hayes brings him west to get the goods on outlaws who've been killing cattle. Oh, yes, and the Sons of the Pioneers lend a hand, too! 53 min.
63-1411 *$14.99*

Romance On The Range (1942)
You can't get good help nowadays, as an Easterner trader learns to her dismay when it's discovered her trusted foreman is in fact a fur felon using the post to smuggle pelts! He'll be the one skinned after Roy Rogers gets through with him! "Gabby" Hayes, Sally Payne co-star. 53 min.
63-1431 Was $19.99 *$14.99*

Song Of Texas (1943)
An ex-rodeo champ, now working as a rancher's hired hand, wants his visiting daughter to think he's the spread's owner. It's up to Roy Rogers and his pals to help pull off the charade in this classic sagebrusher. With Sheila Ryan, Barton MacLane, and Bob Nolan and the Sons of the Pioneers. 59 min.
01-5092 Was $19.99 *$14.99*

King Of The Cowboys (1943)
Rodeo performer Roy Rogers trades his hat for that of special government agent, doing his all for the war effort by infiltrating a ring of saboteurs holed up in a tent-show. Songs include "I'm an Old Cowhand," "Gay Rancheros" and "Red River Valley." 53 min.
10-7091 Was $19.99 *$14.99*

Silver Spurs (1943)
John Carradine co-stars alongside Roy and Trigger as a wily snake in the grass who's trying to fleece Roy's boss out of his oil-rich land. One of "The King of the Cowboys'" best also features Yakima Canutt, Smiley Burnette and Kermit Maynard. 55 min.
10-7093 *$14.99*

Texas Legionnaires (1943)
Looks like Roy Rogers isn't going to have the restful homecoming he was counting on, because the tension between the local cattlemen and sheepmen is coming to a boil! Ruth Terry, the Sons of the Pioneers. AKA: "Man from Music Mountain." 60 min.
10-7286 Was $19.99 *$14.99*

Idaho (1943)
A cheerful cowpoke and a rough and ready rancher vie for the same woman's hand—the daughter of a retired thief turned philanthropist. Roy Rogers, Smiley Burnette. 51 min.
62-1236 Was $19.99 *$14.99*

The Cowboy And The Señorita (1944)
Roy Rogers and Dale Evans, in their first film together, have their hands full when a hornswoggler sets out to rustle a gold mine Dale is keeping for her cousin. With Fuzzy Knight, Guinn "Big Boy" Williams. 53 min.
01-5081 Was $19.99 *$14.99*

Song Of Nevada (1944)
Roy Rogers, Dale Evans and Trigger discover the beauty of the wide open Nevada territory...and also the evil that lurks within. 60 min.
01-5093 Was $19.99 *$14.99*

The Yellow Rose Of Texas (1944)
Roy Rogers and Trigger are "rollin' on the river" when they join a showboat crew to help recover stolen money and clear the good name of Dale Evans' father. 54 min.
09-1075 Was $19.99 *$14.99*

Lights Of Old Santa Fe (1944)
Oh, no! A sneaky rodeo owner has his eyes on "Gabby" Hayes' show, and on Dale Evans, too! Can trick rider Roy Rogers rescue Dale from the cad and expose his schemes in time? With Richard Powers, Roy Barcroft. 78 min.
10-1147 Was $19.99 *$14.99*

Hands Across The Border (1944)
Roy Rogers shoots, sings and slugs as he helps a pretty rancher avenge her paw's death and rides Trigger in a race to save her stables. Ruth Terry, Guinn "Big Boy" Williams, Onslow Stevens co-star. 52 min.
10-1341 Was $19.99 *$14.99*

San Fernando Valley (1944)
When the good folk of the Valley are browbeaten by some bad guys, they whistle for Roy to mop 'em up and croon a few tunes for good measure. Roy also receives his first screen smooch (from his character's kid sister, however). 74 min.
10-7092 Was $19.99 *$14.99*

Utah (1945)
When Eastern musical star Dale Evans decides to sell the Utah ranch she's never seen in order to finance her new stage show, it's up to foreman Roy Rogers to get her to travel out West and change her mind. Lots of laughs, songs and action; even "Gabby" Hayes sings! Complete, uncut version; 78 min.
01-5128 Was $19.99 *$14.99*

Bells Of Rosarita (1945)
When crooks try to swindle Dale Evans out of her ranch and travelling circus, Roy Rogers and "Gabby" Hayes ride to her rescue, along with an all-star cavalry: Red Barry, Wild Bill Elliott, Rocky Lane and Sunset Carson. 68 min.
10-5000 Was $19.99 *$14.99*

Along The Navajo Trail (1945)
Roy Rogers enlists the aid of a band of prairie Gypsies to ride down and rope the rascally rannies twisting the ranchers' arms! Singin' and a-shootin' with Dale Evans, Gabby Hayes, and the Sons of the Pioneers. 60 min.
10-7619 🗨*$14.99*

Don't Fence Me In (1945)
Dale Evans plays a magazine photographer researching a legendary gunslinger who turns out to be "Gabby" Hayes! Roy Rogers and Gabby later team up to tackle some gangsters. The Sons of the Pioneers croon the title tune. 71 min.
10-7841 🗨*$14.99*

Sunset In El Dorado (1945)
Unusual sagebrush outing, in which Dale Evans visits a frontier ghost town where her grandmother was once a dancehall queen. There, Dale imagines herself as her relative, in a "film-within-a-film," and meets up with Roy Rogers. Gabby Hayes, Margaret Dumont also star. 54 min.
10-9283 🗨*$14.99*

My Pal Trigger (1946)
Roy Rogers' personal favorite of his films. When a jealous horse breeder frames him for the killing of Gabby Hayes' stallion, Roy is forced to flee with his own pregnant mare. Years later, atop the now-grown Trigger, Rogers returns to set thing right. Dale Evans, Jack Holt co-star. 79 min.
01-1096 Was $19.99 *$14.99*

Roll On Texas Moon (1946)
Cattlemen and sheepmen are locked in a bitter feud for grazing space...and it's up to Roy Rogers to prevent riot on the range. Double-R-bar derring-do with Dale Evans, "Gabby" Hayes, Bob Nolan and the Sons of the Pioneers. 67 min.
10-1248 Was $19.99 *$14.99*

Heldorado (1946)
Roy Rogers is out to clean up the Vegas strip as a rough-riding Ranger after a mob that's been bilking the revenuers. Hit the trail with Dale Evans, "Gabby" Hayes, Paul Harvey, Clayton Moore. 70 min.
10-1249 Was $19.99 *$14.99*

Rainbow Over Texas (1946)
There may be a rainbow, but when Roy Rogers returns to his hometown he finds, instead of a pot of gold, a band of ornery owlhoots out to fix a local Pony Express race. With Dale Evans, "Gabby" Hayes and Sheldon Leonard. 65 min.
63-1952 🗨*$14.99*

Song Of Arizona (1946)
"Gabby" Hayes has a passel of trouble running his boys' ranch, especially from a lad who wants to emulate his outlaw pa. It's up to Roy Rogers and his six-gun skills to set things right. Dale Evans, Lyle Talbot. 68 min.
65-5006 Was $19.99 ***$14.99***

Home In Oklahoma (1946)
A boy stands to be swindled out of his inheritance, and a cold-blooded killer will go scot free, unless Roy Rogers can crack this prairie puzzler. Dale Evans, "Gabby" Hayes, Bob Nolan and the Sons of the Pioneers. 72 min.
65-5007 Was $19.99 ***$14.99***

Under Nevada Skies (1946)
Roy Rogers rides into six-shootin' action against would-be uranium prospectors trying to force a small tribe off their ore-rich reservation. With Dale Evans, "Gabby" Hayes and the Sons of the Pioneers. 68 min.
65-5013 Was $19.99 ***$14.99***

Young Bill Hickok (1947)
Roy stars as the young frontier lawman. While trying to solve a string of stagecoach robberies, Roy uncovers the plans of a mysterious foreign power to gain land rights to California. With "Gabby" Hayes and Jacqueline Wells (alias Julie Bishop). 60 min.
01-5090 Was $19.99 ***$14.99***

Springtime In The Sierras (1947)
Roy Rogers goes against a mysterious destroyer of nature—who kills deer—in this superior Western adventure. Andy Devine, Sons of the Pioneers and Trigger. 52 min.
09-1580 Was $19.99 ***$14.99***

Bells Of San Angelo (1947)
Roy Rogers roughs 'em up, as he plays a border patrol officer who has to round up smugglers. Of course, it ain't easy, and he gets to throw a few punches in the course of things. Andy Devine, Dale Evans, and the Sons of the Pioneers also star. 77 min.
21-3042 Was $19.99 ***$14.99***

On The Old Spanish Trail (1947)
Roy Rogers teams up with an opera-singing(!) Robin Hood vigilante from Mexico to put an end to an owlhoot's international nastiness in this rousing adventure. With Tito Guizar, Jane Frazee, Andy Devine and the Sons of the Pioneers. 75 min.
65-5002 Was $19.99 ***$14.99***

Apache Rose (1947)
Trail-busting excitement by the ton as Roy Rogers reveals a rich vein of "black gold"...and the web of deceit and death connected with its concealment. Dale Evans and the Sons of the Pioneers. 75 min.
65-5011 Was $19.99 ***$14.99***

Under California Stars (1948)
Roy Rogers and Bob Nolan and the Sons of The Pioneers, plus Trigger, "The Smartest Horse in the Movies." Trigger's kidnapped! Will Roy save him in time? 71 min.
09-1057 In Trucolor ***$14.99***

Night Time In Nevada (1948)
A remorse-ridden wrangler, in an attempt to make amends to the daughter of the man he killed, tries to rustle Roy Rogers' cattle for a payoff. After catching him in the act, Roy rides to set things right. Andy Devine, Adele Mara, Grant Withers co-star. 67 min.
10-1247 Was $19.99 ***$14.99***

Grand Canyon Trail (1948)
When a shifty engineer discovers that Roy Rogers' silver mine isn't as depleted as everyone thinks, he works up a swindle...but you can bet that Roy doesn't need the SEC to handle this "inside trader!" Jane Frazee, Andy Devine, Robert Livingston. 67 min.
10-1338 Was $19.99 ***$14.99***

The Gay Ranchero (1948)
Roy rides to wrangle the rannies who are trying to take over an airport by sabotage and other treacherous, low-down means. With Jane Frazee, Tito Guizar, Andy Devine. 72 min.
10-1339 Was $19.99 ***$14.99***

Eyes Of Texas (1948)
They're upon Roy Rogers as he shoots the lid off a swindle run by rannies who use attack dogs to do their dirty work. Andy Devine, Bob Nolan and the Sons of the Pioneers. 70 min.
65-5008 Was $19.99 ***$14.99***

The Far Frontier (1948)
There's a gang of deadly desperadoes running the most deadly ring of all...smuggling deported owlhoots onto our soil! Only Roy Rogers and Trigger can close the door on 'em. Andy Devine, Clayton Moore, and the Riders of the Purple Sage. 53 min.
65-5012 Was $19.99 ***$14.99***

Down Dakota Way (1949)
Roy Rogers and his friends return to Roy's hometown only to discover that his old schoolteacher has chosen to align herself with her outlaw son. Can Roy bring him to justice? Will she be redeemed? Dale Evans co-stars. 67 min.
63-1088 In Trucolor ***$14.99***

Bells Of Coronado (1949)
This time around, Roy's an undercover agent of an insurance company, trying to catch a group of uranium thieves. Wild Western action in this oater! 67 min.
63-1188 In Trucolor ***$14.99***

The Golden Stallion (1949)
Trigger's in trouble, as Roy comes up against a ring of diamond smugglers. Will Trigger be saved before it's too late?!!! 67 min.
63-1191 In Trucolor ***$14.99***

Susanna Pass (1949)
Roy sets off on the trail of two escaped convicts, ending up in the town of Susanna. Only problem is, one of the convicts is in cahoots with a crooked newspaper owner! Western action abounds! 67 min.
63-1193 In Trucolor ***$14.99***

North Of The Great Divide (1950)
Roy Rogers and Penny Edwards in an exciting tale set in the Great Northwest. A shifty operation is out to endanger an Indian tribe by killing their salmon. Roy to the rescue!! 67 min.
63-1078 Was $24.99 ***$14.99***

Trigger, Jr. (1950)
Between bouts with a gang of extortion-minded thieves, and helping a young boy get over his fear of horses, Roy's got himself one full action-packed day! 67 min.
63-1189 In Trucolor ***$14.99***

Twilight In The Sierras (1950)
Roy's a rough-and-tumble state parole officer after a gang of counterfeiters...but after he gets hold of them, they'd better watch out! 67 min.
63-1190 In Trucolor ***$14.99***

Trail Of Robin Hood (1950)
When B-Western star-turned-Christmas tree rancher Jack Holt faces bankruptcy thanks to a crooked tree wholesaler, it's up to Roy Rogers and an all-star posse of cowboys (Rex Allen, "Rocky" Lane, Monte Hale, Tom Tyler) to save the day. 67 min.
63-1192 In Trucolor ***$14.99***

Sunset In The West (1950)
The title may be a bit obvious, but there's plenty of surprises in this action-filled Roy Rogers tale that finds him playing a deputy who helps the sheriff—and his pretty niece—put the kibosh on a gang of gunrunners. Songs include "Rollin' Wheels" and "When a Pretty Girl Passes By"; with Penny Edwards, Will Wright, and Gordon Jones as Splinters. 67 min.
63-1953 ***$14.99***

Heart Of The Rockies (1951)
Roy is called on to oversee a highway construction project that could divulge the truth about a rancher's illegal acquisition of his land. Co-stars Penny Edwards. 67 min.
05-1261 ***$14.99***

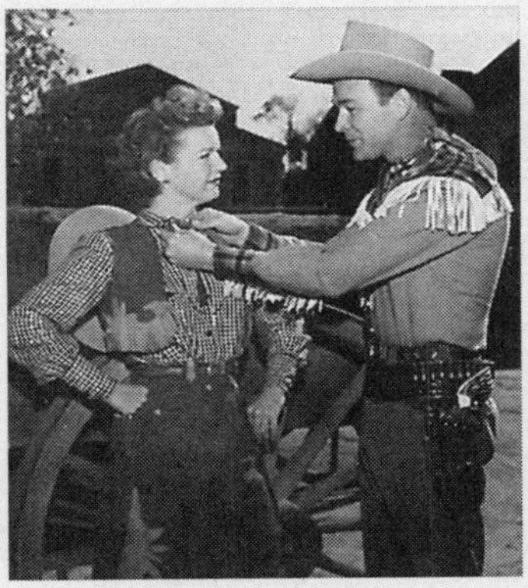

The Roy Rogers Show
Join "King of the Cowboys" Roy Rogers and "Queen of the West" Dale Evans—along with comical sidekick Pat Brady, animal allies Trigger, Buttermilk and Bullet, and the rest of the Double-R Bar Ranch gang—in their beloved 1951-57 TV western series. Each tape features two episodes and runs about 50 min.

The Roy Rogers Show, Vol. 1
In "The Minister's Son," a government agent works undercover to nab counterfeiters, while "The Unwilling Outlaw," finds a bank's embezzling bookkeeper bamboozling the authorities into thinking another employee is doing the deed.
10-7020 Was $19.99 ***$14.99***

The Roy Rogers Show, Vol. 2
It's up to Roy to debunk the ghostly legend of "One Arm Johnny" in "'M' Stands for Murder." Then, "The Train Robbery" follows Roy's discovery of a crooked postmaster and his ornery cronies.
10-7519 Was $19.99 ***$14.99***

The Roy Rogers Show, Vol. 3
Roy and Dale take a "Ride in the Death Wagon" to help a sweet old lady who lost her money for a new clinic to a crook posing as a guard, and Pat Brady's picture winds up on a wanted poster in "Shoot to Kill."
10-7520 Was $19.99 ***$14.99***

The Roy Rogers Show, Vol. 4
Overhearing a talk between Roy and Dale, some crooks search for the book that was said to contain a "Hidden Treasure." Then, "Boys' Day in Paradise Valley" tells about the special day local kids became town officials, and how one boy's uncle uses the occasion to dupe an elderly man out of property.
10-7521 Was $19.99 ***$14.99***

The Roy Rogers Show, Vol. 5
"Outlaw's Girl" follows the kidnapping of Dale and her waitress pal by the woman's blackhat boyfriend, and in "Ghost Gulch," a rancher is conned by a greedy, gold-seeking fellow settler.
10-9952 ***$14.99***

The Roy Rogers Show, Vol. 6
Roy comes to the aid of a sheriff whose brother heads up a gang scheming to make off with a prospector's fortune in "Bullets and a Burro." Also, "The Double-crosser" features a mayor blackmailed into covering for a gang of outlaws.
10-9953 ***$14.99***

The Roy Rogers Show, Vol. 7
Pat Brady for sheriff? It happens in "Flying Bullets," as new lawman Pat then tries to catch a mountaineer's murderer. Next, "Death Medicine" is an exciting story about Roy and Dale's rescue of a kidnapped man in need of insulin.
10-9954 ***$14.99***

The Roy Rogers Show, Vol. 8
In "Haunted Mine of Paradise Valley," Roy and Dale try to help a prospector's widow locate a map to the mine of her late husband. Plus, a wedding is interrupted by the groom's search for his father's killer in "The Feud."
10-9955 ***$14.99***

The Roy Rogers Show, Vol. 9
Can Roy prove a man innocent of a shooting in which his gun was the murder weapon in "Loaded Guns"? Also, some crooks find an "Outlaw's Return" after his release from jail gives them a perfect scapegoat for their shenanigans.
10-9956 ***$14.99***

The Roy Rogers Show, Vol. 10
A travelling sideshow's whip-cracker is accused of murdering his boss in "Carnival Killer," while Part Brady winds up buying a run-down town with one inhabitant in "Ghost Town Gold."
10-9957 ***$14.99***

The Roy Rogers Show, Vol. 11
Some fur-hungry robbers entrap a trapper, while his two children are left stranded in their cabin, in "The Young Defenders." Next, Roy tries to help a youngster who sees an outlaw gang as the way to escape his strict father in "Dead End Trail."
10-9958 ***$14.99***

The Roy Rogers Show, Vol. 12
When there's "Violence in Paradise Valley," you can bet Roy and company will ride in to set things right. Next, "Badman's Brother" is about a sinister saddle tramp who uses his kid brother as a cover for his murderous deeds.
10-9959 ***$14.99***

The Roy Rogers Show, Vol. 13
Why would someone shoot "The Mayor of Ghost Town," and can Roy and Dale avoid being the mysterious gunman's next targets? Then, "Blind Justice" features a blind prospector who uses Roy's dog, Bullet, as a guide, but the man becomes the target of a scheming veterinarian.
10-9960 ***$14.99***

The Roy Rogers Show, Vol. 14
A young Charles Bronson guest stars in "The Knockout," which tells how Roy, Dale and Pat help an elderly woman save her boxing grandson from a group of creeps, while "The Ride of the Ranchers," features Roy's rescue of a rancher's home from a group of ruffians.
10-9961 ***$14.99***

The Roy Rogers Show, Vol. 15
Both Dale and an unsuspecting Easterner are given "The Run-a-Round" in a complicated swindle that could cost Dale her ranch, until Roy can save the day. Next, Roy has some female trouble on his hands when he must stop a fiendish female banker in "The Lady Killer."
10-9962 ***$14.99***

The Roy Rogers Show, Vol. 16
The chief of the Acuna Indians is found murdered next to a silver mine belonging to his tribe in "The Silver Fox Hunt." Plus, Roy is mugged, his clothes are swiped, and he's taken hostage and forced to take part in a bank robbery in "The Mingo Kid." Talk about your bad days!
10-9963 ***$14.99***

The Roy Rogers Show, Vol. 17
Dale has "Money to Burn"—literally—when she discovers that the used stove she's purchased has stolen loot stashed inside! And, "The Milliner from Medicine Creek" is suspected along with her grandfather in a plot to rob a Wells Fargo office.
10-9964 ***$14.99***

The Roy Rogers Show, Vol. 18
Charged to deliver a mine's payroll money, a parson is duped by a phony man of the cloth in "Backfire." Plus, "Last of the Larabee Kid" follows a murdered lawman's son out for vengeance against the blackhats who killed his pappy.
10-9965 ***$14.99***

The Roy Rogers Show, Vol. 19
Roy and Dale team to help an elderly woman catch some rannies out to snatch her land in "The Set Up." Then, a conniving woman weds and kills a miner, then goes after his son, who holds part of a map to the "Treasure of Howling Dog Canyon."
10-9966 ***$14.99***

The Roy Rogers Show, Vol. 20
In "The Desert Fugitive," an innocent man is mistaken for his ornery twin brother in the theft of government documents, while some cattle rustlers avoid authorities by transporting the contraband beef in trucks in "Phantom Rustlers."
10-9967 ***$14.99***

The Roy Rogers Show, Vol. 21
Dale seeks Roy's help in stopping her young nephew from idolizing a famous gunfighter in "Go for Your Guns," while "Outlaws' Town" involves Roy's and Pat's journey to find some blackhats in an area where the law has no power.
10-9968 ***$14.99***

The Roy Rogers Show, Vol. 22
In "Peril from the Past," gunslingers tell a bank clerk that they'll reveal his shady past unless he helps them with a robbery, and "Dead Men's Hills" has Roy, Dale and Pat trying to keep the murderer of a sheriff from escaping to the desert.
10-9969 ***$14.99***

The Roy Rogers Show, Vol. 23
Convinced he's innocent of the murder of his prospective father-in-law, Dale helps a young man stage a "Jailbreak." Next, Roy revokes the license of "Doc Stevens' Traveling Store," which is actually a front for a gang of crooks.
10-9970 ***$14.99***

The Roy Rogers Show, Vol. 24
A teenage aritst is taken in when he takes in a group of felons who seek lodging in his family's home in "Strangers," and "Hard Luck Story" has Roy investigating an insurance company with questionable policies.
10-9971 ***$14.99***

The Roy Rogers Show, Vol. 25
Featured are the episodes "Bad Neighbors," which finds Roy and Dale in the middle of a land feud, and "Quick Draw," in which a stagecoach robbery inspires a sheepherder to join a posse in order to get to his brother-in-law, who happens to be the robber.
10-9972 ***$14.99***

The Roy Rogers Show, Vol. 26
Featured are the episodes "The Big Chance," about Roy and pals rescuing Pat Brady and the "jeepnapped" Nellybelle, and "Outcast of Paradise Valley," involving two boys who head down the criminal road when they can't find jobs.
10-9973 ***$14.99***

The Roy Rogers Show, Vol. 27
Featured are the episodes "The Secret of Indian Gap," in which a gold mine robber uses a 10-year-old orphan with a rifle to keep Roy and Dale at bay, and "The Peddler from Pecos," about a government agent who is killed by beaver poachers.
10-9974 ***$14.99***

The Roy Rogers Show, Vol. 28
Featured are the episodes "Gun Trouble," about a teenager who is ordered by a criminal to kill Roy, and "The Hermit's Secret," in which Roy and Dale investigate an invalid who killed a man and framed the dead man's uncle-in-law.
10-9975 ***$14.99***

The Roy Rogers And Dale Evans Show: This Is Our Country (1962)
Take a musical trip across the good old U.S. of A. with Roy and Dale, plus guests Cliff Arquette and the Sons of the Pioneers, in "This Is Our Country," an episode of the Western duo's short-lived ABC variety series. 55 min.
09-1440 ***$14.99***

Roy Rogers Scrapbook, Vol. 1
A silver-starred collection of memo-Roy-bilia including "The Roy Rogers Riders Club Prayer," movie previews, song clips, home movies with Dale Evans, and Roy's first TV show.
10-7435 Was $19.99 ***$14.99***

Roy Rogers Scrapbook, Vol. 2
More rare film trailers, song clips and stray bullets with Roy and Dale. Includes an episode of his TV show with Roy doing commercial spots.
10-7436 Was $19.99 ***$14.99***

Roy Rogers Gift Set
Hey, pardners, round up four of Roy's best adventures ("Bells of Coronado," "The Golden Stallion," "Susanna Pass," "Twilight in the Sierras") and corral yourself a $10 savings!
63-1412 ***$49.99***

The Roy Rogers Collection
Rustle up a herd of hard-hitting action with this boxed collector's set featuring eight of Roy's finest: "Bells of Coronado," "Down Dakota Way," "The Golden Stallion," "North of the Great Divide," "Susanna Pass," "Trail of Robin Hood," "Trigger, Jr." and "Twilight in the Sierras."
63-1756 Save $32.00! ***$79.99***

Roy Rogers Deluxe Collector's Edition
It's the best bargain since the Double R-Bar Burger: Roy's classic film, "The Golden Stallion"; reproductions of the movie's original theatrical poster and lobby card; the "Roy Rogers: King of the Cowboys" documentary and accompanying autobiographical book; and a tribute CD featuring Roy performing with such stars as Clint Black, Randy Travis and Willie Nelson, all in a special boxed set.
63-1757 ***$79.99***

Please see our index for these other Roy Rogers titles: *The Dark Command • Son Of Paleface*

Radio Ranch (1935)
Gene Autry's the ranch owner whose radium-rich property is coveted by some crooks, and the fight leads both parties to the underground kingdom of Murania in this feature-length version of Gene Autry's action-packed "Phantom Empire" serial. With Betsy King Ross, Frankie Darro, Smiley Burnette. 70 min.
10-7538 Was $19.99 *$14.99*

Oh, Susanna! (1936)
Gene Autry is in deep trouble in this adventure. A killer has stolen his name and identity, and it's up to Gene and sidekick Smiley Burnette to prove his innocence. 55 min.
01-5095 Was $19.99 *$14.99*

Man Of The Frontier (1936)
Gene Autry signs on as a ditch-rider in the Red River Valley to find out who has been dynamiting irrigation projects. AKA: "Red River Valley." 56 min.
01-5100 Was $19.99 *$14.99*

Ride, Ranger, Ride (1936)
Texas Ranger Gene Autry does some scouting work for the Army and helps them get an ammunition shipment past some renegade Comanches. Solid western action with Smiley Burnette, Monte Blue, Chief Thundercloud. 54 min.
01-5123 Was $19.99 *$14.99*

Guns And Guitars (1936)
An action-packed Western saga starring Gene Autry as a cowboy who turns sheriff of a town after he finds the dastardly dudes responsible for killing the town's former lawman. Dorothy Dix, Tom London and Smiley Burnette also star. 58 min.
10-9163 *$14.99*

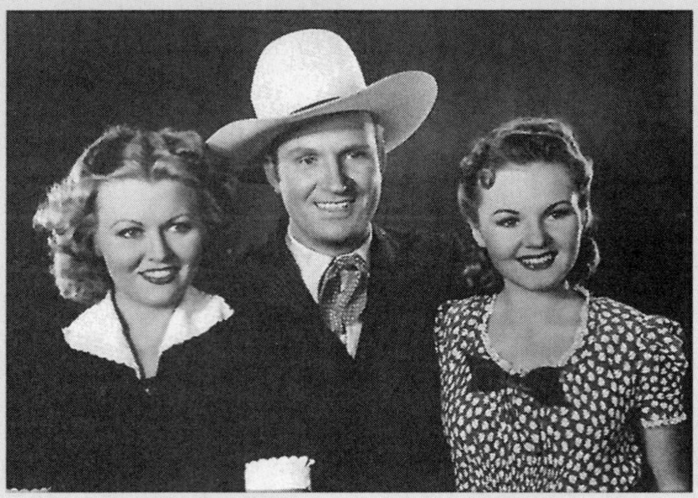

Gene Autry

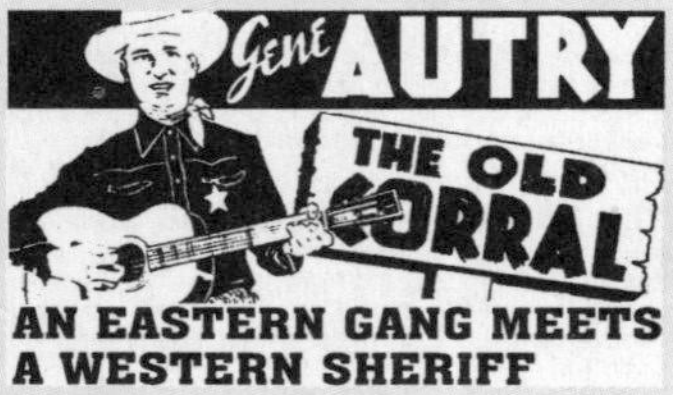

The Old Corral (1936)
Singing sheriff Gene Autry has to deal with big-city blackhats when some Chicago mobsters (!) head out west to track down a murder witness. And if that's not enough, this action-packed oater also features the Sons of the Pioneers (with a young Roy Rogers); Smiley Burnette, Hope Manning, Lon Chaney, Jr. also star. 54 min.
62-1263 Was $19.99 *$14.99*

The Big Show (1936)
Filmed on location at the Texas Centennial in Dallas, this unusual Gene Autry outing finds him in a dual role: an egotistical film cowboy named Tom Ford and his good-natured stunt double (named, of course, Gene Autry). The fun starts when Ford is booked to appear at the Texas fair and Autry agrees to fill in for him. With Smiley Burnette, Kay Hughes, The Light Crust Doughboys and The Sons of the Pioneers (whose numbers include a young Roy Rogers). 56 min.
62-1267 Was $19.99 *$14.99*

Round-Up Time In Texas (1937)
Gene Autry and Smiley Burnette bring a herd of horses to the diamond fields of Africa, and Gene is framed on a charge of diamond smuggling. 56 min.
01-1084 Was $19.99 *$14.99*

The Old Barn Dance (1937)
Gene Autry is a radio singer/cowboy whose sponsor turns out to be a tractor company! Gene and Smiley Burnette have to use some horse sense to get the ranchers to stick with good old-fashioned horsepower. Look for a young Roy Rogers. 56 min.
01-5094 *$14.99*

Springtime In The Rockies (1937)
Gene Autry and Smiley Burnette find themselves in the middle of a range war when they take the side of sheep herders moving into cattle territory. 56 min.
01-5096 *$14.99*

Yodelin' Kid From Pine Ridge (1937)
Gene Autry sings, lassos, rides, sings and gets the bad guys in this Western adventure complete with sidekick Smiley Burnette, pretty ranch owner Betty Bronson and a band of cattle rustlers. 52 min.
01-5097 *$14.99*

Public Cowboy Number One (1937)
Gene Autry and faithful sidekick Smiley Burnette use crimefighting tactics of the Old West to corral a band of modern-day cattle rustlers who hijack trucks. 55 min.
01-5098 Was $19.99 *$14.99*

Rootin' Tootin' Rhythm (1937)
Cattle rustlers are after Gene Autry's herd, so he and sidekick Smiley Burnette assume the indentities of some dead outlaws in order to work their way into the gang. The scheme works...until the "dead" bad guys show up! Monte Blue, Armida also star. 53 min.
01-5099 Was $19.99 *$14.99*

Git Along, Little Dogies (1937)
Gene Autry in an exciting Western adventure about an oil well being drilled in the middle of cattle country. Lots of good songs and yodelling with the words of "Red River Valley" on the screen so you can sing along. 54 min.
09-1357 Was $19.99 *$14.99*

Boots And Saddles (1937)
Gene Autry is a ranch foreman whose boss turns out to be a British youngster. Gene also has to contend with an unscrupulous competitor, the colonel's feisty daughter, a barn fire and the well-meaning blunders of sidekick Smiley Burnette. 59 min.
21-3044 Was $19.99 *$14.99*

Man From Music Mountain (1938)
Gene Autry and sidekick Smiley Burnette foil a worthless gold-mining stock swindle in this rip-roarin,' rootin'-tootin' oater. 54 min.
17-1030 Was $19.99 *$14.99*

Colorado Sunset (1939)
Gene Autry and his cow-punching pals swallow their pride when Smiley Burnette spends their land stake on a sissy dairy ranch, but it's a man's job after all when racketeers demand a payoff from them. With screen Tarzans Buster Crabbe and Elmo Lincoln. 58 min.
10-7666 *$14.99*

Blue Montana Skies (1939)
The fur really flies when a dead man's clue puts Gene Autry and Smiley Burnette on the trail of pelt smugglers from across the border in this action-filled outing. Gene croons "Rockin' in the Saddle All Day," "I Just Want You" and "'Neath the Blue Montana Sky." With June Storey, Tully Marshall, Glenn Strange. 56 min.
10-8221 *$14.99*

Melody Ranch (1940)
Advertised as a musical more than a western in order to broaden Gene Autry's appeal, this modern-day frontier drama finds singing radio star Autry being made an honorary sherrif during a visit to his Arizona hometown, then being called on to act the part when crooks disrupt the festivities. Ann Miller, Vera Vague, Gabby Hayes and Jimmy Durante, as Gene's announcer, co-star. Songs include "Call of the Canyon," "What Are Cowboys Made Of?" and the title tune. 84 min.
62-5048 *$14.99*

Gaucho Serenade (1940)
Gene Autry has a South of the Border odyssey, and while he doesn't come back with a snazzy bumper sticker for his car, he and sidekick Smiley Burnette do manage to help old amigo Duncan Renaldo save his son from some shifty businessmen. Olé! With June Storey, Smith Ballew. 66 min.
11-2308 *$14.99*

Back In The Saddle (1941)
Along with singing what came to be his signature tune, "Back in the Saddle," Gene Autry finds plenty of time to croon while putting the kibosh on some no-goods out to swindle him out of the copper discovered on Autry's ranch. With Smiley Burnette, Mary Lee and Edward Norris. 71 min.
11-2276 *$14.99*

Bells Of Capistrano (1942)
When rodeo owner Virginia Grey's business is threatened by some rapscallions, in come Gene Autry and Smiley Burnette to ring the bad guys' bells and set things right. This was Autry's last film before beginning a four-year military stint. With Morgan Conway, Joe Strauch, Jr. 73 min.
11-2277 *$14.99*

Sioux City Sue (1946)
In his first movie since leaving the Army, Gene Autry plays a singing cattle rancher (that's a cattle rancher who sings, not a rancher of singing cattle) who is brought to Hollywood by a female talent scout. To Gene's dismay, they want him to supply the voice of an animated crooning donkey! What's worse, some blackhats are out to flood Autry's spread. With Lynne Roberts, Sterling Holloway. 69 min.
62-5053 *$14.99*

Trail To San Antone (1947)
Unusual oater outing for Gene Autry finds the cowboy trying to help a handicapped jockey who wishes to ride Champion in a big race. Trouble ensues when Champion is led away by a wild mare (who hasn't been there?), and Gene must track them down from the air. Peggy Stewart, Sterling Holloway co-star. 67 min.
08-1548 *$14.99*

The Last Round-Up (1947)
It's Gene Autry to the rescue of a tribe of Indians who must leave their land when it's marked for part of an aqueduct construction project. With Jean Heather, Bobby Blake, Frank Morgan, Jay Silverheels and Champion, Jr. 77 min.
10-8219 *$14.99*

Loaded Pistols (1948)
Guns-a'blazin' Western actioner finds Gene Autry safeguarding a young cowpoke wrongly accused of murder, while dogging the real killers. Gene also finds time to sing "Loaded Pistols," "Blue Tail Fly" and more. Co-stars Chill Wills, Barbara Britton. 79 min.
10-7095 *$14.99*

Riders Of The Whistling Pines (1949)
Gene Autry must salvage his reputation and clear his name after being wrongly accused of poisoning cattle by a ring of outlaws (Douglass Dumbrille, Damian O'Flynn and Clayton Moore) who are destroying the timberlands. 70 min.
05-1266 Was $19.99 *$14.99*

Beyond The Purple Hills (1950)
Sheriff Gene Autry finds an old friend murdered and arrests the victim's son. But since the son is Wyatt Earp-to-be Hugh O'Brian (his film debut) Gene knows he can't be guilty and sets out to bring the real killer to justice. With Pat Buttram, Don Beddoe. 69 min.
10-8222 *$14.99*

Mule Train (1950)
Part of the Museum of Modern Art's permanent film collection, this Gene Autry rouser has our hero and sidekick Pat Buttram helping a pal keep a valuable cement claim from crooked businessman Robert Livingston. All this, and the title song, too! 69 min.
10-8223 *$14.99*

Rim Of The Canyon (1951)
Gene Autry in a double role: as the marshal who corrals a gang of crooks, and as his son, who must face the same gang years later. A thrill-packed "change of pace" Western. 70 min.
10-1148 *$14.99*

The Gene Autry Collection, Series 1
It's a six-shooter full of savings with this collector's set of classic Autry oaters: "Back in the Saddle," "Bells of Capistrano," "Gaucho Serenade," "Melody Ranch," "Sioux City Sue" and "Trail to San Antone."
11-2279 Save $50.00! *$39.99*

Prairie Pals (1942)
A scientist in a "B" Western? Why not? Cowboys have fought Indians, fought locusts, fought Dix...you remember Richard Dix, don't you? So in this Bill "Cowboy Rambler" Boyd outing, some deputies try to free a kidnapped scientist. Art Davis, Kermit Maynard and Lee Powell also star. 60 min.
10-8029 Was $19.99 *$14.99*

Tumbleweed Trail (1942)
The rugged trio known as the Frontier Marshals (Art Davis, Lee Powell, Bill "Cowboy Rambler" Boyd) combat all sorts of danger and bad guys while riding that "Tumbleweed Trail" in this thrilling oater. Marjorie Manners, Jack Rockwell and Charles King co-star. 55 min.
10-8485 *$14.99*

Texas Man Hunt (1942)
Bill "Cowboy Rambler" Boyd and Art Davis are radio gossip columnists called the "Winchells of the Prairie" who begin sending out scoops over the airwaves about a group of spies. When the spies decide to take them off the air for good, sheriff Lee Powell tries to stop them. 60 min.
10-9147 Was $19.99 *$14.99*

Rolling Down The Great Divide (1942)
Cattle rustlers use short-wave radio signals to track down lost steers and claim them for themselves in this unique sagebrush saga. Bill "Cowboy Rambler" Boyd and Art Davis are the heroes out to cause interference with the crooks' plans. With Glenn Strange. 59 min.
10-9387 *$14.99*

Raiders Of The West (1942)
Posing as entertainers, two range detectives are hired by a leader of a gang of outlaws and are soon captured by the authorities. A friend of theirs tries to get them out of the predicament in this western saga. With Bill Boyd, Art Davis and Lee Powell.
68-9171 Was $19.99 *$14.99*

The Singing Outlaw (1937)
Roving cowboy Bob Baker witnesses a gundown involving a singing cowpoke and a U.S. marshal. When the marshal dies, Baker takes his identity and soon finds himself in all sorts of predicaments, from trying to stop cattle rustlers and romancing a rancher's daughter. Joan Barclay and Fuzzy Knight also star. Directed by Joseph H. Lewis ("The Big Combo"). 56 min.
10-9848 *$14.99*

Western Trails (1938)
The goodfolk of a one-horse town have been bullied about by bare-faced bad guy Carlyle Moore; but Bob Baker, plumb tuckered of this shoddy treatment, slaps on his irons and eighty-sixes that plug-ugly pronto. Co-stars Marjorie Reynolds and Smoky the dog as Wimpy the dog. 58 min.
10-7175 Was $19.99 *$14.99*

Prairie Justice (1938)
U.S. marshal Bob Baker dons disguises in order to uncover his father's killer. Dorothy Fay, Hal Taliafero co-star. 58 min.
10-7798 Was $19.99 *$14.99*

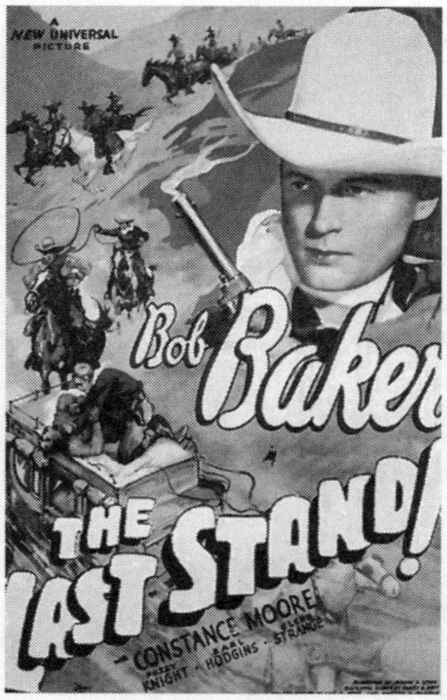

The Last Stand (1938)
In order to find out who killed his father, Bob Baker impersonates a cattle rustler and discovers who is responsible for the dastardly deed when he hangs out with the outlaw gang. Constance Moore and Fuzzy Knight also star. 57 min.
10-8366 Was $19.99 *$14.99*

Outlaw Express (1938)
There's shootouts and expert action sequences galore in this thrilling Western adventure about a cavalry officer out to find the killer who has murdered pony express riders and finds a land-swindling conspiracy linked to the crimes. Bob Baker, Don Barclay and Leroy Mason star. 56 min.
68-8994 Was $19.99 *$14.99*

The Three Mesquiteers

The Law Of The 45s (1935)
The first movie to feature the "Three Mesquiteers" characters (although only two of them are included), this rare oater has Tucson Smith ("Big Boy" Williams) and Stony (Al St. John) investigating the disappearance of a British businessman who was looking to buy Pine Canyon Valley property. The boys soon uncover a deadly land scheme run by a shady attorney. Molly O'Day co-stars. 56 min.
68-9029 Was $19.99 ***$14.99***

The Three Mesquiteers (1936)
The rousing first effort in the popular Western series finds Robert Livingston and Ray Corrigan being discharged from an Army hospital, then traveling West for a new life. When they encounter an outlaw gang, they team with cattlemen and motorcycle-riding Syd Saylor to stop them. 61 min.
09-5133 Was $19.99 ***$14.99***

Ghost Town Gold (1937)
It's a race against time for the Three Mesquiteers as they ride hell-for-leather to return a cache of sawbucks stolen from a bank on the brink of foreclosure. With Robert Livingston, Ray Corrigan and Max Terhune. 57 min.
10-7137 Was $19.99 ***$14.99***

Heart Of The Rockies (1937)
There's a kind of hush all over the plains tonight when Herman's Mountaineers give a leg up to the Three Mesquiteers, who are caught in a flap with park rangers over the death of a bear. Robert Livingston, Ray Corrigan and Max Terhune star. 58 min.
10-7179 Was $19.99 ***$14.99***

Come On, Cowboys (1937)
Life is a carnival, but in this Three Mesquiteers sagebrush saga, it's a carnival of deceit. A carny owner uses the fairway as a front and Bob Livingston, Ray Corrigan and Max Terhune will have no parts of it. 53 min.
10-7914 Was $19.99 ***$14.99***

The Trigger Trio (1937)
Ray "Crash" Corrigan, Max Terhune and Ralph Byrd—aka The Three Mesquiteers—try to thwart a killer who was instrumental in bringing an outbreak of hoof and mouth disease upon the territory. Buck the Great Dane is amazing in this whoopee-ti-yi-yo saga. 55 min.
10-7919 Was $19.99 ***$14.99***

Roarin' Lead (1937)
The Three Mesquiteers—Bob Livingston, Ray Corrigan and Max Terhune—square off against a group of slimeballs who try to bilk an orphanage out of money. A rock-'em-sock-'em rouser! 57 min.
10-7921 ***$14.99***

Range Defenders (1937)
It's the Three Mesquiteers to the rescue, as Bob Livingston, Ray Corrigan and Max Terhune attempt to save some sheepherders who are being driven off their land by a greedy cattle baron. With Eleanor Stewart. 56 min.
10-9381 ***$14.99***

Wild Horse Rodeo (1937)
Loads of gunslinging action in this tale of The Three Mesquiteers (Bob Livingston, Ray Corrigan, Max Terhune), a prized rodeo stallion and the evil rustlers who try to steal it. Look for Roy Rogers (using the name Dick Weston) in a small singing role. 53 min.
21-3004 ***$14.99***

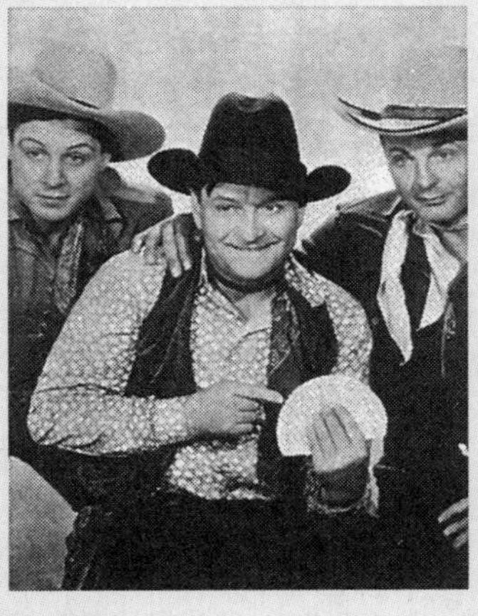

The Riders Of The Whistling Skull (1937)
The Three Mesquiteers (Bob Livingston, Ray Corrigan, Max Terhune) help a young woman track down her missing father in a lost Indian city of gold in this action-packed Western that predated "Raiders of the Lost Ark" by a good 45 years. 53 min.
62-1169 Was $19.99 ***$14.99***

Hit The Saddle (1937)
To rustle wild horses from a federally protected area, a crooked cattleman paints his steed to look like a wild stallion, and then tramples a nosy sheriff under hoof and pins the crime on an innocent nag. Stars the Three Mesquiteers (Bob Livingston, Max Terhune and Ray Corrigan) and a young Rita Cansino (Hayworth). 54 min.
63-1493 ***$14.99***

Gunsmoke Ranch (1937)
In this entertaining outing for the Three Mesquiteers, the trio of western heroes (Ray Corrigan, Bob Livingston, Max Terhune) tackles a shady organization known as "Paradise Land Syndicate," whose principals cash in on flood survivors. With Julia Thayer, Kenneth Harlan.
68-9067 Was $19.99 ***$14.99***

Call The Mesquiteers (1938)
The Three Mesquiteers—Ray Corrigan, Bob Livingston and Max Terhune—go after thieves bilking the area natives out of silk. Authorities begin suspecting the trio of being involved in the robberies, but the son of a medicine show doctor supplies information that leads them to the crooks. With Lynn Roberts. 55 min.
09-5116 Was $19.99 ***$14.99***

The Purple Vigilantes (1938)
No, it's not a film about Prince's bodyguards. It's actually about a band of purple-hooded gunmen who wipe a Western hamlet clean, then partake in its riches. Who ya gonna call to stop 'em? The Three Mesquiteers, of course! Bob Livingston, Ray Corrigan and Max Terhune star.
10-8054 Was $19.99 ***$14.99***

Riders Of The Black Hills (1938)
A valuable racehorse is stolen, and who should happen to have an identical steed but the Three Mesquiteers? Can Bob Livingston, Ray Corrigan and Max Terhune clear their names and track down the real cayuse-smugglers? With Roscoe Ates, Ann Evers. 54 min.
63-1492 ***$14.99***

Outlaws Of Sonora (1938)
It's "double trouble" for the Three Mesquiteers when an outlaw who is a dead ringer for Bob Livingston frames the true-blue hero for murder, and Ray Corrigan and Max Terhune must help clear his name. 56 min.
63-1494 ***$14.99***

The Kansas Terrors (1939)
Bob Livingston returns to the "Three Mesquiteers" series (after being spelled by John Wayne) and, with old pardner Raymond Hatton, journeys to a Caribbean island. There they team up with Mesquiteer-to-be Duncan Renaldo to overthrow a cruel dictator (holy Bay of Pigs!). With Howard Hickman, Jacqueline Wells. 54 min.
63-1500 ***$14.99***

Covered Wagon Days (1940)
When Duncan Renaldo's brother is framed by silver smugglers for killing their uncle, Renaldo and his Three Mesquiteer compadres, Raymond Hatton and Bob Livingston, race to save him from a date with the firing squad. Kay Griffith co-stars. 54 min.
63-1498 ***$14.99***

Heroes Of The Saddle (1940)
The Three Mesquiteers as pappies? It could happen as Bob Livingston, Raymond Hatton and Duncan Renaldo try to adopt an old pal's orphaned daughter and come up against a crooked adoption racket. With Patsy Lee Parsons, Byron Foulger. 54 min.
63-1499 ***$14.99***

Under Texas Skies (1940)
When Bob Livingston returns home he finds his pa murdered and gunman Bob Steele accused of the crime. The two Bobs, though, join forces with Rufe Davis as the new Three Mesquiteers to find the rannies who really committed the crime. With Henry Brandon, Rex Lease, Lois Ranson. 54 min.
63-1501 ***$14.99***

The Trail Blazers (1940)
The bad guys had better brush up on their Morse code, because Three Mesquiteers Bob Steele, Bob Livingston and Rufe Davis are joining forces with the Cavalry to make sure a new telegraph system gets set up in this wired-for-action outing. Pauline Moore co-stars. 54 min.
63-1502 ***$14.99***

Lone Star Raiders (1940)
When an old woman tries to save her horse ranch by selling steeds to the Army, and some crooks do their best (or worst) to sabotage the sale, it's up to the Three Mesquiteers to save Granny's spread. Bob Livingston, Rufe Davis, Bob Steele, Sarah Padden star. 54 min.
63-1503 ***$14.99***

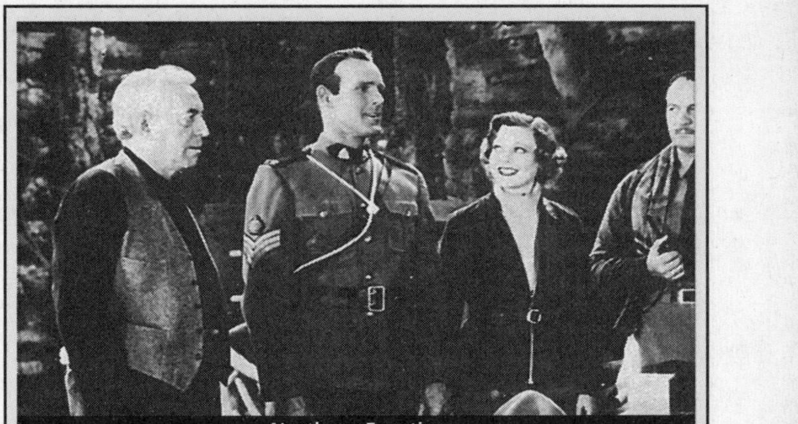

Northern Frontier

Kermit Maynard

His Fighting Blood (1935)
Kermit Maynard is a Mountie whose "fighting blood" is as red as his uniform when he goes undercover to recover some missing funds. With Polly Ann Young, Paul Fix, and The Fighting Constables (one of whom is future Frankenstein monster Glenn Strange!). 54 min.
62-1031 Was $19.99 ***$14.99***

Northern Frontier (1935)
In this Northwest Mounties adventure, tumbleweed hero Kermit Maynard disguises himself as a black hat in order to infiltrate a gang of counterfeiters. Eleanor Hunt and Walter Brennan also star in this stunt-filled spectacular. 56 min.
68-8993 Was $19.99 ***$14.99***

Trails Of The Wild (1935)
The action never stops when Canadian Mountie Kermit Maynard and pal Fuzzy Knight investigate the trouble on Ghost Mountain and encounter a murderer and a kidnapped miner and his daughter. With Billie Seward, Monte Blue. 61 min.
68-9037 Was $19.99 ***$14.99***

Wilderness Mail (1935)
Kermit Maynard plays a Canadian Mountie who treks to the Pacific Northwest to deliver the mail and has a series of exciting adventures in the process. Fred Kohler, Sr., Syd Saylor also star. 65 min.
68-9038 Was $19.99 ***$14.99***

Phantom Patrol (1936)
A mystery writer on retreat in the Rockies gets more inspiration than he counted on when he's kidnapped and replaced by a sinister scalawag! Will Mountie Kermit Maynard ride to his aid? Will he ever! Joan Barclay, Paul Fix co-star. 60 min.
10-7296 Was $19.99 ***$14.99***

Song Of The Trail (1936)
Kermit Maynard stars as a rodeo star in love with a girl whose father is a rancher. A gang of outlaws tries to grab the father's ranch in their effort to corner all the property in the area. 61 min.
62-1029 Was $19.99 ***$14.99***

Timber War (1936)
An underhanded manager of a California lumber mill is bribed to ruin the mill by giving workers paycuts so another mill can take over its operation. Cowboy Kermit Maynard gets involved and soon reveals the manager's devious plan to the mill's owner. Lucille Lund, Lawrence Gray also star. 55 min.
68-9012 Was $19.99 ***$14.99***

Wildcat Trooper (1936)
A Northern adventure in which Kermit Maynard plays the Mountie who gets in the middle of a rivalry between fur traders that also involves a mysterious criminal known as "the Raven." Fuzzy Knight, Jim Thorpe and Hobart Bosworth also star. 60 min.
68-9020 Was $19.99 ***$14.99***

Whistling Bullets (1937)
Top-drawer horse opera with Texas Ranger Kermit Maynard slipping one over on jailbirds by posing as one of their own to get the goods on a stash of missing loot. Co-stars Jack Ingram and Maston Williams. 58 min.
10-7140 Was $19.99 ***$14.99***

Roaring Six Guns (1937)
Kermit Maynard takes a tougher approach on protecting his property when his partner and his fiancée's father try to take it from him. Mary Hayes and Sam Flint co-star. 57 min.
10-7781 Was $19.99 ***$14.99***

Wild Horse Round-Up (1937)
A wild bunch of Western hooligans tries to take advantage of a railroad's new route, but six-shootin' Kermit Maynard is hot on their trail. Betty Lloyd and Dickie Jones co-star. 58 min.
10-7782 Was $19.99 ***$14.99***

Galloping Dynamite (1937)
Gold is discovered, but the crooked foreman tries to hush it up so that he can buy the ranch land cheap. Texas Ranger Kermit Maynard must unravel the plot and ensure that the land is returned to its proper owner. 54 min.
62-1030 Was $19.99 ***$14.99***

Valley Of Terror (1937)
Kermit Maynard is framed for rustling! Who protects the ranch now? Terrific all-around matinee actioner. 59 min.
62-5032 Was $19.99 ***$14.99***

The Fighting Texan

Fighting Texan (1937)
A feud between two ranches leads to murder and an accusation that a new partner in one of the enterprises is responsible for the killing. Can the accused (played by Kermit Maynard) clear his name? Elaine Shepard, Frank LaRue also star. 58 min.
68-8978 Was $19.99 ***$14.99***

Code Of The Mounted (1939)
Jim Thorpe makes an appearance in this lively, set-in-Canada saga in which a tough-as-nails troublemaker accused of killing a fur trapper escapes prison to join his partner in a gang led by a female crook. Kermit Maynard tries to catch the murderer and stop the gang. Robert Warwick co-stars. 60 min.
68-8973 Was $19.99 ***$14.99***

Circle Of Death (1935)
The sole survivor of an Indian massacre is a little baby. Raised by Indians, he later discovers gold on his land, only to have some white men try to steal it from him. Co-stars Montie Montana, Yakima Canutt and Princess Ateenah.
62-1130 Was $19.99 ***$14.99***

Desert Guns (1936)
Cowboy Conway Tearle battles a group of hombres out to dupe the locals out of water rights. Margaret Morris, Charles K. French also star. 60 min.
08-1575 ***$14.99***

The Sombrero Kid (1942)
Don "Red" Barry plays a man who was adopted by a U.S. marshal when he was young, and after the marshal is later murdered by the town boss, "Red" swears vengeance. 56 min.
62-1036 Was $19.99 ***$14.99***

The Outlaw Gang (1949)
Indians and land owners square off after a series of killings at a ranch in this oater starring Don "Red" Barry, Robert Lowery and Julie (Betty) Adams. AKA: "The Dalton Gang." 60 min.
10-9993 ***$14.99***

Song Of The Gringo (1936)
This larrupin' landmark features Tex Ritter in his first starring role, as a green sheriff who is tutored in the way of the gun by an ex-train robber. Joan Woodbury, Fuzzy Knight, Monte Blue co-star. 62 min.
10-7275 *$14.99*

Tex Rides With The Boy Scouts (1937)
Bestowed with the official seal of the Boy Scouts of America, this exciting horse opry stars Tex Ritter, who's always prepared to break the news to any two-bit outlaw, as a sharp-shooter helped by a Boy Scout troop in bringing to bay gold rustlers. Co-stars Marjorie Reynolds. 57 min.
10-7119 Was $19.99 *$14.99*

Sing, Cowboy, Sing (1937)
Mack Sennett resident loonies Al St. John, Snub Pollard and Chester Conklin lend comic relief to this superior sagebrusher with Tex Ritter headin' the bad guys off at the pass (I hate that cliché) who've just robbed a wagon train. 59 min.
10-7122 Was $19.99 *$14.99*

Trouble In Texas (1937)
A rash of rodeo robberies plagues the Old West, and lawman Tex Ritter and gal Friday Rita Cansino (later Hayworth) have their hands full roundin' up rannies Yakima Canutt and Charles King in this Western chock full of two-fisted action. 64 min.
10-7123 *$14.99*

Arizona Days (1937)
Whirlwind action under Western skies as Tex Ritter joins the minstrel show to rescue the group from a gang of bullies who are trying to destroy it. 56 min.
17-1050 *$14.99*

Mystery Of The Hooded Horsemen (1937)
The "Masked Raiders" are a gang of hooded and robed outlaws who are trying to steal all of the land rights from the local ranchers. When one of his friends is murdered, Tex steps in and vows to bring the criminals to justice.
62-1037 Was $19.99 *$14.99*

Hittin' The Trail (1937)
The Tombstone Kid takes advantage of his resemblance to Tex Ritter to frame Tex for his crimes. Tex must corral the outlaw and restore his good name. With the Range Ramblers. 57 min.
62-1225 Was $19.99 *$14.99*

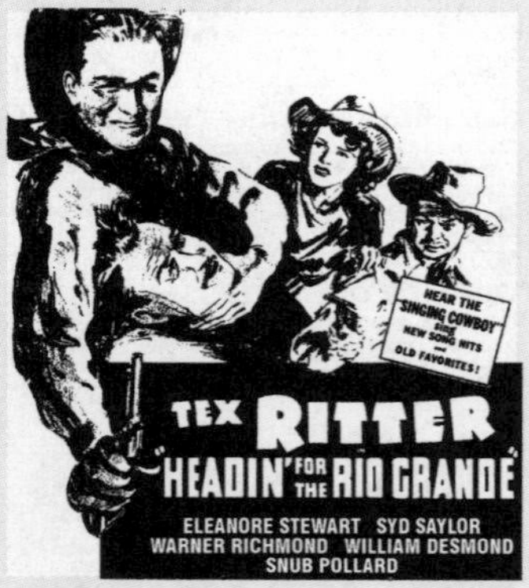

Headin' For The Rio Grande (1937)
Tex Ritter got his boots wet starring in this exciting sagebrusher as an ol' cowhand from the Rio Grande, pinin' for his hometown and lilting out such lovelies as "Campfire Love Song," "Night Herding Song" and "Jailhouse Lament." 61 min.
10-7121 Was $19.99 *$14.99*

Riders Of The Rockies (1938)
Comedy turns to real drama as Tex Ritter and sidekick Pee Wee become rustlers to catch a border gang. 56 min.
08-1093 *$14.99*

Utah Trail (1938)
How can you jail suspected rustlers when the missing cattle has simply vanished into thin air? Tex Ritter gets on the case, and he attempts to sniff out the sidewinders' startling secret! Horace Murphy, Snub Pollard also star. 60 min.
10-7276 Was $19.99 *$14.99*

Rollin' Plains (1938)
With a bit of singing, a bit of sleuthing and a lot of old-fashioned horse sense, Tex Ritter settles a water dispute between sheepmen and cattle ranchers and captures a slippery killer. With Snub Pollard, White Flash. 61 min.
10-7608 *$14.99*

Frontier Town (1938)
After Tex Ritter wins all the major prizes at the rodeo with his roping abilities, the seedy sponsors of the competition try to frame him for murder. With help from Snub Pollard and Horace Murphy, Tex tries to halt their efforts. Songs include "Yip, Yow, I'm an Eagle" and "Streets of Laredo." 60 min.
10-9048 *$14.99*

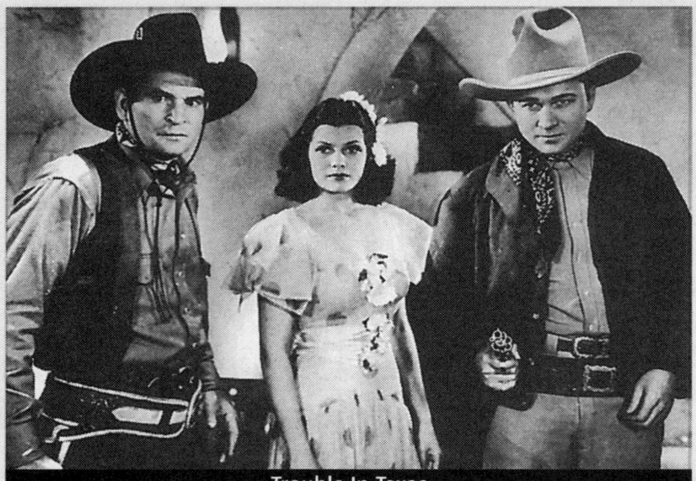

Trouble In Texas

Tex Ritter

Where The Buffalo Roam (1938)
Tex Ritter goes into action when a good-for-nothing desert rat decides to go over the authorities' limit for hunting buffalo. Horace Murphy and Snub Pollard also star. 61 min.
10-9047 *$14.99*

Starlight Over Texas (1938)
After several bloody Indian raids, Tex Ritter goes on the investigation route and finds that a group of white arms smugglers are the real culprits—and they're also responsible for the murder of a sheriff. Salvatore Damino and Carmen LeRoux also star.
68-9215 *$14.99*

Westbound Stage (1939)
Cowpoke favorite Tex Ritter is assigned to guard a shipment of cash on a stagecoach and gets himself involved in finding a gang that slaughtered an entire patrol. Nelson McDowell, Muriel Evans also star. 56 min.
10-9164 *$14.99*

The Man From Texas (1939)
Tex Ritter stars, going to bat for a young cowpoke accused of rustling. Tex has no choice but to track the kid down once he betrays his trust. 55 min.
62-1237 Was $19.99 *$14.99*

Roll, Wagons, Roll (1939)
Tex Ritter is at his trailblazin' best as he steers a wagon train through safe passage to the rugged Oregon frontier. It's pistols, prairie perils, and plunkin' the git-box with Nelson McDowell, Muriel Evans. 52 min.
10-7274 Was $19.99 *$14.99*

Down The Wyoming Trail (1939)
Reliable western hero Tex Ritter battles bad guys and warbles some super songs in this sagebrush saga. Tex takes it to rustlers who are terrorizing farmers during the winter. With Horace Murphy, Charles King. 52 min.
10-8024 Was $19.99 *$14.99*

Take Me Back To Oklahoma (1940)
Tex Ritter comes to the aid of the female owner of a stagecoach line being harassed by unscrupulous competitors. Classic Western action with Tex and sidekick Arkansas Slim and lots of songs, including "You Are My Sunshine." 63 min.
09-1660 Was $19.99 *$14.99*

The Cowboy From Sundown (1940)
Hoof-and-mouth disease a thing of the past? Not in this sagebrush adventure in which lawman Tex Ritter tries to quarantine the ranches in the area, fearing the disease will spread. The ranchers are not happy and plan to stop Ritter's efforts. Carleton Young, Glenn Strange co-star.
10-9131 Was $19.99 *$14.99*

Rainbow Over The Range (1940)
This Tex Ritter effort from Monogram features Tex as a U.S. marshal looking for horse thieves who are robbing animals from the cavalry. During the course of his investigation, Tex meets a school teacher who may have a connection to the crimes. Slim Andrews, Dorothy Fay also star.
68-9170 Was $19.99 *$14.99*

Rhythm Of The Rio Grande (1940)
Singing cowpoke Tex Ritter is out to avenge his pal's murder and travels to Cinco Valley to try to get the job done. Tex finds that a Mexican thug has harmed the settlers there—the same thug could have also done the dirty deed to Tex's pal! With Suzan Dale and Warner Richmond.
68-9219 *$14.99*

The Golden Trail (1940)
Tex Ritter and sidekick Slim Andrews tackle a group of black hat claim-jumpers out to kill prospectors who struck it rich. Turns out the creeps are in cahoots with a swindling county clerk. Inna Guest and Patsy Moran also star.
68-9218 *$14.99*

Riding The Cherokee Trail (1941)
Take a wild trip on the Cherokee Trail in this sagebrusher about a Texas Ranger whose Idaho fishing vacation has him entangled in a murder case. Oh, well. Boise will be Boise! Tex Ritter and Jack Roper star. 53 min.
08-1735 *$14.99*

Arizona Trail (1943)
Tex Ritter teams with Dennis Moore to play stepbrothers with old problems who set aside their differences to help a rancher stop a nasty landgrabber. Fuzzy Knight and Erville Anderson also star in this thrilling sagebrush tale.
10-9049 *$14.99*

Gangsters Of The Frontier (1944)
Tex Ritter and company help spring the good folk of Red Rock, who've been held at gun's point and forced to work the mines by two brothers. Through a clever ruse, the corrupt kin are duped into squaring off against each other in a bloody showdown. Co-stars Dave O'Brien. 56 min.
10-7120 Was $19.99 *$14.99*

Dead Or Alive (1944)
The Texas Rangers make out like a band of nasties to snuggle up to another band of nasties who've been terrorizing a Western community. With Tex Ritter, Dave O'Brien and Guy Wilkerson. 56 min.
10-8413 Was $19.99 *$14.99*

Whispering Skull (1944)
One of the most thrilling efforts in the popular "Texas Rangers" series finds the Rangers out to nab a phantom killer who strikes at night. The murder of a small-time sheriff puts the Rangers on the killer's trail. With Tex Ritter, Dave O'Brien, Dave Wilkerson. 55 min.
10-9272 *$14.99*

Three In The Saddle (1945)
Tex Ritter and the Rangers gallop to the aid of a lady rancher whose under pernicious pressure from a sneaky stagecoach magnate to sell off her land! Singin' and six-guns by the saddleful with Dave O'Brien, Guy Wilkerson. 61 min.
10-7273 Was $19.99 *$14.99*

Marked For Murder (1945)
Preaching that the farmer and the cattleman should be friends, Tex Ritter and the Texas Rangers stop a range feud. Kermit Maynard and Dave O'Brien ride shotgun. 58 min.
10-7389 Was $19.99 *$14.99*

Frontier Fugitives (1945)
Tex Ritter, Dave O'Brien and the rest of the Rangers ride to search for an Indian pack accused of slaying a trapper...but are these redskinned renegades the real article? Guy Wilkerson, Lorraine Miller co-star. 58 min.
10-7569 Was $19.99 *$14.99*

Flaming Bullets (1945)
Tex Ritter leads the Texas Rangers in corraling a pack of culprits with a devious scheme: busting convicts out of the pokey, then collecting the cash reward. The rascally Ritter and pals Dave O'Brien and Guy Wilkerson prove why they were tops in the Texas field. 55 min.
10-8033 Was $19.99 *$14.99*

The Bold Caballero (1936)
Exciting screen adaptation of the Zorro legend. Robert Livingston plays a fop, who, in his secret identity of Zorro, wages war against the corrupt California governor. Heather Angel is the love interest and Sig Ruman is at his most villainous. 69 min.
17-1074 Was $19.99 *$14.99*

Wild Horse Rustlers (1943)
Unusual sagebrusher in which a ranch foreman is mistaken for his identical twin, a Nazi agent, and is accused of sabotaging the U.S. government's horse procurement plan. With help from his friends, the cowboy tries to set the record straight while stopping his sinister sibling. Bob Livingston and Lane Chandler star. 58 min.
10-9537 *$14.99*

Beyond The Law (1930)
A saloon that sits right on the California-Nevada border has become a refuge for rustlers, robbers and other varmints from both states, until Lane Chandler ambles in to show these rapscallions no one's beyond the law. Early oater also stars Robert Frazer, Charlie King.
68-9105 Was $19.99 *$14.99*

Hurricane Horseman (1931)
Lane Chandler is a gunsmith roaming the West repairing firearms who puts his expertise to good use when he attempts to rescue a Spanish woman being held for ransom by a group of outlaws. Lew Chandler, Marie Quillan, Walter Miller star. 59 min.
09-5120 Was $19.99 *$14.99*

Guns For Hire (1932)
An interesting precursor to "The Man Who Shot Liberty Valance," in which a rancher and cowpoke get into a scuffle over a card game that ends in a shoot-out and the cowboy left dead in the street. Did the rancher do it or was there an unseen assassin responsible for the deed? Lane Chandler, Sally Darling and Neal Hart star. 58 min.
68-8981 Was $19.99 *$14.99*

Wyoming Whirlwind (1932)
An enigmatic criminal known as "The Wolf" snags the payroll from a country ranch, but it's soon learned that the crook is the rightful owner of the ranch, cheated out of it years earlier by its current owner. Lane Chandler, Adele Tracy and Yakima Canutt star.
68-9021 Was $19.99 *$14.99*

Texas Tornado (1932)
Superior B western saga with Lane Chandler as a Texas Ranger caught in a series of dangerous situations involving local cattle rustlers, false identities and a big city gambler. Doris Hill and Yakima Canutt also star. AKA: "Ranch Dynamite."
68-9163 Was $19.99 *$14.99*

The Lone Bandit (1934)
From "The Phantom Rider" series comes this rock 'em, sock 'em sagebrusher in which a mysterious bandit seems to know where and when cash is about to be swiped. Lane Chandler, Wally Wales and Slim Whitaker star. 55 min.
10-9843 *$14.99*

The Outlaw Tamer (1934)
Who is the masked bandit sought by a posse and saved by a female saloon-keeper after being shot? There's no shortage of shooting, riding or fancy stuntwork in this enthralling sagebrush entry starring Lane Chandler, Janet Morgan and J. P. McGowan.
68-8995 Was $19.99 *$14.99*

Western Gold (1937)
When gold shipments from Union officials get rerouted before they land in headquarters in the North, a Civil War soldier launches an investigation that leads to an old friend. Smith Ballew, Heather Angel and Paul Fix star. AKA: "The Mysterious Stranger." 60 min.
10-8438 Was $19.99 *$14.99*

Roll Along, Cowboy (1937)
Smith Ballew, one of radio's first singing cowboys, stars in a Zane Grey tale of ranch workers who help their boss keep her land from a band of robber barons. 55 min.
62-5186 Was $19.99 *$14.99*

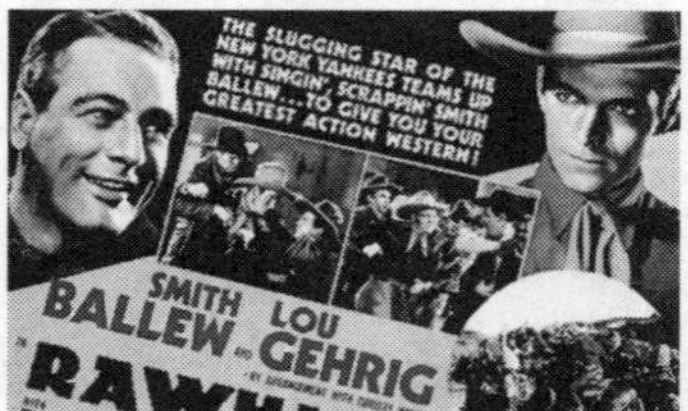

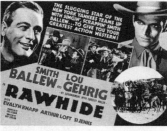

Rawhide (1938)
The "Pride of the Yankees," Lou Gehrig, made his only film appearance in this B-oater about an ex-ballplayer who heads out West to start a ranch, only to meet with opposition from some crooked cattlemen. Smith Ballew co-stars as a lawyer/singing cowpoke who helps Lou strike out the baddies. 60 min.
21-3010 Was $19.99 *$14.99*

Panamint's Bad Man (1938)
A gang of outlaws have been holding up gold-laden stagecoaches, and hero Smith Ballew masquerades as one of the bandits in order to corral them. With Noah Beery, Evelyn Daw. 62 min.
62-1149 Was $19.99 *$14.99*

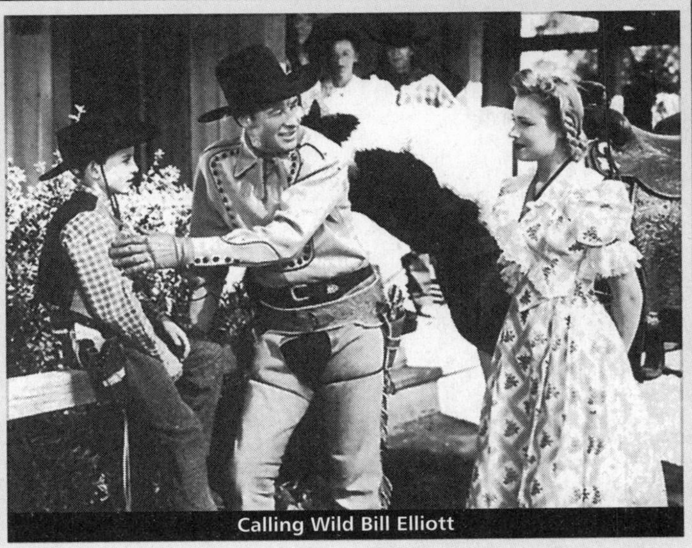

Calling Wild Bill Elliott

Wild Bill Elliott

Frontiers Of '49 (1939)
A nasty land thief is doing no good down in the Spanish territory of the American Southwest, so Cavalry officer Wild Bill Elliott heads into action. Luana de Alcaniz, Charles King also star. 54 min.
10-8260 Was $19.99 *$14.99*

Return Of Daniel Boone (1941)
Bill Elliott is a descendant of legendary frontiersman Daniel Boone who inherits his relative's best characteristics: bravery and a sense of what's right. When two land-snatchers try some slick swindles, young Dan goes to the rescue. Starring Bill Elliott, Betty Miles and Dub Taylor. 60 min.
10-8070 Was $19.99 *$14.99*

Across The Sierras (1941)
Wild Bill Hickok (Wild Bill Elliott) and his sidekick storekeeper, Mitch (Dick Curtis), are hunted by a group of no-gooders, and Wild Bill turns to his gunslinging prowess to stop them. Dub Taylor, Luana Walters, Richard Fiske co-star.
10-8392 *$14.99*

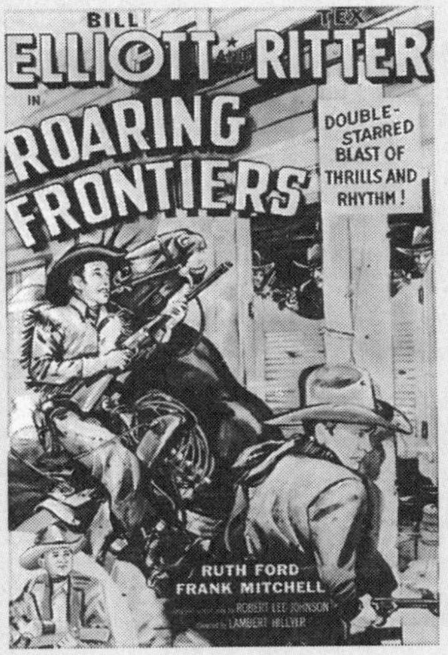

Roaring Frontiers (1941)
A marshal goes to a small town to investigate the murder of the local sheriff, but soon discovers that his suspect may be innocent. When a lynch mob goes after the supposed killer, the marshal uses sagebrush justice to stop the real bad guy. Wild Bill Elliott and Tex Ritter star.
10-8402 *$14.99*

Death Valley Manhunt (1943)
Wild Bill Elliott decides to retire, but is called into action when an oil company harasses settlers. With Gabby Hayes, Anne Jeffreys and Weldon Heyburn. 55 min.
05-1270 Was $19.99 *$14.99*

Bordertown Gunfighters (1943)
A callous cardsharp and his crew are swindling the folks of a Mexican town with their crooked lottery scheme...but their number comes up when Wild Bill Elliott and Gabby Hayes get on the trail! Anne Jeffreys, Ian Keith co-star. 56 min.
10-7630 Was $19.99 *$14.99*

Calling Wild Bill Elliott (1943)
In the kind of gum-beating episode that earned him his nickname, George "Gabby" Hayes brags about his supposed friendship with Wild Bill Elliott just before the hero himself rides into town. With Anne Jeffreys, Herbert Heyes. 55 min.
63-1590 *$14.99*

The Great Stagecoach Robbery (1945)
A sensitive sagebrush saga starring "Wild Bill" Elliott as the cowboy who helps a young boy get over his romanticized remembrances about his criminal father. Bobby (Robert) Blake and Alice Fleming also star. 56 min.
10-9042 *$14.99*

The Plainsman And The Lady (1946)
Rousing Western story starring "Wild Bill" Elliott as a cattleman who launches a deadly rivalry with a stagecoach owner when he decides to open a Pony Express route. Joseph Schildkraut, Andy Clyde, Don "Red" Barry and Vera Ralston also star.
10-9043 *$14.99*

The Fabulous Texan (1947)
Sprawling story of two Confederate officers (William Elliott, John Carroll) who return to postbellum Texas and soon run afoul of the ruinous carpetbaggers. With Catherine McLeod, Andy Devine, Albert Dekker. 97 min.
10-7701 Was $19.99 *$14.99*

Wyoming (1947)
After paying his dues as a series star, William Elliott did a few big-budget gems, including this one about a Wyoming pioneer who survives rustlers and hard-hearted women to become the territory's top rancher. With Vera Ralston, "Gabby" Hayes, Albert Dekker and Maria Ouspenskaya. 84 min.
10-7702 Was $19.99 *$14.99*

Hellfire (1948)
A gambler intent on capturing a female desperado infiltrates her gang, but must save her from other bandits in a Western thriller. William Elliott, Marie Windsor, Forrest Tucker star. 90 min.
63-1132 Was $39.99 *$14.99*

The Showdown (1950)
In his last Western for Republic, "Wild Bill" Elliott plays a man who signs up with a wagon train in order to find out who among the other members of the party is his brother's killer. Will Elliott catch the killer before he's discovered? Walter Brennan, Marie Windsor, Jim Davis co-star. 86 min.
63-1591 *$14.99*

The Longhorn (1951)
Wild Bill Elliott is riding herd on Herefords that he's driving to mate with Texas Longhorns. Good idea? Sure sounds that way to a pack of rustlers who want to hijack that hamburger on the hoof! No bum steers with Phyllis Coates, Myron Healey. 70 min.
10-7223 Was $19.99 *$14.99*

The Range Busters

The Range Busters (1940)
Two-thirds of the Three Mesquiteers reunite in this, the first of the Range Busters series. Ray "Crash" Corrigan and Max "Alibi" Terhune team up with John "Dusty" King to uncover the identity of the "Phantom," who's been bumping off townsfolk left and right. 53 min.
10-7110 *$14.99*

Trailing Double Trouble (1940)
When the Range Busters see a man gunned down, they decide to take care of the baby in his wagon. But while they're trying to track down the killers, they're accused of the crime! "Crash" Corrigan, "Dusty" King and "Alibi" Terhune star. 56 min.
09-1857 Was $19.99 *$14.99*

West Of Pinto Basin (1940)
Robbing stages has been a cakewalk for a wily band of thieves ever since a sneaky bank employee has been leaking vital info. But the righteous Range Busters clog up the leak with lead and bulldog the bandits lickety-split. Ray Corrigan, John King, Max Terhune star. 60 min.
10-7112 Was $19.99 *$14.99*

Trail Of The Silver Spur (1941)
A mysterious killer is on the loose, eliminating all claims to a gold-rich mine, and it's up to The Range Busters ("Crash" Corrigan, "Dusty" King, "Alibi" Terhune) to corral the ranny. 58 min.
10-1165 *$14.99*

Fugitive Valley (1941)
Wild Western excitement as the Range Busters infiltrate a gang of outlaws known as "The Whip," in order to halt its reign of terror over the Arizona countryside. With Ray Corrigan, John King, Max Terhune. 61 min.
10-1252 *$14.99*

Saddle Mountain Roundup (1941)
When a cattleman turns up dead, and you're seeing red, who ya gonna call? Range Busters! Everyone's a suspect and only Ray Corrigan, John King and Max Terhune can unravel the tangled mystery in this Western whodunit. 60 min.
10-7130 Was $19.99 *$14.99*

Tumbledown Ranch In Arizona (1941)
The rip-roarin' Range Busters are out to prove the innocence of a squatter whose frame-up for murder "coincides" with his refusal to let the railroad come through his land! Hooves are a-thunderin' with "Crash" Corrigan, "Dusty" King, "Alibi" Terhune. 60 min.
10-7261 Was $19.99 *$14.99*

The Kid's Last Ride (1941)
The Range Busters saddle up when the brothers of a hanged outlaw seek the sentencing judge's family...and they have revenge on their devious minds! Can Crash, Dusty and Alibi defuse the deadly situation? Ray Corrigan, John King, Max Terhune star. 55 min.
10-7263 Was $19.99 *$14.99*

Wrangler's Roost (1941)
Ray Corrigan, John King and Max Terhune, as the Range Busters, uncover a devious plot involving robberies and an impostor deacon in this rousing Western epic. With Forrest Taylor and Gwen Gaze. 57 min.
10-8030 Was $19.99 *$14.99*

Tonto Basin Outlaws (1941)
The Range Busters ("Crash" Corrigan, "Dusty" King, Max "Alibi" Terhune) get involved in stopping a cattle rustling scandal after they enlist with Teddy Roosevelt's Rough Riders. 60 min.
10-8364 Was $19.99 *$14.99*

Underground Rustlers (1941)
The Range Busters are commissioned by the government to bring down corrupt bankers who are trying to corner the gold market. "Crash" Corrigan, "Alibi" Terhune, "Dusty" King. 58 min.
62-1240 Was $19.99 *$14.99*

Arizona Stagecoach (1942)
A small stage line can't fend off the gang of raiders that are drying up their business...so the call goes out to the Range Busters to hand out some frontier justice. Ray Corrigan, Max Terhune, John King. 58 min.
65-5009 Was $19.99 *$14.99*

Thunder River Feud (1942)
A pair of ranchers are being goaded into a blood battle by pernicious polecats who want to claim the spoils after they wipe each other out! It's up to the Range Busters to expose the schemers and make peace on the prairie. Ray Corrigan, John King, Max Terhune star. 56 min.
10-7262 Was $19.99 *$14.99*

Boot Hill Bandits (1942)
These are not just any ol' bandits. These are the Boot Hill Bandits, and they're out to kick some Western can. Only the famed Range Busters can halt these hooligans who have been looting the stagecoach. "Crash" Corrigan, "Dusty" King and "Alibi" Terhune are the good guys. 58 min.
10-8048 *$14.99*

Texas Trouble Shooters (1942)
The formidable trio of Ray "Crash" Corrigan, John King and Max Terhune head to the Lone Star State, where they try to lasso some malicious no-gooders. 55 min.
10-9041 *$14.99*

Rock River Renegades (1942)
Six-guns go blazing in this Range Busters adventure with the no-nonsense trio facing a ruthless outlaw contingent led by a slick, ornery cuss causing all sorts of trouble for the Rock River residents. Ray "Crash" Corrigan, John King and Max Terhune star, along with John Elliott and Weldon Heyburn as the memorable lead louse. 56 min.
68-9002 Was $19.99 *$14.99*

Texas To Bataan (1942)
Wartime oater has the Range Busters commissioned by the Army to bring a herd of horses to the Philippines. While there, the boys manage to uncover a Japanese spy on the base and bring some Old West justice to the Far East. "Dusty" King, "Alibi" Terhune, David Sharpe star. 56 min.
09-1063 Was $24.99 *$14.99*

Trail Riders (1942)
The Range Busters are called in to clean up the town of Gila Springs when a gang of blackhats gun down the marshal. With John "Dusty" King, Max "Alibi" Terhune, David "Davy" Sharpe. 55 min.
09-1067 *$14.99*

The Haunted Ranch (1943)
The Range Busters ("Dusty" King, Dave Sharpe, "Alibi" Terhune). A shipment of gold is missing after Reno Red is murdered. The bad guys want folks to think that Red's ranch is haunted so that they can look for the gold, and the Range Busters mop up the mystery terrorists of the West.
17-1035 Was $19.99 *$14.99*

Cowboy Commandos (1943)
The Range Busters (Ray "Crash" Corrigan, Max "Alibi" Terhune, Dennis "No Nickname" Moore) help the war effort by lassoing some Nazi spies. Includes the song "I'll Get the Fuhrer, Sure as Shootin'." 53 min.
10-7802 Was $19.99 *$14.99*

Two-Fisted Justice (1943)
Better make that "six-fisted justice," pardner, when Range Busters John King, David Sharp and Max Terhune are hired by Wells Fargo to head into the wild frontier town of Dry Gulch and set the local lawbreakers on the straight and narrow. With Gwen Gaze, Charlie King.
68-8669 Was $19.99 *$14.99*

Black Market Rustlers (1943)
The Range Busters ride once more after Crash's old buddy is killed by dealers in black market beef. Six-gun vengeance is assured. Ray Corrigan, Dusty King, Max Terhune. 56 min.
62-1239 Was $19.99 *$14.99*

Land Of Hunted Men (1943)
No, it's not the first "B" Western set in Greenwich Village and Key West! It's the Range Busters (Ray "Crash" Corrigan, Dennis Moore and Max "Alibi" Terhune) going after a group of ornery riders who've been swiping payroll cash. Phyllis Adair also stars. 58 min.
68-8984 Was $19.99 *$14.99*

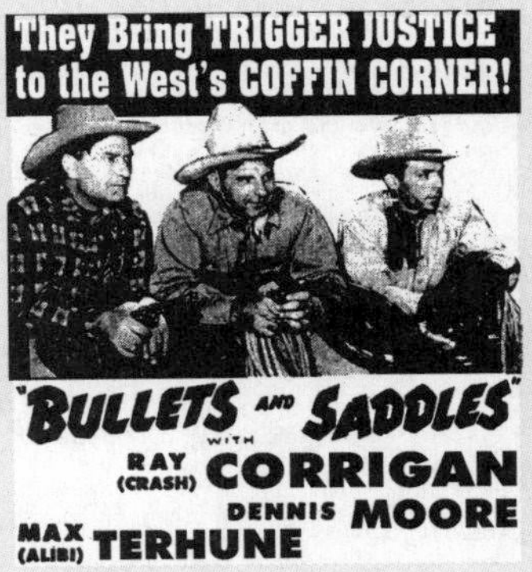

Bullets And Saddles (1943)
The rousing Range Busters (Ray "Crash" Corrigan, Dennis Moore and Max "Alibi" Terhune) go head-to-head against a Midas-minded land baron who plans to purchase the territory's surrounding ranches in order to get the right-of-way when a railroad line is constructed. Glenn Strange also stars in this slam-bang adventure, the final film in the series.
68-8968 *$14.99*

Hopalong Cassidy Enters (1935)
And white-haired whitehat William Boyd debuts as Clarence E. Mulford's veteran cowpoke whose limp earned him the nickname "Hopalong" (and was rarely seen after this film), in the first of over 60 movies made over 13 years. Here Boyd and the gang of the Bar 20 Ranch must stop a crooked foreman's cattle-rustling pals from starting a range war. With James Ellison, Charles Middleton and George "Gabby" Hayes. 73 min.
10-1192 *$14.99*

Eagle's Brood (1935)
The second film in the "Hopalong Cassidy" series finds William Boyd, as sheriff Cassidy, promising an outlaw who saved his life that he'll find the man's kidnapped grandson, whose parents were murdered for their money. Jimmy Ellison, William Farnum, Joan Woodbury and George "Gabby" Hayes also star. 59 min.
10-1701 *$14.99*

Hopalong Cassidy Returns (1936)
With a powerful and (for a "Hoppy" film) brutal ending that puts it among the series' best, this early entry finds Cassidy falling for glamorous dance hall owner Evelyn Brent, unaware that she's the head of a ruthless gang of outlaws. With George "Gabby" Hayes, Stephen Morris (later Morris Ankrum). 74 min.
10-1655 *$14.99*

Trail Dust (1936)
There's plenty of dust—and justice—kicked up when Hopalong Cassidy, "Gabby" Hayes and James Ellison saddle up and take on some low-down rannies out to keep a cattle drive from reaching its goal. Look for a pre-sidekick days Al St. John as one of the bad guys. 77 min.
10-1653 *$14.99*

Bar 20 Rides Again (1936)
Hopalong Cassidy and his Bar 20 cowpokes must pluck the plans of a chicken-hearted cattle rustler named Purdue, who's out to make himself into a frontier Napoleon, in this exciting sagebrush thriller. Jimmy Ellison, Harry Worth, and George "Gabby" Hayes as "Windy" also star. 63 min.
10-1684 *$14.99*

Three On The Trail (1936)
William Boyd's Hopalong Cassidy jumps into action when a town's sheriff turns his head after a group of cattle-rustling stagecoach thieves wreak havoc. James Ellison, Onslow Stevens and "Gabby" Hayes also star. 67 min.
10-1689 *$14.99*

Call Of The Prairie (1936)
The call is a cry for help when a group of outlaws causes all sorts of trouble, and Hopalong Cassidy and his pals are pressed into action to save the day. Jimmy Ellison, Muriel Evans, "Gabby" Hayes and Chill Wills and the Avalon Boys also star. 65 min.
10-7807 *$14.99*

Rustler's Valley (1937)
It was the lawyer who really pulled the bank job...and Hopalong Cassidy is determined to prove it, while saving the ranch and the girl. With George "Gabby" Hayes, Russell Hayden and Agnes Glenn. 58 min.
09-1078 *$14.99*

Texas Trail (1937)
Set during the Spanish-American War, this unusual entry in the "Hopalong Cassidy" series finds Hoppy and the Bar 20 boys helping out the Army by rounding up horses for the Rough Riders to use. With Russell Hayden, "Gabby" Hayes. 59 min.
10-1656 *$14.99*

Borderland (1937)
What's this? Heroic Hopalong Cassidy drinking and being mean to kids? Not to worry, Western fans—it's all due to Hoppy's undercover identity, part of a scheme to flush out an outlaw gang plaguing the border territories. "Gabby" Hayes and Jimmy Ellison (in his final film in the series) co-star. 82 min.
10-1658 *$14.99*

North Of The Rio Grande (1937)
Odds are those directions'll put you in Texas, pardner, and that's where Hopalong Cassidy finds himself when he poses as an outlaw to bring in the crooks who killed his brother. With Russell Hayden, "Gabby" Hayes, and Lee J. Cobb (his film debut). 67 min.
10-1659 *$14.99*

Hills Of Old Wyoming (1937)
These hills are alive—with the sounds of a shady deputy who's using half-breed Indians to run his cattle-rustling scheme. It's up to Hopalong Cassidy and sidekicks George "Gabby" Hayes and Russell Hayden to catch the owlhoots and smooth things between cattlemen and Indians. 82 min.
10-1663 *$14.99*

Hopalong Rides Again (1937)
Hopalong Cassidy's got a bone to pick with the head of a cattle-nabbing gang who poses as a paleontologist to learn about the Bar 20's plans to move 1,000 head of cattle through rustler territory. "Gabby" Hayes, Russell Hayden, Harry Worth also star. 63 min.
10-1702 *$14.99*

Pride Of The West (1938)
A stagecoach robbery sends Hopalong Cassidy and pals Windy and Lucky on a hunt for the culprits. The clues point to a shady land baron named Nixon, but how could anyone named Nixon be a crook? Gabby Hayes, Russell Hayden, James Craig also star. 54 min.
10-1132 *$14.99*

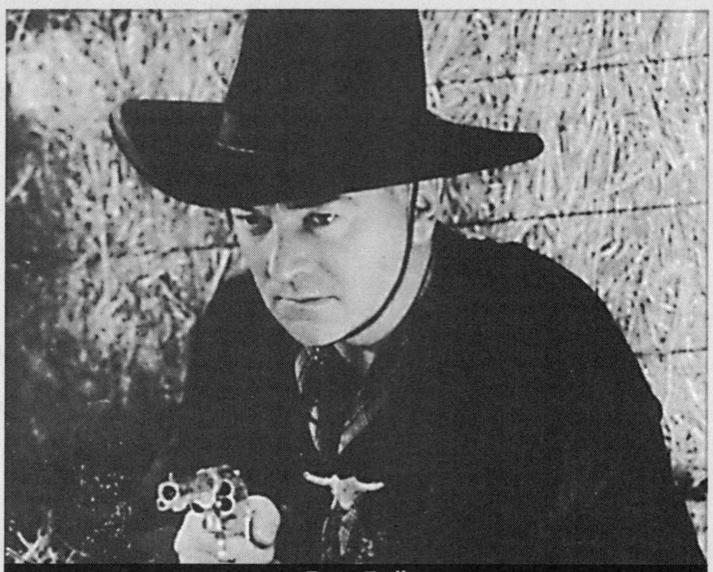
Texas Trail

Hopalong Cassidy

The Frontiersman (1938)
When schoolmarm Evelyn Venable and her charges (played by the St. Brendan Boys Choir) are threatened by perennial B-western bad guy Roy Barcroft and his gang of cattle thieves, Hopalong Cassidy and sidekicks "Gabby" Hayes and Russell Hayden show them that, on the frontier, the three R's stand for "Ropin' Rascally Rustlers." 75 min.
10-1149 *$14.99*

In Old Mexico (1938)
It's anything but a "fiesta" when Hopalong Cassidy, "Gabby" Hayes and Russell Hayden head south of the border and have to solve a friend's murder in this frontier whodunit. With Jane Clayton. 68 min.
10-1654 *$14.99*

Heart Of Arizona (1938)
Notorious lady outlaw Belle Starr gets out of jail and tries to fly right as a rancher, but when things go wrong only Hopalong Cassidy can set them right in this heartfelt frontier drama. "Gabby" Hayes, Natalie Moorhead also star. 68 min.
10-1657 *$14.99*

Cassidy Of Bar 20 (1938)
That's "Cassidy" as in "Hopalong," pardner, who rides into danger when he helps an old flame whose ranch is being terrorized by rustlers. Russell Hayden, Nora Lane, Robert Fiske also star. 58 min.
10-1673 *$14.99*

Partners Of The Plains (1938)
One of the stronger installments of his series finds Hopalong Cassidy lending his services to an English lady who has inherited a ranch and taking care of her pesky little villain problem. Harvey Clark, Russell Hayden, Gwen Gaze also star.
10-1695 *$14.99*

Bar 20 Justice (1938)
Hopalong Cassidy won't be able to do much hopping when he goes underground, helping a pretty mine owner who's plagued by ore theft. Will Hoppy manage to give the bad guys the shaft? With George "Gabby" Hayes, Gwen Gaze. 68 min.
17-1021 *$14.99*

Law Of The Pampas (1939)
The action is *extremely* south of the border—all the way down in Argentina, to be precise—when Hopalong Cassidy and sidekicks Lucky (Russell Hayden) and Fernando (Sidney Toler) travel there to deliver cattle and wind up foiling a shifty ranch foreman's romantic schemes. Sidney Blackmer, Steffi Duna also star. 71 min.
10-1193 *$14.99*

The Renegade Trail (1939)
There's a bigger danger after Hopalong Cassidy than the average owlhoots in this adventure; there's also the amorous advances of a jailbird's wife! With "Gabby" Hayes, Charlotte Winters. 58 min.
10-1194 *$14.99*

Range War (1939)
Angry cattlemen have united in an effort to make sure the railroad doesn't come through...and Hopalong Cassidy must saddle up and ride into the fray if peace on the prairie is going to be kept. Russell Hayden, Britt Wood, Betty Moran also star. 66 min.
10-1342 *$14.99*

Silver On The Sage (1939)
When rustlers pillage the herds on the Bar 20 Ranch, Hopalong Cassidy goes undercover as an Eastern dude in a local gambling den whose owner is part of an elaborate cattle-stealing scheme. With Ruth Rogers, Stanley Ridges, "Gabby" Hayes. 68 min.
10-1651 *$14.99*

Sunset Trail (1939)
When a rancher is murdered, Hopalong Cassidy goes undercover as an Eastern dude in order to flush out the rannies responsible in this hard-ridin "Hoppy" oater. With "Gabby" Hayes, Russell Hayden, Charlotte Wynters.
10-1675 *$14.99*

Three Men From Texas (1940)
The men are Hopalong Cassidy, Russell Hayden and Andy Clyde, and their mission in this frontier actioner is to keep bad guy Morris Ankrum from gaining control of the Texas-Mexico border. 77 min.
10-1195 *$14.99*

The Showdown (1940)
A European villain is pulling the strings of a horse-stealing operation, and Hopalong Cassidy and sidekick Russell Hayden are ready for a showdown for justice. With Morris Ankrum, Jan Clayton; look for B-oater hero Kermit Maynard. 65 min.
10-1316 *$14.99*

Stagecoach War (1940)
What's worse than a gang of stagecoach robbers? How about a gang of *singing* stagecoach robbers? It's a musical war on the prairie, and only Hopalong Cassidy can change these outlaws' tune. With Russell Hayden, Julie Carter. 60 min.
10-1674 *$14.99*

Santa Fe Marshal (1940)
Every December 24th he comes down the jailhouse chimney and...oh, wait, that's the Santa Claus Marshal. Hopalong Cassidy knows who's naughty and nice, however, when he rides into town in the guise of a medicine show member to break up an outlaw ring. With Russell Hayden, Marjorie Rambeau, Britt Wood. 66 min.
10-7336 *$14.99*

Hidden Gold (1940)
Actually, the gold's out in the open, as are the villainous plans of the rannies who swipe it from miners and stagecoaches. Before you can say "Eureka!," though, Hopalong Cassidy and Russell Hayden show up to deliver some 24-karat justice. With Britt Wood, Ruth Rogers, Roy Barcroft.
50-6305 *$14.99*

In Old Colorado (1941)
With hard-working ranch owner Ma Woods about to lose her spread thanks to her foreman's underhanded doings, it's up to Hopalong Cassidy and his pals to save the day. With Russell Hayden, Andy Clyde, Margaret Hayes. 64 min.
10-1343 *$14.99*

Stick To Your Guns (1941)
That's just what Hopalong Cassidy and the Bar 20 gang do when one their friends has trouble with rustlers raiding his ranch in this hard-hitting Hoppy tale. With Brad King, Andy Clyde, Jacqueline Holt, and Tom London as "Waffles." 63 min.
10-1652 *$14.99*

Wide Open Town (1941)
It's not tourism and coffee bars, but rustling, gambling and other illegal activities that keep this town open, until Hopalong Cassidy, Andy Clyde and Russell Hayden ride in to straighten things up and close down the crooks. With Evelyn Brent as villainous Belle Langtry. 79 min.
10-1667 *$14.99*

Secrets Of The Wasteland (1941)
It's no secret that Hopalong Cassidy will always fight on the side of the right, as seen here when he and sidekicks Brad King and Andy Clyde help a group of Chinese immigrants settle their land and fend up some scurrilous saddlesores out to swindle them out of a gold mine claim. With Soo Young, Barbara Britton. 53 min.
10-1685 *$14.99*

Pirates On Horseback (1941)
A gambling tycoon attempts to defraud a cowpoke causing Hopalong Cassidy, Lucky Jenkins and California to come to his defense. A highlight of the sagebrush saga is a terrific fistfight between Hoppy and the gambler. Russell Hayden, Andy Clyde and Morris Ankrum co-star. 69 min.
10-1688 *$14.99*

Outlaws Of The Desert (1941)
The Wild West meets the Middle East when Hopalong Cassidy, Andy Clyde and Brad King are sent to Arabia to buy horses and wind up getting mixed up with a sheik and foiling a kidnapping scheme. Look for future "Cisco Kid" Duncan Renaldo as "Sheik Suleiman." 68 min.
10-7332 *$14.99*

Riders Of The Timberline (1941)
Hopalong Cassidy heads off a bunch of pesky Easterners who are trying to take over some valuable land (Just who do they think they are, anyway?). He also manages to stop them from blowing up a dam. With Brad King, Andy Clyde and J. Farrell McDonald.
10-7333 *$14.99*

Border Vigilantes (1941)
The vigilantes are hired to help a mining town save its silver from being hijacked by a passel of blackhats, but it's up to Hopalong Cassidy and his compadres Lucky and California to uncover the connection between the two groups and save the miners' strike. Russell Hayden, Andy Clyde, Victor Jory also star. 66 min.
10-7334 *$14.99*

Doomed Caravan (1941)
That's just what damsel-in-distress Minna Gombell's wagon line will be, thanks to the nefarious schemes of some rascally businessmen out to corner the wagon train business, unless Hopalong Cassidy can save the day. With Andy Clyde, Russell Hayden, Morris Ankrum. 62 min.
10-7335 *$14.99*

Border Patrol (1943)
Texas Ranger Hopalong Cassidy tries to stop a ruthless mine owner who uses Mexicans illegally as slave laborers. Andy Clyde, Russell Simpson, Duncan Renaldo and a debuting Robert Mitchum star. 65 min.
10-7331 *$14.99*

False Colors (1943)
A friend of Hopalong Cassidy is murdered by some owlhoots and replaced by a substitute so the bad guys can claim a ranch and its water rights. Can Hoppy expose the impostor and bring the killers to justice? With Andy Clyde, Douglas Dumbrille, Robert Mitchum and Jimmy Rogers (Will's son) as himself. 64 min.
09-1726 *$14.99*

The Leather Burners (1943)
No, it's not kids putting their dads' initials on wallets for Christmas gifts: it's fast-paced frontier action as Hopalong Cassidy and Andy Clyde attempt to get the goods on a scheming rustler who's turned an abandoned mine into an underground cattle pen. With Victor Jory, George Givot, and early appearances by Robert Mitchum and George Reeves. 67 min.
10-1196 *$14.99*

Hoppy Serves A Writ (1943)
That is, if bad guy Robert Mitchum will let him! Hoppy's a Texas sheriff who must figure out a way to lure the outlaw Jordan Brothers gang (whose members include Victor Jory, George Reeves, and a young Mitchum) out of Oklahoma so they can be brought to justice. Andy Clyde also stars. 70 min.
10-1197 *$14.99*

Colt Comrades (1943)
No, it's not another book about the old days of Baltimore football by Art Donovan. It's Hopalong Cassidy and sidekick Andy Clyde as oil prospectors whose discovery of an underground well threatens bad guy Victor Jory's local water monopoly. Look for George Reeves and Robert Mitchum in early screen roles.
10-1251 *$14.99*

Texas Masquerade (1943)
It's not a frontier Halloween party, but Hopalong Cassidy and Andy Clyde nonetheless give some two-fisted "treats" to a gang of masked riders out to "trick" local ranchers out of their land. With Jimmy Rogers, Don Castello. 57 min.
10-1337 *$14.99*

Bar 20 (1943)
The title, as every good western fan knows, refers to Hopalong Cassidy's ranch, and in this action-packed oater Hoppy's plans to buy some cattle for his spread hit a snag when he first must corral a gang of stagecoach robbers. Helping Cassidy are Andy Clyde and future Superman George Reeves; with Victor Jory, Dustin Farnum and Robert Mitchum (playing a good guy for once). 58 min.
10-1401 *$14.99*

Lost Canyon (1943)
When Hopalong Cassidy's friend Breezy is wrongly accused of robbing a bank and flees into the hills, Hoppy rides into town to prove his buddy's innocence and catch the real crooks. With Jay Kirby, Andy Clyde and Lola Lane.
10-7330 *$14.99*

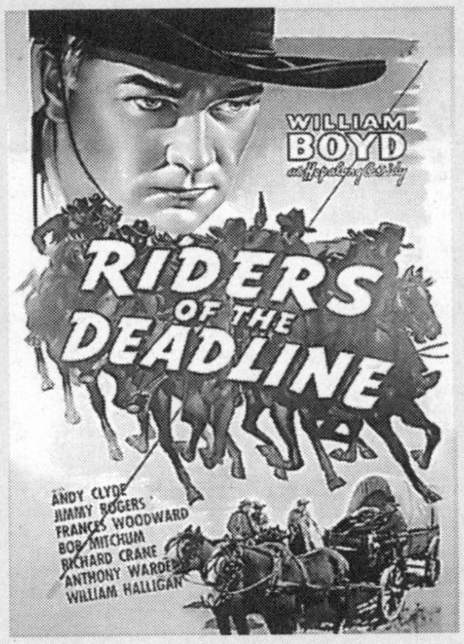

Riders Of The Deadline (1943)
No, it's not the Movies Unlimited catalog writers on horseback! It's Hopalong Cassidy and the Bar 20 Ranch gang saddling up to clear a young man after he gets mixed up with gamblers. With Andy Clyde, Jimmy Rogers, and a young Robert Mitchum as a bad guy. 72 min.
11-1314 *$14.99*

Lumberjack (1944)
Hopalong Cassidy is more than just "O.K." when he heads up to the High Sierras to make sure a logging company owner's widow can fulfill her contracts and get the timber delivered on time. Not only that, he finds her husband's killers, to boot! With Ellen Hall, Andy Clyde, Jimmy Rogers. 65 min.
10-1668 *$14.99*

The Mystery Man (1944)
With that all-black outfit, it's no mystery that the man is Hopalong Cassidy. Here he's a rancher who whips out his pistols and his fists to deal with some rascally rustlers. With Andy Clyde and Jimmy Rogers.
10-7298 *$14.99*

Devil's Playground (1946)
The title refers to a canyon that's said to be haunted, but when they're called in to investigate a bank robbery and attempted murder, Hopalong Cassidy and his compadres will show the bad guys they don't stand a ghost of a chance. Andy Clyde, Rand Brooks, Elaine Riley also star. 68 min.
11-1195 *$14.99*

The Marauders (1947)
One of the last—and best—of the "Hopalong Cassidy" westerns finds black-hatted hero William Boyd and compadres Andy Clyde and Rand Brooks settling the score with a band of murderous owlhoots who've driven a whole frontier town out so they can dig for oil. With Ian Wolfe, Mary Newton. 64 min.
11-1211 *$14.99*

Dangerous Venture (1947)
An archeological dig uncovers a fortune in gold at a Native American burial site, but some rannies plan to make off with the treasure by staging raids while dressed in Indian garb. Can Hopalong Cassidy prove the Indians' innocence and corral the crooks? With Andy Clyde, Rand Brooks, Betty Alexander. 52 min.
11-1252 *$14.99*

Unexpected Guest (1947)
The western action is mixed with mystery in this Hopalong Cassidy tale. When members of California's family, gathered at the estate of a late relative to claim their inheritance, begin turning up murdered, it's up to Cassidy to find the enigmatic killer. With Andy Clyde, Rand Brooks, Una O'Connor. 60 min.
11-1289 *$14.99*

False Paradise (1947)
What's "false" in this western is the spiel that a slick-tongued banker gives a retired professor and his daughter so he and his criminal colleagues can buy their silver-rich land for a song. It's up to Hopalong Cassidy, Lucky and California to teach the crooks that they're "livin' in an owlhoots' paradise." With Andy Clyde, Rand Brooks, Cliff Clark. 60 min.
11-1290 *$14.99*

Borrowed Trouble (1948)
A teacher who protests the building of a saloon near her schoolhouse is kidnapped and Hopalong Cassidy must ride to the rescue. With Andy Clyde, Rand Brooks and Helen Chapman. 58 min.
11-1176 *$14.99*

Sinister Journey (1948)
It's indeed a sinister—and dangerous—journey for Hopalong Cassidy when he has to go undercover to bring a band of murderous outlaws to justice. Also stars Andy Clyde, Rand Brooks. 60 min.
11-1196 *$14.99*

Silent Conflict (1948)
When one of Hopalong Cassidy's cowhands falls under the spell of a hypnotist and gets involved with some dubious activities, Hoppy is put on the spot to try to stop him and his new pals. Andy Clyde, Rand Brooks and Don Haggerty co-star. 60 min.
11-1212 *$14.99*

The Dead Don't Dream (1948)
When three dead people turn up at a frontier hotel, it's up to Hopalong Cassidy to chase down the killers. Instead of meeting Hoppy in the center of town at high noon, however, the bad guys lead him through dark, closed-in alleys at night (a western noir?). Andy Clyde and Rand Brooks also star.
11-1251 *$14.99*

Strange Gamble (1948)
William Boyd made his final screen appearance as Hopalong Cassidy with this frontier thriller which finds Hoppy and sidekicks Lucky and California hot on the trail of a counterfeiting ring working in Silver City. Andy Clyde, Rand Brooks, Elaine Riley also star. 64 min.
11-1313 *$14.99*

Hopalong Cassidy Six-Shooter Collection 1
"Hoppy" days are here again with this collector's set that includes "In Old Mexico," "Renegade Trail," "Rustler's Valley," "Silver on the Sage," "Stick to Your Guns" and "Trail Dust."
10-1660 Save $20.00! *$69.99*

Hopalong Cassidy Six-Shooter Collection 2
Put some savings in your saddlebags with this set of six classic Cassidy oaters: "Borderland," "Heart of Arizona," "Hopalong Cassidy Returns," "North of the Rio Grande," "Range War" and "Texas Trail."
10-1661 Save $20.00! *$69.99*

Hopalong Cassidy Six-Shooter Collection 3
Fill your chamber full of timeless Saturday matinee action with the one and only Hopalong Cassidy. This special set includes "Bar 20 Justice," "Hills of Old Wyoming," "Outlaws of the Desert," "Riders of the Deadline," "Sinister Journey" and "Three Men from Texas."
10-1664 Save $20.00! *$69.99*

Hopalong Cassidy Six-Shooter Collection 4
Take aim at saving yourself some dough with this set featuring six of Hoppy's best: "Doomed Caravan," "The Frontiersman," "Hidden Gold," "Hopalong Cassidy Enters," "Lumberjack" and "Wide Open Town."
10-1669 Save $20.00! *$69.99*

Hopalong Cassidy Six-Shooter Collection 5
There's lots of Cassidy classics in the corral with this money-saving set that includes "Cassidy of Bar 20," "The Leather Burners," "Santa Fe Marshal," "The Showdown," "Stagecoach War" and "Sunset Trail."
10-9506 Save $20.00! *$69.99*

Hopalong Cassidy Six-Shooter Collection 6
Six of Hopalong's hardest-hitting frontier dramas—"Bar 20 Rides Again," "Hoppy Serves a Writ," "Law of the Pampas," "The Marauders," "Secrets of the Wasteland" and "Texas Masquerade"—have been rounded up into a money-saving collection.
10-1686 Save $20.00! *$69.99*

Hopalong Cassidy Six-Shooter Collection 7
You'll roll a lucky "7" when you get this Hoppy collection that includes "Border Patrol," "Borrowed Trouble," "Call of the Prairie," "Pirates on Horseback," "Silent Conflict" and "Three on the Trail."
10-1687 Save $20.00! *$69.99*

Hopalong Cassidy Six-Shooter Collection 8
Hop, hop, hop your way back to the Golden Age of Hollywood westerns with this six-tape collection that features the one and only Hopalong Cassidy starring in "Colt Comrades," "The Dead Don't Dream," "Lost Canyon," "Mystery Man," "Partners of the Plains" and "Riders of the Timberline."
10-1696 Save $20.00! *$69.99*

Hopalong Cassidy Six-Shooter Collection 9
The movies' original "Man in Black," Hopalong Cassidy, protects the Wild West from the scum of the prairie in six vintage oaters: "Bar 20," "Border Vigilantes," "Eagles Brood," "False Colors," "Hopalong Rides Again" and "Unexpected Guest."
10-1703 Save $20.00! *$69.99*

Hopalong Cassidy Six-Shooter Collection 10
Lasso yourself some savings by purchasing this six-tape collector's set that includes the Cassidy faves "Dangerous Venture," "Devil's Playground," "False Paradise," "In Old Colorado," "Pride of the West" and "Strange Gamble."
10-1715 Save $20.00! *$69.99*

The Law West Of Tombstone (1938)
Tim Holt, in his Western debut, stars as a young gunslinger who falls in love with the daughter of the town's two-bit judge, who's been dispensing justice from the local saloon. With Evelyn Brent, Allan Lane. 72 min.
05-1295 Was $19.99 *$14.99*

Under The Tonto Rim (1947)
After his stage is robbed, stagecoach operator Tim Holt goes undercover to catch the culprits. Two-fisted Western adventure, based on a Zane Grey story, also stars Nan Leslie, Richard Martin. 61 min.
10-7771 *$14.99*

Wild Horse Mesa (1947)
Zane Grey's story is the basis for this sagebrush saga in which cowboy Tim Holt tries to locate thousands of horses being hidden in the mountains. The responsible party is a group of crooks who have killed Holt's girlfriend's father. Nan Leslie, Richard Martin and Jason Robards, Sr. also star. 60 min.
66-6059 *$14.99*

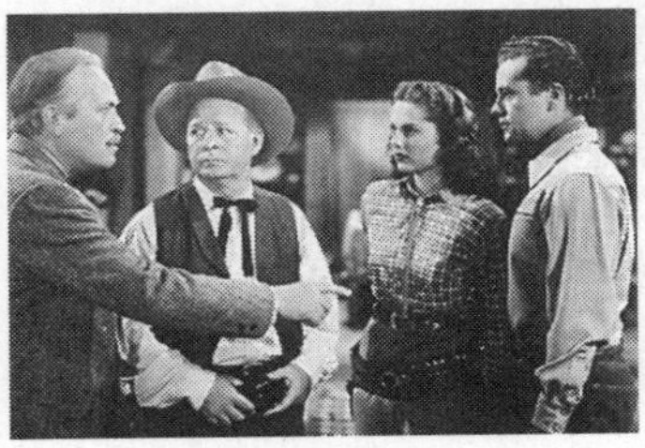

Thunder Mountain (1947)
First-rate adaptation of Zane Grey's story stars Tim Holt as a college grad who tries to stop a family feud that's been fanned by a group of sly crooks out to dupe the local farmers. Holt and gal pal Martha Hyer, a member of a rival family, stop the dirty work and try to make peace. With Richard Martin, Steve Brodie. 61 min.
66-6070 *$14.99*

Hot Lead (1951)
Tim Holt and partner Richard Martin try to avenge the death of a close friend with fisticuffs and smarts. 60 min.
10-7777 Was $19.99 *$14.99*

The Pecos Kid (1935)
The title character is the son of land owners who were killed and robbed of the deed to the famous Pecos Ranch and Mine, which was granted to them by the King of Spain. Years after their death, the Pecos Kid returns to find the killers and make them pay. Fred Kohler, Jr., Ruth Findlay and Roger Williams star.
68-8996 Was $19.99 *$14.99*

Toll Of The Desert (1936)
A tough lawman confronts his outlaw father who deserted him when he was a youngster. Nifty stuntwork highlights this action-packed saga. Fred Kohler, Jr., Betty Mack co-star. 58 min.
10-7801 Was $19.99 *$14.99*

The Mysterious Rider (1938)
From the pen of Zane Grey comes this rouser about a masked rider of the plains who helps homesteaders regain their land from a lowdown owlhoot. Douglas Dumbrille, Russell Hayden, Sydney Toler star. 74 min.
10-1161 *$14.99*

Frontier Law (1943)
A gang of cowboys rides into town to clear a friend charged with murder and put the real coyotes in the hoosegow. Great B-actioner stars Russell Hayden, Dennis Moore, Fuzzy Knight. 55 min.
10-7997 Was $19.99 *$14.99*

Saddles And Sagebrush (1943)
Russell Hayden, Dub Taylor, and Bob Wills and the Texas Playboys star in this enthralling Western programmer with shooting, singing and fun!
10-8272 Was $19.99 *$14.99*

Silver City Raiders (1943)
A group of landowners are about to be duped off their turf when a scheming land-office operator claims he owns the territory. Russell Hayden, Bob Wills, Dub Taylor and Alma Carroll star in this thrilling oater. 55 min.
10-8273 Was $19.99 *$14.99*

'Neath Canadian Skies (1946)
"B" Western great Russell Hayden plays a hard-riding Mountie sergeant who saves a group of miners terrorized by Yukon nasties. Inez Cooper and Kermit Maynard also star. 41 min.
09-2103 Was $24.99 *$14.99*

North Of The Border (1946)
Two-fisted cowpoke Russell Hayden "takes off" to the Great White North in this frontier actioner set in a Canadian fur trapping town. When the friend he was supposed to meet is found murdered, Hayden is charged with the crime and has to set his own trap for the real culprits. With Lyle Talbot, Inez Cooper. 43 min.
09-2207 Was $24.99 *$14.99*

Where The North Begins (1947)
Action and romance blend in this exciting tale of a Mountie who falls in love with a girl, then sets out to stop a gang of ornery outlaws. Russell Hayden, Jennifer Holt and Denver Pyle star. 42 min.
10-1588 *$14.99*

Wanderer Of The Wasteland (1945)
Zane Grey's novel inspired this cowboy saga starring James Warren as a young man driven to find the killer of his father. When Warren finally finds the murderer, he has second thoughts on revenge after realizing he's in love with the man's niece. Richard Martin, Audrey Long and Robert Clarke co-star. 65 min.
66-6060 *$14.99*

God's Country (1946)
Fugitive Robert Lowery hides out in a remote mountain community and helps the residents fend off the schemes of a nasty neighboring lumber baron. Light-hearted western tale is notable for a supporting turn by Buster Keaton as a coonskin-capped cook who runs afoul of the local wildlife. With Helen Gilbert, William Farnum. 64 min.
09-5334 Was $19.99 *$14.99*

Death Valley (1946)
The incredible desert heat turns gold prospectors into enemies, sending their search for booty into a nasty cat-and-mouse game. Robert Lowery and Nat Pendleton star. 72 min.
17-9049 *$14.99*

Call Of The Forest (1949)
Robert Lowery (filmdom's original Batman), Ken Curtis of "Gunsmoke" and Chief Thundercloud star in this daring cowboys and Indians exploit. 74 min.
10-7605 Was $19.99 *$14.99*

Under Colorado Skies (1947)
Those skies are getting pretty dark for bank clerk Monte Hale, who's accused of being part of a bank robbery ring, but is really taking the rap for his fiancée's brother. Can Monte clear things up? With Adrian Booth, Paul Hurst, and the Riders of the Purple Sage, who perform "San Antonio Rose." 65 min.
63-1803 *$14.99*

Outcasts Of The Trail (1949)
When the grown daughter of a reformed stagecoach robber is accused in taking part in a heist, Monte Hale rides in to find the real crooks and clear the woman's and her father's names. With Jeff Donnell, Paul Hurst, Roy Barcroft. 61 min.
63-1802 *$14.99*

The Marshal's Daughter (1953)
Tex Ritter strums her theme, cowpokes Preston Foster, Johnny Mack Brown and Buddy Baer turn up just to play poker, and her tin star papa is no less than Hoot Gibson! Is it any wonder croonin' cowgirl Laurie Anders ("Ah luv those wide open spaces!") has what it takes to clean up a frontier town in this song-filled oater that co-stars Anders' TV cohort, Ken Murray? 71 min.
10-7541 Was $19.99 *$14.99*

Two-Gun Man From Harlem (1938)
Rare all-black sagebrush classic, from when jazz master Herb Jeffries was Herbert Jeffrey, "the Black Tom Mix." Here, he hogties some randy rustlers and clears himself of a trumped-up murder charge. Mary Whitten, Mantan Moreland, Stymie Beard also star. 60 min.
01-1419 Was $19.99 *$14.99*

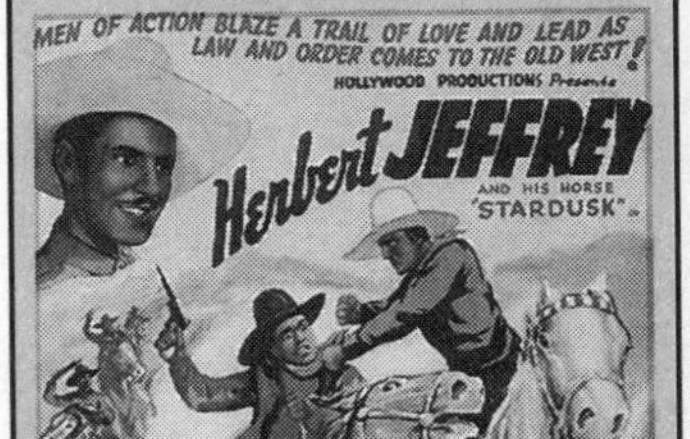

Harlem Rides The Range (1939)
Exciting all-black Western saga tells entertaining story of singing cowboy who's out to foil dastardly outlaws who stole the deed to a uranium mine. Stars Herbert Jeffrey, Clarence Brooks.
08-5023 *$14.99*

The Bronze Buckaroo (1939)
Herbert Jeffrey, Lucius Brooks and Artie Young, three of the best-known black cowpokes, star in this action-jammed sagebrush saga, in which they avenge the death of a friend's father. 57 min.
10-1373 *$14.99*

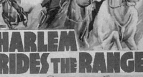

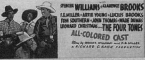

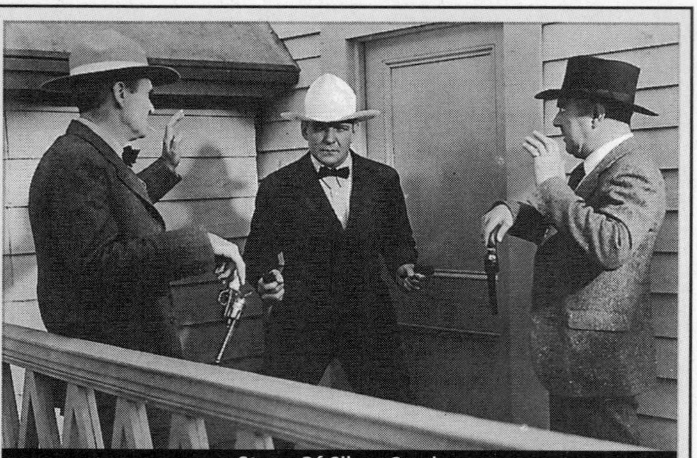

Stone Of Silver Creek

Buck Jones

Border Law (1931)
One of Buck Jones' finest outings finds the heroic cowboy going undercover to find the scoundrel who murdered his brother. Lupita Tovar, Frank Rice and Don Chapman also star. 62 min.
10-8263 Was $19.99 *$14.99*

The Fighting Sheriff (1931)
The sheriff fights with outlaws and is involved in a battle of the sexes when he joins a pretty debutante. Thrilling oater that mixes action and romance with style stars Buck Jones, Loretta Sayers, Robert Ellis.
10-8940 *$14.99*

South Of The Rio Grande (1932)
Buck Jones is an ol' cowhand from...well, you know where. Action-packed tale has the cowpoke serving as captain in the Mexican army. With Mona Harris, Paul Fix. 61 min.
10-7885 Was $19.99 *$14.99*

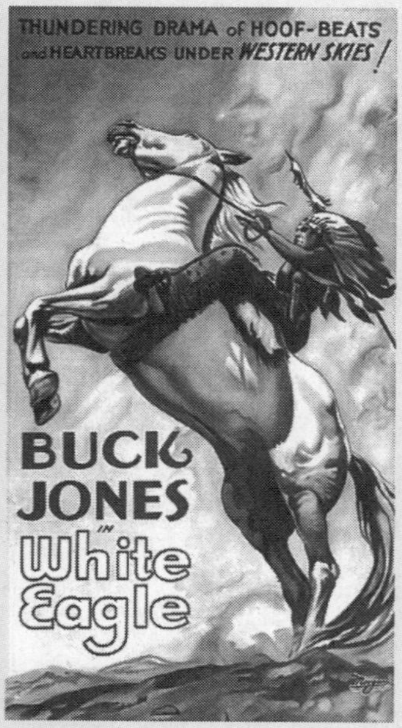
THUNDERING DRAMA of HOOF-BEATS and HEARTBREAKS UNDER WESTERN SKIES!
BUCK JONES IN
White Eagle

White Eagle (1932)
American Indian Buck Jones rides a blue streak across the West as a Pony Express rider, then must clear the name of the local tribe, who is being blamed for the theft of the mail service's finest horses. Jones later reprised the role in a Columbia serial. Co-stars Barbara Weeks, Jason Robards, Sr., Jim Thorpe and Ward Bond. 64 min.
10-9166 Was $19.99 *$14.99*

Unknown Valley (1933)
An offbeat "B" Western in which Buck Jones attempts to find his lost father while living in a desolate area of the desert. Cecelia Parker, Carlotta Warwick also star. 64 min.
10-8262 Was $19.99 *$14.99*

Stone Of Silver Creek (1935)
Buck Jones stars as T. William Stone, owner of a local gambling hall who plays matchmaker for the local parson and then gets help from the good preacher in discovering who's been stealing Jones' gold, in this entertaining frontier drama. With Niles Welch, Noel Francis. Also included on this program are a cartoon, newsreel, and a chapter from Buck's 1933 serial "Gordon of Ghost City." 83 min. total.
07-2567 *$14.99*

Border Brigands (1935)
That border is the one between Canada and the United States, and red-blooded Mountie Buck Jones crosses it—and the line between the law and the outlaw—when he joins a gang of crooks undercover to flush out his brother's killer. Fred Kohler, Lola Andre co-star. Also included on this program are a cartoon, newsreel, and a chapter from Buck's 1933 serial "Gordon of Ghost City." 77 min. total.
07-2568 *$14.99*

The Ivory-Handled Gun (1935)
Interesting sagebrush drama starring Buck Jones and Walter Miller as rival sheepmen who carry on the bitter feud begun by their fathers, leading to a final gunfight that change both men's lives forever. With Charlotte Wynters. Also included on this program are a cartoon, newsreel, and a chapter from Buck's 1933 serial "Gordon of Ghost City." 80 min. total.
09-5121 *$14.99*

The Crimson Trail (1935)
Stand-out Buck Jones oater finds the perennial hero in a tale about two ranch owners at each other's throats, each believing the other to be a rustler. But love cures all when one's nephew falls for the other's daughter. 58 min.
10-8411 Was $19.99 *$14.99*

Law For Tombstone (1937)
And that law arrives in the infamous frontier town in the two-fisted form of Buck Jones, who gets some help from gunslinger Doc Holliday in stopping a stagecoach-robbing ring operating out of Tombstone. With Harvey Clark, Muriel Evans, Earle Hodgins; co-directed by Jones. Also included on this program are a cartoon, newsreel, and a chapter from Buck's 1933 serial "Gordon of Ghost City." 81 min. total.
07-2566 *$14.99*

Boss Of Lonely Valley (1937)
Two saddle scalawags rip off the estates of dead people. When they try to pull a fast one on Buck Jones' gal pal, the cowboy puts an end to their plans. With Muriel Evans, Harvey Clark. 55 min.
08-1605 *$14.99*

Black Aces (1937)
Buck Jones, one of cowboy fans' favorite heroes, is a shy tenderfoot who gets teased by all the other cowpokes. Then he gets a burst of courage and changes his tune. Charles King and Kay Linaker also star. 59 min.
10-8037 Was $19.99 *$14.99*

Empty Saddles (1937)
These saddles won't be empty for long, as rival cattlemen and sheepherders are gearing up for an all-out range war, and only Buck Jones can put things right. Also stars Charles Middleton and silent screen beauty Louise Brooks. 65 min.
10-8484 Was $19.99 *$14.99*

California Frontier (1938)
A U.S. Army captain and the eldest son of a persecuted Mexican family battle racist desperadoes in the California territory. Buck Jones, Milburn Stone and Carmen Bailey star. 54 min.
10-7603 Was $19.99 *$14.99*

Frontier Scout (1939)
George Houston stars here as Wild Bill Hickok, sent by Ulysses S. Grant on a mission that might turn the tide of the Civil War. Great gobs o' gunplay with Ben Marion, Al St. John and Dave O'Brien. 60 min.
10-7297 Was $19.99 *$14.99*

Trigger Pals (1939)
A gang of rustlers is disrupting the settlers, and three sagebrush musketeers set out to stop them. Singing cowboy Art Jarrett teams with Lee Powell and Al St. John in this thrilling western winner. 60 min.
10-8483 Was $19.99 *$14.99*

Six Gun Rhythm (1939)
Radio cowpoke Tex Fletcher's only screen appearance was as a pro football star who returns to his Texas home when his father's killed by outlaws and scores a touchdown for justice. Fletcher also sings five songs in his own inimitable style. 57 min.
62-1035 Was $19.99 *$14.99*

Lure Of The Wasteland (1939)
A rare color sagebrush outing starring Grant Withers as a fed posing as a prisoner in order to get a convict to tell him where a fortune in stolen bonds is hidden. Karl Hackett, Marion Arnold and Snub Pollard also star in this exciting shoot-out spectacle. 52 min.
68-8988 Was $19.99 *$14.99*

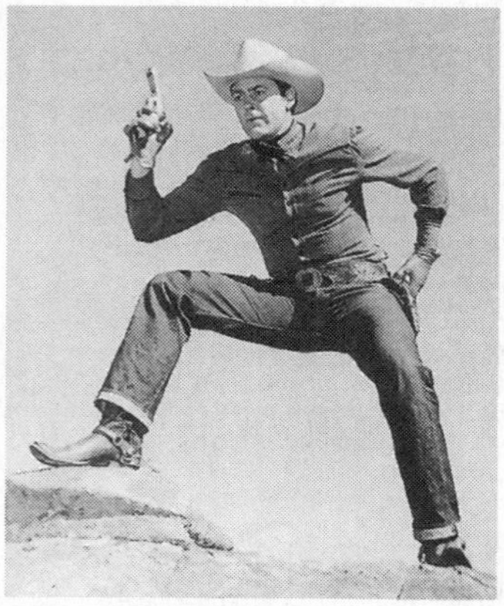

Silver City Kid (1944)
When he learns that a crooked local banker is tapping into ore from a silver mine to (figuratively) line his pockets, mine foreman Allan "Rocky" Lane digs deep to make sure justice pans out. Peggy Stewart, Wally Vernon and "Twinkle" Watts also star. 56 min.
63-1804 *$14.99*

Oklahoma Badlands (1948)
Legendary stunt man Yakima Canutt directs Allan "Rocky" Lane in this land rush saga about a dirty newspaper publisher who masterminds a scheme to drive a pretty rancher off her claim. With Mildred Coles. 59 min.
10-7644 Was $19.99 *$14.99*

Carson City Raiders (1948)
Stunt-filled western yarn with Allan "Rocky" Lane as an express company agent who rids the townspeople of Carson City of a group of crooks led by the town's nefarious banker. Eddy Walker and Frank Reicher also star; features some amazing action scenes directed by Yakima Canutt. 60 min.
10-9039 *$14.99*

Death Valley Gunfighters (1949)
Allan "Rocky" Lane is the western hero who helps miners from Death Valley who are duped out of their silver mine by an outlaw gang. With George Cheseboro, Jim Nolan and Forrest Taylor.
10-1708 *$14.99*

Bandit King Of Texas (1949)
The title rapscallion is selling phony deeds to Lone Star State property to would-be settlers, and it's up to Allan "Rocky" Lane, riding in on faithful Black Jack, to knock the crown off the "king's" head. With Eddy Waller, Helene Stanley. 60 min.
63-1805 *$14.99*

Rough Riders Of Durango (1951)
Allan "Rocky" Lane stars in this sagebrusher that finds him helping some ranchers swindled in an elaborate scheme that left them bankrupt after taking out loans to cover their stolen wheat shipments. Denver Pyle, Ross Ford and Aline Towne co-star.
10-1707 *$14.99*

Captive Of Billy The Kid (1952)
Five of Billy the Kid's compadres are set to regroup in order to piece together parts of a map that leads to the Kid's hidden cash. When some of the associates are discovered to be dead and parts of the map are found to be missing, Allan "Rocky" Lane steps in to solve the mystery. Clayton Moore, Roy Barcroft and Grant Withers also star.
10-1709 *$14.99*

The Marshal Of Cedar Rock (1953)
A rotten railroad agent is buying up cheap land by the barrelful, and doesn't care who he has to hurt to do it...but you can bet Allan "Rocky" Lane is going to derail his sidewinding schemes! Phyllis Coates, Roy Barcroft, Kenneth MacDonald co-star. 54 min.
10-1336 *$14.99*

Black Cyclone (1925)
In a story that closely mirrors real-life incidents, cowboy Guinn Williams joins forces with a wild horse fighting bad guys and helping western heroines. Kathleen Collins and Rex, Williams' horse, also star. Silent with music score.
68-9152 Was $19.99 *$14.99*

Thunder Over Texas (1934)
Some sneaky carpetbaggers want to take advantage of the railroad comin' through town, and Big Boy Williams must hogtie them before it's too late. 52 min.
62-1220 Was $19.99 *$14.99*

Danger Trails (1935)
Guinn "Big Boy" Williams rides once more, to avenge the honor of a pert prairie blossom and rout the rannies raiding her ranch. Gobs o'gunplay in this sagebrush sensation! Marjorie Gordon, Wally Wales co-star. 62 min.
10-7200 Was $19.99 *$14.99*

Cowboy Holiday (1935)
The tree is ready, the egg nog is out and the tinsel is shiny. Problem is, a mean-spirited hombre known as the Juarez Kid is causing all sorts of trouble for a lawman whose job is threatened if he doesn't stop him. Guinn "Big Boy" Williams tries to help his lawman pal in this story that includes secret caves, hidden gold and ancient mines. With Janet Chandler. 56 min.
68-8974 Was $19.99 *$14.99*

Big Boy Rides Again (1935)
The estranged rodeo star son of a rancher receives a reconciliation letter from his father and joins his partner on the trail to meet him. But Dad is mysteriously poisoned after completing his will—a will that leaves the son $50,000 in hidden cash. Facing hoodlums and masked intruders, the compadres try to find the loot. With Guinn "Big Boy" Williams and Charles K. French. 55 min.
68-9023 Was $19.99 *$14.99*

Lucky Boots (1936)
A pair of eager Easterners head for the Pecos to take over their pa's dude ranch...but a pack of banditos with their eyes on the gold buried beneath it want them packing! It's up to Guinn "Big Boy" Williams to dole out some prairie justice! Frank Yaconelli co-stars. AKA: "Gun Play." 60 min.
10-7196 Was $19.99 *$14.99*

Sunset Pass (1946)
Taken from Zane Grey's story, this exciting western adventure features James Warren as a lawman who must make some tough decisions when he discovers that one of the train robbers working along the Arizona border is his girlfriend's younger brother. Nan Leslie, John Laurenz and Jane Greer also star. 55 min.
66-6058 *$14.99*

Ride 'Em Cowgirl (1939)
This tuneful oater stars Dorothy Page as a cowgirl branded an outlaw after she retrieves cash stolen from her pa by a crook. In order to get the story straight, she must enter a race and expose the real criminal. With Milton Frome, Vince Barnett. 50 min.
08-1578 *$14.99*

The Singing Cowgirl (1939)
Singing rage Dorothy Page, the female answer to Gene Autry, helps an 8-year-old orphan win back the family ranch from the polecats who killed his kinfolk. Dave O'Brien co-stars. 60 min.
10-7397 Was $19.99 *$14.99*

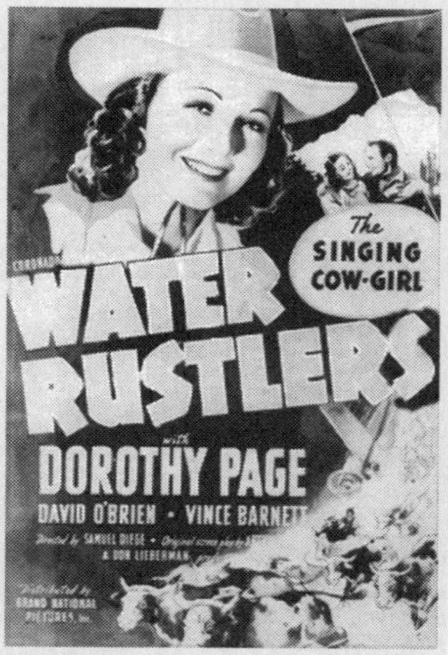
The SINGING COW-GIRL
WATER RUSTLERS
with DOROTHY PAGE
DAVID O'BRIEN · VINCE BARNETT

Water Rustlers (1939)
Dorothy Page, the Singing Cowgirl, goes after the gang who closed the dam gates, thereby killing the grass, the cattle and, soon, the townspeople. With Dave O'Brien. 55 min.
62-1293 Was $19.99 *$14.99*

Bob Steele

Near The Rainbow's End (1930)
In his first talking western, Bob Steele is a third generation cattle rancher who rises above his own mistrust of sheepherders to clear up a violent land squabble. 56 min.
10-7390 *$14.99*

Oklahoma Cyclone (1930)
In this early outing, Bob Steele saddles up, shoots, slugs, and even sings as the leader of a happy-go-lucky band of bronco busters. Enjoyable oater also stars Nita Ray, Al St. John, Slim Whitaker. 64 min.
10-7271 Was $19.99 *$14.99*

Land Of Missing Men (1930)
Bob Steele is a cowpoke who uncovers a devious scheme by black hats to get rid of an entire town of good people—including the daughter of a dying man. Bob decides to trail the killers in hopes of putting an end to their murderous ways. Al St. John and Caryl Lincoln also star in this early talkie frontier film.
68-9201 *$14.99*

Ridin' Fool (1931)
Short in height but plenty tall in the saddle, curly-haired Bob Steele uses his formidable equestrian skills to save his friends from evil bandoleros. With Josephine Velez. 58 min.
10-7749 Was $19.99 *$14.99*

Riders Of The Desert (1932)
Bob Steele plays a college lad who turns in his books for bullets when he returns to his frontier home to help locate stolen loot. With Gertrude Messenger, Al St. John. 63 min.
09-1062 Was $19.99 *$14.99*

South Of Santa Fe (1932)
Trouble's a-brewin' for Saturday matinee idol Bob Steele when he runs afoul of a band of renegades while combing the Mexican border in this high-caliber Western actioner. 60 min.
10-7097 Was $19.99 *$14.99*

Young Blood (1932)
Fisticuffs and gunfights galore as "Robin Hood of the Range" Bob Steele robs from the rich and gives to the poor, while helping a foreign actress who's being blackballed by the townswomen. Co-stars Charles King, Helen Foster. 59 min.
10-7098 Was $19.99 *$14.99*

Man From Hell's Edges (1932)
Bob Steele is mighty burned up when he's framed for a sagebrush slaying...so he breaks jail to set after the genuine bushwhackers and bring them to prairie justice! Nancy Drexel, Julian Rivero also star. 63 min.
10-7272 Was $19.99 *$14.99*

Hidden Valley (1932)
Journeying to a mysterious valley far from human intruders, Bob Steele searches for a buried treasure. Will it be gold, or something really valuable—a recipe for million-dollar Ranch dressing? 60 min.
10-7392 Was $19.99 *$14.99*

Texas Buddies (1932)
Former military pilot Bob Steele flies straight from Wild Blue Yonder to Wide Open Spaces, where he uses his trusty monoplane to round up bad guys. Gabby Hayes co-stars. 57 min.
10-7394 Was $19.99 *$14.99*

Law Of The West (1932)
Tips for rustlers and rogues: 1.) Be prompt; the noon stage is. 2.) Politeness counts; robbery is a people business! 3.) Remove kerchief, then spit. 4.) Stay clear of that Bob Steele, tireless lawman. Co-stars Ed Brady. 50 min.
10-7545 Was $19.99 *$14.99*

Son Of Oklahoma (1932)
A man is killed while his wife and son are kidnapped by a nasty saddle rat. The son escapes the meanie, takes refuge with a Mexican family and, years later, while seeking the location of a lost gold mine, draws the interest of the kidnapper. Bob Steele, Josie Sedgwick and Carmen Laroux star. 63 min.
68-9007 Was $19.99 *$14.99*

Breed Of The Border (1933)
Bob Steele stars as a race car driver who's hired by an outlaw who needs an escort across the Mexican border. But Bob does an about-face and turns the crook over to the law. 53 min.
10-7102 Was $19.99 *$14.99*

Galloping Romeo (1933)
What muzzle through yonder window breaks? Must be that heartthrob on horseback, Bob Steele, stepping off his romantic paces with co-star Doris Hill. 59 min.
10-7395 Was $19.99 *$14.99*

Fighting Champ (1933)
Cowpunching gives way to cowboy punching for feisty Bob Steele when he climbs into the boxing ring and takes on all comers. With Kit Guard and Gabby Hayes. 57 min.
10-7396 Was $19.99 *$14.99*

Trailin' North (1933)
A Texas Ranger (Bob Steele) heads far north to Canada, where he joins the Mounties and helps them get their man. Doris Hill, Arthur Rankin and George "Gabby" Hayes star. 57 min.
10-8269 Was $19.99 *$14.99*

The Gallant Fool (1933)
Top-shelf horse opry with Bob Steele as a man wrongly accused of murder who slips away from the long arm of the law so he can clear his name. With George Hayes, Arletta Duncan, John Elliott. 60 min.
10-8412 Was $19.99 *$14.99*

A Demon For Trouble (1934)
Cowboy Bob Steele has a devil of a time stopping the scheme of outlaws in his territory. First they buy all the land around, then they kill the sellers to steal their money back. Gloria Shea, Lafe McKee, and Don Alvarado also star. 58 min.
10-7339 Was $19.99 *$14.99*

The Rider Of The Law (1935)
Cowboy Bob Steele acts like a tenderfoot from the East in order to snag a group of dastardly outlaws in this western wonder. Gertrude Messinger and Earl Dwire also star; Robert N. Bradbury, Steele's father, directs. 56 min.
08-1550 *$14.99*

Kid Courageous (1935)
Top-drawer Western with Bob Steele in full cry of some disreputable henchman-types who've swiped a shipment of ore. Co-stars Renee Borden. 58 min.
10-7176 Was $19.99 *$14.99*

Western Justice (1935)
Bob Steele is ready and able to slap leather against a pack of avaricious land-grubbers who are out to drive hapless settlers back East! Pistols 'n punches aplenty with Renee Bordon, Julian Rivero. 55 min.
10-7268 Was $19.99 *$14.99*

No Man's Range (1935)
Robert N. Bradbury directs his son, cowboy Bob Steele, in the tale of a lawman with a fair knowledge of dynamite who passes himself off as a renegade to trap some criminals. With Buck Connors. 55 min.
10-7748 Was $19.99 *$14.99*

Trail Of Terror (1935)
Government agent Bob Steele gets the goods on a gang of seedy outlaws by posing as one of them. Forrest Taylor, Beth Marion co-star in this first-rate sagebrusher. 59 min.
10-8265 Was $19.99 *$14.99*

Smokey Smith (1935)
Two elderly settlers are brutally gunned down, and when stalwart Bob Steele and sidekick Gabby Hayes find out the killings were a mistake, they try to snag the creeps who did the deed. Mary Kornman also stars. 55 min.
10-9380 *$14.99*

Tombstone Terror (1935)
Top-notch "B" sagebrusher in which Bob Steele plays twins and—you guessed it!—one's good and one's bad! When good Bob impersonates bad Bob, he learns that his sibling is part of a crime ring. There's all sorts of exciting developments, fights and more. Talk about your "Maximum Bob"! With Gabby Hayes and Kay McCoy.
68-9209 *$14.99*

Alias John Law (1935)
After a feud between a group of black hats and a marshal, Bob Steele is deputized. But soon the head of the gang is impersonating him, trying to snag some much-desired land that really belongs to Steele. Bob's got to stop him and his group, and gets some help from his deaf pardner who reads lips with a telescope. With Roberta Gale, Buck Connors and Earl Dwire.
68-9211 *$14.99*

The Kid Ranger (1936)
After discovering that he's shot an innocent man in his quest for an outlaw gang, Bob Steele vows to never rest till he dispenses frontier judgment to the real rannies. Six-shootin' sagebrush saga also stars William Farnum. 60 min.
09-2030 Was $24.99 *$14.99*

Cavalry (1936)
Trying to impress the young lady he's taken a hankerin' to, Bob Steele leads troopers waging war against insurgent Indians, evil rustlers and just about anybody wearing a black hat. 63 min.
10-7099 Was $19.99 *$14.99*

The Last Of The Warrens (1936)
The Warren-Selby family feud of Kentucky fame receives a Western motif, with Bob Steele paying off old scores after his pa was nearly killed by lowdown sidewinder Kent Selby. Co-stars Charles King and Charles K. French. 60 min.
10-7104 Was $19.99 *$14.99*

Border Phantom (1936)
Bob Steele keeps the border clean in this rousing Westerner, stopping an Oriental baddie from bringing in Chinese brides from Mexico (didn't know they made Chinese brides in Mexico, did you?). 58 min.
21-3006 Was $19.99 *$14.99*

Gun Lords Of Stirrup Basin (1937)
In this first-class cattle drama, Bob Steele is about to marry a homesteader's daughter when trouble begins. A sleazy lawyer urges the area cattlemen that they'll be in trouble if the homesteaders put a dam on a nearby river, and Steele must intervene to save the day. With Louise Stanley, Karl Hackett. 55 min.
08-1570 *$14.99*

Arizona Gunfighter (1937)
Bob Steele is no-nonsense gunmaster Colt Ferron, taking on some of the West's most ornery characters in this two-fisted sagebrusher. With Jean Carmen, Ted Adams. 55 min.
08-1572 *$14.99*

The Gun Ranger (1937)
What with a lax court system cutting the ground out from under him, straight-shooting sheriff Bob Steele casts his tin star aside, takes the law into his own hands and doesn't give a whit about such hogwash as "The Bill of Rights." Co-stars Eleanor Stewart and John Merton. 56 min.
10-7103 Was $19.99 *$14.99*

Lightnin' Crandall (1937)
Bob Steele wants nothing more than to hang up his holsters and live in peace...but he's force to strap 'em on again to settle the score between feuding ranchers at his Arizona retreat! Rootin' tootin' action with Lois January, Frank LaRue.
10-7195 Was $19.99 *$14.99*

Ridin' The Lone Trail (1937)
Early outing for Bob Steele stars him as a six-shooter-slingin' savior to a stagecoach line beset by bandits and a passel of other problems. Claire Rochelle, Charles King co-star. 56 min.
10-7198 Was $19.99 *$14.99*

Sundown Saunders (1937)
Bob Steele finds that the ranch that he's won in a palomino race is more trouble than it's worth, thanks to the evil efforts of a desperado who wants the spread for his own! Frontier fling co-stars Earl Dwire, Ed Cassidy. 63 min.
10-7212 Was $19.99 *$14.99*

The Red Rope (1937)
A sinister secret society is out to murder and terrorize a town's ranchers...and they always leave a scarlet-stained rope with their victim to-be! Count on Bob Steele to hogtie these harbingers of hate! Lois January, Forrest Taylor co-star. 56 min.
10-7267 Was $19.99 *$14.99*

Doomed At Sundown (1937)
Clowning cowpoke Bob Steele gets serious after his father is knifed and sets out to find the creep responsible for the deed. Lorraine Hayes and Warner Richmond also star in this wild western outing. 60 min.
10-8439 Was $19.99 *$14.99*

The Trusted Outlaw (1937)
Cowboy Bob Steele is the last member of an infamous outlaw family who plans to return home after years away and get married and go straight. Unfortunately, Bob is ambushed, kills one of his attackers in self-defense and soon learns his girl's fixin' to marry someone else. He gets a chance to make good when he faces robbers on a payroll patrol. Lois January co-stars. 57 min.
68-9014 Was $19.99 *$14.99*

Thunder In The Desert (1938)
Bob Steele roosts a spell at his dead uncle's ranch, discovers Unc was actually murdered, then sets out to settle the score with the culprits in this two-fisted shoot-'em-up. Co-stars Don Barclay and Louise Stanley. 56 min.
10-7100 Was $19.99 *$14.99*

Paroled To Die (1938)
It's "48 Hrs." on the frontier, as Bob Steele plays a rancher who has been framed for a bank robbery...and must team up with a government agent to uncover the real rascal before it's too late! Varmints and violence with Kathleen Eliot, Karl Hackett. 55 min.
10-7270 Was $19.99 *$14.99*

Durango Valley Raiders (1938)
Cowboy Bob Steele sets up a clever decoy to capture a busy masked bandit known only as "The Shadow." Sagebrush sleuthing with Louise Stanley, Ted Adams. 56 min.
10-7714 Was $19.99 *$14.99*

Feud Maker (1938)
A fork-tongued schemer gains the ear of both sides of a range war to keep the violence raging, and to grab up cheap land when the participants are dead. Bob Steele rides to the rescue; with Karl Hackett. 55 min.
10-7715 Was $19.99 *$14.99*

Colorado Kid (1938)
Bob Steele, the mucho macho Western star, is accused of murder. Of course, he had nothing to do with it, and counts on his pal to help him out of a jam. Marian Weldon and Karl Hackett also star. 56 min.
10-8051 Was $19.99 *$14.99*

Desert Patrol (1938)
After a lawman is killed by a murderous gang of outlaws, pal Bob Steele does some investigating, infiltrates the hombres and tries to put a stop to their reign of terror. Marion Weldon and Rex Lease also star.
68-9068 Was $19.99 *$14.99*

Mesquite Buckaroo (1939)
Trouble's a-cookin' when Bob Steele is challenged to a rodeo duel. His opponent starts getting cold feet before the competition, though...and takes drastic, dangerous steps to make sure Bob'll never weigh in! Frontier fracas features Carolyn Curtis, Frank LaRue. 59 min.
10-7266 Was $19.99 *$14.99*

Riders Of The Sage (1939)
Not the tale of those brave lads who brought the first really good poultry seasoning to the West, but a spicy frontier adventure starring Bob Steele. With James Whitehead. 57 min.
10-7751 Was $19.99 *$14.99*

Feud Of The Range (1939)
Bob Steele is the whitehat who takes on a gang of creeps involved in looting, burning and killing in order to benefit from the arrival of the railroad. Jack Ingram, Rychard Cramer and Charles King also star. 55 min.
55-3063 *$19.99*

El Diablo Rides (1939)
A damsel in distress who draws on would-be rescuers...jumpy jaspers living in fear of the Federales...what's going on? Bob Steele is determined to find the answer. 57 min.
62-1235 Was $19.99 *$14.99*

Smoky Trails (1939)
Rarely seen Bob Steele western in which the cowboy hero is out for revenge after his father's untimely death. The key to the culprit may be a rider he finds who is being chased by some outlaws. Jean Carmen and Ted Adams also star.
68-9168 Was $19.99 *$14.99*

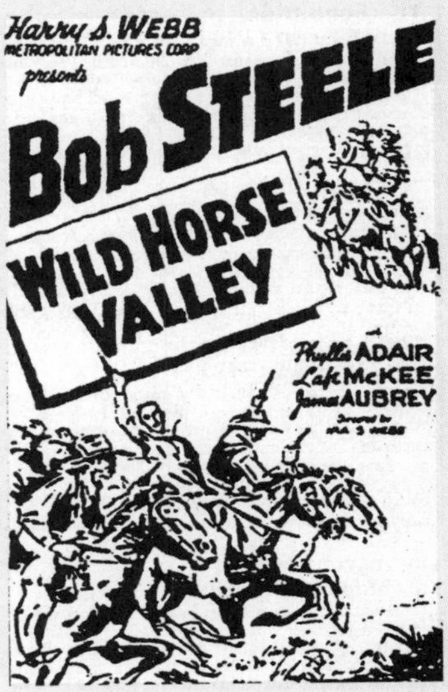

Wild Horse Valley (1940)
A treacherous horse thief nabs a prize Arabian stallion from owner Bob Steele, who then goes on the trail of the missing steed. But when it escapes from its captors into Wild Horse Valley, Bob has to find it before they do. Phyllis Adair, George Chesebro, Buzz Barton also star. 57 min.
68-9018 Was $19.99 *$14.99*

The Navajo Kid (1941)
Bob Steele is an adopted Indian out to find the killer of his foster father. After getting his revenge, he's arrested by a sheriff who, it turns out, has a secret in his past. Syd Saylor and Charles King co-star. 55 min.
09-9296 *$14.99*

Pinto Canyon (1941)
The good news for the cattle thieves is that all the beef on the hoof they've been snatching is bringing top dollar. The bad news is that they're doing their rustling in sheriff Bob Steele's jurisdiction! With Louise Stanley, Kenne Duncan. 55 min.
10-7269 Was $19.99 *$14.99*

The Law Rides (1943)
A booty of gold coins turns up, sparking an onslaught of murder and robbery among the money-grubbin' owlhoots. Leave it to the ever-upright, ever-present Bob Steele to turn the tables and run the baddies out of town. Co-stars Harley Wood.
10-7101 Was $19.99 *$14.99*

The Utah Kid (1944)
Saddle-blazin' sagebrush saga with Hoot Gibson and Bob Steele as two square-shootin' troubleshooters who take on a passel of rodeo renegades. With Ralph Lewis, Beatrice Grey. 55 min.
10-7421 Was $19.99 *$14.99*

Northwest Trail (1945)
It's up to steadfast Canadian Mountie Bob Steele to blaze a passage through that trail, accompanying a young woman delivering her uncle's payroll and helping her battle wolves and outlaws. With Joan Woodbury, Madge Bellamy, John Litel; shot in Cinecolor. 63 min.
01-1097 *$14.99*

Wildfire (1945)
Wildfire, a proud and free stallion, is marked by ranchers because he leads the wild pack. Bob Steele is torn between stopping rustlers or saving the horse's life. With Sterling Holloway. 57 min.
62-1222 Was $19.99 *$14.99*

Six Gun Man (1946)
Tally up the gunshots as U.S. marshal Bob Storm comes out firing against a scurrilous band of cattle rustlers. Bob Steele is the thundering do-gooder; with Syd Saylor, Jimmie Martin. 59 min.
10-7753 Was $19.99 *$14.99*

GEORGE HOUSTON
THE LONE RIDER in Ghost Town
AL Fuzzy ST. JOHN

The Lone Rider In Ghost Town (1941)
Is the abandoned town really haunted by vengeful spooks...or is it just a front for sinister sidewinders? That's what the Rider and Fuzzy are hell-bound to find out! Wild west wonderment with George Houston, Al St. John, Budd Buster. 64 min.
10-7207   Was $19.99   *$14.99*

The Lone Rider In Frontier Fury (1941)
"Lone Rider" George Houston is falsely accused of murdering a rancher and must clear his name and find the culprit responsible for the deed. Al St. John and Karl Hackett also star. 55 min.
10-9414   *$14.99*

The Lone Rider And The Bandit (1942)
George Houston assumes the guise of "The Lone Rider" and impersonates a musician in hopes of finding why local miners are being terrorized. He discovers that the miners are being forced into signing away their savings to some bad hombres. Al St. John, Dennis Moore star. 54 min.
09-5125   Was $19.99   *$14.99*

The Adventures Of The Masked Phantom (1938)
A brother-sister team of mine owners is being terrorized by a crooked foreman, and only the Masked Phantom can save them! A masked crusader of the Plains, his deadly knives spell doom for the crooks. Aiding him are Boots, the Wonder Dog, and his two sidekicks. 56 min.
09-1630   Was $19.99   *$14.99*

Rodeo King And The Señorita (1951)
Singing cowboy Rex Allen unravels a scheme by a crooked partner in a Wild West show to bankrupt the business and solves an old murder in this fine remake of Roy Rogers' "My Pal Trigger." With Buddy Ebsen. 67 min.
10-7617   Was $19.99   *$14.99*

Silver City Bonanza (1951)
Singing cowpoke Rex Allen and sidekick Buddy Ebsen use a seeing-eye dog to help them track down a blind man's killer. There's a bonanza of action in this oater, including an undersea chase and a haunted ranch. "Weeeel, doggie!" Mary Ellen Kaye also stars. 67 min.
63-1807   *$14.99*

Colorado Sundown (1952)
Rex Allen and his musical horse Koko foil a murder and land fraud caper masterminded by a crooked brother and sister, yet the cowboy still has time to sing "Pine Valley Stage" and "Down by the Riverside." With Slim Pickens. 67 min.
10-7544   *$14.99*

Border Saddlemates (1952)
Two-fisted veterinarian Rex Allen sets out to smash a counterfeiting ring that's running bogus bills across the border in fox cages, and you can bet Rex'll see those coyotes get their shots! Slim Pickens, Roy Barcroft also star. 67 min.
63-1806   *$14.99*

Shadows Of Tombstone (1953)
An underhanded lawman joins forces with a saloonkeeper to run a western town using dastardly means. Stranger Rex Allen tries to put an end to their power, while a reporter writes about the incidents that occur. Slim Pickens, Roy Barcroft, Jeanne Cooper co-star.
10-1710   *$14.99*

Iron Mountain Trail (1953)
While trying to investigate the reason why the mail is so slow (some things never change), Rex Allen heads to California, where he discovers some bad dudes are behind the problem. This leads to a showdown between Allen and Koko the Miracle Horse on land and the black hats by ship to see which mode of postal delivery is quicker. With Slim Pickens, Roy Barcroft and Grant Withers. 55 min.
10-9133   *$14.99*

The Phantom Stallion (1954)
This tale of a wagonmaster and his adventures travelling out West is filled with rousing sagebrush action. Rex Allen stars as the frontier hero; with Slim Pickens, Carla Balenda and Don Haggerty.
10-1711   *$14.99*

The Lone Rider In Cheyenne (1942)
An innocent man's been up for the slaying of a prison guard...and only the Rider and Fuzzy stand between him and an appointment with the gallows! Fist-flyin' frontier fury with George Houston, Al St. John, Roy Barcroft star. 59 min.
10-7206   Was $19.99   *$14.99*

Border Roundup (1942)
The Lone Rider follows a trail of death and deceit left by devious rannies who have their sights on a lost mine. With George Houston, Fuzzy St. John, Smoky Moore. 57 min.
62-1241   Was $19.99   *$14.99*

Overland Stagecoach (1942)
An exciting entry in "The Lone Rider" series in which Rider Bob Livingston and sidekick Al St. John are out to nab a masked gunman responsible for a stagecoach heist. With Dennis Moore, Julie Duncan. 61 min.
10-9336   Was $19.99   *$14.99*

Raiders Of Red Gap (1943)
The Lone Rider saves the day...and just in time, too. Fuzzy is about to be shot, mistaken for a notorious outlaw. Bob Livingston, Al St. John star. 56 min.
09-1076   Was $24.99   *$14.99*

Wolves Of The Range (1943)
After gunmen drive innocent ranchers off their cherished land, the Lone Rider calls on his riding and shooting abilities to trap these two-legged varmints. Bob Livingston and Al St. John star.
17-3012   Was $19.99   *$14.99*

Death Rides The Plains (1944)
Crooked lawyer sells ranch over and over again, killing prospective buyers and stealing their money. The Lone Rider and Fuzzy team up to bust the racket. Bob Livingston stars. 53 min.
09-1069   Was $19.99   *$14.99*

Law Of The Saddle (1944)
The law of the saddle is disrupted when the newly-elected sheriff joins forces with a pack of outlaws and wreaks havoc all over town. Only Lone Rider Bob Livingston can get to the bottom of the evil. With Al "Fuzzy" St. John, Betty Miles. 59 min.
10-8072   Was $19.99   *$14.99*

Silver Stallion (1941)
A beautiful horse fends off predatory animals and the elements to protect its children. With David Sharpe, Black Jack the Horse and Captain Boots (as Boots the Police Dog). 60 min.
10-7800   Was $19.99   *$14.99*

Last Of The Duanes (1941)
Rip-roaring filming of Zane Grey's story, starring George Montgomery as a cowpoke who kills someone in self-defense, saves a woman from a couple of black hats, then joins the Texas Rangers to find a pack of outlaws. Eve Arden, Francis Ford star. 57 min.
10-7971   Was $19.99   *$14.99*

King Of The Royal Mounted (1936)
This action-packed precursor to the Republic serial made four years later stars Robert Kent as a member of the Royal Mounted Police who tries to stop an unscrupulous lawyer from swindling a beautiful young woman out of a lost ore mine. Based on a Zane Grey story, this film also stars Rosalind Keith and Frank McGlynn. 61 min.
68-8983   Was $19.99   *$14.99*

A THUNDERING DRAMA OF THE FRONTIER DAYS IN THE WEST!
"THUNDER TRAIL"
GILBERT ROLAND MARSHA HUNT CHARLES BICKFORD MONTE BLUE BILLY LEE

Thunder Trail (1937)
Two brothers are separated when their parents are killed. One is adopted by outlaws, the other by a good family. Reunited years later, they face each other as criminal and lawyer—both in love with the same woman. Gilbert Roland, Charles Bickford star. AKA: "Thunder Pass." 53 min.
10-1591   *$14.99*

Song Of Old Wyoming (1945)
Cowboy Eddie Dean is hired by a black-garbed "Lash" LaRue to scuttle a statehood movement in the Wyoming Territory, but he has a change of heart when he meets one of the pro-Unionists. In color. 65 min.
10-7365   Was $19.99   *$14.99*

Wild West (1946)
Singing cowboy Eddie Dean, his horse Flash, the Texas Rangers and "Lash" LaRue turn out to string telegraph lines across the prairie, and with help from Uncle Sam's horsesoldiers, fight off some outlaw saboteurs. Rarig! In color. 73 min.
10-7363   Was $19.99   *$14.99*

Caravan Trail (1946)
Rare color cowboy horse-opry stars singin' Eddie Dean and Al "Lash" LaRue. The new town marshal interrupts the revenging of his best friend's murder to sing the songs "Wagon Wheels," "Crazy Cowboy Song" and "Too Pretty to Be Lonesome." 53 min.
10-7364   Was $19.99   *$14.99*

Colorado Serenade (1946)
Warbling Eddie Dean and his daredevil sidekick Nevada (David Sharp) trade slugs with a lawless punk who's terrorizing a frontier town. All-color cowboy musical features songs "Home on the Range" and "Riding to Rawhide." 68 min.
10-7366   Was $19.99   *$14.99*

Driftin' River (1946)
After Army horses are hijacked and soldiers investigating the incident are murdered, Eddie Dean and sidekick Roscoe Ates get into action, trying to find the no-goodnicks responsible. Shirley Patterson, Lee Bennett also star; includes the song "Driftin' River." 59 min.
10-9538   *$14.99*

Wild Country (1947)
U.S. marshal Eddie Dean takes out after the dirty low-down I. Stanford Jolley, who's wanted for the murder of a sheriff and now has his gun-sights set on the dead man's daughter. Co-stars Roscoe Ates and Peggy Wynn. 57 min.
10-7558   Was $19.99   *$14.99*

West To Glory (1947)
A pernicious passel of perfidious prairie rats have their beady eyes set on the fabulous gems of a Mexican rancher...and it's up to Eddie Dean and Roscoe "Soapy" Ates to corral the conniving crew! Dolores Castle, Gregg Barton co-star. 61 min.
10-7568   Was $19.99   *$14.99*

Range Beyond The Blue (1947)
Sheriff Eddie Dean and deputy Soapy (Roscoe Ates) rescue a pretty saloon-owner out of trouble, after a group of outlaws steals her gold shipments. 53 min.
10-7811   Was $19.99   *$14.99*

Check Your Guns (1948)
Eddie Dean's got his hands full, trying to outlaw guns to bring peace to his varmint-riddled town... and trying to uncover a corrupt judge who's dispensing ammo to a passel of wrongdoing rannies! Roscoe Ates, Nancy Gates co-star. 55 min.
10-7570   Was $19.99   *$14.99*

Black Hills (1948)
A hungry rancher hits it big when he finds a gold vein under his land...but all it buys is a bullet from a greedy barkeep! Eddie Dean and Soapy Ates ride to set things right; Shirley Patterson, Terry Frost co-star. 60 min.
10-7582   Was $19.99   *$14.99*

The Tioga Kid (1948)
Eddie Dean takes dual roles here, playing a Texas Ranger out to nab a band of rustlers as well as one of the outlaws. Andy Parker and the Plainsmen provide the "nighttime on the prairie" music. 54 min.
10-7814   Was $19.99   *$14.99*

The Hawk Of Powder River (1948)
Eddie Dean gets to the bottom of a plot that involves a beautiful outlaw gang leader with a murderous streak. Jennifer Holt plays the strapping villainess. 54 min.
10-7815   Was $19.99   *$14.99*

Tornado Range (1948)
U.S. Land Office representative Eddie Dean and sidekick Soapy (Roscoe Ates) try to temper the twister of turmoil brewin' on the range between homesteaders and ranchers. Co-stars Jennifer Holt, George Chesebro. 56 min.
10-8047   Was $19.99   *$14.99*

Code Of The Red Man (1942)
Chief Thundercloud and Princess Bluebird star in this fascinating western adventure in which Indians and cowboys try to stop a wild stallion. 63 min.
09-5273   Was $19.99   *$14.99*

Phantom Of Santa Fe (1936)
"Tarzan" creator Edgar Rice Burroughs produced this colorful tumbleweed tale in which a Santa Fe mission is attacked and robbed of its treasure. Area residents think it's the work of an enigmatic figure known as "The Hawk." Is he responsible? And just who is this mysterious person? Norman Kerry, Nena Quartaro and Frank Mayo star. 55 min.
68-8997   Was $19.99   *$14.99*

Riddle Ranch (1936)
Frank Gorshin would be envious of the riddles posed in this Western whodunit in which the murder of a card dealer, a Mexican desperado, a fixed horse race and an innocent cowpoke accused of murder are the primary elements. David Worth, June Marlow and Fred "Snowflake" Toones star. 63 min.
68-9000   Was $19.99   *$14.99*

Buzzy Rides The Range (1940)
Ornery ring toters use trucks to transport lassoed cattle herds, prompting a female rancher's young brother to help government agents go undercover to stop them. Buzzy Henry, Dave O'Brien and Claire Rochelle star in this lively oater. 60 min.
68-8969   Was $19.99   *$14.99*

American Empire (1942)
Deception, intrigue and violence combine in this fast-paced melodrama about the rise of a cattle empire in post-Civil War Texas. Richard Dix and Preston Foster star in this Western treat. 85 min.
17-1102   Was $19.99   *$14.99*

Arizona Bound (1941)
The first film in the "Rough Riders" series shows how lawman Buck Jones, sharpshooting reverend Tim McCoy, and ranchhand Raymond Hatton join forces to stop stagecoach robbers backed by a crooked town boss. With Dennis Moore, Luana Walters. 57 min.
62-1226   *$14.99*

Forbidden Trails (1941)
The Rough Riders (Tim McCoy, Buck Jones, Raymond Hatton) have their hands full when a pair of vengeance-seeking ex-cons come a-gunnin'. 60 min.
08-1088   *$14.99*

Gunman From Bodie (1941)
A murderous band of rustlers and an abandoned baby are the elements that test the fighting (and parenting) skills of Tim McCoy, Buck Jones and Raymond Hatton in this "Rough Riders" outing. With Dave O'Brien, Christine McIntyre. 63 min.
21-3001   *$14.99*

The ROUGH RIDERS "WEST OF THE LAW" BUCK JONES TIM McCOY RAYMOND HATTON and "SILVER"

West Of The Law (1942)
The Rough Riders hit the trail in order to smash an outlaw mob that preys upon peace-loving prospectors. Is the crusading newspaper editor the owlhoots' victim...or is his connection far more shocking? Tim McCoy, Buck Jones, Raymond Hatton star. 58 min.
09-2045   Was $19.99   *$14.99*

Ghost Town Law (1942)
Tip-top oater sprinkled with generous doses of mystery and slam-bang Western action, as the Rough Riders come to scratch with hooded bandits who've deep-sixed two marshals. Stars Buck Jones, Tim McCoy and Raymond Hatton. 62 min.
10-1259   Was $19.99   *$14.99*

Riders Of The West (1942)
Saddle up with the Rough Riders as they square off against a connivin' cattle rustler who's shaking down farmers in an attempt to take over their tracts. The action comes at a gallop with Buck Jones, Tim McCoy, Raymond Hatton. 58 min.
10-7299   Was $19.99   *$14.99*

Down Texas Way (1942)
When Rough Rider Raymond Hatton is accused of killing the town banker, Buck Jones and Tim McCoy go undercover to catch the true culprits (come on, you knew Ray wasn't innocent!). Luana Walters and screen Frankenstein monster Glenn Strange co-star. 57 min.
10-7599   Was $19.99   *$14.99*

Below The Border (1942)
The Rough Riders hightail it south to help a Mexican family discover who's been stealing their cattle and jewelry. Great Western adventure with Buck Jones and Tim McCoy. 57 min.
62-1295   Was $19.99   *$14.99*

Dawn On The Great Divide (1942)
In what turned out to be his last film before his death, Buck Jones leads Rough Riders Rex Bell and Raymond Hatton into action against what they think are hostile Indians. It turns out ruthless white hombres are wearing war paint and feathers to crash a railroad settlement. Complete and uncut version.
10-9138   *$14.99*

MOVIES UNLIMITED

The Texan (1932)
When he gets mixed up in a scheme to fix horse races, Buffalo Bill, Jr. must race against time to clear his name and bring the real bad guys to justice. With Lucille Browne, Jack Mower.
68-9108 Was $19.99 *$14.99*

Rawhide Romance (1933)
Dude ranch cowboy Buffalo Bill, Jr. has fallen in love with a girl (thus breaking B-Western Hero Law #6), and as a result doesn't notice that some owlhoots have been robbing the ranch's guests. Can Bill get his head out of the clouds long enough to bring the crooks down to Earth? 47 min.
09-2206 Was $19.99 *$14.99*

Lightning Bill (1934)
After the owner of a ranch is threatened by a gang of hot-shot outlaws, one of his workers decides to take matters into his own hands and nab the nasty desperadoes. Alma Rayford and Nelson McDowell join Buffalo Bill, Jr. in this entertaining oater.
68-8986 Was $19.99 *$14.99*

Whirlwind Rider (1935)
A nasty crook threatens to take away the property of the daughter of a dead rancher. Buffalo Bill, Jr. tries to put a stop to the creep and his cronies, but finds himself facing all sorts of dirty tricks. Wild western action also stars Jack Long and Jeane Boutell (who didn't do my income tax—check!!).
68-9164 Was $19.99 *$14.99*

Trail To Mexico (1946)
Jimmy Wakely is a cowpoke who finds trouble on the way to Mexico and uses his wits and strength to stop it. Two-fisted Western action with one of the great "B" Western stars! Lee White and Julian Rivero also star. 55 min.
10-9156 Was $19.99 *$14.99*

Range Renegades (1948)
Sheriff Jimmy Wakely thought his hands were full keeping law and order in town. But things get worse when his deputy becomes involved with the leader of a gang of outlaw women. Dub Taylor, Jennifer Holt and Arthur "Fiddlin'" Smith also star. 54 min.
10-8061 Was $19.99 *$14.99*

Brand Of Fear (1949)
Crooning cowpoke Jimmy Wakely mixes gee-tar and guts as he punches out the rannies who tried to rustle the land of an innocent lady. Gail Davis and the great Dub Taylor also star. 56 min.
10-8045 Was $19.99 *$14.99*

Across The Rio Grande (1949)
Stolen ore is smuggled across the border and Jimmy Wakely is the man who must try to put a stop to the activity. Dub Taylor, Riley Hill, Terry Frost and Polly Bergen (in her film debut) co-star. 55 min.
10-9132 Was $19.99 *$14.99*

Bells Of San Fernando (1947)
In this Western drama of Old California's Dons and Señoritas, the whip-snapping aristocrat is the persecutor of the peasants, not their salvation. Monte Blue, Donald Woods star; co-scripted by Reanult Duncan (Duncan "Cisco Kid" Renaldo). 75 min.
09-2002 Was $19.99 *$14.99*

Raiders Of Sunset Pass (1943)
Because the men are away winning WWII, the Women's Army of the Plains is formed to save a rancher's cattle from rustlers. Joining Jennifer Holt and the mostly female cast (there really was a cowboy shortage in Hollywood at the time) are Smiley Burnette and Eddie Dew. 57 min.
10-7337 Was $19.99 *$14.99*

The Red Stallion (1947)
A cowboy trains a horse for racing, then the animal saves the cowpoke and his grandmother from ruin by winning the big race. Robert Paige, Jane Darwell, Big Red the Horse. 81 min.
10-7565 Was $19.99 *$14.99*

Desert Gold (1936)
Fine rendition of the Zane Grey classic stars Buster Crabbe as the chief of an Indian tribe that zealously guards the ore rich deposits beneath their land. Frontier adventure with Robert Cummings, Marsha Hunt, Tom Keene. 59 min.
10-7291 *$14.99*

Arizona Thunderbolt (1936)
A circus performer and his piano-playing sidekick team up to stop a gang of rustlers terrorizing the big top in this sagebrusher. Joe Cook, Robert Cummings, Buster Crabbe, June Martel star. AKA: "Arizona Mahoney." 60 min.
10-8217 Was $19.99 *$14.99*

Drift Fence (1936)
Inspired by a Zane Grey story, this exciting oater stars Buster Crabbe and Tom Keene in a tale of a man who infiltrates a group of cattle rustlers in order to find the murderer of his friend. Katherine DeMille and Glenn Erikson also star.
10-8416 *$14.99*

Arizona Raiders (1936)
Narrowly escaping a frontier "necktie party," outlaw Buster Crabbe teams up with sidekicks Raymond Hatton and Johnny Downs for exciting, and at times comical, Western adventures. 59 min.
17-1073 *$14.99*

Forlorn River (1937)
Rip-roarin' rendition of the Zane Grey standard stars Buster Crabbe as the canny cowpoke who wrests a sleepy Nevada town from the grip of an outlaw gang. Also stars Syd Saylor, June Martel, Chester Conklin. 62 min.
10-7292 *$14.99*

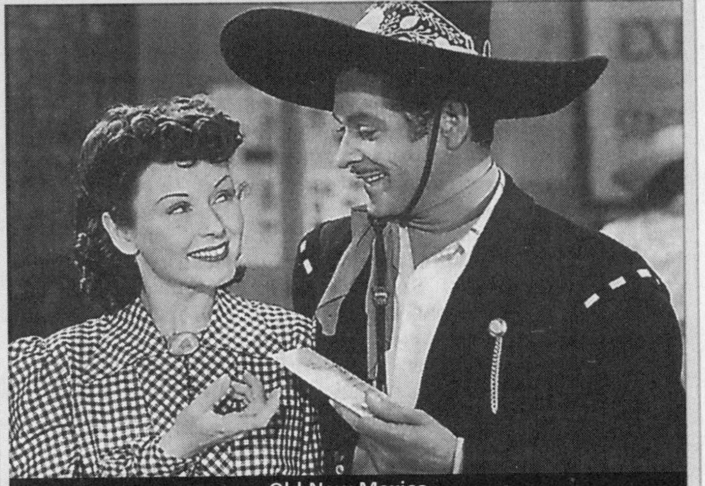

Old New Mexico

The Cisco Kid

The Daring Adventurer (1945)
After a four-year absence from the screen, O. Henry's frontier hero, the Cisco Kid, was revived by Monogram Pictures. Duncan Renaldo's first turn as the character with whom he would forever be associated finds him and sidekick Pancho (Martin Garralaga) caring for a little girl while searching for her rancher father's killer. With Cecilia Callejo, Roger Pryor. AKA: "The Cisco Kid Returns." 65 min.
08-1562 *$14.99*

South Of Rio Grande (1945)
When a close friend is arrested by a ruthless dictator and his men, Cisco (Duncan Renaldo) and Pancho (Martin Garralaga) confront the despot in this enthralling adventure. With Francis McDonald and Armida and the Guadalajara Trio. 62 min.
08-1541 *$14.99*

Old New Mexico (1945)
The ever-suave Duncan Renaldo and the ever-befuddled Martin Garralaga are back as Cisco and Pancho, here "kidnapping" Gwen Kenyon from a stagecoach to save her from a false murder charge and ferret out the real killer. AKA: "In Old New Mexico." 60 min.
17-1028 Was $19.99 *$14.99*

The Gay Cavalier (1946)
Gilbert Roland takes over in the role of the Cisco Kid in a sagebrush adventure that focuses on Cisco's rescuing a woman about to marry a supposedly wealthy suitor and finding outlaws who robbed a mission-bound stagecoach of gold. With Martin Garralaga, Nacho Galindo. 55 min.
08-1565 *$14.99*

South Of Monterey (1946)
A police captain and his tax collector accomplice devise a land-swindling scheme in a small western town. The Cisco Kid learns of the plan and tries to put a stop to it with help from sidekick Pancho. With Gilbert Roland, Martin Garralaga and Frank Yaconelli. 55 min.
08-1568 *$14.99*

Beauty And The Bandit (1946)
Gilbert Roland and Martin Garralaga star as the Cisco Kid and Pancho in this adventuresome outing, as they return the deed to a homestead to a lady in jeopardy. Frank Yaconelli, Vida Aldana also star. 77 min.
10-7624 Was $19.99 *$14.99*

Riding The California Trail (1947)
A young woman being swindled out of her inheritance by a duplicitous uncle is helped by the Cisco Kid (Gilbert Roland) and Pancho (Martin Garralaga). With Frank Yaconelli, Inez Cooper. 55 min.
08-1566 *$14.99*

Robin Hood Of Monterey (1947)
The Cisco Kid comes to the rescue when a woman murders her husband and frames her stepson for the crime. Gilbert Roland, Chris-Pin Martin, Evelyn Brent star. 55 min.
08-1567 *$14.99*

King Of The Bandits (1948)
For his final turn under the sombrero of the Cisco Kid, Gilbert Roland must clear his name when an imposter leaves him taking the blame for a string of stagecoach robberies. With Cris-Pin Martin as Pancho, Angela Greene, Anthony Warde. 60 min.
10-7810 Was $19.99 *$14.99*

Satan's Cradle (1948)
Cisco and Pancho help a frontier street-corner preacher who's been run out of Silver City by an ornery widow who happens to own just about everything in town. Their search leads to a mine where they learn the secret behind the town's corruption. Duncan Renaldo, Leo Carrillo and Ann Savage star. 60 min.
08-1540 *$14.99*

Daring Caballero (1949)
Cisco and Pancho stop by Del Rio Mission, returning a young boy who has run away. When they discover that the boy's father is slated to be executed in the morning, the heroes rescue him, then try to find the real crook who stole $90,000 from a bank and killed a teller. With Duncan Renaldo, Leo Carrillo, Kippee Valdez. AKA: "Guns of Fury." 66 min.
08-1538 *$14.99*

The Gay Amigo (1949)
This rousing adventure finds Duncan Renaldo's Cisco Kid and Leo Carrillo's Pancho targeted as outlaws, with the cavalry closing in fast. Cisco and Pancho must find the real culprits in order to get out of trouble with the military. 55 min.
08-1563 *$14.99*

The Girl From San Lorenzo (1950)
Accused of murder and robbing stagecoaches near Cactus Wells, the Cisco Kid and Pancho must clear their names before they get taken to the pokey. Duncan Renaldo, Leo Carrillo and Jane Adams star. AKA: "Don Amigo." 60 min.
08-1539 *$14.99*

The Cisco Kid: Four-Pack
This four-pack includes Duncan Renaldo as the Cisco Kid in "Daring Caballero," "The Girl from San Lorenzo," "Satan's Cradle" and "South of Rio Grande."
08-1542 Save $20.00! *$39.99*

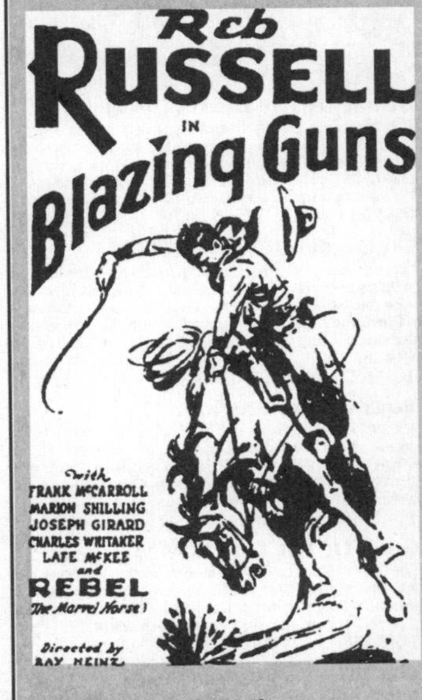

Blazing Guns (1934)
Imagine waking up after being bushwhacked in fight to find your horse gone, you're dressed in an outlaw's clothes, and the law thinks you're guilty of murder! That's what happens to Reb Russell in this sagebrush thriller, and it'll take more than blazing guns to clear his name. With Frank McCarroll, Vivian Shilling.
10-7935 Was $19.99 *$14.99*

The Man From Hell (1934)
Former football hero Reb Russell straps on the boots and holster for this rousing rock-'em-sock-'em western that finds him as a sheriff who dons a disguise to uncover the town's corrupt mayor. Fred Kohler, Ann Darcey also star. 55 min.
10-8187 Was $19.99 *$14.99*

Border Vengeance (1934)
After discovering 40 head of cattle are missing, a rancher is murdered, but the wrong family is accused of the crimes and forced to flee over the border. Reb Russell, Mary Jane Carey and Julian Rivero star in this sagebrush spectacle. 57 min.
68-8966 Was $19.99 *$14.99*

Arizona Badman (1935)
Cowpoke Reb Russell worms his way into a knot of heavies, then single-handedly takes the bullies by the horns in this exciting B horser. Co-stars Lois January and Tommy Bupp. 58 min.
10-7142 Was $19.99 *$14.99*

Cheyenne Tornado (1935)
No, it's not Clint Walker in an Irwin Allen disaster movie. It is an action-packed oater starring Reb Russell as a cowpoke who attempts to stop a group of cattlemen attempting to force a sheepherder and his family off their home on the range. Roger Williams, Victoria Vinton also star. 61 min.
68-8972 Was $19.99 *$14.99*

Outlaw Rule (1935)
Reb Russell is the western hero known as "the Whistler," a U.S. marshal and cattlemen's association detective, out to help a rancher accused of killing a sheriff. There's excitement aplenty as the Whistler fights, faces rattlesnakes and encounters an impersonator and more! 60 min.
68-9039 Was $19.99 *$14.99*

Thunderbolt (1936)
When some devious deputies steal a gold shipment and kill a boy's pa, the child and his heroic dog, Thunderbolt, set out to bring the larcenous lawmen to justice. Kane Richmond, Bobby Nelson and Lobo the Marvel Dog star.
68-9111 Was $19.99 *$14.99*

It Happened Out West (1937)
"It" refers to the devious doings by some crooks trying to swindle an Arizona dairy rancher out of her silver-rich land, until New York banker Paul Kelly arrives to foreclose their schemes. With Judith Allen, Leroy Mason. 56 min.
09-5322 *$14.99*

Songs And Saddles (1938)
A ranch belonging to a cowboy's pal and benefactor is the target of an underhanded banker who wants to swipe it from under his nose. Can the friends turn the tables on the banker? Gene Austin and Joan Brooks star in this surprise-filled prairie tale. 65 min.
68-9008 Was $19.99 *$14.99*

Rawhide Terror (1934)
Years after a young boy disappeared into the desert, laughing hysterically, after witnessing his parents' murder by bandits, a crazed gunman surfaces and begins killing outlaws. The maniac wears a strip of rawhide across the middle of his face and has a laugh that's similar to the youth's. Art Mix and Edmund Cobb star in this unusual mix of shocks and saddles.
68-9207 *$14.99*

Timber Terrors (1935)
Resolute Mountie John Preston lives up to the "always gets his man" motto by tracking down his partner's killers in this exciting Northern frontier thriller. With Marla Bratton, William Desmond, and "Dynamite" the Wonder Dog. 59 min.
09-5004 Was $19.99 *$14.99*

The Irish Gringo (1936)
While Irish eyes are smiling, the Irish Gringo is blasting away. This famous gunslinger is blamed for killing a man who knows the secret of the Lost Dutchman mine. The real culprits are a gang of long riders who pinned the deed on the Gringo. Now, his Irish temper's out of control! Pat Carlyle, William Farnum and Elena Duran.
68-8982 Was $19.99 *$14.99*

Call Of The Rockies (1931)
No, it's not a phone in the Coors Field bullpen. It's the promise of the American frontier that draws a wagon train of settlers out West. But are the three strangers that join the train mere wanderers, or outlaws out to bushwhack them? Ben Lyon, Russell Simpson, Marie Prevost star.
68-9107 Was $19.99 *$14.99*

Jaws Of Justice (1933)
After an old prospector is done away with by the treacherous spy who is after his "Lost Lode," it falls to the courageous German shepherd Kazan to help Kincaid of the Mounties bring the killer to Yukon justice. Stars Richard Terry, Lafe McKee. 55 min.
09-1952 Was $19.99 ***$14.99***

Son Of The Plains (1931)
Cowboy Bob Custer brings charisma to his role of a deputy sheriff trying to track down the Polka Dot Kid, an outlaw responsible for a series of daring robberies. Doris Phillips also stars.
68-9161 Was $19.99 ***$14.99***

Mark Of The Spur (1932)
Bob Custer plays the foreman on a cattle ranch who gets a chance to get tougher when his boss puts him in the company of the ranch's meanest dude. He soon falls for the boss's daughter, but Custer finds more trouble in the form of the boss's nasty, long-lost son. Lafe McKee and Lillian Rich also star.
68-9205 ***$14.99***

Vengeance Of Rannah (1936)
Thrilling oater starring Bob Custer as the cowpoke who comes through when thieves and cattle rustlers start trouble. With Victoria Vinton and Rin Tin Tin, Jr., the legendary pooch. 57 min.
09-5279 Was $19.99 ***$14.99***

Ambush Valley (1936)
There's lots of action in this rousing saddle saga starring Bob Custer as the hero who woos a Western gal and topples the bad guys in his inimitable style. Eddie Phillips and Wally Wales also star. 60 min.
10-9143 Was $19.99 ***$14.99***

Secret Valley (1937)
When she discovers that her husband is a powerful gangster, a Western woman travels to the Nevada ranch of Richard Arlen. Soon, hubby's gangster cronies are out to find his wife and Arlen is put on the defense. 60 min.
68-9035 Was $19.99 ***$14.99***

Gunners And Guns (1935)
A rancher's daughter's plans to marry her father's foreman hit a snag when two crooks from Daddy's past bust out of a Chicago jail and stop at the homestead to claim the loot from their last heist together. Can the would-be groom and his horse put things right? Edmund Cobb, Edna Aselin and Black King, "the horse with the human brain," star. 57 min.
68-9027 Was $19.99 ***$14.99***

Kid From Gower Gulch (1949)
Spade Cooley plays a cowboy crooner who enters the rodeo—knowing little of the danger. Bob Gilbert co-stars. 56 min.
10-7791 Was $19.99 ***$14.99***

The Silver Bandit (1950)
C&W singer/bandleader Spade Cooley stars as a gallant greenhorn who is out to deal justice to the mysterious badman of the title. Ballads 'n bullets to spare with Bob Gilbert, Virginia Jackson. 54 min.
10-7294 Was $19.99 ***$14.99***

Border Outlaws (1950)
Government agent Bill Edwards goes undercover at Spade Cooley's dude ranch to get the goods on a band of masked outlaws led by the Phantom Horseman in this thrilling B-western. With Bill Kennedy, Maria Hart.
68-9114 Was $19.99 ***$14.99***

Wings Of Adventure (1930)
After landing in Mexico, aviator Rex Lease is forced into joining a gang of south-of-the-border bandits. Rex may have a new lease on life, but he's still a good guy at heart, so he rescues a señorita in distress. Clyde Cook and Armida also star in this western thrill-a-thon.
68-9202 ***$14.99***

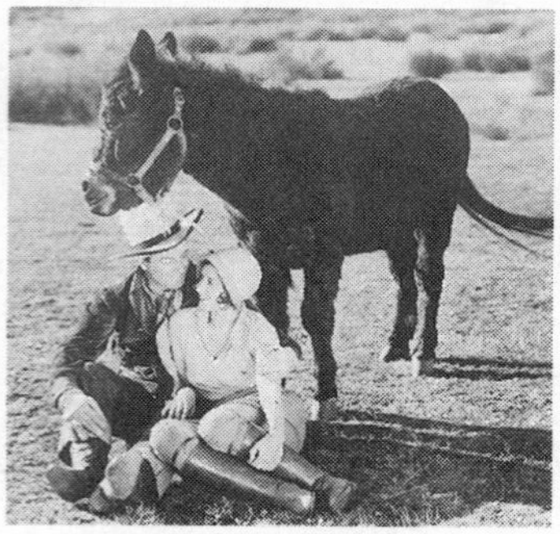

In Old Cheyenne (1931)
A hidden horse thief is using subterfuge to spirit away the stallions from the stables...and it's up to Rex Lease to uncover the rustler and bring him to six-gun justice! Dorothy Gulliver, Jay Hunt co-star. 59 min.
10-7279 ***$14.99***

Pals Of The Range (1935)
Sent up the river on trumped up charges, clean-as-a-hound's-tooth Rex Lease cops a heel outta the clink to collar the real crooks in this fists-a-flyin' horse opry. Co-stars Yakima Canutt and George Chesebro. 57 min.
10-7178 Was $19.99 ***$14.99***

The Cowboy And The Bandit (1935)
It's "Trading Places," sagebrush-style, as a cowpoke and desperado wind up having their identities mistaken...and develop a fast friendship after their tastes of life on the other side of the law. Rex Lease, Bobby Nelson, Janet Morgan star. 57 min.
10-7202 Was $19.99 ***$14.99***

The Ghost Rider (1935)
Shootin' irons meet the supernatural, as deputy Rex Lease gets otherworldly assistance in cleaning up the town from a six-shootin' spectre! Phantoms ride the frontier with Ann Carol, Lloyd Ingraham. 56 min.
10-7281 Was $19.99 ***$14.99***

Rough Riding Ranger (1935)
Rex Lease and Yakima Canutt star in this thrill-a-second adventure about a ranching family threatened by a mysterious stranger. With Johnny Luther's Cowboy Band. 56 min.
10-7804 Was $19.99 ***$14.99***

Cyclone Of The Saddle (1935)
A range war erupts and Rex Lease uses his heroics to settle the score. Meanwhile, while the fight ensues, Lease and Janet Chandler form an attraction. An exciting, romantic sagebrush story, co-starring Bobby Nelson and Yakima Canutt.
10-8374 Was $19.99 ***$14.99***

The Silver Trail (1937)
A cowboy with a penchant for wandering tries to stop a stagecoach robbery, but the female bandit involved in the heist gets away. Later, he attempts to locate his friend, a miner, but no one seems to know what's happened to him. Can the distaff desperado help him find his pal? Rex Lease, Mary Russell and Ed Cassidy star. 58 min.
68-9005 Was $19.99 ***$14.99***

The Prairie (1947)
A young woman, the lone surviving member of a family killed by Sioux Indians, is rescued by settlers heading toward Louisiana Territory. The presence of the woman brings about tension between the family's two sons, both of whom want to win her affections. Lenore Aubert, Alan Baxter and Jack Mitchum star in this gripping James Fenimore Cooper tale. 80 min.
68-8998 Was $19.99 ***$14.99***

The Man From Texas (1948)
James Craig is the El Paso Kid, who walks the line between helping a poor widow and getting involved with robbing bankers. Johnnie Johnston, Una Merkel and Lynn Bari also star in this audacious oater. 71 min.
10-8261 ***$14.99***

Sundown Riders (1948)
After years of sidekicking for Hopalong Cassidy, Jay Kirby and Andy Clyde teamed up with Russell Wade to form the Sundown Riders, a trio of cowobys who tackle outlaws with their riding and shooting abilities. This exciting sagebrush feature was shot on 16mm in Kodachrome for a remarkable $30,000. 56 min.
10-9849 ***$14.99***

Adventures Of Gallant Bess (1948)
A rodeo cowboy captures a wild mare and trains it for show, but his dreams of stardom cause trouble between him and his girl in this Western drama. Cameron Mitchell, Audrey Long, Fuzzy Knight star. 73 min.
21-3035 Was $19.99 ***$14.99***

Outlaws Of Texas (1950)
Lois Lane as an outlaw? Yep. In this sagebrusher, Phyllis Coates is the leader of a gang of thieves who must be stopped by sheriff Whip Wilson and sidekick Andy Clyde, who go undercover to stop the nasties. Terry Frost, Stanley Price also star. 60 min.
10-8442 Was $19.99 ***$14.99***

The Luck Of Roaring Camp (1937)
The arrival of an orphaned baby has a profound effect on the residents of a California gold mining town in this frontier drama based on the Bret Harte short story. Charles Brokaw, Ferris Taylor, Joan Woodbury and Owen Davis, Jr. star.
10-7228 Was $19.99 ***$14.99***

King Of The Stallions (1942)
Chief Thundercloud heads a largely Indian cast in this Western saga of a vicious wild stallion who threatens both the herd and the locals...unless Thundercloud can bring him to heel. Dave O'Brien, Princess Bluebird, Iron Eyes Cody. 63 min.
10-7203 Was $19.99 ***$14.99***

The Rangers Take Over (1943)
Dave "Tex" O'Brien is a Texas Ranger expelled from the group by his commander-father. In retaliation he joins a band of cattle rustlers, but must decide between the law and crime when his father is captured. Tense Western action. 56 min.
09-1631 Was $19.99 ***$14.99***

Return Of The Rangers (1943)
In order to corral a group of cattle rustlers, the Texas Rangers pretend it's Halloween and don disguises. Things get complicated when a Ranger is accused of murder, but his compadres help him out and the trio ride to the rescue. Dave O'Brien, Jim Newill and Guy Wilkerson star. 60 min.
10-1678 ***$14.99***

Fighting Valley (1943)
Down in the valley, trouble's a-brewing. A large company is taking nasty measures to control the ore smelting business. The Texas Rangers, Tex O'Brien and Jim Newill, are out to right the wrongs. With Guy Wilkerson. 60 min.
10-8195 Was $19.99 ***$14.99***

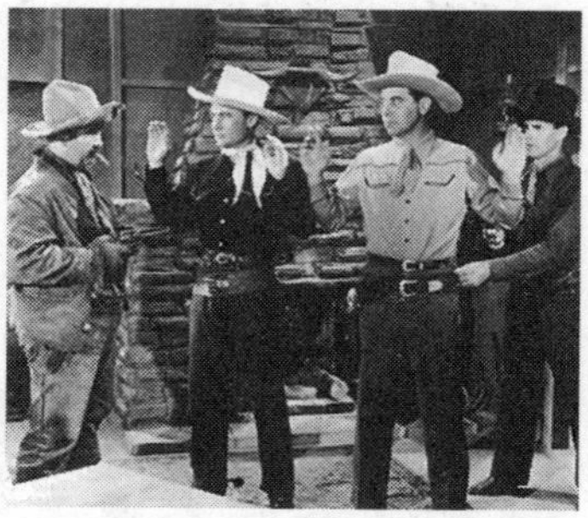

Brand Of The Devil (1944)
The merciless Devil's Brand Gang has stolen many a steer and killed many a cowpoke...and it's up to the Texas Rangers to make sure they're roped, thrown, and tied! Trail-bustin' action with "Tex" O'Brien, Guy Wilkerson, James Newill, Kermit Maynard. 56 min.
09-2031 Was $24.99 ***$14.99***

Gunsmoke Mesa (1944)
"Texas Rangers" Dave O'Brien, Jim Newill and Guy Wilkerson go into action against a notorious black hat who has killed his cousin and the man's wife and nabbed their baby and their gold. Gunplay and galloping rule the day when the Rangers come to the rescue! 59 min.
10-1677 ***$14.99***

Boss Of The Rawhide (1944)
A band of murderous owlhoots ride into an ill wind when they brush with the Texas Rangers (Dave O'Brien, Jim Newill and Guy Wilkerson), who also manage to knock out some musical numbers in between skirmishes. 57 min.
10-7145 Was $19.99 ***$14.99***

Guns Of The Law (1944)
The Texas Rangers try to stop an ornery lawyer (do you know any other kind?) who attempts to swindle a family out of a potential fortune in property. Jim Newill, Jack Ingram and Dave O'Brien star. 56 min.
10-8258 Was $19.99 ***$14.99***

The Pinto Bandit (1944)
A horse thief is causing all sorts of trouble, but the Texas Rangers, led by Dave "Tex" O'Brien, ride to the rescue. Jim Newill, Guy Wilkerson and Mady Lawrence. 56 min.
10-8259 Was $19.99 ***$14.99***

Spook Town (1944)
The residents of a Texas town are terrorized by a mysterious ghost. The sighting prompts the Texas Rangers to investigate the situation. Charles King, Jr., Dick Curtis, Tex O'Brien and James Newill star. 55 min.
55-3042 ***$19.99***

Outlaw Roundup (1944)
Tex O'Brien puts the blocks to an attempted stagecoach hijack. When the leader of the gang springs jail, the Texas Rangers assemble for the final showdown. 51 min.
62-1223 Was $19.99 ***$14.99***

Rex Bell

Broadway To Cheyenne (1932)
West meets East as Rex Bell plays a cowpoke who comes East and gets caught up in the excitement of the Big City. But back home, Marceline Day is being cheated, and Rex must return to see that justice is done. Gabby Hayes also stars. AKA: "From Broadway to Cheyenne." 45 min.
62-1194 Was $19.99 ***$14.99***

Rainbow Ranch (1933)
Rex Bell didn't put in hard time boxing in the Navy to head home and find his ranch dried out, his girl stolen and his uncle killed! Watch out when he takes his vengeance at the end of a shootin' iron! Cecilia Parker, Robert Kortman co-star. 54 min.
10-7211 Was $19.99 ***$14.99***

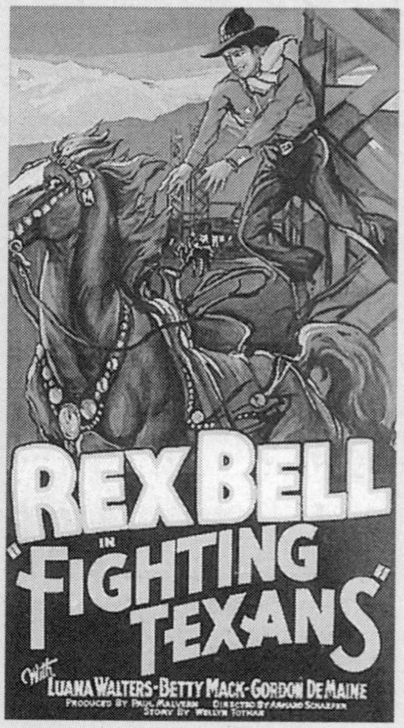

Fighting Texans (1933)
Rex Bell is out to save a dirt town from bankruptcy by convincing the folks to back an oil well. Trouble starts when the local bankers start losing their skepticism about the scheme, and want a piece of the action! Luana Waters, Betty Mack co-star. 60 min.
10-7277 Was $19.99 ***$14.99***

Diamond Trail (1933)
A pack of jewel smugglers from back East are fishing for a frontier fence...and Rex Bell must pass himself off as a greenhorn reporter to get the goods on the gem-smuggling gang! Frances Rich, Bud Osborne co-star. 58 min.
10-7278 Was $19.99 ***$14.99***

Lucky Larrigan (1933)
Comedic sagebrusher about a polo star who heads west to follow his girlfriend. Rex Bell, Helen Foster and George Chesebro star. 56 min.
10-8270 Was $19.99 ***$14.99***

Tonto Kid (1934)
Rex Bell stars in a tale of a delinquent youth who tries to go straight. Ruth Mix is his love interest in this Western saga of gold, greed and revenge. 50 min.
62-1193 ***$14.99***

Saddle Aces (1935)
A murderer and a safecracker slide out of their handcuffs and escape from authorities while being held on a train. The fleeing criminals land on a ranch where they join forces to help a young woman being taken by swindlers. Rex Bell, Ruth Mix and Roger Williams star. 56 min.
68-9004 Was $19.99 ***$14.99***

Gunfire (1935)
One of Rex Bell's best finds the cowboy excelling in his trademark, exciting style, tackling the bad guys through tough-as-nails fistfights and explosive shoot-outs. There's also some interesting, three-dimensional characters in this one, along with strong female characters. 56 min.
68-9166 Was $19.99 ***$14.99***

Fighting Pioneers (1935)
Wild western saga finds Rex Bell as a Cavalry officer trying to halt guns from being sold to an Indian tribe at war with settlers. Leading the Indians is a female warrior. With Ruth Mix and Earl Dwire.
68-9212 ***$14.99***

Stormy Trails (1936)
There are dark clouds on the horizon for frontier stalwart Rex Bell, who faces a false murder charge pinned on him by a passel of owlhoots out to grab his land. With lightning fists and thundering gunplay, Rex fights to weather the storm and clear his name. Bob Hodges, Lois Wilde also star. 58 min.
10-9330 Was $19.99 ***$14.99***

Men Of The Plains (1936)
Trains with gold shipments are being pilfered near a small town by a gang of dastardly prairie snakes. A 10-gallon detective investigates the crime and discovers that the town's bank president may be in on the shady dealings. Rex Bell, Joan Barclay, Charles King star. 62 min.
68-8990 Was $19.99 ***$14.99***

Law And Lead (1937)
Heroic Rex Bell tries to capture a baddie who's been posing as his reformed outlaw pal and falls in love with a woman who happens to be the crook's daughter. Wally Wales and Harley Wood also star. 60 min.
09-5123 Was $19.99 ***$14.99***

The Idaho Kid (1937)
Rex Bell plays the title character, a young cowboy caught between his real pa, who has been feuding with him, and the stepfather who raised him. Throwing a wrench into the Kid's relationships is the fact that both dads are embroiled in a fight over water rights. Dave Sharpe, Earl Dwire and Marian Schilling co-star. 60 min.
10-9341 Was $19.99 ***$14.99***

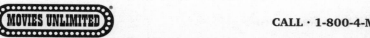

Billy The Kid In Texas (1940)
Bob Steele originated the role of the famed outlaw in this '40s oater series that made Billy out to be a basically good-hearted type. Here, Steele protects a town from rascally rustlers. With Al "Fuzzy" St. John. AKA: "Battling Outlaw." 44 min.
21-3017 Was $19.99 *$14.99*

Billy The Kid's Range War (1940)
After some owlhoots try to frame him, Bob Steele discovers a crooked lawman is pulling the strings in their operation. Meanwhile, an outlaw tries to get a steamship line a contract by hijacking a stagecoach. This exciting western tale also stars Al St. John, Joan Barclay and Carleton Young. 60 min.
68-9024 Was $19.99 *$14.99*

Trigger Men (1941)
Outlaw Billy the Kid and his two-fisted friends fulfill a dying U.S. marshal's mission and try to stop the ornery gang that has taken over a border town. Bob Steele, Al St. John and Phyllis Adair star in this surefire sagebrusher. AKA: "Billy the Kid's Fighting Pals." 55 min.
10-9074 Was $19.99 *$14.99*

Billy The Kid In Santa Fe (1941)
For his last time out as Billy, Bob Steele is on the run when he's falsely accused of murder. With the ever-scruffy Al St. John, Rex Lease. 60 min.
21-3018 Was $19.99 *$14.99*

Blazing Frontier (1941)
Has Billy the Kid (Buster Crabbe) jumped back to the side of the outlaws when he and compradre Fuzzy (Al St. John) join forces with some crooked railroad officials? Don't worry, fans, it's just a plot by the Kid to bring the land-swindling lawbreakers to justice. With Marjorie Manners, Kermit Maynard.
08-1699 *$14.99*

Sheriff Of Sage Valley (1942)
Larry "Buster" Crabbe plays two roles in this thrilling western yarn. He's Billy the Kid, the famous outlaw, who is mistakenly appointed mayor of a Western town and promises to keep it clean. Soon, however, he's confronted by his oily twin brother, gambler Kansas Ed. Al St. John, Tex "Dave" O'Brien also star.
10-8935 *$14.99*

Law And Order (1942)
Billy'd do his poor ma proud...he winds up doubling for a U.S. Cavalry officer! Sound the charge with this fun series entry starring Buster Crabbe and Fuzzy St. John. 60 min.
21-3013 Was $19.99 *$14.99*

Fugitive Of The Plains (1943)
When outlaws turn a young woman into a criminal, Billy the Kid saves the day. Buster Crabbe stars as the western legend; with Karl Hackett, Jack Ingram. 56 min.
08-1688 *$14.99*

Cattle Stampede (1943)
Billy the Kid (Buster Crabbe) and sidekick Fuzzy Jones (Al St. John) go head-to-head against a rustler who schemes to purchase cattle at reduced prices. Frances Gladwin and Charles King also star in this action-packed western. 58 min.
09-5265 Was $19.99 *$14.99*

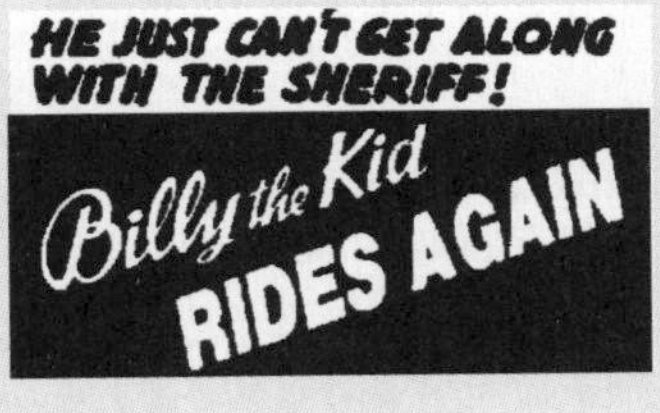

HE JUST CAN'T GET ALONG WITH THE SHERIFF!
Billy the Kid
RIDES AGAIN

The Kid Rides Again (1943)
Things aren't going swimmingly for Buster Crabbe as he is once more forced to dodge a posse of a corrupt sheriff with whom "he just can't get along." Al St. John is once more at Buster's side. AKA: "Billy the Kid Rides Again." 60 min.
21-3011 Was $19.99 *$14.99*

Western Cyclone (1943)
A gang of ornery outlaws frames Billy the Kid (Buster Crabbe) for murder and the kidnapping of a young girl. Crabbe has to clear his name by finding the girl, then joins forces with pardner Al St. John to lasso the creeps. With Marjorie Manners, Charlie King.
68-9221 *$14.99*

Renegades (1943)
A mining town's crooked mayor is trying to buy out a bankrupt group of ranchers who don't know that their land is full of oil. It's up to Billy the Kid (Buster Crabbe) and his sidekick Fuzzy come to town and save the day. Al St. John co-stars. AKA: "The Renegade."
82-1050 *$19.99*

Panhandle Trail (1944)
When a con artist tries to swindle two children out of their inherited mine, Billy the Kid (Buster Crabbe) trots to the rescue. Al St. John, John Merton also star in this superior sagebrusher. 52 min.
08-1689 *$14.99*

Fuzzy Settles Down (1944)
The Kid's grizzled sidekick has had it with life on the run and just wants to settle down, but Billy is more than determined to show him the error of his ways. Buster Crabbe, Al St. John. 60 min.
21-3015 Was $19.99 *$14.99*

Frontier Outlaws (1944)
Even "Billy the Kid" had to grow up someday, and in this first entry in the retitled "Billy Carson" series, Buster Crabbe is once more put in the position of producing the real varmint or being guest of honor at a "necktie party." With the irrepressible Fuzzy St. John. 60 min.
21-3019 *$14.99*

Thundering Gun Slingers (1944)
In a trail of dust, buckaroo Billy Carson (Buster Crabbe) rides out on the trail of a gang of black hats who've bamboozled his uncle out of his land. Co-stars Fuzzy St. John and Kermit Maynard. 59 min.
10-7136 Was $19.99 *$14.99*

Rustlers' Hideout (1944)
Buster Crabbe stars in this rousing sagebrush saga in which cowboy Billy Carson faces rustlers, card sharks and business frauds. With Al St. John, Lane Chandler. 60 min.
10-9331 Was $19.99 *$14.99*

Wild Horse Phantom (1944)
Exciting western yarn starring Buster Crabbe as Billy Carson, who battles some ornery landsnatchers out to dupe a group of honest ranchers. Al St. John and Elaine Morey co-star. 56 min.
10-9332 Was $19.99 *$14.99*

Devil Riders (1944)
Billy Carson has a devil of a time convincing the townsfolk that he isn't an outlaw, but just a guy interested in delivering frontier justice to a crooked lawyer. Buster Crabbe, Al St. John star. 60 min.
21-3014 Was $19.99 *$14.99*

Oath Of Vengeance (1944)
Cowpoke Billy Carson (Buster Crabbe) isn't the swearing type, but he does vow to help a fellow cowboy who's been accused of murder in this series entry. Fuzzy St. John and Mady Lawrence co-star.
68-9069 Was $19.99 *$14.99*

The Drifter (1944)
That's "Drifter" as in "Drifter Davis," a bank robber who uses his uncanny resemblance to Billy Carson (yes, Buster Crabbe plays both roles) to make himself rich while making things hot for the outlaw-turned-do-gooder. With Al "Fuzzy" St. John, Kermit Maynard.
68-9113 *$14.99*

His Brother's Ghost (1945)
In this "Billy Carson" actioner, Fuzzy St. John's lookalike brother is ambushed and slain by outlaws...and Fuzzy has them convinced he's returned from the dead as he and Billy (Buster Crabbe) bring them to frontier justice. Charles King, Archie Hall. 54 min.
10-1238 *$14.99*

Lightning Raiders (1945)
When an ornery pack of mail rustlers (come to think of it, have you ever seen any female rustlers?) swipes an important letter for Fuzzy, it's up to Billy Carson to track down the missing missive and the postal pilferers! Buster Crabbe, Al St. John star. 61 min.
10-7572 Was $19.99 *$14.99*

Shadows Of Death (1945)
Power-packed chapter in the Billy Carson series starring Buster Crabbe and Al "Fuzzy" St. John, about outlaws who murder to learn the route of the new railroad so they can cash in on the land boom. 60 min.
10-7692 *$14.99*

Border Badmen (1945)
Oh, they're bad, bad, border badmen...meanest men on the whole border. Badder than ol' King Kong, meaner than a junkyard dog. Only Buster Crabbe and Fuzzy Knight can stop them from closing on cattle barons. 58 min.
10-8028 Was $19.99 *$14.99*

Gangster's Den (1945)
One of Buster Crabbe's final turns as Billy, this episode is regarded as one of the series' finest entries. Billy once again proves that to live outside the law, you still must be honest. With Al St. John. 60 min.
21-3020 Was $19.99 *$14.99*

Prairie Bad Men (1946)
The proprietor of a travelling medicine show is troubled by bad men seeking a special treasure map. Buster Crabbe's Billy Carson and Fuzzy St. John's Fuzzy Jones come to his rescue in this sagebrusher with comedy. Patricia Knox also stars. 55 min.
08-1690 *$14.99*

Overland Riders (1946)
When Billy the Kid begins causing trouble, Billy Carson (Buster Crabbe) and Fuzzy Jones (Fuzzy Knight) ride in to save the day (But wasn't Billy Carson really Billy the Kid? Don't ask us to explain it!) in this great "B" western. With Patti McCarty, Slim Whitaker. 53 min.
10-9844 *$14.99*

Prairie Rustlers (1947)
"They're cousins...identical cousins," and one of them is Billy Carson (Buster Crabbe), accused of a murder committed by his doppelganger. Billy has to track down the rascally relative and bring him to justice. With Al St. John, Kermit Maynard. 55 min.
10-9285 *$14.99*

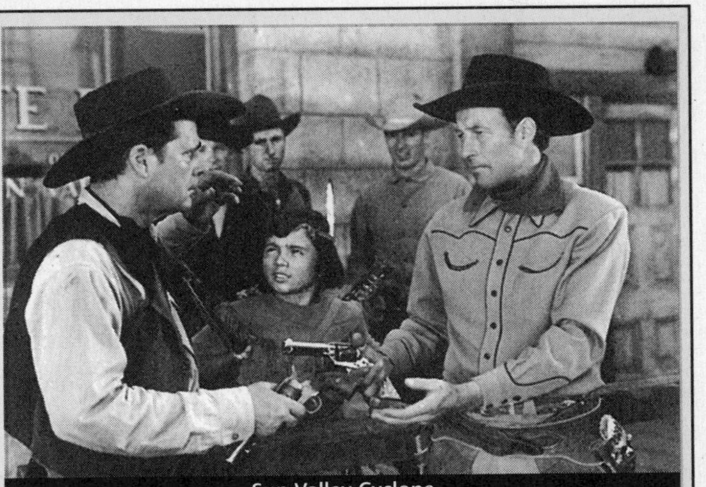
Sun Valley Cyclone

Red Ryder

Tucson Raiders (1944)
The first of the popular "Red Ryder" B-Westerns finds Red (Wild Bill Elliott) and his Indian pal Little Beaver (Bobby Blake) bringing a corrupt governor to justice. With George "Gabby" Hayes, Ruth Lee, and series semi-regular Alice Fleming as the Duchess.
10-8396 *$14.99*

Sheriff Of Las Vegas (1944)
Red Ryder and Little Beaver hunt the killers of a local judge and clear the name of his prodigal son. It's not swinging with the Rat Pack at The Sands, but it's a living. William Elliott and Bobby Blake star. 55 min.
10-7691 Was $19.99 *$14.99*

Cheyenne Wildcat (1944)
Join Red Ryder (Wild Bill Elliott) and Little Beaver (Bobby Blake) as they use their wits to foil a group of ornery outlaws, while Red is caught between the love of two different ladies. Alice Fleming and Peggy Stewart also star.
10-8397 *$14.99*

Marshal Of Reno (1944)
Red Ryder (Wild Bill Elliott) tries to settle the score between townships feuding over which will be the county seat. Bobby Blake is Little Beaver, Alice Fleming the wily Duchess, and Gabby Hayes takes the "sidewindin' crockercrookers" to task.
10-8398 *$14.99*

Lone Texas Ranger (1945)
A six-shooting sagebrusher featuring Bill Elliott as Red Ryder, who discovers that a sheriff has been using his position to shield illegal activities like gambling and murder. When Red pulls the cover off the crooked, albeit beloved, lawman, Red has to face the admiring townspeople. With Bobby Blake and Alice Fleming. 55 min.
10-9129 *$14.99*

Sun Valley Cyclone (1946)
Red Ryder (Wild Bill Elliott) barrels after a horse rustling ring that's preying on the U.S. Cavalry. Roller coaster action with Bobby Blake, Monte Hale and Rex Lease. 56 min.
10-7689 Was $19.99 *$14.99*

Conquest Of Cheyenne (1946)
Wild Bill Elliott and Bobby Blake saddle up as Red Ryder and Little Beaver to bring a passel of owlhoots to justice. 55 min.
10-7706 Was $19.99 *$14.99*

Sheriff Of Redwood Valley (1946)
Making his final appearance as Red Ryder, Bill Elliott restores the good name of a man branded with a long-ago crime and snoops out the real culprits. With Bobby Blake, Bob Steele. 56 min.
10-7690 *$14.99*

Stagecoach To Denver (1946)
A band of money-grubbin' profiteers are out to kill the child that stands between them and their ill-gotten gains...unless Red Ryder and Little Beaver can put 'em down. Allan Lane, Bobby Blake. 53 min.
65-5010 *$14.99*

Homesteaders Of Paradise Valley (1947)
A group of pioneering families need to construct a dam to make their little ploy of heaven complete... and a pack of sinister sidewinders are out to blow their dreams to bits! Only Red Ryder and Little Beaver can carry the day in this sagebrush sensation. Allan Lane, Bobby Blake star. 59 min.
10-7571 Was $19.99 *$14.99*

Oregon Trail Scouts (1947)
For all those who thought he just bought the little rascal outright from Spanky McFarland, here's the real story of how Red Ryder hooked up with sidekick Bobby Blake. Allan Lane stars. 58 min.
05-1289 Was $19.99 *$14.99*

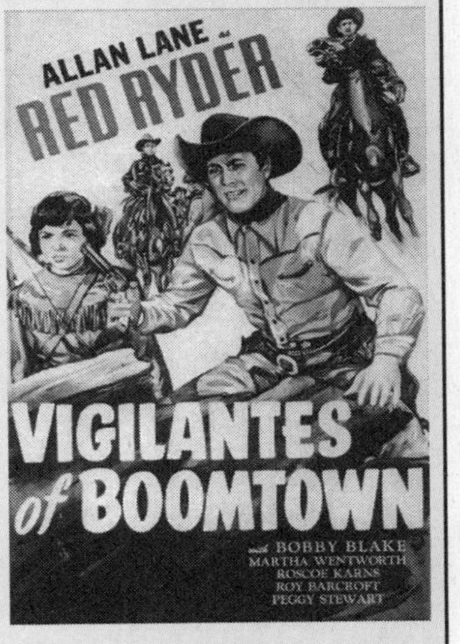

ALLAN LANE
RED RYDER
VIGILANTES of BOOMTOWN
with BOBBY BLAKE
MARTHA WENTWORTH
ROSCOE KARNS
ROY BARCROFT
PEGGY STEWART

Vigilantes Of Boomtown (1947)
A prizefight between heavyweight champ James J. Corbett and Bob Fitzsimmons brings Red Ryder and Little Beaver to Carson City, but bank robbers and a kidnapping threaten to put Red out for the count. Allan Lane, Bobby Blake, Roy Barcroft star. 45 min.
10-1150 *$14.99*

Ride, Ryder, Ride! (1949)
Making his debut as heroic Red Ryder, Jim Bannon joins forces with a lady newspaper publisher to clean up a lawless town. With Peggy Stewart, Emmett Lynn, and Don Kay Reynolds (aka Little Brown Jug) as Little Beaver. 58 min.
10-8006 Was $19.99 *$14.99*

Roll, Thunder, Roll (1949)
A gang of outlaws have a deadly new weapon in their arsenal of mayhem...dynamite! Can Red Ryder (Jim Bannon) and Little Beaver (Little Brown Jug) stop them, or do they get blowed up real good? With Glenn Strange, Nancy Gates. 60 min.
10-8009 Was $19.99 *$14.99*

The Cowboy And The Prizefighter (1950)
The cowpoke is Jim Bannon as Red Ryder, the pugilist is Don Haggerty, and together they'll knock out the crooked fight fixers responsible for Haggerty's pa's murder. With Little Brown Jug, John Hart. 60 min.
10-7987 Was $19.99 *$14.99*

The Fighting Redhead (1950)
In what proved to be the "Red Ryder" series' final entry, star Jim Bannon comes to the aid of a woman tracking her father's killer. With Peggy Stewart, Don Kay Reynolds. 55 min.
10-7996 Was $19.99 *$14.99*

All movies in this section are either rated R or Soft X and are intended for mature audiences only. They are not XXX-rated.

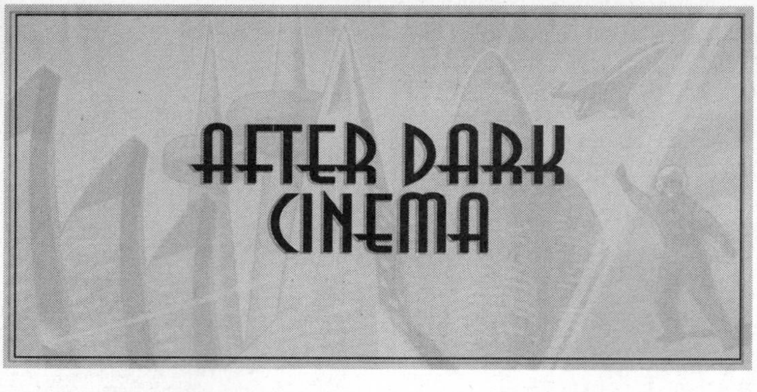

Testing The Limits (2000)
A romantic weekend retreat in the mountains turns into an erotic exploration of new limits for a couple, thanks to a chance encounter with a beautiful fashion photographer and her crew, in this sultry softcore drama. With a bright young cast. Unrated version; 101 min.
07-2894 *$39.99*

Casting Couch (2000)
Sure, you've heard all the stories, but what *really* happens to beautiful young actresses in Hollywood agents' and filmmakers' offices? Now you can see the uncensored true story, through steamy "interviews" that turn into erotic encounters racier than any fiction writer could concoct. Holly Sampson, Everett Rodd, Stacie Marie star. 85 min.
75-5070 *$59.99*

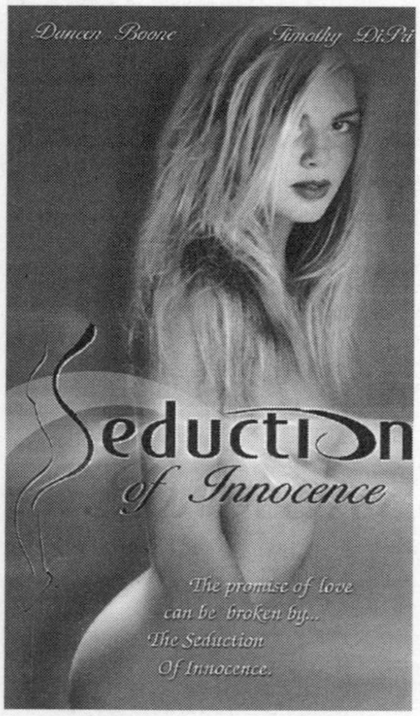

Seduction Of Innocence (2000)
Gorgeous Daneen Boone is a young co-ed attending the Topacre Academy, a school specializing in turning girls into successful women. When Boone gets the hots for a professor, her fantasies run rampant. And when they become realities, she learns some sensuous lessons about love and life. With Timothy DiPri, Jennifer Behr. Unrated version; 94 min.
21-9205 *$49.99*

Mistress Frankenstein (2000)
When sexually repressed Baroness Helena Frankenstein is killed in an accident, scientist husband Victor tries to use a new brain to bring her back to life. But the brain he uses comes from a lesbian nympho, and the new Helena must have sex with every gal she meets. Darian Caine, Victoria Vega star.
73-9370 *$19.99*

Zorrita: Passion's Avenger (2000)
In this erotic thriller the mark of the Z stands for "zexy and zeductive," as the beautiful masked swordswoman known as Zorrita fights for freedom—and pleasure—in old California. Shauna O'Brien, Venessa Blair, Jesse Coleman star. Unrated director's cut; 93 min.
75-5071 *$59.99*

Passion's Obsession (2000)
A female private eye is hired to track down a missing male model whose looks arouse every woman he meets. Entering an erotic underworld, will the sexy P.I. get her man...and when she does, will she "get her man"? C.C. Costigan, Dave Roth star. Unrated director's cut; 93 min.
75-5074 *$59.99*

Fast Lane To Malibu (2000)
School is out for the summer and Brian and Zack are looking for a good time. When word of a sorority sex party hits, the two college boys take to the road for a rockin' trip to ecstasy where every stop turns out to be as wild as the last. So, hop in the convertible and head for the beach! Featuring a bright young cast. Unrated version; 96 min.
07-2916 *$39.99*

The Bare Facts Video Guide
At long last—nudity! It's the biggest "Bare Facts" yet: a 928-page directory to 3,500 actresses and everything they've ever done, minus clothing. New entries include Gillian Anderson, Angie Everhart, Heather Graham, Alex Kingston, Charlize Theron, Peta Wilson and lots more. Featuring extensive cross-referencing, this guide is a must for VCR owners.
ZZ-1013 *$24.99*

The Ultimate Attraction (2000)
Super-sensual sex farce about the Body Beautiful Gym, an exercise facility about to go bankrupt. Personal trainers Gabriela Hall and David Cielens try to attract new membership with a hands-on, alluring approach, and the joint soon becomes the hottest workout spot in town. Jacqueline Lovell (Sara St. James), Taylor St. Claire and John La Zar also star. Unrated version; 91 min.
21-9212 *$49.99*

Beauty Betrayed (2000)
Two cops are on the trail of a murderer after the body of a famous model is found. However, all they have to go on is a mysterious sexual videotape featuring the victim, and the bad blood between her and another model. The officers then realize that they must do whatever it takes to solve the crime in this steamy thriller. Featuring a bright young cast. Unrated version; 93min.
07-2947 *$39.99*

Erotica:
An Intimate Portrait (2000)
Penthouse and Hustler centerfold Azlea is featured with four other incredibly sexy women who are going to make you drool as they share their private fantasies with you. So after you manage to roll your tongue back into your mouth, relax and watch these beauties soak up the pleasure. 70 min.
69-5309 *$19.99*

Andromina:
The Pleasure Planet (2000)
What astronaut would pass up a chance to land on this wanton world where arousing alien women await to meet your every need? Well, three tired star pilots arrive at Andromina, only to find it female-free, and set out to return with the most beautiful babes in the galaxy in this sexy sci-fi romp. Morgan Kelly, John Matrix, Sam Phillips star. Unrated director's cut; 90 min.
75-5076 *$59.99*

Virgins Of Sherwood Forest (2000)
The Merry Men are merrier than usual when sexy, contemporary Nina is transported back to Jolly Olde England and she and a host of young beauties decide to bear arms—and bare all!—and help lazy Robin Hood defeat the Sheriff of Nottingham's evil sister. Gabriella Hall, Shannan Leigh and Amber Newman star in this sensual swashbuckling adventure. Unrated director's cut; 93 min.
75-5081 *$59.99*

NoAngels.com
(Director's Cut) (2000)
Five gorgeous women create the ultimate erotic website and soon find themselves in over their heads—in profits and sizzling new recruits! Penthouse Pet Nicole Martiano, Zoe Paul and Laural Dunne star in this lust connection that's so hot, it'll have you rebooting. Director's cut includes eight minutes of extra footage. 90 min.
75-5090 *$69.99*

Sensual Sensations (2000)
Five beautiful international models from Czechoslovakia, Scandinavia, China, Italy and Germany make some of their erotic fantasies come true at a sexy slumber party featuring plenty of teddy bear fights, all set to the beat of hot music from General Degree, Reggae Sam and others. Starring Roxanne Hill, Caroline, Molly Steele, Dina Marie Vannoni and Shannon Leigh. 58 min.
76-7477 *$19.99*

Naked Wishes (2000)
If your wish has been for an erotic, fun-filled comedy, it's just been granted. A sex therapist finds an old bottle in a trunk of junk from his late uncle—a bottle with a beautiful genie inside! Convinced that her new "master" was her lover in a past life, the delectable djinn turns his life upside-down. Chandra Marie, Jeff Kueppers, Jennifer Marks star. Unrated version; 99 min.
76-9119 *$39.99*

Sexual Chemistry (2000)
Robert, a chemist working on a new sex-enhancing drug, uses himself as a guinea pig—and turns into a woman! The problem is that he keeps shifting from man to woman at the most inopportune times, like when he-she's about to have sex. Things get even trickier when his mother stops in to see him. Wild sex fantasy with Stephanie Lafleur, Chanda Marie. Unrated version; 97 min.
76-9123 *$39.99*

House Of Love (2000)
Melinda, a documentary filmmaker, one day comes across a colossal Hollywood mansion that is home to a large group of nubile, seductive women running a high-class bordello. She decides to take her cameras inside the house in order to learn all about the women and the famous men who frequent their abode. What Melinda discovers may change her forever. Featuring a bright young cast. Unrated version; 90 min.
07-2961 *$39.99*

The Bare Wench Project (2000)
A sensuous spoof of—duh!—sends four curvaceous coeds to Bare Wench Mountain, where they encounter fun-filled terror. That's after some skinny-dipping, campfire carousing and lots of other carnal stuff, of course. Nikki Fritz, Lorissa McComas, Julie K. Smith, Julie Strain and Andy Sidaris star. Unrated version; 76 min.
82-5199 *$89.99*

Virtual Girl (2000)
When a computer whiz perfects some new sexual software that the last programmer died working on, cybersex with a virtual woman becomes possible. But when he realizes that it is difficult to differentiate between real and imaginary people within the program, he finds that a virtual vixen is dangerously obsessed with him in this hi-tech tale. Charlie Curtis and Miche Rene Straub star. 90 min.
82-5229 *$59.99*

Suck It And See (1999)
What started as a CD project from England is turned into an incredible meshing of sound and vision featuring seven provocative music videos, all for adults only. It's late 1960s and early 1970s hedonism in a modern setting in a wild, dialogue-free program inspired by the CD from Howie B and the Pussyfoot label. 40 min.
02-9151 *$14.99*

The Key To Sex (1998)
Charged with caring for his boss's lavish Hollywood home while he's away on a weekend trip, a young office assistant plans to use the mansion for a wild party—unaware that his co-workers have some plans of their own for the place—in this racy tale with a bright young cast. 86 min.
07-2721 *$39.99*

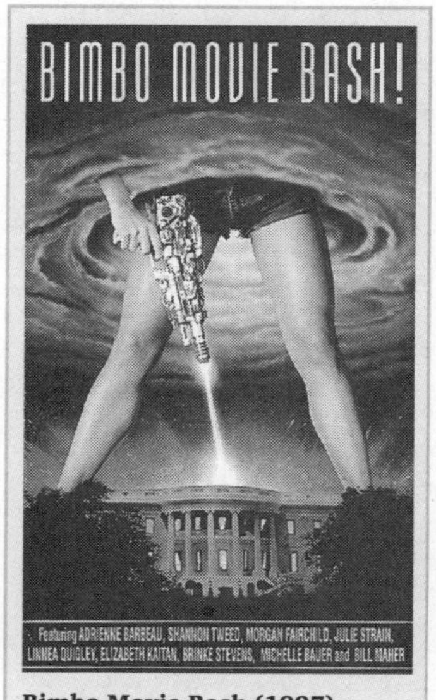

Bimbo Movie Bash (1997)
From the archives of producer Charles Band comes a salute to cinematic blonde bombshells and bubbleheads. Included in provocative scenes are such favorites as Adrienne Barbeau, Shannon Tweed, Brinke Stevens, Linnea Quigley, Julie Strain and Morgan Fairchild—yeah, that's right, Morgan Fairchild. Also featured, in a pre-"Politically Incorrect" turn, is Bill Maher. Nudity abounds. 90 min.
75-5013 Was $69.99 *$14.99*

The Story Of X (1998)
This breezy, no-holds-barred chronicle of the sex film industry is hosted by Buck Henry and features scores of clips, interviews and behind-the-scenes footage from the earliest days of silent stag films to the adult videos, Internet sites and CD-ROMs of today. Russ Meyer, Dave Friedman, Al Goldstein, Marilyn Chambers and Camille Paglia are among those interviewed for this Playboy production. 82 min.
07-2693 *$19.99*

The Price Of Desire (1998)
What price will a couple pay for the ultimate in erotic fulfillment? For Mac and Monica, their desire to have another man make love to Monica while her husband watches leads to a threesome that threatens to tear their marriage apart in this steamy "adults only" drama. 87 min.
07-2722 *$39.99*

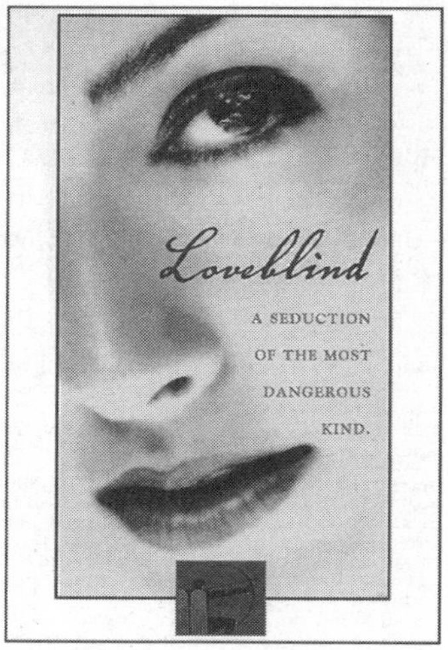

Loveblind (1999)
An engaged couple share their beachfront house with a photographer and his stunning model, and what develops is a summer filled with erotic couplings and an exploration of forbidden passions, in this steamy Playboy production with a bright young cast. Unrated version; 99 min.
07-2750 Was $39.99 *$19.99*

Life Of A Gigolo (1998)
Danielle, an attractive journalist, decides to follow Gage, a handsome male prostitute, for a story she's working on. Soon, she finds herself drawn to him and his seedy lifestyle. So much, in fact, that she begins walking the streets to get a taste of the life of a street-walker first-hand. Uncut, unrated version; 91 min.
07-2737 Was $39.99 *$19.99*

Inside Club Wild Side (1998)
Joe, an aspiring filmmaker, is drawn to his new roommate Tina, an actress wannabe who makes her living as a dancer at an L.A. strip club. Joe is also drawn into Tina's wild lifestyle, but can he avoid getting pulled into a world of kink that can turn dangerous? Uncut, unrated version; 99 min.
07-2738 Was $39.99 *$19.99*

Surrender (1999)
A beautiful young woman learns the meaning of "surrender" when she gives herself away to a mysterious force that leads her through a series of intensely erotic encounters. Follow her sensual odyssey in this steamy Playboy production with a bright young cast. Unrated version; 95 min.
07-2762 Was $39.99 *$19.99*

Word Of Mouth (1999)
A beautiful, high-priced call girl who caters to the city's most influential men becomes the subject of a filmmaker's latest work, but will his obsession with her and her clients take them both too far? Follow their dangerous passions in this steamy Playboy thriller with a bright young cast. Unrated version; 93 min.
07-2780 *$39.99*

The Seventh Sense (1999)
A beautiful, blind cellist learns about more than just music from her teacher, as she is taken into a world of seductive pleasures and senses-awakening sensations in this steamy "adults only" drama. With a bright young cast. Unrated version; 98 min.
07-2810 *$39.99*

Hollywood Sins (1999)
The sordid side of the entertainment industry is exposed in this steamy drama about a Hollywood agent who is seduced by his boss's beautiful wife and finds himself ensnared in a web of eroticism, deception and blackmail. With a bright young cast. Unrated version; 92 min.
07-2858 *$39.99*

Web Of Seduction (1999)
A pair of housewives who are neglected financially and sexually by their husbands come up with a twisted scheme to bump off each others' spouses and gain a valuable art collection in the process, but things go awry in this steamy thriller. With a bright young cast. Unrated version; 90 min.
07-2813 *$39.99*

The Awakening Of Gabriella (1999)
Leaving her small-town home behind her, beautiful young Gabriella heads to Hollywood full of dreams of stardom and happiness. What she finds waiting for her, though, are a mysterious, rich man and his seductive servant, who introduce Gabriella to a world of erotic discovery and sensual obsession. With a bright young cast. Unrated version; 94 min.
07-2727 *$39.99*

Temptations (1999)
How're you gonna keep 'em down on the farm...especially when heated libidos and long-dormant passions erupt between a couple struggling to save a family farm from going out of business. Watch as temptations become too much to resist in this steamy "adults only" drama with a bright young cast. Unrated version; 95 min.
07-2826 *$39.99*

Corporate Fantasy (1999)
The action goes from boardroom to bedroom when a group of amorous admen who make a habit of seducing their female co-workers set their sights on a beautiful new employee, unaware that she has her own agenda for putting them in their place, in this steamy adult drama with a bright young cast. Unrated version; 101 min.
07-2838 *$39.99*

The Big Hustle (1999)
A hard-boiled thief with a passion for money and beautiful women may have bitten off more than he can chew when he winds up in Dutch with a powerful crime boss—thanks to the attentions of the gangster's beautiful girlfriend—in this steamy, erotic thriller with a bright young cast. Unrated version; 92 min.
07-2851 *$39.99*

Hot Club California (1999)
Three gorgeous sisters snag $100,000 that literally falls from the sky and use the cash to move from Detroit to California and their uncle's hot beach club. But when the mob boss whose money the gals "intercepted" tracks them down, they have to outwit him to stay alive in this sexy thriller. With a bright young cast. Unrated version; 106 min.
07-2875 *$39.99*

Forbidden Highway (1999)
Get ready for a long, hot trip down the road of taboo desires with this steamy thriller about a gorgeous woman named Cherry who rips off a mob boss and flees to Las Vegas. A hit man is sent to bring back the money—and her corpse—leaving Cherry to use her sensual body to persuade her pursuer to spare her. With a bright young cast. Unrated version; 106 min.
07-2879 *$39.99*

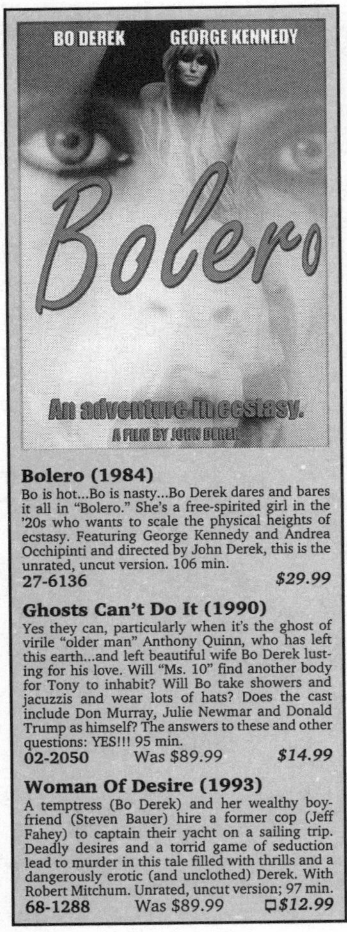

Bolero (1984)
Bo is hot...Bo is nasty...Bo Derek dares and bares it all in "Bolero." She's a free-spirited girl in the '20s who wants to scale the physical heights of ecstasy. Featuring George Kennedy and Andrea Occhipinti and directed by John Derek, this is the unrated, uncut version. 106 min.
27-6136 *$29.99*

Ghosts Can't Do It (1990)
Yes they can, particularly when it's the ghost of virile "older man" Anthony Quinn, who has left this earth...and left beautiful wife Bo Derek lusting for his love. Will "Ms. 10" find another body for Tony to inhabit? Will Bo take showers and jacuzzis and wear lots of hats? Does the cast include Don Murray, Julie Newmar and Donald Trump as himself? The answers to these and other questions: YES!!! 95 min.
02-2050 Was $89.99 *$14.99*

Woman Of Desire (1993)
A temptress (Bo Derek) and her wealthy boyfriend (Steven Bauer) hire a former cop (Jeff Fahey) to captain their yacht on a sailing trip. Deadly desires and a torrid game of seduction lead to murder in this tale filled with thrills and a dangerously erotic (and unclothed) Derek. With Robert Mitchum. Unrated, uncut version; 97 min.
68-1288 Was $89.99 □*$12.99*

I'm Watching You (1998)
Super-sensual thriller starring Jacqueline Lovell (Sara St. James) as a gorgeous painter's model who enlists innocent Lori Dawn Messuri to join her in promiscuous sessions of phone sex and voyeurism from artists' lofts. The women's relationship grows scorchingly close, but when Messuri witnesses a murder, danger ensues. Unrated version; 96 min.
07-2905 *$39.99*

A Place Called Truth (1997)
From "Red Shoe Diaries" creator Zalman King comes a psychological thriller where a kinky love triangle threatens a family's future, as love, lust and power lead to a web of deception. Audie England, Brion James and Valerie Perrine star. 95 min.
12-3292 □*$49.99*

Shame, Shame, Shame (1997)
A beautiful Ph.D. candidate discovers that her on-camera sexual experiments unlock secrets hidden deep in her past in this seductive tale from softcore auteur Zalman King. Audie England, Heidi Schanz, Olivia Hussey, Valerie Perrine and Costas Mandylor star. 87 min.
12-3293 □*$49.99*

Intimate Obsession (1992)
A bored, wealthy and beautiful woman lands a new lover while her lawyer husband worries over a promotion. Soon the two find seduction a game...one that leads them into a web of danger and betrayal. Sizzling erotic thriller for adults stars Jodie Fisher, James Quarter and Richard Abbott Booth. 80 min.
19-3409 *$89.99*

The 12th Annual AVN Awards Show (1995)
Has it really been that many years since Adult Video News first feted the world of XXX video? Wow! Now, join adult stars like Janine, Ashlyn Gere, Sunset Thomas, Lacy Rose and Kylie Ireland as they partake in the glittery Las Vegas presentation. Features scenes from nominated films, the stars in and out of their clothing and lots more. Wow! 120 min.
19-3780 *$19.99*

Adult Video News Awards (1998)
Check out the most coveted awards of the adult film industry as they pay tribute to the sexy superstars that burn up the small screen. Watch as Playboy goes backstage and gets exclusive interviews with such award-winners as Stephanie Swift, Jeanna Fine, Jenna Jameson and others, as well as a sneak peak at their winning performances and the behind-the-scenes festivities. Robert Schimmel hosts.
07-2665 *$19.99*

Business For Pleasure (1996)
In this Zalman King production, a wealthy businessman desiring to ignite his passions indulges in a wild sexual triangle with a gorgeous, no-nonsense executive and his right-hand man. The result is a scorching odyssey in which the boardroom and bedroom intertwine. Gary Stretch, Caron Bernstein, Joanna Pacula and Jeroen Krabbe star. 97 min.
27-7140 *$99.99*

Eve's Beach Fantasy (1997)
For beautiful young Eve, a summer vacation at the beach becomes an erotic education in the sand, as an array of handsome men (one more than one gorgeous woman) help her explore new vistas in sexuality in this steamy softcore fantasy. April Adams, Brendan Claybourn, Gigi Finnel star. 95 min.
46-8025 Was $59.99 *$14.99*

Bikini Goddesses (1996)
From the creator of "Beach Babes from Beyond" comes this sweaty sex comedy in which a young man staying at his father's European hotel accidentally releases three gorgeous sex goddesses who have been trapped in a sundial for centuries. The lad gets an incredible indoctrination into the world of sensuality as the gals blow the cobwebs off. Alton Butler stars. 80 min.
50-5296 *$24.99*

Sahara Heat (1990)
In this European sex saga, a small village is the setting for unbridled lust as Lea, a woman with wanton sexual desires, and Alfred, her macho lover, experience scorching lust between them. Lea's interest in photography leads her to a journey of sexual ecstasy without any bounds. Fiona Gelin, Enzo Decaro star. Unrated version; 90 min.
50-5466 *$19.99*

Cybersex Kittens (1996)
Two computer geeks realize their wildest fantasies when they accidentally find a way to get beautiful women to act totally uninhibited. These gals can't do enough for their new boyfriends, and things really get hot when a woman hires a private detective to look into their activity. Shannyn Smedley and Gloria Lusiak star. 80 min.
50-5467 *$19.99*

Maui Heat: Swimsuit Edition (1996)
Get ready to feel the heat of the sun full blast, as five of the most unbelievably beautiful women fulfill their hottest fantasies during the annual swimsuit edition shoot on Maui's white sand beaches for World Sport Magazine. With Kimberly Dawson, Kimberly Rowe, Kim Hayes and Michael Anderson. 92 min.
50-5888 Was $49.99 *$19.99*

The Blue Angel (1997)
Sexually-charged remake of the classic Marlene Dietrich film. A college professor confiscates an erotic film featuring a nightclub artist named Lola from his students. But when the professor watches the film, he becomes obsessed with Lola, and soon enters into her world of depravity. Raine O'Connor stars. 94 min.
50-8226 *$24.99*

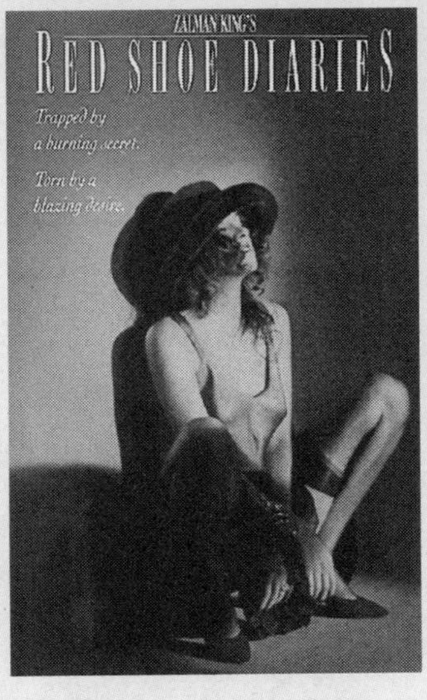

Red Shoe Diaries (1992)
Scorching drama from "Wild Orchid" auteur Zalman King tells the story of a woman who seeks an opportunity to have an affair with a mysterious stranger...a stranger who is perfect in every way. This lusty sexcursion, presented in the uncut, unrated introductory film, stars David Duchovny, Billy Wirth and Brigitte Bako. Uncut, unrated version; 107 min.
63-1574 Was $89.99 □*$14.99*

Red Shoe Diaries: The Game (1994)
Three erotically-charged stories from Zalman King's "Red Shoe Diaries" include "The Game," about a board game with sensual powers; "The Cake," focusing on how a birthday cake adds sugar to a relationship; and "Like Father, Like Son," about a man who enjoys a liaison with his father's older lover. With David Duchovny, Jennifer McDonald and Arielle Dombasle." 77 min.
67-9013 □*$19.99*

Red Shoe Diaries 5: Weekend Pass (1995)
Three lusty tales of eroticism ignite in this "Red Shoe Diaries" installment which features headline-making model Paula Barbieri taking on a pool hustler, a beautiful bounty hunter (Claire Stansfield) encountering her quarry, and an Army recruit (Ely Pouget) playing a kinky game with a drifter while on furlough. 86 min.
63-1771 Was $89.99 □*$14.99*

Red Shoe Diaries 6: How I Met My Husband (1995)
Forget blind dates, the personals and church covered dish suppers; the encounters in this "Red Shoe" trilogy are a good deal hotter. See what happens when a mechanic helps a sexy heiress keep her cars, and herself, in tune; when strangers have a moonlight roundelay on the streets of Paris; and when a woman "into leather" meets the man of her dreams. David Duchovny, Charlotte Lewis, Neith Hunter, Raven Snow star. 85 min.
63-1809 Was $89.99 □*$14.99*

Red Shoe Diaries 7: Burning Up (1995)
Two scorching erotic excursions are presented in this volume hosted by "Red Shoe" veteran David Duchovny. In "Runway," a model and photographer dabble in uninhibited encounters which lead to lesbian liaisons and more, while "Kidnap" follows a businesswoman fulfilling a kidnapping fantasy with a cowboy crook. Matt LeBlanc ("Friends"), Amber Smith, Udo Kier. Unrated version; 90 min.
63-1860 □*$14.99*

Red Shoe Diaries: Girl On A Bike (1995)
Featured in this "Red Shoe" installment are "Girl on a Bike," in which a man pursues his perfect woman on the streets of Paris; "Written Word," about two people who finally meet after exchanging sexy letters; and "Borders of Salt," involving a risqué rendezvous on a train. With David Duchovny, Robbi Chong, Sofia Shinas, Brent Fraser and Geraldine Cotte. 78 min.
67-9014 □*$19.99*

Night Of Abandon: Red Shoe Diaries (1996)
Watch as a trio of beautiful women abandon their inhibitions and give themselves over to absolute pleasure in three seductive stories: "Night of Abandon," "Liar's Tale" and "In the Blink of an Eye." Erika Anderson, Ann Cockburn, Daniel Leza star, with a special appearance by David Duchovny. 86 min.
63-1893 Was $79.99 □*$19.99*

Red Shoe Diaries: Luscious Lola (2000)
Three more lascivious stories from Zalman King feature a shy woman who indulges her fantasies as "Luscious Lola"; a husband who lets his wife sleep with another man because of his own inabilities in "Mercy"; and a couple on the rocks spend a startling and passionate weekend at "The Last Motel." Perrey Reeves, Christina Fulton, Heidi Mark star. 87 min.
67-9031 *$19.99*

Red Shoe Diaries: Four On The Floor (2000)
Another trio of sexy yarns sizzles on the screen in this installment of the series. Two couples spend some "quality time" together in an abandoned house in "Four on the Floor"; a patient's couch time with "The Psychiatrist" leads to very physical therapy; and a rock star eases one of his dancers' anxieties in "Emily's Dance." Rachel Palmieri, Denise Crosby, Freedom Williams star; hosted by David Duchovny. 85 min.
67-9032 *$19.99*

Body Heat (1999)
Her name is Kaoru Sakurazana, and she ranks among the top sweeties of Japanese adult video queens. Here she displays the assets that helped her get on top: a gorgeous face, perky personality and knockout body that measures 36-23-35. A hand fan won't do when Kaoru tempts you—better turn the air conditioning on full blast! 50 min.
53-6839 *$19.99*

Night Of The Living Babes (1991)
Two sex-starved yuppies got more than they bargained for when they paid a visit to Madame Mondo's Fantasy Palace. The sultry staff are actually zombie nymphos...and they absolutely will not stop! Michelle McClellan, Connie Woods, Andrew Nichols and Cynthia Clegg star. 60 min.
59-8019 *$39.99*

Wild Malibu Weekend (1994)
An awesome array of curvaceous dazzlers are featured in this risqué romp in which a group of gals looking to compete on the "Bikini Showdown" TV game show, with high stakes movie deals and money awaiting the winners, arrive at the show's producer's mansion, and everything goes wild. Playboy centerfold Barbara Moore and Penthouse Pet Stevie Jean star. 82 min.
84-5045 *$19.99*

Sunset Strip (1991)
A strip club is the place where a young woman learns how to strut her stuff in this sexy, erotic story filled with sensuous exotic dancing. With Jeff Conaway, Michelle Foreman and Shelley Michelle, the body double for Julia Roberts in "Pretty Woman." 95 min.
86-1059 Was $29.99 *$14.99*

The Many Loves Of Jennifer (1991)
Jennifer is a frustrated housewife, unhappy with her marriage to her executive husband. So she decides to get in touch with her own sensuality and takes off an erotic excursion that leads to sex with the gas company woman, a rendezvous in a porn theater and a one-night stand with a bar patron. This scorcher stars porn legend Sharon Kane; with Biff Malibu, Leanna Fox. 83 min.
84-5007 *$19.99*

The Erotic Adventures Of The Three Musketeers (1994)
Scorching "adaptation" of the Alexandre Dumas classic in which the trio of swashbucklers tackle the evil Cardinal Falwell, who has exposed the Queen's infidelity in 17th-century France. Sexy escapades ensue with Martine Helene, Britt Morgan and Francesca Lee. Steamy, unrated version; 105 min.
69-5270 *$89.99*

Desire: An Erotic Fantasy Play (1996)
Tender, sensual drama set in Northern California, where the arrival of a precocious and mysterious woman helps change the lives of two other women, one who has a fear of letting go romantically, the other who explores her fantasies through a diary. Monique Parent, Anthoni Stewart and Debora Kay star. Unrated version; 90 min.
69-5280 *$29.99*

Intimate Deception (1996)
An unhappily married artist with a deadly secret in his past soon discovers that nothing remains hidden forever when a new neighbor and a beautiful model both begin drawing him into a sinister climax. Suspenseful and erotic thriller stars George Saunders, Lisa Boyle. 96 min.
70-5109 Was $29.99 *$19.99*

The Gift (1998)
A torrid tale of heavy passion and rediscovered love from Candida Royalle's continuing line of erotic tales tailor-made for women. A visit to her old home reignites the passions of a woman who thought she would never love again. Shanna McCullough, Mark Davis, Micki Lynn and Diane Cannon star. 80 min.
70-7405 *$49.99*

The Bridal Shower (1998)
A sensuous softcore drama told from a women's perspective. Five ladies share with each other their deepest sexual fantasies. Watch them come to life in a bridal shower that ends up being more than just a celebration. Featuring Nina Hartley, Melissa Hill, Sharon Kane and Porsche Lynn. 80 min.
76-7404 *$49.99*

Naked Instinct (1993)
Two gorgeous women can't seem to control their cravings for sexual encounters with younger men. In order to try to stop her uncontrollable desires, one of the women tells her therapist about her and her friend's excursions seeking romantic liaisons. Deanne Power, Michelle Bauer and Albert Mitchell star in this scorcher. Unrated version; 90 min.
73-9052 Was $59.99 *$29.99*

One Million Heels B.C. (1996)
Move over, Raquel! Here come "scream queens" Michelle Bauer, Jerica Fox and Cierra Knight in a wild look at primitive pulchritude. An earthquake in Southern California unearths a sexy cavegal who is befriended by two strippers who introduce her to such modern delights as hot tubs, silky lingerie and high, high heels! Full frontal nudity abounds. 35 min.
73-9162 *$39.99*

Bangers (1995)
A stripper with a heart of gold is forced to sink to the ultimate low and dance in sleazy bars and sell her body to live. She is then raped and abused by a strange horde of creatures created by an insane scientist. Kitten Natividad, a Russ Meyer favorite, stars in one of her most revealing efforts. AKA: "Zombie Ninjas." 84 min.
73-9242 *$19.99*

Beach Babe Experiment (1994)
Annie, a pretty college student, starts a research project in which she analyzes the world of "beach babes." She seeks out the blonde bombshells in the skimpiest bikinis and soon gets a lesson from them as they teach her how to drive men wild. Zesty, sexy comedy stars Pamela Sanderson, Nina Ahlin and Tonya Wedlake.
73-9270 *$19.99*

Killer Sex Queens From Cyberspace (1997)
The Prometheus Corporation has developed (and quite well, we might add) a computer-generated prostitute who can produce incredible sexual feelings through virtual means. She's just a love machine, but when something goes awry in the wiring, there's danger. Will Robinson. Lorissa McColbs, Glorri-Ann Gilbert and Danni Ashe star.
73-9279 *$29.99*

The Erotic Witch Project (1999)
This sexually-charged take-off on the hit horror film sends three gorgeous gal pals into the New Jersey woods in search of the infamous Erotic Witch. With camcorders in hand, the women find themselves taken in by an erotic spell that pushes their libidos to the haunting limit, leading to sizzling encounters of every sort. Katie Keane, Darian Caine and Victoria Vega star. Unrated version; 90 min.
73-9323 *$19.99*

Titanic 2000 (1999)
Leo and Kate are nowhere to be found on this re-creation of the legendary ship, but who would want them with Vladamina on board? She's a lesbian vampire in search of the perfect first mate—female preferred—to join her for a sensuous feast of blood. Sex, satire and more are in store—without, thankfully, Celine Dion! Tammy Parks, Tina Krause star. Unrated version.
73-9326 *$19.99*

Virtual Encounters (1996)
A beautiful, successful advertising executive decides her love life needs a kick, so she checks out Virtual Encounters, an interactive boutique where patrons can play any role in different steamy cyber-sex scenarios. Elizabeth Kaitan and Penthouse Pets Cathleen Raymond, Michelle Barry and Sarah St. James star. Unrated version; 84 min.
75-5006 Was $89.99 *$14.99*

Virtual Encounters 2 (1998)
Meet the lover of your dreams at Virtual Encounters, a computerized sex club where virtual reality takes the students of a nearby college into new realms of erotic exploration. Sizzling sequel stars Ethan Hunt, Brandy Davis, Jill Tompkins and Chrissy Styler. 83 min.
75-5024 Was $59.99 *$14.99*

Cyberotica (1999)
Seven unfulfilled beauties decide to take a sensual cyber-trip by wearing a headset that sends them into a virtual reality where sex is best. Soon, they are indulging in their wildest fantasies, delving into an erotic world they never knew existed. Marie Hopkins and Kim Evans star in this sexcursion dripping with carnal close encounters. Unrated version; 70 min.
73-9328 *$19.99*

Lesbos Slaughter, Vol. 1: The Strange Case Of The Phone-Sex Strangler (1999)
The notorious Phone Sex Strangler is on the loose, so women should beware of this deranged murderer. The culprit happens to be a beautiful woman with a penchant for death and kinky sex. See her lure bi-curious females into her apartment—then strike! Misty Mundae and Liz Bathory star. 80 min.
73-9332 *$29.99*

Lesbos Slaughter, Vol. 2: Satan's Hostages (1999)
A Satanic cult looking for new virgins may have found the proper subjects with two pretty women, one of whom is a lesbian, the other very bi-curious. As the sex sizzles, the Satanists get close to the new carnal couple, who are trying some daring erotic experiments. Misty Mundae and Liz Bathory star. 80 min.
73-9333 *$29.99*

Girl Explores Girl: The Alien Encounter (1999)
If extraterrestrial lesbians are your idea of an out-of-this-world time, look no further than this sizzling space saga. Two aliens hoping to save their dying world land on Earth; one becomes a female, the other male. But when the female E.T. discovers that it prefers lovemaking with members of the same sex, Reese's Pieces start to melt with her liaisons. Katie Keane and Victoria Vega star. Unrated version; 80 min.
73-9327 *$19.99*

Bikini Bistro (1995)
When some gals try opening their own restaurant but face eviction thanks to a lack of clientele, all it takes is dressing the waitresses in the skimpiest of bikinis to get the customers lined up around the block. Wild and risqué romp stars Amy Lynn Baxter, Joan Gerardi, and Marilyn Chambers as herself. Ultra-sexy, unrated version; 84 min.
74-3015 *$49.99*

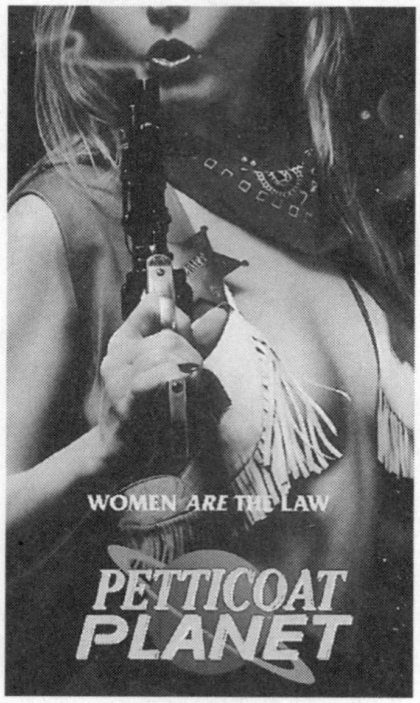

Petticoat Planet (1996)
Come ride a little spacecraft along with space jockey Steve Rogers that's orbiting a desert planet. It is run by beautiful women—only women—so Steve's in for lots of fun, some sexy surprises and incredible interplanetary hanky-panky. Petticoat Planet—woo-woo! With Troy Vincent, Elizabeth Kaitan ("Slavegirls from Beyond Infinity"). Unrated version; 78 min.
75-5011 Was $89.99 *$14.99*

Exotic House Of Wax (1997)
There's no Vincent Price lurking around this wax museum, but there are some priceless beauties who come to life, as the historical tableaus turn into displays of carnal desires with the sexiest statues you've ever seen. Erotic fantasy stars Josie Hunter, Jacqueline Lovell. 90 min.
75-5016 *$14.99*

Lolida 2000 (1997)
The dawning of a new millennium has brought with it the banning of all sexual activities and explicit art, but a government censor named Lolida finds her own sexuality awakened by a trilogy of stories she monitors in this erotic sci-fi drama. Jacqueline Lovell, Gabriella Hall star. 90 min.
75-5018 *$14.99*

Lurid Tales: The Castle Queen (1997)
Thanks to a strange machine he thinks is an arcade game, a young man is sent back in time to 17th-century England. There he finds himself in the middle of a heated rivalry for a lavish castle—and for the seductive lady of the estate—in this bawdy and erotic tale of lust and power. Shannon Dow Smith, Kim Dawson star. 85 min.
75-5019 Was $59.99 *$14.99*

The Exotic Time Machine (1998)
Take the ultimate pleasure trip with two time travellers who want to find out what sexual secrets await them in the past. Among the stops are the court of Marie Antoinette and the Middle East during the days of the Arabian Nights. Gabriella Hall, Joseph Daniels and Nikki Fritz star in this kinky fantasy. Unrated version; 80 min.
75-5022 Was $59.99 *$14.99*

Submission: A Forbidden Fantasy (1996)
In this kinky tale of S&M and B&D, a young executive is drawn to a mysterious young woman whose influence in a large corporation could help his future. The man soon gets an indoctrination into the woman's kinky world, where forbidden fantasies are played out in her dungeon. With Mistress Raven (a real life dominatrix), Bryan Leder. 90 min.
76-7370 *$39.99*

Cabin Fever (1994)
Produced with couples and women in mind, this steamy look at an encounter between a streetwise handyman and a beautiful, older artist is filled with sensuous moments and unadulterated passions. Playful teasing leads to lusty lovemaking in this unusual program. With Judd Dunning and Belinda Farrell. 45 min.
76-7152 Was $29.99 *$19.99*

The Voyeur (1994)
An erotic comedy filled with titillation, teasing and intimate moves, from the same smart folk who gave you "Cabin Fever." See what happens when a couple takes a sensual game to new heights. Designed for women and couples, this program offers a fresh perspective on eroticism. With Kim Dawson and Al Sapienza. 45 min.
76-7153 Was $59.99 *$19.99*

The Hottest Bid (1995)
From the producers of "Cabin Fever" and "The Voyeur" comes this super-charged erotic story about a young woman named Jessica who bids on a canine companion at a charity auction. Jessica falls for the dog's handsome owner, but after learning he's having an affair with a friend, she seeks help from a lawyer friend, and passions ignite. Gwen Somers, Lenore Andriel star.
76-7160 Was $59.99 *$19.99*

The Night That Never Happened (1998)
An impromptu bachelor party leads to a night filled with sleek limos, a kinky strip club, lesbian liaisons, wild drinking and, finally, kidnapping, in this erotic story. James Wellington, Colleen McDermott and Lisa Boyle ("Friend of the Family") star in this scorcher. 83 min.
07-2687 *$39.99*

Pleasurecraft (1999)
What's long and hard and full of spacemen? The starship Prometheus, of course, and its crew is ready to risk interstellar war when they refuse to turn over their "cargo"—three beautiful women being sent to the planet Hutan as brides—in this softcore sci-fi romp. Juan Carlos, Brandy Davis, Amber Newman star. Unrated version; 85 min.
75-5042 *$59.99*

Timegate: Tales Of The Saddle Tramps (1999)
Two gorgeous visitors to a historic frontier town are accidentally transported back to the days of the Wild West. When they're mistaken for workers at the local bordello, the women set out to show the cowboys just how "wild" the west can really be! Sexy sci-fi romp stars Amy Lindsay, Kim Yates, Michelle Bauer. 88 min.
75-5048 *$59.99*

Sexual Outlaws (1994)
John and Lisa, who appear to be a staid middle-class couple, are actually publishers of a sexual fantasy magazine. But when Lisa responds to a personal ad, and her pen pal turns out to be a suspect in a murder, Lisa's fantasies suddenly turn dark. Mitch Gaylord, Erika West, Kimberly Dawson star in this super-erotic suspenser. Uncut, unrated version; 90 min.
76-9059 Was $89.99 *$14.99*

Major Rock (1998)
Steamy sex and action mix in this erotic exciter that shows what happens when five gorgeous centerfolds and the sister of the vice president of the United States are held captive by Nicaraguan rebels. The president calls on tough guy Major Rock and his special team to rescue them. Don Fisher, Tabitha Stevens star. Unrated version; 90 min.
76-9113 Was $39.99 *$14.99*

Teenage Tupelo (1995)
A way-out, nudity- and-music-filled journey from cartoonist-filmmaker John Michael McCarthy, who also stars as the son who was abandoned by a mother intent on having sex with a loser rock-and-roller. Then things get really weird, with catfights, strippers, a tour through Tupelo and exotic dancer Topsy Turvy. With D'Lana Tunnell, Dawn Ashcroft.
79-5910 Was $24.99 *$19.99*

Shandra: The Jungle Girl (1999)
She hails from the jungles of Brazil and when there's a full moon she pleasures her victims to death, draining their sexual essences. How can Shandra be stopped? Four biologists try to capture this gorgeous, leopardskin-clad wild woman, but she's too much for anyone to handle! Lisa Throw, Lisa Comshaw and Venesa Taylor star. Unrated; 80 min.
75-5053 *$59.99*

Dungeon Of Desire (1999)
With help from a magical chastity belt, a gorgeous photographer and her two models are transported back to the 15th century. They soon come face to face with a ruthless captain of the guard and get into lots of hot water before they meet a magician who can help them. Michelle Turner, Regina Russell and Amber Newman star. Unrated version; 90 min.
75-5058 *$59.99*

DVD VIDEO
ASK ABOUT OUR GIANT DVD CATALOG!

Hotel Exotica (1998)
Prepare yourself for the vacation of a lifetime when you check out who's checking in at this otherworldly resort. The guests may come to relax, but there's precious little of that going on! Sexy sci-fi softcore fun with Dutch Flaherty, Ahmo Hight, Landon Hall and Taylor St. Claire. Unrated version; 90 min.
75-5034 Was $59.99 *$14.99*

Veronica 2030 (1998)
In this steamy sci-fier, Veronica is a futuristic love android who discovers the pleasures of human desire. The trouble is that if she has too much fun, she can short circuit! Julia, Joseph Roth and Nikki Fritz star. Unrated director's cut. 88 min.
75-5037 Was $59.99 *$14.99*

Lip Service (1999)
The sexy private eyes who work for the L.I.P. Service always manage to get their man—in more ways than one—in this steamy thriller that finds them looking for a kidnapped adult film actress. Zoe Paul, Michelle Turner, Elina Madison star. Unrated director's cut; 90 min.
75-5062 *$59.99*

Diary Of Lust (1999)
The carnal cattle on this milk farm are just aching to have their udders squeezed and...oh, sorry, that was "Dairy of Lust." This steamy outing follows a sultry sex researcher to a majestic European castle, where she finds an ancient diary and falls under the psychic sway of its erotic entries. Michelle Flotow and Mia star. Unrated version; 85 min.
75-5068 *$59.99*

Squishy Does Porno (1995)
Unusual adult odyssey about a Los Angeles porn star who decides to leave her decadent lifestyle and head to New Orleans, where she plans to create her own erotic films. NOTE: Suggested for mature audiences only. 30 min.
76-7361 *$24.99*

Hot Line (1995)
Shannon Tweed is a radio disc jockey who has a way with getting callers to tell their innermost erotic fantasies. Three of these titillating tales unfold in this scorching production. 90 min.
81-9050 *$14.99*

Hot Line 2 (1996)
Join Shannon Tweed and Tanya Roberts for a trio of torrid stories told to sultry female disc jockeys. Included are "Hung Jury," about two sequestered jurors whose illicit relations solve a murder case; "Double Exposure," in which a detective falls for his on-the-spot mark; and "Highest Bidder," a story of double-crosses involving a husband, wife and male escorts.
81-9023 *$14.99*

Hot Line 3 (1996)
Tanya Roberts turns in "Sheena's" loincloth for a set of headphones as she plays the sexy disc jockey hostess for these three hot stories. A writer's job as "The Sitter" for a businessman's daughter turns into a sizzling time; four femmes in "The Brunch Club" share each other's intimate secrets; and pre-med students cram for more than exams in "Sleepless Nights."
81-9025 *$14.99*

Lady In Blue (1999)
Special Investigations detective Kira Reed uses her assets on her latest assignment, going undercover in a strip club where a shooting took place. She's introduced to a seamier side of life, involving exotic dancing, prostitution and more, but will she give into her darkest desires? With Larry Gund and Jyl Dillon. Unrated version.
81-9079 *$89.99*

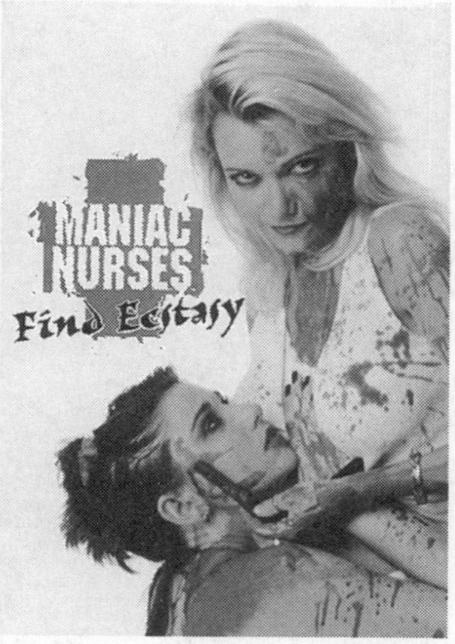

Maniac Nurses Find Ecstasy (1996)
From the wacky crew at Troma comes this nudity-filled shocker from Hungary. The film focuses on Sabrina, a beautiful gal held captive by an army of man-hating feminist terrorists. Sabrina learns she has become an important part in a devious plan hatched by the terrorists' leader, a dominatrix. Unrated version; 93 min.
46-8018 Was $59.99 *$14.99*

Wild Child (1991)
The gorgeous Laurie discovers that her weekend pool party takes a wild turn when the guests decide to get naked and partake in naughty escapades. A gem for lovers of gorgeous gals in and out of bikinis. With Jennifer Irwin, Trystan Moore. 80 min.
84-5001 *$19.99*

Wild Child 2: A Toy To Play With (1996)
Jamie is an expert at designing high-tech computer games. When her new program is stolen, she joins forces with her two lingerie-loving roommates to track it down. Their way of recovering the stolen goods is sexy, funny and revealing. Swimsuit model Julie Skiru and Playboy models Stephanie Champlin and Cherilyn Shea star. AKA: "Silk N' Sabotage." 83 min.
84-5044 *$19.99*

Alien Files (1999)
When the crew of a spacecraft that recently returned to Earth begins to act strangely, special officers of the FBI's "Alien Files" arm investigate the behavior. What they discover is an alien life force, released by the sexual energies of the female crew members, that can shift from body to body. Gabriella Hall, Kira Reed star. Unrated version; 98 min.
82-5123 *$99.99*

Sexual Roulette (1997)
Erotic reversal on the "Indecent Proposal" story follows a man who loses his life's savings while vacationing with his wife in Las Vegas. The beautiful casino owner offers him $40,000 if he'll spend the night with her, but will his jealous wife find comfort in another man's arms? Tane McClure, Tim Abell, Gabriella Hall star. 94 min. Uncut, unrated version.
83-1128 Was $99.99 *$14.99*

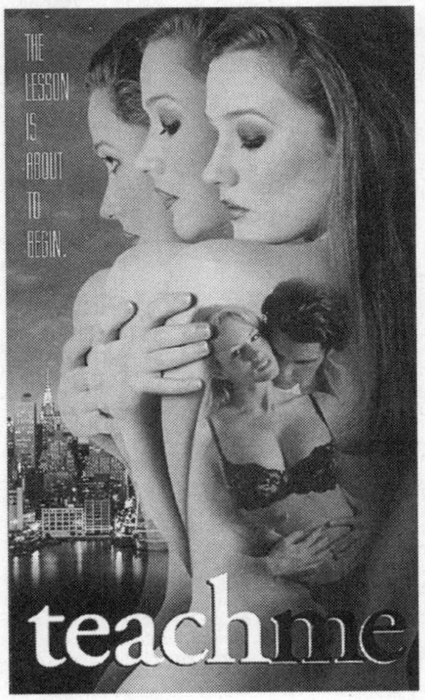

Teach Me (1997)
An education in eroticism awaits a beautiful young woman who seeks to improve the passion in her marriage, as a female author of sensual novels guides the wife into new and formerly taboo realms of love-making. Playboy model Shannon Leahy, Raasa Leela Shields star. Uncut, unrated version; 95 min.
83-1185 Was $99.99 *$14.99*

Ambitious Desires (1995)
A stripper, a recent college graduate and a waitress decide to make a go of it in Hollywood, but soon realize that casting couches are the first stop on the way to stardom. Penthouse Pet Julie Strain, Kay Keyboard and Joyce Hathaway are the gals who play the Tinseltown game in a most erotic way. 60 min.
83-4025 *$29.99*

Bikini Summer (1991)
What could be more fun than a summer at a beach house with some party dudes and some bikini-clad babes? If you can't think of anything either, then just watch the sexy, zany, racy, loopy fun that occurs at this beach house! Shelley Michelle, David Millburn star. 90 min.
86-1050 Was $29.99 *$14.99*

Bikini Summer 2 (1992)
A wild assortment of gorgeous gals—in and out of bikinis—will dazzle you in this wacky, racy comedy about a Malibu beach house and its inhabitants. Jessica Hahn ("Hi, Honey!"), Avalon Anders, Melinda Armstrong and Jeff Conaway star. 87 min.
86-1060 Was $19.99 *$14.99*

Bikini Summer 3: South Beach Heat (1997)
When the makers of a new fragrance called Mermaid Body Splash head to the sun and fun capital of the world, Miami Beach, to hold a bikini contest whose winner will be their spokesperson, you can bet there'll be loads of sexy, wacky, loopy, racy shenanigans. Heather-Elizabeth Parkhurst, Tiffany Turner, Tonya Goodson star. 84 min.
86-1117 ❑*$59.99*

Tales Of Erotica (1995)
Four heralded filmmakers explore the world of sensuality in a kinky quartet of tales. In Susan Seidelman's Oscar-nominated "The Dutch Master," Mira Sorvino enters a sexy 17th-century world she's seen in a painting; Cynda Williams is a whirlpool bath salesman's kinky customer in "Wet," by Bob Rafelson; Ken Russell's "The Insatiable Mrs. Kirsch" shows what happens when a young writer is obsessed with a randy woman; and Melvin Van Peebles' "Vroom, Vroom, Vroom" mixes voodoo, lust and leather-clad bikers. AKA: "Erotic Tales." 103 min.
68-1805 Was $89.99 ❑*$14.99*

Surf, Sand & Sex (1995)
The world's most famous houseguest, Kato Kaelin, is featured in this steamy sexual comedy in which a group of hot-to-trot honeys discuss their sensual adventures while sunning on the beach. Kato plays a car mechanic in a titillating fantasy sequence that's more stimulating than a lube job...or a day of watching Court TV. With Kim Dawson. Unrated version; 80 min.
84-5034 *$29.99*

Jurassic Women (1995)
Mammoth-breasted women, martial arts and sci-fi combine as two astronauts crash land on the planet Kenon, where beautiful women use their karate skills to fight sex-craving cavemen. When a Jurassic Woman falls for one of the spacemen, his partner gets jealous and plots to kill them. Jan-Michael Vincent, Grace Renn star. 90 min.
84-5035 *$59.99*

Nightmare Sisters (1987)
This erotic comedy stars scream queens Linnea Quigley, Brinke Stevens and Michelle Bauer as a group of sorority babes who turn into sexually dynamic vampires during a seance and soon seek their school's hottest hunks for blood and pleasure. Lots of nudity and wacky hijinks ensue in this classic for the "Femme Fatales" set.
20-5215 *$39.99*

The Turn On (1989)
The producer of the legendary "Emmanuelle" films brings you this torrid tale about a medical researcher who invents a device that can control sexual behavior. After experimenting on lab mice, he decides to use it on the world's hottest women. Based on a popular French comic strip; with Florence Guerin and Jean-Pierre Kelfon. 80 min.
21-9031 Was $89.99 *$14.99*

Honey (1983)
A house is populated with all sorts of characters: a voluptuous mistress; a sexual athlete; a dance instructor. Then a gorgeous young woman takes a journey that turns into a glimpse of fantasy desire. The amazing Clio Goldsmith ("The Gift") stars in this Euro sizzler; with Fernando Rey and Catherine Spaak. 90 min.
47-1165 *$19.99*

Caged Women (1983)
Laura Gemser, the exotic star of the "Emanuelle" films, plays a reporter who poses as a prostitute in order to investigate a prison where everything is wild. The prisoners are women seeking love and lust in this sizzling shocker. AKA: "Emanuelle in Hell," "Emanuelle Reports from Women's Prison." 97 min.
47-1255 Was $29.99 *$14.99*

Midnight Gigolo (1986)
In this scorching European sex tale, "Emmanuelle" star Laura Gemser plays a woman whose passions have been unfulfilled by her doctor husband. An illicit affair with a patient leads Gemser into a secret world in which she performs sex acts with a number of partners. Directed by Joe D'Amato ("Trap Them and Kill Them"). AKA: "Christina." 90 min.
59-7040 Letterboxed *$99.99*

The Belt (1989)
In the tradition of "The Story of O" comes this kinky study of a sado-masochistic relationship between an American teacher and a beautiful Italian woman. The woman gives the teacher a belt and requests that she whip him as part of foreplay. Their union eventually reaches new depths of depravity. James Russo, Eleonora Brigliadori star. 90 min.
59-7046 *$99.99*

The Immoral One (1980)
A woman suffering from amnesia reconstructs her life from audiotapes and discovers that she has a sordid past and was involved in prostitution and unusual romantic entanglements. Follow the events that led to her amnesia, and meet such characters as her auto racing lover, her younger, endangered sister and a blackmailing madam. Sylvia Lamo stars in this sophisticated European sizzler. 90 min.
83-3015 *$29.99*

Assault Of The Killer Bimbos (1987)
They're lethal, they're deadly, but above all, they're bimbos! A trio of young women take to the open road in a wild cross-country driving spree that adds up to racy, zany fun. Christina Whitaker, Tammara Souza, Griffin O'Neal, Elizabeth Kaitan star. 85 min.
75-5005 *$14.99*

Joy: Chapter II (1985)
In the tradition of the "Emmanuelle" series comes this sensuous tale of a woman named Joy who searches for her lover in a jungle paradise where she's drugged, ravaged by guests at a perverse party and encounters sexual liaisons that are on an otherworldly level of intensity. This classic of European erotica stars Brigitte Lahaie, Isabelle Solar. 92 min.
84-5002 *$39.99*

Slave Girls From Beyond Infinity (1987)
Tell me, what's a slave girl to do? With tongue planted firmly in cheek, this sci-fi adventure details the exploits of two charming chattels imprisoned on a spacecraft who escape to an uncharted planet. Stars Elizabeth Cayton, Brinke Stevens and Cindy Beal. 80 min.
75-5001 *$14.99*

Sorority Babes In The Slimeball Bowl-O-Rama (1987)
Some gorgeous college coeds discover a bowling trophy with a genie inside...a bloodthirsty genie who's been waiting eons for vengeance! Comedy, horror, sex and 7-10 splits; what more can a moviegoer want? Linnea Quigley, Andas Jones, Brinke Stevens and Michelle Bauer (billed as Michelle McClellan) star in this nudity-filled opus. 80 min.
75-5003 *$14.99*

Galactic Gigolo (1988)
This E.T. won't phone home; he's having too much fun on Earth. A playboy from beyond the stars has landed to sample the local flora and fauna (and Florence and Fanny and Francine) in this outrageous sci-fi satire with some out-of-this-world nude scenes. Ruth Collins, Karen Nielsen and Lisa Petruno star. 80 min.
75-5004 *$14.99*

Hate And Love (1983)
In this sizzling Swedish scorcher, two rival white slavery rings carry on a dangerous feud involving flesh and blood. Among the participants are an ex-lawyer convicted for malpractice who works as a gigolo in Paris and the woman he rapes in a forest, then kidnaps. Marilyn Lamour (aka "Olinka") and Gabriel Pontello star. 90 min.
59-7100 *$29.99*

Emily (1982)
The film that was a sensation around the world stars Prince Andrew paramour Koo Stark as a teenager who returns from a boarding school to learn her mother has become a prostitute. She soon discovers her own sexuality with interludes with her school teacher, an older woman and a distinguished gentleman. Sarah Brackett co-stars; music by Rod McKuen. 83 min.
84-5006 *$19.99*

What Do You Say To A Naked Lady? (1984)
Indiana's Ponderosa Sun Club is famous for its annual "Nudes-A-Poppin'" competition, and this filming of the racy 1984 festivities features a then-unknown Tim Allen interviewing the bountiful beauties entered in the "Fabulous Go-Go," "Custom Body Painting" and "Miss Nude Galaxy" events. There's also a talk with adult movie star Hyapatia Lee. 53 min.
08-8370 *$14.99*

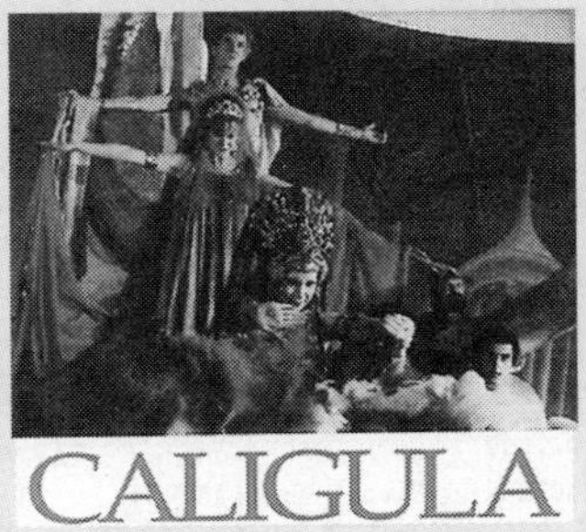

Caligula (1980)
The complete, uncut version of the incredible sexual epic that may be the most controversial film of all time. Astounding decadence, uncensored sex and explicit violence meet in this kinky look at the reign of Caligula, depraved ruler of Rome. Malcolm McDowell, John Gielgud, Peter O'Toole and Helen Mirren star along with a bevy of wild and willing newcomers in this Bob Guccione-Penthouse production. 148 min.
47-1199 Unrated *$59.99*

Caligula, Part II—Messalina: Empress Of Love (1981)
Nothing is sacred in this madcap satire of ancient Rome. Raunchy, no-holds-barred attacks on the citizenry, the nobles and the gods fill this soft adult circus with slapstick hilarity. Anneka di Lorenzo, Vittorio Caprioli star. AKA: "Messalina: Empress of Rome." 90 min.
50-1414 *$19.99*

The Orgies Of Caligula (1984)
No-holds-barred look at the last days of Rome's Emperor Caligula, highlighted by violence and sex supplied by his beautiful slaves, trained in the art of eroticism. Robert Gligorev, Aldo Valli and Sandra Venturini star in this Italian spectacle. AKA: "Caligula's Slaves." 93 min. Dubbed in English.
59-7044 *$89.99*

Caligula: The Untold Story
You've heard all about him. Now see the full, shocking story behind the maniac who ruled Ancient Rome and subjected his people to depraved cruelties and bizarre sexual practices. This compellingly erotic and explicit drama stars screen Emmanuelle Laura Gemser, David Cain, Oliver Finch. 91 min.
20-5153 *$19.99*

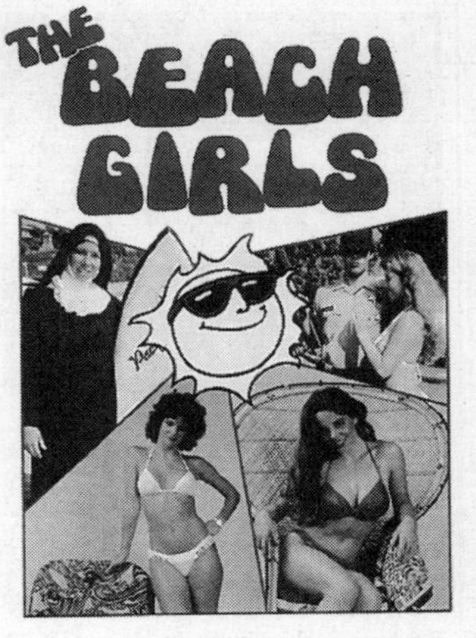

The Beach Girls (1982)
Three—count 'em—three voluptuous coeds show a young student the joys of summer living through playful seduction. Debra Blee, Jeana Thomasina, Adam Roarke and Val Kline star in this sizzling sex comedy filled with gorgeous bikini clad—and unclad—women! 91 min.
06-1146 *$14.99*

Video Vixens (1984)
The boob tube has never been bouncier as a free-thinking network executive decides to put on an awards show that accents the "jiggle." Robyn Hilton and Sandy Dempsey star in this ribald farce. 84 min.
47-1330 *$14.99*

Party Plane (1989)
Welcome to Condor Skyways, an airline where everything is perfect, from the sensuous flight attendants to the outrageous freebies that come with your ticket. Strap yourself into your sofa and take off to the friendly skies of sexiness. Kent Stoddard and Karen Annarino star. 81 min.
47-2028 Was $89.99 *$14.99*

Julia (1974)
Hotter than July! Sylvia Kristel, star of "Emmanuelle" and "Private Lessons," plays a young woman discovering the joys of a sensual lifestyle while on a vacation in the Swiss Alps. Jean-Claude Bouillon also stars. 83 min.
16-1043 *$19.99*

The Boob Tube (1975)
If you think TV is ordinary, check out Station KSEX, where the only thing more shocking than the programs is the hanky-panky between staff members. Naughty, funny softcore sizzler features Louis Lane and Sharon Kelly (porn star Colleen Brennan). 75 min.
16-1130 *$19.99*

The Happy Hooker Goes To Washington (1977)
The sweet Miss, played by Joey Heatherton, serves her country the only way she knows how! George Hamilton, Rip Taylor and Billy Barty co-star. 93 min.
19-7016 *$59.99*

The Happy Hooker Goes Hollywood (1980)
The City of Angels proves uproarious and sexy to Xaviera, as she gets involved with slick movie producers. Martine Beswick, Adam West, Phil Silvers, Chris Lemmon star. 85 min.
19-7017 *$19.99*

Fairy Tales (1979)
An enchanting fantasy musical for adults. The exploits of Little Bo Peep, Snow White and Jack & Jill have never been as risqué as in this early Charles Band effort. Features the sensual talents of Linnea Quigley, Annie Gaybis, Idy Tripoldi and Mariwin Roberts, plus Sy Richardson, Martha Reeves, Nai Bonet and Professor Irwin Corey. 76 min.
03-1029 *$14.99*

I Like The Girls Who Do (1973)
Cute and racy German sex farce chockfull of curvaceous, naked frauleins. The story tells of a young man who will inherit a fortune from his rich uncle if he sleeps with all of the uncle's girlfriends. Monica Mark and Birgit Bergen star.
73-9359 *$19.99*

Naughty Nymphs (1975)
"Naughty" indeed is this racy tale of sexual hospital escapades and nubile nurses that stars the sultry Sybil Danning and an all-European cast. See the film about which the Philadelphia Inquirer said, "adult situations, profanity, nudity." 78 min.
75-7077 *$19.99*

Centerfold Girls (1974)
This softcore favorite from the waning days of drive-ins features a top-notch cast that includes Tiffany Bolling, Jennifer Ashley, Andrew Prine and Aldo Ray. The story involves a group of gorgeous models who become the targets of a demented serial killer. These angels are soon to be dead centerfolds! 88 min.
03-1105 *$14.99*

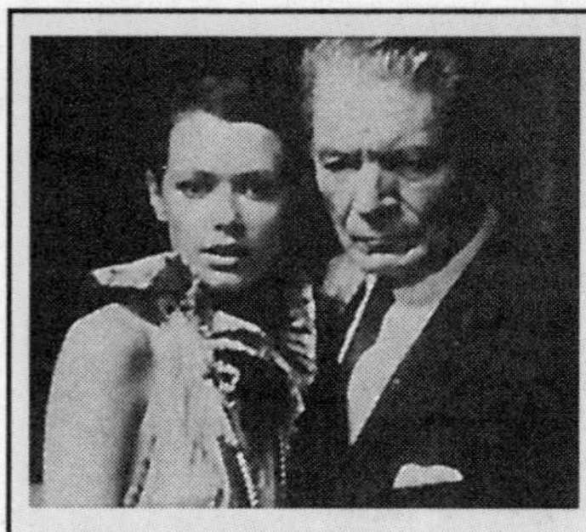

Emmanuelle (1974)
The original erotic classic stars sultry Sylvia Kristel in the title role of the love-starved and sexually frustrated wife of a French embassy official in Thailand. Follow Emmanuelle on an odyssey to explore—and shatter—the frontiers of her sexuality with a variety of male and female lovers. Alain Cuny, Marika Green also star; Just Jaeckin ("The Story of 'O'") directs. 92 min. In French with English subtitles.
53-9610 *$19.99*

Emmanuelle (Dubbed Version)
Also available in a dubbed-in-English edition.
02-1036 *$19.99*

Emmanuelle 2: Joys Of A Woman (1975)
Gorgeous Sylvia Kristel stars in this exotic, erotic sequel to "Emmanuelle." Here she's in Thailand, seeking (as always) to satisfy her insatiable sexual appetite. With Umberto Orsini, Caroline Laurence and future screen "Emmanuelle" Laura Gemser. 92 min. In French with English subtitles.
53-8857 *$19.99*

Emmanuelle 2: Joys Of A Woman (Dubbed Version)
Also available in a dubbed-in-English edition.
06-2612 Was $69.99 *$19.99*

Emmanuelle 5 (1986)
A continuation of the ever-popular erotic series stars gorgeous Monique Gabrielle as the woman of pleasure who is abducted off her yacht by an Arab sheik and forced into a world of white slavery. Can she escape his harem of enslaved, beautiful women? With Charles Foster. Uncut, unrated version; 73 min.
21-9012 Was $89.99 *$14.99*

Emmanuelle 6 (1992)
The "Emmanuelle" saga continues in this exotic, erotic sexcursion that finds the luscious Emmanuelle and a group of gorgeous models in trouble with a nasty drug dealer during a trip into the Amazon jungle. Nathalie Uher, Jean Rene Gossart and Tamira star in this sizzler. 80 min.
21-9021 Was $89.99 *$14.99*

Emanuelle, Queen Of The Desert (1975)
No, Terence Stamp doesn't play the title role here. The stunning Laura Gemser is desert beauty Emanuelle, who becomes the prize in a battle between mercenary soldiers and must use her wits and her body to stay alive. With Angelo Infanti, Gabrielle Tinti. 92 min.
78-3034 *$19.99*

Black Emanuelle (1976)
Laura Gemser is back as the legendary beauty who travels to Africa on a phtoto assignment, but soon finds time to explore her sexuality with a couple who love exotic experimentation. Filled with nudity, lesbian scenes, fantasy sequences and even a sequence involving a rugby team. Karin Schubert also stars. AKA: "Emanuelle in Africa." 85 min.
04-1462 *$29.99*

Emmanuelle's Revenge (1976)
Emmanuelle is hell-bent on a mission fueled by vengeance and love, using her feminine wiles and sexuality to track down her sister's killer. Rose Marie Lindt, George Eastman, Karole Annie Edel star. AKA: "Blood Vengeance."
16-1205 *$29.99*

Emanuelle On Taboo Island (1976)
Lovely Laura Gemser plays the heated beauty who finds romance and lust (but not, unfortunately, seven stranded castaways) on an uncharted island. Paul Giusti and Arthur Kennedy also star. 88 min.
58-1039 *$14.99*

Emmanuelle's Silver Tongue (1976)
And it's a cinch the rest of her body is just as valuable, too, in this erotic roundelay that finds Emmanuelle jumping from her current lover's bed to help a repressed young heir become a man (if you know what we mean and we think you do). Carmen Villani, Nadia Cassini, Roberto Cenci star. AKA: "Ecco Lingua d'Argento." 86 min.
59-7024 *$29.99*

Emmanuelle In Egypt (1977)
Cleopatra had nothing on this lusty lady, as lovely Laura Gemser has an erotic odyssey along the banks of the Nile that could put a smile on the Sphinx. Softcore erotica at its best. AKA: "Naked Paradise." 86 min.
14-6067 *$19.99*

Emanuelle Around The World (1977)
Take a whirlwind tour into new worlds of sexuality when the lovely Emanuelle attempts to stop a white slavery ring. Laura Gemser stars as Emanuelle, with Kristine DeBell and Karin Schubert. AKA: "Emmanuelle, Perché Violenze Alle Donne."
20-1012 *$29.99*

Emanuelle's Daughter (1977)
Gorgeous Laura Gemser pays her lover to kill her husband, releasing her from his cruel sexual treatment, and takes the man's teenage daughter under her wing. Gabrielle Tinti, Livia Russo and Gordon Mitchell co-star. AKA: "Emanuelle the Queen," "Emanuelle, Queen of Sados." 91 min.
39-1963 *$29.99*

Emmanuelle In The Country (1978)
Luscious Laura Gemser is the title character, a lustful lady who cares for the sick in a remote country hospital—in her own special, sexy way. With Aldo Ralli. AKA: "Country Nurse." 82 min.
69-1004 *$19.99*

Emmanuelle In Soho (1981)
See Emmanuelle visit London and commit some nono's as she turns Soho into uh-oh and strings men along like yo-yo's. Wake us up before she go-go's. Mandy Miller, Julie Lee star. 90 min.
46-5287 Was $59.99 *$29.99*

Forever Emmanuelle (1982)
A sensual, beautiful young woman is the focus of a documentary film being shot in the Philippines, and along the way she sets out on her own voyage of erotic discovery. Steamy drama stars Annie Belle, Al Cliver, and the real Emmanuelle, Emmanuelle Arsan. 89 min.
47-1132 *$29.99*

Emanuelle And Joanna (1986)
Two sisters...one a quiet, withdrawn sophisticate, the other a ball of smoldering, decadent eroticism. When they enter each other's private worlds, the result is a veritable explosion of sexual abandon and wanton pleasures. Shery Buchanan, Paola Montenero star. 90 min.
03-1585 *$29.99*

Emmanuelle (1993)
Enter the erotic world of Emmanuelle in this stylishly sensual series produced for European cable TV in 1993. Sylvia Kristel, the original "Emmanuelle," is featured along with alluring beauties Marcella Wallerstein and Krista Allen-Moritt ("Liar Liar" and billed as Sandra Allen), and former James Bond George Lazenby. These uncensored, unrated films tell how Emmanuelle uses a mystic perfume to help people sexually. Each tape runs 90 min.

The Secret World Of Emmanuelle
Emmanuelle suffers amnesia after a car accident and relates her past sexual encounters to a psychoanalyst, offering viewers a chance to explore her fantasies, sensual desires and hedonistic behavior.
59-7033 *$99.99*

The Legend Of Emmanuelle
After her husband dies, a friend of Emmanuelle's inherits his luxurious estate, but comes into conflict with her mother-in-law, a sexy, elegant woman. Emmanuelle enters into her friend's body and uses her sexual abilities to help and please both women.
59-7034 *$99.99*

Emmanuelle's Magic
Emmanuelle tries to help a sculptor's wife who has discovered that her husband has fallen in love with one of his creations. By using her magical perfume, Emmanuelle discovers other women need her aid, so a little same-sex counseling is in order.
59-7035 *$99.99*

Emmanuelle Forever
Emmanuelle uses her new powers to help Falcon, a young rock star who needs to be taught that love and lust can go hand in hand. At the same time, Emmanuelle seeks to find the perfect love and attain total sensual gratification.
59-7036 *$99.99*

Emmanuelle's Love
When she discovers that her friend, Sarah, is being exploited by her philandering husband, Emmanuelle uses her magic potion to help her. Sarah, who has a disfigured face, is turned into a beautiful woman by the perfume and soon regains her inheritance that her hubby swindled. Then Emmanuelle gets herself involved in a dangerous love triangle.
59-7037 *$99.99*

Emmanuelle's Perfume
When Emmanuelle's friend Sam, a hot-shot screenwriter, finds himself falling in love with a high-class woman, Emmanuelle uses her magic perfume to help guide him through the relationship. 90 min.
59-7039 *$99.99*

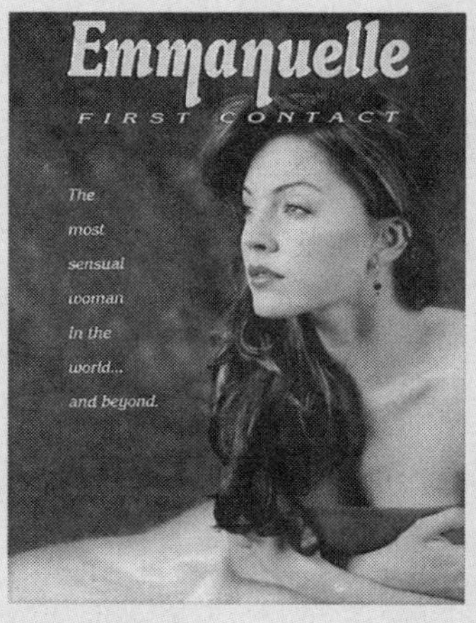

Emmanuelle: First Contact (1995)
Krista Allen Morrit shows it all in this intergalactic sextravaganza that casts her as the legendary lady of lust, demonstrating to a group of aliens how to get it on, Earthling style. Emmanuelle literally goes around the world to different exotic locales to show off her erotic powers. With Chandra, Paul Michael Robinson. AKA: "Emmanuelle in Space," "Emmanuelle, Queen of the Galaxy." Unrated version; 93 min.
21-9199 *$49.99*

Lust Combo (1970)
Get a first-hand look at the "rock and roll lifestyle" with this erotic composition about a trio of horny musicians who get involved with a pair of bored housewives and a "French" chick after playing in a Southern roadhouse. There's "strip spin-the-bottle" and other games awaiting them. Linda LaLane, Cheri Parks and Scott Randall star.
79-5992 Was $24.99 *$19.99*

Love Boccaccio Style (1970)
An all-star adult cast that includes John Holmes, Candy Samples and Marsha Jordan is featured in this erotic salute to sex, Renaissance style. Witty dialogue, lusty ladies, ribald romping and lots of nudity abound as plague survivors amuse themselves by telling risqué tales while congregating in a castle.
79-5994 Was $24.99 *$19.99*

Massage Parlor (1972)
A classy massage parlor movie? Well, sort of. A man searches for a sexy masseuse he once had a session with, launching a search which brings him into contact with gorgeous massage specialists throughout Germany. This European delight stars Elizabeth Volkman and Mai Ling Chang as an Asian beauty.
79-5997 Was $24.99 *$19.99*

Sex On The Groove Tube (1972)
Sean S. Cunningham, who would go on to create the "Friday the 13th" series, co-directed this Miami-based bit of debauchery about two female roommates with different views on sex. One's a nympho, the other's a voyeur who gets in trouble when she sticks her head where it doesn't belong. With XXX legends Fred Lincoln and Harry Reems, and Sheila Stuart.
79-5999 Was $24.99 *$19.99*

The Godson (1971)
An ambitious young man finds babes, violence and lust when he tries to make it in the world of organized crime. Lois Mitchell and Uschi Digart star in this bullet-filled, breasts-a-blazing sinematic story.
79-5283 Was $24.99 *$19.99*

The Notorious Cleopatra (1970)
Jealousies, passion and sex explode in this exposé of the erotic world of ancient Rome, where Cleopatra, Marc Antony and Julius Caesar make history in and out of their bedrooms. Sonora, Johnny Rocco and Jay Edwards star in this titillating affair that gives new meaning to the term "toga party." 88 min.
79-5281 Was $24.99 *$19.99*

Sweet Bird Of Aquarius (1970)
The dawning of the new age hasn't helped a frigid wife, so her spouse has a bright idea: why not go to a nudist colony where sex is hot, hot, hot! Soon, wifey discovers it takes more than one fellow to unlock her sensual key, and her hubby is not happy. With Susanne Robinson, Thomas Wood. 90 min.
79-5137 *$19.99*

Swinging Swappers (1970)
At a fancy cocktail party, two pals sit around and talk about the other guests' sexual proclivities. The escapades in this German-made spectacle include a wife setting up her husband in an adultery "sting" with a masseuse, two bank robbers and their comely hostage, and more. With Carl Heing Bauer.
79-6000 Was $24.99 *$19.99*

The Hawaiian Split (1971)
An erotic suspenser with such early 1970s sex icons as Uschi Digart and Rene Bond. Narcotics, nymphomaniacs, explosives and mobsters play a part in this story of Louie, a drug-runner with heroin stashed in his surfboard who finds himself in and out of beds and trouble when he heads to Hawaii to complete a deal. With Lindsey Hillard, Kathy Hilton.
79-6004 Was $24.99 *$19.99*

Carnal Knowledge (1970)
A birthday party for a pimp attended by a few of his fellow flesh peddlers and some of their top "working girls" turns into an orgy of drugs, sex and naked bodies in this psychedelic romp that has nothing at all to do with the 1971 Jack Nicholson film. Paul Jones, Sally Beck and the legendary John Holmes star.
79-6030 Was $24.99 *$19.99*

Who Killed Cock Robin? (1970)
The death of an egotistical young man prompts an investigation by a cop, who quickly learns of the man's active sex life and sleazy ways. After meetings with a stripper, lesbians and a pretty student, the cop finds out he's being followed—by the person who may hold the key to the mystery! A real sleazefest!
79-6039 Was $24.99 *$19.99*

Teaser (1973)
The gorgeous Becky is a college student by day and a naughty, teasing stripper by night. Her flirtatious manner makes the gals hot, hot, hot, but one day they get her into a whole lot of trouble. Rene Bond and Becky Sharpe star.
79-5692 Was $24.99 *$19.99*

My Sister's Business (1970)
Little sister learns from her prostitute sibling what sex and life are all about in this softcore scorcher from the genre's not-so innocent days. Constance Sirtfem and LuAnn Cox star. 65 min.
79-5139 *$19.99*

Daughters Of Joy (1972)
The French Revolution is the backdrop for this sexy story about a member of a theatrical troupe who inherits an inn which soon becomes a bawdy spot to stop. Spies, traitors, gorgeous women and all sorts of intrigue play a part in the ribald proceedings.
79-5865 Was $24.99 *$19.99*

Love Bavarian Style (1972)
"Love Bavarian Style...truer than the black, red and orange." If you're seeking huge Alps, check out this tribute to Teutonic lust in which a city gal takes over a hotel in the mountains and welcomes all sorts of liederhosen-less ladies and guys to the joint. There's lots of bed-hopping, naked frauleins that'll get you going "yodel-lay-he-and-her!"
79-5866 Was $24.99 *$19.99*

The Bedroom (1972)
A young teacher is nominated to be "dean of students" at a boy's school, but his superiors think it's best that he get married first. The problem is that Teach is extremely shy, so he decides to try a crash course on seducing women. Ole Soltoft stars in this Swedish sexploiter.
79-5872 Was $24.99 *$19.99*

Deep Jaws (1976)
P.G. Dartmouth thinks it's curtains for his movie studio. Sex and disaster films are the rage, and he doesn't produce them. Then his chesty wife gets a government contract and his secretary arranges a sex film shoot with the cash. P.G. gets to audition the actresses, wifey gets it on with a government bigwig, and things get out of hand. David Kelly stars.
79-5688 Was $24.99 *$19.99*

The Dicktator (1974)
When overpopulation threatens the world, a pill is invented to make men sterile for a year. When things go awry with the pill and no one can get pregnant, it's learned that only five men remain virile in the world. And they're a Peruvian shepherd, a Jewish drag queen, a black student, a Russian political prisoner and a stoned Chinese man. Rene Bond stars.
79-5689 Was $24.99 *$19.99*

Wild, Free And Hungry (1970)
These adjectives describe the characters in this heated fantasia of passions involving motorcycles, speed-boat racing, mobsters, a carnival and some extremely horny women. Gary Graver, Barbara Caron and Jane Tsentas star. 88 min.
79-5233 *$19.99*

Diamond Stud (1970)
This early X-rated item is set in the "Gay '90s" and tells the story of "Diamond Jim," who was as at home with wheeling and dealing as he was with dance-hall gals. There's catfights, gem smuggling, action and carnal experiences in this David F. Friedman opus.
79-5193 *$19.99*

Honey Britches (1971)
Extra-sleazy hillbilly hoedown about a group of cons who swipe some jewels and, while on the run, land in a Carolina shack occupied by a moonshiner and his hot but frustrated wife. When the thieves take a liking to the missus, breasts, lust and pitchforks ensue. With Ashley Brookes. AKA: "Shanty Town Honeymoon."
79-5833 Was $24.99 *$19.99*

I Want More (1970)
A sordid exposé on the wild goings-on in Tinseltown, where a classified ad in an underground newspaper can get all the kinks out. Witness a North Carolina couple into voyeurism, a motorcycle gang that practices free love, a nympho hitcher that takes on four guys, a barber with an unusual specialty and others. With sex queen Marsha Jordan and Sandra Olsen.
79-5835 Was $24.99 *$19.99*

Swedish Fly Girls (1970)
Classic European sex tale from Denmark that played for years in drive-ins in the 1970s. Flight attendant Christa has relations with a host of men, including a suave Italian, a young artist and a handsome Australian lawyer who wants to help her in a bitter rivalry against her ex-hubby. With Birte Tove, Clinton Greyn.
79-5870 Was $24.99 *$19.99*

The Sexpert (1972)
A nerdy guy longs to become a ladies' man, but since he has no luck with the ladies this seems impossible. After a series of sexy and zany encounters with a stripper, a hayseed honey, a married woman and a virgin, he heads to a wild, drug-filled party. Will that experience turn the "Ordinary Joe" into "Casanova Joe"?
79-5868 Was $24.99 *$19.99*

The Ribald Tales Of Robin Hood (1974)
A dandy David F. Friedman production that adds sizzle to the "Robin Hood" legend. The merry men are merrier than ever, Maid Marian wants to frolic in Sherwood Forest, and Robin is a dashing hunk. Lusty men and bawdy wenches abound.
03-1037   Was $24.99   *$19.99*

Confessions Of A Young American Housewife (1974)
While searching for sexual fulfillment, a suburban housewife turns to a young couple and their turned-on sexually active friends. Jennifer Wells, Rebecca Brooke and Chris Jordan star. Joe Sarno ("Inga") directs. 83 min.
03-1133   *$24.99*

Salon Kitty (1976)
Notorious sexploitation saga from Tinto Brass ("Caligula") delves into the decadence of the Third Reich with a story set in a Berlin brothel in 1939. That's where Nazi soldiers partake in all sorts of perverse pleasures—while they're being spied on by military officials. Ingrid Thulin, Helmut Berger and Theresa Ann Savoy star in this march on the wild side.
03-1263   *$29.99*

The Key (1983)
From Italian erotic maestro Tinto Brass comes a torrid tale of an aging professor who persuades his sexually unsatisfied wife to get involved with his son-in-law. When his daughter approves of her hubby's liaisons, a game of sexual deception begins with powerful, carnal consequences. Banned by the Catholic Church, the film stars Stefania Sandrelli, Frank Finlay; features a score by Ennio Morricone. 109 min.
59-7103   *$29.99*

The Sensuous Nurse (1979)
You've never seen "tender loving care" like this before, as sultry Ursula Andress plays a nurse hired to "take care of" an elderly millionaire by his greedy heirs. With Jack Palance and Luciana Paluzzi, this is the complete, uncut version of the film which features sequences with full-frontal nudity. 81 min.
04-1298   Was $59.99   *$29.99*

Ilsa, She-Wolf Of The S.S.: Collector's Edition (1975)
Graphic sexual shockfest about a Nazi "medical camp" run by that high-stepping honey, that torture-loving Teutonic titwillow, Ilsa, the Bitch of Buchenwald. Shocking acts of violence and nudity abound! Not for the squeamish! Dyanne Thorne stars. Includes the theatrical trailer. 96 min.
14-8000   Letterboxed   *$14.99*

Ilsa: Harem Keeper Of The Oil Sheiks: Collector's Edition (1976)
Ilsa is back—and your VCR will never be the same! She's involved with a devious Arab sheik in the slave trade, kidnapping and torturing the world's most beautiful women. Bizarre and excessive tortures (wild booby-traps, deadly tarantulas and more!). Blonde bombshell Dyanne Thorne and two beautiful black henchwomen will whip you into a frenzy. Includes the theatrical trailer. 91 min.
14-8003   *$14.99*

Ilsa, The Wicked Warden: Collector's Edition (1978)
With lash in hand and fire in her heart, the ferocious fraulein brings her flair for flagellation to South America to oversee the onslaught of heinous atrocities committed upon the female felons that take part in her "game" of torture. Stars Dyanne Thorne. AKA: "Wanda the Wicked Warden," "Greta the Torturer." Includes the theatrical trailer. 94 min.
14-8004   Letterboxed   *$14.99*

Ilsa Trilogy: Collector's Editions
Whip up a tidy savings with all three "Ilsa" drive-in classics, starring Dyanne Thorne.
14-8005   Save $5.00!   *$39.99*

Miranda (1985)
Lusty sensual comedy from Tinto Brass ("Salon Kitty") concerning the gorgeous owner of a secluded country inn located in Italy. When she decides to take a steady lover from among her inn's staff and frequent clients, Miranda sets out to make her choice by taking each of them to bed. Gorgeous Serena Grandi ("The Grim Reaper") stars with Andrea Occhipinti and Andy J. Forest. 90 min.
59-7102   *$29.99*

What Do You Say To A Naked Lady? (1970)
You'll be surprised what people *do* say when "Mr. Candid Camera" himself, Allen Funt, hosts this ribald film that goes where the TV show never could, with racy stunts and lots of "good clean fun." 90 min.
04-1784   *$14.99*

Malibu High (1979)
The hippest high school around is the setting for this softcore crime drama about a high school student who decides the best way to get good scores on her tests is to score with her teachers. Soon, however, the teacher's pet finds herself in trouble with a mobster. Jill Lansing and Katie Johnson star. 92 min.
08-1118   *$79.99*

Hollywood Babylon (1972)
Inspired by the notorious book by Kenneth Anger (who later sued the movie's makers), this film depicts some of Hollywood's wildest sex scandals and seediest situations. Among the personalities covered are "Fatty" Arbuckle, Erich von Stroheim and Rudolph Valentino. With Uschi Digart, Cindy Hopkins.
10-1291   Was $24.99   *$19.99*

Catherine & Co. (1976)
Sizzling sex farce featuring Jane Birkin as a gorgeous British woman whose attempts to become a chef in Paris is disrupted because her sexual activities. Soon, her bedroom dalliances lead her into the world of prostitution, and she becomes everyone's favorite madam. Jean-Pierre Aumont, Jean-Claude Brialy also star in this risqué European romp. 85 min.
15-1004   *$12.99*

Oh! Calcutta! (1972)
The sensational play has been filmed and turned into a funny and titillating movie, filled with nudity, music and witty observations about sex. John Lennon, Jules Feiffer, Kenneth Tynan, Sam Shepard and Robert Benton are among the writers who contributed to sketches, while Bill Macy and Mark Dempsey are featured in the cast. 120 min.
15-1009   *$29.99*

The Yum-Yum Girls (1978)
An innocent young woman comes to New York to fulfill her dreams of a modeling career, but all too soon her naiveté is shattered by the glamour world's seamy underside. Sensual drama that "bares all" stars Judy Landers, Michelle Daw; look for Tanya Roberts ("Sheena"); Hosted by Ginger Lynn Allen. AKA: "Bright Lights." 89 min.
19-7044   *$19.99*

Ginger (1970)
Every man wanted her; nobody could tame her! The original sexy sleuth, Cheri Chafaro, fights against drugs and prostitution. 90 min.
27-6003   *$19.99*

The Abductors (1971)
Cheri Caffaro, the amazing blonde bombshell dazzles as Ginger, a hit-girl with a body that'll knock you dead. She's up against kidnappers—and they have their hands full! 90 min.
27-6004   *$19.99*

Girls Are For Loving (1973)
Ginger's got a knack for serious undercover work—under the covers. Here she squares off against a wild female bombshell. Cheri Caffaro. 90 min.
27-6002   *$19.99*

The Swinging Cheerleaders (1974)
Gimme a "Z!" Gimme an "A!" Gimme an "N!" Gimme a "Y!" What've ya got? Yep, and "sexy, racy and wacky," to boot! When these booster gals shake their pom poms, the football squad is inspired to try for the big score. Too bad there's no game! Colleen Camp, Rosanne Katon star. 91 min.
27-6018   Letterboxed   *$14.99*

The Pom Pom Girls (1976)
Robert Carradine and Jennifer Ashley star as two California teens bent on getting the most out of their remaining days of high school in this funny, racy romp that features a fractured football game and loads of comely cheerleaders. With Rainbeaux Smith, Lisa Reeves, James Gammon. 91 min.
46-5363   Was $79.99   *$14.99*

Revenge Of The Cheerleaders (1976)
Bricka bracka firecracker, sis boom bah! Comedy and nudity, rah, rah, rah! Wacky, zany, uninhibited teenage cheerleaders stop at nothing to keep their condemned high school open. Stars David Hasselhoff, Cheryl Smith, Rainbeaux Smith, and the legendary Carl Ballantine. 86 min.
47-3147   Was $39.99   *$29.99*

Satan's Cheerleaders (1977)
Scarier than "Porky's"! Funnier than "The Exorcist"! Four lovely high school cheerleaders are kidnapped by the school janitor, secretly a member of a Satanic cult. More horror, comedy, football action and beautiful girls than any one film has a right to have. John Ireland, Yvonne DeCarlo, John Carradine star. 92 min.
08-1316   *$19.99*

That exquisite moment of a girl's sexual awakening

Bilitis

IS A YOUNG GIRL. A FILM BY DAVID HAMILTON

ORIGINAL MUSIC by FRANCIS LAI starring PATTI D'ARBANVILLE MONA KRISTENSEN, BERNARD GIRAUDEAU JAMES KOHLER and MATHIEU CARRIÈRE

David Hamilton

Bilitis (1977)
The sexual awakening of a young woman is the focus of this gorgeously filmed, super-sensual tale from acclaimed photographer David Hamilton ("Laura"). Patti D'Arbanville is the French nymphette who discovers the joys of sex during a memorable summer vacation. With Bernard Giraudeau, Mona Kristenson. 95 min.
03-1090   *$29.99*

Laura (1979)
This controversial and sensual coming-of-age tale from David Hamilton ("Bilitis") focuses on a young woman's affair with a 40-year-old sculptor, who happens to be her mother's former lover. Gorgeously shot in the South of France, the film stars Maud Adams, Dawn Dunlap and James Mitchell. 95 min.
53-1139   *$29.99*

A Summer In St. Tropez (1981)
David Hamilton, the master of erotic photography, presents another alluring essay on the joys of young womanhood. In the South of France, a group of beauties lives together in a country house where they share their innocence and intimate desires. This effort from the director of "Bilitis" offers lush photography, soothing music and a gorgeous cast. 60 min.
44-1031   *$29.99*

Tendres Cousines (Tender Cousins) (1983)
Master erotic filmmaker David Hamilton ("Bilitis") focuses on the frothy, soft-focused sex in a French farmhouse in 1939. Teenage cousins get involved with some of the older folks in this softcore delight. Anja Shute, Thierry Tevini star. 92 min. In French with English subtitles.
22-6046   Letterboxed   *$29.99*

Tendres Cousines (Dubbed Version)
Also available in a dubbed-in-English edition. 90 min.
47-1209   *$29.99*

Little Lips (1978)
A famous writer returns home from the war, but is deeply distressed by what he's seen and over the loss of his lover. After meeting a teenager on the verge of becoming a woman, he believes his life has been changed. But his love turns into an obsession that could eventually destroy him. Katya Berger and future director Michele Soavi star in this European sizzler. 77 min.
20-5011   *$29.99*

Butterflies (1973)
From Joe Sarno, the erotic auteur behind such classics as "Flesh and Lace" and "Inga," comes this made-in-Germany gem starring gorgeous Marie Forsa as a restless farmgirl who seeks fame and fortune as a fashion model in the city. She becomes involved with nightclub owner Harry Reems, but when she learns of his infidelities, she gets it on with one of his girlfriends. 105 min.
27-1142   *$19.99*

Mafia Girls (1976)
Gangsters go gung-ho for sex in this soft adult classic starring Serena in her debut role. She teams with French superstar Claudine Beccarie to get intimately involved with a mobster chief named "the General" and his associates. 87 min.
36-1001   *$29.99*

Squeeze Play (1979)
Tired of being ignored by their baseball-playing boyfriends, a group of gorgeous women form their own softball team and challenge the guys to a game that quickly becomes a sexy competition where "anything goes." Jenni Hetrick, Jim Metzler and Al Corley star.
44-1108   Was $59.99   *$14.99*

Cry Uncle (1971)
Jacob Masters is hired to clear an eccentric millionaire of the murder of his mistress but, somehow everything goes wrong. Not to worry, though; no one takes him seriously anyway. A racy, hilarious softcore spoof of private eye movies with Paul Sorvino and Allen Garfield; directed by John Avildsen. 85 min.
46-5208   *$14.99*

H.O.T.S. (1979)
Meet Boom Boom, Honey, Teri and Melody. These sultry sorority sisters have the H.O.T.S. for every B.M.O.C., and to quell a rival sorority they use the only means they know how: a strip touch football game. Stars Playboy Playmates Susan Kiger and Pamela Sue Bryant. 95 min.
47-1625   *$29.99*

H.O.T.S. (Letterboxed Version)
Also available in a theatrical, widescreen format.
08-8856   *$14.99*

The Hitchhikers (1972)
This drive-in fave stars blonde and bodacious "Hee-Haw" honey Misty Rowe as a hitcher who uses her body to get her way in an all-girl commune and then joins a hippie guru in a series of highway hold-ups. There's amorality a-plenty in this wild sexploiter featuring Norman Klar and Linda Avery and directed by "Gator Bait" creators Ferd and Beverly Sebastian.
31-3016   Was $24.99   *$19.99*

Fiona (1977)
She's the headline-making British temptress whose sexploits outdid any fictional film. Now, Fiona Richmond stars in her own story, a racy softcore romp that traces her adventures as stewardess, writer, and all-around "boy toy." Anthony Steele, Victor Spinetti co-star. AKA: "Hardcore." 82 min.
35-5039   *$29.99*

Dracula Sucks (1979)
Everyone's favorite vampire is out for a lot more than blood in this funny, sexy spoof of the "Dracula" legend. Adult cinema superstars John Holmes, Jamie Gillis, Annette Haven and Seka star. 90 min.
48-1141   Was $29.99   *$14.99*

Virgin Cowboy (1975)
A cowboy on a mission to deliver a green suitcase and coat to a bordello owner named Minnie gets into all sorts of trouble when a group of hombres arrive in town. One of the madams takes a liking to the cowboy, and the two set out on a sexy and dangerous trip through the Wild West. Liz Renay and Brent Zeller star in this sagebrush sexploiter. 80 min.
50-5143   Was $24.99   *$19.99*

Marina (1970)
Torrid sex drama in which an older couple, well-experienced in a hedonistic lifestyle, seduce a young brother and sister into their world of sensual delights. Athena Prezaki and Lisa Vern star. 65 min.
50-5371   Was $24.99   *$19.99*

The Exhibitionists (1977)
Smoldering European sex film in which an underground artist and his new bride discover that their relationship would probably work best if another woman was involved with them. With Italian sex queen Lili Carati, Asha Wilson and Mircha Craven. AKA: "Look at Me." 85 min.
50-5814   *$19.99*

Sweet Georgia (1972)
After watching softcore screen queen Marsha Jordan portray a sex-starved frontier gal who turns to some raunchy ranch hands for attention when her alcoholic husband ignores her, you'll be sure to have Georgia on your mind. (And we didn't even mention the naked women on horseback or the pitchfork fight!) 60 min.
62-1348   *$19.99*

Sandra:
The Making Of A Woman (1970)
Join Sandra as she leaves her alcoholic father and seeks freedom of all sorts (especially sexual!) in this erotic odyssey. Her journey to find self-fulfillment leads her to San Francisco, where she encounters lesbian lovers, men wearing bras and motorcyclists. With Monica Gayle, Daryll Largo. 90 min.
79-5144 Was $24.99 *$19.99*

The Toy Box (1971)
Sordid, sensational orgy of thrills involving a group of monsters from outer space who land on Earth in hopes of stimulating sexual arousal in humans. Once that's accomplished, the aliens slurp the humans' brains. Urgh. The ads screamed: "A Pandora's Box of Freudian Depravity!" And we're not arguing. With Ann Myers and Evan Steel.
79-5180 Was $24.99 *$19.99*

The Joys Of Jezebel (1970)
A scorching biblical sexventure about the Phoenician princess married to Ahab, king of Israel, whose conduct lands her in hell after being killed by Joshua. There she strikes a devious carnal deal in this "molten morass of emotions." A David F. Friedman production.
79-5190 Was $24.99 *$19.99*

Beyond Love And Evil (1971)
Erotic drama involving a young man who attempts to rescue his true love from a sex-seeking madman in a castle. Will the pleasures inside the castle prove too great for him? With Souchka, Fred Saint-James.
67-5036 *$14.99*

Marsha,
The Erotic Housewife (1970)
Marsha Jordan, adult film's first superstar, plays the title role, a gorgeous young bride who discovers that her husband is having a lengthy affair with another woman. Her way of getting hubby back on the right track is the stuff of erotic legend.
79-5225 *$19.99*

Island Of Lost Girls (1973)
An exploitation favorite focusing on a group of sleazy fellows who run a white slavery ring, wheeling and dealing women from their home base in the Orient. Brad Harris, Tony Kendall and Monica Pardo star.
68-8516 *$19.99*

Vampire Ecstasy (1973)
The ultimate erotic vampire movie, Joe Sarno's bloodlust epic tells of a beautiful medieval vampire who lives in a castle in modern-day Germany where she seeks female plasma. Four women meet at the castle, unaware of the orgiastic rituals performed there and the sensual lesbian acts needed to keep the baroness' spirit alive. With Nadia Henkowa, Marie Forsa. 103 min.
73-9255 *$19.99*

Daddy Darling (1970)
A real sleaze-a-rama from pioneer exploitation director Joe Sarno. A young design student is obsessed with her father, but when he remarries she decides to delve into depravity with encounters with her painting teacher, a young man and even her stepmother. With Gio Petré, Helle Louise. 96 min.
79-5207 Was $24.99 *$19.99*

Double Features

Britt Blazer/Golden Gate Pay-Off
"Britt Blazer" is a special operative out to bust a seedy porn mogul who has kidnapped the daughter of a businessman and filmed her in the act of sex with some of his henchmen. In "Golden Gate Pay-Off," a San Francisco effort from the early 1970s featuring interracial liaisons, a gambler's girlfriend sleeps around to help pay off his debts.
79-6099 Was $24.99 *$19.99*

Robot Love Slaves/The Good Fairy
Candy Samples is featured in the incredible "Robot Love Slaves," a sensitive tale of a creepy scientist who resurrects dead women with a vacuum cleaner hose while his wife has an illicit affair. And "The Good Fairy" helps lonely men by magically making sweeties appear in their bedrooms for their pleasure. They just don't do it like they did it in the '70s.
79-6100 Was $24.99 *$19.99*

Panty Party/Harvey Swings
Ultra-sultry shenanigans ensue when a lingerie salesman has his own "Panty Party," readying two pretty models for a buyers' show in his own special way. Adult film star legend Rene Bond stars. And klutzy Harvey and his gal pal joins some swingers for fun and erotic games in "Harvey Swings." These are two prime examples of 1970s softcore.
79-6102 Was $24.99 *$19.99*

My First Time/I'm No Virgin
A young woman, curious about the birds and the bees, seeks excitement with a group of way-out swingers in "My First Time." And after trouble at home, a college student finds a kinky way of life when she goes to live with a group of coeds in "I'm No Virgin," featuring the legendary Rene Bond. A double dose of '70s sleaze!
79-6104 Was $24.99 *$19.99*

Lei'd In Hawaii/Ski Party
Go beachside and get snowed in these two Seventies softcore spectacles. In "Hawaii," two sexy debutantes get involved with Tiki, whom they learn is looking for pretty gals for human sacrifices. And the slopes don't get as much action as the lodge's bedrooms as a group of co-eds show off some sexy moves in a wild "Party."
79-6125 Was $24.99 *$19.99*

Four In Bed/
Marriage American Style
The "Four in Bed" are a quartet of sweeties who take to strip poker in order to get a shy guy into the sack. See how flush he gets when sex is in the cards! And Uschi Digart persuades Donna Young to get out of "Marriage" and into something big and hot—and we're not just talking bras.
79-6126 Was $24.99 *$19.99*

Winter Sports/West Valley PTA
Tune in for more ski-time sexiness in "Winter," where some randy dudes fake injury in order to meet, greet and get to know chicks off the slopes. And a swimming instructor has the time of his life with some lessons in "West Valley PTA," a tribute to sexy valley girls—before there were valley girls.
79-6128 *$19.99*

Model Hunter/Classified Sex
Two swinging lesbian chicks get into nude modeling but soon find a sleazy con artist improvising scenes in "Model Hunter." And such adult film stalwarts as Rick Cassidy, Cyndee Summers and Ric Lutz star in "Classified," a look at swapping, swinging and more, American style.
79-6130 Was $24.99 *$19.99*

Two Goes Into One/
One For The Money
Join sexpo faves Donna Young ("Wild Honey") and Sandy Dempsey ("Country Hooker") in a tale of a therapist whose specialty is sex...with his curvaceous patients! And in "One for the Money," get ready for "the show," as a woman learns about sexual experience by practicing what she reads in "The Picture Book of Sexual Love."
79-6129 Was $24.99 *$19.99*

The Female Frenzy Of
Doctor Studley/Spread It Around
For a taste of the real bizarre stuff, '70s sexploitation style, try "Doctor Studley," complete with boom mikes, characters named Mrs. Lovella Dick and lots of nudity in montage form. Also, unsatisfied housewives tickle their tingle in "Around."
79-6131 Was $24.99 *$19.99*

Motel For Lovers/
Splendor In Bed
Leave the light on in this "Motel," where sexy babes and hunky guys get together under the covers for some uninhibited sexcapades. See Suzanne Fields ("Flesh Gordon") lead the way for a "four-star" time. And there's "Splendor" all over the place as an adulterous hubby, his hot-to-trot spouse and a virginal maid explore carnal possibilities.
79-6132 Was $24.99 *$19.99*

Alley Cat/
Karen And The Carpenter
Witness Sandy Dempsey as an aspiring actress whose sexual desires supersede her career desires—which are quite big, too. "Flesh Gordon's" Suzanne Fields also stars. And a woman named "Karen" asks a hunk to fix her car, then witnesses her girlfriends give him a close inspection.
79-6133 Was $24.99 *$19.99*

Shot On Location/
Blue Movie Madness
See what happens when a group of filmmakers and performers shoot on "Location" and everyone goes wild, unleashing their innermost desires. Featured are adult regulars Rene Bond, Ric Lutz and Sandy Dempsey. Also, a veteran adult actress shows a young woman the tricks to working "Blue."
79-6134 Was $24.99 *$19.99*

The Ranch Hand/
Love From Paris
A double-D dose of sex siren Marsha Jordan! Marsha's the owner of a ranch who takes in a writer trying to find out what life is like as a "Ranch Hand" and shows him how to "ride 'em, cowboy." Also, the mountainous Marsha and her swinging hubby get their friends hot when they show them wild footage from their sex-drenched getaway in "Love from Paris." Jackie Vernon does not appear.
79-6488 Was $24.99 *$19.99*

The Executives' Wives/
3 Phases Of Eve
"The Executives' Wives" will do anything so their husbands can get ahead, even if it means bedding down the executives at their spouses' company. Treachery, back-stabbing and housewives with bodacious bodies are what it's all about; Barbara Mills stars. Also, Sandi Carey is "Eve," a woman with three personalities, all with different sexual desires.
79-6489 Was $24.99 *$19.99*

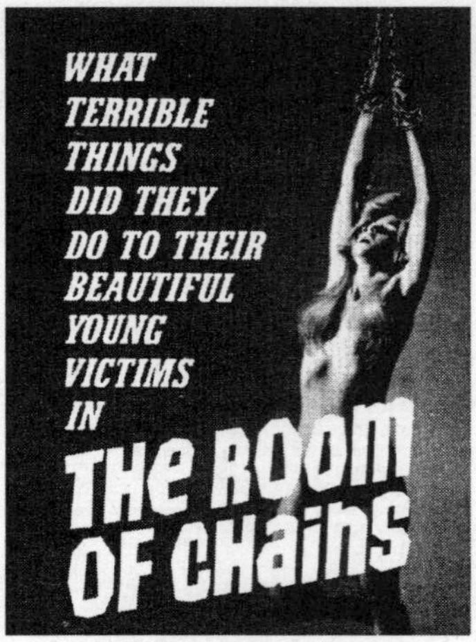

The Room Of Chains (1972)
This delightfully deranged dandy involves a married fellow who happens to have a gay lover. The couple enjoy kidnapping pretty women and torturing them in a cellar while classical music plays. Their sidekick is a creepy henchman with a weird haircut and even weirder skin. This French import stars Oliver Neal, Jack Bernard and Evelyn Kerr. 68 min.
79-5480 *$19.99*

Touch Of Sweden (1971)
Uschi Digart, the mammoth madam of sex movies, stars and narrates this knockout erotic tale about a Hollywood sex kitten who decides to help humanity by becoming a nurse. Little does she realize how wild things can get under the hospital sheets! Sexploitation regulars Sandy Dempsey and Sandi Carey also make this "Touch" one of the most erotic you'll ever find.
79-6221 Was $24.99 *$19.99*

Teach Me (1971)
A silly, saucy German sex comedy set in the 19th century and focusing on a groom-to-be who tells a prostitute about the past sexual events in his life at his bachelor party. Among the experiences: being whipped by his nanny, masturbation in military school and lots more. Puns and perverse situations abound along with some Teutonic titwillows. Dubbed in English.
79-6222 Was $24.99 *$19.99*

Country Love (1972)
It's a lascivious love-in, '70s-style, with big-boobed Maria Arnold getting frustrated with hubby John Cambridge. A trip to a nearby hippie commune gets Maria hot again, especially after an encounter with a cool black dude. Meanwhile, John fantasizes about Maria in some kinky situations. Finally, an all-out orgy with another couple lights the couple's fire again.
79-6426 Was $24.99 *$19.99*

Changes (1970)
Before he revolutionized the porn world with "Deep Throat," director Gerard Damiano delivered this documentary on the sexual revolution, featuring interviews and some scorching encounters. Among those talking: Screw Magazine's Jim Buckley and Al Goldstein; stripper Carol Barr; a theater manager who discuss sex in the cinema; and the owner of a "model studio." Adults only!
79-6427 Was $24.99 *$19.99*

Getting Into Heaven (1970)
Uschi Digart, billed here as "Marie Marceau," shows why she was one of softcore's top stars in this nudity-drenched teaser in which she plays Heaven, a movie star wannabe. With roommate Sin (Jennie Lynn), she goes to incredibly sexy lengths to get roles in the movies from a sleazy producer. Digart is showcased in all of her bountiful glory. Whew!
79-6429 Was $24.99 *$19.99*

Lord Farthingay's Holiday (1970)
Here's a carnal entry in which a stuffy British lord is mistakenly offered a bevy of hooker beauties while visiting a Beverly Hills mansion for a quiet vacation. The butler accidentally calls "tease" entertainers instead of "teas," and soon m'lord and the mansion help as well are shagging such sweeties as Sandy Dempsey, Donna Young and Alida Tennant.
79-6436 Was $24.99 *$19.99*

Tuck Me In (1970)
Softcore diva Kim Pope excels as the daughter of a famous movie star father who decides she wants to be in pictures. But while she climbs the showbiz ladder of success, Dad can't keep his hands out of her best friend's cookie jar and eventually marries her, making for a strange rivalry. In black and white with a psychedelic color sequence, this is a wild New York sleazefest!
79-6443 Was $24.99 *$19.99*

Frankie And Johnnie...
Were Lovers (1975)
Early adult faves Rene Bond and Ric Lutze shine in this sexsational effort from XXX director Alan Colberg ("Tapestry of Passion"). Bond's Frankie, an aspiring songstress whose boyfriend Johnnie (Lutze) is a car junkie with a taste for speed. But Johnnie also loves sex and has the hots for Frankie's gal pal, played by Cyndee Summers. Hot stuff!
79-6526 Was $24.99 *$19.99*

A Fairy Tale For Adults (1970)
Outrageous tale of homosexuality, lesbianism and kinkiness about a "flamboyant" fashion designer who, with only a short time to live, wills his estate to three female assistants...providing "they stick to their own kind." Forman Shane, Phyllis Stangel star. 78 min.
79-5215 *$19.99*

The Van (1976)
In order to snag some hot women, a teenager purchases a van. Soon, the gals start clinging to him—but not the girl he really wants. Meanwhile, his friend borrows some of his payment money to ward off loan sharks. Can the young man with a van beat the bad guys and get the girl? Stuart Getz, Danny DeVito star. AKA: "Chevy Van." 90 min.
78-1169 *$14.99*

Massage Parlor Wife (1971)
She was a bored housewife. And in order to get over her boredom, she took a job. But what kind of job? Secretary? No! Keypunch operator? Nah! Retail operations director for a video store? Uh-uh! Damn! This horny honey took a job as a masseuse in one of the town's hottest massage parlors. See what goes on behind closed doors at the local rub-down room. With Jen Gilliam and Steve Rogers.
79-5285 Was $24.99 *$19.99*

Sexual Customs
In Scandinavia (1971)
The climate may be cooler, but the sex is definitely scorching in this sexposé of Scandinavian morals. All sorts of hanky-panky occurs—usually involving gorgeous blondes like Ingrid Peterson—and, while some of the carnal customs appear staged, the others are sure to astound you. Ulla, go to verk! 80 min.
62-1369 *$19.99*

The Love Garden (1971)
A freelance journalist who has the hots for his lesbian neighbor tries to bed her after hiring her as his private secretary. The writer scores and gets her all excited, making her lover jealous at the same time. But the gal learns "once you go lesbo, it's hard to say no," so she decides to stick to her girlfriend. Barbara Mills and Jason Scott star.
79-6092 Was $24.99 *$19.99*

Candy Stripe Nurses (1974)
Curvaceous candy-stripers Candice Rialson and Robin Mattson, along with their duties of tending to the sick and infirmed, get mixed up with basketball players, drug scandals and other dramas in this softcore sizzler from producer Roger Corman, with nude scenes that'll melt your thermometer. Also stars the great Dick Miller. AKA: "Sweet Candy." 82 min.
53-1210 Was $19.99 *$14.99*

Sex And
The Lonely Woman (1970)
Scorching erotic melodrama in which an escapee from an island prison finds refuge in the house of a frustrated wife. The convict and the woman carry on a steamy affair, much to the chagrin of her husband—who happens to be in charge of the prison—and his sleazy friend.
79-5798 Was $24.99 *$19.99*

Psyched By The 4-D Witch (1970)
Erotic horror fantasy about a young female descendant of a Salem witch whose experiments with sexual black magic conjure up a sorceress from the past. The witch offers the young woman a special sexual high called "the Astral Orgasm" through strange fantasies, but there's an unspoken price to pay for the ecstasy. This is a campy, bizarre shocker—don't see it ripped!
79-5811 Was $24.99 *$19.99*

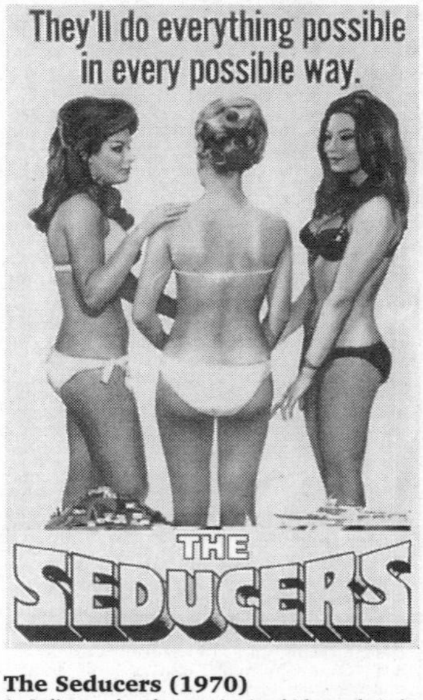

The Seducers (1970)
An Italian-produced sexcursion in which a yacht is the site for a number of wild sexual shenanigans, including lesbianism, threesomes, a prostitute making it with a virgin and an incestuous relationship involving a mother and her son. With Rosalba Neri, Ewa Thulan. AKA: "Sensation."
79-5143 Was $24.99 *$19.99*

CB Hustlers (1978)
That's a big 10-4, good bodies! When the he-men hauling cargo across America in their big rigs need a special kind of "rest stop," the lovely ladies known as the "CB Hustlers" are ready to meet them with their vans for some pedal-to-the-metal lovin'. Risqué road comedy stars Edward Roehm, Tiffany Jones. AKA: "Hot Box Highway." 77 min.
55-3008 *$19.99*

When Women Had Tails (1970)
Take a hilarious look at caveman days, when the women with tails took their primal partners in hand and together discovered sex. Wacky "adults only" comedy stars the sultry Senta Berger; co-written by Lina Wertmuller. 99 min.
59-5072 *$19.99*

When Women Played Ding Dong (1971)
Welcome to the Stone Age, when men were cavemen and women were WOW! This lost entry in the "When Women..." series tells of a battle between the cave dwellers and the water dwellers, with a gorgeous, scantily-clad, promiscuous primitive named Listra as top prize. Nadia Cassini and Howard Ross star in a ding dong delight. 95 min.
79-5382 Was $24.99 *$19.99*

When Women Lost Their Tails (1975)
More Cro-Magnon carnality in this racy look back to prehistoric times. It's "survival of the horniest," with lovely Senta Berger starring. 94 min.
59-5079 *$19.99*

Shame Of The Jungle (1975)
Raunchy and outrageous animated adults-only spoof of the famed jungle lord and his girlfriend, trying to cope in a one-time idyllic world now overrun by sex-crazed animals and an evil queen. Created by French-Belgian cartoonist Picha; featuring the voice talents of John Belushi, Bill Murray, Christopher Guest and Johnny Weissmuller, Jr. 73 min.
59-7002 Was $79.99 *$14.99*

The Danish Connection (1970)
John C. Holmes is detective Johnny Wadd in this softcore suspenser that find Wadd in Hawaii. He's involved in intrigue with an eclectic group of characters like a perverted physician, gals named Mata Horny, Hot Fudge and Half Breed, and a panty-sniffing professor. Rick Cassidy and Rene Bond co-star.
79-5690 Was $24.99 *$19.99*

Danish And Blue (1970)
John Holmes is featured in this softcore saga about a young American man trying to tackle his sexual problems with a romp through Copenhagen. Once in the Danish city, he becomes enamored with a black girl—who turns out to be a man; watches a kinky menage a trois that turns into a rollicking fivesome; and finds the aphrodisiac power of Danish pastries.
79-5691 Was $24.99 *$19.99*

Sex And The Single Vampire (1971)
The legendary John Holmes is Count Spatula, whose home is visited by a group of groovy swingers who want to have sex in a haunted house. The Count spies on them as they're engaged in hanky-panky, then gets into the act himself. A rare softcore outing for Holmes, this one also features Sandy Dempsey.
79-5963 Was $24.99 *$19.99*

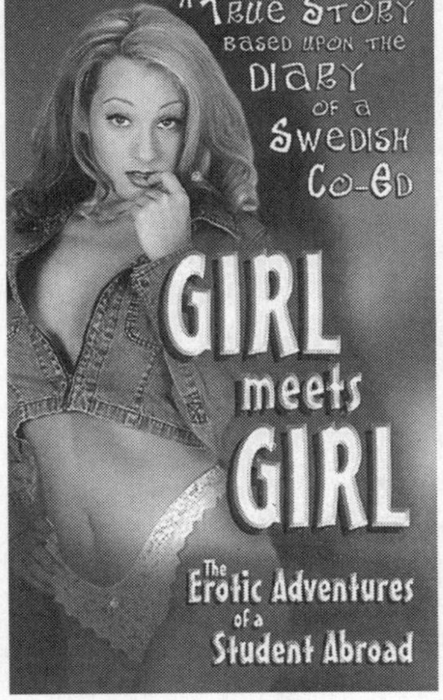

Girl Meets Girl (1974)
Marie Forsa, the lovely star of "Butterflies," plays a Swedish coed who wants to experience the ultimate in erotic encounters when she goes to live with her attractive aunt. Unable to control her desires, Forsa seduces a slew of her aunt's female friends in a series of heated trysts. Softcore sex master Joe Sarno directs this European teaser. AKA: "Bibi." 105 min.
73-9254 *$19.99*

The Story Of "O" (1975)
The classic tale of erotica is brought to the screen by Just Jaeckin ("Emmanuelle"). Corinne Clery stars as "O," who surrenders her body to the men in her life in an orgy of domination, pleasure and pain. With Udo Kier, Anthony Steel. 97 min.
31-1039 Was $39.99 *$19.99*

Fruits Of Passion: The Story Of "O" Continued (1981)
Based on a novel by "Story of 'O'" author Pauline Reage, this sensual drama is set in 1920s Hong Kong. A beautiful British woman, eager to please a decadent lover, enters into a world of sexual submission in an elegant brothel. Arielle Dombasle and Klaus Kinski, Germany's ball of smoldering eroticism, star. AKA: "Flowers of Passion." 82 min. In Cantonese and French with English subtitles.
08-8854 Letterboxed *$19.99*

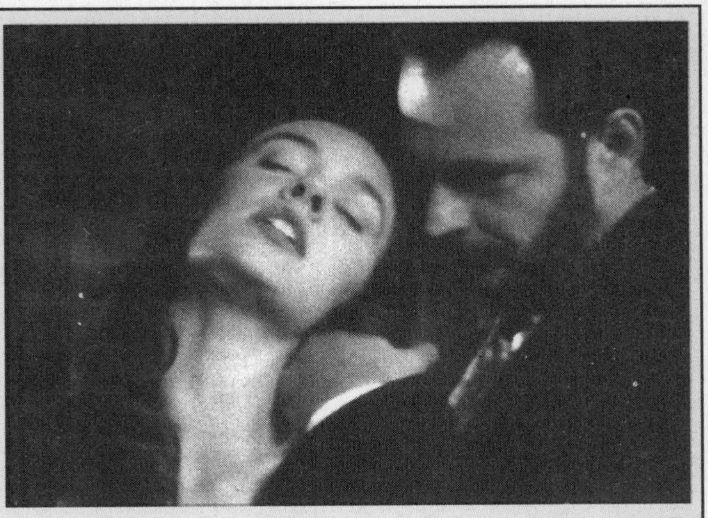

THE STORY OF O
The Series

The Story Of O: The Series (1992)
Elegantly produced series from Pauline Reage's notorious novel of a woman's experiences in the world of sado-masochism, bondage and discipline. "O" is a photographer who, in order to please her lover, René, submits to his kinky desires by becoming a submissive partner in his fantasies. With Claudia Cepeda as "O" and featuring lots of nudity. Each tape runs about 50 min.

The Story Of O, Vol. 1
In order to capture Rene's complete attention, "O" agrees to learn of his sado-masochistic needs by taking a part in a series of kinky rituals with him and others at a secluded mansion.
84-5019 Was $39.99 *$24.99*

The Story Of O, Vol. 2
"O" receives a harsh initiation into the secret world of her lover by being ready, willing and able to have sex and be whipped, tortured and humiliated at his—or other men's—whim.
84-5020 Was $39.99 *$24.99*

The Story Of O, Vol. 3
The indoctrination into S&M continues as "O" is put in a cell and forced into sex and torture sessions with a series of men. She learns the importance of her experience and the depth of her need for Rene and decides to continue satisfying his desires after she leaves the mansion.
84-5021 Was $39.99 *$24.99*

The Story Of O, Vol. 4
"O" prepares for more sexual adventures, and, while desiring the gorgeous model Jacqueline, she reminisces about her past lesbian experiences. Rene introduces "O" to Sir Stephen, a wealthy S&M practitioner.
84-5022 Was $39.99 *$24.99*

The Story Of O, Vol. 5
Sir Stephen makes "O" his total slave and indoctrinates her into an even more stringent world of S&M than Rene showed her, a world of total obedience. Rene tells "O" that Sir Stephen's desires take priority over his, and, to oblige her lover, "O" agrees to be totally dominated by her new master.
84-5023 Was $39.99 *$24.99*

The Story Of O, Vol. 6
"O's" involvement with Jacqueline draws Rene into a menage-a-trois, while Sir Stephen's interests in "O" draw her into a world where she consents to having herself permanently marked and branded. She also becomes concerned that Rene doesn't love her anymore.
84-5024 Was $39.99 *$24.99*

The Story Of O, Vol. 7
Sir Stephen takes "O" to a house where she assimilates into a feminist society and immerses herself into lesbian relations. Although she experiences a new type of fulfillment, she remains a slave thanks to Sir Stephen's orders.
84-5025 Was $39.99 *$24.99*

The Story Of O, Vol. 8
Sir Steven tells "O" he doesn't want to "see her without fresh marks." He offers her to Eric, a handsome associate who, after scorching sex, falls in love with her. When Eric tells Sir Stephen of his love, "O" is punished for three days. At the same time, Rene and Jacqueline fall in love.
84-5026 Was $39.99 *$24.99*

The Story Of O, Vol. 9
Rene takes Jacqueline to Sir Stephen's mansion and Jacqueline's younger sister, Nathalie, joins them. Soon, Nathalie falls in love with "O," while Rene professes his love for Jacqueline. Also, "O" begins to question her devotion to the world of bondage.
84-5027 Was $39.99 *$24.99*

The Story Of O, Vol. 10
Nathalie observes her sister and "O" in a torrid liaison, but "O" is deeply hurt when she realizes Rene loves Jacqueline. Sir Stephen offers "O" to "The Commander," who takes her as his slave to a party. There, while facing humiliation by being ignored by the partygoers, "O" reconsiders the choices she's made in her life.
84-5028 Was $39.99 *$24.99*

The Story Of O Complete Set
All 10 tapes in "The Story of O" series are available in one deluxe set. Now, follow "O's" complete adventures in this erotic epic. 500 min. total.
84-5029 Save $30.00! *$219.99*

Sex And The Law (1970)
A "Confidential Report"-styled mix of reality and fiction from Denmark about the world of pornography. A filmmaker experimenting with sexy movies gets thrown in jail for her efforts, while "man-on-the-street" interviews present Scandinavian views on porn, plus there are film-within-a-film episodes on fetishism, voyeurism and fantasies. Great, Danes!
79-6059 Was $24.99 *$19.99*

Is There Sex After Marriage? (1972)
Sex kitten extraordinaire Candy Samples plays the best friend of a woman in the doldrums from her unexciting marriage. Candy gets her pal to explore some new avenues of sensuality, while unhappy hubby gets acquainted to porno theaters and hookers for diversions. The answer to the title's question, then, is "yes"...but not necessarily between spouses. With Steven Keats, Lori Brown.
79-5844 Was $24.99 *$19.99*

All The Young Wives (1973)
Shot in the South, this rural sexploitation gem tells of Big Jim, the most powerful man in town, who uses his machismo to seduce the wife of one the town's residents while he's away hunting. Meanwhile, Big Jim's spouse is galloping in bed with a horse trainer. Sparks fly when Jim finds out about his wife's whereabouts! With Jerry Richards, Edmund Genest.
79-5845 Was $24.99 *$19.99*

A Man With A Maid (1973)
Racy softcore romp, based on the infamous novel of Victorian erotica. A young man is awakened to the pleasures of the flesh after a visit to his father's mistress and, with some help from his butler and maid, turns his home into a "seduction palace" equipped with all manner of exotic gadgets. Martin Long, Diana Dors and Sue Longhurst star. AKA: "The Groove Room," "Victorian Passions," "What the Swedish Butler Saw." 83 min.
62-1343 *$19.99*

The Good, The Bad And The Beautiful (1970)
The cruelty and perversions of politicos are laid bare in this shocking sexposé about a wealthy senate candidate in the middle of a blackmail plot involving his ex-hippie wife, his sexy maid and a sleazy chauffeur. Lots of skin and some surprising plot developments populate this winner with Kate Wilson and bondage model Elizabeth Aubert.
79-5933 Was $24.99 *$19.99*

The Adult Version Of Jekyll & Hyde (1971)
Forget Fredric March, Spencer Tracy and Jerry Lewis! Here's a lewd and lascivious version of Robert Louis Stevenson's classic story, produced by David Friedman. Instead of turning into Mr. Hyde, however, the not-so-good doctor transforms into Miss Hyde, a lesbian with a penchant for murder and sex.
79-5126 Was $24.99 *$19.99*

The Hand Of Pleasure (1971)
The people who gave you "Terror at Orgy Castle" delve into depravity once again, presenting a tale of an American student in London who gets involved in helping smash Dr. Dreadful and his "Hand of Pleasure": two women-turned-sex-crazed-zombies who love CIA agents to death. Will the student be turned homosexual by the not-so-good Dr.'s "sex transference machine"?
79-5668 Was $24.99 *$19.99*

Marquis De Sade's Justine (1977)
In this kinky adaptation of the Marquis De Sade's story, former British tabloid cover girl Koo Stark plays Justine, an innocent living in a convent with her promiscuous sister and sexually aggressive Mother Superior. Justine's sister travels to London in order to become a prostitute, leaving Justine with a pastor who assaults her. With Martin Potter. AKA: "Cruel Passion." 93 min.
59-7030 *$89.99*

Justine De Sade (1979)
The Marquis De Sade's epic work "Huguette Boisvert" is brought to life in this lavish, erotic drama that depicts the life of a young, innocent country girl who is brought into the sadistic practices of the Marquis. With Alice Arno, Mauro Parenti, Yves Arcanel. 90 min. Dubbed in English.
55-3023 *$19.99*

Dark Prince: Intimate Tales Of Marquis De Sade (1997)
A no-holds-barred look at the 18th-century French nobleman whose name became synonymous with bizarre sex. The story concerns a young woman whose search for her missing sister leads her into de Sade's world of pain and pleasure. Will she surrender to his twisted desires to learn her sister's fate? Nick Mancuso, Janet Gunn and John Rhys-Davies star. Uncut, unrated version includes nine minutes of extra, ultra-kinky footage. 96 min.
21-9144 *$59.99*

The Long Swift Sword Of Siegfried (1971)
The ages-old Germanic legend is reworked into a softcore sizzler by producer David Friedman. Handsome knight Siegfried battles villains and dragons to save his king and for the love of the beautiful Kriemheld. Sybelle Danninger (later known as Sybill Danning), Lance Boyle and Heidi Ho star.
79-5218 Was $24.99 *$19.99*

The Exotic Dreams Of Casanova (1970)
Casanova's stud-like descendant is an egotistical movie star of spaghetti westerns who throws one wild Valentine's Day party. A costume orgy with Casanova and members of Swingers International ensues at his Hollywood mansion, and before long everyone's without clothing, including busty Uschi Digart. With Johnny Rocco and Jane Louise.
79-5311 Was $24.99 *$19.99*

Roseland (1970)
Way, way, way-out hippie fantasia about a redneck who gets his mind expanded in a bizarre land where he encounters nudity, bondage, porno movies, strippers, Busby Berkeley-styled dancers, Biblical characters and mean-spirited psychiatrists. If Fellini dropped acid and visited late-'60s Haight-Ashbury, he might have been inspired to make a movie like this. With E. Kerrigan Prescott.
79-5383 *$19.99*

Teenage Bride (1970)
Charlie is having problems with his wife and has a beautiful mistress on the side. Things get even worse when his college dropout stepbrother stops in on his way to Florida. Hoping to make things better, the stepbrother has a romp with Charley's wife *and* mistress! Despite the title, there's no teenage bride here, but there is a hot, young Sharon Kelly, who became porn star Colleen Brennan.
79-5317 Was $24.99 *$19.99*

Love In The Third Position (1971)
Made-in-Sweden softcore sizzler from Joe Sarno that takes a look at the steamy sex lives of a beautiful blonde fashion photographer and her friends. When the photographer makes a play for a male model, her female assistant's jealousy sets in motion a series of roundelays involving group sex, lesbianism, seduction and decadence. With Lillian Malmkvist.
79-5864 Was $24.99 *$19.99*

The Frightened Woman (1971)
Before "The Story of O" whipped everyone into a frenzy, this sexplicit story welcomed moviegoers into the wild world of sadomasochism. An S&M aficionado finds that the new participant in his weekend master-slave sessions is willing to take her submissive role to new levels...if her master can realize his true dominance! Dagmar Lassander, Philippe Leroy star. 93 min.
83-3013 *$29.99*

Fourplay (1972)
A moviemaking couple consider what their sexy next film will be while making love in a field. Among the plotlines they consider (and you witness) are: a young virgin being seduced by an older man; an attractive woman's liaison with her hubby's chauffeur; a hood who tricks his boss's wife into bedding him; and more. With David Anthony, Greta Hartog.
79-5860 Was $24.99 *$19.99*

Satan's Children (1974)
Outrageously sordid mix of horror and homosexploitation in which teen runaway Bobby is raped by a carload of guys, then settles in with volleyball-playing cultists. The guys think he's gay, but a girl who thinks he's cute helps him leave the cult and exact revenge on his dysfunctional family members. Stephen White, Kathleen Archer star.
79-5824 Was $24.99 *$19.99*

Private Arrangement (1970)
Step aside, "Love Boat." This sleazeathon takes place on a ship where a group of gals and guys go gonzo for sex. The oceanic orgy turns serious when Emily, a lesbian, is lost. Will the passengers interrupt their persistent deck-pounding to try and find her? Lyna Lor and the titanic Edii Swenson (aka Uschi Digart) star.
79-5938 Was $24.99 *$19.99*

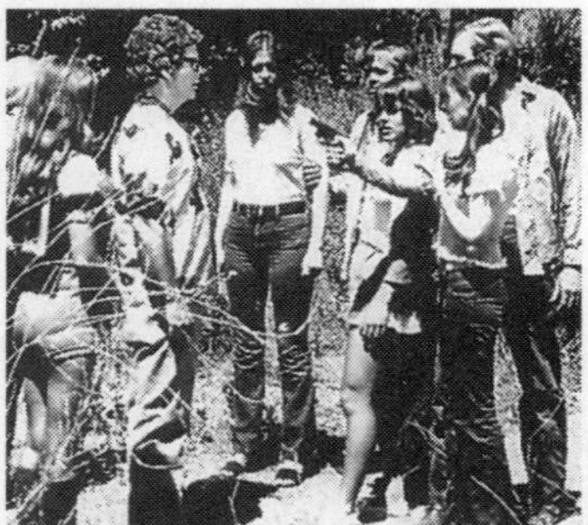

convicts women

Convict's Women (1970)
Two convicts escape prison and go on a rampage, raping women and pillaging in a nearby town. Soon, their repressed libido gets the best of them, as they take women hostages in a ghost town and demand $100,000 for their release. A sordid rural sexploiter! AKA: "Bust Out."
79-5284 Was $24.99 *$19.99*

Caged Woman (1970)
In a genre populated by low-budget entries, this could be the lowest budgeted of them all. The sleaze factor is sky-high, however, in this survey of female inmates who succumb to their sexual desires while behind bars. There's lesbianism, sex with guards and group sex. What women-in-prison fan could ask for anything more? With Tess Drake, Bill Jones, Nan Beal.
79-5944 Was $24.99 *$19.99*

Country Hooker (1971)
Future porn queen Rene Bond stars in this sex-filled flick about two gorgeous gals who solicit musicians for sex when their employer's club is about to be closed. This wild, "admission restricted" movie featuring gals whose "sensuous bodies drive men wild" also stars Sandy Dempsey, Marie Arnold.
79-5310 Was $24.99 *$19.99*

Midnight Plowboy (1971)
Smitten by some city girls who visited his Pa's farm, plowboy Junior goes to the big city and winds up staying at a brothel. He trades rolls in the hay for rolls in the bed and soon acts as a chauffeur for their "Rent-a-Bang" travelling sexual roadshow. John Tull, Nancee and Debbie Osborne star.
79-5314 Was $24.99 *$19.99*

The Pigkeeper's Daughter (1972)
Homespun sex comedy from moonshine territory about the amply endowed 19-year-old daughter of a pigkeeper who becomes a burden for Ma because she hasn't been hitched yet. Little does Ma know that the gal has been getting it on with a hunky farmhand. Terry Gibson, Patty Smith and John Keith star.
79-5315 Was $24.99 *$19.99*

The Takers (1971)
To celebrate their win in a streetfight, two bikers pick up a couple of chicks, take lots of drugs and go on a crime spree that leads to a house where they rape a housewife. Rough sexploiter stars Susan Apple and Deborah Borroli.
79-5405 Was $24.99 *$19.99*

College Corruption (1970)
There's lots of simulated sex, collegiate-style, in this raunchy exposé of what really happened on campus in the swinging 1970s. Debbie, a virgin, and Fran, a party gal, are roommates in a college dorm. Debbie, who is much desired by Bill, Fran's boyfriend, is forced into a lesbian tryst with the female dean, then seeks sexual help from Bill.
79-5945 Was $24.99 *$19.99*

Voluptuous Vixens 76 (1975)
A group of students engaged in an exhaustive study of sex gets to know their subject first-hand as they delve into group sex, cucumbers, outdoor lovemaking and a roundelay with a nerd named Sebastian who carries a butterfly net around. This German spectacle features several top European beauties.
79-5952 Letterboxed *$19.99*

Swedish Wildcats (1972)
British sexpot Diana Dors plays Madame Margareta, an aging hooker and ringmaster of a kinky sex show that features her two gorgeous nieces. When one of the girls meets a nice man and decides to go her own way, the not-so good madame is put on the spot. Naked masked performers, voyeurism, lesbianism and S&M are supplied in this Euro-titillator.
79-5953 Was $24.99 *$19.99*

Trader Hornee (1970)
A large-scale erotic romp from H.G. Lewis collaborator David F. Friedman tells the story of one Hamilton Hornee, who takes an expedition to Africa to find a child kidnapped 15 years earlier and comes across Algona, the White She-Goddess. Buddy Pantsari, Elisabeth Monica star. AKA: "Legend of the Lost Goddess." 105 min.
79-5073 Was $24.99 *$19.99*

A Woman In Love (1970)
A troubled man rapes his innocent fiancée when he begins to imagine her having sex with other men. Soon, he can't tell what is fact or fiction, as his sexual delusions become stranger and stranger. An arty erotic sexcursion starring Audrey Campbell and Phillip R. Allen. 94 min.
79-5101 Was $24.99 *$19.99*

Ann And Eve (1970)
An erotic drama from Sweden about a youthful bride-to-be who takes a holiday with a cynical lesbian film critic (and murderess) that leads to debauchery, degradation with a dwarf, a dinner with naked entertainers and other highlights. Marie Liljedahl ("Inga") and Gio Petré star in this steamy story. 89 min.
79-5107 Was $24.99 *$19.99*

The Golden Box (1970)
After a pianist is murdered, two of his ex-mistresses search for a box containing a secret code that holds the key to treasures. They find the killers, and also partake in a nude gin rummy game and seduce a bellboy, in this wild erotic odyssey. With Marsha Jordan, Ann Myers and Jim Gentry. 79 min.
79-5280 *$19.99*

Wham—Bam—
Thank You, Spaceman (1973)
A pair of aliens from Uranus plan to invade Earth, but first they must scope out the planet to study its inhabitants' sexual desires. The aliens head to Hollywood and encounter how the swinging set lives. A way-out sex farce with John Ireland and Dyanne Thorne (of "Ilsa" fame). AKA: "Erotic Encounters of the Fourth Kind."
79-5286 Was $24.99 *$19.99*

Country Cuzzins (1970)
When moonshine's around, anything can—and will—happen. A wealthy cousin invites the Peabodys to the city, but she doesn't realize what effects some "likker" and horniness will have. Future XXX-star Rene Bond sizzles as an aspiring country singer who loves taking suggestive showers with garden hoses. With John Tull.
79-5309 Was $24.99 *$19.99*

Sassy Sue (1972)
Hillbilly hanky-panky of the hottest kind about a family that includes a lecherous, corncob-puffin' Pa; his wife, who enjoys watching her husband's adulterous encounters; and their virginal hayseed-of-a-son. One day, Pa invents a customized outhouse seat and gets to measure the gals' rears who buy them. Sharon Kelly (later porn star Colleen Brennan) stars.
79-5316 Was $24.99 *$19.99*

Tobacco Roody (1970)
A sexploitation take-off on "Tobacco Road" involving one oversexed family: Pa loves moonshine and his adopted teenage daughter; Ma swaps her body for rent money with the landlord; and their two busty daughters are curious about the birds and the bees. The sex is hot, the characters cartoonish and the hay itchy. Dixie Donovan, Johnny Rocco star.
79-5318 Was $24.99 *$19.99*

Southern Comforts (1971)
A travelling con man adept at beauty contest scams is invited to the manor of a wealthy Southern colonel when his car goes kaput. The colonel persuades the scam artist to promote a contest at his place, and soon all sorts of backwoods beauties strut their stuff. See those nekkid babes do all sorts of naughty things! With Judy Angel and Wendy Gayle.
79-5319 Was $24.99 *$19.99*

Tanya (1976)
Originally advertised as "Tanya, Sex Queen of the S.L.A.," this flick puts a sexy spin on the Patty Hearst story, detailing the exploits of the 20-year-old daughter of a newspaper heir as she's kidnapped by a group of motley revolutionaries. She's soon partaking in sexual encounters with all of them. Marie Andrews, Sasha Gibson star. 78 min.
79-5322 Was $24.99 *$19.99*

The Devil's Garden (1970)
Powerfully perverse sexual drama in which a woman searches for her lost husband in the jungle and is soon held hostage by people into S&M, lesbianism, drugs, interracial sex and strange sexual practices. Sandra Carey and "Baroness Helene DeSade" star.
79-5460 Was $24.99 *$19.99*

The Black Bunch (1970)
Three native women in Africa seek revenge against the culprits who massacred the people of their village. In order to get their hands on guns, the trio will do anything, including partaking in sexual practices with the members of an expedition they meet. Yvonne, Betty Barton and Gladys Bunker star. 80 min.
79-5461 Was $24.99 *$19.99*

Swinging Wives (1972)
Dr. Knut Nielson (yeh, right) supervised this German-made pseudo-documentary that shows what happens when the spouses of disinterested husbands get bored and want sex—any way they can get it! They turn to hooking, massage, even nude bridge to satisfy themselves. With Gale Mayberrie and Ron James.
79-5384 *$19.99*

Moonlighting Mistress (1971)
Softcore sensual mystery from Germany involving a self-centered executive who tries to murder his wealthy, aging wife in order to hop in the sack regularly with his young, blonde mistress. Intriguing plotting and lots of nudity help make this one a real sizzler. Harold Leipnitz and Ruth Maria Kubitchek star.
79-5386 *$19.99*

While The Cat's Away (1972)
With circulation falling, Expose Magazine changes its focus from the sex lives of movie stars to the sex lives of suburban couples. What they find when they spy on a typical American housewife is lots of extra-marital encounters. Chuck Vincent's risqué farce features Kathryn Ford and Calvert DeForest (AKA Larry "Bud" Melman of "Late Night" fame).
79-5387 *$19.99*

The Dirty Mind Of
Young Sally (1970)
Howard Stern, move over! Gorgeous redhead Sharon Kelly (co-star of "Supervixens" and AKA porn star Colleen Brennan) plays a pirate radio station disc jockey whose antics really heat up the airwaves. When Sally gets into the act with her listeners, she's wilder than Dr. Ruth! C.D. La Fleure also stars. AKA: "Innocent Sally."
79-5391 *$19.99*

Kidnapped Coed (1974)
A criminal in debt with the mob kidnaps a young woman for $250,000 in ransom money. But his devious plan takes a turn for the worse when he encounters a group of hoods who rape the woman and a deranged farmer with a pitchfork. Jack Canon and Leslie Ann Rivers star.
79-5395 Was $24.99 *$19.99*

Tower Of Love (1973)
Three nymphomaniacal honeys agree to take some cash and participate in a festival in the small country of Croatavia. The catch is that they must obey the country's weird rules and wear chastity belts. In order to satisfy their sexual desires, the gals play strip poker and erotic billiards. When chastity time is over, the native stud satisfies them. Jean Pascal stars. 80 min.
79-5396 *$19.99*

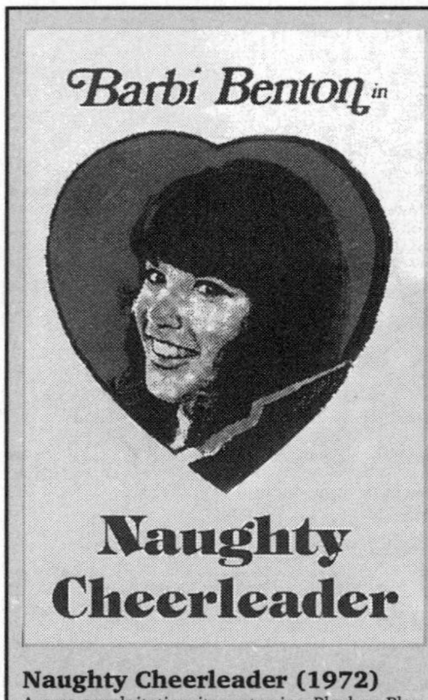

Naughty Cheerleader (1972)
A rare sexploitation item starring Playboy Playmate Barbi Benton as a sex kitten from Scranton whose sexual misadventures take her to Boston (where she and an old sea captain do the nasty) to Miami (where she's paid $3000 to have sex while impersonating Miss Luxembourg) to Italy (where she learns about the casting couch). Klaus Kinski, Clyde Ventura, Broderick Crawford and Lionel Stander also star; look for Ed Begley, Jr. as a bellhop. AKA: "How Did a Nice Girl Like You Get Into This Business?" 85 min.
79-5846 Was $24.99 *$19.99*

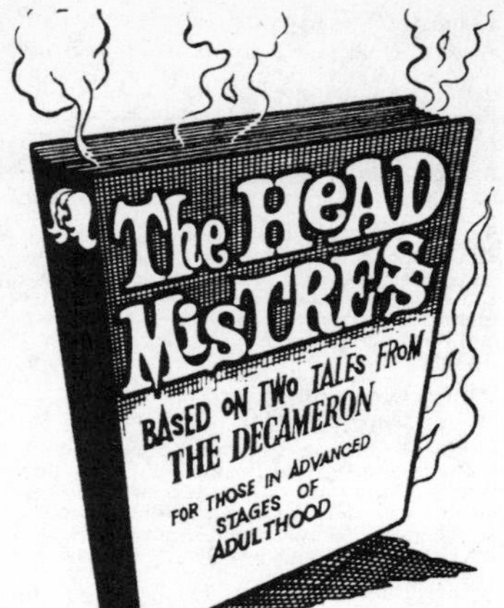

The Head Mistress (1970)
Lavish nudie classic set in a 17th century girl's school where the student are greeted by a number of initiations into the world of sex. There's lots of kinky scenes here, including some heated lesbian liaisons, as the blonde head mistress gets into the act with her students and the new, hunky gardener. With Bermuda Schwartz and Marsha Jordan (using a fake name). 70 min.
79-5129 *$19.99*

The Erotic Adventures Of
Hansel And Gretel (1971)
Hansel's a stud and Gretel is his virginal wife-to-be in this kinky comedy in which the couple encounter the amply endowed Countess Helga during a weekend getaway. Soon, Helga spins a sensual web over the two which includes bondage, chastity belts and more! With Dagobert Walter and Francy Fair.
79-5459 Was $24.99 *$19.99*

Secrets Of
A Door-To-Door Salesman (1974)
A delightful and zesty sex farce involving a door-to-door vacuum cleaner salesman who manages to land the big sale and the curvaceous customers at the same time. Sue Longhurst and Brendan Price star in this amorous adventure filled with lovely British birds.
79-5528 Was $24.99 *$19.99*

Gabrielle (1970)
In this groovy sex film, a gorgeous gal named Gabriella swims nude, reads "The Prophet" and talks about sexual freedom for an underground documentary. Meanwhile, Mom gets it on with the pool boy and Dad, who has the hots for his daughter, goes to bed with a hippie chick. See what happens when this family tunes out and turns on. Gabriella Caron and Luanna Robers star.
79-5547 Was $24.99 *$19.99*

Quiet Days In Clichy (1970)
Inspired by Henry Miller's novel, this unusual erotic drama tells of a self-indulgent American choreographer living in Denmark who joins his pal in pursuit of beautiful women in France. They take a young Parisian mademoiselle as their sexual plaything. Artistic and sensual, this makes a fascinating companion piece to "Henry and June." Paul Valjean stars. AKA: "Not So Quiet Days."
79-5616 Was $24.99 *$19.99*

The All-American Woman (1973)
A daring exploiter in which the sexual problems of a typical American family is revealed. There's Mom and Dad, adolescent Jimmie and teenager Debbie. When Mom's sister, a frigid high fashion model comes to live with them, she decides that some sexual experimentation is in order. And the family is more than happy to oblige her. Marilyn James stars.
79-5687 Was $24.99 *$19.99*

Just The Two Of Us (1970)
Hot lesbian drama concerning Denise and Adria, two lonely housewives who carry on an illicit affair while their husbands are at work. When Adria falls in love with a young actor, Denise gets jealous and will do just about anything to win her lover back. Elizabeth Plumb and Alisa Courtney star in Barbara Peeters' ("Humanoids from the Deep") film.
79-5403 Was $24.99 *$19.99*

Young Lady Chatterley (1977)
When Cynthia Chatterley, at the age of 20, becomes the new owner of the Chatterley estate, the servants and staff give her a "warm" welcome and she obliges by discovering her womanhood in erotic situations with the gardener, the maid and a hitchhiker. This Howard Stern favorite stars the incredible Harlee McBride. Unrated, uncut version; 100 min.
27-6884 Was $39.99 *$19.99*

The Loves Of
Lady Chatterley (1992)
Delve into the world of Lady Chatterley, a beautiful woman who has everything except sex because her husband is an invalid. But hubby has a plan: bail out her ex-lover from prison and give him a job as a stable boy. Of course, he does more than fetch the hay when he gets together with his exotic ex. Malu stars in this European sex effort. 80 min.
50-5477 *$19.99*

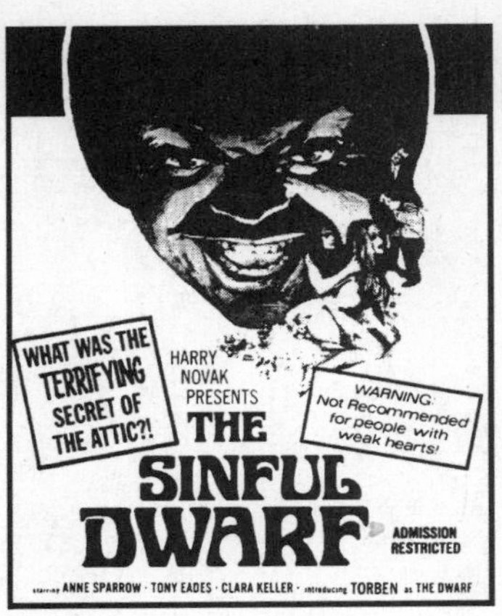
WHAT WAS THE TERRIFYING SECRET OF THE ATTIC?!
HARRY NOVAK PRESENTS
THE SINFUL DWARF
WARNING: Not Recommended for people with weak hearts!
ADMISSION RESTRICTED
starring ANNE SPARROW · TONY EADES · CLARA KELLER · introducing TORBEN as THE DWARF

The Sinful Dwarf (1972)
If you're "bashful," do not see this disturbing sexual shocker about a demented dwarf who kidnaps young women staying at his mother's boarding house and tortures and degrades them for his own amusement. A newly married couple discovers the dwarf's disturbing desires when the bride is held prisoner. Call him "Sleazy"! With Peter Gaumont and Torben as "The Dwarf." 92 min.
79-5393 Was $24.99 ***$19.99***

The Wild Scene (1970)
A psychologist specializing in strange sexual cases finds that her own life has its share of weirdness when she goes underground to investigate her college student's daughter's revolutionary activities and gets sucked into a world of prostitutes, orgies, drugs, nude swimming parties and more. Richard Tate, Alberta Nelson and Anita Eubank star. 96 min.
79-5410 Was $24.99 ***$19.99***

The Swingin' Pussycats (1972)
Philander Manor is the home of sexual fun and games for the family that lives there—along with her friends. Engaged in all sorts of hanky panky are three swingin' siblings, a painter specializing in erotic art, an Italian pornographer and others. Features scenic locations, aphrodisiac water and lots of lusty lovemaking. Marianne Lebeau, Andrea Rau star. 88 min.
79-5429 Was $24.99 ***$19.99***

The Swinging Coeds (1976)
Arousing anthology from Europe with some supersexy stories: a Kansas City gal teaches a group of lovers how Americans make it; a governess involved with her boss gets caught by his wife; a woman doubles as an office worker and masseuse; an aspiring actress has some kinky auditions; and more!
79-5448 ***$19.99***

Office Girls (1972)
Sizzling sexposé of office morals with the young, hot-looking chicks harassing the older men. It's not politically correct, but it certainly is sultry as wanton lust near the water cooler gets an extremely close examination, European-style. AKA: "Eros in the Office."
79-5455 Was $24.99 ***$19.99***

Oddly Coupled (1970)
Nerdy gas station attendant Hobart devotes his life to his pet fish, but when three gorgeous gals kidnap him for their hefty roommate his life gets a major turnaround. The fish fantasies continue, but now there's nudes galore, courtesy of gal kidnappers. The incredible Uschi Digart is featured in a non-speaking but impressive role. AKA: "Fish for All."
79-5457 Was $24.99 ***$19.99***

Terror At Orgy Castle (1971)
Smarmy sexual encounters blend with shocks in this terror tale about a couple who decide to cap off their European vacation with a few nights in a haunted medieval castle. They meet a servant named Igor and the Countess Dominova, and witness freaky ceremonies, orgies, nude black masses and other macabre events.
79-5664 Was $24.99 ***$19.99***

The All-American Girl (1972)
Meet Debbie, a gal on a mission to discover life's erotic pleasures. She promised Mom she wouldn't "go all the way," but that doesn't include experimentation. First, she entices the local bookworm, then she teases an older man, has a liaison with the bookworm's mother and finds self-love. Peggy Church stars in this super-smarmy affair.
79-5686 Was $24.99 ***$19.99***

The Harrad Experiment (1973)
An experimental college where "free and open sexual relations" between students are encouraged is the setting for this infamous softcore drama. Tippi Hedren and James Whitmore head the faculty, and the student bodies on display include then-unknowns Don Johnson, Laurie Walters, Bruno Kirby and Victoria Thompson.
20-1022 ***$29.99***

Love All Summer (Harrad Summer) (1974)
This sequel to "The Harrad Experiment" shows what happens when a group of students graduating from Harrad College take their knowledge of sexuality home and put it to use. Richard Doran, Laurie Walters, Bill Dana and Marty Allen star. AKA: "Student Union." 95 min.
59-7021 ***$29.99***

Pornography Prostitution USA (1970)
Scorching pseudo-documentary look at prostitutes and their lusty lifestyles, filmed with hidden microphones and cameras. Different types of hookers are featured: high-class call girl, streetwalker, nude model, porno actress and lesbian women of the night. 88 min.
79-5446 ***$19.99***

Confessions Of A Frustrated Housewife (1970)
Super-steamy erotic story starring Carroll Baker as the wife of a sexually troubled Italian industrialist who is told to chase after younger women to solve his problems. While Dad's away, his son and Mom get involved in an illicit affair. Adolfo Celi and Femi Benussi ("Hatchet for a Honeymoon") also star in this scorching tale.
79-5454 Was $24.99 ***$19.99***

Jet Set Swingers (1970)
Surprise, surprise! If it isn't Metropolitan Opera star Anna Moffo displaying her beauty in the most unlikely fashion in this European sexploiter about high-living lovers who journey from bed to bed. The film boasts "the impact of 'Tango'" and "the sensuality of 'Emmanuelle.'" With Gianna Macchia. AKA: "La Ragazzia Di Nomo Giulio." Dubbed in English.
79-6198 Was $24.99 ***$19.99***

Her And She And Him (1972)
Stylishly sensual sample of European erotica about an aspiring model in Paris who becomes a participant in a relationship with a ravishing lesbian. When her female lover becomes too possessive, the model takes a job with a homosexual painter and his handsome assistant. Then the sparks really fly! Astrid Frank, Nicole Debonne star. 90 min.
83-3014 ***$29.99***

My Bare Lady (1963)
Don't look for any Shavian wit or Lerner and Loewe songs in this early nudie comedy from England, as the bicycling heroine is injured in a mishap and taken in to rest at a nudist colony. Wonder how long it will be before she's "converted" to the joys of naturalist living? Carl Conway, Bridget Leonard star. 62 min.
62-1362 ***$19.99***

The Stewardesses (1969)
These high-flying, swinging sweeties live life to the fullest...in or out of the cockpit! Sex, drugs, and violence are their layover activities...with every willing and able man around! 90 min.
62-1625 ***$19.99***

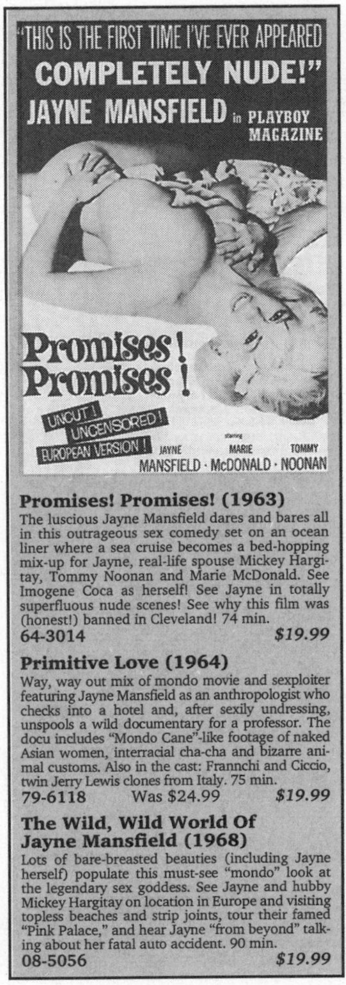
"THIS IS THE FIRST TIME I'VE EVER APPEARED COMPLETELY NUDE!"
JAYNE MANSFIELD in PLAYBOY MAGAZINE
Promises! Promises!
UNCUT! UNCENSORED! EUROPEAN VERSION!
starring JAYNE MANSFIELD · MARIE McDONALD · TOMMY NOONAN

Promises! Promises! (1963)
The luscious Jayne Mansfield dares and bares all in this outrageous sex comedy set on an ocean liner where a sea cruise becomes a bed-hopping mix-up for Jayne, real-life spouse Mickey Hargitay, Tommy Noonan and Marie McDonald. See Imogene Coca as herself! See Jayne in totally superfluous nude scenes! See why this film was (honest!) banned in Cleveland! 74 min.
64-3014 ***$19.99***

Primitive Love (1964)
Way, way out mix of mondo movie and sexploiter featuring Jayne Mansfield as an anthropologist who checks into a hotel and, after sexily undressing, unspools a wild documentary for a professor. The docu includes "Mondo Cane"-like footage of naked Asian women, interracial cha-cha and bizarre animal customs. Also in the cast: Franchi and Ciccio, twin Jerry Lewis clones from Italy. 75 min.
79-6118 Was $24.99 ***$19.99***

The Wild, Wild World Of Jayne Mansfield (1968)
Lots of bare-breasted beauties (including Jayne herself) populate this must-see "mondo" look at the legendary sex goddess. See Jayne and hubby Mickey Hargitay on location in Europe and visiting topless beaches and strip joints, tour their famed "Pink Palace," and hear Jayne "from beyond" talking about her fatal auto accident. 90 min.
08-5056 ***$19.99***

Nine Ages Of Nakedness (1969)
Take a tour of female pulchritude throughout history in this softcore comedy from British girly filmmaker Harrison Marks, as topless beauties from the Stone Age to the Space Age strut their stuff in an attempt to save Marks' ancestors from "feminophobia." All this, plus Charles Gray ("Rocky Horror Picture Show") as the narrator! 88 min.
03-1035 ***$19.99***

All The Way Down (1968)
The Hollywood strip scene is the setting for this sexploiter about a pair of lesbians who excel in a stage act. A fresh approach is needed, so the barmaid with the mammoth mammaries is recruited to partake in the titillating theatrics. With Pat Barrington and Joe Weldon.
03-1597 Was $24.99 ***$19.99***

What's Up Front (1964)
And we're not talking cigarette commercials here! A meek door-to-door drummer gets a new lease on life by becoming a travelling bra salesman, and his clientele includes some of the most buxom babes imaginable. Racy comedy from the creator of "Eegah!" stars Tommy Holden, Marilyn Manning. 90 min.
15-5064 ***$19.99***

The Scavengers (1969)
A raw, brutal tale of a band of Confederate soldiers who tear through a small Kentucky town to rob a Yankee payroll, either raping or killing someone every minute that they wait. Jonathan Bliss, John Riozzi and Uschi Digart star in this softcore serving of savagery and sex. AKA: "Rebel Vixens."
39-1717 Was $24.99 ***$19.99***

Cargo Of Love (1968)
A sordid tale of white slavery focusing on a woman who is drugged and taken to an estate where a pair of New York sisters make sure male guests get exactly what they want. And mostly what they want is to subject the women to torture, degradation and floggings. Can the newest slave get out alive? Sheba Britt and Gloria Izzizary star.
50-5134 Was $24.99 ***$19.99***

My Body Hungers (1967)
After her sister is strangled with a black lace garter belt, a woman decides to find the killer by taking a job at her sibling's place of employment—a strip club. Eventually, she draws the attention of a wealthy mama's boy who may be the culprit. Gretchen Rudolph and John Aristedes star in this seamy Joe Sarno production.
50-5136 Was $24.99 ***$19.99***

Dominique In Daughters Of Lesbos (1969)
A no-holds-barred look at a secret society comprised exclusively of lesbians and their kinky world of S&M, B&D, same-sex love and degradation of men.
50-5137 Was $24.99 ***$19.99***

I Want You (1968)
Take a walk on the wild side with Wanda, a lesbian madam who makes sure her clients and gals get everything they want. From interracial sex to S&M, from lesbianism to orgies, Wanda tries to please everyone—and make lots of money on the side, too. Linda Burns, Tanya and Sophia star in this roughie about perversity and blackmail.
50-5138 Was $24.99 ***$19.99***

1,000 Shapes Of A Female (1963)
A New York art gallery owner commissions a group of Greenwich Village artists to paint a collection of nudes. Each artist has their own unusual technique—from using their hair as a brush to body-painting to stomping on a canvas with paint-covered feet—for immortalizing their gorgeous nude models in this beatnik-era Barry Mahon ("Some Like It Violent") softcore drama. With Dan Craig.
50-5142 Was $24.99 ***$19.99***

I Am Curious (Yellow) (1967)
Controversial softcore film from Sweden that heralded a new era in the cinema's depiction of sensuality. Lena Nyman is an actress playing a sociologist in a film, whose character questions people on the street about sex and politics, and we bear witness to their innermost thoughts and desires. Features several sizzling scenes with female and male nudity. 95 min. In Swedish with English subtitles.
53-6041 Was $59.99 ***$24.99***

Artist's Studio Secrets (1964)
Poor Percy Green. He's an artist who only gets turned on when his female models are clothed, so his wife makes sure the lovelies parading before his palette all show up undressed in this masterpiece of campy Sixties softcore. 78 min.
62-1252 ***$19.99***

Bunny Yeager's Nude Camera (1963)
Pioneering female glamour photographer Bunny Yeager turns her lens on some of the hottest schlagers ever filmed, as the sexiest models in Miami strut their stuff for a girlie magazine shoot. Classic "nudie" drama features Rusty Allen, Allison Louise Downe; from the director of "Cuban Rebel Girls." 62 min.
62-1359 ***$19.99***

Bunny Yeager's Nude Las Vegas (1964)
Playboy photographer Bunny Yeager and her husband, Bud Irwin, play themselves in this risqué Barry Mahon effort in which reel life mirrors real life. The story concerns Peggy, Bunny's friend, who has lost $1,000 gambling in Vegas. With help from a nudie magazine, Bunny has an idea how to get the cash back: shoot a pictorial featuring Peggy and the gals of Glitter Gulch.
79-5620 Was $24.99 ***$19.99***

Erotic Touch Of Hot Skin (1964)
Classic French nudie of two passionate couples pairing up in every permutation possible. When the hot skin really heats up, anything can happen—even murder! With Fabienne Dali and Sophy Hardy. 77 min.
62-1276 ***$19.99***

Revenge Of The Virgins (1966)
For those of you who liked the thrilling mountainside action of "The Treasure of the Sierra Madre," but felt the bandits should have been replaced by a tribe of topless Indian maidens proficient in the art of combat...have we got a film for you!!! Outrageous softcore western romp with the villains packing their very own ".44s." 53 min.
62-1335 ***$19.99***

The Lusting Hours (1967)
The world of prostitution is exposed in this no-holds-barred erotic essay that looks at the underbelly of brothels. See orgies, lesbian lovemaking, whippings and Park Avenue prostitutes. With Anna Riva, Julien Marsh. 73 min.
70-6186 Was $24.99 ***$19.99***

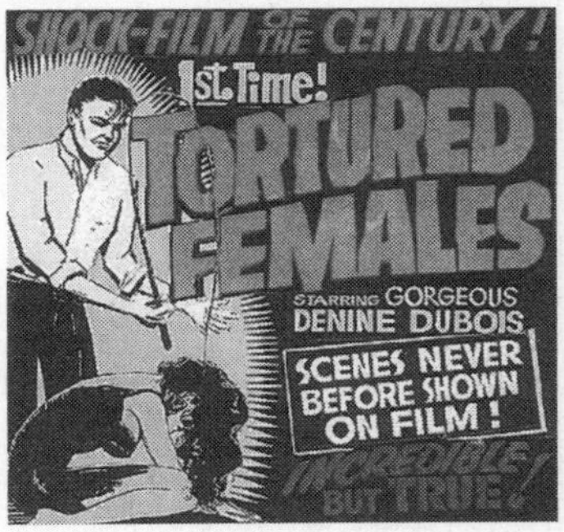
SHOCK-FILM OF THE CENTURY!
1st Time!
TORTURED FEMALES
STARRING GORGEOUS DENINE DUBOIS
SCENES NEVER BEFORE SHOWN ON FILM!
INCREDIBLE! BUT TRUE!

Tortured Females (1965)
Gorgeous, huge-chested Denine Dubois plays a young woman whose trip to the country turns terrifying when she's apprehended by a nasty trucker who assaults her and takes her to the operator of a white slave ring. Soon, she's whipped into submission while watching the fate of other prisoners. Will she ever escape this life of humiliation?
50-5144 Was $24.99 ***$19.99***

Inga (1968)
This classic drive-in sizzler tells of a virginal 17-year-old who comes to live with her free-spirited, sexually liberated aunt after her parents die in a car accident. While there, Inga gets it on with her relative's younger lover while experiencing the ultimate ecstasy of womanhood. Marie Liljedahl stars in this saucy Swedish import. Dubbed in English.
77-7023 Was $24.99 ***$19.99***

Campus Swingers (1969)
A drive-in classic from Germany in which super-sexy coeds slither and seduce their ways to good grades with the professors while wooing fellow students. Filled with sideburns, zoom shots, enticing young women and filmed on location "with participating students and their guardians." With Ingrid Steeger, Evelyne Traeger.
79-5038 ***$29.99***

Help Wanted: Female (1968)
Weird sexual acts, S&M-inspired sequences and hallucinogenic hijinks highlight this seedy study of a bad girl who picks up a guy who gives her more than she bargained for. A prime example of the adults-only drugs-and-sex-gone-amok genre of the Sixties.
79-5046 Was $24.99 ***$19.99***

The Minx (1969)
Sex, lies and corruption in the corporate world, as a group of executives try to blackmail the officers of another company with photos depicting their promiscuity. The wife of the mastermind of the blackmailing scheme hires a detective to find her hubby in uncompromising positions, too. With Jan Sterling, Robert Rodan and music by The Cyrkle.
79-5067 Was $24.99 ***$19.99***

Fly Now, Pay Later (1969)
There's slavery, lesbianism, S&M, whippings and more in this depraved story of a drug ring that uses a new mind-blowing drug on beautiful stewardesses. Charlotte Rouse, Shep Wild and Cherie Walters star. 75 min.
79-5068 Was $24.99 ***$19.99***

Women Of The World (1963)
Beneath the glamorous clothes and the make-up, what are women really like? This bold look at the feminine species from "Mondo Cane" director Gualtiero Jacopetti looks at the "window girls" of Hamburg, Hong Kong's "children of the night," "Swedish beach babes" and more sorts of women, many of whom expose themselves for the first time. Peter Ustinov hosts.
79-5025 Was $24.99 ***$19.99***

The Defilers (1964)
Loosely based on John Fowles' "The Collector," this classic exploitationer tells the story of two wealthy, pot-smoking creeps who terrorize and imprison a young woman who has recently moved to L.A. from Minnesota. Snatched, snared and strapped, she tries to salvage her dignity. Mai Jansson, Jerome Eden star in this David F. Friedman production. 69 min.
79-5029 Was $24.99 ***$19.99***

Doris Wishman

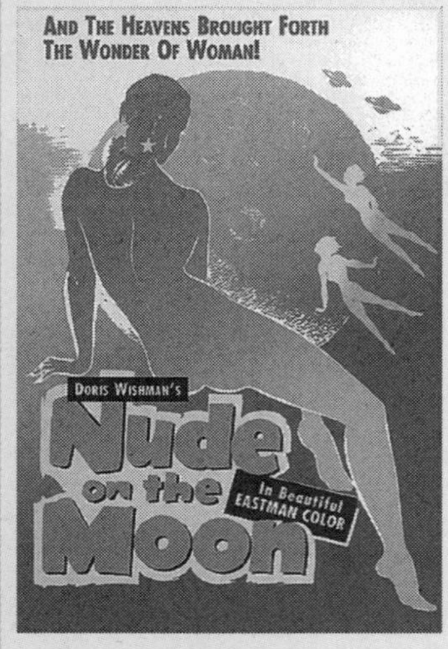
AND THE HEAVENS BROUGHT FORTH
THE WONDER OF WOMAN!
DORIS WISHMAN'S
Nude
on the
Moon
In Beautiful
EASTMAN COLOR

Nude On The Moon (1961)
A whacked-out Doris Wishman nudie classic about two scientists who travel to the moon and discover a group of "moon dolls" who sport antennae and beehive hairdos...and nothing else! Way, way out stuff, featuring the poignant song "I'm Mooning Over You (My Little Moon Doll)." 83 min.
79-5585 Was $24.99 ***$19.99***

Blaze Starr Goes Nudist (1963)
Baltimore's brazen ecdysiastic sensation, portrayed in the Paul Newman film "Blaze," made her screen debut in this Doris Wishman softcore romp as a stripper who takes time off from her wildly sexy routines to visit a nudist colony. See Blaze take it all off in her pulchritudinous prime. AKA: "Blaze Starr: The Original."
79-5022 ***$19.99***

Gentlemen Prefer Nature Girls (1963)
A Doris Wishman nudie classic about a man fired from his job after his boss discovers he's a nudist. After taking a job at the nudist colony he frequents, the man joins forces with a business associate to lure his former boss to the place and show him the carefree nudist lifestyle. Lon Axelon, William Mayer star.
79-5679 Was $24.99 ***$19.99***

Diary Of A Nudist (1964)
A classic early '60s "nudist" film from sexploitation master Doris Wishman ("Double Agent 73"). A female investigative reporter goes undercover (and unclothed) at the Sunny Palms Lodge, where members lounge, soak up the sun, play shuffleboard and swim in the nude.
79-5000 ***$24.99***

My Brother's Wife (1965)
Doris Wishman directed this sordid sexploitative melodrama, told in flashback form, about the recollections of a torrid menage a trois involving a man, his oversexed sister-in-law and his girlfriend. There's lots of black lingerie and a lascivious lesbian scene. June Roberts, Sam Stewart, Darlene Bennett star. 72 min.
79-5003 Was $24.99 ***$19.99***

Bad Girls Go To Hell (1965)
A naive small-town girl travels to New York. Dreaming of fame, but bereft of money, talent and common sense, she is easy prey for sex-seeking lechers and lesbians in this egregious softcore melodrama by Doris Wishman.
79-5586 Was $24.99 ***$19.99***

Another Day, Another Man (1966)
What a difference a day makes, especially in the life of Ann, whose struggle to make ends meet when her husband becomes ill forces her into the world of prostitution. Doris Wishman directed this on-the-edge sexploitationer starring Tony Gregory, Barbi Kemp and lots of hanging plants.
79-5042 ***$19.99***

A Taste Of Flesh (1967)
Doris Wishman's bizarre "ruffie" tells the sordid tale of a pair of assassins who take over the apartment of a lesbian couple, which leads to double-crosses, exotic sex and, finally, murder. Cleo Nova and Layla Peters star. 70 min.
79-5032 Was $24.99 ***$19.99***

Indecent Desires (1967)
Strange sexual mumbo-jumbo occurs when a poor schnook uses a magic ring and a doll he finds in a trashcan to control the sexy gal he's obsessed with. When he wears the ring, he can do things to the doll that the gal can feel, including caressing, fornicating and hurting. Sharon Kent stars; directed by Doris Wishman (under the name "Louis Silverman").
79-5444 Was $24.99 ***$19.99***

The Amazing Transplant (1970)
Notorious exploitation thriller (directed by a pseudonymous Doris Wishman) about a young man who thinks a penis transplant from his dying friend will help his non-existent sex life, but finds that the operation only adds to his already confused state of mind. An amazing movie, starring Juan Fernandez, Larry Hunter and early X-rated film star Kim Pope.
79-5436 Was $24.99 ***$19.99***

Deadly Weapons (1970)
Well, what would you call a 70-plus-inch bustline? The unbelievably-endowed Chesty Morgan steals the screen (no one else could squeeze on with her!) as she uses her cannonball convexities to fight mobsters in this drive-in classic, which also features the legendary Harry Reems. Doris Wishman directs. 76 min.
79-5584 Was $24.99 ***$19.99***

Double Agent 73 (1974)
Chesty Morgan is the special agent, assigned to stop members of a dope-smuggling ring, who has a camera implanted in her gigantic "secret weapons." In order to snap the pictures to identify the bad guys, she must unsnap her bra and let those monsters loose. Doris Wishman directs. 73 min.
79-5583 Was $24.99 ***$19.99***

The Immoral Three (1972)
A tempting trio of illegitimately-born sisters have one year to avenge their mother's murder and claim a $3,000,000 inheritance in softcore filmmaker Doris Wishman's action-packed, sex-soaked saga. Cindi Boudreau, Sandra Kay star. AKA: "Hotter than Hell."
70-3147 Was $24.99 ***$19.99***

Keyholes Are For Peeping (1972)
Notorious cult classic starring Sammy Petrillo ("Bela Lugosi Meets a Brooklyn Gorilla") as a phony marriage counselor who tries to help a group of goofy patients. Meanwhile, the Spanish superintendent can't help but peeking at the building's sexy tenants. Philip Stahl also stars in Doris Wishman's incredible nudie farce. 77 min.
79-5425 ***$19.99***

Let Me Die A Woman (1978)
Notorious exploitation item from director Doris Wishman that lets you "see a man become a woman before your very eyes!" This mondo movie features real transsexuals, grisly surgery footage, a lively discussion of dildoes and a case study of a former sailor now known as Debbie. Dr. Leo Wollman hosts and offers an amazing lecture on the subject. 77 min.
79-5534 Was $24.99 ***$19.99***

Wild Honey (1969)
An 18-year-old farm girl loses her virginity to a farmhand, much to her strict father's displeasure. He then tries to rape her, and she heads for Los Angeles. There she gets involved with the hippie scene, filled with LSD, orgies, prostitution and more!
79-5146 ***$19.99***

The Games Men Play (1968)
When there's an outbreak of bubonic plague, six couples find themselves quarantined in a seedy hotel. Soon, they explore a number of sexual interests, and their relationships change as their sexualities are explored. Maria Antinea, Elsa Daniel star. 92 min.
79-5070 Was $24.99 ***$19.99***

That Tender Touch (1969)
A young orphan is almost raped, so she turns her attentions to a sexual relationship with an older woman. When the girl meets and marries a sensitive man, the lesbian affair ends...until a chance meeting at a party. Sue Bernard, Bee Tompkins star in this sexually powerful tale. 88 min.
79-5074 Was $24.99 ***$19.99***

Over 18...And Ready (1968)
A porno filmmaker and his lesbian talent agent wife lure young women into their web of kinkiness in this lurid shocker that's been called a "more bounce to the ounce show." With Mary M'Rea, Larry Martinelli. Formerly "18...and Ready."
79-5090 Was $24.99 ***$19.99***

Henry's Night In (1969)
A henpecked husband finds an 18th-century diary which features a formula for invisibility. Soon, he's an unseen superstud who seduces a group of gorgeous gals. "More mammary manipulation than any other film in motion picture history!" With Forman Shane, Barbara Kline. 75 min.
79-5091 Was $24.99 ***$19.99***

Hot-Blooded Woman (1965)
A ravishing blonde newlywed is raped by a hobo gang after she dances for them, so her husband sends her to a psychiatrist who has her put into a mental hospital in order to cure her exhibitionist desires. Risqué drama stars Gregg Pappas and Beverly Oliver.
79-5092 Was $24.99 ***$19.99***

Sock It To Me Baby (1968)
No, it's not a documentary on "Rowan & Martin's Laugh-In," but a seedy sexploitation item about a middle-aged fellow who lusts after his teenage niece, unaware that his sexually bored wife has been involved with the sweet young thing already. With Ileen Wreffer, Larry Hunter, Illia Souvern. 80 min.
79-5077 Was $24.99 ***$19.99***

Rio Nudo (1969)
No, this isn't a softcore version of a Wayne/Hawks western, but rather an unflinching look at Rio De Janeiro's Wed light district. Prostitutes, orgies and exotic dancers are featured in a "Mondo Rio" filled with wildly sensual sights and sounds. AKA: "Rio Uncensored."
79-5088 Was $24.99 ***$19.99***

Career Bed (1969)
A horny stage mother causes all sorts of trouble for her sexy, young, aspiring actress daughter, seducing producers, photographers and even her future son-in-law in order to get the best for her child...and herself! Liza Duran, Honey Hunter, James David star; directed by Joel Reed ("Bloodsucking Freaks"). 79 min.
79-5089 Was $24.99 ***$19.99***

Kitten In The Cage (1968)
Kinky erotic drama about a gorgeous woman on the run from jewel thieves who want her to lead them to a cache of stolen gems. She hides out with a lesbian go-go dancer, eventually submitting to the dancer's desires, before she is caught and sadistically tortured by the thieves. Miriam Eliot stars. 79 min.
79-5093 Was $24.99 ***$19.99***

Naughty New Orleans (1962)
The Crescent City is the site for a group of hubba-hubba strippers to sensuously strut their stuff. There's Stormy and Rita Parker, Pork Chops and Kidney Stew, Aluette and Carla: an amazing array of gals who give new meaning to the phrase "Big Easy."
79-5094 ***$19.99***

Jenny, Wife/Child (1965)
A sexy country wife seduces a young and innocent farmhand after she discovers that her husband is having an affair with the local slut. A real sleazy sexploitationer from down South!
79-5152 ***$19.99***

The Love Commune (1969)
Fifteen—count 'em—15 hot-to-trot female dropouts take to a one-room commune, and they soon experience kinky sex and drugs, hippie style. A real Sixties artifact, this one contains lots of nudity and far-out stuff.
79-5160 Was $24.99 ***$19.99***

Crazy Wild And Crazy (1965)
A charming and sexy nudie cutie about an amateur photographer who wants to break into the erotic film-making game, so he buys a movie camera, hires 20—count 'em, 20—fantastically proportioned women and really goes to town! 63 min.
79-5176 ***$19.99***

The Agony Of Love (1966)
A suburban housewife, bored with a dull married life, rents her own apartment to indulge in her sexual fantasies. And soon she's really into the kinky stuff, from S & M to orgies to prostitution. Then hubby attends the same orgy! With Pat Barrington, Sam Taylor.
79-5178 Was $24.99 ***$19.99***

Hot Spur (1968)
Savage, sex-filled Western opus about a Mexican boy who witnesses a group of disturbed cowpokes rape his teenage sister. After she dies from the incident, the boy seeks revenge, and he gets it years later when he takes a job at the group leader's ranch. James Arena, Joseph Mascolo and Virginia Gordon star in this Bob Cresse ("Love Camp 7") production. 91 min.
79-5163 ***$19.99***

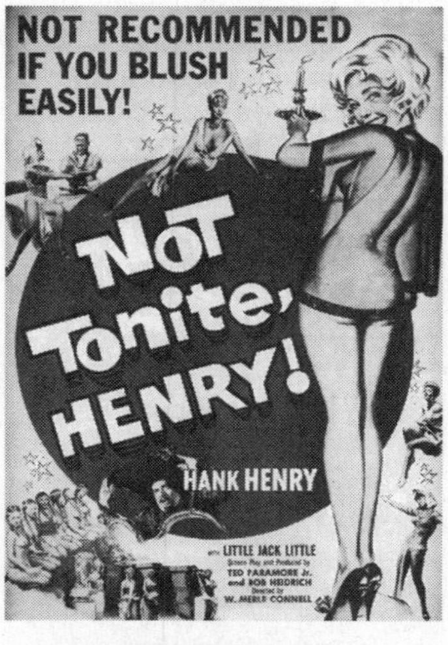
NOT RECOMMENDED
IF YOU BLUSH
EASILY!
Not
Tonite,
HENRY!
HANK HENRY
LITTLE JACK LITTLE

Not Tonight, Henry! (1960)
Classic "nudie cutie" in which Henry, tired of his frigid wife, fantasizes about some of the hottest ladies in history, including Cleopatra, Pocahontas and Lucrezia Borgia. Comic Hank Henry stars as Henry.
79-5189 Was $24.99 ***$19.99***

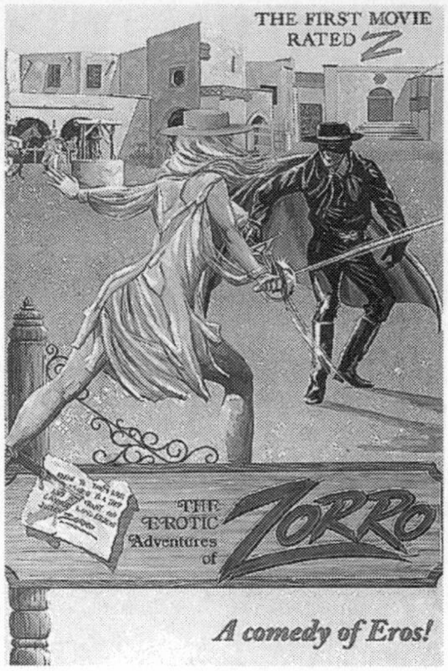
THE FIRST MOVIE
RATED Z
THE
EROTIC
Adventures
of
ZORRO
A comedy of Eros!

The Erotic Adventures Of Zorro (1969)
"Out of the night, when the full moon is bright" comes this sex-mad swordsman who takes off everything but his mask while seducing the señoritas of Old California. This racy rendition of the swashbuckling sensation is offered in its uncut, "Z"-rated glory, complete with the infamous "snake attacking the woman" scene. 102 min.
79-5240 Was $24.99 ***$19.99***

Suburban Pagans (1968)
Welcome to Suburbia, home of Family Values. But in this film, the lid of Suburbia is blown open—wide open—to reveal love cults, wife-swapping, lesbianism and much, much more.
79-5187 ***$19.99***

The Big Snatch (1968)
A savage sexcursion from producer David F. Friedman involving a carnal-seeking kook who, along with his mute henchman, kidnaps five gorgeous gals and forces them to perform degrading sexual acts. Their revenge is sweet...in a real sicko way!
79-5191 Was $24.99 ***$19.99***

Eat, Drink And Make Merrie (1969)
A horny young woman takes on all interested parties in a boarding house populated by horny men. Her younger sister watches her sibling's sexual escapades and tries to emulate her. Adrianne, Judy Farr and Chris Meyer star. 64 min.
79-5208 ***$19.99***

Surfside Sex (1967)
Hang 10 with this hippie-era sexploiter about two groovy couples who go for a beachfront frolic in the nude, then come across a secluded house inhabited by an eccentric writer. Kinky couplings, LSD trips and a surprise visit from the writer's snobby fiancée play parts in this scorching, unpredictable drama.
79-5238 Was $24.99 ***$19.99***

Acapulco Uncensored (1968)
Hidden cameras reveal the seamier side of one of the world's wildest cities. For the first time, see Acapulco uncovered, where young women perform all sorts of incredibly perverse acts in the secret houses of pleasure. 71 min.
79-5239 Was $24.99 ***$19.99***

Hip, Hot And 21 (1967)
The incredible Lorna Maitland, star of Russ Meyer's "Lorna," is featured in this shocking sexploitationer about a Southern belle who falls into a life of sin, sex and drugs when she arrives in the big city with her new husband. Diane Darcel, Pat Crenshaw co-star. 78 min.
79-5212 ***$19.99***

Wanda: The Sadistic Hypnotist (1969)
Watch the satanic Wanda whip guys and gals into a frenzy in this sordid mix of sex, sadomasochism and the supernatural. Katharine Shubeck is the ruler of a cult where kinky activities and hypnotism go hand in hand, in a nudity-filled thriller not for the squeamish. Dick Dangerfield and Janine Sweet also star. 75 min.
79-5223 ***$19.99***

Erika's Hot Summer (1969)
Erica Gavin, of "Vixen" fame, excels in this spectacularly sensual tale, playing a woman who seeks the ultimate pleasure. She eventually finds the proper man, and the two perform some of the most erotic sex ever captured for the camera. But there's that problem with the man's other girlfriend. Walt Phillips and Merci Montello also star.
79-5229 Was $24.99 ***$19.99***

Scare Their Pants Off! (1968)
That's the plan two bored but oversexed guys have for getting gals. They use terror, drugs and special effects to persuade the babes to have sex with a guy with a distorted face, make love to a fake Tibetan guru and experience torture by a pair of fascists. Gee, what's wrong with those classes at the Learning Annex?
79-5230 ***$19.99***

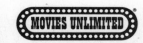

The Immoral Mr. Teas (1958)
The groundbreaking softcore romp from director Russ Meyer that started the sex-in-movies explosion. Mr. Teas is that man-next-door who likes to look at women...nude women...and as his immorality peaks, so will yours. Bill Teas, Ann Peters, Dawn Dennelle star. 63 min.
34-1008 **$59.99**

Eve And The Handyman (1961)
A classic early nudie comedy from director Russ Meyer about a repressed and lonely handyman who gets a taste of female company when he comes in contact with "the modern art world" and its fantastically-figured models. Eve Meyer and Anthony-James Ryan star in this film that's sex-sationally different!
34-1015 **$59.99**

Wild Gals Of The Naked West (1962)
Well, whoopee-ti-yi-yo, get along, big dogies! Russ Meyer's Western spoof is a-whoopin' with wenches with wild whoppers, shoot-outs, ornery villains and more! Evil Snake Wolf and buxom galpal Goldie Nuggets are headed off at the pass by a five-foot-tall hero with a three-foot gun. The movie that promises blazing bras...and delivers! With Judie Williams. AKA: "The Immoral West and How It Was Lost."
34-1013 **$59.99**

Lorna (1964)
Forget compromise. Forget artistic surrender. Director Russ Meyer has none of that in this tale of an insatiable, fully developed girl in women's clothing whose erotic urges are too much for her husband. Lorna Maitland, a lust-driven Euro-sexpot, stars in the title role. 78 min.
34-1002 **$59.99**

Mudhoney (1965)
Lorna Maitland, that Teutonic titwillow from Germany, is back and in the sack in this Russathon of backwoods ribaldry. Hate, love, and the bodacious Rena Horton play supporting roles. AKA: "Rage of Flesh." 92 min.
34-1003 **$59.99**

Motor Psycho (1965)
From the same Meyer-ian mold as "Faster, Pussycat! Kill! Kill!" comes this whirlpool of wayward desires, lurid libidos and snake bites. Three motorcycle-riding creeps lead a violent and sadistic spree until a young veterinarian and a busty Cajun gal say "Enough!" and try to stop them! Brutal! Shocking! Stars Alex Rocco, Haji, Holle K. Winters. 73 min.
34-1014 **$59.99**

Mondo Topless (1966)
Or, "Thanks for the Mammaries." Bazoombas, whoppers, jugs, breasts, bubbles, headlights, zingers, sallies, schlagers, double-barrels. An exotic expose of erotic excess: Strippers In Heat. Meet Babette Bardot, Sin Lenee, Darla Paris and Darlene Gray. Life's not over past 40, it's just beginning to bounce. 61 min.
34-1004 **$59.99**

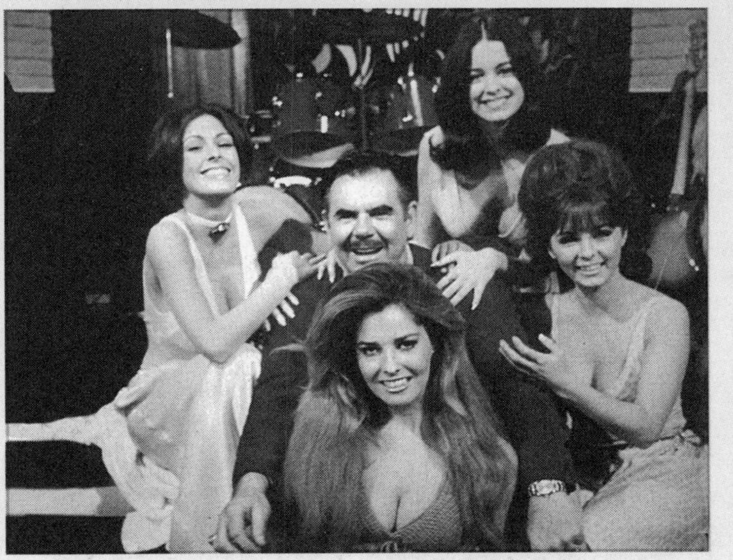

Russ Meyer

Faster, Pussycat! Kill! Kill! (1966)
A new breed of superwomen—some butch, some bitch, all bountiful—go at it in this heated Meyer melodrama about the nasty side of femininity. They came from go-go bars and elsewhere into the desert. To battle. And tantalize. And tempt. And kill! Kill! Tura Santana, Stuart Lancaster, Lori Williams star; title song by The Bostweeds. 83 min.
34-1009 **$59.99**

Common-Law Cabin (1967)
This is a scorching, sexually satisfying survey of Big Women, Big Appetites and Big Trouble. Meet Alaina Capri (42-24-36), Babette Bardot (42-24-36), and Adele Rein (42-24-36)—three innocent girls trapped in heavenly womanly bodies. 70 min.
34-1011 **$59.99**

Good Morning... And Good-Bye (1968)
Russ Meyer tackles contemporary relationships and gets a handful. Go-go dancers, nudes, swervy-curved teenage honeys and haunting seductresses populate the proceedings. Carol Peters and Haji star. 80 min.
34-1010 **$59.99**

Finders Keepers... Lovers Weepers (1968)
A couple of thugs get theirs when they involve themselves in a strip joint and a pack of Wild Women rearin' to go. Russ socks it to Suburbia, and not a stone or gal with big bangers is left unturned. 72 min.
34-1012 **$59.99**

Cherry & Harry & Raquel (1969)
Narcotics smuggling, Russ Meyer-style. Dune buggies, big gals, macho men, blazing guns. Bosom-vast Uschi Digart and Mrs. Soul star with Charles Napier—all done in a way you've got to ad-Meyer. 71 min.
34-1006 **$59.99**

Vixen (1969)
A landmark sex film. Erica Gavin is it: blowsy and bitchin' gal of the woods sure to whet your...er...whatever. A lusty lesbian sequence, the fish dance and more. A landmark sex film! 70 min.
34-1007 **$59.99**

Beyond The Valley Of The Dolls (1970)
Hollywood soap operas get shattered in Russ Meyer's outrageous chronicle of an all-girl rock group's rise to fame and their eventual seduction by sex, drugs and rock and roll. Dolly Reed, Cynthia Myers and Marcia McBroom play the members of the Carrie Nations band. Erica Gavin, Edy Williams and Charles Napier also star in this cult classic, written by Meyer and film critic Roger Ebert. 109 min.
04-1183 **$19.99**

Blacksnake! (1972)
Long-unseen Russ Meyer epic is set on a Caribbean island in the 1800s which is run by a tyrannical, whip-cracking leader named Lady Susan. A black slave who has been the target of cruel punishment decides to lead a revolt against her. Anouska Hempel, David Warbeck and Percy Herbert star in this savage epic Russ fans will surely "ad-Meyer." AKA: "Sweet Suzy." 83 min.
34-1016 Letterboxed **$59.99**

Supervixens (1975)
You won't believe Charles Napier as the rugged Harry, tempting the tenacious torsos of the likes of Uschi Digart, Shari Eubank, Haji and Sharon Kelly. Shocking in its frankness, startling in its violence, busting with female delights, a hilarious Russ Meyer classic!! 106 min.
34-1005 **$59.99**

Up! (1976)
How far can a movie go? A parade of dictators and Greek choruses, Martin Borman and muscular men, cops and robbers and killer fish. Plus, huge, Huge HUGE WOMEN! Kitten Natividad, Margo Winchester, Candy Samples, and other double-bubbled babes delight in this far-out flick. 80 min.
34-1001 **$59.99**

Beneath The Valley Of The Ultravixens (1979)
Prepare to be blown away by this outrageous look at Everytown, U.S.A.—where the bad are bad, the good are good, the ugly are ugly the big are enormous! Ferment your thoughts in phenomenally-busted femmes Flovilla Thatch, Lola Langusta and Junkyard Sal. With "Kitten" Natividad; co-written by Roger Ebert. 93 min.
34-1000 **$59.99**

Sex Freedom In Germany (1969)
It's been called "The 'Mondo Cane' of Way-Out German Sex Practices," but that's underestimating the kinky sexcursions captured here. From lesbian liaisons to homosexual priests! Sensual communes to male prostitutes! Strippers with whips to other carnal perversions that must be seen to be believed! It's all here—and more!! 79 min.
79-5078 Was $24.99 **$19.99**

Moonlighting Wives (1964)
Sizzling exposé about an unhappy housewife who has a new career in mind: prostitution. Joining her in her new occupation are a crew of other despondent homemakers who do more than just stuff envelopes to earn extra cash. Joan Nash, Diane Vivienne and noted belly dancer Fatima star in this Joe Sarno production. 80 min.
79-5079 Was $24.99 **$19.99**

Dracula, The Dirty Old Man (1968)
This has been called "the ultimate nudie horror comedy," and it's easy to see why. A descendant of the famous bloodsucker is joined by his servant in search of beautiful virgins during their trip to America. When the vampire's aide falls in love with one of the victims, look out! Bill Whitton, Vince Kelly, Ann Hollis star. This is the rare, uncut print. 71 min.
79-5082 Was $24.99 **$19.99**

Space Thing (1968)
An outrageous sexy sci-fi story about the sultry crew of sadistic lesbians commanded by Captain Mother. Set in the year 2069, this erotic adventure features explorations into space, sex and campy humor. Produced by David Friedman; With Paula Pleasure, Steve Stunning. 69 min.
79-5083 Was $24.99 **$19.99**

Brand Of Shame (1968)
A sexciting erotic Western that's guaranteed to put you back in the saddle again. A madam and her gang of lovely prostitutes offer the heroes and bad guys service with a smile in this sensuous sagebrush saga that features stagecoaches, horny gunmen, lesbians and whipping. A David Friedman production.
79-5085 Was $24.99 **$19.99**

Hot Thrills And Warm Chills (1966)
A wild sexploitation item featuring Lorna Maitland of Russ Meyer fame and buxomy Rita Alexander. Four hot women—all street gang refugees—try to pull off a dangerous heist in Rio during Mardi Gras. Complete with a Latin garage band soundtrack. 80 min.
79-5086 Was $24.99 **$19.99**

Rent-A-Girl (1965)
A career woman joins a modeling agency, but she discovers that the place is actually a house of ill repute...and the pimps continually pocket the cash! She really regrets her new occupation when she partakes in an orgy where she's whipped and branded!
79-5148 Was $24.99 **$19.99**

Dr. Sex (1964)
A nudie with the cuties, this sexy comedy tells the story of an ever-horny psychiatrist and his group of exotic and erotic patients. Taking their turns on the couch are strippers, naked female ghosts, real live mannequins and more. All presented in warm, fleshtone color! AKA: "The Strange Loves of Dr. Sex."
79-5030 Was $24.99 **$19.99**

Aroused (1966)
A distraught bartender who has been killing prostitutes is tracked down by one of his victim's lovers, who recruits a young cop to investigate the case. Wild sex drama stars Steve Hollister, Fleurett Carter and Janine Lenon. 78 min.
79-5103 **$19.99**

Country Girl (1968)
A group of city slickers land in the boondocks and get some good ol' country hospitality when they decide to engage in kinky sexual swapping. This is Southern Gothic of the sordid sort, featuring wild and willing hillbilly horniness. With Marie Campbell and Jean Wilson. 65 min.
79-5105 **$19.99**

Brazen Women Of Balzac (1969)
There's nothing droll about the stories in this erotic West German opus about some frisky, big-breasted frauleins who are featured in a wild case of mistaken identity and orgies. With Drew Zimmerman.
79-5109 Was $24.99 **$19.99**

The Lustful Turk (1969)
The amorous title character loves gals, and he has scores of them in his harem. Filmed on desert locales, this David Friedman production shows what happens when he raids Europe for their most desirable women.
79-5127 **$19.99**

Confessions Of A Sexy Photographer (1969)
Two horny guys have an idea on how to get girls: set up an all-babe photo shoot and the women will flock to see them. The plan works, and soon the hottest models around pose provocatively in this erotic European import.
79-5289 Was $24.99 **$19.99**

The Commuter Game (1969)
Advertised as "the first inside look at what really goes on inside those apartments," this seedy sexathon tells the story of two suburban husbands who rent an apartment in the city as a place to take the chicks they meet. Soon, their wives get into the act, and lesbianism, swapping and other acts of kinkiness become the name of the game.
79-5106 **$19.99**

Starlet (1968)
One of the groundbreaking films of the adult genre, David Friedman's production offers a sexposé of the adult film industry, detailing a pretty young woman who seeks stardom but finds sleazy producers and downtrodden souls in the business. Features some explicit sex scenes and Stuart Lancaster, the "old man" of Russ Meyer movies fame.
79-5128 **$19.99**

A Smell Of Honey, A Swallow Of Brine (1966)
Sharon was hot, beautiful and manipulative! She teased men to their limits, then accused them of rape, ruining their lives in the process. Eventually, Sharon met her match in the form of Tony, the man who gave her a taste of her own medicine. Stacy Walker stars in this sexploitation milestone from producer David F. Friedman. 70 min.
79-5031 Was $24.99 **$19.99**

The Girl Grabbers (1968)
Seedy, sexploitative look at a ring of girl smugglers and rapists who prowl the streets of New York. After his girlfriend is raped, a man infiltrates the gang of thugs responsible for the deed. Paul Cox, Jackie Richards star. 89 min.
79-5069 Was $24.99 **$19.99**

Sinderella And The Golden Bra (1964)
We all know about the famous Cinderella fairy tale, right? Well, here's the "Sinderella" story, in which the Prince must search for the woman whose breasts fit the golden bra! Mountains of merriment and song ensue with Suzanne Sybele, Bill Gaskin and Sidney Lassick. AKA: "Cindy and Her Golden Dress." 81 min.
79-5098 Was $24.99 **$19.99**

The Ultimate Voyeur (1969)
He's a Peeping Tom whose sexual fantasies have become stranger and stranger, so he picks up a troubled young girl who, he hopes, can deliver the ultimate thrill. She plays his perverse partner and things get even kinkier. A truly sordid affair!
79-5102 Was $24.99 **$19.99**

Lust Weekend (1967)
A truly depraved piece of sleaze-arama from the early days of sexploitation, directed by Ron Sullivan (Henri Pachard of adult film fame). Kidnapping, degradation, sexual enslavement and depravity play a part in this tale of a happily-married couple whose lives are shattered when they become involved with a sadistic cult. Claire Adams stars. AKA: "Lost Weekend." 70 min.
79-5247 Was $24.99 **$19.99**

The Notorious Concubines (1969)
Set in 13th-century China, this one-of-a-kind epic tells of the lives and loves of a sexually unfulfilled people near the end of the Sung Dynasty. Murder, seduction and revenge are the elements you can find in this lavish historical-action-martial arts-nudie experience from Japan. With Tomoko Mayama. 90 min.
79-5248 Was $24.99 **$19.99**

Venus In Furs (1967)
The "other" version of the Sacher-Maschoch classic is a sexplicit journey into depravity and bondage. Meet Venus, the goddess of pleasure who rules an empire of sordid pleasures. Man's darkest fantasies collide in this story of hatred and desire about a whip-happy matron. With "Elinore" and Shep Wild. 65 min.
79-5249 Was $24.99 **$19.99**

The Girl With The Hungry Eyes (1967)
She was the girl who played both sides of the fence, a true-blue bisexual who goes on a rampage when her oversexed girlfriend runs off with a man. See what she does to get her gal pal back. There's catfights, lesbian encounters and more in this titillator starring Cathy Crowfoot and Vicky Dee. 85 min.
79-5251 Was $24.99 **$19.99**

The Acid Eaters (1968)
Get into the groove with this film filled with anti-social significance. A group of thrill-seeking businessmen go hog wild when they find a cache of LSD. Soon they're way out on a trip filled with non-stop sexual kicks. Bric Wall and Buckie Buck star in this rare David F. Friedman adult happening. 69 min.
79-5252 **$19.99**

Girls Come Too (1963)
This is actually two movies that were edited together: a nudie classic by Irving Klaw called "Nature's Sweethearts," with Marie Stinger, and scenes of "Pickles and Beaver," a 1966 sex film. You can thank the Supreme Court's decision that complete nudity is no longer obscene, which inspired the producers.
79-5145 **$19.99**

Heat Of Madness (1966)
A nudie photographer with a sexual problem gets a job on "Great Sex Murders" magazine and goes to town, placing models in all sorts of weird bondage and crime settings. The fake violence confuses him even more, leading to a near-rape and violence. Sordid psychological stuff starring Kevin Scott and Jennifer Laird. 81 min.
79-5312 Was $24.99 ***$19.99***

Pagan Island (1960)
What do you do when you land on a remote island populated exclusively by gorgeous, large-breasted native women? Well, not much, since the women hate men and have you figured as their next human sacrifice! Luckily, one nubile native gal wants to save you. A naughty, shot-in-Florida nudiethon from Barry Mahon which also features a giant clam.
79-5332 Was $24.99 ***$19.99***

The Office Party (1968)
The sexy secretaries of the Harris Company decide to throw a party and it gets way out of hand. Soon, they're engaging in sex with their bosses, while the office boy tries on a bra and a gay janitor gets it on in a closet with another guy. Dianne Davis and Larry Tanner partake in this promiscuous party. 74 min.
79-5385 Was $24.99 ***$19.99***

She Mob (1968)
Big Shim—"the bitchiest dyke in the world"—hires a man to satisfy five hot-to-trot prison escapees. When the stud plots to kidnap Big Shim's "property," the red-hot mama goes wild, using lingerie and whips for revenge. Marni Castle stars in this outrageous flick that exposes "erotic sex practices of the butches and dykes of the weird world!" 79 min.
79-5388 Was $24.99 ***$19.99***

Fandango (1969)
When a group of gold prospectors decide to take the beautiful women of pleasure of the Fandango Saloon away from a lecherous gang of outlaws, the ornery crooks don't take it so easily. Shootings and kidnappings ensue, with the gals and good guys battling against the nasty criminals. Sexciting Western exploiter.
79-5434 ***$19.99***

Behind Locked Doors (1969)
This journey into degradation tells of a group of party girls stranded on a highway who seek refuge in an old home nearby. Little do they realize that it's the headquarters of the demented Mr. Bradley, whose love research includes forceful torture, lesbianism and more. Joyce Denner, Eve Reeves star. 80 min.
79-5439 Was $24.99 ***$19.99***

Unholy Matrimony (1968)
A magazine editor hires a woman to pose as his wife in order to investigate a story on sexually swinging couples. Soon, the two are hot on the trail of amorous housewives, swapping games, kinky pool parties and LSD experimentation. 78 min.
79-5442 ***$19.99***

The Nude Scrapbook (1964)
A successful photographer of nudes reviews his best work and they come to life, all displaying their amazing bodies for his (and your) pleasure. If you like blondes, brunettes and/or redheads, you're sure to want to flip through this scrapbook. 64 min.
79-5449 Was $24.99 ***$19.99***

The Bed... And How To Make It (1966)
A popular motel is the place where young Ellen discovers kinky sex and the strange desires adults have when she takes a job at her aunt and uncle's establishment. Working as a maid, Ellen gets involved in steamy affairs that lead to blackmail and danger.
79-5421 Was $24.99 ***$19.99***

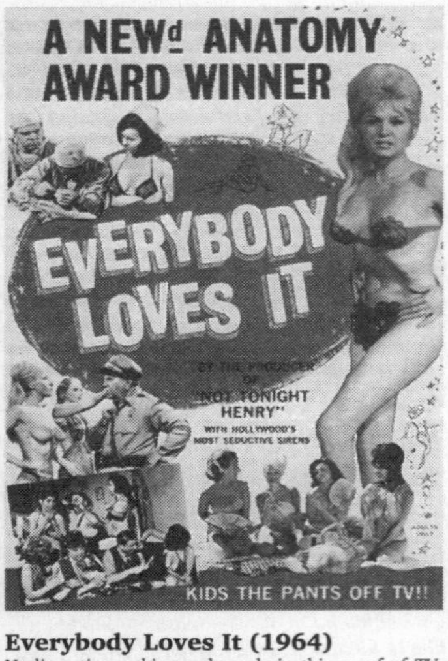

Everybody Loves It (1964)
Nudie-cutie wackiness abounds in this spoof of TV, circa the early 1960s. Sexy skits satirize "Combat!," "Naked City," "Ben Casey" and others. Chockfull of naughty humor, naked bodies and comic sketches, this recently discovered gem features Little Jack Little of "Not Tonite, Henry" fame.
79-5390 Was $24.99 ***$19.99***

White Slaves Of Chinatown (1964)
The first of the notorious "Olga" movies introduces the warped woman who lures gals of all sorts to her New York brownstone and subjects them to drugs, beatings and other unspeakable tortures until they do her bidding. Produced by "Glen or Glenda's" George Weiss (who appears as an abortion doctor) this cinematic sickie inspired two sequels (in the same year!) and stars Audrey Campbell. 70 min.
79-5660 Was $24.99 ***$19.99***

Olga's Girls (1964)
Sadistic madam Olga is back in business in this follow-up to "White Slaves of Chinatown." When she's not busy pushing heroin and prostitution, Olga dons her black leather "cape of persuasion" and brutally abuses her girls with blowtorches, machetes and a nail-laden vise-bed called "the Enforcer." Audrey Campbell, Eva Denning star. 72 min.
83-3006 Was $39.99 ***$29.99***

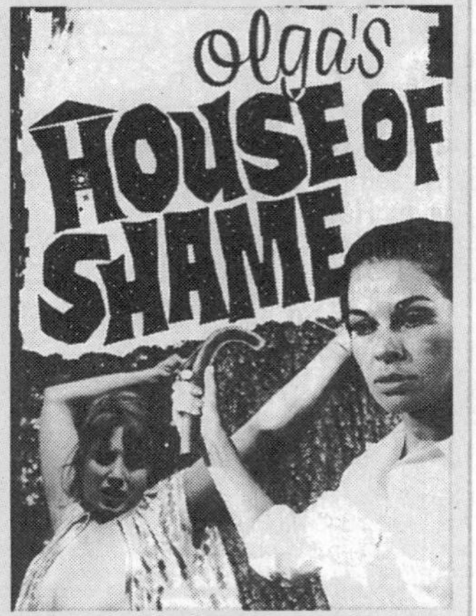

Olga's House Of Shame (1964)
The third installment in the "Olga" series finds that ogre-like sadist taking her torture chamber to upstate New York, where, with help from her brother and scantily-clad helpers, she goes to work on her captive women, using soldering irons, a wire brush, "horse discipline," an electric chair and more. A truly demented effort starring Audrey Campbell and Alice Davis.
79-5659 Was $24.99 ***$19.99***

Olga's Dance Hall Girls (1966)
Perhaps the strangest in the outré "Olga" series, this number shows how evil Olga and a creepy cohort recruit suburban housewives to host their dance hall parties. The parties evolve into orgies and catfights, then Olga leads satanic rituals where the women get naked. With Mary Victoria, Lucie Eldredge.
79-6122 Was $24.99 ***$19.99***

The Swap (1966)
Two women feeling neglected by their husbands decide to try the swinging thing, seducing college boys, getting involved in "exchange clubs" and partaking in all sorts of debauchery. Loraine Claire and Stella Britton star in this Joe Sarno sizzler.
79-5450 Was $24.99 ***$19.99***

The Unsatisfied (1966)
American film distributors got their hands on this European thriller and added some spicy nude scenes for domestic audiences. The story is about teenagers involved in drugs, murder and sex, but you'll check it out for a slew of topless cuties, a striptease sequence and the like. With Rita Cadillac.
79-5451 Was $24.99 ***$19.99***

Strange Rampage (1967)
Miss Anne Howe and her amazing 48-inchers and Bunny Ware are the stars of this perverse potboiler presenting sex-seeking secretaries, schoolteachers and go-go dancers who go to great lengths to degrade themselves, then go after men of all sorts in the evening hours.
79-5477 ***$19.99***

Scream Of The Butterfly (1965)
Extremely rare, classic sexual melodrama starring the amazing nymph Nelinda Lobato as Marla, a nubile thrillseeker who hops from bed to bath to beachfront with her Latin lover and husband, whom she plots to murder. Eber Lobato directed; Ray Dennis Steckler photographed, so you know this must be good. 78 min.
79-5479 ***$19.99***

The Secret Sex Lives Of Romeo & Juliet (1969)
Shakespeare's classic love story gets a sexually-charged treatment with Romeo as a studly sort, Juliet a gorgeous nympho, and all sorts of hanky-panky amongst the gentlefolk of Verona. With Tiffany Lane, Antoinette Maynard and Stuart Lancaster of Russ Meyer movies fame.
79-5402 ***$19.99***

Eve And The Merman (1964)
A different angle on the "Mr. Peabody and the Mermaid" and "Splash" story, this nudie-cutie stars nudist princess Lori Dawson as the young woman who has all sorts of sexy experiences when she meets a merman on a tropical isle. Featuring Johnny Salvo, Marcia Le Roux and that new sensation, the topless bathing suit!
79-5407 ***$19.99***

Love Toy (1968)
After he loses everything he has in a card game, the father of a teenage girl consents to the wealthy winner's request: to have one night with his daughter. The night of lust is filled with all sorts of ultra-kinky events, including spanking, milk-licking, an incestuous menage-a-trois and more.
79-5428 Was $24.99 ***$19.99***

The Walls Have Eyes (1969)
Explosive sexploiter about a voyeuristic owner of a motel who loves checking out his guests through one-way mirrors. He spies on adulterous liaisons of all sorts, including a hot lesbian affair, but when he tries to blackmail one of his subjects, he's in for real trouble. 60 min.
79-5489 ***$19.99***

House On Bare Mountain (1962)
"Hollywood models meet the monsters!," proclaimed the ads. Now you can meet this extremely rare nudie horrorfest about "Granny Good," a demented old coot (played by Bob Cresse) whose charm school for buxom babes is a front for her bootlegging operation and a party in which Frankenstein, Dracula, the Phantom of the Opera and some werewolves are participants. 61 min.
79-5503 Was $24.99 ***$19.99***

Festival Girls (1962)
A film producer discovers a gorgeous, half-drowned model near his hotel and casts her in a movie called "Blond Dynamite." At the Venice Film Festival, the movie winds the top prize, but a woman recognizing the producer as a con artist causes all sorts of trouble. Sizzling tale stars Alex D'Arcy and Barbara Valentin, co-stars in "The Horrors of Spider Island." 72 min.
79-5512 Was $24.99 ***$19.99***

To Ingrid With Love, Lisa (1968)
European arthouse arouser finds attractive fashion designer and repressed lesbian Lisa taking gorgeous, blonde smalltown girl Ingrid under her wing, showing her the fashion industry and confiding in her about her dissatisfaction with men. Eventually, the two have a scorching sapphic liaison in this supercharged and tender film from director Joe Sarno.
79-5537 Was $24.99 ***$19.99***

All The Loving Couples (1969)
Classic Sixties sexploiter about a couple, new to swinging L.A., who discover that the party they are attending is really for wife-swapping. Will they partake in trading mates and the orgy that follows? Bet the lava lamp on it! Norman Alden, Gloria Manon star.
79-5545 Was $24.99 ***$19.99***

It's Hot On Sin Island (1964)
In a desperate need to raise some cash to keep their yacht, two men run a charter cruise, and their passenger list includes five pretty schoolteachers. It's anchors aweigh—and clothes, too—as our two sailors are dazzled by the purveyors of reading, writing and nudity. Pauly Dash and Dick Lynn star. 60 min.
79-5546 Was $24.99 ***$19.99***

Two Roses And A Golden Rod (1969)
A nubile young lady has the hots for her porno screenwriter dad, causing much friction between the girl and her mother. After she manages to unwittingly seduce her father and mom throws her out, she seeks consolation with a lesbian girlfriend. And Dad gets involved there, too. John Alderman and Lisa Grant star in this Albert Zugsmith production.
79-5553 Was $24.99 ***$19.99***

The Slave (1967)
A dose of depravity from Europe about a woman who finds her marriage threatened when explicit photos she took when she was a teenager resurface. In order to keep things quiet, the woman must submit to the kinky sexual whims of her blackmailers. Claude Cerval and Vera Valmont star. 67 min.
79-5555 Was $24.99 ***$19.99***

The Sexploiters (1965)
An ultra-kinky shockathon from Bob Cresse ("Love Camp 7") focusing on a suburban housewife seeking thrills in New York City who joins a prostitution ring that's fronted by a model agency. Along with her co-workers, the woman teases her clients to ecstasy, but learns to appreciate the pleasures of other women after some perverse encounters. 69 min.
79-5558 Was $24.99 ***$19.99***

Some Girls Do (1967)
A gal from the farm arrives in New York City looking for sexual adventures and finds it when she rooms with two women who are into everything: lesbianism, prostitution, S&M and other forms of kinkiness. When the country gal learns how nasty men could be, she seeks an alternative lifestyle...and revenge! Joanna Fair, Cupcake McGirk star. 76 min.
79-5560 Was $24.99 ***$19.99***

Massacre Of Pleasure (1966)
Seamy sexploitation from Bob Cresse ("Love Camp 7") in which women are captured by a Parisian crime operation and given a choice: submit to their captors' sadistic demands or die. But some of the captive women begin to enjoy their S&M lifestyle. The newspaper ads read: "A shattering step forward in the sensual revolution of motion picture-making." 67 min.
79-5561 Was $24.99 ***$19.99***

The Warm, Warm Bed (1966)
A wild exposé of suburbia from schlockmeister supreme Barry Mahon in which the secrets of orgy-goers, stewardesses, sleazy salesmen, and bored housewives and their spouses are revealed in all of their sordid glory.
79-5810 Was $24.99 ***$19.99***

Oona (1969)
A lonely businessman arrives home one day to find his wife in bed with the beautiful hitchhiker he picked up and bedded a few days earlier. The three partake in a menage-a-trois, then the fireworks begin. Ming Toy Epstein, Lilla Allen and John Marshall star. 65 min.
79-6189 Was $24.99 ***$19.99***

For Members Only (1962)
A nudist camp delight, this zesty English comedy tells the story of Jane, a pretty woman who inherits her grandfather's property, which includes the Avonmore Sun Camp. She has plans to sell the nudist colony, but is persuaded to spend some time there by a handsome lawyer and member. What follows is a hedonist's delight. With Shelley Martin. AKA: "Pussycat Paradise."
79-5830 Was $24.99 ***$19.99***

She's Doing It Again (1968)
An inventor invites employees of an auto company to his lakefront home and sexual games and deceit ensue when one of the workers talks his wife into seducing their host, while the other wife takes it upon herself to try the same plan. Bob February, Carol Gian and Lisa Milone star in this sensual, all-swapping drama.
79-5837 Was $24.99 ***$19.99***

Hollywood's World Of Flesh (1963)
Legendary schlockmeisters Bob Cresse and Lee Frost are the creators of this seedy look at what goes on behind the scenes in Tinseltown. See casting couches, nude models, sex clubs, poolside orgies, Japanese bathhouses and more. With Joanne Stewart and Mai Chi.
79-5607 Was $24.99 ***$19.99***

Chained Girls (1965)
The "truth" about lesbians is revealed in this wicked exposé on femmes and dykes in New York City. The film takes a "factual" slant on the gay culture, revealing lesbians cruising for partners, seducing other women, getting married, grappling in catfights and initiating young women into the Daughters of Lesbos Society. June Roberts stars in this one-of-a-kind effort.
79-5602 Was $24.99 ***$19.99***

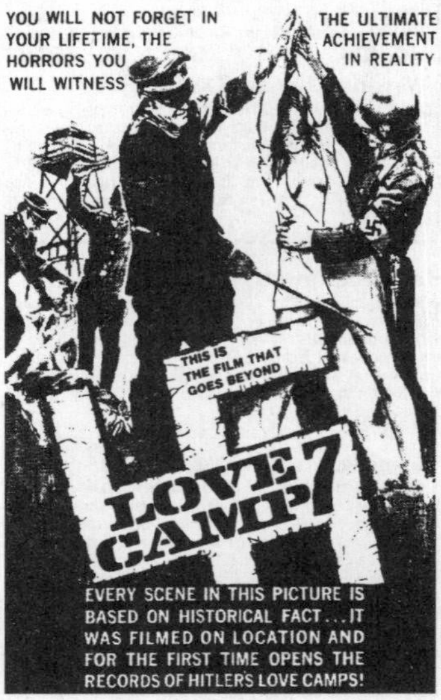

Love Camp 7 (1968)
Notorious sexploitation effort from Bob Cresse and David F. Friedman concerns a WWII German prison camp where all sorts of perverse experiments occur. Two WAC officers attempt to infiltrate the compound and rescue the female scientist being tortured there. Not for the squeamish, the film features lesbianism, S&M practices and orgy sequences. With Maria Lease. 95 min.
79-5542 Was $24.99 ***$19.99***

S.S. Experiment (1976)
Notorious exploiter set in a secret camp in Nazi Germany where German officers mate with prisoners in cruel sexual experiments for "the improvement of the race." A Nazi sergeant falls in love with a French prostitute and joins forces with the other inmates to stop the camp's commandant. Giorgio Cerioni stars in this not-for-the-squeamish shocker. Unrated version; 90 min.
20-1047 ***$29.99***

Helltrain (1977)
Take a train excursion packed with young women who have volunteered to keep Hitler's officers happy with sexual encounters. When the train stops to pick up female prisoners who have taken sides against the Nazis, trouble ensues between a former cabaret singing faithful and a prisoner who was once her childhood friend. Monica Swinn stars. AKA: "S.S. Helltrain." Unrated version; 90 min.
59-8020 ***$29.99***

Sin In The Suburbs (1964)
After discovering that her mother is involved in an adulterous affair, a pretty high school student seeks help from a neighbor. While their trusting bond grows into a deep relationship, a secret sex club for the area's pleasure-seeking women is started. Soon, Mom discovers that her daughter is a member! Alice Linville and Campbell star; sexploitation pioneer Joe Sarno directs. 82 min.
79-5398   Was $24.99   *$19.99*

Indian Raid, Indian Made (1969)
You'll be doing "tomahawk chops" after you witness this wild sex romp starring Morganna, baseball's notorious, big-breasted "kissing bandit." The wacky plot involves secret agents, moonshine stills, Indians in bikinis and more. A one-of-a-kind sexperience featuring Tiffany Lace and Miss Nude Galaxie Dawn Diano.
79-5313   Was $24.99   *$19.99*

Substitution (1969)
Stereo store salesman Harry learns the method of "cosmic substitution" and now has the ability to imagine that his wife has been replaced by the gorgeous, incredibly endowed gals he works with. The parade of 26 stacked starlets doesn't stop in this "adults only" nudie-cutie. Chuck Sailor, Patrice Nastasia star.
79-5321   Was $24.99   *$19.99*

The Curious Dr. Humpp (1967)
Curious exploitation fans will not want to miss this outrageous Argentinean-made study of a twisted doctor who invents an aphrodisiac that turns people into insatiable sex fiends. Aided by robotic monsters and a brain in a jar, Dr. Humpp tries to dominate the world through sex...while isolating the lesbians in a separate room! 87 min.
79-5296   Was $24.99   *$19.99*

Satan In High Heels (1962)
A carnival stripper takes some cash from her drug addict hubby, heads for New York and gets a job at a nightclub, where she carries on an affair with her new lover's son and gets her former husband involved in a murder plot. Meg Myles, Grayson Hall, Sabrina and Del Tenney star in this seedy sexploitationer. 89 min.
79-5298   Was $24.99   *$19.99*

Sexy Probitissimo (1963)
There are 18—count 'em, 18—of Italy's top strippers on hand for this anecdotal arouser featuring the greatest and weirdest moments in "take-it-off" history. See the gals lose their clothes for Dr. Frankenstein and his monster! See a young lady seduce a vampire! See a sexy astronaut excite aliens! See stuff you'll never see anywhere else! 64 min.
79-5300   Was $24.99   *$19.99*

Mini-Skirt Love (1967)
How warped are the morals of the mod world? Well, Auntie sure is hip to the swinging scene, but does she take things too far when she makes it with her imprisoned sister's teenage son? And what happens when mom goes out from behind bars? Marie Brent and Donny Lee star in this taboo-shattering tale of titillation.
79-5186   Was $24.99   *$19.99*

Mundo Depravados (1967)
What do you get when you cross a sexploitation flick with a "mondo" movie? Why, something like this notorious shocker starring stripper Tempest Storm as the gal who volunteers to wiggle her way into the arms of a murderer in order to capture him. With the obscure comedy team of Johnnie Decker and Larry Reed, this nudie watchimicallit must be seen to be believed. 73 min.
79-5294   Was $24.99   *$19.99*

AN EROTIC OBSESSION... FOR LOVE IN TRIPLICATE!

ODD TRIANGLE
AN ADULT FILM

Odd Triangle (1969)
Scorching lesbian erotica ensues when Allison, a gorgeous woman disgruntled by her marriage, befriends a sexy suburban housewife named Janet, whose erotic stories ignite hidden passions. The two get it on and soon welcome the involvement of Winnie, a young guide with mature desires.
79-5401   Was $24.99   *$19.99*

Kiss Me Quick (1964)
Perhaps the world's first nudie comedy-horror-sci-fi film, this outrageous enterprise tells the story of an effeminate alien from an all-male planet and a wacky scientist named Dr. Breedlove, who manufactures women. There's appearances from Frankenstein, Dracula and a mummy, as well as lots of naked women! AKA: "Dr. Breedlove."
79-5174   *$19.99*

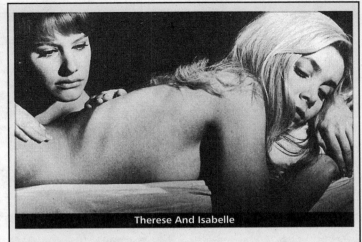
Therese And Isabelle

Radley Metzger

The Dirty Girls (1964)
The erotic trials and tribulations of a Parisian prostitute are the focus of Radley Metzger's look at lust-filled l'amour near the Champs-Elysees. Among the streetwalker's acquaintances are a shy student, a client who prefers her in strange costumes, a man who turns violent during sex and an American businessman. And that's not to mention the ladies. Reine Rohan and Denise Roland star. 78 min.
83-3004   *$29.99*

The Alley Cats (1965)
An exercise in Euro-erotica from Radley Metzger tells of the lusty liaisons shared by a group of young swingers. A woman who becomes aware of her fiancé's unfaithfulness searches for love—and finds it in discos and other colorful locales, with handsome men and willing women. Anne Arthur, Sabrina Koch and Uta Levka star. 83 min.
83-3005   Letterboxed   *$29.99*

Carmen, Baby (1967)
Radley Metzger's titillating take on the "Carmen" story stars the exquisite Uta Levka as a sultry cafe waitress whose sexual manipulation of the men in her life—including a cop, a con and a rock star—leads to danger and, eventually, tragedy. One of Metzger's early softcore smashes, the film is famous for its highly-charged "bottle" scene. With Doris Arden. 90 min.
83-3002   Letterboxed   *$29.99*

Therese And Isabelle (1968)
Two young girls experience awakening sexuality in the heated atmosphere of a French girls' boarding school in this sensitive softcore drama. Essy Persson, Anna Gael star in Radley Metzger's classic tale of lesbian love. Restored, extra kinky version; 118 min. Filmed in English.
27-6250   Letterboxed   *$29.99*

Camille 2000 (1969)
Radley Metzger's slick, sensual adaptation of Alexandre Dumas' "The Lady of the Camellias" tells of a beautiful, kept woman who uses her abilities in the bedroom to interest a nobleman while longing for a commoner. This scorcher showcases chic settings, lots of mirrors and the incredible Daniéle Gaubert. 115 min.
83-3001   Letterboxed   *$29.99*

Riverboat Mama (1969)
This gal knows how to go rollin' on the river! She's a hot-blooded woman with desires for men and women. All aboard this ride through the worlds of lesbianism, nymphomania, prostitution and more.
79-5182   *$19.99*

Escapades In Mexico (1969)
Two high school kids—a guy and a girl—think they're going to find the time of their lives when they hitchhike to Mexico. But things get quite scary when a group of violent thugs pick them up, leading to a ride of horror and fear. There's orgies, whorehouses and brutality in this rough-and-tough sexploitation epic. Olé? No way!
79-5183   *$19.99*

Free Love Confidential (1967)
Take a trip back to the "Swingin' Sixties" for this sordid shocker about a group of bored housewives who pose for some provocative nude pictures, then have to battle a tough lesbian to get them back. This way-out flick is filled with groovy gals who groove once too often. With Karen Miller and Yvette Corday.
79-5184   *$19.99*

For Love And Money (1967)
Female spies reap a harvest of weird sex in this seething sleuth-a-thon spiked with sex, sex, sex. An agency specializing in dirty tricks and blackmail uses gorgeous gals to carry out the dirty work. See how they get their man in the most compromising of situations.
79-5231   *$19.99*

The Lickerish Quartet (1970)
Stylishly kinky erotic tale from Radley Metzger focusing on a man, his wife and the man's stepson who see a porno film starring a gorgeous woman, who becomes the fantasy of each. The family finds the motorcycle-riding woman in a nearby town, and they each get a chance to realize their sexual desires. Silvana Venturelli, Frank Wolff star. Newly remastered version includes the original theatrical trailer. 90 min.
83-3000   Letterboxed   *$29.99*

Little Mother (1971)
Radley Metzger's controversial, sexual take on the life of Eva Peron features beautiful Christiane Kruger as a former prostitute who uses political clout and seduction to marry the president of a small country. When she discovers she is dying of an incurable disease, Kruger schemes to have an ex-lover kill her to help her husband's re-election. Siegfried Rauch, Mark Damon co-star. AKA: "Blood Queen." 95 min.
83-3020   Letterboxed   *$29.99*

Score (1973)
It's mate-swapping, Radley Metzger-style, as the maestro of chic screen sex captures the exploits of two suburban couples involved in wicked carnal games. Their heated roundelays lead to a kinky confrontation where sexual preferences head off into lesbian and bisexual directions. Lynn Lowry, Claire Wilbur and Calvin Culver star. 89 min.
83-3003   Letterboxed   *$29.99*

The Princess And The Call Girl (1984)
It's a kinky twist in the old tale when a socialite and a high-priced prostitute change places for two days, and discover that each world contains its share of sensual pleasures and beautiful people. Carol Levy and Shannah Hall star in Radley Metzger's exquisite piece of erotic entertainment. 90 min.
27-6212   Was $29.99   *$19.99*

Radley Metzger 3-Pack
"The Alley Cats," "The Dirty Girls" and "Therese and Isabelle" are also available in a boxed collector's set.
70-5164   Save $30.00!   *$59.99*

Naked Pursuit (1968)
A young man who unintentionally killed a cop flees his captors and travels to the coast where he rapes a young, emotionally distressed woman. But the rape has an interesting effect on the woman, leading her to reassess her life.
79-5435   Was $24.99   *$19.99*

The Girl From S.I.N. (1966)
Schooled in the art of karate and Oriental love, special agent Poontang Plenty is given the assignment of retrieving a stolen formula for invisibility. Working for the evil Dr. Sexus, Poontang uses torture and her incredible bod to try to complete the assignment. With Joyanna and Sal Rogge. 67 min.
79-5392   Was $24.99   *$19.99*

Felicia (1969)
A gorgeous photographer lures young models into her New York apartment in order to seduce them. A loving lesbian relationship with one leads to bondage, domination and danger, as the two women go wild in the sheets.
79-5432   Was $24.99   *$19.99*

Forbidden Flesh (1968)
Rollicking raucherama from schlockmeister Barry Mahon depicting the forbidden sexual liaison between a swinging salesman and an inquisitive virgin from Tennessee. Strippers, society orgies, lesbians: the salesman uses lots of tales to titillate the lovely young woman.
79-5399   *$19.99*

Two Girls For A Madman (1968)
A maniacal creep takes off from his psychiatrist's office in a frenzy and terrorizes a ballet student and her boyfriend while on the road. After a rough sexual encounter with the psycho, the woman recommends (!!) him to a girlfriend, saying "he was all man." This deranged blast from the past also features drugs, orgies and folk singers. With Toni France and Jean Weston. 78 min.
79-5302   *$19.99*

The Muthers (1968)
Luscious Marsha Jordan stars in this thrill-seeking epic of titillation in the suburbs. The wives really swing when their husbands are away, partaking in kinky sensual shenanigans the likes of which have rarely been topped in sex picture history. Kathy Williams also stars in this sexploitationer. 74 min.
79-5234   Was $24.99   *$19.99*

After The Ball Was Over (1967)
A rough-and-tough sexual drama about a woman who inherits a small fortune and becomes a playgirl. She eventually marries a suave wheeler-dealer, but strange things begin to happen. She's bombarded with porno films, advances, and pills, and is raped, leading to a an explosive finale. 64 min.
79-5235   *$19.99*

The Wonderful World Of Girls (1965)
Stop the world...I wanna get on! That's what a middle-aged man says when he keeps getting into ribald situations with naked gals...lots of them! His experiences are the stuff of fantasies...until the wife finds out about them!
79-5175   Was $24.99   *$19.99*

Diary Of A Swinger (1967)
Through a series of flashbacks, a young woman's descent to the edge of madness is traced as she's forced into a series of kinky sexual encounters which include sadism, lesbianism and group sex. Not for the squeamish, this ruffie stars Joanna Cunningham ("Miss Cavalcade") and was directed by John and Lem Amero ("Blonde Ambition").
79-5179   Was $24.99   *$19.99*

The Ramrodder (1969)
A stud-cowpoke falls in love with a gorgeous Indian squaw and must prove his love for her in order to win the trust of the woman's tribe. Trouble rears its ugly head when a white man rapes an Indian woman and the cowpoke is blamed. A sweltering sagebrush saga starring Jim Gentry and Kathy Williams, complete and uncut with the infamous "whipping scene." 89 min.
79-5241   Was $24.99   *$19.99*

Thar She Blows! (1969)
All hands on deck for this naughty nautical tale of a seaside strumpet who's got a sizzling siren song for any able-bodied seaman who comes across her path. There she is, off the stern...just ready to be harpooned! Shari Mann, Lori Brown and Stuart Lancaster star in this uncut, newly restored version, now with the complete "spanking scene." 77 min.
79-5242   *$19.99*

Mr. Peter's Pets (1962)
A pet store owner discovers he can change himself into any member of the animal kingdom. He adopts the shape of a friendly canine and goes spying in women's homes for prospective "owners." A truly outrageous sexploiter from producer David F. Friedman. 70 min.
79-5243   *$19.99*

The Sex Killer (1967)
A young mannequin factory worker spies on sunbathers in his New York apartment building and has a girlfriend that he loves very much: a mannequin's head. When he gets laughed at, the fellow decides to get a real woman...whom he strangles. Weird shocker directed by Barry Mahon ("Rocket Attack, U.S.A."). 55 min.
79-5303   Was $24.99   *$19.99*

The Love Cult (1966)
In the tradition of Manson, Jim Jones and David Koresh comes Eric the Great, a hypnotist-turned-"minister" with sex on his mind, a bevy of beautiful followers, and a doctrine of "your body can become the Temple of the Beginning and the Climax of Now." But when he seeks more power, he takes the cult thing too far! 65 min.
79-5304   Was $24.99   *$19.99*

SHE CAME ON THE BUS

She Came On The Bus (1969)
All hell breaks loose when a suburban housewife and her girlfriend are held prisoner by a group of sadistic thugs and their horny girlfriends. A violent nudie film that'll satisfy fans of tease and terror.
79-5151   Was $24.99   *$19.99*

Take Me Naked (1966)
Michael and Roberta Findlay, the pioneers of screen perversion, offer one of their most unsettling epics with this story of a drunken Peeping Tom whose fantasies involve his fleshy neighbor, played by Roberta herself. The scumbag eventually gets to meet the gal of his dreams, but his depraved urges get the best of him. With Kevin Sullivan and Michael Findlay.
79-5667 Was $24.99 ***$19.99***

The Touch Of Her Flesh (1967)
When a man learns that his wife is involved with another woman, he goes on a rampage against all members of the opposite sex, killing go-go dancers, prostitutes, his wife and her lover in truly bizarre ways. Suzanne Marre, Angelique, Robert West star in this "ruffie" from Michael and Roberta Findlay. AKA: "Way Out Love." 75 min.
79-5033 Was $24.99 ***$19.99***

The Sin Syndicate: The Story Of The Zero Girls (1968)
They were young and gorgeous...and they worked for the Mob. This is the shocking story of the Zero Girls, masters of bedding down figures for Mob operations. Gorgeous gal strippers and exotic dancers! They better do their job, or Rocky, the head of operations, has it in for them. Sensationalistic sleaze from Michael and Roberta Findlay. 80 min.
79-5060 ***$19.99***

The Kiss Of Her Flesh (1968)
Schlockmeisters Roberta and Michael Findlay top their other excursions into depravity with this disturbing sex-and-violence foray. If tire iron and lobster claw mayhem, electrical earring wiring, incestuous lesbian lust, nymphomania, naked women and blowtorch shenanigans are your cup of tea, then kiss this "Flesh" hello. With Mr. Findlay himself (billed as "Robert West").
79-6121 Was $24.99 ***$19.99***

1,000 Pleasures (1969)
Another journey into depravity from Michael and Roberta Findlay, this sordid affair involves a man who murders his wife and drives around with her body in his car. He picks up two lesbian hitchhikers who make him their love slave. Extremely bizarre S&M-oriented tale with lots of nudity features Marie Brent and eerie flute music.
79-5045 Was $24.99 ***$19.99***

The Filth Shop (1969)
No, it's not an exposé of the inner workings of Excitement Video. Instead, this film looks at the other filth shops throughout the country—the ones preying on the world flesh trade, drugging and forcing innocent young women into their lair of perversity and paid pleasure. Susan Sex and Lover Lee stars. 63 min.
79-6191 Was $24.99 ***$19.99***

Way Out Topless (1967)
It's a wild trip around the U.S.A., where you'll meet some of the hottest topless dancers and see them do their thing. Travel to Baltimore, Washington, D.C., and other spots where the women are wild and willing to drop their tops for your pleasure. With Jenny Long, Sue Johnson and Pussy Kate.
79-6193 Was $24.99 ***$19.99***

Five Wild Girls (1965)
Two sisters and their not-so kissin' cousins duke it out over guys, sex and cash when they try to find the fortune Grandpa left before he passed on. As the stakes get higher, the sex gets hotter in this red-hot regional roundelay of passions run amuck!
79-6196 Was $24.99 ***$19.99***

Elysia (1933)/Unashamed (1937)
A rare find, this early nudie effort was filmed at California's Elysian Valley in the 1930s. The warm weather welcomes "naturalists" of all sorts, having fun in the warm California sun. Also included is "Unashamed," another nudist camp frolic with Barbara "Pinky" Pound.
79-5199 Was $24.99 ***$19.99***

Ten Days In A Nudist Camp (1954)
This carnal compilation of "naturist camp" footage of the '30s, '40s and '50s shows that things were as wild in the good old days as they are in contemporary times. It's a best-of three-decade delight that'll make you yell, "Take it off!"
79-5716 Was $24.99 ***$19.99***

Garden Of Eden (1954)
A strange professional nudie movie, featuring legit actors like R.G. Armstrong and Arch Johnson and directed by Max Noesseck ("Dillinger"). A wealthy old grouch forces his daughter and granddaughter out of his mansion and into a nudist camp, then tries to have his daughter declared an unfit mother. With Mickey Knox, Jamie O'Hara.
79-5876 Was $24.99 ***$19.99***

Nudist Life (1956)
The intricate complexities and subtle social structure of 1950s nudist colony life is depicted in this titillating exploiter in which sun worshippers walk, talk, snack and partake in other activities. There's also ping-pong and volleyball—all captured at Florida's Fair-View Gardens. Produced by George Weiss, producer of "Glen or Glenda." AKA: "Nature Girl's Frolics."
79-5642 Was $24.99 ***$19.99***

Nature's Paradise (1957)
The United Kingdom's first nudie movie is a color wonder, a tale of a pretty female nudist who persuades her pal to join her at England's Spielpastz nudist camp. There, badminton, chess and a violin are played sans clothes and an American fellow shows off his wares to the girls. A highlight is the "Venus Contest" and a visit to the "6th World Nude Contest." With Anita Love.
79-6432 Was $24.99 ***$19.99***

Forbidden Paradise (1959)
The true story of "the origin of nudist cults" are documented in this phony "factual study" filled with the sort of things it purportedly exposes. Lots of nude bathing and romping in natural settings can be found in this European production.
79-5427 Was $24.99 ***$19.99***

As Nature Intended (1961)
Classic nudie epic detailing the naked adventures of five free spirits who frolic and swim through exotic places throughout the world...even Stonehenge! With Jackie (34-22-34) Salt, Petrina (35-23-34) Forsyth, Bridget (38-24-36) Leonard and the incredible Pamela (39-23-36) Green, a delight playing ping-pong, showering or just relaxing on a hammock. 58 min.
79-5002 Was $24.99 ***$19.99***

Lust For The Sun (1961)
Mix a travelogue with lots of lovely naked women and you'll get this nudist delight. Bare sun worshippers frolic in the sun and the snow, sharing in a love for nature and naughtiness. Whether getting a tan or constructing a snowman, the au naturel arousers are sure to impress you. Produced by Werner Kunz.
79-5430 Was $24.99 ***$19.99***

ACTUALLY FILMED IN A NUDIST COLONY
ADULTS ONLY
Nature's Paradise

Shangri-La (1961)
A jolly good nudist camp flick from Merry Olde England. Join in the fun at Shangri-La, where naked patrons run rampant, play volleyball and take sunbaths. It's a nudist flick with a difference. 68 min.
79-5155 Was $24.99 ***$19.99***

Have Figure, Will Travel (1963)
Carol is a nudist from Canada; Sue is a nudist from Australia. Along with non-nudist Marge, they take a yacht tour of the East coast's finest clothing-optional camps, from Sunshine Park in Mays Landing, New Jersey, to Delray, Florida's, Sunny Acres. Will Marge succumb to her pals' liberated lifestyle? Will the girls take showers and roll around in mud? We're not telling! With Susan Baxter, Carol MacKenzie.
79-6434 Was $24.99 ***$19.99***

Naked Complex (1964)
A camp classic, this nudie film details the plight of a handsome race car driver who is absolutely frightened of women. Unable to cope, he leaves society by bailing out of an airplane and lands on a nudist colony populated by naked, big-breasted women, instead. Roy Savage and Mary Margaret star along with members of the Sun Beach Club, "one of the most beautiful nudist resorts in Tampa, Florida."
15-9002 ***$19.99***

Take Your Clothes Off And Live (1964)
The nudist flick hits Europe and it will never be the same! A group of pals talk about their nudist summer in the South of France, where the "Sun Club" partakes in all sorts of fleshy activities, including a trip to a nudist colony.
79-5452 Was $24.99 ***$19.99***

The Beast That Killed Women (1965)
The nudist camp seems so peaceful: men and women frolic stark naked in the sun. And then it happened! The place is terrorized by an apelike creature! Look out, gals. Time to double up on those cots! This Barry Mahon production features "Miami Beach's Most Lovely Nudists." 60 min.
79-5306 ***$19.99***

Nudes On Tiger Reef (1965)
A theatrical director persuades his leading lady to make a nudie movie instead of playing summer stock in this naked gal-laden comedy that features nude softball, nude scuba and other unclothed activities. With Sande Johnsen and Nadja Swenson, directed (and narrated!) by noted B-movie auteur Barry Mahon. 64 min.
79-5408 Was $24.99 ***$19.99***

Nudists Galore (1965)
A humorous "peep show" sex farce in which a math teacher puts away the rulers and compasses in order to visit a nudist camp. There he witnesses naked people romping around, playing games and partaking in athletic events. His fantasies soon take over when his pillows turn into women. With Henry Crawford, Joanne Maguire. AKA: "Pussy Galore."
79-6205 Was $24.99 ***$19.99***

Nudes, Nudists And Nudism
Get back to nature, nudist style, by taking in this compilation of trailers, loops and shorts (and longs) made during the nudist colony heyday. This celebration includes men and women frolicking, playing sports, enjoying the sun. Ah, the good old days.
79-5568 Was $24.99 ***$19.99***

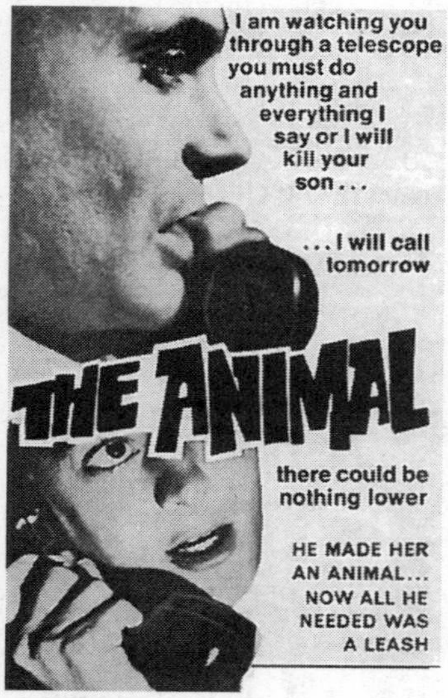
I am watching you through a telescope you must do anything and everything I say or I will kill your son...
...I will call tomorrow
THE ANIMAL
there could be nothing lower
HE MADE HER AN ANIMAL... NOW ALL HE NEEDED WAS A LEASH

The Animal (1968)
Thought lost for decades, this depraved sexploiter from R.L. Frost ("The Defilers") tells of a drug-taking sadist who becomes obsessed with a wealthy woman. After forcing her to cater to his bizarre fantasies, they meet at a local hotel where things get kinkier...and more frightening! David Holmes and Virginia Gordon star. Features the infamous color ending. In Danish with English subtitles.
79-6528 Was $24.99 ***$19.99***

Fluctuations (1969)
What do you get when you mix karate, S&M, whippings and kinky liaisons? Well, you get this perverse piece of erotica in which a number of characters live sexually alternative lifestyles. Delve into their wild worlds with this no-holds-barred bonanza. Sherry Martin, Carla Pompeii and Eric Carlson star. 70 min.
79-6194 Was $24.99 ***$19.99***

The Pick-Up (1968)
This incredibly rare David Friedman-Bob Cresse production is as sleazy as the day it was released—and much more fun! Set in Las Vegas, the film tells of two couriers who track down the two gals who stole cash they're carrying for the mob. Once caught, the gals are subjected to all sorts of depraved torture. With Friedman, Creese, Wes Bishop. In Danish with English subtitles.
79-6529 Was $24.99 ***$19.99***

The Adolescent (1967)
A winner from the Asian erotic cinema of the 1960s tells of a teenage girl who, after watching her mother making love to a stranger and being raped by her cousin's boyfriend, becomes sexually obsessed with her attacker. When he is killed in an accident, she and her cousin seek solace in each other's arms. Dubbed in English.
79-5615 Was $24.99 ***$19.99***

Mister Mari's Girls (1967)
Mister Mari is a millionaire who helps sexy women...for a price! Witness Stella, a junkie desperate enough for a fix that she dances nude for Mari. Then there's Dirk, the lesbian in love with the sightless Barbara. And young Diana, made pregnant by her English tutor. Be amazed at what happens when these women all congregate at Mari's place!
79-5661 Was $24.99 ***$19.99***

Sisters In Leather (1969)
A group of tough-talking, lesbian biker babes pick up a young married executive, then try to draw his wife into their lurid little lair. After champagne orgies and a nude bike ride, the executive decides he's had enough, so he calls on the Motorcycle Studs for help. An awesome exploiter from Manuel S. Conde featuring chesty Pat Barrington.
79-5682 Was $24.99 ***$19.99***

Common Law Wife (1963)
In the tradition of "Mudhoney" and "Shanty Tramp" comes this look at hillbilly lust centering on the brutish Uncle Shuggie, who gets rough with his live-in lover, then sends out for a new companion—his stripper niece named Baby Doll. The ladies don't take a liking to each other, and the stage is set for a feisty fight between hubba-hubba hellcats. Lacy Kelly stars.
79-5678 Was $24.99 ***$19.99***

Deadly Organ (1967)
From the creator of "The Curious Dr. Humpp" comes this gem, a tale of a creepy monstrosity who terrorizes naked women and swingers at local nightclubs in Argentina. His method involves plunging syringes into the heaving bosoms of the local sluts. Gloria Prat stars. AKA: "Feast of Flesh." Dubbed in English.
79-6213 Was $24.99 ***$19.99***

The Love Captive (1969)
Naked gals and nasty monsters highlight this one-of-a-kind sleazefest in which a blonde babe stays too late at the Harry Houdini torture exhibit at a Greenwich Village museum and falls victim to a werewolf, a vampire, a gorilla, naked gals and weird bongo music. Charlotte Russe stars; directed by Larry Crane ("All Women Are Bad").
79-6214 Was $24.99 ***$19.99***

West End Jungle (1962)
Set in London's West End in the swingin' early 1960s, this sexposé surveys the prostitution trade that prospered after there was a crackdown on streetwalking, forcing hookers to become erotic dancers hired out by businessmen or to display their wares in apartment windows. Terry James stars; directed by nudie filmmaker Arnold Louis Miller.
79-6217 Was $24.99 ***$19.99***

The Layout (1969)
Kinky couplings with many women and only one man highlight this Joe Sarno sexploitation sizzler involving two sexy interior designers, one of their troublesome nieces and her roommate, a sexually active male contractor and lots of lascivious interludes. Susan Thomas, Betty Whitman and Rene Howard star in this look at wanton "Designing Women."
79-6218 Was $24.99 ***$19.99***

The Bizarre Ones (1967)
A kinky sex drama from Ron Sullivan (later Henri Pachard of XXX fame) about a sexy, bondage-obsessed babe who picks up a hitchhiker, has sex with him and leaves him chained up sans pants. She soon gets involved with a group of hippie S&M fans who use mechanical objects and keep her bound until that annoyed hitcher returns for revenge. Claire Eclair stars.
79-5738 Was $24.99 ***$19.99***

Relations (1968)
After he's in a car accident with a group of hippies, a married man is visited by one of those involved, a beautiful teenage girl. The two partake in lurid liaisons, but when the man discovers the girl is still with her young boyfriend, he tries to bribe her to stay exclusively with him. Gertie Jung stars in this erotic Danish delight.
79-5803 Was $24.99 ***$19.99***

Hedonistic Pleasures (1969)
Alleged sexumentary that takes a look at the underground sexual activities in Hollywood, featuring a bisexual girl who placed a classified ad from a vibrator's perspective; an acid party; belly-dancing; a model studio, where drugs and sex mix; and a kinky therapy session. With Pat Barrington and Sharon Wells.
79-5843 Was $24.99 ***$19.99***

Summer Of '69 (1969)
The hit single by Bryan Adams is nowhere to be found here, but a whole lot of hot sex is, as a carnal coed uses her sexy body to seduce her history teacher, then her dorm roommate. Reading, writing and 'rithmetic take back seats to sultry encounters that include a "daisy chain" and other orgiastic delights.
79-5849 Was $24.99 ***$19.99***

Foursome (1969)
Down-and-dirty British sexploitation about a country boy named Ted who travels to London to find his sister. He's indoctrinated into the brutal world of big city street life when he encounters pimps, prostitutes, drunken bar patrons, strippers and a kinky woman into whips and leather. With Quinn O'Hara. AKA: "Sweet and Sexy."
79-5856 Was $24.99 ***$19.99***

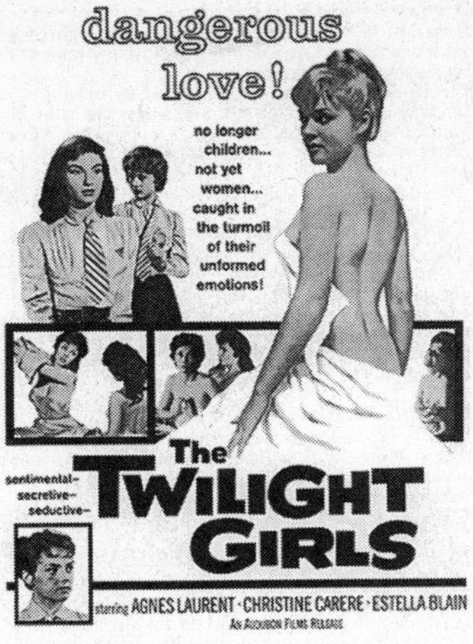

dangerous love!
no longer children... not yet women... caught in the turmoil of their unformed emotions!
sentimental- secretive- seductive-
The TWILIGHT GIRLS
starring AGNES LAURENT · CHRISTINE CARERE · ESTELLA BLAIN
AN AUDUBON FILMS RELEASE

The Twilight Girls (1961)
This controversial account focusing on the sexual intrigue at an all-girl school was originally censored in New York due to the explicit nature of its lesbian scenes. Seeking to make a new life for herself following a family scandal, a new student encounters dangerous love and her own blossoming womanhood. Agnes Laurent, Elga Andersen, Estella Blain, Georgina Spelvin, and Catherine Deneuve (as Catherine Dorleac) star. 61 min.
83-3010 ***$29.99***

Spiked Heels And Black Nylons (1967)
If you're looking for something outrageous in your adult viewing, look no further than this one, a story set at Club Lesbos, a brothel where women service men, but long for women to satisfy their needs. The women, most dressed in garter belts and lingerie, are watched over by a nasty madame named Reba. With Cherry Jones, Bill Thurman and Shirley Boyd.
79-6440 Was $24.99 ***$19.99***

50,000 B.C. (Before Clothing) (1963)
This nudie-cutie tells of a down-and-out burlesque comic who is mistakenly hurled back to the caveman days by way of a time-travelling taxi cab. The funnyman is in for a field day as he meets naked babes, a slave girl with a French accent and an unfriendly giant. Charlie Robinson, Audrey Campbell ("Olga") and Gigi Darlene star; from the director of "The Smut Peddler."
79-6527 Was $24.99 ***$19.99***

Anything Once (Or Twice If I Like It) (1969)
Lesbians involved in the world of show business are exposed in this smarmy smut-a-thon focusing on a group of aspiring actresses involved in a play. When creepy men can't stop their carnal come-ons, the gals turn to each other for some tender love and understanding. Linda Boyce, Liz Cole and sometime Warhol star Louis Waldon star.
79-6537 Was $24.99 ***$19.99***

A Bride For Brenda (1968)
It's a lesbian love-in when recently deflowered Brenda discovers that new roommates Jane and Millie are a couple who'd like to indoctrinate her in their sapphic ways. After a Central Park frolic, the three gals go at it—and soon Brenda's gonna marry Jane! At the wedding, Brenda's former male pal is forced to partake in a kinky celebration—and we're not talking nude Alley Cat either.
79-6425 Was $24.99 ***$19.99***

Freedom To Love (1969)
From West Germany comes this revealing documentary in which sexologists Phyllis and Eberhard Kronhausen set out to prove their theories on sexual freedom by using four dramatized case studies. Among them: a car mechanic learns of his girlfriend's secret life; lesbian lovers are outed; and a troubled marriage is saved by swingers. All this and Hugh Hefner and an early adult cartoon, too.
79-6428 Was $24.99 ***$19.99***

The Improbable Mr. Wee Gee (1960)
Move over, Mr. Teas! Here comes the daffy, sex-driven Mr. Wee Gee, a photographer with a penchant for the pretties who really wants one gal to love. And he finds his true love in the form of a mannequin! But when she's carted off to Europe, Wee Gee takes off for a series of amorous adventures in London, Paris and other spots. With Dick Richards, "Red" Kane and Mary Rooney. 75 min.
79-6182 Was $24.99 ***$19.99***

Her Private Hell (1967)
The kinky inner workings of the swinging European fashion world of the 1960s are bared in this mod masterwork that might have been titled "Ready Not-to-Wear." Trace the sexploits of beautiful Lucia Modunio, a hot-to-trot poser who decides to pose nude after she's desired by both a photographer and his younger assistant. Little did she know that the work would appear in a nudie magazine!
79-6431 Was $24.99 ***$19.99***

The Ice House (1969)
Ultra-sleazy account of a Casanova who gets bonked on the head and becomes a homicidal maniac, picking up and killing strippers and then depositing the corpses in an icehouse he runs. When his twin brother detective begins looking for the missing women, the psycho kills him and assumes his identity! David and Robert Story, Kelly Ross and British pin-up fave Sabrina star; look quickly for future porn legend John Holmes. AKA: "Love in Cold Blood," "The Passion Pit."
79-5975 Was $24.99 ***$19.99***

Happening In Africa (1969)
Sensual mix of travelogue and erotic drama focusing on a writer-photographer in his 40s who is joined by a beautiful younger woman on a wildlife trip to East Africa. As both of them come to terms with their troubled past, can the woman forget her problems by posing nude for the photographer? Darr Poran, Carrie Rochelle star.
79-5996 Was $24.99 ***$19.99***

Pandora And The Magic Box (1965)
Sexploitation maestro Joe Sarno has some sexy fun with this erotic spoof of Italian muscleman sagas, Greek mythology and burlesque. "Sin in the Suburbs'" Alice David (Linville) is the mighty Aphrodite, the goddess of love who narrates the tale of three heroes and their adventures with King Minos, his nympho wife and slave-girl Pandora. With Marlene Denes.
79-5998 Was $24.99 ***$19.99***

Desire Under The Palms (1969)
Sexploitation sultan Joe Sarno helmed this hot New York production centering on a housewife whose aspiring writing career and sexual fantasies get a real charge after she reads a girlie magazine. A meeting with a sex psychologist leads to some lascivious liaisons of her own with some of the shrink's kinky disciples. Ulla Jenson, Susan Martin star.
79-6087 Was $24.99 ***$19.99***

Pretty But Wicked (1965)
A mixture of a Brazilian sex film shot in 1963 and American footage with nudie veteran June Roberts, this sexploiter involves orgies, rape, prostitution and stalking. The story tells of the strange odyssey of a young clerk named Edgar, bribed to marry a wealthy industrialist's daughter while in love with someone else. Jece Valadao stars.
79-6089 Was $24.99 ***$19.99***

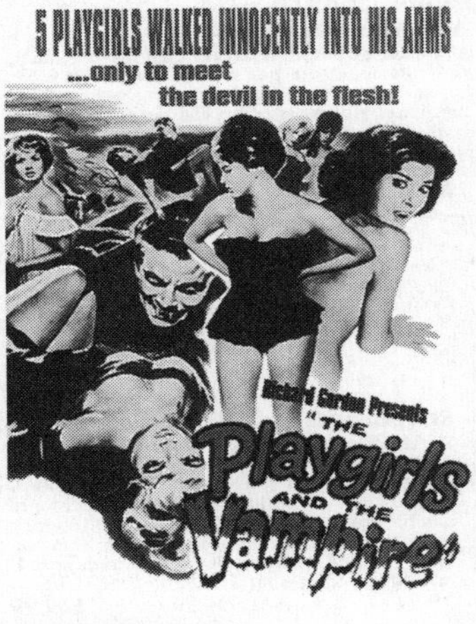

5 PLAYGIRLS WALKED INNOCENTLY INTO HIS ARMS
...only to meet the devil in the flesh!
Richard Gordon Presents
"THE Playgirls AND THE Vampire"

The Playgirls And The Vampire (1960)
Legendary European sex and horror shocker tells of a group of five showgirls who take refuge in a creepy castle during a storm. The place is inhabited by a bloodsucking count and his even nastier brother, who become very fond of the scantily-clad guests—and their blood. Features a controversial striptease sequence! With Walter Brandi, Lyla Rocca.
79-6113 Was $24.99 ***$19.99***

The Soul Snatcher (1965)
While her roommates take part in nude modeling sessions, Kathy has problems adjusting to New York City. One day, she sees a strange premonition: a man in tux and tails, making fun of her. He appears at a party and offers her fun and romance if she wears a pair of golden shoes. She makes the deal, changing her life for the best...until she takes off her shoes. Diane Webster stars.
79-6123 Was $24.99 ***$19.99***

Lust And The Flesh (1965)
After Myra, a virgin, is sexually attacked, she and her new husband look to make things better on an island vacation. They meet Bob, an artist, and Helen, a nympho. The combo of the couples leads to a number of sensual encounters including mate-swapping and lesbianism. Joe Perry, Maureen Conway star. 80 min.
79-6187 Was $24.99 ***$19.99***

Mondo Oscenita (World Of Obscenity) (1966)
From the folks who gave you the lovely "Olga" movies comes this lurid look at the wilder side of men and women, comprised of the sickest scenes from those films, as well as "Nudes of All Nations," "Sunswept" and others. This shocker features forbidden material, so beware! 71 min.
79-6188 Was $24.99 ***$19.99***

Suburbia Confidential (1966)
This exposé of sexual behavior in the suburbs follows the erotic activities of a group of oversexed people who live just beyond the city limits. There's the woman who has a thing for the TV repairman and milkman, a fellow who loves cross-dressing, a gal into bondage sessions with the carpet salesman and more. This A.C. Stephen outing features Helena Clayton and 20 minutes of rarely-seen footage.
79-6485 Was $24.99 ***$19.99***

Motel Confidential (1967)
Check in to "Motel Confidential" and check out what's going on in the sex lives of...well, everyone! There's a lecherous boss and his bra-popping secretary, an unhappily married couple trying to put spice into their love life, an exercise enthusiast who gets it on with the bellboy and, in a rarely seen 16-minute segment, two newlyweds and a drunk. Pat Neice stars; A.C. Stephen directs.
79-6482 Was $24.99 ***$19.99***

Lady Godiva Rides (1968)
A.C. Stephen's campy softcore classic features the legendary Marsha Jordan as the famed long-haired equestrian. Joining up with Tom Jones (no, not the singer) for a trip to America, the pair meet up with all manner of nudie cuties and Wild West outlaws (historians take note). The ads noted that the good Lady "blew the lid off the Wild West."
62-1339 Was $24.99 ***$19.99***

College Girls (1968)
Marsha Jordan, that wowsome starlet of '60s erotica, stars in an A.C. Stephen survey of sex, collegiate style. Here comes Miss Jordan as Fluff, a student who does some extra activities to get a passing biology grade. She's joined by a bevy of bodacious coeds who love to experiment with drugs and classmates of both male and female persuasions. Features 12 minutes of restored footage.
79-6479 Was $24.99 ***$19.99***

Office Love-In (1968)
The love lives of office workers are revealed in all of their raging hormonal glory in this A.C. Stephen production. Follow the sexual adventures of the workers of Date-A-Mate, who can't seem to stay out of the bedroom. Among them: Kathy Williams, who loves her boss and his son; and Lynn Harris, who tries to cure a co-worker of his homosexuality. All this and Marsha Jordan (billed as "Carol Saunders") as a lesbian, too.
79-6483 Was $24.99 ***$19.99***

The Divorcee (1969)
Sultry Marsha Jordan is the titular character, a woman who finds her hubby engaged in sex with another woman, then goes on a sex romp. She beds down a host of partners, including her divorce lawyer, a wealthy playboy, her sado-masochistic dentist and her best friend's hubby. You'll scream "Marsha! Marsha! Marsha!" when you witness Jordan in action. A.C. Stephen directs.
67-1011 Was $24.99 ***$19.99***

Wrong Way (1972)
Becky Sharpe and Lynn Harris are two gals picked up by creeps posing as geologists(?!) after they have car trouble on a secluded road. But this is truly a road to nowhere, littered with rapists, bikers, a psycho hippie cult and two slave-traders delivering a prostitute to a Mexican brothel. This sordid sex and sadism saga was produced by A.C. Stephen ("Orgy of the Dead").
79-6486 Was $24.99 ***$19.99***

The Erotic World Of A.C. Stephen
His real name was Stephen Apostolof, but softcore fans can really get to know Ed Wood compadre and "Orgy of the Dead" director A.C. Stephen through this salute to such softcore classics as "Lady Godiva Rides," "The Divorcee," "Class Reunion" and "Beach Bunnies." Here are clips, shorts, outtakes and more from the ultra-sexy Stephen oeuvre.
79-6477 Was $24.99 ***$19.99***

The Tale Of The Dean's Wife (1969)
Things sure are groovy in this lusty love-in set on a college where the dean can't seem to get a grip on the hedonistic pleasures his campus offers. There's go-go dancing, LSD-taking, protesters and even the dean's oversexed wife partaking in the extra-curricular activities. With Christine Murray.
79-5842 Was $24.99 ***$19.99***

The Marriage Dropouts (1969)
Sizzling sexposé of hanky-panky in typical American families. Son finds Mom making love to another woman; couples try to beat others in a perversion contest; a man spies on his wife while she gets romantic with the paperboys...whew! A hot look at neighborhood naughtiness filmed during the height of the sexual revolution.
79-5739 Was $24.99 ***$19.99***

Sex Circus (1967)
No need to travel to the Big Top to find feats you'll never see anywhere else. Check out this torrid exercise in perversion as a hot lion tamer from Sweden creates a sex club in New York where prostitutes perform only the wildest acts imaginable for kinky customers. The whip-wielding Swede runs the show with a leather hand until an angry cohort seeks the nastiest form of revenge.
79-5740 Was $24.99 ***$19.99***

File X For Sex: The Perverted (1967)
Some of the same people who populate the sleazoid world of Doris Wishman can be found in this depraved "Confidential Report"-style film that looks at why certain people have desires to partake in nymphomania, necrophilia, lesbianism, homosexuality, voyeurism and incest. Features the Bennett Twins.
79-5932 Was $24.99 ***$19.99***

Nymphs Anonymous (1968)
A federation for self-proclaimed nymphomaniacs? You bet, and love-seeking Doreen joins as executive secretary to get in on the action. She has trysts with a vacuum cleaner salesman, her psychiatrist and others...then her hubby finds out. He goes ballistic, shooting all men who have had the pleasure to be involved with the federation. Michele Angelo stars.
79-5936 Was $24.99 ***$19.99***

Swingtail (1969)
While a pretty brunette relates her sordid tales of sex to her director boyfriend, they come vividly to life. You'll learn of the art school dropout's experiences with a black hooker, orgies and carrying on kinky affairs with men. The women eventually go over the line when the director is tied and tortured. But is it real? Karen Park, Lisa La Shawn star.
79-5943 Was $24.99 ***$19.99***

Red Roses Of Passion (1966)
Truly bizarre, ultra-kinky sexploiter about a woman named Carla who joins her friend Enid in visiting a fortune-teller. Soon, both gals join the Daughters of Delphi, a cult of negligee-wearing, rose-fondling nymphos who worship a creepy guy named "God Pan." Carla then punishes her prudish aunt and cousin in a most perverse way. Judson Todd, Jean James star.
79-5955 Was $24.99 ***$19.99***

Sin On The Beach (1963)
Seedy tale of adultery and bed-hopping, French style, set in a resort where a couple go to forget their problems. They soon get involved with the young wife of the resort's dying owner, a bartender and a saucy French maid. When the owner dies mysteriously, everyone begins pointing their finger. With Monique Just, Sylvia Sorente.
79-5990 Was $24.99 ***$19.99***

Shame Shame, Everybody Knows Her Name (1969)
A Greenwich Village go-go dancer named Sharon decides to look for Mr. Right and enlists in a dating agency. But these dates are so kinky, they'd make Jim Lange sweat. There's a guy who hands her over to a lecherous old general, another who gets her drunk so a perverted shutterbug can shoot them "in the act," and a memorable "double date" with her lesbian roommate. Karen Carlson stars.
79-5954 Was $24.99 ***$19.99***

She Should Have Stayed In Bed (1963)
Truly unusual sexploitation item from Barry Mahon ("Cuban Rebel Girls"), in which a man chases a sexy girl around the halls of a high rise populated by nutty, naked women. As the fellow chases the gal around, the other women open their doors and appear naked while he comments to the audience on them. Wow! Mike Baron and Terry Moore star.
79-5621 Was $24.99 ***$19.99***

The Adventures Of Busty Brown (1967)
No use looking for Tige in this tempting thriller. Ms. Brown is a huge-chested private detective working out of San Francisco. In order to find a Chinese girl kidnapped by a crime syndicate, the immensely proportioned investigator poses as a chorus girl to get the goods on the syndicate's chief slimeball. A Barry Mahon production—so you know it's good!
79-5802 Was $24.99 ***$19.99***

Pleasure Plantation (1969)
Steamy sex and sordid activities permeate this seething drama set on a Virginia plantation in the 1860s that's the target of a takeover by a slick entrepreneur and a brothel owner. A New Orleans prostitute, the estate's field boss and the beautiful, mentally retarded sister of the plantation owner all play parts in the complex carnal games. William Scope, Karil Holmes star.
79-5808 Was $24.99 ***$19.99***

A RAGING INFERNO OF EMOTIONS!
Come On BABY, LIGHT MY FIRE

C'Mon Baby Light My Fire (1969)
A goody two-shoes anti-marijuana campaigner is abducted by a group of perverts who take her to the home of a drug kingpin, played by Gerard Damiano of "Deep Throat" fame. Soon, the doors of submission and domination are opened when she's forced to become their sex slave. With Tina Buckley; directed by Lou Campa ("Private Relations").
79-6091 Was $24.99 ***$19.99***

It's A Sick, Sick, Sick World (1965)
Weird sexual practices from around the world are showcased in this globe-hopping shockumentary in the tradition of "Mondo Cane." Travel to Paris, where you'll witness "Prostitute Alley"; London, where women become "ladies of the night" for lack of anything better to do; and other sordid spots. 70 min.
79-6181 Was $24.99 ***$19.99***

This Sporting House (1969)
They don't get much sleazier than this New York-based bit of debauchery directed by Ron Sullivan (later porn director "Henri Pachard"). Three women are recruited by mobsters to work their high-class brothel called Destination. The women, who include a pre-XXX Jennifer Welles (billed as "Lisa Duran") succumb to all sorts of wanton desires—straight, lesbian and more!
79-6539 Was $24.99 ***$19.99***

The Fourth Sex (1962)
The underground lesbian scene in Paris is the focus of this landmark sex film detailing the experiences of a wealthy American woman in Paris named Sand, who enjoys painting her female friends nude. When Sand falls for a handsome man and his sister, she must make some decisions about her desires. Brigitte Juslin, Richard Winckler and Nicole Burgeot star. 82 min.
83-3011 ***$29.99***

Obscene House (1969)
Meet Fat Mamma, a 400-pound madame in a mini-dress, who opens a brothel, employing four fantastic hookers. Visit their training class, where they're taught the proper techniques in dressing and having sex. Then, watch as the gals go to town on their johns, frolicking on beds, in bubble baths and more. Mamma Mia, these gals make Heidi Fleiss look like Marie Osmond! With Dolly Mason.
79-6437 Was $24.99 ***$19.99***

Sex By Advertisement (1967)
This shocking exposé on the world of personal sex ads from Joel Reed ("Bloodsucking Freaks") offers everything the psychiatrist ordered—and then some! Dr. Joanne Ridgefield narrates this look at voyeurism, stag movies, S&M torture, white slavery, transvestites and pretty much every other kinky thing under the sun. With adult superstars Jennifer Welles and Georgina Spelvin.
79-6439 Was $24.99 ***$19.99***

The Libertine (1969)
Catherine Spaak gained international sex symbol status for her alluring performance as Mimi, a sexy widow who discovers that her deceased husband had a secret apartment where he cheated on her. Now, she decides to explore her own sexuality in the same apartment with a number of partners. Will she stop her carousing after she meets handsome radiologist Jean-Louis Trintignant? 90 min. Dubbed in English.
83-3016 ***$29.99***

I, A Woman (1966)
The Swedish sex classic revolutionized American audiences' ideas of an "adult film" and became a box-office sensation. Follow the sexual activities of Siv, from her first experiences through a number of sizzling seductions to a stunning realization about her sensuality. Gorgeous Essy Persson stars in a film noted by a famous scene involving a violin and masturbation. 90 min. Dubbed in English.
79-5610 ***$29.99***

I, A Woman, Part 2 (1971)
A sexual scorcher from Scandinavia starring the gorgeous Gio Petre ("Adam and Eve") as a lonely housewife whose sexual fantasies explode when her husband locks her away in a house filled with precious antiques and no human companionship. This sensual sequel sizzles with chic eroticism.
77-7029 ***$19.99***

The Daughter: I, A Woman, Part III (1973)
The sexual revolution is surveyed in this sexplosive sequel that delves into drugs, lesbianism, racism and more. After she sees her nurse mother in bed with a doctor, Birthe, a teenage girl, goes to a disco and is taken in by a black medical student. But after a lesbian tryst with the student's sister goes sour, Birthe takes a bold route to find happiness. With Inger Sundh.
79-5799 Was $24.99 ***$19.99***

The Playpen (1967)
"Intimate revelations of a tormented journey" are revealed in this hot-to-trot film starring Tiger Lilly as a homespun honey who heads to the big city after her Dad shows off his lechery. There she befriends a lesbian stripper to whom she relates all the wild hillbilly sexual experiences she's had. Jerry Jorden, Corby Drake, Rick Schmidt also star.
79-6540 Was $24.99 ***$19.99***

The Notorious Daughter Of Fanny Hill (1966)
She's the curvaceous child of Fanny Hill, carrying on in her mother's footsteps. Young Kissy Hill loves seducing all sorts of noblemen who arrive at her private room, from the Duke of Roxbury to the Count DeSade, who enjoys being punished. A cute and kinky piece of lasciviousness, with Stacey Walker and Ginger Hale. 74 min.
79-5095 ***$19.99***

Fanny Hill (1969)
The classic tale of a young woman's erotic awakening is transplanted to swinging '60s Stockholm in this sizzling slice of Swedish softcore from director Mac Ahlberg ("I, A Woman"). Diana Kjaer stars as shy, virginal Fanny, whose journey to the big city introduces her to the sex games of the rich and famous of European society. 92 min. Dubbed in English.
20-7056 ***$29.99***

The Young Erotic Fanny Hill (1970)
This is one Fanny that gets a little antsy when she can't get sex. The seductress seeks to live out her fantasies, whether they involve love devices, partner-swapping or other horny young women. Ginny Hamill and Nick Sales star in this erotic enterprise that's sure to delight Fanny fans. 80 min.
79-5142 ***$19.99***

Around The World With Fanny Hill (1974)
She might not break Phineas Fogg's travel record, but it's a cinch the infamous Fanny has a lot more fun. Join the lovely libertine as she seeks sexual pleasure around the globe, from Sweden to Hong Kong to Hollywood and more, in this "adults only" romp by "Fanny Hill" director Mac Ahlberg. Shirley Corrigan, Peter Bonke star. 92 min.
20-7057 ***$29.99***

Invitation To Lust (1968)
A sexually-repressed female anthropologist recounts her incredible story involving an aphrodisiac that transformed her into a sex addict on the prowl for lascivious liaisons. Eventually, she gets too much of a good thing, and even coaxes her medical cohorts into her kinky acts. Jeane Casked, Ela Mitzo and Marco Alius star.
79-6538 Was $24.99 ***$19.99***

The Lullaby Of Bareland (1964)
Come on along and listen to..."The Lullaby of Bareland." And what a lovely tune it is: three sizzling, sexy short films that'll have you humming. "A Weekend with Virginia Bell" offers the bodacious stripper at her best; the ravishing "Anne Howe and The Beatlettes Go Nudist" at a carnal camp; and in "The Super's Dream," a janitor has his fantasies fulfilled. 90 min.
79-6180 Was $24.99 ***$19.99***

Submission (1969)
A male rapist and a sexually repressed young woman pose as domestic help and get hired by a pretty middle-aged fashion designer. When the pair discover some porno films that prove their new boss is a lesbian, the man plans to blackmail her into having sex, while the woman wants to carnally comfort her. With Liza Duran, June Adams and adult star Jennifer Welles.
79-6441 Was $24.99 ***$19.99***

Vibrations (1969)
The vibrations are more than good—they're downright sizzling!—in this raw Joe Sarno study of sex, lesbianism and incest. Julie and Barbara are feuding sisters whose jealousy and hormones rage out of control when a woman named Georgia enters their lives, huge vibrator in tow. The three discover "pleasure so intense, it's akin to torment—exquisite pain."
79-6445 Was $24.99 ***$19.99***

Passion Holiday (1963)
Four Southern gals—a pretty piece of white trash, a blonde secretary, a nightclub singer and a waitress at a greasy spoon—all meet in Miami. And Collins Avenue will never be the same! At a pool, they meet a quartet of studs who later take them to a strip club. The gals are soon taking off their clothes, too, but look out for the mobsters hot on their trail. With Christy Foushee, Linda Hall.
79-6433 Was $24.99 ***$19.99***

Passion In Hot Hollows (1967)
This nasty little sexploiter from Joe Sarno ("Sex in the Suburbs") is set in Hot Hollows, a town going through an economic depression when the residents decide to forget their problems by partaking in a series of sexual liaisons. Jean, the pretty widow running the local hotel; her little sister, Norma Lou; and other townspeople are among the participants. With Britt Hansen, June Daley. 83 min.
79-6197 Was $24.99 ***$19.99***

Sappho Darling (1968)
Albert Zugsmith ("Sex Kittens Go to College") was responsible for the great dialogue in this Swedish teaser about a sweet, young woman named Sappho, who can't make it with men because of terrible things that happened to her mother. Of course, Sappho's gal pals have no problems with the guys—or other gals, for that matter. With Carol Young and Yvonne D'Angers.
79-6438 Was $24.99 ***$19.99***

Watch The Birdie (1965)
Four gorgeous gals looking for some extra cash get lured into a sleazy cheesecake modeling racket headed by a perverted creep named Cullen. The cheesecake turns rancid when cute photo sessions turn into bondage, S&M, lesbian and other kinky excursions for Cullen and his special clients. Wendy Wood, Pamela Sears and character actor Richard B. Shull star. 74 min.
79-6177 Was $24.99 ***$19.99***

Sexus (1964)
A beautiful heiress is kidnapped and held until her wealthy father delivers the ransom. The young woman develops an attraction to one of her captors, but another member of the gang tries to rape her, leading to a deadly triangle. Starring Virginia de Solen, this study in "physical excess" features music by Chet Baker and rousing dances filmed in Elle Et Lui, Paris' famed lesbian nightclub. 88 min.
83-3012 ***$29.99***

Confessions Of A Psycho Cat (1968)
A woman with wanton desires goes about fulfilling her fantasies, ignoring all who stand in her way. She has her sights set on three human targets who will be unwilling participants in lust and humiliation. Eileen Lord and Ed Brandt star in this lurid sexploiter that steps way over the line into depravity, featuring kinky encounters, lesbian liaisons and Jake La Motta.
79-6179 ***$24.99***

The Hookers (1967)
A torrid trio of tales are told in this titillating treatise on prostitutes: an African-American beauty teases her white superiors into paying for her body; a discotheque dancer is lured into the world of hooking by a hustler; and a pretty but bored housewife gets addicted to gambling but has to go to work to pay off her debts to the syndicate. Scorching! Fleurette Carter, Monica Lee star. 70 min.
79-6199 Was $24.99 ***$19.99***

Two Nights With Cleopatra (1954)
A beautiful 19-year-old Sophia Loren plays a dual role in this racy comedy, as both the sultry Queen of the Nile with a "man-a-night" appetite and a blonde slave girl who takes her place temporarily. An all-too-brief skinny-dipping pool scene with Sophia highlights this risqué treat that's so funny you'll laugh your asp off. 77 min.
62-1216 ***$29.99***

Naked Venus (1958)
What a tangled web love weaves! An American boy and a French girl fall in love, but are kept apart because she's a member of a nudist colony! Will they "uncover" true happiness? Patricia Conelle. 80 min.
62-1256 ***$19.99***

The Flesh Merchant (1956)
The sign said "Models Wanted," but the beautiful women who answered didn't know what they were getting into. Soon, they were turning tricks on the streets of Hollywood, with sleazy crooks running the business. Exploitation classic stars Joy Reynolds, Guy Manford and Geri Moffatt. AKA: "The Wild and the Wicked." 90 min.
68-8748 Was $19.99 ***$14.99***

Adam And Eve (1958)
The Biblical story of the world's first man and woman, and that fateful bite from the apple is presented without compromise, with the lead characters naked as nature intended. Former Miss Universe Christiane Martel is the luscious Eve, Carlos Baena the rugged Adam. In Eastman Color.
79-5416 Was $24.99 ***$19.99***

Bagdad After Midnight (1954)
Rock the Casbah with a pair of comics who land in pre-Saddam Bagdad and get to watch a show peppered with a bevy of breasty belly dancers. Lots of sexy, erotic dancing with the likes of Dimples Morgan and burlesque-styled comedy from Dick Kimball and Wally Blair; directed by Phil Tucker ("Robot Monster").
79-5076 ***$19.99***

Tijuana After Midnight (1960)
Travel to Tijuana, the south-of-the-border city where anything can and will happen, in this softcore travelogue from famed B-moviemaker Phil Tucker. You'll get to take in a show of exotic dancers, featuring Rita Ravel and Misty Ayres doing the hoochie-coochie, Mexican-style, replete with pasties and slinky costumes. 60 min.
79-5019 ***$19.99***

Bettie Page

Striporama (1952)
The first film of Bettie Page's "burlesque trilogy" is a risqué blend of comedy and strippers in color! Page, Lili St. Cyr and Georgia Southern star in a story of three comics who try to convince a cultural council that burlesque is a national institution by staging a show. Features Bettie's notorious bubble bath routine in a sheik's harem. NOTE: This rare print is missing its ending—but it doesn't matter!
79-6111 Was $24.99 ***$19.99***

Varietease (1955)
A delightful burlesque movie starring the incredible Bettie Page performing her famous "harem dance," exotic Lili St. Cyr, dancer Chris La Chris and female impersonator Vicki Lynn. Snappy, saucy and spicy, this color Irving Klaw production is a true collector's item. 65 min.
79-5269 Was $24.99 ***$19.99***

Teaserama (1955)
A rare, color burlesque feature, with strippers, dancers and comics at the top of their risqué form. The incomparable Bettie Page is featured in sizzling routines and has 12 costume changes, strip sensation Tempest Storm does her hubba-hubba thing, and funnyman Joe E. Ross is a laugh riot. 69 min.
79-5268 Was $24.99 ***$19.99***

The Classic Films Of Irving Klaw, Vol. 1
Irving Klaw, the pioneer of '40s and '50s fetish films and discoverer of model Bettie Page, is given a kinky salute in this collection of his ground-breaking work. There's spanking, ropes, leather, high heels, shackles and lots more in these bold yet innocent efforts featuring Bettie, Lynn Lyrkle and other not-so-dainty darlings. 60 min.
50-8441 ***$29.99***

The Classic Films Of Irving Klaw, Vol. 2
Bettie Page and pals shake, rattle, roll and whip their way through a second selection of softcore shorts produced by bondage king Irving Klaw. Whether it's metallic cone bras, leather bondage gear, spiked heels or black nylons, these classic—and rarely seen—shorts are sure to amaze you. Page is joined by Jackie Lens, Mya Linn and other pretty models. 60 min.
50-8442 ***$29.99***

America's Pinup Queen: Bettie Page
Throughout the '40s and '50s she was the racy photo and softcore film sex kitten who aroused millions of Americans, and today she enjoys a cult following. This collection of rare "R"-style shorts features Bettie in lingerie, dancing and, yes, even spanking scenes. 53 min.
62-1327 ***$19.99***

Bettie 'N Bondage
Take a walk on the wild side of beloved pin-up fave Bettie Page with these risqué shorts from the '50s and '60s that feature the beautiful Bettie in some painful and combative situations, replete with chains, shackles, spankings and catfights. Included are "Pinup Beauties Battle," "Chastised in High Heels" and "Chained Slave Girls." 55 min.
62-1371 ***$19.99***

Allyson Is Watching
An upscale "escort" girl teaches her moves and tricks to an innocent and inexperienced young woman, but what will the "cost" of her erotic education be? Steamy and compelling softcore thriller stars Caroline Ambrose, James Horan and Jennifer Leigh Hammon. 86 min.
07-2678 *$39.99*

Dr. Yes: The Hyannis Affair
A seductive bitch goddess (Britt Ekland) serves as a proprietor of an exclusive jet-set resort for the rich and lusty. Sizzling softcore sensuality abounds, as Britt tries to keep everyone happy. 97 min.
07-1938 *$19.99*

Babes, Bikes & Beyond
Hot-blooded honeys hover atop their hogs in a sweat-inducing mix of leather, skin and chrome. These easy riders go naked when they're not wearing leather bras and panties or the best in biker lingerie. Harley harlots—start your engines! 52 min.
07-2383 *$14.99*

Candy The Stripper
A stripper named Candy heats up the Mardi Gras when she befriends a handsome stranger. As she takes it off, he learns the tricks of the trade, leading to a sizzling relationship between them. Tracy Vaccaro and Gordon Thomson star. 93 min.
07-1939 *$19.99*

Embrace The Darkness
One of the steamiest vampire tales ever put to film, this erotic chiller follows Galan and Miranda, a vampire couple who journey to L.A. in search of fresh victims. When Galan falls for a beautiful mortal, his jealous partner sets out to ensnare the woman in a web of seduction and otherworldly desires. Kevin Spirtas, Madison Clark, Angelia High star. 93 min.
07-2703 *$39.99*

A Matter Of Cunning
An ambitious, gorgeous female executive uses her looks and her wits to climb to the top of the corporate ladder in this sizzling erotic drama. 92 min.
07-1875 Was $59.99 *$19.99*

Super Boobs, Vol. 1
The biggest, most bodacious strippers of the 1940s and 1950s are showcased in this hubba-hubba collection. See Eleanor Jones, Virginia Bell, Busty Brown and others shake, rattle and swerve in such segments as "Movie Model," "The Sea Siren," "The Forest Nymph," "Slightly High" and "Buxom Blonde." 120 min.
79-6467 Was $24.99 *$19.99*

Super Boobs, Vol. 2
Ha-cha-cha-cha! These sultry sirens of yesteryear exemplify the art of erotic striptease—before strippers were merely silicone-injected porn stars displaying their phony assets! Ya gotta enjoy these "Love Apples" with Bobbie Reynolds! Want to "Caress" Virginia Bell? And see why Busty Brown is "Really Stacked"! 119 min.
79-6468 Was $24.99 *$19.99*

Striptease Girl
Famous stripper Tempest Storm stars in this burlesque bonanza filled with delectable dolls, dancing, prancing, wacky comics and lots of see-through bras. Featuring "a dazzling galaxy of sensational beauties in a riot of mirth and melody."
79-5009 Was $24.99 *$19.99*

Striporama, Vol. 1
The legends of striptease take it off, take it all off for you! Eye-popping ecdysiastic excitement with Sally Rand, Tempest Storm, Scarlett Knight and many more. Includes comedy strips and rare home footage. 50 min.
62-1280 *$19.99*

Striporama, Vol. 2
A second sampling of tassel-tossing teasers from the Golden Age of Burlesque. There's vintage striptease shorts from as far back as 1911's "Dance of All Veils," and among the legendary ladies dancing here are Candy Barr, pin-up queen Bettie Page, and a woman who looks more than a little like Marilyn Monroe (Could it be? You decide!). 53 min.
62-1345 *$19.99*

Striporama, Vol. 3
Take another trip down Mammary Memory Lane with these classic short films with the stars of Burlesque. There's Tempest Storm's "Desert Dance," Jennie Lee ("The Bazoom Girl") in "Sleepy Time Gal" and "Sugar Daddy Strip," a pre-Hollywood Sheree North doing her "Harem Dance," a clip featuring Bettie Page and much more. 50 min.
62-1349 *$19.99*

Hollywood Peepshow
Here's a front-row ticket to burlesque at its best, as some of the world's wildest strippers fling and zing off their clothes in classic, koochie-coo style. See Zabuda, Temptress of the Nile, perform her unbelievable dance. Watch "Texas Cyclone" Dimples Morgan and the always-exciting Tiger Boogie.
15-9009 Was $19.99 *$14.99*

A Night At The Follies
World famous "hubba-hubba girl" Evelyn West wiggles and wows you in this burlesque feature from the world famous Follies Theatre in Los Angeles. She's joined by a host of comics, dancers and other woo-woo gals in this sinuous show. 65 min.
79-5049 Was $24.99 *$19.99*

Tempest Storm: The Queen Of Burlesque
Legendary striptease artist Tempest Storm shows what made her such a hot-shot on the strip circuit with this video that includes a striptease performance, documentary footage of the double-D darling's career and interviews in which she discusses flings with JFK and others. 60 min.
50-8549 *$29.99*

Strip, Strip Hooray (1950)
This Lillian Hunt production captures burlesque the way it was meant to be remembered. Enjoy the scintillating striptease gals on parade here, including Eddie Ware, Wilma Wescott, Blaza Glory, the legendary Tempest Storm and others.
79-5203 Was $24.99 *$19.99*

The Striptease Murder Case (1950)
In New York's Runaway theater, the crowds are being overwhelmed by the strippers and comics while danger lurks behind the klieglights. Two singers are being roughhoused, and the hood responsible is killed. Who did him in? If only the tassels could talk. Dennis Harrison and Janie Ford star.
79-5578 Was $24.99 *$19.99*

Ding Dong: A Night At The Moulin Rouge (1951)
No, it's not the Moulin Rouge in Paris. It's the Moulin Rouge Theatre in Oakland, where a soiree of sexy strippers strut their stuff. From hefty hayseed honeys like the Bell of the Blue Ridge Mountains and a singing hostess with the mostest to a male comedian with pasties and a baseball skit, this one's something to check out! With Illona the Bavarian Orchid. 71 min.
79-5628 *$19.99*

Paris After Midnight (1951)
The legendary striptease artist Tempest Storm makes an early appearance in this burlesque romp about two American GIs who wreak havoc in a French hotel and cabaret filled with sexy French femmes, dancing girls and more. Ms. Storm rehearses her act to piano and bongo accompaniment and talks to a ventriloquist's dummy. Flo Ash and Tandalaye also star.
79-5626 Was $24.99 *$19.99*

B-Girl Rhapsody (1952)
In this stripshow feature, you'll meet the gals who put the "B" in burlesque: Amber Dawn, Ruby Lee, Nona "The Blonde Venus" Carver, Chili Pepper, Ginger "The Atomic Blonde" DuVal and Chrystal Starr. All perform their fabulous routines at L.A.'s New Follies Theatre, along with comedy from wacky comics. 90 min.
79-5548 Was $24.99 *$19.99*

Lili's Wedding Night (1952)
If you love burlesque, you'll savor this incredible feature in which Lili St. Cyr takes a sudsy bath and slips into comfortable clothing, French black dancer Contessa Vera Rickhova "smokes" on stage, and some cowboy cuties are sure to elicit responses of "yippee-i-oh!"
79-5580 Was $24.99 *$19.99*

Love Moods (1952)/ A Bedroom Fantasy (1953)
"God bless Lili St. Cyr," as the legendary strip star is featured in two hubba-hubba short films. See her entice viewers from her boudoir, then take a relaxing bubble bath. Whew! With the Foilettes and the Duponts (no, they're not from Delaware!). 33 min. total.
79-5204 Was $24.99 *$14.99*

Peek-A-Boo (1953)
The sexiest burlesque on Earth is presented in this gem from the golden era of hubba-hubba. The shapely blonde is Sherry Winters, Jennie Lee is bra-ripping in stature, French star Suzette adds the proper European touch and Venus is your girl! 75 min.
79-5327 *$19.99*

A Night In Hollywood (1953)
This is one night burlesque fans will not forget for a long time, a classic example of the bump-and-grind circuit at its peaks, featuring naughty dancers, outlandish routines and wacky comics. Headlining is the incredible Tempest Storm, who's joined by the likes of Wilma Westcott, Dorothy Ates and Jean Carroll.
79-5627 Was $24.99 *$19.99*

Can-Can Follies (1954)
The New Follies Theatre hosts the hottest dancers on the burlesque circuit in this feature offering polka dot dancers, a fan dancer, "a swinger" and a comedienne who gets into the act. Syra the Swiss Doll, Cleo and Carmelita are in the spotlight.
79-5549 Was $24.99 *$19.99*

Merry Maids Of The Gay Way (1954)
Zabouda, Doreen Cannon, Taffy Terrell and Cherri Lee are among the stripping sensations who take the spotlight in this burlesque production. They're cute, they're classy, they're buxom, they're unforgettable.
79-5574 Was $24.99 *$19.99*

Dream Follies (1954)
Written by Lenny Bruce and featuring his mother, Sally Marr, this free-form burlesque bonanza is about a couple of office guys who take to the local hoochy-koochy house when boredom takes its toll. They witness wowsome strippers like Deenah Prince, Rusty Amber, Tarana and Strivena and goofy comics. Phil Tucker ("Robot Monster") directs.
79-5632 Was $24.99 *$19.99*

Shock-O-Rama (1955)
For those who remember the great days of burlesque, this film is a treat! Birdbrain McDuff doesn't have enough cash to attend the girlie show, so he decides to take a peep. And what he sees is a group of gorgeous gals, including a woman taking a bath in a department store window; Diana Ross and her mischievous monkey; and the incredible Tempest Storm and her 44-inch chest.
79-5625 Was $24.99 *$19.99*

Buxom Beautease (1956)
Some of the world's wildest strippers show off their stuff in this crazy collage of koochie-koo from Bettie Page auteur Irving Klaw. There's Tempest Storm, Lili St. Cyr, Blaze Starr and Rita Grable wiggling their bods in their inimitable style. Leave it to cleavage!
79-5494 Was $24.99 *$19.99*

French Peek-A-Boo (1959)
The French...they are a funny race. Witness this wild tale of a detective peeking around a burlesque theater and witnessing can-can girls, gangsters, nude women in clear raincoats and an amazing "Creation of the World" production with naked gals, goofy costumes, animals and symbolism. In French with English subtitles.
79-5633 Was $24.99 *$19.99*

Kiss Me Baby (1961)
You'll want to put the smooch on the sexy strippers showcased here. Gorgeous glamour gals like Midnight, Taffy O'Niel, Joy Ryder and Pat Flannery strut their stuff in classic strip style. 84 min.
79-5200 *$19.99*

My Tale Is Hot (1964)
What would a men's magazine of the 1960s look like if it came to life? Probably something like this nudie-cutie classic, in which the devil enlists a bevy of buxomy babes to seduce "the world's most faithful husband" (played by burlesque comic Little Jack Little) out of his title. Candy Barr leads the large cast. Presented in "Skin-a-Scope."
79-5492 Was $24.99 *$19.99*

Paris Topless (1966)
Check out Paris when it sizzles with stripping great Tempest Storm. She leads the bevy of bodacious women dedicated to making you happy, whether you are in Paris or New York. See them show 'em in a dazzling array of classic stripteases featuring the world's most masterful taker-offers. 62 min.
79-6185 Was $24.99 *$19.99*

Girls Gone Wild, Vol. 1: Deluxe
The girls are running wild in this no-holds-barred program that shows everyday women baring their bods during spring break, at Mardi Gras and other party situations.
50-8290 *$24.99*

Girls Gone Wild, Vol. 2: Mardi Gras Madness
A lot more than beads are on display in this hedonistic hoe-down in the Crescent City. Go to the parties, parades and the streets of the French Quarter where gorgeous gals are seized by the moment and show off their best! 60 min.
50-8292 *$19.99*

Girls Gone Wild, Vol. 3: Spring Break Madness
The babes are wet, wild and beautiful in and out of their bikinis in these uncensored spring break videos. If the MTV spring break broadcasts pique your curiosity, this program will fulfill it, as coeds go carnal for you to see! 60 min.
50-8293 *$19.99*

Girls Gone Wild: Three-Pack
You'll go wild over the money you save with this three-tape set featuring "Deluxe," "Mardi Gras" and "Spring Break."
50-8370 Save $25.00! *$39.99*

Girls Gone Wild: College Spring Break Deluxe
Naughty! Steamy!! Real!!! The gals from colleges around the country are all these and—when they reveal their bodies—so much more! See how candid these cameras can really get.
50-8630 *$19.99*

Girls Gone Wild: Mardi Gras College Co-Eds Deluxe
Welcome to the Big Easy, folks: a place where the booze is flowing, the music is sizzling and the college babes are, er, flashing. Bourbon Street becomes the Avenue of Erotica as sweet-faced university chicks show their beads and more.
50-8631 *$29.99*

Girls Gone Wild: Deluxe Two-Pack
Get two "Girls Gone Wild" programs—"College Spring Break" and "Mardi Gras College Co-Eds"—in this special package.
50-8632 Save $10.00! *$29.99*

Girls Gone Wild: Best Of Spring Break
As proven here, the beach may be the best place to catch the hottest babes in the world. You'll see stunningly simple bikinis and thongs, both on and off these curvaceous co-eds. Hello, dere!
50-8633 *$19.99*

Girls Gone Wild: Best Of Mardi Gras
Ah, the Crescent City. Paul Prudhomme, the New Orleans Saints, Dixieland Jazz...and women walking into town, a-whoopin' and a-whoppin', showing off their whoppers for mere beads. See how wild things can get during Mardi Gras time.
50-8634 *$19.99*

Girls Gone Wild: Best Of Two-Pack
This "Girls Gone Wild" two-pack includes "Best of Spring Break" and "Best of Mardi Gras."
50-8635 Save $10.00! *$29.99*

Stag Reels: 1920s-1930s
This compilation of "smokers" from the old days offers such short, sexy subjects as "A Future Venus" (1926), "The Living Picture" (1928), "Uncle Si and the Sirens" (1927) and others. 60 min.
03-5018 *$24.99*

Grindhouse Follies
Forget "Showgirls," here's the real McCoy! The biggest stars and hottest routines from the Golden Age of Burlesque are featured in these spicy, "adults only" assortments of short films and clips that are as sizzling today as they ever were. Each tape runs about 90 min. There are 24 volumes available, including:

Grindhouse Follies, Vol. 3
They shake, they rattle, they roll and they strip in this unreal collection of take-it-off titillators of the past. See vintage films like "Casbah Mystery," "Hula Fantasies," "Inca Strip," "Tiger Girl" (Rrrowwwwrr!) and more. Hubba hubba! 90 min.
79-5011 Was $24.99 *$19.99*

Grindhouse Follies, Vol. 2
Start whistling, folks. This collection of ripping and stripping shorts from the golden days of burlesque serves up such delights as "Follies Bergere," "Virginia Valentine," "Fan Tease," "Goldilocks Goes Glamorous" and many other mesmerizing memories. 90 min.
79-5012 Was $24.99 *$19.99*

Grindhouse Follies, Vol. 1
It's "tasselmania" and "pasties resistance" with this collection of swervy and seductive dance films from the burlesque of yesteryear. On tap in this tape: Jenny Lee, Doris Delay, Yuma Starr, "H. Bomb," "Persian Cookie" and the inimitable "Sheba Wore No Nylons"! 90 min.
79-5013 Was $24.99 *$19.99*

Grindhouse Follies, Vol. 4
More slinky Sallies strut their sassiness and tassles in your living room: Witness "The Golddigger Tease" (Hey, Dino!), "Jury: No Reservations," "Las Vegas Tease," "Comic Strip" and the favorite "Margie's Tease." 90 min.
79-5055 Was $24.99 *$19.99*

Grindhouse Follies, Vol. 5
Take a gander at "Yukon Belle," "Mohawk War Dance," strippers with parasols and "Escape from a Harem," sure to sexcite even the most staid sheik. 90 min.
79-5056 Was $24.99 *$19.99*

Grindhouse Follies Front-Row Special, Vol. 1
Originally filmed in 3-D, these films give new "hubba" to the term "hubba-hubba." This collection of burlesque shorts from 1953-54 features Tempest Storm (who has her breasts imprinted in cement), and Lili St. Cyr in such films as "Love for Sale," "Madonna and Her Bubbles," "Virgin in Hollywood" and "Bella Starr."
79-5270 Was $24.99 *$19.99*

Grindhouse Follies, Vol. 21
There's an international flair to the sultry strippers delighting you on this tape, displaying their titanic talents. There's Irene Gale ("Oriental Interlude"), Kalantan ("Her Buddha Dance"), Mona ("At the Eve Nightclub in Paris"), Delores Del Raye ("St Louis Woman"), Nelja Ates ("The Turkish Delight") and Amalia Aguilar ("Cuban Devil Drums"). All this and Tempest Storm, too!
79-6457 Was $24.99 *$19.99*

Twisted Sex: Trailers From The Sick, Sick Sixties
Go back in time to the swinging days of the Sexual Revolution, when folks would head to late-night shows at their local theatre or drive-in to see steamy "adults only" fare like the softcore classics whose "coming attractions" are gathered in this series. Each tape runs about 90 min. There are 19 volumes available, including:

Twisted Sex, Vol. 1
The sexploitation films of the wild, wild decade are represented by this collection that includes trailers from such adults-only gems as "The Hookers," "The Tomcat," "Tassel-Go-Go Dancer," "I, A Woman, Part II," "Ride the Wild Pink Horse" and many more. 90 min.
79-5039 Was $24.99 *$19.99*

Twisted Sex, Vol. 2
More nudity-filled teasers from the naked Sixties, including such sexamples as "The Embracers," "Nudes on Tiger Reef," "Some Like It Violent," "Lust and the Flesh," "The Playpen Girls" and more. 90 min.
79-5040 Was $24.99 *$19.99*

Twisted Sex, Vol. 3
Another assortment of trailers promoting the finest in R- and X-rated entertainment. Nudity abounds in such "classics" as "I, A Woman," "Fanny Hill Meets Dr. Erotico," "Sex Club International," "Carny Girl" and "The Art of Marriage" and other delights from the topsy-turvy decade. 90 min.
79-5041 Was $24.99 *$19.99*

The Worst Of Twisted Sex
Turn your living room into your favorite grindhouse by getting this program that offers trailers for such depraved films as "Olga's Massage Parlor," "The Lusting Hour," "Take Me Naked," "The Soul Snatcher," "The Love Toy" and more. Now, all you need is stale popcorn, the scent of industrial-strength disinfectant and chewing gum under your seat.
79-5571 Was $24.99 *$19.99*

Harry Novak's Boxoffice Bonanza Of Sexploitation Trailers And Featurettes, Vol. 1
An amazing amalgam of trailers from the productions of noted schlockmeister Harry Novak, including "The Slave Window," "Mini-Skirt Love," "Mondo Mod," "The Touchables," "Secret Lives of Romeo & Juliet" and many more.
79-5196 Was $24.99 *$19.99*

Harry Novak's Boxoffice Bonanza Of Sexploitation Trailers And Featurettes, Vol. 2
Check out more titillating trailers of one of the pioneers of the softcore sex film. Featured are coming attractions for "Southern Comforts," "Honey Doll Jones," "Tobacco Roody," "Midnight Plowboy," "Erika's Hot Summer" and shorts like "Kittens" and "The Peepers."
79-5197 Was $24.99 *$19.99*

Girls-A-Poppin'
A carnal cornucopia of 1920s, '30s and '40s short films. Included are "Hunting Bare," in which three ladies go hunting; "Neptune's Daughters," featuring four seafaring women; "Perfect Exposure," a look at an all-ladies camera club; and "Christmas Toys," spotlighting sensuous elves. AKA: "Sexcapades." 55 min.
62-1368 *$19.99*

Nudie Classics, Vol. I
Call them "adult films," call them "roadhouse shorts," call them "black-maskers"...these are the racy films that Dad saw in the '30s and '40s. Lots of laughs, (mostly) gorgeous gals and semi-nudity, but no X-rated scenes. 55 min.
62-1080 *$19.99*

Nudie Classics, Vol. II
More frisky films from the heyday of peep shows—1917-1965. All are R-rated, includes: "Feminine Touch," "Hard Work," "Fighting Femmes of Paris," and "Amour Pour Une Femme." 60 min.
62-1170 *$19.99*

Nudie Classics, Vol. III
These naughty nudies are the best smokers you've seen! "A Strip in Rhyme," "Starlet Revue," "Nude Cocktails," "Forbidden" (with pin-up star Bettie Page), "Apple Knockers" (which was rumored to star a young Marilyn Monroe; it doesn't), and "Hollywood Honey," with stripper Virginia Bell, are featured. 55 min.
62-1266 *$19.99*

Flaming Flappers
Featured on this collection are explicit stag reels including "A Free Ride" (1920), "The Magician" (1936), "The Casting Couch" (1928) and the animated "Buried Treasure" (1925). WARNING: Adults only!
03-5019 *$24.99*

60's Bizarro Sex Loops, Vol. 1
This kinky collection of outrageous sex accents weird and wild acts of diversion from the Sixties. Included here are "Turned-On Toes," "I Dreamed I Was a Captive Princess," "Rubber Lovers," "Melinda, The Latex Maid" and more. Tune in, turn on and camp out!
79-5050 Was $24.99 *$19.99*

60's Bizarro Sex Loops, Vol. 2
More kinky and outrageous softcore shorts depicting all manner of strangeness are offered in this truly unusual assortment that includes fetish, catfights, garters, playgirls and vampires.
79-5521 Was $24.99 *$19.99*

60's Bizarro Sex Loops, Vol. 3
Kink out with this selection of deviant sex shorts that offer the full spectrum of perverse behavior. Highlighted here are the classics "The Haunted House" and "The Rack," one of the most disturbing films of its genre.
79-5522 Was $24.99 *$19.99*

Big Bust Loops
Get a bouncy, bountiful blast from the past with these carnal collections of racy shorts and peepshow films from the '50s, '60s and '70s. See top strippers, early adult movie stars and other gargantuan-gazongaed gals show off their "talents" in a variety of revealing outfits and sexy situations. Each tape runs about 90 min. There are 25 volumes available, including:

Big Bust Loops, Vol. 1
79-5034 Was $24.99 *$19.99*

Big Bust Loops, Vol. 2
79-5035 Was $24.99 *$19.99*

Big Bust Loops, Vol. 3
79-5694 Was $24.99 *$19.99*

Big Bust Loops, Vol. 4
79-5695 Was $24.99 *$19.99*

Big Bust Loops, Vol. 5
79-5696 Was $24.99 *$19.99*

Big Bust Loops, Vol. 6
79-5697 Was $24.99 *$19.99*

Big Bust Loops, Vol. 7
79-5698 Was $24.99 *$19.99*

Nudie-Cutie: Shorts, Loops And Peeps
The box says, "Curvaceous cuties and bodacious bouncing babes reveal the utmost in feminine beauty in these spicy peep shows and arcade loops from the '30s, '40s, '50s and '60s." We say, "Nuff said." Each tape runs about 90 min. There are 78 volumes available, including:

Nudie-Cutie, Vol. 1
An amazing collection of yesterday's spicy entertainment, featuring "shorts, loops and peeps" with the nudies of "Feminine Foursome," "Ladder Antics," "Nude Hula," "Chicago Fan Dance" and much more. 90 min.
79-5014 Was $24.99 *$19.99*

Nudie-Cutie, Vol. 2
A further array of arousing actresses is offered in this unbelievable line-up of lascivious ladies enacting "Sun-Kissed Beauties," "Gun Moll," "Let's Make Mary Moan" "On the String" and others. They don't make 'em like this anymore! 90 min.
79-5015 Was $24.99 *$19.99*

Nudie-Cutie, Vol. 3
Take a peep at these "peeps" from olden days when a glimpse of stocking was considered...just the start! Travel from "Tel Aviv" to "Saigon," improve your mind with "Artist's Studio Models," "Bedroom Art Today" and "At the Easel," more. 90 min.
79-5016 Was $24.99 *$19.99*

Nudie-Cutie, Vol. 4
"Drip, Grind and Percolate," "Bronco Busty," "Down in the Mouth," "Lonesome Gal" and "Swinging Frolics" are just a few of the classic examples of nostalgic nudie shorts offered in this enticing program. 90 min.
79-5017 Was $24.99 *$19.99*

Nudie-Cutie, Vol. 5
Witness "Secret Passions," encounter the "Show Off," partake in "Pajama Party Romp," go wild as "Val Takes a Shower," keep cool with the "Steamy Sunbather." All this—and more—in this sampler of vintage sleaze. 90 min.
79-5018 Was $24.99 *$19.99*

Shameless Shorts, Vol. 1
These nudie featurettes were produced as filler for theaters showing sex features, which were typically an hour in length. Running five to 10 minutes each, these color wonders are a rare treat for sexvid collectors. Included here are "Shocking Set," "Naked Fury," "Censored," "Instant Orgy" and more!
79-5274 Was $24.99 *$19.99*

David Friedman's Roadshow Shorts
"The King of Exploitation Movies," legendary producer David F. Friedman, is proud to present these titillating shorts and featurettes shown in movie theatres, burlesque houses, tents and probably even basements in the '30s, '40s and '50s. Each tape runs about 90 min. There are 14 volumes available, including:

Roadshow Shorts, Vol. 1
David F. Friedman, the king of exploitation movies, presents these titillating shorts and featurettes that were originally shown in theaters. Among the films are "They Wear No Clothes," "Congo Cuties," "Playgirl Models," "Nudist of All Nations" and "Why Nudism?"
79-5515 Was $24.99 *$19.99*

Roadshow Shorts, Vol. 2
They'll shock you and make you sweat, these shorts from the '30s, '40s and '50s. Exploitation entrepreneur Dave Friedman presents rare short films like "Model School," "Temple Dance," "Sepia Serins," "Main St. Girl," "Ladies of the Evening" and more.
79-5516 Was $24.99 *$19.99*

David Friedman's Roadshow Trailers
There's 40—count 'em, 40—come-ons for classic exploiters collected on this one-of-a-kind program that shows you how the schlockmeisters sensationally pulled patrons into theaters. Among the trailers are "Dance Hall Racket," "Too Hot to Handle," "Mom and Dad," "Mau Mau," "Souls in Pawn," "Slaves in Bondage" and lots more. 120 min.
79-5581 Was $24.99 *$19.99*

My Fair Dollies
Travel back to the 1920s, where flappers do more than flap, taking their risqué costumes off and revealing their bodies in a style that would delight any gangster of love. 84 min.
50-5474 *$19.99*

Nude On The Ranch
Here's a hoedown you won't want to miss. A group of curvaceous cowgals head to the ranch and soon rip off their clothes while experiencing the ultimate in rest and relaxation. They got boots, they got Stetsons, they got cut-off denims—and then they don't! 60 min.
50-5479 *$19.99*

The Lusty Busty Big Ones
This bountiful tribute to breastacular babes features such cantilevered cuties as Sofia Staks, Meshalynn, Tabitha Stevens and Jordan St. James romping in all of their gigantic glory. 60 min.
50-5550 *$29.99*

Nude Lawyers
This is definitely something you'll never see on Court TV! These lovely, luscious litigators can't wait to get into a judge's chambers and lose their briefs, and you've got a front-row seat in the jury box. "I find the defendants guilty...of being totally bitchin' babes!"
75-7179 *$19.99*

Oil Of L.A.
You can rest assured none of these greasy, gorgeous grapplers will have younger looking skin after slippin' and a-slidin' in an oily battle royal, as they shimmy their things like (petroleum) jelly on springs. 60 min.
76-7003 *$19.99*

Nude Students
The 3 R's turn out to be "racy, risqué and rrrrrrrrrow" in this video featuring some young ladies who like to pursue their studies (in and out of the classroom) in the all-together.
75-7127 *$19.99*

Starlet Screen Test
Now you can catch a great view through a peephole in an agent's office, as 12 different starlets strip down for readings that require nudity. They don't know you're there...and you'll never forget it. 60 min.
14-6094 *$19.99*

Starlet Screen Test II
There's little acting ability on display here, but oooh, what you DO see! A dozen gorgeous women strip for the camera while auditioning for movie roles, and their sensual, smoldering performances are not to be missed. 60 min.
50-2277 *$24.99*

Starlet Screen Test III
Hubba-hubba. See what happens when 10 gorgeous young starlets reveal their spectacular figures in steamy audition sessions. Picture yourself in the director's chair for this full-fledged nude treat. 60 min.
50-2485 *$24.99*

Bikini Patrol
On the patrol for some sexy, sizzling swimwear fun? Look no further than this racy romp that shines the spotlight on gorgeous seaside sweeties modelling the teeniest and tiniest of bikinis. 60 min.
50-8229 *$19.99*

Et L'Amour
A romantic, artful look at a sensual lesbian liaison, in which two women remove each other's clothing in a unique and erotic style. Stylish camerawork and Parisian settings provide extra romantic elements to this unusual and provocative program. 24 min.
76-2026 Was $24.99 *$19.99*

The Miss Nude America Contest
There's no swimsuit competition in this titillating look at beauty au natural. Join Dick Drost, head of Naked City, U.S.A., and his bounty of beautiful babes in the buff for some sexy fun. 78 min.
20-1013 *$29.99*

The Aqua Tape Series, Vol. 1
Just when you thought you've seen it all, here's a collection of shorts from all over the world depicting women seducing, modeling and loving underwater. Three gals check out scuba-diving, lithesome Nikki strips and swims in the Greek Islands, a trio of tootsies try to explore their erotic desires under the sea. It's "H2Ohhh, baby!" 55 min.
50-2691 **$49.99**

The Aqua Tape Series, Vol. 2
Another collection of the greatest hits of sexy gals getting dunked offers a topless scuba session on a coral reef; a Gentlemen's Club magazine modeling session that ends with everyone in the pool; naked underwater nymphs on the prowl; and two gals who appreciate each other's company...especially when wet! 55 min.
50-2692 **$49.99**

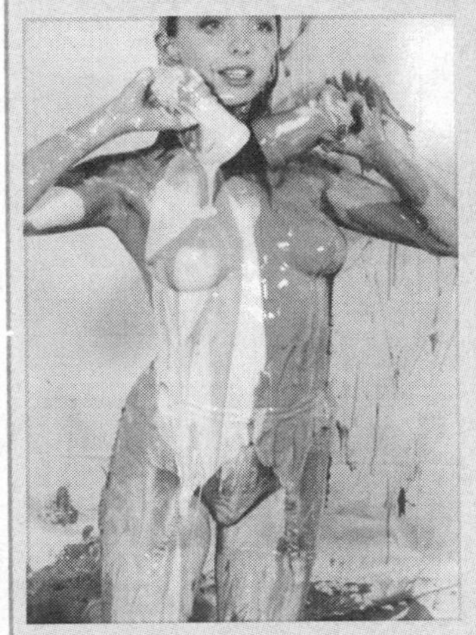

Messy Fun
If you love women getting wet or doused with food or covered in sticky substances, then these tapes are for you. All of the volumes feature gorgeous clothed and unclothed women partaking in dripping, delightfully erotic situations. There are nine volumes available, including:

Messy Fun, Vol. 1: My Friend Shaun
Fans of women who get splashed with—and in—all sorts of substances will appreciate this tape that showers them with risqué fun. Two gals hose each other down at a carwash; a trio of lovelies hit the pit...the mud pit, that is; and body painting takes on a whole new meaning. Contains nudity. 90 min.
50-2486 **$59.99**

Messy Fun, Vol. 2: Just The Facts, Miss
Girls just want to have messy fun in this soppy, sexy program that offers mud volleyball, a food fight, a blonde wearing see-through clothes, and swimming and surprises from a muddy lake. Features nudity. 95 min.
50-2487 **$59.99**

Messy Fun, Vol. 3: Tales Of The Wet And Messy
Looking for some "mudhoney" in your adult entertainment package? Try this video filled with mud massages, an automatic mud device, a whirlpool bath and, for the artists in the audience, a two-girl paint drip. A nude, messy romp! 90 min.
50-2488 **$59.99**

Sloppy, Sopping & Submerged
Splish, splash! These gorgeous gals are doing more than just taking a bath, and you can watch as they get wet—and wild—in a variety of liquids and other gooey substances. Each tape runs about 60 min. There are eight volumes available, including:

Sloppy, Sopping & Submerged, Vol. 1
Five gorgeous English lasses go for the gusto, partaking in all sorts of wild roundelays involving hot and cold substances. See baked bean fights, custard-in-the-face, underwater swims, flour power and more, as these British birds do the unthinkable in and out of their lacy lingerie.
50-2500 **$49.99**

Sloppy, Sopping & Submerged, Vol. 2
Another selection of slippery fun is in store here as two hot tub saleswomen join a pair of adventurous secretaries in wet and wild escapades in "Hot Tubs 'R Us"; food dispensers are used for erotic fun in "The Sales Training Sketch"; a wedding procession follows a bridesmaid into the pool in "The Bride Will Play"; and a wild free-for-all ensues in "Suds 'N Company."
50-2538 **$49.99**

Sloppy, Sopping & Submerged, Vol. 3
It's another incredible wet videoland of fun as two mini-dressed gals fall into the thick brown mud in "The Farmer's Daughter"; a gal gets creamed on the "Pie-Trivia Gameshow"; a pool provides the erotic setting for "Jo's Nighttime Swim"; a "Totally Gratuitous Carwash" gets real sudsy; and airbeds and pancake topping play a part in "The Maple Syrup Sketch."
50-2565 **$49.99**

Sloppy, Sopping & Submerged, Vol. 4
Hubba-hubba, swish-swish! Four gals in schoolgirl-style uniforms take a swim after a tough soccer match in "Schoolgirl Soccer"; "Basic Instinct" is spoofed in "Basic Ingredients," in which the interrogation includes water, chocolate sauce and cream pies; "Mud Limbo Mania" is just what it seems; and gals in designer suits get hosed in "The Drenched Yuppies Awards."
50-2566 **$49.99**

Party Games For Adults Only
Leave the kids at home at this party—it's for adults only! John Byner hosts and it's frivolous fun—Marshmallow Kiss, Body Painting, Ride 'Em Cowboy, Ink Blots and other favorites like Dictionary and Charades. Loads of fun.
07-1225 **$29.99**

Milton Berle Invites You To A Night At La Cage
Boys will be boys...and girls...as "Uncle Miltie" hosts this look at the infamous nightclub revue. "See" Dolly, Diana, Judy, Tina and Marilyn on stage in a wild evening of comedy, song and dance; even Milton keeps the show "dragging" on! 75 min.
07-1525 **$29.99**

The Desires Of Lonely Housewives
Unable to satisfy their desires, these married women will do anything to tickle their fancies, partaking in sexy sessions with male and female neighbors. This scorching video features full-frontal nudity and XXX stalwarts like Rachel Ashley, Selena Steele and Stephanie Rage. 30 min.
50-2693 **$19.99**

Fantasy Centerfold Girls
It's a fantasy (or two) come true when some of the sexiest centerfold models around, including Deborah Ferrari, Michele Frank, Jennifer Lee and "Howard Stern Show" fave Amy Lynn, pose for the camera in and out (but mostly out!) of fabulous outfits. 60 min.
39-5925 Was $19.99 **$14.99**

Nude Secretaries
"Take a letter" becomes "take it off" in this sizzling sexposé of some 9-to-5 nymphs who strip down to show off their "company assets" in ways that would garner a raise from the toughest executive. 60 min.
75-7107 **$19.99**

Nude Secretaries 2: The New Corporation
And what healthy male businessman wouldn't like to launch a "corporate merger" with the sexy stenographers whose "blue chip" bodies are featured on this video. Can they type? Do they know shorthand? Who knows, and who cares?
75-7174 **$19.99**

Nude Golf
These delectable duffers put the "fore" into "foreplay," as they doff their duds for a risqué round of golf in the all-together. Watch them get a good, firm grip on the club handle as they aim for the hole and put it in. 50 min.
19-3719 **$14.99**

Student Bodies
The scholastic cuties on display here are sure to make you yearn for "school days" once more, as an array of sexy young women (each and every one able to matriculate) show off their bodies for your perusal. 60 min.
19-3905 **$14.99**

Pom Pom Girls
Do your "spirits" need a lift? Get ready to root along with the peppy, pulchritudinous women featured in this rousing (and arousing) program, as they shake their pom poms, among other things, in a sexy show of school spirit. 60 min.
19-3906 **$14.99**

Sexy Sorority Sisters
Ever wonder what goes on inside a campus sorority house late at night, when the girls have only each other for companionship? This program gives you an intimate look-see at the sisters' private "pillow talk" sessions, where anything can happen. 60 min.
19-3907 **$14.99**

Spice Home Video's Road Show Featuring Jenna Jameson
She's one of the most popular stars in adult film history, and now you've got a front-row seat as you go on the road with Jenna Jameson. Watch as she gets up-close and personal with her fans, tours some of the country's hottest gentleman's clubs, and even lights up the city of Paris. 85 min.
07-2849 **$19.99**

Carnival In Rio
Brazil's famed carnival is the site for this thrilling program hosted by Arnold Schwarzenegger, who takes you into the middle of the wildest funfest ever captured for the cameras. Sexy sambas, gorgeous women, sensuous costumes (what little of them there is) and Arnold as host!
07-1810 Was $59.99 **$19.99**

Secrets Of Love
Some of the world's greatest erotic literature has been adapted for these beautifully filmed programs that boast nudity, fine production values and intelligent dialogue. Each tape includes two stories and runs about 50 min. There are six volumes available, including:

Secrets Of Love, Vol. 1: The Greenhouse/A Country Villa
In Guy de Maupassant's "The Greenhouse," an older couple are transformed into voyeurs as they observe two young people engage in lovemaking. "A Country Villa" by Anton Chekhov finds a photographer getting involved with a beautiful widow after he rents her villa.
53-6097 **$24.99**

Secrets Of Love, Vol. 2: Augustine/At The Rose Leaf
Written by the Marquis de Sade, "Augustine" tells of a gorgeous lesbian who discovers the joys of the opposite sex when she seduces a handsome man she meets at a costume ball. And a respectable middle-class couple are captivated by the charms of a Turkish-style brothel in Guy de Maupassant's "At the Rose Leaf."
53-6098 **$24.99**

Secrets Of Love, Vol. 3: Mandragora/The Contest
A young medical student smitten with the charms of a virtuous woman uses an erotic drug potion in Niccolo Machiavelli's "The Love Potion." And Geoffrey Chaucer's "The Contest" tells of young students who try to take advantage of an elderly man with a gorgeous young wife.
53-6099 **$24.99**

Secrets Of Love, Vol. 4: The Spanking/The Pupil
After being humiliated by her forewoman, a beautiful weaver takes revenge into her own hands, whipping her boss into an erotic frenzy on St. Innocent's Day in "The Spanking," directed by Harry Kumel ("Daughters of Darkness"). And a wealthy man makes sure his nephew is taught the ways of love in "The Pupil," by Nicolas de la Bretonne.
53-6105 **$24.99**

The Erotic Zone
Tune into a zone where sensuality rules, where the women are beautiful, where the situations are kinky and surprising...tune into "The Erotic Zone." Originally run on Showtime as "Compromising Situations," these tapes will please and tease. Each includes two stories and runs about 60 min. There are six volumes available, including:

The Erotic Zone: The Ring
A tough boxer gets the surprise of his life when he discovers that his new sparring partner is, in fact, a beautiful woman in "The Ring," with Yvette Michelle. And in "Mechanics of Desire," a sexy young woman must decide whether she wants to fulfill her husband's voyeuristic tendencies. Cassandra Leigh ("Midnight Tease") stars. 60 min.
53-8439 **$14.99**

The Erotic Zone: Inspiration
Repressed corporate lawyer Diana Cuevas ("Invasion of Privacy") answers an ad for an "uninhibited artist's model" and has a hot body-painting session in "Inspiration." Then, a bellhop's fantasies about a mysterious actress in a 1950s Hollywood hotel come to life in "The Last Escape." 60 min.
53-8440 **$14.99**

The Erotic Zone: Let Your Fingers Do The Walking
House calls from a gorgeous female electrician, a plucky plumber, sexy Swedish painters and a risqué roofer are just a phone call away in "Let Your Fingers Do the Walking," with Playboy model Donna Spangler. Next, old lovers who haven't seen each other since college meet 20 years later and renew their affair in "The Reunion," featuring former Playmate Carrie Yazel.
53-8566 **$14.99**

Fabulous Flashers
What a feeling you'll get as eight fantastic femmes show what little inhibition they have by unclothing in the most intimate and public places. These ravishing rousers from the West Coast put a new way into sexy wiggling. 60 min.
50-2707 **$19.99**

Fabulous Flashers: Naked In America
Who needs "Breakfast in America" when you can get "Naked in America"? See some of the country's lustiest ladies get naked for your pleasure in this titillating ode to patriotism and nudity in public places. 60 min.
50-5244 **$19.99**

The Best Of Fabulous Flashers
They're fabulous, especially when they strip off their clothes in public, showing everyone their bodies. In this "Best Of" collection, you'll see some of the world's hottest exhibitionists getting naughty and naked. Features 20 minutes of extra-sexy, never-before-seen footage. 60 min.
50-5325 **$19.99**

Fabulous Flashers: Caught In The Act
Public nudism runs rampant as a host of hot-to-trot honies take their exhibitionism to new heights in this sizzling salute to taking it all off where anybody can enjoy it. 60 min.
50-5726 **$19.99**

Uncovered
If blondes are your thing, you should check out this blonde-iful spectacular with Rebecca Wild, Sarah Jane Hamilton and Debi Diamond showing you their "other sides." Sensuous, scintillating sexuality at its wildest are in store in this most unusual treat.
39-5510 Was $39.99 **$14.99**

Bel Air Babes
World-famous covergirls Julia Parton and Kelly Jaye are featured in this sizzling exposé of California's hottest women. See them pleasuring themselves at the pool, in bed and in other situations where they go wild in the sheets. 60 min.
39-5767 Was $19.99 **$14.99**

Best Built Babes Spectacular
They're the top bods in the world and they show off their incredibly stacked figures in this spectacular mix of blondes, brunettes and beaches. Along with "America's #1 Pin-Up," Cindy Margolis, there's Anita Hart and former NFL cheerleader Kimberly Kramer. 60 min.
50-9017 **$24.99**

Sex On The Beach: Spring Break Texas Style
Take a Spring Break you're not likely to forget: a wild romp filled with naked college gals competing in wet T-shirt contests, poolside photo shoots, romps in the sand and bungee jumping, all from South Padre Island, Texas. Features full-frontal nudity. 54 min.
77-9001 **$24.99**

Sex On The Strip: The Lusty Ladies Of Las Vegas
Get naked in Nevada as you explore the sexiest places and personnel of the world's most sexciting city. You'll tour famous strip spots like the Palomino and the Paradise Club, see Miss Nude Universe Venus De Light model for you at home and witness what goes on in a high roller's private suite. The glitter goes on...and so does the array of arresting gals. 60 min.
77-9003 **$24.99**

Swedish Dreamgirls
Say "goo-da voo-day" to a sizzling selection of Scandinavian sweeties, as these blonde bombshells display their beautiful bodies in an array of stunning indoor and outdoor European locales. "Ya, ya, very good." 60 min.
77-9030 **$19.99**

Swedish Dreamgirls 2
This sizzling selection of stunners will have you booking passage for the Arctic Circle. Take your pick of voluptuous hotties from Norway, Denmark and, yes, Sweden, who strut their stuff—right on your TV. Ga-ga-ga-ga. 60 min.
77-9031 **$19.99**

Jenna Exposed!
Sure, adult film superstar, Howard Stern regular and ECW spokeswoman Jenna Jameson has been exposed on video before, but never as in this sizzling behind-the-scenes look at a magazine photo session. See Jenna in lacy lingerie—and less—and find out about her personal side in a revealing interview. 60 min.
77-9024 **$19.99**

Naked At The Lake: Spring Break '98
"You've been such a good girl this week, you deserve a swim. Now take off that itchy robe...and the bikini." You'll be saying these very words as you cheerfully observe these hot vixens bear it all from the hot and sizzling shores of Lake Havasu, Arizona. Adara, Erica, Isabella, and Amanda are the ladies that will leave you breathless. 60 min.
77-9032 **$19.99**

Playboy's Playmates: The Early Years
A sizzling sampling of the many beautiful women who have graced the pages of Playboy over the past three decades which is true "Entertainment for Men." Catch a glimpse of Marilyn Monroe (from the very first issue in '53), Jayne Mansfield and Stella Stevens, plus the magazine's many sensuous centerfolds, film clips and home movies of Hef at play. 70 min.
07-1728 *$19.99*

1993 Playboy Video Playmate Review
1992 proved to be quite a year for feminine beauty and charm, as this salute to the year's Playmates of the Month will bare (and we do mean bare!) out. From January's Suzi Simpson to December's Barbara Moore, this delectable dozen are even hotter in video form. 55 min.
07-1926 *$19.99*

Playboy: 21 Playmates, Vol. 1
Can you pick 21 of Playboy's hottest Playmates? Well, Playboy did, and the winners are in this carnal compilation that will thrill you with its sensuality and beauty. It's an awesome array of ravishing women, a real collector's item. 70 min.
07-2379 *$19.99*

Playboy: 21 Playmates, Vol. 2
More of Playboy's hottest centerfolds are revealed in this sequel to the popular video program. Rekindle your love affair with Playboy's finest in this special collector's presentation that's sure to excite. 60 min.
07-2485 *$19.99*

2000
PLAYBOY
Video
Playmate
Calendar

Playboy Video Playmate Calendars
Who says a calendar is only good for one year? You'll wish the year would never end with these selections of 12 luscious lovelies from the pages of Playboy. There's a different centerfold for each month, each one a stunner to make time stand still. Each tape runs 60 min.

1989 Video Playmate Calendar
44-1557 Was $19.99 *$14.99*

1990 Video Playmate Calendar
44-1670 Was $19.99 *$14.99*

1991 Video Playmate Calendar
44-1767 *$19.99*

1992 Video Playmate Calendar
07-1727 *$19.99*

1993 Video Playmate Calendar
07-1881 *$19.99*

1994 Video Playmate Calendar
07-2029 *$19.99*

1995 Video Playmate Calendar
07-2208 *$19.99*

1996 Video Playmate Calendar
07-2352 *$19.99*

1997 Video Playmate Calendar
07-2466 *$19.99*

1998 Video Playmate Calendar
07-2569 *$19.99*

1999 Video Playmate Calendar
07-2689 *$19.99*

2000 Video Playmate Calendar
07-2796 *$19.99*

2001 Video Playmate Calendar
07-2949 *$19.99*

Inside Out 1
Take a journey through worlds of sexual imagination with this collection of nine short films from Playboy. Each vignette is an erotic adventure with a surprise ending à la "The Twilight Zone," created by such Hollywood mavericks as Lizzie Borden, Tony Randel and Jeff Reiner. 90 min.
07-1803 Was $79.99 *$19.99*

Inside Out 2
A hitchhiker who gets more than just a ride, a sexual "close encounter" with an alien, and a documentary salute to a stripper (played by Kitten Natividad) are just some of the sexy tales on tap in this second sensual sampler of short films. 90 min.
07-1809 Was $79.99 *$19.99*

Inside Out 3
Step into a world where mystery meets eroticism, as Playboy presents such stories as "The Portal," "Dogs Playing Poker," "Tango" and more. Directors include Martin Donovan ("Apartment Zero") and Bernard Rose ("Paperhouse"), and performers include Marilyn Hassert and Greg Louganis. 90 min.
07-1877 Was $79.99 *$19.99*

Inside Out 4
A neglected wife who bares her soul (and body) to a burglar, a bored couple looking for a third person to recharge their love life, and a woman who masquerades as a man's long-lost lover are among the sensual, surprising stories offered in this Playboy production. 90 min.
07-1897 Was $79.99 *$19.99*

Playboy's Erotic Fantasies
Wildly sensuous women and super-handsome men indulge in the wildest and most erotic fantasies ever presented in the Playboy mold, featuring a barrage of stunning Playmates. Gorgeously photographed for maximum impact, these programs are ideal for couples who enjoy the exciting things in life. Each tape runs about 60 min.

Playboy's Erotic Fantasies
07-1813 *$19.99*

Playboy's Erotic Fantasies III
07-1927 *$19.99*

Playboy's Erotic Fantasies: Forbidden Liaisons
07-2275 *$19.99*

Birds In Paradise
Three women find that their prized yacht is about to be repossessed, thanks to a weaselly attorney, and they use their beautiful looks and wits to figure out how to save it. One of their ideas; running the sexiest car wash ever! A feature version of the hit cable series from Playboy, featuring lots of nudity. 97 min.
07-1876 Was $59.99 *$19.99*

Playboy: Playmates In Paradise
Looking for a vacation spot that's a wee bit more exotic than South of the Border? How about letting this video take you to the sun-drenched shores of Jamaica, Puerto Rico and Hawaii with a passel of sexy Playmates romping on the beach in varying states of undress.
07-1883 *$19.99*

Playboy: Ultimate Sensual Massage
Gorgeous production values, lush camerawork and stunning performers will lead you on a discovery of the erotic effects of sensual massage. They'll soothe you, relax you and turn you on! 55 min.
07-1901 Was $29.99 *$19.99*

Playboy: Sensual Pleasures Of Oriental Massage
The centuries-old secrets of Eastern eroticism can be yours through this instructional video that features an arousing array steamy vignettes. See couples practice such relaxing, soothing techniques as Japanese Anma and shiatsu and Chinese "triple heat" massages, and learn how to give your partner the same treatments. 55 min.
44-1827 Was $29.99 *$19.99*

Playboy: Strip
Take a sexy excursion into the world of strippers—gals who take their clothes off, lap dance, romp in a risqué fashion. See some of the wildest women wiggle their way off the stage and into your home, Playboy style.
07-2378 *$19.99*

Playboy's Girls Of The Internet
Take off on the super highway where technology meets titillation and where your imagination is your only boundary. Get down, get loaded with gals you thought were nerds but are really sex kittens. Open these windows to find pleasure.
07-2380 *$19.99*

Playboy International Playmates
If Phineas Fogg had seen these beauties on his round-the-world trip, it would have taken him more than 80 days to complete it! Join Playboy photographers as they travel to Brazil, Germany, Holland, Taiwan, Australia and other lands in search of the world's most beautiful women.
07-1909 Was $19.99 *$14.99*

101 Ways To Excite Your Lover
Who better than Playboy Home Video to present this guide to sensual stimulation for couples? Learn new ways to spice up lovemaking through 101 tips and techniques designed to help you use all five senses and enter new areas of sexuality.
07-1910 Was $29.99 *$19.99*

PLAYBOY
Video
CENTERFOLD
PLAYMATE OF THE YEAR
JODI ANN PATERSON
PLUS PLAYMATE BONUS
BROOKE RICHARDS

Playboy Video Centerfolds
Get acquainted with only the most luscious ladies of Playboy with your very own Video Centerfold, as the camera catches revealing glimpses of each Playmate, without staples getting in the way. There are 20 volumes available, including:

Playboy Video Centerfold: Pamela Anderson
07-1797 *$19.99*

Playboy Video Centerfold: Playmate 2000: Bernaola Twins
07-2815 *$19.99*

Playboy Video Centerfold: Kerri Kendall
44-1756 *$19.99*

Playboy Video Centerfold: 40th Anniversary Playmate: Anna-Marie Goddard
07-2182 *$19.99*

Playboy Video Centerfold: 45th Anniversary Playmate: Jaime Bergman
07-2713 *$19.99*

Playboy Video Centerfold: The Dahm Triplets
07-2719 *$19.99*

Playboy Video Centerfold: Reneé Tenison: 1990 Playmate Of The Year
44-1724 Was $19.99 *$14.99*

Playboy Video Centerfold: Lisa Matthews: 1991 Playmate Of The Year
44-1797 Was $19.99 *$14.99*

Playboy Video Centerfold: Corinna Harney: 1992 Playmate Of The Year
07-1814 *$19.99*

Playboy Video Centerfold: Anna Nicole Smith: 1993 Playmate Of The Year
07-1928 *$19.99*

Playboy Video Centerfold: Jenny McCarthy: 1994 Playmate Of The Year
07-2106 Was $19.99 *$14.99*

Playboy Video Centerfold: Julie Lynn Cialini: 1995 Playmate Of The Year
07-2277 *$19.99*

Playboy Video Centerfold: Stacy Sanches: 1996 Playmate Of The Year
07-2418 *$19.99*

Playboy Video Centerfold: Victoria Silvstedt: 1997 Playmate Of The Year
07-2536 *$19.99*

Playboy Video Centerfold: Karen McDougal: 1998 Playmate Of The Year
07-2645 *$19.99*

Playboy Video Centerfold: Heather Kozar: 1999 Playmate Of The Year
07-2740 *$19.99*

Playboy Video Centerfold: Jodi Ann Paterson: 2000 Playmate Of The Year
07-2881 *$19.99*

Farrah Fawcett: All Of Me
She was a TV "angel" in the '70s, and she looks just as heavenly today. Actress, sex symbol and poster queen Farrah Fawcett lets all her sensuality show in this uncut, uncensored program that takes you on the set of her Playboy photo shoots, features intimate and revealing interviews, and lets you watch as Farrah presents her own unique style of painting. 72 min.
07-2553 ❑*$19.99*

Jenny McCarthy: The Playboy Years
From the Playboy vaults comes these rare never-before-seen shots of America's sexiest blonde. Jenny is more erotic than ever in world premiere segments, nude footage and director's cuts of her hottest video vignettes. 50 min.
07-2563 *$19.99*

Playboy: The Best Of Pamela Anderson
The tantalizing star of "Baywatch" reveals herself in daring new ways in this Playboy compilation of the best of Pam, including 20 minutes of unseen footage. The former Playmate from British Columbia will wow you with a pictorial so wild, Mitch may even take a time out from saving the beach from international drug smugglers to watch. 55 min.
07-2322 *$19.99*

Playboy: The Best Of Anna Nicole Smith
She's gone from small-town Texas girl to Playmate of the Year to blue jeans model to film/TV actress, and now you can see the pulchritudinous Anna Nicole in all her glory, thanks to this sizzling sampler of her hottest Playboy video footage.
07-2364 *$19.99*

Playboy: The Best Of Jenny McCarthy
The blonde, bodacious star of MTV's dating game, "Singled Out," shows you the goods that led to her fame and the title of 1994's Playboy Playmate of the Year. The Chicago native will dazzle you with her charm, talent and incredible looks. 60 min.
07-2416 *$19.99*

Playboy's Girls Of Hooters
The gals from Hooters rip off their orange and white uniforms to display the bodies that made this national chain a sensation. Fresh from their Playboy pictorial, these waitresses will wallop you with their wanton looks, lusty style and delicious demeanor. 52 min.
07-2209 *$19.99*

Playboy Celebrity Centerfold: Jessica Hahn
"Hi-ya, Hiney!" Her Playboy photo shoots won her legions of fans, and now newsmaker, Howard Stern regular and "Love Phone" hostess Jessica Hahn comes to life in a sizzling centerfold video that bares all. "I love you guys!" 50 min.
07-1908 *$19.99*

Playboy Celebrity Centerfold: Dian Parkinson
The sexy spokesperson from "The Price Is Right" uncovered her own version of the "Showcase Package" in a scorching magazine spread, and on this video dynamic Dian displays a body that is a prize in its own right. "Come on down!" 50 min.
07-2022 *$19.99*

Playboy Celebrity Centerfold: LaToya Jackson
We predict you'll find this one a thriller, as Michael's big sister unveils herself for the camera. Say, say, say: she's a pretty young thing whose sizzling sensuality will knock you off the wall. You won't be able to stop 'til you get enough! Talk about a babe in LaToya land.
07-2189 *$19.99*

Playboy Celebrity Centerfold: Patti Davis
First she excited the world—and annoyed her parents—by writing erotic books. Then she posed for Playboy. Now she's taken her act to home video for an extremely revealing portrait. See the controversial daughter of Ronald and Nancy Reagan in a video that'll do wonders for your "executive branch." 50 min.
07-2228 *$19.99*

Playboy Celebrity Centerfold: Shannon Tweed
The queen of erotic thrillers is featured in all her titillating glory in this Playboy special. She's the companion of Gene Simmons of Kiss fame; the star of such movies as "Indecent Behavior" and "Illicit Behavior"; and her "Bare Facts Video Guide" entry lists over 50 notations! Now, Shannon's seductive private side is revealed in segments shot throughout Hollywood and Los Angeles. 55 min.
07-2458 *$19.99*

Playboy's Celebrities
They may be celebrities, but they showed no qualms about baring it all for Playboy. This is a collection of the hottest celebrity shoots in the video series, including Pamela Anderson, Donna D'Errico, Carmen Elektra, Erika Eleniak, Jessica Hahn, Jenny McCarthy, Dian Parkinson, Anna Nicole Smith, Shannon Tweed and more.
07-2766 *$19.99*

Playboy: Love, Sex & Intimacy...For New Relationships
Because relationships have become more complicated in the 1990s, Playboy has fashioned this erotic guide to some of the most important aspects of sexuality. Sections include "Beautiful Beginnings," "Creating Intimacy," "Seduction Everlasting" and "Creative Love-making." All are illustrated by gorgeous performers in sensual situations. 55 min.
07-2190 Was $29.99 *$19.99*

Playboy: Making Love Series
From the magazine that revolutionized America's bedroom habits comes this innovative instructional series that features top sex therapists and authors discussing ways couples can improve their relationships and their lovemaking.

Playboy: Making Love, Vol. 1: Arousal, Foreplay And Orgasm
07-2354 *$19.99*

Playboy: Making Love, Vol. 2: Tantric Lovemaking
07-2471 *$19.99*

Playboy: Hot Latin Ladies
Some of the most gorgeous señoritas in the world are exposed for Playboy cameramen in this spicy program. Among the hot tamales featured are Playmates Maria Checa, Samantha Torres and Stacy Sanches. It's muy sexy!
07-2411 *$19.99*

Playboy's Playmates: Bustin' Out
Bustin' out? What on Earth are these women bustin' out of, jail? Well, whatever these hot playmates are bustin' out of, Jenny McCarthy, Karen McDougal, Stacy Sanches and more than a handful of others will be bustin' onto your TV screen in a "bust of" collection of well-endowed scenes with Playboy's bustiest babes.
07-2957 *$19.99*

Playboy's Really Naked Truth
Forget "The Real World." Forget "Survivor." These babes are going to show everyone what reality-based TV is all about as they get into their birthday suits for the camera, making immunity challenges the last thing on anyone's mind. You'll wish you were stranded on an island with these girls for a lot longer than 40 days! 56 min.
07-2958 *$14.99*

Playboy's Sexcetera
There's no need to ramble on and on about wanting to see the hottest, sexiest moments from the cable documentary series on sexual practices. The best excerpts from the show are right here waiting for you. Whether it's erotic, romantic sex you're looking for, or something a little kinky, you'll certainly find it with these lusty ladies and gentlemen. 56 min.
07-2959 *$19.99*

Playboy's Twins & Sisters Too
Get a double helping of sexiness as Playboy presents this fetching look at sultry twin sisters. They talk about the fun and danger they've had as twins, then reveal their similarities and differences. Find out the naked truth about twin sisters today! 60 min.
07-2486 *$19.99*

Playboy: The Girls Of Hawaiian Tropic—Naked In Paradise
Tans, tremendous ta-tas and terrific personalities are found in this torrid tape featuring a Dream Team of Hawaiian Tropic supermodels taking off their skimpy swimsuits and showing off their firm bodies, all against the backdrop of the gorgeous Hawaiian islands. 60 min.
07-2276 *$19.99*

Playboy's Real Couples: Sex In Dangerous Places
Following a nationwide search, the six couples assembled for this video decided that they would share their most intimate sexual moments on video for the world to see. The results are truthful and titillating, as the couples enact their wildest fantasies. 55 min.
07-2324 *$19.99*

Playboy's Real Couples II: Best Sex Ever
Are the steamy, passion-filled encounters re-enacted by the actual participants on this provocative Playboy program truly the best ever? Watch and decide for yourself, as real people show what real eroticism is all about. 55 min.
07-2529 *$19.99*

Playboy's Girls Of Radio: Talk, Rock & Shock
The sexiest gals you never see are now strutting their stuff for you, making microphones melt and the control room reach new temperatures. There's Howard Stern faves, the ever-sultry Seka and other sensuous sirens, all out of their clothes and on the air for you.
07-2332 *$19.99*

Playboy's Sisters
Talk about sibling ribaldry! Sisters of Playboy Playmates and gorgeous gals-next-door allow you to take a steamy look at their kin and decide what the family resemblance really is. Just when you thought the lascivious lady featured is "10," along comes her "11" sister!
07-2353 *$19.99*

Playboy's Rising Stars And Sexy Starlets
Check out some of the most gorgeous rising stars in Hollywood today. You've seen them in "Naked Gun 33 1/3," "Johnny Mnemonic," "Baywatch" and "NYPD Blue," but you've never witnessed them like this. Featured is model Lisa Boyle ("Daytona Beach") and other stunners. 60 min.
07-2417 *$19.99*

Best Of Playboy's Strip Search
Who better to take you on a tour of some of North America's finest gentleman's clubs than the fine folks at Playboy Video? You've got a front-row seat as the hottest and sexiest dancers strut their stuff from Atlanta, Los Angeles, Sacramento, Tampa and Toronto.
07-2528 *$19.99*

Playboy's Girlfriends
It's a mysterious bond of intimacy and shared secrets that men don't understand. Now Playboy lets you explore the world of female friendship in an erotic exposé that features gorgeous girlfriends opening up to each other as only girls can.
07-2714 *$19.99*

Playboy's Girlfriends 2
Sexy second serving in the Sapphic series further examines the sensual secret relationships that blossom between female friends who take their closeness to new levels. Playmates Kristi Cline, Tishara Cousino and Kimberly Spicer head the cast of beautiful buddies. 52 min.
07-2850 *$19.99*

Playboy's Erotic Weekend Getaways
Put some "oomph" into your love life with this arousing collection of wild weekend sojourns that are sure to take you away from the hectic world and into the bed of lust and romance. Couples stop at spas, wintry resorts, desert locales and the beach for intimate sex-play of the erotic kind. 53 min.
07-1967 Was $29.99 *$19.99*

Sensual Fantasy For Lovers
The line between imagination and reality becomes finer when five couples engage in their wildest fantasies and show you how to get your sex life in high gear in the process. Sexual games are played, romantic moments are shared, secret desires are revealed in this Playboy production. 55 min.
07-2104 Was $29.99 *$19.99*

Playboy: College Girls
You'll give these students straight A's in every subject imaginable! Forget reading, writing and 'rithmetic; remember these risqué, ravishing beauties from such schools as Arizona State, Rutgers University, North Carolina University and other institutions of higher yearning...er, learning. 55 min.
07-2183 *$19.99*

Playboy's Freshman Class
They're away from Mommy and Daddy for the first time, they're all alone in that stuffy dorm room, and now they're ready to break loose and get wild and dirty. Playboy examines every curve and every inch of these beautiful vixens who know that there are more important things in college than frat parties and classes.
07-2673 *$19.99*

Playboy's Girls Of Spring Break
Florida's Daytona Beach is the backdrop for this "A+" pictorial of cute co-eds who enjoy partying at the beach and matriculating sans clothing. Boasting more beauties than you can shake a tassel at, this dazzler features all-American nude fun in the sun.
44-1788 *$19.99*

Playboy's Women Behaving Badly
And we're not just talking leaving the toothpaste cap off or going into the express lane with more than 12 items! No, sir, these used-to-be-good girls get nasty in some provocative vignettes. A pair of passionate painters turn their bodies into works of art; a male stripper inspires his female audience to take the stage themselves; a shower room is the setting for a soapy "three-for-all," and more. 57 min.
07-2601 *$19.99*

Playboy: Wet & Wild
For instant fabulous babes, just add water! In the Playboy tradition of erotic adventure comes a passel of Playmates in each volume finding new and exciting ways to get wet, as a variety of soft, clingy fabrics slowly, slickly append themselves to each and every curve and contour. Each tape runs about 60 min. There are eight volumes available, including:

Playboy: Wet And Wild: The Locker Room
07-2191 *$19.99*

Playboy: Wet And Wild: Hot Holidays
07-2333 *$19.99*

Playboy: Wet And Wild: Bottoms Up
07-2436 *$19.99*

Playboy: Wet And Wild
44-1595 *$19.99*

Playboy: Sexy Lingerie
A collection of racy overviews of lacy underthings, from the magazine that started it all. See a bevy of Playmates model the latest, sheerest and sexiest boudoir fashions ever seen in these series of sessions and vignettes that bring those paper dolls to life. Each tape runs about 60 min. There are six volumes available, including:

Playboy: Sexy Lingerie
44-1584 Was $19.99 *$14.99*

Playboy: Sexy Lingerie II
44-1725 Was $19.99 *$14.99*

Playboy: Sexy Lingerie III
44-1796 Was $19.99 *$14.99*

Playboy's Sexy Lingerie: Dreams & Desire
07-2227 Was $19.99 *$14.99*

Playboy's Women Of Color
Many of the world's most exotic beauties are represented in a scorching tribute to women of all colors. Hosted by Reneé Tenison, 1990's Playmate of the Year, this program features Jamaica's Venice Kong, West Indian, Cherokee and Irish dazzler Stephanie Adamas and others. Share their fantasies in unimaginably colorful ways. 50 min.
07-2229 Was $19.99 *$14.99*

Playboy's Strip Search: Backstage
There's no business like show business, especially when show business is naked business! You've earned the ultimate backstage pass to the best strip clubs in America, as Playboy takes you on a tour to meet the most beautiful exotic dancers in the world. From g-strings to pole dancing, you'll quickly learn how very important it is to be a VIP. 56 min.
07-2960 *$19.99*

Playboy's Voluptuous Vixens
Gals with gargantuan globes are the focus of this sexy spectacle. See incredibly endowed sweeties in kinky situations in a hotel, playing musical instruments and in a bubble bath. Along the way, film director Russ Meyer, one of the world's leading "big breast" authorities, comments on his lifelong love of the subject. With Stacy Sanches, Carrie Westcott, Kimber West. 60 min.
07-2501 *$19.99*

Playboy's Voluptuous Vixens II
You knew there'd be a second volume; after all, all good things come in pairs! Julie K. Smith and the pulchritudinous Pandora Peaks are among the amply-contoured cuties who display their "breast" assets in a variety of sexy spots. Legendary filmmaker and mammary maven Russ Meyer is also on board to offer his unique insight into the subject. 60 min.
07-2596 *$19.99*

Playboy's Girls In Uniform
There's something about a beautiful gal in a uniform...and a lot more when she's out of it! Let Playboy prove it, as they show you a foxy fighter pilot, a randy wilderness ranger, a nasty nurse and many more vivacious vixens who demonstrate that the best thing about uniforms is taking them off! 55 min.
07-2530 *$19.99*

Playboy's Shagalicious British Babes
Blimey, why did we ever leave the "mother country" with beautiful birds like this running around? You've never seen a "British Invasion" like this, as Playboy's cameras present eight of England's loveliest lasses who don't mind going "the full Monty" to show off their "crown jewels." Yeah, baby! 58 min.
07-2861 *$19.99*

Playboy's Girls Next Door: Naughty And Nice
If the females in the old neighborhood had been this hot, we never would have moved away! The Playboy folks have turned their cameras on some gorgeous gals next door, both "naughty" and "nice," and caught them in some revealing situations. Imagine—it's all just next door! 57 min.
07-2589 *$19.99*

Playboy's Naturals
Science may indeed be wonderful, but the pulchritudinous Playmates on display in this video will remind you that there's just no substitute for Mother Nature. Filmed at the Playboy Mansion, the program offers a wide array of beauties whose bodies are all that...and all natural. 54 min.
07-2607 *$19.99*

Playboy's Night Calls
"Intercourse, Pennsylvania, you're on the air!" with the hot, hot hostesses of the Playboy Channel's top-rated phone-in show. Join Juli Ashton and Doria as they listen to the wildest dreams and erotic experiences of callers from across America, and watch them act out their own fantasies before the cameras. 58 min.
07-2620 *$19.99*

Playboy's Babes Of Baywatch
Sand, surf and sex add up to one red-hot video featuring the luscious lifesavers from the phenomenally successful TV series. Playboy models and "Baywatch" beauties Traci Bingham and Marliece Andrada are your hostesses for a look at sizzling photo and video shoots featuring them as well as Pamela Anderson Lee, Donna D'Errico, Carmen Electra, Erika Eleniak and others.
07-2629 *$19.99*

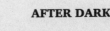

Playboy's Blue Collar Babes
Actually, these nine-to-five foxes don't keep their collars on long enough to tell what color they are, but who's complaining? These are women who play as hard as they work, and you're invited to watch them do both, from some construction-site cuties who take their attraction to new heights to a policewoman who shows off what's behind the badge. 51 min.
07-2779 *$19.99*

Playboy's Playmate Erotic Adventures
The four-color fantasy women from Playboy step out of their centerfolds to bring to life a series of steamy, sexy stories that take you to the limit of your imagination—and beyond. Deanna Brooks, Kristi Cline, Victoria Fuller, Layla Roberts and Rebecca Scott are some of the Playmates sharing their adventures with you.
07-2795 *$19.99*

Playboy's Club Lingerie
So, what's this club got that the local VFW post doesn't? How about a host of seductive Playmates, including Deanna Brooks, Vanessa Gleason, and 45th Anniversary Playmate Jaime Bergman, sashaying across the screen in the sexiest lingerie? It's a lively, lacy display that'll have you ready to become a member. 60 min.
07-2812 *$19.99*

Playboy's wildwebgirls.com
Isn't modern technology wonderful? The world's most gorgeous women are now just a mouse click away, and in this Playboy video you'll visit the websites of Raylene, Janine, Devon and other sexy cyber-beauties and see just how "interactive" the Internet can be. 56 min.
07-2824 *$19.99*

Playboy's Girls Of Mardi Gras
It's the country's biggest, wildest annual party, and who better than Playboy to show you the uncensored revelry (and ribaldry) that turns the Big Easy into...well, the Big Easy. Watch as bayou babes shed their inhibitions (and their clothes) for a handful of beads. 57 min.
07-2836 *$19.99*

PLAYBOY's
Sex
COURT

Playboy's Sex Court
"Here comes the judge" takes on a whole new meaning with these carnal cases from the popular cable TV series. Centerfold fave Julie Strain lays down the law—and anything else that comes across her bench—with the able assistance of bountiful bailiff Alexandra Silk. 52 min.
07-2860 *$19.99*

Playboy's Lusty Latin Ladies
Talk about your "Latino heat"! Southern California's top Spanish radio personalities, the Baka Boyz, host this "muy caliente" look at Hispanic honies who will take your breath away quicker than a jalapeño pepper. 60 min.
07-2877 *$19.99*

Playboy's Playmates Revisited
Get ready to steam up your den with the return of these Playboy beauties from the past. Playmates of the Year India Allen, Barbara Edwards, Lillian Muller and Kathy Shower, plus other classic vixens, will show you that some things get better with age.
07-2647 *$19.99*

Playboy's Asian Exotica
What is it about the women of the Far East that has entranced Western men for centuries? You just may find out by joining Playboy for an erotic video tour of the Orient and an up-close and intimate look at beautiful Asian women. Inscrutable? Maybe. Intense? You bet!
07-2704 *$19.99*

Playboy's Cheerleaders
The gals on the sidelines take center stage in this steamy video from Playboy that's sure to raise spirits. Watch former NFL cheerleaders and other gorgeous women shake their pom-poms and demonstrate some risqué routines you'll never see at a halftime show.
07-2465 *$19.99*

Playboy's Blondes, Brunettes, Redheads
Let's not split hairs; whether you're a gentleman who prefers blondes, or gets red-hot for redheads, or thinks black is where it's at, there's an appropriately-tressed temptress to suit you in this video. Playmates Shae Marks, Julia Schultz and Kimber West are your hostesses for a sexy look at all shades of feminine beauty. 53 min.
07-2644 *$19.99*

The Girls Of Scores
It's the sizzling Manhattan gentleman's club that's a favorite of Howard Stern and his radio cronies, and now Playboy takes you behind the doors at Scores to see why it's the talk of the airwaves. Meet the beautiful women who dance there in candid interviews, and watch them put on an arousing private performance. Best of all, there's no tipping on video! 55 min.
07-2720 *$19.99*

Playboy's Playmate Pajama Party
Leave the "Twister" and "Mystery Date" at home, because the games at this pajama party are of a decidedly more adult nature. You've got a video invitation to the legendary Playboy Mansion for a sexy soiree, with a guest list that includes former Playmates Jaime Bergman, Alexandria Karlsen and Stacy Sanches and the one and only Hugh Hefner. 60 min.
07-2725 *$19.99*

Playboy's Tales Of Erotic Fantasies
A mechanic learns about "body work" from a beautiful customer; an athlete finds a surprise waiting for him in the showers; and a hot oral hygienist gives her patient a very thorough "exam." These are just some of the sizzling fantasies brought to life in this Playboy production. 53 min.
07-2734 *$19.99*

Naughty Amateur Home Videos
"Be it ever so horny, there's no place like home," as you'll see with this outrageous collection of do-it-yourself exhibitionism culled from the popular Playboy TV series. Watch as ordinary women (well, maybe not *that* ordinary!) pose, strip and more for the video cameras. 55 min.
07-2761 *$19.99*

Playmates Of The Year: The '80s
Okay, so the '80s stuck us with New Coke, Milli Vanilli and Dan Quayle. The decade also gave us the 10 lovely video centerfolds spotlighted here, the voluptuous victors who won the coveted "Playmate of the Year" crown. From 1980's Dorothy Stratten to 1989's Kimberly Conrad, they're all here! 60 min.
44-1640 *$19.99*

Playmates Of The Year: The '90s
From the Internet to the Oval Office, sex was everywhere in the '90s, and who better than Playboy to take you back through the decade? This vivacious video salute spotlights such memorable Playmates of the Year as Renee Tennison, Anna Nicole Smith, Lisa Matthews, Jenny McCarthy and six more sexy sweeties. 110 min.
07-2771 *$19.99*

Playboy's Strip Search
No, you don't have to strip and get searched. All you have to do is join your hostess, adult film star Lexus, for a cross-country tour of the most popular gentlemen's clubs and let Playboy's cameras search out the hottest, sexiest performers. The featured ladies include adult stars Brittany Andrews, Shayla LaVeaux, Kylie Ireland, Serenity and many more. 60 min.
07-2772 *$19.99*

Playboy's No Boys Allowed (100% Girls)
You won't find a Y chromosome anywhere in camera range on this video, as Playboy presents the hottest girl-girl action in its archives. Watch as eight lovely ladies, including former Playmates and hosts Julie Cialini and Carrie Westcott, demonstrate that boys aren't necessary for the games they like to play. 60 min.
07-2878 *$19.99*

Playboy's Sexy Girls Next Door
Following a national talent hunt, Playboy has compiled their favorite findings in this scorching sextravaganza featuring America's hottest gals-next-door. These purebred pretties will wow you with their urge to undress. 54 min.
07-2904 *$19.99*

Playboy's Girls Of Hedonism
Gorgeous Playboy Playmates are off to Hedonism III, the wild resort in Runaway Bay, Jamaica, for the vacation of a lifetime. You'll certainly feel the heat as the world's most beautiful women romp around in the world's most notorious clothing-optional adult getaway. The sexual freedom that the girls experience proves that a vacation is all they ever wanted. 56 min.
07-2915 *$19.99*

Playboy's Best Of College Girls
These intellectually inclined babes have been culled from the finest clips of Playboy's college series. Carmen Electra and a whole crew of cute coeds will have you wishing you were a freshman again!
07-2950 *$19.99*

STAR SHAPES

Star Shapes
Let your wildest fantasies come true as top nude photographer Ron Harris directs this excursion into total eroticism. See models pose in their raw nakedness, captured for the cameras by Harris. A stunning salute to the female form! 60 min.
50-5478 *$19.99*

Star Shapes: A Woman's Desire
This unique erotic sexperience offers a bevy of naked natural beauties lying in different provocative positions as the camera captures them in all of their glory and electronic music plays in the background. Then get ready to meet a few of the sweeties as they model kinky clothing, then get naked while being interviewed, all courtesy of photographer Ron Harris. 50 min.
50-5721 *$19.99*

Star Shapes: Female Passions
Photographer Ron Harris takes you to the outer limits of your imagination in this erotic video in which a group of natural sweeties expose their bodies, then enjoy themselves and each other in spectacularly erotic sessions. 60 min.
50-5722 *$19.99*

Star Shapes: Secret Fantasies
Enjoy a group of awesome women in their rawest, most intimate moments. The incredible beauty of these natural wonders are first revealed, and then they pose, play and model provocatively for ace photographer Ron Harris—and you! 60 min.
50-5723 *$19.99*

Star Shapes: Wild Women
Simple yet sexy. Naked and naughty. Blondes with brunettes. Redheads with blondes. The possibilities are endless. And they're all explored in this video filled with gorgeous, natural women exploring each other's sensuality. 60 min.
50-5796 *$19.99*

Star Shapes: Sexy Curves
It's "WARNING: CURVES AHEAD" in this sizzling collection of the most seductive models from the "Star Shapes" series, but these aren't the kind of curves you have to grip the wheel to get through...just get a firm grasp on the remote control and get ready to hit "pause." 60 min.
50-8071 *$19.99*

Private Moments
Three scorching tales of erotica comprise this arousing anthology: "Kate and Leigh" is about a forbidden lesbian affair; "A Marriage" involves the adulterous adventures of a photographer and his wife; and "One Night Stand" shows how a meeting at a singles bar can lead to a feverish roundelay. 95 min.
07-1940 *$19.99*

Nude Cigar Smoking
See three hubba-hubba honeys teach you the ins and outs of cigar smoking. Minus the clothing, but with plenty of flavor, these three gals will wow you with their wild ways of enjoying the good life, smoking style. 45 min.
10-1682 *$14.99*

Marilyn Chambers' Bedtime Fantasies
The ever-steamy star of "Behind the Green Door" plays a writer whose sexy stories come to life in the most sensuous ways imaginable. A group of the world's hottest models, including Kimberly Taylor and Julia Parton, are featured. 60 min.
50-5285 *$24.99*

Marilyn Chambers' All My Best
Adult film legend Chambers hosts this series of erotic vignettes in which such sweeties as Kerry, Ann Goodman and Princess take part in steamy liaisons. Even Marilyn gets into the act in one of them! 60 min.
50-5326 *$24.99*

Marilyn Chambers' Private Fantasies
Chambers shows you why she's an erotic film legend as she's featured in scorching scenes from "The Babysitter," set in the 1950s, and "The Doctor Is In," which will make you feel quite healthy. Wild stuff! 50 min.
50-5475 *$19.99*

Marilyn Chambers' More Private Fantasies
Porn princess Marilyn Chambers lets you take a look at more wild fantasies as she's featured in "Caught in the Act," a bondage romp with Mistress Tantala, and "Bachelor Party," playing the prize at a wild farewell to the single life. 50 min.
50-5476 *$19.99*

Marilyn Chambers' Incredible Edible Fantasies
Join former "Ivory Snow" girl Marilyn Chambers as she explores the sensual link between sex and food. Marilyn leads you on a gourmet's delight, filled with sweet treats and even sweeter women. 60 min.
50-5480 *$19.99*

Marilyn Chambers' Wet & Wild Fantasies
The high priestess of adult films allows her wettest and wildest fantasies to go wacko as beautiful women take off their clothes and enjoy outdoor fun in hot tubs, flume rides and playing volleyball. With Ginette, Kerry and Ann Goodman. 60 min.
50-8056 *$19.99*

Big & Busty Centerfolds
It may take two hands to handle a Whopper, but it only takes one to put this tape in your VCR and be amazed at these whoppers! The bodacious boobs of Kimberly Kupps, J.R. Carrington, Kia and Olivia are presented in all their fleshy glory in this tremendous titillator. 60 min.
50-5242 *$24.99*

Big & Busty Covergirls
Get ready for "the big ones," and we don't mean earthquakes! Sydnee Steele, Danielle Rogers, Rebecca Wilde and Candi Hill are among the seven vivacious vixens gettin' ready, willing and, not surprisingly, buck naked, just for you. 60 min.
50-5908 *$19.99*

Big & Busty Vixens
If you're a vixen watcher who likes them big and busty, this is the video for you! They don't come much bigger, bustier, or more vixeny (vixenish?) than Brittany Andrews, Geanna, Leanna Hart, Shay Sweet, Candi Hill and Sana Fe, whose sexy bodies are on ample display. 60 min.
50-8070 *$19.99*

Big & Busty Divas
No, it's not Joan Sutherland, Beverly Sills and Cecilia Bartoli making their softcore debuts. In fact, we're not sure if the buxom babes featured in this video can sing a note, but once you see Gina Ryder, Sydnee Steele, Melanie Stone, Tiffany Minx and others show off their Rigolettos, you won't care. 60 min.
50-8274 *$19.99*

The Best Of Big & Busty
If it's bodacious, bra-busting babes you desire, look no further than this curvaceous compilation, a bona fide, boob-filled bonanza. Brittany Andrews, Ruby, Sana Fe, Rebecca Wilde, Nina Hartley and Geanna are among the dumpling displayers highlighted. 90 min.
50-8553 *$19.99*

Sexy World: Cabo San Lucas
Tired of those travelogues that show boring old castles and museums? Take a tasty trip to Mexico's hottest beach resort, where you'll visit nude beaches, a wild bikini contest at Sammy Hagar's Cabo Wabo Club, two sexy shipmates who take part in a naked marlin fishing trip (yes, the marlins are naked, too!), and much more. 55 min.
50-8213 *$19.99*

Scream Queens Naked Christmas
"Deck the halls with bodacious bodies, fa-la-la-la-la, la-la-la-AAAHHH!" You'll be singing the praises of scream queens Debbie Rochon, Christine Cavalier and Susan White with this video made during and for the feature film "Santa Claws" as they celebrate the Christmas spirit that's sure to ring your chimes. 60 min.
50-5338 *$14.99*

Hollywood Scream Queen Hot Tub Party
Take some of Hollywood's hottest scream queens and give them a party in a hot tub where they take it all off. You're in for the wildest, wickedest splash celebration ever, as lovelies Monique Gabrielle, Michelle Bauer, Linnea Quigley, Melissa Moore, Kelli Maroney star and get down and soapy. Includes scenes their movies.
73-9053 *$39.99*

The Best Of Sex And Violence
An orgy of Kung Fu killers, samurai thrillers, car crashes, monster mashes, big breasts, hairy chests, wild stunts, gorgeous dolls and much more. Filmdom's sexiest and most violent movie moments are shown here from such films as "Terminal Island," "Tourist Trap," "Zombie" and more! Hosted by John Carradine. 90 min.
20-1016 *$39.99*

SEDUCTIVE CELEBRITY SKINS
BARED BEYOND BELIEF!
EXPOSING!
URSULA ANDRESS
BRIGITTE BARDOT
JACQUELINE BISSET
SYBIL DANNING
PHYLLIS DAVIS
USHI DIGARD
CLAUDIA JENNINGS
NASTASSIA KINSKI
ORNELLA MUTI
JOAN PRATHER
LAURIE WALTERS
EDY WILLIAMS
and many more...
FAMOUS T&A
A RARE LOOK AT THE BARE BEGINNINGS
OF TODAY'S STARS

Famous T And A
Sybil Danning hosts this much-requested salute to the film world's sexiest actresses in their hottest nude scenes. See Ursula Andress undressed...Uschi Digart de-clothed...Edy Williams at her wildest...Brigitte Bardot looking bodacious...Nastassia Kinski showing her skinski...and lots more! 70 min.
20-1031 *$29.99*

NUDE HOUSE WIVES

OF AMERICA

Nude Housewives Of America, Vol. 1
Whether they're dusting the table, vacuuming or polishing the brass, these hotsy-totsy housewives will whip you into an erotic frenzy. They tease and titillate and tempt in this nudity-filled, sensuous salute to horny homemakers. 80 min.
75-7098 *$19.99*

Nude Housewives Of America, Vol. 2
Your home a mess again? Well, let the nude housewives go to work, as they sweep, dust and tidy up wearing nothing more than an apron and a smile...and sometimes even less!
75-7128 *$19.99*

Simply Sex: How To Get Pleasure Without A Man
They like men, but, hey, what's wrong with getting it on with women, too. You'll see a group of gorgeous gals teaching each other the ins and outs of lesbian loveplay in this scorching look at sapphic love. 70 min.
50-5548 *$29.99*

Buttman's Favorite Rio Carnival Parties, Vol. 1
Welcome to Rio, the scene of the wildest party of all time: Carnival! And Buttman is running rampant, shooting the sexiest stuff with the hottest, horniest native gals with the most delightful rears. Go wild at the torrid tusses captured for keepsake on this spontaneous program featuring full-frontal nudity. 90 min.
76-7068 Was $39.99 *$29.99*

Buttman's Favorite Rio Carnival Parties, Vol. 2
Welcome to Rio, land of exotic, erotic sights, sounds and rears! Join the Tsar of Tush as he searches for the world's most perfect posteriors in the wild sight of Carnival. Gals oblige the Buttman as he delves his camera farther and deeper to uncover the world's hottest heinies. With lots of nudity. 90 min.
50-2536 *$29.99*

Buttman At Nudes-A-Poppin', Vol. 1
A host of gorgeous gals get undressed at the Ponderosa Sun Club's 1991 Nudes-A-Poppin' festival, and Buttman captures them in all their glory (focusing particular attention on their luscious round rumps) as they take part in such contests as "Miss Go-Go," "Miss Showstopper" and "Miss Nude Galaxy." With Honey Melons, Alisha Loveroe and Tina Fox. 120 min.
76-7069 *$29.99*

Buttman At Nudes-A-Poppin', Vol. 2
The toreador of tush travels to Roselawn, Indiana, where he and his crew capture a parade of pretties provocatively posing for the cameras. There are 46 females frolicking and getting naked. Hoosiers, hooters and hienies—what a combo! This tape runs an amazing 140 minutes!
50-8066 *$39.99*

Buttman At Nudes-A-Poppin', Vol. 3
The bendover babes are back and John "Buttman" Stagliano has got them! There's 40 frisky felines who love displaying their ample wares and Stag's camera enjoys going shopping. See who takes home the trophy for the most titanic...well, you'll see! 120 min.
50-8067 *$39.99*

Buttman At Nudes-A-Poppin', Vol. 4
John Stagliano has a penchant for capturing the most intimate parts of the world's wildest women, and this tape showcases his unique talents. He's loose in Indiana for an intimate inspection of provocative posers and tantalizing teasers. This tape runs an impressive 140 minutes!
50-8068 *$39.99*

Prairie Gals
Well, whoopee-ti-yi-ya, fellows. Here's the lowdown on the most lascivious ladies on the prairie, a contingent of carnal cowgals ready and willin' to take off their hats and suedes and give y'all a titillatin' time. So mosey on over to Movies Unlimited and get the video that reveals "How the West Was Fun." 60 min.
19-3825 *$14.99*

Big-Busted Goddesses Of L.A.
They dance, they pose and they strip in an amazing revue that sexposé a bevy of Tinseltown's most titillating and top-heavy tootsies. It's D-Cup City with Tammy Reynolds, Janette Littledove, C.C. Moore, Keisha and 44DD Kim Watson. Full nudity featured here! 60 min.
50-2316 *$24.99*

Sweaters On Parade
In a video that would get Ed Wood excited, a host of lovely ladies don their sweaters and get wet, get dunked and have their garments shrunk. This program takes you into the dressing sessions, some bath tub action and a pool party. There's eight audacious models in 60 sweater ensembles. 85 min.
50-2937 *$39.99*

An Evening With Kitten
She's the woman whose 18-hour bra gave up after 20 minutes! Russ Meyer leading lady and softcore legend Kitten Natividad stars in an erotic burlesque revue, shaking, strutting, jutting her way through encounters with such characters as Dracula, Bruce Lee and the Incredible Bulk. 30 min.
15-5065 *$19.99*

American Striptease
Cheer for the red, white and very blue in this sexy video that features 16 sensational gals rippin' and strippin' for you. This program will make you feel proud to be an American! 60 min.
19-3377 Was $19.99 *$14.99*

Unmasked Fantasies
Costumes meet carnality when gorgeous women masquerade in all sorts of disguises—cops, secretaries, catwomen, nurses—and act out your innermost fantasies. The mystery women of your desires are alive and dancing in alluring ways in this sizzler.
19-3454 *$19.99*

European Strip Search
Travel to the hottest exotic clubs in Europe where anything can—and does—happen. Chochotte in Paris...Meerwik Castle in Holland...The Solumbo Club in Hamburg. This is one tour that's sure to sizzle, as the wildest continental cuties show you all! 60 min.
19-3500 *$19.99*

Takin' It Off, Vol. 1
Let 'er strip! This scorching sexposé of the world of striptease artists is hosted by erotic temptress Hyapatia Lee, who demonstrates why she was once Miss Nude World. Porsche Lynn and Trixy Tyler also take it all off in this nudity-laden night of naughtiness. 60 min.
35-5047 Was $19.99 *$14.99*

Nude Pole Dancer Championship
Man, these poles are lucky—they have some of the country's wildest dancers hanging, writhing and swinging all over them. In this steamy competition from the Deja Vu Showgirls club in Minneapolis, hot pole dancers do their thing to win the coveted championship award. 55 min.
39-4049 *$14.99*

Showgirl U.S.A. Championship
Everything you want, these gals got it right in the U.S.A. Where better than Las Vegas to hold the eighth Deja Vu Showgirl of the Year contest, as the sexiest women to ever strut their stuff onstage show off their talents—in every sense of the word? 55 min.
39-4075 *$14.99*

All-American Stripteasers
When the music's on, the clothes come off in this sweaty soiree to a land where the hottest babes have the freedom to bump and grind to a pulsating rock score. Is this a great country, or what? Tabitha Stevens, Roxy Ryder and Kaitlyn Ashley star.
39-5770 Was $19.99 *$14.99*

40 Plus
Filmed in exotic locales around the world, this program features full-chested femmes in different stages of undress. Among the superstars who expose themselves here are Candy Samples, Uschi, Raquel Rios, Kelly Stewart and Raven. Even the Wonderbra cannot contain the mighty mammaries on tap! 60 min.
50-2589 *$29.99*

Naked By Nature
From the producer of the "Fabulous Flashers" series comes this exposé of steamy models taking it all off in the great outdoors. You'll yell "koo-loo-koo-koo-koo-koo-koo-koo" when they get wild in the wilds. 55 min.
50-5319 *$19.99*

Naked By Nature 2
A group of earthy, erotic gals decide to explore the joys of nature—and show off their bodies in the process. The Great Outdoors has never been greater, as these pretties get naked in the woods, on a hammock, near the beach and by the rocks. 60 min.
50-5724 *$19.99*

Cyber Strippers
Choose the gal on the Internet and—poof!—she becomes real and strips for you! Racquel, Cleo, Missa, Destiny and Matilda waltz into your cyberspace fantasies in such a hot-to-trot, totally nude way that your mouse will squirm! 60 min.
50-5983 *$19.99*

Strip Teasers
This is the tape where the "teasing" stops and the stripping starts. A pulchritudinous collection of lissome lasses take to the stage, and take off their wardrobe, in a racy revue that is sure to arouse. 60 min.
69-5071 *$19.99*

Strip Teasers II
"Take it off...take it all off!!" You'll be amazed as 10 duds-doffing darlings slowly, tantalizingly, deliciously reveal their bountiful treasures. The lovely and legendary Ginger Lynn serves as your hostess. 60 min.
69-5080 *$19.99*

Las Vegas Strippers
You'll be rolling a "lucky 7" with this video, as seven sexy gals who put the "strip" in "Vegas strip" display their winning bodies for the camera. Jill Kelly, Rebecca Bardoux, Sydnee Steele, Malita and others all on one video? It's a better bargain than a $3.99 all-the-shrimp-cocktail-you-can-eat buffet! 60 min.
50-5632 *$19.99*

Las Vegas Strippers 2
Siegfried and Roy, David Cassidy, that woman who manages the perfume store and curators at the Liberace Museum, step aside. Here comes the latest attractions from Las Vegas and they're something to behold. Adult director Stuart Canterbury exposes XXX sensation Ashlyn Gere, Olga Stone and others in this sizzler that's more exciting than a wrestling-themed hotel-casino. 60 min.
50-8309 *$19.99*

The Private Dancer: Every Man's Secret Desire
Ever want to witness a private dance from a woman who was so gorgeous she seemed unattainable to you? Well, if so, now's your chance to enjoy the show as a group of gorgeous women take it all off. This turn-on is sure to delight as women let men experience their secret desire. 60 min.
50-5482 *$19.99*

Amateur Nude Strippers
They've been curious long enough—now it's time to take it off! See a batch of gorgeous gals unloosen their dresses, rip off their bras, let down their panties and show you what they've got. A splendid time is guaranteed for all nudity lovers. 60 min.
50-5249 Was $24.99 *$19.99*

Amateur Nude Strippers 2
These sweeties didn't know anything about stripping until the producer put a camera on them. But after watching this sensual soiree, you'll think they're all pros. Get hip to the rip and strip scene in this sexy evening of erotic entertainment. 55 min.
50-5318 *$19.99*

Amateur Nude Strippers 3
Hello, casting couch...goodbye, clothes! See some willing participants in this video take it all off for the first time, hoping to make an impression. We're not talking impressions of Bill Clinton or Jackie Mason, either. They dance, they wiggle, they get naked, they show you that they have the right stuff. 60 min.
50-5732 *$19.99*

Amateur Nude Strippers 4
Forget the money—these gals strip for the love of the art form! You can see it all as eight luscious ladies strut their stuff for the first time before the cameras...and take off their clothes, to boot. 60 min.
50-8069 *$19.99*

Amateur Nude Strippers: Nude Millennium
Bodies like these come around only once in a thousand years! If the Y2K bug didn't blow up your TV and VCR, settle back and enjoy the show, as tantalizing tyro temptresses take it all off and usher in the new millennium the right way: nude! 60 min.
50-4285 *$19.99*

Nude Fantasy Strip-Off
When is the last time you've been whipped—as in whipped cream? Well, if gals with large gazongas getting chocolate syrup, ketchup, whipped cream and other goodies smeared all over their bods is a turn-on, you've come to the right strip-off. And you thought Ann-Margret was hot with the baked beans all over her in "Tommy"! 60 min.
50-5725 *$19.99*

Hot Sexy Strippers 2
Join Catalina L'Amour, Christina Love, Lovette and Cannibal for a tape of concocting phony stripper names...er...sexy, erotic interludes dedicated to fans of gorgeous, naked women. 60 min.
50-5728 *$19.99*

Starlet Strippers
Even Nathaniel Hawthorne would give these naughty chicks a scarlet "A"—for "Awesome"! Enjoy these six sexy (not to mention stunning) women reveal all and show it for the camera...and you. Better get that cold shower all ready to go... Danni Ashe, Sara St. James, Lana and Taylor St. Claire are some of the babes. 60 min.
50-5907 *$19.99*

The Private Dancer: Getting Naked
They are private dancers and when they dance for you, they love getting naked. They are knockouts, both physically and facially, and creative, too, performing their dance routines in and out of costumes, dancing dirty to the music. 60 min.
50-5999 *$19.99*

Hot Chicago Escorts
If you think the biggest thing in the Windy City is Roger Ebert, you're wrong! These Midwestern madams are enough to make Michael Jordan miss a slam dunk, Mark Grace flub a ball at first base and Tony Amonte fan on a breakaway. See why Chicago is their kind of town in this titillating excursion boasting a bountiful cast! 60 min.
50-8310 *$19.99*

Sexy Adventures
The setting may be spare—somewhere in the desert, near a bombed-out building—but the gals are sure lovely. See Kimberly Maddox, Amber and Debbie naked (except for an occasional piece of combat garb or leopard-skin jacket) and ready to go. Look at those canteens! 55 min.
50-8468 *$19.99*

Nude Reflections
Mirror, mirror, on the wall...who's the hottest babe of them all? Well, how about all of them? This incredible array of wild women shows you how intimate gals can get with their reflections. Included are such sweeties as Taimee Hannum, Linda O'Neill, Chase and Kimberly Maddox. 55 min.
50-8649 *$19.99*

Sex On The Saddle: Wicked Women Of The Wild West
Whoopee yi-ti-yo, get along not-so-little dogies! Check into the Dry Gulch Ranch, where a sultry slew of feisty Western femmes comes in a-ridin' and a-rompin', soapin' and scrubbin' their bodies for all to see. As the sun sets, the gals explore themselves and each other in and out of the spurs. Julia Parton stars, with Malika Kinison serving as hostess. Uncut version; 60 min.
77-9004 *$24.99*

Gorgeous Girls Of Goldfingers I
No, it's not Honor Blackman or Shirley Eaton. It is a slew of sultry dancers, slithering, ripping and stripping on the stages of some of the premier gentlemen's clubs in the world. See all sorts of pretty women in and out of their exotic costumes, delighting audiences with their erotically charged dancing. 60 min.
84-5030 *$24.99*

Gorgeous Girls Of Goldfingers II: Miss Topless New York
See a slew of ultra-sexy strippers compete for a large cash prize and the title of Queen of Adult Entertainment in this sizzling program. Doing intimate gymnastics with poles and donning and doffing the wildest of costumes, these curvaceous cuties are sure to stun you with their looks and moves. 60 min.
84-5046 *$19.99*

Night Vamps (1998)
Glori-Ann Gilbert serves as your hostess for an evening of lust, sex and bodacious blondes that's sure to get you excited. Joining Ms. Gilbert are Penthouse Pet Kelly Jaye and adult stars Brittany Andrews and Lovette.
73-9278 *$19.99*

Striptease College Girls
Welcome to Strip Tease College, a university where stripping takes precedence over reading, writing, 'rithmetic, even lunch! Prof. Long G. Stringheimer resides over S.T.C., making sure gals like Eurora Bare, Lotta Class and Dimples Pratt keep studying by doing the koochie-koo wearing pasties and bikinis. A cheesecake classic.
15-9003 Was $19.99 *$14.99*

Shower Girls
If it's suds and showers that turn you on, look no further than this video that's bubbling over with excitement. A group of soapy dishes wash, wiggle and go wild in a nudes-a-poppin' presentation that gives new meaning to the term "Spray and Wash." 60 min.
75-7099 *$19.99*

Shower Girls II
Just when you thought it was safe to step back in the shower, those wet and wild shower gals are back to get you (and themselves) in a lather, as they take to the tub in an aquatic, erotic display loaded with H2Oh...oh...oh! 60 min.
75-7108 *$19.99*

Hot Body Hall Of Fame: Christy Carrera
Ruth, DiMaggio, Mays, Schmidt, Ashburn...Carrera?! This ain't no Cooperstown, but it is just as revered a place...at least to fans of the "Hot Body" series. And perky, perfectly stacked blonde Christy is a well-deserved entrant, showing off what got her there in several nude photo sessions. 55 min.
50-5332 *$19.99*

Hot Body Hall Of Fame: Johnny Luv
She may have a name like a guy, but after watching this torrid tape you'll have no question what Johnny's sex is. Love to Luv her baby in candid conversations and private posing sessions, along with Dottie, Spice and Danielle. 55 min.
50-5688 *$19.99*

Hot Body Hall Of Fame: Summer Leigh
Bring back those lazy, hazy, crazy days of Summer...Leigh, that is. This stunning blonde bombshell is a worthy addition to the Hall of Fame, and you'll see some erotic examples of Summer's "body" of work as she lounges at the pool, gets a lesson in billiards from Morgan Hills, and romps with cowgirl Heather Monroe. 55 min.
50-8080 *$19.99*

Hot Body Competition: Beverly Hills Miniskirt Madness Contest
Ready to see 14 sexy models show off skirts so short the hemline is practically even with the navel? Then join the crowd at St. Marks Night Club for a dazzling display of barely-clad beauties, including Toni, Asia, Chanel, Sandy and others. 55 min.
50-5157 *$19.99*

Hot Body Competition: Summer Wet T-Shirt Finals
Twenty-one—count 'em—twenty-one gorgeous women compete for the "Summer Wet T-Shirt Finals" in this sextravaganza. Sana Fay, April, Angela and Tyler are just a few of the sweeties getting drenched and naked for your enjoyment. 55 min.
50-5380 *$19.99*

Hot Body Video Magazine: Eye Candy
Sara St. James ("Femalien") is the featured female on this hot video. Joining sensual Sara are Stacy Moran, Heather Bankx, Ashley Phillips and amateur discoveries Jasmine, Kennedy and Bailey. 55 min.
50-5381 *$19.99*

Hot Body Competition: Malibu Miniskirt Finals
The skirts don't get any mini-er, the gals any hotter, and the undergarments any more invisible in this sultry salute to shortened fashion that's sure to keep you hot. Contestants in this carnal pageant include Daniela, Brandee, Avalon Anders and others. 55 min.
50-5690 *$19.99*

Hot Body Competition: Beverly Hills Hot Legs Contest
Into gams, wheels, pins, stems, legs? If so, you can't get lustier or leggier than this video featuring such super-duper models as Tara, Donniel, Susan, Crystal, Katt, Crickett and others. Legs are diamonds in this one! 55 min.
50-5695 *$19.99*

Hot Body Competition: Miss Grande Chest Contest
If a gallant tribute to breasts is your thing, then this video is for you. The "Hot Body" people have gathered together nine busty babes whose dangerous curves will "knock" you right off your feet. Kelsie Chambers, Reno Lynn and Chesty Chelsea are among the ladies just waiting to bust out of your TV set. 55 min.
50-5858 *$19.99*

Hot Body Competition: Miss Black Hot Body Competition
Once you go black, you never go back. These seven Nubian princesses will have you drooling for more when they tear it up in your living room. Brandy, Genevieve, Jade, Deja, Jasmine, and others will show you why brown sugar tastes so good. 55 min.
50-5861 *$19.99*

Hot Body Video Magazine: Summer Heat
Blonde and bodacious Summer Leigh shows off her greatest assets in this tantalizing tape. Sweltering along with her are Jessica; Annetta, a foreign firecracker; and Juliette, an adult film star with a wowsome figure. 55 min.
50-5689 *$19.99*

Hot Body Video Magazine: The Best Of IV
There's an amazing array of alluring ladies in this Hot Body hoedown featuring covergirls, feature models, amateur discoveries, Hall of Fame members and more. There's Taylor St. Clare, Alana, Jessica, Sara St. James, Mallesia Renee and others. 55 min.
50-5693 *$19.99*

Hot Body Competition: Beverly Hills Short Shorts
Who wears short shorts? The Southern California cuties who parade around in a captivating contest on this video, that's who! Watch as Eden, Debi, Andrea, Karissa, Renee Ryan and other short-clad sweeties show off their assets before the camera in a luxurious Beverly Hills backyard. 55 min.
50-8081 *$19.99*

Hot Body Competition: Hot Booty Contest
It's a competition whose pulchritudinous participants know that being the frontrunner isn't as good as bringing up the rear. Eight gals with their best features behind them put their...reputations on the line as viewers get to pick the top bottom. 55 min.
50-8313 *$19.99*

Hot Body Competition: Contest Girl Of The Year
We're not exactly sure which year the title refers to, but when one video offers you over 60 stunning models strutting their stuff in wet T-shirts, miniskirts, lingerie and even less in five foxy competitions, plus backstage peeks and a "private" nude dance scene, does it really matter? 55 min.
50-8148 *$19.99*

Hot Body Competition: Disappearing Lingerie Contest
No need to shout "Abracadabra," "Alakazam" or even "By the hoary hosts of Hoggoth!" to have these undies vanish. Watch as Angel Veil, Charli, Kalua, Ericka and five other sexy models make their clothes fly off their bodacious bodies, without the use of magic. 55 min.
50-8224 *$19.99*

Hot Body Competition: Erotic Asians Contest
Meecy, micy, oh-so-spicy! Take a tantalizing tour of the Pacific Rim—without ever leaving Los Angeles—with this look at nine Asian-American temptresses. Join Thai, Maliya, Marissa, Tia, Maitai and December, and answer for yourself the question, "Is it true what they say about Oriental girls?" 55 min.
50-8364 *$19.99*

Hot Body Competition: Cream Of The Crop
This sizzling compilation reviews six contests featuring 45 naked "Hot Body" models, as well as backstage footage, private dance action and a countdown to the "Girl of the Year." Featured models are Karissa, Bridget, Tanya Danielle and Bambi. 55 min.
50-8465 *$19.99*

Hot Body Competition: Lusty Latinas
Looking for a saucy, sizzling South of the Border treat that's less fattening than fajitas? Come to the 20/Twenty Club in Cabo San Lucas, Mexico, and watch as nine sexy señoritas prove that a beautiful body—especially a beautiful nude body—speaks a universal language. 55 min.
50-8083 *$19.99*

Hot Body Video Magazine: Bouncy Blondes
Gentlemen prefer blondes, and so will you after watching more than eight of the hottest goldy-locked babes dish up the good stuff. Get ready to feel naughty watching Cleo, Chase, Tish, and others fulfill your wildest fantasies in the privacy of your own home. 55 min.
50-5857 *$19.99*

Hot Body Video Magazine: The Underwear Affair
Imagine your favorite lingerie catalog suddenly coming to life, as sexy models sashay before your eyes in the most revealing and arousing of unmentionables. Join hostess and European cover girl Patricia for a lacy, racy affair. 55 min.
50-8079 *$19.99*

Hot Body Special: Sizzling Swimsuits & Less
The suits must really be sizzlin', because these gals can't wait to get out of them! Watch as 12 Hot Body models demonstrate the fine art of swimwear removal; a Jacuzzi encounter with Alex and Danni D'Vine gets really hot and bubbly; witness a dressing-room bikini fashion show by Alissa Anderson and Mason Marconi; and much more. 55 min.
50-8149 *$19.99*

Hot Body Competition: 10th Anniversary Contest
Has it really been that long since the first "Hot Bodies" video was released, presenting the world with astonishingly endowed models in exotic locales strutting their stuff? How time flies! In celebration of this momentous occasion, see an amazing contest and dance footage of Megan, Shayla, Cassandra Knight, Eve Ellis, Courtney and Genesis (post-Peter Gabriel, of course!). 55 min.
50-8575 *$19.99*

The Girls Of Tuxxedo: Swimsuit Edition
There's no tuxedos on view on this program (and precious little in the way of swimsuits, for that matter), as 14 exotic beauties pose in wet T-shirts, sexy lingerie, and sometimes nothing at all, in an erotic array of vignettes that are wet and wild. WARNING: Contains full frontal nudity; adults only. 45 min.
20-5268 *$24.99*

Love Scenes, Vol. 1
The ultimate couple's foreplay video, this erotically-charged program features superhunks (including Playgirl centerfolds) and beautiful women in four sexy vignettes. A male dancer learns about casting couches in "Las Vegas Audition"; a woman takes the plunge with a "Palm Springs Pool Man"; go on a shoot with "The Model"; and celebrate with the "Private Party Stripper." The endings are up to you! WARNING: Contains full nudity. 100 min.
50-2230 *$39.99*

Love Scenes, Vol. 2
Five more super-sizzling segments feature hunky guys and gorgeous women in erotic situations. A newspaper writer lusts after a mountain man in "Mountain Cabin Fever"; an engagement celebration moves from a club to a hot tub in "Dirtier Dancing"; a "Doctor's Examination" leads to an exchange between a black athlete and a nurse; and more. You supply the endings! WARNING: Contains full nudity. 110 min.
50-2418 *$39.99*

Love Scenes, Vol. 3
The third nudity-filled, tantalizing entry in this series includes "Motorhome Odyssey," in which dinner and passionate dancing lead to love in a motor home; "High School Reunion," featuring a lusty liaison for some horseback riders; "The Voyeur," about a Nordic hunk and his TV producer paramour; "The Ultimate Birthday Party," which is just that for a female executive; and more! 100 min.
50-2517 *$39.99*

Love Scenes, Vol. 4
The foreplay fantasies continue in "Semester Break," in which an erotic dance number leads to a candlelit bath; a French waiter and a pretty diner take a shower in "Foreign Service"; a writer helps out a woman in need in "Mediterranean Holiday"; a hunky trainer and a divorcée get close in "Moving Experiences"; and a "Shipwrecked Sailor" is helped by a Hawaiian beauty. 115 min.
50-2878 *$39.99*

The All-Conference Nude Workout
They're hot, they're naked and they're exercising. See a collection of the country's sexiest collegians in and out of aerobic gear, putting oomph into sensuality in a number of lively, lusty workouts. 60 min.
19-3671 Was $19.99 *$19.99*

Naked, Fit & Frisky
The world's wildest nude workout is now on video—and outdoors, too! Witness nude models Amy Robins, Amber and Destiny in aerobic workouts guaranteed to knock your danskins off. 60 min.
50-5472 *$19.99*

Totally Nude Busty Workout
If you thought June was busting out all over, wait until you check out the erotic exercisers bending, stretching, jumping and working out with weights on this program. The danskins can't hold the pulchritude on display in this ode to keeping in shape, sans clothing. 60 min.
50-5720 *$19.99*

Totally Nude Aerobics
Exercise and eroticism mix as a bevy of beauties get out of their danskins and work their booties off. See them bend, stretch, bump and grind, sans clothing. Watch as their muscles tighten, beads of sweat pour off their bodies and more. 55 min.
50-5981 *$19.99*

Nude Basketball
If you want to witness some of the finest globes trotting, check out this bonanza of breasts. The gargantuan gals will make you cheer as they take to the court, bouncin', bouncin', bouncin' all over the place. It's blondes against brunettes in a wild shoot-out with so much sex appeal even Marv is sure to turn red—in or out of the lingerie. Yes! 60 min.
50-8240 *$19.99*

Nude Football
"42DD, hut, hut, hut." It's the wildest gridiron game since they stopped wearing leather helmets. It's an exciting football frolic where the participants are busty babes who love to get their backfields in motion with a game of two-hand touch. Join the huddle when their skimpy uniforms come off and they get barer than Terry Bradshaw's dome. 60 min.
50-5998 *$19.99*

Nude Tennis
If you liked Janine and Julia Ann in "In-Flight Fantasies," wait 'til you see them take to the court in a tempting, tantalizing tennis session where "love" is more than just a score and the racquet covers aren't all that's coming off! 50 min.
19-3923 *$14.99*

Nude Models Private Sessions
Six gorgeous nude models allow you to uncover their sensual desires in this nudity-filled exposé. See them rip and strip for the cameras—and your pleasure! With Terri Moore, Glori Gold and Cori Lane. 60 min.
84-5037 *$19.99*

Nude Models Private Sessions 2
Just when you thought it was safe to cool off from the previous "Private Sessions," here comes another scorcher in which a half-dozen curvaceous cuties take it all off for the cameras, striking provocative poses that are sure to entice you into their world of carnality and beauty. 60 min.
84-5038 *$19.99*

Nude Models Summerhouse
Paul answers a "roommate wanted" ad in the newspaper and soon finds himself moving in with three gorgeous, shapely models. It doesn't take long for Paul to enjoy watching his new housemates have fun in the pool, the sauna, kitchen and bedroom. With Glori Gold, Cori Lane and Paul Short; music by the Ohio Players. 60 min.
84-5039 *$19.99*

Erotic Confessions
Get ready to travel into exotic new worlds of sensual pleasure and erotic secrets waiting to be revealed. Your hostess is beautiful author Jacqueline Stone (Playboy Playmate Ava Fabian), who shares with you candid letters from her fans. Watch as their sexiest fantasies come to life in these collections of provocative vignettes.

Erotic Confessions: Desire
86-1110 Was $59.99 *$14.99*

Erotic Confessions: Intrigue
86-1111 Was $59.99 *$14.99*

Erotic Confessions: Passion
86-1112 Was $59.99 *$14.99*

Erotic Confessions: Pleasure
86-1113 Was $59.99 *$14.99*

Erotic Confessions: Intimacy
86-1122 *$39.99*

Erotic Confessions: Taboo
86-1123 *$39.99*

Erotic Confessions: Ecstasy
86-1124 *$39.99*

Erotic Confessions: Seduction
86-1125 *$39.99*

Lessons In Love

Lover's Guide, Vol. 1
Sensuous lovemaking is demonstrated and taught in this scorching primer on how to enjoy the ultimate in physical intimacy. Learn new and enthralling ways to please your mate in this provocative program. 60 min.
19-3422 *$14.99*

Creative Loving: The Art Of Love In 3-D
The art of the Kama Sutra has thrilled and informed practitioners for centuries. Now you can learn its secrets in an erotic video produced by the London Institute of Human Sexuality, filled with sensuous couplings. Presented in 3-D; includes two pairs of glasses. 60 min.
19-3453 Was $19.99 *$14.99*

Stripping For Your Lover
The hottest performers in the world—Janine and Julia Ann of "Blondage" fame—show you all the moves to get your guy in the groove, demonstrating the right way to take off the clothes, lingerie and other accouterments and have a real turn-on of a time. Check out the pair who have shattered records—and taboos—around the world! Unedited edition; 60 min.
19-3826 *$19.99*

The Lover's Guide To Sexual Ecstasy
This guide to complete fulfillment features four beautiful couples demonstrating sensual techniques that enrich lovemaking. Includes an exclusive instruction on the Grafenberg (G-Spot) orgasm. Contains full-frontal nudity. 75 min.
50-2420 *$39.99*

The Lovers' Guide: Advanced Sexual Techniques
Noted therapist Dr. Andrew Stanway helps you zero in on ways to make sex better in this program that features nudity and intimate positions. Among the subjects covered are fantasies, sex games, safe sex, creative lovemaking positions and more. 60 min.
50-2527 *$29.99*

The Lovers' Guide: Better Orgasms
This program is designed for men, women and couples and, through explicit demonstrations and extensive nude sexplay, demonstrates important tips on achieving better orgasms. With information supplied by Dr. Andrew Stanway, you'll learn everything you wanted to know about the subject. 60 min.
50-2528 *$39.99*

Intimate Secrets: How Women Love To Be Loved
Gals just want to have fun—and they show you how in this scorching sex education soiree filled with steamy demonstrations and luscious nudity. Women's most intimate lovemaking secrets are revealed. 60 min.
50-2492 Was $34.99 *$29.99*

The World Of Good, Safe & Unusual Sex: The Video
The entire sex universe is covered in this lusty look at using alternative methods to improve bedroom fun, as XXX stars Lois Ayres, Taija Raye and Angel Kelly demonstrate exhibitionism, fetishism, lesbianism, oral sex, safe sex, transsexualism, masturbation, mud wrestling and other interests. Includes explicit footage. 60 min.
50-2579 *$29.99*

The Sensual Massage Video
Soothe, relax and sexually arouse your partner after watching this titillating instructional tape in which adult stars Tracy Adams, Keisha and Gina Fine offer tips on caressing, touching, extending massage to sexplay using Oriental methods, finding hot spots and more. 60 min.
50-2580 *$29.99*

Encyclopedia Sexualis: The Video
The popular sex guide is transformed into a horny how-to that focuses on such topics as anal eroticism, fellatio, masturbation and "despunta," the mere description of which is illegal in some states. Leading sex therapists offer advice, and adult performers Jessica Wylde, Angel Kelly and Tiffany Blake are your guides. Features explicit material. 60 min.
50-2581 *$29.99*

Over Forty: The Best Sex Of Your Life
You don't have to be a young whipper-snapper to enjoy the joy of sex. Those over 40—or those who prefer sex with over-40 partners—can enjoy active, passionate and erotic lives with help from this video. Adult stars Ona Zee, Nina Hartley and Janet Tyrone are featured. The program includes explicit material.
50-2582 *$29.99*

Interracial Sex: The Video
This sizzling exposé of interracial sex studies the lust between the races and the psychology behind the practice. Adult performers Lacey Logan, Jeannie Pepper and Kim Parker enact erotic scenes of interracial loving to give you a better understanding. Features explicit footage. 60 min.
50-2585 *$29.99*

Sexual Positions: The Video
The world-famous book by Hans Richter has been turned into a sizzling and informative video program that gives viewers an intimate look at sexual positions throughout the world and how using them can improve your sex life. Nothing is taboo, as men and women will learn how to reach new peaks of arousal. Features explicit sequences. 60 min.
50-2586 *$29.99*

The Couples Guide To Great Sex Over 40, Vol. 1
According to this series, you don't have to be a young whipper-snapper to have great sex. This volume focuses on four middle-aged and senior couples who talk about and demonstrate some of the techniques that work. Included are segments on positions, oral sex and overcoming problems. WARNING: Contains full nudity; adults only.
50-5146 *$29.99*

The Couples Guide To Great Sex Over 40, Vol. 2
Avenues to better sex through diet and exercise and how to adjust to menopause are just a few of the topics touched on in this informative video, designed for middle-aged and senior couples. WARNING: Features explicit demonstrations and nudity; adults only.
50-5147 *$29.99*

Sexual Fantasies
This program will help you achieve living your sexual fantasies by imagining your wildest erotic dreams. Communicating desires, wants and needs is important between couples, and Aja, Champagne, Carol Cummings and other XXX performers demonstrate new ways to realize your fantasies. Features explicit material. 60 min.
50-2583 *$29.99*

THE Kama Sutra OF VATSYAYANA

The Kama Sutra Of Vatsyayana
Now you and your loved one can experience the ultimate pleasures of sex thanks to this program dedicated to the third century teachings of Vatsyayana. Total sexual fulfillment is the focus of this video that takes you from kissing, caressing and fondling to more elaborate techniques. Features explicit footage. 60 min.
50-2587 *$29.99*

Kama Sutra
The ancient Kama Sutra, the exotic primer of sex and sexual positions, is the basis for this erotic, informative video. Learn the secrets that could change your life involving 30 different positions. WARNING: Contains nudity and sexual situations; adults only. 47 min.
59-7107 *$29.99*

The Orgasm Workout
Designed for women and men who want to improve their sex lives, this special workout offers info and tips on exercise techniques that can help men prolong ejaculation and women achieve a quicker and more fulfilling orgasm. Live action and special effects combine to help couples reach their carnal peaks. 43 min.
59-7105 *$29.99*

How To Give Pleasure To A Woman By A Woman
They are women, hear them roar, as they show you how to score...with another woman! XXX stars Sarah-Jane Hamilton and Tami Monroe show you all sorts of ways to pleasure a female companion, from kissing and undressing to caressing, romantic interludes and much more. It's alluring and educational, too! 60 min.
50-2612 *$24.99*

The Big O: An Erotic Guide To Better Orgasms
Women and men can learn how to have joyful, ecstatic orgasms thanks to this video in which attractive couples demonstrate techniques to improve viewers' sex lives. Learn how to "tune in" for climaxes, experience multiple orgasms and how to help your partner appreciate pleasure. Features explicit footage and nudity. 60 min.
50-5444 *$29.99*

Erotic Massage
This relaxing video offers important instruction on how to mix massage and sensuality to soothe and stimulate at the same time. Learn how to get into the back, feet, neck, face and genital areas. NOTE: This title includes nudity and scenes of genital massage. 60 min.
50-5163 *$29.99*

How To Seduce Your Lover Forever
The body's incredible potential for passionate response is explored by real couples and sex therapist Diana Wiley. This video offers tips on heightening sensitivity, building arousal and making oral love a total body experience. WARNING: Contains explicit instruction; adults only.
50-5151 *$19.99*

Joys Of Masturbation: The Video
A score of techniques and tips for self-pleasuring are showcased in this no-holds-barred guide to masturbation. Using adult performers like Lacey Logan, Sharon Mitchell and Kim Parker as the participants, this program titillates and teaches in sizzling fashion. Features explicit footage. 60 min.
50-2584 *$29.99*

The Secrets Of Self-Pleasuring And Mutual Masturbation
This primer on self-pleasuring shows you the ins and outs of masturbation. Witness how men and women can reach new sexual heights through masturbation by using fingers, vibrators, and jets of water. Features nudity and explicit scenes. 30 min.
50-5445 *$19.99*

Masturbation Memoirs, Vols. 1 & 2
This innovative instructional video will give new insights into the art of sexual self-pleasure for females. Six mature women show you different techniques, including how to achieve a full G-spot orgasm. 70 min.
50-5949 *$39.99*

The Complete Guide To Sex Toys & Devices
Want all the bells and whistles when you achieve orgasm? Why not check out this video devoted to experiencing new pleasure levels using vibrators, lotions, leather, domination accessories and other items? So, just get out your bottle of Emotion Lotion and turn on. Features explicit material. 60 min.
50-5363 *$29.99*

Ancient Secrets Of Sexual Ecstasy For Modern Lovers
Enhance your lovemaking skills by using this video as your guide and letting it show you dynamic techniques in the Tantric style. Included are ancient secrets of extended, full body orgasm; how to awaken the Goddess spot on women; and more. Experts and couples schooled in Tantric skills are featured. Recommended for adults only. Unedited director's cut; 90 min.
50-5546 *$39.99*

Leather For Lovers
If you and your sweetie are "into leather," then this sexy, three-part instructional series is for you. Learn how tight leather on your body and the power of submission and domination can enhance your sex life. Each volume runs about 65 min.

Leather For Lovers, Vol. 1
Visit a San Francisco leather store and check out the various apparel that they have to offer, as well as a woman-on-woman demonstration of dominance and submission. 60 min.
50-5959 *$29.99*

Leather For Lovers, Vol. 2
Take a dirty look at the underground world of a leather fashion show with Dr. Patti Britton, Ph.D., as well as a demonstration of how to be a successful dominatrix. 65 min.
50-5960 *$29.99*

Sex: A Lifelong Pleasure: The Male Orgasm
Discover how to not only control your orgasm, but how to extend it and prevent premature ejaculation with proven techniques and interviews and insight from well-informed doctors. 60 min.
50-5963 *$39.99*

Sex: A Lifelong Pleasure: The Female Orgasm
Learn about masturbation, techniques of increased arousal, erotic fantasies, and other methods to prolong the female orgasm and the essence of female sexual response. 60 min.
50-5964 *$39.99*

Well Sexy Women
The joy of safe sex for lesbians is discussed and demonstrated fairly explicitly in this program. Experts talk about the essentials of safe, loving gay sex while six lesbians enact sensual situations in erotic style. Filmed in England, this program pulls no punches in dealing with its subject. WARNING: Contains full nudity; adults only. 50 min.
78-5053 Was $39.99 *$24.99*

Come Play With Me: Sex Games For Couples
Learn more satisfying ways to gain pleasure with your partner and have a longer, more productive sex life. Includes live demonstrations by couples of erotic games you can play to have more fun in the bedroom. 81 min.
50-5950 *$29.99*

Secrets Of Female Sexual Ecstasy
Discover new and exciting ways to enhance your sexuality through intimacy, passion and emotional connection with help from this video. Sexperts Charles and Caroline Muir offer their wisdom on the subjects, and attractive couples demonstrate techniques involving erotic kissing, ejaculatory control, G-spot massage and more. WARNING: Contains nudity and sexual situations; adults only. 80 min.
50-8096 *$39.99*

Dr. Suzy: America's Sexiest Therapist
World-famous sex therapist Dr. Susan Block takes you through the bare essentials of carnal pleasure in these revealing and informative instructional videos made with couples in mind. Each tape runs about 60 min.

Foot Fetish Primer
Explore the erotic world of feet and shoes as Dr. Suzy recounts her own personal awakening to the sensuality of her feet, as well as teaching her audience the wonderful pleasures of foot massages, toe-sucking, foot worship, and more.
50-5956 *$39.99*

Wet On Wet: The New Bi-Sexual Female
See for yourself how women can gain pleasure with another woman, and what they can show men about doing the same to them. Includes various techniques for strap-on dildos, positions, and more.
50-5957 *$29.99*

A Woman's Guide To Loving Sex
This video offers lessons in love from leading sexual therapist Tricia Barnes. Geared to women, the program features sections on understanding and appreciating bodies, the role of romance in sexuality, using imagination in the bedroom and enjoying sex in menopausal years. WARNING: Contains nudity and sexual situations; adults only. 52 min.
50-8102 *$29.99*

Maximum Performance: The Man's Guide To Penis Enlargement & Potency Techniques
Lots of men worry about it, but what really can be done to increase penile size and enhance your sexual performance? This groundbreaking video looks at the truths and fallacies behind mechanical devices, surgical and medical options, diet and vitamins and more. WARNING: Contains nudity; adults only. 60 min.
50-5375 *$39.99*

The Complete Guide To Sexual Positions
Learn to experiment with different sexual positions, and bring new flavor and joy to your love life. Includes methods to prolong intercourse, achieve deeper penetration, and locating the coveted "G-Spot." 60 min.
50-5953 *$29.99*

THE COMPLETE GUIDE TO
ORAL LOVEMAKING
THE LOVER'S KISS
DR. PATTI BRITTON
PH.D. F.A.A.C.S.
Escalate Your Passion
To The Highest
Level of Sexual Ecstasy

The Complete Guide To Oral Lovemaking
Men can realize new methods to bring their lovers to explosive climaxes, and women will learn to make the most of his pleasure, with this video that has over 50 live demonstrations and techniques, all fully-indexed with fact-filled narration. 60 min.
50-5954 *$29.99*

She's Safe!
This video includes a series of instructional safe sex programs for lesbian women that just happen to be sensual and sexually explicit. Erotica and education merge in such efforts as "Safer Sister," "Girls Will Be Boys," "Current Flow" and "Jill Jacks Off." 55 min.
78-9006 Was $29.99 *$19.99*

Penthouse: Fire And Ice
A bevy of spectacular Penthouse models turn it on and take it off in a series of arousing episodes. Whether you like your Pets sensuous and romantic or gonzo and on-the-edge, you'll be happy with this torrid tape. 60 min.
19-2525 *$19.99*

Penthouse: Lost Treasures
From the Penthouse archives comes this collection of raw, incredibly hot footage that's never been seen before. Featuring more than a dozen Penthouse Pets, video tape will ensure you one sweltering time. 60 min.
19-2526 *$19.99*

Penthouse: Secret Lives, Secret Desires
Award-winning filmmaker Andrew Blake takes you to an erotic world the likes of which you won't believe. This video features an array of stunning women who share their fantasies and secret lives. 77 min.
19-2757 *$24.99*

Penthouse: Passport To Paradise
Can't afford a Hawaiian vacation? Unable to see enough gorgeous women in skimpy bikinis to make your day? Here's the next best thing: a sun-kissed collection of sexy Penthouse pets posing in (and out of) the latest swimwear on the shores of the Aloha State. Featuring Janine Lindemulder. 60 min.
19-3261 *$19.99*

Penthouse: Pet Of The Year Playoffs
Everyone's a winner in Bob Guccione's annual parade of perfectly proportioned Pets, gathered within these videos featuring each year's lovely and lusty line-up. So get up-close and personal with the marvelous models and cast your vote for your favorite "Pet of the Year" hopeful. Each tape runs about 60 min.

Penthouse: 1991 Pet Of The Year Playoff
19-3263 *$19.99*

Penthouse: 1992 Pet Of The Year Playoff
19-3358 *$19.99*

Penthouse: 1993 Pet Of The Year Playoff
19-3487 *$19.99*

Penthouse: 1994 Pet Of The Year Playoff
19-3637 *$19.99*

Penthouse: 1996 Pet Of The Year Playoff
19-3961 *$19.99*

Penthouse: 1997 Pet Of The Year Playoff
19-4003 *$19.99*

Penthouse: 1998 Pet Of The Year Play-Off
19-4029 *$19.99*

Penthouse: 1999 Pet Of The Year And Friends: Nikie St. Gilles
19-4053 *$19.99*

Penthouse: Satin & Lace
Fans of lovely ladies and luscious lingerie will have a field day with this truly ravishing "film strip." Some of Penthouse's most dynamic models will tantalize you with their sizzling moves in see-through, sensual bedroomwear. A voyeur's delight! 60 min.
19-3281 *$19.99*

Penthouse: Satin & Lace II—Hollywood Undercover
Get the steamy inside story on Tinseltown's most alluring women with this special Penthouse video. Hear from gorgeous lingerie-clad models and actresses about what goes on behind studio doors and on the infamous "casting couch." 60 min.
19-3406 *$19.99*

Penthouse: Ready To Ride
A tantalizing combination of sizzling cycles and sexy women is presented in Penthouse's salute to "taking it on the road." The gals wear leather, boots, thongs...and, often, nothing...in this rebel-rousing program. See the Penthouse Pets become "wild things" when they hit the highway with chrome! 60 min.
19-3312 *$19.99*

Penthouse: Pet Of The Year Winners '92—Brandy And Amy Lynn
A sizzling sexposé of the prestigious Penthouse Pet of the Year competition. This intimate look at two of the world's sexiest models, winner Brandy and runner-up Amy Lynn will wow you as they pose and strut for the camera. 60 min.
19-3323 *$19.99*

Penthouse: Pet Of The Year Winners '93—Julie Strain And Mahalia
Two amazing models show you why they have been chosen as Penthouse's cream of the crop. Julie Strain, featured in many pictorials and sizzling movies, becomes the "Pet of the Year," while Mahalia is the numero-uno (with a capital "ooo") runner-up. 45 min.
19-3440 Was $24.99 *$19.99*

Penthouse: Pet Of The Year Winners '94—Sasha Vinni And Leslie Glass
"Glasnost" took on a whole new meaning when ravishing Russian-born Sasha Vinni was chosen as Penthouse Pet of the Year, while the statuesque Leslie Glass earned the prestigious title of runner-up. Both ladies are seen up close and very personal in this sexy video pictorial. 60 min.
19-3533 *$24.99*

Penthouse: Pet Of The Year Winners '95—Gina LaMarca And Natalie Smith
There's scorching never-before-seen footage of gorgeous Pet of the Year winner Gina LaMarca in action. Pouty-lipped, cutey-pie face, bodacious body: she's everything a man could want...and more! Also, meet ravishing runner-up Natalie Smith. 60 min.
19-3754 *$19.99*

Penthouse: 25th Anniversary Pet Of The Year Spectacular
The most ravishing Pets from Penthouse's 25 years are showcased in this sexy salute. Check out Penthouse Pets from the earliest days of Bob Guccione's magazine to the present, including the 25th Anniversary Pet, Leigh Anderson. 60 min.
19-3587 *$19.99*

Penthouse: 2000 Pet Of The Year Play-Off
What a way to close out a millennium! Six of the sexiest, sultriest models to ever grace the pages of Penthouse show off the beautiful bodies that got them there as they compete for the coveted title of Pet of the Year. 60 min.
19-4061 *$19.99*

Penthouse: Pet Of The Year 2000
"What light through yonder window breaks?" This Juliet may not do a balcony scene, but Penthouse's millennial Pet of the Year is a beauty worthy of a Shakespearean sonnet, and she's joined by fellow Pets Aimee Sweet and Alexus Winston for some erotic vignettes that are masterpieces in their own right. 57 min.
50-8379 *$19.99*

Penthouse: Forum Letters, Vol. 1
Taken from the pages of Penthouse Magazine, this tape offers erotic dramatizations of letters describing sensual encounters. Check out six incredible tales of passion, filled with surprises, unusual situations and lots of heat. 80 min.
19-3400 Was $79.99 *$29.99*

Penthouse: Forum Letters, Vol. 2
"Dear Penthouse; I never thought this sort of thing could happen to me, but..." Once again the amazing true sexual experiences of real people (and you know they're true, or else they wouldn't print them!) are brought to vivid life on video. Window washers, nurses and even a bride are among the carnal correspondents. 60 min.
19-3532 *$29.99*

Penthouse: The All-Pet Workout
Ever wonder how those pulchritudinous Penthouse Pets stay in such fabulous shape? Well, why not let comedian Mark Pitta take you on a behind-the-scenes look at the sexiest exercise sessions ever, as the gals pump, stretch and really work out (sometimes in the nude). 60 min.
19-3405 *$19.99*

The Girls Of Penthouse, Vol. 2
Ready for a second helping of the sexiest Penthouse Pets ever captured on video? Enjoy this collection of lushly-filmed vignettes with some of the world's most seductive women turning their fantasies into reality. 60 min.
19-3486 *$19.99*

The Girls Of Penthouse, Vol. 3
Want to know the most intimate secrets of the beauties who pose for Penthouse magazine? Now's your chance as blondes, redheads and brunettes let you in on their fantasies—then act them out for you! Ravishing, rambunctious and radiant: these women have it all! 60 min.
19-3752 *$19.99*

Penthouse: The Art Of Desire
A super-stylish sexual excursion that's perfect for couples, this feature from award-winning adult director Andrew Blake ("Night Trips") focuses on a gorgeous museum curator who is searching for the ultimate erotic thrill. In the art underworld, she finds a forbidden world populated by passionate artists and insatiable models. 80 min.
19-3401 Was $79.99 *$29.99*

Penthouse: The Great Pet Hunt
Join Penthouse photographer Earl Miller as he searches for the country's most sensuous women in the hottest clubs around. They're exotic dancers whose beauty remains unknown...until this tape exposes them totally for the public. 60 min.
19-3324 *$19.99*

Penthouse: The Great Pet Hunt, Part II
They were born in the U.S.A., and now they get naked in the U.S.A., showing off their fabulous faces and great bods for Penthouse and you. The Pet Hunt is on, and America's hottest women, including Amber Lynn and Sandi Korn, are the catches! 60 min.
19-3441 *$19.99*

Penthouse: 25th Anniversary Swimsuit Video
There's 16 sexy Penthouse Pets on hand for this spectacular tropic teaser in which these sultry, swimsuit-clad sweeties strut their stuff in lush locales, then let their sensual desires take over. Super-steamy unedited version; 60 min.
19-3501 *$19.99*

Penthouse: Swimsuit Video 2
Some of Penthouse's most spectacular models take to the sun in skimpy swimsuits to dazzle and delight you. The tropic locations have never been so hot, as the Pets pose provocatively in and out of their thongs and bikinis. 60 min.
19-3663 *$19.99*

Penthouse: Sexiest Amateur Video Centerfolds
They're young, hot, sexy...and willing to pose totally naked for the Penthouse camera crew. Witness wicked amateurs striking sexy poses, getting in touch with their sensual bodies. The women run the gamut here: blonde, brunette and redhead. And gorgeous, more gorgeous and even "gorgeouser." 60 min.
19-3530 *$19.99*

Penthouse: Sexiest Amateur Video Centerfolds 2
They may be "everyday people," but there's nothing everyday about the fabulous female bodies on display in this second steamy serving of amateur video centerfolds. Could that stunning beauty be one of your neighbors? Watch and find out! 60 min.
19-3962 *$19.99*

Penthouse: International Amateur Video
The famed magazine travels around the world to bring you the hottest amateur videos, Penthouse style. See the smashing sirens from Europe's most exotic places, showing us their pretty natural passports. 60 min.
19-3757 *$19.99*

Penthouse: Dream Girls
Dream a little dream of them! Some of Penthouse's most ravishing models seduce with their charms, bodies and overwhelming carnality in this program that allows you to enter a world where erotic fantasy and reality mesh. 60 min.
19-3531 *$19.99*

Penthouse: Forbidden Fantasies
Journey to an exotic harem, witness an interactive sexcapade, travel back to the 1950s for a sensual blast from the past, and partake in other provocative experiences in this scorching Penthouse program in which wild fantasies turn into reality. 60 min.
19-3624 *$29.99*

Penthouse: Party With The Pets
If you want to party all the time, this one's for you. A group of gonzo Penthouse Pets show you the wildest ways to have fun as they partake in mudfights, pajama parties, photo shoots and other outrageous experiences. 60 min.
19-3636 *$19.99*

Penthouse: Kama Sutra II: The Art Of Making Love
The ancient secrets of the sexual manual known as the Kama Sutra are taken to a new level in this program. Demonstrated by gorgeous and handsome models, the once-taboo learnings of love are brought to viewers with frankness and powerful sensuality. 60 min.
19-3664 Was $29.99 *$19.99*

Penthouse: Women In & Out Of Uniform
When it comes to uniforms, these Penthouse Pets can really fill them out. And when it comes to slipping out of them, it's likely you won't find anyone sexier. Leather, lace, police accouterments, black nylons: see them get it on and get it off. 60 min.
19-3753 *$19.99*

Penthouse: Showgirls Of Penthouse
And what a show it is, as the Penthouse cameras give you a front-row seat to some of the hottest dancers from the country's top gentlemen's clubs performing and revealing all for their audience. Let Sunset, Kia, Roxy and the other girls strut their stuff for you and appear in sexy video centerfolds. 60 min.
19-4004 *$19.99*

Penthouse: Lingerie Party
Here's your invitation to a lively, lacy affair, as those beautiful Penthouse Pets strip down to their skivvies for a sexy soiree, showing up in their "unmentionables"...and their lingerie, too. 60 min.
50-8347 *$19.99*

Penthouse: Earl Miller's Girls Of Europe
Penthouse's leading photographer, Earl Miller, zooms in on some of the continent's most incredible models, who go to sextraordinary lengths to make your fantasies come true. You'll go ooh-la-la with the exotic lookers on display in this steamy production. 60 min.
19-3822 *$19.99*

Penthouse: Pet Rocks
They're lean, they're mean and they love to rock out. See the gorgeous gals of rock revel in the music and sexy situations. A searing amalgamation of guitar riffs—and hip, naked chicks. 60 min.
19-3756 *$19.99*

Penthouse: The Art Of Massage
Who better than the people of Penthouse Magazine to bring out this video that shows couples the basic skills for an erotic and stimulating massage session, with sexy couples demonstrating the techniques? "Aye, there's the rub." 60 min.
19-3878 *$29.99*

Penthouse: All Access
Go behind the scenes of Penthouse's hottest videos and meet some of the world's wildest women at their most uninhibited. See what happens during a video shoot before the cameras roll, and check out the revealing highlights and silly bloopers. 60 min.
19-3955 *$19.99*

Penthouse: Wild Weekend With The Pets
Oh, they're having a party! And everybody's sweating, watching a quartet of Penthouse Pets prep, entertain and get naked for you, their private partygoer. The eats are great, the brews are cold and the Pets are, well, perfect! 60 min.
19-3956 *$19.99*

Penthouse: Behind The Scenes
See what goes on when the lights are off and the cameras aren't rolling, as Penthouse Pets go on display in their uncensored splendor, posing, getting dressed and getting undressed for all the world to see. 60 min.
19-3981 *$19.99*

Penthouse: Centerfold Auditions
The ads went out, and now it's time to take a look at the raw and unadulterated collection of vixens who have the bodies...and the courage to show them off. They're seductive, alluring, and have no problem opening themselves up to any and every possibility. Don't be shy; they aren't. 60 min.
19-4027 *$19.99*

Penthouse: Keys To Fantasy
Beautiful lawyer Priscilla Brewer inherits an exquisite Victorian mansion. When she arrives, she discovers that there are exotic ghosts still living out their deepest fantasies long after their time, and her own sensual dreams are awakened in the process, in this softcore drama. 60 min.
19-4028 *$19.99*

Penthouse: Girls Of The Zodiac
We predict there's twelve months worth of provocative pin-up cuties in your future, courtesy of this Penthouse program features a seductive Pet for each sign of the zodiac. There's temping Taurus Page Summer, arresting Aries Julia Garvey, lovely Libra Nikie St. Gilles, vivacious Virgo (don't look at us, that's her sign!). Leslie Glass, and more. 60 min.
19-4059 *$19.99*

Penthouse: Luscious Ladies
If you have a fantasy woman, it's likely she (or, at least, her type) will be found on this tantalizing tape. See a group of gorgeous Penthouse Pets do everything they can to make your hottest fantasies come true. There's blondes, brunettes, redheads and gals of every stature in store for the true fantasy fans out there. 60 min.
19-4032 *$19.99*

Penthouse: Confessions
Wondering what those sultry Penthouse girls could possibly have to confess? Find out, as a delectable dinner party turns into a fantasy-fulfilling feast for the senses, as a bevy of beautiful models let their erotic imaginations run wild. 60 min.
19-4005 *$19.99*

Penthouse: Lipstick Girls
It's "La Ronde," Penthouse-style, as a lipstick is passed from one lusty woman to another. Follow the beauties as they experience a series of spectacularly sensual encounters at a beauty salon, in a photo shoot and more. Pets Lydia Schoen, Dyanna Lauren and others are featured. 60 min.
19-4031 *$19.99*

Penthouse: Tropical Spice
No, it's not a new Spice Girl. It's really one spicy girl after another, as a passel of pulchritudinous Penthouse models parade their beauty before you, all taking place in a steamy tropical locale that the ladies make even steamier. 60 min.
19-4034 *$19.99*

Penthouse: Amazing Amazon Beauties
Contrary to Greek myth, not all Amazons are one-breasted, warlike man-haters. Join such towering temptresses as former Pet of the Year Julie Strain and Pet Roxy as they serve as sexy inspirations for a beautiful artist. 60 min.
19-4035 *$19.99*

Penthouse: Behind The Scenes At The Swimsuit Calendar Photo Shoot
You're invited to an up-close and personal look at the photo session of Penthouse's red-hot swimsuit calendar, as such stunning models as Amy Lynn, Leslie Glass, Julia Garvey and Pet of the Year Paige Summers are seen on location in a tropical paradise posing for one steamy shoot after another. 60 min.
19-4036 *$19.99*

Penthouse: 30 Pets 60
To celebrate the 30th anniversary of Penthouse magazine, this special compilation, culled from some of their most popular videos, offers an up-close and *very* intimate look at 30 of the sexiest Penthouse Pets of all time. Julie Strain, Amy Lynn, Janine Lindemulder, Raquel Darien and others are here for your pleasure. 60 min.
19-4056 *$19.99*

Penthouse: Sultry Sensations
It's risqué fun under the Central American sun, as you join a passel of pulchritudinous Penthouse babes as they pose in an erotic photo shoot along the Costa Rican shore. 60 min.
19-4057 *$19.99*

Penthouse: Harlots Of Hell
An auto accident leaves a man stranded in the middle of nowhere, but the seemingly empty house he comes to turns out to be occupied by a bevy of devilishly delicious damsels. Is he imagining it, or are these seductive spectres part of an erotic nightmare? Pet of the Year Juliet Cariaga and Pets Julia Garvey, Aimee Sweet and others head the cast in this sensual fantasy from Penthouse. 60 min.
50-8708 *$19.99*

Penthouse: Casting Call
And when that call goes out from Penthouse, you can be sure that only the sexiest, sultriest women will even make it through the front door! Follow a group of would-be Pets and see for yourself if they "have what it takes," and treat yourself to a peek at former Pets Leslie Glass, Amy Lynn and Gina Marca. 60 min.
53-7559 *$19.99*

Penthouse: Sun, Surf & Centerfolds
It's a racy recipe for sexy summer fun, and Penthouse has whipped up a tasty treat for you with this video romp. Join a host of sizzling centerfolds as they pose for the camera in (and out of) revealing swimwear. 60 min.
19-4060 *$19.99*

EE7
Duck! Here come two of the world's most astonishing big-busted gals, facing each other in a competition involving secret agents and not-so-secret pulchritude. In this corner: Beverlee Hills, an incredible bra-straining presence. And in the other corner: Melissa Mounds, Russ Meyer sidekick, bouncing, bouncing, bouncing! EE-Oh! 90 min.
50-2423 Was $29.99 *$24.99*

Big Busty Whoppers
Her name is Whoppers. Wendy Whoppers. And she's got some of the largest hooters around. They wanted to call her house "Hooterville." Along with pals like Rebecca Wild and Summer Knight, Wendy shows you a wowsome display of her ample anatomy. It takes about eight hands to handle these whoppers! 60 min.
50-2591 *$29.99*

Humongous Hooters
No, it's not an extra-large restaurant with shapely waitresses. It's a celebration of celebrations for mammary lovers who love their mammaries large. Letha Weapons, Wendy Whoppers, Lili Xene and Holly Body let it all hang out. 60 min.
50-5352 *$29.99*

The Busty Bombshells
If you've got a hankering for gorgeous gals with mucho mammaries, check out this tape with triple-E star Chrissy Maxx, dark beauty Cassandra Curves, Devon DeRay and Lori Wagner. 60 min.
50-5588 *$29.99*

Big Bust Solo Passion
Put the words "double" and "D-cup" together, and you get the sexiest bunch of big-breasted women since the "Cross Your Heart" bra. Filmed by internationally-known adult director Bert Rhine, these beautiful, fully developed nymphs display themselves in ways you've never imagined. 60 min.
50-5877 *$29.99*

Heavenly Hooters
The naughty Napali Video girls are back to showcase their God-given talents (both of them) in this new video that features Tawny Peaks, Lovette, Bunny Bleu, Kayla Kleevage and Busty Brittany. Ever wonder if their names are real, too? Decide for yourself. 60 min.
50-5878 *$29.99*

Bigger And Better: The Busty Babes Of Napali Video
Nice cans, and we don't mean soup... Lisa Lipps is the star of this hoard of hotties that will bring new meaning to the phrase "well-endowed." Along for the ride are Chrissy Canfield, Christina, Letha Weapons and Spontaneous Xtasy. Aren't their names cool? 60 min.
50-5938 *$29.99*

Babewatch: Hot Bodies
Filmed in the U.S. and British Virgin Islands, this look at some of the world's hottest bodies features a host of Penthouse stunners, including Loni Mallory, Linda Johnson, Jill Shawntai and Howard Stern favorites Amy Lynn Baxter and Kimberly Taylor. See them with (and without) skimpy bathing suits and revealing thongs. 50 min.
42-2909 *$19.99*

The Best Of Real Sex
The hottest, frankest and funniest stories from the groundbreaking HBO documentary series have been gathered on a "best of" video program that's definitely "for adults only." Get an up-close look at the Miss Nude World contest; explore the world of S&M devotees; learn about the life of a peep show girl; and more. 88 min.
44-2097 *$14.99*

The Best Of Sex Bytes
Take a sensual detour off the information superhighway with this collection of steamy cybersex adventures from the popular HBO series. See how the computer revolution is letting people around the world connect in a variety of arousing ways, explore new frontiers of erotic art, and more. 60 min.
44-2098 *$14.99*

The Best Of Taxicab Confessions
The meter's running—and so's the video camera—in this collection of revealing real-life tales from the streets of New York. Culled from HBO's Emmy-winning series, the uncensored looks at taxi drivers and their passengers include five pleasure-seeking girls, a guy talking about his "sex addiction," a women looking for her cheating boyfriend, and others. 60 min.
44-2099 *$14.99*

Edenquest
Get ready for a trip to Paradise, as some of the world's most beautiful women take you on a sensual getaway to the most glamorous vacation spots from around the globe. It's an exotic, erotic odyssey you won't want to miss. Each tape runs about 60 min.

Edenquest: Pamela Anderson
The bountiful "Baywatch" and "Barb Wire" star is joined by a bevy of international swimsuit models for a seaside adventure in the South Pacific playground of Bora Bora.
19-3929 *$14.99*

Edenquest: Anna Nicole Smith
Paradise Island more than lives up to its name when the buxom jeans model, magazine centerfold and film star sets sail with a comely crew for a romp along the beach.
19-3930 *$14.99*

Edenquest: Sandra Taylor
A visit to Maui with Playboy cover girl Sandra Taylor and her girlfriends, in which they sun and play along the sandy shores, will have you saying "Wowie!"
19-3931 *$14.99*

Eight Babes A Week
Take a behind-the-scenes look at a nude photography studio as the models prepare for their sensuous sessions. See them get in—and out of—all sorts of costumes. So, whether you like your blonde, redhead or brunette undressed or dressed as a nurse, firefighter or bikini-clad temptress, you're in luck! 60 min.
50-5315 *$19.99*

The Best Exotic Dancers In The U.S.A.
Travel to an international resort where beautiful models, actresses and dancers compete for recognition as the best exotic dancers in the U.S.A. Off go the evening gowns, on comes the lingerie, then off goes the skimpy stuff, as the gals take it all off for your pleasure. 60 min.
50-5349 *$14.99*

Mammazons: Megabust Amateurs
A sultry slew of sensuous sweeties with sizable, natural breasts are the focus of noted British photographer Richard Thornbury's camera in this provocative program. Amateur models of all colors are featured, letting loose their undergarments and getting nasty. Alexis St. John and Lisa Simpson, minus saxophone, star. 60 min.
50-5435 *$29.99*

Mammazons II: Double-D Housewives
Eight of the largest mammary glands you'll ever see have been gathered in this erotic new video shot by internationally known nude photographer Richard Thornbury. All natural, with no implants whatsoever, these hot housewives have a lot to do in front of you when their husbands aren't around. 60 min.
50-5876 *$29.99*

Wrasslin' She-Babes Of The Fifties
They're fabulous, they're fierce, they're topless (sometimes) and they're female! Check out some classic catfighting action with these collections of gal grapplers giving their all in (and sometimes out of) the ring.

Wrasslin' She-Babes, Vol. 1
They're wild, they like to pull hair, and they wear tight tights. They're women of the mat, mauling and brawling, in vintage matches. See Gorgeous Lindy vs. Clare Mortison, Blonde Ballerina vs. June O'Day, Lillie Bitters vs. June Myers and more. 90 min.
79-5010 *$24.99*

Wrasslin' She-Babes, Vol. 2
Ladies and gentlemen, welcome to the wildest women wrestlers of the 1950s, a collection of tough gals going the distance in difficult grappling competition. If you're into hair-pulling, face-smashing, foot-stomping and more, this amazing selection of female gladiator action is just for you! 90 min.
79-5582 Was $24.99 *$19.99*

Wrasslin' She-Babes, Vol. 3
Look out, "Wild Women of Wongo"! Stand back, "Kansas City Bomber"! Here comes a slew of tough-as-nails tootsies, grapplin', wrasslin' and stompin' each other to smithereens. On hand are a tag-team tournament matching Rita Boucher and Barbara Owens against Lillian Ellison and Patti Neilson, plus Deanna Lane, Terry Clement, Shirley Erwin and midgets in contests.
79-6072 Was $24.99 *$19.99*

Wrasslin' She-Babes, Vol. 4
Take down, go behind, ouch! The ladies of wrestling lay it on the line in this collection that pits Rusty against Maria, Colleen against Rusty, Irma against Blanche, plus heavy and husky gals and Amazons on the mat. WARNING: This tape is for adults only. 120 min.
79-6073 Was $24.99 *$19.99*

Wrasslin' She-Babes, Vol. 5
Look out, here come more grappling gals! Included are mud-wrestling matches with Rene against Ursula, and Aggie against Inga, rough stuff with Margo and Stella, a she-cat showdown and more. WARNING: This tape is for adults only. 120 min.
79-6074 Was $24.99 *$19.99*

Wrasslin' She-Babes, Vol. 6
A real grab-bag of grappling delights awaits fans of femme fighting in this program. See headscissors, Spice Williams and Rosalyn in a topless bout, nude sessions with Sandy Partlow, Cheryl Day, Lynn Black and Gail Gardner, a "Battle Royale" and Joan Velez against Cheryl Day. WARNING: This tape is for adults only. 120 min.
79-6075 Was $24.99 *$19.99*

Wrasslin' She-Babes, Vol. 7
In this wild compendium of ladies' wrestling, Patti Stegert and Lena Blaine go hog wild, Casey Carr and Sharon Lee square off, Rene and Delia do damage to each other, and topless matches feature Uschi Digart, Cheryl Day and others. WARNING: This tape is for adults only. 120 min.
79-6076 Was $24.99 *$19.99*

Wrasslin' She-Babes, Vol. 8
Let's get ready to RRRRRRUUUUUUMMMMMMBLE! Aficionados of mighty Aphrodites wrestling it out will appreciate such stars as Cheryl Day and Jackie West tag-teaming against Jane O'Brien and Sharon Lee, Tanya West meeting such competitors as Sonja and Casey Carr and topless matches which include a black-against-white tourney. WARNING: This tape is for adults only. 120 min.
79-6077 Was $24.99 *$19.99*

Wrasslin' She-Babes, Vol. 9
Nasty! Brutal! Outrageous! If you like your women's wrasslin' way, way out, check out this tape that'll really put a hold on you. Sylvia Hackney battles Sara Lee, who nobody doesn't like; Kitty and Gail wail; a "Battle Royale" will wow you; and there's topless bouts, too. WARNING: This tape is for adults only. 120 min.
79-6078 Was $24.99 *$19.99*

Wrasslin' She-Babes, Vol. 10
The accent is on wrestling and cat-fighting in the nude in this compilation, in which Gail Gardner wrassles Lynn Black, Sally Black and Sheila Mather scratch at each other, Sally and B.J. wrestle nude, Lori and Sandy get some cat-scratch fever and more. WARNING: This tape is for adults only. 120 min.
79-6079 Was $24.99 *$19.99*

Wrasslin' She-Babes, Vol. 11
See them wiggle, see them waggle, see them wrestle. Sonja faces Marlene, Miss Germany goes up against a big Sallery in a topless match, Uschi meets J.B. (sans clothing), Cheryl Day grapples Sylvia Hackney, and Kim and Delilah square off in a match minus Samson. WARNING: This tape is for adults only. 120 min.
79-6080 Was $24.99 *$19.99*

Wrasslin' She-Babes, Vol. 12
Watch out for the turnbuckle, tootsie! Madam, don't get your face slammed on the mat! Hey, sweetie, look out for that scissor-hold! The gals are meaner, leaner and nastier than ever in this furious selection of femme free-for-all fighting featuring topless Spice Williams and Rosalyn Royce, a nude three-girl fracas and lots more. WARNING: This tape is for adults only. 120 min.
79-6081 Was $24.99 *$19.99*

Wrasslin' She-Babes, Vol. 13
See pretties push, pull hair and prance wildly in "Go Go Gotcha," "Blonde and Brawny," "Black Silk Stockings on Zebra 1, 2, 3," "Bleached Blonde Battle," "Rusty vs. Sheila" and more.
79-6105 Was $24.99 *$19.99*

Wrasslin' She-Babes, Vol. 14
These gals can't wait to rip into each other. And when you see them, in all their cat-scratching glory, you'll forget the "Gorgeous Ladies of Wrestling" ever existed. Check out "Naughty Blonde," "Be More Gentle," "Indian Giver," "The Body Press" and more.
79-6106 Was $24.99 *$19.99*

Wrasslin' She-Babes, Vol. 15
They're fierce, they're fabulous, they're topless (sometimes) and they're femmes. They razzle, dazzle and wrestle in this selection of slugging, hair-pulling and grappling moves from the 1950s and 1960s. There's Toni and Little "E", Dixie and Jonnie, Linda and Anita and others. 120 min.
79-6169 Was $24.99 *$19.99*

Wrasslin' She-Babes, Vol. 16
Take yourself out to the brawlgame. Take yourself out with the crowd. Buy you some scratchin' and kickin' and smacks. You won't care if you ever come back. Oh, it's root, root, root for Terri, Lisa and housewives slugging it out in front of their kids. If they don't win it's a shame. For it's one, two, three counts you're out at the old brawlgame!
79-6170 Was $24.99 *$19.99*

Wrasslin' She-Babes. Vol. 17
It's female fighting at its most ferocious with 1950s and 1960s superbitches battling each other in ferocious fighting action, with and without their clothing. Along with some color footage from London, there's B&W winners such as Ditte against Colette. 120 min.
79-6171 Was $24.99 *$19.99*

Evolutionary Masturbation: An Intimate Guide To The Male Orgasm

Put the "love" back in "self-love" with this frank and revealing guide to male masturbation. Handsome nude models demonstrate exercises and movements designed to heighten arousal and self-awareness and bring you to new dimensions in eroticism. 50 min.

50-1246   *$39.99*

Uranus: Self Anal Massage For Men

Get a little behind in your lovemaking by watching this intimate and uncensored video course in anal eroticism. Tips on exercises to tighten and tone muscles, rhythmic breathing, the best positions for massaging and more are offered and demonstrated. 40 min.

50-1247   *$39.99*

Fire On The Mountain: An Intimate Guide To Male Genital Massage

This guide to Taoist erotic massage teaches 25 genital strokes that can be practiced by oneself or by gay or straight couples. Teacher Joseph Kramer shows you how to spread energy throughout the body, allowing you to feel an intense aliveness. Featuring extensive nudity, this program shows that there's something beyond the four-minute orgasm. 45 min.

50-2544   *$39.99*

Kama Sutra Of Gay Sex

The erotic arts of the Kama Sutra are explored by gay men in this sensual and informative program. Six handsome and physically impressive models help show you the secrets of intimate, loving and safe sex between men in exciting style. Includes nudity and explicit scenes. 55 min.

50-5320   *$39.99*

Ultimate Pleasures: An Erotic Exploration Of The Art Of Tantra

Learn how to achieve sexual ecstasy and multiple orgasms without ejaculation when you use the techniques featured on this program. A doctor shows a young man the secrets of the ancient art of Tantra in an incredible homoerotic journey. 55 min.

50-8199   *$29.99*

AMG: The Fantasy Factory

The Athletic Model Guild (AMG) produced many erotic shorts featuring actors without shorts during the 1950s. This retrospective includes famous male models like Jim Paris, Monte Hansen, Ed Fury and Joe Dallesandro (of Warhol film fame), starring in original films. Also, top model Joe Leitel recalls the early days at AMG. 60 min.

50-2596   *$39.99*

AMG: The Fantasy Factory Revisited

A fun-filled tribute to the Athletic Model Guild, featuring short movies produced by Bob Mizer from 1955 to 1970. Rarely seen, this compilation offers prime examples of male photography, nudity, hunky models and even color! 60 min.

50-2597   *$39.99*

AMG: A Third Visit

A look back at the erotica of yesteryear, showcasing a collection of films from the Athletic Model Guild. There's he-men galore in store, as nostalgia, superb physiques and innocence make a muscular combination for fans of the male form everywhere. 60 min.

50-2598   *$39.99*

Wrestle

Tight, sinewy, spectacularly muscled men grapple each other in the nude in this rugged, sweat-dripping program. With strong wills and magnificently structured bodies, the guys go at it furiously, igniting scenarios similar to Greco-Roman wrestling tournaments of yesteryear. Loaded with naked hunks. 50 min.

50-2783   *$39.99*

Sirocco

It's not a promo tape for a new car. It is a scorching journey in which eight men of different races take to the sands of the African desert and explore their desires while swimming, writhing in the sand and hiking together sans clothing. See them explore the rugged terrain—including themselves! Features full nudity. 50 min.

50-2890   *$29.99*

Trance

The creators of "Sirocco" present this steamy excursion into masculine sensuality. Set in South Africa, the video tells of a witch doctor whose sexual spell brings out the desires of six perfectly sculptured men. Gorgeously filmed, this nudity-filled effort offers an exotic turn-on. 50 min.

50-2916   *$39.99*

Interludes

They think they're alone now...it doesn't appear there's anyone else around. They think they're alone now...time for them to get really down. Eight spectacularly chiseled men invite you to take matters into your own hand with this revealing, nudity-filled primer on intimate self-pleasures.

50-2943   *$29.99*

Viz

Water, water everywhere, and not a drop to drink. But there's certainly enough to bathe with in this erotic journey, set in a Turkish bath in Budapest. A selection of European male models frolic in a swimming pool, enjoy a water fountain and partake in wet massages. This nudity-filled tape is from Hungary—and proud of it! 55 min.

50-2944   *$29.99*

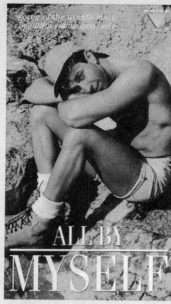

All By Myself

Dim the lights and savor the vision of seven of the world's most beautiful young men as they explore their sensuality and sexuality, all by themselves, just for you. 55 min.

50-5906   *$29.99*

Whatever You Say, Sir

A group of studly buck privates and their commanding officers discover their cigs and mags are confiscated after returning to base following training exercises. The incident sends the military men into a frenzy that's only relieved when they release their sexual energies. Shane Thomas and Rick Chase star in this nudity-filled tale of all-male "maneuvers." 60 min.

50-8189   *$29.99*

The Big Shot

This big shot is also a hot shot, an ugly duckling in high school who has become a self-possessed stud. At a photo shoot, he meets an old flame, but won't delve into that turf again unless the circumstances are right...or at least kinky and sexy enough! Clay Maverick and Michael Crawford star in this steamy all-male tale brimming with nudity. 60 min.

50-8190   *$29.99*

The Pool: Shooting With Tom Bianchi

Tom Bianchi, one of the top photographers of the male form, takes you on an intimate trip populated by stunning, muscular models. Tom's photo shoot becomes a hotbed of activities featuring gold medalists in same-sex-pair body building at the Amsterdam Gay Games. 55 min.

50-8200   *$29.99*

Blue Jeans Fantasy

If your fantasies involve hunky men in and out of tight blue jeans and denim shorts, you've got to get this video! A handsome young man, haunted by an encounter with another hunk in the mountains, finds a pair of the man's blue jeans and enters into a fantasy where seven sinewy he-men let their feelings go. 55 min.

50-8201   *$29.99*

Muscle Fantasies, Vol. 1: Worship

Three men in solo fantasies will enthrall fans of sinewy bodies, leather clothing, chains and masterful attitudes. See what happens with a biker lured into a fantasy warehouse; a bodybuilder who wants his plumber to watch; and an athlete who loves to show it off for a surveillance camera. 75 min.

50-8203   *$29.99*

Muscle Fantasies, Vol. 2: Wrestlers

Muscular hunks in and out of their trunks are showcased in this sizzling, nudity-filled program that features erotic extended matches. See punishment-pounding action at its most outrageous. 55 min.

50-8204   *$29.99*

Dream Boys

Dream a big dream with these heavenly hunks. Six statuesque studs get naked for a steamy photography session. They're surfers, weight-lifters, models and boxers and they aim to please with their day in front of the cameras. From the people who gave you "Love Scenes." 57 min.

50-8302   *$24.99*

Gay To Z Of Sex

This irreverent and scorching look at gay sex offers hot activities coordinated to the letters of the alphabet. Featuring such top models as Johan Paulik, the program illustrates almost every type of hunky move known to he-mankind. 120 min.

50-8494   *$29.99*

Those Moments Together

Witness 10 of the most phenomenally beautiful men committing acts of erotic passion together. Whether making love means to you slow and easy, hot and passionate, or fast and furious, nothing is more enticing than seeing these guys fulfill their wildest fantasies. 55 min.

50-5905   *$29.99*

Erotic Couples: A Guide To Gay Intimacy

The focus is on two couples who show you how to enjoy erotic encounters through communication and negotiation, while keeping it safe. Inspired by the LA Shanti workshops, this video offers explicit depictions of sexual situations between men and is designed for those who want to explore the intimate side of a relationship. WARNING: Includes nudity. 55 min.

50-5705   *$29.99*

Vulcan: Fresh And Cheeky Young Guns

Eight of Slovakia's hunkiest examples of young manhood are showcased in this stunning European erotic production. These foreign men will lure you into their special realm of manhood. Features full nudity. 55 min.

50-8085   *$29.99*

Savage Hearts

An octet of awesome young men from South Africa take you on a sensual trip to the dark continent, where lurid sensuality is sure to seduce you. The producers of "Sirocco" offer this sexy study of burgeoning manhood, Cape Town-style. Features full nudity. 50 min.

50-8086   *$29.99*

Angelic Interludes

Matthew's dreams become reality in this dazzling journey into the world of forbidden sensuality. Matthew imagines excursions to an Eastern European sauna, a trip through the woods, and a photo session turned sultry. Spectacular specimens of youthful manliness are featured! Features full nudity. 55 min.

50-8087   *$29.99*

Hazy Days Of Summer

It's a day in the park in gay old England. Seven of the country's most adorable men celebrate the times, the fine weather and each other in this steamy ode to what makes Britain great. Roll out these not-so lazy, hazy days of summer! Features full nudity. 56 min.

50-8088   *$29.99*

Aroused

A group of men living together explores the possibilities of sexual liaisons in this spectacularly sensuous fantasy. Close proximity leads to heated encounters in a scorching video spotlighting a host of hot hunks. Features full nudity. 55 min.

50-8089   *$29.99*

You're Gorgeous

European men sizzle in a feisty document of solo studs in heat! These young men hail from Hungary and Czechoslovakia and offer tastier treats than the best goulash you ever tasted. Spicy, too! Features full nudity. 84 min.

50-8090   *$29.99*

The Calling

Super-charged phone calls turn into real sexual interludes for seven super-toned he-men in this hot-to-trot video. Mysterious phone sex calls only get the men on the receiving end curious about the pleasures that await on the other end of the line. And when a real meeting is in order, bells are sure to be rung! Features full nudity. 84 min.

50-8091   *$29.99*

Where The Boys Are: The Director's Cut

The pride of Britain's young gay men take off to Portugal's Algarve coast for a romp that's sure to please. See the Brits explore their new surroundings with wonderful lust and a sense of adventure! Features full nudity. This 74-minute tape includes 20 minutes of special footage.

50-8093   *$29.99*

Ibiza: Unzipped

Join a group of stunning studs on a Mediterranean island vacation where their desires run rampant. Hunky bodies and handsome faces set against the picturesque locales are sure to make you intoxicated with this exotic, erotic program. 62 min.

50-8183   *$29.99*

A Private Party

Welcome to Billy's special private party, a swinging soiree attended only by the hottest hunks around. The festivities get way out of control when the guests each bring a buddy along. The clothes soon come off and lustiness abounds! 55 min.

50-8186   *$29.99*

Alone At Last

Want to steer your sexual pleasures in a solo way? Check out this incredible video boasting the talents of super-hunks Ryan Block, Randy White and Danny Bliss. See them survey their pleasure zones with delight. 50 min.

50-8187   *$29.99*

Freshman Yoga

The tight, muscular, glistening bodies of young men as they flex and stretch in seemingly impossible positions are featured in this sweat-inducing program. Spiritually enhancing and erotic, this video is just what Yoga Bare-It ordered. 55 min.

50-8202   *$29.99*

Solo Male Ecstasy

Discover an explosive, natural way to achieve incredible orgasms with this video that offers 40 genital massage techniques, techniques on prolonging orgasm and tips on increasing sexual self-confidence. Features information provided Anthony A. Zaffuto and no-holds-barred demonstration. 60 min.

50-5252   *$39.99*

Bulges And Buns

Some of America's hunkiest men are showcased in this sizzling program that offers them posing in skimpy shorts, micro-swimsuits and even in the nude. See them shower, stretch, exercise and reveal their tremendous physiques in provocative settings. 85 min.

50-5276   *$29.99*

Aussie Dreams

Love Sydney? How about other parts of Australia, like its beaches? Well, if you've got a hankering for hunks and Down Under, this video presents both: muscular he-men in skimpy bathing suits getting naked in Australian hot spots. Sure to make you hop like a kangaroo. 50 min.

50-5305   *$29.99*

Kalahari

The hot sands of the Kalahari get even hotter when this group of international hunks take a rafting trip down the Orange River and trek through the desert. Sexual tensions among the men grow to a fever pitch, and temptations lead to scorching erotic encounters. You'll never want to go out of Africa again! Features full-frontal nudity. 50 min.

50-5321   *$39.99*

My First Time

You'll always remember your first time. And now six strapping young men show you their first time, unforgettable liaisons portrayed in provocative detail for the camera. See how these erotic encounters shaped their futures and helped them experience the thresholds of adulthood. Sir Ian McKellen narrates; features extensive nudity and sexual situations. 45 min.

50-5322   *$29.99*

The Wrestle Club

You won't find Hulk Hogan, Ric Flair or even the Goon in this club. You will find a group of naked athletes who join two pals in a weekly wrassling match that's sure to excite you. Filled with full frontal nudity, this video gives new meaning to the term "take down, go behind." 50 min.

50-5441   *$29.99*

true love takes many different forms
Sunshine after the rain

Sunshine After The Rain

Eight young men who have grown up together share the joys of adulthood at the end of the summer. The octet of awesome hunks has a series of erotic experiences sure to change their lives forever. With Johan Paulik, Matthew Anders and Dano Sulik. 65 min.

50-5589   *$29.99*

Mad About The Boy

From England come these scorching tales of young men in love. A jock and a studious college student find each other; two best friends discover they are attracted to each other; and a male hooker falls for one of his clients; and a young man has a tryst with his family's gardener. 82 min.

50-5590   *$39.99*

Snow-Balls

Eight fabulous young Czech men discover a stylish ski resort to be a hotbed for sensual activities in this sizzling European program. See fantasies fulfilled in showers, between student and teacher and menage-a-trois situations. 55 min.

50-5591   *$29.99*

Summer, The First Time

After a fight with his girlfriend, Ryan encounters a young man at the beach who is having his own problems with an unfaithful lover. The two men soon carry on an intense affair as their passions simmer. 85 min.

50-5592   *$39.99*

Young Americans

You'll wave more than the flag for these patriotic college hunks taking a trip to the mountains of Southern California for some rest and relaxation. These college guys forget the books and drop their clothes for risqué fun in the sun. Features full nudity. 55 min.

50-8084   *$29.99*

L'Albergo
Filmed on the gorgeous Italian Riviera, this program proves spicier than roasted red peppers. See a group of Euro-hunks discover the joys of first love in a coming-of-age essay filmed with eroticism. With Dario D'Alba, Ettore Tosi. 65 min.
50-8499 $29.99

Close Shave
A group of Italy's hottest studs go through the daily ritual of rising out of bed, shaving, washing and pleasuring themselves in this extremely rugged blast of macho, macho men. Riccardo and Marc Lacoma star in this program that features guys taking it off...taking it all off! 60 min.
50-8500 $29.99

Getting Straight
A ranch for wayward young men serves as the backdrop for this erotic excursion where the fellows can solve their problems naturally—sans clothes, of course. Tony Donovan, Ethan Marc and Scott Lyons star in this rock 'em, sock 'em sensual story. 60 min.
50-8580 $29.99

Knaked Knights
Four strapping warriors are thrown into a dungeon after their assault on the castle fails. Stripped of their armor, these heroic he-man must depend only on their muscular bodies to escape the monster in the moat and the kingdom's most sinewy strongmen. Fans of fresh faces and awesome physiques will love this knight life! With Playgirl model Rod Dupree. 90 min.
73-9271 $49.99

Rendezvous At The Golden Gate & Breakfast
There's more than muffins on the menu at the San Francisco inn where lovers Bo and Matt decide to go to for a romantic getaway. Soon, they find that there's room at the inn for other gay men who want to explore their wildest fantasies. Check in and check out some amazing encounters! Features full nudity. 55 min.
66-8092 $29.99

Buff Bachelor Party Weekend
Wedding bells are about to ring, so a gang of hunky fellows group together for one last getaway. The weekend turns into a lost weekend—lost in terms of clothing, as the hunks play all sorts of risqué games leading to their undressing. All the sizzling fun ends in a torrid naked food fight. If you love the naked male form, this fun tape is for you. 75 min.
73-9177 $39.99

Naked Football League
Are you ready for some naked football? You'll want to make a pass at the hunky heroes who doff their uniforms after a tough day on the gridiron and get their backfields (and "frontfields") in motion. There's no penalty for enjoying this salute to awesome athleticism that eventually lands in the locker rooms and showers. 75 min.
73-9186 $39.99

Gymnastikos: Power And Grace
The male form is celebrated in this artistic, erotic look at hunky gymnasts who perform in the nude on the parallel bars, rings, high bars and pommel horse. See these perfectly developed Eastern Europeans flex their muscles, while dramatic lighting and stunning camera angles capture their grace and ability. 45 min.
78-5052 $39.99

Beefcake Buddies
This outrageous collection of gay short films and loops from the 1960s is sure to delight anyone looking for some campy fun. Included in the hunky hoedowns are three nude men shooting pool; a nude guy balancing a pillow on his head; two cowboys and two Indians, sans clothes, in a shooting match; tattooed musclemen playing ukuleles; and lots more.
79-6010 Was $24.99 $19.99

Man For Man, Vol. 1
A magazine designed for gay men in which eight hunky dudes bare all in a quartet of erotic outings. Do you like gladiator movies? See Hercules get his man. There's also a Victorian melodrama, a tryst between a sculptor and his model, and a night of passion in a London penthouse. Also featured is "Buckingham Place," a gay soap opera, a safer sex workshop and more. 59 min.
01-1894 Was $39.99 $29.99

Man For Man, Vol. 2
In this sizzling sequel, you'll check out the nightlife of Amsterdam; witness a tryst involving a college boy and a cab driver in New Orleans; follow the adventures of the world's first gay detective as he searches for a teenage runaway; take a trip to a dungeon where bondage is practiced; and follow another installment of "Buckingham Place." 55 min.
01-1497 Was $39.99 $29.99

Man For Man, Vol. 3
The third volume of this gay-themed video magazine includes a sensual love story based on the ancient story of Gilgamesh; an erotic encounter between a Spanish poet and a hunky sailor; plus travelogues of Barcelona and Sitges, safe sex information, the third chapter of "Buckingham Place" and more. 60 min.
01-1508 Was $39.99 $29.99

Man For Man, Vol. 4
Among the erotic segments featured in this edition are "Closed Set," a gay love story set in '20s Hollywood; Adam Roberts' look at the street life of modern Berlin; a dramatization of the famous gay romance novel "Teleny," which may have been written anonymously by Oscar Wilde; and more. 84 min.
05-1536 Was $39.99 $29.99

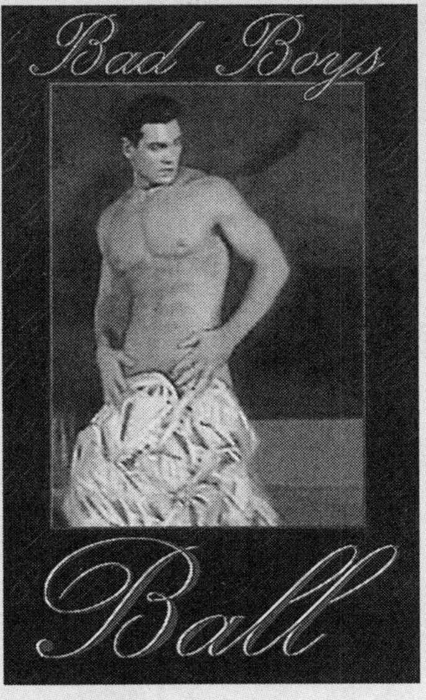

Bad Boys Ball
You can't get any hotter than this amazing turn-on of a tape in which adult film stars Tom Katt, Jeff Hammond and others give an erotic exhibition of their bodies and their moves to an intimate party of fans. The live acts of the XXX stars are captured in the raw, as well as fantasies, including a Roman orgy that must witnessed to be believed. 50 min.
50-2917 $19.99

Mojave
A handsome drifter trying to survive in the windswept Mojave Desert has a series of surreal fantasies in which he gets comfy with some sizzling strangers. His innermost desires taunt him, but eventually lead to his survival in this scorcher. WARNING: This video includes extensive nudity; adults only. 60 min.
50-8695 $29.99

Workin' It Out
A gay bar is the center for some swinging encounters as a hunky bartenders offers only the finest cocktails to the wildest studs. Sonny Markham stars with Joey Morelli and others who are truly "Coyote Gorgeous"! 60 min.
50-8697 $29.99

Military Muscle
Looking for a few good men to watch in military maneuvers, exercising, marching, doing calisthenics, involved in paintball combat and hand-to-hand "techniques"? They're all nude and perfectly sculpted and ready, willing and able for anything. With Bruce Patterson and Thom Bartholemew. 90 min.
73-9218 $59.99

How The West Was Naked
A group of hunky cowpokes show you how good they look in and out of the denim in this erotic ode to the Old West. Eight broncos ride bareback, pitch hay, chase the Indians and take to bullwhip-cracking in this beefcake bonanza. 90 min.
73-9235 $49.99

Naked In The City
The "Boyz in the Hood" becomes the "Boyz in the Nude" in this super-charged salute to the male form. Eight muscle-bound studs are enticed into taking off their clothes and run rampant and naked around the city streets. Their urban journey is the stuff of urban legend, culminating in a wild, flesh-filled free-for-all. 90 min.
73-9251 $49.99

Manifest Fantasies, Vol. 1: College Wrestlers
Fantasies becomes realities when Troy's desires to partake in nude wrestling turns real, as he and his two pals run into a group of hunky collegiate wrestlers. Soon, his private daydreams involve the nude, perfectly-formed grapplers. Features complete nudity; 45 min.
50-5703 $29.99

Manifest Fantasies, Vol. 2: Blue Collar Men
Steve Andrews didn't know that, when he started renovating his home, he'd have a group of hot-to-trot blue collar guys working on different chores, from connecting cable to electrical work. Steve's fantasies take over and he's soon involved with these manly men. And nothing's been added to his cable bill, either! 45 min.
50-5704 $29.99

Manifest Fantasies, Vol. 3: Boot Camp Wrestler
Tommy is bored at army boot camp, so he writes a letter home to his parents. In the midst of it, he drifts off into a series of erotic daydreams involving grappling with his bunkmates, his C.O., and even a stranger he meets on a hike. Don't ask, don't tell...just watch! 55 min.
50-5972 $29.99

Solo Sex: Extended Pleasure For Men
Veteran educator R.M. Karchmer has assembled a group of young male models in order to assist him in demonstrating several masturbation techniques designed to help men raise their physical and mental pleasure to a higher level and experience better and more prolonged sexual gratification. 60 min.
50-8726 $39.99

Maximum Orgasm: Tantric Pleasure For Men
Men are taught to heighten their sexual awareness of themselves in this video through the use of ancient Tantric practices. Topics including prolonged orgasm through ejaculatory control, stimulating the prostate for increased pleasure, and locating unseen energy points of one's own body are explored. 60 min.
50-8727 $39.99

Wide Nude World Of Sports
Spanning the globe to bring you the best in all-nude sporting competitions, this hunk-a-thon offers the thrill of victory and not much agony if you like naked dudes. Eight Playgirl models test their skills and your thrills in Trampoline Dodge Ball, Soccer Skirmish, Naked Mud Wrestling and other games of he-men heroics.
73-9330 $49.99

College Muscle Jocks
More fun than "Animal House," this journey into frat house frolics features a group of groping freshmen who get initiated into their secret society the wildest way possible. From nude gym workouts to towel-snapping shower excursions to pillow fights to stripper parties, these guys know how to party! 90 min.
73-9334 $49.99

Mr. Nude Universe: The Video
Playgirl Magazine presents a sizzling contest in which the world's hottest hunks compete for the title of Mr. Nude Universe. Filmed at the Peppermints Club in Niagara Falls, this program shows you the most astonishing he-men in the world—showing off their greatest assets in the nude! 60 min.
77-9002 $19.99

Hin Yin For Men
Three handsome male models guide you in exploring the ancient methods of self-eroticism designed to enhance spiritual awareness and increase virility. Tastefully photographed yet graphically performed, this tape allows viewers to experience pleasures virtually unknown in the West, including anal and penile massage. New Age expert Neil Tucker hosts. 50 min.
78-5022 $29.99

Naturally Naked
Stunning locations and hunky naked men make for a super-charged erotic combination in this promiscuous program. Witness swimmers, divers, mountain men, desert bikers and other macho men pose and play for you in the great outdoors. From the creators of "Malerotic." 60 min.
78-5047 Was $39.99 $24.99

The Art Of Touch 2
The sensuous sequel to the hit video features six hunky international models who demonstrate the secrets of channeling sexual energy throughout the entire body. These totally nude men guide you on an odyssey exploring sexual heights rarely encountered by Westerners. The tape is presented in 3-D with two pairs of glasses included. WARNING: Contains nudity. 50 min.
78-5044 Was $39.99 $24.99

The Art Of Touch 3: Sports Massage
If you're seeking a soothing yet firm sports massage from a hardy masseur, this tape's for you. See eight physically impressive hunks get rubbed all over their nude bodies, sports-style, in this sweaty, sensuous session. WARNING: Contains nudity. 50 min.
50-2888 $39.99

Hard (1993)
For men who like their all-male erotica hard, this collection of sexy softcore shorts from Great Britain is your cup of tea. Watch an auto mechanic offer "super service" in "Grease My Axle"; there's some funky factory workers in "Machine Room"; "Wild Side" presents a nocturnal dockside roundelay; and a not-quite abandoned building is the setting for "Built." 50 min.
01-1527 $24.99

Billy 2000: Billy Goes Hollywood (2000)
Attention, shoppers! A brand new line of "Billy Dolls" is in stores now, and you'll never imagine what kind of fantasies they elicit until you run to the gift shop and see for yourself. "Cowboy Billy," "Sailor Billy," "Leather Billy" and others are bound to provide hours of playtime fun. Clay Maverick, Thom Barron, Mark Mason others star. 60 min.
50-8724 $29.99

It's Raining Men (2000)
Hallelujah! If you like 'em tall, blond, dark and lean, rough and tough, or strong and mean, then this group of young stallions is just the ticket. Rod Barrett, Jake Armstrong, Jay Strong and others have moved into an apartment together, and they're all more than willing to make each other feel right at home! 60 min.
50-8725 $29.99

Colin's Sleazy Friends
The hit Los Angeles cable show comes to video, with Colin and Dino welcoming such "sleazy" guests as comics Janeane Garofalo, Margaret Cho and Bob Odenkirk; musical acts Korn, Tool and Blink 182; and porn stars Shane, Taylor Hayes and Jasmine St. Clair. 50 min.
10-1729 $19.99

California Girls Amateur Nude Auditions
For the first time anywhere, 16 incredibly cute and gorgeously proportioned models take their clothes off and reveal what makes a California girl a California girl. The auditions are jam-packed with nudity, so don't miss a second of them. 60 min.
50-5253 $24.99

Erotic Bloopers
You won't be able to decide whether to get hot or go ha-ha while watching this assortment of erotic sequences where something wacky occurs at the least expected moments. Sharon Kane, Gigi and Taylor St. Claire star in the steamy scenarios at the pool table and in the kitchen that lead to silliness. 60 min.
50-2927 $24.99

In-Flight Fantasies
No, we're not talking about a bag of peanuts that's easy to open! The high-flying honeys on display here will take your sexual dreams to new heights of eroticism, as the sensual stewardesses and foxy flight crew of Fantasy Air give their passengers true "first-class" treatment. Janine, Julia Ann star. 50 min.
19-3972 $14.99

Love In Hot Leather
In the tradition of Woody Allen's "What's Up, Tiger Lilly?" comes this hilarious film that's actually a German softcore movie with new dubbing. Nudity and laughs abound in a story of a detective searching for a book on the sex lives of famous people. AKA: "Love in Leather Pants." 90 min.
78-3027 $14.99

The Epic Adventures Of White Panties, Vol. 1: Texas Roommates
They come from the Lone Star State, but they'll make you feel like a star and anything but lonely as these Texas roommates lasso you into their realm of seduction with their incredible dancing abilities. The white panties will captivate, but when they come off, things get spicier than that five-alarm chili. 57 min.
50-5468 $19.99

Ginger Lynn Allen's Lingerie Gallery, Pt. 1
Ginger Lynn Allen, aka porn star Ginger Lynn, reveals some of her hottest fantasies in this lusty program that offers several sizzling vignettes. See Ginger and beautiful supermodels in the military, as an Indian maiden, in a 1930s speakeasy, and as Marilyn Monroe. 30 min.
07-2118 $14.99

Ginger Lynn Allen's Lingerie Gallery, Pt. 2: Private Screening
Ginger and her supermodel friends are back in a second spicy serving of erotic fantasies, revealing their perfect bodies while acting out the stories of Zorro, Aladdin, Beauty and the Beast, and more. 30 min.
07-2219 $14.99

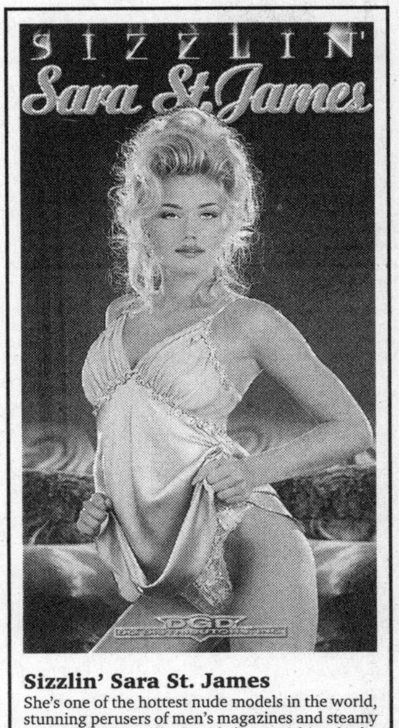

Sizzlin' Sara St. James
She's one of the hottest nude models in the world, stunning perusers of men's magazines and steamy videos like "Femalien" with her ravishing body, strawberry blonde hair and gorgeous face. She's done it all—including XXX films under the name Jacqueline Lovell—and here she shows you why she's a sizzler in a show-all program. 55 min.
50-8612 $19.99

60's Go-Go Chicks
Check out this far-out collection of fetching go-go dancers of the super-psychedelic 1960s. See them thrill in tassels and G-strings, gyrating to acid rock and other far-out music. Psych-out with some amply endowed chicks that are real humdingers.
79-5131   Was $24.99   *$19.99*

Private Passions: Sensual Secrets
Pssst...do you wanna hear a secret? How about a *sensual* secret? How about the most intimate, most erotic, innermost thoughts and fantasies of 20 beautiful models? Well, it's no secret that you'll enjoy this tantalizing Edward Holzman video that's overflowing with private passions made public. With Lorissa Mccombs, Stevi conrad and Sarah St. James. 60 min.
50-5633   *$19.99*

Private Passions: Playful Pleasures
Fantasies of the most feverish kind are on display in this kinky program from award-winning photographer Edward Holzman. From a revolving couch tryst involving six naked women to a lusty lesbian make-up session that turns into a make-out session, this video is full of scintillating surprises. 60 min.
50-5730   *$19.99*

Private Passions: Secret Moments
Jail. Water. Massage. Bath. Snow. Lesbians. Put them all together and you have this titillating treat, a collection of carnal fantasies captured by photographer Edward Holzman. Secret moments are sensual moments here. 60 min.
50-5731   *$19.99*

Private Passions: Dark Dreams
A bevy of beautiful babes takes you to the next erotic level in this fantasy-filled program that's heavy on the self-pleasure and lesbian liaisons. Witness a trio of titillators in a shower, a leather-clad lady in a cage, a make-up session that turns torrid and lots more. 60 min.
50-5749   *$19.99*

Private Passions: Carnal Visions
A number of stunning nymphettes let their fantasies go wild in this salute to sensuality. Director Ed Holzman captures stunning women at their most playful, with baby oil, entangled in silk ribbons, taking baths and partaking in a leather-clad motorcycle fantasy. With Sara St. James, Barbara Doll. 60 min.
50-5750   *$19.99*

Private Passions: Sexy Interludes
Sultry music, dimly lit rooms, and goddesses of love populate this video from director Edward Holzman. Watch some of the most beautiful naked women in the world show you their stuff as you listen to their secret thoughts. With Barbara Doll, Lorissa McComas, Stevi Conrad and Elizabeth Bowmont. 60 min.
50-5862   *$19.99*

Private Passions: Lustful Pleasures
What's your pleasure? Whether it's blondes, brunettes or both, you're sure to find it on this video featuring beautiful models disrobing and displaying their bodies for your erotic edification. 60 min.
50-8249   *$19.99*

Private Passions: Erotic Wishes
This "Private Passions" program features sequences with lesbian lust, handcuffs, delightful dancing and sensual encounters that are sure to keep everyone's erotic wishes fulfilled. Provocative performers include Sara St. James, Stevi Conrad, Renee Taylor and Lorissa McCombs. 55 min.
50-8467   *$19.99*

Private Passions: Strange Desires
If you're curious about how far women's fantasies can go, this video's for you. See a bevy of gorgeous women displaying their wanton lust in a number of scorching sequences. You're unwrapped in silk; partaking in oily, nude massages; taking a sensual bath; trying on different hats; and more! With Sarah St. James, Cory St. James, Stevi Conrad. 60 min.
51-1012   *$19.99*

EuroFlash
Ooh-la-la. If you love gorgeous women from Europe revealing their ravishing bodies and lovely faces, this video is just for you. See these Euro-sweeties take it all off on a farm, pirouette in ballet tutus and get wild, foreign style. They're all natural, too! 60 min.
50-5748   *$19.99*

EuroFlash: Lusting For America
Filmed in Czechoslovakia, this awesome look at Europe's most erotic women will wow you with its incredible cast. See them model in provocative, all-naked poses, taunting you seductively using their hottest assets. Czech out this sizzling video and enjoy all the best Europe has to offer. 60 min.
50-5798   *$19.99*

EuroFlash: Foreign Fantasies
They're all natural and all European, these curvaceous cuties who tantalize you in a series of steamy, intimate scenarios. They take soapy showers with one another; get real close in special touching sessions; and enjoy exploring their most private places. 60 min.
51-1011   *$19.99*

Hot Las Vegas Escorts
Who says a gal with a good head on her shoulders can't find a well-paying job in Las Vegas (Are you listening, A.G.?). Here are a host of hotsy-totsies with enough juice to make Glitter Gulch glitter for decades to come. Among them are Lisa Gayle, Tiffany Burlingame, Michelle Davis and Nikki Nova. 60 min.
50-5989   *$19.99*

Hot Miami Escorts
What's hotter than the Florida sands, wilder than a night on South Beach, and easier to get than Marlins tickets? How about Alexxus, Blake, Flower, Liz and Taylor, five Sunshine State sexpots who sashay before your eyes on this video? Forget about "Miami Vice"; this is Miami NICE! 60 min.
50-8212   *$19.99*

Hot New Orleans Escorts
What's spicier than a jambalaya platter covered in hot sauce? Hot about spending a night along the banks of the Mississippi with these "Big Easy" babes (well, they're not that big) who are ready to jazz up your life in a vivacious video strip session? 60 min.
50-8275   *$19.99*

Nude Pool Party
Everybody into the pool—without the bikinis, please! See what happens when a group of gorgeous dolls doff their swimwear for an incredible party where skin is in. These dolls don't need a pool boy to have fun! Just a little sun, a little lotion and a lot of loving! 60 min.
50-8311   *$19.99*

Suze Randall's Erotic Eye
Top photographer Suze Randall allows you to watch one of her closed-set sessions with nine of the hottest, nastiest nude models around. Ashley Lauren and Emma star in a kinky shoot, and blonde beauty Sara St. James poses provocatively, while Lydia Schore, Chasey Lane and others are sure to wow you as well. 60 min.
50-2877   *$24.99*

Suze Randall's Super Sexy
The world's top nude photographer takes you into the world of the top female adult stars in this sleek and sensuous video. Jenna Jameson, Lisa Ann, Nikki Dial, Nikki Tyler and Shauna Harris are among the sweeties that'll make you happy here. 60 min.
50-5988   *$19.99*

Suze Randall's Super Sexy Too
That's "too" as in "too sexy for words," as you join Randall for a sizzling second sampling of beautiful women, posing before the cameras in revealing sessions. With Jenna Jameson, Juli Ashton, Lexus, Renee, Damian Wolff and many more. 60 min.
50-8195   *$19.99*

Suze Randall's Super Sexy Newcomers
It's more of what you've come to expect from Suze Randall: hot young women running around in the buff! This romp features the exotic Zdenka, a contestant in the Penthouse Pet of the Year Playoff for 2001.
50-8721   *$19.99*

Valley Of The Busty Babes
There's more than one valley in this video, Charlie...and more hills than Rome. California's famed San Fernando Valley is the setting for a sexy display of pulse-pounding pulchritude, as buxom beauties Krista, Jasmine Aloha, Misty Regan, Sa Renna Lee and others put the "boob" back in "boob tube." 60 min.
50-8118   *$29.99*

Busty Babeville USA
Carolyn Monroe plays host to a hot-to-trot parade of prominently boobed babes in this fantasy-filled world of wild women. Included are Lacey Legends, Celeste, Busty Dusty and Raylene. You've never been anywhere like "Busty Babeville USA" before! 60 min.
50-8198   *$29.99*

Naked Outlaws
No, it's not Johnny Cash and Willie Nelson in the buff (and aren't we all glad for that!). It's a risqué round-up of some of the loveliest lasses this side of Dodge City, a-whoopin' and a-wailin' out of their duds in a frisky frontier frolic that'll have any cowpoke in sight saying "Yeee-HAH!" 60 min.
50-8230   *$19.99*

Lingerie Land
This is one attraction you won't find at Disneyland! Get ready for a revealing ride through a land of luscious ladies in lacy lingerie...then get ready to watch the ladies doff their undies and really strut their stuff. Want to ride again? 60 min.
50-8248   *$19.99*

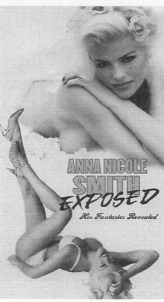

ANNA NICOLE SMITH EXPOSED
Her Fantasies Revealed

Anna Nicole Smith: Exposed
Behind the glamour, beautiful face and unbelievable body lie some of the most erotic fantasies that you will ever see. Dim the lights and take a look at Anna Nicole Smith's most passionate dreams come true, as well as behind-the-scenes footage, heavenly photo sessions, and more. 50 min.
86-1134   *$24.99*

The Daily Star Page 3 Girls
England's Daily Star newspaper publishes photos of gorgeous models in their tabloid every day. On this program, six pretty "page three gals" head to Portugal for a calendar shoot, and their bikinis don't stay on long for the sessions! Who needs the Philadelphia Journal with these gals? With Lisa Chilcott, Gaynor Goodman, Lisa Bangert, Justine King and Michelle Collins. 55 min.
59-7073   *$29.99*

Liquid Passions
An alluring array of Aphrodites go splish-splash in this program of watery wenches strutting their stuff. You won't get hosed with these lovely ladies, who are in their element when drenched while scantily clad or naked. Jessica Lee, Zoe Paul and Cory Lane star. 60 min.
50-8582   *$19.99*

California Dreams
Exotic women in sensual settings are the name of the game in this sensual soiree that sets new standards for erotica and nude art. It's a sizzler! 55 min.
50-8624   *$19.99*

Wild Bikinis
Everyone's invited to the beach for an oceanfront view of Jessica Lee and a host of others as they showcase all of their "Wild Bikinis." These gorgeous women are so frisky that they are also going to show you the wild things underneath their bikinis, but don't let the heat that they generate get to your head! 60 min.
50-8647   *$19.99*

Beverly Hills Bordello
This scorching series centers on the women and the clients involved with the Beverly Hills Bordello, a classy house of ill repute run by the stylishly sexy Madame Winston. Each tape features three sizzling stories guaranteed to titillate.

Beverly Hills Bordello: Love Lessons
Includes "Performance," "Love Lessons" and "Research."
81-9046   *$14.99*

Beverly Hills Bordello: Temptations
Includes "In the Clinches," "Divine Inspiration" and "The Witness."
81-9047   *$14.99*

Beverly Hills Bordello: Things Your Wife Won't Do
Includes "The Bachelor Party," "Things Your Wife Won't Do" and "Janet and the Professor."
81-9048   *$14.99*

Beverly Hills Bordello: Girl Friends
Includes "Taboo," "Adultery...Cyber Style" and "Wish List."
81-9049   *$14.99*

Beverly Hills Bordello: Gift Set
Get a package of kinky sexual encounters when you collect four volumes of "Beverly Hills Bordello" in this special, attractive gift set.
81-9072   Save $10.00!   *$49.99*

PERFECT 10
THE CONNOISSEUR'S MAGAZINE

MODEL OF THE YEAR VIDEO

Dazzling Top Models Compete In Exciting Sporting Events

THE WORLD'S MOST BEAUTIFUL WOMEN!

Perfect 10: Model Of The Year
From the magazine that gives you beautiful, naked women who are 100% natural comes this program in which 20 gorgeous gals compete for the title of "Model of the Year"—and $500,000 in cash. Represented by the top agencies, these gals show they're not all looks, as they also compete in different sporting events, too. 55 min.
50-8367   **$19.99**

Bare Naked Amateurs: Naughty & Nice
If you have a hankering to see that girl next-door or the sweet secretary naked and posing provocatively for the camera, you've got the right video here. Ten sexy gals reveal their greatest assets when the red light goes on! 55 min.
50-5852   **$19.99**

Bare Naked Amateur Models
They're bare! They're naked! They're amateur! They're models! You were expecting maybe Fully Clothed Professional Car Dealers? We didn't think so. Plucked from the local junior college, these coeds will coerce you into taking fantasies to the next level. They major in titillation! 55 min.
50-5853   **$19.99**

Bare Naked Amateur Screentest
The producers of this video placed an ad for models, but didn't mention the nude part of the requirements. Witness these sweeties' reaction to the request and how the gorgeous young women allow their exhibitionist side to shine. 55 min.
50-5854   **$19.99**

Bare Naked: Ladies And Lace
Ten alluring beauties show off their silky bods against the sheets of forbidden pleasures. Such sirens as Becky Sunshine, Dina Maris, Ashley Anderson and Suzanne Longo are among the featured sweeties who strut their stuff in this lacy affair. 55 min.
50-8710   **$19.99**

Dream Girls: Innocence Lost
Twelve hot-to-trot teasers turn you on when the camera focuses on them. Their innocence is suddenly lost when they allow themselves to become prisoners of their own wild fantasies—steamy scenarios sure to make you sweat! 55 min.
50-5855   **$19.99**

Dream Girls On The California Riviera
The California Riviera is a gorgeous beach near La Jolla where a newspaperman decides to stop while looking for a story. Soon, his fantasies turn real as three gorgeous blondes appear and strip totally naked. They sunbathe, they spread suntan lotion all over, and they tantalize our intrepid reporter! A scorcher with lots of full frontal nymphette nudity! 60 min.
76-7067   **$19.99**

Dream Girls: Lady Love
If scorching lesbian scenes are to your liking, check out this program that features an incredible array of luscious ladies, including Playboy model Claudine Jennings, Penthouse Pet Laura Stone and starlet Kathleen Raymond. There's full-frontal nudity galore and scintillating situations! 56 min.
76-7307   **$19.99**

Bikini Magazine: Maui
Sunny Maui is the place where gorgeous gals meet a bikini contest that's a real "Maui Wowie!" Tammy Strickland, Kim Stys, Allison China and Carla Holmes are among the featured sweeties in flesh-featuring swimsuits who parade their stuff. 50 min.
42-2908   **$19.99**

Dream Girls
Dream a little dream with these hot-to-trot honeys from the porn field who show you how to get nice and nasty. Sara St. James, Brittany Andrews and Jill Kelly are the gals dreams are made of—your dreams, thanks to this arouser. 45 min.
39-5768   Was $19.99   **$14.99**

Castaways On Jungle Jane's Island
Forget Gilligan and the Skipper. Here's the wildest island adventure yet, as the captain and his three-cutie crew encounter cannibals, cream pie tortures, a breastacular Jungle Jane, mud baths, sexy pantyhose shots and nude proceedings on a remote Caribbean isle. 75 min.
50-2886   **$49.99**

Cheerleaders vs. The Magic Bottle
After Fawn is rejected from cheerleader tryouts, she finds a magic bottle and begins casting mischievous spells on her school's pom-pom girls. With the spell cast, one gal continually destroys her pantyhose, another keeps covering her body with gooey substances and the third keeps stretching her clothes out of shape. Dunkings, pie and pudding—not for the family! 63 min.
50-2965   **$39.99**

Girls Of Russia
Comrades, take note: Russia's greatest exports are women! Now, a legion of ladies from Moscow to Minsk show you enough sexiness to melt the tundra. They'll turn you on so much, you'll be willing to take the next ship to Siberia to meet them.
48-1192   **$19.99**

Aphrodite Of Asia: Miori Maijima
Osaka's Miori Maijima was named the "Adult Video Girl of the Year" and it's easy to see why in this provocative program. See the lovely Ms. Miori at home, showing why she's thrilled men around the world with her gorgeous face and bosomy body! 45 min. In Japanese with English subtitles.
53-6716   **$24.99**

Virgin Assassin
Japanese adult star Yurika Ohnishi is a sexy killer-for-hire who likes to mix murder and mayhem with kinky pleasures. Using her surveillance lap-top camera in new and creative ways, Ohnishi shows you what's hot under that trench coat of hers. 70 min.
53-6771   **$24.99**

Maiko Yuuki
If you're seeking an incredible Japanese model who's not shy and willing to share her innermost excitement scenarios with you—uh-oh, better get Maiko! If you're willing to delve deep into your libido and let one of Asian's wildest women take over—uh-oh, better get Maiko! Don't delay: if you hit your "Brolin point"—uh-oh, better get Maiko! 50 min.
53-6838   **$19.99**

Bauko Eichi: Naughty Girl
Lithesome adult model Bauko Eichi shows you why she is in such demand with this personal account of her fantasies and innermost thoughts. See her bathing in milk, stretching in the nude and clad in a see-through nightgown. This is one Eichi you'll love to scratch! 50 min.
53-6925   **$19.99**

Mina Kawai: Mugen (Desire)
She may be short in stature but she's huge in sensual desire. Japanese adult star Mina Kawai as a college girl who will stun you with her amazing figure once she gets out of her school uniform. Long legs, broad shoulders, sumptuous bosom: Mina graduates Magna Cum Laude without taking a test! 50 min.
53-6926   **$19.99**

Madoka Ozawa: Madonna.JP.X
While at home, Japanese sex star Madoka Ozawa decides to get dressed in a number of different ways in order to fulfill her fantasies. She's a prostitute, a nymph, a beauty pageant contestant and more. No matter what she wears, this ravishing Tokyo native shows she's anything but a virgin! 50 min.
53-6927   **$19.99**

Jun Kusanagi: GTO-Seduction
Gorgeous Japanese adult model Jun Kusanagi welcomes viewers into her private world where she wears designer underwear, allures you with welcome kisses and teases you with a plastic bottle. 55 min.
53-6937   **$19.99**

Sally Yoshino: Showing Off
Spectacular Asian beauty Sally Yoshino is showcased in all of her glory in this video that offers her fantasies brought to life. She poses in a white room with nothing but a see-through veil and offers her insight on massages. Sally shows all! 55 min.
53-6938   **$19.99**

Chinatsu Ito: Private Expression
Lovely Japanese adult star Chinatsu Ito shows why her innocent demeanor and knock-out body have wowed men the world over. At a resort, she offers you a peek at her curvaceous figure and cute face while relaxing in the most sensual ways. 55 min.
53-6939   **$19.99**

My Wife's Lover (1992)
Ultra-sexy Hong Kong drama about a frustrated married couple seeking new outlets for their sexuality. After deciding to try extra-marital affairs, the wife decides on a female photographer for her lover, but the woman is also desired by the husband. Tung Ling and Lam Wai star in this debauched domestic drama. 88 min. In Cantonese with English subtitles.
53-6289   Letterboxed   **$49.99**

My Wife's Lover (Dubbed Version)
Also available in a dubbed-in-English edition.
53-6801   **$59.99**

Sappho: Femme-A-Femme
The joys of lesbian love are shown in this steamy video that offers a number of the world's top XXX-rated stars involved in all-female encounters. Check out the likes of Kimberly Carson, Tracey Adams, Danielle, Barbara Dare and Sabrina Dawn enjoying themselves—and each other—in sensuous settings. 60 min.
50-2694   **$19.99**

Sappho: The Desire Of Women
Lesbian love at its wildest is the focus of the multi-story survey of sex, all-gals style. In "An Artist's Desire," a sculptress falls for her hot model; "College Memories" finds two former classmates reminiscing and getting it on in bed; and "Virgin Experience" shows what happens when a sexy model submits to a gorgeous pal. With Taylor Wayne, Savannah, Rachel Ryan, Racquel Darrian. 60 min.
50-5173   **$24.99**

Girlfriends: Women Who Love Women
The accent is on lesbian encounters in this amorous anthology in which gals explore the world of similar-sex situations. They may be secretaries, college girls and housewives, but their libidos are ready for a carnal change-of-pace. With Sunset Thomas, Nikki Dial, Debi Diamond, Madison and Tesse Ferre. 55 min.
50-2945   **$24.99**

Love In Sampan (1992)
A young woman discovering the joys of sex for the first time seeks true love on a journey that takes her into the bedrooms of men and women alike. Filled with sensuous couplings of the straight and lesbian kind, this film features the sensuous Tamami Hirori. 90 min. In Cantonese with English subtitles.
53-6290   Letterboxed   **$49.99**

A Chinese Torture Chamber Story (1994)
The unsettling, true story of a beautiful peasant girl who becomes a concubine for a pharmacist. When his wife discovers the affair, she has her arrested on a murder charge, and the young beauty must endure incredible tortures developed in the Yu and Sung Dynasties. This not-for-the-squeamish cinematic experience stars Yvonne Yung Hung and Ng Kai Wah. 93 min. In Cantonese with English subtitles.
53-6291   Letterboxed   **$49.99**

Intimate Desire (1997)
A stirring and sensual love story from Hong Kong, with Miho Nomoto and Rebaca Chang as two beautiful women brought together by chance who come to depend on each other in an increasingly intimate relationship. Dubbed in English.
53-6544   **$19.99**

Exotic Erotica Series: Set 1
Three sizzling "Category III" films—which means "adults only" in Hong Kong—are offered in this boxed set. Included are "A Chinese Torture Chamber Story," "Love in Sampan" and "My Wife's Lover."
53-6288   Save $70.00!   **$79.99**

Exotic Erotica Series: Set 2
This three-tape set includes a trio of Hong Kong titillators: "Angel Heart," "Sex and the Emperor" and "Vietnamese Lady."
53-6319   Save $70.00!   **$79.99**

Cherry Blossom Paradise (1997)
A gorgeous, innocent Japanese woman, on vacation in Hong Kong, faces a series of strange and sensual experiences that awaken her sexuality in this steamy drama featuring top centerfold model Miho Nomoto. Dubbed in English.
53-6541   **$19.99**

In Lonely Venus (1999)
Gorgeous Akira Itazura is moody and quite a bit shy, so she keeps her sexual fantasies to herself. See how she deals with her sensuality with a beach ball, fishnet, in her greenhouse and in the privacy of her bedroom. 60 min.
53-6788   **$24.99**

Erotic Bodies (1999)
This carnal collection features six Asian beauties exposing their awesome bodies for your delight. See them in intimate situations, getting in touch with their sensuality and themselves, as they discuss life, their hobbies, men and, of course, sex. 60 min.
53-6789   **$24.99**

Dream Catcher (1999)
Cute and cuddly erotic model Yuka Asato is featured in this vignette-filled frolic that allows you into her private fantasy world. See Yuka try on nurse outfits and lingerie and enjoying the nectars of fruit in a most interesting way. 60 min.
53-6826   **$19.99**

The X Temptation (1999)
Top Asian adult video star Miho Nomoto reveals her wildest fantasies in this x-citing x-cursion teeming with titillation. See why Ms. Nomoto is one of the most sizzling stars of the Orient in this x-posé! 50 min.
53-6837   **$19.99**

Nippon Love Letters (1999)
Six gorgeous Asian women invite you to delve into their personal lives and sensual experiences with this provocative look at lust in the East. With the streets of Tokyo, the cherry blossom tress of Kyoto and Mount Fuji's waterfalls as your background, these women reveal their inner passions and amazing bodies. 60 min.
53-6827   **$19.99**

Hotlanta Nites I: Big Boobs Of Atlanta
It's the host of the 1996 Summer Olympics, the Town That Ted Helped Build and the former home of Phil Myre and the Flames. The city is also known as the adult entertainment capital of the South, and this program looks at the gorgeous Southern belles with the heaving bosoms. You'll do more than whistle "Dixie" after watching this one. 60 min.
84-5047   **$19.99**

Making Of The Carousel Girls Calendar
Some of the most remarkable women in the world pose for this erotic calendar, and now you can go behind the scenes as Philip Mond and a group of models prepare and pose in scorching settings, wearing little or no clothing at all. Featured are Penthouse Pet Sasha, Julie Smith and Sam Philips (and some lovely carousel horses). 90 min.
50-2704   **$24.99**

Naked Fantasies
Nine stunning women live out their fantasies in this provocative program that delivers a series of heated pleasures you won't soon forget. Among the steamy gals here are Amy Rochelle, Ashley Rhey and Gretchen Marie. 60 min.
50-2706   **$19.99**

Precious Moments (1999)
The focus is on lovely Minori Aoi, whose nostalgic feelings of her college days allow you to reminisce with her as she plays a number of different games in her sportswear or spends summers at a spa. See her wear a skimpy kimono, hugging a teddy bear—and less! 60 min.
53-6828   **$19.99**

Yoko's Secret Diary (1999)
A young woman living far from home keeps a diary detailing her wildest sexual fantasies, and gets to live out these intimate desires in a series of sequences involving water, a rabbit costume, a schoolgirl uniform and a boxing outfit. 50 min. In Japanese with English subtitles.
53-6770   **$24.99**

Mysterious Obsession (1999)
Gorgeous exotic model Manami Suzuki plays an office secretary whose longing for her ever-travelling boyfriend leads her to seek pleasure in other ways. She tries long, hot, sensual showers and some hot office alternatives, but things really sizzle when she cruises into a masquerade party that will surely keep your eyes wide open. 70 min.
53-6770   **$24.99**

First Pin-Up Girl Of China: Keung Ka-Ling (1999)
Keung Ka-Ling, an Asian fave, struts her stuff as the pin-up queen whose desires could turn Hong Kong inside-out. See why the pretty, wonderfully endowed beauty commands such attention in this erotic delight. 50 min.
53-6840   **$19.99**

Haruki Mizuno: Breathless (1999)
Japanese sizzler Haruki Mizuno, one of Asia's most sensual nude models and stars, shows why she has captured the attention of the world with this lusty excursion. She acts out her fantasies, which include dressing like an 18th-century chambermaid, acting like a nurse caring for her imaginary patient and trying on her collection of pink underwear. 55 min.
53-6866   **$19.99**

Shu Kei
VIVA! Island Girl 春回大地

Shu Kei: Viva! Island Girl (2000)
Shu Kei, who dazzled audiences in "Sex and Zen II," shows you why she became one Asia's top sex starlets. The Taiwanese-born sweetie frolics under a waterfall, enjoys herself at a lodge and shows off her dynamite body on the catwalk in this effort, filmed before she retired from doing nude scenes. 70 min.
53-6772   **$24.99**

Electric Blue

The popular soft adult series from the 1980s returns in top form. These videos feature a host of gorgeous models baring all for the cameras in provocative photo sessions. Each tape runs about 55 min.

Electric Blue:
Nude Hot Models, File 1
Features Tina Reid, Jo Phillips, Alison Browne, Tara Jackson and Vicky Lee.
78-9032   *$19.99*

Electric Blue:
Nude Hot Models, File 2
Features Debbie Jay, Emma Nixon and Cathy.
78-9033   *$19.99*

Electric Blue:
Nude Hot Models, File 3
Features Karen Drummond, Julie Whelan, Nicole Simmons and Belinda Cox.
78-9034   *$19.99*

Electric Blue:
Nude Hot Models, File 4
Features Sharon, Fanny and Russian model Lana.
78-9035   *$19.99*

Hunting The Nylon Jungle
Leg lovers around the world will appreciate this tribute to nylon. Take a lingering glimpse into women who will drive you wild with their long appendages draped in artificial coverings of the sheer, white and black style. Rayne, Taylor St. Clair and Kelly O'Dell star; includes nudity. 60 min.
50-5701   *$29.99*

Swimming The Secretarial Pool
Get ready to take a dip in a place where the temperature's hot: the office! Join these sexy secretaries, dressed in spiked heels and shiny nylons, who aim to please. Kelly O'Dell, Brittany Andrews, Denisa and Stephanie Rage are among the boss's favorite babes here; includes nudity. 60 min.
50-5702   *$29.99*

Nina Hartley's
Big & Busty Knockouts
Adult porn sensation Nina Hartley brings you some of the hottest big-breasted gals around, all displaying their ample assets for your enjoyment. Ruby, Chandler (not the guy from "Friends"), Rebecca Lords and Mustang Sally Layd are the featured femmes. 60 min.
50-5727   *$19.99*

Fantasy Flights

Become a sky king when you watch these incredible models—many of them featured on Playboy videos—make your fantasies take flight. They pose totally naked in and out of vintage planes, get into kinky fantasies in the air control tower, and even enjoy some passenger-flight attendant lesbian liaisons. With Michelle Adams, Ivy Kimberly, Missy Dykes, Cindy Rich. 60 min.
50-5984   *$19.99*

Hot & Busty
Country Line Dancing
Well, yee-hah! Ride the wild cowgals who love to country dance to ecstasy in this rompin', stompin' scorcher. With their Stetsons and denim undies, the gals go gonzo, stepping out and taking off their clothes in a sexy style that would make Annie Oakley blush. Jessica Wells and Tara Monroe star. 60 min.
50-2791   *$19.99*

Naked Girls On
A Summer Holiday
These naked gals are hot, hot, hot. See these Southern California cuties drop their skivvies for your delight in the Miss Nude Independence contest. Our forefathers never had this in mind when they signed the Declaration of Independence...or did they? With Alexis Taylor, Meshalynn, Catherine D'Lish and others. 60 min.
50-8709   *$19.99*

Samantha Fox: Calendar Girl
The 1980s fave is featured in her gorgeous glory in this video that mixes sounds and sensuality. Featured is a look at the photo shoot for her 1997 calendar, never-before-seen Playboy shots and live footage of Sam performing "Do You Want Me Baby?," "It Takes Two," "Say What You Want" and more. Includes nudity. 51 min.
59-7020   Was $24.99   *$14.99*

Traci Bingham: Exposed
Traci, you're out of uniform! Get ready for some too-hot-for-TV fun with "Babewatch," er..."Baywatch" lifeguard Traci Bingham, as she and a host of other lovely lifesavers have some full-on, get-down, sexy fun in the sun. 60 min.
59-7053   *$29.99*

Topless Darts
G'day, mates. Welcome to the hottest thing to hit Down Under since Jacko did the battery commercials. It's topless darts played by sensuous Sheilas in bars. See these gals try to hit the bull's eye using their talents and naked body English. Aye, aye, aye! 52 min.
59-7071   *$29.99*

Sextoons

Hilarious, carnal collection of animation featuring 15 inventive cartoons, ranging from early examples of erotic artwork to more recent sexy shorts. 78 min.
53-6042   Was $29.99   *$19.99*

Dream Babies

They're the hottest African-American models in the world, and here they strut their stuff for you. See them model in skimpy swimsuits and dance in hot, erotic style. There's topless teasers galore in this sexy extravaganza. 75 min.
54-9095   *$19.99*

Erotic Heat

The heat is on—and so are the 10 gorgeous ladies who take part in the series of sexy vignettes that comprise this carnal collection. From an exercise session that turns from "workout" to "make out" to a group of bawdy babes' dessert party, there's something here that's sure to raise your temperature. 60 min.
69-5291   *$14.99*

Erotic Heat 2: Hot Salsa

Here's a spicy, red-hot treat that won't upset your stomach. Feast yourself on an appetizing selection of eight wanton, willing women who seek to satiate their carnal cravings in a variety of exotic settings. 60 min.
69-5292   *$14.99*

Tight Moves

The gals are doing the exercising, but you'll get the workout, as you watch this pulse-pounding program. Follow nine knockouts who turn their gym into an erotic free-for-all, from sweat-drenched sauna sessions to a massage that rubs them—and you, the viewer—the right way. 60 min.
69-5293   *$14.99*

Visions & Voyeurism

Pandora Peaks is sure to astound you with her incredible body and teasing nature in this salute to the female form. The bodacious Ms. Peaks shows off all, and now you can see the curves that captivated famed camera-snappers Russ Meyer and Harry Langdon in this odyssey of a provocative six-day photo shoot. 100 min.
69-5299   *$19.99*

City Girls: The Girls Of Atlanta

This video is sure to get your Buckhead going! Five Southern belles put the "t" and "a" in Atlanta as you watch them in the office, at home, and in some spicy private moments. If Sherman had seen this video, it's a cinch he would have dropped the torch. 60 min.
69-5301   *$19.99*

Auditions From Beyond

Check out the auditions of the hottest stars for such Surrender Cinema sizzlers as "Hotel Exotica," "Femalien" and "Lolida 2000." Witness Jacqueline Lovell, Venesa Talor, Nikki Fritz and Lisa Shaw. Find out what it takes to "Surrender." Unrated version; 90 min.
75-5051   *$59.99*

Intimate Sessions: Set

Enter the worlds of women trying to sort out their sexual fantasies and problems with a therapist in intimate sessions. Each volume in this four-tape set features three women who explore their desires. Included are "Secret Lives," "Therapy With a Twist," "Throes of Passion" and "Voyeur." Monique Parent, Nikki Fritz and Caroline Key Johnson star. Uncut, unrated version. NOTE: Individual volumes available at $49.99 each.
81-9087   Save $50.00!   *$149.99*

The Blue Note Collection

If you want your MTV uncensored and filled with erotic music videos from Preacher Keen, Solinger, Suite Jane and Marc Benno. Nudity abounds in these wild videos featuring gorgeous models.
84-5003   *$19.99*

Lovescapes

In the tradition of "Red Shoe Diaries" comes this multi-part erotic excursion that takes you into a sensuous realm where the most unusual fantasies become reality. Here, a young woman obeys her lover's every wish; a vixen treats her workout partner to an unusual exercise regimen; and a Peeping Tom gets more than he can handle. 80 min.
84-5004   *$19.99*

Erotic Fantasies:
The Uncut Versions

These models want to get into the movies so bad they'll do anything—anything!—to win a coveted role. See what sensuous lengths they'll scale when they act out their most outrageous fantasies just for you. Uncensored...and sizzling! 60 min.
84-5005   *$19.99*

Nude Bowling Party

Move over, Johnny Petraglia. Here comes a quartet of gorgeous gals who know how to score on the bowling lanes. Watch them strike out when their clothes come off and they thrust their balls down the alley. Who cares if they're not wearing the right shoes? Enjoy! Taryn Carter, Tammy Parks and Sara St. James star. 60 min.
84-5033   *$19.99*

Featured Star Index

Index

Q

R

S

MOVIES UNLIMITED®

Z

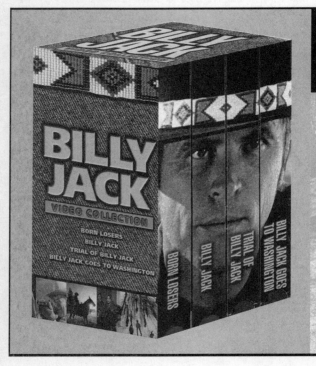

1. Ordered By (Please print or place peel-off label below)

☐ Mr.
☐ Mrs. ☐ Ms.

Customer Number
(from mailing label) _____

Address _____ Apt. # _____

City _____ State _____ Zip _____

Phone No. (____) _____ E-mail address _____

Movies Unlimited Inc.
3015 Darnell Road
Philadelphia, PA 19154

2. Items Ordered

Catalog Number	Page #	Movie Title	Qty.	Price Each	Total
	—				
	—				
	—				
	—				
	—				
	—				
	—				
	—				

3. Shipping Method (Please check one)

Please add appropriate per item charges to the base shipping charge.
All charges in addition to base charge of $5.00.

☐ **Standard Shipping:** .50¢ per item additional.
☐ **2nd Day Air*:** $3.00 per item additional.
☐ **Canadian Postage:** $3.00 per item additional.
☐ **Foreign Postage:** $9.00 per item additional.

*Applies to shipping time only. Does not expedite processing of order.
 Domestic orders only.

Standard shipment sent UPS, US Mail or equivalent. Shipments to post office boxes must be sent by US mail. Attention schools, libraries and institutions: we are happy to accept valid purchase orders. All tapes available in NTSC VHS only.

Source Code: **#602**   Prices In This Book Good Thru **12/31/01.**

4. Payment Method (Please check one)

☐ **Check or Money Order Enclosed**
☐ **Visa** ☐ **MasterCard**
☐ **American Express** ☐ **Discover/Novus**

Credit Card Number:
| | | | | | | | | | | | | | | | |

Expiration Date (Month/Year) | | | — | | |

Signature _____

Charge orders will NOT be sent without signature.

5	**Total Order**	
6	**Base Shipping Charge**	**$5.00**
7	**Per Item Shipping Charge** ____# of Items x $____	
8	**Sales Tax** (PA residents add 7%)	
9	**Credit Due You**	
10	**GRAND TOTAL**	

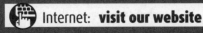

4 Easy Ways To Order!

 Phone: **1-800-4-MOVIES**

Our toll-free line is open 24 hours a day, 7 days a week. Before calling, it's a good idea to fill out your order form so you can refer to it during your call. Please have your credit card number and expiration date handy. **Please note this number is for placing orders only. See information to the right for customer service number.**

 Fax: **1-215-637-2350**

You can transmit your completed order to us anytime day or night. Please sign the order form where indicated and include your credit card number and expiration date.

✉ Mail: **send order form**

You can mail your order with a credit card number and expiration date, personal check, U.S. drawn bank draft or money order.

☞ Internet: **visit our website**

Our web address is: **www.moviesunlimited.com**

NOTE: Prices on our website may vary from prices in our printed catalogs. Coupons and special incentives are not valid on internet orders.

Ordering Information:

How To Send Payment:
Payment for your order should be in the form of a check, postal money order, express money order, bank draft or credit card (Visa, MasterCard, American Express or Discover/Novus). Credit cards not charged until order is shipped. Personal checks will delay orders for up to four weeks until check clears. Foreign payments in U.S. funds only. Returned checks subject to $15.00 processing charge.

Pennsylvania State Residents:
Be sure to include correct 7% Sales Tax (includes city surcharge). Tax rate subject to change according to state or local laws.

Delivery Time:
Most orders shipped within 3 working days. Allow two to six weeks for back ordered items.

Out Of Stock Items:
If we are temporarily out of stock, we will inform you as to availability within three weeks. When an item is permanently out of stock we will credit your Movies Unlimited account or refund your money.

Questions About An Order:
Our staff will be happy to answer your questions or inquiries between 9 a.m. and 9 p.m. ET, Monday to Friday or Saturday between 9 a.m. and 5 p.m. at 1-800-668-4344. We cannot accept collect calls. Customers outside of the U.S. call 215-637-4444.

Foreign Shipments:
When shipment is made to countries other than the U.S., payment may be made by credit card (Visa, MasterCard, American Express or Discover/Novus), International Money Order (U.S. Funds only), or by check. Checks must be drawn on an American bank. Canadian customers, be sure your rate of exchange is correct. Please include per item additional postage plus base shipping charge (see below). We cannot guarantee safe delivery on foreign shipments. Customer is responsible for all tariffs imposed by importing country. All tapes on VHS NTSC only. We do not offer PAL tapes.

Shipping Charges:
Due to increased postal, UPS and insurance rates we have restructured our shipping charges. Please add $5.00 base charge **plus** additional per item charges based on the adjoining chart to cover the costs of postage, insurance and handling. Shipments to Post Office Boxes must be sent by Standard Shipping. Please check the appropriate method of shipment on the order form. Charges computed by adding $5.00 **plus** appropriate per item charge based on method of shipment:

STANDARD SHIPPING: 50¢ per item additional (plus base $5.00 shipping charge.) Standard shipment sent by United Parcel Service, U.S. Mail (Priority or First Class) or equivalent.

2nd DAY AIR: $3.00 per item additional (plus base $5.00 shipping charge). TWO DAY SERVICE APPLIES TO SHIPPING TIME ONLY. DOES NOT EXPEDITE PROCESSING OF ORDER. TWO DAY SERVICE AVAILABLE IN CONTINENTAL U.S. ONLY.

CANADIAN POSTAGE: $3.00 per item additional (plus base $5.00 shipping charge).

FOREIGN POSTAGE: $9.00 per item additional (plus base $5.00 shipping charge).

Mailing List:
The Movies Unlimited mailing list is occasionally made available to very carefully screened companies who offer products and services which may be of interest to our customers. If you prefer NOT receiving these mailings, please send a note with your name and address to: Movies Unlimited, 3015 Darnell Road, Phila., PA 19154. Allow 6-8 weeks for your request to be processed.

Video Movie Guarantee:
If you should receive a video that is defective or improperly manufactured, return it to us with a copy of the invoice and an explanation of the defect within 30 days and it will be replaced with an acceptable copy of the same title. Videos are not exchangeable, except on a title-for-title basis. Movies Unlimited reserves the right to impose a restocking fee on titles returned that are not defective.

Rights On Video Movies:
All programs licensed for home and non-theatrical use only. Broadcast in any form and duplication are prohibited. All prices, taxes and shipping & handling charges subject to change without notice. Prices in this catalog supersede any previous catalog. Not responsible for typographical errors. All offers void where prohibited by law.

© MOVIES UNLIMITED INC. 2000

4 Easy Ways To Order!

 Phone: 1-800-4-MOVIES

Our toll-free line is open 24 hours a day, 7 days a week. Before calling, it's a good idea to fill out your order form so you can refer to it during your call. Please have your credit card number and expiration date handy. **Please note this number is for placing orders only. See information to the right for customer service number.**

 Fax: 1-215-637-2350

You can transmit your completed order to us anytime day or night. Please sign the order form where indicated and include your credit card number and expiration date.

 Mail: send order form

You can mail your order with a credit card number and expiration date, personal check, U.S. drawn bank draft or money order.

Internet: visit our website

Our web address is: www.moviesunlimited.com

NOTE: Prices on our website may vary from prices in our printed catalogs. Coupons and special incentives are not valid on internet orders.

Ordering Information:

How To Send Payment:
Payment for your order should be in the form of a check, postal money order, express money order, bank draft or credit card (Visa, MasterCard, American Express or Discover / Novus). Credit cards not charged until order is shipped. Personal checks will delay orders for up to four weeks until check clears. Foreign payments in U.S. funds only. Returned checks subject to $15.00 processing charge.

Pennsylvania State Residents:
Be sure to include correct 7% Sales Tax (includes city surcharge). Tax rate subject to change according to state or local laws.

Delivery Time:
Most orders shipped within 3 working days. Allow two to six weeks for back ordered items.

Out Of Stock Items:
If we are temporarily out of stock, we will inform you as to availability within three weeks. When an item is permanently out of stock we will credit your Movies Unlimited account or refund your money.

Questions About An Order:
Our staff will be happy to answer your questions or inquiries between 9 a.m. and 9 p.m. ET, Monday to Friday or Saturday between 9 a.m. and 5 p.m. at 1-800-668-4344. We cannot accept collect calls. Customers outside of the U.S. call 215-637-4444.

Foreign Shipments:
When shipment is made to countries other than the U.S., payment may be made by credit card (Visa, MasterCard, American Express or Discover/Novus), International Money Order (U.S. Funds only), or by check. Checks must be drawn on an American bank. Canadian customers, be sure your rate of exchange is correct. Please include per item additional postage plus base shipping charge (see below). We cannot guarantee safe delivery on foreign shipments. Customer is responsible for all tariffs imposed by importing country. All tapes on VHS NTSC only. We do not offer PAL tapes.

Shipping Charges:
Due to increased postal, UPS and insurance rates we have restructured our shipping charges. Please add $5.00 base charge **plus** additional per item charges based on the adjoining chart to cover the costs of postage, insurance and handling. Shipments to Post Office Boxes must be sent by Standard Shipping. Please check the appropriate method of shipment on the order form. Charges computed by adding $5.00 **plus** appropriate per item charge based on method of shipment:

STANDARD SHIPPING: 50¢ per item additional (plus base $5.00 shipping charge.) Standard shipment sent by United Parcel Service, U.S. Mail (Priority or First Class) or equivalent.

2nd DAY AIR: $3.00 per item additional (plus base $5.00 shipping charge.) TWO DAY SERVICE APPLIES TO SHIPPING TIME ONLY. DOES NOT EXPEDITE PROCESSING OF ORDER. TWO DAY SERVICE AVAILABLE IN CONTINENTAL U.S. ONLY.

CANADIAN POSTAGE: $3.00 per item additional (plus base $5.00 shipping charge.)

FOREIGN POSTAGE: $9.00 per item additional (plus base $5.00 shipping charge.)

Mailing List:
The Movies Unlimited mailing list is occasionally made available to very carefully screened companies who offer products and services which may be of interest to our customers. If you prefer NOT receiving these mailings, please send a note with your name and address to: Movies Unlimited, 3015 Darnell Road, Phila., PA 19154. Allow 6-8 weeks for your request to be processed.

Video Movie Guarantee:
If you should receive a video that is defective or improperly manufactured, return it to us with a copy of the invoice and an explanation of the defect within 30 days and it will be replaced with an acceptable copy of the same title. Videos are not exchangeable, except on a title-for-title basis. Movies Unlimited reserves the right to impose a restocking fee on titles returned that are not defective.

Rights On Video Movies:
All programs licensed for home and non-theatrical use only. Broadcast in any form and duplication are prohibited. All prices, taxes and shipping & handling charges subject to change without notice. Prices in this catalog supersede any previous catalog. Not responsible for typographical errors. All offers void where prohibited by law.

---

1. Ordered By (Please print or place peel-off label below)

☐ Mr.
☐ Mrs. ☐ Ms.

Customer Number (from mailing label)

Address _____ Apt. # _____

City _____ State _____ Zip _____

Phone No. ( ) _____ E-mail address _____

Movies Unlimited Inc.
3015 Darnell Road
Philadelphia, PA 19154

2. Items Ordered

Catalog Number	Page #	Movie Title	Qty.	Price Each	Total
—					
—					
—					
—					
—					

3. Shipping Method (Please check one)

Please add appropriate per item charges to the base shipping charge.
All charges in addition to base charge of $5.00.

☐ **Standard Shipping:** .50¢ per item additional.
☐ **2nd Day Air*:** $3.00 per item additional.
☐ **Canadian Postage:** $3.00 per item additional.
☐ **Foreign Postage:** $9.00 per item additional.

Applies to shipping time only. Does not expedite processing of order. Domestic orders only.

Standard shipment sent UPS, US Mail or equivalent. Shipments to post office boxes must be sent by US mail. Attention schools, libraries and institutions: we are happy to accept valid purchase orders. All tapes available in NTSC VHS only.

Source Code: #602 Prices In This Book Good Thru **12/31/01.**

4. Payment Method (Please check one)

☐ **Check or Money Order Enclosed**
☐ **Visa** ☐ **MasterCard**
☐ **American Express** ☐ **Discover/Novus**

Credit Card Number:

Expiration Date (Month/Year)

Signature _____
Charge orders will NOT be sent without signature.

5 Total Order		
6 Base Shipping Charge		$5.00
7 Per Item Shipping Charge ____ # of Items x $____		
8 Sales Tax (PA residents add 7%)		
9 Credit Due You		
10 GRAND TOTAL		